Women and Entrepreneurship

The International Library of Entrepreneurship

Series Editor: David B. Audretsch
*Max Planck Institute of Economics, Jena, Germany
and Ameritech Chair of Economic Development
Indiana University, USA*

1. Corporate Entrepreneurship and Growth
    Shaker A. Zahra

2. Women and Entrepreneurship: Contemporary Classics
    *Candida G. Brush, Nancy M. Carter, Elizabeth J. Gatewood, Patricia G. Greene and Myra
    M. Hart*

Future titles will include:

The Economics of Entrepreneurship
Simon C. Parker

Entrepreneurship and Technology Policy
Albert N. Link

Entrepreneurship and Economic Growth
A. Roy Thurik and Martin Carree

Technological Entrepreneurship
Donald S. Siegel

New Firm Startups
Per Davidsson

Wherever possible, the articles in these volumes have been reproduced as originally published
using facsimile reproduction, inclusive of footnotes and pagination to facilitate ease of reference.

For a list of all Edward Elgar published titles visit our site on the World Wide Web at
www.e-elgar.com

Women and Entrepreneurship:
Contemporary Classics

Edited by

Candida G. Brush
President's Chair in Entrepreneurship and Chair, Entrepreneurship Division, Babson College, USA

Nancy M. Carter
Vice President, Research Catalyst, Inc., New York, NY, USA and Richard M. Schulze Chair in Entrepreneurship, University of St Thomas, USA

Elizabeth J. Gatewood
Director, Office of Entrepreneurship and Liberal Arts, Wake Forest University, USA

Patricia G. Greene
Dean, Undergraduate School and President's Endowed Chair in Entrepreneurship, Babson College, USA

and

Myra M. Hart
MBA Class of 1961 Chair of Entrepreneurial Management, Harvard Business School, USA

THE INTERNATIONAL LIBRARY OF ENTREPRENEURSHIP

An Elgar Reference Collection
Cheltenham, UK • Northampton, MA, USA

Published by
Edward Elgar Publishing Limited
Glensanda House
Montpellier Parade
Cheltenham
Glos GL50 1UA
UK

Edward Elgar Publishing, Inc.
136 West Street
Suite 202
Northampton
Massachusetts 01060
USA

A catalogue record for this book is available from the British Library

ISBN-13: 978 1 84542 259 2
ISBN-10: 1 84542 259 7

Printed and bound in Great Britain by MPG Books Ltd, Bodmin, Cornwall

Contents

Acknowledgements

Introduction   Candida G. Brush, Nancy M. Carter, Elizabeth J. Gatewood, Patricia G.
            Greene and Myra M. Hart

PART I   THEORY

1. Sue Birley (1989), 'Female Entrepreneurs: Are They Really Any
    Different?', *Journal of Small Business Management*, **27** (1),
    January, 32–7   3
2. Candida G. Brush and Robert D. Hisrich (1991), 'Antecedent
    Influences on Women-owned Businesses', *Journal of Managerial
    Psychology*, **6** (2), 9–16   9
3. Candida G. Brush (1992), 'Research on Women Business Owners:
    Past Trends, a New Perspective and Future Directions',
    Entrepreneurship Theory and Practice, **16** (4), Summer, 5–30   17
4. Eileen M. Fischer, A. Rebecca Reuber and Lorraine S. Dyke
    (1993), 'A Theoretical Overview and Extension of Research on
    Sex, Gender, and Entrepreneurship', *Journal of Business Venturing*,
    8 (2), March, 151–68   43
5. Barbara Bird and Candida Brush (2002), 'A Gendered Perspective
    on Organizational Creation', *Entrepreneurship Theory and
    Practice*, **26** (3), Spring, 41–65   61
6. Margaret J. Greer and Patricia G. Greene (2003), 'Feminist Theory
    and the Study of Entrepreneurship', in John E. Butler (ed.), *New
    Perspectives on Women Entrepreneurs*, Chapter 1, Greenwich, CT:
    Information Age Publishing, 1–24   86

PART II   HUMAN CAPITAL AND COGNITION

7. Donald L. Sexton and Nancy Bowman-Upton (1990), 'Female and
    Male Entrepreneurs: Psychological Characteristics and Their Role
    in Gender-related Discrimination', *Journal of Business Venturing*,
    5 (1), January, 29–36   113
8. Karyn A. Loscocco, Joyce Robinson, Richard H. Hall and John K.
    Allen (1991), 'Gender and Small Business Success: An Inquiry into
    Women's Relative Disadvantage', *Social Forces*, **70** (1), September,
    65–85   121

9.　Carin Holmquist and Elisabeth Sundin (1988), 'Women as Entrepreneurs in Sweden: Conclusions from a Survey', in Bruce A. Kirchhoff, Wayne A. Long, W. Ed McMullan, Karl H. Vesper and William E. Wetzel, Jr. (eds), *Frontiers of Entrepreneurship Research 1988*, Chapter 35, Wellesley, MA: Babson College and Alberta: University of Calgary, 626–42　　　　　142

10.　Elizabeth J. Gatewood, Kelly G. Shaver and William B. Gartner (1995), 'A Longitudinal Study of Cognitive Factors Influencing Start-up Behaviors and Success at Venture Creation', *Journal of Business Venturing*, **10**, 371–91　　　　　159

11.　Nancy M. Carter, William B. Gartner, Kelly G. Shaver and Elizabeth J. Gatewood (2003), 'The Career Reasons of Nascent Entrepreneurs', *Journal of Business Venturing*, **18**, 13–39　　　　　180

PART III　SOCIAL CAPITAL

12.　Howard Aldrich (1989), 'Networking Among Women Entrepreneurs', in Oliver Hagan, Carol Rivchun and Donald Sexton (eds), *Women-owned Businesses*, Chapter 5, New York, NY: Praeger, 103–32　　　　　209

13.　Ronald S. Burt (1998), 'The Gender of Social Capital', *Rationality and Society*, **10** (1), February, 5–46　　　　　239

14.　Linda A. Renzulli, Howard Aldrich and James Moody (2000), 'Family Matters: Gender, Networks, and Entrepreneurial Outcomes', *Social Forces*, **79** (2), December, 523–46　　　　　281

PART IV　FINANCIAL CAPITAL

15.　E. Holly Buttner and Benson Rosen (1989), 'Funding New Business Ventures: Are Decision Makers Biased Against Women Entrepreneurs?', *Journal of Business Venturing*, **4**, 249–61　　　　　307

16.　Susan Coleman (2000), 'Access to Capital and Terms of Credit: A Comparison of Men- and Women-owned Small Businesses', *Journal of Small Business Management*, **38** (3), July, 37–52　　　　　320

17.　Ingrid Verheul and Roy Thurik (2001), 'Start-Up Capital: "Does Gender Matter?"', *Small Business Economics*, **16**, 329–45　　　　　336

18.　Nancy M. Carter, Candida G. Brush, Patricia G. Greene, Elizabeth Gatewood and Myra M. Hart (2003), 'Women Entrepreneurs Who Break Through to Equity Financing: The Influence of Human, Social and Financial Capital', *Venture Capital*, **5** (1), 1–28　　　　　353

19.　Patricia G. Greene, Candida G. Brush, Myra M. Hart and Patrick Saparito (2001), 'Patterns of Venture Capital Funding: Is Gender a Factor?', *Venture Capital*, **3** (1), 63–83　　　　　381

PART V   STRATEGIC CHOICE

20. Nancy M. Carter, Mary Williams and Paul D. Reynolds (1997),
     'Discontinuance Among New Firms in Retail: The Influence of
     Initial Resources, Strategy, and Gender', *Journal of Business
     Venturing*, **12** (2), March, 125–45   405

21. Jennifer E. Cliff (1998), 'Does One Size Fit All? Exploring the
     Relationship Between Attitudes Towards Growth, Gender, and
     Business Size', *Journal of Business Venturing*, **13**, 523–42   426

22. Alexandra L. Anna, Gaylen N. Chandler, Erik Jansen and Neal P.
     Mero (2000), 'Women Business Owners in Traditional and Non-
     traditional Industries', *Journal of Business Venturing*, **15**(3), 279–
     303   446

23. Lisa K. Gundry and Harold P. Welsch (2001), 'The Ambitious
     Entrepreneur: High Growth Strategies of Women-owned
     Enterprises', *Journal of Business Venturing*, **16**, 453–70   471

PART VI   PERFORMANCE

24. Arne L. Kalleberg and Kevin T. Leicht (1991), 'Gender and
     Organizational Performance: Determinants of Small Business
     Survival and Success', *Academy of Management Journal*, **34** (1),
     March, 136–61   491

25. Radha Chaganti and Saroj Parasuraman (1996), 'A Study of the
     Impacts of Gender on Business Performance and Management
     Patterns in Small Businesses', *Entrepreneurship Theory and
     Practice*, **21** (2), Winter, 73–5   517

26. John Watson (2002), 'Comparing the Performance of Male- and
     Female-controlled Businesses: Relating Outputs to Inputs',
     Entrepreneurship Theory and Practice, **26** (3), Spring, 91–100   520

PART VII ENVIRONMENTAL

27. Eleanor Brantley Schwartz (1976), 'Entrepreneurship: A New
     Female Frontier', *Journal of Contemporary Business*, **5** (1), Winter,
     47–76   533

28. Lars Kolvereid, Scott Shane and Paul Westhead (1993), 'Is it
     Equally Difficult for Female Entrepreneurs to Start Businesses in
     All Countries?', *Journal of Small Business Management*, **31** (4),
     October, 42–51   563

29. Ted Baker, Howard E. Aldrich and Nina Liou (1997), 'Invisible
     Entrepreneurs: The Neglect of Women Business Owners by Mass
     Media and Scholarly Journals in the USA', *Entrepreneurship and
     Regional Development*, **9** (3), July–September, 221–38   573

30. Richard J. Boden, Jr (1999), 'Gender Inequality in Wage Earnings
     and Female Self-employment Selection', *Journal of Socio-
     Economics*, **28**, 351–64   591

Acknowledgements

The editors and publishers wish to thank the authors and the following publishers who have kindly given permission for the use of copyright material.

Academy of Management and Copyright Clearance Center for article: Arne L. Kalleberg and Kevin T. Leicht (1991), 'Gender and Organizational Performance: Determinants of Small Business Survival and Success', *Academy of Management Journal*, **34** (1), March, 136–61.

Blackwell Publishing Ltd for articles: Sue Birley (1989), 'Female Entrepreneurs: Are They Really Any Different?', *Journal of Small Business Management*, **27** (1), January, 32–7; Candida G. Brush (1992), 'Research on Women Business Owners: Past Trends, a New Perspective and Future Directions', *Entrepreneurship Theory and Practice*, **16** (4), Summer, 5–30; Lars Kolvereid, Scott Shane and Paul Westhead (1993), 'Is it Equally Difficult for Female Entrepreneurs to Start Businesses in All Countries?', *Journal of Small Business Management*, **31** (4), October, 42–51; Radha Chaganti and Saroj Parasuraman (1996), 'A Study of the Impacts of Gender on Business Performance and Management Patterns in Small Businesses', *Entrepreneurship Theory and Practice*, **21** (2), Winter, 73–5; Susan Coleman (2000), 'Access to Capital and Terms of Credit: A Comparison of Men- and Women-owned Small Businesses', *Journal of Small Business Management*, **38** (3), July, 37–52; Barbara Bird and Candida Brush (2002), 'A Gendered Perspective on Organizational Creation', *Entrepreneurship Theory and Practice*, **26** (3), Spring, 41–65; John Watson (2002), 'Comparing the Performance of Male- and Female-controlled Businesses: Relating Outputs to Inputs', *Entrepreneurship Theory and Practice*, **26** (3), Spring, 91–100.

Elsevier for articles: E. Holly Buttner and Benson Rosen (1989), 'Funding New Business Ventures: Are Decision Makers Biased Against Women Entrepreneurs?', *Journal of Business Venturing*, **4**, 249–61; Donald L. Sexton and Nancy Bowman-Upton (1990), 'Female and Male Entrepreneurs: Psychological Characteristics and Their Role in Gender-related Discrimination', *Journal of Business Venturing*, **5** (1), January, 29–36; Eileen M. Fischer, A. Rebecca Reuber and Lorraine S. Dyke (1993), 'A Theoretical Overview and Extension of Research on Sex, Gender, and Entrepreneurship', *Journal of Business Venturing*, **8** (2), March, 151–68; Elizabeth J. Gatewood, Kelly G. Shaver and William B. Gartner (1995), 'A Longitudinal Study of Cognitive Factors Influencing Start-up Behaviors and Success at Venture Creation', *Journal of Business Venturing*, **10**, 371–91; Nancy M. Carter, Mary Williams and Paul D. Reynolds (1997), 'Discontinuance Among New Firms in Retail: The Influence of Initial Resources, Strategy, and Gender', *Journal of Business Venturing*, **12** (2), March, 125–45; Jennifer E. Cliff (1998), 'Does One Size Fit All? Exploring the Relationship Between Attitudes Towards Growth, Gender, and Business Size', *Journal of Business Venturing*, **13**, 523–42; Richard J. Boden, Jr (1999), 'Gender Inequality in Wage Earnings and Female Self-employment Selection', *Journal of Socio-Economics*, **28**, 351–64; Alexandra L. Anna, Gaylen N. Chandler, Erik Jansen and Neal P. Mero

(2000), 'Women Business Owners in Traditional and Non-traditional Industries', *Journal of Business Venturing*, **15**, 279–303; Lisa K. Gundry and Harold P. Welsch (2001), 'The Ambitious Entrepreneur: High Growth Strategies of Women-owned Enterprises', *Journal of Business Venturing*, **16**, 453–70; Nancy M. Carter, William B. Gartner, Kelly G. Shaver and Elizabeth J. Gatewood (2003), 'The Career Reasons of Nascent Entrepreneurs', *Journal of Business Venturing*, **18**, 13–39.

Emerald Group Publishing Limited (http://www.emeraldinsight.com/jmp.htm) for article: Candida G. Brush and Robert D. Hisrich (1991), 'Antecedent Influences on Women-owned Businesses', *Journal of Managerial Psychology*, **6** (2), 9–16.

Greenwood Publishing Group, Inc. for excerpt: Howard Aldrich (1989), 'Networking Among Women Entrepreneurs', in Oliver Hagan, Carol Rivchun and Donald Sexton (eds), *Women-owned Businesses*, Chapter 5, 103–32.

Carin Holmquist and Elisabeth Sundin for their own article: (1988), 'Women as Entrepreneurs in Sweden: Conclusions from a Survey', in Bruce A. Kirchhoff, Wayne A. Long, W. Ed Mc-Mullan, Karl H. Vesper and William E. Wetzel, Jr. (eds), *Frontiers of Entrepreneurship Research 1988*, Chapter 35, 626–42.

Information Age Publishing, Inc. for excerpt: Margaret J. Greer and Patricia G. Greene (2003), 'Feminist Theory and the Study of Entrepreneurship', in John E. Butler (ed.), *New Perspectives on Women Entrepreneurs*, Chapter 1, 1–24.

Journal of Contemporary Business for article: Eleanor Brantley Schwartz (1976), 'Entrepreneurship: A New Female Frontier', *Journal of Contemporary Business*, **5** (1), Winter, 47–76.

Sage Publications Ltd for article: Ronald S. Burt (1998), 'The Gender of Social Capital', *Rationality and Society*, **10** (1), February, 5–46.

Springer Science and Business Media for article: Ingrid Verheul and Roy Thurik (2001), 'Start-Up Capital: "Does Gender Matter?"', *Small Business Economics*, **16**, 329–45.

Taylor and Francis Ltd (http://www.tandf.co.uk/journals) for articles: Ted Baker, Howard E. Aldrich and Nina Liou (1997), 'Invisible Entrepreneurs: The Neglect of Women Business Owners by Mass Media and Scholarly Journals in the USA', *Entrepreneurship and Regional Development*, **9** (3), July–September, 221–38; Patricia G. Greene, Candida G. Brush, Myra M. Hart and Patrick Saparito (2001), 'Patterns of Venture Capital Funding: Is Gender a Factor?', *Venture Capital*, **3** (1), 63–83; Nancy M. Carter, Candida G. Brush, Patricia G. Greene, Elizabeth Gatewood and Myra M. Hart (2003), 'Women Entrepreneurs Who Break Through to Equity Financing: The Influence of Human, Social and Financial Capital', *Venture Capital*, **5** (1), 1–28.

University of North Carolina Press for articles: Karyn A. Loscocco, Joyce Robinson, Richard H. Hall and John K. Allen (1991), 'Gender and Small Business Success: An Inquiry into Women's Relative Disadvantage', *Social Forces*, **70** (1), September, 65–85; Linda A. Renzulli, Howard Aldrich and James Moody (2000), 'Family Matters: Gender, Networks, and Entrepreneurial Outcomes', *Social Forces*, **79** (2), December, 523–46.

Every effort has been made to trace all the copyright holders but if any have been inadvertently overlooked the publishers will be pleased to make the necessary arrangement at the first opportunity.

In addition the publishers wish to thank the Library at the University of Warwick, UK, and the Library of Indiana University at Bloomington, USA, for their assistance in obtaining these articles.

Introduction

Women's entrepreneurship is an important contributor to economic development, wealth creation and innovation around the world (Diana Project, 2005). The size and growth of this phenomenon has attracted significant attention from academics, practitioners and policymakers. For example, according to the US Bureau of the Census, in 1972 only 4.6 percent of all US businesses were women-owned and these businesses generated about .03 percent of all business receipts. In 1999 there were 9.1 million women-owned businesses (38%), employing 27.5 million workers with reported revenues of almost $3.6 trillion (US Bureau of the Census, 2001). By 2003 women were clearly recognized as a driving force in the US economy, whether measured by the number of businesses owned, the revenues generated, or the number of people employed. Other countries around the world report similar numbers emphasizing the importance of these women and the businesses they start in a variety of geographies (Diana Project, 2005). Unfortunately, the research and dissemination of information about female entrepreneurship lags their growth and impact worldwide. Why is this the case?

One explanation is that prior to 1980 the vast majority of entrepreneurial businesses were started by men. Therefore, early research about entrepreneurship investigated motives, characteristics, behaviors and activities of men and their businesses: this practice mirrored that of the larger field of business or management-related research. Because women were less active and certainly less visible as entrepreneurs, it is not surprising that research focused on the male population. Coupled with this situation was an underlying assumption that entrepreneurial behavior was not gender specific. Until 1990, the entrepreneurship literature treated behavior as consistent across populations. This belief negated the importance of studying women entrepreneurs as a separate population (Brush, 1992).

But there has been a recent shift in this thinking. More current entrepreneurship research has found that there are distinct variations among groups of entrepreneurs. Entrepreneurs start with unique sets of motivation, human capital, social networks, and tangible resources (Cowling and Taylor, 2001; Renzulli et al., 2000; Carter et al., 2003). And some of these variations are related to the founder's sex (Brush et al, 2004). It is no longer appropriate to conclude that findings about male entrepreneurs apply equally to women nor that the development of women separate studies are superfluous. Public awareness of this fact led to the development of government policy reports in many countries, similar to those prepared by the US Small Business Administration (SBA Office of Advocacy, 2004). In addition, major research collaborations such as the Global Entrepreneurship Monitor (GEM) (Acs et al., 2005; Minniti et al., 2005) and the Panel Study of Entrepreneurial Dynamics (PSED) (Gartner et al., 2004) have conducted separate analyses of women. However, academic attention to the phenomenon remains limited and fragmented. Though the absolute and proportionate numbers of women entrepreneurs continue to rise, their economic contributions grow significantly, and public policy and research collaboratives investigate their motives and performance, scholars interested in undertaking new research still have a relatively small research base upon which to build.

This volume addresses that knowledge gap. It offers a collection of articles that provides an overview of women's entrepreneurship. The selected articles reflect major theoretical approaches, identify the driving questions, provide examples of a variety of the methodologies, and offer important findings to date. Most important, this volume offers a tool for researchers who seek to understand the many outstanding questions, those not yet asked and those not yet answered. It is intended to advance our understanding of women entrepreneurs and the businesses they create by bringing together many different perspectives, findings and methods that address women's entrepreneurship. Because research and knowledge are built cumulatively, this compendium also provides a launching pad for future scholastic work.

History of the Field

The earliest published work about women's entrepreneurship is credited to Schwartz (1976) in her article that examined characteristics, motivations, attitudes, and barriers of women entrepreneurs. The early publications that followed Schwartz were largely descriptive in nature, examining many of the same personal and business demographics that had been identified as relevant in studies of men entrepreneurs (Kent et al., 1982). While descriptive work is often dismissed as insignificant, it was necessary to describe women as entrepreneurs before delving into explanations and predictions about their behavior. Most studies that built directly on Schwartz (1976) centered on personal characteristics, which were generally explored through the lens of human capital. Acquired traits, for example education and experience, were those most often investigated. These studies were often complemented by research on psychological traits, motivations, and risk-taking propensity. A stream of research by Hisrich and O'Brien (1981, 1982) and then Hisrich and Brush (1983,1984, 1985, 1987) provided the benchmark human capital characteristics subsequently used to anchor most other early research in this field. Other researchers concentrated on the psychological measures of women entrepreneurs (Sexton and Bowman, 1986). This line of research was thoroughly summarized by Brush (1992) who proposed an 'integrated approach' to explaining the linkages between women entrepreneurs and their personal and professional lives.

Notably, the issues addressed and the research findings were remarkably similar across geographic boundaries. In Britain women were found to have education and experiences levels similar to male business owners (Watkins and Watkins, 1983; Birley et al., 1987), but to have very different cumulative educational and work experience patterns (Watkins and Watkins, 1983). In Sweden, Holmquist and Sundin (1988) used a similar questionnaire to Hisrich and Brush (1984) to identify characteristics of women entrepreneurs in that country. These authors also explored differences according to the sex of the entrepreneur and found some robust differences between men and women in terms of business and industry choices.

Other studies examined the ventures owned by women. Researchers examined strategic industry choices and access to resources (Hisrich and O'Brien, 1982; Watkins and Watkins, 1983), as well as challenges, including finding capital, and functional business skills (Pellegrino and Reece, 1982). Early studies concluded that some of the unique challenges women entrepreneurs encountered were related to their personal attributes (Cuba et al., 1983) and others to the firm characteristics (Brophy, 1989). Other research found that the concept of barriers could be expanded to include the suppliers of resources (Pellegrino and Reece, 1982; Buttner and Rosen, 1988, 1989). Another group of researchers examined networks and their impact on resource exchanges and acquisition (Aldrich, 1989; Aldrich et al., 1989). Overall, the question about the relationship between women's professional and personal lives emerged as critical (Honig-Haftel and Martin, 1986; Geoffee and Scase, 1983; Longstreth et al., 1987).

Towards the early 1990s feminist theory emerged as a lens through which to examine women's entrepreneurship. Specifically, questions about whether theories based on male-centered notions and research of entrepreneurship held true for women and minorities. This line of research resulted in a variety of typologies and explanations (Stevenson, 1986; Geoffee and Scase, 1983; Smith et al., 1982). Other studies explored the possibilities of gendered management (Chaganti, 1986; Neider, 1987).

In summary, a review of the field of women's entrepreneurship reveals an emerging body of work that shows progress by addressing multiple levels of analysis as well as an increased sophistication in the formulation of research questions and the choices of methodologies applied.

Selection of the Articles

Many of the articles in this volume were drawn from *Women Entrepreneurs, Their Ventures, and the Venture Capital Industry: An Annotated Bibliography* (Gatewood et al., 2003), which was developed as a baseline reference to encourage and support further research on women's entrepreneurship. The bibliography contains approximately 300 articles from the top entrepreneurship journals, including *Entrepreneurship Theory and Practice, Journal of Business Venturing, Journal of Small Business Management, Entrepreneurship and Regional Development, Journal of Developmental Entrepreneurship, International Small Business Journal,* and *Small Business Economics.* Additional sources included *Journal of Business Ethics* because of that journal's history of including publications about women and *Frontiers of Entrepreneurship Research,* the referred proceedings from the annual Babson Entrepreneurship Research Conference. The selection of articles in this volume represents an updated review that includes new articles published between 2002 (the end of the review cycle for the annotated bibliography) and mid-2004. The final database reviewed included approximately 370 articles. Each of the five members of the Diana Project reviewed the articles and selected the set deemed most appropriate for the collection. The criteria included whether or not the article would be considered 'important' or 'influential'. The results were compiled and a preliminary list of approximately fifty articles was produced. The list was reviewed by all five editors and an iterative review focused upon the extent that the articles covered the field, the types of issues discussed, methodology, theory and the contribution to understanding women's entrepreneurship.

Organization

The first set of papers in this volume focuses on theoretical approaches to female entrepreneurship while the second set is organized by a framework adapted from Diana Project publications (Greene et al., 2001).

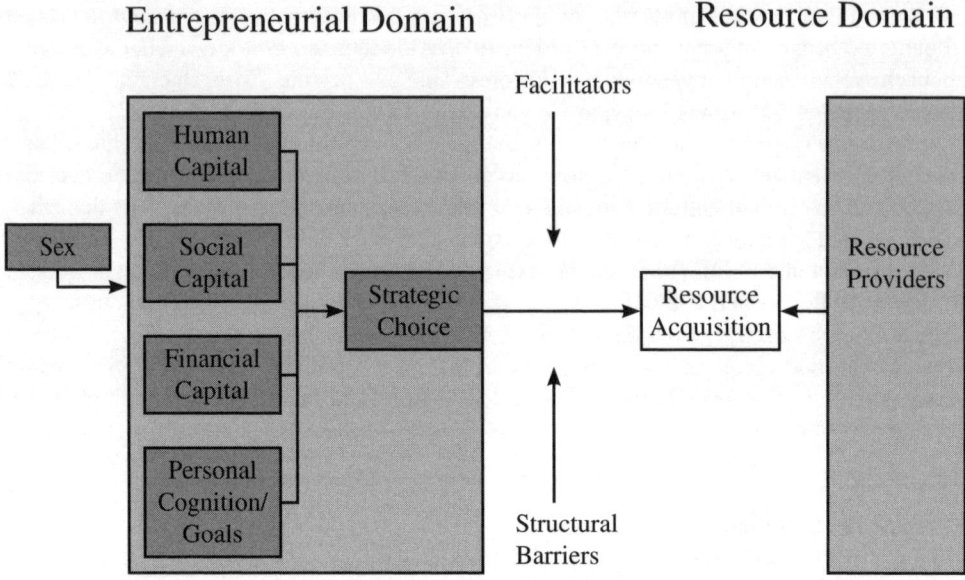

Figure 1   *Organizational Framework*

This framework delineates important constructs and relationships derived from the review of more than three hundred articles, and includes both supply and demand aspects of the entrepreneurial domain, an approach consistent with a long lineage of research (Thornton, 1999). Sex is the defining variable in a framework that explores personal cognitions, human capital, social capital, and financial capital as well as strategic choices that entrepreneurs make. The framework includes environmental effects that can facilitate or hinder business creation or growth. While business performance is not an explicit concept in the framework, we added a selection of papers focusing on performance in order to explore not only entrepreneurial inputs and process, but entrepreneurial outcomes as well.

Part I   *Theory*

The first set of papers introduces the theoretical frameworks for studying women's entrepreneurship. Birley (1989), a pioneer in the field, asked if there really are gender differences between men and women entrepreneurs. She concluded that gender roles, as well as culture and situation, have a significant impact on entrepreneurial activities. Brush and Hisrich (1991) follow up on this investigation, adding the critical dimension of entrepreneurial growth. Each of these papers finds both similarities and differences between men and women entrepreneurs, with Brush and Hisrich (1991) concluding that many of the factors that contribute to business success and survival are the same regardless of gender. Brush (1992), in one of the most cited papers in the field, advanced the discussion by reviewing 57 studies about women entrepreneurs, examining the issues, and again describing both similarities and differences. She then made a significant theoretical contribution by positing an integrated perspective that connects a woman entrepreneur's professional and family life, suggesting this integration as having an important impact on both entrepreneurial approaches and outcomes.

Feminist theory also has useful applications in this field of study and was applied to many of the questions within women's entrepreneurship. Fischer, Reuber and Dyke (1993) used liberal and social feminist theory to examine differences, focusing on sex-based discrimination and the potential existence of 'meaningful socialized gender differences'. The authors conclude with mixed evidence for their hypotheses. Bird and Brush (2003) continued along this line to suggest an 'organizational creatrix' model, using three theoretical anchors to expand the feminine perspective on organizational creation. This work articulated both masculine and feminine views of organizational creation and suggested that successful organizations would have a relative balance of feminine and masculine perspectives in both the start-up process and the venture characteristics. And finally, Greer and Greene (2003) expanded the discussion to include three perspectives of feminist theory, Liberal, Marxist, and Radical, to question both existing social and economic systems, with the suggestion of a need for a more inclusive view of gender.

Part II   Human Capital and Cognition

Human capital is a critical concept in the entrepreneurial domain of our organizational framework. Studies of human capital include trait psychology, motivational theories, and learning as measured by achieved attributes such as experience and education. We have included studies of personal cognition within this section in order to capture the range of individual aspects of the entrepreneur. Sexton and Bowman-Upton (1990) examined the relation of psychological characteristics and role in gender discrimination, again supporting previous findings that some things are different by sex, yet some are the same. They concluded there are more similarities than differences between men and women entrepreneurs, but notably women rate lower on scales measuring energy level and risk-taking while higher on autonomy and change.

Loscocco, Robinson, Hall, and Allen (1991) continued the study of differences, using the individual characteristics of both the owners and the businesses to explain different outcomes (sales and incomes). While focusing on individual entrepreneurs, these authors also raised the question of structural disadvantages, identifying the industrial sectors in which women tend to start their businesses as a potential barrier to high growth and value creation.

We have challenged the practice of making inferences about women's entrepreneurship based on theories and samples consisting of predominately male respondents. We have similar concerns about the ability to generalize from studies conducted only in the US or even in North America to the rest of the world. Holmquist and Sundin (1988) recognized the importance of women entrepreneurs to the Swedish economy. They examined characteristics of the women entrepreneurs in that society, including gender roles and choice of businesses and linked these to social and economic outcomes. While these authors used a predominately female sample, they drew a male comparison group in order to tease out gender-based differences.

Gatewood, Shaver, and Gartner (1995) used cognitive factors to predict persistence in the start-up process and new venture creation success. These authors found differences in both internal and external attributions while Carter, Gartner, Shaver, and Gatewood (2002) questioned how the decision to become an entrepreneur may be shaped by human capital (particularly experience), and whether the gendered socialization of experience results in the development of unique capabilities suited to entrepreneurial careers.

Part III   Social Capital

The discussion on social capital has increased over the past few as it has gained recognition as an important tool in the acquisition of resources. Social capital is now seen as a 'key facilitator of [other] resources' (Aldrich, 1999; Maula, Autio and Murray, 2003). Aldrich (1989) anchors much of the discussion within entrepreneurship about social capital by presenting an organizational schema for networks that includes categories of work, family, and organized social life. He concludes that the ability to connect to resources is different for women and that this has consequences for business formation, survival, and growth. Burt's (1998) discussion of social capital describes it as the 'contextual complement to human capital'. However, Burt questions whether differences really are based on gender differences or are determined by insider-outsider relationships. Renzulli, Aldrich, and Moody (2000) fine-tune this conversation by focusing on information and social support networks, with a particular interest in the heterogeneity of those networks. They concluded that the network itself is a more useful explanatory variable than is gender.

Part IV   Financial Capital

Financial capital is one of the most heavily researched segments of the framework. It is also often considered to be the single greatest obstacle to women's entrepreneurship. Buttner and Rosen (1989) were interested in debt capital and examined bank loan officers' perceptions to understand gender stereotyping. They found no evidence that gender-based stereotypes influence decisions of those loan officers, but found that women were perceived by the loan officers to be less entrepreneurial. Coleman (2000) did not find banking discrimination based upon gender, but did uncover a disconnect between the types of businesses bankers need to fund (larger and more established firms) and those owned by women (usually a smaller average size of firm). Coleman also found that the terms of the loans (interest rates and collateral) tend to be different depending on the gender of the entrepreneur. These same basic questions were explored by Verheul and Thurik (2001) from a Dutch perspective with similar results. The authors also concluded that the types of business, management, and entrepreneurial experiences were more relevant to the lending decision than the sex of the entrepreneur.

Greene, Brush, Hart, and Saparito (2001) and Carter, Brush, Greene, Gatewood, and Hart (2003) moved the discussion of financial capital for women entrepreneurs from debt to equity, beginning with the question of why women-owned businesses stay smaller than those owned by men. These papers focused specifically on equity seeking and equity funded businesses to learn about growth models. The questions explored included the disparity between potential investment opportunities in women-owned businesses and actual equity deals done with women entrepreneurs.

Part V   Strategic Choice

Strategic choice reflects the aspirations and conscious business choices of women entrepreneurs. These key decisions take place before actual start-up, when a woman decides upon the type of business to launch, including the industrial sector, and establishes her goals for the growth and profitability of the business. Questions about strategic choice often include the factors that influence growth strategies, the effect of industrial sector upon growth, and the influence of financing patterns. Carter, Williams and Reynolds (1997) examine how strategic choice is shaped by experience and how those experiences may be a result of gendered socialization. The pathway described suggests that socialization leads to unique capabilities, which subsequently influence choice of a particular strategy.

Cliff (1998) continues the discussion of business size, applying the liberal and social feminist theories introduced by Fischer et al. (1993). Cliff explores both the personal and economic issues regarding establishment of success thresholds and the actual growth of the business. Anna, Chandler, Jansen, and Mero (2000) consider entrepreneurial intention as it relates to choice of industry, business model, and commitment to growth adding a deeper examination of the choice of an entrepreneurial career. And finally, Gundry and Welsch (2001) focus upon women business owners with high growth businesses to examine the attributes of both founder and venture, adding to our understanding of the strategic paths related to growth.

Part VI Performance

Strategic choices affect performance. The statistics drawn from national sources of data around the world consistently show that women-owned businesses are generally smaller, whether measured in terms of revenue or number of employees, than businesses owned by men (Diana Project, 2005). However, Kalleberg and Leicht (1991) find that size is not a predictor of survival and that women-owned businesses, while smaller, are not more likely to go out of business or be less successful. Chaganti and Parasuraman (1996) extend this question to look at goals, strategies, management practices, as well as performance, and find no significant gender differences if measured by return on assets (ROA). We conclude this section with Watson's (2002) careful examination of previous findings on the underperformance of female-owned businesses as compared to male-owned businesses. Watson's methodology includes controlling for input variables in order to better understand performance when considered as a variety of output measures.

Part VII Environmental

The environment includes externalities that both enhance and impede entrepreneurial behaviors and processes for women business owners. Most of the research focuses on the obstacles or perceived barriers that the environment poses. Eleanor Brantley Schwartz's (1976) pioneering article, 'Entrepreneurship: A New Female Frontier', was exploratory research that provided the foundation for the descriptive individual characteristics, motivations, and attitudes of the women business owners. While Schwartz found few gendered differences in the individual level variables, she recognized the structural factors in the environment that had different effects on women and men entrepreneurs. For instance, until the Equal Credit Act was enacted in 1975 married women in the United States could not get credit in their own names. In a similar vein, it was not until US federal regulations recognized women business owners (1978), that the US Small Business Administration captured descriptive statistics about women-owned businesses at a national level (The Bottom Line, 1978).

The environment for women entrepreneurs is global and this global context is explored in the work of Kolvereid, Shane, and Westhead (1993). While controlling for the effect of the home country, these authors addressed interesting questions about availability of resources, turbulence, hostility, and uncertainty and concluded that national differences may be greater than gender differences when considering how the entrepreneurial process works.

Baker, Aldrich, and Liou (1997) examined media coverage to understand the context in which women entrepreneurs operate. They found that within the United States, even as the numbers of women entrepreneurs was increasing, the coverage in the popular press was moving in the opposite direction. The same was true for academic articles. Over the course of the years studied (1982–1995), the coverage of women business owners in academic articles declined. The authors conclude with a consideration of androcentrism; a suggestion that the traditional ways of doing business are 'natural'.

The final paper in this volume recognizes female self-employment as an important labor market consideration and explores the impact of gender inequality in wage returns. Boden (1999) combines issues of environment and performance to illustrate how structural inequity influences women's decisions to leave wage employment and start businesses.

Conclusions

Researchers in the field of women's entrepreneurship have made notable progress over the past three decades. They are now beginning to build a relevant body of knowledge. Significant advances have been made in understanding women entrepreneurs and their businesses. However, gaps remain in both theory and application. There is clearly much more work to be done.

Questions remain not only about research topics, but also about who should be conducting the research. Historically, research on entrepreneurship has been scant. Over the past decade, rigorous research and theory development has emerged in the more general entrepreneurial domain, and these accomplishments have spawned departments of entrepreneurship and more scholarly training in this area. Despite these accomplishments, women's entrepreneurship is still perceived as a subset of entrepreneurship and consequently, studies in this area are sometimes viewed as less important. The size and contribution of women's entrepreneurship as a social and economic phenomenon is undeniable and calls for additional research.

References

Acs, Z., P. Arenius, M. Hay and M. Minniti (2005), Global Entrepreneurship Monitor. *2004 Executive Report*, Babson College and London Business School.

Aldrich, Howard E. (1999), *Organizations Evolving*, Thousand Oaks, California, Sage Publications.

Aldrich, H. (1989), 'Networking among women entrepreneurs', in O. Hagan, C. Rivchun and D. Sexton (eds), *Women-owned businesses*, pp. 103–32, New York: Praeger.

Aldrich, H., P.R. Reese, P. Dubini, B. Rosen and B. Woodward (1989), 'Women on the verge of a breakthrough?: Networking among entrepreneurs in the United States and Italy', in R.H. Brockhaus, Sr., N.C. Churchill, J.A. Katz, B.A. Kirchhoff, K.H. Vesper and Wm. E. Wetzel, Jr. (eds), *Frontiers of Entrepreneurship Research*, pp. 560–74, Boston, MA: Babson College.

Anna, A. L., G.N. Chandler, E. Jansen and N.P. Mero (2000), 'Women business owners in traditional and non-traditional industries', *Journal of Business Venturing*, **15**(3), 279–303.

Baker, T., H.E. Aldrich and N. Liou (1997), 'Invisible entrepreneurs: The neglect of women business owners by mass media and scholarly journals in the U.S.A.', *Entrepreneurship and Regional Development*, **9**, 221–38.

Bird, B.J. and C.G. Brush (2003), 'A gendered perspective on organizational creation', *Entrepreneurship Theory and Practice*, **26**(3), 41–65.

Birley, S. (1989), 'Female entrepreneurs: Are they really any different?', *Journal of Small Business Management*, **27**(1), 32–37.

Birley, S., C. Moss and P. Saunders (1987), 'Do women entrepreneurship require different training?', *American Journal of Small Business* **12** (1), 27–35.

Boden Jr., R.J. (1999), 'Gender inequality in wage earnings and female self-employment selection', *Journal of Socio-Economics*, **28**(3), 351–64.

Brophy, D.J. (1989), 'Financing women owned entrepreneurial firms', in O. Hagan, C. Rivchun and D. Sexton (eds), *Women Owned Businesses*, 55–76, New York: Praeger.

Brush, C.G. and R.D. Hisrich (1991), 'Antecedent influences on women-owned businesses', *Journal of Managerial Psychology*, **6**(2), 9–16.

Brush, C.G. (1992), 'Research on women business owners: Past trends, a new perspective and future directions', *Entrepreneurship Theory and Practice*, **16**(4), 5–30.

Brush, C.G., N.M. Carter, E.J. Gatewood, P.G. Greene and M.M. Hart (2004), *Clearing the Hurdles: Women Building High Growth Businesses*, Upper Saddle River, NJ: Financial Times-Prentice Hall.

Burt, R.S. (1998), 'The gender of social capital', *Rationality and Society*, **10**(1), 5–47.

Buttner, E.H. and B. Rosen (1988), 'Bank loan officers' perceptions of characteristics of men, women and successful entrepreneurs', *Journal of Business Venturing*, **3**(3), 249–58.

Buttner, E. H. and B. Rosen (1989), 'Funding new business ventures: Are decision makers biased against women entrepreneurs?', *Journal of Business Venturing*, **4**(4), 249–61.

Carter, N.M., C.G. Brush, P.G. Greene, E.J. Gatewood and M.M. Hart (2003), 'Women entrepreneurs who break through to equity financing: The influence of human, social and financial capital', *Venture Capital International Journal*, **5**(1).

Carter, N.M., W.B. Gartner, K.G. Shaver and E.J. Gatewood (2002), 'The career reasons of nascent entrepreneurs', *Journal of Business Venturing*, **18**, 13–39.

Carter, N.M., M. Williams and P.D. Reynolds (1997), 'Discontinuance among new firms in retail: The influence of initial resources, strategy and gender', *Journal of Business Venturing*, **12**(2), 125–45.

Chaganti, R. (1986), 'Management in women-owned enterprises', *Journal of Small Business Management*, **24**(4), 18–29.

Chaganti, R. and S. Parasuraman (1996), 'A study of the impact of gender on business performance and management patterns in small businesses', *Entrepreneurship Theory and Practice*, **21**(2), 73–5.

Cliff, J.E. (1998), 'Does one size fit all? Exploring the relationship between attitudes towards growth, gender, and business size', *Journal of Business Venturing*, **13**(6), 523–42.

Coleman, S. (2000), 'Access to capital and terms of credit: A comparison of men- and women-owned small businesses', *Journal of Small Business Management*, **38**(3), 37–52.

Cowling, M. and M. Taylor (2001), 'Entrepreneurial women and men: Two different species?', *Small Business Economics*, **16**(3): 167–75.

Cuba, R., D. Decenzo and A. Anish (1983), 'Management practices of successful female business owners', *American Journal of Small Business*, **8**(2), 40–45.

Diana Project (2005), *The Diana International Project: Research on growth oriented women entrepreneurs and their businesses*, Stockholm, Sweden: ESBRI Forthcoming. See http://www.esbri.se/diana.asp

Fischer, E.M., A.R. Reuber and L.S. Dyke (1993), 'A theoretical overview and extension of research on sex, gender, and entrepreneurship', *Journal of Business Venturing*, **8**(2), 151–68.

Gartner, W., K. Shaver, N.M. Carter and P.D. Reynolds (eds) (2004), *Handbook of Entrepreneurial Dynamics: The Process of Business Creation*, Thousand Oaks, California, Sage Publications.

Gatewood, E.J., K.G. Shaver and W.B. Gartner (1995), 'A longitudinal study of cognitive factors influencing start-up behaviors and success at venture creation', *Journal of Business Venturing*, **10**(5), 371–91.

Gatewood, E.G., N.M. Carter, C.G. Brush, P.G. Greene and M.M. Hart (2003), *Women Entrepreneurs, Their Ventures, and the Venture Capital Industry: An Annotated Bibliography*, Stockholm: ESBRI (ISBN 91-973286-3-4), reprinted in Chinese, 2003.

Geoffee, B. and R. Scase (1983), 'Business ownership and women's subordination: A preliminary study of proprietors', *The Sociological Review*, **31**(4), 625–48.

Greene, P.G., C.G. Brush, M.M. Hart and P. Saparito (2001), 'Patterns of venture capital funding: Is gender a factor?', *Venture Capital: An International Journal of Entrepreneurial Finance*, **3**(1), 63–83.

Greer, M.A. and P.G. Greene (2003), 'Feminist theory and the study of entrepreneurship', in J.E. Butler (ed.), *Women Entrepreneurs*, pp. 1–24, Greenwich, CT: Information Age Publishing.

Gundry, L.K. and H.P. Welsch (2001), 'The ambitious entrepreneur: High growth strategies of women-owned enterprises', *Journal of Business Venturing*, **16**(5), 453–70.

Hisrich, R.D. and C.G. Brush (1983), 'The woman entrepreneur: Implications of family educational, and occupational experience', in J.A. Hornaday, J.A. Timmons and K.H. Vesper (eds), *Frontiers of Entrepreneurial Research*, pp. 255–70, Boston, MA: Babson College.

Hisrich, R.D. and C.G. Brush (1984), 'The woman entrepreneur: Management skills and business problems', *Journal of Small Business Management*, **22**(1), 30–37.

Hisrich, R.D. and C.G. Brush (1985), 'Women and minority entrepreneurs: A comparative analysis', in J.A. Hornaday, E.B. Shils, J.A. Timmons and K.H. Vesper (eds), *Frontiers of Entrepreneurial Research*, 566–87, Boston, MA: Babson College.

Hisrich, R.D. and C.G. Brush (1987), 'Women entrepreneurs: A longitudinal study', in N.C. Churchill, J.A. Hornaday, B.A. Kirchhoff, O.J. Krasner and K.H. Vesper (eds), *Frontiers of Entrepreneurial Research*, pp. 187–99, Boston, MA: Babson College.

Hisrich, R.D. and M. O'Brien (1981), 'The woman entrepreneur from a business and sociological perspective', in K.H. Vesper (ed.), *Frontiers of Entrepreneurial Research*, pp. 21–39, Boston, MA: Babson College.

Hisrich, R.D. and M. O'Brien (1982), 'The woman entrepreneur as a reflection of the type of business', in K.H. Vesper (ed.), *Frontiers of Entrepreneurial Research*, pp. 54–67, Boston, MA: Babson College.

Holmquist, C. and E. Sundin (1988), 'Women as entrepreneurs in Sweden – conclusions from a survey', in B.A. Kirchhoff, W.A. Long, W.E. McMullan, K.H. Vesper and W.E. Wetzel (eds), *Frontiers in Entrepreneurial Research*, pp. 625–37, Boston, MA: Babson College.

Honig-Haftel, S. and L. Martin (1986), 'Is the female entrepreneur at a disadvantage?', *Thrust*, **7**(1, 2), 49–65.

Kalleberg, A. L. and K.T. Leicht (1991), 'Gender and organizational performance: Determinants of small business survival and success', *Academy of Management Journal*, **34**(1), 136–61.

Kent, C.A., D.L. Sexton and K.H. Vesper (1982), *Encyclopedia of Entrepreneurship*, Englewood Cliffs, Prentice Hall.

Kolvereid, L., S. Shane and P. Westhead (1993), 'Is it equally difficult for female entrepreneurs to start businesses in all countries?', *Journal of Small Business Management*, **31**(4), 42–51.

Longstreth, M., K. Stafford and T. Mauldin (1987), 'Self-employed women and their families: Time use and socioeconomic characteristics', *Journal of Small Business Management*, **25**(3), 30–37.

Loscocco, K.A., J. Robinson, R.H. Hall and J.K. Allen (1991), 'Gender and small business success: An inquiry into women's relative disadvantage', *Social Forces*, **70**(1), 65–85.

Maula, M.V.J., E. Autio and G.C. Murray (2003), 'Prerequisites for the creation of social capital and subsequent knowledge acquisition in corporate venture capital', *Venture Capital: An International Journal of Entrepreneurial Finance*, **5**(2): 117–34.

Minniti, M., P. Arenius and N. Langowitz (2005), 'Global Entrepreneurship Monitor', *2004 Report on Women and Entrepreneurship*, Babson College and London Business School.

Neider, L. (1987), 'A preliminary investigation of female entrepreneurs in Florida', *Journal of Small Business Management*, **25**(3), 22–9.

Pellegrino, E.T. and B.L. Reese (1982), 'Perceived formative and operational problems encountered by female entrepreneurs in retail and service firms', *Journal of Small Business Management*, **20**(2), 15–25.

Renzulli, L.A., H. Aldrich and J. Moody (2000), 'Family matters: Gender, networks, and entrepreneurial outcomes', *Social Forces*, **79**(2), 523–46.

Schwartz, E. (1976), 'Entrepreneurship: A new female frontier', *Journal of Contemporary Business*, **5**(1), 47–76.

Sexton, D.L. and N.B. Bowman (1986), 'Validation of a personality index: Comparative psychological characteristics analysis of female entrepreneurs, managers, entrepreneurship students and business students', in R. Ronstadt, J.A. Hornaday, R. Peterson and K.H. Vesper (eds), *Frontiers of Entrepreneurship Research*, pp. 40–51, Boston, MA: Babson College.

Sexton, D.L. and N. Bowman-Upton (1990), 'Female and male entrepreneurs: Psychological characteristics and their role in gender related discrimination', *Journal of Business Venturing*, **5**(1), 29–36.

Small Business Administration, Office of Advocacy (2004), *The Small Business Economy*, Washington, D.C.: US Government Printing Office.

Smith, N.R., G. McCain and A. Warren (1982), 'Women entrepreneurs really are different: A comparison of constructed ideal types of male and female entrepreneurs', in K.H. Vesper (ed.), *Frontiers of Entrepreneurship Research*, pp. 68–77, Boston, MA: Babson College.

Stevenson, L. (1986), 'Against all odds: the entrepreneurship of women', *Journal of Small Business Management*, **24**(4), 30–36.

Thornton, P.H. (1999), 'The sociology of entrepreneurship', *Annual Review of Sociology*, **25**, 19–46.

US Bureau of the Census (2001), *Women Owned Businesses: 1997 Economic Census survey of Women-Owned Business Enterprises*, Washington, DC.: US Government Printing Office.

United States Department of Commerce (1979), *The Bottom Line: Unequal Enterprise in America*, US Task Force Report on Women Business Owners, Washington, DC.

Verheul, I. and R. Thurik (2001), 'Start-up capital: Does gender matter?', *Small Business Economics*, **16**(4), 329–45.

Watkins, J.M. and D.S. Watkins (1983), 'The female entrepreneur: Her background and determinants of business choice: some British data', in J.A. Hornaday, J.A. Timmons and K.H. Vesper (eds), *Frontiers of Entrepreneurship Research*, pp. 271–88, Boston, MA: Babson College.

Watson, J. (2002), 'Comparing the performance of male- and female-controlled businesses: Relating outputs to inputs', *Entrepreneurship Theory and Practice*, **26**(3), 91–100.

Part I
Theory

[1]

FEMALE ENTREPRENEURS: ARE THEY REALLY ANY DIFFERENT?

by Sue Birley

ABSTRACT: FEMMES-ENTREPRENEURS: SONT-ELLES VRAIMENT DIFFERENTES?

Cet article se penche sur un ensemble d'études récentes consacrées aux femmes-entre-preneurs, afin de les comparer aux données disponibles concernant leurs contreparties masculines. La différence majeure ainsi mise en évidence réside dans le type d'entreprise engagée par les hommes et les femmes, ces dernières choisissant le plus souvent les sociétés de service ou de vente au détail.

The entrepreneurial sector is now viewed as a significant factor in the design of strategies for economic recovery and growth in many nations. In the United Kingdom, for example, the Department of Trade and Industry was recently re-named the Department of Enterprise. Increasingly, all sectors of the population are urged to consider self-employment. In the education sector alone, many "Start-Your-Own-Business" programs have been designed for students, for the unemployed, for managers, for ethnic minorities, and for women. This rapid growth in the segmentation of the market has, however, been based on a history of research which has drawn evidence almost entirely from male entrepreneurs.

Recent estimates indicate that more than one-third of the new firms founded in the United States are owned by women,[1] yet, as a number of studies have observed, the data regarding female entrepreneurs is limited.[2] Moreover, the studies which have been conducted are often based upon small, convenience samples which may have had a significant influence on outcomes.[3]

Throughout history, according to the norms of particular cultures, the roles of men and women in society have tended to be quite different. The nature of these roles is gradually changing in Western economies. More and more women are completing university and postgraduate education. They are also working full-time in greater numbers. It is important, therefore, to ask what effect these changes are having on the supply of female entrepreneurs, and

Dr. Birley is Philip and Pauline Harris Professor of Entrepreneurship and Director of Research at the Cranfield School of Management, UK. She also heads the Cranfield Entrepreneurship Research Centre. She is a member of the editorial board of the *Strategic Management Journal*, the *International Small Business Journal*, the *Journal of Business Venturing*, and the *European Management Journal*. She is also chairman of a venture consulting firm in London.

[1] G. Gregg, "Women Entrepreneurs: The Second Generation," *Across the Board* (January 1985), pp. 1-18.

[2] J. Watkins and D. Watkins, "The Female Entrepreneur: Background and Determinants of Business Choice—Some British Data," *International Small Business Journal* (Summer 1984), pp. 21-31.

L. A. Stevenson, "Against All Odds: The Entrepreneurship of Women," *Journal of Small Business Management* (October 1986), pp. 30-36.

[3] J. Curran, "Bolton Fifteen Years On: A Review and Analysis of Small Business Research in Britain, 1971-1986," paper presented to the *Ninth UK National Small Firms Policy and Research Conference* (Gleneagles: 1986).

perhaps more important, are female entrepreneurs significantly different from their male counterparts?

The premise of this article is that the nature of any business (i.e., its trading relationships with customers, suppliers, bankers, and advisors) is "set at the start."[4] Cooper's model[5] is used to analyze the factors which influence the initial entrepreneurship decision and to develop a theory to apply to female entrepreneurs. Cooper's model incorporates three broad categories of influence:

1. "Antecedent influences" incorporate aspects of the entrepreneur's background which affect motivation, perceptions, skills, and knowledge. They include genetic factors, family influences, education, and previous career experiences.

2. The "Incubator Organization" describes the types of organization for which the entrepreneur worked immediately prior to start-up. Characteristics include geographic location, type of skills and knowledge acquired, contact with other budding entrepreneurs, and experience in a small business setting. In addition, Cooper cites the well-known "push" and "pull" factors, such as job loss (push) and desire for independence (pull).

3. "Environmental Factors" include prevailing economic conditions (particularly the availability of venture capital), role models, and access to support services.

ANTECEDENT INFLUENCES

Motivation

It is clear from the literature that the motivation of female entrepreneurs are similar in most respects to those of their male counterparts. Of the four motivations identified by Goffee and

Scase,[6] three—avoiding low-paid occupations, escaping supervision, and the constraint of subservient roles (in the incubator organization)—are directly comparable. Further, the fourth, that of rejecting male-imposed identities had had found little support in the literature. It would seem that females are motivated by the same need for money, wish to be independent, and identification of business opportunities as their male counterparts.[7] In fact, Chaganti notes that when traditional personality tests are conducted, no significant differences emerge with regard to achievement motivation, autonomy, persistence, aggression, independence, non-conformity, goal-orientation, leadership, or locus of control.[8] On only one important factor do males and females appear to differ significantly: self-confidence.[9]

Despite this apparent lack of self-confidence, few women are satisfied with work which merely provides "pin money," whether it be as an employee or through self-employment.[10] As Rimmer and Popay noted a decade ago, only 8 percent of the male labor force in the United Kingdom consisted of sole providers for the "typical" family.[11]

[4]S. Birley, "New Ventures and Employment Growth," *Journal of Business Venturing*, vol. 2 (1987), pp. 156-165.

[5]A. C. Cooper, "Strategic Management: New Ventures and Small Business," *Long Range Planning*, vol. 14, no. 5 (1981), pp. 39-45.

[6]R. Goffee and R. Scase, *Women in Charge: The Experiences of Female Entrepreneurs* (London: George Allen and Unwin, 1985).

[7]J. C. M. Gerritson, C. Beyer, and M. S. El-Namaki, "Female Entrepreneurship Revisited: The Trait Approach Disputed," *RVB Research Paper*, (March 1987); L. Hertz, *The Business Amazons* (London: Deutsch, 1986).

[8]R. Chaganti, "Management in Women-Owned Enterprises," *Journal of Small Business Management* (October 1986), pp. 18-29. See also H. Welsch and E. Young, "Male and Female Entrepreneurial Characteristics and Behaviors: A Profile of Similarities and Differences," *International Small Business Journal* (Summer 1984), pp. 11-20; J. F. DeCarlo and P. R. Lyons, "A Comparison of Selected Personal Characteristics of Minority and Non-Minority Female Entrepreneurs," *Journal of Small Business Management* (October 1979), pp. 22-29; and F. T. Waddell, "Factors Affecting Choice, Satisfaction, and Success in the Female Self-Employed," *Journal of Vocation Behavior*, vol. 23 (1983), pp. 294-304.

[9]M. C. Berry, "Targeting More Aid to Women Entrepreneurs," *Venture* (May 1980), pp. 294-304.

[10]G. Joseph, *Women at Work: The British Experience* (Oxford: Philip Allen, 1983); and C. E. Scott, "Why More Women Are Becoming Entrepreneurs," *Journal of Small Business Management* (October 1986), pp. 37-44.

[11]L. Rimmer and J. Popay, "The Family at Work," *Employment Gazette* (June 1982).

Family Background

Watkins and Watkins concluded that while the backgrounds of their sample of 58 men and 43 women were substantially different, a closer examination of the data revealed similarities in sibling position, fathers' occupations and general level of education.[12] Regarding age, Birley, Moss, and Saunders[13] found the women entrepreneurs in their sample to be younger than the men. These results must be viewed with caution, however, because the sample was small and drawn solely from a population which had participated in enterprise training.

Marital Status

Most of the literature regarding family background which identifies differences between males and females concentrates on the entrepreneur's marital status. Thus, while Curran reported that roughly similar proportions of male and female enterprise owners were married, divorced, or separated, he concluded that "the apparent support for the notion that self-employment among women is an alternative to marriage or to dependence upon males [as reported] in Watkins and Watkins, and Goffee and Scase is a function of the non-random approaches to sample construction."[14]

In a study of 34 female entrepreneurs, Cromie detected different reasons for creating businesses between married and single women.[15] However, after further examination of the data, he concluded that the differentiating factor was not, in fact, marriage but parenthood. For mothers, self-employment or entrepreneurship affords a greater opportunity for the flexibility necessary to combine domestic and employment responsibilities.[16] This point is underlined by Hertz, who comments that "this explains the great disparity between the number of female executives who choose to be mothers (only 39 percent), and the entrepreneurial women in this study, of whom as many as 74 percent are mothers."[17] Further, in her study of the personality types of women in management, Vinnicombe found them to fall mainly into the categories of "Visionaries" and "Catalysts," in contrast to their "Traditionalist" male colleagues. She concludes that these differing types explain the problems which women encounter with "organizational rigidity" and suggests that "starting their own business, working part-time, and staying at home are the kinds of coping strategies women managers are adopting."[18]

THE INCUBATOR ORGANIZATION

In his study of new ventures, Cooper saw the incubator organization as the immediate previous employer of the entrepreneur. While this definition may be too narrow, the underlying assumption that previous experience influences the nature of entrepreneurial choice is pertinent. However, the nature of the skills and knowledge of the unemployed, the student, or the housewife may be quite different from those of a previously employed male in his mid-30s. Thus, although Stevenson notes that most women gain their first managerial experience in their own

[12]Watkins and Watkins, "The Female Entrepreneur." See also D. D. Bowen and R. D. Hisrich, "The Female Entrepreneur: A Career Development Perspective," *Academy of Management Review* (April 1986), pp. 393-407.

[13]S. Birley, C. Moss, and P. Saunders, "The Difference Between Small Firms Started by Male and Female Entrepreneurs Who Attended Small Business Courses," *Entrepreneurship Research* (Babson, Mass.: 1986).

[14]Curran, "Bolton Fifteen Years On."

[15]S. Cromie, "Towards a Typology of Female Entrepreneurs," paper presented to the *Ninth UK National Small Firms Policy and Research Conference* (Gleneagles: 1986). See also R. D. Hisrich and C. Brush, "The Woman Entrepreneur: Management Skills and Business Problems," *Journal of Small Business Management* (January 1984), pp. 30-37.

[16]K. McDermott, "The '80s Decade of Women Entrepreneurs," *D & B Reports* (July/August 1985), pp. 14-16, 34.

[17]Hertz, *The Business Amazon.*

[18]S. Vinnicombe, "Drawing Out the Differences Between Male and Female Working Styles," *Women in Management Review* (Spring 1987). For a discussion of this issue, see M. Longstreth, K. Stafford, and T. Mauldin, "Self-Employed Women and Their Families: Time Use and Socioeconomic Characteristics," *Journal of Small Business Management* (July 1987), pp. 30-37.

businesses, this is not the case for many employed, skilled males, and it may beg the definition of the term "managerial."

Craig, Garnsey, and Rubery caution that the value of traditional women's work must be reassessed: it probably should not be classified as "unskilled."[19] The important issue, therefore, is not so much the type of prior employment as the type of prior experience. Taking this view, it is clear that "women make the same entry choices as men—i.e., all enter sectors open to them given their background, age, economic and family status, education, experience, and career opportunities.[20] For example, Hertz found that while many of the women in her sample had not been employed, 81 percent had nevertheless gained "relevant experience."[21]

Business Choice

It is not surprising that many women enter markets which are "not traditionally male dominated"—the service industry and, most commonly, retailing.[22] This is a pattern which is seen on both sides of the Atlantic. In the United Kingdom, statistics in the 1987 *Employment Gazette* show that:

1. Females account for 45 percent of the employed population.
2. Total female employment is growing
3. Part-time female employment is 42 percent of all female employment.
4. The service sector accounts for 65.7 percent of female employment. [23]

In the U.S., the 1986 report on the *State of Small Business* found that

women-owned businesses were growing much faster than male-owned businesses in the "traditional areas of retail and service" for three reasons: (1) increased participation of women in the labor force in general; (2) a growing trend among firms to contract out services; and (3) flexible working hours.[24]

Finally, in Canada, 95.9 percent of females starting businesses in 1985 entered either the service or retail industries.[25]

ENVIRONMENTAL FACTORS

It is clear from the literature that it may take many years for the motivation to start a new firm and to develop an associated product idea to come to fruition. The corollary to this is that the supply of entrepreneurs is not a fixed quantity, but can be influenced by external factors. On a national level, the role of national culture, acceptable norms of behavior, new networks for assistance and advice, and traditional family relationships all clearly influence individual attitudes. Moreover, the visibility of attractive role models (Ted Turner, Richard Branson of Virgin Atlantic, Laura Ashley, Mary Kay), and the much-publicized success of management buy-outs have made significant contributions to shaping national attitudes toward entrepreneurial behavior. Beyond this, Cooper suggests that the prevailing economic climate is also an important factor in determining the number of people who finally decide to move into self-employment. Thus the mere fact that many large firms have substantially reduced their employee base, and that management at all levels can no longer look to the large firm as a source of long-term security, has meant that many have sought self-reliance

[19]C. Craig, E. Garnsey, and J. Rubery, "Payment Structures and Small Firms: Women's Employment in Segmented Labour Markets," *Department of Employment Research Paper*, no. 48 (1984).
[20]R. Chaganti, "Management in Women-Owned Enterprises."
[21]Hertz, *The Business Amazons.*
[22]D. D. Brown and R. D. Hisrich, "The Female Entrepreneur: A Career Development Perspective," *Academy of Management Review* (April 1986), pp. 393-407; C. E. Scott, "Why More Women Are Becoming Entrepreneurs," *Journal of Small Business Management* (October 1986), pp. 37-44.
[23]*Employment Gazette* (January 1987).

[24]*The State of Small Business: Annual Report of the President* (Washington, D.C.: Government Printing Office, 1986).
[25]*The State of Small Business: Annual Report on Small Business in Ontario* (Toronto: Ontario Government Bookstore, 1986).

through the ownership of their own firms.

The general environmental factors which contribute to an increase in the supply of female entrepreneurs are subtle and part of a general change in society's attitudes to male and female roles, both at home and at work. In their study of the entrepreneurial role of women in developing countries, El-Namaki and Gerritson identified numerous barriers to women's entry into industry and entrepreneurship. They conclude that these barriers are formidable, constituting a never-ending circle: "secondary position of women → little or no education → no work in the formal sector → informal sector → no chance of improving life conditions → daughters needed to help in the house . . . ."[26]

Although until recently many of the same behavioral, societal, legal and other barriers as these have also prevailed in most Western countries, recent evidence from the United Kingdom and the United States paints a more optimistic picture. Positive role models, affirmative action, increased travel, increased media coverage, and the changing nature of education have all contributed to a more supportive environment, and an increase in the number of women considering self-employment. Yet the question remains: do women differ from men in their ability to translate an idea into a business, given the environment which they encounter as they begin to gather resources?

Barriers

In their study of 20 women with one or more years of experience in the operating of a retail or service firm in the U.S., Pellegrino and Reece found that women did not experience any serious formative problems, or any

obstacles unique to their sex.[27] This general conclusion is supported by Bradley and Saunders in their study of 300 female owners registered in the "Pink Pages."[28] Although some reported particular difficulties in qualifying for loans because of a lack of collateral, this is also a problem encountered frequently by male entrepreneurs, and it is difficult to validate differences without detailed knowledge of the particular business plan. The *State of Small Business* (1986) reports that the female entrepreneurs' access to capital does not differ from that of men, although women did seem to depend more heavily on personal savings. Hertz underlines this point in her comparative study of British and American women entrepreneurs who found no real financial discrimination, which she concludes was because of sound business plans.[29] Gumpert reports the view of Helen Charov, founder and president of Goodspeed Systems, Inc., that bankers and investors are "equally uncompromising for men and women."[30] Beyond this, there is little data on women's use of the various assistance networks available, although evidence from the United States points to a strong correlation between involvement in the American Women's Economic Development Council and sales performance.[31]

On the issue of discrimination, Hertz's results are particularly interesting. Fully 60 percent of her respondents considered that to succeed, women had to be "better" than men—a better business person, more confident, and

[26]M. S. S. El-Namaki and J. C. M. Gerritson, "The Entrepreneurial Role of Women in Developing Countries: Entry and Performance Barriers," *RVB Research Paper* (March 1987).

[27]E. T. Pellegrino and B. L. Reece, "Perceived Formative and Operational Problems Encountered by Female Entrepreneurs in Retail and Service Firms," *Journal of Small Business Management* (April 1982), pp. 15-24.

[28]D. B. Bradley and H. L. Saunders, "Problems Women Face in Entrepreneurial Development," *Proceedings of Small Business Institute Directors Association* (San Antonio: February 1987).

[29]Hertz, *The Business Amazons*.

[30]D. E. Gumpert, "Wanted: Women Entrepreneurs for High-Tech Opportunities," *Working Women* (December 1985), pp. 37-39.

[31]R. N. Carter, "New Women Entrepreneurs Mean Business," *Review of Business* (Winter 1980), pp. 9-10.

better at absorbing stress. Moreover, it is interesting to note that 40 percent of Hertz's respondents felt that, far from being discriminated against, being a woman gave them a positive advantage over men.[32] This conclusion is supported by Gumpert, who found discrimination not to be a serious obstacle for high-tech women entrepreneurs.[33] By contrast, the only study which found significant problems for women is that of Goffee and Scase, which took as its theme the assumption of women's "subordination," and her responses to it.[34]

CONCLUSION

Individual motivations, family background, education, and work experience (as distinct from employment experience) are all factors which influence the decision to start a business, the choice of market, and the environment within which the business operates. Most of the empirical evidence to support these assumptions has been drawn from studies of male entrepreneurs.

Almost all of the studies of female entrepreneurs describe basic backgrounds and characteristics, with some comparisons drawn between female entrepreneurs and female executives.[35] However, background data often ignore the more subtle factors of "different cultural conditioning and experiences."[36]

From the evidence presented, it is proposed that while Cooper's model of entrepreneurship holds true for both men and women, the factors which contribute to the supply of entrepre-

neurs are also situationally and culturally bound. For any "minority" group, its position in society will be a significant factor in determining individual attitudes to entrepreneurial activity. Until very recently, the major role of women was seen in most Western economies by both men and women to be that of wife and mother. Indeed, even should they take employment, this was almost always in addition to their role as homemaker. It is not surprising, therefore, that the market-entry choices of female entrepreneurs differ from those of men. Moreover, whereas women often draw heavily on their experience as homemakers for ideas and for "managerial" experience, they have lacked many of the basic commercial networks which are associated with prior employment. Without this credibility base, many have failed to reach the starting gate.

However, the role of men and of women is changing rapidly within Western economies. As McDermott notes, "the exploding number of small businesses owned by women reflects both social and economic transformations. Women have crossed a wider range of economic barriers than at any time since World War II."[37] It is clear that women are beginning to feel more confident about their own skills, to build their own commercial networks, to establish credibility with customers, suppliers, and bank managers, and to start successful, albeit "traditional" (i.e., service and retail) businesses. The growth of women-owned businesses is a reflection of a changing society, and does not appear to reflect differences between the sexes in skills or motivation. It is likely that the profile of women entrepreneurs in the future will continue to match their changing situation, and move even closer to that of their male colleagues.

[32]Hertz, *The Business Amazons.*
[33]Gumpert, "Wanted: Women Entrepreneurs."
[34]Goffee and Scase, *Women in Charge.*
[35]D. L. Sexton and C. A. Kent, "Female Executives and Entrepreneurs: A Preliminary Comparison," *Entrepreneurial Research* (Babson, Mass.: 1981), pp. 40-55.
[36]N. R. Smith, G. McCain, and A. Warren, "Women Entrepreneurs Really Are Different: A Comparison of Constructed Ideal Types of Male and Female Entrepreneurs," *Entrepreneurship Research* (Babson, Mass.: 1982), pp. 68-77.

[37]McDermott, "The '80s Decade of Women Entrepreneurs."

[2]

VOLUME 6 NUMBER 2
1991

ANTECEDENT INFLUENCES ON WOMEN-OWNED BUSINESSES

Candida G. Brush and Robert D. Hisrich

While in 1972 fewer than 5 per cent of all US businesses were owned by women (US Bureau of Census, 1972), women-owned enterprises now account for more than 25 per cent of all small businesses[2]. Women, in fact, are starting businesses at twice the rate of men[2]. The recent increase in women-owned businesses is reflected by the fact that 75 per cent of women business-owners had owned their enterprises for less than ten years[3]. In the decade between 1972 and 1982, the number of self-employed women grew by 69 per cent, a rate of five times that of men[4]. From 1980 to 1985, women-owned non-farm sole proprietorships increase by 47.4 per cent, while men-owned non-farm sole proprietorships increased by only 31 per cent[5].

Despite this growth in the number of women-owned businesses, most remain small in terms of gross receipts, with the national average being $15,647 in 1985[5]. In addition, women-owned businesses tend to have fewer employees than those owned by men[5].

Given the short history and small size of most women-owned enterprises, there has been little research on factors affecting their growth. Research on women-owned enterprises instead has concentrated on describing characteristics of the business owner and the venture, while overall entrepreneurship research has addressed business management factors and the relationship between characteristics of women business-owners and venture success. Much of this literature, while not focused specifically on the woman business-owner,

suggests that the success of the enterprise is tied to the background and previous experience of the entrepreneur.

The notion of antecedent influences derives from a model which also includes two other broad components, incubator organisation and environmental factors, which together contribute to the decision to start a new venture[6]. While some studies have investigated the importance of antecedent influences in creation of women-owned businesses[7-11], none have examined the possible linkages between antecedent influences and survival or growth of women-owned enterprises. This article examines this notion in an attempt to determine key factors important to venture survival and growth by analysing the growth of 191 women-owned enterprises over a six-year period.

BACKGROUND

Research on Women Business-owners

Interest and research on women as business-owners is not only increasing but is now focusing on a wide range of issues. While earlier studies focused on the background, motivations, characteristics and business ventures of the woman entrepreneur, recent research has broadened to include investigations of such areas as management practices and overall business characteristics.

One early study of 20 female entrepreneurs identified several major motivations for starting a business; the need to achieve, the desire to be independent, the need for job satisfaction and economic necessity. These female entrepreneurs tended to have an autocratic style of management, with their

Journal of Managerial Psychology, Vol 6 No 2, 1991, pp 9-16, © MCB University Press
0268-3946

JOURNAL OF
MANAGERIAL
PSYCHOLOGY

major problem during start-up being credit discrimination. Underestimating operating and/or marketing costs was a subsequent problem[7].

Another study focusing on demographic characteristics, motivations and business problems of 21 women entrepreneurs found that they had particular problems with collateral, obtaining credit, and overcoming society's belief that women are not as serious as men about business[12].

The characteristics of women entrepreneurs and differences by type of business were explored in another study. The results indicated that women entrepreneurs had very supportive parents and husbands and were older and more educated than either the general populace or the respondents in previous studies. Female entrepreneurs in non-traditional business areas (finance, insurance, manufacturing and construction) also differed from their counterparts in more traditionally "female" business areas (retail and wholesale trade), with those in the more traditional areas having particular difficulty in acquiring external financial sources[13].

A study of 20 female entrepreneurs with one or more years operating a retail or service firm indicated that female entrepreneurs had problems in obtaining funds to start and operate the business as well as operational problems in the areas of record keeping, financial management, and advertising[14].

A nationwide study of women entrepreneurs indicated that the woman entrepreneur is typically the first-born child of middle-class parents who starts her first business venture in the service area at the age of 35 after obtaining a liberal arts degree and raising children. Typical weaknesses were in finance, marketing and business operations[9].

The basic characteristics, problems and prescriptions for success for women entrepreneurs who start and develop a new venture, as well as the mechanisms needed for doing this, were also researched. In addition to presenting methods for a potential entrepreneur, assessing their risk-taking ability and feelings on independence and control, aspects of starting a business such as developing a business plan, obtaining a bank loan or venture capital, and establishing a support system and network were discussed[15].

An examination of the management techniques of 58 women business-owners found 82 per cent of female entrepreneurs having no written plans or policies with experience in the field being related to sales and profits[16]. This finding is consistent with previous findings for all entrepreneurial organisations[17].

Another study examined the demographic and personality characteristics of 52 Florida women entrepreneurs. The women entrepreneurs surveyed had a high energy level and strong skills in influencing others. Personality and demographic profiles were generally consistent with other studies with respondents rating high on achievement, owning service businesses and being predominantly college-educated. Also, most of the business structures were informal[18]. However, a study assessing the locus of control of 108 Arizona women-owned real estate businesses found these businesses to be highly structured with objectives for growth established[19].

One study of 174 successful business-owners, comparing the psychological traits of female entrepreneurs with males, found that females were no less psychologically effective than males in the vocational pursuits of initiating, growing and managing a business venture[20]. A study of 154 Atlanta, Georgia, women entrepreneurs indicated that Georgia women entrepreneurs are essentially the same as women business-owners in other parts of the country in terms of motivation, business characteristics and backgrounds[21].

Time usage of women entrepreneurs was investigated in a study that found women with families have more problems allocating time between family and business[22]. This study also suggested the attempts to manage these two jobs may account for the lower profitability of some women-owned businesses.

A study of male and female new firm founders in Minnesota also found women entrepreneurs to be well-educated and about 30 years of age at the time of venture start-up. The small business founders who had a mentor, had 16 years of education, and prepared a business plan were also more likely to be successful[23].

A study on the career transitions of women to entrepreneurship found motivations differed by age group, with those under 30 years old being motivated by dissatisfaction with previous work experience while those over 30 were more frequently driven by a desire to be their own boss[10].

An in-depth study of the strategic management techniques of eight women entrepreneurs found that women practised niche or image-oriented marketing strategies, were conservative in financial practices,

VOLUME 6 NUMBER 2
1991

preferred to maintain small (versus large) businesses, had formalised structures and often employed self-learning to improve weak business skills[24]. Finally, the findings of a nationwide longitudinal study profiled the typical established enterprise as an eight-year-old service firm, employing ten or fewer employees and earning average revenues of less than $500,000 per year[25]. The biggest problems were cash flow, lack of time for administrative activities, and personnel. The entrepreneur averaged $50,000 personal income, maintained a controlling interest and was generally 40 years old with two children. About 30-40 per cent had failed or were out of business over the six-year period investigated while continuing ventures increased revenues at an average of 7 per cent per year.

RESEARCH ON BUSINESS SUCCESS FACTORS

Several studies have indicated the importance of previous experience in the field of the venture as a key to enterprise success. One study noted that the success of both entering and surviving was derived from prior experience while another found experience and education highly correlated to profits[26]. These findings were supported by those of a study of 1,000 companies (less than 5 per cent of which were female-owned) examining the characteristics of CEO's and corporate financial performance. The companies who had a founder who was well-educated tended to experience higher growth[27]. Similarly, a survey of 51 semiconductor firms found strong support for a causal relationship between early experience in organisational functions as an important basis for the entrepreneurs' perceived set of distinct competences, and also for their view of the manner in which the firm can successfully compete. In addition, a significant relationship was found between the level of formal education of the entrepreneur and the degree to which the firm followed the strategy of "first mover" — first in the market[28].

A study of the organisational effectiveness of 31 managers concluded that the entrepreneur must know the business, industry and organisation, and recommended that entrepreneurs should not enter a business in which they lacked experience. Also, communication, innovation and market orientation were likewise found to be important at business start-up[29].

Several other studies also indicated the importance of certain business skill competences. A longitudinal study of 218 men who left large firms to become self-employed indicated that those who were successful were able to develop new business skills and wear "several hats"[30]. A final study of 192 profitable and not so profitable businesses in Canada found that the firm's ability to manage cash effectively and ability to innovate were key performance factors[31].

Cooper *et al.*[32] studied 1,190 entrepreneurs and the survival and failure of their firms over a three-year period. This large-scale study found few systematic relationships between entrepreneurial types and survival/discontinuance variables, but did note differences in entrepreneurs (survivors were more often college graduates, middle-aged and male), differences in the process of starting new ventures (survivors were more often "pulled" rather than "pushed" to entrepreneurship and had full-time partners) and differences in the business (surviving businesses had more money and capital and were less likely to be retailing).

In 52 new technical firms in New York, performance was positively correlated with entrepreneurial experience and previous management level of occupational experience, while education level was negatively related. An opportunistic orientation was also marginally related to success[33]. Finally, a study comparing 32 unsuccessful and 38 successful entrepreneurs found psychological profiles in the two groups did not differ significantly. However, successful entrepreneurs were more often involved in production activities and had greater business knowledge before start-up[34].

Even though these areas of research have provided insights into the nature and characteristics of the woman entrepreneur and her venture, as well as the general entrepreneurial factors affecting venture performance, several important questions remain unanswered such as: what are the factors that affect the future success of women-owned ventures? What is the impact of the background of the woman entrepreneur on the growth and ultimate success of her business?

RESEARCH DESIGN

In an attempt to provide answers to these questions and, in effect, to determine the impact on growth of the antecedent influence of the woman founder, a questionnaire consisting of a variety of scaled, open-ended,

JOURNAL OF
MANAGERIAL
PSYCHOLOGY

rank order, dichotomous and multiple choice questions was sent to 344 women entrepreneurs who were able to be identified five years after a nationwide random sample of 468 women entrepreneurs. For a detailed discussion of the changes that occurred in these women-owned businesses over the five-year period refer to an earlier work by Hisrich and Brush[25]. Characteristics of the business, personal entrepreneurial considerations and demographic factors were assessed. For this study, discriminant analysis was used to determine factors affecting high/low growth classification of the business of the women entrepreneurs.

DEMOGRAPHIC COMPOSITION AND BACKGROUND

The typical woman entrepreneur operating an established venture is 46 years old, married, has two children over 20 years old and has operated her typically service-oriented business for eight years. She is college-educated, usually in the area of liberal arts, and has had occupational experience in the service area. Her personal income averages $50,000 per year and she maintains a controlling interest in the business which is typically her first entrepreneurial effort.

The characteristics of an established venture owned by the typical woman business owner are: gross revenues of $100,000, start-up funding mainly through personal assets, and a total investment of $5,000 at start-up. This is consistent with statistics from the US Small Business Administration that indicate women often start their venture with less than $10,000; about half the amount used by men[5]. Most ventures rely on profit reinvestment and bank loans for current financing. The biggest business problems are lack of adequate time for administrative activities, cash flow, and personnel. The planning is conducted by the entrepreneur alone and is frequently strategic in nature.

These findings indicate that the majority of the businesses operated by women entrepreneurs have been "moderately successful", having increases in revenues of about 7 per cent per year. Similar to findings by Cooper *et al.*[32] between 30 and 40 per cent of the original sample had failed or were no longer being operated by the founder. This is a much lower failure rate than the frequently mentioned national average figure of 75 per cent of all new businesses failing in the first five years. While the failure rate may be lower, the size of the typical woman-owned enterprise

Previous occupational experience
Previous experience in the field of the venture
Nature of most recent occupation
Education
Level of education attained
Field of undergraduate study
Field of graduate education study
Business skills
Financial skills
Dealing with people
Marketing and sales
Idea generation — product innovation
Business operations
Organising and planning
Personal factors
Achievement motivation
Job satisfaction motivation
Opportunity motivation
Independence motivation
Age of entrepreneur at start-up
Mentor (yes or no)

TABLE I.
Antecedent Influences of the Woman Business-Owner

remains small with ten or fewer employees and gross revenues of less than $500,000. However, the geographic and market scope of the business is expanding with the woman entrepreneur continuing to improve her business skills while practising strategic planning.

GENERAL FINDINGS

Respondents were initially classified into groups based on their venture's performance over the six-year period occurring between the two surveys. "Growth" included several factors such as an increase in sales and income, but was primarily measured by an increase in number of full-time employees.

Discriminant analysis was used to determine if group classification could be

Variable	Coefficient
Any previous experience in field	0.57106**
Opportunity motivation	0.32574*
Financial skills	0.61481*
Dealing with people skills	0.41035*
Idea generation-product development	0.36907*
Business operation skills	−0.33875*
*p= <0.05; **p= <0.10	

TABLE II.
Standardised Discriminant Function Coefficients in Business and out of Business Analyst

VOLUME 6 NUMBER 2
1991

Actual group	Number of cases	Predicted	Group membership
Group 1. Out of business	39	6 (15.4%)	33 (84.6%)
Group 3. In business	133	11 (8.3%)	122 (91.7%)
Percentage of "grouped" cases correctly classified = 74.42			

TABLE III.
Classification Results in Business and out of Business

predicted by the antecedent-influences of the woman entrepreneur. Consistent with *Cooper's model, antecedent influences were defined generally by four groups of variables*: education, occupational experience, personal factors, and business skills (see Table I).

In the analysis, 172 valid cases were examined. First a two group linear discriminant analysis was conducted between those in business and those out of business. The goal was to determine which variables were important to the survival of the woman-owned enterprises.

Table II shows all the variables that entered the stepwise discriminant function. The standardised coefficients indicating the relative importance of the variables in the function clearly show that financial skills and previous experience ($p = <0.05$) in the area of the venture made the greatest contributions. The overall discriminant function with a Wilks Lambda of 0.835 and a statistically significant chi square value of 11.898.

The original cases used to develop the function were then classified. The results (depicted in Table III) indicate that the percentage of respondents correctly classified is 74.4 per cent. The proportional chance criterion was then used to assess prediction accuracy. If one did not use the function, proportional chance of accurate classification would be 0.75 per cent making the classification at 74 per cent not acceptable at a statistically significant level.

This gives rise to the question: given that the business of the woman entrepreneur survived, which variables were important to greater growth and which ones were not? A second linear discriminant analysis was run between the no growth and growth businesses. The standardised coefficients of all the variables that enter the function are shown in Table IV. Financial skills and previous experience in the area of the venture along with independence motivation made the greatest contribution, with four of the seven variables highly significant.

The overall function yielded a Wilks Lambda of 0.6149 and a statistically

significant chi square. Table V indicates that the percentage of respondents correctly classified was 84.2 per cent. When the proportional chance criteria is applied to assess accuracy, the percentage correctly classified would be 71 per cent making the classification percentage of the function acceptable.

DISCUSSION

Clearly the overall results of this study support those of previous ones. This study shows that the woman entrepreneur who has previous experience in the field of her venture has a better chance of successfully expanding her venture than the woman who does not. This supports the general contention of previous works[26].

Of lesser significance, yet still important to the successful establishment of women-owned businesses, were other *business skills* — dealing with people, idea generation and business operations skills. The importance of strength in idea generation and dealing with people to business establishment supports previous findings that innovation, market niche and creativity are keys to success[24]. Implicit in a strong opportunity motivation is the importance of looking to the need in the market rather than being caught up in satisfying more personal needs for

Variable	Coefficient
Any previous experience in field	0.7157*
Independence motivation	−0.7936*
Financial skills	−0.8722*
Dealing with people skills	0.4521**
Organising and planning skills	0.4841**
Level of education	0.5130**
Major field of graduate study	0.3711**
*$p = <0.001$; **$p = <0.05$	

TABLE IV.
Standardised Discriminant Function Coefficients: No Growth versus Growth Businesses

JOURNAL OF
MANAGERIAL
PSYCHOLOGY

Actual group	Number of cases	Predicted	Group membership
Group 2. No growth	47	44 (93.6%)	3 (6.4%)
Group 3. Growth	10	6 (60%)	4 (40%)
Percentage of "grouped" cases correctly classified = 84.21			

TABLE V.
Classification Results: No Growth versus Growth

achievement or intrinsic self-reward in the early stages of developing a business. This supports previous findings of there being little relationship between psychological attributes (risk taking, achievement, level of control) and financial performance[27].

The correlation of business operations skills with the out of business group is an enigma. Perhaps this is an issue of the relative importance of this skill to the other skills. In other words, the emphasis for the woman entrepreneur needs to be on creating the idea, seeking the opportunity and obtaining cash resources before concentrating on day-to-day operations. This supports previous speculation that these factors are important to the process of venture growth[32].

Experience in the field of the venture is also a key predictor of growth versus no growth. The level of education and, to a lesser degree, major field of graduate study are also important and support previous research findings that educational level is correlated to success of the business venture[27].

The fact that independence, motivation and financial skills were related to no growth in women-owned businesses is somewhat surprising. However, this again may be due to relativity in the context of other important business skills (dealing with people, organising and planning) related to growth businesses. We can speculate that women entrepreneurs who learn to manage their businesses through people, and learn to organise and plan are more successful. These women probably have learned to delegate financial tasks, while the women entrepreneurs who did not experience growth tend to rely more on their personal expertise in running their business. It appears that for a woman entrepreneur to expand her enterprise, she must learn to manage people, delegate and plan. This supports previous findings that more succesful entrepreneurs are able to wear several hats and learn new skills[28].

CONCLUSION

The findings of this study indicate that the antecedent influences of the woman entrepreneur do in fact affect business survival and growth. For the woman entrepreneur establishing a venture, previous experience in the field of the venture, financial skills, strength in dealing with people, and idea generation combined with market opportunity motivation are keys to survival. In differentiating between no growth and low growth ventures some of the same antecedent influences are important: previous experience in the area of the venture and dealing with people. In addition, ability to organise and plan and the educational field of study are contributing factors to growth of the woman-owned enterprise.

The fact that antecedent influences do impact on the success and growth of the woman-owned enterprise supports other findings, suggesting that the key skills needed in expanding a venture may not be gender-based. The antecedent influences of the successful woman entrepreneur are similar to those of successful male entrepreneurs with the factors contributing to success and survival being the same.

The implications of these findings should be looked at in terms of both survival and growth. In terms of survival, two things are important. First, the aspiring woman business-owner should, above all, try to gain experience in the field of her proposed venture. This is an important factor, even though there will continue to be exceptions to the rule as was the case of the nurse who started a multi-million dollar fashion accessories manufacturing business.

Second, the woman entrepreneur should make every effort to obtain strong financial skills. Financial controls and cash management are crucial to new venture survival along with dealing with people, negotiating, managing, and personal selling. The woman entrepreneur should be careful to assess her motivations for starting the venture. A desire for independence will not

VOLUME 6 NUMBER 2
1991

always guarantee success. Creating an idea and being motivated by the opportunity to have that idea succeed in the market are also important factors in achieving venture success[17,35].

Once the business has survived, the findings of our study suggest that in addition to the necessity of occupational experience, the strategic origins correlated to growth (versus no growth) are slightly different. The more successful woman entrepreneur often has a higher level of education. In addition, since different business skills are important in differentiating between no growth and growth enterprises women business-owners with a broader perspective, those who are able to manage and delegate by working through people, have a better chance of success. Consistent with Cooper's model, this study also supports the previous findings that a large number of the women entrepreneurs had planned strategically[25]. Also, a high percentage (80 per cent) of the women entrepreneurs had attended seminars in order to learn business skills and 65 per cent had utilised expert advice. Given this propensity and the skills need, consultants, teachers and small-business advisers should offer women business-owners instruction in cash management and work on developing their financial and interpersonal skills.

While the present study offers valuable insight into the success of women-owned enterprises, further research is needed, particularly on the effects of Cooper's model on survival and growth. Some specific questions need to be addressed. What are the characteristics (geographic location, products, size) of organisations that employ women who become entrepreneurs? Are these organisations similar or different from those that "incubate" male entrepreneurs? What is the relationship of incubator organisation experience to survival and growth of women-owned business? Finally, how do ventures created by women coming from a full-time work status survive and grow compared to those of women who were either not working, employed part-time or unemployed? Answers to these and other questions will provide the framework for understanding the effects of different types of occupational experiences and assess the similarities and differences between men and women in the process of venture creation, growth and success.

References

1. US Bureau of Census, *Survey of Women-owned Businesses*, Washington DC , 1972.

2. US Government Printing Office, *State of Small Business: A Report of the President*, Washington DC, 1985.

3. US Department of Commerce, *The Bottom Line — Unequal Enterprise in America, Report of President's Task Force on Women Business Owners*, Washington DC, 1979.

4. US Small Business Administration, *Annual Report for Year 1984*, Washington DC, 1984.

5. US Small Business Administration, *Small Business in the American Economy*, Office of Advocacy, 1988.

6. Cooper, A.C., "Strategic Management: New Ventures and Small Business", *Long Range Planning*, Vol. 14 No. 5, 1981, pp. 39-45.

7. Schwartz, E.B., "Entrepreneurship: A New Female Frontier", *Journal of Contemporary Business*, Winter 1979, pp. 47-76.

8. Geoffee, R. and Scase, R., *Women in Charge: The Experiences of Female Entrepreneurs*, George Allen and Unwin, London, 1985.

9. Hisrich, R.D. and Brush, C.G., "The Woman Entrepreneur: Implications of Family, Educational and Occupational Experience", *Proceedings*, 1983 Conference on Entrepreneurship, April 1983, pp. 255-70.

10. Kaplan, E., "Women Entrepreneurs: Constructing a Framework to Examine Venture Success and Failure", *Proceedings*, 1988 Conference on Entrepreneurship, 1988, pp. 643-65.

11. Birley, S., "Female Entrepreneurs: Are They Really Different?", *Journal of Small Business Management*, Vol. 27 No. 1, January 1989, pp. 32-7.

12. Hisrich, R.D. and O'Brien, M, "The Woman Entrepreneur from a Business and Sociological Perspective", *Proceedings*, 1981 Conference on Entrepreneurship, 1981, pp. 21-39.

13. Hisrich, R.D. and O'Brien, M., "The Woman Entrepreneur as a Reflection of the Type of Business", *Proceedings*, 1982 Conference on Entrepreneurship, June 1982, pp. 54-67.

14. Pellegrino, E.T. and Reece, B.L., "Perceived Formation and Operational Problems Encountered by Female Entrepreneurs in Retail Service Firms", *Journal of Small Business Management*, April 1982, pp. 15-24.

15. Hisrich, R.D. and Brush, C.G., *The Woman Entrepreneur: Starting, Managing, and Financing a Successful New Business*, Lexington Books, Lexington, Ma, 1986.

JOURNAL OF
MANAGERIAL
PSYCHOLOGY

16. Cuba, R., Decenzo, D. and Anish, A., "Management Practices of Successful Female Business Owners", *American Journal of Small Business,* Vol. VIII No. 2, October-December 1983, pp. 40-5.

17. Stevenson, H. and Gumpert, D., "The Heart of Entrepreneurship", *Harvard Business Review,* March-April 1985, pp. 85-94.

18. Neider, L., "A Preliminary Investigation of Female Entrepreneurs in Florida", *Journal of Small Business Management,* Vol. 25 No.3, July 1987, pp. 22-9.

19. Mescon, T.S., Stevens, G.E. and Vozikis, G.S., "Women as Entrepreneurs: An Empirical Evaluation", *Wisconsin Small Business Forum,* Vol. 2 No. 2, Winter 1983-1984, pp. 7-17.

20. Sexton, D. and Bowman-Upton, N., "Sexual Stereotyping of Female Entrepreneurs: A Comparative Psychological Trait Analysis of Female and Male Entrepreneurship", *Proceedings,* 1988 Conference on Entrepreneurship, 1988, pp. 654-5.

21. Scott, C.E., "Why More Women are Becoming Entrepreneurs", *Journal of Small Business Management,* Vol. 24 No. 4, 1986, pp. 37-44.

22. Longstreth, M., Stafford, K. and Mauldin, T., "Self Employed Women and Their Families: Time Use and Socio-economic Characteristics", *Journal of Small Business Management,* Vol. 25 No. 3, 1987, pp. 30-7.

23. Egge, K., "Expectations vs Reality Among Founders of Recent Start-ups", *Frontiers in Entrepreneurs — Proceedings of the Babson College Conference on Entrepreneurship,* April 1987, pp. 322-36.

24. Chaganti, R., "Management in Women-Owned Enterprises", *Journal of Small Business Management,* Vol. 2 No. 4, 1984, pp. 18-29.

25. Hisrich, R.D. and Brush, C.G., "Women Entrepreneurs: A Longitudinal Study", *Frontiers in Entrepreneurship — Proceedings of the Babson College Conference on Entrepreneurship,* April 1987, pp. 187-99.

26. Vesper, K.H., *New Venture Strategies,* rev. ed., Prentice-Hall, Englewood Cliffs, NJ, 1990, pp. 27-55.

27. Begley, T.M. and Boyd, D.P., "Company and Chief Executive Officer Characteristics Related to Financial Performance in Smaller Businesses", *Frontiers in Entrepreneurship: Proceedings of the Babson College Conference on Entrepreneurship,* 1985, pp. 452-66.

28. Boeker, W., "Strategic Origins and Environmental Imprinting at Founding", *Academy of Management Proceedings — Best Papers,* New Orleans, 1987, pp. 150-3.

29. Smith, K.G. and Gannon, M.J., "Organizational Effectiveness in Entrepreneurially and Professionally Managed Firms", *Journal of Small Business Management,* Vol. 25 No. 1, 1987, pp. 14-21.

30. Kemelgor, B.H. , "A Longitudinal Analysis of the Transition from 'Organizational Man' to Entrepreneur", *Academy of Management Proceedings — Best Papers,* 1985, pp. 67-70.

31. Chaganti, R. and Chaganti, R., "A Profile of Profitable and Not so Profitable Small Businesses", *Journal of Small Business Management,* Vol. 21 No. 3, 1983, pp. 43-51.

32. Cooper, A.C., Dunkelberg, W.C. and Woo, C.Y., "Survival and Failure: A Longitudinal Study", *Proceedings,* 1988 Conference on Entrepreneurship, 1988, pp. 225-37.

33. Stuart, R.W. and Abetti, P.A., "Field Study of Technical Ventures-Part III: The Impact of Entrepreneurial and Management Experience on Early Performance", *Proceedings,* 1988 Conference on Entrepreneurship, 1988, pp. 177-93.

34. Lorrain, J. and Dussault, L., "Relation between Psychological Characteristics, Administrative Behaviors, and Success of Founders at the Start-Up Stage", *Proceedings,* Conference on Entrepreneurship, 1988, pp. 150-64.

35. Timmons, J., *New Venture Creation,* 2nd Ed., Richard, D. Irwin, Homewood, Illinois, 1985.

Robert D. Hisrich is Professor of Entrepreneurial Studies at Tulsa University, Oklahoma, and Candida G. Brush is a doctoral student at Boston University, Massachusetts, USA.

[3]

1042-2587-92-164$1.50
Copyright 1992 by
Baylor University

Research on Women Business Owners: Past Trends, a New Perspective and Future Directions

Candida G. Brush

The number of women starting and owning their own businesses has grown dramatically over the past decade. Concurrent with this trend, there has been an increase in the number of research studies focusing on or including women business owners in their samples. This paper reviews empirical research studies on women business owners and their ventures, classifies the studies in a framework, and summarizes trends emerging from this research. To guide future research, a new perspective on women-owned businesses is proposed and research questions, methods, and implications are discussed.

The increase in women business owners[1] is apparent in the U.S. economy. Since 1970, the percentage of businesses owned by women has increased from 5% to 30%, (*New Economic Realities*, 1988), representing nearly three million of the nation's 12 million small businesses (*Report to the President*, 1985). According to the Internal Revenue Service, from 1977-1985, the number of women-owned sole proprietorships nearly doubled from 1.9 million to 3.3 million, an increase of about 9.4% per year versus 4.3% for men during the same period (*New Economic Realities*, 1988). Estimates are that women are starting businesses at a rate more than twice that of men (*New Economic Realities*, 1988). Similarly, a recent survey released by the Census Bureau notes that the number of women-owned firms has increased from 2.6 million in 1982 to 4.1 million in 1987; a 57% increase (*Nation's Business*, April, 1991).

Even though a smaller percentage of women are self-employed overall, about 8.6%

---

1. The discrepancies in definitions, interpretation of terms, and availability of data create difficulties in accurately identifying the number of female business creators and owners. A statement by the Small Business Administration supports this: "There is no total count of female operated businesses in the U.S." (*Report to the President*, 1985, p. 295). The Internal Revenue Service and the Bureau of Census collect different information on women business owners, and the Small Business Administration estimates the number of businesses operated by women based on a combination of this data. Further, researchers do not often distinguish between "small business owner" (one who is self-employed but did not create or innovate a new venture [Sexton & Bowman, 1984]), and "entrepreneur" in the classical sense (one who takes the initiative, organizes the social and economic resources and accepts the risk of failure [Shapero, 1975]). Given so few studies on women entrepreneurs or women business owners in general, it is difficult to know whether the lack of this distinction has made a difference in the results of the research studies. For purposes of this paper, the term "woman business owner" will be used to encompass the other terms noted above.

versus 14.6% for men (Haber, Lamas, & Lichtenstein, 1987), women-owned businesses are contributing revenues, services, and jobs to the economy. It was estimated in 1988 that women-owned businesses had contributed more than $250 billion to the national economy by 1983 (*New Economic Realities,* 1988). Gross receipts of women-owned businesses are on the increase as well, rising from a .3% ($23 billion) contribution to national gross receipts in 1972, to more than 10% ($98 billion) in 1986 (Thierren, Carson, Hamilton, & Hurlock, 1986). Similarly, the SBA reports that receipts from women-owned sole proprietorships grew by $31 billion between 1977 and 1987 compared to a decline of over $8 billion for men (*The State of Small Business,* 1990).

Despite the tremendous growth in the number of women-owned enterprises and their increasing aggregate impact on society and the economy, there are few studies researching women business owners in general, comparing them to other groups of employed or non-working women, or comparing them to men. Most of the research to date on business ownership has focused on males (Collins & Moore, 1964; Roberts, 1968; Hornaday & Aboud, 1971; Kent, Sexton, & Vesper, 1982). This is not surprising since a higher percentage of men have started and operated their own businesses. Even though women have owned their own enterprises throughout history (Anderson & Zinsser, 1988), public policy and popular press interest in the phenomenon of women as business owners is relatively recent.

Investigation of women business owners as academic research subjects developed during the past decade. The earliest studies emerged in the late 1970s, and sought to distinguish the psychological and sociological characteristics of women business owners from male business owners, assuming there were few differences between males and females (Schrier, 1975; Schwartz, 1976). Other studies focused on women in male-dominated industries (Hisrich & O'Brien, 1981).

The largest study in the U.S. was produced by the President's Interagency Task Force (*The Bottom Line,* 1979) and identified instances of discrimination and barriers encountered by women business owners in their attempts to start new businesses. Since the completion of this report, the topic of women business owners has emerged as an area of more popular interest and research effort.

Research over the past ten years has shown there are similarities between male and female business owners across demographic characteristics, business skills, and some psychological traits (Hagan, Rivchun, & Sexton, 1989). However, differences between male and female business owners have been found in educational and occupational background, motivations for business ownership, business goals, business growth, and approaches to business creation. To date, these differences have been recognized but not fully explained.

This paper proposes a new perspective that offers a basis for interpreting unexplained gender-based differences between male and female business owners. This perspective, referred to as the "Integrated Perspective," is rooted in psychological and sociological theories that submit women's social orientations are more focused on relationships. This new perspective suggests that women view their businesses as an interconnected system of relationships instead of a separate economic unit in a social world (Kent, Sexton, & Vesper, 1982). This system of relationships composing the business is "integrated" into the woman business owner's life. The woman business owner is at the center of a network of various relationships that include family, community, and business. In other words, when a woman starts or acquires her own business, in her view she is not creating/acquiring a separate economic entity, rather she is "integrating" a new system of business-related relationships into her life.

In order to show the need for this new perspective and to substantiate its roots, this paper first reviews academic research on women business owners and their ventures, and

Table 1

Journals Publishing Studies on Women Business Owners, 1977–1991

Journals	Number of Articles	Percent
Frontiers of Entrepreneurship Research		
(Proceedings of the Babson College Conference)	14	24.5%
Journal of Small Business Management	14	24.5%
Entrepreneurship Theory and Practice		
(formerly *American Journal of Small Business*)	5	9%
Journal of Business Venturing	5	9%
USASBE Proceedings	3	5%
Other (*Entrepreneurship and Regional Development*,		
ICSB Proceedings, *Academy of Management Journal*,		
Sociological Review, Wisconsin Small Business Forum,		
book chapters)	16	28%
Total	57	100%

summarizes trends emerging from the findings of previous studies. Second, the Integrated Perspective is described, and questions and implications for future research on women business owners are discussed. This review is representative but not comprehensive and is limited to academic research in the field of entrepreneurship.

RESEARCH ON WOMEN BUSINESS OWNERS

Articles published since 1975 were identified by reviewing past issues of entrepreneurship journals such as the *American Journal of Small Business*,[2] *Journal of Business Venturing*, and the *Journal of Small Business Management*.[3] In addition, book chapters, other relevant journals such as the *Academy of Management Journal*, the conference proceedings including the Babson College Proceedings, *Frontiers of Entrepreneurship Research*, and United States Association for Small Business and Entrepreneurship (USASBE) Conference Proceedings were identified from bibliographies. A total of 57 empirical articles were reviewed and evaluated for this discussion.

Generally, only a small percentage of studies in the field of entrepreneurship have focused on women and their businesses. For instance, the 1987 issue of *Frontiers of Entrepreneurship Research*, which categorized the 227 studies published between 1980 and 1987 by topic, showed that only 13 published studies investigated women and minorities (Churchill & Hornaday, 1987). While this appears to be a relatively small percentage, in fact this publication has included a very high number of studies of women business owners compared to the other popular journals. Table 1 reflects the number of articles researching women business owners in entrepreneurship journals and conference proceedings in recent years.

---

2. This journal is now called *Entrepreneurship Theory and Practice*.
3. These publications are generally accepted as those focusing on aspects of business ownership and entrepreneurship (Brockhaus, 1988). Conference proceedings include United States Association for Small Business and Entrepreneurship, and International Conference for Small Business.

In order to examine the major trends emerging from previous studies, the 57 articles were classified according to Gartner's (1985) framework for new venture creation. This framework was selected because it clearly identifies the four key components of venture creation and ownership—individual, environment, organization, and process[4]—which are common to most entrepreneurship frameworks (Vesper, 1980; Kent, Sexton, & Vesper, 1982; Timmons, 1985; Stevenson & Gumpert, 1985). Classification of articles was based on title, purpose, and major research theme as stated in the papers. Table 2 contains a listing of authors who have conducted studies on women business owners and is organized by topic according to Gartner's (1985) framework.

Consistent with most research in entrepreneurship, the greatest number of studies of women business owners have focused on the "individual": demographic background, psychological characteristics, motivations, and educational and occupational experiences (Churchill & Hornaday, 1987).

Recent studies have investigated aspects of the organization such as strategy, problems, and management style. Start-up activities, such as acquisition of capital and networking behaviors, are other new areas of research. Only three studies have examined environmental factors (economic) as they related to women-owned businesses.

METHODOLOGY EMPLOYED IN RESEARCH ON WOMEN BUSINESS OWNERS

The most popular research design was survey, with the majority of these being descriptive studies. As indicated in Table 3, 36 studies employed a cross-sectional research design, nine of which were national in scope, while the remaining studies were limited to a particular state or region. Twelve studies employed in-depth personal interview techniques, two were longitudinal, and three utilized archival or secondary data bases. The prevalence of descriptive cross-sectional research is not surprising, given that the objectives of early efforts investigating women business owners were to describe their characteristics and activities, similar to early research on males (Kent, Sexton, & Vesper, 1982).

A minority of the studies reported the use of random sampling techniques, with the majority choosing convenience samples of women business owners who were personally known to the researcher, such as SBDC clients, students, women's networking, or business associations (see Table 3). This is to be expected in that there are no comprehensive national listings of women business owners, and more inclusive state lists have only been collected within the past five years. Further, nearly 50% of the studies sampled only women business owners and did not use a comparison group, whereas nearly 26% did use men as a comparison group. The more recent studies have contrasted women business owners to other groups, men or women executives, while earlier studies compared women business owners to what was known about male business owners (see for example, Schrier, 1975; Humphreys & McClung, 1981; Hisrich & Brush, 1982).

Consistent with research on male entrepreneurs, the bulk of the research to date has centered on individual characteristics (Kent, Sexton, & Vesper, 1982). As a result, the primary theory bases used have come from psychology (see for example, Waddell,

---

4. The components of this model include several variables, most of which have been empirically researched. Generally, "individual" includes demographics, background, educational and occupational experiences, and psychological characteristics. "Organization" includes strategy elements, internal organization characteristics, type of business, structure, and problems. "Process" includes opportunity identification, resource acquisition, organization building, managing of the business, and responding to the environment. "Environment" includes resources, government, legal, industry, and technology factors (Gartner, 1985, p. 702).

Table 2

Research on Women Business Owners Classified in Gartner's New Venture Creation Framework*

Individual	Environment	Organization	Process
Schrier (1975)	Buttner & Rosen (1988)	Gomolka (1977)	Sexton & Bowman (1986)
Schwartz (1976)	Buttner & Rosen (1989)	Humphreys & McClung	Longstreth, Stafford &
The Bottom Line (1978)	Riding & Swift (1990)	(1981)	Mauldin (1987)
DeCarlo & Lyons (1979)		Hisrich & O'Brien (1982)	Egge (1987)
Charbonneau (1981)		Pellegrino & Reece (1982)	Nelson (1987)
Sexton & Kent (1981)		Cuba, DeCenzo & Anish	Carsrud, Gaglio & Olm
Humphreys & McClung		(1983)	(1987)
(1981)		Chaganti (1986)	Olm, Carsrud & Alvey
Hisrich & O'Brien (1981)		Hisrich & Brush (1984,	(1987)
Welsch & Young (1982)		1987)	Cromie & Hayes (1988)
Smith, McCain & Warren		Neider (1987)	Aldrich, Reece & Dubini
(1982)		Kemp (1988)	(1989)
Hisrich (1983)		Brush & Hisrich (1988)	Smeltzer & Fann (1989)
Hisrich & Brush (1983)		Brush (1990)	Nelson (1989)
Mescon, Stevens & Vozikis		Kalleberg & Leicht (1991)	Chrisman, Carsrud, DeCastro
(1983–4)			& Herron (1990)
Watkins & Watkins (1983)			Stoner, Hartman & Arora
Waddell (1983)			(1990)
Geoffee & Scase (1985)			
Hisrich & Brush (1985)			
Honig-Haftel & Martin			
(1986)			
Scott (1986)			
Pearson, Bracker &			
Mescon (1986)			
Sexton & Bowman (1986)			
Carsrud & Olm (1986)			
Hisrich & Brush (1987)			
Birley, Moss & Sanders			
(1987)			
Neider (1987)			
Longstreth, Stafford &			
Mauldin (1987)			
Masters & Meier (1988)			
Moryia, Judd & File (1988)			
Kaplan (1988)			
Holmquist & Sundin (1988)			
Sexton & Bowman-Upton			
(1990)			
Scherer, Brodzinski &			
Wiebe (1990)			
Holmquist & Sundin (1990)			
Dugan, Feeser & Plaschka			
(1990)			

* Four studies were classified under two headings because they addressed two aspects: Humphreys & McClung, 1981; Sexton & Bowman, 1986; Longstreth, Stafford, & Mauldin, 1987; and Neider, 1987.

1983; Sexton & Bowman, 1986), and trait and psychoanalytic theories are most often employed. For measures, Rotter's Locus of Control Scales, Edwards Personality Schedule, and Jackson Personality Inventory are commonly used (see Table 4). More recently, social interaction and network theories from sociology have been the basis for investi-

Table 3

Design and Sample Selection in Research on Women Business Owners

Research Design		Number	Percent
Mail Survey, Cross sectional		36	63%
Local/State Region	27		
National	8		
Multi-Country	1		
Personal Interview		12	21%
Archival, Database		3	5%
Longitudinal (national)		2	4%
Case Studies		2	4%
Phone Interview		1	1.5%
Experimental Design		1	1.5%
Total		57	100%

Samples		Number	Percent
U.S. Women Business Owners		26	46%
Men & Women Business Owners		14	25%
Women Business Owners from U.S.			
and/or Foreign Countries		7	12%
Women Business Owners & Other Groups		7	12%
Women Managers	3		
Minorities	2		
Students	1		
Part-time WBOs	1		
Other Samples (Loan Officers, Students)		3	5%
Total		57	100%

gation of start-up processes (see for example, Carsrud, Gaglio, & Olm, 1987; Aldrich, Reece, & Dubini, 1989; Nelson, 1989).

It is notable that one-third of the studies in this review neither explicitly stated that the research was connected to a theory base nor did they indicate if they were exploratory or designed to generate theory (see Table 4). Further, many of the studies using scales and measures from the field of psychology did not explicitly note the linkage between the theory and the research.

Statistical analysis techniques employed have been consistent with the descriptive focus of the research with nearly one-half of the studies reporting only frequency distributions. Again, it is the more recent works that have employed regression analysis, factor, cluster, or discriminant techniques. Qualitative studies employing qualitative analysis are similarly more recent and also few in number.

In sum, the methodologies employed most often for research on women business owners have been cross-sectional surveys that used convenience samples, analyzed data with descriptive statistics, and frequently did not link the research to a theory base. In short, rigor is lacking in much of this work. Other methodological problems noted were similar to those described by Stevenson (1986) and included infrequent instrument validation, reliance on a single convenience sample, and one source and method of data collection. Many studies tended to generalize behaviors and characteristics of women

Table 4

Theory Bases and Statistical Analysis Used in Research on Women Business Owners

Stated Theory Base	Number	Percent
None Stated*	22	39%
Psychology Theories (i.e. Trait, Psychoanalytic Theory)	15	26%
Sociology (i.e. Network, Social Interaction)	10	17%
Exploratory (Grounded Theory)	6	11%
Business Strategy & Policy (Problem Solving, Decision-making)	4	7%
Total	57	100%

Statistical Analysis Techniques	Number	Percent
Descriptive Statistics	25	44%
Descriptive and χ^2, or Correlation, or t-test	17	30%
Multiple Regression, MANOVA, ANOVA	6	11%
Factor, Cluster, Discriminant Analysis	4	7%
Qualitative Analysis	4	7%
Logit Model	1	1%
Total	57	100%

* Many articles did not explicitly link the empirical study to a theory. Instead, the research was frequently justified by a "lack of information about women business owners." It is these studies that are in this category.

business owners across different types of women, such as new business creators and family business successors, and business characteristics such as age, industry, and size.

Despite these problems, there are several instances of careful and rigorous work in more recent studies. For example, work matching samples of males and females to examine psychological traits (Welch & Young, 1982; Carsrud & Olm, 1985; Sexton & Bowman, 1986; Masters & Meier, 1988) has proved fruitful in distinguishing particular areas where men and women business owners do differ. Particular issues affecting women business owners have been highlighted in careful qualitative work by Cromie & Hayes (1988); whereas cross-cultural sampling (Aldrich, Reece, & Dubini, 1989), development of a logit model (Kalleberg & Leicht, 1990), and testing of social interaction theory (Nelson, 1989) are representative of high quality methodological work. While the bulk of the research to date has not been rigorously performed, it appears there is a trend toward more careful methodology based on these more recent studies.

GENERAL FINDINGS EMERGING FROM RESEARCH ON WOMEN BUSINESS OWNERS

Individual Characteristics of Women Business Owners

It is generally agreed that women business owners are more similar to than different from men across psychological and demographic dimensions such as motivations (independence, achievement, job satisfaction) for starting a business (Schrier, 1975; Schwartz, 1976; Welsch & Young, 1982; Geoffee & Scase, 1985; Hisrich & Brush,

1983; Chaganti, 1986; Longstreth, Stafford, & Mauldin, 1987). The majority of studies examining personality and psychological characteristics have employed reliable and valid instruments to compare samples of males and females. These studies conclude that women business owners are more similar than different from males across personality factors (Sexton & Bowman, 1986), risk-taking propensity (Masters & Meier, 1988), and psychological characteristics (Welsch & Young, 1982; Dugan, Feeser, & Plaschka, 1990). Sexton and Bowman (1986, 1990) have found in the course of several years' research that the only significant gender-based trait differences are that women business owners reflect a lower risk-taking propensity and energy level.

In spite of these conclusions, it is notable that many of the standard psychological instruments employed by researchers to measure entrepreneurial traits of women business owners are derived from research on samples of male entrepreneurs (Hurley, 1991). For example, McClelland's (1961) work on need for achievement as a motivation for entrepreneurship emerged from research on men. Similarly, Collins and Moore's (1969) work on motivations investigated male founders of manufacturing firms and concluded that these individuals had unresolved fears of their fathers which motivated them to pursue autonomy through business creation. Measuring instruments flowing from this work were similarly developed using samples of males (Kent, Sexton, & Vesper, 1982). The fact that these instruments were developed on male populations suggests that they may not fully explain the personality traits of female business owners.

Some demographic characteristics of women business owners also are similar to those of men. For example, marital status (married), age (30–45), birth order (first born) (Charbonneau, 1981; Watkins & Watkins, 1983; Hisrich & Brush, 1983; Sexton & Kent, 1983; Mescon, Stevens, & Vozikis, 1983/4; Honig-Haftel & Martin, 1986; Neider, 1987), and having a self-employed father (Hisrich & Brush, 1983; Watkins & Watkins, 1983; Birley, Moss, & Sanders, 1987) are not significantly different between women and men business owners. However, it is notable that a higher proportion of males tend to be married than females (Stevenson, 1986), and a higher percentage of spouses of male business owners did not work compared to spouses of female business owners (Honig-Haftel & Martin, 1986).

Differences between male and female business owners in individual characteristics have been noted especially in background factors such as work experience and education. Several studies found that women business owners had previous work experience in teaching, retail sales, office administration, or secretarial areas (Hisrich & Brush, 1983; Welsch & Young, 1983; Scott, 1986; Neider, 1987) rather than executive management, scientific, or technical positions more typical of men (Watkins & Watkins, 1982; Stevenson, 1986). Likewise, research on career paths has found that for women, careers are more frequently interrupted (Kaplan, 1988; Cromie & Hayes, 1988), and that men more often had previous work experience in self-employment (Kalleberg & Leicht, 1990).

The educational level of women business owners is comparable to men (Birley, Moss, & Sanders, 1987), but the fields of study differ widely. Most often women have pursued undergraduate studies in liberal arts rather than business, engineering, or technical subjects (Hisrich & Brush, 1983; Watkins & Watkins, 1983; Scott, 1986; Honig-Haftel & Martin, 1986; Neider, 1987).

While the general business management skills of men and women business owners have been reported not to vary significantly (Birley, Moss, & Sanders, 1987), women business owners feel that social adroitness and interpersonal skills are their strongest assets (Smith, McCain, & Warren, 1982; Hisrich & Brush, 1984). Likewise, self-assessed competence in financial skills has been frequently rated lower by females than males (Hisrich & Brush, 1984; Chaganti, 1986).

Early research found the personal timing and circumstances for business start-up/acquisition is similar for males and females in that economic necessity was a frequent condition (Schrier, 1975; Schwartz, 1976). However, more recent studies have found men more often become business owners out of a desire to be an entrepreneur (Scherer, Brodzinski, & Wiebe, 1990) or not work for someone else (Swayne & Tucker, 1973), while for women the dominant impetus is a desire to create employment that allows flexibility to balance work and family (Geoffee & Scase, 1983; Scott, 1986; Chaganti, 1986; Kaplan, 1988; Holmquist & Sundin, 1988; Brush, 1990). One recent study proposes that interest in helping others is a key motivator for women to become business owners (Thompson & Hood, 1991).

Few studies have investigated differences in individual characteristics across groups of women. Research in this area has found that women do face different issues and problems depending on a woman's stage of personal life cycle (Kaplan, 1988), region or industry of location (Holmquist & Sundin, 1988), and role perceptions in business ownership (Geoffee & Scase, 1985).

It can be concluded that women business owners are more different from than similar to men in terms of individual level factors such as education, occupational experience, motivations, and circumstances of business start-up/acquisition. The next section will consider the organizational level factors in women-owned businesses.

Organization Characteristics of Women-Owned Businesses

Several studies have reported on the characteristics of businesses owned by women, but few have explored the strategy, problems, and structure of their enterprises. Descriptive methodologies comparing women-owned businesses to what is known about male-owned businesses are the most common types of studies. Investigation of the characteristics of the businesses owned by women shows these to be predominantly service-oriented (Schrier, 1975; Smith, McCain, & Warren, 1982; Hisrich & Brush, 1983; Cuba, Decenzo, & Anish, 1983; Scott, 1986; Neider, 1987); small in terms of revenues and employees (Cuba, Decenzo, & Anish, 1983; Hisrich & Brush, 1983; Welsch & Young, 1984; Scott, 1986); and young—less than five years old (Hisrich & Brush, 1983; Cuba, Decenzo, & Anish, 1983; Scott, 1986). Comparable to male-owned businesses, women most often choose sole proprietorships as the preferred form of business structure (Hisrich & Brush, 1983; Cuba, Decenzo, & Anish, 1983; Mescon, Stevens, & Vozikis, 1983/4).

Strategic management aspects of women-owned businesses have been rarely investigated, but differences from male-owned enterprises have been noted with regard to management style, which has been described as more "feminine" (Chaganti, 1986), informal (Cuba, Decenzo, & Anish, 1983), and participative (Neider, 1987). This parallels in-depth case research of high-level women executives that found women emphasized openness in communications, participative decision making, and less hierarchical organizational structures (Helgesen, 1990). On the other hand, one study did find women-owned businesses to be structured, formal, and well-planned (Mescon, Stevens, & Vozikis, 1983/4), but this may have been a function of the sample which consisted of women-owned real estate firms averaging 15 years old.

Business goals is another area where women-owned businesses differ from those that are male owned. Women business owners frequently note that they pursue social goals, such as customer satisfaction (Holmquist & Sundin, 1989; Moriya, Judd, & File, 1988; Hisrich & Brush, 1987; Chaganti, 1986), *together* with economic goals, such as profit and growth, emphasized by male-owned firms (Kent, Sexton, & Vesper, 1982; Stevenson & Gumpert, 1985).

The great disparity in financial performance between male- and female-owned businesses also suggests profit and growth may not be the main goal of these enterprises. Several studies note sales of women-owned businesses tend to be less than $500,000 annually (Hisrich & Brush, 1983, 1987; Cuba, Decenzo, & Anish, 1983; Welsch & Young, 1983; Longstreth, Stafford, & Mauldin, 1987).[5] Longitudinal research shows the average gross revenues of women-owned businesses to be about $100,000 a year, with sales growth averaging 7 percent a year, whereas the average for male-owned small businesses is closer to $500,000 annually (Hisrich & Brush, 1987). These statistics may reflect a desire by women-owned businesses to focus on goals other than growth and performance.

Problems of women-owned businesses have been investigated and described in several studies, most finding women not to experience any serious formative problems unique to their gender (Pellegrino & Reece, 1982). While problems hiring and maintaining employees, managing time, and delegating are typical of both male- and female-owned enterprises (Pellegrino & Reece, 1982; Cuba, DeCenzo, & Anish, 1983; Hisrich & Brush, 1987), problems in managing conflict between personal and work responsibilities are more frequently mentioned by women business owners (Geoffee & Scase, 1983; Honig-Haftel & Martin, 1986; Scott, 1986; Neider, 1987).

Financial aspects of venture start-up and management are without a doubt the biggest obstacles for women. Obtaining start-up financing and credit (Schwartz, 1976; Charbonneau, 1981; Pellegrino & Reece, 1982; Hisrich & Brush, 1984; Neider, 1987; Olm, Carsrud, & Eddy, 1988), cash flow management in early operations (Hisrich & Brush, 1984; Scott, 1986), and financial planning (Hisrich & Brush, 1984) have been noted in several studies.

While financial problems are also common to male-owned businesses, they may not always be the biggest obstacle (Chrisman & Leslie, 1984). One recent study comparing start-up problems of male and female business owners found no significant differences in types or amount of pre-venture assistance required (Chrisman, Carsrud, DeCastro, & Herron, 1990). Nevertheless, it has been suggested that financial difficulties are exacerbated for women who have not had experience in finance, or rate themselves weak on financial skills (Hisrich & Brush, 1984). Further, it is proposed that women have difficulty penetrating informal financial networks (Olm, Carsrud, & Alvey, 1988) due to their lack of experience and skills (Aldrich, 1989; Hurley, 1991). Several studies have reported that women used only personal assets at start-up and have employed no or minimal external funding (Honig-Haftel & Martin, 1986; Neider, 1987; Hisrich & Brush, 1987; Olm, Carsrud, & Alvey, 1988). Moreover, women frequently start their businesses with half the amount employed by male business owners (an average of $11,000 versus $22,000) (Hisrich & Brush, 1987; Brush, 1990).

Consistent with male-owned enterprises, financial problems of women-owned businesses do seem to vary by stage of development. A longitudinal study by Hisrich and Brush (1987) found early problems in obtaining outside financing were diminished after the business had developed a track record. The same study found that as women's businesses got older, the priorities of problems shifted from purely financial to general business management issues, such as personnel and marketing, which is consistent with findings for male-owned businesses. Delegating responsibility was another general management problem reported frequently by established women-owned businesses (Cuba,

---

5. These studies support aggregate statistics as noted by the Small Business Administration in *Small Business in the American Economy*, chapter 4, pp. 117-164.

Decenzo, & Anish, 1983; Neider, 1987). Similarly, a longitudinal study investigating survival rates of male- and female-owned businesses found women-owned businesses are not more likely to fail (Kalleberg & Leicht, 1991).

In sum, organizational characteristics of women-owned businesses are more different than similar to male-owned businesses. While form of business and general business problems over the life cycle of the enterprise do not vary widely by gender of the owner, there are wide differences in sales levels, management styles, goals and severity of financial obstacles at start-up.

Process of Creating or Acquiring a Business

Activities involved in identifying an opportunity, acquiring resources, and building a business have been investigated in only a few studies (see Table 2). The area of most research is networking, a means of obtaining information and resources important to business development (Carsrud, Gaglio, & Olm, 1986).

The existence or non-existence of networks at start-up is not a distinguishing characteristic of women-owned businesses (Carsrud, Olm, & Gaglio, 1989). Similarly, the process of building networks of contacts does not appear to differ across gender (Aldrich, Reece, & Dubini, 1989). The information needs of women business owners (Nelson, 1987) and the degree of planning and importance of personal versus impersonal information are also very similar between male- and female-owned businesses (Smeltzer & Fann, 1989).

On the other hand, differences in network compositions and size have been identified in research. One rigorous study of Italian and U.S. male and female business owners found notable differences in the composition of networks—those of women business owners were made up of a greater proportion of females (Aldrich, Reece, & Dubini, 1989). Researchers note that women are seeking to build their own ''female'' networks where they gain both social and instrumental support (Smeltzer & Fann, 1989). Likewise, women tend to have smaller networks, which may limit their access to low-cost facilities or transportation (Aldrich, 1989).

In the area of support systems, there is evidence that women business owners tend to have many strong supporters (Hisrich & Brush, 1983; Olm, Carsrud, & Alvey, 1988; Smeltzer & Fann, 1989) and in particular, a spouse or significant other seems to be an important factor for successful women business owners (Sexton & Kent, 1981; Hisrich & O'Brien, 1981; Hisrich & Brush, 1983; Nelson, 1987). It is difficult to say if the support systems of women differ from those of males because there have been few studies of men exploring this issue.

The limited number of studies investigating the steps in the process of business acquisition or creation make it difficult to identify well-defined trends. However, it has been proposed in a comprehensive examination of women-owned businesses in 24 countries (including the U.S.) that because of different occupational, social, and educational experiences, women may follow various approaches to venture creation that may result in different steps, different problems, and different business outcomes (Brush, 1990).

Environmental Factors Affecting Women-Owned Businesses

The relationship of environmental factors to women and their enterprises is the area where the fewest studies have been completed. The issue of possible credit discrimination against women business owners has been examined in three recent studies (Buttner

& Rosen, 1988; Buttner & Rosen, 1989; Riding & Swift, 1990). While lending institutions still perceive women business owners to be less successful than men (Buttner &
Rosen, 1989), loan officers did not note any differences by gender in the objective
quality of business plans prepared by males and females (Buttner & Rosen, 1989).
Furthermore, a large Canadian national study found that terms of loans granted to male
and female business owners did not vary significantly (Riding & Swift, 1990), and
concluded it was the banking relationship that differed by gender.

Given the scarcity of studies of environmental factors and their relationship to
women-owned businesses, it is difficult to draw substantive conclusions. The focus on
financial institutions as possible sources of differences between male- and female-owned
enterprises is logical given the previously mentioned financial problems experienced by
women. However, the impacts of political, cultural, technological, and social factors do
remain to be studied (Hurley, 1991).

A NEW PERSPECTIVE ON WOMEN-OWNED BUSINESSES

We can conclude from the above discussion that there are more differences than
similarities between male- and female-owned businesses. As noted by Sexton (1989),
this review found that most studies agree that there are few gender-based differences in
certain psychologically based entrepreneurial traits. Furthermore, some motivations,
demographic characteristics, basic business skills, problems, planning, and terms of
outside financing do not vary significantly by gender.

On the other hand, women business owners differ greatly from males in several
areas. Significant differences have been found in reasons for business start-up/
acquisition, timing and circumstances of start-up, educational background, work experience, and business skills. More differences are apparent in business goals, management styles, business characteristics, and growth rates. These variations suggest that
women perceive and approach business ownership differently than men. To unify these
differences, a new perspective for thinking about women-owned businesses is proposed,
one that looks at the business through the eyes of women.

The basis of this perspective is similar to a cooperative systems view (Barnard,
1938), which assumes the organization to be a consciously coordinated system of activities conditioned by communication, cooperation, and common purpose. Organizational theorists have discussed this view of organizations as it relates to business strategy
(Chaffee, 1985), but this idea has not been frequently employed in entrepreneurship.

This paper suggests that women perceive their businesses as "cooperative networks
of relationships" rather than separate economic units. In this conception, business
relationships are integrated rather than separated from family, societal, and personal
relationships. The business is "integrated" into the woman business owner's life. This
"integrated" perspective offers explanations for many of the differences between male-
and female-owned businesses as well as suggests future directions for research.

Foundations of the Integrated Perspective

The world consisting of multiple socially constructed realities created through social
interactions, language, knowledge and experience has been espoused by sociologists
(Berger & Luckman, 1967). Similarly, the theory that women perceive a different reality
due to their situation and experiences has been empirically investigated in psychological
studies (Miller, 1976; Gilligan, 1982), and written about in studies of female managers
(Hennig & Jardim, 1977). A popular book by Helgesen (1990) borrowed from Mintz-

berg's (1973) methodology to investigate perceived roles of women managers. This work found that women emphasized interpersonal connections, were guided by intuition and opportunity, and dealt with work and family matters simultaneously.

The main theme of this psychological research is that women's "reality" is characterized by connectedness and relationships (Gilligan, 1982) rather than the autonomy and logic more typical of men's reality. This stream of literature further argues that women's social orientations are directed towards cultivating strong relationships rather than achieving independence (separateness) and position (Gilligan, 1982). A woman's identity is defined in the context of a relationship with decisions situationally determined. Women's personal reality is "web-like," connecting family, work, and community relationships. Men's reality is seen as separate and autonomous, with decision making being logical and rule-based (Gilligan, 1982).

Recent work in sociology by Aldrich (1989) supports the idea that women business owners may view their social relations differently than men by placing more emphasis on building interpersonal relationships. Aldrich (1989) goes on to suggest that the causes for this "different view of reality" emanate from social structures: the workplace, marriage, family, and organized social life. He suggests that not only do women still face a limited range of job opportunities, primarily in the service sector, but also have limited access to upper-level management experience, which similarly limits opportunities in entrepreneurship (Nieva, 1985; Cromie & Hayes, 1988; Aldrich, 1989; Gould & Parzen, 1990). In addition, women are more likely to have primary responsibility for domestic responsibilities, work part-time, and have interrupted careers (Larwood, Stromberg, & Gutek, 1985; Aldrich, 1989; Gould & Parzen, 1990). In social life, women's social networks are frequently a function of their children (i.e. parent-teacher associations, school committees) and they are often excluded from informal business networks and professional business clubs (Gould & Parzen, 1990). Thompson & Hood (1991) argue that women's view of their business's corporate social performance is different from men's because of their psychological make-up and sociological experiences. Research by Hurley (1991) suggests not only that women's perspectives on entrepreneurship are different, but also that new female-based theories need to be employed in sociology to investigate business ownership by women.

Despite sociological and psychological evidence that women's internalized systems of thinking and social and work experiences vary from men's leading to a different view of reality, the bulk of the research on women business owners assumes a view of business ownership rooted in men's view of reality, which is characterized by autonomy, logic, and rule-based decision making. Studies on women business owners have been based on male-derived psychological traits (Stevenson, 1986) and focus on structural factors (political, economic, cultural) as they affect male populations (Hurley, 1991). Furthermore, this research has explored business creation and performance based on the assumption that the venture is viewed as a separate economic entity designed primarily to achieve profit through competitive advantage and the creator of the business is assumed to follow a logical sequence of steps (see for example, Hagan, Rivchun, & Sexton, 1989).

If we acknowledge this evidence on women's view of reality from sociology and psychology, it is logical to assume women would view their businesses differently from men. A closer look at the empirical studies of women business owners reviewed herein supports this idea (Holmquist & Sundin, 1988). The "Integrated Perspective" is proposed as a new basis for investigating women-owned businesses (see Table 5). The main premise of this perspective is that many women business owners conceive of their businesses as a cooperative network of relationships rather than primarily as a separate profit-making entity. As such, these cooperative relationships become integrated into a

Table 5

An Integrated View of Factors in Women's Business Ownership

Dimension	Interpretation	Empirical Support
Individual		
Owner/founder role	Coordinator; center of web of relationships	Smith, McCain, & Warren, 1982 Geoffee & Scase, 1983 Longstreth et al., 1987 Aldrich, 1989 Holmquist & Sundin, 1990
Motive for start-up or business ownership	Create a job; have flexibility in family & work; response to social issue	Schwartz, 1976 *The Bottom Line*, 1978 Hisrich & O'Brien, 1982 Geoffee & Scase, 1983 Chaganti, 1986 Kaplan, 1988 Scott, 1989 Birley, 1989 Thompson & Hood, 1991
Decision making	Situation determined; intuitive	Hisrich & Brush, 1987 Neider, 1987 Dugan, Feeser, & Plaschka, 1990
Personal success	Balance between work & family, in relationships	Schwartz, 1976 Humphreys & McClung, 1981 Neider, 1987 Holmquist & Sundin, 1988
Organization		
View of business	Cooperative network of relationships	Chaganti, 1986 Brush, 1990 Holmquist & Sundin, 1990
Business goals	Economic & non-economic; social contribution	Chaganti, 1986 Hisrich & Brush, 1987 Kaplan, 1988 Moriya, Judd, & File, 1988
Structure	Network; team	Schwartz, 1978 Chaganti, 1986 Hisrich & Brush, 1987 Neider, 1987
Performance	Customer & employee satisfaction	Hisrich & Brush, 1987 Mescon et al., 1983–4
Planning	Cooperative, informal, intuitive	Cuba et al., 1983 Hisrich & Brush, 1987
Process		
Activities in creating/ acquiring a business	Simultaneous; construction of business relationships	Honig-Haftel & Martin, 1986 Longstreth et al., 1987 Kaplan, 1988 Aldrich et al., 1989 Nelson, 1989 Brush, 1990
Management style	People orientation	Chaganti, 1986
Obstacles	Conflict of work & family	Hisrich & Brush, 1982, 1987 Scott, 1986 Honig-Haftel & Martin, 1986 Neider, 1987 Kemp, 1988 Brush, 1990
Environment		
Perspective	Family, work & society are integrated	Aldrich, 1989

woman's life along with her family and community relationships. The women business owner is at the center of these various mutual relational interactions and her role is to bring these connections together. This perspective suggests different interpretations of the variables across the four main dimensions involved in venture creation or acquisition (see Table 5), and begs different questions for future research.

DIRECTIONS FOR FUTURE RESEARCH

Individual Dimensions

View of business. The main assumption of the integrated perspective, that women business owners view their businesses as a cooperative network of relationships, is suggested by current studies. Research has found there is considerable crossover between business and personal dimensions of life in the case of women business owners, which suggests these are connected (Stoner, Hartman, & Arora, 1990). While this also has been alluded to in some studies (Chaganti, 1986; Aldrich, 1989; Brush, 1990; Holmquist & Sundin, 1990), further investigation through field research or case studies would be the first step in refining this proposed viewpoint. Questions of interest include:

1. How do women business owners view their businesses? Is there variation in perspective of the business across types of women business owners based on dimensions such as age, location, work experience, life cycle stage, or cultural background?
2. Is the perspective that women business owners have of their business similar or different from that of male business owners? If so, how do perspectives of businesses vary between male and female business owners?
3. What are the implications for the differences in perspectives (if any) between males and females across business strategy, goals, and performance of their enterprises?

Role. The commonly accepted role for business creators is to be the initiator, innovator, or creator (Vesper, 1990). While women business owners may in fact initiate or create their own businesses, they may conceive of their role as a coordinator of relationships (Aldrich, 1989). Their role is to facilitate and enable others to make contributions (Shaef, 1985). Research questions of interest are:

1. How do women business owners view their primary role in business operations? How is this role related to other roles that women business owners assume?
2. What are the implications of the perceived roles of women business owners for business operations and performance? For family, community and the woman business owner?

The nature of these questions could be explored in field research similar to Helgesen's methodology (1990). Further, the use of "role set theory" (Bird, 1989) may be an appropriate theoretical framework to employ.

Motive. Even though it is a popular notion to "be an entrepreneur," there are several empirical studies suggesting that women business owners are motivated to create or own their own businesses out of a desire to have flexibility in their work and family (Geoffee & Scase, 1983; Chaganti, 1986; Birley, 1989; Holmquist & Sundin, 1990). Women are motivated by job frustration (Kaplan, 1988) rather than a desire to express themselves by becoming an entrepreneur (Geoffee & Scase, 1983). For example, Lynn Wilson, who heads a large public relations firm, notes in a recent issue of *Nation's Business*, "I never considered being an entrepreneur.'' She started her $250 million firm because she wanted to have flexibility in her family and work (Nelton, 1990a, p. 17).

There is also some evidence that social issues or problems are the impetus for women to begin businesses. Cathy Leibow started Baby Minder Finders, a private child-care referral service, when she encountered problems locating a day-care provider for her own infant (Leibow, 1991). Research questions of interest include:

1. What factors lead to the decision of women business owners to become business owners? Are these factors similar or different from males? What is the effect of these factors on the start-up process? Are there differences for male and female business owners?
2. Do women business owners differ from men in motivations for business creation/ ownership across age, family life cycle, or background?

Although testing of motivations has been done using existing psychological theories and instruments, more study of motivations of women business owners is needed. As noted earlier, many of the instruments previously used have been based on psychological motivations of males (Hurley, 1991; Stevenson, 1986). Instead, motives such as "flexibility," "necessity," "social contribution," "affiliation" (Gilligan, 1982) might be tested on carefully selected samples of male and female business owners and matched samples of different groups of women business owners, such as venture creators and acquirers.

Decision making. Normative literature in entrepreneurship suggests that a logical stepwise decision-making process is best for women business owners (see, for example, Hagan, Rivchun, & Sexton, 1989), yet there is no evidence that women follow this model. Rather, many women business owners seem to have an "intuitive" (Hisrich & Brush, 1987; Dugan, Feeser, & Plaschka, 1990) or team approach (Chaganti, 1986) to decision making. Similarly, Helgesen (1990) comments that women managers typically seek lots of information, trade ideas with people and let it "jell" before making a choice. Further, women business owners quoted in the popular press have noted "women are more willing to allow people to be involved in decision-making" (Nelton, 1990a, p. 20). Research questions of interest are:

1. How do women business owners make critical decisions? How do they frame decisions and make choices?
2. Is the decision-making process of women business owners similar or different from that of male business owners?

Decision theories from strategic management such as decision framing (Tyversky & Khaneman, 1981), incremental decision making (Lindblom, 1959), or rational decision making (March & Simon, 1958) would offer useful approaches to test and investigate these issues. Comparative case studies or longitudinal analysis of a single business owner in a company also might be appropriate methodologies.

Success. Personal success in business is frequently synonymous with high income and wealth. However, for many women business owners there is evidence to suggest that they view personal success as achieving a balance between family and work (Schwartz, 1976; Humphreys & McClung, 1981; Neider, 1987; Holmquist & Sundin, 1990). This interpretation of success is consistent with the earlier proposed motive for acquiring or starting a business as well. In the integrated view, family, social, and business relationships are connected, thus suggesting that measures of success should not be achievement of personal wealth. Thompson & Hood (1991) note that women business owners frequently measure success by helping others and self-fulfillment rather than just profits. Questions of interest might include:

1. How do women business owners measure personal success? Do women business owners view personal success in the same way that male business owners view it?

2. Is there variation in the view of success across different types of women business owners based on location, education, experience, or life cycle stage?

The first step in exploring these questions might be field research to examine the dimensions of personal success as perceived by women business owners. Second, these dimensions might be tested on other groups, such as women managers, non-working women, and male business owners.

Organization

Business goals. Business goals for small businesses are assumed to be primarily economic (Kent, Sexton, & Vesper, 1982). However, research suggests that a balance between economic and non-economic goals may be a more accurate description for women-owned businesses (Chaganti, 1986; Hisrich & Brush, 1987; Kaplan, 1988). Such goals as customer satisfaction (Kaplan, 1988), to make the firm the best (Chaganti, 1986), or to help others (Thompson & Hood, 1991) have been frequently mentioned. Kalleberg and Leicht (1991) found women business owners placed more emphasis on quality than males. Relatedly, one woman business owner was quoted as saying "my progress is not generated by a quest for money or a quest for being bigger—but a quest for being better" (Nelton, 1990a, p. 19). Questions of interest are:

1. What are the primary business goals of women-owned businesses? To what degree are these economic or non-economic goals?

2. How do these goals arise and do these goals vary over the life cycle of the business or by type of business?

3. To what degree do women- and men-owned businesses have similar or different goals? What are the implications of these goals for business operations and performance?

Structure. While many small businesses are conceived of as hierarchical structures, many women-owned businesses have been characterized as networks or teams, loosely and informally structured (Schwartz, 1976; Neider, 1987). Watkins and Watkins (1983) suggested that males replicated the business in which they had experience. Because many women business owners have not had previous venture-creation experience (Hisrich & Brush, 1983), lack high-level executive experience, and have interrupted careers, they frequently structure their organizations differently from men, in a flexible, personal manner where a team philosophy predominates (Chaganti, 1986). Questions of interest include:

1. How do women business owners organize their businesses and allocate responsibilities among employees?

2. Do women business owners employ different structure and design dimensions from male business owners?

3. What are the implications of any differences in structure and design dimensions on business operations of male- and female-owned businesses?

Business performance. Typically business performance is measured in economic or financial terms (Brush & VanderWerf, 1991). However, there is empirical evidence that suggests women-owned businesses earn less money (Hisrich & Brush, 1987; Brush, 1990) and often do not grow as rapidly as male-owned businesses (Kalleberg & Leicht,

1991). Sexton (1989) notes that growth is a choice; it is likely that many women business owners choose not to grow their businesses, instead pursuing other goals. As one woman business owner recently noted, "growing is more than growing in size; it's growing in knowledge and ability to do what you do better—it's growing in a lot of ways" (Nelton, 1990a, p. 19). Hence, the assessment of business performance for women-owned businesses should include not only financial measures, but should incorporate other measures such as employee satisfaction, social contributions, goal achievement, and effectiveness. Questions of interest include:

1. How is business performance measured by women business owners? How is this similar or different from male business owners?
2. Does interpretation of business performance vary across groups of women business owners?
3. What are the perceptions of business performance of women-owned businesses from the viewpoint of employees? customers? community?

Planning. Relatively little research has been done on planning in women-owned businesses. Normative literature suggests that the process should be a linear and stepwise progression (Hagan, Rivchun, & Sexton, 1989). Some research has found that many women business owners do not plan (Cuba et al., 1983), while other research has found that many do plan, and the process is often participative (Hisrich & Brush, 1987). In terms of distinct competence and competitive advantage, customer service and quality are most often mentioned (Kalleberg & Leicht, 1991). Research questions of interest are:

1. How do women business owners conceive of planning? What is the content and process of their planning activities?
2. Does planning vary for male- and female-owned businesses? If so, what are the implications for business operations and performance?

Process

Activities involved in business start-up acquisition. Although the business-creation process is generally prescribed as a sequential series of steps (Kent, Sexton, & Vesper, 1982), some studies of women business owners have found that the process by which women business owners create or acquire their own business is simultaneous rather than sequential (Geoffee & Scase, 1983; Kaplan, 1988). Because women business owners frequently have interrupted careers (Kaplan, 1988) and have primary responsibility for the children (Aldrich, 1989), the business creation process is often intertwined or simultaneous with managing a family (Brush, 1990). This in turn requires a strong support system of relationships (Hisrich & Brush, 1987; Nelson, 1989; Smeltzer & Fann, 1989). In fact, recent articles in *Nation's Business* noted that most women business owners refuse to sacrifice their personal life to business (Nelton, 1990a, p. 22; 1990b, p. 32), pointing out the interconnection between work and family. Moreover, a large proportion of women business owners are homebased (Honig-Haftel & Martin, 1986; Kemp, 1988), making it possible for business and household management to occur simultaneously. Research questions of interest are:

1. How do women business owners create or acquire their own businesses? What is the role of family and business relationships in this process?
2. What are the effects of various background factors such as family life cycle stage, cultural background, or education and occupational experience on the process of venture creation or acquisition?

3. What are the similarities and differences in the process between male and female business owners?

Theories that might be applied include the life path model of Shapero & Sokol (1982) and the network approach (Aldrich et al., 1989).

Management style. Investigations have found that women business owners have a personalized and people-oriented management style (Chaganti, 1986), while dealing with people is considered a prime strength (Hisrich & Brush, 1983; 1987). Similarly, the popular press describes women business owners as offering flexibility: flex-time and multiple career ladders are practices typical in many women-owned businesses (Nelton, 1990b). Research questions of interest include:

1. What are the management approaches of women business owners? How are they similar or different from male business owners?
2. What is the relationship of management style to perceptions of job satisfaction by employees? to overall business performance?

Obstacles. Financial obstacles as well as other problems in business creation/ownership have been investigated and it is commonly agreed that women do not face different financial obstacles from men (Buttner & Rosen, 1990; Chrisman et al., 1990). However, one obstacle frequently mentioned by women business owners is the conflict between work and family (see, for example, Pellegrino & Reece, 1982; Hisrich & Brush, 1983, 1987; Honig-Haftel & Martin, 1986; Neider, 1987; Brush, 1990). Research questions of interest are:

1. How do work/family conflicts arise and how do women business owners manage these?
2. What is the role of expectations of employees, family, and other stakeholders in operations and performance of women-owned businesses?
3. How do women business owners view relationships with work and family and is this similar or different from the perspective of males? for other groups of women?

Environment

Integrated perspective. While very little research has been done investigating environmental factors, the integrated perspective suggests that women business owners do not view the environment as a separate element; rather, they see themselves as embedded in the environment which is conceived of as a network of relationships in work, family, and society (Aldrich, 1989). Questions of interest include:

1. To what degree do women business owners view the environment as connected to their business, work, and family? Do male and female business owners view the environment in the same manner?
2. What is the effect of different work, family, social, and cultural experiences on the environmental perspective of women business owners?
3. What is the role of women's associations and groups in establishing relationships and networks for women business owners? Do these associations perform the same functions as organizations that are not gender-based?
4. What are the political, governmental, technological, and economic factors that encourage or discourage women's business ownership?
5. What are the structural barriers (noted by Aldrich, 1989) faced by women busi-

ness owners and are these similar or different for male business owners? How do women manage these and how do these impact business performance?

The transactional relationship of women business owners and the environment might be investigated using a resource dependence theory (Pfeffer & Salancik, 1978) to examine the impact of environmental factors on resource acquisition (capital, information). Further, the effect of environmental and societal changes such as women's rights, legal decisions for equal and minority rights, advances in home and office communications, and the greater acceptance of women in the workforce, need to be investigated for their impact on women's business ownership (Hurley, 1991).

CONCLUSION

This paper has reviewed 57 articles presenting empirical research on women business owners. The discussion concluded that women business owners are similar to males across some basic demographic factors, problems, and business characteristics, but they differ widely from male business owners across individual dimensions related to education, work experience, skills, approach to venture creation/acquisition, business goals, problems, and performance. It is suggested that the major reason for these differences is that women conceive of their businesses differently than men which in turn leads to different approaches and outcomes for performance. This is consistent with previous work from the fields of psychology and sociology that theorizes that women have a different reality from men rooted in their situation and experiences. This paper proposes that women view their businesses as a cooperative network of relationships rather than a separate economic entity. When a woman starts or acquires a business, the set of business relationships are "integrated" into her life. This new view, the "integrated perspective," has implications across the four main components of business creation—individual, organization, process, and environment dimensions—and redirects the focus of our research on this topic.

While this new perspective challenges the assumptions about conceptions of a business underlying previous research, this view is similar to theories of organizations as cooperative systems. Not only does the integrated perspective capture the perception most women business owners have of their ventures, but it also offers explanations for the differences in the motivations, activities at start-up, business goals, and performance between male and female business owners.

The implications for viewing women-owned businesses as a system of cooperative relationships should encourage new measures of motivations for women who become business owners, and in turn these will suggest different dimensions of the start-up acquisition process to be explored. Similarly, the linkages between work and family, where personal and business goals are intertwined and both economic and non-economic goals are pursued, suggests different performance measures will need to be considered. For example, the performance of women-owned businesses as a group may need to be measured in terms of social contributions, innovative management practices, customer satisfaction, quality of customer services, job security, social responsiveness, business goal achievement, and employee satisfaction as well as growth in sales, and increase in employees and profits.

The idea that business problems are a combination of balancing family and work issues implies that different training approaches also may be important. For example, attention to cultivation and maintenance of personal relationships, development of negotiation skills, and formulation of cooperative strategies may need to be included in business management courses along with a discussion of identification of critical economic, technical, and facilities resources, industry analysis, and competitive strategies.

In addition, investigation of the simultaneous, often interrupted and participative process by which women business owners create/acquire and manage their businesses may yield new information about start-up and management techniques. In other words, what can be learned from the experiences of women business owners? One scholar recently noted that women's attitudes about team-building and consensus are much more geared to leading a business through the growth stages than men's (Nelton, 1990a, p. 19). If this is true, women business owners can suggest prescriptions for success in moving a business through the life cycle that might be useful for smaller businesses in general. Similarly, the fact that women frequently handle many varied life roles simultaneously implies that they may be better equipped to manage the conflicting demands of business ownership, or may be able to educate male business owners on the topic of successful "coping" strategies.

Finally, a study of the conditions leading to the integrated perspective should allow for a better understanding of the various structural antecedents encouraging business ownership as well as the barriers faced by women business owners and how these are similar or different from those faced by males. As suggested in Brush (1990), at least two different approaches (deliberate and evolutionary) to business ownership have been noted internationally. Each approach has different structural considerations, obstacles, and outcomes. Further consideration of these should provide insights into possible changes in public policy and assistance programs.

The number of women business owners is expected to increase rapidly in the next decade and they are expected to make a great impact on the workplace (*The State of Small Business*, 1990; Nelton, 1990b). For researchers, it is time to use a new lens to guide our research on the activities of women business owners and recognize a view that considers the integrated nature of relationships important to women business owners.

REFERENCES

Aldrich, H. (1989). Networking among women entrepreneurs. In O. Hagan, C. Rivchun, & D. Sexton, *Women-owned businesses*, pp. 103-132. New York: Praeger.

Aldrich, H., Reece, P. R., & Dubini, P. (1989). Women on the verge of a breakthrough?: Networking among entrepreneurs in the U.S. and Italy. *Entrepreneurship and Regional Development, 1*(4), 339-356.

Anderson, B. S., & Zinsser, J. P. (1988). *A history of their own*, vol. 1. New York: Harper & Row.

Barnard, C. (1938). *The functions of the executive*. Cambridge, MA: Harvard University Press.

Berger, P. L., & Luckman, T. (1967). *The social construction of reality*. New York: Anchor Press.

Birley, S. (1989). Female entrepreneurs: Are they really different? *Journal of Small Business Management,* 27(1), 32-37.

Birley, S., Moss, C., & Sanders, P. (1987). Do women entrepreneurs require different training? *American Journal of Small Business,* Summer, 27-35.

Brockhaus, R. (1988). Entrepreneurship research: Are we playing the correct game? *American Journal of Small Business, 12*(3), 55-61.

Bruno, A. V., & Tyebjee, T. T. (1982). The environment for entrepreneurship. In C. A. Kent, D. L. Sexton, & K. H. Vesper (Eds.), *Encyclopedia of entrepreneurship*, pp. 288-314. Englewood Cliffs, NJ: Prentice Hall.

Brush, C. G., & VanderWerf, P. (1992). A comparison of methods and sources for obtaining estimates of new venture performance. *Journal of Business Venturing, 7*(2), 157-170.

Brush, C. G. (1990). Women and enterprise creation: Barriers and opportunities. In S. Gould & J. Parzen, (Eds.), *Enterprising women: Local initiatives for job creation,* pp. 37-58. Paris: OECD.

Brush, C. G., & Hisrich, R. D. (1988). Women entrepreneurs: Strategic origins impact on growth. In B. A. Kirchoff, W. A. Long, W. Ed. McMullan, K. H. Vesper, & W. E. Wetzel, Jr. (Eds.), *Frontiers of entrepreneurship research,* pp. 612-625. Wellesley, MA: Babson College.

Buttner, E. H., & Rosen, B. (1988). Bank loan officers' perceptions of the characteristics of men, women and successful entrepreneurs. *Journal of Business Venturing, 3*(3), 249-258.

Buttner, E. H., & Rosen, B. (1989). Funding new business ventures: Are decision-makers biased against women entrepreneurs? *Journal of Business Venturing, 4*(4), 249-261.

Carsrud, A. L., Olm, K. W., & Eddy, G. (1985). Entrepreneurship: Research in quest of a paradigm. In D. L. Sexton & R. Smilor (Eds.), *The art and science of entrepreneurship,* pp. 367-378. Cambridge, MA: Ballinger.

Carsrud, A. L., & Olm, K. W. (1986). The success of male and female entrepreneurs: A comparative analysis of the effects of multi-dimensional achievement motivation and personality traits. In R. Smilor & R. Kuhn (Eds.), *Managing take-off in fast growth firms,* pp. 147-162. New York: Praeger.

Carsrud, A. L., Gaglio, C. M., & Olm, K. W. (1986). Entrepreneurs, mentors, networks and successful new venture development: An exploratory study. In R. Ronstadt, J. A. Hornaday, R. Peterson, & K. H. Vesper (Eds.), *Frontiers of entrepreneurship research,* pp. 229-235. Wellesley, MA: Babson College.

Chaganti, R. (1986). Management in women-owned enterprises. *Journal of Small Business Management, 24*(4), 18-29.

Charbonneau, J. (1981). The woman entrepreneur. *American Demographics,* June, 21-23.

Chrisman, J., & Leslie, J. (1989). Strategic administrative and operating problems: The impact of outsiders on small firm performance. *Entrepreneurship Theory and Practice, 13*(3), 37-52.

Chrisman, J., Carsrud, A. L., DeCastro, J., & Herron, L. (1990). A comparison of assistance needs of male and female pre-venture entrepreneurs. *Journal of Business Venturing, 5*(4), 235-248.

Cromie, S., & Hayes, J. (1988). Towards a typology of female entrepreneurs. *The Sociological Review, 36*(1), 87-113.

Collins, O. F., & Moore, D. G. (1969). *The enterprising man.* East Lansing: Michigan State University Press.

Cuba, R., Decenzo, D., & Anish, A. (1983). Management practices of successful female business owners. *American Journal of Small Business, 8*(2), 40-45.

DeCarlo, J., & Lyons, P. R. (1979). A comparison of selected personal characteristics of minority and non-minority female entrepreneurs. *Journal of Small Business Management,* December, 22-29.

Dugan, K. W., Feeser, H. R., & Plaschka, G. R. (1990). A comparison of personality characteristics among women entrepreneurs and the general female population. In T. W. Garsombke & D. J. Garsombke (Eds.), *Proceedings of the U.S. Association for Small Business and Entrepreneurship,* pp. 88-94.

Egge, K. (1987). Expectations vs. reality among founders of recent start-ups. In N. C. Churchill, J. A. Hornaday, B. A. Kirchoff, O. J. Krasner, & K. H. Vesper (Eds.), *Frontiers of Entrepreneurship Research,* pp. 322-326. Wellesley, MA: Babson College.

Gartner, W. B. (1985). A conceptual framework for describing the phenomenon of new venture creation. *Academy of Management Review, 10*(4), 696-706.

Geoffee, R., & Scase, R. (1983). Business ownership and women's subordination: A preliminary study of female proprietors. *The Sociological Review*, *31*(4), 625-648.

Gilligan, C. (1982). *In a different voice*. Cambridge, MA: Harvard University Press.

Gomolka, E. (1977). Characteristics of minority entrepreneurs and small business enterprises. *American Journal of Small Business*, 2(1), 178-184.

Gould, S., & Parzen, J. (Eds.). (1990). *Enterprising women: Local initiatives for job creation*. Paris: OECD.

Haber, S., Lamas, E., & Lichtenstein, J. H. (1987). On their own: The self-employed and others in private business. *Monthly Labor Review*, May, 16-23.

Hagan, O., Rivchun, C., & Sexton, D. (1989). *Women-owned businesses*. New York: Praeger.

Helgesen, S. (1990). *The female advantage: Women's ways of leadership*. New York: Doubleday.

Hennig, M., & Jardim, A. (1977). *The managerial woman*. New York: Anchor.

Hisrich, R. D. (1983). The woman entrepreneur in Puerto Rico. *Commercio y Production*, May-June, 42-46.

Hisrich, R. D., & O'Brien, M. (1981). The woman entrepreneur from a business and sociological perspective. In K. H. Vesper (Ed.) *Frontiers in entrepreneurship research*, pp. 21-39. Wellesley, MA: Babson College.

Hisrich, R. D., & O'Brien, M. (1982). The woman entrepreneur as a reflection of the type of business. In K. H. Vesper (Ed.), *Frontiers in entrepreneurship research*, pp. 54-77. Wellesley, MA: Babson College.

Hisrich, R. D., & Brush, C. G. (1983). The woman entrepreneur: Implications of family, educational, and occupational experience. *Frontiers in entrepreneurship research*, pp. 255-270. Wellesley, MA: Babson College.

Hisrich, R. D., & Brush, C. G. (1984). The woman entrepreneur: Management skills and business problems. *Journal of Small Business Management*, 22(1), 30-37.

Hisrich, R. D., & Brush, C. G. (1985). Women and minority entrepreneurs: A comparative analysis. *Frontiers in entrepreneurship research*, pp. 566-572. Wellesley, MA: Babson College.

Hisrich, R. D., & Brush, C. G. (1987). Women entrepreneurs: A longitudinal study. *Frontiers in entrepreneurship research*, pp. 187-189. Wellesley, MA: Babson College.

Holmquist, C., & Sundin, E. (1988). Women as entrepreneurs in Sweden—Conclusions from a survey. *Frontiers of entrepreneurship research*, pp. 643-653. Wellesley, MA: Babson College.

Holmquist, C., & Sundin, E. (1990). What's special about highly educated women entrepreneurs? *Entrepreneurship and Regional Development*, 2, 181-193.

Honig-Haftel, S., & Martin, L. (1986). Is the female entrepreneur at a disadvantage? *Thrust: The Journal for Employment and Training Professionals*, 7, 49-64.

Hornaday, J. A., & Aboud, J. (1971). Characteristics of successful entrepreneurs. *Personnel Psychology*, 24, 55-60.

Humphreys, M. A., & McClung, J. (1981). Women entrepreneurs in Oklahoma. *Review of Regional Economics and Business*, 6, 13-20.

Hurley, A. (1991). Incorporating feminist theories into sociological theories of entrepreneurship. Presented at the Annual Academy of Management Meetings, Entrepreneurship Division, Miami, Florida, August.

Kalleberg, A., & Leicht, K. T. (1991). Gender and organizational performance: Determinants of small business survival and success. *Academy of Management Journal, 34*(1), 136-161.

Kaplan, E. (1988). Women entrepreneurs: Constructing a framework to examine venture success and business failures. In B. A. Kirchoff, W. A. Long, W. Ed. McMullan, K. H. Vesper, & W. E. Wetzel, Jr. (Eds.), *Frontiers of entrepreneurships research*, pp. 625-637. Wellesley, MA: Babson College.

Kent, C. A., Sexton, D. L., & Vesper, K. H. (Eds.). (1982). *Encyclopedia of entrepreneurship.* Englewood Cliffs, NJ: Prentice Hall.

Kemp, P. R. (1988). The marketing activities of female entrepreneurs in home-based businesses. In H. J. Lasher, E. Maliche, G. Roberts, & R. Scherer (Eds.), *Entrepreneurship: Bridging the gaps between research and practice*, pp. 57-63. USASBE, Monterey, CA.

Larwood, L., Stromberg, A. H., & Gutek, B. A. (1985). *Women and work: An annual review*, vol. 1. Beverly Hills, CA: Sage Publications.

Leibow, C. (1991). Necessity mothers a child care invention. *Nation's Business*, June, p. 8.

Lindblom, C. E. (1959). The science of muddling through. *Public Administration Review, 19,* 79-88.

Longstreth, M., Stafford, K., & Mauldin, T. (1988). Self-employed women and their families: Time use and socio-economic characteristics. *Journal of Small Business Management, 25*(3), 30-37.

March, J. G., & Simon, H. A. (1958). *Organizations*. New York: John Wiley and Sons.

Masters, R., & Meier, R. (1988). Sex difference and risk-taking propensity of entrepreneurs. *Journal of Small Business Management, 26*(1), 31-35.

McClelland, D. (1961). *The achieving society*. Princeton: D. Van Nostrand.

Mescon, T. S., Stevens, G. E., & Vozikis, G. S. (1983-1984). Women as entrepreneurs: An empirical evaluation. *Wisconsin Small Business Forum, 2*(2), 7-17.

Miller, J. B. (1976). *Toward a new psychology of women*. Boston: Beacon Press.

Mintzberg, H. (1973). *The nature of managerial work*. New York: Harper and Row.

Moriya, F. E., Judd, B. B., & File, K. M. (1988). Are women business owners the new breed of entrepreneurs? In H. J. Lasher, E. Maliche, G. Roberts, & R. Scherer (Eds.), *Entrepreneurship: Bridging the gaps between research and practice*, pp. 84-87. USASBE, Monterey, CA.

Nation's Business (1991). Women business owners: What's really new, April, p. 24.

Neider, L. (1987). A preliminary investigation of female entrepreneurs in Florida. *Journal of Small Business Management, 25*(3), 22-29.

Nieva, V. F. (1985). Work and family linkages. In L. Larwood, A. H. Stromberg, & B. A. Gutek (Eds.), *Women and work: An annual review*, vol. 1, pp. 162-190. Beverly Hills, CA: Sage Publications.

Nelson, G. (1987). Information needs of women entrepreneurs. *Journal of Small Business Management,* 25(1), 38-44.

Nelson, G. (1989). Factors of friendship: Relevance of significant others to female business owners. *Entrepreneurship Theory and Practice, 13*(4), 7-18.

Nelton, S. (1990a). The challenge to women. *Nation's Business*, July, 16-21.

Nelton, S. (1990b). Making an impact on the workplace. *Nation's Business*, August, 32.

New economic realities: The rise of women entrepreneurs. (1988). A Report of the Committee on Small Business, House of Representatives, Second Session, (June 28), Washington, DC: U.S. Government Printing Office.

Olm, K., Carsrud, A., & Alvey, L. (1988). The role of networks in new venture funding of female entrepreneurs: A continuing analysis. In B. A. Kirchoff, W. A. Long, W. Ed. McMullan, K. H. Vesper, & W. E. Wetzel, Jr. (Eds.), *Frontiers of entrepreneurship research*, pp. 658-659. Wellesley, MA: Babson College.

Pellegrino, E. T., & Reece, B. L. (1982). Perceived formative and operational problems encountered by female entrepreneurs in retail and service firms. *Journal of Small Business Management*, April, 15-24.

Riding, A. L., & Swift, C. S. (1990). Women business owners and terms of credit: Some empirical findings of the Canadian experience. *Journal of Business Venturing, 5*(5), 327-340.

Schaef, A. W. (1985). *Women's reality.* New York: Harper & Row.

Scherer, R. F., Brodzinski, J. D., & Wiebe, F. (1990). Entrepreneur career selection and gender: A socialization approach. *Journal of Small Business Management, 28*(2), 37-43.

Schrier, J. W. (1975). The female entrepreneur: A pilot study. Milwaukee, WI: The Center for Venture Management.

Schwartz, E. B. (1976). Entrepreneurship: A new female frontier. *Journal of Contemporary Business,* Winter, 47-76.

Scott, C. E. (1986). Why more women are becoming entrepreneurs. *Journal of Small Business Management, 24*(4), 37-44.

Sexton, D. L. (1989). Research on women business owners. In O. Hagan, C. Rivchun, & D. L. Sexton (Eds.), *Women-owned Businesses*, pp. 183-193. New York: Praeger.

Sexton, D. L., & Kent, C. A. (1981). Female executives and entrepreneurs: A preliminary comparison. In K. H. Vesper (Ed.), *Frontiers of entrepreneurship research*, pp. 40-46. Wellesley, MA: Babson College.

Sexton, D. L., & Bowman, N. (1984). Entrepreneurship and education: Suggestions for increasing effectiveness. *Journal of Small Business Management, 22*(2), 18-25.

Sexton, D. L., & Bowman, N. (1986). Validation of a personality index: Comparative psychological characteristics analysis of female entrepreneurs, managers, entrepreneurship students, and business students. *Frontiers of entrepreneurship research*, pp. 18-25. Wellesley, MA: Babson College.

Sexton, D. L., & Smilor, R. W. (Eds.). (1986). *The art and science of entrepreneurship.* Cambridge, MA: Ballinger.

Sexton, D. L., & Bowman-Upton, N. (1990). Female and male entrepreneurs: Psychological characteristics and their role in gender related discrimination. *Journal of Business Venturing, 5*(1), 29-36.

Shapero, A. (1975). Entrepreneurship and economic development. Wisconsin Project ISEED, Ltd., Center for Venture Management, Summer, pp. 185-192.

Shapero, A., & Sokol, L. (1982). The social dimensions of entrepreneurship. In C. A. Kent, D. L. Sexton, & K. H. Vesper (Eds.), *Encyclopedia of entrepreneurship*. Englewood Cliffs, NJ: Prentice Hall.

Smeltzer, L. R., & Fann, G. L. (1989). Gender differences in external networks of small business owners/managers. *Journal of Small Business Management, 27*(2), 25-32.

Smith, N. R., McCain, G., & Warren, A. (1982). Women entrepreneurs really are different: A comparison of constructed ideal types of male and female entrepreneurs. *Frontiers of entrepreneurship research,* pp. 68-77. Wellesley, MA: Babson College.

Stevenson, H., & Gumpert, D. E. (1985). The heart of entrepreneurship. *Harvard Business Review,* March-April, 85-94.

Stevenson, L. A. (1986). Against all odds: The entrepreneurship of women. *Journal of Small Business Management, 24*(4), 30-36.

Stoner, C. R., Hartman, R. I., & Arora, R. (1990). Work-home conflict in female owners of small business: An exploratory study. *Journal of Small Business Management, 28*(1), 30-38.

Swayne, C., & Tucker, W. (1973). *The effective entrepreneur.* Morristown, NJ: The Learning Press.

The bottom line: Unequal enterprise in America. (1979). Report of the President's Taskforce on Women Business Owners (U.S. Department of Commerce: Washington, DC), pp. 90-93.

Therrien, L., Carson, T., Hamilton, J. O'C., & Hurlock, J. (1986). What do women want? A company they can call their own. *Business Week,* (December 22), 60-62.

Thompson, J. K., & Hood, J. N. (1991). A comparison of social performance in female-owned and male-owned small businesses. Presented at the Annual Academy of Management Meetings, Entrepreneurship Division, Miami, Florida, August.

Timmons, J. (1985). *New venture creation,* 2nd ed. Homewood, IL: Richard D. Irwin, Inc.

Tyversky, A., & Khaneman, D. (1981). The psychology of choice. *Science, 211*(30), 453-458.

U.S. Department of Labor. (1987). Employment and earnings statistics. Bureau of Labor Statistics, October.

U.S. Department of Labor. (1983). Time of change: 1983 handbook on women workers. Women's Bureau Bulletin #298, Washington, DC: U.S. Government Printing Office.

U.S. Small Business Administration. (1984). *Annual report for year 1984.* Washington, DC: U.S. Government Printing Office.

U.S. Government Printing Office. (1985). *Report of the president on small business.* Washington, DC: U.S. Government Printing Office.

U.S. Government Printing Office. (1988). *Small business in the American economy.* Washington, DC: U.S. Government Printing Office.

U.S. Government Printing Office. (1990). *The state of small business.* Washington, DC: U.S. Government Printing Office.

Vesper, K. H. (1980). *New venture strategies.* Englewood Cliffs, NJ: Prentice Hall.

Waddell, F. T. (1983). Factors affecting choice, satisfaction and success in the female self-employed. *Journal of Vocational Behavior, 23*(3), 294-304.

Watkins, J., & Watkins, D. (1983). The female entrepreneur: Background and determinants of business choice—Some British data. In J. A. Hornaday, J. A. Timmons, & K. H. Vesper (Eds.), *Frontiers of entrepreneurship research,* pp. 271-288. Wellesley, MA: Babson College.

Welsch, H. B., & Young, E. C. (1982). Comparative analysis of male and female entrepreneurs with respect to personality characteristics, small business problems, and information source preferences. *Proceedings—International Council for Small Business,* pp. 2-10.

Wortman, M. S., Jr. (1987). Entrepreneurship: An integrating typology and evaluation of the empirical research in the field. *Journal of Management, 13*(2), 259-279.

Candida G. Brush is a doctoral candidate in the Boston University School of Management.

Acknowledgments to Margarete Arndt, Ray Bagby, Radha Chaganti, Frank Hoy, Amy Hurley, Pieter VanderWerf, and three anonymous reviewers for their helpful suggestions and comments on earlier drafts of this manuscript.

[4]

A THEORETICAL OVERVIEW AND EXTENSION OF RESEARCH ON SEX, GENDER, AND ENTREPRENEURSHIP

EILEEN M. FISCHER
York University

A. REBECCA REUBER
University of Toronto

LORRAINE S. DYKE
Carleton University

EXECUTIVE SUMMARY

With the rising number of women-owned businesses has come a considerable amount of research, and even more speculation, on differences between male and female entrepreneurs and their businesses. To date, these findings and speculations have been largely atheoretical, and little progress has been made in understanding whether such differences are pervasive, let alone why they might exist. Thus public policy-makers have had little guidance on such difficult issues as whether or not unique training and support programs should be designed for women versus men. Moreover, lenders who finance new and growing firms have little to go on but their own "gut instinct" in assessing whether women's and men's businesses are likely to run in similar ways, or whether they might be run in different but equally effective ways.

The lack of integrative frameworks for understanding the nature and implications of issues related to sex, gender, and entrepreneurship has been a major obstacle. Two perspectives that help to organize and interpret past research, and highlight avenues for future research, are liberal feminism and social feminism.

Liberal feminist theory suggests that women are disadvantaged relative to men due to overt discrimination and/or to systemic factors that deprive them of vital resources like business education and experience. Previous studies that have investigated whether or not women are discriminated against by lenders and consultants, and whether or not women actually do have less relevant education and experience, are consistent with a liberal feminist perspective. Those empirical studies that have been conducted provide modest evidence that overt discrimination, or any systematic lack of access to resources that women may experience, impedes their ability to succeed in business.

Address correspondence to Eileen M. Fischer, Faculty of Administrative Studies, York University, North York, Ontario, Canada M3J 1P3.

The authors gratefully acknowledge the financial assistance of the Social Sciences and Humanities Research Council of Canada and the National Centre for Management Research and Development, and the research assistance of Hans Aggarwal and Gavin Bogle.

Journal of Business Venturing 8, 151–168
© 1993 Elsevier Science Publishing Co., Inc., 655 Avenue of the Americas, New York, NY 10010

0883-9026/93/$6.00

152   E.M. FISCHER ET AL.

Social feminist theory suggests that, due to differences in early and ongoing socialization, women and men do differ inherently. However, it also suggests that this does not mean women are inferior to men, as women and men may develop different but equally effective traits. Previous entrepreneurship studies that have compared men and women on socialized traits and values are consistent with a social feminist perspective. These studies have documented few consistent gender differences, and have suggested that those differences that do exist may have little impact on business performance.

While this interpretation of past findings is relevant to the question of if and how female and male entrepreneurs differ, there are still large gaps in our knowledge. In particular, only one study (Kalleberg and Leicht 1991) has systematically explored whether or not potential differences related to discrimination or socialization affect business performance; the study used limited measures of business performance, and assessed only a restricted range of male/female differences. This article reports on a study that explored other potential differences related to discrimination and to socialization (which are hypothesized based on liberal and social feminism) and looked at their relationship to a more comprehensive set of business performance measures.

The study indicates that for a large, randomly selected sample of entrepreneurs in the manufacturing, retail, and service sectors, there were few differences in the education obtained by males and females, or in their business motivations. Women entrepreneurs were, however, found to have less experience in managing employees, in working in similar firms, or in helping to start-up new businesses. Women's firms also were found to be smaller than men's, to have lower growth in income over two years, and to have lower sales per employee. Regressions undertaken to examine predictors of a range of business performance indicators suggest that women's lesser experience in working in similar firms and in helping to start-up businesses may help to explain the smaller size, slower income growth, and lesser sales per employee of their firms.

For policy-makers, this article suggests that systemic factors that afford women less access to experience must be addressed. Support for classroom training or related advisory activities may not be warranted; there is little evidence that women lack access to relevant classroom education. However, programs that help increase women's access to hands-on experience in starting firms or in working in the industry in which they hope to set up business does seem advisable. In-class education or counseling would not seem to compensate for lack of real-world experience, which suggests that any available funds should be directed more toward initiatives centered on apprenticeship programs than toward those centered on classroom teaching.

Implications for lenders and investors are less clear cut, but suggest that whatever innate differences may exist between men and women are irrelevant to entrepreneurship. While women's businesses do not perform as well as men's on measures of size, they show fewer differences on other, arguably more critical business effectiveness measures—growth and productivity—and no differences on returns. Discrimination against women-owned businesses based on these findings would clearly be both unethical and unwarranted. The fact that women appear to obtain similar growth, productivity, and returns, in fact, suggests that they may be compensating for experience deficits in ways that current research does not illuminate. While more systematic inquiry is required to assist in understanding why men's and women's firms may differ in some predictable ways, this study would suggest that lenders and investors wishing to assist small businesses should focus on evaluating the amount and quality of the business and non-business experience of entrepreneurs, and consider sex an irrelevant variable.

For entrepreneurs, this research reinforces the notion that acquiring relevant industry and entrepreneurial experience is of considerable importance if they seek to establish large firms and/or to achieve substantial firm productivity and returns. In particular, helping in the start-up of firms and spending extended periods of time in the industry of choice appear to yield subsequent rewards in the performance of any individual's firm. Future research is needed to investigate whether or not other types of business experience or non-business experience might bring additional benefits in terms of positive impact on future business performance, but the indication of the current work is that one's sex per se is neither a liability nor an asset.

INTRODUCTION

Research on sex and gender differences in entrepreneurial characteristics and performance has received and continues to receive a considerable amount of attention (see recent contributions by Belcourt et al. 1991; Buttner and Rosen 1988, 1989; Chrisman et al. 1990; Fagenson 1990; Kalleberg and Leicht 1991; Riding and Swift 1990; Sexton and Bowman-Upton 1990). The empirical findings and recommendations that have been reported are diverse and often contradictory; while many studies suggest that there are few differences between the experiences and needs of female and male entrepreneurs (e.g., Buttner and Rosen 1989; Chrisman et al. 1990; Riding and Swift 1990), other investigations seem to confirm the existence of relevant male/female differences in traits (e.g., Sexton and Bowman-Upton 1990), in experiences, and in needs (e.g., Belcourt et al. 1991).

In the broader entrepreneurship literature, highly disparate empirical findings have led to calls for theory-driven research (Low and MacMillan 1988). Articulating and testing theories, rather than merely accumulating empirical findings, allows for a more systematic development of knowledge. Research on sex and gender differences in entrepreneurship needs such a theoretical overview if future studies are to be reconciled with previous ones, and if progress is to be made in understanding the extent to which relevant differences exist and what, if anything, should be done to address them.

Sexton and Bowman-Upton (1990) recently made a start toward introducing greater rigor in this area by outlining some of the major theories about sex-related discrimination. Much, however, remains to be done to develop our understanding of (1) relevant sex- or gender-related differences in personal characteristics and firm performance and (2) the related issue of the nature, extent, and implications of sex-based discrimination. This article introduces two major theoretical perspectives drawn from the feminist literature and draws on them to consolidate the previous research on sex and gender in the entrepreneurship literature. These two perspectives, liberal feminism and social feminism, arose from similar motivations: to understand the bases of, and work toward the elimination of, the lesser status of women in society. They draw, however, on distinct theoretical underpinnings and contain distinct views on the origins, nature, and implications of male/female differences. The alternative viewpoints these theories provide are useful in raising sensitivity to some persistent, unquestioned assumptions that seem to be latent in past entrepreneurship research. Such assumptions may account for the frequent "null findings" and apparent empirical discrepancies that have been reported. Reviewing past studies in light of these two theories also helps to clarify what research is required to fill in gaps in our knowledge and develop a firmer basis for managerial and policy decisions related to male/female differences in entrepreneurship.

The article proceeds by outlining the key distinctive aspects of liberal feminist and social feminist theories. Because the focus of this article is on consolidating past research, the emphasis is not on exploring detailed nuances of the theories but rather on showing how each relates to previous work, and on tracing out further hypotheses that arise from such a review. The article describes a study undertaken to test these hypotheses. Finally, it suggests some implications of the theories and findings for researchers and practitioners.

LIBERAL FEMINIST AND SOCIAL FEMINIST THEORIES

Agreement is far from complete on how the numerous diverse versions of feminism should be grouped and characterized. There is, however, some consensus that liberal feminism and

154   E.M. FISCHER ET AL.

social feminism constitute two of the major distinct categories of feminist thought (cf. Black 1989; Jaggar 1983).

   Liberal feminism (hereafter referred to as LF) is rooted in liberal political philosophy. This philosophy encompasses basic beliefs in the equality of all beings, and in human beings as essentially rational, self-interest-seeking agents. Rationality is assumed to be a purely mental capacity, and is regarded as what is especially valuable about human beings. Individual psychological differences resulting from differences in social opportunities are acknowledged, but rationality, the human essence, is viewed as a capacity for which every human being has the same potential.

   LF, then, is based on the premise that women are equally capable of rationality and thus are as fully human as men. The theoretical explanation for observed differences in the achievements of men and women is that women have less frequently realized their full capabilities only because they were deprived of essential opportunities such as education. Observed psychological differences are posited not to be innate, but rather grounded in the ways that women's socialization discourages them from developing their full capacities for reason. Physical differences between men and women are regarded as irrelevant, as rationality is seen as having no physical basis, and women and men are assumed to be equal in their rational capacity.

   LF hypothesizes that as women gain access to equal opportunities, women and men will actualize their potential rationality more equally and thus observed psychological differences will diminish or disappear, resulting in widespread androgyny. An implicit assumption of LF is that women will evolve to become more like men, because the basis for any extant difference is taken to be women's relative deprivation. Before this can happen, LF argues that both legal discrimination and the more insidious forms rooted in tradition must be identified and eradicated. For instance, the tendency for women to be encouraged to take less "practical" types of education and to enter jobs that require fewer technical skills is seen to diminish their opportunities for acquiring experience conducive to founding and running larger, financially more lucrative firms.

   Social feminism (hereafter referred to as SF) has somewhat more diverse theoretical roots, ranging from social learning theory to psychoanalysis. SF holds that there are differences between males' and females' experiences from the earliest moments of life that result in fundamentally different ways of viewing the world. It argues that female experiences are an equally valid basis for developing knowledge and organizing society (Calas and Smircich 1989). In contrast to LF thought, men and women are not considered essentially the same; among men and among women, shared experiences are assumed to help define a group-based rationality or mode of knowing. Neither the male nor the female mode of knowing is regarded as innately superior or more functional for society. Further, feminists in this tradition tend to subscribe to the view that "distinctions of gender, based on sex, structure virtually every aspect of our lives and indeed are so all-pervasive that ordinarily they go quite unrecognized" (Jaggar 1983, p. 85).

   It should be noted that, largely through the insights of SF, a distinction between sex and gender is now widely recognized. A person's sex is regarded to be based strictly on those physiological differences that make them either male or female. A person's gender, however, is based on differences in social experience, which typically begin to occur from the moment of birth, due to caregivers' reaction to the observed sex of a child (cf. Chodorow 1978). It must be noted, though, that caregivers and others who interact with a person throughout their lifespan will vary somewhat in their reactions to a male versus a female, and thus a person's gender is not completely determined by their sex. That is, there will be considerable within-sex, as well as between-sex, variation in experiences.

Due to the deep cultural embeddedness of experiential differences for women and men, androgyny is generally *not* considered feasible in SF. Neither is it considered desirable; a central premise of SF is that, although women's experiences and ways of knowing have been denigrated, their knowledge may be conducive to equally societally functional behaviors. SF posits that it is essential to recognize the ways in which knowledge is gendered and to gain legitimacy for that feminine knowledge that has been suppressed or marginalized. This involves both identifying gender differences and exploring their implications for individual behavior and societal well-being.

PREVIOUS RESEARCH

Much of the foregoing research on sex and gender pertaining to North American or British samples can be classified as consistent with either LF or SF. Some studies (e.g., Kalleberg and Leicht 1991) appear to test certain hypotheses consistent with each theoretical position. The hypotheses derived from these theories need not be logically contradictory as LF and SF are not in complete conflict despite their differing assumptions about the bases and implications of male/female differences.

Research Consistent with LF

Research that is implicitly consistent with LF tacitly assumes or explicitly seeks evidence of overt or systemic sex-based discrimination. Several studies that have looked for evidence of sex-based discrimination have not included men as respondents. Rather, women alone have been questioned about their characteristics and experiences, and their perceptions of discrimination have been assumed to be accurate (see, for instance, Belcourt et al. 1991; Goffee and Scase 1983; Hisrich and Brush 1984). Latent hypotheses that women are relatively disadvantaged cannot, however, be tested empirically when men are not included as respondents. Thus, such studies can only help to develop hypotheses relevant to LF by suggesting the obstacles that may exist. The most common beliefs discerned regarding disadvantages women entrepreneurs face include the following

1. They receive unequal treatment when they deal with lenders and other resource providers (Belcourt et al. 1991; Goffee and Scase 1983; Hisrich and Brush 1984; Humphreys and McClung 1981; Stevenson 1986).
2. They are less likely to have a relevant education (Belcourt et al. 1991; Hisrich and Brush 1984; Watkins and Watkins 1983).
3. They are less likely to have relevant management, industry, and entrepreneurial experience (Belcourt et al. 1991; Hisrich and Brush 1984; Watkins and Watkins 1983).

It should be noted that while the first suggestion points to overt discrimination against women, the latter two point to more systemic disadvantages that women may face.

Empirical studies that actually compare women with men, either by documenting resource providers' (i.e., lenders and consultants) perceptions of female versus male entrepreneurs or by studying female and male entrepreneurs empirically, can be used to draw more concrete inferences regarding the overt discrimination posited by LF. These studies offer limited evidence of overt discrimination against women entrepreneurs by resource providers. Buttner and Rosen (1988) did find that bank loan officers perceive men to have significantly more of the characteristics of successful entrepreneurs than do women. However, Buttner and Rosen (1989) found that, in an experimental setting, loan officers were not more likely to extend loans to hypothetical male entrepreneurs than to hypothetical female entrepreneurs to whom identical business plans were attributed.

In a direct empirical comparison of experiences obtaining bank loans, Riding and Swift (1990) found that when a sample of males and females matched according to business age, size, growth rate, and organizational form were compared, lenders showed no difference in rates of loan approvals, cosignature requirements, requirements for loan collateral, and interest rates on loans and lines of credit. The only apparent sex-based difference was that women were given higher collateral requirements for lines of credit. A study of "pre-entrepreneurial" men and women who received consulting advice from a small business development center showed that the two groups were virtually identical in terms of the amount and type of assistance they received, their satisfaction with that assistance, and their propensity to initiate ventures after receiving advice (Chrisman et al. 1990). Taken as a whole, these studies suggest that women may experience relatively less overt discrimination than has been suggested. However, Reuber, et al. (1991) did detect some evidence that consultants may unconsciously offer different types of guidance to female versus male entrepreneurs. Presented with descriptions of the same business problem facing a man versus a women, the consultants they studied offered a greater quantity of advice to women, but offered more complex advice to men.

Studies relevant to the question of systemic biases that may work against women include those that empirically compare educational and experiential opportunities of men versus women. With regard to education, Birley et al. (1987) found no significant differences in the education of men and women who had enrolled in small business training courses. Evidence based on this small, non-random sample of pre-entrepreneurs, however, does not fully address the question of whether actual male and female entrepreneurs differ in regard to education or experience, or whether these differences are associated with success. While a number of "women-only" studies have speculated that men and women entrepreneurs have approximately equivalent education (cf. Hisrich and Brush 1984), there is still little empirical evidence that this is true.

With regard to business experience, Birley et al. (1987) found that their sample of pre-entrepreneurs did not differ in prior experience. Kalleberg and Leicht (1991), however, found that women in three industries (restaurants, computer sales and software, and health-related businesses) tended to have less industry-specific experience and to have started fewer businesses, but that equal numbers of men and women had been self-employed prior to starting their own business. Interestingly, these authors found no difference in the likelihood that men's and women's firms would survive or succeed. Given evidence that the number of new ventures an entrepreneur has been involved in is related significantly to firm performance (e.g., Stuart and Abetti 1990), it is curious that the men's and women's firms in all three industries were equally likely to survive and grow. It must be noted, however, that the measures of experience (number of years an individual had been in an industry and whether or not the individual had been self-employed before acquiring current business) and of success (growth in the logarithm of gross earnings) used by Kalleberg and Leicht are not as extensive as those found elsewhere in the entrepreneurship literature; this measurement limitation may be related to the "no difference in success" finding. Taken together, these studies relevant to the systemic disadvantages posited by LF are inconclusive. Those that offer some direct empirical evidence comparing men and women are either based on non-representative samples or offer mixed evidence.

Research Consistent with SF

Research consistent with SF implicitly or explicitly posits that there are inherent differences in the traits and/or experiences of men and women that give rise to differences in observed entrepreneurial behaviors or outcomes. Values are one category of psychological difference that has been explored. Fagenson (1990) compared male and female entrepreneurs and organizational employees with respect to their scores on the Rokeach value survey. She found that the majority of terminal values (e.g., compassion) and instrumental values (e.g., self-actualization) were not statistically different for male and female entrepreneurs; most significant differences found were related to occupation (entrepreneur versus employee) rather than to gender.

Sexton and Bowman-Upton (1990) looked at a range of psychological characteristics including tendency to conform, energy level, interpersonal affect level, risk-taking propensity, social adroitness, value placed on autonomy, value placed on change, tendency to avoid harm, and need for succorance. They did find some significant differences in personal values, noting that relative to women, men scored lower on value placed on autonomy and change. They also found that men scored higher on energy level and risk-taking propensity. They concluded, however, that there is greater similarity than difference between male and female entrepreneurs as many of the other bases on which they compared them showed no significant differences.

Male and female entrepreneurs also have been expected to differ in their level of self-confidence (Birley 1989). Kalleberg and Leicht (1991), however, found no difference in either the self-confidence or the internality of locus of control between the 878 men and 261 women entrepreneurs they studied. In terms of management strategy, they found male entrepreneurs likely to offer a wider range of products and services and women entrepreneurs more likely to emphasize quality. The male and female respondents were equally likely to characterize their strategy as based on innovation.

Other potentially relevant differences have not been examined through direct comparisons of male and female entrepreneurs within a single study. For instance, entrepreneurial motivations have not been directly empirically compared for men and women, although male/female differences in these traits have been posited (Bowen and Hisrich 1986). Extrapolating from gender differences in socialization, women might be expected to be less opportunistic and more craft-oriented, drawing on Smith's distinction (Smith and Miner 1983).

Although the amount of literature investigating male/female differences has been modest, it generally tends to suggest that there are few significant differences in characteristics relevant to entrepreneurship. As these studies largely stop short of examining the relationship of differences that do exist to business performance, it is difficult to assess how important to business outcomes any extant differences may be. Only Kalleberg and Leicht's (1991) recent study, which fortunately used a relatively large and representative sample, sheds some light on this question. They hypothesized and found, consistent with an SF perspective, that women and men manifest at least one difference in strategic thinking: they differ in their emphasis on product range versus product quality. However, they report that, in the three industries they studied, men's and women's businesses are equally likely to survive and be successful. This suggests that whatever male/female differences exist in these groups are not determinative of business performance.

Discussion of Previous Findings

This literature review illustrates that most studies can be categorized as having implicit assumptions consistent with either LF and SF theories. To the extent that these studies' results may be taken as tests of LF theories, they provide mixed evidence that discrimination (overt or systemic) against female entrepreneurs is pervasive. Insofar as LF hypotheses concerning systemic disadvantages faced by women are supported, Kalleberg and Leicht's (1991) study calls into question whether these disadvantages are sufficiently great to cause women to be less successful in business.

Equally limited support may be inferred for hypotheses concerning socialized gender differences, consistent with SF. Only a few psychological differences have been detected when samples of men and women have been directly compared. There is some support for the SF hypothesis that women will not perform in a fashion inferior to men simply because they differ; the Kalleberg and Leicht study suggests that male/female differences in product range and product quality emphases are unrelated to business performance.

As was noted above, however, Kalleberg and Leicht's study used rather limited measures of business performance. Their findings should not, therefore, be considered conclusive evidence either that systemic disadvantages faced by women do not impact business performance, or that male/female differences are unrelated to business performance. This suggests that a study that, like Kalleberg and Leicht's, uses a large representative sample, but that also uses a wider range of measures of success would be useful in order to consolidate and extend past research findings.

Moreover, the literature review above points out the need for a study to examine certain implicit hypotheses, consistent with either LF or SF, that have been inadequately addressed in empirical entrepreneurship studies. Three hypotheses derived from the extant literature are discussed below.

LF-H1:   Women will have less entrepreneurially relevant formal education than men, and their firms will therefore be less successful.

Following LF, because women are systematically less likely to have access to valuable, self-potential-maximizing opportunities, they will be less likely to obtain the same degree of relevant formal education that would help them in running their own businesses.

LF-H2:   Women will have less entrepreneurially relevant experience than men and their firms will therefore be less successful.

Again, because women are systematically less likely to have access to valuable opportunities, they will be less likely to obtain the same amount of relevant experience that would help them in running their own businesses.

SF-H1:   Women will differ from men in their entrepreneurial motivation, a trait previously linked to entrepreneurial success.

The different socialization men and women are subjected to due to their observed sex will condition them to differ in many characteristics, including motivations generally considered relevant to entrepreneurship.

The study reported below both builds on Kalleberg and Leicht's work and tests these hypotheses.

STUDY OVERVIEW AND METHODOLOGY

To consolidate and extend our understanding of sex, gender, and entrepreneurship along the lines discussed above, this study was designed so as to include extensive measures of both education and experience that could pick up subtle but pervasive systemic constraints on women. An attempt also was made to use a psychometrically valid measure of entrepreneurial motivations that could be simply and readily scored. Further, a range of criterion business-performance measures was included so that relationships between sex or gender differences and business performance could be carefully examined. Attempts also were made to ensure that a sufficiently large and representative sample was obtained to allow for valid male/female comparisons.

Sample

A random sample of 908 manufacturing firms (split equally between food and furniture manufacturers), 908 retail firms (split equally between food and furniture retailers), and 908 service firms (split equally between computer services and management and public relations services) was obtained from Dun and Bradstreet. The industries within each sector were chosen based on the assumption that if women were to be found in the sector, they would be more likely to be concentrated in these industries than in many others. Although this data source provides one of the best-defined populations of entrepreneurial firms currently available (Kalleberg et al. 1990), it has the limitation of a lag in listing new businesses, which results in a bias toward older firms (Aldrich et al. 1989). To address this, the sample was drawn disproportionately from newer firms, with 10% of the sample one year old or less. In addition, firms were excluded from selection if (1) they had parent companies, branches, or subsidiaries (thus excluding firms where the owner-manager is more likely to be controlled externally); or (2) their Dun and Bradstreet record had not been updated in the preceding 16 months.

The final usable sample consisted of 136 (11 female) manufacturing firm owners, 156 (29 female) retail firm owners, and 216 (20 female) service firm owners, with response rates of 14.9%, 17.9%, and 23.8%, respectively. These response rates are low, despite the fact that a follow-up postcard was sent one week after the questionnaires were mailed in an effort to increase response rates. Low response rates were expected, and reflect the unwillingness of entrepreneurs to respond to lengthy mail surveys. The initial samples drawn were large in anticipation of low response rates, and the aggregate numbers are sufficient for statistical analyses. To assess the representativeness of this sample, data obtained from Dun and Bradstreet for all firms contacted was used. Characteristics on which responding firms (i.e., the sample obtained) versus all firms contacted (i.e., the sampling frame) could be compared using Dun and Bradstreet data included number of employees, sales, geographic location, sector, and year of start-up. At the .05 level of significance, the sample did not differ from the sampling frame with respect to number of employees, level of sales, or geographic location. However, there was a significant difference between the sample and sampling frame

160   E.M. FISCHER ET AL.

with respect to year of start-up and sector: younger firms were overrepresented in the sample relative to the sampling frame, service firms are overrepresented, and manufacturers are underrepresented. The low response rates, coupled with these biases in the sample, suggest that caution be exercised in overgeneralizing findings of this study, particularly to very mature firms or to firms in the manufacturing sector.

Procedure

The survey and cover letter were mailed to the firm owners at their business addresses. The instructions said: "Please fill this out if you are the business owner. If more than one person owns this business, it should be filled out by an owner responsible for managing the firm's strategic direction." Completed questionnaires were returned in an enclosed postage-paid addressed envelope.

Measures

Education

Education was measured first by asking "What is the highest level of education you have obtained?" and offering respondents the options ranging from "grade school," to "graduate degree." To more fully explore education, they also were asked "Have you had any prior education (courses or seminars)" in each of six functional areas: marketing; finance; personnel; accounting; production; and business strategy? For each functional area, subjects could respond: "a little," "some," or "a lot." These categories, while not as precisely differentiated as ideally would be desirable, should capture respondents' relative levels of training in each area.

Experience

Experience was measured in several ways. Respondents were asked how many years, in total, they had owned a business of any kind; how many years they had operated their current business; how many years, in total, they had been responsible for managing employees; how many years they had worked in other firms with a product or service similar to their current firms'; and how many new businesses, in total, they had helped to start-up.

Motivation

Motivation was measured using several items reflecting the range of entrepreneurial motivations listed in the literature, including but not limited to the opportunist versus crafts motivations (Smith and Miner 1983). These items had been previously developed and pre-tested by the authors in a previous study of a non-random sample of 104 business owners. (A working paper on this measure is available from the authors.) In both the pre-test and this study, the 15 questions regarding motivations for starting or being in business loaded on five factors with an eigenvalue greater than 1 in factor analyses.

The first factor was labeled "financial motives" and consisted of four items with a factor loading of greater than .5 (one item with a loading of less than .5 was dropped from further analysis), each relating to making the business more profitable or valuable. The second factor was labeled "lifestyle motives" and consisted of three items each relating to

TABLE 1 Factor Loading for Items Measuring Entrepreneurial Motivations

Item Wording	Factor 1 Financial Motives	Factor 2 Lifestyle Motives	Factor 3 Social Recognition Motives
Please indicate the importance to you of each of the following goals . . .			
Making my business grow.	.68605	−.12977	.21632
Increasing the profitability of my business.	.78192	.02636	.12051
Earning a good living from the business.	.54352	.23744	.08645
Improving my product or service.	.54837	−.03081	.13154
Achieving a balance between work and family.	.01128	.66758	.16643
Spending more time in leisure activities.	−.01155	.67031	.08565
Avoiding high stress in my life.	.00174	.76304	.01263
Making my name known in the community.	.22240	.29572	.54694
Building something to pass on to my heirs.	.01454	.14814	.61115
Diversifying my range of business activities.	.06288	−.03387	.72866
Expanding my professional network.	.17889	−.04647	.70989

enhancing quality of life outside of work. The third factor was labeled "social/recognition motives" and consisted of four items pertaining to increasing reputation or connections in the business community. The fourth factor was labeled "intrinsic motives" and contained two items related to being challenged by and enjoying work. The final factor, a single item, was labeled "independence motive" and related to being one's own boss. The internal consistency reliability (coefficient α) for the four multiple item factors was .62, .59, .62, and .42, respectively. These reliabilities are modest, due both to the preliminary state of development of the scale and the small number of items, particularly in the fourth factor; the reliabilities of the first three are acceptable for research of this kind (Nunnally 1970). The semantic correspondence of the first factor to the opportunistic orientation, and of the second and third to the craft orientation, seem also to suggest that these factors have some validity. The item loading on each of the first three factors were, accordingly, formed into subscales to assess dimensions of entrepeneurial motivation. The items in the other two factors were dropped from further analysis because of their questionable reliability. The factor loadings for those items that were used in the analysis, grouped according to the subscales developed, are displayed in Table 1.

Business Performance

Business performance was assessed using four categories of indicators collected from the sample. The first category was size, and included measures of total number of employees, current income, and current sales. The second category was growth, and included measures of change over two years in number of employees, income, and sales. The third category was productivity, and included calculations of income per employee and sales per employee. The final category was returns, and included calculations of income per owner and income per sales (i.e., margin). To ensure that industry heterogeneity within sector did not affect the results of analyses that involved these performance indicators, each indicator was con-

TABLE 2   Comparisons of Females and Males on Education Variables

	Males		Females	
	Mean	SD	Mean	SD
General education[a]	3.3	1.3	3.5	1.2
Marketing education[b]	1.7	.8	1.6	.9
Finance eduation[b]	1.7	.8	1.5	.9
Personnel education[b]	1.5	.8	1.4	.9
Accounting education[b]	1.7	.8	1.8	.9
Production education[b]	1.5	.8	1.1	.6[c]
Strategy education[b]	1.8	.8	1.6	.9

[a]Measured as a continuous variable with a highest score of 6.
[b]Measured as a continuous variable with a highest score of 3.
[c]*t* test of female/male difference significant at .01 level.

verted to a standardized (z-score) measure representing the firm's performance relative to other firms in the same industry and sector.

Analyses

To test the hypotheses, *t* tests comparing means for male and female subjects on all education, experience, and motivations measures were first conducted. Then, *t* tests comparing means for males and females on all performance indicators were undertaken. Finally, regressions using as independent variables the experience, expertise, and motivation measures that differed significantly for men and women were performed for each performance indicator.[1]

RESULTS

Table 2 shows the comparisons of females and males with respect to education. It indicates that there were few significant sex differences in education, other than that men had more production-related business education.

Table 3 reflects female/male comparisons on the experience variables. Female/male differences in relevant experience are more pronounced. Overall, men appear to have spent more years managing employees, to have had more experience in similar firms, and to have helped to start more businesses.

Table 4 shows the results of comparisons of female and male motivations for business owners in all sectors. The only significant difference is that women have stronger financial motivation. This suggests that, relative to men, women are somewhat more opportunistically oriented but no more craft-oriented. This result is somewhat unexpected.

Table 5 displays the results of comparisons of females' and males' business performance for each category of variables. In the size category, men's businesses consistently outperform women's; their firms have more employees, higher annual sales, and higher annual income. In the growth category, men's firms exhibited a higher two-year growth in

---

[1]At the suggestion of one reviewer, information on marital status, number of children, and age also was analyzed. Analyses of variance revealed no significant differences between males and females with respect to age or number of children, but showed that men were significantly more likely to be married. However, marital status showed no relationship to any performance indicator in analyses of variance.

TABLE 3 Comparisons of Females and Males on Experience Variables

| | Males | | Females | |
	Mean	SD	Mean	SD
# Years owned a business	11.9	8.5	10.3	7.3
# Years owned current business	8.6	7.3	7.3	6.5
# Years managed employees	15.9	9.7	11.1	7.5[a]
# Years in similar firms	4.0	5.7	1.9	4.7[b]
# Firms helped to start	2.8	2.6	2.0	2.6[c]

[a] *t* test of female/male difference significant at .001 level.
[b] *t* test of female/male difference significant at .01 level.
[c] *t* test of female/male difference significant at .05 level.

income. In terms of productivity, men's firms exhibited higher levels of sales per employee. There were no differences between the returns exhibited by men's and women's firms.

Table 6 illustrates the results of multiple linear regressions (with all variables forced to enter) predicting the performance variables. Note that the independent variables included in regressions are only those on which men and women in the sample were found to differ significantly, as only these variables, if any, should explain *differences* in women's and men's firms' performance. Note also that the education and motivation variables were scaled as metric variables for purposes of analysis.

As can be seen, across all the regressions, the education, experience, and motivational variables on which men and women were found to differ together account for an almost negligible portion of the variance in firm performance. The production education variable is positively related to number of employees (on which men's businesses outperform women's) but negatively related to change in income over two years (on which men's firms also outperform women's). Thus, having more education in production does not seem to provide men with a clear advantage. Similarly, while men have more experience managing employees, this seems if anything to be a disadvantage to them, as this variable is negatively related to change in employees over two years and change in sales over two years. Men's greater number of years spent in a similar business does seem to contribute to the better performance of their firms in terms of size; years in similar business is positively related to annual sales and annual income; moreover, the same variable is positively related to income per employee, sales per employee (on which, again, men's firms outperform women's), and income per owner. Having greater experience in helping to start firms also appears to be an asset to men, given that the number of firms an individual helps to start is positively related to number of employees and annual sales.

TABLE 4 Comparisons of Females and Males on Motivation Variables

| | Males | | Females | |
	Mean	SD	Mean	SD
Financial motivation[a]	24.9	2.8	25.7	2.2[b]
Lifestyle motivation[c]	15.0	3.5	15.5	3.8
Social/recognition motivation[c]	16.8	5.2	16.0	4.5

[a] Highest possible score: 28.
[b] *t* test of female/male difference significant at .05 level.
[c] Highest possible score: 21.

TABLE 5 Comparisons of Females and Males on Business Performance Variables[a]

	Males Mean	SD	Females Mean	SD
# of Employees	.3	1.0	−.2	.6[b]
Annual sales	.0	1.0	−.3	.4[c]
Annual income	.0	1.0	−.2	.5[b]
2-year change in employees	−.0	.9	.0	1.2
2-year change in sales	.0	1.0	−.0	.9
2-year change in income	.0	1.0	−.2	.6[b]
Income per employee	−.0	.9	.1	.9
Sales per employee	.0	1.0	−.3	.4[c]
Income per owner	.0	1.0	−.1	.5
Margin	−.0	1.0	−.0	.7

[a]Using z-scores standardized by sector.
[b]t test of female/male difference significant at .05 level.
[c]t test of female/male difference significant at .001 level.

DISCUSSION

The particular LF and SF hypotheses tested here received mixed support. The prediction of LF-H1—that women would have less access to relevant education—is not supported in terms of general education. The only significant difference in relevant education appears to be that men have more production training than women. Whether or not this extra training benefits men is questionable, as production education is positively related to one performance variable (number of employees) but negatively related to another (change in income over two years).

TABLE 6 Standardized Regression Coefficients

	Production Education	Financial Motivation	# Years Managed Employees	# Years in Similar Business	# Firms Helped Start	R^2 for Regression
# Employees	.09[a]	−.05	.02	.03	.15[b]	.03
Annual sales	.07	.00	.06	.19[b]	.10[c]	.06
Annual income	.06	.04	.01	.25[b]	.02	.07
2-year change in employees	.08	.02	−.10[a]	.02	.02	.01
2-year change in sales	−.01	−.00	−.13[c]	.00	.03	.01
2-year change in income	−.11[c]	.02	−.06	−.01	.01	.01
Income per employee	.05	.04	.00	.25[b]	.00	.06
Sales per employee	.02	.05	.05	.21[b]	−.00	.05
Income per owner	.06	.04	.00	.25[b]	.01	.07
Margin	−.01	.10[a]	−.07	.04	.02	.01

[a]Coefficient significant at .05 level.
[b]Coefficient significant at .001 level.
[c]Coefficient significant at .01 level.

The prediction of LF-H2—that women would have less access to experience—appears to be somewhat more substantiated; women did have less experience than men in managing employees, working in similar firms, and helping to start other businesses. The fact that managing employees is negatively related to change in employees and change in sales over two years suggests that women's relative lack of experience in this area is not impeding their performance. The findings that years in similar business is positively related to annual sales, income, income per employee, income per owner, and sales per employee, and that the number of businesses a person has helped to start is positively related to number of employees and annual sales, offer more support for this hypothesis. They suggest that women are disadvantaged to the extent they are subject to systemic forces that lessen their opportunities for such experiences.

The prediction of SF-H1—that there would be between-sex differences in motivation—received some support. Women did differ from men in that they had greater financial motivation. However, this finding is somewhat surprising in that most social feminist theory suggests that women might, if anything, be more lifestyle-oriented (in keeping with having a greater concern for the well-being of other people in their lives). It might be argued, however, that women entrepreneurs exhibit stronger financial motivations because having greater financial success is important to their ability to take care of their dependents. Alternatively, it may be that, relative to the general population of women, those drawn to entrepreneurial careers have stronger financial motives. In any event, the fact that financial motivation was significantly related to only one performance variable (margin) suggests that this character difference has a modest effect on any behaviors that affect performance.

Taken together, these findings offer some insights into why men's firms may outperform women's (primarily in terms of size); women's relative lack of experience is a factor, although the small percentage of variance explained in each criterion variable suggests that other factors also must be considered. From an LF perspective, it would be logical to consider relevant opportunities other than experience or education that are systematically less available to women and that impede them from starting large firms or growing their firms rapidly. From an SF perspective, it would make sense to explore psychological gender differences (other than motivations) that may explain either why women are more likely to prefer smaller firms or why they are predisposed to start smaller firms.

It also is worth noting that, although women lack the experience in similar firms, which is positively related to income per employee and income per owner, their firms do not perform poorly relative to men's on these measures. The possibility that women's socialization leads them to manage their firms in a way that offsets the impact of lesser exposure to similar businesses (which would be consistent with SF theory) is an interesting one. However, this possibility is merely speculative and would require more research to substantiate or disconfirm.

CONCLUSIONS

The theoretical perspectives introduced in this study help to organize both assumptions and findings from the foregoing research on sex, gender, and entrepreneurship. They also offer guidance as to how to explore these topics further without resorting to atheoretical attempts to explain puzzling data.

While performance differences exist and the reasons for them need to be explored further, some of the variables discussed in previous research either fail to differ as expected or fail to relate to performance as expected. Further exploration based on LF theory would

166   E.M. FISCHER ET AL.

lead researchers to look for sources of overt or systemic bias against women that have been previously neglected. For instance, customer or supplier biases affecting their willingness to do business with firms run by women might be studied. Studies based in SF would focus on male/female differences that have not yet been explored. For instance, as Bowen and Hisrich (1986) suggest, a logical next step would be to investigate gender differences in management styles and how they may affect firm performance.

Some guidelines for future research arise from the insights developed in both LF and SF theory:

1. If the existence of male/female differences is being posited, empirical evidence comparing women and men drawn from the same population at the same time is necessary; otherwise, situational or temporal factors may invalidate comparisons between women studied in one setting at one time and men studied in another setting at another time.
2. If evidence is being sought that hypothetical sex or gender differences exist and that they are relevant to firm performance, then including criterion measures of performance as well as independent measures of the differentiating characteristics in a single study is necessary. Unless such measures are taken, and the appropriate analyses performed, it is dangerous to speculate that differences that are detected are relevant to business performance.
3. Similarly, if evidence of overt or systemic discrimination is argued to be relevant to the relative business performance of men and women, studies should assess both opportunities to which women are thought to lack access and the aspects of business performance that are thought to be affected. Otherwise, it may be incorrectly inferred that the opportunities to which women lack access actually prevent them from performing well in business.

It must be acknowledged, of course, that both LF and SF theory may not be substantiated by future research; this may account for the mixed support found for hypotheses derived from these theories thus far. However, before such a conclusion is drawn, it is important to recognize that the studies reviewed above were not designed specifically as tests of the LF and SF theories, and that the hypothesis tested in this research are not the only ones that would be generated by a more sustained and systematic effort to apply these theories in this domain. At least as a theoretical point of departure for future research, these theories hold promise.

The empirical results of this study also make an incremental contribution to the building knowledge pool in this area. Particularly taken together with the results of Kalleberg and Leicht (1991), they suggest that sex differences in in-class education may not be of critical importance. However, these findings suggest that more investigation of men's and women's differential access to real-world experience is warranted, and that there may be as yet undefined male/female socialization differences that lead men and women to run their firms in different but equally effective ways.

A notable limitation of this study is the low response rate. The possibility that our sample is unrepresentative in that it contains an unduly high proportion of those with the time or willingness to respond must be acknowledged. Another issue may be the self-selection of highly educated women into entrepreneurial ventures. Perhaps many women did or do lack access to relevant education, and only those who were relatively privileged in this regard even attempt to start firms, and thus show up in the samples studied. These factors constrain the generalizability and interpretation of findings. Nonetheless, the theories outlined and the incremental empirical findings gleaned are of value to those who wish to pursue research in this area.

From a policy-maker's perspective, this research suggests that the key resource they might seek to provide potential women entrepreneurs is access to apprenticeship in the industry in which they hope to set up their firms. From investors' or lenders' perspectives, differential treatment of men and women would clearly be unwarranted. Although men's and women's firms do differ in some aspects of performance, there is no strong evidence that women's firms are impeded by the owners' relative lack of education or experience.

For entrepreneurs, this research suggests that for both men and women, the best way they can prepare themselves to do business in a particular sector or industry is to gain experience in that setting, and to seek out exposure to business start-ups.

REFERENCES

Aldrich, H., Kalleberg, A., Marsden, P., and Cassell, J. 1989. In pursuit of evidence: Sampling procedures for locating new businesses. *Journal of Business Venturing* 4:367–386.

Belcourt, M., Burke, R., and Lee-Gosselin, H. 1991. *The Glass Box: Women Business Owners in Canada*. Ottawa, Canada: The Canadian Advisory Council on the Status of Women.

Birley, S. 1989. Female entrepreneurs: Are they really any different? *Journal of Small Business Management* 27:32–37.

Birley, S., Moss, C., and Saunders, P. 1987. Do women entrepreneurs require different training? *American Journal of Small Business* 12(1):27–36.

Black, N. 1989. *Social Feminism*. Ithaca, NY: Cornell University Press.

Bowen, D. and Hisrich, R. 1986. The female entrepreneur: A career development perspective. *Academy of Management Review* 11(2):393–407.

Buttner, E.H. and Rosen, B. 1988. Bank loan officers' perceptions of the characteristics of men, women and successful entrepreneurs. *Journal of Business Venturing* 3:249–258.

Buttner, E.H. and Rosen, B. 1989. Funding new business ventures: Are decision makers biased against women? *Journal of Business Venturing* 4:249–261.

Calas, M. and Smircich, L. 1989. Using the "F" word: Feminist theories and the social consequences of organizational research. Presented at the Annual Meeting of the Academy of Management, Washington, D.C.

Chodorow, N. 1978. *The Reproduction of Mothering*. Berkeley, CA: University of California Press.

Chrisman, J., Carsrud, A., DeCastro, J., and Herron, L. 1990. A comparison of the assistance needs of male and female pre-venture entrepreneurs. *Journal of Business Venturing* 5:235–248.

Fagenson, E. 1990. The values of organizational and entrepreneurial men and women: Occupational role and/or gender related differences. Presented at the Academy of Management Conference, San Francisco, CA.

Goffee, R. and Scase, R. 1983. Business ownership and women's subordination: A preliminary study of female proprietors. *Sociological Review* 31:625–648.

Hisrich, R. and Brush, C. 1984. The women entrepreneur: Management skills and business problems. *Journal of Small Business Management* 22(1):30–37.

Humphreys, M. and McClung, J. 1981. Women entrepreneurs in Oklahoma. *Review of Regional Economics and Business* 6(2):13–21.

Jagger, A. 1983. *Feminist Politics and Human Nature*. NJ: Rowman and Allenheld.

Kalleberg, A. and Leicht, K. 1991. Gender and organizational performance: Determinants of small business survival and success. *Academy of Management Journal* 34:136–161.

Kalleberg, A., Marsden, P., Aldrich, H., and Cassell, J. 1990. Comparing organizational sampling frames. *Administrative Science Quarterly* 35:658–688.

Low, M. and MacMillan, I. 1988. Entrepreneurship: Past research and future challenges. *Journal of Management* 14(2):139–161.

Nunnally, J. 1970. *Introduction to Psychological Measurement*. New York, NY: McGraw Hill.

Reuber, A.R., Dyke, L., and Fischer, E. 1991. Gender role stereotypes regarding women business

168 E.M. FISCHER ET AL.

owners: Impacts on external resource provision by consultants. *Canadian Journal of Administrative Sciences* 8:244–250.

Riding, A. and Swift C. 1990. Women business owners and terms of credit: Some empirical findings of the Canadian experience. *Journal of Business Venturing* 5:327–340.

Sexton, D.L. and Bowman-Upton, N. 1990. Female and male entrepreneurs: Psychological characteristics and their role in gender-related discrimination. *Journal of Business Venturing* 5:29–36.

Smith, N. and Miner, J. 1983. Type of entrepreneur, type of firm and managerial motivation: Implications for organizational life cycle theory. *Strategic Management Journal* 4:325–340.

Stevenson, L. 1986. Against all odds: The entrepreneurship of women. *Journal of Small Business Management* 24(4):30–36.

Stuart, R. and Abetti, P. 1990. Impact of entrepeneurial and management experience on early performance. *Journal of Business Venturing* 5:151–162.

Watkins, J.M. and Watkins, D.S. 1983. The female entrepreneur: Her background and determinants of business choice—Some British data. In J.A. Hornaday, J.A. Timmons, and K.H. Vesper, eds., *Frontiers of Entrepreneurship Research*. Wellesly, MA: Babson College, pp. 271–288.

[5]

1042-2587-02-263$1.50
Copyright 2002 by
Baylor University

A Gendered Perspective on Organizational Creation

Barbara Bird
Candida Brush

Literature on the creation of organizations is often cast within a masculine gender framework. This paper draws from three theoretical perspectives to develop a new perspective that broadens the view of organizational creation by encompassing the relative balance of feminine and masculine perspectives in the entrepreneur's venture start-up process and new venture attributes. We elaborate the relatively less visible feminine and personal perspective and compare this with the traditional or masculine perspective. Important to the discussion is the distinction between biology (sex: male and female, man and woman) and socialized perspectives (gender: masculine and feminine). While research and the general public often use the concept of gender loosely to signify sex, we follow a more precise feminist distinction. The paper advances new concepts of gender-maturity (an individual difference) and gender-balance (an organizational quality).

Organizations are created out of pre-emergent conditions (Carter, Gartner, & Reynolds, 1996; Hansen, 1995), which are essentially the processes of organizing and assembling interdependent actions into sensible sequences that generate sensible outcomes (Weick, 1979). As they take form, organizations identify, acquire and exchange resources with other firms and individuals (Gartner, 1993), and contribute to household, local, regional, national, and even international economies. The emergence of new organizations and the role of founder(s) or entrepreneurs in this process is a topic of continuing fascination for scholars (Bull & Willard, 1993; Sexton & Kasarda, 1992; Katz & Gartner, 1988; Shane & Venkataraman, 2000).

Historically, an array of definitions characterize entrepreneurship; for instance, risk bearing (Knight, 1921), initiative taking, (Shapero & Sokol, 1982), opportunism, (Kirzner, 1985), innovation (Baumol, 1993), and carrying out new combinations (Schumpeter, 1934). One of the core attributes of entrepreneurship is the creation of new organizations (Bygrave, 1993; Gartner, 1985, 1993; Katz & Gartner, 1988; Low & MacMillan, 1988). Organizational creation includes but is not limited to committing resources to an opportunity (Bruno & Tyebjee, 1982; Shaver & Scott, 1991; Shane & Venkataraman, 2000), coordinating and establishing routines (Liebenstein, 1968; Nelson & Winter, 1982), and sequencing events for enactment, selection, and retention of routines and resources (Carter et al., 1996; Gartner, 1993; Weick, 1979).

While accepted as generic, the historical descriptions of the entrepreneur's activities and resulting ideal forms of new organizations are decidedly masculine. Entrepreneurship has been a "man's" domain. Schumpeter (1934) describes the entrepreneur as *captain of industry,*[1] while Hebert and Link (1982) celebrate the *key man.* Liebenstein (1968) describes the *hero who perceives the gaps and connects markets,* and Knight's (1921) entrepreneur was a capitalist, a special social class and an *active businessman*

---

1. While the word captain can refer to men and women, in 1934 it is likely to have been largely a reference to men.

who directed economic activity. The literature of psychology also describes entrepreneurs as "men." Collins and Moore (1964) devote a book to the empirical study of male entrepreneurs and business hierarchs in *The Enterprising Man,* and note that *"the men who travel the entrepreneurial way are, taken on balance, not remarkably likable people"* (p. 244). McClelland (1961) defines the entrepreneur as the *"man who organizes the firm (the business unit) and/or increases its productive capacity"* (p. 205). In addition, tycoon histories focus exclusively on stories of *"successful businessmen"* (Livesay, 1982), and practitioner literature frequently refers to "exploitation" of opportunities by successful men such as Bill Gates, Donald Trump, and Henry Ford. More recently it has become de riguer to avoid sex- and gender-specific references when attempting to generalize, so these blatant biases are no longer highly visible.

The male-derived emphasis not only pervades these definitions and descriptions but also underpins the expected process of new venture creation, generally conceived as sequential, profit maximizing, and strategically and competitively focused. Steps in the entrepreneurial process can be clearly laid out—the entrepreneur searches for and evaluates an opportunity, often due to extra "alertness" (Kirzner, 1985), then acquires resources and builds an organization. This is followed by strategically growing the company in order to harvest wealth (profits) and power (Baumol, 1993; Ronen, 1983; Stevenson, Roberts, & Grosbeck, 1994). These processes are inherently rational and instrumental—they assume that the entrepreneur has access to needed information and through better preparation and careful analysis may be able to implement a unique innovation and achieve personal gain (Bull & Willard, 1993). The individual entrepreneur is motivated by achievement and power (McClelland, 1961; Smith, 1967), with attendant qualities of moderate risk, individual effort, need for instrumental feedback, and need for influence over others while maintaining autonomy. It is argued that the innovating entrepreneur is seen as a driven individual whose hand is forced by the pursuit of new profits (Baumol, 1993, p. 202). Furthermore, the new organization has primarily or solely an economic purpose (Cole, 1965; Kirzner, 1983; Schumpeter, 1934), is centralized and dominated by the entrepreneur (Cooper, 1981), and has a clear chain of command or hierarchy (Churchill & Lewis, 1983; Greiner, 1972).

Even recent discussions of the entrepreneurial process emphasize the rational economic assessment in the discovery process that is based on the belief of the value of resources, the cost efficiency of pursuing some opportunities rather than others, and success based on exploitation, more commonly associated with male than female behavior (Shane & Venkataraman, 2000). "Entrepreneurs tend to see logic rather than the guts of their own actions" (Sexton & Smilor, 2000, p. xvi). Yet, it is not surprising that characterizations of entrepreneurs and their resulting organizations are masculine in character. Until recently, the predominant population involved in entrepreneurial activities was men. For instance, in the U.S. until 1970, less than 4.6% of all small companies were women-owned (*The State of Small Business,* 1987). Between 1970 and 1980 this also was true in European countries, where female participation rates in self-employment hovered around 5-6% (Ducheneaut, 1997). Hence, the bulk of theory was developed and tested on samples of male entrepreneurs (Brush, 1992).

In spite of this explanation for the dominance of male-derived theories of organizational creation, the effect of this emphasis creates two dilemmas. First, as useful and explanatory as these approaches are for men, we cannot be sure they adequately reflect the organizing process and organizations of women. While these approaches cover much variance among male entrepreneurs, their application to the female entrepreneurs is open to question. Limited empirical research shows that women do not follow sequential steps in venture creation (Brush, 1990), consequent of interrupted careers (Kaplan, 1988) and primary responsibility for family and children (Aldrich, 1989). Similarly, organizational structures of women's firms are described as horizontal network (Chaganti, 1986; Westerberg, 1996), policies often have relational or nurturing aspects (Holmquist & Sundin, 1990), and decision making is participative (Chaganti, 1986). Moreover, a study of new retail firms showed that women manage their businesses differently, using different strategies (Carter et al. 1996). These differences emerging from research on women-owned/founded businesses suggest that the theoretical literature may be incomplete, not including aspects of women's organizing, and therefore is less relevant to women business owners (Cliff, 1998). While this was easily rationalized when the populations of women entrepreneurs were comparatively small, today women business owners number nearly 38% of U.S. businesses (NFWBO, 2000), and internationally constitute more than 20% of all businesses in a majority of OECD countries (Ducheneaut, 1997).

The second dilemma is found at a broader level, where the omission of "feminine" aspects in theoretical discussions of new ventures and venture creation processes raises the risk that our studies may suffer a lack of construct validity (Kerlinger, 1973). Here we must distinguish between sex (male/man and female/woman) and gender (masculine and feminine).[2] Cultures comprise masculine and feminine qualities and values anchored in culturally defined roles for men and women (Hofstede, 1980). Depending on the situation, a man may behave in a feminine way (e.g., bringing home-baked cookies to his employees) or a women in a masculine way (e.g., taking her employees to a hockey game) (Bem, 1974; Duchenaut, 1997). In the context of organizational creation, it is reasonable to assume that masculine and feminine aspects will be incorporated into the organizing process and new venture for both men and women. In other words, the process is gendered in nature. This gap in theory exists because the feminine aspects of organizational creation and feminine dimensions of new ventures are not well articulated, and if articulated, not identified as feminine (Fondas, 1997). We recognize the extensive literature on diversity (Jackson et al., 1992), organizational feminism (Calas & Smircich, 1992; Gottfried & Weiss, 1994; Martin, Knopoff, & Beckman, 1998) and women's leadership role in existing organizations (Rosener, 1995), however attention to "feminine" aspects of organizing or creating new ventures is sparse.

We address these two dilemmas by offering an articulation of an alternative organizing process that is gendered in nature, often combining masculinities (Cheng, 1996) and femininities, and applicable to both men and women. We argue that the gendered perspective of the founder(s) influences the organizing process and resultant new organization. Our purpose is neither to focus exclusively on women entrepreneurs and their organizing processes nor to deconstruct and reconstruct existing theory.

Our theoretical stance is that individuals (e.g., founders) make a difference in how organizing takes place and what results from organizing. Founders' values, intention, and social capital (e.g., prior experience and social networks) can critically impact the way a venture is created and how that organization operates (Bird, 1989; Cooper & Jimeno-Gascon, 1992; Shaver & Scott, 1991). Our focus is on the individual's internalized and enacted gender perspective, which is not isomorphic with biological sex or even sexual preference. Gender perspective is a mental (cognitive and affective) framework, often unconscious, which colors or conditions perception, values, and behavior and is likely learned through an interaction of biology and social influence. The perspective can be approached in terms of masculine and feminine "ideal types," recognizing that the gender perspective of any individual will be complexly and multiply influenced. Of course, other impersonal factors are critically important to venture start-ups, including cultural, temporal, and industrial conditions within which the founder embeds the new venture.

---

2. In doing so, we run counter to current practice in many research studies where respondents are asked to respond to gender (M or F) and "gender" is equated with biological sex. Feminist theorists and research on sex, however, draw distinctions between biology and socialized self- and role-concepts.

We approach gender perspective from three theoretical roots—Jungian psychology, cognitive and moral development, and feminist theory—to cover much of the cognitive and perceptual domain from depth psychology to political framing. We synthesize these into five gender perspective dimensions that interact and influence the "gendering" of the organizing process and resultant new organization. Given that masculine or "creator" organizing processes are well explicated, we focus our attention on an archetypal feminine or "creatrix" process and organizational attributes at the other end of the gender spectrum. That is, while some form of gender balance is most likely in practice, we highlight the less obvious and less articulated feminine aspects. We suggest that the gendered nature of new venture creation and operations is less visible, in part due to limited exposure of "successful" women-led ventures and their creators in media and literature (Baker, Aldrich, & Liou, 1997). Hence the gendered nature is more discernible only when one is ready to see it, most apparent when looking under the surface of the enterprise, and relatively invisible at the level of the firm or populations of firms. Following this, we discuss gendered maturity, a core individual difference that influences "feminine" forms of organizing. We conclude with implications and suggestions for future research.

FEMININE AND MASCULINE PERSPECTIVES

Jungian Psychology

Carl Jung (1951/1971a) postulated the existence of masculine and feminine principles as core components of personality. He argued that one's ego or conscious identity as man or woman (socialized and articulated in a cultural and temporal context) was balanced by an unconscious unarticulated complement. For men it is the inner feminine or "anima" and for women, the inner masculine or "animus." These conscious and unconscious currents function to help us become more individuated (i.e., differentiated and complex) as personalities, and structure our relationship to the "opposite sex" (Sanford, 1980). The anima and animus are archetypes that are collective and not personal; they have cross-cultural and cross-historical meanings. The anima is associated with Eros (the principle of love) and the positive and negative associations with a generalized mother (e.g., life-giver, nurturer, manipulator); the animus is associated with Logos (the principle of discrimination and cognition) and the positive and negative associations with a generalized father (e.g., protector, provider, tyrant). In all cultures, everyone is somehow touched by both masculine and feminine energies and sex at birth determines which becomes conscious through socialization and where we begin our process of individuation.

Other interpreters of Jung (de Castillejo, 1973; Woodman, 1982), add aspects to the feminine such as diffuse awareness, holism, slower pace, meandering spiral patterns, and present-centered time frame. The masculine is elaborated with focused awareness, analysis, faster pace, direct pathways, and past and future time frames.

In sum, the Jungian view highlights differences in personality components where the masculine is discriminating, goal oriented, drawn to explaining, improving, and providing, and the feminine is nurturing, holistic, and accepting. While there are other psychological approaches to gender, the Jungian approach offers an initial perspective on how the masculine and feminine worldviews (in Western developed economies) differ.

Moral Development

Psychologists other than Jungians contribute to this deeper appreciation of the feminine and masculine. In her research on moral development, Carol Gilligan (1982, 1988) points out differences in the worldviews of women and men. highlighting the issue of interpretation. Having a hierarchical and legalistic view, the masculine looks to social conventions and rules to guide moral decisions. Responsibility begins with responsibility to self and then extends outward to others. Responsibility is thus seen as "a limitation of action, a restraint of aggression, guided by the recognition that his actions can have effects on others, just as theirs can interfere with him" (Gilligan, 1982, p. 37). Rules serve to limit or constrain aggressive or intrusive behavior making "life in the community safe, protecting autonomy through reciprocity, extending the same consideration to others and self" (p. 38). The justice orientation idealizes reciprocal rights and equal respect of individuals in contrast to inequality and oppression (Gilligan & Attanucci, 1988). It considers one's role responsibilities, duties, standards, rules, and principles, including what is fair. It manifests in how decisions are justified and whether values, principles, and standards are maintained. In this way moral judgment is impersonal, abstract, and formal (Tronto, 1987).

The feminine, in contrast, sees the world as a network or web of relationships and is guided in moral decision making by the desire to preserve connections. Thus, "awareness of the connection between people gives rise to a recognition of responsibility for one another" (Gilligan, 1982, p. 30). For the feminine, responsibility "signifies response, an extension rather than a limitation of action. Thus it connotes an act of care rather than the restraint of aggression" (p. 38). The care perspective idealizes attention and response to others' needs and the problem of detachment or abandonment (Gilligan & Attanucci, 1988). It considers maintenance of relationships and interdependencies and helping others to benefit, avoid harm, or recover from harm. It is seen in descriptions of what happens and whether relationships are maintained or restored. In this way the ethic of care is personal, particular, and tied to concrete circumstances and action (Tronto, 1987).

Empirical research shows that most people reflect both the justice and caring orientations when faced with moral conflicts but tend to be more focused on one or the other. Furthermore, nearly all men focused on justice in rationalizing their decisions whereas nearly equal numbers of women focused on justice as on caring (Gilligan & Attanucci, 1988). Other research suggests that the differential application of the justice or caring orientation depends on the type of dilemma one is facing (Walker, de Vries, & Trevethan, 1987), where women tend to propose real-life dilemmas of care more than dilemmas of justice, while the opposite is true for men (Bebeau & Brabeck, 1994, Jack & Jack, 1988). Other empirical and conceptual work critiques Gilligan and her colleagues on methodology and for justifying behaviors of subjugation (Puka, 1990, 1994).

In sum, the gendered moral perspective, while open to controversy, distinguishes differences in world interpretation where the masculine is rule based, legal, and hierarchical and the feminine relies on relational decision making and care.

Feminist Theory

Feminist theory provides us with another critical perspective on the feminine principle. Feminist theory is characterized by a tension between efforts to identify and articulate a uniquely feminine voice for a multitude of phenomena and efforts to deconstruct gender as an important individual difference (Alcoff, 1988; Belenky, Clinchy, Goldberger, & Tarule, 1986; Ferguson, 1984, 1991; Fletcher, 1994). The voice perspective "opposes the identities and coherencies contained in patriarchal theory in the name of . . . a different and better way of thinking and living" (Ferguson, 1984, p. 321). The deconstruction perspective steps back from masculine versus feminine comparisons and contrasts to "loosen the hold of gender on life and meaning" (Ferguson, 1991, p. 321). Deconstruction focuses on a political reinterpretation of organizational phenomena and points to the dominance of some perspectives (e.g., males, whites, and developed economies) and the silencing of other perspectives. The feminine voice emphasizes the need to speak with and listen to women's perspectives to direct political change.

Scholars have woven these into critiques of existing organizational forms (for the most part mature and large entities) and reports of feminist alternatives. Acker (1990, 1992), Ferguson (1984), and Ramsey and Calvert (1994) condemn bureaucracy and hierarchy in particular for their objectification of workers, separation and subsequent formalization of personnel management, and resistance to seeing human problems in organizations as structural rather than merely poor person-job fit. These issues reflect the shadow of bureaucratic "strengths" identified by Weber (1947) and originally applied to organizations in a different zeitgeist with considerably fewer women in the workplace and even fewer in leadership than are found in contemporary American and European enterprise. While bureaucracy need not emerge out of an entrepreneurial venture, the shadow of bureaucracy lingers as organizations grow and bring on "professional" management (Flamholtz, 1990). Acker (1990) argues that existing organizational logic has implicit gender distinctions, symbols, interactions, and identities, and these make jobs and hierarchies abstract and separate from the people who work and live within them. Furthermore, "the absence of sexuality, emotionality, and procreation in organizational logic and organizational theory is an additional element that both obscures and helps to reproduce the underlying gender relations" (p. 151). For example, lack of attention to these "facts of life" results in family-unfriendly workplaces. Even when emotional phenomena are addressed by organizations, it is usually as emotional labor (Martin et al., 1998; Rafaeli, 1989; Rafaeli & Sutton, 1989), something used instrumentally to serve the organization.

Ferguson (1984) proposes a feminist alternative that would "undermine the chain of command, equalize the participants, subvert the monopoly on information and secrecy of decision-making, and essentially seek to democratize the organization" (p. 209). Building on Ferguson's work, Ramsey and Calvert (1994) outline basic dimensions for a feminist vision of organizing. Hierarchy is recognized as limiting organizational responsiveness and damaging individuals largely because status and position are relatively permanent; the alternative has temporary and shifting power relationships' which are more responsive to internal organizational concerns as well as external ones. The feminist alternative replaces ranking with linking, enacts leadership as central in a web rather than at the top of the hierarchy, and advocates power-with and cooperation instead of power-over and competition, thus "embracing collectivist decision-making, member empowerment, and a political agenda of ending women's oppression" (Ferree & Martin, 1995).

In the feminist ideal, leaders are characterized more by affiliation motivation (associated with interest in appreciating and developing others [Boyatizis, 1991; Harlos, 1995] paired with power motivation (associated with serving a social rather than personal good) rather than by a more traditional characteristic of achievement motivation (associated with individual contribution) paired with personal or social power (McClelland, 1961). The feminist perspective also shifts from preeminence given to organizational needs and values to individual needs and values, and from top-down empowerment to self-determination. It recasts maturity and healthy identity as embedded in interpersonal relationships rather than in autonomy. Finally, it embraces inclusion of the whole person, especially "private" aspects such as emotion, sexuality, race, and family issues in the organization rather than excluding these from overt consideration (Martin et al., 1998; Mumby & Putnam, 1992; Ramsey & Calvert, 1994; Taylor, 1995). While contemporary American and European management have found the value in some of these alternatives (but not all), there is strong resistance to identifying them as having a feminine source (Fondas, 1997).

In sum, the feminist deconstruction and political perspective suggests that male-founded bureaucratic organizations objectify work, through symbols and identity, which suppresses the feminine voice. An alternative feminist bureaucracy is based on affiliation, self-determination, social good, and equality. We conclude that these three perspectives on masculine and feminine "ideal types" can be distilled and focused into five dimensions of gender perspective relevant for examining new venture creation. These dimensions are the concepts of reality, time, action/interaction, power, and ethics.

Table 1 shows these dimensions listed as opposite ends of a continuum, as a link to the ideal types of gender. However they are best conceived as independent elements in the weaving-of-new-organizations creation process. There is no element that is primary, and each interacts with others and with factors not considered here (e.g., personalities and age of the principal(s), family influences, history, culture, economy, and industry structure) to produce a wide variety of entrepreneurial organizing. For example, one can compete playfully or strategically in an empowering or controlling way in the pursuit of a goal or just for fun. The gender perspective of founders may have an important and heretofore relatively invisible impact on both the process of venture creation and the attributes of the newly created organizations.

PROCESS OF ORGANIZATION CREATION—TOWARD A FEMININE VIEW

The process of starting a new organization has been described as involving as many as 57 discrete steps (Swayne & Tucker, 1973). These can be reduced to five broad not necessarily sequential activities: (1) locating an opportunity and forming the intention to start a venture (Cole, 1965; Glade, 1967; Reynolds, 1991); (2) accumulating resources including capital, technology, and talent to pursue the opportunity (Vesper, 1990); (3) allocating or deploying resources and establishing procedures for their use in producing and marketing products and services (Becker & Gordon, 1966; Cole, 1965; Shaver & Scott, 1991; Vesper, 1990); (4) building an organization, developing structure, establishing routines (Churchill & Lewis, 1983; Cole, 1965; Liebenstein, 1968); and (5) responding strategically to task and larger environments to survive, grow, and harvest values created (Cole, 1965).

Table 1

Gender Perspectives on the Entrepreneurial Process

Dimensions	Traditional (Masculine)	Personal (Feminine)
Concept of Reality	Focused consciousness	Diffuse awareness
	Analysis	Appreciation
	Separable nature	Interconnected nature
	Knowledge as control	Knowledge as caring
Time	Future	Present
	Faster pace	Slower pace
	Linear	Circular or spiral
Action/Interaction	Rational	Emotional
	Strategic, grounded in goals and reason	Personal, influenced by familial history and biology
	Competitive	Cooperative, caring
	Aggressive, violent	Harmonizing
	Distant	Empathic
Power	Mastery over others	Self-mastery
	Used for self	Used for others
	Centralized	Shared
Ethics	Responsibility as control over self	Responsibility as a response to others, circumstances
	Restrain aggression/limit behavior	Preserve relationships/repair harm
	Right and laws	Caring and fairness

The traditional process of starting a new venture shows a linear process typical of what is prescribed to potential entrepreneurs (Stevenson et al., 1994; Timmons, 1985) and which is often found in studies of entrepreneurial behavior (Swayne & Tucker, 1973), including studies of the behavior of women founders. These traditional processes are in keeping with a masculine perspective. Finding a *distinctly feminine process and a distinctly feminine form of organization creation* requires us to look at the five gendered dimensions from the other end of the spectrum (irrespective of the sex of the entrepreneur) and their impact on these processes. Thus, our focus is to articulate or give greater voice to the feminine side of these continua.

When the process is interpreted as feminine and the *concept of reality* includes less focused and more diffuse concepts of venturing, marketing, and organizing, the founder's reasons for venturing may not sound completely rational, strategic, or thought-through, and participants, including the founder, may feel confused, ambivalent, or lacking clear direction. The ways that entrepreneurs and their teams work through their ambivalence and confusion become data to understand the period of business incubation and the process of organizational creation. When knowledge is associated with caring more than control, the process of organizational creation may be more open, with more information shared rather than held closely, especially with those who are seen as caring about the venture's birth (e.g., family, friends, investors, customers, etc.)

When the *orientation toward time* is more present than future, there may be difficulty in writing a business plan with a 3-5-year horizon, and greater difficulty in negotiating terms of leases, loans, and employment. When the temporal orientation is more circular than linear, with loops of intention and effort circling back to earlier intention, there may be a perception of lack of progress. As a result, the process may take longer than a linear approach and the iteration may contribute to perceptions of lack of direction.

When *actions and interactions* are more emotional, personally motivated, relational, cooperative, and caring the venture created will likely reflect idiosyncrasies of the founder. For example, a venture formed to complement the founder's family situation (i.e., accommodating or assimilating the expectations and needs of one's spouse, parents, and children) is more likely to be a home-based business or a part-time business. Even if a full-time, off-site business is created, there may be a preference for policies favoring families, community involvement, and individuals' personal need fulfillment.

With a more feminine, less instrumental, orientation toward interaction, the founder may attempt to preserve relationships with "old timers" and partners even when they no longer serve the singular focus of organizational survival, growth, or profit. Such policies and practices can give rise to distinct organizational cultures and relative competitive (dis)advantages.

When the *power motive* of the founder is self-mastery or contributing to the social good more than dominance or self-benefit, the venture may have a different pattern of growth, a different ideology, and, as a result, a different emergent culture with relative strengths and weaknesses. Policies and practices may be created to extend self-mastery to others, for example through empowerment, to engage others in decision making, and to extend benefits to others (e.g., stock benefits, matching contributions to employees' charities, and reaching out to business "neighbors"). Likewise, there would be a greater likelihood and ease in establishing strategic alliances and other cooperative arrangements.

Finally, with a more feminine *ethic,* the entrepreneur is likely to be more responsive to others and less self-controlled. The organizing process is likely to be more open to negotiation and conciliation with apparent aggressors and less likely to apply the rule of law. Such a venture may obtain legal advice later and less frequently than more masculine/traditional forms and may be less likely to litigate and more likely to mediate conflicts. As a result of a feminine power and ethic, fewer secrets would be maintained.

Figure 1

Model of Gender Impacts on New Venture Creation

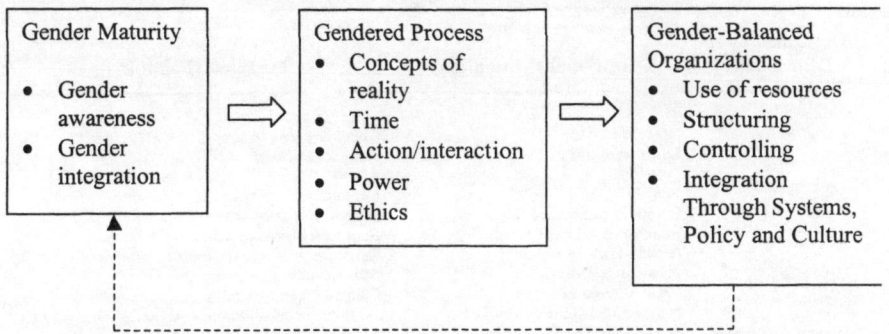

To the extent that the feminine perspective is active in organizing a new venture, the result of that process is likely to have distinct attributes. Figure 1 shows the relationship between the gendered process and its antecedents (**gender maturity**) and consequences (**gender-balanced** organizations).

"GENDERED" ATTRIBUTES OF NEW VENTURES

Organizations are characterized by an array of dimensions and attributes, but generally important in the early stages of organizational creation are four aspects: use of resources; structure; control; and integration through systems, policies, and culture (Churchill & Lewis, 1983; Katz & Gartner, 1988; Kotter, 1978; Scott, 1987; Scott & Bruce, 1987; Schein, 1985; Jelinek & Litterer, 1995). For each of these aspects there are gendered manifestations shown as continua in Table 2. We posit an "ideal" form[3] that is more distinctly feminine or personal and drawn primarily from cases of women-owned organizations. However, it is important to note that the personal/feminine attributes are also found in organizations initiated by men. Furthermore, not all women-founded organizations will have feminine characteristics. New ventures will most often comprise a combination of masculine/traditional and feminine/personal characteristics. However, the relative balance of these will vary based on variables previously discussed and others presented in the next section. Furthermore, we postulate that organizational scholars and practitioners can recognize and implement more personal/feminine features once these are framed as "gendered." That is, since some contemporary organizations work well with networks and flat structures, for example, entrepreneurs and organizational designers may wish to consider other personal/feminine possibilities.

Finally, while all dimensions can characterize any organization, in a newly created one, the values and gender perspective of the entrepreneur drive the purpose or mission of the organization, its policies, structure, and practices. New organizations, by virtue of their newness and smallness, have fewer stakeholders, minimal resource commitments, and few constraints imposed by institutionalization of procedures (Aldrich, 1999). Thus there is more freedom for the entrepreneur to create an organization consistent with

---

3. Akin to an ideal type, which is "pure," unrealistic and extreme to contrast with its "ideal" opposite or complement.

Table 2

Gender Impacts on New Venture Organizations

Organizational Dimensions	Traditional (Masculine)	Personal (Feminine)
Use of Resources	"Lease" people Low commitment Promoter	Commit to people High commitment Trustee
Structure	Formal Decisions centralized in entrepreneur Boundaries between people, jobs clear Growth leads to hierarchy	Informal Participative decisions Boundaries between people, jobs fuzzy Resists growth; growth leads to struggles to stay flat
Controlling	Personal control Financial control Dominant coalition of similars	Sharing control Cultural control No dominant coalition or coalition of diverse others
Integration Through Systems Culture Policies	Value is success for self & firm Policies instrumental toward goal Transactional	Value is well being for self & others Policies relational Accommodating

his/her conscious or unconscious gendered perspective and to create a venture with relative gender balance or imbalance. Arguably, the feminine form of organization is most likely to be seen in these early stages of an organization rather than in established organizations where "generations" of leaders, most of whom were men following traditional approaches, have each left their imprint on the administrative and cultural history of the organization.

Resource Use

How resources are used will differ based on the gendered perspective of the entrepreneur. The traditional/masculine approach to resources is to find ways to obtain and use them by leveraging rather than sacrificing the founder's own resources (e.g., use other people's money rather than sell your house). The traditional entrepreneur makes a short-term commitment to an opportunity and a minimal commitment of resources, renting rather than buying, and hiring contingent or contract workers rather than employing full-time staff, all designed to have lower risk and greater flexibility (Stevenson, 1985). The value of resources is perceived differently by the entrepreneur and the owner of the resources. When deciding whether to exploit an opportunity, the entrepreneur employs a rational process in assessing the price of resources, with the goal of capturing entrepreneural profit (Casson, 1982; Shane & Venkataraman, 2000). The traditional entrepreneur is encouraged to shift resources, making incremental commitments until a highly profitable and sustainable advantage is found (Bhide, 2000). By way of contrast, some ventures are founded with a more personal approach, where the individual is fully at risk and makes a deeper personal commitment to both the opportunity and the resources, including employees. The personal/feminine venture is likely to be self- or family-funded, with the intention of a long-term involvement (Cliff, 1998). The personalized version of the entrepreneur is likely to persist longer in a marginal business because it is personal to him/her and because people employed and invested matter to him/her. The difference between these two types is exemplified in companies "built to flip"—fast-growth venture-capital-funded enterprises where values and people are temporary—compared to those "built to last"—those founded on core values meant to infuse work with meaning and a legacy for company permanence (Collins, 2000).

Chantal Cookware, founded by Heida Thurlow[4] provides an illustration of the feminine dimension with regard to use of resources. Chantal was founded on a principle of lasting personal relationships, ones that are not severed even when an employee leaves. For example, a young sales manager left to pursue a career-growth opportunity with another housewares manufacturer. Heida proclaimed "In a way, he'll always remain a part of the family. He'll always stay in touch. I know we'll go and have dinners with him in San Francisco at the Gourmet Show. I know we will know what's going on in David's life."

Likewise, Thurlow makes a personal commitment to assisting with her employees' long-term financial security. Unlike many small and founder-led firms, Chantal has a 401 (k) program[5] and Thurlow is committed to getting her employees involved.

I want to make people feel that they are important, that their health is important. I truly feel that I want them to know that their health is important to me, that their future is important to me, that their retirement is important me. I don't know if you saw the picture. I think it's now in the copy room. It was a drawing that the guy who presented the 401K plan to us had in his brochure. It's a picture, a drawing of a little pleasure boat and two or three retired people with their fishing poles and different races and everybody is smiling. It says something important—to prepare for your retirement, to remember to save for the golden years. I had that picture blown up into a poster and I'm trying to tell people how important it is to me. Anybody that has worked for me or with me for twenty, thirty years, when they retire I would want them to not have to worry where their living, where their income would be coming from.

The feminine perspective makes a longer-term, deeper, and personal commitment to resources. Entrepreneurs anchored here more than the traditional/masculine end of the continuum, care about resources and their continuity. This may account, in part, for the greater likelihood of repayment of micro-loans made to women than those made to men in developing economies (Ducheneaut, 1997).

Structure

The structure of an organization articulates the relationships, roles, and principles that shape the organization (Kotter, 1978; Scott, 1987). Specialization divides work and resources according to some logic (e.g., function, geography, customer, etc.) to allow economies of scale. Formalization objectifies the structure, facilitating the interaction of organizational participants, while informal structures such as norms and expectations bind and integrate patterns of behavior within the organization. A premise of new venture growth and development is the formation of hierarchy and structures (Churchill & Lewis, 1983; Flamholtz, 1990). The faster the growth and the more ties to institutional sources of funding, the more formalized the structure is expected to be (Bhide, 2000).

---

4. Data on Chantal, Berner International, Rand Corporation, and Flight Time were obtained as part of a systematic study of successful women executives and entrepreneurs and included two questionnaires, several hours of interviews with the founder, a day of observation, and interviews with key subordinates and outsiders.

5. A 401(k) is an employer-sponsored retirement savings plan that allows employees to make pre-tax contributions, often matched by the employer.

Hierarchy distances ownership, management, and operations from one another along lines of control, and channels communication.

The feminine/personal organization would manifest in a structure that balances the need for boundaries and separation with the advantages of inclusiveness and trust. This form is thus more open, less secretive, with flatter hierarchy, resembling a network of partnerships whether or not that is the legal structure of incorporation. When hierarchy exists, it would be grounded in values other than control. For example, individuals who have a creative capacity for generating synergy with others (a higher form of value creation) will likely be seen as equally or more important than those with control over money, information, and other tools of control.

Recent studies by Helgeson (1990) show the feasibility of a web-like organizational form even among large firms. Research on women-owned ventures shows that structure may be web-like, interconnected rather than hierarchical (Brush, 1992). Among entrepreneurs, both male and female, this may be even more common, especially in Internet and virtual firms. A flatter, interconnected structure is also a means of revitalizing flagging enterprises. Lars Kolind (Hagstrom, 1995) led the revival of the Oticon A/S lagging hearing aid business by mandating a vision that included "despecializing" people while maintaining their excellent specialties, dropping departmental structure in favor of projects, creating a physical space that allowed flexibility as project teams disbanded and reformed, and using computers to rid the firm of most paper. In the reformed "spaghetti organization," everyone has several "jobs" and everyone belongs to one pool of resources. The organizing dimensions of project, specialty, and people (coaching and personal development) function to coordinate and use resources, but no manager has control.

> There is no control of working hours and employees decide themselves for how long and when they have vacations. There is little control of projects and the situation is rather chaotic. Most projects eventually find themselves phased into the electronic project information system, but there are still no specific mechanisms in place to restrain a project leader from over-spending on and over-staffing a particular project. The "spaghetti" of organization is seen to illustrate the disorderly links between, and boundaries around, people in the organization. Also a pot of boiling spaghetti gives a distinct impression of chaos. However, fishing out a single strand of spaghetti one can easily follow it to the end. This is similar to how projects can be readily identified and followed in Oticon's organization (p. 5).

Today Oticon employs 1500 people and sells its products to 100 countries worldwide and is by most measures, successful.

Control

Traditionally, decision-making systems are centralized in the individual entrepreneur or a "dominant coalition" of familiars (Baker & Aldrich, 1994) and usually are rationalized by research and analysis, although organizational politics can enter, especially as the firm increases in size. Traditional controls are financial in nature, attending to the maxim "cash is king" and oriented toward time-related goals (Gersick, 1994). Strategic but fast decision making is valued. In traditional control paradigms, non-disclosure agreements and other legal action protect boundaries.

Decision-making systems in a feminine/personal organization reflect shared control and wider participation in the process, validated by intuition and feelings. These systems are more open with less distinct boundaries. Some feminist organizations proactively seek a diversity of voices in decision making. Feminine controls are interpersonal or cultural in nature, resting on more intuitive and emotionally salient perspectives. Decisions often take longer than in more traditional systems. Because the feminine/personal organization is more open and less secretive, legal action is perceived as a last resort after interpersonal mediation fails.

Quality control and the use of reward systems are other ways that control operates in traditional and personal ventures. Traditional quality control involves measurement and statistics whereas the more personal approach involves education. Again, Chantal offers a good example. Quality control is critical to this small business and an internal quality control function has been established. The firm found that one of its long-term suppliers in Germany was no longer providing the quality controls Chantal needed. Rather than looking for an alternative supplier, the firm decided to take the time to teach quality control methods to their German collaborator. The CEO, Heida Thurlow, attempts to institutionalize this way of thinking:

> My mission always has been treating people with respect. Whether it's the people on the team or the customers or the suppliers. It's even written in our manual. If anybody comes to the office to sell something I want these people to be treated with respect and if they have an appointment, if something comes up that you can't see them at the appointed time, do not let them wait longer than fifteen minutes."

Likewise, traditional reward systems link performance to financial and career rewards. A more personal approach looks to individual growth. Employees are valued for their willingness and ability to express their uniqueness in appropriate ways and to make the sacrifices necessary to be a team player, as well as the more traditional metrics of productivity. Efforts to encourage employee development and learning are typical. Georgia Berner (Berner International) encourages and pays for employees to take foreign language classes and attend school for advanced degrees in addition to trade workshops and training seminars. She believes that "educating" her employees develops them as people which makes the company overall more effective in its business dealings.

Integration Through Systems, Policies, and Culture

The culture of a new venture hinges largely on the values of the entrepreneur. These provide the sense of what "ought" to be (Schein, 1985). Traditional entrepreneurial values include financial success (survival, profits, and wealth), power in demonstrations of personal efficacy and business competitive advantage, personal or ego gratification seen in autonomy accorded the self-employed, and the tendency to hire people more like the founder than different from him (Bird, 1989, Baker & Aldrich, 1994). In growing or mature ventures, there is an effort to formalize systems, provide tangible incentives and rewards, and prescribe objective work rules for particular roles and responsibilities. In part, this is done through the articulation of formal planning processes. The extent to which planning processes, systems, and roles are formalized depends on the external demands for legitimacy, often generated by venture capitalists, funders, or other stakeholders (Stone & Brush, 1996; Bhide, 2000).

A feminine organization would reflect different values, culture, and social relations. As suggested earlier, values might be more existential than driven toward definable goals, reflective of the personal values of the founder and oriented toward well-being, cooperation and caring, self-determination, and preservation of relationships. Indeed, if the personal perspective follows contemporary feminist thinking, there will be a commitment to hire, retain, and give voice and power to a greater diversity of individuals than does the traditional perspective. However, as the feminine organization ages, the greater affiliation and less instrumental social networks could result in less cumulative diversity because the organization has fewer replacement hires and less opportunity to draw upon even greater heterogeneity.[6] In contrast to the traditional venture, the personal venture would have fewer work rules and less formalized separation of roles. Because it is personal and not primarily aimed at wealth creation, it would have fewer external investors, less need for external financial legitimacy,[7] and thus might engage in formal planning later than more masculine ventures.

Values feed into the entrepreneur's vision for the venture (Bird & Brush, 2000; Collins & Lazier, 1995). The vision of a traditional new venture would include content such as becoming the leader in an industry or market, setting standards, gaining a reputation, making employee-owners millionaires, and going public. Feminine perspective ventures would have visions with more "heart," focused more internally on the firm and its well being and the quality of relationships both internal and external.

The routines, systems, and culture of Rand Construction illustrate some of the feminine dimensions, particularly since the industry is populated with traditional masculine firms. Founder and CEO Linda Rabbit operates her business with a team structure. No one operates alone and teams keep changing as needs of clients and projects change. Rabbit is an active member of the teams and there is little hierarchy in her 40-person firm, where people gain status by "being good to their customers and by having a following, a group of believers who want you to work on their project." In addition, Rabbit breaks industry norms by bringing together the field staff and the office people once a year to do strategic planning. Industry norms keep the field staff excluded from this level of input.

Another example is Georgia Berner, president of Berner International, a producer of air doors. The routines and systems are informal and flexible. For instance, each week Berner holds a meeting of staff, but anyone can come. It is an open meeting, where she sits at the back of the room. The discussion is led by the person(s) that have issues to discuss. Subcommittees and task forces are formed and disbanded depending on how issues are decided by the group. Berner gets involved for clarification on issues, and on strategic topics. New systems are put in place as a result of the meeting. Similarly, the workspace is completely open, which is a physical manifestation of the openness of the culture. Berner states her vision as "becoming the name in the marketplace for solving customers' problems by producing, selling, and servicing the highest quality of air doors and related products, for the lowest possible cost—in a cooperative, respectful environment of team work and mutual support."

Policies are the rules or courses of action that guide specific decisions (e.g., vacation policies, promotion policies; Selznick, 1957). Policies are mechanisms intended to guarantee consistent actions throughout the organization and across time (Hofer & Schendel, 1978). Policies may cover financial procedures, operations guidelines (e.g. manufacturing), marketing and customer contact, information sharing and disclosure, and decision making (Andrews, 1987). Policies guide performance through reward structures, whether they are contingent on performance or individually or collectively based (Aldrich, 1999). Traditional policy orientation establishes formal and psychological contracts with employees to limit and channel authority and discretion, and treats employees as instruments of the organization within their zone of acceptance (Thompson, 1967). These policies are often monitored through objective and subjective personnel evaluations

---

6. Thanks to Becky Reuber for pointing this out in an early review of this paper.
7. There may be need for external social legitimacy, a sense of belonging to a community of businesses and network organizations but there is no apriori reason to think that this might impact formal planning. (Again, thanks to Becky Reuber for pointing this out.)

(Bretz, Milkovich, & Read, 1992; Latham & Wexley, 1981). A similar approach is traditionally used with other stakeholders such as vendors and customers.

At the other end of the spectrum we might find a more feminine or personal policy orientation that would include agreements containing considerable flexibility to accommodate the biological, familial, and even spiritual needs of employees, and sharing of authority and even ownership; the sharing might even extend to other organizational stakeholders. Thus the feminine firm would be likely to have flexible working hours and places, allow personal leave for family issues, and offer generous and flexible benefits. For example, Flight Time, a Boston-based charter flight business, serves as intermediary between airlines with excess flight space and customers who want to book flights. The jobs are stressful, but founders keep turnover low through selected policies and practices. The firm is very competitive with salaries and benefits, including a 401(k), profit sharing, a corporate apartment for employees visiting from distant offices. Patti Zinkowski, founder and CFO says "We have a little bit of golden handcuffs . . . auto and house loans to employees and now we're looking at ESOP." To help stressed staff, Flight Time has a gym, massage therapist, and personal trainers on site. The firm has also instituted an unpaid sabbatical after ten years.

> I recognize there's a burn out point. It seems like eight to ten years. So we say after ten years take a sabbatical. We have one guy that's going to go off and write a book. We had another woman whose sister was very sick and she decided to take almost a year off to sit with her sister with her whole deal of cancer. I took a year off. I went and rode my horses competitively all last year. I came back in April and bingo I can see the whole thing from a fresh eye. So we encourage them, if you're feeling this way, and we recognize the signs. You know you're just not happy, you come in late, or you're just dragging your feet. Go away for a little while and then come back.

While not a written policy, the hiring practices of feminine/personal ventures take on a humanism. Heida Thurlow (Chantal) has purposely hired "a little United Nations," seeking a diverse workforce represented by many ethnic, racial, linguistic, and physical abilities. Her hires have included individuals from shelters for abused women, Lighthouse for the blind, and refugee organizations. Like Thurlow, Berner's (Berner International) vision includes diversity and compassion in hiring. She has hired two women from a women's shelter where she serves on the board and one woman, from Bosnia, who did not speak English well.

We have described the feminine attributes of the new venture, attributes that tend to be unrecognized by the literature and not part of the normative approach to new venture creation (Bhide, 2000; Timmons, 1999). The feminine/personal is one end of a continuum with masculine/traditional at the other. We now turn to individual differences that might determine which end of the continuum or what mix of personal and traditional an entrepreneur might choose. From this enactment, spring the venture process and the new organization.

GENDERED MATURITY

While traditional approaches to entrepreneurship tend to dominate the academic literature, there is increasing attention to more personal approaches (e.g., Martin et al., 1998), particularly in popular (normative) media such as *Inc.* and *Fast Company*. Based on this, we believe that contemporary organizations, especially new ventures, often embody feminine/personal features without violating the economic, political, and technical imperatives addressed by the traditional process and environmental demands.

These organizations balance the traditional imperatives with more personal, existential, and relational features of the feminine. We believe that a critical individual difference, gendered maturity, may underlie these balanced approaches.

Not all founders are prepared to act out of their feminine capacity. Contributing as necessary to the creation of a balanced organization is the founder's gendered maturity. This we conceive as an individual's adult awareness of gender as an influence on behavior and social constructions and his or her conscious integration of both gender qualities in self-concepts, social roles, and behavior. In Jungian terms the male becomes conscious of and makes use of his usually unconscious feminine qualities and the female her usually unconscious masculine qualities. In terms of moral development, rights and laws are balanced with care and compassion. In power, there is a blend of separation and inclusion organizationally. Gendered maturity is the conscious integration, acceptance, appreciation, and enactment of qualities of both genders. It is conceptually analogous to emotional intelligence (Goleman, 1995) and psychological androgyny (Bem, 1974; Blanchard-Fields, Suhrer-Roussel, & Hertzog, 1994; Hall, Workman, & Marchioro, 1998; Stake, 1987). Gendered maturity is expected to result in the use of gender-balanced processes in new venture creation and the creation of relatively gender-balanced organizations. Thus gendered maturity is an individual level variable and gender-balance a process and organizational variable.

Gender maturity is a consequence of an entrepreneur's developmental experiences, including formal education, which points to the pervasive effect of gender. Courses, books, and public speakers address issues of feminism and masculinity in the U.S. At the same time, management scholarship has raised awareness of the impact of gender in the workplace and new ventures (Brush, 1992; Calas & Smircich, 1992; Chaganti, 1986; Fletcher, 1994; Helgesen, 1990, 1995; Mumby & Putnam, 1992, and others). Still, there is evidence that the feminine contribution to contemporary thought often disappears as "feminine" (Fondas, 1997). So the question of gender awareness remains.

In the United States, the historical milieu or zeitgeist in which an individual comes into conscious adulthood can have an "imprint" on the values and attitudes and gender awareness she or he enacts in later years as a business founder (Braungart & Braungart, 1984; Mannheim, 1952; Sheehy, 1995). This is also true in other countries that have seen changes in how women and the feminine are valued. Every age cohort "experiences shared formative social conditions at approximately the same point in their lives and . . . holds a common interpretive framework shaped by historical circumstances" (Whittier, 1995). This zeitgeist includes the degree to which gender-relevant laws have been passed to treat men and women equally (e.g., laws regarding community property, inheritance, etc.). It includes the degree to which women have been accepted in positions of leadership and men accepted in positions of service.

Historical zeitgeist also includes the relative and dynamic position of individuals with regard to social change issues such as "women's liberation" in the U.S. (e.g., the publication of Betty Friedan's *Feminine Mystique* in 1963) and women's rights following the 1991 global conference on women in Beijing. It also includes the recent attention in the U.S. on issues of masculinity (Palmer, 2000) and "reverse discrimination," where men fear career limitations due to sexual preferences for women and seek freedom from sexual harassment by men and women.

Even if cognizant of the differences, some founders have not integrated their feminine and masculine sides. Integration stems from social and psychological factors. Recall that for men, the feminine is relatively unconscious and for women the masculine is more unconscious and adult development includes the task of integrating these and other unconscious and unexpressed aspects of oneself (Jung 1928/1971b). Integration of the feminine means giving it equal weight and voice within the psyche, a formidable task in societies where both the feminine and the inner world of the unconscious have been undervalued, ignored, and even punished in years and eras past (Eisler, 1988). It is particularly formidable in the externally driven competitive world of business.

Many people are socialized from early childhood to support only the masculine model (Izraeli & Adler, 1994). Masculine views are unconsciously absorbed by both men and women; for instance, it is widely accepted that focus, analysis, goal-direction, control through knowledge, and rapid growth are important to organizational success (Hofer & Schendel, 1978; Kanter, 1983; Porter, 1985). We have yet to recognize or praise the value of diffused awareness, deep feelings, spiraling pathways, caring knowledge, affiliation, and satisfying balanced lives in a lifestyle business venture, nor do we find much praise for organizational policies and practices that share resources and knowledge and diffuse control and responsibility.

In the U.S. this has translated into a narrow band of appropriate gendered behavior in business. For years American women were expected to "dress for success" (which meant obscuring their sexuality) and encouraged to conduct business with the same laser-like focus and aggression that successful men appear to have. Consequently, women competed with each other for token, "queen bee" positions in the hierarchy and thereby reinforced the power of dominance. On the other hand, men were expected to withhold expression of any feminine perspectives for fear of being seen as ineffectual, effeminate, or gay (Mindell, 1995). The organization was "masculine" and men and women were expected to integrate, understand, and enact the masculine views to be accepted (Henning & Jardim, 1977). Because of this, it is likely that the masculine will predominate in the less gender-aware and gender-integrated individual, whether the person is male or female. However, less aware and less integrated females might manifest a largely feminine perspective.

It is not the purpose of this paper to fully operationalize gendered maturity. However, as conceived here it can be approached by measures of psychological androgyny (Bem, 1974; Blanchard-Fields et al., 1994) and attitudes toward gender. As we begin to look for individual differences in gendered maturity, we might begin to see the founding process occurring in different ways and with different outcomes than we have seen in the literature to date. Where individuals have higher degrees of gendered maturity, organizations and processes exhibit higher degrees of gender-balance.

Proposition 1: The greater the gendered maturity of an entrepreneur, the greater the likelihood of the venture process and outcome having a balance of traditional and personal qualities.

Proposition 2: The less gender-mature a female entrepreneur, the more likely her venture process and outcome is skewed to one of the extremes.

Proposition 3: The less gender-mature a male entrepreneur, the more likely his venture process and outcome is skewed to the traditional/masculine extreme.

IMPLICATIONS

We have argued that there is a feminine side to new venture creation, grounded on three theoretical perspectives. These theoretical views were synthesized into five dimensions that elaborate the feminine or personal and masculine or traditional ends of the spectrum with regard to how venture creation proceeds. We then extended this spectrum to new venture organizations with an emphasis on articulating the more silent feminine/personal end. Finally, because entrepreneurs and ventures are likely to manifest both masculine and feminine attributes, we proposed two new constructs, gendered-maturity and gender-balance, to describe individuals and ventures, respectively. As a result, we can see how individuals may be more or less able to include the feminine or personal perspective in their ventures, and some of the consequences of a gender-balanced firm. Clearly, entrepreneurial behavior will be affected by the gender maturity of the individual and the firm he or she creates.

If we were to frame entrepreneurial behavior research with a gendered lens, we might consider the impact of the feminine when looking at the process of organizing, leading, and growing a nascent enterprise. New considerations might usefully include: (1) the degree to which the entrepreneur engages in self-reflection in order to maintain a balance between personal and work priorities; (2) whether and how they create policies and practices that would enable and encourage employees to engage in their own reflection to achieve balance; (3) how aversive or easy it is for the entrepreneur to build an empowered workforce, delegating, training, and rewarding increasing management and leadership competence, rather than shedding "old timers"; (4) the degree of balance toward the external environment from solely opportunistic, competitive, and acquisitive to socially responsible; and (5) whether and how charitable actions of the entrepreneur are part of the venture and extended by policies to support these actions in employees.

Thus, by looking for and measuring the feminine/personal and traditional/masculine dimensions of individuals and process, research might identify ways that men and women behave similarly and differently. This would resolve the two dilemmas introduced earlier that entrepreneurship theory may not reflect the realities of women and that our conceptualizations of entrepreneurship lack construct validity. Extended to gender perspectives of the new organization, research might begin to address the impact of gender skewness and balance on strategy. For example, is a feminine, masculine, or balanced venture more or less likely to set calendar-based plans, use gantt charts, aim at growth, use boards of directors, engage in formal or informal alliances, require nondisclosure and noncompetitive agreements of employees and advisors? Finally, when faced with economic downturns, how do gendered ventures respond?

In addition, when founders and ventures are "sorted" on gender maturity and gender balance, researchers and practitioners may also extend the model to look at performance differences. At this point researchers and practitioners would need to review performance through the gender lens. What are the gendered perspectives on venture survival, success, growth, and founder and team satisfaction?

Finally, the model may extend a feedback loop from the gender-balanced organization to the creation of gender-balanced individuals. Employees and other stakeholders and associates of the gender-mature entrepreneur and his or her gender-balanced enterprise may arrive at greater awareness and integration of the traditional/masculine and personal/feminine perspectives.

LIMITATIONS

The model we propose is admittedly ethnocentric based on the developmental and psychological models of the United States and Europe. The psychology, development, and zeitgeist of men and women in other cultures do vary in important ways. For example, some cultures value masculinity and power distance. In these cultures individual initiative influences social and economic development as well as opportunities for gender balance; other cultures are more communal with different social and economic impacts for gender balances (Hofstede, 1980, 1991; Sundin, 1996; Holmquist, 1996).

The social, familial, and work roles, responsibilities, and rights held by men and women vary widely across cultures (Aldrich, 1989; Lerner, Brush, & Hisrich, 1997; Ducheneaut, 1997). The degree to which family responsibilities and family wealth are shared by both men and women, the degree to which occupations are open and accessible to both men and women, and the degree to which social groups, networks, clubs, and athletics are open to both genders will permit greater opportunity for gender balance in how one organizes a new venture and the attributes of the new organization. For example, in Sweden 90% of jobs as typists, nurses, or housekeepers are filled by women and 60% of work in the public sector (government) is done by women, compared to less than 25% of those starting businesses (Holmquist, 1996). Thus even Sweden, with its social support for women, shows occupational segregation. Relatedly, in some countries 30-40% of the self-employed are women (e.g., Canada, U.S., Australia), while in other countries the percentage is below 20% (e.g., Ireland, Turkey, Greece; Ducheneaut, 1997). In other countries, such as Syria and Afghanistan, women have limited rights to inherit and limited opportunities to work outside their father's or husband's homes. Therefore the culture of origin of the founder needs, at least for now, to qualify the gendered model.

Even industry "culture" may play a role in allowing a more gender-balanced entrepreneurial process and new venture forms. For example, feminine/personal organizations may be more frequent in low-technology niches and in industries anchored on caring and service. Technology-driven firms tend to be highly competitive and characterized by a sense of urgency and pressure for growth that is foreign to the feminine/personal model, while service, health care, nursing, child care, education, and the arts are areas more compatible. Notwithstanding these differences, the norm of new business creation and survival is the traditional/masculine. Due to the social desirability of the legitimacy conferred by this norm it may be difficult to find feminine or gender-mature founders or feminine or gender-balanced organizations. As a result we don't know how frequently these patterns may be enacted. Seen from the outside, all firms have marketing, financing, and human resource needs, often encompassed in a fairly standard template dictated by legal and financial requirements. In this way, most successful firms are similar. What we don't see is how the firms are structured, how they operate, and what spirit possesses them. To see this we need to look below the surface into the heart of the venture where we might find gender-mature leaders and processes. We need to look for them. We need to expect more than or other than business-as-usual.

REFERENCES

Acker, J. (1990). Hierarchies, jobs, bodies: A theory of gendered organizations. *Gender & Society*, 4(2), 139-158.

Acker, J. (1992). Gendering organizational theory. In A. Mills & P. Tancred (Eds.), *Gendering organizational analysis*. Newbury Park: CA: Sage.

Alcoff, L. (1988). Cultural feminism versus post-structuralism: The identity crisis in feminist theory. *Signs: Journal of Women in Culture and Society, 13*(3), 405-436.

Aldrich, H. (1989). Networking among women entrepreneurs. In O. Hagan, C. Rivchun, & D. E. Sexton (Eds.), *Women owned businesses*, pp. 103-132. New York: Praeger.

Aldrich, H. (1999). *Organizations evolving*. London: Sage Publications.

Andrews, K. (1987). The concept of corporate strategy, Homewood, IL: Richard D. Irwin.

Baker, T., & Aldrich, H. (1994). Friends and strangers: Early hiring practices and idiosyncratic jobs. In Bygrave (Eds.), *Frontiers of entrepreneurship research 1994*. Wellesley, MA: Babson College.

Baker, T., Aldrich, H., & Liou, N. (1997). Invisible entrepreneurs: The neglect of women business owners by mass media and scholarly journals in the US. *Entrepreneurship and Regional Development*, 9, 221-238.

Baumol, (1993). Formal entrepreneurship theory in economics: Existence and bounds. *Journal of Business Venturing, 8*(3), 197-210

Bebeau, M., & Brabeck, M. (1994). Ethical sensitivity and moral reasoning among men and women in the professions. In B. Puka (Ed.), *Caring voices and women's moral frames,* pp. 240-259). New York: Garland.

Becker, G. S., & Gordon, G. (1966). An entrepreneurial theory of formal organizations, Part I: Patterns of formal organizations. *Administrative Sciences Quarterly,* Dec, 315-344.

Belenky, M. F., Clinchy, B. M, Goldberger, N. R., & Tarule, J. (1986). *Women's ways of knowing: The development of self, voice, and mind.* New York: Basic Books.

Bem. S. L. (1974). The measurement of psychological androgyny. *Journal of Consulting and Clinical Psychology, 42,* 155-162.

Bhide, A. (2000). *The origin and evolution of new business.* New York: Oxford Press.

Bird, B. J. (1989). *Entrepreneurial behavior.* Glenview, IL: Scott Foresman.

Bird, B. J., & Brush, C. (2000). Vision of women entrepreneurs and executives: A hint for the new millennium. Paper presented at the USASBE conference, San Antonio, TX.

Blanchard-Fields, F., Suhrer-Roussel, L., & Hertzog, C. (1994). A confirmatory factor analysis of the Bem Sex Role Inventory: Old questions, new answers. *Sex Roles, 30*(5-6), 423-457.

Boyatzis, R. (1991). The need for close relationships and the manager's job. In D. Kolb, I. Rubin, & J. Osland (Eds.) The Organizational Behavior Reader (5th Ed.). Englewood Cliffs, NJ: Prentice-Hall.

Braungart, R. G., & Braungart, M. M. (1984). Life course and generational politics. *Journal of Political and Military Sociology, 12*(1), 1-8.

Bretz, R., Milkovich, G., & Read, W. (1992). The current state of performance appraisal research and practice: Concerns, directions, and implications. *Journal of Management,* June, 326.

Bruno, A., & Tyebjee, T. (1982). The environment for entrepreneurship. In C. Kent, D. Sexton, & K. Vesper (Eds.), *The encyclopedia of entrepreneurship,* pp. 288-307. Englewood Cliffs, NJ: Prentice Hall.

Brush, C. G. (1990). Women and enterprise creation. In S. Gould, & J. Parzen (Eds.), *Women, entrepreneurship and economic development,* pp. 37-50. Paris: Organization for Economic Cooperation and Development (OECD).

Brush, C. G. (1992). Research on women business owners: Past trends, a new perspective and future directions. *Entrepreneurship Theory and Practice, 16*(4), 5-30.

Bull, I., & Willard, G. E. (1993). Towards a theory of entrepreneurship. *Journal of Business Venturing, 8,* 183-195.

Bygrave, W. D. (1993). Theory building in the entrepreneurial paradigm. *Journal of Business Venturing, 8,* 255-280.

Calas, M. B., & Smircich, L. (1992). Re-writing gender into organization theorizing: Directions from feminist perspectives. In M. Reed & M. Hughes (Eds.), *Re-thinking organizations: New directions in organizational research.* London: Sage.

Carter, N. M., Gartner, W. B., & Reynolds, P. D. (1996). Exploring start-up event sequences. *Journal of Business Venturing, 11,* 151-166.

Casson, M. (1982) *The entrepreneur.* Totowa, NJ: Barnes & Noble Books.

Chaganti, R. (1986). Management in women-owned enterprises. *Journal of Small Business Management, 24*(4), 18-29.

Cheng, C. (1996). *Masculiniites in organizations*. Thousand Oaks, CA: Sage.

Churchill, N. C., & Lewis, V. (1983). Five stages of business growth. *Harvard Business Review,* May-June, 30-50.

Cliff, J. E. (1998). Does one size fit all? Exploring the relationship between attitudes toward growth, gender, and business size. *Journal of Business Venturing,* 13, 523-542.

Cole, A. (1965). An approach to the study of entrepreneurship: A tribute to Edwin Gay. In H. D. Aitken (Ed.), *Explorations in entrepreneurship*. Cambridge, MA: Harvard University Press.

Collins, J. (2000) Built to flip? *Fast Company,* March, 131-145

Collins, J., & Lazier, W. (1995). *Managing the small to mid-sized company*. Chicago: Irwin.

Collins, O. E., & Moore, D. G. (1964). *The enterprising man*. East Lansing, MI: MSU Business Studies.

Cooper, A., & Jimeno-Gascon, F. (1992). Entrepreneurs, process of founding and new firm performance. In D. Sexton & J. Kasarda, 301-340, *The State of the Art of Entrepreneurship*. Boston: PWS Kent.

de Castillejo, I. C. (1973). *Knowing woman: A feminine psychology*. New York: Harper.

Ducheneaut, B. (1997). Women entrepreneurs in SME's, A report prepared for the OECD conference on women entrepreneurs in small and medium enterprises: A major force for innovation and job creation. Paris: OECD.

Eisler, R. (1988). *The chalice and the blade: Our history, our future*. San Francisco: Harper & Row.

Ferguson, K. E. (1984). *The feminist case against bureaucracy*. Philadelphia: Temple University Press.

Ferguson, K. E. (1991). Interpretation and genealogy in feminism. *Signs: Journal of Women in culture and Society, 16*(2), 321-338.

Ferree, M., & Martin, P. (1995). Doing the work of the movement: Feminist organizations. In M. Ferree & P. Martin (Eds.), *Feminist organizations,* pp. 3-23. Philadelphia: Temple University Press.

Flamholtz, E. (1990). *Growing pains: How to make the transition from an entrepreneurship to a professionally managed firm*. San Francisco: Jossey-Bass.

Fletcher, J. K. (1994). Castrating the female advantage: Feminist standpoint research and management science. *Journal of Management Inquiry, 3*(1), 74-82.

Fondas, N. (1997). Feminization unveiled: Management qualities in contemporary writings. *Academy of Management Review, 22,* 257-282

Gartner, W. B. (1985). A conceptual framework for describing the phenomenon of new venture creation. *Academy of Management Review, 14*(4), 696-706.

Gartner, W. B. (1993). Words lead to deeds: Towards an organizational emergence vocabulary. *Journal of Business Venturing, 8*(3), 231-240.

Gersick, C. (1994). Pacing strategic change: The case of a new venture. *Academy of Management Journal, 37*(1), 9-45.

Gilligan, C. (1982). *In a different voice: Psychological theory and women's development*. Cambridge, MA: Harvard University Press.

Gilligan, C. (1988) Remapping the moral domain: New images of self in relationship. In C. Gilligan, J. Ward, & J. Taylor (Eds.), *Mapping the moral domain: A contribution of women's thinking to psychological theory and education,* p. 3-20. Cambridge, MA: Harvard University Press.

Gilligan, C., & Attanucci, J. (1988). Two moral orientations: Gender differences and similarities. *Merrill-Palmer Quarterly, 34*(3), 223-237.

Glade, W. P. (1967). Approaches to a theory of entrepreneurial formation. *Explorations in Entrepreneurial History, 4*(3), 245-259.

Goleman, D. (1995). *Emotional intelligence.* New York: Bantam.

Gottfried, H., & Weiss, P. (1994). A compound feminist organization: Purdue University's council on the status of women. *Women and Politics, 14*(2), 23-44.

Greiner, L. (1972). Evolution and revolution as organizations grow. *Harvard Business Review, 50*(4), 37-46.

Hagstrom, P. (1995). Oticon A/S: Project 330. Boston: Harvard Business School Publishing (case 9-195-141).

Hall, R., Workman, J., & Marchioro, C. (1998). Sex, task, and behavioral flexibility effects on leadership perceptions. *Organizational Behavior and Human Decision Processes, 74*(1), 1-32.

Hansen, E. (1995). Entrepreneurial networks and new organization growth. *Entrepreneurship Theory and Practice, 19*(4), 7-19.

Harlos, K. P. (1995). Beauty and the beast: Radical feminist theory and power in organizations. Paper presented to the Academy of Management, Vancouver, BC.

Hebert, R. F., & Link, A. N. (1982). *The entrepreneur: Mainstream views and radical critiques.* New York: Praeger Press.

Helgesen, S. (1990). *The female advantage: Women's ways of leadership.* New York: Currency/Doubleday.

Helgesen, S. (1995). *The web of inclusion.* New York: Currency/Doubleday.

Henning, M., & Jardim, A. (1977). *The managerial woman.* New York: Anchor/Doubleday.

Hofer, C., & Schendel, D. (1978) *Strategy formulation: Analytical concepts.* St Paul, MN: West Publishing.

Hofstede, G. (1980). *Culture's consequences: International differences in work related values.* Beverly Hills, CA: Sage Publications.

Hofstede, G. (1991). *Cultures and organizations: Software of the mind.* London: McGraw-Hill.

Holmquist, C. (1996). The female entrepreneur—Woman and or entrepreneur? In *Aspects of women's entrepreneurship,* pp. 87-114. Stockholm: Swedish National Board for Industrial and Technical Development.

Holmquist, C., & Sundin, E. (1990). What's special about highly educated women entrepreneurs? *Entrepreneurship and Regional Development, 2,* 181-193.

Izraeli, D., & Adler, N. J. (1994). Competitive frontiers: Women managers in a global economy. In N. J. Adler & D. N. Izraeli (Eds.), *Competitive frontiers: Women managers in a global economy,* p. 2-21. Cambridge, MA: Blackwell Press.

Jack, D., & Jack, R. (1988). Women lawyers: Archetype and alternatives. In C. Gilligan, J. Ward, & J. Taylor (Eds.), *Mapping the moral domain: A contribution of women's thinking to psychological theory and education,* p. 263-288. Cambridge, MA: Harvard University Press.

Jackson, S. E., & Associates (1992) *Diversity in the workplace: Human resource initiatives.* New York: Guilford Press.

Jelinek, M., & Literer, J. (1995). Toward entrepreneurial organizations: Meeting ambiguity with engagement. *Entrepreneurship Theory and Practice, 19*(3), 137-168.

Jung, C. G. (1971a). Aion: Phenomenology of the self. In J. Campbell (Ed.), *The portable Jung,* pp. 139-162. New York: Penguin. (Original work published 1951.)

Jung, C. G. (1971b). The relations between the ego and the unconscious. In J. Campbell (Ed.), *The portable Jung*, pp. 70-138. New York: Penguin. (Original work published 1928.)

Kanter, R. B. (1983). *The changemasters: Innovations and entrepreneurship in the American corporation.* New York: Simon & Schuster.

Kaplan, E. (1988). Women entrepreneurs: Constructing a framework to examine venture success and business failures. In B. A. Krichoff, W. A. Long, W. E. McMullan, K. H. Vespers, & W. E. Wetzel, Jr. (Eds.), 625-637, *Frontiers of Entrepreneurship Research.* Wellesley, MA: Bobson College.

Katz, J., & Gartner, W. B. (1988). Properties of emerging organizations. *Academy of Management Review, 13,* 429-441

Kirlinger, F. N. (1973). *Foundations of behavioral research, 2nd ed.* New York: Holt Rinehart.

Kirzner, I. (1985). *Discovery and the capitalist process.* Chicago: Univ. of Chicago Press.

Knight, F. (1921). *Risk uncertainty and profits,* New York: Houghton Mifflin.

Kotter, J. (1978). *Organizational dynamics: Diagnosis and intervention.* Reading, MA: Addison-Wesley.

Latham, G., & Wexley, K. (1981). *Increasing productivity through performance appraisal.* Reading, MA: Addison-Wesley.

Lerner, M., Brush, C., & Hisrich, R. (1997). Israeli women entrepreneurs: An examination of factors affecting performance. *Journal of Business Venturing, 12,* 315-339.

Liebenstein, H. (1968). Entrepreneurship and development. *American Economic Review, 58,* May.

Livesay, H. C. (1982). Entrepreneurial history. In C. Kent, D. Sexton, & K. Vesper (Eds.), *The encyclopedia of entrepreneurship,* pp. 1-15. Englewood Cliffs, NJ: Prentice Hall.

Low, M., & MacMillan, I. (1988). Entrepreneurship: Past research and future challenges. *Journal of Management, 14*(2), 139-161.

Mannheim, K. (1952). The problem of generations. In P. Kecskemeti (Ed.), *Essays on the sociology of knowledge.* London: Routledge & Kegan Paul.

Martin, J., Knopoff, K., & Beckman, C. (1998). An alternative to bureaucratic impersonality and emotional labor: Bounded emotionality at The Body Shop. *Administrative Science Quarterly, 43,* 429-469.

McClelland, D. C. (1961). *The achieving society.* Princeton, NJ: Van Nostrand.

McClelland, D. (1961). *The achieving society.* New York: Free Press.

Mindell, P. (1995). *A woman's guide to the language of success: Communicating with confidence and power.* Englewood Cliffs, NJ: Prentice Hall.

Mumby, D., & Putnam, L. (1992). The politics of emotion: A feminist reading of bounded rationality. *Academy of Management Review, 17*(3), 465-489.

Nelson, R., & Winter, S. (1982). *An evolutionary theory of economic change.* Cambridge, MA: Belknap Press.

NFWBO (2000). Women owned businesses in the United States. National Foundation of Women Owned Business: Silver Springs, MD.

Palmer, K. (2000). In academia, males under a microscope. *The Washington Post,* September 12, C4.

Porter, M. E. (1985). *Competitive advantage.* New York: Free Press.

Puka, B. (1990). The liberation of caring: A different voice for Gilligan's "different voice." *Hypatia, 5*(1), 58-82.

Puka, B. (1995). *Caring voices and women's moral frames.* New York: Garland.

Rafaeli, A. (1989). When cashiers meet customers: An analysis of the role of supermarket cashiers. *Academy of Management Journal, 32,* 245-273.

Rafaeli, A., & Sutton, R. (1989). The expression of emotion in organizational life. In L. L. Cummings & B. M. Staw (Eds.), *Research in organizational behavior, 11,* 1-42. Greenwhich, CT: JAI.

Ramsey, V. J., & Calvert, L. M. (1994). A feminist critique of organizational humanism. *Journal of Applied Behavioral Science, 30*(1), 83-97.

Reynolds, P. D. (1991). Sociology and entrepreneurship: Concepts and contributions. *Entrepreneurship Theory and Practice, 16*(2), 47-70.

Ronen, J. (Ed). (1983). *Entrepreneurship.* Lexington, MA: Lexington Books.

Rosener, J. B. (1995). *America's competitive secret: Utilizing women as a management strategy.* New York: Oxford Press.

Sanford, J. A. (1980). *The invisible partners: How the male and female in each of us affects our relationships.* New York: Paulist Press.

Schein, E. H. (1985). *Organizational culture and leadership.* San Francisco: Jossey-Bass.

Schumpeter, J. A. (1934). *The theory of economic development.* Cambridge, MA: Harvard University Press.

Scott, W. R. (1987). *Organizations: Rational, natural and open systems.* Englewood Cliffs, NJ: Prentice Hall.

Scott, W. R., & Bruce, R. (1987). Five stages of growth in small businesses. *Long Range Planning, 20*(3), 45-52.

Sexton, D., & Kasarda, J. (1992). *The State of the Art of Entrepreneurship.* Boston: PWS Kent.

Sexton, D., & Smilor, R. (2000). *Entrepreneurship 2000.* Chicago: Upstart Publishing.

Shane, S., & Venkataraman, S. (2000). The promise of entrepreneurship as a field of research. *Academy of Management Review, 25*(1), 217-226.

Shapero, A., & Sokol, L. (1982). The social dimensions of entrepreneurship. In C. Kent, D. Sexton, & K. Vesper (Eds.), *The encyclopedia of entrepreneurship,* pp. 72-90. Englewood Cliffs, NJ: Prentice Hall.

Shaver, K., & Scott, L. (1991). Person, process, choice: The psychology of new venture creation. *Entrepreneurship Theory and Practice, 16*(2), 23-47.

Sheehy, B. (1995). *New passages.* New York: Ballantine.

Smith, N. R. (1967). *The entrepreneur and his firm: The relationship between type of man and type of company.* Lansing, MI: Bureau of Business and Economic Research, Graduate School of Business Administration, Michigan State University.

Stake, J. (1997). Integrating expressiveness and instrumentality in real-life settings: A new perspective on the benefits of androgyny. *Sex Roles, 37*(7-8), 541-564.

The State of Small Business (1987). Washington, D.C.: US Government Printing Office.

Stevenson, H. H. (1985). A new paradigm for entrepreneurial management. In J. Kao & H. Stevenson (Eds.), 30-61, Entrepreneurship: What it is and how to teach it. Cambridge, MA: Harvard Business School.

Stevenson, H. H., Roberts, M. J., & Grosbeck, H. I. (1994). *New business ventures and the entrepreneur.* Burr Ridge, IL: Irwin.

Stone, M., & Brush, C. (1996). Planning in ambiguous contexts. *Strategic Management Journal, 17*(8), 633-652.

Sundin, E. (1996) Women's entrepreneurship: A reflection of society at large. In *Aspects of women's entrepreneurship,* pp. 63-86. Stockholm: Swedish National Board for Industrial and Technical Development.

Swayne, C., & Tucker, W. (1973). *The effective entrepreneur.* Morristown, NJ: General Learning Press.

Taylor, V. (1995). Watching for vibes: Bringing emotions into the study of feminist organizations. In M. Ferree & P. Martin (Eds.), *Feminist organizations,* pp. 223-233. Philadelphia: Temple University Press.

Thompson, J. D. (1967). *Organizations in action.* New York: McGraw-Hill.

Timmons, J. A. (1985). *New venture creation, 2nd edition.* Homewood, IL: Irwin.

Timmons, J. A. (1999). *New venture creation: Entrepreneurship for the 21st century.* Boston: Irwin.

Tronto, J. (1987). Beyond gender difference to a theory of care. *Signs, 12*(4) 644-663.

Vesper, K. E. (1990). *New venture strategies.* Englewood Cliffs, NJ: Prentice Hall.

Walker, L., de Vries, B., & Trevethan, L. (1987). Moral stages and moral orientations in real-life and hypothetical dilemmas. *Child Development, 58,* 842-858.

Weber, M. (1947). *Theory of social and economic organization.* New York: Free Press

Weick, K. E. (1979). *The social psychology of organizing, 2nd edition.* Reading MA: Addison-Wesley.

Westerberg, L. (1996). How do entrepreneurs in female sectors express value? In NUTEK, pp. 225-242. Stockholm: Swedish National Board for Industrial and Technical Development.

Whittier, N. (1995). Turning it over: Personnel change in the Columbus, Ohio women's movement, 1969-1984. In M. Ferree & P. Martin (Eds.), *Feminist organizations,* pp. 223-233. Philadelphia: Temple University Press.

Woodman, M. (1982). *Addiction of perfection: The still unravished bride.* Toronto: Inner City Books.

Barbara Bird is Associate Professor of Management in the Kogod School of Business at American University.

Candida Brush is Director-Council for Women's Entrepreneurship and Leadership and Director-Entrepreneurial Institute at Boston University.

The authors are grateful to Jennifer Cliff, Per Davidson, and Becky Reuber for their detailed and thoughtful comments and suggestions and to Bob Baum, Kathy Getz, and the anonymous reviewer for additional comments on this paper.

[6]

FEMINIST THEORY
AND THE STUDY
OF ENTREPRENEURSHIP

Margaret J. Greer and Patricia G. Greene

ABSTRACT

This paper applies three perspectives of feminist theory, Liberal, Marxist, and Radical, to research on entrepreneurial women. The paper discusses each perspective and reviews the appropriate entrepreneurship literature using those perspectives. We then discuss three early examples of feminist theory in entrepreneurship research, the works of Brush (1992), Hurley (1991), and Fisher, Reuber, and Dyke (1993). These studies each represent an important step forward in incorporating gender as an analytic category in the study of entrepreneurship. We contend that future research on women in entrepreneurship would benefit from a thorough grounding in wider sociological scholarship on women's economic activity and in more complete applications of feminist theory.

INTRODUCTION

This paper begins by asking the question, why should we turn to feminist theory to learn about entrepreneurship? Feminist theory is the specific

New Perspectives on Women Entrepreneurs, pages 1–24
Copyright © 2003 by Information Age Publishing
All rights of reproduction in any form reserved.

2   M.J. GREER and P.G. GREENE

area of social theory that addresses relations of gender. Feminist theory has also supplied a rich tradition of analyzing relations of gender and of class, making it a first choice for researching the economic activity of women and men. The study of women engaging in activities categorized as self-employment, small business ownership or entrepreneurship has grown along with their numbers over the last two decades. However, as other researchers have noted, work in this relatively new field of study often lacks a specific theoretical framework either of feminism or of entrepreneurship (Barrett, 1994; Brush, 1992; Hurley, 1991).

We seek to correct this situation in two ways. The first section of the paper discusses the three major subfields of feminist theory (Liberal, Marxist and Radical) and reexamines existing literature on women entrepreneurs using these theories. The second part of the paper examines several specific efforts to use feminist theory in entrepreneurship research. These works include Brush's (1992) "integrated perspective" which focuses on the woman business owner as embedded in an environment of networked work, family, and society relationships, Hurley's (1991) epistemological review of the collection of entrepreneurial knowledge, and Fisher, Reuber, and Dyke's (1993) use of social feminism to better understand discrimination against women business owners. We have essentially two critiques of these endeavors to date: First: there is a lack of integration between the well-established field of study on women in the labor force and the rapidly expanding body of work concerning women entrepreneurs. Secondly, the applications of feminist theory done so far tend to be piecemeal and do not adequately apply any one focus from feminist theory to the study of women entrepreneurs. The article concludes with some suggestions for a more thorough and effective utilization of feminist theory in the study of entrepreneurship.

FEMINIST THEORY: LIBERAL, MARXIST, RADICAL

As a place to begin a feminist analysis, it is useful to look at categorizations of feminist theory. While there are various sub fields in feminist theory and different ways of classifying them, we will rely on a division of feminist theory into Liberal, Marxist and Radical. We take this approach, in part, because both liberal feminism and Marxist feminist have been widely used within the field of sociology to analyze women's economic activity. The following section outlines the major tenets of these perspectives and reviews research on women entrepreneurs that have drawn on the perspective or to which the perspective is applicable.

Liberal Feminism

The goal of liberal feminism historically has been the elimination of explicit legal and institutional barriers to women's participation in society on an equal basis with men. Liberal feminism regards men and women as equal, autonomous individuals. Thus, the solution to women's lesser achievements is to remove barriers to women's participation, notably in education and employment. The removal of legal barriers allows men and women to be free as individuals, moving ahead based on their talents, skills and willingness to work. The earliest emphases of liberal feminist concerned the citizenship rights of women (Jagger, 1983; Sapiro, 1994). The Married Women's Property Acts of the nineteenth century and the Woman Suffrage Campaign of the nineteenth and twentieth centuries are classic examples of these efforts. More recent liberal feminist reforms continue to focus on barriers in education and employment; 1970s efforts to increase equality in the labor force by removing gender as an explicit job qualification in a wide variety of occupations is clearly both liberal and feminist. Liberal feminism rests on the premise that biological sex should not preclude the equal rights afforded to individuals in a democratic society; thus, men and women can be regarded as essentially the same.

While existing research on women business owners is not consistently organized according to any particular feminist framework, much of this research can be viewed from a feminist perspective. Since the entrepreneurship literature that considers gender often includes both a focus on legal and institutional barriers and recognition that findings from this research rarely support gendered differences in psychological or demographic profiles, this body of work fits well with a liberal feminist view.

The entrepreneurial behavior of women is not now constrained by law. Historically laws existed that prohibited women from owning property, operating a business or borrowing money. However, over time these laws have been repealed and do not directly contribute to limitations on women's business ownership in the United States. We can see the positive effects of liberal legal reforms in terms of entrepreneurship in the fact that more women are choosing to be entrepreneurs. By 2002 the number of women-owned businesses reached a total of 6.2 million majority owned businesses, representing almost 34% of all U.S. businesses. These numbers represent an increase of 16% from the 1992 census data (Center for Women's Business Research, 2001). In addition, the level of revenues generated increased 33% over the same time period. It is estimated that in 2002 women-owned businesses employed 9.2 million people and generated almost $1.15 trillion in sales (Center for Women's Business Research, 2002). However, the legacy of earlier laws restricted the economic behavior of women did contribute to the development of institutional and social

4   M.J. GREER and P.G. GREENE

practices that continue to constrain entrepreneurial behavior. As a result, the number, size, type and scope of women-owned businesses are still often less than those owned by men. The institutional barriers that contribute to this situation are related to gender differences in: (1) education, (2) work experiences, (3) networks, and (4) access to capital.

The education of women business owners is relevant both to the level and the type of education. The educational background of women business owners has been taken into account in most studies on women entrepreneurs. These studies share the fairly robust conclusion that the female entrepreneur is most often a college graduate (Bowen & Hisrich, 1986; Brush, 1992; Devine, 1994; Hisrich & Brush, 1983, 1987). However, the impact of the education remains in question. An analysis of PUMS data (Public Use Microsample Data) concludes that education and other human capital characteristics such as age and work experience were significant predictors of self-employment status (Carr, 1996). However, previous education does not seem to predict the eventual performance of the business (Allen & Carter, 1996).

The types of educational programs that women select or are placed in are important to their labor market activities. Hisrich (1986) described the educational background of female entrepreneurs as more likely to be in liberal arts, as compared to male entrepreneurs having a degree in business or engineering. Hisrich and Brush (1987, p. 190) also found a preponderance of liberal arts degrees, concluding that for women entrepreneurs "Engineering and science were infrequent areas of study." Indeed, women remain underrepresented in science and engineering related educational programs (Vetter, 1992). However, in 1997 female students in 1998 accounted for approximately 20% of engineering students (Society of Women Engineers, 2002).

This lack of scientific and technological education may make women's entry into technologically sophisticated businesses less likely, and it is these kinds of businesses that may generate the greatest income and profits. Women are more likely to start retail and service oriented businesses that, while they may be successful on other dimensions, do not routinely become as financially lucrative as businesses focused more on development and presentation of technology (Anna, Chandler, Jansen, & Mero, 2000; Brush, 1992, 1999; Brush & Hisrich, 1991; Loscocco & Robinson, 1991; Loscocco, Robinson, & Hall, 1992; Wharton, 1989). In one of the earliest studies on women who start "nontraditional" businesses, Hisrich and O'Brien (1981) found them to be even more highly educated than women owners of gender traditional types of businesses. Overall, however, many questions remain on how educational levels of the population of women business owners vary by industry.

Women's work experiences also shape their entrepreneurial behaviors. Occupational segregation, although slowly decreasing over the last three decades, remains a basic fact of the labor market (Reskin & Padavic, 2002). Women are much more likely to work in retail and service sectors than in manufacturing, construction, and other industrial sectors. This segregation occurs both across and within occupations. For instance, women working in construction will be more likely to work in smaller, less lucrative types of jobs such as wallpapering and interior painting (Loscocco & Robinson, 1991). There is no legal barrier to participation in higher paying trades. However, institutional barriers of custom can be insidiously effective in proscribing certain activities to either gender. For instance, many trade apprentice programs are strongly gendered along traditional lines, with cross-gendered attendance discouraged by family and friends. Hisrich and Brush (1983) found the previous work experience of women entrepreneurs to be primarily in the areas of teaching, middle management, and secretarial and to be highly correlated to the type of business started: 90% service, 7% financial, and only 3% in manufacturing. The educational and occupational choices made by young men and women are enacted into gender related constraints on work experiences that affect the types of businesses women start (Brush, 1992; Bowen & Hisrich, 1986; Robinson & Sexton, 1994).

Not only the type of her work experience but also her vertical placement in the authority structure has a direct effect on a woman's entrepreneurial activity. Women are less likely to hold top management positions in corporate environments. Currently women hold 15.7% of the corporate office positions in the Fortune 500 (Catalyst Census of Women Corporate Officers and Top Earners, 2002).

These are the positions where the general management experience most conducive to learning about running an entire business is gained. The "glass ceiling" remains an institutional limiting factor to gaining the general knowledge and experience that could be leveraged to entrepreneurial success (Moore & Buttner, 1997). Hisrich and Brush (1983) reported that 42% of their sample of entrepreneurial women became involved in the new venture due to job frustration in their previous position. For women, these previous positions are more likely to lead to experience in areas such as human resources where relational competencies, particularly those involved in employer-employee relations, are both an input and outcome of the position (Liou & Aldrich, 1995). These functional areas are often not those that will result in knowledge that will ultimately be helpful in the overarching activities of owning a small business. The long standing occupational segregation of women leads women entrepreneurs to feel particularly deficient in business functions to which they

6   M.J. GREER and P.G. GREENE

remain less exposed, for example, finance, marketing, and planning (Bowen & Hisrich, 1986; Hisrich & Brush, 1983; Kalleberg & Leicht, 1991).

Social and professional networks are the sources of all types of resources and assistance, both instrumental and expressive, for entrepreneurs. Few differences typically exist between the process of network creation by men and women (Aldrich, Reese, & Dubini, 1989; Brush, 1992). The ongoing discussion has centered largely on the size of the network, gender composition differences between men and women's networks, and the source of those network contacts, whether family or professional (Aldrich, 1989; Aldrich & Reese, 1994; Aldrich et al., 1989; Baines & Wheelcock, 1998; Brush, 1992; Smeltzer & Fann, 1989). Aldrich et al. (1989), studying the personal networks of women entrepreneurs in the United States and in Italy, found that in both places the networks were predominately male.

This research has only begun to deal with issues of relative power and influence differences between men's and women's networks. It is probable that male entrepreneurs share networks with higher status professionals in various fields, such as banking and law, than do women. Network contacts who have higher social and economic power can be of greater assistance during business start-up, as well as important sources of ongoing referrals.

Access to capital also limits women's entrepreneurial behaviors. There are many compounding factors resulting in a shortage of funds available to women for both the establishment and growth of their business. Start-up and business growth, however, are two extremely different types of situations; the capital needs and sources are different for each, and institutional factors at play are different by gender for each as well. These issues are discussed below.

It is unusual for a business start-up to be financed by a commercial bank loan. Most small businesses start with funds borrowed from family and friends. Start-up funds may also be obtained through second mortgages of a home or a personal bank loan. It is under conditions such as these when gender differences become more evident, one reason being that women are less likely to have a home mortgage solely in their name. The question of whether women are less likely to receive such a bank loan than a male business owner is a difficult one. Using a hypothetical business plan, Buttner and Rosen (1989) found no differences in bank funding decisions whether the borrower was male or female, although in an earlier study they found an interaction effect between gender of the entrepreneur, business sex-type (traditional or nontraditional for the gender of the owner), and gender of the funding decision maker (Buttner & Rosen, 1988b). Buttner and Rosen (1988a) also found that women entrepreneurs were perceived by loan officers as less entrepreneurial and less likely to be successful than male entrepreneurs. Riding and Swift (1990) found that many perceived funding decision differences could be accounted for by characteristics of the business. However, after controlling for those business characteristics, Riding and Swift did find that in their sample the collateral requirements for a line of credit were higher for women than for men. However, the original finding of no significant difference in access to debt financing is supported by more recent studies as well (Haynes & Haynes, 1999). Liberal feminist reforms have been very successful in rooting out many kinds of overt gender discrimination at the organizational level. As the above research shows, the kinds of discrimination that remain tend to be more subtle, more difficult to identify, and more complex, but no less effective.

The process of applying for a loan is an indicator of the stereotype of women business owners as less likely to be successful. The institutional structure of many homes and financial institutions still results in the registration of many family assets in a male spouse's name. The wage gap also contributes to the lower loan acceptance rates for women. Women's earnings continue to be significantly less than those of men in similar jobs. This wage differential contributes both to the amount of personal savings that can be accumulated, and to the level of assets that can then be shown on a loan application. Finally, difficulty in acquiring start-up financial capital affects the type of business started. Service businesses, as well as smaller retail businesses, require lower levels of start-up funds than those in manufacturing, construction, mining or agriculture. Thus, difficulties in obtaining start-up credit contribute to the channeling of women into ownership of types of business that are generally of a less financially lucrative nature.

Research shows fewer gender differences for the acquisition of financial capital from banks for existing businesses. A liberal feminist interpretation of this would be that once women have demonstrated their ability to achieve on a par with men, in this case by successfully establishing a new business, they will be treated more equally with men by the institutions of society. The remaining differences in loan acceptance rates are due to lesser collateral and capital accumulation that accrues to the types of business, retail and service, which are more likely to be owned by women (Buttner & Rosen, 1988a, 1988b, 1989, 1992; Greene 1995; Riding & Swift, 1990).

Research on women business owners and equity investments has been almost nonexistent but is beginning to emerge. Over the last 30 years women owned or led businesses received approximately 2.4% of the funds invested as venture capital (Greene, Brush, Hart, & Saparito, 2001). Whereas, 6,362 companies received funds between 1991 and 1996, only 31 of these deals were with women owned firms (Seegull, 1998). However, evidence supports an increasing trend, with 1998 investments in women owned or led firms reported at 4.1% (Greene et al., 1999). The primary reasons given for the gendered difference are similar to those discussed for issues of constrained growth and access to debt, the type of businesses

8   M.J. GREER and P.G. GREENE

being created, and lack of memberships in relevant networks (Carter, Greene, Brush, Hart, & Gatewood, 2003; Greene et al., 1999).

The liberal feminist analysis of labor market activity is useful for pointing out the persistence of legal and institutional barriers to gender equality. However, the liberal insistence of seeing men and women as equal under the law can also be counterproductive when it obscures ways in which men and women are not the "same" based upon their opportunities and resources. In addition to these kinds of differences, there is another important way in which women and men tend not to be the same, that is, in the balance of work and family labor. The gendered division of labor in the workplace and in the home is highly pertinent to systematic differences in economic achievement between women and men, including entrepreneurial activity. For a feminist analysis of the gendered division of labor in the workplace and in the home, we turn to Marxist feminism.

Marxist Feminism

One of the important contributions of Marxist feminism has been the analysis of women's domestic labor as a kind of productive, though unpaid, work. Marxist feminism has this focus partly in response to the contention from Marx and early Marxists that differences in social class serve as a kind of "master" inequality and that if economic injustice can be eliminated, other kinds of social inequality, such as those of gender and race, also will have been erased. Marxist feminism makes a strong claim that the relationship between a woman's domestic labor and her market labor is a key determinant in understanding the disadvantaged economic position of women compared to men. Today, it is well understood that women still do the majority of housework and childcare in most U.S. families. Though there has been some recent progress in men's participation in domestic labor, at least for some groups, the traditional pattern remains strongly in place (Baca Zinn, & Eitzen, 2002; Coltrane, 2000; Kemp, 1994: Pleck, 1977; Reskin & Padavic, 2002). Marxist feminism suggests two remedies for this inequity. The first is a call for the socialization of housework and child care along with fully equal labor force participation by women resulting in a union with men in the development of a working-class consciousness.

Another strategy offered is the demand that wages should be paid to homemakers in order to recognize the long ignored economic contribution of women's domestic labor to capitalism (Sokoloff, 1981; Tong, 1989). The importance of recognizing household labor as part of the output of nations receives more mainstream attention from a source far removed from Marxist feminism. Gary S. Becker, 1992 Nobel laureate and professor at the University of Chicago authored an Economic Viewpoint in *Business*

Week magazine (Oct. 16, 1995) in which he stated, "ignoring household labor distorts growth statistics and robs those who stay at home—mostly women—of self-esteem." Together, the strategies proposed under Marxist feminism are meant to achieve a two-pronged goal: radically altering the terms under which women's labor is analyzed and squarely planting the work of women in the analysis of capital.

The relationship between patriarchy and capitalism is the central theme of much of the later Marxist feminist analysis. Hartmann (1976, p.138) defines patriarchy as "a set of social relations which has a material base and in which there are hierarchical relations between men, and solidarity among them, which enable them to control women." The understanding of this shared material base, the ideological bases of patriarchy and capitalism, as well as the mutually reinforcing nature of the two systems, leads to a more complete understanding of women's labor force positions (Sokoloff, 1981). Both the gender system of male domination and the class system of economic domination require the subordination of women in the labor market and their unpaid domestic labor in the home.

A Marxist-Feminist approach to studying female business owners raises different types of questions than those suggested by Liberal Feminism. Carrying forward the key relationship between paid labor and domestic labor leads us to compare women to women and women to men. Is the typical "double day" of the female employee the same for female entrepreneurs? Do female entrepreneurs have different ways of coping with the double day? And secondly, are the typical differences in the distribution of domestic and market labor between female and male entrepreneurs the same as they are for wage and salary workers? Or does entrepreneurship affect the gendered division of labor in the home in somewhat different ways than other kinds of employment?

The greater need of women to balance work and family commitments may make entrepreneurship more appealing than wage and salary work to some women. Though self-employment often requires long workweeks, it also can offer the possibility for greater flexibility in structuring the workday. Some studies of wage and salary workers show that it is the scheduling of work hours rather than the total number of hours worked that causes the most stress for people combining work life and family life (Eichardus, & Glorieux, 1994; Longstreth, Stafford, & Mauldin, 1987; Voydanoff, 1987). The entrepreneurial intention, or state of mind directing entrepreneurial behavior, may combine with other beliefs, habits, values, and goals to be oriented toward control over work and family issues (Anna & Chandler, 2000; Bird, 1992).

Only a few studies in entrepreneurship explicitly address these questions. Some make the claim that entrepreneurship should break down the patriarchal home-workplace relationships common to employed women.

10   M.J. GREER and P.G. GREENE

One study in particular, though not Marxist scholarship, focuses on issues germane to the perspective. Goffee and Scase (1983) recognize the potential for business ownership to reproduce an oppressive system of dependent patriarchal relationships as opposed to providing a path for women's economic liberation. They contend that material and ideological effects of entrepreneurship are gendered, resulting in women business owners increasingly questioning the structure of societal gender relationships.

Specific differences between entrepreneurial women and wage and salary women have been examined less than the posited differences between entrepreneurial men and women. Women who report themselves as self-employed are more likely to be married and have children than the average woman who works for a wage or salary (Devine, 1994; Greene & Johnson, 1995). This suggests that self-employed women are more likely to be combining work and family labor and facing the conflicts such combinations often entail. Research on the balance of domestic and market labor among self-employed women has been done by Longstreth et al. (1987). These authors analyzed the amount of time spent in domestic labor per week, the number of hours spent in market labor per week, as well as the level of assistance received from a spouse, children, or domestic hired help. This study compared part-time to full-time self-employed women and found few differences in their likelihood to have help at home whether from husbands or others.

Stoner, Hartman, and Arora (1990) more specifically examined the conflict between the domestic and market spheres for female business owners, questioning whether self-employment, with a perceived nature of autonomy or control over working conditions, allows the self-employed to limit work-home role conflicts. These authors find significant levels of work-home role conflict for women business owners, regardless of marital or parental status.

The influence of domestic attachments upon the entrepreneurial behavior of women and men has been explored in the entrepreneurship literature through studies of the effect of being married, of having a working spouse in the household, and of having preschool children in the household. Again, while these questions were not posed in the setting of a Marxist Feminist framework, the findings of these studies can be examined within this framework. Brush (1992), in her comprehensive study of research on female entrepreneurs, reports findings that male entrepreneurs are slightly more likely to be married than female entrepreneurs (Stevenson, 1986). Male entrepreneurs are also more likely to have a spouse who does not work outside the home (Honig-Haftel & Martin, 1986). Another study found that being married has a negative impact on the earnings of self-employed women, whereas they had positive impacts on the earnings of self-employed men (Clain, 2000). These findings suggest that male entrepreneurs are indeed less involved in domestic labor than female entrepreneurs. Brush (1992) also cites evidence to suggest that for women a desire for a work situation that provides flexibility for family and work responsibility contributes to their decision to become business owners (Chaganti, 1986; Goffee & Scase, 1983; Scott, 1986).

Radical Feminism

This area of feminist theory covers a group of approaches united by the common theme that women and men are essentially different. Differences are innate, psychological, emotional, and typically attributed at least to some degree to basic distinctions in reproduction of the species. Women's bodily experiences in conception, pregnancy, birth and lactation are thought to induce a variety of characteristics such as a connectedness with others and with nature, nurturance and a lack of aggression, while men's more removed reproductive role leads them to be more separated from others, to see themselves as atomized individuals. Radical feminism does not look at these essential differences as benign but rather as central to the oppression of women by men (Daly, 1984; Firestone, 1972; Millett, 1970; Tong, 1989). Male dominance is maintained, then, by systematically ranking the difference between women and men in such a way that men have more power (socially, economically, politically, occupationally, symbolically) and women have less. The practical implications of radical feminism range from the need for separatist communities, to the call for equal male participation in childrearing, to the contrary demands for technological means that would liberate women from the necessity of childbearing on one hand, as well as a ban to reproductive technologies on the other.

Radical feminist has not been widely used to analyze economic activity. However, the assumption of innate difference, rather than sameness, between women and men typically underlies research than compares women and men entrepreneurs. Behavioral differences and outcomes, however, remain difficult to separate from outcomes resultant from inherent traits, those developing from a woman's socialization, and those, the most likely case, which develop from a combination of many inputs. A final question to address is whether separatist economic activities play a role in the phenomena of entrepreneurial women. While again, although it is difficult to separate the impact of these organizations by outcome, the role of gender separatist organizations must be considered.

One recent work more directly exemplifies the type of approach that may be taken under the radical feminist approach. Bird and Dreyfus (1995) develop a model of the organization creatrix, emphasizing the need for more "feminine" metaphors than had previously been used to describe entrepreneurial activities. The research questions driving the paper are not unique: "How do women founders architect their ventures differently than their male peers? What effect do these differences play in venture outcomes?" (p. 3). However, the authors draw from Jungian psychology to propose that biological, natural, and possibly divine sources are the basis for differences in masculine and feminine experiences and attributes. These differences have the potential for explaining subsequent entrepreneurial differences, including motivation, structure, and strategic plans and goals.

The question of gender separatist entrepreneurial activities is one that is essentially untouched within this body of literature. In the United States, and increasingly in other countries as well, there are programs that are strictly for women, for example training programs, funding sources, business incubators. These programs almost never operate with a complete lack of male involvement. However, the separatist ideology plays strong in that the intent of the program design is to function in a significantly different way from the already existing masculine derived models. The use of the term feminine is not to connote weak or lesser, but to recognize and emphasize the unique strengths of women that can contribute to their business success. Johnson (1995) examined the trend toward microlending organizations in the United States that supported only women business owners. These mutual aid organizations were created to fill the funding gap left by banks and venture capital groups to whom the size and type of the women's businesses were not attractive.

The practice of lending only to women for self-employment activities has also received much attention through the activities of the Women's World Banking (WWB) program (Cuff, 1990; Gorman, 1990). WWB is a not-for-profit financial institution. Inaugurated in 1979, WWB operates as a global network of local organizations with activities in more than fifty countries. WWB describes itself as an embodiment of a key paradigm for the 1990s, "showing that low-income women entrepreneurs are restructuring the global economy" (WWB, 1992, p. 1). The WWB justifies its focus on women business owners by saying, "...A dollar or rupee or peso in the hands of a woman gets into the mouths, medicine, and schoolbooks of her children. Once empowered economically, women are courageous change agents in and beyond their local communities" (WWB, 1992, p. 2). While the WWB does not go on to posit what happens to a dollar, rupee, or peso in the hands of a man, the language and practices of the program correspond with the tenets of the radical feminist perspective, women as connected with others, demonstrating a priority placed on nurturing activities.

Programs targeting women and equity investments are also increasing. Springboard 2000 is actually a series of events being held across the United States to match women led businesses with equity capital providers, largely venture capitalists. This program is in partnership with groups such as the National Women's Business Council and the Forum for Women Entrepreneurs. The stated intent is to serve as a "national initiative designed to increase investment channels and facilitate deal flow for women led high-tech and life sciences companies" (Business Wire, 2000).

The approach to questions regarding economic advancement evident in the behaviors of entrepreneurial women is tightly confounded in the ideological approach to the phenomena. Who determines the desired outcome toward which we are measuring progress? As discussed earlier, a founding assumption of the liberal feminist approach is that men and women should be regarded as essentially the same and equally free to progress based on talents, skills, and willingness to work. While this does not explicitly assume that male defined and modeled economic behaviors are the ideal, the question of, "Progress toward what?" is too seldom raised. The theme found throughout most of the entrepreneurship literature measures female business owners according to their differences from male business owners and uses measures derived from studies often consisting predominately or even entirely of males (Barrett, 1994; Brush, 1992; Stevenson, 1990).

THE INTERSECTION OF GENDER, RACE, AND SOCIAL CLASS

One of the most important foci of current feminist work is how gender, social class and race or ethnicity operate at the structural level to affect individual lives (Collins, 1989; Feiner, 1994; Gonzalez, 1987; Hartsook, 1997; Hooks, 1984, 1994; Rothenberg, 1995). There is a long established pursuit in the study of the sociology of entrepreneurship that is highly relevant to the race, gender and class concentration in feminist study. That is the tradition of empirical and theoretical study of the economic behavior of minority groups (Waldinger, Aldrich, Ward, & Associates, 1990). This research can be traced from the writings of Weber (1989 [1904]) and Sombart (1914) on religion to more contemporary work by Bonacich and Modell (1980), Butler (1991); Portes and Bach (1985), Light (1980), Zhou (1992), and Sanders and Nee (1987, 1992, 1996) on race and ethnicity. These works develop the concepts of middleman minority theory and/or ethnic enclave theory or apply frameworks derived from those theories. The theoretical explanations are grounded in a situation of a minority population turning to certain types of self-employment activities in order to avoid falling to the bottom of the economic barrel. The retail and service industries are the primary sectors of economic activities for these populations.

Few of the works on ethnic entrepreneurship deal in any systematic way with issues of gender. One of the first exceptions to this is the work of

14   M.J. GREER and P.G. GREENE

Phizacklea (1988) who analyzes the intersection of race and ethnicity with gender in her study of economic behavior of immigrant women. Phizacklea (1988, p. 22) describes ethnic business as predominately male controlled, achieving success due to "social structures that give easier access to female labor subordinated to patriarchal control mechanisms." However, the intersection between race or ethnicity and gender and entrepreneurship is just beginning to receive any research attention.

Alcorso (1993) and Carr (1993) furthered this work by illustrating the strong effect of patriarchal systems within family businesses owned by members of minority groups. Discussing such topics as overlapping family and business roles for women, business divisions of labor (Alcorso, 1993), decision making, and payment arrangement (Carr, 1993), these authors recognize the confounding nature of group memberships and the effect of those memberships on economic behaviors. And finally, Dallalfar (1994) emphasizes gender as a definitive factor in determining entrepreneurial behavior given differential access to ethnic community resources. Based on two case studies within the Los Angeles Iranian community, Dallalfar finds that the merging of the public and private spheres of the Iranian entrepreneurial women is of significant import to their businesses. One example of this is that the business setting is often in the home, making the home a site of convergence of domestic and market activity. All the literature to date suggests that for ethnic groups with strong patriarchal structures, entrepreneurial women work in an environment strongly characterized by the connection between their domestic and market labor.

This body of literature has recently been expanded to include the early findings of the Panel Study for Entrepreneurial Dynamics (PSED) (Reynolds, 2000). The PSED focused upon the identification and analysis of nascent entrepreneurs, those individuals actually in the process of starting their business. The findings of the PSED are notable as to differences found regarding entrepreneurial activity by gender, race or ethnicity, and age (Reynolds, Carter, Gartner, Greene, & Cox, 2002).

USING FEMINIST SCHOLARSHIP IN THE STUDY OF ENTREPRENEURSHIP

Feminist theoretical ideas are not completely missing from the study of entrepreneurship; however, there are two unusual characteristics in this body of work. There are no really thorough applications of any one complete theory to entrepreneurship research. The practical applications that do exist often borrow ideas from a range of scholarship on gender, applying various degrees of theoretical vigor, while at the same time proffering newly named theories for use within their own discipline based on these eclectic borrowings. In this section we address three of the most comprehensive efforts in this area to date (Brush, 1992; Fischer et al., 1993; Hurley, 1991).

Brush (1992) summarizes fifty-seven works concerning women entrepreneurs to conclude that there are few gender-based differences between women and men entrepreneurs in regard to psychological traits and motivations linked to entrepreneurial success, as well as to most business skills, types of problems encountered, planning, and outside financing. However, Brush reports significant differences in reasons that women and men give for business start-up or acquisition, for the timing and circumstances of start-up, in type of educational background, work experience, and some business skills. Additionally, gender differences are apparent in business goals, management styles, business characteristics and growth rates. Theoretically, Brush advances an "integrated perspective" based on theories of social interaction and psychological studies (Berger & Luckman, 1967; Gilligan, 1982). Though incomplete from the point of view of feminist analysis of women's economic activity, Brush's perspective represents significant progress toward an adequate inclusion of gender in the study of entrepreneurship.

The development of the integrated perspective is a reaction to traditional entrepreneurship research which "has explored business creation and performance based on the assumption that the venture is viewed as a separate economic entity designed primarily to achieve profit through competitive advantage and the creator of the business is assumed to follow a logical sequence of steps" (Brush, 1992, p. 17). Brush describes the integrated perspective approach to studying women business owners as based on the conception of businesses as a cooperative network of relationships rather than emphasizing profit-making motives for the creation of businesses. While Brush does not explicitly frame the integrated perspective in terms of feminist theory, the guiding assumptions of the perspective suggest it. Brush's emphasis is on women's different way of defining and conducting business, one in which business, family, social and personal relationships are mingled into a network of relationships. Brush explicitly suggests that reasoning through the integrated perspective contributes to a better understanding of differences between male and female owned businesses. Brush is not alone in recognizing that entrepreneurship research has been based on models of male economic activity (Barrett, 1994; Stevenson, 1986).

The integrated perspective offers an explanation for how women business owners take both paid, economic labor and unpaid, domestic labor into account in structuring their lives. Drawing out its connections to the Marxist feminist analysis of women's labor could enrich this analysis. The integrated perspective takes for granted the relationship between patriarchy and capitalism without elucidating it. One assumption of the integrated perspective seems to be that women taking on new business ventures would continue to be solely or primarily responsible for family labor. No attention is given to the possible disruption of gendered domestic, as well as economic, arrangements which starting a business might precipitate for women and their families. Brush generates an important list of future research questions to explore the integrated perspective, only one of which refers to male perspectives on domestic life. Brush's integrated perspective implies that it is plausible to continue the separation of domestic and economic activity at least as far as men are concerned. This is a good point at which to reflect that the gender system applies to the labor of both men and women. The integrated perspective is limited by suggesting that the relationship between domestic and economic activity affects only women and that it is legitimate to continue to analyze men's economic activity as if it is completely separated from family labor.

Hurley's (1991) approach to the application of feminist theory to entrepreneurship is largely epistemological. She sets forth the goals of feminist theory as reappraising what counts as knowledge, what knowledge is produced and the methods used in the production of knowledge. Drawing heavily from Calas and Smircich (1992), she approaches the existing body of literature through steps of "revising," identifying where women have been absent as researchers and as subjects; "reelection," a constant consideration of how knowledge is constructed; and "rewriting," a deconstruction and reconstruction of writings in organization theory clearly recognizing patriarchal assumptions. Hurley brings out several relevant points about historical entrepreneurship research, explicitly establishing the male biased foundation of this area of study. She illustrates a conceptual development based on the material labor and ideology of men. This development basically ignores similar economic activities of women since these are often integrated with a woman's domestic environment. Like Brush, Hurley considers the importance of gender-based realities, based on different social frames and values. She recognizes patriarchy as a form of male dominant gender relations and suggests the desirability of changing the patriarchal system.

Hurley's framework of sociological entrepreneurship research is based on how the environment affects entrepreneurship, beginning with McClelland's (1961) work on the need for achievement. The environment is defined to include effects on founding rates, political factors and state policies, cultures, and spatial location. In addition, a particularly interesting point is to question how business schools train nascent entrepreneurs for a male, profit-oriented, growth-oriented economic entity. Hurley continues with a critique of existing work in this field. However, while her suggestions for future research are anchored in feminist methods, she stops short of analyzing the theoretical explanations and/or implications of future research in entrepreneurship.

Fischer et al. (1993) make one of the most noted efforts to date to apply feminist theory to women's entrepreneurial activity. Using a liberal feminist perspective, they examine the effects of discrimination against women business owners. They also examine the effects of gender socialization, drawing on a theoretical perspective called "social feminism" which was put forward by Black (1989). While liberal feminism does provide one kind of framework for viewing the operations of the labor market, we argue that social feminism is a limited theoretical categorization with two central weaknesses: (1) It is not really a distinct theory but is assembled from too many divergent sources. (2) Pursuing this particular set of ideas does not lead to greater knowledge or clarity regarding movement toward change.

Social feminism is a combination of ideas about gender socialization pieced together with elements of psychological and philosophical theory about innate differences between men and women in personality makeup or moral development. While this echoes a central claim of radical feminism, Black's (1989) original formulation did not include radical feminism as a source. Women and men are conceptualized as essentially different, with the proviso that this inherent difference does not mean that one gender is superior and the other inferior. Rather, they have differing experiences and modes of rationality that are "equally valid." In our view a major weakness of the social feminism focus on the different but equally valid natures of men and women is that it ignores very real material inequalities between men and women. Fischer et al. (1993) offer social feminism as a major school of feminist theoretical thought, along with liberal feminism. The contrasting idea between the two seems to grow from the distinction about whether men and women are the "same" or whether they are "different." The debate about whether and to what degree an irreducible gender difference exists in human nature is an ongoing one in feminist theory. At the same time, the arguments about sameness or difference have been called a blind alley when it comes to reducing the disadvantages of women relative to men (MacKinnon, 1987). A key problem with both sameness and difference arguments is that both are judged in relation to a male-defined standard; both conceal the guiding principles of man as the measure of all things.

Even if we leave aside this important idea at the heart of differing theoretical perspectives, there is another problem that comes from the lack of theoretical distinction in social feminism. That is, the study of socialization does not stand in contrast to liberal feminism. In fact, ideas about gender role socialization coexist quite nicely within the framework of liberal feminism. Socialization explains how human beings internalize the values and learn the expected behaviors of their society, and how they develop a sense of self. These explanations are widely used in sociology and psychology to describe the microsocial, interpersonal processes by which we come to accept as necessary and natural the use of knives and forks as well as the subordinate status of women and the superordinate status of men. Socialization can be seen as both reflecting and perpetuating discrimination. In fact, liberal feminism implies that if socialization were simply more egalitarian, for example, if boys were taught to be more sensitive and girls to be more aggressive, this would result eventually in the reduction of economic inequality between men and women.

A third shortcoming in the conceptualization of socialization in social feminism is that socialization appears to be a process that takes place and is concluded early in life. One of the elementary ideas about socialization is that socialization is a lifelong process, and its effects are cumulative. This makes attributing differences in the economic activity of adults to socialization an untidy undertaking. For example, studies show that women entrepreneurs have less supervisory experience than men. The subsequent question is how do we account for the effects of early socialization that may have contributed to the lesser supervision in the first place, and the effects of workplace socialization of women to be supervised rather than supervisors?

IMPLICATIONS FOR FUTURE RESEARCH

We propose that the study of women entrepreneurs needs to begin with the understanding that gender does not apply only to women. The U.S. labor force is still highly gender segregated and gender stratified; it is essential to understand how the entrepreneurial activity of both men and women is gendered. As many of the earlier works cited show, this perspective is gaining ground in organizational and entrepreneurial research. Calas and Smircich (1992, p. 229) use feminist theory with organization theory to "rethink our field." They describe earlier, still rampant, literature on women in management which equates the following: "gender = sex = women = problem" with a resulting focus on how to solve the problem.

Gender is not a problem to be fixed or eliminated; like social class and race, gender is a basic element of human social interaction and, importantly, stratification. This article is another step away from seeing gender as a problem that has to be fixed and toward a more inclusive view of gender in entrepreneurial research. For instance, we know that women owned businesses typically are smaller and earn less money than those owned by men. A traditional approach to entrepreneurship would focus on how to assist women business owners with growth and income generation, two areas where they typically lag behind. A more feminist and sociological approach recognizes the additional validity of a low growth, less aggressive approach to earnings, along with the importance of business survival as a criterion of business success.

In our view, the greatest omission in the application of feminist theory to entrepreneurship is in the area of Marxist feminism. All feminist theories have a political goal—the elimination of oppression. Marxist theory is the most developed theory explaining the links between patriarchy and capitalism. Capitalism is a system built on a structure of dominance and subordination that maintains privileges for some groups over others. From this perspective it matters little whether women and men are presumed to be different or to be the same; either ideological position can be used to justify inequality. Our economy depends on what has been referred to elsewhere as the "work-family role system" which reinforces the traditional, gender division of labor in both the workplace and the home (Pleck, 1977). Marxist feminism posits this division as the primary mechanism that keeps inequality in place. We cannot separate the outcomes of economic endeavors from domestic realities. This seems a rich possibility for exploring the origins and meanings of gender differences in entrepreneurial activities. For example, are women entrepreneurs purposely limiting business size in an attempt to keep a viable balance between work and family obligations? Or are they held back from business expansion by family obligations and expectations? How do entrepreneurial men deal with the balance of work and family obligations and family expectations? Marxist feminism also suggests that one pertinent focus for this study should be how entrepreneurial activity reinforces or disrupts the gendered division of labor in twenty-first century capitalist patriarchy.

ACKNOWLEDGMENT

The authors wish to thank Howard Aldrich, Mary Barrett, Barbara Bird, Candida Brush, Margaret Johnson and Pat Seitz for their insightful comments and suggestions.

REFERENCES

Alcorso, C. (1993, Fall). And I'd like to thank my wife: Gender dynamics and the ethnic family business. *Australian Feminist Studies, 17*, 93–108.

Aldrich, H. (1989). Networking among women entrepreneurs. In O. Hagen, C. Rivchun, & D. Sexton (Eds.), *Women-owned businesses* (pp.103–122). New York: Praeger.

20 M.J. GREER and P.G. GREENE

Aldrich, H., & Reese, P.Y. (1994, March 9–11). *Gender gap, gender myth: Does women's networking behavior differ significantly from men's?* Paper presented at the 1994 Global Conference on Entrepreneurship, INSEAD, Fontainebleau, France.

Aldrich, H., Reese, P.R., & Dubini, P. (1989). Women on the verge of a breakthrough: Networking among entrepreneurs in the United States and Italy. *Entrepreneurship & Regional Development, 1,* 339–356.

Allen, K.R., & Carter, N.M. (1996). Women entrepreneurs: Profile differences across high and low performing adolescent firms. In P.D. Reynolds, S. Birley, J.E. Butler, W.D. Bygrave, P. Davidsson, W.B. Gartner, & P.P. McDougall (Eds.), *Frontiers of entrepreneurship research* (pp. 98–99). Wellesley, MA, Babson College.

Anna, A.L., G.N. Chandler,G.N., Jansen, E., & Marco, N. (2000). Women business owners in traditional and non-traditional industries. *Journal of Business Venturing 15*(3), 279–303.

Baca Zinn, M., & Eitzen. D.S. (2002). *Diversity in families* (6th ed.). New York: Harper Collins College Publishers.

Baines, S., & Wheelcock, J. (1998). Working for each other: Gender, the household and micro-business survival and growth. *International Small Business Journal, 17*(1), 16.

Barrett, M. (1994). Feminism and entrepreneurship: Reflections on theory and an Australian study. In *International Council for Small Business: Proceedings of the 39th World Conference: Small Business and its Contribution to Regional and International Development.* Strasbourg.

Becker, G.S. (1995, Oct. 16). Economic viewpoint. *Business Week.*

Berger, P.L., & Luckman, T. (1967). *The social construction of reality.* New York: Anchor Press.

Bird, B.J. (1992). The operation of intentions in time: The emergence of the new venture. *Entrepreneurship Theory and Practice, 17*(1), 11–20.

Bird, B., & Dreyfus, C. (1995). *Organization creatrix* (Working paper). Washington, DC: The American University.

Black, N. (1989). *Social feminism.* Ithaca, NY: Cornell University Press.

Bonacich, E., & Modell, J. (1980). *The economic basis of ethnic solidarity: Small business in the Japanese-American community.* Berkeley: University of California Press.

Bowen, D.D., & Hisrich, R.D. (1986). The female entrepreneur: A career development perspective. *Academy of Management Review, 11,* 393–407.

Brush, C. (1999). Women's entrepreneurship. *Proceedings, The Second ILO Enterprise Forum.* International Small Enterprise Programme. International Labour Office.

Brush, C. (1992). Research on women business owners: Past trends, a new perspective and future directions. *Entrepreneurship Theory and Practice, 16*(4), 5–30.

Brush, C.G., & Hisrich, R.D. (1991). Antecedent influences on women-owned businesses. *Journal of Managerial Psychology, 6,* 9–16.

Butler, J.S. (1991). *Entrepreneurship and self-help among Black Americans: A reconsideration of race and economics.* Albany: SUNY Press.

Business Wire. (2000, Jan. 24). *Springboard 2000.* Redwood City, CA: Author.

Buttner, E.H., & Rosen, B. (1988a). Bank loan officers' perceptions of the characteristics of men, women, and successful entrepreneurs. *Journal of Business Venturing, 3,* 249–258.

Buttner, E.H., & Rosen, B. (1988b). The Influence of entrepreneur's gender and type of business on decisions to provide venture capital. *Proceedings*, Southern Management Association, Atlanta.

Buttner, E.H., & Rosen, B. (1989). Funding new business ventures: Are decision makers biased against women entrepreneurs? *Journal of Business Venturing, 4*, 249–261.

Buttner, E.H., & Rosen, B. (1992). Rejection in the loan application process: Male and female entrepreneurs' perceptions and subsequent intentions. *Journal of Small Business Management, 30*(1), 58–65.

Calas, M.B., & Smircich, L. (1992). Re-writing gender into organization theorizing: Directions from feminist perspectives. In M. Reed & M. Hughes (Eds.), *Rethinking organization* (pp. 227–253). London: Sage Publications.

Carr, D. (1996). Two paths to self-employment? *Work & Occupations, 23*(1), 26.

Carr, J. (1993). Negotiating patriarchy: Gender and ethnic patterns of small business ownership. *Australian Feminist Studies, 17*,109–126.

Carter, N., Greene, P.G., Brush, C.G., Hart, M.M., & Gatewood, E. (2003). Women entrepreneurs breaking through to equity markets: The influence of human, social, and financial capital. *Venture Capital, 5*(1).

Catalyst. (2002). *The 1998 census of women corporate officers and top earners of the fortune 500.*

Center for Women's Business Research. (2001). *Breaking the boundaries: The continued progress and achievement of women owned businesses.* Washington, DC: CWBR.

Center for Women's Business Research. (2002, August 27). New analysis documents employment and revenue distribution of women-owned firms in 2002. www.womensbusinessresearch.org.

Chaganti, R. (1986). Management in women-owned enterprises. *Journal of Small Business Management, 24*,18–29.

Clain, S.H. (2000). Gender differences in full-time self-employment. *Journal of Economics and Business, 52*(6), 499–513.

Collins, P.H. (1989). The social construction of black feminist thought. *Signs, 14*, 4.

Coltrane, S. (2000). Modeling and measuring the social embeddedness of routine family labor. *Journal of Marriage and the Family, 62.*

Cuff, D.F. (1990, November 13). Helping women abroad get started in business. *The New York Times.*

Dallalfar, A. (1994). Iranian women as immigrant entrepreneurs. *Gender and Society, 8*(4), 541–561.

Daly, M. (1984). *Pure lust: Elemental feminist philosophy.* Boston: Beacon Press.

Eichardus, M., & Glorieux, I. (1994). The search for the invisible hours: The gendered use of time in a society with a high labour force participation of women. *Time and Society, 3*, 5–27.

Feiner, S.F. (1994). *Race and gender in the American economy.* Englewood Cliffs, NJ: Prentice-Hall.

Fischer, E.M., Reuber, A.R. & Dyke, L.S. (1993). A theoretical overview and extension of research on sex, gender and entrepreneurship. *Journal of Business Venturing, 8*, 151–68.

Firestone, S. (1972). *The dialectic of sex.* London: Paladin.

Gilligan, C. (1982). *In a different voice.* Cambridge, MA: Harvard University Press.

22   M.J. GREER and P.G. GREENE

Goffee, R., & Scase, R. (1983). Business ownership and women's subordination: A preliminary study of female proprietors. *Sociological Review, 31*, 625–647.

Gonzalez, R.M. (1987). Distinctions in western women's experience: Ethnicity, class and social change. In S. Armitage & E. Jameson (Eds.), *The women's west*. Norman: University of Oklahoma Press.

Gorman, C. (1990, June 4). Women start taking credit. *Time, 135*(23).

Greene, P.G. (1995, March). *Women entrepreneurs: A consideration of capital types.* Paper presented at the IC² Conference. Immigrant and Minority Entrepreneurship: Building American Communities, University of Texas at Austin.

Greene, P., Brush, C., Hart, M., & Saparito, P. (2001). Patterns of venture capital funding: Is gender a factor? *Venture Finance, 3*(1), 63–83.

Greene, P.G., & Johnson, M.A. (1995). Social learning and middleman minority Theory: Explanations for self-employed women. *National Journal of Sociology, 9*, 59–84.

Hartmann, H. (1976). Capitalism, patriarchy and job segregation by sex. *Signs, 1*(3), 137–169.

Hartsook, N.C.M. (1997). *Money, sex and power: Toward a feminist historical materialism.* Northwest University Press.

Haynes, G.W., & Haynes, D.C. (1999). The debt structure of Small businesses owned by women in 1987 and 1999. *Journal of Small Business Management, 37*(2), 1–19.

Hisrich, R.D., & Brush, C.G. (1983). The woman Entrepreneur: Implications of family, educational, and occupational experience. In J. Hornaday, J.A. Timmons, & K.H Vesper (Eds.), *Frontiers of entrepreneurship research* (pp. 255–270). Wellesley, MA: Babson College.

Hisrich, R.D., & Brush, C.G. (1987). Woman entrepreneurs: A longitudinal study. In N.C. Churchill, J.A. Hornaday, B.A. Kirchhoff, O.J. Krasner, & K.H. Vesper (Eds.), *Frontiers of entrepreneurship research* (pp. 187–199). Wellesley, MA: Babson College.

Hisrich, R.D., & O'Brien, M. (1981). The woman entrepreneur from a business and sociological perspective. In K.H. Vesper (Ed.), *Frontiers of entrepreneurship research* (pp. 21–39). Wellesley, MA: Babson College.

Hooks, B. (1984). *Feminist theory from margin to center.* Boston: South End Press.

Hooks, B. (1994). *Teaching to transgress.* New York: Routledge.

Hurley, A.E. (1991, August). *Incorporating feminist theories into sociological theories of entrepreneurship.* Paper presented at the Annual Meetings of the Academy of Management, Miami, FL.

Jagger, A.M. (1983). *Feminist politics and human nature.* NJ: Rowan and Allenheld.

Johnson, M.A. (1995). *Women entrepreneurs in the United States: Explaining gendered trends and nontraditional business financing.* Paper presented at the IC² Conference, Immigrant and Minority Entrepreneurship: Building American communities, University of Texas at Austin.

Kalleberg, A.I., & Leicht, K.T. (1991). Gender and organizational performance: Determinants of small business survival and success. *Academy of Management Journal, 34*,136–161.

Kemp, A.A. (1994). *Women's work.* Englewood Cliffs, NJ: Prentice-Hall.

Light, I. (1980). Asian enterprise in America: Chinese, Japanese and Koreans in small business. In S. Cummings (Ed.). *Self-help in urban America: Patterns of minority economic development* (pp. 33–57). Port Washington, NY: Kennikat Press.

Liou, N., & Aldrich, H.E. (1995, August). *Women entrepreneurs: Is there a gender-based relational competence?* Paper presented at the American Sociological Association meetings, Washington, DC.

Longstreth, M., Stafford, K., & Mauldin, T. (1987). Self-employed women and their families: Time use and socioeconomic characteristics. *Journal of Small Business Management, 25,* 30–37.

Loscocco, K.A., & Robinson, J. (1991). Barriers to women's small business success in the United States. *Gender and Society, 5,* 511–533.

Loscocco, K.A., Robinson, J., & Hall, R.H. (1991). Gender and small business success: An inquiry into women's relative disadvantage. *Social Forces, 70,* 65–86.

MacKinnon, C. (1987). Feminism unmodified. Cambridge, MA: Harvard University Press.

McClelland, D.C. (1961). *The achieving society.* Princeton, NJ: D. Van Nostrand.

Millett, K. (1970). *Sexual politics.* Garden City, NY: Doubleday.

Moore, D.P., & Buttner, E.H. (1997). *Women entrepreneurs: Moving beyond the glass ceiling.* Thousand Oaks, CA: Sage.

Phizacklea, A. (1988). Entrepreneurship, ethnicity and gender. In S. Westwood & P. Bhachu (Eds.), *Enterprising women* (pp. 21–33). New York: Routledge.

Pleck, J.H. (1977). The work-family role system. *Social Problems, 24,* 417–427.

Portes, A., & Bach, R.L. (1985). *Latin journey.* Berkeley: University of California Press.

Reskin, B.F., & Padavic, I. (2002). *Women and men at work* (2nd ed.). Thousand Oaks, CA: Pine Forge Press.

Reynolds, P.D. (2000). National panel study of U.S. business startups: Background and methodology. In J.A. Katz (Ed.), *Advances in entrepreneurship, firm emergence, and growth* (Vol. 4, pp. 153–227). Stamford, CT: JAI Press.

Reynolds, P.D., Carter, N.M., Gartner, W., Greene, P.G., & Cox, L. (2002). *The entrepreneur next door.* Kansas City, MO: Kauffman Center for Entrepreneurial Leadership.

Riding, A.L., & Swift, C.S. (1990). Women business owners and terms of credit: Some empirical findings of the Canadian experience. *Journal of Business Venturing, 5,*327–340.

Robinson, P.B., & Sexton, E.A. (1994). The effect of education and experience on self-employment success. *Journal of Business Venturing, 9*(2), 141–156.

Rothenberg, P.S. (1995). *Race, class and gender in the United States.* New York: St. Martin's Press.

Sanders, J.M., & Nee, V. (1996). Social capital, human capital, and immigrant self employment. *American Sociological Review, 61,* 231–249.

Sanders, J.M., & Nee, V. (1992). Problems in resolving the enclave economy debate. *American Sociological Review, 57,* 415–418.

Sanders, J.M., & Nee, V. (1987). Limits of ethnic solidarity in the enclave economy. *American Sociological Review, 52,* 745–773.

Sapiro, V. (1994). *Women in American society.* Mountain View, CA: Mayfield Publishing Company.

24   M.J. GREER and P.G. GREENE

Scott, C.E. (1986, October). Why more women are becoming entrepreneurs. *Journal of Small Business Management, 24,* 37–44.

Seegull, F. (1998). *Female entrepreneurs' access to equity capital.* Cambridge, MA: Harvard Business School Working Paper.

Smeltzer, L.R., & Fann, G.L. (1989). Gender differences in external networks of small business owner/managers. *Journal of Small Business Management, 28*(2), 25–32.

Sokoloff, N.J. (1981). *Between money and love.* New York: Praeger Press.

Society of Women Engineers. (2002). Based upon statistics from the National Science Foundation and the Bureau of the Census. (www.swe.org)

Sombart, W. (1914). *The Jews and modern capitalism* (Trans. by M. Epstein). New York: E.P. Dutton.

Stevenson, L. (1990). Some methodological problems associated with researching women entrepreneurs. *Journal of Business Ethics, 9,* 440–446.

Stevenson, L.A. (1986). Against all odds: The entrepreneurship of women. *Journal of Small Business Management, 24,* 30–36.

Stoner, C.R., Hartman, R.I., & Arora, R. (1990, Jan.). Work-home role conflict in female owners of small businesses: An exploratory study. *Journal of Small Business Management,* pp. 30–38.

Tong, R. (1989). *Feminist thought.* Boulder, CO: Westview Press.

Vetter, B.M. (1992). *What is holding up the glass ceiling? Barriers to women in the science and engineering workforce* (Occasional Paper 92-3). Washington, DC: Commission on Professionals in Science and Technology.

Voydanoff, P. (1987). *Work and family life.* Beverly Hills, CA: Sage.

Waldinger, R., Aldrich, H., Ward, R., & Associates. (1990). *Ethnic entrepreneurs.* Newbury Park, CA: Sage.

Weber, M. (1989/1904). *The Protestant ethic and the spirit of capitalism.* London: Unwin Hyman.

Wharton, A.S. (1989). Gender segregation in private-sector, public sector, and self-employed cccupations, 1950–1981. *Social Science Quarterly, 70,* 923–940.

Zhou, M. (1992). *Chinatown: The socioeconomic potential of an urban enclave.* Philadelphia: Temple University Press.

Part II
Human Capital and Cognition

Part II
Political Parties and Corruption

[7]

FEMALE AND MALE ENTREPRENEURS: PSYCHOLOGICAL CHARACTERISTICS AND THEIR ROLE IN GENDER-RELATED DISCRIMINATION

DONALD L. SEXTON
Ohio State University

NANCY BOWMAN-UPTON
Baylor University

EXECUTIVE SUMMARY

There is good news and bad news about actual gender-related managerial differences. The good news is that some do exist. The bad news is that they are overused as the basis for sexual stereotyping.

The increase in the number of female entrepreneurs in the United States has been paralleled by an increase in academic research related to their activities. Published research studies of the female entrepreneur have ranged from psychological and demographic studies to perceived start-up obstacles. These studies gave rise to the perception that although male and female entrepreneurs possessed similar socioeconomic backgrounds, motivations, and techniques, the female business owners have been subjected to gender-related discrimination. More recently, research studies have addressed the question, "Is the object of discrimination the woman or is it the type of firm she tends to initiate?"

Studies have shown that both females and males possess the characteristics required for effective performance as managers. Yet negative attitudes toward females still exist. Trait analyses studies have found more similarities than differences between the two groups. However, a gap still exists between the actual traits of women business owners and the perception of those traits by others. This gap is even more significant when the impact of the traits on occupational choices is considered.

The use of psychological traits as a predisposition to initiate a business as an occupational choice has been well established. In this study, the psychological traits of growth oriented female and male entrepreneurs were measured and tested for significant differences.

One hundred five female owners of businesses that rate in the top 10% with respect to sales and number of employees were compared with those of similar male business owners. No significant differences were found on five of the nine traits that were measured. The females did score significantly lower on traits related to energy level and risk taking. They also scored significantly higher on the traits related to autonomy and change. These scores indicate that female entrepreneurs are less willing

Address correspondence to Dr. Donald L. Sexton, College of Administrative Sciences, Ohio State University, 1775 College Road, Columbus, OH 43210.

Journal of Business Venturing 5, 29–36

0883-9026/90/$3.50

30　　D. L. SEXTON AND N. BOWMAN-UPTON

than male entrepreneurs to become involved in situations with uncertain outcomes (risk taking) and have less of the endurance or energy level needed to maintain a growth-oriented business.

The significantly higher scores by the female entrepreneurs on the traits associated with autonomy and change directly refute the perceptions of females found to exist in earlier studies. In addition, the lack of a significant difference on the traits related to social adroitness and to succorance between the two groups belies the "emotionality" label often attributed to females.

This study shows that the psychological propensities of female and male entrepreneurs are more similar than they are different. While some differences did exist, they would not be expected to affect the person's ability to manage a growing company. Hence, as stated earlier, gender-related psychological traits related to managerial differences do exist. However, they do not provide a basis for sexual stereotyping.

> A modification of the Jackson Personality Inventory and the Personality Research Form-E test instruments was administered to similar groups of 105 female entrepreneurs and 69 male entrepreneurs. All of the entrepreneurs sampled were founders of those 10% of the firms in the United States that have reached annual sales levels of $100,000 and have five or more employees. The two groups had similar scores on five traits. The females scored significantly lower on two traits related to risk taking and energy level and higher on two traits related to autonomy and change. No evidence was found to support the perceptions that females may be lacking in the attributes necessary to initiate and manage a business.

A lthough figures vary, it is estimated that women currently own 28% of all the businesses in the United States and are projected to own 50% by the year 2000 (House of Representatives Report No. 100–736, 1988, p. 2). Concomitant with the growth of female entrepreneurship has been the researchers' interest in her. Initial studies focused on the demographics of the female entrepreneur and her organization (Schwartz 1976; Sexton and Kent 1981), perceived obstacles to start-up and success (Hisrich and O'Brien 1982; Pellegrino and Rees 1982; Humphries and McClung 1981; Hisrich and Brush 1984), and analyses of traits or psychological characteristics (DeCarlo and Lyons 1979; Smith et al. 1982; Waddell 1984). A perception arose that although male and female entrepreneurs possess similar socioeconomic backgrounds, motivations, and personality traits, female business owners are subjected to gender-related discrimination, especially by financial institutions. This prompted a series of comparative analyses of male and female entrepreneurs to determine if significant differences do exist (Welsch and Young 1984; Sexton and Bowman-Upton 1986; Cromie 1987; Fagenson and Coleman 1987) and studies of the actions and perceptions of lending officers toward women business owners (Birley et al. 1986; Bowman-Upton et al. 1987; Olm et al. 1988; Buttner and Rosen 1988). The former studies revealed the differences were few. The latter sparked a debate centered around the question: "Is the object of discrimination the woman or is it the type of firm she tends to initiate?" According to Brophy (1989), women have difficulty obtaining financing for their firms because they tend to pursue life-style rather than growth-oriented business ventures. Might not there be a bias toward both? Psychologists and social researchers utilizing techniques for discerning the more subtle forms of gender bias have revealed a "lingering but potentially potent bias in people's beliefs, feelings and actions regarding women" (Myers 1986). These results are mirrored in a number of studies concerning male and female attitudes toward women managers (Schein 1973, 1975; Heilman and Guzzo 1978; Donnell and Hall 1980; Dubno 1985; Sutton and Moore 1985). Discrimination does exist and research designed to reveal evidence of it is necessary. But what is also needed is a better understanding of the origin of these attitudes and research that will refute them.

ORIGINS OF GENDER-RELATED DISCRIMINATION

A number of models have been proposed to explain why we practice gender-related discrimination. Monopsonistic exploitation theory would propose that men collude to discriminate against women so there will be less competition for well-paying jobs (Madden 1975; Bergman 1983). Serious doubts toward this theory have been espoused by Hamermesh and Rees (1984). Statistical discrimination occurs when the characteristics of a group (which are factual and objective) are attributed to an individual, regardless of his or her own personal characteristics (Thurow 1975). Statistical discrimination has been found to be neither particularly rational nor efficient (Bielby and Baron 1986).

A similar form of discrimination, error discrimination, occurs when an individual is assigned characteristics based on false stereotypes and assumptions about the group of which he or she is a member (Heilman 1984). Further, once an individual elaborates a stereotype, he or she is primed to expect differences on a wide variety of characteristics, including some for which no real sex differences exist (Martin 1987). Fisher (1987) calls attention to the fact that individuals may be discriminated against

> . . . not necessarily because of their own personal characteristics, but because of either the actual or perceived characteristics of the group to which they are assigned. It is a matter of 'guilt by association' . . .

Sex role orientation theories predict discrimination based on the perceived and actual trait differences between males and females. Kovach (1983) proposes that male employers determine which jobs should be "female" based upon their knowledge of these traits. Bielby and Baron (1986) provide strong evidence that some employers reserve some jobs for men and others for women based on their perceptions of group differences between the sexes. It has been found that we tend to exaggerate the amount and extent of differences between the sexes because we accept as real both actual and perceived differences (Unger 1979; Martin 1987).

PERCEPTIONS AND ATTITUDES TOWARD WOMEN IN BUSINESS

Despite studies indicating that males and females both have characteristics required for effective performance as managers (Lirtzman and Wahba 1972; Donnell and Hall 1980; Stephens and DeNisi 1980), negative attitudes toward females still exist (Dubno 1985; Sutton and Moore 1985). Traits attributed to women, such as emotionality (Goleman 1988), gentleness, sensitivity, passiveness, and lack of logic, compose stereotypes that have been shown to be effective obstacles to employment, promotion, and salary increases (Heilman and Guzzo 1978; Chacko 1982; Rosenstein and Hitt 1986).

In a study of bank loan officers' perceptions of male and female entrepreneurs, Buttner and Rose (1988) found that women were perceived as less entrepreneurial than men. Female entrepreneurs were evaluated significantly lower on dimensions related to leadership, autonomy, risk-taking propensity, readiness for change, endurance (energy level), and low need for support (succorance). Further, they were rated as more emotional.

Contrary to these perceptions, actual trait analyses find more similarities between the sexes than differences (Goffee and Scase 1985). Women seem to possess similar motivations as men for need for money, need for independence, and seizing an opportunity (Hertz 1986). Chaganti (1986) notes that no significant differences between the sexes have emerged concerning need for achievement, autonomy, persistency, aggression, independence, nonconformity, goal orientation, self-confidence, leadership, and locus of control.

32 D. L. SEXTON AND N. BOWMAN-UPTON

There seems to be a gap between actual traits of women in business and perceptions of those traits. This may be significant when one considers the impact of the traits in occupational development.

PERSONALITY AND OCCUPATION

The use of traits in vocational development theory is best described by Holland (1959), who theorized that individuals would select occupations and work environments that suit their personality types. Subsequent studies have shown that traits and values play an important role in occupation choice (Bordin et al. 1964; Thumin 1965; Singer and Abramson 1973). Further, a number of studies have used the instruments utilized in this study area to predict occupations and effectiveness in that occupation (Siess and Jackson 1971; Winegardner 1978; Bridgewater 1982).

A plethora of studies comparing the traits or psychological characteristics of entrepreneurs to others has been published. Vocational development theory would suggest that these traits predisposed the individual to enter a career. While possessing the trait would in no way imply success in vocational pursuits related to initiating, growing, and managing a business, there does seem to be a correlation between possessing these characteristics and entrepreneurial endeavors. It is not a far leap to assume that women are not suited for entrepreneurship because they do not possess the necessary traits or psychological characteristics.

METHODOLOGY AND ANALYSIS

The sample comprised 105 female members of the Houston Entrepreneurial Resource Service and 69 male entrepreneurs from the Columbus, Ohio, area. The samples were not randomly selected. In each case, they were members of the audience at a meeting in which the authors were speaking. While this situation may lend itself to a response-set bias, such as a socially desirable response style, the instrument used was designed to control it (Jackson 1974, 1976). Unusually high or low responses on the desirability scale alert the researcher to this response set.

The definition of an entrepreneur used in the study is that he or she is an owner of a business with five or more employees and annual sales in excess of $100,000. This definition excludes self-employed professionals, those engaged in part-time ventures, and small-business owners. It represents a group of entrepreneurs who have achieved a company size that exceeds 90% of the firms in the United States (State of Small Business 1987).

The composition of the firms in the sample by type of industry reveals a fairly even distribution with the exception of manufacturing. In general, females were clustered in the service area and males in manufacturing, but this is somewhat representative of the population in general (Hisrich and Brush 1984). The average ages of the entrepreneurs were relatively close (females, 41 years; males, 39 years). Although the males were on the average slightly younger, they had been in business about four years longer.

The instrument utilized was a modification of the Jackson Personality Inventory and the Personality Research Form-E (Jackson 1974, 1976). Both instruments have been reviewed as highly psychometrically sound assessment devices (Neill and Jackson 1976; Hogan 1978). The modified instrument has been validated in earlier studies (Sexton and Bowman 1984). It consists of nine substantive scales and two validity scales. The nine substantive scales are bipolar, each containing equal numbers of true-keyed and false-keyed statements. Bi-

TABLE 1 Trait Description of the Personality Scales

Conformity: A low scorer normally refuses to go along with the crowd, is unaffected and unswayed by others' opinions, and is independent in thought and action.

Energy level: A high scorer is active and spirited, possesses reserves of strength, does not tire easily, and is capable of intense work or recreational activity for long periods of time.

Interpersonal affect: A lower scorer is emotionally aloof, prefers impersonal to personal relationships, displays little compassion for other people's problems, has trouble relating to people and is emotionally unresponsive to those around him/her.

Risk taking: A high scorer enjoys gambling and taking a chance, willingly exposes self to situations with uncertain outcomes, enjoys adventure having an element of peril, and is unconcerned with danger.

Social adroitness: A high scorer is skillful at persuading others to achieve a particular goal, is diplomatic but occasionally may be seen as manipulative of others, and is socially intelligent.

Autonomy: A high scorer tries to break away and may be rebellious when faced with restraints, confinement, or restrictions; enjoys being unattached, free, and not tied to people, places, or obligations.

Change: A high scorer likes new and different experiences, dislikes and avoids routine, may readily change opinions or values in different circumstances, and adapts readily to changes in environment.

Harm avoidance: A low scorer enjoys exciting activities especially when danger is involved, risks bodily harm, and is not concerned with personal safety.

Succorance: A low scorer does not need the support nor frequently seeks the sympathy, protection, love, advice, or reassurance of other people and has difficulty confiding in others.

polarity allows the scales to be viewed on a continuum. For example, a low score on energy level not only reflects the absence of traits related to high energy level but also traits associated with a low energy level. The scales measure traits related to conformity, energy level, interpersonal affect, risk taking, social adroitness, autonomy, change, harm avoidance, and succorance. Definitions or description of persons scoring high or low on a particular scale are shown in Table 1.

A multivariate analysis of variance was used to test differences between the group means. The resultant F test indicated significant differences on four scales. Two multiple comparison tests, Scheffe's multiple comparison tests, Scheffe's multiple comparison procedure for all main effect means and Bonferroni's t test of differences between means, were used. Both tests were made at the .05 alpha level. As can be seen in Table 2, female

TABLE 2 Comparison of Group Means

Scale	Female	Male
Conformity	6.4095	6.9565
Energy level	14.6286*	16.0000
Interpersonal affect	10.0857	9.8551
Risk taking	12.3333*	14.1884
Social adroitness	11.8000	11.5362
Autonomy	10.7048*	8.5362
Change	10.4190*	9.1884
Harm avoidance	8.5048	8.1449
Succorance	4.9714	5.3913

*Significant at $p < .05$ level.

34   D. L. SEXTON AND N. BOWMAN-UPTON

entrepreneurs scored significantly lower than male entrepreneurs on the scales of energy level and risk taking. Significantly higher scores for the females were found for the scales of autonomy and change. There were no significant differences on the remaining five scales.

DISCUSSION

It has been noted that discrimination may occur when we align sex roles on perceived trait differences. Further, we tend to exaggerate these differences. In this study female entrepreneurs were found to score similarly to males on conformity, interpersonal affect, social adroitness, harm avoidance, and succorance. The insignificant differences between the groups on interpersonal affect and succorance belies the "emotionality" label attributed to females (Goleman 1988). Since the scores were relatively low, they indicate the absence of traits associated with a high scorer, one of which is emotionalality.

Females scored significantly lower on energy level and risk taking. Yet their scores are still high relative to published norms. Obviously it requires a great deal of energy to maintain a growth-oriented business. Although the risk-taking scale was designed to measure four facets of risk (monetary, physical, social, and ethical), it correlates highest with monetary risk (Jackson et al. 1972). This study would indicate that female entrepreneurs are less willing to get involved in situations with uncertain outcomes where financial gain is involved. As noted by Buttner and Rosen (1988), bank loan officers perceived females as having less endurance and risk-taking propensity than males and successful entrepreneurs. While this may be true, it may also be that the perception is exaggerated.

Females scored significantly higher on the scale's autonomy and change. This refutes directly the perceptions noted by Buttner and Rosen (1988). In this sample, females have a higher need for independence and a stronger desire for new and different experiences.

This study has shown that male and female entrepreneurs possess similar traits. Two noticeable differences are in risk taking and energy level. If female entrepreneurs are perceived as lacking the attributes necessary to initiate and manage a venture, they were not revealed here. Our knowledge of actual traits of female entrepreneurs should allow us to perceive them in a more objective manner.

REFERENCES

Bergman, B. 1983. Women's plight: Bad and getting worse. *Challenge* 31 (March-April):22–26.

Bielby, W. T., and Baron, J. N. 1986. Sex segregation within occupations. *American Economic Review* 76(1):43–47.

Birley, S., Moss, C., and Saunders, P. 1986. The differences between small firms started by male and female entrepreneurs who attended small business courses. In R. Ronstadt, et al., eds., *Frontiers of Entrepreneurship Research*. Wellesley, MA: Babson College.

Bordin, E. S., Nachman, B., and Segal, S. J. 1963. An articulate framework for vocational development. *Journal of Counseling Psychology* 10 (Summer:107–117.

Bowman-Upton, N., Carsrud, A., and Olm, K. 1987. New venture funding for the female entrepreneur. In N. Churchill et al., eds., *Frontiers of Entrepreneurship Research*. Wellesley, MA: Babson College.

Bridgewater, C. 1982. Personality characteristics of ski instructors and predicting teacher effectiveness using the PRF. *Journal of Personality Assessment* 46 (March):163–166.

Brophy, D. J. 1989. Financing the women-owned entrepreneurial firm. In O. Hagen et al., eds. *Women-Owned Businesses*. New York: Praeger.

Buttner, H., and Rosen, B. 1988. Bank loan officers' perceptions of the characteristics of men, women and successful entrepreneurs. *Journal of Business Venturing* 3(3):249–258.

Chacko, T. I. 1982. Women and equal employment opportunity: Some unintended effects. *Journal of Applied Psychology* 67:119–123.

Chaganti, R. 1986. Management in women-owned enterprises. *Journal of Small Business Management* 24(4):18–29.

Cromie, S. 987. Motivations of aspiring male and female entrepreneurs. *Journal of Occupational Behavior* 8:251–261.

DeCarlo, J., and Lyons, P. 1979. A comparison of selected personality characteristics of minority and non-minority female entrepreneurs. *Proceedings*. Atlanta: Academy of Management.

Donnell, S., and Hall, J. 1980. Men and women as managers: A significant case of no significant difference. *Organizational Dynamics* 8(4):60–77.

Dubno, P. 1985. Attitudes toward women executives: A longitudinal approach. *Academy of Management Journal* 28(1):235–239.

Fagenson, E. A., and Coleman, L. L. 1987. What makes entrepreneurs tick: An investigation of entrepreneurs' values. In N. Churchill et al., eds., *Frontiers of Entrepreneurship Research*. Wellesley, MA: Babson College.

Fisher, C. C. 1987. Toward a more complete understanding of occupational sex discrimination. *Journal of Economic Issues* 21(1):113–137.

Goffee, R., and Scase, R. 1985. *Women in Charge: The Experiences of Female Entrepreneurs*. London: George Allen and Unwin.

Goleman, D. 1988. In the liberated 80s sexual stereotypes are alive and well. *New York Times* August 23, 11.

Hamermesh, D. S., and Rees, A. 1984. *The Economics of Work and Pay* (3rd ed.). New York: Harper and Row.

Heilman, M. C. 1984. Information as a deterrent against sex discrimination: The effects of application sex and information type on preliminary employment decisions. *Organization Behavior and Human Performance* 21 (April):174–86.

Heilman, M. E., and Guzzo, R. A. 1978. The perceived cause of work success as a mediator of sex discrimination in organization. *Organizational Behavior and Human Performance* 21:346–357.

Hertz, L. 1986. *The Business Amazons*. London: Deutsch.

Hisrich, R., and Brush, C. 1984. The woman entrepreneur: Management skills and business problems. *Journal of Small Business Management* January: 33.

Hisrich, R., and O'Brien, M. 1982. The women entrepreneur as a reflection of the type of business. In K. H. Vesper, ed., *Frontiers of Entrepreneurship Research*. Wellesley, MA: Babson College.

Hogan, R. 1978. Personality research form. In O. K. Buros, ed., *The Eighth Mental Measurement Yearbook*. Highland Park, IL: Gryphon Press.

Holland, J. 1959. A theory of vocational choice. *Journal of Counseling Psychology* 6 (Spring): 35–44.

House of Representatives Report No. 100-736. 1988. *New Economic Realities: The Rise of Women Entrepreneurs*. Washington, D.C.: U.S. Government Printing Office.

Humphries, M., and McClung, J. 1981. Women entrepreneurs in Oklahoma. *Review of Regional Economics and Business* 6:13–20.

Jackson, D. 1974. *Personality Research Form Manual*. Goshen, NY: Research Psychologists Press.

Jackson, D. 1976. *Jackson Personality Form Manual*. Goshen, NY: Research Psychologists Press.

Jackson, D., Hourany, L., and Vidmar, N. 1972. A four-dimensional interpretation of risk taking. *Journal of Personality* 40 (September):487.

Kovach, K. A. 1983. Squelching stereotypes: Ending sex discrimination from cradle on. *Management World* 12 (December):44–53.

Lirtzman, S., and Wahba, M. 1972. Determinants of coalition behavior of men and women: Sex roles of situational requirements. *Journal of Applied Psychology* 56:406–411.

Madden, J. 1975. Discrimination—A manifestation of male market power. In C. Lloyd, ed. *Sex Discrimination and the Division of Labor*. New York: Columbia University Press.

Martin, C. L. 1987. A ratio measure of sex stereotyping. *Journal of Personality and Social Psychology* 52(3):489–499.

36   D. L. SEXTON AND N. BOWMAN-UPTON

Myers, D. G. 1986. *Psychology.* New York: Worth Publishers, Inc.

Neill, J. A., and Jackson, D. N. 1976. Minimum redundancy item analysis. *Educational and Psychological Measurement.*

Olm, K., Carsrud, A., and Alvey, L. 1988. The role of networks in new venture funding for the female entrepreneur: A continuing analysis. In B. Kirchhoff et al., eds., *Frontiers of Entrepreneurship Research.* Wellesley, MA: Babson College.

Pellegrino, E. T., and Rees, B. L. 1982. Perceived formative and operational problems encountered by female entrepreneurs in retail and service firms. *Journal of Small Business Management* 20(2):15–24.

Rosenstein, J., and Hitt, M. 1986. Experimental research on race and sex discrimination: The record and the prospects. *Journal of Occupational Behavior* 7:215–226.

Schein, V. 1973. The relationship between sex role stereotypes and requisite management characteristics. *Journal of Applied Psychology 57:95–100.*

Schein, V. 1975. Relationships between sex role stereotypes and requisition management characteristics among female managers. *Journal of Applied Psychology* 60:340–344.

Schwartz, E.B. 1976. Entrepreneurship: A new female frontier. *Journal of Contemporary Business* 53:47–75.

Sexton, D. L., and Bowman, N. 1984. Personality inventory for potential entrepreneurs: Evaluation of a modified JPI/PRF-E test instrument. In J. Hornaday, F. Tarpley, Jr., J. Timmons, and K. Vesper, eds., *Frontiers of Entrepreneurship Research.* Wellesley, MA: Babson College.

Sexton, D. L., and Bowman-Upton, N. 1986. Validation of a personality index: Comparative psychological characteristics analysis of female entrepreneurs, managers, entrepreneurship students and business students. In R. Ronstadt, J. Hornaday, R. Peterson, and K. Vesper, eds., *Frontiers of Entrepreneurship Research.* Wellesley, MA: Babson College.

Sexton, D. L., and Kent, C. A. 1981. Female executives vs. female entrepreneurs. In K. H. Vesper, ed., *Frontiers of Entrepreneurship Research.* Wellesley, MA: Babson College.

Siess, T. F., and Jackson, D. N. 1971. Vocational interests and personality: Evidence from the personality research form. In P. McReynolds, ed., *Advances in Psychological Assessment* Vol. 2. Palo Alto, CA: Science and Behavior Books, Inc.

Singer, H. A., and Abramson, P. R. 1973. Values of business administrators: A longitudinal study. *Psychological Reports* 33 (August):43–46.

Smith, N., McCain, G., and Warren, G. 1982. Women entrepreneurs really are different: A comparison of constructed ideal types of male and female entrepreneurs. In K. Vesper, ed., *Frontiers of Entrepreneurship Research.* Wellesley, MA: Babson College.

State of Small Business: A Report of the President. 1987. Washington, D.C.

Stephens, G. E., and DeNisi, A. S. 1980. Women as managers: Attitudes and attributions for performance by men and women. *Academy of Management Journal* 23:355–361.

Sutton, C., and Moore, K. 1985. Executive women: 20 years later. *Harvard Business Review* (September-October):42–66.

Thumin, F. 1965. Personality characteristics of diverse occupational groups. *Personnel Guidance Journal* 45 (July):468–470.

Thurow, L. 1975. *Generating Inequality.* New York: Basic Books, Inc.

Unger, R. K. 1979. Toward a redefinition of sex and gender. *American Psychologist* 34:1085–1094.

Waddell. F. T. 1984. Factors affecting choice, satisfaction, and success in the female self-employed. *Journal of Vocational Behavior* 23:294–304.

Welsch, H., and Young, E. 1984. Male and female entrepreneurial characteristics and behaviors: A profile of similarities and differences. *International Small Business Journal* 2(4):11–20.

Winegardner, J. 1978. Prediction of vocational outcome using the personality research form. Master's thesis, University of Montana.

[8]

Gender and Small Business Success: An Inquiry into Women's Relative Disadvantage*

KARYN A. LOSCOCCO, *State University of New York at Albany*
JOYCE ROBINSON, *State University of New York at Albany*
RICHARD H. HALL, *State University of New York at Albany*
JOHN K. ALLEN, *Allen Associates*

Abstract

Even among a successful group of small business owners, women generate lower sales volumes and derive less income than their male counterparts. Alternative explanations of women's relative disadvantage are evaluated systematically. The characteristics of the owner and the small business that differ between genders explain the discrepancy in financial success, with the smaller size of women's businesses emerging as the major explanatory factor. Women's lack of experience and their concentration in the least profitable industries contribute strongly to the gender discrepancy as well. The processes through which the female small business owner generates sales and derives income are quite similar to those of her male counterpart, but even successful women are not as well positioned to exploit business opportunities as their male counterparts because of their structural disadvantages both within and outside of the business arena.

This article compares the financial success of established female and male small business owners, a topic that merges issues of gender and class. Advanced technology and the expansion of the service sector — two hallmarks of postindustrial society — have combined to foster considerable business growth in the U.S. economy. Between 1980 and 1987, businesses with fewer than 100 employees created 12 million new jobs, while during this same period Fortune 500 companies eliminated three million jobs (Ritzer 1989). Women, in particular, have been turning to small business ownership in ever-increasing numbers.

* *The study on which this research is based was partly supported by a grant from the State University of New York Research Foundation and by Allen Associates. We gratefully acknowledge the help of Monika Reuter, Anne Roschelle, Gene Shackman, and Nicholas Loscocco during various stages of data collection and analysis. We are indebted to James Jaccard, Kevin Leicht, and Arne Kalleberg for their comments and generous advice. Direct correspondence to Karyn Loscocco, Department of Sociology, SS 340, State University of New York at Albany, Albany, NY 12222.*

66 / *Social Forces* 70:1, September 1991

During the 1980s the number of self-employed women increased five times faster than the number of self-employed men and three times faster than the number of female employees (American Demographics 1985; U.S. Small Business Administration 1986).

Small business ownership has always been attractive to groups whose access to good jobs is limited by discrimination (Bonacich 1973; Borjas 1986; Light 1972). Thus, women appear to be the "new immigrants" (Committee on Small Business 1984) opting for the small business arena as a way of escaping their well-documented labor force disadvantage (England et al. 1988; Fox & Hesse-Biber 1984). Yet small businesses owned by women are not as successful as those owned by men, even when they operate in the same industry (Loscocco & Robinson 1991).

There are a number of possible reasons for women's relative lack of financial success. These can be broadly categorized as a function of individual differences brought to the small business sector or differences in the businesses themselves. Thus, differences in material "class resources" (Light 1984) such as financial and human capital brought to the business arena may be largely responsible for the gender discrepancy in economic success. For example, it has been suggested that women enter the ranks of small business owners with fewer of the skills important to small business success (Hisrich & Brush 1984). Alternatively, differences between the characteristics of the businesses of male and female owners may explain women's lesser success. It may be that female-owned businesses suffer from liabilities of both smallness and newness (U.S. Small Business Administration 1985). While past research on small business motivation and success has offered these and other explanations, there has been, to our knowledge, no attempt to evaluate systematically their relative explanatory power.

Given the tremendous growth in small business ownership among women, it is surprising that minimal research has been devoted to evaluation of the success of the female small business owner. Consistent with the general literature on small business ownership, past studies on women and small businesses have tended to assess women's motivation for choosing the small business arena. Such research suggests that women have motivations similar to those of men for starting their own businesses, although women are more likely to enter ownership in response to lack of opportunity in the labor market (Bender 1980; Cromie 1987; Humphreys & McClung 1981). Female owners, like their male counterparts, tend to have an internal locus of control — or the belief that they determine their own fate — and tend to value autonomy and achievement (Cromie 1987; Humphreys & McClung 1981; Schwartz 1976). While some gender differences in personality traits among female and male small business owners have been revealed, the patterns do not indicate that women are less well suited to small business ownership (e.g., Smith, McCain & Warren 1982). Unfortunately, most studies of the female owner are based on very small samples (Cuba, DeCenzo & Anish 1983; DeCarlo & Lyons 1979; Humphreys & McClung 1981; Pellegrino & Reece 1982). There have been few attempts to make systematic comparisons of female-owned and male-owned small businesses (e.g., Kalleberg & Leicht 1991).

Gender and Small Business Success / 67

This investigation draws from diverse literatures to frame examination of the determinants of success among a sample of well-established female and male small business owners who belong to the Smaller Business Association of New England (SBANE). Since women are still less likely than men to engage in small business ownership and more likely to fail when they do (U.S. Small Business Administration 1985), our gender comparison of successful businesses drawn from the same membership group provides a unique perspective on the question of whether and why women owners fail to achieve the same success as their male counterparts. Because we have data on a number of personal as well as business characteristics, we are able to assess the relative power of explanations that emphasize one or the other type of influence. Our study aims at providing a better understanding of this increasingly important but insufficiently studied sector of the economy. In addition, this study addresses in yet another context the continued debate about the relevance of gender to work-related outcomes.

Success Among Small Business Owners

Research suggests four major categories of variables — reflecting either personal or business characteristics — that affect the success of small business firms. First, *human capital* has been highlighted as a prerequisite for small business success. The more skills and experience that the individual brings to ownership, the more likely it is that the business will be successful (Bender 1980). Those with money to invest overcome one of the major obstacles to success — difficulty securing capital (Aldrich & Auster 1986; Shapero 1983). A second major theme of past research on small businesses is that the *personal characteristics* of owners affect the success of their businesses. McClelland's classic study (1961), though controversial (e.g., Frey 1984; Mazur & Rosa 1977), identifies successful businesspeople as having a high need for achievement. It has also been argued that the key to entrepreneurial success is taking risks (Stevenson & Gumpert 1985). Those who become small business owners appear to have especially strong needs for being their own boss as well as an internal locus of control (Brockhaus 1982; Kets de Vries 1977), traits that have been linked to economic success (Kalleberg & Leicht 1991). Small business owners themselves emphasize the importance of making a strong commitment to the business (Goffee & Scase 1985; Pellegrino & Reece 1982; Scase & Goffee 1982).

Another important personal dimension is the *family situation* of the owner. Research suggests that many small business owners benefit from the tangible and emotional support of family members in running their businesses (e.g., Aldrich et al. 1983; Scase & Goffee 1982). Thus, a lack of family support may place small business owners at a disadvantage. Alternatively, heavy family responsibilities may detract from the owner's ability to devote time to the enterprise, thereby detracting from business success.

Features of the business itself — reflecting organizational context and structure — is the third major category of key influences on its vitality. The industry or product market in which a business is found is one such determinant. An organization's product market tends to determine technologies,

68 / *Social Forces* 70:1, September 1991

competition, and business problems (Kalleberg & Berg 1987), thereby affecting the relative chances for business success. Lieberson and O'Connor's classic study (1972) emphasizes that type of industry affects organizational performance. This is likely to be true for small firms as well as large ones. In fact, there is evidence of variation in gross business receipts across industries in the small business sector (Loscocco & Robinson 1991).

Among structural characteristics of the business, the size and age of small business firms have been emphasized as particularly important features of the economic outcomes. Research has shown that firm size is one of the single greatest predictors of income among small capitalists (Aldrich & Weiss 1981). Liabilities of newness place very young firms at a distinct disadvantage because they lack both an established client or customer base and proven organizational structures (Stinchcombe 1965). Research seems to indicate, however, that beyond the very early years of a business's life, age does not contribute to success. In fact, there appear to be liabilities of "old age" as well as of newness (Aldrich & Auster 1986). It has also been argued that the growth of companies is due to size much more than to age (Birch 1987). Therefore, age may not explain variation in success among established small businesses (e.g., Kalleberg & Leicht 1991; Meyer & Zucker 1989).

We have identified several key characteristics of both the business owner and of the business itself that are likely to affect economic success in the small business arena. We now turn to an examination of these issues in the context of gender.

GENDER AND SMALL BUSINESS SUCCESS

Each of the categories of determinants of small business success described above has been offered as a possible explanation for women's relative disadvantage to men in the arena of small business capitalism. These explanations house the responsibility for business outcomes either in the individual (human capital, personal attitudes, and family situation) or in the business itself (industry and business characteristics), corresponding loosely to gender versus job models in the sociology of work (Feldberg & Glenn 1979).

Gender models predict that the work outcomes of women differ from those of men because of individual differences that are brought to the work situation, although the two major strands of this model differ in their explanatory focus (Loscocco 1990). According to the traditional perspective, gender differences in work outcomes are expected and are explained on the basis that, prior to their entry into a particular work position, women and men have had different socialization, training, and other experiences that ultimately shape their experience of work (see review in England & McCreary 1987).

Consistent with the traditional strand of the gender model is the assertion that female small business owners' failure to achieve levels of success comparable to those of male owners stems from women's relative lack of human capital. In fact, women report that they lack the managerial and technical skills that are so important to small business success (Humphreys & McClung 1981; U.S. Department of Commerce 1978). Additionally, it has been argued that women have less access to financial capital. Although banks are traditionally reluctant to lend to small business owners, it appears that their reluctance is heightened when a woman is at the helm (Committee on Small Business 1984; Hisrich & Brush 1984; Humphreys & McClung 1981). Furthermore, because of past credit discrimination, women's lower earning power, and their traditional economic dependence on men, women are likely to have fewer material resources than men to invest in a business (Committee on Small Business 1988). Finally, gender differences in socialization experiences (Bowles & Gintis 1976; Marini & Brinton 1984) may result in women lacking the attitudes, such as risk taking and internal locus of control, that are deemed important to small business success.

The structural-feminist strand of the gender model predicts gender differences on the basis of women's position in both economic and noneconomic spheres rather than on the basis of human capital, socialization, or personal orientation (e.g., Eisenstein 1979; Hartmann 1976; Sokoloff 1988). In particular, this perspective points to women's primary responsibility for the home as a major factor that places women at a disadvantage relative to the men with whom they share a particular kind of work experience (e.g., Goldberg 1984). Supporting the feminist strand of the gender model, findings show that women are at the same time less likely than men to have help with their businesses and more likely to have domestic responsibilities that pull them away from the business (Goffee & Scase 1985; Watkins & Watkins 1983). These results lead to the identification of women's domestic commitments as a probable cause of their lesser economic success (Hisrich 1989; Loscocco & Robinson 1991).

An alternative view that derives from structural or job models is that the nature of the business itself has an impact on the economic success of women and men that supersedes their personal characteristics (Feldberg & Glenn 1979; Kohn & Schooler 1983). From this perspective, gender differences in economic outcomes are attributable to differences in business characteristics. Identification of the business context as a primary cause of the male-female discrepancy in sales and profits is consistent with this model. Research has suggested that the concentration of women in highly competitive, low-growth industries explains their relative lack of success as small business capitalists (Humphreys & McClung 1981; Kalleberg & Leicht 1991; Loscocco & Robinson 1991). Moreover, women's businesses tend to be both smaller and newer than men's (U.S. Small Business Administration 1986). These factors — especially the former — may explain women's lesser success in small businesses.

There are two important avenues of investigation in the study of gender and small business success. First, it is important to ascertain which of the factors identified above goes furthest toward explaining women's tendency to achieve less economic success than their male counterparts in the small business arena. While gender models emphasize personal characteristics, job models identify aspects of work-related structure as primary determinants of work outcomes. Second, it is important to assess whether the processes through which various individual and structural determinants affect the economic success of female and male business owners are similar or different. The notion that the processes differ for women and men is consistent with gender models of work outcomes. Women's unique socialization experiences and different positions in the social structure may mean, for example, that even when women share an entrepreneurial orientation with men, it does not translate as readily into financial success. Structural or job models, on the other hand, suggest that any and all gender differences in outcomes can be explained by differences in individual and business characteristics. The implication is that if women shared men's characteristics, they would achieve comparable levels of success.

As Feldberg and Glenn (1979) argue, there has been a tendency to assign primary causal status to gender in discussions of women and work outcomes but to the work situation in similar studies of their male counterparts. There is a clear need for integrated models of work outcomes that allow for the joint influence of personal and structural characteristics (Feldberg & Glenn 1979). Thus we consider the possibility that aspects of gender and features of the business contribute jointly to the small business success of both women and men. To the extent that there are parallels between employment and ownership, we would expect to find that both individual and structural influences are operative but that structural factors have greater explanatory power (Lowe & Northcott 1988; Reskin & Hartmann 1986). Cross-gender comparison of the specific effects of human capital, business context and structure, personal attitudes, and family situation variables allows us to assess the extent of similarity or difference in the *processes* through which sales and income are generated among small capitalists. On the basis of past comparisons of female and male employees (e.g., Loscocco 1990; Miller 1980), we expect to find considerable gender similarity in the effects of specific determinants.

Data and Variables

THE STUDY

This model is evaluated through analysis of data that come from a pilot study of small businesses in the New England area. Questionnaires were mailed to the 1,742 members of the Smaller Business Association of New England (SBANE), a trade organization representing many different industries. A letter ensuring confidentiality and urging participation in the study was provided by the president of SBANE. Respondents were asked to provide information about the nature and structure of their operation, as well as their personal background and their attitudes toward their work. A second mailing was made to those who did not respond within a few weeks. We received useable information from the owners of 540 firms. Our low response rate (31%) is probably due to the mail survey method (Babbie 1983) and the tremendous time pressure on the small business owner. Unfortunately, budget constraints prohibited us from alternative methods of soliciting cooperation for this pilot project. Clearly, our results must be judged with this low response rate in mind.

Our sample is representative of the SBANE membership on key dimensions such as industry distribution, size, and age of company. Yet comparisons of our sample with Massachusetts census data reveal key differences in terms of industry concentrations. The SBANE sample includes a much larger number of manufacturing organizations and a much smaller number of retail firms.[1]

Similarly, while these owners characterize the SBANE membership, they are a rather elite group of small business employers. A startling 53% have postgraduate education and another 31% are college graduates. This education level is probably explained by the lure of the well educated to high-technology firms, which are particularly prevalent in the Boston area, and to the concentration of colleges and universities in New England. Furthermore, the majority of our respondents have turned to ownership from professional jobs (19%) and managerial jobs (60%). It is also important to keep in mind that the mere existence of these small employers makes them a highly select group. As others have concluded, "nearly all small organizations disappear within a few years" (Starbuck & Nystrom 1981:xiv) and "hundreds of thousands of organizations die each year" (Aldrich & Auster 1986:173). The presumably many New England women and men whose businesses have failed are not represented here.

Given our goal of determining how female and male small business owners compare, this sample is useful. If women who are extremely successful in the small business sector differ from their male counterparts in achievement levels and processes, this suggests that there are serious limits to women's opportunity in the small business arena. We would expect gender differences to be even more pronounced among less elite groups of small business owners.

THE VARIABLES

In our society the success of a small business is typically defined as profitability and indexed by the company's sales volume or gross business receipts (e.g., Kalleberg & Leicht 1991; Loscocco & Robinson 1991). While every small business owner may not define success in this way, we choose this societal measure because it provides the best indicator of possible gender inequality. Some might argue that women are redefining the concept of business success (e.g., Wojahn 1986), yet any such redefinition comes at the price of lesser economic success.

Personal success is almost always assessed by income. Sociological studies of gender stratification emphasize income inequality. In keeping with this emphasis on income as the best index of social standing, studies of the small business or small capitalist class have also used personal income as a key outcome (e.g., Aldrich & Weiss 1981; Wright & Perrone 1977).

Accordingly, we use two indicators of the success of the small business owner: (1) business success is tapped by sales volume (measured in units of $10,000), and (2) personal success is presented by income (measured in units of $1,000).

We include the following aspects of the capital — human and otherwise — that the owner brings to his or her small business: age, educational level, bank loans, and years of experience in the industry.

Business context is tapped by industry dummy variables. Although there is some question as to whether, in these days of mergers, industry remains a meaningful concept (Kalleberg & Berg 1987), we expect that it does continue to be relevant for small businesses in the same basic geographical region. Based on the sample distribution, the following categories are included: wholesale trade; retail trade; finance, insurance, and real estate; business services; and other services, with manufacturing as the omitted category in the regression equations (Tables 2 and 3).[2]

72 / *Social Forces* 70:1, September 1991

The size of the company is measured by the log of the number of full-time employees. Before taking the log, employee size was increased by 1 for each business. This was done to permit the transformation and to account for the owner's labor (see Aldrich & Weiss 1981). Company age is measured in years.

Personal orientation is tapped by such owner attitudes as risk-taking proclivities and internal locus of control, in keeping with the emphases of past studies (e.g., Brockhaus 1982; Kalleberg & Leicht 1991; Kets de Vries 1977). These attitudes are measured by single items that tap the importance of taking chances (ranging from 4 = very important to 1 = not at all important) and the extent of agreement that the "outcomes of my business ventures are largely influenced by my own efforts" (ranging from 5 = strongly agree to 1 = strongly disagree). Although we have attitudinal measures of business commitment, we include the average number of hours that the owner reports devoting to the business, which has an objective referent.[3]

Past research suggests that greater domestic responsibilities, as reflected in family status and role strain, diminish women's relative success as small business owners (e.g., Hisrich 1989). Accordingly, family situation is assessed by marital status (1 = married, 0 = not married), number of dependent children, and role strain, or tension between business and family life. Role strain is the unweighted average (α=0.72) of four items tapping the desire for more personal time, difficulty managing time between business and personal life, having too many tasks to handle oneself, and feeling that one does not have enough time (where 5 = high role strain and 1 = low role strain).

Results

Analysis begins with a descriptive comparison of the female and male small business owners in this sample. Then we turn to a series of equations in which sales and income were regressed on gender and groups of variables entered sequentially: these reflect human capital, business environment and structure, personal attitudes, and family situation. By examining the change in the relationship between gender and the dependent variables with each subsequent group of variables entered, we are able to assess the power of each category to explain the tendency toward less economic success among female small business owners. Finally, we investigate whether economic success is determined in similar or different ways among male and female small business owners. We estimated sets of regression equations, each of which included a product term representing the interaction between gender and a given predictor variable, with all main effect variables controlled.[4]

DESCRIPTIVE RESULTS

Table 1 presents descriptive statistics for the dependent variables as well as each category of predictor variables for the female and male samples of small business owners. It shows, as expected, that women average lower sales volume and income from their small businesses than men. While the typical woman generates $1,346,900 in sales and takes home $51,340 in income, her male counterpart has $3,414,300 in sales volume and derives $95,240 in income.

Gender and Small Business Success / 73

TABLE 1:   Means, Standard Deviations, and Percentages of Selected Variables

	Women			Men		
	Mean	S.D.	% Distrib.[a]	Mean	S.D.	% Distrib.[a]
Success						
Income (in $1,000)	51.34*	45.26		95.24*	56.18	
Sales (in $10,000)	134.69*	225.24		341.43*	338.09	
Human and financial capital						
Age (years)	43.54*	7.78		49.75*	10.24	
Education	4.69	1.45		4.58	1.60	
Years in industry	11.78*	7.46		20.15*	11.23	
Bank loans (1=yes)	.37	1.22		.51	1.47	
Industrial context						
Wholesale			5.4			10.4
Business services			64.9			35.4
Finance and real estate			8.1			7.5
Retail			3.6			5.3
Other services			3.6			5.1
Manufacturing			14.4			36.3
Business characteristics						
Size (no. full-time emplys.)	5.10*	3.56		14.44*	4.01	
Age (years)	13.78*	25.42		23.72*	25.05	
Personal orientation						
Internal locus of control	4.38	.78		4.28	.77	
Risk taker	2.86*	.87		2.64*	.89	
Hours devoted to business	54.28	12.32		55.79	10.36	
Family situation						
Married (1=yes)	.61*	.49		.88*	.32	
No. of dependent children	1.01	1.16		1.18	1.18	
Role strain	2.96*	.67		2.77*	.62	
Previous occupation						
Owner			7.0			5.7
Executive			16.5			28.6
Middle management			33.9			29.9
Lower management			3.5			3.6
Professional			27.8			16.0
Worker			4.3			3.9
Homemaker			3.5			0.0
Military			3.5			12.4

(N=442)

[a] Distribution across variable categories
* Indicates significant difference between samples (p ≤ .05, two-tailed test)

74 / *Social Forces* 70:1, September 1991

The human capital variables show clearly that these small capitalists —
women as well as men — are a very select group. The vast majority of both
women and men have secondary and postsecondary educations. In addition,
both genders tend to come from the managerial and professional ranks,
although men are somewhat more likely to have been executives and women
more likely to have been middle or lower-level managers and professionals.
When it comes to experience in the industry, however, men have an advantage.
The average male has been involved in some capacity in his current industry for
a longer period of time than his female counterpart. In addition, the typical man
is six years older than the typical woman. There is no significant difference in
the use of bank loans as start-up capital.

Table 1 does reveal some gender differences in industry distributions. While
the majority of establishments in both samples are concentrated in business
services and manufacturing, male-owned establishments are distributed more
evenly across the two industries, whereas female-owned ones are concentrated
much more heavily in the business services. Women's establishments are both
smaller and newer than men's.

The men and women in this sample do not evidence much difference in the
attitudes that they bring to business ownership, a result which suggests that
personal orientation variables will contribute little to understanding the gender
discrepancy in business success. For example, women are virtually as likely as
men to report an internal locus of control, or the belief that they determine
business outcomes. Furthermore, there is no significant difference in the number
of hours per week that women and men devote to the business. However,
women are more likely than men to espouse risk taking. Given the greater
obstacles facing women in the small business arena (Committee on Small
Business 1988), perhaps those with a propensity for risk taking are more likely
to take on ownership.

There are similarities as well as differences in the personal situations of
these women and men of SBANE. The mean number of dependent children is
strikingly similar. Moreover, though this is not shown in the table, 43% of the
women and 40% of the men have no dependent children. Yet the men are
considerably more likely than the women to be married, a fact which indicates
that the personal situation of men may offer greater tangible and emotional
support. Given the continued definition of the domestic sphere as women's
responsibility (Fox & Nickols 1983; Pleck 1985), it is not surprising that women
experience greater tension than men between business and family.

GENDER AND SMALL BUSINESS SUCCESS

We turn now to an examination of the extent to which these different types of
variables explain the gender discrepancies in sales and income. Table 2 presents
results from regressions of sales and income on gender, to which the five sets
of variables — human capital, business context, business characteristics, owner
attitudes, and personal situation — were added sequentially. The difference in
the gender coefficient from one column to the next represents the amount that
is mediated by the additional set of variables. Column 2 shows that aspects of
human capital do partially explain the tendency of these women to attain lesser

Gender and Small Business Success / 75

business success. Women's relative lack of experience in the industry (i.e., years in industry) is the major aspect of human capital that accounts for their lower sales and income, as experience mediates most of the total gender effect.

Controlling for human capital differences that might affect the type of business chosen, business context does in fact mediate part of the gender difference in sales and income. That is, women's operation in the least profitable product markets, such as business services, explains part of their disadvantage.

Yet comparison of the gender coefficients in columns 3 and 4 reveals that women's concentration in the business services industry accounts for their lesser success only because business services firms tend to be small. In fact, the major reason for the relative lack of success of these women is that their businesses are generally smaller in size than the men's businesses (i.e., size mediates most of the difference between the gender effects in columns 3 and 4). This finding is consistent with previous research which demonstrates that size is the single greatest predictor of income among small capitalists (Aldrich & Weiss 1981). The importance of size is not surprising, since economic success and growth go hand in hand. In fact, size is often used as an indicator of success (U.S. Small Business Administration 1985).

Columns 5 and 6 reveal that, contrary to the expectations of the traditional strand of the gender model, personal attitudes explain little of the gender discrepancy in sales and income, with human capital, business context, and business size controlled. Since the women in this sample did not evidence substantially less of an entrepreneurial orientation than their male counterparts, personal attitudes are inadequate explanations of the revealed gender discrepancy in business success.[5]

Family situation does explain part of the gender difference in income, although it masks some of the gender difference in sales. Role strain is the major explanatory variable for income among the indicators of family situation. Recognizing that family situation might cause role strain, we estimated an alternative model 6 that includes marital status and the number of dependent children but omits role strain. Neither of the family variables explained the gender discrepancy in income. This finding indicates that differences in family situation between genders per se are less relevant than gender-linked difficulties in balancing family and business demands. With marital status controlled, there is a slightly greater gender discrepancy in sales, because marriage is negatively correlated with sales among women and many women are not married.

Among this sample of established, highly educated members of the Smaller Business Association of New England, we have seen that characteristics of both the business and the owner explain part of the gender difference in business success. The possibility remains that gender differences in the processes through which small capitalists achieve success also account for the male-female discrepancies in sales and income. To gain a more complete understanding of how women and men compare, we turn to the results of the analyses of gender interaction. Table 3 presents coefficients obtained from regressions of sales and income on significant interaction terms ($p<.05$) and all main effect covariates. Where there is a significant difference by gender, the coefficients for men and women are shown.

TABLE 2: Unstandardized (Standardized) Coefficients Obtained from Regression of Measures of Sales and Income on Gender and Individual and Structural Determinants

	Sales					
	1	2	3	4	5	6
Gender	-206.74**	-134.64**	-86.86**	-12.53	-9.54	-12.57
	(-.259)	(-.169)	(-.109)	(-.016)	(-.012)	(-.016)
Human and financial capital						
Age		.57	.69	-.72	-.60	-1.29
		(.017)	(.021)	(-.022)	(-.018)	(-.040)
Education		3.12	11.87	1.75	1.76	3.84
		(.015)	(.057)	(.008)	(.008)	(.018)
Years in industry		7.95**	5.22**	2.63*	2.67*	2.78*
		(.268)	(.176)	(.089)	(.090)	(.094)
Bank loans (1=yes)		16.18	8.91	-4.78	-5.74	-6.45
		(.070)	(.038)	(-.021)	(-.025)	(-.028)
Industrial context						
Wholesale			-20.22	108.98**	107.88**	117.28**
			(-.018)	(.097)	(.096)	(.104)
Business services			-266.44**	6.34	5.81	14.05
			(-.401)	(.010)	(.009)	(.021)
Finance and real estate			-70.62	162.49**	161.47**	166.26**
			(-.057)	(.132)	(.131)	(.135)
Retail			-140.73*	37.58	36.12	44.67
			(-.093)	(.025)	(.024)	(.030)
Other services			-215.48**	-12.49	-16.27	-2.96
			(-.140)	(-.008)	(-.011)	(-.002)
Business characteristics						
Size (log)				171.52**	173.11**	173.79**
				(.747)	(.754)	(.757)
Age				-.24	-.19	-.22
				(-.018)	(-.015)	(-.017)
Personal orientation						
Internal locus of control					10.29	11.46
					(.024)	(.027)
Risk taker					.70	1.36
					(.002)	(.004)
Hours devoted to business					.69	1.13
					(.023)	(.037)
Family situation						
Married (1=yes)						-10.89
						(-.013)
No. of dependent children						-8.77
						(-.031)
Role strain						-29.18
						(-.056)
Constant	341.43**	130.50	263.17**	-160.64*	-255.97*	-170.47
Adjusted R^2	.065	.134	.244	.585	.583	.584

(N=442)

* $p \leq .05$ ** $p \leq .01$

Gender and Small Business Success / 77

TABLE 2: Unstandardized (Standardized) Coefficients Obtained from Regression of Measures of Sales and Income on Gender and Individual and Structural Determinants (Continued)

	Income					
	1	2	3	4	5	6
Gender	-43.91**	-29.54**	-27.52**	-17.51**	-16.75**	-13.47*
	(-.318)	(-.214)	(-.199)	(-.127)	(-.121)	(-.097)
Human and financial capital						
Age		.34	.31	.13	.16	.08
		(.061)	(.055)	(.024)	(.029)	(.015)
Education		3.49*	3.61*	2.25	2.45	2.48
		(.096)	(.100)	(.062)	(.068)	(.068)
Years in industry		1.48**	1.41**	1.07**	1.08**	1.14**
		(.288)	(.274)	(.209)	(.209)	(.221)
Bank loans (1=yes)		1.46	.44	-1.32	-1.71	-1.59
		(.036)	(.011)	(-.033)	(-.043)	(-.040)
Industrial context						
Wholesale			-13.82	3.31	2.48	2.59
			(-.071)	(.017)	(.013)	(.013)
Business services			-15.30**	20.68**	19.73**	21.15**
			(-.133)	(.179)	(.171)	(.183)
Finance and real estate			16.30	47.29**	45.89**	46.29**
			(.076)	(.221)	(.214)	(.216)
Retail			-24.22*	-.35	-1.31	.57
			(-.093)	(-.001)	(-.005)	(.002)
Other services			-20.93	5.99	3.26	5.84
			(-.078)	(.022)	(.012)	(.022)
Business characteristics						
Size (log)				23.04**	24.02**	23.23**
				(.578)	(.603)	(.583)
Age				-.07	-.04	-.03
				(-.029)	(-.017)	(-.015)
Personal orientation						
Internal locus of control					7.52**	7.62**
					(.102)	(.103)
Risk taker					1.27	1.52
					(.020)	(.024)
Hours devoted to business					.14	.29
					(.027)	(.055)
Family situation						
Married (1=yes)						6.68
						(.045)
No. of dependent children						2.33
						(.048)
Role strain						-10.08**
						(-.112)
Constant	95.24**	31.63*	42.52**	-14.16	-62.03**	-48.56*
Adjusted R^2	.099	.188	.212	.411	.418	.429

(N=442)

78 / Social Forces 70:1, September 1991

TABLE 3: Unstandardized Coefficients Obtained from Regression of Sales and Income on Individual and Structural Determinants: Small Business Owners

	Sales	Income
Human and financial capital		
Age	-1.27	.04
Education	3.16	2.55
Years in industry	2.75*	1.21**
Bank loans (1=yes)	-7.38	-1.54
Industrial context		
Wholesale	124.65**	2.30
Business services	18.34	21.25**
Finance and real estate	187.91**	46.76**
Retail	46.42	.36
Other services	8.74	6.78
Business characteristics		
Size (log)		23.29**
Men	186.05**	
Women	110.43**	
Age	-.03	-.05
Personal orientation		
Internal locus of control	7.41	7.29**
Risk taker	4.32	1.35
Hours devoted to business	1.35	.30
Family situation		
Married (1=yes)	-2.91	
Men		15.68*
Women		-8.02*
No. of dependent children	-7.06	2.23
Role conflict	-27.99	-9.85**
Constant	-224.54**	-55.52*
Adjusted R²	.60	.43

(N=442)

* p ≤ .05   ** p ≤ .01

Gender and Small Business Success / 79

Table 3 shows that almost all of the processes through which individual and business characteristics affect the financial success of a small business capitalist are the same for women and men. The results suggest that variables emphasized in past research, such as industry,[6] business size, and owner experience affect the financial success of both genders, as has been found in other studies comparing very different types of small businesses (Kalleberg & Leicht 1991). The significant difference in the effect of marital status on income suggests that the feminist strand of the gender model's emphasis on family roles is important. Apparently, married men experience greater pressure than single men to draw income from the business in order to provide for their families, whereas marriage does not affect the income of women in this way. Single women derive more income than married women. These findings point to structured gender differences in the roles of men and women, as men derive less income benefit from having a spouse than women do, at least partly because women have less earning power than men (Glenn 1987). Furthermore, as the descriptive statistics indicate, the single women in our sample are more likely than the single men to be heads of households, and this heightens the financial need relative to their married counterparts.

Particularly noteworthy is the finding that, while business size is clearly the major determinant of economic success among both female-owned and male-owned small businesses, size brings greater sales volume to male-owned than to female-owned businesses. These women are less successful than their male counterparts not only because their businesses tend to be smaller but also because they do not derive as much financial benefit from size.

The results displayed in Table 3 offer support for both structural and process explanations of gender differences in small business success among this elite group of small business owners. While there is evidence that the business-success levels of women would be much more comparable to those of men if they had the same personal and business characteristics, there is also evidence that size, a key business characteristic, translates into less success among women than among men. To investigate this further, we assigned to females the male mean levels of the predictor variables and solved the sales regression equation for women. If women were to acquire the same structural positions as men, they would generate $2,640,500 in sales. This figure represents an increase of $1,293,600 in sales volume. Yet women would still achieve considerably less financial success than men, who average almost $3,500,000 in sales.

Clearly, then, process differences are also important. To take a closer look, we estimated how large the typical female-owned business would have to be (assuming average levels of all other characteristics and using the coefficients for females) to generate the same level of sales as the average male-owned business. These calculations show that, to attain men's average sales volume, women's businesses would have to grow to a size of 34 employees. Note that the average size of the men's businesses is 14 employees.

80 / *Social Forces* 70:1, September 1991

Discussion and Conclusions

The results of this inquiry into women's relative lack of success as small business owners offers additional support for models of work outcomes that combine structural and individual explanations of work outcomes, even in the realm of self-employment. Consistent with past research comparing female and male employees, we find that structural explanations of gender differences are somewhat more important than those focusing on individual characteristics. In this sample of highly educated and experienced small business owners, the industry and size of the business exert major influences on business outcomes. The greatest part of women's lesser success as small business owners can be explained by their tendency to operate smaller businesses in less-profitable industries. The findings highlight the importance of human capital as well. Even among a highly qualified sample of women, their relative lack of industry-specific experience puts them at a disadvantage relative to their male counterparts.

Among this rather select sample, personal orientation and family situation explain little of the gender difference in sales. We speculate that those with an entrepreneurial orientation and a manageable home life have been selected into this sample of successful small business owners. Such variables probably explain gender discrepancies in success among individuals who are just starting out in business or who operate on the margins of the small business sector.

The difference in income, but not sales, between genders remained with all structural and personal variables controlled. In addition, we were not able to explain as much of the variance in income as in sales. Finally, family situation (i.e., role strain) explains part of the gender difference in income, although it has no effect on sales. We submit that income determination in the small business sector is a personal process likely to be affected by considerations (e.g., total family income and personal goals) that we were unable to assess. Our findings underscore the need to modify traditional models of income inequality to fit the small business context. Future theories must model the decision-making processes used by small business owners to determine their incomes to elucidate why female business owners enjoy less personal success than comparable males.

Given the marked gender difference in levels of economic success, it is noteworthy that there are relatively few differences in the effects of specific determinants of sales and income between the female and male samples. Thus, the processes through which the female small business owner generates sales and derives income are similar to those of her male counterpart. Women's levels of success would be more comparable to those of their male counterparts if they were able to attain the same structural positions.

Still, there are limits to these women's business and personal success that go beyond the characteristics of the businesses themselves. Our analyses show that the relationship between business and family differs in ways that are consistent with the traditional ideology of the married male as "good provider" (Bernard 1981). Moreover, we found that size brought greater financial returns to male-owned than to female-owned businesses. More detailed study of comparable female-owned and male-owned firms is necessary to identify the reasons for this gender discrepancy.

Gender and Small Business Success / 81

Aldrich and Auster's discussion (1986) of the relationship between business size and effectiveness suggests fruitful avenues for such investigation. These authors explain that smaller firm size is a detriment in four key areas: (1) raising capital, (2) securing employees, (3) complying with government regulations, and (4) dealing with tax laws. We posit that small size may be of particular disadvantage to women when it comes to the first two activities. There is considerable anecdotal evidence that financial institutions prefer to deal with men. Even very successful businesswomen have difficulty securing expansion capital (Committee on Small Business 1988; Hisrich & O'Brien 1981). Thus, if bankers feel that very small businesses represent too great a risk, they are likely to perceive an even greater risk when such businesses are owned by women. In addition, it appears that women tend to fill the niches in the small business sector that are unattractive to white men (Loscocco & Robinson 1991). This indicates that a very small female-owned business is apt to have even greater difficulty attracting and retaining employees than a male-owned business of the same size.

Given the importance of business size as a predictor of economic success, it is imperative that future research uncover the reasons for the tendency of women's businesses to be smaller than men's. In particular, research must evaluate the possibilities that women keep their businesses small because of their inability to gain expansion capital or to balance work and family.

Although we cannot confidently generalize the results of this study to national populations of successful small business owners, we are encouraged by the fact that many of the results are consistent with the tenets and findings of past research. We expect that if the industry mix, background characteristics, and success levels of these owners had been more similar to the Massachusetts and national populations, the gender discrepancies revealed in our analyses would have been even stronger. Given the many barriers to women's success as small business owners (Aldrich 1989; Hisrich 1989; Loscocco & Robinson 1991), the women in our sample are probably an even more select group than the men and are thereby likely to compare relatively favorably.

From a policy standpoint, these results are both discouraging and encouraging. They are discouraging because the disadvantages of women relative to those of men transcend class. Even highly select, successful female small business owners do not enjoy the same level of business and personal success as male small business owners. The results are encouraging because they suggest that some of the major causes of women's relative disadvantage can be addressed programmatically. If the major obstacles are removed from their paths, qualified women are likely to achieve levels of success that are comparable to men's when these women enter the ownership ranks. Of course, further research is needed to identify the precise mechanisms through which greater equality can be achieved, and commitment to putting such mechanisms in place must be made before this theoretical possibility can become a reality.

82 / *Social Forces* 70:1, September 1991

Notes

1. Unfortunately we were unable to find census data on the personal characteristics of the Massachusetts small business population.

2. Additional measures of business context, such as the amount of domestic competition and the number of suppliers and customers, were highly correlated with industrial category. For example, domestic competition had a positive effect on sales and income, because it is greatest in the most lucrative manufacturing industry. Therefore, we have omitted additional indicators of business context in order to avoid problems associated with multicollinearity.

3. Although we use hours devoted to the business as an indicator of commitment, it is important to note that family responsibilities, in particular, might limit the amount of time an owner can devote to the business, regardless of how important it is to him or her. Given that women continue to shoulder the lion's share of domestic responsibilities, regardless of the number of hours they work outside the home (Fox & Nickols 1983; Pleck 1985), this may be particularly true for women.

   Because of the controversy surrounding the importance of need for achievement to success (Frey 1984; Mazur & Rosa 1977) and the fact that it did not contribute to the explanatory power of preliminary models, it was omitted from the final model.

4. The full set of analyses was run using both pairwise and listwise deletion of missing data. The overall patterns were remarkably similar, with pairwise results providing a slightly more conservative accounting of significant effects. To maximize our sample size, then, we present the pairwise results. Cases with missing data on the gender variable were always omitted, given the central importance of gender comparisons. The 15 cases with missing data on sales or income were assigned the gender-appropriate mean.

5. Of course the possibility still exists that women are less likely to go *into* business than men because of gender differences in entrepreneurial orientation.

6. We performed an *F*-test to assess whether the industry dummy variables made a significant contribution to the explained variance in the dependent variables. The test showed that industry has a significant effect on both sales and income for women and men.

References

Aldrich, Howard. 1989. "Networking Among Women Entrepreneurs." Pp. 103-32 in *Women-Owned Business*, edited by O. Hagan, C. Rivchun, and D. Sexton. Praeger.

Aldrich, Howard, and Ellen R. Auster. 1986. "Even Dwarfs Started Small: Liabilities of Age and Size and Their Strategic Implications." Pp. 165-98 in *Research in Organizational Behavior*, vol. 8, edited by Barry M. Staw and Larry L. Cummings. JAI Press.

Aldrich, Howard, John Cater, Trevor Jones, and Dave McEvoy. 1983. "From Periphery to Peripheral: The South Asian Petite Bourgeoisie in England." Pp. 1-32 in *Research in the Sociology of Work: Peripheral Workers*, edited by Ida Harper Simpson and Richard L. Simpson, vol. 2.

Aldrich, Howard, and Jane Weiss. 1981. "Differentiation Within the United States Capitalist Class: Workforce Size and Income Differences." *American Sociological Review* 46:279-90.

American Demographics. 1985. "Entrepreneurial Eighties." 7:11.

Babbie, Earl. 1983. *Survey Research Methods*. Wadsworth.

Bender, Henry. 1980. *Report on Women Business Owners*. American Management Association.

Bernard, Jessie. 1981. "The Good-Provider Role: Its Rise and Fall." *American Psychologist* 36:1-12.

Birch, David. 1987. *Job Creation in America: How Our Smallest Companies Put the Most People to Work*. Free Press.

Bonacich, Edna. 1973. "A Theory of Middleman Minorities." *American Sociological Review* 38:583-94.

Gender and Small Business Success / 83

Borjas, George J. 1986. "The Self-Employment Experience of Immigrants." *Journal of Human Resources* 21:485-506.

Bowles, Samuel, and Herbert Gintis. 1976. *Schooling in Capitalist America: Educational Reform and the Contradictions of Economic Life.* Basic Books.

Brockhaus, Robert H. 1982. "The Psychology of the Entrepreneur." Pp. 39-57 in *Encyclopedia of Entrepreneurship*, edited by Calvin A. Kent, Donald L. Sexton, and Karl H. Vesper. Prentice Hall.

Committee on Small Business. 1984. *Women Entrepreneurs: Their Success and Problems.* Government Printing Office.

____. 1988. *New Economic Realities: The Rise of Women Entrepreneurs.* Government Printing Office.

Cromie, Stanley. 1987. "Motivations of Aspiring Male and Female Entrepreneurs." *Journal of Occupational Behaviour* 8:251-61.

Cuba, Richard, David DeCenzo, and Andrea Anish. 1983. "Management Practices of Successful Female Business Owners." *American Journal of Small Business* 8:47-56.

DeCarlo, James F., and Paul R. Lyons. 1979. "A Comparison of Selected Personal Characteristics of Minority and Nonminority Female Entrepreneurs." *Journal of Small Business Management* 17:22-29.

Eisenstein, Zillah R. 1979. "Developing a Theory of Capitalist Patriarchy and Socialist Feminism." Pp. 5-40 in *Capitalist Patriarchy and the Case for Socialist Feminism*, edited by Z. Eisenstein. Monthly Review Press.

England, Paula, George Farkas, Barbara Kilbourne, and Thomas Dou. 1988. "Explaining Occupational Sex Segregation and Wages: Findings from a Model with Fixed Effects." *American Sociological Review* 53:544-58.

England, Paula, and Lori McCreary. 1987. "Gender Inequality in Paid Employment." Pp. 286-320 in *Analyzing Gender: A Handbook of the Social Science Research*, edited by Beth B. Hess and Myra M. Ferree. Sage.

Feldberg, Roslyn L., and Evelyn Nakano Glenn. 1979. "Male and Female: Job Versus Gender Models in the Sociology of Work." *Social Problems* 26:525-35.

Fox, Karen D., and Sharon Y. Nickols. 1983. "The Time Crunch: Wife's Employment and Family Work." *Journal of Family Issues* 4:61-82.

Fox, Mary Frank, and Sharlene Hesse-Biber. 1984. *Women at Work.* Mayfield.

Frey, R. Scott. 1984. "Need for Achievement, Entrepreneurship and Economic Growth: A Critique of the McClelland Thesis." *Social Science Journal* 21:125-34.

Glenn, Evelyn N. 1987. "Racial Ethnic Women's Labor: The Intersection of Race, Gender and Class Oppression." Pp. 46-73 in *The Hidden Aspects of Women's Work*, edited by Christine E. Bose. Praeger.

Goffee, Robert, and Richard Scase. 1985. *Women in Charge: The Experience of Female Entrepreneurs.* Allen & Unwin.

Goldberg, Roberta. 1984. "The Determination of Consciousness Through Gender, Family and Work Experience." *The Social Science Journal* 21:75-85.

Hartmann, Heidi. 1976. "Capitalism, Patriarchy, and Job Segregation by Sex." *Signs* 1:137-69.

Hisrich, Robert D. 1989. "Women Entrepreneurs: Problems and Prescriptions for Success in the Future." Pp. 3-32 in *Women-Owned Businesses*, edited by Oliver Hagan, Carol Rivchun, and Donald Sexton. Praeger.

Hisrich, Robert D., and Candida G. Brush. 1984. "The Woman Entrepreneur: Management Skills and Business Problems." *Journal of Small Business Management* 22:30-37.

Hisrich, Robert D., and Marie O'Brien. 1981. "The Woman Entrepreneur From a Business and Sociological Perspective." In *Proceedings, 1981 Conference on Entrepreneurship*, 21-39. Babson College.

84 / *Social Forces* 70:1, September 1991

Humphreys, Marie Adele, and Jacquetta McClung. 1981. "Women Entrepreneurs in Oklahoma." *Review of Regional Economics* 6:13-21.

Kalleberg, Arne L., and Ivar Berg. 1987. *Work and Industry*. Plenum Press.

Kalleberg, Arne L., and Kevin T. Leicht. 1991. "Small Business Success and Survival: Individual and Structural Determinants of Organizational Performance." *Academy of Management Journal*. In press.

Kets de Vries, Manfred F.R. 1977. "The Entrepreneurial Personality: A Person at the Crossroads." *Journal of Management Studies* 14:34-57.

Kohn, Melvin L., and Carmi Schooler, with the collaboration of Joanne Miller, Karen A. Miller, and Ronald Schoenberg. 1983. *Work and Personality: An Inquiry into the Impact of Social Stratification*. Ablex.

Lieberson, Stanley, and James F. O'Connor. 1972. "Leadership and Organizational Performance: A Study of Large Corporations." *American Sociological Review* 37:117-30.

Light, Ivan. 1972. *Ethnic Enterprise in America*. University of California Press.

____. 1984. "Immigrant and Ethnic Enterprise in North America." *Ethnic and Racial Studies* 7:195-216.

Loscocco, Karyn A. 1990. "Reactions to Blue Collar Work: A Comparison of Women and Men." *Work and Occupations* 17:152-77.

Loscocco, Karyn A., and Joyce Robinson. 1991. "Barriers to Small Business Success Among Women." *Gender and Society*. In press.

Lowe, Graham S., and Herbert C. Northcott. 1988. "The Impact of Working Conditions, Social Roles and Personal Characteristics on Gender Differences in Distress." *Work and Occupations* 15:55-77.

Marini, Margaret Mooney, and Mary C. Brinton. 1984. "Sex Typing in Occupational Socialization." Pp. 192-232 in *Sex Segregation in the Workplace: Trends, Explanations, Remedies*, edited by Barbara F. Reskin. National Academy Press.

Mazur, Allan, and Eugene Rosa. 1977. "An Empirical Test of McClelland's 'Achieving Society' Theory." *Social Forces* 55:769-74.

McClelland, David C. 1961. *The Achieving Society*. Free Press.

Meyer, Marshall W., and Lynne G. Zucker. 1989. *Permanently Failing Organizations*. Sage.

Miller, Joanne. 1980. "Individual and Occupational Determinants of Job Satisfaction." *Sociology of Work and Occupations* 7:337-66.

Pellegrino, Eric T., and Barry L. Reece. 1982. "Perceived Formative and Operational Problems Encountered by Female Entrepreneurs in Retail and Service Firms." *Journal of Small Business Management* 20:15-24.

Pleck, Joseph H. 1985. *Working Wives, Working Husbands*. Sage.

Reskin, Barbara F., and Heidi Hartmann. 1986. *Women's Work, Men's Work: Sex Segregation in the Job*. National Academy Press.

Ritzer, George. 1989. "The Permanently New Economy: The Case for Reviving Economic Sociology." *Work and Occupations* 16:243-72.

Scase, Richard, and Robert Goffee. 1982. *The Entrepreneurial Middle Class*. Croom Helm.

Schwartz, Eleanor Brantley. 1976. "Entrepreneurship: A New Female Frontier." *Journal of Contemporary Business* 5:47-75.

Shapero, Albert. 1983. "Pre-venture Capital: A Critical but Neglected Issue." *The Entrepreneurial Economy* 2:3-4.

Smith, Norman R., Gary McCain, and Audrey Warren. 1982. "Women Entrepreneurs Really Are Different: A Comparison of Constructed Ideal Types of Male and Female Entrepreneurs." Pp. 68-77 in *Frontiers of Entrepreneurship Research — 1982*. Babson College.

Gender and Small Business Success / 85

Sokoloff, Natalie J. 1988. "Contributions of Marxism and Feminism to the Sociology of Women and Work." Pp. 116-31 in *Women Working*, edited by Ann H. Stromberg and Shirley Harkess. Mayfield.

Starbuck, William H., and Paul Nystrom. 1981. "Designing and Understanding Organizations." Pp. ix-xxii in *Handbook of Organizational Design*, edited by Paul Nystrom and William H. Starbuck. Oxford University Press.

Stevenson, Howard H., and David E. Gumpert. 1985. "The Heart of Entrepreneurship." *Harvard Business Review* 63:85-94.

Stinchcombe, Arthur L. 1965. "Social Structure and Organizations." Pp. 142-93 in *Handbook of Organizations*, edited by James G. March. Rand McNally.

U.S. Department of Commerce. 1978. President's Interagency Task Force on Women Business Owners. *The Bottom Line: Unequal Enterprise in America*. Government Printing Office.

U.S. Small Business Administration. 1985. *The State of Small Business: A Report of the President*. Government Printing Office.

____. 1986. *The State of Small Business: A Report of the President*. Government Printing Office.

Watkins, Jean, and David Watkins. 1983. "The Female Entrepreneur: Background and Determinants of Business Choice — Some British Data." *International Small Business Journal* 2:21-31.

Wojahn, Ellen. 1986. "Why There Aren't More Women in This Magazine." *Inc.* July:45-48.

Wright, Erik Olin, and Luca Perrone. 1977. "Marxist Class Categories and Income Inequality." *American Sociological Review* 42:32-55.

[9]

WOMEN AS ENTREPRENEURS IN SWEDEN
CONCLUSIONS FROM A SURVEY

Carin Holmquist, University of Umeå
Elisabeth Sundin, University of Linköping

ABSTRACT

This paper presents some results from our extensive questionnaire to 1,500 female and and 300 male entrepreneurs in Sweden. The
respondents were selected from 18 strata, each stratum representing a
marital status and a line of business. Questions were asked on the
background of the entrepreneurs, on their business, on results, on the
motives for going into business and on attitudes to entrepreneurship -
especially for women. The paper also presents the general findings
from the first part of our study, the statistics on all female
entrepreneurs, 64,420 women, in Sweden in 1980. Finally we discuss
the differences between male and female entrepreneurs.

PRESENTATION OF THE STUDY

Women are very active participants in the Swedish economic
system. The law provide equal opportunities for women and in an
international perspective the number of women in the labour force is
high.

In practice, however, women are occupied in traditional fields
and in low level jobs. There are, for instance, few female leaders in
industry. Male and female worlds are separated by invisible but efficient barriers.

The main arguments for encouraging women to become entrepreneurs are the need for entrepreneurs, the need for a more androgynous
leadership and women's need for self-fulfillment and independence.

The entrepreneurial world is by tradition male-dominated. The
drives associated with entrepreneurial behavior coincide to a large
extent with those traditionally attributed to men. As an example we
may take McClelland's "need for achievement". Women's world has traditionally been focused around the family, the household and social
relations. In this context the drive is more for "need for affiliation" - the type of drive that is commonly attributed to the female
species.

In the following model the two worlds – of entrepreneurs and of women – are pictured as diametrically different. There are few overlaps.

FIGURE 1
A MODEL OF WOMEN ENTREPRENEURS

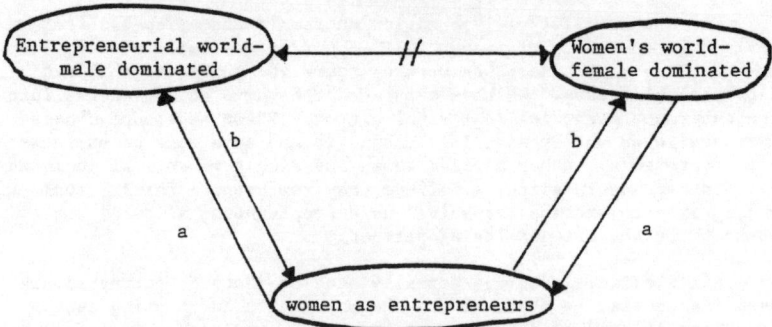

Women as entrepreneurs represent an anomaly in the traditional gender role pattern. They are positioned between two cultures – women's world and the entrepreneurial world. We are interested in how these women adapt to their unique position. Here we may find at least three types of behaviour:

a) women bring into entrepreneurship some of their experiences from the women's world

b) women adapt fully to the culture of the entrepreneurial world and bring these experiences into the women's world

c) a totally new culture is defined – separated from both traditional cultures.

The aim of our study was to find out whether female entrepreneurship is a means for society to fill the need for entrepreneurs and for women to achieve equality with men.

Our study is planned so that we cover a wide array of questions. We study female entrepreneurship at three levels and we believe that these taken together will give a full and relevant picture of the Swedish situation. The study consists of two parts: first a descriptive study of national material and second a study at the organizational and individual level.

PART 1 - SURVEY OF NATIONAL STATISTICS FOR 1980

This is a national study and we incorporated all Swedish women who in 1980 stated that they were "working in their own business". Our total figure is far higher than that of other official statistics, owing to our having considered all Swedish women.

Our data consist of information on female entrepreneurs from every single community of Sweden (279), on ages of female entrepreneurs, on line of business, on working hours, on number of children and on marital status. We have separated the women entrepreneurs into three subgroups according to marital status. These subgroups consist of women with an entrepreneurial husband in the same line of business (co-entrepreneurs), other married women and single women. We included the co-entrepreneurs since we believe they represent a fairly usual way for women to express themselves as entrepreneurs, allowing the husband to be the outward-facing partner.

Since official sources normally used to identify entrepreneurs proved inadequate, we chose to use the population and housing census. This census is conducted every fifth year and provides basic information on all Swedish residents.

We selected information on women who had stated in the 1980 census that they worked in a business of their own. The number stating this was 64,420, a much higher figure than the official 43,000. The co-entrepreneurs are a likely reason for the discrepancy.

Number of Entrepreneurs

In 1980 there were 64,420 women entrepreneurs in Sweden. They were of the following types:

TABLE 1
NUMBER OF FEMALE ENTREPRENEURS IN SWEDEN 1980

Married, co-entrepreneurs	30,308	47%
Married, other entrepreneurs	23,759	37%
Unmarried	10,325	16%
Total	64,420	100%

It should be noted that "married" is used for women living on a permanent basis with a man, regardless of the juridical status.

As can be seen from Table 1 the co-entrepreneurs are by far the biggest group, comprising almost 50%.

Marital Status

Table 1 showed that only 16% of the female entrepreneurs are unmarried. This is a low rate compared to the marital status of all Swedish women. Even when excluding the co-entrepreneurs, a group that by definition is married, this holds true. Consequently it seems as if women entrepreneurs are married to a greater extent than are other Swedish women.

TABLE 2
MARITAL STATUS OF WOMEN ENTREPRENEURS
FIGURES IN THOUSANDS

	Total female population	%	Women entre-preneurs	%	Women entre-preneurs (excl. working with husband)	%
Married	2,043	63	54	85	24	70
Single	1,213	37	10	15	10	30
Total	3,256	100	64	100	34	100

Number of Children

In the following table we find that women entrepreneurs tend to have relatively many children. The co-entrepreneurs are different from the other groups, but also other groups of female entrepreneurs have many children compared to women in general.

TABLE 3
NUMBER OF CHILDREN WOMEN 16 - YEARS
PERCENTAGES

	0	1	2	3+	
Co-entrepreneurs	51%	21%	21%	7%	100%
Other female entrepreneurs	60%	20%	16%	4%	100%
Total population	74%	12%	10%	4%	100%

Line of Business

In our material we have included women working in farming, i.e., if it is of a business type. For comparison with male entrepreneurs we have to exclude these women, thus obtaining the following table:

TABLE 4
LINE OF BUSINESS FOR DIFFERENT GROUPS OF
FEMALE AND MALE ENTREPRENEURS - PERCENTAGES

	Men	Women Total	Co-entre- preneurs	Other married	Single
Line of business					
Manufacturing	13%	11%	15%	8%	7%
Construction	23%	6%	11%	2%	1%
Trade etc.	30%	45%	46%	44%	45%
Transport	16%	5%	9%	2%	3%
Service	18%	33%	19%	44%	44%
Total	100%	100%	100%	100%	100%

Compared to men, women entrepreneurs are more often active in
commerce, restaurants and service and less often in manufacturing,
construction and transport. These dramatic differences are more
obvious when we notice that the co-entrepreneurs more often have a
line of business resembling the male pattern, while women running a
business without the involvement of a husband are more likely to be
different. For instance we may note that hair-stylists account for
less than half a percent of co-entrepreneurs while, the remaining
women entrepreneurs have more than 20% working in this line of business. The most "typical" line of business for women entrepreneurs in
all groups is food retailing.

The concentration to a few lines of business is especially
marked for the women not working as co-entrepreneurs. The distribution over the most important lines of business, in terms of number of
women entrepreneurs, is presented in Table 5.

As can be seen, 14 lines of business occupy 58.49% of the
female entrepreneurs. None of these 14 lines is in industrial production, building, construction or consultancy. These fields of business
life are thus much less common for women entrepreneurs than those with
a traditional female representation, such as retailing and service.

Even if women entrepreneurs are concentrated to a few lines of
business, the fact is that female entrepreneurship is also very
widespread in terms of types of business. We searched the 232 lines
(4-position SNI-code) included in our census material to find out the
types of business lacking women entrepreneurs. The result was that
only 16 out of 232 lines lacked women entrepreneurs. Of these most
are monopolies (e.g., cigarette production) and the rest are "strange"
lines (e.g., artistic activity, not specified).

TABLE 5
NUMBER OF ENTREPRENEURS IN THE MOST COMMON
LINES OF BUSINESS AND PERCENTAGES OF TOTAL ENTREPRENEURS
TOTAL POPULATION (N = 64,420)

Line of Business	Number of Entrepreneurs	%
Hair-stylist and beauty care	7,867	12.21
Food retailing	5,729	8.89
Garment retailing	4,426	6.87
Farming and agriculture	3,761	5.84
Restaurants and cafes	2,531	3.93
Health care and nursing	2,207	3.43
Tobacconist and newspaper retailing	2,002	3.11
Goods transportation	1,619	2.51
Artistic activity	1,427	2.22
Transportation of people	1,359	2.11
Jewelry and leisure goods retailing	1,295	2.01
Retailing with non-specified home equipment	1,285	1.99
Flower retailing	1,093	1.70
Gardening	1,076	1.67
Total	37,677	58.49

We thus concluded that women entrepreneurs are spread over almost all lines of business, although the distribution is not quite even. It is important to bear in mind this double picture of female entrepreneurship - on the one hand a concentration, on the other a wide distribution - when we analyze the phenomenon further.

Geographical Distribution

There are many similarities in the patterns of distribution between female entrepreneurs as a group and the total population. But there are great differences within the group of female entrepreneurs, for instance the rate of unmarried entrepreneurs is extremely high in the Stockholm region. The regions with high rates of entrepreneurship and low rates of employment seem to be located in the northern part of Sweden and in highly industrialized areas in other parts.

Briefly, we may conclude that four lines of business are predominant in almost every region: hair-stylist/beauty-care, food retailing, garment retailing and farming. These four lines include the three most common in every region. The big cities are a little different in that farming is less common, while consultancy is frequent only in these areas.

PART 2 THE QUESTIONNAIRE

This part aimed at finding out how women entrepreneurs behave and with what attitudes they face their entrepreneurial task. Information was collected on the individual as well as on the organizational level.

The method was a questionnaire. It was sent to a sample of 1,500 women and 300 men. The sample was stratified, each stratum consisting of a certain marital status and a certain type of business. The questions are comprehensive and include type of business, size of enterprise, organization, outcomes, background of the entrepreneur, domestic and social relations and attitudes to work, family and entrepreneurship. The questions were sequenced according to the model shown below.

FIGURE 2
A MODEL FOR RELATING FACTUAL CIRCUMSTANCES AND ATTITUDES

Background of entrepreneur   Attitudes I

Time   Character of business   Attitudes II

Outcomes: social/economic   Attitudes III

As is clear, the model relates the experience of the women to their attitudes, and these are seen as interacting over time. In the following we will present some results in the order given by the model.

Background of Entrepreneur

We found a rather conventional background for the female entrepreneurs. They report being from a fairly entrepreneurial background, having previous experience in the line of business they came to choose and with a rather low figure for higher education. As an example we present the occupation of parents and husbands of female entrepreneurs:

TABLE 6
OCCUPATION OF PARENTS AND HUSBANDS OF WOMEN ENTREPRENEURS
PERCENTAGES

Professional status	Mother	Father	Husband
Working in the home	53.1	0.5	–
Owner manager	9.9	21.1	54.6
Farmer	7.4	19.2	5.3
Assisting in the family firm	2.9	0.2	–
Privately employed			
–at a high level	2.3	13.1	12.3
–at a low level	18.5	35.5	19.1
Publicly employed			
–at a high level	1.6	2.3	4.6
–at a low level	4.1	7.3	3.7

By far the most common situation is that the entrepreneur's mother has been a housewife and the most common occupation for the entrepreneur's father was that he was privately employed at a low level. Considering farming, which in many respects is an occupation resembling entrepreneurship, we find an even higher figure for the group of entrepreneuring fathers: 40% are self-employed. The high proportion of husbands working as entrepreneurs is due to our including the female co-entrepreneurs who, by definition, have a husband as the other co-entrepreneur. As previously noted, half the population of female entrepreneurs are co-entrepreneurs and so is the respondent group.

Two things should be noticed. The first is that it is essential to remember that most of our respondents grew up when it was common for the mother to be a housewife if the family could afford it. Today in Sweden as many as 85% of women with children under 7 are working, part- or full-time, and often in the public sector. The second thing to notice is that there is a high proportion of mothers of entrepreneurs who have been self-employed. In fact many more female entrepreneurs have had self-employed mothers than have male entrepreneurs.

Attitudes Before Going Into Business

One of the most obvious attitudes is the motive for starting a business. We asked the respondents to choose between a number of motives or state other motives. When analyzing the material we have summarized the answers according to the type of motive – push or pull factors.

Pull-factors are motives that see the new situation as attractive and positive, i.e., to actively seek the new opportunity expecting a positive change. Push-factors are quite the opposite. These motives are connected with a currently bad situation that demands a change. Emigration is an example that can hold both types of motives, pull-factors being the search for a new and rich future, push-factors being famine and lack of work in the native country. Of course there are some difficulties in separating the two kinds of motive.

TABLE 7
PUSH- AND PULL-FACTORS OF FEMALE ENTREPRENEURS
PERCENTAGES

Push-factors		Pull-factors	
Unemployment	1.5	Monetary motives	4.4
Passive entering			
(inheritance)	7.4	Self fulfillment	
Discontent	3.0	– to test ideas	5.3
Opportunity to stay in		– to realize old ideas	6.7
this type of business	11.7	– to develop knowledge	12.9
Family reasons	39.0	– to be one's own boss	45.3
		Altruistic motives	10.4
Total	62.4		85.0

As can be seen the total is more than 100% which is because the respondents could choose more than one alternative. The pull-factor motives as a group amount to 85%, while the push-factor motives have a lower total percentage. The single most stated reason was to be one's own boss - a reason we have placed under the heading of self-fulfillment.

We also notice the high figure for family reasons, a motive we have placed under the push-factor grouping. The women's ambition to combine private life and working life is obvious in this motive. The relatively low percentage given for inheritance of a business - more women stated altruistic motives than inheritance as a motive for starting a business - is notable since it is common to speak of women entrepreneurs as passively entering business when their fathers or husbands die.

Another finding is that 41% stated that it was not a big step to go into business and even more women, 66%, stated that it was not a difficult decision. Consequently we argue that the action orientation of the entrepreneur is manifested also in this female group; they see the decision to go into business as a big one but do not find it hard to make the decision.

Character of Business and of the Entrepreneur's Work

It is common to consider women entrepreneurs as having a rather small turnover and – as noticed in part 1 – concentrated to some typical areas. First we may notice that 57% of the respondents had established the business on their own initiative while 33% established a business together with someone else.

It is often claimed that female entrepreneurship is a new phenomenon. As we have argued elsewhere there is clear evidence of a long history of women as entrepreneurs. The questionnaire supports the idea of a long history, as 14% of the companies were more than 38 years old and more than half had existed for more than 14 years.

Almost 50% of the respondents stated that they had employed personnel, often just a few persons. The turnover of the companies was in one third of the cases so low that it could not be the primary source of income. This is related to the fact that it is common, especially in entrepreneurial regions, for women to have a business on a part-time basis. One third of the women entrepreneurs run their business on a part-time basis. If we set the limit to SEK 300,000 as a minimum turnover for full-time income we find that 43% of the entrepreneurs could live on their business.

The type of business of the respondents was to a large extent provided by the selection criteria, i.e., we divided the population of female entrepreneurs into strata and made a random sample in each stratum. The questionnaire showed no discrepancies from the overall pattern stated in part 1 – for instance the women we had a priori placed in the stratum "hairdressers" proved to be in that line of business.

As to the entrepreneurial task we found that more than half the respondents work more than full-time, 40 hours a week. Many of those working less than full-time have another job too.

The women list a lot of different tasks when asked about the nature of their work. The traditional role of small businessmen is to perform a multitude of tasks, and this also holds true for female entrepreneurs. As the most important task one third of the women state that they do a number of different things, and one third state that they are mainly in production. We may note that only 16% state that they mainly have supportive tasks, such as cleaning and book keeping.

Attitudes to Being in Business

When asked to describe the goals of their business the women could choose more than one alternative and were asked to mark the single most important goal, which were as follows:

TABLE 8
MOST IMPORTANT GOALS STATED BY FEMALE ENTREPRENEURS
PERCENTAGES

Satisfied customers	39%
Increased turnover	17%
Job creation for the entrepreneur	14%
Increased profitability	7%
More customers	7%

The social goals are obvious although we notice that women are not negative to increased profit as well as turnover.

The female entrepreneurs were asked how they viewed their experience as entrepreneurs. Questions were asked on job satisfaction as well as on social rewards from the entrepreneurial effort. In general we wish to emphasize the positive experience of the female entrepreneurs.

For instance women entrepreneurs to a very large extent find the attitudes of others to be highly encouraging. Customers, banks, employees and other entrepreneurs are all very supportive. There is more neutral attitude from the public sector but it is not seen as negative. This positive experience is also shown in the working situation where female entrepreneurs say that they seldom feel frustrations and worries – one exception is the fact that many of them state that they worry about the future as an entrepreneur.

Another dimension of the attitudes to being in business is how female entrepreneurs combine business life and private life. The following table shows factors stated as contributing to satisfaction in life.

TABLE 9
RANKING OF ALTERNATIVES OF MOST SATISFYING FACTORS IN LIFE
THE MOST COMMON ALTERNATIVES
PERCENTAGES

Work in the company	29%
Children/grandchildren	22%
Partner	18%
Family, other persons	17%
Home	16%
Other people	7%
Hobbies	6%
Outdoor activities	6%
Sports	5%

The respondents could choose more than one alternative and the most common are the job in the company, the children and the partner – in that order. As with other entrepreneurs it seems that female entrepreneurs have little time for other activities than the company and the family – their work is their hobby.

Social and Economic Outcomes and Attitudes to These

The economic outcome has been discussed when we noticed that many women entrepreneurs had a low turnover. Another measure of economic outcome is the salary from the company. Seventy percent of the women state that they have less than SEK 50,000 net a year, a modest salary. More than half the entrepreneurs believe they would earn more in another job. However the respondents do not complain over the salary and one third believe that the future will bring financial improvement.

The social outcomes have been discussed above, for instance the goals for the business and the job satisfaction. Another measure of social rewards is the responses provided on the most positive/negative experiences encountered in entrepreneurship.

TABLE 10
MOST POSITIVE AND NEGATIVE EXPERIENCES IN ENTREPRENEURSHIP
PERCENTAGES

Positive:

Freedom/independence	67%
Professional pride	9%
Socially rewarding	8%
A variety of things	7%
Great fun!	5%
Combination with family	4%

Negative:

Never free	40%
Financial responsibility	17%
Nothing is negative!	14%
Personal/social responsibility	12%
Paper-work/bureaucracy	9%
A variety of things	8%

Again we find a typical entrepreneurial pattern. The women state that the most positive experience is the freedom, and that the most negative experience is that of never being free! The entrepreneurial spirit is also obvious in the answers saying that it is simply great fun to be in business, and that there is nothing negative in entrepreneurship.

A Comparison Between Male and Female Entrepreneurs

        We have emphasized the general entrepreneurial traits of the
female respondents. There are also many similarities between male and
female entrepreneurs in our study. Since the questionnaire was sent
to many more women than men it is hard to compare on an even basis.
For instance the male respondents were mainly from Stockholm and consequently may differ from female respondents in other respects than
gender differences. One example of this is that there are more
entrepreneurs with immigrant backgrounds in the male group – immigrant
entrepreneurs are more common in the Stockholm region.

        The motives for starting a business are somewhat different
since the men stress the economic outcome more. Men also provide more
motives than women do. One important difference is in part-time
entrepreneurship. While as many as 35% of the women work part-time,
only 7% of the men work less than full-time.

        Women entrepreneurs more often handle bookkeeping while men
more often deal with advertising. A higher proportion of male
entrepreneurs, 85% compared to 62% for women, view themselves as
leaders of the company. This observation is consistent with other
studies showing a reluctance on the part of women to regard themselves
as leaders. An interesting difference is shown in attitudes to female
leaders:

TABLE 11
OPINIONS ON WOMEN AS LEADERS
STATED BY MALE AND FEMALE ENTREPRENEURS
PERCENTAGES

| | Yes | | No | | No opinion | |
	Women	Men	Women	Men	Women	Men
Women have better employee relations	47	23	16	34	37	43
Women are worse leaders	2	4	81	65	17	31

        As can be seen, men are more reluctant to reveal an opinion on
female leaders.

        For a full comparison of female and male entrepreneurs we chose
to compare for special types of business, trade and transport. This
group exhibits the same characteristics for women and men – in age,
marital status and so on. The only really distinguishing factor apart
from gender is that more men live in Stockholm.

This comparison proved to be very interesting. As is shown, there were some differences on the aggregate level, for instance in the rate of part-time entrepreneurship. This and other differences, in business volume as in attitudes, tend to vanish when we break down the population into more similar groups. This we hold to be the usual gender trap — comparing female hair stylists with male machinery producers, i.e., comparing male/female and type of business intertwined.

A Comparison With Other Studies

We have drawn on other studies of e.g., leadership attitudes and on job satisfaction for comparison. In this paper, however, we shall limit the discussion to a comparison with a study made by Goffee and Scase. They propose female entrepreneurship to be of four types according to the following model:

FIGURE 3
TYPES OF FEMALE ENTREPRENEURS
(SOURCE: GOFFEE R & SCASE R: WOMEN IN CHARGE, LONDON 1985, PAGE 55)

| | | Attachment to Conventional Gender Roles | |
		High	Low
Attachment to Entrepreneurial Ideals	High	Conventional	Innovative
	Low	Domestic	Radical

The conventional type sees herself as a woman and an entrepreneur, and hence has to cope with the norms of these two roles at the same time. She chooses conventional lines of business such as restaurants and retailing. The innovative type has broken with the conventional gender role and hence often chooses a business in a more male area such as marketing. The domestic type does not see herself as a real entrepreneur, it is just an activity on the side, like a little pottery or a small beauty parlor in the home. The radical type, finally, breaks both role patterns and often tries to form alternatives, for instance in women's cooperatives in trade.

When we started our study we did not have access to the Goffee & Scase study. However, we have analyzed our respondents' answers by scanning the questions on goals and motives. Then we classified the alternatives provided if they indicated low/high attachment to traditional gender roles and to traditional entrepreneurial ideals. For example the alternative "a way of combining family and work" shows a high attachment to conventional female roles. We found the following distribution in the two groups of male and female entrepreneurs.

TABLE 12
ATTACHMENT TO CONVENTIONAL GENDER ROLES FOR WOMEN
PERCENTAGES

	Women	Men
High	54%	30%
Low	46%	70%

It might seem surprising that many men exhibit a high attachment to conventional female roles, but it is consistent with studies of Sweden in an international perspective that show equality to be higher than in other countries.

TABLE 13
ATTACHMENT TO ENTREPRENEURIAL IDEALS
PERCENTAGES

	Women	Men
High	7%	7%
Low	93%	93%

We notice that few respondents give evidence of strong attachment to conventional entrepreneurial ideals, which again might be attributable to national culture.

Summarizing we found that the Goffee & Scase matrix gave the following distribution in our population:

TABLE 14
TYPES OF ENTREPRENEURS
PERCENTAGES

Conventional type

Women 3%
Men   2%

Innovative Type

Women 4%
Men   5%

Domestic type

Women 21%
Men   15%

Radical Type

Women 72%
Men   78%

Again, we note that there are small differences between male
and female entrepreneurs. The largest group is the radical type, a
fact that suggests that the Goffee & Scase matrix might have to be
reformulated when used in another cultural context. The conventional
roles as we see them from the common theories are more often broken in
some cultures. For instance the radical feminist business type seen
in Great Britain is less common, if even present, in Sweden.

DISCUSSION

As a conclusion of part 1 we may stress the concentration to
ten lines of business even if half of the women do not work in these
lines. We also note that big cities, especially Stockholm, are different and that entrepreneurial regions for women coincide with
entrepreneurial regions for men.

The main characteristic of women entrepreneurs as found in this
study is diversity. Female entrepreneurs are present everywhere, in
almost every line of business, in every county, with all kinds of
marital status, with six children or none, aged 19 or 65.... The only
everpresent characteristic is being female.

Another observation is that the female entrepreneurs are invisible as entrepreneurs - to themselves as well as to others. This is
an astonishing fact considering that one in every four entrepreneurs
is a woman and considering the widespread pattern of female entrepreneurship. The women entrepreneurs have not been observed - but they
have existed and still do exist.

Another tendency is that female entrepreneurs seem to be adaptable. The diversity discussed above indicates that the typically
feminine does not exist as a specific category - except as in the key
word adaptation. Women working with their husbands probably adapt to
the business chosen by their men - thus giving a different pattern.
This differing pattern could also be explained by women persuading
their men to adapt, but the most likely explanation is mutual adjustment where women consider the family situation as a whole.

From part 2 the most encouraging conclusion is that the female
entrepreneurs seem to be satisfied with entrepreneurship. This is so
even if there are indications of a less than good economic result.
This is not a group that portrays itself as underprivileged; rather
it is full of energy and enthusiasm. The sense of independence and
self-reliance is strong.

Another conclusion from the questionnaire is that female
entrepreneurs exhibit entrepreneurial characteristics as these are
described in other studies of small business and entrepreneurship.

From comparisons between male and female entrepreneurs we conclude that we must avoid the gender trap and stop comparing for more than one thing at a time. There are differences between male and female entrepreneurs but these must be separated according to level of analysis.

On the aggregate level there are differences of a structural type. There is a difference between a female hair-dresser and a male machine producer, but this difference to a large extent is due to their being hairdresser and machine producer. It is in this more basic fashion that the gender differences work - already in the choice of line of business. The material imperative is very strong, i.e., when working in a specific line of business you have to adjust to the conditions of this line regardless of your sex. These differences on the aggregate level are also seen in the aggregate attitudes on gender roles. These attitudes control norms for lifestyles and choice of work. The existing working life pattern strengthens the gender roles.

When we look at the individual level we find differences between men and women in more general views on gender roles, while at the same time we find women in traditional male lines of business behaving very much like male entrepreneurs and vice versa. Consequently, if we want to change gender role patterns we have to start on the aggregate level, for instance encouraging boys and girls to make educational choices from individual rather than gender preferences. Trying to change typically feminine occupations into more masculine behaviour is less useful in the long run.

Finally, we wish to stress the conclusion that a very common prejudice against women must be attacked. This is the myth that all women are alike. We wish to stress the individuality of the female entrepreneurs. No one would dream of forcing the 64,420 inhabitants of a city into the same pattern, but this is frequently done with female entrepreneurs (the number stated is the number of Swedish female entrepreneurs). It goes without saying that such a large group consists of many subgroups.

[10]

ELSEVIER

A LONGITUDINAL STUDY OF COGNITIVE FACTORS INFLUENCING START-UP BEHAVIORS AND SUCCESS AT VENTURE CREATION

ELIZABETH J. GATEWOOD
University of Houston

KELLY G. SHAVER
College of William and Mary

WILLIAM B. GARTNER
San Francisco State University

EXECUTIVE SUMMARY

The purpose of this study was to explore whether certain cognitive factors of potential entrepreneurs (as measured by a personal efficacy scale and the kinds of reasons people offer for their decision to undertake efforts to start a business) can be used to predict their subsequent persistence in business start-up activities and in new venture creation success. Two hypotheses were tested:

H1: *Potential entrepreneurs who offer internal and stable explanations for their plans for getting into business (e.g., "I have always wanted to own my own business") should be more likely to persist in actions that lead to successfully starting a business.*
H2: *Potential entrepreneurs with high personal efficacy scores should be more likely to persist in actions that lead to successfully starting a business.*

The beginning pool of subjects for this research consisted of 142 consecutive preventure clients (47 women, 95 men) of a Small Business Development Center between October 1990 and February 1991. As part of their initial consultation, these individuals were asked to explain their decision to enter business. These responses were coded on the basis of a detailed procedure derived from the attributional model (Weiner 1985). Potential entrepreneurs also responded to a locus-of-control questionnaire: Paulhus (1983) Spheres of Control Scale. In February 1992, all 142 people were sent a follow-up

Address correspondence to Elizabeth J. Gatewood, SBDC, University of Houston, 5th Floor, 1100 Louisiana Street, Houston, TX 77002.

Journal of Business Venturing 10, 371–391
© 1995 Elsevier Science Inc.
655 Avenue of the Americas, New York, NY 10010

0883-9026/95/$9.50
SSDI 0883-9026(95)00035-7

questionnaire designed to assess the extent of their new venture development activity in the intervening year. Responses from 85 individuals were available for this analysis.

The follow-up questionnaire listed 29 separate activities involved in starting a business. These activities were grouped into five major categories: gathering market information, estimating potential profits, finishing the groundwork for the company, structuring the company, and setting up business operations. The measure of success at getting into business was operationalized by the question: "Have you completed the first sale (defined as having delivered the product or service and collected the payment from your customer)?"

An analysis of the results found that H1 (internal/stable attributions, e.g., "I have always wanted to be my own boss") was supported for female potential entrepreneurs, whereas external/stable attributions (e.g., "I had identified a market need") were significant for male potential entrepreneurs. SIC code classifications revealed no significant differences in the sorts of businesses being contemplated by women and men. H2 (personal efficacy) was not supported.

Those activities that focused on setting up business operations (e.g., purchasing materials, hiring employees, producing the product/service, distributing the product) distinguished potential entrepreneurs who had started businesses from those who had not.

We believe that one of the important features of this research is the use of a longitudinal research design. By measuring attributions before these potential entrepreneurs had started (or not started) their businesses, we can make stronger claims for a causal relationship between initial attributions and each individual's subsequent success or failure in business start-up. Given all of the events and activities that occur between an individual's attributions for getting into business and the actual start-up, the attributional findings about male and female potential entrepreneurs have important implications for future research and practice. Men and women do have different reasons for getting into business that appear to be significant indicators of their future ability to start a business successfully. We believe that the development of measures focusing on details of the attributional model (i.e., perceptions of skills, abilities, the difficulty of the task, luck, and the value of the opportunity) will likely lead to a more comprehensive and accurate conception of the factors that influence entrepreneurial persistence. We offer some suggestions for how the use of an attributional model might influence the selection, counseling, and training of potential entrepreneurs.

INTRODUCTION

Creating a new business is a process fraught with difficulty and failure (Reynolds and Miller 1992; Van de Ven 1992b; Venkataraman et al. 1990). We suggest that the cognitive orientation (i.e., ways of thinking) of potential entrepreneurs will have a significant influence on their willingness to persist in entrepreneurial activity in the face of these difficulties. For example, it seems reasonable to assume that individuals who believe they can control the environment through their actions will be more likely to persist in entrepreneurial activities when difficulties in the start-up process are encountered (Brockhaus and Horwitz 1986). This study will explore two kinds of cognitive factors that might influence entrepreneurial persistence. One cognitive factor concerns the reasons that potential entrepreneurs offer when contemplating getting into business. Weiner, Russell, and Lerman (1978) note that three dimensions of causal explanation—the locus of causality (which is not the same construct as the locus of control), the stability of the presumed causes, and the intentions of the actors in the situation—will have significant effects on persistence. For example, individuals will persist in an activity if they attribute the reasons for their successes to internal, stable, and intentional factors while attributing their failures to external, variable, or accidental factors. Research in a variety of educational and occupational settings has indicated the importance of these three dimensions [see (Weiner 1985) for a review]. Building on this literature we argue that potential entrepreneurs who offer internal/stable reasons (e.g., "I've always wanted to own my own business," "I want the autonomy and independence to do what I like through self-employment") are more likely to persist through the difficulties and failures of getting into business.

The second cognitive factor that will be studied is the personal efficacy dimension of locus of control (Collins 1974; Levenson 1981; Rotter 1966; Strickland 1989). The idea behind exploring locus of control as a predictor is a view of successful entrepreneurs as people who have an intense desire to control their own destinies, at least in an economic sense. Thus, individuals with a high locus of control would be likely to persist in starting a business (Brockhaus and Horwitz 1986).

CONCEPTUAL DEVELOPMENT

The focus of this research is on some of the individual level factors (cognitions and actions) that influence the process of starting a new business. A number of researchers have labeled this time period in an organization's life as organizational emergence (Gartner 1993; Gartner, Bird, and Starr 1992), the preorganization (Hansen 1990; Katz and Gartner 1988), the organization in vitro (Hansen and Wortman 1989), prelaunch (McMullan and Long 1990), and start-up (Van de Ven, Angle, and Poole 1989; Vesper 1990). Previous research on the process of starting a business indicates that entrepreneurial activities and the results of these activities are complicated, chaotic, and prone to failure (Bygrave 1989; Cooper and Gascon 1992; Longsworth 1991). The primary focus of this study was to discover what cognitive factors might influence an individual's persistence in entrepreneurial activities despite the uncertain odds of start-up success.

The underlying premise of this research is that some individuals are more likely to start a business, no matter what difficulties they encounter, because of their cognitive orientation regarding the nature of the business start-up. An entrepreneur's persistence influences two aspects of the process of starting a business: (1) the activities undertaken to start a business, and (2) success at starting a business. In general, one would assume that the more time and effort one devotes toward accomplishing a task, the more likely it is that the achievement of this task will occur. Yet, the start-up of a business appears to consist of problems and difficulties that are unforeseen at the outset and often uncontrollable once these activities are undertaken (Van de Ven et al. 1989). Success at getting into business is, therefore, not only due to the amount of time and effort devoted to entrepreneurial activities, but also to some exercise of will toward achievement of this elusive goal. If one views persistence in terms of the adage, "Where there's a will, there's a way," then it becomes a plausible assumption that potential entrepreneurs with the will (the "right" cognitive orientation) to get into business will find a way to achieve this objective.

Shaver and Scott (1991) suggest that certain cognitive factors of potential entrepreneurs are likely to affect their subsequent success. Recognizing that the start-up of an organization is composed of a series of discontinuous changes (Bygrave 1989), Shaver and Scott specify that:

> No matter how the sequence from initial idea to new company is segmented, the social cognition approach argues that the explanations potential founders offer for prior segments will affect the likelihood of the final discontinuous change (p. 34).

In other words, how entrepreneurs think about themselves and their situation will influence their willingness to persist towards the achievement of their goal. This study looks at two different cognitive factors likely to have some bearing on an entrepreneur's persistence at

374   E.J. GATEWOOD ET AL.

TABLE 1   Causes of Success and Failure

	Locus of Causality	
Stability	Internal	External
Stable	Ability	Task Difficulty
Variable	Effort	Luck

starting a business: the explanations offered for wanting to try, and the individual's belief about personal efficacy.

Attributions of Causality

The social psychological study of the attribution of causality is based on the work of Heider (1958), who first argued that task performance would depend on the balance between personal force – the capabilities associated with the individual, and environmental force – the dispositional characteristics of the external surroundings. Key elements of personal force are ability, intention, and effort. Key elements of the environmental force are task difficulty and luck. The success or failure of an intentional action depends on the relationships among ability, effort, task difficulty, and luck. These four causes can be arrayed in a two-by-two table (Table 1). One dimension represents what is known in the literature (Weiner 1986) as locus of causality (not to be confused with *locus of control* to which we refer below). Presumed locus of causality is either internal to the person or external. The other dimension represents the presumed stability of the factor involved. Presumed stability is either stable or variable. For example, ability is internal and stable, whereas luck is external and variable. A substantial amount of research has confirmed the influence of these dimensions on perceptions of likely success in a variety of domains (see Weiner 1985). Particularly important for the present purposes is the consistent finding that higher levels of achievement motivation are associated with the presence of internal and stable attributions for task success. Entrepreneurial success has often been linked to achievement motivation [see a review by Johnson (1990)], so it is reasonable to expect that attribution processes will also be linked to entrepreneurial behavior. The attribution principles involved in Weiner's model have been generalized beyond contemporary American culture to societies, such as in the People's Republic of China, usually considered to have economic and social conditions dramatically different from those in the United States (Stipek, Weiner, and Li 1989). In short, the attributional model appears sufficiently robust to be extended from educational achievement settings to entrepreneurship, and from a capitalist economic structure to other economic systems.

The four specific causes – ability, effort, task difficulty, and luck – are attributed only after the fact of a success or failure. In prospective research, like that reported here, it is pointless to ask people to explain a success or failure that has not yet occurred. On the other hand, the causal *dimensions* of stability and locus can be used to characterize a person's account of plans for the future as well as the person's explanations for events in the past. Moreover, we believe that the dimensions used in the explanation of plans are the more likely dimensions to be used in the later explanations offered for the outcome.

What should be ascertained from this discussion of attribution theory is that internal/ stable attributions of success will significantly affect entrepreneurial persistence. If this reasoning is correct, then:

> *H1:* Potential entrepreneurs who offer internal and stable explanations for their plans for getting into business should be more likely to persist in actions that lead to successfully starting a business.

Locus of Control

The logic for using locus of control as a measure for identifying potential successful entrepreneurs was specified by Brockhaus and Horwitz (1986) in their review of the psychology of the entrepreneur:

> Individuals who cannot believe in their ability to control the environment through their actions would be reluctant to assume the risks that starting a business would entail (p. 27).

Although many investigators have used locus-of-control scales to study entrepreneurs, (e.g., Ahmed 1985; Begley and Boyd 1987; Brockhaus 1980; Cromie and Johns 1983; Venkatapathy 1987), the results of these studies have been mixed (Brockhaus and Horwitz 1986). In most of these studies locus of control has been assessed with the Rotter (1966) Internal-External Locus of Control Scale. One reason for the empirical confusion regarding locus of control might be that the Rotter measure is multidimensional, and not all of its dimensions are equally plausible as predictors of entrepreneurial activity. For example, several factor analyses of the Rotter scale have identified a "political responsiveness" factor and a "personal efficacy" factor (e.g., Collins 1974; Levenson 1981; see also a review by Strickland 1989). Whereas beliefs about personal efficacy make intuitive sense as possible predictors of entrepreneurial behavior, beliefs about the responsiveness of the political system seem less clearly related to entrepreneurial activity. Shaver and Scott (1991) suggested that the Paulhus (1983) Spheres of Control Scale subscale specific to personal efficacy was a preferable alternative for research in entrepreneurship. Paulhus (1983) describes several validity studies of the entire 30-item Spheres of Control subscale of 10 items. On the chance that prior inconsistencies in locus-of-control research might have been instrument-specific, we used the Paulhus SOCS Personal Efficacy subscale. We suggest the following hypothesis:

> *H2:* Potential entrepreneurs with high personal efficacy scores should be more likely to persist in actions that lead to successfully starting a new business.

Other Factors Influencing Start-Up Success

Although a certain cognitive orientation toward entrepreneurship might influence one's readiness to persist in entrepreneurial action, previous research has shown that some entrepreneurial activities (e.g., planning, networking, selling, finding resources) are more likely to result in a successful start-up than are others (Cooper 1993; Duchesneau and Gartner 1992; Hills 1984; Van de Ven et al. 1984; Vesper 1990). Being willing and able to persist in entrepreneurial activities may not lead to the successful creation of a business if persistence merely results in potential entrepreneurs engaging in the wrong activities. For example, a critical activity in starting a business is likely to be "finding potential customers." If a potential entrepreneur devotes a substantial amount of time to planning, but no time to finding potential customers, a new business may not be created. We suggest that entrepreneurial activities are, therefore, an important mediating variable between an entrepreneur's cognitive orientation and subsequent start-up success.

We undertook a review of the entrepreneurship literature (e.g., Duchesneau and Gartner 1992; Gartner 1988; Gartner and Starr 1993; Timmons 1990; Van de Ven et al. 1984; Vesper 1990) to identify specific entrepreneurial activities that might lead to the successful start-up of a business. Using the list of activities generated from this literature review, we engaged a focus group of SBDC counselors in a discussion and evaluation of these activities in terms of their perceived efficacy in real-world settings. From these discussions we generated a summary list of 29 separate entrepreneurial activities (see Appendix 1) grouped into five major categories: gathering market information, estimating potential profits, finishing the groundwork for the business, developing the structure of the company, and setting up business operations. Rather than propose a series of hypotheses of which activities might be significant for successfully starting a business, we sought to measure these activities in the study and to see which activities proved to be significant.

Finally, we sought to explore gender as a mediating factor that might influence the cognitive orientations of these potential entrepreneurs, their entrepreneurial activities, and start-up success. Overviews of the effect of gender in entrepreneurship have offered mixed results (Bird 1993; Brush 1992), though Brush (1992) suggests that the results from a comprehensive study of women-owned businesses in 24 countries shows that women follow different approaches to venture creation because of different occupational, social, and educational experiences. Some studies (Brush 1990; Chaganti 1986; Geoffe and Scase 1983; Scott 1986) have found that women business owners are motivated to create their own businesses out of a desire to have flexibility in their work and family schedules, and that the process of business founding may be different for female entrepreneurs (Belcourt, Bourke, and Lee-Gosselin 1991; Fischer, Reuber, and Dyke 1993; Sexton and Bowman-Upton 1990). Yet, other studies have not found gender to be a significant differentiating characteristic. The need for achievement, independence, job satisfaction, and economic necessity seemed to be shared by men and women, alike (Chaganti 1986; Hisrich and Brush 1983, 1985; Longstreth, Stafford, and Maudlin 1987; Schwartz 1979). This controversy in the literature precludes our offering specific hypotheses regarding the role that gender might play in our research, but it also suggests that gender will need to be taken into account in our analysis of the data.

METHOD

Subjects

The beginning pool of participants for this research consisted of 142 individuals (47 women, 95 men) who were preventure clients of a Small Business Development Center (SBDC) in a large southwestern metropolitan area between October 1990 and February 1991. None of these consecutive 142 participants refused to complete the initial questionnaires. Preventure clients of an SBDC are obviously different from the general population in that they have taken one concrete step in the direction of organizing a new business venture. They are also different from sophisticated repeat-entrepreneurs who would not require the services offered by SBDCs. On the other hand, SBDC clients represent an important segment of the population to which we hope our findings will generalize – individuals seeking to start businesses.

As part of their initial consultation at the SBDC, all 142 preventure clients were asked to explain the reasons why they chose to enter business and to complete a locus of control scale. These two measures (described in detail below) were the psychological variables involved in the study.

In February of 1992 all 142 participants were sent a follow-up questionnaire designed to assess the extent of their new venture development activity during the intervening year. This follow-up questionnaire asked for the hours devoted to each of 29 business start-up activities and asked whether there had been sales, whether the entrepreneur was involved full-time in the business, and whether there were additional employees of the business. Individuals who did not return this questionnaire were sent a second one. Individuals who

TABLE 2 Reasons for Getting Into Business

1st Reason		2nd Reason		1+2 Combined		
#	%	#	%	#	%	
53	37%	15	17%	68	29%	I had identified a market need
34	24%	7	8%	41	18%	I wanted the autonomy and independence to do what I like through self-employment
14	9%	27	30%	41	18%	I wanted to make more money
15	11%	19	21%	34	16%	I wanted to use my knowledge and experience
11	8%	6	7%	17	7%	Enjoyment through self-employment
3	2%	8	9%	11	5%	I wanted to show I could do it
12	9%	8	8%	20	7%	Other (e.g., opportunity to learn, needed a job, an opportunity to be creative, provide jobs for others, avoid taxes, God's will)
142	100%	90	100%	232	100%	Totals

did not return the second questionnaire were then sent a third questionnaire by certified mail, and an attempt was made to contact them by telephone. Of the 142 participants, 30 individuals could not be reached by mail or phone, and 27 individuals who were contacted did not complete the follow-up questionnaire.

Initial Attributional Coding

To examine the relationship between attributional processes and business success, we asked all 142 potential entrepreneurs to tell us why they want to enter business. Specifically, we explained that we were interested in their decision-making processes, and then we asked them the two questions shown below:

1. What business are you thinking of starting?
2. Why would you start this business?

All answers to the question, "Why would you start this business?" were subjected to attributional coding and were subsequently analyzed. To conserve space, we report only a summary of people's first two answers in Table 2. Some potential entrepreneurs gave more than five explanations.

All verbatim answers to the "Why?" question were coded according to a detailed procedure derived from the attributional model described previously. This coding protocol is an extension of attributional coding procedures first described by Harvey et al. (1980). Two of the authors of this study, each acting independently, first separated every answer into the number of separate explanations it contained. Then for each separate explanation, the coder first decided whether the explanation identified a factor internal to the person or a factor in the external environment. Once the internal/external decision had been made, the coder then decided whether the explanation identified a stable characteristic (one that would not, or could not, change in the immediate short-term) or a variable characteristic (one that would, or could, change in the immediate short-term). For example, "I have always wanted to be my own boss" is an internal-stable reason for going into business, whereas "there is a large market demand for this product" is an external stable reason for going into business.

As a result of the three-step coding process, each separate explanation was first identified and then placed into one of the four coding categories constructed from the combination of internal/external and stable/variable. Reliabilities for coding were computed separately for each step in the process. The Pearson correlations reflecting intercoder reliability for parsing answers into separate explanations was 0.95; reliability for the internal/external step was 0.95; reliability for the stable/variable step was 0.85. These reliabilities show a very high degree of agreement in the content coding. The few disagreements in coding that did arise were resolved by discussions among all three authors.

Based on previous research on the importance of attributions for success (Weiner 1985), the primary measures for the present study were the numbers, for each individual in the study, of internal/stable attributions and external/stable attributions offered in their statements answering the question "Why would you start this business?" It was predicted that this attribution measure would be related to persistence, both in terms of sustained business start-up activity and in terms of actually getting into business. In other words, we predict that potential entrepreneurs who gave internal/stable attributions for getting into business would persist in the activities involved in starting a business and that persistence would lead to starting a business that actually made sales.

Locus of Control

Empirically, locus of control has in the entrepreneurship literature been assessed using the Rotter (1966) Internal-External Locus of Control Scale. As has been argued elsewhere (Shaver and Scott 1991), this measure is not well-suited to the study of the founding of new business ventures. A better alternative is the Paulhus (1983) Spheres of Control Scale, specifically, the subscale having to do with personal efficacy. As noted earlier, this subscale has sufficient reliability and validity and has the added advantage of containing only 10 items, thus minimizing the time that subjects must devote to its completion.

Assessment of Business Start-Up Activity

The follow-up questionnaire began with a listing of the 29 separate activities involved in starting a business, grouped into the categories described earlier. Recall that the categories were: gathering market information (six items), estimating potential profits (four items), finishing the groundwork for the business (three items), developing the structure of the company (seven items), and setting up business operations (nine items). Respondents were asked to indicate which of the 29 separate activities they performed, and to provide an *estimate* of the hours they had devoted to each activity. Respondents were also asked to give an estimate of the total hours per week they were currently spending on the business activities described earlier.

Success at Getting Into Business

The measure of success at getting into business was operationalized by the question: "Have you completed the first sale (defined as having delivered the product or service and collected the payment from your customer)?" If respondents answered affirmatively as to whether or not they were in business, then they were asked to provide the date of their first sale and the number of their full-time and part-time employees. First sale was used as the measure of successfully getting into business based on Katz and Gartner's (1988) properties of emerging organizations framework. They offer theoretical justifications for using measures of exchange (i.e., date of first sale) as appropriate indicators of successful business start-up. In addition,

TABLE 3 Comparisons of Respondents to Nonrespondents

Subject gender:	Females		Males	
Response:	NonResp	Respond	NonResp	Respond
n^a:	15	31	40	54
Age category[b]	3.20	3.45	2.80	3.11
	(1.01)	(1.23)	(0.97)	(0.74)
Experience category[c]	1.73	1.87	2.50	2.11
	(1.16)	(1.15)	(1.45)	(1.31)
Education category[d]	3.27	3.61	3.53	3.98
	(1.28)	(1.28)	(1.13)	(1.11)
Spheres of Control	56.47	56.65	57.13	56.82
	(8.63)	(6.40)	(9.26)	(6.09)
Business pers-stable	0.93	1.39	0.80	1.07
	(1.28)	(1.20)	(0.82)	(1.01)

Note: Figures in parentheses are standard deviations.
[a] Numbers of nonrespondents reduced by two missing cases.
[b] Age categories: 1 (under 21), 2 (21 to 29), 3 (30 to 39), 4 (40 to 49), 5 (50 to 59), 6 (60 and over).
[c] Experience as years in field: 1 (<1 year), 2 (1 to 3 years), 3 (3 to 5 years), 4 (>5 years).
[d] Education categories: 1 (not a high school grad), 2 (high school grad), 3 (some college), 4 (college degree), 5 (some graduate school), 6 (graduate degree).

Reynolds and Miller's (1992) study of new firm gestation indicators concludes that "Date of first sale appears a suitable indicator of 'birth' if only one event is to be used" (p. 405).

RESULTS

In Appendix 2 we provide a detailed description of the plan used for data analysis.

Representativeness of the Respondents

The final sample of 85 respondents constituted nearly 60% of the total of 142 individuals who participated in the initial assessment of reasons for entering business, and nearly 76% of the individuals for whom there were valid addresses or telephone numbers. Comparisons of the 85 respondents to the 57 nonrespondents on various demographic measures are shown in Table 3. These mean scores were subjected to a 2 × 2 (Subject Gender × Response) analysis of variance, which revealed no significant differences between respondents and nonrespondents. The relatively high response rate and the lack of differences between the two groups gives us confidence that the respondents were representative of the total sample.

Cognitive Factors and Business Start-Up Activities

Pearson correlations among the two cognitive factors (internal/stable attributions and Spheres of Control scores) and the five category measures of business start-up activity are shown in Table 4. All significance tests are two-tailed, based on 85 subjects. Two features of these correlations are immediately apparent. First, among the business start-up activities, the first four—assessing the market, estimating the profits, completing the groundwork, and structuring the company—were all highly intercorrelated. But only one of these (assessing the market) was significantly correlated with setting up business operations. The second feature of the correlations is that the Spheres of Control Scale scores were not correlated with any organizing activity, whereas personal attributions correlated significantly with structuring the company.

380   E.J. GATEWOOD ET AL.

TABLE 4   Correlations Among Business Start-Up Activities and Psychological Variables

	PRO	GRD	STR	OPE	SOC	ATT
Assessing market	0.70^c	0.30^b	0.49^c	0.32^b	−0.07	0.16
Estimating profits (PRO)		0.52^c	0.81^c	0.18	0.02	0.13
Completing groundwork (GRD)			0.46^c	0.12	0.02	0.15
Structuring company (STR)				0.16	0.07	0.27^b
Setting up operations (OPE)					0.02	0.10
Spheres of Control score (SOC)						0.04
Personal stable attributions (ATT)						

Note: Significance tests are two-tailed, based on $n = 85$.
$^a p < .05$.
$^b p < .025$.
$^c p < .001$.

This is especially interesting given the fact that the attribution measure has a highly restricted range, whereas the locus of control measure has a substantial range.

Business Start-Up Activity and Getting Into Business

The five categories of business start-up activities can be considered part of the process that takes place between the intention to start a business and making the first sale. As we noted earlier, this process may be quite different for females than for males. Consequently, we examined the five categories of business start-up activity separately for females and males, also considering whether sales have actually been made. The five business start-up activity category scores are shown in Table 5 separately for females and males who have, or have not, made sales.

The activity measures are properly regarded as a within-subjects variable, so we performed a $2 \times 2 \times 5$ (Gender × Sale × Activity) multivariate analysis of variance, with repeated measures on the last factor. Because the various activity measures were differentially correlated with one another, a multivariate statistical test was appropriate. The analysis revealed no significant interaction between gender and either entrepreneurial activity or sales. There was a significant interaction between sales and activity, Wilks' lambda = 0.84, $p <$

TABLE 5   Mean Scores for Business Start-Up Activities by Gender and Sales

Subject Gender:	Females		Males	
Sales:	No Sales	Sales	No Sales	Sales
n:	20	11	38	16
Assess market	12.05	39.77	23.61	25.19
	(13.55)	(85.73)	(43.52)	(15.48)
Estimate profits	10.88	22.30	26.43	25.55
	(15.03)	(45.10)	(54.78)	(26.81)
Complete ground work	54.00	79.50	71.54	54.58
	(154.41)	(106.83)	(166.53)	(71.05)
Structure company	8.83	12.56	24.73	22.77
	(17.04)	(17.45)	(76.03)	(31.19)
Set up operations	3.45	58.16	3.56	65.01
	(9.49)	(71.85)	(12.16)	(89.92)

Note: Figures in parentheses are standard deviations.

.01 (approximate F = 3.80, with 4 and 78 *df*)[1]. This interaction is best understood by examining the differences between activity levels of respondents who made sales and respondents who had not made sales. For four of the activity categories this difference score (mean activity score for those with sales minus the mean activity score for those without sales) was low, or even negative (assessing market difference = 11.50 hours, estimating profits different = 3.16 hours, completing groundwork difference = −0.076 hours, structuring company difference = −0.64 hours). Indeed, a 2 × 2 × 4 (Gender × Sales × Activity) MANOVA on these four activities showed no significant sales × activity interaction. For the remaining category, however, there was an impressive difference between respondents with sales and respondents without sales (mean difference = 58.7 hours). This difference is even more impressive expressed as a ratio than as a mean difference: Compared to respondents without sales, respondents with sales devoted 17.8 times the hours to setting up business operations.

Some elements in the setting up operations category, such as installing and adjusting the product or service, or training customers, would be expected to occur only in very rare cases unless sales had been made. Consequently, it might be the case that the sale/no sale difference for the category could be an artifact produced by the greater time devoted to activities that would normally only follow sales. To check this possible explanation, we examined the activity mean scores for all elements of the category (Table 6). A 2 × 2 (Gender × Sale) multivariate analysis of variance of the elements shown in Table 6 revealed a significant multivariate effect for sale, Wilks' lambda = 0.67, $p < .001$ (approximate F value = 3.95, with 9 and 73 *df*). Examination of the corresponding univariate tests revealed a significant sale effect for every separate element except the first one—securing a location. Therefore, respondents who made sales differed from those who did not make sales on activities that normally precede sales (e.g., purchasing supplies, leasing equipment) as well as on activities that normally follow sales (e.g., installation and adjustment, training of customers).

Cognitive Factors and Getting Into Business

Hypotheses regarding the two cognitive factors (attributions, beliefs in personal efficacy) included in the research can be tested directly in two ways. First, the cognitive factors can be correlated to each of the five general categories of business start-up activity. These correlations appear in Table 4. As noted before, all of these correlations were positive, but only the correlation between attributions and structuring the company reached conventional levels of significance. The second direct way to test the relationship between attributions and success at starting a business is to compare respondents who made sales to respondents who did not make sales, and ask whether these two groups of individuals had different attributional patterns at the beginning of this process. Mean scores for the attributions and the Spheres of Control scores are shown in Table 7.

Each cognitive factor was subjected to a 2 × 2 (Gender × Sales) analysis of variance. For personal stable attributions there was a significant interaction between gender and sales, $F(1, 81) = 5.41$, $p < .025$. Among female respondents, but not among male respondents, the personal stable attributions were higher among those who subsequently made sales than among those who did not subsequently make sales. Almost the reverse pattern was obtained for external stable attributions, which also showed a significant interaction between gender

---

[1] In this design, both the Pillai-Bartlett trace and the Hotelling trace produce exactly the same approximate F value as the Wilks' lambda, so we have elected to use the more familiar Wilks measure.

TABLE 6 Mean Scores for Elements in Setting up Operations by Gender and Sales

Subject Gender:	Females		Males	
Sales:	No Sales	Sales	No Sales	Sales
n:	20	11	38	16
Secure a location	1.00	9.91	9.90	9.06
	(2.77)	(23.99)	(31.01)	(16.01)
Purchase supplies	2.65	8.73	1.24	31.44
	(5.59)	(11.92)	(4.25)	(59.35)
Lease equipment	1.35	4.76	0.76	20.19
	(3.92)	(8.09)	(2.79)	(27.05)
Hire employees	1.05	26.36	1.18	38.13
	(3.69)	(72.43)	(6.50)	(80.35)
Produce prd./serv.	11.50	101.46	1.42	65.56
	(36.31)	(299.51)	(6.66)	(130.76)
Distrib. prd./serv.	2.25	63.84	0.90	162.13
	(8.96)	(178.54)	(4.18)	(453.87)
Market prd./serv.	9.25	160.45	15.29	191.13
	(35.78)	(237.73)	(81.03)	(372.43)
Install and adjust	0.00	32.36	0.63	28.88
	(0.00)	(90.01)	(3.89)	(59.97)
Train customers	2.00	30.09	0.68	41.56
	(8.94)	(89.83)	(3.90)	(149.31)

Note: Figures in parentheses are standard deviations.

and sales $F(1, 81) = 3.96$, $p < .05$. Males who had subsequently made sales showed the highest frequency of external stable attributions. Finally, the analysis of Spheres of Control scores produced no significant differences.[2]

There are two possible explanations for the attributional differences. First, there is the stereotyped view that females start service businesses (where presumably sheer persistence is more important than know-how or outside financing), whereas males start technological businesses in which external forces are more important than internal desires. This alternative can be tested by comparing the SIC code distributions for females and males. If the stereotype is true, and is the explanation for our differences, then the female respondents should have been under-represented in such areas as manufacturing and transportation (both capital-intensive) and overrepresented in service businesses. We combined the manufacturing and transportation SIC categories (all codes beginning with 2 or 3) into a single cell; maintained wholesale and retail business as a second cell (codes beginning with 5); combined finance, insurance, and real estate (codes beginning with 6) with the two service categories (codes 7 and 8); and examined the participation of females and males in each of the three cells. The chi-squared analysis showed no significant difference in the participation of females and

---

[2] Paulhus (1983) reports several cross-validation samples in which the subscale alpha reliabilities range from 0.75 to 0.80. In our sample, the entire personal efficacy subscale produced an alpha reliability of only 0.48, suggesting that the scale might have been operating differently in our context. For this reason, we elected to factor analyze responses on the (sub)scale. A principle components factor analysis with varimax rotation produced four factors (respectively four items, three items, two items, and one item) that together accounted for 65% of the variance. Only the first of these had a satisfactory Chronbach's alpha (0.78). This four-item factor, which we call Diligence, included "when I get what I want it's usually because I worked hard for it," "My major accomplishments are due to my hard work and ability," "When I make plans I am almost certain to make them work," and "I can learn almost anything if I put my mind to it."

Both control measures (the 10-item scale and the four-item Diligence subscale) were subjected to a 2 × 2 (Gender × Sales) analysis of variance. The results of these analyses revealed no significant differences based on gender, sales, or their interaction for either the 10-item or four-item measure of locus of control.

TABLE 7 Mean Scores for Psychological Variables by Gender and Sales

Subject Gender:	Females		Males	
Sales:	No Sales	Sales	No Sales	Sales
n:	20	11	38	16
Personal stable	1.10	1.91	1.18	0.81
	(1.11)	(1.22)	(1.04)	(0.91)
External stable	0.45	0.27	0.37	0.81
	(0.69)	(0.47)	(0.59)	(0.83)
Spheres of Control	57.30	55.46	56.76	56.94
	(6.85)	(5.48)	(5.91)	(6.70)

Note: Figures in parentheses are standard deviations.

males across the three cells, χ^2 (2, N = 82) = 1.30, p = NS. Thus, the differential importance of personal attributions to women does not appear to be related to the general kinds of businesses being started by men and women.

A second explanation for the attributional differences, also based on a stereotyped view of females and males in the workforce, is that females can afford the "luxury" of following their internal desires, because in doing so they would become the second breadwinner in a family. In contrast, males, who by this view are the primary breadwinners in a family, would need to concentrate on the external environment in order to ensure the success of their planned businesses. The difficulty with this alternative is that it leads us to expect consistently more external attributions from men regardless of whether or not they had actually made sales, but there was no gender main effect on external stable attributions.

Alternative Conceptions of Getting Into Business

Throughout the article we have defined "getting into business" as having made a sale and collected money from a customer. There are, however, other ways in which an entrepreneur's seriousness toward getting into business might be measured, such as hours devoted to the business or hiring employees. We examined both of these alternative ways of assessing an entrepreneur's seriousness about the business. Specifically, we first split the sample into those respondents devoting 30 or more hours per week to the business and those devoting 29 or fewer hours per week. A 2 × 2 (Gender × hours) analysis of variance on personal stable attributions showed the same interaction obtained with sales as the cross-cutting variable, $F(1,80) = 3.71$, $p < .06$. A similar Gender × Hours analysis of variance on external stable attributions produced a strong trend comparable to the interaction obtained with sales as the cross-cutting variable, $F(1,80) = 2.91$, $p < .10$. Next, we split the data according to the presence of at least one full-time employee (who might be the founder) or at least one part-time employee who is not the founder. A 2 × 2 (Gender × Employee) analysis of variance on personal stable attributions showed a nearly significant interaction comparable to that obtained with sales $F(1,81) = 3.65$, $p < .06$. A similar Gender × Employee analysis of variance on external stable attributions showed a nearly significant interaction comparable to that obtained with sales, $F(1,81) = 3.80$, $p < .06$. Thus, despite the fact that the particular individuals involved changed slightly from one grouping to another, the overall attributional results remain essentially the same: whatever the definition used for "getting into business," females who successfully start businesses have higher internal stable attributions, whereas males who successfully start businesses have higher external stable attributions.

DISCUSSION

The Value of an Attributional Approach for Research and Practice

The use of attributional measures to predict entrepreneurial persistence in business start-up activities and in business start-up success shows much promise as a viable approach to understanding the cognitive factors that influence potential entrepreneurs. The following discussion highlights the results and offers some suggestions for how the use of an attributional approach might be of benefit to research and practice.

The attributional measures used in this study—counts of the number of internal/stable and external/stable causes—proved significant for predicting both persistence in activities and persistence for success in business creation. We found that the internal attribution measure was significantly correlated to some entrepreneurial activities measured in this study—structuring the company. We also found that the attributional measure was useful for predicting success at getting into business. Females with internal and stable reasons for getting into business (e.g., "I've always wanted to own my own business," "I want the autonomy and independence to do what I like through self-employment") were more likely to start businesses that generated sales. Males with external and stable reasons for getting into business (e.g., "I had identified a market need") were more likely to start businesses that generated sales.

The finding that females with internal and stable reasons for getting into business are more likely to start a business that generates sales runs counter to a view of entrepreneurs as opportunists. In the attributional framework, opportunities are external causes for getting into business (i.e., opportunities are not internal characteristics of individuals.) We believe that a more detailed exploration of the perceptions of entrepreneurial success or failure using the attributional framework outlined in Table 1 will lead to a better understanding of the causes of entrepreneurial persistence. For example, because internal and stable attributions suggest a focus on internal needs and abilities, the result about internal/stable attributions and success at getting into business seems to indicate that females undertake entrepreneurial activity because they perceive they have the desire, skills, and abilities to be successful, and women stop entrepreneurial activity when they perceive they don't have the desire, skills, and abilities to be successful. If this is true, then, training programs might be of value for enhancing female potential entrepreneurs' perceptions of their desires for starting a business, as well as their abilities at successfully starting a business.

Individuals who enter business for internal/stable reasons such as "I wanted the autonomy and independence to do what I like through self-employment" may also have more knowledge of the value of entrepreneurship versus those that fail. It is likely that individuals who perceive a high payoff (e.g., financial, emotional, social) for getting into business may be more likely to persist at difficult tasks than those who perceive fewer rewards. The relationship between the types of efforts undertaken (for example, efforts to explore the value of the opportunity by spending time marketing and getting customer orders) and perceptions of the value and difficulty of the entrepreneurial opportunity might also be explored. Results presented in Table 6 suggest that undertaking marketing activities influences efforts to begin operations. It is likely that individuals who have undertaken more activities to understand the market might have more favorable perceptions of the value of the opportunities they face and more favorable perceptions of their abilities to complete successfully the tasks required.

Other aspects of the attribution framework might also be explored for clues to why some potential entrepreneurs start businesses and why others do not. For example, entrepreneurs must believe that their abilities and effort can meet the perceived demands of the tasks involved in starting a business. Research may find that individuals stop entrepreneurial activity because they perceive that the necessary tasks required to get into business are too difficult. Or research may explore whether there is an interactive effect between a potential entrepreneur's perceptions of skills, abilities, and task difficulty. For example, successful entrepreneurs may choose "easier" new ventures that *match* their skills and abilities to the perceived difficulty of getting into business. Or successful entrepreneurs who perceive they lack the skills or abilities to be successful at a difficult new venture may *shift* their attention to easier opportunities (less difficult tasks).

The findings about female and male potential entrepreneurs offers additional evidence that gender makes a difference (Belcourt, Bourke, and Lee-Gosselin 1991; Brush 1992; Fischer, Reuber, and Dyke 1993; Sexton and Bowman-Upton 1990). Our findings are consistent with those that have found that women decide to become entrepreneurs for such reasons as self-fulfillment (Thompson and Hood 1991) and as a way to actualize personal goals that focus on family (Birley 1989, Chaganti 1986; Orr 1992). Moreover, our results contribute to the view that gender is not merely a demographic descriptor of the characteristics of a sample of entrepreneurs, but an important differentiating factor. If female and male potential entrepreneurs with similar success in starting ventures have persisted for different reasons, then selection and training need to account for this difference.

For example, assuming that new venture success depends on both personal commitment and a viable market opportunity, entrepreneurship training might be used to enhance a potential entrepreneur's strengths with complementary skills and knowledge. Training for females who offer internal/stable reasons for getting into business might be oriented toward identifying viable market opportunities. On the other hand, training for males who offer external/stable reasons for getting into business might be oriented toward exploring their personal commitment toward entrepreneurship. We believe that training that recognizes the different reasons for why successful potential entrepreneurs are willing to persist in entrepreneurial activity is more likely to result in the creation of successful and sustainable new firms because such training builds on a potential entrepreneur's strengths by affirming a person's reasons to persist.

In summary, the attributional framework is based on a substantial body of theory and empirical research that can be adapted to the particular needs and issues of entrepreneurship researchers. Using the attributional framework offers a new way to think about the specific causes of entrepreneurial persistence, as the interaction between locus of causality (internal/external) and stability (stable/variable): ability, effort, task difficulty, and luck. Besides the benefits for improving research on entrepreneurs by grounding these explorations in a rich base of prior theory and empirical evidence, we believe the application of the attributional framework to entrepreneurial problems is likely to influence the selection, counseling, and training of potential entrepreneurs. For example, perceptions of the difficulty of getting into business can be changed through exposure to cases, stories and interactions with successful entrepreneurs (e.g., If that person can get into business, then I can get into business too!). And in many instances, appropriate exposure to the difficulties of entrepreneurship may help individuals to decide not to pursue this endeavor. Especially in light of the results for attributions, the low predictive validity of the Paulhus Spheres of Control personal efficacy subscale comes as a surprise. Obviously the low reliability of this scale in our sample reduces the measure's potential for predictive validity. In the future it might be better to develop locus-of-control items specific not only to personal efficacy, but also to the domain of entrepreneurial business.

386   E.J. GATEWOOD ET AL.

Business Start-Up Activities

The results from this study show that both groups (those who were successful and those who were not successful at getting into business) devote the same amount of time to gathering information, estimating profits, completing know-how, and structuring the company. Yet those individuals who were successful at getting into business take the next step and devote effort to beginning operations (see Tables 5 and 6). This result suggests a number of lines of inquiry.

Because both successful and unsuccessful entrepreneurs devote nearly the same amount of time to exploring an opportunity – gathering marketing information, estimating potential profits, finishing the groundwork, and structuring the company – the critical difference between success and failure at getting into business, might be the nature of the opportunity itself. It is likely that not all opportunities that entrepreneurs encounter are similar. Some opportunities are likely to be "bad" opportunities (new ventures with a low probability of sufficient rewards for the efforts and investments necessary), whereas other opportunities are likely to be "good" opportunities. Successful entrepreneurs may be luckier than unsuccessful entrepreneurs (encounter better opportunities) or successful entrepreneurs may perceive opportunities differently than unsuccessful entrepreneurs.

As we suggested earlier, individuals who are successful at getting into business might have skills and abilities that better match the opportunities they face than unsuccessful entrepreneurs. Successful entrepreneurs may be wise to begin operations because they have the necessary capabilities. Unsuccessful entrepreneurs may be wise to abandon efforts to begin operations because they lack the necessary skills.

Future research might also focus on how potential entrepreneurs go about solving certain kinds of new venture tasks. For example, successful entrepreneurs may perceive the scale of certain tasks differently than unsuccessful entrepreneurs. Successful entrepreneurs may be more global in confronting the tasks of getting into business, or they may accomplish tasks better by breaking them into smaller pieces. Unsuccessful entrepreneurs may be overwhelmed by the number and difficulty of the tasks they face because they lack an ability to break down this complex experience into a series of small accomplishable achievements.

Some behaviors that entrepreneurs undertake are likely to be more beneficial for getting into business than others. Some behaviors, such as selling, are likely to improve a potential entrepreneur's knowledge of the value and difficulty for achieving a given opportunity. In addition, effort expended on some activities is likely to improve one's skills and abilities so that some tasks become easier to accomplish over time.

We believe that a critical aspect of business start-up behavior involves the interplay of action and its effect on knowledge. Individuals successful at getting into business appear to be eager learners who use new knowledge to adapt to new and changing circumstances. A study of entrepreneurial activities necessitates a methodology that identifies behaviors over time and the events that both influence and are influenced by these activities (Van de Ven 1992a, 1992b).

CONCLUSIONS

We believe that one of the important features of this research is the use of a longitudinal research design. By measuring attributions *before* these potential entrepreneurs had started (or not started) their businesses, we can make stronger claims for a causal relationship between these initial attributions and each individual's subsequent success in starting a venture. Given all of the events and activities that occur between an individual's attributions for getting into business and the actual start-up, the finding that female potential entrepreneurs who offered internal and stable attributions ("I want to be my own boss") for getting into business, and male potential entrepreneurs who offered external and stable attributions ("I had identified a market need"), actually succeeded at getting into business, is a significant result. Attributions matter. If research in entrepreneurship is going to focus on the individual, and if researchers believe that the attitudes, motivations, intentions, and cognitions of entrepreneurs are an important factor in determining entrepreneurial success, then prospective research designs must become the norm, rather than the exception.

REFERENCES

Ahmed, S.U. 1985. nAch, risk-taking propensity, locus of control, and entrepreneurship. *Personality and Individual Differences* 6:781–782.

Begley, T.M., and Boyd, D.P. 1987. Psychological characteristics associated with performance in entrepreneurial firms and smaller businesses. *Journal of Business Venturing* 2(1):79–93.

Belcourt, M., Burke, R., and Lee-Gosselin, H. 1991. *The Glass Box: Women Business Owners in Canada*. Ottawa: The Canadian Advisory Council on the Status of Women.

Bird, B.J. 1993. Demographic approaches to entrepreneurship: the role of experience and background. *Advances in Entrepreneurship, Firm Emergence, and Growth*. 1:11–48.

Birley, S. 1989. Female entrepreneurs: are they really different? *Journal of Small Business Management* 27(1):32–37.

Brockhaus, R.H. 1980. Risk-taking propensity of entrepreneurs. *Academy of Management Journal* 23:509–520.

Brockhaus, R.H., and Horwitz, P.S. 1986. The psychology of the entrepreneur. In D.L. Sexton and R.W. Smilor, eds., *The Art and Science of Entrepreneurship*. Cambridge, MA: Ballinger, pp. 25–48.

Brush, C.G. 1990. Women and enterprise creation: barriers and opportunities. In S. Gould and J. Parzen, eds., *Enterprising Women: Local Initiatives for Job Creation*. Paris: OECD.

Brush, C.G. 1992. Research on women business owners: past trends, a new perspective and future directions. *Entrepreneurship: Theory and Practice* 16(4):5–30.

Bygrave, W.D. 1989. The entrepreneurship paradigm (II): chaos and catastrophes among quantum jumps. *Entrepreneurship: Theory and Practice* 14(2):7–30.

Chaganti, R. 1986. Management in women-owned enterprises. *Journal of Small Business Management* 24(4):18–29.

Collins, B.E. 1974. Four components of the Rotter Internal-External scale: belief in a difficult world, a just world, a predictable world, and a politically responsive world. *Journal of Personality and Social Psychology* 29:381–391.

Cooper, A.C. 1993. Challenges in predicting new firm performance. *Journal of Business Venturing* 8(3):241–254.

Cooper, A.C., and Gascon, F.J.G. 1992. Entrepreneurs, processes of founding, and new firm performance. In D.L. Sexton and J.D. Kasarda, eds., *The State of the Art of Entrepreneurship*. Boston: PWS-Kent, pp. 301–340.

Cromie, S., and Johns, S. 1983. Irish entrepreneurs: some personal characteristics. *Journal of Occupational Behavior* 4:317–324.

Duchesneau, D.A., and Gartner, W.B. 1990. A profile of new venture success and failure in an emerging industry. *Journal of Business Venturing* 5(5):297–312.

Fischer, E.M., Reuber, A.R., and Dyke, L.S. 1993. A theoretical overview and extension of research on sex, gender, and entrepreneurship. *Journal of Business Venturing* 8(2):151–168.

Gartner, W.B. 1988. "Who is an entrepreneur?" is the wrong question. *American Journal of Small Business* 12(4):11–32.

388 E.J. GATEWOOD ET AL.

Gartner, W.B. 1993. Words lead to deeds: toward an organizational emergence vocabulary. *Journal of Business Venturing* 8(3):231–240.

Gartner, W.B., Bird, B.J., and Starr, J.A. 1992. Acting as if: differentiating entrepreneurial from organizational behavior. *Entrepreneurship: Theory and Practice.* 16(3):13–31.

Gartner, W.B., and Starr, J.A. 1993. The nature of entrepreneurial work. In S. Birley and I.C. MacMillan, eds., *Entrepreneurship Research: Global Perspectives.* Amsterdam: North-Holland, pp. 35–67.

Hansen, E.L. 1990. Entrepreneurial networks: their effect on new organization outcomes. Unpublished Doctoral Dissertation. Knoxville, TN: University of Tennessee.

Hansen, E.L., and Wortman, M.S. 1989. Entrepreneurial networks: the organization in vitro. In F. Hoy, ed., *Best Papers Proceedings.* Washington, DC: Academy of Management, pp. 69–73.

Harvey, J.H., Yarkin, K.L., Lightner, J.M., and Town, J.P. 1980. Unsolicited interpretation and recall of interpersonal events. *Journal of Personality and Social Psychology* 35:55–568.

Heider, F. 1958. *The Psychology of Interpersonal Relations.* New York: Wiley.

Hisrich, R.D., and Brush, C.G. 1983. The woman entrepreneur: implications of family, educational, and occupational experience. *Frontiers of Entrepreneurship Research.* Wellesley, MA: Babson College, pp. 255–270.

Hisrich, R.D., and Brush, C.G. 1985. Women and minority entrepreneurs: a comparative analysis. *Frontiers of Entrepreneurship Research.* Wellesley, MA: Babson College, pp. 566–572.

Johnson, B.R. 1990. Toward a multidimensional model of entrepreneurship: the case of achievement motivation and the entrepreneur. *Entrepreneurship: Theory and Practice* 14(3):39–54.

Katz, J.A., and Gartner, W.B. 1988. Properties of emerging organizations. *Academy of Management Review* 13(3):429–441.

Levinson, H. 1981. Differentiating among internality, powerful others, and chance. In H.M. Lefcourt, ed., *Research With the Locus of Control Construct: Assessment Methods.* Vol. 1. New York: Academic Press, pp. 15–63.

Longsworth, E.K. 1991. *The Anatomy of a Start-Up.* Boston: Inc. Publishing.

McMullan, W.E., and Long, W.A. 1990. *Developing New Ventures.* San Diego, CA: Harcourt Brace Jovanovich.

Orr, E. 1992. Assessment of Title II Demonstration Projects for Women Business Owners. Washington, DC: Small Business Administration. Contract SBA 4137-WIB89.

Paulhus, D. 1983. Sphere-specific measures of perceived control. *Journal of Personality and Social Psychology* 44:1253–1265.

Reynolds, P., and Miller, B. 1992. New firm gestation: conception, birth, and implications for research. *Journal of Business Venturing* 7:405–418.

Rotter, J.B. 1966. Generalized expectancies for internal versus external control of reinforcement. *Psychological Monographs* 80(Whole No. 609).

Sexton, D.L., and Bowman-Upton, N. 1990 Female and male entrepreneurs: psychological characteristics and their role in gender-related discrimination. *Journal of Business Venturing* 5:29–36.

Shaver, K.G., and Scott, L.R. 1991. Person, process, choice: the psychology of new venture creation. *Entrepreneurship: Theory and Practice* 16(2):23–45.

Stipek, D., Weiner, B., and Li, K. 1989. Testing some attribution-emotion relations in the People's Republic of China. *Journal of Personality and Social Psychology* 56:109–116.

Strickland, B.R. 1989. Internal-external control expectancies: from contingency to creativity. *American Psychologist* 44:1–12.

Timmons, J. 1990. *New Venture Creation.* 3rd ed. Homewood, IL: R.D. Irwin.

Thompson, J.K., and Hood, J.N. 1991. A comparison of social performance in female-owned and male-owned small businesses. Presented at the Annual Academy of Management Meetings, Entrepreneurship Division, Miami, Florida, August.

Van de Ven, A.H. 1992a. Suggestions for studying strategy process: a research note. *Strategic Management Journal* 13:169–188.

Van de Ven, A.H. 1992b. Longitudinal methods for studying the process of entrepreneurship. In D.L. Sexton and J.D. Kasarda, eds., *The State of the Art of Entrepreneurship*. Boston: PWS-Kent Publishers, pp. 214–242.

Van de Ven, A.H., Hudson, R., and Schroeder, D.M. 1984. Designing new business start-ups: entrepreneurial, organizational, and ecological considerations. *Journal of Management* 10:87–107.

Van de Ven, A.H., Venkataraman, S., Polley, D., and Garud, R. 1989. Processes of new business creation in different organizational settings. A.H. Van de Ven, H.L. Angle, and M.S. Poole, eds., *Research on the Management of Innovation*. New York: Harper and Row, pp. 221–297.

Venkatapathy, R. 1984. Locus of control among entrepreneurs: a review. *Psychological Studies* 29: 97–100.

Venkataraman, S., Van de Ven, A.H., Buckeye, J., and Hudson, R. 1990. Starting up in a turbulent environment: a process model of failure among firms with high customer dependence. *Journal of Business Venturing* 5:277–296.

Vesper, K.H. 1990. *New Venture Strategies*. 2nd ed. Englewood Cliffs, NJ: Prentice Hall.

Weiner, B. 1985. An attributional theory of achievement motivation and emotion. *Psychological Review* 92:548–573.

Weiner, B., Russell, D. and Lerman, D. 1978. Affective consequences of causal ascriptions. In J.H. Harvey, W. Ickes, and R.F. Kidd, eds., *New Directions in Attribution Research*. Vol. 2. Hillsdale, NJ: Lawrence Erlbaum Associates, pp. 59–90).

APPENDIX 1   Client Follow-up Questionnaire

This questionnaire is a follow-up to your visit(s) to the Small Business Development Center (SBDC). As part of your visit approximately a year ago, we asked you to indicate the reasons you were considering going into business for yourself. At that time, we noted that your answers could help us improve out services to clients, but to do that we need to find out what kinds of activities you have been involved in since visiting the SBDC. Would you please take a few moments to tell us about your activities and the progress of your business?

1. Listed below are activities that might be involved in trying to start a business. Would you please place a check mark in the space before *any* activities you undertook during the past year? then for each checked activity, please *estimate* the total number of hours you spent on that activity.

a. Gathering Marketing Information: Hours

_____ on the industry   _____
_____ on who would be my customers   _____
_____ on firms that could be my suppliers   _____
_____ on the *existing* competitors to my product or service   _____
_____ on possible entrants (my *potential* competitors)   _____
_____ on products or services that could serve as a substitute for mine   _____

b. Estimating My Potential Profits:

_____ gathering information on the cost of raw materials, wages, and salaries   _____
_____ gathering information on costs for rents, leases, equipment   _____
_____ making sales/revenue projections   _____
_____ establishing a price for my product or service   _____

c. Finishing the Groundwork for My Product or Service
_____ getting the know-how or technical expertise to make the product or deliver the service   _____
_____ refining the business idea, enhancing or improving the business idea   _____
_____ getting into the business network (joining trade organizations, bulletin boards, or clubs)   _____

(*continued*)

390 E.J. GATEWOOD ET AL.

APPENDIX 1 *Continued*

d.   Developing the Structure of My Company:
_____   developing financial statements (income and cash flow statements, break-even analysis)   _____
_____   seeking financing   _____
_____   gathering information on legal requirements (permits, licenses, legal corporate entity)   _____
_____   arranging for legal assistance or accounting assistance   _____
_____   developing goals and objectives (business plan, organization structure, strategic plan)   _____
_____   choosing a business name, legally incorporating, getting state and federal tax numbers   _____
_____   developing a logo and letterhead, printing stationery and business cards   _____

e.   Setting up Business Operations:
_____   securing a location
_____   purchasing raw materials and supplies   _____
_____   purchasing or leasing equipment or furniture   _____
_____   hiring and training employees, developing personnel policies   _____
_____   producing the product or service package   _____
_____   distributing the product or service   _____
_____   marketing the product or service   _____
_____   supporting customers with installation and adjustment of the product   _____
_____   supporting customers with training on the product or service   _____

2.   Approximately how many hours per week are you now devoting to the business described   _____
            on the other side?

3.   If you have completed your first sale (delivered the product or service and collected the   _____
            payment from your customer), please tell us the DELIVERY DATE:

4.   Including yourself, how many full-time employees does your business now have?   _____

5.   Including yourself, how many part-time employees does your business now have?   _____

6.   If the business you have been describing here is NOT the same business you discussed
            with us in your visit to the SBDC, please tell us what the business is:

APPENDIX 2 Overall Analysis Plan

Wherever there were analysis choices to be made, we chose the route that would retain the maximum number of subjects. Two such choices were necessary. First, there was the question of missing data. Four subjects checked business activities in which they had participated, but provided no hour estimates for those activities. In each of these instances, the overall mean score for the particular activity checked was inserted, so that the case could be retained.

The second analysis choice that could have reduced the sample arose because of the assumptions underlying the statistical tests to be used. Specifically, the correlation procedures and multiple analyses of variance (MANOVAS) assume that the underlying distributions of scores are essentially normal in form. But whenever individuals are asked to indicate how many hours they might have spent on each of 29 separate activities during the preceding year, the result is likely to be a distribution with a substantial positive skew. There is a logical lower limit (zero hours), but the upper limit might be in excess of 2000 hours (eight hours per day for 240 working days devoted to only one activity), and indeed, we received several activity time estimates that exceeded 1000 hours. Either the data from such outliers can be excluded, or the data can be transformed to reduce the variance and minimize the positive skew of the distributions. Eliminating any scores that exceeded $+3.5$ standard deviations from the overall mean would have reduced the number of cases by 9, and more importantly would have cost us valuable information from individuals who were particularly active in their attempts to establish a business. For this reason, we elected to retain all cases, using a square root transformation (appropriate when the means and variances are proportional) to reduce the skewness of the distributions. Analyses were performed on both the transformed and the nontransformed scores, and in all cases the two methods produced equivalent statistical conclusions. Consequently, to keep as close to the original data as possible, we report below only the nontransformed scores.

As noted earlier, the 29 business organizing activities were grouped into five major categories. To simplify presentation of the results, an average score was computed for each category. This score was computed by adding up the hours a respondent spent on any activity in the category and then dividing by the number of separate activities in the category, whether or not a particular respondent had performed all activities. In this way, the average hours spent on completing the groundwork, for example, can be directly compared to the average hours spent structuring the company, despite the fact that the former category contains only three elements whereas the latter category contains seven elements. Dividing by the number of elements assumes, of course, that all elements within a category are at the same level of specificity, and this assumption may not be justified. To examine this possibility, we conducted parallel analyses of the *sums* of activity in each of the five categories. This analysis produced the same results as those reported below for the category means. Finally, we conducted multiple analyses of variance on the elements within each category, and report the mean scores for elements on which there were substantial differences across subject groups.

Our first hypothesis, that internal stable attributions will be positively related to venture creation, is clearly directional. But our other expectations for the outcome of the study could not be stated as directional predictions. Consequently, to minimize confusion we have elected to use two-tailed statistical tests throughout.

[11]

ELSEVIER   Journal of Business Venturing 18 (2003) 13–39

JOURNAL
of BUSINESS
VENTURING

The career reasons of nascent entrepreneurs[☆]

Nancy M. Carter[a,*,1], William B. Gartner[b], Kelly G. Shaver[c,2],
Elizabeth J. Gatewood[d,3]

[a]*Graduate School of Business, University of St. Thomas, TMH 470-1000 LaSalle Ave., Minneapolis,
MN 55403-2005, USA*
[b]*Lloyd Greif Center for Entrepreneurial Studies, Bridge Hall One, Marshall School of Business,
University of Southern California, Los Angeles, CA 90089-0801, USA*
[c]*Psychology Department, College of William and Mary, Williamsburg, VA 23187, USA*
[d]*Johnson Center for Entrepreneurship and Innovation, Indiana University, 501 Morton Street, Suite 108,
Bloomington, IN 47404, USA*

Received 30 April 2001; received in revised form 30 October 2001; accepted 30 October 2001

Abstract

This paper explores the reasons that nascent entrepreneurs offered for their work and career choices and compares those responses to the reasons given by a group of nonentrepreneurs. Six separate factors accounted for 68% of the variance: self-realization, financial success, roles, innovation, recognition, and independence. The factor scores of nascent entrepreneurs and nonentrepreneurs were not significantly different on self-realization, financial success, innovation, and independence. Nascent entrepreneurs rated reasons concerning roles and recognition significantly lower than nonentrepreneurs. Finally, gender differences in reasons also emerged; male nascent entrepreneurs and nonentrepreneurs rated financial success and innovation higher than did females, regardless of their group of origin.
© 2002 Elsevier Science Inc. All rights reserved.

[☆] A version of this paper was presented at the Babson/Kauffman Entrepreneurship Research Conference, Wellesley, MA, June 2000.
* Corresponding author. Tel.: +1-651-962-4407; fax: +1-651-962-4410.
E-mail addresses: wgartner@marshall.usc.edu (W.B. Gartner), nmcarter@stthomas.edu (N.M. Carter), kgshav@attglobal.net (K.G. Shaver), gatewood@indiana.edu (E.J. Gatewood).
[1] Tel.: +1-651-962-4407; fax: +1-651-962-4410.
[2] Tel.: +1-757-221-3885; fax: +1-757-221-3896.
[3] Tel.: +1-812-855-4248; fax: +1-812-855-2751.

14   N.M. Carter et al. / Journal of Business Venturing 18 (2003) 13–39

1. Executive summary

This paper explores the reasons that nascent entrepreneurs offered for their work and career choices and compares these responses to the reasons given by a group of nonentrepreneurs.

A substantial concern about the validity of research on the reasons for business start-up has hinged on the problem of retrospection, that is, interviewing entrepreneurs about their reasons for entrepreneurship long after they are in business. To address this concern we examined the reasons that individuals offered for choosing independent business start-up while they were in the initial stages of forming a business. In addition, our research compared these nascent entrepreneurs with a representative comparison sample of individuals who were not actively engaged in independent business creation.

Based on prior research, we identified six categories of reasons that individuals give for starting businesses: The first category, *innovation*, involved reasons that describe an individual's intention to accomplish something new; the second category, *independence*, described an individual's desire for freedom, control, and flexibility in the use of one's time; *recognition* described an individual's intention to have status, approval, and recognition from one's family, friends, and from those in the community; *roles* described an individual's desire to follow family traditions or emulate the example of others; *financial success* involved reasons that describe an individual's intention to earn more money and achieve financial security; and *self-realization* described reasons involved with pursuing self-directed goals.

We offered a number of ideas that support the view that nascent entrepreneurs have similar reasons for career choice as working age adults in the general population. Based on this viewpoint, we tested the following hypothesis:

Hypothesis 1: Nascent entrepreneurs and a comparison group of nonentrepreneurs have similar scores on the six kinds of career reasons (innovation, financial success, independence, recognition, roles, and self-realization).

Research on the differences between men and women indicated that there are significant differences in their career choices, and that theoretical models that described the career paths of men are less suited to the experiences of women. There appeared to be significant differences in the reasons that compel men and women to pursue entrepreneurial careers, especially if more weight was given to the results of prospective studies. Therefore, we suggested:

Hypothesis 2: Women (nascent entrepreneurs and the comparison group) rate the six kinds of career reasons differently than men (nascent entrepreneurs and the comparison group).

The data for this research were obtained from the Panel Study of Entrepreneurial Dynamics (PSED), a national database of nascent entrepreneurs who were in the process of starting companies. The analysis was conducted on the reduced PSED data set of 558 nascent entrepreneurs and comparison group participants. Eighteen items from the mail survey of the PSED database (items G1a–r) were selected for coding and analysis. We first tested the predictive validity of our model by subjecting the data to a principal components factor analysis (listwise deletion of missing values, varimax rotation) with the analysis directed to produce six factors. The rotation required eight iterations to converge. The six factors that were produced account for more than 68% of the variance and show truly remarkable similarity to the theoretical dimensions—only two of the items were out of place.

The Group × Reasons interaction tested the primary hypothesis of the research, that nascent entrepreneurs and a comparison group have similar scores on career reasons. The ANOVA revealed a significant Group × Reasons interaction, $F(5,2770) = 28.25$, $P < .0001$. The findings provided mixed support for accepting Hypothesis 1. There was no significant difference between nascent entrepreneurs and the comparison group on four of the scales (self-realization, financial success, innovation, and independence). There was a significant difference between nascent entrepreneurs and the comparison group on two of the scales (recognition and roles). The analysis also showed a significant main effect for group, with overall scores lower for nascent entrepreneurs than for the comparison group $F(1,554) = 5.57$, $P < .02$, but this difference was most likely a consequence of the significant interaction.

In addition to the significant Group × Reasons interaction, the $2 \times 2 \times 6$ (Group × Gen-Gender × Reasons) repeated measures ANOVA on the weighted scale values also showed a highly significant main effect difference among the reasons' mean scores, with independence having the overall highest scores and roles having the overall lowest scores, $F(5,2770) = 292.20$, $P < .0001$. This ordering of the six sets of reasons made it clear that the significant differences between nascent entrepreneurs and the control group occurred on scales that were rated as less important by both groups (such as roles). On scales that were highly rated (such as independence, financial success, and self-realization), there were no significant differences between the two groups. Finally, the analysis showed a small but significant difference between men and women, with men having higher scores on financial success and innovation than women, regardless of their group of origin, $F(5,2770) = 2.67$, $P < .02$. This finding partially supported Hypothesis 2. It is important to note that although the score women assigned to financial success was lower than that given by men, women still saw financial success as an important reason in career choice and equal in their ranking to self-realization.

Nascent entrepreneurs are both similar to, and different from, the general population. Entrepreneurs were similar to nonentrepreneurs on four scales: independence financial success, self-realization, and innovation. Both entrepreneurs and nonentrepreneurs rated independence, financial success, and self-realization as more important than recognition, innovation or roles. The differences that were found between nascent entrepreneurs and nonentrepreneurs were on the scores that both groups ranked lower than the others: roles and recognition. Nascent entrepreneurs offered reasons for getting into business that were less likely to take the validation of others into account. There were differences in reasons for career choice by gender. Males (entrepreneurs and nonentrepreneurs) rated financial success and innovation higher than females (entrepreneurs and nonentrepreneurs) as a reason for choosing a career.

An issue that should not be underestimated in this study is the fact that this research was based on interviews with a representative sample of individuals in the process of starting a business and that this sample of nascent entrepreneurs was compared to a control group that is generalizable to the population of the United States. These nascent entrepreneurs were offering reasons for getting into business before the success (or failure) of their efforts was determined. Because these findings are based on prospective reasons, rather than retrospective reasons, we believe the results of this study should take precedence over any previous studies where retrospective reasons for start-up were offered. The overall results of our research argue against considering entrepreneurs to be qualitatively different from individuals who pursue other career options.

2. Introduction

The creation of new independent businesses accounts for between one fourth to nearly one third of the variation in economic growth in many industrialized countries (Davidsson et al., 1994; Reynolds, 1994; Reynolds and Maki, 1990; Reynolds et al., 2000). Discovering the factors that influence an individual's choice to pursue independent business creation might, therefore, lead to insights that would have an impact on economic growth and development. There is a long history of specifying various personal characteristics, cognitions, and social conditions that influence an individual's choice to pursue entrepreneurial activity (Aldrich, 1999; Carroll and Mosakowski, 1987; Gartner, 1988, 1989; Katz, 1992; Kolvereid, 1996a,b; Krueger et al., 2000; Shaver and Scott, 1991; Simon et al., 2000). This article focuses on a specific set of cognitions, namely the reasons individuals offer for undertaking entrepreneurial activity.

A substantial concern about the validity of research on reasons for business start-up has hinged on the problem of retrospection, that is, interviewing entrepreneurs about their reasons for entrepreneurship long after they are in business (Gartner, 1989; Shaver and Scott, 1991). Retrospective accounts, particularly when describing prior intentions, have been shown to have a significant self-justification bias. Such bias seriously undermines any confidence that the initial reasons an individual gives for an action accurately describes their undertaking subsequent actions, or outcomes of those actions (Golden, 1992; Huber and Power, 1985). To address this concern we examined the reasons that individuals offered for choosing independent business start-up while they were in the initial stages of forming a business. These nascent entrepreneurs offered prospective accounts for their choice of entrepreneurship, rather than retrospective reminiscences. In addition, our research compared these nascent entrepreneurs with a representative comparison sample of individuals who were not actively engaged in independent business creation.

This article is structured in the following manner. Prior research on reasons that entrepreneurs offered for starting businesses is explored and summarized. An attempt is made to link these prior research efforts to theories that might explain the reasons for choosing entrepreneurship versus other types of work. Based on the results of previous empirical studies of entrepreneurial reasons, and the theoretical justifications generated, variables were identified for use in a questionnaire. Hypotheses are offered for why nascent entrepreneurs would rate reasons for starting new businesses differently from (or similarly to) other individuals' ratings of reasons about their work careers. The critical problem of ret-

N.M. Carter et al. / Journal of Business Venturing 18 (2003) 13–39   17

rospective reporting was remedied by using data from the PSED. The PSED is a survey of individuals who were identified while they were in the process of starting their businesses. The survey also collected information from a comparison group identified in such a way that the individuals in the group represented the population of individuals in the United States. Responses from the nascent entrepreneurs and the comparison group were analyzed, described, and discussed. Implications for research and practice are offered.

3. Prior research and hypotheses

As outlined in Kolvereid (1996a), the reasons that potential entrepreneurs offer for getting into business should have a significant influence on whether they actually engage in entrepreneurial activity (Ajzen, 1991; Krueger and Brazeal, 1994; Krueger and Carsrud, 1993). Reasons that individuals offer for getting into business (or not) matter, because reasons are traditionally considered to be the basis of intentions (Anscombe, 1956; Shaver, 1985). New businesses are not created by accident. The effort and time involved in starting a business would suggest that entrepreneurial actions are clearly intentional. Indeed, a number of studies of the new venture creation process described individuals persisting at a variety of activities over a period of months, or years, in order to achieve the creation of a new firm (Carter et al., 1996; Gatewood et al., 1995; Reynolds and Miller, 1992; Reynolds and White, 1997). When obstacles arise in connection with any of these activities, entrepreneurs must find ways to overcome them. In summary, new venture creation is action that involves repeated attempts to exercise control over the process, in order to achieve the desired outcome. By this description, new venture creation constitutes a sort of behavior that social psychologists, for nearly 50 years, have regarded as intentional (Heider, 1958).

3.1. Reasons for getting into business

Academic research on the reasons entrepreneurs offer for starting businesses has a long history of prior empirical and theoretical efforts. We offer a chronology of the progression of these efforts as a way to show how we have extended ideas from this previous research and how we arrived at the reasons for the variables used in the present study. Many of the initial research efforts on reasons entrepreneurs offer for starting businesses stemmed from work undertaken by Sari Scheinberg and colleagues. This research has been labeled as the Society of Associated Researchers of International Entrepreneurship (SARIE) research (Alange and Scheinberg, 1988; Birley and Westhead, 1994; Blais and Toulouse, 1990; Dubini, 1988; Scheinberg and MacMillan, 1988; Shane et al., 1991). Initially, the theoretical justification for the list of reasons used in these empirical studies (Scheinberg and MacMillan, 1988) was based on a wide variety of sources, such as: need for independence (Friberg, 1976; Hofstede, 1980), need for material incentives (Friberg, 1976), desire to escape or avoid a negative situation (Collins and Moore, 1955; Cooper, 1971; Friberg, 1976; Hagen, 1962; Shapero, 1975), need for social approval (Friberg, 1976; Maslow, 1943; McClelland, 1961; Vroom, 1967), and a drive to fulfill personal values or norms (Friberg, 1976). A list of 38 statements (reasons), based loosely on different aspects of these theories, was generated for the SARIE research. Scheinberg and MacMillan (1988) sought to discover the differences among entrepreneurs in how they might rate these reasons. Over 1400 independent business owners/founders in 11 countries were surveyed. Subsequent explorations of this data began a quest to develop what might be labeled as an "empirically based" theory about the reasons entrepreneurs offered for business creation.

Scheinberg and MacMillan (1988) conducted a factor analysis of the 38 items and found six broad factors of reasons for business creation that they called: need for approval, perceived instrumentality of wealth, communitarianism, need for personal development, need for independence, and need for escape. In comparing entrepreneurs by country, they found that the reasons for business creation varied. For example, U.S. and Australian entrepreneurs scored highest on the "need for independence" factor, whereas entrepreneurs from Italy, Portugal, and China scored highest on "communitarianism." Scandinavian countries, such as Sweden, Norway, and Denmark had entrepreneurs who offered low scores on the instrumentality of wealth factor. In a follow-up study, Shane et al. (1991) sought to extend the model developed by Scheinberg and MacMillan (1988) by focusing on nationality and gender of the entrepreneur. In hopes of improving the response rate, they reduced the original 38 "reasons" items to 21 and added two questions on tax considerations. They surveyed 597 owner–managers in three of the 11 countries, Great Britain, New Zealand, and Norway, and identified four broad factors that explained an entrepreneur's reasons for business creation. They called these four factors: recognition, independence, learning, and roles. They identified a number of nationality and gender differences but no overall main effect for any specific item. Based on these two previous explorations, Birley and Westhead (1994) administered a questionnaire with 23 reasons items to 405 owner–managers of independent businesses in the United Kingdom. A factor analysis of the 23 reasons produced seven factors that the authors labeled: need for approval, need for independence, need for personal development, welfare considerations (in terms of contributing to a sense of community), perceived instrumentality of wealth, tax reduction, and following role models. Each of these studies involved surveys of individuals who had already started firms.

Although the preponderance of research exploring the reasons entrepreneurs offer for starting new business can be attributed to the SARIE efforts, there have been other academic studies on the topic. Kolvereid (1996a) explored the reasons given for self-employment versus organizational employment using a group of 372 Norwegian business-school graduates. He designed a classification scheme that posited 11 types of reasons for choosing between self-employment and organizational employment: security, economic opportunity, authority, autonomy, social environment, work load, challenge, self-realization, participation in the whole process, avoid responsibility, and career. He found that individuals who were self-employed were more likely to choose economic opportunity, authority, autonomy, challenge, self-realization, and participate in the whole process, compared to those choosing organizational employment. Although many of Kolvereid's classifications were consistent with those of the SARIE studies, his effort did not build directly on these earlier studies. His research methodology however, was consistent with the earlier retrospective approach—surveying people years after their occupational choices had been made.

N.M. Carter et al. / Journal of Business Venturing 18 (2003) 13–39   19

In one of the few prospective studies on reasons offered for getting into business, Gatewood et al. (1995), asked 142 preventure clients from a small business development center (SBDC) their reasons for choosing to start a business. Most respondents provided no more than two distinct answers to this open-ended question. Although there were obviously differences in individual wording, six kinds of answers accounted for 93% of the first two reasons offered, and five of the categories reflected the categories of the SARIE studies. These reasons were identification of a market need (29% of the total), autonomy and independence (an additional 18%), a desire to make more money (18%), a desire to use knowledge and experience (16%), the enjoyment of self-employment (7%), and a desire to show that it could be done (5%).

All of these studies suggest that entrepreneurs offer a variety of reasons for getting into business. Table 1 displays our attempt to synthesize the reasons generated by the SARIE studies and the research of others as a way to show the continuity that exists among these prior research efforts. The listing, shown in Table 1, is intended as a post hoc parsimonious synthesis of the SARIE studies, which essentially became an empirically derived theory of the reasons entrepreneurs offer for getting into business. The order of the categories listed in Table 1 corresponds to the order of the factor weights in each related empirical analysis.

The first category in Table 1, labeled innovation, involves reasons that describe an individual's intention to accomplish something new (McClelland, 1961; McClelland and Winter, 1969). The category contains items Shane et al. (1991) considered as "learning" and what Birley and Westhead (1994) and Sheinberg and MacMillan (1988) considered as "need for personal development." The second category, independence, describes an individual's desire for freedom, control, and flexibility in the use of one's time (Schein, 1978; Smith and Miner, 1983). Items in this category were consistently identified in all three of the SARIE studies. The third category we labeled recognition and combined two categories of items from the previous research: recognition and need for approval. Items in this category describe an individual's intention to have status, approval, and recognition from one's family, friends, and other people in the community (Bonjean, 1966; Nelson, 1968). The fourth category, roles, contains items from Shane et al. (1991) that describe an individual's desire to follow family traditions or emulate the example of others (Hofstede, 1980). The last category, financial success, involves reasons that describe an individual's intention to earn more money and achieve financial security (Knight, 1987). Although Shane et al. (1991) did not find a financial success factor, the other two studies (Birley and Westhead, 1994; Scheinberg and MacMillan, 1988) did, which they labeled as "perceived instrumentality of wealth."

In addition to the five categories identified from the SARIE studies and described in Table 1, evidence in previous research on gender in entrepreneurship (e.g., Brush, 1992; Carter, 1997; Fischer et al., 1993) led us to believe a sixth factor, self-realization, should be added to the classification scheme. There is evidence that men are more likely to seek to create financial wealth, whereas women are more likely to pursue other types of goals that center on personal interests. Women are seen as experiencing more complexity in making career choices because of their need to balance employment, childcare, and housing. Fulfilling multiple roles requires women to consider time and space constraints as they make

20   N.M. Carter et al. / Journal of Business Venturing 18 (2003) 13–39

Table 1
Categories of entrepreneurship reasons

	Innovation	Independence	Recognition	Roles	Financial success
Schienberg and MacMillan (1988)	Need for personal development m. To develop an idea for product/business h. To keep learning c. To be innovative and in the forefront of new technology *. Direct contribution to success of company	Need for independence *. Control of my own time b. To have greater flexibility for private life f. Freedom to adapt my own approach to work	Need for approval e. Be respected by friends l. Achieve something and get recognition a. Achieve higher position in society *. Increase status of family *. Have more influence in community		Perceived instrumentality of wealth k. Desire to have high earnings *. Needed more money to survive g. Give self and family security *. Access to indirect benefits
Shane et al. (1991)	Learning m. To develop an idea for a product c. To be innovative and in the forefront of new technology h. To continue learning	Independence *. To control my own time b. To have greater flexibility for my personal and family life f. To have considerable freedom to adapt my own approach to work	Recognition a. To achieve a higher position for myself in society *. To have more influence in my community e. To be respected by friends l. To achieve something and get recognition for it *. To increase the status and prestige of my family	Roles d. To continue a family tradition *. To have more influence in my community i. To follow the example of a person I admire	
Birley and Westhead (1994)	Need for personal development c. To be innovative and be in the forefront of technological development m. To develop an idea for a product h. To continue learning	Need for independence f. To have considerable freedom to adapt my own approach to my work b. To have greater flexibility for my personal and family life *. To control my own time	Need for approval a. To achieve a higher position for myself in society e. To be respected by friends *. To increase the status and prestige of my family l. To achieve something and get recognition for it k. Desire to have high earnings *. To have more influence in my community	Follow role models i. To follow the example of a person I admire	Perceived instrumentality of wealth g. To give myself, my spouse, and children security *. To contribute to the welfare of my relatives

The letters (a–m) in correspond to the item letters used in our analyses (presented in Table 2). The table, therefore, links the questions used in this study with those of prior research.

*Item not used in subsequent analyses for this research.

N.M. Carter et al. / Journal of Business Venturing 18 (2003) 13–39   21

economic and social decisions in concert (Gilbert, 1997). One explanation for gender differences in career development is that differing societal expectations for men and women lead to divergence in work preferences (Harriman, 1985). Sex-role socialization experiences teach young girls what roles are appropriate, or not. These experiences are seen as constricting career choices, compromising career potential (Gottfredson, 1981) and influencing women's beliefs, attitudes and self-conceptions that ultimately affect their work interests and choices (Farmer, 1997). Several studies of choices involving the start-up of a business support this perspective (Brush, 1992; Buttner and Moore, 1997; Carter, 1997; Gatewood et al., 1995), but others provide evidence that the entrepreneurial career choice is gender blind (Fagenson, 1993). Adding variables to constitute a self-realization factor, therefore, seemed to be an appropriate way to test which viewpoint was more plausible. Moreover, adding this factor appeared to offer a more comprehensive list of the types of reasons that might differentiate between nascent entrepreneurs and others.

3.2. Are the career reasons of nascent entrepreneurs different?

A cursory review of the literature may lead to the conclusion that entrepreneurs offer different reasons for getting into business than other people give for having jobs. Many of the prior studies implicitly assumed a difference, but only Kolvereid (1996a) directly compared the reasons of entrepreneurs with the reasons given by adults choosing other careers. Unfortunately, his study was retrospective in nature. We could find not one prospective study that compared the reasons of individuals in the process of getting into business with the career reasons of other individuals. The validity of retrospective surveys of successful entrepreneurs for accurately ascribing the prospective reasons offered by nascent entrepreneurs is doubtful. As suggested earlier, such retrospective reminiscences are likely to be biased and inaccurate depictions of what may have actually occurred in the past (Golden, 1992; Huber and Power, 1985). In addition, it is unlikely that surveys of established business owners would accurately capture the diversity of ratings on career reasons. Surveying successful entrepreneurs about their retrospections of start-up reasons could have a significant "left-censored" bias. Specifically, entrepreneurs who attempted to start businesses but quit, or those who started businesses that no longer exist, would not be in the sample. Such samples may reflect only a small proportion of the individuals who represent the phenomenon of interest.

We believe that—*when questions are asked before the fact*—the reasons offered by potential entrepreneurs for getting into business will not be significantly different from the reasons offered by a similar comparison group of individuals in other types of careers. Such reasons as to lead, to achieve something, to earn income, to grow and learn, to challenge oneself, to be respected, to attain a higher position for oneself, would likely be the kinds of reasons that anyone might offer for choosing any kind of job (Fagenson, 1993; Kanter, 1977; Powell, 1988). In this way, the differences among entrepreneurs may be as great as the differences among nonentrepreneurs, and vice versa (Gartner, 1985; 1988). Even setting aside the retrospective bias argument, we believe that the previous findings of differences between the career choice reasons of entrepreneurs and others are flawed. They are likely to represent a historical artifact. We speculate that the "job of entrepreneurship" as a career, has changed over time. The SARIE studies were originally undertaken in the mid-1980s and early 1990s, and the samples used involved entrepreneurs from a variety of countries. At that time in history, an individual's chance of self-employment as a career probably reflected an option perceived as more of an "outlier" than other career choices. In the current decade, the choice of entrepreneurship as a career in the United States is likely to be perceived quite differently compared to 20 years ago. Entrepreneurship, today, may be perceived to be more like other jobs.

As a starting point for comparing nascent entrepreneurs to people in the general population, we follow a logic that assumes that the prospective reasons of these nascent entrepreneurs are *not* different than the reasons of others. Therefore, we suggest the following hypothesis:

Hypothesis 1: Nascent entrepreneurs and a comparison group have similar scores on the six kinds of career reasons (innovation, financial success, independence, recognition, roles, and self-realization).

3.3. Gender differences in reasons for getting into business

Research on the differences between men and women indicate that there are significant differences in their career choices, and that theoretical models that describe the career paths of men are less suited to the experiences of women (Farmer, 1997; Farmer et al., 1995; Larwood and Gattikers, 1989). Some studies of job preferences revealed that women want work that is intellectually stimulating and provides opportunities for personal and professional growth (Bigoness, 1988; Brenner and Tomkiewicz, 1979). Brush (1992) found women business owners tend to balance economic goals with other kinds of goals, such as personal enjoyment and helping others. Sexton and Bowman-Upton (1990) found that female business owners scored lower on energy level and risk taking and higher on autonomy and change than male business owners. Fischer et al. (1993) found that on three motivational factors (financial, lifestyle, and social/recognition) women scored higher than men on financial motivation, a result they found "somewhat unexpected" (p. 162). Buttner and Moore (1997) found that "pull factor" reasons, such as seeking challenge and self-determination, were more important to women than to men. Conversely, in a comparison of the values of entrepreneurs and managers, Fagenson (1993) found more similarities among women and men than differences. Women were found to value equality more than men, and men tended to value family security more than women, but the greater differences were found between entrepreneurs and managers. Entrepreneurs were found to value self-respect, freedom, a sense of accomplishment, and an exciting life more than did managers.

Although the findings are mixed, there appear to be significant differences in the reasons that compel men and women to pursue entrepreneurial careers, especially if more weight is given to the results of prospective studies like those of Gatewood et al. (1995) and Carter (1997). In their study of preventure clients, Gatewood et al. found that nascent women entrepreneurs who offered internal reasons (e.g., "I always wanted to be my own boss") and

N.M. Carter et al. / Journal of Business Venturing 18 (2003) 13–39   23

nascent men entrepreneurs who offered external reasons (e.g., "I had identified a market need") were more likely to start businesses than entrepreneurs who gave other types of reasons. In a study of 92 nascent entrepreneurs, Carter used a list of reasons similar to the list of reasons used in this study and generated a set of four factors: autonomy or independence, task interest, wealth or income, and a desire to stay in the community. She found that nascent men entrepreneurs rated wealth and prestige higher than nascent women entrepreneurs. Both men and women rated the autonomy factor higher than the other factors. Women appeared to place a higher value on staying in the community, relative to their rating on wealth.

Extrapolating from these findings, we argue that the reasons men and women offer for choosing careers are different whether they choose self-employment, or another career option. We hypothesize:

Hypothesis 2: Women (nascent entrepreneurs and the comparison group) rate the six kinds of career reasons differently than men (nascent entrepreneurs and the comparison group).

Taken together, our hypotheses suggest that reasons offered by entrepreneurs for getting into business will be similar to the reasons offered by nonentrepreneurs for having jobs, but in either case the reasons given by women will differ from those given by men. Implicit in these two hypotheses is our belief that any differences between entrepreneurs and nonentrepreneurs in their career reasons may be driven by differences in a failure to account for the proportion of gender in the samples. Typically, men started businesses at rates that were two to five times higher than women (Reynolds et al., 2000). Previous samples of entrepreneurs were likely to have significantly more men than women compared to a sample of people who have jobs. The proportion of men and women needs to be recognized when analyzing samples of entrepreneurs and nonentrepreneurs. If the gender variable is controlled, there may not be any differences in reasons between entrepreneurs and others, but women may offer different reasons than men.

4. Method

4.1. Sample

The data for this research were obtained from the PSED, a national database of individuals who were in the process of starting companies. The Institute for Social Research at the University of Michigan administers the PSED (, http://projects.isr.umich.edu/psed/). Detailed descriptions of the methods and sampling used to generate the PSED can be found in Reynolds (2000). PSED data used in this study involve three different samples of individuals, all of whom were initially identified through a random-digit dialing (RDD) telephone survey procedure conducted in two phases.

In the first phase, Market Facts Inc., telephoned households through their TeleNation surveys, which involve a minimum of 1000 completed interviews of adults (500 female, 500 male) 18 years of age or older over a 3-day period. Up to three attempts were made on each selected telephone number. During 1998 to 1999, through successive waves of phone calls, an initial sample of RDD calls were made, totaling 31,261 individuals (15,662 females and 15,599 males). Two questions in the telephone screening were designed to identify people who might be starting businesses (either as autonomous start-ups or as something being done in cooperation with a current employer).

• Are you, alone or with others, now trying to start a business?
• Are you, alone or with others, now starting a new business or new venture for your employer? An effort that is part of your job assignment?

A respondent could answer "no" or "yes" to either question, thereby placing him- or herself into one of four categories (no start-up activity, start-up activity in conjunction with an employer, autonomous start-up activity, or both kinds of start-up activity). For purposes of this research, only individuals falling into the autonomous start-up category were considered eligible for the designation "nascent entrepreneur." Two additional questions asked in the telephone screening were used to separate those people actively involved in autonomous start-up from those who were perhaps thinking about it, but not actively involved. These questions inquired (a) whether the respondent anticipated becoming an "owner" (in whole or in part) of the business being developed, and (b) whether there had been any ongoing business organizing activity during the immediately preceding 12 months. Affirmative answers to both questions were necessary for individuals to be considered "nascent entrepreneurs." The result was a total of 1494 nascent entrepreneurs (561 females, 933 males) eligible for the longer telephone interviews conducted by the University of Wisconsin Survey Research Laboratory (UWSRL).

In the second phase of the research, respondents who met the inclusion criteria were called by the UWSRL and were interviewed extensively by telephone. At the conclusion of these telephone interviews, participants were sent a detailed mail questionnaire. One of the early questions in the telephone interview asked whether the business being organized had achieved sufficient cash flow for 3 months to pay expenses and the owner–manager's salary. If the answer was affirmative, as it was for some 27% of the people contacted (Reynolds, 2000), then the activity was considered an "infant business" no longer in the organization stage and the respondent was dropped from the overall telephone interview sample.

4.1.1. Oversample of women

The Entrepreneurial Research Consortium (ERC), which consisted primarily of academic institutions, financed the original data collection for the PSED. Additional financial support was later obtained from the National Science Foundation (NSF), but these funds were earmarked for the specific purposes of generating a telephone oversampling of women and minorities. (Note: As the funds for oversampling of minorities arrived well into the research process, the only oversampling included in the present data set was the oversampling for women.) The 1494 eligible nascent entrepreneurs (NEs) noted above consequently fell into the four categories formed by the intersection of respondent gender with source of support (ERC or NSF). The ERC funds were used to collect information from both female and male respondents, whereas the NSF funds were used to collect telephone information *only* from females. Interviews were completed with 148 ERC females (51.41% of the original group of eligible NE females), 222 ERC males (46.64% of the originally eligible NE males), 154 NSF females (56.62% of the originally eligible NE females) and 45 of the 457 NSF males. Although the NSF funds were intended for interviewing only females, sometimes females screened by Market Facts reported on start-up activities that were being undertaken by males in the household. When UWSRL conducted the phone interview, the person most responsible for the start-up initiative was asked to provide information on the start-up. A comparison of variables that identified the sex of the founder of a solo start-up or that of team members, the first names of respondents, and interview notes made at the conclusion of the phone interview were used to ascertain the correct identification of the respondent's sex.

At the end of the telephone interview, respondents were asked to volunteer their first name and address, so that they could be sent a mail questionnaire and a US$25 payment for taking part in the telephone interview. Not all respondents agreed to provide a name and address. Respondents were also offered a payment of an additional US$25 for completion of the mail survey. Some respondents who agreed to answer the mail questionnaire did not, and some respondents did not answer all of the questions we used. Thus, our sample consisted of nascent entrepreneurs starting independent business ventures who answered questions on the mail questionnaire that were of interest in the present study. The category sizes were as follows: 108 ERC females, 149 ERC males, 97 NSF females, and 30 NSF males. The total of 384 represented an overall response rate for our questions of 39% of the originally eligible individuals engaged in start-up activities.

The comparison group for the present research was the initial comparison group of 119 females and 104 males. However, this comparison group actually included four people (two females and two males) who at the 1-year follow-up interview indicated that they had started businesses. We eliminated these four people from the comparison group on the grounds that their answers to the "reasons" questions most probably dealt with their intended start-up, rather than their (current) work for others. The resulting group of 219 completed a shorter version of the telephone interview, with 174 (89 female, 85 male) also completing the questions of interest here.

4.2. Use of weights

The PSED data set comes with "post-stratification weights for each respondent based on estimates from the U.S. Census Bureau's Current Population Survey (Reynolds, 2000). The post-stratification scheme was based on gender, age, household income, and the four National Census Regions [Northeast, South, Midwest, and West]. The scheme produces a total of 144 cells for weighting adjustments" (p. 177). The weights are essential for drawing conclusions intended to generalize to the entire U.S. population. According to Reynolds (p. 181), "any analysis should be completed with a weighted sample. . .. This is a reflection of the number of procedures employed in the sampling and data collection that increased the yield and efficiency of the procedures." Details about the creation and application of weights in this research are described in Appendix A.

4.3. Measures of reasons

Eighteen items from the mail survey of the PSED database (items G1a–r) were selected for coding and analysis. Twelve of these items were adopted from the SARIE survey. Ten are a subset of the 14 items Shane et al. (1991, p. 445) found significant in their factor analysis comparing the reasons of entrepreneurs in Britain, New Zealand, and Norway. From their findings we selected and adapted items with factor scores greater than .50 from each of their four factor constructs. Three items represent innovation (m—to develop an idea for a product, c—to be innovative and in the forefront of technology, h—to grow and learn as a person) (alphabetic designations as listed in Tables 1 and 2). Two items represent independence (b—to have greater flexibility for my personal and family life, f—to have considerable freedom to adapt my own approach to work). Three items represent recognition (a—to achieve a higher position for myself in society, e—to be respected by my friends, l—to achieve something and get recognition for it). Moreover, two items represent roles (d—to continue a family tradition, i—to follow the example of a person I admire). We also adapted two items from other SARIE studies (Birley and Westhead, 1994; Scheinberg and MacMillan, 1988) having to do with financial success (g—to give myself, my spouse, and children financial security; k—to earn a larger personal income). In addition to these two items, we added two items to the financial success category (n—to have a chance to build great wealth or a very high income; j—to build a business my children can inherit). Finally, we added four items (items o, p, q, r) to represent the pursuit of self-realization that can motivate individuals to become entrepreneurs (o—fulfill a personal vision; p—to lead and motivate others; q—to have the power to greatly influence an organization; r—to challenge myself).

The 18 items were asked in the following manner. For the nascent entrepreneurs, the items were preceded by this question: "To what extent are the following reasons important to you in establishing this new business?" For the comparison group, the items were preceded by this question: "To what extent are the following important to you in your decisions about your work and career choices? " Both groups responded to each item on a 1 to 5 scale: 1, *to no extent*; 2, *little extent*; 3, *some extent*; 4, *great extent*; 5, *to a very great extent*.

4.4. Corrections for missing item responses

The total number of respondents for the 18 questions varied by question, from a low of 578 for the item having to do with "build a business my children can inherit" to a high of 586 for two of the items, one of which was "financial success." Across the 18 items, different respondents omitted different items. The result was that there were only 558 individuals who answered all 18 items. It is these 558 people (384 nascent entrepreneurs, 174 comparison

N.M. Carter et al. / Journal of Business Venturing 18 (2003) 13–39   27

Table 2
Factor loadings for reasons items: six factor solution, $N = 558$

G1 #	Factor:	1 Self-Realization	2 Financial Success	3 Roles	4 Innovation	5 Recognition	6 Independence
	Sum of squared rotated loadings:	2.60	2.41	1.98	1.98	1.75	1.50
	Percentage variance accounted for:	14.43	13.40	11.01	10.98	9.72	8.32
	Cronbach α:	.78	.76	.73	.63	.60	.58
r	To challenge myself	**.77**	[a]				
o	To fulfill a personal vision	**.68**					
h	Grow and learn as a person	**.66**					.37
p	To lead and motivate others	**.65**			.33		
q	Power to influence an organization	**.41**			.48		
k	Earn a larger personal income		**.81**				
g	Financial security		**.80**				
n	Build great wealth, high income		**.66**		.35	.38	
j	Build business children can inherit		**.61**[b]		.31		
d	To continue a family tradition			**.78**			
i	Follow example of a person I admire	.38		**.72**			
e	To be respected by my friends			**.64**		.60	
c	Innovative, forefront of technology				**.78**		
m	To develop an idea for a product				**.72**		
l	Achieve something, get recognition					**.78**	
a	Gain a higher position for myself		.31	.32		**.54**	
b	Get greater flexibility for personal life						**.79**
f	Free to adapt my approach to work	.34					**.68**

[a] Factor loadings smaller than .30 have been suppressed.
[b] Cronbach alpha shown for this factor is with item j removed to increase the reliability of the remaining scale.

28   *N.M. Carter et al. / Journal of Business Venturing 18 (2003) 13–39*

group individuals) whose answers were factor analyzed to determine the underlying structure of the items.

5. Analysis and results

5.1. Model testing

As noted earlier, the 18 items in this section of the PSED were developed on the basis of prior research to reflect six categories of the reasons people might choose one career path over another: innovation (items c, h, m), independence (items b, f,) recognition (items a, e, l), roles (items d, i), financial success (items g, j, k, n), and self-realization (items o, p, q, r). See Table 2 for a listing of the reasons items.

We first tested the predictive validity of this model by subjecting the data to a principal components factor analysis (listwise deletion of missing values, varimax rotation) with the analysis directed to produce six factors. The analysis was conducted on the reduced PSED data set of 558 nascent entrepreneurs and comparison group participants. Because the test of validity intended no between-group contrasts, the factor analysis was conducted on raw scores, not weighted scores. This analysis accounted for a total of over 68% of the variance, and the rotation required eight iterations to converge. The six factors produced showed truly remarkable similarity to the theoretical dimensions—only two of the items (h and e) were out of place. As shown in Table 2, the first factor, self-realization, involved five items (Cronbach α reliability of the scale=.78), the second, financial success, involved three items (Cronbach α=.76 for the three-item scale, dropping item j), the third, roles, involved three items (α=.73), and the remaining factors (innovation achievement, recognition, and independence) had two items apiece (α levels, respectively, .63, .60, and .58). Two of the 18 items (q and e) had cross-loadings that exceeded the usual rejection criterion of ±.40, but in each case the Cronbach α for the scale would have been reduced or eliminated by dropping them. To retain as many items as possible, we used this reliability criterion (which led us to drop item j), rather than the cross-loading criterion. It is always difficult to obtain high Cronbach α levels when scales consist of only two items, and because the last three scales were an identical match to their conceptual counterparts, we elected to use them despite their marginal reliabilities. To test the hypotheses we calculated values for each of the six reason scales by summing the items in each scale and dividing by the number of items associated with the scale.

5.2. Comparisons of reasons

Because the number of participants was reduced due to missing data on the reasons questions, the mail questionnaire weights to be applied to factor scores prior to conducting the ANOVA were adjusted so that they summed to 205, 179, 89, and 85, respectively. The weighted scores, by groups, are shown in Table 3, which also indicates the number of participants in each group and the standard deviation of the adjusted mail questionnaire

N.M. Carter et al. / Journal of Business Venturing 18 (2003) 13–39

Table 3
Mean scores for six weighted[a] reasons by groups

	Nascent entrepreneurs		Comparison group		Total
	Female $n=205$ wt$_{S.D.}$ = 0.28	Male $n=179$ wt$_{S.D.}$ = 0.30	Female $n=89$ wt$_{S.D.}$ = 0.38	Male $n=85$ wt$_{S.D.}$ = 0.71	
Independence					
M	4.23	4.10	4.06	4.18	4.15
S.D.	1.78	1.34	1.76	2.97[b]	1.89
Financial success					
M	3.68	3.92	3.77	3.98	3.82
S.D.	1.74	1.37	1.54	2.66	1.78
Self-realization					
M	3.67	3.56	3.77	3.68	3.65
S.D.	1.59	1.21	1.54	2.43	1.63
Recognition					
M	2.76	2.71	3.34	3.33	2.92
S.D.	1.44	1.31	1.66	2.84	1.74
Innovation					
M	2.61	2.74	2.70	2.91	2.71
S.D.	1.54	1.31	1.45	2.37	1.62
Roles					
M	1.96	1.88	2.94	2.98	2.24
S.D.	1.12	.90	1.49	2.42	1.48

[a] Each individual's reasons factor scores were multiplied by the individual's demographic weight for the mail questionnaire, with the original mail questionnaire weights corrected to sum to the total *n* by group and gender. Thus within each of the four Group × Gender cells, the mean of the corrected weights is 1.0.

[b] The larger standard deviations for weighted means in this column reflect the fact that as a group, it also has the highest standard deviation for mail questionnaire weights.

weights. The weights were more variable among males in the comparison group than among participants in any of the other three groups, so the standard deviations of weighted factor scores were also higher in this group. High within-subject variability, of course, acts to reduce the likelihood of finding statistically significant differences across groups, so the ANOVA on weighted scale values can be regarded as a relatively conservative test of the hypotheses.

The weighted scores were subjected to a 2 × 2 × 6 (Group × Gender × Reasons) analysis of variance with repeated measures on the reasons variable. The primary hypothesis of the research was tested by the Group × Reasons interaction, as weighted score patterns of entrepreneurs were compared with the weighted score patterns of the comparison group participants. The ANOVA revealed a significant Group × Reasons interaction, $F(5,2770)=$ 28.25, $P < .0001$. On four of the clusters of reasons for occupational choice—self-realization, financial success, innovation, and independence—the largest mean difference between participant groups (averaged across gender within group) was less than .15. On the remaining two clusters of reasons, recognition and roles, scores for nascent entrepreneurs (both female and male) were substantially lower than comparable scores for the comparison group (.6 lower for recognition, over 1 point lower for roles). The findings provide mixed support for accepting Hypothesis 1 that nascent entrepreneurs and a comparison group have similar sets of reasons for their career choices. There was no significant difference between nascent entrepreneurs and the comparison group on four of the scales (self-realization, financial success, innovation, and independence). There was, however, a significant difference between nascent entrepreneurs and the comparison group on two of the scales (recognition and roles). Men in the process of starting a business assigned the lowest score of either group, across all reasons categories to the role scale. Apparently, the influence of role models on their career choice is minimal compared to other reasons.

It is important to note that this group-based difference on motives having to do with public views of one's behavior (external validation and roles) was a very robust finding. For example, if the analyses were conducted using the unweighted mean scores from the six scale values, rather than the weighted scores, there was a significant Group × Reasons interaction; with the same two clusters of reasons showing a difference between nascent entrepreneurs and people in the comparison group. Or, if the factor analysis was conducted so that the "minimum eigenvalue" criterion was used to terminate the factor analysis, rather than specifying the six factors that tests the theoretical criterion, the result was four factors (accounting for 58% of the variance) instead of the six reported here. One of those four factors consisted of items e, d, i, and a (four of the five items that constituted Factors 3 and 5 in the six-factor solution). A $2 \times 2 \times 4$ (Group × Gender × Reasons) repeated measures ANOVA computed on these four reasons categories showed a significant Group × Reasons interaction with the only difference occurring on the e–d–i–a cluster, with the scores for nascent entrepreneurs again lower than those for comparison individuals.

In addition to the significant Group × Reasons interaction, the $2 \times 2 \times 6$ repeated measures ANOVA on weighted scale values also showed a highly significant main effect difference among the six types of reasons, with independence having the overall highest scores and roles having the overall lowest scores, $F(5,2770) = 292.20$, $P < .0001$. This ordering makes it clear that the significant differences between nascent entrepreneurs and the control group occurred on the scales that were rated as less important to both groups (such as roles). On scales that were highly rated (such as independence achievement, financial success, and self-realization), there were no significant differences between the two groups. It should also be noted that the mean scores for the nascent entrepreneurs tended to be lower overall than scores in the control group $F(1,554) = 5.57$, $P < .019$. This difference, however, is most probably attributable to the two scales shown to be significantly different in the Group × Reasons interaction.

Finally, the analysis showed a small but significant difference between men and women on some of the weighted scale values, with men having higher scores on financial success and innovation than women, regardless of their group of origin, $F(5,2770) = 2.67$, $P < .02$. This finding partially supports Hypothesis 2 that women would have differences in the six kinds of reasons compared to men.

N.M. Carter et al. / Journal of Business Venturing 18 (2003) 13–39   31

Although the score women assigned to financial success was lower than that given by men, women still saw financial success as an important reason in career choice, equal in importance to them as self-realization. As illustrated in Table 3, the score for women on financial success, like the score for men, is their second highest ranking, exceeded only by the desire for independence. This finding supports the results of Fischer et al. (1993) who found that financial success motivated women. Similarly, it is noteworthy that the mean score that nascent women entrepreneurs gave independence was the highest assigned by all groups, across all reasons. This is similar to the results of Carter (1997), who found that both men and women starting businesses desired autonomy and independence, but for women it was their highest work value. Similarly, Gatewood et al. (1995) found that nascent women entrepreneurs often reported "want[ing] to be my own boss" as the reason for starting their ventures, and Buttner and Moore (1997) found self-employed women were most motivated by self-determination.

6. Discussion

Implicit in prior research on the reasons entrepreneurs offer for getting into business was an assumption that entrepreneurs pursued entrepreneurial activity because of greater interest in such reasons as financial success, independence, and self-actualization. Entrepreneurs were assumed to offer such reasons because they wanted "more of" these reasons than individuals who were pursuing jobs. Entrepreneurs wanted more financial success, more independence, and more self-actualization than others. Yet, surprisingly, prior studies offered no specific tests of this assumption. Previous studies were typically retrospective (surveying only successful entrepreneurs long after they had started their firms) and often failed to compare the reasons of entrepreneurs with other individuals. Are the reasons for starting businesses similar for nascent entrepreneurs compared to the general population?

The present study reveals that nascent entrepreneurs were both similar to, and different from, the general population. Entrepreneurs were similar to nonentrepreneurs in the kinds of reasons they offered for career choice on self-realization, financial success, innovation, and independence. Both entrepreneurs and nonentrepreneurs rated independence, financial success, and self-realization as more important than recognition, innovation or roles. In fact, as measured by a composite of the six scales, nonentrepreneurs scored higher than nascent entrepreneurs on these dimensions. Overall, these findings argue against considering entrepreneurs to be qualitatively different from individuals who pursue other career options. In reasons for career choice, entrepreneurs do not seem to fit the stereotype held about them in the popular wisdom (Shaver, 1995).

The two between-group differences that were obtained were on the scale values that both nascent entrepreneurs and nonentrepreneurs ranked low: roles and recognition. By comparison to the nonentrepreneurs, nascent entrepreneurs offered reasons for getting into business that were less influenced by external validation from others: the respect of friends, family traditions, the examples of others, achieve something and get recognition, and gain a higher position for myself.

There were differences in reasons for career choice by gender. Males (entrepreneurs and nonentrepreneurs) rated financial success and innovation higher than females (entrepreneurs and nonentrepreneurs) as a reason for choosing a career. This finding was consistent with previous research by Carter (1997) and Gatewood et al. (1995).

In summary: (1) nascent entrepreneurs were more similar to nonentrepreneurs than they were different. The primary exception is in terms of desiring recognition or external validation: nascent entrepreneurs were less likely to do so; and (2) males were different from females. Males were more likely to seek financial success and opportunities to create new products or technology than women.

6.1. Concerns

There might be a concern that the way the reasons for career choice were presented to the nascent entrepreneurs and the control group influenced their responses. Nascent entrepreneurs were asked "To what extent are the following reasons important to you in establishing this new business?" while the comparison group was asked "To what extent are the following important to you in your decisions about your work and career choices?" The nascent entrepreneurs were asked to offer a prospective account of their reasons for undertaking the new task of developing a new business, while the comparison group may have interpreted their question to account for their decision to stay in their current job, rather than provide reasons for why they would decide to choose a career. Although there may be some semantic nuances between the ways these two questions were presented, we believe that those individuals in the comparison group were offering a logic for their current career *choice*: their reasons for staying in their current position would reflect their reasons for choosing to stay in their current position.

Given that the control group of individuals was selected to represent the population of adults in the United States, it should contain a certain number of individuals who report being self-employed. When screened during the Market Facts interview, these individuals would have responded that they were not at the time of the interview, "alone or with others attempting to start a new business." Instead, these individuals may have been self-employed for a number of years. We would expect their responses to the *reason* questions to reflect their present work status, as managers/owners of the businesses, rather than as nascent entrepreneurs explaining why they are considering self-employment as a career option. As owners, their responses should be similar to others in the control group.

To test this supposition we first determined if there were self-employed individuals in the control group. Both nascent entrepreneurs and control group respondents were asked about their occupational status during their phone interviews. Specifically, respondents were asked, "In terms of current work activity, are you involved in any of the following?" Response options included: working for others (full time vs. part time); a small business owner or self-employed; a manager of a business; a homemaker; retired; student (full time vs. part time); or unemployed. Multiple responses for the categories were allowed. Thirty-nine individuals in the control group reported they were small business owners or self employed, and of these, 16 indicated they also worked full time for others while being self-employed.

N.M. Carter et al. / Journal of Business Venturing 18 (2003) 13–39   33

To determine whether these individuals might change the outcome of the analyses, we removed the self-employed individuals from the control group data and reran the factor analysis and repeated measures analysis of variance. The factor structure remained essentially the same, and the six-cluster repeated measure analysis (weighted) revealed the same reasons by group interaction as before, $F(5,2570) = 24.89$, $P < .0001$, and the same reasons by gender interaction as before $F(5,2570) = 2.83$, $P < .02$. The findings generated from all of these analyses offer remarkably similar results.

6.2. Implications

If one agrees with the generalizability of this sample of nascent entrepreneurs and the comparison group, these findings offer an important answer to some questions about differences between entrepreneurs and nonentrepreneurs. Overall, it would appear that nascent entrepreneurs offer reasons for starting businesses that are similar to the reasons offered by nonentrepreneurs for choosing jobs: independence, self-realization, financial success, innovation. Business start-up or "a job in an organization" are both pathways to meeting the same goals. This finding has significant implications for research and practice.

We believe that the findings presented here challenge prior beliefs and theories that suggest that individuals will choose entrepreneurship because they desire higher levels of financial success, self-realization, and independence compared to other individuals. The evidence presented here does not support this view. The desire for financial success, self-realization, and independence is important it seems, to nearly everyone, not just to nascent entrepreneurs. We would hope that one important message from the evidence presented here is that nascent entrepreneurs are not, in terms of their reasons for career choice, very different than others.

These findings should be encouraging evidence for those who suggest that there may be other kinds of cognitive and behavioral factors that affect an individual's decision to start a firm versus the choice of some other career. For example, Krueger et al. (2000) argued that perceived self-efficacy and perceived feasibility of accomplishing new business creation would have a significant impact on career choice. From our perspective, this argument is one about the likely effectiveness of a process, rather than a difference in the intent behind the process. Entrepreneurship educators should take note. The perception of the feasibility of business creation can be modified through education, training, and feedback (Gatewood, 1993; Gatewood et al., 2001). Individuals can be taught knowledge, skills, and behaviors to improve their effectiveness in the tasks necessary for business creation. Knowledge and skills may have more of an impact on an individual's choice of starting a business than any assumed innate desire. Greater insights about the factors influencing an individual's choice to pursue entrepreneurial activity could lead to better designed economic growth and development programs.

The consistency of the factors generated in this study of nascent entrepreneurs to those reported in the previous retrospective studies (Birley and Westhead, 1994; Scheinberg and MacMillan, 1988; Shane et al., 1991) give us confidence in the validity of the items associated with the six factor solution (self-realization, financial success, roles, innovation, recognition, and independence). Given that the 18 items used in this study did not completely correspond to the 23 items used by Birley and Westhead (1994) and Shane et al. (1991) or the 38 motivational items used in Scheinberg and MacMillan (1988), the degree of consistency can be viewed as some triumph. We believe that any differences in the results between the present and previous studies are more likely a function of sample selection. For example, although Birley and Westhead (1994) and Shane et al. (1991) used the same items for analysis, their factor results were different. Shane et al. (1991) did not find a consistent factor for entrepreneurs in their three-country study on the financial success items. We believe that the sampling procedures used in the PSED mitigates any affects on the factor analyses that might be caused by a selection bias, either in the selection of nascent entrepreneurs or in the selection of the comparison group.

The selection of a sample of individuals to represent nascent entrepreneurs and the sample of individuals to represent the general population is critical. This study surveyed entrepreneurs in the process of starting firms, and their reasons are likely to offer a concurrent logic for their actions. It is doubtful whether surveying individuals who had successfully started businesses would accurately capture the diversity of ratings on career reasons. As we noted earlier, a sample of successful entrepreneurs surveyed about their retrospections of start-up reasons may have a significant "left-censored" bias, in that all entrepreneurs who attempted to start businesses but quit, or who started businesses that no longer exist, would not be in the sample. In addition, retrospective "stories" may tell us more about the present views of entrepreneurs than about views they held at the time of venture creation (Golden, 1992; Huber and Power, 1985). Given these two important limitations, it is not surprising that studies involving successful entrepreneurs produced some of the "facts" that are now called into question by an improved methodology. Finally, this study not only surveyed individuals in the process of starting firms, it also provided a comparison group whose characteristics generalized to the population of individuals in the United States. We believe that this attention to the characteristics of the sample of entrepreneurs and the comparison group is an important standard for other researchers who desire to make generalizations about their findings.

6.3. Speculations

Our speculation that previous research findings about the reasons individuals give for starting a business may be flawed because of their retrospective bias, or because of their historical setting, appear to be supported. Nascent entrepreneurs are not unlike others making career choices, perhaps in large part because the "job of entrepreneurship" as a career choice has changed. Similarly, the fact that we found only limited differences in the reasons between men and women (only differences on *some* of the reasons) may also be time dependent. The finding may be a harbinger that career paths and interests of men and women are converging. Differences in gender may represent a social milieu that reflects a moment in time that, as time passes, will likely change. The findings presented here, therefore, should be viewed in the context of time and place (Aldrich, 1999).

N.M. Carter et al. / Journal of Business Venturing 18 (2003) 13–39   35

Some scholars may disagree with our perspective that an entrepreneur's retrospective reasons for starting a business may not be an accurate depiction of that entrepreneur's reasons at the time of start-up. It might be plausible that the reasons entrepreneurs offer are stable over a long period of time. We suggest that both views will be subject to testing when longitudinal data from the PSED becomes available.

It should also be noted that at the time of submission of this article, no determination had been made regarding the outcome of the start-up efforts of the nascent entrepreneurs that were sampled for this study. Based on prior longitudinal studies of nascent entrepreneurial efforts (Carter et al., 1996; Gatewood et al., 1995; Reynolds and Miller, 1992; Reynolds and White, 1997), there is a high probability that many of these nascent entrepreneurs will not be successful in starting their companies. It might be plausible that the scores and ratings of reasons offered by nascent entrepreneurs who successfully start businesses may be different from nascent entrepreneurs who give up, or are still trying. In addition, successful nascent entrepreneurs may have scores and ratings of reasons that are different from the comparison group. An analysis of forthcoming longitudinal data from the PSED should offer insights about this issue.

7. Conclusions

These research results provide evidence that the reasons nascent entrepreneurs offered for starting a business are very similar to the career reasons of other individuals on such dimensions as self-realization, financial success, innovation and independence. The career reasons of nascent entrepreneurs were more similar to individuals choosing jobs, than they were different.

One issue that should not be underestimated in this study is the fact that this research is based on interviews of a representative sample of individuals in the process of starting a business. Moreover, the reasons offered for getting into business are prospective, rather than retrospective. These nascent entrepreneurs are offering their reasons for getting into business *before* the success (or failure) of their efforts are determined. Because these findings are based on prospective reasons, rather than retrospective accounts, we believe the results of this study should take precedence over previous studies where retrospective explanations for start-up have been offered. In short, the stereotype of the highly independent, financially driven, self-actualized entrepreneur may be nothing more than a distillation of the retrospective stories that entrepreneurs have told researchers in the past. In addition, this study systematically compared nascent entrepreneurs to a representative sample of nonentrepreneurs, a comparison that no other study, heretofore, has accomplished. The choices involved in sampling individuals to represent entrepreneurs matter, and any challenges to the findings presented here will require as thoughtful a process as this study for identifying individuals who are starting businesses. The identification of a comparison group matters as well, and questions about the generalizability of a study's findings necessitates some way to link the characteristics of the comparison sample to the population at large. We believe that this study marks a turning point in research on entrepreneurship, particularly for research on individuals involved in the process of starting businesses.

Acknowledgements

This material is based upon work supported by the National Science Foundation under Grant No. 9809841. Any opinions, findings, and conclusions or recommendations expressed in this material are those of the author(s) and do not necessarily reflect the views of the National Science Foundation.

The authors thank Paul Reynolds, Coordinator of the Entrepreneurial Research Consortium (ERC), for his tireless efforts on the Panel Study of Entrepreneurial Dynamics (PSED); Elizabeth Crosby and Nikhil Aggarwal for their research assistance; and two anonymous reviewers for their comments and insights during the revision process. The ERC has provided support for the development of the PSED with supplemental funding from the National Science Foundation [Nancy M. Carter, Principal Investigator, Grant SBR-9809841]. Support for the development and analysis of the PSED data used in this study was provided to Kelly G. Shaver and William B. Gartner from the Kauffman Center for Entrepreneurial Leadership. Support for the preparation of this paper was provided to Kelly G. Shaver and Nancy M. Carter from the Entrepreneurship and Small Business Research Institute (ESBRI).

Appendix A. Application of weights

When Reynolds (2000) states that "any analysis" should use weighted scores, we understand him to mean any analysis that involves comparisons between or among groups of respondents, where such factors as gender and nascent status are used to define the groups. By contrast, when there are *no* comparisons *across* demographically defined groups, the weights are superfluous. Specifically, for example, for the within-subjects factor analysis of the reasons variables, weights were not applied to the variable scores. Once the factor analysis (which was based on a total, nonsubdivided sample) was done, however, we applied the weighting system to the resulting factor scores, as we were then going to compare those factor scores across demographically defined groups of respondents.

The actual weights used in the PSED data set were significantly modified from the original Market Facts weights (Reynolds, 2000, p. 177). Specifically, because 144 weighting categories were too many for the size of the sample, this number was reduced to 32 (the factorial combination of two levels of respondent sex, four Census regions, two levels of household income, and two levels of respondent age). Second, the final weights were computed separately for the comparison group and for females and males within the entrepreneur groups. This was done to take into account the fact that the selection probabilities within the entrepreneur groups were different for females and males (because of the NSF-male empty interview cell). Within demographic groups the weights have always been normalized, so that the sum of weights for any particular subsample (e.g., nascent

N.M. Carter et al. / Journal of Business Venturing 18 (2003) 13–39   37

entrepreneur males) was equal to the total number of respondents in that subsample. Thus the phone interview weights sum to the number of respondents in the phone interviews, and the mail interview weights sum to the (smaller) number of participants who returned the mail survey. Following this logic, we modified the mail questionnaire weights in each of the four (nascent/comparison by female/male) respondent categories to reflect the fact that not all people who returned the mail questionnaire actually answered all items of interest to us. Thus our weights, like those for the overall phone survey and the overall mail survey, summed to the final cell sizes: 205 nascent females, 179 nascent males, 89 comparison group females, 85 comparison group males.

References

Ajzen, I., 1994. The theory of planned behavior. Organ. Behav. Hum. Decis. Processes 50, 179–211.

Alange, S., Scheinberg, S., 1988. Swedish entrepreneurship in a cross-cultural perspective. Frontiers of Entrepreneurship Research, Wellesley, MA: Babson College, 1–15.

Aldrich, H.E., 1999. Organizations Evolving. Sage, London.

Anscombe, G.E.M., 1956. Intention. Basil Blackwell, London.

Bigoness, W., 1988. Sex differences in job attribute preferences. J. Organ. Behav. 9, 139–147.

Birley, S., Westhead, P., 1994. A taxonomy of business start-up reasons and their impact on firm growth and size. J. Bus. Venturing 9, 7–31.

Blais, R.A., Toulouse, J.M., 1990. National, regional or world patterns of entrepreneurial motivation? An empirical study of 2,278 entrepreneurs and 1,733 non-entrepreneurs in fourteen countries on four continents. J. Small Bus. Entrepreneurship 7, 3–20.

Bonjean, C.M., 1966. Mass, class and the industrial community: a comparative analysis of managers, businessmen, and workers. Am. J. Sociol. 72 (2), 149–162.

Brenner, O.C., Tomkiewicz, J., 1979. Job orientation of males and females: are sex differences declining? Pers. Psychol. 32, 741–749.

Brush, C.G., 1992. Research on women business owners: past trends, a new perspective and future directions. Entrepreneurship Theory Pract. 2 (1), 1–24.

Buttner, E.H., Moore, D.P., 1997. Women's organizational exodus to entrepreneurship: self-reported motivations and correlates with success. J. Small Bus. Manage. 35 (1), 34–46.

Carroll, G.R., Mosakowski, E., 1987. The career dynamics of self-employment. Administrative Sci. Q. 32, 570–589.

Carter, N.M., 1997. Entrepreneurial processes and outcomes: the influence of gender. In: Reynolds, P.D., White, S.B. (Eds.), The Entrepreneurial Process. Westport, CT: Quorum Books, pp. 163–178.

Carter, N.M., Gartner, W.B., Reynolds, P.D., 1996. Exploring start-up event sequences. J. Bus. Venturing 11 (3), 151–166.

Collins, D.F., Moore, D.G., 1955. The Enterprising Man. Double Day, New York.

Cooper, A., 1971. The Founding of Technologically Based Firms. Center for Venture Management, Milwaukee, WI.

Davidsson, P., Lindmark, L., Olofsson, C., 1994. New firm formation and regional development in Sweden. Reg. Stud. 28 (4), 395–410.

Dubini, P., 1988. The influence of motivations and environment on business start-ups: some hints for public policies. J. Bus. Venturing 4, 11–26.

Fagenson, E.A., 1993. Personal value systems of men and women entrepreneurs versus managers. J. Bus. Venturing 8, 409–430.

Farmer, H.S., 1997. Gender differences in career development. In: Farmer, H.S. & Associates (Eds.), Diversity and Women's Career Development. Thousand Oaks, CA: Sage Publications, pp. 127–160.

Farmer, H.S., Wardrop, J., Anderson, M., Risinger, R., 1995. Women's career choices: focus on science, math and technology careers. J. Couns. Psychol. 42, 155–170.

Fischer, E.M., Reuber, A.R., Dyke, L.S., 1993. A theoretical overview and extension of research on sex, gender, and entrepreneurship. J. Bus. Venturing 8, 151–168.

Friberg, M., 1976. Is the salary the only incentive for work? (in Swedish). Sociol. Forsk. 1.

Gartner, W.B., 1985. A framework for describing and classifying the phenomenon of new venture creation. Acad. Manage. Rev. 10 (4), 696–706.

Gartner, W.B., 1988. Who is an entrepreneur? is the wrong question. Am. J. Small Bus. 12 (4), 11–32.

Gartner, W.B., 1989. Some suggestions for research on entrepreneurial traits and characteristics. Entrepreneurship Theory Pract. 14 (1), 27–38.

Gatewood, E.J., 1993. The expectancies in public sector venture assistance. Entrepreneurship Theory Pract. 17 (2), 91–95.

Gatewood, E.J., Shaver, K.G., Gartner, W.B., 1995. A longitudinal study of cognitive factors influencing start-up behaviors and success at venture creation. J. Bus. Venturing 10, 371–391.

Gatewood, E.J., Powers, J.B., Shaver, K.G., Gartner, W.B., 2001. The effects of perceived entrepreneurial ability on task persistence (Working paper).

Gilbert, M.R., 1997. Identity, space and politics: a critique of the poverty debates. In: Jones, J.P., Nast, H.J., Roberts, S.M. (Eds.), Thresholds in Feminist Geography: Difference, Methodology, Representation, pp. 29–45.

Golden, B., 1992. The past is the past—or is it? The use of retrospective accounts as indicators of past strategy. Acad. Manage. J. 35 (4), 848–860.

Gottfredson, L., 1981. Circumscription and compromise: a developmental theory of occupational aspirations. J. Couns. Psychol. 28, 545–579.

Hagen, E.E., 1962. On the Theory of Social Change: How Economic Growth Begins. Dorsey Press, Homewood, IL.

Harriman, A., 1985. Women/Men/Management. Praeger, New York.

Heider, F., 1958. The Psychology of Interpersonal Relations. Wiley, New York.

Hofstede, C., 1980. Culture's Consequences: International Differences in Work Related Values. Sage, Beverly Hills, CA.

Huber, G., Power, D., 1985. Retrospective reports of strategic-level managers: guidelines for increasing their accuracy. Strategic Manage. J. 6, 171–180.

Kanter, R., 1977. Men and Women of the Corporation. Basic Books, New York.

Katz, J.A., 1992. A psychological cognitive model of employment status choice. Entrepreneurship Theory Pract. 17 (1), 29–37.

Knight, R.M., 1987. Can business schools produce entrepreneurs? Frontiers of Entrepreneurship Research, 603–604.

Kolvereid, L., 1996a. Organizational employment versus self-employment: reasons for career choice intentions. Entrepreneurship Theory Pract. 20 (3), 23–31.

Kolvereid, L., 1996b. Prediction of employment status choice intentions. Entrepreneurship Theory Pract. 21 (1), 47–58.

Krueger Jr., N.F., Brazeal, D.V., 1994. Entrepreneurship potential and potential entrepreneurs. Entrepreneurship Theory Pract. 19 (3), 91–104.

Krueger, N.F., Carsrud, A.L., 1993. Entrepreneurial intentions: applying the theory of planned behavior. Entrepreneurship Reg. Dev. 5 (4), 315–330.

Krueger, N.F., Reilly, M.D., Carsrud, A.L., 2000. Competing models of entrepreneurial intentions. J. Bus. Venturing 15, 411–432.

Larwood, L., Gattikers, U., 1989. A comparison of the career paths used by successful men and women. In: Gutek, B., Larwood, L. (Eds.), Women's Career Development, pp. 129–156.

Maslow, A.H., 1943. A theory of human motivation. Psychol. Rev., 370–396 (July).

McClelland, D.C., 1961. The Achieving Society. Free Press, New York.

McClelland, D.C., Winter, D.G., 1969. Motivating Economic Achievement. Free Press, New York.

Nelson, J.I., 1968. Participation and integration: the case of the small businessman. Am. Sociol. Rev. 33 (3), 427–438.

Powell, G., 1988. Women and Men in Management. Sage, Beverly Hills.

Reynolds, P.D., 1994. Autonomous firm dynamics and economic growth in the United States 1986–1990. Reg. Stud. 28 (4), 429–442.

Reynolds, P.D., 2000. National panel study of U.S. business startups: background and methodology. In: Katz, J.A. (Ed.), Advances in Entrepreneurship, Firm Emergence, and Growth, vol. 4, Stanford, CT: JAI Press, pp. 153–227.

Reynolds, P.D., Maki, W.R., 1990. Business volatility and economic growth. Final Project Report. Small Business Administration, Contract SBA, Washington, DC, 3067-OA-99, May 1990.

Reynolds, P.D., Miller, B.A., 1992. New firm gestation: conception, birth, and implications for research. J. Bus. Venturing 7, 1–14.

Reynolds, P.D., White, S.B., 1997. The Entrepreneurial Process. Greenwood Publishing, Westport, CT.

Reynolds, P.D., Hay, M., Bygrave, W.D., Camp, S.M., Autio, E., 2000. Global Entrepreneurship Monitor: 2000 Executive Report. Kauffman Center for Entrepreneurial Leadership, Kansas City.

Schein, E.H., 1978. Career Dynamics: Matching Individual and Organizational Needs. Addison-Wesley, Readings, MA.

Scheinberg, S., MacMillan, I.C., 1988. An 11-country study of motivations to start a business. In: Kirchoff, B.A., Long, W.A., McMullan, W.E., Vesper, K.H., Wetzel, W.E. (Eds.), Frontiers of Entrepreneurship Research, Wellesley, MA: Babson College, pp. 669–687.

Sexton, D.L., Bowman-Upton, N., 1990. Female and male entrepreneurs: psychological characteristics and their role in gender-related discrimination. J. Bus. Venturing 5, 29–36.

Shane, S., Kolvereid, L., Westhead, P., 1991. An exploratory examination of the reasons leading to new firm formation across country and gender. J. Bus. Venturing 6, 431–446.

Shapero, A., 1975. The displaced uncomfortable entrepreneur. Psychol. Today, 83–88 (November).

Shaver, K.G., 1985. The Attribution of Blame: Causality, Responsibility, and Blameworthiness. Springer-Verlag, New York.

Shaver, K.G., 1995. The entrepreneurial personality myth. Bus. Econ. Rev. 41 (3), 20–23.

Shaver, K.G., Scott, L.R., 1991. Person, process, choice: the psychology of new venture creation. Entrepreneurship Theory Pract. 16 (2), 23–45.

Simon, M., Houghton, S.M., Aquino, K., 2000. Cognitive biases, risk perception, and venture formation: how individuals decide to start companies. J. Bus. Venturing 15 (2), 113–134.

Smith, N.R., Miner, J.B., 1983. Type of entrepreneur, type of firm, and managerial innovation: Implications for organizational life cycle theory. Frontiers of Entrepreneurship Research. Wellesley, MA: Babson College, 51–71.

Vroom, V.H., 1967. Work and Motivation. Wiley, New York.

Part III
Social Capital

[12]

NETWORKING AMONG
WOMEN ENTREPRENEURS
Howard Aldrich

In 1985 women constituted 45.6 percent of the wage and salaried labor force, but only 33.4 percent of the self-employed. About 9 percent of employed men were self-employed compared to only 5.6 percent of employed women. The average male-owned business was about seven times as large as the average female-owned business, based on average annual dollar receipts (Small Business Administration 1986). Although women entrepreneurs are now increasing their share of the business population rapidly, and therefore increasing their share of business receipts, a sizable gap remains.

A substantial portion of the difference between men and women entrepreneurs' achievements can be traced to the opportunities open to each and the constraints on each. In particular, women entrepreneurs are embedded in different personal and social networks than men, with far-reaching consequences for their rates of business formation, survival, and growth.

IMPORTANCE OF LINKAGES AND RELATIONSHIPS IN FOUNDING BUSINESSES

The formation of new businesses is a result of motivated entrepreneurs with access to resources finding niches in opportunity structures. On the demand side, opportunity structures contain the environmental resources that can be exploited by new businesses as they seek to carve out niches for themselves. On the supply side, motivated entrepreneurs need access to capital and other resources so that they can take advantage of perceived opportunities. In short, entrepreneurship

104 / NETWORKING

involves value creation through mobilizing resources in response
to opportunities.   Note a central issue in this formulation:
entrepreneurship requires linkages or relations between key
components of the process.

Entrepreneurs must establish connections to resources and
niches in opportunity structures. The behavior required of them
differs from that of traditional managers in one important way.
Entrepreneurs are driven by opportunity seeking behavior, not by
a simple desire to invest resources (Stevenson 1984).
Entrepreneurs, in contrast to managers, thrive on unsettling and
turbulent conditions.   Their greatest gains are made when
discontinuities and gaps appear in society's economic fabric,
making traditional modes of doing business or traditional
products and services obsolete.   Even under normal conditions,
hidden opportunities for linking new products or services to
untapped markets may be available, if only entrepreneurs could
obtain information about where they lie.

Freely available and widely shared information is not the
basis for a very profitable venture. Successful start-ups and
business growth depend on specialized or unique knowledge not
widely available.   Otherwise, others quickly imitate the new
business, and any advantage gained is temporary, at best.   Thus,
a key question for entrepreneurship research is, "How do
potential and active entrepreneurs obtain the information they
need?"

Entrepreneurs must discover possibilities and mobilize
resources more effectively than others. People most often follow
very repetitive cycles of activities, with daily routines
dominating their lives. People absorbed in their own activities-
-not well-connected to other people--thus often let profitable
opportunities slip by unnoticed.   Mobilizing resources requires
entrepreneurial contacts, knowledge, and confidence. Mobilizing
resources also involves asking others to raise money, labor, and
effort for a venture with an uncertain future.

Unlike earlier approaches to entrepreneurship, the picture
drawn here focuses on entrepreneurs as embedded in a social
context, channeled and facilitated, or constrained and inhibited,
by their position in social networks (Aldrich and Zimmer 1986;
Granovetter 1985). We must see entrepreneurship as intimately
linked to other aspects of life, especially pre-entrepreneurial
careers and nonworkplace relationships.

The literature on work and careers indicates that women are
more likely than men to have access to a limited range of jobs,
to be shunted to jobs with little chance of promotions rather
than to positions with significant responsibilities, and to
experience tokenism in upper-level jobs.   The literature on
marriage and the family indicates that women are more likely than
men to have domestic responsibilities, work parttime, and have

interrupted careers. The literature on organized social life shows that women are significantly segregated from men in much of their nonwork life. The literature on gender differences in socialization and roles suggests that women view relationships in a different light than men. Women see responsibilities and commitments where men see mostly opportunities and rights, although the differences are not great and thus should not be overstated.

This chapter reviews the depth and pervasiveness of the differences identified in these literatures. The issue is whether the networks women construct, or are embedded in, are different in important respects from men's and the consequences networks have for women's entrepreneurial behavior.

NETWORK PROPERTIES

The starting point for studying entrepreneurship through social networks is a relation or transaction between two people. Relations may be treated as containing (1) communication content, or the passing of information and advice from one person to another; (2) exchange content, or goods and services; and (3) normative content, or the expectations persons have of one another because of some special characteristic or attribute, such as moral support provided by close friends. The strength of ties depends on the level, frequency, and reciprocity of relations between persons. Ties can vary from simple, one-purpose relations to multiplex, all-purpose relations.

Relations between pairs of individuals--entrepreneurs, customers, suppliers, creditors, or inventors--whatever their content and whatever a person's social role, could be extended indefinitely. A central interest of network analysts, therefore, has been finding ways of setting meaningful limits to the scope of a social unit under discussion. The concepts of personal network and social network provide us with some tools for setting such boundaries.

Personal Networks

A personal network, or role set, consists of all those persons with whom an entrepreneur has direct relations. For entrepreneurs, we could think of partners, suppliers, customers, venture capitalists, bankers, other creditors, distributors, trade associations, and family members.

106 / NETWORKING

Direct Ties

The simplest kind of personal network just includes direct ties linking an entrepreneur with persons with whom she has direct dealings, as shown in figure 5.1. Five persons are shown, with the entrepreneur in the center. The network in this example includes three men and two women, a ratio supported by some research on women entrepreneurs. Typically, these are persons the entrepreneur meets on a face-to-face basis, and from whom she obtains services, advice, and moral support.

When we use the term networking as a verb, describing entrepreneurial behavior, we are usually thinking of special relations within personal networks--a network built on strong ties, relations entrepreneurs can count on. By contrast, weak ties are superficial or casual, and people typically have little emotional investment in them.

Figure 5.1 Personal Network Example: Direct Ties between an Entrepreneur and Her Network

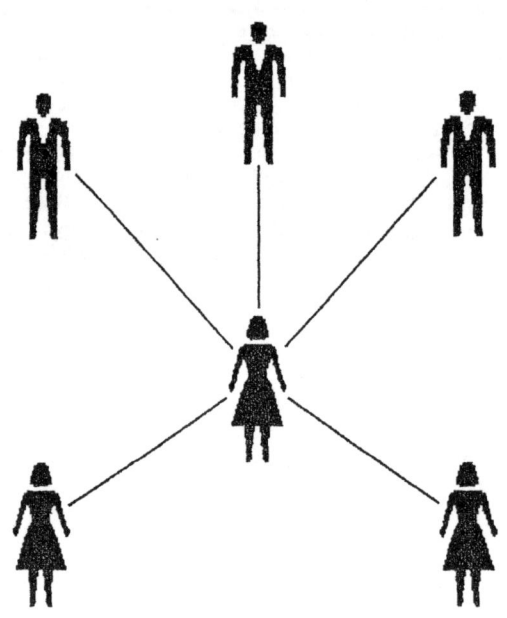

Networking is often mentioned because people feel the need to distinguish networking behavior from ordinary business behavior. For example, picture behavior at two extremes: First, one-of-a-kind, quick and dirty, market-mediated transactions between people who never expect to see each other again (e.g., buying a magazine at a corner newsstand in downtown Cleveland). And second, contact between two persons who expect to see each other frequently and who are in a relation for the long term (e.g., taking a machine-tool shop owner to lunch to discuss specifications for a new piece of equipment you need). The first behavior is just a straightforward pragmatic transaction between people whose personal characteristics count for very little. It does the job, in most circumstances, and can be an efficient way of doing business. However, there are three problems associated with market-mediated transactions: opportunism, uncertainty, and exit.

First, opportunism is always a possibility. The other party, expecting never to deal with you again, may engage in "self-disbelieved" statements of competence or performance (Williamson 1981). Second, the problem of opportunism is heightened under conditions of uncertainty. It may be impossible to predict all the conditions under which a contract will have to be carried out, or to know precisely all the specifications a piece of equipment will have to meet. Third, when problems crop up, the other party may simply exit the situation, leaving you in the lurch (Hirschman 1972). The other party may simply walk out on you instead of joining you to talk things over or negotiate.

Networking, by contrast, refers to the expectation that many times both parties are investing in a long-term relation. Consider three benefits that follow from creating a social context in which people expect to deal with each other frequently over an extended period: trust, predictability, and voice, rather than exit.

First, regardless of what popular fiction says about business, trust is an important component of business dealings. Portrayals of double-dealing in works like "How to Succeed in Business Without Really Trying" or "Dallas" are mostly figments of Hollywood writers' imaginations. Business would grind to a halt if parties always treated each other the way J. R. Ewing treats his business associates. Trust is enhanced--purely through self-interest--under conditions when people feel there is a good chance of dealing with each other again.

Second, predictability is increased when long-term relations are established. The inherent uncertainty in a situation is not reduced, but what is reduced is the uncertainty about whether the other party will do something to assist you when things do not go according to plan. Uncertainty is also reduced when your network contacts tell you where to go for assistance.

108 / NETWORKING

Third, people are more likely to use voice rather than exit in response to problems when relations are implicitly long term. Voice means making one's complaints known and negotiating over them, rather than sneaking silently away.

Thus, networking with one's direct ties to turn them into strong ones is first and foremost a way of overcoming some of the liabilities inherent in purely marketlike transactions with other people. Networking involves expanding one's circle of trust. In network terms, relations of trust are strong ties, as opposed to casual acquaintances, who are weak ties.

Indirect ties

Direct ties, especially strong ones, are significant not only for the persons directly linked to entrepreneurs but also for the indirect access they provide to people beyond entrepreneurs' immediate contacts. Indirect links can be considered by specifying how many steps removed from entrepreneurs we wish to include. Including indirect ties takes us closer to the essence of networks, as we begin to see how entrepreneurs can leverage their direct connections by judicious choice of contacts who have access to others. Figure 5.2 shows an entrepreneur, labeled B, linked to her direct ties, who in turn are linked to several other people with information or resources of value. In addition to strong direct ties to A, C, and D, shown as solid lines, one of her direct ties is weak, shown as a dotted line to E.

Figure 5.2 Three Interconnected Personal Networks: Weak and Strong Ties

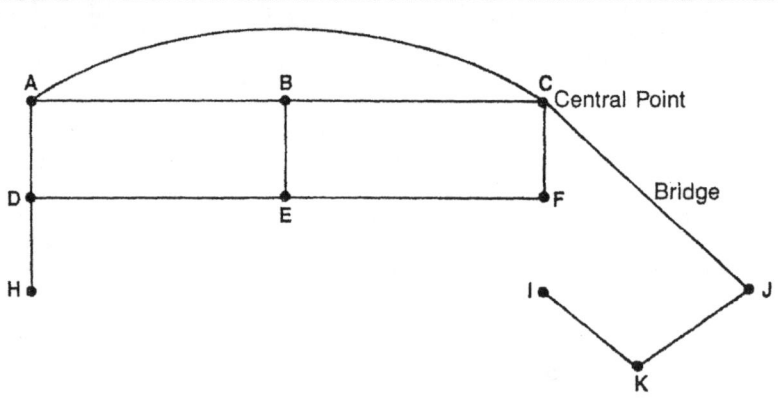

Indirect ties enable entrepreneurs to substantially increase their access to information and resources, multiplying by many times over what is available through their direct ties.

Figure 5.2 also illustrates three aspects of entrepreneurs' personal networks: density, reachability, and diversity.

<u>Density</u>. The density of a network refers to the extensiveness of ties between persons, and is measured by comparing the total number of ties present to the potential number that would occur if everyone in the network were connected to everyone else. The simplest measure of density just considers the presence or absence of a tie, but more sophisticated measures take account of the strength of ties. In figure 5.2, the number of persons in entrepreneur A's direct personal network is four, including A, B, C, and D, and the maximum possible number of ties is given by the formula $(N)*(N-1)/2$, or $(4)(3)/2=6$. (The ties could be AB, AC, AD, BC, BD, and CD.) As this is also the actual number present--all four persons directly know each other--density is 100 percent.

<u>Reachability</u>. Reachability refers to the presence of a path between two persons. Persons can be ranked by how many intermediaries a path travels before one person is indirectly linked with another. Some people are completely isolated from others, as no path can be constructed to link them. For most of us, however, there probably is a path to many other people, although it may be quite lengthy. In figure 5.2, all persons have paths between them, with the longest between G and K--a path made up of six relations (GF, FE, EB, BD, DI, and IK).

Fairly short paths are responsible for the often-heard comment, "Isn't it a small world!" when two apparent strangers meet and discover they have a mutual friend. Travers and Milgram (1969) studied the small world phenomenon experimentally. Arbitrarily chosen persons in Nebraska were given letters to send to a target person in Boston, with the restriction that the letters had to be channeled only through persons known to the senders. Out of 296 starts, 64 letters reached the target person, with the mean number of intermediaries being 5.2.

Consider for a moment how many ties it might take to reach the entire United States work force of roughly 100 million people. Some simple mathematics shows that, in theory, each of us is no more than four steps away from anyone else in the work force. Assume that each of us knows 100 other people, that these 100 people also know 100 people, and as they each know 100 people, we are two steps away from 100 times 100, or 10,000 people. In three steps, we reach 10,000 times 100, or 1 million people, and in four steps, 1 million times 100, or 100 million people! Obviously the small world phenomenon is not an everyday

110 / NETWORKING

occurrence, but usually we do not dig that deeply (nor can we)
into the ties of strangers we meet. Two constraints limit our
ability to extend the reachability of our ties: (1) there will
be some "unknowns" between us and a target, so that we do not
know whom to start with, and (2) networks are lumpy--many of the
100 people known to our friends are also known to us, and so our
personal networks turn back in on us.

     Diversity. The diversity of an entrepreneur's network is
crucial to the scope of open opportunities. People with whom we
have weak ties, such as casual acquaintances, are less likely to
know one another than are persons with whom we have strong ties,
such as close friends. Therefore, a personal network made up of
a person's direct and indirect weak ties is a low-density
network, with many persons unknown to each other. A personal
network made up of a person's strong ties is a high-density
network with most persons known to each other (Granovetter 1973).
Of course, most personal networks include a mix of weak and
strong ties; the relative balance of weak to strong is crucial.

     An entrepreneur may have a small group of friends she knows
well, each of whom knows the others quite well, such as the
network centered on person A in figure 5.2. Information known to
one person in this group is rapidly diffused to the others, and
the entrepreneur learns little from talking to C beyond what she
already knows from talking to D. She may also have many casual
acquaintances, each of whom also has a circle of close friends,
such as person B's weak tie to E in figure 5.2. These close
friends of her casual acquaintances (F and H) are unlikely to be
known to her, and thus her only possible ties to them are through
the casual acquaintance. Thus, if either F or H has information
of value, her only possible access to the information is through
her weak tie.

     Individuals with few weak ties "will be deprived of
information from distant parts of the social system and will be
confined to the provincial news and views of their close friends"
(Granovetter 1982). Alternatively, having enough diversity in
one's strong ties, such that one's immediate network includes
strongly linked people who have ties to very different parts of
the social system, could provide information channels otherwise
unavailable. For example, in figure 5.2, D is strongly tied to
B, and provides B with an indirect channel to I, who is in a very
different network.

     Research on job searches by white-collar professionals has
documented that lack of access to the information provided by
weak ties puts people at a competitive disadvantage in the labor
market. They obtain only redundant information from close
acquaintances who travel in the same circles as the job seeker.
People with a more diverse personal network, connected to distant

WOMEN-OWNED BUSINESSES / 111

others via weak (or possibly strong) ties, have access to a wider range of information and resources.

Successful entrepreneurs are more likely, therefore, to be found in positions connected to lots of diverse information sources. Information about new business locations, potential markets for goods and services, sources of capital or potential investors, and innovations is likely to be spread widely among individuals. Other things being equal, someone with a small set of overlapping ties is at a disadvantage when competing for information with someone with a large set of divergent ties.

Social Systems as Networks

Personal networks are constructed from the viewpoint of a particular individual. The concept of a social network is much broader. It can include the local community, a region, or an industry. In examining social networks, we start from a population under study and identify the totality of all persons connected by a certain relationship. Given a bounded system, we identify all the links between people within the boundaries.

This way of thinking about networks alerts us to the way personal networks either interconnect and overlap, or stand in isolation from one another. Entrepreneurs might enjoy extensive connections within a limited region of a total network, but lack the indispensable relation needed to discover essential information in another region. Information and resources can be thought of as mapping onto networks. Networks can be thought of as the thread or channel along which information and resources flow.

Most of the concepts necessary to analyze social networks have already been introduced, including density, reachability, and diversity. Two additional concepts are important: centrality, and broker roles.

Centrality. The centrality of a person in a network is determined by two factors: (1) the total distance from that person to all other persons following along all paths leading outward from that person; and (2) the total number of other persons that person can reach. The more persons who can be reached and the shorter the aggregate distance to these persons, the higher the centrality of a person. Figure 5.3 illustrates a social network, with person C in a central role, directly linked to four other people.

Persons who have extensive ties to different parts of a network can play key roles in entrepreneurial processes. They can serve three important functions: (1) they may serve as communication channels between distant persons; (2) they may

112 / NETWORKING

provide brokerage services linking third parties to one another
by transferring resources; and (3) if they are dominant or high-
status individuals, they may serve as role models for others or
may use their positions to direct the behavior of others.

   Brokers.   Brokers are people who link persons having
complementary interests, transferring information or resources,
and otherwise facilitating the interests of persons not directly
connected to one another. For example, venture capitalists are
probably as important for their broker role as for the funds they
provide to struggling entrepreneurs. They bring together
technical experts, management consultants, and financial planners
to supplement an entrepreneur's limited knowledge and experience.
   Some social settings facilitate brokerage, and some
associations and organizations are themselves brokers in the
roles they play. Many voluntary associations, trade
associations, public agencies, and other organizations increase
the probability of people making contact with one another. The
complex pattern of social organization in the Silicon Valley, for
instance, illustrates the synergistic effects of brokers, central
meeting points (bars and restaurants), and family and friendship
networks in supporting high start-up rates (Rogers and Larson
1984).

Figure 5.3   Social Network

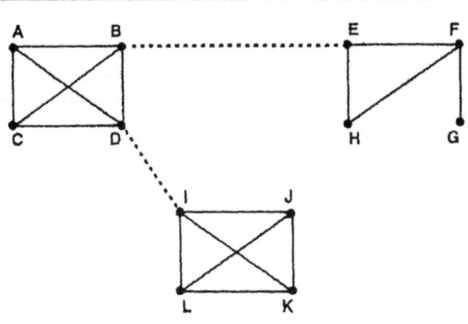

LEGEND:

Strong Ties _____
Weak Ties ......

Bridges. Bridges are links joining two regions of a network that would otherwise have little, if any, contact with each other. For example, in figure 5.3, a bridge between C and J links two otherwise isolated sections of the network. Bridges in social networks play a role analogous to those Kanter (1977) identified in the opportunity structures of organizations--they allow people to leap over otherwise unbridgeable gaps in their development.

Personal networks and social networks are simple but powerful ideas, allowing us to conceptualize the opportunities and constraints facing entrepreneurs in the pursuit of their goals. Applied to the situation of women entrepreneurs they provide new insight into several related issues: why the proportion of women in the entrepreneurial population is so low, why women entrepreneurs are concentrated in certain limited sectors of the economy, why women-owned businesses grow more slowly than men's and, perhaps, what adaptive strategies women entrepreneurs might pursue as they enter business.

CHARACTERISTICS OF WOMEN'S NETWORKS

Whether just starting a business or trying to keep one alive and growing, entrepreneurs' personal networks and their positions in larger social networks affect their access to information and advice, resources, and social support. To what extent do women's networks differ from men's? Is there any reason to believe that women and men are embedded in networks different enough to affect rates and types of entrepreneurship? A careful reading of the social science literature on sex differences in work and occupations, family life, and organized social life, suggests that the answer is a qualified "yes."

In many respects, women inhabit a "female world" that only partially overlaps the "male world" (Bernard 1981). In many important regions of social life, divisions and barriers limit the reach and diversity of women's networks. Some evidence suggests that women even view social relations in a different way than men, leading to different networking behaviors. Within the boundaries of the female world, relational solidarity among women may enhance certain aspects of entrepreneurial activities, and so ultimately the net costs of limited reach and diversity must be balanced against the benefits of strong ties and increased density. Whether the balance is positive or negative cannot be ascertained with presently available knowledge.

Bowen and Hisrich (1986) concluded that research on women entrepreneurs had

114 / NETWORKING

contributed little to the development of a theory of
female entrepreneurs' careers. Entire areas have been
overlooked in the design of the research, most notably
life and career stages and non-work adult history.

Differential Access: Divisions and Barriers

Men have historically occupied the central economic
positions in our society, and have enjoyed dominant positions in
other spheres, as well. To analyze women entrepreneurs' network
potential, we need to examine the extent to which the female and
the male worlds interpenetrate. How high are the barriers to
men's networks, and what changes are occurring?

The presence of formidable divisions and barriers to women's
networking would suggest the possibility that women's ambitions
and level of activity may be the same as men's, but opportunity
structure constraints may produce different consequences for
them. Moreover, barriers in the work world may have had the side
effect of propelling women into self-employment, much as has
happened for immigrant groups in American society (Light 1972).

The following three key life events affect the networks
women enter into or construct: the workplace, marriage and
family, and organized social life.

The Workplace: Careers, Jobs, and Authority

Almost no one, man or woman, enters entrepreneurship fresh
out of school. Most people become entrepreneurs in their mid-30s
to mid-40s, after a decade or two of working for someone else.
During these formative years, employees are accumulating
experience and becoming embedded in personal and social networks
that they subsequently draw on in starting and running their own
businesses. We have overwhelming evidence that sex roles affect
working careers--from the choice of college majors and subsequent
occupations to the levels of authority achieved in firms (Reskin
and Hartmann 1986). Sex segregation is the norm in most
occupations, firms, and industries; few women are at the top.

Women's careers are different from men's and are likely to
remain different for some time (Gutek and Larwood 1987). At
least four differences have been identified:

1. Expectations about the appropriateness of jobs for men
    and women are different. These expectations or
    perceptions affect the occupations for which men and
    women prepare.

2. Wives are generally more willing to move or otherwise
    adapt to their husbands' career needs. Some might see
    this as a rational strategy for a couple to pursue if
    their goal is to maximize joint income and career

development. Husbands tend to receive better job
offers and move up faster than their wives. U.S.
Census Bureau figures show that women today, on
average, earn about 64 percent as much as men.

3.   Parenting and domestic roles are defined differently
for husbands and wives. A mother's role requires
substantially more time and effort than a father's,
thus affecting the time each has to invest in career
development (Berk 1979).

4.   Women are faced with workplace discrimination and
stereotyping which place more constraints on their
career advancement than men face (Kanter 1977).

College majors. More women are entering occupations
traditionally sex-stereotyped for men, but the large differences
that have existed for many years have produced sizable sex
differences for people in their mid-30s and older. For example,
at the University of California, Berkeley, the ratio of men to
women in the math program has just recently approached balance--
about 40 percent of the undergraduate majors are women, but less
than one in five students in the graduate program are women
(Parker 1988).
    In 1986 the U.S. Department of Education compared the
percent of bachelor's and master's degrees awarded to women in
scientific and professional fields in 1983 versus 1973, and found
substantial changes (Wall Street Journal, March 26, 1986). The
figures for master's degrees show near parity in some fields--
advertising, 22 versus 55 percent; and journalism, 35 versus 54
percent; approaching parity in others--pharmacy, 22 versus 37
percent; personnel management, 7 versus 39 percent; law, 8 versus
36 percent; accounting 9 versus 34 percent; and larger gaps in
still other fields--engineering, 2 percent in 1973 versus 9
percent in 1983; data processing, 5 versus 21 percent; banking
and finance, 3 versus 28 percent; computer and information
sciences, 11 versus 28 percent; and business and management, 5
versus 29 percent. Figures for bachelor's degrees are slightly
lower. Assuming these trends continue, in a few years the
occupational distribution for women college graduates who are
under 35, as well as women with postgraduate degrees, will look
substantially different from that for women over 35. Two network
implications stand out: (1) Placement and recruitment networks
in these professions have heretofore processed graduating classes
that were almost entirely male. Will young women get into the
pipelines necessary to give them the connections that could
someday lead to entrepreneurial careers? (2) Young women in
these professions are unlikely to find senior women in their
firms to serve as mentors. Will networks emerge outside of their
firms to bring pools of young women professionals into contact

116 / NETWORKING

with the small coterie of experienced women in their fields, or will men assume the role of mentoring them?

Occupational sex segregation. A large proportion of the female labor force is concentrated in a limited number of "female" occupations. In 1980 48 percent of all women worked in occupations that were at least 80 percent female (Rytina and Bianchi 1984). Of the ten largest occupations for women in 1980, nine were more than 70 percent female (women made up 43 percent of the total labor force then), and all of the ten largest occupations for men were at least 70 percent male. As with college majors, occupational sex segregation has diminished over the past decade, especially for young white women in professional and managerial jobs (Beller 1984). Even in these occupations, however, the index of dissimilarity for occupational sex segregation was about 50, meaning that half of all women would have to change occupations to achieve equal representation with men across the occupational distribution.

Some theorists have suggested that women have different conceptions of careers than men; marriage, children, and family life are a much more conscious part of the career plan for women than for men. Career conceptions affect women's choices of occupations, work settings, and so forth. The differences are great enough to lead some theorists to speak of "dual development" models of career development (Gutek and Larwood 1987).

Roos and Reskin (1984) argued that occupational sex segregation persists in white-collar jobs partly because information networks are sex segregated. Women are largely outside the informal networks through which men obtain desirable jobs. Women must rely on formal means, such as intermediary agencies. Because they have traditionally been concentrated in lower-level sales and service jobs, women share job information with friends and acquaintances looking for work, thus channeling them into similar jobs. Ensel and Lin (1982) found that "women who found high-status jobs were more likely than men to have used mere acquaintances and indirect contacts (weak ties)" with males. This finding is consistent with the conventional wisdom that "women who want to progress in their careers in male occupations need men's help either as sponsors or at least as intermediaries" (Roos and Reskin 1984; see also Marsden 1987, and Marsden and Hurlbert 1988).

In her study of 186 persons who had recently changed jobs in the Research Triangle Area of North Carolina, Campbell (1988) found that men had a small but statistically significant advantage in the range of their occupational contacts (as measured across nine specific occupations). However, diversity--

measured by the range of prestige scores for persons known--did
not differ by sex.

    Industry statistics on sex segregation.   Women are
concentrated in personal and professional services, finance,
insurance and real estate, communications, and retail trade,
largely because these industries employ large numbers of clerical
and sales workers, most of whom are women (Reskin and Hartmann
1986). Little can be learned about the consequences for women's
networking at this aggregate level, however, because the major
industrial categories are so heterogeneous. We can learn more by
looking at specific industries important to entrepreneurship.
    Women are underrepresented in some industries crucial to
growing firms' access to capital. The 1986 Venture Capital
Association directory showed that only 7 percent of the partners
and associates at venture capital firms were women. Many of the
largest firms had no female partners. A 1983 survey by the Equal
Employment Opportunity Commission found the 39 percent of bank
officials and managers were women, but only 1 percent of bank
presidents were women. In 1985 Institutional Investor reported
that about 25 percent of all professionals on Wall Street were
women, but only 1 percent of Wall Street partners were women.
Seglin (1986), in his interviews with women in venture capital
firms, found that women felt they were taken seriously as
professionals, but many said they had experienced problems in the
past because of their sex.
    Women are found in increasing proportions in the financial
services sector. In 1986 the Wall Street Journal reported the
following percentages of women in the management ranks of major
financial services firms: American Express, 37 percent;
BankAmerica, 64 percent; Chemical Bank, 34 percent, and Wells
Fargo Bank, 58 percent. Very few of these women, however, are in
top management positions. Women are especially underrepresented
in the management ranks of industrial firms. In 1985 they held
only 7 percent of the management jobs at DuPont and 8 percent at
General Motors. Proportions are slightly higher in the high
technology sector among big corporations: AT&T, 32 percent;
General Electric, 6 percent; IBM, 16 percent; and Xerox, 23
percent. In the retail and media sectors, women were slightly
better represented in management positions, but seldom in the
higher ranks.

    Firm level statistics.   Implications drawn solely from
occupational and industry distributions are somewhat misleading
because they do not reflect the actual working environment of
women within firms, where many are segregated into sex-typed jobs
and relegated to positions with little authority. Such jobs

118 / NETWORKING

limit cross-sex contacts that would extend women's networks into the masculine world.

In studying firms in California, Baron and Bielby (1984) found that of over 400 work organizations, 59 percent were perfectly segregated by sex--no women and men shared the same job title. In the remaining 41 percent, the median amount of segregation was 84.1 percent, as measured by the index of dissimilarity. Therefore, men and women are still unlikely to be found working side by side in the same occupation in the same firm.

Women not only tend to work in sex-stereotyped jobs within firms, but also work in jobs with little authority (Wolf and Fligstein 1979). Baron and Bielby (1984) noted that

> We repeatedly encountered instances of sex-segregation of jobs leading to gender-specific promotion lines--an orderly progression through jobs of successively greater authority and responsibility for men and dead-end careers for women.

A 1979 national survey of 1,708 top executives found just eight women in the group. A follow-up survey of 300 top women executives three years later found them in substantially lower positions than the men surveyed earlier, and earning $24,000 less, on average (Sussman 1979; Korn/Ferry 1982). A study by Bailey and Burrell (1980) found that seven years after graduating from Harvard Law School, 25 percent of the men but only 1 percent of the women were partners in law firms. The same study also examined class of 1972 graduates from Harvard's schools of public health, dentistry, design, divinity, education, and arts and sciences. Women graduates had consistently lower salaries, and apparently fewer responsibilities, than male graduates, regardless of marital or family status.

If males at the top of hierarchies refrain from informal training of their female subordinates, then women have less effective networks. When they leave firms to start their own businesses, they face a "network deficit" in competing with men who have enjoyed direct access to the power in organizational hierarchies.

Marriage and Family
Most women entrepreneurs must balance family and work responsibilities in ways that men do not. Fischer and Oliker (1983) examined the impact of marriage and children on women's networks in an interview study of 1,050 adults living in 50 localities in northern California. They asked people to name the people from whom they had, did, or could receive social exchanges such as giving personal advice, helping with odd jobs, and

lending money. They were also asked to describe these direct personal network contacts. Men and women tended to name about the same number of persons (18.6 for men and 18.4 for women), but there were substantial sex differences by stage of life cycle.

Young unmarried men and women had about the same number of persons in their networks. However, married women, especially those with children, had significantly fewer persons in their networks. In particular, they had fewer co-workers as close associates. When young, childless working wives knew people, they were much less likely to have met them at work, and much more likely to have met them through their husbands, than working husbands were to have met associates through their wives. Working women thus appear to be assisting in supporting their husbands' networks. However, the contacts women make through their husbands may not always be supportive of them.

The critical period for entrepreneurs' life cycles is the late 20s and early 30s. This is when they accumulate resources and contacts that might sustain a business founding. These are precisely the years when married women are disadvantaged. Their networks are structured more by their husbands' associations than their own. Under some circumstances, women may make valuable contacts through their husbands' networks. In Fischer and Oliker's (1983) study, unmarried women under 36 had the same pattern in their personal networks as men.

Fischer and Oliker's results lead to the prediction that a disproportionate fraction of women entrepreneurs will be single or divorced, because such women would be more likely to have personal networks that are work-related. A survey of about fifteen hundred men and women who had received MBAs from the University of Texas over a 60-year period found that women workaholics reaped fewer rewards than their male counterparts and were more likely than the men to be single, divorced, or married several times. A total of 52 percent of the women and only 17 percent of the men were single (Diamond 1987).

A study of 90 Newton, Massachusetts, women in high prestige careers found that having children made a substantial difference in the sex composition of a woman's reference group (Zanna, Crosby, and Loewenstein 1987). Among married women without children, 50 percent had an all-male reference group and 30 percent had an all-female reference group. Among married women with children, only 14 percent had an all-male reference group and 59 percent had an all female reference group. The others had mixed-sex reference groups. Wellman (1985) also found that having children significantly reduced cross-sex contacts for women, compared to men. These differences reflect, in part, the pull of the "female world" on women with children in the form of play groups and PTA functions.

120 / NETWORKING

In a pilot study conducted in the Research Triangle Area of
North Carolina, Aldrich, Rosen, and Woodward (1987), examined the
sex composition of entrepreneurs' networks by measuring what
proportion of the persons in the network were male. Among the 24
women, an average of 68 percent of the five closest people in
their strong-tie network were men. The male entrepreneurs
reported 86 percent of their strong ties as men. Some of those
interviewed were women and men who were just starting or not yet
thinking about going into business. Among the women interviewed,
only 50 percent of their strong-tie network were men, compared to
the 89 percent reported by men. Although these results are based
on a small number of cases, they show that many women are linked
to men in their strong tie networks. The results also suggest,
however, that sex composition of strong-tie networks is worth
pursuing as a possible factor affecting business start-up rates.

Because women's careers are more likely to include
interruptions for child rearing, and because other barriers
prevented many women from beginning their careers earlier, they
start businesses with fewer years of work experience than men.
In the pilot study conducted in the Research Triangle Area of
North Carolina, Aldrich, Rosen, and Woodward found 38 percent of
the 24 women business owners reported fewer than ten years' work
experience. Only 11 percent of the 132 male business owners had
fewer than ten years' experience. Campbell (1988) found that
changing locations because one's spouse had moved to a different
job depressed the reach and diversity of women's networks. She
also found that having children under six significantly reduced
the number of persons in different occupations known to women, as
well as reducing the prestige of the highest prestige person
reached in their direct ties. Work-related networks have fewer
years to mature for women than for men because of their domestic
obligations.

The same Research Triangle study also found that family
responsibilities affect women's networking. Women invest about
the same number of hours per week in building and maintaining
networks. However, these hours represented a much higher
fraction of their available time for women than for men. This
finding suggests that trade-offs and sacrifices are being made in
other aspects of their lives. Kalleberg's (1985) study of 411
business owners in three Indiana communities found that women
were more likely than men to say that business had affected their
home life negatively. About equal proportions of men and women
said that managing the time between family and business was
"always a problem." According to Hisrich and Brush (1986),

> men usually have outside advisors (lawyers,
> accountants) as their most important supporters, with
> the spouse being secondary. Women consider their

spouses to be their most important advisors, close
friends next most important, and business associates
third.

This occurs because wives have not had the opportunity to build
up work-related personal networks in the same way as their
husbands. Women may also interpret questions about "support"
differently than men, with women focusing more on emotional
support and men on instrumental support.

One research project on unemployed women uncovered evidence
suggesting that spouses and other members of women's personal
networks are often indifferent or hostile to their employment.
Ratcliff and Bogdan (1988) found that over half of the unmarried
women they spoke to, and two-thirds of the married women,
received clear messages from their immediate networks expressing
disapproval or hostility to women's employment. Only a minority
reported strong and consistent support for their working. "The
conflict between their own employment and the anti-employment
messages they receive from others represents a substantial burden
for many women" (Ratcliff and Bogdan 1988).

In contrast to Ratcliff and Bogdan's results, Kalleberg
(1985) found that men were more likely than women to report that
others discouraged them from becoming self-employed. For men and
women, the greatest encouragement came from spouses, clients, and
friends. Men were more likely than women to report that they
were encouraged by their parents or siblings.

Organized Social Life

Informal networks centered around work-related after-hours
socializing and nonwork related voluntary associations'
activities are an important source of information and alliances.
Women often lack full access to such opportunities. In the past,
many professional associations and unions routinely barred women
from membership. A National Research Council report in 1986
concluded that "even today, some elite professional clubs in
which important contacts are nurtured do not accept women as
members, and women attending meetings there must literally use
the back stairs" (Schafran, 1981).

Sex-segregated occupational networks put women at a
disadvantage, as numerous studies have documented. Martin's
(1978) study of police officers found that male officers
discussed opportunities for transfers to desirable assignments in
off-hours activities when women officers were not present. Ortiz
and Covel (1978), studying female school administrators, found
that "even women who used formal networks effectively were barred
from informal networks" (Reskin and Hartmann 1986). Kaufman's

122 / NETWORKING

(1977) research on informal academic networks found that women's networks included fewer highly ranked colleagues than men's.

Just as work organizations tend to be highly segregated by sex (Baron and Bielby 1984), so too are voluntary associations. McPherson and Smith-Lovin (1986) studied 815 face-to-face voluntary associations meeting locally in ten communities in Nebraska. They found that almost one-half of all groups were all female, and one-fifth all male. The effects of work status were quite different for men and women. Employed women were much less likely to belong to all female groups than employed men were to belong to all male groups. This finding partially reflects strategic networking by women and is partly a reflection of the dominance of heavily male groups in the civic and professional arena (e.g., the Chamber of Commerce) which business women must join.

The level of cross-sex contact was uniformly low in all voluntary associations studied. In none of the 11 groups was a woman likely to meet more than 15 men. The typical female membership generated potential contact with 29 other members, less than four of whom were male. However, the chances of cross-sex contact were higher in business and professional associations, in which a woman could have contact with 39 other members, 14 of whom were male.

McPherson and Smith-Lovin (1986) noted that these averages are a mix of rather dissimilar types. The "average woman" is actually a statistic combining many women whose association memberships are almost entirely within the traditional female world (housewives' social clubs) and a few who belong to male-dominated groups. These few women belong to associations where they may have token status (Kanter 1977), but they may also have a rich network of cross-sex contacts.

Even more strongly than in the work world, the voluntary association sector divides men and women into separate domains, where weak ties of acquaintanceship are generated within the traditional female and male worlds.

> In this arena, as in so many others, separate is probably not equal. The few members of either sex who belong to sex-integrated voluntary associations have key positions, which may provide <u>bridges</u> between the male and female domains (McPherson and Smith-Lovin 1986; italics added).

Thus in three regions within which social networks are constructed--the worlds of work, marriage and family, and organized social life--sex divisions and barriers exist, although conditions are changing. The generation of women in college today will face a rather different world than women currently in their mid-30s to mid-40s--the cohort producing today's women entrepreneurs. These women are subject to forces producing gaps in their personal networks and to barriers limiting their access to important regions of the social networks they inhabit.

Differential Investments: Responsibilities and Obligations

Within the past two decades, a sizable literature has grown up on gender differences in socialization. Sex roles are no longer seen as the result of immutable genetic programming, but rather as a consequence of the interplay between nature and nurture. Without reviewing all of the gender/sex roles literature, we discuss two issues relevant to gender, networks, and entrepreneurship: the moral ambiguity of entrepreneurship for women, and women's possibly differing views of commitment in social relationships.

The Moral Ambiguity of Entrepreneurship

Stewart (1987) has noted the moral ambiguity of entrepreneurship, both in our culture and in some persons' views of entrepreneurs. Entrepreneurs are highly valued for their creativity and innovativeness, but the way they accumulate wealth may leave them open to charges of opportunism and self-seeking behavior. Men and women may evaluate such behavior differently.

Entrepreneurs are often in bridging roles--places or points in an economic system where there are discrepancies in evaluations between persons or groups. Such market imperfections exist because information is not widely or freely circulated, giving entrepreneurs an opportunity for profit.

The "male" style is to treat such gaps opportunistically, keeping knowledge of how to bridge them to oneself, until profits are made. Instead of exploiting such discrepancies, another response might be to help those on both sides to bridge the gap, without asking for compensation. Such altruism benefits the parties involved, and perhaps the larger system, but does little more for go-betweens than enhancing their prestige or moral standing.

Might women be tempted to play this role--that of the uncompensated go-between? As Hochschild (1983) noted, "many studies have told us that women adapt more to the needs of others and cooperate more than men do. These studies often imply the existence of gender-specific characteristics that are inevitable if not innate." However, Hochschild and others (e.g. Kanter 1977) argue that women rely on "emotion work"--behavior that affirms, enhances, and celebrates the well-being and status of others. This is one of the few resources left to women by men who use their power and authority to dominate social

124 / NETWORKING

relationships. Emotion work is also a response to men's lack of training in making their emotions a resource, whereas women learn emotional skills at an early age.

Perhaps one reason women systematically underbid on contracts, assume weak bargaining positions, and hesitate in taking full advantage of opportunities lies in their ambivalent feelings about the entrepreneurial role. Pursuit of weak ties, and cultivation of strong ties with brokers or other central people in social networks, requires a single-minded commitment to an instrumental rather than an affective approach to relationships.

A recent study has examined the significance of strong ties in women's networks. Lynne Zucker, in a study which is not yet completed, is examining Jessie Bernard's (1981) ideas about the "female world" and the extent to which it circumscribes women's social relations. Zucker gave her sample of men and women adults, from the west side of Los Angeles and the Hyde Park area of Chicago, the task of sending a message to a contact person they did not know. In half of the cases, the respondent was told that the contact person could be reached by using anyone with whom the respondent was acquainted. In the other half of the cases, respondents were restricted to passing the message on via a person of the same sex. The contact people were drawn from three groups: one-third each from the female world, the male world, and the sex neutral world. Tentative results for the restricted condition suggest that the female world is most tightly linked, with the shortest paths being found when women are restricted to using female acquaintances to reach a contact person in the female world, such as a child care person. The male world does not look as tightly linked, although men using only other men to reach contact persons who are males tend to follow shorter paths than women using only men.

Gender Differences in Views of Relationships

Some writers (e.g., Gilligan 1982) have concluded that there is a distinctly female approach to social relationships. Whereas men tend to see situations in terms of what they might gain personally from them and are willing to subordinate affective considerations to ones of effectiveness, women often are not. Women, unlike men, are more likely to think of what all parties to a situation gain and lose, and give greater weight to affective considerations. The hypothesized differences should not be overdrawn, but they are germane to observations many observers have made of women entrepreneurs.

Women entrepreneurs often report that one of the hardest things for them to learn was to treat business dealings in primarily instrumental terms, placing their own interests paramount in a situation. Whether the situation involves dealing with poorly performing subordinates, negotiating a new contract with a customer, or just engaging in self-promotion, women entrepreneurs say that they feel uneasy in putting personal feelings aside.

How is this relevant to networking? Concern for the other party's emotional well-being and feelings toward you is appropriate for strong ties, where mutual expectations are high that a relationship will be a multiplex one. Women's strong ties might be richer and more stable than men's, giving women an advantage in situations where social support is important. Multiplex strong ties also increase the likelihood that multilink paths can be sustained, thus increasing general reachability within women's networks.

However, entrepreneurs can afford only a limited number of strong ties in their personal networks. Strong ties demand cultivation and maintenance and by definition are fairly limited in number. Frequent meetings, phone calls, letters, ceremonial occasions and other investments in strong ties simply cannot be spread out over very many people.

Thus, women entrepreneurs might be disadvantaged if they apply a strong tie orientation to weak ties and invest too much in them. Weak ties are, in an emotional sense, superficial ones, not needing intense commitments. Weak ties require only very infrequent freshening, and many can be allowed to lapse without either party feeling offended. Otherwise, a woman entrepreneur risks spending much of her time on relationship matters, rather than business ones.

CONCLUSIONS AND STRATEGIC IMPLICATIONS

Networks are a crucial component of the entrepreneurial process, as entrepreneurs are embedded in social contexts that channel and facilitate, as well as constrain and inhibit, their activities. The concepts of network analysis--personal network, social network, strong ties, weak ties, density, reachability, diversity, and brokers--provide a rich vocabulary for describing relations between persons. Applied to the entrepreneurial process, they suggest ways in which persons gain or lose ground in their struggle to found and run their own businesses.

Based on the assumption that women are disadvantaged to the extent that they are excluded from significant social relationships, three spheres relevant to entrepreneurship were reviewed: work, marriage and family, and organized social life. The evidence suggests that divisions and barriers within these spheres significantly limit the reach and diversity of women's networks. Women may view social relationships in a slightly

126 / NETWORKING

different light than men, placing more emphasis on
responsibilities and obligations.

These tentative conclusions have two implications for women
considering founding a business, or attempting to increase their
firms' competitive positions. First, women need to more
systematically plan and monitor their networking activities.
Second, women should attempt to increase the diversity of their
networks.

Planning and Monitoring Network Activities

Many of the divisions and barriers limiting the reach and
diversity of women's networks are unplanned, institutionalized
structures and processes that can be overcome by women with
proper planning (Welch 1980). However, barriers that are
supported and enforced, such as discriminatory hiring and
promotion policies, require collective action beyond the
resources of any individual. There are two major activities
women entrepreneurs should perform in planning and monitoring
their networks.

Chart the Present Network
A good place for women to begin is with an inventory of
current ties. Starting with their strong ties, they should list
the persons to whom they would go if they had business problems
and needed someone whom they could trust to both give advice and
support and to hold the conversation in confidence. Next, women
should inventory their weak ties. An entrepreneur may have
listed only four or five people under strong ties; however, the
weak ties personal network should be substantially larger.
Female business owners should place them into categories
according to the relationship they have to the business and which
resources or sources of information they represent.

Assess the Level of Network Activity
The next step is examining how active the businesswoman has
been in maintaining and expanding the circle of trust represented
by persons in the strong-tie network. When was the last time she
saw them? How frequently did she see them in the past year? Has
she phoned them recently or sent a note? As important as her
strong ties might be to her, weak ties are equally significant.
How many lunch dates has she had in the past month with persons
she did not know personally but who are of value to her business
(Welch 1980)? Has she been seeing only people she knows as
friends? Women who fall short in this area should make a list of
ideas of where and how to meet those (unknown) people who are
important to the success of their businesses. For women, this

list ought to specifically include cross-sex contacts (i.e., include men in positions of importance) to compensate for the high proportion of same-sex contacts most people make.

Women can put themselves in the paths of important people by joining or attending meetings of trade and professional associations, civic groups, cultural institutions, charities, and other voluntary associations (Welch 1980). They need to join, attend, participate, and volunteer; to take on committee assignments and responsible jobs to make themselves more visible. They should be aware, however, of the tendency of these groups to be sex-segregated.

Finding people to play broker or bridging roles allows them to economize on the maintenance of their personal networks. These people substantially extend the reach of entrepreneurs' networks at the cost of maintaining only one more direct tie. A businesswoman might find brokers by asking five or six people she knows only casually (weak ties) to suggest someone with an expertise in the area in which she needs help. It is not a good idea to ask strong ties to suggest someone, as the reason for getting to know a broker well is to break out of personal network.

When a woman entrepreneur finds a potential broker, she should invite that person out to lunch and pick up the tab. By following the suggestions in Bixler (1984) she can project a professional image when dealing with weak ties and potential brokers who will not have preformed ideas about her.

Increasing Network Diversity

The great danger facing all business persons is that the daily struggle to cope with pressing problems and expected routines gradually eliminates time and energy spent in innovative activity (Mintzberg 1974). Entrepreneurs need to set aside time for purely "random" activities--things done with no specific problem in mind. Attending cocktail parties, dinner engagements, get-togethers after work or on weekends, and other sociable occasions, can lead to chance connections increasing their weak ties networks.

Check Network Density

Entrepreneurs can quickly check on whether they may be sacrificing diversity for density in personal networks by looking at the lists of persons generated for their strong tie inventories. How many of them know one another? The answer will probably be 50 percent or higher. (In the study of the Research Triangle, density was about the same for men and women entrepreneurs: 55 percent for women and 58 percent for men.)

128 / NETWORKING

Then, they can do the same thing for their lists of weak ties.
If that answer is also 50 percent or higher, entrepreneurs may be
involved in networks that are too ingrown and insulated to be of
maximum benefit.

One way to increase diversity in a network is by consciously
trying to increase the age range of persons in it. Because the
occupational distribution for younger women is significantly more
like that for men than the distribution for older women, female
business owners should make an effort to include younger women in
their networks. Younger women are likely to have the connections
with men who can help overcome gaps in women entrepreneurs'
personal networks caused by previously encountered sex barriers.

Assertiveness and an instrumental orientation pay off in
building personal networks and are especially important in
increasing network diversity. Entrepreneurs must be self
promoting and explain to others how their product or service or
skills complement the listener's. This establishes a common
ground. The next step is to arrange follow-up meetings with
people who have something to offer. By playing a broker role
women entrepreneurs can bring people together whose needs are
complementary and take credit for the results.

Finally, women must break into the "old boys" network by
deliberately invading male turf whenever possible. A "new girls"
network will create strong ties and promote social support; but
with less than one in three businesses owned by women, and most
of the major corporate and financial centers of power controlled
by men, sex-segregated separate networks are a decided handicap
for women. Many divisions and barriers will only fall under the
combined assault of individual effort and concerted collective
action by women and men determined to make entrepreneur a sex-
neutral term.

REFERENCES

Aldrich, H., and C. Zimmer.   "Entrepreneurship through Social
    Networks." In The Art and Science of Entrepreneurship, edited
    by D. L. Sexton and R. W. Smilor.   Cambridge, Mass.:
    Ballinger, 1986, 3-23.

Aldrich, H., B. Rosen, and W. Woodward. "The Impact of Social
    Networks on Business Foundings and Profit." In Frontiers of
    Entrepreneurship Research--1987, edited by N. Churchill, J.
    Hornaday, O. J. Krasner, and K. Vesper.   Wellesley, Mass.:
    Babson College, 1987, 154-68.

Bailey, S., and B. Burrell.   Second Century Radcliffe News
    (Winter 1980).

Baron, J. N., and W. T. Bielby. "A Woman's Place Is with Other
   Women: Sex Segregation in the Workplace." In *Sex Segregation
   in the Workplace: Trends, Explanations, Remedies*, edited by B.
   Reskin. Washington, D.C.: National Academy Press, 1984, 25-55.

Beller, A. H. "Trends in Occupational Segregation by Sex and
   Race, 1960-1981." In *Sex Segregation in the Workplace:
   Trends, Explanations, Remedies*, edited by B. Reskin.
   Washington, D.C.: National Academy Press, 1984, 11-26.

Berk, S. F. "Husbands at Home: Organization of the Husband's
   Household Day." In *Working Women and Families*, edited by K. W.
   Feinstein. Beverly Hills, Calif.: Sage Publications, 1979,
   125-58.

Bernard, J. *The Female World*. New York: Free Press, 1981.

Bixler, S. *The Professional Image*. New York: Putnam, 1984.

Bott, E. *Family and Social Network*, 2 ed. New York: Free
   Press/MacMillan, 1971.

Bowen, D. D., and R. D. Hisrich. "The Female Entrepreneur: A
   Career Development Perspective." *The Academy of Management
   Review* 11 (April 1986): 393-407.

Campbell, K. "Gender Differences in Job-Related Networks." *Work
   and Occupation* 15 (May, 1988): 179-200.

"College Majors." *Wall Street Journal*. 26 March 1986.

Diamond, E. "Theories of Career Development and the Reality of
   Women at Work." In *Women's Career Development*, edited by B.
   Gutek and L. Larwood. Beverly Hills, Calif.: Sage
   Publications, 1987, 15-27.

Ensel, W. M. and N. Lin. "Social Resources and Strength of Ties:
   Gender Differences in Status Attainment." Paper presented at
   the annual meeting of the American Sociological Association,
   Toronto, August, 1982.

Fischer, C. S., and S. J. Oliker. "A Research Note on
   Friendship, Gender, and the Life Cycle." *Social Forces* 62
   (September 1983): 124-33.

Gilligan, C. *In a Different Voice*. Cambridge, Mass.: Harvard
   University Press, 1982.

130 / NETWORKING

Gore, S. "The Effect of Social Support in Moderating the Health Consequences of Unemployment." *Journal of Health and Social Behavior* 19 (1978): 157-65.

Granovetter, M. "Economic Action and Social Structure: The Problem of Embeddedness." *American Journal of Sociology* 91 (November 1985): 481-510.

_____. "The Strength of Weak Ties." *American Journal of Sociology* 78 (May 1973): 1360-80.

_____. "The Strength of Weak Ties: A Network Theory Revisited." In *Social Structure and Network Analysis*, edited by P. V. Marsden and N. Lin. Beverly Hills, Calif.: Sage Publications, 1982, 105-30.

Gutek, B., and L. Larwood. *Women's Career Development*. Beverly Hills, Calif.: Sage Publications, 1987.

Hisrich, R. and C. Brush. *The Woman Entrepreneur*. Lexington, Mass.: Lexington Books, 1986.

Hirschman, A. O. *Exit, Voice, and Loyalty.*. Cambridge, Mass.: Harvard University Press, 1972.

Hochschild, A. *The Managed Heart*. Berkeley: University of California Press, 1983.

Kalleberg, A. *Entrepreneurship in the 1980s: A Study of Small Business in Indiana*. Bloomington, Ind.: Center for Survey Research, 1985.

Kanter, R. *Men and Women of the Corporation*. New York: Basic Books, 1977.

Kaufman, D. "Women and the Professions: Can What's Preached Be Practiced?" *Soundings* 60 (Winter 1977): 410-27.

Korn/Ferry International. *International Survey of Women Senior Executives*. New York: Korn/Ferry, 1982.

Light, I. *Ethnic Enterprise*. Berkeley: University of California Press, 1972.

McPherson, J. M., and L. Smith-Lovin. "Sex Segregation in Voluntary Associations." *American Sociological Review* 51 (February 1986): 61-79.

WOMEN-OWNED BUSINESSES / 131

Marsden, P. V. "Core Discussion Networks of Americans." _American Sociological Review_ 52 (February 1987): 122-31.

Marsden, P. V., and J. S. Hurlbert. "Social Resources and Mobility Outcomes: A Replication and Extension." _Social Forces_ 66 (June 1988): 1038-59.

Martin, S. "Sexual Politics in the Workplace: The International World of Policewomen." _Symbolic Interaction_ 1 (Spring 1978): 44-60.

Mintzberg, H. _The Nature of Managerial Work_. New York: Harper & Row, 1974.

Ortiz, F., and J. Covel. "Women in School Administration: A Case Analysis." _Urban Education_ 13 (1978): 213-36.

Parker, R. "Women Still Seek Roles as PC Industry Leaders." _InfoWorld Industry_, 22 February 1988: 1.

Ratcliff, K. S., and J. Bogdan. "Unemployed Women: When 'Social Support' Is Not Supportive." _Social Problems_ 35 (February 1988): 54-63.

Reskin, B. _Sex Segregation in the Workplace: Trends, Explanations, Remedies_. Washington, D.C.: National Academy Press, 1984.

Reskin, B., and H. Hartmann. _Women's Work, Men's Work: Sex Segregation on the Job_. Washington, D.C.: National Academy Press, 1986.

Rogers, E. M., and J. K. Larson. _Silicon Valley Fever: Growth of High-Technology Culture_. New York: Basic Books, 1984.

Roos, P. A., and B. F. Reskin. "Institutional Factors Contribution to Sex Segregation in the Workplace." In _Sex Segregation in the Workplace: Trends Explanation, Remedies_, edited by R. Reskin. Washington, D.C.: National Academy Press, 1984, 235-60.

Rytina, N. F., and S. M. Bianchi. "Occupational Reclassification and Changes in Distribution by Gender." _Monthly Labor Review_ 107 (March 1984): 11-17.

Schafran, L. H. _Removing Financial Support From Private Clubs That Discriminate Against Women_. New York: Women and Foundations Corporate Philanthropy, 1981.

132 / NETWORKING

Seglin, J. "Can Old Boys Change?" Venture (July 1986): 60-66.

Small Business Administration. The State of Small Business: A
Report of the President. Washington, D.C.: United States
Government Printing Office, 1986.

Stevenson, H. "A Perspective on Entrepreneurship," No. 9-384-
131. Boston: Harvard Business School, 1984.

Stewart, A. "Running Hot for Competitive Markets: Collective
Entrepreneurship, Personal Authority." Ph.D. diss., York
University, Toronto, 1987.

Sussman, J. A. International Executive Profile: A Survey of
Corporate Leaders. New York: Korn/Ferry, 1979.

Travers, J., and S. Milgram. "An Experimental Study of the Small
World Problem." Sociometry 32 (1969): 425-43.

Venture Capital Association. Directory. 1986.

Welch, M. S. Networking: The Great New Way for Women to Get
Ahead. New York: Harcourt Brace Jovanovich, 1980.

Wellman, B. "Domestic Work, Wage Work, and Network." In
Understanding Personal Relationships: An Interdisciplinary
Approach, edited by S. Duck and D. Perlman. Beverly Hills,
Calif.: Sage Publications, 1985, 159-91.

Williamson, O. "The Economics of Organization: The Transaction
Cost Approach." American Journal of Sociology 87 (November
1981): 548-77.

Wolf, W., and N. D. Fligstein. "Sex and Authority in the
Workplace: The Causes of Sexual Inequality." American
Sociological Review 44 (April 1979): 235-52.

Zanna, M. P., F. Crosby, and G. Loewenstein. "Male Reference
Groups and Discontent Among Female Professionals." In Women's
Career Development, edited by B. A. Gutek and L. Larwood.
Beverly Hills, Calif.: Sage Publications, 1987, 28-41.

[13]

THE GENDER OF SOCIAL CAPITAL

Ronald S. Burt

ABSTRACT

Legitimacy affects returns to social capital. I begin with the network structure of social capital, explaining the information and control benefits of structural holes. The holes in a network are entrepreneurial opportunities to add value, and persons rich in such opportunities are expected to be more successful than their peers. Accumulating empirical research supports the prediction. However, women here pose a puzzle. The entrepreneurial networks linked to early promotion for senior men do not work for women. Solving the gender puzzle is an occasion to see how network models of social capital can be used to identify people not accepted as legitimate members of a population, and to describe how such people get access to social capital by borrowing the network of a strategic partner.

KEY WORDS: • gender • legitimacy • social capital • social networks • structural holes

Introduction

There is a delightfully descriptive word in Yiddish, mishpokhe, that refers to people who are 'one of us'. The word is specifically about extended family, but it is popularly used to refer to people who are one of us. Rosten (1989, 338) illustrates with Chase Manhattan Banks's advertising campaign built around the slogan 'You have a friend at Chase Manhattan'. In a window of the bank next to a Chase Manhattan branch there appeared a sign: '—BUT HERE YOU HAVE MISHPOKHE!'

This paper is about people who are not mishpokhe, the outsiders who are not one of us. In other words, this article is about each of us at one time or another. No matter who you are, there are certain projects in which you are an insider, mishpokhe, and others in which you are an outsider. Example outsiders are an economist arguing the merits of his model to an audience of sociologists, an American pitching a deal to a Japanese investor, a woman arguing the merits of a business policy to a

Rationality and Society Copyright © 1998 Sage Publications (London, Thousand Oaks, CA and New Delhi), Vol. 10(1): 5–46. [1043–4631(199802)10:1; 5–46; 003216]

6   RONALD S. BURT

sexist male, a baby-faced youngster proposing a new theory to a seasoned pro, a manager representing her group's interests on a team composed of managers from another group. The list is as infinite as the differences among us.

I study outsiders to understand how legitimacy affects returns to social capital. In the interpersonal politics of competition, legitimate members of the population, mishpokhe, are twice advantaged. Investors are more likely to believe they understand the motives and probable actions of someone like themselves, which means they feel more confident in predicting the future behavior of mishpokhe. Second, it is easier for investors to trust mishpokhe because his or her reputation among us will be tarnished if investors are treated poorly.

The key for outsiders breaking into the game is to borrow social capital rather than build it. Legitimate members of a population succeed by building their own social capital. Illegitimate members of the population have to borrow. In my analysis, based on a probability sample of senior managers in one of America's leading computer and electronic equipment manufacturers, the illegitimate members of the population turn out to be women and young men. The young men eventually compete as legitimate members of the population when they enter the more senior ranks (like an assistant professor promoted to a position with tenure). Women remain illegitimate across the senior ranks. My concern is the network mechanism by which illegitimate members of a population gain access to social capital, but the results raise a broader question about the gender of social capital. Is it a man's game? I argue that it is not, but I cannot dismiss the question. I begin with an introduction to social capital as a network phenomenon, explaining the information and control benefits of structural holes.

The Network Structure of Social Capital

Some people enjoy higher incomes. Some are promoted faster. Some are leaders on more important projects. As a factor responsible for such inequality, there are two ways to understand social capital: relative to human capital, and as a form of network structure.

The human capital story is that inequality results from differences in individual ability. The usual evidence is on general populations, as is Becker's (1975) pioneering analysis of income returns to education, but the argument is widely applied by senior managers to explain who gets to the top of corporate America—managers who make it to the top are smarter, or better educated, or more experienced. Human capital is surely necessary to success, but it is useless without the social capital of opportunities in which to apply it.

Cast in diverse styles of argument, social capital can be distinguished in its etiology and consequences from human capital (e.g. Coleman 1990; Bourdieu and Wacquant 1992; Burt 1992; Putnam 1993; Lin 1998). With respect to etiology, social capital is a quality created between people whereas human capital is a quality of individuals. Investments that create social capital are therefore different in funda-mental ways from the investments that create human capital (see Coleman 1988, 1990, for elaboration). I focus in this paper on consequences, a focus in network analysis for many years (see Breiger 1995, for an integrative review of contemporary research on inequality and social structure). With respect to consequences, social capital is the contextual complement to human capital. Social capital predicts that returns to intelligence, education and seniority depend in some part on a person's location in the social structure of a market or hierarchy. While human capital refers to individual ability, social capital refers to opportunity. Some portion of the value a manager adds to a firm is his or her ability to coordinate other people: identifying opportunities to add value within an organization and getting the right people together to develop the opportunities. Knowing who, when, and how to coordinate is a function of the manager's network of contacts within and beyond the firm. Certain network forms deemed social capital can enhance the manager's ability to identify and develop opportunities. Managers with more social capital get higher returns to their human capital because they are positioned to identify and develop more rewarding opportun-ities.

Structural Holes

Structural hole theory gives concrete meaning to the social capital metaphor. The theory describes how social capital is a function of the brokerage opportunities in a network. The following is a brief synopsis (from Burt 1997a) sufficient to set the stage for the subsequent gender results (see Burt 1992, for detailed discussion).

The structural hole argument draws on several lines of network theorizing that emerged in sociology during the 1970s, most notably Granovetter (1973) on the strength of weak ties, Freeman (1977) on betweenness centrality, Cook and Emerson (1978) on the power of having exclusive exchange partners, and Burt (1980) on the structural autonomy created by network complexity. More generally, sociological ideas elaborated by Simmel (1922) and Merton (1957), on the autonomy generated by conflicting affiliations, are mixed in the hole argument with traditional economic ideas of monopoly power and oligopoly, to produce network models of competitive advantage. In a perfect market, one price clears the market. In an imperfect market, there can be multiple prices because of disconnections between individuals, and holes in the structure of the market, which leaves some people unaware of the benefits they offer one another. Certain people are connected to certain others, trusting certain others, obligated to support certain others, dependent on exchange with certain others. Assets get locked into suboptimal exchanges. How an individual is positioned in the structure of these exchanges can be an asset in its own right. That asset is social capital, in essence a story about location effects in differentiated markets. The structural hole argument defines social capital in terms of the information and control advantages of being the broker in relations between people otherwise disconnected in social structure. The disconnected people stand on opposite sides of a hole in social structure. The structural hole *is an* opportunity to broker the flow of *information* between people, and *control* the form of projects that bring together people from opposite sides of the hole.

Information benefits. The information benefits are access, timing and referrals. A manager's network provides access to information well beyond what he or she could process alone. It provides that information early, which is an advantage to the manager acting on the information. The network that filters information coming to a manager also directs, concentrates and legitimates information received by others about the manager. Referrals get the manager's interests represented in a positive light, at the right time, in the right places.

The structure of a network indicates the redundancy of its information benefits. There are two network indicators of redundancy. The first is cohesion. Cohesive contacts—contacts strongly connected to each other—are likely to have similar information and therefore provide redundant information benefits. Structural equivalence is the second indicator. Equivalent contacts—contacts who link a manager to the same third parties—have the same sources of information and therefore provide redundant information benefits.

Non-redundant contacts offer information benefits that are additive rather than redundant. Structural holes are the gaps between non-

THE GENDER OF SOCIAL CAPITAL 9

redundant contacts (see Burt 1992, 25–30, on how Granovetter's 1973, weak ties generalize to structural holes). The hole is a buffer, like an insulator in an electric circuit. A structural hole between two clusters in a network need not mean that people in the two clusters are unaware of one another. It simply means that they are so focused on their own activities that they have little time to attend to the activities of people in the other cluster. A structural hole indicates that the people on either side of the hole circulate in different flows of information. A manager who spans the structural hole, by which I mean a manager who has strong relations with contacts on both sides of the hole, has access to both information flows. The more holes spanned, the richer the information benefits of the network.

Figure 1 provides an example. James had a network that spanned one structural hole. The hole is the relatively weak connection between the cluster reached through contacts 1, 2 and 3, and the cluster reached through contacts 4 and 5. Robert took over James's job and expanded the social capital associated with the job. He preserved connection with both clusters in James's network, but expanded the network to a more diverse set of contacts. Robert's network, with the addition of three new clusters of people, spans 10 structural holes.

Information benefits in this example are enhanced in several ways. The volume is higher in Robert's network simply because he reaches

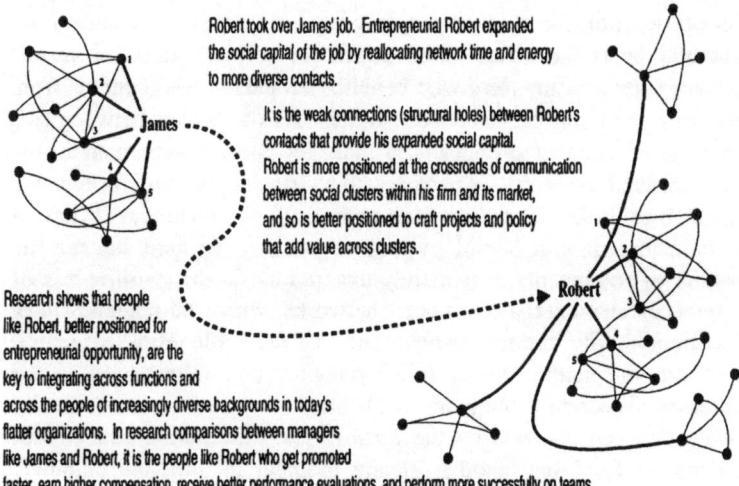

Robert took over James' job. Entrepreneurial Robert expanded the social capital of the job by reallocating network time and energy to more diverse contacts.

It is the weak connections (structural holes) between Robert's contacts that provide his expanded social capital. Robert is more positioned at the crossroads of communication between social clusters within his firm and its market, and so is better positioned to craft projects and policy that add value across clusters.

Research shows that people like Robert, better positioned for entrepreneurial opportunity, are the key to integrating across functions and across the people of increasingly diverse backgrounds in today's flatter organizations. In research comparisons between managers like James and Robert, it is the people like Robert who get promoted faster, earn higher compensation, receive better performance evaluations, and perform more successfully on teams.

Figure 1. The network structure of social capital

more people indirectly. Also, the diversity of his contacts means that the quality of his information benefits is higher. Each cluster of contacts is a single source of information because people connected to one another tend to know the same things at about the same time. Non-redundant clusters provide Robert with a broader information screen, and therefore greater assurance that he will be informed of opportunities and impending disasters (access benefits). Further, since Robert's contacts are only linked through him at the center of the network, he is the first to see new opportunities created by needs in one group that could be served by skills in other group (timing benefits). He stands at the crossroads of social organization. He has the option of bringing together otherwise disconnected individuals where in the network it would be rewarding. And because Robert's contacts are more diverse, he is more likely to be a candidate for inclusion in new opportunities (referral benefits). These benefits are compounded by the fact that having a network that yields such benefits makes Robert more attractive to other people as a contact in their own networks.

Control benefits. The manager who creates a bridge between otherwise disconnected contacts has a say in whose interests are served by the bridge. The disconnected contacts communicate through the manager, giving the manager an opportunity to adjust his or her image with each contact (the structural foundation for managerial robust action, Padgett and Ansell 1993). More, the sociological theories of Simmel and Merton describe the role of people who derive control benefits from structural holes (see Burt 1992, 30–2, for review). It is the *tertius gaudens* (literally 'the third who benefits'), a person who benefits from brokering the connection between others. As the broker between two otherwise disconnected contacts, a manager is an entrepreneur in the literal sense of the word—a person who adds value by standing between others (Burt 1992, 34–6; see Martinelli 1994, for historical review of the term in economic sociology). There is a tension here, but not the hostility of combatants. It is merely uncertainty. In the swirling mix of preferences characteristic of social networks, where no demands have absolute authority, the *tertius* negotiates for favorable terms. Structural holes are the setting for *tertius* strategies, and information is the substance. Accurate, ambiguous or distorted information is strategically moved between contacts by the *tertius*. The information and control benefits reinforce one another at any moment in time and cumulate together over time.

Networks rich in structural holes present opportunities for entrepreneurial behavior. The behaviors by which managers develop these opportunities are many and varied, but the opportunity itself is at all times defined by a hole in the social structure around the manager. In terms of the structural hole argument, networks rich in the entrepreneurial opportunities of structural holes are entrepreneurial networks, and entrepreneurs are people skilled in building the interpersonal bridges that span structural holes.

Predicted Social Capital Effect

Managers with contact networks rich in structural holes know about, have a hand in, and exercise control over, the more rewarding opportunities. They monitor information more effectively than it can be monitored bureaucratically. They move information faster, and to more people, than memos. These entrepreneurial managers know the parameters of organization problems early. They are highly mobile relative to people working through a bureaucracy, easily shifting network time and energy from one solution to another. More in control of their immediate surroundings, entrepreneurial managers tailor solutions to the specific individuals being coordinated, replacing the boiler-plate solutions of formal bureaucracy. There is also the issue of costs; entrepreneurial managers offer inexpensive coordination relative to the bureaucratic alternative. In sum, managers with networks rich in structural holes operate somewhere between the force of corporate authority and the dexterity of markets, building bridges between disconnected parts of the firm where it is valuable to do so. They have more opportunity to add value, are expected to do so, and are accordingly expected to enjoy higher returns to their human capital. The prediction is that in comparisons between otherwise similar people like James and Robert in Figure 1, it is people like Robert who should be more successful.[1]

The social capital difference between James and Robert can be measured by the relative extent to which their contact networks are constrained. Network constraint C is an index, computed from the structure of relations around a person, that varies from 0 toward 100 with the extent to which the person's relations are directly or indirectly concentrated in a single contact (see Appendix for detailed discussion). Constraint is lower in large networks. It is higher in dense or hierarchical networks. The range of network constraint scores across the sample managers to be discussed is illustrated by the 20 to 54 difference between Robert and James, respectively, in Figure 1.

Evidence of the Predicted Social Capital Effect

Three lines of empirical evidence emerged in sociology during the 1970s to support the argument that structural holes are a competitive advantage. First, laboratory experiments have been used to show that resources distributed through a small-group exchange network accumulate in people with exclusive exchange relations to otherwise disconnected partners (e.g. Cook and Emerson 1978; Cook et al. 1983; Markovsky et al. 1988). Second, census data have been used to describe how producer profit margins increase with structural holes in the producer network of transactions with suppliers and customers. Burt (1983) describes the association in 1967 with profits in American manufacturing markets defined at broad and detailed levels of aggregation, and extended the results into non-manufacturing through the 1960s and 1970s (Burt 1988, 1992). Burt et al. (1996) extend the results through the 1980s. Using profit and network data on markets in other countries, similar results have been found in Germany during the 1970s and 1980s (Ziegler 1982; Burt and Freeman 1994), Israel during the 1970s (Talmud 1992, 1994), Japan in the 1980s (Yasuda 1993), and Korea in the 1980s (Jang 1997).

Third, and most relevant to the evidence to be presented here, survey data have been used to describe the career advantages of having a contact network rich in structural holes. The earliest and most widely known is Granovetter's (1973, 1974) demonstration that white-collar workers find better jobs, faster, through weak ties that bridge otherwise disconnected social groups. Lin worked with several colleagues to present evidence of the importance of ties to distant contacts for obtaining more desirable jobs (e.g. Lin et al. 1981; Lin and Dumin 1986; Lin 1998). Similar empirical results appear in Campbell et al. (1986), Marsden and Hurlbert (1988), and Flap and De Graaf (1989). Moving to the top of organizations, Burt (1992, 1997a, b), Burt et al. (1997) and Podolny and Baron (1997) present survey evidence from probability samples of managers. Senior managers with networks richer in structural holes are more likely to get promoted early, receive more positive job evaluations, and take home higher compensation.

Working with more limited data, Gabbay (1997) shows how promotions occur more quickly for sales people with strong-tie access to structural holes (cf. Meyerson, 1994, on manager income as a function of strong ties; Pennings et al. 1997, on accounting firm survival as a function of strong partner ties to client sectors), and Sparrowe and Popielarz (1995) innovatively reconstruct past networks around managers to estimate an event-history model of how structural holes in yesterday's network affect the likelihood of promotion today. The benefits that accrue to individuals aggregate to the management teams on which they serve. Studying quality management teams in several midwest manufacturing plants, Rosenthal (1996) shows that the teams composed of employees with more entrepreneurial networks are significantly more likely to be recognized for their success in improving the quality of plant operations (cf. Krackhardt and Stern 1988, on higher group performance with cross-group friendships between students; Ancona and Coldwell 1992, on team success as a function of the teams external network; Fernandez and Gould 1994, on organizations in broker positions within the national health policy arena being perceived as more influential).[2]

These results are consistent with Coleman's (1988, 1990) use of a network metaphor to motivate his social capital explanation of why certain children perform better in school. Children perform better if they have a constrained network in which friends, teachers and parents are all strongly connected to one another. The imagery is the same as in structural hole theory, a small network of interlocked relations constrains action. Constraint from parents and teachers has positive long-term consequences for children, forcing them to focus on their education (cf. Hirschi 1972, on the negative consequences of network constraint from delinquent friends). However, at some point on the way to becoming an adult, the child shaped by the environment becomes responsible for shaping the environment. Constraint, positive for children, is detrimental to adults, particularly adults charged with managerial tasks at the top of their firm (see Portes and Landolt 1996, for more diverse examples).

Women Pose a Puzzle

Figure 2 contains illustrative evidence of the predicted social capital effect and evidence on women that seems to contradict the predicted effect. I have network, background and performance data on senior managers with one of the largest American firms in electronic components and computing equipment. The respondents are a probability sample of the more than 3000 people just below the rank of vice-president (the firm employs more than 100,000 employees). The managers are all employed in the same firm, but their firm is the size of a small city, scattered across separate parts of the country, and diverse corporate functions (sales, service, manufacturing, information systems, engineering, marketing, finance and human resources). Company personnel records on all managers in the study population were combined with survey network data on a representative sample of 284 managers who completed survey questionnaires for the study in the fall of 1989 (Burt 1992, 118–26).

The horizontal axis in Figure 2 is a network constraint measuring the

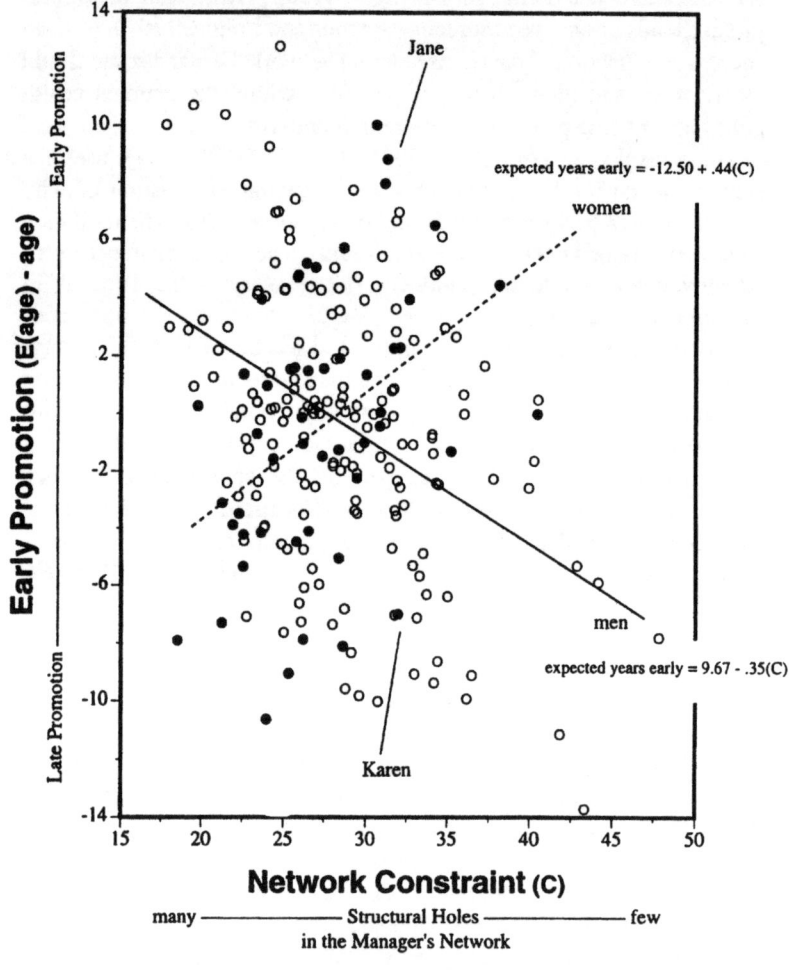

Men (o ; *r* = -.40, *t* = -5.4, *p* < .001)   Women (• ; *r* = .42, *t* = 3.1, *p* = .001)
All Displayed Managers (*r* = -.23, *t* = -3.4, *p* < .001)

Figure 2. Gender difference in social capital effect

lack of social capital. Each manager described his or her network of key contacts within and beyond the firm: (i) Contacts were identified with nine name-generator questions on diverse kinds of relations such as informal discussion and socializing, political support, critical sources of buy-in for projects, authority relations to supervisor and promising subordinates, and so on. (ii) Relations with and between contacts were distinguished by name-interpreter questions into four categories of emotional closeness and a correspondence model was used to scale the categories from zero (distant or total strangers) to one (especially close). Some managers have sparse networks of disconnected contacts (minimum density is .07). Others have dense networks of interconnected contacts (.82 maximum density). On average, the manager networks are as dense as observed in other studies (e.g. .47 average density across the managers, versus .42 average density for Americans with more than a high school education in the 1985 General Social Survey of Americans). Managers with networks rich in structural holes—like Robert in Figure 1—have low-constraint networks and so appear to the left of the graph in Figure 2. Managers like James in Figure 1 are at the other extreme, to the right of the graph.

The vertical axis in Figure 2 is early promotion. Financial compensation in this study population is too closely tied to job rank to measure the relative success of individual managers. Time to rank provides a criterion variable. Whether promoted internally or hired from the outside, people promoted to senior rank in large organizations have several years of experience preceding their promotion. For reasons of competence and legitimacy, a certain amount of time must pass before people are ready for promotion to senior rank (see Merton's 1984, theoretical analysis of the socially expected duration associated with time in a role, entry to the role, and exit; Burt 1992, 196–7, on using socially expected durations to measure competitive success). How much time, is an empirical question the answer to which differs between individual managers.

To identify early-promotion factors in the population, I predicted age at promotion to current rank from the kind of work a manager does (rank, function and plant location) and personal background (education, race, gender and seniority; see Burt 1992, 126–31, for details). The human-capital diversity question is whether women or minorities wait longer for their promotions. There are no level or slope differences between white and non-white managers. There is a significant level difference between men and women, reflecting efforts to bring women into the senior ranks. The average woman promoted to these ranks is

3 years younger than a comparable man.[3] Women arrive at their senior ranks significantly earlier than comparable men. The point of the results to be presented is that the women arrive by a very different route.

Residuals from the regression prediction are the vertical axis in Figure 2. The residuals distinguish managers by how early they were promoted relative to their peers. Expected age at promotion, E(age), is the average age at which a manager with a specific personal background (education, race, gender and seniority) is promoted to a specific rank within a specific function (rank, function and plant location). Early promotion is the difference between when a manager was promoted to his or her current rank and a human capital baseline model predicting the age at which similar managers are promoted to the same rank to do the same work; E(age) −age. A score of −5.5, for example, indicates a manager promoted 5.5 years behind similar managers promoted to the same job. Managers promoted earlier than expected are at the top of the graph in Figure 2. Managers promoted late are at the bottom.[4]

Gender Difference in Returns to Social Capital

The graph includes senior men (hollow dots) and their female colleagues (solid dots). The aggregate association between early promotion and network constraint is clearly negative (−3.4 t-test), but it is a compound of two very different effects.

Early promotion for the men has the expected negative correlation with constraint (−5.4 t-test). Early promotions in Figure 2 go to senior men with more social capital, i.e. to the men with the entrepreneurial networks rich in the information and control benefits of structural holes. Constraint varies in the graph from 17 to 48 points around a mean of 28. The −.35 slope for men in the graph means that each point of additional constraint is associated with an average promotion delay of 4 months (−5.4 t-test, $p < .001$).

The reverse is true for women (3.1 t-test). Trace the slopes for men and women back to the hypothetical case of a manager whose contacts are so scattered that he or she has zero network constraint. Such a manager, if a man, would reach senior rank 10 years early (9.67 regression intercept). The same manager, if a woman, would be 12.5 years late (−12.50 intercept). The implication, contrary to the predicted social capital effect, is that women do better with a small network of interconnected contacts.

THE GENDER OF SOCIAL CAPITAL 17

Consistent Gender Difference

The first question is whether the gender difference is real. Graphs in Figure 3 show a consistent gender difference across different kinds of

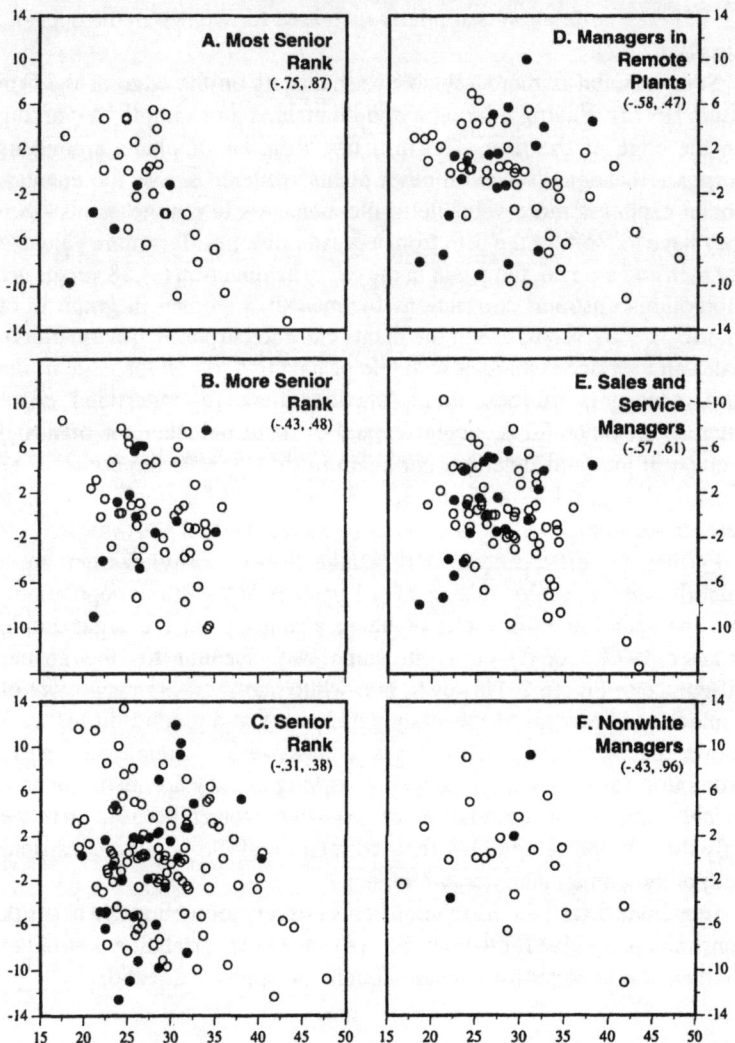

Figure 3. Gender difference is consistent
(same axes as in Figure 2, solid dots are women, correlation is listed for men then women)

managers. Graphs A, B and C show the consistent difference across job ranks. At the senior rank, early promotion has a negative correlation with network constraint for men, positive for women ($-.31$ versus $.38$). At the most senior rank in the study population, the greater value of social capital is indicated by the increased negative correlation for men ($-.75$). The correlation is similarly increased for women in the opposite direction ($.87$).

Social capital is more valuable to managers on the edge of the firm (Burt 1997a). Having a job at a remote plant is an example of working on the edge of the firm. The firm has a cluster of plants around its corporate headquarters, with other plants scattered across the country. Social capital is more valuable to the managers in remote plants since they have to monitor the firm from a greater distance. It is more valuable for men and women, but again in the opposite direction ($-.58$ versus $.47$ promotion-constraint correlations for men than women in graph D of Figure 3; $-.32$ versus $.38$ in the plants close to corporate headquarters). Sales and service is another example of having a job on the edge of the firm. Managers in these field functions have to understand client interests in other firms. Social capital is more valuable for men and women in the field function, but again in the opposite direction ($-.57$ versus $.61$ in graph E of Figure 3; $-.32$ versus $.38$ for employees not in sales or service).

Further, the difference is more gender than minority. Women are a minority among senior managers (14 percent of the study population), and the social complications of being a minority in the organization (Kanter 1977, 206 ff) could in some way account for the gender difference in Figure 2. However, non-white managers are even more of a minority (8 percent of the study population), and graph F in Figure 3 shows that network constraint has a negative association with early promotion for non-white managers—as long as they are men. I cannot reliably estimate the correlation for non-white women because there are only three in the sample, but their correlation of $.96$ is more consistent with other women than non-white men.

I conclude that (i) the correlation between early promotion and network constraint is positive for women, and (ii) where the correlation is stronger for men, it is stronger for women—but in the opposite direction.

Three Reasons Why Women Should Be Different

There are arguments with which one could make sense of the gender difference (Milkman and Townsley 1994, provide general review). I discuss three popular lines of argument to show how the arguments do not account for the gender difference in this population.

Social support. One line of argument focuses on emotional differences between men and women. Where men are drawn to the rough and tumble of an entrepreneurial network, women are argued to be more comfortable in a small circle of supportive mutual friends. People perform better where they are more comfortable. Therefore, men can thrive in an entrepreneurial network and women do better with clique networks.[5] The women in Figure 2 hold senior corporate positions, so they could be argued to have risen above emotional differences that elsewhere distinguish men from women. But if there is a preference for cliques, I should see women more often in cliques. In fact, the senior women have no tendency to build more dense networks (0.2 *t*-test), and a significant tendency to build larger networks (2.4 *t*-test)—which means less, not more, constrained networks than men (−2.0 *t*-test).[6] In other words, the women have no less access than men to the information and control benefits of structural holes that advance men's careers (cf. Ibarra 1997). They differ in how the firm reacts to their access.

Pink collar jobs. A second line of argument focuses on how women are treated. Women end up in 'pink collar' jobs, low-opportunity jobs are more often held by women. This is a rich literature in sociology. An exemplar is Baron and Bielby's work showing women concentrated in certain kinds of less attractive jobs (e.g. Baron and Bielby 1985; Baron et al. 1986; Bielby and Baron 1986; cf. Cohen et al. 1995).

Of course, averages across all jobs in a large organization need not describe jobs at the top. The sample women in this study population are randomly scattered across ranks (4.33 chi-square, 3 d.f., $p = .23$), corporate functions (10.86 chi-square, 10 d.f., $p = .15$), and 29 combinations of rank and function (32.63 chi-square, 28 d.f., $p = .25$).[7] It would be difficult to explain the Figure 2 difference between men and women with an argument about women working in jobs different from those in which men work.

Moreover, there is no gender difference in the constraint of the corporate authority networks that define their jobs. To study social capital and network content following Podolny and Baron (1997), I computed constraint from different kinds of relations (Burt 1997c). The managers in this firm describe a behavioral distinction between their personal discussion relations (confiding, socializing, career advice) and the corporate authority relations that define their jobs (supervisor and essential sources of buy-in). The tendency reported previously for women to have less constrained networks is only true of personal discussion networks. Men and women in these senior ranks are no differently constrained in their networks of authority relations (0.5 *t*-test), and are no different in the irrelevance of that constraint to early promotion (1.4 *t*-test for slope difference between women and senior men).

Combat-birth metaphor. A third line of argument focuses on women reacting to how they are treated. Women with dense networks of female colleagues have a competitive advantage in breaking through the 'glass ceiling' into the senior ranks. Such women can better look out for one another's interests—speaking up for one another in the other's absence, and informing one another of developing opportunities.[8] The sample women do include a higher proportion of other women among their key contacts (9.2 *t*-test; see Kanter 1977; Brass 1985, Ibarra 1992 for similar evidence). Excluding spouses, 31 percent of the average woman's network is other women—45 percent of her personal discussion network (cf. McPherson and Smith-Lovin 1987, on induced versus choice homophily). Men cite women more in proportion to the population. Women are 14 percent of the study population and 13 percent of the average man's contacts (13 percent of all non-kin contacts, 13 percent of personal discussion non-kin contacts).

However, preference for female contacts does not explain the gender difference in Figure 2. Two reasons: First, there is no tendency for women citing a higher proportion of other women to have more constrained networks (0.1 *t*-test). Women in constrained and unconstrained networks equally prefer other women as contacts. It is men who show an effect of gender preference. Men in constrained networks include significantly fewer women among their contacts (-2.7 *t*-test). Second, early promotion has no association with a preference for women. Women with constrained networks tend to be promoted early (3.1 *t*-test in Figure 2). The prediction is unaffected by the extent to which the woman includes other women among her contacts (3.0 *t*-test for network constraint, -0.2 *t*-test for proportion women in her network). Senior men with constrained networks tend to be promoted late (-5.4 *t*-test in Figure 3). This prediction too is unaffected by the extent to which the man includes women among his contacts (-5.2 *t*-test for constraint, 0.9 *t*-test for proportion women in his network).

From Gender to Legitimacy and Borrowed Social Capital

I solved the gender puzzle by looking more closely at the networks around the women. What I found is illustrated in Figure 4 with a comparison between two of the women, Jane and Karen (pseudonyms). To make their network differences more obvious, neither woman is included in the sociogram of her network. If you turn back to Figure 2 you can see Jane and Karen indicated one above the other in the data. Network constraint is similar for them, so they are at about the same point on the horizontal axis of Figure 2. They are very different on the vertical axis. The two women hold the same rank in the firm, but Jane was promoted 9 years earlier than other women in her line of work with the same personal background. Karen was promoted 7 years late. I am looking for something in their networks to explain the promotion difference. Aggregate constraint is the same for both women. The component variables in network constraint are displayed in Figure 4. The explanation is not size. Jane's eight contacts are similar to Karen's nine. The explanation is not density. The average strength of relation between contacts is .36 in both networks.

Hierarchy Indicates Borrowed Social Capital

The difference is hierarchy. A network is hierarchical to the extent that links between contacts are indirect through a central person (other than the manager him or herself). Measurement details are given in the Appendix (Figure 9 is a quick reference). Jane's network is hierarchical because so many of her contacts are connected through Sam (a pseudonym). Sam has especially close ties with all but two of Jane's contacts, and close ties with the remaining two. More, there would be few relations between contacts if Sam were removed from the network. In contrast, Karen's contacts are connected directly. With respect to hierarchy in the networks of the other sample managers, Jane's network is two standard deviations above average. Karen's is three standard deviations below average.

I also know something about the contacts in each network. I know from Karen's network questionnaire that her network is concentrated in her immediate work group. Her boss, contact 5, is the most central contact in her network. He has especially close relations with three of the four other contacts, and close relations with another four. Contacts 3, 4, 6, 7, 8 and 9 are all other people who work with Karen under her boss.

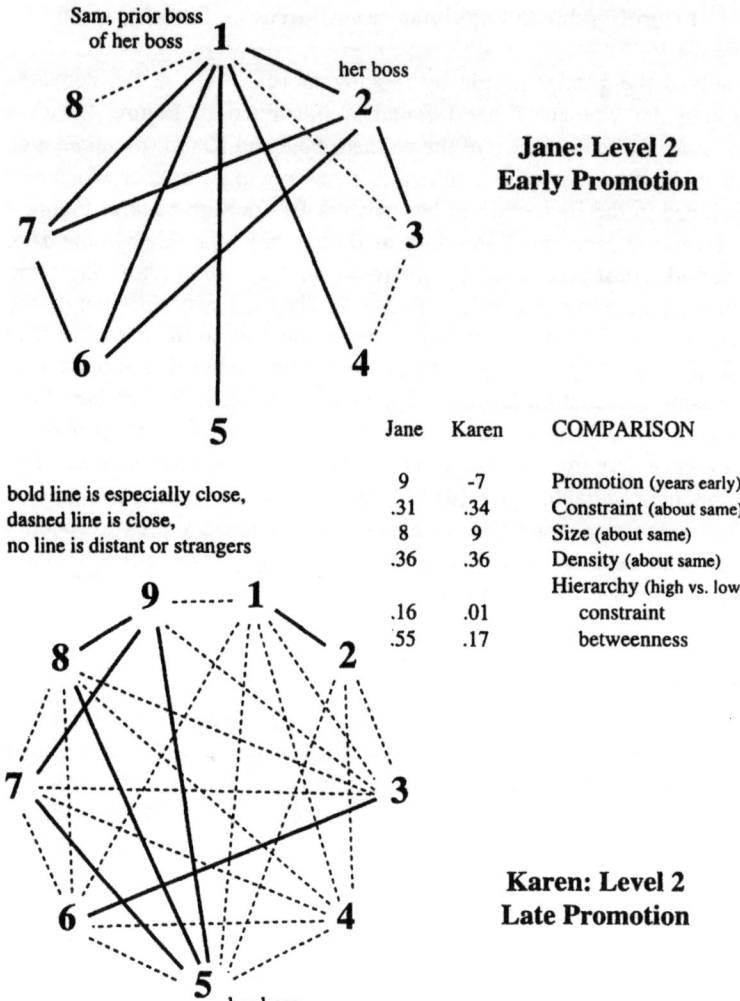

bold line is especially close,
dasned line is close,
no line is distant or strangers

Figure 4. Discovering hierarchy

	Jane	Karen	COMPARISON
	9	-7	Promotion (years early)
	.31	.34	Constraint (about same)
	8	9	Size (about same)
	.36	.36	Density (about same)
			Hierarchy (high vs. low)
	.16	.01	constraint
	.55	.17	betweenness

Jane's network has a broader reach. From her questionnaire, I know that only two of her eight contacts are from her work group; contact 3 and her boss, contact 2. Jane's other ties are essential sources of buy-in beyond her group (contacts 1, 4, 5 and 6), and people further removed who Jane cites as valuable sources of support and advice. The key to this network is understanding Sam's role in it. Sam is Jane's sponsor in the

THE GENDER OF SOCIAL CAPITAL   23

organization.[9] Jane's boss maintained a strong relation with his prior boss, Sam. On her boss's recommendation, Jane represented her group in a project under Sam's direction. Sam was impressed with Jane and took her under his wing, brokering introductions to other senior managers. Senior managers dealing with Jane felt that they were dealing indirectly with Sam, which greatly simplified Jane's work with them.

The hierarchy in Jane's network indicates borrowed social capital. The point is illustrated in Figure 5. At the top of Figure 5 is the dyad between a new manager and a sponsor. The sponsor's network,

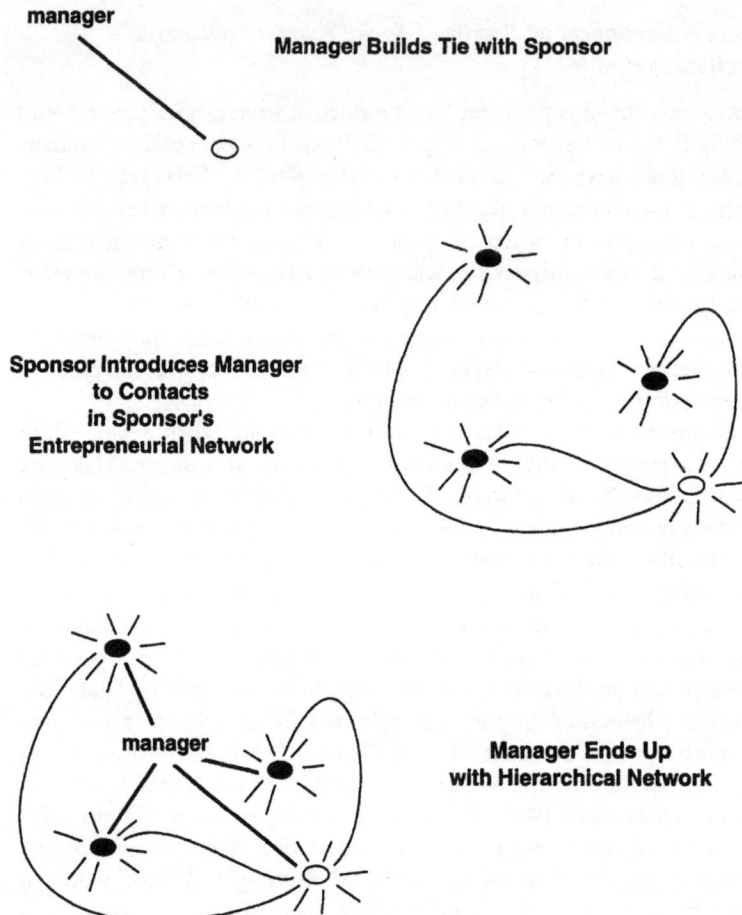

Figure 5. Hierarchical network indicates a borrowed entrepreneurial network

displayed in the middle of Figure 5, is composed of strong ties to disconnected contacts. In other words, the sponsor has social capital in the form of an entrepreneurial network rich in structural holes. When the sponsor introduces the manager to his key contacts at the bottom of Figure 5, the manager ends up with a hierarchical network. The same would not be true if the sponsor had a clique network (connect the three contacts in the middle sociogram). Introducing the manager to the sponsor's already connected contacts would only expand the clique to one more member. Everyone is before and after connected to everyone else.

Success Contingent on Borrowed Social Capital Indicates a Legitimacy Problem

Borrowing social capital can be a productive strategy (Raider and Burt 1996). Every manager needs a sponsor at one time or another. Company leaders don't have time to check into the credibility of everyone making a bid for broader responsibilities. They are looking for fast, reliable cues about managers on whom they do not already have information. A manager deemed suspect for whatever reason—a new hire, someone just transferred from another country, a new addition to a cohesive group—needs an established insider to provide the cues, sponsoring the manager as a legitimate player to open the mind of a contact not ready to listen seriously to the manager's proposal.

Borrowed social capital is especially obvious when relationships cross corporate or cultural boundaries. It is official in Japan. There are industry-specific directories of people available to help outsiders develop relations with Japanese firms.[10] The people in these directories are usually retired corporate executives who prefer the active life of consulting to life in a window seat. These people bring no technical skills, for they were too long at the top to know the technical details of their industry. They bring connections. Without the proper personal connections, outsiders don't do business in Japan. Corning Glass is a concrete illustration. Corning has a history of joint ventures that give Corning access to a market where the partner firm is established. Nanda and Bartlett (1990) offer illustrative examples in the United States and Europe (see Gulati 1995, for more systematic evidence of third-party effects on alliances), but I particularly enjoy their quote from a Corning executive commenting on the result of Corning's alliance with the Japanese firm Asahi (Nanda and Bartlett 1990, 14):

> When our salespeople began calling on the Japanese TV set manufacturers, we felt

as if a veil came over them when they dealt with us. Their relationships with their Japanese suppliers ran very deep, while they were very distant with us. Last week, Asahi people escorted me to a meeting with the worldwide TV tube manager of a large Japanese company and introduced me properly to him. We had extremely fruitful conversation. I wouldn't have even been able to meet him and discuss issues between us if it were not for the Asahi connection.

It is one thing to occasionally borrow social capital to succeed in a new venture. It is another to have to borrow social capital for all your ventures. If borrowing social capital is a strategy through which suspect outsiders (however suspect outsiders are defined in a study population) get access to the benefits of social capital, then a category of people for whom success depends on borrowing social capital is a category of people deemed suspect.

The women in Figure 2 seem to be just such a category of people. Jane and Karen illustrate a systematic pattern. Promotions come earlier to women with more hierarchical networks (2.6 t-test, $p = .01$), which means that promotions come earlier to women who borrow social capital.

Combine that point with the results in Figures 2 and 3. There are two strategies for building social capital. The direct strategy is to build your own social capital by establishing strong ties to disconnected groups in the firm and beyond. The results in Figures 2 and Figure 3 show that building your own is not a productive strategy for women in this organization. Women who have entrepreneurial networks are promoted late. The alternative strategy is to borrow the social capital of someone, a sponsoring strategic partner, already connected to disconnected groups in the firm and beyond. This is the route by which women in this firm get promoted. The fact that women fall behind when they build their own social capital, and move ahead when they borrow social capital, implies that they have a legitimacy problem in this firm.

My interpretation of that implication is that the gender difference in Figure 2 is not a difference between men and women in particular so much as it is a generic difference between insiders and outsiders—where the insider–outsider distinction is, in this study population, correlated with gender. Here are four points to support my interpretation:

Hierarchy versus size and density. Hierarchy—indicating borrowed social capital—is alone responsible for the positive association across women between network constraint and early promotion. The results in Table 1 separate network size, density and hierarchy components in the social capital effect for the senior men and women in Figure 2.

Table 1. Components in the social capital effect

	Senior men		Women			100 Least legitimate		Women and Entry-Rank Men		
Multiple correlation:	.40	.49	.42	.46	.37	.72	.41	.22	.37	.28
Intercept	9.67	2.35	−12.50	−.98	3.98	−9.39	7.21	−6.34	−2.45	1.67
Network constraint (C)	−.35 [−.40] (−5.4)	—	.44 [.42] (3.21)	—	—	—	—	.20 [.22] (2.3)	—	—
Network size (number of contacts)	—	.48 [.27] (3.8)	—	−.43 [−.18] (−1.4)	−.55 [−.23] (−1.6)	.27 [.13] (1.5)	−.20 [−.10] (−1.0)	—	−.27 [−.14] (−1.5)	−.30 [−.15] (−1.6)
Network density (average tie between contacts)	—	−.21 [−.43] (−5.7)	—	.10 [.21] (1.6)	−.01 [−.02] (−0.1)	.01 [.01] (0.1)	−.22 [−.44] (−4.1)	—	.08 [.17] (1.8)	−.00 [−.01] (−0.1)
Network hierarchy (Constraint from many concentrated in one contact)	—	−.21 [−.23] (−3.0)	—	.37 [.35] (2.6)		.69 [.80] (7.9)		—	.34 [.30] (3.2)	
Betweenness concentrated in one contact	—				.13 [.25] (1.7)		.11 [.24] (2.2)			.10 [.23] (1.9)

Note: These are ordinary least-squares estimates of row variables predicting early promotion. Standardized estimates appear in [brackets] and routine *t*-tests appear in (parentheses). The row variables are described in the Appendix.

The aggregate negative correlation for senior men between early promotion and network constraint is a composite of effects consistent with direct access to social capital: Larger networks are associated with early promotion (3.8 *t*-test). Less dense networks are associated with early promotion (−5.7 *t*-test). Less hierarchical networks are associated with early promotion (−3.0).

The aggregate positive correlation for women is the effect of only one constraint component; hierarchy. The women promoted early with constrained networks in Figure 2 were not promoted because they focused their attention on a small number of contacts (negligible −1.4 *t*-test for network size in Table 1), nor because they built dense networks of interconnected contacts (negligible 1.6 *t*-test for network density in Table 1). It is because they have more hierarchical networks (2.6 *t*-test for network hierarchy in Table 1, $p = .01$).

Size-sensitive hierarchy. Second, the hierarchy effect is stronger with hierarchy measures that reflect the volume of social capital borrowed. Betweenness hierarchy measures the extent to which there exists one contact who brokers connections between other contacts in a network. Betweenness does not vary with the number of brokered connections (see Figure 9 in the Appendix; betweenness hierarchy is 100 in all three hierarchical networks, regardless of network size). In contrast, constraint hierarchy increases linearly with the size of a hierarchical network. In other words, betweenness hierarchy measures the extent to which a manager has borrowed social capital, while constraint hierarchy measure the volume of structural holes in the borrowed social capital. The results in Table 1 show stronger early promotion associations with constraint hierarchy; i.e. early promotion is more likely with borrowed richer in structural holes.

Sponsor legitimacy. The third bit of supporting evidence concerns the source of borrowed capital. Analysis elsewhere shows that the boss makes a poor sponsor (Burt 1992, Ch. 4). Supervisors are expected to sponsor their subordinates. What they say about their subordinates reflects on their own work. Competent bosses usually say positive things about their subordinates. Having a more distant strategic partner means that there are two people in different places sponsoring the manager when new opportunities arise. This adds a corroborating external voice to the boss's sponsorship. The strategic partner around whom the hierarchical network is built has to be sufficiently close to sponsor the manager, but sufficiently distant to lie untarnished by day-to-day arguments, and speak with an authoritative voice of ostensible objectivity.

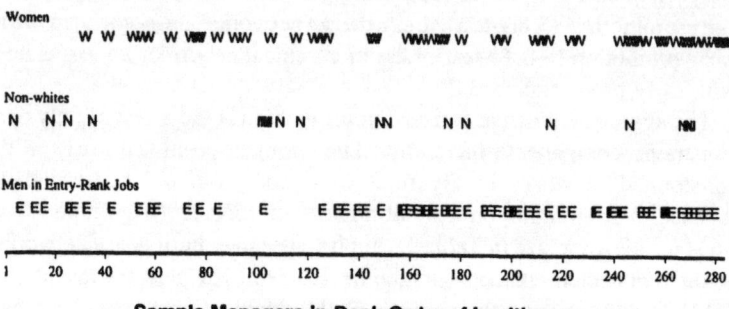

	Mean Rank		Rank ($p = .01$; $< .001$ for entry rank)	
			Most Senior	94
All	143		More Senior	116
			Senior	131
Education ($p = .54$)			Entry	172
College or less	132			
Graduate	145		**Function** ($p = .86$)	
			Sales	136
Race ($p = .54$)			Service	145
White	143		Manufacturing	161
Nonwhite	141		Engineering	134
			Marketing	145
Sex ($p < .001$)			MIS	128
Men	135		Finance	146
Women	177		Human Resources	130
Seniority ($p = .12$)			**Plant Location** ($p = .55$)	
Recent hire	139		Core	146
Long with the firm	146		Remote	134

Figure 6. Detecting diversity problems

Illegitimate men. Fourth, the pattern of effects suggesting that women face a legitimacy problem in the firm also occur for a category of men who are more obviously suspect as senior managers.

There is a two-step network test for diversity problems. First, rank managers by their legitimacy, where legitimacy can be measured by the extent to which their success does not depend on borrowed social capital.[11] The 284 respondent managers are ranked on the horizontal axis of Figure 6. The managers to the left are people for whom early promotion is primarily associated with having a large network of disconnected contacts. Hierarchy is just another form of network constraint. Managers to the right of Figure 6 are the people for whom early promotion is associated with having a large hierarchical network organized around a central contact. For these managers, hierarchy is a competitive advantage indicating that they have indirect access to social capital through a central contact. Table 1 contains estimates of social capital effects for the managers in ranks 185 through 284 (the 100 least legitimate managers in the sample). Early promotion is dramatically dependent on hierarchy (7.9 t-test, $p < .001$).

The second step is to look for kinds of managers that are as a group low in the legitimacy rank order. I tested for differences between numerous categories of managers, but found significant differences for only two; women and entry-rank men. Mean ranks are reported at the bottom of Figure 6 for the categories of managers used to define strata in the sampling frame. I tested for differences on two variables: position in the legitimacy rank-order, and the legitimacy measure on which the rank-order is based. Only women and entry-rank men stand out as categories significantly different in legitimacy from other managers.

The gender difference at the bottom of Figure 6 tells me something that I already know; namely, women have less legitimacy than men in this study population. The average man is at rank 135 among the 284 sample managers. The average woman is significantly lower at rank 177.

The other significant distinction is job level. The highest legitimacy scores on average are for men in the most senior jobs. However, they are not significantly higher than other managers (1.1 t-test). The men who stand apart are in the lowest level of this study population; men who have just entered the population of senior managers. Their average rank in the legitimacy rank-order is 172, significantly lower than other managers (4.5 t-test, $p < .001$). Up to this point in the paper, I have not included entry-rank men in the regression equations predicting early promotion because they are so clearly distinct from other senior men. Adding them to the women in Table 1 yields an even more significant association between early promotion and network hierarchy (see the last three columns in Table 1).

This is an important point because it means that the gender difference in Figure 2 and Figure 3 extends beyond women to at least one category of men. Entry-rank men are the new arrivals to the senior manager population (akin to assistant professors just hired from graduate school). They are senior managers in the firm, but they have only just entered senior management. They have to establish their legitimacy as members of the senior management. Similar stories can be told about other groups. Non-whites are an obvious minority within the firm, and have a historical claim to not being accepted at the top of the white establishment. However, the structural analysis shows no significant legitimacy difference between white and non-white managers in this population. It is women and youngsters who are deemed suspect.

Not all women and entry-rank men are illegitimate. Three categories of minority managers are distinguished at the top of Figure 6; non-whites, women and entry-rank men. Each N in the graph at the top of Figure 6 marks a rank held by one of the non-white managers. There is no significant legitimacy difference between white and non-white managers because non-white managers are so widely spread across the rank order. Some are at the top of the rank order, others are at the bottom. Each W marks a rank held by a woman and each E marks a rank held by a man in an entry-rank job. The Ws and Es are concentrated at the bottom of the rank order, as indicated by the averages for women and entry-rank men at the bottom of Figure 6. But look at the spread of Ws and Es across the whole rank order. The Ws and Es to the left of the graph are women and entry-rank men who are accepted as legitimate players—in the sense that their odds of early promotion increase with the extent to which they have their own entrepreneurial network.

Conclusion: Network Forms of Social Capital

In conclusion, the network form of social capital varies with legitimacy. Key distinctions are illustrated in Figure 7. Providing security but no access to structural holes, a network untended degenerates into a clique—an interconnected set of mutual friends. The information and control benefits of structural holes that constitute social capital lie in two directions away from a clique. One direction is for a manager to *build* his or her own social capital with strong ties to otherwise disconnected groups. This leads to the entrepreneurial network in Figure 7, associated with more successful senior men in this chapter's study population. Senior men compete through entrepreneurial networks for direct access to the information and control benefits of structural holes. Anything less than the direct access of an entrepreneurial network is associated with less successful senior men. The alternative is to *borrow* the social capital of an established manager who has strong ties to otherwise disconnected groups. This leads to the hierarchical network in Figure 7, associated with more successful women and entry-rank men in this chapter's study population.

Figure 8 contains summary evidence for the distinctions in Figure 7. The top graph shows that senior men, women and entry-rank men have

THE GENDER OF SOCIAL CAPITAL 31

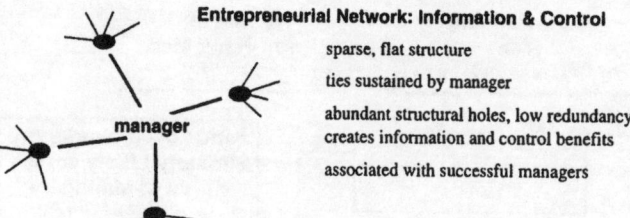

Entrepreneurial Network: Information & Control

sparse, flat structure

ties sustained by manager

abundant structural holes, low redundancy, creates information and control benefits

associated with successful managers

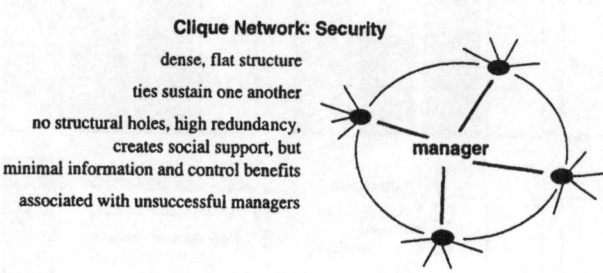

Clique Network: Security

dense, flat structure

ties sustain one another

no structural holes, high redundancy, creates social support, but minimal information and control benefits

associated with unsuccessful managers

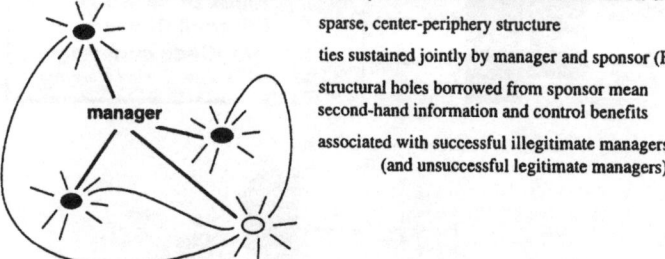

Hierarchical Network: Sponsored Access to Information & Control

sparse, center-periphery structure

ties sustained jointly by manager and sponsor (Fig. 5)

structural holes borrowed from sponsor mean second-hand information and control benefits

associated with successful illegitimate managers (and unsuccessful legitimate managers)

Figure 7. Network forms of social capital

the same kinds of networks in the study population. I divided the manager networks into four kinds. Flat structures (constraint hierarchy below average) are distinguished from hierarchical structures (average or higher constraint hierarchy). Flat structures are divided into entrepreneurial networks (constraint below average) versus clique networks (average or higher constraint). Hierarchical structures are divided into those in which the boss is the central contact versus others.[12] Managers in this firm are encouraged to 'network'. Entrepreneurial networks are the mode in Figure 8, and the distribution of networks among senior men is the same among women and entry-rank men. In fact, kinds of

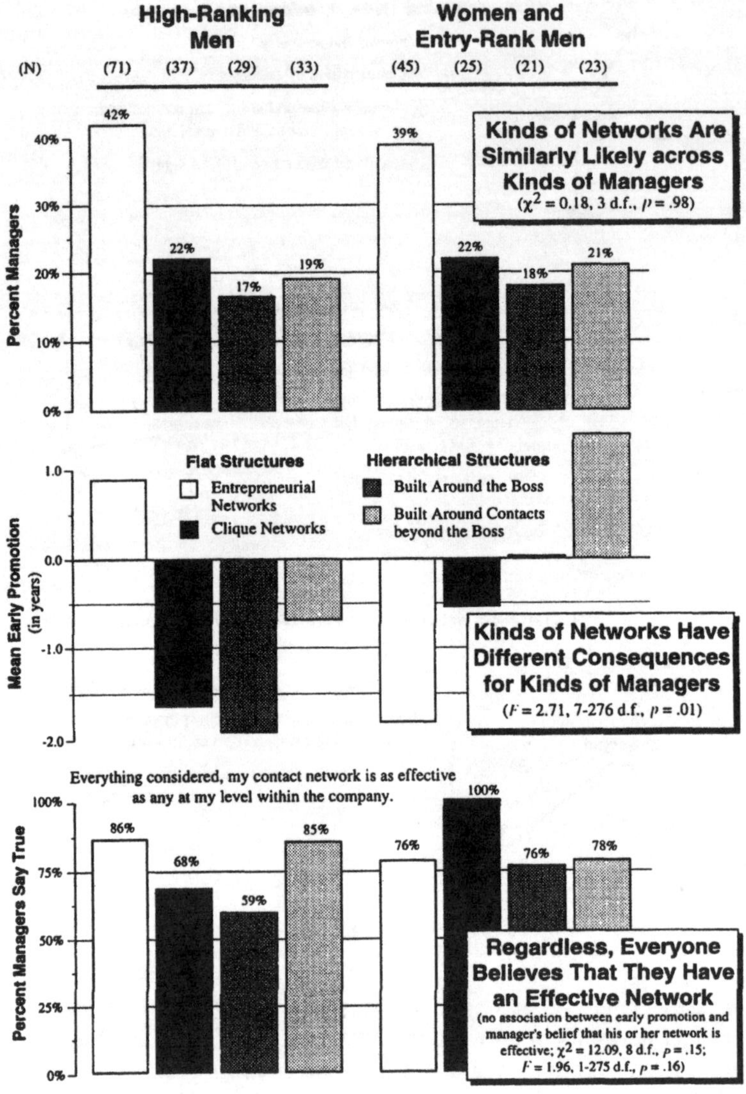

Figure 8.

networks occur in similar proportions among every kind of manager within the firm.[13] This is an important point for observers who claim that certain kinds of people tend to build certain kinds of networks (e.g. women build cliques, men build entrepreneurial networks). Figure 8 shows that women and entry-rank men build the same networks built by senior men.

What is different between managers is what happens to them as a consequence of their network. In the middle of Figure 8, entrepreneurial networks are the only form associated with early promotion for senior men. Promotions come late to senior men in cliques, or worse, senior men whose contacts are borrowed from their boss. At the other end of the legitimacy continuum, entrepreneurial networks are the worst choice for women and entry-rank men looking for early promotion. Promotions come significantly late when they build their own entrepreneurial network.

What began as an empirical puzzle for the structural hole argument, is resolved as richer empirical support. The difference between entrepreneurial and hierarchical networks is further empirical support for the central premise of the argument; namely, social capital is a matter of access to the information and control benefits of structural holes. Women and entry-rank men are exceptions that prove the rule. They do not have equal access to the benefits of social capital, but the network conditions that benefit their careers indirectly are the same network conditions that directly benefit the careers of senior men. The positive correlation between early promotion and network constraint for women and entry-rank men is a reduced-form coefficient. It is the combination of a strong relation to a sponsor and the entrepreneurial network of the sponsor. The two combine to define a hierarchical network around the manager, and it is access to the sponsor's entrepreneurial network that is associated with early promotion. A strong relation to a sponsor with a clique network does not lead to early promotion. The fact that hierarchy, not density, is associated with the success of women and entry-rank men means that borrowing is only as valuable as the network you borrow. Whether a manager has direct access to structural holes, or indirect access through the borrowed network of an entrepreneur, he or she has social capital to the extent that he or she has access (direct or indirect) to structural holes.

Optimum Networks

There is a practical implication for individuals: Pick a network for what it can do, not for the kind of people who pick it. The managers studied here seem oblivious to the value of their networks. The third panel in Figure 8 shows the percentage of managers in each category who said that 'their network was as effective as any at my level within the company'. The negligible test statistics in the figure show no differences between managers. Entrepreneurial networks are optimum for senior men, but those with hierarchical networks are as enthusiastic about their networks. Hierarchical networks are optimum for women and entry-rank men, but those with entrepreneurial networks (the worst choice for these managers) are as enthusiastic about their networks.

If there is optimizing behavior here, it is difficult to see. Kinds of networks have career implications for kinds of managers, but kinds of networks are randomly distributed across kinds of managers, and managers are poor judges of whether their network is right for their job. Ignorant of social capital theory, managers often look to successful colleagues for behavioral guidelines. The point illustrated in Figure 8 is that people should pick a network for what it can do, not for the kind of people who pick it. Where legitimacy is not an issue, competition is through entrepreneurial networks for direct access to the information and control benefits of structural holes. Where legitimacy is an issue, the optimum strategy is to compete through a hierarchical network for indirect access to the structural holes in an established person's network.

There is also a practical implication for the firm. The distinction between network forms of social capital in Figure 7 provides a useful diagnostic of diversity problems within a labor market. The people needed to support an idea have to take seriously the entrepreneurial manager to whom the idea is attributed. Certain categories of people (defined by gender, race or other attributes) are in certain organizations not taken seriously as a source of ideas. Returns to social capital can be used to sort managers into those accepted as legitimate players in the population versus those deemed suspect. The latter, 'illegitimate entrepreneurs', have to borrow the social capital of a sponsor to benefit from the information and control advantages of structural holes. Women and entry-rank men in this papers study population are most likely to be promoted early when they build their network within the entrepreneurial network of a strategic partner beyond their boss. Even working within the limits of a clique network, or their boss's network, is preferable to building their own entrepreneurial network (in terms of early promotion). The fact that women and entry-rank men fall behind when they build their own social capital, and move ahead when they borrow social capital, indicates that they have a legitimacy problem in this firm. It is one thing to occasionally borrow social capital to succeed in a new venture. It is another to have to borrow social capital for all your ventures. If borrowing social capital is a strategy through which suspect outsiders get access to the benefits of social capital, then a category of people for whom success depends on borrowing social capital is a category of people deemed suspect. The social capital analysis provides more than a method of identifying groups of people deemed suspect. Instead of distinguishing people by broad attributes of age, race, gender and treating everyone as equal within the same category, the network analysis provides a manager-specific measure of legitimacy (Figure 6). Legitimacy is keyed to the social situation of a person, not to the person's attributes. This is a powerful shift in the analysis of diversity problems.

APPENDIX
Network Constraint Components

Network constraint (a function of size, density and hierarchy) measures the concentration of relations in a single contact (Burt 1992, 50 ff). Contact-specific constraint, the extent to which manager i's network is concentrated in the relation with contact j is defined as follows: $c_{ij} = (p_{ij} + \Sigma_q p_{iq} p_{qj})^2$, for $q \neq i,j$, where p_{ij} is the proportion of i's relations invested in contact j. Measuring indirect connections, the sum $\Sigma_q p_{iq} p_{qj}$ is the portion of i's relations invested in contacts q who are in turn invested in contact j. The sum in parentheses is the proportion of i's relations directly or indirectly invested in i's relationship with contact j. The sum of squared proportions, $\Sigma_j c_{ij}$, is a network constraint index C measuring the concentration of direct and indirect relations in one contact. I multiply the constraint index C—as well as the density and hierarchy components below—by 100 to discuss social capital effects per point of constraint.

I use the relative contributions of the size, density and hierarchy components to make inferences about diversity problems. Results in Table 2 and Figure 9 illustrate the associations between the components, the aggregate, and early promotion. The regression results in Table 2 predict early promotion for the senior men in Figure 2. The hypothetical networks in Figure 9 illustrate how constraint varies with size, density and hierarchy. Relations, usually continuous, often asymmetric, are simplified in Figure 9 to binary and symmetric. Also, the figure only displays relations between contacts. Relations with the respondent manager are not presented.

Size

Constraint is more severe in smaller networks because they contain few alternative contacts to provide information, and play against one another. An increasing number of contacts decreases, on average, the proportional strength of relations, p_{ij}, in the constraint model. In the first column of Figure 9, a manager citing three disconnected contacts has a constraint of 33, which decreases to 20 for the manager citing five contacts, and 10 for the manager citing ten. At maximum density in the second column of Figure 9, constraint is 93 for the manager citing three strongly connected contacts, 65 for the manager citing five such contacts, and 36 for the manager citing ten.

There are two size variables in Table 2. The simpler is number of contacts. The second variable, C-size, is the size component in the constraint model. This measures the extent to which a manager's relations are concentrated in a single contact. The two size variables covary. As the number of contacts increases, the proportion of a manager's network allocated to any one contact decreases (−.86 correlation). Both size variables have significant associations in Table 2 with early promotion (3.9 t-test in model I, versus −3.2 in model II).[14]

Table 2. Components in the social capital effect for senior men

Network variables	I	II	III	IV	V
Multiple correlation:	.51	.48	.47	.54	.49
Intercept	−.79	10.26	2.88	12.06	2.35
Size:					
Number of contacts	.49	—	.22	.05	.48
	[.27]		[.12]	[.03]	[.27]
	(.39)		(1.3)	(0.3)	(3.8)
C-size	—	−.47	—	—	—
		[−.23]			
		(−3.2)			
Density:					
Average relation between contacts	−.12	−.12	—	−.11	−.21
	[−.25]	[−.25]		[−.22]	[−.43]
	(−3.1)	(−3.3)		(−3.0)	(−5.7)
C-density	—	—	−.34	—	—
			[−.19]		
			(−1.9)		
Hierarchy:					
Constraint from many concentrated in one contact	—	—	—	—	−.21
					[−.23]
					(−3.0)
Betweenness concentrated in one contact	−.09	−.10	−.11	—	—
	[−.27]	[−.29]	[−.33]		
	(−3.6)	(−3.9)	(−4.5)		
C-hierarchy	—	—	—	−1.51	—
				[−.43]	
				(−4.7)	

Note: These are ordinary least-square estimates of row variables predicting early promotion. Standardized estimates appear in [brackets] and routine t-tests appear in (parentheses). The row variables are explained in the text.

	Entrepreneurial Networks	Clique Networks	Hierarchical Networks
Small Networks			
size	3	3	3
density	0	100	67
hierarchy	0	0	7
constraint	33	93	84
from:			
A	11	31	44
B	11	31	20
C	11	31	20
Larger Networks			
size	5	5	5
density	0	100	40
hierarchy	0	0	25
constraint	20	65	59
from:			
A	4	13	36
B	4	13	6
C	4	13	6
D	4	13	6
E	4	13	6
Still Larger Networks			
size	10	10	10
density	0	100	20
hierarchy	0	0	50
constraint	10	36	41

NOTE: — Network density, hierarchy, and constraint scores are multiplied by 100 to match computer output

Figure 9. Constraint = f(size, density, hierarchy) (network scores are multiplied by 100; hierarchy is constraint then betweenness)

Density

Constraint is more severe in more dense networks because dense networks contain, in effect, fewer alternative contacts. Strongly interconnected contacts are more likely to have the same information, and are more difficult to play against one another. Density increases the indirect connections component in the constraint model ($\Sigma_q p_{iq}p_{qj}$). For all sizes, density is 0 in the first column of Figure 9, and 100 in the second column of the figure. At each size, constraint is much higher in the second column of Figure 9 than in the first column.

There are two network density variables in Table 2. The more familiar of the two is the average strength of relation between contacts, which is presented in Figure 9. The other, C-density, measures the extent to which a manager's strongest relations are with contacts strongly tied to other of the manager's contacts. This is the density component in the constraint model.[14] The two density variables are correlated (.42), and have similar negative correlations with early promotion ($-.33$ and $-.35$ respectively). Both density variables have negative associations with early promotion (-3.1 t-test in model I, -1.9 in model III).[15]

Hierarchy

Constraint is more severe in more hierarchical networks because hierarchical networks contain, in effect, fewer alternative contacts. A network is hierarchical to the extent that it is organized around one of the contacts. A manager is more constrained when one central contact has exclusive relations with the manager's other contacts (see Burt 1992, 56–62, on the constraint-significance of the difference between exclusive and strong relations, building on the small-group experiments with exchange networks). The central contact gets the same information available to the manager and cannot be avoided in manager negotiations with each other contact. More, the central contact can be played against the manager by third parties because information available from the manager is equally available from the central contact since manager and central contact reach the same people.

Hierarchy and density both increase, but in different ways, the indirect connections component in the constraint model ($\Sigma_q p_{iq}p_{qj}$). Density measures the average strength of indirect connection. Hierarchy measures the concentration of indirect connection through one contact. No one contact is more connected than others in the minimum and maximum density networks in the first two columns of Figure 9. Hierarchy is zero. In the third column, one contact is strongly connected to all others, who are otherwise disconnected from one another (except through the manager citing them who is not reported in the sociograms). The hierarchy is evident in the relative levels of constraint posed by individual contacts. Contact A poses more severe constraint than the others because network ties are concentrated in A. Note how constraint increases with hierarchy and density. Constraint is high in the dense and hierarchical three-contact networks (93 and 84 points, respectively). Constraint is 65 in the maximum-density five-contact network and 59 in the hierarchical network, even though density is only 40 in the hierarchical network. In the ten-contact networks, constraint is lower in the maximum-density network than it is in the hierarchical network (36 versus 41), and density is only 20 in the hierarchical network. In short, density and hierarchy are correlated, but distinct, components in network constraint.

There are three network hierarchy variables in Table 2. All measure the extent to which a manager's network is concentrated in the hands of one contact. (i) The first variable measures the extent to which constraint is concentrated in the hands of one contact.[16] *Constraint hierarchy is zero in the first two columns of Figure 9* (because all contacts poses equal constraint) and non-zero in the third-column networks (because contact A is the disproportionate source of constraint by dint of A's exclusive connections with the other contacts). Constraint hierarchy increases with network size because the difference between minimum and maximum constraint is larger in larger hierarchical networks (as reported in the third column of Figure 9; 7 in the three-contact hierarchical network, 25 in the five-contact network, and 50 in the ten-contact network). (ii) The second hierarchy variable is Freeman's (1977) betweenness index, also displayed in Figure 9. Betweenness measures the extent to which one contact stands between all others. It varies from 0 in the first two columns of Figure 9 (because no contact stands between the others), to its 100 maximum in the column-three networks (because contact A provides the only connection between contacts, putting aside the manager). Independent of network size, betweenness hierarchy equals 100 in all of the networks in the third column of Figure 9.[17] (iii) The third hierarchy variable, C-hierarchy, is the hierarchy component in the constraint model.[14] This measures the extent to which a manager's contacts concentrate their relations in one central contact and covaries with betweenness hierarchy (.57 correlation with betweenness hierarchy versus .23 correlation with constraint hierarchy). Their differences notwithstanding, all three hierarchy variables have significant negative associations with early promotion (*t*-tests at the bottom of Table 1 vary from −3.0 to −4.7).

The results in Table 2 show that size, density, and hierarchy make significant independent contributions to the social capital effect on early promotion. At the same time, the three components covary to define social capital. If I predict early promotion from all seven variables in Table 2, I get a .56 multiple correlation. I get almost the same level of prediction without the two size variables (.55 multiple correlation), or without the two density variables (.52), or without the three hierarchy variables (.45). Judging from the multiple correlations, the hierarchy variables make the most independent contribution to social capital. The summary point is that all three network constraint components matter, and they covary to define social capital. This need not always be true. Hierarchy is the critical component for identifying minority managers deemed suspect (Figure 6).

NOTES

1. I focus on rewards to the individual manager (Brass 1992; Lazega 1994; Breiger 1995, review related works). I assume that managers with entrepreneurial contact networks add value to their firm, and therefore receive from the firm compensation in

one form or another that is above average. The more general argument is to describe how the firm is shaped by managers searching for early information to resolve corporate and market uncertainties. For that more general argument, see Stinchcombe (1990).

2. There is a process element missing in these studies that can be seen in other styles of analysis. Historical accounts offer a glimpse of the process by which brokers built bridges across structural holes (e.g. Padgett and Ansell 1993; on Cosimo Medici's rise to power in Renaissance Florence as a broker between conflicting interests; DiMaggio 1992, esp. pp. 129–30, on the creation of New York's Museum of Modern Art and the role of Professor Paul Sachs's strong ties to the previously disconnected worlds of museums, universities, and finance). Ultimately, there is no substitute for direct observation. Kotter's (1982) cases illustrate the information and control advantages of an entrepreneurial network in performing the two tasks of the successful general manager; reading the organization for needed business policy, and knowing what people to bring together to implement the policy. Mintzberg (1973) is similarly rich in case material on the central importance to managers of getting their information live through personal discussions rather than official channels. Sutton and Hargadon (1996) offer rich detail on an institutional case (cf. Allen and Cohen, 1969 on gatekeepers). They describe a firm, IDEO, that relies on brainstorming to create product designs. The firm's employees work for clients in diverse industries. In the brainstorming sessions, technological solutions from one industry are taken where useful to other client industries where the solutions are rare or unknown. The firm makes its margin by brokering the flow of technology between industries. Sutton and Hargadon's evidence on IDEO offers process detail that corroborates the more authoritative, but static, survey evidence of the social capital value of structural holes.

3. The exact zero-order difference is 3.4 years (4.0 t-test), which is 3.1 years in a multiple regression holding constant the other variables in the age regression equation (3.9 t-test), and 2.8 years in the same regression excluding sample men older than the oldest women (3.8 t-test).

4. Tests for the statistical significance of social capital effects are adjusted downward for degrees of freedom lost in defining early promotion as a residual score (ordinary least-squares t-tests are multiplied by .97, the square root of 268/284, to decrease t-tests in proportion to the lost degrees of freedom). Most of the background variables have little association with age at promotion, but I take the conservative route of holding them all constant to define early promotion.

5. Kanter (1977), South et al. (1982), Brass (1985), Maniero (1986), and Ibarra (1992, 1997) provide illustrative kinds of evidence for this argument, but the argument seems more widely circulated in the business press; e.g. Klieman's (1980, 25, 28) popular book on women's networks:

> To know that, on the job, there are a handful of people with your best interests in mind, who are there to lean on, to share information with, who care about what happens to you—especially when so often the Big Bosses are invisible and do not care—can make moving ahead on the job a real possibility. And the road to better jobs, better pay, better working conditions need not be so filled with frustration, barriers, and lack of information. Instead, it can have good feelings—and positive results—connected with it. .... Through networking, you will find the group support you now lack, a circle of friends who understand the reality of working 9 to 5. .... 'We really respect each other,' a middle-management woman says of the four women in her company at her level who share problems and insights.

'When there's trouble, we give advice. It doesn't mean anyone has to take it. But they know they have a friend. You've got to have a friend.'

6. That women do not more often build cliques still leaves the question of women performing better in cliques because they are more emotionally comfortable in a clique. The question is answered later, where density is a negligible factor in early promotions going to women in more constrained networks.

7. My sampling obscures the tendency for women in this study population to be human resource managers (though there are no significant differences in the proportions of kinds of managers in the sample and study population, Burt 1992, 120). Women are a minority in the study population (14 percent). They are less of a minority in the sample (18 percent) because I drew a minimum of five women from each of 32 categories in the sampling frame. There is no tendency in the study population for men and women to work in different functions (3.71 chi-square, 7 d.f, p = .81), except in human resources (29.92 chi-square, 1 d.f., $p < .001$)—5 percent of the senior men are HR managers versus 12 percent of the senior women. The HR gender difference is negligible in the sample (0.50 chi-square, 1 d.f., p = .83). The HR gender difference notwithstanding, the difference in Figure 2 between sample men and women cannot be attributed to women working in jobs different from men because men and women in the sample are equally likely to work in each kind of job (holding constant the relative numbers of sample men and women).

8. Again, Klieman (1980, 14–15) provides tradebook illustration of the argument:

As a direct result of the past decade, during which women have lobbied for equal rights and representation, many corporations named one woman to a top post, local governments put one woman in a high position, and the media have one or two women in visible spots. Women, one by one, are getting more responsible jobs, and their tasks and the weight of what they do hang heavier on them just because they are women. Because they are 'token', it isn't politic for them to show any doubts or confusion, as a man in the same position might do. These women, then, are spearheading the formation of business and professional networks throughout the United States. By joining forces with one another, they give and get mutual support and also provide the climate for more women to enter management. . . . Women have always shared job information, but by joining formal or informal networks we commit ourselves to helping other women.

9. Sponsor is my word, not Jane's. I telephoned Jane in 1993, four years after the original study, in the course of preparing the graphic in Figure 4 for an MBA course. I identified Jane and Karen from the sample data distributions because they nicely illustrated the hierarchy association with early promotion, but I wanted more information on Jane to bring her to life for the business students. I called the telephone extension I had for her from the original study, and was transferred to her new number. I explained the nature of the call, and was graciously given a better understanding of Sam's role in her work at the time of the study.

10. I am grateful to James E. Schrager for calling my attention to these directories. Professor Schrager's knowledge of them comes from their importance in his work arranging partnerships between American and Japanese firms through his firm, Great Lakes Consulting Group.

11. The legitimacy variable is based on subsampling (Finifter 1972). Table 1 contains regression equations predicting early promotion from network size, density and hierarchy. The regression coefficient for hierarchy, call it b, indicates the extent to which success depends on borrowed social capital (holding constant size and density,

the measures of direct access to the social capital of structural holes). Delete a manager from the sample, and re-estimate the equation to get a new estimate bi with manager i deleted. If bi is more positive than b, then hierarchy is more associated with early promotion without the deleted manager, which means that borrowed social capital is less critical to the manager's success. If bi is less positive than b, then hierarchy is less associated with early promotion without the deleted manager, which means that borrowing social capital is more critical to the manager's success. Repeat this procedure for each manager. The legitimacy criterion variable is $bi - b$. Positive values indicate managers who have direct access to social capital (left of Figure 6). Negative values indicate managers whose success depends on borrowed social capital (right of Figure 6).

12. Boss centrality is a continuous variable. For this illustration, I computed the ratio of constraint posed by the boss over the average contact-specific constraint c_{ij} in a manager's network, then looked for a cut-off that highlighted the benefits of a hierarchical network and divided the hierarchical networks into two categories of roughly equal numbers of managers. The cut-off is one. A hierarchical network is built around the boss if the boss poses more constraint than the average contact in the network.

13. The chi-square statistic in Figure 8 shows that the kinds of networks are independent of the distinction between senior men versus women and entry-rank men. They are similarly independent of a distinction between men and women (4.10 chi-square, 3 d.f., $p = .25$), a distinction between people long with the firm in their function versus people more recently hired (1.22 chi-square, 3 d.f., $p = .75$), a distinction between the four job ranks (3.80 chi-square, 9 d.f., $p = .92$), and a distinction between the eight functional areas (23.96 chi-square, 21 d.f., $p = .30$).

14. Given contact-specific constraint, c_{ij}; $(p_{ij})2 + 2p_{ij}(\Sigma_q p_{iq}p_{qj}) + (\Sigma_q p_{iq}p_{qj})2$, $q \neq i,j$, the aggregate constraint index, C, is a sum of three variables; $\Sigma_j(p_{ij})^2 + 2\Sigma_j p_{ij}(\Sigma_q p_{iq}p_{qj}) + \Sigma_j(\Sigma_q p_{iq}p_{qj})^2$. The first variable in the expression, C-size in the text, is a Herfindal index measuring the extent to which manager i's relations are concentrated in a single contact. The second variable, C-density in the text, is an interaction between strong ties and density in the sense that it increases with the extent to which manager i's strongest relations are with contacts strongly tied to the other contacts. The third variable, C-hierarchy in the text, measures the extent to which manager i's contacts concentrate their relations in one central contact.

15. The density component in network constraint, C-density, is less useful for distinguishing size and density effects. It includes size variance because relations are measured as proportions. Number of contacts is correlated .08 with density, $-.67$ with C-density. The stronger correlation between size and C-density affects the results in Table 2. Number of contacts has a 3.9 t-test association with early promotion in model I holding density constant, which drops to a 1.3 t-test in model III when C-density is held constant.

16. This is the Coleman–Theil inequality index applied to contact-specific constraint scores, and is the hierarchy variable in the original structural hole analysis of these data (for reasons given there, Burt 1992, 70 ff). The index is the ratio of $\Sigma_j r_j \ln(r_j)$ divided by $N \ln(N)$, where N is number of contacts, r_j is the ratio of contact-j constraint over average constraint, $c_{ij}/(C/N)$, and c_{ij} is the level of constraint contact j poses for the manager. The index equals zero if all contact-specific constraints equal the average. It approaches 1.0 to the extent that all constraint is from one contact.

17. Let b_j equal the mean indirect connection from manager i through contact j between

two other contacts k and q: $\Sigma_k \Sigma_q z_{ij} z_{jk} z_{jq} /([N-1][N-2])$, $j \neq k,q$ and $k \neq q$. Betweenness hierarchy is the ratio of $\Sigma_j (b\text{max} - b_j)$ divided by $N-1$, where $b$max is the largest value of b_j in the manager's network. One contact will have b_j equal to $b$max. When all other b_j are zero, the $(b\text{max} - b_j)$ sum to $N-1$ and the index is 1.0. When all b_j are equal, the $(b\text{max} - b_j)$ sum to 0.0 and the index is 0.0. I tried Freeman's aggregation with contact-specific constraint scores, but obtained weaker results than reported in Table 2 for the Coleman–Theil model. I tried the Coleman–Theil aggregation with betweenness scores b_j, but obtained weaker results than reported in Table 2 for the Freeman model. I therefore report both aggregation models in Table 2.

REFERENCES

Allen, Thomas J. and Saul Cohen. 1969. 'Information Flow in R&D Labs.' *Administrative Science Quarterly* 14: 12–19.

Ancona, Deborah G. and David F. Caldwell. 1992 'Bridging the Boundary: External Activity and Performance in Organization Terms.' *Administrative Science Quarterly* 37: 634–65.

Baron, James N. and William T. Bielby. 1985. 'Organization Barriers to Gender Equality: Sex Segregation of Jobs and Opportunities.' In *Gender and the Life Course*, ed. by Alice Rossi, pp. 233–51. New York: Aldine.

Baron, James N., Alison Davis-Blake and William T. Bielby. 1986. 'The Structure of Opportunity: How Promotion Ladders Vary Within and Among Organizations.' *Administrative Science Quarterly* 31: 248–73.

Becker, Gary. 1975. *Human Capital*. Chicago: University of Chicago Press.

Bielby, William T. and James N. Baron. 1986. 'Men and Women at Work: Sex Segregation and Statistical Discrimination.' *American Journal of Sociology* 91: 759–99.

Bourdieu, Pierre and Loïc J.D. Wacquant. 1992. *An Invitation to Reflexive Sociology*. Chicago: University of Chicago Press.

Brass, Daniel J. 1985. 'Men's and Women's Networks: A Study of Interaction Patterns and Influence in an Organization.' *Academy of Management Journal* 28: 327–43.

Brass, Daniel J. 1992. 'Power in Organizations: A Social Network Perspective.' In *Research in Politics and Society*, eds Gwen Moore and J.A. Whitt, pp. 295–323. Greenwich, CT: JAI Press.

Breiger, Ronald L. 1995. 'Socioeconomic Achievement and Social Structure.' *Annual Review of Sociology* 21: 115–36.

Burt, Ronald S. 1980. 'Autonomy in a Social Topology.' *American Journal of Sociology* 85: 892–925.

Burt, Ronald S. 1983. *Corporate Profits and Cooptation*. New York: Academic Press.

Burt, Ronald S. 1988. 'The Stability of American Markets.' *American Journal of Sociology* 93: 356–95.

Burt, Ronald S. 1992. *Structural Holes: The Social Structure of Competition*. Cambridge, MA: Harvard University Press.

Burt, Ronald S. 1997a. 'The Contingent Value of Social Capital.' *Administrative Science Quarterly* 42: 339–65.

Burt, Ronald S., Joseph E. Jonnolta and James T. Mahoney. 1997. 'Personality Correlates of Structural Holes.' *Social Networks* 19: in press.

Burt, Ronald S. and John H. Freeman. 1994. 'Market Structure Constraint in Germany.' Graduate School of Business, University of Chicago.

Burt, Ronald S., Yuki Yasuda and Miguel Guilarte. 1996. 'Competition, Contingency and the External Structure of Markets.' Paper presented at an INSEAD conference on 'Organizations in Markets' in Fontainebleau, France.

Campbell, Karen E., Peter V. Marsden and Jeanne Hurlbert. 1986. 'Social Resources and Socioeconomic Status.' *Social Networks* 8: 97–117.

Cohen, Lisa E., Joseph P. Broschak and Heather A. Haveman. 1995. 'And Then There were More? The Effect of Organizational Sex Composition on Hiring and Promotion.' Paper presented at the annual meetings of the Academy of Management.

Coleman, James S. 1988. 'Social Capital in the Creation of Human Capital.' *American Journal of Sociology* 94: S95–20.

Coleman, James S. 1990. *Foundations of Social Theory*. Cambridge, MA: Harvard University Press.

Cook, Karen S. and Richard M. Emerson. 1978. 'Power, Equity and Commitment in Exchange Networks.' *American Sociological Review* 43: 712–39.

Cook, Karen S., Richard M. Emerson, Mary R. Gillmore and Toshio Yamagishi. 1983. 'The Distribution of Power In Exchange Networks: Theory and Experimental Results.' *American Journal of Sociology* 89: 275–305.

DiMaggio, Paul. 1992. 'Nadel's Paradox Revisited: Relational and Cultural Aspects of Organizational Structure.' In *Networks and Organizations*, ed. Nitin Norhia and Robert G. Eccles, pp. 118–42. Boston: Harvard Business School Press.

Fernandez, Roberto M. and Roger V. Gould. 1994. 'A Dilemma of State Power: Brokerage and Influence in the National Health Policy Domain.' *American Journal of Sociology* 99: 1455–91.

Finifter, Bernard M. 1972. 'The Generation of Confidence: Evaluating Research Findings by Random Subsample Replication.' In *Sociological Methodology, 1972*, ed. Herbert L. Costner, pp. 112–75. San Francisco: Jossey-Bass.

Flap, Hendrik D. and Nan D. De Graaf. 1989. 'Social Capital and Attained Occupational Status.' *Netherlands Journal of Sociology* 22: 145–61.

Freeman, Linton C. 1977. 'A Set of Measures of Centrality Based on Betweenness.' *Sociometry* 40: 35–40.

Gabbay, Shaul M. 1997. *Social Capital in the Creation of Financial Capital*. Champaign, IL: Stipes.

Gargiulo, Martin and Mario Benassi. 1993. 'Informal Control and Managerial Flexibility in Network Organizations.' INSEAD Working Paper.

Granovetter, Mark S. 1973. 'The Strength of Weak Ties.' *American Journal of Sociology* 78: 1360–80.

Granovetter, Mark S. [1974] 1995. *Getting a Job*. Chicago: University of Chicago Press.

Granovetter, Mark S. 1985. 'Economic Action, Social Structure, and Embeddedness.' *American Journal of Sociology* 91: 481–510.

Gulati, Ranjay. 1995. 'Social Structure and Alliance Formation Patterns: A Longitudinal Analysis.' *Administrative Science Quarterly* 40: 619–52.

Hirschi, Travis. 1972. *Causes of Delinquency*. Berkeley, CA: University of California Press.

Ibarra, Herminia. 1992. 'Homophily and Differential Returns: Sex Differences in Network Structure and Access in an Advertising Firm.' *Administrative Science Quarterly* 37: 422–47.

Ibarra, Herminia. 1997. 'Paving an Alternate Route: Gender Differences in Managerial Networks.' *Social Psychology Quarterly* 60: 91–102.

Jang, Ho. 1997. *Market Structure, Performance, and Putting-Out in the Korean Economy.* PhD thesis, Department of Sociology, University of Chicago.

Kanter, Rosabeth M. 1977. *Men and Women of the Corporation.* New York: Harper and Row.

Klieman, Carol. 1980. *Women's Networks: The Complete Guide to Getting a Better Job, Advancing Your Career, and Feeling Great as a Woman Through Networking.* New York: Lippincott and Crowell.

Kotter, John P. 1982. *The General Managers.* New York: Free Press.

Krackhardt, David and Robert N. Stern. 1988. 'Informal Networks and Organizational Crisis: An Experimental Simulation.' *Social Psychology Quarterly* 51: 123–40.

Lazega,. Emmanuel. 1994. 'Analyse de réseaux et sociologie des organizations.' *Revue Française de Sociologie* 34: 293–320.

Lin, Nan. 1998. *Social Resources and Social Action.* New York: Cambridge University Press (forthcoming).

Lin, Nan and Mary Dumin. 1986. 'Access to Occupations Through Social Ties.' *Social Networks* 8: 365–85.

Lin, Nan, Walter Ensel and John Vaughn. 1981. 'Social Resources and Strength of Ties: Structural Factors in Occupational Status Attainment.' *American Sociological Review* 46: 393–405.

Maniero, L.A. 1986. 'Coping with Powerlessness: The Relationship of Gender and Job Dependency To Empowerment-strategy Usage.' *Administrative Science Quarterly* 31: 633–53.

Markovsky, Barry, David Willer and Travis Patton. 1988. 'Power Relations in Exchange Networks.' *American Sociological Review* 53: 220–36.

Marsden, Peter V. and Jeanne Hurlbert. 1988. 'Social Resources and Mobility Outcomes: A Replication and Extension.' *Social Forces* 66: 1038–59.

Martinelli, Alberto. 1994. 'Entrepreneurship and Management.' In *The Handbook of Economic Sociology*, eds Neil J. Smelser and Richard Swedberg, pp. 476–503. Princeton, NJ: Princeton University Press.

McPherson, J. Miller and Lynn Smith-Lovin. 1987. 'Homophily in Voluntary Organizations: Status Distance and the Composition of Face-to-face Groups.' *American Sociological Review* 52: 370–9.

Merton, Robert K. [1957] 1968. 'Continuities in the Theory of Reference Group Behavior.' In *Social Theory and Social Structure*, pp. 335–440. New York: Free Press.

Merton, Robert K. 1984. 'Socially Expected Durations: A Case Study of Concept Formation in Sociology.' In *Conflict and Consensus*, eds Walter W. Powell and Richard Robbins, pp. 262–83. New York: Free Press.

Meyerson, Eva M. 1994. 'Human Capital, Social Capital and Compensation: The Relative Contribution of Social Contacts to Managers' Incomes.' *Acta Sociologica* 37: 383–99.

Milkman, Ruth and Eleanor Townsley. 1994. 'Gender and the Economy.' In *The Handbook of Economic Sociology*, eds Neil J. Smelser and Richard Swedberg, pp. 600–19. Princeton, NJ: Princeton University Press.

Mintzberg, Henry. 1973. *The Nature of Managerial Work.* New York: Harper and Row.

Nanda, Ashish and Christopher A. Bartlett. 1990. 'Corning Incorporated: A Network of Alliances.' *Harvard Business School Case 9–391–102.* Boston, MA: Harvard Business School Press.

46   RONALD S. BURT

Padgett, John F. and Christopher K. Ansell. 1993. 'Robust Action and the Rise of the Medici, 1400–34.' *American Journal of Sociology* 98: 1259–319.

Pennings, Johannes M., Kyungmook Lee and Arjen van Witteloostuijn. 1997. 'Intangible Resources and Firm Mortality: A Study of Professional Services Firms.' *Academy of Management Journal* 100: in press.

Podolny, Joel M. and James N. Baron. 1997. 'Relationships and Resources: Social Networks and Mobility in the Workplace.' *American Sociological Review* 62: 673–93.

Portes, Alejandro and Patricia Landolt. 1996. 'The Downside of Social Capital.' *The American Prospect* 16: 18–21.

Putnam, Robert D. 1993. Making Democracy Work: Civic Traditions in Modern Italy. Princeton: Princeton University Press.

Raider, Holly J. and Ronald S. Burt. 1996. 'Boundaryless Careers and Social Capital.' In *The Boundaryless Career*, eds Michael B. Arthur and Denise M. Rousseau, pp. 187–200. New York: Oxford University Press.

Rosenthal, Elizabeth A. 1996. *Social Networks and Team Performance*. PhD thesis, Graduate School of Business, University of Chicago.

Rosten, Leo. 1989. *The Joys of Yinglish*. New York: McGraw-Hill.

Simmel, Georg. [1922] 1955. *Conflict and the Web of Group Affiliations*. (trans. by Kurt H. Wolff and Reinhard Bendix). New York: Free Press.

South, Scott J., Charles M. Bonjean, William T. Markham and Judy Corder. 1982. 'Social Structure and Intergroup Interaction: Men And Women of the Federal Bureaucracy.' *American Sociological Review* 47: 587–99.

Sparrowe, Raymond T. and Pamela A. Popielarz. 1995. 'Weak Ties and Structural Holes: The Effects of Network Structure on Careers.' Department of Management, University of Illinois-Chicago.

Stinchcombe, Arthur L. 1990. *Information and Organizations*. Berkeley, CA: University of California Press.

Sutton, Robert I. and Andrew B. Hargadon. 1996. 'Brainstorming Groups in Context: Effectiveness in a Product Design Firm.' *Administrative Science Quarterly* 41: 685–718.

Talmud, Ilan. 1992. 'Market Power, Political Power, and State Support: The Case of Israeli Industry.' In *Research in Politics and Society*, eds Gwen Moore and J.A. Whitt. Greenwich, CT: JAI Press.

Talmud, Ilan. 1994. 'Relations and Profits: The Social Organization of Israeli Industrial Competition.' *Social Science Research* 23: 109–35.

Yasuda, Yuki. 1993. *A Comparative Structural Analysis of American and Japanese Markets*. PhD thesis, Department of Sociology, Columbia University.

Ziegler, Rolf. 1982. *Market Structure and Cooptation*. Munich: University of Munich, Institut für Soziologie.

RONALD S. BURT is the Hobart W. Williams Professor of Sociology and Strategy at the University of Chicago. His interests concern network theory applied to the social organization of competition.

ADDRESS: Graduate School of Business, University of Chicago, Chicago, IL 60637, USA [email: ron.burt@gsb.uchicago.edu]

[14]

Family Matters: Gender, Networks, and Entrepreneurial Outcomes*

LINDA A. RENZULLI, *University of North Carolina at Chapel Hill*
HOWARD ALDRICH, *University of North Carolina at Chapel Hill*
JAMES MOODY, *Ohio State University*

Abstract

In this article, we explore several factors that may have an effect on business start-ups, focusing on possible gender differences. We conceptualize social capital as inhering in people's relations with others and examine the association between men's and women's social capital and their likelihood of starting a business. Two aspects of respondents' social capital are highlighted: the extent to which their business discussion networks are heterogeneous and the extent to which they contain a high proportion of kin. We show that a high proportion of kin and homogeneity in the network, rather than a high proportion of females in the network or being female, are critical disadvantages facing potential small business owners.

Historically, men have enjoyed several advantages over women in their life chances. For example, men have had, on average, higher occupational status, a higher rate of self-employment, and higher incomes than women (Reskin 1993). Female-dominated occupations have been devalued, in part, because Americans consider work done by women less valuable, less important, and less difficult (England 1992). Men have also owned and controlled the great majority of businesses. In 1990 the self-employment rate[1] for men was 12%, whereas it was only 6% for women (Devine 1994). However, in the past several decades, women have made gains in occupational status, income, and business ownership. Many women are now employed in traditionally male occupations, and the pay gap between men and

A draft of this article was presented at the 1998 Conference on Entrepreneurship, Insead, Fontainebleau, France. We thank Rachel Rosenfeld, Jeremy Reynolds, and the two reviewers for their helpful comments on earlier drafts. Direct correspondence to Linda A. Renzulli, University of North Carolina at Chapel Hill, Department of Sociology, CB #3210 Hamilton Hall, Chapel Hill, NC 27599. Telephone: 919-962-5044. E-mail: linda_renzulli@unc.edu.

524 / *Social Forces* 79:2, December 2000

women has decreased (Reskin 1993). In addition, female business ownership has
risen dramatically. Since the 1970s, women have experienced a sixfold increase in
their share of U.S. businesses (Baker, Aldrich & Liou 1997; Devine 1994).

In this article, we explore the effects that social networks may have on women's
inroads into business ownership, using unique social network data from a
longitudinal sample of owners and potential owners in the Research Triangle Park
area of North Carolina. We examine the actions of *nascent entrepreneurs* — persons
who are seriously attempting to start a business, a category that includes persons
who are not currently business owners as well as existing owners. We focus on
social capital in business start-up, following Lin's (1999) conception of social capital
as channels of access to resources that inhere in someone's social relations. Such
ties provide differential incubation prospects for new business ideas, depending
on the quality of the information and resources flowing through them. Indeed,
few founders begin their businesses as solo endeavors (Reynolds & White 1997).
Instead, they draw upon support and assistance from others to whom they are tied
by personal and professional connections.

The viability of a new venture depends, in part, on how well nascent
entrepreneurs gauge the environment in which they choose to start a business and
on how well they can capture resources in order to survive after start-up. We argue
that the diversity and composition of nascent entrepreneurs' social networks provide
access to information and resources that change the likelihood of starting a
business. We examine men's and women's networks and focus specifically on
heterogeneity and kin composition, because much of the network literature points
to gender differences in these dimensions of personal networks. Research has shown
that men tend to have more diverse networks than do women, which, in turn, may
provide subtle advantages to men.

Social Capital

Theorists have disagreed over the definition and interpretation of the term *social
capital* (for the multiple definitions and usage, see Bourdieu 1986; Burt 1997;
Coleman 1988; Lin 1999; Putnam 1993). Bourdieu (1986) and Putnam (1993)
used the group as the level of analysis in their arguments that groups collectively
enhance their members' life chances through social capital. By contrast, Lin (1999)
used the individual as the unit of analysis to argue that social capital is instrumental
for business and work in a way similar to that of human capital investments.
Coleman (1988) seemed to use the term with both a collective and individual
referent. He saw social capital as a resource for social action that could lead to the
acquisition of other forms of capital, human and physical. Similarly, Burt defined
social capital as a quality created between people, and Sik and Wellman (1999)
referred to valuable social ties as "network capital." We use *social capital* to indicate

Gender, Networks, and Entrepreneurial Outcomes / 525

the relationship characteristics of a person's ties to others who may provide access to important resources.

Arguments concerning the value of social capital suggest that part of the difference in business start-up rates between male-owned and female-owned businesses might be explained by differences in social capital accumulation created through ties. Interpersonal connections are a significant informal source of information about opportunities and available resources for occupational mobility and improved life chances (Campbell 1988; Campbell, Marsden & Hurlbert 1986; Marsden & Hurlbert 1988). By extension from these arguments, social capital can play a similar role in business start-ups. If there are consistent differences between the social networks in which men and women are embedded, and if such information affects business start-ups, then a partial explanation for differential start-up rates by gender could be found in people's differential possession of social capital.

We are specifically interested in the effects of network composition and heterogeneity on the likelihood of an individual's attempt to start a business. We focus on information and social support networks. These are very different from resource, exchange, or joint-venture organizational networks, which involve the flow of tangible capital resources. Our theoretical interest rests in the immediate circle of discussion partners surrounding a nascent entrepreneur, defined as a set of alters with whom a given entrepreneur discusses business matters. Such persons have the potential to influence nascent entrepreneurs' recognition of business opportunities, as well as the quality of their economic decision making. A key characteristic of such networks, affecting the types and quality of information obtained, is the relationship heterogeneity of the alters.

Our hypotheses thus focus on the informational and social support resources provided by business discussion networks, guided by three principles. First, people can maximize the value of the information they receive if they have low redundancy among the alters in their discussion network (Granovetter 1973). Therefore, the greatest returns to social capital occur for nascent entrepreneurs with many nonredundant ties. Second, kinship ties — by virtue of their common origin in the family — are likely to generate information drawn from a homogeneous pool. Kinship ties thus provide lower levels of new information (Marsden 1990). Third, access to information about opportunities and social support from peers are key bridges between one's intention to start a business and actually doing so (Denison, Swaminathan & Rothbard 1994).

Before explaining the rationale for our hypotheses, we review the central concepts of social network analysis relevant to gender differences. We illustrate our two major independent variables — heterogeneity and composition — and explain their theoretical significance.

526 / *Social Forces* 79:2, December 2000

GENDER AND NETWORKS

Researchers have found that men and women are embedded in different social networks and have suggested that network differences lead to divergent economic consequences (Popielarz 1999). Several studies have shown that women tend to nominate more kin as people with whom they "discuss important matters" (Marsden 1987; Moore 1990). In fact, women in the same social situation as men tend to have more homogeneous networks in terms of kin composition (Marsden 1987; Moore 1990), either because of induced homophily or choice homophily (McPherson & Smith-Lovin 1987).

In studies of business owners, researchers have replicated many of the findings from surveys of the general population. Evidence from a limited number of surveys suggests that men and women business owners resemble the general public in the composition of their personal networks. For example, using the Research Triangle Entrepreneurial Development Study (EDS), Renzulli (1998) found that women business owners included more kin in their business discussion networks than did men. By contrast, men owners included more coworkers in their networks than did women.

Researchers have interpreted gender differences in network composition as posing a disadvantage for women in the business world (Liao & Stevens 1994; Moore 1990). Women who include greater proportions of kin in their discussion networks may secure greater social support than men, but at the cost of sacrificing the necessary instrumental support needed for economic achievement (Fischer & Oliker 1983; Hurlbert 1991). Social support provides the emotional strength owners and managers need to cope with daily exigencies, but such ties may also limit the diversity and reach of women's networks.

However, despite men and women owners' differences in network characteristics, researchers have not found differences in the *consequences* of these characteristics for how owners use their networks (Katz & Williams 1997). Reese and Aldrich (1995) found that networking activity, defined as the time spent building and maintaining business contacts, was not essential to business survival. Furthermore, they found that survival rates and general economic performance were not significantly related to global measures of networking activity. Aldrich, Elam, and Reese (1997) reported that women owners were just as aggressive as men in searching for advice and assistance through their networks and just as successful in obtaining what they sought. These findings suggest that the type of information and support provided by business discussion networks may have little impact on the survival of businesses after they are founded. However, the likelihood of business start-up may still depend on network heterogeneity and composition.

Gender, Networks, and Entrepreneurial Outcomes / 527

HETEROGENEITY

Granovetter (1973, 1974) argued that people who have contacts in more places (a greater range) have greater access to resources and information. Heterogeneity is the most direct indicator of the diversity of an individual's interpersonal environment. High diversity implies integration into several spheres of society, which is often advantageous for instrumental action (Marsden 1987). Networks that are diverse help people reach other social realms and avoid redundant information. A redundant relation is one in which the same information or resource could be obtained from other relations (Burt 1992). A given piece of information obtained from a member of a heterogeneous network is likely to be unique because actors in the network draw information from different sources. However, most people's relations are within clusters containing people who are similar to themselves along multiple dimensions, such as race, sex, and age (Blau 1994).

The more heterogeneous someone's discussion networks, the greater the likelihood that they can obtain nonredundant or diverse information (Blau 1977). For example, Popielarz (1999) argued that an organization's demographic mix affects a member's opportunity to form network ties with dissimilar others. Heterogeneity may increase potential owners' social capital by deepening or extending their knowledge through indirect ties to others beyond their immediate circle. A heterogeneous network may also compensate for an individual's biased or incomplete perceptions and raise expectations for business start-up.

Hypothesis 1: The greater the heterogeneity in an individual's discussion network, the greater the likelihood he or she will start a new business.

KIN COMPOSITION

The concept of network composition refers to the precise mixture of alters in a social network (Marsden 1987, 1990). Whereas heterogeneity captures the mere diversity of network alters, the concept of composition captures the type and mix of alters as well. The category of kin includes spouse, parents, siblings, and in-laws; that of nonkin includes friends, neighbors, coworkers, consultants, and group or association members. Figure 1 illustrates the possible difference between the extent of heterogeneity and the percentage of kin in someone's discussion network. Networks A and B have the same heterogeneity scores: each actor reaches the same number of diverse alters. The two networks, however, differ in their composition. Network A has a higher proportion of coworkers and network B has a higher proportion of kin. Thus, both concepts, heterogeneity and composition, are crucial in understanding someone's personal discussion network.

528 / *Social Forces* 79:2, December 2000

FIGURE 1: Heterogeneity and Composition

Network A

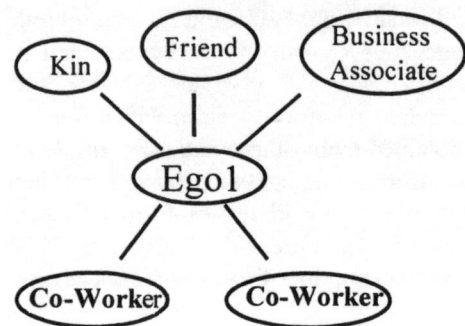

Composition = 2/5 coworker
1/5 kin

$$\left[\left(\frac{1\text{ kin}}{5}\right)^2 + \left(\frac{1\text{ business associate}}{5}\right)^2 + \left(\frac{2\text{ coworkers}}{5}\right)^2 + \left(\frac{1\text{ friend}}{5}\right)^2\right] = .72$$

Network B

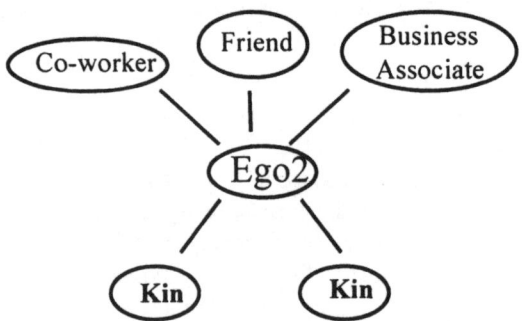

Composition = 1/5 coworker
2/5 kin

$$\left[\left(\frac{2\text{ kin}}{5}\right)^2 + \left(\frac{1\text{ business associate}}{5}\right)^2 + \left(\frac{1\text{ coworker}}{5}\right)^2 + \left(\frac{1\text{ friend}}{5}\right)^2\right] = .72$$

Note: For heterogeneity, see equation 1.

Gender, Networks, and Entrepreneurial Outcomes / 529

Previous research has suggested that kin ties are less likely than nonkin ties (especially coworker ties) to provide instrumental resources and unique information (Fischer & Oliker 1983; Moore 1990; Wellman 1990; Wellman, Carrington & Hall 1988; Wellman & Wortley 1990). For example, family members are much more likely to share information with each other than are nonkin members. Therefore, if individuals have a large proportion of kin members in their network, they may be at a disadvantage in the business community because their social ties are more inward-looking. A high proportion of kin in a network may indicate a high level of redundancy in information sources.

Hypothesis 2: The greater the proportion of kin in an individual's discussion network, the lower the likelihood he or she will start a new business.

OTHER FACTORS

Our two hypotheses focus exclusively on social capital for business start-up. We concentrate on heterogeneity and kin composition because the main thesis of our article is that quality of ties facilitates business start-up. Because men and women also differ in the number of women in their networks, our analysis takes into account the gender composition of nascent entrepreneurs' networks.[2]

Our analysis also includes factors such as life stage, employment status, and human capital to fully specify our model and ensure that our results are not spurious. We discuss previous research in which these factors have been the focus of analysis, and we comment on the effects of these other factors, but we do not present formal hypotheses about them.

Across entrepreneurial samples, researchers have found that the average age of business owners is generally greater than that of employees (Aldrich, Elam & Reese 1997; Aldrich, Renzulli & Langton 1998; Carter 1997). A nascent or established owner's age is important because throughout their life course, people pick up additional contacts and social support through their involvement in associations, work, and family activities. Marriage and parenthood are life-stage events that may also affect ownership. The presence of a spouse indicates that a respondent has a social tie to at least one other person and thus is not a social isolate. A tie to a spouse can, in turn, link respondents to others who can provide information and possible resources.

Marriage is not only a tie but also a potential constraint on economic activities due to gender-based expectations. For example, single women are similar to married men, and unlike married women, in their ability to allocate their time to business activities with little regard to domestic responsibilities (Starr & Yudkin 1996). Thus, it would seem likely that single female owners could begin and pursue business start-up activities more easily than their married counterparts. However, according to a Wisconsin study and data from the Current Population Survey, female owners are at least as likely to be married as are male owners (Carter 1997; Devine 1994). Because these studies focus on respondents' current employment, rather than the process of moving into new employment, we do not know whether their results will hold for people in the process of starting a business. Children can also constrain someone's likelihood of entering self-employment. Married people with children are likely to face the competing demands of family life and business ownership and be more constrained in how much time they can devote to business than are nonparents (Shelton & Daphne 1996).

A person's employment status may also influence business start-up chances. Prior employment histories can affect a person's likelihood of following through on intentions to be self-employed by raising or lowering their stock of human capital and their career expectations. Thus, career histories and specific career trajectories push or pull someone into self-employment. Although some research points to unemployment as a push factor into self-employment (Evans & Leighton 1989; Storey 1991, 1994), other data reveal that the great majority of new owners have full-time employment directly prior to ownership (Aldrich, Renzulli & Langton 1998; Carter 1997; Manser & Picot 1999; Reynolds & White 1997).

Starting a business is a process that includes intentions or serious thought about business ownership. Thus, people who had an idea or inclination toward self-employment are more likely to actually move into the nascent stages of ownership if other influences are present (Carter 1997). However, intentions do not always come to fruition. Many people think about starting a business but never actually go through the stages to become an owner (Carter 1997; Reynolds & White 1997). Nevertheless, intentions are a first step toward ownership and thus should be included in analyses of start-ups.

Human capital is the investment in technical skills and knowledge that boosts someone's earning power (Becker 1964). People invest time and money in their education so that they will be able to negotiate for better jobs and more income based on their skills (Lin 1999). Thus, sociologists and economists alike have used years of education to measure human capital. In the case of business owners, some research has found that they have about the same level of educational attainment as the general public (Aldrich, Renzulli & Aldrich 1998; Gartner 1988), whereas others have found contrary results (Reynolds & White 1997).

Previous research has shown that women tend to have more ties to women than to men (McPherson & Smith-Lovin 1986; Popielarz 1999). Even though women have made substantial gains in occupational status and authority over the past few decades, they still on average occupy more disadvantaged positions than men do (Reskin 1993). Thus, if someone's ties are primarily to other women, this could also be a disadvantage in the business community for gathering information and other resources.

Research Design

The data consist of a panel of individuals in the early stages of business formation, owners of established organizations, and people providing services to new organizations. We tracked respondents over a two-year period, from 1990 to 1992.

DATA

We use data from the Research Triangle Entrepreneurial Development Study to explore the networks of nascent entrepreneurs and business owners. Participants were located in the Research Triangle area of North Carolina, an area previously studied by Aldrich et al. (1989), Campbell (1988), Kalleberg et al. (1990), and others. Campbell (1988) analyzed gender differences in job-related networks by contacting people through the firms that employed them in the region. Kalleberg et al. (1990) and Aldrich et al. (1989) used the same region to study differences in the coverage of various organizational sampling frames. Luger and Goldstein (1991) found that economic development efforts in the Research Triangle area were similar to programs in other regions that attempted to promote growth through science parks. Based on these studies and others, we believe the Research Triangle area of North Carolina is a valuable laboratory in which to study business start-up and growth.

The respondents in this sample were selected from people with entrepreneurial or business activity memberships and involvement, drawn from organizations in Durham and Wake Counties, North Carolina,[3] participants in technical-college small business classes in Wake County, and a random sample of new business owners in Wake County. The sample thus includes information on current small business owners (those with an active business) and two groups of people qualifying as nascent entrepreneurs: people actively trying to start a business and those who are thinking about becoming business owners. According to Reynolds and White (1997), our sample includes nascent entrepreneurs because we have included people who have taken action in the first steps toward business ownership, such as joining a business organization and taking an entrepreneurial class. Reese (1993) conducted analyses in which she included a dummy variable for her randomly drawn subsample, contrasting it with her purposively drawn subsamples, and showed that sample source was not a statistically significant predictor of network composition or networking activities.[4]

Two waves of information were collected, the first between 1990 and 1991 and the second in 1992 (see Reese 1993 and Reese & Aldrich 1995 for a full description of the data). Phase 1 of the first wave was a short mailed questionnaire, and phase 2 involved an in-depth telephone interview with those who returned the questionnaire. In the first phase, 659 questionnaires were mailed out and 444 returned. Telephone interviews were completed for 353 of the respondents who returned a mailed questionnaire. The survey thus had a completion rate of 67% of those who received a mailed questionnaire and a response rate of 54% of the original sample who completed a mailed and telephone questionnaire. We used only those wave 1 respondents who completed a phone interview, as they were asked the social network questions we used to construct our independent variables.

For the second wave (collected in 1992), a mailed questionnaire was sent to all the people who had completed a mailed questionnaire in wave 1. All respondents were also telephoned. Of the 353 who had completed the mailed and telephone questionnaire in wave 1, we received at least some follow-up information on 328 respondents, for a follow-up rate of 93%. These rates are comparable to those in other studies of entrepreneurs (Birley, Cromie & Myers 1990; Cooper & Dunkelberg 1987; Kalleberg 1987; Kalleberg 1986). See Table 1 for the demographic characteristics of our sample.

VARIABLES

We present information on the coding and definition of all variables in Table 2. For the dependent variable and the four central independent variables, we present additional information below.

Business Start-Up

We used the second wave of data to obtain information about business start-ups. Two groups of people were identified on the basis of their business status at wave 1 — business owners and nonowners. Interviewers asked the business owners a series of questions to tap additional business start-ups as well as new business start-ups.[5] Interviewers asked the nonowners if they had started or bought a business since wave 1. Fifty-two respondents started a new business between wave 1 and wave 2 of our interviews. Of the respondents already in business at wave 1, 16% had started a new business by wave 2. Of the respondents who were not owners at wave 1, 31% had started a new business by wave 2.

To measure business formation, we constructed a dichotomous variable for start-up in wave 2 that indicated whether respondents from wave 1 had started a business by wave 2. We have information on 276 cases for business start-up events between wave 1 and wave 2.[6]

Gender

Gender was measured with a dichotomous variable, taking the value 1 for male and 0 for female respondents.

Heterogeneity

Interviewers in the first wave of data asked respondents about the people with whom they talked about business. The respondents were asked the following: "Now I would like to talk about your business contacts. Please tell me the first five people with whom you feel especially willing or able to discuss your ideas for a new business or your ideas about representing or running your current business." The five people with whom respondents talked about business matters are "strong ties,"[7] and we will refer to these people as the "business discussion network."

Networks are composed of people with many different attributes. An investigator needs to decide which dimension of heterogeneity is relevant, as a person's network can be heterogeneous in some respects and homogeneous in others (Blau 1977; Marsden 1987). For example, someone can have a network made up of all kin members, and that network is homogeneous with respect to kin. Yet each of the kin members may have a different occupation, and thus the network is heterogeneous with respect to occupation. Because we were interested in whether potential owners gleaned information from multiple sources, we focused on the differing social dimensions within which relationships with alters arose: work, friendship, family, and membership groups.

Moore (1990) and other researchers have used separate OLS models for each relationship type to measure absolute network composition. By contrast, we prefer to use a general measure of heterogeneity, because it is a concise measure of network diversity. We asked respondents their relationship to each of the persons in their discussion network. Respondents could list up to three relationship categories for each alter (similar to the General Social Survey format). For the heterogeneity measure, we categorized an alter by using the first relationship the respondent named. The name generator provided six categories that make up the absolute composition of business discussion networks: kin, friends, coworkers, business associates, consultants, and fellow group or association members. We defined network heterogeneity as the probability of randomly choosing people with two different attributes from the possible six attributes. We calculated it as follows:[8]

$$
1 - \left[\left(\frac{\# \text{ kin}_i}{\text{total}} \right)^2 + \left(\frac{\# \text{ business associates}_i}{\text{total}} \right)^2 + \left(\frac{\# \text{ coworkers}_i}{\text{total}} \right)^2 \right.
$$
$$
\left. + \left(\frac{\# \text{ consultants}_i}{\text{total}} \right)^2 + \left(\frac{\# \text{ friends}_i}{\text{total}} \right)^2 + \left(\frac{\# \text{ group members}_i}{\text{total}} \right)^2 \right].
$$
\hfill (1)

A heterogeneity score equal to 0 indicates a perfectly homogeneous network, whereas a heterogeneity score approaching 1 indicates a more heterogeneous network.

Proportion of Kin

We measured the percentage of kin members that ego nominated in the business discussion network as the ratio of kin to all persons named. As we note above, respondents had the opportunity to classify each alter into three relation categories.

534 / *Social Forces* **79:2, December 2000**

TABLE 1: Demographic Characteristics of Respondents in Wave 1 Who Were Followed Up in Wave 2

Characteristic	Men	Women
Education		
High school or less	8.0 (20)	12.4 (12)
2 years of college	6.8 (17)	22.7 (22)
Bachelor's degree	48.2 (121)	37.1 (36)
Master's degree	26.3 (66)	22.7 (22)
Ph.D. degree	10.8 (27)	5.2 (5)
Race		
White	94.8 (237)	91.8 (89)
Black	3.6 (9)	8.2 (8)
Other	1.6 (4)	0
Family status		
Married	84.5 (212)	69.1 (67)
Single	15.5 (39)	30.9 (30)
Number of children		
0	50.4 (113)	64.8 (57)
1-4	43.4 (109)	32.0 (31)
5+	.8 (2)	0
Run own business		
Currently an owner	77.7 (195)	72.2 (70)
Currently not an owner	22.3 (56)	27.8 (27)
Intend to start a business	29.2 (73)	22.7 (22)
Source of respondent		
Random sample	8.8 (22)	16.5 (16)
Organizational rolls	91.2 (229)	83.5 (81)
Industry		
Manufacturing	7.2 (18)	7.2 (7)
Business services	17.5 (44)	18.6 (18)
Consulting services	16.3 (41)	7.2 (7)
Retail	11.6 (29)	20.6 (20)
Other (R&D, computers, real estate)	25.1 (63)	18.6 (18)
Work history		
Number of years employed full-time		
0	12.8 (30)	24.2 (22)
1-5	25.5 (60)	24.2 (22)
6-11	61.7 (145)	51.8 (47)
Number of years self-employed		
0	33.2 (78)	38.5 (35)
1-5	38.3 (90)	36.2 (33)
5-11	28.5 (67)	25.3 (23)
Start-up between waves 1 and 2	19 (40)	15 (11)

TABLE 1: Demographic Characteristics of Respondents in Wave 1 Who Were Followed Up in Wave 2 (Continued)

Characteristic	Men	Women
Mean age	42	40
N	251	97

Note: Figures preceding those in parentheses are percentages, and those in parentheses are total numbers.

We coded an alter as kin if the respondent classified him or her as kin as the first, second, or third relation type to ensure that we captured all kin alters.[9]

Total Number of People in the Network

The total number of people with whom respondents discuss business is a crude measure of the number of direct contacts but does not limit respondents to listing strong ties. Interviewers asked the respondents to indicate the total number of people with whom they discussed aspects of starting or running a business. The mean number of people was 8.8 and the mode was 5, but the data were highly skewed, with an interquartile range of 3 to 10.[10]

Results

We tested the hypotheses about network characteristics and business start-up in two steps. First we computed descriptive statistics for gender and network characteristics. Then we used multivariate logistic regression models to predict start-up by gender and network characteristics.

GENDER AND NETWORK CHARACTERISTICS AT WAVE 1

Our analyses only weakly confirm previous studies showing that gender is related to network characteristics.[11] Because the distributions of heterogeneity and proportion of kin are discontinuous in very small networks (less than 5), it is important to evaluate the size of each person's business network. Therefore, we explored whether the distribution of number of alters nominated by men and women was the same. The mean number of alters nominated by men and women was 4.7. About 82% of men and 84% of women nominated 5 business discussion ties (the difference between men and women is not statistically significant). Men and women have the same number of diverse alters and similar heterogeneity scores. The mean heterogeneity score for men is .45 and for women is .49, a

536 / *Social Forces* **79:2, December 2000**

TABLE 2: Variables and Coding for Business Discussion Network

	Definition	Coding
Dependent Variable		
Business start-up	Respondents who started or bought a business between waves 1 and 2	0 = didn't start a business by wave 2 1 = started a business by wave 2
Independent Variables		
Social capital variables		
Heterogeneity score	Probability that each alter in the network will have a different relation to respondent from that of all other alters	Range of 0 to 1 (theoretical) where 0 = completely homogeneous network, 1 = absolutely heterogeneous network
Proportion of kin	Number of kin mentioned / total number of alters mentioned (as a function of the number of alters) at wave 1	0-.80 (observed) 0-1 (possible)
Total number in network	Total number of people with whom respondents discuss business at wave 1. Open-ended question not solicited through the name generator.	Range of 0 to 200 (mean = 8.8, mode = 5)
Proportion of female alters	Number of females mentioned / number of alters mentioned (as a function of the number of alters) at wave 1	0-1 (observed)
Life stage		
Marital status	Respondent married at wave 1	0 = not married, 1 = married
Age	Age of respondent at wave 1	22-78 (mean = 41.2)
Presence of children	Total number of children 18 years old or younger living with nascent or established owner	Range of 0 to 8 (mean = .86, s.d. = 1.1)
Human capital		
Education	Level of education attained	4 dummy variables: 1= some college 1 = Bachelor's degree 1 = Master's degree 1 = Ph.D. degree 0 = Other education level, for each dummy

TABLE 2: Variables and Coding for Business Discussion Network
          (Continued)

	Definition	Coding
Human capital (cont'd)		
Work history	The respondent's work history over the past 10 years: number of years employed full time and number of years self-employed	Continuous variables: Employed: range of 0 to 11 years (mean = 5.2, s.d. = 3.9) Self-employed: range of 0 to 11 years (mean = 3.3, s.d. = 3.7)
Stage of business ownership	Running own business at wave 1	0 = no, 1 = yes
Continuity of business ownership	Running same business at wave 2	0 = no, 1 = yes
Intent to start a business	At wave 1, respondent planned to start a business in the future	0 = no plans, 1 = plans

statistically insignificant difference, as Table 3 shows. Women and men differ substantially in the proportion of female alters in their business networks (.48 versus .18, respectively).

Bivariate analysis, however, supports the typical finding that women nominate more kin in their networks than do men (Marsden 1987; Moore 1990; Renzulli 1998). Fifty-six percent of women nominate one or more kin as part of their business discussion network, compared with only 40% of men. The average proportion of kin for men is .14 and for women is .20, as shown in Table 3, and the difference is statistically significant. The proportion of kin for men and women in this sample was lower than in Wellman (1992a), who found that 55% of men and women named kin in their active networks. Moore (1990), using the General Social Survey, found that the proportion of kin in personal discussion networks was .51 for men and .58 for women. We believe that we found a smaller proportion of kin in our respondents' networks because they were specifically asked to name alters in their *business* networks. General discussion networks may draw more heavily on kin because they often provide emotional support, whereas business networks may draw less heavily on kin and more heavily on other kinds of ties that provide instrumental support.

START-UP BY GENDER AND NETWORK CHARACTERISTICS

In the final part of our analysis, we used logistic regression in two steps to test our hypotheses about the association between discussion network characteristics and business start-ups. We first ran a baseline model (model 1) without any network

TABLE 3:   Mean Network Characteristics for Men and Women in
Business Discussion Network

	Men	Women
Number of business discussion	4.68	4.70
alters nominated	(.84)	(.75)
Heterogeneity score	.45	.49
	(.21)	(.19)
Proportion of kin	.14***	.20
	(.21)	(.23)
Proportion of females	.18***	.48
	(.21)	(.27)

Note: Standard deviations are in parentheses.

*** p < .001 (one-tailed tests)

variables in order to predict start-ups, and then we added the network variables in model 2. The nested models show that the addition of the network variables significantly increases explanatory power from model 1 to model 2. Table 4 shows the results of the multivariate models for start-ups.

As predicted by hypothesis 1, we found that network heterogeneity significantly increased the odds of starting a business, net of intentions, demographic characteristics, and other control variables.[12] The coefficient for heterogeneity's effect on start-up is positive, indicating that diverse ties in a network facilitate the start-up process. In fact, a perfectly heterogeneous network increased the odds of starting a business by a factor of five, net of all other variables (significant at the .05 level, one-tailed). This supports our contention that heterogeneous discussion networks serve as an important resource for nascent owners.

Hypothesis 2 was also confirmed. With respect to kin, we found that the greater the proportion of kin in respondents' networks, the less likely they were to start a new business between the two waves of our study. For a unit increase in the proportion of kin, the chances of starting a business at wave 2 decreased by a factor of .05, net of other network characteristics, individual variables, work history, and human capital variables. In other words, a business network that changes from zero kin to all kin will reduce the odds of a person starting a new business by 95%. We interpret this result as suggesting that the information that kin provide and the time it takes to maintain kin ties create disadvantages for people contemplating a business start-up. Net of the network variables, the gender of a respondent had no significant effect on the likelihood of starting a new business.

When we tested for the possible effect of the gender composition of a respondent's network, we found that adding the proportion of females did not

Gender, Networks, and Entrepreneurial Outcomes / 539

TABLE 4: Logistic Analysis for Business Start-Ups

Predictor Variables	Model 1 No Network Variables			Model 2 Full Model		
	Coefficient	S.E.	Odds Ratio	Coefficient	S.E.	Odds Ratio
Intercept	−3.51	1.23		−3.89	1.44	.00**
Social capital						
Heterogeneity	—	—	—	1.65	.96	5.23†
Proportion kin	—	—	—	−3.02	1.22	.05*
Proportion female	—	—	—	.67	.89	1.96
Total network size	—	—	—	.00	.01	1.00
Individual variables						
Married	−.01	.49	.99	.13	.51	1.14
Gender (male = 1)	.04	.46	1.04	.22	.55	1.25
Age	.03	.02	1.04	.03	.02	1.03
Number of children	.02	.16	1.02	.01	.17	1.01
Human capital						
Some college	−.59	.87	.56	−.53	.92	.59
Bachelor's degree	.19	.63	1.21	−.08	.67	.93
Master's degree	.04	.68	1.04	−.16	.72	.85
Ph.D. degree	.54	.81	1.72	.22	.86	1.25
Running own business at wave 1	.46	.62	1.58	.44	.65	1.56
Running same business at wave 2	−.65	.51	.52	−.73	.54	.48
Intent to start a business at wave 1	1.21	.41	3.37*	1.22	.41	3.37**
Work history						
Employed	.01	.07	1.01	.01	.08	1.01
Self-employed	.01	.08	1.01	−.02	.08	.98
−2 log-likelihood (N = 246)		219.39†			209.926*	

† p < .10   * p < .05   ** p < .01 (two-tailed tests)

significantly change our findings. Proportion of females is not significant, nor does it change the significant negative effects of proportion of kin. Therefore, we are confident that it is the type of relation individuals have to the alters in their personal networks, rather than the gender of the alters, that has the greatest impact on the likelihood of becoming an entrepreneur. We suspect that the proportion of women in our respondents' networks does not significantly affect business start-ups because respondents named people with whom they had discussed business and thus may have named only people (male or female) who have some business knowledge.

We found that the gender of our respondents did not affect the likelihood of business start-up: men and women are equally likely to start a business (in Table 4, gender is not statistically significant). Our sample of owners and nascent owners probably eliminates most women who have been occupationally steered away from business ownership or blocked from considering ownership because of other gender-related factors. According to our data, network composition, rather than gender, is a key obstacle for starting a business. Thus, we find that what differentiates people at this level of interest in ownership is their networks and not their gender.

Among the other variables we included, only intentions had a significant impact on start-ups. Individual variables such as age, education, marital status, and number of children did not significantly affect the likelihood of start-up. Our sample was fairly homogeneous with respect to education and marital status, and this lack of variation undoubtedly played a role in reducing the explanatory power of such factors. Also, because we followed respondents over a fairly narrow time period, factors associated with life-course events were less likely to be significant in our models. A person's work history also did not significantly affect start-ups. But intentions do matter.

Having intentions to start a business at wave 1 significantly increased the likelihood of actually starting one, raising the odds by a factor of 3.4 in both the fully specified model and the restricted model, net of all other variables. People who said they were going to start a business were very likely to carry their plans through. In keeping with the unpredictable world of entrepreneurship, we note that a few people who were neither running a business nor even contemplating a start-up in our first wave nevertheless went on to actually start one.

Conclusion and Discussion

Over the last few decades, women-owned businesses have greatly increased as a proportion of all businesses. We suspect that the observed trend toward a greater number of female-headed businesses stems from an increase in women's social capital. That is, increasing occupational opportunities for women may well be generating increased heterogeneity in the composition of their social networks. The composition of women's discussion networks, especially women with entrepreneurial interests, might have changed in the past few decades. We believe that historical research on trends in women's social networks may lead to a better understanding of the relative increase in female-owned businesses.

In this article, we used a sample of Research Triangle area owners and potential owners, gathered in the early 1990s, to examine the association between the characteristics of owners' and nascent entrepreneurs' social capital and the likelihood that they would start a business. We followed Lin's (1999) and Portes's (1998) conceptions of social capital as inhering in people's relations with others

Gender, Networks, and Entrepreneurial Outcomes / 541

and focused on the degree to which respondents' business discussion networks were heterogeneous and contained kin members. We treated discussion networks as conduits for information about economic opportunities as well as sources of social support for people who might be hesitant about attempting to start a business.

We found that networks spanning multiple domains of social life apparently provide nascent entrepreneurs with greater access to multiple sources of information than do more homogeneous networks and thus enable them to make the transition from idea to action. Our analyses show that actors with networks that draw information from multiple sources — those with high heterogeneity and a low percentage of kin — are much more likely to start a new business than are those with more homogeneous networks. Evidently, the increased social support provided by kinship ties does not offset the loss of information due to restrictions on network range. Our finding complements research showing that the most valuable social capital a person can mobilize is found via dissimilar ties (Popielarz 1999).

The received wisdom on the relationship between gender and social network composition is replicated in our data. We found that women tended to have more homogeneous networks than men with respect to kin. The network effects we observed held *net* of gender differences, and in analyses not shown here we found no significant interactions between network composition and owner gender. This implies that although men's and women's discussion networks differ in their composition, the mechanisms that link network range and entrepreneurial activity are similar across the sexes. A central conclusion of our study is that networks made up of a greater proportion of kin create disadvantages in entrepreneurial start-up *regardless* of gender. Therefore, based on our results, we conclude that a high percentage of kin in people's networks, rather than their gender or the gender composition of their networks, is a critical disadvantage facing potential owners.

We also found that intentions to start a business may be an impetus for people to mobilize and use their social capital. Although most people who initially reported that they intended to start a business in the near future did not actually do so, enough people did carry through on their intentions to suggest that intentions to start one might affect the extent to which people call upon their networks for assistance. Further research should examine the relationship between intentions and use of social networks.

Future research in network analyses of business ownership should look at the content of the information that passes between individuals and the alters to whom they are tied. Our analysis shows that network composition and heterogeneity are important influences on business start-up, implying that the information found in heterogeneous networks with nonkin ties is unique and useful to nascent entrepreneurs. However, we have not captured the content of ties with our network measurements; that is, we do not know what people are actually talking about when

542 / *Social Forces* **79:2, December 2000**

they meet with the alters in their networks. Instead, we have the characteristics of the network as a whole.

Research on the content of ties by Podolny and Baron (1997) shows the importance of looking at tie content for performance and mobility in firms. They showed that consistent role expectations within dense intrafirm networks affect an employee's likelihood of moving to higher levels. Outside the relatively closed boundaries of firms, however, role expectations may be less important than nascent entrepreneurs' ability to recognize potential resource providers and sustain ties with them. Nevertheless, the content of tie information and the level of role expectations may play a powerful role in the business community.

This article provides insights derived from a unique sample of owners and nascent entrepreneurs. Like all such samples, there are limitations based on sample size and geographic specificity. Although such limitations constrain the generalizability and statistical power of our work, we feel the general processes identified are grounded in a conceptual frame that is not context-specific. Heterogeneous social ties are an important resource that people can tap to improve their life chances. Thus, we suspect that research on business start-ups in other regions should find similar outcomes.

Notes

1. The self-employment rate is calculated as the percentage of people 16 and older who reported themselves as self-employed in a nonagricultural sector.

2. Thanks to an anonymous reviewer who pointed out that some readers may see gender composition as a competing hypothesis to kin composition as a disadvantage in business ownership.

3. The sample was drawn from membership lists for the following organizations: the Council for Entrepreneurial Development, a private nonprofit entrepreneurship promotion based in Durham, North Carolina; six private nonprofit business networking organizations; participants in Wake Technical Community College Small Business Center classes; and a local chapter of the National Association of Women Business Owners. To check on possible sample selection bias, a random sample of businesses registered in Wake County in 1990 was drawn.

4. In analyses not shown here, we replicated and extended Reese's (1993) test for possible selection bias in our sample. We found that sample source was not a significant predictor of our dependent variable, as the groups did not significantly differ from one another.

5. Thirteen respondents were lost because they refused to participate further at the end of wave 1.

6. To check for bias in nonresponse, we created a new test variable, coding the missing cases for the start-up variable as 1 and the others as 0. We then regressed the missing data variable on the independent network variables (proportion of kin, heterogeneity, and network size) and gender. The results (not shown here) were not significant,

Gender, Networks, and Entrepreneurial Outcomes / 543

indicating that respondents who did not answer the business start-up questions in wave 2 are not significantly different from those who did. Thus we are confident that our results are not influenced by selection bias.

7. The respondents were restricted to naming a maximum of five alters. This restriction limits the inferences we can draw about weak ties, as research has shown that using the name generator method elicits reasonably strong ties (Marsden 1987). Because we asked the respondents to tell us about their business networks, a focused subsample of their networks, we believe that having five named alters will provide an accurate account of the business discussion network. Asking for just five alters may introduce distortions in the data; however, the six relation types were evenly distributed over the five alters. We found no pattern across any of the five alters for any of the relationship types. Thus, there is no reason to suspect that the general pattern changes beyond five people, and thus we do not suspect our data were distorted by limiting the number of alters to five.

8. "Except for modifications due to sampling without replacement or an effort to take into account the true range of possible values for a given number of categories, [our measure of heterogeneity] is basically the same as the Index of Qualitative Variation described by Mueller and Schuessler" (Lieberson 1969:852).

9. Multiplex ties for kin members and partners in the business were not great in this sample and were not more common for women. Only 13% of men named a kin alter as a partner, which was very similar to the 9% of women who did so.

10. The variable had a range of 0 to 200 and was slightly skewed, with a small number of high values. We corrected for skewness by logging the size of the network. However, logging it did not significantly change the results; therefore, for ease of interpretation we used the raw size of the network. The mean of 8.8 is reasonable, considering other findings of general network size by Fischer (1982) and Wellman (1992b). Their studies found a mean range of 11 to 17. Because our question was only about business networks, a lower mean is plausible.

11. Multivariate analyses regressing heterogeneity and proportion of kin on gender are not shown here.

12. We ran models that would test the interaction effects of gender with the other variables, curvilinear effects of age, and influence of industry. However, the interactions, curvilinear age effects, and industry were not significant and therefore were not included in the final model.

References

Aldrich, Howard, Amanda Elam, and Pat Ray Reese. 1997. "Strong Ties, Weak Ties, and Strangers: Do Women Business Owners Differ from Men in Their Use of Networking to Obtain Assistance?" Pp. 1-25 in *Entrepreneurship in a Global Context*, edited by Sue Birley and Ian MacMillan. Routledge.

Aldrich, Howard E., Arne L. Kalleberg, Peter V. Marsden, and James Cassell. 1989. "In Pursuit of Evidence: Five Sampling Procedures for Locating New Businesses." *Journal of Business Venturing* 4:367-86.

Aldrich, Howard E., Linda Renzulli, and Nancy Langton. 1998. "Passing On Privilege." *Research in Social Stratification* 17:291-317.

544 / *Social Forces* 79:2, December 2000

Baker, Ted, Howard E. Aldrich, and Nina Liou. 1997. "Invisible Entrepreneurs: The Neglect of Women Business Owners by Mass Media and Scholarly Journals in the United States." *Entrepreneurship and Regional Development* 9:221-38.

Becker, Gary S. 1964. *Human Capital.* University of Chicago Press.

Birley, Sue, Stan Cromie, and Andrew Myers. 1990. *Entrepreneurial Networks: Their Creation and Development in Different Countries.* Cranfield School of Management.

Blau, Peter M. 1977. *Inequality and Heterogeneity: A Primitive Theory of Social Structure.* Free Press.

————. 1994. *Structural Contexts of Opportunity.* University of Chicago Press.

Bourdieu, Pierre. 1986. "The Forms of Capital." Pp. 241-58 in *Handbook of Theory and Research for the Sociology of Education,* edited by John G. Richardson. Greenwood Press.

Burt, Ronald S. 1992. *Structural Holes: The Social Structure of Competition.* Harvard University Press.

————. 1997. "The Contingent Value of Social Capital." *Administrative Science Quarterly* 42:339-65.

Campbell, Karen E. 1988. "Gender Differences in Job-Related Networks." *Work and Occupations* 15:179-200.

Campbell, Karen E., Peter V. Marsden, and Jeanne S. Hurlbert. 1986. "Social Resources and Socioeconomic Status." *Social Networks* 8:97-117.

Carter, Nancy. 1997. "Entrepreneurial Processes and Outcomes: The Influence of Gender." Pp. 163-77 in *The Entrepreneurial Process: Economic Growth, Men, Women, and Minorities,* Paul D. Reynolds and Sammis B. White. Quorum.

Coleman, James S. 1988. "Social Capital in the Creation of Human Capital." *American Journal of Sociology* 94:S95-S121.

Cooper, Arnold, and William Dunkelberg. 1987. "Old Questions, New Answers and Methodological Issues." *American Journal of Small Business* 11:11-23.

Denison, Daniel R., Anand Swaminathan, and Nancy Rothbard. 1994. "Networks, Founding Conditions, and Imprinting Processes: Examining the Process of Organizational Creation." Paper presented at the meeting of the Academy of Management, August 15, Dallas, Texas.

Devine, Theresa J. 1994. "Characteristics of Self-Employed Women in the United States." *Monthly Labor Review* 17(3):20-69.

England, Paula. 1992. *Comparable Worth.* Aldine de Gruyter.

Evans, David S., and Linda S. Leighton. 1989. "Some Empirical Aspects of Entrepreneurship." *American Economic Review* 79:519-35.

Fischer, Claude S. 1982. *To Dwell among Friends.* University of Chicago Press.

Fischer, Claude S., and Stacey J. Oliker. 1983. "A Research Note on Friendship, Gender, and the Life Cycle." *Social Forces* 62:124-33.

Gartner, William B. 1988. "Who Is an Entrepreneur? Is the Wrong Question." *American Journal of Small Business* 12:11-32.

Granovetter, Mark S. 1973. "Strength of Weak Ties." *American Sociological Review* 78:1360-80.

————. 1974. *Getting a Job: A Study of Contact and Careers.* Harvard University Press.

Hurlbert, Jeanne. 1991. "Social Circle and Job Satisfaction." *Work and Occupation* 18:415-30.

Gender, Networks, and Entrepreneurial Outcomes / 545

Kalleberg, Arne L. 1986. "Entrepreneurship in the 1980s: A Study of Small Business in Indiana." Pp. 157-89 in *Entrepreneurship and Innovation*, edited by Gary Libecap. JAI Press.

Kalleberg, Arne L., Peter V. Marsden, Howard E. Aldrich, and James Cassell. 1990. "Comparing Organizational Sampling Frames." *Administrative Science Quarterly* 35:658-88.

Katz, Jerome A., and Paula M. Williams. 1997. "Gender, Self-Employed and Weak-Tie Networking through Formal Organizations." *Entrepreneurship and Regional Development* 9:183-97.

Liao, Tim Futing, and Gillian Stevens. 1994. "Spouses, Homophily, and Social Networks." *Social Forces* 73:693-707.

Lieberson, Stanley. 1969. "Measuring Population Diversity." *American Sociological Review* 34:850-62.

Lin, Nan. 1999. "Building a Network Theory of Social Capital." *Connections* 22:28-51.

Luger, Michael I., and Harvey A. Goldstein. 1991. *Technology in the Garden: Research Parks and Regional Economic Development*. University of North Carolina Press.

Manser, Marilyn E., and Garnett Picot. 1999. "The Role of Self-Employment in U.S. and Canadian Job Growth." *Monthly Labor Review* 122:10-25.

Marsden, Peter V. 1987. "Core Discussion Networks of Americans." *American Sociological Review* 52:122-31.

———. 1990. "Network Data and Measurement." *Annual Review of Sociology* 16:435-63.

Marsden, Peter V., and Jeanne Hurlbert. 1988. "Social Resources and Mobility Outcomes: A Replication and Extension." *Social Forces* 66:1039-59.

McPherson, J. Miller, and Lynn Smith-Lovin. 1986. "Sex Segregation in Voluntary Associations." *American Sociological Review* 51:61-79.

———. 1987. "Homophily in Voluntary Organizations: Status Distance and the Composition of Face-to-Face Groups." *American Sociological Review* 52:370-79.

Moore, Gwen. 1990. "Structural Determinants of Men's and Women's Personal Networks." *American Sociological Review* 55:726-35.

Podolny, Joel M., and James N. Baron. 1997. "Resources and Relationships: Social Networks and Mobility in the Workplace." *American Sociological Review* 62:673-93.

Popielarz, Pamela A. 1999. "Organizational Constraints on Personal Network Formation." *Research in the Sociology of Organizations* 16:263-81.

Portes, Alejandro. 1998. "Social Capital: Its Origins and the Application in Modern Sociology." *Annual Review of Sociology* 24:1-24.

Putnam, Robert D. 1993. *Making Democracy Work: Civic Traditions in Modern Italy*. Princeton University Press.

Reese, Pat Ray. 1993. "Entrepreneurial Networks and Resource Acquisition: Does Gender Make a Difference?" Ph.D. dissertation, Department of Sociology, University of North Carolina.

Reese, Pat Ray, and Howard E. Aldrich. 1995. "Entrepreneurial Networks and Business Performance." Pp. 124-44 in *International Entrepreneurship*, edited by Sue Birley and Ian C. MacMillan. Routledge.

546 / *Social Forces* 79:2, December 2000

Renzulli, Linda. 1998. "Small Business Owners, Their Networks, and the Process of Resource Acquisition." Master's thesis, Department of Sociology. University of North Carolina at Chapel Hill.

Reskin, Barbara. 1993. "Sex Segregation in the Workplace." *Annual Review of Sociology* 19:241-70.

Reynolds, Paul D., and Sammis B. White. 1997. *The Entrepreneurial Process: Economic Growth, Men, Women, and Minorities*. Quorum.

Shelton, Beth Ann, and John Daphne. 1996. "The Division of Household Labor." *Annual Review of Sociology* 22:299-322.

Sik, Endre, and Barry Wellman. 1999. "Network Capital in Capitalist, Communist, and Post-Communist Countries." Pp. 225-54 in *Networks in the Global Village*, edited by Barry Wellman. Westview Press.

Starr, Jennifer A., and Marcia Yudkin. 1996. "Women Entrepreneurs: A Review of Current Research." Center for Research on Women, Wellesley College, Research Report.

Storey, David J. 1991. "The Birth of New Firms—Does Unemployment Matter?" *Small Business Economics* 3:167-78.

———. 1994. *Understanding the Small Business Sector*. Routledge.

Wellman, Barry. 1990. "The Place of Kinfolk in Personal Community Networks." *Marriage and Family Review* 15:195-228.

———. 1992a. "Men in Networks: Private Communities, Domestic Friendships." Pp. 74-114 in *Men's Friendships*, edited by Peter M. Nardi. Sage Publications.

———. 1992b. "Which Ties Provide What Kinds of Support." *Advances in Group Processes* 9:207-35.

Wellman, Barry, Peter J. Carrington, and Alan Hall. 1988. "Networks as Personal Communities." Pp. 80-85 in *Social Structures: A Network Approach*, edited by Barry Wellman and S.D. Berkowitz. Cambridge University Press.

Wellman, Barry, and Scot Wortley. 1990. "Different Strokes from Different Folks: Community Ties and Social Support." *American Journal of Sociology* 96:558-88.

Part IV
Financial Capital

[15]

FUNDING NEW
BUSINESS VENTURES:
ARE DECISION MAKERS
BIASED AGAINST
WOMEN ENTREPRENEURS?

E. HOLLY BUTTNER and BENSON ROSEN
University of North Carolina

EXECUTIVE SUMMARY

Women have been leaving large corporations in increasing numbers in recent years to start their own businesses. However, they have not been succeeding at the same rate as their male counterparts. One potential barrier to a successful new venture is access to startup capital. Anecdotal evidence suggests that women starting their own businesses may have more difficulty obtaining financial support than men. In a loan decision simulation, this study systematically tested the allegations of female entrepreneurs that bank loan officers are more likely to grant loans, to make a counteroffer, and to make larger counteroffers to male entrepreneurs compared to female entrepreneurs under identical circumstances.

Loan officers usually make funding decisions on the basis of information gathered from an interview and a business plan, while venture capitalists often screen proposals on the basis of a business plan alone. A second purpose of this study was to determine whether the mode of presentation— business plan versus business plan with interview—increased the male or female entrepreneur's probability of successfully obtaining a loan.

A third purpose of this study was to examine the effects of the decision maker's previous experience on funding decisions. The recommendations of (experienced) loan officers versus (inexperienced) undergraduate students were compared in order to determine how experience and accountability influence loan decisions.

The study consisted of a 2 × 2 × 2 research design with three independent variables. Loan officers and undergraduate students either read a business plan, or read a business plan and watched a videotape of an interview between a loan officer and a male or female entrepreneur who was seeking a loan to start a business. Participants then indicated the likelihood that they would recommend approval of the loan, make a counteroffer of a smaller amount, and the magnitude of the counteroffer.

There was no evidence that sex stereotypes influenced business funding decisions. With respect

Address correspondence to Dr. E. Holly Buttner, University of North Carolina at Greensboro, Bryan School of Business and Economics, 366 Bryan Building, Greensboro, NC 27412.

The authors wish to thank Dr. Rollie Tillman and the Frank Hawkins Kenan Institute for Private Enterprise, Chapel Hill, NC for grant support for this research project.

Journal of Business Venturing 4, 249–261
© 1989 Elsevier Science Publishing Co., Inc., 655 Avenue of Americas, New York, NY 10010

0883-9026/89/$3.50

to the amount of counteroffer, a significant three-way interaction was obtained between entrepreneurial gender, presentation format, and participant status. Loan officers made larger counteroffers to the female compared to the male when they read the business plan and watched the interview. Students made larger counteroffers to the male compared to the female when they read the business plan and observed the interview. Loan officers were significantly more cautious and conservative than students in their funding decisions.

Failure to support allegations of bias against women entrepreneurs is discussed in terms of possible unrealistic expectations regarding the ease of obtaining startup capital. Further research is needed to examine this explanation.

One implication of these findings is that female entrepreneurs should seek opportunities to meet with loan officers to present their business proposals. In the interview, the female has the opportunity to address questions of motivation and competence. On the other hand, bankers may make more impartial decisions when relying on information in the business plan alone, where financial considerations would have greater weight. Finally, the results suggest that studies using students as proxies for bank loan officers have very limited generalizability.

INTRODUCTION

Women have been leaving large corporations in growing numbers during the past 10 years. In a *Fortune* survey of business school graduates who earned MBAs in 1976, 30% of the women reported that they had left their jobs in large corporations (Taylor 1986). Many of these women abandoned organizational careers in order to start new ventures. Between 1980 and 1985, the number of businesses owned by women increased 47% to 3.7 million. However, there is evidence that businesses founded by women have not succeeded at the same rate as businesses founded by men. In 1985, women owned 28% of all sole proprietorships, yet received only 12% of revenues (SBA 1988). One potential barrier to new business formation is access to startup capital. Anecdotal evidence suggests that women who aspire to start their own business may have more difficulty in obtaining financial support than men.

Survey findings reported by Hisrich and O'Brien (1982) suggest that bank loan officers may be influenced by the gender of the entrepreneur, favoring males over females, in evaluating loan applications. Twenty-seven percent of the female entrepreneurs who responded to the survey cited discrimination as a major or moderate obstacle in starting and operating a business. One respondent commented that, "Banks give the impression that women should not be operating a business. Therefore they give us the run around." Another respondent complained that she had to " . . . furnish 100% collateral for a working capital loan, which the bank would not have required from a man with (her) experience" (Hisrich and O'Brien, 1982). In another study, a female venture capitalist reported that, "Some men are prejudiced against working with women entrepreneurs. There are very few deals done with women. I've only seen two in eight years" (Seglin 1986, p. 66).

Funding Decision Criteria

Consideration of an applicant's gender in determining the level of funding for a new venture would be both unethical and illegal. Recently, a number of studies have examined the factors that venture capitalists and bankers consider in awarding venture capital. Shilit (1987) found that venture capitalists' decisions about financing a business startup depend on the level of risk, the potential return, the experience of the management team, and whether the venture capitalists could recover their investment should the business go bankrupt. Similarly, MacMillan, Siegel and Narasimha (1985) surveyed venture capitalists to determine the criteria they used to evaluate prospective enterpreneurs. They found that qualities of the entrepreneur including endurance, experience, and ability to manage risk ultimately determine whether the venture is funded.

With respect to the decision criteria bankers use to determine the level of capital available for aspiring entrepreneurs, Jones (1982) identified the following factors: collateral, credit history, management experience, and financial position. In another survey of reported decision criteria (Ulrich and Arlow 1981), bank loan officers ranked the importance of 30 possible variables affecting their decisions about entrepreneurial loan applications. Factor analysis yielded four factors: (1) financial soundness of the business, (2) cost of granting and monitoring the loan, (3) risk, and (4) exposure time to loan maturity.

Jackowicz and Hisrich (1987) used Kelly's Personal Construct theory to develop a repertory grid of the factors bank loan officers use to evaluate an entrepreneur's loan application. The factors used to evaluate loan applications were: the experience and track record of the applicant, level of risk involved, clarity of the company's planning, quality of the business plan, profitability, collateral, and the nature of the need for the loan (e.g., to expand operations versus to overcome setbacks).

In summary, it appears that there are many variables that influence decisions of venture capitalists and loan officers. Some of these variables relate to the business, e.g., its financial position and risk, while other variables concern the entrepreneur's experience, ability to manage risk, and endurance. The intuitive decision process that venture capitalists and loan officers use combines a variety of factors into a loan decision.

Research evidence suggests that male and female entrepreneurs do not differ on attributes associated with entrepreneurial success. Research by DiCarlo and Lyons (1979) showed that female entrepreneurs differed significantly from women in the general population on the entrepreneurial attributes: need for achievement, independence, leadership, autonomy, aggressiveness and (lack of) conformity. Thus, any difference in treatment of female entrepreneurs cannot be attributed to actual differences in entrepreneurial attributes.

In spite of the failure to find major differences between male and female entrepreneurs, it is still possible that sex stereotypes influence the decision for approval of an entrepreneurial loan. To the extent that venture capitalists and loan officers consider personal qualities of the entrepreneur such as ability to manage risk, managerial experience and endurance, sex stereotypes depicting women as lacking in these critical entrepreneurial attributes can influence funding decisions. Recent research (Buttner and Rosen 1988a) has shown that bank loan officials do see women relative to men as lacking important entrepreneurial characteristics including leadership, risk-taking propensity, endurance and ability to change. An important extension of this line of research is to determine whether sex stereotypes influence actual decisions, leading to favored treatment for male entrepreneurs compared to female entrepreneurs in otherwise identical circumstances.

The Influence of Gender on Funding Decisions

Considerable research has demonstrated that gender influences business decisions. Schein (1973, 1975) found that males were seen as more fit than females to hold managerial positions. In other studies, males were treated more favorably than females in decisions concerning selection, job assignment, promotion, development, and performance evaluation (Deaux and Taynor 1973; Dipboye, Arvey and Terpstra 1977; Heilman 1983; Rosen and Jerdee 1973, 1974a, 1974b; Shaw 1972; Terborg and Ilgen 1975). Extrapolating from research examining the influence of sex stereotypes on business decisions suggests that bias against female

252   E. H. BUTTNER AND B. ROSEN

entrepreneurs is a real possibility. The first objective of the present study is to systematically investigate possible sex bias in funding decisions.

Presentation Format

Funding decisions made by loan officers are usually made on the basis of a business plan and an interview with the entrepreneur. Venture capitalists, on the other hand, receive many requests for venture capital and must screen proposals on the basis of a business plan alone. Research has shown that in situations where a decision is required and information is ambiguous or incomplete, decision makers will fall back on stereotypes (Pheterson, Kiesler and Goldberg 1971; Terborg and Ilgen 1975; see Nieva and Gutek 1980 for a review). Since the business plan provides only an outline of the business and a brief biography of the entrepreneur, respondents may be more likely to fall back on sex stereotypes than when they have the additional information about the entrepreneur provided in the interview. On the other hand, the gender of the entrepreneur is obvious in the interview. Stereotypes of women lacking qualities of successful entrepreneurs may become salient.

The second objective of the study was to determine whether possible bias in decisions to support entrepreneurs is more likely in situations where the decision maker only examines a business plan versus situations where the decision maker also interviews the entrepreneur.

The Effect of Respondent Type on Funding Decisions

A third purpose of this study was to examine the effect of the decision makers' previous experience on funding decisions. Students are occasionally substituted for business professionals in research. In several studies (Bernstein, Hakel and Harlan 1975; Dipboye, Fromkin and Wiback 1975; Hakel, Dobmeyer and Dunnette 1970; Landy and Bates 1973), students exhibited a leniency bias in evaluations when compared to their business professional counterparts. Experienced bankers, who have responsibility for evaluating entrepreneurial loans and accountability for their decisions, may make more conservative decisions than students. Our third objective was to compare the responses of students to bank loan officers. This provided an opportunity to examine how experience and personal accountability influence loan decisions.

METHODOLOGY

Sample

The sample consisted of two groups: 51 commercial loan officers (40 males and 11 females) at two mid-sized southeastern banks, and 69 undergraduate business administration students (34 males and 35 females) at a large southeastern university. Average age was 34.2 years for the loan officers and 22.1 years for the students. Loan officers had an average of 5.6 years experience in their jobs. None of the students had actual experience with bank lending decisions.

Procedure

Loan officers were divided into two groups. A business decision-making simulation was mailed to the first group of 33 loan officers. The loan officers were asked to imagine that

GENDER BIAS IN FUNDING NEW BUSINESS VENTURES   **253**

they had just received a business plan from an entrepreneur requesting a loan of $50,000 to start a business.

The Business Plan

The business plan described a toxic waste disposal venture. The entrepreneur proposed to contract with local governments and businesses to dispose of toxic chemical waste. The entrepreneur was depicted as having extensive experience in biochemistry. The plan included a description of the business, marketing strategy, organizational structure, financial projections, and the entrepreneur's resume and personal financial statement. The entrepreneur requested a loan of $50,000 to cover startup costs.

The business plan was based on extensive conversations with biochemists experienced in chemical waste disposal. In addition, several loan officers were consulted in the development of the plan to ensure the plan's realism.

Two business plans were created. The gender of the entrepreneur was manipulated in alternate versions of the business plan by changing the first name on the resume and financial statement. A resume with a photograph was placed in the beginning of the business plan read by those subjects who did not see the interview. To strengthen the gender manipulation, the entrepreneur was frequently referred to by name in the business plan.

Loan officers received only one version of the business plan (from either a male or a female entrepreneur) and responded to a series of questions regarding their evaluation of the loan request. Then participants completed the simulation by providing background information and answering questions to check the manipulation of the entrepreneurial gender variable. Finally, they returned their evaluation in a post-paid return envelope. Thirty-one loan officers returned the simulation for a response rate of 94%.

The Videotaped Interview

The videotape consisted of an interview between either a male or a female entrepreneur and a loan officer. In the interview, the entrepreneur described the business, provided background about experience and education, described expectations about the business' operations, and requested a $50,000 loan. The script and the videotape were reviewed by an experienced bank loan officer to ensure that topics typically covered in an interview were included. To enhance the realism of the interview, videotaping was conducted in the office of a loan officer after banking hours.

Five actors were employed; one male played the role of the loan officer, and two males and two females played the entrepreneurial role. Four versions of the interview were produced: two versions with male actors and two with female actresses in the entrepreneurial role. To determine which male and female entrepreneurial versions were most comparable in quality of acting, four groups of undergraduate business students independently viewed the videotapes. The undergraduates rated the actors and actresses on dimensions of attractiveness, likability, energy, sincerity, believability and overall quality of the acting. Two versions featuring the actor and actress whose ratings were most similar were selected. There were no significant differences in the ratings of the male and female actors playing the role of the entrepreneur on any of the six dimensions. We therefore concluded that the acting quality was comparable in the two versions of the interview used in the experiment. Any differences in funding decisions could be attributed to the entrepreneur's gender rather than acting ability.

254   E. H. BUTTNER AND B. ROSEN

The second group of 20 loan officers participated in the simulation in their offices. Each loan officer read the business plan and then viewed a five-minute videotape of a loan application interview between a bank officer and either a male or female entrepreneur. At the close of the interview, participants evaluated the loan request and provided background information.

In the second phase of the study, students were recruited from an undergraduate business policy course. Although the students had taken finance courses, none had any commercial lending experience. The students were divided into two groups. The first group of 43 students was asked to assume the role of a bank loan officer and to read a business plan developed by an entrepreneur who was eager to start a toxic waste business. After reading the business plan, participants evaluated the loan request and provided background information.

The second group of 26 students was given the same instructions. In addition to reading the business plan, this group also viewed a videotape of either a male or female entrepreneur's interview with the loan officer. They then completed the questions about their evaluation and background information.

In summary, there were four groups of participants: loan officers who either read a business plan or read the plan and watched the interview, and students who read the plan only or read the plan and observed the interview.

Independent Variables

The three independent variables were: (1) gender of the entrepreneur, (2) presentation format—business plan only versus business plan and interview, and (3) experience of the participant—loan officer (experienced) versus student (inexperienced). In half the simulations, the entrepreneur was male; in the other half, the entrepreneur was female. The second independent variable, presentation format, was manipulated by randomly assigning loan officers and students into two experimental groups: one group read the business plan only, and the other group read the business plan and viewed the videotape.

Dependent Variables

Three dependent variables were measured: (1) likelihood of granting the $50,000 loan, (2) likelihood of making a counteroffer of a smaller amount, and (3) the size of the counteroffer. Respondents indicated the likelihood of approving the loan on a seven-point scale ranging from a 1 for "highly unlikely" to a 7 for "highly likely."

After responding to the first question, participants were informed that banks frequently will not approve the original request of an entrepreneur but may make a counteroffer of a smaller amount. Participants were then asked to indicate, on a similar seven-point scale, the likelihood that they would approve a counteroffer for the entrepreneur. Respondents indicated, in dollars, the size of the counteroffer for the new business loan. In an open-ended question, participants indicated what concerns they would have in granting the loan. Finally, subjects completed a short background questionnaire and responded to a question to check the manipulation of the gender of the entrepreneur.

In summary, the study consisted of a 2 × 2 × 2 research design with three independent variables. Loan officers or students evaluated a business proposal by reading a business plan only or reading the plan and watching an interview of either a male or a female entrepreneur. Respondents participated in only one version of simulation. Loan officers in

TABLE 1   Effect of Entrepreneurial Gender, Mode of Presentation, and Respondent Type on Funding Decisions (Means and Standard Deviations)

	Loan Officers				Students			
	Male Entrepreneur		Female Entrepreneur		Male Entrepreneur		Female Entrepreneur	
Dependent Variable	BP[1]	Int.[2]	BP	Int.	BP	Int.	BP	Int.
Likelihood of granting the loan[3]	1.46	2.00	1.36	1.67	3.74	4.50	3.89	4.25
(s.d.)	.66	1.79	.50	1.00	1.32	.97	1.29	.93
Likelihood of a Counteroffer[3]	2.54	2.82	2.64	3.56	3.95	4.00	3.76	4.13
(s.d.)	1.71	1.72	1.69	1.67	1.24	1.32	1.60	1.36
Amount of the Counteroffer ($)	13,068	12,725	9,458	22,778	28,000	36,944	30,929	25,000
(s.d.)	16,770	11,789	12,279	18,559	12,711	13,097	10,550	16,329

[1]Business plan only.
[2]Business plan plus interview.
[3]Likelihood was indicated on a scale from 1 (highly unlikely) to 7 (highly likely).

the same branch received only one version of the business plan or viewed only one version of the interview, usually at the same time, and were unaware that other versions existed. Comparisons of the likelihood of granting the loan, likelihood of counteroffer, and amount of the counteroffer across the eight experimental conditions provided a test of the influence of the entrepreneur's gender, the respondent's status (banker or student), and the format of presentation on funding decisions.

RESULTS

Manipulation Check

Participants were asked at the beginning of the response form to write the name of the entrepreneur. Two loan officers did not write the name of the entrepreneur on the question-naire. Therefore, their responses were omitted from further analysis. All other participants correctly identified the entrepreneur by name.

A second preliminary analysis examined possible effects attributable to the respondent's gender. No main or interactive effects were found for likelihood of granting the loan or for likelihood of making a counteroffer. All subsequent analyses were conducted with male and female respondents combined.

Gender of the Entrepreneur

Our first objective was to examine whether sex stereotypes influence funding decisions. Table 1 shows the means for likelihood of granting a loan, likelihood of a counteroffer, and amount of the counteroffer for the male and female entrepreneurs across the two modes of presentation for loan officers and for students. Respondents were equally likely to approve

256   E. H. BUTTNER AND B. ROSEN

TABLE 2   Results of 2 × 2 × 2 ANOVA Analysis

Independent Variable	Likelihood of Approval	Likelihood of Counteroffer	Amount of Counteroffer
Entrepreneurial Gender (A)	.36	.41	.05
Mode of Presentation (B)	4.91*	1.74	1.87
Respondent Type (C)	124.60**	12.49**	28.81**
A × B	.51	.61	.01
A × C	.15	.56	1.74
B × C	.09	.42	.72
A × B × C	.04	.07	5.94*

*$p < .05$.
**$p < .01$.

the male and female entrepreneur's loan application ($\overline{X} = 3.02$ for the male entrepreneur versus $\overline{X} = 3.05$ for the female). Similarly participants were equally likely to make a counteroffer to the male and female entrepreneur ($\overline{X} = 3.39$ for the male; $\overline{X} = 3.57$ for the female). Finally, there was no significant difference in the magnitude of the counteroffer ($\overline{X} = \$23,695$ for the male; $\$22,721$ for the female). Table 2 shows that when data was pooled across both bankers and students and across the business plan and video-interview experimental conditions, there was no evidence that lending decisions were significantly influenced by the entrepreneur's gender.

Interaction of Entrepreneur's Gender and Presentation Format

Our second objective was to examine the special conditions where the entrepreneur's gender would influence loan decisions. We looked for a possible interaction between entrepreneurial gender and mode of presentation (business plan versus business plan and interview) on funding decisions. There was no significant interaction between presentation format and entrepreneurial gender for likelihood of making an offer, likelihood of making a counteroffer, or for amount of counteroffer.

Loan Officers versus Students

Our third objective was to examine possible differences between experienced loan officers and (inexperienced) business students. Loan officers ($\overline{X} = 1.60$) were significantly less likely to award a loan to the entrepreneur compared to students $\overline{X} = 4.01$; $F = 124.60, p < .01$). Loan officers were also less likely to make a counteroffer ($\overline{X} = 2.83$ versus $\overline{X} = 3.95$ for students; $F = 12.49, p < .01$). Finally, loan officers made counteroffers of a smaller amount ($\overline{X} = \$14,084$) than did students ($\overline{X} = \$29,246$; $F = 28.81, p < .01$). Clearly, loan officers were considerably more cautious and conservative compared to students in their funding decisions.

Interaction of Entrepreneurial Gender, Presentation Format, and Type of Respondent

The ANOVA design permitted examination of possible three-way interactions among the experimental variables. There was no significant interaction of the independent variables on likelihood of awarding the loan or on likelihood of making a counteroffer. However, there was a significant interaction with respect to the amount of the counteroffer ($F = 5.94$; $p < .02$).

When loan officers only reviewed the business plan, they gave the male entrepreneur a slightly but not significantly larger counteroffer than the female. However, when they had the opportunity to observe the entrepreneur in the interview, the loan officers made a larger counteroffer to the female entrepreneur. Students, on the other hand, slightly but not significantly favored the female entrepreneur when they read the business plan, but after watching the interview, they made a larger award to the male entrepreneur. This interaction is illustrated in Figure 1.

Finally, the open-ended responses regarding the concerns of the loan officers in granting the loan were content-analyzed (Weber 1985). Loan officers cited adequacy of collateral most frequently as a concern (by 61% of loan officers), followed by (lack of) management experience (47%), the company's liability in toxic waste cleanup (41%), riskiness of the venture (24%), and environmental threats such as competition and regulatory changes (22%). No mention of the entrepreneur's gender was made for either the male or the female version of the simulation.

In summary, we found no evidence that the male entrepreneur was favored over the female in funding decisions. There was also no evidence that sex stereotypes were heightened when participants only read the business plan. As expected, we found that loan officers were significantly more cautious than students in making funding decisions. Finally, we found a significant three-way interaction between entrepreneurial gender, presentation format, and participant's experience for the magnitude of the counteroffer. Gender of the entrepreneur had the strongest influence on counteroffers in the business plan and videotape interview conditions. Loan officers made larger counteroffers to the female compared to the male when they read the business plan and watched the interview. Students made larger counteroffers to the male compared to the female when they read the business plan and observed the interview.

DISCUSSION

In the Hisrich and O'Brien survey (1982), female entrepreneurs reported that women were frequently victims of bias in business funding decisions. Although a number of studies (Jackowicz and Hisrich 1987; Jones 1982; Shilit 1987; Ulrich and Arlow 1981) have identified financial and managerial factors considered by bankers when evaluating loan applications, including collateral, potential return, level of risk, and entrepreneur's past experience, gender was not considered in the research designs. Accordingly, prior to the present study, allegations of bias against women entrepreneurs have not been studied systematically.

Our first objective was to determine whether, relative to males with identical qualifications, loan requests from female entrepreneurs would receive less chance of support and lower levels of funding. Our second objective was to examine the effect of additional information about the entrepreneur's gender, available in the application interview, on funding decisions. We also examined whether loan officers would be more cautious than students in making funding decisions.

Our first analysis failed to find significant differences in the likelihood of approving a loan, or the amount of the loan based on the gender of the entrepreneur. In this controlled experiment, where financial data and business prospects were identical, there was no evidence of sex bias in funding decisions. Other investigations of the criteria loan officers use in

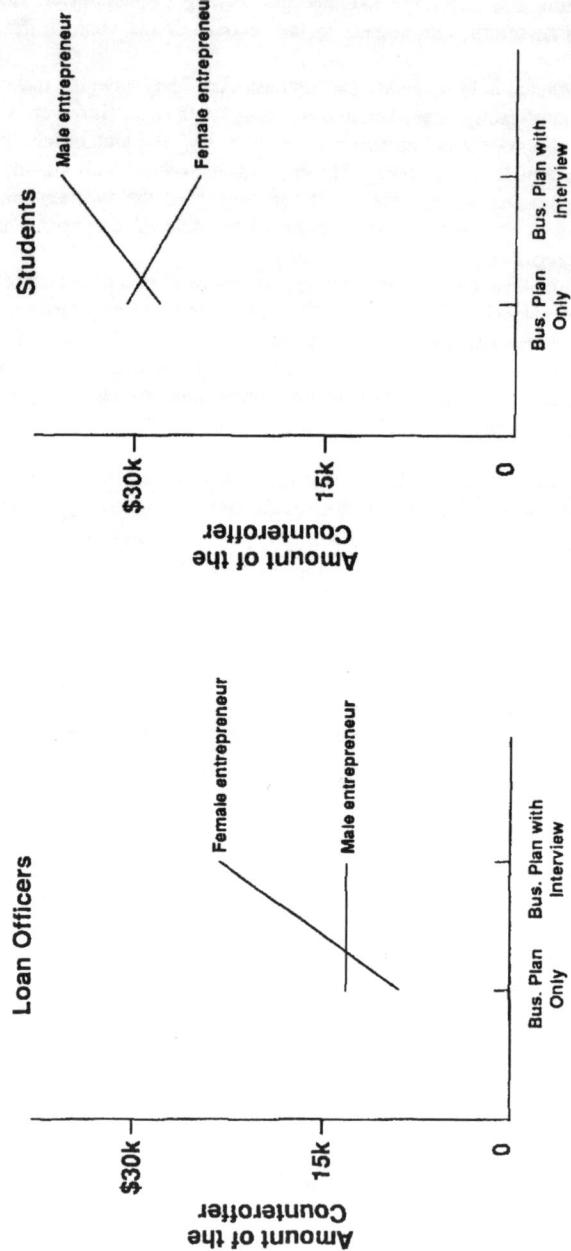

FIGURE 1   Interaction effect of entrepreneurial gender, presentation format, and respondent type on amount of counteroffer.

making loan decisions have highlighted the importance of financial considerations (Jackowicz and Hisrich 1987; Jones 1982; Shilit 1987; Ulrich and Arlow 1981). It appears that financial data in the business plan were more important than gender in determining the magnitude of startup loans. This finding should come as good news for bankers and aspiring female entrepreneurs. The results indicated that, other things equal, bankers are not significantly influenced by sex stereotypes in funding decisions.

The allegations of bias reported by female entrepreneurs in the Hisrich and O'Brien (1982) study may not be valid. Perhaps the female participants in the Hisrich and O'Brien survey were reacting to one-of-a-kind situations where their proposals were rejected due to lack of collateral, poor business prospects, or some other business-related problem. Our findings suggest that when business prospects are identical, bankers do not accord special treatment to male entrepreneurs.

Loan officers were extremely conservative in their funding decisions. It is possible that some female entrepreneurs do not realize the difficulty in securing financial support for a business startup. Accordingly, they may be more likely to be surprised by having their loan request denied. If the reason for rejection is not clearly communicated, then the female entrepreneur may attribute the rejection to sex bias. The female entrepreneurs' attributions that the denial is based on gender rather than qualifications and business prospects may account for the discrepancy between Hisrich and O'Brien's survey findings and the results of our systematic experiment. Future research should explore possible differences in male and female entrepreneurs' expectations about obtaining startup loans. If female entrepreneurs have higher expectations concerning loan awards, then denials may be perceived as sex bias rather than loan officers' conservatism.

When we examined the influence of entrepreneurial gender and mode of presentation, we found that across both samples of participants, mode of presentation did not influence funding decisions. The loan officers were extremely cautious about approving the loan; none of the bank officers approved the application. Therefore, it is not surprising that we found no difference in the likelihood of approval. However, we did find a difference in treatment of the male and female entrepreneurs when participants made recommendations regarding the magnitude of counteroffer. When we partitioned the sample according to loan officers versus students, a triple interaction was obtained for the amount of the counteroffer dependent variable. When loan officers made their evaluations based on the business plan only, the magnitude of the counteroffer was quite similar for both the male and the female entrepreneurs. However, when loan officers reviewed the business plan and observed the loan application interview, they made larger counteroffers to the female compared to the male entrepreneur. Perhaps in the interview condition, loan officers were surprised and impressed by the female's knowledge and enthusiasm about the business. The unexpected performance of the female entrepreneur in the interview may have led bankers to inflate her performance and reward it accordingly. This explanation is consistent with the findings of Bigoness (1976) and Hamner, Baird and Bigoness (1974), who found that high-performing females were rated more positively and seen as more deserving of a reward than comparably performing males.

The implications of these findings are quite different for female entrepreneurs and for bank loan officers. The large counteroffer awarded to the female entrepreneur in the business plan and interview condition suggests that female entrepreneurs should seek out opportunities to meet with their loan officers whenever possible. Perhaps in the interview situation, women can offset or counter questions about their motivation and competence to carry out their business plans.

On the other hand, from the bank loan officer's perspective, more impartial decisions

260   E. H. BUTTNER AND B. ROSEN

are likely when based on the business plan only. In the business-plan-only condition, decisions are more likely to reflect financial considerations, unbiased by the entrepreneur's gender.

Our results showed that the loan officers were significantly more cautious than the students in funding decisions. The differences between loan officers and students in likelihood of approval and level of funding is not surprising. This finding is consistent with the works of Bernstein, Hakel and Harlan (1975), Dipboye, Fromkin and Wiback (1975), Dobmeyer and Dunnette (1970), and Landy and Bates (1973), which showed that students exhibit a leniency bias in evaluations. The results do suggest that findings based on using students as proxies for loan officers have very limited generalizability. Future research needs to determine the extent to which inexperienced loan officers are influenced by the gender of the entrepreneur in decisions about provision of startup capital.

Finally, we found no differences in funding decisions as a function of respondents' gender in our combined sample of loan officers and students. In an earlier study, we found that female loan officers rated women in general significantly higher on the entrepreneurial attributes (leadership, endurance, and autonomy), and lower on need for support than did male loan officers (Buttner and Rosen 1988a). Further investigation is needed to determine whether male and female loan officers differ in their decisions about male and female entrepreneurs' business proposals.

To control for the possible effect of the nature of the business on the funding decision, we used only one business. It is possible that differences in the nature of businesses initiated by male and female entrepreneurs may influence loan officers' decisions. Hisrich and Brush (1983) found that the majority (90%) of ventures initiated by the female entrepreneurs in their sample were service businesses, while only 3% of the women were operating manufacturing companies. Ronstadt (1984) reported that 77% of all entrepreneurial businesses in the United States are service-oriented, while 16% are in manufacturing. It appears that women are initiating service-oriented businesses more frequently than are men. If service businesses have less attractive loan potential, then their female initiators may experience more difficulty obtaining funding than males starting other types of businesses. In a preliminary study, Buttner and Rosen (1988b) found a triple interaction between entrepreneurial gender, business sex-type, and gender of the decision maker on funding decisions. Male participants were most supportive of male entrepreneurs seeking to start a traditionally male business, and were more supportive of a female initiating a traditionally female business than one starting a male-typed business. Since undergraduate business students assumed the role of loan officers, the study should be replicated using loan officers as participants.

One practical application of our research findings could be to develop training materials for helping bank loan officers to identify and overcome possible sex bias in funding decisions. Bank loan officers could be asked to view simulated loan application interview tapes similar to our experimental materials and to make loan recommendations. In a workshop format, decisions could be compared for loan officers who viewed the male and female versions of the tape. The simulation results provide a vivid illustration for those likely to be involved with funding new ventures that decisions should be based on the quality of the business plan and the skills of the entrepreneur, not on gender and tradition.

REFERENCES

Bernstein, V., Hakel, M., and Harlan, A. 1975. The college student as interviewer: A threat to generalizability? *Journal of Applied Psychology*, 60:266–268.

Bigoness, W. 1976. Effect of applicant's sex, race, and performance on employers' performance ratings: Some additional findings. *Journal of Applied Psychology*, 61:80–84.

Buttner, E., and Rosen, B. 1988a. Bank loan officers' perceptions of the characteristics of men, women, and successful entrepreneurs. *Journal of Business Venturing*, 3:249–258.

Buttner, E., and Rosen, B. 1988b. The influence of entrepreneur's gender and type of business on decisions to provide venture capital. *Proceedings*, Southern Management Association, Atlanta.

Deaux, K., and Taynor, J. 1973. Evaluation of male and female ability: Bias works two ways. *Psychological Reports*, 32:261–262.

Dipboye, R., Arvey, R., and Terpstra, D. 1977. Sex and physical attractiveness of raters and applicants as determinants of resume evaluations. *Journal of Applied Psychology*, 62:288–294.

Dipboye, R., Fromkin, H., and Wiback, K. 1975. Relative importance of applicant sex, attractiveness, and scholastic standing on evaluation of job applicant resumes. *Journal of Applied Psychology*, 60:39–43.

Hakel, M., Dobmeyer, T., and Dunnette, M. 1970. Relative importance of three content dimensions in overall suitability of job applicants' resumes. *Journal of Applied Psychology*, 54:65–71.

Hamner, W., Kim, J., Baird, L., and Bigoness, W. 1974. Race and sex as determinants of ratings by potential employers in a simulated work-sampling task. *Journal of Applied Psychology*, 59:705–711.

Heilman, M. 1983. Sex bias in work settings: The lack of fit model. In L. Cummings and B. Staw, eds., *Research in Organizational Behavior*. Vol. 5. Greenwich, CT: JAI Press, pp. 269–299.

Hisrich, R., and Brush, C. 1983. The woman entrepreneur: Implications of family, educational, and occupational experience. In J. Hornaday, J. Timmons, and K. Vesper, eds., *Frontiers of Entrepreneurship Research*. Wellesley, MA: Babson College Center for Entrepreneurial Studies, pp. 255–270.

Hisrich, R., and O'Brien, M. 1982. The woman entrepreneur as a reflection of the type of business. In K. H. Vesper, ed., *Frontiers of Entrepreneurship Research*. Wellesley, MA: Babson College Center for Entrepreneurial Studies, pp. 54–67.

Jackowicz, A., and Hisrich, R. 1987. Intuition in small business lending decisions. *Journal of Small Business Management*, 25:45–52.

Jones, N. 1982. Small business commercial loan selection decision: an empirical evaluation. *American Journal of Small Business*, 6:41–49.

Landy, F., and Bates, F. 1973. Another look at contrast effects in the employment interview. *Journal of Applied Psychology*, 58:141–144.

MacMillan, I., Siegel, R., and Narasimha, P. 1985. Criteria used by venture capitalists to evaluate new venture proposals. *Journal of Business Venturing*, 1(1):119–128.

Nieva, V., and Gutek, B. 1980. Sex effects on evaluation. *Academy of Management Review*, 5:267–276.

Pheterson, G., Kiesler, S., and Goldberg, P. 1971. Evaluation of the performance of women as a function of their sex, achievement, and personal history. *Journal of Personality and Social Psychology*, 19:114–118.

Ronstadt, R. 1984. Ex-entrepreneurs and the decision to start an entrepreneurial career. In J. Hornaday, F. Tarpley, Jr., J. Timmons, and K. Vesper, eds., *Frontiers of Entrepreneurship Research*. Wellesley, MA: Babson College Center for Entrepreneurial Studies, pp. 437–460.

Rosen, B., and Jerdee, T. 1973. The influence of sex-role stereotypes on evaluations of male and female supervisory behavior. *Journal of Applied Psychology*, 57:44–48.

Rosen, B., and Jerdee, T. 1974a. The influence of sex role stereotypes on personnel decisions. *Journal of Applied Psychology*, 59:9–14.

Rosen, B., and Jerdee, T. 1974b. Effects of applicant's sex and difficulty of job on evaluations of candidates for managerial positions. *Journal of Applied Psychology*, 59:511–512.

Schein, V. 1973. The relationship between sex role stereotypes and requisite management characteristics. *Journal of Applied Psychology*, 57:95–100.

Schein, V. 1975. The relationships between sex role stereotypes and requisite management characteristics among female managers. *Journal of Applied Psychology*, 60:340–344.

U.S. Small Business Administration. 1988. *Report on the State of Small Business*. Washington, D.C.: U.S. Government Printing Office.

[16]

Access to Capital and Terms of Credit: A Comparison of Men- and Women-Owned Small Businesses
by Susan Coleman

This article compares access to capital for men- and women-owned small businesses using data from the 1993 National Survey of Small Business Finances. Findings reveal that women-owned firms are less likely to use external financing as a source of capital. It does not appear, however, that lenders discriminate against women on the basis of gender in terms of access to capital. A second part of this study examines the terms under which women obtain credit to determine whether they are at a relative disadvantage from that perspective. Findings reveal that women-owned firms paid higher interest rates than men for their most recent loans. In addition, women-owned service firms were more likely to put up collateral than men-owned service firms.

Small businesses are an important source of economic growth and job creation. According to the U.S. Small Business Administration, there were over 22 million small businesses in 1994 employing 53 percent of the workforce (*Facts About Small Business* 1997). Small firms account for 50 percent of the gross domestic product and the majority of new jobs created. In terms of innovation, it is estimated that small firms produce twice as many product innovations per employee as large firms, creating new products, services, lines of business, and industries.

Access to capital is a critical issue for small businesses. Without sufficient capital, small firms are unable to develop new products and services or grow to meet demand. Insufficient liquidity is a frequently cited cause of small business failure. Unlike larger publicly held firms, small firms typically cannot access the traditional capital markets (Ang 1991; Weinberg 1994). Instead, small firms are heavily dependent on bank loans, trade credit, and "informal" sources of financing such as personal savings, credit cards, home equity loans, and loans from family and friends (Ang 1992; Ang, Lin, and Tyler 1995; Berger and Udell 1995; Binks and Ennew 1996; Cole and Wolken 1996; Petersen and Rajan 1994).

Small businesses owned by women represent an increasingly important part of the small business sector. The National Women's Business Council (1996) estimates that women-owned businesses represent one-third of all businesses, and that the number of women-owned firms is growing twice as fast as firms in total. The same study estimates that women-

Dr. Coleman is an assistant professor of finance at the University of Hartford in Hartford, Connecticut. Her research interests include small firm finance and women-owned firms.

owned businesses employ almost six million people and are adding jobs much more rapidly than firms on average. A number of researchers have found that acquiring capital and dealing with financial institutions is particularly difficult for women business owners. Reasons cited include the small size of most women-owned firms (Coleman and Carsky 1997; Fabowale, Orser, and Riding 1995; Riding and Swift 1990); lack of financial sophistication (Brophy 1989; Brush 1992; Hisrich and Brush 1984; Loscocco and Robinson 1991); risk aversion (Chaganti 1986; Olsen and Currie 1992); and possible discrimination (Brush 1992; Neider 1987).

This study had three goals. First, it compared men and women-owned businesses in terms of their usage of various external credit products. Second, it identified firm characteristics or variables, including gender, that predict the likelihood of a firm using these same external credit products. Finally it examined terms of credit, including interest rate and collateral requirements, to determine whether lending conditions imposed on women business owners are more stringent than those imposed on men. The study also explored how the length of the relationship a firm has with a financial institution impacts on terms of credit.

The value of this study is that it uses a large national sample of both women and men-owned small businesses to explore differences between the two. Although a number of prior studies have been done on women-owned firms and their access to capital, most of the studies have been based on small samples or samples of women-owned firms only. In addition, by separating the issue of access to capital from terms of credit, this research addresses the concern that although women-owned firms may have similar access to external debt, they may obtain it under less favorable lending terms. If that is the case, it may affect their willingness to use external debt capital and its perceived accessibility.

The structure of the article is as follows. First, issues pertaining to access to capital for small businesses in general and women owned businesses in particular are discussed. Since a key issue may be the greater risk associated with small business lending, the next section describes strategies used by financial institutions to control or minimize risk. Discussions of the research methodology, data set, and results follow. The article concludes with a discussion of the study findings.

Access to Capital

As noted above, capital is one of the key ingredients enabling small businesses to innovate, grow, and create jobs. In the case of larger companies, growth, geographic expansion, and new product development are often funded by issuing stocks or bonds, alternatives which are not generally available to small privately held companies. Prior research has noted that banks are a major source of external capital for small firms. Using the 1993 National Survey of Small Business Finances, Cole and Wolken (1996) found that banks provided 60 percent of the dollar value of credit used by firms in the survey. Thirty-six percent of the firms in the survey obtained credit from a bank. Cole and Wolken (1995) found, however, that women-owned businesses were less likely to use banks as a source of capital than were men.

A study by the National Foundation of Women Business Owners (1996) found that 48 percent of small businesses used some form of bank credit. They found that women were slightly less likely than men to use bank credit, but the real distinction regarding credit usage came with size. Only one-third of the smallest firms used any type of bank credit. These findings mirror the results obtained by Coleman and Carsky (1996a, 1996b, 1997) who found that women-owned businesses were significantly less likely to use external debt capital than men-owned businesses. When size and age of the firm were held constant, however, there were no significant differences between men and women in the use of most credit products. The authors concluded that women-owned businesses may be less attractive to banks and other potential creditors precisely because they are small and viewed as being more risky.

In studies involving relatively small samples of men- and women-owned firms, Buttner and Rosen (1989, 1992) did not find evidence of discrimination in the lending process. Using a much larger sample of Canadian firms, however, Riding and Swift (1990) found that women were required to put up more collateral than men. In another study involving a large number of Canadian small businesses, Fabowale, Orser, and Riding (1995) found no gender differences in loan approvals or terms of credit, but they did find that women were less satisfied than men with their banking relationship. In sum, these prior studies seem to suggest that although women small business owners may not face outright discrimination in the lending process, their relationships with banks and other financial institutions are different from the relationships male owners have with them.

At least three different theories have been put forth to explain why women owners may have greater difficulty obtaining debt capital than men. First, some researchers contend that there may be adverse discrimination in the lending process that places women at an unfair disadvantage (Brophy 1989; Brush 1992; Neider 1987; Riding and Swift 1990; Scherr, Sugrue, and Ward 1993). According to this view, women are either unfairly denied credit or discouraged in the credit application process with the end result that they are less likely to obtain loans. In addition, women may not network as effectively as men (Aldrich 1989; Brush 1992). As a result, they may not have the same access to sources of information and capital.

Others contend that women are more risk averse than men and thus less likely

to take on debt (Brown and Segal 1989; Chaganti 1986; Collerett and Aubry 1990; Olsen and Currie 1992; Scherr, Sugrue, and Ward 1993). According to this hypothesis, women avoid debt and are reluctant to put up the collateral that may be required to obtain a loan (Carter and Cannon 1992).

A third theory contends that women-owned businesses use less debt because they don't need it. Women-owned firms tend to be smaller and more heavily concentrated in service lines of business (Chaganti 1986; Kallenberg and Leicht 1991; Loscocco and Robinson 1991). Because they are small, they may be able to finance their needs using personal resources. In addition, many service businesses do not have much in the way of assets to be financed because the principal resource is the human capital of the owner; financial capital requirements for businesses of this type may be relatively modest.

One goal of this research is to examine differences between men- and women-owned businesses in their use of credit and specific credit products. This research examines the effect of explanatory variables, including gender, to determine whether women are less likely to use external credit than men.

Minimizing Risk

From a creditor's perspective, the primary objective in lending money is capital recovery, ideally within the desired timeframe and with an acceptable return on capital. If women are perceived to be riskier borrowers than men, they may be denied credit or offered it under less favorable terms.

In general, lenders prefer borrowers who have a track record of profitability, some degree of longevity, and assets that can be used as collateral (Cole and Wolken 1995; Ennew and Binks 1995; Weinberg 1994). To the extent that women-owned businesses fail to meet these requirements, they may be at a relative disadvantage. Prior research indicates that women-owned firms are, in fact, smaller, newer, and less profitable than men-owned businesses (Coleman and Carsky 1996a, 1996b, 1997; Riding and Swift 1990). In addition, they tend to be more heavily concentrated in service businesses, which may not have assets that can be used as collateral.

In addition to problems of size, age, and profitability, small privately held firms are plagued with the problem of asymmetric information or incomplete flows of information between the borrower and the lender (Ang 1992; Berger and Udell 1995; Ennew and Binks 1995; Petersen and Rajan 1994; Stiglitz and Weiss 1981; Weinberg 1994). Privately held firms do not publish the same quantity or quality of financial information that publicly held firms are required to produce. As a result, information on their financial condition, earnings, and earnings prospects may be incomplete or inaccurate. Faced with this type of uncertainty, a lender may deny credit, sometimes to firms that are creditworthy but unable to document it. Prior research has suggested that women network less effectively than men (Aldrich 1989; Brush 1992) and that they find financial management, which includes the preparation of financial statements, an area of weakness (Brophy 1989; Brush 1992; Hisrich 1989; Pellegrino and Reece 1982). Either of these factors could affect women business owners' ability to communicate effectively with lending institutions.

Lenders have several tools at their disposal to help them minimize the risks of dealing with potential borrowers. First, the interest rate on loans to riskier borrowers can be raised to reflect the greater uncertainty of repayment (Berger and Udell 1995). In a study using data from the 1987 National Survey of Small Business Finances, Petersen and Rajan (1994) found that smaller firms do pay higher rates of interest than larger companies.

Collateral requirements represent a second possible strategy for reducing uncertainty and managing risk. If the bor-

rower fails to pay, the lender takes the collateral and either manages it or liquidates it to pay off the loan. Again, using data from the 1987 National Survey of Small Business Finances, Ang, Lin, and Tyler (1995) found that 69 percent of firms included in the survey pledged some form of personal collateral. Several other researchers have also noted that a high percentage of loans are granted on a collateralized basis (August et al. 1997; Berger and Udell 1995; Boot, Thakor, and Udell 1991) and that these loans are associated with riskier borrowers. In some instances, small firms can actually signal their creditworthiness by offering collateral (Binks and Ennew 1996; Chan and Kanatas, 1985; Leeth and Scott 1989).

A third strategy for managing risk is to develop long-term relationships with borrowers. Over time, lenders have the opportunity to gather information on the firm and its principals. This type of informal knowledge regarding the firm enables the lender to make better decisions on credit applications. Berger and Udell (1995) found that there was an inverse relationship between the interest rate charged and length of relationship—the longer the relationship, the lower the rate of interest. Blackwell and Winters (1997) also found that firms with longer-term banking relationships were monitored less frequently and charged lower rates of interest. When Petersen and Rajan (1994) examined the effect of length of relationship on availability and cost of credit, they found that firms that concentrated their borrowing with one bank had greater access to credit and paid lower interest rates.

Another goal of this study is to determine whether women obtain credit under less favorable terms than men. This may be the case if lenders view them as riskier borrowers. To that end, differences in interest rate charged and collateral requirements are examined. In addition, we explore the impact of length of relationship on terms of credit.

Sampling Methodology

This study examined the impact of various characteristics, including gender, on access to various types of debt capital. In addition, it examined differences in terms of credit (including interest rates and collateral) and the impact of the length of relationship between lender and borrower.

Data for the study were drawn from the 1993 National Survey of Small Business Finances (NSSBF) conducted by the Federal Reserve Board and the U.S. Small Business Administration. This study included a national stratified random sample of privately owned small businesses having fewer than 500 employees. Businesses were contacted in advance of the survey to determine eligibility and the name of the appropriate contact person. This was followed by a telephone survey lasting approximately 50 minutes. Over 4,000 small businesses were interviewed representing a 50 percent response rate. Balance sheet and income statement data were collected as well as information on the firm's use of financial services and financial service providers.

Statistical Results

Univariate Tests

Differences between men-owned and women-owned small businesses were explored using the *t*-test. Table 1 presents the results. Prior research indicates that women-owned businesses are smaller and newer than men-owned businesses (Coleman and Carsky 1996a, 1996b, 1997; Devine 1994). Chi-square analysis was used to determine differences between men and women in the use of various credit products. Prior research has also noted that women are less likely to use external financing than men (Cole and Wolken 1995; Coleman and Carsky 1996a, 1997). Women rely more heavily on informal and personal sources of financing such as savings, loans from family and friends, and credit cards.

Table 1
Characteristics of Men-Owned
and Women-Owned Small Businesses

	Men	Women	*t*-Statistic	Probability for *t*-Statistic
Number	3,797	840		
Firm Age*	15.84	12.92	-5.6511	0.0000
1992 Sales*	$4.1 million	$1.6 million	-5.7126	0.0000
1992 Employees*	34.5	18.5	-6.8077	0.0000
Percent in Sole Proprietorships*	30.3	40.6	5.7920	0.0000
Percent in Service Businesses*	32.26	40.95	4.8279	0.0000

*Differences between men and women were significant at the .01 level.

The sample used for this study included 3,797 men-owned businesses and 840 women-owned businesses. The women-owned businesses were significantly younger and smaller than the men-owned businesses, as is reflected in Table 1. In addition, women-owned businesses were significantly more likely to be sole proprietorships, with over 40 percent of women-owned businesses taking this organizational form. From a lending and borrowing perspective, this distinction is important because sole proprietorships were much smaller than other organizational forms in terms of sales volume. The average sales for sole proprietorships in this sample were $341,497 compared to average sales of $3,055,794, $5,000,754, and $5,872,327 for partnerships, S-corporations, and corporations, respectively. Women were also significantly more likely to be in service businesses than men; over 40 percent of women-owned businesses were in service businesses compared to less than one-third of men-owned businesses.

Table 2 examines the characteristics of the most recent loan granted and reveals significant differences between men and women business owners. Women were significantly less likely to have applied for a loan during the previous three years —only 35 percent sought external funding compared to 45 percent of the men. In addition, women were significantly less likely to be granted a loan if they did apply. Women applied for significantly smaller loans, less than half of what men applied for. Finally, women paid significantly higher interest rates than men, if granted a loan. However, there were no significant differences between men and women in terms of collateral requirements.

Table 3 examines the use of six types of credit products and reveals that women-owned businesses were significantly less likely to use certain products, including lines of credit, financial leases, and equipment loans. They were significantly more likely to use business credit cards, however. It is noteworthy that although only 26 percent of women-owned businesses used lines of credit, over 40 percent used business credit cards.

Multivariate Tests

Logistic regression was used to determine the relationship between the use of various types of credit products and

Table 2
Most Recent Loan:
Difference between Men and Women-Owned Businesses

	Men	Women	Statistic	Probability
Percent applied in last 3 years**	45.11	35.00	X^2=28.665	0.000
Approved**	85.46	78.57	X^2=9.080	0.003
Loan amount*	$1.1 million	$4.1 million	t=-2.5002	0.0125
Percent with interest rate over index**	1.302	1.707	t=4.2258	0.0000
Percent with collateral required	71.00	72.11	X^2=0.123	0.726
Relationship length**	9.41	8.00	t=4.2489	0.000

*Differences between men and women were significant at the .05 level.
**Differences between men and women were significant at the .01 level.

Table 3
Difference between Men and Women
in the Usage of Bank Credit Products

Credit Product	Men (Percent)	Women (Percent)	Chi-Square	Probability for Chi-Square
Line of credit*	37.87	25.60	45.191	0.000
Financial lease*	16.64	11.55	13.487	0.000
Commercial mortgage	9.43	8.33	0.985	0.321
Vehicle loan	26.99	25.71	0.576	0.448
Equipment loan*	20.07	15.71	8.739	0.004
Business credit card*	35.90	40.95	7.558	0.006
Other loans	14.22	13.69	0.160	0.689

*Differences between men and women were significant at the .01 level

small business explanatory variables. Like ordinary least squares regression, logistic regression describes the relationship between a dependent variable and a series of independent variables. When the dependent variable is a binary variable, however, logistic regression is generally preferable to ordinary least squares (Aldrich and Nelson 1984; Cramer 1991; Demaris 1992; Tansey et al. 1996). A series of stepwise logistic regression models was developed using different dependent variables for credit products and the same set of independent variables. In each case, the logistic regression model took the following form:

$$\text{Credit Product} = a + B_1\text{FIRMAGE} + B_2\text{LOG OF 92 SALES} + B_3\text{PARTNERSHIP} + B_4\text{SCORPORATION} + B_5\text{CORPORATION} + B_6\text{FEMALE} + B_7\text{SIC} + E$$

Dependent variables represent the use or nonuse of (1) lines of credit; (2) financial leases; (3) commercial mortgages; (4) motor vehicle loans; (5) equipment loans; and (6) "other" loans which include personal loans used for business purposes. In each instance, the dependent variable was coded with a yes or no response.

Independent variables represent the (1) age of the business; (2) size of the business; (3) gender of the owner; (4) organizational form; and (5) SIC classification. Table 4 provides descriptions of the independent variables.

Age and size variables (FIRMAGE, LOGSALES) were used as control variables because prior research suggests that larger, more established firms are more likely to receive loans than smaller, newer companies (Ang 1992; Cole 1996; Cole and Wolken 1995; Coleman and Carsky 1996a; Ennew and Binks 1995; Fabowale, Orser, and Riding 1995; Riding, Haines, and Thomas 1994; Scherr, Sugrue, and Ward 1993; Weinberg 1994).

Variables representing organizational form (PROP, PARTNER, SCORP, CORP) were included to determine whether businesses that have adopted the corporate form of organization have an advantage in accessing credit over firms that have not. Corporations and S-corporations have the advantage of limited liability which may encourage greater risk-taking and willingness to assume debt. Sole proprietorships and partnerships, on the other hand, have unlimited liability, and their owners and partners are personally liable in the event

Table 4
Independent Variables Used in Logistic Regression Analysis

Variable	Description
FIRMAGE	Number of years the firm has been in existence
LOGSALES	Log of 1992 sales
PROP	Coded as "1" for a sole proprietorship; "0" for all other forms; omitted as reference
PARTNER	Coded as "1" for a partnership; "0" for all other forms
SCORP	Coded as "1" for an S-corporation; "0" for all other forms
CORP	Coded as "1" for a corporation; "0" for all other forms
FEMALE	Coded as "1" for women-owned businesses; "0" for men-owned businesses. (The NSSBF defines a woman-owned firm as one which is at least 50 percent owned by a woman or women).
SIC	Coded as "1" for service businesses; "0" for non-service businesses

of bankruptcy or default (Brigham 1992; Osteryoung, Newman, and Davies 1997). This distinction may discourage proprietorships and partnerships from undertaking high levels of debt.

The SIC variable distinguishes between service and non-service businesses. Prior research indicates that service businesses are less likely to be candidates for bank loans because they often lack assets that can be used as collateral (Hisrich 1989, Riding, Haines, and Thomas 1994).

FEMALE was included as a variable to capture gender differences in the use of various types of credit products.

As noted above, Table 3 reveals significant differences between women and men-owned businesses in the usage of various credit products. Those tests, however, were based on univariate analysis and did not control for differences in key aspects of the business such as size, age, organizational form, and industry. Multivariate analysis does control for these factors in examining their impact on the likelihood of obtaining various types of loan products. The results are presented in Table 5. Three major findings stand out. First, the variable FIRMAGE is consistent-

ly significant and negative, revealing that younger firms are more likely to obtain loans than larger ones. Although at first glance one might expect younger firms to be at a relative disadvantage, it stands to reason that younger firms that are still growing are more likely to need capital than larger firms that have matured and generate larger amounts of cash.

A second major finding is that the variable representing size, LOGSALES, is consistently significant and positive, indicating that larger firms (in terms of sales volume) are more likely to use external loans than smaller firms. This finding is consistent with prior research suggesting that lenders prefer larger, well-established companies over smaller ones (Ang 1992; Cole and Wolken 1995; Riding, Haines, and Thomas 1994; Weinberg 1994). It may also confirm the idea that capital requirements for very small companies are relatively modest, making it unnecessary for these firms to seek external debt capital.

A third noteworthy finding is that the gender variable was not significant for any of the models. This indicates that lenders do not discriminate against

Table 5
Results of Logistic Regressions: Use of Credit Products
(Coefficient Estimates)

Significant Independent Variables	Line of Credit	Financial Lease	Commercial Mortgage	Motor Vehicle	Equipment	Other
FIRMAGE		-0.0122**		-0.0131**	-0.0116**	-0.0098**
LOGSALES	0.5418**	0.3775**	0.1776**	0.1265**	0.2451**	0.1429**
PARTNER	0.3036*			-0.3689*		
SCORP		0.3256*	-0.4375**		0.2590**	-0.2401*
CORP		0.5568**	-0.5483**		0.3105**	
FEMALE						
SIC		0.4656**	-0.2588*		0.1981*	

*Significant at the .05 level.
**Significant at the .01 level.

women on the basis of their gender in providing access to capital. However, more complex models may allow men and women to vary in the relative importance of the different predictors of these credit products. Indeed, prior research suggests that men and women have different experiences when attempting to obtain loans.

To test for this, each of the six credit models was run for men only and then for women only. This produces the best possible fit for these variables as measured by the combined chi-square. The combined chi-square for the two groups was then compared to the original chi-square for the entire group to determine whether there were significant differences by credit product. The difference in chi-squares obtained using this method was significant in the models for line of credit ($p=.045$) and leases ($p=.026$). For each of these, a second model was constructed using the original independent variables and a matching set of variables representing the interaction of each independent variable and gender in an attempt to capture differences between the experiences of male and female busi-

ness owners. The model took the following form:

$$\text{Credit Product} = a + B_1\text{FIRMAGE} + B_2\text{LOGSALES} + B_3\text{PARTNERSHIP} + B_4\text{SCORPORATION} + B_5\text{CORPORATION} + B_6\text{SIC} + B_7\text{FEMALE} + B_8\text{GENAGE} + B_9\text{GENSIZE} + B_{10}\text{GENPART} + B_{11}\text{GENSCORP} + B_{12}\text{GENCORP} + B_{13}\text{GENSIC} + E$$

The original independent variables (B_1-B_7) were forced into the model, and the interaction variables were added using a stepwise procedure. Results revealed that none of the newly created interaction variables were significant for the line of credit model. For the lease model, however, the variable GENSCORP was significant and positive, indicating that women-owned S-corporations are significantly more likely to have leases than men-owned S-corporations (see Table 6).

The final piece of analysis examined the relationship between small business explanatory variables and interest rates and collateral requirements. In addition, the

Table 6
Expanded Model: Lease

Independent Variables	Parameter Estimate
INTERCEPT**	-7.0426
LOGSALES**	0.3707
PARTNER	0.1822
SCORP	0.2981
CORP**	0.6075
FIRMAGE**	-0.0122
SERV**	0.4599
FEMALE	-0.2309
GENSCORP*	0.5457

*Significant at the .05 level.
**Significant at the .01 level.

impact of length of relationship on interest rates and collateral requirements was explored. In order to examine variables having an impact on interest rate, a stepwise regression model was constructed using the interest rate on the most recent loan (MRLINT) as the dependent variable and the variables detailed in Table 4 as independent variables. In addition, the following independent variables were added to the model: (1) LOGMRL: amount of the most recent loan; (2) MRLCOLT: coded as "1" if collateral was required for the most recent loan and "0" if collateral was not required; and (3) RELATE: length of owner's relationship with the primary financial institution. The interest rate model took the following form:

$$MRLINT= a + B_1LOGMRL$$
$$+ B_2MRLCOLT + B_3RELATE$$
$$+ B_4FIRMAGE + B_5PARTNERSHIP$$
$$+ B_6SCORPORATION$$
$$+ B_7CORPORATION + B_8FEMALE$$
$$+ B_9SIC + E$$

Collateral requirements were examined using two stepwise logistic regression models, one having collateral requirements for the most recent loan (MRLCOLT) as the dependent variable and a second using collateral requirements on lines of credit from the primary lending institution as the dependent variable (COLL1). In the second collateral model, LOGBAL (the log of the balance on the line of credit) was substituted for LOGMRL. These models took the following form:

$$MRLCOLT= a + B_1LOGMRL$$
$$+ B_2MRLINT + B_3RELATE + B_4FIRMAGE$$
$$+ B_5PARTNERSHIP + B_6SCORPORATION$$
$$+ B_7CORPORATION + B_8FEMALE$$
$$+ B_9SIC + E$$

and

$$COLL1= a + B_1LOGBAL + B_2RELATE$$
$$+ B_3FIRMAGE + B_4PARTNERSHIP$$
$$+ B_5SCORPORATION$$
$$+ B_6CORPORATION + B_7FEMALE$$
$$+ B_8SIC + E$$

Table 7
Terms of Credit
(Coefficient Estimates)

Significant Independent Variables	MRLINT	MRLCOLT	COLL1
FIRMAGE		0.0131**	
LOGMRL	-0.1245**	-0.3084**	
LOGBAL			-0.3163**
PARTNER			
SCORP	-0.1284*		-0.5510**
CORP		-0.3220*	-0.7768**
FEMALE	0.2618**		
SIC			0.2218*
MRLCOLT	0.3172**		
MRLINT		-0.4543	
RELATE	-0.0170**		

*Significant at the .05 level.
**Significant at the .01 level.

Table 7 presents the results on the relationship between interest rate charged, collateral requirements, and length of relationship. As shown, higher interest rates were associated with smaller loans, higher collateral requirements, and shorter banking relationships. These findings are consistent with work done by Petersen and Rajan (1994) who found that length of relationship affects both the availability and the cost of credit. Berger and Udell (1995) and Blackwell and Winters (1997) also found that banks charge lower interest rates to firms with whom they have had longer relationships. Table 7 also reveals that the variable representing gender was significant and positive, indicating that women paid significantly higher interest rates than men on their most recent loan.

Table 7 also shows the results on predictors for collateral requirements using the dependent variables MRLCOLT (use of collateral for most recent loan) and COLL1 (collateral requirements). For both models, the size of the loan was significant and negative, indicating that smaller loans have higher collateral requirements. In addition, the variable representing organizational form was significant and negative for both collateral models, suggesting that unincorporated firms face higher collateral requirements.

For the MRLCOLT model, firm age was significant and positive, indicating that older firms are more likely to put up collateral. In addition, the variable representing interest rate (MRLINT) was significant and negative, indicating that firms supplying higher collateral borrow at lower interest rates. These findings support the work of Binks and Ennew (1996) and Leeth and Scott (1989) who suggest that having collateral can be used to signal creditworthiness and to obtain more favorable credit terms.

In the COLL1 model, the SIC variable was significant and positive, suggesting that service businesses face higher collateral requirements. These findings are consistent with prior research demonstrating that lenders require higher collateral from potentially riskier borrowers including smaller borrowers, unincorporated firms, and service firms that lack specific collateral associated with the business (August et al. 1997; Berger and Udell 1995; Boot, Thakor, and Udell 1991). The variable representing gender was not significant for either collateral model.

As in the case of the six credit product models above, separate regressions were run for men-only and women-only groups using the MRLINT, MRLCOLT, and COLL1 models. There was a significant difference in the change in chi-square for the COLL1 model ($p=.047$). Again, gender variables were created to test for significant interactions in a model taking the following form:

$$COLL1 = a + B_1 LOGBAL + B_2 RELATE$$
$$+ B_3 FIRMAGE + B_4 PARTNERSHIP$$
$$+ B_5 SCORPORATION$$
$$+ B_6 CORPORATION + B_7 SIC$$
$$+ B_8 FEMALE + B_9 GENBAL$$
$$+ B_{10} GENRELATE + B_{11} GENAGE$$
$$+ B_{12} GENPART + B_{13} GENSCORP$$
$$+ B_{14} GENCORP + B_{15} GENSIC + E$$

Table 8 presents the results from this analysis. The variable GENPART was significant and negative, indicating that the women-owned partnerships in the sample were least likely to put up collateral. In addition, the variable GENSERV was significant and positive, indicating that women-owned service firms were significantly more likely to put up collateral than men-owned service firms.

Discussion

The results of this study confirm the findings of prior research (Cole and Wolken 1995; Coleman and Carsky 1996a, 1997). Women-owned businesses are significantly smaller and newer than those owned by men. In addition, they are less likely to use external financing as

Table 8
Expanded Model: COLL1

Independent Variables	Parameter Estimate
INTERCEPT**	4.4725
LOGBAL**	-0.3202
PARTNER	0.5041
SCORP**	-0.4594
CORP**	-0.6762
FIRMAGE	-0.0032
SERV	0.1077
RELATE1	0.0131
FEMALE	0.0282
GENPART**	-1.4705
GENSERV*	0.6482

*Significant at the .05 level.
**Significant at the .01 level.

a source of capital. It does not appear, however, that lenders discriminate against women on the basis of gender in giving them access to capital. Rather, it appears that lenders discriminate on the basis of firm size, preferring to lend to larger and, one would assume, more established firms. This preference may put women-owned firms at a disadvantage given that they are half the size of men-owned firms on average. The findings of this study, however, particularly those from the logistic regressions for use of credit products (Table 5), suggest that, with size and firm age held constant, women-owned firms have the same access to the most frequently used credit products as men. This confirms the prior work done by Fabowale, Orser, and Riding (1995) using a large sample of Canadian firms. The findings of this research are additionally important, however, because they are based on a large national sample of both men- and women-owned small firms in the U.S. where the banking system is considerably more fragmented and less centralized than in Canada.

This study examined the terms under which women obtain credit to determine whether they are at a relative disadvantage. The results revealed that higher interest rates are associated with smaller loans and female borrowers (see Table 7) and that women-owned service firms have higher collateral requirements than men-owned service firms (see Table 8). Taken together, these findings suggest that women obtain credit under less favorable terms than men, confirming prior work done by Riding and Swift (1990) but refuting Fabowale, Orser, and Riding (1995), both of which used samples of Canadian firms. This study is the first to examine terms of credit obtained by women-owned firms using a large sample of U.S. small businesses. Differences between the banking systems in Canada and the United States may possibly account for some of the discrepancies between these findings and those of Fabowale, Orser, and Riding (1995). In addition, a possible weakness of these findings is that gender may be highly correlated with some other variable affecting interest rates and collateral requirements that is not included in the NSSBF database. If that is the case, gender may be significant only because of its correlation with an important variable that has not been specified.

Length of relationship with the financial institution does appear to affect the terms of credit. As seen in Table 7, shorter relationships were associated with higher interest rates, as previously found by Berger and Udell (1995) and Blackwell and Winters (1997). As shown in Table 2, women business owners have shorter relationships with their primary financial institutions than do men. This suggests a possible strategy for women business owners who tend to have smaller companies and smaller loans—developing a relationship with a primary financial institution may help them to offset their size disadvantage and the problems of asymmetric information to obtain more favorable lending terms.

These results also show that collateral was associated with loans to smaller firms, unincorporated firms, and women-owned firms in service businesses. Many women-owned firms fall into all three of these categories, suggesting that women who want loans from financial institutions need to be prepared to provide some type of collateral to counteract the perceived riskiness of their firms. If their businesses do not have sufficient assets, they need to come to terms with their own willingness to pledge personal assets and accept the risk entailed in doing so.

By separating the issue of access to credit from terms of credit, the results of this study demonstrate that although women-owned firms have comparable access to credit, they do not obtain it on the same terms as do men-owned firms. This difference may affect their willingness to seek out external credit as well as their perceptions of its availability.

References

Aldrich, Howard (1989). "Networking among Women Entrepreneurs," in *Women-Owned Businesses*. Ed. Oliver Hagan, Carol Rivchun, and Donald Sexton. New York: Praeger.

Aldrich, John H., and Forrest D. Nelson (1984). *Linear Probability, Logit, and Probit Models*. Newbury Park, California: Sage Publications.

Ang, James S. (1991). "Small Business Uniqueness and the Theory of Financial Management," *The Journal of Small Business Finance* 1(1), 1-13.

——— (1992). "On the Theory of Finance for Privately Held Firms," *The Journal of Small Business Finance* 1(3), 185-203.

Ang, James S., James Wuh Lin, and Floyd Tyler (1995). "Evidence on the Lack of Separation between Business and Personal Risks among Small Businesses," *The Journal of Small Business Finance* 4(2/3), 197-210.

August, James D., Michael R. Grupe, Charles Luckett, and Samuell M. Slowinski (1997). "Survey of Finance Companies, 1996," *Federal Reserve Bulletin* (July), 543-556.

Berger, Allen N., and Gregory F. Udell (1995). "Relationship Lending and Lines of Credit in Small Firm Finance," *Journal of Business* 68(3), 351-381.

Binks, Martin R., and Christine T. Ennew (1996). "Growing Firms and Credit Constraint," *Small Business Economics* 8, 17-25.

Blackwell, David W., and Drew B. Winters (1997). "Banking Relationships and the Effect of Monitoring on Loan Pricing," *The Journal of Financial Research* 20(2), 275-289.

Boot, Arnoud W.A., Anjan V. Thakor, and Gregory F. Udell (1991). "Secured Lending and Default Risk: Equilibrium Analysis, Policy Implications and Empirical Results," *The Economic Journal* (May), 458-472.

Brigham, Eugene F. (1992). *Fundamentals of Financial Management*, 6th edition. Fort Worth, Texas: Dryden Press.

Brophy, David (1989). "Financing Women-Owned Entrepreneurial Firms," in *Women-Owned Businesses*. Ed. Oliver Hagan, Carol Rivchun, and Donald Sexton. New York: Praeger.

Brown, Stanley A., and Phyllis Segal (1989). "Female Entrepreneurs in Profile," *Canadian Banker* (July-August), 32-34.

Brush, Candida G. (1992). "Research on Women Business Owners: Past Trends, a New Perspective and Future Directions," *Entrepreneurship Theory and Practice* (Summer), 5-30.

Buttner, E. Holly, and Benson Rosen (1989). "Funding New Business Ventures: Are Decision Makers Biased Against Women Entrepreneurs?" *Journal of Business Venturing* 4, 249-261.

——— (1992). "Rejection in the Loan Application Process: Male and Female Entrepreneurs' Perceptions and Subsequent Intentions," *Journal of Small Business Management* (January), 58-65.

Carter, Sara, and Tom Cannon (1992). *Women as Entrepreneurs*. San Diego. Calif.: Academic Press Limited.

Chaganti, Radha (1986). "Management in Women-Owned Enterprises," *Journal of Small Business Management* (October), 18-29.

Chan, Yuk-Shee, and George Kanatas (1985). "Asymmetric Valuations and the Role of Collateral in Loan Agreements," *Journal of Money, Credit, and Banking* 17(1), 84-95.

Cole, Rebel A. (1996). "New Evidence from Small Businesses on the Benefits of Lending Relationships," paper presented at the 1996 Financial Management Association Annual Meeting, New Orleans, Louisiana, October.

Cole, Rebel A., and John D. Wolken (1995). "Financial Services Used by Small Businesses: Evidence from the 1993 National Survey of Small Business Finances," *Federal Reserve Bulletin* (July), 629-666.

——— (1996). "Bank and Nonbank Competition for Small Business Credit: Evidence from the 1987 and 1993 National Surveys of Small Business Finances," *Federal Reserve Bulletin* (November) 983-995.

Coleman, Susan, and Mary Carsky (1996a). "Financing Small Business: Strategies Employed by Women Entrepreneurs," *The Journal of Applied Management and Entrepreneurship* 3(1), 28-42.

——— (1996b). "Women Owned Businesses and Bank Switching: The Role of Customer Service," *The Journal of Entrepreneurial and Small Business Finance* 5(1), 75-84.

——— (1997). "Banks as a Source of Small Business Capital: A Comparison of Men and Women Owned Small Businesses," paper presented at the Annual Meeting of the Academy of Entrepreneurial and Small Firm Finance, Honolulu, Hawaii, October.

Collerett, P., and P. Aubry (1990). "Socio-Economic Evolution of Women Business Owners in Quebec," *Journal of Business Ethics* 9, 417-22.

Cramer, J.S. (1991). *The Logit Model*. London: Edward Arnold.

Demaris, Alfred (1992). *Logit Modeling: Practical Applications*. Newbury Park, Calif.: Sage Publications.

Devine, Theresa J. (1994). "Characteristics of Self-Employed Women in the United States," *Monthly Labor Review* (March), 20-34.

Ennew, Christine T., and Martin Binks (1995). "The Provision of Finance to Small Businesses: Does the Banking Relationship Constrain Performance?" *The Journal of Small Business Finance* 4(1), 57-73.

Fabowale, Lola, Barbara Orser, and Allan Riding (1995). "Gender, Structural Factors and Credit Terms between Canadian Small Businesses and Financial Institutions," *Entrepreneurship Theory and Practice* 19(4), 41-65.

Hisrich, Robert D. (1989). "Women Entrepreneurs: Problems and Prescriptions for Success in the Future," in *Women Owned Businesses*. Ed. Oliver Hagan,

Carol Rivchun, and Donald Sexton. New York: Praeger.

Hisrich, Robert D., and Candida Brush (1984). "The Women Entrepreneur: Management Skills and Business Problems," *Journal of Small Business Management* (January), 30-37.

Kallenberg, Arne L., and Kevin T. Leicht (1991). "Gender and Organizational Performance: Determinants of Small Business Survival and Success," *Academy of Management Journal* 34, 136-161.

Leeth, John D., and Jonathan A. Scott (1989). "The Incidence of Secured Debt: Evidence from the Small Business Community," *Journal of Financial and Quantitative Analysis* 24(3), 379-394.

Loscocco, Karyn A., and Joyce Robinson (1991). "Barriers to Women's Small Business Success in the United States," *Gender & Society* 5, 511-532.

National Foundation for Women Business Owners (1996). *Capital, Credit and Financing*. Silver Spring, Md.: The National Foundation for Women Business Owners.

National Women's Business Council (1996). *Expanding Business Opportunities for Women*. Washington D.C.: National Women's Business Council.

Neider, Linda (1987). "A Preliminary Investigation of Female Entrepreneurs in Florida," *Journal of Small Business Management* (July), 22-29.

Olsen, Shirley F., and Helen M. Currie (1992). "Female Entrepreneurs: Personal Value Systems and Business Strategies in a Male Dominated Industry," *Journal of Small Business Management* (January), 49-57.

Osteryoung, Jerome S., Derek L. Newman, and Leslie George Davies (1997). *Small Firm Finance*. Fort Worth, Texas: Dryden Press.

Pellegrino, Eric T., and Barry L. Reece (1982). "Perceived Formative and Operational Problems Encountered by Female Entrepreneurs in Retail and Service Firms," *Journal of Small Business Management* (April), 15-24.

Petersen, Mitchell A., and Raghurum G. Rajan (1994). "The Benefits of Lending Relationships: Evidence from Small Business Data," *The Journal of Finance* 49(1), 3-38.

Riding, Allan, George H. Haines, and Roland Thomas (1994). "The Canadian Small Business-Bank Interface: A Recursive Model," *Entrepreneurship Theory and Practice* (Summer), 5-24.

Riding, Allan L., and Catherine S. Swift (1990). "Women Business Owners and Terms of Credit: Some Empirical Findings of the Canadian Experience," *Journal of Business Venturing* 5, 327-340.

Scherr, Frederick C., Timothy F. Sugrue, and Janice B. Ward (1993). "Financing the Small Firm Start-Up: Determinants of Debt Use," *The Journal of Small Business Finance* 3(1), 17-36.

Tansey, Richard, Michael White, Rebecca G. Long, and Mark Smith (1996). "A Comparison of Loglinear Modeling and Logistic Regression in Management Research," *Journal of Management* 22(2), 339-358.

U.S. Business Administration (1997). *Facts About Small Business* [Online]. http://www.sba.gov/ADVO/stats/fact 1.html. Accessed December 9.

Weinberg, John A. (1994). "Firm Size, Finance, and Investment," *Federal Reserve Bank of Richmond Economic Quarterly* 80(1), 19-40.

[17]

Start-Up Capital: "Does Gender Matter?"

Ingrid Verheul
Roy Thurik

ABSTRACT. Female and male entrepreneurs differ in the way they finance their businesses. This difference can be attributed to the type of business and the type of management and experience of the entrepreneur (indirect effect). Female start-ups may also experience specific barriers when trying to acquire start-up capital. These may be based upon discriminatory effects (direct effect). Whether gender has an impact on size and composition of start-up capital and in what way, is the subject of the present paper. The indirect effect is represented by the way women differ from men in terms of type of business and management and experience. The direct effect cannot be attributed to these differences and is called the gender effect. We use of a panel of 2000 Dutch starting entrepreneurs, of whom approximately 500 are female to test for these direct and indirect effects. The panel refers to the year 1994. We find that female entrepreneurs have a smaller amount of start-up capital, but that they do not differ significantly with respect to the type of capital. On average the proportion of equity and debt capital (bank loans) in the businesses of female entrepreneurs is the same as in those of their male counterparts.

1. Introduction

Developed countries are undergoing a fundamental shift away from a managed economy and toward an entrepreneurial economy (Audretsch and Thurik, 2001). Economic activity is moving from large, incumbent firms toward small, new ones. There is a growing literature about how and why the developed countries are undergoing this fundamental shift (Brock and Evans, 1989; Admiraal, 1996; Audretsch and Thurik, 2000).

The speed of this industrial transformation process has varied considerably across countries and industries (Carree et al., 2001; Thurik, 1999).

Centre for Advanced Small Business Economics
Faculty of Economics
Erasmus University Rotterdam
P.O. Box 1738
3000 DR Rotterdam
The Netherlands
E-mail: verheul@few.eur.nl; thurik@few.eur.nl

Increasingly, evidence becomes available that this transformation has to be promoted (Gavron et al., 1998). Empirical evidence shows that those countries and industries that are lagging behind in this process experience lower growth and productivity levels and higher levels of unemployment (Thurik, 1996; Carree and Thurik, 1999; Audretsch and Thurik, 2000).

Entrepreneurship seems to be a driving force in economic development. However, entrepreneurship itself cannot be a determinant of growth. It is an ill-defined, at best multidimensional concept. Understanding its role requires the decomposition of the concept (Wennekers and Thurik, 1999). Dimensions of entrepreneurship are smallness, competition, deregulation, innovation, co-operation, variation, turbulence and motivation (Audretsch and Thurik, 1999, 2001). Deregulation and variation are essential dimensions. Low barriers should enable a broad variety of entrepreneurs to enter the market. Diversity in terms of products, processes, forms of organisation and targeted markets should leads to a selection process where customers are at liberty to choose according to their preferences.

This process where entrepreneurs seek for better products, processes, forms of organisation and markets can only thrive under enabling rather that constraining public policies (Audretsch and Thurik, 2001). Therefore, it is important that all potential entrepreneurs are able to play a role in securing maximum diversity and in taking maximum advantage of free competition. No group of potential entrepreneurs should experience any barrier for starting or developing a business. From this perspective it is worth noting that female entrepreneurs are still underrepresented.

The desire of women to be economically independent leads to their increasing participation in the labour market and an increasing number of

330 *Ingrid Verheul and Roy Thurik*

female entrepreneurs (Koper, 1993). Moreover, contextual factors, like social structures, family and organized life influence the access women have to entrepreneurial opportunities (Brush and Hisrich, 1999).

In spite of the growing number of female entrepreneurs, the share of female entrepreneurs is still disproportionally low when compared to their participation rate. This share accounts for approximately thirty percent of the total number of entrepreneurs in the Western world (OECD, 1998) whereas more than forty percent of employees is female. Considering the backward position of female entrepreneurs and the need for diversity, it is important to pay attention to specific barriers for female entrepreneurs, like the combination of social and economic responsibilities and the consequences of these specific barriers for female entrepreneurship. Furthermore, it is important to investigate whether the impact of general barriers, like the acquisition of financial resources, differs between female and male entrepreneurs.[1]

Entrepreneurs may meet several obstacles when starting a business like unexpected or fierce competition, delayed customer payments and limited access to financial resources. Indeed, acquiring financial capital is often referred to as an important problem for entrepreneurs (Hughes and Storey, 1994; EIM, 1998; OECD, 1998). Entrepreneurs starting up a business usually have little equity to finance their business with, while debt capital is difficult to acquire. Banks are often reluctant to lend money to small businesses because of low expected profit margins, asymmetrical information and high risks (EIM, 1998). Most starting entrepreneurs use their own money for financing their business. However, when the amount of financial capital needed is higher, more external capital is needed. External capital is an important source also for small enterprises (OECD, 1998). Bank loans in particular are much relied upon. This is also put forward by Riding and Swift stating that "It is well known that small businesses rely heavily on banks for both short- and long-term debt capital" (Riding and Swift, 1990, p. 329). Other important sources of external finance are family members, suppliers and other business partners (Van Uxem and Bais, 1996). These sources will not be explicitly investigated in the present study.

Considerable sums of public money are spent to diminish alleged debt gaps, particularly for small expanding firms and start-ups. Subsidised loans and loan guarantees are the most common instruments of government assistance programs to support small and new businesses. The idea is that capital markets do not provide adequate funds for small and new businesses. There are differing views whether the resulting debt gaps influences the probability of survival. In Cressy's analysis (Cressy, 1996) this is not the case whereas in that of Evans and Jovanovic (1989) and Bates (1990) it is. In the present paper we focus on the specific situation of female start-ups.

In the literature much attention is paid to financial problems of female entrepreneurs. This may have to do with the size of their businesses. It is often reported that the start-up size of businesses run by women is smaller than that of businesses run by men (Carter and Rosa, 1998; OECD, 1998; Stigter, 1999). A variety of reasons is brought forward for the smallness of the enterprises run by women. First, female entrepreneurs usually have a smaller amount of equity capital available because of lower salary payments in earlier jobs, discontinuities of earlier jobs or because family property is usually registered in the name of the husband. Second, the amount of start-up capital may also be related to the sector where an entrepreneur operates (ENSR, 1996). Women often start in sectors with low capital requirements, like the service sector. Banks are often reluctant to lend money to these sectors characterised by a high mobility. Finally, women are more likely to be risk avers than men (ENSR, 1996). This can also be an explanation for the smaller size of the businesses of female entrepreneurs.

Apart from the amount of start-up capital, female and male entrepreneurs may differ with respect to the capital structure of their business. Clearly, a distinction can be made between equity and debt capital. Finance theorists have argued about whether there exists an optimal capital structure for small firms in terms of both debt and equity (Hughes and Storey, 1994). Market imperfections, like taxes, bankruptcy costs, agency costs (monitoring) and the signalling effect (information asymmetry leading to information costs) have been brought forward as determinants of the firm's optimal capital structure (Van der Wijst and Thurik, 1996). In practice, the ensemble of market imperfections leads to a trade-off between equity and debt financing.

In the neo-classical tradition, the trade-off theory describes the optimum in terms of a trade-off between tax advantages of debt and the increase in expected bankruptcy costs. The agency theory gives an alternative explanation, independent of taxes and bankruptcy costs, which is based on minimising agency costs. Myers' Pecking Order Theory uses elements from both the trade-off theory and the agency theory. According to the Myers' Pecking Order Hypothesis the financing of projects is undertaken first by using internal resources, then debt and equity as a final resort. Holmes and Kent have developed a "Restricted Pecking Order Theory" (Holmes and Kent, 1991). This theory can be applied to small firms by assuming that small firms usually are not able to issue shares and owner-managers want to be in control of their business. As a consequence, small businesses are unlikely to use (external) equity. Furthermore, this theory is applicable only in case entrepreneurs have a genuine choice between equity and debt capital in the sense that they have personal equity available and relevant access to credit. The existence of an optimal capital structure is no longer debated in the theory of finance. The remaining issue is essentially an empirical one, i.e. whether, or under which set of circumstances – including the size of the firm – the various determinants are of sufficient economic importance.

In reality, a wide variation in the patterns of finance across small firms is to be expected, due to differences in the life cycle position of firms, size and strategies towards independence and growth (Hughes and Storey, 1994). In fact, the seemingly irrational behaviour of those running small businesses may increase this variation. D'Amboise and Muldowney even state that "The goals of the small business person are vague, inadequately defined, pragmatic and short-ranged" (D'Amboise and Muldowney, 1988, p. 231).

In the literature there is little consensus about the differences in the composition of financial capital between female and male entrepreneurs. Some state that female and male entrepreneurs do not differ with respect to the amount of their

own resources used (Rosa et al., 1994). Others conclude that female entrepreneurs make more use of their own resources and less of debt financing with the exception of money borrowed from family and friends (Carter and Rosa, 1998; Honig-Haftel and Martin, 1986; Neider, 1987; Hisrich and Brush, 1987; Olm et al., 1988; Johnson and Storey, 1993). Moreover, men may have better access to formal sources of debt financing, like banks and private financial institutions (OECD, 1998) and informal financial networks (Olm et al., 1988; Riding and Swift, 1990). In the present study our focus will be on the proportion of bank loans because of the relative importance of bank loans within the total amount of debt finance used by small businesses.

It can be concluded from the literature that female and male entrepreneurs differ with respect to the way in which they finance their businesses. However, there is ambiguity about the determinants and the direction of these differences. To investigate the differences between female and male entrepreneurs and their causes the present paper deals with the following question: *"What is the impact of gender on financial capital?"* We will discriminate between the *amount* of capital and its *composition*. The amount of financial capital refers to total investment in the start-up venture. With respect to the composition of capital a distinction is made between equity and debt. In this paper we will concentrate on internal equity, which is equity provided by the entrepreneur, as we assume that starting entrepreneurs, who are the subject of this study, are hardly in a position to acquire external equity through stock market quotation. Moreover, we also focus on a particular type of debt, namely bank loans. As can be deducted from the literature bank loans are an important source of debt capital for starting entrepreneurs. One has to bear in mind that internal equity and bank loans together do not add up to the total amount of financial capital used to start a venture. Other types of finance include external equity (although this is not very likely) and debt capital provided for by suppliers, other business partners and family and friends (F-capital).

Moreover, the impact of gender on financial capital can be *direct* or *indirect*. The indirect effect refers to differences between male and female entrepreneurs with respect to the type of business and their type of management and experience. Below, this is referred to as *"the female profile"*. The direct effect cannot be attributed to these differences and can be called a *gender effect*, i.e. female and male entrepreneurs with the same characteristics differ with respect to the way in which they finance their businesses. Both effects are depicted in Figure 1. To our knowledge, this paper represents the first discrimination between direct and indirect effects of gender on the amount and composition of financial capital.

2. Differences between male and female entrepreneurs

2.1. *Introduction*

"No two entrepreneurs are the same'. Entrepreneurs differ with respect to the sector they work in, their background and experience, the size of their enterprises, etc. This applies to female as well as to male entrepreneurs. It is interesting to investigate in what way female and male entrepreneurs differ. For instance, they may differ because their societal opportunities are unevenly distributed or as a result of a different upbringing.[2] The present chapter focuses on differences between female and male entrepreneurs with respect to their experience and education, the time they spend on running their business, networking, sector, firm size and entrepreneurial characteristics. Differences between male and female entrepreneurs with respect to these factors will be used to construct the "female profile". Of course there will be other factors that can be used making up

the female profile. However, this paper deals only with those factors that are most likely to have impact on the amount and composition of financial capital. Moreover, the availability of these factors in the data set is also an important reason for the selection of factors. The present chapter deals with differences between male and female entrepreneurs with respect to these factors. In the next chapter differences with respect to these factors are captured in terms of a set of hypotheses.

2.2. *Experience and education*

Male and female entrepreneurs differ with respect to experience and education (Brush, 1992). The *level* of education of female and male entrepreneurs is roughly identical, whereas the *type* of education differs (Van Uxem and Bais, 1996; Birley, Moss and Saunders, 1987). Male entrepreneurs are more likely to have completed a technical schooling, while the education of female entrepreneurs usually is more economical, administrative or commercial of nature. Moreover, female entrepreneurs usually are more specialised in personal services (Van Uxem and Bais, 1996).

The *length* and *type* of experience of women and men in the labour market vary considerably. Men are more likely to have been employed prior to the start-up of their business and tend to have more working experience (Van Uxem and Bais, 1996; Welsch and Young, 1982). Differences in type of experience are related to differences in type of education. Female entrepreneurs are more likely to be experienced in fields like teaching,

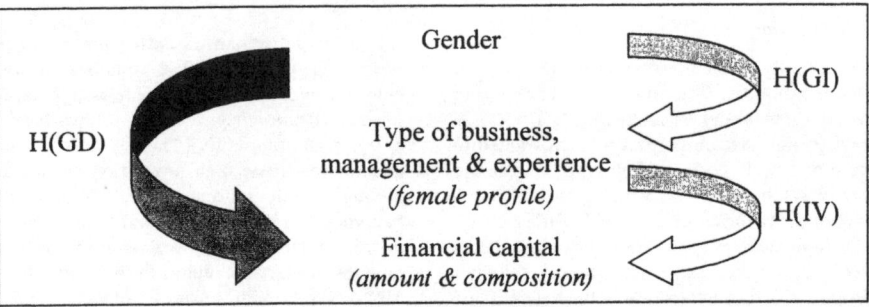

Figure 1. Direct and indirect impact of gender on business finance and hypotheses.

sales, administration and personal services (Hisrich and Brush, 1983; Scott, 1986; Neider, 1987; Welsch and Young, 1982) as opposed to management, sciences and technology (Watkins and Watkins, 1983; Stevenson, 1986). Men are also more likely to have earlier entrepreneurial experience (Fischer et al., 1993, Kalleberg and Leicht, 1991). Additionally, they have more industry experience and experience with human resource management, financial management and the application of modern technologies (Fischer et al. 1993, Van Uxem and Bais, 1996).

2.3. *Part-time entrepreneurship*

Male entrepreneurs work more often on a full-time basis when compared to their female counterparts (OECD, 1998). More than half of the enterprising women carry out other activities besides running their own business, like being employed or taking care of their family (Stigter, 1999). Of those female entrepreneurs who work part-time in their business, approximately half is part-time entrepreneur due to household activities, whereas only a small percentage of the male part-time entrepreneurs have similar obligations (Van Uxem en Bais, 1996). Male entrepreneurs work more often on a part-time basis in their own business as a result of having another enterprise or having other employment (Stigter, 1999). Female entrepreneurs have "double assignments"; i.e. they are running an enterprise and a household at the same time. These "double assignments" may limit the time female entrepreneurs spend on their businesses (Loscocco, 1991; Tigges and Green, 1992).

2.4. *Networking*

Only recently female entrepreneurs started acknowledging the importance of networking activities (Moore and Buttner, 1997). There is a general feeling that in the past women wanted to prove they could "do it on their own". There are several ways in which networking activities can be measured (Aldrich et al., 1987; Birley et al., 1991). Indicators proposed are (1) the tendency to network, (2) the size of the network (number of people), (3) the composition of the network and (4) the time spend on networking.

The tendency to network does not differ sig-

nificantly between female and male entrepreneurs. Women understand the importance of using a network (Hansen and Allen, 1992). The size of the networks used by male is similar to that used by female entrepreneurs (Cromie and Birley, 1990). However, in a discussion on the differences in network compositions and size, Brush refers to Aldrich (1989) who states that women usually engage in smaller networks consisting primarily of women (Brush, 1992). Men spend more time developing and maintaining networks (Cromie and Birley, 1990). Household activities of women ("double assignments") and other social obligations may lead to more isolation than men usually experience (Moore and Buttner, 1997). This implies that women spend less time on networking. Moreover, the members of both formal and informal networks are not always open to accepting women.

2.5. *Sector*

Male and female entrepreneurs work in different sectors. Female entrepreneurs are overrepresented in the retail- and service sectors, in particular in personal services (OECD, 1998). Male entrepreneurs are overrepresented in manufacturing, wholesale trade and financial services (Van Uxem and Bais, 1996). Within sectors, female entrepreneurs are often found in supporting jobs or occupations. The businesses of female entrepreneurs can be characterised as "supporting services", like secretarial, translation and processing activities (Van Uxem and Bais, 1996).

2.6. *Size*

By and large, female entrepreneurs have smaller businesses than men. The smallness of female entrepreneurial activity can be related to the sector of their business, e.g. sectors with low barriers to entry, high competition and low profit margins, and the relatively high proportion of part-timers among female entrepreneurs. Their smallness becomes manifest in several ways, like low returns, a small workforce (if any) and a small amount of start-up capital (Van Uxem and Bais, 1996). The main business objective of male entrepreneurs is growth so that they can reap the fruits of increasing returns. However, growth is

merely a secondary objective for female entrepreneurs (Van Uxem and Bais, 1996). This can be
related to the situation where their business is not
the only means of earning a living. Most female
entrepreneurs have an earning partner.

2.7. Entrepreneurial characteristics

Men and women have different values. This is
concluded in a study by Sexton and Bowman-
Upton (1990) about the extent to which men and
women possess entrepreneurial characteristics,
like perseverance, autonomy, propensity to take
risks and readiness to change. Although the differences with respect to entrepreneurial characteristics are rather small, it is reported that men
put a higher value on perseverance and risk and a
lower value on autonomy and change than women
do. Moreover, women value their own entrepreneurial characteristics lower than men (Van Uxem
and Bais, 1996). This is the case especially with
regard to taking risk, industry knowledge and
technological knowledge. The lack of confidence
of female entrepreneurs in their own entrepreneurial capabilities may be attributed to a relatively negative self-perception. Social and cultural
factors play an important role in maintaining this
negative self-image of women, like the subordinate role of women in large parts of the world and
internalised gender specific images and values
(Hofstede, 1991).

3. Hypotheses

Hypotheses can be formulated relating differences
between male and female entrepreneurs to the
amount and composition of financial capital. The
manner in which these hypotheses are formulated
is displayed in Figure 1. Hypotheses of type H
(IV) refer to the impact of the intermediary
variables on financial capital in terms of differences between male and female entrepreneurs.
Hypotheses of type H (GI) refer to the relation
between gender and the intermediary variables.
Hypotheses of type H (GI) and H (IV) together
make up the indirect effect of gender on financial
capital, while hypotheses of type H (GD) reflect
the direct effect of gender on financial capital.

Hypotheses have been formulated regarding the
effect of gender on the total amount of financial

capital, the proportion of equity, which in this
paper refers to internal equity, and the proportion
of bank loans. One has to bear in mind that
internal equity and bank loans do not necessarily
add up to the total amount of financial capital.
This indicates that equity and bank loans are not
entirely complementary and there is another effect
of gender on the residual category of financial
capital, including for instance F-capital.

The hypotheses formulated below are coded
using abbreviations. These abbreviations are
clarified in Table I.

Financial management experience and financial capital

Female entrepreneurs are more likely to have less
experience with financial management than male
entrepreneurs because women usually have less
opportunity to accumulate management experience
due to the vertical segregation of the labour
market. Prospective entrepreneurs with little
experience of financial management maybe
assumed to be unaware of the way in which they
can acquire financial capital and of whom they can
contact for help and advice. Entrepreneurs with
financial management experience are assumed to
be able to use their earlier experience to convince
credit managers of banks to invest in their venture.
This might also be valid when attempting to
convince business angels and venture capitalists.
Moreover, tax shields can be an incentive to
use bank loans for financing the business.
Entrepreneurs with financial experience may be

TABLE I
Abbreviations used

Abbreviation	Description
IV	Intermediary variables
PT	Part-time entrepreneurship
S	Services
FM	Financial management experience
RA	Risk attitude
N	Networking
GI	Indirect effect of gender
GD	Direct effect of gender
A	Amount of financial capital
E	Proportion of equity
B	Proportion of bank loans

better informed about these tax incentives. Financial management experience may also involve knowledge about the importance of free cash flows for entrepreneurs. Constraints on financial resources may hinder a flexible response on market fluctuations. Interest payments on bank loans corrode free cash flows. In that case entrepreneurs will be inclined to use personal resources for financing their business. Finally, financial management might be associated with a sufficient amount of personal savings based upon success in earlier jobs and investments. The following hypotheses are formulated:[3]

H (GI=FM)	Female entrepreneurs have less experience with financial management than their male counterparts
H (IV=FM, A)	Experience with financial management leads to a higher amount of financial capital
H (IV=FM, E)	Experience with financial management leads to a higher proportion of equity in the total amount of financial capital
H (IV=FM, B)	Experience with financial management leads to a higher proportion of bank loans in the total amount of financial capital

Part-time entrepreneurship and financial capital
Female entrepreneurs are more likely to work on a part-time basis than male entrepreneurs. Women often try to combine work- and household responsibilities. Part-time entrepreneurship usually goes together with a smaller business involving relatively few investments and requiring a small amount of financial capital. Part-timers are supposed to bring in a high proportion of equity, because they are able to, having resources out of their other activities, and they are willing to, having their risks spread among various activities. Additionally, banks may have a limited inclination to support part-timers. Part-time entrepreneurship can have a signalling effect. By working part-time, the entrepreneur gives a signal that the business is not important or successful enough to merit all the entrepreneurs resources. This means that outside parties, like banks, can be expected to be

more cautious when deciding whether or not to invest in the venture. This leads to the following hypotheses:

H (GI=PT)	Female entrepreneurs work on a part-time basis more often than their male counterparts
H (IV=PT, A)	Part-time entrepreneurship leads to a smaller amount of financial capital
H (IV=PT, E)	Part-time entrepreneurship leads to a higher proportion of equity in the total amount of financial capital
H (IV=PT, B)	Part-time entrepreneurship leads to a smaller proportion of bank loans in the total amount of financial capital

Networking and financial capital
Having contact with other entrepreneurs can lead to the exchange of relevant information. Female entrepreneurs spend less time networking than their male counterparts, which may deprive them of important information concerning the acquisition of finance. Network activities are assumed to improve the entrepreneur's view on his or her goals and future activities and hence his or her capital requirements. Network activities are assumed to lower barriers when acquiring bank loans. We have no a priori hypothesis about the influence of networking on the proportion of equity in the total amount of financial capital. The following hypotheses are formulated:

H (GI=N)	Female entrepreneurs more often spend less time networking than their male counterparts
H (IV=N, A)	Networking leads to a higher amount of financial capital
H (IV=N, E)	No a priori hypothesis
H (IV=N, B)	Networking leads to a higher proportion of bank loans in the total amount of financial capital

Sector and financial capital
Female entrepreneurs are more likely to work in the service sector. This sector is characterised by relatively small initial investments requiring a

small amount of financial capital. The service sector is generally associated with low investments in tangible assets, like machines and buildings and high investments in intangibles, like human capital and customer relations. In case of bankruptcy, the former have a high value in second hand markets, the latter a low value, if any. Investment in the service sector is less attractive for banks. Therefore the service sector is associated with a low proportion of debt (bank loans). We have no a priori hypothesis about the influence of the service sector on the proportion of equity in the total amount of financial capital. The following hypotheses are formulated:

H (GI=S) Female entrepreneurs work in the service sector more often than their male counterparts

H (IV=S, A) Entrepreneurial activities in the service sector require a smaller amount of financial capital

H (IV=S, E) No a priori hypothesis

H (IV=S, B) Entrepreneurial activities in the service sector lead to a smaller proportion of bank loans in the total amount of financial capital.

Size and financial capital
Enterprises of female entrepreneurs generally are smaller than those of male entrepreneurs. A smaller amount of financial start-up capital is assumed to make equity financing more likely compared to debt financing. An analysis of the financial structure of small businesses indicates that the bulk of their funds are personal savings of the owner-manager and retained profits from business operations (Kotey, 1999). This corresponds with the views of Weston and Brigham who state that small firms tend to start out using only owners' resources (Weston and Brigham, 1981). Several reasons can be brought forward for the reliance of owners of small businesses on personal resources for the financing of their business. First, the availability of equity is not likely to vary considerably between entrepreneurs. Generally, as the scale of the business increases, the amount of personal resources will not suffice and the use of bank loans and other types of external finance will have to be taken into consideration. Thus, equity decreases with size,

because banks require some sort of buffer capital and this buffer decreases proportionally as size increases. Second, autonomy is an important motive for starting up a business (Van Uxem and Bais, 1996). Entrepreneurs are reluctant to loose control of the business in an early stage by pursuing a bank loan. However, as the business starts to grow the need for debt capital will increase, eventually leading to the acquisition of external capital and a loss of control. A third reason is related to Myers' Pecking Order Theory. According to this theory the financing of projects is undertaken first by using internal resources, then debt and finally external equity (stock market). The Restricted Pecking Order Theory by Holmes and Kent can be applied to small businesses assuming that small businesses are rarely in a position to issue shares to acquire external capital. In case of start-ups there is no basis for a stock market quotation. It has also been noted that entrepreneurs starting a business set great value on being in control of their business, thereby partly minimising their need of external financial capital (debt as well as equity). Moreover, internal resources, in the shape of retained earnings, play an important role in the Pecking Order Theory. However, these funds are by definition not available for starting firms. Accordingly, starting entrepreneurs will have to finance their business with other internal resources: personal resources, i.e. internal equity. Finally, there is a supply side reason for the capital structure of small firms. Banks are reluctant to lend to starting small businesses, because they do not possess audited financial statements, they do not have many business assets that can be easily evaluated or used as collateral and have little repayment history or records of profitability (Berger and Udell, 1998). Moreover, the fixed cost element of transactions puts small businesses at a disadvantage in raising external finance (Chittenden et al., 1996). The impact of the leverage effect on small businesses is not clear and no evidence has been found in the literature. The following hypotheses are formulated:

H (GI=A) Female entrepreneurs generally have smaller businesses than their male counterparts

H (IV=A, E) A small amount of financial

H (IV=A, B)　A small amount of financial capital leads to a smaller proportion of bank loans in the total amount of financial capital

Risk attitude and financial capital

Women are assumed to be more risk avers than men and risk aversion implies a reliance on equity instead of bank loans. This is confirmed by Kotey and Meredith who state that risk aversion of entrepreneurs leads to dependency on personal equity as a source of finance (Kotey and Meredith, 1997) and Carland who claims that a higher risk taking propensity and a better understanding of the risks inherent in investments leads to the use of more debt finance (Carland et al., 1989). Debt financing increases the financial risk of the firm because interest payments on debt are to be paid when due, irrespective of the firms' profitability or liquidity levels. Moreover, debt financing involves the risks of fluctuating interest rates, redemption and liability. The following hypotheses can be derived:

H (GI=RA)　Female entrepreneurs have a lower propensity to take risks than their male counterparts

H (IV=RA, A)　The propensity to take risks leads to a higher amount of financial capital

H (IV=RA, E)　The propensity to take risks leads to a smaller proportion of equity in the total amount of financial capital

H (IV=RA, B)　The propensity to take risks leads to a higher proportion of bank loans in the total amount of financial capital

Direct effect

The direct effect of gender on financial capital cannot be explained using intermediary variables. However it can be interpreted in the following way. Female entrepreneurs may have less confidence in their entrepreneurial capabilities than male entrepreneurs, leading to the start-up of smaller enterprises. Moreover, it is possible that female entrepreneurs have other ambitions than

capital leads to a higher proportion of equity in the total amount of financial capital

male entrepreneurs or set more value on "quality" instead of "quantity". They serve a niche market or focus on customer satisfaction rather than strive after growth of their business through diversification. A possible supply side reason for the smaller firms of women is the conservative attitude of male businessmen and entrepreneurs or, more important, that of bankers.

Female entrepreneurs may have less personal financial resources than male entrepreneurs. For instance this is due to discontinuity of past labour relations, leading to a smaller proportion of equity within the total amount of financial capital. Finally, female entrepreneurs may experience difficulties acquiring bank loans for instance due to discrimination based on images of women not being adequately equipped for entrepreneurship. The remaining hypotheses are:

H (GD, A)　Gender has a negative direct impact on the amount of financial capital

H (GD, E)　Gender has a negative direct impact on the proportion of equity within the total amount of financial capital

H (GD, B)　Gender has a negative direct impact on the proportion of bank loans within the total amount of financial capital

4. Empirical analyses

4.1. *Data source*

To investigate the impact of gender on financial capital and to test the hypotheses dealt with in the previous chapter, use is made of a panel of 2,000 Dutch firms that have started their business in the first quarter of 1994. Approximately 1,500 are male and 500 are female. This is a reasonable representation of the average distribution of female and male entrepreneurs in most OECD-countries (OECD, 1998). The panel is set up and implemented by EIM Business and Policy Research in Zoetermeer. The data consist of questions concerning the process of starting-up, the period prior to the start-up phase and the shape of the prospective business. The focus is on the background of the entrepreneur (education and experience), the motives for starting up a firm, financial data and investments, management bottlenecks and expectations. The panel is set up in the year 1994. For the present analyses the results are used of the first questionnaires sent out in 1994. Follow-up questionnaires were distributed to map developments in the years after start-up.[4]

The national character of the data set limits the extent to which the conclusions can be generalized since the financial support of start-ups, the operating procedures of financial institutions and other institutional barriers to entry may differ between countries.

4.2. *Description of variables*

From the data source described in the previous paragraph, the following variables are selected for the empirical analyses. The dependent variables

TABLE II
Description of variables

	Description	Variable name	Measurement	Average	Std. deviation
1	Amount of start-up capital	Start-up capital (A)	Observations are given one out of 7 different amounts in thousands of Dutch guilders[a]	48.51	93.36
2	Proportion of equity in total amount of start-up capital	Proportion equity (E)	Observations are ordered according to classes 1 to 12[b]	8.40	4.38
3	Proportion of bank loans in total amount of start-up capital	Proportion bank loans (B)	Observations are ordered according to classes 1 to 12[b]	3.62	3.68
4	Whether the entrepreneur works in the service sector or in non-services	Services (S)	Dummy variable: services = 1 and elsewhere = 0	Percentage (dummy variable = 1) = 25	
5	The extent to which an entrepreneur is willing to take risks	Risk attitude (RA)	Observations are ordered according to classes 1 (very weak) to 5 (very strong)	3.81	0.79
6	Whether the entrepreneur is engaged in other activities besides the own business	Part-time (PT)[c]	Dummy variable: part-time = 1 and full-time = 0	Percentage (dummy variable = 1) = 50	
7	The extent to which an entrepreneur has contact with other entrepreneurs	Networking (N)	Observations are ordered according to classes 1 (never), 2 (sometimes) and 3 (regularly)	1.57	0.71
8	The extent to which an entrepreneur had previous experience with financial management	Financial management (FM)	Observations are ordered according to classes 1 (no experience) to 4 (much experience)	2.06	0.98
9	Whether the entrepreneur is male or female	Gender	Dummy variable: female = 1 and male = 0	Percentage (dummy variable = 1) = 27	

[a] The following amounts in thousands of Dutch guilders have been selected: (1) 5, (2) 17.5, (3) 37.5, (4) 75, (5) 175, (6) 375 and (7) 500.
[b] Classes 1 to 12 refer to the following percentages: (1) 0%, (2) 1–10%, (3) 11–20% . . . (11) 91 < 100% and (12) 100%.
[c] In the present empirical analyses part-time entrepreneurship is defined by performing other activities besides running a business. This is in contradistinction to many other studies where usually someone is considered to be a part-time entrepreneur when working less than 40 hours per week. This is a time-based definition. As a rule, entrepreneurs who engage in other activities besides entrepreneurship work less than 40 hours a week. However, exceptions have to be taken into account.

are the amount of start-up capital, the proportion of equity and the proportion of bank loans in the total amount of start-up capital. The amount of financial capital is both a dependent variable and an explanatory variable when explaining the composition of financial capital. The description and measurement of the variables is presented in Table II.

The correlation between the explanatory variables is presented in Table III, as a test of multicollinear distortions. Generally, the correlation coefficients are low. The highest absolute value of the Pearson correlation coefficients of Table III is that of the start-up capital and part-time entrepreneurship, being 0.20. One may conclude that, although most values are significantly differing from zero, this is not relevant considering their small values. Furthermore, experiments omitting variables in a pseudo stepwise fashion did not reveal any suspicion of multicollinear distortions.

4.3. *Analyses*

The hypotheses formulated in the previous section are tested using multiple regression analyses to determine the direct and indirect impact of gender on the amount and composition of start-up capital. Single bilateral correlation is used to test whether there is a connection between gender and the other explanatory variables of start-up capital.

In Table IV the correlation between gender and the intermediary variables is presented. All hypotheses of type H (GI) are supported at a 5% level of significance. The following profile can

be constructed of the female entrepreneur in comparison with the male entrepreneur: female entrepreneurs are more likely to work part-time, more likely to work in the service sector, they are more averse to risk, have less experience with financial management, spend less time on networking and start smaller businesses.

Regression analysis is used to determine the direct and indirect impact of gender on the total amount of start-up capital and the proportion of equity and bank loans in the total amount of start-up capital. The results are presented in Tables V, VI and VII, respectively. A distinction is made between taking into account all explanatory variables, the intermediary variables (the female profile) or just the gender dummy variable. β's refer to the coefficients of the explanatory variables. The number of observations is smaller in case the intermediary variables are taken into account because they are not always available.

From the intermediary variables column in Table V we conclude that the amount of start-up capital is lower if firms are operating in the service sector, if entrepreneurs are risk averse, if they operate on a part-time basis, if they do not indulge in networking and if they have no earlier experience with financial management. All these effects are significant at the 5% level. Hence, this implies that all hypotheses are supported. From the gender column we conclude that women start their business with a smaller amount of start-up capital than men. From the all variables column we conclude that in a joint analysis the intermediary variables effect and the gender effect remain present. This implies that a negative effect of

TABLE III
Pearson correlation between explanatory variables

	Start-up capital	Services	Risk attitude	Part-time	Networking	Financial management	Gender
Start-up capital	1.00	−0.12**	0.08**	−0.20**	0.09**	0.16**	−0.13**
Services	−0.12**	1.00	−0.03	0.07**	−0.07**	−0.11**	0.14**
Risk attitude	0.08**	−0.03	1.00	−0.06*	0.06*	0.15**	−0.09**
Part-time	−0.20**	0.07**	−0.06*	1.00	0.01	−0.03	0.08**
Networking	0.09**	−0.07**	0.06*	0.01	1.00	0.13**	−0.10**
Financial management	−0.16**	−0.11**	0.15**	−0.03	0.13**	1.00	−0.15**
Gender	−0.13**	0.14**	−0.09**	0.08**	−0.10**	−0.15**	1.00

** Correlation is significant at the 0.01 level (2-tailed).
* Correlation is significant at the 0.05 level (2-tailed).

TABLE IV
Correlation between gender and the intermediary variables

Intermediary variables	Direction of correlation	Hypothesis
Services	Positive	H (GI=S)
Risk attitude	Negative	H (GI=RA)
Part-time	Positive	H (GI=PT)
Networking	Negative	H (GI=N)
Financial management	Negative	H (GI=FM)
Start-up capital	Negative	H (GI=A)

gender on the amount of start-up capital can be separated in a direct and indirect effect. The direct effect can be found in the all variables column, whereas the indirect effect can be inferred from the results of the correlation between gender and the intermediary variables (Table IV) and the effect of the intermediary variables on the amount of start-up capital. The indirect effect can also be associated with the difference between the β's of the total and the direct effect of gender on the amount of start-up capital. The indirect effect can be explained using the intermediary variables, i.e. the female profile. The direct effect cannot be explained by the female profile. The following interpretation can be given. Female entrepreneurs may have a lack of confidence in their entrepreneurial capabilities when compared to male entrepreneurs. Moreover, women may have less equity than men or they fear that they will meet with discrimination when they apply for a bank loan. Below, the composition of the start-up capital will be discussed.

The regression results of the analysis on the proportion of equity are presented in Table VI. From the intermediary variables column we conclude that the proportion of equity in the total amount of start-up capital is higher if entrepreneurs are risk averse, if they work on a part-time basis, if they have networking contacts with other entrepreneurs and if they have a smaller amount of start-up capital. The only effect not significant at the 5% level is that of networking for which no a priori hypothesis was formulated. No a priori hypothesis has been formulated with respect to the effect of services on the proportion of equity and no significant effect has been found in the analysis. From the gender column we conclude that gender has no significant effect on the proportion of equity. From the all variables column it can be concluded that in a joint analysis the intermediary effects remain present and a gender effect appears. The total effect of gender on the proportion of equity, which is not significant, can be separated in a direct and indirect effect. The direct effect can be found in the all variables column, whereas the indirect effect can be inferred from the results of the correlation between gender and the intermediary variables (Table IV) and the effect of the intermediary variables on the proportion of equity. The indirect effect can also be associated with the difference between the β's of the total and the direct effect of gender on the proportion of equity. Neglecting the intermediary variables one is inclined to conclude that gender has no influence on the proportion of equity. However, when the female profile is taken into account, it can be concluded that female entrepreneurs are less able to acquire equity than their

TABLE V
β- and t-values in a linear regression analysis on the total amount of start-up capital

	All variables		Intermediary variables		Gender		Hypothesis
	β-value	t-value	β-value	t-value	β-value	t-value	
Services	−16.77	−3.32	−18.76	−3.73	0	0	H (IV=S, A)
Risk attitude	4.67	1.67	5.34	1.91	0	0	H (IV=RA, A)
Part-time	−36.54	−8.41	−37.56	−8.64	0	0	H (IV=PT, A)
Networking	9.47	3.09	10.11	3.29	0	0	H (IV=N, A)
Financial management	11.84	5.20	12.71	5.60	0	0	H (IV=FM, A)
Gender	−16.84	−3.34	0	0	−27.11	−5.69	H (GD, A)
R^2	0.09		0.085		0.017		
N	1757		1757		1913		

TABLE VI

β- and *t*-values in a linear regression analysis on the proportion of equity in the total amount of start-up capital

	All variables		Intermediary variables		Gender		Hypothesis
	β-value	*t*-value	β-value	*t*-value	β-value	*t*-value	
Services	−0.11	−0.45	−0.17	−0.69	0	0	H (IV=S, E)
Risk attitude	−0.57	−4.27	−0.55	−4.12	0	0	H (IV=RA, E)
Part-time	1.36	6.47	1.47	6.37	0	0	H (IV=PT, E)
Networking	0.01	0.69	0.12	0.80	0	0	H (IV=N, E)
Financial management	0.37	3.40	0.40	3.67	0	0	H (IV=FM, E)
Start-up capital	−0.01	−9.69	−0.01	−9.52	0	0	H (IV=A, E)
Gender	−0.57	−2.36	0	0	−0.05	−0.23	H (GD, E)
R^2	0.108		0.105		0.000		
N	1627		1627		1760		

male counterparts. The gender effect that female entrepreneurs have a smaller proportion of equity may be caused by relatively little personal resources as a means of financing the business.

The regression results of the analysis on the proportion of bank loans are presented in Table VII. From the intermediary variables column we conclude that the proportion of bank loans in the total amount of start-up capital is lower if entrepreneurs are risk averse, if they work on a part-time basis, if they do not engage in networking activities, if they have experience with financial management and if they have a small amount of start-up capital. Apart from the effect of financial management and networking all effects are significant at the 5% level: hypotheses H (IV=FM, B) and H (IV=N, B) are not supported. Moreover, hypothesis H (IV=S, B) has not been supported

in the analysis: no significant effect of the service sector on the proportion of bank loans has been found. As with the proportion of equity, on average, gender has no impact on the proportion of bank loans. This can be read from the gender column. From the all variables column we conclude that in a joint analysis the intermediary variables effect remains present and a small gender effect, significant at the 10% level, appears. This implies that the total effect of gender, which is insignificant, can be divided in a direct and indirect effect. The direct effect can be found in the all variables column, whereas the indirect effect can be inferred from the results of the correlation between gender and the intermediary variables (Table IV) and the effect of the intermediary variables on the proportion of bank loans. The indirect effect can also be associated with the

TABLE VII

β- and *t*-values in a linear regression analysis on the proportion of bank loans in the total amount of start-up capital

	All variables		Intermediary variables		Gender		Hypothesis
	β-value	*t*-value	β-value	*t*-value	β-value	*t*-value	
Services	−0.27	−1.14	−0.24	−0.10	0	0	H (IV=S, B)
Risk attitude	0.70	5.29	0.67	5.12	0	0	H (IV=RA, B)
Part-time	−1.09	−5.20	−1.07	−5.14	0	0	H (IV=PT, B)
Networking	0.02	0.11	0.01	0.07	0	0	H (IV=N, B)
Financial management	−0.15	−1.36	−0.16	−1.51	0	0	H (IV=FM, B)
Start-up capital	0.01	7.39	0.01	7.27	0	0	H (IV=A, B)
Gender	0.43	1.79	0	0	−0.20	−0.85	H (GD, B)
R^2	0.121		0.12		0.001		
N	1169		1169		1269		

difference between the βs of the total and the direct effect of gender on the proportion of bank loans. Neglecting the intermediary variables one is inclined to conclude that gender has no influence on the proportion of bank loans. However, when the female profile is taken into account, it can be concluded that female entrepreneurs have a higher proportion of bank loans in the total amount of start-up capital. This can be interpreted in the following way. Female entrepreneurs may be more successful in convincing credit managers of banks of their ideas and capabilities than male entrepreneurs. Here one has to bear in mind that the data do not allow for women entrepreneurs who did not succeed in acquiring bank loans or for the "price" of bank loans to be included in the analysis.

The distinction between a direct and indirect effect appears to be vital for understanding the impact of gender on the composition of the start-up capital. In the case of the total amount of start-up capital, leaving out the separation between direct and indirect does not lead to incorrect conclusions about the impact of gender. However, it does cover up the reasons why female entrepreneurs use less start-up capital than male entrepreneurs.

5. Summary and conclusions

The focus of this study is on the differences between female and male entrepreneurs with respect to the amount and composition of financial capital. Using a panel of 2000 Dutch start-ups (1994) we find that female entrepreneurs have a smaller amount of start-up capital than their male counterparts, but that they do not significantly differ with respect to the composition of financial capital. On average the proportion of equity and the proportion of bank loans in the businesses of female and male entrepreneurs is the same. This does however not imply that gender has no impact on the composition of financial capital. When investigating the impact of gender on the size and composition of the start-up capital a distinction is made between an indirect and direct effect. The indirect effect is represented by the way women differ from men in terms of type of business and management and experience. The profile of female entrepreneurs differs from that of male entrepre-

neurs: female entrepreneurs are more likely to work part-time, more likely to work in the service sector, they are more averse to risk, have less financial management experience and spend less time networking. The direct effect cannot be attributed to these differences and is called a gender effect. When corrected for the indirect effect, i.e. the female profile, the direct effect tells us that female entrepreneurs have a smaller amount of start-up capital, a smaller proportion of equity and a higher proportion of bank loans. This direct effect can be interpreted as follows. The smaller amount of financial capital of female entrepreneurs may be attributed to a lack of confidence in their own entrepreneurial capabilities, which discourages female entrepreneurs to start with a large amount of financial capital. Moreover, female entrepreneurs may have different ambitions and objectives than male entrepreneurs. For instance, female entrepreneurs are more likely to attach value to "quality" instead of "quantity" aspects of life. Female entrepreneurs may have more problems acquiring financial capital, i.e. equity and debt capital. The smaller proportion of equity may be attributed to female entrepreneurs having less personal resources they can use to finance their business with. For instance this may be due to discontinuity of past labour relations. Contrary to what is generally assumed, our investigation suggests that women are able to acquire a larger proportion of bank loans. Here one has to bear in mind that the data do not allow for women entrepreneurs who did not succeed in acquiring a bank loan or for the "price" of bank loans to be included in the analysis.

It can be concluded that when separating the total impact in a direct and indirect component gender has impact on the amount as well as the composition of financial capital. Consequently, merely focusing on the total impact of gender on financial capital can lead to misleading conclusions. The impact of gender on the amount of capital is likely to be overestimated because part of the negative total effect can be attributed to the female profile. When controlled for the female profile a smaller negative (direct) effect remains. In case of the proportion of equity and bank loans, when not controlled for the female profile there is no significant effect of gender on the composition of capital. However, when properly controlled for the effect of gender on equity is negative, whereas the effect on bank loans is positive.

Clearly, the present study is based on Dutch data and cannot be easily generalized to other countries. To improve knowledge of female entrepreneurship future studies should focus on international data that enable a comparison of gender issues in different countries. Moreover, the empirical analysis can be expanded to include more (and other) explanatory variables of start-up capital. Factors that could provide additional information are the age and marital status of the entrepreneur, the number of previous businesses owned (entrepreneurial experience), motives for starting up a business and self-confidence. The latter variable may be difficult to measure and can probably only be captured through self-rating. Additionally, the study should focus not only on businesses that are in the first phase of the (business) life cycle. Next to start-up ventures established businesses should be taken into account because these businesses have a track record that is important for the acquisition of debt capital from financial institutions. Recent spectacular changes in the European stock exchange landscape (the advent of specialized stock exchanges for smaller and high-risk ventures and the merger activities) are not thought to affect the reach of our conclusions. In the present study we deal with very small firms with an average start-up capital of less than 50,000 Dutch guilders. The entrepreneurial climate however may change in Europe due to the extension of venture capital type markets. This long-term effect may also influence the ability of very small start-ups to attract capital.

Research on the impact of gender should not be confined to financial capital. The impact of gender on organizational issues may even be more illuminating than that on financial capital. Female entrepreneurs are often considered to have a different organizational approach than male entrepreneurs. Moreover, organization can be a variable that intermediates between gender and financial capital. In this sense there will be an indirect effect of gender through organization on financial capital.

Differences between male and female entrepreneurs can also express themselves through other aspects of entrepreneurship like the use and composition of labour, the use of knowledge related factors (input factors) and growth rates and survival rates of the firm (output factors). When taking into account output factors, it can be expected that female entrepreneurs use their smaller amount of capital more effectively, i.e. they use less capital for given output levels. Thus, female entrepreneurs have a smaller amount of financial capital when compared to male entrepreneurs and this may imply that they make more efficient use of their relatively scarce resources.

Extending the analysis of the impact of gender to other input factors than financial capital, and taking into account output factors as well will result in a better understanding of differences in the way male and female entrepreneurs operate. Moreover, expansion of the number of intermediary variables in the analysis will create better insight in the gender-based differences and the specific nature of female entrepreneurship.

Acknowledgement

The authors would like to thank Robert Cressy, Stijn Goossens, Peter Risseeuw, Heleen Stigter, Frits van Uxem, Erik Vermeulen, Nico van der Wijst and an anonymous referee for their comments on an earlier version of the present paper. Earlier versions have been read at the Doctoral Seminar on Entrepreneurship Research in Barcelona (October 1999) and at the RENT XIII Conference in London (November 1999). The authors acknowledge the financial support of the VSB Fund Schiedam, as well as the Trust Fund Rotterdam.

Notes

[1] Female entrepreneurship is not only important because of the need for diversity. Entrepreneurship is an important opportunity to combine work- and household responsibilities (OECD, 1998). Moreover, female entrepreneurs can play an important role in the fulfilment of contemporary needs, because they often start in relatively new and experimental industries.

[2] Adherents of "liberal feminism" believe that women differ from men due to unevenly distributed opportunities in society caused by numerous forms of discrimination. Adherents of "social feminism" believe that women and men differ as a result of a different upbringing (socialisation). Boys and girls are being taught different values leading to different life styles and ideals. See Mills and Voerman, 1997 and Fischer et al., 1993.

344   Ingrid Verheul and Roy Thurik

[3] One has to bear in mind that in this paper a distinction is made between internal equity (equity provided for by the entrepreneur) and bank loans. This leaves a residual category of capital, including mainly F-capital. Equity and bank loans are not entirely complementary. The implication of hypotheses H (IV=FM, E) and H (IV=FM, B) is that experience with financial management may lead to a lower proportion of F-capital. In case of the impact of financial management experience on the use of F-capital it can be said that financial experience is associated with a touch of professionalism, making the use of F-capital less likely.

[4] Further information on the data set used in the empirical analysis can be obtained through EIM Business and Policy Research, Zoetermeer, The Netherlands (+31 79 3413634).

References

Admiraal, P. H. (ed.), 1996, *Small Business in the Modern Economy*, Oxford: Basil Blackwell Publishers.

Aldrich, H., 1989, 'Networking Among Women Entrepreneurs', in O. Hagan, C. Rivchun and D. Sexton (eds.), *Women-Owned Businesses*, New York: Praeger, pp. 103–132.

Aldrich, H., B. Rosen and W. Woodward, 1997, 'The Impact of Social Networks on Business Foundings and Profit: A Longitudinal Study', in D. P. Moore and E. H. Buttner (eds.), *Women Entrepreneurs: Moving Beyond the Glass Ceiling*, London & New Delhi: Sage Publications.

Amboise, G. d' and M. Muldowney, 1988, 'Management Theory for Small Business: Attempts and Requirements', *Academy of Management Review* 13(2), 226–240.

Audretsch, D. B. and A. R. Thurik, 2000, 'Capitalism and Democracy in the 21st Century: From the Managed to the Entrepreneurial Economy', *Journal of Evolutionary Economics* 10(1), 17–34.

Audretsch, D. B. and A. R. Thurik, 1999, 'Entrepreneurship and Unemployment in the Knowledge Economy', in *Innovation and Economic Development: The Role of Entrepreneurship and Small and Medium Enterprises*, Proceedings of the 44th ICSB World Conference, Edizione Scientifiche Italiane, Cdrom.

Audretsch, D. B. and A. R. Thurik, 2001, 'What is New About the New Economy: Sources of Growth in the Managed and Entrepreneurial Economies', *Industrial and Corporate Change*, forthcoming.

Bates, T., 1990, 'Entrepreneur Human Capital Inputs and Small Business Longevity', *The Review of Economics and Statistics* 72(4), 551–559.

Berger, A. N. and G. F. Udell, 1998, 'The Economics of Small Business Finance: The Roles of Private Equity and Debt Markets in the Financial Growth Cycle', *Journal of Banking and Finance* 22, 613–673.

Birley, S. J., S. Cromie and A. Myers, 1991, 'Entrepreneurial Networks: Their Emergence in Ireland and Overseas', *International Small Business Journal* 10(1), 237–251.

Birley, S., C. Moss and P. Saunders, 1987, 'Do Women Entrepreneurs Require Different Training?', *American Journal of Small Business*, 27–35.

Brock, W. A. and D. S. Evans, 1989, 'Small Business Economics', *Small Business Economics* 1, 7–20.

Brush, C. and R. D. Hisrich, 1999, 'Women-owned Businesses: Why Do They Matter?', in Z. J. Acs (ed.), *Are Small Firms Important? Their Role and Impact*, Dordrecht: Kluwer Academic Publishers, pp. 111–127.

Brush, C. G., 1992, 'Research on Women Business Owners: Past Trends, a New Perspective and Future Directions', *Entrepreneurship Theory and Practice* 17(4), 5–30.

Carland, J. W., J. C. Carland and C. D. Aby, 1989, 'An Assessment of the Psychological Determinants of Planning in Small Businesses', *International Small Business Journal* 7(4), 23–34.

Carree, M. and A. R. Thurik, 1999, 'Industrial Structure and Economic Growth', in D. B. Audretsch and A. R. Thurik (eds.), *Innovation, Industry Evolution and Employment*, Cambridge University Press, pp. 86–110.

Carree, M., A. van Stel, A. Wennekers and A. R. Thurik, 2001, 'Economic Development and Business Ownership: An Analysis Using Data of 23 OECD Countries in the Period 1976–1996', *Small Business Economics*, forthcoming.

Carter, S. and P. Rosa, 1998, 'The Financing of Male- and Female-owned Businesses', *Entrepreneurship & Regional Development* 10, 225–241.

Chittenden, F., G. Hall and P. Hutchinson, 1996, 'Small Firm Growth, Access to Capital Markets and Financial Structure: Review of Issues and an Empirical Investigation', *Small Business Economics* 8, 59–67.

Cressy, R. C., 1996, 'Are Business Startups Debt-Rationed?', *Economic Journal* 106, 1253–1270.

Cromie, S. and S. Birley, 1990, 'Networking by Female Business Owners in Northern Ireland', *Journal of Business Venturing* 7(3), 237–251.

EIM, 1998, Kleinschalig Ondernemen 1998: *Structuur en Ontwikkeling van het Nederlandse MKB*, Zoetermeer.

ENSR, 1996, *The European Observatory for SME's; Fourth Annual Report*, Zoetermeer: EIM.

Evans, D. and B. Jovanovic, 1989, 'An Estimated Model of Entrepreneurial Choice under Liquidity Constraints', *Journal of Political Economy* 97(4), 808–827.

Fay, M. and L. Williams, 1993, 'Gender Bias and the Availability of Business Loans, *Journal of Business Venturing* 8, 363–376.

Fischer, E. M., A. R. Reuber and L. S. Dyke, 1993, 'A Theoretical Overview and Extension of Research on Sex, Gender, and Entrepreneurship', *Journal of Business Venturing* 8, 151–168.

Gavron, R., M. Cowling, G. Holtham and A. Westall, 1998, *The Entrepreneurial Society*, London: Institute for Public Policy Research.

Hansen, E. L. and K. R. Allen, 1992, 'The Creation Corridor: Environmental Load and Pre-Organization Information-Processing Ability', *Entrepreneurship Theory and Practice* 17(1), 57–65.

Hisrich, R. D. and C. G. Brush, 1987, 'Women Entrepreneurs: A Longitudinal Study', in N. C. Churchill, J. A. Hornaday, B. A. Kirchhoff, O. J. Krasner and K. H. Vesper (eds.), 'Frontiers of Entrepreneurship Research', Wellesley, MA: Babson College, pp. 187–199.

Hisrich, R. D. and C. G. Brush, 1984, 'The Woman Entrepreneur: Management Skills and Business Problems', *Journal of Small Business Management* **22**(1), 30–37.

Hisrich, R. D. and C. G. Brush, 1983, 'The Woman Entrepreneur: Implications of Family, Educational and Occupational Experience', in *Frontiers in Entrepreneurship Research*, Wellesley: Babson College, pp. 255–270.

Hofstede, G., 1991, *Cultures and Organizations*, London: Harper Collins Publishers.

Holmes, S. and P. Kent, 1991, 'An Empirical Analysis of the Financial Structure of Small and Large Australian Manufacturing Enterprises', *Journal of Small Business Finance* **1**(2), 141–154.

Honig-Haftel, S. and L. Martin, 1986, 'Is the Female Entrepreneur at a Disadvantage?', *Thrust: The Journal for Employment and Training Professionals* **7**, 49–64.

Hughes, A. and D. J. Storey, 1994, *Finance and the Small Firm*, London and New York: Routledge.

Johnson, S. and D. J. Storey, 1993, 'Male and Female Entrepreneurs and Their Businesses', in S. Allen and C. Truman (eds.), *Women in Business: Perspectives on Women Entrepreneurs*, London & New York: Routledge.

Kalleberg, A. and K. Leicht, 1991, 'Gender and Organizational Performance: Determinants of Small Business Survival and Success', *Academy of Management Journal* **34**, 136–161.

Koper, G., 1993, 'Women Entrepreneurs and the Granting of Business Credit', in Allen, S. and C. Truman (eds.), *Women in Business: Perspectives on Women Entrepreneurs*, London and New York: Routledge.

Kotey, B., 1999, 'Debt Financing and Factors Internal to the Business', *International Small Business Journal* **17**(3), 11–29.

Kotey, B. and G. G. Meredith, 1997, 'Relationships among Owner/Manager Personal Values, Business Strategies and Enterprise Performance', *Journal of Small Business Management* **32**(2), 37–64.

Loscocco, K. A., 1991, 'Gender and Small Business Success: An Inquiry into Women's Relative Disadvantage', *Social Forces* **70**(1), 65–85.

Moore, D. P. and E. H. Buttner, 1997, *Women Entrepreneurs: Moving Beyond the Glass Ceiling*, London and New Delhi: Sage Publications.

Neider, L., 1987, 'A Preliminary Investigation of Female Entrepreneurs in Florida', *Journal of Small Business Management* **25**(3), 22–29.

OECD, 1998, *Women Entrepreneurs in Small and Medium Enterprises*, OECD Conference Paris 1997.

Olm, K., A. Carsrud and L. Alvey, 1988, 'The Role of Networks in New Venture Funding for the Female Entrepreneur: A Continuing Analysis', in B. A. Kirchoff, W. A. Long, W. E. McMullan, K. H. Vesper and W.E. Wetzel (eds), *Frontiers of Entrepreneurship Research*, Wellesley, MA: Babson College.

Riding, A. L. and C. S. Swift, 1990, 'Women Business Owners and Terms of Credit: Some Empirical Findings of the Canadian Experience', *Journal of Business Venturing* **5**, 327–340.

Rosa, P., D. Hamilton, S. Carter and H. Burns, 1994, 'The Impact of Gender on Small Business Management: Preliminary Findings of a British Study', *International Small Business Journal* **12**(3), 25–32.

Scott, C. E., 1986, 'Why More Women are Becoming Entrepreneurs', *Journal of Small Business Management* **24**(4), 37–45.

Sexton, D. L. and N. Bowman-Upton, 1990, 'Female and Male Entrepreneurs: Psychological Characteristics and Their Role in Gender-Related Discrimination', *Journal of Business Venturing* **5**, 29–36.

Stevenson, L. A., 1986, 'Against All Odds: The Entrepreneurship of Women', *Journal of Small Business Management* **24**(4), 30–37.

Stigter, H. W., 1999, *Vrouwelijk Ondernemerschap in Nederland 1994–1997*, Zoetermeer: EIM.

Thurik, A. R., 1999, 'Entrepreneurship, Industrial Transformation and Growth', in G. D. Libecap (ed.), *Advances in the Study of Entrepreneurship, Innovation, and Economic Growth*, JAI Press, pp. 29–65.

Thurik, A. R., 1996, 'Small Firms, Entrepeneurship and Economic Growth', in P. H. Admiraal (ed.), *Small Business in the Modern Economy*, Oxford: Basil Blackwell Publishers, pp. 126–152.

Tigges, L. M. and G. P. Green, 1992, *Small Business Success Among Men and Women-Owned Firms*, Rural Sociological Society Association Paper.

Van der Wijst, N. and A. R. Thurik, 1996, 'Determinants of Small Firm Debt Ratios: An Analysis of Retail Panel Data', in Z. J. Acs (ed.), *Small Firms and Economic Growth, Volume I, The International Library of Critical Writings in Economics*, Cheltenham and Brookfield: Edward Elgar Publishing Company, pp. 639–649.

Van Uxem, F. W. and J. Bais, 1996, *Het starten van een bedrijf: ervaringen van 2000 Starters*, Zoetermeer: EIM.

Watkins, J. M. and D. S. Watkins, 1983, 'The Female Entrepreneur: Her Background and Determinants of Business Choice – Some British Data', in J. A. Hornaday, J. A. Timmons and K. H. Vesper (eds.), *Frontiers of Entrepreneurship Research*, Wellesley, MA: Babson College.

Welsch, H. P. and E. Young, 1982, 'The Information Source of Selection Decisions: The Role of Entrepreneurial Personality Characteristics', *Journal of Small Business Management* **20**(4), 49–57.

Wennekers, S. and A. R. Thurik, 1999, 'Linking Entrepreneurship and Economic Growth, *Small Business Economics* **13**(1), 27–55.

Weston, J. F. and E. F. Brigham, 1981, *Managerial Finance*, 7th ed., Hinsdale: Dryden Press.

[18]

VENTURE CAPITAL, 2003, VOL. 5, NO. 1, 1–28

Women entrepreneurs who break through to equity financing: the influence of human, social and financial capital

NANCY M. CARTER, CANDIDA G. BRUSH,
PATRICIA G. GREENE, ELIZABETH GATEWOOD
and MYRA M. HART

(Final version accepted 2 July 2002)

This is one of the first efforts to systematically study attributes of women business owners and their equity financing strategies. The study explored the factors associated with the use of equity capital in women led firms. Hypotheses examined the influence of human and social capital on the likelihood of seeking equity funding, access to funding sources, bootstrapping techniques and development of financial strategies. Data for this study came from a survey of 235 US women business owners conducted by the National Foundation for Women Business Owners from a sample identified by Dun and Bradstreet. Results showed only graduate education significantly influenced the odds of using outside equity financing. Social capital had no direct effect on increasing likelihood of using equity but influenced the use of bootstrapping techniques. Network diversity was positively related to the use of personal sources of funding, while professional advisor relationships were negatively related to personal sources of financing. Our research suggests women obtaining higher levels of education may increase their likelihood of obtaining funding. Further, during the bootstrap phase, utilizing social capital is an asset.

Keywords: equity capital; financing strategy; woman entrepreneur

Introduction

Over the last decade rapid expansion of the US venture capital industry substantially increased the equity financing available to firms with high

Nancy M. Carter, Richard M. Schulze Endowed Chair in Entrepreneurship, University of St. Thomas, TMH 470, 1000 LaSalle Avenue, Minneapolis, Minnesota 55403-2005, USA; email: nmcarter@stthomas.edu. *Candida G. Brush*, Associate Professor of Strategy and Policy and Research Director, Entrepreneurial Management Institute, Boston University, 595 Commonwealth Ave, Boston, MA 02215, USA; email: cgbrush@bu.edu. *Patricia G. Greene*, Ewing Marion Kauffman/Missouri Chair in Entrepreneurial Leadership, Henry W. Bloch School of Business and Public Administration, University Missouri—Kansas City, 5100 Rockhill Road, Kansas City, MO 64110-2499, USA; email: greenep@umkc.edu. *Elizabeth Gatewood*, Jack M. Gill Chair of Entrepreneurship, The Johnson Centre for Entrepreneurship and Innovation, Kelly School of Business, Indiana University, 501 N. Morton, Suite 108, Bloomington, IN 47404, USA; email: gatewood@indiana.edu. *Myra M. Hart*, Class of 1961 Professor of Management Practice, Harvard Business School, Harvard University, 313 South Hall, Boston, MA 02163, USA; e-mail: mhart@hbs.edu

Venture Capital ISSN 1369-1066 print/ISSN 1464-5343 online © 2003 Taylor & Francis Ltd
http://www.tandf.co.uk/journals
DOI: 10.1080/1369106032000082586

growth potential and large capital needs. Since 1994, the annual funds raised and invested by independent venture capital firms grew every year (Fineberg 1998, Mason and Harrison 1999). The National Venture Capital Association reported that venture capital raised in 2000 alone reached $103 billion, an increase of more than 113% from 1999 (Thompson Financial Securities Data 2000). The number of deals increased from 1166 in 1995 to 5380 in 2000 (Taylor 2001). During the last decade high net worth individuals, known as angels, also invested an additional $20 billion to $30 billion (Sohl 1999). The crash of the dot.coms slowed the raising and investing of venture capital in 2001 but did not stop it. Venture capital investments for 2001 were reported as $37.7 billion, representing 3224 investments at an average investment of $11.7 million per company (www.nvca.org, 20 February 2002).

Funding for high growth firms comes from multiple sources, including private venture capital partnerships, partnerships affiliated with financial corporations and investment banks, corporate venturing programmes, SBIC's, individuals, and direct investments from banks and financial corporations. The role of venture backed companies, as a major engine for economic growth is indisputable (Mason and Harrison 1999). More than 50% of the 544 initial public offerings on the NASDAQ in 1999 were venture backed, up from 20% in 1998 (Thompson Financial Securities Data 1999).

In spite of the increased availability of equity funds, venture capital investment in US women-led businesses was a small percentage of overall investment. In 1998 women led firms had about 4.1% of all venture capital investments, up from about 2.5 % between 1991 and 1996 (Greene *et al.* 1999). VentureOne reported that this number rose to just 5% in 1999. This finding is startling because in 2002 there were 6.2 million majority-owned, privately-held women-owned businesses in the US, employing nearly 9.2 million workers and generating nearly $1.5 trillion in sales, up 40% nation wide from 1997 (Centre for Womens Business Research 2002).[1] Though women acquired greater access to business debt in the past five years and established a strong record of reinvestment of business earnings (Coleman 2000), they have not yet accessed the large pool of equity capital currently available in the US.

In 2000, an initiative led by the National Women's Business Council and the Forum for Women Entrepreneurs sought to stimulate investment in US women-owned businesses by launching six Springboard 2000 venture forums in Silicon Valley, the Mid-Atlantic region, and Boston. From an applicant pool of over 1700, the forums chose 175 women-led businesses to present to the venture capital community. By early 2001 the companies reportedly had raised over half a billion dollars. The early success of the Springboard participants raised the question of why some women succeed in securing equity funding and others had not?

Knowledge, capabilities and an effective network have been shown to be key to equity financing. Greene *et al.* (1997) identified human capital and social capital as critical components of entrepreneurial knowledge and capabilities. Both types of capital are important because they represent initial 'endowments' that provide the basis for acquiring other sorts of resources, like physical capital (i.e. assets and facilities), organizational capital and financial capital (Brush *et al.* 2001). The broad question driving this study is whether higher levels of human and social capital are associated with particular financial strategies women use for securing equity capital? Specifically, the human and social capital framework proposed by Greene *et al.* (1997) is drawn upon to develop hypotheses about whether women who succeed in acquiring equity capital have higher levels of human capital and social capital which they use to leverage loans and bootstrapping, two aspects of financial capital, to acquire equity investments.

Background and hypotheses

Venture capital research has focused primarily on the venture capitalist's investment process, strategy, and the relationship of the equity provider to the venture backed firm. Fewer articles emphasized the entrepreneur or the entrepreneurial firm. Mason and Harrison (1999) characterized this research approach as focusing on the supply side of the equation where the perspective of the venture capitalist, or the venture capital industry, is the central concern. Studies examined the strategies of venture capital firms (Swartz 1991, Gupta and Sapienza 1992), the 'value added' to entrepreneurial firms by venture capitalists (Sapienza 1992), the effects of team processes in the partnership (Watson *et al.* 1995), and venture capitalist's perceptions of serial entrepreneurs (Wright *et al.* 1997). More recent studies employed experimental design techniques and cognitive theory to assess venture capitalist decision-making processes (Zacharakis and Shepherd 2001).

Studies about the influence of angels, or informal investors, have taken a similar tack. Although fewer in number because angels often do not want to be identified, and in the US are not members of a national organization of institutional venture capital firms, these studies have also emphasized the perspective of the investor rather than the entrepreneur. Studies compared angels and non-angels (Freear *et al.* 1994a), examined the effects of angel financing in different sized firms (Mason and Harrison 1995a), and the role of informal equity in the financing process and the economy (Freear *et al.* 1994b, Mason and Harrison 1995b).

Less research has examined the demand side, or the approaches taken by firms seeking venture capital. A noteworthy exception is a study by Sapienza and Korsgaard (1996) that investigated ways entrepreneurs managed information flows that influenced investors. Industry overviews have explicitly pointed out that future research opportunities lay in studying public policy and examining factors that influence variations in the ability of some populations of firms to obtain venture capital (Timmons and Sapienza 1992, Timmons and Bygrave 1997). To date, populations of entrepreneurs including women and minorities, remain understudied (Freear *et al.* 1997). Research about sex of the business owner and financing has focused exclusively on access to debt capital (Buttner and Rosen 1988, Riding and Swift 1990, Coleman 2000). A recent literature review (Gatewood *et al.* 2002) found no single academic study that examined the factors that affect women entrepreneurs' access to, or utilization of, outside equity funding. This suggests that what we know about the seeking, utilization and strategies of obtaining equity capital is based on the experiences of men. There is presently no knowledge of the factors related to successfully seeking and obtaining equity capital by women entrepreneurs. A better understanding of how women business owners finance their businesses would expand knowledge of the equity capital process. The lack of research samples including or focusing on women business owners required the study to draw on contiguous bodies of literature for hypothesizing the influences of human, social and financial capital. Figure 1 displays the conceptual model that guided the hypotheses.

Human capital

Industry pundits and researchers point to human capital as the single most important factor for venture capital investment. Human capital consists of achieved attributes that lead to increased levels of productivity (Becker 1964). It not only derives from investments in formal education, occupational experiences and training (Carter *et al.* 1997), but also extends to judgement, insight, creativity, vision and intelligence (Dollinger 1994). The more specific human capital is to the nature of the entrepreneurial venture, the greater the likelihood of the businesses' success (Cooper *et al.* 1994, Pennings *et al.* 1998).

Muzyka *et al.* (1996) and Smart (1999) showed a direct relationship between venture investment and the strength of the management team,

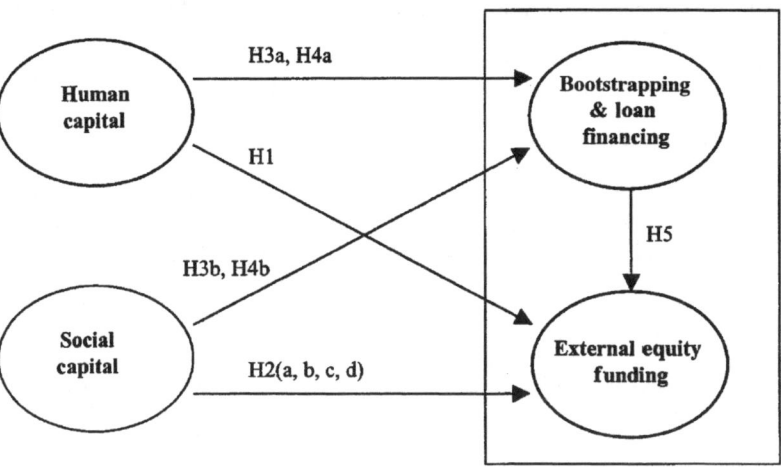

Figure 1.   Accessing financial equity

in terms of capabilities and industry experience. Some comparisons have shown that women and men entrepreneurs had similar levels of education (Birley *et al.* 1987), but that the content of their education differed. Hisrich and O'Brien (1982), Hisrich and Neider (1987), Brush and Hisrich (1991) and Brush (1992) described women entrepreneurs as college educated and/or having more education than their wage and salary counterparts. Historically, women were more likely to have a liberal arts education instead of training in business, sciences or engineering (Hisrich and Brush 1983, Honig-Haftel and Martin 1986, Brush 1992, Carter and Allen 1997)—the background preferred by outside investors. But graduate education, regardless of content, may inspire confidence in investors, especially if augmented by specific business training or work experience.

Besides education and training, human capital derives from work experience. For entrepreneurs three dimensions of work experience are especially important: industry, management, and start-up. Research has shown a robust positive relationship between prior work experience in the same industry or line of business and venture survival/success (Cooper *et al.* 1988, Bruderl *et al.* 1992, Cooper *et al.* 1994, Carter *et al.* 1997). Women business owners appeared to have less industry experience than their male counterparts, and investors may undervalue what they do have (Brophy 1992). Carter *et al.* (1997) provided empirical evidence showing that women business owners had fewer years of industry experience than their male counterparts, and other research showed women tended to be segregated within retail, service, finance and real estate sectors (Women in Business 1998). They were less visible in other areas, such as manufacturing and high technology, where they could acquire the industry expertise sought by prospective funders.

Women were less likely to gain human capital through experience in executive or technical management (Watkins and Watkins 1984, Stevenson 1986). Catalyst[2] reported in 1998 that 11.1% of the total board seats in Fortune 500 companies were held by a woman, while only 3.8% of the highest ranking positions in these companies (e.g. Chairman, Vice-Chair, CEO, President, COO, SEVP and EVP) were held by a woman. Of these, women held mostly staff positions, while men held line positions (responsible for profit-and-loss). Similarly, women lacked relevant human capital gained in starting new ventures (Cromie and Birley 1991, Carter *et al.* 1997). A study of Canadian small firms showed only 30% of women and 57% of men previously owned businesses (Cliff 1998).

To the extent that investors rate 'management' in capital-seeking companies more favourably if they have experience in founding a venture, and a strong track record in marketing, management, and leadership decision-making (Fried and Hisrich 1988, Wright *et al.* 1997), women with these experiences should have a higher probability of funding success than women without these experiences. Women having strategic decision-making experience, a business or technical degree, or previous experience in founding new ventures, therefore, should be more likely to meet the management standards of venture capitalists and secure equity funding for their businesses:

H1:   Women entrepreneurs with higher levels of human capital are more likely to secure outside equity funding than women with lower levels of human capital.

Social capital

The success of the entrepreneur in raising equity capital may also depend on who she knows, or her amount of social capital. Social capital is a form of non-economic knowledge separate from the foundation of human capital. Distinct from formal learning or instruction, it nevertheless directly impacts the economic behaviours of individuals (Kelly 1994). Social capital emerges from the norms, networks, and relationships of the social structure in which an individual lives, potentially producing useful resources for business through the development of sets of obligations and expectations, information channels, and social norms that reinforce certain types of behaviours (Coleman 1988). A critical source of social capital is an individual's social network. Networks provide a conduit for the exchange of information and resources that can enhance the success and survival of an entrepreneur's business. Social networks allow entrepreneurs to gain access to opportunities and resources, save time, and tap into advice and moral support that may otherwise be unavailable. Social networks also are important for venture capital firms. Bygrave (1992) described the venture capital industry as a closed network, geographically concentrated, and tightly interconnected. It is widely recognized that the core of a venture capital firm's livelihood is deal flow, which the principals learn about through their network of informal contacts (Bygrave 1992, Alimansky 2000). The success of VC firms depends on who, as well as what, the principals know.

The overlap of the entrepreneur's network structure with the venture capitalists' may be an important factor in determining the likelihood that the entrepreneur will be able to find private equity funding (Tybee and Bruno 1984, Bygrave 1988, Fiet 1991, Sargent and Young 1991, Freear *et al.* 1992, Fiet, 1996). Most venture capitalists invest in deals brought to them or referred by people they know. Few deals originate from plans received 'over the transom'. Therefore entrepreneurs seeking venture capital increase their odds of receiving it when they know the venture capitalists or those who shepherd deals to them. (See *Inside the Silicon Valley Money Machine*, by Melanie Warner, Fortune, 1998, for a look at how extensive the overlap can be between investors and investees.) The greater the overlap of networks between the venture capitalists and the entrepreneur, therefore, the higher the probability that the entrepreneur can tap into the private equity markets to gain access to financial resources and also to gain access to critical knowledge and expertise. Aldrich (1989, p. 112) argued that, 'venture capitalists are probably as important for their broker role as for the funds they provide to struggling entrepreneurs. They bring together technical experts, management consultants, and financial planners, who supplement an entrepreneur's limited knowledge and experience.'

The question is whether some women business owners have better access to the investor network than other women business owners. Research suggests women might be underrepresented in the venture capital social networks. Social network theory posits that people tend to interact with people like themselves. This preference, or 'homophilous' propensity, leads to segregated networks (Brass 1985). Studies showed that the networks of women entrepreneurs conformed to this propensity and are predominately female (Aldrich 1989, Aldrich *et al.* 1989, Brush and Hisrich 1991). Conversely, networks in the investment industry are predominately male. A review of Pratt's *Guide to Venture Capital Sources* (2000) indicated that only 529 of the more than 6086 venture capitalists were women (Hart *et al.* 2002). With these odds, the likelihood that the network of a female entrepreneur will contain female equity investors is remote. To make the critical connections in the investment community, women entrepreneurs may need to rely on alternative networking strategies.

Network diversity

One compensating strategy women entrepreneurs can adopt is to have a wide range of contacts in their social networks. Research showed that when networks contain people from a variety of work backgrounds, especially those beyond the immediate work group, they tended to be more powerful (Blau and Alba 1982, Brass 1984). The work and social background diversity in the network provides a higher probability that the entrepreneur will receive non-redundant information. Aldrich (1989, p. 111) argued that, 'information about new business locations, potential markets for goods and services, sources of capital or potential investors, and innovations is likely to be spread widely among individuals'. Other things being equal, someone with a small set of overlapping ties is at a disadvantage when competing for information with someone with a large set of diverse ties. Contacts with individuals with a variety of backgrounds, including varying socio-demographic and intra-personal characteristics, enhance the richness of the information exchanged, attitudes formed, and interactions that individuals experience (McPherson *et al.* 2001). In other words, having a diverse or large set of ties in their network may help women entrepreneurs connect to different parts of a social system and open information channels inaccessible to those women with a small set of immediate network ties. By extension, one can argue that women entrepreneurs with wide ranging, diverse networks are more likely to have contacts that will connect them to equity capital markets than women without diverse networks. Women business owners who expand the diversity of their networks gain social capital and enhance their probability of accessing equity financing:

H2a: Women entrepreneurs with more diverse social networks are more likely to secure outside equity financing than women with less diverse social networks.

Network tie strength

Network diversity enhances the chances of accessing a wide array of resources. But the likelihood that the contacts will deliver value or resources depends on the strength of the tie, or the nature of the relationships between the network members. Individuals draw both instrumental resources like materials or physical resources, as well as expressive resources such as friendship, from their network contacts (Ibarra 1993, Brush *et al.* 2001). Women are thought to prefer strong ties that are expressive and characterized by emotional intensity, mutual confiding and intimacy. They more often turn to family and friends than to casual acquaintances like work associates. The apparent disadvantage of strong ties is that they offer a restricted range of knowledge and experiences beyond that already known by the entrepreneur and those close to her. Weak ties, conversely, act as 'bridges' connecting to non-overlapping resources (Granovetter 1973). Burt (1992) found that among male and female managers, women needed strong strategic sponsors who could convey cues signalling women's legitimacy as key players among their weak ties.

Some network relationships involve the exchange of multiple resources, providing instrumental value, like career advice, as well as friendship. Mentors are one example. The strong relationship that develops between a mentor and a protégé increases the likelihood that the protégé will be connected to and benefit from the mentor's own network contacts (Ibarra 1993). Aldrich (1989) suggested that for women, such multiplex strong ties could substantially increase the general reachability within their networks.

Extrapolating from these findings one can argue that women entrepreneurs with multiplex strong ties in their networks, especially in the form of mentors, would be more successful seeking equity investments than women without these ties. Although a woman business owner's first inclination may be to turn to family and friends since they provide emotional support, these relationships are unlikely to yield contacts that would connect them to the equity markets. Weak ties like attorneys, accountants, bankers and technical consultants are more likely to represent bridges into the investment community. But weak ties may not be willing to signal to the market that the woman entrepreneur is a legitimate player, and her business a worthy investment. Weak tie sponsors may have little motivation to expend their own reputation capital to advance the interests of the women entrepreneur. However, mentors can impart legitimacy, provide morale support and friendship, and chauffeur women to capital markets. Mentors who have entrepreneurial experience are particularly beneficial to entrepreneurs. Aldrich and Reese (1997) found that advice from other entrepreneurs in their line of work paid the highest dividends for business owners:

H2b: Women entrepreneurs with greater reliance on friends and family (strong ties) are less likely to secure outside equity funding than women with lower reliance.

H2c: Women entrepreneurs with greater reliance on professional business advisors (weak ties) are more likely to secure outside equity funding than women with lower reliance.

H2d: Women entrepreneurs with greater reliance on mentors or other business owners (multiplex strong ties) are more likely to secure outside equity funding than women with lower reliance.

Financing strategy

Obtaining the necessary financing to start and grow a business is generally considered one of the entrepreneur's major problems. While the emphasis in this study is on securing equity capital, it is rarely the only source of capital used by entrepreneurs. Capital comes from many sources, including personal savings, banks, government programs, venture capital funds, and business angels. Drawing on each of these sources has different ramifications for the business and the business owner. The choice of an appropriate capitalization structure and decisions about the sequencing of capital sources are widely acknowledged as important to venture success. Scheer *et al.* (1993) suggested that new ventures should follow Myer's Pecking Order where firm's finance their businesses in hierarchical fashion. Florin and Schulze (2000) extended this logic and argued that the most common financing strategy for IPO firms begins with the founding team's reliance on personal savings, bank loans, and/or government programmes. As the businesses in their sample grew, they used bootstrapping techniques to build the business while they gained the additional experience and legitimacy desired by external stakeholders. Bootstrapping involves the use of personal and internally generated funds for business investment, the control of costs and the delay of capital expenditure until such funds are available. Often it involves a high reliance on internally generated retained earnings, leasing of equipment, customer advances, second mortgages and even use of credit cards to finance the operation. Cash flow or retained earnings subsequently fuels the business as owners position the venture for success in the private equity markets. The question is what role human and social capital play in accessing the funding sources that seemingly position the firm for acquiring equity capital.

Debt financing

According to the 'Pecking Order Hypotheses', debt will be included among the first sources of funding entrepreneur's seek in financing their business. This may be from 'quasi' external sources like credit cards, or from more formal sources like banks or other larger institutional providers. There is conflicting evidence on women's experiences in accessing debt financing. Some empirical studies have shown that women entrepreneurs have less access to debt financing from institutions, suffer from weaker collateral positions, and believe that they have been discriminated against or received unequal treatment by financing institutions (Goffee and Scase 1983, Hisrich and Brush 1984, Olm *et al.*1988). There are other studies however, that show little evidence of obvious discrimination against women (Buttner and Rosen 1988, 1989). Particularly when samples of men and women have been matched on key variables like business age, firm size, and growth rate, few differences in access to debt are identified (Riding and Swift 1990). Authors of the latter study noted that collateral requirements for women were higher and that women were less satisfied with their banking experiences. These results were supported in a recent study by Coleman (2000), who found no difference in women's ability to obtain loans, but found women were required to provide higher levels of collateral and pay higher interest rates. Brush (1992) found that while there seem to be some differences regarding the likelihood of obtaining bank funds for growth, this difference lessened as a woman business owner's venture matured and she developed a business track record. Similarly, Carter and Allen (1997) found that availability of capital through private and personal banking sources related to size of women-owned businesses.

It seems plausible that the discrepancies in the studies may relate to differences in the level of the entrepreneurs' human and social capital. Indeed, Gundry and Welsch (2001) found human capital factors such as intention, greater scanning of the environment and more disciplined approach to management distinguished high growth from low growth women led ventures. As women acquired critical work experience, their difficulties in accessing debt financing for their businesses appeared to abate. Furthermore, ventures are seldom funded by a single source, hence experience in obtaining debt or other types of financing would provide a stronger foundation for securing equity capital. Similarly it is expected that the more extensive and diverse the business owners' social networks, the higher their odds of being introduced to the favourable banking relationships necessary for loan approval:

H3a: Women entrepreneurs with higher human capital are more likely to use outside debt as part of their financing strategy than women with lower human capital.

H3b: Woman entrepreneurs with higher social capital are more likely to use outside debt as part of their financing strategy than women with lower social capital.

Bootstrap financing

In addition to debt financing, bootstrapping appears to be a critical component to venture financing success. Like Florin and Schulze (2000), Van Osnabrugge and Robinson (2000) saw bootstrapping as an effective strategy for financing a new enterprise's growth that build on personal equity and debt. If successful in using bootstrapping, the enterprise purportedly is better positioned to receive private equity investments in later stages of development. Freear *et al.* (1991) identified bootstrapping as the most likely source of initial equity for 94% of new technology-based firms, and Bhide (1992) found it the preferred source by more than 80% of the 500 fastest-growing privately held firms in the US.

Bootstrapping can free the venture from excessive debt loads that may constrain the company in its early years and hamper its growth. Bootstrapping may be an effective means of preparing a venture for getting outside investments at a later time. These arguments indicate that some funding sources provide the basis for acquiring other sources. Personal investment may precede bootstrapping, which in turn creates the opportunity to acquire outside equity investments at a later date.

Effective bootstrapping depends on both the human capital and social capital of the management team. Whether it involves managing internal cash flow, sharing premises with others, bartering underused services, or forming partnerships and business alliances, managerial skills and social networks are foundational to effective bootstrapping techniques.

The extent to which women effectively use bootstrapping to position their business for outside funding is unclear. No studies were found that examined women business owners' experience in using bootstrapping to effectively grow their companies. Intuitively though, it would appear that women business owners who have industry, management and start-up work experience, together with diverse social networks, are better equipped to effectively use bootstrapping to position their businesses as attractive investment opportunities for outside investors than women business owners without these experiences and networks. Such human and social capital can provide women knowledge of bootstrapping strategies, capabilities, access to leasing opportunities, access to credit from vendors, or business alliances needed to generate revenue and reduce costs—all bootstrapping techniques that can minimize business risk and demonstrate the hustle that outside equity investors reward:

H4a: Women entrepreneurs with higher human capital are more likely to use bootstrapping techniques to finance their businesses than women with lower human capital.

H4b: Women entrepreneurs with higher social capital are more likely to use bootstrapping techniques to finance their businesses than women with lower social capital.

Despite our arguments about the role of human and social capital in debt and bootstrap financing there is little empirical evidence to document the process or sequencing for developing an appropriate financing strategy for entrepreneurs aspiring to use private equity to fuel their business' growth. Van Osnabrugge and Robinson (2000) supported the contention by Florin and Schulze (2000) that sequencing of funding sources is critical in determining subsequent investment by equity investors. Based on their argument it is suggested that a careful and well-disciplined financing strategy during the start-up could increase the chances of the firm's later success and increase the venture's access to outside investors. It can be argued that women who use debt and bootstrapping will be more likely to be successful in securing equity financing than women who do not use these financing techniques. The use of debt and bootstrap financing position the business for subsequent equity investment:

H5:   Woman entrepreneurs that use debt and bootstrapping techniques to finance their early stage businesses are more likely to secure outside equity funding than women who don't use these financing techniques.

Methodology

Sample

A survey method was used to administer a questionnaire with 'closed' responses to women business owners via a telephone interview. Potential respondents for this study came from a survey of US women business owners conducted by the National Foundation for Women Business Owners (NFWBO) in 2000. Since women who seek and/or acquire equity capital appear to be few, a sampling procedure was adopted to maximize the probability of finding representatives of this elusive population. Respondents were women who owned firms identified by Dun and Bradstreet and who met one or more of the following criteria: business operated within an industry associated with venture capital; located in one of the top states for venture capital activity (CA, MA, PA, TX, DC); or showed 15% or more revenue growth over each of the past three years. Some respondents also self-identified as having sought or received equity capital in response to a notice on the NFWBO web site. Total Dun and Bradstreet listings that met the criteria were 4878 women-owned businesses. Of the total, 2145 were eliminated from the sample for the following reasons: 183 listed contact persons who were not owners or co-owners; 494 listed wrong telephone number or disconnects; 595 phone listings were fax machines; 24 were deaf or presented other language barriers for the interviewer; 78 of the listings were duplicate phone numbers; 338 of the businesses owners were reported as not being available during the study dates; and 433 of the numbers were never contacted because of cost constraints in the study. Of the 2733 qualified listings, 1686 refused to be interviewed; 65 terminated the interview prematurely; 747 had multiple busy signals or the interviewer reached an answering machine; 235 interviews were completed. All data were collected by telephone interview.

Characteristics of the sample are shown in table 1. Almost 40% of the women were between 45 and 54 years of age, and few were non-white; approximately two-thirds (64%) of the businesses operated in the service sector. The majority of the businesses reported annual revenues of less than $250 000 (62%), and less than 18% reported sales totalling $1 million or higher. Nearly 45% indicated they had 10 or fewer full-time employees and 41% reported less than $50 000 capital available in their businesses.

Measures

In the phone survey, interviewers first asked respondents general questions about important issues they currently faced in their businesses, followed by

Table 1. Means, standard deviations, and percentage distribution of sample characteristics

	Total sample
Number of firms	235
Founder's age	
Under 35	10%
35–44	31%
45–54	39%
55–64	14%
65+	6%
Founder's ethnicity	
White	92%
Black	3%
Hispanic	3%
Asian/Pacific Islander	2%
Industry sector	
Biomedical	3%
Information Technology/Internet	9%
Manufacturing	12%
Telecommunications	10%
Service/Education	66%
Sales revenue	
Under $50 000	29%
$50 000–$99 999	16%
$100 000–$249 999	17%
$250 000–$499 999	13%
$500 000–$999 999	7%
$1–$3.9 million	14%
$4–$5.9 million	–
$7–$9.9 million	2%
$10 million +	2%
Capitalization	
Under $50 000	41%
$50 000–$99 999	15%
$100 000–$499 999	25%
$500 000–$999 999	7%
$1 to $4.9 million	10%
$5 million or more	2%
Employees	
Full-time employees	
0	35%
1–10	45%
11–25	9%
more than 25	11%

questions about their intended business growth strategies and about advisors they consulted regularly. Interviewers then described two basic kinds of financing available to businesses—debt and equity. Respondents were asked whether they had ever obtained an equity investment in their business either from individuals or institutions such as an SBIC or a venture capital firm.

Equity funding

The dependent variable (whether the business received equity funding) was a dummy variable coded one (1) for yes and zero (0) for no. Forty respondents (17%) reported receiving equity investments.

Human capital

Four measures of human capital were considered; two reflecting education and two experience: (1) educational attainment; (2) financial acumen; (3) prior experience in starting new ventures; and (4) prior senior managerial or executive experience.

Educational attainment. Educational attainment was measured from a question about whether the respondent had any graduate school training or advanced degree(s) (1=yes, 0=no)

Financial acumen. One aspect of financial knowledge was assessed by asking respondents how much formal education and training in finance they possessed on a four-point scale ranging from none (0) to extensive (4).

Start-up experience. Prior business start-up experience was measured from a question asking how many other businesses the respondent had started or owned prior to this business. It was reasoned that it was more relevant to know whether or not they had start-up or ownership experience rather than the total number of experiences. There is likely only incremental knowledge gained from multiple experiences. The use of both measures would result in multicollinearity. The variable was coded one (1) if the respondent had started or owned a prior business and zero (0) if she had not had prior start-up or ownership experience.

Managerial experience. Prior managerial experience was assessed by noting whether an owner had held a senior management or executive level position prior to becoming a business owner. Respondents indicated which of 10 occupational categories best described the position they held before becoming a business owner. Responses to the occupational category 'senior manager or executive' were dummy coded with one (1) representing top-level managerial experience and (0) if no top-level experience.

Social capital

Two aspects of social capital were considered: network diversity and the strength of the relationships between the entrepreneur and others they relied on for advice.

Network diversity. One dimension of network diversity was assessed using the number of different kinds of contacts the business owner consulted regularly on general business issues. During the interview respondents were asked about nine different types of outside advisors. Diversity was measured by counting the number of different kinds of advisors they indicated consulting regularly.

Network tie strength. Network tie strength was considered to be a measure of the relationship between the business owner and those she relied on for general business advice. Strength was measured by classifying different types of outside advisors into three categories: weak, multiplex, and strong ties. Professional business experts like attorneys, accountants, financial consultants, general business consultants, or bankers were considered as strangers or weak ties. Two categories of weak ties were further delineated: (1) foundational service providers and (2) professional advisors. Bankers, attorneys or accountants were considered foundational providers. Whether or not owners relied on these providers was dummy coded (1=yes, 0=no). Reliance on professional business advisors—on financial consultants or general business consultants—also was dummy code (1=yes, 0=no).

The rationale for segmenting the two forms of weak ties was that the business owner has a different relationship with the two set of advisors. Foundational service providers are a necessary part of doing business. Professional advisors, on the other hand, typically require the entrepreneur to expend additional resources for their counsel.

Fellow business owners or informal mentors were classified as multiplex ties (1=yes, 0=no), and friends and family were considered strong ties (1=yes, 0=no).

Financing strategy

It is believed that the financing strategy business owners adopt can help them secure equity capital for growing their business. Two aspects of financing strategy can be focused on, the use of loans and bootstrapping techniques. During the phone interview, respondents were asked to indicate which of 14 types of financing they used to meet capital needs. Four of the 14 had to do with equity investments from external sources. These items were used to corroborate the dependent variable. The remaining ten items were used to assess the influence of loans and other bootstrapping techniques on the dependent variable, odds of securing external equity investments:

- *Loans.* Three of the 10 items asked about different types of loans owners use to finance their businesses: (1) loan guarantees from the US Small Business Administration or other sources; (2) personal bank loans; or (3) business/commercial bank loans. A dummy variable was created indicating whether the respondent reported using any of the three (1=yes; 0=no).
- *Bootstrapping.* Following the lead of Van Osnabrugge and Robinson (2000), the remaining seven items were classified into four categories of bootstrapping activities. The categories represented options owners could use for developing their businesses, as well as for minimizing or meeting the need for capital.

- *Retained earnings.* One item assessed whether respondents used business earnings to finance the business (1=yes, 0=no). Using retained earnings may delay the need for external investments and preserve owners' control over the business as long as possible.
- *Personal sources.* One item assessed whether respondents contributed personal financial resources to financing their business or received money from families or friends (1=yes, 0=no). By investing their own or family and friends' money, entrepreneurs may stave off outside investors and have greater control while proving the business concept, establishing relationships with customers and suppliers, and getting the products or services ready for roll out.
- *Leasing.* To lessen the need for capital, entrepreneurs may choose to minimize expenses within the venture. One option is to lease equipment instead of buying. Responses to the question of whether the owners leased equipment were dummy coded (1-yes; 0=no).
- *Credit.* In addition to minimizing the need for capital, bootstrapping can also be used to meet the need for capital. Four items dealt with how owners used credit or factoring of accounts receivables to raise capital quickly or to meet short-term material costs. A dummy variable (1=yes, 0=no) was created for assessing whether the owners used business credit cards, personal credit cards, vendor credit, or selling/pledging accounts receivables.

Analyses

A series of equations was used to test the hypotheses. First each bootstrapping technique on measures of human and social capital was regressed to test the hypotheses that women with higher levels of these resources have an increased probability of using each of the bootstrapping options than women with lower levels of these resources, and that the resources increased the probability of their securing equity investments. To test the hypotheses that use of bootstrap financing will increase the odds of securing equity investment, equity funding on bootstrapping was regressed after controlling for the effects of social and human capital. Because the dependent variables are dichotomous, logistic regression analyses were used, controlled for industry and firm size. It was reasoned that there are investment possibilities in all industries but some may offer more opportunities than others. Similarly, larger businesses may be more attractive investment propositions for equity investors. Although the sampling procedure sought to increase the number of women's businesses attractive to equity investors by selecting those with aggressive growth rates, firm size still varied substantially. As such, the two variables as covariates in each of the models were included.

Results

Table 1 presents descriptive statistics associated with the sample. The largest percentage of women in the sample was between ages 35 and 54

(39%) and had businesses in the service/education sectors of the economy (66%). Only 3% of respondents reported having businesses in the biomedical sector, and less than 10% in information technology or internet related sectors. Despite the over sampling technique used to identify high growth potential businesses, the firms were relatively small in size with 45% having between one and 10 full-time employees, and 40% being capitalized at less than $50 000.

Table 2 presents descriptive statistics for the explanatory and dependent variables and a correlation matrix. A third of the women reported having a graduate degree, and 28% reported senior managerial experience. Almost 50% said they had prior start-up or ownership experience. Fifty-eight percent (58%) reported relying on foundational advisors like bankers, attorneys, and accountants. Twenty-nine percent (29%) relied on a business mentor, some of who were business owners. Less than 20% consulted professional counsellors like management or financial advisors regularly, and only about 15% said they consulted family and friends regularly.

Three-fourths of the women said they relied on retained earnings to meet their business capital needs, approximately two-thirds (65%) reported relying on credit, and 46% used loans. The percentage relying on credit in this study was remarkably similar to the percentage (61%) reported by the Federal Reserve Board (*Federal Reserve Bulletin* 1996). Approximately 40% said they contributed personal resources or those from family or friends, and just over a third (35%) indicated using leasing to meet the capital needs of the business. The data indicated that only 17% of the owners interviewed (n=40) had secured outside equity to finance their business.

Logistic regression analyses results

Table 3 displays the results of the seven models used to test the hypotheses. The results provide mixed support for the hypotheses that human capital influences the financial strategies for women owned firms, specifically equity, debt, or bootstrapping techniques (H1; H3a; H4a). After controlling for firm size (number of full time employees) and industry sector, only prior start-up/ownership experience and graduate education significantly influenced women entrepreneurs' financing strategies. Prior start-up/ ownership experience had an effect on the odds of using bootstrapping, but in the opposite direction expected. Woman entrepreneurs without start-up/ownership experience were more likely to use credit ($b=-0.772$, $p<0.05$) and retained earnings ($b=-0.671$, $p<0.05$) to finance their businesses than women with these experiences. This suggests that women with start-up experience move away from the typical reliance on credit cards and the slow growth achieved through using retained earnings to satisfy their firms' capital needs. Women entrepreneurs with at least some graduate education were more likely to use equity funding ($b=1.121$, $p<0.01$) than women without. Prior studies had found business, science and engineering education as most relevant for an entrepreneur's success (Roberts 1991). Our findings show that after controlling for firm size and

Table 2. Descriptive statistics and correlation matrix

	Mean	SD	1	2	3	4	5	6	7	8	9	10	11	12	13	14	15	16
Full time employees (log)	−0.47	3.28																
Human capital																		
1 Finance knowledge	2.51	1.02	0.16†															
2 Startup/ownership experience	0.47	0.50	0.14†	0.08														
3 Senior managerial experience	0.28	0.45	0.28§	0.15†	0.17‡													
4 Graduate education	0.33	0.47	0.16‡	0.03	0.02	0.07												
Social capital																		
5 Network diversity	1.62	1.41	0.22§	0.11	0.12	0.12	0.16†											
Network tie strength																		
6 Weak ties-foundational advisors	0.58	0.49	0.26§	0.05	0.02	0.01	−0.04	0.53§										
7 Weak ties-professional advisors	0.18	0.38	0.08	0.03	0.19‡	0.14†	0.21§	0.48§	0.00									
8 Multiplex strong ties-mentors	0.29	0.45	−0.03	0.03	0.01	0.08	0.13†	0.54§	0.01	0.15†								
9 Strong ties—family	0.16	0.37	0.15†	0.04	−0.02	−0.17‡	−0.04	0.32§	−0.07	0.01	0.10							
Bootstrap financing																		
10 Loans	0.46	0.50	0.31§	0.08	0.14†	0.08	−0.02	0.08	0.10	0.01	0.02	−0.08						
11 Credit	0.65	0.48	0.13	0.03	−0.09	0.12	0.04	0.13	0.05	0.03	0.01	0.06	0.15†					
12 Retained earnings	0.75	0.43	−0.06	−0.03	−0.15†	0.01	−0.03	−0.04	0.03	−0.04	0.00	0.01	−0.22§	−0.01				
13 Personal sources	0.41	0.49	−0.12	−0.05	0.08	0.00	0.12	0.10	−0.09	0.01	0.06	0.06	−0.03	0.03	−0.16†			
14 Leasing	0.35	0.48	0.47§	0.14†	0.11	0.22§	0.06	0.12	0.15†	0.04	−0.09	−0.10	0.28§	0.03	−0.13†	0.01		
Equity financing	0.17	0.38	0.31§	0.13†	0.15†	0.25§	0.26§	0.22§	0.06	0.18§	0.16†	−0.05	0.02	0.05	−0.10	0.20†	0.26§	

†p < 0.05.
‡p < 0.01.
§p < 0.001.

Table 3. Results of logistic regression analyses

	Loan	Credit	Bootstrap financing				Equity financing	
			Retained earnings	Personal sources	Leasing			
Intercept	−0.444	0.823	1.327	0.568	−1.157†	−4.423§	−5.223§
	(0.515)	(0.517)	(0.5622)	(0.506)	(0.588)	(0.886)	(1.195)
Number of employees	0.203§	0.072	0.001	−0.131‡	0.304§	0.255§	0.279‡
	(0.054)	(0.053)	(0.057)	(0.052)	(0.065)	(0.091)	(0.103)
Industry sector							
Biomedical	−1.703	6.338	−0.478	−0.184	0.841	1.566	1.177
	(1.191)	(14.584)	(0.958)	(0.956)	(1.020)	(1.135)	(1.194)
Information-technology/Internet	−1.4382†	−0.984	0.439	1.013	−0.409	1.796‡	1.569†
	(0.658)	(0.562)	(0.702)	(0.579)	(0.670)	(0.681)	(0.737)
Manufacturing	−0.802	−0.534	0.018	0.306	0.306	1.689§	1.523†
	(0.484)	(0.462)	(0.503)	(0.465)	(0.517)	(0.594)	(0.647)
Telecommunications	−0.530	−0.443	6.312	0.701	−1.273	−0.111	0.117
	(1.042)	(0.960)	(16.213)	(1.015)	(1.268)	(1.359)	(1.465)
Human capital							
Finance knowledge	0.114	−0.032	−0.059	−0.172	0.133	0.339	0.381
	(0.156)	(0.156)	(0.167)	(0.153)	(0.172)	(0.228)	(0.247)
Startup/ownership experience	0.467	−0.772†	−0.671†	0.565	0.161	0.454	0.296
	(0.315)	(0.322)	(0.340)	(0.318)	(0.349)	(0.474)	(0.505)
Senior management experience	0.284	0.593	0.105	0.055	0.536	0.638	0.576
	(0.375)	(0.394)	(0.401)	(0.368)	(0.397)	(0.478)	(0.519)
Graduate education	−0.119	−0.094	−0.186	0.650	0.046	1.121‡	0.937†
	(0.348)	(0.353)	(0.372)	(0.340)	(0.379)	(0.454)	(0.478)
Social capital							
Network diversity	−0.064	0.352	−0.390	0.539†	0.410	0.339	0.028
	(0.262)	(0.291)	(0.277)	(0.266)	(0.286)	(0.340)	(0.364)

Continued

Table 3. Continued

	Bootstrap financing					Equity financing	
	Loan	Credit	Retained earnings	Personal sources	Leasing		
Network tie strength							
Weak ties—foundational advisors	0.164 (0.515)	-0.289 (0.523)	0.798 (0.555)	-1.032† (0.511)	-0.407 (0.577)	-0.427 (0.725)	0.113 (0.757)
Weak ties—professional counselors	-0.053 (0.589)	0.025 (0.626)	0.577 (0.638)	-1.366† (0.614)	-0.690 (0.648)	-0.406 (0.817)	0.431 (0.877)
Multiplex strong ties—mentors	0.262 (0.493)	-0.319 (0.504)	0.702 (0.539)	0.012 (0.475)	-1.188† (0.564)	0.243 (0.643)	0.574 (0.699)
Strong ties—family	-0.428 (0.557)	-0.026 (0.561)	0.676 (0.604)	-0.432 (0.532)	-0.400 (0.629)	-0.109 (0.778)	0.129 (0.839)
Bootstrap financing							
Loans							-0.653 (0.523)
Credit							0.322 (0.540)
Retained earnings							-0.061 (0.550)
Personal sources							1.098† (0.518)
Leasing							0.966 (0.546)
-2 Log likelihood	254.576	250.280	228.596	260.942	218.992	142.676	133.150
Goodness of fit	215.198	203.973	205.463	217.377	210.489	226.494	186.768
Cox and snell—R^2	0.162	0.107	0.055	0.124	0.242	0.245	0.279
Model chi-square	37.429§	23.99†	12.006	28.104‡	58.830§	59.720§	69.246§

Referent category=services/education; †$p<0.05$; ‡$p<0.01$; §$p<0.001$.

industry sector, any graduate education was associated with using equity investments as part of the financial strategy for the firm. This suggests that graduate education, regardless of the content basis, may be more valuable for women seeking equity funding than previously suspected.

The results also provided mixed support for the hypotheses that women with higher levels of social capital use loans, bootstrap financing and equity funding (H2a, b, c, d; H4b). Only the use of personal sources and leasing were impacted by social capital, and mostly in unexpected directions. As expected, the more diverse a woman's social network, the higher the odds she used personal sources as a bootstrapping technique to meet the capital needs of her business ($b=0.539$, $p<0.05$). But, the higher the likelihood that women relied on foundational advisors ($b=-1.032$, $p<0.05$) and professional counsellors ($b=-1.366$, $p<0.05$), the lower the odds that they used personal sources as part of their financial strategies. Similarly, the effect of mentors on leasing was unexpected. As the likelihood that a women entrepreneur consulted with a mentor regularly, their odds of using leasing to bootstrap finance their business decreased ($b=-1188$, $p<0.05$). Networking had no significant main effect on securing equity financing or loans. This finding is very surprising given the robust nature of the assumption that equity deals are generated through relationships.

The last column in table 3 displays the results of estimating a model assessing the effects bootstrapping financing had on the odds of securing external equity funding after controlling for firm size, industry sector, human capital, and social capital (H5). Although the model chi-square (69.246, $p<0.001$) indicated that the data fit the model, there was limited support for the hypothesis. Only the use of personal financial resources was associated with using outside equity financing after the covariates are controlled ($b=1.098$, $p<.05$). The significance of the model is more attributable to firm size and industry sector.

Conclusions and implications

Resource decisions are the most important decisions entrepreneurs make, for example, where to obtain resources, which to acquire, and how they will be used (Hart 1995). The research questions in this paper addressed which factors affect the financial strategies of women led firms. Of specific interest were the factors associated with equity capital. The study built on a conceptual model of the funding process and examined the relationships among the acquisition of external equity and human capital, social capital, and two other forms of financial capital—debt financing through loans and bootstrapping. The relationships among human capital and social capital were also examined in predicting the odds of using loans or bootstrapping techniques and equity infusions. The results provided mix support of the hypotheses but did increase our understanding of several crucial relationships.

Westhead and Wright (1998) found that entrepreneurs with start-up experience were more likely to have used funds from personal savings, friends, and family to finance their new ventures. Our results showed that prior start-up or ownership experience did not influence the use of personal sources or loans, but did influence other bootstrapping techniques—but in an unexpected direction. Women without start-up/ownership experience were more likely to have used credit and retained earnings; women with this experience were less likely to use those financing options. It may be that lack of start-up experience limits some women entrepreneurs to the use of easily attainable credit, such as personal credit cards and trade credit, and internally generated funds. No other of our measures of human capital impacted the odds of using loans or bootstrapping techniques.

Human capital effects on equity financing were different than anticipated. It is widely noted that previous experience and education are key to entrepreneurial success (Cooper *et al.* 1994) and that venture capitalists consider human capital factors as primary in funding decisions (Smart 1999). However in our sample, only one type of human capital, graduate education, affected the odds of women entrepreneurs using equity capital to fund their firms. This finding only partially supports existing literature. Muzyka *et al.* (1996) and Smart (1999) found a relationship between managerial proficiencies and equity capital investments. Similarly, Fried and Hisrich (1988) and Wright *et al.* (1997) found previous decision-making experience important in meeting the management standards of venture capitalists. No significant effect of prior business start-up/ownership or senior management experience was found on the odds of women entrepreneurs using equity capital to fund their businesses.

Social capital had no direct effect on increasing the odds of using equity or loans in the financial strategy but did influence certain bootstrapping techniques. Interestingly, most of those relationships were in a negative direction. Women entrepreneurs who did not use foundational and professional advisors were more likely to use personal sources (savings, family and friends) to finance their businesses than women who used these types of advisors. It may be that the use of advisors provided greater knowledge of and access to other forms of financing. Women who did not use business mentors were more likely to use leasing as part of their financing strategy than women with mentors. Leasing options frequently are provided through the sales force of equipment manufacturers, a financing resource that comes to the entrepreneur rather than sought out by her. The presence of a diverse network of supporters was not associated with loans, equity financing, or most bootstrapping techniques. Only the use of personal sources was associated with the diversity of the woman entrepreneur's network. However the average number of network categories of contacts reported by the respondents was 1.7, which may indicate fairly limited networks overall.

Previous research has demonstrated the importance of a diverse network for successful financial strategies (Blau and Alba 1982, Brass 1984, Aldrich 1989), but the apparent inability of our sample to use this social capital to increase the odds of equity financing calls for further examination of this issue. One possible explanation involves the timing of the network's impact. The diversity and the strength of the women entrepreneur's network may contribute more during the deal generation phase of the investment process. The entrepreneur's use of her network may get the venture to a point of contact, but the characteristics of the top management team and the firm, its business model and potential, may ultimately have a more direct effect on the investment decision. In this way the network contribution may be felt earlier in the funding process and may be less direct. Future research should carefully examine what happens after the woman's network provides bridges to initial contacts in the venture capital industry. What screens and reviews occur in the due diligence process that follows? And how does network diversity affect or influence this process? The effect of variety, density and reachability of advice channels (Aldrich 1989) on success at various phases of development and funding is a topic for future investigation. Alternatively, the extent to which some women's social networks lead to funding success may also be affected by the nature of the venture capital industry. Research shows that the venture capital industry in the United States is highly concentrated with several large firms controlling the bulk of capital (BenDaniel *et al.* 2000). The firms are also geographically concentrated, male dominated, and with limited professional diversity. A survey of 145 venture capitalists from 98 firms found that 36% were located in California, and 80% were on the East and West coasts (Smart *et al.* 2000). In addition 63% had MBA degrees from one of three schools (Stanford, Harvard and Wharton). Because the industry is, small, geographically concentrated, and male dominated, and men typically have men in their networks, it is less likely that the networks of women entrepreneurs will overlap with equity-investors who can assist them in securing equity investment. The extent to which some women overcome these network structural characteristics and obtain funding is a topic for future investigation.

It was hypothesized that bootstrapping and loan financing provide a foundation for gaining experience and legitimacy that position ventures to secure equity financing. This hypothesis was only partially supported. Only one type of bootstrapping, the use of personal resources, was associated with the use of outside equity funding. Size and industry sector were more important in explaining the model than other financing techniques. This may indicate that the women in this sample had been successful in securing later stage capital, rather than seed or start-up, and had grown their companies to that point with personal resources. A research topic of interest may be the sequencing of various financial strategies by women led firms.

There are limitations to this study. The number of women respondents who reported receiving equity funding was small. The sample is also biased toward ventures more likely to be interested in and interesting to a provider of equity investment. However, these limitations impact the general-izeability of the results to the population of women-owned firms. This paper makes no pretence of doing so, instead finding this sample valuable for understanding an understudied topic—women entrepreneurs and equity financing.

In future research, it would be useful to more tightly specify the definition of equity funding. The median amount reported in this sample was $50 000, a very small amount for institutional venture capital, and indeed suggests an angel type of equity investment. Finally, the response rate is low and the survey methodology adopted may have impacted the findings. Face-to-face interviews or other methods for collecting the data may produced alternative results. However, this is the first study that we are aware of which has systematically examined venture funded women-owned business. Venture funded women-owned businesses are an elusive population, one both difficult to identify, locate and survey. The lack of knowledge about this population of entrepreneurial firms makes the insights we might gain about this sample and methodology worthwhile. This study contributes to the extremely small body of research regarding women's financing strategies, and offers results explaining why some women secured equity capital while others did not.

The understanding of women entrepreneurs and access to equity financing is at a very early stage. It is important to understand the factors that lead to successful acquisition of outside funding. Subsequent studies might research the effects of social networks, human capital and bootstrapping on the due diligence process, timing, amount of investment, and stages of capital infusion. A better understanding of the timing of the process would allow consideration of where and when the actual value of the human and social resources are created and contributed. A breakdown of the process into steps might show the identification of potential fall-out points for women entrepreneurs, ultimately resulting in direction for educational and training programmes. Extended research on the interactions between measures of human and social capital will advance understanding of the entrepreneur, characteristics of the venture, and the equity financing process. Finally, future research should include a variety of populations not typically receiving equity capital such as different races and ethnic groups, to insure our understanding of venture growth and wealth creation is not limited to certain groups.

This paper addresses the gap in the research by approaching the equity funding issue from the perspective of the demand side—the firms seeking venture capital. Wright and Robbie (1998) pointed out that venture capitalists in the US and UK were beginning to look outside their usual markets for increased opportunities. Women-owned businesses would appear to represent an untapped market for these equity investors. Women entrepreneurs in general are more highly educated, and those with growth aspirations for their businesses are increasingly acquiring education and experiences that foster more sophisticated capital structures.

Acknowledgements

Support for the study was provided by the Kauffman Center for Entrepreneurial Leadership. Data collection by the National Foundation for Women Business Owners was underwritten by Wells Fargo.

Notes

1. Recently released figures based on the 1997 US Census indicate a lower number of women-owned businesses, a discrepancy that resulted from the adoption of different qualifying criteria. To be considered 'women-owned' under the new definition requires 51% ownership, $1000 minimum annual revenues (up from the previous criterion of $500), and that the business be privately held. The US Census reported that the new criteria showed women own 26% of all US businesses, or 5.4 million.
2. Catalyst is a leading, nonprofit research and advisory organization, with offices in New York and Toronto, which works to advance women in business and the professions.

References

Aldrich, H., 1989, Networking among women entrepreneurs. In O. Hagan, C. Rivchun and D. Sexton (eds) *Women-Owned Businesses* (NY: Praeger) 103–132.

Aldrich, H. and Reese, P.R., 1997, Gender gap, gender myth: does women's networking behaviour differ significantly from men's? In S. Birley, I. MacMillan (eds) *Entrepreneurship in a Global Context* (International Business & the World Economy, 5) (London: Routledge).

Aldrich, H., Reese, P.R. and Dubini, P., 1989, Women on the verge of a breakthrough: networking among entrepreneurs in the United States and Italy. *Entrepreneurship &Regional Development*, 1, 339–356.

Alimansky, B, 2000, Eight ways to ruin your chances of raising equity capital. *Journal of Private Equity*, Summer, 3(3), 78–83.

Becker, G.S., 1964, *Human Capital* (NY: Columbia University Press).

BenDaniel, D., Reyes, J. and d'Angelo, M., 2000, Concentration in the venture capital industry. *Journal of Private Equity*, Summer, 7–13.

Bhide, A., 1992., Bootstrap finance: the art of start-ups. Harvard Business Review, Nov.-Dec., 109-117.

Birley, S., Moss, C. and Saunders, P, 1987, Do women entrepreneurs require different training? *American Journal of Small Business*, 12, 27–35.

Blau, J.R. and Alba, R.D., 1982, Empowering nets of participation. Administrative Science Quarterly, 27, 363-379.

Brass, D.J., 1984, Being in the right place: a structural analysis of individual influence in an organization. *Administrative Science Quarterly*, 29, 518–539.

Brass, D.J., 1985, Men's and women's networks: a study of interaction patterns and influence in an organization. *Academy of Management Journal*, 28, 327–343.

Brophy, D., 1992, Financing the new venture: a report on recent research. In D.L. Sexton and J. Kasarda (eds) *The State of the Art of Entrepreneurship* (Boston: PWS Kent) 387–401

Bruderl, J. Preisendorfer, P. and Ziegler, R., 1992, Survival chances of newly founded business organizations. *American Sociological Review*, 57, 227–242.

Brush, C., Greene, P. and Hart, M., 2001, From initial idea to unique advantage: the entrepreneurial challenge of constructing a resource base. *Academy of Management Executive, Special issue on Strategic Management and Entrepreneurship*, 15, 64–80.

Brush, C.G., 1992, Research on women business owners: past trends, a new perspective and future directions. *Entrepreneurship Theory and Practice*, 16, 5–30.

Brush, C.G. and Hisrich, R.D., 1991, Antecedent influences on women-owned businesses. *Journal of Managerial Psychology*, 6, 9–16.

Burt, R.S., 1992, *Structural Holes: The Social Structure of Competition* (Cambridge, MA: Harvard University Press).

Buttner, E.H. and Rosen, B.H., 1988, Bank loan officer's perceptions of characteristics of men, women and successful entrepreneurs. *Journal of Business Venturing*, 3(3), 249–258.

Buttner, E.H. and Rosen, B.H., 1989, Funding new business ventures: are decision-makers biased against women entrepreneurs? *Journal of Business Venturing*, 4(4), 249–261.

Bygrave, W.D., 1988, The structure of the investment networks of venture capital firms. *Journal of Business Venturing*, 3(2), 137–157.

Bygrave, W.D., 1992., Venture capital returns in the 1980's. In D.L. Sexton and J. Kasarda (eds) *The State of the Art of Entrepreneurship* (Boston: PWS Kent) 438–462.

Carter, N.M. and Allen, K.R., 1997, Size determinants of women-owned businesses: choice or barriers to resources? *Entrepreneurship and Regional Development*, **9**, 211–220.

Carter, N.M., Williams, M. and Reynolds, P.D., 1997, Discontinuance among new firms in retail: the influence of initial resources, strategy and gender. *Journal of Business Venturing*, **12**, 125–146.

Centre for Women's Business Research, 2002, *Women-owned businesses in the United States: A fact sheet, Silver Spring* (MD: Centre for Women's Business Research).

Cliff, J.E., 1998, Does one size fit all? Exploring the relationship between attitudes towards growth, gender and business size. *Journal of Business Venturing*, **13**, 523–542.

Coleman, J., 1988, Social capital in the creation of human capital. *American Journal of Sociology*, **94**, S95–S120.

Coleman, S., 2000, Access to capital and terms of credit: a comparison of men-and women-owned small businesses. *Journal of Small Business Management*, **38**, 48–52.

Cooper, A.C., Dunkelberg, W.C. and Woo, C.Y., 1988, Survival and failure: a longitudinal study. *Frontiers of Entrepreneurship Research* (Wellesley, MA: Babson College) 225–237.

Cooper, A.C., Gimeno-Gascon, F.J. and Woo, C.Y., 1994, Initial human and financial capital as predictors of new venture performance. *Journal of Business Venturing*, **9**, 371–395.

Cromie, S. and Birley, S., 1991, Networking by female business owners in Northern Ireland. *Journal of Business Venturing*, **8**, 237–251.

Dollinger, M. 1994, *Entrepreneurship: Strategies and Resources* (Boston, Mass: Irwin).

Fiet, J.O., 1991, Network reliance by venture capita firms and business angels: An empirical and theoretical test. In N.C. Churchill, W.D. Bygrave, J.G. Covin, D.L. Sexton, K.H. Vesper and W.E. Wetzel, Jr (eds) *Frontiers of Entrepreneurship Research* (Boston, MA: Babson College) 445–455.

Fiet, J.O., 1996, Fragmentation in the market for venture capital. *Entrepreneurship Theory & Practice*, **21**, 5–20.

Fineberg, S. 1998b, Venture capital financing reaches another high. *Venture Capital Journal*, July, 37–40.

Florin, J. and Schulze, B., 2000, Born to go public? Founder performance in new, high growth, technology ventures. Babson College-Kauffman Foundation Entrepreneurship Conference, Wellesley, MA, June.

Freear, J., Sohl, J. and Wetzel, W.E. Jr, 1991. Raising venture capital to finance growth. In N.C. Churchill, S. Birley, W.D. Bygrave, D.F. Muzyka, C. Wahlbin and W.E. Wetzel, Jr. (eds) *Frontiers of Entrepreneurship Research* (Wellesley, MA: Babson College).

Freear, J., Sohl, J. and Wetzel, W.E. Jr, 1992. The investment attitudes, behaviour, and characteristics of high net worth individuals. In N.C. Churchill, S. Birley, W.D. Bygrave, D.F. Muzyka, C. Wahlbin and W.E. Wetzel, Jr (eds) *Frontiers of Entrepreneurship Research* (Wellesley, MA: Babson College) 374–387.

Freear, J. Sohl, J. and Wetzel, W.E. Jr, 1994a, Angels and non-angels: are there differences? *Journal of Business Venturing*, **9**, 109–123.

Freear, J., Sohl, J. and Wetzel, W.E. Jr, 1994b, The private investor market for venture capital. *The Financier: ACMT*, **1**, 7–15.

Freear, J. Sohl, J. and Wetzel, W.E. Jr, 1997, The informal venture capital market: milestones passed and the road ahead. In D.L. Sexton and R.W. Smilor (eds) *Entrepreneurship 2000* (Chicago: Upstart Publishing) 47–49.

Fried, V. and Hisrich, R.D., 1988, Venture capital research: past, present & future. *Entrepreneurship Theory and Practice*, **13**, 15–29.

Gatewood, E., Brush, C.G., Carter, N.M., Greene, P.G. and Hart, M., 2002, *Venture Capital, Women's Entrepreneurship and High Growth Ventures: An Annotated Bibliography* (Stockholm: Entrepreneurship and Small Business Research Institute).

Goffe, R. and Scase, R., 1983, Business ownership and women's subordination: a preliminary study of female proprietors. *Sociological Review*, **31**, 625–648.

Granovetter, M., 1973, The strength of weak ties. *American Journal of Sociology*, **6**, 1360–1380.

Greene, P., Brush, C. and Brown, T., 1997, Resource configurations in new ventures: relationships to owner and company characteristics. *Journal of Small Business Strategy*, **8**, 25–40.

Greene, P., Brush, C., Hart M. and Saparito, P., 1999, An exploration of the venture capital industry: is gender an issue? In P.D. Reynolds, W. Bygrave, S. Manigart, C. Mason, G.D. Meyer, H. Sapienza, and K.G. Shaver (eds) *Frontiers of Entrepreneurship Research* (Wellesley, MA: Babson College).

Gundry, L. and Welsch, H., (2001), The ambitious entrepreneur: high growth strategies of women-owned enterprises. *Journal of Business Venturing*, **16**, 453–470

Gupta, A.K. and Sapienza, H. 1992, Determinants of venture capital firms' preferences regarding the industry diversity and geographic scope of their investments. *Journal of Business Venturing*, **7**, 347–362.

Hart, M., 1995, Founding resource choices: influences and effects. Doctoral dissertation. Harvard Graduate School of Business.

Hart, M., Brush, C., Greene, P, Gatewood, E. and Carter, N., 2002, Women of the venture capital industry: Do they make a difference? Babson College-Kauffman Foundation Entrepreneurship Research Conference, Boulder, CO, June.

Hisrich R.G. and Brush, C.G., 1983, The women entrepreneur: implications of family, educational and occupational experience. In N.C. Churchill, S. Birley, W.D. Bygrave, D.F. Muzyka, C. Wahlbin and W.E. Wetzel, Jr (eds) *Frontiers of Entrepreneurship Research* (Wellesley, MA: Babson College).

Hisrich, R. and Brush, C. B., 1984, The women entrepreneur: management skills and business problems. *Journal of Small Business Management*, **22**, 30–37.

Hisrich, R.G. and Neider, L., 1987, A preliminary investigation of female entrepreneurs in Florida. *Journal of Small Business Management*, **25**, 22–29.

Hisrich, R.G. and O'Brien, M., 1982, The women entrepreneur as a reflection of the type of business. In N.C. Churchill, S. Birley, W.D. Bygrave, D.F. Muzyka, C. Wahlbin and W.E. Wetzel, Jr (eds) *Frontiers of Entrepreneurship Research* (Wellesley, MA: Babson College).

Honig-Haftel, S. and Martin, L., 1986, Is the female entrepreneur at a disadvantage? *Thrust: The Journal for Employment and Training Professionals*, **7**, 49–64.

Ibarra, H., 1993, Personal networks of women and minorities in management: a conceptual framework. *Academy of Management Journal*, **18**, 56–87.

Kelly, M., 1994, Towanda's triumph: social and cultural capital in the transition to adulthood in the urban ghetto. *International Journal of Urban and Regional Research*, 18 March, 88–111.

Mason, C. and Harrison, R., 1999, Venture capital: rationale, aims, and scope. *Venture Capital*, **1**, 1–46.

Mason, C.M. and Harrison, R.T., 1995a, Informal venture capital and the financing of small and medium sized enterprise. *Small Enterprise Research*, **3**, 33–56.

Mason, C.M. and Harrison, R.T., 1995b, Closing the regional equity capital gap: the role of informal venture capital. *Small Business Economics*, **7**, 153–172

McPherson, M., Smith-Lovin, L. and Cook, J.M., 2001, Birds of a feature: homophily in social networks. *Annual Review of Sociology*, **27**, 415–44.

Muzyka, D., Birley, S. and Leleux, B., 1996, Tradeoffs in the investment decisions of European venture capitalists. *Journal of Business Venturing*, **11**, 273–287.

Olm, K., Carsrud, A. and Alvey, L., 1988, The role of networks in new venture funding for the female entrepreneur: a continuing analysis. In B.A. Kirchoff, W.A. Long, E. McMullan, K.H. Vesper and W.E. Wetzel Jr (eds) *Frontiers of Entrepreneurship Research* (Wellesy, MA: Babson College).

Pennings, J.M., Lee, K. and Witteloostuijn, A.V., 1998, Human capital, social capital and firm dissolution. *Academy of Management Journal*, **41**, 425–440.

Riding, A. and Swift, C., 1990, Women business owners and terms of credit: some empirical findings of the Canadian experience. *Journal of Business Venturing*, **5**, 327–340.

Roberts, E.B., 1991, *Entrepreneurs in High Technology* (NY: Oxford University Press).

Sapienza, H., 1992, When do venture capitalists add value? *Journal of Business Venturing*, **7**, 9–28.

Sapienza, H. and Korsgaard, M.A., 1996, Procedural justice in entrepreneur-investor relations. *Academy of Management Journal*, **39**, 544–574.

Sargent, M. and Young, J.E., 1991, The entrepreneurial search for capital: a behavioural science perspective, *Entrepreneurship & Regional Development*, **3**, 237–252.

Scherr, F.C., Sugrue, T.F. and Ward, J.B., 1993, Financing the small firm startup: determinants of debt use, *Journal of Small Business Finance*, **3**, 17–36.

Smart, G., Payne, S. and Yuzaki, H., 2000, What makes a successful venture capitalist? *Journal of Private Equity*, Fall, 7–29

Smart, G.H., 1999, Management assessment methods in venture capital: an empirical analysis of human capital valuation. *Venture Capital*, **1**, 59–83.

Sohl, J.E. 1999, The early-state equity market in the USA. *Venture Capital*, **1**, 1–20.

Stevenson, L.A., 1986, Against all odds: the entrepreneurship of women. *Journal of Small Business Management*, **24**, 30–36.

Swartz, J., 1991, The future of the venture capital industry. *Journal of Business Venturing*, **6**, 89–92.

Taylor, J., 2001, Venture-backed Companies Account for Half of all IPO's in 1999. Available online at: http://www.nvca.org/VEpress01_07_00ahtml

Thomson Financial Securities Data, 1999, Venture investments reach a record. *National Venture Capital Association*. Available online at: http://nvca.org/80299nr.html.

Thomson Financial Securities Data, 2000, Venture capital investments achieve record level in 2000, torrid pace relaxed in fourth quarter. *National Venture Capital Association*. Available online at: www.nvca.org

Timmons, J. A. and Bygrave, W.D., 1997, Venture capital: Reflections and projections. In D.L. Sexton and R. Smilor (eds) *Entrepreneurship 2000* (Chicago, IL: Upstart Publishing).

Timmons, J.A. and Sapienza, H., 1992, Venture capital: the decade ahead. In D.L. Sexton and J. Kasarda (eds) *The State of the Art of Entrepreneurship* (Boston: PWS Kent).

Tyebjee, T.T. and Bruno, A.V., 1984, A model of venture capitalist investment activity. *Management Science*, **30**, 1051–1076.

Van Osnabrugge, M. and Robinson, R.J., 2000, *Angel Investing: Matching Start-up Funds with Start-Up Companies* (San Francisco: Jossey-Bass).

Warner, M., 1998, Inside the silicon valley money machine, *Fortune*, 28 Oct, 128–140.

Watkins, J. and Watkins, D., 1984, The female entrepreneur: background and determinants of business choice—some British data. *International Small Business Journal*, **2**, 21–31.

Watson, W., Ponthieu and Critelli, J., 1995, Team interpersonal effectiveness in venture partnerships and its connection to perceived success. *Journal of Business Venturing*, **10**, 393–411.

Westhead, P. and Wright, M., 1998, Novice, portfolio, and serial founders in rural and urban areas. *Entrepreneurship Theory & Practice*, **22**, 63–100.

Women in Business, 1998, A report on statistical information about women-owned businesses prepared by the US Small Business Administration's Office of Advocacy, October. Available online at: http://www.sba.gov/advo/stats/wib.html.

Wright, M. and Robbie, K., 1998, Venture capital and private equity: a review and synthesis. *Journal of Business Finance and Accounting*, **25**, 521–570.

Wright, M., Robbie, K. and Ennew, C., 1997, Venture capitalists and serial entrepreneurs. *Journal of Business Venturing*, **12**, 227–249.

Zacharakis, A.L. and Shepherd, D.A., 2001, The nature of information and overconfidence on venture capitalist's decision-making. *Journal of Business Venturing*, **16**, 311–332.

[19]

VENTURE CAPITAL, 2001, VOL. 3, NO. 1, 63–83

Patterns of venture capital funding: is gender a factor?

PATRICIA G. GREENE, CANDIDA G. BRUSH,
MYRA M. HART and PATRICK SAPARITO

Since the early 1980s, new ventures with high growth potential and large capital needs have found an ever-increasing pool of venture capital available to support their growth. However, the flow of venture capital investment to women-led businesses remains meager in spite of the fact that in the US and Europe an increasing number of businesses are owned by women. The apparent disparity between potential investment opportunity and actual deals made between venture capital firms and women-led businesses raises the question of whether gender is an issue. The majority of venture capital studies investigate equity funds flows, investor criteria and the nature of the investor-investee relationship. Research on women entrepreneurs focuses on psychological dimensions, business characteristics and performance. Questions about the intersection of gender and venture capital financing are largely unexamined. This exploratory study utilizes longitudinal data to track US venture capital investments by proportion, stage, industry and gender. The descriptive statistics and our analysis of the findings suggest several hypotheses to explain the apparent gender gap.

Keywords: gender; structural barriers; human capital; strategic choice

Introduction

Venture capital-backed companies are recognized as engines for economies (EVCA 1993, Mason and Harrison 1999). The worldwide expansion of the venture capital industry in recent years has provided increased equity financing opportunities for growing entrepreneurial firms. Venture capitalists contribute to innovation, job creation, economic growth and industrial renewal, not only through their financial investments, but also through the managerial expertise and deal making leverage they provide to their portfolio companies (Mason and Harrison 1999). Concurrently, however, the increased sophistication of limited partners, venture capital firm investment specialization, and growing investment fund size has intensified competition among venture capital firms and raised the bar for entrepreneurs seeking equity capital (Timmons and Bygrave 1997).

An earlier version of this paper was presented at the 1999 Babson Kauffman Entrepreneurship Research Conference, Columbia, South Carolina, USA.
Patricia G. Greene, University of Missouri- Kansas City, Henry W. Bloch School of Business and Public Administration, 5100 Rockhill Road, Kansas City, MO 64110-2499, USA; e-mail: greenep@umkc.edu;
Candida G. Brush, Boston University, USA; *Myra M. Hart*, Harvard University, USA;
Patrick Saparito, Department of Management, Whittemore School of Business and Economics, University of New Hampshire, Durham, NH 03824-3593, USA.

Venture Capital ISSN 1369-1066 print/ISSN 1464-5343 online © 2001 Taylor & Francis Ltd
http://www.tandf.co.uk/journals
DOI 10.1080/13691060010024737

Factors distinguishing entrepreneurial firms that receive equity funding from those which do not has received only limited scholarly attention (Wright and Robbie 1998). Research has explored many aspects of the investment process; deal generation, screening, valuation, deal structure, monitoring, and exit (Wright and Robbie 1998, Timmons and Sapienza 1992, Fried and Hisrich 1988). Major factors associated with successful equity acquisition are identified as management aspects—quality of the team, capabilities, experience, and staying power (Bruno and Tyebjee 1985, Sahlman and Stevenson 1985, MacMillan *et al.* 1985, MacMillan *et al.* 1987, Hisrich and Jancowicz 1990, Amit *et al.* 1990, Sweeting 1991, Gupta and Sapienza 1992, Hall and Hofer 1993, Muzyka *et al.* 1996. But, despite significant research that investigates the role of gender in access to debt capital, there is no parallel stream of research that considers gender, either as an independent or analysis variable in studies of equity capital. This gap leads us to consider pressing questions regarding the role and participation of women in the venture capital funding process, the absolute and proportional amounts of venture capital invested in businesses owned or led by women, and the relative success of male and female-led businesses in securing investment. Furthermore, there is very little information available about male/female participation in venture funding sorted by industry or stage of investment.

Background

Timmons and Sapienza (1992) offer a history of the US Venture Capital Industry, pointing out that in 1979 there were approximately 225 venture capital firms managing $2.9 billion, and by 1989 there were 674 managing $33.4 billion. Currently the US based National Venture Capital Association (NVCA) reports that in 1999 $46.5 billion of venture capital was raised with $48.3 billion invested in 6336 deals, a 151.6% increase over 1998 (Thompson Financial Securities Data 1999).

The venture capital industry in the UK is second only to the US in terms of investing activity and the industry is growing rapidly throughout Europe and the rest of the world (Wright and Robbie 1998). Since 1983 the UK venture capital industry has invested more than 35 billion pounds in approximately 19 000 firms. The British Venture Capital Association reports 1999 investments of 7.8 billion pounds in 1358 companies (BVCA 2000). The pattern is similar in the rest of Europe, with venture capital funds raised in 1997 amounting to 1.5 times that of 1996 (Fineberg 1998a, Mason and Harrison 1999).

Changes are also notable in the types of investments pursued. While the 1980s marked a trend toward investments at the seed stage (approximately 44% of US investments), the 1990s showed that the majority of venture capital firms are now investing in later stages of venture development (Timmons and Sapienza 1992, NVCA 1999). The industrial sector, once focused primarily on computer hardware and energy products, has broadened considerably. Investments in 1999 were in internet specific businesses (38.8%), communications (17.3%), computer software and services (15.5%), consumer related (3.5%), medical/health (5.0%), semiconductor and electrical related (3.6%), biotechnology (2.5%), computer hardware (2.7%), industrial/energy (1.5%) and a broad category of other products (9.0%) (Thompson Financial Securities Data 2000).

This pattern is quite similar in Europe where 1996 statistics report that 'engineering' sector companies received the most venture capital (European Venture Capital Association 1997) and over 1 billion pounds were invested in high tech companies in 1999 (British Venture Capital Association 2000). More than 470 high tech companies in electronics, medical, biotechnology and communications received funding, accounting for 43% of the total number of companies backed (British Venture Capital Association 1999).

Against this backdrop, the industry faces several challenges (Wright and Robbie 1998, Timmons and Bygrave 1997). These include trends towards stronger gatekeepers, increased deal size, more competition for better deals among venture capital firms, greater specialization and focus on industry sectors, more institutional investors, increased co-investing and shorter time frames for exit. It is suggested that the industry dynamics are becoming more competitive, causing venture capital firms to develop distinct competencies and advantages. Strategies utilized by VC firms to achieve these include concentration on quality of management and market potential of portfolio companies, taking a more active role in ventures, continuing to use contacts, devising creative deal structures and harvesting alternatives, and developing strategic partnerships (Timmons and Bygrave 1997). It is less clear how these trends and strategies will impact women-owned businesses and their involvement in and with the venture capital industry.

To support our discussion of women and venture capital, we reviewed all issues of *Journal of Business Venturing* published between 1991 and 1998, identifying 29 studies on venture capital. We also included the four literature reviews from *State of the Art of Entrepreneurship* (Bygrave 1992, Timmons and Sapienza 1992) and *Entrepreneurship 2000* (Brophy 1997, Timmons and Bygrave 1997). With the exception of the four literature reviews, all articles were empirically based. Only two articles examined the European venture capital industry (Ooghe et al. 1991, Manigart 1994). As noted in earlier reviews (Fried and Hisrich 1988), research falls into three major streams: (1) the relationship between the investor and the venture capital firm (Sapienza 1992, Sapienza and Korsgaard 1996); (2) the operations and decision processes of the venture capital firm, particularly pertaining to the search/screen and evaluation activities (Runkha et al. 1992, Hall and Hofer 1993, Fiet 1995, Norton 1995, Zacharakis and Meyer 1995); and (3) the relationship between the entrepreneurial company and the venture capital firm (Rosenstein et al. 1993, Elango et al. 1995, Busenitz et al. 1997, Wright et al. 1997).

The majority of the studies we reviewed were focused on the venture capital firm's investment process, strategy, and relationship to the entrepreneurial firm; with fewer articles investigating the actual entrepreneurial firm. Even fewer studies consider the relationship between the investor and venture capital firm, although this topic is examined in the literature reviews (Bygrave 1992, Timmons and Sapienza 1992, Brophy

1997, Timmons and Bygrave 1997). Strategies of venture capital firms are considered in some empirical works (Swartz 1991, Gupta and Sapienza 1992), while other authors explore the 'valued added' to entrepreneurial firms from venture capitalists (Sapienza 1992), the effects of team processes in the partnership (Watson *et al.* 1995), and venture capitalists perceptions of serial entrepreneurs (Wright *et al.* 1997).

As Mason and Harrison (1999) and Wright and Robbie (1998) before us, we conclude that the majority of research, regardless of research stream or theoretical framework, approaches venture capital studies from the perspective of the venture capitalist, or the venture capital industry, which is the supply side. Less often does research examine the demand side, or the approaches taken by firms seeking venture capital. Indeed, industry overviews explicitly point out that future research opportunities lie in studying public policy, industry competitiveness and venture capital firm operations and strategies (Timmons and Sapienza 1992, Timmons and Bygrave 1997), and examination of the factors influencing variations in the ability of some populations of firms to obtain venture capital. Furthermore, none of the samples we reviewed indicated that women-owned businesses were included in the samples of entrepreneurial venture firms.

Women-owned firms

The dramatic growth in presence, size and contributions of women-owned businesses has attracted significant attention over the past 10 years. From 1987–1996, the number of women-owned businesses grew by 78%, well above the 48% growth posted by all US businesses (SBA 1996). In 1992 (SBA 1996) it was estimated that more than 600 000 women-owned firms had sales greater than $1 million (Women Owned Businesses: The New Economic Force 1992). In 1996, women owned 36% of US businesses, employed 26% of the total work force and generated $2.3 trillion in revenues or 16% of total US revenues (NFWBO 1998). The 8.5 million women-owned businesses reported in 1997 represents a net gain of 5.8%. Employment gains (28%) and revenue growth (34.8%) from 1996–1997 represent an even greater impact on the economy than does the sheer growth in the number of such firms. As of 1999, there were 9.1 million women-owned businesses generating more than $3.6 trillion in sales, and employing more than 27.5 million workers (NFWBO 1999). If past performance is a reliable indicator, it is expected these newly formed women-owned businesses will have a better than average survival rate.[1]

Trends are similar in European countries. For example, the Netherlands reports women comprise 34% of all self-employment, while in Finland, Denmark, Spain, the UK and Belgium the percentage is over 25% (Ducheneaut 1997). Likewise, the numbers of women-owned businesses have increased over the past decade between 10–20% in different countries. As in the US, European women's participation in various industry sectors has similarly expanded from service and retail to other areas, such as health care, high technology and business services.

Paralleling the growing presence of women-owned businesses, academic research on women entrepreneurs and their businesses has accelerated. Studies examine various levels of analysis: individual, firm and environmental factors, as well as processes that influence women's entrepreneurship (Brush 1992, 1997). Yet, research on financing of women-owned businesses, access and use of debt and equity capital, financing strategies and their relationship to growth and performance of women-owned firms is extremely limited. Studies examining issues of gender and financing focus exclusively on access to debt capital (Buttner and Rosen 1988, Riding and Swift 1990, Coleman 2000).

In recent years bank financing has become more accessible to women-owned businesses. US Government initiatives (e.g. the Small Business Administration's Women's Pre-qualification Loan Programme), private banking programmes (e.g. Wells Fargo Bank and BankBoston programmes for women business owners), women's business organizations (e.g. Women Inc.), and training programmes and centres have increased availability and accessibility to commercial credit since 1995. In the US in 1998, more than 52% of women business owners had a line of bank credit, compared to 59% of men business owners. Approximately one third had credit of $50 000 or more, 16% had $100 000–500 000 and 7% have credit lines in excess of $500 000 (NFWBO 1998).

Reports on women's access to bank funding in Europe are not as positive. A study commissioned by the French Ministry of Industry which compared women's access to financing in France to that of the UK, Germany, Spain and Italy found that women in all countries who start venture in retailing, services, or who take over a family business are more likely to receive financing (Mahot 1998). Studies carried out in the Netherlands, Germany and the UK show that women start ventures with smaller loans than men, and that they have less recourse to bank finance, often relying on their own financing (Fourth Annual Report 1996). Another study from the UK in 1993 found that 55% of men had recourse to bank loans compared to only 33% of women (Johnson and Storey 1995). Some countries have put into place programmes to help women acquire funding, one being the Local Employment Initiative, a direct subsidy for women provided by the European Commission. The UK and France also have had special funds reserved for women's enterprises (Mahot 1998).

Hence, research findings on the relationship between gender and access to debt financing are inconclusive. A study of the role of initial firm resources on start-up success showed that women-owned firms had less access to financial resources than did their male counterparts (Carter *et al.* 1997). A follow up study showed that availability of capital through private and personal banking sources was related to the size of women-owned businesses (Carter and Allen 1997). Similarly, Buttner and Rosen (1988) found that bankers perceived men to be higher on characteristics associated with successful entrepreneurship than women, while a similar study in New Zealand showed parallel results (Fay and Williams 1993). In contrast, a study of access to bank financing in Canada showed few differences where firm age, size and growth rate were controlled (Riding and Swift 1990).

However, these authors did note that collateral requirements for women were higher, and that women were less satisfied with their banking experience. A recent study supports this, in that a comparative study of men and women utilizing bank debt found that access did not differ by sex, but terms of credit did, with women more frequently being required to present collateral, and paying higher interest rates (Coleman 2000). Although there are attempts to understand the relationship between gender and access to debt financing, our literature review found no academic studies examining women's access to or utilization of equity funding in their ventures. What explains the gap in scholarly research examining gender in venture capital financing decisions, and women-owned businesses access to equity capital? In part, this can be explained by the low levels of participation. Despite the growth in female entrepreneurship and improvement in women's access to debt capital, private equity and venture capital remains unfamiliar to most women entrepreneurs. Of the approximately 1900 companies that received $11.4 billion of venture capital in 1997, less than 2.5% were woman-owned. (Pratt 1998, Seegul 1998). As noted in the Wall Street Journal, November 28, 1997:

> Last year (1996), 1200 new firms got venture financing, the growth serum for many entrepreneurial success stories; only 30 were run by women, according to the Small Business Administration. A recent private study estimates that 2% of the $33 billion venture capitalists invested between 1991 and 1996 went to female-run firms.
>
> (Stout 1997)

A private study of the venture capital industry, conducted by Venture One for Aurora Venture Partners in 1996, indicated that of the 6362 companies that received venture funding from 1991 through 1996, only 31 deals were with women-owned businesses (Seegull 1998). The Small Business Administration's estimates of venture capital deals in 1997 support this finding.

Many explanations are offered for the venture community's apparent disinterest in women-owned businesses. Choice of industry, firm size, size of capital requirements, growth expectations, and ownership/control issues are among the business reasons suggested. Venture capital dollars were invested predominantly in computer software, hardware and services, medical, health and biotechnology; and communications. There is also a suggestion of a geographic impact (Wright and Robbie 1998). More than 35% of the US funds were invested in California firms, primarily in Silicon Valley (Pratt 1998). In contrast, female entrepreneurs are heavily concentrated in the service (51%) and retail (18%) sectors, and most of their firms are small. In 1997, 84% had revenues less than $100 000.[2] Approximately 60% of female entrepreneurs started their businesses with $5000 or less—most of which came from personal savings. The predominant industry choices of female entrepreneurs appear to be mismatched with the industry preferences of venture capitalists. A hypothesis is that venture capitalists seek to avoid risk while gaining returns and are likely to avoid diseconomies involved in disproportionate monitoring and due diligence associated with certain populations:

> The combination of a perceived unacceptable risk/return relationship and investment diseconomies pose special problems for firms of varying types of ownership, many of which carry an extra burden of prejudgment with them as they approach the financial community. These include women-owned and minority-owned firms, and family businesses, franchises, and micro-businesses†
>
> (Brophy 1997: 7)

An alternative explanation suggests that women are involved in different social networks, which may cause differential access to equity capital (Aldrich 1989). The historically male composition of the venture capital community indicates that there may be network gaps that present serious access challenges for women.

No matter what the explanation, there is evidence that the venture capital community may be missing many good opportunities to invest in women-owned businesses. With almost 40% of all US firms being owned by women, more than 600 000 having revenues of greater than $1 million in 1992, significant revenue gains, and positive track records, it was expected that increasing numbers of women-owned firms would be funded by venture capitalists. However, of the IPOs brought to market between 1995–1998, only 2% were venture funded women-owned businesses (Seagull 1998). It begs the question, 'Why are so few women-owned businesses funded by venture capital?'

Theoretical framework

Theoretical frameworks previously applied in this field of study include agency, procedural justice, decision theory and industrial economics. We organize this discussion around a theoretical framework adapted from Fried and Hisrich (1988), Timmons and Sapienza (1992) and Timmons and Bygrave (1997) (see figure 1). We propose that the reasons so few women-owned businesses are funded by venture capital fall into three categories: structural barriers, human capital and strategic choice.

Structural barriers

The institutional environment of the venture capital industry is described as a close network, that is geographically concentrated, and tightly interconnected (Bygrave 1992). Success of the VC firm is dependent on what they know and who they know—where tight interconnectedness leads to better information increasing the firm's legitimacy. The life's blood of the venture capital firm is the deal flow, which firms learn about through their contact networks in other firms (Bygrave 1992). The overwhelming majority of venture capitalists is male and has significant experience in the industry (Timmons and Sapienza 1992). Hence the rules, beliefs and practices created in this environment are predominantly 'male'. Feminist theory suggests that men and women are shaped by different societal experiences. Men are socialized to be masterful, dominant, and competi-

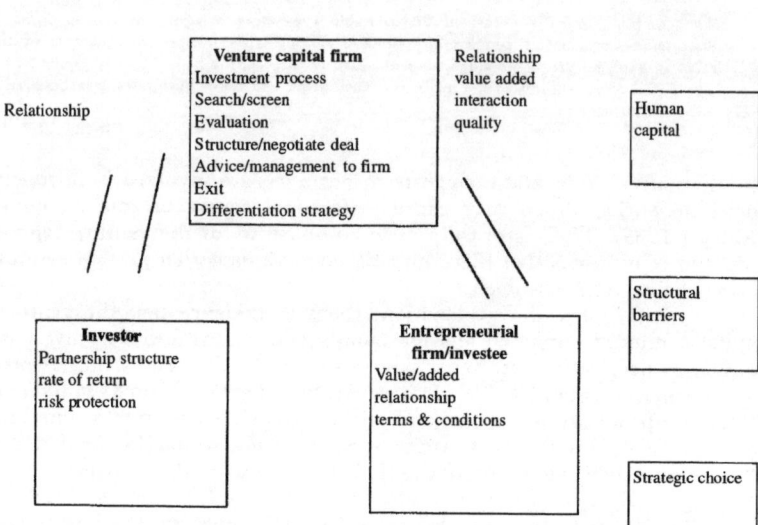

Source: Adapted from Fried and Hisrich 1988, Timmons and Sapienza 1992, Timmons and Bygrave 1997.

Figure 1.   Theoretical framework.

tive; while women are socialized to be nurturing and relational (Gilligan 1982, Aldrich 1989).

It is argued that men emphasize economic values and quantitative success measures whereas women assign more importance to social values and qualitative success measures (Cliff 1998). Following this logic, it might be argued that women are not socialized to negotiate, compete and structure deals in accordance with the institutional norms of the predominantly male venture capital industry. Instead, women are entering an environment constructed by men, one that reflects male beliefs and practices. Consequently, women and their ventures may be perceived as less legitimate in the eyes of prospective funders. The view that women are less serious about their ventures, make 'riskier' investments, and are less likely to pay back loans may be based on these perceptions (NFWBO 1996, Brush 1997). Reports from OECD support this notion, where women are considered untalented at business and therefore less attractive for financial risk (Ducheneaut 1997). If this is true, venture capitalists would expend more time and money costs to complete the due diligence, creating diseconomies in the venture capitalist-entrepreneur relationship, and the venture capitalists would have less incentive to fund women-owned firms (Brophy 1992).

Social network theory offers an alternative explanation. The theory argues that the presence or absence of social ties, such as access or membership in associations, plays a key role in business success. Research shows that men and women have different networks. Women tend to have more women in their networks and men, predominantly men (Aldrich 1989). Women also have more kin ties and are more likely to name their spouses first in their networks than men. Women may be excluded from formal networks in the corporate environment by virtue of job position and may also participate in different informal networks (Moore and Buttner 1997). By extension, one can argue that women are outside the formal, predominately male 'venture capital' network. Consequently, it may be harder for female entrepreneurs to make the connection, to get in the door, or gain attention for their 'deal'.

Human capital

Human capital refers to the stored knowledge and skills of individuals (Becker 1964). For women, occupational segregation by industry sector or level of managerial experience may decrease the chances of women gaining requisite capabilities needed to demonstrate management competence to equity providers. Women's participation in the retail, service, finance and real estate sectors is strong, yet in other areas, such as manufacturing and high technology, women are less visible. For instance, women still comprise fewer than 16% of all US undergraduates in engineering (*Wall Street Journal* 1994, Brush 1997), and are highly concentrated in clerical and sales jobs or administrative positions with fewer employed in production, transportation, or agriculture (United Nations 1991). Hence, the differential backgrounds and industry work experience of women may decrease the likelihood of women starting businesses in sectors attractive to venture capitalists. The US Small Business Administration reports that women-owned firms comprise almost 20% of the share of service businesses, with their share in all other industry sectors less than 10% (Brush 1997, Women in Business 1998). In contrast, high proportions of venture capital investments are made in the computer software, telecommunications, medical instruments and devices and industrial products areas (Timmons and Sapienza 1992, Boston Globe 1999, EVCA 1999, BVCA 2000).

Besides differences in women's work-force experience by sector, other statistics show that women are often limited in leadership and managerial experience. Reports show an average of 25% of all managers in Fortune 200 companies are female (*Wall Street Journal* 1994a) with some companies having only 7% female managers. Similarly, less than 5% of the vice-presidents and executives of major companies are female, and fewer than 5% of the board members of Fortune 1000 companies are women (*Wall Street Journal* 1994). In France, 54% of women business owners have some work experience compared to 70% of men (Ducheneaut 1997). Additionally, a study of Canadian small firms showed that 9% of women had business degrees versus 23% of men, whilst 30% of women and 57% of men had previously owned businesses (Cliff 1998). Further, in Europe women typically have experience in lower management positions or in the service sector, rather than in high-level decision-making jobs or manufacturing industries (Ducheneaut 1997). In comparison, research shows that venture capitalists rate 'management' in capital seeking companies more favourably if they have experience in founding a venture, a strong track record in marketing management, engineering and leadership decision-making (Wright *et al.* 1997, Fried and Hisrich 1988). The lower probability that women have strategic decision-making experience, a business degree, an engineering degree, or previous experience in founding may hinder their ability to meet management standards of venture capitalists.

Social learning theory offers a complementary perspective. Social learning can occur through the development or observation of behaviour in others, often referred to as role models. The individual's socialization process, which occurs in the family setting, transforms norms, language, aspirations, and career preferences through observational learning and modelling (Bandura 1977). While the most influential role models are family members, the prevalence and visibility of successful examples can be helpful to entrepreneurs. For men, examples of successful venture capital funded male-owned firms are pervasive. However, for women, success stories are less visible. Baker *et al.* (1997) reported in a comprehensive survey of business periodicals between 1982 and 1995 that about 4% of the articles covered women. Similarly, a review of business school cases on entrepreneurship showed only 10% featured women as the chief decision-maker. Hence women have fewer professional role models, thereby possibly making it more difficult for them to learn how to engage in equity financing practices.

Strategic choice—do women choose not to seek venture capital?

Growth is a strategic choice that entrepreneurs may or may not elect to pursue (Churchill and Lewis 1983), and is a function of the entrepreneur's aspirations, product/market strategy, and context (Sexton and Bowman-Upton 1991). Furthermore, choices about resources, capital structures, and complex resource combinations are critical determinants of growth strategy (Greene and Brown 1997).

Part of the strategic choice issue is that maintaining control of the business may be more important to women than to men. It is argued that women value relationships, social policies, strong interpersonal sensitiv-ities, and have high concern for others (Gilligan 1982, Cliff 1998). In debt or other types of growth financing, ownership of the business remains with the entrepreneur. Typically in equity financing, venture capitalists will expect not only between 15–30% annual returns but also anywhere from 20–75% ownership of the business (Bygrave 1992). Because women entrepreneurs may view a dramatic shift in ownership structure as detrimental to the relationships they have with employees and partners, venture capital financing may be less attractive as an option. Preferences for debt financing are also supported by government and bank programmes which target women. This financing mechanism employs different evaluation criteria (i.e. assets, collateral, track record and ability to pay back). Hence women may choose to pursue debt financing rather than equity because access is easier.

While statistical differences between men and women in terms of whether they want to grow or not were insignificant in Cliff's (1998) study, she did find differences in the pace of growth. Female business owners tended to be more careful and conservative, taking into account personal and business risks whereas men planned to expand more rapidly. This is supported by research in Europe that finds women more likely to operate small ventures that are not capital intensive (Ducheneaut 1997). Venture capitalists expect a funded venture to grow rapidly in terms of sales and profits, so the VC firm can exit within 5 years (Timmons and Bygrave 1997). In contrast, women may choose not to seek venture capital because the terms of rapid growth and expansion may be contrary to their strategic pacing.

To summarize, we develop an over-arching conceptual framework that not only builds on previous work, but also adds theoretical explanations that might explain differences in venture capital investments between men and women led ventures.[3] This study seeks to provide empirical evidence on the proportion, size and scope of venture capital investments in women-led businesses. We pose the following questions to guide this study.

What is the proportion of venture capital funded businesses led by women? This question is related to that of strategic choice. By better understanding the proportion of women led ventures receiving venture capital funding, we advance our understanding of the types of businesses and growth strategies adopted and applied by women led business. We do, however, recognize that this study does not address the women led businesses that are unsuccessful in attempts to obtain venture capital investments.

Are there variations in venture capital funded men and women- led businesses by industrial sector? Venture capital funding is concentrated in specific industrial sectors. Meaningful participation in these sectors is largely predicated upon related stocks of human capital, especially educational and work experiences. A broader range of industrial sector participation by women-led businesses would suggest broader acceptance of different levels and types of human capital.

Do stages of investment for venture capital vary for men and women-lea venture capital funded businesses? Participation in the venture capital industry is largely predicated upon membership in related corridors or networks. We suggest that women business owners start with different types of people in their networks and therefore take more time to enter into venture capital networks. Therefore it seems likely that venture capital funding would come at a later stage for their business, allowing time for network development.

Following is a description of our methodology and the results of our analysis. We discuss theoretical explanations for our findings, concluding with implications and future research directions.

Research design and methodology

Data for this research study was provided by the Kauffman Centre for Entrepreneurial Leadership through its strategic partnership with the National Venture Capital Association (NVCA) and Venture Economics, a subsidiary of Securities Data Corp. The data was collected by the National Venture Capital Association for more than 30 years in an annual survey that was originally intended for political purposes to lobby Congress on behalf of the industry on matters of taxation and regulation (Brophy 1997). All data refers to US investments and the database continues to be updated on a quarterly basis. Survey participants indicated multiple investments in companies each year. However, as noted by MacMillan *et al.* (1985) and as is the case with many publicly available data sets, this data set suffered some common limitations—i.e. completeness of responses, and definitional purity (Phillips and Dennis 1997). This is due to the unwillingness of respondents to disclose financial information in some years, as well as the pre-computer collection methodology used to set up the data files. Our choice of this data set is in part a response to the current lack of large sample longitudinal data examining gender comparisons in entrepreneurship (Aldrich and Baker 1997).

This exploratory study reports on the first phase of a longer-term project that investigates women's access to and use of equity financing. This phase of the project reports on responses from companies that were coded according to gender of firm owner or top management, year of first investment, stage at first investment, and industrial sector. The original data was not coded for gender. Therefore we screened 21 845 entries and coded male or female by first name or title (Mr/Mrs/Ms). Entries for which gender was not apparent by either criterion were coded '2', used to establish frequencies, and set aside for future investigation and consideration. The file also contains multiple entries for each firm. After we converted the data files from an Excel format to SPSS, we visually reviewed every record and deleted duplicates. In order to determine whether the firm is led by a male or female, we screened according to job title, selecting the highest-ranking role for each firm as the representative. In cases where both Chairman and President/CEO were listed, we chose the latter, reasoning that management capabilities was one of the key determinants in the decision to fund a new venture (MacMillan *et al.* 1985, Hisrich and Jancowicz 1990). Almost half of the investments either were not identifiable by individual characteristics due to either first names that were not gender specific or both first name and title were missing.

These two screening processes, conducted by two researchers, resulted in a reduction of our total sample to 16 412 records. Each record represented an investment in a company, for which there could be multiple investments in a single company. While a gender comparison of total capital invested in individual companies would be ideal, the information was not available in this data set or others considered(should this be a footnote. Our descriptive statistics consider the 30 year time period, but because an extremely small number of investments in women-led ventures occurred prior to 1988, our statistical analysis focused on years 1988–1998.

Our choice to truncate the analysis reduced the sample to 4306. Stages of investment are represented as 'early stage' (0), 'expansion' (1), 'later stage' (2), buyout/acquisition (3) and other (4). Although this data set includes a longitudinal array of investments per firm, this phase of the project is limited to the analysis of the first investment recorded for each firm. Standard SIC codes are used for industry representation.

What is the proportion of venture capital funded businesses led by women?

To address this research question, we ran frequencies and descriptive statistics on the entire data set of 16 412 investments. Of the investments in firms since 1953, 2.4% (392) were to companies identifiable as women led, while 46.8% (7684) firms were headed by men. While we were able to identify the numbers of investments in women-led businesses funded by year, space limitations did not allow a conservative way to present the data for each of the 30 years. However, general trends show that: from 1957–1980 there was no year in which there were more than 3 female-led firms receiving investments. From 1981–1987 the frequency range was 4–33. The peak of 33 was in 1987 representing 4.1% of the investments reported, coincident with the highpoint of the 1980s venture capital market. During this year 547 investments were reported by male-led firms (223 were unidentifiable).

Between 1988 and 1998 the number of investments in women-led firms ranged from a low of 9 in 1993 to ever increasing numbers of 43 (3.8% of deals) in 1996; to 52 (3.5%) in 1997, and 54 (4.1%) in 1998. This data suggests female-led firms are participating in the recent overall upswing in venture capital funding (Timmons and Bygrave 1997). In fact, the percentages shown here are slightly higher than reported in the popular press—which, as noted above, stated that approximately 30 women-owned businesses were funded by venture capital (or 2.5% of the total). Table 1 presents an aggregate of this time period for the frequency of venture capital investments.

Are there variations in venture capital funded men-and women-led businesses by industrial sector?

In order to examine differences in gender by industrial sector, we examined the frequency distribution and conducted chi-squared-tests on those for

Table 1. Frequency of firm acquisition of venture capital from 1988–1998.

	Frequency	Percent	Valid percent	Cumulative percent
Male	4016	48.4	48.4	48.4
Female	290	3.5	3.5	51.9
Unidentified	3992	48.1	48.1	100.0
Total	8298	100.0	100.0	

which gender was determined. As table 2 shows, no investments were made in either agriculture or mining sectors. Additionally, no investments were made in women-led firms in construction, public administration, or finance, insurance, real estate (FIRE) sectors. Women-led businesses were more often found in the service sector and male-led businesses were more often found in the manufacturing sector.

The characteristics of the frequency distribution are supported by the results of the t-tests reported in table 3 and show significant differences

Table 2. Frequency of firm acquisition of venture capital funding by gender and industry from 1988–1998.

Industry	Male (No./%)	Female (No./%)	Total	Chi-Squared/ significance
Construction	3	0	3	0.338
	0.1	0		0.625
Manufacturing	1097	77	1174	1.817
	40.3	35.6		0.178
Transportation	1	1	2	5.342
	0	0.5		0.021
Wholesale	152	10	162	0.351
	5.6	4.6		0.553
Retail	62	7	69	0.808
	2.3	3.2		0.369
FIRE	0	0	0	na
	0	0		
Services	1405	121	1526	1.540
	51.6	56.0		0.215
Public admin.	1	0	1	0.079
	0	0		0.778
Total	2721	216	2937	
	99.9	99.9		

Differences in sample size are due to missing data. Data is presented only for firms for which gender of owner is identifiable and SIC code is reported.

Table 3. Results of t-tests on industrial sector (SIC) by gender, years 1988–1998.

Variable	Male Mean	SD	N	Female Mean	SD	N	T-value
Agriculture	0.0000	0.0000	2721	0.0000	0.0000	216	[a]
Mining	0.0000	0.0000	2721	0.0000	0.0000	216	[a]
Construction	1.103E-03	3.319E-02	2721	0.0000	0.0000	216	0.488
Manufacturing	0.4032	0.4906	2721	0.3565	0.4801	216	1.348
Trans/comm	3.675E-04	1.017E-02	2721	4.630E-03	6.804E-02	216	−2.313**
Wholesale	5.586E-02	0.2297	2721	4.630E-02	0.2106	216	0.593
Retail	2.279E-02	0.1492	2721	3.241E-02	0.1775	216	−0.898
FIRE	0.0000	0.0000	2721	0.0000	0.0000	216	[a]
Services	0.5164	0.4998	2721	0.5602	0.4975	216	−1.241
Public admin	3.675E-04	1.917E-02	2721	0.0000	0.0000	216	0.282

*$p < 0.05$ **$p < 0.01$ ***$p < 0.001$ (two-tailed tests).
[a]T-values could not be computed for either agriculture or mining sectors since there are no firms in these cells and thus the standard deviations of both groups are zero.

between the genders in only one industrial sector, transportation/ communications.

Do stages of investment for venture capital vary for men and women led venture capital funded businesses?

As reported in table 4, we classified the firms by stage of investment for the years 1988–1998. Significant differences between the genders were found in the early stage and for buyout/acquisition investments. The majority (62.8%) of investments in women-led businesses were provided as seed capital while 55.3% of all VC investments in firms led by men were made in the seed round. The buy-out acquisition stage represented approximately 14% of all investments in male-led businesses, but not quite 8% of those made in women-led firms. Expansion and later stage investments were very similar in number for both male and female led firms.

Results of the t-tests reported in table 5 support that the differences found are significant in two of the investment stages. Women are more likely to report 'early stage' whereas men are significantly more likely to report buyout/acquisition investments.

Table 4. Frequency of firm acquisition of venture capital by gender and stage from 1988–1998.

Stage	Male (No./%)	Female (No./%)	Total	Chi-Squared/ Significance
Early stage	2221	182	2403	6.050
	55.3	62.8	55.8	0.014**
Expansion	840	61	901	0.002
	20.9	21.0	20.9	0.965
Later stage	347	23	370	0.175
	8.6	7.9	8.6	0.675
Buyout/acquisition	587	23	610	9.959
	14.6	7.9	14.2	0.002***
Other	18	1	19	0.066
	0.4	0.3	0.4	0.797
Total				

Differences in sample size are due to missing data. Data is presented only for firms for which gender of owner is identifiable and SIC code is reported.

Table 5. Results of t-tests on investment stage by gender, years 1988–1998.

Variable	Male Mean	SD	N	Female Mean	SD	N	T-value
Early stage	0.5533	0.4972	4014	0.6276	0.4843	290	−2.461**
Expansion	0.2093	0.4068	4014	0.2103	0.4083	290	−0.44
Later stage	8.645E-02	0.2811	4014	7.931E-02	0.2707	290	0.419
Buyout/ acquisition	0.1462	0.3534	4014	7.931E-02	0.2707	290	3.159***
Other	4.484E-03	6.682E-02	4014	3.448E-03	5.872E-02	290	0.257

Discussion

Even this first phase of our study shows that the proportion of venture capital investments in women-led businesses over the past 30+ years is extremely small. Earlier reports note that about 2% of the deals receiving venture capital were women-led firms and our data shows overall similar results. Whereas the data in this study shows the overall percentage for the past 30 years as 2.4%, the last few years provides indications of a positive and increasing trend with women-led ventures receiving up to 4.1% in 1998. Nevertheless, the proportion of women-led businesses receiving venture capital is still extremely small considering their overall participation in the US economy, owning almost 40% of all businesses. This raises serious questions about women's access to growth and expansion capital. Why is this number so small? Considering that barriers in women's ability to start ventures, to enter any industrial sector, and even obtain debt financing have nearly disappeared (Coleman 2000), this significant disparity is of great interest, especially given that the role of venture capital in innovation, job creation, economic growth and industrial renewal is recognized, and that venture backed companies play a significant role in the development of our modern industrial economy (Mason and Harrison 1999).

The lack of significant differences between industrial sectors supports the strength of the supply side of the industry. Venture capital dollars are attracted to specific industries in order to best maintain the risk/reward ratios most desirable to the equity investors. In part, the lack of gender differences is due to the extremely small participation of women in agriculture, construction, finance, insurance and real estate. Notably, the predominant industry choices of female entrepreneurs appear to be mismatched with the industry preferences of venture capitalists. Female entrepreneurs historically were heavily concentrated in the service and retail sectors. As of 1990, women-owned businesses comprised less than 10% of all firms in construction, mining and manufacturing; and agriculture, forestry and fishing (*The State of Small Business* 1992: 265). In the wholesale and retail trade, and transportation, communications and public utilities, women comprised less than 15%. Only in the finance, insurance and real estate, and services sectors did the share of women-owned businesses reach 20%. Statistics show that women are acquiring or staring businesses in construction, wholesale trade, transportation, agribusiness and manufacturing at up to 3 times their male counterparts (NFWBO 1999). For instance, between 1987 and 1992 the numbers of women-owned firms grew by 94% in construction, 87% in wholesale and 77% in transportation (*The State of Small Business* 1992). However, progress is slow. By 1998 70% of women-owned businesses were still in service and retail sectors, with an additional 10.2% in fire, insurance and real estate (SBA 1998).

However, the significant difference in transportation and communications is of interest. Arguably, these might be considered technology businesses. Historically technology businesses are responsible for innovations, and typically grow faster and bigger (Kirchhoff 1994). There is still a question about the participation of women in technology businesses, as founders and/or leaders. A report by the National Women's Business Council (NWBC 1998) shows women are more often serving in management positions, the change being 21% in 1998–1999. While the majority of these are not venture capital funded, it might be expected that more women led internet ventures will be seeking capital in the future, and whether or not there will be differences in amount and stage of funding between men and women-led ventures in the same technology sectors remains to be seen.

Consideration of stage of development shows that the bulk of women-led businesses are being funded at early stage, with a greater number of male-led businesses receiving buy/out and acquisition funding. It is possible that women led firms are younger, consistent with data showing the growth in women's business ownership over the past decade (US SBA 1998). Earlier stage investment might be considered more 'risky' especially if the venture is in the market and product development stage, because the company has not entered its accelerating growth stage, most often still incurring losses (Mason and Harrison 1999). What is less clear is whether or not there might be disparities in the amount of funding based on gender, due to perceived risk and/or diseconomies of extra due diligence as suggested by Brophy (1997). This study did not have the data to investigate whether the amounts of seed funding were equivalent by gender, which is a question for future investigation. This suggests that even for women led growth-oriented firms, as in those likely to be funded by venture capital, growth by acquisition may not a primary strategy. This is definitely an area to be pursued with future research.

Conclusions, implications, and future research

We sought to map the past and current state of venture capital financing of women led businesses. This research provides initial results of our continuing analysis. Our methodology involved re-coding, re-formatting and examining each record in an extensive data set of 21 845 records by gender and firm. This resulted in a data set of, resulting in 16 412 firm records. Although this process was conducted manually by two separate researchers, there is the possibility of coding error, considering the size of the data set, its age, and the multiple parties that entered the data. However, with these limitations in mind, in this first attempt to analyse venture capital investments by gender, we believe our findings are notable and important.

Overall, we find that the percentage of investments in women-led businesses over the past 30 years is indeed extremely small. Because an extremely small number of investments were made in women-led firms prior to 1988, we limited our analysis to the current decade, 1988–1998. However, our data suggests that the trend is changing very slowly—recent statistics show more women have acquired venture capital in the past 5 years than in previous years. The disproportionately low level of female participation in venture capital financing has been reported in the popular press, but we found the industry distribution of those investments actually made were surprising.

We propose three theoretical approaches to further investigating potential disparities in venture capital funded ventures by gender. The structural barriers approach suggests that women-led ventures might face either institutional or social network barriers making it more difficult for them to gain access to institutional venture capital funders. A study comparing the process of deal origination and screening by gender of the leader would provide information about whether this is the case. Alternatively, the human capital approach might study the leadership skills, background and social learning of men and women-led ventures in the same industry to determine if there are differences in terms of size, stage and growth of investment. Finally, the strategic choice approach could be studied by examining growth aspirations and product/market strategies of men and women-led ventures seeking venture capital and actually funded. This would yield information as to whether the growth and competitive goals of men and women-led firms actually differed. In addition, further analysis of other questions regarding the size and stage of investments, geographic dispersion of investments, composition of management team, goals and performance for women-led businesses independently and compared to men, both in the US and in Europe, should occur in the future. While our study focused exclusively on the US, we were unable to identify a single study on venture capital from Europe that included or analysed funding of women-led ventures. Clearly this is an important research opportunity. Women are active participants in the global economy, and it is important to understand the ways they contribute, in addition to any barriers and opportunities existing in these environments

Notes

1. In the US, 72% of the women-owned firms operating in 1991 were still in business 3 years later. This compares favourably with 66% survival rate for all firms. From Weeks, J., 1998 NFWBO. A Study on Women Entrepreneurs in SMEs in APEC Region: Report from the United States. December, 1998.
2. National Foundation for Women Business Owners, *1996 Facts on Women-Owned Businesses: State Trends.*
3. Literature and statistics are reported for women-owned businesses, however, when a venture receives venture capital, most often the founder/manager must give up a significant portion of ownership. It is more appropriate in this context to refer to ventures as women-led, even though it is likely they still maintain some ownership, we cannot be sure.

References

Aldrich, H., 1989, Networking among women entrepreneurs, in O. Hagan, C. Rivchun, D. Sexton (eds) *Women-Owned Businesses* (NY: Praeger), pp. 103–132.
Amit, R., Glosten, L. and Muller, E., 1990, Entrepreneurial ability, venture investments and risk sharing. *Management Science*, **36**, 1232–1245.

Baker, T., Aldrich, H. and Liou, N., 1997, Invisible entrepreneurs: the neglect of women business owners by mass media and scholarly journals in the US. *Entrepreneurship and Regional Development*, **9**, 221–238.

Bandura, A., 1977, *Social Learning Theory* (Englewood Cliffs, NJ: Prentice Hall).

Becker, G., 1964, *Human Capital* (NY: Columbia University Press).

Boston Globe, 2/14/99.

British Venture Capital Association, 2000, *Key Facts About Venture Capital in the UK*. (London: BVCA).

Brophy, D., 1992, Financing the new venture: a report on recent research, in D. L. Sexton and J. Kasarda (eds) *The State of the Art of Entrepreneurship* (Boston: PWS Kent), pp. 387–401.

Brophy, D., 1997, Financing the growth of entrepreneurial firms, in D. L. Sexton and R. Smilor (eds) *Entrepreneurship 2000* (Chicago, ILL: Upstart Publishing), pp. 5–28.

Bruno, A. and Tyebjee, T., 1985, The entrepreneurs' search for capital. *Journal of Business Venturing*, **1**, 61–74.

Brush, C. G., 1992, Research on women business owners: past trends, a new perspective and future directions. *Entrepreneurship Theory and Practice*, **16**, 5–30.

Brush, C. G., 1997, Women-owned businesses: obstacles and opportunities, *Journal of Developmental Entrepreneurship*, **2**, 1–24.

Brush, C. G., 1998, A resource perspective on women's entrepreneurship: research, relevance and recognition, Proceedings of the Organization for Economic Cooperation and Development (OECD) *Conference on Women in Small and Medium-Sized Enterprises: A Major Force in Innovation and Job Creation* (Paris, France: OECD), pp. 155–168.

Busenitz, Moesel, Fiet and Barney, 1997, The framing of perceptions of fairness in the relationship between venture capitalists and new venture teams. *Journal of Business Venturing*, **3**, 249–258.

Buttner, E. H. and Rosen, B. H., 1988, Bank loan officer's perceptions of characteristics of men, women and successful entrepreneurs. *Journal of Business Venturing*, **3**, 249–258.

Bygrave, W. D., 1992, Venture capital returns in the 1980's, in D. L. Sexton and J. Kasarda (eds.) *The State of the Art of Entrepreneurship* (Boston: PWS Kent), pp. 438–462.

Carter, N. M. and Allen, K. R., 1997, Size determinants of women-owned businesses: choice or barriers to resources? *Entrepreneurship and Regional Development*, **9**, 211–220.

Carter, N. M., Williams, M. and Reynolds, P. D., 1997, Discontinuance among new firms in retail: the influence of initial resources, strategy and gender. *Journal of Business Venturing*, **12**, 125–146.

Churchill, N. C. and Lewis, V., 1983, The five stages of small business growth. *The Harvard Business Review* (May/June), 30–50.

Cliff, J. E., 1998, Does one size fit all? Exploring the relationship between attitudes towards growth, gender and business size. *Journal of Business Venturing*, **13**, 523–542.

Coleman, S., 2000, Access to capital and terms of credit: a comparison of men and women—owned businesses. *Journal of Small Business Management*, **38**, 37–52.

Ducheneaut, B., 1997, *Women Entrepreneurs in SME's. Report prepared for the OECD Conference on Women Entrepreneurs in Small and Medium Sized Enterprises: A Major Force for Innovation and Job Creation* (Paris, France: OECD).

Elango, B., Fried, V., Hisrich, R. and Polonchek, A., 1995, How venture capital firms differ. *Journal of Business Venturing*, **10**, 157–79.

European Venture Capital Association, 1999, *Regional Investment Patterns* (EVCA: Zaventem).

Fay, M. and Williams, L., 1993, Gender bias and the availability of business loans. *Journal of Business Venturing*, **8**, 363–376.

Fiet, J., 1995, Reliance upon informants in the venture capital industry, *Journal of Business Venturing*, **10**, 195–224.

Fineberg, S., 1998a, Fund-raising blitzes in first half. *Venture Capital Journal*, August, 38–40.

Fineberg, S., 1998b, Venture capital financings reach another high. *Venture Capital Journal*, July, 37–40.

Fried, V. and Hisrich, R. D., 1988, Venture capital research: past, present and future. *Entrepreneurship Theory and Practice*, **13**, 15–29.

Gilligan, C., 1982, *In a Different Voice: Psychological Theory and Women's Development* (Cambridge, MA: Harvard University Press).

Greene, P. and Brown, T., 1997, 'Resource needs and the dynamic capitalism typology. *Journal of Business Venturing*, **7**, 8–17.

Gupta, A. K. and Sapienza, H., 1992, Determinants of venture capital firms' preferences regarding the industry diversity and geographic scope of their investments. *Journal of Business Venturing*, **7**, 347–362.

Hall, J. and Hofer, C., 1993, Venture capitalist's decision criteria in new venture evaluation. *Journal of Business Venturing*, **8**, 25–42.

Hisrich, R. and Jancowicz, A. 1990, Intuition in venture capital decisions: an exploratory study using a new technique. *Journal of Business Venturing*, **5**, 49–62.

Johnson, S. and Storey, D., 1995, Male and female entrepreneurs and their businesses: a comparative study, in S. Allen and C. Truman (eds) *Women in Business. Perspectives on Women Entrepreneurs* (London: Routeledge Press), pp. 70–85.

Kirchhoff, B., 1994, *Entrepreneurship and Dynamic Capitalism* (Westport CT: Praeger Press).

MacMillan, I., Siegel, R. and Subba Narasimha, P., 1985, Criteria used by venture capitalists to evaluate new venture proposals. *Journal of Business Venturing*, **1**, 119–128.

MacMillan, I., Zeman, L. and Subba Narasimha, P., 1987, Criteria distinguishing successful from unsuccessful ventures in the venture screening process. *Journal of Business Venturing*, **2**, 122–137.

Mahot, P., 1988, Funding for Women: a real – though disputed – problem, in *Women Entrepreneurs in Small and Medium Enterprises* (Paris : OECD), pp. 217–225.

Manigart, S., 1994, What drives the creation of a venture capital firm? *Journal of Business Venturing*, **9**, S25–S41

Mason, C. and Harrison, R., 1999, Venture capital: rationale, aims, and scope. *Venture Capital*, **1**, 1–46.

Moore, D. P. and Buttner, E. H., 1997, *Women Entrepreneurs: Moving Beyond the Glass Ceiling* (Thousand Oaks, CA: Sage Publications).

Muzyka, D., Birley, S. and Lelux, B., 1996, Trade-offs in the investment decisions of European venture capitalists. *Journal of Business Venturing*, **11**, 273–287.

National Foundation for Women Business Owners, 1996, *Women Owned Businesses in the United States: 1996 Fact Sheets* (Silver Spring, MD: NFWBO).

National Foundation for Women Business Owners, 1998, *Business Financing & Confidence Survey* (Silver Spring, MD: NFWBO).

National Foundation for Women Business Owners and Catalyst, 1998, *Paths to Entrepreneurship: New Directions for Women in Business* (Silver Spring, MD: NFWBO).

National Foundation for Women Business Owners, 1998, *Capital, Credit and Financing: An Update* (Silver Spring, MD: NFWBO).

National Venture Capital Association, 1999; http://www.nvca..org

National Women's Business Council, 1998; http://www.nwbc.org

Norton, E., 1995, Venture capital as an alternative means to allocate capital: an agency-theoretic view. *Entrepreneurship Theory and Practice*, **20**, 19–30.

Ooghe, H., Manigart, S. and Fassian, Y 1991, Growth patterns in the European venture capital industry, *Journal of Business Venturing*, **6**, 381–404.

Pratt, S. E., 1998, The organized venture capital community, in *Pratt's Guide to Venture Capital Sources*, edition 75–79 (NY: Securities Data Publishing).

Phillips, B. and Dennis, W. D., 1997, Databases for small business analysis, in D. L. Sexton and J. Kasarda (eds) *The State of the Art of Entrepreneurship* (Boston: PWS Kent), pp. 341–359.

Riding, A. and Swift, C., 1990, Women business owners and terms of credit: some empirical findings of the Canadian experience. *Journal of Business Venturing*, **5**, 327–340.

Rosenstein J., Bruno, W., Bygrave, W. and Taylor, N., 1993, The CEO, venture capitalists and the board. *Journal of Business Venturing*, **8**, 99–114.

Ruhnkha, J., Feldman, H. and Dean, T., 1992, The living dead phenomenon in venture capital investments. *Journal of Business Venturing*, **7**, 137–156.

Sahlman, W. and Stevenson, H., 1985, Capital market myopia. *Journal of Business Venturing*, **1**, 7–30.

Sandberg, W., Schweiger, D. M. and Hofer, C. 1988, The use of verbal protocols in determining venture capitalists decision process. *Entrepreneurship Theory and Practice*, **13**, 7–20.

Sapienza, H., 1992, When do venture capitalists add value? *Journal of Business Venturing*, **7**, 9–28.

Sapienza, H. and Korsgaard, M. A., 1996, Procedural justice in entrepreneur-investor relations. *Academy of Management Journal*, **39**, 54–74.

Seegull, F., 1998, Female entrepreneurs' access to equity capital. *Harvard Business School*, working paper.

Sexton, D. L. and Bowman-Upton, N., 1991, *Entrepreneurship: Creativity and Growth* (New York: MacMillan).

Small Business Administration, 1996, *The State of Small Business* (Washington, DC: US Government Printing Office).

Swarz, J., 1991, The future of the venture capital industry. *Journal of Business Venturing*, **6**, 89–92.

Sweeting, R., 1991, UK venture capital funds and the funding of new technology based-businesses: processes and relationships. *Journal of Management Studies*, **28**, 601–622.

Timmons, J. A. and Sapienza, H., 1992, Venture capital: the decade ahead, in D. L. Sexton and J. Kasarda (eds) *The State of the Art of Entrepreneurship* (Boston: PWS Kent), pp. 402–437.

Timmons, J. A. and Bygrave, W. D., 1997, Venture capital: reflections and projections, in D. L. Sexton and R. Smilor (eds) *Entrepreneurship 2000* (Chicago, IL: Upstart Publishing), pp. 29–46.

Thomas, P., 1991, When Mars decides to invest in Venus's promising start-up. *Wall Street Journal*, February 24, 1999, B1.

Thompson Financial Securities Data., 1999, Venture investments reach a record. National Venture Capital Association; http://nvca.org/80299nr.html

United Nations, 1991, *The World's Women 1970–1990: Trends and Statistics* (New York: United Nations).

US Small Business Administration, 1998, Women in business, office of advocacy, APEC women entrepreneurs report: United States/first draft, 28 December, Washington, DC.

US Small Business Administration (1982–1996) *The State of Small Business: A Report of the President* (Washington DC: US Government Printing Office).

Watson, W., Ponthieu L. and Critelli, J., 1995, Team interpersonal effectiveness in venture partnerships and its connection to perceived success. *Journal of Business Venturing*, **10**, 393–411.

Weeks, J. R., 1998, A study on women entrepreneurs in SMEs in the APEC region: report from the United States. Asia-Pacific Economic Cooperation Project No. SME 02/98 (Silver Spring, MD: NFWBO).

Wright, M. and Robbie, K., 1998, Venture capital and private equity: a review and synthesis. *Journal of Business Finance & Accounting*, **25**, 521–570.

Wright, M. Robbie, K. and Ennew, C., 1997, Venture capitalists and serial entrepreneurs. *Journal of Business Venturing*, **12**, 227–249.

Zacharakis, A. and Meyer, D., 1995, A lack of insight: do venture capitalists really understand their own decision processes? *Journal of Business Venturing*, **13**, 57–76.

Part V
Strategic Choice

[20]

DISCONTINUANCE AMONG NEW FIRMS IN RETAIL: THE INFLUENCE OF INITIAL RESOURCES, STRATEGY, AND GENDER

NANCY M. CARTER
Marquette University

MARY WILLIAMS
Widener University

PAUL D. REYNOLDS
Babson College

EXECUTIVE SUMMARY

Women-owned businesses represent one of the fastest growing segments of the U.S. economy. Their rate has increased more than six-fold since 1970. Despite this growth rate, the number of firms owned by women still lags behind that of men, and the sales and income of women-owned firms are significantly lower than those of men-owned firms.

The discrepancy between the number of businesses owned by women and men and their economic success has been a popular theme among researchers. Some have suggested that performance differentials result from disparate structural positions women and men occupy in work and society, whereas others attribute the differences to deep rooted interpersonal orientations.

This study examines whether the performance differences can be explained by variations in initial resources and founding strategy. We test whether women have fewer start-up resources, and if they do,

Address correspondence to Nancy M. Carter, College of Business Administration, Marquette University, Milwaukee, WI 53233.

The initial data collection in Pennsylvania, completed in 1986 at the University of Pennsylvania Snider Entrepreneurial Center, was sponsored by the Appalachia Regional Commission and the Pennsylvania Department of Commerce. The initial data collection in Minnesota, completed in 1986–87 at the University of Minnesota for Urban and Regional Affairs, was sponsored by 10 state, regional, and local agencies in Minnesota. The 1991–92 follow-up data collection has been a joint effort of the Marquette University Center for the Study of Entrepreneurship, University of Minnesota Carlson Entrepreneurial Center, and University of Pennsylvania Snider Entrepreneurial Center.

The authors thank Howard E. Aldrich, Candida Brush, Patricia G. Greene, Margaret Greer, and A. Rebecca Reuber for insightful comments on earlier versions of the article.

0883-9026/97/$17.00
PII S0883-9026(96)00033-X

126   N.M. CARTER ET AL.

whether they can compensate for these deficiencies through their founding strategy. Recent work in social psychology argues that strategic choice is shaped by experiences to which individuals have been subjected, and that women and men have fundamentally different socialization experiences. We test the assumption that if the strategy that women-owners adopt exploits the unique capabilities they derive from their social-ization, they can improve the performance of their firms and ward off discontinuance.

We examine the discontinuance pattern of 203 new firms in the retail industry. This industry was selected because women entrepreneurs often choose to operate in this industry, giving us a basis for com-paring women-owned and men-owned firms. We classify the firms into six strategy archetypes. The arche-types range from a broad focus where founders emphasize multiple strategic foci simultaneously to nar-rowly targeted differentiation strategies. We assume that the experiential base of women entrepreneurs limits their successfully executing pricing strategies. We hypothesize that women-led firms decrease the odds of discontinuing by adopting one of two strategy types: (1) narrow differentiation strategies that seek to satisfy a narrow segment of the market and that do not rely on "pricing," or (2) broad "generalists" strategies that emphasize service and quality but not pricing, and take advantage of women's capability for handling multiple stakeholders simultaneously.

The results offer support for using an integrative model to explain the performance of women-owned firms. Women-owned firms have higher odds of discontinuing than men-owned firms, and women appear to have fewer resources to start their businesses. Women owners were less likely to have instrumen-tal experience from working in the retail industry and start their businesses on a smaller scale then men but were no less likely then their male counterparts to have access to credit from formal financial institu-tions, or to be disadvantaged by starting fewer other new businesses. Despite some apparent situational disadvantage, resource deficiencies do not appear to affect the odds of women-owned businesses discon-tinuing as much as they do men-owned initiatives.

The findings indicate support for the supposition that women owners can use founding strategy to decrease the odds of discontinuing business. A broad generalists strategy that represents a multi-focused approach was found to benefit women-owned businesses most. Overall, the results suggest that men use prior business experience and human capital to affect the survival status of their businesses. Women ap-pear to find strategic choice more beneficial.

Future research is recommended to further elaborate the integrative model. Special attention should be given to developing alternatives to measures traditionally used in gender research. Many researchers charge that those typically used reflect male derived measures. Similarly, greater attention should be given to understanding why the scale of women-owned businesses at start-up is substantially smaller than that of men, since scale has been shown to be related to subsequent growth and survival. © 1997 Elsevier Science Inc.

INTRODUCTION

Accumulating evidence documents the rapid rise in the portion of women-owned businesses in the U.S. economy. Their share of all businesses grew by over 550% between 1972 and 1987 (Clark and James 1992). Despite this proportionate growth, by 1987 women owned only one in three firms, and the economic scale of their businesses was substantially smaller than those owned by men (Clark and James 1992; Devine 1994).

The discrepancy between the number and economic success of women- and men-owned firms has stimulated considerable commentary among researchers and public policy makers. Some have suggested that performance differentials result from women having fewer re-sources or assets with which to create a firm (Cromie and Birley 1991), less access to opportu-nities, different managerial styles and intentions (Brush 1992; Kaplan 1988), and less benefi-cial social networks to assist the start-up process (Reese 1992). Others, however, have documented few differences between the needs and experiences of men and women entrepreneurs that would explain the differences in firm performance (Buttner and Rosen 1988; Kalleberg and Leicht 1991; Sexton and Bowman-Upton 1990).

Inconsistencies in the empirical findings have been attributed to inadequate research design, but varying assumptions also characterize the research efforts. Some have assumed that performance differences relate to variations in structural positions women and men occupy in work and society, whereas others attribute differences to deep rooted interpersonal orientations. Liou and Aldrich (1995) refer to these two perspectives as situational versus dispositional. Situational proponents argue that gender-based differences can be attributed to variations in the power and opportunities accorded men and women. According to this perspective, women are seen as having been denied equal access to opportunities in labor markets and organizations and thus have been hindered in acquiring the skills and capabilities necessary to compete at the same level with men. Once equal access is ensured, gender-based differences in performance seemingly disappear.

Alternatively, dispositional explanations contend that women and men have different experiential backgrounds and ways of thinking that derive from variations in their education and socialization patterns. These differences are seen as shaping the way women and men construct and interpret reality and influence the formation of their values and intentions. According to this perspective, variations in performance can be attributed to owner's motives and intentions.

Until recently, the situational and dispositional perspectives have been posed as competing models. Researchers now theorize that a collaborative or integrative approach that incorporates both perspectives offers a better explanation of gender-based differences. For example, from an extensive review of the literature, Liou and Aldrich (1995) concluded that both disposition and situation shape women's development of a relational competence. This competence, which they define as "the ability to develop and maintain long-term associations with others on the basis of mutual trust, exchange, and support," may affect the strategies women adopt and ways in which they operate their businesses (1995, p. 1). Fischer, Reuber, and Dyke (1993) take the argument further and suggest that women's socialization processes may lead them to manage their firms in ways that offset sex-based discrimination or systematic bias. In other words, women may use dispositional characteristics to overcome situational barriers. The issue then, is not which of the two models best explains and predicts performance, but how they contribute jointly to a more robust explanation of the phenomenon.

THEORY AND HYPOTHESES

In this study we adopt an integrative model to examine performance differences between women- and men-owned businesses in the retail industry. We test whether dispositional characteristics can be used to overcome or moderate deficiencies that arise from situational differences. Recognizing that dispositional characteristics are the accumulation of influences beginning in childhood and spanning adulthood and work career, we use the implementation and execution of the firm's "founding strategy" as a surrogate measure. We believe this is one aspect of management where women's reliance on dispositional characteristics will be most obvious.

Research has established the linkage between strategy and new ventures' performance and survival (Sandberg and Hofer 1987; Romanelli 1989; Keeley and Roure 1990; McDougall and Robinson 1990; Stearns et al. 1995). Implicit in these studies is the argument that an effective strategy hinges on the alignment between the organization's internal capabilities and resources and challenges offered by the external environment. For new ventures, the entrepreneur's human and financial capital are seen as major sources of the firm's internal capabilities. If the situational background of women results in them having fewer of these resources to start their businesses, the question becomes whether they exploit dispositional capabilities to compensate for the deficiencies. For example, to what extent might the relational competence identified by Liou and Aldrich (1995) be used by women to construct and implement a strategy for dealing with customers, competitors, and suppliers that effectively offsets other resource deficiencies?

We use the odds of discontinuing business as the measure of firm performance and data from new ventures in the retail industry. Businesses in retail were chosen for several reasons. First, new ventures founded by women are more prevalent in retail than in any other industry except service (Clark and James 1992; Zellner et al. 1994). This provides us with a sufficient number of women-led firms to compare with those founded by men. In some industries, (e.g., manufacturing), the paucity of women-owned firms precludes meaningful comparisons. Second, the retail industry has been characterized as having attenuated career tracks and lower capital requirements than other industries (except selected services) (Clark and James 1992). Thus, the resource requirements necessary to establish businesses in this industry should be attainable by both women and men. Third, we limit our sample to one industry, because research shows that significant strategy-industry interactions exist in predicting new firm performance and survival (Keeley and Roure 1990; Sandberg and Hofer 1987; Stearns et al. 1995).

Start-Up Resources

A key supposition in entrepreneurship research is that a firm's resources at start-up are critical determinants of success and survival. Research has focused on two sets of resources, those intangible assets individuals bring with them to the entrepreneurial process in the form of human capital, and the entrepreneur's ability to secure tangible resources from the environment (e.g., capital, partners, employees, suppliers).

Human Capital

Human capital derives from investments individuals make in themselves, often through education (formal and occupational experiences) and training. Presumably, the more specific the human capital to the nature of the new firm start-up, the higher the likelihood of success. Researchers have found a positive relationship between entrepreneurs' prior experience in the industry with success of the new firm (Cooper and Bruno 1977; Van de Ven, Hudson, and Schroeder 1984).

In orthodox economic theory, the acquisition of human capital is viewed as almost entirely under the individual's control, but barriers are seen as impeding women in acquiring adequate levels of human capital. Research supporting this hypothesis finds that in comparison to men, women entrepreneurs are less likely to have experiences gained from owning prior businesses or working in private firms (Cromie and Birley 1991); are more likely to have pursued undergraduate studies in liberal arts rather than technical disciplines like business or engineering (Honing-Haftel and Martin 1986); have careers that are more frequently interrupted (Kaplan 1988); and are less likely to be part of start-up teams for high-growth new firms (Reynolds 1993). To the extent that deficiencies in human capital render new firms vulnerable, those begun by women are more likely to have higher odds of discontinuing than those started by men.

Access to Resources

In addition to systemic barriers, overt discrimination has been viewed as restricting women's access to critical opportunity structures and resources in the external environment. Two sets of resources particularly critical for start-up efforts are access to financial resources and level of human resources. Access to capital markets has been regarded as among the most important resources denied women. Tigges and Green (1994) suggested three reasons why women may be disadvantaged in capital markets: (1) they tend to have less experience and equity in their businesses than men; (2) they may be discriminated against by resource lenders on the basis of outmoded gender role beliefs; and (3) their belief that they will receive differential treatment may reduce the rate of lending applications among women business owners.

Empirical studies that have tested these assumptions present mixed findings. Some researchers have found that women entrepreneurs have access to less external financing, weaker collateral positions, and believe that they have been discriminated against or received unequal treatment by financing institutions or other resource providers (Goffee and Scase 1983; Hisrich and Brush 1984; Olm, Carsrud, and Alvey 1988). Others, however, have found little evidence of obvious discrimination against women (Buttner and Rosen 1988). Particularly when samples of men and women have been matched on key variables like business age, firm size, and growth rate, few differences in resource access have been identified (Riding and Swift 1990).

The number of employees and whether there are start-up partners also have been seen as critical resources. Birley (1986) demonstrated the importance of the scale of human resources in her finding that the employment size at start-up influences the extent to which businesses will survive and grow. Typically, the scale of women-owned firms has been smaller than that of men-owned firms. This difference has been attributed to the motives or intentions of women owners. Women have been viewed as focusing on goals other than growth and economic performance (Brush 1992). But if women have been limited in acquiring adequate financial resources to start their businesses either because they haven't taken on partners to increase the resource base or are denied access to formal lending, they would seem less able to take on costs associated with hiring and training employees.

H1: High levels of human capital and access to outside resources decrease odds of businesses discontinuing.

H2: Women-owned firms have lower levels of human resources and less access to financial resources from outside sources than men-owned businesses, increasing the odds they will discontinue.

Women's Style

Over the past two decades a considerable body of research has addressed women's segregation in the workplace. Increasingly, interests concerned with determining women's "relative worth" within organizations have turned to identifying the styles of leading and managing exhibited by women, and why those styles are particularly useful at this time in history (Astin and Leland 1991). Sheppard's (1992) work on how women in management view themselves as women and as organizational members is representative of this trend. Studying a small, but purposive sample, Sheppard found that women managers and professionals view themselves as "humanistic" and "personal oriented" as opposed to "cost oriented." Their management style was described as being service oriented with an emphasis on persuasion, appeasement, and maintaining good relations. Sheppard characterized women's decision-making as having a strong "relational" component and as being embedded within a particular context.

Sheppard's findings complement those of earlier studies. Neider (1987) found that women perceive themselves as having better human relations skills, which allow them to deal effectively with employees and customers. Others have found that women have a "feminine" style of leadership, which fosters participative decision-making and may translate into employee satisfaction and increased performance (Chaganti 1986; Hisrich and Brush 1984). Some have speculated that the skills women attain in running a household and the broad range of experiences they acquire as they follow spouses and raise children result in a diverse experiential base that transfers to their business management style (Scott 1986).

One area where differences resulting from variations in women's and men's socialization patterns may be most evident is in their choice and execution of the firm's competitive strategy. Recent work on information-processing theories from social psychology argue that strategic choice is limited by individual's belief structures or cognitive maps (Walsh and Fahey 1986). Belief structures are shaped by the experiences to which individuals have been subjected. If women develop distinctive styles of leadership or management as a result of their particular socialization patterns, we would expect their implementation and execution of strategy to reflect those unique competencies.

Predicting precisely how the choice and execution of strategy differs across gender requires speculation. Few empirical studies have related the competencies or managerial styles men and women derive from their socialization patterns to strategy and new firm performance. We rely on related research to formulate hypotheses.

Mapping Style to Strategy

Differences in the attributes that result from women's and men's socialization patterns can be mapped to the distinction between "specialist" and "generalists" strategies. Researchers have used this classification scheme to predict appropriate strategies for new ventures. The specialist perspective maintains that new businesses should seek a niche in the marketplace where they can avoid direct competition with larger, more established firms. According to this perspective, new firms lack adequate resources for effective organizational learning, and this "liability of newness" (Stinchcombe 1965) limits the firms' ability to compete on the basis of price (Deeks 1976; Stegall, Steinmetz, and Kline 1976). Advocates of this perspective caution that new ventures should become specialists by targeting narrow market segments that have been overlooked by larger firms and serve those customers through specially designed, high quality products or services (Broom and Longenecker 1971; Cohen and Lindberg 1974; Hosmer 1957).

Alternatively, other researchers have argued that broad strategies will lead to better survival chances for new ventures. Biggadike (1976) contended that entrepreneurs must adopt an aggressive posture when entering markets and match the broad appeal offered by competitors. Researchers concurring with this generalists perspective have argued that new ventures penalize themselves unless they compete head to head with the market leaders, including competing on the basis of price (Cooper, Willard, and Woo 1986; MacMillan and Day 1987; Miller and Camp 1985). To successfully implement a pricing strategy requires the knowledge to achieve efficiencies and cost savings across the entire value chain of the firm's operation. Typically, the firm must keep its per unit costs low, minimize spending on unnecessary operating expenses, and have sufficient resources for broad-scale marketing (Porter 1985).

Predicting which of the two perspectives best prescribes strategies for women-owned businesses presents a dilemma. An essential distinction between the approaches concerns the firm's resource base. The generalists approach with its emphasis on pricing requires firms to have adequate resources to market effectively and knowledge of how to achieve cost-efficiencies in order to sustain adequate profits. The resources women bring to the start-up process appear insufficient for such an approach. Women have lower levels of instrumental skills gained from industry experience and fewer financial resources to achieve a sufficient presence in the marketplace. These deficiencies make it unlikely they can successfully execute a strategy that relies on pricing where adequate profits must be sustained by achieving cost efficiencies and marketing prowess.

Instead, their resource bases seem more amenable to a specialist strategy that relies on relational competencies. Narrow strategies that reflect a service orientation, emphasize a particular area of expertise or specialty, or target a narrow segment of the market would seem more judicious. Such strategies would exploit women's "cooperative network of relationships" while embedding them in market niches where they are less likely to attract the attention of larger competitors.

But does the generalists approach necessarily require an emphasis on pricing? The diverse skills women gain from integrating their "web-like" connections among family, work, and community (Brush 1992) argue for developing effective broad-based strategy. Broad strategies that emphasize quality, service, and responsiveness to the varying needs of diverse customer bases correspond closely to the socialization patterns of women. To the extent that broad strategies can be developed that avoid emphasizing pricing, women entrepreneurs should be able to compensate for resource deficiencies and increase the likelihood of their business's success or survival.

Research by Kalleberg and Leicht (1991) illustrates the dilemma in predicting whether women-owned firms are better suited for executing generalists or specialist strategies. They found that men were more likely to build a strategy around offering a wide range of products and services. However, only women-owned businesses that adopted the generalists strategy were less likely to have discontinued. Women were more likely to emphasize quality, but women who adopted this strategy were no more likely to have gone out of business than men who adopted a quality emphasis. Kalleberg and Leicht's (1991) findings may be attributable to a lack of statistical power. The discontinuance rate among the businesses in their sample was very low. They concluded that their data collection strategy resulted in successful, viable businesses being overrepresented in the sample. Second, the firms Kalleberg and Leicht studied were not necessarily new ventures, our interest in the present study. The average age of the companies they studied was 13.19 years. It is unclear whether the strategy differences they detected arise from variations in the firm's initial founding strategy or strategic adaptations entrepreneurs made over time.

To investigate whether women-owned new ventures use a broad generalists strategy to compensate for resource deficiencies or adopt narrow specialist strategies, we offer competing hypotheses. We reason that strategy affects the performance and survival of new firms, and if within the same industry women-owned and men-owned businesses behave differently after variations in resources have been controlled, gender-role socialization accounts for the differences. We contend that strategies that avoid price competition will lower the odds of women-owned businesses discontinuing and allow women-owned firms to overcome resource deficiencies. But because the literature presents contradictory evidence for predicting women's strategy choice beyond its insight on price, we adopt an exploratory approach.

H3: Strategy decreases odds of businesses discontinuing.

H4: Women-owned firms that use a "specialist" strategy that seeks to satisfy a narrow segment of the market and does not rely on "pricing" have lower odds of discontinuing.

H5: Women-owned firms that use a broad "generalists" strategy that emphasizes service and quality and does not emphasize pricing have lower odds of discontinuing.

H6: Women-owned firms use strategic choice to lower odds of discontinuing and reduce resource deficiencies.

METHODS

Sources of Data

Data for assessing characteristics of new ventures were collected via a survey of new firms in two midwestern states in 1986 (Reynolds and Freeman 1987; Reynolds and Miller 1988). A stratified random sample ensured that all regions of the state were represented. The sample was based on firms listed in the Dun's Market Identifier files as between one to six years old just prior to the survey. Phone call verification excluded all listings that were not new, autonomous, and active; about one-half of the listings qualified. Each eligible new firm was sent a mail questionnaire three times, with a reminder postcard between the first and second mailings. Instructions included with the questionnaire asked that the survey be completed by a person that had major responsibility for starting the firm and is active in the management of the firm. Any of the founders could qualify. Phone interviews were completed with about half of those not returning the mail questionnaire. Final response rate was 69%. The data were developed on more than 2,500 new firms representing all industry sectors. We limit our analysis in the present study to the the 203 retail firms in the sample.

Subsequent phone interviews were completed in 1992 to verify status of the respondents from the initial survey. Five categories of responses were noted: (1) firms that were still in operation at the time of the follow-up survey; (2) firms that we could confirm were out of business; (3) firms that were "dormant" at the time of the follow-up survey; (4) firms that had been "sold or merged"; and (5) firms, that despite multiple follow-ups using phone directories (four to six calls) and site visits, we were unable to contact. Since it is difficult to judge whether firms that are dormant or those that are sold or merged can be classified as surviving for the present analysis, we disregarded firms in these two categories from the analysis. Furthermore, our persistence in contacting the firms in the sample gave us confidence in categorizing those we were unable to contact as discontinued firms. The result of the paring was a sample where all businesses represented were founded by the current owner.

Measures

Gender Composition of the Founding Team

New ventures may be founded by individual entrepreneurs or by teams of entrepreneurs, and a team of founders may be composed of women and men. We divided our sample into the following gender designations: (1) those in which the majority (greater than half) of the team members were men; (2) those in which the majority (greater than half) of team members were women. Using this method, women staring a new venture by themselves are classified as "women-owned" and men starting alone, "men-owned." Of the businesses designated as women-owned, 34 were started by one individual, 25 were founded by a team of entrepreneurs. Of the men-owned businesses, 67 were started by one entrepreneur, 77 were founded by a team. There is no statistical difference in composition of founding team by gender (chi-Square = 3.42, $p < .07$). Approximately one-third of the businesses in the study were headed by women, a number slightly higher than the percentage reported by Kalleberg and Leicht (1991).

Firm Age

The year in which the owner of the new firm first made a resource commitment to the firm also was included in the analysis as a control. All firms in the sample were six years or less in age when the first wave of data was collected in 1986. We assumed that firms that were one year of age may have differential probability of survival from firms that were six years of age in 1986. If our assumption is true, we would expect the age to be significant and negative (e.g., older firms in 1986 would have lower rates of discontinuance by 1992). By using firm age as a covariate, we partial out the effect of age at the time the firm enters into the risk set. Age was measured as the number of months since founding.

Resources

Two categories of resources entrepreneurs bring to the firm at the time of founding were considered: tangible and intangible. Tangible resources represent resources that can be secured by the individual and used to launch the firm. Intangible resources are properties of individuals that have accrued through experience and education.

Two types of tangible resources were considered: (1) size of the organization at the time of founding and (2) access to financial resources. Size was measured in two ways. Whether the business was started as a sole proprietorship rather than with partners (a start-up team) was seen as providing access to a smaller resource base. Responses were coded 1 if started without partners, 0 if a start-up team was present. The second measure of size was the number of full-time employees. To reduce the skewness and produce a more symmetrical distribution, we use the log of size as the variable measure. Whether or not the businesses used formal sources to provide capital for start-up was used as a proxy for access to financial resources. As noted by Tigges and Green (1994) this variable does not measure access to credit markets, because the sample only includes entrepreneurs who succeeded in establishing businesses. Those denied access to credit sources may not be in the sample. Instead, the variable measures whether or not the businesses rely on formal sources for capital as opposed to financing start-up from other sources (e.g., personal equity stakes). Responses were coded 1 if loans were obtained from banks or other formal lending institutions and 0 if these formal sources did not provide any of the capital infusion.

Two indicators of intangible resources were used to test hypotheses. Since the unit of analysis is the business, the indicators are aggregate values when the firm is founded by a group or team. The first indicator is the extent to which members of the founding team have prior experience starting new ventures. The variable was calculated as the percent of the founding team that had helped start at least one other new firm prior to the current venture. The second indicator is the extent to which team members have experience working in the same industry as that of the new venture. To create a more symmetrical distribution, experi-

134   N.M. CARTER ET AL.

ence was measured as the square root of the total number of years team members had worked in the retail industry.

Strategy

The questionnaire method of data collection we used relies on key informants to indicate the focus of the firms' competitive strategy. As architects of the founding strategies, the survey respondents are uniquely qualified to assess strategic intentions. Respondents to the survey questionnaire were asked to indicate on a four-point scale ranging from critical (1), to insignificant (4) the importance of 13 attributes of competitive strategy to their firms' strategic focus. These items were chosen for their correspondence to previously identified strategy attributes and their appropriateness to new ventures.

In previous analyses (Carter et al. 1994) these 13 measures were shown to be associated with six strategic attributes: market sensitivity, technology, product distinctiveness, site appeal, service, and price. Appendix 1 displays the items from the questionnaire sorted by their factor loadings and Cronbach alpha reliability coefficients associated with each factor. Assuming that strategy consists of a composite or bundle of actions rather than an emphasis on one dimension, Carter et al. (1994) subjected the strategic attributes from the factor analysis to a cluster analysis to discern strategy archetypes. These procedures are consistent with the prevailing conceptualization in the literature that strategy is a multidimensional construct. The six strategy archetypes as defined by the extent to which they emphasize the strategy attributes are described in Appendix 2.

Results from the original six-cluster solution determined by Carter et al. (1994) were used to classify the retail firms in the present study into one of the six strategy archetypes. The cluster centroid means for each strategy dimension from the original analysis (see Carter et al. 1994, p. 32) were used as initial starting values in an iterative partitioning analysis (SPSS Quick Cluster). This procedure sorts each retail firm in the sample according to its emphasis on the six strategy attributes and assigns the firm to the closest centroid vector of the original six-cluster solution. This approach assumes that the original structure identified by Carter et al. adequately represents the strategy archetypes used by new ventures across industries and avoids the construction of a typology unique to the retail industry. In related research, Stearns et al. (1995) ranked the six strategy archetypes from broad to narrow depending on the number of strategy dimensions emphasized in each archetype. Appendix 2 presents the strategies from broadest in scope to narrowest according to the number of dimensions emphasized.

In retail, few businesses adopt the technology value or equivocator strategy. Only two businesses head by women pursued these strategies, and neither of those firms discontinued during the time of the study. Because our intent is to determine the odds of businesses discontinuing, we eliminated firms that pursued equivocator and technology value strategies.

RESULTS

Data Analyses

We first use descriptive statistics and *t*-tests to compare women-owned and men-owned firms in the sample. Second, we use a series of equations in which the firm's survival status is regressed on groups of variables entered sequentially. Because the dependent variable is dichotomous, we use logistic regression analysis. We use a step-down regression approach

TABLE 1 Means, Standard Deviations, and Percentage Distribution of Predictor Variables

Variables	Women-Owned			Men-Owned		
	Mean	SD	%	Mean	SD	%
Discontinuance	.34[a]	.48		.22[a]	.41	
Firm characteristic						
Age (months)	48.98	20.61		47.06	22.17	
Resource access						
Credit from formal sources	.51	.50		.51	.50	
Number of employees	4.34	5.30		8.99	14.89	
(measured as logarithm)	.45[b]	.38		.64[b]	.49	
Start-up team	.48	.50		.57	.50	
Owner characteristics						
% Prior start-up experience	30.17	44.61		32.64	43.99	
Years industry experience	4.53	6.44		7.92	9.54	
(measured as square root)	1.46[b]	1.55		2.09[b]	1.89	
Strategy						
Super achievers			32.88			43.14
Quality proponent			10.47			10.98
Price			13.17			12.41
Niche purveyor			43.48			32.88

[a] Indicates significant differences between samples (*t*-test $p \leq .01$).
[b] Indicates significant differences between samples (*t*-test $p \leq .001$).

where the control variable, organization size, is entered in the first step, followed by groups of main effects variables. This method introduces variables as "sets" and allows us to examine the relationship between the resource variables, strategy, gender, and the dependent variable as each set of explanatory variables is entered. We then include product terms representing the interaction between gender and resources, and gender and strategy, with all main effect variables controlled. This allows us to test whether women-owned business's use of strategic choice improves the fit of the model after all other variables are controlled.

Because the strategy variable is categorical, we used deviation contrasts. This approach compares each level, or factor, of the strategy variable to the pooled effect of all levels. For example, if the pooled effect of strategy is statistically significant as indicated by the Wald chi-square value, the effect of each strategy type can be evaluated in comparison with the average effect of all strategies.

Descriptive Analysis

Descriptive statistics for the dependent variable and predictor variables for women-owned and men-owned firms are presented in Table 1. Appendix 3 presents correlation coefficients of all variables in the study. Table 1 shows that within the retail industry, women-owned firms have a higher rate of discontinuing than men-owned firms. More than one-third of the women-owned firms discontinued during the time frame of the study. Just over 20% of the men-owned firms ceased operation.

Age of the businesses was included in the study as a control variable. It was expected that age may differentially affect the probability of survival. To the extent that this effect may exist, it does not appear to relate to gender of the founding team. On average, the firms

136   N.M. CARTER ET AL.

in the sample have been operating for four years, and the length of time women-owned firms had been in business was no different than that of men-owned firms.

The resource variables indicate mixed support for the supposition that women-owned firms have fewer resources at the time of start-up than men-owned firms. As expected, men-owned businesses have significantly more employees at start-up, but they are no more likely to start with partners than women and there were no apparent differences in access to sources of financial credit. Women-owned firms were no less likely to rely on outside financial credit. Approximately 50% of all firms in the sample rely on credit from formal financial institutions.

The expectation that women-owned firms possess a lower stock of human capital at start-up received some support. As predicted, businesses headed by women have significantly fewer years of experience working in the retail industry. However, men-owned firms are no more likely to benefit from knowledge acquired from founding other new ventures than women-owned firms. On average, 30% of the founding team in women-owned firms had experience in starting previous businesses; 33% of the entrepreneurs in men-owned firms had such background.

Regression Analyses

Table 2 presents results from six logistic regression analyses. The extent to which each set of variables improves the fit of the model is evaluated by the chi-square improvement.

The results displayed in column 1 indicate that when firm age is entered in the first step it has no significant impact on the survival of new firms in the sample (Wald = 2.46; $p <$ .12). The findings in column 2 display the results of main effects tests. The findings provide support for hypotheses 1 and 3 (Model chi-square improvement = 20.15; $p < .001$). Hypothesis 1 stated that high levels of human capital and access to outside resources decrease odds of businesses discontinuing. Experience in starting other businesses (B = $-.01$; $p < .01$), experience working in the industry (B = -0.31; $p < .001$), starting the business with partners (B = -0.34; $p < .05$), and having employees (B = -0.69; $p < .05$) all decrease the odds of discontinuing. Only access to formal lending sources (B = 0.01; $p < .92$) was not statistically significant. The results indicate that both the human capital founding teams bring to the start-up process and the scale of the business at start-up explain the odds of discontinuing.

The results also support H3, indicating that the founding strategy adopted by start-ups affects the odds of discontinuance. The findings show that broad strategies significantly affect discontinuance, but narrow strategies have no apparent effect. The two broad strategies, super achievers and quality proponents, both emphasize multi foci simultaneously. The major difference between the strategies is their emphasis on pricing. The super achiever strategy promotes seeking a flexible and responsive position in the market by emphasizing characteristics of site location, exploiting advanced technology, and emphasizing the quality of their distinctive products and services relative to the price charged. The quality proponents strategy emphasizes service and distinctiveness, and deemphasizes price. The findings indicate that the super achievers strategy (B = -0.73; $p < .001$) decreases odds of discontinuing, whereas implementation of a quality proponent strategy (B = 1.12; $p < .001$) increases odds of discontinuing business. Evidently, the absence of a pricing emphasis renders start-ups vulnerable to competition. This finding supports earlier studies that argued new ventures must match the broad appeal offered by competitors, including competing on the basis of price.

Column 3 in Table 2 shows the effect of adding gender to the model. The coefficient is positive and statistically significant, indicating that women-owned businesses have a higher

DISCONTINUANCE AMONG NEW FIRMS IN RETAIL **137**

TABLE 2 Determinants of Log Odds of Discontinuing Business

Step Variables	1 b	SE	2 b	SE	3 b	SE	4 b	SE	5 b	SE	6 b	SE
1. Firm age	−0.01	0.01	−0.02[c]	0.01	−0.02[c]	0.01	−0.02[c]	0.01	−0.02[c]	0.01	−0.02	0.01[d]
2. Resources												
Prior start-up experience			−0.01[e]	0.00	−0.01[e]	0.00	0.01[e]	0.00	−0.01[c]	0.01	−0.01[d]	0.00
Industry experience			−0.31[f]	0.08	−0.27[f]	0.08	−0.33[f]	0.10	−0.35[f]	0.11	−0.36[f]	0.11
Start-up team			−0.34[d]	0.15	−0.37[c]	0.15	−0.38[d]	0.16	−0.37	0.17	−0.37	0.18
Number of employees			−0.69[d]	0.33	−0.61	0.33	−0.34	0.36	−0.29	0.41	−0.30	0.41
Credit for formal sources			0.01	0.13	0.00	0.13	0.06	0.14	0.16	0.16	0.17	0.16
Strategy												
Super achievers			−0.73[f]	0.22	−0.70[c]	0.22	−0.76[f]	0.24	−1.18[f]	0.32	1.14[f]	0.32
Quality proponent			−1.12[f]	0.28	1.15[f]	0.28	1.34[f]	0.31	1.59[f]	0.37	1.56[f]	0.36
Price competitor			−0.09	0.28	−0.11	0.28	−0.12	0.31	−0.02	0.33	−0.02	0.33
Niche purveyor			−0.30	0.21	−0.33	0.21	−0.45	0.23	−0.39	0.26	−0.39	0.26
3. Gender												
Women's firms					0.32[d]	0.14	0.04	0.27	0.01	0.28	0.04	0.29
4. Resource by gender												
Prior start-up experience × women's firms							0.01[e]	0.00	0.01[f]	0.00	0.02[e]	0.01
Industry experience × women's firms							−0.05	0.10	−0.04	0.11	−0.04	0.11
Start-up team × women's firms							0.48[e]	0.16	0.40[d]	0.17	0.41	0.22
Number of employees × women's firms							0.44	0.37	0.43	0.41	0.42	0.41
Credit from formal sources × women's firms							−0.10	0.14	−0.03	0.16	−0.03	0.16
5. Strategy by gender												
Super achievers × women's firms									−1.05[f]	0.28	−1.04[f]	0.32
Quality × women's firms									0.43	0.36	0.57	0.40
Price competitor × women's firms									0.39	0.33	0.31	0.35
Niche purveyor × women's firms									0.22	0.26	0.15	0.28
6. Resource by strategy by gender												
Team by SA × women's firms											−0.07	0.25
Experience by SA × women's firms											−0.01	0.01
Constant	−0.66	0.27	1.04[c]	0.40	1.08[c]	0.41	0.95[d]	0.42	0.82	0.43	0.83	0.43
2-Log likelihood	438.98		375.04[c]		369.87[a]		351.12[b]		336.18[b]		335.37	

[a] Model chi-square improvement significant at 0.05.
[b] Model chi-square improvement significant at 0.01.
[c] Model chi-square improvement significant at 0.001.
[d] $p < 0.05$.
[e] $p < 0.01$.
[f] $p < 0.001$.

probability of discontinuing than men-owned businesses after resources differences are controlled. The inclusion of gender with the other main effect variables significantly improves the overall fit of the model (Model chi-square improvement = 5.17; $p < .02$).

Column 4 displays the results associated with testing H2 that women-owned firms have lower levels of human resources and less access to financial resources, increasing the odds they will discontinue. The inclusion of the product terms to the equation significantly improves the overall fit of the model (Model chi-square improvement = 18.75; $p < .002$). An examination of the coefficients reveals that only two resources contribute significantly to the model improvement. Only prior start-up experience and whether the business was started by a team differentially affected the odds of women and men-owned businesses discontinuing. The means associated with the resource by gender interactions are displayed in Figures 1 and 2.

Contrary to expectations, the lack of prior start-up experience does not differentially

138 N.M. CARTER ET AL.

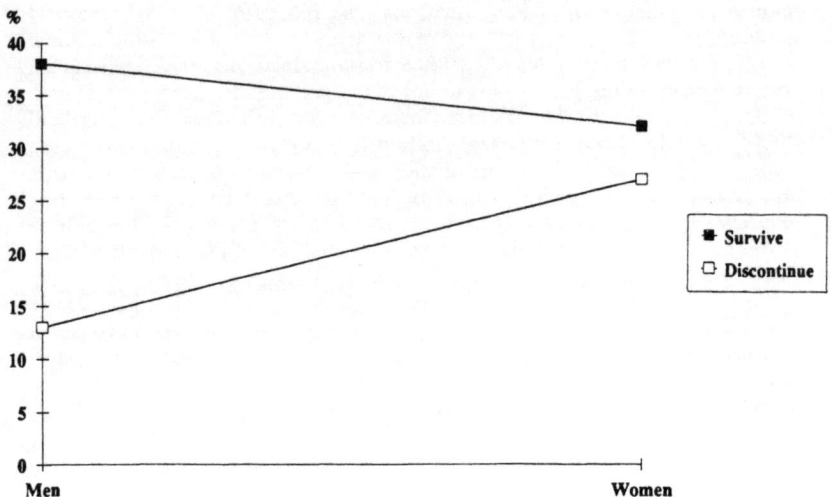

FIGURE 1 Prior start-up experience.

affect the survival status of women-owned businesses. On average, almost 27% of the start-up team in women-owned firms that discontinued had prior start-up experience compared with 32% of the teams in surviving businesses. The probability of men-owned businesses surviving is significantly enhanced by owner's prior experience in starting new businesses. Only 13% of the start-up team in men-owned businesses that discontinued had started other firms. In businesses that survived, almost 38% of each team had prior start-up experience. It appears that men-owned businesses utilize experience gained in starting previous new ventures to enhance the survival chances of their businesses. Such knowledge does not appear to benefit women-owned businesses in the same way.

The supposition that women-owned businesses would be differentially disadvantaged by starting their businesses without partners was not supported. Figure 2 indicates that neither form of start-up impacted odds of survival for women-owned businesses. On the other hand, men-owned businesses in retail appear disadvantaged by having start-up partners. Men-owned businesses, on average, were more likely to be founded by a team. But the higher the probability that men-owned businesses was started by partners, the higher the odds of the business discontinuing. In men-owned businesses that discontinued, 73% had been started by a team.

Means tests presented earlier showed that founders of women-owned businesses had fewer years of industry experience and fewer employees than men-owned businesses. The coefficients associated with these resources indicate that these deficiencies do not differentially affect women-owned firms. Apparently, the negative impact of having inadequate numbers of employees and fewer years of industry experience is shared by women- and men-owned businesses.

The findings displayed in column 5 of Table 2 report the test of H5. Adding the product terms of strategy and gender to the equation significantly improves the fit of the model (Model chi-square improvement = 14.93; $p < .002$). The supposition that a gender-strategy interaction predicts probability of retail businesses surviving beyond that explained by the

DISCONTINUANCE AMONG NEW FIRMS IN RETAIL **139**

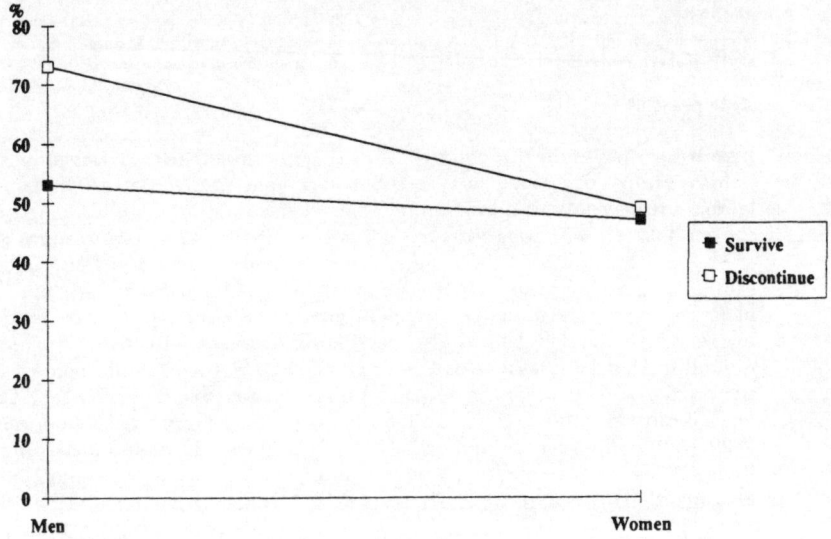

FIGURE 2 Start-Up team.

business's initial resource base is supported. We predicted that women-owned firms that pursue a generalists strategy that emphasizes service and quality, but not price, would have lower odds of discontinuing. This strategy is best represented by quality proponents. The coefficient associated (B = 0.43; $p < .24$) with this parameter is not statistically significant. Instead, the results indicate that only the interaction between super achievers, a generalists strategy that does include a pricing emphasis, significantly contributes to the model improvement (B = -1.05; $p < .001$). Figure 3 displays the means associated with the interaction. The results reveal that the nature of the strategy-gender interaction was not as expected. Women-owned businesses that adopt a super achievers strategy have a significantly higher probability of surviving. Of the surviving women-owned firms, 46% reported pursuing the super achievers strategy. Only 6% of those that discontinued were pursuing the generalists strategy. For men-owned businesses, the choice of strategy made little difference in their odds of discontinuing business.

Column 6 reports the results of adding terms to represent the three-way interaction among the two significant resource by gender interactions and the super achievers strategy by gender interaction. The three-way terms were added to assess whether women can use strategic choice to compensate for resource deficiencies and reduce odds of discontinuing. The three-way interactions did not significantly contribute to improvement of the model (Model chi-square improvement = 0.82; $p < .66$). There was no support for H6.

DISCUSSION

An integrative approach that incorporates both the situational and dispositional perspectives was used to examine the role that initial resources, founding strategy, and gender play in predicting new firm discontinuance. The results indicate that women-owned retail businesses

140   N.M. CARTER ET AL.

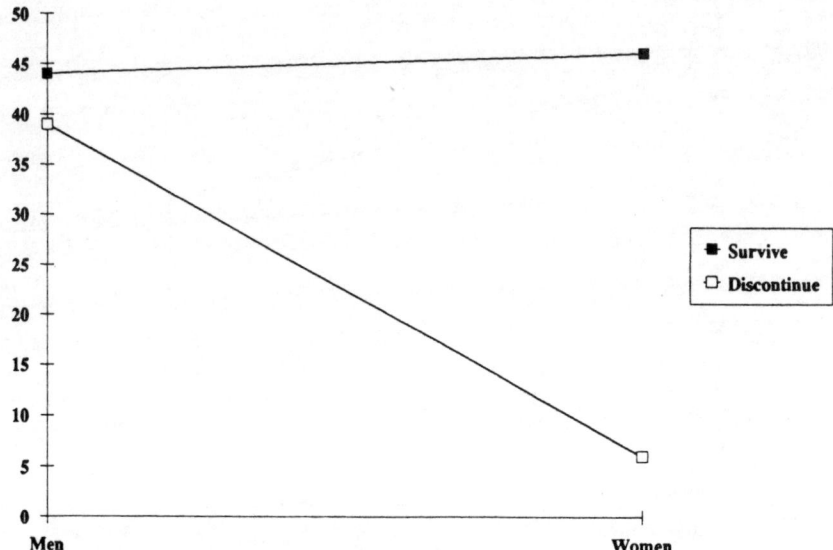

FIGURE 3   Super achievers strategy.

have higher odds of discontinuing than those owned by their male counterparts and that the lack of human and financial resources significantly increase the odds of businesses discontinuing. Despite there being some evidence that women have fewer resources to start their businesses, the resource deficiencies do not appear to differentially affect the survival of their businesses relative to those owned by men. The founding teams of men-owned businesses were more likely to have greater experience working in the industry than the founders of women-owned businesses. Men also were more likely to start their businesses on a larger scale with more employees then women. On the other hand, women were no less likely to have access to credit from formal financial institutions, nor were they at a disadvantage from starting fewer other new businesses. Only the lack of experience starting other new ventures and having a start-up team differentially predicted discontinuance for women- and men-owned businesses.

Contrary to expectations, the lack of prior start-up experience had a much greater impact on predicting the odds of men-owned businesses discontinuing than those owned by women. Low levels of prior experience significantly increased the odds of men-owned business discontinuing. Knowledge gained from starting previous businesses did not differentiate the survival status of women-owned businesses. Similarly, men-owned businesses did not appear to derive a benefit from being started by a team. We had expected that partners would bring additional human and financial resources to the start-up process, which would affect chances of surviving and that women would have less access to such resources. Men-owned businesses were more likely to be started by a team, but these same businesses had higher odds of discontinuing. Having a start-up team does not appear to affect the survival status of women-owned businesses. Perhaps the addition of partners in men-owned businesses increases overhead costs beyond that which can be supported by the business. As partners draw on revenues for personal support, the burden on the business may be too high.

The results indicate that broad-based strategies are more effective in retail than narrow niche strategies. Previous research had suggested that by adopting a narrow specialist strategy new ventures might be able to secure a protected position in the market where they would be overlooked by larger competitors. Such strategies do not appear to effect survival status in retail. The findings also support the supposition that women-owned firms can decrease odds of discontinuance through strategic choice. Founding strategy was portrayed as representing differences in women's and men's belief structures that derived from variations in their socialization patterns. By choosing a founding strategy that fit their particular competencies, women appear to manage their businesses in ways different from men and with different outcomes. Our analyses show that strategy is more important for the success of women's businesses than for men's.

Unexpected was the finding that the most beneficial strategy for women-owned businesses in retail appears to be the super achievers strategy. It may be that the effectiveness of the super achievers strategy reflects the fact that women are particularly adept at "scrambling" to give the customers whatever they want whenever they want it. By emphasizing multiple strategy foci simultaneously and "being all things to all people," businesses headed by women may be able to ward off discontinuance. Kalleberg and Leicht (1991) refer to this approach as a thrashing process whereby organizations adapt to high environmental uncertainty by trying a variety of approaches in order to stay in business.

Alternatively, it might be argued that the effectiveness of the generalists strategy reflects women's relational orientation. Women were seen as emphasizing cooperative networks among family, society, and person. The ability to juggle expectations from many quarters may be the underpinning of effectively executing the super achievers strategy.

CONCLUSIONS

This study adds to the knowledge pool about the effects of gender on organizational performance. The use of situational and dispositional perspectives in an integrative model provides an explanation for some of the contradictions in the literature. The findings suggest that whereas men use human and financial resources to enhance the chances of their firms' survival, women find strategic choice more beneficial.

Although the findings are supportive of the integrative model, future research should respond more fully to challenges that measures traditionally used in gender research reflect male-derived measures. Greater attention should be given to the development of measures that appropriately represent both spheres of gender. Similarly, alternative measures of access to financial resources are needed to provide additional insight into the question of the existence of systematic barriers and may reveal stronger support for the theory of situational factors determining business discontinuance rates. Additionally, other forms of human capital like skills needed to interface effectively with critical stake holders such as customers and suppliers may better represent the theory.

In addition, subsequent analyses should extend to other sectors of the economy. We chose to limit this study to one industry to control for extraneous influences and to ensure an adequate sample size to test hypotheses. Because the retail industry is characterized by attenuated career tracks and lower capital requirements for starting a business, differences between genders is less likely than would be found in other industries. Thus, the findings are probably a conservative representation of gender-related situational disadvantages. Future efforts should examine the effect of strategy in overcoming situational resource deficiencies specific to other industries.

142   N.M. CARTER ET AL.

APPENDIX 1

Factor Analysis of New Firm Competitive Strategy Associated with Factor Dimensions

Competitve Aspects Emphasized	Descriptive
Factor 1 *alpha* = 0.63 Fast response to changes in markets (0.81) Serve those missed by others (0.69) More effective marketing/advertising (0.68)	Market sensitivity Knowledge of the market emphasized to reach and respond quickly to key customer needs.
Factor 2 *alpha* = 0.81 Develop new/advanced technology (0.92) Utilize new/advanced technology (0.87)	Technology Emphasize process or product technology by developing or using new or advanced technology.
Factor 3 *alpha* = 0.61 More contemporary, attractive products (0.76) Distinctive goods/services (0.71) More choices (0.64)	Product distinction Seek to distinguish the firm from others in the market place by providing unique products or services.
Factor 4 *alpha* = 0.71 Superior location/customer convenience (0.84) Better, more attractive facilities (0.83)	Site appeal Attractiveness and convenience of facilities and location emphasized.
Factor 5 *alpha* = 0.68 Better service (0.86) Quality products/services (0.81)	Service Provide a higher level of service than competitors.
Factor 6 Lower prices (0.93)	Price Sell products or services at a lower price than competitors.

APPENDIX 2

Strategy Archetype Descriptions

1. *Super Achievers*—Firms pursuing this strategy strive to promote multiple strategic attributes simultaneously. New ventures adopting this strategy attempt to be all things to all people. They seek a flexible and responsive position in the market by emphasizing characteristics of their site location, exploiting advanced technology, and by emphasizing the quality of their distinctive products and services relative to the price charged. This strategy is broad based in its efforts to exploit a diverse set of resources.
2. *Quality Proponents*—Firms adopting this strategy also have a penchant for a broad market. Quality Proponents are much like Super Achievers except they do not emphasize price as an integral strategic foci. This strategy emphasizes service and distinctiveness.
3. *Equivocators*—Firms adopting this strategy fail to emphasize any particular strategy focus. This strategy may be analogous to Porter's (1985) description of firms "stuck in the middle." At best ambivalent, uncertainty seemingly characterizes strategy formation in these new ventures. Because a distinct strategic emphasis is absent, this strategy can be considered neither broad or narrow.
4. *Price Competitors*—This strategy reflects new ventures' attempts to rely on a combination of marketing/advertising and low price to attract customers. This strategy appears to be the most flexible since pricing and advertising can be changed quickly in response to competitor actions.
5. *Niche Purveyors*—These firms emphasize site qualities. Attractive facilities at superior, convenient locations are seen as creating customer value. By coupling convenience with exceptional or unique products at competitive prices, firms pursuing this strategy narrow their scope and attempt to secure a distinctive foothold in the competitive landscape by focusing on a narrow segment of the population.
6. *Technology Value*—Firms adopting this strategy pursue a narrow differentiation approach. They attempt to distinguish themselves by making price-competitive products through the use and/or development or new technology. This strategy is narrow based as technology products and services limit the market segment they seek to serve.

DISCONTINUANCE AMONG NEW FIRMS IN RETAIL **143**

APPENDIX 3[a]
Correlation Matrix

Variables	1	2	3	4	5	6	7	8	9	10	11
1. Out of business		−0.05	−0.02	−0.05	0.02	−0.06	−0.26^b	−0.40^b	0.17	0.06	0.34^b
2. Firm age	−0.12^c		0.06	−0.11	0.23^c	−0.16	−0.21^c	0.09	−0.09	−0.13	0.18^c
3. Firm size	−0.14^c	−0.04		0.04	0.18^c	−0.21^c	−0.09	−0.01	−0.32^b	0.28^b	−0.09
4. Credit resources	0.03	−0.09	0.01		0.02	−0.09	−0.08	−0.01	−0.29^b	0.27^b	−0.09
5. Start-up team	0.16^b	0.08	0.28^b	−0.04		−0.10	−0.34^b	−0.04	−0.12	0.08	0.07
6. Prior start-up experience	−0.23^b	−0.18^b	0.27^b	−0.04	0.10		0.31^b	0.11	0.03	−0.08	−0.08
7. Industry experience	−0.20^b	−0.01	0.10	0.15^c	−0.17^b	−0.06		0.25^b	−0.13	−0.08	−0.12
8. Super achievers	−0.04	0.01	0.07	−0.06	0.04	0.18^b	0.10		−0.27^b	−0.61^b	−0.24^b
9. Price	−0.06	−0.02	−0.04	0.03	−0.14^c	−0.19^b	0.03	−0.33^b		−0.34^b	−0.13
10. Niche	−0.05	0.02	0.02	−0.05	0.11	−0.03	−0.15^c	−0.62^b	−0.27^b		−0.30^b
11. Quality	0.21^b	−0.03	−0.10	0.14^c	−0.08	−0.04	0.02	−0.31^b	−0.13^c	−0.25^b	

[a] Correlations for women's businesses are above the diagonal, those for men below the diagonal.
[b] $p < 0.01$.
[c] $p < 0.05$.

REFERENCES

Astin, H.S., and Leland, C. 1991. *Women of Influence, Women of Vision*. San Francisco, CA: Jossey-Bass Publishers.

Biggadike, R.E. 1976. *Corporate Diversification: Entry, Strategy and Performance*. Boston, MA: Harvard University Press.

Birley, S. 1986. The small firm—set at the start. In R. Ronstadt, J.A. Hornaday, R. Peterson, and K.H. Vesper, eds., *Frontiers of Entrepreneurship Research*. Wellesley, MA: Babson College.

Broom, H.M., and Longenecker, J.G. 1971. *Small Business Management*, 3rd ed. Cincinnati, OH: South Western.

Brush, C. 1992. Research on women business owners: Past trends, a new perspective and future directions. *Entrepreneurship Theory and Practice* 16(2):5–30.

Buttner, E.H., and Rosen, B. 1988. Bank loan officers' perceptions of the characteristics of men, women and successful entrepreneurs. *Journal of Business Venturing* 3(3):249–258.

Carter, N.M., Stearns, T.M., Reynolds, P.D., and Miller, B. 1994. New venture strategies: Theory development with an empirical base. *Strategic Management Journal* 15(1):21–41.

Chaganti, R. 1986. Management in women-owned enterprises. *Journal of Small Business Management* 24(4):18–29.

Clark, T.A., and James, F.J. 1992. Women-owned businesses: Dimensions and policy issues. *Economic Development Quarterly* 6(1):25–40.

Cohen, T., and Lindberg, R.A. 1974. *Survival and Growth: Management Strategies for the Small Firm*. New York: AMACOM.

Cooper, A.C., and Bruno, A. 1977. Success among high-technology firms. *Business Horizons* 20(2):16–23.

Cooper, A.C., Willard, G.E., and Woo, C.Y. 1986. Strategies of high performing new and small firms: A reexamination of the niche concept. *Journal of Business Venturing* 1(3):247–260.

Cromie, S., and Birley, S. 1991. Networking by female business owners in Northern Ireland. *Journal of Business Venturing* 7(3):237–251.

Deeks, J. 1976. *The Small Firm Owner-Manager*. New York: Praeger.

Devine, T.J. 1994. Characteristics of self-employed women in the United States. *Monthly Labor Review* 117(3):20–34.

Fischer, E.M., Reuber, A.R., and Dyke, L.S. 1993. A theoretical overview and extension of research on sex, gender, and entrepreneurship. *Journal of Business Venturing* 8(2):151–168.

Goffee, R., and Scase, R. 1983. Business ownership and women's subordination: A preliminary study of female proprietors. *Sociological Review* 31(4):625–648.

144 N.M. CARTER ET AL.

Hisrich, R., and Brush, C. 1984. The women entrepreneur: Management skills and business problems. *Journal of Small Business Management* 22(1):30–37.

Honing-Haftel, S., and Martin, L. 1986. Is the female entrepreneur at a disadvantage? *Thrust: The Journal for Employment and Training Professionals* 7:49–64.

Hosmer, L. 1957. Small manufacturing enterprises. *Harvard Business Review* 35(6):111–122.

Kalleberg, A., and Leicht, K. 1991. Gender and organizational performance: Determinants of small business survival and success. *Academy of Management Journal* 34(1):136–161.

Kaplan, E. 1988. Women entrepreneurs: Constructing a framework to examine venture success and business failures. In B.A. Kirchoff, W.A. Long, W.E. McMullan, K.H. Vesper, and W.E. Wetzel, Jr., eds., *Frontiers of Entrepreneurship Research*. Wellesley, MA: Babson College.

Keeley, R., and Roure, R. 1990. Management, strategy, and industry structure as influences on the success of new firms: A structural model. *Management Science* 36(10):1256–1267.

Liou, N., and Aldrich, H.E. 1995. Women entrepreneurs: Is there a gender-based relational competence? Presented at the 1995 American Sociological Association meeting, Washington, DC.

MacMillan, I.C., and Day, D.L. 1987. Corporate ventures into industrial markets: Dynamics of aggressive entry. *Journal of Business Venturing* 2(1):29–40.

McDougall, P., and Robinson, R.B., Jr. 1990. New venture strategies: An empirical identification of eight "Archetypes" of competitive strategies for entry. *Strategic Management Journal* 11(6):447–467.

Miller, A., and Camp, B. 1985. Exploring determinants of success in corporate ventures. *Journal of Business Venturing* 1(1):87–105.

Neider, L. 1987. A preliminary investigation of female entrepreneurs in Florida. *Journal of Small Business Management* 25(3):22–29.

Olm, K., Carsrud, A., and Alvey, L. 1988. The role of networks in new venture funding for the female entrepreneur: A continuing analysis. In B.A. Kirchoff, W.A. Long, W.E. McMullan, K.H. Vesper, and W.E. Wetzel, Jr., eds., *Frontiers of Entrepreneurship Research*. Wellesley, MA: Babson College.

Porter, M.E. 1985. *Competitive Advantage*. New York: The Free Press.

Reese, P. 1992. Resource acquisition: Does gender make a difference? Presented at the Second Annual Global Entrepreneurship Research Conference, London.

Reynolds, P.D., and Freeman, S. 1987. *1986 Pennsylvania New Firm Survey*. Washington, DC: Appalachia Regional Commission.

Reynolds, P.D., and Miller, B. 1988. *1987 Minnesota New Firm Survey*. Minneapolis, MN: University of Minnesota Center for Urban and Regional Affairs.

Reynolds, P.D. 1993. High performance entrepreneurship: What makes a difference? Working paper. Milwaukee, WI: Marquette University.

Riding, A., and Swift, C. 1990. Women business owners and terms of credit: Some empirical findings of the Canadian experience. *Journal of Business Venturing* 5(5):327–340.

Romanelli, E. 1989. Organization birth and population variety: A community perspective on origins. In L.L. Cummings and B.M. Staw, eds., *Research in Organizational Behavior*. Greenwich, CT: JAI Press Inc.

Sandberg, W.R., and Hofer, C.W. 1987. Improving new venture performance: The role of strategy, industry structure, and the entrepreneur. *Journal of Business Venturing* 2(1):5–28.

Scott, C. 1986. Why more women are becoming entrepreneurs. *Journal of Small Business Management* 24(4):37–44.

Sexton, D.L., and Bowman-Upton, N. 1990. Female and male entrepreneurs: Psychological characteristics and their role in gender-related discrimination. *Journal of Business Venturing* 5(1):29–36.

Sheppard, D. 1992. Women manager's perceptions of gender and organizational life. In A.J. Mills and P. Tancred, eds., *Gendering Organizational Analysis*. Newbury Park, CA: Sage Publications.

Stearns, T.M., Carter, N.M., Reynolds, P.D., and Williams, M. 1995. New firm survival: Industry, strategy and location. *Journal of Business Venturing* 10(1):23–42.

DISCONTINUANCE AMONG NEW FIRMS IN RETAIL **145**

Stegall, D.P., Steinmetz, L.L., and Kline, J.B. 1976. *Managing the Small Business*. Homewood, IL: Irwin.

Stinchcombe, A. 1965. Social structure and organizations. In James G. March, ed., *Handbook of Organizations*. Chicago, IL: Rand McNally.

Tigges, L.M., and Green, G.P. 1994. Small business success among men- and women-owned firms in rural areas. *Rural Sociology* 59(2):289–310.

Van de Ven, A., Hudson, R., and Schroeder, D. 1984. Designing new business start-ups: Entrepreneurial, organizational, and ecological considerations. *Journal of Management* 10(1):87–107.

Walsh, J.P., and Fahey, L. 1986. The role of negotiated belief structures in strategy making. *Journal of Management* 12(3):325–338.

Zellner, W., King, R.W., Byrd, V.N., DeGeorge, G., and Birnbaum, J. 1994. Women entrepreneurs. *Business Week* (April 18):104–110.

[21]

DOES ONE SIZE FIT ALL? EXPLORING THE RELATIONSHIP BETWEEN ATTITUDES TOWARDS GROWTH, GENDER, AND BUSINESS SIZE

JENNIFER E. CLIFF
University of British Columbia

EXECUTIVE SUMMARY

To help explain the typically smaller size of businesses headed by women, this study examines a relatively unexplored dimension on which male and female entrepreneurs are expected to differ: their attitudes towards growth. An increasing number of scholars believe that the growth of a venture is at least partially determined by the entrepreneur's motivations and intentions, yet very few have investigated whether gender differences exist. Quantitative and qualitative analyses of data collected through personal interviews with 229 small business owners in the Greater Vancouver area of British Columbia, Canada, provide novel insights into the factors affecting an entrepreneur's growth decision and desired pace of expansion.

Although male and female entrepreneurs seem equally likely to desire business growth, there appear to be important differences with respect to how they wish to expand. The qualitative findings suggest that female entrepreneurs are more likely to establish maximum business size thresholds beyond which they would prefer not to expand, and that these thresholds are smaller than those set by their male counterparts. These thresholds represent the size that the entrepreneur is comfortable managing—the size that enables him/her to maintain control of the organization, devote a reasonable amount of time and energy to the firm, and/or balance work and personal life. The attainment of such size thresholds appears to be a key trigger in the no-growth decision. Female entrepreneurs also seem to be more concerned than male entrepreneurs about the risks associated with fast-paced growth and tend to deliberately adopt a slow and

Address correspondence to Jennifer E. Cliff, Faculty of Commerce & Business Administration, University of British Columbia, 2053 Main Mall, Vancouver, BC V6T 1Z2, Canada.

I would like thank Allen Lehman, Jodi McFarlane, John Oesch, Jane Olsen, and Indira Prahst for their assistance in data collection; Amy Ewert for her help with data entry; Howard Aldrich, Candida Brush, and Patricia Greene for their valuable comments on earlier drafts of this article; and especially Nancy Langton for her supportive supervision throughout this project. I gratefully acknowledge financial support from S.S.H.R.C.C. Grant No. 412-93-0005. An earlier version of this article was presented at the August 1996 Academy of Management meetings in Cincinnati, Ohio.

0883-9026/98/$19.00
PII S0883-9026(97)00071-2

steady rate of expansion. Thus, for female entrepreneurs in particular, personal considerations appear to override economic considerations in the business expansion decision

These findings have important implications for policy-makers, financial capital providers, researchers, and entrepreneurs. For policy-makers, the finding that female entrepreneurs appear to be particularly concerned about growing in a controlled fashion that does not exceed their maximum business-size threshold suggests that a smaller-sized firm with a slower growth rate may be a deliberately chosen, desirable state for many women business owners. As a result, government programs designed to increase the size and/or growth rate of female-owned firms may not achieve the expected level of demand; moreover, these programs may be considered unsatisfactory by participants if they do not explicitly address women's expansion concerns.

The desire expressed by female entrepreneurs about not letting growth get "out of control" also has important implications for financial capital providers. This managed approach to business expansion may result in ventures that are able to out-survive those headed by entrepreneurs pursuing more risky, high-growth strategies. Thus, banks might view women as better loan risks, given their more cautious attitudes toward growth.

Further research is needed to more fully investigate the existence of gender differences in entrepreneurs' attitudes towards growth and whether such differences can, in turn, affect venture performance. If, for example, a positive relationship is found between the emphasis placed on growing in a manageable manner that does not exceed the maximum business-size threshold and the long-term survival of the firm, entrepreneurs may benefit from increased awareness of the favorable outcomes of a more cautious attitude to growth. This would require recognition that one approach to business ownership—the desire to head a large, quickly growing enterprise—may not necessarily fit all. © 1998 Elsevier Science Inc.

INTRODUCTION

Understanding the factors that influence business performance lies at the heart of much work on management and organizations. Studies comparing the performance of male- and female-owned firms consistently show that businesses headed by women tend to be smaller than those headed by men, whether size is measured by gross revenues, number of employees, or profit level (Fischer 1992; Fischer, Reuber, and Dyke 1993; Kalleberg and Leicht 1991). There is also some evidence that they grow less quickly than those owned by men[1] (Cooper, Gimeno-Gascon, and Woo 1994; Fischer et al. 1993). Since size and growth are typically used as criteria for evaluating organizational success (Venkatraman and Ramanujam 1986), previous studies comparing male- and female-owned firms have been directed primarily at providing explanations that can account for the "poorer performance" of businesses headed by women.

The common assumption underlying many of these studies seems to be that the smaller size and slower growth rates of female-owned enterprises is a "problem": if they could, women would want to grow their businesses as quickly and have them become as large as those headed by men. A number of authors have begun to challenge the idea that the growth of an organization is a naturally occurring phenomenon, proposing instead that expansion is at least partially determined by the entrepreneur's motivations and intentions for the business (e.g., Bird 1988; Cooper 1993; Davidsson 1991; Herron and Robinson 1993; Kolvereid 1992; Sexton 1989a). The results of several empirical investigations indicate that many female business owners deliberately choose to keep their companies small (e.g., Goffee and Scase 1985; Kaplan 1988; Lee-Gosselin and

---

[1] Kalleberg and Leicht (1991), however, found no significant gender differences in gross earnings growth. Fischer et al. (1993) found significant gender differences for income growth but not for sales or employment growth.

Grisé 1990) or have conservative growth expectations (e.g., Belcourt, Burke, and Lee-Gosselin 1991; Chaganti 1986). All of these studies, however, have utilized women-only samples.

A recent comparative investigation conducted in Norway (Kolvereid 1992) found that male entrepreneurs were more likely to state positive growth intentions than female entrepreneurs, but that the difference was not statistically significant. In interpreting the results, the author cautioned that the lack of statistical significance "may be country specific, since Norway is an egalitarian country where the male-female differences are not particularly strong" (1992, p. 218). Given this caveat, and the scarcity of other comparative investigations, it is too soon to draw any firm conclusions on the existence of gender differences in entrepreneurs' growth intentions. Thus, the primary objective of this study is to question the assumption that men and women are equally motivated to expand their businesses, by exploring the relationship between an entrepreneur's gender and his/her attitudes toward growth. In doing so, I hope to offer fresh insights into the reasons behind the smaller size and slower growth of female-owned firms.

The article is presented in two sections. In the first section, I use data collected through personal interviews with 229 small business owners in the Greater Vancouver area of British Columbia, Canada, to test hypotheses regarding gender differences in entrepreneurs' resources available for expansion, valued placed on growth, and expansion intentions. In the second section, I present the results of a qualitative analysis that was conducted to reconcile the lack of quantitative empirical support for the theory-driven hypotheses with my interviewing experiences. Based on these findings, I develop the notion of maximum busines-size thresholds and offer a series of propositions regarding the existence of gender differences in such thresholds as well as the desired pace of growth.

CONCEPTUAL BACKGROUND

Bird (1988), Cooper (1993), Davidsson (1991), Herron and Robinson (1993), Kolvereid (1992), and Sexton (1989a) have recently argued that small business performance is influenced by the motivations, aspirations, and intentions of the entrepreneur. Sexton, for example, proposed that the growth of a new business venture does not occur naturally but is instead determined by the owner: "Those in control of the firm may initiate, foster, nurture, or prune growth in accordance with their own propensity for growth and their abilities to manage it" (1989a, p. 137). He defined propensity for growth as an entrepreneur's intent to expand the organization, and ability to manage growth as the degree to which he/she can obtain resources and develop the organization. Although Sexton (1989b) argued that there are no *psychological* reasons to believe that female entrepreneurs will have a lower propensity for business expansion, liberal and social feminist theories provide *sociocultural* reasons for expecting gender differences. Figure 1 presents an overview of the conceptual framework.

Gender Differences in Resources for Expansion

Liberal feminist theory posits that if women had equal access to the opportunities available to men—such as education, work experience, and other resources—they would behave similarly (Unger and Crawford 1992). Although no significant gender differences have been reported in the educational backgrounds of entrepreneurs (Birley,

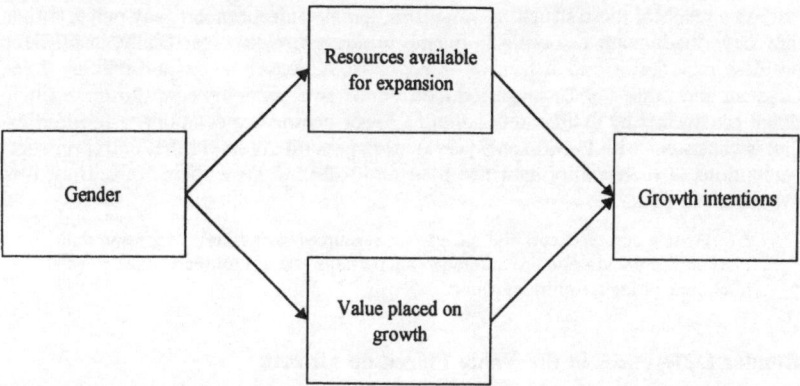

FIGURE 1   A model of gender differences in entrepreneurs' growth intentions.

Moss, and Saunders 1987; Fischer et al. 1993), female entrepreneurs tend to have less industry, management, and prior business start-up experience[2] (Carter, Williams, and Reynolds 1995; Fischer et al. 1993; Hisrich and Brush 1983; Kalleberg and Leicht 1991; Watkins and Watkins 1983). Women who lack relevant experience may question their ability to manage a quickly growing enterprise and may therefore purposely limit the expansion of their firms. Lee-Gosselin and Grisé (1990, p. 431), for example, suggested that the minimal prior business experience of the female entrepreneurs they interviewed contributed to their modest growth expectations.

In addition to differences in their prior business experience, male and female entrepreneurs tend to face very different domestic demands. Despite the fact that women are entering the workforce and starting new businesses at an increasing rate, they are still more likely to be the "primary parent, emotional nurturer, and housekeeper" (Unger and Crawford 1992, p. 474). Unlike their male counterparts, female entrepreneurs are not usually relieved of their domestic responsibilities when they start a business (Belcourt 1991; Belcourt et al. 1991; Goffee and Scase 1985) and are thus more likely to face conflicting demands between their professional and personal lives (Allen and Truman 1992; Buttner 1993; Goffee and Scase 1985; Stevenson 1990; Stoner, Hartman, and Arora 1990). This conflict may be manifested in the adoption of reduced growth intentions. Goffee and Scase, for example, found that many of the female business owners they interviewed were reluctant to expand because "business growth would create demands on their time and life-styles which would threaten the pattern of family and conjugal relationships" (1985, p. 122). In contrast, the primary family responsibility of men—to be a good provider (Unger and Crawford 1992)—is compatible with heading a growing firm.

---

[2] Birley, Moss, and Saunders (1987) found no significant gender differences in industry-related experience, and Kalleberg and Leicht (1991) and Carter, Williams, and Reynolds (1995) did not find that women were less likely to have prior experience in starting a business. The latter study, however, used an aggregate measure based on the experience of the founding team (which could have included male partners). If measured on their own, the women may have had less prior start-up experience. As will become evident in the methods section, the characteristics of my sample are more similar to that of Fischer et al. (1993), who reported significant gender differences for industry, management, and prior start-up experience.

As a result of these structural variations, female entrepreneurs may perceive that they have inadequate resources to pursue business growth—specifically, insufficient business experience and a lack of freedom from household responsibilities. Lee-Gosselin and Grisé (1990) suggested that female entrepreneurs adapt to these situational constraints by deliberately adopting lower growth expectations, a proposition that is consistent with Davidsson's (1991) more general argument that entrepreneurs' perceptions of their ability influence their motivation to grow their firms. Thus, it is hypothesized that:

> *H1:* Female entrepreneurs will have fewer resources for business expansion than male entrepreneurs, and this difference will partially account for the weaker growth intentions of female entrepreneurs.

Gender Differences in the Value Placed on Growth

Social feminism also offers a compelling argument for anticipating gender differences in growth intentions. This theoretical perspective asserts that women have different—yet equally valuable and effective—qualities, values, and ways of thinking due to variations in early and ongoing socialization processes (Black 1989). Men are expected to possess high levels of agentic qualities such as self-assertion, self-expansion, and the urge to master, whereas women are expected to possess high levels of communal qualities such as selflessness, a concern for others, and interpersonal sensitivity (Eagly and Wood 1991). Empirical studies indicate that men tend to place a greater emphasis on economic values and quantitative, nonambiguous measures of achievement and success, such as status and wealth; women tend to assign more importance to social values and qualitative, ambiguous measures of achievement and success, such as personal fulfilment and strong interpersonal relations (Travis et al. 1988; Unger and Crawford 1992; Williams 1987).

In the context of business ownership, the above-noted findings suggest that male and female entrepreneurs will differ in the value attached to business expansion. Given that men face strong societal pressures to be competitive, masterful, and dominant, male entrepreneurs will likely emphasize size as a measure of business success. In contrast, given that women are expected to be more concerned about the quality of interpersonal relationships, female entrepreneurs will likely measure success by less objective criteria. Anecdotal evidence is provided in the following quote by Amy Miller, a Texas-based entrepreneur who is often featured in the business media:

> Our success lies not in bottom-line growth but in our ability to meet challenges adequately: our responsiveness to our communities' changing needs, our continued commitment to innovative employee training and motivation, and our commitment to constant improvement in service standards. That progress can occur with or without increasing the number of stores or the sales per store. In theory, of course, success would lead to an increase in those numbers—but the most important signs of success would still not be visible to the outside observer (1995, p. 21).

Similarly, in her literature review, Brush (1992) noted that women business owners tend to pursue a balance between economic goals, such as profit and growth, and noneconomic goals, such as product quality, personal enjoyment, and helping others.

Since theories of motivation posit that values influence intentions (e.g., Locke 1991), gender differences in the value placed on business expansion will likely contribute

528   J.E. CLIFF

TABLE 1   Descriptive Statistics for the Businesses Studied

Variables	Total (n = 229)				Male-headed (n = 141)		Female-headed (n = 88)	
	Mean	SD	Min	Max	Mean	SD	Mean	SD
Retail	0.14	0.34			0.09	0.28	0.22**	0.41
Business services	0.41	0.49			0.40	0.49	0.42	0.50
Personal services	0.08	0.27			0.06	0.25	0.10	0.31
Manufacturing	0.20	0.40			0.21	0.41	0.17	0.38
Wholesale	0.18	0.39			0.24	0.43	0.09**	0.29
Years firm owned	11.5	8.5	0.1	42.6	12.4	9.5	10.0*	6.3
# of employees[a]	20.1	35.4	0.0	323.0	25.3	42.5	11.8**	15.9
# of owners[b]	2.0	2.1	0.5	21.0	2.0	1.8	1.9	2.4

[a] Calculated by summing the number of full-time employees plus half the number of part-time employees (temporary staff, unpaid workers, and subcontractors were not included in the total).
[b] Calculated by summing the number of full-time owners plus half the number of part-time owners (silent partners were not included in the total).
Differences between male-headed and female-headed firms significant at * $p < .05$ and ** $p < .01$, respectively.

to differences in the growth intentions of male and female entrepreneurs. More specifically, it is expected that women will be less likely to express a desire to grow their firms since expansion may interfere with other, less objective yet equally cherished goals. In their in-depth study of female business owners in Britain, for example, Goffee and Scase (1985, p. 70) found that many of these women regarded growth as "very risky" because it would deter them from achieving their goal of developing an "employer-employee relationship based upon trust and mutual respect." As such, it is hypothesized that:

> *H2:* Female entrepreneurs will attach less value to business expansion than male entrepreneurs, and this difference will partially account for the weaker growth intentions of female entrepreneurs.

METHOD

Sample

These hypotheses were tested on a sample consisting of 141 small businesses headed by men and 88 small businesses headed by women in the Greater Vancouver area of British Columbia, Canada.[3] Table 1 presents descriptive statistics for the sampled businesses. Consistent with other comparative studies, there were significant gender differences in terms of industry concentration, years in business, and firm size. The women were more likely to head retail and service firms (74% of female-headed firms versus 55% of male-headed firms) and less likely to head manufacturing and wholesale firms (26% of female-headed firms versus 45% of male-headed firms). The women had owned their firms for less time than the men, averaging 10.0 versus 12.4 years, respectively, and their businesses were less than half the size of those headed by men, averaging 11.8 versus 25.3 full-time equivalent employees, respectively.

In general, the firms in this study are older and larger than those reported elsewhere in the entrepreneurship literature, a difference that can be attributed in part to the sampling procedure. The sample was drawn for a larger investigation into the human re-

---

[3] A business was deemed to be headed by a woman if the primary active owner was female.

source management strategies of small business owners.[4] To obtain the sample, the principal investigator of the larger study selected the entire population of female-headed firms and a random sample of male-headed firms in the manufacturing, wholesale, retail, business service, and personal service industries that were listed in the 1994 Greater Vancouver Contacts Target Marketing database as having greater than five employees. Research assistants attempted to reach the primary contact person by telephone or facsimile to determine whether the company met the selection criteria and to solicit participation in the study. Firms were excluded if: (1) they were franchises, branches, or subsidiaries; (2) they were no longer in business; (3) the owner was untraceable or not involved in the management of the company; or (4) the owner had participated in our pilot study. This resulted in a total of 574 eligible firms; 229 owners agreed to participate, resulting in a respectable response rate of 40%.[5]

Data Collection

The data for this and the larger human resource practices investigation were collected through structured, personal interviews with the primary active owner of the sampled firms. These were conducted by a team of seven interviewers that included myself, the principal investigator of the larger study, and five research assistants. Most of the interviews were conducted on the participant's business premises and typically took between 50 and 80 minutes to complete. The main part of the survey instrument included questions on: the nature, structure, size, and profitability of the company; human resource practises, policies, and hiring intentions; the background of the owner; and the interplay between work and personal domains. A series of open-ended questions tapping the owner's goals, definitions of success, and growth intentions was posed at the end of the interview. I used an open-ended format for these questions because the extant literature on women business owners has been criticized for its reliance on structured surveys and predefined measures that provide limited opportunities for entrepreneurs to express their own perceptions of, and approaches to, business ownership (Allen and Truman 1992; Belcourt et al. 1991; Brush 1992; Stevenson 1990).

Measures of the Constructs

Five variables served as indicators of an entrepreneur's resources for growth. Business education was measured by whether the participant possessed a business-related college diploma or university degree. Management experience was measured by whether the participant had managerial responsibility in either of the two most recent positions prior to owning the current business. Industry experience was measured by whether the participant had worked in or had owned another firm in the same industry as his/her current business. Prior business ownership experience was measured by whether the participant had previously owned another enterprise. Freedom from household responsibilities was

---

[4] Nancy Langton and Howard Aldrich are the principal and co-principal investigators, respectively, of this larger study. The study is one of several projects being conducted by the Entrepreneurship Research Alliance at the University of British Columbia under S.S.H.R.C.C grant no. 412-93-0005.

[5] This response rate was calculated by dividing the number of completed interviews by the number of people who were interviewed, who refused to participate, and who did not respond to our faxes after repeated attempts.

TABLE 2   Gender Differences in Resources Available for Expansion, Value Placed on Growth, and Growth Intentions

Variables	Male-headed firms ($n = 141$)		Female-headed firms ($n = 88$)	
	Mean	SD	Mean	SD
Resources available for expansion				
Business degree	0.23	0.42	0.09**	0.29
Management experience	0.79	0.41	0.73	0.45
Industry experience	0.71	0.46	0.63	0.49
Business ownership experience	0.57	0.50	0.30***	0.46
Level of household responsibilities	10.5	11.5	16.2*	22.8
Value placed on growth				
Size a measure of business success	0.32	0.47	0.20*	0.41
Growth intentions				
Desire to grow	0.80	0.40	0.72	0.45
Plan to hire	0.76	0.43	0.74	0.44

Differences between male-headed and female-headed firms significant at * $p < .05$, ** $p < .01$, and *** $p < .001$, respectively.

measured by the estimated average number of hours spent on housework and child care per week.

The value attached to business expansion was measured by whether the participant stated size as a measure of business success. This was determined by content-analyzing responses to the open-ended question, "What factors do you consider in determining whether or not your business is successful?" If such criteria as sales level, number of customers, number of employees, market share, or growth were mentioned, the participant was deemed to have size as a business success measure.

Two variables served as indicators of growth intentions: whether the participant wanted to grow the business and whether he/she planned on hiring new employees in the year following the interview. These are very similar to those used by Kolvereid (1992).

RESULTS

The hypotheses derived from liberal and social feminism posit that gender differences in entrepreneurs' growth intentions can partially be explained by differences in the resources available for business expansion and the value attached to growth, respectively. I followed Baron and Kenny's (1986) suggestions for testing such mediated propositions: prior to examining whether resources and values mediated the relationship between gender and growth intentions, I examined whether there were significant gender differences in the explanatory and dependent variables. Table 2 presents the results of the chi-squared and *t*-tests (correlations are presented in the Appendix).

Consistent with the first part of H1, the liberal feminist argument, female participants possessed fewer resources for business expansion than their male counterparts. The women were significantly less likely to possess a business degree (9% of women versus 23% of men) and prior business ownership experience (30% of women versus 57% of men). The women also exhibited less freedom from domestic responsibilities, devoting approximately one-and-a-half times as many hours to housework and child care as the men (16.2 hours/week for women versus 10.5 hours/week for men). No gender differences were found in participants' managerial and industry experience. Consistent with the first part of H2, the social feminist argument, female participants attached less value to business expansion that their male counterparts: the women were significantly less likely to measure success by the size of their firm (20% of women versus 32% of men).

Although the women had fewer resources available for, and placed less value on, business expansion, they were just as likely to have positive growth intentions. No significant differences were observed for the proportion of male and female participants who stated that they wanted to grow their firm (72% of women and 80% of men) nor in the proportion who planned on hiring in the year following the interview (74% of women and 76% of men). Thus, H1 and H2, in their entirety, were not supported.

DISCUSSION

Given the consistently reported smaller size of female-owned firms, the strength of theoretical arguments propounding the notion of intentionally driven business growth, and the case for gender differences derived from applications of feminist theory, the lack of differences in the growth intentions of male and female entrepreneurs are not only surprising but also require an explanation. Sampling bias is one possibility: because firms with greater than five employees were selected for the larger human resources management study, growth-oriented female entrepreneurs may have been overrepresented in this investigation.[6] Although this explanation may account for the lack of gender differences in growth intentions, my recollection of the comments made by participants during their interviews suggested that the women in the sample—even if more expansion-oriented than other female entrepreneurs—did differ from the men in their attitudes toward growth. To help reconcile my interview experiences with the null findings from the theory-driven quantitative analysis, I decided to content-analyze qualitative data obtained from the responses to other open-ended questions.

This exercise resulted in rich descriptions of the growth decision as well as a set of inductively developed propositions regarding the relationship between attitudes toward growth, gender, and business size. Although the presentation of theory-testing and theory-building in one article departs from normative standards, it is not without precedent: see, for example, Elsbach (1994) and Sutton and Rafaeli (1988). Knowledge advances through cycles of deduction and induction, and researchers have been encouraged to "embark on a new phase of theory-building" when "empirical observations do not confirm a theory" (Sutton and Rafaeli 1988, p. 471).

QUALITATIVE ANALYSIS

Methods

The qualitative phase of data analysis consisted of content-analyzing responses to two questions, "How do you want to grow?" and "Why don't you want to grow?", which were asked after receiving a participant's reply to the more general question, "Do you want to grow the business?" As such, qualitative data on attitudes toward growth were analyzed for both types of entrepreneurs: those who did want to grow their firms and those who did not.

---

[6] I would like to thank one of the anonymous reviewers for pointing out this possible interpretation.

The content analysis was conducted in three stages. First, based on a subset of 70 interviews that were completed early on in the data collection period, I created initial categories of responses for both questions. Next, the face validity of my initial classification systems was evaluated by the principal investigator of the larger human resource management study and one of our research assistants, which resulted in the development of more clearly differentiated categories. Finally, all of the interviews were coded. To help minimize potential bias, I trained a second coder who was blind to both the gender of the participant and to my specific hypotheses. Our level of interrater agreement was approximately 85%, which suggests that the emergent categories fit the data. Any differences were resolved by discussion and, when necessary, by referral to the principal investigator of the larger investigation.

Chi-squared tests of independence were conducted to explore the existence of gender differences. As part of the inductive phase of the analysis, I also drew on excerpts from informal discussions held with some of the participants after the structured interviews. These excerpts were interpreted directly and offer a more holistic portrayal of entrepreneurs' attitudes toward growth as well as vivid illustrations of the themes that emerged from the content analysis.

Findings from Those Who Did Not Want to Grow: Considerations in the Growth Decision

Table 3 presents the emergent thematic categories, classification criteria, representative interview excerpts, frequencies, and chi-squared results for the responses of those who did not intend to expand their firm. The emergent thematic categories capture the factors that participants considered when deciding whether to grow. The majority of these factors reflect personal rather than economic considerations.

The most frequently reported no-growth reason is a case in point. When asked why they didn't want to expand, the majority (58.5%) replied that they had reached a size that they were comfortable managing—one that enabled them to maintain control over the organization, required a reasonable amount of time and energy, and/or allowed them to balance work and personal life. Illustrative statements include the following:

> I am very comfortable with the balance in my life. To improve upon things how they are now is more important than to expand at this point. I don't know if I'm the type of person who would be good in running a business twice as large. I'm at my limit.
> —*Female, personal services sector, has owned business for over 7 years*

> No, [I don't want to grow], not as fast as I have. I want to stabilize it . . . because growth is so hard and I'm tired of it. At first you have a lot of energy, but I'm at a point where I don't want it to be my whole life. I want my freedom.—*Female, retail sector, has owned business for over 9 years*

> [It's] a matter of control. Growth without stress would be okay.—*Male, business services sector, has owned business for over 19 years*

This type of response was interpreted as revealing the existence and attainment of a "maximum business-size threshold"—the optimal size beyond which an entrepreneur would prefer not to expand. In contrast to the tenets of standard microeconomic theory, assessments of marginal costs and prices are noticeably absent from participants' descriptions of the factors affecting the optimal size of their firms. Consistent with the

TABLE 3　Thematic Categories, Classification Criteria, and Representative Interview Excerpts for Participants' No-Growth Reasons[a]

Thematic Category	Classification Criteria	Representative Interview Excerpts	Proportion Citing Reason			χ^2
			Overall (n = 53)	Men (n = 28)	Women (n = 25)	
Threshold size reached	Participant believes is at his/her limit; doesn't think he/she would be able to handle growth, manage a larger firm, or maintain control; doesn't have the energy or time to grow the business; would not enjoy managing a growing business; wants a better balance between work and personal life.	"I couldn't handle it . . . [I] had two stores for a while . . . [it] takes up too much time . . . [a] second store is more than double the work." "[It's] a matter of control. Growth without stress would be okay." "Because growth is so hard and I'm tired of it. At first you have a lot of energy, but I'm at a point where I don't want it to be my whole life—I want my freedom." "I know what it takes and I'm not prepared to pour that much into it at this point in my life."	58.5	35.7	84.0	12.68**
Lack of emphasis placed on growth	Participant doesn't measure success by size; has run a large company before and is not interested in doing it again.	"[I'm] not concerned with it . . . it doesn't matter to me." "My self-actualization does not depend on how many people work for me." "We've been there, done that."	30.2	35.7	24.0	0.86
Willing to trade off growth for other business goals	Participant is willing to trade-off growth to accomplish other business objectives such as quality, profitability, or customer service.	"I want more quality, not quantity." "Big isn't necessarily best." "More stores doesn't necessarily mean more profits." "The key thing we offer clients is hands-on involvement. If we grew we would just be managers."	24.5	17.9	32.0	1.43
Costs and hassles associated with growth	Participant believes growth is costly, causes human resource problems, legal problems, or other hassles.	"Too many government hassles, particularly in a small business. You have increased personal and financial or responsibility." "You face tax problems . . . there is a lot of paperwork." "Union employees made too much per hour including benefits."	17.0	14.3	20.0	0.31
Exogenous factors preventing growth	Participant attributes lack of growth to market forces, poor economic conditions, or other external factors.	"You need a good economy and market to expand." "There's not a lot of growth potential." "[The] business is going through a bad time."	13.2	25.0	0.0	7.20*
No long-term interest in business	Participant wants to retire, close, or sell the business.	"I want to retire." "I'm tired of what I'm doing [running this business]."	5.7	10.7	0.0	2.84

[a] Column percentages sum to more than 100% because the categories were not mutually exclusive, and participants often provided several reasons for not wanting to grow. Pearson chi-square values significant at **$p < .01$ and *$p < .001$, respectively (Fisher's exact test used when at least one expected cell frequency was less than 5).

growth deterrents identified by Davidsson (1989), personal considerations—such as the fear of reduced control and the expectation of heavier workloads—tend to predominate. Interestingly, a significantly greater proportion of female participants attributed their lack of growth intentions to having attained their maximum business-size threshold: 84.0% of the women but only 35.7% of the men stated this no-growth reason.

The next two most frequently reported no-growth reasons are consistent with the theoretical argument that entrepreneurs' growth intentions are influenced by the value they place on business expansion. When asked why they didn't wish to expand, approximately one-third (30.2%) provided reasons indicating that they placed little emphasis on growth. Some didn't measure success by the size of their firms, as reflected by the entrepreneur who replied, "My self-actualization does not depend on how many people work for me." Others had managed large companies before and were not interested in doing it again: in the words of one entrepreneur, "We've been there, done that." No significant gender differences were found for this reason.

Approximately one-quarter (24.5%) indicated that they were willing to trade growth for other, more highly valued, business objectives. Responses such as "I want more quality, not quantity" and "More stores doesn't necessarily mean more profits" reveal a belief that expansion may interfere with other goals such as product quality, profitability, or customer service. No significant gender differences were found in the proportion citing this reason for electing not to grow.

The final three categories of no-growth reasons were each provided by less than one-fifth of participants who did not wish to expand. Seventeen percent replied that they were unwilling to assume responsibility for the additional financial and administrative responsibilities associated with business growth. One entrepreneur, for example, stated, "You face tax problems . . . there is a lot of paperwork." No significant gender differences were found in the proportion citing this reason.

Slightly more than 13% attributed their lack of growth intentions to exogenous factors, such as strong competitive forces or poor economic conditions, that were preventing them from expanding: as one entrepreneur succinctly put it, "You need a good economy and market to expand." In contrast to the other no-growth reasons, this type of response seems to suggest that business expansion is actually desired by the entrepreneur and would be pursued if environmental conditions were more favorable. Interestingly, none of the women yet one-quarter of the men cited this no-growth reason: a statistically significant gender difference.

Finally, 5.7% stated that they did not wish to expand because they had no long-term interest in the venture: they planned on retiring, closing, or selling the business. No significant gender differences were found for this reason.

Findings from Those Who Wanted to Expand:
The Pace of Business Growth

Whereas the above responses of participants who did not wish to grow increase our understanding of the factors affecting the expansion decision, the responses of those who did wish to grow offer insights into gender differences in the desired pace of business growth. In response to the question, "How do you want to grow?", 11.4% emphasized that they wanted to expand, but only in a cautious, controlled, or manageable manner. The following quotes are indicative of this type of response:

[I want to grow] but gradually—we knew we would run into problems if we kept on growing. I had to stop things for awhile. I spent a lot of time fixing internal things. —*Female, business services sector, has owned business for over 5 years*

Yes in volume but in a smart way—cautiously. I want to become a small- to medium-sized company. I don't want more 25 employees.—*Female, manufacturing sector, has owned business for over 16 years*

[I want to grow] a little, yeah. I'm not planning to be a giant. I don't want to be spending that much time on the business. I want to spend the least time possible to have the business profitable. If you grow too fast, you could very well bust it.—*Female, personal services sector, has owned business for less than 1 year.*

A chi-squared test revealed a marginally significant gender difference: 17.5% of the women but only 8.0% of the men ($\chi^2 = 3.62$, 1 df, $p < 0.10$) responded with statements such as these. Thus, although there do not appear to be any significant gender differences in terms of *whether* male and female entrepreneurs want to expand (H1 and H2 were not supported), there do seem to be important differences with respect to the *manner* in which they wish to grow. Female business owners appear to be more careful and conservative, purposely striving for a controlled and manageable rate of growth.

This deliberately chosen slower pace reflects a concern about the risks and negative outcomes associated with expanding too quickly. These risks and negative outcomes tend to be personal rather than economic, such as the belief that fast-paced expansion will place inordinate demands on the entrepreneur's time and energy. This theme is consistent with the concept of maximum business size thresholds that emerged through the content analysis of participants' no-growth reasons. It is also echoed in the following quotes by participants who offered their own explanations, during informal discussions after the structured interviews, for the existence of gender differences in entrepreneurs' growth attitudes:

We heard that a lot of men grow, build, and sell [their business]. They seem to find it easier to take risks. Women tend to be more careful, to hold back more, are not as interested in becoming a global company. Instead, they seem to want to do well managing what they've got, doing it methodically and carefully.—*Female, business services sector, has owned business for over 6 years*

Most men in this type of business would go out for venture capital, get on the stock exchange, get millions of dollars and then squander it. I never wanted that approach. I want to grow slowly and do meaningful things. I'm willing to do slow and steady growth rather than erratic, high-risk growth. I know that I'm changing the paradigm for people, making a difference. . . . It's not about the money but the satisfaction. . . . In a lot of ways this holds women back. . . . I'm not a big risk-taker.—*Female, business services sector, has owned business for over 12 years*

Any gals that I know in business want to manage their risks. They're not stupid like we are. They are a lot more conservative. I don't know many women owners, but I don't know any that have failed either. But I have known men that have failed. My wife and I have often been at loggerheads over the business. Unfortunately she let me do what I wanted [try to grow the business].—*Male, wholesale sector, has owned business for over 12 years*[7]

---

[7] Rather ironically, a telephone follow-up conducted approximately 1 year after the interview revealed that this participant was no longer in business.

EMERGENT PROPOSITIONS REGARDING THE RELATIONSHIP BETWEEN ATTITUDES TOWARDS GROWTH, GENDER, AND BUSINESS SIZE

As outlined in Glaser and Strauss's (1967) discussion of how to generate theory, the propositions developed in this section are grounded in the interplay between deduction, experience, and induction. These propositions not only elucidate previously unexplored considerations in the expansion decision of entrepreneurs, they also advance understanding of the reasons behind the smaller size of female-owned firms.

Maximum Business-Size Thresholds

One novel insight to emerge from the qualitative analysis of participants' no-growth reasons addresses the question of when entrepreneurs decide not to expand as well as the nature of the causal relationship between growth intentions and business size. It appears that many entrepreneurs express a desire to stop growing upon attaining the maximum business size threshold that they have established for the enterprise. This threshold represents the optimum or ideal size that the entrepreneur is comfortable managing—the size that allows them to maintain control over the organization, requires a reasonable amount of time or energy, and/or permits them to achieve a balance between work and personal life. The existence of such a threshold implies that the relationship between growth intentions and business size is bicausal: growth intentions not only influence the size of the firm, as suggested in several models of small business performance (e.g., Cooper 1993; Davidsson 1991; Herron and Robinson 1993), but these intentions are themselves dependent on the existing size of the organization.

This discovery of the bicausality between size and intentions is not entirely without theoretical precedent in the entrepreneurship literature. Herron and Robinson (1993), for example, suggested that a venture's performance affects an entrepreneur's motivation. Similarly, Davidsson (1991) and Kolvereid (1992) advanced the more specific proposition that a negative relationship exists between business size and an entrepreneur's growth aspirations: entrepreneurs heading smaller firms are hypothesized to have stronger growth aspirations than those heading larger firms. The results of this investigation extend this line of work by explicating a potential mechanism underlying the proposed relationship between performance and motivation.

The notion that growth intentions are dependent upon the existing size of the firm is also consistent, at a more fundamental level, with control theory models of behaviour. Control theory models of behavior, such as those proposed by Carver and Scheier (1981) and Klein (1989), posit that "the feedback loop is the fundamental building block of action" (Klein 1989, p. 151). The basic feedback loop works as follows: individuals compare information about their current status to a referent standard or goal; if a discrepancy is detected, the individual is motivated to take action to reduce the discrepancy. Although control theory models are intended to explain individual-level behavior, at least one entrepreneurship researcher has implicitly incorporated the central tenets of such models in the explanation of an organizational-level phenomenon. Cooper (1993), for example, suggested that the decision to remain in business may depend upon the minimum threshold level of performance established for the enterprise: if the firm is operating below this level, the entrepreneur may decide to discontinue in pursuit of better opportunities elsewhere.

Analogously, in terms of the expansion decision, the results of this study suggest that entrepreneurs compare the existing size of their firms with their maximum business size thresholds: if the existing size falls short of the threshold, they will desire further growth; if the threshold has been reached, they will no longer wish to expand. To summarize, the preceding discussion suggests that:

> *P1:* An entrepreneur's growth intentions are dependent on whether the firm has reached his/her maximum business-size threshold.

Gender Differences in Entrepreneurs' Maximum Size Thresholds and Desired Rate of Growth

The results of the qualitative analysis also point to the existence of gender differences in entrepreneurs' maximum business-size thresholds. Almost 85% of female participants, but only 36% of male participants, attributed their lack of growth intentions to having attained the ideal size that they are comfortable managing. This result suggests that male and female entrepreneurs may differ in the likelihood of establishing maximum size thresholds for their firms. More specifically, it is proposed that:

> *P2:* Female entrepreneurs will be more likely than male entrepreneurs to establish a maximum business-size threshold for their enterprise.

The following two comments made by participants during informal discussions after their structured interviews raise another intriguing possibility—that even if male entrepreneurs do establish size thresholds, they may be unable to stop growing once these thresholds have been reached:

> Men are so concerned about beating others. They're so competitive. Even if they don't start off wanting to be big, if their buddies are doing well, they have to do better because of their ego.—*Female, manufacturing sector, has owned business for over 11 years*

> I think a large part of why male-owned businesses go skyrocketing and then collapse is ego. Men are driven so hard by ego that they don't realize that they should stop. They can't.—*Female, business services sector, has owned business for over 10 years*

A further insight into the existence of gender differences in entrepreneurs' maximum business-size thresholds is indicated by the characteristics of the sampled firms. Despite the fact that the female-headed firms were less than half the size of the male-headed firms, statistically equivalent proportions of women and men (28% and 20%, respectively) stated that they did not want to grow their firms. Moreover, the average size of firms headed by participants who did not wish to expand was smaller for the women than the men, averaging nine versus 14 full-time equivalent employees respectively. Thus, it appears that gender differences exist in the ideal-sized firm desired by entrepreneurs. More specifically, it is proposed that:

> *P3:* Female entrepreneurs will have smaller maximum business-size thresholds than male entrepreneurs.

Male and female entrepreneurs appear to differ not only with respect to their maximum business-size thresholds but also in terms of the speed at which they strive to attain their ideal size. The qualitative findings of this investigation suggest that female entrepreneurs are more concerned than their male counterparts about the risks associated with fast-paced business growth, and thus deliberately strive to expand in a controlled and manageable manner. As such, it is proposed that:

> *P4:* Female entrepreneurs will desire a slower rate of business growth than male entrepreneurs.

Taken together, the three preceding propositions imply the following explanation to partially account for the smaller size of female-owned firms. Firms headed by women tend to be smaller than those headed by men because female entrepreneurs are more concerned than their male counterparts about growing in a cautious, controlled manner that does not exceed their maximum business-size threshold. This argument assumes that P1 holds—that attaining the maximum business-size threshold triggers the decision not to grow—and that this decision, in turn, influences the resultant size of the firm. Thus, the smaller size and slower growth rate of enterprises headed by women is at least in part a conscious choice of many female entrepreneurs.

CONCLUSION

A common finding in the entrepreneurship literature, and one that was supported by the results of this study, is that businesses owned by women tend to be smaller than those owned by men. Given the value placed on size in North American society, this outcome is typically interpreted as an indicator of the poorer performance of female-owned firms, and several investigations have been conducted to determine the cause of this "problem." The overarching question driving these studies seems to be: Do women have what it takes to become "successful" entrepreneurs? (Stevenson 1990). The underlying assumption appears to be that male and female entrepreneurs are equally motivated to run large, quickly growing enterprises. This study explored the validity of this assumption by examining entrepreneurs' attitudes toward expansion.

Based on applications of liberal and social feminist theory, I argued that female entrepreneurs would be less likely to state positive growth intentions than male entrepreneurs because they have fewer resources available for, and attach less value to, business expansion. The quantitative results did not fully support this conceptual perspective: although female participants did have less prior business ownership experience and less freedom from domestic responsibilities, and were less likely to measure success by the size of their firms, they were just as likely as male participants to desire growth.

Consistent with Sutton and Rafaeli's (1988) recommendations regarding the pursuit of scientific knowledge, a subsequent qualitative analysis was conducted to help make sense of this lack of empirical support. The emergent themes led to the development of novel propositions concerning the determinants of an entrepreneur's growth intentions and desired pace of expansion. It is proposed that many entrepreneurs establish a maximum business-size threshold for their firms, the attainment of which triggers the desire to curtail continued growth. A greater proportion of female entrepreneurs is expected to set such size limits, and these will likely be smaller than those established by their male counterparts. It also appears that female entrepreneurs express greater concern about the risks associated with fast-paced growth; as such, it is proposed that women desire a slower rate of expansion than men. These arguments may help account for the smaller size of female-owned firms.

The limitations of this study suggest several avenues for future research. First, the propositions regarding entrepreneurs' maximum business-size thresholds were based solely on the remarks of those participants who did not want to grow. Thus, further studies are needed to explore whether entrepreneurs who *do* want to grow also establish maximum size thresholds, whether being below such thresholds motivates the pursuit of continued expansion, and whether there are any gender differences. Second, the proposition regarding gender differences in the desired rate of expansion was based on responses to an open-ended question: all participants were not asked specifically about the importance placed on growing in a controlled, manageable manner. As such, further research is needed to determine whether the observed gender difference reflects a true difference in the growth orientations of male versus female entrepreneurs, or merely a difference in the rhetoric used by men versus women to describe their attitudes toward expansion. Third, due to the cross-sectional research design, it is not possible to claim that the observed gender differences in attitudes toward growth can partially account for the smaller size of female-owned firms. Such an inference awaits the results of longitudinal investigations.

Despite its limitations, this study makes a number of contributions to the emerging literature on gender and entrepreneurship. First, it addresses the criticism that existing gender studies are largely atheoretical (Allen and Truman 1992, 1993; Brush 1992; Fischer et al. 1993) by presenting a conceptual argument, based on applications of liberal and social feminist theory, for anticipating that male and female entrepreneurs will differ in their expansion intentions. Second, by posing open-ended questions in the data collection phase rather than relying on predefined measures, it captures entrepreneurs' approaches to growth "in their own voices." Third, it is one of very few comparative investigations of entrepreneurs' attitudes toward expansion; as such, it offers novel insights into the reasons behind the smaller size and slower growth of businesses headed by women.

This investigation also makes an important contribution to the broader entrepreneurship literature. In response to the need for increased understanding of mechanisms in general (Herron and Robinson 1993, p. 292) and what triggers the desire for no growth in particular (Kolvereid 1992, p. 220), the qualitative findings reported herein elucidate a previously unexplored aspect of the expansion decision. For many entrepreneurs—particularly women—the decision to grow appears to be dependent on whether the firm has reached the owner's maximum business-size threshold.

Although further research is needed on the relationship between attitudes toward growth, gender, and business size, the results of this study suggest that many female entrepreneurs deliberately choose to limit the growth rate and size of their firms. One size—large—does not necessarily fit all.

REFERENCES

Allen, S., and Truman, C. 1992. Women, business and self-employment: A conceptual minefield. In S. Arber and N. Gilbert, eds., *Women and Working Lives*. London: Macmillan, pp. 162–174.

Allen, S., and Truman, C. 1993. Women and men entrepreneurs: Life strategies, business strategies. In S. Allen and C. Truman, eds., *Women in Business: Perspectives on Women Entrepreneurs*. London: Routledge, pp. 1–13.

Baron, R., and Kenny, D. 1986. The moderator-mediator distinction in social psychological research: Conceptual, strategic, and statistical considerations. *Journal of Personality and Social Psychology* 51(6):1173–1182.

540 J.E. CLIFF

Belcourt, M. 1991. From the frying pan into the fire: Exploring entrepreneurship as a solution to the glass ceiling. *Journal of Small Business and Entrepreneurship* 8(3):49–55.

Belcourt, M., Burke, R., and Lee-Gosselin, H. 1991. *The Glass Box: Women Business Owners in Canada.* Ottawa: Canadian Advisory Council on the Status of Women.

Bird, B. 1988. Implementing entrepreneurial ideas: The case for intention. *Academy of Management Review* 13(3):442–453.

Birley, S., Moss, C., and Saunders, P. 1987. Do women entrepreneurs require different training? *American Journal of Small Business* Summer 12:27–35.

Black, N. 1989. *Social Feminism.* New York: Cornell University Press.

Brush, C. 1992. Research on women business owners: Past trends, a new perspective, and future directions. *Entrepreneurship Theory and Practice* Summer 16:5–30.

Buttner, H. 1993. Female entrepreneurs: How far have they come? *Business Horizons* March–April 36:59–65.

Carter, N., Williams, M., and Reynolds, P. 1995. Discontinuance among new firms in retail: The influence of initial resources, strategy and gender. Working paper, Marquette University, Milwaukee, WI.

Carver, C., and Scheier, M. 1981. *Attention and Self-Regulation: A Control Theory Approach to Human Behavior.* New York: Springer-Verlag.

Chaganti, R. 1986. Management in women-owned enterprises. *Journal of Small Business Management* 24(4):18–29.

Cooper, A. 1993. Challenges in predicting new firm performance. *Journal of Business Venturing* 8:241–253.

Cooper, A., Gimeno-Gascon, F.J., and Woo, C. 1994. Initial human and financial capital as predictors of new venture performance. *Journal of Business Venturing* 9:371–395.

Davidsson, P. 1989. Entrepreneurship—and after? A study of growth willingness in small firms. *Journal of Business Venturing* 4:211–226.

Davidsson, P. 1991. Continued entrepreneurship: Ability, need, and opportunity as determinants of small firm growth. *Journal of Business Venturing* 6:405–429.

Eagly, A., and Wood, W. 1991. Explaining sex differences in social behavior: A meta-analytic perspective. *Personality and Social Psychology Bulletin* 17(3):306–315.

Elsbach, K. 1994. Managing organizational legitimacy in the California cattle industry: Construction and effectiveness of verbal accounts. *Administrative Science Quarterly* 39:57–88.

Fischer, E. 1992. Sex differences and small-business performance among Canadian retailers and service providers. *Journal of Small Business and Entrepreneurship* 9(4):2–13.

Fischer, E., Reuber, R., and Dyke, L. 1993. A theoretical overview and extension of research on sex, gender, and entrepreneurship. *Journal of Business Venturing* 8:151–168.

Glaser, B., and Strauss, A. 1967. *The Discovering of Grounded Theory.* Chicago, IL: Aldine.

Goffee, R., and Scase, R. 1985. *Women in Charge: The Experiences of Female Entrepreneurs.* London: George Allen and Unwin.

Herron, L., and Robinson, R. 1993. A structural model of the effects of entrepreneurial characteristics on venture performance. *Journal of Business Venturing* 8:281–294.

Hisrich, R., and Brush, C. 1983. The women entrepreneur: Implications of family, educational, and occupational experience. *Frontiers of Entrepreneurship Research.* Wellesley, MA: Babson College, pp. 255–270.

Kalleberg, A., and Leicht, K. 1991. Gender and organizational performance: Determinants of small business survival and success. *Academy of Management Journal* 34(1):136–161.

Kaplan, E. 1988. Women entrepreneurs: Constructing a framework to examine venture success and failure. *Frontiers of Entrepreneurship Research.* Wellesley, MA: Babson College, pp. 643–653.

Klein, H. 1989. An integrated control theory model of work motivation. *Academy of Management Review* 14(2):150–172.

Kolvereid, L. 1992. Growth aspirations among Norwegian entrepreneurs. *Journal of Business Venturing* 7:209–222.

Lee-Gosselin, H., and Grisé, J. 1990. Are women owner–managers challenging our definitions of entrepreneurship? An in-depth survey. *Journal of Business Ethics* 9:423–433.

Locke, E. 1991. The motivation sequence, the motivation hub, and the motivation core. *Organizational Behavior and Human Decision Processes* 50:288–299.

Miller, A. 1995. The knockout lesson. *Inc.* June:21–22.

Sexton, D. 1989a. Growth decisions and growth patterns of women-owned enterprises. In O. Hagan, C. Rivchun, and D. Sexton, eds., *Women-Owned Businesses.* New York: Praeger, pp. 135–150.

Sexton, D. 1989b. Research on women-owned businesses: Current status and future directions. In O. Hagan, C. Rivchun, and D. Sexton, eds., *Women-Owned Businesses.* New York: Praeger, pp. 183–193.

Stevenson, L. 1990. Some methodological problems associated with researching women entrepreneurs. *Journal of Business Ethics* 9:439–446.

Stoner, C., Hartman, R., and Arora, R. 1990. Work–home role conflict in female owners of small businesses: An exploratory study. *Journal of Small Business Management* 28(1):30–38.

Sutton, R., and Rafaeli, A. 1988. Untangling the relationship between displayed emotions and organizational sales: The case of convenience stores. *Academy of Management Journal* 31(3):461–487.

Travis, C., McKenzie, B., Wiley, D., and Kahn, A. 1988. Sex and achievement domain: Cognitive patterns of success and failure. *Sex Roles* 19(7/8):509–525.

Unger, R., and Crawford, M. 1992. *Women and Gender: A Feminist Psychology.* New York: McGraw-Hill.

Venkatraman, N., and Ramanujam, V. 1986. Measurement of business performance in strategy research: A comparison of approaches. *Academy of Management Review* 11(4):801–814.

Watkins, J., and Watkins, D. 1983. The female entrepreneur: Background and determinants of business choice—Some British data. *Frontiers of Entrepreneurship Research.* Wellesley, MA: Babson College, pp. 271–288.

Williams, J. 1987. *Psychology of Women: Behavior in a Biosocial Context.* New York: W.W. Norton and Company.

APPENDIX Correlation Matrix for Male-Owned and Female-Owned Firms[a]

Variables	1	2	3	4	5	6	7	8	9	10	11	12	13	14	15	16
1 Retail		−0.45	−0.18	−0.24	−0.17	0.12	0.06	−0.07	−0.17	0.01	−0.22	−0.08	−0.10	−0.06	−0.16	−0.00
2 Business services	−0.25		−0.29	−0.39	−0.27	−0.15	−0.13	0.14	0.21	−0.05	0.28	−0.00	0.10	0.08	0.08	−0.02
3 Personal services	−0.08	−0.21		−0.15	−0.11	−0.02	−0.01	−0.09	−0.11	−0.13	0.11	0.08	−0.05	−0.08	−0.12	0.12
4 Manufacturing	−0.16	−0.42	−0.14		−0.14	0.06	0.03	0.06	−0.04	0.07	−0.21	0.08	0.10	−0.15	0.22	−0.01
5 Wholesale	−0.17	−0.48	−0.15	−0.29		0.03	0.11	−0.10	0.04	0.10	0.00	−0.05	−0.12	0.23	−0.06	−0.08
6 Years firm owned	−0.01	−0.20	−0.07	0.09	0.20		0.18	−0.06	0.04	−0.02	0.05	−0.17	−0.07	−0.13	−0.16	0.00
7 Number of employees	0.10	−0.18	−0.12	0.10	0.11	0.20		0.13	−0.06	0.01	0.04	−0.04	0.23	−0.17	0.02	0.19
8 Number of owners	0.06	−0.05	−0.09	−0.13	0.19	0.02	0.14		−0.03	0.01	0.10	−0.05	0.01	0.10	0.15	−0.06
9 Business degree	0.02	−0.02	0.14	−0.03	−0.03	−0.17	0.13	0.08		0.10	0.00	0.02	0.06	−0.16	−0.06	−0.17
10 Management experience	−0.16	0.02	−0.01	0.09	0.00	−0.35	−0.05	−0.01	0.07		−0.05	−0.04	0.12	0.18	−0.10	0.04
11 Industry experience	−0.08	0.07	0.04	−0.09	0.03	0.10	0.09	0.03	−0.10	0.06		−0.09	−0.01	0.16	−0.12	−0.09
12 Prior ownership experience	0.00	−0.03	0.09	−0.02	0.01	−0.10	−0.07	−0.12	−0.01	−0.05	−0.03		0.16	0.01	0.23	0.06
13 Hours on housework	−0.04	0.01	−0.01	0.10	−0.08	0.00	−0.06	0.00	0.10	0.19	−0.05	−0.05		0.04	0.19	0.10
14 Size measure of success	0.06	0.22	0.01	−0.21	−0.10	−0.23	−0.12	0.07	0.03	0.05	−0.03	−0.04	0.03		0.07	0.17
15 Intend to grow	0.02	0.00	−0.02	−0.05	0.03	−0.17	0.18	−0.03	−0.03	0.05	−0.01	−0.12	0.11	0.07		0.08
16 Plan to hire	−0.01	0.02	−0.06	0.09	−0.07	−0.13	0.22	−0.06	0.11	−0.04	0.08	−0.04	0.01	0.10	0.22	

[a] Correlations for male-owned firms are below the diagonal and those for female-owned firms are above. Coefficients are for Pearson product-moment correlations when both variables are continuous and for Spearman rank-order correlations when at least one variable is categorical. Coefficients with an absolute value greater than 0.17 for male-owned firms and 0.21 for female-owned firms are significant at $p < .05$.

[22]

WOMEN BUSINESS OWNERS IN TRADITIONAL AND NON-TRADITIONAL INDUSTRIES

ALEXANDRA L. ANNA
United States Air Force Academy

GAYLEN N. CHANDLER
Utah State University

ERIK JANSEN
Department of Systems Management,
Naval Postgraduate School

NEAL P. MERO
Department of Management & Decision Sciences,
Washington State University

EXECUTIVE SUMMARY

Small businesses continue to grow in importance to the national economy. According to the Small Business Administration, America's 22 million small businesses generate more than half of the nation's Gross Domestic Product and are the principal source of new jobs. The National Foundation for Women Business Owners reported that between 1987 and 1994, the number of women-owned businesses grew by 78% and women-owned firms accounted for 36% of all firms. Although the growth in the number of women-owned businesses is encouraging, the size of such businesses remains small in terms of both revenues and number of employees, especially in comparison to male-owned businesses. One explanation for this disparity is that female business ownership is concentrated primarily in the retail and service industries where businesses are relatively smaller in terms of employment and revenue as opposed to high technology, construction, and manufacturing.

One of the most fruitful streams of research in women's occupational choice has been based on

Address correspondence to Alexandra L. Anna at HQ USAFA/DFM, 2354 Fairchild Drive, Suite 6H94, USAFA, CO 80840-5701; (719) 333-4405; Fax: (719) 333-2944; E-mail: AnnaAL.DFM@USAFA.AF.MIL

This research was funded in part by the Ewing Marion Kauffman Foundation and the Center for Entrepreneurial Leadership. An earlier version of this paper was presented in the Entrepreneurship Division of the National Academy of Management Meeting held in Cincinnati, August, 1996. We acknowledge comments and contributions by several anonymous reviewers.

0883-9026/00/$–see front matter
PII S0883-9026(98)00012-3

social learning theory. Specifically, self-efficacy has been found to relate to both type and number of occupations considered by college men and women, and with regard to traditional and non-traditional occupations. Entrepreneurship researchers have also used social learning theory to study entrepreneurial intentions. This study builds on that background of women's career development and entrepreneurial intentions to examine differences between traditional and non-traditional women business owners. We examine 170 women business owners in various traditional and non-traditional businesses in Utah and Illinois. Questionnaires were the primary method of collecting data, in addition to 11 in-depth interviews from a sample of the survey respondents. Using a careers perspective, based on social learning theory, we hypothesized that women in these two different categories of industries would differ on levels of self-efficacy toward entrepreneurship or venture efficacy, their career expectations and their perceived social support. A second analysis was also done that explored the relationship between the same independent variables and success or performance of the business. The results offer support for using this integrative model to understand differences between women in traditional and non-traditional industries. The first analysis revealed that significant differences exist between the two groups on several of the independent variables. Traditional business owners had higher venture efficacy for opportunity recognition, higher career expectations of life balance and security and they reported that the financial support received from others was more important to them than those in non-traditional businesses. On the other hand, the non-traditional owners had higher venture efficacy for planning and higher career expectations for money or wealth than the traditional group.

The second analysis explored whether success, as measured by sales, was affected by differences in venture efficacies, career expectations, or perceived support received by women in traditional businesses as compared to those in non-traditional ones. This analysis revealed that traditional women business owners might have different factors that contribute to their success than non-traditional owners. Specifically, for the traditional owners, venture efficacies for opportunity recognition and economic management as well as the career expectation of autonomy and money (or wealth) were positively related to sales. For the same group efficacy toward planning and the need for security were negatively related to sales. For the non-traditional women, venture efficacy toward planning and the career expectation of autonomy were positively related to sales while the expectation of money or wealth was negatively related. Also for the same group, the perceived importance of the emotional and financial support was negatively related to sales.

In the past, most of the entrepreneurial research has used predominantly male samples of entrepreneurs. Those that include women entrepreneurs generally are comparative, between men and women. This study's comparison of two groups of women entrepreneurs offers a unique contribution to the field.

Future research is recommended to further understand how venture efficacy and career expectations affect the decision to start a new business in a particular industry. It would be particularly beneficial to study venture efficacy and career expectations of prospective women entrepreneurs prior to the start of the business. Similarly, greater attention should be given to understanding how venture efficacy develops in different individuals. © 1999 Elsevier Science Inc.

INTRODUCTION

The National Foundation of Women Business Owners (NFWBO) reports that although there has been tremendous growth in the number of women in non-traditional industries, two out of three women-owned firms remain in the retail trade and service sectors (NFWBO 1994). The concentration of women in these types of businesses is not surprising, given that they represent traditional areas of employment for women (Birley 1989; Bowen and Hisrich 1986; Brush 1987; Hisrich and Brush 1986; Hisrich and Brush 1984; Loscocco and Robinson 1991; Scott 1986; Smith, Smits, and Hoy 1992). In their study of barriers to women's small business success, Loscocco and Robinson (1991) suggest that "women's influx into small capitalism results from their movement into expanding, but highly competitive, industrial niches that are relatively unattractive to men" (1991:511). Their analyses found that women-owned businesses are concentrated in traditional female-typed fields with lower average business receipts than male-typed fields. Loscocco and Robinson (1991) categorize the retail and service industries as female-typed, and the manufacturing, construction, and high technology as male-typed.

As women increasingly enter the ranks of business founders, it is important to develop an understanding of how or if women business owners in various industries differ. Understanding women's experiences can help us better understand the education and training needs of potential women entrepreneurs. In her review of research on women business owners, Brush (1992) suggests that few studies have looked at differences in individual characteristics between groups of women. More often the focus has been on looking at similarities and differences between men and women. The purpose of this study is to investigate individual level differences between women business owners in construction, high technology, or manufacturing sectors that historically have been male dominated, and women business owners in the more traditional retail or service sectors. As indicated by Bowen and Hisrich (1986), a careers perspective is likely to produce fruitful insights on how to encourage women to venture into non-traditional industries to start their businesses. This study uses both a more traditional careers perspective and a more applied occupational choice perspective to investigate these two groups of women entrepreneurs: traditional and non-traditional.

Some attempts have been made to develop a theory of women's entrepreneurial careers (Bowen and Hisrich 1986), however most of the entrepreneurial career development research has been based primarily on career patterns of male entrepreneurs (Diamond 1989; Gallos 1989). The issue of women's career development has received more attention in the organizational behavior literature (Gutek and Larwood 1989; Konek and Kitch 1994; Nieva and Gutek 1981). In addition, some of these researchers have specifically studied why women select or choose to enter traditional or non-traditional occupations (Moore and Rickel 1980). One of the most prolific areas of research into women's selections of occupations has been in the vocational counseling area with the application of Bandura's (1977) theory of self-efficacy to the study of career behaviors (Hackett and Betz 1981). In the entrepreneurship arena, Boyd and Vozikis (1994) have examined the role of self-efficacy in the development of entrepreneurial intentions. This study examines differences between women who start businesses in both traditional and non-traditional fields by pulling together the career development and self-efficacy research. Our basic research objectives are to explore the possibility that differences in career orientations and types of venture efficacy distinguish women business owners in traditional industries from those in non-traditional industries. In addition, we want to examine the relationship between career orientations and venture efficacy and the success of the business owner.

The literature on career and occupational choice revolves around three main themes. The first theme shows that individual competencies or efficacies toward certain skills seem to be related to occupational choices that people make. The second theme shows that individual motives or desired outcomes appear to influence career decisions. Finally, the third theme shows that choices people make are often restricted or modified by the individual's context. The next section will examine each of these three themes as they apply to entrepreneurship.

COMPARING WOMEN BUSINESS OWNERS IN DIFFERENT INDUSTRIES USING A CAREERS PERSPECTIVE

As the number of women in the work force increases, the subject of women's career development has become increasingly important (Gutek and Larwood 1989). For many years women were considered casual workers who only stayed in the labor force until they got married and had children. There was little need for a theory of women's careers, as there weren't many to speak of. As suggested by Gutek and Larwood (1989), "men had careers; women had temporary employment or jobs that took second place to family interests and obligations" (1989:8).

A considerable amount of research has been done on organizational careers. Some of this research has been translated to entrepreneurial careers and the issue of women's career development has become a research area on its own. Dyer (1994) suggests that a comprehensive theory of entrepreneurial careers should contain four sub-theories: career choice, career socialization, career orientation, and career progression. This study focuses on a couple of aspects of women's careers. First, it is about the careers of women entrepreneurs, not of women on more conventional career paths. Second, the focus is on women who start traditional or non-traditional businesses, it is not a comparison of male and female entrepreneurs. Therefore, we focus primarily on the sub-theory of career orientation, which is useful in understanding why women choose to own a traditional business as compared to a non-traditional business.

Women's Career Development in Traditional vs. Non-traditional Occupations

The study of careers has been through many changes over the last 20 years, for both men and women. Specifically, for women the focus has gone from one where women were expected to choose homemaking as a career, through one where women worked until marriage and/or children, to one of studying women who choose non-traditional careers—pioneers (Gutek and Larwood 1989). Some researchers have suggested that as more women enter the labor force, they will behave more like men in their career development. Others suggest that women's careers are different and likely to remain so in the near future (Gallos 1989; Powell and Mainiero 1992). Some of the reasons for this difference include: differential expectations for men and women, family career progress, parental role expectations, and external constraints (discrimination, stereotypes, etc.). Gutek and Larwood (1989) assert that this difference does not mean that every study of women's careers should include a comparison with men. There are many internal dynamics to women's career experiences that should be examined.

Researchers have looked at the difference between women in traditional and non-traditional occupations from many different angles or perspectives. One study found that women in non-traditional professions (like business), participated more in competitive sports as children and reported more male playmates and fewer female playmates than did women in traditional professions (Coats and Overman 1992). The same study also examined forms of encouragement by fathers and mothers and their relationship to type of profession. In a more individual oriented type of study, Moore and Rickel (1980) examined characteristics of women in traditional and non-traditional managerial roles. Their study found that women in non-traditional business roles were more achieving, emphasized production more, saw themselves as having characteristics more like managers and men, and saw no self-characteristics which conflicted with those ascribed to male managers, contrary to women in traditional roles.

One of the most fruitful areas of occupational preference research has been in the vocational counseling area. In their model of women's career development based on social learning theory, Hackett and Betz (1981) suggest that primarily "as a result of socialization experiences, women lack strong expectations of personal efficacy in relationship to many career-related behaviors and thus, fail to fully realize their capabilities and talents in career pursuits" (1981:326). In an empirical test of their model, Betz and Hackett (1981) found that self-efficacy expectations were related to both the type and number of occupations considered by college men and women, and with regard to traditional and non-traditional occupations. Although men had approximately equal self-efficacy for either class of occupation, women had higher levels of self-efficacy for traditional occupations and lower levels for non-traditional occupations.

Several studies have followed up on this stream of research (Fiorentine 1988; Mathieu, Sowa, and Niles 1993; Nevill and Schlecker 1988; Whiston 1993). Whiston's (1993) findings extended the Hackett and Betz (1981) research by examining self-efficacy and its relationship to working with people or working with things. She found that employed women have higher self-efficacy for tasks associated in working with people than for tasks associated in working with things. In yet another extension of this research, Mathieu, Sowa, and Niles (1993) examined differences in career self-efficacy. Women who already expressed preference for a non-traditional career had significantly higher scores on a measure of career self-efficacy than women with traditional career preferences. The self-efficacy concept has been shown to be an important influence on these types of decisions and may also differentiate between women in traditional and non-traditional types of businesses.

The psychology literature has explored the relationship between self-efficacy, intentions, and behavior (Fishbein and Ajzen 1975). Intentions are hypothesized to be the link between beliefs and subsequent behavior (Fishbein and Ajzen 1975). People form attitudes about performing a specific behavior. These attitudes are developed from the individual's beliefs that performing that specific behavior will result in certain outcomes, as well as his or her normative beliefs about the behavior. Several entrepreneurship researchers have used this theory to specifically explore the concept of entrepreneurial intentions. Bird (1988) developed a model of entrepreneurial intentionality grounded in cognitive psychology theory that tried to predict or explain human behavior. Applying this theory to new venture creation, Bird (1988) suggested that individuals are predisposed to entrepreneurial intentions based upon a combination of personal and contextual factors.

Subsequently, other researchers have seen a need to incorporate the concept of self-efficacy into Bird's model of entrepreneurial intentionality. More recently in the social psychology literature, Ajzen (1991) developed the theory of planned behavior, which suggests that perceived behavioral control is an important determinant of intentions and, ultimately, behavior. He points out that perceived behavioral control is very similar to the notion of self-efficacy (Bandura 1977). Both concepts refer to an individual's perceived ability to attain a given goal or behavior. Krueger and Carsrud (1993) includes a related variable called perceived feasibility in his model of the formation of entrepreneurial intentions. Finally, Boyd and Vozikis (1994) revise Bird's (1988) original model of entrepreneurial intentions to include self-efficacy. In their discussion of the model, they suggest that career development theory is a framework within which the role of self-efficacy can be studied as it relates to the development of entrepreneurial intentions and behavior. The following discussion of three themes is built around the basic influences on an individual's feeling of self-efficacy toward entrepreneurship. The first theme is venture efficacy, which specifically discusses self-efficacy in the specific domain of entrepreneurship. The second theme is career expectations, which goes back to the original link between beliefs, attitudes, intentions, and behaviors. Career expectations are those beliefs individuals have about the consequences of performing a certain behavior. Finally, the third theme is individual context, which is similar to Bird's (1988) contextual factors.

Theme 1: Venture Efficacy

As used in Bandura's (1977) social learning theory, self-efficacy is a specialized judgment. It is a construct that varies with the individual's context. In considering self-efficacy in the context of owning and running one's own business venture, there are several types of skills and abilities that must be assessed. In the context of this study, self-efficacy is referred to as venture efficacy.

Several specific efficacy domains have been identified in the entrepreneurship literature as important in founding businesses and may be useful in differentiating women who choose to operate businesses in traditional vs. non-traditional industries. First is the perceived ability to recognize a business opportunity. Vesper (1994) states that entrepreneurs must be able to generate and screen ideas. Chandler and Jansen (1992) refer to the ability to recognize and envision taking advantage of opportunity as entrepreneurial competence. Timmons et al (1987) suggests that this ability is the core of entrepreneurship. We refer to this specific venture-efficacy as opportunity recognition.

Second, when an entrepreneur has launched the business, the ability to manage the business and its employees and deliver a quality product on time is crucial to the survival and growth of the venture. Chandler and Jansen (1992) refer to this ability as managerial competence. Vesper (1994) distinguishes managerial competence into two important areas. First, managing employees involves more human/conceptual competencies. Next, managing the cash flow and efficiency of operations involves more economic management competencies. For women these financial management skills have been identified as an area of weakness, often due to educational background (Collerette and Aubry 1990; Stevenson 1986). We refer to these two types of venture efficacy as efficacy for economic management and human/conceptual competence.

In discussing planning for entrepreneurs, Vesper (1994) suggests that plans can take many different forms and serve many purposes. Although Vesper suggests that the planning phase may be the least necessary, Rieke (1993) suggests that for women, putting together a business plan to obtain financing is a troublesome step, and that it may differentiate between women who start larger, more progressive ventures and those who bootstrap. In addition, Castrogiovanni (1996) considers how varying degrees of planning relate to planning benefits and, ultimately, business survival. This type of efficacy is referred to as planning. We believe that perceived venture efficacies in each of these areas may differentiate between women who choose opportunities in traditional versus non-traditional industries.

Theme 2: Career Expectations

In trying to understand why some women choose to become entrepreneurs in traditional vs. non-traditional industries, it is useful to examine motives for business start-up or venture formation. A common thread that runs through models of venture formation is the importance of the reasons leading to business start-up (Shane, Kolvereid, and Westhead 1991). Gartner (1989) argues that there are individual differences among those who start ventures, the types of organizations they create, the environment surrounding the venture, and the process by which it is started, as opposed to a universal theory of new venture formation. Differences have been found in the reasons for new business formation between men and women (e.g., Hisrich and Brush 1984). Shane, Kolveried, and Westhead (1991) found that choice seemed to be the function of an interaction of gender and nationality. It is likely that within gender there may exist different motives or reasons for new formation that are related to the type of business started.

In the vocational literature Brooks and Betz (1990) found marked and consistent gender differences in outcome valences and the likelihood of choosing specific male and female dominated occupations, which varied according to the traditionality of the occupation. Some researchers (Birley 1989; Hisrich and O'Brien 1982; Loscocco and Robinson 1991) have suggested that entrepreneurship opportunities also are subject to gender segregation. Thus, it is possible that motives may be related to the type of business started, just as they are to career choice.

Katz (1992) suggests that Schein's career anchors model is well suited for research in entrepreneurial careers because it is one of the few models that consider self-employed individuals. Schein defines a career anchor as "that element in our self-concept that we will not give up, even if forced to make a difficult choice" (1978:158). In Schein's (1978) career anchor model he proposes that certain aspects of a person's career self-image serve as a guiding force for career decisions. Part of this image may be based on individual assessment of competencies and an assessment of their motives or goals. Schein identifies several types of career anchors: security, autonomy, technical/functional, managerial, service, challenge, life style, and identity. He also specifically identifies a separate anchor called the entrepreneurial/creativity anchor. In his research he found that the group of individuals with this anchor was clearly very different from the other more managerial type of anchor groups. The dream of founding one's own business leads these individuals to leave traditional organizations or keep them only as a sideline while they build their enterprise.

Derr (1984) also used a career anchors perspective to specifically identify different types of entrepreneurs that fall under the entrepreneurial anchor, and Derr found that different types of entrepreneurs have distinctly different motives and types of businesses. Researchers have given considerable thought to how entrepreneur's careers differ from managerial careers (Derr 1984; Dyer 1994; Katz 1992; Scherer, Brodzinski, and Wiebe 1990), but the possibility that different career expectations or anchors affect the entrepreneurs choice of business has yet to be studied.

The concept of a career orientation is similar to that of person-organization fit, which has been considered more often in the organizational literature (Cable and Judge 1996; Chatman 1989). In discussing how people select their environments, Cable and Judge (1996) suggest, "'job seekers' prefer organizations that have the same 'personality' as they do" (1996:294). Lovelace and Rosen (1996) focus attention on race and sex in organizational fit by exploring the differences in organizational experiences faced by female and minority managers and those faced by white male managers. Derr's (1984) description of different types of entrepreneurs would suggest that business owners take part in the same type of self-selection. This career anchors perspective is used to examine differences among women who have started businesses in both traditional and non-traditional industries.

Theme 3: Individual Context

A closely related issue with career expectations, venture-efficacy, and social learning theory is the support received by potential entrepreneurs. Bandura (1986) suggests that structural and institutional arrangements allow social bias to influence outcomes regardless of perceived self-efficacy. An important aspect of the individual context is how much support the entrepreneur receives (Aldrich, Reese, and Dubini 1989; Chrisman, Carsrud, DeCastro, and Herron 1990). This support may be in the form of financing, encouragement, or hands-on operational support.

Enactive attainment, or actual profits and losses, to an entrepreneur in any particular industry, is an influential source of efficacy information (Bandura 1986). Another important source of self-efficacy information is verbal or social persuasion (Bandura 1986). This social persuasion can range from positive encouragement of friends and family to professional support from bankers and accountants. From a.social learning theory perspective, people who are persuaded verbally that they possess the skills and talent to achieve certain goals are more likely to put forth greater effort than those who may have self-doubts (Bandura 1986). For women venturing into non-traditional types of businesses, this social persuasion or support may be relevant in ways that are different from those that apply to women taking a more traditional path.

From an entrepreneurship perspective, the support construct has focused primarily on networking, or obtaining information and resources that are important to starting and developing a business (Brush 1992). In her review of research on women business owners, Brush (1992) found that women business owners tend to have many strong supporters. For many women business owners a spouse or significant other is an important factor in maintaining a successful business (Nelson 1989). In addition to this more personal type of support, there are also some environmental types of support that are important for entrepreneurs. This type of support comes from bankers, accountants, lawyers, small business development counselors, and other professionals.

The value of assistance from personal associates to the female business founder appears to have mixed results (Hisrich and Brush 1986; Stoner, Hartman, and Arora 1990) Based on his empirical study of the relevance of significant others to female business owners, Nelson (1989) hypothesizes that female owners look to those most qualified in their given area of business for help. In some cases spouses or significant others are valued for the emotional support provided, and in other cases the same individuals provide more pragmatic support, like money or labor.

Greenberger and Sexton (1988) suggest that "social supporters can be valuable in changing attitudes" (p. 7). If the potential entrepreneur sees that the important people in her life believe in her idea, then that person begins to believe more strongly in herself. The different type and level of support received by women entrepreneurs may vary by industry. The gender compositions of important networks, trade associations, and other industry type organizations will represent the gender composition of the industry. Gaining access to these support systems may be more difficult for non-traditional owners. Thus, the importance of support, whether it is emotional, financial or operational, may be different for non-traditional women business owners than for their more traditional counterparts.

Venture-efficacy, career expectations, and support received from the individual's context are factors that potentially influence the choice of women entrepreneurs to pursue businesses in traditional vs. non-traditional industries. They may also influence the success of that venture. This research explores those questions.

METHODS

Due to the limited research on the experience of women business owners in traditional vs. non-traditional industries, we used survey methodology supported by qualitative methods to provide more detail about women's experiences and decisions (Strauss and Corbin 1990). The qualitative data that was gathered through interviews was used to provide a richer discussion of items not easily answered in the survey. Interviews were recorded and transcribed for analysis.

Experimental Sample and Procedures

Questionnaires were mailed to a total of 369 women business founders in Illinois and 240 women business founders in Utah. Both lists came from each states' individual chapter of the National Association of Women Business Owners (NAWBO). Respondents were asked how they started their business and those who responded with "inherited it" were not included in the analysis. The data were collected from the two samples during the same time period. The effective response rate was 27.9% (N = 170) for the entire sample of business owners. The response rate for Utah (39.1%) may be higher than for Illinois (20.5%) because the correspondence was mailed out under the auspices of the University of Utah, and women business owners may be more willing to take the time to respond to a survey from an educational institution in their home state. Also, the Utah chapter of the NAWBO published a letter in their monthly newsletter that solicited people to respond to the survey. The sample used for most analyses in this study was 143 as 27 surveys had some missing data. Analyses using sales as a dependent variable are based on a sample of 103 because 40 respondents did not report total sales information that will be discussed in a later section.

To assess potential differences within the sample caused by the variety of states, t-tests analyses were conducted to measure all independent and dependent variables. There were significant differences (p $\leq$ 0.05) between the Utah and Illinois samples in the age of the company, age of the owner, venture-efficacy for human competence, and sales. These differences indicate that, on average, women business owners in Illinois operated businesses that were better established and more mature. To control for these differences, state and business ages are included as control variables in each analysis.

Interviews were conducted from the sample of survey respondents. After the completed surveys were received, arrangements were made to interview 11 (9 from Utah and 2 from Illinois) business owners. The authors recognize the disparity between the number of interviews conducted in Utah vs. the number conducted in Illinois, however more interviews were conducted in Utah simply because of cost, accessibility, and the time availability of the respondents. The analysis of the interview data was consistent with recommendations by Strauss and Corbin (1990) for the combined use of quantitative and qualitative data. Qualitative data is used "to illustrate or clarify quantitatively derived findings" (p. 18). These results will be presented in the discussion section to provide a richer understanding of the survey results.

Demographic Characteristics of Respondents

The sample is predominantly comprised of Caucasian women, married or partnered, and over the age of 40. Over half of the sample have no children living at home, 15% have one child at home and 16% have two children living at home. Businesses range in age from 1 year to 51 years with the mean age being 7.74 years. Businesses in this sample represent a variety of both traditional and non-traditional industries.

Dependent Variables

Sales

Measuring financial performance of an organization is a problematic issue (Venkatraman and Ramanujam 1986). There are additional challenges faced when measuring financial performance or success in entrepreneurship research. Chandler and Hanks (1993) suggest that new ventures are usually privately held with no obligation to divulge performance information, and traditional financial measures of performance are often unavailable. In general these traditional measures of performance have been developed for large, publicly held firms, not for small privately held emerging firms (Chandler and Hanks 1993).

Additionally, in a study of womens' motivations toward entrepreneurship, Buttner and Moore (1997) also suggest that perhaps traditional economic measures of success make women-owned businesses appear to be less successful than male-owned businesses. This may be because women-owned businesses tend to be smaller and slower growing (Buttner and Moore 1997). In a study of womens' career paths, Larwood and Gattiker (1989) have suggested that women may look to outcomes other than business growth to a measure their success. Some of these outcomes may be challenge, personal growth or balance (Buttner and Moore 1997). Survival rates of male and female owned businesses are comparable (Kalleberg and Leicht 1991). However, the way women run their businesses to achieve what they define as success may mean that the traditional measures of business success or performance do not adequately represent success for female entrepreneurs (Buttner and Moore 1997).

Nonetheless, following the entrepreneurship literature and Chandler and Hanks' (1993) recommendation, data on sales and sales growth was asked for in the survey, in addition to some open-ended questions regarding motivation for becoming an entrepreneur. Sales data was asked for in two different ways from the owners. First, the survey asked respondents for the last three years of exact sales figures. These numbers would have been used to estimate growth for the business (Chandler and Hanks 1993). Unfortunately, the majority of respondents failed to provide this information. In many cases, respondents gave only one or two of the three years of figures requested. Many gave no exact sales figures. However, as a back-up performance measure (Chandler and Hanks 1993), broad categories were used for the total sales for the most current year of data. This allowed the owner the option of not having to divulge specific information. Although not ideal, several studies have found evidence that supports the reliability of founder-reported performance measures (Brush and Vanderwerf 1992; Chandler and Hanks 1993). Other studies of entrepreneurs have used similar measures of business performance: (1) size of business, (2) profitability (i.e., Was your business profitable?), (3) gross revenues in categories for the previous year and (4) an open-ended question about the owner's monthly income (Brush and Hisrich 1991; Brush and Vanderwerf 1992; Lerner, Brush, and Hisrich 1997). Sales figures used here represent the total pre-tax sales for each business in the most recent year (in this case 1994) as reported by the respondents. Sales, as the dependent variable, were also controlled for by the age of the company (Chandler and Hanks 1993) and state the business was located in.

Business Type

Each business was identified as traditional or non-traditional depending on whether the venture was in an industry traditionally entered by women entrepreneurs or one not traditionally entered by women. To determine this we developed a list of female and male dominated industries based on a review of the literature (Carter 1990; Hisrich and Brush 1984, 1982; Hisrich and O'Brien 1982; Konek and Kitch 1994; Long 1989; Loscocco and Robinson 1991; OECD 1990; Plas and Wallston 1983; Smith, Smits, and Hoy 1992) categorizing certain types of businesses as either traditionally or not traditionally pursued by women entrepreneurs. Previous researchers have found that male and female dominated industries and businesses possess objective organizational characteristics that differentiate them from each other (Hisrich and O'Brien 1984; Loscocco and Robinson 1991; Smith, Smits, and Hoy 1992). Using these characteristics, we categorized the main business activity of the respondents (1 for traditional and 2 for non-traditional). To support the validity of our classification scheme we reviewed US Census Data reporting on the characteristics of business owners by industry sector (SIC Code). The 54 businesses classified by us as traditional come from industries which on average have 42% women ownership. Businesses from industries classified by us as non-traditional have on average 17% women ownership. The results of this review of owner characteristics by industries represented in our sample are provided in Table 1. As a final means of supporting the construct validity of our measure, respondents were asked to give their perceptions of the gender composition of their respective industry. Women business owners operating businesses in industries identified by us as non-traditional perceived that the industry was comprised of 87% male and 12% female owners. Respondents in industries identified as traditional perceived 67% male and 33% female ownership. These results support our traditional and non-traditional categorization scheme.

Independent Variables

Consistent with variables thought to be important in career choice and success of entrepreneurial ventures, three major categories of independent variables were considered: venture efficacy, career expectations, and the importance of support or individual context received for the venture. The correlation matrix, including means and standard deviations for each measure, is provided in Table 2.

TABLE 1 Number of Respondents by Type of Business

SIC Codes	Business Description	Percent of Women Owners in Industry Sector	Business Type Classified for This Study (T = Traditional/ NT = Non-traditional)	No. of Women Respondents in that Business Type
56 & 59	Traditional Retail (apparel, crafts, hobby, etc.)	46	T	11
653	Real Estate Sales	46	T	6
47	Travel Services	35	T	7
72 & 73	Traditional Service (secretarial, personal services)	43	T	21
80	Health Care Services	37	T	4
82	Education & Training	61	T	5
79	Artists & Writers	26	T	2
52 & 55	Non-traditional Retail (cars, auto parts, recreational vehicles, etc.)	12	NT	12
75	Non-traditional Service (auto repair)	7	NT	6
20-39	Manufacturing	21	NT	11
15	Construction	6	NT	9
87	Management Consulting, Computer Consulting, Marketing, or Public Relations	21	NT	21
62	Financial Services	17	NT	12
42	Transportation (Trucking)	8	NT	4
50 & 51	Wholesale Distributors	19	NT	7
48	Telecommunications	24	NT	2
64	Insurance	17	NT	3

Venture Efficacy

Two aspects of Schein's career anchors typology are especially relevant to the study of entrepreneurial choices and success. These aspects include the perceived technical and managerial competencies (efficacies) that have been found to be important factors (anchors) in career choice. In their self-efficacy approach to the career development for women, Hackett and Betz (1981) suggest that already existing measures could easily be adapted for use in assessing self-efficacy. Similar self-perceived technical-functional and managerial competencies were already developed in the entrepreneurial literature (Chandler and Jansen, 1992), and, therefore, this research uses those previously established measures. These measures were developed to differentiate between types of competencies important in the founding and success of entrepreneurs. One objective of this research is to further the development of these venture-efficacy measures. The earlier discussion provided a theoretical base for a four-factor venture-efficacy model (e.g., Chandler and Jansen 1992). The self-efficacy items use a 7 point Likert format. The scales and their alphas are reported in Table 3. The items were written as scales with an a priori four-factor structure. We used LISREL VII to assess the goodness of fit of a four factor venture efficacy model with respect to two criteria: (1) the Goodness of Fit Index (GFI), and (2) the root mean square residual (RMSR). GFI is somewhat analogous to R2; the GFI of 0.92 means that 92% of the total variance and co-variance is

TABLE 2 Correlation Matrix

Variable	Mean	S.D.	1	2	3	4	5	6	7	8	9	10	11	12	13	14	15
1. State	0.38	0.49															
2. Age of Company	8.74	7.80	0.43														
3. Sales	5,232	18,551	0.32	0.09													
4. V.E. Planning	5.00	1.28	0.01	-0.13	-0.07												
5. V.E. Opportunity Recognition	5.60	0.91	0.03	0.11	0.17	0.01											
6. V.E. for Human Competence	6.06	0.66	0.19	0.20	0.17	0.15	0.27										
7. V.E. for Economic Mgt.	5.82	0.95	0.14	0.15	0.12	0.24	-0.01	0.24									
8. C.E. for Challenge	4.36	0.84	-0.09	-0.14	0.07	0.28	0.08	0.04	0.13								
9. C.E. for Autonomy	4.55	0.80	-0.07	-0.02	0.02	0.23	0.11	0.19	0.08	0.09							
10. C.E. for Security	3.56	1.54	0.02	-0.08	-0.23	0.04	-0.02	0.08	0.09	0.09	0.06						
11. C.E. for Entrepreneurship	3.74	1.09	0.18	-0.05	0.05	0.03	0.09	0.03	-0.12	0.22	0.10	0.13					
12. C.E. for Life Balance	3.90	1.07	-0.12	-0.12	-0.04	0.17	0.06	0.02	0.14	0.27	0.44	0.10	0.09				
13. C.E. for Money	4.01	0.90	-0.02	-0.02	-0.08	-0.07	0.17	0.02	-0.02	-0.05	0.18	0.16	0.08	0.16			
14. Importance of Operational Support	3.17	1.88	0.14	0.11	0.04	-0.01	-0.06	-0.05	-0.07	0.12	0.05	-0.02	0.06	0.09	-0.01		
15. Importance of Emotional Support	3.94	1.51	-0.01	-0.02	-0.01	0.04	-0.02	-0.03	-0.07	0.08	0.16	-0.05	0.06	0.10	-0.10	0.47	
16. Importance of Financial Support	3.52	1.97	0.07	-0.05	0.07	-0.04	0.05	-0.04	-0.11	0.16	0.02	0.09	0.07	0.08	0.01	0.34	0.24

* N = 143 for all correlations except those with sales where N = 103. Correlations greater than 16 (>19 for sales) are significant at p < 0.05.

292 A.L. ANNA ET AL.

TABLE 3 Confirmatory Factor Analysis: Venture Efficacies

Item	Factor 1	Factor 2	Factor 3	Factor 4
Opportunity Recognition				
SA1 Perceive unmet needs	0.724	0.000	0.000	0.000
SA2 Recog. Successful goods	0.733	0.000	0.000	0.000
SW1 Seize opportunities	0.854	0.000	0.000	0.000
Alpha = 0.81				
Formal Planning				
SA3 Write formal plans	0.000	0.817	0.000	0.000
SA4 Vision into strategy	0.000	0.728	0.000	0.000
SW3 Comm. Objectives in writing	0.000	0.637	0.000	0.000
Alpha = 0.77				
Economic Management				
SA6 Manage expenses	0.000	0.000	0.880	0.000
SA7 Control business costs	0.000	0.000	0.844	0.000
SW5 Manage cash flow	0.000	0.000	0.773	0.000
Alpha = 0.87				
Human/Conceptual Competence				
SA10 Supervise, influence, lead	0.000	0.000	0.000	0.696
SW9 Organize & motivate	0.000	0.000	0.000	0.794
SW11 Keep org'n running smoothly	0.000	0.000	0.000	0.551
Alpha = 0.71				

explained by the four-factor model. RMSR for this model is 0.049; which supports a strong fit (Byrne 1989). The factor loading matrix (see Table 3) represents the most parsimonious solution found with LISREL analysis. In the factor loading matrix each of the items loads on its expected factor. Coefficient α (Cronbach 1960) was calculated for each of the venture efficacies; all of the αs ≥ 0.71, which is considered acceptable for research purposes (Nunnally 1978). The Phi Matrix (see Table 4) for the four-factor model shows interfactor correlations. It appears that the venture efficacy factors are not highly correlated and provide evidence of good discriminant validity between the factors.

Career Expectations

A list of expected or desired outcomes was compiled from research on women entrepreneurs and the types of outcomes they expected to receive from business ownership (Hisrich and Brush 1986; Lee-Gosselin and Grise 1990). The list of expectations are a sense of achievement, job satisfaction, independence, money/wealth, security, power, status/prestige, balance between work and nonwork life, challenge, and personal control. Many of these expectations reflect career anchors identified by Schein (1987) such as the security, autonomy, challenge, life-style, money, and entrepreneurial anchors (a creative aspect identified by Schein and colleagues). Participants were asked to rate the

TABLE 4 Phi Matrix: Venture Efficacies

	OPPREC	PLAN	ECONMGT
PLAN	0.12		
ECONMGT	0.03	0.28	
HUMCOMP	0.23	0.26	0.32

importance of challenge, autonomy, security, and money to them in operating their business using a 5-point Likert scale with 1 representing expectations "not important at all" and 5 representing expectations that were "very important". Life balance was a two-item measure constructed from participant responses to questions about the importance of their expectations about life balance and personal control. This measure was used to capture the aspect of career anchors that Schein (1987) identified as important in the integration of work and family concerns. Entrepreneurship measures the importance of accomplishment that is a potential factor in motivating entrepreneurs. It considers the achievement and status that comes with being identified with an organization, product, or service. Responses to two items, the importance of achievement and the importance of status, were combined to create this entrepreneurship anchor. Scores for life balance and entrepreneurship represent the mean value for the participant's response to both items used in the measure's construction.

Measures of Support

A final set of variables considers the support received by participants in initiating their business venture. This focuses on the role of others in supporting entrepreneurs. Three types of support were considered. "Operational support" represents the amount of support provided in the way of advice and or expertise. "Emotional support" considers the encouragement provided the participants by others. "Financial support" is the importance of the financial resources provided by others. Respondents were asked to identify the most important individual(s) who supported their efforts in each area and rate the importance of that contribution on a 1-5 scale with 1 representing "mildly important" to 5 representing support that was of "critical importance". Operational, emotional, and financial support measures indicate the respondents perceived importance of these contextual factors to their entrepreneurial venture.

RESULTS

To assess the differences between women who have chosen to operate businesses in traditional industries and those who operate in non-traditional industries, a multivariate analysis of co-variance (MANCOVA) was used. In this context MANCOVA allowed us to simultaneously test the differentiating effect of all variables while controlling for intercorrelations between variables (Bray and Maxwell 1985). This also allowed us to treat our control variables, state and age of business, as co-variates to control for their effects. The MANCOVA analysis showed a significant difference exists between the dependent variables for women business owners in traditional and non-traditional areas with a Wilk's multivariate test of significance $F(13,127) = 4.08$, $p < 0.001$. Uni-variate tests of differences showed women business owners in traditional businesses had higher venture-efficacy for opportunity recognition [$F(1,139) = 6.90$, $p < 0.01$], higher career expectations of life balance [$F(1,139) = 4.67$, $p < 0.05$] and security [$F(1,139) = 4.95$, $p < 0.05$], and reported the financial support received from others was more important [$F(1,139) = 6.92$, $p < 0.01$], than women business owners in non-traditional businesses. Conversely, women business owners in non-traditional businesses had higher venture-efficacy for planning [$F(1,139) = 5.53$, $p < 0.05$] and higher expectations for profit [$F(1,139) = 3.40$, $p < 0.05$] than women business owners in traditional businesses. Means and standard deviations for each variable by business type are provided in Table 5.

TABLE 5 Means and Standard Deviations for Independent Variables

	Traditional		Nontraditional		Total	
	Mean	S.D.	Mean	S.D.	Mean	S.D.
V.E. Planning	4.68	1.17	5.20	1.20	5.00	1.21
V.E. Opportunity Recognition	5.83	0.71	5.45	0.88	5.60	0.84
V.E. for Human Competence	6.11	0.60	6.02	0.70	6.06	0.66
V.E. for Economic Mgt.	5.87	0.72	5.78	1.07	5.82	0.95
C.E. for Challenge	4.36	0.70	4.37	0.92	4.36	0.84
C.E. for Autonomy	4.66	0.61	4.47	0.90	4.55	0.80
C.E. for Security	3.88	1.09	3.34	1.74	3.55	1.54
C.E. for Entrepreneurship	3.69	1.52	3.78	0.69	3.74	1.09
C.E. for Life Balance	4.14	0.72	3.75	1.21	3.90	1.07
C.E. for Money	3.84	1.02	4.11	0.80	4.00	0.90
Importance of Operational Support	3.16	1.83	3.18	1.91	3.17	1.88
Importance of Emotional Support	4.18	1.28	3.79	1.63	3.94	1.51
Importance of Financial Support	4.00	1.40	3.21	2.22	3.52	1.97

Our second analysis explored whether success, as measured in sales, was affected by differences in venture-efficacies, career expectations, or support received by women business owners in traditional industries as compared to those in non-traditional ones. Independent variables were entered in sets representing the control variables (state and age of the business), type of business (traditional or non-traditional), three venture-efficacy variables, six career expectation variables, and three support variables using hierarchical regression analysis. To test for the moderating effect of type of business on the relationship between sales and the sets of independent variables, cross-product terms were created by multiplying each independent variable by type of business (1 or 2). These variables were entered in sets after entering·the control variables and main effect terms. The results for this hierarchical regression analysis are reported in Table 6.

Fifty-four percent of the variance in sales can be explained by the independent variables used in the regression analysis. The addition of the cross-product variable sets, including venture-efficacy and career expectation, by business type terms resulted in a significant improvement in model fit over the model with just the control variables and main effect terms. This analysis suggests that women business owners operating businesses in traditional areas may have different factors that contribute to their success (sales) than women owners of non-traditional businesses. However, the high level of multi-collinearity that exists due to using cross-product terms created from a dichotomous variable makes interpretation of β weights difficult. One approach to analyzing

TABLE 6 Hierarchical Regression Results

Variable Sets Entered in the Model	Delta R^2	F For Model Comparison	DF For Model Comparison	Total R^2	F
Control Set				0.10	5.67**
Business Type (BT)	0.02	2.51	1,99	0.12	4.67**
Venture Efficacy (VE) Set	0.04	1.16	4,95	0.16	2.68*
Career Expectation (CE) Set	0.10	1.93	6,89	0.26	2.42**
Support (SU) Set	0.02	0.83	3,86	0.28	2.11*
VE X BT Set	0.10	3.07*	4,82	0.38	2.46**
CE X BT Set	0.13	3.51**	6,76	0.51	3.05**
SU X CE Set	0.03	1.39	3,73	0.54	2.92**

Note: N = 103; *p < 0.05; **p < 0.01.

TABLE 7 Comparison of Beta Weights for Independent Variables

Independent Variable	Traditional		Nontraditional		Comparison
	Non-Std Beta	Std Beta	Non-Std Beta	Std Beta	*t*-test for Delta Between Betas
V.E. Planning	−7,840.41	−0.26	542.69	0.10	−14.43**
V.E. Opportunity Recognition	14,621.07	0.35	561.07	0.07	27.88**
V.E. Human Competence	−4,536.29	−0.09	−412.21	−0.05	−8.74**
V.E. Economic Mgt	8,786.18	0.23	−4.47	0.00	17.82**
C.E. for Challenge	798.37	0.02	−270.63	−0.04	1.65
C.E. for Autonomy	11,298.54	0.24	712.23	0.10	17.09**
C.E. for Security	−14,754.86	−0.56	186	0.03	−19.72**
C.E. for Entrepreneurship	2,209.33	0.11	145.84	0.01	2.77**
C.E. for Life Balance	−3,930.83	−0.10	−179.51	−0.04	−5.38**
C.E. for Money	6,530.84	0.22	−1,788.29	−0.21	11.83**
Importance of Operational Support	−753.77	−0.05	2.16	0.00	−0.97
Importance of Emotional Support	−1,375.05	−0.06	−1,207.39	−0.25	−0.25
Importance of Financial Support	4,860.95	0.20	−528.54	−0.17	7.90**

Note: For Women in Traditional Industries: Model $R^2 = 0.60$ F = 2.28*; For Women in Nontraditional Industries: Model $R^2 = 0.47$ F = 2.84**; *p < 0.05; **p < 0.01.

these interaction effects is to dichotomize the sample based on the moderator variable used in the analysis (Jacccard, Turrisi, and Wan 1990). This allows us to compute separate slopes for each dependent variable for women owners in traditional industries and compare those slopes to women business owners in non-traditional industries. We can then conduct a test of the statistical significance of the difference between the two slopes by using the formula provided by Jacccard, Turrisi, and Wan (1990). Although there are limitations to this approach, such as the loss of statistical power and increased possibility of a type two error (Jacccard, Turrisi, and Wan, 1990), it does allow us to better analyze potential differences identified by the regression analysis. Table 7 provides the β weights for each independent variable by business type and the results of the t-test of statistical significance between those weights. Both models account for a significant portion of the variance (60% for traditionals and 47% for non-traditionals) in sales.

Results shown in Table 7 support the conclusion from the hierarchical regression analysis that the effect of the venture-efficacies and career expectancies variables shows different relationships with sales for women business owners in traditional industries as compared to those in non-traditional industries. For women business owners in traditional industries, venture-efficacies for opportunity recognition and economic management, as well as career expectations of autonomy and money as outcomes from the entrepreneurial venture, were positively related to sales. For this same group, venture-efficacy for planning and the importance of security as an expected outcome were negatively related to sales. For women in non-traditional industries, efficacies in planning and the career expectation of autonomy were positively related to sales, while expectation of money was negatively related. Interestingly, the importance of emotional and financial support was negatively related to sales for this non-traditional group.

DISCUSSION

This is the first empirical study examining factors related to the type of field in which female founders venture. The results indicate venture-efficacy, career expectations, and perceived support measures differentiate between women who have started businesses

296 A.L. ANNA ET AL.

in traditional and non-traditional industries. Although the qualitative data gathered from interviews with five women in traditional bussinesses and six women in non-traditional businesses cannot adequately represent the entire sample, they helped to shed more light on the findings from the survey (Strauss and Corbin 1990) and provide direction for future study.

Differences between Non-traditional and Traditional Women Business Owners

Using a career choice perspective, we proposed that differences in venture-efficacy, career expectations, and importance of types of support might exist between women business owners in traditional and non-traditional industries, and this was supported by the MANCOVA. When the geographic location and the age of the company are controlled for, women owners in non-traditional industries had higher efficacy for planning than those in traditional industries. It is likely that non-traditional industries have higher entry barriers, and, thus, more planning is required to start a non-traditional business.

Women in traditional industries reported higher levels of perceived ability to recognize opportunities. The qualitative findings also suggested that some traditional owners may be more motivated by opportunities presented by their individual situations than by opportunities found by a more deliberate search process. This is consistent with research findings suggesting that the ability to recognize opportunity may be contingent on familiarity with the industry (e.g., Timmons et al. 1987). By definition women, on average, have spent more time in traditional than in non-traditional settings, and they thus would be more confident in their ability to recognize opportunities in traditional settings.

The quantitative analysis also indicated that women who have started businesses in non-traditional industries have a higher expectation of money as an outcome of their business ownership. This finding is consistent with Loscocco and Robinson's (1991) suggestion that businesses in non-traditional industries tend to be more lucrative in terms of sales and growth. Buttner and Moore (1997) also found that women owned businesses in more traditional industries were smaller and experienced slower growth. A prospective entrepreneur seeking wealth or money would tend to start a business in a more non-traditional setting.

Women in traditional businesses had stronger career expectations of security and of a balance between the demands of work and home. In the interviews their references to money tended to be more in regard to money as a means of achieving the end, which was security or balance. The finding that women in traditional industries are more likely to seek security suggests that even though they are willing to start a venture, a high need for security may keep them from venturing too far afield into industries of which they are less familiar.

Women in traditional businesses perceived higher levels of financial support than their counterparts in non-traditional businesses. It appears that there is less perceived support as women venture into industries that are traditionally "less acceptable" for women. These non-traditional women described their frustration in trying to secure loans and venture capital from banks and other organizations. They still felt as though the financial institutions did not take them seriously as they sought funding in their non-traditional ventures.

Success and Type of Business

The regression analyses revealed that the relationship between certain types of venture-efficacy, career expectations, support, and sales or success is different for women in traditional and non-traditional businesses. Although some of these findings were confusing, the interview data yielded some insights to clarify these quantitative results.

As suggested in the previous section, women in non-traditional industries showed higher venture-efficacy for planning than traditionals. The regression analyses also showed that planning was strongly related to sales within this non-traditional group. Most experts on strategy and small business consultants would likely agree that a well-thought out business plan will lead to a more successful business. One non-traditional owner described her secretary's failed attempt to start a more traditional secretarial services business. She attributed that failure to a lack of analysis of the market, or careful up-front planning.

The finding that autonomy was important for those in non-traditional industries was further supported with interview responses. Each non-traditional owner described the importance of her ability to "call the shots". For the owner of an actuarial firm, the need for autonomy was so dominant that it was her impetus for leaving her old company and becoming an independent consultant.

The finding that for non-traditionals the expectation of making money was negatively related to sales was initially puzzling. The same is true of the findings of the negative relationship between sales and financial support. Again, the qualitative data helps to make more sense of these findings. For non-traditionals, a consistent theme in starting their businesses was that it was a financial necessity; but they then described how money has become secondary to the fun and challenge of owning their own businesses. One owner, who pushed herself into business because of the death of her husband, described herself as reluctant and hesitant at the beginning of her career as an independent business owner. Several years after that initial start-up, her attitude has changed and she now describes the excitement she feels at watching the technology involved in her printing business change on a regular basis and how fun her business has become. Another non-traditional owner commented on how her priorities had changed so that "her goals in life were first, to do something interesting and second to make money doing that". Although the need or goal to make more money was the impetus for start-up, the fun and excitement of the business eventually began to overshadow it.

Another theme from the non-traditional owners was the difficulty in getting financial support from lending institutions. This is consistent with the finding that financial support received from others was less of an important factor for women owners of non-traditional businesses. When asked what they thought could be done to encourage other women to start their own companies, each said that making start-up capital more accessible was critical. Many of these non-traditional owners reported that they financed their business through credit cards and personal loans. Financial support from others had been less important to their success. We believe that the boundaries between financial and social support are somewhat blurred, as the owners in both categories received not only money from family members, but also encouragement and hands-on help in the business when necessary.

Within the group of traditional owners, venture-efficacy for opportunity recognition and economic management had strong positive relationships with sales success, while venture-efficacy for planning had a negative relationship. When asked how they

298 A.L. ANNA ET AL.

got started, all six of the traditional business owners described a scenario of being in the right place at the right time and an opportunity presenting itself to them. The owner of a gift basket shop used the term "divine intervention" to describe how she got started. The owner of a real estate business, said she "happened into it." The non-traditional owners described a more deliberate process, precipitated by some event that forced them to seek an alternative situation. Shapero (1984) described these transitional events as "pushes" and "pulls", and this may be the most useful way of summarizing differences between the traditional and non-traditional women owners found in this study. For this sample, the traditional women owners experienced "pulls"—events that draws a person away from one situation into entrepreneurship. The non-traditionals' experienced more "pushes"—negative events that force a person into looking for entrepreneurial opportunities (e.g., discontent with their previous situation, or change in their family situation). This may also help us understand why there is a negative relationship for women in traditional businesses between venture-efficacy for planning and success. An opportunity arises in a familiar area or industry and the barriers to entry are lower than most non-traditional industries. These factors enable the prospective entrepreneur to move more quickly with less need for careful and deliberate planning to overcome obstacles faced by women entering non-traditional industries. They came across an opportunity and jumped in with both feet first. However, the traditional owners did recognize that their lack of planning impacted their success in the first few years of their businesses. They often found that they had to learn how to do things, like book-keeping, on their own and quickly.

The positive relationship between the career expectation of money and venture-efficacy for economic management is more direct and straightforward. Clearly of an individual desires to make money and has confidence in her abilities to manage the finances of her business, it is more likely that she will actually be successful. Social learning theory would also suggest that as a result of vicarious experience of being successful, or making a profit, one's efficacy for that skill would also increase (Bandura 1986).

Implications and Future Directions

Research done in the entrepreneurship field has been predominantly samples of male entrepreneurs. This study has identified several aspects of the female entrepreneurial experience and has sought to identify and validate factors that may differentiate women entering traditional industries from those entering non-traditional ones. The results indicate that there are differences between these two groups. There are a number of possible directions for future research on the relationship between venture-efficacy, career expectations, and perceived support and whether a woman starts a business in a traditional or non-traditional industry.

This research supported the construct validity of the venture-efficacy scales and their usefulness in differentiating among types of entrepreneurs. It also proved to be useful in explaining differences in the success of those entrepreneurs. Future researchers should include these scales and consider using a longitudinal design that examines how venture-efficacies affect prospective entrepreneurs' choices as venture options are considered. This study used these efficacies to examine differences, but the choices had already been made.

We found that women in traditional industries had a desire for some level of security, while women in non-traditional industries were more likely to have the expectation of money. One question for future research is how the propensity for risk-taking relates to the type of business started. Traditional investment theory provides a rule of thumb that the higher the risk, the higher the rate of return on an investment, and conversely, the lower the risk, the lower the rate of return. Perhaps traditional owners are more averse to taking risks than non-traditionals.

There are some inherent weaknesses in the research. The data are cross-sectional; thus, we can examine patterns of results only after the fact. Although this research has explored the relationships between venture-efficacy, career expectations and support, and the type of business started, the cross-sectional design makes it impossible to provide evidence that a certain level of venture-efficacy or specific career expectations will lead to an individual starting one type of business or another. A longitudinal design that follows prospective entrepreneurs and business owners to either business start-up or abandonment of the idea is required to develop evidence for causality. Richer data would come by analyzing women who are going through the process of starting businesses in traditional and non-traditional fields.

In addition, we recognize that using sales as a dependent variable is problematic because of reasons discussed previously. However, our results do indicate that for women entrepreneurs economic performance measures may not capture the idea of business success. More research is needed to find out how these women define success for themselves and how that definition compares with their male counterparts'. In the future, researchers need to consider the issue of non-economic, self-perceived definitions of success. How does the individual answer the question, "How do I know if I have been successful in my business?"

Clearly, more in-depth data needs to be gathered on how the career expectations, perceived support, and venture-efficacy of women are related to the type of venture they have created. However, the interview data gathered in this study seem to support the quantitative findings of these specific dimensions. These results have implications for educators and policy makers. This study suggests that individual context and support for women entrepreneurs varies widely, as do perceived entrepreneurial competencies. All prospective women business owners should not be viewed equally. Opportunities for entrepreneurial education should be diverse and accessible for both prospective entrepreneurs and those already involved in business ventures. Both the qualitative and quantitative analyses reveal that the women in this sample perceive that their competencies in certain skill areas are low. Whether or not the precipitating event for women is a "push" or a "pull" may affect the type of entrepreneurial skill training that is needed to raise venture efficacy. Small business development centers need to develop packages that can teach entrepreneurship skills in short, concentrated sessions and at convenient times.

The number of women owned businesses continues to grow and the number of new jobs created by these businesses also increases. Currently, women business owners employ more than 11 million employees (NFWBO 1994). Included among the trends predicted by the NFWBO (1994) are that business receipts will grow strongly, sales will increase, and more women will move into non-traditional businesses. The NFWBO also suggests that despite the growth in numbers and economic power, barriers to increased growth remain. One of the major barriers is obtaining capital. In this study, all the interviewees expressed their frustration over the lack of access to capital and the difficulties in the actual process of securing capital. Not only is money or financial support not easily available, but dealing with lending institutions can be problematic. This was especially

300 A.L. ANNA ET AL.

obvious to the non-traditional owners. Funds could be set aside and designated specifi-cally for programs that encourage women to enter non-traditional industries. If increas-ing the number of jobs is important for the economy, this is a critical barrier that policy makers and educators need to address.

There is clearly much that we do not know. Given the differences in financial re-wards, should women be encouraged to start more businesses in non-traditional indus-tries? If they should be encouraged, what can be done to provide additional support? What can be done to cultivate stronger efficacy perceptions? The study suggests numer-ous rich possibilities for research extensions that would have practical as well as aca-demic interest.

REFERENCES

Ajzen, I. 1991. The theory of planned behavior. *Organizational Behavior and Human Decision Processes* 50:179–211.

Aldrich, H., Reese, P.R., and Dubini, P. 1989. Women on the verge of a breakthrough: Net-working among entrepreneurs in the United States and Italy. *Entrepreneurship and Re-gional Development* 1:339–356.

Bandura, A. 1977. *Social Learning Theory.* Englewood Cliffs, NJ: Prentice-Hall.

Bandura, A. 1986. *Social foundations of thought and action: A social cognitive theory.* Englewood Cliffs, NJ: Prentice-Hall.

Betz, N.E., and Hackett, G. 1981. The relationship of career-related self-efficacy expectations to perceived career options in college women and men. *Journal of Counseling Psychol-ogy* 28(5):399–410.

Bird, B. 1988. Implementing entrepreneurial ideas: The case for intention. *Academy of Manage-ment Review* 13:442–453.

Birley, S. 1989. Female entrepreneurs: Are they really any different? *Journal of Small Business Management* 27(1):32–37.

Bowen, D.D., and Hisrich, R.D. 1986. The female entrepreneur: A career development perspec-tive. *Academy of Management Review* 11(2):393–407.

Boyd, N.G., and Vozikis, G.S. 1994. The influence of self-efficacy on the development of entrepre-neurial intentions and actions. *Entrepreneurship: Theory and Practice* 18:63–77.

Bray, J.H., and Maxwell, S.E. 1985. *Multivariate analysis of variance.* Beverly Hills, CA: Sage Pub-lications.

Brooks, L., and Betz, N.E. 1990. Utility of expectancy theory in predicting occupational choices in college students. *Journal of Counseling Psychology* 37(1):57–64.

Brush, C. 1987. Women and enterprise creation. In Organization for Economic Co-Operation and Development, *Local initiatives for job creation: Enterprising women,* pp. 37–55.

Brush, C. 1992. Research on women business owners: Past trends, a new perspective and future directions. *Entrepreneurship: Theory and Practice* 16(4):5–30.

Brush, C., and Vanderwerf, P. 1992. A comparison of methods and sources for obtaining estimates of new venture performance. *Journal of Business Venturing* 7(2):157–170.

Buttner, H.E., and Moore, D.P. 1997. Women's organizational exodus to entrepreneurship: Self-reported motivations and correlates with success. *Journal of Small Business Manage-ment* 35(1)34–46.

Byrne, B.M. 1989. *A primer of LISREL: Basic application and programming for confirmatory factor analytic models.* New York: Springer.

Cable, D.M., and Judge, T.A. 1996. Person-organization fit, job choice decisions, and organiza-tional entry. *Organizational Behavior and Human Decision Processes* 67(3):294–311.

Carter, S. 1990. The dynamics and performance of female-owned firms in London, Glasgow, and Nottingham. *Journal of Organizational Change Management* 2(3):54–64.

Castrogiovanni, G.J. 1996. Pre-startup planning and the survival of new small businesses: Theoretical linkages. *Journal of Management* 22(6):801–822.

Chandler, G.N., and Hanks, S.H. 1993. Measuring the performance of emerging businesses: A validation study. *Journal of Business Venturing* 8(5):391–408.

Chandler, G.N., and Jansen, E. 1992. The founder's self-assessed competence and venture performance. *Journal of Business Venturing* 7(3):223–236.

Chatman, J. 1989. Improving interactional organizational research: A model of person-organization fit. *Academy of Management Review* 14(3):333–349.

Chrisman, J., Carsrud, A., DeCastro, J., and Herron, L. 1990. A comparison of assistance needs of male and female pre-venture entrepreneurs. *Journal of Business Venturing* 5(4):235–248.

Coats, P.B., and Overman, S.J. 1992. Childhood play experiences of women in traditional and non-traditional professions. *Sex Roles* 26(7/8):261–271.

Collerette, P., and Aubry, P. 1990. Socio-economic evolution of women business owners in Quebec. *Journal of Business Ethics* 9(4/5):417–422.

Cronbach, L.J. 1960. *Essentials of psychological testing.* New York: Harper.

Derr, C.B. 1984. Entrepreneurs: A careers perspective. Paper presented at the meeting of the Academy of Management, Boston, MA.

Diamond, E.E. 1989. Theories of career development and the reality of women at work. In B. Gutek and L. Larwood, eds., *Women's Career Development.* Newbury Park, CA: Sage Publications.

Dyer, W.G. 1994. Toward a theory of entrepreneurial careers. *Entrepreneurship: Theory and Practice* 19(2):7–21.

Fiorentine, R. 1988. Sex differences in success expectancies and causal attributions: Is this why fewer women become physicians? *Social Psychology Quarterly* 51(3):236–249.

Fishbein, M., and Ajzen, I. 1975. *Belief, attitude, intention, and behavior: An introduction to theory and research.* Reading, MA: Addison-Wesley.

Gallos, J.V. 1989. Exploring women's development: Implications for career theory, practice, and research. In M.B. Arthur, D.T. Hall, and B.S. Lawrence, eds., *Handbook of Career Theory.* New York: Cambridge University.

Gartner, W.B. 1989. "Who is an entrepreneur?" Is the wrong question. *Entrepreneurship: Theory and Practice* 12(4):47–68.

Greenberger, D.B., and Sexton, D.L. 1988. An interactive model of new venture initiation. *Journal of Small Business Management* 26(3):1–7.

Gutek, B.A., and Larwood, L. 1989. *Women's Career Development.* Newbury Park, CA: Sage.

Hackett, G., and Betz, N.E. 1981. A self-efficacy approach to the career development of women. *Journal of Vocational Behavior* 18:326–339.

Hisrich, R.D., and Brush, C.G. 1984. The woman entrepreneur: Management skills and business problems. *Journal of Small Business Management* 22(1):30–38.

Hisrich, R.D., and Brush, C.G. 1986. *The Woman Entrepreneur.* Lexington, MS: Lexington Books.

Hisrich, R.D., and O'Brien, M. 1982. The woman entrepreneur as a reflection of the type of business. In K.H. Vesper, ed., *Frontiers of Entrepreneurship Research.* Wellesley, MA: Babson Center for Entrepreneurial Studies, pp. 54–77.

Jaccard, J., Turrisi, R., and Wan, C.K. 1990. *Interaction Effects in Multiple Regression.* Newbury Park, CA: Sage Publications.

Kalleberg, A. and Leicht, K. 1991. Gender and organizational performance: Determinants of small business survival and success. *Academy of Management Journal* 34:136–161.

Katz, J. 1992. Modeling Entrepreneurial Career Progressions: Concepts and Considerations. Unpublished manuscript.

Konek, C.W., and Kitch, S.L. 1994. *Women and Careers.* Thousand Oaks, California: Sage.

Krueger, N., and Carsrud, A.L. 1993. Entrepreneurial intentions: Applying the theory of planned behavior. *Entrepreneurship & Regional Development* 5:315–330.

302 A.L. ANNA ET AL.

Larwood, L., and Gattiker, U.E. 1989. A comparison of the career paths used by successful men and women. In B.A. Gutek, and L. Larwood, eds., *Women's Career Development*. Newbury Park, CA: Sage.

Lee-Gosselin, H., and Grise, J. 1990. Are women owner-managers challenging our definitions of entrepreneurship? An in-depth survey. *Journal of Business Ethics* 9(4/5):423–433.

Lerner, M., Brush, C., and Hisrich, R. 1997. Israeli women entrepreneurs: An examination of factors affecting performance. *Journal of Business Venturing* 12:315–339.

Long, B. 1989. Sex-role orientation, coping strategies, and self-efficacy of women in traditional and non-traditional occupations. *Psychology of Women Quarterly* 13(3):307–324.

Loscocco, K.A., and Robinson, J. 1991. Barriers to women's small-business success in the United States. *Gender and Society* 5(4):511–532.

Lovelace, K., and Rosen, B. 1996. Differences in achieving person-organization fit among diverse groups of managers. *Journal of Management* 22(5):703–722.

Mathieu, P.S., Sowa, C.J., and Niles, S.G. 1993. Differences in career self-efficacy among women. *Journal of Career Development* 19(3):187–196.

Moore, L.M., and Rickel, A.U. 1980. Characteristics of women in traditional and non-traditional managerial roles. *Personnel Psychology* 33(2):317–333.

National Foundation for Women Business Owners 1994. *A Compendium of National Statistics on Women Business Owners in the U.S.: Data Report.* Silver Springs, MD: NFWBO.

Nelson, G. 1989. Factors of friendship: Relevance of significant others to female business owners. *Entrepreneurship: Theory and Practice* 13(4):7–18.

Neville, D.D., and Schlecker, D.I. 1988. The relation of self-efficacy and assertiveness to willingness to engage in traditional/non-traditional career activities. *Psychology of Women Quarterly* 12(1):91–98.

Nieva, V.F., and Gutek, B.A. 1981. *Women and work: A psychological perspective.* New York: Praeger.

Nunnally, J.C. 1978. *Psychometric theory.* New York: McGraw Hill.

Organization for Economic Co-Operation and Development (OECD) 1987. *Local initiatives for job creation: Enterprising women.* Paris: OECD.

Plas, J.M., and Wallston, B.S. 1983. Women oriented toward male dominated careers: Is the reference group male or female? *Journal of Counseling Psychology* 30(1):46–54.

Powell, G.N., and Mainiero, L.A. 1992. Cross-currents in the River of Time: Conceptualizing the complexities of women's careers. *Journal of Management* 18(2):215–237.

Schein, E. 1978. *Career Dynamics: Matching Individual and Organizational Needs.* Reading, MA:Addison Wesley.

Schein, E. 1987. Individuals and careers. In Lorsch, J. W., ed., *Handbook of Organizational Behavior.* Englewood Cliffs, NJ: Prentice-Hall, Inc.

Scherer, R.F., Brodzinski, J.D., and Wiebe, F.A. 1990. Entrepreneur career selection and gender: A socialization approach. *Journal of Small Business Management* 28(2):37–44.

Scott, C.E. 1986. Why more women are becoming entrepreneurs. *Journal of Small Business Management* 24(4):37–44.

Shane, S., Kolvereid, L., and Westhead, P. 1991. An exploratory examination of the reasons leading to new firm formation across country and gender. *Journal of Business Venturing* 6:431–446.

Shapero, A. 1984. The entrepreneurial event. In C.A. Kent, D.L. Sexton, and K.H. Vesper, eds., *Encyclopedia of Entrepreneurship.* Lexington, MA: D.C. Heath and Company.

Smith, P., Smits, S.J., and Hoy, F. 1992. Female business owners in industries traditionally dominated by males. *Sex Roles* 26(11/12):485–496.

Stevenson, Lois A. 1986. Against all odds: The entrepreneurship of women. *Journal of Small Business Management* 24(4):30–36.

Stoner, C.R., Hartman, R.I., and Arora, R. 1990. Work-home role conflict in female owners of small business: An exploratory study. *Journal of Small Business Management* 28(1):30–38.

Strauss, A., and Corbin, J. 1990. *Basics of Qualitative Research.* Newbury Park, CA: Sage Publications.

Timmons, J.A., Muzyka, D.F., Stevenson, H.H., and Bygrave, W.D. 1987. Opportunity recognition: The core of entrepreneurship. In N.C. Churchill, J.A. Hornaday, B.A., Kirchoff, O.J. Kransner, and K.H. Vesper, eds., *Frontiers of Entrepreneurship Research.* Wellesly, MA: Babson Center for Entrepreneurial Studies, pp. 109–129.

Venkatraman, N., and Ramanujam, V. 1986. Measurement of Business Performance in strategy research: A comparison of approaches. *Academy of Management Review* 11(4):801–814.

Vesper, K.H. 1994. *New Venture Experience.* Seattle, Washington: Vector Books.

Whiston, S.C. 1993. Self-efficacy of women in traditional and non-traditional occupations: Differences in working with people and things. *Journal of Career Development* 19(3):175–186.

[23]

ELSEVIER

THE AMBITIOUS ENTREPRENEUR: HIGH GROWTH STRATEGIES OF WOMEN-OWNED ENTERPRISES

LISA K. GUNDRY
DePaul University, Chicago, Illinois

HAROLD P. WELSCH
DePaul University, Chicago, Illinois

EXECUTIVE SUMMARY

During the last two decades, researchers have sought to develop categories of entrepreneurs and their businesses along a variety of dimensions to better comprehend and analyze the entrepreneurial growth process. Some of this research has focused on differences related to industrial sectors, firm size, the geographical region in which a business is located, the use of high-technology or low-technology, and the life-cycle stage of the firm (i.e., start-up vs. more mature, formalized companies). Researchers have also considered ways in which entrepreneurs can be differentiated from small business managers. One of these classifications is based on the entrepreneur's desire to grow the business rapidly. This is the focus of our study.

To date, the media have paid considerable attention to rapidly growing new ventures. However, still lacking are large-scale research studies guided by theory through which we can expand our knowledge of the underlying factors supporting ambitious expansion plans. Some research has identified factors that enhance or reduce the willingness of the entrepreneur to grow the business. Factors include the strategic origin of the business (i.e., the methods and paths through which the firm was founded); previous experience of the founder/owner; and the ability of the entrepreneur to set realistic, measurable goals and to manage conflict effectively.

Our study attempted to identify the strategic paths chosen by entrepreneurs and the relation of those paths to the growth orientation of the firm. The entrepreneurs sampled in this study are women entrepreneurs across a wide range of industrial sectors. Recent reviews of entrepreneurship research have suggested the need for more studies comparing high-growth firms with slower-growth firms to better delineate their differences in strategic choices and behaviors.

Our study sought to answer the following questions: What characterizes a "high growth-oriented

Address correspondence to Dr. Lisa K. Gundry, DePaul University, Department of Management, 1 East Jackson Blvd., Chicago, IL 60604; (312) 362-8075; Fax: (312) 362-6973; E-mail: lgundry@wppost.depaul.edu

Journal of Business Venturing **16**, 453–470
© 2001 Elsevier Science Inc.   All rights reserved.
655 Avenue of the Americas, New York, NY 10010

0883-9026/01/$–see front matter
PII S0883-9026(99)00059-2

454   L.K. GUNDRY AND H.P. WELSCH

entrepreneur?" Is this distinction associated with specific strategic intentions, prior experience, equity held
in previous firms, the type of company structure in place, or success factors the entrepreneur perceives
are important to the business? Do "high growth" entrepreneurs show greater entrepreneurial "intensity"
(i.e., commitment to the firm's success)? Are they willing to "pay the price" for their own and their firm's
success? (i.e., the "opportunity costs" associated with business success and growth). Other relationships
under investigation included different patterns of financing the business' start-up and early growth. Do
"high-growth" entrepreneurs use unique sources of funding compared with "lower-growth" entrepreneurs?

Eight hundred thirty-two entrepreneurs responded to a survey in which they were asked to describe
their growth intentions along nineteen strategic dimensions, as well as respond to the foregoing questions.
Some of the strategic activity measures included adding a new product or service, expanding operations,
selling to a new market, and applying for a loan to expand operations. Actual growth rates based on
sales revenues were calculated, and average annualized growth rates of the industrial sectors represented
in the sample were obtained. This study showed that high-growth-oriented entrepreneurs were clearly
different from low-growth-oriented entrepreneurs along several dimensions. The former were much more
likely to select strategies for their firms that permitted greater focus on market expansion and new technol-
ogies, to exhibit greater intensity towards business ownership ("my business is the most important activity
in my life"), and to be willing to incur greater opportunity costs for the success of their firms ("I would
rather own my own business than earn a higher salary while employed by someone else").

The high-growth–oriented entrepreneurs tended to have a more structured approach to organizing
their businesses, which suggests a more disciplined perception of managing the firm. In summary, results
showed the group of high-growth–oriented entrepreneurs, labeled "ambitious," as having the following dis-
tinctions: strategic intentions that emphasize market growth and technological change, stronger commitment to the success of the business, greater willingness to sacrifice on behalf of the business, earlier planning for the growth of the business, utilization of a team-based form of organization design, concern for
reputation and quality, adequate capitalization, strong leadership, and utilization of a wider range of financing sources for the expansion of the venture. *The purpose in uncovering these differences is to enable*
entrepreneurs and researchers to identify more clearly the attributes of rapid-growth ventures and their
founders and to move closer to a field-based model of the entrepreneurial growth process which will help
delineate the alternative paths to venture growth and organizational change.   © *2001 Elsevier Science Inc.*

INTRODUCTION

Throughout the history of entrepreneurship research, there have been many attempts
to categorize entrepreneurs according to a variety of dimensions. These categories have
included industry, size, region, age, capital (labor) intensity, high- or low-technology,
stage of life cycle, gender, personality type, and numerous others. A particular stream
of research has evolved that has attempted to categorize or differentiate small business
owners from "pure" entrepreneurs, i.e., the former who were satisfied with the status
quo versus the latter who desired to grow their businesses more rapidly. The focus of
this research study is on the entrepreneurs whose businesses have exhibited high growth.
We examine the strategic growth intentions, commitment level, opportunity costs, structure, and success factors that may distinguish these types of ventures from those with
lower growth outcomes. Merz, Weber, and Laetz (1994) noted the chief weakness of
many studies on the entrepreneurial growth phenomena was that they rarely compare
high or rapid-growth firms with low- or no-growth firms. Even though more is known
about high-growth firms, it is unclear whether the observations reported are similar or
different for low-growth firms. The present research attempts to fill this gap.

The theoretical model we develop follows a pattern of growth literature developed
by Davidsson and Wiklund (1999); Wiklund (1998); Davidsson (1989, 1991); Greening,
Barringer, and Macy (1996); Krueger and Carsrud (1993); Ward (1993); Kolveried

(1992), and Gibb and Davies (1990). The study reported here extends the decision models to start a business (as chosen by the founder) to the decision to grow the business by the same entrepreneur or her successors. To date, most of the research attention has focused on rapidly growing new ventures. However, there is a paucity of theoretically guided, quantitative, and rigorous literature that discusses the underlying factors supporting such expansion plans.

Attributes of High-Growth Entrepreneurs and Organizations

For many entrepreneurs, the greatest satisfaction of owning a business lies in working closely with customers and employees. Inevitably, as the business grows, the owner's role changes. Jack Ferner, former dean at Wake Forest University, noted, "Many entrepreneurs would rather limit growth than give up those satisfactions. My experience has been that for every one who has dreams of grandeur and size and billions of dollars, there are probably five that prefer to remain small" (Barrier 1996). Another perspective was described by John Thorne of Carnegie Mellon University: "I think there is an argument in many industries that if you don't grow, you can't hold good people, you're not going to stay in touch with the technology or the marketing trends" (Barrier 1996).

As the field of entrepreneurship has developed, firm growth has been almost implicitly construed as a condition or assumption of entrepreneurship. Researchers have examined behaviors, intentions, and goals of entrepreneurs in an attempt to differentiate this group from small business managers. Carland et al (1984) differentiated between "small business owners" and "entrepreneurs," with the latter category focusing on growth and innovation. Moderate growth firms were identified by Ginn and Sexton (1990), who contrasted them to the sample of *Inc*'s 500 fastest growing firms of the year. Thus, a partial replication for Carland's conceptualization was established. Moore and Buttner (1997) described "traditional" and "modern" entrepreneurs, with the former being small and slow-growing. Birch (1987) studied two groups of small firms that he labeled "income substitutors" and "entrepreneurs." He found that entrepreneurs intended to grow their organizations significantly, and he concluded that those organizations were responsible for a major proportion of job creation over several periods ranging from 1969 to 1985. Other scholars have identified growth-oriented ventures based on the goals established by the entrepreneurs, such as creating jobs for others (Vesper 1993) and innovative strategic practices (Carland et al. 1984), and have suggested that entrepreneurs have, per se, a growth orientation (Sexton and Bowman 1985).

According to Davidsson (1989, 1991), firm growth is an indication of continued entrepreneurship. Incorporating a multidimensional approach and utilizing a sample of 400 Swedish entrepreneurs, Davidsson (1989) attempted to identify the factors that enhanced or reduced the willingness to grow. Among his findings were that most firms favored growth: 62% favored moderate growth in the number of employees, and 87% favored growth in sales. The perception of what growth will bring over time had an impact on actual growth.

If the decision to start a business is a choice made by the founder, it may be assumed that the decision to grow the business is a choice made by the same person. In a study of Norwegian entrepreneurs, Kolvereid (1992) adopted a multilevel approach looking at the relationships among the entrepreneur's motives to start the business, education, experience, industry, localization, characteristics of the organization and its environment, the firm's history of growth, and the entrepreneur's growth aspirations.

456   L.K. GUNDRY AND H.P. WELSCH

On the basis of a sample of 250 Norwegian entrepreneurs, the research uncovered significant relationships between the entrepreneur's education and the industry as well as a number of organizational variables, including past growth in both revenue and number of employees, in relation to an entrepreneur's aspirations to grow their firm. No significant relationships emerged between growth aspirations of entrepreneurs and their experience, gender, location, or size of business as measured by employee count. Kolvereid (1992) concluded that there were significant relationships between willingness to grow and expectations concerning employee well-being, control, independence, workload, and achievement motivation. This study provided valuable insights; however, as Davidsson (1991) concluded, there are likely to be many situational influences unique to each firm that influence growth willingness and intention.

Other studies have attributed differences between high-growth–oriented enterprises and low-growth–oriented enterprises to factors such as strategic origins, previous experience, and the ability of the entrepreneur to establish goals for staff and effectively handle disputes and conflict (Brush and Hisrich 1991). Baum (1995) tested a structural equation model and concluded that entrepreneurial tenacity was related to firm growth. The present study was designed to identify some of these situational influences to gain a clearer picture of the paths that high-growth firms follow. Building on the work of Kolvereid, Baum, and others, this study was designed to extend the empirical examination of entrepreneurial growth orientation by comparing the strategic activities in which entrepreneurs are engaged, along with several attitudinal and structural factors in order to further delineate differences between high-growth and low-growth firms.

The present study extends the literature on growth intention by including a large sample of women entrepreneurs across industrial sectors in well-established firms with significant sales. Although the focus on women entrepreneurs has greatly increased in recent years, few studies have included women-owned firms. To locate and study such firms requires substantial effort and cost (Eggers and Leahy 1993). According to a study published by the National Foundation for Women Business Owners (1994), 21% of women-owned firms reported that maintaining the growth and competitiveness of their firms is a significant challenge. In their comprehensive review of current research on women entrepreneurs, Starr and Yudkin (1996) suggest the need for more studies of women-owned-businesses to help define preconditions and strategies for growth.

This study attempts to extend the research on women entrepreneurs beyond the examination of the link between gender and entrepreneurial (personal) characteristics (such as propensity to take risks, degree of independence desired, locus of control, etc.). Such research, although it is valuable in describing women entrepreneurs, tells us little about the differences that exist *among* women entrepreneurs, whose businesses may be differentiated by size, industry, strategic intent, and performance. The present research examines critical elements in the entrepreneurial process, including strategies for growth and organizational design.

RESEARCH PROPOSITIONS

Strategic Intentions of High-Growth and Low-Growth Entrepreneurs

What constitutes an entrepreneur's willingness to grow? How are growth intentions implemented? What are the next steps that an entrepreneur takes when he or she is motivated to grow the venture? Kim and Mauborgne (1997) found that the difference between the high-growth companies and their less successful competitors lay in each group's strategy. However, specific strategic choices may not be available to the entrepreneurial community, nor are they communicated well so that they can be more readily operationalized. Hoy, McDougall, and Dsouza (1992) noted that research is incomplete regarding how the strategies of high-growth firms differ from those with slower growth. Therefore, for the purposes of the present study it was important to identify a pool of specific strategic intentions along which high-growth and low-growth firms could be compared. The strategic activities measured in this study are derived from Schumpeter's (1954) theory of new combinations associated with enterprise growth. These five characteristics included industrial reorganization, introduction of new methods of production, opening of new markets, opening of new sources of supply, and the introduction of new goods. The following hypothesis is proposed.

> *H1:* Entrepreneurs in high-growth firms will exhibit greater strategic growth and expansion intentions than entrepreneurs in low-growth firms.

Entrepreneurial Intensity and Growth

Because there are various types of entrepreneurs (e.g., life-style, part-time, serial, temporary, etc.) with varying levels and types of motivations (e.g., strong achievement orientation, moderate level of independence, etc.), it is important to measure the degree of commitment of the entrepreneur. In the present study, this is identified as high *entrepreneurial intensity*. There is a lack of empirical work on entrepreneurial motivation, particularly in the stages beyond start-up, that contribute to sustained entrepreneurship (Bhave 1994; Kuratko, Hornsby, and Naffziger 1997). Although commitment to the entrepreneurial endeavor can be described as the passion required for entrepreneurial success, it is further characterized in this study as a single-minded focus to work towards the growth of the venture, often at the expense of other worthy and important goals. Presumably, entrepreneurial intensity would be positively related to growth intentions, but circumstances such as growing markets, socialization, incompetence, self-efficacy, and other factors may lead to conditions where even intensely-motivated entrepreneurs may not be willing to grow the company. Or, alternatively, nonintense entrepreneurs may have strong growth intentions based on competitive advantages, a unique product, or joint venture efforts that fall into their lap. For the purpose of this study, however, it is construed that "planned growth" requires a heavy dose of concentrated effort, as suggested by Bracker, Keats, and Pearson (1988) and Lyles et al. (1993). Thus, the following proposition is developed:

> *H2:* Entrepreneurs in high-growth firms can be differentiated from entrepreneurs in low-growth firms in the degree of entrepreneurial intensity they display.

Opportunity Costs and Firm Growth

Commitment to a planned direction is often measured by the sacrifices an entrepreneur is willing to undergo to achieve a particular goal. Because most, if not all, entrepreneurs suffer from a scarcity of resources, certain penalties would have to be paid in order to meet desired objectives of business growth. Amit and Cockburn (1995) found that the lower the opportunity costs for individuals, the more likely they were to undertake entrepreneurial activity. However, are entrepreneurs in high-growth firms more willing to incur these costs while entrepreneurs in slower-growth firms try to reduce them? Specifically, what sacrifices would a growth-oriented entrepreneur be willing to make in pursuit of a growth strategy? The following is proposed:

> *H3:* Entrepreneurs in high-growth firms can be differentiated from entrepreneurs in low-growth firms in their willingness to incur the opportunity costs of their strategic pursuits.

Structuring the Firm for Growth

Previous studies have determined a link between organization structure and firm performance. For example, organically structured entrepreneurial firms were found to have the highest performance (Covin and Slevin 1988). Additionally, Caruana, Morris, and Vella (1998) found that increased centralization limits entrepreneurial behavior. Therefore, it was of interest in this study to determine whether the structures entrepreneurs employed in high-growth ventures tend to differ from those found in low-growth ventures. Centralization would be greater in a functional structure, for example, than in a team-based structure that permits greater delegation and flexibility. The following proposition is developed:

> *H4:* Entrepreneurs in high-growth firms will utilize more organic organization structures than entrepreneurs in low-growth firms.

Strategic Success Factors Perceived by Entrepreneurs

Following the work of Storey (1989), Hills and Narayana (1989), and others, we examined the perceived success factors of high-growth-oriented entrepreneurs and compare these factors to the perceptions of slower-growth entrepreneurs. These factors, as noted in the aforementioned research, include the leader's vision, a market-driven focus, product and service quality, and the reputation of the business. Building on this work, we propose the following:

> *H5:* Entrepreneurs in high-growth firms perceive strategic success factors to be of greater importance to their organization than do entrepreneurs in low-growth firms.

Financing Start-Up and Growth Strategies

In a study of 30 rapid-growth firms, Hambrick and Crozier (1985) found that high levels of financial resources are needed for rapid growth. In another study, the goal orientation of the entrepreneur and the odds of firm success were the most important predictors of the capital structure of the firm, which suggests that the characteristics of the entrepreneur play a key role in capital structure decisions (Chaganti, DeCarolis, and Deeds 1995). Thus, this study includes measures of the type and frequency of financial resources (equity and debt) utilized by the respondents to determine whether high-growth-oriented entrepreneurs report a distinctive pattern in the capital structure of their firms:

> *H6:* Entrepreneurs in high-growth firms are more likely to utilize a greater variety of financing resources at start-up and growth than entrepreneurs in the lower-growth firms.

METHOD

Participants

Eight-hundred thirty-two women business owners responded to a survey developed by the authors in conjunction with the state's department of commerce and community affairs. The firms were randomly sampled by industrial sector from Dun's Marketing Database. The entrepreneurs who responded represented all industrial classifications, including: service (35%), wholesale trade (14%), construction (14%), retail trade (9%), manufacturing (9%), professional service (6%), finance/insurance (3%), transportation (3%), and agribusiness (1%). Forty-two percent of firms reported annual sales greater than $1 million; 12% had sales of $500,000 to $1 million; 18% had sales of $250,000 to $500,000; 20% had sales of $100,000 to $250,000; and 18% had sales less than $100,000 per year. More than 50% of the women entrepreneurs had been established in business over 10 years; 12% had been in business less than five years. Overall, most entrepreneurs were age 45 to 54 (33%) and 35 to 44 (31%). Nearly 10% were 25 to 34 years of age, and 19% were 55 to 64 years of age. Nearly 70% of the sample had at least a post-secondary education, while 20% had four-year college degrees and 21% had completed some post-graduate work. The average number of years of experience in the industry in which the firm operated was 16, and the average number of years of overall business experience was 18.

Overview and Procedure

The following variables of interest were assessed via a written, confidential instrument: strategic growth and expansion intentions, degree of entrepreneurial intensity, the willingness to incur opportunity costs, organizational structure in use, perceived importance of strategic success factors, financial resources used during start-up and growth, and demographic characteristics of the entrepreneurs and their firms. All items except demographic measures used a Likert-type five-point response format.

Measures

High-Growth and Low-Growth Sample Categorization

In the present study, high-growth-oriented ("ambitious") entrepreneurs are differentiated from low-growth-oriented ("status quo") entrepreneurs by actual firm growth rates as measured by sales growth. The utilization of sales growth as a valid indicator of firm growth has been well documented in entrepreneurship research (Ginn and Sexton 1989; Hoy, McDougall, and Dsouza 1992). Feeser (1987) suggested that sales growth be used for research on the growth strategies of firms because it tends to reflect the inflationary pressures of the time being studied, is familiar to business executives, and reflects long-term and short-term changes in the firm and the environment (Hoy, McDougall, and Dsouza 1992). Similarly, Neiswander and Fulton (1989) found that CEOs measure growth through firm sales. The industry growth rates for the sample population of firms was also obtained for this study. As Dsouza (1990) stated, high-growth firms may be differentiated by selecting those firms whose sales growth exceeds the average growth rate of their industries. Previous research has established that the growth rate of the industrial sector to which firms belong can serve as a gauge of the growth rate of particu-

460 L.K. GUNDRY AND H.P. WELSCH

lar firms (Cooney and Bygrave 1994; Wijewardena and Tibbits 1999). Studies have also utilized a calculation of current sales (Eggers, Leahy, and Churchill 1994) or previous year's sales (Ensley and Banks, 1994) to estimate growth rates.

The purpose of the current study is to depict a particular set of strategic intentions and activities rather than the long-term effects of those strategies occurring over more than one stage of the growth of these companies. Data collected over a long period of time could be misleading, as the organizations could presumably be going through more than one stage of growth during the measured interval. Thus, the growth rates calculated in this study are a fairly accurate reflection of what the firms experienced at the stage in their life cycle studied in comparison with what is going on in their industries during that period of time. Previous research has also compared CEO behaviors within specific growth phases (Eggers, Leahy, and Mikalachki 1997), further documenting the validity of this approach.

Variables Assessed

The variables were operationalized as follows.

Strategic Growth and Expansion Intentions were defined as the degree to which entrepreneurs intend to actively engage in specific strategies to grow and expand their firms. On the basis of Miles and Snow's (1978) Typology of Strategy, activities measured included adding a new product or service, expanding operations, selling to a new market, and applying for a loan to expand operations. Recently, Pistrui (1999) termed these series of entrepreneurial behaviors reflecting strategic characteristics "implementable attributes of planned growth" (IAPG). The IAPG serves to operationalize the Schumpeterian characteristics described earlier by identifying the specific types of new combinations entrepreneurs tend to pursue. Nineteen strategic intentions were thus measured in this study.

Entrepreneurial intensity is the degree to which entrepreneurs are willing to exert maximum motivation and effort towards the success of their venture. The Entrepreneurial Intensity (EI) scale was adapted from the Entrepreneurial Profile Questionnaire (EPQ) , successfully implemented in a variety of research sites in the United States, Mexico, Russia, Poland, Romania, and Hungary (Pistrui, Liao, and Welsch 1998; Welsch and Pistrui 1993; Welsch and Roberts 1994). A sample item measuring this construct is, "my business is the most important activity in my life." *Opportunity Costs* were operationalized as the extent to which entrepreneurs are willing to incur personal and professional sacrifices for the sake of the venture (i.e., "I would rather own my own business than pursue another promising career").

Organizational structure is measured by the configuration selected by entrepreneurs to coordinate people and tasks (functional, product/market, team-based, a combination, or none in place at all). Also measured in this study was the perceived importance entrepreneurs attached to strategic success factors, such as those cited in research by Storey (1989) and Hills and Narayana (1989): competent leadership, market/product focus, hiring technical staff, and attracting financing. Respondents were also asked to indicate the *financing sources* they used to start and grow their ventures, including several equity and debt sources. Finally, *demographic* characteristics were measured, including sales revenues, industry, years of experience, and the equity the entrepreneurs held in previous ventures.

RESULTS

Strategic Growth and Expansion Activities

Growth rates of the firms were statistically computed using sales revenues over a two-year period. The average annualized growth rate for the population was calculated over a multi-year period as 5.03%. Examination of the growth rates by industrial sector for the three largest industrial sectors represented in the sample (i.e., business/professional/technical service, wholesale/distribution, and construction) showed an average growth rate of 6%. A tertial split on the entire sample was performed, and the upper and lower thirds were included for analysis. The "high-growth-oriented" group achieved a growth rate of 23% or higher, while the "low-growth-oriented" group's rate was 5% or lower. The "moderate growth" group (growth rates of 6 to 22%) was dropped from the analysis to obtain a clearer bifurcation in the sample, so as to better differentiate the high-growth and low-growth orientations. The growth rate of the firms labelled "high-growth" greatly exceeded the average annualized industry growth rate.

The differences between the high-growth entrepreneurs and low-growth entrepreneurs on the set of nineteen strategic growth intentions (IAPG) is presented in Table 1. The data were submitted to a factor analysis using principal components extraction and varimax rotation. This yielded a five factor solution, as indicated through our interpretation of the scree plot and the eigenvalues greater than 1.0. Factor 1 accounted for 40.2% of the variance and the remaining four factors accounted for an additional 29%. The factors are: Market Expansion, Technological Change, Search for Financing, Operations Planning, and Organizational Development. A multivariate analysis of variance test was conducted to compare differences between the two groups, and it was highly significant (overall $F = 33.00, p < 0.001$). These differences illustrate the entrepreneurial focus placed within these two groups of firms for the next two years. As demonstrated, the two most highly-rated set of growth actions intended by high-growth-oriented entrepreneurs were market expansion (mean = 4.10) and technological change for the firm (mean=3.87), thus supporting Hypothesis 1.

Entrepreneurial Intensity and Opportunity Costs: Commitment to the High-Growth Venture

A factor analysis of the items measured utilizing varimax rotation was conducted, and a two-factor solution was obtained. Items loading on *entrepreneurial intensity* included: "I do whatever it takes to establish my business," "I will do whatever it takes to make my business a success," "There is no limit to how long I would give a maximum effort to establish my business," and "My business is the most important activity in my life." Items loading on *opportunity costs* included: "I would rather own my own business than earn a higher salary employed by someone else," "I would rather own my own business than pursue another promising career," "I am willing to make significant personal sacrifices in order to stay in business," and "I would work somewhere else only long enough to make another attempt to establish my firm." The scale reliabilities were strong: for *Entrepreneurial Intensity* alpha was 0.81, and for *Opportunity Costs* alpha was .75.

Next, a discriminant analysis to predict growth orientation (high or low) was run on the composite scores of both variables. The primary objectives of a discriminant analysis are to find the dimension or dimensions along which groups differ (Tabachnik and Fidell 1989). The resulting chi-square tests were significant: for *Entrepreneurial Inten-*

462 L.K. GUNDRY AND H.P. WELSCH

TABLE 1 Factor Analysis of Strategic Growth Intentions[a,b]

Strategic Growth Intention	Factor Loading	High-Growth Entrepreneurs (n = 240)	Low-Growth Entrepreneurs (n = 263)	Univariate F
Factor 1: Market Expansion		4.10	3.04	113.56***
Adding a new product or service	0.75			
Selling to a new market	0.82			
Expanding distribution channels	0.64			
Expanding advertising and promotion	0.63			
Researching new markets	0.72			
Expanding scope of operating activities	0.63			
Factor 2: Technological Change		3.87	2.99	64.54***
Acquiring new equipment	0.70			
Computerizing current operations	0.74			
Upgrading computer systems	0.77			
Replacing present equipment	0.76			
Factor 3: Search for Financing		3.55	2.53	75.24***
Seeking additional financing	0.87			
Seeking professional advice	0.56			
Applying for a loan	0.87			
Factor 4: Operations Planning		3.45	2.22	114.64***
Adding operating space	0.79			
Expanding current facilities	0.74			
Redesigning layout	0.65			
Adding specialized employees	0.46			
Factor 5: Organizational Development		3.01	2.14	58.59***
Training of employees off-site	0.80			
Redesigning work methods	0.67			

*** $p < 0.001$.
[a] A multivariate analysis of variance between groups on these factors yielded an overall F of 33.00 ($p < 0.001$).
[b] Varimax rotation.

sity, $\chi^2 = 21.68$ ($p < 0.001$); for *Opportunity Costs* $\chi^2 = 22.04$ ($p < 0.001$). The mean score on the scale for *Entrepreneurial Intensity* in the high growth group was 4.11; for the low-growth firms it was 3.70. On the *Opportunity Costs* scale, the mean for low-growth firms was 3.60, and for the high-growth firms it was 3.99. Thus, the scores on entrepreneurial intensity and opportunity costs can successfully predict the high-growth-orientation or low-growth-orientation of the entrepreneurs sampled. Thus, both Hypotheses 2 and 3 are supported.

Organizational Structure and Growth Orientation

The organizational structures selected by the entrepreneurs sampled are presented in Table 2. Although one-third of both high-growth and low-growth entrepreneurs reported a functional structure in place, the high-growth entrepreneurs were nearly twice as likely to utilize a team-based structure in their organizations ($\chi^2 = 10.84$, $p < 0.05$). Among the low-growth businesses, 34% reported no structure in place at all. Thus, Hypothesis 4 is supported.

Strategic Success Factors and Entrepreneurial Growth

Entrepreneurs were asked to rate ten factors based on their perception of the importance of the factor's contribution to the strategic success of the business. The responses

TABLE 2   Organizational Structure of High-Growth and Low-Growth Firms

	High-Growth Firms ($n = 240$)	Low-Growth Firms ($n = 263$)
Organization design[a]		
Functional (grouped by skill)	32%	33%
Product/market (grouped by output)	10%	16%
Team-based	28%	15%
Combination (one or more of above)	1%	2%
None at all	29%	34%

[a] Chi square = 10.38; $p < 0.05$

are shown in Table 3. The pattern of response is similar, in terms of which factors were perceived as more important within each group of entrepreneurs. However, the strength of response, or emphasis, is significantly different, according to a multivariate analysis of variance test (overall $F = 4.37, p < 0.001$). Overall, high-growth-oriented entrepreneurs attached much greater importance to the success factors than did low-growth entrepreneurs. Specifically, the four factors perceived by high-growth entrepreneurs as contributing most strongly toward the growth of their ventures were: the reputation or image/identity of the business, available cash, product/service focus, and competent leadership. Thus, Hypothesis 5 is supported.

Financing Strategies of High-Growth and Low-Growth Entrepreneurs

Table 4 illustrates the financing strategies used by high-growth and low-growth entrepreneurs to start and to expand their businesses. Significant differences were found in the following sources: Family, friends, and relatives (measured as one source) were more likely to be used by high-growth entrepreneurs at start-up (53 vs. 43%, respectively; $\chi^2 = 3.90, p < 0.05$), although there were no differences in the utilization of that source at expansion. The Small Business Administration (SBA) Loan Program was significantly more likely to be a source for high-growth entrepreneurs at expansion ($\chi^2 = 3.73, p < 0.05$). In fact, high-growth entrepreneurs were twice as likely as low-

TABLE 3   High-Growth and Low-Growth Entrepreneurs' Perceived Importance of Success Factors

Factor	High-Growth Entrepreneurs ($n = 240$)	Low-Growth Entrepreneurs ($n = 263$)	Univariate F
Available cash	4.56	4.26	8.95**
Competent leadership	4.41	4.14	5.11*
Competent technical people	4.20	3.81	9.82**
Competent sales people	4.24	3.90	6.76**
Market focus	4.14	3.66	22.67**
Product/service focus	4.46	4.00	24.17***
Financing sources	3.94	3.52	11.14***
Reputation/image/identity	4.82	4.61	12.29***
Location	3.50	3.46	0.09
Strategic planning	4.14	3.58	26.23***

Note: A multivariate analysis of variance (MANOVA) between groups on these factors yielded an overall F of 4.37 ($p < 0.001$).
* $p < 0.05$; ** $p < 0.01$; *** $p < 0.001$.

TABLE 4 Financing Sources Utilized by High-Growth and Low-Growth Entrepreneurs

	High-Growth Entrepreneurs		Low-Growth Entrepreneurs	
Financing Source	Start-up (%)	Expansion (%)	Start-up (%)	Expansion (%)
Commercial banks	49	64	55	69
Family, friends, and relatives	53*	39	43	32
SBA loan program (Small Business Administration)	5	8*	3	3
Illinois developmental finance authority	0.5	3	0	1
Dept. commerce/community affairs	2	3	0	0
Commercial finance companies	6	10	7	11
Personal savings	94**	79	86	75
Leasing companies	20*	23	12	18
Private equity investors (Angels)	4	5	3	3
Venture capital firms	0.5	2	0.5	1
Local/municipal revolving loans	3	4	2	3
Women's finance initiative	1	3	0.5	0.1

* $p < 0.05$; ** $p < 0.01$.

growth entrepreneurs to use the SBA. Personal savings were more likely to be used at start-up by high-growth entrepreneurs (χ^2=6.85, $p < 0.01$), and leasing companies were more likely to be used by this group at start-up (χ^2=4.74, $p < 0.05$). No differences were found between the groups on the use of the state's department of commerce and community affairs loan program, private equity investors (angel financing), banks, finance companies, venture capital firms, local/municipal revolving loan programs, and the Women's Finance Initiative (a state-based program). Hypothesis 6, that high-growth firms are likely to utilize a greater variety of financing resources at start-up and growth, is therefore only partially supported.

Entrepreneurial and Organizational Characteristics of High-Growth and Low-Growth Firms

The entrepreneurial and organizational characteristics of the high-growth and low-growth firms are illustrated in Table 5. Entrepreneurs in high-growth firms had significantly fewer years of industry experience ($F = 23.16$; $p < 0.001$) and significantly fewer years of experience in business overall ($F = 7.72$; $p < 0.01$). In addition, they held equity in more firms than low-growth entrepreneurs ($F = 4.51$; $p < 0.05$).

The industrial classifications for the firms show that both types of firms tended to have similar representation in the service sector (33–36%), with relatively equal breakdowns across other industries. For women-owned firms, many of the industries are non-traditional, such as transportation, manufacturing, and construction.

DISCUSSION AND CONCLUSIONS

The high-growth-oriented entrepreneurs in this study were clearly differentiated from the low-growth–oriented entrepreneurs along several dimensions. Figure 1 depicts a model of the "ambitious," high-growth–oriented entrepreneur constructed from the findings of this research. The "ambitious" entrepreneurs are similar to those identified

TABLE 5 Entrepreneurial and Organizational Characteristics of High-Growth and Low-Growth Firms

Characteristic	High-Growth ($n = 240$)	Low-Growth ($n = 263$)	t Value
Years of experience in industry	13.2	17.5	4.83***
Years of business experience	17.2	19.9	2.78**
Number of firms in which entrepreneur has held equity	2.2	1.5	2.31*
Business description (Industry)			
Service organization	36%	33%	
Retail	7%	9%	
Finance/insurance/real estate	3%	2%	
Transportation	2%	5%	
Professional services	5%	8%	
Distributor/wholesale	15%	11%	
Manufacturer	8%	8%	
Construction	14%	14%	
Agribusiness	0%	1%	
Other	8%	7%	

* $p < 0.05$; ** $p < 0.01$; *** $p < 0.001$.

by David Birch as *gazelles*, having an annual growth rate of at least 20%. When the strategic intentions of high-growth entrepreneurs were compared with those of slower-growth entrepreneurs, a striking set of differences emerged along all five sets (factors) of strategic orientations. High-growth–oriented entrepreneurs were significantly more likely to pursue (in order of importance) *market expansion* (e.g., adding a new product or service and expanding advertising and promotion, etc.); *technological change* (e.g., acquiring new equipment and computerizing current operations); *search for financing* (e.g., seeking professional advice and applying for loans); *operations planning* (e.g., expanding current facilities); and *organizational development* (e.g., off-site training of employees). Further, our findings suggest that the key strategic success factors perceived by high-growth–oriented entrepreneurs are the reputation (image) of their firms, a strong focus on the quality of the product or service, available cash to grow the business, and effective leadership. While these differences were statistically significant, more research should be done to determine the nature and direction of the strategic success factors over time. They serve as gauges by which the entrepreneurs can "monitor" their success in achieving their growth goals. Hoy, McDougall, and Dsouza (1992) stated that more research is needed to understand how the strategies of high-growth companies differ from the strategies of firms with slower growth. Merz, Weber, and Laetz (1994) added that detailed comparative measurement of strategies pursued by small firms is also needed. Moreover, Davidsson and Wiklund (1999) have underscored the need for more research to further our understanding of this phenomenon. Our findings thus contribute to the work in this area and suggest some of the strategic distinctions among these firms.

It was proposed that high-growth entrepreneurs exhibit greater intensity towards business ownership and would be willing to incur greater opportunity costs. Tests confirmed that these two dimensions did in fact discriminate among entrepreneurs on the basis of actual growth rates. Ambitious entrepreneurs were significantly more motivated to do whatever it takes to grow their enterprises and to make the necessary sacrifices to ensure the success of their businesses. This result reveals the nature of entrepre-

FIGURE 1   Attributes of high-growth entrepreneurs and their firms.

neurial motivation at a more established stage in the venture creation process, extending the work in this area beyond the pre-launch or launch stages (Bhave 1994).

   The high-growth entrepreneurs were significantly more willing to incur opportunity costs associated with venture growth. They desired to own and grow their businesses despite earning less than they could elsewhere and would readily give up a more promising career for business ownership. Perhaps these entrepreneurs are more pragmatic than their overly optimistic counterparts who may "want it all" and believe that opportunity costs do not influence growth objectives. High-growth entrepreneurs, therefore, would put aside some of their personal or family goals and incur sacrifices and penalties, pursuing a "delayed gratification" model of behavior because they are committed to the growth of their ventures. However, neither group in our study perceived owning their business as more important than spending time with their families. This finding is intriguing and may be attributable to the sample, in this case women entrepreneurs. Previous research has suggested that women business owners often founded their businesses to better balance (or control) their time spent on work and family (Starr and Yudkin 1996 and others). Even though we might expect high-growth–oriented entrepreneurs to desire to harvest their businesses eventually, this study did not show such a goal. Perhaps the psychological investment in and commitment to the business demonstrated by these women entrepreneurs preclude their intention to harvest the business in the foreseeable future. Recent findings from a qualitative study by Cliff (1998) suggest that women entrepreneurs prefer a managed approach to business growth, rather than following more risky growth strategies. However, our study discloses that some women entrepreneurs deliberately select high-growth–oriented strategies. This supports our assertion that differences *among* women entrepreneurs are of research interest and that future studies should further examine variables across categories (strategic or other) of women-owned businesses.

The high-growth–oriented entrepreneurs also tended to have a more structured organization, suggesting a more disciplined approach to management. Although both groups utilized functional structures (as is common in smaller organizations), the "ambitious" entrepreneurs were nearly twice as likely to use team-based structures, which can better position their firms to respond rapidly to changes in the external environment. This finding lends support to Gilmore and Kazanjian's (1989) position that to achieve and maintain high growth, a structured decision-making approach to team building would permit information sharing and delegation. Nearly 35% of low-growth entrepreneurs utilized no design at all, suggesting that these business owners, and possibly their employees as well, may be called on to perform "hat tricks" in carrying out a wide variety of unassigned tasks with little coordination among them. While this highly informal approach to organization design is likely to be found in fledgling firms in the early stages of business evolution, it is ineffective for more established firms engaged in expansion.

Entrepreneurial and organizational characteristics of the firms studied suggest that the individuals in the high-growth group had less experience in the industry in which their firm operated, and fewer years of overall business experience. Although the average years of experience (14) was substantial, the "ambitious" entrepreneurs tended to plan for growth earlier in the life of their businesses. They also tended to have held equity in more firms than did the low-growth entrepreneurs. This suggests that "ambitious" entrepreneurs engaged in greater scanning of the environment, such as opportunity recognition behaviors.

Recommendations for Future Research

Several questions are raised by this study. The first is the aspiration level of the entrepreneur herself. Is the high-growth entrepreneur driven to seek higher levels of attainment inherently or as a result of previous successes, such as equity held in previous, or concurrent, enterprises? Also, the cross-sectional nature of the study has caught entrepreneurs in various stages of their firm's life cycle. It is possible in future research to control the stage of respondents and investigate the relationship to growth intention. Future work may also be done to examine the convergent and discriminant validity of the scales used in this study. Finally, we have identified "ambitious" entrepreneurs relative to one another (i.e., within a sample of 832). Are other definitions possible, such as those companies that seek venture capital? Focusing on that group, however, might result in ignoring the rich implications found for entrepreneurs who are seeking to "make it on their own." Monroe, Price, and Neck (1997) identified a group of very high growth ventures as "Fast Trac Super Gazelles," which were characterized as early stage organizations reporting a 100% increase in annual gross sales. Future research should consider such further distinctions among growth-oriented ventures to delineate them more clearly.

Researchers may also consider examining growth orientation within a cultural context. Kolvereid (1991) compared samples of Norwegian, British, and New Zealander entrepreneurs and found that the Norwegian entrepreneurs did not aspire to grow their firms, at least at the same rate as the other groups. Although the sample in the present study was large and represented several ethnic and cultural groups within the United

468 L.K. GUNDRY AND H.P. WELSCH

States, it would be interesting to expand the research in this area to include cross-cultural comparisons of entrepreneurial growth strategies and intentions.

This research has attempted to highlight some of the differences that exist between "ambitious" and "less ambitious" entrepreneurs. Uncovering these relationships allows researchers to discern more clearly the influence of strategic growth intentions in the entrepreneurial process and to observe the underlying attributes of entrepreneurs and the strategic actions they select that permit venture growth and organizational change.

REFERENCES

Amit, R., and Cockburn, I.E. 1995. Opportunity costs and entrepreneurial activity. *Journal of Business Venturing* 10(2):95–106.

Barrier, M. 1996. Can you stay small forever? *Nation's Business* 10:34R.M

Baum, J.R., 1995. The relation of traits, competencies, motivation, strategy, and structure to venture growth. In P.D. Reynolds et al., eds., *Frontiers of Entrepreneurship Research.* Wellesley, MA: Babson College.

Bhave, M. 1994. A process model of entrepreneurial venture creation. *Journal of Business Venturing* 8:223–242.

Birch, D. 1987. *Job Creation in America.* New York, NY: Free Press.

Bracker, J., Keats, B., and Pearson, J. 1988. Planning and financial performance among small firms in a growth industry. *Strategic Management Journal* 9:591–603.

Brush, C.G., and Hisrich, R.D. 1991. Antecedent influences on women-owned businesses. *Journal of Managerial Psychology* 6:9–16.

Carland, J., Hoy, F., Boulton, W., and Carland, J.A. 1984. Differentiating entrepreneurs from small business owners: A conceptualization. *Academy of Management Review* 9(2):354–359.

Caruana, A., Morris, M.H., and Vella, A.J. 1998. The effect of centralization and formalization on entrepreneurship in export firms. *Journal of Small Business Management* 36(1):16–29.

Chaganti, R., DeCarolis, D., and Deeds, D. 1995. Predictors of capital structure in small ventures. *Entrepreneurship: Theory and Practice* 20(2):7–18.

Cliff, J.E. 1998. Does one size fit all? Exploring the relationship between attitudes towards growth, gender, and business size. *Journal of Business Venturing* 13(6):523–542.

Cooney, T., and Bygrave, W. 1997. The evolution of structure and strategy in fast-growth firms founded by entrepreneurial teams. In P.D. Reynolds et al., eds., *Frontiers of Entrepreneurship Research.* Wellesley, MA: Babson College.

Covin, J.G., and Slevin, D.P. 1988. The influence of organization structure on the utility of an entrepreneurial top management style. *Journal of Management Studies* 25(3):217–234.

Davidsson, P. 1991. Continued entrepreneurship: Ability, need, and opportunity as determinants of small firm growth. *Journal of Business Venturing* 6:405–429.

Davidsson, P. 1989. Entrepreneurship and after? A study of growth willingness in small firms. *Journal of Business Venturing* 4:211–226.

Davidsson, P., and Wiklund, J. 1999. Suitable approaches for studying small firm growth. *Babson College/Kauffman Foundation Entrepreneurship Research Conference*, Columbia, S.C.: University of South Carolina.

Dsouza, D.E. 1990. *Strategy types and environmental correlates of strategy for high-growth firms: An empirical study.* Doctoral Dissertation, Georgia State University.

Eggers, J., and Leahy, K. 1993. *Entrepreneurial Leadership Initiative: Research Overview.* San Diego, CA: Center for Creative Leadership.

Eggers, J., Leahy, K., and Churchill, N.C. 1994. Stages of small business growth revisited: Insights into growth path and needed leadership/management skills in low and high growth companies. In P.D. Reynolds et al., eds., *Frontiers of Entrepreneurship Research.* Wellesley, MA: Babson College.

Eggers, J., Leahy, K., and Mikalachki, A. 1997. Challenges of managing rapidly growing Companies. In P.D. Reynolds et al., eds., *Frontiers of Entrepreneurship Research.* Wellesley, MA: Babson College.

Ensley, M., and Banks, M. 1994. An empirical investigation of the impact of formal Strategic planning in extremely high-growth ventures. In P.D. Reynolds et al., eds., *Frontiers of Entrepreneurship Research.* Wellesley, MA: Babson College.

Feeser, H.R. 1987. *Incubators, entrepreneurs, strategy and performance: A comparison of high and low growth high tech firms.* Doctoral Dissertation, Purdue University.

Gibb, A., and Davies, L. 1990. *Frameworks Aimed at the D Development of Possible Growth Models.* United Kingdom: Durham Business School.

Gilmore, T.N., and Kazanjian, R.K. 1989. Clarifying decision making in high-growth ventures: The use of responsibility charting. *Journal of Business Venturing* 4(1):69–83.

Ginn, C.W., and Sexton, D.L. 1989. Growth: A vocation choice and psychological preference. In R. Brockhaus et al., eds., *Frontiers of Entrepreneurship Research.* Wellesley, MA: Babson College.

Ginn, C.W., and Sexton, D.L. 1990. Growth: A vocation choice and psychological preference. In R. Brockhaus, et al., eds., *Frontiers of Entrepreneurship Research.* Wellesley, MA: Babson College.

Greening, D., Barringer, B., and Macy, G. 1996. A qualitative study of managerial challenges facing small business geographic expansion. *Journal of Business Venturing* 11:233–256.

Hambrick, D.C., and Crozier, L.M. 1985. Stumblers and stars in the management of rapid growth. *Journal of Business Venturing* 1:31–45.

Hills, G.E., and Narayana, C.L. 1989. Profile characteristics, success factors and marketing in highly successful firms. In R. Brockhaus, et al., eds., *Frontiers of Entrepreneurship Research.* Wellesley, MA: Babson College.

Hoy, F., McDougall, P., and Dsouza, D. 1992. Strategies and environments of high-growth firms. In D. Sexton and J. Kasarda, eds., *The State of the Art of Entrepreneurship.* Boston, MA: The Coleman Foundation, PWS-Kent.

Kim, W.C., and Mauborgne, R. 1997. Value innovation: The strategic logic of high growth. *Harvard Business Review* 75(1):102–112.

Kolvereid, L. 1992. Growth aspirations among Norwegian entrepreneurs. *Journal of Business Venturing* 5:209–222.

Kruger, N., and Carsrud, A. 1993. Entrepreneurial intentions: Applying the theory of planned behaviour. *Entrepreneurship & Regional Development* 5:315–330.

Kuratko, D.F., Hornsby, J.S., and Naffziger, D.W. 1997. An examination of owner's goals in sustaining entrepreneurship. *Journal of Small Business Management* 35(1):24–33.

Lyles, M., Baird, I., Orris, J., and Kuratko, D. 1993. Formalized planning in small business: Increasing strategic choices. *Journal of Small Business Management* 31:38–50.

Merz, G., Weber, P.B., and Laetz, V.B. 1994. Linking small business management with entrepreneurial growth. *Journal of Small Business Management* 32(4):48–60.

Miles, R.E., and Snow, C.C. 1978. *Organizational Strategy, Structure, and Process.* New York: McGraw-Hill.

Monroe, S.R., Price, C., and Neck, H. 1997. Growing "super gazelles": An empirical Study of entrepreneurial training strategies and venture hyper-performance. In P.D. Reynolds et al., eds., *Frontiers of Entrepreneurship Research.* Wellesley, MA: Babson College.

Moore, D., and Buttner, E. 1997. *Women Entrepreneurs: Moving Beyond the Glass Ceiling.* Thousand Oaks, CA: Sage.

National Foundation for Women Business Owners. 1994. *Credibility, Creativity and Independence: The Greatest Challenges and Biggest Rewards of Business Ownership Among Women.* Silver Spring, MD: NFWBD.

Neiswander, D., and Fulton, M.E. 1989 Successful growth management. In R. Brockhaus et al., eds., *Frontiers of Entrepreneurship Research* Wellesley, MA: Babson College.

470   L.K. GUNDRY AND H.P. WELSCH

Pistrui, D. 1999. *Growth intentions and expansion plans of new entrepreneurs in transforming economies: An investigation into family dynamics, entrepreneurship and enterprise development.* Technical Report: Universitat Autonoma de Barcelona.

Pistrui, D., Liao, J., and Welsch, H. 1998. Entrepreneurial expansion plans: An empirical Investigation of infrastructure predictors. Paper presented at Research in Entrepreneurship (RENT XII). Lyon, France: November 26–27.

Schumpeter, J. 1954. *Can Capitalism Survive?* New York, NY: Harper and Row.

Sexton, D.L., and Bowman, N. 1985. The entrepreneur: A capable executive and more. *Journal of Business Venturing* 1:129–140.

Starr, J., and Yudkin, M. 1996. *Women Entrepreneurs: A Review of Current Research.* Wellesley, MA, Center for Research on Women.

Storey, M.J. 1989. *Inside America's Fastest Growing Companies.* N.Y.: John Wiley and Sons.

Tabachnick, B.G., and Fidell, L.S. 1989. *Using Multivariate Statistics.* Cambridge: Harper & Row.

Vesper, K. 1993. *New Venture Mechanics.* Englewood Cliffs, NJ: Prentice Hall.

Ward, E. 1993. Motivation of expansion plans of entrepreneurs and small business managers. *Journal of Small Business Management* 31(1):32–38.

Welsch, H., and Pistrui, D. 1993. Entrepreneurship commitment and initiative in Romania. Paper presented at Research in Entrepreneurship VII, Budapest, Hungary, November 25–26.

Welsch, H., and Roberts, J. 1994. Predictors of growth and expansion initiatives of Russian entrepreneurs in a post-socialist environment. Paper presented at the International Council of Small Business. Strasbourg, France: June 27–29.

Wijewardena, H., and Tibbits, G.E. 1999. Factors contributing to the growth of small manufacturing firms. *Journal of Small Business Management* 37:88–95.

Wiklund, J. 1998. *Small firm growth and performance: Entrepreneurship and beyond.* Doctoral Dissertation, Jonkoping International Business School.

Part VI
Performance

[24]

© Academy of Management Journal
1991, Vol. 34, No. 1, 136–161.

GENDER AND ORGANIZATIONAL PERFORMANCE: DETERMINANTS OF SMALL BUSINESS SURVIVAL AND SUCCESS

ARNE L. KALLEBERG
University of North Carolina at Chapel Hill
KEVIN T. LEICHT
Pennsylvania State University

In this study, we examined several hypotheses on how the survival and success of small businesses headed by men and women are related to industry differences, organizational structures, and attributes of owner-operators. We found that businesses headed by women were not more likely to go out of business, nor less successful, than those owned by men. Our analyses are based on data collected annually over a three-year period from an initial group of 411 companies in the computer sales and software, food and drink, and health industries in South Central Indiana.

Recent research on entrepreneurship, management, and organizations has underscored the importance of understanding better the conditions that promote business survival and success. Although organizational survival has been studied for many years (e.g., Mayer & Goldstein, 1961), research on this topic grew rapidly in the late 1970s and 1980s, largely as a result of an increase in business failures, bankruptcies, and hostile takeovers during that period (Cameron, Sutton, & Whetten, 1988: 5; Meyer, 1988; Whetten, 1987). The focus on survival contrasts with that of most research on organizational performance in the 1960s and early 1970s, which emphasized the success and development of large organizations (Cameron & Whetten, 1983; Goodman & Pennings, 1977). Many large organizations managed to survive during the 30 years of uninterrupted growth that marked the postwar era but were permanent failures that consistently performed poorly (Meyer & Zucker, 1989).

An important issue in research on organizational survival and success is the relevance of gender to the performance of small businesses. The rate of growth in self-employment has recently been greater among women than

The University of North Carolina's Institute for Private Enterprise provided financial support for this study. Indiana University's Center for Survey Research collected the data used. We are grateful to the following people for their constructive comments on earlier versions of this article: Howard Aldrich, Glenn Carroll, Robert Kaufman, Peter Marsden, Toby Parcel, Paul Reynolds, Donald Tomaskovic-Devey, Catherine Zimmer, and this journal's reviewers.

men; women experienced an increase of 35 percent from 1977–82, compared to 12 percent for men (Hisrich & Brush, 1984). Nevertheless, men are still more likely than women to be self-employed. Moreover, researchers and others commonly assert that businesses owned by men are more successful than those owned by women (Aldrich, 1989; Cuba, Decenzo, & Anish, 1983). Indeed, in 1985, the average man-owned business had seven times the average annual receipts of the average woman-owned business (U.S. Small Business Administration, 1986). Data on the relative survival chances of businesses headed by men and by women are sparser than those on success, but descriptions of the disadvantages women face in small business led us to expect them to fail more often than men. In view of the importance of this topic, it is surprising that there is little empirical evidence on how gender differences affect organizational performance. Few studies have directly compared male and female entrepreneurs, and we were unable to locate any studies that examined the determinants of organizational survival and success separately for businesses headed by men and women. We addressed these issues by examining the mechanisms that help to explain business survival and success. Our analysis is based on a group of small businesses in three industries—food and drink, computer sales and software, and health—in South Central Indiana during the period 1985–87.

THEORETICAL ISSUES

Survival and success are distinct aspects of performance that are determined by different processes. Two recent studies have suggested that conclusion.[1] Blau's (1984) investigation of New York architecture firms showed that large firms were more likely to survive but that smaller ones were more profitable. Moreover, Carroll and Huo's (1986) study of newspapers suggested that their survival was more strongly related to institutional environmental variables, such as political turmoil, but that their success was more strongly related to task environmental variables, such as the number of skilled employees in the local labor market.

Explaining Organizational Survival and Success

Much of the recent research on organizational performance has been at the macro level of analysis and has used a population ecology approach (e.g., Hannan & Freeman, 1977). Ecologists generally focus on survival and tend to neglect differences in success among surviving organizations. Population ecologists assume that organizations do not have much control over their survival or failure and that strong inertial forces prevent them from changing their forms to fit their environments better. Selection of particular organization forms by environmental characteristics is thus the fundamental process explaining differences in survival within organizational populations.

---

[1] Also see a discussion in Meyer and Zucker (1989: 72–74).

Changes in these populations result from turnover among units, not from their transformation or adaptation.

A second line of research on the two dimensions of organizational performance has focused on micro-level determinants. Scholars have assumed that differences in survival and success depend on organizations' abilities to adapt their internal structures to the contingencies associated with their technologies or task environments (e.g., Child, 1972; Pfeffer & Salancik, 1978). Successful organizations are those that best adapt to fit the opportunities provided and constraints imposed by their environments. Such adaptation depends a great deal on the choices and actions an organization's leaders make. Leaders differ in the extent to which they have the psychological traits, experience, and skills needed to accomplish the entrepreneurial and managerial tasks necessary for organizational survival and growth (Cummings, 1988).

Macro and micro perspectives on survival and success are complementary. Organizational ecologists have identified the kinds of structures or environments that are more and less conducive to the survival of certain organizational forms. But ecologists tend to ignore—or at least downplay—the actions of organizational leaders. Studies of entrepreneurs fill this gap and help explain why some organizations are more successful than others, but these microscopic approaches generally ignore the environmental characteristics that affect performance. Our multilevel model of the two dimensions of organizational performance incorporates explanatory variables from both levels of analysis: macro characteristics describing organizations and their environments and micro variables describing entrepreneurs' personal characteristics.

Organizational Age and Performance

The relation between an organization's age and its survival and success illustrates the divergence of the two dimensions of performance. We would expect an organization's age to be generally positively related to its survival. Carroll (1983) concluded that the most common finding of the major empirical studies of mortality is that the death rate of business organizations declines with increasing age; organizations are more likely to die in the first few years of their operation. Young organizations and organizational forms suffer liabilities of newness involving both internal processes, such as coordinating and defining roles and developing trust and loyalty among employees, and external problems like acquiring resources and stabilizing supplier and customer relationships (Stinchcombe, 1965). By contrast, the liabilities of newness are not likely to matter as much once organizations are past a certain age. Therefore, we did not expect an organization's age to be necessarily related to its success (Meyer & Zucker, 1989).

> Hypothesis 1: A company's age will be positively related to the probability of its survival but unrelated to its success.

The Effect of Gender Differences on Organizational Performance

Men usually occupy dominant positions in the economy and labor force. Some observers have argued that entrepreneurship is an exception to this general pattern and suggested that self-employment enables women to overcome discrimination and other employment difficulties (Cromie & Hayes, 1988). However, most writers have maintained that self-employed women are still disadvantaged relative to self-employed men because women face barriers associated with education, families, and workplaces (Aldrich, 1989; Goffee & Scase, 1983). The paucity of research on how gender differences affect organizational performance has hindered a resolution of this issue. Almost all our knowledge of entrepreneurship and the success or failure of small businesses comes from studies of men; there is very little hard information on woman entrepreneurs and their businesses, although several authors have called for more information on them (Bowen & Hisrich, 1986; Cromie & Hayes, 1988; Cuba et al., 1976; Hisrich & Brush, 1984; Schwartz, 1976; Wilkens, 1987). The few extant studies of woman entrepreneurs are based on very small or unsystematically selected samples: Goffee and Scase (1983) studied 23 woman proprietors; 86 women who owned businesses in Oklahoma returned Humphreys and McClung's (1981) questionnaires; Pellegrino and Reece (1982) randomly selected 20 woman entrepreneurs; and Schwartz (1976) studied 20 women.

Our second hypothesis examines whether there actually are differences in the two dimensions of organizational performance related to the gender of a business's owner-operator.

> Hypothesis 2: Businesses owned and operated by women
> are less likely to survive and be successful than those
> headed by men, ceteris paribus.

Our remaining hypotheses are contingent upon Hypothesis 2: if we found that businesses headed by women were indeed less likely to survive, be successful, or both, we would seek to explain why. If women's businesses performed no worse than men's, there would be no female disadvantage to explain and we instead would try to identify the processes that determine the performance of small businesses, regardless of their owners' genders.

Gender differences affecting organizational performance may be produced in two major ways. First, there may be differences between businesses headed by men and women in the level of an independent variable: for example, if small businesses perform less well than large ones and businesses headed by women are generally smaller, then those businesses will perform less well on the average than men's (again, ceteris paribus). Such a pattern would show an additive effect of gender. Second, there may be gender differences in the process by which an independent variable is related to the two dimensions of performance: for example, a year of work experience may enhance survival or success more for men than women. In that case, there would be an interaction between gender and the independent variable. We have little basis on which to predict specific interaction effects a priori because of the scarcity of past research on these issues. Hence, although we tested for the presence of interactions, we state our hypotheses regarding gender differences in terms of additive effects. We frame these hypotheses around variables at the three main levels of analysis included in our model of organizational performance: industry, company, and individual entrepreneurs.

Industrial differences. Self-employed women—like their counterparts who work for someone else—are segregated into certain kinds of work. Businesses owned by women are concentrated in retail sales and in personal and educational service industries, the so-called female ghetto. In 1982, about half of all women entrepreneurs were in service industries, and another 30 percent were in retail trade (U.S. Small Business Administration, 1986). Companies in the service and trade industries generally have lower growth rates and less success (measured by earnings or returns on investment) than businesses in other industries, in part because services and trades are highly labor-intensive and there is a lot of competition among sellers in their product markets (Humphreys & McClung, 1981).

Restricting the industries studied to three groups in which women were prominent prohibited our assessing the impact of industrial gender segregation on business survival and success. However, we could examine within-industry differences in the survival and success of businesses headed by men and women. Within a broad industry group, such as health-related businesses or eating and drinking establishments, there is a second tier of gender segregation. Businesses owned by women tend to be in highly female-typed fields, and those fields may be especially crowded or competitive. Women's concentration in those fields may account for the gender difference in the earnings of small businesses even within industries—in 1980, the average receipts of businesses owned by women in the food and drink industry were 61.4 percent of those owned by men (Loscocco & Robinson, 1989).

> Hypothesis 3: Product market characteristics such as the
> size of an industry and the extent of competition within it
> help to explain why businesses headed by women are less
> likely to survive and be successful than those headed by
> men.

Organization size. Companies headed by women generally employ fewer people than those headed by men (Charboneau, 1981; Humphreys & McClung, 1981). Since women's businesses are generally smaller, they are more exposed to liabilities of smallness than companies headed by men. These liabilities include difficulties in raising capital, meeting government regulations, and competing for labor with larger organizations that pay more and offer greater benefits (cf. Aldrich & Auster, 1986). The smallness of businesses headed by women may help to explain why they perform less well than those headed by men.

> Hypothesis 4: Businesses headed by women are smaller
> than those headed by men, and that explains in part why

*the former are less likely to survive and be successful
than the latter.*

Personal attributes. Differences in the personal attributes of men and women constitute a final set of reasons why businesses headed by women may perform less well than those owned by men. Several studies have suggested that men and women do not differ significantly on many of the psychological attributes thought to characterize successful entrepreneurs; these attributes include work values like independence and motivations such as a need for achievement and a willingness to take risks (Humphreys & McClung, 1981; Pellegrino & Reece, 1982; Schwartz, 1976). Those studies did not compare male and female business owners directly, but we saw little reason to question their conclusions about the absence of gender differences in work values and psychological motivations. We focused instead on two types of personal attributes that we thought were more plausible explanations for any observed gender-based differences in business survival and success.

First, women generally have less business experience than men. The importance of experience for the two dimensions of organizational performance is well documented: for example, a 1974 Dun and Bradstreet study showed that lack of experience and management skills was a contributing factor in 9 of 10 business failures (cf. Humphreys & McClung, 1981; Schwartz, 1976). Moreover, Humphreys and McClung reported that 45 percent of the women they surveyed mentioned lack of previous business experience as a major or moderate obstacle to business success. And Cuba and colleagues (1983) found that women in their study group with more experience than other women had more successful businesses, in terms of sales and profits. Those findings suggest a fifth hypothesis:

> Hypothesis 5: *Entrepreneurs who are women have less business experience than those who are men, and this discrepancy accounts in part for why companies headed by women are less likely to survive and be successful than those headed by men.*

Second, women are generally thought to be less likely than men to engage in innovative behaviors. Innovation is regarded as essential to small business growth and development (Wilkens, 1987), and men are often seen as more apt than women to innovate. For example, none of the 468 women entrepreneurs Hisrich and Brush (1984) surveyed reported that their business was based on a product innovation or modification; rather, the majority founded their businesses using an established or slightly modified product for an existing market.[2]

> Hypothesis 6: *Businesses headed by women are less likely to innovate, and this difference explains in part why they*

---

[2] However, Hisrich and Brush did not have a group of men with whom they could compare their results for women.

are less likely to survive and be successful than those
headed by men.

There are a number of possible explanations for why women may tend
to avoid innovative products and services. One reason is the social disapproval girls are likely to incur for straying from socially accepted, gender-
normative patterns of behavior and the encouragement and tolerance that
boys typically receive for engaging in innovative play and nonconforming
behavior (e.g., Papalia & Olds, 1981). Unfortunately, our data did not permit
us to test this explanation directly. Another possible reason for male-female
differences in innovative behavior—one that we can examine with these
data—is that women are less confident than men of their ability to succeed
in business.

> Hypothesis 7: Women have less confidence than men in
> their business ability and are less apt to feel that they can
> influence the performance of their business, and these
> differences explain in part why companies headed by
> women are less likely to survive and be successful than
> those headed by men.

RESEARCH DESIGN AND METHODS

Testing these hypotheses required data meeting certain key criteria. The
data needed to be longitudinal, since organizational survival and success are
dynamic processes. The organizations studied had to be systematically selected from a well-defined population (cf. Kalleberg, Marsden, Aldrich, &
Cassell, 1990). Moreover, longitudinal information had to be collected on the
characteristics of those organizations, their leaders, and their industries. Our
data generally meet these requirements.

A Longitudinal Study of Small Businesses in Indiana

To generate such data, we conducted a longitudinal study of a group of
small businesses in Indiana.[3] We investigated businesses located in Bloomington, Indianapolis, Evansville, Fort Wayne, Lafayette, Terre Haute, and
several other Indiana cities; 12 counties in all are represented. The businesses studied—eating and drinking establishments, computer sales and
software companies, and health-related businesses—are fairly typical of
businesses found throughout the United States. In the health industry, the
largest percentage of the companies studied provided nutrition counseling,
physical treatments, health food, and exercise. All of the businesses in the
food and drink industry served food, though almost all of them also provided
other products and services. Over three-quarters served alcoholic beverages,
about 40 percent offered catering, a third provided banquet facilities, and
about a quarter provided entertainment. In the computer industry, about
three-quarters of the companies sold software and about 65 percent sold or

---

[3] Kalleberg (1986) provides an overview of the study and its main findings.

rented hardware. In addition, almost 80 percent provided systems consultation, 63 percent furnished education services, and nearly half provided word or data processing services.

Sampling procedures. Our primary sampling frame was the telephone book's yellow pages (cf. Freeman & Hannan, 1983). In contrast to businesses emphasizing commercial, business, or producer markets, consumer-oriented businesses like those studied here are likely to be listed in this source, as they are oriented toward local markets and provide services and products to individuals in their communities. Our methods of selecting organizations from the yellow pages differed by industry. Since there were so many businesses listed in the food and drink industry, we randomly selected companies. On the other hand, the yellow pages identified relatively few businesses in the other two industries, so we included all of them as potential respondents. In addition, in the health industry we supplemented the yellow pages with other sources, such as lists provided by networking groups for entrepreneurs who are women.

Data collection. We gathered information in 1985, 1986, and 1987 on characteristics of industries, companies, and owners. In each company, we interviewed the person who both owned the business and had some responsibility for organizing its day-to-day activities. Graduate students and professional staff interviewers of the Center for Survey Research at Indiana University conducted telephone interviews with these people. In general, these owner-operators were very busy, as they were often involved in all aspects of their companies operations, and we had difficulty completing some interviews. Given this pool of respondents, we believe our response rates to be respectable: in 1985, we completed 136 interviews in computer companies, a response rate of 68 percent; 127 in health-related businesses (63.5%); and 148 in eating and drinking establishments (55%).[4]

In wave 2 (1986), we completed 286 interviews in the three industries; 34 companies had gone out of business. The two main reasons for nonresponse were that the owner-operator of a business was persistently unavailable (51%) and that an owner-operator refused to participate (20%). In wave 3 (1987), we sought to reinterview all 377 original owner-operators who did not go out of business in 1986, and we completed 310 interviews. We completed more interviews in wave 3 than in wave 2 (310 vs. 286) for several reasons.[5] First, we improved our follow-up procedures in the third wave of

---

[4] These response rates were computed as the number of completed interviews divided by the number of people who were interviewed, who refused, who were out of town throughout the study, and who were persistently unavailable after repeated tries. The response rates exclude people with nonworking telephone numbers, businesses with no eligible owners, and people who were ineligible for other reasons.

[5] In wave 2, we completed 103 interviews in the computer industry (a 76 percent response rate), 98 in food and drink (67%), and 85 in health-related businesses (66%). In wave 3, we completed interviews with 106 people in the computer industry, 112 in food and drink, and 92 in health.

TABLE 1
Summary of Businesses Studied

	Businesses Headed by Men			Businesses Headed by Women		
Industry	N	Number of Failures	Percentage of Failures	N	Number of Failures	Percentage of Failures
Food and drink	106	15	14	42	7	17
Computers	122	23	19	14	1	7
Health	84	12	14	43	7	16
Totals	312	50	16	99	15	15
χ^2		1.19			0.82	
df		2			2	

interviews. Second, we conducted an abbreviated interview in wave 3 with another key informant if the original one was unavailable, while in wave 2 we only interviewed the same people we had interviewed initially.[6] By 1987, an additional 31 companies had gone out of business, for a total of 65 during our study period. The death rate of 8 percent per year among the companies studied is similar to that Reynolds found in his study of new firms in Minnesota (eg., Reynolds & Miller, 1989).

Table 1 summarizes the numbers of firms we studied headed by men and by women in each of the three industries. Not surprisingly, businesses headed by men outnumbered those headed by women in each industry. Nevertheless, nearly a quarter of the businesses had women heading them, with the highest proportion in the health industry and the lowest in the computer industry. Table 1 also lists the number of companies that went out of business in each industry-gender group. We examine these patterns of survival and failure in more detail below.

Measures of Organizational Survival and Success

Organizational survival is a fundamental aspect of performance and a necessary condition for sustained business success. Organizational death takes many forms, including dissolution, merger, and reorganization. Unfortunately, our data do not allow us to distinguish among the different processes that ideally should be analyzed separately in a study of dissolutions (Freeman, Carroll, & Hannan, 1983): complete dissolution, bankruptcy, relocation, sale to a larger company, and so on. In this study, we defined a company as out of business at the time of the second or third wave of interviews (1986 or 1987) if the telephone number used in the previous wave (1985 or 1986) was no longer operative and we were unable to find a new, valid number for the business. This is a reasonable assumption for small businesses, especially in these industries: small companies generally do not

---

[6] Of the 310 interviews in wave 3, 282 were with the same person previously interviewed in a company and 28 were with another knowledgeable person in the company.

move far geographically (Birch, 1987) and, when they do move, tend to keep the same telephone number to maintain contacts with customers.

Surviving companies differ in the degree to which they are successful. Success can be measured in a variety of ways: by accounting-based indicators of financial performance, such as returns on investment; by market-based indicators of financial performance, like market share; and by stakeholders' evaluations of performance, such as the degree of satisfaction they express.[7] Our measure of success was based on a company's gross earnings, the only quantitative indicator of success available in the data set. We experimented with various additional possibilities, most notably a rough measure of profits based on respondents' perceptions of whether their business profits had increased, decreased, or remained the same during the previous two years. This variable was unrelated to the probability of survival when we added it to the model reported in Table 4.

Growth in the logarithm of gross earnings during the study period was our measure of success. In each wave of interviews, owner-operators reported their company's gross business earnings for the prior year. In our analysis, we regressed gross earnings in later periods (1986 and 1987) on initial (1985) gross earnings. Controlling for level of earnings at the beginning of the study period avoided confounding a company's initial resources with its earnings at the end of the period.

Measures of Independent Variables

Table 2 presents means and standard deviations for all the independent variables used in our analysis. Table 3 presents correlations among the variables.

Industries. Our first two industrial measures are indicators of the sizes of the business populations in the same industries and geographical areas as the respondents'; we obtained data for these measures from *County Business Patterns* (U.S. Department of Commerce, 1983–1986). The first measure is the number of businesses with employees in a respondent's industry and county lagged one year; thus, wave 1 data represent 1984 values, wave 2 data, 1985 values, and wave 3 data, 1986 values. These counts include firms of all sizes, both incorporated and unincorporated, in each industry and each of the 12 counties represented in the data set. The percentage of change in industry size represents change in the number of businesses in Indiana in a respondent's industry, also lagged one year. These measures tap different things, so the correlations between them are low: –.06 for men's businesses and .05 for women's (see Table 3).

Our other industry-based measure is a perceptual one; we asked for entrepreneurs' perceptions of the extent of competition in the product market in which their businesses operated and how much of a problem compe-

---

[7] For discussions of these dimensions of performance, see Venkatraman and Ramanujam (1986).

TABLE 2
Means and Standard Deviations for All Variables

Variables	Businesses Headed by Men		Businesses Headed by Women	
	Means	s.d.	Means	s.d.
Industry				
Food and drink	0.35	0.48	0.41	0.49
Health	0.26	0.44	0.44	0.50[d]
Competition[a]	1.79	0.52	1.75	0.55
Size[a]	585.41	596.80	763.70	587.95[d]
Percent change in size[a]	0.07	0.65	0.02	0.09
Company				
Incorporation[a]	0.73	0.44	0.64	0.46[d]
Gross earnings[a,b]	10.72	0.80	10.51	0.85[d]
Size[a,b]	1.78	1.12	1.20	0.97[d]
Age[a]	13.19	15.17	10.55	11.59[d]
Number of products and services	0.43	0.22	0.38	0.21[d]
Edge is quality	0.23	0.42	0.30	0.46[c]
Innovations[a]	0.46	0.27	0.43	0.26
Owner-operator				
Age[a]	44.49	11.35	44.96	10.65
Years in industry[a]	15.22	11.07	12.17	9.43[d]
Prior self-employment	0.23	0.42	0.22	0.39
Involvement in other business[a]	0.38	0.48	0.18	0.37[d]
Confidence	4.09	1.09	4.09	1.02
Internal locus of control	4.70	0.98	4.64	1.06
N	878		261	

[a] This is a time-varying explanatory variable, that is, a variable whose values differ for each time period.

[b] This variable was measured as a logarithm.

[c] The difference between men and women is significant at $p < .05$, two-tailed test.

[d] The difference between men and women is significant at $p < .01$, two-tailed test.

tition was for them. We averaged responses to four questions: "How much competition would you say there is in your market?", for which responses ranged from 1 = none to 4 = a great deal; "My business has been affected by increased competition from large businesses" and "My business has been affected by increased competition from small businesses" (1 = yes, 0 = no); and "How much of a problem for you is competition?" 1 = no problem at all to 5 = a great problem). The competition scale has a reliability (Cronbach's alpha) of .57. Less than 3 percent of the variation in this measure lies between industries, with the rest due to differences among companies within these industry categories.

Companies. We measured a company's age in years since its founding. In 1985, the average age of the companies headed by men (13.2) was greater than that of those headed by women (10.5). These rather high average ages suggest that the companies studied were all relatively successful ones. Cuba and colleagues (1983) measured the success of a business by whether it had survived for 5 years, a feat they termed "remarkable" in the U.S. economy.

TABLE 3
Correlation Matrix[a]

Variables	1	2	3	4	5	6	7	8	9	10	11	12	13	14	15	16	17	18	19
1. Out of business		.01	.03	.01	.09	.06	.01	.01	.03	−.07	−.05	−.09	.06	−.02	.04	−.08	.02	−.02	−.10
2. Gross earnings[b]	−.10		.19	−.27	.08	−.23	−.01	.36	.34	.08	.13	−.04	.11	−.04	.02	.07	−.15	−.01	−.01
3. Food and drink	−.02	−.01		−.75	.13	.10	−.05	.24	.32	.35	.27	.23	.06	.43	.27	−.04	−.13	−.01	−.04
4. Health	−.01	.07	−.43		−.17	.25	−.01	−.37	−.48	−.25	−.49	−.04	−.08	−.24	−.17	−.04	.08	−.16	−.03
5. Competition	.03	.02	−.04	−.15		.04	.01	.13	.24	.10	.19	.16	.10	−.03	.12	−.06	.12	−.03	−.01
6. Industry size	−.03	.04	.34	.40	−.07		.05	−.19	−.21	−.09	−.20	.16	−.13	.04	−.12	−.21	−.04	−.19	−.04
7. Percent change in industry size	−.03	−.02	−.06	−.05	.04	−.06		.00	.02	−.07	.03	−.02	−.01	−.05	−.05	−.03	−.01	.04	.04
8. Incorporation	−.08	.08	.09	−.39	.18	−.05	.04		.48	−.04	.35	.00	.18	−.06	−.11	.03	.05	.07	−.01
9. Size[b]	−.06	.19	.10	−.34	.20	−.06	.05	.43		.23	.43	.06	.26	.02	.19	.10	.13	.14	−.07
10. Company age	−.08	.08	.04	.12	.04	.11	−.05	.06	.11		−.18	.14	−.03	.44	.65	.05	−.11	.00	−.16
11. Number of products or services	.02	−.03	−.04	−.27	−.03	−.25	.02	.12	.20	−.18		−.13	.17	−.02	−.08	.03	.06	.08	.08
12. Edge is quality	−.06	.06	.20	−.05	−.02	.07	.01	.07	.10	−.01	.03		.03	.17	.08	−.25	−.10	−.02	.03
13. Innovations	.03	.03	−.05	−.03	.13	.02	.02	.13	.26	−.11	.17	.05		−.15	.01	−.03	.10	.03	.06
14. Owner's age	−.01	−.05	.14	−.01	−.05	.02	−.06	−.04	.01	.39	−.12	.08	−.15		.59	−.03	−.18	.17	−.01
15. Years in industry	−.07	.10	−.01	−.04	.00	−.07	−.03	.13	.17	.46	−.03	.04	−.04	.59		−.01	−.05	.05	−.07
16. Prior self-employment	.06	−.01	.09	−.11	.04	.03	.07	.10	.14	−.09	.07	.10	.00	.06	−.10		−.07	.22	−.02
17. Involvement in other business	.07	.04	−.01	−.05	.10	.08	.00	.13	.15	−.06	.10	−.02	.08	−.07	−.12	.23		.02	−.03
18. Confidence	−.10	.07	.00	.08	−.11	.09	.03	−.04	.07	.06	−.06	−.03	.14	.04	.08	.02	.04		.23
19. Internal locus of control	−.01	.09	.09	−.05	.00	.03	.02	.04	.03	−.03	.06	.00	.01	−.01	.01	−.03	.08	.06	

[a] Correlations for men's businesses are below the diagonal and those for women's businesses are above. Correlations greater than .12 for women and .07 for men are significant at $p < .05$, two-tailed test.
[b] This variable was measured as a logarithm.

Our measure of an organization's size was the logarithm of the number of its full-time employees.

Our measure of innovation was based on respondents' reports of which of the following six types of innovations they had engaged in during the two prior years: new products, new services, new advertising techniques, new management or organizational structures, physical changes, and other innovations. We averaged the types of innovations reported in each wave of the survey.

Finally, several variables were included in our analysis as controls. First, we recorded whether or not companies were incorporated (0 = no, 1 = yes). Incorporation is an indicator of the extent to which a business is institutionalized and has certain legal and financial protections that may inhibit dissolution. Second, we measured generalism and specialism by summing the number of products or services a company provided and dividing by the number of possible products or services that were represented by the businesses studied. Third, respondents were asked an open-ended question about whether there was anything about their business that they felt gave them an edge over their competitors. From responses to this question, members of the research team coded whether or not a company's edge was a high-quality product or service. The resulting measure allowed us to assess the importance to the owner-operators studied of quality, a characteristic many observers have seen as crucial for business excellence (Peters & Waterman, 1982).

Entrepreneurs. Table 2 indicates that the average age in 1985 of both the men and women interviewed was between 44 and 45. We used two measures of experience: the number of years a respondent had been in an industry and whether or not he or she had been self-employed before acquiring the current business (1 = yes, 0 = no).

Two measures of personal attributes were used: respondents' assessments of how successful they were in business and an indicator of internal locus of control (Brockhaus, 1982). For the first of these measures, our measure of confidence, we summed responses to two statements: "I have a better idea about running my business than most of my competitors" and "Compared to others, I feel I am very successful in my present business" (5 = agree, 3 = undecided, 1= disagree). To assess locus of control, we used responses to the statement, "I feel that outcomes of my business ventures are largely influenced by my own efforts," made on the same scale.

Our models also included a measure of whether respondents were involved in other businesses (1 = yes, 0 = no), a rough control for competing demands on the entrepreneurs' time. We expected that people who spread themselves over many businesses might be unable to devote sufficient attention to the company of interest.

Analytic Strategy

All longitudinal studies of organizational mortality will contain censored data, that is, data on organizations that do not die during the period of observation. Our data set illustrates variable-age censoring, in which censoring has no relationship to the age of a company. This contrasts with fixed-age censoring, in which all organizations censored at the end of an observation period are the same age, and with cohort-varying fixed-time censoring, in which several birth cohorts are followed until a fixed point in calendar time (Carroll, 1983).

Both left and right censoring characterize our design. The left censoring occurred because organizations that were founded at the same time as those studied but failed before 1985 were not included. We also did not add companies in the second and third waves of data collection. Thus, successful, viable businesses are necessarily overrepresented because the data are from a cross-section followed over time. Although we could not adjust statistically for the bias introduced by left censoring, we were sensitive to this source of sample bias and consider some of its implications for our findings in the concluding section. The right censoring occurred because we did not observe businesses for their whole lives; those surviving in 1987 may die eventually, but we did not control for the times of their deaths. To control for right censoring, we used a discrete event history analysis (Allison, 1984). The dependent variable for our analysis of survival was the discrete-time hazard rate, or the probability that a firm would go out of business in either 1986 or 1987. Ordinary-least-squares regression was inappropriate for estimating such a probability, which varies between 0 and 1, so we used the logarithmic odds of going out of business (the "logit" transformation) and estimated the effects of our explanatory variables on the hazard rate by logistic regression analysis. Our estimation model is $\log [P(t)/1 - P(t)] = a(t) + \Sigma b_i x_i + \Sigma c_j x_j(t)$, where $a(t)$ is a constant that compares events occurring in 1986 as opposed to 1987, b_i is a set of coefficients of the independent variables (x_i) that do not vary over time (i denotes a particular such independent variable), and c_j is a vector of coefficients of the independent variables $[x_j(t)]$ that do change over time (j represents each such time-varying explanatory variable). The values of the time-varying explanatory variables differ for the different time periods. The time-varying explanatory variables are identified in Table 2 (Allison, 1984; Aldrich, Zimmer, & McEvoy, 1989: 928).

Event history analysis controls for right-censored cases by a unique data structure. We created one data record for each year a firm was in business. Each record contains a dichotomous variable coded 0 if a firm was in business and 1 if it had dissolved by the end of the year. Our units of analysis are thus business-years. Our 411 organizations yielded 1,139 business years. Censored observations—those from organizations that were in business throughout the period—contributed a maximum of three business-years to the data set; businesses failing in 1987 contributed two; and those dying in 1986 contributed one. This data structure solved the problem of bias due to right censoring since all information collected on surviving businesses was used. The data structure also allowed us to take into account changes in some of the explanatory variables that occurred during the three-year period.

RESULTS

Determinants of Survival

Table 1 provides initial evidence on our second hypothesis. Contrary to the first part of Hypothesis 2, women were not more likely than men to go out of business: 16 percent of businesses headed by men failed, compared to 15 percent of those headed by women ($\chi^2 = .002$, 1 df, n.s.). Business failure also did not differ significantly by industry, as the nonsignificant chi-square values at the bottom of Table 1 indicate.

The issue of gender differences is examined further in Table 4, which presents the results of our analysis of the determinants of the probability of whether or not a company went out of business in either 1986 or 1987.[8] The nonsignificant coefficient for gender in the last column of Table 4 reinforces our conclusion that businesses headed by men and women were equally likely to go out of business during the study period.

In Table 4, we report results separately for businesses headed by men and women and for both together. Overall tests of significance (likelihood ratio F-tests) showed that gender-specific coefficients did not improve the explanatory power of the model; indeed, only one variable, prior self-employment, had different effects for men and women. The absence of significant interaction suggests that the processes underlying the survival of businesses headed by men and women are similar. It is not surprising that we found little interaction by gender, given the event-history structure of our data: for men, only 50 of 878 business-years resulted in a company going out of business; for women, only 15 of 261 years involved failure. The statistical power to detect gender interactions available to us was thus very low.

For men, the coefficient of the period variable was significant, indicating that businesses headed by men were more likely to go out of business in 1986 than in 1987. Including this period constant in our model controlled for unmeasured variables that differ across time periods, such as unemployment rates.

Industries. As the results shown in Table 1 indicate, there were no overall differences among industries in the probability of business survival. Nor did the effects of the explanatory variables vary much among industries. Consistent with our earlier expectations, the results shown in Table 2 indicate that the businesses headed by women we studied were in larger popu-

---

[8] In preliminary analyses, we considered and rejected other variables not presented here. These included measures of owner-operators' personal characteristics such as their commitment to work, the importance they placed on various aspects of work, sole ownership of the business of interest, and educational attainment. We also experimented with indicators of types of business problems. Adding these potential independent variables did not enhance our models, and their inclusion did not seem essential on theoretical grounds. Cases with missing data on any of independent variables that appear in Table 4 were assigned the mean of that variable for the valid cases.

TABLE 4
Industrial, Organizational, and Individual Determinants of Log Odds of Going Out of Business

Independent Variables	Men's Businesses		Women's Businesses		Totals	
	b	Standard Error	b	Standard Error	b	Standard Error
Industry						
Food and drink	−0.13	0.26	0.58	0.70	−0.03	0.22
Health	−0.15	0.30	0.27	0.72	−0.14	0.25
Competition	0.10	0.15	0.55	0.32*	0.20	0.13
Size	0.00	0.00	0.00	0.00	0.00	0.00
Percent change in size	−1.09	0.47*	1.70	3.29	−0.93	0.45*
Company						
Incorporation	−0.39	0.20*	−0.04	0.41	−0.29	0.17*
Gross earnings[a]	−0.14	0.08*	−0.04	0.21	−0.10	0.07
Size[a]	−0.05	0.09	0.16	0.20	−0.03	0.08
Age	−0.02	0.01*	−0.05	0.03*	−0.03	0.01**
Number of products or services	−0.12	0.41	−2.21	1.28*	−0.26	0.36
Edge is quality	−0.38	0.24	−0.92	0.44*	−0.46	0.20*
Innovations	0.63	0.31*	0.68	0.77	0.61	0.27*
Owner-operator						
Woman					0.04	0.17
Age	0.01	0.01	0.01	0.02	0.01	0.01
Years in industry	0.00	0.01	0.02	0.02	0.00	0.01
Prior self-employment	0.32	0.18*	−0.56	0.50	0.17	0.16[b]
Involvement in other business	0.32	0.17*	−0.07	0.43	0.26	0.15*
Confidence	−0.19	0.07**	−0.01	0.16	−0.16	0.06**
Internal locus of control	0.01	0.08	−0.13	0.11	−0.04	0.06
Period—1986 or 1987	0.51	0.16**	0.21	0.31	0.42	0.13**
Intercept	5.31		3.30		4.87	
N	878		261		1,139	
χ^2	946		231		1,133	
df	858		241		1,118	

[a] This variable was measured as a logarithm.
[b] The difference between men and women is significant at $p < .10$.
 * $p < .05$, one-tailed test
 ** $p < .01$, one-tailed test

lations than the businesses headed by men, though the rate of change in industry size was similar for all the businesses studied. Companies headed by men in rapidly growing industries were less likely to have gone out of business, an effect that was not observed for companies headed by women. We speculate that a positive rate of growth in an industry reflects enhanced opportunities and expanding markets, conditions likely to promote survival. Alternatively, decrease in industry size could signal that business conditions in general were not good.

Table 2 indicates that the level of competition was similar for businesses headed by men and women. However, within industries, women in highly competitive markets were more likely to have gone out of business. This finding provides some support for Hypothesis 3, though the coefficient of competition for women was not significantly different from that for men.

Companies. Older companies were less likely to go out of business, supporting Hypothesis 1. Also consistent with our reasoning that survival and success are distinct aspects of performance is the finding that gross earnings were unrelated to survival for women's businesses. Earnings enhanced survival for businesses headed by men, though the effect was not a particularly strong one.

Companies headed by women were smaller than those headed by men: the mean for the latter is 12 employees, compared to 6 for the former, a finding supporting the first part of Hypothesis 4 (cf. Charboneau, 1981; Humphreys & McClung, 1981). However, we found no evidence that smallness was a liability for either men's or women's businesses. The absence of a size effect on survival is not unreasonable considering that the model controls for variables highly correlated with size, such as incorporation status. To assess the possibility that the correlations of size were confounding the effects of size, we reestimated the pooled model excluding all company-level variables except size (analyses not shown). The effect of size was negative and significant at $p < .10$.

Companies headed by men offered a wider range of products and services than those headed by women. Generalists were less likely to have gone out of business than specialists, but only among women's businesses. Generalism may reflect an organizational adaptation to high environmental uncertainty (Wholey & Brittain, 1986: 522–524). This adaptation could be described as a thrashing process in which companies try a variety of different products or services in order to stay in business.

Businesses headed by men were more likely to be incorporated than those headed by women (Table 2). Incorporated businesses headed by men were less likely to go out of business; the coefficient of incorporation was also negative, though nonsignificant, for women's businesses.

Moreover, women were somewhat more likely to feel that quality gave them an edge over their competitors (Table 2). Women who reported that the quality of their products and services gave them an edge were less likely to have gone out of business during this period; the coefficient for men is in the same direction but is not statistically significant. This finding also confirms the idea that quality is of key importance as expressed in many popular books on management (e.g., Peters & Waterman, 1982).

Finally, contrary to the expectations expressed in the first part of Hypothesis 6, men were not more likely to report business innovations than women (Table 2). This finding suggests that previous discussions of a male-female innovation gap have been misguided. A possible methodological reason for our finding is the broadness of our innovation measure, which was not restricted to major or dramatic changes. In any event, Table 4 suggests that the businesses headed by men that frequently engaged in innovative behaviors were less likely to survive than other businesses headed by men; innovation was unrelated to survival among women's businesses. We speculate that organizations scoring high on our broad measure of innovation may be marginal ones that are seeking to find a formula for success by trying new things, a phenomenon similar to the thrashing about noted above. This result also confirms the idea that staying close to familiar products is better than introducing a wide variety of products and services.

Personal attributes. The first part of Hypothesis 5, which says that men have more business experience than women, received mixed support: men reported that they had spent more time in their current industries, but similar proportions (22 and 23%) of men and women had been self-employed prior to owning their current businesses (see Table 2). Nevertheless, businesses run by entrepreneurs with greater experience in an industry were not more likely to survive, a finding contrary to the expectations expressed in Hypothesis 5, as is the finding that prior self-employment is positively related to going out of business for men. The latter result is, however, consistent with a common theme in the entrepreneurship literature: entrepreneurs typically fail, often many times, before achieving success. Further support for this is provided by the finding (not shown) that the men studied had been self-employed more times on the average than the women; among people who were previously self-employed, men were self-employed an average of 1.98 times, compared to 1.24 times for women, a statistically significant difference. It may be, then, that men are more likely than women to take the risks associated with repeated attempts to start new businesses.

Contrary to the first part of Hypothesis 7, the results in Table 2 indicate that male and female entrepreneurs appear to be equally confident and to have similar opinions about their ability to influence business outcomes through their own efforts. The men who were more confident in their business abilities in 1985 were less likely to go out of business. That relationship offers some support for the second part of Hypothesis 7, though the difference between men and women is not significant. We speculate that the confidence effect might reflect the impact of entrepreneurs' personal efforts on their success. A plausible alternative explanation is that we tapped respondents' awareness that their businesses were either successful or in trouble in 1985, perceptions that may have been validated in the next several years, and that men perceived their survival chances more accurately.

Finally, men were much more likely than women to be involved in businesses other than the one studied. Table 4 indicates that businesses headed by men who were involved in other companies were more likely to fail, but outside involvement was unrelated to business survival of women. One possible interpretation for that difference is that involvement in other businesses is a proxy for an entrepreneur's degree of dependence on a company. By this argument, men are less dependent on their businesses (see Table 2) and thus less likely to be willing to absorb extra hours to keep them going.

Summary. Companies headed by women were no more likely to go out of business than those headed by men, contrary to Hypothesis 2. Moreover, the processes generating survival did not differ by gender: only one variable—previous self-employment—had significantly different effects on survival for businesses headed by men and women. A company's age was positively related to its survival regardless of the gender of its owner-operator (cf. Hypothesis 1). Size was unrelated to survival for both men's and women's businesses, contrary to Hypothesis 4.

The remaining effects were observed for only one gender: competition increased the death rate among businesses headed by women, and rapid changes in industrial populations increased the survival chances of businesses headed by men (Hypothesis 3); incorporation and high gross earnings enhanced survival only among businesses owned by men; generalism and an emphasis on quality decreased the probability of failure only among women's businesses; innovations were positively related to failure only among men's businesses, contrary to Hypothesis 6; confidence enhanced survival only for men, partially supporting Hypothesis 7; a prior history of self-employment increased the probability of going out of business only among men, contrary to Hypothesis 5; and being involved in other businesses decreased chances of survival only for men.

Determinants of Success

Businesses headed by men had a higher level of gross earnings than those headed by women: mean earnings for the former were nearly $54,000, compared to about $46,000 for the latter. However, that discrepancy does not necessarily mean that men's businesses were more successful than women's in terms of our indicator of success, growth in earnings from one year to the next. We examined change in earnings by regressing gross business earnings in later periods on initial earnings and a set of independent variables. The coefficient of initial earnings represents the stability in earnings during the period. The coefficients of the other explanatory variables in the model denote the impacts of the independent variables on changes in earnings. Table 5 presents these results.

As with survival, there was no gender difference in success, contrary to Hypothesis 2. Moreover, the models do not differ significantly for men and women; results of a global F-test for gender interactions ($F = .989$, with 19 and 1,099 df) were not significant at $p < .05$, and only one variable—involvement in another business—had a significant interaction with gender. Hence, we report coefficients for a pooled model as well as coefficients from models estimated separately for men and women.

Industries. Businesses headed by men in the health industry had higher earnings growth than those in computers, but there were no other differences among industries. There was also very little interaction by industry, so we again present results from models pooled across the three industries. Con-

TABLE 5
Industrial, Organizational, and Individual Determinants of Growth in Business Earnings

Independent Variables	Men's Businesses		Women's Businesses		Totals	
	b	Standard Error	*b*	Standard Error	*b*	Standard Error
Gross earnings, 1985	0.58	0.03**	0.65	0.05**	0.61	0.02**
Industry						
Food and drink	0.12	0.07	0.15	0.15	0.16	0.06**
Health	0.20	0.08*	0.12	0.15	0.20	0.07**
Competition	−0.05	0.04	0.02	0.07	−0.04	0.04
Size[a]	−0.00	0.05	−0.11	0.08	−0.03	0.04
Percent change						
in industry size	−0.03	0.03	−0.06	0.42	−0.03	0.03
Company						
Incorporation	0.09	0.06	0.12	0.10	0.11	0.05*
Size[b]	0.07	0.02**	0.14	0.05**	0.08	0.02**
Age	0.00	0.00	−0.01	0.01	0.00	0.00
Number of products						
or services	0.13	0.10	−0.26	0.24	0.11	0.09
Edge is quality	0.03	0.05	−0.02	0.09	0.01	0.04
Innovations	−0.02	0.08	−0.07	0.15	−0.02	0.07
Owner-operator						
Woman					−0.05	0.05
Age	−0.01	0.00**	−0.01	0.00	−0.01	0.00**
Years in industry	0.00	0.00	0.00	0.01	0.00	0.00
Prior self-						
employment	−0.04	0.05	0.01	0.10	−0.02	0.05
Involvement in						
other business	0.04	0.05	−0.22	0.11*	−0.01	0.04[c]
Confidence	0.01	0.02	−0.04	0.04	0.01	0.02
Internal locus						
of control	0.03	0.02	−0.02	0.04	0.02	0.02
Period—1986 or 1987	−0.03	0.04	−0.04	0.08	−0.03	0.04
Intercept	0.33		0.61		0.28	
N	878		261		1,139	
Adjusted R^2	.42		.53		.45	

[a] This statistic represents size multiplied by 1,000.
[b] This variable was measured as a logarithm.
[c] The difference between men and women is significant at $p < .10$.
  * $p < .05$, one-tailed test
 ** $p < .01$, one-tailed test

trary to Hypothesis 3, none of our industry variables (industry size, change in industry size, and competition) were related to changes in earnings for either men or women.

Companies. Consistent with the second part of Hypothesis 1, a company's age was unrelated to its earnings growth for both men's and women's businesses, providing further support for the view that survival and success are distinct aspects of performance.

A company's size was positively related to its earnings growth for both men's and women's businesses. Since businesses headed by women are generally smaller (Table 2), size helps contribute to male-female differences in earnings growth (cf. Hypothesis 4). The absence of a gender gap in success suggests that other mechanisms help to offset women's business-size disadvantage.

Contrary to Hypothesis 6, innovations were unrelated to earnings growth for both men's and women's businesses. In addition, neither the generalist-specialist distinction nor an emphasis on quality enhanced growth in business earnings for either group.

Personal attributes. Experience was unrelated to short-term business success for men and women. This finding fails to support the second part of Hypothesis 5: men's businesses were not more successful because men have more experience. Whether an entrepreneur had been previously self-employed was also unrelated to growth in business earnings.

These results also fail to support the second part of Hypothesis 7: both our confidence scale and our indicator of locus of control were unrelated to earnings growth. These data thus provide no support for the view that men are better able than women to translate confidence in their business abilities into business success.

Older male entrepreneurs were less successful than younger ones; we observed that discrepancy also for women, though for the latter the age coefficient is not statistically significant. Since our model controls for experience, this negative age effect may reflect a lessening of older entrepreneurs' ability to keep up with the pressures of small business ownership. Finally, women who were involved in other businesses were less successful, though involvement in other businesses had no impact on earnings growth for men.

Summary. There were no differences in earnings growth between businesses headed by men and women, contrary to Hypothesis 2. Moreover, the processes underlying growth in earnings appear to be similar, since only one variable, involvement in another business, had a significantly different effect on success for men and women.

Old organizations were not more successful than young ones, regardless of the owner-operator's gender, confirming the last part of Hypothesis 1. Large organizations, whether headed by men or women, were more successful than small ones in the sense of having growth in earnings (cf. Hypothesis 4).

Several other variables had significant effects for only one gender: men's businesses in the health industry had higher earnings growth than those in computers, but otherwise none of the industry variables had an impact on earnings growth, contrary to Hypothesis 3; an entrepreneur's age was negatively related to growth in earnings among men; and only companies headed by women who were involved in other businesses experienced less earnings growth than other businesses studied. Earnings growth was unrelated to experience, innovation, and confidence for both men and women, contrary to Hypotheses 5, 6, and 7.

CONCLUSIONS AND IMPLICATIONS

That women entrepreneurs are disadvantaged relative to their counterparts who are men is a common theme in discussions of entrepreneurship and organizational performance. Authors frequently point to the barriers women face in small business raised by socialization practices, educational experiences, family roles, lack of networks of business contacts, and so on. Disadvantages experienced by women in all these areas are widely believed to result in higher failure rates and lower growth rates for women's businesses. As with many accepted "facts" in the entrepreneurship literature, however, these claims and assumptions have rarely been subjected to empirical testing; very few carefully constructed studies have directly compared the performance of businesses headed by men and women.

This study helps to fill this gap in our knowledge about the effects of gender on organizational performance. We examined the determinants of survival and success among small businesses headed by men and by women using longitudinal data. Our findings sharply challenge the conventional wisdom regarding women's inferiority in entrepreneurship: the women's businesses we studied were no more likely to fail—and were just as successful—as the men's. Moreover, we found that the determinants of survival and success operated in much the same way for men and women, suggesting that the processes underlying small business performance are similar irrespective of an entrepreneur's gender.

The scarcity of previous sound research on gender differences in organizational performance and entrepreneurship cautions us against drawing premature conclusions based on these results. Our data have several obvious and important limitations. Our study group was restricted to three industries, which made it impossible for us to assess whether businesses headed by women are less likely to survive because they are often in service industries with high failure rates. Perhaps a more serious problem is our oversampling of successful businesses. Left censoring introduces bias into our results, and that bias may vary systematically by gender. For example, it could be that businesses headed by women are more likely to fail in general, but those that survive may be unusually successful and thus similar to businesses headed by men.

Our measures of survival and success were also far from ideal. We would have preferred to have had more objective information on profits, market share, and other indicators of business success, though there is evidence that subjective assessments of success made by key informants converge considerably with objective measures (Venkatraman & Ramanujam, 1986). We also would have liked to have known more precisely the circumstances under which the vanished companies went out of business—whether they were bought by a larger company, went bankrupt, moved to another state, and so on. It would also have been desirable to have had more precise and objective information on our industrial and organizational independent variables.

Our inability to explain more of the variation in business survival and success may have another cause. To a large and unknown degree, essentially random processes that defy measurement and study may determine these dimensions of performance (Kaufman, 1985). It may also be the case that our study did not cover a sufficiently long time period; the years 1985, 1986, and 1987 did not vary dramatically in business cycles and conditions. We intend to survey the respondents to this study in the future, hoping that a long time lapse may reveal greater impacts of our industrial, organizational, and individual variables on their organizations' survival and success than emerged here.

Our suggestive findings will, we hope, encourage others to pursue these issues using richer data sets. Further research is necessary to test more rigorously some key implications of our results for theories of gender, entrepreneurship, and organizational performance. Thus, it may be that an owner's gender has little relevance to the survival and success of small businesses because competitive market mechanisms govern those processes. That view is consistent with an ecological, demand-side perspective that explains entrepreneurial survival and success on the basis of the structure of opportunity in an industry. If opportunity structures pull people into starting businesses in particular niches, an entrepreneur's gender shouldn't matter much in determining the survival and success of the business. By contrast, if characteristics related to the supply of entrepreneurs primarily govern the performance of small businesses, women may more often be pushed into lower-quality opportunities—by family constraints, lack of business contacts, or poor occupational options—and hence may be prone to poorer business performance than men. Future research needs to examine which of those scenarios better describes entrepreneurship among women.

Our results also suggest that the processes underlying small business performance are generally similar for men and women. Despite the widely shared assumption that women are less apt than men to innovate, for example, we found no evidence of women's being less likely to do this in their businesses. Moreover, we found no evidence that men were more confident of their business abilities.

On the other hand, we did find hints that different market approaches may pay off differentially for women and men. In particular, a generalist orientation and an emphasis on quality appear to be more salient to the survival chances of businesses headed by women, though the differences between men and women on those dimensions were not statistically significant. Our finding that women's businesses in competitive markets are more likely than men's to fail suggests a possible reason for the importance of those characteristics; the edge provided by high quality and the flexibility made possible by generalism may be particularly important in helping women to compete in the small business arena.

Future comparative research needs to address systematically these speculations. Such research should be based on samples of businesses carefully selected from well-defined populations and followed over time. Such studies need to recognize that survival and success are divergent aspects of performance determined by processes at several levels of analysis, including the industrial context of an organization, the organization itself, and the individual entrepreneur.

REFERENCES

Aldrich, H. E. 1989. Networking among women entrepreneurs. In O. Hagan, C. Rivchun, & D. Sexton (Eds.), *Women-owned businesses:* 103–132. New York: Praeger.

Aldrich, H. E., & Auster, E. 1986. Even dwarfs started small: Liabilities of age and size and their strategic implications. In B. M. Staw & L. L. Cummings (Eds.), *Research in organizational behavior,* vol. 8: 165–198. Greenwich, CT: JAI Press.

Aldrich, H. E., Zimmer, C., & McEvoy, D. 1989. Continuities in the study of ecological succession: Asian businesses in three English cities. *Social Forces,* 67: 920–944.

Allison, P. D. 1984. *Event history analysis: Regression for longitudinal event data.* Beverly Hills, CA: Sage Publications.

Birch, D. L. 1987. *Job creation in America: How our smallest companies put the most people to work.* New York: Free Press.

Blau, J. 1984. *Architects and firms.* Cambridge, MA: MIT Press.

Bowen, D. D., & Hisrich, R. D. 1986. The female entrepreneur: A career development perspective. *Academy of Management Review,* 11: 393–407.

Brockhaus, R. H. 1982. The psychology of the entrepreneur. In C. A. Kent, D. L. Sexton, & K. H. Vesper (Eds.), *Encyclopedia of entrepreneurship:* 39–57. Englewood Cliffs, NJ: Prentice-Hall.

Cameron, K. S., Sutton, R. I., & Whetten, D. A. (Eds.). 1988. *Readings in organizational decline: Frameworks, research, and prescriptions.* Cambridge, MA: Ballinger.

Cameron, K. S., & Whetten, D. A. 1983. *Organizational effectiveness: A comparison of multiple models.* New York: Academic Press.

Carroll, G. R. 1983. A stochastic model of organizational mortality: Review and reanalysis. *Social Science Research,* 12: 303–329.

Carroll, G. R., & Huo, Y. P. 1986. Organizational task and institutional environments in evolutionary perspective: Findings from the local newspaper industry. *American Journal of Sociology,* 91: 838–873.

Charboneau, F. J. 1981. The woman entrepreneur. *American Demographics,* 3(6): 21–23.

Child, J. 1972. Organizational structure, environment, and performance: The role of strategic choice. *Sociology,* 6: 1–22.

Cromie, S., & Hayes, J. 1988. Towards a typology of female entrepreneurs. *Sociological Review,* 36: 87–113.

Cuba, R., Decenzo, D., & Anish, A. 1983. Management practices of successful female business owners. *American Journal of Small Business,* 8(2): 40–46.

Cummings, L. L. 1988. Organizational decline from the individual perspective. In K. Cameron, R. Sutton, & D. Whetten (Eds.), *Readings in organizational decline: Frameworks, research, and prescriptions:* 417–424. Cambridge, MA: Ballinger.

Freeman, J., Carroll, G. R., & Hannan, M. T. 1983. The liability of newness: Age dependence in organizational death rates. *American Sociological Review,* 48: 692–710.

Freeman, J., & Hannan, M. T. 1983. Niche width and the dynamics of organizational populations. *American Journal of Sociology,* 88: 1116–1145.

Goffee, R., & Scase, R. 1983. Business ownership and women's subordination: A preliminary study of female proprietors. *Sociological Review,* 31: 625–648.

Goodman, P. S., & Pennings, J. M. 1977. *New perspectives on organizational effectiveness.* San Francisco: Jossey-Bass.

Hannan, M. T., & Freeman, J. 1977. The population ecology of organizations. *American Journal of Sociology,* 82: 929–964.

Hisrich, R. D., & Brush, C. 1984. The woman entrepreneur: Management skills and business problems. *Journal of Small Business Management,* 22(1): 30–37.

Humphreys, M. A., & McClung, H. 1981. Women entrepreneurs in Oklahoma. *Review of Regional Economics and Business,* 6(2): 13–20.

Kalleberg, A. L. 1986. Entrepreneurship in the 1980s: A study of small business in Indiana. In G. Libecap (Ed.), *Advances in the study of entrepreneurship, innovation, and economic growth,* vol. 1: 157–189. Greenwich, CT: JAI Press.

Kalleberg, A. L., Marsden, P. V., Aldrich, H. E., & Cassell, J. W. 1990. Comparing organizational sampling frames. *Administrative Science Quarterly,* 35: 658–688.

Kaufman, H. 1985. *Time, chance, and organizations.* Chatham, NJ: Chatham House.

Loscocco, K. A., & Robinson, J. 1989. *Barriers to small business success among women.* Albany, NY: State University of New York at Albany.

Mayer, K., & Goldstein, S. 1961. *The first two years: Problems of small business growth and survival.* Small Business Research Series no. 2. Washington, DC: U.S. Government Printing Office.

Meyer, A. D. 1988. Organizational decline from the organizational perspective. In K. Cameron, R. Sutton, & D. Whetten (Eds.), *Readings in organizational decline: Frameworks, research, and prescriptions:* 411–416. Cambridge, MA: Ballinger.

Meyer, M. W., & Zucker, L. G. 1989. *Permanently failing organizations.* Newbury Park, CA: Sage Publications.

Papalia, D. E., & Olds, S. W. 1981. *Human development.* New York: McGraw-Hill Book Co.

Pellegrino, E. T., & Reece, B. L. 1982. Perceived formative and operational problems encountered by female entrepreneurs in retail and service firms. *Journal of Small Business Management,* 20(2): 15–24.

Peters, T. J., & Waterman, R. H., Jr. 1982. *In search of excellence.* New York: Harper & Row Publishers.

Pfeffer, J., & Salancik, G. R. 1978. *The external control of organizations.* New York: Harper & Row Publishers.

Reynolds, P. D., & Miller, B. 1989. *New firm survival: Analysis of a panel's fourth year.* Unpublished paper, University of Minnesota Center for Urban and Regional Affairs, Minneapolis, MN.

Schwartz, E. B. 1976. Entrepreneurship: A new female frontier. *Journal of Contemporary Business,* 5: 47–76.

Stinchcombe, A. L. 1965. Social structure and organizations. In J. G. March (Ed.), *Handbook of organizations:* 142–193. Chicago: Rand McNally Publishers.

U.S. Department of Commerce. 1983–1986. *County business patterns.* Washington, DC: U.S. Government Printing Office.

U.S. Small Business Administration. 1986. *The state of small business: A report of the president.* Washington, DC: U.S. Government Printing Office.

Venkatraman, N., & Ramanujam, V. 1986. Measurement of business performance in strategy research: A comparison of approaches. *Academy of Management Review,* 11: 801–814.

Whetten, D. A. 1987. Growth and decline processes in organizations. *Annual Review of Sociology,* 13: 335–358.

Wholey, D. R., & Brittain, J. W. 1986. Organizational ecology: Findings and implications. *Academy of Management Review,* 11: 513–533.

Wilkens, J. 1987. *Her own business: Success secrets of entrepreneurial women.* New York: McGraw-Hill Book Co.

Arne L. Kalleberg is a professor in and the Chair of the Department of Sociology, University of North Carolina at Chapel Hill. His current research uses national samples of work organizations and their employees in the United States and Norway to examine issues related to organizational sources of economic inequality, organizational commitment, performance, and economic and sociological aspects of employment contracts.

Kevin T. Leicht is an assistant professor of sociology at the Pennsylvania State University. His research interests include the organizational context surrounding U.S. labor relations, organizational determinants of technological change and innovation, and the political economy of deindustrialization. He is currently doing research on state-level direct investment in high-technology development and the economic consequences of unionization for unorganized workers.

[25]

1042-2587-97-212$1.50
Copyright 1997 by
Baylor University

A Study of the Impacts of Gender on Business Performance and Management Patterns in Small Businesses

Radha Chaganti
Saroj Parasuraman

There is extensive comparative research on management patterns in women-owned businesses (WOBs) and men-owned businesses (MOBs), but the results are mixed. Some earlier studies pointed to lower performance for WOBs (Cuba, DeCenzo, & Anish, 1983; Hisrich & Brush, 1984, 1987; Loscocco, Robinson, Hall, & Allen, 1991), while others observed similar levels (Fischer, Reuber, & Dyke, 1993; Kalleberg & Leicht, 1991). Further, women are reported to place greater emphasis on non-financial and personal goals, stressing financial goals less (Hisrich & Brush, 1987; Kaplan, 1988), though Fischer and colleagues (1993) reject this. Researchers have not analyzed strategies of WOBs versus MOBs, except for Kalleberg and Leicht (1991), who pointed out that WOBs perceived quality as their competitive edge. Finally, studies suggest that WOBs relied less on systematic practices (Brush, 1992; Cuba et al., 1983; Hisrich & Brush, 1987). We add to this research by examining gender differences in performance, goals, strategies, and management practices simultaneously.

SAMPLE AND MEASURES

Dun's Marketing Services generated a sample of 1800 MOBs and 1800 WOBs employing 4 to 99 employees located in the northeastern U.S. A mailed survey with a structured questionnaire yielded 372 useable responses. Since 15% of businesses were not locatable, this yielded a net response rate of 12.3%. One hundred and ninety-four were MOBs and 178 (48%) were WOBs. A significantly higher proportion of WOBs were service firms (50% for WOBs and 37% for MOBs, chi-square = 4.48, p< 0.5), and a significantly greater proportion of MOBs were retail firms (28.8% of MOBs and 19.7% of WOBs, chi-square = 4.89, p < 0.5). The average employment size of WOBs was significantly smaller (10 = WOBs, MOBs = 13) (F = 3.65, p< .05). However, average age of WOBs and MOBs (18.7 years and 18.6 years respectively) was similar. Again, these men and women entrepreneurs did not differ on: founder versus non-founder status (women = 69.7%, men = 60.1%, Chi-sq = 3.43 p < .18); managerial experience (yes = 1, no = 0) (women = .017, men = .022, Chi sq = 2.6 p < .12); or parental ownership of business (yes = 1, no =) (women = .51, Chi-sq = 0.02), but they differed on years of industry experience (women = 13.92 years, men = 15.56 years, F = 19.86, p < .001).

Three performance measures were used: (1) preceding year's sales; (2) 3-year growth in employment; and (3) 3-year average return on assets (ROA). For goals, respondents rated

Table 1

Descriptive Statistics Study Variables

Variables	Women-Owned Firms		Men-Owned Firms		Alpha	Univ.F[1]
	Mean	Std Dev	Mean	Std Dev		
GOALS						
Achvmt	4.52	0.50	3.99	1.06		37.03***
Fin Perf	4.25	0.60	3.99	0.98		7.20**
STRATEGIES						
Cost eff	3.05	0.72	3.05	0.71	0.66	0.00
Custzn	0.49	0.59	0.51	0.50		2.14
Quality	4.26	0.85	4.02	0.83		5.96*
MANAGEMENT PRACTICES						
Formalizn	2.13	0.55	2.04	0.52	0.86	3.39
Opn Plng	4.00	0.75	4.05	0.79	0.74	0.49
Res Plang	3.52	0.83	3.53	0.90	0.69	0.02
Spczn	0.30	0.32	0.39	0.34	0.61	3.12
PERFORMANCE						
Sales	545.54	741.23	1205.94	2248.70		12.61***
EmpGth	93.82	278.15	66.06	120.22		1.33
ROA	14.02	16.35	16.36	17.57		0.04

Note: $* = p < .05$ $** = p < .01$ $*** = p < .001$

[1] = *MANCOVAs controlled for owner's industry experience, and firm's employment size, and industry sector.*

importance of seven goals on a 5-point scale, and two factors, viz, (1) achievement, and (2) financial goals were produced. For strategies business owners were asked to rate firm's promotion expenses, labor and material costs, prices, and product quality relative to key competitors' on a 5-point scale, and customization of products was measured as 1 - mostly customized, and 0 = mostly standardized. One strategy factor, namely cost efficiency, was produced, and product quality and customization were single-item measures. Three management practice were included: (1) formalization, measured as use of written reporting in five areas (3-point scale); (2) use of long-range planning horizon for seven types of decisions (5-point scale); and (3) staff specialization, measuring the hiring (=1) versus non-hiring (= 0) of trained personnel in six areas. Single factors were produced for formalizaton and staff specialization, while two planning factors were produced: (1) operations planning and (2) resource planning. Cronbach alphas for the factors ranged between 0.88 and 0.61.

RESULTS

Table 1 presents the descriptive statistics and univarate Fs from the multivariate analysis of covariance (MANCOVA). Industry sector, firm size, and owner manager's years in the industry were covariates.

On business performance, WOBs had significantly smaller annual sales ($741,230 versus $1,205,940 respectively; $F = 12.61$, p. $< .000$), agreeing with prior research (Hisrich & Brush, 1984; Loscocco et al., 1991). However, employment growth and ROA were similar, which was in line with other research (Fischer et al., 1993). Regarding goals, women's ratings for both achievement goals and financial goals (4.52 and 4.25, respectively) were significantly higher than for men (3.99 for both types of goals) ($F = 37.03$, $p < .000$ for achievement goals), and ($F = 7.21$, $p < .01$ for financial goals). This concurs with Hisrich and Brush (1984) and Kaplan (1988), who pointed out that non-financial goals would be more important for women, and with Fischer and colleagues (1993), who found women's financial motivation to be stronger. On strategies, women business owners emphasized product quality to a greater degree (women = 4.26, men = 4.03, $F = 5.96$, $p < .05$), but there were no differences on customization (women = 0.59, men = 0.51, $F = 2.14$ $p < .21$), or cost efficiency (women = men = 3.05, $F =$). In contrast to prior findings (Cuba et al., 1983; Hisrich & Brush, 1984), differences were significant on the four management practices.

REFERENCES

Brush, C. G. (1992). Research on women business owners: Past trends, a new perspective and future directions. *Entrepreneurship Theory and Practice, 16*(4), 5-30.

Cuba, R., DeCenzo, D., & Anish, A. (1983). Management practices of successful female business owners. American *Journal of Small Business, 8*(2), 40-45.

Fischer, E. M., Reuber, A. R., & Dyke, L. S. (1993). A theoretical overview and extension of research on sex, gender and entrepreneurship. *Journal of Business Venturing, 8*, 151-168.

Hisrich, R. D., & Brush, C. G. (1984). The women entrepreneur: Implications of family, educational and occupational experience. *Journal of Small Business Management, 22*(1), 30-37.

Hisrich, R. D., & Brush, C. G. (1987). Women entrepreneurs: A longitudinal study. In *Frontiers of entrepreneurship research*, pp. 187-189, Wellesley, MA: Babson College.

Kalleberg, A., & Leight, K. T. (1991). Gender and organizational performance. Determinants of small business survival and success. *Academy of Management Journal, 34*, 136-161.

Kaplan, E. (1988). Women entrepreneurs: Constructing a framework to examine venture success and business failures. In *Frontiers of entrepreneurship research*, pp. 625-637, Wellesley, MA: Babson College.

Loscocco, K. A., Robinson, J., Hall, R. H., & Allen, J. K. (1991). Gender and small business: An inquiry into women's relative disadvantage. *Social Forces 70*, 65-85.

[26]

1042-2587-02-263$1.50
Copyright 2002 by
Baylor University

Comparing the Performance of Male- and Female-Controlled Businesses: Relating Outputs to Inputs

John Watson

Previous research has found that female-owned businesses generally underperform male-owned businesses on a variety of measures such as sales and profit. Further, this under-performance appears to persist even after controlling for demographic differences. However, previous studies have tended to limit their assessment of performance to output measures (sales or profit, for example) without relating these output measures to appropriate inputs (such as total assets or owner's equity). This would appear to be a significant oversight.

After controlling for industry, age of business, and the number of days a business operated, this study finds no significant differences between male- and female-controlled businesses with respect to total income to total assets (TITTA), the return on assets (ROA), or the return on equity (ROE). Interestingly, if the control variables are removed, there is evidence to suggest that female-controlled businesses outperform male-controlled businesses.

Studies examining and comparing the performance of male- and female-owned businesses have generally found that female-owned businesses underperform male-owned businesses (Du Rietz & Henrekson, 2000). Liberal feminist theory (Fischer, Reuber, & Dyke, 1993) suggests that small and medium enterprises (SMEs) run by women will exhibit poorer performance because women are overtly discriminated against (by lenders, for example) or because of other systematic factors that deprive women of important resources (for example, business education and experience). By way of contrast, social feminist theory (Fischer et al., 1993) suggests that men and women are inherently different by nature. These differences do not imply that women will be less effective in business than men, but only that they may adopt different approaches, which may or may not be as effective as the approaches adopted by men.

The majority of research to date appears to have adopted a liberal feminist theory perspective in the sense that the researchers have attempted to explain the apparent underperformance of female-owned businesses by examining the systematic differences between male and female entrepreneurs. The assumption (sometimes implicit) in these studies is that if demographic differences are controlled for (thereby removing the effects of any bias against female entrepreneurs) there should be no significant difference in the relative performances of male- and female-owned businesses (Anna, Chandler, Jansen, & Mero, 2000). Unfortunately, even after controlling for demographic differences, the majority of prior research has still found that female-owned businesses underperform relative to male-owned businesses (Kalleberg & Leicht, 1991; Cooper, Gimeno-Gascon, & Woo, 1994; Rosa, Carter, & Hamilton, 1996; Fasci & Valdez, 1998; Du Rietz & Henrekson, 2000).[1] However, it is conceivable that the performance measures used by previous studies (as discussed in the following section) may have contributed to this finding.

This study takes a social feminist theory perspective and assumes that male and female entrepreneurs are likely to be equally effective in business, although they may adopt different approaches. In order to adequately test this proposition it is critical to use an appropriate measure of performance. The next section examines the issue of performance measurement and develops three hypotheses for testing.

PERFORMANCE MEASUREMENT AND HYPOTHESES

As noted by Palepu, Healy, and Bernard (2000, p. 9-3) the "starting point for a systematic analysis of a firm's performance is its return on equity (ROE)." Return on assets (ROA) is an important determinant of ROE because it shows how much profit a company is able to generate for each dollar of assets invested (Palepu et al., 2000). Although ROE and ROA are commonly used to assess the performance of large companies, research into SME performance has tended to focus on sales or profit, or growth in sales or profit (see, for example, Kalleberg & Leicht, 1991; Fischer et al., 1993; Cooper et al., 1994; Rosa et al., 1996; Fasci & Valdez, 1998; Du Rietz & Henrekson, 2000). While there is no doubting the importance of sales and profit to a business, it is equally important to relate these output measures to measures of inputs (namely assets or equity) when making comparisons of business performance. This may be particularly relevant when comparing the performance of male- and female-controlled businesses. It has been suggested that females, as a group, may be more risk averse than males (Sexton & Bowman Upton, 1990; Powell & Ansic, 1997; Jianakoplos & Bernasek, 1998; Barber & Odean, 2001). This being the case we might expect that females, on average, will devote fewer resources to their business ventures, thereby reducing their exposure (risk) should things go wrong. Further, based on 229 interviews with small-business owners in the Greater Vancouver area, Cliff (1998, p. 523) concluded that:

> female entrepreneurs are more likely to establish maximum business size thresholds beyond which they would prefer not to expand, and that these thresholds are smaller than those set by their male counterparts. . . . Female entrepreneurs also seem to be more concerned than male entrepreneurs about the risks of fast-paced growth and tend to deliberately adopt a slow and steady rate of expansion.

Given the discussion above, it seems reasonable to expect that businesses controlled by females will (on average) have lower sales, profits, assets, and owner's equity, compared to businesses controlled by males. This gives rise to the following two hypotheses:

H1: Female-controlled businesses (on average) will generate lower outputs measured in terms of total income and profits, compared to male-controlled businesses.

---

1. Du Rietz and Henrekson (2000) found that after controlling for industry the underperformance for female entrepreneurs disappeared for three variables (increased profitability, increased number of employees, and increased number of orders), but not for a fourth (increased sales). Chell and Baines (1998), in a U.K. study of 104 micro-businesses, found that after controlling for industry there was no significant difference in sales between male- and female-owned businesses.

H2: Female-controlled businesses (on average) will have lower levels of inputs measured in terms of total assets and owner's equity, compared to male-controlled businesses.

Social feminist theory would suggest that while females may take a different approach to business (for example they may be more cautious in terms of the resources they commit to their ventures and in growing their businesses) they are likely to be as effective as males (provided performance is measured appropriately). This gives rise to the following hypothesis:

H3: On average, there will be no significant difference between male- and female-controlled businesses in terms of total income to total assets (TITTA), return on assets (ROA), and return on equity (ROE).

Chandler and Hanks (1994) suggested that profitability measures such as ROE and ROA may not be appropriate for start-up firms or where data were self-reported. However, these are not major concerns for this study for two reasons. First, approximately 75% of the sample firms in this study are at least five years old. Second, this study uses a database developed from surveys conducted on behalf of the Australian Federal Government and specifically aimed at providing a better understanding of the growth and performance of Australian SMEs. As a result, the sample used was highly representative of Australian SMEs and was based on very good response rates (typically over 90%), a significant advantage over many previous studies.

DATA

The data used in this study have been taken from the 1994-95, 1995-96, 1996-97, and 1997-98 Business Growth and Performance Surveys (also known as the Business Longitudinal Survey) undertaken by the Australian Bureau of Statistics (ABS). The surveys were designed to provide information on the growth and performance of Australian employing businesses for the federal government. For confidentiality reasons, information on all large businesses (those employing more than 200 people) was excluded from the dataset made available to researchers outside the ABS.

The ABS Business Register was used as the population frame for the surveys. For the 1995-96 survey a representative sub-sample of the original 1994-95 survey was selected and this sub-sample was then used for the remaining surveys. To maintain a representative sample over the four periods, the ABS added additional firms to each of the subsequent surveys to replace firms that had ceased operations during the preceding period.

All employing businesses in the Australian economy were included in the scope of the survey except for businesses of the following kind: government enterprises; libraries; museums; parks and gardens; private households employing staff; agriculture, forestry and fishing; electricity, gas, and water supply; communication services; government administration and defense; education; and health and community services.

Data collection was through self-administered questionnaires, copies of which can be obtained from the ABS. Because the ABS can legally enforce compliance with its data requests (under the Census and Statistics Act 1905) response rates were very high (typically in excess of 90%).

Table 1 describes the dataset used for this study. With respect to the initial survey in 1994-95, responses were received from 8,375 businesses. However, 3,436 businesses were excluded for the purposes of this study because they did not have a single major

Table 1

Data Selection Process

	1994-95 Data	Pooled Data
1. Businesses Active in 1994-95	8,375	8,375
2. Less businesses with more than 1 key decision maker or no sex response	3,436	3,436
Businesses Active in 1994-95 with 1 key decision maker	4,939	4,939
3. Businesses Active in 1995-96 with 1 key decision maker		3,109
4. Businesses Active in 1996-97 with 1 key decision maker		3,180
5. Businesses Active in 1997-98 with 1 key decision maker		3,288
	4,939	14,516
6. Less businesses with no income	16	90
	4,923	14,426
Male	4,594	13,551
Female	329	875
	4,923	14,426

decision maker,[2] or the sex of that decision maker was not reported. This left 4,939 businesses that could be analyzed based on the sex of the major decision maker for the period 1994-95. A similar process was used for the subsequent surveys, resulting in usable responses of 3,109, 3,180, and 3,288 in 1995-96, 1996-97, and 1997-98, respectively.

On examining the data it was found that 16 businesses surveyed in 1994-95 (and 90 businesses across the four surveys) had no income (sales or other income). These businesses were excluded from the dataset on the assumption that they had probably not yet formally commenced trading.[3] Therefore, the final dataset had 4,923 firms in the 1994-95 period (of which 4,594 were controlled by a male and 329 were controlled by a female) and 14,426 firms pooled across the four surveys (of which 13,551 were controlled by a male and 875 were controlled by a female).

RESULTS

As there were very few differences between the results from the 1994-95 data and the pooled data, only the results for the pooled data are reported in the following discussion and tables. However, where there were any notable differences these will be referred to in the footnotes.

Table 2 provides details on the two output measures (total income and profit) and the two input measures (total assets and owner's equity) used in this study to compare the performance of male- and female-controlled businesses. The results in Table 2 provide strong support for hypothesis 1; both total income and profit (output measures) were significantly higher (on average) for the male-controlled businesses. Similarly, the results in Table 2 provide strong support for hypothesis 2; both total assets and owner's equity (input measures) were significantly higher (on average) for the male-controlled businesses.

---

2. Businesses with more than one owner are included in this study provided there is only one major decision maker.
3. Including these firms did not alter the results.

Table 2

Output/Input Measures: Mean Results for Male and Female Controlled Businesses

Output/Input Measures	Mean		Significance Level
	Male	Female	
Total Income	$6,158,168	$1,661,729	.000
Profit	$354,181	$22,314	.000
Total Assets	$4,432,502	$734,070	.000
Owner's Equity	$1,509,569	$158,866	.000

It would appear that males tend to invest more heavily in their businesses. But does the extra investment pay off? Is the higher profit in the male-controlled businesses disproportionately higher, relative to the additional investment, such that the additional investment is more than justified? Or are the higher profits simply in line with the higher levels of resources invested (risked) in those businesses? This issue is addressed by examining the TITTA, ROA, and ROE achieved by the male- and female-controlled businesses in this study (that is, by relating both total income and profit [output measures] to total assets and owner's equity [input measures]). However, an examination of the histograms for each of these performance measures (with a normal curve fitted) suggested they were not normally distributed. For this reason the log of each of these performance measures is also examined. However, there were 1,164 firms (1,071 male-controlled and 93 female-controlled) with reported losses. Therefore, for the purposes of examining profitability, the sample firms were split into two groups: profitable and unprofitable. Businesses with zero profit (122) were excluded. For the unprofitable group the absolute amount of the loss was examined (in relation to total assets or total equity). As the sample size in this study is relatively large, 0.01 (1%) will be used throughout the remainder of this paper as the appropriate significance level in determining whether there are differences in the relative performances of male- and female-controlled businesses.

The results in Table 3 show no significant difference in the relative performances of male- and female-controlled businesses as measured by TITTA, ROA, ROE,[4] or the log of TITTA. However, in terms of profitability, there was some evidence to suggest that female-controlled businesses outperformed male-controlled businesses in this study. For profitable businesses, both the log of ROA and the log of ROE indicated that the female-controlled businesses significantly outperformed the male-controlled businesses.[5] For unprofitable businesses there was no significant difference between male- and female-controlled businesses.

While the results in Table 3 provide some support for hypothesis 3 there is evidence to suggest that, for profitable firms, the female-controlled businesses outperformed the

---

4. However, as noted previously, the TITTA, ROA, and ROE numbers were not normally distributed, and this could have contributed to the finding of no significant difference. It is for this reason that the natural log of each of these performance measures is also examined.
5. In the 1994-95 data, there was no significant difference between male- and female-controlled businesses with respect to the log of ROE.

Table 3

Mean Results for Various Performance Measures: Comparing Male- and Female-Controlled Businesses

| | Mean | | Significance |
Performance Measure	Male	Female	Level
All Firms			
Total income to total assets (TITTA)	10.5392	10.1048	.960
Profit to total assets (ROA)	0.3744	0.5478	.197
Profit to total equity (ROE)	0.7824	1.8938	.334
Log of total income to total assets (Log TITTA)	1.1583	1.2406	.142
Profitable Firms			
Profit to total assets (ROA)	0.5398	0.8339	.048
Log of profit to total assets (Log ROA)	−1.6369	−1.3604	.000
Profit to total equity (ROE)	1.0139	2.5461	.321
Log of profit to total equity (Log ROE)	−0.6930	−0.5015	.005
Loss Making Firms			
Absolute loss to total assets (ABROA)	0.5902	0.6373	.920
Log of absolute loss to total assets (Log ABROA)	−2.0283	−1.9877	.759
Absolute loss to total equity (ABROE)	1.7095	1.3829	.674
Log of absolute loss to total equity (Log ABROE)	−0.9210	−1.0729	.248

male-controlled businesses. However, the results in Table 3 do not control for a number of potentially very important confounding variables that would be expected to affect SME performance. For example, the performance measures reported in Table 3 do not control for industry risk. As noted by Anna et al. (2000, p. 299):

> Traditional investment theory provides a rule of thumb that the higher the risk, the higher the rate of return on an investment, and conversely, the lower the risk, the lower the rate of return.

To control for industry-based risk, the businesses in this study have been grouped into the following industries: mining; manufacturing; construction; wholesale trade; retail trade; accommodation, cafes, and restaurants; transport and storage; finance and insurance; property and business services; cultural and recreational services; and personal and other services.

Similarly, controlling for age of business is also important because age affects performance in two ways. First, younger firms tend to have lower sales (and, therefore, lower profits) than older, more established businesses. Second, and perhaps more importantly, ROA will be enhanced in older firms because, other things being equal, their assets will have been depreciated more than those of younger firms. It would be preferable to have market values for all assets, but because this is not possible it is important (in assessing business performance) to control for age of business. In this study businesses have been grouped into the following age categories: less than two years; two years to less than five years; five years to less than ten years; ten years to less than twenty years; and over twenty years.

Finally, Fasci and Valdez (1998) found that hours dedicated to the business on a weekly basis, a measure of input to the business, contributed significantly to earnings.

Although expected, the finding confirmed the importance of including this variable as a control in any evaluation of firm performance. In this study businesses have been classified into two groups: those operating less than five days per week and those operating five or more days per week. This provides some control over a potentially important additional input to the business: the owner's human (as opposed to financial) capital.

Because this paper is not trying to explain differences in performance, (that is, it does not take a liberal feminist theory perspective) many of the variables found in previous studies (for example, experience or education of the owner) have not been included. In keeping with a social feminist theory perspective, the only variables that are included in this study are those considered appropriate for a proper assessment of performance (rather than an explanation for differences in performance).

Tables 4 to 6 present the results of analyzing the variance (ANOVA) in the performance measures for all firms and for profitable firms only (as reported in Table 3) by: industry; age of business; the number of days a business operates; and the sex of the owner (to see if the sex of the owner has any residual explanatory power). To minimize repetition, the remainder of this paper will only report on the log of the respective performance measures, because these are deemed to be the more robust.[6]

Table 4 presents the ANOVA results for the log of TITTA. Table 4 shows that both industry and age of business were significant in explaining the variance in performance for the businesses in this study. The number of days the business operated was not significant and whether a male or female controlled the business continued to be not significant.

Table 5 presents the ANOVA results for the log of ROA for profitable firms. Table 5 shows that industry, age of business, and the number of days the business operated were all significant in explaining the variance in performance for the profitable businesses in this study. However, whether a male or female controlled the business was no longer significant.

Table 6 presents the ANOVA results for the log of ROE for profitable firms. Table 6 shows that both industry and age of business were significant in explaining the variance in performance for the profitable businesses in this study. The number of days the business operated was not significant and whether a male or female controlled the business was no longer significant.

For the unprofitable firms, the ANOVA results for the log of ABROA and the log

Table 4

ANOVA of Log TITTA to Various Business and Owner Demographics

Source of Variation	Sum of Squares	DF	Mean Square	F	Sig of F
Industry	1453.543	10	145.354	77.077	0.000
Age of business	269.066	4	67.267	35.669	0.000
Days business operated	6.703	1	6.703	3.555	0.059
Sex	2.764	1	2.764	1.466	0.226

6. The results for the other performance measures did not alter the conclusions of this paper.

Table 5

ANOVA of Log ROA (Profitable Firms) to Various Business and Owner Demographics

Source of Variation	Sum of Squares	DF	Mean Square	F	Sig of F
Industry	348.397	10	34.84	14.96	0.000
Age of business	390.964	4	97.741	41.968	0.000
Days business operated	28.943	1	28.943	12.427	0.000
Sex	10.971	1	10.971	4.711	0.030

of ABROE confirmed the results reported in Table 3. That is, whether a male or female controlled the business continued to be not significant in explaining performance.

The results presented in Tables 4-6 provide strong support for social feminist theory, because, after controlling for industry, age of business, and the number of days the business operated, there was no significant variation in business performance that could be attributed to the sex of the person in control of the business. Female entrepreneurs appeared to devote fewer resources to their businesses but their profitability for each dollar of equity (or assets) invested was the same as for male-controlled businesses. In other words, females (on average) may take a different approach to business, in terms of the amounts of capital they are able or prepared to invest, but, in terms of the return they earn on their invested capital, they are no less effective than males.

CONCLUSIONS AND DIRECTIONS FOR FUTURE RESEARCH

The purpose of this study was to compare the relative performance of businesses controlled by males with those controlled by females. In assessing performance, this study, unlike most previous studies, related output measures (total income and profit) to input measures (total assets and owner's equity). A significant advantage of this study, is that it used a database developed from surveys conducted on behalf of the Australian Federal Government and specifically aimed at providing a better understanding of the

Table 6

ANOVA of Log ROE (Profitable Firms) to Various Business and Owner Demographics

Source of Variation	Sum of Squares	DF	Mean Square	F	Sig of F
Industry	143.235	10	14.323	7.06	0.000
Age of business	494.227	4	123.557	60.905	0.000
Days business operated	0.591	1	0.591	0.291	0.589
Sex	1.666	1	1.666	0.821	0.365

growth and performance of Australian SMEs. As a result, the sample used was highly representative of Australian SMEs and was based on very good response rates.

The results indicated that female-owned businesses had significantly lower total income and profits compared to male-controlled businesses. However, there were also significantly fewer resources invested in the female-controlled businesses compared to the male-controlled businesses. When business outputs were related to inputs (and after controlling for industry, age of business, and the number of days the business operated), the results indicated that there were no significant differences in the performances of male- and female-controlled businesses. Interestingly, before including the control variables, there was evidence to suggest that female-controlled businesses outperformed the male-controlled businesses in this study.

This finding provides strong support for social feminist theory. It suggests that females may take a different approach to business in that they are likely, on average, to use fewer resources in their ventures. However, their overall performance, in terms of TITTA, ROA, and ROE, is likely to be the same as for males. In other words, this study suggests that differences in the relative performances of male- and female-controlled enterprises reported by previous studies may not have been caused by the inability on the part of females to put resources to effective use. Rather, it would appear that females are just as effective as males in using resources, but that females, on average, use fewer resources per firm. The reasons why females use fewer resources in their ventures is an issue that warrants further careful examination. There are at least two possible explanations for this phenomenon. First, and in line with a liberal feminist perspective, it could be argued that females have fewer resources to invest because they tend to earn less (and, therefore, will have lower levels of savings available for investment) and because females are discriminated against by lenders. Second, and in line with a social feminist theory perspective, it could reasonably be argued that females generally tend to commit fewer resources to their businesses because they are more risk averse. Interestingly, Coleman (2000) found that female-owned firms paid higher interest rates than male-owned firms for their most recent loans, and female-owned service firms were more likely to put up collateral than male-owned service firms. This may also explain why women are likely to commit fewer resources to their businesses and may be more risk averse. This could be a useful area for further investigation, since there has been relatively little work undertaken to date into the differences between males and females in terms of the way they operate their businesses and their attitudes to business risk.

REFERENCES

Anna, A. L., Chandler, G. N., Jansen, E. & Mero, N. P. (2000). Women business owners in traditional and non-traditional industries. *Journal of Business Venturing, 15*(3), 279-303.

Barber, B. M., & Odean, T. (2001). Boys will be boys: Gender overconfidence, and common stock investment. *The Quarterly Journal of Economics, 116*(1), 261-292.

Chandler, G. N., & Hanks, S. H. (1994). Founder competence, the environment, and venture performance. *Entrepreneurship Theory and Practice, 18*(3), 77-89.

Chell, E., & Baines, S. (1998). Does gender affect business "Performance"? A study of microbusinesses in business services in the UK. *Entrepreneurship & Regional Development, 10,* 117-135.

Cliff, J. E. (1998). Does one size fit all? Exploring the relationship between attitudes towards growth, gender, and business size. Journal of Business Venturing, 13(6), 523-542.

Coleman, S. (2000). Access to capital and terms of credit: A comparison of men- and women-owned small businesses. *Journal of Small Business Management, 38*(3), 37-52.

Cooper, A. C., Gimeno-Gascon, J. F., & Woo, C. (1994). Initial human and financial capital as predictors of new venture performance. *Journal of Business Venturing, 9*(5), 371-395.

Du Rietz, A., & Henrekson, M. (2000). Testing the female underperformance hypothesis. *Small Business Economics, 14*(1), 1-10.

Fasci, M. A., & Valdez, J. (1998). A performance contrast of male- and female-owned small accounting practices. *Journal of Small Business Management, 36*(3), 1-7.

Fischer, E. M., Reuber, R. A., & Dyke, L. S. (1993). A theoretical overview and extension of research on sex, gender, and entrepreneurship. *Journal of Business Venturing, 8*(2), 151-168.

Jianakoplos, N.A., & Bernasek, A. (1998). Are women more risk averse? *Economic Inquiry, 36*(4), 620-630.

Kalleberg, A. L., & Leicht, K. T. (1991). Gender and organizational performance: Determinants of small business survival and success. *Academy of Management Journal, 34*(1), 136-161.

Palepu, K. G., Healy, P. M., & Bernard, V. L. (2000). *Business analysis and valuation: Using financial statements.* Cincinnati: South-Western College Publishing.

Powell, M., & Ansic, D. (1997). Gender differences in risk behaviour in financial decision-making: An experimental analysis. *Journal of Economic Psychology, 18*(6), 605-628.

Rosa, P., Carter, S., & Hamilton, D. (1996). Gender as a determinant of small business performance: Insights from a British study. *Small Business Economics, 8,* 463-478.

Sexton, D. L., & Bowman-Upton, N. (1990). Female and male entrepreneurs: Psychological characteristics and their role in gender-related discrimination. *Journal of Business Venturing, 5*(1), 29-36.

John Watson is Associate Professor of Accounting and Finance at The University of Western Australia.

Part VII
Environmental

[27]

Journal of Contemporary Business   *Winter 1976*

ENTREPRENEURSHIP: A NEW FEMALE FRONTIER

Eleanor Brantley Schwartz
The Cleveland State University

What man has not yearned to create a profitable venture as his own
boss? Most of our major corporations are such dreams made reality.
Today, something new is on the "profitable venture horizon" -- i.e.,
women, in increasing numbers, also want to start their own companies.

Why would women risk entrepreneurship when statistics show that about
72 percent of all new ventures fail within the first 2 years? A Dun
and Bradstreet survey revealed a 6 percent rise in small business failures for 1974; dollar losses surpassed $3 billion.[1] New, inexperienced
firms accounted for most of the losses; specifically, companies 5 years
old or less were responsible for 60 percent of the total failures.

Sufficient capital, sound ideas and hard work are not always enough
to make a profitable new venture. However, the simple fact that
thriving self-employed people are still around is testimony enough
that the odds are surmountable; and, increasingly, women want to take
their chances.

ENTREPRENEUR DEFINED

Basically, the entrepreneur is an innovative individual who creates
and builds a business from nonexistence. The entrepreneur assumes
responsibility for not only the development and management of the
enterprise but also for the risk of gain or loss from the venture.
Classical economists viewed entrepreneurs as capitalists who financed
and directed factors of production into marketable products. Now
it is believed that entrepreneurs should have certain personal characteristics in addition to being risk-takers and manager/owners.[2] For
instance, a corporate manager who supervises and performs delegated

47

tasks is not an entrepreneur, although he or she may perform entrepreneurial tasks.[3] Often, the entrepreneur is not the best manager
for a company as it matures since he or she generally may be "unable to
allocate administrative responsibility and to set up procedures and
controls." Problems typically arise "after a new company reaches sales
of $6 million."[4]

THE STUDY

While female corporate executives/managers have been the subject of recent research, little attention has been given to female entrepreneurs.[5]
In contrast, the entrepreneurial behavior of males has been researched
extensively with conclusions rendered regarding the characteristics,
psychology and management styles of these male entrepreneurs. The purpose of this study is to discern the set of characteristics, motivation
and attitudes of female entrepreneurs; e.g.,

● Who is the female entrepreneur? Do women who start their own business
possess characteristics similar to those of men who start their own
business?
● Why do some women shun the security of more traditional paths to
strike out on their own?
● How do women view themselves in their entrepreneurship role? How
do her attitudes toward her entrepreneurial role compare to the general
essentials of entrepreneurship concluded from research on male entrepreneurs?
● How do women perceive the attitudes of males and females (e.g.,
lenders, investors, suppliers, customers, employees) who do business
with or work for them?
● What deterrents to success can women identify as unique to them as
females (in contrast to their male counterparts)?
● Can women develop the qualities considered essential to entrepreneurship?

To determine answers to these questions, we reviewed literature from
1958 to 1975 on male entrepreneurs, and 25 female entrepreneurs were
interviewed, either in person, by telephone or by mail. Twenty female
entrepreneurs participated in the survey; this represented an 80 percent
response. The female entrepreneurs were not characterized by geographic
location and they represented a variety of businesses, although most
of them fell within the "services" category. (See Table 1.) No attempt

Table 1

Basic Characteristics of Respondents

Category	Number in Category	Percentage in Category
Business		
Artist's agent	1	5
Restaurant owner	1	5
Beauty shop owner	2	10
Dressmaker	1	5
Jewelry designer	1	5
Insurance/financial consultant	1	5
Freelance filmmaker	1	5
Antique dealer	1	5
Dress shop owner	2	10
Gift shop owner	1	5
Florist	1	5
Cosmetics franchisee	1	5
Book/music store owner	1	5
Employment contractor (secretarial, clerical, services-- temporary and permanent)	2	10
Business/research services consultant	1	5
Travel agent	1	5
Advertising & PR agent (firm handles multiple range of business problems--e.g., management, marketing, data processing, communications, personnel training)	1	5
Total	20	100%
Pre-entrepreneur Background		
Secretary	2	10
Teacher (high school)	1	5
Housewife	4	20
Banking	1	5
Administrative management	5	25
Retailing (buyer)	1	5
Advertising	1	5
Neither housewife nor employed before entrepreneurship	5	25
Total	20	100%

49

Table 1 (cont.)

Category	Number in Category	Percentage in Category
Education		
High school graduate	4	20
Some college	5	25
College graduate	7	35
Some post-graduate credits	1	5
Graduate degree:		
1. Fine Arts;		
2. Business Administration	3	15
Total	20	100%
Age Range		
20-25	1	5
26-30	6	30
31-40	8	40
41-50	4	20
51-over	1	5
Total	20	100%
Marital status		
Married	8	40
Unmarried	12	60
(5, single; 7, divorced)		
Total	20	100%

50

was made to eliminate businesses traditionally dominated by females
(such as beauty shops). Most of the questions provided an opportunity
to comment or qualify one's answer and added a qualitative dimension.

The goal of the study was to develop a better understanding of female
entrepreneurs--the kind of women, as compared to the kind of men, who
become entrepreneurs--and what they go through to build and maintain
a new business. This understanding can help determine the special
education and training needs of self-employed women and of those who
want to become self-employed. As a result, educational programs to
provide needed skills to existing and potential female entrepreneurs
can be planned better. And, importantly, many of the 7.2 million
women who head families may see broader directions for career opportunities.[6]

THE FINDINGS

The study focused on perspectives from the female entrepreneurs as
they correlated to or contrasted with the findings of research literature on male entrepreneurs. Perceptions of the surveyed female entrepreneurs are presented as major findin s and then related to research
on male entrepreneurs in the discussion that follows.

● Finding #1. Major motivators for becoming entrepreneurs were perceived to be the need to achieve, the desire to be independent, the need
for job satisfaction and the necessity -- economically.

Discussion: Some researchers have concluded that most entrepreneurs
have a long, lonely and difficult road; those who follow it must be a
special breed. Numerous studies offer insight into the psychology and
characteristics of male entrepreneurs. They generally conclude that
individuals with entrepreneurial drive are not drawn randomly from the
population. On the contrary, they are likely to be found in certain
social structures, to possess common behavioral traits and to emerge
especially when the economy displays certain characteristics.[7]

For instance, "social marginality"[8] appears to be one of the most likely
forces motivating a man to set up his own business.[9] The owner/manager
role is chosen to develop an acceptable self-identity. Discrepancy
between perceived ability in one's self and work roles available creates
an inconsistency resolved only in being one's own boss.[10] For example,

51

an "educationally unsuccessful" person from a modestly well-off family
needs "paper qualifications" for corporate management mobility. Rather
than accepting a corporate situation with less status, he develops his
own business.[11]

Some research presents evidence that entrepreneurs are motivated strongly by an almost overwhelming ego (desire to succeed, self-esteem)[12] and
perhaps, ultimately, self-fulfillment needs. Safety and physiological
needs of entrepreneurs tend to be low, but need for self-esteem is great.
Self-esteem needs must be satisfied almost entirely before self-actualization factors motivate. Once met, the entrepreneur may seek to self-
actualize through other new ventures to build from scratch. The entrepreneur may talk about retiring, but seldom does. If the business is
sold, usually another one is started eventually.[13]

Almost all studies on entrepreneurs show the desire for independence
as a motivation to become one's own boss. Entrepreneurs tend to strongly
dislike authority, especially when they feel they can do a better job
than their superiors.

However, perhaps, the strongest research-supported motivator is the need
for achievement--the desire to do well--not for social prestige, but for
a feeling of accomplishment.[14] A high need for achievement leads people
to:

"behave in most of the ways they should behave if they are to fulfill
the entrepreneurial role successfully....The achievement motive should
lead individuals to seek out situations which provide moderate challenge to their skills, to perform better in such situations, and to
have greater confidence in the likelihood of their success. It should
make them conservative where things are completely beyond their control,
as in games of chance, and happier where they have some opportunity of
influencing the outcome of a series of events by their own actions and
of knowing concretely what those actions have accomplished...Finally,
it should encourage them to value money not for itself but as a measure
of success."[15]

Although the entrepreneurs often think they are motivated by money,
in reality, it is "the achievement of creating an organization" that
motivates them. Money is but a criterion of the degree of success.[16]

To determine if females are motivated differently than male entrepreneurs, the entrepreneurs surveyed were asked to rank from "insignificant" to "considerably strong" the role of the following motivators
in their decision to start their own business: achievement, independence, status, money, power, competition, affiliation,[17] security and
job satisfaction. (See Table 2.) Many of the respondents included
the rationale for their rankings, and the responses showed that women
who decided to start their own business are motivated the same as men
who do. Just as in Schreier's study,[18] a significant number of women
indicated that economic necessity was a basic reason. (None of the
respondents started their business as a hobby.) Some female entrepreneurs were heads of household and felt they went into business out of
economic necessity (they felt they could make more money on their own
than in working for someone else). However, most of the respondents,
just as the male entrepreneurs, seemed to be motivated primarily by
achievement and self-actualizing needs. "Ability versus opportunity"
reasons given for leaving a corporate position could lead to the conclusion that "social marginality" was also a major motivator.

Interestingly, significantly more than half of the respondents had
a management, or semiadministrative, position for 2 or more years before
going into business for themselves. They left for achievement, independence or job satisfaction needs; e.g., one entrepreneur commented,
"I started my own business mainly because I couldn't get the kind of
job I felt my background warranted." Another entrepreneur got only
so far; management was unwilling to give her more challenge, "I could
not achieve my personal career goals. I got frustrated, definitely
bored, and left to be my own boss." Another relatively new entrepreneur left her management position after 4 years because:

"Much of the work I could not justify as meaningful. I found myself
on a treadmill, my creativity and initiative suppressed; everything
had to be done the 'organization's way.' I was miserable. Rather than
thwart my goals to succeed, I set up my own company."

Another entrepreneur left a well-paying corporate position to set up
her own company because:

"I got tired of being promoted again and again only to find the job
had been narrowed or that I reported to someone on the 'totem hierarchy' lower than my male predecessor did." Other comments, such as

53

Table 2

Perceived Motivation for Starting Own Company
(Responses shown in numbers and percents)

	Insignificant N	Insignificant %	Weak N	Weak %	Significant N	Significant %	Considerable N	Considerable %	Strong N	Strong %
Achievement	0	0	1	5	2	10	3	15	14	70
Independence	1	5	1	5	1	5	2	10	15	75
Status	5	25	12	60	1	5	1	5	1	5
Money	0	0	1	5	16	80	2	10	1	5
Power	15	75	3	15	1	5	1	5	0	0
Competition	2	10	3	15	11	55	3	15	1	5
Affiliation	12	60	5	25	2	10	1	5	0	0
Security	5	25	4	20	8	40	2	10	1	5
Job satisfaction	0	0	0	0	2	10	15	75	3	15

the following, further supported female entrepreneurs' needs for achievement, independence and job satisfaction:

"I wanted to be master of my own fate. I deliberately went after the education, technical and business; and, more important, gained experience in other people's companies to ready myself for the big step."

"I feel like I've earned something by the sweat of my brow."

"Being my own boss is a continual learning experience. It's forced me to be creative when I thought I couldn't be. I've had to shift gears when things went wrong. I must depend on my own sense of self confidence and courage. Besides, it's a great feeling to break new ground."

"I wasn't getting anywhere. I was frustrated and depressed, though I told myself to 'keep smiling.' I didn't want to lose sight of my goal, but after so long I couldn't persevere any longer. I left and set up my own business. I no longer have 'just a job.' And I've proved to myself that a woman can do almost anything if she wants to badly enough. Women's place, no matter what anyone says, is where she *wants* to be."

I figured I'd never make it to the top of a corporation, so I just decided to create my own."

Research by Professor Eugene Jennings[19] highlighted a tendency for women high-achievers to become disenchanted in a mature organizational environment. While some high achievers (male and female) can compromise with corporate requirements, one type of person cannot. Jennings found that after 10 years, and often less in management, female high achievers had learned how to carry authority and to manage profit objectives. Many of them made $20,000 to $40,000 and were managers of a branch office, department or zone but at this point, left the company. Three alternatives, according to Jennings, were likely to attract high female achievers:

- One's own business
- Small, service-oriented corporations that require initiative and creativity
- Staff position (perhaps in the same corporation) in, for example, planning, advertising, personnel or some aspect of finance

- Finding #2. The most important personality traits for success as an entrepreneur were thought probably to be strong ego and achievement

55

drives.

Discussion: An almost "consuming desire to succeed," "capacity to
work hard for long hours" and "willingness to forego immediate satisfactions for future gain" were considered to be absolutely necessary
to "make it" as an entrepreneur. (See Table 3.) Not only were these
items self-requirements, but also entrepreneurs want to hire (in the
words of one of them) "only energetic achievers who are unafraid to
work 18-hour days and really want to get ahead." As many as half
of the respondents believed an entrepreneur could overcome most
"reasonable" economic barriers if the personality makeup combined a
strong desire to succeed with willingness to work hard (see Finding #6).

The majority of respondents felt that not only must entrepreneurs want
to succeed but also that they must be confident they have what it takes
to achieve the results they want. In a *New York Times* study, a female
entrepreneur expressed this self-confidence as well as an intuitive
ability to read the market: "....My guts just told me this was the right
thing to do. I can't say why. And I always find a way to come out on
my feet. There's something in my nature that just doesn't allow me to
fail."[20]

Almost all of the female entrepreneur respondents felt they and other
entrepreneurs are nonconformers. Evaluations, decisions and actions
are made in terms of what the entrepreneur wants or thinks must be done.[21]
They believe their success requires aggressive determination to "make
things happen." "Being an entrepreneur just simply requires a certain
amount of toughness," said one entrepreneur. Interestingly, one researcher emphasized a necessity for strong empathy to balance ego
toughness. A weak ego and strong empathy combination was found to result in a "nice guy" who is inadequately assertive to fight the new
firm's survival battle. A strong ego with weak empathy is sufficiently
assertive, but insensitivity to needs and feelings of others causes
resistance to seemingly "bulldozer" tactics. An individual with both
weak ego and weak empathy is a follower-type.[22] These female entrepreneurs indicated comfortableness with their highly developed aggressiveness and leadership behavior, although they also indicated awareness that many traditionally oriented people often are not comfortable
with this determination and assertiveness. A substantial majority

56

Table 3

How Female Entrepreneurs Perceive Importance of
Behavioral Traits that Tend to Characterize Entrepreneurs
(Responses shown in numbers and percents)

Traits	Degree of Entrepreneurial Importance					
	Very Important		Important		Unimportant	
	N	%	N	%	N	%
Intense desire to succeed	16	80	4	20	0	0
Self-discipline and perserverance (willingness to work hard, endure stress/pressure and loneliness of entrepreneurial role)	18	90	2	10	0	0
Drive for independence	13	65	4	20	3	15
Need for achievement	15	75	5	25	0	0
Assertive (confident, determined, competitive)	17	85	2	10	1	5
Action-oriented (decisive, makes things happen, does the job now)	19	95	1	5	0	0
Goal-oriented (quantifiable and realistic; every moment counts toward the goal)	18	90	1	5	1	5
High energy level (stamina)	17	85	2	10	1	5

57

Figure I

How Well Entrepreneurs Perform Managerial Functions

FUNCTION	ACTIVITY	DEFINITION	ENTREPRENEURIAL PERFORMANCE (Poor → Excellent)
Planning	Forecast	Establish where present course will lead	
	Set objectives	Determined desired end results	
	Develop strategies	Decide how and when to achieve goals	
	Program	Establish priority sequence & timing of steps	
	Budget	Allocate resources	
	Set procedures	Standardize methods	
	Develop policies	Make standing decisions on important recurring matters	
Organizing	Establish organization structure	Draw up organization chart	
	Define relationships	Define liaison lines to facilitate coordination	
	Create position descriptions	Define scope, relationship, responsibilities and authority	
	Establish position qualifications	Define qualifications for each person in each position	
Staffing	Select	Recruit qualified people for each position	
	Orient	Familiarize new people with the situation	
	Train	Make proficient by instruction and practice	
	Develop	Help improve knowledge, attitudes and skills	
Directing	Delegate	Assign responsibility and exact accountability for results	
	Motivate	Persuade and inspire people to take desired action	
	Coordinate	Relate efforts in most effective coordination	
	Manage differences	Encourage independent thought and resolve conflicts	
	Manage change	Stimulate creativity and innovations in achieving goals	
Controlling	Establish reporting system	Determine what critical data are needed, how and when	
	Develop performance standards	Set conditions that will exist when key duties are well done	
	Measure results	Ascertain extent of deviation from goals and standards	
	Take corrective action	Adjust plans, counsel to attain standard and replan	
	Reward	Praise, remunerate	

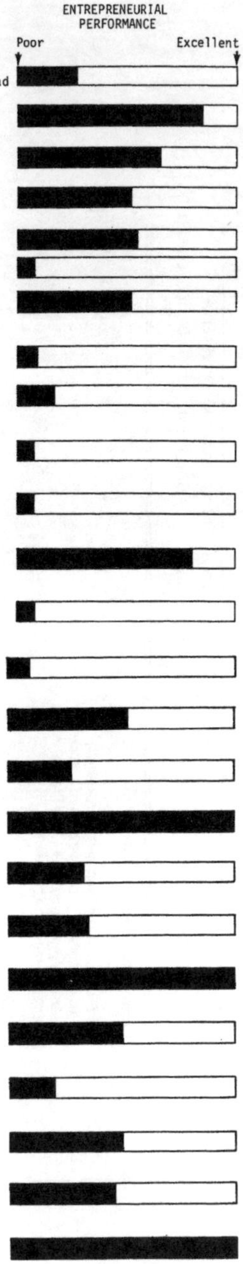

Source: Charles B. Swayne and William R. Tucker, *The Effective Entrepreneur*, (New Jersey: General Learning Press, 1973), pp. 40, 41.

acknowledged that an entrepreneur must be able to endure high levels of stress. Said one respondent, "The entrepreneur must be able to maintain control in unusual situations and still be innovative after intensive demands."

● Finding #3. Most of the women entrepreneurs tend to closely watch and control their business operations, thus leaning toward an autocratic management style.

"Maximizing sales and controlling costs is a major concern," said one of the women entrepreneurs reflecting the view of all the entrepreneurs surveyed. "I must maintain an adequate cash position." Research shows that the leadership style most characteristic of male entrepreneurs in the first stages of their company's growth also tends to be autocratic. Although male entrepreneurs tend to have a "Theory Y" style, neither Theory X nor Y appears to be a better entrepreneurial style.[23] Fighting survival in an uncertain environment, however, most entrepreneurs tend to make decisions in favor of sales, production or costs over "people" considerations. A business name must be established, consumer acceptance gained, competitors combatted; the major goal is to create a profitable base and, therefore, survival. The company depends on the drive and resources of the entrepreneur, so authority revolves around the entrepreneur, who, incidentally, rarely delegates well anyway.[24] As the organization matures, a more balanced approach appears to emerge among the male entrepreneurs. People increasingly are recognized as essential to the company, though many of them may not commit the same energy to their jobs as the entrepreneur. On the other hand, entrepreneurs are eternally aware that not even one unproductive employee can be afforded. The "basic design of a small business is its lean and thin structure."[25]

In general, research (see Figure I, for example) shows male entrepreneurs to be fair to good planners and intuitive, keen market analysts. Short-term plans are stressed with concentration on tactical plans to achieve them. Less time may be devoted to organizing and staffing, except in selecting good personnel. The entrepreneurs in this study recognized the importance of all the management functions, especially planning and staffing (see Finding #5). Generally, persuasive leaders tend to motivate and control their support people effectively.

As a company matures, a leadership crisis may occur.[26] Emphasis must
move from an entrepreneurial to a managerial orientation.[27] Research
indicates that most entrepreneurs are unsuited tempermentally to manage
as the firm moves into a stage[28] that needs professional management (see
Figure II). For the organization to remain effective, the entrepreneur
must delegate--decentralize control--and adapt to sophisticated management. Few entrepreneurs can so drastically change their management
style.[29] In cases in which the entrepreneur is concerned "with specifics
and views the business as an extension of himself," the company as it
matures needs a professional manager concerned with "integration of
systems and the long-range planning necessary for long-term growth."[30]
The female entrepreneurs surveyed in this study had not been in business
long enough to draw any conclusions about how their management style
might evolve as their businesses mature. Only one comment was made
which may be a clue, "I'm a builder, not a manager."

● Finding #4. The initial and major barrier experienced was felt to be
be credit discrimination during the capital formation stage. Many
of the responding female entrepreneurs said credit was denied just because they were women. In general, however, they found that once
established both women and men would do business with them.

Discussion: In an open-end question,[31] the respondents were asked to give
the biggest obstacle(s) they had encountered, which was unique to them
as females, in getting their business off the ground. See Table 4 for
the barriers indicated most often.

Putting together the necessary capital was felt to be the greatest
challenge. Though they recognized that this also was possibly true for
males, women felt that it was more of a barrier for them. The major
sources of initial capital reported included their own savings; loans
(or gifts) from husband, father or relative; and bank loans. Many of
them felt that, generally, of commercial loan sources, clearing banks
had the lowest interest rates and simplest procedures for getting a loan.
Said one female entrepreneur, "Banks determine the entrepreneurs of
tomorrow." She stresses that banks, in general, need to be more lenient
toward small business. She found the small entrepreneur stands a better
chance with a smaller bank: "In the process of growing itself, the bank
is more willing to take a chance." The general consensus of those who

Figure II
Entrepreneurial Effectiveness Versus Growth

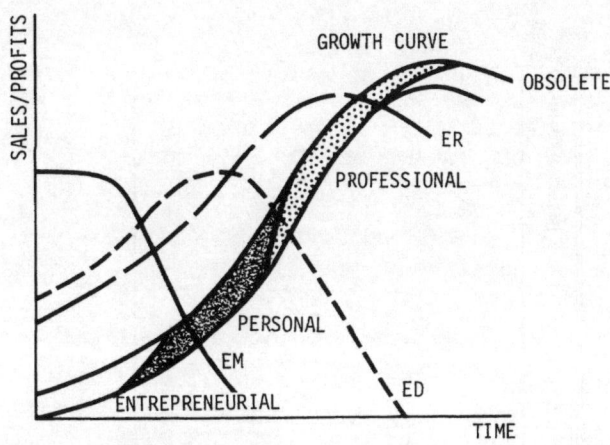

ER-Effectiveness of That
   Very Rare Entrepreneur
   Who Delegates and Can
   "Manage" in the Traditional Sense

ED-Effectiveness of Those
   Entrepreneurs Who
   Can Delegate

EM-Effectiveness of Most Entrepreneurs

Source: Charles B. Swayne and William R. Tucker,
         The Effective Entrepreneur
         (New Jersey: General Learning Press, 1973), p. 19.

Table 4

Major Barriers Experienced Most Frequently
By New Female Entrepreneurs

Barriers	Times mentioned
Obtaining lines of credit	17
Weak collateral position	11
Lack of business training and knowledge	13
Lack of management experience (staffing, supervising, directing)	12
Lack of respect for women	3
Demands of the company affecting stability of marriage	9
Overcoming some of society's belief that women are not as serious as men about business matters	4

62

had experienced difficulty obtaining credit was that, because of the Equal Credit Opportunity Act,[32] future female entrepreneurs would not be as likely to have this problem "just because they are women." All of the respondents felt it absolutely essential to establish and maintain a good credit rating.

Research shows that the odds against any new entrepreneur obtaining venture capital are high--perhaps as high as 50 to 1. Lack of knowledge and communication of information on the venture capital process among entrepreneurs, capital sources and intermediaries were often major impediments. Not only do new entrepreneurs not have access to all venture capital sources, but also government tax and regulatory policies can impede the flow of venture capital.[33] Importantly, most venture capital financiers weigh the entrepreneur's management capabilities as much as the merit of the venture idea. Consequently, entrepreneurs should have business plans, financial requirements and repayment proposals well thought out, with a professional appearance (typed, etc.). Useful persons to consult in the mechanics of starting a business include an accountant and lawyer. A company's profitability depends to a large extent, on strategic accounting, taxation and legal arrangements.[34]

Those respondents who saw their biggest obstacle as overcoming their lack of training and business knowledge indicated they had to learn basic things such as how to:

"....tackle business problems as a leader.
.....wade through confusing and often hazy details to get at the crux of the business problem.
.....compensate for lack of experience (a) from no formal education in schools of business and finance, and (b) at management levels in the business world itself.
.....deal with available sources of credit and financing.
.....negotiate contracts and, in some cases, deal with unions.
.....wade through the myriad laws and regulations on how business must report its activities."[35]

Lack of management experience (staffing, supervising, directing) did not concern the respondents as much as lack of access to credit and need for more business knowledge. A number of respondents had learned

63

that "acquiring an efficient working team is a trial and error process." They pinpointed three critical principles important to building an effective workforce: (1) good selection procedures, (2) incentives to motivate good performers to stay with the firm and (3) prompt dismissal of inefficient people.

Almost all the respondents would not marry unless the "partner could understand and fit into the female entrepreneur's business owner role." Combining the demands of marriage, and especially a family, with the demands of a business seemed hazardous to both the marriage and the business unless the partner was understanding and cooperative when the business had to take a dominant role. However, the entrepreneurs married to such a partner felt that their husband's understanding and support was a decided asset. A small percentage of the respondents said their business caused their divorce. Many unmarried women said they had little time for frivolous dating or a social life, but expressed no regret for the business's erosion into their personal lives.

● Finding #5. The greatest common mistake the majority of the female entrepreneurs felt they had made was underestimating the cost of operating their business and marketing their product or service.

Discussion. The respondent's biggest fiasco was "running out of money," which was felt to result largely from a lack of experience in handling money. Almost equally blamed was that they "did not plan well enough." The general consensus was that everything had to be soundly planned for-- from the cost of marketing to the building up of the marketing organization. As expressed by one respondent, "You have to have an idea, but you also have to have the capital and management if you are to succeed with the idea. The idea must be marketed, and this costs money. The capital goes fast, at first, with no income. But regardless of how good the product or service is, you have to have customers. You can't cut marketing costs easily, or taper them down quickly, if you want to get where you want to go. Instead, you must plan carefully and then through good management handle your financial affairs prudently."

The importance of managing money is supported further by a recent quote of a female entrepreneur in the moving and storage business, "Building equity is top priority now. We got through a very rough winter because

I know how to handle cash."[36] Lack of experience and success in handling money is a major problem for male entrepreneurs also.[37] Inept management has been shown to be the major cause for business failure; the Dun and Bradstreet 1974 survey showed it to be the contributing factor in nine out of every ten failures. Modern operations, and particularly today's uncertain economic conditions, demand management expertise. Inexperienced entrepreneurs are apt to go under quickly. The Dun and Bradstreet survey showed key management problems responsible for the following percents (as shown in Table 5) of this total failure rate:

Table 5
Key Management Problems

Key problem	Percent of total failure rate
Lack of experience in the line	15%
Lack of managerial experience	14%
Unbalanced experience	22%
Incompetence	40%

Companies with small financial reserves were involved in approximately 68 percent of the total failures. The difficulties of striking out on one's own have increased because of rising costs, expensive credit and an uncertain business climate.

● Finding #6. The female entrepreneurs strongly felt that women, just as men, have entrepreneurial qualities to some extent and in some combination. They believe that these abilities can be developed with an understanding of the qualities important to entrepreneurship.

Discussion: The respondents felt, almost unanimously, that women who demonstrate entrepreneurial characteristics and inclinations have as good a chance to become successful entrepreneurs as men who have these traits and desires. They have to learn, just as do men, how to create and take advantage of business opportunities and solve business problems. As one of the female entrepreneurs pointed out, "The rules of the game must be known before either a man or a woman can play the game." Ambition, high self-esteem, energy, competitiveness, achievement motivation, willingness to assume risk and a high need for

65

independence were considered necessary qualities for entrepreneurial
success. Women have these potentials, which, under the proper conditions, can be developed. Generally all the respondents felt about themselves as this female entrepreneur, "I have never for a minute thought
I couldn't do something just because I'm a woman. Or that I should be
a certain way just because I'm a woman. I'm a person first. I always
intended to be in a business of my own in some form at some time.
I don't think it was a new or urgent derive that impelled me into busi-
ness--just a simple ambition that had been with me as long as I can
remember." Increasingly, research shows that neither sex exclusively
possesses a certain aptitude or ability. Where women generally excell,
there are men who also excell and vice versa.[38]

Research supports the notion that entrepreneurial abilities can be
developed in male adults (based on researcher/psychologist David Mc-
Clelland's work in India).[39] McClelland found the "need for achievement" to be the major force motivating entrepreneurship among males.
Three factors were found to be important in the development of achievement motivation in males: (1) the parent's high achievement standards;
(2) encouragement and warmth in the home; and (3) a nondominating,
nonauthoritarian father. Females traditionally have been thought to be
motivated by a "need for affiliation or external social approval"
rather than by an "internalized desire to excell."[40] Little research
has been done specifically on the development of achievement needs and
entrepreneurial behavior in females. However, a few studies have been
conducted on development of achievement needs in career-oriented women
in a corporate environment. For example, sociologist Jean Lipman-
Blumen showed that career women tend to have a dominant or dissatisfied
mother (or equal dominance between the parents). The female tends to
pursue a domestic life style if the father is dominant. A dissatisfied mother's influence is stronger than a dominant father, however.
Neither the parent's income, occupation or education, nor number of
siblings or mother's career was found to have any relationship in
shaping career versus domestic goals.[41]

Margaret Henning studied 125 U.S.-Canadian female corporate presidents
and vice presidents and found that these achieving women tended to be
either only children or the oldest in an all-girl family; had strong
self-esteem; and were close to their fathers. Because their parents

66

had the same ambitions for them as for a son, they grew up with the
same choices boys have. They were not a "girl's girl"; rather, they
liked intellectually serious girls. They dated males who respected
a woman's intellect. Once in the business world, they became a protege
of a male executive several levels higher in the company and related
to him as they once had to their father (e.g., role model and security
base).[42] Another study indicated that only moderate levels of warmth
and permissiveness, coupled with high achievement expectations by
parents, facilitated female achievement behavior. It was postulated
that if females are oversocialized with too much warmth or too much
restrictiveness, they tend to develop conforming, dependent (traditionally feminine) behavioral patterns. Further, fathers may be
particularly important in encouraging independence and achieving behavior in females, especially if the mothers are traditional women.
Achievement behavior can be reinforced or negated by other adults,
e.g., as in the case of teachers who react negatively to task-oriented
behavior in bright girls but positively to socially oriented behavior.[43]

Interestingly, research also shows that females achieve well during
early school years, but their achievement efforts tend to diminish as
they reach adolescence and adulthood.[44] Doing well in school does not
appear to make a female more intellectual or interested in intellectual
pursuits. On the other hand, school as a contributing factor to later
work achievement does not promote better school performance among
males.[45] Perhaps this is because society has not expected women to
"succeed" or wield power in the business world, but to be "feminine"--
i.e., submissive, unassertive, emotional and sociable. These expectations can become self-fulfilling prophecies. To succeed in the business
world, qualities such as determination, assertiveness and objective and
analytical thinking are needed, whether male or female. The problem
has been that a man with these traits is a "great guy" while a woman
traditionally has been "unfeminine." This has put many nontraditionally
achieving women into a doublebind. A frustration expressed by one
respondent who was a corporate manager before setting up her own company
was having to tread a thin line between "too little assertion" to get
results and too much assertion "for a woman." Another respondent, also
a corporate manager before becoming an entrepreneur, said,

"Soon after I married I knew the little bride's role was not for me.
I committed myself to a career. I soon ran straight into conflict

with my desire to succeed and other expectations of what I should and
should not be like. While trying to resolve my achievement-femininity
conflict, I reduced my efforts to avoid successful competition with
my male peers. For a while, it was easier to internalize their low
expectations of me than to swim upstream. Fortunately, I decided this
was dishonest to myself and what I wanted. When I kept running into
people--men and women--who saw my achieving behavior as offensively
overaggressive (and with the encouragement of my husband), I left the
company to go into business for myself."

Willingness to risk generally is conditioned by how a person sees the
costs versus the benefits of a particular action. Until the last 5
to 10 years, most women have perceived the risks as being unworthy of
the costs of surmounting the significant barriers to success. A female
entrepreneur said,

"Women are still a minority in the business world because their expectations haven't been there for as long as men's have. As attitudes continue they change--women will become inspired as they watch other women
succeed and as they themselves get more technical training and experience
as well as get used to thinking and doing for themselves. They'll not
be so afraid to take on responsibility or of making mistakes. They'll
no longer be caught between 'fear of failure' and 'fear of success.'"[46]

Just as more women now are moving into the management mainstream, more
women are likely to assume the risks of entrepreneurship. Most people--
men or women--are more self confident and willing to risk when they
understand a situation, their role in it, and have a reasonable chance
to succeed.

IN PERSPECTIVE

The entrepreneur must be able to spot opportunistic changes in the market and economy, risk the capital needed to implement them and develop
and manage a growing small business. This demands certain abilities
whether the entrepreneur is male or female. Interviews with female
entrepreneurs indicate little difference in the basic makeup of female
and male entrepreneurs. Female entrepreneurs are special people--just
as their male counterparts--who work, achieve, fight for their judgments and sacrifice private time and emotional energy. Once proven
knowledgeable and professional, women entrepreneurs felt they received

the same respect and admiration, for the most part, as a man. The women interviewed communicated extreme confidence in their abilities and
comfortableness with their aggressive drive to compete successfully--
an attitude that probably helps create their good business relationships and overall high productivity.

Some evidence exists that entrepreneurial characteristics can be developed. Perhaps what is first required is an understanding of the
qualities that are essential to entrepreneurship; the social and psychological factors that encourage or inhibit entrepreneurial drive; and the
business tools and concepts the entrepreneur must learn in order to
succeed. David McClelland has postulated the need for achievement as
the entrepreneur's primary motivator. The needs of high-achievement
motivation have been traced back to early childhood. Interestingly,
most researchers hypothesized a greater female need for affiliation
than achievement. Traditionally, women have been socialized to "achieve"
in directions other than owning and managing their own business (e.g.,
wife, mother or supportive--affiliative--role in an "acceptable"--cul-
turally approved--occupation for women). Thus, for entrepreneurship
to attract many women, and for them to be successful entrepreneurs,
these women will have to be resocialized first. An appraisal of currently changing female attitudes reflects more independent thinking
about what they can and cannot do and should or should not be, and a
strong indication of more of an achievement orientation outside the
traditionally "feminine" areas. Certainly, the old myths no longer
hold true. (See Figure III.) On the other hand, many women will not
ever want to live around the clock with their work to the extent they
would if they owned their own business and had to live with make-or-
break decisions. But, then, neither do many men.

Moreover, while achievement motivation is essential, it alone is not
enough. Skills are needed to transform desires and hopes into overt
actions. Similarly, skills without motivation are unlikely to gain
success. Those interested in developing entrepreneurial ability need
to focus on both the appropriate psychological makeup and functional
skills (ability to handle money, find risk capital, market, manage,
etc.).[47]

More research needs to be done to help women assess their entrepreneurial potential and education needs. It also could assist the

Figure III

Women and Work: Myths and Facts

Over time several reasons have been advanced to explain women's general failure to advance into more responsible, better paid jobs, despite the fact that they constitute 38 percent of the labor force. *On closer examination many of these explanations turn out to be more myth than fact.*

"Women are intellectually unsuited for professional work"

Studies show that two-thirds as many females as males among 11th grade students tested have engineering aptitude. Women's lack of professional and technical training does not follow from a deficit in potential ability, but rather from education, counselling and general socialization processes that direct women away from such careers.

"Women are physically unsuited for many jobs"

Specific aptitudes, including finger dexterity and hand-eye coordination, required for a number of crafts, are found as frequently among female as male students. As to weight lifting ability, men on the average are stronger than women, but clearly there is some overlapping, with some women being stronger than some men. (The Equal Employment Opportunity Commission is taking an increasingly critical look at any claim of sex as a "bona fide occupational qualification.").

"Women are emotionally unsuited for executive work"

Even professional opinion is divided on this point, but doctors point out that men as well as women have physical/emotional problems which interfere with their work. They assert that it is not the case that all women have difficulty performing work during menstrual periods or menopause. And studies by Dr. Estelle Ramey of Georgetown Medical School have proved repeatedly that women stand up to stress, on average, better than men do.

"Women don't have to support families"

Most women *do*, in fact, work to support themselves or others. 19 percent of working women are widowed, separated or divorced; 22 percent are single; and 25 percent have husbands with annual incomes below $7,000.

"Women have a higher rate of absenteeism"

Two major studies show there is a very little over-all difference between men and women in this regard. In one study, the annual time lost due to illness or injury was 5.6 days for women, 5.3 days for men; in the other, it was 5.3 days for women, 5.4 days for men.

"Women aren't seriously attached to their jobs"

Over-all *turnover* rates are indeed higher for women because they are disproportionately represented in lower occupations, where turnover is highest for both sexes. When compared with men in similar occupations, however, women's turnover rates are only marginally different. In terms of *occupational mobility*, men change jobs more frequently than women (10 percent vs. 7 percent). Women's *work life expectancy* is, on average, only 25 years compared with 43 years for men. However, between 1900 and 1960 it more than tripled (from 6.3 years to 20.1 years), and it is still increasing rapidly.

* * * * * * *

Clearly, there is evidence that tends to overthrow or seriously modify many of these preconceptions. One must conclude, therefore, that the real reasons for the failure of qualified women to advance more on an equal footing with men are to be sought in cultural biases and structural discrimination in employment.

Source: "Women & Business: Agenda for the Seventies," Business Environment Studies (General Electric, New York, New York), March 1972, p. 7.

entrepreneur in general by refocusing upon the special training needs
of the small business owner and manager. For instance, most business
schools train people to fit into a corporate environment. This is of
l.ttle help to the entrepreneur; administration of a small company is
largely different. Just to mention only two ways: short-term planning
is emphasized over long-term planning; and the entrepreneur needs to
be more of a generalist (know a little about everything) than the
corporate executive.

Advice from these experienced entrepreneurs to other women who want to
start their own business emphasized the all-consuming need for money
(and energy), especially during the start-up period; a real interest
in the business; the ability to risk and sacrifice friends, sports or
hobbies; the need for those who live with them to understand them;
and a continuing willingness to modify the product or service to what
the customer wants.

Many of the entrepreneurs previously employed confided an "identity
crisis" during the first year on their own. Suddenly they were no
longer defined by salary, title or tasks assigned by others. "Employee
benefits" were nonexistent--i.e.paid vacations, sick leave, medical care
or pension plans. No one said, "you're getting in over your head," or
"you're not doing the job right," or whatever. If the work situation
is not exactly right, it is the responsibility of the owner/boss to
change it. Most of the problems are directly traceable to the owner,
anyway. In the words of one of the interviewees, "Some aspects of owning your own business are good, some bad; but almost all are of your
own doing." The entrepreneur is free from "being bossed," meetings,
office politics and any other activities which may have been done in
a corporate setting. On the other hand, the entrepreneur has to become a good "self-manager." Unproductive days are no longer paid for
by someone else.

Other general points to consider before starting a business include:

●....*Know the business and its market extremely well*--Who are the
customers? Where is the market? What is the growth potential? Bankruptcy can come all too quickly to those who know little about the
business they go into.

71

●....*Investigate similar businesses and other expert sources of information.* Seek the advice of people who have accomplished what you aspire to do. A major source of information for the beginning entrepreneur as well as the established small business owner is the Small Business Administration. The SBA not only offers free advice but also provides booklets, checklists and films and holds seminars and workshops on all facets of starting a business. Also, a trade association can be a valuable source of information for industry growth trends, capital equipment, new technology, operating ratios and/or other pertinent data.[49] Local and state Chambers of Commerce also can be helpful in providing information on site locations and labor.

●....*Provide adequate and sound financing.* This requires some sound thinking and hard arithmetic. What are goals for the business immediately? Five years from now? What is the breakeven position? What is the immediate profit potential? What are goals for profit improvement? In the start-up stage, "seed" money is needed to cover things such as supplies, equipment and space needs, and costs of employees as well as accounting and legal services. Figure "normal" operating expenses (plus one's own salary) and then adjust upward (the amount experts recommend ranges from 25 percent to 50 percent) to cover unforeseen costs. Determine business volume needed to cover these expenses. What capital is needed to generate enough income to yield a "reasonable" profit after expenses? Keep in mind that insufficient starting capital ranks close to lack of managerial experience as a major reason for new business failures. Once the money needed and where it can be secured has been determined, then "shop" for it. Conventional sources of financing can be uninterested in providing funds during the highly speculative start-up period. Reward potential is often difficult to ascertain. To obtain sufficient financing during this stage, the entrepreneur generally must invest a substantial part of personal net worth.

Another major reason for small business failures, and one to guard against in one's own planning, is investing too much capital in fixed assets. These "frozen" dollars may not be available when needed for a crisis in opportunity. Obviously, sound and balanced financial planning is crucial.

●....*Good credit-granting practices.* Before extending credit, one should ask, "Can I afford it--do I have enough capital?" and "Do I know how to collect?" A general rule often given is to have enough capital

72

available to equal 1-1/2 month's credit sales.

●....*Analyze continuously for strengths and weaknesses.* Lack of business and managerial experience is one of the major reasons for small business failures. But even with experience, there is no assurance of success. However, one basic that is needed includes "balance" --good business plans (sound, realistic, measurable objectives, alternatives to achieve them, good controls), intimate knowledge of productivity methods applicable to the business, expertise in handling finances and expert buying and selling ability (e.g., hard questions that must be answered constantly: "What sells?" "At how fast a turnover?" "For what markup?"). Objectivity must be a rule on a day-to-day basis in each aspect of the business's operation. Well-selected management consultants, as well as the use of legal and accounting advisers, can be valuable in assessing policies, plans, projects and, in general, in viewing the business in true perspective.

In final perspective, the mood of the mature 1970s supports the increased involvement of women in all facets of our society, and especially in business. A redefinition of sex roles in America has been taking place. Men and women have begun to share the pressures and excitement of the working world. Increasingly, more options are opening up for both sexes. Entrepreneurship is a new frontier for women, offering unlimited opportunities. The extent to which women have, in the past, assumed an entrepreneurial role is statistically difficult to determine. However, the Census Bureau is conducting the first nationwide headcount of women in business for the U. S. Department of Commerce's Office of Minority Business Enterprise. Information is being gathered on partnerships, sole proprietorships and corporations. The report will break down various categories of geographic areas, industry and employment. While the 1970 Census reported 1,060,000 self-employed women, the new survey (base year 1972) will show for the first time how many women actually own businesses. And it is highly probable that in the next decade we will see the emergence of many more female owners/managers of small businesses. Successful women entrepreneurs will attract other women to the entrepreneurial role.

FOOTNOTES

[1]*Dun and Bradstreet Small Business Survey* (1975).

[2]Michael Palmer, "The Application of Psychological Testing to Entrepreneurial Potential," *California Management Review* Vol. 13, No. 3, pp. 32-38.

[3]Herbert E. Kierulff, "Can Entrepreneurs Be Developed?" *MSU Business Topics* (Winter 1975), p. 40.

[4]"Venture Capital and Management," *Boston College Management Seminary Proceedings* (28-29 May 1970), p. 83.

[5]A recent pilot study, *The Female Entrepreneur* (1975), was conducted by James W. Schreier at the Wisconsin Center for Venture Management. His study included an examination of entrepreneurial activity among Milwaukee, Wisconsin women who started their own businesses.

[6]As of March 1975

[7]In addition to personal motivations and characteristics, individuals tend to become entrepreneurs in proportion to entrepreneurial opportunity; i.e., rising income per capita in an expanding economy leads to investment opportunity. In turn, increased investment promotes entrepreneurial growth. Also, high levels of change combined with economic expansion (as, for example, the 10- to 15-year period after World War II) provides entrepreneurial opportunities.

[8]Discontinuity between how one perceives oneself and roles available to him in society. For a review of the "social marginality" concept, see H. P. Dickie-Clark, *The Marginal Situation* (Routledge & Kegan Paul, 1966).

[9]O. F. Collins, D. G. Moore and D. B. Unwalla, "The Enterprising Man," *MSU Business Topics* (1964).

[10]Second-generation entrepreneurs appear to have a much lower level of social marginality than their parents. Frequently they admit that if they had not inherited it, they would not have created the business. See Charles B. Swayne and William R. Tucker, *The Effective Entrepreneur* (New Jersey: General Learning Press, 1973), p. 14.

[11]A socially marginal person with a blue-collar background is believed to be more likely to choose an extreme political ideology or trade union role than to become an owner/manager.

[12]According to A. H., Maslow *Motivation and Personality* (Harper & Row, 1954), ego needs involve self-esteem (self-respect, self-confidence, autonomy) and reputation (status, recognition, appreciation, and respect of others).

[13]Swayne, *The Effective Entrepreneur*, Chapter 3.

[14]David C. McClelland, J. W. Atkinson, R. A. Clark and E. L. Lowell *The Achievement Motive* (New York: Appleton-Century-Crofts, Inc., 1953).

[15]David C. McClelland, *The Achieving Society* (Princeton, N. J.: Van Nostrand, 1961), p. 238.

[16]Ralph M. Hogdill, *Individual Behavior and Group Achievement* (Oxford University Press, 1969) Chapter 5.

[17]Affiliation was included because traditionally women have been labeled as having high affiliation needs in contrast to high achievement needs. See Finding #6.

[18]The women surveyed in the Schreier's study, *The Female Entrepreneur*, started their businesses (1) out of economic necessity (whether prompted by a specific financial crisis or a family crisis--e.g., a divorce), (2) as a hobby or (3) because they saw a marketing opportunity and seized it.

[19]As reported by John Cunniff, "Obstacles for Female Managers" (by Professor Eugene Jennings, Michigan State University), *Atlanta Journal* (11 July 1975).

[20]Joan Lipman, "Female Entrepreneurs Like Del Goetz Make 'Man's Work' Pay Off," *New York Times*, Volume 219, p. 1, 19.

[21]Schreier's study, *The Female Entrepreneur*, showed a tendency for entrepreneurs not to communicate what is on their mind...not that they do not mean to, but because they just do not think to do it.

[22]Swayne, *Effective Entrepreneur*, p. 25.

[23]Douglas McGregor, *The Human Side of Enterprise* (New York: McGraw-Hill, 1960).

[24]Robert Black and Jane Mouton, *The Managerial Grid* (Houston, Texas: Gulf Publishing Company, 1964).

[25]Swayne, *Effective Entrepreneur*, p. 14.

[26]Rohrer, Hibler, Replogh, *Managers for Tomorrow* (New American Library, 1969), p. 258.

[27]Richard Ivan Henderson, "The Best of Two Worlds: The Entrepreneurial Manager," *Journal of Small Business Management*, p. 5.

[28]According to economic life-cycle models, a business develops through four stages: (1) birth and struggle for survival, (2) adolescence and rapid growth, (3) maturity and (4) senescence and death.

[29]Larry E. Greiner, "Evolution and Revolution as Organizations Grow," *Harvard Bsuiness Review* (July-August 1972), p. 39.

[30]Swayne, *Effective Entrepreneurship*, p. 16.

[31]The question asked the respondents was: "Aside from general obstacles to entrepreneurial success for anyone (e.g., unfavorable economic climate, governmental restrictions, and so on), what particular barriers have you experienced which you feel were unique to you as a female entrepreneur?

[32]The Equal Credit Opportunity Act (effective 28 October 1975), prohibits discrimination against credit applicants on the basis of sex or marital status. It covers all those who regularly extend credit to individuals, including banks, finance companies, department stores, credit card issuers and government agencies, such as the Small Business Administration.

75

[33]"Venture Capital and Management," *Proceedings* (Second Annual Boston College Management Seminar, 28-29 May 1970), p. 52.

[34]Ibid.

[35]New female entrepreneurs expressed amazement at learning the seeming endlessness of regulations that affected them at city (e.g., business license, zoning restrictions), state (e.g., sales and income taxes, workers'compensation) and federal (e.g., payroll tax, social security, income tax, unemployment tax) levels, for example.

[36]Lipman, "Female Entrepreneurs," p. 1, 19.

[37]"Venture Capital and Management."

[38]A nonprofit, New York-based firm with twelve testing facilities across the country that has tested for differences in male and female aptitudes since 1922. Thousands of men and women of all ages have been tested; however, the largest sample has been young high school graduates.

[39]David C. McClelland, "Achievement Motivation Can be Developed," *Harvard Business Review*, Volume 43, Number 6 (November-December 1965)

[40]Aletha Huston Stein and Margaret M. Bailey, "The Socialization of Achievement Orientation in Females," *The Psychological Bulletin 80* (November 1973), pp. 345-366.

[41]Jean Lipman-Blumen, "What Shapes a Woman's Wish for a Career or To Be A Full-time Housewife?" *Scientific American* (May 1973).

[42]Margaret Henning (Ph.D. diss. Simmons College).

[43]See U. Bronfenbrenner, "Some Familial Antecedents of Responsibility and Leadership in Adolescents," in L. Petrullo and B. M. Bass, eds., *Leadership and Interpersonal Behavior* (New York: Holt, 1961), pp. 239-271; and W. C. Becker, "Consequences of Different Kinds of Parental Discipline," in M. L. Hoffman and L. W. Hoffman, eds., *Review of Child Development Research*, Vol. 7 (New York: Russell Sage, 1964), pp. 169-208.

[44]Jean D. Grambs and Walter B. Waetjen, "Being Equally Different: A New Right for Boys and Girls," *The National Elementary Principal*, Vol. XLVI, No. 2 (November 1966), p. 63.

[45]Ibid., p. 62.

[46]See Matina S. Horner, "Toward an Understanding of Achievement--Related Conflicts in Women," *Journal of Social Issues 28* (1972), pp. 157-176.

[47]Douglas E. Durand, "Training and Development of Entrepreneurs: A Comparison of Motivation and Skills Approaches," *Journal of Small Business Management*, Vol. 12, No. 4 (12 October 1971), p. 26.

[48]Ibid.

[49]A full listing of trade associations can be found in *National Trade and Professional Associations of the United States* (Washington, D.C.: Columbia Book Publishers).

[28]

IS IT EQUALLY DIFFICULT FOR FEMALE ENTREPRENEURS TO START BUSINESSES IN ALL COUNTRIES?*

by Lars Kolvereid, Scott Shane, and Paul Westhead

Do men and women face the same environmental conditions for business start-up across different countries? A large body of literature now explains that organizations face different environments as measured by differences in resources, technology, information, and external relationships (Tsai, MacMillan, and Low 1991). Moreover, environmental differences are perceptual as well as objective, and business people act in response to the perceptual environment (Tosi, Aldag, and Storey 1973; Tsai, MacMillan, and Low 1991).

Little work has examined how perceptions of the environment influence business formation of male and female entrepreneurs across countries. While the organizational theory literature has identified four characteristics of organizational environments relevant to ven-

ture formation: munificence, resource availability, hostility, and uncertainty (Tsai, MacMillan, and Low 1991), no one has investigated whether these environmental characteristics are perceived differently by male and female entrepreneurs. Nor do we know whether these perceptions differ between male and female entrepreneurs across countries.

There is evidence that these characteristics influence entrepreneurs in general. Environmental munificence, which measures the worth of the venture opportunity, encourages business formation (Covin and Slevin 1989, Dandridge 1982). Resource availability, which reflects the presence of labor, capital, and market demand, increases venture success (Cooper and Dunkelberg 1981; Dubini 1989; Holt 1987; Olofsson, Petterson, and Wahlbin 1986; Freedman 1983; Dandridge 1982). Environmental hostility, which reflects the fierceness of competition, discourages new venture formation (Covin and Slevin 1989, Holt 1987), and the uncertainty of the business environment inhibits business formation (Bull and Winter 1991, Bearse 1982). However, most of this research has been carried out in the United States using samples of predominantly male entrepreneurs.

Dr. Kolvereid is professor of management at Bodo University in Bodo, Norway. His research interests are in entrepreneurship in Scandinavia and Eastern Europe.

Dr. Shane is assistant professor of strategic management at Georgia Institute of Technology in Atlanta. His research interests are in cross-cultural and international issues in entrepreneurship and corporate venturing.

Dr. Westhead is senior lecturer at Cranfield University in the United Kingdom. His research focuses on start-up businesses in the United Kingdom.

*Acknowledgements: We would like to thank the Sol C. Snider Entrepreneurial Center at the Wharton School of the University of Pennsylvania, the Graduate School of Business and Public Management at Victoria University of Wellington, New Zealand, and the Royal Norwegian Ministry for Industrial Affairs for the financial support that made this research possible. We would also like to thank the Society of Associated Researchers in Entrepreneurship under whose auspices the data for this study were collected.

A small body of literature suggests that these environmental factors are perceived differently by male and female venture initiators. Female venture initiators have more trouble getting access to capital (Hisrich and O'Brien 1981, Collerette and Aubry 1990) perhaps because of a lack of confidence shown by banks, suppliers, and clients (Schwartz 1975, Lee-Gosselin and Grise 1990). They find it more difficult to get business training (Hisrich and Brush 1984; Knight and Gilbertson, forthcoming; Lee-Gosselin and Grise 1990) and have more trouble attracting qualified labor (Knight and Gilbertson, forthcoming).

No research has yet examined perceptions of the business start-up environment across countries. However, unemployment rates, distribution of labor skills, rates of economic growth, availability of capital, interest rates, sources of capital, and proximity of producers and customers all vary from nation to nation. While within nations, environmental influences on business formation vary by location (Denison and Alexander 1986). If perceptions of the environment vary by country, there is a clear need to control for this effect in cross-national research.

HYPOTHESIS AND METHODOLOGY

The hypothesis tested here is:

Controlling for the effect of country, do female entrepreneurs perceive the business start-up environment to be characterized by greater resource scarcity, turbulence, hostility, and uncertainty than do male entrepreneurs?

Survey Instrument

This study is part of a Society for Associate Researchers in International Entrepreneurship (SARIE) project on new business formation started in 1986. At that time, an international group of researchers collected data from 2,278 venture initiators and 1,733 non-venture initiators in 14 countries. In 1989, the research group decided to develop an abbreviated and improved version of the original questionnaire, aimed at the development of a new international database. This database was developed to look at the performance, growth, and characteristics of new ventures across national boundaries. In order to increase response rates from the original pilot study conducted by an international research group (Scheinberg and MacMillan 1988), the questionnaire was dramatically reduced.

The questionnaire contains items concerning the entrepreneur and the organization, reasons leading to start-up, perceptions of the start-up environment, and attitudes toward entrepreneurship. This study looks at the environmental section of the SARIE survey only. This section consists of 23 items, each of which described a possible state of the environment at the time of the start-up. The questions covered the availability of resources (labor, machines and equipment, suppliers, customers, and capital), the environmental complexity and diversity (range of incentives, the number of new businesses, and the complexity involved in targeting the market), the rate of change in the environment (the stability of price, price-cost margin, and technology), and the degree of perceived hostility and uncertainty (the number of business failures, political uncertainty). Respondents were asked to indicate the degree to which they agreed to each statement along a five-point Likert-type scale ranging from strongly disagree to strongly agree with the statement provided.

Sample

Data were collected from venture initiators in Great Britain, Norway, and New Zealand. Only independent, for-profit businesses with at least one employee in addition to the owner were included. Also, they had to have received their first orders between 1986 and 1989. This definition has been widely used in previous studies of new firm formation (Cross 1981; Storey 1982; Scheinberg and MacMillan 1988; Dubini 1989; Blaise, Toulouse, and Clement 1990).

In New Zealand the survey was mailed to 500 venture initiators who were randomly selected from government records on new ventures. Sixty-four were returned undeliverable; 138 responses were received, for a response rate of 28 percent. In Norway, the target sample of new firms was identified using the Bryde's Trade Register (a list of all new ventures). The questionnaire was translated into Norwegian and back translated into English to ensure accuracy. It was then mailed to all new businesses started in 4 (out of 19) counties in Norway. Of the 1,146 questionnaires mailed out, 108 were returned undelivered or insufficiently answered. After one reminder, 250 venture initiators answered the questionnaire, for a response rate of 24 percent. In Great Britain, the target sample was abstracted from industrial trade directories. The questionnaire was mailed to 1,000 venture initiators. A total of 209 were returned completed, yielding a response rate of 21 percent.

When evaluating the response rates, one should bear in mind the difficulties involved in defining the sample frame and finding accurate lists of new firms. A high proportion of businesses approached failed to be independent companies but rather were co-ops, subsidiaries, or franchises. In addition, several businesses had a number of owners or partners but no employees. Therefore, we suspect that many of the venture initiators who did not respond to the questionnaire chose not to because they did not fit our criteria for new firm founders. The demographics of the venture initiators in our study are surprisingly similar given their establish-ment in different countries by different founders. No statistically significant differences were found in the distribution of venture initiators across industries either by country or by gender. Similarly, there appeared to be no significant differences in employment by nationality or gender. The locations where they started are also similar. Table 1 shows a demographic profile of the entrepreneurs in our study.

A comparison of male and female respondents was undertaken. Venture initiators who ran their companies as couples were excluded from the analysis. There were fewer female entrepreneurs in the sample than male entrepreneurs (table 1). This illustrates a dilemma researchers are faced with when investigating differences across gender among entrepreneurs. On one hand, if a random selection approach is used, the sample must be relatively large to allow for gender comparisons when women account for only 8 to 12 percent of the new businesses initiated. On the other hand, if stratified sampling is applied, the stratification process itself may introduce errors.

DATA ANALYSIS

In many cross-cultural surveys, significant differences are often found on individual items not because the people in the different countries differ on the degree to which they hold a belief, but because they have different interpretations of the questions. To ensure that respondents in the three countries were answering the same questions, we factor analyzed the 23 environmental influence questions. Factor analysis shows the extent to which people answering a question are likely to answer that question in the same way they answered similar questions. If the same factors appear in all three countries, it is more likely that the interpretations of

Table 1
DEMOGRAPHIC PROFILE OF THE BUSINESSES SURVEYED

	Great Britain		New Zealand		Norway	
Number of respondents						
Total	209		138		250	
Male	192	(92%)	122	(88%)	219	(88%)
Female	17	(8%)	16	(12%)	31	(12%)
Mean number of partners at start-up						
Male	2.1		2.5		2.5	
Female	1.9		2.1		1.6	
Industry sector*						
Farming, fishing and mining						
Male	1	(0.5%)	6	(4 %)	8	(3 %)
Female	0	(0 %)	1	(0.7%)	1	(0.4%)
Manufacturing						
Male	80	(38%)	11	(8 %)	31	(12%)
Female	9	(4%)	3	(2.1%)	2	(1%)
Construction						
Male	16	(8%)	12	(9%)	38	(15 %)
Female	0	(0%)	0	(0%)	1	(0.4%)
Services						
Male	95	(45%)	77	(56%)	136	(54%)
Female	8	(4%)	12	(9%)	27	(11%)
Location of Business*						
Rural						
Male	63	(30%)	12	(9%)	111	(44%)
Female	7	(3%)	3	(2%)	21	(8%)
Minor City						
Male	114	(55%)	35	(25%)	74	(30%)
Female	9	(4%)	5	(4%)	9	(4%)
Major City						
Male	14	(7 %)	52	(38%)	26	(10 %)
Female	1	(0.5%)	6	(4%)	1	(0.4%)
Capital						
Male	1	(0.5%)	9	(7%)	1	(0.4%)
Female	0	(0 %)	2	(1%)	0	(0 %)
Mean number of employees at start-up						
Male	2.2		2.2		2.7	
Female	1.9		1.3		2.4	
Mean age of business initiator (years)						
Male	42.9		40.2		38.6	
Female	41.2		43.1		38.1	
Highest education level achieved*						
Compulsory						
Male	68	(33%)	39	(28%)	28	(11%)
Female	3	(1%)	10	(7%)	8	(3%)
Professional						
Male	79	(38%)	42	(30%)	107	(43%)
Female	10	(5%)	3	(2%)	20	(8%)
University						
Male	31	(15%)	19	(14%)	60	(24 %)
Female	3	(1%)	2	(1%)	1	(0.4%)
Graduate Study						
Male	13	(6 %)	7	(5 %)	19	(8 %)
Female	1	(0.5%)	1	(0.7%)	2	(0.8%)

*The total number of respondents in each category may not equal the total number of respondents listed for each country because some respondents did not answer all questions.

the questions are consistent across the countries.

The factor analyses yielded three factors which were consistent across the three countries, containing 9 of the 23 questions. Only items which loaded .4 or better on one of the factors were included, and only factors composed of three or more items were kept. The three factors found were: labor availability, stability, and hostility/uncertainty. Further analysis pertains only to the questions which loaded on one of the factors. Table 2 shows the questions that compose these factors and their loadings.

We believe these results are strong, not just because the items load on the same factors across the three countries, but because there is agreement with previous researchers using a similar survey in other countries. The three items which compose the resource availability factor are used by Dubini (1989). Although she conducted her study in Italy three years before ours, and the other items she used were different from ours, the resource availability items form the same factor in both studies. Unfortunately, no other research is available to check the validity and reliability of the other factors.

In our research, we did not develop factor scores. Since our a priori belief was that there would be significant differences across gender as well as nationality, we did not believe that factors created to be consistent across nations would necessarily be consistent across gender. This reasoning turned out to be correct. Factor analysis by gender would not have yielded the same factors as factor analysis by nationality. Therefore, in this study, the factor analysis was treated just as a means of ensuring similarity of interpretation of questions across countries. Individual questions were analyzed separately.

Multiple analysis of variance (MANOVA) was conducted to determine the effect of gender, nationality, and the gender-nationality interaction on the nine remaining environmental items as the dependent variables. MANOVA is particularly appropriate under the present circumstances where the objective is to analyze the effect of different categorical variables (nationality, gender, and the interaction between nationality and gender) on a number of dependent variables (nine environmental factors) simultaneously.

Results

Table 3 shows that there are no significant gender-country interactions, but there are significant national and gender differences among the responses. However, further examination of the data (using ANOVA) shows that the gender differences are restricted to one item of the questionnaire.

Significant country differences are found for items making up all three factors. On the labor availability factor, skilled labor was perceived as being more readily available in Norway than in the other two countries. There were no significant gender-based differences on these items and no significant gender-nationality interactions.

On the second factor, stability, there were also significant country differences. Norwegian entrepreneurs faced significantly more stable sales in their industry than New Zealand entrepreneurs who, in turn, faced more stable sales than British entrepreneurs. A similar pattern is found for the stability of the price-cost margin. Again no significant gender differences or gender-nationality interactions were found.

The third factor, hostility/uncertainty, shows significant gender differences on the perception of political uncertainty in the country. Female entrepreneurs perceived higher political uncertainty

Table 2
FACTOR LOADINGS OF THE ENVIRONMENTAL PERCEPTION ITEMS FOR
BRITISH, NEW ZEALAND, AND NORWEGIAN ENTREPRENEURS*

	Britain	New Zealand	Norway
Labor Availability			
Skilled labor available	.82	.81	.77
Managerial labor available	.86	.81	.85
Labor skilled in new technologies available	.76	.75	.77
Stability			
Annual sales in my industry relatively stable	.73	.82	.77
The price-cost margin in my industry relatively stable	.68	.74	.75
The technology used in my industry relatively stable	.60	.65	.61
Hostility/Uncertainty			
Large number of business failures in the area that I live	.84	.68	.77
Large number of business failures in my industry	.83	.68	.77
Political uncertainty in the country	.68	.77	.74

*This table is based upon a separate Varimax factor analysis of responses for each country. All factors have eigenvalues greater than 1.0. Only items which loaded on the same factor for all countries are included. Only factors on which at least three items loaded are reported. Only items which loaded greater than .4 were accepted.

than male entrepreneurs. No significant country differences or country-gender interactions were found on perceptions of political uncertainty. Significant national differences were found on perceptions of business failures in the area in which the entrepreneur lives and in his or her industry. On both items, British and New Zealand entrepreneurs perceived greater numbers of business failures than Norwegian entrepreneurs. Table 4 indicates one significant gender-nationality interaction. British female entrepreneurs perceived a greater number of business failures in the area in which they lived than did Norwegian male entrepreneurs. Tables 4 and 5 show these data.

These data show relatively few significant gender differences in perceptions

Table 3
PERCEPTIONS OF THE BUSINESS START-UP ENVIRONMENT BY COUNTRY AND GENDER*
(MANOVA)

Test	Gender X Country	Country	Gender
Pillais	0.044 (1.278)	0.119 (3.617***)	0.039 (2.320**)
Hotellings	0.045 (1.283)	0.128 (3.644***)	0.041 (2.320**)
Wilkes	0.957 (1.281)	0.884 (3.630***)	0.961 (2.320**)

* Entries in table are coefficients and (F-ratios): *** indicates $p < .01$; ** indicates $p < .05$; * indicates $p < .10$ (in two-tailed tests).

Table 4
PERCEPTIONS OF THE START-UP ENVIRONMENT BY COUNTRY AND GENDER
BY ITEM (ANOVA)[a]

	Gender X Country	Country	Gender
Labor Availability			
Skilled labor available	1.050	9.031***	1.879
Managerial labor available	1.575	1.402	1.153
Labor skilled in new technologies available	1.948	1.886	1.163
Stability			
Annual sales in my industry relatively stable	0.779	5.262***	0.438
The price-cost margin in my industry relatively stable	0.737	8.079***	0.001
The technology used in my industry relatively stable	0.342	1.493	0.030
Hostility/Uncertainty			
Large number of business failures in the area that I live	3.019**	6.132***	1.764
Large number of new business failures in my industry	0.078	2.420*	0.025
Political uncertainty in the country	0.956	1.880	5.229**

[a] Entries in table are F statistics. Significance of F: *** indicates $p < .01$, ** indicates $p < .05$, * indicates $p < .10$.

Table 5
MEAN VALUES OF PERCEPTIONS OF THE START-UP ENVIRONMENT FOR
MALE AND FEMALE ENTREPRENEURS IN THE THREE COUNTRIES

	All Countries		Great Britain			New Zealand			Norway		
	M	F	All	M	F	All	M	F	All	M	F
Labor Availability											
Skilled labor	2.84	3.10	2.59	2.56	2.94	2.70	2.70	2.56	3.24	3.19	3.48
Managerial labor	2.71	2.56	2.47	2.46	2.63	2.75	2.80	2.27	2.86	2.89	2.69
Technical labor	2.58	2.49	2.36	2.34	2.56	2.53	2.57	2.07	2.80	2.81	2.69
Stability											
Stable sales	3.22	3.36	3.84	2.81	3.19	3.32	3.34	3.20	3.55	3.55	3.54
Stable margins	3.34	3.40	3.01	3.00	3.13	3.31	3.33	3.13	3.66	3.65	3.69
Stable technology	3.27	3.30	3.08	3.07	3.19	3.45	3.42	3.60	3.37	3.39	3.19
Hostility/Uncertainty											
Failures in area	2.44	2.58	2.62	2.57	3.19	2.54	2.54	2.27	2.29	2.26	2.39
Failures in industry	2.40	2.41	2.62	2.62	2.56	2.42	2.38	2.40	2.22	2.20	2.33
Political uncertainty	2.43	2.73	2.44	2.40	2.94	2.79	2.76	2.80	2.32	2.29	2.57

of the influence of the environment on business formation. Many more significant national differences are found. Surprisingly, few significant interactions of gender and nationality were discovered, and the interaction effect in the MANOVA analysis was insignificant. While conclusions of this study are tentative because of the relative similarity of the three countries studied, the study shows that gender is not as important as nationality in differentiating environmental influences.

RESEARCH LIMITATIONS

The snapshot survey methodology is not without its limitations and its critics (Mason 1989). Despite attempts to produce a logical and thorough survey of new firm founders in each of the countries, the methodology can be questioned on several counts. First, the target sample of new firm founders was different in each of the countries studied because of the necessity of using different data sources. However, in each of the countries, only those firms satisfying criteria of independence, for-profit status, date of start-up, and number of employees were included. Second, better response rates could have been achieved had a direct face-to-face personal survey approach been adopted. However, the choice of a postal survey approach was based on time and resource constraints and the need to begin examining cross-national trends in new business formation. Third, the surveys only gained responses from venture initiators whose firms had survived through 1990. The surveys can say nothing about the characteristics of the businesses which had not survived. But, since we are only interested in comparing cross-national and gender differences among surviving firms, this limitation is acceptable. Fourth, like many other studies, this is a retrospective study which relied upon the mem-

ory of the founders for the recall of specific circumstances, such as environmental conditions at the time of start-up. Fifth, because of the relatively low response rates, we caution readers against extrapolation of the findings or drawing any generalized conclusions. Finally, there is a danger that the relatively low number of female entrepreneurs in the sample may have influenced the results.

DISCUSSION

Even though no previous research has focused on gender differences in perceptions of the business environment in general terms, several more specific aspects of the environment have been investigated. For example, several studies have reported complaints of gender bias in new venture financing (Hisrich and Brush 1987, Hisrich and O'Brien 1982, Humphreys and McClung 1981, Pellegrino and Reese 1982). In a study to determine whether these accusations were justified, Buttner and Rosen (1989) found that loan officers showed no gender bias. Buttner and Rosen (1992) also failed to find a gender bias in the securing of other forms of capital for a new business. The findings of the present research support those reported by Buttner and Rosen (1989, 1992), suggesting that male and female entrepreneurs in western countries do not face very different business environments.

Even though the items used to measure perceptions of the environment in the present research are descriptive in nature, some of them also capture the evaluative/affective dimension. The political uncertainty item, the only item to which male and female entrepreneurs scored differently, is probably the item containing the strongest evaluative/affective flavor. A possible explanation may be that men and women do not perceive their environment very differently but tend to evaluate it differently. This effect may be due to differences in the value systems of men and women.

One policy implication of this study is that if governments seek to promote venture formation, their policies should differ across countries. If the environmental influences that promote business formation differ across countries, policies designed to promote venture formation are unlikely to be importable. However, these policies can be the same for male and female entrepreneurs.

This study also suggests that further research on female venture formation should be encouraged. The conclusions developed from such study should take into account the cultural beliefs about women prevalent in the society under investigation. Despite the relatively weak effect of gender reported here, we need to continue our pursuit of theories of venture formation by categorizing business initiators into types and examining differences between these types. Among areas that we need to examine are differences between old and young, technical and non-technical, international and domestic, and large and small venturers. The evidence on national differences found here suggests that if we follow Gartner's (1985) advice and develop conditional theories of venture formation rather than universal ones, we will learn more about what promotes business formation.

REFERENCES

Bearse, P. (1982), "A Study of Entrepreneurship by Region and SMSA Size," in *Frontiers of Entrepreneurship Research 1982*, ed. K. Vesper, Wellesley, Mass.: Babson College.

Blaise, R., J. Toulouse, and B. Clement (1990), "International Comparisons of Entrepreneurial Motivation Based on Personal Equation, Hierarchical Analysis, and Other Statistical Methods," in *Proceedings of the 39th World Conference for Small Business*, ed. R.

Gomolus and W. Ward, Washington, D.C.: International Council for Small Business.

Buttner, E.H., and B. Rosen (1989), "Funding New Business Ventures: Are Decision Makers Biased Against Women Entrepreneurs?" *Journal of Business Venturing*, 4 (July), 249-261.

_____ (1992), "Rejection in the Loan Application Process: Male and Female Entrepreneurs' Perceptions and Subsequent Intentions," *Journal of Small Business Management* 30 (1), 58-65.

Bull, I., and F. Winter (1991), "Community Differences in Business Births and Business Growths," *Journal of Business Venturing* 6 (1), 29-44.

Collerette, P., and P. Aubry (1990), "Socioeconomic Evolution of Women Business Owners in Quebec," *Journal of Business Ethics*, 9 (2), 417-422.

Cooper, A., and W. Dunkelberg (1981), "A New Look at Business Entry: Experiences of 1,805 Entrepreneurs," in *Frontiers of Entrepreneurship Research 1981*, ed. K. Vesper, Wellesley, Mass.: Babson College.

Covin, J. and D. Slevin (1989), "Strategic Management of Small Firms in Hostile and Benign Environments," *Strategic Management Journal* 10 (1), 75-87.

Cross, M. (1981), *New Firm Formation and Regional Development*. Farnborough: Gower.

Dandridge, T. (1982), "Encouraging Urban Entrepreneurship," in *Frontiers of Entrepreneurship Research 1982*, ed. K. Vesper, Wellesley, Mass.: Babson College.

Denison, D., and J. Alexander (1986), "Patterns and Profiles of Entrepreneurs: Data from Entrepreneurship Forums," in *Frontiers of Entrepreneurship Research 1986*, ed. R. Ronstadt, J. Hornaday, R. Peterson, and K. Vesper, Wellesley, Mass.: Babson College.

Dubini, P. (1989), "Motivational and Environmental Influences on Business

Start Ups: Some Hints for Public Policies," *Journal of Business Venturing* 4 (1), 11-36.

Freedman, A. (1983), "New Technology Firms: Critical Location Factors," in *Frontiers of Entrepreneurship Research 1983*, ed. J. Hornaday, J. Timmons, and K. Vesper, Wellesley, Mass.: Babson College.

Gartner, W. (1985), "A Conceptual Framework for Describing the Phenomenon of New Venture Creation," *Academy of Management Review* 10 (4), 696-706.

Hisrich, R., and C. Brush (1987), "Women Entrepreneurs: A Longitudinal Study," in *Frontiers of Entrepreneurship Research 1987*, ed. N.C. Churchill, J.A. Hornaday, B.A. Kirchhoff, O.J. Krasner, and K.H. Vesper, Wellesley, Mass.: Babson College.

Hisrich, R., and M. O'Brien (1981), "The Woman Entrepreneur from a Business and Sociological Perspective," in *Frontiers of Entrepreneurship Research 1981*, ed. K. Vesper, Wellesley, Mass.: Babson College.

Holt, D. (1987), "Network Support Systems: How Communities Can Encourage Entrepreneurship," in *Frontiers of Entrepreneurship Research 1987*, ed. N.C. Churchill, J.A. Hornaday, B.A. Kirchhoff, O.J. Krasner, and K.H. Vesper, Wellesley, Mass.: Babson College.

Humphreys, M., and J. McClung (1981), "Women Entrepreneurs in Oklahoma," *Review of Regional Economics and Business* 6 (2), 13-20.

Knight, R., and D. Gilbertson (forthcoming), *Entrepreneurship in New Zealand*.

Lee-Gosselin, H., and J. Grise (1990), "Are Women Owner Managers Challenging Our Definitions of Entrepreneurship? An In-Depth Survey,"

Journal of Business Ethics 9 (2), 423-433.

Mason, C.M. (1989), "Explaining Recent Trends in New Firm Formation in the UK: Some Evidence from South Hampshire," *Regional Studies* 23(4), 331-346.

Olofsson, C., G. Petterson, and C. Wahlbin (1986), "Opportunities and Obstacles: A Study of Start-Ups and Their Development," in *Frontiers of Entrepreneurship Research 1986*, ed. R. Ronstadt, J. Hornaday, R. Peterson, and K. Vesper, Wellesley, Mass.: Babson College.

Pellegrino, E., and B. Reese (1982), "Perceived Formative and Operational Problems Encountered by Female Entrepreneurs in Retail and Service Firms," *Journal of Small Business Management* 20 (April), 15-24.

Scheinberg, S., and I. MacMillan (1988), "An Eleven Country Study of the Motivations to Start a Business," in *Frontiers of Entrepreneurship Research 1988*, ed. B. Kirchhoff, W. Long, W. McMullan, K. Vesper, and W. Wetzel, Wellesley, Mass.: Babson College.

Schwartz, E. (1975), "Entrepreneurship, A New Female Frontier," *Journal of Contemporary Business* 5, 47-76.

Storey, D.J. (1982), *Entrepreneurship and the New Firm*. London: Croon Helm.

Tosi, H., R. Aldag, and R. Storey (1973), "On the Measurement of the Environment: An Assessment of the Lawrence and Lorsch Environmental Uncertainty Questionnaire," *Administrative Science Quarterly* 18, 27-36.

Tsai, W., I. MacMillan, and M. Low (1991), "Effects of Strategy and Environment on Corporate Venture Success in Industrial Markets," *Journal of Business Venturing* 6 (1), 9-28.

[29]

ENTREPRENEURSHIP & REGIONAL DEVELOPMENT, 9 (1997), 221–238

Invisible entrepreneurs: the neglect of women business owners by mass media and scholarly journals in the USA

TED BAKER, HOWARD E. ALDRICH and NINA LIOU

CB#3210, Department of Sociology, UNC-CH, Chapel Hill, NC 27599-3210, USA. email: bak@email.unc.edu; howard_aldrich@unc.edu; nliou@gibbs.oit.unc.edu; Home page: http://www.unc.edu/~healdric/

We examine a paradox: gains in women's business ownership in the USA have been extraordinary, whereas popular press coverage has actually declined, and academic articles on women owners are also exceedingly rare. We offer three simple explanations for this: (1) the media no longer consider women's business 'news'; (2) scholars are not interested in women's firms because they are mostly small and relatively unimportant; and (3) documented differences between men and women owners are few and thus reporters and scholars no longer look for them. Two dissenting voices, however, complicate the picture: small but significant gender differences have been found in studies of social behaviour and leadership; and, advocacy groups have strongly asserted that women owners possess unique advantages. Why haven't these voices been heard? We argue that androcentrism has clouded our perceptions of gender differences and blinded journalists and academics in two ways: (1) women's distinctive contributions have been muted as they have adapted to institutions of business that were already gendered, and (2) the search for distinctive contributions by women owners has been thwarted by assumptions that traditional ways of doing business are 'natural'.

Keywords: women; entrepreneur; androcentrism; gender; sex; business owner.

1. Introduction: the paradox

Some of the greatest gains achieved by US women in recent decades have been in business ownership, but media and academic attention to this progress and its consequences have been meager at best. Paralleling similar gains in the UK, Germany and other European nations (Cromie and Birley 1992, Marlow 1996, ENSR 1995), US women have achieved a six-fold increase in their percentage share of business ownership. However, as is shown in this paper, this phenomenal growth – this gender revolution in business ownership – has gone largely unnoticed by major US newspapers. Attention to women owners has actually decreased over the past decade. Similarly, despite burgeoning academic interest and writing about 'women's issues' and gender, little scholarly effort has been directed towards the study of women's business ownership. Academic articles on women business owners are still rare, and mainstream entrepreneurship journals pay little attention to gender issues. The discrepancy between achievements in business ownership and lack of attention to them poses a paradox for us: why has women's spectacular progress in business ownership been virtually *invisible*.

Our attempt to resolve the paradox is organized into four parts: (1) a description of the issue; (2) the development of a straightforward, gender-neutral explanation of what we observe; (3) a review of some dissident voices, rebutting our gender-neutral interpretation and arguing for more attention to gender differences; and (4) a call for more subtle research in the area of gendered differences in business ownership.

First, we demonstrate the extent of the paradox through detailed examination of patterns of popular newspaper and scholarly coverage of women's business ownership in the USA. We find that the paradox is powerful: a huge wave of women owners has flooded the US business landscape, but very few authors have taken notice. The patterns of neglect hold for two major national newspapers, for the general business press, and for scholarly business and entrepreneurship journals.

Second, we offer some simple, common-sense explanations that treat the paradox as largely unproblematic. If women are taking advantage of emerging ownership opportunities by creating firms that mimic men's, the story is simply old news. In the absence of a convincing demonstration that women's ownership of business really matters, reporters and scholars will ignore them. Additionally, élite academic journals tend to focus on patterns and issues important to large businesses, and a majority of women-owned firms are still small 'lifestyle' businesses – typically sole proprietorships. Documented differences between men and women owners are few and thus reporters and scholars no longer look for them.

Third, we review two sets of dissenting voices that have been raised, by scholars researching sex and gender issues, and by women's advocacy groups. Some scholars argue that there really are systematic empirical differences in the work-related behaviour of men and women. Likewise, some women's advocacy groups assert that women business owners are not only different but also possess unique advantages over men. If such gendered differences really exist, then women's rapid growth in ownership could result in distinctive differences between how women and men run their businesses. We argue that dissenting voices have been ignored because of 'androcentrism' (Bem 1993), in the form of the taken-for-granted notion that the traditional male-centred business model is the 'neutral' or 'normal' model. Androcentrism has lulled journalists and scholars into assuming that women and men business owners are interchangeable. This has in turn allowed the scant literature on differences to remain satisfied with documenting a few demographic differences between women's and men's businesses, and explaining the differences as a result of women owner's lesser qualifications in terms of human, social and financial capital.

Finally, we draw on the scholarly literature regarding gendered differences in social behaviour, and on writings on difference by women's business advocates, to highlight a variety of understudied areas where gendered empirical differences in ownership practices might be found. We conclude by speculating about what may be lost to a nation's economy when new approaches to business are disregarded.

2. The quiet revolution: media and academic silence about the growth in women's ownership

The origins of this study were in casual conversation when it was realized that the common-sense question, 'how do women run businesses differently from men?' could not be answered. A cursory review suggested that very few papers published in entrepreneurship journals had approached this as an empirical question requiring a comparative design. It was difficult to find empirical studies of what women owners actually do, regardless of whether men were also studied. We were also struck by Joline Godfrey's (1992) letter to George Gendron, Editor-in-Chief of *Inc. Magazine*, noting that the annual competition for 'Entrepreneur of the Year' included remarkably few women. Beginning with a working hypothesis that women owners were seriously under-represented in the academic literature, we decided to explore whether this was also true for the popular press.

Twenty-five years ago, an absence of articles on women's business ownership would have raised few eyebrows. As recently as 1970, women owned only about 5% of all the businesses in the USA. However, since 1970, growth has been rapid and steady. Women's proportional participation in entrepreneurship has been growing during a time in which entrepreneurship in general has flourished: by 1992, the Department of the Census estimated that women owned about 6.4 million businesses in the USA, representing over 33% of the US total of just under 19.3 million firms (US Department of Commerce 1996). Although the proportion of firms owned by women in EU nations is evidently not as high as in the USA, recent statistics none the less suggest that women are increasing their level of ownership in Europe as well. Kovalainen (1996), for example, noted that about 30% of the non-agricultural entrepreneurs in Finland are women. The 1995 ENSR report stated that the proportion of women starters was about 27% of the total across the EU (ENSR 1995: 91).

We conducted searches of indexes representing popular and scholarly outlets for coverage of US women's business ownership over time (detailed descriptions of the search methods are provided in the Appendix). Patterns of coverage for three groups were studied: general business periodicals, élite national newspapers and academic journals because of the varying time periods and periodicals covered by the indexes used, and also because we wanted to see whether overall patterns held for sub-groups of publications.

2.1 General business periodicals

Between 1982 and 1995, the number of articles on business ownership issues increased by more than five-fold, from 258 to 1326. The number of articles on women business owners also increased, but only by a factor of approximately 3, from 82 to 260 articles. Consequently, the proportion of ownership articles on women actually fell, from about 32% in 1982 to 20% in 1995. The long-term trend is shown in Figure 1. The number of articles on women in general, regardless of content, also increased substantially from 1982 to 1995, rising from 333 to 3,258. Thus, the decline shown in Figure 1 is not a result of the business media becoming more conservative or paying less attention to women's issues. Instead, the decline represents a shifting of article content, proportionately away from ownership and towards other issues, such as equal employment opportunity, family/work conflicts and sexual harassment.

2.2 Élite national newspapers

The underlying mix of articles in the Information Access Company index that we used (see Appendix for details) expanded and changed during the period being considered, and this may partially account for the results in Figure 1. Moreover, the data in Figure 1 begin in 1980 and show a decline thereafter, but tell us nothing about what happened during the 1970s, when women's business ownership first took off.

**Business and Academic Index: Percent of Ownership
Articles Focusing on Women**

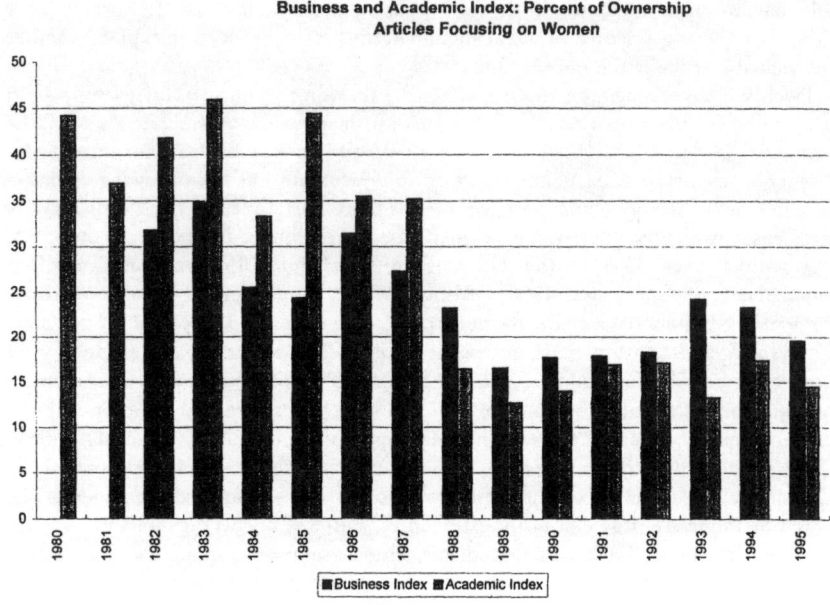

Figure 1. **Business and academic index: percentage of ownership articles focusing
on women.**

We therefore examined two élite national newspapers: *The New York Times (NYT)*
and *The Wall Street Journal (WSJ)* for which a longer time series is available.

The *NYT* index is incomplete prior to 1981, but as shown in Table 1, the data for
the 1970s fits very well with the long-term trend in the *NYT*'s coverage of women's
business issues for the 1980s and 1990s. The percentage of all business ownership
articles that specifically mentioned women increased slowly over this period, to a
maximum of about 4% in the early 1990s. Thus, the *NYT* only slightly increased
its coverage during the period of explosive growth in women's business ownership.

The low level of interest in women's business ownership was not driven by declining
interest in either business issues or women's issues. The number of articles on business
ownership remained almost constant over this period, at about 2,500 per year from
1981–1994. The number of articles covering 'women' in some way rose slightly in the
NYT, from 12,017 in 1981 to 14,145 in 1994. Note that this is in contrast to the five-
fold increase noted in the general business periodicals index.

The pattern of the *WSJ*'s coverage of women business owners was very similar to
what we have described for the *NYT*. As shown in Table 1, the *WSJ* published few
articles on women owners, proportionately, in the late 1970s and early 1980s, and then
increased its coverage slightly.

Table 1. Business ownership articles mentioning or focusing upon women.†

Year	Percentage business articles mentioning women				Percentage business articles with women as main focus					
	ETP	JBV	AMR	AMJ	WSJ	NYT	ETP	JBV	AMR	AMJ
1969	‡	‡	‡	6	‡	1	‡	‡	‡	0
1970	‡	‡	‡	3	‡	2	‡	‡	‡	0
1971	‡	‡	‡	11	‡	1	‡	‡	‡	0
1972	‡	‡	‡	0	‡	1	‡	‡	‡	0
1973	‡	‡	‡	10	0	1	‡	‡	‡	2
1974	‡	‡	‡	11	0	0	‡	‡	‡	3
1975	‡	‡	‡	19	0	1	‡	‡	‡	4
1976	10	‡	2	39	1	1	10	‡	0	14
1977	10	‡	6	34	0	2	10	‡	0	13
1978	11	‡	7	40	1	1	5	‡	2	13
1979	11	‡	4	30	1	2	5	‡	2	16
1980	0	‡	7	40	2	3	0	‡	2	10
1981	6	‡	7	53	2	3	6	‡	2	16
1982	8	‡	8	29	0	2	4	‡	3	13
1983	3	‡	10	50	1	3	3	‡	2	17
1984	7	‡	7	43	4	3	3	‡	2	15
1985	0	0	10	39	4	3	0	0	5	11
1986	11	8	10	39	5	3	0	0	6	8
1987	25	0	6	28	1	4	17	0	4	2
1988	36	11	3	35	4	3	18	5	3	8
1989	43	8	8	45	2	3	14	8	4	8
1990	33	20	7	26	1	3	0	12	4	5
1991	17	5	4	22	2	3	17	5	4	4
1992	11	26	24	40	3	4	11	4	16	9
1993	24	24	19	29	4	4	6	10	14	3
1994	25	20	9	48	5	4	20	8	9	14

†All numbers rounded to nearest integer.
‡Not available.

2.3 Academic journals

Across a broad spectrum of academic journals, between 1980 and 1995, the annual number of articles on business ownership issues – regardless of gender – increased by more than three-fold, from 129 to 447 articles. The number of articles on women business owners changed only slightly over that period, fluctuating at around an average of about 70 articles per year. Consequently, the proportion of ownership articles on women *fell* substantially, from about 44% in 1980 to 14% in 1995. The long-term trend is shown in Figure 1.

The number of articles on women in academic journals covered by the Information Access Company (IAC) index, regardless of content, increased substantially from 1980 to 1994, rising from 792 to almost 7,000. Thus, the decline shown in Figure 1 is not a result of academic researchers paying less attention to women's issues. Instead, the decline represents an actual shifting of article content, proportionately *away* from ownership and towards other issues regarding women.

2.4 Management and entrepreneurship journals

We chose four US academic journals for further investigation, based on their reputations as publication outlets for articles on entrepreneurship and business ownership: the *Academy of Management Journal* (*AMJ*), the *Academy of Management Review* (*AMR*), *Entrepreneurship: Theory and Practice* (*ETP*) and the *Journal of Business Venturing* (*JBV*). These journals have recently published more articles that at least mention gender/sex than they did in the 1980s. Our measure of 'mentioning' gender is quite generous, giving a journal credit for any article that collected data on the sex of subjects, even if sex was not included in the analysis. For three of the four journals, however, the proportions are still quite small. In the entrepreneurship journals *JBV* and *ETP* (Table 1), about one in six of the articles in the last decade has mentioned gender/sex, and in *AMR*, about one in ten has mentioned gender/sex. Only in *AMJ* have articles mentioning gender/sex figured prominently, averaging about 30% in the late 1970s and about 35% over the last ten years.

Using a more restrictive coding than merely 'mentioning' gender/sex, the total number of articles with gender as the main focus of interest was recorded as shown in Table 1. The absolute number of articles falling into this category by journal is as follows: *JBV*: 13; *ETP*: 24; *AMR*: 30; *AMJ*: 120. Even in the *Academy of Management Journal*, only 26% of the 457 articles that mentioned gender/sex actually used it as an independent variable. Clearly, gender/sex has *not* been a major issue of interest in any of these four journals.

Of the 187 articles with gender as a main focus, the number which had studied women *as owners of businesses* was counted. For the four journals, the totals were: *ETP*: 10; *JBV*: 10; *AMR*: 1; *AMJ*: 1. Thus, for the two entrepreneurship journals, 20 of the 37 articles with gender/sex as a central focus dealt with ownership, but these 37 articles represented only 7% of all the articles published in that period. For *AMR* and *AMJ*, the two articles on women owners were lost in the 2,650 papers published over the period of our investigation.

European researchers apparently have no more interest in women-owned firms than do Americans. Although we did not conduct the same thorough search through major publication outlets as we did for US sources, we picked two that were recent and broad in scope. First, the authors examined the first four Annual Reports produced by the European Observatory for SMEs in 1993, 1994, 1995 and 1996 (see ENSR (1995) for reference). We found: in the 1993 report, one overt reference to gender; in the 1994 report, one page devoted to 'women and entrepreneurship'; and in the 1995 report, one page on 'entrepreneurial background', devoted mostly to 'female starters'. All three reports contained major reviews of trends and policies regarding labour markets, education, business training needs, and so forth, and none of the sections mentioned women. Thus, in approximately 1300 pages of text, tables, and figures, women occupied about 0.0002% of the space in the first three volumes. Only in the 1996 report was a separate section introduced on women owners, covering 21 pages, and that section will be dropped in the 1997 report.

Second, we examined a comprehensive review of entrepreneurship and small business research in 16 European nations, prepared by experts in each nation (Landström *et al.* 1996). In the sixteen chapters, three references to research on women were found: a study carried out in Ireland in 1987; 3 studies from Norway, focusing mainly on family issues; and 3 studies in the UK. This review of these two extensive sources on national developments in research on entrepreneurship and small business convinced us that European scholars view this field through a gender-lens very similar to that of American scholars. As Holmquist and Sundin (1989: 1) noted, 'entrepreneurial theories are created by men, for men, and are applied to men'.

2.5 Summary of findings

Our review of business periodicals shows that coverage of women as business owners and entrepreneurs declined between 1982 and 1995. Coverage in two national newspapers changed slightly, with the *NYT* increasing its percentage of business ownership articles mentioning women to around 4%, and the *WSJ* recently showing an increase to slightly higher levels. Our review of academic journals indicates that coverage of women in general increased substantially between 1982 and 1995, but coverage of women as entrepreneurs and owners declined substantially. Coverage of women in general in four entrepreneurship and management journals changed slightly, with only the *AMJ* publishing a substantial number of papers on women in the 1990s. Over 85% of the articles published in the two entrepreneurship journals over the period studied made no mention of women, whether as employees or owners. More importantly, women as owners and entrepreneurs were simply *invisible* in these four journals – only 22 of the 3206 articles published over the study period featured women owners or entrepreneurs.

3. Simple explanations for the silence

We present three simple explanations for women owners' relative invisibility: (1) the media only cover what editors and reporters consider to be 'news', and women's business is no longer 'news'; (2) scholars are interested in economically important entities, and women's firms are small and relatively unimportant; and (3) documented differences between men and women owners are few and thus reporters and scholars no longer look for them. After reviewing these three explanations, we will examine two lines of argument that claim gender differences are not only visible but also consequential for work-related behaviour. We believe that these two lines of inquiry have been inadequately pursued because of androcentric assumptions built into journalistic and scholarly work.

3.1 Media inattention

Perhaps there is good news in our findings: women's ownership of businesses does not get much coverage in popular business journals and newspapers because it is no longer novel or new. As opportunities for business ownership and entrepreneurship have opened up to them, women have responded by rapidly increasing their percentage ownership of US businesses, and are moving – on this measure – towards parity with men. Back in the late 1970s, or very early 1980s, when the two broadest series (Figure 1) begin and also show their highest levels of coverage, women business owners were still remarkable. However, as their numbers have grown and time has passed, women proprietors have simply slipped silently into the generic category of 'business owners' and disappeared.

News gathering routines are likely to ignore stories that don't lead to copy that stands out, as McCarthy *et al.* (1996) argued in their study of media coverage of demonstrations in Washington, DC. Newsworthy 'pegs' on which to hang a story must refer to notorious, consequential, extraordinary, or culturally resonant events. As Scollard (1995: 77) noted, 'routine fascination' with women who are successful entrepreneurs (and executives) 'has become as passé as frying two eggs easy over for breakfast every morning'. As women business owners have become taken-for-granted, gender has ceased to be a salient or newsworthy dimension of business ownership stories. The slight increase in newspaper coverage may simply be a result of the greater number and increasing variety of women's businesses. Articles are written when interesting things happen concerning some of these businesses, not because they are run by women.

3.2   Scholarly disinterest

Lack of coverage of women business owners by academic journals is also easy to understand. Mass media fascination with an issue seems to affect the choices that academic authors make about what topics to study (Barley *et al.* 1988), and declining media coverage may have reduced overall scholarly interest. Moreover, reward systems in business schools have systematically favoured research that focuses on large firms, preferably Fortune 500 firms and others whose stock is publicly traded. Such firms are overwhelmingly managed by men executives (Blau and Ferber 1986, Reskin and Padavic 1994). In 1995, women only held about 10% of the 6,274 positions available on the boards of Fortune 500 firms, although more than 80% of Fortune 500 firms had at least one woman on their board (*Women's Business Exclusive* 1995). Within business schools, research on small and family-owned businesses has sometimes been dismissed as trivial. Elite academic journals tend to focus on patterns and issues related or important to large businesses. Thus, we are not surprised to see that *AMJ* and *AMR* have all but ignored women entrepreneurs and business owners. As more women build large firms, they and their businesses will become more central to mainstream academic business research.

Just as business school curricula and management journals reflect the needs of large and growing firms, so too do the leading entrepreneurship journals. Since the early 1980s, a great deal of entrepreneurship research in the USA and Europe has been oriented to economic dynamism and job growth (Birch 1979, Davis *et al.* 1993, Davidsson *et al.* 1996). Leading entrepreneurship researchers have repeatedly attempted to distinguish between 'entrepreneurial' versus 'lifestyle' businesses, or between 'small business' versus 'entrepreneurship' (Reynolds 1993). The entrepreneurship literature has shown less concern with 'lifestyle' businesses and sole proprietorships than with fast-growing, job-generating enterprises. Only about 20% of women-owned businesses in the USA have any employees, a figure remarkably similar to the average of 22% of women-owned firms in the EU that have employees (ENSR 1995: 92). Some research has found that women are more likely to become self-employed for 'lifestyle' reasons such as attempts to balance work and family (Brush 1992, Elam 1997, Marlow and Strange 1994, Starr and Yudkin 1996). Consequently, we are not surprised to find that women have been invisible in entrepreneurship journals. As more women's businesses grow rapidly and generate large numbers of jobs, they will perhaps get more attention from entrepreneurship researchers.

3.3 Limited findings of gendered differences in ownership style and practices

If researchers were to document substantial differences between how women and men practice business ownership, sex/gender issues might become very hard to ignore. Gender would become particularly salient if, as some women's business advocates claim, women's leadership style was shown to provide women with a significant business advantage (Helgensen 1995) or if empirical findings showed 'styles of success' that strongly differentiated between successful women and men (Stover 1995). Instead, very few systematic empirical differences have been uncovered, either between women and men business owners or between the businesses that they run. The strongest differences uncovered have been demographic, with few 'style' differences documented.

The short list of differences between *businesses* shows that women's businesses, on average, are: (1) younger, (2) smaller, (3) more likely to be in retail or services, and (4) more likely to be sole proprietorships than are businesses owned by men (Brush 1992, Starr and Yudkin 1996; US Dept. of Commerce 1996). Comparing *owners* by gender, women tend to: (1) have less experience in their firm's industry, (2) have less experience as managers, (3) be more likely to have liberal rather than technical education, and (4) be more likely to start businesses to gain flexibility. Overall, 'along many psychological and demographic characteristics, women entrepreneurs are more similar to than different from men' (Starr and Yudkin 1996: 11; see also Birley 1989). Moreover, neither the differences in women's businesses, nor the differences in the characteristics that they bring to ownership, appear to convey clear 'advantages'. Rather, it appears that women approach business ownership similarly to men, but that they often bring less human, social, or financial capital to bear when they come to business ownership, due largely to structural differences in the overall position of women and men in US society.

An institutional market-oriented approach would predict that women business owners behave much like men. All entrepreneurs, men and women alike, operate their firms in a business environment structured by laws, standard practices, norms of behaviour, and a complex set of institutional contingencies to which owners adapt if their businesses are to persist. For example, Holmquist (1996) suggested that the effects of gender are primarily limited to women's choice of industries in which to operate. In a study of Swedish entrepreneurs, she found tangible gender differences overall, but when she focused on a specific industry, behavioural differences between men and women business owners all but disappeared. As Holmquist (1996: 107–108) explained, 'to be able to work in a specific industry, the entrepreneur has to adapt to the rules of the industry, regardless of gender'.

A market-based perspective thus sees differences among men and women, and individual differences between men and women, as fundamentally subordinated to economic and institutional requirements. Although 'odd' behaviour is occasionally associated with fabulous entrepreneurial success, indulgence of personal difference at the expense of responding to business needs is more likely to be a recipe for failure. As Campbell (1960) noted, most variations from established practices are deleterious. According to this view, business is business, for men and women alike.

4. Complicating the simple explanations

Despite huge growth in the numbers of women business owners, few findings of interesting gender differences have emerged and national media and academic interest in women business owners has dwindled. We have presented a series of simple explanations that we think are reasonably powerful in resolving this paradox.

However, our claim for a simple resolution of the paradox is substantially at odds with two sets of voices that have grown increasingly bold over the past two decades: academics writing about sex and gender roles, and advocates offering arguments about women owners' distinctive advantages. We now turn to an examination of these voices.

4.1 Academic research on gendered differences in social behaviour

Sociologists and others have investigated a variety of structural or contextual explanations of gendered differences in behaviour. These explanations differ from the dispositional arguments of many psychologists by stressing differences in men's and women's current social circumstances that account for observed differences in patterns of behaviour. Fairly strong evidence supports arguments regarding consequential differences in women's role requirements and how they integrate them (Brush 1992, Kolvereid *et al.* 1993). By contrast, recent investigations into gender differences in use of social networks (Aldrich *et al.* 1996) and in access to financing (Schragg *et al.* 1992, Buttner and Rosen 1992, Van Auken *et al.* 1993, Loscocco and Robinson 1991, Neider 1987, Read 1994), have produced limited evidence of convincing gender differences.

Arguments that men's and women's social behaviours differ are also common across a variety of psychological and social psychological orientations, including bio-social (Buss 1995, Nielsen 1994, Udry *et al.* 1992, Wilson and Daly 1992), Freudian, feminist reformed Freudian, cognitive developmental (Chodorow 1978, Gilligan 1982, Miller 1976) and gender role (Eagly 1995, Eagly and Wood 1991, Eagly *et al.* 1992, 1995) approaches.

In a review of meta-analytic studies of sex differences in social behaviour, Eagly and Wood (1991: 315) 'challenged the consensus view-point in psychology that women and men behave either equivalently or so nearly identically that any differences are trivially small'. They found patterns of gendered behavioural differences whose magnitude is evidently typical of other research findings in psychology. Their largest and most robust finding – holding even in organizational contexts – was that women tend to have more democratic and participative leadership styles than men, who are more likely to display autocratic and directive styles. Small to moderate and reasonably consistent gendered differences were found, supporting the notion that women in groups tend to be more 'socially skilled, emotionally sensitive', 'expressive', and more 'concerned with personal relationships than men'. Women were also found to be 'more concerned than men about the social aspects of interaction and others' feelings' while men in groups tend to focus on task completion and more tangible outcomes (Eagly and Wood 1991: 307).

Sociological and psychological approaches both raise questions about the contexts that influence whether overall gendered differences will be expressed as gendered differences in particular types of behaviour. In a review of meta-analytic studies of sex differences in social behaviour, Eagly and Wood (1991) noted that little of the psychological research on sex differences had examined behaviour in *any* work organizations, where gender differences may be less predictive and formal role requirements more salient than in the laboratory studies frequently conducted by social psychologists. Indeed, in later meta-analyses, Eagly and her colleagues (Eagly *et al.* 1992, 1995, Eagly 1995) found consistent and non-trivial average differences between men and women in organizational leadership behaviour and how they were evaluated, but these differences were generally smaller than in those found in studies focusing on non-work contexts. Apparently, organizational contexts diminished – but did not extinguish – gendered behavioural differences.

What workplace contexts permit the most free expression of gender differences? Relatively small gendered differences in behaviour would be expected among employees in the same jobs in large, formalized organizations. The play of gender differences is probably more likely among employees in smaller organizations with less formalized job systems and role requirements than in larger organizations (Baker and Aldrich 1994). We would expect owners of small and medium-sized businesses to possess the greatest freedom from corporate hierarchy and formal role requirements. A strong expression of gendered behavioural differences would be possible between men and women business owners.

Therefore, whatever the differences between men and women, they should be increasingly embodied within the ranks of entrepreneurs and their firms. Our intent is not to engage in gender polarization or to essentialize the nature of behavioural differences between men and women (Bem 1993). Even where gendered behaviour differences have been found, there is a great deal of overlap between men and women, and variability within each sex generally dwarfs the behavioural differences between the sexes. None the less, differences do exist.

4.2   Advocates for women's business ownership

Women's business advocates tend to ignore the similarities between men and women, as well as the variation among women. These advocates constitute a committed force fighting against the invisibility of women business owners. Many of the contrasts claimed in the practitioner and policy-oriented research closely mirror the differences found in more narrowly-focused academic work. The main difference is that advocates characterize almost all differences as if they were large. In addition, context-specific behavioural differences are often represented as essential sexual distinctions.

We review a number of exemplars of policy-oriented writing to show the style of thinking that they represent. Helgensen (1995) argued that successful women owners, compared to men, (1) tend to communicate directly, rather than through hierarchical channels, (2) emphasize process, not just goals, (3) use health of relationships as an important criterion by which to judge business success, (4) do not compartmentalize their lives and identities into work and domestic spheres, and (5) are scornful of 'excessive' concern with rank, position and perks. The National Foundation for Women Business Owners issued a report on 'Styles of Success', a survey of 127 women and men conducted in 1994 (Stover 1995). The report suggested that men and women think differently and have correspondingly different styles of management.

Kearney and White (1994) claimed that men in business are oriented to tasks and women are oriented to relationships, and White argued that these different orientations, combined with 'an automatic, unthinking tendency to prefer to be surrounded by people like ourselves' (White 1995: 75) result in potential and actual problems when men manage women, or women manage men. In contrast, Scollard (1989, 1995) downplayed gendered differences in managing people, but claimed that with the exception of small numbers of very high level corporate executives and founders of large successful firms, women are hampered in business by fear of taking risks, and therefore usually found and build only small firms. Similarly, Stolze (1989, 1995) alleged that women's businesses are smaller and less successful than men's because women fear losing control if they accept money from outside investors.

In summary, the practitioner literature presents plausible descriptions of differences in how women and men think about their businesses and the people in them, how the businesses fit into their lives, and how they judge whether a business is successful. The first two columns of Table 2 summarize some of the differences between men and women suggested by the research we have reviewed. Column three describes the stereotypically similar – but often exaggerated – set of differences claimed by proponent researchers.

4.3 Androcentrism and why the dissenting voices have been ignored

We complicated our three simple explanations for the invisibility of women business owners by reviewing arguments from sex and gender scholars and women's business advocates, claiming that significant gender differences really do exist. Why, then, does invisibility persist?

We suggest that women are rendered invisible by a particular form of reification labelled androcentrism (Bem 1993). Reification of social constructions is a common and probably functionally necessary aspect of social life (Berger and Luckmann 1966), but it can have deleterious consequences. The concept of 'androcentrism', a specific

Table 2.   Descriptions of difference: academic and advocate literature.

Academic literature		Advocate/policy literature
Women	Men	Women entrepreneurs
Mothering	Non-mothering	Non-hierarchical communication
Nurturing	Ethics of justice	Emphasize process
Relational	Separation	Evaluate business by relationships
Connected	Tangible outcomes	Integrated work/family lives
Selfless	Task completion	Scornful of hierarchy and perks
Ethics of care	Dominant	Fear of risks
Feelings	Controlling	Fear of losing control
Interaction	Independent	Internally directed
Sensitive	Agentic	Instinct
Friendly	Leadership style:	Sensitivity
Integrate role requirements	autocratic and directive	Values
Expressive		Emphasize relationships
Leadership style:		
democratic/participative		

type of reification, describes the taken-for-granted notion that the traditional male-centred business model is the 'neutral' (or 'normal' or 'natural') model. We suspect that androcentrism affects both business owners and the scholars and journalists who study business owners.

Many authors have claimed that academic researchers wear androcentric blinkers. Gendered norms and values have been shown, in various contexts, to affect even disciplined observers' interpretations and explanations. For example, McGrayne (1993) argued that women scientists who teamed with men in research projects have been repeatedly overlooked by the Nobel Prize committee because of stereotypic assumptions about women's place. Calàs (1993) argued that management theorists' conceptions of 'charismatic leadership' have been based implicitly upon male leaders and ignore leadership characteristics associated with femininity. Calàs and Smircich (1992) asserted the presence of a more general gender bias in organization studies, and Hurley (1991) claimed that entrepreneurship research has historically been biased toward men, with writers ignoring gender-based realities.

Our own simple explanations are androcentric. We argued above that because men *and* women are subject to common institutional and economic structures, they adapt by behaving similarly and creating similar businesses. Playing by the same rules in the same game, women's ownership behaviour looks much like men's ownership behaviour. In short, they become isomorphic because they have adapted to, or been selected by, the environment they share in common (DiMaggio and Powell 1983).

However, our explanation of isomorphism ignores the historical fact that women owners enter a business world largely constructed and dominated by men. Thus, the simple structural explanation exemplifies androcentric reification. Men and women play by identical rules, but the rules were written, over long periods of time, by men.

Of course, androcentrism would not matter were there not reason to believe that an institutional business world constructed by women would differ in some way from that constructed by men, or that – given the chance – some women would approach business ownership differently from men. Is there a basis for such beliefs? Our review above of recent writings on gender differences leads us to suspect that under looser institutional constraints, women's ownership behaviour *would* differ more from men's. A careful look may find gender differences that have survived or even flourished and we now consider some hypotheses regarding gender differences that may well be consequential for the long-term viability of the business population.

5. Directions for future research on gendered differences in business ownership

In this section we suggest directions for future research on gendered differences in ownership that go beyond demographic comparisons by drawing on some of the evidence and claims about gendered behaviour that were reviewed in Table 2. Regardless of whether these differences provide *an advantage or a disadvantage*, they should be interesting to reporters, academics, and women's business proponents alike. If future research fails to uncover interesting differences, it will speak to the powerful ability of the marketplace to render dispositional differences moot.

5.1   Differences in leadership

One of the most robust findings of the gender differences literature is that women use leadership styles that are democratic and participative, compared to men's more autocratic and directive styles (Eagly and Wood 1991). Researchers could search for direct evidence of this difference through comparative study of organizational decision-making. Do women-owned firms have more people involved in decision processes, on average, than men-owned firms? Do they have distinctive decision-making processes that result in different decisions? In any industry undergoing significant changes, do men-owned firms respond differently than women-owned firms, on average, to the changes?

5.2   Nurture and social sensitivity

If women are more nurturing, relational, and socially sensitive than men, we would expect this to be reflected across a wide variety human resource practices. For example, do women-owned firms establish more 'family-friendly' policies, including flexible working arrangements and support for employees who balance work and family concerns? Are women-owned firms able to make productive use of employees who might be viewed as 'problems'? Do women-owned firms draw upon a broader population of potential employees than men-owned firms?

5.3   Role integration and balance

If women tend to be motivated to ownership by a desire to achieve integration and balance across role requirements, thus placing less value on rapid growth, then 'smallness' means something different for women-owned than for men-owned businesses (Cliff 1995). Are women's businesses on average more likely to be small through choice, rather than through lack of competence, compared to men's? Are small businesses owned by women more successful than small businesses run by men who have tried but failed to develop their businesses, controlling for industry?

5.4   New organizational forms

A burgeoning literature describes the increasing importance of hybrid and network form of organization (Powell 1990). These new forms are generally characterized as less hierarchical than traditional businesses, constructed using many ties between relationally connected firms and individuals. The skills that these new forms are said to demand sound a lot like the attributes that are claimed to differentiate women from men: 'there is little disagreement about what business must become: less hierarchical, more flexible and team oriented, faster and more fluid. In my opinion, one group of people has an enormous advantage in realizing this new vision: women' (Peters 1990: 216, quoted in Fletcher 1995: 2). Following this argument, are women-owned businesses particularly successful when they are organized in hybrid and network forms? Are women's hybrid organizations – or their parts of network firms – more successful than men's hybrid and network firms?

6. Summary and conclusions

We have described a powerful paradox of women's business ownership in the USA today, demonstrating that despite spectacular gains, women business owners have remained virtually invisible in journalistic and academic discourse. We offered simple solutions to the paradox, and then suggested that the simple solutions could be improved by taking account of discordant voices.

We then argued that androcentrism muted these voices. Women have had to adapt to institutions of business ownership which are *already gendered*, in the sense of having been built and dominated by men. Additionally, efforts to find evidence of women's distinctive contributions to business ownership may have been retarded by an assumption that the traditional model of business ownership is gender neutral and 'natural'. Perhaps greater differences will be found in the future, with the huge increases in women's entrepreneurship, because an increasingly heterogeneous group of women is being drawn into ownership (Starr and Yudkin 1996).

New businesses add to the diversity of organizational solutions available to a society (Aldrich and Fiol 1994), enhancing economic vitality and expanding the variety of workplaces available. Conceivably, even in the absence of institutional pressures, women would build businesses just like men's. If – for whatever reason – women-owned businesses are really just like those owned by men, then diversity will not increase as women increase their ownership share. Something may have already been lost, if – in response to institutional and market pressures – women have merely mimicked men and created businesses in a traditional mould. However, we also wonder whether women are offering new ways of managing, new solutions to problems, and they just aren't being noticed. Very little scholarly empirical research has focused on this question. We suggest that entrepreneurship researchers consider the question still open, and design research that explores whether there are really are distinctive differences, or merely deceptive distinctions (Epstein 1988).

References

Aldrich, H. E. and Fiol, M. C. 1994 Fools rush in? The institutional context of industry creation, *Academy of Management Review*, 19: 645–670.

Aldrich, H. E., Elam, A. B. and Reese, P. R. 1996 Strong ties, weak ties, and strangers: do women business owners differ from men in their use of networking to obtain assistance?, in Birley, S. and MacMillan, I. (eds), *Entrepreneurship in a Global Context* (London: Routledge), 1–25.

Baker, T. and Aldrich, H. E. 1994 Friends and strangers: early hiring practices and idiosyncratic jobs, *Frontiers of Entrepreneurship Research* (Wellesley, MA: Babson College).

Barley, S., Meyer, G. and Gash, D. C. 1988 Cultures of culture: academics, practitioners and the pragmatics of normative control, *Administrative Science Quarterly*, 33(1): 24–60.

Bem, S. 1993 *The Lenses of Gender: Transforming the Debate on Sexual Inequality* (New Haven, CT: Yale University Press).

Berger, P. L. and Luckmann, T. 1966 *The Social Construction of Reality* (New York: Doubleday).

Birch, D. 1979 *The Job Generation Process: Final Report to Economic Development Administration* (Cambridge, MA: MIT Program on Neighborhood and Regional Change).

Birley, S. 1989 Female entrepreneurs: are they really any different? *Journal of Small Business Management*, 27(1): 32–37.

Blau, F. E. and Ferber, M. A. 1986 *The Economics of Women, Men, and Work* (Englewood Cliffs, NJ: Prentice-Hall).

Brush, C. G. 1992 Research on women business owners: past trends, a new perspective and future directions, *Entrepreneurship Theory and Practice*, 16(4): 5–30.

Buss, D. M. 1995 Psychological sex differences: origins through sexual selection, *American Psychologist*, 50(3): 164–168.

Buttner, E. H. and Rosen, B. 1992 Rejection in the loan application process: male and female entrepreneurs' perceptions and subsequent intentions, *Journal of Small Business Management*, 30(1): 58–65.

Calàs, M. 1993 Deconstructing 'Charismatic Leadership': re-reading Weber from the darker side, *Leadership Quarterly* 4(3/4): 305–328.

Calàs, M. and Smircich, L. 1992 Re-writing gender into organization theorizing: directions from feminist perspectives, in Reed, M. and Hughes, M. (eds) *Rethinking Organization* (London: Sage), 227–253.

Campbell, D. T. 1960 'Blind variation and selective retention in creative thought as in other knowledge processes', *Psychological Review*, 67: 380–400.

Chodorow, N. 1978 *The Reproduction of Mothering* (Berkeley, CA: University of California Press).

Cliff, J. 1995 Does one size fit all? Exploring the relationship between attitudes towards growth, gender, and business size. Unpublished paper, Faculty of Commerce and Business Administration, University of British Columbia.

Cromie, S. and Birley, S. 1992 Networking by female business owners in Northern Ireland, *Journal of Business Venturing*, 7: 237–251.

Davidsson, P., Lindmark, L. and Olofsson, C. 1996 The extent of overestimation of small firm job creation – an empirical examination of the 'regression bias'. Paper presented at the 41st ICSB World Conference, Stockholm, June.

Davis, S. J., Haltiwanger, J. and Schuh, S. 1993 Small business and job creation: dissecting the myth and reassessing the facts. Working Paper No. 4492, National Bureau of Economic Research, Cambridge, MA.

DiMaggio, P. J. and Powell, W. W. 1983. The iron cage revisited: institutional isomorphism and collective rationality in organizational fields, *American Sociological Review*, 48: 147–160.

Eagly, A. H. 1995 The science and politics of comparing women and men, *American Psychologist*, 50: 145–158.

Eagly, A. H. and Wood, W. 1991 Explaining sex differences in social behavior: a meta-analytic perspective, *Personality and Social Psychology Bulletin*, 17: 306–315.

Eagly, A. H., Karau, S. J. and Makhijani, M. G. 1995 Gender and the effectiveness of leaders: a meta-analysis, *Psychological Bulletin*, 117: 125–145.

Eagly, A. H., Makhijani, M. G. and Klonsky, B. G. 1992 Gender and the evaluation of leaders: a meta-analysis, *Psychological Bulletin*, 111(1): 3–22.

Elam, A. B. 1997 Small business ownership as a more flexible work option. Paper presented at University of North Carolina Department of Sociology Entrepreneurship Seminar, April.

ENSR (European Network for SME Research) 1995 *Third Annual Report: The European Observatory for SMEs* (Zoetermeer, The Netherlands: EIM Small Business Research and Consultancy).

Epstein, C. 1988 *Deceptive Distinctions* (New York: Russell Sage).

Fletcher, J. K. 1995 Radically transforming work for the 21st Century: a feminist reconstruction of 'Real' Work. Paper presented at the 1995 Academy of Management Meeting, Vancouver, BC, August.

Gilligan, C. 1982 *In a Different Voice: Psychological Theory and Women's Development* (Cambridge, Mass: Harvard University Press).

Godfrey, J. 1992 *Our Wildest Dreams: Women Entrepreneurs Making Money, Having Fun, Doing Good* (New York: HarperCollins).

Helgesen, S. 1995 One key strength of women: an emphasis on relationships, *Small Business Forum*, Vol. 13 Spring: 70–72.

Holmquist, C. 1996 The female entrepreneur: woman and/or entrepreneur, in *Aspects of Women's Entrepreneurship* (Stockholm: Swedish National Board for Industrial and Technical Development), 107–108.

Holmquist, C. and Sundin, E. 1991 The growth of women's entrepreneurship: push or pull factors? in Davies, L. and Gibb, A. (eds) *Recent Research in Entrepreneurship: The Third International EIASM Workshop: 1989* (Aldershot, UK: Avebury).

Hurley, A. E. 1991 Incorporating feminist theories into sociological theories of entrepreneurship. Unpublished paper presented at the Annual Meeting of the Academy of Management, Miami, Florida.

Kearney, K. G. and White, T. I. 1994 *Men and Women at Work* (NJ: Career Press).

Kolvereid, L., Shane, S. and Westhead, P. 1993 Is it equally difficult for female entrepreneurs to start businesses in all countries? *Journal of Small Business Management*, 31(4): 42–51.

Kovalainen, A. 1996 Female entrepreneurship in Finland and the Nordic countries, in *Aspects of Women's Entrepreneurship* (Stockholm: Swedish National Board for Industrial and Technical Development), 143–154.

Landström, H., Frank, H. and Veciana, J. (eds) 1996 *Entrepreneurship and Small Business Research in Europe – An ECSB Survey* (Aldershot, UK: Avebury).

Loscocco, K. and Robinson, J. 1991 Barriers to women's small-business success in the United States, *Gender and Society*, 5: 511–532.

Marlow, S. and Strange, A. 1994 Female entrepreneurs: success by whose standards?, in Tanton, M. (ed.), *Women in Management, A Developing Presence* (London: Routledge), 172–185.

Marlow, S. 1996 Women in self employment – do they mean business?, Unpublished working paper, April 1996, Leicester Business School, UK.

McCarthy, J. D., McPhail, C. and Smith, J. 1996 Images of protest: dimensions of selection bias in media coverage of Washington demonstrations, 1982 and 1991, *American Sociological Review*, 61(3): 478–499.

McGrayne, S. B. 1993 *Nobel Prize Women: Their Lives, Struggles and Momentous Discoveries* (New York: Birch Lane Press).

Miller, J. B. 1976 *Toward a New Psychology of Women* (Boston: Beacon Press).

Neider, L. 1987 A preliminary investigation of female entrepreneurs in Florida, *Journal of Small Business Management*, 25(3): 22–29.

Nielsen, F. 1994 Sociobiology and sociology, in Hagan, J. and Cook, K. S. (eds), *Annual Review of Sociology 20* (CA: Annual Reviews Inc.), 267–303.

Peters, T. 1990 The best new managers will listen, motivate, support: isn't that just like a woman?, *Working Woman*, Vol. 15 September: 216–217.

Powell, W. W. 1990 Neither market nor hierarchy: network forms of organization, in *Research in Organizational Behavior*, vol. 12 (Greenwich, CT: JAI Press), 295–336.

Read, L. 1994 Raising finance from banks: a comparative study of the experiences of male and female business owners, *Frontiers of Entrepreneurship Research* (Wellesley, MA: Babson College), 361–372.

Reskin, B. and Padavic, I. 1994 *Women and Men at Work* (Thousand Oaks, CA: Pine Forge Press).

Reynolds, P. 1993 High performance entrepreneurship: what makes it different?, in *Frontiers of Entrepreneurship Research* (Wellesley, MA: Babson College), 88–103.

Schragg, P., Yacuk, L. and Glass, A. 1992 Study of barriers facing Alberta women in business, *Journal of Small Business and Entrepreneurship*, 9(4): 40–49.

Scollard, J. R. 1989 *Risk to Win: A Woman's Guide to Success* (New York: MacMillan).

Scollard, J. R. 1995 Management has become unisex – but managing risks hasn't, *Small Business Forum*, Vol. 13 Spring: 76–79.

Starr, J. and Yudkin, M. 1996 Women entrepreneurs: a review of current research, Monograph published by Center for Research on Women, Wellesley, MA CRW 15.

Stolze, W. J. 1989 *Startup: An Entrepreneur's Guide to Launching and Managing a New Venture* (New York: Rock Beach Press).

Stolze, W. J. 1995 A very important gender-related issue is control, *Small Business Forum*, Spring: 80–82.

Stover, C. 1995 Styles of success: research on gender differences in management styles, *Small Business Forum*, Vol. 13 Spring: 52–69.

Udry, R. J., Kovenock, J. and Morris, N. 1992 A biosocial paradigm for women's gender roles. Paper presented at annual meeting of the Population Association of America, Denver, CO, April.

US Department of Commerce 1996 1992 Economic census: survey of women-owned businesses, US Government Printing Office, Washington, DC.

Van Auken, H., Gaskill, J. and Kao, S.-S. 1993 Acquisition of capital by women entrepreneurs: patterns of initial and refinancing capitalization, *Journal of Small Business and Entrepreneurship*, 10(4): 44–55.

White, T. I. 1995 Men and women judge subordinates differently, *Small Business Forum*, Vol. 13 Spring: 74–76.

Wilson, M. and Daly, M. 1992 The man who mistook his wife for a chattel, in Markow, J. H., Cosmides, L. and Tooby, J. (eds), *The Adapted Mind: Evolutionary Psychology and the Generation of Culture* (Oxford: Oxford University Press), 289–322.

Women's Business Exclusive 1995 Most Fortune 500 companies have women on boards, 3(7): 4–5.

Appendix. Indexes used.

General business press: Information Access Company's (IAC) computerized Business and Company Index, both the full index (ASAP) and the Backfile. This index covers over 1,000 periodicals, back to 1982, with coverage more complete in later years.

Academic journals: IAC's Academic Index, which covers over 1600 journals and other periodicals, back to 1980, with coverage more complete in later years.

Elite newspapers: Lexis/Nexis electronic database, which covers the *NYT* fully back to 1980 and partially back to 1969, and covers the *WSJ* fully back to 1989 and partially back to 1973.

Search routines: The same routine was used in each index to develop measures of: (1) articles about business ownership, regardless of gender; (2) articles mentioning women, regardless of other content; and (3) articles about ownership that mentioned women. All articles that mentioned any of the following words were searched for by year:

1 Business ownership: entrepreneur(s), entrepreneurial, entrepreneurship, owned business(es), businessman, business man, businessmen, business men, business woman, businesswoman, business women, businesswomen, business owner(s).

2 Women: woman, women, womyn, female(s).

3 Women and business ownership: the same terms as in the business ownership search were searched for, but with the modifying adjectives: 'woman', 'women', or 'female' combined with the terms, except for those that already had woman as part of the term.

Elite management and entrepreneurship journals: For *AMR*, *AMJ*, *ETP*, and *JBV*, all issues were searched through for refereed papers, including research notes, classifying articles into one of five categories:

1   no mention of gender/sex;
2   demographic data on gender/sex collected, but not reported;
3   gender/sex composition of sample reported, but not used in analysis;
4   controlled for gender/sex of subjects in analysis; and
5   used gender/sex as an independent variable in analysis.

For the last category, papers were further classified by whether gender/sex was the main issue of interest, and of those, whether ownership was the focus of the article.

[30]

ELSEVIER

Journal of Socio-Economics 28 (1999) 351–364

The Journal of
**Socio-
Economics**

Gender inequality in wage earnings and female self-employment selection

Richard J. Boden, Jr

*Department of Marketing, College of Business Administration, The University of Toledo,
Toledo, OH 43606-3390 USA*

Abstract

Female self-employment has risen strongly over the last few decades and has become an important labor market development. The few studies that have examined women's decision to become self-employed indicate that this decision is complex. Women are more likely than men to shoulder family-related obligations, especially child rearing, and there is evidence that this affects some women's propensity to become self-employed. Also, women have yet to achieve full economic parity with men in wage employment. This paper specifically examines how gender inequality in wage earnings may precipitate some women's selection out of wage employment and into self-employment. We find that women's lower wage returns to observed worker characteristics have a positive and significant effect on women's decision to switch from wage employment to self-employment. © 1999 Elsevier Science Inc. All rights reserved.

1. Introduction

Female self-employment in the United States has risen substantially over the last two decades, as chronicled by Devine (1994a), and must be regarded as a significant labor market phenomenon. However, female self-employment is as yet a thinly researched topic, and many empirical issues have not been addressed. Some of the more notable studies include Carr (1996) and Boden (1996) that uncover systematic gender differences in self-employment selection processes, including the unique, positive influence that having young children has on women's selection into self-employment. Boden (1999) finds that nonpecuniary

---

* Corresponding author. Tel.: +1-419-530-2042; fax: +1-419-530-2098.
E-mail address: rboden@pop3.utoledo.edu (R.J. Boden)

1053-5357/99/$ – see front matter © 1999 Elsevier Science Inc. All rights reserved.
PII: S 1053-5357(99)00026-8

352   *R. J. Boden / Journal of Socio-Economics 28 (1999) 351–364*

aspects of self-employment—e.g., flexible working hours—are especially attractive to women who have young children, whereas parental status has no discernable effect on men's reasons for becoming self-employed. Devine (1994b) analyzes inter-temporal changes (between 1975 and 1987) in self-employed women's observed skill levels relative to their wage-sector counterparts, as well as well as changes in women's wage returns to skill and their implication for the rise in female self-employment. In this paper, we directly examine how gender differences in returns to skill in wage employment influence women's propensity to select out of wage employment and into self-employment.

2. Data description

The analyses described below are based on longitudinally matched CPS data—from the March Income Supplements—for the paired reference years of 1987 to 1988, 1988 to 1989, 1989 to 1990, 1990 to 1991, and 1991 to 1992.[1,2] Specifically, these analyses are based on matched observations on white men and white women who were wage workers in one year (the base year) and either self-employed or employed in the wage sector in the following year. (Employment status corresponds to individuals' respective jobs of longest duration in each of the two years. Also, both incorporated and unincorporated workers are classified as self-employed for the purposes of this paper.) The exclusion of data on minorities is made in the interest of reducing unobserved heterogeneity in worker attributes. Also, data on minorities are sparse even in the full CPS cross-sections, and attrition only exacerbates this problem in matched CPS data on minorities. The restriction based upon employment status as well as other screens applied to the matched data are discussed later in this paper.

There are precedents for using matched CPS data for analyses of transition into self-employment—e.g., Evans and Leighton (1989) and Boden (1996). Of course, there are other sources of data on self-employed workers. Indeed, these alternative data series are longitudinal by design, and include the Census Bureau's Survey of Income and Program Participation (SIPP), the National Longitudinal Surveys (NLS), and the Panel Study of Income Dynamics (PSID). However, although the majority of women who enter self-employment do so from wage employment, women's transition rate from wage employment to self-employment—the focus of this paper—is very small (less than 2%). As a result, the volume of observations in each of the latter data series is inadequate for the present purposes. By contrast, the number of observations on female workers in matched CPS data for any given year is several times that of the SIPP, NLS, or PSID data.

3. Theoretical framework

The behavior modeled in this paper should be interpreted in the context of the following static, discrete-choice framework, which is similar to the partial equilibrium framework described by Evans and Leighton (1989). Women are assumed to have chosen to participate in the labor force for at least two consecutive periods and are employed in period t (or the "base year") as wage workers. Their decision to become self-employed or remain in wage employment in period t + 1 (the "terminal year") reflects the solution to an expected utility maximization problem. Their utility functions include expected earnings (or expected lifetime earnings discounted to year t + 1), leisure, and nonpecuniary employment attributes as arguments. Expected earnings, whether from wage employment or self-employment, are assumed to be a function of the usual set of human capital attributes—viz., human capital developed through formal education and employment experience. Expected self-employment earnings, however, are further assumed to be a function of the financial scale at which they enter self-employment, in deference to Evans and Jovanovic (1989). Women will choose to become self-employed or remain in wage employment in year t + 2 according to which of these two alternatives yield a higher level of expected utility.

A wage-employment attribute of central importance to this paper is the gender difference in wage returns to skill. It is impossible to positively identify the sources of this difference, but it is assumed that it is partly a manifestation of employer discrimination. It is further assumed that women have at least crude knowledge of the extent to which their wages are greater or less than those of otherwise comparable men, and that women's discount in wage returns to skill is a negative argument in their utility functions. That is, employer discrimination—or women's perception thereof—is a source of disutilty (or "resentment") for female wage workers. As a result, the greater the excess of men's wage returns to skill over women's, the lower women's utility derived from wage employment will be, and the more likely they will be, other things equal, to switch from wage employment to self-employment.

4. The Model

An equation of self-employment entry was estimated using probit regression. The dichotomous dependent variable in this equation assumes a value of unity for women who switched from wage employment in the base year to self-employment in the terminal year, and assumes a value of zero for women who remained in wage employment for each of two consecutive years. The regressors in this equation are:[3]

WORKEXP1: imputed years of work experience, calculated as age minus years of schooling minus 6;

SOMECOLL: a dummy variable that assumes a value of unity for women with one to three years of college;

COLLPLUS: a dummy variable that assumes a value of unity for women with four or more years of college;

WEARN1: total annual wage earnings during the base year (in nominal dollars);

FAMINC1: total income by other family members during the base year (in nominal dollars);

NWINC1: total nonwage income (i.e., the sum of rental, dividend, interest, and trust income) during the base year (in nominal dollars);

KIDSU61: a dummy variable that assumes a value of unity for women with at least one child under the age of six (in the terminal year), and a value of zero, otherwise;

MULTEMP1: a dummy variable that assumes a value of unity for women who had two or more different employers in the base year;

WAGEDIF1: a measure of gender differences in returns to skill in the wage sector during the base year (in nominal dollars).

The opportunity cost of abandoning wage employment for self-employment is captured, in part, by WEARN1. Evans and Jovanovic (1989) and Evans and Leighton (1989) find that wealthier workers are more likely to become self-employed, other things equal, so NWINC1 is included as a proxy measure of women's wealth—a variable that is not explicitly captured by the CPS. The earnings of other family members in the base period—FAMINC1—are specified as a regressor under the assumption that the greater these earnings are, the more likely women will be to entertain the risk of entering self-employment. Boden (1996, 1999) finds that women who have at least one young child are more likely to become self-employed, other things equal, hence the inclusion of KIDSU61 in the model.

This equation was estimated for observations restricted to white women who: (a) were employed as wage workers in their job of longest duration in the base year; (b) had some wage earnings in the base year, but no self-employment earnings in that year; (c) were employed either in the wage sector (with no self-employment earnings) or self-employed in the terminal year (according to their job of longest duration); and (d) worked at least 40 h in each year. Other exclusions from the data analyses include records on workers who were in the military or employed as private household workers or in the agricultural sector in either year t or year t + 1. A total of 41, 266 observations met these criteria, and of the 41,266 women in this research sample, a total of 793 (or 1.92%) switched from wage employment to self-employment.[4] (Additional tabulations of the matched CPS data reveal that over two-thirds of newly self-employed women were previously employed in the wage sector.) There are solid antecedents for the restricted scope of the data used to estimate our probit regression equation— e.g., Evans and Leighton (1989) and Boden (1996)— but it should be emphasized that this equation does not represent a general model of female self-employment selection.[5]

The variable capturing gender differences in base-year returns to skill in the wage sector—WAGEDIF1—is defined as follows:[6]

$$\text{WAGEDIF1}_{it} = \exp(\mathbf{a}_{mt}\mathbf{x}_{it}) - \exp(\mathbf{a}_{wt}\mathbf{x}_{it}) \tag{1}$$

where:

$\mathbf{x}_{it}$ is a vector of the i-th woman's wage-determining personal attributes and relevant control variables (in year t);

$\mathbf{a}_{mt}$ is a vector of OLS parameter estimates from a model of the natural logarithm of hourly wage earnings (in year t) estimated for data on male wage workers;

$\mathbf{a}_{wt}$ is a vector of OLS parameter estimates from a model of the natural logarithm of hourly wage earnings (in year t) estimated for data on female wage workers.

WAGEDIF1 roughly corresponds to the returns-to-skill portion of the standard wage-gap decomposition attributable to Oaxaca (1973). WAGEDIF1 is specified as a proxy for women's assessment of their hourly wages relative to those of otherwise comparable men.

Table 1
Probit parameter estimates for model of women's selection into self-employment from wage employment

Variable	Estimate	Standard error	Variable mean	Variable description
INTERCEPT	−2.461900	0.046840		
WORKEXP1	0.008643	0.001446	19.113	Years of Work Experience (Imputed)
SOMECOLL	0.129460	0.036400	0.25745	Dummy Variable: 1 to 3 years College
COLLPLUS	0.200920	0.039550	0.22767	Dummy Variable: 4 or More Years College
WEARN1	−7.574e−06	1.102e−06	15,602	Total Base-Year Wage Earnings (in Dollars)
FAMINC1	2.211e−06	5.336e−07	28,246	Base-Year Income of Other Family Members (in Dollars)
NWINC1	1.235e−05	2.920e−06	831.5	Base-Year Nonwage Income (in Dollars)
KIDSU61	0.272740	0.040250	0.16006	Dummy Variable: Has at Least One Child Under Age Six
MULTEMP1	0.082355	0.042520	0.14734	Dummy Variable: Two or More Different Employers in Base Year
WAGEDIF1	0.043927	0.011000	2.23300	Imputed Gender Difference in Base-Year Hourly Wage Returns to Skill (in Dollars)
Number of Observations		41,266		
Dependent Variable Mean		0.0192		
Log-Likelihood		−3,822.64		
Model Chi-Squared		193.20		

(The estimates for the wage earnings equations—that were used to construct WAGEDIF1—are presented in the appendix of this paper.) It should be noted that the variable WAGEDIF1 is correlated with the other regressors in our probit regression equation, including (imputed) years of work experience. However, the exclusion of work experience from this equation would result in a blatant upward bias in the probit parameter estimate for WAGEDIF1.[7]

5. Probit regression results

Table 1 displays our probit regression parameter estimates. All of the parameter estimates have the expected signs and are significantly different from zero at a confidence level of more than 95%. These estimates indicate that the greater women's total base-year wage earnings are (as measured by WEARN1), the less likely they are to switch to self-employment, other things equal. The wealthier women are (as captured by the proxy variable NWINC1), the more likely they are to enter self-employment–a finding consistent with those obtained for men by Evans and Leighton (1989) and Evans and Jovanovic (1989). Also, women with young children are, other factors held constant, more likely to enter self-employment, a finding consistent with Boden (1996). Most importantly, as hypothesized, women's propensity to switch to self-employment is positively related to the imputed discount in their wage-sector returns to skill (relative to men's). In fact, if the mean value of WAGEDIF1 were equal to zero, women's rate of transition from wage employment to self-employment would be about 25% lower.[8]

Table 2 displays the mean values of the regressors for women who switched to self-

356   *R. J. Boden / Journal of Socio-Economics 28 (1999) 351–364*

Table 2
Mean values of probit model regressors for switched to self-employment in year t + 1 or remained in wage employment in year t + 1

Variable	Remained in wage employment in year t + 1	Switched to self-employment in year t + 1	Variable description
WORKEXP1	19.0588	21.8752	Years of Work Experience (Imputed)
SOMECOLL	0.25706	0.27743	Dummy Variable: 1 to 3 Years College
COLLPLUS	0.22687	0.26860	Dummy Variable: 4 or More Years College
WEARN1	15,623.86	14,507.00	Total Base-Year Wage Earnings (in Dollars)
FAMINC1	28,149.24	33,169.12	Base-Year Earnings of Other Family Members (in Dollars)
NWINC1	810.13	1,922.08	Base-Year Nonwage Income (in Dollars)
KIDSU61	0.15887	0.22068	Dummy Variable: Has at Least One Child Under Age Six
MULTEMP1	0.14731	0.14880	Dummy Variable: Two or More Different Employers in Base Year
WAGEDIF1	2.22683	2.54657	Imputed Gender Difference in Base-Year Hourly Wage Returns to Skill (in Dollars)
Number of Observations	40,473	793	

employment in year t + 1, and, separately, for women who remained in wage employment in year t + 1. Compared to women who remained in the wage sector in year t + 1, women who switched to self-employment were wealthier and more likely to have young children. They also were better educated, had more years of work experience, and earned, on average, an estimated 32 cents an hour less than otherwise comparable men. The latter patterns are consistent with the notion that a "glass ceiling"—an invisible barrier to women's progress—in the wage sector results in some women selecting into self-employment. In fact, Devine (1994b) finds that self-employed women have higher levels of observed measures of skill than female wage workers and that this disparity in average skill levels tended to rise with the rise in the female self-employment rate. Devine construes her findings as consistent with— but by no means definitive evidence of—the presence of a glass ceiling for women in wage employment.

A measurement issue should now be addressed. The CPS data that were used to support this study lack explicit data on job tenure and years of work experience. For this study, years of work experience were calculated as age minus years of education minus six. It is well known that this proxy measure of work experience may systematically overstate actual years of work experience for women. To the extent that this is true, this would imply that there is a downward bias in estimated wage returns to work experience for women relative to the estimated returns for men. However, the relatively low standard error of the parameter estimate for WAGEDIF1—*after controlling for years of work experience*—suggests that WAGEDIF1's measured effect on women's propensity to enter self-employment is not merely an artifact of correlation between WAGEDIF1 and unobserved gender differences in years of work experience.

6. Conclusions

Employer discrimination and the "glass ceiling" that allegedly limits women's ascent in wage employment have received much popular attention. It is entirely plausible that women who feel thwarted in their progress in the wage sector will be more likely to entertain the notion of becoming self-employed. This paper presents evidence that gender inequality in wage returns to observed worker attributes—a possible manifestation of employer discrimination—may indeed positively influence some women's decision to leave wage employment for self-employment.[9] This does not mean that gender inequality in the wage sector is an important source of the recent increase in female self-employment, however. Women become self-employed for a wide variety of reasons, and in this paper we have examined one very specific, potential factor.

Now, entering self-employment is a risky and often costly proposition, and it would be irresponsible to suggest that self-employment is a solution to the problem of labor market discrimination against women or minorities. But if self-employment is a preferred alternative for some women who are treated unfairly in the wage sector, then policies designed to promote women's economic parity with men should not overlook the self-employed. For instance, a woman's lesser exposure to managerial or supervisory experience in wage employment may indicate a need for remedial training and/or some form of mentoring support for self-employed women.

Likewise, women's prospects for success in self-employment could also be improved by policies designed to promote women's access to external sources of capital, including commercial loans. This is because women may face more binding wealth constraints on the initial (and subsequent) capitalization of their business ventures. Evans and Jovanovic (1989) and several subsequent studies have established a positive relationship between men's individual wealth and their propensity to enter self-employment and success in self-employment. Table 2 indicates that the average nonwage income (a proxy for individual assets or wealth) of women who switched from wage employment to self-employment is over twice that of women who remained in wage employment. This, and the positive and statistically significant parameter estimate for nonwage income reported in Table 1, suggest that Evans' and Jovanovic's model applies to women as well as men. Moreover, Boden (1996) finds that the average nonwage income of men is substantially greater than that of women, perhaps a manifestation of women's lower wage earnings and diminished opportunities to accumulate wealth. So wealth or liquidity constraints on women's self-employment selection and earnings may be especially binding, and the viability of women's business ventures may be particularly tied to their access to external sources of capital.

Appendix: annual wage earnings model specification and earnings

Tables A.1(a) and A.1(b) summarize the OLS parameter estimates for log (nominal) hourly wage earnings equations that were estimated separately for men and women for each of the five base years in the sample.[10,11] (These estimates were used to calculate the variable

358   *R. J. Boden / Journal of Socio-Economics 28 (1999) 351–364*

WAGEDIF1.) The regressors in these equations–mean values of which appear in Table A.2–are as follows:

WORKEXP1:   is imputed years of work experience, calculated as age minus years of schooling minus 6;

WEXP_2:   is the square of WORKEXP1;

SOMECOLL: is a dummy variable that assumes a value of unity for workers with one to three years of college;

COLLPLUS: is a dummy variable that assumes a value of unity for workers with four or more years of college;

NEVMAR: is a dummy variable that assumes a value of unity for workers who were never married;

KIDSU61:   is a dummy variable that assumes a value of unity for workers with at least one child under the age of six (specified to control for any associated absence from the labor force);

U100_1:   is a dummy variable that assumes a value of unity for workers employed in firms with fewer than 100 employees;

MULTEMP1:   is a dummy variable that assumes a value of unity for workers who had two or more different employers in the base year;

PROFESNL: is a dummy variable that assumes a value of unity for workers employed in selected professional occupations in the base-year;[12]

MANAGER: is a dummy variable that assumes a value of unity for workers employed in managerial, administrative, or supervisory occupations in the base-year;[13]

CLERSERV: is a dummy variable that assumes a value of unity for workers employed in selected clerical, administrative support, and service occupations in the base-year;[14]

MANUFACT, RETAIL, and SERVICES are dummy variables that assume values of unity for workers employed in the manufacturing, retail trade, or services industry divisions, respectively, in the base year. MSA1 is a dummy variable that assumes a value of unity for workers who reside in an identifiable metropolitan statistical area. NRTHCNTL, SOUTH, and WEST are dummy variables that assume values of unity for workers who reside in the North Central, South, and West census regions, respectively.

The March Income Supplement data of the CPS do not provide for determination of hours worked in workers' respective jobs of longest duration. Although the data allow for determination of earnings in workers' respective jobs of longest duration during the reference year, data on hours pertain to total hours worked in the reference year, including, in the case of about 15% of the men and women in the matched sample data used here, hours worked in jobs other than the job of longest duration. This matter was handled as follows. The dependent variable in the equations summarized in Tables A.1(a) and A.1(b) is the natural logarithm of total reference-year wage earnings divided by total hours worked in the reference year (where the latter was calculated as the product of hours per week usually worked and number of weeks worked). A potential problem with this resolution is that some of the regressors in the wage equations—viz., the industry and occupation dummy vari-

R. J. Boden / *Journal of Socio-Economics 28 (1999) 351–364*

Table A.1(a)
OLS parameter estimates for log hourly wage earnings equations for men, base years 1987, 1988, 1989, 1990, and 1991

Variable	1987		1988		1989		1990		1991	
	Estimate	Standard error[a]	Estimate	Standard error[a]	Estimate	Standard error[a]	Estimate	Standard error[a]	Estimate	Standard error[a]
INTERCEPT	1.95050	0.03114	2.04450	0.03229	2.06750	0.03089	2.07740	0.03034	2.07570	0.03148
WORKEXP1	0.04154	0.00199	0.03680	0.00208	0.03697	0.00194	0.03550	0.00195	0.03715	0.00203
WEXP_2	-0.00073	0.00004	-0.00063	0.00004	-0.00063	0.00004	-0.00060	0.00004	-0.00063	0.00004
SOMECOLL	0.14710	0.01535	0.15861	0.01503	0.17487	0.01428	0.16088	0.01349	0.13012	0.01395
COLLPLUS	0.33709	0.01757	0.38576	0.01732	0.36231	0.01679	0.37748	0.01601	0.35975	0.01690
NEVMAR	-0.25022	0.02200	-0.25259	0.02317	-0.24833	0.02126	-0.21411	0.02091	-0.24932	0.02053
KIDSU61	0.00583*	0.01557	0.00229*	0.01521	0.01311*	0.01456	0.01611*	0.01499	0.03565*	0.01512
U100_1	-0.21339	0.01328	-0.18678	0.01335	-0.18011	0.01305	-0.18015	0.01247	-0.18491	0.01313
MULTEMP1	-0.08937	0.01873	-0.09833	0.01780	-0.09405	0.01808	-0.10125	0.01731	-0.10061	0.01928
PROFESNL	0.12795	0.02469	0.18861	0.02122	0.16907	0.02109	0.15520	0.02274	0.17343	0.02110
MANAGER	0.19049	0.01696	0.17769	0.01643	0.18812	0.01635	0.20472	0.01590	0.22765	0.01687
CLERSERV	-0.16751	0.01908	-0.16961	0.01938	-0.17272	0.01768	-0.17282	0.01669	-0.14843	0.01767
MANUFACT	-0.01935*	0.01359	-0.03345	0.01331	-0.03912	0.01304	-0.06715	0.01320	-0.02692*	0.01386
RETAIL	-0.26047	0.01853	-0.30012	0.01967	-0.28386	0.01852	-0.30958	0.01832	-0.29193	0.01881
SERVICES	-0.20954	0.01844	-0.22950	0.01852	-0.23477	0.01786	-0.19698	0.01618	-0.17298	0.01689
MSA1	0.15887	0.01311	0.14814	0.01382	0.15862	0.01338	0.16970	0.01305	0.16081	0.01344
NRTHCNTL	-0.05551	0.01525	-0.06858	0.01513	-0.09222	0.01501	-0.07482	0.01455	-0.07252	0.01528
SOUTH	-0.12012	0.01561	-0.15998	0.01553	-0.15648	0.01531	-0.13235	0.01529	-0.11036	0.01566
WEST	0.00191	0.01833	-0.04553	0.01924	-0.03800	0.01629	-0.03564	0.01707	-0.02846*	0.01808
Number of Obs.	8,295		8,394		8,829		8,769		8,500	
Dep. Var. Mean	0.2293		0.2338		0.2385		0.2411		0.2446	
R-Squared	0.4139		0.4196		0.4123		0.4098		0.4021	

[a] Standard errors are corrected for heteroskedasticity.
* Not significantly different from zero at 95-percent or greater level of confidence.

Table A.1(b)
OLS parameter estimates for log hourly wage earnings equations for women, base years 1987, 1988, 1989, 1990, and 1991

Variable	1987		1988		1989		1990		1991	
	Estimate	Standard error[a]	Estimate	Standard error[a]	Estimate	Standard error[a]	Estimate	Standard error[a]	Estimate	Standard error[a]
INTERCEPT	1.80160	0.03226	1.77540	0.03761	1.81780	0.03340	1.85500	0.03136	1.88190	0.03380
WORKEXP1	0.02402	0.00182	0.02470	0.00185	0.02413	0.00177	0.02784	0.00159	0.02644	0.00183
WEXP_2	-0.00042	0.00004	-0.00045	0.00004	-0.00041	0.00003	-0.00048	0.00003	-0.00049	0.00004
SOMECOLL	0.18895	0.01505	0.19902	0.01607	0.19275	0.01514	0.20309	0.01394	0.18927	0.01496
COLLPLUS	0.40518	0.01798	0.44199	0.02084	0.46040	0.01725	0.46126	0.01685	0.43844	0.01882
NEVMAR	-0.08644	0.02105	-0.06887	0.02116	-0.07601	0.02158	-0.02616*	0.01810	-0.07756	0.02213
KIDSU61	0.04879	0.01807	0.04326	0.01844	0.07509	0.01809	0.06067	0.01709	0.03841	0.01826
U100_1	-0.17386	0.01263	-0.14878	0.01378	-0.14323	0.01284	-0.17878	0.01243	-0.17426	0.01285
MULTEMP1	-0.08391	0.01825	-0.08061	0.01872	-0.07669	0.01760	-0.05329	0.01767	-0.11000	0.02042
PROFESNL	0.16823	0.02956	0.09198	0.02975	0.13580	0.02659	0.13833	0.02766	0.09106	0.03697
MANAGER	0.16088	0.01947	0.17573	0.02105	0.20173	0.01808	0.16035	0.01958	0.16911	0.01733
CLERSERV	-0.11647	0.01475	-0.10284	0.01540	-0.09088	0.01464	-0.10847	0.01378	-0.09253	0.01482
MANUFACT	-0.10441	0.01977	-0.07074	0.02038	-0.12124	0.02055	-0.10964	0.01913	-0.07494	0.02069
RETAIL	-0.35758	0.01955	-0.35507	0.02123	-0.38161	0.01901	-0.41028	0.01879	-0.35471	0.01998
SERVICES	-0.17153	0.01594	-0.15199	0.01672	-0.14836	0.01554	-0.12829	0.01541	-0.09907	0.01668
MSA1	0.15583	0.01331	0.19203	0.01477	0.19197	0.01370	0.15278	0.01378	0.18309	0.01387
NRTHCNTL	-0.08028	0.01598	-0.08681	0.01657	-0.11427	0.01617	-0.13743	0.01518	-0.10564	0.01602
SOUTH	-0.11085	0.01575	-0.14333	0.01720	-0.14560	0.01614	-0.13809	0.01529	-0.13302	0.01634
WEST	-0.04661	0.01932	-0.08829	0.01990	-0.05825	0.01797	-0.08206	0.01822	-0.04123	0.01963
	Number of Obs.	7,794	Number of Obs.	8,054	Number of Obs.	8,504	Number of Obs.	8,580	Number of Obs.	8,334
	Dep. Var. Mean	0.1921	Dep. Var. Mean	0.1958	Dep. Var. Mean	0.2024	Dep. Var. Mean	0.2071	Dep. Var. Mean	0.2123
	R-Squared	0.2922	R-Squared	0.2770	R-Squared	0.3035	R-Squared	0.3174	R-Squared	0.2892

[a] Standard errors are corrected for heteroskedasticity.

* Not significantly different from zero at 95-percent or greater level of confidence.

Table A.2
Mean values of regressors in log hourly wage equations

Variable	1987		1988		1989		1990		1991	
	Men	Women	Men	Women	Men	Women	Men	Women	Men	Women
WORKEXP1	18.914	18.617	19.013	18.886	19.484	19.206	19.456	19.085	19.617	19.729
WEXP_2	541.80	532.55	549.50	537.16	562.09	550.57	555.48	539.06	553.80	558.15
SOMECOLL	0.18975	0.22530	0.20503	0.22871	0.20976	0.23060	0.25009	0.29685	0.26906	0.30214
COLLPLUS	0.24316	0.21298	0.24756	0.22411	0.25326	0.23166	0.24062	0.23065	0.25047	0.23770
NEVMAR	0.24569	0.22363	0.24839	0.21033	0.24646	0.21872	0.24575	0.22005	0.24388	0.20290
KIDSU61	0.19433	0.15987	0.19168	0.16017	0.19459	0.15793	0.18828	0.16352	0.19788	0.15875
U100_1	0.36239	0.37657	0.35823	0.37807	0.35587	0.36583	0.36447	0.36270	0.35647	0.36537
MULTEMP1	0.14876	0.15473	0.14629	0.15483	0.15019	0.14746	0.14346	0.14534	0.13365	0.13511
PROFESNL	0.08174	0.04157	0.08649	0.04520	0.08767	0.04810	0.08621	0.05245	0.08812	0.04572
MANAGER	0.15226	0.11406	0.15904	0.11622	0.15902	0.12147	0.16250	0.12179	0.15941	0.13019
CLERSERV	0.14008	0.44791	0.13915	0.44214	0.14248	0.44062	0.14563	0.43730	0.15659	0.44288
MANUFACT	0.29259	0.14729	0.28223	0.14899	0.28293	0.14922	0.27187	0.14103	0.26988	0.13499
RETAIL	0.15057	0.20798	0.15142	0.20226	0.16299	0.20355	0.15657	0.19732	0.16212	0.20302
SERVICES	0.21230	0.44419	0.20050	0.45394	0.21293	0.45473	0.21713	0.46375	0.22106	0.47372
MSA1	0.74045	0.72825	0.74279	0.72672	0.75513	0.73307	0.74866	0.73811	0.74376	0.73098
NRTHCNTL	0.27920	0.28881	0.27853	0.28234	0.26707	0.27364	0.27027	0.27762	0.28106	0.27850
SOUTH	0.29005	0.28496	0.29009	0.28905	0.26719	0.27199	0.26719	0.27429	0.26659	0.26686
WEST	0.15793	0.16243	0.16059	0.15893	0.18439	0.18297	0.19250	0.18415	0.18071	0.17375

ables—pertain to workers' respective jobs of longest duration. Fortunately, however, workers with wage earnings from jobs other than their job of longest duration comprise a relatively small proportion of the matched sample data used in this paper, and even among these workers, a majority of their reference-year wage earnings were from their respective jobs of longest duration.

Notes

1. The CPS is a monthly survey of approximately 60, 000 households and roughly 100, 000 household members that serves as the source of household-based labor force statistics, such as the unemployment rate. Every March, the CPS includes a supplementary set of questions that elicit data on the characteristics of individuals' jobs of longest duration and sources of income in the previous year. The resultant data files are also known as Annual Demographic Files. Because up to 50% of households—and almost the same percentage of household members—are interviewed in two consecutive years, it is possible to match these subsets of CPS cross-sectional data to obtain two-year panel data. In practice, the match rate for individuals ("person records") is less than 50% because of migration of individuals out of interviewed households and because some entire households become "non-interview" households in the subsequent year. This attrition obviously could result in all manner of biases in estimates based upon matched CPS data. However, Peracchi and Welch (1995) find that biases in estimates of transition rates between labor market statuses—a measurement issue of fundamental relevance to this paper—are not so problematic after controlling for gender, age, and labor market status in the base year.
2. Records were matched on month-in-sample, household identification number, then line number. In addition, person records qualified for matching only if sex and race were the same between years t and $t + 1$, and if the absolute value of age in year $t+1$ minus age in year t was less than or equal to two. No attempt was made to match person records that did not match on line number. The SAS programs used to read the hierarchical CPS March Income Supplement files, to match CPS person records between adjacent years, as well as the LIMDEP programs used to estimate the self-employment selection and wage earnings models described in this paper are available from the author.
3. The model was estimated with a set of dummy variables to control for different years, but the parameter estimates for these variables were very insignificant and inclusion of these dummy variables contributed little to the goodness of fit of the model. Also, the values of parameter estimates for the other regressors proved to be robust to inclusion or exclusion of dummy variables for year.
4. Boden (1996) reports a corresponding self-employment entry rate for white men of approximately 3%.
5. In this paper, class of worker in the job of longest duration during the March Income Supplement reference year is used to classify workers by employment status, whereas Evans and Leighton (1989) use class of worker during the survey reference week.

R. J. Boden / Journal of Socio-Economics 28 (1999) 351–364 363

6. WAGEDIF1 is a measure of gender differences in hourly wage returns to observed worker characteristics. The probit equation presented in this paper was also estimated with a variable that measures gender differences in *annual* wage returns to worker characteristics (with annual hours worked treated as endogenous using two-stage least squares to obtain parameter estimates for men's and women's annual wage earnings equations). The probit parameter estimate for this variable was likewise found to be positive and significant at a confidence level in excess of 95%.

7. A regression of WAGEDIF1 on the other regressors in Eq. (1) obtained an R-squared of 0.3420, with years of work experience, alone, accounting for just under 20% of the variation in WAGEDIF1. This regression indicates that each additional year of work experience results in a 5.6 cents increase in WAGEDIF1. Although the inclusion of years of work experience in Eq. (1) lowered the value of the probit parameter estimate for WAGEDIF1, the value of this estimate proved to be robust with regard to inclusion and exclusion of the other regressors in Eq. (1). These regression results are available from the author.

8. This statement is based upon the fact that $\partial P(SELFEMP = 1)/\partial WAGEDIF1 = \Phi(\mathbf{xa})*a_6 = 0.001895$, where $\Phi(\mathbf{xa})$ is the standard normal density function evaluated at the inner product of $\mathbf{a}$, the vector of probit parameter estimates, and $\mathbf{x}$, the vector of mean values of the regressors in the probit equation.

9. It does not necessarily follow that gender earnings differences in self-employment are necessarily smaller than they are in the wage employment. Both Carr (1996) and Boden (1996) suggest that nonpecuniary factors— especially flexibility of hours— play a relatively important role in women's decision to enter self-employment. And in this paper, it is assumed that the disutility of employer discrimination (or perceptions, thereof)–independent of expected self-employment earnings—is an impetus for (some) women's selection out of wage employment and into self-employment. Moreover, gender differences in the quality of wage employment experience (including exposure to managerial decision making) and access to start-up capital may well have an adverse impact on women's self-employment earnings potential.

10. The observations used in the estimation of these equations were subjected to the same screens imposed upon the data used to estimate the probit model of female self-employment entry.

11. As in the case of the probit model of self-employment entry, these wage equations were first estimated with a set of dummy variable regressors to control for year. These variables were dropped from these wage equations for exactly the same reasons they were excluded from the probit model.

12. Workers in this occupation group include: (a) architects and surveyors, (b) natural scientists and mathematicians, (c) computer systems analysts and scientists, and (d) workers employed in other professional specialty occupations.

13. Workers in this occupation group include: (a) managers and administrators, (b) salaried workers, (c) workers employed in management-related occupations, (d) sales supervisors and proprietors, and (e) production supervisors.

14. Workers in this occupation group include: (a) computer equipment operators, (b) secretaries, stenographers, and typists, (c) financial records processors, (d) other

clerical and administrative support workers, (e) protective service workers, (f) food service workers, (g) cleaning and building service workers, and (h) personal service workers.

References

Boden, R. (1999). Flexible working hours, family responsibilities, and female self-employment selection. *Am J Econ Socio 58*(1), 71–83.

Boden, R. (1996). Gender and self-employment selection: an empirical assessment. *J Socio-Econ 25*(6), 671–82.

Carr, D. (1996). Two paths to self-employment? Women's and men's self- employment in the United States, 1980. *Work and Occupations 23*(1), 26–53.

Devine, T. (1994a). Changes in wage-and-salary returns to skill and the recent rise in female self-employment. *Am Econ Rev 84*(2), 108–13.

Devine, T. (1994b). Characteristics of self-employed women in the United States. *Monthly Labor Review 117*(3), 20–34.

Evans, D., & Jovanovic, B. (1989). Estimates of a model of entrepreneurial choice under liquidity constraints. *J Polit Econ 97*(4), 808–27.

Evans, D., & Leighton, L. (1989). Some empirical aspects of entrepreneurship. *Am Econ Rev 79*(3), 519–35.

Oaxaca, R. (1973). Male-female wage differentials in the urban labor market. *Int Econ Rev 14*(4), 693–709.

Peracchi, F., & Welch, F. (1995). How representatives are matched cross-sections? Evidence from the current population survey. *J Econometrics 68*(1), 153–79.

Name Index

Abetti, P. 48
Aboud, J. 18
Abramson, P.R. 116
Acker, J. 66
Adler, N.J. 77
Admiraal, P.H. 336
Ahmed,S.U. 163
Ajzen, I. 184, 450
Alange, S. 184
Alba, R.D. 359, 374
Alcoff, L. 65
Alcorso, C. 99
Aldag, R. 563
Aldrich, H.E. 22, 23, 26, 27, 29, 31, 34, 35, 51,
    62, 64, 69, 72–4, 78, 90, 91, 98, 123, 124, 127,
    128, 131, 183, 201, 210, 226, 282, 284, 287–9,
    322, 323, 326, 358–60, 374, 375, 387–9, 392,
    407, 408, 453, 492, 494, 495, 497, 504, 582,
    583, 587
Alexander, J. 564
Alimansky, B. 358
Allen, J.K. 517
Allen, K.R. 89, 340, 357, 385
Allen, S. 429, 432, 442
Allen, T.J. 274
Allison, P.D. 504
Alvey, L. 26, 27, 409
Amboise, G. d' 338
Amit, R. 382, 475
Ancona, D.G. 247
Anderson, B.S. 18
Andrews, K. 74
Ang, J.S. 320, 323, 326, 327
Angle 161
Anish, A. 25, 27, 122, 492, 517, 519
Anna, A.L. 89, 94, 520, 525
Anscombe, G.E.M. 184
Ansell, C.K. 244, 274
Ansic, D. 521
Arlow 309, 315, 317
Arora, R. 31, 95, 429, 453
Arvey, R. 309
Astin, H.S. 409
Attanucci, J. 65
Aubrey, P. 322, 451, 564
Audretsch, D.B. 336

August, J.D. 323, 331
Auster, E. 495
Auster, E.R. 123, 124, 127, 137

Babbie, E. 126
Baca Zin, M. 93
Bach, R.L. 98
Bailey, S. 224
Baines, S. 91, 521
Baird, L. 317
Bais, J. 337, 339–41, 343
Baker 392
Baker, T. 64, 72, 73, 282, 390, 582, 583
Bandura, A. 390, 448, 450, 451, 453, 465
Banks, M. 478
Barber, B.M. 521
Barley, S. 580
Baron, J.N. 115, 224, 228, 246, 253, 300
Baron, R. 433
Barrett, M. 87, 98, 100
Barrier, M. 473
Barringer, B. 472
Bartlett, C.A. 258
Bates, F. 310, 318
Bates, T. 337
Baum, J.R. 474
Baumol 61, 62
Bearse, P. 563
Bebeau, M. 65
Becker, G. 240, 389
Becker, G.S. 67, 288, 356
Beckman, C. 63
Begley, T.M. 163
Belcourt, M. 45, 47, 164, 173, 427, 429, 432
Belenky, M.F. 65
Bem, S. 574, 583, 584
Bem, S.L. 63, 76, 77
BenDaniel, D. 375
Bender, H. 122, 123
Berg, I. 124, 127
Berger, A.N. 320, 323, 331, 333, 343
Berger, P.L. 28, 100
Berk, S.F. 221
Bernard, J. 136, 219, 230
Bernard, V.L. 521
Bernasek, A. 521

Bernstein, V. 310, 318
Betz, N.E. 448, 450, 452, 457
Bhave, M. 475, 484
Bhide, A. 70, 71, 73, 75, 362
Bielby, W.T. 115, 224, 228, 253
Biggadike, R.R. 410
Bigoness, W. 189, 317
Binks, M.R. 320, 322, 323, 326, 331
Birch, D. 124, 473, 580
Birch, D.L. 500
Bird 31
Bird, B. 427, 428, 450, 451
Bird, B.J. 63, 73, 74, 94, 96, 161, 164
Birley, S. 5, 24, 31, 48, 49, 114, 173, 184–6, 193,
    200, 201, 290, 339, 340, 357, 406, 408, 409,
    428, 429, 447, 573, 581
Bixler, S. 233
Black, N. 46, 102, 430
Blackwell, D.W. 323, 331, 333
Blais, R.A. 184
Blaise, R. 565
Blanchard-Fields, F. 76, 77
Blau, F.E. 580
Blau, J. 492
Blau, J.R. 359, 374
Blau, P.M. 285, 291
Boden, R. 591, 592, 594, 595, 597, 602, 603
Bogdan, J. 227
Bonacich, E. 98, 122
Bonjean, C.M. 186
Boot, A.W.A. 323, 331
Bordin, E.S. 116
Borjas, G.J. 122
Bourdieu, P. 241, 282
Bourke, R. 164, 173
Bowen, D.D. 89, 90, 91, 219, 447, 448, 494
Bowles, S. 125
Bowman, N. 17, 21, 23, 24, 116, 473
Bowman-Upton, N. 45, 49, 114, 164, 173, 189,
    341, 390, 407, 521
Boyatizis, R. 66
Boyd, D.P. 163
Boyd, N.G. 448, 450
Brabeck, M. 65
Bracker, J. 475
Bradley, D.B. 7
Brass, D.J. 254, 273, 274, 359, 374
Braungart, M.M. 76
Braungart, R.G. 76
Brazeal, D.V. 184
Breiger, R.L. 241, 273
Brenner, O.C. 189
Bretz, R. 75
Bridgewater, C. 116

Brigham, E.F. 327, 343
Brittain, J.W. 507
Brock, W.A. 336
Brockhaus, R. 19
Brockhaus, R.H. 123, 128, 160, 161, 163, 503
Brodzinski, J.D. 25, 452
Brooks, L. 452
Broom, H.M. 410
Brophy, D. 321, 322, 357, 383, 387, 388, 392,
    397
Brophy, D.J. 114
Brown, S.A. 322
Brown, T. 390
Bruderl, J. 357
Bruno, A. 382, 408
Bruno, A.V. 61, 358
Brush, C.G. 20, 23–7, 31–5, 37, 47, 62, 72–4, 76,
    78, 86, 87, 89–93, 95, 96, 98, 100, 101, 116,
    122, 125, 164, 226, 318, 321–3, 337–40, 355,
    357, 359–62, 385, 388, 409–11, 429, 430, 432,
    442, 447, 448, 452, 453, 456, 459, 474, 492,
    494, 496, 517, 519, 564, 570, 580–82
Bryne, B.M. 459
Bull, I. 563
Burke, R. 428
Burrell, B. 224
Burt, R.S. 241–4, 246, 248, 249, 252, 253, 258,
    261, 272, 275, 282, 285, 360
Busenitz, M. 383
Buss, D.M. 582
Butler, J.S. 98
Buttner, E.H. 27, 28, 35, 45, 48, 90–92, 114, 115,
    118, 188, 189, 198, 309, 318, 322, 340, 355,
    362, 385, 389, 407, 409, 429, 455, 463, 473,
    570, 582
Bygrave, W. 478
Bygrave, W.D. 61, 161, 355, 381, 383, 384, 387,
    391, 393

Cable, D.M. 452
Calàs, M. 46, 63, 76, 101, 103, 585
Calvert, L.M. 66
Camp, B. 410
Campbell, D.T. 581
Campbell, K. 222, 226
Campbell, K.E. 246, 283, 289
Cannon, T. 322
Carland, J. 473
Carland, J.W. 344
Carr, D. 89, 591, 603
Carr, J. 99
Carree, M. 336
Carrington, P.J. 287
Carroll, G.R. 183, 492, 493, 494, 499, 504

Carsky, M. 321, 322, 323, 326, 331
Carson, T. 18
Carsrud, A.L. 22, 23, 26, 27, 184, 424, 450, 453, 472
Carter, N. 93, 287, 288, 429
Carter, N.M. 61, 89, 99, 184, 186, 188, 189, 198, 199, 202, 356, 357, 362, 385, 414
Carter, S. 322, 337, 338, 521
Caruana, A. 476
Carver, C. 439
Cassell, J.W. 497
Casson, M. 70
Castrogiovanni, G.J. 451
Chacko, T.I. 115
Chaganti, R. 4, 24, 25, 31–3, 35, 62, 63, 76, 96, 115, 164, 173, 321, 322, 410, 476
Chan, Y.-S. 323
Chandler, G.N. 89, 94, 455–7, 520, 522
Charboneau, F.J. 495, 507
Charbonneau, J. 24, 26
Chatman, J. 452
Chell, E. 521
Cheng, C. 63
Child, J. 493
Chittenden, F. 343
Chodorow, N. 46, 582
Chrisman, J. 35, 45, 48, 453
Churchill 19, 20
Churchill, N.C. 62, 67, 69, 71, 390, 478
Clain, S.H. 95
Clark, T.A. 406, 408
Clement, B. 565
Cliff, J. 586
Cliff, J.E. 63, 70, 357, 388–91, 484, 521
Clinchy, B.M. 65
Coats, P.B. 449
Cockburn, L.E. 475
Cohen, L.E. 253
Cohen, S. 274
Cohen, T. 410
Coldwell, D.F. 247
Cole, A. 62, 67
Cole, R.A. 320–22, 324, 326, 327, 331
Coleman, J. 358
Coleman, J.S. 241, 247, 282
Coleman, L.L. 114
Coleman, S. 321, 323, 324, 326, 331, 355, 362, 385, 386, 396, 528
Collerette, P. 322, 451, 564
Collins, B.E. 161, 163
Collins, D.F. 184
Collins, J. 70, 74
Collins, O.F. 18, 24, 62
Collins, P.H. 98

Coltrane, S. 93
Cook, K.S. 241, 246
Cooney, T. 478
Cooper, A. 62, 63, 184, 290, 427, 428, 439, 563
Cooper, A.C. 4, 6, 8, 11, 12, 13, 15, 161, 163, 356, 357, 374, 408, 410, 521
Corbin, J. 455, 463
Covel, J. 227
Covin, J.G. 476, 563
Cox, L. 99
Craig, C. 6
Cramer, J.S. 324
Crawford, M. 428, 429
Cressy, R.C. 337
Cromie, S. 5, 23, 24, 29, 114, 122, 163, 290, 340, 357, 406, 408, 494, 573
Crosby, F. 225
Cross, M. 564, 565
Crozier, L.M. 476
Cuba, R. 25, 26, 34, 122, 494, 494, 496, 501, 517, 519
Cuff, D.F. 97
Cummings, L.L. 493
Curran 5
Currie, H.M. 321, 322

Dallalfar, A. 99
Daly, M. 96, 582
Dandridge, T. 563
Daphne, J. 288
Davidsson, P. 183, 427, 428, 437, 439, 472–4, 483, 580
Davies, L. 473
Davies, L.G. 327
Davis, S.J. 580
Day, D.L. 410
de Castillejo, I.C. 63
De Graaf, N.D. 246
de Vries, B. 65
Deaux, K. 309
DeCarlo, J. 114, 122
DeCarolis, D. 476
DeCastro, J. 453
DeCenzo, D. 25, 27, 122, 492, 517, 519
Deeds, D. 476
Deeks, J. 410
Demaris, A. 324
Denison, D. 564
Denison, D.R. 283
Dennis, W.D. 392
Derr, C.B. 452, 453
Devine, T. 591, 592, 596
Devine, T.J. 89, 95, 96, 281, 282, 288, 324, 406
Diamond, E. 225

Diamond, E.E. 448
DiCarlo 309
Dickie-Clark, H.P. 560
DiMaggio, P. 274
DiMaggio, P.J. 585
Dipboye, R. 309, 310, 318
Dobmeyer, T. 310, 318
Dollinger, M. 356
Donnell, S. 114, 115
Dreyfus, C. 96
Dsouza, D. 475, 477, 483
Du Rietz, A. 520, 521
Dubini, P. 22, 23, 27, 91, 184, 453, 563, 565
Dubno, P. 114, 115
Ducheneaut, B. 62, 63, 71, 78, 79, 388, 389, 391
Duchesneau, D.A. 163
Dugan, K.W. 24, 32
Dumin, M. 246
Dunkelberg, W. 290, 563
Dunnette, K. 310, 318
Dyer, W.G. 449, 452
Dyke, L.D. 164, 173
Dyke, L.S. 517, 521
Dyke, R.S. 86, 87, 407, 427

Eagley, A. 430
Eagley, A.H. 582, 583, 586
Eggers, J. 474, 478
Eichardus, M. 94
Eisenstein, Z.R. 125
Eisler, R. 77
Eitzen, D.S. 93
Elam, A. 284, 287
Elam, A.B. 580
Elango, B. 383
El-Namaki, M.S.S. 7
Elsbach, K. 434
Emerson, R.M. 241, 246
England, P. 122, 124, 281
Ennew, C.T. 320, 322, 323, 326, 331
Ensel,W.M. 222
Ensley, M. 478
Epstein, C. 587
Evans, D. 337, 592, 594, 595, 597, 602
Evans, D.S. 336

Fabowale, L. 321, 322, 326, 332
Fagenson, E. 45, 49
Fagenson, E.A. 114, 188, 189
Fahey, L. 410
Fann, G.L. 27, 34, 91
Farmer, H.S. 188, 189
Fasci, M.A. 521, 525
Fay, M. 385

Feeser, H.R. 24, 32, 477
Feiner, S.F. 98
Feldberg, R.L. 124–6
Ferber, M.A. 580
Ferguson, K.E. 65, 66
Fernandez, R.M. 247
Ferree, M. 66
Fidell, L.S. 479
Fiet, J. 383
Fiet, J.O. 358
File, K.M. 25
Fineberg, S. 354, 382
Finifter, B.M. 275, 281, 282, 288
Fiol, M.C. 587
Fiorentine, R. 450
Firestone, S. 96
Fischer, C.S. 224, 225, 284, 301
Fischer, E.M. 86, 87, 100, 102, 164, 173, 186,
    189, 198, 340, 350, 407, 427, 429, 442, 517,
    519, 520, 521
Fishbein, M. 450
Fisher, C.C. 115
Flamholtz, E. 66, 71
Flap, H.D. 246
Fletcher, J.K. 65, 76, 586
Fligstein, N.D. 224
Florin, J. 361, 363
Fondas, N. 63, 66, 76
Fox, K.D. 130, 138
Fox, M.F. 122
Freear, J. 355, 358, 362
Freedman, A. 563
Freeman, J. 492, 498, 499
Freeman, J.H. 246
Freeman, L.C. 241, 273
Freeman, S. 412
Frey, R.S. 123, 138
Friberg, M. 184
Fried, V. 357, 374, 382, 387, 390
Fromkin, H. 310, 318
Fulton, M.E. 477

Gabbay, S.M. 246
Gaglio, C.M. 22, 27
Gallos, J.V. 448
Garnsey, E. 6
Gartner, W.B. 20, 61, 69, 99, 162, 163, 166, 183,
    188, 288, 452, 571
Gascon, F.J.G. 161
Gatewood, E. 93, 356
Gatewood, E.J. 184, 186, 188, 189, 198–200, 202
Gattiker, U.E. 455
Gattikers, U. 189
Gavron, R. 336

Gerritson, J.C.M. 7
Gersick, C. 72
Gibb, A. 473
Gilbert, M.R. 188
Gilligan, C. 28, 29, 32, 64, 65, 100, 230, 387,
	390, 582
Gilmore, T.N. 485
Gimeno-Gascon, F.J. 427
Gimeno-Gascon, J.F. 521
Ginn, C.W. 473, 477
Gintis, H. 125
Glade, W.P. 67
Glaser, B. 439
Glenn, E.L. 124–6
Glenn, E.N. 135
Glorieux, I. 94
Goffee, R. 4, 8, 23, 25, 31, 34, 47, 95, 96, 115,
	123, 164, 361, 409, 427, 429, 431, 494
Goldberg, P. 310
Goldberg, R. 125
Goldberger, N.R. 65
Golden, B. 183, 188, 201
Goldstein, H.A. 289
Goldstein, S. 491
Goleman, D. 76, 115
Gonzalez, R.M. 98
Goodman, P.S. 491
Gordon, G.67
Gorman, C. 97
Gottfredson, L. 188
Gottfried, H. 63
Gould, R.V. 247
Gould, S. 29
Granovetter, M. 210, 216, 241, 243, 283, 285,
	360
Green, G.P. 340, 409, 413
Greenberger, D.B. 453
Greene, P. 92, 354, 355, 390
Greene, P.G. 92, 93, 95, 99
Greening, D. 472
Greiner, L. 62
Grisé, J. 428, 429, 430, 459, 564
Grosbeck, H.I. 62
Gulati, R. 258
Gumpert, D.E. 7, 20, 25, 123
Gundry, L. 362
Gupta, A.K, 355, 382, 384
Gutek, B. 220, 222, 310
Gutek, B.A. 29, 448, 449
Guzzo, R.A. 114

Haber, S. 18
Hackett, G. 448, 450, 457
Hagan, O. 18, 29, 34

Hagen, E.E. 184
Hagstrom, P. 72
Haines, G.H. 326, 327
Hakel, M. 310, 318
Hall, A.287
Hall, J. 114, 115, 382, 383
Hall, R. 76
Hall, R.H. 89, 517
Hambrick, D.C. 476
Hamermesh, D.S. 115
Hamilton, D. 521
Hamilton, J. O'C. 18
Hamner, W. 317
Hanks, S.H. 455, 456, 522
Hannan, M.T. 492, 498, 499
Hansen, E. 61
Hansen, E.L. 161, 340
Hargadon, A.B. 274
Harlan, A. 310, 318
Harlos, K.P. 66
Harriman, A. 188
Harrison, R. 381, 382, 384, 396, 397
Harrison, R.T. 354, 355
Hart, M. 92, 359, 373
Hart, M.M. 93
Hartman, R. 429
Hartman, R.I. 31, 95, 453
Hartmann, H. 125, 126, 220, 223, 227
Hartzook, N.C.M. 98
Hayes, J. 23, 24, 29, 494
Haynes, D.C. 92
Haynes, G.W. 92
Healey, P.M. 521
Hebert, R.F. 61
Heider, F. 184
Heilman, M. 319
Heilman, M.C. 115
Heilman, M.E. 114, 115
Helgensen, S. 581, 583
Helgesen, S. 25, 28, 31, 32, 72, 76
Hennig, M. 28
Henning, M. 77
Henrekson, M. 520, 521
Herron, L. 453
Herron, N. 427, 428, 439, 442
Hertz 5, 6
Hertz, L. 115
Hertzog, C. 76
Hesse-Biber, S. 122
Hills 163
Hills, G.E. 476, 478
Hirschi, T. 247
Hirschman, A.O. 213
Hisrich, R.D. 18, 20, 23–27, 32–5, 47, 89, 90, 91,

114, 116, 122, 125, 128, 137, 219, 226, 308,
309, 315, 317, 318, 319, 321, 323, 327, 337,
338, 340, 357, 359, 361, 374, 382, 383, 387,
390, 392, 409, 410, 429, 447, 448, 452, 453,
459, 474, 492, 494, 496, 517, 519, 564, 570
Hitt, M. 115
Hochschild, A. 229
Hofer, C. 74, 77, 382, 383
Hofer, C.W. 407, 408
Hofstede, C. 184, 186
Hofstede, G. 63, 78, 341
Hogan, R. 116
Holland, J. 116
Holmes, S. 338
Holmquist, C. 25, 29, 31, 32, 63, 78, 79, 579,
581
Holt, D. 563
Honig-Haftel, S. 24, 26, 34, 35, 95, 338, 357,
408
Hood, J.N. 25, 29, 32, 33, 173
Hooks, B. 98
Hornaday, J.A. 18, 19, 20
Hornsby, J.A. 475
Horwitz, P.S. 160, 161, 163
Hosmer, L. 410
Hoy, F. 447, 456, 475, 477, 483
Huber, G. 183, 188, 201
Hudson, R. 408
Hughes, A. 337, 338
Humphreys, M.A. 20, 32, 47, 122, 124, 125,
494–6, 507
Humphries, M. 114
Huo, Y.P. 492
Hurlbert, J.S. 222, 246, 283, 284
Hurley, A. 24, 26, 28, 29, 32, 36
Hurley, A.E. 86, 87, 100, 101, 585
Hurlock, J. 18

Ibarra, H. 253, 254, 274, 360
Ilgen 309, 310
Izraeli, D. 77

Jaccard, J. 462
Jack, D. 65
Jack, R. 65
Jackowicz, A. 309, 315, 317
Jackson, D. 116, 118
Jackson, D.N. 116
Jackson, S.E. 93
Jaggar, A. 46
Jagger, A.M. 88
James, F.J. 406, 408
Jancowicz, A. 382, 392
Jang, H. 246

Jansen, E. 89, 457, 520
Jardim, A. 28, 77
Jelinek, M. 69
Jennings, E. 541
Jerdee, T. 309
Jianakoplos, N.A. 521
Jimeno-Gascon, F. 63
Johns, S. 163
Johnson, B.R. 162
Johnson, M.A. 95, 97
Johnson, S. 338, 385
Jones, N. 309, 315, 317
Jovanovic, B. 337, 594, 595, 597
Judd, B.B. 25
Judge, T.A. 452
Jung, C. 64, 76

Kalleberg, A.226, 227, 407, 411, 413, 421, 427,
455, 517
Kalleberg, A.L. 23, 24, 33, 44, 45, 47–51, 58, 91,
122–4, 128, 135, 289, 290, 322, 340, 497, 521
Kanatas, G. 323
Kanter, R. 188, 219, 221, 228, 229
Kanter, R.B. 77
Kanter, R.M. 252, 254, 274
Kaplan, E. 24, 25, 31, 33, 34, 62, 408, 427, 517,
519
Kasarda, J. 61
Katz, J. 61, 69, 452
Katz, J.A. 162, 166, 183, 284
Kaufman, D. 227
Kaufman, H. 513
Kazanjian, R.K. 485
Kearney, K.G. 583
Keats, B. 475
Keeley, R. 407, 408
Kelly, M. 358
Kemp, A.A. 93
Kemp, P.R. 34
Kenny, D. 433
Kent, C.A. 18, 20, 24, 25, 27, 33, 34, 114
Kent, P. 338
Kerlinger, F.N. 63
Kets de Vries, M.F.R. 123, 128
Khaneman, D. 32
Kiesler, S. 310
Kim, W.C. 474
Kirchhoff, B. 396
Kirzner, I. 61, 62
Kitch, S.L. 448, 456
Klein, H. 439
Klieman, 274, 275
Kline, J.B. 410
Knight, F. 61

Knight, R.M. 186
Knopoff, K. 63
Kolvereid, L. 183–5, 427, 428, 433, 442, 452,
    472–4, 485, 582
Konek, C.W. 448, 456
Koper, G. 337
Korsgaard, M.A. 355, 383
Kotey, B. 343, 344
Kotter, J. 69, 71
Kotter, J.P. 274
Kovach, K.A. 115
Kovalainen, A. 575
Krackhardt, D. 247
Krueger, N. 450, 472
Krueger, N.F. 183, 184
Krueger, N.F. Jr. 184
Kuratko, D.F. 475

Laetz, V.B. 472, 483
Lamas, E. 18
Landholt, P. 247
Landy, F. 310, 318
Langton, N. 287, 288
Larson, J.K. 218
Larwood, L. 29, 189, 220, 222, 448, 449, 455
Latham, G. 75
Lazega, E. 273
Lazier, W. 74
Leahy, K. 474, 478
Lee-Gosselin, H. 164, 173, 427–9, 430, 459, 564
Leeth, J.D. 323, 331
Leibow, C. 32
Leicht, K.T. 23, 24, 33, 44, 45, 47–51, 58, 91,
    122–4, 128, 135, 322, 340, 407, 411, 413, 421,
    427, 455, 517, 521
Leighton, L. 592, 595, 602
Leland, C. 409
Lerman, D. 160
Lerner, M. 78, 456
Levenson, H. 161, 163
Lewis, V. 62, 67, 69, 71, 390
Li, K. 162
Liao, J. 478
Liao, T.F. 284
Lichtenstein, J.H. 18
Liebenstein, H. 61, 67
Lieberson, S. 124, 301
Light, I. 98, 122, 220
Lin, J.W. 320, 323
Lin, N. 222, 246, 282, 288, 298
Lindberg, R.A. 410
Lindblom, C.E. 32
Link, A.N. 61
Liou, N. 64, 90, 282, 407, 408

Lipman-Blumen, J. 552
Lirtzman, S. 115
Literer, J. 69
Livesay, H.C. 62
Locke, E. 430
Loewenstein, G. 225
Long, B. 456
Long, W.A. 161
Longenecker, J.G. 410
Longstreth, M. 24, 26, 94, 95, 164
Longsworth, E.K. 161
Loscocco, K.A. 89, 122, 124–7, 137, 321, 322,
    340, 447, 448, 452, 456, 463, 495, 517, 519,
    582
Lovelace, K. 452
Low, M. 45, 61, 563
Lowe, G.S. 126
Luckman, T. 28, 100
Luger, M.I. 289
Lyles, M. 475
Lyons 309
Lyons, P. 114, 122

MacKinnon, C. 102
MacMillan, I. 45, 61, 308, 382, 392, 563–5
MacMillan, I.C. 410
MacMillan, I.D. 184
Macy, G. 472
Madden, J. 115
Mahot, P. 385
Mainiero, L.A. 449
Maki,W.R. 183
Maniero, L.A. 274
Manigart, S. 383
Mannheim, K. 76
Manser, M.E. 288
March, J.G. 32
Marchioro, C. 76
Marlow, S. 573, 580
Marsden, P.V. 222, 246, 283, 284, 285, 291, 295,
    301, 497
Martin, C.L. 115
Martin, J. 63, 66, 75
Martin, L. 24, 26, 34, 35, 95, 338, 357, 408
Martin, P. 66
Martin, S. 227
Martinelli, A. 244
Maslow, A.H. 184, 560
Mason, C. 381, 382, 384, 396, 397
Mason, C.M. 354, 355
Masters, R. 23, 24
Mathieu, P.S. 450
Mauborgne, R. 474
Mauldin, T. 24, 26, 94, 164

Mayer, K. 491
Mazur, A. 123, 138
McCain, G. 24, 25, 122
McCarthy, J.D. 580
McClelland, D. 24, 62, 66
McClelland, D.C. 101, 123, 184, 186, 541
McClung, J. 20, 32, 47, 114, 122, 124, 125, 494–6, 507
McCreary, L. 124
McDermott 8
McDougall, P. 407, 475, 477, 483
McEvoy, D. 504
McGrayne, S.B. 585
McMullan, W.E. 161
McPherson, J.M. 228, 254, 284, 288
McPherson, M. 359
Meier, R. 23, 24
Meredith, G.G. 344
Mero, N. 89
Mero, N.P. 520
Merton, R.K. 242, 249
Merz, G. 472, 483
Mescon, T.S. 24, 25
Meyer, A.D. 491
Meyer, D. 383
Meyer, M.W. 124, 491, 493
Meyerson, E.M. 246
Mikalachki, A. 478
Miles, R.E. 478
Milgram, S. 215
Milkman, R. 252
Milkovich, G. 75
Miller, A. 410, 412
Miller, B. 160, 167, 499
Miller, B.A. 184, 202
Miller, J. 126
Miller, J.B. 28, 582
Millett, K. 96
Mills 350
Mindell, P. 77
Miner, J. 49, 52
Miner, J.B. 186
Mintzberg, H, 28, 233, 274
Modell, J. 98
Monroe, S.R. 485
Moore, D. 473
Moore, D.G. 18, 24, 62, 184
Moore, D.P. 90, 188, 189, 198, 340, 389, 455, 463
Moore, G. 284, 287, 291, 295
Moore, K. 114, 115
Moore, L.M. 448, 449
Moriya, F.E. 25
Morris, M.H. 476

Mosakowski, E. 183
Moss, C. 5, 24, 339
Muldowney, M. 338
Mumby, D. 66, 76
Muzyka, D. 356, 374, 382
Myers, A. 290
Myers, D.G.114

Naffziger, D.W. 475
Nanda, A. 258
Narasimha, P. 308
Narayana, C.L. 476, 478
Neck, H. 485
Nee, V. 98
Neider, L. 24, 25, 32, 33, 35, 321, 322, 338, 410, 582
Neill, J.A. 116
Neiswander, D. 477
Nelson, F.D. 324
Nelson, G. 22, 23, 27, 34, 453
Nelson, J.I. 186
Nelson, R. 61
Nelton, S. 32–5, 37
Neville, D.D. 450
Newman, D.L. 327
Nickols, S.Y. 130, 138
Nielsen, F. 582
Nieva, V. 310
Nieva, V.F. 29, 448
Niles, S.G. 450
Northcott, H.C. 126
Norton, E. 383
Nunnally, J. 53
Nystrom, P. 127

Oaxaca, R. 594
O'Brien, M. 18, 27, 89, 114, 137, 308, 315, 317, 357, 452, 456, 570
O'Connor, J.F. 124
Odean, T. 521
Olds, S.W. 497
Oliker, S.J. 224, 225, 284
Olm, K. 338, 361, 409
Olm. K.W. 22, 23, 26, 27
Olofsson, C. 563
Olsen, S.F. 321, 322
Ooghe, H. 383
Orr, E. 173
Orser, B. 321, 322, 326, 332
Ortiz, F. 227
Osteryoung, J.S. 327
Overman, S.J. 449

Padavic, I. 90, 93, 580

Padgett, J.F. 244, 274
Palepu, K.G. 521
Palmer, K. 76
Papalia, D.E. 497
Parker, R. 221
Parzen, J. 29
Paulhus, D. 163, 166, 170
Pearson, J. 475
Pellegrino, E.T. 7, 26, 35, 114, 122, 123, 323, 494, 496, 570
Pennings, J.M. 246, 356, 491
Peracchi, F. 602
Perrone, L. 127
Peters, T. 586
Peters, T.J. 507
Petersen, M.A. 320, 323, 331
Petterson, G. 563
Pfeffer 36
Pfeffer, J. 493
Pheterson, G. 310
Phillips, B. 392
Phizacklea, A. 99
Picot, C. 288
Pistrui, D. 478
Plas, J.M. 456
Plaschka, G.R. 24, 32
Pleck, J.H. 93, 104, 130, 138
Podolny, J.M. 246, 253, 300
Poole 161
Popay, J. 4
Popielarz, P.A. 246, 284, 285, 288, 299
Porter, M.E. 77, 410, 422
Portes, A. 98, 247, 298
Powell, G.N. 449
Powell, M. 521
Powell, W.W. 585, 586
Power, D. 183, 188, 201
Pratt 359
Pratt, S.E. 386
Price, C. 485
Puka, B. 65
Putnam, L. 66, 76
Putnam, R.D. 241, 282

Rafaeli, A. 66, 434, 441
Raider, H.J. 258
Rajan, R.G. 320, 323, 331
Ramanujam, V. 427, 455, 500, 512
Ramsey, V.J. 66
Ratcliff, K.S. 227
Read, L. 582
Read, W. 75
Reece, B.L. 7, 122, 123, 323, 494, 496
Reece, P.R. 22, 23, 26, 27, 35, 360

Rees, A. 115
Rees, B.L. 114
Reese, B. 570
Reese, P. 406
Reese, P.R. 453
Reese, P.Y. 91, 284, 287, 289, 300
Renzulli, L. 284, 288, 295
Reskin, B. 580
Reskin, B.F. 90, 93, 126, 220, 222, 223, 227, 282, 288
Reuber, A.R. 48, 86, 87, 164, 173, 407, 427, 517, 520
Reynolds, P. 160, 167, 429, 580
Reynolds, P.D. 61, 67, 99, 183, 184, 190, 192, 193, 202, 203, 282, 288, 289, 408, 412, 499
Rickel, A.U. 448, 449
Riding, A. 321–3, 326, 327, 332, 355, 362, 385, 409
Riding, A.L. 28, 45, 48, 91, 337, 338
Rieke 451
Rimmer, L. 4
Ritzer, G. 121
Rivchun, C. 18, 29, 34
Robbie, K. 376, 382, 384, 386
Roberts 18
Roberts, E.B. 369
Roberts, J. 478
Roberts, M.J. 62
Robinson, J. 89, 90, 122, 124, 125, 127, 137, 321, 322, 495, 517, 582
Robinson, R. 427, 428, 439, 442, 447, 448, 452, 457, 463
Robinson, R.B. Jr. 407
Robinson, R.J. 362
Rogers, E.M. 218
Romanelli, E. 407
Ronen, J. 62
Ronstadt, R. 318
Roos, P.A. 222
Rosa, E. 123, 138
Rosa, P. 337, 338, 521
Rosen, B. 28, 35, 45, 48, 91, 92, 114, 115, 118, 226, 309, 318, 32, 355, 362, 385, 407, 409, 452, 570, 582
Rosener, J.B. 63
Rosenstein, J. 115, 383
Rosenthal, E.A. 247
Rosten, L. 239
Rothbard, N. 283
Rothenberg, P.S. 98
Rotter, J.B. 161, 166
Roure, R. 407, 408
Rubery, J. 6
Ruhnkha, J. 383

Russell, D. 160

Sahlam, W. 382
Salancik 36
Salancik, G.R. 493
Sandberg, W.R. 407, 408
Sander, S. J.M. 98
Sanders, P. 24
Saparito, P. 92
Sapienza, H. 355, 382, 384, 387, 389
Sapiro, V. 88
Sargent, M. 358
Saunders, H.L. 7
Saunders, P. 5, 339
Scase, R. 4, 8, 23, 25, 31, 34, 47, 95, 96, 115,
    123, 164, 361, 409, 427, 429, 431, 494
Schafran, L.H. 227
Scheier, M. 439
Schein, E. 452, 457, 459, 460
Schein, E.H. 69, 73, 186
Schein, V. 114, 309
Scheinberg, S. 184, 185, 186, 193, 200, 201, 564,
    565
Schendel, D. 74, 77
Scherer, R.F. 25, 452
Scherr, F.C. 322, 326, 361
Schlecker, D.I. 450
Schragg, P. 582
Schreier, J.W. 560, 561
Schrier, J.W. 18, 20, 23, 25
Schroeder, D. 408
Schulze, B. 361, 363
Schumpeter, J.A. 61, 62, 475
Schwartz, E. 564
Schwartz, E.B. 18, 23, 25, 26, 32, 33, 114, 122,
    164, 494, 496
Scollard, J.R. 580, 584
Scott 164
Scott, C. 410
Scott, C.E. 24–6, 96, 340, 447
Scott, J.A. 323, 331
Scott, L. 61, 63, 67
Scott, L.R. 161, 163, 183, 184, 198
Scott, W.R. 69
Seegull, F. 92, 386, 387
Segal, P. 322
Seglin, J. 223, 308
Selznick 74
Sexton, D. 61, 62, 427, 428
Sexton, D.L. 17, 18, 20, 21, 23, 24, 27–9, 34, 45,
    49, 114, 116, 164, 173, 189, 341, 390, 407,
    453, 473, 477, 521
Sexton, E.A. 90
Shaef 31

Shane, S. 61, 62, 70, 184–6, 193, 200, 201, 452
Shapero, A. 35, 61, 123, 184, 465
Shaver, K. 61, 63, 67
Shaver, K.G. 161, 163, 166, 183, 198
Shaw 309
Sheehy, B. 76
Shelton, B.A. 288
Shepherd, D.A. 355
Sheppard, D. 409
Shilit 308, 315, 317
Siegel, R. 308
Siess, T.F. 116
Sik, E. 282
Simmel, G. 242
Simon, H.A. 32
Simon, M. 183
Singer, H.A. 116
Slevin, D.P. 476, 563
Smart, G. 375
Smart, G.H. 356, 374
Smeltzer, L.R. 27, 34, 91
Smilor, R. 62
Smircich. L. 46, 63, 76, 101, 103, 585
Smith, N. 49, 52, 114
Smith, N.R. 24, 25, 62, 122, 184
Smith, P. 447, 456
Smith-Lovin, L. 228, 254, 284, 288
Smits, S.J. 447, 456
Snow, C.C. 478
Sohl, J.E. 354
Sokol, L. 35, 61
Sokoloff, N.J. 93, 94, 125
Sombart, W. 98
South, S.J. 274
Sowa, C.J. 450
Sparrowe, R.T. 246
Stafford, K. 24, 26, 94, 164
Stake, J. 76
Starbuck, W.H. 127
Starr, J. 474, 484, 580, 581, 587
Starr, J.A. 161, 163, 287
Stearns, T.M. 407, 408, 414
Stegall, D.P. 410
Steinmetz, L.L. 410
Stern, R.N. 247
Stevens, G. 284
Stevens, G.E. 24, 25
Stevenson 5
Stevenson, H. 25, 210, 382
Stevenson, H.H. 62, 68, 70, 123
Stevenson, L. 47, 98, 429, 432, 441
Stevenson, L.A. 20, 22, 24, 29, 32, 95, 100, 340,
    357, 451
Stewart, A. 229

Stiglitz 323
Stigter, H.W. 337, 340
Stinchcombe, A. 410
Stinchcombe, A.L. 124, 493
Stipek, D. 162
Stolze, W.J. 584
Stone, M. 73
Stoner, C. 429
Stoner, C.R. 31, 95, 453
Storey, D. 385
Storey, D.J. 337, 338, 565
Storey, M.J. 476, 478
Storey, R. 563
Stover, C. 581, 583
Strange, A. 580
Strauss, A. 439, 455, 463
Strickland, B.R. 161
Stromberg, A.H. 29
Stuart, R. 48
Sugrue, T.F. 322,326
Suhrer-Roussel, L.76
Sundin, E. 25, 29, 31, 32, 63, 78, 579
Sussman, J.A. 224
Sutton, C. 114, 115
Sutton, R. 66, 434, 441
Sutton, R.I. 274, 491
Swaminathan, A. 283
Swartz, J. 355, 384
Swayne, C. 25, 67, 68
Swayne, C.B. 560
Sweeting, R. 382
Swift, C.S. 28, 45, 48, 91, 92, 321–3, 332, 337, 338, 355, 362, 385, 409

Tabachnik, B.G. 479
Talmud, I. 246
Tansey, R. 326
Tarule, J. 65
Taylor 308
Taylor, J. 354
Taylor, V. 66
Taynor, J. 309
Terborg 309, 310
Terpstra, D. 309
Thakor, A.V. 323, 331
Thierren, L. 18
Thomas, R. 326, 327
Thompson, J.D. 74
Thompson, J.K. 25, 29, 32, 33, 173
Thumin, F. 116
Thurik, A.R. 336, 338
Thurow, L. 115
Tibbets, G.E. 478
Tigges, L.M. 340, 409, 413

Timmons, J. 20, 163
Timmons, J.A. 68, 75, 355, 381–4, 387, 389, 391, 393, 451, 463
Tomkiewicz, J. 189
Tong, R. 93, 96
Tosi, H. 563
Toulouse, J. 565
Toulouse, J.M. 184
Townsley, E. 252
Travers, J. 215
Travis, C. 430
Trevethan, L. 65
Tronto, J. 65
Truman, C. 429, 432, 439, 442
Tsai, W. 563
Tucker, W. 25, 67, 68
Tucker, W.R. 560
Turrisi, R. 462
Tyebjee, T. 61, 358, 382
Tyler, F. 320, 323
Tyversky, A. 32

Udell, G.F. 320, 323, 331, 333, 343
Udry, R.J. 582
Ulrich 309, 315, 317
Unger, R. 428, 429
Unger, R.K. 115

Valdez, J. 521, 525
Van Auken,H. 582
Van de Ven, A. 408
Van de Ven, A.H. 160, 161, 163
Van der Wijst, N. 338
Van Osnabrugge, M. 362, 363
Van Uxem, F.W. 337, 339–41, 343
Vanderwerf, P. 33, 456
Vella, A.J. 476
Venkatapathy, R. 163
Venkataraman, S. 61, 62, 70, 160
Venkatraman, N. 427, 455, 500, 512
Vesper, K.H. 18, 20, 24, 25, 31, 33, 34, 67, 163, 451
Vetter, BJ.M. 89
Vinnicombe, S. 5
Voerman 350
Voydanoff, P. 94
Vozikis, G.S. 24, 25, 448, 450
Vroom, V.H. 184

Wacquant, L.J.D. 241
Waddell, F.T. 20, 114
Wahba, M. 115
Wahlbin, C. 563
Waldinger, R. 98

Walker, L. 65
Wallston, P.S. 456
Walsh, J.P. 410
Wan, C.K. 462
Ward, A. 472
Ward, J.B. 322, 326
Ward, R. 98
Warren, A. 24, 25, 122
Waterman, R.H. Jr. 507
Watkins, D. 5, 24, 33, 47, 125, 340, 357, 429
Watkins, J. 5, 24, 33, 47, 125, 340, 357, 429
Watson, W. 355, 384
Weber 315
Weber, M. 66, 98
Weber, P.B. 472, 483
Weick, K.E. 61
Weinberg, J.A. 320, 322, 323, 326, 327
Weiner, B. 160, 162, 166
Weiss 323
Weiss, J. 124, 127, 128, 131
Weiss, P. 63
Welch, F. 602
Welch, M.S. 232, 233
Wellman, B. 225, 282, 287, 295, 301
Welsch, H. 114, 362, 478
Welsch, H.B. 23–5
Welsch, H.P. 339, 340
Wennekers, S. 336
Westerberg, L. 62
Westhead, P. 184–6, 193, 200, 201, 373,452
Weston, J.F. 343
Wexley, K. 75
Wheelcock, J. 91
Whetton, D.A. 491
Whiston, S.C. 450
White, S.B. 184, 202, 282, 288, 289
White, T.I. 583, 584
Whittier, N. 76
Wholey, D.R. 507
Wiback, K. 310, 318
Wiebe, F. 25
Wiebe, F.A. 452
Wijewardena, H. 478

Wiklund, J. 472, 483
Wilkens, J. 494, 496
Willard, G.E. 61, 62, 410
Williams, J. 430
Williams, L. 385
Williams, P. 429
Williams, P.M. 284
Williamson, O. 213
Wilson, M. 582
Winegardner, J. 116
Winter, D.G. 184
Winter, F. 563
Winter, S. 61
Winters, D.B. 323, 331, 333
Wojahn, E. 127
Wolf, W. 224
Wolken, J.D. 320–22, 323, 326, 331
Woo, C. 521
Woo, C.Y. 410, 427
Wood, W. 430, 582, 586
Woodman, M. 64
Woodward, W. 226
Workman, J. 76
Wortley, S. 287
Wortman, M.S. 161
Wright, E.O. 127
Wright, M. 357, 373, 374, 380, 373, 374, 376, 382, 384, 386, 390

Yasuda, Y. 246
Young, E. 114, 339, 340
Young, E.C. 23–5
Young, J.E. 358
Yudkin, M. 287, 474, 484, 580, 581, 587

Zacharakis, A.L 355, 401
Zanna, M.P. 225
Zellner, W. 408
Zhou, M. 98
Ziegler, R. 246
Zimmer, C. 210, 504
Zinsser, J.P. 18
Zucker, L.G. 124, 491

Volunteerism

The Directory
of Organizations,
Training, Programs
and Publications

The Points of Light Initiative: Community Service as National Policy

"From now on in America, any definition of a successful life must include serving others."

—President George Bush
June 22, 1989

Objective: A Nation Transformed by Service

The *Points of Light Initiative* is a movement to engage all individuals, groups and organizations in America in direct and consequential action to solve community problems. The President's three-part strategy to make community service national policy of the highest priority is as follows:

1. *The call to claim society's problems as your own:* To call every American and every American family, corporation, firm, school, place of worship, union, club or association to engage in helping to solve our most critical social problems.

2. *Identify, enlarge and multiply what is working:* To identify successful and promising community service projects and initiatives, bring news of their existence to other communities and multiply them throughout the nation.

3. *Discover, encourage and develop leaders:* To discover, encourage and develop individuals who are "points of light" and to convince all Americans that a life that includes serving others is a meaningful, adventurous and successful life.

Volunteerism

The Directory
of Organizations,
Training, Programs
and Publications

Third Edition

Formerly entitled *Community Resources Directory,* 2nd Edition

Harriet Clyde Kipps, Editor

With forewords by

Barbara Bush, *First Lady of the United States*
John Glenn, *U.S. Senator from Ohio*
Eugene M. Lang, *Founder, "I Have a Dream" Foundation*

R. R. BOWKER

VOLUNTARISM and VOLUNTEERISM

No book on voluntary action is complete without an attempt at clarification of the difference between these two terms.

Voluntarism—action by a large entity (corporation, national leader) that goes beyond the bounds of duty to help relieve the problems of society; e.g., a corporation agreeing to adapt some of its jobs to handicapped persons with special needs, or a successful individual "adopting" a class of underprivileged children and challenging them with a promise of paid college educations.

Volunteerism—action by an individual or a group, giving time and energy, to help another individual or group; e.g., an adult working with a child who is deprived of a role model to help him or her through the difficult "growing up" years, or a successful family helping another family get through some hard times through friendship and understanding.

Published by R. R. Bowker,
a division of Reed Publishing (USA) Inc.
Copyright © 1991 by Reed Publishing (USA) Inc.
All rights reserved
Printed and bound in the United States of America

International Standard Book Number   0-8352-2739-1
International Standard Serial Number   0000-1325
Library of Congress Catalog Card Number   83-25349

ISBN 0-8352-2739-1

9 780835 227391

Contents

FOREWORDS

The Most Peculiar People in the World... xi
  by Barbara Bush, First Lady of the United States

The Spirit of Volunteerism in America xii
  by John Glenn, U.S. Senator from Ohio

Voluntarism and the Human Spirit xiii
  by Eugene M. Lang, Founder and Chairman,
  "I Have a Dream" Foundation

INTRODUCTION

Background xv
Scope of This Edition xv
Preparation of This Edition xvi
Information Gathering xvi
Other Features xxi
Acknowledgments xxi

HOW TO USE THIS BOOK xxii

Model Listings xxii
Abbreviations and Symbols xxiv

MESSAGE TO VOLUNTEERS

1. Overview and Definition of the Volunteer Center xxv
2. The Volunteer's Rights and Responsibilities xxvi
3. Diversity of Roles for Volunteers xxvi
4. Alternatives Where Volunteer Centers Do Not Exist xxvii
5. Contact Information for Volunteer Centers and
   Other Resources xxvii

   Nationwide Hotline. Nationwide Contacts for Youth Volunteers.
   Governors' Offices. Local Volunteer Centers

READINGS FOR VOLUNTEERS

The Hidden Face of Volunteering xxxviii
What...Life Without Volunteers xxxix

I. ADMINISTRATIVE/ORGANIZATIONAL RESOURCES

Administration
General 3
Accountability 7
Career Exploration 9
Evaluation/Surveys/
  Reports 9
Local Center 10
Philosophy of Volunteerism 14
Recognition 15
Recruitment/Orientation 18
Volunteer/Center/Agency
  Relations 21

Business/Industry Involvement
General 22
Adopt-A-School 31
AIDS 31
Arts 32
Businesses 33
Children/Youth 33
Civic Affairs 35
Crime Prevention 35
Disaster 36
Drugs/Alcohol 37
Education 37
Employee Support 40
Employment 40
Entrepreneurship 42
Environment 44
Families 45
Funding 46
Handicapped 46
Health 49
Homeless 49
Housing 50
Literacy 50
Nutrition 51
Offenders 53
Older Person 54
Pet Therapy 54
Recreation/Sports 55
Transportation 56

Citizenship
Children/Youth 57
Children/Youth–Handicapped 60

Communications & Public Relations
General 61
AIDS 67
Arts 68
Children/Youth 68
Domestic Abuse 70
Drugs/Alcohol 70
Handicapped 71
Health 72
Homeless 73
Image 74
Justice 75
Mental Health 76
Nutrition 76
Outreach 77

Community Services
General 79
Community Action
  Programs 91
Fraternal Organizations 92
Military 93
Rural 93
Students 93
Tenants/Residents 94
Urban 95

Funding/Fund-Raising/Related Services
General 97
AIDS 105
Arts 106
Auctions 107
Businesses 107
Children 108
Drugs 110
Education 110
Families 112
Handicapped 112
Health 114
Homeless 115
Housing 116
In-Kind 117
Justice 118
Nutrition 119
Recreation 119
Self-Help 119
Walks/Races 119

Governors' Offices on Volunteerism
General 122   By State   122-153

Information & Referral
General 155   Drugs/Alcohol 168   Housing 174   Sexual Abuse 177
AIDS 160   Employees 168   Law Enforcement 174   STD 178
Arts 161   Families 169   Mental Health 174   Suicide Prevention 179
Cancer 161   Handicapped 170   Minorities/Women 175   Women 180
Children/Youth 161 Health 171   Nutrition 176   120/80 180
Consumer/Legal Rights 163   Health/Emergencies 171   Older Person 176
Domestic Abuse 165 Homeless 173   Receration/Sports 177

Leadership Development/Boards
General 181   Disaster 196   Health 200   National Service 203
Arts 188   Domestic Abuse 196   Homeless 201   Older Person 203
Children/Youth 189 Drugs/Alcohol 197   Housing 201   Parents 204
Civic Affairs 195   Education 197   Law Enforcement 202   Tenants/Residents 204
Communications & PR 195   Ethnic Groups 198   Literacy 202   Transportation 205
Crime Prevention 195   Handicapped 199   Military 203   Welfare Reform 205

National Service/Points of Light Initiative
General 206

Private Sector Initiatives Offices
General 209   By Agency   210-220

Self-Help
General 221   Drivers 223   Homeless 224   Prisoners/Ex-Offenders 226
AIDS 222   Drugs/Alcohol 223   Housing 224   Tenants/Residents 226
Children/Youth 222 Families 224   Intergenerational 225
Communications & PR 223   Former Mental Patients 224   Older Person 225
Crime Prevention 223   Handicapped 224   Parents 225

Training/Conferences/Teaching
General 228   Communications & PR 289   Handicapped 303   Military 319
Accountability 274 Community Services 290   Health 304   Older Person 319
AIDS 274   Crime Prevention 292   Homeless 306   Older Volunteer 319
Armed Forces 275   Domestic Abuse 294   Housing 307   Parenting 320
Arts 276   Drugs/Alcohol 295   I&R 307   Philosophy 320
Boards 277   Education 296   Interfaith 308   Recruitment 321
Business/Industry 281   Entrepreneurship 299   Internships 309   Self-Help 323
Career Exploration 281   Environment 300   Justice System 314   Students 324
Center/Agency 282   Ethnic Groups 300   Leadership 317   Tenants/Residents 328
Children/Youth 283 Families 301   Literacy 318
Civic Affairs 286   Funding 301   Mental Health 318

Volunteers
Advocates 330   Armed Forces Members–   Ethnic Groups 383   Persons with AIDS 424
Alternative Sentencing   Navy 348   Families 385   Police Offices 425
  Offenders 337   Armed Forces Members–   Former Drug Addicts 388   Prisoners/Ex-Offenders 429
Alumni 341   Veterans 353   Former Mental Patients 388   Professionals 431
Armed Forces Members–   Celebrities 354   Fraternal Organizations 390   Role Models 447
  General 341   Church/Synagogue   Handicapped 392   Role-Players 450
Armed Forces Members–   Members 354   Homeless 395   Self-Help 451
  Air Force 342   Civic Groups 375   Intergenerational 395   Staff Support 459
Armed Forces Members–   Counselors 377   Low-Income 395   Students 461
  Army 344   Docents 378   Older Person 396   Teams 494
Armed Forces Members–Naval   Drivers 379   Parents 413   Tenants/Residents 499
  Reserve 348   Employees 382   Peers 424   Unemployed 502
                                                                                 Union Members 502

II. SUBJECT-SPECIFIC RESOURCES

AIDS
General 508   Education 514   Home Care/Hospices 520   Psychosocial Support 522
Children/Youth 510 Employment 516   Housing 520   Self-Help 523
Clinics/Hospitals 511   Ethnic Groups 517   I&R 520
Communications & PR 513   Funding 518   Nutrition 521

Arts/Cultural Enrichment

General 524
Adopt-A-School 525
Business/Industry 526
Children/Youth 526

Crafts 526
Ethnic Groups 527
Exhibits 528
Festivals 529

Funding 532
Handicapped 532
History/Museums 532
Intercultural 537

Legal Services 538
Mental Health 538
Music/Dance/Theatre 538
Older Person 541

Business Assistance

General 542
Children/Youth 546

Funding 548
Legal Rights 548

Minorities/Women 548
Self-Help 549

Citizenship

Children/Youth 551

Civic Affairs

General 552
Advocacy 556
Children/Youth 557
City/County Goals 557

Education 560
Evaluation/Surveys/Reports 561
Law Enforcement 561
Minorities/Women 561

Older Person 562
Peace 563
Physical Environment 566
Tenants/Residents 566

Training 567
Voting 567
21st Century 568

Consumer Services/Legal Rights

General 571
AIDS 575
Arts 575
Children/Youth 575
Cooperatives 576
Credit/Finances 577

Entrepreneurship 578
Ethnic Groups 578
Handicapped 578
Health 579
Homeless 579
Housing 579

I&R 579
Low-Income 580
Minorities/Women 580
Nutrition 580
Older Person 581
Prisoners 581

Recreation/Sports 582
Tenants/Residents 582
Transportation 582

Day Care/Head Start

General 583
Arts 585
Crisis 585

Curriculum 586
Ethnic/Bilingual 586
Evaluation 586

Family Day Care 586
Handicapped 587
Home 588

Homeless 589
Latchkey 589
Military 589

Disaster Response/Emergency Preparedness

General 590

Drug Abuse/Alcoholism

General 598
AIDS 601
Alcohol 601
Children/Youth 603

Communications & PR 605
Drugs–General 605
Drugs–Crime Watch 609
Drugs–Drug-Free Zones 610

Funding 611
Homeless 612
Minorities/Women 612
Prescriptions 612

Self-Help 612
Teen Pregnancy/Parenting 613
Transportation 613

Education

General 615
Adopt-A-School 620
Adult 623
AIDS 625
Career Exploration 625
Curriculum Enrichment 626

Dropout Prevention 629
Ethnic/Bilingual 631
Funding 633
Handicapped 634
Home 634
Homeless 635

Library Services 635
Military–Active/Veterans 638
Parent Involvement 638
Prisoners/Ex-Offenders 639
Reading 639
Scholarships 640

School Volunteers 641
Tutoring 645
Vocational/Alternative 649

Employment

General 652
AIDS 655
Career Exploration 655
Children/Youth 656

Handicapped 658
Homeless 659
Low-Income 659
Military–Active/Veterans 659

Minorities/Women 659
Older Person 660
Prisoners/Ex-Offenders 661
Psychosocial Support 662

Self-Help 662

Health

General 663
Advocacy 664
Blood/Organ Donation 664
Cancer 665
Children/Youth 667
Clinics 668
Diabetes 668

Education 669
Emergencies 669
Exercise 670
Funding 671
Health Fairs 671
Heart Disease 673
Homebound 673

Homeless 673
Hospices 674
Hospitals 675
I&R 677
Lung Disease 678
Military–Active/Veterans 679
Older Person 679

Self-Help 680
STD 680
Stroke 681
Transportation 681
Women 681
120/80 681

Housing

General 682	Funding 685	Low-Income 687	Revitalization 692
AIDS 684	Handicapped 686	Older Person 689	Rural 694
Cooperatives 684	Homeless 686	Rental 690	Self-Help 694
Discrimination 685	I&R 687	Repairs/Maintenance 691	

Law Enforcement/Crime Prevention

General 697	Education 713	Legal Rights 719	Self-Help 723
Advocacy 701	Employment 717	Offenders 719	Sentencing 723
Children/Youth 702	Facilities 717	Older Person 719	Sexual Abuse 726
Crime Watch 708	Families 717	Parents 719	Staff Support 728
Domestic Abuse 712	Funding 718	Re-Entry 720	Victims 729
Drugs/Alcohol 712	I&R 718	Recreation 723	

Literacy

General 732

Mental Health

General 739	Children/Youth 743	I&R 744
Advocacy 739	Communications & PR 743	Re-Entry 744
Centers/Hospitals 740	Foster Care 744	Self-Help 745

Nutrition

General 747	Consumer/Legal Rights 748	Food Banks 750	I&R 757
AIDS 747	Delivery 748	Food Production 754	Older Person 757
Children/Youth 747	Education 749	Homeless 755	On-Site 758
Communications & PR 748	Families 750	Hunger 756	Self-Help 759

Physical Environment

General 760	Demographics 768	Energy 772	Solid Waste 779
Air Pollution 762	Earth Day 769	Land Use 774	Toxic Waste 780
Beautification 762	Ecology 770	Recycling 777	Water Pollution 780
Conservation 766	Education 771	Revitalization 777	Wildlife/Pets 782

Psychosocial Support Services

General 785	Families 791	Military 793	Prisoners 795
AIDS 789	Handicapped 792	Older Person 793	Victims 795
Children/Youth 789	Health 792	Parents 794	
Disaster 790	Homebound 792	Peers 794	
Employees 790	I&R 792	Pet Therapy 795	

Recipients

Children/Youth 796	Homebound 872	Minorities/Women 895	Prisoners/Ex-Offenders 914
Ethnic Groups 823	Homeless 873	Older Person 895	Tenants/Residents 915
Families 825	Intergenerational 887	Persons with AIDS 912	Victims 916
Handicapped 842	Military-Active/Veterans 888	Police/Court Officers-Respite 912	Women 916

Recreation & Sports

General 917	Ethnic Groups 922	Handicapped 923	Olympics 926
Arts 918	Facilities 922	Homeless 925	Parks/Forests 927
Children/Youth 918	Funding 923	I&R 925	Prisoners/Ex-Offenders 929
Cycling 922	Gardening 923	Older Person 925	Safety 929

Teenage Pregnancy/Parenting

General 930

Transportation & Safety

General 935	Consumer/Legal Rights 937	Drugs/Alcohol 938	Low-Income 939
Children/Youth 936	Crime Prevention 937	Handicapped 938	Older Person 939
Commuters 937	Cycling 937	Health 938	

Welfare Reform

General 940

III. ANNOTATED BIBLIOGRAPHY 943

Organization Name Index 1103   **Geographic Index** 1137

Volunteerism

The Directory
of Organizations,
Training, Programs
and Publications

The Most Peculiar People in the World...

by Barbara Bush
First Lady of the United States

> These Americans are the most peculiar people in the world. You'll not believe it when I tell you how they behave. In a local community in their country a citizen may conceive of some need which is not being met. What does he do? He goes across the street and discusses it with his neighbor. Then what happens? A committee begins to function on behalf of the need. You won't believe this, but it's true; all of this is done without reference to any bureaucrat. All of this is done by private citizens on their own initiative!
>
> —Alexis de Tocqueville

Although de Tocqueville is probably the most-quoted non-American on American volunteerism, I never tire of the sheer delight he expresses in the passage above. Coming from a foreign visitor, it's like someone other than a member of your family telling you how great you are.

Please bear in mind that this Frenchman's book, *Democracy in America*, was written during a period (1835–1840) when "leisure time" in America as we know it today was virtually nonexistent. Stories about sunup to sundown toil during the nineteenth century can be found in every medium. To impress our visitor as they did, our forefathers must have been very talented in budgeting their time.

Today, with shorter work weeks, instant worldwide communication, machines that do a lot of our work faster, and longer life spans, volunteerism in America has gone far beyond what de Tocqueville touted a century and a half ago. Wouldn't he be surprised to know that in 1987, Arkansas—one of our most sparsely populated states—had more than 175,000 volunteers donating almost five million hours, saving the state nearly $70 million? This phenomenon is multiplied 50 times across America!

If this kind of caring warrants de Tocqueville's designation of "the most peculiar people in the world," I think we should accept the title proudly as the compliment it is—a tribute to the volunteer spirit of America!

This book is intended to tap into that spirit. Its thousand pages represent only the "tip of the iceberg," but it can provide ideas for all of us as we work to improve the quality of life in our communities.

The Spirit of Volunteerism in America

by John Glenn
U.S. Senator from Ohio

There is a destiny that makes us brothers. None goes his
way alone. What we send into the lives of others comes
back into our own.

—Edwin Markham

Volunteerism—the notion of individuals giving to the
community so that all may enjoy a piece of the American
dream—is a national tradition. But never before have we had
so many people giving of themselves to help others. And
with increasing budget pressures and decreasing government
services, never have such efforts been more needed.

It is apparent that the challenges of the 1990s will be a continuation of the ones we face today. As our society grapples
with the complex issues of AIDS, drug abuse, teenage pregnancy, illiteracy, and eldercare, we turn to the legion of
America's volunteers whose example shows that individuals
can make a difference in what appear to be impossible
circumstances.

It is dangerous, however, to proceed under the assumption
that volunteerism is *the* solution to our mounting domestic
problems. Government has a clear obligation to provide support services backed up by dollars, and not just rhetoric to
demonstrate its commitment to those with the greatest need.
We cannot abandon our responsibility to the disadvantaged in
the name of volunteerism.

I am pleased to endorse *Volunteerism*, which links limited
resources to those with the greatest need. I am confident that
a teamwork approach, combining the commitment of government and the ambition of America's volunteers, can and
will make a difference for tomorrow and beyond.

Voluntarism and the Human Spirit

by Eugene M. Lang

Founder and Chairman, "I Have a Dream" Foundation

How lovely to think that no one need wait a moment. We can start now. We can start changing the world.

—Anne Frank

The contents of this book, distilled to their essence, characterize voluntarism as the noblest expression of the human spirit—its goodness, compassion and sense of justice. More than that, voluntarism is displayed as an assertion of personal worth.

In its most significant aspect, voluntarism starts with a refusal to be intimidated by any social involvement merely because the problem is vast. Magnitude or complexities must not immobilize or depreciate the ability of any person to contribute meaningfully to solutions. Archimedes said, "Give me a place to stand and I can move the earth." This principle of leverage works for every person that adopts a place for serving others.

In seeking that place to stand, the spirit of voluntarism urges that the heart lead the head. From the profusion of human problems—individual, systemic, sociological, economic, environmental—voluntarism urges us to reach out to embrace the concern that is most disturbing and that most deeply excites our consciences.

Whatever concern we embrace, it should be realized that all social issues are inevitably interconnected. Accordingly, voluntarism in any area of human need expands the horizon of individual capacity, motivation and opportunity for fulfilling service. The experience of voluntarism also develops an ability to cope effectively with the unexpected. While it may seem to violate the canons of sound management, trying to outguess the future, however thoughtful the plan, can be a poor trade-off for an opportunity to respond immediately to a present human need.

For the community, voluntarism is an essential leavener of the human condition. The ripple effect of each act of service —as a multiplier in attracting the resources and inspiring the energies of others—is incalculable. Anne Frank wrote in her diary, "How lovely to think that no one need wait a moment. We can start now. We can start changing the world."

Introduction

Volunteerism is the third edition of what has become the standard guide to information on volunteer involvement in specific areas of the human services and the physical environment, and to resource groups and training events to assist volunteer managers in their efforts. Previous titles were *Community Resource Tie Line* for the first edition and *Community Resources Directory* for the second edition.

Volunteerism is comprised of three parts: Administrative/Organizational Resources; Subject-Specific Resources; and Annotated Bibliography. The first two parts consist of a combined total of 35 sections. Each section has components in three fields of concern to volunteer managers: (1) national organizations; (2) training programs; and (3) individual program profiles. The bibliography includes over 2,000 listings. The fact that little of this appears elsewhere in the literature makes *Volunteerism* a singular reference for this field.

For the first time, a "Message to Volunteers" has been included to help volunteers understand why *Volunteerism* addresses volunteer administrators, and to lead them to sources of volunteer opportunities.

Background

Volunteerism began as a slim volume, the *Green Sheets*, first distributed in 1969. It contained 27 pages of references to national organizations and federal agencies willing to provide technical and financial resources of relevance to the volunteer manager. In less than three years, the *Green Sheets* had become the primary reference for the field of volunteerism and had grown to over 300 pages of such resource groups, adding annotations of manuals, guides, and other publications, made available at the request of the *Green Sheets* editor.

A need for more in-depth information in two significant areas of volunteerism became apparent through requests from the field: training for volunteers and examples of local volunteer programs. In the late 1970s, to meet these needs, two additional volumes were developed: the *Training Blue Book*, providing detailed descriptions of courses and other training events designed for volunteer administrators and volunteers both on and off college and university campuses; and the *Pure Gold Pages*, offering details of volunteer organization and management in local projects in cities, towns, and small communities across the country.

The three volumes were combined in 1980 in a 600-page loose-leaf version entitled *Community Resource Tie Line*, now known as the first edition of *Volunteerism*. It had become the hallmark of references for volunteerism across the country, and was used in several foreign countries as "a perfect example of what one country can do." In 1984 the second edition was published with over 900 pages and renamed the *Community Resources Directory* (the second edition of *Volunteerism*). For that edition, the color designations for the sections were replaced by more descriptive titles for these sections. Although the name of the publication and the arrangements of the sections have changed, the purpose of the directory remains the same. This, the third edition, is named *Volunteerism*, the title that will be used for all future editions.

Scope of This Edition

Volunteerism has three major parts: (1) administrative/organizational resources, with sections on recruitment, funding, local centers, evaluation, communications, business/industry involvement, leadership, boards, and so on; (2) subject-specific areas, with sections on day care, education, the homeless, AIDS, employment, health, psychosocial support, teenage pregnancy, recreation, and so forth; and (3) an extensive annotated bibliography.

The first two parts consist of a combined total of 35 sections, each of which provides information in three distinct areas of concern to volunteer managers: (1) national, federal, state and regional resource groups; (2) training courses and events both on and off college and university campuses; and (3) individual local volunteer programs. The sections are arranged alphabetically. In every case they address this question: *WHO is doing WHAT for WHOM across the country?*

Administrative/Organizational Resources

The WHO   is a national-level or federal service-providing resource group.

The WHAT   is a service relevant to volunteer programs, either free or at nominal cost.

For WHOM   indicates the volunteer program leader/manager.

The WHERE   is anywhere in the nation.

Training Courses and Events

The WHO	is a college, university, national organization, federal agency, state office, or community organization.
The WHAT	is a training event, ranging from a half-day seminar on a specific issue such as fund-raising to a full academic course leading to a degree in volunteer administration.
For WHOM	indicates volunteer coordinators, volunteers, agency executives, board members, business/industry representatives, and foundation executives.
The WHERE	is a meeting place anywhere in the nation, on or off campus.

Individual Local Volunteer Programs

The WHO	is an organization ranging from the national and federal level to an informal group rallying around a concern at the local level—each serving as a sponsor or an implementer of a volunteer effort, and the volunteers themselves, who come from all walks of life.
The WHAT	represents the type of volunteer program the sponsor helps to create to address a community concern, for example, public relations, health, information and referral, and education.
For WHOM	indicates the recipient of the services provided by the volunteer program, for example, older persons, drug addicts, the handicapped, prison inmates.
The WHERE	is any community in the nation (city, town, village, or hamlet) where volunteers come together to address a need and help improve the quality of life in that community.

Annotated Bibliography

Part III is an extensive Annotated Bibliography (over 2,000 entries). Although arranged alphabetically by subject and by title within each subject, administrative/organizational resources and subject-specific areas are not separated as in the first two parts.

Each annotation provides the title, date published, type, subject, length, cost, and source of the publication. Publications available from the groups in Part I and Part II are listed after their entries. Items from publishers and others not operating volunteer-related programs, but which are considered relevant for volunteer managers, are included.

Cross-Referencing

To assist the user, there is some cross-referencing. A full description of each program is given in each of the *two major parts* of the book. A second subject area within the *same part* (e.g., a health program for older persons) carries a full description in one of the sections only (health), with a referral to the program in the other section (older person). However, it is in the best interest of the user to screen all subjects with relevance to his or her area of concern; for example, a leader operating or planning to start a *health* (1) program for *older persons* (2) involving *professional volunteers* (3) has three points of reference from which to draw information.

Indexes

In response to many requests from the field, a Geographic Index is now included, in addition to the Organization Name Index. Users are encouraged to consult these indexes to locate specific organizations, agencies, programs, and so forth.

Preparation of This Edition

To further ensure the viability of *Volunteerism*, leaders in the field familiar with this reference were called on for suggestions that they might have for improvement. Brian O'Connell of Independent Sector, Henry Smith of United Way, Winifred Brown of the Mayor's Office in New York City who is also a member of the Board of VOLUNTEER: The National Center, and Milton Boyce of National 4-H in the U.S. Department of Agriculture responded, and their suggestions are incorporated in the third edition of *Volunteerism*.

Based on these suggestions from leaders in the field and unsolicited ones from volunteer managers across the country, the format of this edition of *Volunteerism* is a significant departure from that of the second edition. Instead of three major sections (resources, training, profiles), this edition has two major parts: administrative/organizational resources and subject-specific resources. Within each part are individual sections, each containing resources, training, and profiles in the area represented. The combined parts create 35 "mini-manuals," enabling the volunteer manager to have a self-contained reference in a given area of concern; for example, management, training, and program examples in the same area of education are in one location rather than in three separate sections as in past editions. This is a time-saving feature of this new edition.

The practice of retaining selected entries from the small percentage of nonresponders during the updating process continues as in previous editions, but only after there was reasonable certainty through a routine check that the program still exists and/or the idea imparted is self-contained and useful in the overall coverage of a given area. The retained entries are indicated with a symbol (*). Entries prepared by organization or authorized source not previously listed add 40–50 percent to the number of resources in *Volunteerism*.

Information Gathering

Four basic forms, shown on the following pages, were used to gather information—one for administrative/organizational resources, one for training courses and events, one for individual local volunteer programs, and one for annotationed publications.

There were no "lists" of categories; conversely, program leaders could submit programs in any category they wished.

(continued on p. xxi)

Four-One-One
Community Green Sheets

7304 Beverly Street ● Annandale ● Virginia ● 22003 ● (703) 354-6270

RESOURCE GROUPS: NATIONAL, FEDERAL & REGIONAL LEVELS
(See "Program Profiles" form for describing local programs)

Organization/Agency Name _____

Street/PO Box _____

City/State/Zip Code _____

Contact for Additional Information:

Name _____ Phone _____

> *Please provide a brief description of organization/agency **objective(s)** and an overview of your **services**. We are interested in knowing what type of information, materials or assistance you provide that can help the volunteer program manager. Please send copies of any **printed materials** that you have developed, as well as annotations of any publications that are "on the drawing board" at this time. Include costs, if any, and publication dates where available. Copies of your current **annual report** and **institutional brochure** would be very helpful.*

Objectives:

Services:

> *Thank you for providing information. Volunteer Leaders will benefit from your expertise. Please call us if you would like information about other resource groups or local volunteer programs.*

Administrative/organizational resource groups are not necessarily volunteer organizations, per se, but operate in the fields covered by *Volunteerism*. Each organization contacted is required to answer "yes" to the question: "Will you assist a local volunteer program leader free or at a nominal cost?"

Four-One-One
Training Blue Book

7304 Beverly Street ● Annandale ● Virginia ● 22003 ● (703) 354-6270

Title of Training Program:

Location:

Date(s):

Credits:

Sponsor(s):

Contact for Additional Information:

Name _____ Telephone _____

Institution / Organization _____

Mailing Address _____

City, State, Zip Code _____

DESCRIPTION OF TRAINING PROGRAM

Please give a description of your course, workshop, seminar or other training activity, telling briefly how it was developed, sponsor/funding source, curriculum, credit/certification status, plans for evaluation, follow-up, continuation. We are interested in knowing about participation by staff, volunteers, and administrators, sources of faculty, etc. Please send copies of printed materials designed for the training activity.

THANK YOU FOR PROVIDING THE INFORMATION. OTHER PEOPLE WILL BENEFIT FROM YOUR EXPERIENCES.
PLEASE CALL US IF YOU WANT INFORMATION ON THE EXPERIENCES OF OTHER GROUPS.

Training events and courses, both on and off campuses, are required to be relevant for volunteerism, in areawide, regional, statewide or nationwide activities. *Not* included: in-house training in a specific program (which is mentioned instead in the program profile itself).

Four-One-One
Community Program Profiles

7304 Beverly Street • Annandale • Virginia • 22003 • (703) 354-6270

Name of Program:

Location:

Purpose:

Sponsor(s):

Contact for Additional Information:

Name _____ Telephone _____

Organization _____

Mailing Address _____

City, State, Zip Code_____

DESCRIPTION OF PROGRAM

Please give a description of your program, telling briefly when it began, how it operates, funding source, its goals and accomplishments. We are interested in knowing what types of work your volunteers do, the number of volunteers, kinds of training, supervision of volunteers, etc. Please send copies of any printed materials you have developed, e.g. training manuals, operation guidelines, recruitment brochures, etc.

THANK YOU FOR PROVIDING THE INFORMATION. OTHER PEOPLE WILL BENEFIT FROM YOUR EXPERIENCES.
PLEASE CALL US IF YOU WANT INFORMATION ON THE EXPERIENCES OF OTHER GROUPS.

Individual local volunteer programs are included if they indicate a benefit to the local community, either as a direct service program designed by a local group, or as a model program designed at the national level for suggested implementation at the local level (the latter often through chapters, affiliates, or local offices of national organizations or federal agencies, e.g., the Red Cross Clown Corps program for youth, or ACTION's Retired Senior Volunteer Program).

PUBLICATIONS
Be sure to enclose review copies.

Title:

Author/Editor (if applicable):

Publication date (if known):

Annotation:

Cost (if any):

Title:

Author/Editor (if applicable):

Publication date (if known)':

Annotation:

Cost (if any):

Title:

Author/Editor (if applicable):

Publication date (if known):

Annotation:

Cost (if any):

Please copy this form or attach additional sheets if needed. Thank you.

Annotated Bibliography contributors were asked to submit only those publications that were
relevant to the operation of a volunteer program and that were free or inexpensive (with a few
exceptions to fill a gap that otherwise would be neglected). Publications include the slick ones from
a highly structured national or federal group as well as the locally oriented manuals or guides
developed by the local group.

Following space for the contact information, a small paragraph was included asking for pertinent details such as when the program began, the number of volunteers, how volunteers were involved, funding sources, sponsors, and a brief description of how the program operates.

The remaining two-thirds of the form was blank, to encourage a narrative rather than a structured question-and-answer format. This resulted in many different styles of reporting, but also elicited the actual scope and tone of the program. The task here was to assure clarity, contacting the program for more information when necessary, and editing for obvious structural deficiences.

Other Features

Agencies, organizations, corporations, and other sponsors or participants that do not have individual entries but are mentioned or described briefly within an entry are included in the Organization Name Index.

Programs for which a response was not received in time to include the designated changes, or for which no response was received but where there is reasonable certainty that it still exists, have been retained for the ideas they impart. The entries retained have the symbol (*) immediately following the program name in the entry.

Although a few audiovisuals have been evident in the two previous editions, this edition reflects the changing times and the wider use of this medium. These items are listed in the bibliography and identified at the beginning of the annotation. Often carrying a higher cost than a publication, most audiovisuals include permission for the purchaser to rent the item to constituents. As many as possible have been reviewed. Those not reviewed are from organizations known to produce widely used and accepted materials.

Acknowledgments

The valuable assistance of the many information contributors to this edition of *Volunteerism* is gratefully acknowledged, with a special *Thank You!* going to volunteer centers and Governors' Offices on Volunteerism. The assistance of many individuals is also gratefully acknowledged, with several who made major contributions mentioned here:

First Lady Barbara Bush not only for lending her thoughts on volunteers to *Volunteerism*, but also for her long years of devotion to and promotion of volunteerism.

Senator John Glenn for acknowledging voluntary action as an appropriate activity for recognition by the federal government, especially in his honoring of "Young Heroes" in past years.

Eugene M. Lang for inspiring a nation to come forward and assure the benefit of higher education to deserving young people who otherwise would not have the opportunity.

Milton Boyce, Winifred Brown, U.S. Representative Cardiss Collins, U.S. Senator Dave Durenberger, Pat Hall, the late Harriet Naylor, Brian O'Connell, Helga Roth, Ivan Scheier, Eunice Kennedy Shriver, and Henry Smith, long-standing professionals in the volunteer field, for providing advice and assistance.

Greg Petersmeyer and Clark Kent Ervin of the White House Office of National Service for the documentation of department efforts in the areas of Private Sector Initiatives (agencies working with the private sector); National Service (a national public/private effort to rally youth and others to volunteerism); the Thousand Points of Light Initiative (which recognizes one "point of light" each day among individuals, groups, and organizations across the nation); Diane Moore, Director of the White House Office of Presidential Inquiries, for her assistance in clarification of information on volunteerism available through the Executive Offices of the President; and Surgei Shurygin of the Soviet Embassy for verification of Soviet-American information in the Arts/Cultural Enrichment section of *Volunteerism*.

Arthur Walters and Charles Kipps for ensuring a quiet and pleasant place in which to work; Dennis Barnett, Barbara Baroody, John William Clyde, Kay Drake, Susan Ellis, Dave Miller, Anita Rodriguez, Keith Westerfield, and Nancy Yde for their generous assistance with research needs; Glenn Kipps for the hundreds of miles he traveled gathering information; and Ginger Kipps for exhaustive collaboration in editing and refining *Volunteerism*.

Marjory Avery, Elizabeth Blake, Stephen Cheek, Joseph Creed, Eric Dew, Dinia Duncan, Kimse Duncan, Jay Figer, Haralabos (Bob) Gekas, Daniel L. Grindstaff, Arthur W. Hazlett, James Heivilin, Vincent Heivilin, Steve Higgins, Warren Hull, Margaret Ann Jess, Senora Johnson, Mark Kimbro, Charles Leighton, Theron McCulloch, Kent Miller, Rodney Sean Monteith, Julie Morton, George Plank, Jason Plank, Randall Forrest Riker, Barbara Rodriguez, Charles R. Scott, Clarke Spillers, Rita Wenderoth, Kay Wilson, Madeline Wolson, and Tami Zilberfarb for their interest, assistance, and encouragement.

Finally, deep gratitude to R. R. Bowker for recognizing the dearth of information in the volunteer field for individuals, groups, agencies, and organizations seeking assistance in their efforts to improve the quality of life in the communities, and for becoming the conduit through which the information provided in *Volunteerism* can flow to the communities and their volunteer leaders. Special thanks to Bowker's talented professional staff—especially Iris Topel, whose dedication in editing has assured the highest degree of accuracy for users of *Volunteerism*. Most of all, sincere appreciation to Bowker for its ability to select the right person to facilitate *Volunteerism*—Marion Sader, whose direction has made this work a far better resource.

The editors invite the users of *Volunteerism* to submit information on resource groups, training events, program profiles and/or publications with relevance to volunteerism as possible sources of additional listings. Comments on or suggestions for improvement of *Volunteerism* are always welcome. Please write to Editor, R. R. Bowker, 121 Chanlon Road, New Providence, NJ 07974.

How to Use This Book

Model listings are shown below for each of the individual sections of *Volunteerism*.

Administrative/Organizational Resources
(National/Federal)

> 1 — **INTERNATIONAL ASSOCIATION OF JUSTICE VOLUNTEERISM (IAJV)**
> 2 — *(formerly National Association of Volunteers in Criminal Justice)*
> **University of Wisconsin/Milwaukee**
> 3 — Criminal Justice Institute
> Box 786
> Milwaukee, WI 53201
> 4 — TEL: 414-229-6092
> 5 — *Objectives:* To improve the juvenile and criminal justice systems through citizen participation.
> 6 — *Services:* Carries out the mission of early pioneers in volunteerism—to bring together localized volunteer throughout the country in a national movement; seeks to carry out this mission by working to unify, strengthen and coordinate the efforts of various local programs and join them with other local programs across the nation and Canada; sets specific goals including:
> • Establishing guidelines for effective citizen
>
> programs; provides organizational support for IAJV activities through its national office located at the University of Wisconsin-Milwaukee, Division of Outreach and Continuing Education, Criminal Justice Institute.
> 7 — *Publications:* IAJV In Action; Membership Resource Directory
> 8 — *Founded:* 1976

1. **Name of Organization.** The formal name is given. *The, Inc.*, and so on are omitted in most entries (included only for organizations such as 70001, or when it is an integral part of an acronym, or where organizations specifically requested that it be included).
2. **Former Name.** This information is given to assist users when an organization with a familiar name changes its name.
3. **Address.** The permanent national headquarters is given or the address of the chief official for groups that have no permanent office.
4. **Telephone/Fax/Toll-Free Numbers.** These are listed when furnished by the organization.
5. **Objectives.** A brief mission statement is provided for quick reference.

6. **Services.** The organization's objectives are expanded here to assist the user who finds the objective to be relevant to his or her area of concern. The entry length varies according to information provided by the organization and the overall relationship to volunteerism, citizen participation, and private sector initiatives.
7. **Publications.** Only the titles of the publications offered by the organization are given, and most appear in the Annotated Bibliography.
8. **Founding Date.** This is the date the organization was founded; it is listed when furnished by the organization.

Training Courses and Events
(National, Federal, Statewide, and Regional)

> 1 — **VOLUNTEER MANAGEMENT SEMINARS**
> **American University**
> Division of Continuing Education
> 2 — McKinley Building
> Washington, DC 20016
> TEL: 202-686-6150
> 3 — *Credit:* CEUs; Volunteer Manager Certification (partial fulfillment)
> 4 — *Sponsor:* American University
> 5 — *Contact:* See individual seminars for contact persons
> *Description:* These seminars can be taken individually, or selected as part of the 12 hours of instruction required to complete the Volunteer Management Certification program (see above). Topics covered in Fall 1983:
> **Organizational Theory and Behavior for Volunteer**
> 6 — **Managers:** a six-part seminar (Course 760) that serves
>
> conception and execution of successful promotional campaigns. This seminar is in the regular Professional Development Program. (Contact: Ann Gilbert)
>
> Additional Volunteer Management Seminars are planned; preference is given to those taking a seminar for certification. CEUs are available for individual seminars; inquire.
> 7 — *Publications:* Conference Proceedings

1. **Title of Training Event.** The title of the seminar, workshop, course, is given.
2. **Training Provider, Address and Telephone Number.** The college/university, volunteer center, state office, federal agency, national organization, consulting service, lo-

cal chapter, or other training provider is given together with address and telephone number. The title and the provider are listed in the indexes.

3. **Credit.** Credit is listed when the information is provided. No credit is shown when provider indicates that there is no credit. In all others, the word "inquire" is used to indicate that this must be determined by the *Volunteerism* user.

4. **Sponsor.** Sponsors other than the training provider are included when this information is supplied.

5. **Contact.** The contact person is listed. In cases where a symbol (*) follows the title of the program, the contact person may have changed; see Abbreviations and Symbols for explanation.

6. **Description.** The content of the program is described based on the subject matter, sophistication, and information submitted about the program.

7. **Publications.** Only those publications offered through the event are listed; most of these publications are included in the Annotated Bibliography.

Individual Local Volunteer Programs
(including model and demonstration programs)

```
 1 — TRANSITIONAL VOLUNTEERS ARE...
 2 — Voluntary Action Center
      United Way of Central Massachusetts
      9 Walnut Street, Room 930
 3 —  Worcester, MA 01608
      TEL: 617-754-5366
      Purpose: To help clients at the point of
      rehabilitation toward taking full responsibility for
 4 —  their own actions; to help human service agencies
      expand and improve their services.
 5 — Sponsor: United Way/Voluntary Action Center
 6 — Contact: Barbara M. Stewart, Assistant Director
      Description: Recognizing trends in the direction of
      deinstitutionalization and a slightly more
 7 —  enlightened attitude from some agencies toward

      offered another workshop. Such brainstorming
      sessions are held periodically as needs arise.
 8 — Publications: Transitional Volunteers Are...
 9 — Founded: 1975
```

1. **Title of Local Volunteer Program.** The title of the program is given.

2. **Name of Organization.** The local (90 percent), state, or federal implementer of the program is given under the program title. Both the organization and the title are listed in the indexes.

3. **Address and Telephone Number.** The address and telephone number are what was current at the time the information was submitted.

4. **Purpose.** A brief mission statement is provided.

5. **Sponsor.** Sponsors other than the program implementers are listed when included with the information. All others list the implementer as sponsor (but users should inquire).

6. **Contact.** The name of the person to contact is listed. In cases where the program title is followed by a symbol (*), the contact person may have changed. See Abbreviations and Symbols for explanation.

7. **Description.** The description expands on the purpose, telling briefly how the program began, how it operates, its funding source, its goals and accomplishments, how volunteers are involved, how it trains and supervises volunteers, and so on.

8. **Publications.** Titles of publications offered by this group are listed; most are listed in the Annotated Bibliography.

9. **Founding Date.** This is the date the *project* was started. It is listed when it is furnished by the organization. If operated by a national organization described in Part I of *Volunteerism*, the organization's founding date is given there, and it may differ from that of the project.

Annotated Bibliography

```
 1 — SIMPLE ACTS OF KINDNESS
 2 — (1989)—an overview of the growth of community-
      based volunteer activities in areas of advocacy,
      counseling, and support networking on behalf of
      AIDS victims and their families; includes ten
 3 —  stories by volunteers relating how they have made a
      difference in the lives of people with AIDS—either
      by volunteering or by organizing volunteers;
      describes five model volunteer programs.
4, 5 — 128pp. $5.00. United Hospital Fund, 55 Fifth
 6 —  Avenue, New York, NY 10003-4392. 212-645-2500
```

1. **Title of Publication.** This is the title of the publication except when a series of small but useful, related pamphlets are offered from the same source.

2. **Date.** The date is included when it is provided or can be determined. When no date is available, the designation "undated" is used.

3. **Annotation.** The contents of the publication is described, varying in length according to the relevance and scope of the publication.

4. **Number of Pages.** Since a requirement for listing is submitting a review copy of each publication, page numbers are provided except where noteworthy providers to past editions who send advance annotations of new publications fail to add or do not yet know the number of pages.

5. **Cost.** Cost is listed when given by the publication provider or, if not given, when it can be determined through follow-up. Unpriced materials are included only when the provider is known to publish relevant materials that are free or inexpensive, or that are not available elsewhere.

6. **Name, Address, and Telephone Number of Organization, Corporation, Publishing House, and so forth.** The name of the publication provider is listed as submitted (often directing the user to a warehouse or distribution center). The name of the provider but not the publication is also listed in the Organization Name Index.

Indexes

Two comprehensive indexes—the Organization Name Index and the Geographic Index—have been included to provide maximum assistance to the user who requires more detail than the Contents can furnish.

The Organization Name Index provides quick reference to an organization or its affiliates. All entries are listed alphabetically, each with page numbers. This is especially useful for those seeking specific entries such as Junior Leagues, American Red Cross chapters, or specific government resources.

The Geographic Index shows the entries, each with page numbers, arranged by state, with cities ordered under the state headings.

ABBREVIATIONS AND SYMBOLS

Federal Government Abbreviations

ACTION	ACTION: The Federal Volunteer Agency	GSA	General Services Administration
CPSC	Consumer Product Safety Commission	HHS	Department of Health and Human Services
DEd	Department of Education	HUD	Department of Housing and Urban Development
DEn	Department of Energy	NASA	National Aeronautics and Space Administration
DoA	Department of Agriculture	NCUA	National Credit Union Administration
DoC	Department of Commerce	NEA	National Endowment for the Arts
DoD	Department of Defense	NEH	National Endowment for the Humanities
DoI	Department of Interior	OMB	Office of Management and Budget
DoJ	Department of Justice	OPM	Office of Personnel Management
DoL	Department of Labor	PS	Postal Service
DoT	Department of Transportation	SBA	Small Business Administration
DTreas	Department of the Treasury	VA	Veterans Administration
EPA	Environmental Protection Agency		

State Abbreviations

Alabama	AL	Kentucky	KY	Ohio	OH
Alaska	AK	Louisiana	LA	Oklahoma	OK
Arizona	AZ	Maine	ME	Oregon	OR
Arkansas	AR	Maryland	MD	Pennsylvania	PA
California	CA	Massachusetts	MA	Puerto Rico	PR
Colorado	CO	Michigan	MI	Rhode Island	RI
Connecticut	CT	Minnesota	MN	South Carolina	SC
Delaware	DE	Mississippi	MS	South Dakota	SD
District of Columbia	DC	Missouri	MO	Tennessee	TN
Florida	FL	Montana	MT	Texas	TX
Georgia	GA	Nebraska	NE	Utah	UT
Guam	GU	Nevada	NV	Vermont	VT
Hawaii	HI	New Hampshire	NH	Virgin Islands	VI
Idaho	ID	New Jersey	NJ	Virginia	VA
Illinois	IL	New Mexico	NM	Washington	WA
Indiana	IN	New York	NY	West Virginia	WV
Iowa	IA	North Carolina	NC	Wisconsin	WI
Kansas	KS	North Dakota	ND	Wyoming	WY

Symbols

One symbol is used in this resource. It follows the name in the entry affected, both in the text and in the indexes.

*The organization response was not received in time to include changes designated, the organization did not respond but the editor is reasonably certain that it still exists and has retained it for the idea it imparts, or it is not operating but has had significant impact and the organization maintains staff and materials for response to inquiries about its operation.

Message to Volunteers

Volunteerism is humanism in its most compassionate form
Volunteerism—is the best of every religion
It is an extended hand to a voiceless plea

A sun on the worst of days
A lighted candle on the darkest night
A selfless spirit—in a selfish world

It is that small voice that whispers from our heart—
reminding us that we all share this small Blue Marble
for so little time—that to give it meaning, we must
share our love.

—Cliff Robertson
Academy Award Winning Actor,
Writer and Director

Over the years, editors of *Volunteerism* have responded to the questions: "Where can I go to Volunteer?" and "How do I find my hometown in your book?" While explaining the purpose of the book—*to assist the volunteer manager*—we also recognized that the need of potential volunteers is to find satisfying volunteer assignments. To help, we developed "state lists" and responded to phone calls and letters with referrals to local volunteer centers and other sources. We are well aware of the wisdom of the well-known leader who said:

"Millions of Americans serve their communities in countless ways. But for those millions, there are millions more who want to help, *but do not know how to get started.* And at the same time, tens of thousands of volunteer programs involving other millions of individuals need volunteers, *but do not know where to find them.*"

—Ruby Sills Miller, 1971
Distinguished Volunteer Leader
and Author

Today, we are still grappling with this dilemma, because no central national source exists to help volunteers get started. With this new section, "Message to Volunteers," suggested by Brian O'Connell of Independent Sector, we hope to do a better job in helping you get started. At last, *Volunteerism* will have something in it for *you*, the volunteer! It won't be "just for volunteer managers" anymore.

This section is designed to assist individuals, groups, or corporations seeking volunteer opportunities. It is a long-awaited section to help volunteers understand why this directory addresses the volunteer administrators, and to show how potential volunteers can find satisfying assignments in their communities.

It discusses five topics: (1) the purpose of the local volunteer center, (2) rights and responsibilities of volunteers, (3) diversity of volunteer roles, (4) alternatives when no volunteer center exists in the community, and (5) specific contact information, which describes a national hotline for volunteers operated by ACTION: The Federal Volunteer Agency, and includes a list of Governors' Offices on Volunteerism, and a list of local Volunteer Centers, each with addresses and telephone numbers.

1. OVERVIEW AND DEFINITION OF THE VOLUNTEER CENTER

Given the relatively few centers that exist (only 380 across the country), and the variety of names used, many volunteers are not aware of this service. In spite of the existence of volunteer centers for more than 30 years, volunteers have been surprised to learn, in numerous instances, that the volunteer center is just blocks away from their homes. Although Centers were reorganized in the mid-80s under the name "Voluntary Action Center (VAC)," many prefer to retain previous familiar names for everyday operations; for example, Crusade of Mercy, Hand-Up Volunteer Center, Community Help Line, Volunteer Connection. And they can be found in United Way, Chamber of Commerce, American Red Cross, local government (in one case state government), and other offices as well as being totally autonomous. A complete list of Centers appears below to help alleviate the name problem, and to put the information at your fingertips. To demonstrate the services provided by these Centers, a generic description follows:

Volunteer Center is a generic term for a nonprofit organization whose primary mission is to promote volunteering within the community that it serves. The Volunteer Center serves as a *clearinghouse* for volunteer efforts and should not be confused with a "volunteer program" in which individuals serve an agency. The Volunteer Center *refers* volunteers to those volunteer programs.

If someone wants to volunteer, but does not know where to go, where their special skills are needed the most, or when volunteer opportunities are available, they should contact the local Volunteer Center. The Centers refer an estimated half million new volunteers each year who, based on national studies, are likely to provide more than 100 million total hours of service in a given year, worth at least $800 million to the nation.

In addition to recruiting and referring volunteers, the Centers assist local volunteer managers by offering area-wide training, promotion, advocacy, planning, information sharing, administrative support and other services.

As you can see, Centers strive to place you, the volunteer, in an assignment that will be mutually beneficial and enjoyable for all. It is good to keep in mind, however, that finding the right volunteer role can be as difficult as finding the ideal job. Many factors affect the success of the relationship—some that are not apparent at the outset. With perseverance, and open channels of communication, you can play a vital and satisfying role as a volunteer.

2. THE VOLUNTEER'S RIGHTS AND RESPONSIBILITIES

This listing emphasizes the need for all participants in the volunteer relationship—the volunteer, the agency, and the recipient—to have a mutual respect and a desire to cooperate.

It Is Your Right...

· To be assigned a job that is worthwhile and challenging with freedom to use existing skills or develop new ones.

· To be trusted with confidential information that will help you carry out your assignments.

· To be kept informed through house organs, attendance at staff meetings, memoranda, and so on, about what is going on in the organization.

· To receive orientation, training, and supervision for the job you accept and to know why you are asked to do a particular job.

· To expect that your time will not be wasted by lack of planning, coordination, and cooperation within the organization.

· To know whether your work is effective and how it can be improved; to have a chance to increase understanding of yourself, others, and your community.

· To indicate when you do not want to receive telephone calls or when out-of-pocket costs are too great for you.

· To be reimbursed for out-of-pocket costs, if it is the only way you can volunteer.

· To declare allowable nonreimbursed out-of-pocket costs for federal (some state and local) income tax purposes if volunteering with a charitable organization.

· To expect valid recommendation and encouragement from your supervisor so you can move to another job—paid or volunteer.

· To be given appropriate recognition in the form of awards, certificate of achievement, and so forth, but even more

important, recognition of your day-to-day contributions by other participants in the volunteering relationship.

· To ask for a new assignment within the organization.

It Is Your Responsibility...

· To accept an assignment of your choice with only as much responsibility as you can handle.

· To respect confidences of your sponsoring organization and those of the recipients of your services.

· To fulfill your commitment or notify your supervisor early enough that a substitute can be found.

· To follow guidelines established by the organization: codes of dress, decorum, and so on.

· To decline work not acceptable to you; not let biases interfere with job performance; not proselytize or pressure recipient to accept your standards.

· To use your time wisely and not interfere with performance of others.

· To continue only as long as you can be useful to recipient.

· To refuse gifts or tips, except when recipient makes or offers something of nominal value as a way of saying "thank you."

· To stipulate limitations: what out-of-pocket costs you can afford, when you might be willing to contribute hours beyond your usual ones, and so forth.

· To use reasonable judgment in making decisions when there appears to be no policy or policy not communicated to you—then, as soon as possible, consult with supervisor for future guidance.

· To provide feedback, suggestions, and recommendations to supervisor and staff if these might increase effectiveness of program.

· To be considerate, respect competencies, and work as a team with all staff and other volunteers.

3. DIVERSITY OF ROLES FOR VOLUNTEERS

Whether one is comfortable working in a one-to-one relationship or working behind the scenes, or whether one helps set policies, there is a place for volunteering in the community. Below are examples of the diversity of volunteer roles:

Direct Service Volunteering provides service through one-to-one or small-group relationships; e.g., friendly visitor, mental health aide, youth group leader.

Indirect Service Volunteering provides staff support or clerical assistance so direct service can take place.

Direct Action or Advocacy Volunteering organizes and works for change in services or systems affecting others; e.g., demanding adequate housing, welfare rights, prison reform, or improved services for the elderly. It might mean fighting for higher personnel standards, supporting a budget, and intervening on a consumer complaint.

Administrative Volunteering provides services for carrying out a program; e.g., managing, researching, consulting, advising, assessing needs, planning and training development, planning expansion or curtailment of services, and making recommendations to decision- and policy-making bodies.

These roles often overlap; for example, a direct service volunteer may become an advocate when intervening with "the system" on behalf of the person being helped. A policy-making volunteer asked to help with planning or research becomes an administrative volunteer, and so on. Many volunteers enjoy the diversity of such occasional "cross-overs."

4. ALTERNATIVES WHERE VOLUNTEER CENTERS DO NOT EXIST

A Voluntary Action Center (VAC) is a unique and needed service if a community is to find you and other volunteers, match each with a satisfying job, train them, keep records, mediate, and so forth. However, many communities do not have such a center, and other organizations are called on to provide this service. A good place to contact is one of the more than 3,000 United Way offices across the country. Because of the varied names of these offices, it is best to contact the Mayor's Office, Chamber of Commerce, or other communitywide resource if a United Way office is not listed in the telephone directory. There are a like number of local Red Cross offices across the nation. If neither exists in your community, consult the list of Governors' Offices on Volunteerism (GOV) in item 5 below for assistance. If a GOV is not listed for your state, your governor's staff may be able to assist you. Also, consider the following ideas to help find points of contact as you seek a volunteer role in your community. Each should suggest an existing group or program in your area to contact for information:

AIDS programs
Big Brother/Big Sister
"boarder babies" (hospital nurseries with abandoned infants)
child day-care centers
civic and fraternal associations (Junior Leagues, Lions' Clubs)
Clown Corps, a youth program of the Red Cross; other Red Cross programs
Congressmen's offices
credit unions
drug prevention efforts
Give Five (a nationwide program developed by Independent Sector)
handicapped groups (Special Olympics, schools for the deaf, blind)

homebound elderly/handicapped (errands, meals-on-wheels, visits)
homeless (housing, literacy, employment)
hospitals and hospices
juvenile justice system (probation or court volunteer)
labor unions
libraries (bookbinding, storytelling)
literacy programs (reading, English as a Second Language)
local welfare departments
police departments (neighborhood watch, victim assistance)
prisons (visiting, teaching, family liaison)
schools (dropout prevention, tutoring, latchkey programs)
sports (Little League coach, swim meet timekeeper)
teen centers; teen pregnancy/parenting/family-oriented programs
Veterans Administration hospitals
VISTA, Foster Grandparents, RSVP (Retired Senior Volunteer Program), and other programs of ACTION: The Federal Volunteer Agency
Y.E.S. (Youth Engaged in Service)—a program of the National Service Office of the White House
youth groups (4-H, YM–YWCA, Boy Scouts, Girl Scouts, Boys and Girls Clubs, Head Start)

These are only a few of the opportunities waiting for you —to test a career, to earn employment credit, to help a program succeed, to make one person's life better, and—the bottom line—to help your community become a better place in which to live.

5. CONTACT INFORMATION FOR VOLUNTEER CENTERS AND OTHER RESOURCES

The following information provides opportunities for exploring volunteerism at national, state, and local levels.

Nationwide Hotline on Volunteer Opportunities (Toll-Free) 800-424-8867

This hotline is publicized in the media to assist potential volunteers in locating volunteer opportunities. The hotline is located at ACTION: The Federal Volunteer Agency, 1100 Vermont Avenue, NW, Washington, DC 20525.

Nationwide Contacts for Youth Volunteers

StarServe Launched by President Bush in December 1990, this program is a Points of Light Initiative designed by the Love Foundation for American Music and funded by Kraft General Foods Foundation. It provides educators with materials and ideas for the classroom to involve children and youth in grades 4 through 12 in volunteer projects. Contacts:

• Kraft, c/o Fowler & Associates, Gale Kong, Director, StarServe (202-842-2600)

• White House Office of National Service, Schelly Reid (202-456-6266)

• United Way of America, Young America Cares, Diane Landis (703-836-7100)

• Love Foundation for American Music, Mike Love (213-201-8800)

• National VOLUNTEER Center, Kay Drake (703-276-0542)

Super Volunteers! Launched in 1985, this program works with children and youth ages 4 to 17 in major youth organizations (Boy Scouts, Camp Fire, 4-H Youth, Girl Scouts, Girls' and Boys' Clubs, Head Start, Red Cross Youth, Special Olympics, YM-YWCA, and such independent groups as the Small World News Team and the Southern Maryland Athletic Club). Its purpose is to help leaders build teams of youth volunteers to work with local government, the schools, and other youth groups. Contact: Harriet Clyde Kipps (703-354-6270)

Governors' Offices on Volunteerism

The Governors' Offices on Volunteerism provide support to local volunteer centers and other volunteer groups through training for administrators and volunteers, information gathering and sharing on the state's volunteer efforts, development and distribution of relevant materials, and other technical assistance on-site and by mail or telephone. Those in existence at press time are listed here.

These offices are members of the Assembly of State Offices on Volunteerism, which changes location each year. For 1991, that contact is: Ms. Norma W. Johnson, Executive Director, Kentucky Office of Volunteer Services, 275 East Main, #6W, Frankfort, KY 40621 (502-564-4357).

If your state does not show a Governor's Office on Volunteerism in the list, contact the Assembly above to see if one is under way, or contact your Governor's office directly to learn where in your state's government the issues of national service, private sector initiatives, and volunteerism are addressed.

Alabama. Governor's Office of Volunteerism, 560 S. McDonough Street, Montgomery, AL 36130 (205-242-3020)

Arkansas. Arkansas Division of Volunteerism, 1300 Donaghey Building, PO Box 1437, Little Rock, AR 72203-1437 (501-682-7540)

California. Governor's Office on Volunteerism, 2800 Meadowview Road, Sacramento, CA 95832 (916-427-4542)

Colorado. Office of Voluntary Citizen Participation, 1313 Sherman, Room 419, Denver, CO 80203 (303-272-7531)

Connecticut. Governor's Council on Voluntary Action, 80 Washington Street, Hartford, CT 06106 (203-566-8320)

Delaware. Division of Volunteer Services, 156 S. State Street, PO Box 1401, Dover, DE 19901 (302-736-4456)

Florida. Florida Department of Health & Rehabilitation Services, 1323 Winewood Boulevard, Building 1 #217, Tallahassee, FL 32301 (904-488-2761)

Georgia. Georgia Office of Volunteer Services, 100 Peachtree Street #1200, Atlanta, GA 30303 (404-656-9790)

Hawaii. Governor's Statewide Volunteer Services, State Capitol, Room 444, Honolulu, HI 96813 (808-548-8539)

Idaho. Idaho Volunteer, PO Box 6756, Boise, ID 83707 (602-774-0103)

Idaho. Volunteer Bureau/United Way Services, 6164 Emerals, Boise, ID 83704 (208-344-1411)

Illinois. Governor's Office of Voluntary Action, 100 W. Randolph, 16th Fl., Chicago, IL 60601 (312-814-2789)

Indiana. Governor's State Voluntary Action Programs, State Capitol, #117, Indianapolis, IN 46204 (317-633-4085)

Iowa. Governor's Office for Volunteers, State Capitol, Des Moines, IA 50319 (515-281-8304)

Kentucky. Kentucky Office of Volunteer Services, 275 East Main, #6W, Frankfort, KY 40621 (502-564-4357)

Louisiana. Volunteer Services Coordination Bureau, 150 Riverside Mall, Baton Rouge, LA 70801 (602-263-7701)

Maine. Maine State Office of Volunteerism, State House Station #73, Augusta, ME 04333 (207-289-3771)

Maryland. Governor's Office on Volunteerism, 301 W. Preston Street, Suite 1506-A, Baltimore, MD 21201 (301-225-4496)

Massachusetts. Executive Office of Community Development, 100 Cambridge, Room 1104, Boston, MA 02202 (617-727-4258)

Minnesota. Minnesota Office on Volunteer Services, 500 Rice Street, St. Paul, MN 55155 (612-296-4731)

Mississippi. Office of Voluntary Citizen Participation, 301 W. Pearl Street, Jackson, MS 39203-3091 (601-949-2027)

Missouri. Missouri Volunteers, 600 E. 22nd Street, Springfield, MO 65806 (417-866-2707)

Nevada. Nevada Office of Community Services, 1100 E. William, Suite 117, Carson City, NV 89710 (702-885-4420)

New Hampshire. Governor's Office on Volunteerism, State House Annex, 410E, Concord, NH 03301 (603-271-2121)

New Jersey. New Jersey Office of Volunteerism, State House, W. State Street, CN001, Trenton, NJ 08625 (609-292-9069)

New Mexico. Governor's Office, State Capitol, Santa Fe, NM 87503 (505-827-3031)

New York. Governor's Office for Voluntary Service, Two World Trade Center, 57th Fl., New York, NY 10047 (212-587-2555)

North Carolina. Governor's Office of Citizen Affairs, 116 W. Jones Street, Raleigh, NC 27603 (919-733-5017)

North Dakota. North Dakota Division of Volunteer Services, State Capitol, Bismarck, ND 58505 (701-224-2310)

Ohio. Ohio Office of Volunteerism, 30 E. Broad Street, Columbus, OH 43266-0401 (614-466-5087)

Oklahoma. Oklahoma Division of Community Affairs, 6601 Broadway Extension, Building #5, Oklahoma City, OK 73116 (800-522-8573)

Oregon. Special Projects, State Capitol Building #254, Salem, OR 97310 (503-378-4584)

Oregon. State Community Services/D-HR Volunteer Program, Public Services Building, Salem, OR 97310 (503-378-4729)

Pennsylvania. PennSERVE: Governor's Office of Citizen Participation, 333 Market Street, 9th Fl., Harrisburg, PA 17120 (717-783-4517)

Rhode Island. Volunteers in ACTION, 160 Broad Street, Providence, RI 02903 (401-421-6547)

South Carolina. Division of Volunteer Services/Governor's Office, PO Box 11450, Columbia, SC 29211 (803-734-0442)

South Dakota. Governor's Office, 500 E. Capitol, Pierre, SD 57501 (605-733-3661)

Tennessee. Tennessee Department of Human Services, 400 Deadrich Street, Nashville, TN 37219 (615-741-4614)

Texas. Governor's Office of Community Leadership/Volunteer Services, PO Box 12428, Capitol Station, Austin, TX 78711 (512-463-1782)

Vermont. NUCVA/Vermonters Is Volunteer Administration, Vermont College/Continuing Education, Montpelier, VT 05602 (802-223-8800)

Virginia. Virginia Department of Volunteerism, 23 Governor Street, Richmond, VA 23219 (804-786-1431)

Washington. Washington State Center for Voluntary Action, 9th & Columbia, Building MS/GH-51, Olympia, WA 98504-4151 (206-753-0548)

West Virginia. Department of Welfare Volunteer Program, 1900 Washington Street East, Charleston, WV 25305 (304-348-7980)

Wyoming. Wyoming Volunteer Assistance Corps, PO Box 3963, University Station, Laramie, WY 82071 (307-766-6310)

Local Volunteer Centers

A typical local volunteer center is described in Item 1 above. Over 300 centers exist across the country. The umbrella organization for local volunteer centers is VOLUNTEER: The National Center, 1111 North 19th Street, Arlington, VA 22209 (703-276-0542). This office can keep you informed of new centers as they are established. Those in existence at press time are listed below.

Alabama

United Way Volunteer Center, 407 Noble Street, PO Box 1122, Anniston, AL 36202 (205-236-8229)

United Way Volunteer Center, 3600 Eighth Avenue South, Suite 504, Birmingham, AL 35222 (205-251-5131)

Volunteer Center of Morgan County, 303 Cain Street, NE, Suite D, PO Box 986, Decatur, AL 35602-0986 (205-355-8628)

Volunteer Information & Referral Center, 408 W. Main Street, PO Box 405, Dothan, AL 36302 (205-792-4792)

Volunteer Action of the Eastern Shore, 150 S. Green Road, Suite P, PO Box 61, Fairhope, AL 36533 (205-928-0509)

Volunteer Center of Huntsville & Madison, 1101 Washington Street, Huntsville, AL 35801 (205-539-7797)

Volunteer Mobile, 2504 Daughin Street, Suite K, Mobile, AL 36606 (205-479-0631)

Voluntary Action Center/Information & Referral, 2125 E. South Boulevard, PO Box 11044, Montgomery, AL 36116-0044 (205-284-0006)

Alaska

Volunteer Services, 341 W. Tudor Road, Suite 106, Anchorage, AK 99503-6638 (907-562-4483)

Volunteer Action Center, PO Box 74396, Fairbanks, AK 99707-4396 (907-452-7000)

Arizona

Volunteer Center of Maricopa County, 1515 E. Osborn Road, Phoenix, AZ 85014 (602-263-9736)

Volunteer Center of Yavapai County, 107 N. Cortez, Room 208, Prescott AZ 86301 (602-776-9908)

Volunteer Center, 877 S. Alvernon, Tucson, AZ 85711 (602-327-6207)

Arkansas

United Way Voluntary Action Center, PO Box 3257, Little Rock, AR 72203-3257 (501-376-4567)

California

Volunteer Center of Kern County, 601 Chester Avenue, Bakersfield, CA 93301 (805-734-6364)

Community Action Volunteers in Education, West 2nd & Cherry Streets, Chico, CA 95929-0750 (916-895-5817)

Volunteer Center of Contra Costa County, 1070 Concord Avenue, Suite 100, Concord, CA 94520 (415-246-1050)

Volunteer Bureau of Fresno, 2140 Merced Street, Suite 102, Fresno, CA 93721 (209-449-1479)

Volunteer Center of Orange County N., 2050 Youth Way, Building 2, Fullerton, CA 92635 (714-526-3301)

Volunteer Action Center of Nevada County, 10139 Joerschke Drive, Grass Valley, CA 95945 (916-272-5041)

Volunteer Center Orange County West, 16168 Beach Boulevard, Suite 121, Huntington Beach, CA 97647 (714-375-7751)

La Mirada Volunteer Center, 12900 Bluefield Avenue, La Mirada, CA 90638 (213-943-0131)

Lake County Community Resource Center, 375 S. Main Street, PO Box 1776, Lakeport, CA 95453 (707-263-3333)

Volunteer Center of Los Angeles, S. Central, 8812 S. Main Street, Los Angeles, CA 90003 (213-753-1315)

Volunteer Center of Los Angeles, City Hall, 200 N. Spring Street, Los Angeles, CA 90012 (213-485-6984)

Volunteer Center of Los Angeles W., 11646 W. Pico Boulevard, Los Angeles, CA 90064 (213-445-4200)

Volunteer Center of Los Angeles E/NE, 133 N. Sunol Drive, Los Angeles, CA 90063-1429 (213-267-1325)

Volunteer Center of Los Angeles, 2117 W. Temple Street, 3rd Fl., Los Angeles, CA 90026 (213-484-2849)

Volunteer Center of Orange County W., 15055 Adams Street, Suite A, Midway City, CA 92655 (714-898-0043)

Volunteer Center Stanislaus, 2125 Wylie Drive #4, Modesto, CA 95355 (209-524-1307)

Monrovia Volunteer Center, 119 W. Palm Avenue, Monrovia, CA 91016-2888 (818-357-3797)

Volunteer Center of Monterey Peninsula, 801 Lighthouse Avenue, Monterey, CA 93940 (408-373-6177)

Volunteer Center of Napa County, 1820 Jefferson Street, Napa, CA 94559 (707-252-6222)

Volunteer Center of Alameda County, 1212 Broadway, Suite 622, Oakland, CA 94612 (415-893-6239)

Volunteer Center of San Fernando Valley, 8134 Van Nuys Boulevard, #200, Panorama City, CA 91402 (818-908-5066)

Volunteer Center of San Gabriel Valley, 3301 Thorndale Road, Pasadena, CA 91107 (818-792-6118)

Volunteers Involved for Pasadena, 234 E. Colorado Boulevard, Suite 508, Pasadena, CA 91101 (818-405-4073)

Valley Volunteer Center, 333 Division Street, Pleasanton, CA 94556 (415-462-3570)

Volunteer Center of Gr. Pomona Valley, 436 W. Fourth Street, Suite 201, Pomona, CA 91766 (714-623-1284)

Volunteer Center of Riverside, 2060 University Avenue, #206, Riverside, CA 92507 (714-686-4402)

Volunteer Center of Sacramento, 8912 Volunteer Lane, #140, Sacramento, CA 95826-3221 (916-368-3110)

Volunteer Center/United Way of Salinas Valley, PO Box 202, Salinas, CA 93902 (408-424-7644)

Volunteer Center/United Way of San Diego County, 4699 Murphy Canyon Road, PO Box 23543, San Diego, CA 92123 (619-492-2090)

Volunteer Center of San Francisco, 1160 Battery Street, San Francisco, CA 94111 (415-982-8999)

Volunteer Exchange of Santa Clara County, 1310 S. Bascom Avenue, Suite B, San Jose, CA 95128-4502 (408-286-1126)

Volunteer Center of San Mateo County, 436 Peninsula Avenue, San Mateo, CA 94401 (415-342-0801)

Volunteer Center of Marin County, 70 Skyview Terrace, San Rafael, CA 94903 (415-479-5660)

Volunteer Center of Orange County, Central/S., 1000 E. Santa Ana Boulevard, Suite 200, Santa Ana, CA 92701 (714-953-5757)

Volunteer Center of Santa Cruz County, 1110 Emeline Avenue, Santa Cruz, CA 95060 (408-423-0554)

Volunteer Center of Sonoma County, 1041 Fourth Street, Santa Rosa, CA 95404 (707-573-3399)

Voluntary Action Center, PO Box 878, S. Lake Tahoe, CA 95731 (916-541-2611)

San Joaquin Volunteer Center of United Way, PO Box 1585, Stockton, CA 95201 (209-943-0870)

Volunteer Center/S. Bay Harbor–Long Beach, 1230 Cravens Avenue, Torrance, CA 90501 (213-212-5009)

Tulare Volunteer Bureau, 115 South M Street, Tulare, CA 93274 (209-688-0539)

Volunteer Center of San Fernando Valley, 6851 Lennox Avenue, Van Nuys, CA 91405 (818-908-5066)

Volunteer Center of Victor Valley, 15561 Seventh Street, Victorville, CA 92392 (619-245-8592)

City of Visalia Volunteer Services Program, 417 N. Locust, Visalia, CA 93291 (209-738-3483)

Colorado

Center for Information & Volunteer Action, 400 E. Main Street, Aspen, CO 81611 (303-925-7887)

Volunteer Boulder County, 3305 N. Broadway, Suite 1, Boulder, CO 80301 (303-444-4904)

Volunteer Center of Mile High United Way, 2505 Eighteenth Street, Denver, CO 80211-3907 (303-433-6060)

Volunteer Resource Bureau of United Way of Weld, 1001 Ninth Avenue, PO Box 1944, Greeley, CO 80632 (303-353-4300)

Connecticut

United Way Volunteer Center of E. Fairfield, 75 Washington Avenue, Bridgeport, CT 06604 (203-334-5106)

Volunteer Bureau of Gr. Danbury, 337 Main Street, Danbury, CT 06810 (203-797-1154)

Volunteer Center for Capitol Region, 99 Woodland Street, UW Building, Hartford, CT 06105 (203-247-2580)

Voluntary Action Center of Gr. New Haven, 70 Audubon Street, New Haven, CT 06510 (203-785-1997)

Voluntary Action Center of Mid-Fairfield, 83 East Avenue, Norwalk, CT 06051 (203-852-0850)

Voluntary Action Center of SE Connecticut, 12 Case Street, Suite 302, Norwich, CT 06360 (203-887-2519)

Volunteer Center of SW Fairfield County, 62 Palmer's Hill Road, Stamford, CT 06902 (203-340-7714)

Delaware

Delaware Division of Volunteer Services, 156 S. State Street, PO Box 1401, Dover, DE 19903-1401 (302-736-4456)

District of Columbia

Volunteer Clearinghouse of DC, 1313 New York Avenue, NW, #303, Washington, DC 20005 (202-638-2664)

Florida

Volunteer Services of Manatee County, 1001 Third Avenue West, Bradenton, FL 34205 (813-746-7117)

Volunteer Center of Volusia-Flagler, 3747 Volusia Avenue, PO Box 1306, Daytona Beach, FL 32124 (904-253-0563)

Volunteer Broward, 1300 S. Andrews Avenue, PO Box 22877, Ft. Lauderdale, FL 33335 (305-522-6761)

Voluntary Action Center of Lee County, 2243C McGregor Boulevard, PO Box 2829, Fort Myers, FL 33902 (813-334-0405)

Volunteer Center of Alachua County, 220 N. Main Street, PO Box 14561, Gainesville, FL 32602 (904-378-2552)

Volunteer Jacksonville, 1600 Prudential Drive, Jacksonville, FL 32207 (904-398-7777)

Volunteer Center of United Way/Central FL, 1825 N. Gilmore Avenue, PO Box 51, Lakeland, FL 33802 (813-686-6171)

United Way's Center for Voluntarism, 600 Brickell Avenue, Miami, FL 33131 (305-579-2300)

Volunteer Center of Collier County, 955 Creech Road, Naples, FL 33940 (813-649-4747)

Volunteer Service Bureau of Marion County, 520 SE Fort King, Suite C-1, Ocala, FL 32671 (904-732-4771)

Volunteer Center of Central Florida, 1900 N. Mills Avenue, Suite 1, Orlando, FL 32803 (407-896-0945)

Volunteer Pensacola/Volunteer Action Center, 7 North Coyle Street, Pensacola, FL 32501 (904-438-5649)

Volunteer Service Bureau of Palm Beach, 3700 N. Broadway, SE Bank, 2nd Floor, Riviera Beach, FL 33404 (407-881-9503)

Volunteer Center of Sarasota, 1750 Seventeenth Street, Sarasota, FL 34234 (813-366-0013)

Volunteer Action Center, 5200 Sixteenth St. North, PO Box 13087, St. Petersburg, FL 33733 (813-527-7300)

United Way Volunteer Center, 851 Johnson Avenue, PO Box 362, Stuart, FL 34995 (407-220-1717)

Volunteer Tallahassee, 307 E. Seventh Avenue, Tallahassee, FL 32303 (904-222-6263)

Volunteer Center of Hillsborough County, 4023 N. Armenia Avenue, Suite 300, Tampa, FL 33607 (813-878-2500)

Volunteer Center South, 101 W. Venice Avenue, Suite 25, Venice, FL 34285 (813-484-4305)

Georgia

Voluntary Action Center of United Way, 500 North Slappey Boulevard, PO Box 3609, Albany, GA 31706 (912-883-6700)

Volunteer Resource Center, PO Box 2692, Atlanta, GA 30371 (404-527-7346)

Help Line, 630 Ellis Street, Augusta, GA 30902 (404-826-4460)

Voluntary Action Center/Hand-Up, 206 Pine Street, SW, PO Box 631, Calhoun, GA 30703 (404-629-7283)

Volunteer Center, 1425 Third Avenue, PO Box 1157, Columbus, GA 31902 (404-596-8657)

Voluntary Action Center of NW Georgia, 305 S. Thornton Avenue, Suite 2, Dalton, GA 30720 (404-226-4357)

Volunteer Gainesville, 430 Pryor Street SE, PO Box 1193, Gainesville, GA 30503 (404-535-5445)

Volunteer Macon, 2484 Ingleside Avenue A103, Macon, GA 31204 (912-742-6677)

Voluntary Action Center of United Way, PO Box 9119, Savannah, GA 31412 (912-234-1636)

Volunteer Thomasville, 144 E. Jackson Street, PO Box 1540, Thomasville, GA 31799 (912-228-3190)

Volunteer Houston County, PO Box 266, Warner Robbins, GA 31099-0266 (912-922-0161)

Hawaii

Voluntary Action Center of Oahu, 200 N. Vineyard Boulevard, #603, Honolulu, HI 96817 (808-536-7234)

Idaho

United Way Volunteer Connection, 1975 Broadway, Suite B, Boise, ID 83706 (208-345-7777)

Lewis-Clark Volunteer Bureau, 413 Main, Room 210, Lewiston, ID 83501 (208-746-0136)

Illinois

Volunteer Center/NW Suburban Chicago, 306 W. Park Street, Arlington Heights, IL 60005 (312-398-1320)

Volunteer Center/UW/Crusade of Mercy, 560 Lake Street, Chicago, IL 60601-1499 (312-906-2422)

Volunteer Center of Knox County, 140 E. Main Street, Galesburg, IL 61401 (309-343-4434)

Volunteer Center for Lake County, 2020 O'Plaine Road, Green Oaks, IL 60048 (708-816-0065)

VAC of Rock Island & Scott County, 1417 Sixth Avenue, Moline, IL 61265 (217-245-4557)

United Way Volunteer Center, 1802 Woodfield Drive, PO Box 44, Savoy, IL 61874 (217-352-5151)

Community Volunteer Center, Lincoln Land Community College, Springfield, IL 62794-9256 (217-786-2430)

Voluntary Action Center/DeKalb County, 1606 Bethany Road, Sycamore, IL 60178 (815-758-0818)

Volunteer Development Unit/DuPage County, 421 N. County Farm Road, Wheaton, IL 60187 (312-682-7586)

Indiana

Volunteer Services/Information & Referral, 646 Franklin, PO Box 827, Columbus, IN 47202 (812-376-0001)

Volunteer Action Center, 101 NW First Street, PO Box 18, Evansville, IN 47701 (612-269-8822)

Volunteer Connection, 227 E. Washington Boulevard, Fort Wayne, IN 46802 (219-420-4263)

Window Community Volunteer Center, 223 S. Main Street, Goshen, IN 46526 (317-325-8240)

VAC of the Lake Area, 221 W. Ridge Road, Griffin, IN 46319 (217-245-4557)

Volunteer Action Center, 1828 N. Meridan Street, Indianapolis, IN 46202 (317-923-1466)

Volunteers in Community Services/Howard County, 210 W. Walnut Street, Kokomo, IN 46901-4512 (317-457-4481)

Greater Lafayette Volunteer Bureau, 301-1/2 Columbia Street, Lafayette, IN 47901 (317-742-8241)

VAC of St. Joseph County, 914 Lincolnway West, South Bend, IN 46601 (309-734-6364)

Volunteer Action Center, 721 Wabash Avenue, Suite 502, Terre Haute, IN 47807 (812-232-8822)

Iowa

Volunteer Bureau of Story County, 510 Fifth Street, Ames, IA 50010 (515-232-2736)

Volunteer Bureau of Council Bluffs, 40 Pearl Street, Council Bluffs, IA 51503-0817 (712-323-1673)

United Way of Central IA Volunteer Center, 1111 Ninth Street, Suite 300, Des Moines, IA 50314 (515-246-6545)

Voluntary Action Center of Muscatine, 113 Iowa Avenue, Muscatine, IA 52761 (319-263-0959)

Volunteer Action Center of IA Great Lakes, 1713 Hill Avenue, Spirit Lake, IA 51360 (712-336-4444)

Cedar Valley United Way Volunteer Center, 3420 University Avenue, Waterloo, IA 50702 (319-235-6211)

Kansas

Volunteer Center of Wyandotte County, 710 Minnesota Ave., PO Box 17-1042, Kansas City, KS 66117 (913-371-3674)

Roger Hill Volunteer Center, Po Box 116, Laurence, KS 66044 (913-865-5030)

Volunteer Center of Johnson County, 5311 Johnson Drive, Mission, KS 66205 (913-432-0766)

Volunteer Center of Topeka, 4125 Gage Center Drive, Suite 214, Topeka, KS 66604 (913-272-8890)

United Way Volunteer Center, 212 N. Market, Suite 200, Wichita, KS 67202 (316-267-1321)

RVIA District #569, PO Box 1998, Wichita, KS 67201 (316-261-5313)

Kentucky

Volunteer Center of Frankfort/Franklin County, 401 W. Main Street, PO Box 183, Frankfort, KY 40602 (502-227-7702)

Volunteer and Information Center, 236 N. Elm Street, PO Box 2009, Henderson, KY 42420 (502-831-2273)

Voluntary Action Center, 2029 Bellefonte Drive, Lexington, KY 40503 (606-278-6258)

Volunteer Connection, 334 E. Broadway, PO Box 4488, Louisville, KY 40204-0488 (502-583-2821)

Volunteer Center, 920 Frederica Street, #108, PO Box 123, Owensboro, KY 42302 (502-683-9161)

Louisiana

Volunteer Baton Rouge, 8776 Bluebonnet Boulevard, Baton Rouge, LA 70810 (504-767-1698)

Volunteer Center of Lafayette, PO Box 52074, Lafayette, LA 70505 (318-233-1006)

Volunteer Center of SW Louisiana, 715 S. Ryan, Suite 201, Lake Charles, LA 70601 (318-439-6109)

United Way of NE Louisiana Volunteer Center, 1300 Hudson Lane, Suite 7, Monroe, LA 71201 (318-325-3869)

Volunteer & Information Agency, 4747 Earhart Boulevard, Suite 111, New Orleans, LA 70125 (504-488-4636)

Maine

Center for Voluntary Action for Gr. Portland, 233 Oxford Street, Portland, ME 04102 (207-874-1015)

Maryland

Volunteer Center of Frederick County, 22 S. Market Street, Frederick, MD 21701 (301-663-9096)

Anne Arundel County Community Services, 101 Crain Highway, Suite 505, Glen Burnie, MD 21061 (301-787-6880)

Prince Georges Voluntary Action Center, 6309 Baltimore Avenue, Suite 305, Riverdale, MD 20737 (301-779-9444)

Montgomery County Volunteer Center, 50 Monroe Street, #400, Rockville, MD 20850 (301-217-9100)

Massachusetts

Voluntary Action Center/United Way of Mass. Bay, Two Liberty Square, Boston, MA 02109 (617-482-8370)

VAC/United Way of Pioneer Valley, 184 Mill Street, PO Box 3040, Springfield, MA 01102-3040 (413-838-2691)

Volunteer Service Bureau of Taunton, 4 Court Street, PO Box 416, Taunton, MA 02780 (508-824-3985)

Volunteer Resources/United Way of Central Mass., 484 Main Street, Suite 300, Worcester, MA 01608 (508-757-5631)

Michigan

Alpena Volunteer Center, Alpena Community College, 666 Jackson Street, Alpena, MI 49707 (517-356-9021)

Voluntary Action Center, 2301 Platt Road, Ann Arbor, MI 48104 (313-971-5852)

Volunteer Bureau of Battle Creek, 182 W. Van Buren Street, Battle Creek, MI 49017 (616-965-0555)

Volunteer Action Center of Bay County, 1308 Columbus Avenue, Bay City, MI 48708 (517-893-6060)

Center for Volunteerism/UCS, 1212 Griswold at State, Detroit, MI 48226-1899 (313-226-9429)

Volunteer Center of United Way, 202 E. Boulevard Drive, #110, Flint, MI 48503 (313-232-8121)

Volunteer Center of the United Way of Kent County, 500 Commerce Building, Grand Rapids, MI 49503-3165 (616-459-6281)

Voluntary Action Center of Gr. Kalamazoo, 709-A Westnedge Street, Kalamazoo, MI 49007 (616-382-8350)

Voluntary Action Center of Gr. Lansing, 6035 Executive Drive, #105, Lansing, MI 48911 (517-887-8004)

Voluntary Action Center of Midland County, 220 W. Main Street, #17, Midland, MI 48640-5137 (517-631-7660)

Southwestern Michigan Voluntary Action Center, 1213 Oak Street, Niles, MI 49120 (616-683-5464)

Voluntary Action Center of Saginaw County, 118 E. Genesee, Saginaw, MI 48607 (517-755-2822)

SW Michigan Volunteer Center, 508 Pleasant Street, St. Joseph, MI 49085 (616-983-0912)

Minnesota

Bemidji Area Volunteer Center, 300 Bemidji Avenue, Bemidji, MN 56616 (218-759-2802)

Voluntary Action Center, 424 W. Superior Street, #402, Duluth, MN 55802 (218-726-4776)

United Way's Voluntary Action Center, 404 S. Eighth Street, Minneapolis, MN 55404 (612-340-7532)

Volunteer Connection, 903 W. Center, Suite 200, Rochester, MN 55902 (507-287-2244)

United Way's Voluntary Action Center, 26 N. Sixth Avenue, Suite 20, PO Box 698, St. Cloud, MN 56302 (612-252-0227)

Voluntary Action Center of the St. Paul Area, 251 Starkey Street, Suite 127, St. Paul, MN 55107 (612-227-3938)

Community Volunteer Service of St. Croix Valley, 1965 Greeley Street, Stillwater, MN 55082 (612-439-7434)

Mississippi

Volunteer Center of United Way, 843 N. President Street, PO Box 23169, Jackson, MS 39225-3169 (601-354-1765)

Volunteer Jackson County, 3510 Magnolia Street, PO Box 97, Pascagoula, MS 39567 (601-762-7662)

Missouri

Voluntary Action Center, 111 S. Ninth Street, Suite 200, Columbia, MO 65201 (314-449-6959)

Voluntary Action Center E. Jackson County, 10901 Winner Road, Suite 102, Independence, MO 64052 (816-252-2636)

Volunteer Center/Heart of America United Way, 605 W. 47th Street, Suite 300, Kansas City, MO 64112 (816-531-1945)

Voluntary Action Center, 401 N. 12th Street, PO Box 188, St. Joseph, MO 64502-0188 (816-364-2381)

Voluntary Action Center/United Way of Gr. St. Louis, 1111 Olive, St. Louis, MO 63101 (314-421-0700)

Montana

Community Help Line, 113 Sixth Street N., Great Falls, MT 59401 (406-761-6010)

Nebraska

United Way of the Midlands Volunteer Bureau, 1805 Harney Street, Omaha, NE 68102 (402-342-8232)

Scotts Bluff County Volunteer Bureau, 1721 Broadway, Room 409, Scotts Bluff, NE 69361 (308-632-3736)

Nevada

United Way Volunteer Bureau, 1055 E. Tropicana, #300, Las Vegas, NV 89119 (702-798-4636)

Voluntary Action Center/United Way of N. Nevada, 500 Ryland Street, PO Box 2730, Reno, NV 89505-2730 (702-322-8668)

New Hampshire

Monadnock Volunteer Center, 331 Main Street, Keene, NH 03431 (603-352-2088)

Voluntary Action Center, 102 N. Main Street, Manchester, NH 03102 (603-668-8601)

New Jersey

Volunteer Center of Camden County—CPAC/HSC, Seventh & Linden Streets, Camden, NJ 08102 (609-541-3939)

Volunteer Bureau/Bergen County, 64 Passaic Street, Hackensack, NJ 07601 (201-489-9454)

Volunteer Center of Mercer County, 3131 Princeton Pike, Building #4, Lawrenceville, NJ 08648 (609-896-1912)

VSC of United Way of Central NJ, 32 Ford Avenue, PO Box 210, Milltown, NJ 08850 (201-147-3727)

Voluntary Action Center of Morris County, 36 South Street, Morristown, NJ 07960 (201-538-7200)

Volunteer Center of Gr. Essex County, 303-309 Washington Street, 5th Fl., Newark, NJ 07102 (201-622-3737)

Volunteer Center of Atlantic County, 101 S. Shore Road, PO Box 648, Northfield, NJ 08225 (609-646-5528)

Volunteer Action Center of Passaic County, Two Market Street, Paterson, NJ 07501 (201-279-8900)

Volunteer Center of Monmouth County, 188 E. Bergen Place, Red Bank, NJ 07701 (201-741-3330)

Volunteer Center of Somerset County, 205 W. Main Street, 4th Fl., PO Box 308, Somerville, NJ 08876-0308 (201-725-6640)

New Mexico

Volunteer Center of Albuquerque, 302 Eighth Street, NW, PO Box 1767, Albuquerque, NM 87103 (505-768-1077)

Volunteer Involvement Service, College of Santa Fe, LaSalle B-108, Santa Fe, NM 87501 (505-473-1000)

New York

Volunteer Center of Albany, 340 First Street, Albany, NY 12206 (518-434-2061)

Voluntary Action Center, Vestal Parkway E. at Jensen Road, PO Box 550, Binghamton, NY 13902 (607-729-2592)

Volunteer Center of United Way of Buffalo/Erie County, 742 Delaware Avenue, Buffalo, NY 14209 (716-887-2692)

Volunteer Connection, 22 W. Third Street, PO Box 95, Corning, NY 14830 (607-936-3753)

Nassau County Voluntary Action Center, 320 Old Country Road, Garden City, NY 11530 (516-535-3897)

Voluntary Action Center, 65 Ridge Street, Glens Falls, NY 12801 (518-793-3817)

Voluntary Action Center of Suffolk County, 90 High Street, Huntington, NY 11743 (516-549-1867)

Volunteer Service Bureau/United Way of Chautauqua County, 101 E. Fourth Street, PO Box 1012, Jamestown, NY 14702-7012 (716-483-1562)

Mayor's Voluntary Action Center, 61 Chambers Street, New York, NY 10007 (212-566-5950)

United Way Volunteer Connection, 55 St. Paul Street, Rochester, NY 14604 (716-454-2770)

Voluntary Action Center, City Hall on the Mall, Rome, NY 13440 (315-336-5638)

Volunteer Center/Human Services Planning, 152 Barrett Street, Schenectady, NY 12305 (518-372-3395)

Volunteer Center of Syracuse/Onondaga County, 115 E. Jefferson Street, Suite 300, Syracuse, NY 13202 (315-474-7011)

Volunteer Center of Rensselaer County, 502 Broadway, PO Box 156, Troy, NY 12181 (518-272-1000)

Voluntary Action Center of Gr. Utica, 1644 Genesee Street, Utica, NY 13502 (315-735-4463)

Volunteer Service Bureau of Westchester, 470 Mamaroneck Avenue, White Plains, NY 10605 (914-948-4452)

North Carolina

Volunteer Service Bureau, 50 S. French Bread Avenue, Asheville, NC 28801 (704-255-0696)

Moore County Volunteer Services Center, PO Box 905, Carthage, NC 28327 (919-947-6395)

United Way/Voluntary Action Center, 301 S. Brevard Street, Charlotte, NC 28202 (704-372-7170)

Volunteer Center of Gr. Durham, 119 Orange Street, Durham, NC 27701 (919-688-8977)

Cumberland County VAC, PO Box 2001, Fayetteville, NC 28302 (919-323-8643)

Voluntary Action Center of Greensboro, 1301 N. Elm Street, Greensboro, NC 27401 (919-373-1633)

Volunteer Center of Vance County, 414 S. Garnett Street, PO Box 334, Henderson, NC 27536 (919-492-1540)

Volunteer Center, 475 S. Church Street, PO Box 487, Hendersonville, NC 28793 (704-692-8700)

Volunteer Center of Gr. High Point, 305 N. Main St., McPherson Center, High Point, NC 27260 (919-883-6171)

Dare Voluntary Action Center, PO Box 293, Manteo, NC 27954-0293 (919-473-2400)

United Way of Wake County/Voluntary Action Center, 1100 Wake Forest Road, PO Box 11426, Raleigh, NC 27511 (919-833-5739)

United Way of Cleveland County/Volunteer Division, PO Box 2241, Shelby, NC 28150 (704-482-7344)

Volunteer & Information Center, PO Box 333, Supply, NC 28462 (919-754-4766)

Volunteer Center/United Way, 311 W. Fourth Street, Winston-Salem, NC 27101 (919-723-3601)

North Dakota

Missouri Slope Areawide United Way, PO Box 2111, Bismarck, ND 58502 (701-255-3601)

United Way of Cass-Clay, 315 N. Eighth Street, PO Box 1609, Fargo, ND 58107-1609 (701-237-5050)

United Way/Community Services, 323½ De Mers Avenue, PO Box 207, Grand Forks, ND 58206-0207 (701-775-0671)

Ohio

Volunteer Center, 500 W. Exchange Street, Akron, OH 44302 (216-744-3701)

Voluntary Action Center of United Way, 618 Second Street, NW, Canton, OH 44703 (815-453-9172)

Volunteer Bureau/Geauga Information Line, 107 Water Street, Chardon, OH 44024 (216-729-7931)

Voluntary Action Center/United Way–Community Chest, 2400 Reading Road, Cincinnati, OH 45202 (513-762-7171)

First Call for Help/CIVAC of United Way, 3100 Euclid Avenue, Cleveland, OH 44115 (216-391-1010)

CALLVAC, 370 S. Fifth Street, Columbus, OH 43215 (614-221-6766)

Voluntary Action Center of United Way, 184 Salem Avenue, Dayton, OH 45406 (513-225-3066)

United Way/Hamilton–Fairfield Area, 323 N. Third Street, Hamilton, OH 45011 (513-863-0800)

United Way Voluntary Action Center, 20 North Mechanic, Lebanon, OH 45036 (513-932-3987)

Volunteer Lima/Churchpeople for Change, 326 W. McKibben Street, Lima, OH 45801 (419-229-6949)

Volunteer Center of Richland County, 35 N. Park Street, Mansfield, OH 44902-1711 (419-525-2816)

Medina County Organization on Volunteering, 113 E. Homestead Street, Medina, OH 44256 (216-725-3926)

Volunteer Center of Huron County, 258 Benedict Avenue, Norwalk, OH 44857 (419-663-1179)

Voluntary Action Center of Erie County, 108 W. Shoreline Drive, Sandusky, OH 44870 (419-627-0074)

Volunteer Service Bureau, 616 N. Limestone Street, Springfield, OH 45503 (513-322-4262)

United Way/Voluntary Action Center, One Stranahan Square, Suite 141, Toledo, OH 43604 (419-244-3063)

CONTACT Community Connection, PO Box 1403, Warren, OH 44482-1403 (216-395-5255)

Volunteer Registry, 215 S. Walnut Street, Wooster, OH 44691 (216-264-9473)

Oklahoma

Tulsa Volunteer Center, 1430 S. Boulder, Tulsa, OK 74119 (918-585-5551)

Oregon

Voluntary Action Center/YMCA, 2055 Patterson, Eugene, OR 97405 (503-686-9622)

Volunteer Bureau of Gr. Portland, 718 W. Burnside, #404, Portland, OR 97209 (503-222-1355)

Pennsylvania

Voluntary Action Center of United Way, 520 E. Broad Street, Bethlehem, PA 18018 (215-691-6670)

Franklin County Volunteer Center, 60 S. Third Street, Chambersburg, PA 17201 (717-261-1133)

Volunteer Center of Clearfield County, 103 N. Front Street, PO Box 550, Clearfield, PA 16830 (814-765-1398)

COVE/Council on Volunteers for Erie County, 110 W. Tenth Street, Erie, PA 16501-1466 (814-456-6248)

Volunteer Center, 546 Maclay Street, Harrisburg, PA 17110 (717-238-6678)

Volunteer Center of Lancaster County, 630 Janet Avenue, Lancaster, PA 17601 (717-299-3743)

Volunteer Action Council, 7 Benjamin Franklin Parkway, Philadelphia, PA 19103 (215-568-6360)

Volunteer Action Center of United Way, 200 Ross Street, #105, Pittsburgh, PA 15219 (412-261-6010)

Voluntary Action Center of NE Pennsylvania, 225 N. Washington Avenue, Scranton, PA 18510 (717-347-5616)

Voluntary Action Center of Centre County, 1524 W. College Avenue, #8, State College, PA 16801-2175 (814-234-8222)

Tracanna Volunteer Resource Center, 58 E. Cherry Avenue, Washington, PA 15301 (412-225-3322)

Volunteer Action Center, 9 E. Market Street, Wilkes-Barre, PA 18711-0351 (717-822-3020)

Volunteer Center of York County, 800 E. King Street/United Way Building, York, PA 17403 (717-846-4477)

Rhode Island

Volunteers in Action, 160 Broad Street, Providence, RI 02903 (401-421-6547)

South Carolina

United Way Volunteer Center, 114 W. Greenville Street, PO Box 2067, Anderson, SC 29622 (803-226-1078)

Volunteer & Information Center, 706 Bay Street, PO Box 202, Beaufort, SC 29901-0202 (803-524-4357)

Voluntary Action Center of Trident United Way, PO Box 20696, Charleston, SC 29413-0696 (803-760-6930)

Voluntary Action Center of the Midlands, 1800 Main Street, PO Box 152, Columbia, SC 29202 (803-733-5400)

Volunteer Greenville, 301 University Ridge, Suite 5300, Greenville, SC 29601-3672 (803-232-6444)

Voluntary Action Center, PO Box 4759, Hilton Head Island, SC 29938 (803-785-6646)

Oconee Volunteer & Information Services, 409 E. North First Street, PO Box 1828, Seneca, SC 29679 (803-882-9744)

United Way of Piedmont Valley Volunteer Center, 101 East St. John Street, #307, PO Box 5624, Spartanburg, SC 29304 (803-582-7556)

Volunteer Sumter, PO Box 957, Sumter, SC 29151 (803-775-9424)

South Dakota

Volunteer & Information Center, 304 S. Phillips, Suite 310, Sioux Falls, SD 57102 (605-339-4357)

Yankton Volunteer Center and Information, PO Box 851, Yankton, SD 57078 (605-665-6067)

Tennessee

Volunteer Center, 451 River Street, PO Box 4029, Chattanooga, TN 37405 (615-265-0514)

Volunteer—Johnson City, 200 E. Main Street, #202, PO Box 1443, Johnson City, TN 37605 (615-926-0010)

Volunteer—East Tennessee State University, Student Activities Center, PO Box 21040A, Johnson City, TN 37614 (615-929-5675)

Volunteer Kingsport, 1701 Virginia Avenue, Kingsport, TN 37664 (615-247-4511)

Volunteer Center of United Way of Gr. Knoxville, 1514 E. Fifth St., PO Box 326, Knoxville, TN 37901-0326 (615-523-9135)

Volunteer Center of Memphis, 263 S. McLean Boulevard, Memphis, TN 38104 (901-276-8655)

Volunteer Center—United Way of Nashville, 250 Venture Circle, Nashville, TN 37228 (615-256-8272)

Texas

Volunteer Center of Abilene, PO Box 3953, Abilene, TX 79604 (915-676-5683)

United Way Voluntary Action Center, 2207 Line Avenue, PO Box 3069, Amarillo, TX 79116-3069 (806-376-6714)

Volunteer Resource Center of Brazoria County, PO Box 1959, Angleton, TX 77516 (409-849-4404)

Volunteer Center, Southeast, 401 W. Sanford, Arlington, TX 76011 (718-860-1613)

Capital Area Volunteer Center, 5828 Balcones, Suite 205, Austin, TX 78731 (512-451-6651)

Volunteer Action Center of SE Texas, PO Box 2945, Beaumont, TX 77704 (409-898-2273)

Volunteer Resource Center, 1301 Los Ebanos, Suite B-3, Brownsville, TX 78520 (512-544-0321)

Volunteer Center of Coastal Bend, 1721 S. Brownlee Boulevard, Corpus Christi, TX 78404 (512-887-4543)

Volunteer Center of Dallas County, 2816 Swiss, Dallas, TX 75204 (214-744-1194)

Volunteer Bureau of United Way, 1918 Texas Street, PO Box 3488, El Paso, TX 79923 (915-533-2434)

Volunteer Center, Northeast, c/o Stripling & Cox, 7600 Grapevine Highway, Fort Worth, TX 76118 (817-284-8800)

Volunteer Center of Metropolitan Tarrant County, 210 E. Ninth Street, Fort Worth, TX 76102-6494 (817-878-0099)

Volunteer Center, West, 210 E. Ninth Street, Fort Worth, TX 76102 (817-878-0095)

Volunteers in Service to Others, PO Box 607, Gainesville, TX 76240 (817-668-6403)

Volunteer Center of Texas Gulf Coast, 3100 Timmons Lane, Suite 100, Houston, TX 77027 (713-965-0031)

Volunteer Center of Longview, 500 E. Whaley Street, Longview, TX 75606 (214-758-2374)

Volunteer Center of Lubbock, 1706 23 Street, #101, Lubbock, TX 79411 (806-742-0551)

Volunteer Resource Center, 2217 Primrose, McAllen, TX 78504 (512-630-3003)

Volunteer Center of Midland, 1030 Andrews Highway, #207, PO Box 2145, Midland, TX 79702 (915-697-8781)

Volunteer Center of Plano, 301 W. Parker Road, Suite 213, Plano, TX 75023 (214-422-1050)

United Way Volunteer Center, 700 S. Alamo, PO Box 898, San Antonio, TX 78293-0898 (512-224-5000)

Texarkana Volunteer Center, 3000 Texas Boulevard, Texarkana, TX 75503 (214-793-4903)

Volunteer Center of Tyler, 115 E. Houston, Tyler, TX 75702 (214-592-6342)

Volunteer Center of United Way, 201 W. Waco Drive, PO Box 2027, Waco, TX 76703 (817-753-5683)

Utah

Voluntary Action Center, 236 N. 100 East, PO Box 567, Logan, UT 84321 (801-752-3103)

Weber County Volunteer Center, 2650 Lincoln Avenue, #268, Ogden, UT 84401 (801-625-3782)

United Way Volunteer Center, 60 E. 100 South, PO Box 135, Provo, UT 84603 (801-374-8108)

Voluntary Action Center of Community Services Council, 212 W. 1300 South, Salt Lake City, UT 84115 (801-486-2136)

Vermont

Volunteer Connection of the United Way, One Burlington Square, Burlington, VT 05401 (802-864-7541)

Virginia

Alexandria Volunteer Bureau, 801 N. Pitt Street, Alexandria, VA 22314 (703-836-2176)

Arlington Volunteer Office, 2100 Clarendon Boulevard, Suite 6, Arlington, VA 22201 (703-358-3222)

Volunteer Center of Montgomery County, W. Roanoke at Otey St., PO Box 565, Blacksburg, VA 24060-0565 (703-552-4909)

Volunteer—Bristol, 600 Cumberland Street, 2nd Fl., Bristol, VA 24201 (703-669-1555)

United Way Volunteer Center, 413 E. Market #101, PO Box 139, Charlottesville, VA 22902 (804-972-1705)

Voluntary Action Center of Fairfax County Area, 10530 Page Avenue, Fairfax, VA 22030 (703-246-3460)

Voluntary Action Center of Virginia Peninsula, 1520 Aberdeen Road, Suite 109, Hampton, VA 23666 (804-838-9770)

Voluntary Action Center of United Way of Central Virginia, 1010 Miller Park Square, PO Box 2434, Lynchburg, VA 24501 (804-847-8657)

Voluntary Action Center of Prince William Area, 9300 Peabody Street, Suite 104, Manassas, VA 22110 (703-369-5292)

Voluntary Action Center of South Hampton Roads, 253 W. Freemason Street, Norfolk, VA 23510 (804-624-2403)

Volunteer Center/United Way Services, 233 S. Adam Street, PO Box 227, Petersburg, VA 23804 (804-861-9330)

Voluntary Action Center of SW Virginia, Route 19, SVCC Training Center, PO Box SVCC, Richlands, VA 24641 (703-964-4915)

Volunteer Center of Greater Richmond, 4001 Fitzhugh Avenue, PO Box 6649, Richmond, VA 23230-0649 (804-353-2000)

Voluntary Action Center, 920 S. Jefferson Street, PO Box 496, Roanoke, VA 24003 (703-985-0131)

Washington

Volunteer Center, c/o American Red Cross, 2111 King Street, Bellingham, WA 98225 (206-733-3290)

Volunteer Center of Lewis County United Way, 500 N. Pearl, PO Box 5, Centralia, WA 98531 (206-330-2122)

Volunteer Center of United Way of Snohomish County, 917 134th Street SW, #A-6, Everett, WA 98203-0977 (206-742-5911)

Benton/Franklin Volunteer Center, 205 North Dennis, Kennewick, WA 99336 (509-783-0631)

Voluntary Action Center, 613 S. Second, PO Box 1507, Mt. Vernon, WA 98273 (206-336-6627)

United Way Volunteer Center of King County, 107 Cherry Street, Seattle, WA 98104 (206-461-3751)

United Way's Volunteer Center, PO Box 326, Spokane, WA 99210-0326 (509-838-6581)

Volunteer Center of United Way of Pierce County, 734 Broadway, PO Box 2215, Tacoma, WA 98401 (206-272-4767)

Volunteer Bureau of Clark County, 1703 Main Street, PO Box 425, Vancouver, WA 98660-2607 (206-694-6577)

Greater Yakima Volunteer Bureau, 302 W. Lincoln, Yakima, WA 98902 (509-248-4460)

West Virginia

Volunteer Action Center, 1007 Mary Street, Parkersburg, WV 26101 (304-428-6344)

Wisconsin

Information & Referral Center, 120 N. Morrison Street, PO Box 1091, Appleton, WI 54912 (414-832-6000)

Volunteer Service Bureau/Voluntary Action Center, 431 Olympian Boulevard, Beloit, WI 53511 (608-365-1278)

Volunteer Center, 338 S. Chestnut, Green Bay, WI 54303 (414-435-1101)

Kenosha Voluntary Action Center, 716 58th Street, Kenosha, WI 53140 (414-657-4554)

Voluntary Action Center of United Way of Dane County, 2059 Atwood Avenue, Madison, WI 53704 (608-246-4380)

Volunteer Center of Gr. Milwaukee, 600 E. Mason Street, Suite 100, Milwaukee, WI 53202 (414-273-7887)

Volunteer Center of Waukesha County, 2220 Silvernail Road, Pewaukee, WI 53072 (414-544-0150)

United Way Volunteer Center, 1045 Clark Street, #204, Stevens Point, WI 84321 (715-341-6740)

Wausau Area Volunteer Center, 407 Grant Street, Wausau, WI 54401 (715-845-5279)

Volunteer Center of Washington County, 120 N. Main Street, #340, West Bend, WI 53095 (414-338-8256)

United Way of S. Wood County Volunteer Center, 1120 Lincoln Street, Suite 2, Wisconsin Rapids, WI 54494 (715-421-0390)

Wyoming

Volunteer Information Center, 900 Central, PO Box 404, Cheyenne, WY 82003 (307-632-4132)

The Volunteer Center: Helping the Volunteer Get Started, by Ruby Sills Miller (Dr. Helga Roth, Isolde Chapin, and Harriet Clyde Kipps, eds.) has been a valuable reference in developing this "Message to Volunteers." Now out of print, it may be available in libraries. Also consulted were materials provided by ACTION: The Federal Volunteer Agency, and VOLUNTEER: The National Center.

Readings for Volunteers

The following readings, "The Hidden Face of Volunteering" and "What . . . Life Without Volunteers?," are sample speeches. They were written by the staff of the Committee on Marshalling Human Resources, and have never been delivered. They are included simply to provide inspiration.

THE HIDDEN FACE OF VOLUNTEERING

All of us would agree that volunteering is a good thing to do. If someone asked us why, we'd probably answer "because it's a way to help other people," or "because it's a way to solve problems." Both these statements are true. Volunteering *is* a way to help other people, to feel useful, and to help solve many kinds of individual, community, and national problems. But there's another side of volunteering, a hidden side that no one talks about. In fact, it's a very well-kept secret. Everyone who volunteers knows about it, even if no one will say so.

The secret is this: *Volunteering is good for the volunteer.*

Volunteering is good for the volunteer because of the contact it provides with other people—the companionship, the friendship, the fellowship of working with others on a common goal. No one knows this better than the young mother at home with small children, or the newly retired worker who no longer goes out to an office every day. Both share a sense of isolation from the world outside, and both are among the most likely segments of our society to volunteer—for reasons that may be as simple as the need for companionship that we all share.

Volunteering also offers a way to exercise skills, talents, and experiences not used in regular paid jobs or in other areas of life. Many of us who have found that paid work doesn't meet all our needs do find that volunteering offers an opportunity to pursue personal goals and delve into areas of personal interest. The computer programmer who spends her days working with machines may welcome the change of pace that coaching a girls' soccer team provides. The accountant who juggles numbers may find an outlet for his love of art by serving as a tour guide at the local museum on Saturdays.

Volunteering offers a chance to learn new skills as well. Many a woman can attest that the skills she acquired through years of volunteering when her children were young—skills in organizing, managing, and fund-raising, for example—were exactly the skills that got her hired for a paid position once those children were grown and she was ready to resume an interrupted career or to begin a new one.

Someone said recently that volunteering is a form of continuing education. That certainly can be true for the volunteer who consciously chooses to volunteer in ways that provide opportunities for learning throughout a lifetime. Most of us discover that learning doesn't stop when our formal schooling comes to an end. Indeed, the healthiest, most active adults continue to learn until they die. One of the best ways to ensure this is to volunteer intelligently; that is, to choose the areas we want more knowledge about, and then to immerse ourselves in volunteer work relating to that subject.

The possibilities are endless—volunteering on a rescue squad teaches us emergency medical techniques; working for our political party at the polls expands our understanding of how the political process works; the training given those who staff emergency "hot lines" provides a wealth of information about counseling and human relations. Many museums give intensive training courses for their docents or guides; in a large city the subjects available could include history, architecture, art, science, or transportation. Serving on a school board keeps us in touch with the changing field of education. Volunteering truly is a path to lifelong learning.

We live in a mobile society. Americans move more than anybody—it's in our blood, starting with our immigrant and pioneer ancestors. Moving can be tough, even within the same country. In many ways it means starting all over again. Volunteering can ease that transition. What better way to get to know new people and a new community than by making a phone call offering your services, and getting involved in a volunteer project? Again, this is something that people rarely talk about, but all volunteers who move frequently know.

The last way that volunteering is good for the volunteer is perhaps the hardest way to describe: When you volunteer, you begin to claim power over your life. That is, through thoughtful, serious volunteering, people gain the information, the skills, and the relationships needed to understand how the world works, and to participate in making decisions. Particularly when people volunteer to work on issues of deep concern to them, on problems that touch their own lives, volunteering is an empowering experience.

No one is trying to suggest that the only reason to volunteer is because of what it can do for you. We've just said goodbye to a period in our history some have called the "me decade." No one wants to go back to that, or to recommending narcissism as an approach to or a rationalization for volunteering. But when it is perfectly clear that volunteering *is* good for the volunteer, and when some people don't know that, or are embarrassed to admit it, it's important to point it out, to remind ourselves.

It should not really come as a great surprise. After all, it is an age-old truth of most of the world's religions that in giving we receive and in healing we are healed. But somehow, volunteering has been surrounded with such a halo, such an aura of "do-goodism," that we tend to forget that it's not a one-sided experience.

It's time to show the other side, to share this secret. It's time to let people know that volunteer work is and can be a significant part of their life experience that deserves to be taken seriously, to be protected and strengthened. Volunteering is not just a means of getting things done—it is itself a valuable, enriching experience.

WHAT...LIFE WITHOUT VOLUNTEERS?

Most of us take volunteers for granted. We know, of course, that the teenager wheeling flowers down the hospital corridor is a volunteer, as is the neighbor who rings our doorbell asking for a donation for birth defects. We may even have done some volunteering of our own at one time or another. But mostly we give little thought to volunteers, or to volunteering; we just accept them as a natural part of American life.

Just for a moment, imagine what would happen if, *tomorrow,* all volunteers in America went on strike. Of course this is an unlikely prospect, given the commitment and conscientiousness of most American volunteers. But just for a minute imagine what a walk-out by all volunteers would do to a typical day in a typical American community.

Let's begin close to home, at your community hospital. In the lobby, the gift shop, run by volunteers, is closed. At the desk, there is no one to greet and direct visitors. On the upper floors, things are worse. Not only are the candy stripers gone, but those patients in need of blood transfusions are out of luck—without volunteer blood donors, the shortage would be felt at once.

Down the street, at the home for the elderly, it's even quieter. No one is there to read to the blind, talk with the lonely, or wheel the chairs out into the sun.

Church is quiet, too—no choir; no flowers on the altar; no one to pass the collection plate. At the synagogue, much of the warmth and closeness is gone.

Many museums are closed—without volunteer tour guides, there is no one to run the programs.

At the end of the day, after school or after work, there's very little to do. No community soccer games—how could there be, without volunteer parents to coach, organize, and drive? No scout meetings—who would lead the troops? The alcoholic facing temptation has no AA meeting to turn to; there are no Parents Without Partners meetings for the newly divorced or widowed. Not even the usual choice of television programs is available—without volunteers, the public stations would be off the air.

The point is clear. American civilization as we know it is based, absolutely, on the efforts of volunteers. Trying to imagine doing without those efforts is truly a nightmare. *And that's the way it should be!*

The tradition of people helping people is as old as our nation itself—in fact, we would not exist today were it not for the volunteers who won our freedom from England in the Revolutionary War. The spirit of volunteerism flows like a deep river through the history of our nation. It's what the American dream is all about.

All of us together can keep that dream from turning into the kind of nightmare just described. If you are not already a volunteer—and more than half of all Americans are—ask your neighbor how you can help. Think back on the institutions that have made up your personal universe and ask them how you can best serve: the hospital where your children were born; the library where those children enjoyed Saturday story hours, or where you borrow books; the church or synagogue where you were married.

Contact volunteer organizations in your community and ask how you can become part of an established volunteer program. Call your local voluntary action center and ask for a list of volunteer opportunities. You'll be amazed at how many organizations are looking for people like you. Everyone has a skill to share, a gift of time he or she can give to the community.

Ask your neighbor to volunteer, too. Get the people in your neighborhood together to stage a community spring cleanup of that vacant lot, trashed park, or creek that's been a eyesore in your town. That's the American way—people helping each other to solve the problems close to home.

Don't take volunteers for granted. Imagine what life in America would be like without them. Don't let that nightmare come true—Volunteer!

*"The voluntary association of free men and women
in organizations of their own choosing
for mutually beneficial objectives
lies at the heart of our
democratic society."*

AFL-CIO CONVENTION

1.
ADMINISTRATIVE/ORGANIZATIONAL RESOURCES

ADMINISTRATION

NATIONAL/STATE ORGANIZATIONS

AMERICAN SOCIETY OF DIRECTORS OF VOLUNTEER SERVICES
American Hospital Association
840 North Lake Shore Drive
Chicago, IL 60611
TEL: 312-280-6110
Objectives: To provide an organized structure to advance and develop effective volunteer administration in health care institutions.
Services: Provides long-term skills development for both the new and the experienced volunteer services director; convenes conferences, workshops and institutes which cover such subjects as: the role of the director of volunteer services, the needs and functions of the department of volunteer services, the needs and motivations of volunteers, the development of management skills and techniques, humanism in management, effective time management, effective communications, utilizing human resources, attaining organization objectives, selected volunteer programs, current issues affecting health care institutions; publishes a journal and other materials; makes available *American Hospital Association* publications, including *Hospitals;* provides access to extensive library; sponsors special consultants; convenes annual convention.
Publications: Volunteer Service Magazine; Administration Newsletter; Membership Roster
Founded: 1972

ASSEMBLY OF STATE OFFICES ON VOLUNTEERISM
SEE GOVERNORS' OFFICES ON VOLUNTEERISM

ASSOCIATION FOR VOLUNTEER ADMINISTRATION
PO Box 4585
Boulder, CO 80306
TEL: 303-497-0238
Objectives: To promote Volunteer Administration as a profession; to establish and maintain standards for the field of volunteer administration; to promote the exchange of knowledge and experience; to encourage creative use of volunteers; to work with higher education facilities to develop professional education and training in Volunteer Administration; to promote professional stature among members through meetings, workshops, institutes.

Services: Provides professional certification program which awards C.V.A. (Certified in Volunteer Administration) certificate to qualified candidates; works with educational institutions to design training programs at both the degree and non-degree level; presents National Service Award to three outstanding individuals and/or organizations each year; conducts workshops, institutes and meetings for exchange of information and to engage in problem solving exercises; publishes monthly newsletter, a journal, and other guidelines and certification materials; convenes annually *The International Conference on Volunteer Administration* and several regional conferences.
Publications: Volunteer Administration; AVA Newsletter; Professional Ethics; Conference Guidelines; AVA in the Marketplace
Founded: 1960

ASSOCIATION OF VOLUNTARY ACTION SCHOLARS
Lincoln Filene Center
Tufts University
Medford, MA 02155
TEL: 617-628-5000
Objectives: To provide services to individuals who conduct, make use of, or have a serious interest in research and study of voluntary action - including the nature and characteristics of a voluntary society, voluntary associations, volunteers, and voluntary acts.
Services: Organizes, sponsors and operates conferences, forums, conventions, workshops, symposia to study voluntary action in any form (including consumer action, community development, social movements, religious activities, etc.); sponsors and organizes study panels, research teams, task forces, and other groups of voluntary action scholars; publishes a newsletter, a journal and other periodicals, books, pamphlets, abstracts that may further above-stated objectives.
Publications: Citizen Participation Abstract; Voluntary Action Abstracts; Voluntary Action Research
Founded: 1971

ASSOCIATION OF VOLUNTEER CENTERS
c/o VOLUNTEER - The National Center
1111 North 19th Street, Suite 500
Arlington, VA 22209
TEL: 703-276-0542
FAX: 703-528-6021

Objectives: To promote volunteerism and voluntarism at the local, state and national levels through central volunteer organizations in local communities across the country.

Services: Assists member agencies to recruit and place volunteers in agencies throughout the community; assists these organizations in launching and maintaining successful volunteer programs in all areas of the human services; develops and publishes standards and guidelines for the field of volunteerism, training information, a monthly newsletter, and other materials; convenes annual conference, sometimes jointly with other national voluntary organizations.

Publications: Directory: Volunteer Centers; Notebook; Standards and Guidelines

Founded: 1951

CENTER FOR CREATIVE COMMUNITY
PO Box 2427
Santa Fe, NM 87504-2427
TEL: 505-983-8414

Objectives: To study and encourage volunteerism.

Services: Offers diverse channels through which professionals in volunteer administration may enrich their skills and knowledge as well as options for involvement for others in the volunteer community who wish to enhance their personal volunteering experience; operates through a 10-person Board of Directors from the U.S. and Canada, each with a strong individual history in volunteerism and a commitment to the Center as a focus for outreach; provides options for involvement, including:

Networks
- **National DOVIA (Directors of Volunteers in Agencies) Network** - an exchange of information and ideas among associations of people involved in leadership of volunteers.
- **Library Linkage Network** - linkage for a number of collections on volunteerism for cross-reference and mutual support.

Consulting
- **Circuit Riders** - a clearinghouse for people who want to share special skills and dreams with another community for anywhere from a week to a year on site.
- **Consultants to the Center** - volunteer participation in planning and development of the *Center for Creative Community* (project coordinator in administration, research, or planning).

Professional Growth & Development
- **CHALLENGE Series on Think Tanks on Volunteerism** - an opportunity for practitioners to look at *why* and *what if* issues, in short-term colloquia.
- **Study Tours** - low-cost, self-directed, individualized learning opportunities in Santa Fe.
- **Project Associate Network** - an opportunity to conduct or support discovery in less well-mapped areas of volunteerism; e.g., career tracks, all-volunteer groups, and freelance volunteers.
- **Advanced Training & Consulting Services** - training programs at the Center such as *Winning With Staff, Shaping Your Future in Volunteerism, Empowering the Profession of Volunteer Administration*, etc. (35 subject areas)

Information Sharing
- **Harriet Naylor Memorial Collection on Volunteerism** - the library named in honor of Harriet Naylor, a founder and organizer of volunteerism.
- **Other Collections** - establishment of other collections in North America.

Building Together
- **VOLUNTAS** - the first building designed for and dedicated to volunteers everywhere; a place for seminars, retreats, reflection, and renewal; a museum that expresses the spirit of volunteerism, and more (in planning stage).

Contact: Ivan H. Scheier, Ph.D., Director; Janet Stoker, Administrator

Publications: A Reconsideration of Volunteerism; Shapes &

Scenarios in the Future of Volunteerism; Frontiers 1989 (annual series)

FOUR-ONE-ONE (411)
National Clearinghouse on Volunteerism
7304 Beverly Street
Annandale , VA 22003
TEL: 703-354-6270
FAX: 703-941-4360

Objectives: To provide tools for local volunteer leaders to help them mount, improve or expand volunteer programs; to work with youth ages four to seventeen to instill the spirit of volunteerism in their lives.

Services: Serves as national clearinghouse on volunteerism; provides references to information needed for planning, designing, and managing successful volunteer programs in all areas of human services and community needs; maintains a youth arm, which provides volunteer program information and ideas to teams of youth ages four to 17 who participate in organizations such as *Boy Scouts of America, Girl Scouts of the USA,* and Red Cross Youth, and independent groups of 12 or more youth volunteers; operates a library of 3,000 volumes related to volunteerism; publishes a newsletter for volunteer managers, a newsletter for youth, and edits a 1,000-page volume describing volunteering in America, which includes national/federal resources, training programs, and local program profiles, a series of factual and fictional books for children and youth, and other materials.

Publications: Mirror on Volunteerism; Super Volunteers! Newsletter; Super Volunteers! Booklet Series; Volunteer World; Volunteers! The Learning/Coloring Book; Super Volunteers! The Learning/Coloring Book

Founded: 1969

INDEPENDENT SECTOR
1828 L Street, NW
Washington, DC 20036
TEL: 202-659-4007
FAX: 202-457-0609

Objectives: To act as a meeting ground where the diverse elements in and related to the independent sector can comfortably come together to learn how to improve their performance and effectiveness and how to create a positive national climate for giving, volunteering, and not-for-profit initiative.

Services: Administers specific programs in:

Public Education to improve the public's understanding of the independent sector, its contributions and its problems, including providing information to and making contacts with opinion leaders, the media, educators, the business community and the public.

Communication within the sector to identify shared problems and opportunities through a regular flow of information, including a Sector periodical.

Research to develop a store of knowledge about the Sector and focus/clarify its usefulness, and to identify existing information (and gaps).

Non-Profit Operations and Management to help maximize service to individuals and society by encouraging standards and evaluations, helping to improve internal practices, and promoting basic operational principles.

Government Relations to coordinate the multitude of interconnections between the sector and national, state and local governments, such as pursuing legislation to preserve and enhance the independent sector's ability to serve public needs.

Publications: Corporate Philanthropy; Update; Memo to Members

Founded: 1980

INTERNATIONAL ASSOCIATION OF VOLUNTEER EFFORT
c/o Mary Ripley
10775 Wilkins Avenue
Los Angeles, CA 90024
TEL: 213-470-1867
Objectives: To promote voluntary commitment to human service throughout the world.
Services: Operates through a membership of 350 individuals in 38 nations, including the United States, who are interested in action through voluntary commitment to human service; maintains an international network to encourage volunteer program development and promote understanding through volunteer effort, with a central office that changes location as leadership changes (1990, Bogota, Colombia), and nine regional offices around the world (one in the United States); makes presentations, etc. in French, Spanish and Japanese; corresponds in English; works in cooperation with the *International Council on Social Welfare;* publishes conference proceedings biannually. [Operated initially under the name *International Association for Volunteer Education.*]
Publications: IAVE Conference Proceedings

NATIONAL ASSEMBLY OF VOLUNTARY HEALTH AND SOCIAL WELFARE ORGANIZATIONS
1319 F Street, NW, Suite 601
Washington, DC 20004
TEL: 202-347-2080
Objectives: To foster intercommunication and interaction among national voluntary health and social welfare agencies; to increase the effectiveness of each agency.
Services: Works for good communication among national volunteer health and social welfare agencies; emphasizes that cooperation increases the impact of individual organizations as well as the volunteer community as a whole; holds leadership retreat and convenes annual meeting; publishes monthly newsletter, biennial service directory, and other publications to meet the needs of the voluntary organization.
Publications: Assemblyline; Voluntary Organization Survey; Organization
Founded: 1923

NATIONAL COUNCIL OF PUERTO RICAN VOLUNTEERS
541 South Sixth Avenue
Mount Vernon, NY 10550
TEL: 924-664-0892
Objectives: To organize groups of Spanish-speaking people to help bridge language barriers that affect services and facilities available to them; to provide bilingual volunteers to public and private service organizations.
Services: Provides training and some technical assistance; emphasizes areas of education, legal services, health, social and welfare services, and youth; has cooperative arrangement with National Council of Negro Women; convenes annual meeting.
Founded: 1964

PROJECT SHARE
National Clearinghouse for Improving the Management of Human Services
7830 Old Georgetown Road, Suite 204
PO Box 30666
Bethesda, MD 20814
TEL: 301-231-9539
TOLL FREE: 800-537-3788
Objectives: To help congressional sponsors boost support to Congress for the Volunteer Protection Act (HR 911), and to raise the visibility of the issue.
Services: Co-sponsors: Giant Food, Inc., PO Box 1804 D-599, Washington, DC 20013 - Barry Scher, Vice President

(301-341-4710); Capital Area Community Food Bank, 2266 25th Place, NE, Washington, DC 20018 - Lynn Brantley, Executive Director (202-334-5344)

SOCIETY FOR NONPROFIT ORGANIZATIONS
6314 Odana Road
Suite 1
Madison, WI 53719
TEL: 608-274-9777
Objectives: To provide a forum for exchange of information, knowledge and ideas on strengthening and increasing productivity within nonprofit organizations.
Services: Works with executive directors, staff, board members, volunteers, and others who serve nonprofit organizations to provide a network for sharing experiences and ideas on strengthening and increasing productivity within nonprofit organizations; provides fundraising programs, travel services, and national group insurance plans for nonprofits; offers professional support services, a resource center, speakers, seminars and workshops; maintains a referral service of providers of services and products to nonprofit organizations; publishes a journal, a catalog, occasional papers, books and pamphlets on nonprofit management and leadership.
Publications: Nonprofit World; Directory of Service Providers to Nonprofit Organizations; Resource Center Catalog
Founded: 1983

TECHNICAL ASSISTANCE PROGRAM (TAP)
US/ACTION - The Federal Volunteer Agency
1100 Vermont Avenue, NW
Suite 1100
Washington, DC 20525
TEL: 202-634-9108
TOLL FREE: 800-424-8580
Objectives: To improve the human service efforts which small voluntary and non-profit organizations provide to their communities through the use of volunteers.
Services: Provides training and technical assistance to voluntary and non-profit organizations through the development and exchange of materials and information. TAP develops printed technical materials and training packages on various aspects of volunteerism, awards grants in which training and technical assistance materials are developed, and researches, collects and disseminates information on volunteerism.
Contact: Joseph Bass

US/ACTION - THE FEDERAL VOLUNTEER AGENCY
1100 Vermont Avenue, NW
Suite 1100
Washington, DC 20525
TEL: 202-634-9108
TOLL FREE: 800-424-8580
Objectives: To stimulate and expand voluntary citizen participation through coordination of its efforts with public and private sector organizations and other government agencies.
Services: Provides funding for support of volunteers to non-profit sponsoring organizations and community groups (volunteers are supervised by local project sponsors). Programs include:
● VISTA (Volunteers in Service to America)
● Student Community Service Program (SCSP)
● Retired Senior Volunteer Program (RSVP)
● Foster Grandparent Program (FGP)
● Senior Companion Program (SCP)
● ACTION Drug Alliance
Through grants, provides for the sponsorship of VISTA, SCSP, FGP, RSVP and SCP volunteers; assists with project development upon request of local organizations and agencies. Contact your ACTION State Program Offices or the Office of Public Affairs,

ACTION, 1100 Vermont Street, NW, Washington, DC 20525, telephone 202/634-9108
[Most of above programs are described in appropriate sections throughout this Directory]
Contact: Kay Drake, Public Relations Officer
Publications: ACTION
Founded: 1971

VOLUNTEER - THE NATIONAL CENTER (*formerly National Center for Voluntary Action*)
1111 North 19th Street, Suite 500
Arlington, VA 22209
TEL: 703-276-0542
FAX: 703-528-6021
Objectives: To strengthen and support volunteerism in the United States by helping sustain and creating local resources which encourage volunteer involvement.
Services: Serves as the national leadership organization for volunteering; although not a clearinghouse for volunteer opportunities, works to insure that resources needed to run an effective volunteer program are in place, through five primary areas:
- serving as the parent organization for the nationwide network of some 350 local Volunteer Centers that provide local leadership for volunteering and annually recruit over a half million new volunteers;
- supporting the development of corporate-sponsored employee volunteering, through information-sharing, training, technical assistance and convening services for both individual corporations and the business community as a whole;
- providing "umbrella national services" for individual volunteer leaders: information and technical assistance services, a national conference, *Voluntary Action Leadership,* a quarterly magazine; *Volunteer Readership,* catalog service for publications and promotion items;
- educating the public about the importance of volunteering through such programs as "National Volunteer Week" and the "President's Volunteer Action Awards," sponsored annually in cooperation with the White House;
- demonstrating new, unique and innovative ways to involve people as volunteers, such as the administration of projects which involve unemployed persons as volunteers and physically and mentally challenged high school students as volunteers.
Serves the volunteer community in a number of other capacities, including the training of trainers in a week-long course, and technical assistance to communities and organizations seeking ways to involve volunteers in meaningful roles to solve problems and reach goals.
Contact: Kay Drake, Director of Information Services
Publications: Volunteers from the Workplace; Volunteer Center Development; Voluntary Action Leadership
Founded: 1979

VOLUNTEERS IN PREVENTION, PROBATION, PRISONS
527 North Main Street
Royal Oak, MI 48067
TEL: 313-398-8550
Objectives: To stimulate citizen participation in court and correction programs; to upgrade existing volunteer programs; to improve the criminal justice system for juveniles and adults and to support the development of state organizations in this area.
Services: Sponsors the National Education Training Program developed for both professionals and nonprofessionals; assists in the development of volunteer programs with courts and correctional institutions by furnishing speakers, consultants, workshops, demonstrations, films, literature, tapes, etc.
Publications: VIP Examiner; A Father, A Son
Founded: 1969

TRAINING PROGRAMS

THE HEART OF COMPASSION
Carondolet Management Institute
PO Box 12069
Tucson, AZ 85732
TEL: 602-721-3838
TOLL FREE: 800-726-3888
FAX: 602-721-3985
Credit: Inquire
Contact: David Lee Davidson, Ph.D., Instructor
Description: This training program addresses the special concerns of caregivers who devote their best energies to others, while often neglecting themselves, and thereby placing themselves at high risk for stress and burnout. Through presentations, discussions, group exercises and individual experiential processes, participants in the program:
- Define key characteristics of compassionate caregiving
- Identify basic obstacles to caring and traps in the helping relationship
- Learn effective techniques for self-renewal and relaxation that reduce stress, avoid burnout and generate greater peace and vitality
- Develop a model of compassion that nourishes the caregiver as well as the receiver
- Practice affirmations and visualizations that enhance your self-esteem and effectiveness as a caregiver
- Expand your ability to receive support from others and identify a network of support you can rely on
- Create the essential balance between empathy and detachment, lightness and seriousness
- Reaffirm your inspiration and commitment as a helping professional
Designed for all persons who serve the growth and wellbeing of others, the conference includes the following specific topics:
The Power of Caring
- Compassion, self-renewal and caregiving
- Purpose and themes
The Heart of Compassion
- Dimensions of compassion
- Heart and mind
Obstacles to Compassionate Caregiving
- Our limiting reactions to work and suffering
- Barriers in attitude and self-image
The Process of Self-Nourishment
- Techniques for self-renewal
- Being receptive: issues in receiving support
- Compassion mediation & guided imagery
- The power of detachment and humor
The instructor specializes in promoting the personal and professional development of helping professionals and provides in-house training for hospitals, clinics, universities, school districts, and community agencies. The program has been approved for accreditation by the following: *National Board of Certified Counselors* (7.5 contact hours); *Arizona Nurses Association* (7.8 contact hours); *California Board of Registered Nursing* (7.0 contact hours); *Florida Board of Nursing* (7.0 contact hours); *Iowa Board of Nursing* (7.0 contact hours). For states not listed, this program meets the continuing education requirements in nursing of most states. Inquire about credit for others.
The low-cost program ($69) is conducted in cities across the country and contains an option for a further reduction ($10) when three or more register on the same registration form. Inquire about annual schedule.

INSTITUTE ON VOLUNTEER ADMINISTRATION: A PROPOSAL
SEE TRAINING/CONFERENCES/TEACHING

MANAGEMENT OF VOLUNTEER PROGRAMS IN THE ARMED FORCES
SEE VOLUNTEERS: ARMED FORCES MEMBERS

MANAGEMENT OF VOLUNTEER PROGRAMS/NORWICH
Norwich University Center for Volunteer Administration
Continuing Education
Vermont College
Montpelier, VT 05602
TEL: 802-223-8800 (college); 802-223-3285 (home)
Credit: Certificate
Sponsor: Norwich University
Contact: Carolyn Smith Sprague
Description: The Certificate in Management of Volunteer Programs (CMVP) is earned by attending six one-day sessions and completing a student paper. The sessions cover basic skill areas essential for effective management of volunteers in a nonprofit organization. This program will benefit volunteer coordinators, executive directors, board members, committee chairmen and anyone responsible for volunteer activity either as a paid or unpaid staff member. The sessions are scheduled throughout the academic year and are held on campus at Norwich University. The sessions are:

Session I: Background and Overview of Volunteerism
● historical perspective of volunteerism
● current trends and issues
● ethics and standards
● personal philosophy of volunteerism and career goal examination

Session II: Elements of a Volunteer Program: Basic Steps to Success
● goals and objectives
● plans of action and job design
● recruitment, interviews and placement
● training and supervision
● evaluation

Session III: Communications Makes the Difference
● verbal skills: (1) making a presentation; (2) the open-ended question
● non-verbal communication: body language
● written communiation skills: (1) newsletters; (2) dealing with the media; (3) the CMVP paper
● working with others: (1) mentoring; (2) networking; (3) collaborating

Session IV: The Dollar Issues
● budgets
● grant writing
● fundraising and special events planning

Session V: Working with Boards of Directors and Advisory Councils
● Board/staff relations
● composition of the Board
● planning meetings
● Board committees
● parliamentary procedures
● evaluation techniques

Session VI: Life Skills for Volunteer Managers
● creativity
● delegating responsibilities
● time and stress management
● professional development of the volunteer manager

An integral part of the Certificate in Management of Volunteer Programs is the preparation of a student paper. Each participant works closely with the staff of the Norwich University Center for Volunteer Administration (NUCVA) through the stages of topic choice and development. Student paper guidelines are presented at the first workshop attended by the participant.
Faculty is drawn both from the University and from the community.

INDIVIDUAL PROGRAM PROFILES

VOLUNTEER VOLUNTEER COORDINATORS*
Big Country Retired Senior Volunteer Program
PO Box 5648
Abilene, TX 79608
TEL: 915-692-4645
Purpose: To maintain a totally volunteer program by making the position of Volunteer Coordinator one of the volunteer assignments.
Sponsor: US/ACTION
Contact: Ernestine Shirey, Director
Description: In 1974, Big Country RSVP decided to do something about the fact that too many natural leaders among volunteer groups are never given the opportunity to reach their full potential. Gradually thereafter, whenever a group situation involving volunteers was encountered, program leaders looked for the person within who stood out as the leader and asked him/her to accept the assignment of volunteer volunteer coordinator for the group. The program now has 19 volunteer coordinators, and continues to be on the alert for additional volunteers who would be effective in such a position.
There are 700 volunteers in the program, and the majority operate in group situations. The coordinators serve as liaison between the volunteer group and the office. They recruit volunteers, place them in positions or refer them to the director for placement, and collect volunteer hours to be recorded in the office records. They also help select volunteers for special recognition, and each directs a specific group of volunteers. One coordinator handles a group of over 120 volunteers. Most of the volunteers serve in nutrition centers, nursing homes, senior housing groups, hospitals, nursing schools, health agencies, youth-serving agencies, mental health and many civic organizations.
The volunteer coordinators have proven to be very effective leaders, freeing the office staff for professional tasks that the average volunteer cannot perform. In addition, no funding is needed for the coordinator positions, since it is that person's volunteer assignment. Any expenses incurred (phone, postage, etc.) are considered normal office expenses.
The program area includes Taylor, Jones and Callahan counties which cover a metropolitan city and six rural towns. The coordinators have been especially helpful with recruiting efforts and record-keeping, the latter especially crucial when writing annual grant proposals and requesting local funding. Add to this the additional fulfillment that comes to the volunteers as one of their own assumes the leadership position of coordinator. It follows that this method of operation is obviously beneficial to all concerned - staff, volunteers and volunteer coordinators.
To further undergird the coordinating network now functioning, the staff projects plans for a training event for volunteer coordinators as well as a recognition for them during 1983. The training will include recruitment techniques as well as sharing information on the "how-to's" of retraining current volunteers. Leadership development would be another aspect of the training.
Founded: 1972

ADMINISTRATION: ACCOUNTABILITY

NATIONAL/STATE ORGANIZATIONS

NATIONAL COALITION FOR VOLUNTEER PROTECTION
c/o Capitol Associates
1575 Eye Street, NW
Washington, DC 20005
TEL: 202-544-1880

Objectives: To help congressional sponsors boost support to Congress for the Volunteer Protection Act (HR 911), and to raise the visibility of the issue.

Services: The National Coalition for Volunteer Protection (NCVP) has found that lobbying on the grass-roots level is an effective way to generate support for legislation in Congress. The Volunteer Protection Act (HR911), introduced in 1985, is designed to encourage states to pass laws that limit volunteer liability under certain circumstances. The Act was generated by the American Society of Association Executives and other major volunteer groups including the American Heart Association, the National Parent Teachers Association, and Big Brothers. The initial direct effort was a four-month grass-roots campaign begun in September 1987. A broad range of volunteer-oriented national organizations have become involved, including those who have formally agreed to back the bill (Boys Clubs, American Red Cross, and Little League). In spite of the fact that the bill has not yet passed, by 1989 roughly 25 states had enacted some form of volunteer protection law after the bill was introduced, but many of these are still "patchwork" and inadequate. According to the Director, "The enactment of HR911 would assist these 25 states, as well as those planning to institute protection laws after the bill is passed."

Sponsor: Boys and Girls Clubs of America

Contact: Gordon MacDougall, Executive Director

Publications: Broadening Power Bases (reprint); HR 911: Volunteer Protection Act; S 1430: Volunteer Service Bill; S 520: Volunteer Protection Act

PREPARING FOR AN AGING SOCIETY
Aging Futures Project
United Way of America
701 North Fairfax Street
Alexandria, VA 22314-2045
TEL: 703-836-7100, Ext. 538

Objectives: To help community leaders and service providers construct a detailed picture of the long-term needs of the community's elderly population.

Services: Assists communities in projecting data about the health, financial status, and number of elderly in a given community for as long a period as 70 years, which helps them plan for the human-care needs of future aging populations through a computerized program, *Preparing for an Aging Society* (by 2010, about one-third of America's population will be between 55 and 75 years old); works through a grant from the *U.S. Administration on Aging* to enable 10 cities to pilot the program; links pilot cities' efforts with those of local offices of the federal government's *Area Agencies on Aging* and with those of planning councils and local agencies serving the elderly; serves as a catalyst for public-private partnerships on the issue; incorporates data projected by the program into a new needs assessment planned for late 1990; studies previous projections (a 1987 study called for a 205 percent increase needed for senior day care by 2010) which point to "alternatives to institutionalization for the elderly" such as at-home care, service delivery, and alternative living arrangements; brings together local elder-care agencies and representatives from the *Social Security Administration* among others through the program; maintains a corporate advisory network; issues RFPs (requests for proposal) for elder-care services identified in local needs assessments; provides a demonstration diskette to United Way local offices on request.

Sponsor: United Way of America

Publications: Preparing for an Aging Society

PUBLIC INTEREST COMPUTER ASSOCIATION
1025 Connecticut Avenue, NW
Suite 1015
Washington, DC 20036
TEL: 202-775-1588

Objectives: To assist nonprofit organizations in the installation of effective computer programs.

Services: Provides education and training to nonprofit organizations seeking to upgrade administrative systems through installation of effective microcomputer technology; provides a network of communications among nonprofit users; sponsors classes and workshops on computer applications designed especially for nonprofit organizations; conducts on-site training, consulting, and laboratory training; maintains a library and offers computerized services such as desktop publishing as an alternative to installation when indicated; holds monthly meetings; publishes a newsletter and other materials.

Publications: PICA Newsletter

Founded: 1983

TRAINING PROGRAMS

COMPLETE VOLUNTEER LEGAL LIABILITY WORKSHOP
SEE GOVERNORS' OFFICES ON VOLUNTEERISM: VIRGINIA

MAILER EDUCATION SEMINARS
US/PS - Mailer Education Center
PO Box 836
Windsor, CT 06006-0836
TEL: 203-285-7030 (CT)
TOLL FREE: 800-877-7843 (nationwide)

Sponsor: US/PS - Postal Service

Contact: Mailer Education Coordinator

Description: These seminars are provided on-site nationwide to help nonprofits benefit from a thorough understanding of which of the Postal Service's programs best fits the organization's needs. They are designed to help nonprofits cut costs, improve efficiency, save money, utilize several different mail programs, and share ideas. Attendees include administrative, production, and supervisory personnel involved in an organization's mailing program. Ideally, they should be:

● Seeking practical, cost-effective solutions for lowering mailing costs, increasing productivity, and eliminating wasteful overcosts that affect programs;

● Wanting a clear understanding of the procedures and latest developments in the methodology of an effective mail program; and

● Needing to update present mailroom for maximum efficiency.

Although diversifying all the time, typical seminars include:

Marketing with Direct Mail, which explores why direct response is so popular, how and when to use direct mail, and what makes an effective direct mail piece, as well as the proper use of the direct mail system, bulk sorting, bonded mail houses, etc.

Marketing in the 90's, which integrates various aspects of marketing theory with practical everyday examples using modern communications techniques to help participants understand the factors influencing the marketplace; promotes advertising methods useful for fund-raising campaigns.

Mailing Procedures for Administrative Personnel, which is designed, in part, to help the one-person operation which handles incoming and outgoing mails; teaches how to reduce postal costs, improve mail service, and master all the basic postal services.

Third Class Bulk Mail, which covers all aspects of this necessity for nonprofit organizations, especially in soliciting donations; covers permit imprint, meter license, and precancelled stamps, restrictions, enclosures, cooperative mailings, discounts for various pre-sorts, documentation, preparation, etc.

All seminars incorporate lectures, roundtable discussions, videotapes, films, audio-visual presentations, overhead slides, brochures, reference materials, charts, etc. Complete advance materials are provided on request with fees, training locations, and complete course descriptions.

Publications: Professional Business Seminars

MANAGING YOUR FISCAL RESPONSIBILITIES AS A NONPROFIT: HOW TO AVOID FINANCIAL PITFALLS
SEE TRAINING/CONFERENCES/TEACHING: ACCOUNTABILITY

INDIVIDUAL PROGRAM PROFILES

BASIC ACCOUNTING ASSISTANCE
Virginia Society of Certified Public Accountants
Suite 1010
700 East Main Building
Richmond, VA 23210
TEL: 804-270-5344
Purpose: To help nonprofit organizations struggling with financial questions related to bookkeeping, tax filing, fiscal accountability, etc.
Sponsor: Virginia Society of Certified Public Accountants
Contact: Beth Jacobson
Description: Maintains volunteer program to donate technical assistance to nonprofit organizations.

GROUP SAFETY ASSOCIATION
United Way of California
410 Bush Street
San Francisco, CA 94108-3731
TEL: 415-772-4461
Purpose: To help overcome tight financial straits by combining resources.
Sponsor: United Way of Los Angeles
Contact: Herbert J. Paine, Executive Director
Description: This group was formed to help alleviate the crisis of inadequate or unaffordable liability insurance among California nonprofit organizations. By voluntarily joining forces, and working in cooperation with the United Way plan, the nonprofit organizations can use their combined volume as leverage to obtain affordable and comprehensive coverage at stable rates. The plan was developed in conjunction with the *Kornreich Organization,* a New York-based brokerage firm, and is the result of a collaborative effort between the United Way of California and United Way, Inc., of Los Angeles.
The plan is now open to all California nonprofit community service organizations (with the exception of hospitals and blood banks). It offers several types of insurance, including property, general liability, auto liability, physical damage, workers compensation, and umbrella liability. With approximately 40,000 nonprofit organizations in the state of California, there is great potential for a successful long-term plan which will make its participants less susceptible to insurance market cycles.
The *Group Safety Association* also offers education and technical assistance in risk management to participating nonprofits. The individual organizations will conduct self-assessments every other year and can arrange for consultation and site visits by a risk management consultant when necessary.
Founded: 1988

ADMINISTRATION: CAREER EXPLORATION

TRAINING PROGRAMS

MAKING THE VOLUNTEER EXPERIENCE COUNT
SEE TRAINING/CONFERENCES/TEACHING: CAREER EXPLORATION

NCSL JOB SKILLS DEVELOPMENT SEMINARS
SEE TRAINING/CONFERENCES/TEACHING: CAREER EXPLORATION

SOCIAL LAB
SEE TRAINING/CONFERENCES/TEACHING: INTERNSHIPS

ADMINISTRATION: EVALUATION/SURVEYS/REPORTS

NATIONAL/STATE ORGANIZATIONS

COMMUNITY RESEARCH FORUM*
SEE COMMUNITY SERVICES

COUNCIL ON ECONOMIC PRIORITIES
SEE BUSINESS/INDUSTRY INVOLVEMENT

MINI-GRANTS: RESEARCH IN VOLUNTEERISM
SEE FUNDING/FUND-RAISING/RELATED SERVICES

PREPARING FOR AN AGING SOCIETY
SEE ADMINISTRATION: ACCOUNTABILITY

YOUTH SERVICES TO FRAIL, HOMEBOUND ELDERLY
SEE VOLUNTEERS: STUDENTS

INDIVIDUAL PROGRAM PROFILES

ENVIRONMENTAL SCAN TASK FORCE
SEE LEADERSHIP DEVELOPMENT/BOARDS

TOWNWIDE CENSUS
SEE FUNDING/FUND-RAISING/RELATED SERVICES: EDUCATION

YOUTH EVALUATION SERVICES (Y.E.S.)
Family Services-Woodfield
475 Clinton Avenue
Bridgeport, CT 06605
TEL: 203-368-4291
Purpose: To standardize the method of diagnosing addiction.
Sponsor: United Way of Eastern Fairfield County; Family Service America
Contact: YES Coordinator
Description: Youth Evaluation Services (Y.E.S.) is considered a vital link in the war on drugs since it standardizes the method of diagnosing addiction. Using very sophisticated medical and computerized equipment, Y.E.S. can diagnose physical, emotional, social, and family-oriented factors through one system instead of through many different counselors or case workers. It standardizes which questions are asked to determine levels of addiction. For example, Y.E.S. allows the results of different types of treatment to be measured and evaluated, and defines what is working and what is not. In part, the process includes:
- a series of screening tests administered to the child and to all available family members;
- interviews which focus on the issues of family relationships;
- a treatment plan based on the severity of the problem and

emotional support with the family

The primary benefit of the program is the avoidance of coping with many different resources to determine the most effective course of treatment. Y.E.S. not only maintains updated information about in-patient, residential and out-patient treatment availability, but the staff is knowledgeable about the types of treatment that individual insurance plans will support. Also, Y.E.S. monitors a child for a period of up to 18 months. In addition, it has built a resource bank that can make referrals to families in other parts of the country for local treatment

Between its beginning in April 1989, and September 1989, Y.E.S. served 60 youth from the Bridgeport area.

Y.E.S. was made possible through the United Way with funds received from the Robert Wood Johnson Foundation and the state government.

Publications: What's Working and What Isn't: Evaluating Drug Treatment

Founded: 1989

ADMINISTRATION: LOCAL CENTER

NATIONAL/STATE ORGANIZATIONS

VOLUNTEER LINK
SEE GOVERNORS' OFFICES ON VOLUNTEERISM: DELAWARE

INDIVIDUAL PROGRAM PROFILES

JEWISH VOLUNTEER ASSOCIATION
Jewish Community Federation of Louisville
3630 Dutchmans Lane
Louisville, KY 40205
TEL: 502-451-8840
Purpose: To provide clearinghouse volunteer recruitment and placement for federated social service agencies.
Sponsor: The Jewish Community Federation of Louisville, Inc.
Contact: Jan Rothschild, 502-451-8840
Description: The Jewish Volunteer Association (JVA) is a clearinghouse service for the beneficiary and affiliated agencies of the Jewish Community Federation of Louisville. It was developed by the Federation's Women's Cabinet as a response to the loss of social service staff as Title XX and CETA were dismantled. JVA works with the agencies to develop volunteer positions, recruit appropriate candidates, and place them under the supervision of the requesting agency. Tracking of volunteers and occasional "replacements" keep the system dynamic.

JVA receives consultative services from the staff of the Federation. The line workers who conduct interviews and place volunteers are, themselves, voluntary personnel. An advisory committee meets several times annually to monitor the program.

Nearly 40 volunteers have been placed since JVA started in October, 1982. The individuals represent a wide range of ages (teens through elderly) and a wide range of skills. All participating agencies have had the benefit of receiving volunteers from JVA and have grown very creative in developing volunteer positions.

JVA was started with a seed grant of $2,500. The funds were used to develop an outreach brochure, train staff and volunteers, and purchase supplies for the program. At present, the program has minimal expense.

Volunteer recognition is given by the agency employing the volunteer. Community-wide recognition takes place on an annual basis.

Founded: 1982

VOLUNTARY ACTION CENTER OF CHATTANOOGA
Metropolitan Council for Community Services
451 River Street
PO Box 4029
Chattanooga, TN 37405
TEL: 615-265-0514
Purpose: To serve as the center for the promotion of volunteerism in the community.
Description: The *Volunteer Center* directs the efforts and resources of volunteers to the needs of organized nonprofit agencies and services in the health, recreational, welfare, educational, civic and cultural areas on a community-wide basis. An up-to-date listing of volunteer opportunities, submitted by organizations who utilize volunteers in their operation, is maintained at the Center. This information is used to refer prospective volunteers to the agencies who have registered their needs with the Center.

The Center coordinates the *Management Assistance Program (MAP).* More than 50 community volunteers are available to work as consultants to local nonprofit agencies, sharing their expertise and assisting them with concerns involving the management of their programs.

Each year a series of five workshops is offered utilizing volunteer presenters who are experts in their fields as well as top-notch trainers.

The Center works with several area schools, providing volunteer placements for students as part of their curriculum and also working with the youngsters in finding individual placements. The Center staffs the *Student Board for Community Service,* a youth volunteer organization, with representation from 19 area high schools, which include both public and private, city and county schools.

The Center is an Associate Member of *VOLUNTEER, The National Center,* and serves as a source for up-to-date information concerning volunteerism both locally and nationally.

Books and other educational materials relating to volunteerism are housed at the Center and are available to volunteer managers on a checkout basis. The *Volunteer Center* is a resource for the recognition of the volunteer effort in the community as well as offering training and consultation in volunteer management both on an individual basis and through workshops and seminars.

VOLUNTARY ACTION CENTER OF SOUTH LAKE TAHOE
3333 Sandy Way
PO Box 14254
South Lake Tahoe, CA 95702
TEL: 916-541-2611
Purpose: To assist in resolving community problems and meeting needs through voluntarism; to assist groups and agencies in utilizing volunteers effectively.
Sponsor: City of South Lake Tahoe; C.E.T.A.; El Dorado County Justice System; United Way of Northern Nevada; V.I.S.T.A.; foundations; donations
Contact: Volunteer Services Coordinator
Description: The Voluntary Action Center is a non-profit agency that has been serving South Lake Tahoe since 1974. Each year over 8,000 people in California and Nevada are served by VAC programs. Programs and services of VAC include:
- **Volunteers in Action** - recruits and places people of all ages in volunteer jobs in over 50 local agencies and organizations. Volunteers in Action also provides technical assistance to local agencies and volunteers on effective volunteer programming;
- **Tel-A-Care** - daily phone call or weekly visit to a homebound senior;
- **Family Volunteer Project** - volunteer opportunities for the entire family;
- **Volunteers in Transition** - volunteer opportunities for the disabled;
- **Big Brothers and Big Sisters of the High Sierra** - offers children the opportunity to establish a one-to-one relationship

with an adult;
- **Information and Referral** - comprehensive and accurate information about available human services;
- **Legal Information Service** - provides anyone with general legal information;
- **Tahoe Area Sentencing Alternative Program** - accepts misdemeanor, felony and traffic offenders sentenced by the courts to perform community service work instead of fines and/or jail sentences;
- **VA Connection** - quarterly newsletter;
- **Small Claims Court Advisory Program** - informational workshop on small claims court procedures;
- **Self-Help Library** - reading material on a variety of legal issues;
- **Home Mail Delivery** - for homebound seniors, by referral only; and
- **Medical Equipment Loan** - no charge, by referral only.

Publications: VA Connection
Founded: 1974

VOLUNTARY ACTION CENTER OF THE FAIRFAX COUNTY AREA
10530 Page Avenue
Fairfax, VA 22030
TEL: 703-246-3460

Purpose: To promote, support and increase effective volunteerism in the Fairfax County area.

Description: The *Voluntary Action Center of Fairfax County Area (VAC)* is the primary resource center serving over 250 registered public and private nonprofit organizations. VAC services are designed to strengthen the management skills of volunteer program administrators, organization leaders and volunteers. VAC provides the following:

Consultation Services for volunteer administrators, organization executives and corporate community relations managers about volunteer management issues are available by telephone or appointment, at no charge.

Skills Workshops are offered regularly on topics geared specifically for executives and volunteer administrators. Fees are nominal.

FastTrack Series are power-packed workshops designed especially for the busy volunteer administrator, covering specific management issues in 1-1/2-hour modules. Fees are nominal.

Customized Workshops are designed specifically for your organization upon request and presented at your site. Topics include management and Board of Directors issues.

Clearinghouse Services provide individuals or groups with information about volunteer opportunities. VAC matches and refers potential volunteers using volunteer-designed data base records on current volunteer opportunities.

Recruitment Assistance for selected registered organizations is provided by VAC's weekly press releases.

VAC Update is a bi-monthly newsletter which provides pertinent information on volunteer management issues to executives and volunteer administrators of registered organizations.

Site Visits to targeted registered organizations are performed by VAC staff to help determine community volunteer needs to share information and resources.

VAC Alliance programs are offered to a group of organization representatives three or four times yearly providing technical assistance and networking for mutual needs and concerns.

Management Resource Library provides registered organizations with current books, periodicals, and information on non-profit management issues and resources.

Public Awareness of volunteer service to the community is encouraged by VAC sponsorship of local and national recognition programs. VAC also promotes *National Volunteer Week* events annually in the Fairfax County area.

Advocacy plays a vital role in VAC's commitment to its registered organizations. VAC encourages public support for legislation

favorable to volunteers. VAC promotes a positive overview on the value of volunteer service and the importance of volunteer administrators who coordinate volunteer efforts in the community. *VAC is an associate member of VOLUNTEER - The National Center.* VAC's Executive Director holds a membership in the national *Association for Volunteer Administration (AVA)* and staff members are active members of the *Northern Virginia Association for Volunteer Administration (NVAVA).*

VAC staff works closely with the *Virginia Department of Volunteerism,* the *Metropolitan Coalition of Volunteer Centers,* and other volunteer-referral organizations (such as *Seniors In Action,* a program of the *Fairfax County Area Agency on Aging*) in order to share and provide the most current information on volunteer issues.

Publications: Guide to Services in Volunteer Management

VOLUNTARY ACTION CENTER OF WAKE COUNTY*
United Way of of Wake County
1100 Wake Forest Road
PO Box 11426
Raleigh, NC 27604
TEL: 919-833-5739

Purpose: To provide a central point in Raleigh/Wake County where the needs of individuals and agencies can be met through voluntary action in the areas of health, welfare, education, recreation, culture, civic and other non-profit activities.

Sponsor: City of Raleigh
Contact: Stephen Dudek

Description: The concept of a VAC in the capital city of North Carolina was originated in the late 1960's when civic leaders and representatives of the United Way of Wake County and the Junior League of Raleigh met to discuss the need for a central clearinghouse/resource center for volunteers. It was not until 1973 when the VAC finally established itself with funding from the above mentioned organizations, corporations, individual donations, and grants from city and county governments. By 1980, funding sources were diminishing rapidly. The Board of Directors approached the Raleigh City Council, a major funding source, about the possibility of becoming a part of City Government. In November 1980, the VAC was accepted into the Human Resource Department. County officials consented to allow the VAC to remain in one of its ten office buildings, thus assuring that it could continue its work county-wide.

The VAC serves volunteers and the agencies which use volunteers. Volunteer placement counseling, information on human services, referrals to community organizations, and suggestions for service projects are offered to individuals and to civic, church and neighborhood organizations. Agencies can benefit from training sessions in volunteer management and retention, publicity of volunteer needs, technical aspects concerning their volunteer programs, and volunteer recruitment. VAC staff members also assist as consultants for community needs assessments, development, and program implementation.

The VAC has a corps of volunteers who perform a number of staff functions:
- **Volunteer Advisors** (three on board at present) interview by telephone or in person individuals who wish to volunteer, keep updated agency requests for volunteers, follow-up with volunteer placements, assist community organizations with their service projects, and route donations of material goods to appropriate organizations.
- **Office Assistants** (some work at home) help the Office Manager with typing, telephone answering, filing, and a myriad of other support tasks, benefitting all staff members.
- **A Publicity Coordinator** (who occasionally has an assistant) writes the volunteer needs columns for daily and weekly newspapers and Public Service Announcements for radio and television stations, develops and edits a quarterly newsletter and writes news releases.

- **A Projects Coordinator and Projects Assistants** design, develop and implement special projects designed to increase citizen participation.
- **Graphic Artists** design brochures, covers and art illustrations for VAC publications.
- **Occasional Mailing Assistants** collate, stuff, and staple materials for bulk mailings.

At present, the Director supervises the Volunteer Advisors, Publicity Coordinator, Project Coordinator, and Graphic Artists. However, if future funding permits, an additional paid staff person would be hired to oversee projects and publicity, and would then supervise volunteers working in these areas. The Office Manager assigns work to and supervises office support staff and volunteers who are working on specific office operation projects. Training of new Volunteer Advisors is provided by one individual currently in that position who has been with the VAC for a long period of time. This same individual is also responsible for compiling monthly statistics for all the Advisors and determining which volunteer opportunities should be advertised each week.

The VAC has published a number of books/booklets concerning citizen participation, including *Holiday Hopes,* an annual publication which lists year-round service projects needed by human service agencies, *Job Exploration Through Volunteering,* a manual for youth volunteers, and *Options,* a directory of volunteer opportunities. Currently, the VAC is working on a publication which encourages older adults to volunteer on government boards and commissions and in non profit and government agencies. It will also feature a resource section for those wishing to learn more about the senior years.

Publications: Job Exploration/Volunteering; Options
Founded: 1973

VOLUNTEER BUREAU OF THE OMAHA UNITED WAY
Voluntary Action Center
1805 Harney Street
Omaha, NE 68102
TEL: 402-342-8232 Ext. 531
Purpose: To promote volunteerism among the citizens of Metropolitan Omaha and to encourage their participation through recruitment and referral, training opportunities and recognition.
Sponsor: Voluntary Way of the Midlands
Contact: Jamesena Grimes Moore, Director
Description: The Volunteer Center is a clearinghouse. Through its *Recruitment and Referral Program,* individuals wanting to become a part of the community problem-solving process are matched with one of the more than 200 agencies that are seeking volunteer assistance.
The *Court Referral Program* provides individuals an opportunity for alternative sentencing. These individuals, through a referral and placement process are placed in nonprofit agencies to complete their court-ordered community service hours.
Training opportunities are offered for volunteers and volunteer leaders to help enhance their skills. Consultation regarding the establishment and maintenance of volunteer programs is also provided.
Annually, a *Director's Reception, Recognition Luncheon for Outstanding Volunteers,* and an agency fair, *EXPO,* are held to promote volunteerism.
The *Volunteer Bureau* processes approximately 100-125 persons a week through its services.
Founded: 1954

VOLUNTEER BUREAU OF THE UNITED WAY
United Way of El Paso
Voluntary Action Center
1918 Texas Avenue
PO Box 3488
El Paso, TX 79923-3488
TEL: 915-533-2434

Purpose: To coordinate the volunteer needs and services of the community.
Sponsor: United Way of El Paso
Contact: Vivienne Corn, Director
Description: The Volunteer Center of the United Way, a Voluntary Action Center, was organized in September 1968 as a pilot project of the El Paso Section, National Council of Jewish Women. In May 1971 it became a private, non-profit, tax-exempt agency governed by a Board of Directors. In November 1972 the Volunteer Center became an affiliate of VOLUNTEER - The National Center. At that time it also became a component of, and is now administered by, the United Way of El Paso. It is supervised by an advisory committee composed of members of the United Way Planning Committee and individuals from the general community.
The Volunteer Center is the clearinghouse for persons seeking volunteer jobs, and for the non-profit community agencies needing volunteer help. The Bureau recruits, interviews and refers volunteers to these agencies, maintains files of the continuing volunteer needs of the agencies, and works with the agencies' staffs for effective use of volunteers. The Center also maintains files of clubs and organizations in the community, assists civic groups in finding worthwhile projects, sponsors conferences on volunteer services and conducts a special summertime program for teenage volunteers.
Founded: 1968

VOLUNTEER CENTER OF JOHNSON COUNTY
5311 Johnson Drive
Mission, KS 66205
TEL: 913-432-0766
Purpose: To identify human needs and to help meet these needs by utilizing available County services and volunteers.
Sponsor: United Community Services of Johnson County
Contact: Virginia Bryngelson
Description: The Voluntary Action Center of Johnson County is a non-profit organization dedicated to volunteerism and to identifying human needs. The goal of the Center is to help meet these needs by utilizing available Johnson County services and volunteers.
The Voluntary Action Center recruits, counsels and refers volunteers. It is the Johnson County link for people who want to volunteer, and the agencies that need their help.
The Center encourages any person or group with time available to serve the community through volunteer work. It provides a coordinated and personalized program for recruiting and placing volunteers where they will be happiest and most effective among over 85 charitable agencies, hospitals and schools in Johnson County. Some programs sponsored by VAC include:

- **Friendly Visitor** - Volunteers bring companionship to isolated, lonely elderly persons in their own homes or in nursing homes.
- **Transportation** - Volunteers drive and/or escort elderly and handicapped persons to doctors' offices or other essential appointments.
- **Adult/Juvenile Diversion** - Community service volunteer placements for defendants under 18 as well as adult defendants.
- **Volunteer Awards** - Annually presents certificates of merit to Johnson County organizations and individuals for outstanding volunteer service; also presents Volunteer of the Year award.

VOLUNTEER CENTER OF YORK COUNTY
800 East King Street
York, PA 17403
TEL: 717-846-4477
Purpose: To provide a clearinghouse of volunteer opportunities for residents of York County; to serve as the advocate for volunteerism.

Sponsor: Junior League of York

Contact: Peggy Stoppard, Director

Description: Begun in mid-1986, the *Volunteer Center of York County* is a service of the United Way. The Center's main function is that of community clearinghouse for volunteer opportunitie for both individuals and groups. We work with all ages and types of volunteers. Special programs are for teens and mentally handicapped.

As the advocates for volunteerism in this community, we perform a public education role, and offer free speakers to various community groups.

We published our first annual *York County WishBook* for 1989-90 in cooperative with the *Junior League of York*. This book lists agencies and organizations and their volunteer needs. Response has been very positive. We are a relatively new Center, but are expanding as we become aware of community needs and can recruit and place the volunteers to meet them.

Publications: York County WishBook; We Need You

VOLUNTEER CENTER/UNITED WAY AT WORK
United Way of San Joaquin County
12 East Park Street
PO Box 1585
Stockton, CA 95201
TEL: 209-943-0870

Purpose: To assist the community by serving as a clearinghouse for volunteer involvement.

Contact: Denise Ortega, Director

Description: The *Volunteer Center* places, recruits and screens over 2,000 volunteers each year for 300+ nonprofit organizations. We maintain a *Speakers Bureau,* a *Board Bank,* and offer *Management Assistance Programs (MAP).*

In addition, we facilitate *DOVIA (Directors of Volunteers in Agencies),* a group that networks to share resources and information. We provide self-help workshops and information and referral (I&R).

Also, we hold annual events such as: *The Human Race,* a community fundraiser, raising $50,000+ for over 75 nonprofits countywide. We participate in the *J.C. Penney Golden Rule Awards* luncheon to recognize outstanding volunteers across the county.

United Way at Work offers educational information and volunteer opportunities to corporate employees. This helps the company, the employee, the community at large, and clients who may receive the benefits of volunteer efforts of both individuals and groups. We offer a *Student Volunteer Program* to schools to teach students that volunteering is more than an alternative to punishment - that it is hands-on experience, on-the-job training (OJT), and a valuable asset when applying for jobs, college or military service.

Publications: The Human Race: People In Motion; United Way At Work; Volunteer!

VOLUNTEER NETWORK*
Fifth Avenue Center
507 Nanum
Ellensburg, WA 98926
TEL: 509-925-6967

Purpose: To fill the gaps created by agency cutbacks; to provide the psychological uplift of being needed and productive.

Sponsor: Fifth Avenue Center

Contact: Donna M. Becker

Description: Volunteer Network began approximately ten years ago and has been coordinated by VISTA volunteers. Volunteer Network is under the umbrella of 5th Avenue Center, which receives funding from various sources, including United Way. Volunteer Network encourages volunteers from 18-60, as the RSVP and Youth Volunteer Programs recruit from the other age groups. Many social agencies in the community have lost their funding, so Volunteer Network encourages the use of volunteers in

order to keep these agencies in operation. With an unemployment rate of over 15%, volunteerism can provide the psychological well-being that comes from having a job to do. Volunteer Network is a clearing-house for volunteers and the agencies which can use them.

Founded: 1978

VOLUNTEERS IN ACTION
Kennebec Valley Community Action Program
101 Water Street
Waterville , ME 04901
TEL: 207-873-2122
TOLL FREE: 800-452-8760

Purpose: To coordinate people of various ages, skills and educational backgrounds who want to upgrade their own skills while they give time to a community social services organization.

Sponsor: Kennebec Valley Community Action Program

Contact: Katrine Scholl, Volunteer Coordinator

Description: Volunteers in Action matches volunteers with skills they wish to learn as well as with volunteer positions that need to be filled. Kennebec Valley Community Action Program has many departments and living classrooms where volunteers can receive pre-work or post-work experience in such areas as typing, bookkeeping, interpersonal skills, etc. Departments in which volunteer skills have been matched include: Child Development Center, Energy Education Library, Family Planning, Job Skills Library, Weatherization, WIC, Demand Response, Fuel Assistance, Computer Services, and the Media Department.

In exchange for the volunteer's effort, VIA offers valuable career services. VIA works with volunteers to expand job hunting skills beyond reading the want ads and gives them responsibilities that help develop motivation, career direction, concrete skills, and a feeling of accomplishment.

All volunteers are interviewed by theVolunteer Coordinator to determine specific placement. A tour of the Agency and a two-hour orientation precede on-the-job training.

VOLUNTEERS OF CAPE COD
PO Box 717
Hyannis, MA 02601
TEL: 617-771-7925

Purpose: To provide a central resource for the development, coordination, and organization of volunteer and career related activities in Barnstable County for persons of all ages.

Sponsor: Volunteers of Cape Cod

Contact: Dianne J. Dinger

Description: Volunteers of Cape Cod was first established in July 1980. Additional purposes of VOCC are as follows:

- To recruit potential volunteers to perform volunteer services for any public or private non-profit organization or licensed proprietary health care facility, to provide meaningful volunteer opportunities for said organizations and facilities and to match volunteers according to their interests and skills with desired opportunities.
- To provide leadership and cooperation, to improve the satisfaction of the volunteer experience, including educating organizations and facilities as to the best utilization of volunteers.
- To participate in the training of volunteers and organizations and facilities.
- To sponsor the Retired Senior Volunteer Program (for volunteers aged 60+) and Young Volunteers in Action Program (for volunteers age 14-22) and promote three ACTION programs.
- To develop and implement additional programs related to or using volunteers.
- To perform such other services as the corporation is deemed capable of performing.
- To become the local Voluntary Action Center sponsoring a

Younger Volunteer Program for volunteers age 23-59.
A technical assistance handbook entitled *How To Set Up and Operate a Volunteer Program From A to Z* has been developed by VOCC to provide directors and coordinators of volunteer centers with an accountable system of operation. Since volunteer bureaus themselves are engaged in supporting both the needs of other non-profit organizations and the volunteers, this handbook will focus on procedures for the development and implementation of an internal system of monitoring volunteer placement and volunteer station requests.
Founded: 1980

ADMINISTRATION: PHILOSOPHY OF VOLUNTEERISM

TRAINING PROGRAMS

ARROWHOOD 22: FUTURE CHALLENGES: A UNIVERSAL PERSPECTIVE
SEE TRAINING/CONFERENCES/TEACHING: PHILOSOPHY

CONFERENCE ON PHILOSOPHICAL ISSUES IN VOLUNTEERISM
SEE TRAINING/CONFERENCES/TEACHING: PHILOSOPHY

THE FUTURE OF VOLUNTEERISM: SHAPES AND SCENARIOS
Center for Volunteer Development
Virginia Tech
Cooperative Extensive Service
Blacksburg, VA 24061-0512
TEL: 703-231-6000
Sponsor: Center for Volunteer Development
Contact: Delwyn Dyer, Ph.D.
Description: This workshop addresses *futuring* - "an attempt to predict trends and events which haven't occurred yet, and to control these events, or deflect them in a desired direction" (Dr. Ivan Scheier). Attendees (22 local volunteers and volunteer administrators) were offered an opportunity to learn about some of the purposes, paradoxes, and pitfalls of futuring, as well as strategies for do-it-yourself futurists:
Purposes
- sheer curiosity
- hope (a chance to escape present frustrations and dream of better days)
- to understand the present more fully
- intervention (shape the future in a desired direction)
- help recognize how the future may influence us
Paradoxes
- Just making a prediction tends to change it.
- The easiest predictions are often the most accurate.
- "Backcasting" is the best preparation for forecasting.
- The best way to predict the future (taking a running start from the past) may also be the worst because it underestimates the subtleties of behavior.
- The assumptions that have served us so well in the past may be the greatest barriers to imaginative visualizing of positive futures.
Pitfalls
- Being clear and consistent in what you are predicting about (unit of study).

- Acting as if what you are predicting about is unconnected to the rest of the world.
- Failing to recognize that your unit of study can act upon the environment as well as be acted upon by it.
- Flirting with fantasy by working with overly far-futures.
- Wishful thinking.

The workshop was sponsored by The Center for Creative Community, Santa Fe, and the Center for Volunteer Development, Virginia Tech. The purpose of the workshop was summarized by Dr. Schier like this: "You can't stop a hurricane, but foreknowledge can at least help you prepare for it and soften its impact."
Publications: Shapes and Scenarios in the Future of Volunteerism

NATIONAL FORUM ON A COMMISSION ON VOLUNTEERISM: THE FEDERAL GOVERNMENT AND FUTURE OF VOLUNTEERISM*
Alliance for Volunteerism
3706 Rhode Island Avenue
Mt. Ranier, MD 20822
TEL: 202-347-0340
Credit: Inquire
Sponsor: Alliance for Volunteerism
Contact: Dorothy Height
Description: This conference was convened to bring together leaders in the national volunteering community - Board Chairpersons, staff executives, Washington representatives - to plan together on issues affecting the future of volunteering in the United States. It was not a position-taking conference, but designed to:
- explore the national situation as it relates to volunteerism today.
- examine current legislation and its implications.
- stimulate exchange of information and opinion.
- prepare to provide input to Congress.
- inspire action plans.

Senator Dave Durenberger's revised legislation on a Commission on Volunteerism, and Senator Paul Tsongas' bill to create a Commission on National Service were discussed along with related issues based on a series of "idea papers" provided to participants in advance of the conference, including:
- A Commission on Volunteerism: Pro and Con
- Legislative Update and Analysis
- The Federal Role in Resources for Volunteerism: Current and Future
- Who Speaks for Volunteers and the Voluntary Sector and Who in Government Listens?
- Mapping the Volunteer Sector
- Roles for Citizen Volunteers in the Federal System
- Government Domination/Government Support and Encouragement of Volunteer Programs
- Youth National Service
- Senior National Service

Additional discussion addressed: use of volunteers in federal programs; federal support for private sector volunteerism; citizen participation in federal decision-making, and other matters of interest to Forum participants.
After the first day of presentations by faculty, an opinion-sharing session to provide stimulation, and informal discussions with resource persons, the small group technique was called into play using a four-fold plan: 1) defining the issue; 2) understanding the issue; 3) dealing with the issue; 4) developing recommendations. This was followed by a dialogue with Congressional representatives on recommendations and, finally, the participants' formulation of action plans.
The Forum was co-sponsored by seven national groups, hosted by a State University, and supported by three foundations.

VOLUNTEERS DO MAKE A DIFFERENCE!
SEE GOVERNORS' OFFICES ON VOLUNTEERISM:
DELAWARE

VOLUNTEERS: FACTS AND FICTION
SEE TRAINING/CONFERENCES/TEACHING:
PHILOSOPHY

INDIVIDUAL PROGRAM PROFILES

A MESSAGE FOR THE FUTURE - THE VOLUNTAS TIME CAPSULE
Center for Creative Community
PO Box 2427
Santa Fe, NM 87504-2427
TEL: 505-983-8414
Purpose: To send a message to the future on today's volunteerism.
Description: The *Time Capsule Project* is monitored and administered by experts in the field of volunteerism, who will make the final selections for messages, books, videos, recognition items, etc. that best reflect contemporary volunteerism, based on the following points:

- Good things you see about volunteering today in your program or organization, and in general.
- Challenges, problems, things that need improving in volunteerism today.
- Your prediction of what 2050 will be like as far as volunteering is concerned.
- Your message to the future; advice, encouragement, cautions, or a greeting.

From 150 to 200 messages of about 500 words each will be selected and transferred to paper designed for preservation. They will come from individuals, associations, or organizations involved in volunteerism, including volunteer coordinators and consultants; clergy and lay leadership in church, temple and synagogue; self-help and service club leaders, etc. Each message-sender selected will be asked to recommend others, and to vote on the actual contents of the capsule. Message providers are asked to contribute $100 to the project, part of which is used for scholarships for those who are deemed to have a meaningful message, but cannot finance their contribution.
The first actual time capsule messages were prepared at the *Challenge III* think tank on volunteerism on November 1-3 at the Center in Santa Fe.
Because of the fast pace of change in volunteerism today, the capsule is set to be opened in 2050, rather than in centuries from now as other capsules have been scheduled. According to the creator of the concept, "Some younger people invited to the 1990 launching may still be alive in 2050 for the opening! The rest of us can visualize our children there, or their children..."
Publications: VOLUNTAS: A Message for the Future

ADMINISTRATION: RECOGNITION

NATIONAL/STATE ORGANIZATIONS

ALEXIS DE TOCQUEVILLE SOCIETY PROGRAM
United Way of America
701 North Fairfax Street
Alexandria, VA 22314-2045
TEL: 703-836-7100
Objectives: To recognize individuals who have rendered outstanding service as volunteers.

Services: Recognizes individuals - both locally and nationally - who have been exemplary volunteers; oversees local *Societies* - 100 nationwide as of mid-1990; operates the program in keeping with *Second Century Initiative (SCI)* goals of doubling resources - both human and financial, with a five-year plan reflecting this initiative; provides information on starting and maintaining local *Tocqueville Societies;* convenes a *Board of Governors Tocqueville Society* composed of individuals in business/industry, government, and the nonprofit sector to help in developing local Societies, and to assist existing Societies; recommends specific procedures to attract new members, including:

- Present potential members with a vision of the community as it can be, and help them understand how they can be an integral part of the effort;
- Announce the Society's specific goals, and build momentum with progress reports to members and potential members;
- Sponsor special Society events - such as a victory celebration or a new member recruitment reception;
- Conduct research on an area's growing industries to help build a Society;
- Implement a plan to thank Society members every couple of months throughout the year.

Conducts major campaigns for United Way-supported programs, but recognizing volunteers through special events, in news announcements about United Way activities, on special occasions (Valentine's Day, etc.), and so on is one of the strengths of the program, and the activity that maintains interest and provides a link to the community.
Founded: 1972

GOLDEN RULE AWARDS PROGRAM
J.C. Penney Company
14841 Dallas Parkway
Dallas, TX 75240
TEL: 214-591-1000
FAX: 214-591-2808
Objectives: To recognize groups and individuals across the country who have performed outstanding service in their local communities.
Services: Presents awards to groups and individuals for outstanding volunteer service in the community at large; maintains award panels of involved citizens and community leaders independent of J.C. Penney, who choose thirteen semifinalists at the community level for the local *Golden Rule Award,* selecting three finalists from those to receive specially commissioned sculptures signifying the spirit of volunteerism and $1,000 grants to their volunteer organizations, as well as to the organization of one *Golden Rule Youth Award* winner at the local level, and $250 grants to the remaining ten semifinalists; conducts a national program with all local finalists eligible for the national awards of $10,000 for the top winner's organization, $5,000 to each national semifinalist's organization, and $5,000 to the organization of the national youth volunteer selectee; Eligibility requirements include:

- Must be active in volunteer efforts;
- Must have been done in local community where award is offered;
- Must have provided volunteer services with no more than out-of-pocket reimbursed;
- Must not be a member of Award coordinators' or judging panel's families;
- Must be 18 or under at time of nomination to be eligible for youth award (youth groups qualify for regular *Golden Rule Awards*).

Allows any individual to nominate one candidate, including him/herself, fill out the forms completely, mail by deadline, and prepare to provide additional information upon request to the judges; sets criteria in areas of need, action, initiative, achievement, impact, time and challenge.

Contact: Golden Rule Awards Coordinator
Publications: Golden Rule Awards Program

POINTS OF LIGHT INITIATIVE
SEE NATIONAL SERVICE/POINTS OF LIGHT INITIATIVE

TEMPLE AWARDS FOR CREATIVE ALTRUISM
Institute for Noetic Sciences
PO Box 909
Sausalito, CA 94966
TEL: 415-331-5650
Objectives: To recognize outstanding altruists for a national awards program.
Services: Presents annual awards in September of each year to several persons who exemplify unselfish love and service to others, inspire altruism or the spirit of generosity and caring in others, have sustained commitments to altruistic ideals, have personal qualities that support this commitment, are loving, compassionate, kind and nonviolent in their relationships, and make significant contributions to humanity through consistent actions which benefit others, rather than for isolated acts of heroism or self-sacrifice; divides $25,000 among the recipients (four in 1989 in areas of mental retardation, drugs/alcoholism, the homeless, and AIDS); Seeks award nominations from the public.

TWENTY-FIVE YEAR PRESIDENTIAL AWARD CERTIFICATE PROGRAM FOR VOLUNTEERS IN JUVENILE CRIMINAL JUSTICE
US/Presidential Awards Programs
Office of Public Liaison
Washington, DC 20500
TEL: 202-456-1414
Objectives: To recognize professionals (paid or unpaid) who supervise volunteers, and volunteers in the juvenile and criminal justice systems who meet the criteria of the awards program.
Services: Provides a certificate, signed by the President, to show appreciation for administrative service in the criminal justice volunteer community (supervision of 50 volunteers for at least one year, 10 volunteers for at least five years, etc.), and for the extraordinary volunteer (at least 50 hours a month for a year); represents a tradition involving five Presidents as of 1989 (Presidents Nixon, Carter, Ford, Reagan and Bush); covers service from 1959; distribution is by Volunteers in Prevention, Probation, and Prison (a national organization) or through individuals or offices within a state.
Sponsor: US/White House
Founded: 1968

INDIVIDUAL PROGRAM PROFILES

CHAIRMAN OF VOLUNTEERS GALLERY
American Red Cross
10151 East Eleventh Street
Tulsa, OK 74128
TEL: 918-831-1190
Purpose: To recognize distinguished volunteer leadership in the Tulsa area chapter of the American Red Cross.
Contact: Dorothy Biery, Gallery Project Chairman
Description: A highlight of the 73rd annual meeting of the Tulsa Red Cross chapter was the dedication of the *Chairman of Volunteers Gallery.* In the making for some time, the gallery was dedicated by the Board Chairman and the Gallery Project Chairman. Twenty-one past Chairmen attended the gallery opening, which displays framed photographs of volunteer chairmen who served in Tulsa since its beginning. Plaques were given to three volunteers who provided color portraits, reproductions from old black and white photographs, and black and white portraits

that make up the gallery.
In some cases, family members and friends of deceased chairmen represented them.
The gallery was developed entirely with donations of both funds and time. It will be maintained and operated by volunteers.
Founded: 1989

THE COURANT'S YOUTH LEADERSHIP AWARDS PROGRAM
The Hartford Courant
Hartford, CT 06101
TEL: 203-241-6200
Purpose: To recognize high school students for outstanding service to school and community.
Sponsor: Area churches
Contact: Michael J. Davies, Editor/Publisher
Description: In 1988, *The Courant,* a Hartford publication, began an awards program that recognizes high school students for community involvement as well as academic work and demonstration of leadership qualities. The program is unique in that it is designed not only to present the awards of $250 cash at its annual ceremony, but also to provide ongoing access to an emergency fund for academic or personal obstacles or emergencies the students might encounter after they are in college. The emergency fund was opened with $5,000 in 1989 and will be increased as donations are received from individuals, groups, and other corporations. It is retroactive and available to the initial year's recipients as well as all subsequent award winners. Community involvement takes many forms with the 1989 winners - from volunteering at the *House of Bread* and *St. Elizabeth's House* in Hartford, to volunteer assistance in scout troops, athletic programs, and the National Honor Society. All have agreed that their publicly-declared status as "role models" is a big responsibility, which they intend to live up to throughout their lives. This sums up another purpose of the program described by the sponsoring corporation - to build on teenage community involvement achievements to encourage continuation in the less-supervised, less-structured university and job settings. Students are nominated by the city's *Office of Youth Services* and by community and church leaders, school staff and classmates. Three area high schools were represented among the nine 1989 winners.
Founded: 1988

GIRAFFE PROJECT
120 Second Street
PO Box 759, Langley
Whidbey Island, WA 98260
TEL: 206-221-7989
TOLL FREE: 800-344-TALL
FAX: 206-221-7817
Purpose: To spark a proliferation of responsible, capable, citizens who *stick their necks out* to take on the challenges faced by their communities.
Sponsor: 18 foundations, membership
Contact: John Graham or Ann Medlock
Description: The *Giraffe Project* was started in 1982 to seed the media with stories of real contemporary heroes, ordinary people who are sticking their necks out to make their communities better places to live. They are called *Giraffes.* The intent was to raise the consciousness of other citizens to increase the chances of a better community, a better country and a better world.
By 1990, the project had installed over 400 Giraffes, selected by a volunteer committee out of nominations sent to us from all over the country. Every story the Giraffe Project tells focuses on a very real problem and then shows what can be done by an individual citizen who decides to take responsibility for that problem. Viewers, listeners and readers are constantly being challenged by the Project to become such responsible citizens.

In 1988, the Project developed a youth arm, *Young Giraffes,* which is expected to be a major component by 1991. The Project puts a special emphasis on finding Young Giraffes as role models for their peers and is working on a television cartoon show about a giraffe who guides kids in making ethical, compassionate choices. Textbook publishers and children's magazines are using Giraffe stories regularly.

Stories of Giraffes have reached the Soviet Union. In the winter of 1989, Project officers spent eight days in Moscow, at the invitation of the Soviet state broadcasting agency. They explained Giraffes to the Soviet people through their television, radio and newspapers and helped launch a parallel project there. The Project has termed its Soviet connection *Giraffenost.* The goal of "Giraffes USSR" is to encourage Soviet citizens to accept the freedoms and the responsibilities *glasnost* and *perestroika* offer them. The *Giraffe Project* is assisting in the organization and training of this fledgling organization.

The Project earns almost a third of its annual budget from lecture and workshop fees, memberships, and product sales. The balance comes from foundations, private donors and fundraising appeals to members. The Project and its Giraffes have been featured in the *New York Times, Parade, Christian Science Monitor* and *Time Magazine;* on the ABC, CNN, Fox and CBS television networks; on USA Today, Canadian Broadcasting, Monitor Radio and the Voice of America. A PBS documentary has been shown on most of this country's public television stations.

GBS (Giraffe Broadcasting Service), produces and distributes scripts and recorded public service announcements to radio stations with a combined listening market of over 150 million people. Celebrity volunteers record *Giraffe Spots* and have included Dick Cavett, Chuck Connors, Celeste Holm, John Denver, Dina Merrill, Raul Julia, Eli Wallach, and Candice Bergen. The Giraffe press service sends news of Giraffes to local media, attracting valuable hometown attention and support for the Giraffes' work.

Project officers are frequently speakers and seminar leaders, bringing audiences and workshop participants practical coaching on effective social action. The quarterly *Giraffe Gazette* reports on Giraffes' activities and gives readers inspiration and practical advice on helping their communities. Nomination forms are provided on request.

Publications: Giraffe Gazette; Giraffe Project Information Packet; Giraffe Radio Scripts; Giraffenalia Catalog; Giraffe Membership Kit

Founded: 1982

GOOD SAMARITAN RECOGNITION CEREMONY
St. Paul's Episcopal Cathedral
Genessee Street
Chittenango, NY 13037
TEL: 315-687-6304
Purpose: To recognize volunteers from 50 area churches who serve hot meals to the needy at the *Samaritan Center.*
Sponsor: St. Paul's Episcopal Cathedral and other churches
Contact: Dean William Hale, Rector
Description: The board of directors of the *Samaritan Center,* which serves hot meals to the needy, honored the volunteers who serve the meals with - what else - a recognition dinner. More than 200 people representing 50 of the churches involved with the Center attended. Piano selections were played throughout the evening as *Certificates of Outstanding Service* were presented to volunteers from the Center's clothing shop, maintenance department, home bakers group, cleanup crew, carpentry workers, volunteer administrative aides and weekend volunteers.
In addition to the tasks indicated above, volunteers collect clothing, set out reading materials, and provide a multitude of other services as needed to the homeless, people down on their luck, or those simply unable to make the check last for one more

meal. As many as 200 people are served every afternoon at the Center.
The rector at St. Paul's Cathedral said, "The dinner is a way of saying thank you to all the volunteers. After all of their baking, stirring, slicing and preparing of food for others, we felt that it was time our 'good Samaritans' got served themselves."

NEWSDAY VOLUNTEER RECOGNITION PROGRAM
Newsday Newspapers
235 Pinelawn Road
Melville, NY 11747
TEL: 516-454-2700
Purpose: To honor Long Island individuals or groups who make unique contributions through volunteer service.
Contact: Community Affairs Director
Description: In the spring of 1989, *Newsday* held its first *Volunteer Recognition Ceremony.* There were 38 individual and four group winners chosen from thousands of nominations received by the newspaper. Nominations were in six categories of volunteer service:
- Human Services (food, clothing, job and shelter assistance);
- Community Services (local organizations, fire services, citizenship aid);
- Health Related Services (physical and mental health);
- Education (day care through adult education);
- Arts and Humanities (arts and cultural organizations); and
- Leadership (innovation in organizing programs or motivating volunteers).

A panel of leaders from the community and public service sector served as judges. Group winners included programs in nutrition, AIDS, the arts, and leadership. Winners ranged from a junior high school council to volunteers who had served almost 40 years and donated over 19,000 hours.
The 1989 Ceremony is the landmark activity for a program that the newspaper expects to continue as part of its ongoing, scheduled activities each year.
Founded: 1989

THANK YOU PICKET LINES
United Way of Licking County
21 South First Street
Newark, OH 43055-5664
TEL: 614-345-6685
Purpose: To create and use an innovative event to honor local volunteers.
Sponsor: Volunteer Center of Licking County
Contact: Molly Ingold, President, Communications
Description: Borrowing from the attention-getting picket lines concept used by American workers, members of human service agencies in Licking County, Ohio, "picketed" their volunteers. The picket lines were staged to thank the many volunteers who gave their time, talents, and financial resources to support local human service agencies.
Cosponsored by the *United Way of Licking County* and the *Volunteer Center of Licking County,* the picketers lined up in front two of the county's most popular spots - Newark's Courthouse Square, and the new Indian Mound Mall. To involve the total community, the picketers handed out balloons and chocolate kisses to citizens who passed by the lines. There was music and, for those interested in finding out about volunteer opportunities, colorful brochures from the Volunteer Center.
Picketers came from a variety of human service agencies, United Way-supported as well as others. The public thank you was aimed at all Licking County volunteers. According to United Way officials, inquiries and other evidence following the event indicated that it sparked a new interest in volunteering.

VOLUNTEER AWARDS PROGRAM
Oregon Human Development Corporation
835 NE Twentieth
Portland, OR 97232
TEL: 503-236-9670
Purpose: To recognize volunteers who have assisted the OHD in meeting its goals to improve the lives of low-income groups and farm workers.
Sponsor: Human Development Corporation
Contact: Volunteer Coordinator
Description: This awards program reached across the state to honor individuals and organizations who have volunteered to assist the needy. The *Oregon Human Development Corporation (OHD)* is a private, nonprofit organization that assists low-income groups and farm workers. The awards given included recognition for:
- lifetime volunteer work with low-income groups and farm workers;
- efforts to ease the state's 1988 crisis among farm workers;
- home-school counseling for the needy;
- advocacy for farm workers;
- representation for the Hispanic and the elderly;
- health clinic services for target population; and
- education and job training for farm workers.

Award recipients came from the *Governor's Office,* social service agencies, Hispanic groups, the education field, organizations for the aging, advocacy groups, journalism, labor agencies, church groups, and health clinics, and included the former Governor of Oregon who raised $500,000 through the state to help alleviate the 1988 farmworker crisis.
The *Oregon Human Development Corporation* is based in Portland and has offices in Hermiston, Hillsboro, Klamath Falls, Ontario, Salem and Woodburn. It is part of a network operating in four states - California (parent corporation), Washington, and Hawaii in addition to Oregon.

ADMINISTRATION: RECRUITMENT/ORIENTATION

NATIONAL/STATE ORGANIZATIONS

GIVE FIVE **CAMPAIGN**
Independent Sector
1828 L Street, NW
Washington, DC 20036
TEL: 202-223-8100
FAX: 202-457-0609
Objectives: To establish a national *standard* for individual giving and volunteering: *five hours a week and five percent of income to the causes and charities we care about.*
Services: Works to encourage every citizen to achieve the standard for giving and volunteering based on studies of a 1983 *Task Force of Independent Sector Members* and recommendations of a 1986 national forum comprised of 650 members from corporations, foundations and national organizations; issues a challenge to all Americans to join a five-year nationwide program to increase giving and volunteering; operates with yearly goals to that end, with 1991 goals including:
- To achieve greater public awareness that personal service is essential to a free and caring society, and that everyone can make a difference by generously supporting the causes of his or her choice;
- To show clearly that people who give five percent or more of their income and five or more hours a week are models for a caring society;

- To help voluntary organizations develop their ability to raise money and effectively use boards and other citizen volunteers;
- To encourage foundations and corporate grantmakers to invest more funds in helping voluntary organizations achieve greater capacity to raise money and involve volunteers;
- To help accelerate the birthrate and growth rate of foundations;
- To help fulfill the goal of the *President's Task Force on Private Sector Initiatives,* which called for doubling the involvement of corporations and for achieving an average of two percent of pretax next income for corporate contributions;
- To preserve tax deductions for charitable contributions;
- To double the number of strong, visible *Volunteer Centers;*
- To develop the independent sector's research capacity in topics such as motivations for giving and volunteering; and
- To build a grassroots lobby capable of convincing government officials of the significance of the independent sector.

Works with 30 local *Give Five* coalitions (as of June 1990) at the city, regional or state level in various stages of development or operations, and national organizations, who continue to adopt the program, including as of June 1990:
- American Heart Association
- American Red Cross
- National Society of Fundraising Executives
- National Association for Hospital Development
- United Negro College Fund
- Association for Volunteer Administration
- Girl Scouts
- Association of Junior Leagues
- Girls Clubs
- National Civic League
- National Council for International Visitors
- National 4-H Council
- March of Dimes
- United Way
- VOLUNTEER - The National Center
- Women's Equity Action League

Provides information and technical assistance to foundations, corporations, and individuals, as well as religious denominations, which are looking at *Give Five* as an incentive for increased stewardship; commissions *Gallup Organization* polls, the latest in 1988, which is the first national survey to cover both giving and volunteering behavior of individuals, including exploration of the motivations for giving and for volunteering (2,775 individuals interviewed face-to-face in their homes); uses information from these surveys to plan programs (e.g., 75% of those interviewed believe it is an individual's responsibility to give to charity, and one third of those felt they did not give enough, an encouraging sign for the expansion of *Give Five),* and to inform associates in the field.
Contact: Sandra T. Gray, Vice President, Independent Sector

US/WHITE HOUSE - OFFICE OF NATIONAL SERVICE
SEE NATIONAL SERVICE/POINTS OF LIGHT INITIATIVE

TRAINING PROGRAMS

DEVELOPING YOUR PERSPECTIVE: RECRUITING VOLUNTEERS
SEE TRAINING/CONFERENCES/TEACHING: RECRUITMENT

RECRUITING TECHNIQUES FOR VOLUNTEER ORGANIZATIONS
SEE TRAINING/CONFERENCES/TEACHING: RECRUITMENT

SELECTING AND TRAINING VOLUNTEERS
SEE TRAINING/CONFERENCES/TEACHING

VOLUNTEER INTERVENING FOR EQUITY (VIE)*
SEE TRAINING/CONFERENCES/TEACHING:
RECRUITMENT

VOLUNTEER STAFFING WORKSHOPS*
SEE TRAINING/CONFERENCES/TEACHING:
RECRUITMENT

**VOLUNTEER TRAINING AND RECRUITMENT
CONFERENCE**
SEE TRAINING/CONFERENCES/TEACHING:
RECRUITMENT

INDIVIDUAL PROGRAM PROFILES

DONOR INVOLVEMENT
SEE FUNDING/FUND-RAISING/RELATED SERVICES

END HUNGER PROJECT
SEE COMMUNICATIONS & PUBLIC RELATIONS:
NUTRITION

LOUISVILLE YOUTH INVOLVEMENT COMMITTEE
Metro United Way
334 East Broadway
Louisville, KY 40204-0488
TEL: 502-583-2821
Purpose: To involve the *leaders of tomorrow* in today's community
needs.
Sponsor: Youth Involvement Committee
Contact: Robert C. Reifsnyder, President
Description: As part of its *Second Century Initiative,* Metro
United Way in Louisville has developed a series of youth
initiatives to involve more youth in community problem-solving.
Developed by the agency's *Youth Involvement Committee,* the
initiatives include:
- *A Youth Volunteerism Survey* - 1,200 survey forms distributed
  to students at 30 junior and senior high schools, with
  responses showing that 45.5 percent of the students had
  volunteered within the past two years.
- *A Youth Speakers Bureau* - encouraging young people to
  speak to groups about volunteerism.
- *A Junior Loaned Executive Program* - training teens to assist
  corporate loaned executives in campaign activities during
  United Way's *Pacesetter* season.
- *A Youth Exploring Service (YES) Program* - a booklet listing
  over 250 volunteer opportunities for young people in over 80
  agencies.
- *Youth Volunteer Fairs* - publicizing volunteer opportunities
  for young people at popular sites such as shopping areas.
- *Walkathons* - involving students in raising money to address
  human needs - annual goal, $40,000.
All events are coordinated by Louisville's *Youth Involvement
Committee.*
Publications: A Youth Exploring Service (YES) Program
Founded: 1987

PEOPLE NEED PEOPLE VOLUNTEER FAIR
Prince George's Voluntary Action Center
6309 Baltimore Avenue
Suite 305
Riverdale, MD 20737
TEL: 301-779-9444

Purpose: To bring together motivated individuals and volunteer
agencies in a recruitment setting that eliminates distractions.
Sponsor: Capital Centre
Contact: Mary Reese, Director, or Toynette Spears, Administrative
Assistant
Description: In October 1989, owners of the *Capital Centre*
outside of Washington, DC in Maryland opened its doors to a
Volunteer Fair involving the entire community. One hundred ten
agencies across the metropolitan area were present to discuss
volunteer opportunities with over 3,500 people who were
motivated to help and came for information.
The Fair was organized as a joint effort of the owners of the
Capital Centre and the *Prince George's Voluntary Action Center.
(PGVAC)* The *Capital Centre* site lent instant publicity and
resources to the event. The generous and enthusiastic support of
the corporate community not only benefits the agencies, but gives
citizens the added incentive of seeing significant voluntary action
by a large, well-known corporation.
The very nature of such an event, meeting potential volunteers
face-to-face, provides the personal touch that improves the
recruitment effort. In addition, it gives program coordinators and
interested persons a few moments to decide whether this seems like
a "match" before proceeding to applications, training and
placement. Such unprecedented exposure to a wide range and
number of potential volunteers affords not only an opportunity to
recruit volunteers, but also to educate the public about services
and programs. Emphasis was on the fact that *Volunteers are an
integral part of achieving program goals.*
The PGVAC received more than 260 visits and inquiries. Some
"secrets for success" for attracting so many visitors include
photographs/posters of volunteers in action, giveaways and other
tokens bearing the familiar volunteer logo. Also, PGVAC's
volunteer clown traveled the arena, giving out stickers and other
items.
A program of the *Prince George's County Department of Aging,
Pets on Wheels,* provided two volunteers with their dogs, creating
a great deal of interest for the *Pet Therapy* program. According to
the Department's Volunteer Coordinator, volunteers are natural
publicists for this and the Department's other programs - *Foster
Grandparents, Life Enrichment, Ombudsman,* and the *RSVP
Program.* By sharing experiences and answering questions, they
provide an authentic view of being a volunteer for their respective
programs.
Although Fairs at colleges and universities or at a mall are often
quite successful, the *Capital Centre* eliminated the distraction of
uninterested passersby or students, and included ony motivated
people and the agencies themselves. This makes the ideal
combination.
Publications: VAC News; Make Time. Make Friends. Make A
Difference. *Be A Volunteer!*

PRIME TIME TO END HUNGER
SEE COMMUNICATIONS & PUBLIC RELATIONS:
NUTRITION

PROJECT BLUEPRINT
SEE LEADERSHIP DEVELOPMENT/BOARDS: ETHNIC
GROUPS

THOMAS JEFFERSON FORUM*
One Boston Place
Suite 923
Boston, MA 02108
TEL: 617-723-3098
Purpose: To enrich a student's character and education by
connecting him or her with genuine human needs in the
community.
Sponsor: T.J. Coolidge; Thomas Jefferson Forum
Contact: Jay Davis

Description: A private nonprofit community service program, the Thomas Jefferson Forum helps youth service coordinators in Boston high schools develop their own student volunteer programs. Created in 1986, the Forum's goal is to involve high school students in social service programs to instill concern for their communities, while developing leadership and other skills. Students volunteer three hours each week at specific sites. Their involvement includes soup kitchens, shelters, day care centers, convalescent homes, and special education classes. Specific projects include a harden and sitting area prepared for senior citizens in an unused area next to their complex, and on-site kitchen help to prepare meals for a soup kitchen.

Students have ample opportunity to interact with fellow volunteers and their faculty coordinators through group rap sessions. They also take part in workshops, write about their experiences, and participate in the Forum's annual conference. The conference provides leadership skills training, and brainstorming sessions with volunteers from other schools.

Founded: 1986

VOLUNTEER CONNECTION TELETHON
United Way of Greater St. Louis
1111 Olive Street
PO Box 14507
St. Louis, MO 63178-0507
TEL: 314-421-0700
Purpose: To extend an invitation and the opportunity to volunteer.
Sponsor: Corporate Volunteer Council
Contact: Martin B. Covitz, President
Description: Unlike most telethons, the *Volunteer Connection Telethon* went on the air to request *time* rather than money. It set a national record for volunteer telethons: 468,122 hours of volunteer time pledged. This was more than double its initial goal of 200,000 hours. A rewarding statistic was that over half of the pledges came from people who *had never before volunteered.*
Produced jointly by *United Way of Greater St. Louis, Corporate Volunteer Council, Council of Volunteer Directors,* and *KMOV-TV/Channel 4,* the Telethon had a threefold purpose:
- To demonstrate volunteerism's positive impact on the quality of life in the community;
- To raise the awareness of volunteer needs in the community; and
- To encourage more people to volunteer their time and talents to agencies in need of volunteer assistance.

Volunteers were needed in all phases of the enormous venture, including the telethon's pre- and post-production aspects, as well as on-the-air activities. A three-month time frame was established for pre-production activities to gather information about volunteer needs from local service agencies, run campaigns to promote the telethon among local corporations, produce print pieces to publicize the telethon within the community, and videotape volunteerism vignettes to be shown during the production.
On-the-air requirements ranged from securing financing and on-camera hosts for the two-hour program to using a computer system to connect volunteers with volunteer needs. Promoting among corporate employees resulted in pledges of 150,000 hours before the telethon began. The viewing audience was more than 1.5 million households.
The true success of the telethon came after it was over, when agencies began receiving the volunteer help they needed. In one instance, a small, all-volunteer organization that teaches severely disabled children and adults to ride horses was on the brink of closing services due to a lack of volunteers. *Therapeutic Horsemanship* got the help it needed to continue, with the results of the telethon swelling its ranks of volunteers. Many similar examples verified the success of this method of recruiting volunteers. It is expected to be an annual event.

VOLUNTEER INITIATIVE PROGRAM (VIP)
SEE BUSINESS/INDUSTRY INVOLVEMENT

VOLUNTEER ORIENTATION PROGRAM
National Information Center on Deafness
Gallaudet University
Volunteer Office
800 Florida Avenue, NE
Washington, DC 20002
TEL: 202-651-5606
Purpose: To assist the Information Center on Deafness in all phases of its program
Sponsor: National Information Center on Deafness/Visitors Center
Contact: Cindi Olson
Description: The Volunteer Orientation Program is a one-day orientation to deafness and Gallaudet College for individuals who have been interviewed and screened by the Volunteer Coordinator. All volunteers are required to complete the program which covers such topics as:
- deafness;
- communication;
- functions of Gallaudet University;
- discussion of the role of Alumni Publication Relations;
- the objectives of the National Information Center on Deafness and the Visitors Center; and
- other relevant volunteer placements.

Upon completion, volunteers are assigned to either the Information Center, Visitors Center, or other placement concommittant with their interest and backgrounds. Volunteers have such varied responsibilities as leading tours, responding to inquiries, research for responses or development of new materials; information collection; telephone support, clerical support. Volunteers are given continuing individual attention and guidance by supervisors in all Centers. At the present time, periodic volunteer meetings are scheduled for discussion of topics of concern and as a forum for continued learning related to Gallaudet University and deafness.

VOLUNTEER RESOURCES - AIDS PROGRAM
Whitman-Walker Clinic
1407 S Street, NW
Washington, DC 20009
TEL: 202-797-3576; 202-328-0697 (Spanish)
Purpose: To train, place and provide ongoing support for the Clinic's volunteers.
Sponsor: Whitman-Walker Clinic
Contact: Peter Provost
Description: Volunteer job descriptions in the *Volunteer Resources Department* of the Whitman-Walker Clinic cover 30 distinct positions, providing a wide-range of services within various divisions of the Clinic's AIDS program.
Beginning in 1990 with over 1,500 active volunteers, this department recruits, trains, and places new volunteers and provides ongoing support for them. Orientations for prospective volunteers are held monthly and basic training is held one weekend every other month. Training seminars on a variety of issues, such as death and dying, and grief and healing are held on a regular basis for active volunteers.
Some of the areas in which volunteers are trained to provide care with dignity for persons living with AIDS and HIV infections are: medical services, support services (legal/financial/emotional), housing, education, alcoholism and substance abuse, and others. Volunteer Resources, as in other Clinic programs, coordinates with the community to ensure a unified response to AIDS.
Publications: Volunteer Job Descriptions: AIDS Program

VOLUNTEER SENIOR LEADERS
SEE LEADERSHIP DEVELOPMENT/BOARDS: OLDER PERSON

ADMINISTRATION: VOLUNTEER/CENTER/AGENCY RELATIONS

TRAINING PROGRAMS

ARHA/COUNCIL ON VOLUNTEER TRAINING EVENTS
SEE TRAINING/CONFERENCES/TEACHING: HEALTH

HOW TO WORK EFFECTIVELY WITH VOLUNTEERS
SEE TRAINING/CONFERENCES/TEACHING

SUPERVISING VOLUNTEERS*
SEE TRAINING/CONFERENCES/TEACHING

TRAINING FOR VOLUNTEERS AND VOLUNTEER AGENCIES
SEE TRAINING/CONFERENCES/TEACHING:
CENTER/AGENCY

USING VOLUNTEERS IN YOUR AGENCY
SEE TRAINING/CONFERENCES/TEACHING:
CENTER/AGENCY

VOLUNTEERS: HEROES OF THE 80'S*
SEE TRAINING/CONFERENCES/TEACHING

INDIVIDUAL PROGRAM PROFILES

RESPITE FOR AIDS VOLUNTEERS
Kairos House
114 Douglass Street
San Francisco, CA 94114
TEL: 415-861-0877
Purpose: To help volunteers approaching burnout by providing an evening for retreat once a week in a relaxed setting.
Contact: Father John McGrann, Founder
Description: Almost ten years and more than 4,300 deaths into the local AIDS epidemic, people from cities outside of the Bay Area still marvel at the volunteer response that created the network of AIDS services known as the *San Francisco model*. At a Victorian house founded by a Catholic priest it is clear that the model places a high price on its volunteers. Known as *Kairos House,* it is a place where AIDS volunteers approaching overload and others working with AIDS patients can find relief from the suffering. Leaders in AIDS charities say despair is a common product of a system using up its human resources. Volunteers describe the first sign of approaching burnout as "emotional numbness."
Kairos House has taken one step toward caring for the people on the front-line in the epidemic. It is a place where AIDS caregivers can get a free 15-minute Japanese massage, and where a table full of hors d'oeuvres awaits them. Piano music drifts softly through the rooms, and many volunteers come to just sit and listen to the music. *Kairos House* offers one way to hold on to volunteers approaching burnout or exhaustion. With a recent drop in donations and volunteers throughout AIDS charities, this respite is especially important. According to one AIDS volunteer, "There's a point where there's so much pain, you just shut down." *Kairos House* offers one way of providing the support the San Francisco

model needs to keep its trained volunteers, and to attract new sources of donations and volunteers. Age groups not well represented as volunteers in AIDS charities are teenagers and the elderly, and recruitment efforts are under way to attract those groups.
Founded: 1988

BUSINESS/INDUSTRY INVOLVEMENT

NATIONAL/STATE ORGANIZATIONS

BUSINESS/INDUSTRY PROGRAM
Federation of Protestant Welfare Agencies
281 Park Avenue, South
New York, NY 10010
TEL: 212-777-4800
Objectives: To include the business world in specific phases of the volunteer efforts of the Federation.
Services: Operates two specific services that involve the business community:
- **Technical Assistance Program** - a cooperative project linking nonprofit organizations with major business corporations who are willing to provide management expertise and leadership for education/credit seminars.
- **A Bridge to the Business World** - an activity to foster corporate/community outreach programs of employee participation as volunteers in the community.
Founded: 1922

CENTER FOR CORPORATE PUBLIC INVOLVEMENT
1001 Pennsylvania Avenue, NW
Washington, DC 20004
TEL: 202-624-2425
Objectives: To provide assistance and guidance to life and health insurance companies in using resources effectively for community projects.
Services: Conducts a social reporting program concerning community projects, company contributions, voluntarism, employment of women and minorities, health, and social investments. Sponsors health education and promotion programs. Focuses on education in areas of AIDS, the elderly, health, housing, hunger, the homeless and hard-to-employ individuals. Sponsors a Socially Responsive Investment Technical Advisory Group and a Corporate Public Involvement Committee.
Publications: Response; Social Report
Founded: 1971

COUNCIL OF BETTER BUSINESS BUREAUS
1515 Wilson Boulevard
Arlington, VA 22209
TEL: 703-276-0100
Objectives: To assist the consuming public; to help maintain confidence in the private enterprise system.

Services: Provides free binding arbitration of business consumer disputes using community volunteers as arbitrators; testifies before Congress on consumer issues; maintains the Philanthropic Advisory Service (PAS) which checks non-profit corporations to determine how much of contributions are actually used for cause, and how much for management; places public service announcements, a 30-minute radio program (Conversation for Consumers), and other mini-series, mini-programs, and announcements on behalf of the consumer, including "Auto-Line," a national arbitration capability putting consumer and manufacturer in direct touch; publishes an extensive series of consumer information booklets which are offered to the public.
Publications: CBBB Annual Report
Founded: 1970

COUNCIL ON ECONOMIC PRIORITIES
30 Irving Place
New York, NY 10003
TEL: 212-420-1133
TOLL FREE: 800-822-6435
Objectives: To assist public interest groups, concerned individuals and others in determining the extent of involvement by business/industry in human service matters.
Services: Compiles and makes available information on corporate interest and activities in consumer-related issues; conducts research on the corporate social responsibility activities of corporations; rates and compares such activities and analyzes them as to their economic impact; offers speakers bureau services; publishes monthly newsletter, an annual magazine, and a number of other periodicals for distribution.
Publications: CEP Newsletter; CEP Reports; CEP Studies Series; Shopping for a Better World
Founded: 1969

INTERFAITH CENTER ON CORPORATE RESPONSIBILITY
475 Riverside Drive, Room 566
New York, NY 10115
TEL: 212-870-2293
Objectives: To develop and share information related to the degree of social responsibility demonstrated by large corporations, through a church-related coalition.
Services: Provides a channel for cooperation with other organizations with an interest in business/industry corporate

responsibility record; participates in campaigns on 15 issues including South Africa infant formula abuse, nuclear weapons, church investors, and other challenges; runs campaigns against corporate abuse; conducts discussions with government, business/industry, foundations, universities, and interested groups and individuals for input into monthly *Corporate Examiner;* also publishes research papers and transcripts of public hearings; maintains library.
Publications: Corporate Examiner
Founded: 1974

INVOLVEMENT, INC.
1366 Las Canoas Road
Pacific Palisades, CA 90272
TEL: 213-459-1022
Objectives: To enable a corporation to make a contribution to society that is exciting for its employees and vital to the community it serves.
Services: Teaches special skills needed for building and running a corporate volunteer program, such as: program initiation, recruiting, placement, agency liaison training, publicity, fundraising, budgeting and management; specifically:
- recommends a program model appropriate for the corporation (modifying when necessary);
- hires a qualified Volunteer Coordinator who works in the company (in some cases a company employee assigned full time to the program);
- researches community needs and uses the results to make recommendations to the company and employees about projects for involvement;
- helps the employee-volunteers develop a productive relationship with the agencies or groups that are selected for assistance;
- provides ongoing training and support through consultants and materials to the volunteer coordinator, employees, agency, and company management;
- provides a national linkage to other corporations with similar programs. Program is managed entirely by corporate employees working with assistance of Involvement Corps through any of its offices or the national headquarters (see above); informative materials are available from these sources.
Involvement Corps Locations:
Portland, Oregon 503-222-1355
San Francisco, California 415-781-1953
Englewood, Colorado 303-790-1000
Milwaukee, Wisconsin 414-933-4224
Winston-Salem, North Carolina 919-724-7474
[Not a complete list; may or may not be affiliated with above national organization]

NATIONAL ALLIANCE OF BUSINESS
1201 New York Avenue, NW, Suite 700
Washington, DC 20005
TEL: 202-289-2888
Objectives: To team loaned business executives with government and the public; to work toward solving the problem of unemployment in large cities.
Services: Develops and maintains a number of community betterment programs through close collaboration with local government, labor, local industry and community-based organizations, including:
- Regional Service Offices - a network of 10 offices at the local level which serve as the Alliance's "action arm" for local direction and planning of local programs. The Chairman (usually a local senior executive) and an Advisory Board of local business leaders work directly with other community leaders.
- Private Sector Initiative Program - a program enabling businesses to participate in the nationwide employment effort

(also operated by local leaders), and to locate meaningful jobs for the disadvantaged, including needy youth, veterans, ex-offenders and others.
- Summer Youth Program - to enable the disadvantaged student to gain experience and earn income by participating in the summer work force.
Publications: Business Currents; WorkAmerica; NAB Monograph Series
Founded: 1968

NATIONAL FEDERATION OF INTERFAITH VOLUNTEER CAREGIVERS
SEE VOLUNTEERS: CHURCH/SYNAGOGUE MEMBERS

SOCIETY OF CONSUMER AFFAIRS PROFESSIONALS IN BUSINESS
SEE VOLUNTEERS: PROFESSIONALS

US/ADMINISTRATION: THE PRESIDENT'S PRIVATE SECTOR INITIATIVES PROGRAM
SEE PRIVATE SECTOR INITIATIVES OFFICES

TRAINING PROGRAMS

AFFORDABLE MEETINGS
SEE TRAINING/CONFERENCES/TEACHING

BUILDING PARTNERSHIPS WITH CORPORATIONS
South Carolina Association for Volunteer Administration
c/o Hilton Head Hospital Auxiliary
Box 1117
Hilton Head Island, SC 29925
TEL: 803-785-6122 (also below)
Credit: Inquire
Sponsor: South Carolina Association for Volunteer Administration (SCAVA)
Contact: All 803 area codes: Rock Hill, Ann Spencer, 366-4116; Columbia, Carol Taylor, 765-2375; Greenville, Larue Bettis, 298-8484; Charleston, Mary Blanchard, 577-1156; Hilton Head, June Branham
Description: This conference is designed to assist corporations and volunteer-involving community groups in the involvement of employees as volunteers. Workshops include:
Building Partnerships with Corporations: a comprehensive, step-by-step approach to the how-to's of corporate volunteering in a six-hour curriculum which includes:
- internal agency preparation
- identifying and assessing potential corporate resources in the community
- making the approach to the corporation
- building an ongoing mutual support relationship with corporations
- dealing with the special needs and expectations of workers who volunteer
- confronting the problems involved in tapping this new resource
Participants receive workshop and take-home materials to help them assess the readiness to receive or offer corporate volunteers, and to construct a work plan if feasible.
For Corporations Only: a workshop designed to teach corporations how to design, develop, and maintain employee volunteer programs. Course and take-home materials are provided in a portfolio which includes supplementary reading lists and other references.
The Creative Use of Volunteers: Expanding Your Resources: a workshop based on a research project conducted under the auspices

of SCAVA to assess the attitudes of professionals and volunteers working in human service agencies. Participants gain:

- an overview of the issues and challenges present in the traditional professional volunteer relationships
- techniques for working effectively with volunteers
- skills in involving volunteers in policy-making and as advocates.

An information-sharing session is an integral part of this session.
Risks and Rewards: a workshop covering the legal rights and responsibilities of volunteers and board members, including charitable immunity, insurance, liability for acts and ommissions, privileged communications, confidentiality and duty to report.
Basic Skills: a session for the new Volunteer Service Director, which is helpful also to the veteran director. Topics covered include:

- How to Develop a Volunteer Program
- Roles and Responsibilities of Volunteer Directors
- Staff Development
- Basic Needs Assessment
- Planning
- Job Descriptions
- Orientation
- Training
- Recruiting
- Recognition
- Retention

Faculty is drawn from the fields of education, nonprofit organizations, law and state government (in this case the Governor's Council on Volunteerism). Technical assistance is provided for those wishing to activate the workshop learning experience, or improve an existing program.

CREATIVE INVOLVEMENT FOR PRODUCTIVE COMMUNITIES
SEE TRAINING/CONFERENCES/TEACHING: BUSINESS/INDUSTRY

"UNITED WAY AT WORK" CONFERENCE
United Way of Central Carolinas
301 South Brevard Street
Charlotte, NC 28202-2317
TEL: 704-372-7170
Credit: Certificate of Completion
Sponsor: United Way of America's Resource Development Division
Contact: Donald C. Sanders, President
Description: "United Way at Work" programs ensure that interaction continues between a United Way and a company's employees and management. They serve to personalize United Way for employees, educate them about United Way, link workers seeking volunteer opportunities with local human-service agencies and services, and recognize companies' support of United Way. United Way at Work programs can be as diverse as the companies where they take place.
This conference was coordinated in 1989 by the United Way of Central Carolinas in Charlotte, North Carolina. Approximately 70 representatives from local companies and staff from 30 United Way-supported agencies in the greater Charlotte area attended.
Using information published in United Way of America's report, *The Future World of Work,* the conference helped company staff establish a dialogue with agency representatives.
One focus in the area served by United Way of Central Carolinas was on child care, since that surfaced as one of the greatest needs of residents. Company staff and agency representatives found this means of brainstorming on the issue both practical in that many people concerned with the issue were brought together, and more satisfying, since the personal contact enabled immediate followup of questions and concerns.

INDIVIDUAL PROGRAM PROFILES

BERKS SCHOOLCASTING*
SEE COMMUNICATIONS & PUBLIC RELATIONS

BLOCKBUSTER COMMUNITY SERVICE PROGRAM
Blockbuster Entertainment Corporation
10460 Miller Road
Dallas, TX 75238
TEL: 214-503-9222
FAX: 214-503-2377
Purpose: To provide customers with free films on topics of community concern.
Description: Blockbuster believes that video stores should have something to offer besides entertainment. It can act as a forum to address national issues and educate the public on the dangers facing our communities through a program of free films.
Under the program, Blockbuster members can check out any of 40 titles in the store's community service library. The collection is available in July 1989 in 750 stores nationwide. It includes a variety of family-oriented films falling under such categories as health, education, safety and quality of life, and specific areas such as drug abuse, heart disease and crime.
Videos in the library are made available through private firms and civic organizations - many addressing crucial public issues like AIDS, alcoholism, drugs and safety. Titles include: *Crackdown on Drugs,* endorsed by the National Federation of Parents for Drug-Free Youth; *How to Save Your Child's Life,* an instructional cassette that leads the viewer through the four critical stages in an infant or child respiratory emergency; *Buckle Up: Seat Belt Safety,* endorsed by the General Motors Corporation; *Home First Aid,* featuring Dr. Henry Heimlich, who discovered the Heimlich Maneuver; and *Straight Up,* starring Lou Gossett, who guides a young boy through a world that constantly tempts children with drugs and alcohol.
According to a spokesman from the American Council for Drug Education, "Kids between the ages of 12 and 18 are bombarded with decisions every day, and services like these can educate and inform them on many dilemmas they face."

BUSINESS CONCENTRATION TOWARD CHARITIES
Theodore Roosevelt National Bank
1201 New York Avenue, NW
Washington , DC 20005
TEL: 202-371-1201; 202-546-3400
FAX: 202-371-8233
Purpose: To provide service based on Theodore Roosevelt's quote: "...this Country will not be a permanently good place for us to live in unless we make it a reasonably good place for *all* of us to live in."
Contact: Harold J. Fischer, President and CEO
Description: Theodore Roosevelt National Bank is a newly-established National Bank (so new that the address for the recently-occupied bank building in the heart of Washington, DC was not yet in the local telephone book at press time). It has embarked on a unique concept of business concentration toward charities and non-profit organizations. The bank features a collection of memorabilia devoted to Teddy Roosevelt, the nation's 26th president. In the bank president's words, "He (Teddy Roosevelt) was an activist and a maverick, and that's what we want to be."
Theodore Roosevelt National Bank will target charitable, non-profit organizations, offering personalized deposit and account services not available from other banks. One service will make use of the spacious atrium to host fund-raising events for client social service organizations.
In addition to the major fundraisers for the non-profit and charitable clients, the bank offers numerous direct-involvement programs in the metropolitan area, many planned at the beginning

of the bank's organization stage to enable ongoing evaluation and a smooth transition into the bank's regular program. These programs include:

Special Student Advisory Board - advisors from junior and senior high schools in the area charged with advising the bank on youth banking affairs.

Promotion of the Champ Cookie Program - a program for children/youth in which the youngsters own their own bakery and learn about being entrepreneurs, founded by a police officer to help deter drug-related and other crime.

Special Home Mortgage Affordable Housing Program - a program focusing on FHA products, especially the FHA 203(k) program, which enables low- and moderate-income people to own their own homes.

Major Christmastime Fundraiser - a program involving the sale of hundreds of sturdy and educational wooden toys to raise money for needy children and *Special Olympics.*

Advisory Boards for Foreign Customers - a program that will operate like any of the Bank's boards - in an advisory capacity to help provide the best service possible to the targeted group.

It is the Bank's goal to establish one major fund raiser of a non-profit charitable customer at least once per calendar quarter in keeping with the objectives of its *Mission Statement.*

No strangers to charity, bank officials are collectively involved with *The Boy Scouts of America, American Red Cross, So Others Might Eat, Legal Counsel for the Elderly, American Heart Association,* and others. Some of the programs mentioned above are more fully described elsewhere in this book.

BUSINESS INFORMATION AND RESOURCE COUNCIL
SEE GOVERNORS' OFFICES ON VOLUNTEERISM: NEW HAMPSHIRE

BUSINESS/SCHOOL PARTNERSHIP PROGRAM
Community Relations
3830 Richmond Avenue
Houston, TX 77027
TEL: 713-892-6384
Purpose: To involve business in public education.
Sponsor: Houston Independent School District
Contact: Mrs. Terry Chauche, Director
Description: In 1988-89, the *Houston Independent School District (HISD)* had as much real involvement with the business community as any school district in the country. The Houston story differed from other cities, though, in that ours was particularly people-intensive. It also differed in that, along with a number of programs initiated by HISD with the business community, there were a number of organizations outside the HISD that initiated and developed programs. The various programs are not coordinated under any one umbrella.
The *Business/School Partnership Program* was initiated by HISD in 1980 with the support of the *Houston Chamber of Commerce.* It grew progressively from 17 connections in 1980-81 to 682 in 1988-89. In 1986, the chamber started active recruitment efforts to supplement that of the school district.
As to the 1988-89 contributions of the business community to HISD, some were partnerships or adopt-a-school; some were other connections; some were large; some were small; some were HISD-initiated; some were initiated from the outside. All of them involved the business community and HISD schools. Students at risk of dropping out are the target of a majority of the programs. The major thrust continued to be to involve as many business people as possible, as often as possible, directly in the schools. Business people, whatever the activity, serve as motivators, role models, and mentors. They are virtually unanimous in their support of HISD's efforts. There were:
- 682 connections
- 262 businesses and 2,250 business people involved
- 237 schools that had minimal business involvement

- 110 schools that had regular involvement of business people
- 72 substantive partnerships
- $7,000,000 estimated time, fund, and in-kind donations

Not only did 1988-89 see a 15% increase in numbers of businesses and connections, it saw the addition of some very substantive partnerships and significant deepening of several existing partnerships.
Partnerships included Aetna, Allstate Insurance, Altrusa Club, American Airlines, American General Life, American Institute of Architects, American Productivity & Quality Center, and 640 other businesses and organizations.
Founded: 1980

CATCH PROGRAM
SEE VOLUNTEERS: PARENTS

COORS V.I.C.E. SQUAD
Adolph Coors Company
Community Affairs Department
Golden, CO 80401-1295
TEL: 303-277-2197; 303-277-6565
FAX: 303-277-6564
Purpose: To provide supportive services to employees interested in volunteering to help the community.
Sponsor: Adolph Coors Company
Contact: Rosa Bunn
Description: Volunteers In Community Enrichment, dubbed *the V.I.C.E. Squad,* was established in 1985 as a corporate volunteer program within *Adolph Coors Company,* and includes the retiree arm, *Additional Duties for Volunteers in Community Enrichment (A.D.V.I.C.E.).* Over 2,000 employees dedicate their time, talent and enthusiasm to hundreds of charity projects each year.
V.I.C.E. Squad activities range from painting senior citizens' homes to cleaning of government subsidized apartment complexes to supporting the *Old Timers Rodeo.* There is also the *Colorado Special Olympics* where *V.I.C.E. Squad* members host a carnival for athletes, and *Hands and Hearts for Christmas,* when Coors employees and friends hand-knit over 1,000 lap robes to distribute to wheelchair-bound nursing home residents on Christmas Day.
One of the reasons for V.I.C.E.'s success is the members' freedom to choose which projects the group will undertake. V.I.C.E. considers only those projects brought to the group by other members. If a community organization desires V.I.C.E.'s participation on a project, the request must be channeled through a Coors employee.
The criteria for selecting an activity are simple: Is it good for the community? How can Coors assist? Can volunteers be used to support the project?
Sign-up forms are found in Coors lunchrooms and communications centers, or can be obtained by calling V.I.C.E. headquarters (303-277-5363 or 277-3852), although there is never any obligation to participate.
To assist other companies in mounting volunteer programs, Coors offers the benefit of its own experience, speaks about the rewards of a corporate sponsored program, and provides consultation and other assistance to interested companies.
Publications: Coors Volunteers in Community Enrichment Calendar; V.I.C.E. Squad; V.I.C.E. Squad Monthly Activity Guide; Lifesaver Tags

DISTRICT OF COLUMBIA CORPORATE VOLUNTEER COUNCIL
Volunteer Clearinghouse of the District of Columbia
1313 New York Avenue, NW
Washington, DC 20005
TEL: 202-638-2664
Purpose: To find volunteer positions for employees of local business and industry.
Sponsor: Volunteer Clearinghouse of the District of Columbia

Description: Since its formation in 1984, the DC Corporate Volunteer Council has assisted local business and industry in finding satisfying volunteer opportunities for their employees. With over 1,400 programs needing volunteer assistance - from painting houses to bringing cheer to nursing home residents - the Council has never turned away a volunteer.

In addition, the Council brings together community relations officers from the corporations to share ideas and information, which helps make them better prepared to meet the challenges of volunteerism in the area. In summary, overall goals are:

- to promote corporate volunteerism
- to communicate new developments and new opportunities for employee involvement
- to act as a resource for companies or groups expanding existing programs or developing new ones
- to initiate communication between local companies and groups developing special types of projects, workshops and conferences.

The Council operates in cooperation with the Volunteer Clearinghouse of DC, A United Way agency which serves the local area in matching volunteers to opportunities. Services include:

- an information bank on volunteer opportunities available to employees
- a clearinghouse for donated materials when needed
- an advocate for business in its support of community service
- "volunteer opportunity" information for internal company communications
- group projects for employees
- training and consultation services to agencies with which businesses interact

Among the materials it provides to supplement its services are "how-to" resource material on establishing employee volunteer projects, strategies for selling corporate volunteering to top level management, information on corporate volunteer activities in Washington, DC, and information on community relations coordinators and programs.

CVC members come from the entire spectrum of public and private sectors and academe - ranging from a local hotel to a federal agency, to the World Bank. Membership is available to businesses and associations who have an employee volunteer program and/or activities which encourage employees to volunteer or interest in starting an employee volunteer program.

Publications: DC Corporate Volunteer Council (brochure); DC/CVC Packet

FIRST FAMILY VOLUNTEER PROGRAM
First National Bank of Hot Springs
Central and Court
Hot Springs, AR 71901
TEL: 501-321-8000
Purpose: To encourage employees to contribute up to 100 hours (or more) per year of their time to the community.
Description: In 1982, to celebrate the bank's 100th anniversary, the First National Bank of Hot Springs developed the First Family Volunteer Program. The program has not only benefitted Hot Springs, but has also brought a sense of community to the employees of the bank.

Each employee is asked to contribute up to 100 hours of their time to volunteer efforts (more when possible). Incentives motivate employees and recognize them for their participation in different levels of the program. Days off are offered for each 25 hours volunteered, and prizes are awarded. Participation is purely voluntary, and 80 percent of the employees remain on the list. Among the First Family projects are:

Tree Planting/Parks - planting 150 willow oak trees (donated by the bank) on a median strip in the main thoroughfare; making a commitment to "adopt-a-spot" and create a mini-park at a downtown interesection and maintain it year-round.

Library Assistance - helping in a book drive, which was the most successful in the history of the library, and facing books and performing other odd jobs in the library.
Ouachita Children's Center Adoption - organizing activities for a temporary placement shelter for pre-delinquent, neglected or abused children, chaperoning skating parties, preparing special meals, and serving as weekend foster parents. In addition, a fundraising activity, "First Family Night at the Movies," raised $1,100 for the Center's building fund.
County Assistance - saving money for the County by assisting with clerical work in the office of the County Tax Collector from 5:00 to 8:00 p.m. weeknights. In two months, 249 hours of volunteer time finished a job that would have required hiring another governmental employee, and would have taken at least five months to complete.

Other projects included helping with the Red Cross Blood Drive, staff training in CPR, March of Dimes Walk-a-Thon, Red Cross Disaster Services, County Fair, Arts and Crafts Fair, car wash, Radiological Defense Monitors, Barrier Awareness Day, Hot Springs Mall Charity Bazaar, leaf raking service, Salvation Army, and Christmas caroling at nursing homes.

During a two-year period First Family volunteers logged over 7,300 hours, and undertook several new projects, including March of Dimes Rock-a-thon, a painting party for the YWCA, and two new fundraisers.

A committee of employees now plans and oversees all of the projects. Spring 1990 began the ninth year of the First Family Volunteer Program.
Publications: First Family Volunteer Program Packet

HIGH-RISE FIRE RESPONSE TRAINING
Steelcase, Inc.
E. Paris Ave. & 60th St., SE
PO Box 1967
Grand Rapids, MI 49501
TEL: 616-247-2710
FAX: 616-246-4890
Purpose: To assist the local fire department in disaster response methods.
Sponsor: Steelcase, Inc.
Contact: Frank Merlotti, President, or Dale Gipe, Dutton Fire Chief
Description: The 20-member volunteer fire department of Dutton, Michigan, has participated in fire inspections every week for more than two years during construction of Steelcase Inc.'s new Corporate Development Center. Described by the fire chief as "very fire-conscious," the corporation requested this intense inspection activity in preparation for a comprehensive training program that the company has developed for responding to high-rise fires.

The 20 volunteers from the Dutton Fire Department will be instructed in the course at Steelcase by officials there. Since the weekly inspections have familiarized them with the internal structure of the building, training time is used to go beyond any primary explanations of building materials, etc. Dutton works in a "mutual aid" fire response situation with other fire departments such as nearby Kentwood and Gaines Township. All departments expect to benefit from the Steelcase training program either directly or indirectly, in some cases with one fire department being trained and, in turn, training others.

Steelcase is the first corporation in the area to make such an effort to prepare fire personnel should a high-rise fire occur. This will benefit the community at large, since there are many high rises in the area, none of which have taken any responsibility in emergency preparedness.

I AM INVOLVED
Florida Power
101 Fifth Street, South
St. Petersburg, FL 33701
TEL: 813-895-8711
Purpose: To match employee volunteers with community agencies and organizations that need their talents.
Sponsor: Florida Power
Contact: Cindy Bishop, Volunteer
Description: The I Am Involved program of Florida Power is staffed by more than a thousand employees - about 26% of the company's work force - who take part in community volunteer efforts through the company's clearinghouse service to match volunteers with local projects. The agencies and organizations involved include those concerned with social welfare, mental and physical health, education, scientific and civic affairs, and cultural enrichment.

I Am Involved volunteers can work toward raising money for a particular organization by joining the Time is Money part of the program. Donations to different agencies are based on the number of hours of personal time volunteered during one year. Florida Power then issues checks to the organizations and sends them to the employees so they may present the donations themselves. Volunteers contributed more than 10,000 hours in 1988, doubling the hours of the founding year, 1986.

In addition to encouraging employees to join existing programs, Florida Power develops and sponsors programs based on expressed needs in the community. Feedback shows that the efforts of the company have helped both active volunteers by increasing their involvement, and new volunteers who plan to stay involved.
Founded: 1986

INVOLVEMENT CORPS*
Volunteer Center of Greater Milwaukee
600 East Mason Street
Milwaukee , WI 53202
TEL: 414-273-7887
Purpose: To develop effective and efficient employee volunteer programs for corporations desiring to promote community participation.
Sponsor: Greater Milwaukee Voluntary Action Center
Contact: Mary Pat O'Keefe
Description: The Involvement Corps, a program of the Greater Milwaukee Voluntary Action Center (GMVAC) since 1976, is part of a national effort of Involvement, Inc., to guide corporations willing to use their manpower, resources, and knowledge to help meet community needs. Since the national program's founding in California in 1968, hundreds of large and small corporations throughout the country have implemented Involvement Corps corporate volunteer programs.

The Milwaukee Involvement Corps designs a Community Involvement Program (CIP) according to the human and other resources of an individual corporation. Each CIP consists of 8-10 employees who select and plan community service projects and recruit their coworkers as volunteers. The corporate in-house leaders work closely with the GMVAC Involvement Corps Coordinator. The Coordinator teaches CIP members the skills of program initiation, recruiting, placement, agency liaison training, publicity, fundraising, budgeting and management, etc., all tailored to fit an individual company's expectations.

The Involvement Corps maintains a listing of community projects needing volunteers for CIP leaders needing this type of assistance. Program involvement by corporations since 1976 include: Very Special Arts Festival, Milwaukee County Rehabilitation Hospital, Literacy Services, Channel 10 Membership Drive, Wehr Nature Center, Parents Anonymous, Schlitz Audobon Center, Milwaukee Public Schools Recreation, Interfaith Gardening/Produce Project, and others. Corporations have included Surgical Care-Blue Shield, Time Insurance Company, Marine Corporation, First Wisconsin

Bank, Honeywell, A.C. Spark Plug Company, First Savings Bank, and others.

The Involvement Corps conducts seminars for interested corporations, often surveying the corporation's employees in advance. Most corporate officers are surprised to learn that over 50% of their employees are interested in community service projects. Involvement Corps funding comes from United Way and corporate fees.
Founded: 1976

MINORITY ENTREPRENEURSHIP PROGRAM*
Detroit Public Schools
Stevenson Building
10100 Grand River
Detroit, MI 48204
TEL: 313-931-3838
Purpose: To mount an intensive program of curriculum implementation and practical experience to encourage minority students to consider business ownership.
Sponsor: Detroit Public Schools; Development Career Guidance Program
Contact: Felix R. Sloan, Project Director
Description: Recognizing that the plight of minorities in the area of entrepreneurship in business and industry is one deserving attention and positive action, the Detroit Public School System mounted an intensive program to increase the potential of highly-motivated minority students to succeed as business owners. To succeed, voluntary assistance from the business community was crucial, and was quickly obtained through role models, curriculum advice, materials, and the job stations necessary to provide the practical element to the program.

The program design aspired to give minority students some knowledge and understanding of business fundamentals and management and eventually reduce the high incidence of minority business failure. To reach this goal, the curriculum considers the full K-12 program (K-5 Career Awareness; 6-8 Exploration; 9-12 Pursuit of chosen careers in real situations). The 9-12 program includes work study programs, field trips, actual business operation, and counseling to assist senior high students in getting jobs and scholarships to colleges/schools providing a transition to a career in business management and/or ownership.

Each school is responsible for its own program, providing extensive staff training and access to business representatives for curriculum specialists, teachers, and counselors involved in the effort. The Program Director is responsible for orientation of key school personnel and administrators, and outlines each individual's role. The individual school's administrator then assigns staff persons to the project to:
- disseminate information
- help orient other staff
- arrange field trips for students
- notify staff of working dates, etc.
- assist in contacting resource people
- monitor general progress of the program
- serve on the program's task force committee

Students participate in a classroom/work program, usually spending one to two weeks in the classroom and then the same amount of time at the job station.

NEWSDAY VOLUNTEER RECOGNITION PROGRAM
SEE ADMINISTRATION: RECOGNITION

NOXZEMA EXTRAORDINARY TEEN CONTEST
Noxzema Skin Cream
c/o Marina Maher Communications
645 Madison Avenue
New York, NY 10022
TEL: 212-759-7543

Purpose: To honor young women who have volunteered their time, talents and energy to a charitable or socially conscious project that helps others.
Sponsor: Noxzema Skin Cream
Contact: Elsa Shapiro
Description: Young women who care about other people and who do something about it are the focus of the Noxzema Extraordinary Teen Contest (NET) for girls aged 12 to 18 nationwide and in Canada. The first twelve years focused on academic achievement. The 1990 contest is the first to feature the issue of volunteerism. The new focus of NET came about as a result of many changes taking place in our society, and the fact that there are many committed young women devoting their time to causes that help others.

Five finalists are selected on the basis of essays they submit and their level of commitment to their favorite cause. Each entrant provides affidavits and recommendations from adults who are familiar with their efforts.

Finalists are invited to New York City for an all-expense-paid week of activities, culminating in the announcement of a winner selected by a panel of distiguished judges.

The winner receives a total of $10,000 - $5,000 for herself and $5,000 for the charity of her choice. In addition, all finalists are featured in the July 1990 editorial of *TEEN Magazine*. Fifty honorable mention candidates will be recognized as well.

All young women in junior and senior high school are invited to enter NET.
Founded: 1977

QUALITY EDUCATION PROGRAM
UAW-GM Human Resource Center
Region 1-C
Flint, MI 48501
TEL: 313-257-0440
Purpose: To work with business/industry to help students prepare for careers.
Sponsor: United Auto Workers
Contact: Coordinator of Education Activities
Description: The Flint Quality Education Program is operated by the UAW-GM (United Auto Workers-General Motors) Human Resource Center, region 1-C Office. The Center's program is nationwide.

This program does not provide resource persons to go into the schools, per se, but instead brings teachers to the Centers in Flint and Lansing for summer work experience through which they can gain insight into potential career opportunities for students. It is a "partnership" in the sense that, in exchange for gaining such insight, and introducing their students to math-related skills they may need as General Motors workers, the teachers serve as plant trainers and developers of training modules that can be used in General Motors Plants across the country.

The Quality Education Program was one of 16 that received honors in a 1989 awards program conducted by the Michigan Board of Education.
Publications: Employee Training Modules

SALVATION ARMY HAMBURGER SALES DAY
Earl's Hamburgers
301 East Linwood Boulevard
Kansas City, MO 64111
Purpose: To raise funds for the Salvation Army.
Sponsor: Earl's Hamburgers
Contact: Helen Phillips
Description: For the seventh year in a row, Earl's Hamburgers opened its doors at 4:00 a.m. to sell the "just-bigger-than-bite-sized" hamburgers at 1940s prices. The purpose is the same each year - to raise funds for the *Salvation Army*. The owners of the grill and dozens of volunteers cooked, bunned, pickled and sacked burgers for the long line of customers.

This year, however, drawing on experience from previous years when some customers waited over two hours, the Salvation Army's new canteen truck was brought into play - even though nobody ever complained about the long wait. With a capacity of 20 burgers from the canteen truck added to the 55 capacity in the restaurant, waiting time was considerably shorter.

Hamburgers were sold in bags of ten, and over 800 bags were sold by the end of the day, raising more than $2,000.

A favorite charity of Earl's, the owners (a husband-wife team) started the project to recognize the Salvation Army for the food and comfort it provided during the depression of the 1930s - remembered personally by the wife in the ownership team. "It was like a gift of God, and I haven't forgotten it," she said.
Founded: 1982

SAUNDERS B. MOON CHILD DEVELOPMENT CENTER
Saunders B. Moon School Community Resource Advisory Program
8100 Fordson Road
Alexandria, VA 22306
TEL: 703-360-2100
Purpose: To provide child care and instruction to two- to five-year-olds from low-income families.
Sponsor: Local business/industry; donations
Contact: Charlotte H. Branch, Director
Description: After over 25 years of representing the poor in Fairfax County, the Saunders B. Moon Child Development Center was faced with closing in August 1989 after a dispute with Fairfax County. The county provided major funding for the Center ($400,000 per year). The new County contract, offering no increase in budget to care for the 150 children enrolled, stipulated that the Center must increase its staff-pupil ratio before the contract could be validated. Without an increase in funding, Center staff found this requirement to be impossible. This latest problem culminated a two-year dispute with the County in matters of irregular inspections, budget autonomy, etc. The Contract was denied. Undaunted, the Center turned to the community and, with corporate donations and contributions from individuals, six volunteers continued operations. They felt that interruption of the service could affect not only the progress and supervision of the children, but employment of the parents. Although the Center was officially closed, and the County would place some of the children in school programs, too many families who would not be in those programs would be affected, since many of them could not pay a babysitter. The Center is a full-day, year-round operation that specializes in instruction and development of the child.

THE SMALL BUSINESS WAY: SMALL BUSINESSES SUPPORTING UNITED WAY
United Way of Greenville County
824 East Washington Street
PO Box 1086
Greenville, SC 29602-0010
TEL: 803-242-0995
Purpose: To increase contributions from small businesses.
Sponsor: United Way of Greenville County
Contact: Mack D. Hixon, Executive Director
Description: United Way of Greenville County increased contributions from small businesses by 57.2 percent during its 1988 campaign. This achievement resulted from a carefully-structured letter/telemarketing effort: The Small Business Way - Small Businesses Supporting United Way. Chief executive officers at local companies recruited United Way volunteers to telephone small business owners. An additional five volunteers came from Research, Inc., a telemarketing firm which also provided phone bank facilities, solicitation training, and supervision.

Greenville's Small Business Council, an advisory group of nine small-business owners in the County also supported the effort by providing the Council's letterhead, with the Small Business Way

Logo added, for solicitation letters. Thank you letters signed by phone volunteers went to both new and continuing contributors, and to noncontributing businesses thanking them for their time. A training program and a visit to a United Way-funded program were important elements of the campaign for the phone volunteers. Also, to assure a greater likelihood of success, initial calls assigned were to previous donors. This strategy worked: 70.8 percent of former contributors made pledges.
Publications: The Small Business Way Information Packet; Touch A Life - The Small Business Way (poster)
Founded: 1988

SPECIAL MORTGAGE AFFORDABLE HOUSING PROGRAM
Theodore Roosevelt National Bank
1201 New York Avenue, NW
Washington , DC 20005
TEL: 202-371-1201; 202-546-3400
FAX: 202-371-8233
Purpose: To assist the community by providing an affordable housing program.
Description: Only one of two lenders in the Washington area to revive a languishing HUD low-cost housing program (203[k]), *Theodore Roosevelt National Bank* officials see it as a way to help the community. *HUD's Federal Housing Administration* guaranteed mortgage program is designed for moderate- and low-income borrowers. It allows banks to extend acquisition, construction and fixed-rate long-term mortgage financing in one package for borrowers who might not qualify for conventional loans.
Although Roosevelt Bank officials plan to be conservative in the lending program, they feel that, because of the loan limits, they will be making a lot of loans "in the eastern part of town - Northeast, Southeast and Prince George's County" (primarily low-income areas).
With a backlog of repossessed real estate, and a need to accelerate the disposal of it, HUD is pleased with the Bank's expressed plans, and would like to see other area banks follow suit. HUD has made all of its inventory eligible for the three-in-one loans. Nationwide, the program is being used by first-time home buyers to get decent housing at an affordable price. Many are buying two-unit houses, or converting single-family dwellings into two units. In this way, the rental from the second unit often pays a high percentage - sometimes all - of the mortgage. Another benefit of this type of purchase is that the anticipated income from renting the second unit can be used as a part of the potential buyers' income to help meet qualifications of the mortgage.
Roosevelt Bank officials feel that the benefits of the program outweigh the problems, one of which is the requirement for the low- or moderate-income buyer to retain a knowledgeable contractor to bring the home up to *HUD Minimum Property Standards* - no "home handymen allowed." Contractors with proven track records make the transition less problematic for all concerned, according to HUD officials.
Although Roosevelt Bank considers its initial involvement in HUD's 203(k) program an "experiment," the president says, "We think we can make it work."
With skeptic counterparts describing the Roosevelt Bank as a *boutique bank* (fresh fruit and free umbrellas in its antique-filled lobby, extra interest for kid clients who get good grades, home phone numbers on its employees' business cards, etc.), and cautioning that *TLC* "will only get you so far," the Bank moves on toward its program of "charities on the deposit side, and lower income housing on the loan side," winning praise from all quarters of the community along the way.

STRIDE RITE CHILDREN'S CENTER
Stride Rite Corporation
960 Harrison Avenue
Boston, MA 02118
TEL: 617-427-1100
Purpose: To help provide an answer to the vital question, "Who's minding the kids?"
Sponsor: Stride Rite Corporation
Contact: Miriam Kertzman, Director
Description: In response to a community group's request in 1971, the Stride Rite Corporation's philanthropic foundation helped fund a community child-care center. It occurred to the company that this center could include employee children, too, and the facility opened with 30 children - 15 employees' children and 15 children from the community at large. Presently, 50 children are accommodated. An additional day care center opened in early 1983 in Kendall Square, Cambridge, to accommodate employees' and community children at the new corporate headquarters site. The staffers and several volunteers run the center, with personnel costs reduced somewhat through affiliation with high-school and college-intern projects and teacher-training programs.
The center is open from 7 a.m. to 5 p.m. to allow for variance in parents' shifts. After breakfast, the children's activities include math and reading readiness, cooking, drama and field trips. Interns from local hospitals work as teacher aides during their pediatrics rotations, and children are taken on a rotating basis to the pedodontic department at Boston University's Dental School for dental care.
The center occupies former office space on the first floor of the plant, which employs about 700 people. It cost about $25,000 to renovate and equip the initial area, with total start-up costs amounting to about $40,000. The facility has been enlarged several times, with $46,000 in company funding supplemented by government subsidies and non-financial sources of support. For example, a federal program reimbursed 75% of the cost of installing the kitchen; a contract with the state school lunch and nutrition bureau pays about 70% of food costs.
The cost of running the center is about $60 per week, per child. Employee parents pay 10% of their weekly gross pay, and community parents pay the state on a sliding-scale basis. The center is a separate corporation with its own charter, board of directors and insurance. The company has no legal responsibility for its operation.
The company considers industry-sponsored day care extremely cost-effective since the company is already paying for heat, light, telephones, maintenance and other services. Reduction in absenteeism is another plus for the company, as well as the side benefit of access to the children to "wear-test" new shoe designs. Stride Rite has developed a summary of the operation in a free booklet, *How We Do It,* and the director conducts a monthly two-hour information-sharing session for persons interested in visiting the center.
A footnote worth mentioning here is an observation made by a staff member. "Some of us try to be near the Center around noon to see the sheer delight on the children's faces when their parents join them for lunch."
Publications: How We Do It
Founded: 1971

"UNITED WAY AT WORK" PROGRAM
United Way of America
701 North Fairfax Street
Alexandria, VA 22314-2045
TEL: 703-836-7100
FAX: 703-683-7840
Purpose: To ensure that interaction continues between a United Way and a company's employees and management.
Sponsor: United Way of America's Resource Development Division

Contact: Shannon Smith, Manager, Resource Development
Description: The *United Way at Work* program is a model for local United Ways across the country. Approximately 150 United Ways nationwide have *United Way at Work* programs, with an additional 100 in the planning stages. However, except for several basic objectives, they can be as diverse as the companies where they take place. Those basic objectives include:
- aiming to personalize United Way for employees;
- educating employees about United Way;
- linking workers with local human-service agencies and services; and
- recognizing the workers' companies for their support of United Way.

But that is where the similarity ends, simply because rural, urban, suburban and other specific neighborhoods have different types of needs. For example, United Way of Central Carolinas in Charlotte, North Carolina, felt that a conference involving 30 local companies and staff from United Way-supported agencies and 70 representatives from local companies would provide direction. Child care surfaced as the issue to address for the area served by that United Way.

United Way of Lackawanna County in Scranton, Pennsylvania, succeeded in having the Governor proclaim United Way "Workplace Presence Week." They organized week-long awareness activities at local companies, including health fairs where local agencies screened employees' stress levels and blood pressure. Joint events in Lackawanna include food drives and holiday toy collections for needy children.

Companies in the Toledo, Ohio, area participate in United Way of Greater Toledo's program at three levels of involvement. One is through employee group tours of agencies, where agency directors are on hand to meet them. This personal touch brings many employees back to the agencies to volunteer. Another is the company's involvement in planning related to surveys that indicate areas where their services will have the greatest impact. Also, they receive and contribute input to Toledo's quarterly *United Way at Work Newsletter* and United Way posters.

In Des Moines, United Way of Central Iowa has *Employers Mutual Companies* involved not only in annual agency fairs, quarterly lunchtime workshps, and a *United Way at Work* newsletter, but they have created goodwill partnerships with a residence for senior citizens and a local office of the *Association for Retarded Citizens.* Employees visit with service recipients, have potluck meals, engage in pen-pal correspondence, and hold holiday decorating parties through the partnerships.

Among elements found in some of the most successful *United Way at Work* programs are the presence of a *United Way at Work* committee; market research activities; involvement with chief executive officers, presence of employee-assistance programs; and interaction with the top-ranking types of worksites - manufacturing, utility, and banking industries.

UNITED WAY EDITORIAL BOARD
SEE COMMUNICATIONS & PUBLIC RELATIONS

VOLUNTEER INITIATIVE PROGRAM (VIP)
Atlantic Electric Company
1199 Black Horse Pike
Atlantic City, NJ 08401
TEL: 609-645-3500
Purpose: To devote a variety of resources to volunteer mobilization in Southern New Jersey.
Sponsor: Atlantic Electric Company
Contact: VIP Coordinator
Description: Southern New Jersey's social support agencies, operating within the confines of limited financial resources, have come to rely on a steady stream of dedicated volunteers to provide quality services. The agencies' traditional supply of volunteers has greatly diminished in recent years due to lifestyle changes

(working women, aging population, increases in shift work). Non-profit groups now need extraordinary assistance to find, recruit and retain volunteers to fill this gaping hole.

A group of individuals at Atlantic Electric recognized this volunteer shortage as a critical problem concerning the community and embarked on a plan to devote its varied resources to volunteer mobilization. These resources are being used in the company's *Volunteer Initiative Program (VIP)* that recruits and places employees in volunteer jobs, provides leadership and in-kind support for the establishment of the *Volunteer Center of Atlantic County,* and sponsors special volunteer projects with the *New Jersey Division of Youth and Family Services (DYFS)* and the *Literacy Volunteers of America (LVA).*

VIP is helping LVA through a support program involving volunteer recruitment, promotion and training. It has assisted DYFS in special projects, including its Christmas gift drive in which 770 employees pledged gifts. Also, VIP has assumed a leadership role in the pursuit of effective public/private volunteer partnerships in Southern New Jersey.

The Volunteer Center of Atlantic County, established in 1988 with Atlantic's assistance, has received in-kind support in the way of printing, mailing and secretarial services from the company. In September 1988, Atlantic Electric sent more than 15,000 leaflets in its bills to customers on behalf of the Center.

In addition, VIP has compiled a data bank of hundreds of volunteer needs from organizations throughout its Atlantic Electric's eight-county service area. Employees are computer-matched with needs for volunteers and learn how to find out more about specific openings.

In 1989, VIP was a recipient of one of the *Governor's Volunteer Awards.*
Publications: VIP Information Packet
Founded: 1987

WHEELCHAIR WASH
Northside Surgical Supply
1165 Portland Avenue
Rochester, NY 14621
TEL: 716-544-9060
Purpose: To provide a needed service to handicapped persons who use wheelchairs.
Sponsor: Southside Apothecary
Contact: Bernie Huffer
Description: For the sixteenth year, employees of a medical supply company and 23 other businesses and agencies volunteered their labor to clean wheelchairs. After motors and other power components are removed, the chairs are blasted with water, scrubbed by hand with industrial detergent, rinsed, wiped dry by *Boy Scouts,* and then reassembled and checked over for mechanical problems. All labor is free, but owners pay for any parts needed for repair.

Based in the parking lot of *Northside Surgical Supply,* the project took on a carnival air. A tent sheltered some wheelchair owners, while others chose to sit in the sunshine, chatting, sipping pop, nibbling cookies and listening to rock music from the local radio station. Helium balloons decorated the area, and volunteers and wheelchair owners wore bright blue T-shirts commemorating the 16th annual wheelchair wash.

Since owners know that well-functioning wheelchairs often mean the difference between isolation at home and an independent, active life, participation is extensive, with 135 chairs cleaned, checked and/or repaired during the event. According to one owner, "It is very important that we have a chair that is mechanically safe because you can get into some very real problems when you're alone."
Founded: 1973

WOMEN OFF WELFARE (WOW)
SEE VOLUNTEERS: LOW-INCOME

BUSINESS/INDUSTRY INVOLVEMENT: ADOPT-A-SCHOOL

INDIVIDUAL PROGRAM PROFILES

ADOPT-A-SCHOOL
San Jose Unified School District
1605 Park Avenue
San Jose, CA 95110
TEL: 408-998-6000 (schools); 408-279-7900 (Water Co.)
Purpose: To introduce students to the business world while
employees share business talents with students.
Sponsor: San Jose Unified School District
Contact: Gayle Jones (school); Scott Yo (Water Co.); Theresa
Johnson (Chamber of Commerce)
Description: In San Jose, businesses share their human resources,
expertise, technology, equipment, etc., to expose students to the
business world. When appropriate, businesses include written
curricula to be incorporated into classroom teaching. In turn,
students give back to the businesses by performing skits and
musicals or sending pictures and murals.
Every school in the San Jose Unified School District has been
adopted except one, and some have more than one sponsor. The
San Jose program was the first in the area and served as a strong
pilot for other districts to emulate.
Science magnet *Hacienda Valley View Elementary School* was
adopted in 1966 by the *San Jose Water Company.* The school
emphasizes science and maintains an outdoor biology lab designed
to simulate the Santa Clara Valley, with two ponds connected by a
small creek. Aside from maintaining the ecology ponds, the water
company provides curriculum and helps with field trips that focus
on water conservation. Curricula is available for every grade level.
To emphasize saving and conserving water, the first act of the
water company was to install an organic filtering system to avoid
wasting water during cleaning of the ecology ponds. The company
continually places emphasis on the relation of water to the
environment and the importance of conserving it.
Students reciprocate in many ways, including sending pictures,
student stories and murals to water company employees.
Sponsoring businesses benefit by developing business-literate
students for the future and by raising the morale of employees who
volunteer for the program.

BUSINESS/INDUSTRY INVOLVEMENT: AIDS

TRAINING PROGRAMS

AIDS IN THE WORKPLACE
San Francisco AIDS Foundation
333 Valencia Street
PO Box 6182
San Francisco, CA 94101-6182
TEL: 415-861-3397
Sponsor: Local groups
Contact: Education Coordinator
Description: This multi-media education program was developed
with the assistance of top business leaders; provides assistance in
employment situations at any level, as well as health programs by
educators employed in the workplace; consists of:
1. An Epidemic of Fear: Aids in the Workplace - a video tape

using real-life situations to educate managers and employees about
AIDS; includes interviews with medical experts, corporate
managers, employees with AIDS and their coworkers.
2. An Educational Guide for Managers - provides decisionmakers
with information about AIDS and includes a model for educating
employees, and using educational resources effectively.
3. Strategy Manual and Appendix - provides hands-on suggestions
for the development of policies and guidelines for responding to
AIDS in the work environment, and draws on the experience of
companies which have successfully dealt with AIDS in the
workplace.
4. AIDS in the Workplace - a pamphlet developed for distribution
to employees consisting of questions and answers about AIDS.
This program was developed in cooperation with the Business
Leadership Task Force of the San Francisco Bay Area. Members
of the Task Force include Levi Strauss & Co., Pacific Bell,
Mervyn's, Bank of America, Wells Fargo Bank, AT&T and
Chevron Corporation. These businesses and their associated
foundations also funded the development and production of *AIDS
in the Workplace* materials.
This education program is designed as a self-contained training
program for the business community.
A more advanced program, *The Next Step: HIV in the 90s,* begins
where *AIDS in the Workplace* ends. It addresses issues that arise
after policies are in place and AIDS education is underway. These
issues include reasonable accommodation, confidentiality, benefits,
fitness for duty, legal issues, and grief and loss. Inquire about cost
to local businesses of both segments of the training program.
Publications: An Epidemic of Fear: AIDS in the Workplace; An
Educational Guide for Managers; Strategy Manual and Appendix;
Aids in the Workplace

INDIVIDUAL PROGRAM PROFILES

FAMILY LIFE AND AIDS INSTRUCTION PROGRAM
SEE BUSINESS/INDUSTRY INVOLVEMENT: EDUCATION

HIV/AIDS WORKPLACE PROGRAM
American Red Cross Office of HIV/AIDS Education
1709 New York Avenue, NW
Washington, DC 20006
TEL: 202-662-1577; 202-662-1580
FAX: 202-662-1555
Purpose: To provide a means of communication on HIV/AIDS
between employer and employees.
Contact: Carole Kauffman
Description: The Red Cross workplace HIV/AIDS education
program is being used (as of mid-1990) in over 400 local Red
Cross chapters. The program provides employers with the
opportunity to explain or reinforce their policies regarding HIV
infection, including AIDS. The video/discussion portion of the
program combines the delivery of facts and information about how
HIV can and cannot be transmitted with guided group discussions
about employee responses to potential HIV/AIDS-related events in
the workplace.
Additional workplace video scenarios continue to be developed,
along with new discussion guides, and are released to the field as
they become available. Updating is done periodically throughout
each project year.

BUSINESS/INDUSTRY INVOLVEMENT: ARTS

NATIONAL/STATE ORGANIZATIONS

ARTS AND BUSINESS COUNCIL
130 East 40th Street
New York, NY 10016
TEL: 212-683-5555
Objectives: To foster corporate involvement with the arts on a local and national basis; to increase effectiveness of arts managements through corporate volunteers; to create working and mutually-beneficial arts-business partnerships.
Services: Establishes and administers arts programs to benefit both business and arts communities; provides services by specially-trained business executives to assist in problem solving for arts organizations; coordinates national network of business volunteer programs to aid arts managers (e.g., Arts Fare, Business Volunteers for the Arts); maintains extensive data bank and library; conducts advisory service in cable and electronic media; sponsors annual awards program for corporate service to the arts and arts service to the community; aids individual artists through part time job programs.
Publications: Winterfare; ABC Newsletter
Founded: 1973

BUSINESS COMMITTEE FOR THE ARTS
1775 Broadway, Suite 510
New York, NY 10019
TEL: 212-664-0600
Objectives: To encourage all businesses throughout the United States to support the arts; to offer advice to businesses that want to begin supporting the arts; to counsel businesses interested in expanding existing art support programs; to assist businesses interested in developing special arts support projects such as corporate art collecting, a matching gifts program for the arts, museum sponsorship and many other partnerships between business and the arts; to provide the business community and the public with information and statistics about business support to the arts; to encourage communication and cooperation between business, government agencies, foundations and private sector groups interested in supporting the arts; to create public awareness of business support to the arts.
Services: Presents conferences, seminars and workshops for business leaders throughout the United States to increase business support to the arts and to stimulate partnerships between business and the arts; compiles information and statistics about business support to the arts in the United States, the specific needs of American arts organizations, trends in business support to the arts and facts about government and private sector support to the arts; conducts a public service advertising compaign to encourage new and increased business support to the arts; publishes a newsletter, brochures and policy papers to encourage and to assist business support to the arts; honors corporations for their outstanding efforts to support the arts through the annual BCA Business in the Arts Awards jointly sponsored with Forbes Magazine; presents an annual Award to the arts organization that has done the most to stimulate an outstanding partnership between business and the arts; advocates the development of state and community associations to develop business support to the arts; cooperates with government agencies, foundations and private sector groups interested in supporting the arts; invites prominent business leaders to speak at national gatherings and conventions about business support to the arts.
Publications: BCA News; Matching Gift Programs/Arts
Founded: 1967

INDIVIDUAL PROGRAM PROFILES

ADOPT-A-SCHOOL DANCE PROGRAM
National Dance Institute
599 Broadway
11th Floor
New York, NY 10012
TEL: 212-226-0083
Purpose: To provide dance classes to individual school children in New York City schools.
Sponsor: Corporations, foundations and individuals
Contact: Meryl Salzinger, Communications Director
Description: Founded in 1976 by a former principal dancer in the New York City Ballet, the National Dance Institute sends dance instructors to 28 schools in Manhattan, Brooklyn and Queens for an hour a week throughout the school year. In 1988, the Institute started a sponsorship program to help defray expenses of the program. By Fall 1989, eight of the schools its serves were "adopted" by individuals, corporations, and foundations. The Institute sponsor donates $5,000 a year for five years to a specific school, and the school raises another $4,000 each year from other sources.
In addition to the one-hour classes, donors sponsor dance performances throughout the year, including a final event in which children from all participating schools perform. Over 1,000 children danced in the closing performance of the 1988-89 school year, which was held at the Felt Forum in New York's Madison Square Garden.
To keep sponsors interested and involved with their adoptive schools, the Institute invites them to performances and to classes to observe the enthusiasm of the students. Also, donors and school principals are included in "class pictures" and, at the end of the school year, the children in the dance classes write thank-you letters to the sponsors.
Although the Institute's Adopt-A-School program is similar to other arrangements in which individuals or businesses have "adopted" schools, it requires a much smaller donation, thus, according to the program's director, "bringing in a whole group of people who could not otherwise afford to help. For some individual donors, this is their first major gift." Also, corporations and foundations formerly donating less than $5,000 have managed to bring their donations up to the $5,000 level.
Founded: 1976

GRAND RAPIDS SYMPHONY ORCHESTRA
SEE FUNDING/FUND-RAISING/RELATED SERVICES: ARTS

TAE KWON DO CHOREOGRAPHIC PERFORMANCES
Jhoon Rhee Institute of Tae Kwon Do
1258 Wisconsin Avenue, NW
Washington, DC
TEL: 202-USA-1000
Purpose: To demonstrate to youth the discipline and enjoyment of karate.
Contact: Jhoon Rhee
Description: The *Jhoon Rhee Institute of Tae Kwon Do* was the first such group to develop choreographed performances by participants in a karate program. The performers range in age from four to adult, and the performances are offered to schools and nonprofit groups throughout the Washington metropolitan area.
A typical performance is the show provided for the national meeting of *Super Volunteers*. The troupe, in silks, satins and sequins, performed a dance of intricate *Tae Kwon Do* movements with a finale in which the performers took the shape of the American flag. Also, the *Institute* presented a five-year-old *black belt* who, with a seven-year-old partner, performed a dance choreographed by the two youngsters themselves; and had a

number of children and teenagers display their talents in the various levels of *Tae Kwon Do*.

Following the performance, the young participants mingled with the audience to answer questions about their involvement in the program, how their school grades had improved, and how much better they felt, physically, because of the exercise involved. This was followed by a presentation by Jhoon Rhee who talked about shy, withdrawn youngsters who "blossom" in the program - one who was failing in school, and now heads the class - and an 84-year-old participant who was rapidly rising in the levels of the program.

In addition to the performing troupe, a speakers program is maintained, and some scholarships are made available to youngsters who cannot otherwise participate in the program. The constant reminder is that the program is one of discipline and self-esteem, not violence.

BUSINESS/INDUSTRY INVOLVEMENT: BUSINESSES

INDIVIDUAL PROGRAM PROFILES

MIDAS TOUCH
SEE FUNDING/FUND-RAISING/RELATED SERVICES: BUSINESSES

BUSINESS/INDUSTRY INVOLVEMENT: CHILDREN/YOUTH

NATIONAL/STATE ORGANIZATIONS

DISTRIBUTIVE EDUCATION CLUBS OF AMERICA
SEE BUSINESS/INDUSTRY INVOLVEMENT: ENTREPRENEURSHIP

TRAINING PROGRAMS

GOVERNORS' SCHOOL
SEE GOVERNORS' OFFICES ON VOLUNTEERISM: WASHINGTON

INDIVIDUAL PROGRAM PROFILES

BOARDER BABY PROJECT
Gartenhaus Furs
6950 Wisconsin Avenue
Chevy Chase, MD 20015
TEL: 202-656-2800
Purpose: To reduce or eliminate hospital stays of babies abandoned by their drug-addicted mothers.
Contact: Lynne or Patty Gartenhaus
Description: Starting with a fashion show in early 1990, *Gartenhaus Furs* plans to raise $200,000 for a "boarder baby home," which would give priority to the abandoned infants at DC General Hospital. These babies are medically ready to be

discharged, but have no place to go. Most were abandoned by drug-addicted mothers.

Although the DC City Council has taken steps to force the city to take custody of such children soon after they are declared ready for discharge, the caseloads of social workers prohibit any hope of a rapid solution. Since caseload priority is given to abused children who must be removed from their homes, the boarder babies - considered safe as long as they are in the hospital - are not always placed first. During the 1988-90 fiscal years, the child welfare system added only about 30 new foster parents to its rosters. Therefore, *Gartenhaus Furs* is making an effort to "fill in the gap."

According to the founders, however, help is not far away. With the publicity surrounding the babies, many benefits are surfacing. A March 1990 celebrity auction brought out many stars to call attention to the problem - including the world heavyweight boxing champion, who donated his champion's belt. In addition, due to a surge in volunteers in the social services system, by March 1990 more than 230 families either had enrolled in classes, or were awaiting final approval to become foster or adoptive parents for the infants. Unfortunately, this expanded help is accompanied by a dramatic rise in the number of pregnant women using drugs. In one week at a local hospital, 18 of the 29 children born had been exposed to drugs.

The boarder baby home is not expected to be a permanent solution, according to its founders. However, experts warn that the hospital setting during the first year causes children to miss opportunities to bond and they are likely to be developmentally delayed. Plans for the Gartenhaus project are to create a home-like setting and enough volunteers and staff to make each child feel special - in the hope of counteracting the dire prediction of the experts. "Hopefully, foster families will make even that stay a short one," one founder said, "and will create permanent homes and families for the youngsters. The important thing is to remove them from that necessarily sterile setting."

BUSINESS MANAGEMENT/JUNIOR ACHIEVEMENT
SEE BUSINESS/INDUSTRY INVOLVEMENT: ENTREPRENEURSHIP

CHILD IDENTIFICATION PROGRAM
Safeway Stores
Little Rock Division
8109 Highway I-30
Little Rock, AR 72202
TEL: 501-562-3583
Purpose: To demonstrate the spirit of volunteerism through community involvement.
Sponsor: Safeway Stores
Contact: Community Relations Officer
Description: As a matter of policy, Safeway has always recognized its responsibility as a corporate citizen and has urged its employees to become involved in community activities where they live and work. In Little Rock, Arkansas, one community service program that received overwhelming participation was the Child Identification Program in which six area Safeway stores participated. This was a joint effort of Safeway, Pepsi Cola and Channel 4 and involved establishing "Child ID Centers" in the six Safeway stores stores.

The program ran for four consecutive weeks in late fall to be sure as many children as possible would be in the area and could participate.

Parents were invited to bring their children 12 years of age and under. An ID card for each child included a photograph and finger prints, along with vital statistical information. Volunteers experienced in the areas needed prepared the cards. They were developed for parents to keep in the event a child should ever be lost or missing.

The response to the Child ID Program was overwhelming. Almost

10,000 children visited the stores with their parents to be photographed and fingerprinted.

Plans are to make the Child Identification Program an ongoing activity on an as-needed basis.

Publications: Safeway Community Involvement Packet

CHILDREN'S MIRACLE NETWORK TELETHON
SEE FUNDING/FUND-RAISING/RELATED SERVICES: CHILDREN

COMMUNICATING HUMAN NEEDS
SEE COMMUNICATIONS & PUBLIC RELATIONS: CHILDREN/YOUTH

COMMUNITY BLOCK HOMES
Illinois State Board of Education
Instructional Improvement Section
100 North First Street
Springfield, IL 62777
TEL: 217-782-9374
Purpose: To provide help for children in the community should an emergency arise.
Sponsor: McDonald's Restaurants
Contact: Volunteer Coordinator
Description: Community Block Home is a program being sponsored with the cooperation of *McDonald's Restaurants* throughout the State of Illinois. The foundation of the program is a network of homes and businesses that have been approved as safe havens for children in danger. The homes and businesses are recognized by a statewide safety symbol placed in the window. This symbol signals a home where children can find help in an emergency. Block Homes function in cooperation with local elementary schools and law enforcement agencies.

Adults interest in children's wellbeing must qualify to be a Block Home participant, although it is not necessary to be a parent to apply. Some of the volunteers in the program are:

- Adults who are home during the daytime hours
- Small neighborhood businesses that are open during the day
- Senior Citizens

Approved volunteers promise the children in their community that they will provide aid should an emergency arise. The *Block Home Safety Symbol* in the window lets children know they can turn to that home for protection.

DISCOUNT MART SHOPPING CENTER II
SEE VOLUNTEERS: PROFESSIONALS

INDEPENDENT LIVING/HOMELESS YOUTH
The Bridge
1115 Ball, NE
Grand Rapids, MI 49505
TEL: 616-451-3001
Purpose: To offer help to newly-emancipated 16- and 17-year-old youths.
Sponsor: United Way
Contact: Connie Hendershot, Director
Description: In Michigan, *legal emancipation* is the phrase used when a youngster's parents, for whatever reason, ask to be relieved of all legal obligations toward their child and are granted their request. With emancipation, the child suddenly must assume full responsibility for his or her life, no matter how ill-equipped the youngster might be.

In Grand Rapids, the youth can turn to the *Independent Living/Homeless Youth* project sponsored by *The Bridge,* a United Way-sponsored program. The project helps homeless 16- and 17-year-olds find suitable housing, financial assistance, employment, food, clothing, health care, and educational and vocational training.

The youth project was an outgrowth of the concern of staff and volunteers of *The Bridge,* a short-term shelter for homeless individuals. They noticed a disturbing rise in the number of emancipated youths seeking shelter. Most of them appeared to need assistance, and it was felt that hiring a case manager to work one-to-one with individual youths could provide them with the resources they needed, both material and emotional. A three-month period for each youth was considered ample to help them acquire the skills and sense of responsibility needed to survive.

Youths who enter the program agree, in writing, to commit themselves to the program and to follow its rules, including attending school or working 40 hours a week, taking good care of their housing, and maintaining the confidentiality of other program participants.

When the youths leave the program after the three-month period, the case manager meets with each participant once every 30 days for six months to provide follow-up assistance.

To help participants on their way following their stay, *The Bridge* established a pool of funds from which clients can borrow the amount of security deposits for apartments. Funds come from the *Federal Emergency Management Agency (FEMA),* the *State of Michigan,* and other sources. At the same time, staff has been able to negotiate with some local landlords to waive such deposits.

The goal is to assure that each youth, by the end of his or her 90 days, can find housing and employment, and can gain access to appropriate health and human services they might require. In this way, *The Bridge* is enabling teens to accept responsibility for their lives.
Founded: 1987

PHONE PAL
Southwestern Bell
1010 Pine Street
Room 921
St. Louis, MO 63101
TEL: 314-235-9800
Purpose: To provide "latchkey children" and their parents with an added sense of security.
Sponsor: Southwestern Bell
Contact: Darrell Lauer
Description: When Southwestern Bell in St. Louis started "Phone Pal," a program to pair older adults with "latchkey" children - grade schoolers who are alone at home before or after school, it was picked up almost immediately by the Southwestern Bell office in El Dorado, Arkansas.

Phone Pal, started in 1986 at Yokum Elementary School in El Dorado, matches child and adult according to shared interests. They keep in touch regularly by telephone. Phone Pal children are offered a monthly club meeting at the school. According to the principal of the school, the child devlops a sense of responsibility, since the experience of talking to an older adult enhances courtesy, telephone skills, and communication skills in general. It has been determined that a program like Phone Pal works best with grade schoolchildren.

Both partners of the Phone Pal team represent growing segments of the population. Due to increases in the number of working women and single-parent families, more children are returning to empty homes after school. At the same time, the number of homebound seniors is growing. Phone Pal meets needs in both groups: children who need to be cared for and older adults who need someone to care about.
Publications: Phone Pal Information Packet

ROADRUNNER PROGRAM
Capital Metropolitan Transportation Authority
City of Austin
2910 East Fifth Street
Austin, TX 78702
TEL: 512-474-1200

Purpose: To assist youth with transportation expenses by providing a reduced-fair program and other cost-saving features.
Sponsor: City of Austin
Contact: Youth Coordinator
Description: Recognizing that many youth are hindered from pursuing jobs and services available to them due to transportation expense, the *Capital Metropolitan Transportation Authority* decided to try to help. The agency introduced the *Roadrunner Program* for youth 18 years of age and under, which provides a pass for a considerable saving on transportation, and qualifies participants for discounts on items ranging from food to music to miniature golf from more than 20 area merchants.
Young riders can purchase Roadrunner passes by showing one of a number of IDs - including a school report card - at most of the locations that sell regular Capital Metro passes. It is hoped that the cost-saving feature and the support of area merchants will encourage more youth to seek summer employment and pursue social activities that will counteract the practice of idle youth congregating in the neighborhoods with nothing productive to keep them occupied.

SAFE PLACE
Metro Alternative Shelter House (MASH)
536 West Third Street
Lexington, KY 40508
TEL: 606-254-2501
Purpose: To provide a safe place to wait for troubled youths until a trained volunteer arrives from the local center.
Contact: Suzanne Conrad
Description: The *Metro Alternative Shelter House (MASH)* had a problem. When a youth needing help was reported, often they arrived to find the youth gone. In mid-1989 a volunteer in the program suggested *Safe Place,* a project that enlists the help of area businesses to solve the dilemma.
Once designated as a "safe place," a business agrees to provide shelter for troubled youths until a trained volunteer arrives from MASH. Unfortunately, most businesses fail to meet the criteria. The site needs to be:
● a business, not a home;
● highly visible;
● easily accessible;
● open nearly 24 hours a day;
● an appropriate location for a young person to wait; and
● staffed by at least two qualified people at all times.
Summer time is a busy time for the shelter, with schools closed and young people without direction, leading to restlessness. Children are without adult supervision, or spending the whole day in homes which are abusive. Also, summer is a prime time for 14 to 15-year-old runaways.
Because of these problems, MASH continues to try to increase the number of *Safe Places* - especially in the inner city. Male volunteers are best for inner-city locations, and recruitment efforts are underway to increase their numbers.
Although many more *Safe Places* are needed, the present level of assistance has helped. Each business receives a bright, highly visible, yellow and black *Safe Place* sign for window or door. Word is spread through schools and other youth-serving sources to make this sign a recognizable and acceptable means of help for youth.

BUSINESS/INDUSTRY INVOLVEMENT: CIVIC AFFAIRS

INDIVIDUAL PROGRAM PROFILES

COMMUNITY ADVISEMENT BOARD
Acacia Federal Savings Bank
7023 Little River Turnpike
Annandale, VA 22003
TEL: 703-642-3000
Purpose: To involve citizens in advising the bank on community needs.
Contact: Community Reinvestment Act Officer
Description: The *Acacia Federal Savings Bank* has been an active member of the community for many years. Many of its projects are a direct result of recommendations by its all-volunteer *Community Advisement Board,* which is composed of citizens from the surrounding area. The purpose of the Board is to advise the bank on credit needs of the community, including the needs of low- and moderate-income neighborhoods.
The Board is composed of religious, business, educational and political leaders as well as individuals from the neighborhoods. When new members are needed, Acacia notifies the community through various media. All interested persons submit a brief statement outlining their interest and qualifications to the *Community Reinvestment Division* of the bank. When they are notified of their appointments, members meet with the Division's officials. Meetings are held twice a year.

BUSINESS/INDUSTRY INVOLVEMENT: CRIME PREVENTION

NATIONAL/STATE ORGANIZATIONS

CENTER FOR PREVENTION AND TREATMENT OF SEXUAL ABUSE
SEE GOVERNORS' OFFICES ON VOLUNTEERISM: VERMONT

INDIVIDUAL PROGRAM PROFILES

MID-VALLEY ADOLESCENT CENTER*
1610 Court Street, NE
Salem, OR 97301
TEL: 503-364-9152
Purpose: To provide community-based treatment for delinquent adolescent males as an alternative to institutional care, court-committed youth, and residential treatment.
Sponsor: State contract; Juvenile Justice grants; federal funds for in-program teachers
Contact: Jan Rutschman
Description: Mid-Valley is a residential youth care center for delinquent males, ages 13-18, who have been court-committed. Seventeen youth are involved in the three program components: residential, proctor care, and partial residential. Youth care centers aim at keeping youth out of state institutions and at enabling the youth to grow and change. Funds are obtained primarily by contracting to provide those services for the State of Oregon. Miscellaneous amounts are also obtained from other sources.

Volunteers are used as on-line staff, recreational aides, on a volunteer resource board, to add extras on holidays and for special projects, i.e., foster grandparents, a skiing outing, etc. Currently, Mid-Valley has about 20 volunteers.

Volunteers do essentially the same things that on-line (supervision of youth) staff do with the exception of having a caseload and writing reports. Volunteers are especially appreciated for their relationship and fun activities, for which the staff often have difficulty in finding time.

Volunteers of all levels of experience are accepted, including ex-residents and participants in the program. Expansion of the volunteer program is underway and employers are being recruited to help with the Experience-Based Career Education program.

MORRIS COUNTY CHAPLAINCY COUNCIL
SEE VOLUNTEERS: CHURCH/SYNAGOGUE MEMBERS

PARTNERS*
1260 West Baysud
Denver, CO 80223
TEL: 303-777-7000
Purpose: To match volunteers one-to-one with young people who have been referred by courts, schools, police.
Sponsor: 90% private, 10% state funding
Contact: Jeffrey W. Pryor, Executive Director
Description: Partners was founded in 1968 by a Denver businessman and a small group of volunteers who believe that a one-to-one "partnership" with an in-trouble youth would have positive effects on the problem of juvenile delinquency. This concept is the foundation for the Partners program and has resulted in a significant reduction in recidivism and has improved opportunities for youth in the program to lead more successful lives. Partners has nine branches in three states and a Central office. To date, Partners has involved over 15,000 youth and adult volunteers.

Adult volunteers, called Senior Partners, and youth, or Junior Partners, agree to spend a minimum of three hours a week together for one year. During that time the youngsters have an opportunity to strengthen feelings of self-worth, improve academics, decrease delinquent behaviors, and increase abilities to cope with stressful situations.

The relationship formed between the Junior and Senior Partner is aided by Partners' staff which provides supervision and guidance through support groups, counseling and Life Skills, a series of trainings that help the Partnership seek out options and alternatives to situations they encounter. Various activities to aid in the relationship-building are available, such as water sports, hiking, skiing, and educational classes. The staff also refers the Partnerships to community agencies for legal, educational and mental health services as needed.

Involvement of the community is essential to the success of Partners. Interested, caring adults serve as volunteer Senior Partners, assist in fundraising, provide health services, and help in a myriad of other ways. Foundations and corporations offer business and management expertise to Partners' Board of Directors, committees, and staff, thereby strengthening the Partners organization. Partners receives 90 percent of its financial support from local, private contributors.
Founded: 1968

BUSINESS/INDUSTRY INVOLVEMENT: DISASTER

INDIVIDUAL PROGRAM PROFILES

SEWARD RESCUE CENTER
Exxon
Oil Spill Volunteer Response Center
Anchorage, AK 77002
TEL: 907-276-3688 (volunteers); 212-333-1000 (NY)
FAX: 212-333-1348 (NY)
Purpose: To wash and treat otters coated with oil after the Exxon Valdez oil spill.
Sponsor: Exxon Corporation
Contact: Jim Styers, Marine Mammalogist
Description: One hundred volunteers from across the country (one from Germany) wash, dry and help treat oil-coated otters in an Exxon-financed rescue center in Seward, a southern Alaska coastal town. The disaster occured in March 1989 when the Exxon Valdez, a super tanker, ran around and dumped 11.2 million gallons of oil in Prince William Sound, about 125 miles northeast of Seward, spilling into the environment crude oil that was carried 300 miles to the southwest by wind and current. By June 1989, over 800 otters and nearly 23,000 waterfowl had died as a result of the spill.

When rescue centers in Valdez and Homer proved inadequate, the center in Seward was opened in May 1989. Biologists, veterinarians and volunteers work to refine and improve techniques used in the early days of the spill.

Caught in tangle nets off the Kenai Peninsula, otters are flown to the Seward center in groups of six to 10 a day. Once inside the center's network of mobile homes, cages and tanks, they are treated like patients in any hospital. Their progress is charted, some are sent to intensive care, and pregnant females go to a maternity ward. For the first 24 hours after their arrival in Seward, otters are put in cages (they prefer their cages outside), fed and calmed by giving them ice to chew on. When they are ready, they are tranquilized and carried to elaborate washing tables, where one worker holds the head of the 40- to 100-pound animal and two more wash the oil from its fur. The job takes three people about 45 minutes. Drying the otter with dryers takes another 45 minutes. With an hour and a half per otter for the cleaning process, all volunteers are utilized to the fullest extent. Hypothermia is a major cause of death since otters have no layer of fat and need their thick coats to keep warm, so the teams must work quickly to remove the oil. Also, learned the hard way, veterinarians discovered the proper doses of tranquilizers to keep otters from biting their rescuers. Also, by trial and error, they learned that ordinary dishwashing liquid, highly diluted, is best for washing the oil from their fur.

As they recover, otters are placed in big tanks, where they can frolic and eat shrimp, mussels and clams, and need only minimal supervision. As of late May 1989, volunteers and staff saw one pup born. Of the 80 otters at the center up to that time, nine had died. Recovered otters are transferred from Seward to holding pens in a remote inlet called Little Jokolof Bay. Volunteers there feed them and monitor their progress until they are finally released. Camps for volunteers at Little Jokolof are in a remote but spectacular area of Alaska, and campers endure a lot of rain, but temperatures average 40-60 degrees.

In Seward, the dedicated volunteers are faced with scarce accommodations, also. However, many live in a campground near town, tolerating drunks and transients, and getting a shower whenever they can at other workers' accommodations. Others sleep on floors of shared hotel rooms; some live in their cars. At least one has given up a job and is living on savings to help bring the history-making disaster to the best conclusion possible.

Another program identified by the *Oil Spill Volunteer Response Center* involves volunteers who can identify birds to assess damage to local bird populations. Millions of birds, including eagles, live or spend their summers in the affected area. By June 1989, the dead-bird body count had passed 22,000. Volunteers count birds to compare their numbers with those before the spill, and track recovery rates in the future. Because of the controversy surrounding the oil cleanup efforts, per se, volunteers are not used in those operations.
Founded: 1989

VOLUNTEER COMMUNITY BETTERMENT PROJECT
Goodner Brothers Aircraft
Intermountain Regional Airport
Mena, AR 71953
TEL: 501-394-4709
Purpose: To make Polk County a safer place to live.
Sponsor: Goodner Brothers Aircraft
Contact: Albert S. Goodner, Jr.
Description: Goodner Brothers Aircraft is an Arkansas corporation employing 35 people. It is know worldwide for its aircraft painting. From the 1970s, the company has been involved in communty betterment projects - most in the area of emergency preparedness and disaster response.
Many of the company's volunteer efforts are in the area of painting upkeep of fire engines for the local fire company, airplanes, emergency jeeps, power plants, signs and compressed air cylinders for the County's Office of Emergency Preparedness, and other County vehicles. Although Goodner's efforts are primarily in Polk County, the company has not refused communities outside of Polk County. The value of this volunteer effort for the communities was placed at over $8,000 and involved as much as 20% of the paint shop's work force.
Other projects in which Goodner Brothers Aircraft has played a major role included the upgrading of a taxiway at the local airport when the deteriorated runway was being renovated. This enabled the airport to remain open while runway repairs were underway. In addition, corporate-owned aircraft has been made available for various emergencies that have arisen in Polk County, including medical evacuations and search missions, as well as emergencies arising from floods and tornadoes. These volunteer services are innumerable in dollars and cents.
The volunteer efforts of Goodner Brothers Aircraft have enabled Polk County to become one of the best emergency prepared counties in Arkansas.
Publications: Goodner Brothers Aircraft Volunteer Information Packet

BUSINESS/INDUSTRY INVOLVEMENT: DRUGS/ALCOHOL

NATIONAL/STATE ORGANIZATIONS

PHARMACISTS AGAINST DRUG ABUSE
McNeil Pharmaceutical, Division of McNeilab
Johnson & Johnson Subsidiary
Spring House, PA 19477
TEL: 215-628-5000
Objectives: To utilize the facility of American pharmacies to help in the fight against drug abuse.
Services: Works with ACTION, the National Volunteer Agency, in a nationwide program which enables development and distribution of free printed materials on drug abuse by the nation's pharmacists and a public service awareness campaign; involves

spokespersons such as the First Lady, major television personalities, and others who are nationally known; works to expand the pilot project launched in Maine, New Hampshire and Massachusetts in November 1982 to include some 50,000 pharmacies nationwide.

INDIVIDUAL PROGRAM PROFILES

MAKE IT HOME FOR THE HOLIDAYS
Washington Regional Alcohol Program
8720 Georgia Avenue
Silver Spring, MD 20910
TEL: 301-565-4161
Purpose: To bring together all segments of the metropolitan region in a concerted effort to reduce drunk driving during the holidays.
Contact: Susan Morris, Board Chairman
Description: With statistics showing December second only to June for the highest number of motor vehicle fatalities, the *Washington Regional Alcohol Program (WRAP)* and the *Council of Governments' Police Chiefs Committee* launched the *Make It Home for the Holidays* campaign. They joined forces with local business and media organizations to promote safe driving messages urging people to think twice before taking chances behind the wheel. The essence of the campaign was a reminder to citizens that the best present they can give is their safe return home.
One sponsor, *Coors Brewing Company,* provided a *Sober Ride* service during the entire month of December, the height of office parties. With a few restrictions, *Sober Ride* offers a free, no-questions-asked taxi ride home to wary revelers. During the two weeks *Sober Ride* operated in 1988, over 1,000 people used the service. The program is provided only to people who drove their own cars to parties and bars and who are not able to drive themselves home. They are taken only to their homes and not any other place.
All of the region's 21 law enforcement agencies are alerted during the period to help make the highways safe, conducting sobriety checkpoints, organizing "six pack" patrols and setting up radar stop teams to reduce the number of alcohol-related accidents.
Other efforts include 15,000 posters provided by new car dealers and put on display in buildings and businesses throughout the region. In addition, public service announcements produced and aired by WMZQ-radio, and television announcements produced by *Rock Creek Films,* are heard and seen throughout the month. The *Corporate Guide to the Holidays,* published by *Greater Washington Board of Trade,* offers responsible party giving tips to its 1,500 members.
The success of the program is attributed, in part, to the combination of a caring theme, *Make It Home for the Holidays,* and the law enforcement presence - two good reasons not to drive drunk, according to one of the business sponsors.
Publications: Corporate Guide to the Holidays

BUSINESS/INDUSTRY INVOLVEMENT: EDUCATION

NATIONAL/STATE ORGANIZATIONS

BUSINESS ISSUES IN THE CLASSROOM
Constitutional Rights Foundation
601 South Kingsley Drive
Los Angeles, CA 90005
TEL: 213-487-5590

Objectives: To involve business in preparing students to confront the business dilemmas that they will encounter in the future; to complement business visitations with a related classroom format.
Services: Recruits business participants for classroom visits; works with Business Advisory Council comprised of senior-level executives; supports the B-I-C Education Council, which conducts field tests, develops lesson plans, and coordinates activities; publishes *Business Issues in the Classroom* lesson plans with *Economic Supplements to Instructors' Guides.*
Publications: Bill of Rights Newsletter; Business Issues Lesson Plan; B:isiness Issues in the Classroom (audiovisual)
Founded: 1963

INDIVIDUAL PROGRAM PROFILES

AMERIBANC ADOPT-A-SCHOOL PROGRAM
Ameribanc Savings Bank
7630 Little River Turnpike
Suite 932
Annandale , VA 22003
TEL: 703-658-5555 (No. VA)
TOLL FREE: 800-638-7768 (nationwide)
Purpose: To follow through on its belief that *Tomorrow's Future Rests with Today's Youth.*
Description: To help combat the problems of budget cuts and teacher shortages in schools, *Ameribanc Savings Bank* has adopted six elementary schools in southeastern Virginia (Birdneck, Kingston, Tallwood, Providence, Thoroughgood, and Fairlawn schools). The school/business partnership program in the Virginia Beach area began as a pilot in 1984, involving businesses, military commands and civic organizations. The purpose was to utilize available resources in the community in order to add a broader dimension of education.
The program is considered a success in many ways. Businesses are able to increase their visibility while providing valuable services. Schools are able to enrich their curriculum. The community receives better-educated citizens.
Participating organizations provide expertise on many topics ranging from banking and computers to firefighting and water safety. Financial assistance through contributions of materials and equipment, along with sponsorships of school activities, and donations of services is also essential to the success of the partnership between schools and businesses.
Ameribanc's involvement has been very beneficial to all involved, including our bank employees. This is very obvious at the *Hilltop Branch* as they proudly wear their *Rough Reader* T-shirts donated by the bank for participants in Birdneck Elementary School's *Reading Rodeo Round-Up* program.
We have provided guest speakers for topics on money, especially highlighting the importance of saving. Many students opened savings accounts at their sponsored branch offices after our presentations. In addition to doing special learning activies, *Ameribanc* sponsors advertisements in school yearbooks and a gifted and improved student award, and displays children's artwork and hosts school choruses for mini-concerts at the branches.
From a spokesman for the bank: "*Ameribanc* is excited to have this opportunity to work with today's youth and looks forward to continuing our successful partnerships with our schools."

APPLES FOR THE STUDENTS
Giant Food
6300 Sheriff Road
Landover, MD 20785
TEL: 301-341-4100
FAX: 301-341-4582
Purpose: To continue a long-standing commitment to education.
Contact: Odonna Matthews or Barry Scher

Description: Recognizing that many schools have limited dollars for computer equipment, *Giant Food* launched a six-month partnership program to provide free computers to area schools. From October 1989 through April 1990, schools were able to redeem special *Giant Food* register tapes from participating stores for free Apple computers, printers and educational software.
To begin the program, schools were given a checklist providing redemption amounts for each piece of equipment. "Deposits" of register tapes were recorded at *Giant Food,* and "statements" were provided regularly to the schools. Both parties kept the same record of deposits and account balance information.
Many schools worked with their parent-teacher associations to generate community support. Parents spread the word in their jobs to garner tapes from co-workers without children of school-age. Some businesses adopted schools and collected the tapes for the designated school.
The offer was made available to all public, private and parochial schools, grades kindergarten through grade twelve.

BUSINESS/INDUSTRY ADVISORY COUNCIL (BIAC)
Fairfax County Public Schools
Burkholder Administration Center
10700 Page Avenue
Fairfax, VA 22030
TEL: 703-246-2502
Purpose: To involve the business community in education through service on an advisory committee to advise school officials on specific matters.
Sponsor: Fairfax County Public Schools; local businesses
Contact: Robert Spillane, Superintendent of Schools
Description: The *Superintendent's Business/Industry Advisory Council* has 33 members who serve on four committees created to study issues and make recommendations to the school system in the following areas:
- International Education (Arthur Anderson & Co. and SYCOM)
- Teacher Professionalization (Hekiman Laboratories)
- Vocational Education (Dynasty Enterprises of Virginia)
- Outlook 2010 (Bell Atlantic and Squibb Corporation)
A new thrust in 1989 by the Council was students with disabilities, and an additional committee was formed as the year progressed:
- Disabled Workers in the Business Setting (Sovran Bank)
After six years of serving the school system, Council members decided to visit *Thomas Jefferson High School for Science and Technology* to observe the results of the Council's work that started in 1983. The school, which opened its doors in 1985, was supported by the Council with funding through the *Fairfax County Public Schools Education Foundation.* This provided an outstanding example of how cooperation between the public schools and the business community can achieve goals not usually possible for either sector alone. The first class was graduated in June 1989.
The 1990 conference sponsored by the Council is *Outlook 2010* bringing together business and education leaders. It is designed to explore the future - what Fairfax County will look like and what students will need to know in order to be prepared to enter the work force in the year 2010.
The Council grows every year with new businesses stepping forward with ideas and assistance, and an opportunity for young people to reciprocate and learn what cooperation is all about.

EASTERN HIGH SCHOOL'S 500 CLUB
Washington Post
1150 Fifteenth Street, NW
Washington, DC 20071
TEL: 202-334-6130; 202-334-7969
Purpose: To help students reach their academic potential.
Sponsor: Washington Post
Contact: Community Services Coordinator

Description: In 1986, The Washington Post challenged Eastern High's students to reach their academic potential through its Washington Post/Eastern High School Incentive Program (500 Club). As incentive, The Post promised $500 per semester to any student who made no grade less than a B. A freshman who maintains As or Bs throughout high school can therefore earn $4,000 for post-secondary education. The money is held in a special account and sent to the accredited college, trade school or business school where the graduate has been accepted.

In addition, over 30 colleges across the country in partnership with The Post offer matching funds to any 500 Club member graduate who is admitted to their institutions, bringing to $8,000 the amount he or she can earn for college.

To offer additional support, The Post has a Mentor Program, which matches individual students with volunteer Post employees - positive professional role models. In this way the students experience first-hand in a one-on-one relationship what professional life demands. They discuss academic goals, college choices and career decisions. The student observes the mentor at work, which strengthens the partnership further.

And the Post has involved its employees further. Recognizing that personal growth encompasses much more than academic achievements, each school year the 500 Club visits The Post for informal luncheons, receptions, award ceremonies and to participate in seminars designed for their needs (SAT Instruction, Why It's OK To Be Smart, Selecting a College, etc.).

The Post initiated this program because, with today's pressures on youth, now more than ever, students need assurances that academic achievements can make their dreams come true.

Publications: Washington Post/Eastern High School Incentive Program

Founded: 1986

EDUCATION SUPPORT PROGRAM
Dollywood Foundation
700 Dollywood Lane
Pigeon Forge, TN 37863-4101
TEL: 615-428-9498
FAX: 703-941-4360
Purpose: To reduce high school dropout rate by working both at the college-entry level and the elementary level of the school system.
Description: In 1988, Dolly Parton launched a campaign to reduce the high school dropout rate in Sevier County by forming buddy teams of two students to help each other stay in school and graduate. In 1989, a follow-up program provided a college scholarship to each of those students who graduated from any of the three high schools in the county.

The scholarship program has been developed in connection with *Hiwassee College,* with the college offering a $500 scholarship to any student graduating from one of the high schools and applying to the college. If admission qualifications are met, inadequate S.A.T. score or grade point average will be disregarded. In addition, the college will provide financial aid above the $500 scholarship when necessary. This financial assistance is in addition to Dollywood scholarships already funded by the *Dollywood Foundation.*

Through the Foundation plan, each high school recieves a $1500 scholarship to be given to a music or arts student, and another $1200 scholarship to be given to a deserving student on the basis of academics. High school administrators make the final selection. Another program by the Foundation is a curriculum enrichment program in a local elementary school. A $10,000 grant, along with assistance from the P.T.A., the local bank, and others, will allow the school's arts and crafts program to meet its $20,000 budget and continue through 1990. A special bonus is an invitation to all students in Sevier county - 9,000 total - to be guests of Dolly Parton free of charge at *Dollywood* during the *National Crafts Festival.*

The philosophy behind the gift, in Dolly Parton's words, is that "Giving kids the opportunity to excel in their own personal skills such as arts, crafts and entertainment is part of what will motivate them to finish school. That's the primary purpose of the *Dollywood Foundation.*"

FAMILY LIFE AND AIDS INSTRUCTION PROGRAM
Los Gatos Union School District
Los Gatos, CA 95032
TEL: 408-395-5570 (school); 408-356-4111 (hospital)
Purpose: To introduce students to the business world, and provide volunteer opportunities for company employees.
Sponsor: Los Gatos Union School District
Contact: Bob Lowry, Principal, Fisher Middle School
Description: In the fall of 1988, after discussing the Adopt-A-School program with school personnel in the San Jose Unified School District, the Los Gatos School District started a program at Fisher Middle School. The school was "adopted" by Los Gatos Mission Oaks Hospital in October 1988.

School and hospital officials discussed the needs of students in the areas of health. The school sought assistance with its family life and AIDS instruction programs for eighth-graders.

Volunteer pediatricians and other trained staff members from the hospital selected sections of the family life course on human development and birth control and developed courses of instruction. In addition, the hospital provides literature geared to young people on acquired immune deficiency syndrome (AIDS). In turn, the hospital uses the Fisher campus for large meetings, and the Fisher choir sings at hospital events.

Apart from the health resources, the hospital provides costumes for the school's spring musical, and hospital employees are alert for other needs as they communicate with school personnel and work with students. As a result of the program, a number of students have expressed interest in health careers - a definite plus for the hospital as it looks to the future.

PARENT TO PARENT, ATTENTION ON ATTENDANCE
SEE VOLUNTEERS: PARENTS

PARTNERSHIPS
SEE VOLUNTEERS: ARMED FORCES MEMBERS - NAVY

SCHOOL COUNCIL VOLUNTEERS
Harris Bank
503 North Washington Street
Naperville, IL 60540
TEL: 312-420-3500
FAX: 312-420-6670
Purpose: To encourage employees to volunteer for leadership roles in the community.
Sponsor: Harris Bank
Contact: B. Kenneth West, CEO
Description: School Councils are new vehicles in the Chicago area to encourage citizen involvement in the schools. Harris Bank is encouraging its employees to run for local Chicago school council elections. In addition to pointing to school reform as "our one best shot at improving education for the young people in this city," Bank officials are interested in school reform because of the need they have for a bank of qualified employees.

Harris Bank encourages its employees in this effort by allowing release time to campaign and, when elected, to attend meetings called during business hours, as well as arranging flexible work hours to allow the volunteer employee to fill obligations that may arise. Those not elected who are parents of school-age children will be allowed these privileges also at times when parents are important to the issue.

In addition, the Bank trains employees for the responsibilities involved in being a local school council member. Nominees are given ample time to campaign, and other employees are encouraged to work with them on their campaigns. Flexible time, and time off with pay, is offered to employee campaign workers also.

Following Harris' announcement, other Chicago area corporations joined the program.

BUSINESS/INDUSTRY INVOLVEMENT: EMPLOYEE SUPPORT

NATIONAL/STATE ORGANIZATIONS

EMPLOYEE ASSISTANCE PROGRAM CONSORTIUM
Lincoln Center Building
Lincoln, NE 68508
TEL: 402-476-0186
Objectives: To provide free professional counseling for troubled workers and their dependents.
Services: Addresses any personal problems that affect job performance; helps employees to help themselves through the use of professional counselors, psychologists, psychiatric social workers, doctors, and attorneys; covers wide range of problems from marital discord to compulsive habits such as gambling, overeating, and drinking; works as coordinating EAP for several companies and a public school system.

EMPLOYEE ASSISTANCE SOCIETY OF NORTH AMERICA
PO Box 3909
Oak Park, IL 60303
TEL: 312-383-6668
Objectives: To assist managers of employee assistance counseling programs.
Services: Serves as a network for employee assistance programs (EAPs) nationwide; works with individuals in the field of employee assistance, including psychiatrists, psychologists, and managers; facilitates communication among these groups; maintains a file of resumes of employee assistance professionals; conducts research and shares its findings among EAPs; maintains committees on credentialing, ethics, regional affairs and research; publishes a newsletter and a membership list; bring EAP leaders together annually to share experiences and ideas.
Publications: The Source; Who's Who Directory
Founded: 1984

TRAINING PROGRAMS

EMPLOYEE ASSISTANCE PROGRAMS
Chamber of Commerce
801 North Fairfax Street
Alexandria, VA 22314
TEL: 703-549-1000
Credit: None
Sponsor: Alexandria Chamber of Commerce
Contact: Brenda Hunt, Chairman, Health Care Committee
Description: This forum focused on services available to employees, usually through programs that have come to be known as EAPs (Employee Assistance Programs). It defined an EAP as a program designed to provide employees with short-term counseling for problems with family, finances, substance abuse, and jobs. EAPs also serve as referral services - especially if the problem in question requires specialized care, connecting employees to

specialists. When this becomes necessary, the company's insurance usually picks up the tab.

During the course of the forum, the following conclusions, opinions, and facts surfaced based on the experiences of the presenters:
- The average company saves five dollars for every dollar they invest in an EAP.
- A company's bottom line is affected by the health and happiness of its workers.
- Up until a few years ago, most personal problems were ignored by employers until performance plunged so low that drastic action - usually dismissal - had to be taken.
- Managers are starting to realize that good workers are their most important resource.
- With an EAP, employers gain an ally in dealing with employees who are often absent or tardy - confidential counseling instead of the "pink slip."
- Businesses who subscribe to EAPs find that employees are making less use of sick leave and are taking less time off.
- Employers are holding on to valuable workers who otherwise might lose their jobs.
- It's a lot cheaper to rehabilitate someone than to hire and train a new worker.
- Despite the claimed advantages of EAPs, health experts concede that the idea has not yet caught on in the overall business community.
- EAPs have been used mostly by big companies, and are just now starting to trickle down.
- A drawback of EAPs is that some employees are reluctant to divulge personal information to anyone "being paid by the boss."
- EAP staff must be sure that any information given to employers must first be approved by the employee.

Among attendees was the director of AHEAD (Alexandria Health Employee Assistance Division), the assistance program of the Alexandria, Virginia, Community Services Board; a personnel administration and benefits service manager from a small northern Virginia community; a spokesman for an Atlanta-based health care and payroll management firm, and an outpatient coordinator of an addiction-treatment center in a small city. It was determined that the cost to the company to provide the program is $10 to $15 per employee.

BUSINESS/INDUSTRY INVOLVEMENT: EMPLOYMENT

NATIONAL/STATE ORGANIZATIONS

RENT-A-KID REFERRAL SERVICE
Citizens Committee on Youth
2147 Central Avenue
Cincinnati, OH 45214
TEL: 513-632-5200
Objectives: To give very young teenagers the opportunity to gain work experience, acquire references, and earn spending money; to provide homeowners and small businesses a convenient and reasonably-priced source of labor.
Services: Places youths between the ages of 14 and 16 who are enrolled in school; assigns Rent-A-Kids to their own communities to perform odd jobs such as housecleaning, leaf raking, lawn moving, flyer distribution, moving, gardening; allows lower than minimum wage (not less than $2.25/hour) where federal and state minimum provisions do not apply; conducts registration each spring via school counselors and community agencies; provides

services in Cincinnati area only, but sends detailed information about the program to any requesting individual or group.

INDIVIDUAL PROGRAM PROFILES

AIDS IN THE WORKPLACE
United Way of Central Maryland
22 Light Street
PO Box 1576
Baltimore, MD 21203-1576
TEL: 301-547-8000
Purpose: To encourage the business sector to focus on the AIDS issue.
Sponsor: United Way of Central Maryland
Contact: Dana Struke, Director of Workplace Services
Description: In 1988, the United Way brought together representatives from business and specialists from human resources, medical and legal fields to form a volunteer task force on the AIDS issue. From discussions of the kinds of information and assistance area businesses need to address AIDS in the workplace, the task force recommended an in-depth survey. One goal of the survey was to determine how many businesses had policies for employees with AIDS and/or employee AIDS-awareness programs.
Of the 450 businesses which responded to the survey, 84 percent said they did not have an AIDS policy in place and 76 percent said businesses should be involved with the AIDS issue. Half of the respondents said they would like assistance in developing an AIDS policy.
As a result of the survey, the United Way sponsored publication of an AIDS manual designed for businesses wanting practical information. The manual was developed by the Health Education Resource Organization with a $25,000 grant from the United Way. After the manual was published, the United Way held a follow-up conference for the business community.
According to the project's director, "Interacting with businesses about AIDS is a way of providing year-round communications about the disease. In the long run, we hope it will educate employees as well."
Publications: AIDS Manual for Businesses
Founded: 1988

CE-2
Tigard High School
PO Box 23059
Tigard, OR 97223
TEL: 503-684-2255
Purpose: To enable students to test their career choices by volunteering in organizations and agencies reflecting their interests.
Sponsor: Tigard High School
Contact: Garry J. Wagner
Description: An alternative program, *Career Education* - popularly called CE-2 - enables students of Tigard High School to spend a major portion of their time in the community at job sites. Sites are selected according to the students' career interests. The cooperation of employers across the community makes this program possible.
School time away from job sites is spent in the CE-2 learning center at the school. Rather than working in a group, such as a class, each student works on an individualized study program in keeping with career interests. This includes learning projects, journals, survival skills, and job site requirements.
Involving the community in the educational process has many benefits for all concerned. For the student the on-site exploratory activities develop basic skills, help students develop positive work habits and attitudes, foster students' desire to learn, and involves the students in designing their own educational programs.
Although learning plans for students are individualized, an

accountability system continually monitors student behavior. The CE-2 curriculum depends on imaginative use of community resources. Every student project has three facets: basic skills, life skills, and career development.
Upon completion of their site work, students receive credit toward graduation requirements.

HELPING HAND
United Way of Allegheny County & SW PA
200 Ross Street
PO Box 735
Pittsburgh, PA 15230-0735
TEL: 412-261-6010
Purpose: To respond to the needs of the unemployed.
Sponsor: Pittsburgh Steelers Football Club
Contact: L. Stanton Williams, Chief Volunteer Officer
Description: Families who once prospered working in the steel industry in western Pennsylvania are now jobless and struggling to put food on their tables. To respond to the needs of the unemployed, a project called *Helping Hand* was developed by the United Way of Allegheny County. The board president, who is also a director of *PPG Industries,* proposed a plan that would help families and individuals suffering as a result of the area's economic problems.
A *Helping Hand Task Force* was formed to run a one-month fund-raising drive completely separate from the annual United Way campaign. When funds were in hand, the program began distributing vouchers which could be redeemed at various distribution sites for goods and services, with the value of the vouchers depending on the size of the family. Vouchers could be redeemed for food, health care, and help with utility payments. Once the vouchers were redeemed, participating agencies submitted them to *Helping Hand* for reimbursement. At the same time, employment and financial counseling for individuals and families was made available.
A portion of the proceeds was allocated to food banks, health insurance companies, and counseling services, allowing more people to take advantage of the free help. In-kind services also were offered to the program, including an offer from *St. Francis Hospital* to give free medical care to the unemployed. Participants in the program received a catalog detailing the services offered at various social service agencies.
In addition to helping the unemployed, *Helping Hand* has assisted others in need. In response to a string of destructive tornadoes that struck western Pennsylvania, the board voted to allocate $20,000 from the fund to ease the financial crunch on the *Salvation Army* and the *American Red Cross.* To help raise money, collection containers were placed in *McDonald's* restaurants, and WTAE-TV hosted a successful day-long telethon. In addition, *Helping Hand* received grants from foundations and corporations, and individuals gave one-time cash or credit card donations.
Chairman of *Helping Hand* is the president of the *Pittsburgh Steelers Football Club,* and Vice Chairman is the international president of the *United Steelworkers of America.* The body of the Committee included representatives from labor, as well as United Way labor-relations specialists, who knew were help was needed most and how it could be delivered. Overall, the program represents a major community response to problems of people in need, bringing together a broad-based coalition of agencies and individuals dedicated to helping the unemployed.

HOUSTON EX-OFFENDER PROGRAM
National Alliance of Business/Houston
3637 West Alabama
Suite 340
Houston, TX 77027
TEL: 713-627-9600
Purpose: To help ex-offenders obtain immediate employment by preparing them for job-hunting.

Contact: George Trabing
Description: This program is designed to place as much responsibility as possible on the ex-offender himself or herself for future participation as a productive member of the community. Participants are not given jobs, but are provided with skills to find and keep a job.

The one-day workshops offer a five-hour instruction session on how to apply for and interview for a job, followed by a three-hour practice session in which trainees participate in simulated job interviews. Participants are expected to identify job-related skills in their own backgrounds, and set goals for themselves - in this way enhancing their self-confidence and motivation.

More than 100 volunteers assist NAB with the program, many of them making the crucial contacts by telephone with both potential students and potential employers. Others are involved in supervisory and management capacities.

Most participants are referred from individual Parole Board case officers, and by the local Department of Corrections. The majority of the participants come with work skills developed in the vocational, academic, and work experience programs of the correctional facilities.

The instruction is designed to highlight the initial telephone call and the interview itself. Also, instructors emphasize that a prison record is not necessarily a liability which cannot be overcome. Participants are told to re-emphasize their goals in the interview. The key elements to the success of the program are threefold:
- the practical value of the workshop material;
- the dedication and enthusiasm of the staff; and
- the Director's effort to maintain personal relationships with corrections, parole, and probation officials.

The long-term goal is to prepare ex-offenders to find and keep employment. The results of one program show that, of the 719 offenders enrolled, 583 found employment. Much of this success is attributable to the cooperation and direct involvement of local businesses, corporations, and governments. Also, all of the project funding comes from corporate contributions.

MASTER BUILDER GAME
SEE VOLUNTEERS: PROFESSIONALS

STUDENT VOLUNTEER/WORK PROJECT (SV/WP)
National Association of Partners in Education
601 Wythe Street
Suite 601
Alexandria, VA 22314
TEL: 703-836-4880
Purpose: To use volunteerism as a vehicle for providing students with the opportunity to develop, test and extend their interests, skills and talents; to apply the skills developed to paid job situations.
Sponsor: National Association of Partners in Education; Citibank; New York State General Accounting Service; National Alliance of Business
Contact: Carol Pierce
Description: Recognizing the problems low-achieving disadvantaged high school students are likely to encounter in seeking to enter the job market, the National School Volunteer Program of New York City developed a special project aimed at helping to offset these expected difficulties. The Student Volunteer/Work Project locates volunteer work placements for the students to help them develop marketable skills, provides career counseling for the volunteers, and exposes them to employment possibilities.

The student volunteers are placed in day care centers, hospitals, nursing homes, schools and museums. They are required to give a minimum of four hours a week. Each volunteer assignment is approached as if it were a paying job. Training is provided to help the student become proficient in the interviewing process, filling out applications, arranging for appointments, applying for working papers, writing resumes, and determining appropriate work behavior.

Adult volunteers from the School Volunteer Program provide basic skills development through one-to-one tutoring. In addition, school volunteers on released time from their companies provide one-to-one counseling in the area of career development - also serving as role models. The Volunteer Coordinator follows up on interviews and placements, contacts agencies for progress reports, makes site visits and requests student volunteer evaluations. References are maintained for each student to be used for future job applications. Monthly sessions are scheduled for sharing placement experiences for ongoing career awareness.

A challenging assignment for 20 student volunteers was to serve as volunteer job developers for the National Alliance of Business, and approach corporations for summer job pledges for themselves and fellow students. Student volunteers also participated in an employment workshop convened by the School Volunteer Program, the National Alliance of Business, and Citibank. A bank personnel administrator explained how to read want ads, fill out applications, and write resumes. New York State's General Accounting Service led a lecture series on economics to introduce the students to the financial realities of today's society.

Based on the total number of hours given to community service, students receive academic credit.

TEEN OPPORTUNITIES PROMOTE SUCCESS (TOPS)
Birmingham Area Alliance of Business
2027 First Avenue, North
Birmingham, AL 35203
TEL: 205-326-4153
Purpose: To develop jobs for teenaged youth.
Contact: C. Dowd Ritter, AmSouth Bank
Description: For summer 1989, The *Birmingham Area Alliance of Business* completed its most successful job development campaign for the TOPS (Teen Opportunities Promote Success) program in the organization's history. The program involved volunteer efforts of all companies in the *Alliance* as well as cooperation across the community.

To begin the program, a call went out for volunteer executives. A dozen local businesses loaned an executive each. Each executive worked full time for eight weeks. The volunteers developed more than 150 jobs for the youth in some 80 companies.

The success of the program is attributed to the ability of many companies to release an executive for full-time participation in the program. They came from utilities, medical, financial, retail, industry, and church sources, among others.
Founded: 1989

BUSINESS/INDUSTRY INVOLVEMENT: ENTREPRENEURSHIP

NATIONAL/STATE ORGANIZATIONS

DISTRIBUTIVE EDUCATION CLUBS OF AMERICA
1908 Association Drive
Reston, VA 22091
TEL: 703-860-5000
Objectives: To encourage private enterprise and economic awareness through student activities; to promote understanding and appreciation for the responsibilities of citizenship in a free, competitive enterprise system.
Services: Develops and provides instructional aids and activities, exposure to business leaders and practical experience in business; offers ideas for community betterment projects and support of

community activities; maintains a series of State and National Competitions designed to stimulate, motivate and reward student accomplishment, encourage career choices, strengthen occupational commitment; administers a scholarship program to stimulate, assist and encourage students toward higher education; administers student activity areas such as Leadership Development, Civic Participation, Public Information, Program Development, Career Conferences, and Advisor Aids; operates as a "co-curricular" program structured to serve as part of the classroom instructional program through DECA chapters (classes); offers workshops, seminars and publications for development of student competencies; supports state and regional conferences and the National Career Development Conference, which is attended by teachers, and business and industry representatives as well as the students.
Publications: New Dimensions; DECA Newsletter
Founded: 1946

JUNIOR ACHIEVEMENT (JA)
45 Clubhouse Drive
Colorado Springs, CO 80906
TEL: 303-540-8000
Objectives: To teach high school students how the American business system operates; to help them gain practical experience by running a small-scale business of their own.
Services: Enlists adult volunteers from business and industry to implement above objectives; guides 7000 student-run companies through its 254 franchised corporations across the country; publishes bimonthly magazine, annual National Board List, and other materials; convenes annual meeting.
Publications: Partners; Achiever
Founded: 1919

NAWBO SCHOLARSHIP FUND
SEE FUNDING/FUND-RAISING/RELATED SERVICES: BUSINESSES

INDIVIDUAL PROGRAM PROFILES

BUSINESS MANAGEMENT/JUNIOR ACHIEVEMENT
Fairfax County Schools
Vocational, Adult & Community Educ.
7423 Camp Alger Avenue
Falls Church, VA 22042
TEL: 703-698-0400
Purpose: To involve volunteers from business/industry in enabling high school students to run small businesses of their own while learning how the American business system operates.
Sponsor: Junior Achievement (JA); local business/industry; Fairfax County Schools
Contact: Beverly S. Dopler
Description: Guided by adult volunteers from business and industry, high school students in Fairfax County will set up businesses again this fall to produce jewelry, toys, lamps, ash trays, Christmas decorations, etc., or to provide services such as photography, secretarial, advertising and "fix-it." Others will produce newspapers, magazines, radio and TV shows, etc. Business/Industry volunteers work through the local Junior Achievement Corporation to guide the companies run by students. At the beginning of each semester JA staff members conduct orientation meetings in individual schools or, where practical, on an areawide basis, for participating teaches and school personnel. Participating students receive one-half credit per semester, and are required to spend 75 hours in the program as follows:
- Junior Achievement meeting time - 38
- Management training at sponsoring firms - 6
- Marketing of products and services - 20
- Tours of business establishments - 4
- Selected activities such as elementary program, preparation of written reports - 7

Sponsoring firms provide six hours of management training designed to teach students the principles of free enterprise and help them run their own miniature businesses. This enables the young people to see a place in free enterprise for themselves in the future.

Adult volunteers contact students who have completed application forms by phone and through a special mailing to discuss their interests and to follow-up on JA notification of the first company meeting. To maintain their standing in the class for credit purposes, the students must attend 85% of the company meetings, attend six out of eight Board of Directors' meetings, and be actively involved in a Junior Achievement company.

Fairfax County also hosts Project Business, a JA program geared to eighth or ninth grade students. Central to this program is the Volunteer Business Consultant, who leads one class each week in seven business topics including The Nature of Economics, The U.S. Market System, Money and Banking, and others. Each Project Business class is sponsored by a local business firm. Training for consultants and teachers is conducted by the JA Project Business staff. Materials and operating costs are covered by the sponsor, and are designed to develop student enthusiasm for business and economics, and as a "lead-in" to the primary JA program.

CHAMP BAKERY
SEE VOLUNTEERS: POLICE OFFICERS

GREEN LINE ACTION ASSOCIATION
Tuxedo Valet
1715 Seventh Street, NW
Washington, DC 20001
TEL: 202-232-5370
Purpose: To organize business owners affected by the developing metro system, and seek disaster relief to cover extensive loss of business.
Contact: Edward Archie, Owner
Description: When one business owner - operating in the Shaw neighborhood of Washington, DC, in a block that was rendered inaccessible by metro construction - saw his business fall by 50%, he began a process to seek fair and equitable treatment by the city of Washington, DC. His first step was to set up a merchants' organization reflecting the root of the problem, the *Green Line Action Association,* which attracted 33 merchants from the inaccessible area. This organization replaced the once thriving 135-member *Shaw Business and Professional Association.* The small self-help group seeks disaster relief "just like after a hurricane or earthquake."
They are fighting in the face of the opinion of the experts - that, even with help, they will not be able to continue. According to the director of the *Center for Washington Studies,* "Few owners of small businesses survive long disruptions and then stay around long enough to prosper from the changes." Rents skyrocket, and taxes for owners increase drastically when a subway line enters the community, he said.
Motivated by the fact that many of the businesses have been in the family for several generations, the *Green Line Action Association* disagrees. "We are seeing new owners come in when former owners have given up and left, and they expect to get back their investment when the Green Line is completed," he said.
To respond, the City has built two parking lots and a sidewalk to the stores. Although the director of Metro Construction regrets the 90-day closing of the street, he maintains that the five-year subway project had reached a point where safety was paramount, since "running sands" were being encountered - shifting soil that jeopardized the stability of the street overhead during tunneling. Although the Association is optimistic, by mid-1990 the question

of disaster relief was not resolved. Members feel that the important thing is that they have joined in a volunteer effort to help maintain long-standing businesses in the Shaw community.

BUSINESS/INDUSTRY INVOLVEMENT: ENVIRONMENT

NATIONAL/STATE ORGANIZATIONS

ECONET
Stanford University
PO Box AA
Stanford University, CA 94305
TEL: 415-321-1990 (CA); 202-347-1990 (DC)
Objectives: To present coordinated themes for *Earth Day 1990* and beyond.
Services: Econet is a system developed by Stanford University to reach out to all parts of the world with ideas for participation in *Earth Day 1990 and Beyond: Launching a Decade of the Environment* at the local, regional, national, and international levels.
Some of the coordinated themes include planting a billion trees; participating in urban parades and public gatherings; coordinating with school and college teach-ins; educating business and government leaders; participating in clean-up and restoration projects; and "wearing something green." All but the latter are expected to have lasting effect and consciousness-raising value into the next century.
To facilitate involvement across the country, the University opened an east coast office in Washington, DC, called *Earth Day 1990,* a part of *Econet,* which will continue beyond 1990 to help monitor progress. The DC office was launched with an all-day rally on the Mall on April 22 and another the next day at the PEPCO plant in the northeast quadrant of the city.
Numerous environmental organizations have joined with the University in this effort, including the Natural Resource Defense Council, National Audubon Society, United Auto Workers, Earth Island Institute, Environmental Action, Friends of the Earth, Sierra Club, Wilderness Society, National Wildlife Federation, Rainforest Action Network, Renew America, Environmental Defense Fund, Izaak Walton League, Rocky Mountain Institute, Better World Society, Trust for Public Land, Earth First, World Resources Institute, and Hewlett Packard.
Sponsor: United Auto Workers
Contact: Denis Hayes (CA); James Day (DC)

INDIVIDUAL PROGRAM PROFILES

FIGHTING DIRTY!
PhilaPride
123 South Broad
Philadelphia, PA 19107
TEL: 215-545-5823
Purpose: To rally the community to help restore the reputation of a once clean, historic Philadelphia.
Sponsor: KYW-TV
Contact: Paula Young, Executive Director
Description: With the help of *The Daily News, KYW-TV,* the city *Streets and Licenses & Inspection Departments,* and citizens, *PhilaPride* has launched a campaign that will eliminate the new name some people are giving to Philadelphia - *Philthydelphia.* Using innovative terminology to attract attention, the program

calls on neighborhood people, community volunteers, businesses, shop owners, and individuals to join the nonprofit litter-prevention organization in "fighting dirty." Teams are dubbed "MOD (Monarchs of Dirt) Squad" and asked to be on the lookout for *DMZs (Disgusting Mucky Zones)* and report them to the "Top MOD (Marquis of Debris)." This is done by completing a reporting form printed in the daily paper, shooting a videotape of the scene, or taking photographs and mailing the report to *KYW-TV.* Some videos are shown on the TV program.
One victory for a persistent MOD squad was getting the city to clean up a city-owned area that was being used as a dumping ground. After the long battle, "dump watchers" were assigned to stake out the lot and send potential dumpers packing. After chasing away three or four violators, "the word must have spread and they haven't dumped here since."
An outgrowth of the initial neighborhood effort resulted in the volunteers going into other neighborhoods and instructing people on how to conduct dump serveillance and record vital information. The illegal dumping problem is the most troublesome, by far, according to the volunteers. In addition to tires and the usual junk, large appliances, like refrigerators, are dumped at illegal dumping sites. However, with volunteer MOD squads moving across the area from neighborhood to neighborhood, getting license numbers, and turning information over to the police, significant improvement is seen - especially since the word has spread that it is a misdemeanor offense which could result in fines ranging from $2,500 to $10,000.
According to a Streets Department official, "There's nothing so unusual about the approach. It's just a matter of getting organized and spreading the word." *PhilaPride* adds, "Just send in your DMZ reports. The Marquis and his court will do the rest!"

HONEYWELL NEIGHBORHOOD IMPROVEMENT PROGRAM
Honeywell Foundation
Honeywell Plaza
Minneapolis, MN 55408
TEL: 612-870-6411
Purpose: To provide housing choices to people whose alternatives are restricted, and to improve the appearance of the neighborhood.
Sponsor: Honeywell Foundation
Contact: Ray Frellsen
Description: With its general offices located in a relatively small geographic area, Honeywell noted that some 500 families in one neighborhood of this area did not have adequate income to keep their homes in good repair. To assist in meeting this need, Honeywell collaborated with local voluntary organizations and local government units to establish the Neighborhood Improvement Program (NIP), which is 100% funded by corporate contributions.
At the outset, the Program was designed as a two-pronged effort - housing improvement and more effective use of open land.
Since the Neighborhood Improvement Program began in 1971, Honeywell built or renovated 54 living units in the Minneapolis neighborhood surrounding the Honeywell general offices. The company purchased single-family homes, duplexes and fourplexes, then rehabilitated and resold them primarily to people who live in the neighborhood.
The Foundation, acting as a non-profit sponsor, acquires the buildings at a markdown from the Minneapolis Community Development Agency, then renovates and sells them at prices neighborhood residents are able to pay.
In addition to the rehabilitation and resale program, Honeywell assisted more than 100 owners with exterior improvements to their properties. Owner assistance funds have been used for siding repair, fences, cement work, windows, doors, porch repair, roofing, landscaping and paint.
The combination of renovation and repair has proven to be an ideal method of assuring total neighborhood improvement instead

of the disappointing "spotty" effect that is evident when only one or the other is implemented.

In 1978, seven years after the Program began, Honeywell completed the companion phase of the ongoing Program - an eight-acre park. Honeywell Plaza Park is landscaped with trees, flowers, shrubs, pieces of sculpture, a waterfall and reflecting pools. Open during the daylight hours, seven days a week, it was built for the enjoyment of Honeywell employees and neighborhood residents.

A number of activities are held in the park on an ongoing basis. These activities have included free summer concerts by the Minnesota Orchestra, and arts and crafts fairs.

Among the benefits noted by the Foundation in addition to the aesthetic value of the Program are: the rapport developed with other organizations; increased communication with the public; and the Foundation's new understanding of the community through the exchange of information that takes place on a continuing basis. NIP is part of Honeywell's overall plan to help enhance growth and development in the neighborhood by "making changes that are real and can be seen and felt." The Phillips Neighborhood Improvement Association has presented Honeywell with two awards for its work in the neighborhood: a Special Service Award and the Good Neighbor Award.

PERFORMANCE CONTRACTING
United Way of Wyoming Valley
9 East Market Street
Wilkes-Barre, PA 18711-0351
TEL: 717-829-6711
Purpose: To reduce expenses involved in energy consumption.
Sponsor: Exxon
Contact: Charles J. Reynolds, Jr., President
Description: Six volunteer organizations in Wilkes-Barre have pooled their energy-saving potential by *performance contracting.* This is a method that allows agencies to voluntarily come together in order to take advantage of a plan to finance conservation measures with no capital investment.

The agencies jointly enter into a contract with the *National Energy Management Institute (NEMI)* and receive $250,000 worth of energy-saving improvements on their buildings. In return, the agencies use the money they save on energy bills to reimburse NEMI for the energy-conserving improvements ranging from roof insulation to high efficiency boilers and energy-management systems.

Exxon funded the project, which was developed by *United Way of America* and the *Alliance to Save Energy.* According to the Alliance chairman, who is also a U.S. Congressman, "United Way-supported agencies nationwide could save $250 million annually on energy bills through conservation."

SOCIETY BANK/WOLF CREEK ASSOCIATION PARTNERSHIP
Society Bank
Bellbrook, OH 45305
TEL: 513-848-6111
Purpose: To emphasize the bank's commitment to the community through volunteer effort and community partnership.
Sponsor: Society Bank
Contact: Anna Vasilakos, Chairwoman
Description: Society Bank's Community Affairs Department and the Wolf Creek Association have become partners in community service with a commitment to make Wolf Creek a better place in which to live. Wolf Creek is one of the lowest income areas in the city, according to a bank official, with an average yearly income of $7,000.

The first project involved paint brushes and lawn mowers as volunteers from the bank and the association joined forces to spruce up the neighborhood. In addition to cutting grass and clearing debris from three vacant lots, the bank selected two

homes in need of paint owned by senior citizens who could not afford to paint them.

The Society Bank Community Affairs Officer requested two volunteers from each branch office, and received many more - in one instance, all of the employees of a branch. Some Society Bank managers came from as far away as Waynesville, Bellbrook and Fairborn to participate in the Wolf Creek neighborhood cleanup. Nearby Pilgrim Church served lunch for the volunteers.

The cleanup project is just the beginning of the bank's commitment to Wolf Creek, according to a Society officer. A housing development project is also in the works. The bank spent $27,000 to conduct a feasibility study on housing needs in the community. The housing will be in the low- to moderate-income range. Other volunteer projects will be mounted by the partnership as needs arise.

VOLUNTEERS IN PARKS (VIP)
SEE BUSINESS/INDUSTRY INVOLVEMENT: RECREATION/SPORTS

BUSINESS/INDUSTRY INVOLVEMENT: FAMILIES

INDIVIDUAL PROGRAM PROFILES

CHRISTMAS CLEARING HOUSE
The Voluntary Action Center
2125 East South Boulevard
PO Box 11044
Montgomery, AL 36116-0044
TEL: 205-285-0006
Purpose: To provide gifts, food and clothing to indigent families at Christmas time.
Contact: Doci Haslam
Description: The Christmas Clearing House was established in Montgomery, Alabama in 1980. The Clearing House is a central file of families in need who are not able to provide the traditional gifts, food and clothing for their loved ones at Christmas time. These names are placed in the files by the large service providers such as Salvation Army, Pensions and Security and Catholic Social Services.

To be included in the Clearing House, each family must file an application and must be willing to document income, expenses, etc. When the families are registered, the VAC starts a blitz of publicity and asks the clubs, churches, businesses, organizations and individuals to help these families.

In 1980 more than 12,000 people were served and more than 5,000 volunteers participated. In 1981 again more than 12,000 were served and more than 6,000 volunteers gave 53,360 hours. In 1982, 18,000 people were served and approximately 7,000 volunteers were involved.

The Clearing House was established with two goals in mind:
- That more needy people could be served at Christmas.
- That duplication of giving be eliminated.

These goals have been accomplished each year.

Funding for operating the Clearing House has been furnished by the Presidents Council of Montgomery and the Junior League of Montgomery. In 1983 it was funded by the Kiwanis Club of Montgomery. A part-time employee will be added this year. The Clearing House funds are totally separate from the VAC operating budget.

A very important part of the Clearing House is the Christmas Clearing House Fund. A local radio station sponsors this and arrangements are made with a local bank for direct deposits to be made to the fund. It is most successful. In 1981, $8,249 was raised; in 1982, $10,480 was raised.

The Clearing House serves as an example of bringing a community together for a common cause. It spreads the spirit of cooperation.
Founded: 1980

BUSINESS/INDUSTRY INVOLVEMENT: FUNDING

NATIONAL/STATE ORGANIZATIONS

AMERICAN ASSOCIATION FOR CORPORATE CONTRIBUTIONS
SEE FUNDING/FUND-RAISING/RELATED SERVICES

INDIVIDUAL PROGRAM PROFILES

BUSINESS/COMMUNITY INVOLVEMENT PROGRAM
Pies On The Run
Barcroft Plaza
6347 Columbia Pike
Falls Church, VA 22041
TEL: 703-941-A-PIE (2743)
Purpose: To demonstrate to the community that even a new, small business can be responsive in some way right at the start.
Contact: Linda Ambrus, President, or Christina Scheib, Vice President
Description: "One of the first things we did when we opened in Falls Church was to have gift certificates printed to be ready when a community group needed support for a program. Although necessarily a small effort at first, we were very anxious to become part of the community in which we operate." The philosophy of the owner of *Pies On The Run* is that, no matter how small, any business can contribute to the community.

The nature of the business itself suggests concern for the community. *Pies On The Run* emphasizes nutrition, no difficult task since the Vice President in charge of Operations received a degree in nutrition and chemistry from *Seton Hall College* and had planned to become a dietician. The business is aimed at customers who want homestyle meals but don't have the time to cook for themselves. The pies are made with fresh ingredients, without preservatives, and with very little salt. The small company is committed to its employees (seven full time and 20 part time), creating an atmosphere of respect, honesty, fun and safety while helping employees to achieve personal goals.

The community involvement program is expected to grow as the business grows. In the meantime, the new company has involved itself in the community in several ways:
- During the Christmas holidays and January (only two months after it opened) *Pies On The Run* donated 200 pies to *Martha's Table* to help feed the homeless and hungry. Leftover food also has been donated on other occasions.
- In March, over 50 pies were donated to Q107's *Freedom Drive* to help feed the homeless and the hungry.
- In January and February, *Pies On The Run* and *Holmes Intermediate School* work study program for learning disabled children did a joint marketing project - including passing out flyers to local homes and businesses.
- The Pies On The Run owner has visited several local high schools and colleges to discuss the risks and rewards of being an entrepreneur, marketing, and general business issues.

In addition to the above, when *Pies On The Run* is ready for

"neighborhood marketing" (door-hangers, flyers, etc.), the option to distribute the materials is given to a local youth group to provide funds for its scholarship programs, materials acquisitions, team trips, etc. According to the founder, "We have a commitment to the community to give back to those who are less fortunate." The immediate involvement of the company upon opening its first business establishment reflects that statement.

SAFE HOUSE
PO Box 3426
Kingsport, TN 37664
TEL: 615-246-1619
Purpose: To provide emergency shelter for battered women and their children.
Sponsor: Corporate and private donations
Contact: Gail Myers, Executive Director
Description: SAFE House opened in December 1982 as a twenty-four-hour, short-term shelter for battered women and their children. Services include comfort, food, counseling and guidance through the helping system (food stamp, legal aid, medical attention, mental health counseling, etc.). SAFE House is a non-profit, state chartered corporation governed by a board of directors of thirty men and women representatives of the community. Presently, funding is through private and corporate contributions. The goal: to become an agency of Kingsport Area Community Chest plus other area Chests.

Professional staff discusses options with each batterd woman - all decisions being left to the guests - with hope that battering victims will discover their right to live without violence. Paid staff consists of an Executive Director and a House Manager.
- **Area Served** - SAFE House is a regional service and has provided shelter for women and children from Kentucky, West Virginia, and Tennessee since December 1982.
- **Volunteer Staff** - At present, fifteen volunteers provide assistance as Client Advocates, Child Nurturers, Transporters, Office Assistants and Menu Planners/Shoppers. Additional volunteers are being recruited.
- **Volunteer Experience** - Each volunteer receives training and ongoing orientation plus group discussions at will.

BUSINESS/INDUSTRY INVOLVEMENT: HANDICAPPED

NATIONAL/STATE ORGANIZATIONS

MAINSTREAM
1030 Fifteenth Street, NW
Suite 1010
Washington, DC 20005
TEL: 202-898-1400
Objectives: To encourage increased employment opportunities for handicapped Americans; to provide employers, national handicap organizations, federal regulators and other groups with the information that will help mainstream handicapped individuals into the workplace.
Services: Designs and coordinates national demonstration programs that involve handicap organizations and employers in making the training and placement of more disabled persons a reality in a specific metropolitan area; gives companies training in handicap awareness, interviewing and recruiting, job analysis, information on legal incentives for employing handicapped persons; presents forum for employers to discuss their affirmative action concerns and efforts with representatives of national handicap groups; publishes a bimonthly, subscription newsletter,

In the Mainstream, that reports on the legal and practical issues of employing disabled persons; also publishes specific issue brochures and reports; maintains a resource center on handicap employment issues and serves as an information source on handicap employment, disabled individuals, disability service providers and governmental officials.
Founded: 1975

NATIONAL ORGANIZATION ON DISABILITY (NOD)
SEE COMMUNICATIONS & PUBLIC RELATIONS: HANDICAPPED

TRAINING PROGRAMS

WHEELCHAIR RACE COMMUNICATIONS SERVICES
Amateur Radio Emergency Service (ARES)
American Radio Relay League
225 Main Street
Newington, CT 06111
TEL: 203-666-1541
Purpose: To provide radio communications for the "Wheelchair Race of Champions."
Sponsor: Ford Motor Company; Hardee's Restaurants; American Radio Relay League (groups from Winchester, Frederick County, Loudoun County, Fairfax County, and Arlington in Virginia, and District of Columbia)
Contact: David Sumner, Executive Vice President
Description: Ham radio operators are best known for their response and assistance in disasters. They are not CBers. Ham Radio exists primarily for service to the public through emergency service. Licensed by the FCC, they are called in by local, state and federal governments to help in communications emergencies. This makes them a national resource in times of need.
In the annual wheelchair races, HAM operators find that their communications skills are sharpened by using such events for practice and exercise. Skills needed to communicate during special events are similar to those required during an actual emergency. They communicate using radio frequencies normally useful only for short distances by talking through "repeaters" or automatic relay stations, set up, operated, and maintained by the HAMs. These repeater stations must also be licensed by the FCC.
Amateur Radio Emergency Service (ARES) groups from Winchester, Frederick County, Loudoun County, Fairfax County, and Arlington in Virginia, and the District of Columbia provided communications for this first annual 54-mile Race of Champions.

INDIVIDUAL PROGRAM PROFILES

BLUE RIDGE TO THE WHITE HOUSE: WHEELCHAIR RACE OF CHAMPIONS
National Wheelchair Athletic Association
1604 East Pikes Peak Avenue
Colorado Springs, CO 80909-5619
TEL: 303-697-8330
Purpose: To identify United States Olympic representatives for wheelchair long distance road racing.
Sponsor: Ford Motor Company
Description: The first annual "Race of Champions" for long distance wheelchair racers was held in May 1989 in Virginia and Washington, DC. The ten top wheelchair road racing athletes in the world compete for $20,000 in prizes in a grueling, double marathon (approximately 54 miles) endurance race to identify United States Olympics representatives. The race is organized in cooperation with the Mid Atlantic region of the National Wheelchair Athletic Association.
The 1989 race began at 8:00 a.m. in Purcelville, Virginia, and took

the racers along some of Virginia's most scenic countryside, then into Washington, DC, past the national monuments and reflecting pool to the finish line at the Washington Monument. The estimated time of arrival for the winning racer was 12 noon, only four hours later.
Joining many other dignitaries at the finish line was Virginia's Senator Charles Robb and former White House Press Secretary James Brady, as well as members of Congress from each racer's locality and state.
Proceeds from the Blue Ridge to the White House Wheelchair Race of Champions benefits Grafton School (a residential educational facility for seriously handicapped children) and Shalom et Benedictus (a drug and alcohol treatment facility for young adolescents).
The course for the race was laid out by a wheelchair racer - an executive at the Grafton School and the Race of Champions organizer - who tested the course by "running" it himself a month before the event.
Publications: Blue Ridge to the White House Wheelchair Race of Champions

DATA SYSTEMS UNLIMITED
SEE BUSINESS/INDUSTRY INVOLVEMENT: OFFENDERS

KAISER ROLL
Lincoln Del/Storer Cable Communications
4401 West South 80th Street
Bloomington, MN 55420
TEL: 612-888-0222
Purpose: To provide a sports activity for the handicapped while raising funds for nonprofit organizations that specialize in physical rehabilitation.
Sponsor: Lincoln Del/Storer Cable Communications
Contact: Daniel Berenberg or George Stanfield
Description: More than 200 volunteers assist the program sponsor of this event in drawing attention to handicapped athletes, and raising funds to support rehabilitation efforts of three nonprofit health organizations. They help to stage five and ten kilometer races for handicapped and other athletes. Competition is held for able-bodied runners and wheelchair racers.
The program is administered through the Kaiser Roll Foundation, with the goal of making it the prime event of its kind in the country. Among support activities obtained by the Foundation is the tape-delayed cable coverage provided by Storer Cable. Through this community-wide public awareness effort, maximum community awareness is attained.
Volunteers do much more than provide direct delivery of service. They are involved in supervisory, management, public relations, fund-raising, advocacy and self-help capacities.
Beneficiary organizations of the first program were Sister Kenny Institute, Vinland National Center and Courage Center. Although more than two-thirds of project funds come from the corporate sponsor, the balance is raised by the volunteers/staff and/or received in goods and services from across the community. Given the success of the initial effort, Kaiser Roll has become an annual event.

PATOWMACK HERBAL FARM: SUMMER EMPLOYMENT FOR THE HANDICAPPED
Association for Retarded Citizens
Loudoun County Chapter
15 East Market Street
Leesburg, VA 22075
TEL: 703-777-1939
Purpose: To provide jobs for the handicapped while helping the small farmer to find affordable workers.
Sponsor: Patowmack Herbal Farm
Contact: Barbara June Appelgren, Director

Description: When a small farmer found the going rate of $6.00 for farm workers to be too high for her budget, she called the Loudoun County Association for Retarded Citizens. She had heard that advocates for the handicapped are always looking for summer work for them. Although the Association had never placed handicapped teenagers in private sector jobs, the Director felt it was time to experiment with a small group. Six mentally- and physically-handicapped youngsters were sent to Patowmack Herbal Farm to plant, pick and weed garlic crops. The youth were selected because they had demonstrated a high degree of independence. Handicaps ranged from mental retardation and emotional problems to spina bifida and brittle bones. When they first arrived at the farm, much time had to be spent to show them what to do. They were uncertain of themselves and exhibited a low tolerance for teasing, often getting into scraps. They took frequent water breaks, which tended to become times for "goofing off." Some of them had done yard chores, but had only a vague idea of what it means to work regularly - most never having worked a six-hour-long period before. However, with much time and patience freely given by the owners, they were completing assigned tasks, anticipating the next chores and avoiding friction.

For five weeks they worked through muggy days in muddy fields to harvest about 8,000 elephant garlic bulbs - a mild form of garlic prized by chefs which rots if left in the ground too long. In addition to the harvesting, assignments included sorting garlic, weeding sage, mowing lawns, and producing labels on a copying machine and pasting them on vinegar bottles. They were allowed to choose their tasks. At the same time, they reveled in the fresh air, learned about herbs, and "befriending chickens."

Awareness that what they were doing was the way the farm owners made money turned out to be an important concept to the handicapped teens. Also, their own paychecks, at $4.00 an hour, helped them understand what it means to "earn a living." And the parents of the teens, realizing that they will not always be around to support the youngsters, were grateful for the opportunity provided the youngsters to learn an important fact - "if you don't work, you don't get paid."

The Association's coordinator at the job site sees this experience as a major step toward independent living and believes that each of the youngsters in the program will be able to live in a supervised apartment setting - with a couple of them not requiring the supervision at all. She cited a bed and breakfast inn near Winchester, Virginia, that is run entirely by retarded people and feels that people like the owners of Patowmack Herbal Farm help speed the process toward independence for the handicapped.

An added pleasure was to witness the feelings the youth had developed for the Furnace Mountain farm as a special place, and their intentions to return.

SAN FRANCISCO SPECIAL OLYMPICS WINTER GAMES

c/o Shaklee Corporation
444 Market Street
San Francisco, CA 94111
TEL: 415-221-6575

Purpose: To promote physical fitness and provide an experience in skill building and increased confidence for mentally handicapped participants.

Sponsor: Shaklee Corporation

Description: The San Francisco Special Olympics Games began at Soda Springs in 1977 when only five San Francisco athletes could compete. The raw talent and enthusiasm displayed by these five athletes warranted that the winter games program be expanded and become a permanent part of the Special Olympics program. Members of the San Francisco Special Olympics Board approached the Shaklee Corporation for the help needed to expand the program. The Shaklee Corporation agreed to become the corporate sponsor of the Winter Games Program.

In the years following, the Winter Games Program has seen an even more rapid growth pattern. In 1979, 25 athletes and eight

chaperones were active in the California State Special Olympics Winter Games at Dodge Ridge. This represented an increase of five times the original number. Since 1982, over 100 athletes participated in winter activities.

The surrounding communities in the Tahoe area became involved, and volunteer ski instructors and other assistance came from local ski hills, ski shops, and nurses from the community hospital. Equipment was donated by the Boreal Ridge Ski Area, and owners of demonstration vans loaned equipment from various manufacturers.

Besides over ten years of underwriting the costs of this program, Shaklee Corporation has made available many sincere and dedicated personnel to assist as chaperones and to help in the training and supervision of the athletes. These employees volunteer as part of the Shaklee Volunteer Employee Program, SERVE. Also made available to each athlete has been a sports bag or backpack of Shaklee products, including energy bars and skin care products. Official winter games uniforms for the athletes were obtained through Shaklee donations. The official uniform consists of a cap, vest, goggles, after-ski boots, gloves, thermal underwear and gaiters.

The San Francisco Special Olympics is staffed by one paid Executive Director and many volunteers from both the sponsoring corporation and the community. Volunteers are involved in supervisory, management, and public relations activities as well as in training and supervision of the athletes and as chaperones. The programs are coordinated through the Recreation and Parks Department. Ninety percent of the funding comes from the sponsoring corporation with the remaining 10% received in the form of in-kind contributions, both goods and services.

Founded: 1977

TRAINING FOR DISABLED STUDENTS

Roy Rogers Restaurants
Marriott Corporation
1 Marriott Drive
Washington, DC 20058
TEL: 202-380-0000
FAX: 301-897-5181

Purpose: To provide job training and placement for disabled students.

Sponsor: Fairfax County Public Schools

Contact: Robert R. Spillane, Superintendent of Schools

Description: Training personnel from *Roy Rogers Restaurants* are being "loaned" to the *S. John Davis Center of Fairfax County Public Schools* to train disabled students in various aspects of food service. This loan of executives is the result of an agreement between the Restaurant chain and the school system. Students at the Falls Church center are selected for training by Davis Center staff, interviewed by Roy Rogers representatives, and approved for employment by both parties.

Roy Rogers provides equipment, utensils, food products, and training personnel to the Davis Center, while Fairfax County provides seminars to selected management-level employees of Roy Rogers in the day-to-day supervision and instruction of disabled individuals.

Students complete job applications and are interviewed by their prospective managers. Assignments are made as close to students' homes as possible. The training operates on a two- to three-week cycle, with the length of each student's training based on individual performance. Each cycle involves four to six students. After successfully completing the training, each student is assigned to the previously-selected restaurant. Job coaches are provided on-site by the school if necessary. Transportation needs are the responsibility of the Davis Center.

Job development categories addressed by the volunteer trainers include: food preparation worker, salad bar preparation and maintenance worker, deep-fryer cook, and dining room attendant. In the summer of 1989, the program involved about a dozen students who successfully made the transition from training to job. The program was expanded in September of the same year, and continues to grow.

WALKAMERICA
SEE FUNDING/FUND-RAISING/RELATED SERVICES: WALKS/RACES

BUSINESS/INDUSTRY INVOLVEMENT: HEALTH

NATIONAL/STATE ORGANIZATIONS

LEAVE BANK
US/OPM - Office of Information
1900 E Street, NW
Washington, DC 20006
TEL: 202-632-5582
Objectives: To enable workers to donate and receive annual leave for personal emergencies after their own leave is exhausted.
Services: Offers a leave-sharing program "along the lines of a blood bank;" enables workers to donate and receive annual leave for crisis situations when their own leave is exhausted; operates leave banks in six agencies - Internal Revenue Service, Environmental Protection Agency, Defense Nuclear Agency, Farm Credit Administration, National Gallery of Art, and Occupational Safety and Health Commission; enables transfer of leave to another employee designated as a needy recipient; operates under the *Employees Leave Act of 1987,* created when an employee contacted his congressman about a friend who did not have enough leave for an emergency situation; plans a review of the program on October 31, 1993, to determine success/continuation.
Sponsor: US/OPM - Office of Personnel Management
Contact: John P. Cahill, Specialist

INDIVIDUAL PROGRAM PROFILES

COMMUNITY PARTNERS PROGRAM*
Robert Wood Johnson Foundation
Mid-Atlantic Regional Council
20 West Ninth Street
Kansas City, MO 64105
TEL: 816-474-4240
Purpose: To promote improved health services to the medically underserved through implementation of low cost, largely self-supporting neighborhood health centers.
Sponsor: Robert Wood Johnson Foundation
Contact: Jean G. Bacon
Description: Recognizing that responding to the health care needs of the elderly requires a multi-year strategy based on extensive community collaboration and support, the Mid-Atlantic Regional Council, in collaboration with the Robert Wood Johnson Foundation, initiated the Community Partners Program.
Based on the overall health care strategy for the elderly developed by the Mid-Atlantic Regional Council (MARC), the following assumptions provide the foundation for the strategy of the Community Partners Program design:
- Health service needs vary by level of functional status. Healthy elderly need different forms of health services than the moderately or severely impaired.
- Both preventive and treatment-oriented services must exist for the healthy, declining, and frail population groups.

- Health services must be made available in more flexible settings to encourage accessibility.
- Health services capacities should be based upon projections of future need, rather than documentation of the past problems.

Emphasis for development of improved care for the well elderly is almost exclusively on prevention-oriented services. In the case of the declining elderly, prevention emphasis is maintained, but as a supplement to improvement of non-institutional treatment services. For the frail elderly, the emphasis is on development of effective treatment services in both the institutional and non-institutional settings.
Fifteen volunteers assist the five full-time and five part-time staff members. The volunteers are involved in supervisory and project management roles as well as in the direct service capacity. In addition to individual volunteers, project leaders initiate coalitions with other organizations, corporations, and local government units to effect the widest possible community participation.
All of the project's funding comes from foundation grants.

BUSINESS/INDUSTRY INVOLVEMENT: HOMELESS

TRAINING PROGRAMS

GIVE ME SHELTER: DESIGNS FOR URBAN SURVIVAL
SEE TRAINING/CONFERENCES/TEACHING: HOMELESS

INDIVIDUAL PROGRAM PROFILES

CONTINENTAL HOMELESS ASSISTANCE PROGRAM
Continental Airlines
Western Division
1605 California Street
Denver, CO 80202
TEL: 303-398-3000
Purpose: To provide funds for homeless programs in the Colorado area.
Sponsor: Continental Airlines
Contact: James Bacon, Vice President, Western Division
Description: In summer 1989, through its project to help the homeless and hungry, the western division of Continental Airlines presented $30,000 to a project designed to coordinate homeless programs in Colorado. A portion of the funds ($5,000) is earmarked for a planned Denver mission by Mother Theresa, who indicated in a spring 1989 visit that her *Missionary Sisters of Charity* wants to open a Denver mission.
The program was funded by the airline through coupon sales to business customers over a 60-day period. The airline backed up the ticket sales with numerous full-page newspaper advertisements.
In addition to charting its own public service course, and improving its image, the airline looks for "win-win" situations in which it can both help charities and save money for its business customers.
The presentation ceremonies at *Holy Ghost Church,* where the founder of the coordinated program serves as pastor, drew leaders of ten of the groups in the project - representing thousands of volunteers, including the *Salvation Army, Volunteers of America,* the *Mennonite Urban Ministry* and a number of Catholic charities. According to the founder, many corporations have talked about helping the needy, but Continental is the first to act. He added, "Someone has to bridge the gap between those who have and those who do not. We have to keep trying."

Continental's contribution to the homeless brought to $80,000 the amount funneled by the airline into 26 Colorado charitable agencies through its discounted airline coupon program.

HELP THE HOMELESS MILLION DOLLAR SHOOTOUT
SEE FUNDING/FUND-RAISING/RELATED SERVICES:
HOMELESS

OPERATION COVER UP
SEE VOLUNTEERS: OLDER PERSONS

OUTINGS FOR HOMELESS CHILDREN
Columbus Zoo
990 Riverside Drive
Columbus, OH 43221
TEL: 614-645-3550
Purpose: To provide a cultural experience and "some fun" for children at homeless shelters and their families.
Sponsor: Columbus Zoo
Contact: Barbara Boatwright, Docent
Description: Sponsored by local business/industry, a trip to the Columbus Zoo provided diversion for hundreds of homeless children and their families. The trip included admission to Wyandot Lake, an amusement area, following the zoo tour.
Sponsors arranged for bus pickups at designated stops serving six homeless shelter programs, provided 230 chicken lunches, meat, beverages and salads for a picnic at the zoo, disposable diapers, baby food in jars, toys, coloring books and crayons, and prizes for games the children played while at the picnic, as well as volunteers to serve as escorts and guides.
Since many other volunteer groups are working very hard to meet the basic needs of the residents of the shelters, the sponsors felt someone had to reach out to provide a little fun in the process.
The program is expected to be a periodic, ongoing recreation event for shelter residents in the area.
Founded: 1989

SPARE CHANGE PROJECT
SEE FUNDING/FUND-RAISING/RELATED SERVICES:
HOMELESS

BUSINESS/INDUSTRY INVOLVEMENT: HOUSING

NATIONAL/STATE ORGANIZATIONS

LOW-INCOME APARTMENTS PROGRAM
SEE VOLUNTEERS: CHURCH/SYNAGOGUE MEMBERS

MORTGAGE BURNING FUND
SEE FUNDING/FUND-RAISING/RELATED SERVICES:
HOUSING

INDIVIDUAL PROGRAM PROFILES

COMMUNITY BETTERMENT PROGRAM
Carondelet Community Betterment Federation
6408 Michigan Avenue
St. Louis, MO 63111
TEL: 314-752-6339

Purpose: To make Carondelet a better place in which to live, by updating properties and improving the quality of life for those who need assistance.
Sponsor: Carondelet Community Betterment Federation (CCBF)
Contact: Sister Marie Charles Buford
Description: The Carondelet Community Better Foundation (CCBF) operates several programs, the largest being a House Repair Program for Senior Persons living in the service area. Criteria for participation in the program are:
- at least 60 years of age;
- property owner;
- live in service area; and
- document income level.

With an executive director, a volunteer manager, and a staff of four, CCBF completes a minimum of 130 house repair jobs for senior persons. Such jobs consist of any type of house repairs, including windows, painting, replacement of total porches (front or back), building ramps for handicapped persons, concrete repairs, roof repairs, some small tuckpointing jobs. Interior work includes plastering, painting, wall-papering, panelling, flooring replacement or new, door repairs, plumbing, installation of water heaters, basement waterproofing, replacement of stairs, etc.
Through this program, now in its sixth year, property values have improved; senior persons have been assisted to remain in their homes, upkeep their properties and avoid city citations; and community housing stock has improved.
The program also acts as an incentive program. Annually, from 80 to 190 other property owners have improved their own properties since this program began. This was not happening previously. Older houses are also being purchased by younger families for rehabilitation and improvements. Other programs by CCBF are:
- operates a Senior Center;
- provides social services to homebound elderly;
- publishes a newsletter;
- sponsors a businessmen's group; and
- sponsors youth programs in the summer.

Publications: CCBF Newsletter
Founded: 1976

HONEYWELL NEIGHBORHOOD IMPROVEMENT PROGRAM
SEE BUSINESS/INDUSTRY INVOLVEMENT:
ENVIRONMENT

BUSINESS/INDUSTRY INVOLVEMENT: LITERACY

INDIVIDUAL PROGRAM PROFILES

CHAMBER OF COMMERCE LITERACY COUNCIL
Gadsden Chamber of Commerce
One Commerce Square
Gadsden, AL 35904
TEL: 205-543-3472
Purpose: To fight an illiteracy rate estimated at 25 percent among the county's approximately 100,000 residents.
Sponsor: Mid-South Industries
Contact: Dennis Phillips, Council Chairman
Description: The *Gadsden Chamber of Commerce,* enlisted the *United Way,* literacy service providers, and more than 35 other leaders from area businesses, school systems, and industry to form a *Literacy Council* to combat illiteracy in the Gadsden area.
The Chairman of the Council, corporate director of human-resource development of *Mid-South Industries,* and other

members oversee individual literacy efforts in the community. The *United Way* provided venture grants to fund information materials to get the word out about available literacy services. Recognizing the difficulty of encouraging people to ask for help, the materials are carefully developed to make it as easy as possible for people to come forward.

The *Gadsden United Way* also has added a *Literacy Hotline* to its regular *Information & Referral Service.* In addition, it has funded production of a videotape that promotes local literacy assistance programs. The video is distributed to stores, restaurants, and other locations with video monitors, all of whom cooperate fully with the program.

PALS PROGRAM
Gulf State Steel
174 South 26th Street
Gadsden, AL 35904
TEL: 205-543-6100
Purpose: To provide literary assistance to employees and the wider community.
Sponsor: Gadsden Board of Education
Contact: Human Resources Director
Description: Recognizing a considerable literacy problem among employees, *Gulf State Steel* purchased the *IBM Corporation's Principles of the Alphabet Literacy System (PALS)* program. The computer package was installed and set up on-site in a facility where employees could have a quiet place to receive literacy assistance. This approach proved very successful, with employees constantly using the resource.

The *Gadsden Board of Education* saw an opportunity in this corporate effort to avoid duplication of an innovative idea. With help from the *United Way,* arrangements were made with *Gulf State Steel* to allow community residents to take advantage of the facility also. According to United Way officials, "Cooperative ventures such as these help to conserve resources in the fight against illiteracy."

TIME TO READ
Time, Inc.
Corporate Community Relations
Rockefeller Center
New York, NY 10020
TEL: 212-522-1212
Purpose: To combat functional illiteracy through trained volunteer tutors and innovative teaching methods and materials.
Sponsor: Time, Inc.
Contact: TTR Coordinator
Description: Time to Read (TTR) is a model volunteer literacy program that began in 1985 as a Time, Inc. employee volunteer program in New York City. It was launched nationally to address the problem of 27 million Americans who cannot read well enough to fill out a job application, understand a supermarket ad, or read instructions on the job. TTR is not for people who cannot read at all, but for those who lack the skills to read fluently. The program is designed to augment and work in concert with existing literacy programs by providing the needed bridge between basic programs such as *Laubach Literacy* and *Literacy Volunteers of America,* and high school equivalency (GED) programs.

Time To Read works as a community partnership involving local businesses, institutions, and community organizations. Corporate and community volunteers manage the program and provide tutoring. Specially-trained volunteer tutors spend two hours a week for one year with one learner or a group of two to five learners. Learners are recruited through four different settings - schools, prisons, the workplace, and community organizations.

TTR skills are ones that learners "can take home with them" since they work as well with newspapers, magazines, a job application, etc., as they do with school assignments. In addition to instructional materials, each TTR learner and tutor gets a

subscription to *Time* magazine and a choice of one other (*People, Sports Illustrated, Life, Money,* or *Southern Living*).

Between 1985 and 1988, TTR grew from five pilot sites to 35 sites in 12 states. Surveys have shown that up to 71% of the learners improved their reading scores, and 82% said they enjoyed reading more. Almost two-thirds of the volunteer tutors repeat the service for a second year due to its high success rate.

Tutor training involves one 6-hour training session, one 3-hour follow-up training session, and a videotape and manual. In addition to the magazine subscriptions for tutor and learner, instructional materials provided to each tutor include 50 lesson plans with guide, and a loose-leaf manual with activity sheets, and the learner receives an Activity Sheet Pad, a dictionary and a bookbag. Costs are minimal and are borne by the sponsor. Where no sponsor is available, *Time, Inc.* defrays costs through an assistance program.

A special free publication, *The Time to Read Approach to Reading,* details the theory and practice behind TTR.
Publications: The Time to Read Approach to Reading; Time to Read: The Time, Inc. Literacy Program
Founded: 1985

BUSINESS/INDUSTRY INVOLVEMENT: NUTRITION

INDIVIDUAL PROGRAM PROFILES

BLUE RIDGE AREA FOOD BANK*
818 Richmond Avenue
Staunton, VA 24401
TEL: 703-886-3003
Purpose: To reduce food waste, and feed the needy, through distributing donated food to charities.
Sponsor: Corporate and private donations
Contact: Phil Grasty
Description: Blue Ridge Area Food Bank (BRAFB) is a clearinghouse for surplus and non-marketable (but edible products). These products are distributed to non-profit agencies and churches who feed the needy. These agencies become members of the BRAFB and are requested to contribute $.10 per lb., for food received.

BRAFB is a non-profit public supported corporation, which began operations on November 23, 1981 and is currently distributing more than 100,000 lbs. of food per month. The organization operates a main warehouse in Staunton, Virginia, with branch locations in Charlottesville, and Winchester.

At present more than 100 volunteers are involved in the operation of the Food bank, including VISTA and Green Thumb federally funded volunteers.

Volunteers perform many and varied tasks. Some of these include serving on the Board of Directors, assisting with management of branches, working in the warehouse, clerical duties, etc.

Some volunteers are used in the outreach work, calling on potential member agencies and food donors, financial supporters and arranging public relations.

BRAFB utilizes volunteers with varying levels of experience. Training is provided in various skills, such as:
- Clerical
- Public Relations
- Warehousing Skills

One-to-One supervision is given as needed. There is a continuing need for volunteers, both to work on-site and to work with special projects, such as:
- Gleaning

● Canned Food Drives
● Arranging Media Events
● Repacking Food Products, etc.

BRAFB serves an eighteen-county area. A screening and interviewing process is used in placing volunteers.
Founded: 1981

CAPITAL AREA COMMUNITY FOOD BANK
2266 25th Place, NE
Washington, DC 20018
TEL: 202-526-5344
Purpose: To distribute surplus food to area charities.
Sponsor: United Way; churches, foundations, grocery retailers/wholesalers
Contact: Richard Stack, Executive Director
Description: The food bank concept originated in Phoenix about 15 years ago and has since spread across the country. The 1976 Tax Reform Act made it better for grocery businesses to "donate rather than dump" salvageable surplus foods, and helped to proliferate the establishment of food banks. The Capital Area Community Food Bank (CACFB) began operations in mid-1980. CACFB collects overstocked or slightly damaged food products in large quantities from grocery retailers and wholesalers, including Giant and Safeway. This merchandise is usually discarded by the merchants while it is still edible because of laws regarding dating, etc. Through a network of 130 agencies, CACFB volunteers distribute the food without charge.

With the recent cutbacks, many more individuals and families are expected to need this type of private sector help. With the passing of the District of Columbia's *Good Faith Food Donor and Donee Act of 1981,* CACFB expects to be in a position to increase its distribution of food to area charities for redistribution to the needy. In September 1981, the month prior to the passing of the Act, the Bank distributed 88,196 pounds of food, which included items such as baby food, vegetables and condiments.

To avoid resale for profit, return of the item to the store for refund, etc., volunteers and staff stamp individual products with the word "donated." In the area of liability, CACFB has all agencies sign a waiver of liability, and the legislation itself provides additional protection in this area.

In addition to volunteer staffing, CACFB helps finance its organization by charging member agencies $.12 per pound for the food it dispenses. Other funds come from the United Way, churches and foundations.

COMMUNITY PROGRAMS
SEE COMMUNITY SERVICES

END HUNGER PROJECT
SEE COMMUNICATIONS & PUBLIC RELATIONS: NUTRITION

GALLATIN VALLEY EMERGENCY FOOD BANK
317 East Mendenhall
Bozeman, MT 59175
TEL: 406-587-4486
Purpose: To provide emergency food assistance to needy persons by salvaging food stuffs that would otherwise be wasted.
Sponsor: Human Resource Development Council District IX, United Way, Gallatin County Council on Aging, Local Wholesalers and Retailers, and Private Individuals.
Contact: Julie Hintz
Description: The Gallatin Valley Emergency Food Bank is an incorporated, non-profit organization which works in cooperation with the food industry to responsibly collect, store, record, and redistribute surplus and salvaged food stuffs. The Food Bank serves the hungry poor, and non-profit organizations serving congregate meals.

The Food Bank, governed by a nine member Board of Directors began operation January 11, 1982. It is sponsored by the Human Resource Development Council District IX, a community action agency serving three rural counties in southwestern Montana. In order to begin operation, it was necessary to pass legislation allowing wholesalers, retailers, and individuals to donate food items in good faith without being subject to criminal or civil liability. This was accomplished in February 1981 by the former director of the program.

The Food Bank was able to acquire a building for $15.00 a month, two refrigerators and two freezers at no cost, donated repair and construction from refrigeration and electrical contractors, also flooring and office furniture at a minimal expense.

The Food Bank staff has been successful in obtaining funds from VISTA, United Way, and Gallatin County Council on Aging to partially cover expenses of the operation. The staff has also sponsored fundraisers to help offset some of the costs.

The two main purposes for the Gallatin Valley Emergency Food Bank's existence are to eliminate waste and to reduce domestic hunger. By utilizing a seventeen-volunteer staff, the Food Bank collects, stores, records and redistributes food stuffs donated by local businesses, community groups, and individuals. For the most part this food is either surplus or salvaged. Surplus refers primarily to food companies' surplus products - overruns and discontinued products that cannot be sold before their "pull date." This food is edible but does not meet the company's quality control standards. Salvaged food includes edible but not readily marketable products such as food in dented cans, or damaged cases (where food quality is not affected), and crushed loaves of bread and produce that do not meet supermarket standards of attractiveness.

By providing emergency food assistance to needy persons the Food Bank is helping to reduce domestic hunger in these hard economic times. These people are in need of food due to a crisis situation such as loss of spouse, natural disaster, high living expenses with low incomes, or loss of a job. The Food Bank volunteers prepare nutritional three-day food boxes for those needy individuals and families who are faced with the problem of inadequate food budgets.

Food is also given to other non-profit agencies to aid them in serving the poor and needy. Senior Centers, Meals on Wheels, Day Care Centers, the Salvation Army, and homes for the Developmentally Disabled are some of the agencies who have benefited from Food Bank donations. With Food Banks doing the legwork in obtaining food from donors, agencies have more time and funds to concentrate on other activities.

Industry can benefit because of the 1976 Tax Reform Act which allows it to deduct, as a charitable contribution, its manufacturing cost plus one-half of the difference between cost and fair market value on items it contributes. In addition to solving the problem of what to do with surplus and salvaged food, companies are exhibiting their social consciousness by helping to solve the hunger problem in Gallatin County.

In one typical year, the Gallatin Valley Emergency Food Bank recovered approximately $29,326.00 worth of usable yet unsalable food and received approximately $2,146.00 of canned and boxed food from community groups and individuals totalling $31,472.00 worth of food collected and salvaged in the year.

This enabled the Food Bank to provide 549 families (1,497 individuals) with emergency food assistance. On the average, a three-day food box is worth $9.72.

The Food Bank also contributed $13,759.81 worth of food to non-profit agencies serving congregate meals, which has proven to significantly reduce the cost of their food programs.

With Gallatin County's current unemployment rate at 9.7%, persons living below the federal poverty level at 13%, and cutbacks in federal help programs, the Food Bank is seeing an increased need for emergency food assistance. The Director notes, "By keeping this program alive, the Gallatin Valley Emergency Food Bank, together with the local community's support, will continue to 'care for it's own.'"
Founded: 1982

NEIGHBORS HELPING NEIGHBORS
Washington Post
Promotion Department
1150 Fifteenth Street, NW
Washington, DC 20071
TEL: 202-334-4371
FAX: 212-334-4319
Co-sponsors: Giant Food, Inc., PO Box 1804 D-599, Washington, DC 20013 - Barry Scher, Vice President (301-341-4710); Capital Area Community Food Bank, 2266 25th Place, NE, Washington, DC 20018 - Lynn Brantley, Executive Director (202-334-5344)
Purpose: To raise food and money to help feed needy people in the metropolitan area.
Contact: Kathy Soulia
Description: Neighbors Helping Neighbors is a program designed to raise food and money to help feed 160,000 needy people in the Washington, DC metropolitan area. In its second year, this joint project among the *Capital Area Community Food Bank, The Washington Post, Giant Food, Inc.* and the people who live in the metropolitan Washington area was mid-campaign at the time of publication. Washington Post Columnist, Bob Levy, served as official spokesperson.

During the campaign's first-year effort in 1989, the organizations collected more than 250,040 pounds of food and more than $100,000 in cash. The food alone provided 83,346 meals for the hungry.

All costs of the *Neighbors Helping Neighbors* campaign are covered by *The Washington Post* and *Giant Food.* Every dollar donated and all of the food goes directly toward feeding the hungry of the Washington area.

1990 Campaign
The Washington Post kicked off the campaign on Sunday, April 8, 1990, by printing and inserting a grocery shopping bag into every issue, reaching 1,200,000 homes. The bags and the two-page ad published that day encouraged people to do one of two things - either fill out a check and mail it to the *Food Bank,* or fill up a bag with non-perishable goods and drop it at the nearest *Giant Food* store.

The *Post* continued to run in-paper advertising to promote awareness of the Washington-area hunger problem during the three-week campaign and provided 10-second radio broadcast support.

Giant Food, Inc., with more than 180 stores in the Washington area, supported the campaign with: in-store displays featuring posters and food products suggested for the drive, in-store point-of-purchase materials at the checkout and on the shelves, and window posters. *Giant* also placed *Neighbors Helping Neighbors* tags in print and radio advertising.

Giant's stores served as collection sites for the food and *Giant* transported food to the *Food Bank.*

The *Capital Area Community Food Bank* sorted the food and processed the cash donations. The *Food Bank* also handled publicity including news releases to local clergy with an informational flyer that was inserted in church bulletins.

The *Capital Area Community Food Bank* is a nonprofit organization that solicits food, sorts and warehouses it, and distributes it to organizations which feed the hungry. More than 5500 people volunteer at the *Food Bank* each year. About 80% of the volunteers sort through dented cans, crushed boxes and other food that is good to eat but cannot be sold in stores.

Nearly 700 organizations - churches, community groups - come to the food bank and "shop" for their clients. They contribute $.12 per pound, which covers approximately 60% of the *Food Bank's* operating expenses. The rest of its expenses are covered by corporate donations. Approximately 160,000 people, half children, are fed each month.

The *Capital Area Community Food Bank* serves the District of Columbia, south and central Maryland and northern Virginia.
Publications: Tis The Season

TASTE OF THE NATION
SEE VOLUNTEERS: PROFESSIONALS

BUSINESS/INDUSTRY INVOLVEMENT: OFFENDERS

INDIVIDUAL PROGRAM PROFILES

DATA SYSTEMS UNLIMITED
Goodwill Industries of San Francisco
PO Box 548
San Francisco, CA 94101
TEL: 415-362-0778
Purpose: To train disabled adults and offenders and ex-offenders to become qualified computer operators and data entry clerks, and to help them find entry-level career opportunities in this field.
Sponsor: Goodwill Industries of America; IBM
Contact: Judy A. Langley
Description: In 1981, IBM awarded Goodwill the three-year gratis loan of their Computer System 34 for the purpose of providing vocational training to disabled people. It is the second program of its kind in the country, established exclusively for disabled individuals.

In accordance with the agreement with IBM, the program can operate only on a break-even basis, and the equipment cannot be used for money-making ventures or Goodwill business.

The instructor's salary, administrative costs and trainee stipends are funded mostly through student tuitions, which come from the San Francisco Department of Rehabilitation, private rehabilitation, fund-raising sources, and occasionally from students' own resources.

Six staff and 25 volunteers operate the program, with volunteers involved in supervisory and advocacy capacities as well as in direct delivery of services. They have succeeded in involving public, private and corporate sectors in support of the program.

The Industry Advisory Board, made up of personnel and data processing managers from the business community, help in planning and implementing the program.

During the first year, twelve students registered for the class, with eight of them graduating, and three being placed immediately in data processing jobs, and two involved in internships. Based on the success of this size class, the program each year will be limited to twelve students.

To be eligible for the training program, interested disabled individuals must first pass Goodwill's extensive testing to determine their abilities for handling course requirements, their levels of emotional stability, and their motivations to seek and find employment.

In an effort to be of assistance to the wider community also, Goodwill accepts applications from offenders and ex-offenders for the program.
Founded: 1981

BUSINESS/INDUSTRY INVOLVEMENT: OLDER PERSON

INDIVIDUAL PROGRAM PROFILES

ABILITY IS AGELESS
Long Island Lighting Company
175 East Old Country Road
Hicksville, NY 11801
TEL: 516-933-4590
Purpose: To assist senior citizens in obtaining full or part time employment, and to offer other informational, health, education and ancillary services.
Sponsor: WNBC-TV; Long Island Lighting Company; other cooperating companies
Contact: J. Joseph Crowley
Description: In the spring of 1981, Long Island Lighting Company, in conjunction with WNBC-TV, embarked on a program directed toward the holding of a Senior Citizen Job Fair, with the intended purpose of affording all attendees the opportunity to register for full- or part-time positions with Long Island firms. Some 50 companies joined in the effort as well as representatives of the New York State Department of Labor, Long Island State Park Commission, Nassau and Suffolk County senior citizen agencies, local county Bar associations, local hospitals and universities, news media, U.S. Marine Corps, and the U.S. Social Security Administration.
Approximately 3,000 seniors attended the first fair at Bethpage State Park. Each private sector representative had its own area with large tents to register and/or interview potential job seekers. Approximately 1,500 individuals were registered for jobs, and this registry has been maintained by the major sponsor as an ongoing job bank.
As part of the service, educational, health, legal and other applicable information of interest to our senior population is distributed by appropriate agencies. Also, during the course of the fair, entertainment is presented by professionals, and food is provided by major food chains with no cost to participants.
Job pledges are made by private firms at the fair and later in referring to the job bank created by this activity. More than 65 companies participate, answering questions about possible part-time employment as well as regular job openings.
Also, participating companies assist in staging the job fair by lending personnel to serve as volunteers for the arrangements committee and for interviewing job fair attendees seeking part-time employment. All sponsoring committees are asked to seek employment possibilities within their organizations for Job Fair attendees. The expenses of the Job Fair are shared among the participating companies on an assessment basis.
Other volunteers are involved in supervisory and management capacities, fund-raising and public relations. In addition, educational institutions and local and state governments played major roles in the success of the Fair.
Founded: 1981

PARTNERS IN CARING
Telephone Pioneers of America
3841 Green Hills Village Drive
Nashville, TN 37215
TEL: 615-665-8845
Purpose: To get people in companies interested in nursing home patients and to link them with individual nursing homes.
Sponsor: Telephone Pioneers of America
Contact: Suzanne Petrey
Description: The *Partners in Caring* program was initiated to improve services to older Nashvillians. The main goal is to get

people in companies interested in nursing home patients and to link them with individual nursing homes. In the spring of 1989, an initial *pilot* partnership was forged between the patients at *Bordeaux Hospital* and the *Telephone Pioneers,* a volunteer organization of telecommunications employees. Twenty *Pioneers* signed up for the program. Volunteer training is administered before the two sides of the partnership are brought together, and includes:
- how to talk, listen to and look at an older person;
- death and dying concerns;
- the importance of confidentiality; and
- how to handle concerns and suggestions.
Also, the individual nursing homes involved conduct orientations of their own. They provide information about aging issues, and what to expect while volunteering at the nursing home. The volunteers are matched according to their interests and the nursing home's needs, such as staffing the patient information desk, forming a one-on-one family-type relationship with a specific patient, and a wide variety of other jobs. Some volunteers commit to weekly activities, some monthly and some yearly.
According to the director, groups of non-working volunteers of the past are now part of the work force. Without a program like *Partners,* which gets corporations involved, the program would be inadequate or nonexistent. Feedback from the volunteers indicate that they, themselves, benefit personally from the experience.
Founded: 1989

BUSINESS/INDUSTRY INVOLVEMENT: PET THERAPY

INDIVIDUAL PROGRAM PROFILES

PETS FOR PEOPLE
Ralston Purina Company
Checkerboard Square
St. Louis, MO 63164
TEL: 314-982-1000
FAX: 314-982-1211
Purpose: To provide pet therapy and/or pet ownership to senior citizens.
Sponsor: Ralston Purina Company
Description: This program of Ralston Purina Company makes shelter pets available to older persons by working with local participating Humane Societies, which are all-volunteer groups. Pet therapy volunteer programs have long demonstrated the value of bringing together pets and older people, especially nursing home residents or elderly people living alone.
Ralston Purina Company pays initial pet "adoption" fees (up to $100 per adoption), and includes veterinary fees and pet supplies in the service. The corporation donates up to a total of one million dollars each year to the program.

BUSINESS/INDUSTRY INVOLVEMENT: RECREATION/SPORTS

INDIVIDUAL PROGRAM PROFILES

AIR PRODUCTS DEVELOPMENTAL CYCLING PROGRAM
Air Products and Chemicals
PO Box 538
Allentown, PA 18105
TEL: 215-481-8079
Purpose: To teach bicycle safety, maintenance and the fundamentals of riding and racing.
Sponsor: Air Products and Chemicals, Inc.
Contact: Pamela S. Handwerk
Description: The Air Products Developmental Cycling Program is designed to encourage area residents to experience first-hand what the exciting sport of bicycle racing is all about. It continues to be a good example of how industry and recreation work together to provide a worthwhile program for the community.
The program is a corporate-underwritten event, open to people eight years or older who have bicycling interest. Depending on experience, participants are assigned to one of three categories: beginners, intermediate or advanced, where they are taught bicycle safety, maintenance and the fundamentals of riding. All equipment is provided and the coaches are the top racers in North America. The summer climaxes with Air Products night, where participants in the program have their own night of racing.
Graduates of the Developmental Cycling Program are able to participate at a more advanced level. Novice racers can gain the necessary experience and training from coaches who have been recognized nationally.
All training, coaching and racing is done at Lehigh County Velodrome under close supervision by expert instructors. There is no cost to participants, as the program is financed through corporate contributions.
The program enjoys considerable success and has gained national recognition. A number of other velodromes have indicated their intention of duplicating the program. Two graduates of the program have gone on to become the U.S. Junior National Champions.

CAMP GOOD DAYS AND SPECIAL TIMES REBUILDING PROJECT
SEE VOLUNTEERS: UNION MEMBERS

ROBERTS PARK AND PLAYGROUND/LANTRIP SCHOOL PARK*
Sun Company
6200 Savoy Drive
Houston, TX 77001
TEL: 713-974-9800
Purpose: To transform a barren school ground into an award-winning community park with picnic areas, climbing towers, sand lots and gardens.
Sponsor: The Park People
Contact: Walter Erwin
Description: In 1979, The Park People, Inc., called for proposals for park-related projects from its membership. At the same time, the Eastwood Civic Association was embarking on a campaign to improve its neighborhood by becoming involved and providing opportunities for residents of the area to help themselves. The Civic Association determined that a small park and playground at Lantrip Elementary School would benefit the neighborhood, and pledged to rally its membership to construct the playground if funding became available. Houston Independent School District agreed to the concept of placing the playground at the school.

A proposal for the park/playground was prepared for The Park People. This proposal was a short, two-page document that outlined the need for more play sites in inner-city neighborhoods and stressed the importance of the involvement of the community in the actual construction of the project. A grant of $13,000 was requested for the park project.
The Park People presented the Eastwood-Lantrip proposal along with several others to Sun Company for consideration. After examining all of the proposals, Sun Company selected the Eastwood-Lantrip Proposal for funding. The school district was asked to further support the project by awarding the school a $5,000 grant from a special community projects fund.
In March 1980, the plans for the park were completed and construction began. Sixty volunteers assisted with the construction. The East End Progress Association provided valuable assistance in locating heavy equipment at no charge and locating free or discounted material. Lantrip students assisted neighborhood work crews by moving sand, laying bricks, and planting trees and shrubs.
This project - totally volunteer - provides an example of the results that can be attained when local organizations, agencies, and business/industry work together. One Sun employee said: "A primary consideration in the selection was the community involvement that the project would engender."
Founded: 1979

VOLUNTEERS IN PARKS (VIP)
Kansas City Department of Parks and Recreation
3915 East 63rd Street
Kansas City, MO 64130
TEL: 816-561-6630
Purpose: To provide non-skilled and semi-skilled volunteer help in park and boulevard maintenance on a regular, dependable basis.
Sponsor: Kansas City Department of Parks and Recreation; various corporate sponsors
Contact: Phil Thornburg, Volunteer Coordinator
Description: The VIP program is an incentive-based program to encourage ongoing individual and group participation in the non-skilled and semi-skilled routine maintenance of Parks and Recreation properties, facilities, structures, and displays. The program allows for volunteers to work in a location convenient to home or work, the time of day, day(s) of the week, and number of hours available or convenient to them by contacting the manager of the work site.
The VIP program was begun June 21, 1982 and offered as incentives passes to a number of Parks and Recreation facilities/activities as well as passes, discounts, and coupons offered by four local merchants.
Staffing requirements are only the Supervisor of the sections involved such as Park District Managers, Golf Course Supervisors, Florist, etc. The program expenses are minimal and are financed through the Corporate Sponsor Coupon donations and the maintenance budget for paint or other special items. Trash bags, hand tools, etc. are furnished by the volunteer as needed.
Volunteer Duties - VIP's may volunteer for any of a number of projects or suggest an alternative of their own subject to approval. The types of projects listed included weeding of flower beds; litter removal in parks or sections of a boulevard; sweeping and cleaning hard surface walks, courts, and curbs; shrub bed cleaning and leaf removal; painting of restrooms, play equipment, trash containers; glass, trash, and weed removal from playgrounds and sand boxes.
How the Program Operates - The volunteer must schedule the location and time with the appropriate supervisor.
The incentives are cumulative and may be collected as work is completed. Choices of activities are given for some hours to provide maximum appeal to volunteers.
Groups and one-time projects are accommodated by providing the representative the incentives based on the number of hours worked and the number in the group.
Founded: 1982

BUSINESS/INDUSTRY INVOLVEMENT: TRANSPORTATION

INDIVIDUAL PROGRAM PROFILES

BICYCLE SAFETY AND SEAT BELT AWARENESS PROGRAMS
McDonald's of Paragould, Arkansas
One Medical Drive
Paragould, AR 77450
TEL: 501-236-3715
Purpose: To emphasize, demonstrate, and help improve bicycle safety practices and seat belt usage in Paragould.
Sponsor: McDonald's of Paragould; Paragould Police Department
Contact: Community Services Officer
Description: In cooperation with the Paragould Police Department, McDonald's of Paragould mounted two programs: a bicycle safety and engraving program, and a "Buckle Up and Make It Click" seat belt program.

The bicycle program began with a bicycle parade down the main street with over 50 children participating. Prizes were given for the best decorated bikes, and a festive and cooperative spirit prevailed afterwards as bicycle safety was discussed and demonstrated, and bicycles were engraved for identification purposes should they be stolen.

The buckle up program involved the police department also, and included the local hospital as well. Volunteers from the hospital and McDonald's visited local elementary schools to show a film on the benefits of buckling up, demonstrated how to buckle up a car seatbelt, and presented each child with a sticker for a free surprise at McDonald's if they buckled up for seven days in a row.

Both programs were considered a great success, making children aware of the responsibility that goes with owning a bicycle, and bringing seat belt restraint to top-of-mind awareness. The programs will be continued on request. According to McDonald's manager, "If we helped make Paragould just a little safer for our children through these programs, our investment of time and resources is well worth the effort."
Publications: Bicycle Program Packet

CITIZENSHIP

CITIZENSHIP: CHILDREN/YOUTH

NATIONAL/STATE ORGANIZATIONS

BOY SCOUTS OF AMERICA
1325 Walnut Hill Lane
Irving, TX 75038
TEL: 214-580-2000
Objectives: To provide an educational program for boys and young adults; to build character; to train in the responsibilities of participating citizenship, and to develop personal fitness.
Services: Issues national charters to community groups who use the Scouting program as a part of their own youth work, and who have goals compatible with those of the BSA; includes groups from religious, educational, civic, fraternal, business, labor, governmental, corporate, and professional areas, as well as autonomous groups of citizens; operates programs at several levels of ability, including:

- **Tiger Scouting,** which has been developed for seven-year-old boys.
- **Cub Scouting,** which serves boys eight, nine, and ten years of age (at ten, they become Webelos Scouts in preparation for Boy Scouting).
- **Boy Scouting,** which is designed for boys aged 11 through 17 as a vigorous outdoor program and peer group leadership program.
- **Exploring,** which is a contemporary program for young men and women aged 15 through 20 to provide opportunities to learn about adult roles and vocational opportunities in association with business and community partners.

(Varies age limits from those stated above when school grade and other considerations warrant a departure from the general guidelines.)
Involves volunteer adult leaders at all levels of scouting in 415 local councils, 32 areas, six regions, and nationally with volunteer executive boards and committees providing guidance; celebrates Scouting Anniversary Week in February of each year, Scouting Environment Day in April, and Scouting Energy Day in October; publishes three magazines: *Boys' Life* for all boys, *Exploring* for young men and women and Explorer leaders, and *Scouting* for all registered adults in scouting programs.
Receives most of its support from pack, troop and post fees, the sale of scouting equipment, bequests and special gifts (local

programs receive United Way support and have a dues structure for this purpose); fees from local programs help support national training events for leaders, counseling, camping and outdoor facilities, program materials, literature, planning tools, etc.
Publications: Boys' Life; Scouting Magazine; Exploring Magazine; Annual Report to Congress
Founded: 1910

CAMP FIRE
4601 Madison Avenue
Kansas City, MO 64112
TEL: 816-756-1950
TOLL FREE: 800-821-6180
Objectives: To provide an informal education program for young people to help them become self-directed, responsible, caring individuals.
Services: Administers program to children in small group settings in three basic ways:

- **Club Programs** - programs created at the national level and offered to groups who meet on a regular basis with a volunteer leader.
- **Outdoor Programs** - programs created by the national organization and by Camp Fire councils, and including group camping, day camping, resident camping, trips, environmental projects and outdoor recreation.
- **Response Programs** - programs based on researching the needs of young people and creating the content, systems and materials responsive to these needs (developed by Camp Fire councils and the national organization); includes response programs in day care centers, after school recreation programs, tutorial reading programs, job training programs, drop-in centers, campership projects, delinquency prevention projects, in-school enrichment programs, and projects to mainstream the handicapped.

Includes both boys and girls as members, from birth to 21 years of age; divides program into four groupings: Blue Bird (grades 1-3; largest group); Adventure (grades 4-8); Discovery (grades 7 and 8); and Horizon (grades 9-12); supplements these groupings in some Councils with preschool and post-high school programs; delivers programs directly to youth, as well as through sponsoring institutions, church bodies, businesses and other organizations; trains volunteer leaders so that Program Standards are uniform across the country; exercises social/advocacy responsibility through programs in juvenile justice, immunization of children, rape prevention, youth employment, tutoring, tree planting, CPR,

English as a Second Language, and numerous other areas reflecting social concerns within the community.
Promotes volunteerism by demonstrating volunteer leadership through its Councils, and by involving volunteers in management and decision-making.
Publications: Camp Fire Management; Leadership Magazine
Founded: 1910

GIRL SCOUTS OF THE USA
830 Third Avenue
New York, NY 10022
TEL: 212-940-7500
Objectives: To provide an informal education program for girls and adults to inspire high ideals of character, conduct, patriotism and service.
Services: Guides and supports approximately 336 Councils and over 553,000 volunteers; provides assistance through three field centers (Dallas, New York, and Chicago) with each Center recruiting, promoting, and retaining its own adult volunteers; provides opportunity for volunteer activity in areas ranging from policy making at local and national levels to direct service to girls in troops (the volunteer program supports the total girl scout program); involves volunteers as Council board members, community administrators, committee members, neighborhood chairpersons, consultants and supervisors at the administrative level; involves volunteers as troop/camp leaders, learning consultants, recruiters, trainers, fund raisers, project leaders, speakers' bureau members, and numerous other areas at the operational level; maintains salaried staff in the field offices to provide support and guidance, with actual supervision of local staff and volunteers being controlled by the respective local Council; offers financial aid to relevant seminars and courses to qualified volunteer staff.
Publishes instructional materials for distribution to volunteer staff, including *Leader's Digest: Blue Book of Basic Documents, Tips for the Program Consultant, Mix and Match, Directing the Work of Others,* etc.; provides job descriptions for all volunteer appointments, as well as supervision and career guidance for volunteers through clarification of expectations, performance goals, monitoring, coaching, and ongoing evaluation of performance; convenes regional and national meetings.
Publications: GSUSA News; Girl Scout Leader; Environmental Scanning Report
Founded: 1912

GIRLS CLUBS OF AMERICA
30 East 33rd Street
New York, NY 10016
TEL: 212-689-3700 (New York); 317-634-7546 (Indiana)
Objectives: To focus national attention on the special needs of girls; to enable them to achieve responsible and confident adulthood, economic independence and personal fulfillment.
Services: Serves a quarter of a million girls ages 6-18 through over 200 Clubs and various outreach programs, over half belonging to racial and ethnic minority groups and two-thirds coming from families earning under $15,000 a year; currently operates national programs addressing AIDS education, substance abuse prevention, science, math and technology, adolescent pregnancy, and sports and physical fitness; includes among traditional and nontraditional programs initiated by local Clubs activities in drama, the arts, computer science, humanities and life skills; includes 2500 professional staff members and 8,000 volunteers in Girls Clubs buildings, extensions and branches across the country, including volunteer board members from local communities; through local Clubs offers an average of 30 hours a week of programs and activities in an informal educational environment after school, on weekends and during school vacations; has four regional service centers which provide training, technical and organizational assistance to Clubs' professional staff and volunteers.

[All programs developed by Girls Clubs of America are researched, analyzed and evaluated at the National Resource Center, the nation's first and most extensive clearinghouse of its kind for information about girls. It contains library and research facilities and distributes publications and materials to parents, educators, policymakers, women's groups and others concerned with girls.]
Contact: Susan Ellis (Indiana)
Publications: Voice for Girls; We're On The Move; Girls and Substance Abuse; Sporting Chance
Founded: 1945

US/DOA - 4-H YOUTH/EXTENSION SERVICE
South Building
Third Floor
Washington, DC 20250
TEL: 202-447-5853
Objectives: To involve youth and adults, working together, in learn-by-doing educational activities and real-life experiences.
Services: Involves parents, volunteer leaders, and other adults in organizing and conducting projects for community and family settings; operates in counties, towns, and cities through Cooperative Extension Service agents who guide and supervise nearly 600,000 volunteer leaders and other volunteers; serves nearly five million members between the ages of nine and 19 both on farms and in big cities, suburbs, small towns and communities; varies planning to reflect the diversity of the clubs, working in the following areas:
- organized community or neighborhood 4-H clubs;
- special interest or short-term groups;
- school enrichment programs;
- 4-H instructional television;
- camping; and
- individual 4-H members.
Operates an international youth exchange program to work with the 82 countries around the globe that have adapted youth programs similar to 4-H; enlists leadership through the combined efforts of federal, state and county Extension staff, existing leaders, support from the National 4-H Council, and other private support donors.
Founded: 1900

TRAINING PROGRAMS

GOVERNORS' SCHOOL
SEE GOVERNORS' OFFICES ON VOLUNTEERISM: WASHINGTON

INDIVIDUAL PROGRAM PROFILES

BOYS & GIRLS CLUBS OF GREATER WASHINGTON
1320 Fenwick Lane
Suite 800
Silver Spring, MD 20910
TEL: 301-587-4315
FAX: 301-587-8120
Purpose: To help build self-esteem through instilling a sense of belonging, competence, usefulness and influence; to help young people become productive, civic-minded and responsible adults.
Contact: Program Coordinator
Description: The *Boys & Girls Club of Greater Washington* has been providing services for young boys and girls from all backgrounds for over 100 years. There are eight branch *Clubs* in the District of Columbia, Maryland and Virginia. There are nine shelters and residential facilities for neglected, abused and homeless young people, and special services are pioneered to help

youth-at-risk. The organization provides educational assistance, recreational and social opportunities, job training and personalized counseling. Specific programs include:

- *Career Education and Vocational Training Services,* helping young people to complete school and move to college and work with educational and scholarship assistance, computer education, preparation for college, job training and tutoring.
- *Citizenship and Leadership Development Services,* giving youngsters a sense of civic responsibility by becoming involved in the leadership process, with opportunities for planning and decision-making, as well as becoming aware of their heritage, through: *Torch and Keystone Clubs,* special interest groups, and an annual awards program for *Youth of the Year.*
- *Cultural Enrichment Services,* encouraging understanding of many cultures through classes and performances to provide skills and experiences in the visual and performing arts.
- *Personal Development Services,* helping young people plan and set goals and helping them to cope with physical, social, academic and emotional problems.
- *Health and Physical Education Services,* developing and maintaining health through physical fitness and education in team and individual sports, and health education including drug and substance abuse counseling.
- *Social Recreation Services,* teaching youngsters good use of leisure time and helping them get along with peers and make new friends through special co-ed teenage activities, a game room, hobby groups, and outings and special events.
- *Targeting Special Needs,* providing specialized assistance through programs such as the *Teen Parent Self-Sufficiency Program, Targeted Outreach* (youth-at-risk), and *Cities in Schools* (a support team to keep youth in school).
- *Summer Camping,* providing a variety of activities in day camps at eight *Clubs* which include swimming, arts and crafts, building new friendships, learning about careers, etc. *Gift of Summer* scholarship assistance is available when needed.

In addition to volunteer counselors and other direct service individuals and groups, supporters include foundations, businesses and corporations.

Publications: Capital Connection; Project Right Start; Boys & Girls Club Information Packet

CENTER FOR YOUTH SERVICE

921 Pennsylvania Avenue, SE
Washington, DC 20003
TEL: 202-543-5707

Purpose: To offer inner city adolescents a new way of expanding their skills and overcoming their obstacles and deficits.

Sponsor: March of Dimes

Contact: Youth Service Coordinator

Description: The Center for Youth Services (CYS) is a nonprofit, private corporation with a goal of helping youth be the best that they can. Youth become members of CYS through a four-step program which begins with an orientation to the center and the signing of a contract agreeing to do his or her best to complete the program as planned. Next the youth are exposed to a series of seminars on issues such as values, environmental influences, decisionmaking, and employment options. Following the seminars, the youth have an interview with a staff member to determine interests, goals and needs. The result of the interview is a program of services designed especially for the youth.

The opportunities at CYS include an extensive employment program, which includes supervised on-the-job experience, building maintenance training, summer youth employment, and direct placement with follow-up services. The educational component is also an important aspect of CYS. It includes classes in Basic Skills I and II, GED preparation, and tutoring. CYS has had a high success rate in helping students to pass the GED.

In the counseling program, the mental health staff of CYS become involved with nearly all of the young people who use the center.

They are available to discuss personal problems, strengthen self-esteem, and encourage goal-setting. Also, CYS has a health clinic which provides general health care, treatment of sexually-transmitted diseases, and prenatal care.

CYS offers day care free of charge to young people while they participate in center activities or one of the job components. CYS staff also work to provide a wide range of recreational opportunities for youth, including sports teams, table games, and field trips.

CYS is unique in that it allows each youth to create a program to suit his individual needs, concerns and interests.

Since 1985 the March of Dimes has awarded local grants to CYS totaling $19,996 as of early 1989. An additional grant of $10,000 was awarded to CYS to fund the "Male Health Clinic," which promotes sexual responsibility among adolescents and young males through a combined program of education and medical services.

TROOP 400 AND TROOP 391
Boy Scouts of America
National Capital Area Council
Wisconsin Avenue at Cedar Lane
Bethesda, MD 20014
TEL: 301-530-9360

Purpose: To put handicapped scouts into a more competitive and challenging environment through mainstreaming.

Sponsor: Boy Scouts of America

Contact: Stephen Zungali, Program Director; David Henderson, Special Projects Executive for Handicapped Scouting

Description: The National Capital Area Council of the Boy Scouts of America, which covers the Washington, DC, area, has special camps for its 28 troops of disabled scouts. However, until July 1989, an entire troop of disabled scouts had never attended a regular week of camp. At Camp Marriott in Goshen, Virginia, two troops of handicapped scouts joined 200 other campers for a week to "swim, fish and fight off mosquitoes." Troop 400 is from the National Children's Center in northwest Washington, which is a school for autistic and mentally retarded students. Troop 391 is from Gibbs P.A.C.E., a special education program in northwest Washington.

The disabled scouts followed the same program as other scouts to earn merit badges. With disabled scouts, some of the projects took a little longer, but they learned the skills, according to camp staff. By mainstreaming in this way, the handicapped campers are in a more competitive and challenging environment, and scouts who are not disabled find serving as "buddies" a rewarding experience. Leaders found that the disabled scouts worked harder at Camp Marriott than they did the previous year at a special camp. At the special camp many things were done for the scouts, such as having meals delivered to them. At Camp Marriott they had to "rough it" while learning specific skills to get their merit badges, and other scouts eagerly volunteered to assist them.

Observations from the young volunteers indicated that the non-handicapped scouts received as much growth from the experience as did the disabled scouts. The director was pleased with some of the comments of the young volunteer/scouts, including: "They're just like us!" "They don't laugh at you if you make a mistake." "A lot of people treat handicapped people like they're not normal. They're just like normal people."

According to the camp director, "As the week wore on, the line between teacher and pupil became fuzzy as the paired youths laughed and talked about everything from their favorite comedian (Eddie Murphy) to insects." Plans of the National Capitol Area Council is to increase the number of troops of disabled scouts for the next session of regular camp to three or four - until as many of the 28 troops as possible have merged into the regular program.

YOUTH-IN-GOVERNMENT DAY
SEE LEADERSHIP DEVELOPMENT/BOARDS:
CHILDREN/YOUTH

YOUTH SERVICES
American Red Cross
Princeton Area Chapter
182 North Harrison Street
Princeton, NJ 08540
TEL: 609-924-2404
Purpose: To provide students from grades kindergarten through twelve with the opportunity for leadership development while gaining a greater awareness for people in their community.
Sponsor: Princeton Area Chapter, American Red Cross
Contact: Director, Youth Services
Description: Youth Services at the Princeton Area Chapter seeks to provide area youth with the opportunity for leadership development, personal growth, and career exploration through participation in worthwhile volunteer activities. The program strives to furnish young people with the skills needed to become responsible, self-reliant adults and to stimulate them to be lifetime volunteers in service to the community.

Opportunities for growth and development are mainly provided through high school youth involvement in the Youth Teaching Youth program, in which student volunteers teach children at the elementary and middle school levels. This year, the chapter's youth volunteer instructors taught 195 classes to children on topics such as first aid, safety, drug awareness and abuse, babysitting, and components of blood. Currently, twenty-one youth volunteers are active participants in the program, coming from Stuart County Day School, West Windsor-Plainsboro High School, Princeton Day School, and Princeton High School.

Program growth has been noted in the provision of nine youth volunteers to serve as aides at the chapter office on a periodic basis to perform support functions for blood, safety, youth, and secretarial services. Significant progress has also been evidenced in the recruiting of eligible youth blood donors from local public and private high schools to assist in meeting the growing need for blood at the Princeton Medical Center.

Goals for future expansion of Youth Services include the formation of a Youth Advisory Committee to generate new methods of introducing Red Cross services into the schools. Finally, the chapter is investigating methods of further developing leadership among area youth through participation in a Leadership Development Conference, designed to introduce youth to various Red Cross activities and to inspire them to continued community involvement.

CITIZENSHIP: CHILDREN/YOUTH - HANDICAPPED

NATIONAL/STATE ORGANIZATIONS

SCOUTING FOR THE HANDICAPPED
Boy Scouts of America
1325 Walnut Hill Lane
Irving, TX 75062
TEL: 214-659-2127
Objectives: To encourage the inclusion of handicapped youngsters in regular packs, troops, and posts.
Services: Assists with job preparation for handicapped scouts; encourages packs, troops, posts at schools and homes for the handicapped when impossible to include them in local programming; includes scouting for the hearing impaired, the visually impaired, the mentally retarded, and the physically handicapped; publishes manuals in each of the handicap areas, plus numerous other pamphlets, brochures, and program suggestion materials; convenes biennial meeting.

SCOUTING FOR THE HANDICAPPED
Girl Scouts of the USA
830 Third Avenue
New York, NY 10022
TEL: 212-940-7500
Objectives: To make the troop/camp experience for girls with disabilities as much as possible like that of the nondisabled girl.
Services: Provides training and other services to scout troops without designating "special" or different activities for girls with disabilities; encourages leaders to adapt activities to suit abilities and limitations when necessary; includes information about special needs in most program materials.

INDIVIDUAL PROGRAM PROFILES

TROOP 400 AND TROOP 391
SEE CITIZENSHIP: CHILDREN/YOUTH

COMMUNICATIONS & PUBLIC RELATIONS

NATIONAL/STATE ORGANIZATIONS

CITIZENS COMMUNICATION CENTER
Georgetown University Law Center
600 New Jersey Avenue, NW
Washington, DC 20009
TEL: 202-624-8047; 202-624-8057
Objectives: To increase the level of citizen participation and decision-making in the broadcast media.
Services: Aids citizens and groups without resources or technical skills in obtaining media access; educates and trains advocates to assert citizens rights to participation in the media process; provides information on request to individual citizens and community groups regarding the broadcast industry's obligation to the community.

COMMUNITY ADVISORY BOARDS
SEE LEADERSHIP DEVELOPMENT/BOARDS:
COMMUNICATIONS/PR

CORPORATION FOR PUBLIC BROADCASTING
1111 Sixteenth Street, NW
Washington, DC 20036
TEL: 202-955-5100
Objectives: To assure that a voice in public communications is given to the people for whom the service is intended.
Services: Promotes the long-term financing and growth of noncommercial radio and television; identifies areas in which public participation should be developed or expanded (includes volunteerism in these areas); makes grants to local public radio and television stations; presents annual awards for outstanding local radio and television programs; maintains a data bank and publishes findings, handbooks, bibliographies, research reports and other materials to keep the public informed of its activity.
Publications: CPB Report; Public Broadcasting Directory
Founded: 1968

INDIVIDUAL GIVING/VOLUNTEERING CAMPAIGN*
Advertising Council
825 Third Avenue
New York, NY 10022
TEL: 212-758-0400
Objectives: To increase public awareness on the benefits of volunteering.

Services: To work in partnership with the President's Office on Private Sector Initiatives and Independent Sector in a nationwide campaign to encourage voluntary action, including volunteering and voluntary giving; includes print, radio and, beginning in January 1984, TV ads.
Publications: Public Service Advertising; Report to the American People
Founded: 1942

MEDIA ACCESS PROJECT
2000 M Street, NW, 4th Floor
Washington, DC 20036
TEL: 202-232-4300
Objectives: To maximize citizen group ability to gain access to radio and TV audiences; to assure that the broadcast media report fully and fairly on important issues (environment, consumerism, civil rights, the economy, the political process, etc.).
Services: Works to insure that the media fully informs the public on issues that effect them (environment, consumerism, civil rights, the economy, and the political process); advises local and national organizations on increasing responsiveness of the media; represents these groups in their efforts; participates in seminars and conferences designed to increase the effectiveness of citizens in this area; publishes broadcast media guides.
Publications: Taking the Initiative; Corporate Control
Founded: 1971

NATIONAL ASSOCIATION OF BROADCASTERS
1771 N Street, NW
Washington, DC 20036
TEL: 202-429-5300
Objectives: To promote acceptable programming and advertising practices; to inform the public on approaching radio and television stations for public service air time.
Services: Provides guidelines to stations, and information to the public, on opportunities for organizations working for the public good to enhance programs and better serve the community through public interest broadcasting; maintains 21 committees, subcommittees and task forces, including Children's Television, American Improvement, and Television and Radio Political Action.
Publications: NAB Today; Radioactive; NAB Conference Proceedings
Founded: 1922

NATIONAL FRIENDS OF PUBLIC BROADCASTING

c/o Elaine N. Peterson
3315 Hidden Hills Drive
Brookfield, WI 53005
TEL: 414-781-3326
Objectives: To develop and encourage productive cooperation between local volunteer groups and local station management.
Services: Serves in a volunteer capacity to foster public understanding of and participation in public broadcasting; provides a central source of information for volunteers in public broadcasting; encourages and establishes volunteer groups and activities geared to the needs of public broadcasting; publishes a newsletter, a directory, and numerous pamphlets; convenes regional annual conferences; conducts community outreach and awards programs.
Publications: How to be a Friend; NFPB Newsletter; Volunteer Directory
Founded: 1968

TELEVISION INFORMATION OFFICE*

810 Seventh Avenue
Second Floor
New York, NY 10019
TEL: 212-759-6800
Objectives: To provide a "two-way bridge of understanding" between the television industry and the public.
Services: Seeks to provide a bridge of understanding between the television industry and the public; provides members materials for community education; maintains extensive library which includes community-oriented materials, information on the impact television can provide in social, cultural, and promotional areas; publishes newsletter, *Information*, and other materials.
Founded: 1959

TRAINING PROGRAMS

COMMUNICATIONS WORKSHOP/PERSPECTIVES FOR VOLUNTEERS

SEE TRAINING/CONFERENCES/TEACHING: COMMUNICATIONS & PR

GROWING WITH PUBLIC RELATIONS*

SEE TRAINING/CONFERENCES/TEACHING: COMMUNICATIONS & PR

HOW TO PROOFREAD

Fred Pryor Seminars
2000 Johnson Drive
PO Box 2951
Shawnee Mission, KS 66201
TEL: 913-384-6400
TOLL FREE: 800-255-6139
FAX: 913-384-2637
Credit: 0.6 CEUs
Sponsor: Pryor Resources
Contact: Seminar Coordinator
Description: Recognizing the embarrassment and disappointment that follows after errors are discovered "too late" in a newsletter, Pryor has developed a one-day seminar to increase proofreading skills among those responsible for the newsletter and other communication vehicles of an organization. Some of the discussion topics:
- Effective proofreading routines
- Pointers on punctuation
- Hints to eliminate distractions
- Principles to help spot and correct the 12 most common grammatical errors

- Tactics to avoid missing commonly misspelled words
- Courtesy and tact in pointing out mistakes of others
- Strategies for spotting hard-to-see mistakes
- Pointers on "demon pairs" of words
- Tips on catching errors early

In addition, instructors take participants through a 20-point program on power proofreading skills, and a 10-session course in on the basic elements for quick and accurate proofreading, word choice, format and style, word processors and PCs, and other areas.

The Seminar concentrates only on applications that can be used immediately upon the participant's return to the organization. References materials, including the *Proofreading Workbook*, charts, lists, reference forms and other tools, are provided free to participants. The seminar is held in various locations around the country which change from year to year. It is approved for Continuing Education Credits (CEUs) and provides a Certificate upon completion.
Publications: Proofreading Workbook; Pryor Report (newsletter)

MARKET-ABILITY: MARKETING STRATEGIES FOR NONPROFITS

Voluntary Action Center of United Way
United Way of Minneapolis Area
404 South Eighth Street
Minneapolis, MN 55404
TEL: 612-340-7532
Credit: CEUs
Sponsor: Junior League of Minneapolis
Contact: Dr. Lorna Michelson
Description: Recognizing the importance of an effective marketing program for volunteer groups and organizations, the above sponsors developed a training program to help strengthen those in the programs who are responsible for communicating with the media, foundations, other agencies and organizations, and the general public. The program includes introductory sessions for the novice, but includes strategies and other processes to assist the veteran also. Sessions are focused in the following areas:
- Introduction to Marketing Principles;
- Strategies for Resource Development;
- Strategies for Fund-raising Potential; and
- Application of Marketing Principles to the Participant's Own Organization.

The program is designed to benefit Executive Directors, Board Members, Volunteer Directors and other volunteer leaders, as well as the targeted public relations/resource development staff.
Principal presenter is a Board Member/Trainer for the *Junior League of Minneapolis.*

MARKETING FOR VOLUNTARY SERVICE ORGANIZATIONS

SEE TRAINING/CONFERENCES/TEACHING: COMMUNICATIONS & PR

MARKETING STRATEGIES FOR NONPROFIT ORGANIZATIONS

Padgett Thompson
Padgett Thompson Building
PO Box 8297
Overland Park, KS 66208
TEL: 913-451-2900
TOLL FREE: 800-255-4141
Credit: Certificate
Sponsor: Padgett Thompson
Contact: Jan Chrisman
Description: These one-day seminars are based on extensive research, including surveys of nonprofits who have demonstrated success in getting press and airtime, and have developed

community images which attract civic leaders to their boards. The seminar involves directors and managers of such organizations who present real case histories of their experiences in leading and promoting their organizations. A typical seminar includes topics such as:

Power-Marketing Strategies That Will Put You in the Spotlight

- Situation Analysis - what it is and why it should be your first marketing activity
- Should you hire an advertising consultant? Five questions to ask first
- Selecting the most effective approach to your market research
- Five ways to make your telemarketing effort more effective
- The underdog role - how and when to play it
- What to say in the most important line of copy in your direct mail piece
- When integrated marketing works well for nonprofits
- Shoestring tactics to get the most for your marketing dollar
- How to set up and benefit from "deferred giving" programs
- Follow-up strategies you can use to guarantee first-time contributors give again... and again

Tell Your Story: Raising Your Visibility to Gain Support and Funding

- Proven techniques for gaining the support of public officials and funding sources
- Four ways to keep your public service announcements out of the trash - and on the air
- The controlled interview: How to make sure a reporter asks the questions you want to answer
- Why you should never ask for money in public service announcements
- Five facts potential donors want to know about your organization... before they'll give money
- How to avoid the most common PR blunder made by nonprofits
- When to buy media coverage - and when to use PSAs
- Do you use too much jargon? How to find out
- One statement to omit from all your media interviews
- Writing the press release that an editor will use
- Photography: When you should use visuals
- Four facts all press releases must include
- Not every special event should be a fund-raiser... here's why
- When, where and why to hold a press conference

How to Lead with Vision and Authority

- How to get your staff to take over day-to-day operations - so *you* can focus on community relations
- Five ways to get your board to tell you what they really want
- Motivation techniques to wake up a laid-back board
- A clear-cut method to divide your responsibilities from the board's
- Four questions your proposal must answer to earn your board's approval
- When your principles are challenged - how to stick to your beliefs
- Three ways to help your staff deal more professionally with the public
- Setting measurable goals when money is not the issue
- Five ways to turn business contacts into advocates for your cause
- The most common reasons why board members resign... and how to keep yours satisfied

A feature of the program is thorough coverage and intensive discussion of pitfalls - practices which a nonprofit should avoid. Ample time is set aside for sharing ideas among participants in networking sessions. Two publications, *The Nonprofit Manager's Workbook* and *The Media Reference Guide* and a Certificate of Participation are provided. Seminars are held throughout the year in 500 different cities, and can be arranged on-site for an individual organization with pre-seminar consultation to tailor it to the organization's specific needs.

In addition to Padget Thompson trainers, faculty is drawn from

participating nonprofit groups, which have included American Red Cross, Goodwill Industries, Boy Scouts of America, and American Cancer Society.
Publications: The Nonprofit Manager's Workbook; The Media Reference Guide

MEDIA RELATIONS FOR NONPROFIT AND VOLUNTEER ORGANIZATIONS
SEE TRAINING/CONFERENCES/TEACHING: COMMUNICATIONS & PR

PRODUCING, DESIGNING & WRITING NEWSLETTERS
Newsletter Factory
3036 Roswell Road, NE
Marietta, GA 30062
TEL: 404-977-9800
FAX: 404-977-4632
Credit: Certificate of Completion
Sponsor: Newsletter Factory
Contact: Thom Hartmann
Description: This one-day seminar addresses newsletter design, production and editing and has been developed to serve both the beginner and the professional, and to span public, private, and corporate sector communications needs. Areas of learning at the seminar include:

- **How newsletters can be produced inexpensively,** *even if you don't have a computer!* - assembling newsletters on your typewriter, or working with a typesetter without spending a fortune.
- **The seven most common newsletter design mistakes** - what they are, why they're often made, and how to avoid making them yourself.
- **How internal newsletters build a sense of family** with staff, maintain high levels of motivation, and keep staff up to date on new benefits of working for or belonging to your organization.
- **The seven essential components** of every newsletter, and how to make them work for your newsletter.
- **The 27 essential elements of good newsletter copy** which increase readership, creditibility and motivation.
- **The 10 deadly sins of newsletter production,** and how to train yourself so they don't even accidentally creep in.
- **The 29 point checklist** for producing a successful, effective newsletter that people will want to read.

All participants receive an extensive free package of materials containing publications, diskettes, a style manual, and other tools to assist in production of a newsletter. Available only at the seminar or with the video cassette program (see below), this package includes:

- *Producing, Designing and Writing Newsletters Manual;*
- Strunk and White's *The Elements of Style;*
- sample newsletter designs;
- computer newsletter formats (on diskette);
- samples of layout board, non-reproducible blue pencil, and other production tools;
- listings of type libraries;
- copy of *Newsletter Communications;*
- layout grid samples; printer bid form;
- *Computer Virus Detector;*
- free subscription to *Compuserve* with $15 of usage credit;
- *Newsletter Design Guide* showcasing layouts of ten actual newsletters.

These materials are not available separately.
A special session on **Desktop Publishing** provides advice on the array of programs and machines in the marketplace. The session emphasizes the necessity to learn how to choose a system that's easy to use and compatible with current computers (covers both IBM and McIntosh), and how to improve productivity without sacrificing quality. For those without a computer but with plans to

acquire one, this special seminar helps determine what is available, how it works, and how this technology can be used even without an in-house computer system.

Participants receive a certificate upon completion of the seminar. Faculty is drawn from fields of marketing and communications, computer systems, education and journalism.

Reduced registration is available on request for nonprofit organizations (35% of participants at these seminars are from nonprofit groups such as the YMCA, Red Cross, Braille Institute, etc.). Public agencies have included Veterans Administration, Coast Guard, Postal Service and others. Business/industry is always well represented.

Seminars are held in major cities across the country, including Atlanta, Boston, Chicago, New York, Philadelphia and Washington, DC (inquire about other cities, as well as in-house seminars available to groups with ten or more people involved in newsletter publication).

For those who cannot attend, a six-hour audiovisual cassette, with complete materials package, is available (inquire).

Publications: Producing, Designing & Writing Newsletters Manual; Sample Newsletter Design; Computer Newsletter Formats (diskette); Computer Virus Detector; Newsletter Design Guide

PUBLIC RELATIONS ON A SHOESTRING*
SEE TRAINING/CONFERENCES/TEACHING: COMMUNICATIONS & PR

PUBLICITY WORKSHOP
Volunteer Information Center
407 East 17th Street
PO Box 404
Cheyenne, WY 82001
TEL: 307-632-4132
Credit: Inquire
Sponsor: Laramie County Volunteer Information/Action Center; VA Hospital
Contact: Marie Baptiste
Description: Recognizing the importance of media exposure to volunteer programs, the central volunteer organization first queried organizations on needs in this area, then developed a workshop to bring together organization leaders for a knowledge providing and sharing workshop. All aspects of the media (newspapers, television, radio, newsletters, fairs, etc.) joined in efforts to develop a comprehensive plan for recruiting publicity that is effective in educating the public about the goals of the various service-providing organizations. Broad topics include:
- How to get attention of the TV media.
- Any problems that may be encountered in getting publicity.
- Writing and story ideas.

Faculty was drawn from fields of the media, volunteer management, government, business and industry, and education. This is one of a series of workshops on expressed concerns of volunteer managers sponsored by the Volunteer Information Center. Others cover areas of recruiting, interviewing, placing, and supervising and recognizing volunteers, volunteer/staff relations, agency involvement, evaluation, funding and others based on queries to the field.

INDIVIDUAL PROGRAM PROFILES

BERKS SCHOOLCASTING*
Reading and Berks County Chamber of Commerce
541 Court Street
Reading, PA 19601
TEL: 215-376-6766
Purpose: To create a dedicated educational access channel.

Sponsor: Berks County Schools; Berks-Suburban Cable Company; Berks County Chamber of Commerce
Contact: J.F. Horrigan, President
Description: Berks Schoolcasting is an organization of volunteers from local schools, industry and government media personnel who meet monthly during the school year to coordinate the scheduling of locally-produced educational television programs. Membership is open to all public, parochial and private schools and colleges in Berks County as well as to any community group or individual willing to work on a cooperative voluntary basis toward a common goal.

The process began in 1962 when the Chamber of Commerce created the Public School Educational Television Advisory Committee to explore and report on ways in which educational TV involving the local school system might be provided. Although the Committee determined that it was cost-prohibitive, Berks County continued to seek ways to provide the service. The first encouraging move was made by Berks TV Cable Company, who offered to wire two school buildings and interconnect them via the cable system. When Berks County Schools was approached with this offer of free help, officials agreed to purchase the necessary internal equipment for the two schools.

In addition, in 1969, the Superintendent of Schools created the "Berks County Educational Television Subcommittee" to serve as a clearinghouse and monitor of the initial efforts.

As citizen involvement increased, and additional schools began to develop media programs, the Berks Suburban Cable Company continued to assist in wiring buildings. In addition, they provided, and still provide, technical assistance and information on the acquisition and use of television and related equipment. Some of the schools and their programs follow:

Governor Mifflin School District - Sports Program, Cooperation with Community Groups, District Feature Program, In-Service Programs, Seasonal Programs.

Kutztown Area School District - weekly half-hour program transmitted to local community inviting citizens to interact on pre-announced subject with students and an invited volunteer specializing in the week's subject.

Central Catholic High School - oral history project in cooperation with elderly; National/State Political Convention with candidates present.

Several additional school districts, business/industry, and local colleges also develop and present innovative programming through this voluntary effort, thus providing a vehicle for interaction that was created by an unmet need within the community.
Founded: 1962

BLOCKBUSTER COMMUNITY SERVICE PROGRAM
SEE BUSINESS/INDUSTRY INVOLVEMENT

CABLEVISION BY THE PEOPLE*
Berks Community Television
1112 Muhlenberg Street
Reading, PA 19602
TEL: 215-374-3065
Purpose: To enable the people themselves to generate local awareness and information.
Sponsor: American Television and Communications Corporation; the community
Contact: Jerry Richter, Executive Director
Description: A wood carver, without ever leaving his workbench, demonstrates the art of making fine gunstocks and responds to questions from people all over town. Three attorneys, together in a small room, answer questions from and talk with people in widely separated parts of the city. A panel is formed of students involved in a race riot and brought together with school and human relations officials to discuss the problem and respond to the public. Such innovations are part of a community's effort to inform itself, rather than be informed by producers, politicians, public relations

experts, etc., through the television medium.

The Reading Dialogue toward a community-owned television organization began in 1963 when a cable TV franchise was granted to the Reading area, but it was in 1975 when the community itself became involved. To break the cycle of systematic isolation of the elderly, the first exploration was in the area of senior citizens. This was not set up as just another program aimed at old people, but as something they were to do for themselves. The idea was to involve people who had no experience in television, teach them how to use the medium, and provide access to equipment, facilities, and support so that they could develop their own programming.

Regularly-scheduled productions include:

Sing Along: Two senior centers and a State hospital are linked for the program and can see and hear each other talk and sing; many participants, unable to travel, have made lasting friends of both participants and home viewers.

Inside City Hall: This a weekly program with two-way interactive cablecasts arranged between the mayor and city council and citizens; officials have become more aware and responsive, and citizens more interested and involved in the problems of their areas.

Bridging the Generation Gap: This program is a senior citizens "rap" with high school students.

Program topics now consider all ages and groups with experts in arts and culture, health, nutrition, finances, etc., providing access to valuable information in all areas of human services and community needs.

Founded: 1975

"IN THE TRENCHES" AUTHOR SEARCH PROGRAM
Association for Volunteer Administration, Region IV
c/o Voluntary Action Center
1520 Aberdeen Road, Suite 109
Hampton, VA 23666
TEL: 804-838-9770

Purpose: It is a well-known fact that many volunteer programs have very limited budgets, with the bulk of the funding going to the target population designated by the program's charter or bylaws. In many cases, when a volunteer effort could benefit from attendance by staff and/or volunteers in the program, budget constraints prohibit participation. *In the Trenches,* an upcoming book by and for volunteers and volunteer administrators, addresses this issue through its "call for authors."

Launched by Region IV of the Association for Volunteer Administration (AVA-IV), this call for authors represents a unique way to develop a scholarship fund to finance participation in the national conference of the *Association for Volunteer Administration* by volunteer administrators and volunteers who might not otherwise attend. The resulting increased attendance to these events, which include Certification, training, workshops and many other volunteer-related activities for people "in the trenches," benefits not only the individual attendees, but the entire field of volunteerism as well.

Open to AVA members in Region IV, submissions may be stories of success or failure on any area of volunteerism (i.e., program development, problem-solving, recognition, recruitment, public relations, etc.). All articles are written in the first person and may be humorous, dramatic, or simply a factual account. Although open to regional members only, the book will be distributed nationwide.

Each Regional office of AVA develops its own way of raising funds. For other fund-raising ideas, contact the *International Association for Volunteer Administration* (see separate entry).

Contact: Kay Bradley, Chair

LABOR EDITORS ROUNDTABLE
United Way of Franklin County
360 South Third Street
Columbus, OH 43215-5412
TEL: 614-227-2700

Purpose: To foster a United Way-labor union information-sharing forum to help meet the community's human-care needs.

Sponsor: United Way of Franklin County

Contact: Diane Biggs, Labor and Community Services

Description: The United Way receives generous campaign support from workers belonging to some 60 area unions, and also benefits from direct volunteer service by union workers. In turn, the United Way has helped thousands of union members to receive the human-care services they need. This hand-in-hand effort has a long history of working to meet the Columbus area's human-care needs. To build on that productive history, United Way developed an information-sharing program to assure a year-round United Way presence with organized labor. The United Way "Labor Editors Roundtable" brings together newsletter editors from the locals in a United Way setting.

Since the roundtable editors first met in March 1989, several articles have been published about United Way activities. For example, the Ohio AFL-CIO newsletter endorsed the 1989 United Way campaign in a half-page article. The article told readers how many local human-care agencies their contributions helped to support, and described some specific volunteer programs receiving support.

The United Automobile, Aerospace and Agricultural Implement Workers of America also published an informative article describing ways in which United Way addressed workers' problems caused by layoffs, as well as on-the-job issues such as planning for retirement and understanding AIDS in the workplace. The article also pointed out that over 40 members of different unions sit on boards and committees of United Ways and United Way-funded programs.

Since its inception in March 1989, the roundtable has almost doubled - from an initial 12 editors to 23 by September. The United Way maintains regular contact with the editors and the presidents of the locals. According to the Associate Director at United Way, "We think the United Way articles in union newsletters will create a lot of positive reactions from a much wider audience."

Founded: 1989

SPECIALS PROJECT
National Public Radio
2025 M Street, NW
Washington, DC 20036
TEL: 202-822-2848

Purpose: To find new ways of addressing issues of national concern which affect our communities.

Contact: Sallie Bodie, Specials Project Outreach Coordinator

Description: The *Specials Project* is a new approach to public broadcasting. Beginning in September 1990, National Public Radio's (NPR) journalists will examine issues of national concern which affect our communities. To find new ways to address these issues, this inaugural series will be accompanied by an *Outreach Program* to link listeners, schools, businesses and community organizations with their public radio station. Also, the *Specials Project* offers public radio stations around the country an opportunity to serve their local communities.

Outreach Program - A wider audience through outreach is a goal of the *Specials Project.* The *Outreach Program* will help NPR and public readio reach a wider audience by building in support from national educational and youth organizations. Member stations will be encouraged to schedule follow-up programming on the current *Specials Projects* issue in their communities. NPR will support stations by providing contacts, materials, promotion, and activity plans to facilitate local outreach.

The First Specials Project - The 1990 hallmark *Specials* focuses on prejudice as it affects youth. The young people will tell in their own words, how they feel about prejudice. (See separate entry, *Class of 2000: The Prejudice Puzzle,* for more details on this first effort.)

Publications: Specials Project Information Packet

SUPPORT FOR PUBLIC TELEVISION
SEE FUNDING/FUND-RAISING/RELATED SERVICES

UNITED WAY EDITORIAL BOARD
Stateline United Way
431 Olympian Boulevard
Beloit, WI 53511-4211
TEL: 608-365-4451
Purpose: To assist in promotion and publicity for the area's volunteer programs through a board of experts in the media field.
Sponsor: Sears, Roebuck & Company
Contact: F. William Winkelman, Executive Director
Description: Chaired by the manager of *Sears, Roebuck & Company's* Beloit Store, the *United Way Editorial Board* is made up of representatives from radio stations, the newspaper, the cable television channel, and three company newsletters. In addition to setting up a system of ongoing media coverage, editorial board members conduct communications workshops for staff from nonprofit agencies, training them to tailor their written material to fit the needs of each type of media.
The Board's efforts have resulted in regular features in newsletters of more than 25 area companies, announcementes of volunteer opportunities on Beloit's two radio sations, *WBEL* and *WGEZ,* videos from Beloit's public access TV channel about volunteer agency activities, and articles, photos, and public-service advertisements in the *Beloit Daily News.*
In addition, the Board generates press releases and articles for company newsletters which, according to one executive, "are read from cover to cover" by employees. Also, the Board is responsible for maintaining contact with each company's communications staff.
As agency staff become more proficient in issuing their own press materials, the Board focuses on broader issues affecting the community, such as literacy. Also, the Board helps plan volunteer recognition programs each year.
Founded: 1987

VOLUNTEER CONNECTION TELETHON
SEE ADMINISTRATION: RECRUITMENT/ORIENTATION

WMNR RADIO - ACCESS BROADCASTING COMPANY*
Masuk High School
Monroe, CT 06468
TEL: 203-268-9667
Purpose: To deliver quality arts programming, and to make the handicapped highly visible in the community.
Sponsor: CETA (initially); private and corporate donations
Contact: Stewart Nazzaro, General Manager
Description: WMNR-FM is the only radio station in the country that is totally managed by the handicapped. WMNR began operating in January 1980 with a rock music format. Since that time it has switched to a classical and big band jazz format, and emphasizes cultural programming. In addition to an interest in an arts format, talk shows will alternate with public service spots on civic events and local jobs for the disabled. A call-in rider service, for example, helps homebound listeners get to appointments, entertainment programs, etc.
The WMNR crew ranges in age from 14 to 65 and includes alcoholics, amputees, the cerebral palsied, stutterers, etc. The station director is a legally blind albino who is determined to use radio to help other handicapped people combat some of the obstacles he faced when growing up. Many disabled listeners visit the studio to see first hand the accomplishments of the crew. These visitors range from very young children to the elderly, and all have come away with renewed hope and satisfaction.
Because of limited funds, only five of the disabled personnel are actually on the payroll. Both handicapped and able-bodied volunteers are recruited to keep the station operating seven days a week from 7 a.m. to midnight. However, the period from 7 a.m. to 2 p.m. every weekday is reserved for operation by only handicapped staff and volunteers. This was done to make one section of the program unique.
Formerly, WMNR was the local high school's radio club. With a degree in radio and TV from Syracuse University in hand, the present station manager convinced the Board of Education that he could transform it into an actual aired station. With a $52,300 CETA grant, the first program went on the air.
Now that the CETA funding has been depleted, the station is planning to raise $100,000 needed to keep WMNR on the air (each year). WMNR has no commercials, and depends solely on grants and contributions.
To accept donations, the station founded Access Broadcasting Company. Several corporations have talked with the station's officers, and are considering funding assistance. Future plans include increasing WMNR's signal from 600 to 10,000 watts to expand coverage to 450 square miles, enlarging the staff, winning affiliation with National Public Radio and sponsorship by the Corporation for Public Broadcasting. There is no locally-based, arts-oriented radio station in the area, and WMNR plans to fill that need.
Founded: 1980

WXPN-FM RADIO
University of Pennsylvania
3400 Chestnut Street
Philadelphia, PA 19104
TEL: 215-898-7483
FAX: 215-848-6619
Purpose: WXPN-FM is a radio station at the University of Pennsylvania with a staff composed almost entirely of volunteers. It's programming is designed to motivate and inform the community in areas including children's programming, public affairs, and community services. Typical programs include the three 1989 CPB Gold (first place) Award winners below:

- **Children's Programming** - *Kid's Corner,* a live show aimed at listeners six to twelve years of age, which was dropped from a New York public radio station because it felt "there was no place for kids' radio."
- **Community Service** - *WXPN's City-Wide Public Hearing on Drugs* ("an attempt to go beyond the national 'Just Say No' campaign"), which brought together teenagers, community leaders, former addicts, educators and law enforcement officers at the *Free Library of Philadelphia* for a seven-hour public hearing on the city's drug problems.
- **Public Affairs** - *No Bed of Roses,* which reflects difficulties faced by black families traveling through the South before 1964 civil rights legislation (a 30-minute documentary featuring interviews with blacks who vividly remembered traveling in those times).

In addition to the three first place awards (out of eleven awarded by CPB in competition that included 267 public radio stations), an innovation that won a CPB Silver (second place) Award was *Poetry of the Air,* which enabled poets to read their own work, accompanied by music and sound effects and woven into the station's regular programming for a month. The station's manager attributes WXPN-FM's success to a departure from long-standing programming in 1987. Although the changes caused some turmoil at first among listeners and the station's volunteers, the manager feels that their culmination in the prestigious awards has demonstrated the often-rewarding results of taking risks, and reduced the need to "stay with the familiar." According to one volunteer, "WXPN is a treasure to the community."
Sponsor: University of Pennsylvania
Contact: Mark Fuerst, General Manager

COMMUNICATIONS & PUBLIC RELATIONS: AIDS

NATIONAL/STATE ORGANIZATIONS

AMERICA RESPONDS TO AIDS
National AIDS Information Campaign
Centers for Disease Control
1600 Clifton Road, NE #B-68
Atlanta, GA 30333
TEL: 404-329-2384
Objectives: To keep the public informed on the latest information on AIDS.
Services: Provides technical assistance to *Scholastics, Inc.,* the world's largest publisher of supplementary, English-language educational materials, to assist in age-appropriate coverage of AIDS in classroom magazines; coordinates a variety of events with state medical associations on AIDS prevention and AIDS-related resources; distributes public-service announcements (PSAs) to 7,000 radio stations around the country; prepares national satellite news feeds for television and radio broadcasting of basic information on transmission and prevention of AIDS featuring recognized medical professionals; publishes free AIDS brochures in its *What You Should Know About AIDS* series with segments tailored to different audiences (general public, low-income women, parents of teens, inner-city blacks, employees, inner-city Hispanics, and families); works with various state and local groups - including businesses - to plan activities that will coincide with the themes of CDC campaigns.
Contact: AIDS Information Coordinator

THE NAMES PROJECT/AIDS MEMORIAL QUILT
The NAMES Project Foundation
PO Box 14573
San Francisco, CA 94114
TEL: 415-863-5511
Objectives: To confront individuals and governments with the urgency and enormity of the AIDS epidemic and the need for an immediate and compassionate response by revealing the names and the lives behind the global statics.
To build a powerful, positive, creative symbol of remembrance and hope, linking diverse peoples worldwide in the shared expression of our common grief, pain and rage in response to AIDS.
To encourage donations in every community where the *Quilt* is displayed, thereby raising the desperately needed funds for people living with AIDS and their caregivers.
Services: The *NAMES Project* is an international AIDS memorial taking the shape of a huge quilt made up of thousands of individual 3'x6' panels. Each panel remembers the life of someone who has died of AIDS.
The *Project* started as a volunteer organization in 1987, a year and a half after the idea of a quilt as an AIDS memorial was posed by an individual (Cleve Jones) in response to a candlelight memorial service. Jones teamed up with several others to organize the *NAMES Project Foundation.*
The response to the *Quilt* was immediate. People from each of the major cities most affected by the epidemic - New York, Los Angeles and San Francisco - sent panels in memory of their friends and loved ones. Lesbians, gay men and their friends in San Francisco were especially generous, responding to wish lists in the *NAMES Project* workshop's storefront window asking for sewing machines, office supplies, and volunteers.
As awareness of the *Quilt* grew, so did participation. Thousands of individuals and groups from all over the U.S. and from many foreign countries began to send the memorial panels to the San Francisco workshop, to be included in the *Quilt.*

On October 11, 1987, the *NAMES Project* displayed the *AIDS Memorial Quilt* on the Capital Mall in Washington, DC during the *National March on Washington for Lesbian and Gay Rights.* The *Quilt* covered a space larger than two football fields, and included 1,920 panels. A half million people saw the *Quilt* that weekend.
The overwhelming response to the *Quilt* during this inaugural display led to a four-month, 20-city, national tour in the Spring of 1988. The tour raised nearly $500,000 for AIDS direct care services. These funds remained in their communities and were distributed through local organizations. The tour also generated community spirit, as more than 9,000 volunteers nationwide helped the seven-person road crew move and display the *Quilt.* Local panels were added in each city, doubling the size of the *Quilt* to more than 6,000 panels by the end of the tour.
The *Quilt* returned to Washington, DC in October 1988 to be displayed once again in its entirety. Having grown to include 8,288 memorial panels, it was displayed on the Ellipse behind the *White House,* and the reading of the names of the dead continued throughout the entire day.
A second tour through North America brought a large section of the *Quilt* to 19 more cities in the U.S. and Canada in 1989. It was displayed once more - for the final time - on Columbus Day weekend, October 1989. However, smaller displays of the *Quilt* will continue to take place in cities all over the U.S. and around the world. The *Quilt,* which presently contains almost 11,000 panels, has been nominated for the *Nobel Peace Prize.*
The *Quilt* is an ongoing memorial and educational tool; panels continue to be added as the AIDS epidemic continues. As the toll of AIDS deaths globally continues to rise, the *Quilt* is offered as one example of an appropriate, compassionate response to the epidemic. The *Foundation* has a commitment to continue for the duration of the epidemic.
Although springing from an idea of one man, who garnered a handful of volunteers in San Francisco in 1987, the organization has grown to include 22 paid staff members. The staff relies on hundreds of volunteers in the San Francisco area, and hundreds of thousands across the country. Over 30 *NAMES Project Chapters* have sprung up in cities all over the U.S., and these volunteers are the ones who "make it happen" whenever there is a display of the *Quilt* anywhere.
An aspect of the program that gives the *NAMES Project* staff and volunteers a feeling of great pride is the fact that, after seeing a display of the *Quilt,* many people are moved to become involved in their own communities' responses to the epidemic. This often includes volunteering at local AIDS service organizations in their cities. In this way, we foster and encourage volunteerism for AIDS across the country.
Contact: Sue Martin, Director of Development
Publications: Quilt Facts
Founded: 1987

INDIVIDUAL PROGRAM PROFILES

EDUCATION & PREVENTION SERVICES: AIDS PROGRAM
Whitman-Walker Clinic
1407 S Street, NW
Washington, DC 20009
TEL: 202-797-3560; 202-328-0697 (Spanish)
Purpose: To provide HIV-related education and prevention information to targeted communities.
Sponsor: Whitman-Walker Clinic
Contact: Peter Provost
Description: Sunnye Sherman AIDS Education Services is a division of the Whitman-Walker Clinic, a volunteer-based effort enhanced by professional staff. The education program is a multifaceted and multilevel approach to community health

education. The program uses both traditional and nontraditional teaching and counseling methods to provide HIV-related eduation and prevention information. While the focus of all education is on risk behaviors, messages are targeted at specific communities. The service has individual emphasis programs such as:

Project HEART (Healthy Relationship Training) - conducts seminars and workshops where gay/bisexual men examine social and sexual lifestyle issues in the context of HIV and AIDS. The project emphasizes skill building and behavior modification leading to risk reduction and healthy practices.

Street Outreach Teams - delivers HIV/AIDS education on the streets to I.V. drug users and sex industry workers.

The Speakers Bureau - addresses general and specialized audiences in the workplace, community centers, classrooms, and health care settings.

The DC AIDS Information Line - operates four lines functioning seven days a week and answers over 500 calls a month.

The Latino AIDS Services Access Network - operates in conjunction with community outreach, HIV counseling and training, and traditional education as part of a project aimed at serving Spanish-speaking communities.

Education services is named in memory of Sunnye Sherman, who was diligent in her efforts to educate the public about the realities of AIDS through speaking out as a person living with AIDS. She died in 1986.

Volunteers in all Clinic programs receive orientation, training, seminars and workshops. All programs are coordinated with local government and community-based organizations.

HEART STRINGS - MEMPHIS STOP
SEE FUNDING/FUND-RAISING/RELATED SERVICES: AIDS

PROJECT NOVA - AIDS PROGRAM
SEE INFORMATION & REFERRAL: AIDS

COMMUNICATIONS & PUBLIC RELATIONS: ARTS

NATIONAL/STATE ORGANIZATIONS

AMERICAN FEDERATION OF ARTS
41 East 65th Street
New York, NY 10021
TEL: 212-988-7700
Objectives: To work toward spreading enjoyment of the work of many periods and cultures in areas of painting, sculpture, design, architecture, crafts, etc.
Services: Originates traveling exhibits of art and film programs and makes them available to art centers, university and small rural art galleries, museums and other cultural programs; assists centers in developing resources; operates the Museum Management Institute; mounts conferences, workshops, and other training events for museum professionals; offers reduced-rate fine arts insurance and air transportation programs; sponsors annual arts competitions; publishes free information on its more than 20 shows.
Publications: AFA Newsletter; Program and Exhibit Catalog
Founded: 1909

INDIVIDUAL PROGRAM PROFILES

ART FOR KIDS' SAKE
SEE VOLUNTEERS: PROFESSIONALS

SENIOR ACTING PROGRAM OF THE BARN PLAYERS*
Retired Senior Volunteer Program
5165 Merriam Drive
Merriam, KS 66302
TEL: 913-362-3343 (office); 913-341-8834 (home)
Purpose: To provide new challenges and goals to the participants; to enrich the lives of the audience through theatre.
Sponsor: The Barn Players
Contact: Winifred Laas, Secretary-Steering Committee
Description: In September 1978, a group of 25 older persons made up the original production unit of a new offshoot of the *Barn Players Theatre* - the *Senior Acting Program.* The volunteer company organized the Program with a CETA grant and free space provided by Johnson County Community College. Bookings at that time were through the Johnson County Arts Council.
In 1978, the volunteers prepared six 30-minute one-act plays about the process of aging, held rehearsals and began performing for nutrition sites, nursing homes and other senior organizations in the community. Now the plays tour regularly throughout the Greater Kansas City metropolitan area, performing before church, civic and professional groups of mixed ages, Junior College level social studies, as well as senior groups. Over a four-year period, 443 performances were presented to approximately 18,000 people. Plays are designed with touring in mind and require few props and small casts. Originally each play emphasized some aspect of aging - not the condition of being aged. Material of this nature has been more and more difficult to find and recently light comedies have been included in the repertory. Performances are followed by a period of discussion led by a Program member in which the audience participates. Each performance is based on a choice by the booking organization of the play most suited to their needs and runs approximately 20-30 minutes.
The senior volunteers are highly dedicated to the Program and find that much more time is involved in coordinating the activities than was first anticipated. Auditions are held, plays are rehearsed for at least two months, performers must be willing to devote two to three evenings each week for rehearsals, and their schedules must be flexible enough to enable them to perform during the day or evening; discussion leaders must be chosen, plays selected, and publicity released to local radio, TV and newspaper media. One goal of the Program is to be self-sufficient thereby necessitating the requested donation to be increased from the original $10 per performance to $15 and now to $25.
Founded: 1978

COMMUNICATIONS & PUBLIC RELATIONS: CHILDREN/YOUTH

NATIONAL/STATE ORGANIZATIONS

NATIONAL COLLABORATION FOR YOUTH
1319 F Street, NW
Suite 601
Washington, DC 20004
TEL: 202-347-2080
Objectives: To increase public awareness of the needs of youth.
Services: Works to affect public and private policy on the needs of youth; seeks to redirect national resources toward youth development; involves youth in the decision-making processes of programs and institutions affecting their lives; collaborates on areas such as youth employment, education, health, family life, and juvenile justice; works with government and voluntary agencies to improve services for youth; includes in its membership Boy Scouts of America, 4-H Program, Big Brothers/Big Sisters of

America, and the national boards of YMCAs and YWCAs, and works with the *National Assembly of National Voluntary Health and Social Welfare Organizations;* publishes a newsletter and other materials.
Sponsor: Boy Scouts of America
Publications: NCY Today
Founded: 1973

NATIONAL LISTEN AMERICA CLUB
SEE VOLUNTEERS: STUDENTS

PUBLIC AWARENESS ABOUT CHILD CARE (PAACC)
SEE VOLUNTEERS: PARENTS

PUBLIC RELATIONS STUDENT SOCIETY OF AMERICA
33 Irving Place
New York, NY 10003
TEL: 212-995-2230
Objectives: To foster students' understanding of modern theories and procedures of public relations; to instill in them a professional attitude, and to encourage them to adhere to the highest ideals of the practice of public relations.
Services: Works only through *Public Relations Student Society of America (PRSSA)* Chapters chartered at a college or university; brings together students and professional public relations practitioners as part of its education program; leads workshops and other training events throughout the year; convenes annual conference simultaneously with the *Public Relations Society of America.*
Publications: PRSSA Forum; Campus Newsletters
Founded: 1968

INDIVIDUAL PROGRAM PROFILES

BUT I'M DIFFERENT...
Duke Ellington School of the Arts
35th and R streets, NW
Washington, DC 20007
TEL: 202-282-0123
Purpose: To dramatize a somber message: "Teenage pregnancy is a serious problem."
Sponsor: Metropolitan Washington Council of Governments
Contact: Roger Bellamy
Description: Washington, DC teenagers periodically join students from the *Duke Ellington School of the Arts* for workshops designed to enable students to educate each other about pregnancy, unsafe sex, AIDS and substance abuse. In March 1990, the subject was teenage pregnancy.
The Ellington School students also are volunteer counselors at Planned Parenthood of Metropolitan Washington. Before teaching at the workshops, they work to compel their peers to think about the issues. To accomplish this they perform skits. The skit on teenage pregnancy featured two teenagers playing sisters, with the younger sister breaking the news of her pregnancy to her older sister. Although the skit is light so as to amuse as well as teach, the bottom line is the message it hopes will be impressed on the nearly 100 teens usually in the audience - that teen pregnancy is more than just a "cute baby to cuddle."
The workshops are sponsored by the *Metropolitan Washington Council of Governments (COG),* the *Washington Consortium on HIV Infection in Youth,* and the *District of Columbia Independent Living Program.* According to a COG official, the concern is not only the pregnancy itself, but reports of teenagers with sexually-transmitted diseases is increasing. Through experience with the workshops and skits, COG and the other sponsors have learned first-hand that the best people to teach young people are other young people.

Apart from education, the teen counselors talked about self-esteem, telling their peers that, ultimately, each individual is responsible for his actions, "which sometimes means being the oddball. With self-esteem, if you're pressured, you won't give in." Teen volunteer counselors from several high schools were represented at the workshop - *Terrific Peers* from *Rockville High School,* and *Teen Council* of *Coolidge Senior High School,* for example. Others not involved in counseling groups volunteered to lead sessions and help in other ways. Sponsors stayed in the background, since the students did not appear to need any assistance. The teens ranged from 14 to 19 years of age. Other workshops cover other issues, including AIDS and substance abuse. One of the volunteer counselors was very direct about the reasons for his participation: "I do this because I may be saving somebody's life."

CHILDREN'S LITERACY INITIATIVE
SEE TRAINING/CONFERENCES/TEACHING: LITERACY

CHILDREN'S MIRACLE NETWORK TELETHON
SEE FUNDING/FUND-RAISING/RELATED SERVICES: CHILDREN

COMMUNICATING HUMAN NEEDS
United Way of San Antonio and Bexar County
700 South Alamo
PO Box 898
San Antonio, TX 78293-0898
TEL: 512-224-5000
Purpose: To encourage youngsters to explore human needs in their community.
Sponsor: Mervyn's Department Stores
Contact: Richard Alvarado, Director
Description: To develop a rapport with teenagers in the community while encouraging them to explore human needs in their community, a photo-essay contest was launched in San Antonio and Bexar County. Addressing high school students, the contest was sponsored by the *United Way, San Antonio Youth Literacy (SAYL), Women in Communications, Inc. (WICI), Mervyn's Department Stores,* and *Fox Photo.*
Cameras were donated by *Mervyn's,* and film was donated by *Fox Photo.* The teen participants who volunteered for the contest submitted photo entries along with a 50-word essay on community needs to a panel of judges convened by WICI.
Five awards were presented at each participating school (Edgewood, Memorial, Sam Houston, and Fox Tech High Schools). Each of the award-winning entries then became part of a traveling community exhibit.
Designed to benefit youth by making them more aware of their environment and the needs that must be met, the sponsoring organizations found it to be a rewarding event that ignited a renewed interest in education and "opening new horizons for youth."

COMMUNICATIONS & PUBLIC RELATIONS: DOMESTIC ABUSE

NATIONAL/STATE ORGANIZATIONS

NATIONAL COMMITTEE FOR PREVENTION OF CHILD ABUSE
332 South Michigan Avenue
Suite 1250
Chicago, IL 60604
TEL: 312-663-3520
Objectives: To prevent all forms of child abuse, including: nonaccidental injury, physical and emotional abuse and neglect of children.
Services: Operates ongoing national media campaign to create public awareness of child abuse; conducts research on how to prevent abuse; publishes a wide variety of publications for professionals and the lay public on the issue; and organizes concerned citizens into volunteer-based chapters which develop primary prevention programs in their own communities.
Founded: 1972

INDIVIDUAL PROGRAM PROFILES

SCAN (SPOKANE CHILD ABUSE AND NEGLECT PREVENTION CENTER)
South 500 Stone
Spokane, WA 99202
TEL: 509-458-7445
Purpose: Primary child abuse and neglect prevention.
Sponsor: United Way, Spokane Community Mental Health Center
Contact: Sue Hiale, Coordinator
Description: The SCAN Center was established in 1973 to provide direct parent aide services to families with the goal of preventing child abuse and neglect and establishing a positive, nurturing home environment for children. As the number of reports of child abuse and neglect have increased SCAN has become a major resource for prevention and treatment for troubled families.
For the past three years SCAN has been a program area of Spokane Community Mental Health Center. SCAN receives in-kind administrative services and consultation skills from the Mental Health Center. This merger has provided stability and quality to the SCAN program. The SCAN budget and physical location remain separate from the Community Mental Health Center.
United Way of Spokane County funds approximately forty percent of the SCAN budget. Local fund raising events provide a little over twenty percent of the total. It is estimated that in 1990 SCAN will need to receive over $14,000 from foundation and grant requests.
The SCAN program consists of five areas of service delivery, each with the major goal of preventing child abuse and neglect.
The public education aspect of SCAN is an essential means of informing citizens about how to report suspected cases of child abuse and neglect. SCAN provides speakers throughout the community to present information on the definitions, identification and causes of child abuse and neglect. These speakers are specially trained and will speak to any group requesting information. These requests come from schools, service clubs, churches, and the corporate community to name a few. Community resources and opportunities for citizen involvement are also discussed at public presentations.
The professional staff at SCAN presents training to medical, legal and educational personnel regarding prevention, identification and treatment of child abuse and neglect.

Community education and awareness are essential ingredients in the prevention of child abuse and neglect. In 1989 SCAN presented over 200 education sessions in response to local requests. In addition to these on-site presentations, SCAN maintains a resource center which includes films and a wide assortment of materials on child abuse and neglect, community agencies, parenting and related topics.
The SCAN parent aide program provides direct one-to-one services for troubled families, with primary focus on the prevention of child abuse and neglect.
Parent aides are volunteers who are trained in a 30-hour initial training class. The classes emphasize interpersonal relationships, communication skills, problems of parenting and child discipline to prepare volunteers to work individually with a client family. Although this class was previously taught at the local community college, the professional staff at SCAN now presents the training with the assistance of experts throughout the community. After completing the initial training, volunteers are matched on a one-to-one basis with clients. The role of the parent aide is to give nurturing support and model good parenting for clients who are assessed as high risk, or who have already abused or neglected their children. The parent aide is available in times of crisis and commits to three to four hours per week of contact with the client. There are currently 70 volunteers who will serve approximately 175 families during the year.
Clients are referred to SCAN by other community resources such as Child Protective Services, Community Mental Health Center and the Public Health Department. Additionally, approximately forty percent of clients contact SCAN directly for help before any abuse has occurred and volunteers respond to the needs of parents who are seeking help before they hurt their children. SCAN is the only local agency with the stated primary focus of child abuse and neglect prevention.
Client families stay involved with SCAN an average of six months or more. Over half of the clients are single parents. Most clients report an improved relationship with their children as a result of parent aide services. Current research indicates that parent aide programs are the most effective means of preventing child abuse and neglect.
SCAN maintains support groups, two child protection teams, and parent advocates. The SCAN staff includes the program coordinator, a caseworker, secretary and half-time registered nurse. The professional staff provides consultation, motivation, support and training for volunteers. In addition, the staff actively participates in community projects which assess, evaluate or develop resources for the prevention or treatment of child abuse and neglect.
Founded: 1973

COMMUNICATIONS & PUBLIC RELATIONS: DRUGS/ALCOHOL

NATIONAL/STATE ORGANIZATIONS

ENTERTAINMENT INDUSTRIES COUNCIL
SEE VOLUNTEERS: CELEBRITIES

INDIVIDUAL PROGRAM PROFILES

MAKE IT HOME FOR THE HOLIDAYS
SEE BUSINESS/INDUSTRY INVOLVEMENT: DRUGS/ALCOHOL

COMMUNICATIONS & PUBLIC RELATIONS: HANDICAPPED

NATIONAL/STATE ORGANIZATIONS

CHALLENGE INTERNATIONAL (*formerly National Challenge Committee on Disability*)
6719 Lowell Avenue
McLean, VA 22101
TEL: 703-790-1616
Objectives: To make disability a familiar and comfortable issue by closing the communication gap between the public and disabled community.
Services: Mounts a media awareness campaign to change the way in which Americans perceive disabled individuals; promotes positive images of disabled persons in the media through newspaper articles, radio and television news reports, television shows, motion pictures, and advertisements; educates the public about disability issues; serves as a clearinghouse on the needs of the disabled; works with and assists organizations which represent the disabled; maintains a *National Media Council on Disability;* provides internships for disabled persons in media-related fields; offers speakers to community groups; designs school programs and educational materials; publishes printed and video promotional materials; oversees a national network of education, information, and entertainment services for the disabled; awards outstanding accomplishments by and for the disabled; produces public service announcements on disability issues.
Contact: Mary Nemec Doremus, Founder
Founded: 1983

NATIONAL ORGANIZATION ON DISABILITY (NOD)
910 Sixteenth Street, NW
Suite 600
Washington, DC 20006
TEL: 202-293-5960
Objectives: To expand opportunity for America's 35 million persons with physical or mental disabilities, thereby enhancing their contribution to society.
Services: Works with the private sector and government to strengthen public understanding of the unmet needs and potential contribution of disabled persons; fosters the partnership of people from all walks of life in furthering the long-term goals of and for citizens with disabilities, described below:
- Expanded educational opportunity;
- Improved access to housing, buildings, transportation;
- Greater opportunity for employment;
- Greater participation in recreational, social, cultural activities;
- Expanded and strengthened rehabilitation programs and facilities;
- Purposeful application of biomedical research aimed at conquering major disabling conditions;
- Reduction in the incidence of disability through accident and disease prevention;
- Increased application of technology to ameliorate the effects of disability; and
- Expanded international exchange of information and experience to benefit all disabled persons.

Operates two programs in response to the proclamation of the UN General Assembly declaring 1983-1992 as the Decade of Disabled Persons:
- **The Community Partnership Program** promotes awareness and disseminates information on disability programs/issues; advocates partnership and private sector self-help initiatives; supports local committees of disabled and non-disabled volunteers working to improve attitudes toward disabled persons (in more than 1,000 communities); expands access; promotes greater opportunities in education, housing, employment, recreation and transportation; prevents disabling conditions.
- **The Corporate Partnership Program** encourages the business community to expand employment and other opportunities; provides technical assistance and advice to corporations on disability programs.

Supports above programs by providing technical assistance and materials to local groups; acts as a clearinghouse for information; carries out an ongoing public information and awareness program, obtains support from key leaders and groups; sponsors a national Advertising Council campaign; a special $25,000 National Awards Program; and "Friends of the National Organization," a nationwide group of people interested in activities on behalf of the handicapped; publishes a quarterly newsletter, which focuses on program ideas, and *Meeting the Challenge of Disability,* a program manual for local community partnership liaisons and chairpersons; works with 300 national partner organizations; spearheads the U.S. program for the Decade of Disabled Persons; convenes workshops on specific topics and national conferences.
Publications: Community Action Guide; Community Idea Book; NOD Report; Update
Founded: 1982

ORGANIZATION FOR THE USE OF THE TELEPHONE (OUT)
PO Box 175
Owings Mill, MD 21117
TEL: 301-655-1827
Objectives: To make the telephone an accessible instrument of communication to those who are "phone deaf."
Services: Persuades telephone companies to convert public, home and business phones to make them electronically compatible with telephone pick-ups in hearing aids, and to amplify public pay phones; advocates for the installation of Induction Loop Amplification (ILA) systems in places of public gatherings; publishes the OUT-Line on an occasional basis to keep people informed of new developments in this area; publishes various items on the use of the telephone with hearing aids, including *All Telephones Must Work with All Hearing Aids - Everywhere,* which is a guide to action for interested individuals and groups (all materials are free).
Contact: David Saks
Publications: OUT-Line; OUT Annual Report; Telephones and Hearing Aids; All Telephones... Everywhere
Founded: 1973

PRESIDENT'S COMMITTEE ON MENTAL RETARDATION
RO Building
7th & D Streets, SW
Washington, DC 20201
TEL: 202-245-7634
Objectives: To promote public understanding of the mentally retarded; to keep the President informed in this area.
Services: Stimulates individual, group, and media action; fosters cooperation among public and private agencies; recommends federal action where needed; works with the President.

INDIVIDUAL PROGRAM PROFILES

ALEXANDER HUMAN DEVELOPMENT CENTER
VOLUNTEER COUNCIL
SEE VOLUNTEERS: PARENTS

GIVEN OPPORTUNITIES...
Little City Foundation
4801 Peterson Avenue
Chicago, IL 60646
TEL: 312-282-2207
Purpose: To highlight the accomplishments and abilities of people with developmental challenges.
Sponsor: Little City Foundation
Contact: Cable TV Coordinator
Description: The Little City Foundation has developed a national public access cable monthly television program to bring to the attention of the general public the abilities and talents of people with disabilities. The program features individuals who have succeeded as a result of being given an opportunity, or people who have achieved beyond the limits and barriers imposed upon them by society, circumstances, or their disabilities.
The success of the program depends on the willingness of people to volunteer their experiences on camera, and the recommendations provided for follow-up by people across the country.
The Foundation also serves as an information source for professionals, advocates and volunteers in areas of educational, residential, vocational and recreational opportunities available. Begun in fall 1989, this program continually seeks exemplary people who have overcome obstacles so that they can provide positive information to the general public about people with developmental challenges.
Publications: Given Opportunities...

HUG IN
Community Workshop and Training Center
3215 North University
Peoria, IL 61604
TEL: 309-686-3314
Purpose: To conduct an awareness event to inform the community of the needs of handicapped people.
Sponsor: Community Workshop and Training Center, Inc.
Contact: Nikki Vulgaris
Description: In May 1982 volunteers and staff of Community Workshop and Training Center (CWTC) felt that public relations efforts regarding the agency needed to be increased to promote employment and independent living for handicapped persons. With this in mind, something new had to be tried.
The Hug-In developed through agency volunteer recognition items. Earlier in the year, a cartoon figure was adopted which appeared on "hug" cards (Thank You notes) and the volunteer newsletter. In addition, the population (developmentally disabled) is one which requires much positive reinforcement so the Hug-In occurred naturally.
The Hug-In took place in September and was held in downtown Peoria, in an area where people mill during their lunch hour. Buttons were purchased to promote the event, and Hug Coupons were used for advertising time, place, etc.
To establish a crowd, local celebrities, communiity leaders and others were invited to participate as "official" huggers. In addition, since hugging a stranger is uncomfortable for many, we arranged with other organizations to have costume characters. On hand were: Miss Piggy, Cookie Monster, clowns and many others. Other entertainment included a jazz band and the Community Workshop Chorus.
What were the benefits of the Hug-In? It:
- increased CWTC visibility in the community;
- opened doors for placement opportunities with local employers;
- obtained new work contracts for training;
- increased interest by community volunteers to volunteer in the agency;
- opened doors for fundraising. Two local businesses sponsored fundraising events for CWTC.
Founded: 1982

RADIO INFORMATION SERVICE (RIS)
Golden Triangle Radio Information Center
PO Box 3663
Pittsburgh, PA 15230
TEL: 412-434-6023
Purpose: To provide radio reading service to the blind and print handicapped persons; and to provide programs to other stations and cable systems.
Sponsor: Federal/State grants; corporate underwriting; private donations
Contact: Norman H. Russell, General Manager
Description: Radio Information Service, "Pittsburgh's Most Unusual Radio Station," is a radio reading service for the blind and print handicapped. It is headquartered on the campus of Duquesne University and serves the Southwestern Pennsylvania area. Its goal is to provide current printed material such as the daily newspapers, periodicals like *Time* and *People* magazines, current best selling novels and much more to its listeners. There are currently over 100 such stations across the country and several of the shows that RIS produces are marketed to many of these other stations. RIS is an affiliate of National Public Radio's service for the print handicapped.
Originally, 95% of RIS funds came from Federal and State Title XX monies. However, the budget cuts lowered this proportion considerably and the station is now more reliant on corporate and private donations.
RIS operates as a sub-carrier of WDUQ, 90.5 FM. Because of this sub-carrier status, RIS cannot be heard on AM or FM. Special radio receivers which resemble a small table radio are distributed free of charge to the listeners. It is also available on various cable TV and hospital audio systems.
There is a paid staff of four full time and three part time persons as well as over 300 volunteers who generously donate their time and talents to do the reading and other assignments. The RIS volunteers represent a large cross section in terms of age and background. The majority of them are employed as readers. However, jobs as office personnel, producers, engineers and public relations assistants are also available. Internships with RIS are also available to both high school and college students.
Previous experience in any of the above areas is not a prerequisite. What is stressed is reliability and an aptitude for whatever task the volunteer wishes to do. For example, readers should have a pleasant voice and be able to read fluently. All prospective volunteers are asked to complete an application form and those specifically interested in reading are given a voice test to determine the types of materials they read best and their level of fluency in reading aloud.

COMMUNICATIONS & PUBLIC RELATIONS: HEALTH

INDIVIDUAL PROGRAM PROFILES

THE S.O.A.P.S.
SEE INFORMATION & REFERRAL: MINORITIES/WOMEN

COMMUNICATIONS & PUBLIC RELATIONS: HOMELESS

INDIVIDUAL PROGRAM PROFILES

HOUSING NOW!
Community for Creative Non-Violence
425 Second Street, NW
Washington , DC 20001
TEL: 202-393-1909
Purpose: To demand the "American dream" of affordable housing for all.
Sponsor: Community for Creative Non-Violence
Contact: Mitch Snyder
Description: On October 7, 1989, 250,000 homeless persons and their supporters marched through the streets of Washington, DC. The throng included housing advocates, college students, social workers, shelter residents, and children - the latter in a caravan of red wagons who converged on the Capitol. The youngsters presented the House Speaker with hundreds of letters written by the children, asking Congress to help end homelessness.
Many actors and music stars served as masters of ceremonies, spokespersons, and entertainers. Speakers ranged from Coretta Scott King to homeless men who had walked to Washington from New York and Roanoke, Virginia, in marches called a "New Exodus."
While homeless men and women led the main march, the crowd was dominated by college students, organized-labor delegations and church groups participating as a sign of solidarity with those less fortunate.
A major emphasis of the housing march was to make sure that, after housing is provided, support services such as job assistance is offered to help the homeless persons get back to reality.
Publications: Housing Now! Information Packet

PRIME TIME TO END HUNGER
End Hunger Network
7080 Hollywood Boulevard
Suite 105
Hollywood, CA 90028
TEL: 213-465-1377
Information available also from:
Alice Barkus
Volunteer and Outreach Services
United Way of America
701 North Fairfax Street
Alexandria, VA 22314-2045
703-836-7100
Purpose: To focus the power of the communications industry on a current social issue.
Contact: Jerry Michaud, Executive Director
Description: Developed by the *End Hunger Network,* this nationwide recruitment project works with some of television's most popular prime-time shows to motivate millions of viewers nationwide to volunteer their time, talents, and energy to address the country's most serious problems - including hunger, homelessness, and illiteracy.
The project gains commitments from the major television networks to script prime-time shows which will feature episodes about major social concerns, followed by public-service announcements inviting viewers to call a "900" phone number for information on how they can volunteer. Callers hear a recorded message from one of the show's stars and are asked to leave a message stating their name and address. Within two weeks, callers receive a personalized letter and a handbook on volunteering, produced with assistance from the *United Way of America.* The prospective volunteer is first

referred to a local *Volunteer Center.* Where none exists, callers are directed to their community's United Way, or to a local Emergency Food and Shelter office for information about volunteer opportunities.
Considered unusual because the project does not solicit funds from TV viewers, it is expected that 290 million viewers throughout the U.S. could collectively watch these episodes during this initial project's run (December 1-20, 1989). *Prime Time to End Hunger* was launched in October 1989 by President Bush at a White House press conference attended by *End Hunger Network* executives, corporate sponsors, and representatives from United Way of America, VOLUNTEER, and the Emergency Food and Shelter Board.
A packet of information is available from local United Ways, Volunteer Centers, and Emergency Food and Shelter Board offices. The packets include fact sheets, a schedule of project-related broadcasts, sample press releases, tips for local participation, project logo slicks, and information to help local organizations collect volunteer data and conduct project evaluations.
Founded: 1982

STAY THE NIGHT ON MY STREET
Emergency Shelter Council
United Way of the Midlands
1800 Main Street, PO Box 152
Columbia, SC 29202-0152
TEL: 803-733-5400
Purpose: To dispel some of the myths and fears about street people.
Sponsor: Columbia Experimental Theatre
Contact: John L. Heins, Jr., Executive Director
Description: Developed by *Columbia Experimental Theatre* and cosponsored by the *United Way of the Midlands, Stay the Night on My Street* is an original play about the problems of the homeless in the Midlands of South Carolina. It was first presented in 1987 in special recognition of that year as the *International Year of Shelter for the Homeless.* Opening performance was at the *University of South Carolina Law School,* with performances moving among the University and six other locations.
The all-volunteer cast uses comedy and rapidly-shifting scenes to depict the lives of both the haves and the have-nots. Although taking a lighthearted approach, the play points out that the growing occurrence of homelessness is indicative of the failure of existing institutions to break the cycle of poverty and oppression, according to the play's director. The performers hope to dispel some of the myths and fears about street people - some of which performers had held themselves before signing on for the performance. The play features original music by a local musician created for the play.
Performances are followed by informal panel discussions involving community leaders, shelter providers, and homeless individuals. Admission is always free.

COMMUNICATIONS & PUBLIC RELATIONS: IMAGE

NATIONAL/STATE ORGANIZATIONS

HEARTLINE*
National Association of Older Americans*
12 Electric Street
West Alexandria, OH 45381
TEL: 614-775-7634

Objectives: To reestablish a satisfactory level of comfort and security for older Americans, to restore a well-deserved dignity to the elderly image, and to provide individual assistance and vital information to older Americans.
Services: Conducts specialized education and research programs; assists older Americans in dealing with government agencies; offers an insurance policy program to supplement Medicare; provides a pharmaceutical plan; sponsors a travel program; publishes a monthly newsletter, an almanac, and specialized publications on pre-retirement planning.
Publications: Crime Prevention Guide; Almanac for Retirement

NATIONAL MEDIA RESOURCE CENTER ON THE AGING
National Council on the Aging
600 Maryland Avenue
West Wing 100
Washington, DC 20024
TEL: 202-479-1200
Objectives: To supply information to editors, writers and producers in the press, film and broadcasting industries to improve the image of the elderly.
Services: Furnishes items for the media's use; serves as resource to program planners; works with existing networks, and creates additional ones; develops educational programs; stimulates consciousness-raising among the elderly themselves; leads briefings and workshops; draws from major 1974 study on attitudes about older persons; has continuous research and survey program; convenes intermittent conferences.
Publications: Perspective on Aging
Founded: 1950

OLDER WOMEN'S LEAGUE (OWL)
730 Eleventh Street, NW
Suite 300
Washington, DC 20001
TEL: 202-783-6686
Objectives: To bring together people of all ages to support the cause of the underserved elderly.
Services: Maintains a national office and 120 chapters with over 20,000 participants (both men and women) to address the needs of older persons; supports chapters (a minimum of eight persons) through training, technical assistance, printed materials, etc.; enables local chapters to select projects according to needs at their local level; publishes educational materials in areas such as defense and reform of social security, health care insurance, and equity in pensions for women, as well as a regular series of papers, a bimonthly newsletter, action bulletins, statistical reports, videotapes, books, and occasional papers.
Publications: OWL Observe; Gray Papers; Women Take Care
Founded: 1980

INDIVIDUAL PROGRAM PROFILES

THE BEST YEARS
RSVP of Humboldt County
Humboldt State University
Arcata, CA 95521
TEL: 707-826-3372
Purpose: To utilize the television media to inform and educate the four-county area to services available, political issues, special happenings; to present a positive view of the aging.
Sponsor: KVIQ-TV
Contact: Charlotte Tropp, Director
Description: In May 1975, leaders of the Retired Senior Volunteer Program negotiated with KVIQ-TV officials for public service air time on a regular basis, and conducted an active search for older people who would be assets on a planning committee and in actual

production. Through this effort they hoped, through profiles and examples, to present a positive view of aging, to educate older adults in the viewing area about all the services available to them, to inform older adults about current political issues and special happenings important to them, to provide a stimulating and creative volunteer opportunity for older adults. KVIQ viewing area covers Humboldt, Del Norte, Mendocino and Trinity Counties. The resultant biweekly, 30-minute television program shown on Sunday afternoons over the last seven years has covered every conceivable topic, and the program has a very large viewing audience. KVIQ-TV provides all broadcast services including tape, sets, time, audiovisual materials. RSVP, along with nonfederal community resources, provides all out-of-pocket expenses for volunteers.
The television program is generally divided into five segments: News, Focus, Uncommon Knowledge, Upbeat and Mailbag. Volunteers serve as coordinators and hosts, and provide all services including writing, scheduling, visual effects, publicity, guest appearances, producing and directing.
A Best Years committee meets weekly with RSVP and KVIQ staff to plan the shows. The planning committee itself changes frequently and the circle of older guests grows monthly. Appearing on television is a very exciting new growth experience for a lot of people. The shows are taped three days before they are shown to allow for review before airing. KVIQ-TV is a commercial station.
Founded: 1975

CLASS OF 2000: THE PREJUDICE PUZZLE
National Public Radio
2025 M Street, NW
Washington, DC 20036
TEL: 202-822-2000
FAX: 202-822-2329
Purpose: To explore how young people with a variety of backgrounds deal with prejudices and stereotyping.
Contact: Sallie Bodie, Special Project Outreach Coordinator
Description: In 1989, *National Public Radio (NPR)* commissioned *Significance, Inc.* to survey teenage attitudes. This was the first step toward a new ongoing series, *Special Projects* (see separate entry), which will examine national issues which affect our communities. From a series of focus groups formed by the survey team and conducted in four cities across the U.S., NPR learned that "Although most panelists try to draw a rosy picture of race relations, they seemed naive and euphemistic when discussing race relations. Several teens did acknowledge race problems, although they frequently ascribed these race-motivated problems to others." The 1990 project on prejudice features young people telling in their own words how they feel about prejudice. They will talk about issues such as job barriers, the importance of belonging to groups, and the impact of stereotypes and racial incidents. The stories in this series will raise the question of how youth are being prepared to live in the demographically different society of the 21st century. The program finale is a two-hour "national call-in" with a panel to respond live to queries. The finale is designed so that either hour can be aired separately, or delayed for rebroadcast. Segments in the series range from five to 22 minutes. Although the groundwork is done, planning for the initial, week-long series, *Class of 2000: The Prejudice Puzzle,* is in process. *The Prejudice Puzzle* is designed to learn the feelings and attitudes of young people from many walks of life in the area of prejudice. The program is building a strong *Outreach Partnership* of public radio and national organizations with some interest and service in the area of the special issue being explored. With the appeal for *Outreach Partners* barely begun, three organizations are in place - *Very Special Arts,* the *American Library Association,* and *Four-One-One (National Clearinghouse on Volunteerism)* - with an anticipation of hundreds of nonprofits joining the effort. *Outreach Partners* lend their names, state and local contacts, and services in promotion, program support, community involvement,

etc., to a major resource directory being compiled by NPR for distribution to member stations. The stations will be invited to contact these local resources for follow-up local programming on youth and prejudice, and for mounting jointly-sponsored community activities.

Organizations participating as *Outreach Partners* will become part of a nationwide network of community resources available to NPR's 375-plus members. A benefit to the *Outreach Partners* is an increase in visibility in a collaborative effort that will establish new links with public radio and other nonprofits.

One of the responsibilities of the *Outreach Partners* is to "spread the word" by publicizing the *Special* in their communications vehicles, contacting the closest station periodically to find out when *Prejudice Puzzle* programs will air, and the agenda for each program. Through this and other issue specials, NPR members hope to make their communities better places in which to live.

LOS ANGELES POVERTY DEPARTMENT (LAPD)
Art Against AIDS
406 Seventh Street, NW
Third Floor
Washington, DC 20004
TEL: 202-347-1033
Purpose: To help raise money for AIDS research, the homeless, child abuse, poverty, etc.
Sponsor: Local host theatre
Contact: Kevin Williams, Assistant Director
Description: In the sixties, the poverty program (Community Action Agencies) created "street theatre," in which the poor would literally "climb on stage and ad lib a play about life in the poverty community." Usually the setting was a kitchen or dining room with a family around the table. Today's *street theatre* is actually set in the streets. Although a little more sophisticated - the method starts with a script - a lot of angry ad libbing soon takes over. One group making its mark in this setting is the *LAPD (Los Angeles Poverty Department) Acting Troupe.* The troupe has a base of 20 full-time actors, and as many of them travel to other cities as budget allows. The Troupe is composed of formerly homeless actors and actresses who team up with homeless people - on-site - in skits that reflect the local realism of homelessness. The purpose for their existence is to raise money not only for the homeless, but also for AIDS research (*Art Against AIDS*) and other issues, including child abuse and poverty.

A typical example is a play on the homeless presented at the *Arena Stage* in Washington, DC. Four LAPD performers were sent to Washington, and it was their task to enlist performers from the area - preferably from the population being served. The result - all of the actors were either homeless or had once been homeless. They played their parts the only way they knew how: for real, according to the director, who didn't expect so much violence. The scripted lines often gave way to some angry ad libs.

Before performing in a city, the assigned performers talk with experts on AIDS, homeless, or other area that will be addressed in their performance. The casting of people from the streets has resulted in the kind of performance that the media calls "raw and wonderful," with "no preachy moments to stop the momentum." Many media cited the work as a way for mainstream America to learn about life on the street and life on the road - subjects most people know little about. They describe the *LAPD Troupe* and their local volunteer performers as creators of "an underground of rich, elemental interaction among people who are facing a reality that most of us have managed to banish from our lives."

COMMUNICATIONS & PUBLIC RELATIONS: JUSTICE

NATIONAL/STATE ORGANIZATIONS

NATIONAL CENTER FOR COMMUNITY CRIME PREVENTION
PO Box 37456
Washington, DC 20013
TEL: 202-783-6215
Objectives: To administer a program of public education on community crime prevention.
Services: Works under the premise that crime prevention begins in the community with the responsibility shared by criminal justice practitioners and citizens; provides specialized and general training; develops related educational programs; conducts research and makes its findings available; provides general information and an advisory and technical assistance service to support and supplement community crime prevention programs; uses the resources of criminal justice practitioners, educators, and advisors to plan, develop, and implement community crime prevention programs; assists and encourages state and local governments in evaluating the status of their crime prevention standards; makes recommendations based on the government evaluations; publishes a newsletter, *We CAN Prevent Crime*, and other informative materials.
Publications: We CAN Prevent Crime

INDIVIDUAL PROGRAM PROFILES

STOP! THE MADNESS FOUNDATION
1325 W Street, NW
Washington, DC 20009
TEL: 202-483-2771
Purpose: To help make "the system" more responsive to the needs of survivors of victims of homicide.
Sponsor: Gannett Foundation
Contact: Cynthia Harris, Founder
Description: With a grant from the *Gannett Foundation* and successful recruitment of the Democratic and Republican National Committee Chairmen for the board of directors, *Stop! The Madness Foundation,* a public awareness program, opened its doors in April 1988. The founder is the mother of a young victim of homicide in the District of Columbia.

A major thrust of the program involves speaking to community groups around the country, encouraging them to build up their communities and put pressure on the criminal justice system to see that those responsible for violence are kept out of circulation. The theme of the public awareness campaign is: "We are all responsible for stopping the killing." It is an effort to make the public more aware of the seriousness of what they are facing - "illegal guns and drugs among young people for starters."

The project has produced a series of posters and printed materials calling for the end of teenage violence and murder, designed to assist volunteer groups across the country - many led by mothers who had experienced the loss of a child through violence.
Publications: Stop! The Madness Information Packet
Founded: 1988

COMMUNICATIONS & PUBLIC RELATIONS: MENTAL HEALTH

NATIONAL/STATE ORGANIZATIONS

NATIONAL MENTAL HEALTH ASSOCIATION
1021 Prince Street
Alexandria, VA 22314
TEL: 703-684-7722
Objectives: To provide advocacy and public education in areas of mental and emotional disorders.
Services: Conducts public awareness campaigns to effect changes in neighborhood and business community attitudes toward recovered mental patients; works for improved community-based treatment facilities; engages in litigation where a test case seems warranted; handles inquiries through 850 local offices as well as the national office; publishes an extensive list of publications such as *Civil Rights of Patients* and *What Every Child Needs for Good Mental Health, How to Deal with Your Tensions,* and various publications and position statements on services, legislation, rehabilitation, citizen activism, and other areas.
Publications: Civil Rights of Patients; Good Mental Health; How to Deal with Your Tensions; FOCUS
Founded: 1909

INDIVIDUAL PROGRAM PROFILES

MENTAL HEALTH PLAYERS
The Voluntary Action Center
2125 East South Boulevard
Montgomery, AL 36116-0044
TEL: 205-284-0006
Purpose: To raise the consciousness of the community to its role in promoting and fostering the mental health of its citizens.
Contact: Doci Haslam
Description: The Mental Health Players use drama in the form of role-playing to spark the consciousness of the community to its role in promoting and fostering the mental health of its citizens. The intention of the role-played situation is to involve the audience on an emotional level and elicit questions and discussion from the audience regarding their feelings in reaction to the situation.
One, two or three players make up a given skit. They work without scripts. Each skit is role-played spontaneously after a situation is decided on, and with previous input, discussion and direction from the Moderator/Director and the entire troupe of players. Examples of situations that might be role-played are:
- An alcoholic mother in a family.
- A depressed woman and her manic-depressed neighbor.
- A depressed man in the work situation.
- Mid-life crisis between husband and wife.
- A former mental patient's first encounter back with family.
- Teenagers on drugs (their family, their school and their social problems).
- Adult children discussing putting mother in a nursing home.
These experiences lead members of the audience into an awareness usually not recognized before and into some type of action involving the mentally disabled.
Since the formation of the group in 1979, the Players have become increasingly in demand for educational programs for schools, churches, civic and social clubs. They tailor each presentation specifically to meet the needs of each group. There are currently around 15 players and they did about 50 skits during last year. This involved the actual performance time plus travel and practice time. They have also traveled to other parts of the state to conduct training sessions for other organizations who want to start their own players group.
Founded: 1979

COMMUNICATIONS & PUBLIC RELATIONS: NUTRITION

NATIONAL/STATE ORGANIZATIONS

NATIONAL HUNGER COALITION
Food Research and Action Center
1319 F Street, NW
Washington, DC 20004
TEL: 202-393-5060
Objectives: To speak with one voice on child nutrition, food stamps, and elderly nutrition programs.
Services: Seeks increased involvement of food program participants in the policy decision process; acts as a clearinghouse for food program information; promotes stronger regulatory advocacy; assists in regional training in the area of education on food program issues; strengthens linkages with other groups; works on special projects such as Foodless June, Poor People's Food Platform, full funding for food stamps, and others; operates through 50 State Coordinators (plus Puerto Rico and Virgin Islands), 35 Regional Representatives, and seven national organizations, which involve church members, legal services workers, parents, Community Action Agencies, advocates, and food program participants, as well as interested persons and groups from the general community; works through state-wide networks, local organizations, and locally-based national agencies and organizations; convenes regional and national meetings.
Founded: 1970

SOCIETY FOR NUTRITION EDUCATION*
1700 Broadway
Suite 300
Oakland, CA 94612
TEL: 415-444-7133
Objectives: To promote nutritional well-being for all people through education and communication.
Services: Sponsors an annual meeting, conducted in part by volunteers, addressing the above objectives; collects, analyzes and provides information regarding nutrition through: films on nutrition (two for professionals; three for laymen); library facilities (open to all; loans to San Francisco area only); reference lists and annotated bibliographies contract services; in addition, the Society for Nutrition Education sponsors a Public Policy Advisory Council and a Legislative Committee, both of which help to design strategies for community action; publishes a quarterly newsletter and bimonthly journal.
Publications: Journal of Nutrition Education; SNE Exchange
Founded: 1967

INDIVIDUAL PROGRAM PROFILES

END HUNGER PROJECT
United Way of Fresno County
4270 North Blackston Avenue #212
PO Box 5177
Fresno, CA 93755-5177
TEL: 209-224-9202
Purpose: To mount a two-pronged hunger program that collects food for the hungry while educating the public about the root causes of hunger.

Sponsor: Fresno Bee
Contact: Anthony J. Folcarelli, Executive Director
Description: The *End-Hunger Project* took shape when a Fresno newspaper, *Fresno Bee,* decided to sponsor a food drive. The newspaper turned to the United Way of Fresno County for help, requesting the the United Way organize and administer the communitywide effort. The newspaper planned to include in one edition of the paper a grocery bag printed with the words *Share & Care Package.* People would be asked to fill the bags with nonperishable food and drop them off at collection sites throughout the Fresno area for final coordination and distribution by the United Way.

United Way agreed to the newspaper's request for administering the program and, in turn, requested that the paper include with its food-drive coverage additional information about the six major root causes of hunger in the Fresno area based on a survey by Fresno's *Hunger Coalition:*

- Minority, elderly, and seasonal unemployment;
- Insufficient variety of well-paying jobs;
- Educational inadequacies;
- Shift in government priorities;
- Educational barriers to job-skill development; and
- Resource distribution.

United Way saw an excellent opportunity in the *Fresno Bee's* planned coverage of the food drive to publicize and reinforce these root causes.

The newspaper ran a full-page ad promoting the food drive, illustrating the information printed on the grocery bag, and featured a follow-up article, and a front-page photograph of food collected during the drive. To assist the newspaper with expenses of printing the bags, the United Way enlisted KFSN-TV Channel 30 (an ABC affiliate) to share the cost. Thirty-five members of the Grocery Manufacturers Representatives Organization volunteered to pick up the filled bags from the 44 drop-off points and transport them to a warehouse donated for the drive by *Fleming Foods,* a wholesale distributor.

The goal set for the five-day drive was 40 tons of food and $4,000 in contributions. The drive's final tally was 64 tons of food and $7,000. Food was distributed by four organizations to more than 8,000 people, with the remainder and the cash contributions divided among area food banks. The *Fresno Bee* ran a full-page thank you ad after the event, which repeated the area's six causes of hunger and a reminder that work remained to be done to eliminate hunger from the Fresno community. The linking of the food drive *and* the public education effort turned out to be a winning combination.

NEIGHBORS HELPING NEIGHBORS
SEE BUSINESS/INDUSTRY INVOLVEMENT: NUTRITION

PRIME TIME TO END HUNGER
SEE COMMUNICATIONS & PUBLIC RELATIONS: HOMELESS

PRIME TIME TO END HUNGER
VOLUNTEER - The National Center
1111 North 19th Street
Suite 500
Arlington, VA 22209
TEL: 703-276-0542
FAX: 703-528-6052
Purpose: To help volunteering become more visible.
Sponsor: VOLUNTEER - The National Center
Contact: Pamela Warwick
Description: Prime Time to End Hunger is a national initiative to recruit volunteers. It uses the power of prime time television to encourage volunteering. Six prime time shows, representing all three television networks, incorporate themes that reflect today's social issues in the regular programming. Following each show,

viewers are encouraged to call a *900* number to obtain information about how they can volunteer.

Callers are mailed a *Consumer's Guide to Community Service,* which includes a personalized letter and the telephone number of the *Volunteer Center, United Way,* or *Emergency Food and Shelter Board* in their communities.

Prime Time to End Hunger receives support from *VOLUNTEER, United Way of America,* and the *National Emergency Food and Shelter Board* program in partnership with *The End Hunger Network.* Other sponsors include Governors' Offices on Volunteerism.

As a result of this and other media campaigns such as *The Volunteer Connection* and *Time to Care,* thousands of new volunteers have come forward to contribute their time and skills.
Publications: Consumer's Guide to Community Service

COMMUNICATIONS & PUBLIC RELATIONS: OUTREACH

NATIONAL/STATE ORGANIZATIONS

NATIONAL CONFERENCE OF BLACK LAWYERS
SEE VOLUNTEERS: PROFESSIONALS

INDIVIDUAL PROGRAM PROFILES

OUTREACH PLAN: FOCUS ON THE HISPANIC COMMUNITY
United Way of the Capital Area (Hartford)
99 Woodland Street
Hartford, CT 06105-1207
TEL: 203-249-2300
Purpose: To increase United Way involvement among specific ethnic and other groups in its community.
Sponsor: United Way of the Capital Area
Contact: Marilyn Cruz-Aponte, Chair, United Way's Special Constituencies Committee, and Administrative Aide to the Governor, or Dale Gray, United Way
Description: Launched in 1989, the United Way's five-year effort to increase United Way involvement among specific ethnic and other groups begins with an outreach to the Hispanic community. The effort began with a visit by a popular musician to appear in two United Way public-service announcements (PSAs) and a videotape to be used for the first full year's campaign. Songs by the singer, Ruben Blades, encourage positive social action among Hispanic people.

The videotape is in Spanish and features Blades talking about United Way, with students at a Hartford elementary school in the background. The video, partially-funded by Aetna Life Insurance, began showing in the spring of 1990.

The PSAs and videotape are part of a larger agenda of United Way's Special Constituencies Committee. This Committee was created to concentrate communications and community outreach among specific groups. The Hispanic population is one of the largest ethnic groups, and many companies do special marketing to that group.

Other phases of this effort include translation of Health Appeal Drive brochures into Spanish and Polish, which were printed at a Hispanic-owned printshop, then sent with letters to 2,000 Hispanic residents, and the *Plant Together, Harvest Together* theme, which was developed specifically for the Hispanic community, and will continue for the next few years. To facilitate the latter, area elementary schools having a large Hispanic population mounted a poster contest sponsored by the United Way, with a prize and media exposure for the winning poster.

The *Plant Together, Harvest Together* theme was launched in the community with a kickoff luncheon attended by 130 Hispanic professionals from business and human service fields. The keynote speaker at the luncheon praised Hispanics for their history of informal generosity towards those in need, and urged them to make the transition from "generosity to philanthropy."

The Special Constituencies Committee plans similar outreach efforts tailored to other groups, such as the Polish community, during the next few years.

Founded: 1989

COMMUNITY SERVICES

NATIONAL/STATE ORGANIZATIONS

**AMERICAN VALUES: THE COMMUNITY ACTION
NETWORK**
211 East 43rd Street
Suite 1400
New York, NY 10017
TEL: 212-818-1360
Objectives: To bring together individuals interested in solving
critical community social problems.
Services: Serves as a clearinghouse for information on solving
social and community problems; addresses such issues as
addiction, drunk driving, teenage suicide, and child abuse; works
with community leaders, business leaders, and members of the
media; disseminates information on how various communities solve
their problems; sponsors competitions and gives awards for
outstanding performance; conducts national surveys on 20 social
issues most troubling to Americans; publishes a quarterly
newsletter.
Publications: American Values Newsletter
Founded: 1985

CAMPUS OUTREACH OPPORTUNITY LEAGUE (COOL)
SEE VOLUNTEERS: STUDENTS

CENTER FOR PUBLIC SERVICE
SEE TRAINING/CONFERENCES/TEACHING:
INTERNSHIPS

CITIZENS INFORMATION SERVICE*
67 East Madison Street
Chicago, IL 60603
TEL: 312-236-0315
Objectives: To foster more effective citizen participation in
response to community and organizational needs.
Services: Focuses on providing information to citizens - both in
print and in educational classes - that will encourage them to
become involved in the concerns of their communities; develops
library resources and provides information on civic concerns,
government performance in relation to these concerns, and other
community-oriented issues; operates a telephone information
service, a pamphlet shop, workshops and classes (all services and
many publications available in Spanish also).

COMMISSION ON VOLUNTARY SERVICE AND ACTION
SEE VOLUNTEERS: STUDENTS

COMMUNITY CAREERS RESOURCE CENTER
1516 P Street, NW
Washington, DC 20005
TEL: 202-667-0661
Objectives: To help socially-concerned individuals find meaningful
work with nonprofit public interest organizations; to help those
organizations recruit qualified and dedicated staff.
Services: Maintains an extensive nationwide job listing bank,
arranged by region, for community organizers, outreach workers,
VISTAs, and other interested citizens; examines major issues of
concern to community-betterment groups; profiles organizations
that are challenging these issues and interviews the individuals
who are leading the efforts; provides how-to information on
mounting a community program, or making an existing one more
effective; publishes a monthly newspaper with community-oriented
columns, readers forum, reviews, announcements, information on
resource guides and other materials.
Publications: Community Jobs; Survival Planning; Making the
Community a Career
Founded: 1977

COMMUNITY REGENERATION
SEE LEADERSHIP DEVELOPMENT/BOARDS

COMMUNITY RESEARCH FORUM*
505 East Green Street
Suite 210
Champaign, IL 61820
TEL: 217-333-0443
Objectives: To plan and promote improvement of human services
at the community and neighborhood levels (currently directed
toward the juvenile justice system).
Services: Provides technical assistance to communities in program
management areas, including program development, staff training,
citizen involvement, and evaluation; mounts long- and short-term
projects, currently directed toward the juvenile justice system; for
example:
  • *Children in Adult Jails* - assists communities in eliciting
    citizen participation, identifying issues, developing alternative
    programs, monitoring the justice system, etc., to separate
    detained juvenile and adult offenders.

● *Planning Regional Services for Youth* - looks into the cost implications of removing juveniles from adult jails and providing relevant services in the community.
In addition, CRF responds to requests from local organizations faced with a crisis situation involving juvenile offenders, including citizen pressure when residential facilities and/or nonresidential alternatives are deemed inadequate; maintains extensive library collection; works with public or private, urban or rural local programs; publishes *Removing Children from Adult Jails and Lockups: A Citizen's Guide to Action,* and numerous other materials based on past and current projects; conducts workshops and sponsors symposia.
Publications: Removing Children from Jails and Lockups

COPE RETIREE PROGRAM
SEE VOLUNTEERS: OLDER PERSONS

JESUIT VOLUNTEER CORPS: NORTHWEST
PO Box 3928
Portland, OR 97208
TEL: 503-228-2457
Objectives: To volunteer services to help poor and dispossessed persons.
Services: Works with individuals, primarily college graduates, to enable them to volunteer for up to one year to help the needy in finding alternatives to poverty, racism, militarism and other areas, while helping the volunteers to become more loving individuals, and more dedicated to serving others; develops within volunteers a sense of community in which each individual is an integral part of that group and dedicated to its welfare; helps institutions become more involved in constructive social change in the light of Christian principles; places volunteers throughout the country; conducts annual orientation meetings; publishes a newsletter three times a year.
Publications: Focus
Founded: 1956

NATIONAL ASSOCIATION OF NEIGHBORHOODS
(*formerly Alliance for Neighborhood Government*)
1651 Fuller, NW
Washington, DC 20009
TEL: 202-332-7766
Objectives: To enable neighborhood leaders to exchange information.
Services: Works with more than 2,000 neighborhood organizations in 120 cities to provide a network of information about programs, issues, structures, and ethics, and to secure a political voice; promotes its *National Neighborhood Platform* and *Neighborhood Bill of Responsibilities and Rights;* maintains a number of task forces in areas including citizen education, energy, health, housing and community development, neighborhood crime; neighborhood information; participation in human rights, and others; publishes and distributes a bulletin each quarter.
Publications: National Neighborhood Platform; Neighborhood Bill of Responsibilities & Rights; NAN Bulletin
Founded: 1975

NEIGHBORHOOD DEVELOPMENT SERVICES CENTER
Urban Coalition
1120 G Street, NW, Suite 900
Washington, DC 20005
TEL: 202-628-2990
Objectives: To assist community development corporations in their efforts to improve communities.
Services: Operates through a Ford Foundation grant to assist community development groups in revitalization efforts; provides technical assistance to community development corporations undertaking physical and economic development such as new

business start-ups, housing, mixed use development, adaptive reuse projects, etc.; provides technical assistance through mail, phone and on-site visit; conducts workshops on issues vital to communities; publishes a monthly newsletter, neighborhood booklets, and other materials designed to inform and assist neighborhood groups.
Publications: Housing Exchange; Urban Exchange; Urban Education Exchange ; Urban Health Exchange; Neighborhood Exchange
Founded: 1967

RETIRED SENIOR VOLUNTEER PROGRAM
SEE VOLUNTEERS: OLDER PERSONS

STUDENT COMMUNITY SERVICE (SCS) PROGRAM
SEE VOLUNTEERS: STUDENTS

SUPERIOR COUNCIL
Society of St. Vincent de Paul
4140 Lindell Boulevard
St. Louis, MO 63108
TEL: 314-371-4980
Objectives: To promote and practice charity in the community.
Services: Enlists congregation members of the Catholic church in personal volunteer service at the local level; provides financial assistance to the poor, counseling services, volunteer and professional social services, summer camps, salvage bureaus, drop-in centers for the homeless and the aged, and personal visitation; maintains committees on disaster and other concerns that surface in conferences; publishes and distributes a newsletter.
Publications: Ozanam News

VISTA (VOLUNTEERS IN SERVICE TO AMERICA)
US/ACTION - The Federal Volunteer Agency
Volunteers In Service to America
1100 Vermont Avenue, NW
Suite 1100
Washington, DC 20525
TEL: 202-347-2080
TOLL FREE: 800-424-8580
Objectives: To mobilize community resources and increase the capacity of the low-income community to solve its own problems.
Services: Provides full-time, full-year volunteers (ages 18 to 80+) at the request of community groups who serve as local sponsors in the U.S., Puerto Rico, the Virgin Islands and Guam to help mobilize community resources; requires volunteers to be U.S. citizens or permanent residents at 18 years of age, to complete pre-service general and in-service specific training, to respond to needs articulated by the low-income community, and to live among the people they serve while increasing the capacity of the low-income community to solve its own problems; allows recruitment of local low-income volunteers, and requires that the poor community that is being served participate in the development and implementation of the program; provides health insurance and a basic subsistence allowance, with a readjustment allowance at the end of service; authorizes volunteer assignments up to three years; includes service in community project areas such as runaway youth, drug abuse, homelessness, child abuse, literacy, neighborhood revitalization, economic development, farm cooperatives, food gleaning, refugee resettlement, health clinics, nutrition projects, teen-age centers, disaster relief, and low-income seniors; maintains information on former VISTA projects such as a senior citizen-owned pharmacy organized by low-income elderly, a discount buying program, and others.
[VISTA is ACTION's oldest volunteer program, created as part of the Economic Opportunity Act of 1964. College students are permitted to defer college loans while serving in VISTA.]

Contact: Patricia A.E. Rodgers
Publications: Building/One Block at a Time; Serve in the USA/Be a VISTA
Founded: 1964

VOLUNTEERS IN TECHNICAL ASSISTANCE
Volunteers in Technical Assistance
1815 North Lynn Street, Suite 200
Arlington, VA 22209
TEL: 703-276-1800; Cable: VITAINC
TOLL FREE: Telex: 440192 VITAUI
Objectives: To help solve community problems, promote business and fight poverty.
Services: Provides technical assistance to individuals, businesses and community organizations in the U.S. and more than 100 other countries; responds to technical inquiries on wide range of subjects, including energy, farming, small business, water resources, reforestation, soil conservation, food processing and low-cost construction; manages major projects; helps local groups adapt and implement technologies appropriate to their situations; conducts seminars on information resources, microcomputer applications, volunteerism, and other topics; maintains library of 45,000 reference documents on small- to medium-scale technologies; publishes numerous how-to manuals; provides business services, including data base searching, consultants, export promotion; especially active in providing appropriate technical assistance to people in developing countries.
Publications: News
Founded: 1960

VOLUNTEERS OF AMERICA
3813 N. Causeway Boulevard
Metairie, LA 70002
TEL: 504-837-2652
Objectives: To establish programs which are responsive to community need, characterized by programmatic and managerial integrity, and consistent with its Christian commitment.
Services: Provides material and spiritual assistance to those in need without regard to race, color, creed, age, sex or national origin; establishes programs in response to expressed needs across the community; maintains several general purpose programs which:
- Facilitate community response to disasters through coordination of emergency programs.
- Recycle and refurbish clothing and household goods for thrift stores.
- Direct holiday fund drives to benefit disadvantaged people.
Serves families, children, youth, the elderly, the handicapped, drug abusers, alcoholics, offenders and ex-offenders in the following ways:
Families:
- Helps during times of crisis, offering emergency financial aid, free food and clothing and crisis hotlines.
- Provides emergency shelters for families needing a temporary place to stay, for battered women, and for other abused family members.
- Maintains VOA housing complexes that are safe, decent and affordable for low- and moderate-income families.
Children and Youth:
- Provides day care for young children of working parents, which include educational activites and promote social and emotional development.
- Offers foster homes as a substitute family environment for children and youth whose normal family life is disrupted.
- Maintains group homes and boys' ranches to provide structured living environments for social and emotional adjustment.
- Operate summer camps for youths from low-income families.
Handicapped Persons:
- Assists mentally retarded adults through residential facilities

and independent living programs, and sheltered employment program to help develop skills.
- Maintains group homes for emotionally disturbed children where trained house parents provide a positive family environment.
- Provides intensive treatment for autistic children in residential programs.
- Offers a range of community-based support services such as communication centers for deaf people and trained aides for other disabled persons.
Alcoholics and Drug Abusers:
- Provides drop-in centers for public inebriates with food, medical referral, counseling and emergency shelter.
- Operates residential and nonresidential employment programs with job training, or employment in a sheltered environment.
- Offers social or medical model detoxification and psychological and peer group counseling for both adult and adolescent alcoholics and drug users.
- Works to prevent youth alcoholism and drug abuse through education programs.
Older Persons:
- Maintains home repair, homemaker assistance, transportation and senior center programs.
- Provides congregate and home-delivered meals.
- Operates foster grandparent and senior volunteer programs for helping others in need.
- Offers safe and affordable places to live.
- Considers elderly persons who cannot be completely independent with day care, group homes and congregate living facilities.
- Provides professional health care in nursing homes for the aged and chronically ill.
Designs programs specifically for the local communities they serve; operates in approximately 150 communities across the nation.
Publications: Gazette (quarterly); A Ministry of Service...; VOA Annual Report

YOUNG MEN'S CHRISTIAN ASSOCIATION OF THE U.S.
(formerly National Council of the YMCAs)
YMCA
101 North Wacker Drive
Chicago, IL 60606
TEL: 312-977-0031
Objectives: To offer a flexible program approach designed to meet the developing needs of people of all ages, races, religions, and incomes.
Services: Works through 2,048 local groups representing almost 13.5 million members to strengthen families, increase international understanding, promote healthy lifestyles, and develop communities, youth leadership, and adult health enhancement programs; offers group and club activities, facilities for physical and health education and training, youth sports activities, aquatics instruction, camping, parent-child programs, child care, world service work, and counseling; operates the *International Camp Counselor Program* which recruits counselors from other countries to work with youth in the U.S.; maintains a library and database of its activities; publishes a journal, a newsletter, a yearbook/Roster, a directory, and several bulletins, manuals, books and pamphlets.
Publications: Discovery YMCA; YMCA Newsletter; YMCA Yearbook and Official Roster; YMCA Directory; Executive Notes; Program Notes
Founded: 1851

YOUNG WOMEN'S CHRISTIAN ASSOCIATION OF THE U.S.
726 Broadway
New York, NY 10003
TEL: 212-614-2700

Objectives: To provide service programs for women and girls over 12 years of age.

Services: Works through its 4,000 local groups representing two million members to provide programs in health education, recreation, clubs and classes, and counseling and assistance to girls and women in the areas of employment, education, human sexuality, self-improvement, volunteerism, community citizenship, emotional and physical health, and juvenile justice; seeks to make contributions to peace, justice, freedom and dignity for all people; works toward elimination of racism; maintains national advocacy programs on the *Equal Rights Amendment,* sex-based discrimination against women, national policy of full employment, pay for work of comparable value, prevention of teenage pregnancy, protection against violence for all individuals, and child care services; includes men and boys in programs as associates; maintains 44 camps for children; publishes a journal, a newsletter, an annual report, a directory, and several bulletins and other materials.

Publications: YWCA Interchange; Communicator's Exchange; The Print Out; YWCA Directory; Annual Report

Founded: 1858

TRAINING PROGRAMS

AYE SHARE
SEE TRAINING/CONFERENCES/TEACHING

COMMUNITY ACTION TRAINING (CAT)
SEE TRAINING/CONFERENCES/TEACHING:
COMMUNITY SERVICES

COMMUNITY DEVELOPMENT, NEIGHBORHOOD SELF-SUFFICIENCY AND VOLUNTEERISM/VOLUNTEER PROGRAM MANAGEMENT
SEE TRAINING/CONFERENCES/TEACHING:
COMMUNITY SERVICES

COMMUNITY SERVICE
SEE TRAINING/CONFERENCES/TEACHING:
CHILDREN/YOUTH

COOL NATIONAL CONFERENCE
SEE TRAINING/CONFERENCES/TEACHING: STUDENTS

HOME TOWN AWARDS
SEE GOVERNORS' OFFICES ON VOLUNTEERISM:
ILLINOIS

SMALL TOWN SURVIVAL WORKSHOPS
Governor's Office on Volunteer Services/NM
308 Read Street
Santa Fe, NM 87501
TEL: 505-827-8235
Credit: Inquire
Sponsor: GOVS; Community Services Center of Portales
Contact: Pat Hamm Powell
Description: This is one of a series of workshops held in small towns designed to help community leaders identify local needs and methods of solving those problems together. The workshops take the leaders step-by-step through a process that brings together a cross-section of the community to discuss community problems. The workshop is divided into three sections; outlined below:
Getting Started
- The Core Group (a cross section of the community limited to five to fifteen people, with a mechanism for adding new people from time to time)

- The Coordinator (with responsibility to ensure that tasks are being completed satisfactorily and on time, and to structure meeting times and places)
- Frequency of meetings (a decision for the group to make based on the time they can commit)
- Format of Meetings (a meeting plan ranging from problem identification to assignment of activities to volunteers)

Essential Preparation for Setting Up a Public Meeting
- Decide on time and place (a place that is well-known, easily found, and meets space needs)
- Publicizing meeting (making it clear that whole families and people of all ages are welcome)
- Arranging setup for meetings (to symbolize the unity of the group, and ensure that all people can see each other and the front of the room)
- Planning decor (to assure that it attracts and stimulates participation)
- Providing supplies (to be sure that necessary supplies are on hand to avoid distractions in this often underestimated area)

Methods and Techniques for Conduct of Meetings
- The Dynamic Structure (silent generation of ideas in writing; round-robin listing of ideas on newsprint, serial discussion of ideas)
- Brainstorming (a way to get everyone's wisdom focused onto the concern)
- Consensus Categorizing (an organized "brainstorm," focused so people can deal with the issue effectively)
- Setting Priorities (a sorting and ranking of problem identifications or solutions)

The 4 x 4
This technique is employed to organize a lot of diverse material so that it can be used to write a document, give a lecture, plan a grant proposal, or used in other ways.

Problem-Solving Unit (PSU)
This is a method of breaking open a new arena or for moving toward solving persistent problems.

Community Forum
This is a technique employed when large groups are to be assembled, and group leadership has decided to involve the entire assembly in meaningful tasks.

Timelines
This is a graphic device that is quite simple, yet ingenious and very powerful. It is used to structure and coordinate responsibilities, plan events, and/or to record what has transpired.

An Evaluation Technique
This is a tool for reflection on four levels of awareness: Objective Level, Reflective Level, Interpretive Level, and Decisional Level. A training manual, Leaders for a New Day, provides additional steps, charts, and an example of a successful effort in a small New Mexico town that resulted in 19 new programs for one community over a 15-year period.

SOLVING COMMUNITY PROBLEMS BY BUILDING COMMUNITY PARTNERSHIPS
SEE GOVERNORS' OFFICES ON VOLUNTEERISM:
MINNESOTA

"UNITED WAY AT WORK" CONFERENCE
SEE BUSINESS/INDUSTRY INVOLVEMENT

INDIVIDUAL PROGRAM PROFILES

AIR FORCE MEMBERS AS VOLUNTEERS*
SEE VOLUNTEERS: ARMED FORCES MEMBERS - AIR FORCE

AMHERST Y.E.S. (YOUTH ENGAGED IN SERVICE)
SEE VOLUNTEERS: STUDENTS

CALIFORNIA HOUSE

820 East California Boulevard
Pasadena, CA 91106
TEL: 213-449-6950
Purpose: To provide senior adults with opportunities for community service and for social contact.
Sponsor: Assistance League of Pasadena; California House membership
Contact: Marge McIntyre, Director
Description: California House is different from most senior centers, because older people gather there not to receive services, but to give them. Through one of its two major activities, the *Senior Service Volunteer Program,* members of California House donate thousands of hours of volunteer service each year to community agencies.
From 130 to 150 volunteers are involved weekly in the Senior Service Volunteer Program. From 10:00 a.m. to 2:00 p.m., Tuesday through Friday, the sewing and community rooms, the kitchen and the workshop at California House are busy with groups meeting requests from hundreds of different nonprofit agencies. The volunteers help with folding, stuffing, and addressing mailings; make and repair clothing for children; make crafts and educational aids for schools; knit slippers and other articles for hospitals; bake cookies for children and servicemen; create and repair toys, puzzles, teaching aids and other wooden items.
The schedule of activities is announced in a monthly newsletter mailed to each California House member. A steering committee, composed of representatives of each activity group - sewing, woodworking, knitting, etc. - meets several times a year to develop and guide the Senior Service programs.
California House was built in 1965 by the Assistance League of Pasadena, a nonprofit volunteer service organization that provides continuing support to the facility. Members pay an annual fee of $2.50 to belong to California House. A light luncheon is available daily for a nominal fee. Assistance League members prepare and serve a monthly birthday luncheon, which is followed by a speaker, entertainment, or other program. Monthly tours and other special events, such as an annual volunteer recognition tea, also are held for members.
Founded: 1965

CAMPUS MINISTRY

SEE VOLUNTEERS: CHURCH/SYNAGOGUE MEMBERS

CAUSE (COMMUNITY AND UNIVERSITY SERVICES IN EDUCATION)

SEE VOLUNTEERS: STUDENTS

CENTRAL NAUGATUCK VALLEY RETIRED SENIOR VOLUNTEER PROGRAM

SEE VOLUNTEERS: OLDER PERSONS

CHRISTIAN INVOLVEMENT

SEE VOLUNTEERS: CHURCH/SYNAGOGUE MEMBERS

CHRISTIAN SERVICE DEPARTMENT

SEE VOLUNTEERS: CHURCH/SYNAGOGUE MEMBERS

CHRISTIAN SERVICE PROGRAM

SEE VOLUNTEERS: CHURCH/SYNAGOGUE MEMBERS

A CLASS ACT

c/o Jonathan Wiener
144 Kendrick
Brighton, MA 02194
TEL: 617-782-4202
Purpose: To add the dimension of community service to make a class reunion more meaningful.
Sponsor: Harvard University
Contact: Jonathan Wiener
Description: A Class Act was the fifth reunion of 130 graduates of Harvard and Radcliffe class of 1984, but it was a special kind of reunion. The former classmates performed acts of community service at 11 sites in and around Boston to make the reunion more meaningful.
Classmates met at JFK Park in Cambridge for bagels, coffee and work assignments. Transportation to the sites was provided by Harvard and Radcliffe. The 11 sites were chosen because tangible results were possible in three hours of labor.
Projects included beautification in parks and gardens, painting and cleaning at a women's center, assisting at a food bank, yard work at a youth center, etc.
The organizer found the sites by calling service agencies in the area and offering the services of his classmates. Each site was assigned a team leader, and the leaders visited the locations before the work began to talk with the people on-site and plan the work according to their needs.
At the end of the day, the organizer/classmate passed out packets urging them to continue public service work in their communities after the reunion weekend. The packets listed the 11 projects and acknowledged service agencies that helped find the sites, and included information on how to find opportunities to perform service work outside the Boston area.

CLEBURNE COUNTY CARES

Cleburne County Department of Human Services
1521 West Main
Heber Springs, AR 72543
TEL: 501-362-3298
Purpose: To pool resources of community service organizations and civic clubs for the betterment of county residents.
Sponsor: Cleburne County Department of Human Services
Contact: Bob Morris, Executive Director
Description: In 1986, the Cleburne County DHS Administrator determined that, although volunteer efforts were evident in the community, a pooling of resources would result in improved programs and services for the community. In a fall program that year, 24 community leaders met with DHS staff to discuss better use of their time and volunteers. Six weeks later, "Cleburne County Cares" (CCC) opened its doors.
Beginning modestly as a small food bank and used clothing center, the group quietly worked toward their goals without government grants or assistance from county or federal authorities. Individual and organizational membership dues, voluntary contributions, and proceeds from sales of used household goods provided the initial funding. But the community began to do more - one businessman offering free rental space in one of his buildings, a lawyer volunteering to draw up the articles of incorporation and other legal documents gratis, and others stepping forward to help the program grow.
During the first month of operation, 93 persons received food assistance, and used clothing proceeds totaled $89.40. Within a short time, more than 3,000 pounds of food per month was being distributed, and used clothing proceeds averaged $2,000 each month.
The Center rapidly outgrew its initial location and, in 1987, moved to a more centrally located building in downtown Heber Springs. At about the same time, a HUD grant allowed CCC to open an emergency shelter for the homeless, and a full-time volunteer executive director, a retired Air Force Officer, stepped forward. In addition to the homeless shelter, which is in constant use, CCC added a program of providing clothing, blankets and household items to disaster victims.
By 1988 more than 126 volunteers had logged 19,329 hours, distributed more than 60,000 pounds of food to almost 3,000

individuals, and served scores of homeless persons and disaster victims.

There is no paid staff at CCC, and it is receiving an ever-increasing amount of county-wide support. In 1988, CCC was nominated for the President's Volunteer Action Award. According to the director, "The dream lives on and the volunteers of Cleburne County make it all possible."

COMMUNITY BETTERMENT PROGRAM
SEE BUSINESS/INDUSTRY INVOLVEMENT: HOUSING

COMMUNITY FIELD WORK
SEE VOLUNTEERS: STUDENTS

COMMUNITY LABORATORY PROJECT
SEE VOLUNTEERS: STUDENTS

COMMUNITY LEARNING PROGRAM
SEE VOLUNTEERS: STUDENTS

COMMUNITY PROBLEM SOLVING COMMITTEE
United Way of Central Maryland
22 Light Street
PO Box 1576
Baltimore, MD 21203-1576
TEL: 301-547-8000
Purpose: To mount an all-out effort to accelerate community problem-solving.
Sponsor: United Way, local business, labor, government, education, and community leaders
Contact: Mel Tansill, Director of Media Relations
Description: This program was begun in 1989 to develop an extensive community-feedback process to identify the region's most critical human-service needs. Nearly 76,000 area residents worked with the United Way to accelerate community problem-solving. The process included a survey printed on pledge cards distributed during the 1988 campaign, and 12 subsequent town meetings held throughout Baltimore and five surrounding counties.
When the feedback process was completed, the three overall concerns which the community had identified as most pressing were substance-abuse treatment, literacy training and child day care. In response, United Way designated $1 million, in addition to funds to be raised during its current campaign, for programs addressing those concerns.
Both the pledge-card survey and the town meetings provided a comprehensive list of human service issues which had been analyzed in United Way's publication, *Central Maryland Megatrends,* a study of regional demographic trends and related service needs. Also, respondents were given the opportunity to add issues they felt were important but which were not included on the list.
A return of approximately 75,000 pledge card responses prioritizing top issues were received. At the 12 town meetings, a total of approximately 1,000 participants ranked top needs in a voting process. Volunteer leaders and the 30-member Community Problem Solving Committee helped staff conduct the meetings. The agendas began with an explanation of the problem-solving role and objectives, and continued with open discussion of issues and needs.
Although the $1 million dollars was designated for substance-abuse treatment, literacy training, and child day care, it was pointed out that each of these critical needs is linked to other specific concerns. For example, expanded substance-abuse treatment can help relieve problems such as crime, family violence and child abuse, homelessness, and AIDS. Illiteracy contributes to unemployment, and inadequate day care is often detrimental to a child's future.
The Community Problem-Solving Committee continually considers

proposals in the three critical-need areas - 160 through September of 1989. Those evaluated as having the most potential were allocated funds in October 1989. The Committee consists of representatives from local business, labor, government, education, and community leaders.
Publications: Central Maryland Megatrends
Founded: 1989

COMMUNITY PROGRAMS
Marillac House
2822 West Jackson Boulevard
Chicago, IL 60612
TEL: 312-722-7440
Purpose: To provide service for the poor of East Garfield Park.
Sponsor: Chicago Community Trust
Contact: Mrs. Kay Hallagan
Description: Marillac House is committed to the community of East Garfield Park. With unemployment at an all-time peak and government assistance slashed, the families of this community are enormously deprived. Homes are without heat due to impossible utility costs. Fires and eviction are forcing people out on the streets. Crime and violence are commonplace. Meager aid checks and food stamp allotments are snatched from homemakers as they struggle to pay their bills.
Frequently a family is without food for a month due to theft. Marillac House maintains a food pantry five days a week for families in emergency need. The *Emergency Infant Nutrition Program* provides needed formula for babies who have not yet been added to the grant or who have not yet qualified for WIC. Over one hundred infants per month are served through this program. The Chicago Community Trust is funding this program. Donations specifically for infant care are used to purchase disposable diapers and layettes for newborns.
A summer feeding program funded by a private donation supplied breakfast to 1,300 children every morning for eight weeks during the summer of 1982. The private funding replaced resources previously supplied by the Department of Agriculture through the Illinois Department of Education, cancelled by the federal government.
The agency operates Day Care for children of mothers employed or in school. The Child Protection units counsel families under the auspices of the Department of Children and Family Services. Elderly Outreach seeks out senior citizens who are without family and resources to help them survive. Alcoholics Anonymous groups meet regularly and a GED program is offered. Neighborhood recreation programs attract children of all ages.
A new program specifically designed for teen mothers has been funded by the Chicago Community Trust. Its goal is to intervene in the constantly recurring cycle of poverty.

COMMUNITY PROJECTS IN SAINT PAUL
St. Paul/Office of the Mayor
347 City Hall
St. Paul, MN 55102
TEL: 612-298-4323*
Purpose: To provide useful services and programs to St. Paul through volunteer effort.
Sponsor: City of St. Paul
Contact: *George Latimer, Mayor (or specific contacts noted with each program)
Description: Volunteers in St. Paul work in many human service areas, providing financial support as well as useful services and programs, which are especially helpful in the present era of budget cutbacks and financial shortfalls. Examples of community services by volunteers include:
Athletic Boosters: The Northwest Como Boosters Club provides leadership for activities at a neighborhood recreation center and provides financial support. The organization purchases equipment, sponsors an awards banquet, provides coaches, sponsors Halloween

activities, etc. The principal fundraising event is a Booya, another name for a Minnesota Community Beef Stew Cookout.

- [*Specific Contact: Larry McMahon, President, Northwest Como Boosters Club, 1573 Fernwood Street, St. Paul, MN 55117 612-489-2428*]

Friends of the Library: This volunteer group assists the St. Paul Public Library by providing financial support and leadership for programs which the library is unable to provide. In addition, they deliver books to homebound people, arrange and staff "Meet the Author" autographing parties, assist in mailings, conduct fund drives and fund raising events, process paperbacks, and take care of plants.

- [*Specific Contact: Alice Neve, Coordinator of Volunteers, Friends of the Library, 90 West Fourth Street, St. Paul, MN 55102 612-292-6393*]

Como Zoological Society: This group of volunteers assists the Como Zoo financially, and motivates citizen support and legislative approval for capital improvements at the Zoo. Money raised through dues and fund raising events is used to purchase equipment for the Zoo, needed but not included in the budget.

- [*Specific Contact: Steven Hurvitz, President, Como Zoological Society, PO Box 16127, St. Paul, MN 55116 612-770-2311*]

Zoo Outreach and Tour Program: The Docents at the Zoo provide volunteers to staff the office of the Zoo, provide outreach programs, conduct tours of the facility, provide information about the Zoo and the denizens, take Zoo animals into the community, and raise funds for Zoo improvement. The Docents have a cadre of 50 volunteers.

- [*Specific Contact: Marylin Tarasar, Como Park Zoo Docents, 2107 Third Street, NE, Minneapolis, MN 55418 612-789-1269*]

St. Paul Garden Club: This volunteer group assists the Como Park Conservatory financially, helps to plan its programs, purchases equipment for the Conservatory, provides design assistance on the preparation of the Como Park Master Plan, and mounts other volunteer activities to benefit the Conservatory.

- [*Specific Contact: Lee Hallgren, St. Paul Garden Club, 2160 Eleanor Street, St. Paul, MN 55116 612-887-4511*]

Examples of other volunteer efforts developed and implemented to benefit the City are available.

COMMUNITY SERVICE/AWARENESS ACTION
SEE VOLUNTEERS: STUDENTS

CONEJO VALLEY RETIRED SENIOR VOLUNTEER PROGRAM
SEE VOLUNTEERS: OLDER PERSONS

DENISON COMMUNITY ASSOCIATION
SEE VOLUNTEERS: STUDENTS

DOVE, INC.
1112 East Locust
Decatur, IL 62521
TEL: 217-428-6616
Purpose: To use volunteers to meet needs arising from social inequities and personal crises.
Sponsor: 32 area churches
Contact: Fred Spannaus, Executive Director, Ron Butler, Youth Director
Description: Formed in 1970, Dove has four program wings:
- Core Programs (Preschool and Family);
- Youth (Education, Drug Prevention, Career Development);
- Domestic Violence (including Sexual Assault); and
- Retired Senior Volunteer Program.

DOVE has a volunteer force of 700, a staff of 16, and a budget of $220,000. Funding is received from churches, public and private sources.
DOVE uses volunteers in such diverse tasks as preschool

instruction, child care, transportation, tutoring, crisis line response (domestic violence and sexual assault), one-to-one advocacy, group facilitators (women's, men's and children's groups), youth activity leaders, nursing home visitation/advocacy, and aluminum recycling. As the area RSVP agency, Dove also provides senior volunteers to many other organizations.
DOVE also uses VISTA Volunteers (full-time commitment of one year, with a small living allowance) and student interns. Student interns may work in any program area, by agreement between the program director and the educational institution.
The length of orientation varies with the volunteer duties. Examples are 1-2 hours for tutors, 8-10 hours for crisis line response, 16-18 hours for nursing home visitation, and eight days for VISTA Volunteers. Orientation is coordinated by the professional staff, and outside resources are used as appropriate. Training manuals are used where needed.
Many volunteers work in teams under limited supervision by staff. Volunteer meetings ("reflection sessions") are held regularly for all volunteer groups. Volunteers may serve, along with client representatives, on Program Councils, which function as strong advisory committees in each program area.
DOVE recruits volunteer from the Decatur area for all programs. Applicants for VISTA and internships are solicited from throughout the country and undergo a careful screening process.
Founded: 1970

DWIGHT-ENGLEWOOD SCHOOL VOLUNTEER PROGRAM
Dwight-Englewood School
315 East Pallisade
Englewood, NJ 07632
TEL: 201-569-9500
Purpose: To emphasize community involvement as an important activity in the development of the individual.
Contact: James Van Amburg, Headmaster
Description: From its beginning, an educational philosophy that emphasizes community involvement has been the hallmark of the private Dwight-Englewood School. Although it's history of celebrity graduates (George Schultz, Dick Button, Brooke Shields, Edwin Roberts, Michael Gore and others) has caused it be dubbed a "rich" school, its students have always been concerned with social issues. To make that point, graduates who were not celebrities when they came, but made a place in history, include the first director of the U.S. Civil Rights Commission (1947), and the founder of the Englewood Urban League (1891), among others. Once considered a "WASPy place," today the school population includes black, Hispanic, Indian, Pakistani, Iranian, and Armenian students as well as white.
On its one hundredth anniversary in 1989, officials found that volunteering by students is at a higher level than ever. When school officials found that 80% of the students were involved in some type of volunteer project, they decided to formalize it. Today, sophomores are required to take an ethics course, and since 1986 all students have had to complete 40 hours of community service to graduate. To do this, they volunteer at Englewood Hospital, the library, blood banks, food banks, and many other community programs and organizations. Teachers are constantly involved in making students aware of a deep sense of social responsibility. Values and involvement in the wider community are emphasized as strongly as academics "to develop the whole person."

EDUCATIONAL PARTICIPATION IN COMMUNITIES
SEE VOLUNTEERS: STUDENTS

FIELD EDUCATION PROGRAM
SEE VOLUNTEERS: CHURCH/SYNAGOGUE MEMBERS

FIELD EXPERIENCE EDUCATION
SEE VOLUNTEERS: STUDENTS

FRESH FORCE
SEE VOLUNTEERS: STUDENTS

FRIENDSHIP HOUSE
619 D Street, SE
Washington, DC 20003
TEL: 202-547-8880
Purpose: To serve the needs of poor people in Southeast
Washington.
Sponsor: United Way; United Planning Organization; District of
Columbia Office on Aging
Contact: Pete Ward, Executive Director
Description: Founded in 1904, Friendship Center today has 300
volunteers assisting 60 staff members in 12 locations in the
Southeast Washington area. Its primary aim in its 78 years of
existence has been to meet the needs of poor people. Some of the
programs operated by staff and volunteers are:
- **Child Development Center:** an educational program for
  children ages two to ten. In addition to the educational
  program, health screening, outings, and special events are
  arranged by volunteers and parent groups.
- **Services to the Elderly:** a nutrition program operated at five
  locations, with some home delivery of meals. Transportation is
  provided for those who are able to attend the congregate meal
  sites. The program also includes supportive services such as
  escort assistance, counseling, shopping assistance, and
  recreational activities.
- **Neighborhood Housing Center:** a program of financial and
  technical assistance, counseling, prepurchase planning, money
  management, default/delinquent counseling and other services
  to low-income homeowners or renters. The program also
  assists with stabilizing, upgrading and improving the condition
  of homes.
- **Consumer Action Unit** and **Martin Luther King Co-op Food
  Store:** a dual service where bulk buying keeps food prices low,
  and help is available for consumer problems. Consumer
  education programs are held at the co-op showing ways of
  stretching the food dollar, and individuals with emergency
  food needs can obtain free food at this location.
- **Clothing Center:** a center for the collection of good used
  clothing donated by individuals, agencies and businesses and
  available free to the needy.
- **Youth Unit:** a drop-in center for youth which provides a
  multitude of services and youth education programs, e.g.,
  employment counseling and assistance, sex education,
  counseling for teenage parents, tutoring, and special trips to
  local theatres and sports arenas. In addition, this unit
  maintains an after-school care program for children from five
  to eleven years of age.
- **Community Organization Unit:** a program that deals with a
  number of issues including tenant problems, quality of
  education, job counseling and training, etc.

Cooperating services provided for the convenience of local
residents include alcoholic counseling meetings and food stamp
certification. In addition, Friendship House runs summer job
referrals for teenagers, offers credit union services, conducts voter
registration drives, and develops other programs as new needs are
identified. Some 20,000 people benefit from Friendship House
programs each year.
Founded: 1904

GIVE FIVE ALABAMA
SEE GOVERNORS' OFFICES ON VOLUNTEERISM:
ALABAMA

GOALS FOR DALLAS*
2004 Davis Building
1309 Main Street
Dallas, TX 75202
TEL: 214-741-1738
Purpose: To assist citizens in setting goals, developing plans to
achieve goals, and monitoring and facilitating goal achievement
activities.
Sponsor: Individuals, business/industry, foundations
Contact: John Lewis, Director
Description: Goals for Dallas was founded in 1965. The basic
challenge continues to provide an arena in which all the differing
ideas about what should happen in Dallas may be resolved into
one list of goals representing a consensus of community opinion.
Based on these goals, a continual effort works toward the building
of a community that satisfies collective and individual needs of its
citizens.
Goals for Dallas works through a Planning Committee which lays
the groundwork each year for a new *Goals for Dallas* process.
Some 500 volunteers on Goals Achievement Committees in 17
areas of community concern meet in the fall of each year to report
on each of the 205 citizens' goals set in 1977. The 150-member
Planning Committee forms small groups consisting of ten to twelve
members each to explore the various approaches and building
blocks that form the bases for the new Goals for Dallas process.
The work of the 17 Achievement Committees resulted in a series
of published reports covering the following 17 areas of concern:
- Citizen Involvement
- Continuing Education
- Cultural Activities
- The Design of the City
- Economy
- Elementary and Secondary Education
- Energy
- Environment
- Government
- Health
- Higher Education
- Housing
- Human Services
- Public Safety
- Quality of the Citizenry
- Recreation and Leisure Time
- Transportation

In the decade of the eighties, the process of Goals for Dallas
diverged somewhat from the one that worked so well for 15 years.
The increasing rate of change indicates that more is needed than a
collective definition of problems and opportunities, and traditional
plans to achieve goals. A recognition of the "new" Dallas - the
changing nature of its people, politics, resources and organizations
- has indicated that future goals must respond to the "new" Dallas
as well as the successes of 15 years of work. In the meantime,
activities toward goals achievement continue uninterrupted.
In addition to goals achievement activities and planning for the
next decade, Goals for Dallas Trustees and Achievement
Committee Executives meet to deal with long-range needs. Their
Workshop 2000 examined the city in its present state, predicted
change to the year 2000, and assessed the positive and negative
impacts of that change on the future. In addition, meetings are
held by organizations such as the *Dallas Alliance Convocation of
Neighborhoods,* with workshops ranging from neighborhood
leadership to zoning, and providing the opportunity for direct
citizen-public official contact.
The new Planning Committee consists of elected officials, business
people, public administrators, media members, civic leaders,
educators, students, retirees, local groups, association chapters,
long-time Goals workers, newcomers to Dallas, and many other
volunteers. This diversity is reflected, also, in the 17 Achievement
Committees.
Publications: Goals for Dallas; New Goals for Dallas
Founded: 1965

GONZAGA ACTION PROGRAM (GAP)
SEE VOLUNTEERS: CHURCH/SYNAGOGUE MEMBERS

GRAND PEOPLE'S RETIRED SENIOR VOLUNTEER PROGRAM
SEE VOLUNTEERS: OLDER PERSONS

THE GREATER CLEVELAND CONNECTION
SEE VOLUNTEERS: STUDENTS

INDEPENDENCE NEIGHBORHOOD COUNCILS
Neighborhood Councils Service Center
201 West Maple
Liberty on the Square
Independence, MO 64050
TEL: 816-833-4225
Purpose: To improve the quality of life in the community.
Sponsor: Neighborhood Councils Service Center
Contact: Terry Snapp, Communications
Description: Through a network of 64 citizen organizations (42 neighborhoods and 22 citywide committees), the Independence Neighborhood Councils average 345 programs each year aimed at improving the quality of life in the Communities. In 20 major citywide and numerous unique neighborhood areas of concern, local citizens have banded together for the past ten years to carry out a multitude of programs. Activities include health screenings, dental programs, beautification projects, crime prevention activities, CPR training, drug abuse programs, street repair, park development, clean-up efforts, educational programs, Family Fun Festivals, gardening projects, recreation programs, etc.
In their ten-year history, the Councils have grown from 1,003 members the first year to the current enrollment of 21,000 citizens twelve years old and older. However, nearly 74,000 citizens have at some time been involved in some kind of Neighborhood Council activity. There is no charge for membership in the Councils, permitting any interested citizen to participate without concern for a financial obligation.
While the phenomenal growth of this massive volunteer effort had resulted from the infusion of federal funds along with funds from the Mott Foundation, these funds have been curtailed or sharply reduced. Currently, the Councils are almost totally dependent on local funding to support the thousands of hours provided by the volunteer-members, or "good neighbors." To help meet the challenge, the organization has enlisted an executive committee of professionals in financial, fundraising, and administrative affairs in Independence. This committee, chaired by the chairman of the board of a local bank, spends scores of volunteer hours examining the finances of the Councils and seeking ways to put them on a firm financial footing.
The Councils work closely with businesses, city departments, churches, civic organizations, agencies, schools, and other groups - assisting many of them in achieving their goals and carrying out their services more effectively. The Councils see themselves as "servant agencies" with human and other resources to share with other community groups.
In addition to mounting and assisting programs, the Councils provide a vehicle of communication among citizens and their community leaders. They provide monthly neighborhood meetings, citywide committee workshops, rallies, a weekly newsletter, a monthly magazine, TeleNeighbor (a 24-hour hotline), and 42 neighborhood newsletters to help facilitate the communication process between neighborhoods and the institutions and agencies that serve them.
The Councils also have stimulated the economy by bringing $2 million dollars into the area over the past ten years, and helping to create the Neighborhood Assistance Act which provides generous state tax credits for corporations who invest in their communities through the Councils. Through neighborhood and citywide meetings, the Councils identify and recognize those making special efforts to help make the area a better place to live. Examples are: the Youth Appreciation Show, Business-of-the-Month Program, Good Neighbor Month, the Community Builder Award, neighborhood Recognition Banquets, the "Ya Dun Good" award in honor of an exemplary citizen, a citywide Recognition Banquet, etc.
An important side benefit of the Councils' efforts is the cadre of citizens equipped with skills and attitudes of leadership that is developing through the Councils' workshops, conferences, retreats and special courses. Not only do people become better neighbors in their volunteer positions, but many have obtained better jobs and more confidence in other areas. Crime has decreased, health conditions have improved, eyesores have disappeared, vacant lots have turned into gardens, historic sites have been preserved or restored, lives have been enriched as citizens become more effective leaders in their neighborhoods.
Since 1971, representatives from over 1100 communities and 43 nations have visited Independence to learn more about its Neighborhood Councils' activities. In addition, Independence is one of 18 finalists in a selection process spear-headed by pollster George Gallup to find the "All-America City."
Publications: Neighborhood Assistance Act
Founded: 1971

INVOLVEMENT CORPS*
SEE BUSINESS/INDUSTRY INVOLVEMENT

JUNIOR LEAGUE OF DETROIT
32 Lake Shore Road
Detroit, MI 48236
TEL: 313-881-0040
Purpose: To reach out to all young women who demonstrate an interest in and a commitment to volunteerism.
Contact: Kathleen Nesi, Trustee
Description: To celebrate its 75th year in 1989, the *Junior League of Detroit* reflected on the changes since its beginnings in 1914. For years, it appeared to all to be a "private club" with membership only by invitation. African Americans, Jews and other minorities, working women and less-than-affluent women were not invited.
In recent years, a concerted effort has been made to diversify membership. Currently about 25 of the 350 members are minority women. Invitations are no longer required for membership. Interested women simply contact the League themselves. The 1988-89 annual report states that "it reaches out to all young women regardless of race, religion or national origin, who demonstrate an interest in and a commitment to voluntarism." Current projects of the League include:

- **AIDS Volunteer Project** - For this project, the League trains volunteers to work not only with the AIDS patients, but with their families as well. Also, the League maintains a committee for the project to keep abreast of medical and other AIDS issues to find the best way to be helpful to AIDS patients and families as science progresses toward a cure.
- **Barat Human Services** - This special project of the League is an emergency child-care program. Initially, the League raised $60,000 for its operation. They devote untold volunteer hours to taking care of youngsters to keep them from joining the child-abuse statistic.

These are in contrast to its 1914 project of establishing a lunch room for working women in one area of the city. Each member is required to donate at least 75 hours annually to the organization's projects - today, usually in the evening or on weekends to accommodate working women. The League has given some 25,000 volunteer hours and more than $2 million to city projects in its 75-year life.
League volunteers are especially happy to be able to work at all levels of involvement - from a research committee member working 5-10 hours weekly, to a new mother available only 2-3

hours weekly to help with the clerical tasks.

The process of choosing projects begins with the research committee, which conducts surveys to determine the most pressing needs. In 1989, the committee sent proposals to over 100 mental health facilities based on the results of one of the surveys.

A new revelation has surfaced at the League as more and more young women move into the work force. Currently, members over 40 are put on "sustainer" status and are expected to take a less active role. However, research shows that women are more likely to do volunteer work between the ages of 35 and 50, when their children are out of the toddler stage. According to one committee member, "We are losing a whole contingency of volunteers. It would be an improvement to move [the age] up to 50; ideally there would be no age limit at all."
Founded: 1914

THE LEARNING WEB
SEE TRAINING/CONFERENCES/TEACHING:
INTERNSHIPS

LIVINGSTON COUNTY RSVP PROGRAM
SEE VOLUNTEERS: OLDER PERSONS

LUTHERAN SOCIAL SERVICES VOLUNTEER PROGRAM
SEE VOLUNTEERS: CHURCH/SYNAGOGUE MEMBERS

MINDSTRETCHERS
SEE LEADERSHIP DEVELOPMENT/BOARDS:
CHILDREN/YOUTH

MOVE (MOBILIZATION OF VOLUNTEERS)
SEE VOLUNTEERS: STUDENTS

**THE OWL (OUTREACH-WORKING-LEARNING)
PROGRAM**
SEE VOLUNTEERS: STUDENTS

PHI MU SORORITY COMMUNITY SERVICE CHAPTER
SEE VOLUNTEERS: FRATERNAL ORGANIZATIONS

PROJECT OASES
SEE VOLUNTEERS: STUDENTS

PROJECTS IN THE COMMUNITY
SEE VOLUNTEERS: STUDENTS

PUBLIC ASSISTANCE CLIENTS VOLUNTEER
SEE VOLUNTEERS: SELF-HELP

RAMAPO KEY CLUB*
SEE VOLUNTEERS: STUDENTS

REQUIREMENT: SKIP CLASSES
Long Beach Unified School District
701 Locust Avenue
Long Beach, CA 90813
TEL: 213-436-9931
Purpose: To demonstrate school support of volunteerism by releasing high school students during class hours to assist in the community.
Sponsor: Long Beach Unified School District
Contact: Edward Eveland, Assistant Superintendent
Description: Students in Long Beach Unified School District high schools have a better chance of getting good grades if they skip school. This phenomenon involves a pilot project designed to get kids more involved with their community. The pilot project was

instituted in May 1989, releasing 250 seniors from three high schools - Avalon, Millikan and Jordan - for three days into the community to work in community projects pre-selected by the students.

Although many school districts require before- or after-school volunteer service of their high school students, Long Beach is the first in California to allow students class time to serve their communities. If the project is successful, all of the district's seniors will be required to perform at least 15 hours of community service each year during school hours.

The Social Studies department of Millikan School is coordinating the volunteer effort, which is voluntary, but termed "semi-forced optional," since the students have been told it will have a favorable effect on their grades. During their three days, students in the pilot project worked at city halls, police departments, hospitals, parks, schools, the fire department and the animal shelter, with hospitals - especially the Veterans Hospital - the most popular option. Other seniors, about a dozen, went into the back country of their scenic island and planted shrubs to shore up an eroding hillside. Another dozen students helped in elementary school classrooms, tutoring, reading, and playing games with the children. Three students chose the animal shelter, taking pets to visit elderly patients in convalescent homes, working in the kennels, and riding along with animal control officers. The latter were told that junior high school students had been coming on their own to accompany pets to the convalescent homes.

In addition to selecting their assignments, students were required to provide their own transportation. One exception was the Veterans Hospital. With so many students choosing that option, the school bus was used to transport them.

RETIRED SENIOR VOLUNTEER PROGRAM
SEE VOLUNTEERS: OLDER PERSONS

RSVP OF MORRIS COUNTY
SEE VOLUNTEERS: OLDER PERSONS

RSVP OF RAMSEY COUNTY
SEE VOLUNTEERS: OLDER PERSONS

SAN FERNANDO VALLEY INTERFAITH COUNCIL
3370 Perlita Avenue
Los Angeles, CA 90039
TEL: 213-664-6847 (Perlita); 213-254-1555 (Piedmont)
Satellite Office:
6150 Piedmont Avenue
Los Angeles, CA 90042
Purpose: To bring together churches, corporations, volunteers and the entire community to address and resolve issues that adversely affect the community.
Sponsor: Area churches and synagogues
Contact: Barry Smedberg, Executive Director
Description: Twenty-five years ago San Fernando Valley churches and temples joined together to fight Proposition 14, an initiative sponsored by the real estate industry and designed to overturn state and local anti-discrimination housing laws then on the books. Although the battle was lost, group members did not disband, but created an ongoing vehicle for tackling social issues in an interfaith setting. They named the organization the San Fernando Valley Interfaith Council (VIC).

In May 1989, 300 people attended a banquet celebrating the Council's 25 years of existence. VIC remains a largely volunteer organization concerned with the immediate social issues of the day, as well as the deeper problems of intolerance and exploitation. It organizes educational forums on interfaith and interracial issues and sponsors gatherings of the clergy and public discussions on the homeless, gangs, AIDS and other issues. In early 1989, VIC organized the first Valleywide interfaith service honoring Martin

Luther King Jr. Day.

But since the mid-1970s, VIC has become increasingly involved in direct-assistance programs that have increased its budget to $1.5 million, 90% of which comes from government contracts. Programs include:

- **Senior Citizen Centers** - two multipurpose centers (Pacoima and Van Nuys) help solve problems involving housing, transportation, companionship, Social Security, health and other matters for nearly 13,000 elderly people each year.
- **Meals on Wheels** - 218,000 hot meals in the Valley and ten other sites scattered around the area.
- **Food Pantries** - seven pantries distribute emergency groceries to another 160,000 poor people of all ages, and VIC's AIDS Coalition is attempting to gain funding for another food program to help those bedridden with AIDS.
- **Homeless Shelter** - an attempt in 1986 provide a emergency shelter for the homeless by renovating the Fiesta Motel in North Hollywood (purchased for $2.2 million), which resulted in unexpected high expenses and the necessity to turn over operations to the *Los Angeles Family Housing Corporation* for operation.

More than 60 staff members are employed in the various direct-assistance programs, but volunteers remain the key to VIC's success. VIC has 400 paid members, 42 of which are churches, temples or other religious congregations, but about 100 individuals - members and nonmembers alike - contribute more than 4,000 volunteer hours each month (not including board members' time and time spent when emergencies arise).

VIC has no regrets about the shelter effort. According to VIC's vice president, "We managed to get it going... when no one else was willing to take it on. Success in this area is getting something started and raising people's awareness in the process, not making it problem-free."

Programs underway include a Valley hospice for dying AIDS patients. Attention is also given to the Cal State Northridge *United Campus Ministry* program, which is directed by VIC's vice president.

Reaching out to the corporate world - including firms linked to the defense industry, a move that VIC's leadership might in the past have rejected on ideological grounds - is one attempt at reconciliation. Appointing a local representative of the conservative *Church of Jesus Christ of Latter-day Saints* to VIC's advisory board is another move toward reconciliation. The executive director feels that to focus on one group as the bad guys is simplistic: "All of us have a degree of responsibility and each of us is part of the problem as well as the solution."
Founded: 1964

SENIOR PROGRAM
SEE SELF-HELP: INTERGENERATIONAL

SERVICE-LEARNING CENTER
SEE VOLUNTEERS: STUDENTS

ST. MATTHIAS OF SOMERSET COUNCIL NO. 9925
SEE VOLUNTEERS: FRATERNAL ORGANIZATIONS

STUDENT VOLUNTEER SERVICES
SEE VOLUNTEERS: STUDENTS

TAU KAPPA EPSILON (TKE) COMMUNITY PROJECTS
SEE VOLUNTEERS: FRATERNAL ORGANIZATIONS

THURSDAY AFTERNOON PROGRAM (TAP)
SEE VOLUNTEERS: STUDENTS

TIP NEIGHBORHOOD HOUSE/OLDER ADULT VOLUNTEERS
SEE VOLUNTEERS: OLDER PERSONS

TRANSITIONAL VOLUNTEERS ARE...
SEE VOLUNTEERS: FORMER MENTAL PATIENTS

UNIFIED COMMUNITY RESOURCE COUNCIL
Arkansas Office of Volunteerism
Department of Human Services
PO Box 1437
Little Rock, AR 72203-1437
TEL: 501-682-7540
TOLL FREE: 800-482-5850, Ext. 27540
Purpose: To coordinate community projects among community groups and organizations.
Sponsor: Arkansas Office of Volunteerism; local Human Services Offices
Contact: Billie Ann Myers, Director
Description: A Unified Community Resource Council (UCRC) is a council of community groups and organizations based on a program developed by the Arkansas Office of Volunteerism. Each group sends one representative to UCRC meetings to share information, coordinate community projects, and report back to the group. In this way each organization can better serve local needs with limited resources, since much duplication is avoided. A UCRC is made up of local people who can:

- **Care** about community problems and local suffering;
- **Share** community resources; and
- **Coordinate** efforts to help solve community needs. UCRC representatives come from churches, civic clubs, school clubs, fire departments, health groups, government agencies, private businesses, professional clubs, etc.

The efficiency of a community-owned UCRC helps organizations and the community to get more things done with less time and resources expended. It is a "roundtable" for all local groups and can bring unity and strength to the community (large or small) by using the experience of each group in sharing ideas and projects. A UCRC is:

- owned by the community;
- operated independently of state or federal agencies;
- a provider of services to anyone the community wishes to serve;
- a structure for getting things done quickly when the need arises;
- a community problem-solver, and therefore a community resource;
- a central information and resource organizer;
- a focal point for local volunteers;
- a nonprofit structure which can receive assistance, donations, grants, etc. for the benefit of the community;
- an opportunity to network with other groups and UCRCs throughout the state.

The Arkansas Office of Volunteerism serves as a catalyst of the UCRC in that it can provide the organization with program speakers, training workshops for community volunteer projects, or help in forming the URCR.
Publications: UCRC Newsletter

"UNITED WAY AT WORK" PROGRAM
SEE BUSINESS/INDUSTRY INVOLVEMENT

VERMONT INTERNSHIP PROGRAM
SEE TRAINING/CONFERENCES/TEACHING: INTERNSHIPS

VIVA (VERY IMPORTANT VOLUNTEERS IN ACTION)
SEE VOLUNTEERS: OLDER PERSONS

VOLUNTEER SENIOR LEADERS
SEE LEADERSHIP DEVELOPMENT/BOARDS: OLDER PERSON

VOLUNTEER SERVICES PROGRAM/UA
SEE VOLUNTEERS: STUDENTS

VOLUNTEER VOLUNTEER COORDINATORS*
SEE ADMINISTRATION

VOLUNTEERS AT FORT LEAVENWORTH
SEE VOLUNTEERS: ARMED FORCES MEMBERS - ARMY

YOUNG VOLUNTEERS IN ACTION*
SEE VOLUNTEERS: STUDENTS

YOUTH COMMUNITY SERVICE
SEE VOLUNTEERS: STUDENTS

YOUTH COMMUNITY SERVICE
Constitutional Rights Foundation
601 S. Kingsley Drive
Los Angeles, CA 90005
TEL: 213-487-5590
Purpose: To give students an opportunity to select, develop, and administer volunteer projects in the community.
Sponsor: Constitutional Rights Foundation
Contact: Cathryn Berger Kaye
Description: This school-based service program begins with a session aimed at developing leadership prior to assigning students to community projects. The students meet away from the school for an overnight meeting of workshops, discussions, and an opportunity to share experiences and ideas with their peers and selected community leaders. Students from 22 high schools are involved in the process, with the assistance of teacher/sponsors who meet with them regularly following the initial session. Skill development is ongoing throughout the school year, with advisors from the community participating.
The handbook provided to the students emphasizes academic skills in conjunction with leadership tasks, and in some cases academic credit is available.
Student projects have included feeding the homeless, adopting grandparents, painting trash cans, cleaning up graffiti, and many more. Themes are chosen each year, the most current year's being school and communty beautification, children, and senior citizens. One beautification project resulted in an anti-graffiti project called *Wipe-Out Weekend (WOW)*. It was organized by a student and involved no less than 800 painters aged three to 65 years of age covering graffiti on schools, freeway underpasses, park structures, and trash cans at sixty sites around Los Angeles. The project continues, and now includes mural paintings as well as graffiti coverup.
Another project involved immigrants and was called the *Welcome America Project*. It was designed to help immigrants in both school and community.
Youth Community Service is a project of the *Constitutional Rights Foundation*, in cooperation with the *Los Angeles Unified School district*. It receives primary funding from the *Ford Foundation*. The director of the project emphasizes that *leadership* is the goal so that the skills developed will "give students the opportunity to take their own ideas and make them happen."
Publications: YCS Leadership Training Manual
Founded: 1982

YOUTH IN ACTION
United Way of the Capital Area
843 North President Street
Jackson, MS 39225-3169
TEL: 601-948-4725
Purpose: To give students the opportunity to become involved in the *United Way* process and in their communities - using their energy, enthusiasm and idealism to help themselves while helping others.
Contact: Doris Bridgeman
Description: The *Youth In Action* program recruits, refers and recognizes students ages 13 to 24 from public and private junior/senior high schools and colleges in the Capital Area. Students are required to commit at least eight hours a month on a continuous basis, but may also be involved in one-time projects. Students are making a difference in their communities by volunteering in hospitals, nursing homes and other health care facilities, museums, offices, after-school programs, and youth centers on a year 'round basis - they're tutors, teacher assistants for handicapped children, food sorters, entertainers, public speakers and friendly visitors and readers for the elderly.
Young people involved in the *Youth In Action* programs gain personal growth in leadership, responsibility and commitment; knowledge of the community and its needs; opportunities to use their skills, talents and hobbies; career exploration and preparation; and new friendships, both with other volunteers and with those they serve.
United Way and the community benefit from the *Youth In Action* programs also - *United Way* gains a largely-untapped source of new volunteers for today who will likely continue to volunteer and support *United Way* as adults, and the community benefits in both the short-term and the long-term. YIA volunteers are providing a new generation of citizens knowledgeable about community needs and committed to caring for others.
Students also have the opportunity to participate in special projects:
- **Mayor's Summer Youth Program** - Youth ages 13-19 volunteer a minimum of 40 hours during a six-week period (June 11 - July 20). Youth may provide services as candy stripers and junior volunteers in hospitals, work with Y's and Boys/Girls Clubs, museums, with handicapped children, the elderly, in offices and in recreational programs. At the end of the program, the students are recognized by the agency volunteer coordinators, *United Way* and the Mayor in a special ceremony at City Hall. In 1989, over 82 youth provided 5,000 hours of service to the capital area during the six-week period.
- **Intergenerational Program (IGP)** - Junior High School students spend one hour per week reading and visiting with elderly residents at the nursing home across the street from their school. The IGP program gives these students an opportunity to enhance their reading skills while spending quality time with the residents. Sixty-five students participated in this program during the 1989-90 school year. Other schools and nursing homes will be added to the program during the next school year.
- **Youth Advisory Council** - Provides assistance to staff coordinator with recruitment, publicity, and recognition. Two students representing each public and private high school and college in the capital area are asked to serve on the *Council* and serve as Volunteer Coordinators for their respective schools. Students meet once each month from September to May during the school year, participating in workshops, planning special projects, and judging an annual coloring contest for elementary schools sponsored by a local *United Way* agency. Twenty-three students were part of the 1989-90 project.
- **Youth Allocations Committee** - a program in which youth evaluate and make decisions in funding youth programs in their communities. (This program is detailed in a separate entry of this publication.)

YOUTH SERVICES
SEE VOLUNTEERS: STUDENTS

YOUTH VOLUNTEER SERVICES
SEE VOLUNTEERS: STUDENTS

COMMUNITY SERVICES: COMMUNITY ACTION PROGRAMS

NATIONAL/STATE ORGANIZATIONS

NATIONAL CENTER FOR COMMUNITY ACTION*
1328 New York Avenue, NW
Washington, DC 20005
TEL: 202-6678-8970
Objectives: To assure an ongoing program of services to assist
Community Action Agencies; to make information available to
other groups working to eliminate poverty.
Services: Provides technical assistance through field services;
designs and conducts two- and three-day workshops/seminars in
cities throughout the country; maintains a clearinghouse of
information on programs and issues affecting the poor for use by
CAAs and other low-income interest groups; publishes a monthly
journal, a digest of federal funding sources, and *Human Work for
Human Needs,* which capsulizes CAA programs and activities
across the country.
Publications: National Center Reporter; Where the Money Is!;
Human Work for Human Needs

NATIONAL COMMUNITY ACTION FOUNDATION
2100 M Street, NW
Suite 604A
Washington, DC 20037
TEL: 202-775-0223
Objectives: To assist low-income families in becoming
self-sufficient.
Services: Serves as the umbrella organization for community action
agencies that provide services at the local level, such as Head
Start, Meals on Wheels, low-income energy assistance,
weatherization services, emergency food and shelter, and job
training and placement; assists low-income families in becoming
self sufficient and obtaining employment and decent housing; helps
to improve communities by developing local solutions to problems
and stimulating economic development; lobbies for federal
programs that serve the poor, including employment and training,
energy assistance, nutrition, and services to children and senior
citizens; provides information on energy programs for low-income
people, and neighborhood block grants; conducts a program for
communities entitled *How Congress Works;* publishes a newsletter
and periodic research reports.
Publications: How Congress Works Information Packet; NCAF
Newsletter
Founded: 1981

US/HHS - OFFICE OF COMMUNITY SERVICES
US/HHS - Office of the Secretary
PO Box 1182
Washington, DC 20201
TEL: 202-245-7000
Objectives: To provide a range of services and activities having a
measurable and potential major impact on causes of poverty in the
community.

Services: Provides block grants to states toward the above objective
(enabling states to tailor their own programs to meet the needs in
their communities); supports activities designed to assist
low-income people, including the elderly poor and Native
Americans, in:
- securing and retaining meaningful employment;
- attaining an adequate education;
- making better use of available income;
- obtaining and maintaining adequate housing;
- obtaining emergency assistance (food, housing, health services,
  employment services, etc.);
- achieving greater participation in the affairs of the community;
  and
- making more effective use of related programs.
Coordinates and establishes linkages between governmental and
other social services programs to assure effective delivery of such
services to low income individuals; encourages entities in the
private sector to help ameliorate poverty in the community.
Judges proposals based on program objectives stated in program
announcements, project viability, community support, reasonability
of cost, and qualifications of applicant organization and personnel.
[NOTE: Responsibilities for the former Community Services
Administration are now in the Office of Community Services,
D-HHS]
Sponsor: US/HHS - Department of Health & Human Services

INDIVIDUAL PROGRAM PROFILES

VOLUNTEER SERVICES/CAC
Lower Columbia Community Action Council
PO Box 2129
Longview, WA 98632
TEL: 206-425-3430
Purpose: To provide the needed manpower, expertise, skills
necessary to run the various programs of our agency.
Sponsor: Lower Columbia Community Action Council;
Community Services Block Grant Funds
Contact: Merilyn Thompson
Description: Lower Columbia Community Action has its own
volunteer service. Volunteers are used in nearly all programs. The
agency uses over 500 volunteers each year, many of whom work in
more than one program. Any necessary special volunteer training
is done by the person in charge of the program where the
volunteer is used.
The volunteer coordinator takes job descriptions from staff who
are in need of volunteers, recruits the volunteers, and makes
referrals or lists of referrals to the program managers. Volunteers
are then called in to talk about or to train for the position. A
volunteer card is filled out on each volunteer, including a notation
of what kind of work is being done. All volunteers sign a time
sheet and list the hours worked. At the end of the month, these
time sheets are collected, tallied, and a report is sent to the fiscal
office. Four programs are almost entirely run by volunteers:
Friendly Visiting for Seniors, Tele-Assurance for Seniors,
Congregate Meal Sites, and the HELP Warehouse, which serves 30
food banks in a two county area. Some volunteer activites are
described below:
- Longshoremen unload and warehouse all USDA foods.
- Pacific NorthwestBell employees solicit food.
- The Lions have collected food door to door.
- Volunteers deliver meals to congregate and home delivered
  meal sites.
- Volunteers are involved in fundraising
- Four-wheel drive clubs and van clubs deliver food to outlying
  areas.
- Volunteers sort and distribute food.
- Volunteers do office work.
- Volunteers do accounting.

Monthly statistical reports show that many hours are contributed to the function of providing service to others. The Community Action Program is dedicated to community service. Volunteers help reach that goal.

COMMUNITY SERVICES: FRATERNAL ORGANIZATIONS

NATIONAL/STATE ORGANIZATIONS

KIWANIS INTERNATIONAL
3636 Woodrow Trace
Indianapolis, IN 46268
TEL: 317-875-8755
Objectives: To provide community services in several areas of human needs and the physical environment.
Services: Provides assistance to the young and elderly; supports conservation and agriculture, and programs aimed at fighting crime and eliminating drug and alcohol abuse; assists in the development of community facilities; promotes international understanding; sponsors *Key Clubs* for high school students, *Circle K* clubs for college students, and *Builders Clubs* for junior high school students; publishes a magazine, a bulletin and a directory.
Publications: Kiwanis Magazine; Kiwanis Directory; Bulletin for Kiwanis Officers

KNIGHTS OF COLUMBUS
One Columbus Plaza
New Haven, CT 06507
TEL: 203-772-2130
Objectives: To carry programs and projects directed to the benefit of our fellowman.
Services: Serves through development of and involvement in numerous programs and projects to benefit both the Catholic and the wider community; oversees 63 state groups and 8,729 local groups representing almost one-and-a-half million individual members; includes the following programs in its many efforts:
- *Surge with Service:* A family, fraternal and service organization of action under the direction of two men who select others to perform duties as directors of church, community, council, family and youth programs. They, in turn, appoint various committees to plan projects and activities for the council to implement. State and local selection of activities assures progams unique to individual local or state needs. Manuals and handbooks, as well as a volunteer services newsletter, are sent to the men selected to serve as directors.
- *Catholic Information Service:* One purpose of this service is to provide information to non-Catholics to help overcome prejudice and misunderstanding of the Catholic faith. Another is to lead the way for Catholics and non-Catholics to work together in mutual programs for the community. One example of this cooperative effort is the worldwide *Habitat for Humanity* organization in which volunteers from all faiths come together on a single project - affordable housing for the poor. In addition to newspaper supplements and pamphlets for distribution, a correspondence course is offered, as well as individual responses when confidential counsel is requested.
- *College Councils:* This program enables students to become involved in the college and the local community through activities and projects sponsored by the council. As of mid-1990, Councils exist on approximately 100 campuses across the U.S.

- *Columbia Squires and Youth:* Since its early days, the *Knights of Columbus* has been actively concerned about the welfare of youth. *Partnership with Youth* is the theme that motivates ongoing programs in local and state councils - Boy Scout units, CYO sponsorship, CCD trainign, Little Leagues, Big Brothers, 4-H Clubs and many others have been assisted financially and by manpower donated by the Knights. The Order's own youth program, *Columbia Squires,* 0requires Council sponsorship and exists for the purpose of training its young members in the art and techniques of leadership (the junior organization of the Knights).
Publications: Columbia; Knightline; Squires; These Men They Call Knights
Founded: 1882

LIONS CLUB INTERNATIONAL (*formerly Lions International*)
300 22nd Street
Oak Brook, IL 60570
TEL: 312-571-5466
Objectives: To provide community service; to promote better international relations.
Services: Conducts service activities through its 38,400 clubs representing over one-and-one-third million members in areas of citizenship, education, environment, health, speech action and work with the deaf, drug awareness, diabetes research, sight conservation and work for the blind, youth exchange, international understanding and cooperation, international youth camp programs, and others; publishes a magazine, newsletters, bulletins, and other materials.
Publications: Lion Magazine; Club President's Update; District Governor's Update; Lions Club Community Activities Bulletin

LOYAL ORDER OF MOOSE
Mooseheart, IL 60539
TEL: 312-859-2000
Objectives: To respond to community needs, especially in relation to children and the elderly.
Services: Operates a home for aged dependent members and their wives at Moosehaven in Florida; maintains a school and home in Mooseheart, Illinois, for qualified children, especially those who have lost one or both parents; works through more than 4,000 local chapters representing over one-and-three-quarter million members to provide a variety of other community betterment services; publishes monthly magazine.
Publications: Moose Magazine

ROTARY INTERNATIONAL
One Rotary Center
Evanston, IL 60201
TEL: 312-866-3000
Objectives: To conduct community betterment programs and promote high ethical standards in the business community.
Services: Maintains the *Rotary Foundation,* which awards scholarships, sponsors volunteer programs, and makes grants for international development projects; mounts community betterment projects, promotes high ethical standards in business, and the advancement of international understanding, goodwill and peace; works through its more than 23,000 local groups representing over a million members; awards scholarships and grants to outstanding young men and women; publishes a magazine, a Spanish language newsletter, convention proceedings and other materials.
Publications: Rotarian; Revista Rotaria; Rotary Basic Library

U.S. JAYCEES (*formerly U.S. Junior Chamber of Commerce*)
PO Box 7
Four West 21st Street
Tulsa, OK 74121
TEL: 918-584-2481

Objectives: To promote active participation in local community betterment programs.

Services: Provides leadership training for its members (ages 21 to 40) through community service projects; operates several selection programs to recognize outstanding young men in areas of citizenship, health and fitness, and farming; maintains departments in community development, corporate development, public affairs, international affairs and others; publishes a magazine, handbook, guide and other materials.

Publications: Jaycees Magazine; Chapter President's Management Handbook; Officers and Directors Guide

COMMUNITY SERVICES: MILITARY

INDIVIDUAL PROGRAM PROFILES

ARMY COMMUNITY SERVICE
SEE VOLUNTEERS: ARMED FORCES MEMBERS - ARMY

FORT DIX VOLUNTEERS
SEE VOLUNTEERS: ARMED FORCES MEMBERS - ARMY

FORT GORDON VOLUNTEER PROGRAM
SEE VOLUNTEERS: ARMED FORCES MEMBERS - ARMY

FORT SILL VOLUNTEERS
SEE VOLUNTEERS: ARMED FORCES MEMBERS - ARMY

NAVY VOLUNTEERS AT GUANTANAMO BAY
SEE VOLUNTEERS: ARMED FORCES MEMBERS - NAVY

VOLUNTEER PROGRAM - FORT BENJAMIN HARRISON
SEE VOLUNTEERS: ARMED FORCES MEMBERS - ARMY

COMMUNITY SERVICES: RURAL

INDIVIDUAL PROGRAM PROFILES

GAIN (GREATER ACHIEVEMENT THROUGH INVOLVEMENT NOW)
SEE GOVERNORS' OFFICES ON VOLUNTEERISM: SOUTH CAROLINA

RURAL VOLUNTEER SERVICES NETWORK
SEE GOVERNORS' OFFICES ON VOLUNTEERISM: WASHINGTON

COMMUNITY SERVICES: STUDENTS

TRAINING PROGRAMS

COMMUNITY INVOLVEMENT PROGRAM
SEE TRAINING/CONFERENCES/TEACHING: STUDENTS

COMMUNITY SERVICES
SEE TRAINING/CONFERENCES/TEACHING: STUDENTS

EDUCATION AND HUMAN SERVICES COURSE
SEE TRAINING/CONFERENCES/TEACHING: STUDENTS

THE MARSHALL SERVICE UNIT AND VOLUNTEER OUTREACH
SEE TRAINING/CONFERENCES/TEACHING: STUDENTS

INDIVIDUAL PROGRAM PROFILES

CITY YEAR
11 Stillings Street
Boston, MA 02210
TEL: 617-451-0699
Purpose: To provide opportunities for youth to give a year of community service.
Sponsor: Bank of Boston
Contact: Michael Brown or Alan Khazen
Description: The *Bank of Boston, Bain & Company, General Cinemas,* the *Boston Bar Association, General Atlantic Partners,* and the *Equitable* have each donated $100,000 to sponsor a *City Year* team. *City Year* is a privately-funded, Boston-based youth service corps that engages youth in a year-long community service program beginning each September. In addition to corporate sponsors, there is also a "citizens' team" made up of thousands of concerned and generous individuals.
City year youth volunteers work in a variety of settings, including the *Massachusetts Hospital School* (a residential facility for severely disabled children and young adults), Pine Street Inn, and *St. Paul's AME Church* (where teen volunteers converted a former parsonage into a shelter for women and children). In addition, they cleared vacant lots, created playgrounds, repaired houses with the *Neighborhood of Affordable Housing,* and salvaged tons of food at the *Boston Food Bank.*
The age range of *City Year* volunteers is 17 to 22, with many students opting to spend the year just after completing high school and before entering college. Although a local program, the co-founders visualize a national effort with youth choosing volunteer assignments from one large, nationwide catalog.
In addition to funding, the program receives tax-deductible gifts of computers, tools, office furniture, and other needed items.
Founded: 1989

COMMUNITY SERVICE REQUIREMENT
Metro High School
5017 Washington
St. Louis, MO 63108
TEL: 314-367-5210
Purpose: To create a "school without walls" for the students of Metro High School.
Description: When applying for admission at Metro High School, the students are aware of the obligation to community service requirement of the school. There is little or no resistance to fulfilling the service requirement.
The rationale behind this requirement is that the students should give something back to their community. The principal sees even a greater obligation to serve the community in the fact that Metro pupils have many talents.
Orientation is given at the beginning of the year. Students are expected to develop and arrange their own projects as a way of teaching them how to be responsible. They are given a letter of introduction to the site staff, an evaluation form, and contact information for Metro's principal.
Although Metro High School staff originally had to research the community to find volunteer slots for the students, today agencies seek out students, demonstrating the quality of their service and the dedication to their commitments. Calls come from hospitals, day care centers and nursery schools, nursing homes, and many

other agencies. Training is done at the sites. Students volunteer during free time - during free periods in the school day, or after school, on weekends, and during vacations. Fundraisers, such as walkathons and bikeathons, are acceptable as part of the student's service requirement.

Many students work in excess of the 240-hour requirement. Students working 340 hours or more have their names included on the graduation program as *Community Service Honorees.*The principal sees side benefits to the program - meeting a need of individual students who may have no other outlet for their energies and talents, or helping a student who may be unaware of hidden capabilities. An example she likes to cite is about a student basketball player whose assignment was with homeless children at the *Salvation Army.* He expected to feel foolish playing with young children, but instead was looked up to as a role model by children who had never had a role model in their lives. His attitude changed completely, and the experience was mutually beneficial.

COMMUNITY SERVICES PROJECT
Union-Endicott School District
1200 East Main Street
Endicott, NY 13760
TEL: 607-757-2181
Purpose: To recruit, screen and place high school students in community agencies that need them.
Sponsor: Union-Endicott School District
Contact: William E. Dupkanick
Description: The *Community Service Program* of the Union-Endicott School District serves as a volunteer bureau to help fill the needs of local agencies and organizations. Students earn one-half credit for 70 hours of service to the community. Admission to the program is flexible.

The project director may be from the teaching staff or the administrative offices of the school, depending on time and availability. It is the duty of the director to recruit and screen students, make contacts with community service groups that need volunteers, evaluate the students' work, and counsel the student participants.

Students interested in the program are interviewed by the service agency and assigned to a staff member of the agency if accepted. This staff member also provides preservice training for the student. Community work is performed either during free periods in the school day, or after school. Students are responsible for their own transportation.
Founded: 1977

DUO
SEE VOLUNTEERS: STUDENTS

DUTIES TO THE COMMUNITY
SEE VOLUNTEERS: STUDENTS

JESUIT SERVICE PROJECT
SEE VOLUNTEERS: STUDENTS

NEW BREED DRILL TEAM
SEE VOLUNTEERS: STUDENTS

NORTH HIGH COMMUNITY SERVICE PROGRAM
North High School
801 Seventeenth Avenue North
Fargo, ND 58102
TEL: 701-241-4787
Purpose: At North High School, faculty does not get involved in the community service program until the student has decided what kind of work he or she would like to do, and has submitted a proposal to the program supervisor for approval. If the proposal is

not accepted, the program supervisor or other staff person assists the student in finalizing the proposal. By doing this the student chooses to earn up to one credit - one-half credit for every 80 hours of volunteer service.

Participating students have worked in large traditional organizations such as the Red Cross, Chamber of Commerce, or United Way, and smaller programs at hospitals, nursing homes, nursery schools and day care centers. They have also tutored their peers, and served as cross-age tutors in elementary schools. Scheduling is flexible. Students provide their own transportation to service sites, participating during free periods in the school day as well as after school and on weekends.
Sponsor: North High School
Contact: Nancy Murphy

PREVENTION THROUGH ACTION
SEE VOLUNTEERS: STUDENTS

STUDENT VOLUNTEERS
SEE LEADERSHIP DEVELOPMENT/BOARDS: CHILDREN/YOUTH

WESTTOWN SERVICE NETWORK
SEE VOLUNTEERS: STUDENTS

COMMUNITY SERVICES: TENANTS/RESIDENTS

NATIONAL/STATE ORGANIZATIONS

BREAKTHROUGH FOUNDATION
25 Van Ness Avenue
Suite 320
San Francisco, CA 94102
TEL: 415-863-4141
Objectives: To help people improve the quality of their lives and their communities.
Services: Develops community projects that help people change what they feel are unacceptable situations in the quality and conditions of their lives; focuses on serious and violent young crime offenders, substance abusers, and professionals working with the disabled; offers two-year programs to teach people how to start and maintain community development projects to address their problems and to improve their communities; trains workers to help local community groups set up and administer development projects in the US and some countries abroad; sponsors fundraising projects and operates programs of corporate sponsorship, internships, volunteers, youth at risk, and youth sponsorship.
Founded: 1980

CENTER FOR ORGANIZATIONAL AND COMMUNITY DEVELOPMENT (*formerly Citizen Involvement Training Program*)
University of Massachusetts
School of Education
Room 225
Amherst, MA 01003
TEL: 413-545-2038
Objectives: To help local citizen groups and agencies become more effective.
Services: Organizes sessions tailored to individual groups to aid them in responding effectively to issues that range from human

relations to community development to coalition building; strives to make local groups and agencies more effective in reaching their goals; sponsors workshops on topics including: cultural issues, community development, and interorganizational and organizational development; provides consultation services and training materials on organizing, fundraising, the media, and citizen action training; assists groups and organizations in designing, developing and implementing their own conferences; publishes a series of manuals and information packets.
Sponsor: Community Education Resource Center
Publications: Citizen Action Manual Series; COCD Information Packet
Founded: 1985

NATIONAL ASSOCIATION FOR THE SOUTHERN POOR
SEE VOLUNTEERS: SELF-HELP

NATIONAL ASSOCIATION OF COMMUNITY LEADERSHIP ORGANIZATIONS
SEE LEADERSHIP DEVELOPMENT/BOARDS: TENANTS/RESIDENTS

NATIONAL TRAINING AND INFORMATION CENTER*
SEE TRAINING/CONFERENCES/TEACHING: TENANTS/RESIDENTS

COMMUNITY SERVICES: URBAN

INDIVIDUAL PROGRAM PROFILES

CITY VOLUNTEER CORPS
838 Broadway
New York, NY 10003
TEL: 212-475-6444
Purpose: To give high school students, and other youth to age 20, a chance to serve their community.
Sponsor: City of New York
Contact: Jennifer Elias
Description: Operating a full-time volunteer service program since 1984 for youth aged 17 to 20, the City Volunteer Corps (CVC) became aware of the need for a similar program within the high school system. In 1987 a part-time component was added for high school students. The two programs are similar, but address time and other differences in the youth groups:

- **The full-time program** - This program is designed for teams of 10 to 15 youth aged 17 to 20 who perform a wide range of tasks through city agencies and nonprofit organizations. The program, enrolling 700 youth each year, combines service with education, enabling participants to attend GED preparation, Adult Basic Education, English as a Second Language, and college credit courses. They receive an expense stipend each week, and after a year of service are awarded $5,000 in scholarship funds, or $2,500 in cash. During the summer months, they are expected to work side-by-side with high school volunteers, offering the benefit of their longer experience to the younger participants.
- **The part-time program** - Added in 1987, this program enables students to volunteer two afternoons after the class day for a minimum of six hours each week. During the summer, the students work for eight weeks full time with the regular full-time volunteers.

High school students are from economically and ethnically diverse groups. In its first year of operation, eight high schools and a total of 113 students became involved in the community. Students

receive weekly transportation stipends and - at the end of their service - receive $750 scholarships for one semester of involvement, or $2,000 scholarships for working two semesters and two summers. Recruitment has been expanded to include many other schools, including private secular schools and parochial schools. The part time workers have volunteered at Coney Island Geriatric Center, the Salvation Army, numerous latchkey programs, and shelters for the homeless. They are responsible for their own transportation, but are assigned to sites near their schools. Training for all CVC volunteers is provided both on site and at a training camp rated by CVC. All youth are required to keep personal journals describing their volunteer projects, and detailing their roles in them. CVC Field Supervisors are available for help at all times.
Founded: 1984

MINNEAPOLIS URBAN LEAGUE VOLUNTEER SERVICES*
1121 Twelfth Avenue North
Minneapolis, MN 55411
TEL: 612-377-0011
Purpose: Purpose: To provide volunteer support to the League's direct service staff.
Sponsor: Minneapolis Urban League
Contact: Librarian/Historian
Description: Even though volunteers have given countless hours to the Minneapolis Urban League (MUL) on Boards and Advisory Committees, a mechanism for volunteers to provide direct service in MUL's programs had not been established until 1980. During the first year, many avenues were explored to develop and administrate an effective volunteer service. The first step involved directors of the many MUL projects, asking them to provide information to the new Director of Volunteer Services as to where they could best utilize volunteers to allow them to provide more and/or better services to the Minneapolis community.
The goal of providing requested volunteers for all 15 programs was met by the Volunteer Services Director through a campaign that identified and worked with at least 266 sources of volunteer recruitment. These sources included community meetings, inter-agency networks, churches, corporations, social service organizations, volunteer centers, schools, etc. - with a total of 739 contacts made with these sources by mail, telephone and personal visit. This initial effort resulted in 100 volunteers providing over 1100 hours of direct services in both short- and long-term projects. MUL programs receiving volunteer help through this effort included:

- **Street Academy** - an approved alternative educational program for students 16-21 years of age. Volunteers assist teachers in math, English, reading, history, science and physical education classes. In addition, volunteers serve as librarians, workshop consultants, clerical assistants, and mentors.
- **Labor Education and Advancement Program** - an apprentice program set up with the Minneapolis Building Trades Council; volunteers serve as employment counselors, mathematicians, lawyers, etc.
- **Community Organization** - an intervention program that provides advocacy in issues of emerging housing, discrimination, and political awareness. Volunteers serve as voter registrants, lawyers, spokespersons, etc.
- **Health Services** - a health education program that "zeroes in" on existing health problems and issues. Volunteers serve as nurses, doctors and spokespersons.
- **Juvenile Advocacy** - a youth outreach program that provides services to youth between the ages of 12 and 18 who have been involved in crime. This program provides court, employment, and school advocacy. Volunteers provide chaperone and other services.

Other problems the Volunteer Services Director found in

recruitment efforts was the fact that many people do not feel that their own skills and talents can be beneficial to other people. They underestimate the value of the 2-4 hours each week that they could volunteer to a community agency. Also, those who have never volunteered are reluctant to step forward.

To help counteract this problem, the Director emphasizes that agencies today allow the volunteer to use/develop their skills in direct service, with supportive training when indicated. Also, appropriate records on volunteer hours are kept for career advancement, references, and school admission. Opportunities for professional growth are made available through comprehensive continuing education.

Today, MUL's volunteer staff consists of 150 people serving in capacities such as teaching assistants, tutors, health screeners, voter registration campaigners, fundraisers, editors, photographers, writers, hosts and hostesses, membership committee members, as well as in positions in the specific projects listed above. Also, the list of recruitment sources has grown - still including the initial 1980 sources, but adding universities, synagogues, radio, television, newspapers, and the community at large. This wide range of community resources has provided legal and technical volunteer service as well as outreach and clerical volunteer assistance.

URBAN INVOLVEMENT
SEE VOLUNTEERS: STUDENTS

FUNDING/FUND-RAISING/RELATED SERVICES

NATIONAL/STATE ORGANIZATIONS

ALEXIS DE TOCQUEVILLE SOCIETY PROGRAM
SEE ADMINISTRATION: RECOGNITION

**AMERICAN ASSOCIATION FOR CORPORATE
CONTRIBUTIONS**
PO Box 6401
Evanston, IL 60204
TOLL FREE: 800-426-5843
Objectives: To serve as a resource center on fundraising and tax laws.
Services: Serves as a resource center for its 9,500 members (both nonprofit organizations and corporate donors) on fundraising and tax laws; negotiates on behalf of nonprofit organizations for gifts of merchandise; produces a videocassette for workshops; publishes a monthly newsletter and other materials.
Publications: 501(C)(3); Rent-A-Workshop; Give and Take

CATHOLIC CHARITIES USA (*formerly National Conference of Catholic Charities*)
1319 F Street, NW
Washington, DC 20004
TEL: 202-639-8400
Objectives: To serve as the central national organization for Catholic charities in the US.
Services: Works with almost 5,000 individuals and agencies in its capacity as the central national organization for charitable contributions by the Catholic church; provides consultation and information services for a broad array of social problems, including Social Security, unemployment and housing; maintains committees on aging, residential child care, social services, unmarried parents, and women's issues; publishes a newsletter, a journal, a directory, and other materials.
Sponsor: Association of Ladies of Charity of the US
Publications: Charities USA ; Social Thought; Directory of Diocesan Agencies of Catholic Charities
Founded: 1910

COUNCIL ON FOUNDATIONS
1828 L Street, NW
Washington, DC 20036
TEL: 202-466-6512

Objectives: To provide consultative services to member foundations and philanthropic programs.
Services: Advises community, independent, and company foundations and associations and corporations with philanthropic programs in areas of administration, grantmaking, foundation law, regulations, and information to the media; conducts meetings for the purpose of sharing information and keeping participants abreast of current trends in foundation matters and activities; has several committees, including Community Foundations and Educational Programs; publishes bimonthly journal which includes feature articles about developments regarding foundations, a newsletter, handbooks, monographs, an annual report and other materials.
Publications: Foundation News; CF Newsletter
Founded: 1949

DEMONSTRATION PROGRAM
US/ACTION - The Federal Volunteer Agency
1100 Vermont Avenue, NW
Suite 1100
Washington, DC 20525
TEL: 202-634-9108
TOLL FREE: 800-424-8580
Objectives: To provide the means for testing new and innovative ways of using volunteers to address specific community issues or problems.
Services: Provides one-year grants to private non-profit community organizations to test new and innovative program models to respond to a wide range of community needs, including illicit drug use prevention, illiteracy, homelessness, infant mortality, child and family services, victim assistance, and other needs unique to specific communities. These program models are studied for their efficiency and effectiveness in using volunteers, enabling ACTION to develop different methods or models for replication in other settings and to encourage the development of public/private partnerships.
Contact: Philip McLaurin

**FEDERAL ASSISTANCE PROGRAMS RETRIEVAL
SYSTEM (FAPRS)**
US/OMB - Federal Programs Information Branch
Washington, DC 20503
TEL: 202-395-3112

Objectives: To identify federal assistance programs that communities can use to help meet development needs.

Services: Uses a computerized system to generate a list of names and identifying numbers of the applicable federal programs from the *OMB Catalog of Federal Domestic Assistance,* giving the user the option of referring to the *Catalog* for more detail, or obtaining individual program descriptions from FAPRS; works with the Department of Agriculture, which provides access points in every state for FAPRS searches (request referral to closest access point); makes referral to private time sharing companies for direct access to FAPRS in some cases.

Sponsor: US/OMB - Office of Management and Budget

Publications: Catalog of Federal Assistance

FOUNDATION CENTER
79 Fifth Avenue
New York, NY 10003
TEL: 212-620-4230

Objectives: To provide basic factual and descriptive information about foundations and the grants they award.

Services: Acquires, organizes and disseminates information on foundations from its three data bases; arranges for access on-line to these data bases through Lockheed Information Systems, 3251 Hanover Street, Palo Alto, CA 94304 (800-227-1960); conducts Associates Program whereby frequent users of foundation data are given access to special services; works within network of 170 cooperating collections (including DIALOG Telecommunication Services, 800-424-9836) providing free public access to information on grants for the public; publications include *Source Book Profiles,* a quarterly reference resource, *COMSEARCH Printouts,* listing foundation grants by subject categories, and *The Foundation Directory,* offering information on the top 3,000 private foundations; maintains offices in Washington, DC (202-331-1400), Cleveland, Ohio (216-861-1933), and San Francisco, California (415-397-0902).

Publications: Foundation Grants Index; Source Book Profiles; COMSEARCH Printouts; Corporate Foundation Profiles; Annual Grants Index; Directory of Corporate Charity ; Grants to Individuals

FOUNDATION RESEARCH SERVICE (FRS)
Douglas N. Lawson Associates, Inc.
39 East 51st Street
New York, NY 10022
TEL: 212-759-5660

Objectives: To cover many aspects of private sector funding for information and training purposes.

Services: Offers a two-day fund raising course; publishes a research guide, *The Foundation 500,* which lists all grants of $1,000 or more made by the 500 leading foundations in the U.S. in the last tax year of record; tells where (the 50 states, D.C., and international), and in what subject area (e.g., "handicapped") the grant was made; publishes *Data Files* on all 500 foundations, which contain information on individual 990-AR's plus biographical data on foundation trustees; offers the fund raising course in both self-study cassettes and two-day on-site workshop formats; conducts the workshop each month in cities throughout the country.

Publications: Data Files; The Foundation 500

FUND-RAISING INSTITUTE
Box 365
Ambler, PA 19002
TEL: 301-816-0210 (MD)
FAX: 301-816-0811 (MD)

In January 1990 the Fund Raising Institute was absorbed by The Taft Group, 12300 Twinbrook Parkway, Suite 450, Rockville, Maryland 20852 (phone/facsimile numbers above) Initially, the extensive Institute library will remain in Ambler.

Objectives: To study the fund-raising techniques used by nonprofit groups of all types and to report the findings in a series of periodicals, books, and systems.

Services: Draws on experience from groups across the nonprofit field to compile, analyze, synthesize and offer the benefit of the most successful activities of these groups in a step-by-step format; publishes a comprehensive collection of guidance materials in all aspects of fund raising, including a series of very practical manuals and a monthly newsletter for current information to keep the manuals updated.

Publications: Call for Help: How to Raise Philanthropic Funds with Phonothons; Phonothon System ; Solid Gold Fundraising Letters; Capital Ideas; The Art of Asking; The Membership Mystique; Deferred Gifts/How to Get Them

GIVE FIVE CAMPAIGN
SEE ADMINISTRATION: RECRUITMENT/ORIENTATION

GOVERNMENT INFORMATION SERVICES
1611 North Kent Street, Suite 508
Arlington, VA 22209
TEL: 703-528-1082

Objectives: To provide the public with information about sources of federal funding.

Services: Operates a hotline service; conducts seminars to teach grantsmanship techniques; publishes *Local Government Funding Report,* which provides current coverage of federal aid programs and funding sources, and *Congressional Boxscore,* which describes all major legislation introduced in the Congress involving federal funding to local and state governments.

Publications: Local Government Funding; Congressional Boxscore

GRANT INFORMATION SYSTEM
Oryx Press
2214 North Central at Encanto
Phoenix, AZ 85004
TEL: 602-254-6156

Objectives: To provide current information on grants and other funding.

Services: Stores current information on grants awarded by federal, state, and local governments and private foundations, associations, and businesses; provides program information keyed to academic discipline, sponsoring organization, and grant name; includes in data the dollar amount, requirements, restrictions, deadline dates, and renewability; arranges for on-line access to this system through the System Development Corporation, 2500 Colorado Avenue, Santa Monica, CA 90406 (800-421-7729), and DIALOG Information Services, Inc. 3460 Hillview Avenue, Palo Alto, CA 94304 (800-227-1960).

GRANTSMANSHIP CENTER
PO Box 6210
650 S. Spring Street, Suite 507
Los Angeles, CA 90014
TEL: 213-689-9222
TOLL FREE: 800-421-9512

Objectives: To improve skills in grantsmanship in programs seeking funds.

Services: Conducts 250 week-long workshops across the U.S. each year for individuals from nonprofit public and private agencies; training focuses on program planning and development, the identification of appropriate private and public sources of funds, and effective proposals and program ideas; alumni of the training programs are offered services, including proposal critiques and staff consultation; publishes *Grantsmanship Center News,* which includes articles on where to find funds and how to obtain funds, and other publications; maintains library of over 4,000 references and a field office in Washington, DC (202-347-9847).

Publications: Whole Nonprofit Catalog; Grantsmanship Center News
Founded: 1972

INDIVIDUAL GIVING/VOLUNTEERING CAMPAIGN*
SEE COMMUNICATIONS & PUBLIC RELATIONS

MINI-GRANT PROGRAM
US/ACTION - The Federal Volunteer Agency
1100 Vermont Avenue, NW
Suite 1100
Washington, DC 20525
TEL: 202-656-9108
TOLL FREE: 800-424-8580
Objectives: To initiate or improve local public and private non-profit programs that use community volunteers to address local problems.
Services: Awards small (not to exceed $10,000), one-year, non-renewable "seed" grants. The Program deals with a broad range of human problems, especially those related to poverty, and builds community self-reliance by supporting the volunteer-intensive activities of grass roots organizations.
Contact: Joseph Bass
Publications: Mini-Grant Program Guidelines
Founded: 1971

MINI-GRANTS: RESEARCH IN VOLUNTEERISM
Center for Volunteer Development
Virginia Tech
Cooperative Extensive Service
Blacksburg, VA 24061-0512
TEL: 703-231-6000
Objectives: To provide funds for the most needed research in areas of volunteerism.
Services: Maintains a Resource Development Committee which determines the most needed research in the area of volunteerism; conducts studies to explore the areas in which practitioners perceived the greatest need and to determine faculty interest in mounting the research efforts; emphasizes areas of strongest agreement, including organizational issues, motivational issues, gender patterns, and student volunteerism; raises funds to provide mini-grants to faculty who wish to mount research in volunteerism, most recently a project on student community service and one on volunteerism in the Philippines.
Distributes full reports of the research to state offices, individuals and groups.
Contact: Emily Reames, Advisory Council
Publications: Student Community Service: Three Motivational Environments; Helping Patterns Among Filipino Associations in Tidewater Area

NATIONAL ASSOCIATION OF INVESTMENT COMPANIES
915 Fifteenth Street, NW
Washington, DC 20005
TEL: 202-347-8600
Objectives: To keep small minority businesses current on issues that affect their operations.
Services: Assists organizing groups attempting to form or acquire MESBICS (Minority Enterprise Small Business Investment Companies); provides management and technical assistance; monitors regulatory agency actions; conducts periodic professional and management training seminars; collects and disseminates business information; publishes intermittent *Legislative Alerts,* newsletters, bibliographies, and other materials.
Publications: Perspectives-NAIC; NAIC Membership Directory; Legislative Alert
Founded: 1971

PARTNERSHIP BANKCARD SYSTEMS*
3444 Fourteenth Street
Boulder, CO 80302
TEL: 303-447-1718
Objectives: To offer a credit card program to small and medium size nonprofits.
Services: Provides a person-to-person, volunteer-based system of marketing for small and medium size nonprofits (previously served only large groups) involving BankCard holders to increase financial support and improve other areas of outreach; works with its new program for small and medium size nonprofits by:
  ● tailoring program to needs and profile of organization's constituency;
  ● providing support materials for distribution to members and supporters;
  ● training members and supporters in techniques for promoting use of the bankcard, such as "each one reach one" campaigns, distribution of applications at events, reaching out to the community in newsletters and through other means that will maximize income potential; and
  ● becoming an extension of the nonprofit through liaison with banks and offering personalized methods to increase visibility and raise funds.
In addition, Partnership BankCard Systems makes available a special VISA/MasterCard fundraising program enabling cardholders to donate funds passively through a percentage of purchases made with cards affiliated with the nonprofit organization.
Large groups utilizing the bankcard system include Sierra Club, League of Women Voters, Cities of Hope, Juvenile Diabetes Foundation, Foster Parents Plan, American Kidney Fund, and General Federation of Women's Clubs.
Sponsor: American BankCard Services
Contact: Nonprofit Liaison
Publications: The Card Carrying Volunteer
Founded: 1989

TAFT GROUP
12300 Twinbrook Parkway
Suite 450
Rockville, MD 20852
TEL: 301-816-0210
TOLL FREE: 800-424-3761
FAX: 301-816-0811
In January 1990 The Taft Group absorbed the Fund Raising Institute of Ambler, Pennsylvania. Initially, the Institute's library will remain in Ambler.
Objectives: To develop and disseminate information on grants opportunities, nonprofit management and fundraising.
Services: Provides information on application procedures, specific interests or restrictions of foundations, patterns of giving, etc.; publishes a directory, which contains some 450 detailed reports on the nation's top corporate foundations, a number of titles on grantsmanship, a reference which gives biographical data on philanthropic decision makers, and printouts from the Taft Foundation Information System providing, among other information, sample grants.
Publications: Trustees of Wealth; Taft Corporation Directory

TOYOTA MOTOR SALES USA
19001 South Western Avenue
Torrance, CA 90509
TEL: 213-618-5397
FAX: 213-618-7809
Objectives: See specific objectives below.
Services: Serves the community through the following programs:
Corporate Contributions:
Objectives: To provide grants for deserving community organizations.

Services: Program includes financial support to education, health and human services, civic and urban affairs, arts and culture.

Community Relations:
Objectives: To support various community projects and encourage employee volunteerism.
Services: Adopted North High School in Torrance; provides scholarships through the *United Negro College Fund* and *National Hispanic Scholarship Fund;* supports junior golf.
Contact: Tracy Underwood

Toyota USA Foundation:
Objectives: To provide grants which enhance America's academic environment.
Services: Provides funding exclusively to education programs, primarily in the area of pre-collegiate education; places special emphasis on math and science classroom programs. Current endowment is $14 million. Established in 1987. Grants for FY 89 totaled $250,000.
Contact: Kimberly Byron
Contact: See specific contacts or Public Relations Officer
Publications: Guidelines and Application Procedure
Founded: 1967

YOUTH AS RESOURCES
National Crime Prevention Council
733 15th Street, NW, Suite 540
Washington, DC 20005
TEL: 202-393-7141
FAX: 202-638-2928
Objectives: To develop young people's stake and role in the community through sponsorship of youth volunteer efforts.
Services: Funding of youth volunteer efforts in school-based programs was generated by the belief of the *National Crime Prevention Council (NCPC)* that the best way to steer youth in the direction of good citizenship is to involve them in meaningful activities that meet the needs of the community. Some of these programs are funded by the *Lilly Foundation* through NCPC. Others receive guidance from NCPC, but find local foundations or other funding sources.
The program is open to any city. The procedure requires a board of community leaders and youth to head up the program, advertise for and screen proposals, vote on the grants (from $100 to $5,000) to be awarded to host agencies including, but not limited to, schools. The board also monitors the grantees' projects and provides recognition to project participants.
One unique strength of the program is that it is based in the community proper with the youth involved ranging from dropouts to Honor Society members, and from nonjoiners to class and school leaders. Although they may work with adults, the grant requires that the youth themselves develop and manage the projects. Each project is based in the community, although it draws from a wide range of secondary schools and the community at large. The project is based on the premise that teen-operated projects will help the young people grow and learn, and become assets to their communities.
Sponsor: Lilly Foundation

TRAINING PROGRAMS

CHANGING WAYS WE DO BUSINESS: NEW ROLES AND RESPONSIBILITIES
SEE TRAINING/CONFERENCES/TEACHING: FUNDING

FUND-RAISING SUCCESS SEMINAR
Third Sector Press
2000 Euclid Avenue
PO Box 18044
Cleveland, OH 44118
TEL: 216-831-9300
FAX: 216-831-8511
Credit: Inquire
Contact: Alice Randolph, Ph.D., Managing Director
Description: This program focuses on the essentials for success - using marketing and campaigning ideas and strategies - and time management for fund-raising executives. An optional pre-seminar briefing for professionals and board members new to fund raising is made available immediately prior to the seminar. Clinics include:

- Jim Lord's Brochure and Copy Clinic (to which participants may bring copy for critique);
- Kent Dove's Capital Campaign Clinic;
- 16 Ways to Find New Prospects;
- Managing Your Relationships with Your Trustees and CEO;
- How to Write for Fund-Raising Results;
- How to Plan and Conduct Awareness/Cultivation Meetings to Get Top VIPs and Donors Interested and Involved in Your Fund Raising; and
- Advanced Skills in Speaking and Making Presentations.

Workshops during August-December 1990 are held in New York, San Francisco, Boston, Cleveland, Washington, DC, Los Angeles, and Phoenix (schedule available on request for these and later dates). Facilitators are from the corporate fund-raising community and academe, including authors of *The Raising of Money: 35 Essentials Every Trustee Should Know* and *Conducting a Successful Capital Campaign: A Comprehensive Fundraising Guide for Nonprofit Organizations,* both published by the sponsor of the training event.
Publications: The Raising of Money: 35 Essentials Every Trustee Should Know; Conducting a Successful Capital Campaign; The Raising of Money; Philanthropy and Marketing

GRANTSMANSHIP TRAINING PROGRAM
SEE TRAINING/CONFERENCES/TEACHING: FUNDING

GRANTSMANSHIP TRAINING PROGRAM (SHORT COURSE)
Grantsmanship Center
650 South Spring Street
Suite 507
Los Angeles, CA 90014
TEL: 213-689-9222
TOLL FREE: 800-421-9512
FAX: 213-623-5667
Credit: Inquire
Sponsor: Host Organization (more than 200 across the country)
Contact: Workshop Coordinator
Description: This five-day grantsmanship training seminar is jointly sponsored by the Grantsmanship Center and a host organization or agency such as the Virginia Department of Volunteerism. The Grantsmanship Center was founded in 1972, making it the oldest and largest fundraising training organization in the country. To date, the Center has trained over 45,000 staff from public and private agencies, large and small, in all areas of human services.
Designed for both the novice and the experienced grant seeker, this "hands-on" workshop covers:

- all aspects of researching for grants;
- writing grant proposals;
- negotiating with funding sources (foundation, corporate, government, etc.);
- learning proposal writing format;
- searching out funding using materials provided; and

● working in teams to actually develop a proposal.
Group size is limited to 25, so that individual attention and maximum benefit can be assured.

MASTER OF PROFESSIONAL STUDIES DEGREE: FUND RAISING MANAGEMENT
SEE TRAINING/CONFERENCES/TEACHING: FUNDING

PROPOSAL WRITING INSTITUTE*
SEE TRAINING/CONFERENCES/TEACHING: FUNDING

RESOURCE DEVELOPMENT CONFERENCE*
SEE TRAINING/CONFERENCES/TEACHING: FUNDING

INDIVIDUAL PROGRAM PROFILES

ALEXIS DE TOCQUEVILLE SOCIETY
United Way of America
701 North Fairfax Street
Alexandria, VA 22314-2045
TEL: 703-836-7100
Purpose: To work with major givers ($10,000 or more) to encourage high-level giving in their communities.
Sponsor: United Way (local)
Contact: Ruth Maldonado, New Market Development
Description: Alexis de Tocqueville Societies are programs created to work with major donors ($10,000 or more) by asking initial contributors to network with colleagues and business associates in other cities and encourage them to give to the United Way. In 1988, 80 local Tocqueville Societies raised over $41.4 million from 2,725 high net worth individuals - $10 million more than the previous year. By 1989, 95 local United Ways had Tocqueville Societies.
Another way in which major givers have encouraged high-level giving is through challenge matching grants. In Orange, California, for example, Alexis de Tocqueville Society members Peter M. Ochs, President, The Fieldstone Company, and his wife, Gail, have offered a challenge matching grant of $250,000 for each of the past two years to United Way of Orange County to encourage new membership in that community's Tocqueville Society. Also, John C. Haas, retired chairman of Rohm and Haas Company, recently offered his second $1 million challenge matching grant for new Tocqueville Society members contributing $10,000 or more to United Way of Southeastern Pennsylvania in Philadelphia. New Million Dollar Roundtable member Leslie H. Wexner, chairman, The Limited, Inc., Columbus, Ohio, and his mother, Bella Wexner, pledged to match gifts of $5,000 or more from new leadership donors and to match the amount of increase in gifts ranging from $5,000 to $1 million to United Way of Franklin County in Columbus.
Alexis de Tocqueville, the inspiration for the Society, is the Frenchman who came to America in the mid-1800's and, after seeing the phenomenon of Americans joining together to solve community problems whenever the need arises, returned home to write a book, *Volunteering in America*, about his observations.
Founded: 1987

BUSINESS/COMMUNITY INVOLVEMENT PROGRAM
SEE BUSINESS/INDUSTRY INVOLVEMENT: FUNDING

CANDLE LIGHTERS' PROPOSAL LUNCH
Candle Lighters
c/o American Cancer Society
535 Race Street
San Jose, CA 95126
TEL: 408-287-5973

Purpose: To "light the way" for Tri-City based groups who are in need of financial support.
Sponsor: Candle Lighters
Contact: Leanne Garcia, President
Description: The *Candle Lighters* is a women's fund-raising organization created to raise funds for local projects in the San Jose area. A major aspect of the program is a proposal luncheon, when representatives of organizations seeking financial aid for projects present proposals to the membership. Eighty volunteers participated in the 1989 proposal luncheon. After lunch, the membership votes on how the projected funds will be allocated to each of the top projects.
A major annual fundraising event is the *Halloween Ghost House*. In August, members begin to see their plans unfold as they transform the historic Carriage House, located at the Fremont Hub, into a haven of horrors designed to thrill both young and old.
Candle Lighter members donate 50 hours of time per year to the *Ghost House*, with 40 of those hours mandated for on-site services when the *Ghost House* is open. The other 10 are accounted for prior to the opening by participating in work parties doing such things as sewing costumes or construction. The volunteer schedule is set up at the proposal luncheon. Prospective members are required to work at the *Ghost House* before they are installed to give those who are seriously interested an opportunity to learn how the organization works before they join.
No one in the organization escapes hands-on volunteer duties. The 12 members of the board of directors are responsible for helping prepare the meal of hearty energy food for the proposal luncheon.
Founded: 1969

CHARITY PLANE RIDE FOR ORANGE GROVE
Epsilon Sigma Alpha International
Alpha Beta Chapter
1922 Wisteria Drive
Hixson, TN 37421
TEL: 615-756-4719
Also contact:
Barbara Farr
8440 Chambers Road
Chattanooga, TN 37421
Purpose: To raise funds to help the residents of Orange Grove and other programs in the Chattanooga area.
Contact: Betty Jolly
Description: For four cents a pound, Chattanooga area residents can "take to the skies" and get a bird's-eye view of the city. For this once-a-year fund-raising event, many local pilots donate their services as well as airplanes, while area aviation companies contribute fuel. The *Federal Aviation Administration (FAA)* helps to carry out the flight plan for the event, working closely with the *Airport Authority*.
The event is sponsored by the *Alpha Beta Chapter of Epsilon Sigma Alpha International*, a philanthropic organization that is dedicated to the service of others. The organization started the plane-ride project over two decades ago and to date has given over $100,000 in donations to Orange Grove. In 1985, Alpha Beta established the *Wanda Fleming Scholarship Fund* with a $10,000 donation. By 1989 the Fund had grown to $48,000. It supplies meals and transportation for those who otherwise would be financially unable to attend. Local businesses and individuals assure participation by Orange Grove students and residents of *Bethel Bible Village, Chambliss Children's Home, Baptist Children's Home* and others by donating the cost of their rides. In 1988, one of the volunteer pilots offered to match the $10,000 in proceeds from the event, making that year's donation the largest since the program's inception. The pilot offered the same match in 1989, donating over $12,000 for that year, surpassing the previous year's record donation.
The success of the plane ride program is attributed to volunteers,

sponsors and active participation by area residents.
Founded: 1965

CLASS ACTION SUIT
United Way Services of Las Vegas
1055 East Tropicana, Suite 300
PO Box 70720
Las Vegas, NV 89170-0720
TEL: 702-798-4636
Purpose: To obtain financial support from attorneys in the Las Vegas area.
Contact: Garth R. Winckler, President
Description: A suit filed on behalf of *John Doe,* a homeless person, *Jane Doe,* a pregnant teen, *Bob Doe,* an abused child, and *Alice Doe,* a senior citizen was personally "served" by young volunteers to nearly 1,000 Las Vegas attorneys with legal-looking documents that named the attorneys as defendents in a facsimile "class action suit." The cause of action was "failure to adequaely support human-care services," calling on the defendants "to voluntarily provide relief" according to a giving guide based on the defendants' number of years in practice.
The "tongue-in-cheek" effort received local media attention when one of the young volunteers hand-delivered the document to an attorney who is also the president and associate editor of a leading newspaper. In many cases, responses were received in the form of an "Answer to the Complaint," enclosing checks as "repentance" and offering to do better "as long as someone reminds" them. The "class action suit" increased giving by lawyers by 45 percent over the previous year.

CONTINENTAL HOMELESS ASSISTANCE PROGRAM
SEE BUSINESS/INDUSTRY INVOLVEMENT: HOMELESS

DOLLARS FOR SCHOLARS
Citizens' Scholarship Foundation of America
1505 Riverview Road
Box 297
St. Peter, MN 56082
TEL: 507-931-1682
Purpose: To expand access to higher education by involving and assisting the private sector in the support of students and in the encouragement of higher levels of educational achievement.
Contact: John Nadeau, National Director
Description: Dollars for Scholars are volunteer-operated community scholarship programs affiliated with *Citizens' Scholarship Foundation of America (CSFA).* Over 500 chapters nationwide raise money for local students to continue their education beyond high school.
In addition, 300 higher education institutions have joined *CSFA's Collegiate Partner Program* and provide support, and often matching funds, to students with scholarships from a *Dollars for Scholars* chapter. Information regarding starting a chapter in your community is available on request.

DONOR INVOLVEMENT
United Way of South Hampton Roads
109 Main Street
PO Box 2896
Norfolk , VA 23501-2896
TEL: 804-629-0500
Purpose: To directly link donors with human service needs in their communities.
Sponsor: United Way of South Hampton Roads
Contact: Eugene Berres
Description: A new category has been added to the United Way's donor program - donor involvment. This new approach enables the donor to help make the decision about where the donor's money goes. The new category, specific needs, is added to the pledge card

and allows the donor to designate one of six areas for his contribution:
● youth programs;
● health, medical research, and rehabilitation programs;
● elderly, child-care, and family programs;
● military family programs and facilities;
● food, shelter, and emergency assistance; and
● planning solutions to unmet human-service needs.
Examples of specific programs - such as substance abuse and services to the mentally ill - are listed on the back of the pledge card for each need area.
The donor involvement program has changed the agency's allocations system. Although the United Way has had a certification review process where practices are evaluated by allocations volunteers, the new donor involvement approach forces them to be more responsive to donor needs - especially significant since there is greater competition for fewer dollars now.
The donor involvement program includes year-round communications to donors about specific programs and people helped by their contribution. Also a newsletter is sent three times a year to over 110,000 donors who expressed an interest in receiving it.
The pledge card also asks donors if they would be willing to volunteer, and provides space for them to name a specific agency. During the first year, 1,200 donors responded positively. Involving donors in this new approach is facilitating campaign contributions and increasing public understanding of their community problem-solving roles.
Publications: You Make a Difference (3/year)

GIVE FIVE ALABAMA
SEE GOVERNORS' OFFICES ON VOLUNTEERISM: ALABAMA

"IN THE TRENCHES" AUTHOR SEARCH PROGRAM
SEE COMMUNICATIONS & PUBLIC RELATIONS

MATCHING FUNDS PROJECT
RSVP of Utah County
160 East Center
Provo, UT 84601
TEL: 801-373-5510
Purpose: To help meet RSVP's funding needs while meeting the basic human needs of the community.
Sponsor: Retired Senior Volunteer Program (RSVP) of Utah County
Contact: David L. Gardner
Description: A very practical and workable project that helps RSVP generate matching funds and, at the same time, helps agencies who need volunteer coordinators, is being implemented by the RSVP Program of Utah County. RSVP staff actually hire and help supervise volunteer coordinators for many agencies who are either RSVP stations or potential RSVP stations under the conditions that:
● the volunteer coordinator's salary (usually minimum wage) will be applied as matching funds toward RSVP funding needs.
● that all volunteers 60 years old or older automatically will be signed up as RSVP volunteers.
The RSVP Director started the project by submitting individual proposals to the local mental health association, the Utah County Housing Authority, and the Utah County Department of Alcohol and Drugs. In each case the idea was picked up with overwhelming tenacity, and though some people were skeptical, it has now proven itself to be a successful venture. It helps those agencies who do not as yet have volunteer coordinators, and provides RSVP with matching funds and a constant flow of new volunteers.
This special project idea is funded totally from other agencies, with

the exception of perhaps recognition and insurance. The agency involved pays the salary and staff travel of the volunteer coordinator who is hired. In some instances, RSVP picks up some volunteer mileage reimbursments.

In one case, the outside agency involved funnels the cash to pay the volunteer coordinator directly to RSVP and allows RSVP to handle everything, thereby picking up direct cash match.

Through this project, RSVP has taken on greater meaning in the community, boosting its credibility as well as its matching level. Information on the project is available to interested individuals or groups.

RSVP THRIFT SHOP*

605 East Main Street
East Prairie, MO 63845
TEL: 314-649-5243
Purpose: To provide monies for the volunteer program while providing low-cost items to needy people in the community.
Sponsor: US/ACTION; Chamber of Commerce
Contact: Betty Johnson
Description: Initiated in 1975 with a rent-free building and donated racks, tables and other necessities, the RSVP thrift shop has met a community as well as a program need. It is a favorite project of the volunteers because they know it is really needed in the community, and also have the satisfaction of raising funds for their own volunteer program.

Twelve volunteers man the shop five days a week. Donated items for resale are solicited through newspaper, radio and other media advertising. Duties of the volunteer salespersons include mending and repairing the usable household items and clothing received. Items are sold at a very low cost from the downtown location, which is convenient to low-income neighborhoods.

All income from the thrift shop is used for volunteer insurance, special recognition and awards events, volunteer transportation, and other program costs. The Chamber of Commerce pays for utilities and volunteer meals.

Descriptive printed materials have been prepared describing the development and operation of the program, and are available to individuals and groups interested in starting a thrift shop to raise funds for their volunteer programs.
Founded: 1975

SALVATION ARMY HAMBURGER SALES DAY
SEE BUSINESS/INDUSTRY INVOLVEMENT

SIX FRIENDS MEMORIAL FUND
First American Bank
Westover Branch
1701 McKinney Road
Arlington, VA 22205
TEL: 703-284-6550
Purpose: To acknowledge the work of volunteer rescue teams, and to assist in their efforts.
Sponsor: First American Bank
Contact: Rosemary May, Branch Manager
Description: This memorial fund was established in May 1990 by the families and friends of six young men who died in a plane crash on the way home from a fishing trip earlier in the month. During the weeklong vigil until the plane was found, families and friends waiting at a command center set up at *Manassas Municipal Airport,* a local airport in northern Virginia, became aware of the seemingly tireless efforts of volunteer search and rescue teams, the dedication to their jobs and their concern and compassion for survivors. Rescue teams were directed by the *Civil Air Patrol, Virginia Emergency Services,* and the *Appalachian Search and Rescue Conference.* Volunteers from both the community, including a family member of one of the crash victims, and nearby *Fort Belvoir* and other military bases joined the teams. It was the family member who first spotted part of the plane wreckage. The

Virginia State Police were on hand as well, including the State Police Chaplain, throughout the ordeal.
The fund is designated to support search and rescue teams, but is also intended as a tribute to their all-out efforts that are often taken for granted.

THE SMALL BUSINESS WAY: SMALL BUSINESSES SUPPORTING UNITED WAY
SEE BUSINESS/INDUSTRY INVOLVEMENT

SUPPORT FOR PUBLIC TELEVISION
Larchmont Homes
3350 Watt Avenue
Sacramento, CA 95821
TEL: 916-488-4500
Purpose: To raise funds to enable quality public television to continue in the community.
Sponsor: Larchmont Homes
Contact: Donald E. Reed
Description: For the second straight year, about 60 employees of *Larchmont Homes* and affiliated companies volunteered to spend an evening in June 1989 on the telephones at a local television station taking pledges of financial support for the public television programming provided by KVIE-Channel 6. The station's work has received the praise of the entire community, and the financial support provided by the phonathon is expected to help them continue their efforts to provide community-oriented and -approved television.

During the course of the phonathon, the station conducted an auction of donated items, including furniture given for the auction by *Larchmont Homes.*

In addition to representatives of Larchmont Homes, volunteers came from the Channel 6 boosters of the *Ryland Mortgage Corporation, Sacramento Escrow Company, Sierra Western Insurance Agency, Design Center,* and *Runyon Saltzman Weagraff & Siegel.*

Volunteers receive a briefing on public relations and fund-raising techniques before being assigned to three-hour shifts at the telethon.

THREE WAYS TO CARE
United Way of Southeastern Pennsylvania
7 Benjamin Franklin Parkway
Philadelphia, PA 19103-1294
TEL: 215-665-2500
Purpose: To make the allocations process easier for people to understand and offer them a way to channel their money and get satisfaction from the giving process.
Sponsor: United Way of Southeastern Pennsylvania
Contact: Ted Moore
Description: Three Ways to Care uses a donor-involvement approach by marketing three donation categories:
- **Community Care** - the category for undesignated gifts;
- **Targeted Care** - an issue-oriented giving category; and
- **Specific Care** - for gifts designated to specific agencies.

The program builds on the focus of current issues through special media reports, such as homelessness or drug abuse, and gives donors an opportunity to direct their gift toward a special concern to them.

This aspect of the donor program resulted from three years of research by a special committee, which included a focus-group study, a survey of employee campaign chairs, interviews with local human-care agency directors, public forums, and other types of research. A major recommendation - a "targeted care" campaign category - emerged from the committee's efforts. First implemented during the 1988 campaign, *Three Ways to Care* found 16,000 contributors choosing the new "Targeted Care" category for their contributions.

Targeted Care encompasses the following need areas:

- hungry and homeless;
- children and youth;
- the elderly;
- health and rehabilitation;
- families and women;
- self-help; and
- community needs still in the assessment phase.

This method helps the donor find middle ground when he would like to choose an area of concern, but not a specific agency.

The program incorporates a year-round communications element involving a general report to about 135,000 donors, *Report to Contributors,* covering all three giving categories, and two additional reports on the fund distribution of *Targeted Care* and *Specific Care* gifts mailed to donors who designated those categories.

Recently Bell of Pennsylvania produced three-minute video modules in each of the *Targeted Care* categories for use in workplace news programs.

U.S.-BASED JAPANESE CORPORATIONS AND THE UNITED WAY
United Way of America
701 North Fairfax Street
Alexandria, VA 22314-2045
TEL: 703-836-7100
Purpose: To provide a framework through which local United Way organizations can work on behalf of communities with U.S.-based Japanese companies toward a mutually-beneficial relationship.
Sponsor: United Way of America
Contact: Marty Walsh
Description: Since 1987, *United Way of America* has been working to develop a national strategy and resource materials for involving Japanese companies in United Way. This has included training sessions for United Way volunteers and professionals and has initiated contact with major U.S.-based Japanese corporations around the country and in Japan. Individual United Ways have joined the effort to help Japanese executives better understand how United Way works.

According to the *International Corporations* division of United Way, there are several fundamental cultural differences between the U.S. and Japan in matters of volunteerism. In Japan, the government, private industry, and the family take care of human-care needs. Also, the process in making decisions about philanthropy often takes a very long time, since consultation with the headquarters in Japan is mandated.

However, several local United Ways have reached a point of understanding with local Japanese companies. Examples are:

- **Battle Creek, Michigan** - *Nippondenso,* Battle Creek's largest Japanese-owned company, has led the Japanese business community in giving to United Way. In addition, the company was influential in helping to recruit other Japanese companies to participate in the campaign. In addition, the company's director of personnel is a United Way board member, and serves as a liaison with the company's president. Battle Creek's Chamber of Commerce helped lay the groundwork through its international committee.

- **Santa Clara, California** - In 1989, 26 Japanese-business liaisons from area banks and certified public accounting firms formed a community-relations advisory committee in Santa Clara. The volunteer committee members rely on senior Japanese executives for financial consultation and for help in understanding the American culture. The committee has developed Japanese-language materials and sponsored special United Way events. Also, the *Japanese Chamber of Commerce* has endorsed the campaign. Consequently, United Way contributions from the Japanese community almost doubled in 1990.

- **Los Angeles, California** - The United Way and the *Japanese*

Business Association began working together in 1987. Their first joint effort was to develop a Japanese-language United Way brochure that included information about charitable giving in the United States. In 1989, the United Way recruited its first board member from the Japanese business community. According to the senior campaign associate of the United Way, "Japanese executives are very impressed when they look at United Way boards and see key American business leaders as volunteers. They see United Way board membership as a bridge to the community." The Los Angeles United Way plans to encourage Japanese business leaders to assist with planning, marketing, and allocations - "to help increase their understanding of how United Way works."

At United Way of America, it is felt that as more international companies invest in American communities, they challenge United Ways to be marketing-oriented - to listen to and understand different customers. For example, in dealing with the Japanese, it has been found that it is important to be consistent. Plans are to continue to work to increase United Way involvement of Japanese and other foreign-owned companies in the U.S.

YOUTH ALLOCATIONS COMMITTEE
United Way of the Capital Area (Jackson)
843 North President Street
Jackson, MS 39202
TEL: 601-948-4725
Purpose: To evaluate and to make decisions to fund youth programs in their communities.
Sponsor: United Way of the Capital Area
Contact: Mack Mitchell, Chairman
Description: In 1986, the United Way Volunteer Center's *Youth in Action Program* expanded to include a *Youth Allocations Committee.* The students must make a two-year commitment to get the most out of the training provided - making a limited amount of funds benefit the greatest number of people. Students may serve a third year if they desire.

Sixteen senior high schools and eight colleges in the Jackson area endorse and participate in the program. Student allocations committee members attend three orientation sessions to learn about the role and responsibility of volunteers in the community, about United Way and community health and human-care agencies, and acquire a basic overview of the allocation process.

The Chairman is a student, a freshman at Millsaps College. For many students, it is the first time they have volunteered for anything - and the program's process of learning what community services exist and how they work lays a good foundation for future community involvement.

The United Way provides $5,000 in venture grant funds for the committee to distribute. In September of each year students evaluate how effectively funds allocated the previous year were used. Beginning the following March, the students review new applications for funding and attend agency presentations. Final funding decisions are made in April, and United Way funds are distributed by committee members in May.

In 1989-90 the Committee funded eight youth-oriented programs: *Epilepsy Foundation of Mississippi* for its summer camp for children with Epilepsy, *Metro YMCA* for its *Youth Development Program, Metro Boys and Girls Clubs* for various projects, *Exchange Club/Parent Child Center* for its *Teen Parent Education Scholarship Program, Jackson State University/Division of Continuing Education* for training of GED students, and the *Jackson YWCA* for the development of an educational program. In 1988-89 the committee funded seven youth programs, including several offered by local chapters of the Boys and Girls Clubs, a teen center for troubled youth, and church youth groups.
Founded: 1986

YOUTH LEADERSHIP VENTURE FUNDING PROGRAM
SEE VOLUNTEERS: STUDENTS

FUNDING/FUND-RAISING/RELATED SERVICES: AIDS

NATIONAL/STATE ORGANIZATIONS

AMERICAN FOUNDATION FOR AIDS RESEARCH
AmFar
5900 Wilshire Boulevard
Second Floor
Los Angeles, CA 90036
TEL: 213-857-5900
Objectives: To raise funds to support research on acquired immune deficiency syndrome (AIDS).
Services: Focuses research on discovering the causes of AIDS, a disease of immune dysfunction, believed to be transmitted through certain body fluids; organizes state and local fundraising and develops educational programs as a preventative to the spread of the disease, for which the cause is unknown and there is no known cure; works with local groups such as *Art Against AIDS* in Washington, DC, and *LAPD (Los Angeles Poverty Department)* in Los Angeles to raise funds, with a share going to the local host group, a share to *AmFar* for research, and the balance distributed among other local groups across the country; provides speakers to groups and organizations; publishes an educational brochure about AIDS for distribution.
Publications: Facts About AIDS
Founded: 1985

CHAPTER GRANTS PROGRAM
American Red Cross Office of HIV/AIDS Education
AIDS Public Education Program
1709 New York Avenue, NW
Washington, DC 20006
TEL: 202-662-1577; 202-662-1580
FAX: 202-662-1555
Objectives: To help local chapters provide HIV/AIDS education to high-risk populations.
Services: Awards grants to Red Cross chapters for creative and new approaches to HIV/AIDS education; places focus on helping chapters provide community HIV/AIDS education to hard-to-reach, high-risk populations; shares successful programs with other chapters so they can be adapted, if necessary, and used as models for local use; funds programs such as peer counseling in homeless shelters, and education efforts in migrant worker camps, prisons, and schools, with two grants going to evaluation programs using local university resources for assessing effectiveness of local chapter programs; provides chapter mini-grants, which act as seed money to small chapters that lack the resources to begin any sort of community HIV/AIDS education program without assistance.
Contact: Carole Kauffman

INDIVIDUAL PROGRAM PROFILES

ART AGAINST AIDS EXHIBIT
Art Against AIDS
406 Seventh Street, NW
Third Floor
Washington, DC 20004
TEL: 202-347-1033
Purpose: To raise funds for AIDS research and local AIDS programs.
Contact: Kevin Williams, Assistant Director
Description: In May 1990, a group of prominent contemporary artists provided artwork for a local fundraiser to assist in AIDS research, and local AIDS efforts to provide education materials

and programs for the community, and/or care for AIDS patients. In addition to the artists, support comes from First Lady Barbara Bush (honorary chairperson), celebrities including Elizabeth Taylor, half of the members of the Senate, and Leonard Marx, who donated the space for the exhibit. In addition more than 130 local artists have contributed works.
The exhibition and sale are part of a campaign that involves the national organization, *American Foundation for AIDS Research (AmFar)*, with local AIDS program leaders to benefit the local host organization (50%), continuing *AmFar* research programs, and other local AIDS programs needing assistance across the country. Beneficiaries in the Washington, DC area are *Walt Whitman Clinic, Best Friends, Clinical Trials Expanded Access Project, DC Coalition of Black Gay Men and Women, Grandma's House, Us Helping Us,* and *St. Francis Center.*
This national partnership has proven to be an excellent way to "spread the wealth" and provide opportunities at the local level where resources are scarce or nonexistent. The fundraising effort has proven beneficial to all, and the substance of the programs offered to the community in return for their generosity have been both cultural and educational. Within the first two weeks of the show, sales reached $300,000.
Prices vary widely. One work sold for $100,000, with others a twentieth of that amount. Some are in the $15,000-$35,000 price range, while others are priced at a small fraction of those figures. Combined with a gala fundraising dinner at the *National Building Museum* during the last week of the exhibit, the goal for the program is $800,000.
Among artists who contributed works for the exhibit program are Louise Bourgeois, Jasper Johns, Cindy Sherman and Christo. The work of the local contributing artists has been noted as very impressive. According to one visitor to the exhibit, a *Washington Post* staff writer, "It rarely suggests fury, the despair of the dying or the anger of AIDS activists. Instead, its spirit is compassionate, collegial, inclusive."

HEART STRINGS - MEMPHIS STOP
Aid to End AIDS Committee
689 Melrose
Memphis, TN 38104
TEL: 901-458-2437; 901-272-0855
Purpose: To raise funds to help a broader spectrum of AIDS victims in the Memphis area.
Sponsor: Aid to End AIDS Committee
Contact: Allen Cook, ATEAC Secretary
Description: Heart Strings is a show sponsored by the *Design Industries Foundation for AIDS,* headquartered in New York. The national production raises funds around the country during a 30-city tour beginning in early fall each year. It's purpose is to expand financial support for AIDS into the community-at-large, while helping communities to understand AIDS. AIDS organizations in the host community receive 85% of the profits from the stop. The other 15% is earmarked for AIDS care and education in cities skipped by the tour.
The host community is expected to provide volunteers and an estimated $15,000 to $20,000 for local production expenses.
The musical includes a touring company of about 20 performers. Local celebrities and choirs are often added. Just how much the show makes in each city depends upon such factors as ticket prices and corporate sponsorship. Ticket prices are set after the level of financial support from other sources is determined.
In Memphis, the *Aid to End AIDS Committee (ATEAC)* and the *Memphis AIDS Coalition* spearhead local sponsorship of the show. ATEAC's need for more money stems from the group's growing caseload. In 1988, the group paid an average of about $400 per month in direct financial aid to clients. A year later, the tab averaged about $2,000 per month. Financial support can include making rent or utility payments for needy patients or even paying the first month's fee for the AIDS drug AZT.

The group also rents a house in Memphis used as a shelter for homeless AIDS patients. Clients include hemophiliacs who apparently caught the virus through tainted blood or blood products, and women who apparently contracted the virus through heterosexual relations, as well as members of the gay community. For this reason, the community-at-large is included in the effort to supplement the limited amount of money realized from the very targeted (gay) audience.

THE RESPONSE POOL
United Way of Dade County
600 Brickell Avenue, Eighth Floor
PO Box 010790
Miami, FL 33101-0790
TEL: 305-579-2200
Purpose: To fund in-home care for people with AIDS.
Sponsor: Visiting Nurse Association, Hospice, Inc., Health Crisis Network, United Way
Contact: Alexandra Lindsey, Director of Initiatives
Description: The Response Pool supports AIDS services through a community problem-solving fund. In 1985, The Response Pool began funding an in-home care program for people with AIDS - a program jointly operated by the Visiting Nurse Association, Hospice, Inc., and Miami's Health Crisis Network.
Currently, United Way helps fund more than a dozen agencies with AIDS programs ranging from suicide-prevention hotlines to an AIDS education training program for social service professionals.
With approximately 32 percent of Florida AIDS cases occurring in the Miami area - and 12,000 cases of HIV-infection predicted by 1991 - the United Way is prioritizing AIDS in its public-awareness materials as well. Last year, the organization made AIDS a subject in its campaign film, adding to its examples of human-service needs a portrayal of a woman with AIDS.
Founded: 1989

SUPPORT SERVICES - AIDS PROGRAM
Whitman-Walker Clinic
1407 S Street, NW
Washington, DC 20009
TEL: 202-797-3540; 202-328-0697
Purpose: To provide a variety of support services to persons with AIDS and HIV infection.
Sponsor: Whitman-Walker Clinic
Contact: Peter Provost
Description: Support Services is a division of *Whitman-Walker Clinic AIDS Program,* which is a volunteer-based (1,500 overall) effort, enhanced and supported by professional staff. The Support Services Division includes:
Financial Help - The AIDS Foundation administers over 250 memorial funds established by lovers, other family members, and friends of local persons so that donations contributed in their memory will be of service to others. Over $370,000 has been distributed over the past four years. The foundation provides direct financial assistance to persons living with AIDS. Among other things, funding has been granted for housing, food, transportation, moving, entertainment, and funeral expenses. Ninety percent of foundation money goes to direct assistance; the remainder is used for administrative costs.
Emotional Help - Support services include individual and group counseling for persons with HIV infection and for lovers and other family members; social work case management to insure proper coordination with available services; buddies and home companions for help with day-to-day tasks; and referrals for religious, visiting nurse, and hospice services. Home health care workers are employed with the support of the *DC Long Term Care Administration.*
Legal Help - The *Legal Services Project,* with over 200 volunteer attorneys and two full-time attorneys, provides basic estate

planning such as wills, powers of attorney, and living wills. The project also assists clients with public benefits applications and appeals, and with problems involving discrimination, insurance, and debt collection. Persons with HIV infection are welcome to telephone for general legal consultations.
Volunteers in Support Services receive orientation and basic training, and seminars on a variety of issues. All of the clinic's programs are coordinated with local government and community-based organizations.

FUNDING/FUND-RAISING/RELATED SERVICES: ARTS

NATIONAL/STATE ORGANIZATIONS

BREAD AND ROSES
78 Throckmorton Avenue
Mill Valley, CA 90048
TEL: 415-381-0320
Objectives: To donate time and talents to people who "desperately need and appreciate the pleasure and human contact that live entertainment can bring."
Services: Takes free live entertainment to institutions such as convalescent homes, correctional facilities, psychiatric centers, work farms, hospitals, children's homes and similar institutions; produces benefit concerts to raise funds for certain nonprofit organizations; holds two seminars per month to educate other groups on producing benefit concerts; provides information to any individual or group, but performs in California only at the present time. (Operating since 1974, Bread and Roses has found that the performers' benefits are two-fold: bringing enjoyment to others, and having a "sympathetic, noncommercial environment in which to perform.")
Publications: Bread & Roses Handbook; Bread & Roses Newsletter
Founded: 1974

INDIVIDUAL PROGRAM PROFILES

ART FOR KIDS' SAKE
SEE VOLUNTEERS: PROFESSIONALS

GRAND RAPIDS SYMPHONY ORCHESTRA
Grand Rapids, MI 49501
TEL: 616-454-9451
Purpose: To raise funds to keep the Grand Rapids Symphony Orchestra operating.
Contact: Patrick O'Neall, Development Director
Description: Halfway through the *Grand Rapids Symphony Orchestra's* 1989 annual fund-raising campaign, some 243 volunteers had received donations from 875 corporate and individual contributors, reaching more than half of their goal of $1 million. For the all-volunteer orchestra, this indicates that the community is pleased with its program of cultural enrichment for all age groups across the city.
Following this major campaign, volunteers begin to look for new donations at the grass-roots level, primarily from subscribers. Orchestra officials feel that these small gifts are as important as the major ones.
With so many other arts programs seeking funds, accountability has become a major factor for enrichment groups, with a large number of donors wanting to know more about where their dollars are going. This has brought the community's arts groups together

to discuss the overall arts programs for the area and compare notes on ways of maintaining adequate funding. In addition, arts groups are becoming more sensitive to meeting the needs of the community, with more surveys and more proactive response to public opinion as to cultural pursuits that will benefit all individuals and groups.

TEA AND TREASURES
SEE GOVERNORS' OFFICES ON VOLUNTEERISM: RHODE ISLAND

FUNDING/FUND-RAISING/RELATED SERVICES: AUCTIONS

INDIVIDUAL PROGRAM PROFILES

CELEBRITY AUCTION*
c/o Julie Stewart
7821 Manor House Drive
Fairfax Station, VA 22039
TEL: 703-250-7128; 703-691-3400
Purpose: To raise money for 4-H educational programs.
Sponsor: Fairfax County Department of Extension and Continuing Education
Contact: Julie Stewart, Chairman
Description: The 4-H educational programs provide scholarships and educational trips for youth, enabling some to acquire higher education that might not be possible, and broadening their horizons through exposure to communities other than their own. With the State horse program needing $14-$15,000 in educational funds each year for this purpose, 4-H Advisory Committee meetings were consumed with the dilemma of raising money for this worthwhile program.
A lone volunteer, Vice President of one of the Committees, decided that continuing such meetings without some type of simultaneous action would be fruitless. A fundraising auction at the college her son attended had produced a tidy sum for the college's programs. The college students had solicited articles from celebrities for their auction.
After going through the 4-H bureaucratic process for approval, the "go ahead" signal was finally given. The first step was to get 4-H youth and board members involved. Since articles for the auction were not limited to celebrity items, the youth volunteers were given the task of contacting local businesses, agencies and individuals to request items.
At first it was difficult for the young volunteers to accept the rejection that they encountered in many instances, but the Celebrity Auction Chairman (the original volunteer) worked closely with them to further develop their approaches to the potential donors. Board members spread the word among each other and local citizens, causing a chain reaction. Soon the local business community became almost totally involved - and enjoyed it!
The Volunteer Chairman handled the celebrity aspect of the solicitation herself. Armed with a New York newspaper which listed all Broadway plays, stars, and some producers, she typed individual letters to each, signed by her as Chairman, and the 4-H Extension Agent. Senators and Congressmen were telephoned. Gifts ranged from an autographed "Sugar Babies" program from Mickey Rooney, to an autographed copy of *The Real War* from Richard Nixon. Contact with the media produced a dinner date with a popular single newscaster, with a local restaurant donating the dinner. Haircuts, T-shirts, savings accounts, a bushel of fresh corn, magazine subscriptions, and almost anything else that comes to mind has been donated.

YOUTH-IN-ACTION AUCTION
Youth Advisory Commission
170 Santa Maria Avenue
Pacifica, CA 94044
TEL: 415-877-8631
Purpose: To raise sufficient funds for a Summer Beach Cleaning Program; to give youth the opportunity to put on a community auction and to provide jobs for youth.
Sponsor: City of Pacifica
Contact: John W. Deuel
Description: An annual fundraising project executed by Youth Advisory Commission is a televised community auction called The Youth-in-Action Auction. The purposes of the auction are:
● to improve the local beaches through a summer beach cleaning program;
● to hire high school age city youth as part-time beach cleaners to staff the beach crews; and
● to give youth volunteers a variety of community experiences in fundraising and producing a televised auction.
Preparation for the auction begins in early September when the Youth Advisory Commission begins to solicit donations from local merchants and community members. The YAC takes on the jobs of publicity, merchandise inventory, scheduling local dignitaries and personalities as auctioneers, and arranging for youth volunteers to staff the auction.
The auction is held during three consecutive evenings at the City Council Chambers. The Community Cable TV station handles the technical production each night and the YAC coordinates all other activities. On the nights of the auction, each donated item or service is auctioned off by a volunteer auctioneer from one of four tables. Each table has from five to eight items at a time and each item is assigned a number which is written on a chalkboard behind each table for identification purposes. Home viewers who want to bid on an item call into a bank of phones manned by youth volunteers. Each new bid is run up to the table where it is written on the board. Bids are taken until it is decided by the floor director to sell the item. When an entire board is sold off, new items are put up on the table by the inventory manager. The high bid is immediately confirmed on a separate phone, to make sure the item wasn't sold to a phony bid.
To pick up items, the high bidders come in to pick up and pay in an area where items have been marked with the high bidder's name.

FUNDING/FUND-RAISING/RELATED SERVICES: BUSINESSES

NATIONAL/STATE ORGANIZATIONS

NAWBO SCHOLARSHIP FUND
National Association of Women Business Owners
600 South Federal Street
Suite 400
Chicago, IL 60605
TEL: 312-922-0465
Objectives: To encourage young women to become entrepreneurs.
Services: Works to accelerate the growth and stability of businesses owned by women through internships for college students; accepts nominations from colleges based on academic success and the students' desire to own their own businesses; places selected students in six-week internships with local entrepreneurs in its 4,000 local membership areas; provides a stipend (usually about $1,500) for the duration of the internship; offers nominees its general services for potential women business owners, including

workshops and seminars, an information clearinghouse, and referral services, as well as access to its corporate relations and leadership development programs and its data bank of women business owners; publishes a newsletter and a directory.
Contact: Barbara Madro, Administrative Director
Publications: Statement (newsletter); Directory of Women Business Owners
Founded: 1974

INDIVIDUAL PROGRAM PROFILES

MIDAS TOUCH
Volunteers of America of Los Angeles
3600 Wilshire Boulevard
Los Angeles, CA 90010
TEL: 213-389-1500
Purpose: To provide guaranteed small business loans to teens from humble backgrounds.
Sponsor: Volunteers of America of Los Angeles
Contact: Mark Cosman, VP/Corporate Relations
Description: Begun in 1986, MIDAS is a new VOA project which provides guaranteed small business loans to disadvantaged teens who show the potential for business ownership. Partially funded with a $25,000 grant from TRW, MIDAS loans are offered for after-school, weekend and summer businesses which are started by MIDAS graduates.
The first MIDAS TOUCH Seminar was held in August 1986 in Los Angeles, both administered and funded by TRW employees, who led the way for other members of the business community to become involved.
Funded by TRW's Employees Charitable Organization (ECHO), MIDAS '86 had the hands-on participation of TRW employees - from selecting the project's curriculum to recruiting panelists and serving as counselors.
TRW was also a sponsor of the MIDAS program in Huntsville, Alabama, and is still assisting national VOA in its MIDAS program for disadvantaged teens who demonstrate that they can benefit from such career assistance.

FUNDING/FUND-RAISING/RELATED SERVICES: CHILDREN

NATIONAL/STATE ORGANIZATIONS

HEAD START - FAMILY DAY CARE
US/HHS - Administration for Children, Youth and Families
PO Box 1182
Washington, DC 20201
TEL: 202-475-0257
Objectives: To extend the part-time services of *Head Start* to include full-time child care.
Services: With a $1.9 million grant from the US Department of Health and Human Services to the District of Columbia School System, an extension of the long-standing Head Start program was launched in September 1989. The intent of the pilot program is to assist working parents struggling to break away from the welfare rolls who need full time child care, but would like to see their children receive the benefits of the strong educational component of the popular Head Start program as well.
The Department's solution for this model program is to enlist low-income families as full-time day care providers, with a limit of five children in each home compared to 17 in Head Start classes in

the schools. All providers receive training through the school system by early childhood specialists to assure that the educational intent of the Head Start program is as fully utilized as possible in the homes. All materials and supplies, from books to musical instruments, are supplied through the Head Start office. Providers are paid $12 per day per child following completion of their training. The providers are closely supervised, with school monitors assigned to visit the homes weekly. School officials require that the providers keep detailed records on each child's progress and submit monthly reports on their activities.
The element that sets the family program apart from the school program is that it provides a natural setting that makes children feel secure and eager to learn in homes within their neighborhoods. Some volunteer community agencies provide full-day child care in Head Start programs on a limited basis. The *National Child Day Care Association* operates centers in churches, housing projects and community centers in the District, providing full-time care in two of its eight Head Start programs and in the home of one child-care provider.
The Bush administration's 1991 fiscal year request for $500 million increase for Head Start (a 36% increase over 1990) is considered a testament to the success of the program, and its bipartisan reputation (it was begun during the poverty program era of the Kennedy administration). According to a leading organization for children, the *Children's Defense Fund,* "It's made an enormous difference to countless children and families. It's enabled many children to enter school healthy and strong."
The District's program is small. Six day-care providers are operating under the model program. Sixteen similar projects are being tested around the country. Since the project includes an employment element for low-income people, the benefits reach adults and families as well as children.

NATIONAL CENTER ON CHILD ABUSE AND NEGLECT
US/HHS - Administration for Children, Youth and Families
PO Box 1182
Washington, DC 20013
TEL: 703-821-2086
Objectives: To assist state, local and voluntary agencies and organizations in strengthening their capacities in areas of child abuse.
Services: Provides grants for demonstration programs, research into causes, prevention and treatment; funds states for efforts related to child abuse prevention, investigation and treatment; operates the Clearinghouse on Child Abuse and Neglect Information (see separate entry); publishes manuals, available without charge.
Sponsor: US/HHS - Department of Health & Human Services
Founded: 1975

TRAINING PROGRAMS

STUDENT CARE DAY
United Way Services of Cleveland
3100 Euclid Avenue
Cleveland, OH 44115-2577
TEL: 216-881-3170
Credit: Inquire
Sponsor: Cleveland Public Schools
Contact: Cheryle A. Wills, Chairman
Description: Upon returning home from the *United Way Young Leaders Conference* in Washington, DC, in 1987, youth leaders in Cleveland planned *Student Care Day* to follow through on the suggestion in Washington that the more people know about United Way, the more likely they are to support it.
The half-day seminar was designed to spark students' imaginations to develop unique fund-raising ideas. The seminar was held on a college campus in downtown Cleveland, with more than 500

people composed of two or three student leaders and one adult from each of 137 schools in the Greater Cleveland area. Participants ranged from fourth graders to college students. In addition to sparking imaginative ideas, the seminar taught participants leadership skills and cooperation, and gave the students a clear understanding of the kinds of services United Way provides, especially for youth. The program included a video tour of several United Way-supported agencies, as well as the showing of award-winning public-service announcements from United Ways around the country.

Two Cleveland students who had directly benefited from United Way Services talked about their experiences and the importance of student involvement in volunteerism and charitable giving. Two other students performed an original "rap" on the subject to help spark enthusiasm.

During a brainstorming session, students divided into groups of 10 to 15, according to grade level. Each group was asked to create a fund-raising event that would be fun and would be effective in raising money for United Way. Each group was asked to create a poster to promote its event, with posters lining the halls before the conference ended. Ideas ranged from a rap contest and a fashion show to a sledgehammer car smash and a men's wet T-shirt contest. The price for taking part in each event included a contribution for United Way.

Speakers included the United Way's Chairman of the Board of Trustees, and two Cleveland Browns football players. Door prizes were provided by local merchants.

In a followup of the youth seminar, one student commented, "The interaction between east-side, west-side, and inner-city kids was great. The whole day was *excellent*." Another student said, "I wish my whole school could have come today." In general, student evaluations of the program point to repeating the seminar annually, in concert with a youth leadership conference held each year.

Officials see the long-term payoff as an important aspect of the seminar - Cleveland can look forward to a cadre of future volunteer leaders whose training started with the seminar.
Founded: 1987

INDIVIDUAL PROGRAM PROFILES

CHILDREN'S MIRACLE NETWORK TELETHON
KMOL-TV
1031 Navarro
San Antonio, TX 78205
TEL: 512-226-4444
Purpose: To raise money for children's hospitals in the U.S. and other countries.
Contact: Denise F. Barkis, Telethon Coordinator
Description: Six *Marathon Miracle Men* operated phone banks during the entire 22 hours of Austin's 1989 "Children's Miracle Network Telethon" mounted to benefit the *Santa Rosa Children's Hospital* - one of five such hospitals across the state. They anchored a show that involved some 1,000 volunteers of all ages and from all walks of life. The two-day 1989 telethon raised over $900,000 - about $100,000 more than the previous year. The response from individuals was continuous and often accompanied by encouraging statements. Over $200,000 came from three benefactors - *WalMart, Sam's Wholesale Club,* and *Credit Unions for Kids.*

A variety of performers, group skits, and a visit by a child who was badly injured when his father's car backed over him ("I was squished!") but now totally healed through the Children's Hospital's services were some of the activities used to maintain interest. The *Marathon Miracle Men,* who facilitated the program, came from *Jaycees, Kiwanis Club, Knights of Columbus, Lions Club, Optimist Club* and *Rotary Club.*

An unexpected occurrence increased the poignancy of the Telethon

when a co-host left the studio in a rush after receiving a phone call that his 13-year-old son was rushed to Children's Hospital. The *Children's Miracle Network Telethon* was begun in 1982 by the *Osmond Foundation* and is broadcast nationwide to raise money for more than 170 children's hospitals in five countries. KMOL began airing the local show in 1983.
Founded: 1982

FUND FOR NEEDY SCHOOL CHILDREN
1466 Harbert
Memphis, TN 38104
TEL: 901-276-0372
Purpose: To assist in meeting some of the health and welfare needs of economically-disadvantaged elementary school children.
Sponsor: United Way
Contact: Sheryl Bowen
Description: The activities of this volunteer community organization are designed to help meet needs of disadvantaged elementary school children. Working in the public schools with the approval of the elected Board of Education, the superintendent and his staff, the program is directed by a 12-member steering committee, headed by the co-chairman.

As a United Way agency, it receives funds for that part of the program which provides new clothing, shoes, and glasses from United Way. Additional limited foundation and private group donations also contribute to the purchase of glasses. Other phases of its work are supported by funds from the city and county governments and contributions from the general public.

The elimination of hunger in the classroom was one of the main thrusts of the program until the federal program became firmly established. In 1969, Fund volunteers insisted successfully that 40,000 or more school children coming from poverty-income families should be reflected on the free lunch/breakfast roster. Volunteer concern has followed these children as they have been bussed to schools all over the city.

In addition to increasing free lunch participation, the Fund has found the means to meet other needs of some of the children as newborns and later at school. An Infant Formula program supported by funds from city and county governments, and a layette program supported by contributions from the public, are examples. The formula and layette programs are carried out in coordination with the City of Memphis Hospital and the Health Department. The provision of new clothes and shoes is carried out through the Pupil Services Department of the Board of Education. The Fund for Needy School Children began in 1964 with 12 volunteers in four elementary schools seeking out and enrolling eligible children in the national school lunch program. Volunteer activities expanded into all Title I elementary schools and, by 1971, there were more than 400 volunteers in over 50 city and county schools providing a solid base for continuing interest in the program.
Founded: 1964

TEENS AS COMMUNITY RESOURCES*
SEE LEADERSHIP DEVELOPMENT/BOARDS: CHILDREN/YOUTH

YOUTH ALLOCATIONS COMMITTEE
SEE LEADERSHIP DEVELOPMENT/BOARDS: CHILDREN/YOUTH

YOUTH AS RESOURCES
SEE LEADERSHIP DEVELOPMENT/BOARDS: CHILDREN/YOUTH

YOUTH RESOURCES OF SOUTHWESTERN INDIANA
SEE LEADERSHIP DEVELOPMENT/BOARDS: CHILDREN/YOUTH

FUNDING/FUND-RAISING/RELATED SERVICES: DRUGS

INDIVIDUAL PROGRAM PROFILES

BUREAU OF DRUG ABUSE SERVICES GRANTS PROGRAM
Santa Clara County
645 South Bascom Avenue
San Jose, CA 95128
TEL: 408-299-6002
Purpose: To find and fund creative methods among community organizations to get the anti-drug message across.
Sponsor: Santa Clara County
Contact: Lily Alvarez, Assistant Prevention Services Coordinator
Description: A series of $2,000 grants from the Prevention Services Office of the County's Bureau of Drug Abuse Services has enabled social agencies and volunteer groups in Santa Clara County to continue to widen the battle against drug abuse. Tactics range from an *American Indian Youth Sobriety Pow Wow* to a group therapy session for women at Elmwood Rehabilitation Center. Grants have been allotted to organizations in Los Gatos, San Jose, Santa Clara and Mountain View. Funded programs include:

- **American Indian Youth Sobriety Pow Wow** - a program of the *Four Winds Lodge,* an intermediate alcohol recovery residence affiliated with the *Indian Center of San Jose* which includes music, dancing, arts and crafts exhibits in its program designed to appeal to youth never to abuse drugs or alcohol. [This was the second mini-grant to the lodge in 1989. The first paid for a puppet show called *BABES* which is used to educate young children about drug abuse.]
- **Anti-drug Group Therapy** - a series of 15 therapeutic educational sessions by *Lutheran Social Services* for women at *Elmwood Rehabilitation Center.* Topics covered include effect of alcohol on the fetus, ways to reduce drug abuse by children, and community services available to women.
- **Preparing for the Drug-Free Years** - a series of five workshops for parents conducted by Los Gatos Unified School District. Remaining funds were used to develop a brochure listing area organizations that provide information and seminars for parents on drug abuse by children and ways to cope with it.
- **A Clean and Sober Summer** - a rally administered by CASA (Community Against Substance Abuse), a totally-volunteer group, and the Los Gatos *Teen Counseling Center* featuring music, clowns and jugglers, and talks by former drug and alcohol abusers. [Each organization was given a $2,000 mini-grant for its part in the rally.]
- **Drug Abuse and the Foster Child** - two workshops on drug abuse prevention conducted cooperatively by the *Adult and Child Guidance Center* in San Jose and the *Foster Parents Association* in Santa Clara County. [The *Center* also sponsors training sessions in foster parents' homes to help them identify drug abuse in its early stages and learn strategies for managing the resulting problem behavior by the children.]
- **Drug Abuse Prevention: The Asian Way** - a publication for distribution to clients and agencies serving Asian Americans, to be translated in 13 Asian dialects as well as English.
- **Educational materials on drug abuse prevention** - materials developed by Santa Clara County's *Juvenile Hall Medical Clinic* based on group discussions involving input from 30 adolescents in custody working with a clinic consultant and geared toward youth coming into *Juvenile Hall* later.

The grants program was begun by the Bureau when it became evident that standard approaches were not working well enough and "more creative methods are needed to get the anti-drug message across." The Bureau received 28 proposals and gave out 20 grants.

VSPA FUND-RAISING PROGRAMS
Virginia State Police Association
6944 Forest Hill Avenue
Richmond, VA 23225
TOLL FREE: 800-523-5088
Purpose: To mount fund-raising programs to help provide support for volunteer programs around the Commonwealth.
Sponsor: Virginia Department of State Police
Contact: Kyle L. Miller, President
Description: Founded in 1975, the Virginia State Police Association (VSPA) strives to be mutually helpful to one another in an effort to provide a higher degree of professionalism and morale within the Department, and to provide better police services to the citizens of the Commonwealth of Virginia. These services include numerous fund-raising efforts for citizens who support the efforts of the State Police to make our communities better places to live.
Drug abuse resistance efforts are a primary concern of the Association, and contributions for citizen efforts in this area of concern have included:

- Drug Abuse Resistance Education (DARE), which is sponsored by the Virginia Department of State Police, and which is active in nearly 100 school districts
- Virginia Federation of Parents for Drug-Free Youth
- Greater Richmond Informed Parents (GRIP)
- Drugbusters
- Parents' Association to Neutralize Drug and Alcohol Abuse (PANDAA)
- Amherst County DARE Program

In addition to the many drug abuse prevention programs, VSPA contributes to volunteer programs in other areas of concern, such as:

- Portsmouth Family/Community Task Force
- Virginia Beach Council of PTAs
- Sheltered Homes of Alexandria
- Tough Love of Northern Virginia
- South Augusta Babe Ruth League
- Allegheny County ESCAPE Club
- Virginia Special Olympics
- Make-A-Wish Foundation
- Salvation Army
- VSPA Scholarship and Emergency Relief Fund

According to the Association's President, "All fund-raising programs come with problems, but we feel the positive results far outweigh the negative. We are acutely aware of the positive image of the Department of State Police and are making a good faith effort to maintain that image."
Publications: VSPA Annual Report
Founded: 1975

YOUTH LEADERSHIP VENTURE FUNDING PROGRAM
SEE LEADERSHIP DEVELOPMENT/BOARDS: CHILDREN/YOUTH

FUNDING/FUND-RAISING/RELATED SERVICES: EDUCATION

NATIONAL/STATE ORGANIZATIONS

COUNCIL ON LEGAL EDUCATION OPPORTUNITY
1800 M Street, NW
Suite 290, North Lobby
Washington, DC 20036
TEL: 202-785-4840

Objectives: To assist students who come from a background of "cyclical poverty" who would otherwise have little opportunity to attend an accredited law school due to financial and admission credential limitations.

Services: Sponsors Regional Summer Institutes at ABA-accredited law schools to prepare disadvantaged students for law school through a six-week intensive course; provides stipends for law school averaging $2,500 per academic year. (The Council is sponsored by the *Association of American Law Schools,* the *American Bar Association, National Bar Association, Law School Admission Council,* and the *Hispanic National Bar Association.*)

Sponsor: Association of American Law Schools

Publications: CLEO: Advancing Legal Education

I HAVE A DREAM FOUNDATION

31 West 34th Street
New York, NY 10001
TEL: 212-736-1730

Objectives: To motivate disadvantaged grade school students to attend college.

Services: Works to encourage disadvantaged youth to consider college; offers scholarships; oversees local, individually-run *I Have a Dream (IHAD)* projects; provides reading materials, support groups, and counseling services to sponsors of local chapters; provides information and guidance for establishment of local IHAD projects; encourages networking among local project leaders to exchange ideas and experiences; collects and shares information about project ideas; furnishes special funding for program enrichment; provides speakers to local communities; bases program on the first IHAD project started in 1981 by Eugene Lang, who pledged full college scholarships to all sixth graders in a New York City School who finished high school.

Founded: 1985

INDIVIDUAL PROGRAM PROFILES

ADAMS' EXPRESS: A MINI-GRANT PROGRAM
Teaching-for-Excellence Mini-Grant Program
Lynch Elementary School
1901 71st Avenue North
St. Petersburg, FL 33702
TEL: 813-527-7304

Purpose: To develop an innovative solution to the literacy crisis.

Sponsor: Pinellas County School System

Contact: Kay Adams, Second Grade Teacher

Description: After receiving a *Teaching for Excellence* mini-grant from the Pinellas County School System, the second grade class of Lynch Elementary School acquired a camera and a typewriter with a plan to produce a newspaper. The goal was to motivate students who were reluctant readers at the start of the year. According to the teacher, some of the pupils "would rather have gone to the dentist than write a report." At the end of the school year they had become "inquisitive reporters," anxious to write about things they read or experienced.

The metamorphosis is the result of *Adams' Express,* a newspaper that improved with each edition. A month before the end of the year, copies of the third edition were sent to the principal, offices of state and city government officials and the homes of Pinellas County residents.

Subjects tackled by the young reporters ranged from a classmate welcoming his new brother to an assessment of the oil spill in Alaska, and from a reporter's story of a student who was stabbed to a scolding look at parental misconduct at a Little League baseball game.

The mini-grants are made available by the County school system as an incentive for teachers to try innovative teaching approaches. Funds were given to 85 such projects during the 1989 school year at a cost of $115,000 - $50,000 from the school system, and $65,000 from the *Education Foundation,* composed of a group of businesses.

Grants range from $50 to $2,500 and must address a student-based problem.

A pleasant side benefit of the *Adams' Express* newspaper program was that parent involvement increased tremendously after the project began. Pupils' enthusiasm over the paper consumed parents as well. Parents provided much of the production and technical help for the paper. They also served as a "second source" for the young reporters seeking to verify information. When facts get cloudy, according to the young weather reporter, "Ask Mom." Asked what to do when that fails, her answer is "Ask Dad." According to the teacher, "In 19 years of teaching, I have never seen such cooperation from parents."

Over 400 applicants competed for the 85 grants in 1989. Approved programs included improved curriculum for gifted pupils by interaction with Eckerd College and area businesses, swimming and water safety lessons for K-3 pupils; *Project CARES (Children At Risk in Elementary School)* to identify potential dropouts; and a computer lab where volunteers work with "average" students.

EASTERN HIGH SCHOOL'S 500 CLUB
SEE BUSINESS/INDUSTRY INVOLVEMENT: EDUCATION

EDUCATION SUPPORT PROGRAM
SEE BUSINESS/INDUSTRY INVOLVEMENT: EDUCATION

JAMES MADISON NATIONAL COUNCIL
SEE LEADERSHIP DEVELOPMENT/BOARDS: EDUCATION

TOWNWIDE CENSUS
Lincoln School System
Lincoln, RI 02865
TEL: 401-726-2150

Purpose: To involve volunteers in a townside census to help the school system project its needs.

Contact: Kenneth Grew, School Superintendent

Description: Eighteen volunteers responded to a call for 20 volunteers to assist the Lincoln School System in the townwide census needed to help project education needs and qualify for adequate funding. Since 20 or more volunteers are needed to assure the most accurate census possible, and it must be done before school lets out each year, the school board faced a decision of hiring at least two paid persons (at a cost of up to $29,000) or expand the amount of time to wait for more volunteers. The decision was to tap a $25,000 fund that was never spent for a special report on the school's computer system. Since the leftover computer funds must be spent before the school year ends to keep the money, the shortage of volunteers was not the problem it might have been. All census volunteer and paid census-takers undergo a training session with the contractor hired (1989, Alpha Research) to administer the door-to-door census. Since the census must be accurate, it must be completed before school closes and families leave town for summer vacations.

Although the Superintendent felt the school committee expected more volunteers just as he did, he felt that the main concern is to have a valid instrument, and the school committee agreed. "The lesson learned that may be of help to other school systems," he said, "is that a campaign for volunteers must have enough lead time to accomplish goals set." The advent of more women in the job market than ever before, rather than a lack of interest, is considered a primary factor in lower volunteer response.

VOLUNTEERS IN ACTION
SEE FUNDING/FUND-RAISING/RELATED SERVICES: IN-KIND

FUNDING/FUND-RAISING/RELATED SERVICES: FAMILIES

INDIVIDUAL PROGRAM PROFILES

FREE THE CHILDREN (FTC)
409 Ayers Street
Memphis, TN 38105
TEL: 901-521-8084
Purpose: To reduce county welfare rolls 75 percent by 1997.
Sponsor: State of Tennessee
Contact: Bob Cannon, President
Description: The *Free The Children (FTC)* initiative has set a
target date of 1997 to reduce welfare rolls by 75 percent. Basically,
it operates with a small staff, a $300,000 state grant and other
smaller grants, the generosity of strangers, and hundreds of
volunteer hours and in-kind services from Memphis and Shelby
County governments.
The $300,000 grant received in late January 1989 had generated
$3,627 in interest by June, and had paid for nearly $50,000 in
labor costs, more than $8,000 in office expense, and $15,000 for
rent, office furniture, etc. Other grants and the services they have
made possible include:
- **Case Management Work** - funding of seven CSA case workers
  supervised by a veteran social worker ($174,738 Community
  Service Block Grant).
- **Professional Services by Groups** - funding for groups such as
  the *Volunteer Center,* which organizes volunteers for FTC, the
  Memphis Literacy Foundation, which coordinates
  literacy-related programs, and *Porter Leath Children's Center,*
  which helps form home-based day care programs ($183,174
  Community Service Block Grant).
- **Economic Development and Training Coordinator** -
  administrative support for this position (paid through CSA).
- **Nurses** - funding for two Health Department nurses to assess
  health needs of more than 140 families ($60,000 county grant).
- **Scholarships** - funding for the *Memphis Pre-Science Scholars
  Program* - a program for black junior and senior high school
  students interested in health science careers, and for the
  coordinator of the science project, who also administers an
  evaluation program for the entire FTC concept ($1 million
  Henry J. Kaiser Family Foundation grant).
- **Housing** - funding for homeownership programs for low- or
  moderate-income families ($5 million Shelby County Home
  Buyers Revolving Loan Fund grant).
Smaller funds include the *Cliff Tuck Memorial Scholarship Fund*
($928), the *Recreation Playground Equipment Fund* ($550), and
Book Friends ($1,075), the latter of which also collects children's
books (12,000 in early 1989 campaign).
Donations in early 1989 amounted to $25,000, with $5,900 coming
from individuals and $19,300 from a February fund-raiser, the
Coppertone/Maybelline Ladies Tennis Challenge.
In addition, FTC's operations manager continually seeks new
sources of funds, most recently applying to the *Plough Foundation*
for grants for a teen pregnancy program, computer equipment, and
an anti-arson program. Many other needed programs await the
results of his and other staff persons' efforts in a program that
counties across the state and in other states are observing closely
for relevance to their own areas.

U.S. OPEN VOLUNTEER COMMITTEE
SEE FUNDING/FUND-RAISING/RELATED SERVICES:
HANDICAPPED

FUNDING/FUND-RAISING/RELATED SERVICES: HANDICAPPED

NATIONAL/STATE ORGANIZATIONS

**FOUNDATION FOR CHILDREN WITH LEARNING
DISABILITIES**
99 Park Avenue
Sixth Floor
New York, NY 10016
TEL: 212-687-7211
Objectives: To address the needs of learning disabled children; to
increase public awareness of these needs.
Services: Provides direct financial support to programs which
academically and socially aid learning disabled children; sponsors
projects and fund-raising benefits; works closely with a
professional advisory board on all foundation activities; provides
information on programs and progress to any group or individual.
Founded: 1977

HUMAN RESOURCES CENTER
201 I.U. Willets Road West
Albertson, NY 11507
TEL: 516-747-5400
Objectives: To create employment opportunities for the physically
handicapped.
Services: Brings together industry, labor, education and
rehabilitation in a forum to find ways to increase and create job
opportunities for the handicapped (more than 70 major companies
and labor unions involved); provides workshops, seminars and
conferences at the Center and throughout the country; plays key
role in a national and somewhat international information
exchange network on employment of the handicapped; conducts
research on the nature of job placement practices for disabled
persons and publishes its findings; maintains coordinated divisions:
- **Human Resources School** is a specially-designed barrier-free
  facility which offers a tuition-free fully-accredited education
  program for physically-disabled children from pre-school to
  senior high.
- **The Research and Training Institute** conducts national
  demonstration studies in areas such as career education, job
  placement, independent living, attitudes toward the disabled,
  and driver training; disseminates information aimed at
  enhancing the employability and quality of life of persons with
  disabilities.
- **Vocational Rehabilitation Services** provides vocational
  evaluation, counseling, skills training, and placement; serves
  over 600 disabled adults per year between the ages of 17 and
  70.
- **Abilities Inc.** is a work center which demonstrates the
  capabilities of disabled workers (includes fields of banking,
  data processing, electronics, and other clerical and industrial
  operations).
- **Industry-Labor Council** is a membership organization of 84
  major corporations and unions, including Warner-Lambert
  Company, Mobil Oil Corporation, General Electric Company,
  Xerox Corporation, and International Brotherhood of
  Electrical Workers, which assists industry/labor nationwide to
  develop employment opportunities for disabled Americans.
- **Independent Living Project** is a program for senior high
  school students and high school graduates (one of four
  organizations selected for federal grants to develop and
  administrate projects).
Publishes numerous guides and manuals for business, industry, and
labor, for groups and individuals working with the handicapped,
and for the handicapped themselves in areas of education,

placement, work independence, recreation and others (request complete catalog).
Founded: 1952

INDIVIDUAL PROGRAM PROFILES

CPSS FASHION SHOW
SEE VOLUNTEERS: HANDICAPPED

DAISY (FRIEND-RAISER) BALL
Kessler Institute for Rehabilitation Auxiliary
1199 Pleasant Valley Way
West Orange, NJ 07052
TEL: 201-731-3600
Purpose: To raise funds for the Kessler Institute for Rehabilitation.
Contact: Shelly Mandel, President
Description: The annual fund-raising ball of the *Kessler Institute Auxiliary* has come to be known the "Friend-Raiser Ball."
Organizers have found that making friends for the Institute is more fun than raising funds, and once the friends see the work that is done at the Institute, they provide the funds anyway.
One of the goals of the auxiliary is to help the Institute realize its goal in a $2.5 million building campaign. The Auxiliary's pledge is $300,000, and it is ahead of schedule. Another $50,000 remains, and there is a full year-and-a-half before the total is due.
Besides money volunteers from the auxiliary and the community assist in all other areas of the physical rehabilitation operation, as they have since its beginning in 1948. Many came through the efforts of the auxiliary's "friend-raiser" activities. They work for both in-patient and out-patient services, which have been expanded into Bergen, Passaic and Union counties. Volunteer board members help decide the allocation of funds among research projects, educational programs, and advanced equipment. Other volunteers continually study and restructure the many activities of the Institute for maximum benefit and growth. One way of returning something to the community is the Institute's policy to open its auditorium to the general public for community activities.

FLINT AIRSHOW
Bishop Airport Authority
3425 West Bristol Road
Flint, MI 48507
TEL: 313-766-8620
Purpose: To raise funds for Area XIII Special Olympics, while providing entertainment for the community.
Sponsor: US/DoD - Air Force
Contact: Michael W. Mills, Director
Description: The *Flint Airshow* has an economic impact each year of more than $1.5 million to the Flint area, and a major impact on the annual budget of *Area III Special Olympics.* Organizers feel that the show, which features the *United States Air Force Thunderbirds* and is geared toward family entertainment, is a way to give something back to the community for their assistance.
The beginnings of the show are in 1984 when, with virtually no money, a handful of volunteers, and very little support, the City of Flint and Bishop Airport approved plans for the event. Since then the Airshow has grown to be Genesee County's single largest weekend event with a budget of more than $250,000. It includes skydivers, wing-walkers, and other athletic feats as well as airplane maneuvers. The show represents a year's planning and organizing, and 500 volunteers throughout the year. In addition to raising funds, volunteers work with scheduling and other logistical aspects of the show. Planning for the subsequent year begins almost immediately following the close of each show.
The majority of volunteers come from *Area III Special Olympics.*
Other volunteers include the *Genesee County Sheriff's Department*

and its Special Deputies, *125th Combat Support Company of the Michigan Army National Guard, Young Marines, ROTC, Flint Township* and *Flint Police,* Flint businesses, and many others. Beginning with the 1990 show, the future of the *Flint Airshow* is in the hands of the *Bishop Airport Authority.*
The director believes that the fact that the Airshow is financed entirely by corporate sponsorship, advertising, and admission tickets and volunteer staff is a success story of its own.
Founded: 1984

FRED RUFFING MEMORIAL SCHOLARSHIP
Annandale Christian Community for Action (ACCA)
7200 Columbia Pike
Annandale, VA 22003
TEL: 703-256-1378
Purpose: To provide scholarships to handicapped students.
Sponsor: ACCA
Contact: George Davis, Chairman
Description: ACCA awards a scholarship each year to one or more handicapped graduating high school seniors in the Northern Virginia area. The idea for the scholarship grew out of the interest Fred Ruffing, ACCA's Founder, had in the handicapped. He was spearheading a program for the deaf at his workplace at the time of his death.
The *Fred Ruffing Memorial Scholarship* honors the achievements of young persons who have risen to the special challenges in their lives. It is hoped it will give them the leverage needed for tackling the next rung on their educational ladders. It also gives ACCA volunteers an opportunity to establish a model to demonstrate the commitment of the community to education.
By 1989, ACCA had awarded $19,800. Recipients include students with vision, hearing, learning, muscular and paralytic problems. Among the careers they are pursuing are human services, geology, medical records technology, child development, history, economics and math.
Publications: ACCA Annual Report

JAIL 'N BAIL ON CAPITOL HILL
March of Dimes
National Capital Area Chapter
2700 South Quincy Street, Ste 220
Arlington, VA 22206
TEL: 703-824-0111
Purpose: To raise funds to help prevent birth defects.
Sponsor: US Congress Staff; March of Dimes
Contact: Leo Schargorodski, Editor
Description: In December 1988, Capitol Hill staffers were "arrested" by the March of Dimes of the National Capital Area - by agreement - to help prevent birth defects; the "Hill Arrest" involved the incarceration of good-natured volunteers at the Tiber Creek Pub in the Bellevue Hotel on Capitol Hill.
The "jailbirds" were sentenced to calling their friends and business associates, seeking donations for the March of Dimes.
Participating offices included those of Congressmen Oberstar, Whittaker, Hunter, Kyl, Chandler and Ackerman, and of Senator Metzenbaum.
Although many staffers claimed they were "framed" in the "Hill Arrest," the only "record" these ex-cons had to beat was a goal of $12,000 to ensure a healthy birth for all of their newborn and future constituents.
Publications: Jail 'N Bail Report

KAISER ROLL
SEE BUSINESS/INDUSTRY INVOLVEMENT:
HANDICAPPED

U.S. OPEN VOLUNTEER COMMITTEE
School of the Holy Childhood
1150 Buffalo Road
Rochester, NY 14611
TEL: 716-436-9200
Information also available from:
Twigs Volunteers for the U.S. Open
Norma Horn, Chairwoman, Rochester General Hospital
Association
Rochester, NY
Purpose: To raise money for a school for the handicapped (School
of the Holy Childhood), and a birthing center (Rochester General
Hospital Association).
Sponsor: U.S. Open Golf Tournament
Contact: Lynda Kessler Newman, Chairman
Description: Volunteers at the U.S. Open work for pay at the
concession stands - $4.50 an hour. It is a unique way of raising
funds for their service programs, since the entire paycheck goes to
the volunteer project they represent.
The *School of the Holy Childhood* will use the money it raises
either for general education expenses or a planned
20,000-square-foot expansion of its woodworking shop. The
workshop helps residents become independent, since they work for
a wage there. The final decision comes through a school board
vote after the funds are received.
The *Rochester General Hospital Association* set a target of
$15,000 from their U.S. Open volunteers to be applied to its
$700,000 pledge to the *Twig Birthing Center* at the hospital. The
Center is designed to allow a room for mothers and fathers to stay
overnight with their newborns to help develop the initial family
bond with the infant.
In return for their efforts, the volunteers - some in their seventies -
are able to watch the Open when their shifts end.

UNE SOIREE PARISIENNE (AN EVENING IN PARIS)
Outreach & Escort
San Jose, CA 95101
TEL: 408-436-2865
Purpose: To raise funds for a program designed to help disabled
people lead independent lives.
Sponsor: Outreach & Escort
Contact: Terry Bialas, Event Coordinator
Description: Outreach & Escort is a service that finances the
transportation needs and support services that allow disabled
people to lead independent lives. Each year, volunteers and staff
plan a fund-raiser using a theme that mimics an exotic, distant
locale. The 1988 event was a lavish *Far East Fest* featuring Asian
food, music and dance.
The theme for 1989 is *Une Soiree Parisienne* or *An Evening in
Paris,* chosen for the program's tenth anniversary to coincide with
the bicentennial of the French Republic. Much care was taken to
assure that people will savor the tastes, sights and sounds of Paris
in the evening, with four-star French cuisine, and strolling
musicians, singers and can-can dancers providing the
entertainment. American and French flags were displayed, with
both national anthems played while they were being put into place.
The lavish experience costs an individual $89.10, and a group of
ten (one table) $891.00. Both types of reservations are quickly
depleted after announcements are made of the unique cultural
opportunities each year. This event is a major fund-raiser for
Outreach & Escort, which annually serves more than 7,000
disabled people.

WHITE CANE DRIVE
SEE VOLUNTEERS: CIVIC GROUPS

FUNDING/FUND-RAISING/RELATED SERVICES: HEALTH

NATIONAL/STATE ORGANIZATIONS

PROJECT CONCERN YOUTH PROGRAM
SEE VOLUNTEERS: STUDENTS

INDIVIDUAL PROGRAM PROFILES

ARLINGTON HOSPITAL FOUNDATION
Arlington Hospital
Development Office
1701 North George Mason Drive
Arlington, VA 22205
TEL: 703-558-6613
Purpose: To keep pace with ever-changing technology, maintain
the highest quality service, and work hard to control costs.
Contact: James L. Rieder, President
Description: The *Arlington Hospital Foundation* brings together
consumers and providers as partners to help maintain the quality
and affordability of healthcare in Northern Virginia. In 1989,
nearly 7,000 individuals, corporations, service clubs and
foundations contributed toward hospital programs, medical
equipment, nursing scholarships and endowments.
Through programs like *Friends of Nursing,* the *Galen Society,*
Associate Membership, the *Annual Ball,* and the *Golf and Tennis
Tournament,* the community donated $1.44 million to the
Arlington Hospital Foundation.
Accomplishments of the *Foundation* during 1989 include:
- Continuation of the long-standing teaching affiliation with
  Georgetown University;
- Addition of an open heart surgery program;
- Approval of an ambulatory care center (construction to begin
  in 1990);
- Opening of the *Women's Health Connection* in Tysons
  Corner;
- Expanding of the *Arlington Treatment Center* in Harrisonburg
  (addiction treatment); and
- Continuing work through *Arlington Joint Ventures Group,*
  which oversees joint ventures with area hospitals and
  physicians to provide services to local residents, and the
  Arlington Health Services Corporation, which generates
  revenue for the hospital by operating the parking garage on
  the hospital campus.
Without the community as a *partner in healthcare,* many of these
programs would not reach fruition. With community support, the
Foundation continues to work toward providing the best possible
health services to the residents of Northern Virginia. One way the
Foundation "gives back" to the community is to offer members
special benefits such as one hour free parking, a special discount
on mammograms, cafeteria discounts, reduced rates for hospital
seminars, and the *Prime Time 55* (formerly *65 plus*) program with
special seminars and other benefits for older persons, among
others. Full details are available on request.
Publications: Health Reach

BACK ROADS BIKE TREK
American Lung Association of Northern Virginia
9735 Main Street
Fairfax, VA 22031
TEL: 703-591-4131
Purpose: To raise funds to assist the American Lung Association
of Northern Virginia.

Description: The *American Lung Association of Northern Virginia (ALA)* is the beneficiary of a cycling weekend each year in which cyclists raise pledges for each mile of cycling. Called the *Back Roads Bike Trek,* the 1990 event covered 100 miles of the Old Dominion's scenic countryside, from Nokesville to Fredericksburg. Trekkers traveled a mapped route that included lunch on the banks of the Rappahannock, Chancellorsville Battlefield Park, and an overnight stay at the Holiday Inn South's Indoor Recreation Center in Fredericksburg.

Volunteer cyclists are accompanied by trained staff, "sag wagons," mechanical and emergency care, radio support and refreshments. Cyclists must be 18 years of age or older unless accompanied by a parent. They pay a tax-deductible registration fee of $25, which includes all meals, hotel lodging, food along the route, a *Back Roads Bike Trek* T-shirt, maps, accompanying support, and a one-month free membership to all area *Courts Royal* and *Sport and Health* clubs. In addition, volunteer trekkers are required to raise a minimum of $250 in pledges before the trek.

The 1990 event was the fifth annual trek, and each year volunteer support is greater, according to an ALA official. "The volunteers seem to find this a great way to meet and help others while enjoying a sport and comraderie," he said. "Lung disease is a devastating illness, and we never know when or where it will strike next. The funds raised through the trek are helping to cure, and perhaps eradicate, this disease."

SUMMERFEST ART FAIRE
Logan Regional Hospital
Logan , UT 84321
TEL: 801-752-2050
Purpose: To raise funds for the hospital's 24-hour emergency response system for the elderly and disabled.
Sponsor: Logan Regional Hospital
Contact: Marilyn Sedgwik, Chairwoman
Description: Community artists, musicians, merchants and volunteers come together each year in Logan to create and operate *Summerfest Art Faire,* which draws artists, performers and visitors from across the country. The festival is organized by the volunteer directors of *Logan Regional Hospital* with help in 1989 from the *Utah State University Chamber of Music* and many local merchants.

Entertainers included a saxophonist from the *Tonight Show Band,* who performed a free concert, a production of the musical *Carousel* in the historic Capitol Theatre produced by a nationally-known vocalist, a well-known jazz artist, and other celebrities. Additions in 1989 were an antique carousel merry-go-round brought in from another county, and a new "guest artist" display featuring new artists who created and painted for visitors as well as displaying their work. Local artists continued to display their work as in years past, and local restaurants participated by providing food.

The hospital volunteers have found that by organizing this event they help erase the image of "pink ladies" that some people harbor. The program for which all of the effort is expended is *Lifeline,* an electronic system that keeps the hospital in touch with people who may require emergency treatment. Each year the festival attracts more people from out-of-town and out-of-state.

FUNDING/FUND-RAISING/RELATED SERVICES: HOMELESS

INDIVIDUAL PROGRAM PROFILES

HELP THE HOMELESS MILLION DOLLAR SHOOTOUT
Charity Sports
c/o Grubbs Oldsmobile
I-30 & 183 South
Fort Worth, TX 76119
TEL: 817-560-9000
Purpose: To benefit a Fort Worth charity which helps the homeless in the Fort Worth area.
Sponsor: Grubbs Oldsmobile
Contact: Project Director
Description: In summer 1989, *Charity Sports* mounted a golf project designed to help improve and increase the services of a Fort Worth charity working with homeless people in the area. The charity, *Loaves & Fishes,* was founded in 1982 by Franciscans and includes *The Soup Kitchen,* which feeds between 150 and 300 homeless and hungry people daily, employment counseling, and other services.

Charity Sports brings together the business community in a concerted, eight-day effort to help relieve the financial burden of *Loaves & Fishes* so that services can be expanded as needs among the homeless arise. Some of the merchants provided "free shot coupons" to encourage participation, and four participating car dealers - Grubbs Oldsmobile, Longhorn Dodge, Alan Young Buick, and Hilcher Ford - offered new 1989 cars to winners of the competition. As a further incentive, the dealers put the prize cars on display well in advance of the event - a luxury car, a converted van, a pickup truck, and a convertible.

The games were held at four local driving ranges, with shots costing visitors $1 each. The two top contestants each day move into the final competition.

A *Charity Sports* spokesperson said that the needs of the target volunteer organization keep growing, and "it is our hope that the results of our efforts during this event will fill a big part of these needs."

SPARE CHANGE PROJECT
Volunteer Fund Raising Committee
9255 Sunset Boulevard
Suite 620
Los Angeles, CA 90069
TEL: 213-550-6771
FAX: 213-550-7105
Purpose: To raise funds for the Family Assistance Program of Hollywood.
Sponsor: The Ford Group; Business/Industry
Contact: Judith A. Katz or Linda Ford
Description: In November 1987, a group of professional men and women from the business community created the *Spare Change Project,* a campaign to raise funds for the Family Assistance Program (FAP). The Spare Change Project was founded by a public relations agency with the help of friends and associates in the PR and entertainment fields who volunteer their time and resources to develop and implement fund raising activities for FAP.

FAP is a privately-funded organization that was created in 1984 to counsel and assist those homeless families who are willing to do something to help themselves. FAP works with social service agencies, and the Employment Development Department to find jobs and adequate housing for homeless families.

The Spare Change Project promotes its fundraising efforts via a massive public service campaign with public service announcements by celebrities - most recently Martin Sheen and Gregory Hines. The Project is coordinated by a committee of individuals and organizations including advertising agencies, public relations firms, media specialists, graphic artists, entertainers, musicians, fundraisers, and restauranteurs. Funds raised are directed at efforts to work with homeless families in Los Angeles County in areas of employment, training, counscling, housing, education and transportation - helping families once again to become productive members of society.

The Spare Change Project launched its first massive public service campaign during the Summer of 1988 throughout Los Angeles. It included people in the entertainment industry doing radio and television PSAs using very recognizable names of actors, elected officials, comedians, and related personnel as honorary board members, and highlighting over an extended period the plight and needs of homeless families in Los Angeles. The goal was $500,000 for organizations working in a comprehensive way with homeless families. Since that initial successful campaign, many events have been mounted by the Committee, including: a celebrity-studded concert, an art auction (works by Rembrandt, Picasso and others), a celebrity bowling tournament, a restaurant celebration of the Eiffel Tower Centennial, a photo auction of polaroid pictures taken by celebrities (*A Vision of Home*), etc.

Other plans are in progress with the continued collaboration of public relations and advertising firms to create supportive promotional relationships. One film director said, "Our support of FAP has become an important part of our lives. We hope that, more and more, others will feel that way, too."

Publications: Spare Change Project; Spare Change Summary; Spare Change Press Kit
Founded: 1987

FUNDING/FUND-RAISING/RELATED SERVICES: HOUSING

NATIONAL/STATE ORGANIZATIONS

MORTGAGE BURNING FUND
PO Box 762
Annandale, VA 22003
TEL: 703-354-6270
Objectives: To provide crisis assistance when older persons are victims of the "fine print" in equity and other housing loans.
Services: Provides crisis intervention assistance and psychosocial support services to older homeowners in financial trouble regarding their homes; addresses financial documents drawn up "within the law," but containing language that create emergency situations regarding imminent loss of the home; works toward changing legislation to preserve a specified portion of an elderly person's home equity from indebtness no matter how long they live in the house; provides emergency funds when legality is in question but cannot be challenged; maintains a bureau of experts to work with the lender to help the elderly person or persons stay in the home; administers donations from private business/industry to provide crisis intervention when appropriate; provides assistance only after all over avenues are exhausted and only to stabilize the situation; provides counseling when the only alternative for the older person has been deemed by expert legal counseling to relocate.

NATIONAL HOUSING PARTNERSHIP
1126 Sixteenth Street, NW
Washington, DC 20036
TEL: 202-223-4844

Objectives: To stimulate the production by private industry of low- and moderate-income housing through partnerships with community organizations, developers, builders at the local level.
Services: Provides equity capital and joint venture funds to partnerships it forms; provides working capital to single family home builders through its Small Business Investment Company (licensed by Small Business Administration); functions with staff of specialists provided by the National Corporation for Housing Partnerships, its administrative arm; rehabilitates old, and constructs new, buildings for Section 8 programs; works with FmHA in the development of housing for senior citizens and families in rural areas and small communities; publishes various materials on its rural and urban programs; participates in NCHP annual meetings; manages low- and moderate-income housing nationwide.

US/HUD - OFFICE OF FAIR HOUSING AND EQUAL OPPORTUNITY
400 Seventh Street, SW
Washington, DC 20410
TEL: 202-755-7252
TOLL FREE: 800-424-8590
Objectives: To assist rural Americans with supervised credit and technical assistance in four primary areas: housing, farming, community programs, and business/industrial development.
Services: Provides loans and grants to rural Americans, including:
- **Homeownership Loans** - money to buy, build, or improve homes, including housing sites; certain housing debts may be refinanced; for low- or moderate-income.
- **Rural Rental Housing** - loans to build, maintain, and operate rental facilities for low- to moderate-income families.
- **Repair and Rehabilitation Housing Loans** - to make repairs to remove health and safety hazards; for very low income.
- **Self-Help Technical Assistance Grants** - to provide technical assistance to families in self-help homebuilding; grants to public agencies or nonprofit corporations who provide assistance.
- **Farm Ownership Loans** - long-term credit to family size farmers to purchase farms or to make major improvements.
- **Emergency Loans** - credit to farmers and ranchers in designated disaster areas for actual losses to property or production.
- **Water and Waste Disposal Loans and Grants** - to install or improve rural community water systems, sewage disposal systems or solid waste disposal systems.
- **"Other" Community Facility Loans** - credit to build or improve public-use facilities, such as hospitals, fire and police departments, community centers, libraries, schools publicly-owned recreation centers, and other essential community facilities.
- **Business and Industry Loan Guarantees** - guarantees assuring up to 90% repayment of funds from commercial lenders to establish a variety of enterprises in rural areas, including towns up to 50,000 population; interest rates and repayment terms negotiated between lender and borrower.

VIRGINIA PARTNERSHIP FUND AND OTHER PROGRAMS
Virginia Department of Housing & Community Development
State Office Building
205 North 4th Street
Richmond, VA 23219-1747
TEL: 804-786-1575
Objectives: To provide housing assistance for low-income, handicapped and elderly people.
Services: Oversees a number of housing assistance programs to assist special populations, including:
- **Virginia Partnership Fund** - established in 1988 to increase housing opportunities for low-income households throughout

Virginia. Three programs under this fund either directly or indirectly benefit persons with disabilities:

- **Emergency Home Repair Grant** - funds repairs to properties which present an immediate health and safety threat; also funds grants of up to $1,000 per household to be used for accessibility adaptations for people with physical disabilities. [Of the 513 jobs funded by this grant in the past year, 80 of them involved unit adaptations for persons with physical disabilities.]
- **Multifamily Production Loan Program** - provides low-interest loans to developers for the construction of new housing for low and moderate income persons; adheres to Uniform Statewide Building Code which requires that in developments of 21 to 99 units, at least one of those units must be accessible; if more than 100, one unit per 100 or fraction thereof.
- **Congregate Housing Loan Program** - benefits persons who are elderly or disabled, providing up to $250,000 per project to be used to rehabilitate or construct new units for individuals who are not able to function without assistance; includes separate rooms for individuals with a central food preparation area and group dining area.

Works with a federal program available through the Department of Housing and Urban Development (HUD) - *Permanant Housing for the Handicapped Homeless* - which offers funding through states to developers to construct permanent housing for people with disabilities. [When approved, states are required to provide a 50% match and monitor project sponsors.]

Administers Virginia Uniform Statewide Building Code regulations (Section 512.0), which addresses accessibility based on the American National Standard Specifications for making public buildings and facilities accessible to and usable by persons with disabilities.

Brings together representatives of persons with disabilities and the housing industry to discuss changes required by the federal *Fair Housing Amendments Act,* producing proposed amendments agreed to by both groups. Many other activities of the department serve special members of the Commonwealth.

Sponsor: State of Virginia
Contact: Neal J. Barber, Director

TRAINING PROGRAMS

ADOPT-A-FAMILY
Columbus Board of Realtors
200 Town Street
Columbus, OH 43230
TEL: 614-221-5353
Sponsor: Columbus Board of Realtors
Contact: Beverley Halterman, Chairperson
Description: To celebrate *American Home Week* in April 1989, the *Columbus Board of Realtors* initiated a new seminar program, *Adopt-A-Family,* designed to help families earning $15,000 to $24,000 per year to buy homes. It started with five seminars held in various parts of the city, where Realtor and lender volunteers met with potential buyers. Seminars attracted as many as 70 families, 75 to 100 Realtor volunteers, and more than a dozen lender volunteers. The highest attendance was at *Beery Middle School,* where the principal took a personal interest and recruited families. Volunteers work with families one-on-one.

Seminars help families look realistically at their income-debt ratio, and work toward paying off debts to help qualify them for purchasing a home. The 1989 seminars produced 40 families with a potential for home purchase, and the goal is to get at least 25 of them into their own homes. Some will be delayed until their financial situations are better, with volunteers staying with them until they qualify. Six families were "in contract" within 30 days of the last seminar. The volunteer project helped some with down payments and closing costs.

Word spread quickly about the program, and the board continually receives calls from families and volunteer Realtors and lenders who want to be involved. The board hopes to hold the seminar program each year, and plans to suggest similar projects to other boards around the country.

INDIVIDUAL PROGRAM PROFILES

HOMELESSNESS PREVENTION PROGRAM
SEE GOVERNORS' OFFICES ON VOLUNTEERISM: NEW JERSEY

HOUSING PROGRAM OF ACCA
SEE VOLUNTEERS: CHURCH/SYNAGOGUE MEMBERS

FUNDING/FUND-RAISING/RELATED SERVICES: IN-KIND

NATIONAL/STATE ORGANIZATIONS

GIFTS IN KIND
700 North Fairfax Street
Alexandria, VA 22314
TEL: 703-836-2121
Objectives: To encourage non-cash, gifts-in-kind donations from businesses to supplement financial support of voluntary human service organizations.
Services: Provides assistance that enables companies and businesses to give products, goods, services, and other nonmonetary items to voluntary human services organizations and arts and education programs; identifies and selects needy health and human service agencies and arts and education programs as recipients; administers details involving taxes and transportation to facilitate corporate donating; informs the public of the donor's generosity; works to improve efficiency and capacity of this type of supplement to financial support; promotes in-kind giving as an effective means to help donors manage inventory and lower storage costs and warehousing demands; works with the *United Way* to establish local programs to encourage and facilitate gift-giving; assists United Way-operated in-kind programs through technical assistance, publications and workshops.
Sponsor: United Way of America
Publications: Profile: In-Kind Giving
Founded: 1983

INDIVIDUAL PROGRAM PROFILES

GIFTS IN KIND AMERICA
United Way of America
700 North Fairfax Street
Suite 300
Alexandria, VA 22314-2045
TEL: 703-836-2121
Purpose: To help local communities tap potential contributors of goods and services in "their own backyards."
Sponsor: United Way of America
Contact: Daphne Coerse
Description: Gifts In Kind America (GIKA), a new associate program of United Way of America, is designed to add to the national corporate donor base through in-kind gifts - the donation

of goods and services. Through a variety of specially-designed marketing materials, local United Ways are able to develop a program that encourages local businesses to donate goods and services to human-care agencies. Examples of local efforts include:

- **Houston, Texas** - The United Way of the Texas Gulf Coast has incorporated in-kind giving into its annual campaign. Information about contributions of goods and services are included in loaned executives' campaign packets. This reaches small companies who can donate services more easily than large monetary gifts. Printing and advertising are the services most requested by local United Way agencies, followed by skilled labor such as plumbing and electrical work needed by shelters and agencies. A *Gifts In Kind Newsletter* has been developed by the agency to communicate to both agencies and corporations about the benefits in both directions of this type of giving.

- **Seneca Falls, NY** - Even before GIKA surfaced, the United Way of Seneca County received a truckload of clothes from K-mart Corporation (March 1989). A communitywide volunteer effort included a volunteer trucking company, soldiers who volunteered from a nearby army depot, people from 16 local agencies to sort and distribute garments, and a local seamstress who organized several church groups' volunteers to repair some of the clothes (mostly needing zippers, which were requested and received from the *Talon Company* - about 20,000 of them). The many examples of people in crisis and poverty who benefited from the clothing received much local press coverage, which has demonstrated to area businesses how much in-kind gifts can improve the quality of life throughout a rural area such as Seneca County.

There are two levels of GIKA associate membership. Marketing tools are available from GIKA on a year-round basis - camera-ready logo artwork and news releases, public-service print and radio advertisements, and other materials - all of which can be localized.

VOLUNTEERS IN ACTION

1000 Coconut Creek Boulevard
Coconut Creek, FL 33066
TEL: 305-973-2205
Purpose: To assist the community college in continuing to offer programs and services during a time of decreased budgets.
Sponsor: Broward Community College, North Campus, Community Services
Contact: Judy Fink, Coordinator
Description: Volunteers in Action was created in 1981 to develop and train a corps of volunteers to serve Broward Community College, North Campus, in a wide range of volunteer assignments, thereby reducing the current strain on staffing while improving services to students and community. The program is funded primarily by *Community Services - Community Instructional Services (CIS)* and supplemented by a small grant through the college's *Staff and Program Development (SPD)* grant program. The program has grown from August 1981 when one volunteer donated twenty-one hours to a current average of forty-four, donating 650 hours. Volunteers serve in various positions throughout North Campus (i.e., Behavioral Science, and Political Science research assistants, Newspaper editor, Tutors, Advisement and Registration assistants).
Volunteer Assignments - Volunteers are interviewed by the volunteer coordinator and a second time by a department supervisor. The job descriptions allow a volunteer to choose a position most suitable to his/her experience and interests. The interview with a supervisor allows volunteers to further explore their prospective duties, and acquaint themselves with work site and supervisor. If both the supervisor and volunteer are satisfied, an orientation time is set with the Volunteer Coordinator.
The volunteer is expected to be available at least four hours a week for one term. The orientation, which covers general college

information in one half hour, is followed by on-the-job training. Unique volunteer opportunities are available on college campuses. A man volunteers as the hands for a handicapped student - going to class with him to take notes and tests. Although difficult to refrain from helping, this means writing the test answers down right or WRONG! Another is the "eyes" for a blind instructor. Several work in the Career Placement Center, assisting students and community residents with career exploration. The book store, test monitoring, test grading, typing, reading and writing labs also involve volunteers in positions that challenge their skills, allow them to grow and assist the college programs to operate as efficiently and effectively as possible.
Volunteer Staff Recognition - Volunteer/Staff recognition and appreciation are important aspects of the program at *Broward Community College*. The day-to-day "thank you" a volunteer receives and the climate in which they work are the responsibility of the staff. Recognition and reinforcement of this effort is especially important. The coordinator interviews and places the volunteer. Much of the rest of the relationship and job assignment are the responsibility of the staff person. At *Broward Community College* both receive periodic "thank you" notes from the volunteer coordinator. Both receive periodic "comfort conferences" (our term for an evaluation and growth builder). In the second term of volunteering, both volunteer and staff involved with supporting and supervising volunteers receive Broward Community College Coffee Mugs.
In the second year of volunteering both receive a canvas book bag. Certificates were presented at first Annual Recognition Coffee. Broward Community College tie tacks were presented at the second.
The Recognition coffee is short...one hour. The Provost and Dean make very short "thank you" speeches, pins are presented informally rather than in a formal ceremony. The object is food, fun, fellowship and appreciation. The feedback from staff and volunteers has been positive for each Coffee.
The success of this program lies in its organization. Goals and Objectives are written, every job has a written job description, sign-in sheets are used, evaluations - on-going and exit - are conducted, and statistics are recorded. A monthly statistical report is filed, enabling an annual report to be easily compiled with a narrative, both of which are useful for program justification and refunding.
Broward Community College also offers program assistance to area volunteer programs, libraries, social service agencies and schools.
Founded: 1981

FUNDING/FUND-RAISING/RELATED SERVICES: JUSTICE

NATIONAL/STATE ORGANIZATIONS

LAW ENFORCEMENT ASSISTANCE PROGRAM

US/DoJ - Law Enforcement Assistance Agency
Criminal Justice Assistance Div.
Washington, DC 20531
TEL: 202-476-3611
Objectives: To provide assistance to criminal justice programs where a need is indicated.
Services: Provides grants, advisory services, counseling, training, and other services in the major areas of crime control (police, courts, corrections, etc.); requires a letter expressing need for service; includes short-term on-site visits and assistance in evaluation among its services; maintains files on previously-funded

programs such as (1) Corrections Innovations Assistance, (2) Treatment and Rehabilitation for Addicted Prisoners; publishes information concerning available consultative services, and numerous guides, handbooks and other program materials.
Sponsor: US/DoJ - Department of Justice

FUNDING/FUND-RAISING/RELATED SERVICES: NUTRITION

NATIONAL/STATE ORGANIZATIONS

COMMUNITY FOOD AND NUTRITION PROGRAM
US/HHS - Office of the Secretary
PO Box 1182
Washington, DC 20201
TEL: 202-245-7000
Objectives: To help communities counteract the conditions of hunger and malnutrition among the poor.
Services: Provides financial and training assistance to extend and broaden food programs (whether federally-funded or supported by state or local public or private resources); enables local programs to provide services such as emergency foodstuffs to low-income families; emphasizes the design of programs that will stimulate services through other institutions and organizations; suggests that programs include advocacy as an integral part of its program to assure that the views of the poor are heard, involves the poor themselves in planning and operation, and working in one of the following four areas:
- Access - increase participation of the poor in federally-funded programs;
- Self-help - improve the capability of the poor to purchase and produce food efficiently;
- Nutrition and Consumer Education - to improve the understanding of the poor in matters of diet and health;
- Crisis Relief - to improve methods for emergency provision of foodstuffs; publishes detailed instructions regarding this program.

PROJECT CONCERN YOUTH PROGRAM
SEE VOLUNTEERS: STUDENTS

SHARE OUR STRENGTH (SOS)
SEE VOLUNTEERS: PROFESSIONALS

INDIVIDUAL PROGRAM PROFILES

NEIGHBORS HELPING NEIGHBORS
SEE BUSINESS/INDUSTRY INVOLVEMENT: NUTRITION

TASTE OF THE NATION
SEE VOLUNTEERS: PROFESSIONALS

FUNDING/FUND-RAISING/RELATED SERVICES: RECREATION

NATIONAL/STATE ORGANIZATIONS

FUND FOR ADVANCEMENT OF CAMPING
PO Box 8
Hatteras, NC 27943
TEL: 919-986-2163
Objectives: To stimulate and fund innovative projects to benefit the organized camping/outdoor activity experience; to increase the scope and effectiveness of camping for children and youth.
Services: Funds pilot projects and research; provides camping scholarships; sponsors Camping Unlimited, which conducts intergroup projects and activities; publishes quarterly newsletter; convenes semiannual trustee meetings.
Publications: Occasional Papers
Founded: 1965

TURRELL FUND
15 South Munn Avenue
Orange, NJ 07018
TEL: 201-678-8580
Objectives: To promote and support recreation programs for children and youth, with special emphasis on the needy youngster.
Services: Aids youth organizations in setting up and maintaining recreational facilities and programs; provides money for inner-city children to take part in camping expeditions and special cultural activities (other thrusts are juvenile rehabilitation, family service and child guidance); publishes the *Turrell Fund Annual Report* which reviews its year's activities on behalf of youth and children (currently gives priority to requests from the states of New Jersey and Vermont).
Publications: Turrell Fund Annual Report

FUNDING/FUND-RAISING/RELATED SERVICES: SELF-HELP

NATIONAL/STATE ORGANIZATIONS

CAMPAIGN FOR HUMAN DEVELOPMENT
SEE SELF-HELP: TENANTS/RESIDENTS

FUNDING/FUND-RAISING/RELATED SERVICES: WALKS/RACES

INDIVIDUAL PROGRAM PROFILES

AIDS-WALK NEW YORK
GMHC Walkathon
Gay Men's Health Crisis
Old Chelsea Station
PO Box 10
New York, NY 10113
TEL: 212-807-6310

Purpose: To raise funds for the programs of the *Gay Men's Health Crisis.*

Contact: Leif Green, Event Manager

Description: AIDS Walk New York is a ten kilometer fundraising walkathon benefiting *Gay Men's Health Crisis (GMHC).* The funds raised support the many programs and services provided by GMHC, the largest nonprofit AIDS service, education and advocacy organization in the world, and the first organization to confront the AIDS epidemic.

In mid-1990, GMHC was working with 2,800 clients. Services provided include case management, crisis intervention, financial advocacy, legal services, a hot-meal service, and a buddy program, among others.

Most of the work of organizing the *AIDS Walk* each year is performed by volunteers. Each year, hundreds of people donate time to make sure that the Walkathon is a success. Volunteer activities include:

- **Phonebanking (evenings)** - The Walkathon phonebank takes place during the evenings, with fifteen volunteers on duty each telephoning GMHC supporters to ask them to register for the Walk.
- **Tabling on Weekends** - During each weekend in April of each year, volunteers sign up walkers at designated locations.
- **Office Help on Weekdays** - Volunteers are needed on weekdays to send out Walk materials and assist staff with other Walk-related tasks.
- **Walk Day** - In 1990, tasks on the day of the event required 900 volunteers to serve as *Safety Monitors, Registration Volunteers, Checkpoint Workers,* and *Crowd Control Assistants.* Volunteers are credited with completing the full ten kilometers and may raise funds as well.

Corporate and community groups support *AIDS Walk* by forming teams representing them. These groups include fields of advertising, banking, communications, entertainment, fashion, health care, law, public relations, publishing, securities, and transportation, as well as numerous community groups, schools, and government agencies. A lighter side of the team effort comes in the form of "friendly competition." For example, *American Airlines* flight attendants are being challenged by the flight attendants of *TWA* and *PanAm.* Many teams provide T-shirts, breakfasts, and parties for their team members to encourage full participation. Some companies provide each participating employee with a separate corporate donation. Many companies have a "matching grant" policy for employee donations to charity, and often this donation system is used for the Walk.

In addition to assisting GMHC in providing services, Walk funds help in the production and distribution of AIDS prevention and related information, and a portion of the net Walk proceeds - 15% - is used to fund grants to a number of different organizations whose programs assist people affected by HIV-related illnesses. In 1989, more than $3 million was raised for that year's 6.2-mile walk from 125,000 sponsors. Information about participation in *AIDS Walk New York* is available throughout the year.

Publications: Walk Update; AIDS Walk New York Information Package

CHAMPIONS RUN FOR LIFE TORCH RELAY
Jonathan Jaques Children's Cancer Center
Long Beach Memorial Medical Center
2801 Atlantic Avenue
Long Beach, CA 90806
TEL: 213-595-8592
Purpose: To raise money for the Cancer Center, while giving patients a morale boost.
Sponsor: Local corporations and individuals
Contact: Dr. Jerry Finklestein, Director
Description: Almost 100 young cancer patients trotted and wheeled around the circular sidewalk of *Long Beach Aquatic Park* in a relay race held each year to raise funds for the *Jonathan*

Jaques Children's Cancer Center and to give a morale boost to the young patients. The torch relay provides funds for a school reintegration program and psychosocial support services, which were not available before the race program was instituted. Since they were added to the cancer center's agenda, these two programs have made a big difference in the overall treatment of the children. Especially dramatic improvements have been in the social and psychological programs made available by the fundraising effort. The nearly 100 racers from the center - from toddlers to teenagers - carried the torch, which was a gold-painted flashlight adorned with a crown. Hundreds of family members, sponsors, doctors, celebrities (over 40) and volunteers cheered them on.

Each patient ran, walked, rode or wheeled at least an eighth of a mile on the sidewalk around the park's lagoon. The relay's corporate sponsors and benefactors had donated more than $75,000 to set up 13 way stations along the route. Each station had its own rooting section, with all stations cheering in unison as the relay got underway.

The torch relay was followed by a dinner dance and auction. Funds are earmarked for the Cancer Center's endowment fund and its research, education and social programs.

FROM ALL WALKS OF LIFE
AIDS Action Committee
131 Clarendon Street
Boston, MA 02190
TEL: 617-437-6200
Purpose: To raise funds for AIDS service organizations.
Sponsor: Bank of Boston; Shawmut Bank
Contact: Larry Kessler, Executive Director
Description: From All Walks of Life is a 10 kilometer (6.2 mile) walk for AIDS care and research in Massachusetts. The event has become a major source of funds at a time when adequate funding is not forthcoming from federal, state and city sources. The 1989 walk drew nearly 15,000 participants, including some AIDS patients and parents of AIDS patients.

Since its beginning in 1986, the walk has become the single largest fund-raiser for AIDS service organizations in the Commonwealth. The 1989 walk generated $600,000 in grants to 34 AIDS community centers, coalitions, and hospices. The U.S. Surgeon General participated in the 1989 event.

Before the walk there was an aerobic stretch to music led by a fitness instructor, followed by opening ceremonies and a low-cost breakfast. Community support was evident throughout the day. Twenty members of Patriots Trail Council of the Girl Scouts of America made stickers with messages, which were handed out to walkers at water stops. *China Educational Tours of Dorchester* donated a 16-day tour of China to be awarded to the walker earning the highest dollar amount of pledge money. Thirty-six music groups performed along the route - one teen-age group performing *Stop the Madness,* its new single about AIDS. *Creative Gourmets Ltd.* enlisted 200 volunteers to prepare 10,000 vegetable sandwiches on pita bread to be served with a piece of fruit and other food items in sandwich boxes and distributed at the end of the walk. Vendors in the area contributed food for the lunches. Fifty radio stations throughout the state simultaneously broadcast Dionne Warwick's *That's What Friends Are For* at the conclusion of the walk.

Sponsors included the *Bank of Boston, Boston Globe Foundation, Bank of New England, Lotus Development Corporation, John Hancock Financial Services, Digital Equipment Corporation, New England Medical Center Hospitals* and *Shawmut Bank.*

WALKAMERICA
March of Dimes Birth Defects Foundation
National Capital Area Chapter
2700 Quincy Street, Suite 220
Arlington, VA 22206
TEL: 703-824-0111

Purpose: To raise funds to help prevent birth defects.
Sponsor: March of Dimes Birth Defects Foundation (national); local business, industry, and individuals
Contact: S. Ross Hechinger, Honorary Chairman
Description: WalkAmerica is the March of Dimes national walk-a-thon. The national capital area chapter sponsors WalkAmerica annually in April. It is the biggest springtime event in the Washington, DC metropolitan area. Thousands of people come out for a festive day of fun and fellowship, while raising money to fight birth defects.
Whether walkers raise $5 or $5,000 by walking the 30 kilometer event, the money helps to secure a healthier beginning for all of our children.
TeamWalk is people walking together as a team of *WalkAmerica.* It is a very popular volunteer activity with corporations and organizations. Teams adorned in T-shirts and hats show their team pride and take on the competition. Building a team is an organizational activity and is considered a challenge, a way of meeting people with similar concerns and talking about civic involvement, and a way of helping give every baby a healthy start in life. In addition, volunteers say "It is fun!"
In what is called "The Team Recipe," the Teamleader coordinates the team effort, sets team goals, develops strategies to reach goals, and is the "spark" that makes things happen. He or she must first organize a committee to help promote the team, recruit team members, challenge another department or division within the company, and help encourage the registration and fill out cards. This Chapter uses the "Pyramid Method," which asks each person that registers to recruit three other people among family, friends and associates.
Team promotion includes announcements in the Company newsletter, letters from the boss, Company prizes, "Team Barometer" using a wall chart with names of walkers, and close collaboration and cooperation with committees.
Organizational backing is represented by endorsement of top management, a company van to supply refreshments to team along walk route, recognition of walkers by the company after the event, setting a Corporate Challenge in funding goals and challenging another company within the industry classification.
Tips to walkers include: arrive early, dress appropriately, listen to your body, celebrate.
Committee members include U.S. Treasury Department, Virginia Power, DC Public Schools, United Airlines, House of Representatives, Ameritemps, Stouffer Hotels, Hechinger Company, Children's Defense Fund, Sovran Bank, Electrical Workers' Union, and others.
Publications: TeamWalk Team Leader Guide

GOVERNORS' OFFICES ON VOLUNTEERISM

NATIONAL/STATE ORGANIZATIONS

ASSEMBLY OF STATE OFFICES ON VOLUNTEERISM
c/o KY Office of Volunteer Services
275 East Main, #6W
Frankfort, KY 40621
TEL: 502-564-4357
Objectives: To serve as a membership organization and
coordinating point for Governors' Offices on Volunteerism (GOVs)
across the country.
Services: Provides information on the overall goals and objectives
of *Governors' Offices on Volunteerism (GOVs)* in areas of
volunteerism, national service, and private sector initiatives;
maintains profiles of individual GOVs (44 in existence at press
time); answers questions by phone, mail or on-site visit about goals
and objectives, conferences and meetings, contact persons, and
other information and activities of member GOVs; works with
both public and private sector agencies and organizations to assure
that the GOVs make the best use of their time and resources in
helping to improve the quality of life in communities across the
nation.
Contact: Norma W. Johnson, Directory, Kentucky Office of
Volunteer Services

NATIONAL GOVERNORS' ASSOCIATION (*formerly National
Governors' Conference*)
Hall of the States
North Capitol Street
Washington, DC 20001
TEL: 202-624-5300
Objectives: To provide a forum through which governors can
influence the development and implementation of national policy
and apply creative leadership to state problems.
Services: Operates the *Office of State Services,* a vehicle for sharing
information among the states (the 50 states, Guam, American
Samoa, the Virgin Islands, the Northern Mariana Islands, and
Puerto Rico); keeps the federal government informed of the needs
and perceptions of the states; provides technical assistance to
governors on a wide range of issues, including health, education,
welfare reform, information management, and others of concern to
the Governors as new issues arise, especially following changes in
federal government administration; assists in research and
development areas by undertaking demonstration projects and
providing research on important policy issues; maintains a number

of committees in areas including: human resources, energy and
environment, communications, transportation, criminal justice,
economic development, and agricultural and rural development;
works with the *Council of State Planning Agencies* and the
National Association of State Budget Officers; holds two
conferences a year, winter and summer; publishes bulletins, a
directory, conference proceedings, monographs, and other
materials.
Publications: Governors' Bulletin; Policy Positions; Governors of
American States, Commonwealths, Territories; Governors'
Priorities; Conference Proceedings

TRAINING PROGRAMS

EXPLORING NEW FRONTIERS IN VOLUNTEERISM
SEE TRAINING/CONFERENCES/TEACHING

GOVERNORS' OFFICES ON VOLUNTEERISM: ALABAMA

NATIONAL/STATE ORGANIZATIONS

GOVERNOR'S OFFICE ON VOLUNTEERISM/AL
64 North Union Street
Rooms 13-15
Montgomery, AL 36130
TEL: 205-261-3020
Objectives: To promote and support volunteerism in the State of
Alabama.
Services: The state office on Volunteerism was established as a
grassroots citizens movement and it continues to draw from a
broad and diverse spectrum of volunteer leaders in carrying out its
mission.
The Governor's Office on Volunteerism (GOV) is a statewide
resource administered by the Governor of Alabama. GOV services
are available to state and local agencies and organizations in the
public, private and voluntary sectors. GOV goals are:
 • To serve as a statewide advocate regarding issues affecting

volunteers and their respective volunteer organizations.
- To develop and maintain communication with and among the volunteer community and promote greater public and private sector cooperative and coordination of resources.
- To provide training and technical assistance to volunteer leaders, managers, administrators, and community coalitions and volunteers.
- To encourage and participate in volunteer recognition activities and events to increase the visibility and status of volunteers and their accomplishments, and to encourage greater citizen participation in voluntary efforts.
- To strengthen and expand volunteer programs within Alabama state departments and agencies and promote increased citizens' participation in state services.
- To serve as an information clearinghouse on volunteerism.

GOV seeks to serve all organizations and individuals interested in volunteerism. Although GOV does not offer direct service or recruitment and placement of volunteers, the office actively encourages and supports such community activities with professional staff available at all times to respond to questions or requests for information or assistance from across the state.
GOV holds an annual conference directed by a Steering Committee consisting of representatives from all segments of the community. Publications include a quarterly newsletter, a recognition packet, guides, conference reports, and other materials, all free on request.

Contact: Joyce St. John-Marcus
Publications: Volunteer Alabama - Give Five; Volunteer Alabama (quarterly newsletter); Volunteer Alabama Recognition Packet; Volunteers - Our Caring Alabama; Volunteers - The Spirit that Supports Alabama; Bill S. 233 (legislation on volunteer liability); Beyond Promises: A Guide for Rural Volunteer Program Development

TRAINING PROGRAMS

THE SPIRIT THAT SUPPORTS ALABAMA - VOLUNTEERS
SEE TRAINING/CONFERENCES/TEACHING

VOLUNTEERS... OUR CARING ALABAMA
SEE TRAINING/CONFERENCES/TEACHING

INDIVIDUAL PROGRAM PROFILES

GIVE FIVE ALABAMA
Governor's Office on Volunteerism/AL
64 North Union Street
Rooms 13-15
Montgomery, AL 36130
TEL: 205-261-3020
Purpose: To increase charitable giving and volunteering by individuals.
Contact: Donna Huntley, Statewide Coordinator
Description: "Give Five Alabama" is a statewide two-year voluntary initiative developed to promote involvement of individuals in a direct and satisfying way to help other people and address community problems. For charitable agencies it is an opportunity to develop new and enlarged sources of financial and volunteer support. For the public, private and independent sectors, it is an opportunity to come together as the "golden triangle" working for a common cause. The program is based on a standard for excellence in giving and volunteering set by the Governor - five percent of annual household income and five hours of volunteer service each week to causes of one's choice.
Give Five Alabama is a special project of the Governor's Office on Volunteerism. The Governor has designated a lead agency in each

of the 57 counties to serve as the Give Five Liaison. He has appointed a state chairman and a statewide steering committee. Give Five's primary goals are:
- **Goal One** - To establish a climate for giving and volunteering so that society as a whole and individuals in particular are conditioned to the importance of private philanthropy and voluntary service.
- **Goal Two** - To develop a far greater ability of voluntary organizations to raise money and involve volunteers.

Complementary to a national program of the Independent Sector entitled "Daring Goals for a Caring Society," Give Five Alabama is one of only three such statewide efforts. Moving into the forefront as a model program, it is the only effort in the nation initiated by the Governor's Office to adopt the promotion of Give Five as a standard of excellence for all to strive toward in their charitable and volunteer activities. Give Five Alabama has three components:
- Public Awareness (media campaign);
- Comprehensive Data Base (information gathering); and
- Statewide Statistical Survey.

According to the Governor, "As a result of this project, it is hoped that more people in Alabama will be aware of the importance of charitable giving and volunteering, and will be able to apply the concept of Give Five as a standard by which they can measure their own activity. And, that existing efforts by area nonprofits to facilitate volunteering and giving by citizens will be enhanced and the seeds for future activities will be planted in local communities and throughout the state."
Publications: Give Five Communications Portfolio
Founded: 1988

GOVERNORS' OFFICES ON VOLUNTEERISM: ARIZONA

INDIVIDUAL PROGRAM PROFILES

THE VOLUNTEERISM PROJECT
1515 East Osborn Road
Phoenix, AZ 85014
TEL: 602-263-8853
Purpose: To increase the pool of volunteers available to the human services community in order to partially offset reductions in services caused by reductions in public funds.
Sponsor: Community Council, Inc.; the Arizona Department of Economic Security; Valley of the Sun United Way; Volunteer Center of Maricopa County; US/HHS - Department of Health and Human Services
Contact: Irene K. Rasmussen
Description: The Community Council, the Arizona Department of Economic Security, and the Volunteer Center of Maricopa County initiated a project to increase the use of volunteers by public and private agencies. Special assistance has been given by the Valley of the Sun United Way. The goals of the Volunteerism Project are:
- To increase the pool of volunteers available to the human services community in order partially to offset reductions in service caused by reductions in public funds;
- To enable agencies seeking additional volunteers to use and retain these volunteers effectively; and
- To assure that the need for volunteers continues to be communicated in our community, and that adequate numbers of volunteers are continually placed in and retained by agencies.

The Arizona Department of Economic Security contracted with the Community Council for the services of the Director of the

Project. The Valley of the Sun United Way supported the Volunteer Center with two years of special grants to cover the extra intake staff person and extra telephone, supplies, etc. The U.S. Department of Health and Human Services awarded a 17-month grant to the Community Council to do further research and to assist the Volunteer Center to determine demographic and attitude characteristics of volunteers and non-volunteers. The regular funding of the Community Council and the Volunteer Center supported the portion of their core staffs' time which is devoted to the Project. The corporate community has supported the recruitment drive through direct contributions, in-kind services, and volunteer time of their corporate staffs.

GOVERNORS' OFFICES ON VOLUNTEERISM: ARKANSAS

NATIONAL/STATE ORGANIZATIONS

ARKANSAS DIVISION OF VOLUNTEERISM
Department of Human Services
Donaghey Bldg, Ste 1800, Box 1437
Little Rock, AR 72203-1437
TEL: 501-682-7540
Objectives: To encourage volunteerism as a means of community and state problem-solving through promotion, technical assistance and leadership.
Services: Promotes the importance of volunteerism; supports volunteer activities statewide; works with other statewide offices that exist to promote volunteerism; provides non-partisan encouragement for the effective coordination and channeling of voluntary action in order to improve the quality of life for Arkansas citizens; assists in the planning and implementation of its programs through its staff and an Advisory Council appointed by the Governor. Established in 1977 by Act 865, the Office was mandated to:
- Assess and recognize the needs of communities throughout Arkansas and recruit, train and coordinate volunteers and volunteer organizations in meeting those needs.
- Assist in specific projects involving volunteers to meet community needs.
- Provide greater public awareness and recognition of volunteer efforts.
Works to establish a program for voluntary action by the people as well as government action in every community; provides numerous and various services for agencies, organizations, and private citizens of Arkansas, including:
- training and workshops on managing volunteers;
- legislation concerning volunteers;
- recognition of volunteers through certificates and awards ceremonies for both individuals and communities as a whole.
In addition the ADV:
- promotes Arkansas Volunteer Month and National Volunteer Week;
- manages a Volunteer Consultants program;
- provides technical assistance as requested;
- publishes a journal, studies, and other materials; and
- operates an *Information Center* containing its own materials and those of others deemed beneficial to Arkansas volunteer leaders, all either free or available for loan.
Contact: Billie Ann Myers, Director
Publications: Involvement; Volunteers and Insurance: An Arkansas Guide; ADV Resource Library Center; Legislation on Volunteerism (Act 42 and Act 398); Management Bridge: Building a Sound Volunteer Program; Economic Impact of Arkansas

Volunteers; UCRC Organizational Handbook
Founded: 1977

INDIVIDUAL PROGRAM PROFILES

SILVER HAIRED LEGISLATIVE SESSION
Arkansas Division of Aging and Adult Services
Department of Human Services
PO Box 1437
Little Rock, AR 72203
TEL: 501-682-8511
Purpose: To bring attention to the needs of senior Arkansans.
Sponsor: Arkansas Division of Aging and Adult Services; eight Area Agencies on Aging
Contact: Bean Hudson, Advocacy Supervisor
Description: The Silver Haired Legislative Session (SHLS) is a one-day mock session with older Arkansans serving as delegates in a very special session at the State Capitol. The 1988 session was the 6th biennial session conducted to bring attention to the needs of older persons in Arkansas.
The senior "delegates" have the opportunity to write bills, work in committees, speak on the floor of the House Chamber, and vote their opinion. The success rate of a Silver Haired bill or resolution is much higher than for legislation during a real General Assembly session. Only two of the 24 bills and one of the 11 resolutions failed to pass.
During the opening ceremonies, state and elected officials welcomed the delegates and let them know how serious their Silver Haired work is to the General Assembly. They assured the delegates that they would be reading the SHLS bills carefully.
Five Silver Haired committees met in the House committee rooms to discuss bills in six important topic areas: (1) health care cost containment; (2) nursing home reform; (3) transportation issues; (4) taxation and retirement income; (5) alternatives to nursing homes, and (6) consumer concerns. Eight of the 24 bills addressed alternatives to nursing homes and indicated great concern about this issue.
At the close of the program the delegates were reminded that "on August 31 you were legislators, but after the session you should continue to be 'lobbyists' for the interest of the elderly." He added that grassroots support through their group was instrumental in the success of a number of bills, especially in the area of nursing home reform.
The Silver Haired Legislation Session is sponsored by the Arkansas Division on Aging and Adult Services with assistance from the eight Area Agencies on Aging. A complete report of all aspects of the SHLS, including copies of bills that were passed, is available from the Division.
Publications: Silver Haired Legislation Session Report

UNIFIED COMMUNITY RESOURCE COUNCIL
SEE COMMUNITY SERVICES

GOVERNORS' OFFICES ON VOLUNTEERISM: COLORADO

NATIONAL/STATE ORGANIZATIONS

COLORADO OFFICE OF VOLUNTEERISM
State Capitol Building
Room 24
Denver, CO 80203
TEL: 303-866-2595

Objectives: To encourage, promote and advocate for increased volunteer participation in non-profit organizations and government agencies - especially in rural areas - to meet growing human, social and environmental needs throughout Colorado.

Services: The Colorado Office of Volunteerism (COV) was created by Executive Order by the Governor of Colorado in December 1979 to fulfill the purpose stated above. With a decreasing grant from ACTION, and funds from the Governor's Office, the organization was established under the supervision of a twenty-one member Advisory Board and thirteen Regional Directors who act as a local liaison for the state office in regional volunteer activities, projects, programs and concerns of the volunteer community. Activities of the Office of Volunteerism include:

- **Training** - COV sponsors, coordinates and participates in regional organizational and agency workshops on various aspects of volunteer management including recruitment, training, supervision and recognition of volunteers as well as fund raising, marketing, public relations, media and networking.
- **Technical Assistance** - COV gives individual and group technical assistance to government agencies and non-profit organizations on starting or restructuring volunteer programs, funding and grant-writing and other issues related to volunteerism. Technical assistance given in 1981-82 included such organizations as the Colorado Department of Corrections, Young Volunteers in Action Program, USDA National Forest Service and Alternative Homes.
- **Advocacy and Legislation** - COV keeps the volunteer community informed on pending state and national volunteer legislation, regulations benefits and issues related to volunteerism.
- **Education and Public Relations** - COV publishes and mails a quarterly newsletter to approximately 7,000 volunteer organizations. COV encourages and promotes media coverage of volunteer opportunities, training recognition and special events.
- **Recognition** - COV assists in year-round recognition of outstanding volunteers and once each year, during National Volunteer Week, hosts a Volunteer of the Year Awards Banquet honoring thirty outstanding volunteers from Colorado.

Sponsor: Governor's Office
Contact: Ann Hamilton, Executive Director
Publications: Civics
Founded: 1979

GOVERNORS' OFFICES ON VOLUNTEERISM: CONNECTICUT

TRAINING PROGRAMS

CONNECTICUT LEADERSHIP CONFERENCE
Governor's Council on Voluntary Action/CT
80 Washington Street
Hartford, CT 06106
TEL: 203-566-8320
Credit: Inquire
Contact: Alice L. Clive, Volunteer Management and Training Coordinator
Description: Thirty workshops are included in *Connecticut Leadership,* the statewide training event for volunteers and people who work with volunteers, from the nonprofit, public, and private sectors. The1990 session is the thirteenth annual conference and, as with most of our annual conferences, features a keynote

address, information exchange area, early bird networking session, buffet lunch, and a closing reception. Although topics change, a typical conference might include:

- **Paper and Time Management** - Make the most productive use of your time with time-management techniques, identifying and eliminating common time wasters, curing paperwork paralysis, and mastering the art of delegation.
- **Recruiting, Retaining, Recycling and Recognizing Volunteers** - You asked for it... a morning devoted to learning how. The afternoon provides the opportunity to get together in small groups and share successes and solutions to problems. This is a two-session workshop. Attendance both morning and afternoon is required.
- **Corporate Social Responsibility** - To provide the business community with an overview and some specifics of the variety of ways that the private sector can interact with the non-profit to build mutually supportive and beneficial relationships.
- **Conflict Management** - Techniques to resolve conflict constructively.
- **Succeeding with Public Relations** - An approach to creating and communicating your organizational image.
- **Public Speaking** - How to make an effective presentation. This is a two-session workshop. Attendance both morning and afternoon is required. Limited to 15.
- **Assertiveness Training** - Learning methods to communicating your point of view clearly and effectively.
- **Group Decision-Making** - Recognizing and using the full potential of your group for more effective decision-making.
- **Awareness of Attitudes of Racism and How They Affect Volunteerism** - Attitudinal and cultural differences and how they influence behavior.
- **Serving on Boards and Committees: Volunteer Roles and Responsibilities** - An overview of legal and practical considerations for effective service.
- **Leadership for Meetings** - Techniques for running an effective meeting.
- **Stress Management** - Burn-Out - Learn to set priorities, identify sources of support and develop life-coping skills. Topics include differing lifestyles, time-management, relaxation techniques, approaches to stress mediation.
- **Advocacy for Administrators of Volunteer Programs** - Promoting recognition and status for your program and position.

Faculty is drawn from universities, volunteer centers, business/industry, civic groups, state departments, etc. Logistical support is provided by some numerous organizations, associations, businesses/industries, state agencies, colleges universities, volunteer centers, etc.

GOVERNOR'S CONFERENCE ON VOLUNTEERS IN ENERGY*
Governor's Council on Voluntary Action/CT*
80 Washington Street
Hartford, CT 06106
TEL: 203-566-8320
Credit: Inquire
Sponsor: US/ACTION
Contact: Karen S. Lee
Description: The statewide forum on energy is convened by the Governor's Council on Voluntary Action to enable participants to learn about volunteer projects, exchange ideas and volunteers and local and state officials, expand volunteer involvement, and plan for the future.

Preceding the workshops are "Swap Shops" - small groups of participants exchanging ideas, techniques and suggestions for new projects for volunteers. Of the three workshops that follow, participants are asked to select two - one for the morning and one for the afternoon session. Workshop topics are:

- *Workshop A* - **Energy and Crisis Intervention** - Information on both private fuel banks and volunteer involvement in government assistance programs, especially outreach to the elderly and the handicapped.

- *Workshop B* - **Energy Conservation and Your Community** - Successful energy conservation projects done by local groups; programs to encourage individuals to change their energy habits.
- *Workshop C* - **Expanding Your Community's Energy Awareness** - Model awareness campaigns; strategies for the 1980s.

Each workshop includes a section on Energy Issues in the Hispanic Community. Between morning and afternoon sessions, a panel presentation is offered by staff from the Massachusetts Office of Citizen Participation on Fitchburg Action to Conserve Energy. The conference wrap-up - Where Do We Go From Here? - is presented by the Connecticut Governor's Council on Voluntary Action.

Although designed to bring together volunteer leaders and local/state officials, the conference is open to all interested citizens.

During the course of the proceedings, community volunteers active in energy conservation throughout the state are recognized.

GOVERNOR'S YOUTH ACTION CONFERENCE
Governor's Council on Voluntary Action/CT
80 Washington Street
Hartford, CT 06106
TEL: 203-566-8320
Credit: Inquire
Sponsor: Governor's Council on Voluntary Action/Youth Action Committee
Contact: Judy Halpern
Description: Several hundred student leaders and advisors from Connecticut's middle, junior, and senior high schools attend this statewide conference each year to share information about school-sponsored volunteer programs and community needs. The theme at a recent conference was "Youth Can Make a Difference" and participation numbered more than 425. Fifteen workshops were offered, and included the following:

- Working With the Media
- Recruiting, Retaining, Recycling, and Recognizing Volunteers
- Working With the Elderly
- Persons With Disabilities and Their Needs
- Alcoholism - What the Student Volunteer Can Do
- Peer Counseling and You
- Fund Raising - What Works!
- Encouraging Participation in Student Volunteering

In addition to participating in the workshops, students and advisors had the opportunity to discuss ideas, techniques, and project suggestions in regionally grouped swap shops. Each participant also received a packet of resource information about student volunteerism and a copy of a "Youth Can Make A Difference" poster.

The Youth Action Conference is organized by the Governor's Youth Action Committee of the Governor's Council on Voluntary Action and is supported by state funds and contributions from private sources. At the 1982 conference, lunches were provided by the Connecticut General Insurance Company and posters were provided by the Travelers Insurance Company. There is no registration fee for the participants.

Also see "Training for the Municipal Volunteer Coordinator," cosponsored by the Connecticut Conference of Municipalities.

GOVERNORS' OFFICES ON VOLUNTEERISM: DELAWARE

NATIONAL/STATE ORGANIZATIONS

DIVISION OF VOLUNTEER SERVICES
156 South State Street
PO Box 1401
Dover, DE 19901
TEL: 302-736-4456
Objectives: To support and increase volunteerism to alleviate unmet needs in Delaware.
Services: Supports and expands volunteerism in Delaware through professional, structured programs; enables the retired to contribute their vital skills to the public benefit through Retired Senior Volunteer Programs (RSVPs) in New Castle and Sussex Counties and the Foster Grandparents Program on a statewide basis; fulfills unmet needs of nonprofit organizations and State agencies by the matching of volunteers of all ages and walks of life to meet the needs of Delawareans in areas such as human services, education, cultural institutions, etc.; targets efforts to respond to special emphasis areas such as literacy, at-risk children, the homeless, and drug programs; recognizes outstanding contributions of volunteers through annual awards programs and recognition events; specific programs include:

- **The Volunteer Link** - a volunteer clearinghouse which matches potential volunteers (both individuals and groups) with community needs; recruits volunteers through "Volunteers Needed" columns in printed media and PSAs (public service announcements) on electronic media, advertising, participation in community groups, public speaking, etc.; distributes recruitment brochures over a wide area.
- **Governor's Outstanding Volunteer Awards** - recognition for exemplary volunteer service by individuals, organizations, businesses, and youth.
- **Senior Volunteer Services** - ACTION-sponsored volunteer programs for older persons - "Retired Senior Volunteer Program (RSVP)" which is operated in two counties, and "Foster Grandparent Program (FGP)" which is statewide.

Also operates a Corporate Volunteer Program, and provides listings of short- and long-term group projects, works with the Department of Public Instruction to develop volunteer programs within the schools, and develops new programs as unmet needs surface.
Contact: Nancy F. Olsen, Director
Publications: Outstanding Volunteer Awards

VOLUNTEER LINK *(formerly Volunteer Clearinghouse)*
Delaware Division of Volunteer Services
Department of Community Affairs
156 S. State Street, PO Box 1401
Dover, DE 19903
TEL: 302-736-4456; 302-571-2620
Other locations:
Division of Volunteer Services
Carvel State Office Building
810 French Street
Wilmington, DE 19801 571-7620
Dover Public Library
45 South State Street
Dover, DE 19901 736-0677
Eastern Sussex Family YMCA
105 Church Street
Rehoboth Beach, DE 19971 227-8018
Georgetown Public Library

10 W. Pine Street
Georgetown, DE 19947 856-1814
Objectives: To serve as a voluntary action center for the entire state of Delaware.
Services: Historically, *Volunteer Link* began in March 1984 in New Castle County as a pilot project of the *Coalition on Volunteerism* to serve as a countywide volunteer clearinghouse. The *Delaware Division of Volunteerism* was part of the Coalition as was the United Way and other community organizations. Funding was provided through grants.
In September 1986 the program was moved to the State Division of Volunteer Services so that it could grow and better serve Delaware's entire population.
To foster maximum participation, the program has five local contact points - staffed offices in Dover and in Wilmington and three computer-linked satellites in various downstate locations. Over 400 organizations and agencies across the state request individual volunteers and volunteer groups to fill a variety of needs. Volunteers range from student to retiree, from professional to homemaker, and opportunities are available in all areas of interest. Skills and interests are matched by computer to agencies needing assistance. The list of matches is provided to the volunteer, complete with contact persons, addresses and phone numbers, and the volunteer makes the selections for contact.
Sponsor: Delaware Division of Volunteerism
Contact: Marilyn H. Levin, Administrator
Publications: Don't think about it... do it!
Founded: 1984

TRAINING PROGRAMS

VOLUNTEERS DO MAKE A DIFFERENCE!
Delaware Department of Health and Social Services
Division of Mental Health
Delaware State Hospital
New Castle, DE 19720
TEL: 302-421-6011
Credit: Inquire
Sponsor: Coalition on Voluntarism
Contact: Carol A. Wells, CAVS
Description: With a grant from the Delaware Humanities Forum, the Coalition on Voluntarism conducted a participatory conference with the goal of providing a historic overview of voluntarism and to exchange ideas and resources. The decision to provide this opportunity for the volunteer community in Delaware was based on the belief that the voluntary sector will play a crucial role in the next decade in improving delivery of social services in America. Issues addressed include:
Motivation Begins with the Volunteer
- self-image
- risk-taking
- creativity

Upgrading the Volunteer's Status
- support systems
- recognition

Finding the Volunteer's Niche
- improving volunteer/staff relationship
- decision-making for the volunteer

Voluntarism as a Career/A Way to a Career
- continuing education in voluntarism
- the volunteer professional

Power Without Portfolio
- advocacy, a new role
- decision-making

The Next Generation
- voluntarism as a tradition
- citizen participation in the future

A unique and informal tool opened the morning session - a play

presented by the National Council of Jewish Women entitled, The Day the Volunteers Stayed Home. The keynote address was presented by Dr. Ivan Scheier, with other faculty being drawn from the University of Delaware and the Governor's Commission on the Status of Women.
[Coalition members include Junior League of Wilmington, Martin Luther Foundation, Greater Wilmington Development Council, Rotary Club, United Way of Delaware, Retired Senior Volunteer Program (RSVP), National Council of Jewish Women, the Wilmington Mayor's Office, Wilmington Medical Center, and the Delaware Volunteer Coordinators.]

INDIVIDUAL PROGRAM PROFILES

PRESCHOOL DIAGNOSTIC AND DEVELOPMENTAL EDUCATION NURSERIES
54 South State Street
Dover, DE 19901
TEL: 302-736-6038
Purpose: To serve developmentally delayed children and their families.
Sponsor: Delaware Department of Health and Social Services
Contact: Nancy Reihm
Description: PDDEN I opened in January 1973 and PDDEN II in 1980. They are administered by the Division of Public Health, Office of Speech and Hearing Services with funds allocated by the State Legislature and from the Department of Public Instruction (P.L. 89-313 and EHA, Part B, P.L. 94-142). These nurseries are designed to serve children (1 1/2 to 4 years of age) residing in Kent County and nearby areas of lower New Castle County and upper Sussex County, with developmental delays in speech/language, motor, social and/or cognitive skills.
In PDDEN I diagnostic assessment, individualized education plan, speech therapy, individual, family and group counseling services are provided. Activities are designed to enable the staff to observe and assess the child's strengths and weaknesses in order to determine how best to accelerate development. Special diagnostic studies and services are arranged through either the Division of Public Health programs or other agencies. Children may attend this nursery for four months.
PDDEN II is a developmental nursery designed to serve those children who have attended PDDEN I and are not eligible or cannot be served by local education agencies, private nurseries or special programs. Here they receive ongoing educational and developmental programming based on PDDEN I evaluation and observation. The objective here is to raise the child to an optimum level of functioning. The length of time a child remains in this program depends upon the individual needs and progress of the child.
Volunteers work one 2-1/2 period each week and at other times if needed. They assist the teachers in most functions and work with children in small groups and individually. Some volunteers attend Delaware State College as well as workshops with the PDDEN staff. The only supervision needed is a briefing on each new child that enters the program.
Founded: 1973

RSVP OF NEW CASTLE COUNTY
Hudson State Service Center
501 Ogletown Road
Newark, DE 19711
TEL: 302-368-6874
Purpose: To enable people 60 years of age or older to volunteer.
Sponsor: Delaware Department of Community Affairs
Contact: Marion Seibold
Description: RSVP (Retired Senior Volunteer Program) of New Castle County, Delaware, has over 1,000 active members who

serve at over 125 different sites, contributing over 240,000 hours of service to the community each year.

RSVP has been a resource in New Castle County since 1973. One of its unique services is transportation - we provide transportation for nearly 70 seniors each week, to and from their volunteer assignments, with the help of paid and volunteer drivers, and provide mileage reimbursements for nearly 400 members.

While the vast majority of our members serve outside their homes at agencies and organizations, we also try to develop opportunities for homebound seniors to volunteer. About 40 volunteers knit all year long: in December, they donate more than 1,500 items to a dozen different agencies for distribution to needy families. Our five mail groups process over 200,000 items each year for about 25 non-profits.

We have also developed some innovative projects for frail elderly residents of nursing homes, linking them with non-profits that need their expertise.

GOVERNORS' OFFICES ON VOLUNTEERISM: HAWAII

TRAINING PROGRAMS

VOLUNTEER TRAINING PROGRAM FOR VOLUNTEER ADVOCATES
Hawaii Protection and Advocacy Agency
1580 Makaloa Street
Honolulu, HI 96814
TEL: 808-949-2922
Credit: 3 hours (Leeward Community College)
Sponsor: Hawaii Protection and Advocacy Agency
Contact: Patty Henderson
Description: Hawaii's volunteer advocacy program was started in 1974 by the Hawaii chapter of the Association for Retarded Citizens (ARC). Today it is administered by the Hawaii Protection and Advocacy Agency. Training is an important part of the program, which has two components:
- **Citizen Advocates** - volunteers who enter into a one-to-one relationship with the developmentally disabled on a long-term basis.
- **Advocacy for Our Community Volunteers** - citizens who are specialists and work on specific problems for the developmentally disabled.

Since assuming responsibility for the Volunteer Advocacy Program, the Protection and Advocacy Agency has offered 115 training sessions and trained 250 private citizens as volunteer advocates.

In addition, Leeward Community College offers a three-hour credit course on advocacy skills, which is attended by disabled as well as non-disabled volunteers. Kapolani Community College offers a course in self-advocacy as part of its community education program on Advocates for the Rights of the Disabled.

Training programs for advocates attempt to give the volunteers "a mind-set which provides the advocates a reason for staying as an advocate." Recently, ten new trainers were initiated statewide, and 4618 media announcements mentioned one or another component of the citizen advocacy program. These efforts are aimed at making the prospect of being a citizen advocate more attractive, more visible and carrying more prestige.

A trainer's manual for the volunteer advocate in a teaching role, and a self-advocacy handbook for the developmentally disabled themselves have been widely distributed nationally. An important part of the self-advocacy training is developing the ability to train others to be self-advocates.

Other sponsors include H-CAP, Hawaii Office on Aging, and US/ACTION.

INDIVIDUAL PROGRAM PROFILES

HAWAII STATE YOUTH VOLUNTEER BOARD*
Office of the Governor
1270 Queen Emma Street
Honolulu, HI 96813
TEL: 808-548-8539
Purpose: To promote unity among Hawaii's youth service organizations through project collaboration.
Sponsor: Voluntary Action Center; Office of the Governor; youth service organizations
Contact: Dexter T. Suzuki, Coordinator
Description: The Hawaii State Youth Volunteer Board (HSYVB) is an independent organization which works with and is sponsored by the Volunteer Information and Referral Service (a voluntary action center), and Statewide Volunteer Services, Office of the Governor. The Board is composed of selected state leaders from youth service organizations including Key Club, Keywanettes, Youth Against Cancer, and the National Honor Society.

In addition to their work to avoid overlap in services offered by Hawaii's youth service organizations, the Board strives to:
- assist in finding solutions to common problems voiced by all clubs;
- help in designing and implementing innovative and meaningful projects;
- improve volunteer education and training; and
- protect all clubs involved from exploitation.

Since its inception in 1977, Board projects have included:
- **Statewide Litter Campaign** - the Board's first major project. Members of youth organizations converged on three districts, cleaning up the areas and culminating the day with a picnic at a local park.
- **Wellness Celebration** - an Oahu-wide Health Fair held at a local community college. Youth organizations assisted in setting up and providing manpower for the two-day event.
- **Youth Employment Conference** - a meeting designed to address the issue of credit for volunteer experience in job application situations. The conclusion presented to the community and business/industry was that the youth involved in Hawaii's communities on a voluntary basis were developing marketable skills and, therefore, volunteer experience should be recognized by employers. They pushed for two specific policies in this regard. In addition, the Board urged employers to grant an interview to every applicant seeking employment to help them gain confidence in job-seeking efforts.

NORTH SHORE CIVIL DEFENSE TEAM
State of Hawaii
3949 Diamond Head Road
Honolulu, HI 96816
TEL: 808-734-2161
Purpose: To prepare for emergencies and respond to disasters.
Sponsor: State of Hawaii
Contact: Linda Fulp, District Two Coordinator
Description: The 45 volunteers who are responsible for responding to natural disasters on the North Shore of Hawaii use their own vehicles and gas, and respond to an island-wide siren warning system. An initial training program enables volunteers to use the equipment provided, and hard hats and badges are assigned. Fearing that the fact that Hawaii has not experienced a natural disaster in a number of years has created apathy, in mid-1989 the volunteers approached a newly-created, five member *Citizens Advisory Commission* with some concerns they have had for some time about the inadequacy of both equipment and training. The primary concern of North Shore residents is high-wave conditions

which can cause extensive damage and loss of life if warnings are not timely.

Citizens from the community joined the volunteers to ask for modernized equipment and a better means of warning people in areas of high risk, since the island-wide siren system cannot be used for this purpose. Currently, residents in high risk areas are warned about high-wave conditions either by police using bullhorns, or a telephone network which is not effective if people are not at home.

Suggestions from both the volunteers and citizens from the community who attended the meeting to support the volunteers included a stronger public civil defense education program, and a manually-operated secondary siren warning system in areas of high risk on the North Shore. Another concern of all attendees was the lack of emergency drills for students at schools located near beaches. One resident asked for more consistent forecasting - using an existing buoy 250 miles out and an added buoy - to give residents ample time before the warnings to prepare. In the past, residents have had as little as two hours after the warning to evacuate. Both volunteers and residents made the point that, in many areas around the world, it takes a disaster to "loosen the purse strings."

The volunteers were encouraged after the meeting. Besides the benefit of an outlet for their frustrations and an opportunity to connect quickly with a Commission set up to respond, the volunteers were pleased with the backup and support that came from the community. According to one of the volunteers, "We may wind up with the best civil defense program in the country yet!"

OFFICE OF CHILDREN AND YOUTH (OCY)
Hawaii Office of the Governor
PO Box 3044
Honolulu, HI 96802
TEL: 808-548-7582
Purpose: To improve and promote the coordination of all children and youth services in the State of Hawaii and to assist in the resolution of pressing problems affecting children and youth.
Sponsor: Hawaii State Agency
Contact: Genevieve T. Okinaga, Director
Description: There are about 417,900 children and youth in Hawaii from birth through age 24, almost half of the State's total population. Most are too young to vote or mobilize themselves for public action in their own behalf. The Office of Children and Youth (OCY), therefore, was created by the 1976 Legislature with the intent to promote a high level of public concern to better insure the protection and well-being of our youngest population by assisting agencies who provide direct services to them. Thus, the OCY's scope of operation mandated by legislation includes the entire range of programs and agencies who deliver services to children and youth in education, health, social services, welfare, employment, recreation, and others.

Undergirding the extensive duties of OCY as mandated by law are the wide array of OCY activities via fact finding, analysis and mobilizing existing resources to address the problems. OCY duties and responsibilities are mandated by H.R.S. Chapter 581 as amended by Act 207 and Act 187, Session Laws of Hawaii 1976, and Act 297, Session Laws of Hawaii 1980.

The Office of Children and Youth utilizes volunteers to supplement work performance on an as-needed basis. Program staff managers actively pursue appropriate volunteers for specific needs such as professional expertise, clerical abilities, etc. Program staff managers provide orientation, supervision and support to volunteers. One particular area where volunteers are greatly utilized is in Task Forces created by the Office to advise the Director on matters relating to a particular subject area.

Volunteers are called upon for the production of major conferences. For example, in 1979 the International Year of the Child was held in which hundreds of volunteers were involved.

The Office also co-sponsored the Governor's Hawaii State White House Conference on Children and Youth Project which included activities within all four counties and culminated at the State Conference.

The basic operational premise of the Office of Children and Youth has been and will continue to be to encourage and foster community involvement (via volunteers) for OCY projects, which are usually multi-agency endeavors involving both public and private sectors of individuals and agencies. The involvement of community representatives from the initial phase of decision making on project specifications is vital to the educative process leading to the completion of any project. This makes possible use of existing resources from the involved sectors, and even more importantly, the educative process results in a knowledgeable commitment when statewide implementation is sought.
Founded: 1976

GOVERNORS' OFFICES ON VOLUNTEERISM: IDAHO

TRAINING PROGRAMS

STATEWIDE VOLUNTEER MANAGEMENT TRAINING PROGRAM
Idaho Volunteer
1303 West Fort Street
PO Box 6756
Boise, ID 08707
TEL: 208-344-1411
Credit: Inquire
Sponsor: Idaho Volunteer
Contact: Patricia D. Sarriugarte
Description: The Idaho Volunteer Office was established to promote the effective coordination and channeling of voluntary action to improve the quality of life in Idaho. A major activity toward this goal is the annual Statewide Conference on Volunteerism. In addition, separate volunteer management workshops are held annually in each region of the state. The Office strives to provide opportunities for volunteer coordinators to learn new skills, to share and develop their resources and to increase the visibility of volunteer efforts throughout the state.

Upon request from communities, organizations and individuals, other shorter workshops are held on various topics related to the effective management of volunteers.

Format and content will differ and vary according to evaluations from past training events and/or the conduction of training needs assessments. The following is a list of training topics recently requested and provided by the Idaho Volunteer Office.
- Public Relations
- Corporate Involvement
- Styles of Volunteerism
- Supervision
- Developing a Volunteer Management Program
- Assertiveness Training
- Record Keeping and Documentation
- Fundraising and Resource Development
- Recruitment, Interviewing and Placement
- Developing Local Volunteer Clearinghouses
- Personal Effectiveness
- Advocacy/Lobbying
- Boards and Committees
- Developing Volunteer Job Descriptions
- Facilitation and Training of Trainers
- Networking and Coalition Building

- Career Options for Volunteers
- Volunteer/Staff Relationships
- Time Management

"The training is planned only after the requests are in and a consensus of need is drawn from them," according to an Idaho Volunteer spokesperson.

GOVERNORS' OFFICES ON VOLUNTEERISM: ILLINOIS

NATIONAL/STATE ORGANIZATIONS

GOVERNOR'S OFFICE OF VOLUNTARY ACTION
100 West Randolph
16th Floor
Chicago, IL 60601
TEL: 312-814-2789
Objectives: To promote and support volunteerism throughout Illinois.
Services: Formed in 1980 by Governor James B. Thompson, the office basically has three goals:
- to assist not-for-profit organizations;
- to increase volunteerism in public and private agencies; and
- to mount statewide voluntary projects.

More specifically, GOVA assistance includes areas of:
- recruiting, interviewing, placing, guiding and recognizing volunteers
- being or helping someone to be a better Board member
- raising money
- getting publicity
- doing long-range planning
- building partnerships among government, business, labor and the voluntary sector to meet community needs
- setting up a volunteer center.

The Office holds a yearly statewide conference, works with volunteers in state government and does hundreds of consultations, workshops and speeches each year; works with any volunteer or not-for-profit organization requesting assistance by:
- providing in-service training and technical assistance to coordinators of volunteers (involving over 86,000 volunteers in 1989);
- acting as a resource within the Governor's Office for technical assistance, consultation, workshops and support for all voluntary and governmental agencies throughout Illinois;
- stimulating partnerships among labor, business, government and the independent sector;
- co-sponsoring the "Governor's Home Town Awards" program, which recognizes oustanding volunteer efforts in towns throughout Illinois.
- sponsoring a statewide conference, awards programs and other events to promote and recognize voluntary action;
- publishing a quarterly newsletter and other materials as needed; and
- initiating cooperative voluntary efforts with the private sector such as the Literacy Council, food pantries, blood drives and special events.

Also, the Office maintains a volunteer Advisory Council with membership drawn from Spriggs and Company, National Can Corporation, Southern Illinois University, Illinois State Chamber of Commerce, Allstate Insurance, Voices for Illinois Children, Illinois Valley Community College, Mid-Central Illinois District Council of Carpenters, Habilitative Systems, Corporate Management Assistance Program, Lincoln Land Community College, Illinois Dept. of Commerce & Community Affairs, Sears,

Roebuck & Company, University of Illinois, Bright Futures, Vietnamese Community Services, Japanese American Service Committee, Illinois Retail Merchant Association, Cooperative Extension Service, Chicago Special Services, Skokie Valley Volunteer Services, and retirees and professional volunteers. Free membership is provided to the Governor's Office of Voluntary Action, which includes receiving the quarterly newsletter, *Volunteer Illinois,* the volunteer center list, the resource library and workshops, as well as a technical assistance packet on request and a certificate of recognition for exemplary volunteers (all materials are free).
Contact: Diane G. Marks, Public Information Officer
Publications: Volunteer Illinois (quarterly newsletter); Volunteers: Making Illinois Stronger; Welcome Volunteer!; Technical Assistance Packet
Founded: 1980

TRAINING PROGRAMS

HOME TOWN AWARDS
Governor's Office on Volunteerism/IL
Governor's Home Town Awards Program
222 South College
Springfield, IL 62706
TEL: 312-793-2789; 217-782-4311
Credit: Inquire
Sponsor: State of Illinois
Contact: Sue Ellen Stavrand or Kathleen Knox
Description: This conference has a dual purpose: to present the Home Town Awards, and to conduct workshops that might be helpful to people from volunteer organizations and local governments. In the former role, it honors outstanding community projects undertaken by various volunteer organizations and assists communities desiring to initiate such projects. Its second purpose is to offer a forum for those responsible for volunteer programs through workshops with topics such as:
- How to Recruit Volunteers
- Public Relations
- Senior Citizen/Youth Involvement
- Organizing Goals and Objectives
- Fundraising (Proposal Writing; Selecting An Event)
- Press Relations
- Continuing a Community Project
- Local Government Use of Volunteers in Public Service

The Conference is designed for local government officials, Chambers of Commerce, community leaders and volunteers, with a special emphasis on those communities interested in starting a community betterment project. Awards were provided in eight population categories, and five youth areas, with a major award, the Governor's Traveling Silver Cup, concluding the awards portion of the program. A number of mini-"workshops within workshops" addressed specific problems in communities (e.g., Community Alternatives for the Unemployed) in areas of interest both to volunteer coordinators, and to those involved in the community betterment awards program.

Faculty was drawn from fields of fundraising, the media, law enforcement, academe, and volunteer programs. Along with the regular proceedings of the Conference, a Home Town Awards Projects Book is developed following each annual conference.

LIVE '89 (LEADERSHIP IN VOLUNTEERISM EXPERIENCE)
Governor's Office on Volunteerism/IL
100 West Randolph, 26th Floor
Chicago, IL 60601
TEL: 312-814-2789
Credit: Inquire

Sponsor: University of Illinois
Contact: Jeanne Bradner, Director
Description: This conference was a joint effort of education, business and government - the *University of Illinois, Illinois Bell* and the *Governor's Office on Voluntary Action.* The event brought together two students and one faculty member from each of Illinois' four-year colleges to discuss their campus volunteer programs, share in some training programs and create an agenda for strengthening the programs throughout the state. Among topics covered were:

- The future of volunteerism
- The urban scene and the necessity for volunteerism
- Why volunteerism is important to business
- Student volunteerism in the past
- Prejudice reduction ("celebrate the uniqueness of people; do away with guilt")
- Values of the volunteer experience
- Managing conflict

Several sessions were devoted to sharing programs and ideas with each other. On one afternoon of the conference, students took a workbreak and went to Champaign to help paint a social service center and to work with children in a day care center.

At the end of the meeting, students and faculty outlined an agenda for the future, including:

- Establish volunteerism as a priority in Student Affairs
- Train student leaders and volunteers
- Provide a permanent staff to coordinate/advise student volunteerism
- Institute a coordinated program or clearinghouse to facilitate all volunteerism efforts on campus
- Include volunteerism as a part of university social service curricula

Before the program was over the three sponsors had plans underway for LIVE '90 by forming a statewide planning committee of college students and faculty. In addition, *Illinois Bell* instituted a 1990 LIVE Award Program to recognize, stimulate and reward excellence by students and faculty of Illinois four-year colleges and universities. The students, wearing tee shirts emblazoned with LIVE '89, were presented with a testimonial book from leading Illinois corporate and business leaders stressing the importance of community responsibility.

The day the conference opened, the Governor signed HB 2571 to create a campus student volunteer corps on each state university campus. The program is to be administered by the Illinois State Board of Higher Education. GOVA continues to work with the State Board to implement the campus student volunteer corps.

STATEWIDE LEADERSHIP SYMPOSIUM: WORKING TOGETHER TO MAKE VISIONS REALITIES
SEE PRIVATE SECTOR INITIATIVES OFFICES

VOLUNTEER LEADERSHIP: CHALLENGES FOR THE NINETIES
Governor's Office on Volunteerism/IL
100 West Randolph
Sixteenth Floor
Chicago, IL 60601
TEL: 312-814-2789
Sponsor: DuPage County Health Department
Contact: Diane Marks, Public Information Officer
Description: This conference focuses on learning how to recruit and retain volunteers, how to handle stress, and how to build team leadership. It is cosponsored by the *Illinois Community Education Association.* It is designed for health and human services organizations, religious organizations, community groups, advocacy groups and local and state government to enhance the abilities of their directors of volunteers, executive directors, volunteers and board members. Ninety-minute workshops include:

- *Interviews that work* with "tryout" volunteer interviews;

- *Understanding and Managing Change* to help participants become "change facilitators;"
- *I Make A Difference* to help attendees feel good about themselves and what they do;
- *Hitting the Bulls-Eye: Targeting Your Recruiting Messages* to provide help in more effective recruiting;
- *Stress Management* to explore techniques in reducing stress;
- *Making Your Volunteer Program Multilingual* to include volunteers from the black and Hispanic communities;
- *Lobbying in the Illinois Legislature* to foster an understanding of how the legislative process works;
- *Teaming Up For Success In The 90s* to introduce the teamwork management style;
- *Learning Styles: How They Influence Teaching Strategies* with five reinforcing steps of learning to help make teaching more effective;
- *Corporate Partnerships: Hope For The 90s* with successful models of nonprofit-business partnerships;
- *Major Gifts: Yours For The Asking* with ideas on where to look and how to ask for major gifts;
- *Creating Volunteer Opportunities for Young People* describing ways to recruit and involve teens and preteens;
- *Youth Community Service* discussing a 1/2-credit class offered at a high school;
- *7 Steps To A Winning Proposal* with a thorough examination of the step-by-step process of proposal-writing;
- *Conflict Management Styles* involving a survey instrument to help individuals understand conflict situations;
- *Tips And Techniques For Working With Groups* featuring new training and group process activities;
- *Listening To Yourself And Others* including evaluation of participants' listening habits;
- *Training For Technicalities In Mental Health and Corrections Settings* covering confidentiality, regulations and advocacy;
- *Conflict Styles* exploring skills needed to resolve conflict;
- *Recruiting, Retaining and Recognizing Volunteers* presenting "what works and what doesn't;" and
- *Getting Through To People* to improve communication skills.

In addition to the regular proceedings, a breakfast session not only provides an opportunity for networking, but presents adds twelve topics to the agenda, with participants selecting one of twelve sites. Breakfast session topics are:

- *Governor's Office on Voluntary Action;*
- *Intergenerational programs;*
- *Seniors as Volunteers;*
- *Volunteer Centers;*
- *Volunteers in Hospitals and Libraries;*
- *Literacy Volunteers;*
- *Youth Volunteers;*
- *School Volunteers and Programs;*
- *Museum/Historic Site Volunteers;*
- *Domestic Violence Volunteers;*
- *Volunteers in Settings for Seniors; and*
- *Volunteers in State and Local Government.*

Breakfast attendees were asked to bring ten copies of something they wished to share with the nine other members at each table. Display tables were made available for additional materials for general sharing. An Awards Luncheon and an *AVA Certification* session were held on the final day.

Faculty was drawn from the *Veterans Administration, Gateway Foundation, DuPage County Health Department, WICS-TV 20, Social Engineering, The DDR Group, University of Illinois Extension, Community MAP, American Heart Association, Triangle Center, Lincoln Land Community College, Center Point Management, Chicago Public Library, John Howard Association, Mental Health Association in Illinois, CNY Enterprises, Farm Resource Center,* private consultants, and the *Governor's Office on Voluntary Action.*

GOVERNORS' OFFICES ON VOLUNTEERISM: IOWA

NATIONAL/STATE ORGANIZATIONS

STATE VOLUNTEER PROGRAM
Iowa Department of Social Services
Hoover Building
Des Moines, IA 50319
TEL: 515-281-8269
Objectives: To enhance the services provided to the Iowa Department of Social Services through the involvement of volunteers.
Services: The original manual of the Department of Social Services Volunteer Program was written in 1976. At that time volunteers worked only in the Mental Health Institutions. Today volunteers are working in all 99 counties plus juvenile and adult correctional institutions.
The State of Iowa is divided into eight Districts. Each District has from one to five volunteer coordinators who recruit volunteers on the basis of need for the county offices where they are assigned. The need for a volunteer is identified by a staff member, who sends a written request for a volunteer to the coordinator. The coordinator uses this request to develop a volunteer job description and as a tool to recruit the volunteer. Orientation is provided to the volunteer by the volunteer coordinator and any specialized training needed is provided by the staff who made the request for the volunteer. During National Volunteer week, the Department of Social Services hosts a statewide recognition in the Capitol Complex. At this time outstanding volunteers are recognized in Social Services from all over the state.
The volunteer program is funded through federal and state funds. There are 4,000 volunteers, registered with the Department of Social Services, who work an average of 30,000 hours a month. In the Central Office, volunteers work in the Bureau of Communications answering the phone, filing, and as a graphic artist. There is also a team of volunteers in the Community Service Division which operates the adoption exchange program and answers mail from people inquiring about parents and children. In the field, volunteers handle the distribution of cheese and butter commodities. They also operate many food pantries and clothes closet. Other volunteers work to prevent child abuse and, in the case of proven child abuse, to stop it. The training for all of these programs is provided by staff, experienced volunteers and professionals from related fields who volunteer their time.
Sponsor: Iowa Department of Social Services
Contact: J.D. Hall
Founded: 1976

TRAINING PROGRAMS

REGIONAL SEMINARS AND A STATE CONFERENCE ON VOLUNTEERISM
Iowa Governor's Office for Volunteers
State Capitol Building
Des Moines, IA 50319
TEL: 515-281-5492
Credit: Inquire
Sponsor: Governor's Office for Volunteers/IA
Contact: Barbara Finch
Description: With the increase of volunteer involvement in state agencies, unnecessary duplication, lack of preparation for the arrival of volunteers, inexperience of volunteer supervisors, and other problems were considered a distinct possibility if a plan could not be implemented to assure orderly growth. The

Governor's Office for Volunteers is playing a role in this planning effort in a number of ways, including training events such as Regional Training seminars and a State Conference on Volunteerism.
This workshop is designed for state agencies to explore policies and methods of developing an effective volunteer program. Topics include:
● recruitment
● placement
● training
● orientation
● reco gnition
● staff/volunteer relations
● evaluation of performances
Emphasis is placed on the concept of volunteerism. Participants are helped to look critically at development of a volunteer program and the utilization of volunteers who will be necessary with the present budget cuts.
Coordination and cooperation in volunteer programming will be stressed also to assure that serious overlaps in volunteer services will not take place, and to keep an avenue open for exchange of ideas, discussion of problems, and general moral support among volunteer program managers.
In addition to its own training, the Governor's Office for Volunteers provides information on other training efforts for volunteer administrators and volunteers that come to their attention, such as the course on Effective Management of Volunteer Programs conducted by the Des Moines Area Community College.

GOVERNORS' OFFICES ON VOLUNTEERISM: KENTUCKY

TRAINING PROGRAMS

GOVERNOR'S CONFERENCE ON VOLUNTEERISM
Governor's Office on Volunteer Services/KY
Office of the Governor
Frankfort, KY 40601
TEL: 502-564-4357
Credit: CEUs
Sponsor: Commonwealth of Kentucky, Department for Local Government; Governor's Office on Volunteer Services
Contact: Norma W. Johnson
Description: Recognizing the contributions of volunteers in hospitals, libraries, nursing homes, schools, the arts, energy conservation, and with the mentally and physically handicapped, the elderly, delinquents, ex-offenders and their families, and many other areas, the State of Kentucky offers two- to three-day training conferences to provide assistance in skills development for program effectiveness.
The Governor's Volunteer Advisory Council - about a dozen men and women from around the state - coordinate and facilitate the conference, and arrange for evaluation and follow-up to help refine future programs. A recent theme for the annual event was Volunteerism: Today's Luxury or Need? The following subject areas and methods were used to explore this concern:
Beginning a New Volunteer Program - a panel format with 15-minute presentations by the three panel members, followed by a period for comments, and finally an audience/panel open discussion.
Roles for Volunteers within United Way - a movie presentation, followed by panel discussion and audience participation.
Recruiting, Screening and Training Volunteers - a panel discussion

with audience participation.
Community Action Programs - audiovisual presentation and panel discussion.
Special Workshop - Marketing Your Volunteer Programs - audiovisual presentation with handouts and audience discussion.
Revitalizing Your Volunteer Program - panel discussion with audience participation.
Recognition of Volunteers - slide presentation and panel discussion, with time provided for audience comments.
Organizing a Community Project with Volunteers - slide presentation with audience participation, a panel discussion, and ample time for questions and answers.
Some of the workshops are presented more than once due to high interest. In addition, luncheon speakers address topics of current interest such as: The International Year of the Child, and Proposition 13: Its Effect on Human Services. The final session of the day is entitled Forum/Questions and Answers, enabling an overview and an opportunity for participants to voice concerns that may not have been adequately covered during the program. Faculty is drawn from the Governor's staff, the State Department for Human Services, United Way, Red Cross, Voluntary Action Centers, the Mental Health field, Community Action Agencies, ACTION Older Americans Programs, universities, Public Schools Administration, Jaycees, women's clubs, foundations, and individual volunteer programs such as Teens Who Care, as well as officials from other states.
Students desiring Continuing Education Units (CEUs) for this training event must make arrangements in advance.

GOVERNORS' OFFICES ON VOLUNTEERISM: MARYLAND

INDIVIDUAL PROGRAM PROFILES

MARYLAND HUNTER EDUCATION PROGRAM
Tawes State Office Building
Annapolis , MD 21401
TEL: 301-269-3188
Purpose: To train young and inexperienced hunters in an effort to reduce hunting accidents and make hunters aware of their responsibility while afield.
Sponsor: Department of Natural Resources
Contact: Lt. Thomas R. Turner
Description: The program began in 1966 with the primary responsibility of firearms safety. As time passed, the need for more education concerning hunter responsibility, knowledge of game laws and conservation practices, and skills in use of different methods of hunting became necessary. To that end the program evolved into the present day Hunter Education Program.
The program is funded 25% by funds received from Hunting License sales and 75% by funds received from an excise tax on firearms and archery equipment sales.
The primary goal of the program is still to reduce hunting accidents but a fast growing concern is to instill an attitude of responsibility in each hunter and improve hunter/landowner relationships.
The program became mandatory for all first time hunters before they purchase a hunter's license in 1977. Since then, hunting accidents decreased by more than 60%.
The program is coordinated by the Maryland Natural Resources Police and the classes are taught by 384 volunteers. Each volunteer must complete the course as a student, attend a seven (7) hour training session, assist with a class for on the job training, and is then assigned to a team for certification. Retraining workshops are

given annually and each volunteer must attend one session at least every two (2) years.
The program is divided into four (4) regions with a Regional Coordinator responsible for the activity within that region. Supervision and evaluations are conducted by the State Coordinator, the Regional Coordinator, team leaders, Senior Instructors, and occasionally by other DNR members.
Founded: 1966

GOVERNORS' OFFICES ON VOLUNTEERISM: MICHIGAN

TRAINING PROGRAMS

IN-SERVICE TRAINING/STATEWIDE VOLUNTEER DEVELOPMENT
Michigan Statewide Volunteer Development
Department of Social Services
PO Box 30037
Lansing, MI 48909
TEL: 517-373-0920
Credit: Inquire
Sponsor: Michigan Department of Social Services
Contact: Elizabeth Albee Frier
Description: Periodically, as needed, one-day training sessions are offered to volunteer coordinators, directors, and service staff of the Department of Social Services, with guests from other state departments included.
Faculty consists of state DSS office directors with visiting lecturers from other public and private agencies. Topics covered in the program include:
- Overturning Turnover
- Overcoming Staff Hostility
- Recruiting Volunteers
- Training Volunteers
- Stretching Dollars
- Organizing Food Co-ops
- Making Toys out of Trash
- Family-to-Family Program
- Third Party Payees
- Youth Companions
- Cashing in on Cash-off Coupons and Refunds
- Poverty
- Transportation
- Insurance and Liability
- Michigan's Cooperative Volunteer Program
- Fund-raising - Thrift Shops, Used Book Sales
- Parent Aides
Curriculum changes from year to year to respond to emerging needs and delete topics that cease to be relevant.

GOVERNORS' OFFICES ON VOLUNTEERISM: MINNESOTA

TRAINING PROGRAMS

HUMAN SERVICE PROGRAMS: VOLUNTEER LEADERSHIP EMPHASIS AREA
Minnesota Office of Volunteer Services
130 State Capitol
St. Paul, MN 55155
TEL: 612-296-4731
Credit: Associate Degree (90 credits)
Sponsor: Metropolitan Community College
Contact: Laura Lee M. Geraghty
Description: Graduates of Metropolitan Community College's Human Services Programs are expected to have acquired an understanding of the concepts, principles, and skills necessary for entry into a semi-professional position in social welfare and community agencies. The program serves three main purposes:
- to train students for entry level positions in the field of human services.
- to provide in-service or continuing education for working practitioners in humans services
- to provide general education in human services for any interested student.

To earn an Associate Degree with preparation in Human Services, a student must meet the college's distribution requirements, Human Services Core requirements and requirements in one of the emphasis areas (Volunteer Leadership and Management of Non-Profit Agencies; Youth Services; Gerontology). Forty-five of the 90 credits required are in General Education (English, Health, Sociology, Science, Art, Communications, History, etc.).
Twenty-one credits are in the Human Services Core Courses, and the remaining credits are in the selected emphasis area. Following is the curriculum on the volunteerism emphasis area.
Volunteer Leadership and Management of Non-Profit Agencies
- Introduction to Volunteer Leadership and Management, 3 credits.
- Introduction to Management Assistance for Non-Profit Agencies, 3 credits.
- Communication and Leadership, 3 credits.
- Public Relations, Publicity, Recruitment, 3 credits.
- Methods of Planning, 3 credits.
- Personnel Supervision, 3 credits.
- Fiscal Management, 3 credits.
- Field Experience, 6-12 credits.

This curriculum is designed to provide basic knowledge and skills for entry level positions such as coordinator or director of volunteers in settings such as hospitals, churches, community centers, political groups, schools, welfare departments and corrections.
The Human Services Core Requirements include the following foundation courses which must be completed by all students in the Human Services Programs:
- **Human Services 1,** Introduction to Human Services, 3 credits.
- **Human Services 2,** Personal Assessment, 3 credits.
- **Human Services 3,** Community Resources and Agencies, 3 credits.
- **Human Services 4,** Introduction to Counseling and Interviewing, 3 credits.
- **Human Services 5,** Introduction to Group Dynamics, 3 credits.
- **Human Services 6,** Family Counseling, 3 credits.
- **Human Services 7,** Intercultural Aspects of Human Services, 3 credits.

The overall curriculum is designed to provide the student who has a special career objective with a combination of basic human

services skills found in several emphasis areas. In this type of individualized curriculum, field experience of at least six credits is considered an advantage for the student.

REGIONAL VOLUNTEER WORKSHOPS
Governor's Office of Volunteer Services/MN
130 State Capitol
St. Paul, MN 55155
TEL: 612-296-3391
Credit: CEUs
Sponsor: Governor's Office on Volunteerism
Contact: Phyllis A. Acker
Description: The Minnesota Governor's Office of Volunteer Services was established to promote the effective coordination and channeling of voluntary action to improve the quality of life for Minnesota citizens. A major activity toward this goal is the convening of separate annual volunteer workshops in each region. Workshop planners strive to provide opportunities to learn new skills, to share resources with volunteers and volunteer leadership, and to increase the visibility of the value of volunteer efforts in this region.
Content and direction of each workshop is based on the positive evaluations of the previous workshops held in the individual region. These evaluations are provided by attendees, who are volunteers, volunteer coordinators, board members, clergy, and staff who work with volunteers. Since format differs from year to year and from region to region, the following is a composite of components of several of the workshops:
Aspects of Community Relations - for volunteer leaders concerned with the public relations of their programs.
Fundraising and Financing - "how-to's" of grant writing, grassroots fundraising including events and special projects, budgeting, accountability, etc.
Recruitment and Retention of Volunteers - how to find the right volunteers, what influences their decisions to stay or to leave, and how to keep them once you have them.
Boards and Committees - for those who are board members or work with boards and committees and are concerned with improving their effectiveness.
Issues on Volunteerism - how legislation, energy, aging, and other continuing processes affect volunteer programs.
Nontraditional Sources of Volunteers - how to approach untapped populations; how to meet their special needs; how to feel more comfortable working with people of different backgrounds; how to interest youth in volunteering.
Consultations - how to get academic credit for volunteer training; how to deal with the unique aspects of church volunteering, etc.
Volunteer/Staff Teambuilding - how to identify and solve the conflicts in roles and build an effective team.
Potpourri for Volunteers - a smorgasbord of topics on tax laws, insurance coverage, special assignments, benefits of volunteering, energy and how it affects volunteering, etc.
Time Management - how to manage responsibilities and involvements to be most effective.
A Volunteer Perspective - how to develop the skills that volunteers need to bring to a program and that can be transferred from one program to another.
Burnout and Stress: Prevention and Cure - how to handle stress to be most effective; what burnout is all about.
Rural Volunteering: Challenges and Opportunities - how to find solutions to the difficulties encountered by rural volunteer programs.
Volunteer Recognition - how to build effective volunteer recognition into program plans; who needs to be involved.
Evaluation Techniques - how to use surveys; how surveys are developed, distributed and interpreted.
Certification of Volunteer Directors - What is the process? Is there value in it? How does one use it?
The Association of Volunteer Administration (AVA) accepts

attendance at these regional workshops as partial fulfillment of the requirements necessary to qualify for, or to be recertified as, a Certified Administrator of Volunteer Services.

SOLVING COMMUNITY PROBLEMS BY BUILDING COMMUNITY PARTNERSHIPS
Minnesota Office of Volunteer Services
Volunteer for Minnesota
200 Administration Building
St. Paul, MN 55155
TEL: 612-296-4731
TOLL FREE: 800-652-9747 (statewide)
Credit: CEUs
Sponsor: State of Minnesota
Contact: Workshop Coordinator
Description: Grouping learners by community, this workshop is designed to give community leaders the tools to develop new and innovative public/private partnerships at the local level according to the needs and resources within their own communities. Sessions aimed at planning for change through cooperative efforts include:
Coalition Building:
- identifying community leadership;
- developing cooperation and commitment among diverse groups; and
- creating change in response to common goals.

Needs Assessment:
- identifying community needs and determining priorities;
- learning various methods for assessing needs; and
- recognizing resources for assessing needs.

Optional Resources:
- examining existing resources;
- exploring new ways to use or refocus monetary, material, and human resources; and
- networking as individuals and organization

Role of the Volunteer:
- volunteering as a community resource;
- motivating individuals; and
- volunteering in direct service and advisory capacities.

Planning for Community Change:
- preparing strategies for change;
- using power to influence outcomes; and
- understanding and applying the dynamics of community public/private partnerships.

The workshops are based on a process developed by Volunteer for Minnesota, and are conducted over a period of five weeks. Due to limited space and the design of the workshop, priority is given to teams of five to ten leaders from each community, representing a diversity of interests within the community (i.e. business, local government, agriculture, labor, nonprofit agencies, civic and religious organizations, media, academic and volunteer communities, and education organizations). A participant manual that illustrates a process for establishing community based coalitions to work on community concerns is included for workshop purposes and as a "take-home" tool for continued reference.
[The above workshop is Part One of a two-part training series sponsored by the State of Minnesota]

UNIVERSITY PROGRAMS FOR VOLUNTEERS AND ADMINISTRATORS OF VOLUNTEERS
Minnesota Office of Volunteer Services
130 State Capitol
St. Paul, MN 55155
TEL: 612-296-4731
Credit: B.A.; Certificate: credit for past work in volunteer field
Sponsor: Metropolitan State University
Contact: Laura Lee M. Geraghty
Description: Metropolitan State University's (Metro U's) program for volunteers and volunteer administrators is a two-pronged

approach recognizing the various levels of experience among entering students. The basic components are:
- studies for professional development in the volunteer field.
- identification and assessment of skills gained from volunteer work.

People who have been - or intend to be - active in volunteer services in their communities and who wish to gain credit for that experience or gain new learning in the field need not be degree candidates at Metro U. Metro U also has a professional development program for persons who are or who wish to become administrators of volunteers. Either of these programs can be part of Metro U's B.A. program.

Administrator of Volunteers Professional Development Program
Ten competencies lead to the completion of this program - seven required and three elected. Strategies by which competencies are gained (classroom learning, independent study, internships, prior learning), the specific elements of competencies, and levels of competences individualized for each student. Required competency areas are:
- **Volunteerism:** History, Issues and Trends of Volunteerism
- **Written Communication:** General Writing; Writing for Work; Nonfiction Writing
- **General Management:** Management, Education and Supervision of Volunteers; Human Services Administration
- **Public Relations:** Principles of Public Relations
- **Personnel Management:** Overview of Personnel Management; Effective Supervision; Personnel and Industrial Psychology; Supervision Theory Workshop
- **Public Relations:** Principles of Public Relations
- **Program Development:** Program Development in Volunteer Services; Program Development for Volunteer Managers (workshop)
- **Human Relations:** Social Class and Cultural Differences; Human Relations and Cultural Awareness; Sociology: Urbanism and Minorities; Prejudice in America (independent study); Black Culture/Afro-American Experience

Some of the elective competency areas are: Advocacy, Counseling, Fiscal Management, Fund Raising, Grant Writing and Administration, Group Leadership, Human Service or Civic Agency, Interpersonal Communication, Legislative Process, Museum Studies, Public Speaking, Research, and Training.

Volunteer Services Individualized Program
Individualized programs can be developed by students based on their diverse knowledge through volunteer or civic service. Many competencies are achieved through past experience such as work in public policy youth organizations, churches, politics, art and education institutions, etc. With one-to-one advising by faculty, and the listing of competency areas, students assist in selecting courses, independent studies and/or internships.

Bachelor of Arts Degree
Students may use competencies in the volunteer field as part of their Metro U baccalaureate degree program. Students who do not have sufficient transfer credit to enter Metro U may use volunteer competencies for entrance purposes.
Before beginning classes, each student is required to attend a half-day planning workshop and an individual meeting with a faculty member to gain, among other types of assistance, full academic credit for volunteer experiences.

VOLUNTEER PROGRAM MANAGEMENT
Minnesota Office of Volunteer Services
Volunteer for Minnesota
200 Administration Building
St. Paul, MN 55155
TEL: 612-296-4371
TOLL FREE: 800-652-9747 (statewide)
Credit: CEUs
Sponsor: State of Minnesota
Contact: Workshop Coordinator

Description: Presented in a series of eight, day-long training sessions, these workshops are designed with a dual purpose:

- to continue the training of those individuals who participated in Part One, above; and
- to provide fundamental concepts and skills to others who also wish to start, expand, or refine a volunteer program.

The workshops focus on the basic elements and provide specific guidelines for planning and implementing a successful, integrated volunteer program. Content is devoted to covering the key elements in the planning and implementing of effective volunteer programs and citizen participation efforts. Part of the workshop design includes the individualization of those elements and the opportunity to concentrate on specific areas of interest. Topics include:

- Preplanning
- Job Descriptions
- Recruitment
- Placement
- Orientation
- Supervision
- Recognition and Retention
- Program Evaluation

This workshop is Part Two of a two-part training series sponsored by the State of Minnesota.

An informal luncheon session for participants in the Part One workshops on building community partnerships is provided to enable those leaders to share experiences and successes since applying the principles of the Part One workshops on building community partnerships.

GOVERNORS' OFFICES ON VOLUNTEERISM: MISSISSIPPI

TRAINING PROGRAMS

NATIONAL CONFERENCE FOR VOLUNTEER LEADERSHIP*
Mississippi Office of Volunteerism
802 North State Street
Suite 100
Jackson, MS 39201
TEL: 601-949-2010
Credit: Partial fulfillment for AVA Certification
Sponsor: Mississippi Office of Voluntary Participation
Contact: Ruth Wilson
Description: This conference features advanced level workshops, leadership training sessions and seminars for the professional concerned with social and cultural changes affecting the field of volunteerism. Special emphasis is placed on capabilities to meet the challenges presented by current issues. Opening with a keynote address, "Challenges for the Eighties," which explored the coming decade and what is in store for volunteerism, the conference proceeded with three series of workshops over a three-day period:
Workshop Series #1

- **A Marketing Approach for Volunteer Services** - with increasing competition for volunteer involvement, this session looked at marketing strategies to increase citizen participation.
- **Challenges for the Eighties** - a general seminar to discuss the implications of the keynote address.
- **Understanding the National Volunteer Scene** - Who can help? How does one find leading organizations? What services can they offer?
- **Basic Management Skills for Volunteer Leaders** - starting or re-tooling a major effort to involve volunteers; exploring a

systems approach for volunteer program management.
Workshop Series #2

- **A New Look at Staff-Volunteer Relations** - issues, strategies, and concepts to help address the number one problem facing volunteer involvement.
- **Fundraising for Volunteer Programs** - Where's the money? Who has it? What's available?...a look at resources for supporting volunteer programs.
- **Time Management for Managers** - a look at where the manager's time is going and how it can be better utilized.

Workshop Series #3

- **New Recruiting Techniques for the Eighties** - the effect of societal pressures and changes on recruitment of potential volunteers.
- **Problem Solving Techniques for Managers** - specific problem solving techniques and skills for administrators and managers (developed and practiced).
- **The Future of Volunteer and Citizen Involvement** - a look into the crystal ball for the next 25 years.

The conference closed with a plenary session, Issues for the Eighties, which covered:

- Energy shortages;
- Changing roles for men and women;
- Competition for volunteers;
- Firing volunteers;
- Other issues affecting the volunteer field.

Participants included volunteer coordinators, educators, administrators, social workers, religious leaders, correctional professionals, agency directors, board and advisory committee members, legislators, personnel offices, organizational leaders, and others concerned with volunteer involvement. Credit is available toward AVA requirements for Certified Administrator of Volunteer Services.

The University of Southern Mississippi and VOLUNTEER - The National Center are additional sponsors.

GOVERNORS' OFFICES ON VOLUNTEERISM: MISSOURI

TRAINING PROGRAMS

SHOW-ME SEMINARS
Missouri Volunteers
PO Box 563
Jefferson City, MO 65102
TEL: 314-751-3222
Credit: Inquire
Sponsor: Missouri Division of Family Services; Missouri School System; Missouri Volunteer Office; National School Volunteer Program
Contact: Lt. Gov. William C. Phelps, Coordinator
Description: The Show-Me Seminars are an outgrowth of the Missouri Volunteer Program's desire to focus on providing training to specific groups, instead of the volunteer community in general. The first two targeted groups were school volunteer coordinators and staff of the Division of Family Services, with plans begun for a variety of other volunteer groups interested in a marketplace for new ideas.

The school volunteer program began in response to a survey by the Missouri Volunteer Program that targeted 39 school districts interested in starting volunteer programs or wanting to increase their program's effectiveness. Regional seminars for this group were held in four locations across the state in late spring. As a follow-up to the smaller meetings, two major school volunteer seminars were held in the fall in Kansas City and St. Louis for volunteers as well as volunteer leaders in Missouri schools. The day-long school seminars offered six workshops for school volunteers, new volunteer leaders and volunteer leaders with experience. Topics covered were:

- Kindergarten Screening
- Strengthening Your School Volunteer Program
- Volunteers as Tutors
- Setting Up a Volunteer Program for Children with Special Needs
- Starting a New School Volunteer program
- Involving Older School Volunteers

During the summer, workshops for Division of Family Services volunteer leaders were held in five cities to provide in-service training, promote a sharing of ideas about successes and failures, focus on supervision and motivation of volunteers, and offer new insights to enable the Volunteer Division to expand and grow. Overall goals were:

- to expand the number of DFS volunteer programs; and
- to strengthen and promote growth of existing programs.

The nursing home volunteer program was the third target for Show-Me Seminars, with other groups who would benefit from the program being included as time and resources permitted. Publicity about the Seminars resulted in requests from groups needing this type of assistance, thereby eliminating much of the time-consuming groundwork in locating and prioritizing volunteer groups in need of training.

STATEWIDE CONFERENCE ON VOLUNTEERISM VOCAL
Box 563
Jefferson City, MO 65102
TEL: 314-751-2781; 314-751-2421
Credit: Inquire
Sponsor: Volunteer Ombudsman Citizen Action League (VOCAL); Missouri Office for Volunteer Effectiveness (MOVE)
Contact: Lt. Gov. Kenneth J. Rothman,
Description: Using A Team Approach for the theme of the 1980 Statewide Conference on volunteerism, the Missouri Volunteer Ombudsman Citizen Action League (VOCAL) and the Missouri Organization for Volunteer Effectiveness (MOVE) aimed at three groups (the team) in developing the training program:

- **Volunteers** - This valuable resource upon which all volunteer programs depend but do not always provide with new training methods were offered workshops in creative volunteering, volunteer-staff relationships and bridging generation gaps.
- **The New Volunteer Coordinator** - This group which is likely to be unfamiliar with basic structures learned how to lay the groundwork for a volunteer program, involve older adults and supervise by delegation.
- **The Experienced Volunteer Coordinator** - This group, always seeking new methods and innovative ideas, attended workshops on funding, communications and legislation.

Workshops considered each member of the team separately as well as together, with general discussion both before and after the workshop sessions. Workshops were designated with an "A" for volunteers, a "B" for new volunteer coordinators, and a "C" for experienced volunteer coordinator in the first sessions, D, E, & F respectively in the second groups, and G, H & I respectively in the final workshops. Topics covered included:

- **What's in it for me?** - How to get the most from your volunteer job.
- **Before you get your first volunteer** - Laying the groundwork for a volunteer program.
- **How to get a dollar** - Funding/Grantsmanship.
- **How do I fit?** - Volunteers and staff relate to each other.
- **Involving older adults** - An untapped source of volunteers.
- **Calling the shots** - Communication/Assertiveness/Power
- **The Massey Tapes,** "What You Are Is Not Necessarily What

You Will Be" - Bridging generation gaps.
- **Supervision by delegation** - Overworked? Overburdened? Learn to Delegate.
- **Legislation such as** - Bigger and better tax deductions for volunteers.

A team concept from another perspective stresses volunteerism in the public, private and volunteer sectors and how they can help each other. The conference convenes for two days, with faculty drawn from state departments, business and industry, United Way, and the Governor's office on volunteerism (VOCAL). Facilities are provided for state meetings for volunteer coordinators in the Divisions of Family Service, Mental Health and Aging as well as Voluntary Action Centers and Volunteer Centers. Also, MOVE's annual meeting was incorporated into the conference.

This event is deliberately held during volunteer week to demonstrate that the greatest appreciation for the volunteer is adequate training for his/her volunteer assignments. An awards banquet, The Team Approach, was held on the first evening to accommodate those who might not be able to attend the full program.

GOVERNORS' OFFICES ON VOLUNTEERISM: NEW HAMPSHIRE

NATIONAL/STATE ORGANIZATIONS

GOVERNOR'S OFFICE ON VOLUNTEERISM/NH
State House Annex
Concord, NH 03301
TEL: 603-271-3771
Objectives: To encourage and promote volunteerism in New Hampshire.
Services: The Governor's Office on Volunteers (GOV) in New Hampshire was created in 1983 through a federal ACTION grant (five years, decreasing). Today the GOV administrative costs are supported by the Governor's budget. This includes two full-time staff persons, travel and office expense, etc. An annual fund-raising letter supports the programs. GOV programs include:

- Technical assistance to volunteer groups, nonprofits, and business;
- New Hampshire State Conference on Volunteerism (annually);
- Five regional conferences throughout each year;
- Governor's Volunteer Recognition Awards;
- IOU New Hampshire (a teen volunteer program);
- Governor's Dinner for Business and Volunteerism;
- Peg McGarity Award for Outstanding Volunteer Management; and
- *A State of Involvement,* the quarterly newsletter.

All programs are organized by volunteer committees, such as the Business Information and Resource Council (see separate entry). An 18-member Steering Committee supervises the office. The Office holds memberships in *VOLUNTEER - The National Center, AVA (Association for Volunteer Administration), IAVE (International Association for Volunteer Effort),* and the *New Hampshire Council on Fund Raising.* An annual report is published each year and distributed across the state.
Sponsor: Governor's Office on Volunteerism/NH
Contact: Linda Darling, Executive Director
Publications: A State of Involvement (quarterly newsletter); Governor's Recognition Awards; GOV Annual Report; You - The Board Member of a New Hampshire Charitable Corporation; Networking Directory; Business Information and Resource Council (BIRC)
Founded: 1983

TRAINING PROGRAMS

LAKES REGION CONFERENCE ON VOLUNTEERISM - VOLUNTEERS: A CARING RESOURCE; A PRACTICAL PERSPECTIVE
Governor's Office on Volunteerism/NH
State House Annex
Concord, NH 03301
TEL: 603-271-3771
Credit: Inquire
Sponsor: Governor's Office on Volunteerism; The Belknap Mill
Contact: Linda Darling, Executive Director
Description: This one-day training event is one of five regional conferences sponsored each year by the Governor's Office on Volunteerism. It is designed to assist managers and leaders of volunteers in developing skills and resources which can make them more effective. Workshops and presenters have been selected in response to the particular needs of the Lakes Region. Conference agenda includes:

- **The Care and Feeding of Volunteers: From Soup to Nuts** - The uniquely American tradition of volunteerism faces many challenges in today's environment. Realistic goals can be met with innovation and creativity. This workshop looks at the basics of recruitment, retention, and recognition with a new perspective that can often make a difference.
- **Marketing Your Volunteer Program** - This workshop focuses on how a basic marketing approach can be applied to your program to recruit appropriate volunteers, strengthen community appreciation for your program's achievements, and enhance fundraising efforts.
- **Creative Volunteer Recognition** - This is a panel discussion of volunteer recognition: what it is and why it is important. It features inexpensive and creative ideas for rewarding and honoring volunteers.
- **Resource Sharing** - This is an informal exchange event allowing you to share examples of materials you have used successfully for recognition of volunteers and learn about materials used by others.

Facilitators and presenters for the current conference came from Lakes Region Conference Committee, Riverside Communications, Lakes Region General Hospital, New Hampshire Association for the Blind, American Lung Association of New Hampshire, American Red Cross of Greater Central New Hampshire, Belknap-Merrimack Community Action, Lakes Region United Way, Merrimack County RSVP, and the Governor's Office on Volunteerism.

NH STATE CONFERENCE ON VOLUNTEERISM
Governor's Office on Volunteerism/NH
State House Annex
Concord, NH 03301
TEL: 603-271-3771
Credit: Inquire
Contact: Linda Darling, Executive Director
Description: Begun in 1985, the New Hampshire State Conference on Volunteerism is an annual event. A one-day conference, it offers more than 25 workshops and panel discussions. All are facilitated by experts in their fields, preferably from New Hampshire, who volunteer their time. Conference fees are kept to a minimum: $25 in 1990.
Financially, the conference is self-supporting, organized by a volunteer committee, held at a state facility (which is free to state agencies), and all presenters donate their time and travel. Specific workshop topics differ from year to year based on current needs, but usually come under broad areas of volunteer management, operation of a nonprofit organization, fund-raising, legal issues, computers, public speaking, etc. Current workshop topics include:
SESSION I
Operations
- Combining Services, Strengths and Philosophies into One Agency
- Measuring the Impact of Your Volunteer Program
- Marketing Techniques for Volunteer Organizations

Volunteers
- Volunteers: How to Find Them; How to Keep Them
- Understanding Yourself and Others
- Building an Active and Effective Board

Fundraising
- Up and Running (applying for exempt status)
- Fundraising: Your Game Plan
- Starting and Maintaining a Bequest Program
- Using Research to Target Audiences & Identify Donor Potential
- Wellness: What's in It for Me as a Manager and an Individual?

SESSION II
Operations
- You - The Board Member
- Cost Savings with Desktop Publishing
- Measuring the Impact of Your Volunteer Program, Part 2
- The Planning Process: Personnel
- Excellence in Management

Volunteers
- Volunteers: How to Find Them; How to Keep Them, Part 2
- Understanding Yourself and Others, Part 2
- Volunteer Administration Is a Profession
- Sharpen Your Personal Speaking Skills

Finances
- Grant Writing
- An Overview of Corporate Giving: Private Philanthropy for the Public Good
- Budget and Financial Reports at Nonprofit Agencies

SESSION III
Volunteers
- Improve Your Speaking Skills with Practice

Operations
- Cost Savings Through Desktop Publishing, Part 2

Finances
- An Overview of Corporate Giving: Private Philanthropy for the Public Good, Part 2

Panel Discussions
- Proving that Volunteer Programs Count
- Inspiring Volunteers to Succeed
- Interpreting the Laws: Legislation, Liability, Insurance

Facilitators came from National Academy of Volunteerism, University of New Hampshire Extension Service, Home Health and Hospice Care, Small Business Development Center, Mary Hitchcock Memorial Hospital, Walnut Hill Seminar House, Antioch New England, United Way of Greater New Manchester, Holderness School, New Hampshire the Beautiful, William Bigelow Law Offices, Planned Giving Consultants, Dudley Research, Blue Cross and Blue Shield of New Hampshire, Amanuensis, American Lung Association of New Hampshire, Dunfey Group, Norwich University Center for Volunteer Administration - Vermont College, Center for Voluntary Action, Association for Volunteer Administration/Region I, American Red Cross, Toastmasters, New Hampton School, Littleton Hospital, National Extension Homemakers Council, WOKQ Radio, Markem Corporation, Friends of the Norris Cotton Cancer Center, Karen's Climb, Big Brothers/Big Sisters/Exeter, New Hampshire Charitable Fund, Merrill & Broderick, William Hopkins Law Offices, Professional Insurance Agents of New England, A.B. Gile Agency, and the Governor's Office on Volunteerism. Future plans call for a nationally-known keynote speaker, funded by a prime sponsor.

INDIVIDUAL PROGRAM PROFILES

BUSINESS INFORMATION AND RESOURCE COUNCIL
Governor's Office on Volunteerism/NH
State House Annex
Room 410E
Concord, NH 03301
TEL: 603-271-2121
Purpose: To involve the private sector in volunteerism.
Sponsor: Governor's Office on Volunteerism; New Hampshire companies
Contact: Linda Darling, Executive Director
Description: The Business Information and Resource Council (BIRC) is composed of twelve volunteer members from New Hampshire companies. These companies represent a diversity of businesses, geographic areas and sizes, but have one important characteristic in common: they are committed to volunteerism. Several of the companies have received the Governor's Volunteer Recognition Award.
BIRC works in a number of ways to involve the private sector in New Hampshire's volunteer activities. It promotes public/private cooperation ventures that contribute to the enrichment of life in the State. Some of these activities are:
- technical assistance to business;
- selection of business winner of the Governor's Volunteer Recognition Award; and
- Governor's Dinner for business and volunteerism.

One form of technical assistance offered by BIRC to businesses is in helping the business to create an employee volunteer program or to expand their support of the voluntary sector. This assistance includes:
- one-to-one consultation;
- referral to other New Hampshire businesses with volunteer programs;
- use of "modern program" materials;
- publicizing companies' efforts in support of volunteerism;
- supporting the development of partnerships with the voluntary sector.

BIRC emphasizes the benefits of volunteerism to business, since it brings together volunteers, business and government to tackle New Hampshire's toughest problems and help retain that special quality of life. In this way, a business which supports volunteerism gains the loyalty and cooperation of its employees, and the respect of its customers and the community. In short, when business commits to volunteerism, everyone benefits.
As one of the committees of the Governor's Office on Volunteerism, BIRC was established in 1983 by an eighteen-member Steering Committee - the Governor's Committee on Volunteerism - composed of volunteers, volunteer administrators, and business people.
Publications: Business Information and Resource Council (BIRC)
Founded: 1983

GOVERNORS' OFFICES ON VOLUNTEERISM: NEW JERSEY

NATIONAL/STATE ORGANIZATIONS

GOVERNOR'S ADVISORY COMMITTEE ON PRIVATE/PUBLIC VOLUNTEER PARTNERSHIPS/NJ
SEE PRIVATE SECTOR INITIATIVES OFFICES

NEW JERSEY OFFICE OF VOLUNTEERISM
101 South Broad Street
CN 800
Trenton, NJ 08625-0800
TEL: 609-292-9069
Objectives: To support the growth and development of volunteerism throughout the state.
Services: In November 1985 the New Jersey Office of Volunteerism (NJOV) was established within the Office of the Governor in response to concerns by the volunteer community in the State. NJOV was initially funded by a five-year grant awarded by *ACTION, The Federal Volunteer Agency* and by matching State funds. Legislation has been introduced to mandate NJOV and thus ensure the Office a permanent position in New Jersey State Government. NJOV offers various types of services to the volunteer community across the state, including:
Technical Assistance
Statewide Conference - schedules a full-day annual event to provide the opportunity for networking and offer technical assistance to volunteers, program directors, nonprofit agencies, board members, community groups, and corporations active in volunteerism.
Regional/Local Workshops and Conferences - organizes separate conferences in northern and southern New Jersey, as well as numerous regional workshops throughout the state - all tailored to local needs.
Resource Library - houses a statewide volunteer resource library containing books, periodicals, videos, articles, and other resource materials related to the field of volunteerism - available on request.
Other Technical Assistance - develops new programs; maintains existing volunteer programs; provides in-person visits, mail correspondence, and/or telephone consultation regarding training, awards, resources, CompuList, legislation, and other matters related to the New Jersey volunteer community.
NJOV also works to help create new volunteer programs such as DOVIAS (Directors of Volunteers in Agencies) and VACs (Voluntary Action Centers). In addition, NJOV staff members hold membership on several advisory committees, attend local volunteer organization meetings, develop specialized technical assistance material packages, and deliver public speeches at numerous events.
Communications
CompuList - a computerized master registry of volunteer organizations throughout New Jersey serving as a reference guide to agencies and volunteers seeking information about volunteer programs or positions.
Active Volunteer - a statewide quarterly newsletter with a mailing list of over 5,000, which highlights outstanding volunteer efforts, features career volunteer position openings, reports trends in the field, etc.
Other Communications - press releases, brochures, correspondence, reports on timely volunteer topics and issues, speaking agenda, etc.
Recognition
Governor's Volunteer Awards - annual event honoring individuals, groups or causes which help to improve the quality of life in the communities.
Volunteer Administrtor of the Year Award - recognition for outstanding performance in volunteer administration.
New Jersey State Fair - a ceremony highlighting volunteerism at the annual fair, and publicly acknowledging contributions of the State's volunteers.
Special Projects
Statewide Survey - a needs assessment survey designed to gather information about the State's volunteer programs and to help shape the future of NJOV.
SOV Manual - designated as the host state to develop a technical assistance manual that all State Offices on Volunteerism can use to benefit their communities.
Rutgers - holds membership on the University's Advisory Committee on Volunteerism, enabling NJOV to provide input

about curriculum for *The Certificate of Volunteer Management* offered through the Continuing Education Program, School of Social Work, and other volunteer-related courses.
Volunteer Connection - has responsibility to receive telephone calls from across the state and to connect callers with volunteer opportunities as part of a nationwide program which uses the media to educate and recruit people for volunteer projects.
Association for Volunteer Administration (AVA) - holds membership in Region II of AVA, a national association for the profession of volunteer management.
National Assembly of State Offices on Volunteerism (NASOV) - holds membership in this coalition of state government offices of volunteerism, which influences and supports the growth of volunteerism inside and outside of the United States, and works with local and state programs comprised of more than 40,000,000 volunteers.
VACs and DOVIAs - provides technical assistance, leadership, resources, and a voice to the Governor to assist Directors of Volunteers in Agencies and Voluntary Action Centers as they provide the means to carry out many of the NJOV's programs through their vast network and community resources.
To carry out its many programs, NJOV is assisted by the *Governor's Advisory Committee on Private/Public Volunteer Partnerships,* which is an organization of community leaders representing public, private and independent sectors on matters concerning volunteerism. This Committee's goals are:

- Advise and prioritize community needs; identify resources to meet these needs.
- Recognize and reward successful examples of private initiatives and community partnerships; to provide these examples to other communities.
- Identify regulatory and statutory impediments to volunteer activity; explore and suggest legislative solutions.
- Encourage involvement of private sector through partnerships, resources (time, funds, efforts); strengthen and meet needs of New Jersey's communities.

Among the thirty-six members of the Committee are representatives of the Junior Leagues, PTA, Volunteer Bureau, public utilities, the media, Chamber of Commerce, the arts, literacy programs, ethnic groups, Rutgers University, state agencies, National Council of Jewish Women, and the Center for Non-Profits.
Contact: Elizabeth A. Lane, Assistant Director
Publications: New Jersey Office of Volunteerism; Governor's Volunteer Awards; Active Volunteer (newsletter)
Founded: 1985

INDIVIDUAL PROGRAM PROFILES

HOMELESSNESS PREVENTION PROGRAM
New Jersey Office of the Governor
101 South Broad Street
CN 800
Trenton, NJ 08625
TEL: 609-292-9069
Purpose: To enlist assistance the Red Cross, Salvation Army, and other service agencies to locate and help families at risk of becoming homeless.
Sponsor: American Red Cross
Contact: Helen Seitz, Director (state); Tricia Fagan, Director (Rutgers University)
Description: When New Jersey announced that it would administer and fund a "homelessness prevention project" across the State, volunteer organizations, universities, legal services, and others offered to help by referring families-at-risk that came to their attention. This network of volunteer referral organizations has worked so well that it has helped New Jersey's program to be considered a national model, and several other states are emulating

the idea by instituting projects of their own. Maryland, Michigan and Pennsylvania offer emergency mortgage assistance for homeowners. New York and Connecticut offer eviction mediation services for renters, and Virginia has begun a program based on the New Jersey experiment.
Begun in 1984, by 1990 the New Jersey project had assisted 15,000 New Jersey families by paying rents, mortgages and providing the security deposits that often make the difference between shelter and the streets. In one instance, a blind woman with a mentally-handicapped son called an attorney at the *Commission for the Blind* for help, and was put in touch with the state program which paid the back rent and penalties.
According to the initiators, the project was begun to counteract the focus in recent years on opening massive shelters or housing families in dilapidated hotels like the recently-closed Capital City Inn in Washington. Besides, the $4.8 million New Jersey spent on the program last year is cost-effective, since State officials estimate that intervention before a family becomes homeless is three times cheaper than putting the family up in an emergency shelter and 30 times cheaper than a welfare hotel.
The State's program offers one-time assistance for people suffering temporary financial crises but are not eligible for other emergency assistance. For homeowners, the assistance is treated as a loan and a lien is placed on their property. All applicants must demonstrate that they are in imminent danger of eviction or foreclosure and cannot get the money any other way. "The best way to do something about homelessness is to prevent it."
With assistance of *Rutgers, The State University's American Affordable Housing Institute,* which provides studies and statistics, private groups such as the *Elizabeth Coalition to House the Homeless,* which serve thousands of homeless individuals and families, and the volunteer and nonprofit organizations that refer families at risk of becoming homeless, the project is expected to continue.

GOVERNORS' OFFICES ON VOLUNTEERISM: NEW MEXICO

TRAINING PROGRAMS

COALITION FOR VOLUNTEER SUPPORT
Governor's Office on Volunteer Services/NM
308 Read Street
Santa Fe, NM 87501
TEL: 505-827-8235
TOLL FREE: 800-423-2070
Credit: Inquire
Sponsor: Governor's Office on Volunteer Services
Contact: Pat Hamm Powell
Description: Formed by the Governor's Office of Volunteer Services, this Coalition provides the opportunity for input from a wide range of individuals involved in volunteer activities into the plans for GOVS in the coming year. Participants represent all areas of the state and many different types of volunteer programs and activities. Subcommittees are formed around specific topics; examples of their suggestions appear below:
Promotion of Volunteer Activities - Change the image of a volunteer from that of a "slave" to that of someone making a valuable contribution, and encourage everyone to volunteer.
Business - Business and labor need more information about the benefits of encouraging volunteerism, and to examine types of "in-kind" contributions they can make to assist volunteer programs and organizations. Business is well-represented in the President's Private Sector Initiatives Program, which needs

comprehensive coverage at all levels.

Training/Technical Assistance - Training programs available need to be inventoried and shared with groups needing information. An information and referral system could provide packets of information to individuals and groups wishing additional information on selected topics. Volunteer training workshops could be held on a local or regional basis.

Statewide Skillsbank - Development of a statewide skillsbank will require funding, training volunteers, identifying skills to be included, and updating of information. Matching needs with skills on a statewide basis could assist many communities in critical areas.

Volunteer Legislation - An inventory needs to be made of legislation throughout the country related to volunteers. Special legislation should be drawn up to include such items as tax credits and incentives for volunteer time and expense, credit given on an application with the State Personnel Office for volunteer work as well as other related areas.

Recognition - A handbook for managers of volunteers with suggestions for various types of recognition that could be valuable to individual organizations involving volunteers. The information could include types of publicity and suggestions for ongoing recognition. The statewide recognition ceremony should be repeated.

Young Volunteers in Action - Encouraging teenagers to volunteer was identified as a first priority in this area. Volunteer stations should include job descriptions for younger volunteers in areas in which they would be interested and for positions which would be achievable.

Volunteers in State Agencies - A network should be developed of state agencies utilizing volunteers to provide an opportunity for sharing of experiences and information. Employees of state agencies also should be encouraged to volunteer. Work release time would facilitate state employee volunteering.

The meeting considers expectations for the role of Governor's Office of Volunteer Services, as well as the above recommendations for future directions. The initial meeting of this group was held in 1982, the first year of state funding of the GOVs. Many of the initial recommendations have been implemented, and are considered valuable contributions toward the improvement of the quality of life in New Mexico.

VOLUNTEERS: OUR GREATEST NATURAL RESOURCE
New Mexico Statewide Conference on Volunteerism
Governor's Office on Volunteer Services
308 Read Street
Santa Fe, NM 87501
TEL: 505-827-3175
TOLL FREE: 800-432-2070
Credit: AVA Endorsement
Sponsor: Governor's Office on Volunteer Services/NM
Contact: Alice King, Director
Description: This conference involved fourteen 1-1/2-hour workshops, repeated throughout the two-day period based on responses to the registration forms. The keynote address was provided by Cherrie Carapetyan, who also conducted the opening workshop. Workshop topics:

- **Effective Management of the Volunteer Resource** - how to plan, organize, staff recruit/retain, train, supervise/motivate, evaluate/recognize and assess trends...to discover, develop and deploy the volunteer resource.
- **Creative Problem Solving for Small Town Survival** - how to create a core group, set up public meetings, conduct meetings to develop methods for revitalizing small towns through volunteer efforts.
- **Creative Fundraising** - useful techniques in local fundraising for volunteer groups.
- **Marketing Techniques/Membership Development** - how to broaden community support through marketing and expand

that support while surviving outside losses.
- **Stress Management and Burnout** - how to deal with staff and volunteer burnout, including a discussion of symptoms, causes and cures.
- **Advocacy** - how to utilize skills to effectively advocate for a program, person or group.
- **How to Start a Volunteer Program** - the nitty-gritty steps involved in starting a new program.
- **Running Effective Meetings** - the essentials of planning and conducting effective meetings with emphasis on Board Meetings.
- **Cutbacks** - the impact of cutback decisions from the State level and how to deal with cutbacks at the local level.
- **Time Management** - techniques of managing personal time effectively.
- **Media Relations** - methods of maintaining an ongoing relationship between volunteer programs and the community's working press.
- **Newsletters** - how to plan and produce an agency newsletter.
- **International Year of the Disabled** - how to utilize the disabled as volunteers.
- **Prison Advocacy/Reform** - how to become involved in making prison reforms.

These Conferences are held annually with format changes based on the changing times. Timely topics added to recent Conferences include:

Skills for New Mexico: focuses on tying New Mexico's needs through the use of a statewide skills bank, including the use of computers (and how it has worked for 17 years in one community).

Public/Private Partnerships: which focuses on how government entities, businesses and corporations, and non-profit organizations can work together to benefit local communities and the state.

Promoting Non-profits through the Use of Communications: which assists groups in developing good communications with the public through news releases, the electronic media and organizational newsletters.

Volunteer Management and other relevant issues are continued from year to year after a perusal to assure currency and/or alterations to meet current needs.

Faculty for the conference was drawn from across the state of New Mexico and included representatives from volunteer organizations with many years of successful experience.

INDIVIDUAL PROGRAM PROFILES

SAVE OUR WATER*
308 Read Street
Santa Fe, NM 87501
TEL: 505-827-8235
Purpose: To educate citizens about the benefits of conserving water.
Sponsor: The Governor's Office of Volunteer Services/NM and US/ACTION
Contact: Pat Powell
Description: In the past, most communities have turned to water conservation only as a last resort - as an emergency measure in a crisis situation. This project, however, establishes the fact that water conservation is an effective management tool to be used in both short and long term water supply planning.

Save Our Water is based upon the premise that a locally-designed and orchestrated community-wide campaign which features simple, affordable conservation technologies will motivate large numbers of people to take specific water conservation measures in their daily lives; and that the direct participation of local residents in the community effort is essential to the ultimate success of the program.

Volunteer Staff - Volunteers are recruited in each community to

conduct workshops on water conservation, assemble and distribute water conservation kits, handle publicity and promotion, speak to civic and service organizations and a variety of other activities. Volunteers are the essential ingredient for the success of this project because they can approach their neighbors and friends on a equal level, convincing them of the need for conserving water.
Volunteer Experience - There are jobs in this project which can be handled by youth groups, senior citizens - or any other specific group. Volunteers who conduct workshops must have prior experience in this field, or be willing to undergo appropriate training.

GOVERNORS' OFFICES ON VOLUNTEERISM: NEW YORK

NATIONAL/STATE ORGANIZATIONS

GOVERNOR'S OFFICE FOR VOLUNTARY SERVICE/NY
2 World Trade Center
57th Floor
New York, NY 10047
TEL: 212-587-2255
Objectives: To heighten awareness of the opportunities and need for volunteerism in New York State.
Services: Advises the Governor on all matters relating to volunteerism; promotes voluntary activities within state government; serves as an advocate for the voluntary sector on issues which affect their operations; activities include:

- **Development of Public/Private Partnerships** - To identify and address the state's unmet human service needs, public questions are studied and the public, private and voluntary sectors are assisted in the establishment of coalitions around important issues.
- **Encouragement of Corporate Involvement** - To create new opportunities for volunteerism and to increase support for voluntary programs, the corporate community is encouraged to allocate additional human and financial resources to voluntary efforts.
- **Initiation of Pilot Programs** - To implement innovative programs developed in cooperation with public and voluntary agencies, funding sources are identified, supervision and leadership provided, and community resources located.
- **Legislative Task Force** - To advance and strengthen voluntary organizations, legislation impacting on volunteerism is monitored and studied and legislative initiatives undertaken.
- **Governor's Empire State Volunteer Program** - To reinforce and promote the role of volunteerism within state government, technical assistance, training, public awareness efforts and support are provided to state agencies to increase volunteer participation in state programs and activities.
- **Eleanor Roosevelt Community Service Awards** - To recognize voluntary efforts throughout the state, an annual awards program honors local groups for their development of creative projects employing volunteers to provide needed community services.
- **Foster Care Youth Independence Project** - To give aid and support to youth aging out of foster care, volunteers are recruited and trained to serve as mentors and role models to ease the transition to living independently.
- **Private Sector Initiatives Task Force on Alcohol and Drug Abuse** - To attack the critical problem of alcohol and drug abuse, partnerships are facilitated between the business community and human service agencies to develop and implement primary prevention programs targeted to children

in grades K-4.
- **New York State Voluntary Service Corps** - To enrich undergraduate education and provide opportunities to explore careers with government and other service providers, college students are offered volunteer placements in government agencies and community organizations, as well as academic credit for a course on the history and philosophy of volunteerism in America.
- **"Celebrating Our Volunteers" Photo Exhibit** - To celebrate National Volunteer Week, and honor the recipients of the Governor's Volunteer Awards, a photo exhibit of the award winners' activities is opened in the Empire State Plaza along with a celebration attended by State dignitaries and volunteer entertainers.
- **Bi-Annual Statewide Conference** - To promote volunteerism in New York State, delegates from the public, private and voluntary sectors are provided opportunities for training, learning and information sharing on the many aspects of volunteerism.
- **Quarterly Newsletter** - To keep the citizens of New York State informed, *Citizen Involvement* reports on the activities of the Governor's Office for Volunteer Service and provides information on issues of interest to the Voluntary Sector.

Publications: Citizen Involvement (quarterly newsletter); Eleanor Roosevelt Community Service Awards Program; Governor's Office for Voluntary Service

INDIVIDUAL PROGRAM PROFILES

FLAME OF HOPE
SEE VOLUNTEERS: POLICE OFFICERS

GOVERNORS' OFFICES ON VOLUNTEERISM: NORTH CAROLINA

TRAINING PROGRAMS

NORTH CAROLINA/VIRGINIA EXCHANGE: PART ONE
Governor's Office on Volunteerism and Citizen Affairs/NC
116 West Jones Street
Raleigh, NC 27611
TEL: 919-733-2391
Credit: Inquire
Sponsor: Virginia Department of Volunteerism; Governor's Office on Volunteerism and Citizen Affairs
Contact: Arlene Pulley
Description: Initiated by North Carolina's Governor, Virginia and North Carolina engaged in the first segment of a learning experience in the form of an exchange of information on each state's volunteer program. Held in Raleigh, the program provided delegates from each state opportunities to:
- learn about each other's state-sponsored volunteer activities.
- observe North Carolina program operations.
- brainstorm about day-to-day operations of a state office on volunteerism.
- plan for Part Two, a visit by the North Carolina delegation to Virginia's program.

The backgrounds of the two state offices provided a foundation for the meeting:
- The *Virginia Department of Volunteerism* was the first state to enact a *State Government Volunteers Act* to encourage the fullest possible involvement of volunteers in state and local

governments.
- The *Governor's Office of Volunteerism and Citizen Affairs* in North Carolina is the largest staffed and funded statewide volunteerism office in the nation.

Also, program emphases of the two offices is complementary in that Virginia's program concentrates on training, technical assistance, and information dissemination for volunteer-involving agencies; North Carolina's program emphasizes public education and recognition efforts.

The Virginia delegation had an opportunity to observe recognition techniques of the North Carolina office by representing Virginia at Governor Hunt's Volunteer Awards Ceremony in the course of the meeting. The Ceremony was attended by 1,200 North Carolinians. Part Two is the reciprocal visit with Virginia hosting the North Carolina delegation, described below. Information on one or both sessions is made available to interested state offices on volunteerism.

GOVERNORS' OFFICES ON VOLUNTEERISM: OREGON

NATIONAL/STATE ORGANIZATIONS

OREGON STATE VOLUNTEER SERVICES PROGRAM
415 Public Service Building
Salem, OR 97310
TEL: 503-378-3755
Purpose: To increase, extend and enrich services to agency clients through citizen and community involvement.
Sponsor: Federal/state governments; private donations
Contact: Darlene Shen, Volunteer Program Manager
Description: The State of Oregon Volunteer Services Program is a statewide program directed toward developing and coordinating volunteer and community resources needed to enhance and extend agency services for clients of four human services agencies within the Department of Human Resources.

The program staff consists of one state level program manager and at least one Volunteer Services Supervisor field position located in al most every county of the state. Volunteer Services Supervisors work closely with state agency staff to determine the service needs of clients. Once a need is identified, the Volunteer Supervisors are responsible for meeting the need by recruiting, training and placing individual volunteers or working with other community agencies to assist them in providing the needed service.

Currently, over 1,200 volunteers and countless local agencies are working together with the program every month to provide services for local communities. The program provides such services as transportation to medical appointments, one-on-one support for the elderly moving into or out of nursing facilities, assisting individuals looking for employment by providing classes on interviewing skills, resume writing, one-on-one support for the children in foster care, etc. The list of services provided can go on and on depending on the service needs identified in the local community and the resources available to meet the needs.

INDIVIDUAL PROGRAM PROFILES

INTERDIVISIONAL VOLUNTEER PROGRAM
Oregon Department of Human Resources
Post Office Box 628
Hillsboro, OR 97123
TEL: 503-648-0711

Purpose: To incorporate local citizen involvement in many areas of social service delivery with the clientele of the Adult and Family Services, Children's Services, Senior Services and Mental Health Division of the State of Oregon, Department of Human Resources.
Sponsor: State of Oregon, Department of Human Resources, private donations
Contact: Guy Hornbeck, Volunteer Services Supervisor
Description: The Interdivisional Volunteer Program has its origin in the 1967 Harris Amendments to the Social Security Act of 1935. These amendments mandated the use of volunteers in the delivery of services by all public assistance and service programs. The goals of the interdivisional Volunteer Program are:
- To extend, supplement and enrich services to clients.
- To provide the personalized help and interest of a sincere friend.
- To provide opportunity for persons with different life styles and varied socio-economic levels, including clients themselves, to help agency clients.
- To provide first hand information to the public on the nature of the services and problems of the agencies.
- To assist in developing community awareness of social problems and the need for finding appropriate solutions.

The Interdivisional Volunteer Program is funded through Title XIX of the Social Security Act of 1935, State of Oregon General Fund monies, and through private donations.

Volunteers in Washington County participate in activities that range from serving as a "big sister" to a sexually abused girl, to advocating for the needs of nursing home patients, to soliciting and delivering donated food and furniture items to destitute families, to befriending a mentally handicapped adult.

Volunteers in these programs are considered "Agents of the State" and as such are covered by certain Tort Liability immunity and Workman's Compensation Insurance...just like any other "Agent of the State."
Founded: 1967

VOLUNTEER AWARDS PROGRAM
SEE ADMINISTRATION: RECOGNITION

GOVERNORS' OFFICES ON VOLUNTEERISM: PENNSYLVANIA

NATIONAL/STATE ORGANIZATIONS

PENNSERVE: THE GOVERNOR'S OFFICE OF CITIZEN SERVICE
1306 Labor & Industry Bldg.
Harrisburg, PA 17120
TEL: 717-787-1971
FAX: 717-783-5420
Objectives: To inspire all Pennsylvania citizens to engage in some form of community service (with an emphasis on youth).
Services: Provides support and technical assistance in three areas of volunteerism, with an emphasis on youth:
Full-Time Service - supports the development of a full-time youth service corps, with nine Pennsylvania programs under way, including:
- **Pennsylvania Conservation Corps** - the second largest full-time service corps in the nation, where some 8,000 young people have "worked, earned and learned" since 1985 while improving the state's environmental and recreational resources (all unemployed, 50% high school dropouts, 30% receiving public assistance); 70% moved directly from the corps into private sector jobs, the military or back into school.

- **Philadelphia Youth Service Corps** and **Fairmont Ranger Corps** - launched in 1988, provides more than 100 Philadelphia youth with full-time service opportunities.
- **Urban Service Corps Initiative** - Begun in 1989 in Pittsburgh and McKeesport, these state-local partnerships provides corps experiences for 200 youth each year (one state dollar generates three local dollars).
- **Local Corps Incubator Program** - Using *Pennsylvania Conservation Corps* funds, PennSERVE has launched five new local Corps. Selected in July 1990, these Corps began operation in October 1990.
- **Summer Youth Employment and Training Program,** in which PennSERVE works closely with the **Bureau of Job Training Partnership (JTPA)** and the **Service Delivery Association (SDA)** to redirect the $27 million program, allocates funds to integrate non-JTPA eligible youth into the Summer Youth Program, and responds to nationwide inquiries about these programs.

School and College Community Service - supports school- and college-based service-learning programs in a number of ways:

- provided $5,000 minigrants to school-based community service programs;
- encouraged academic credit for community service;
- promoted special events such as the *Day in the Life of Youth Service* at over 300 sites across the state;
- provided technical assistance to school districts to expand community service programs;
- helped launch *Pennsylvania Campus Compact,* a program of the *Pennsylvania Association of Colleges and Universities* involving 30 college Presidents and student community service on campus;
- established a *Pennsylvania Literacy Corps* to enlist and train college students in the fight against illiteracy, which now operates on 13 campuses;
- works with the *Association of Secondary School Principals,* the *School Boards Association,* the *State Education Association,* and the *American Federation of Teachers* to support community service;
- helped initiate a resolution by the State Board of Education to make community service an integral part of the school system, involving every student.

Volunteer Service - serves as an advocate for volunteering throughout Pennsylvania, mounting activities such as:

- conducts surveys on volunteerism;
- sponsors statewide conferences (the first in 1989);
- works with *Department of Labor and Industry's Job Center Initiative* to bring volunteers into the jobs and job training effort for all Pennsylvanians;
- provides technical assistance in support of $50,000 JTPA grant to expand volunteer-to-work program.

PennSERVE provides free packets of information on request to help spread the word about youth community service programs operating in Pennsylvania.
Sponsor: State of Pennsylvania
Contact: John A. Briscoe
Publications: PennSERVE Packet

GOVERNORS' OFFICES ON VOLUNTEERISM: RHODE ISLAND

INDIVIDUAL PROGRAM PROFILES

TEA AND TREASURES
Friends of Linden Place
PO Box 328
Bristol, RI 02809
TEL: 401-253-0390
Purpose: To raise funds for restoration of a historical property for use as an educational and cultural center.
Sponsor: Rhode Island Historical Preservation Commission
Contact: Patricia A. Kenyon, Executive Director
Description: Volunteer appraisers, many of whom operate auctions for historical pieces worth millions of dollars, provided the base for a fund-raising event at the Governor's mansion. The jewelry appraisal volunteer is from the distinguished Tilden-Thurber. The purpose of the program was to provide the means of restoring a historic building, Linden Place, to serve as an educational and cultural center for the area. The Governor's wife and the chairwoman of the Rhode Island Historical Preservation Commission share the chairmanship of the *Friends of Linden Place* honorary board of directors.
Appraisals of small art works, old photos, jewelry, silver and furniture were made at *Tea and Treasures* for a $5 donation to the restoration fund for each appraisal. A $10 additional donation allows guests to join a reception and have tea poured by the Governor's wife and the Historical Preservation Commission chairwoman.
The need for the educational and cultural center has been well established, and fundraisers such as *Tea and Treasures* are helping to make it happen, according to the executive director.

GOVERNORS' OFFICES ON VOLUNTEERISM: SOUTH CAROLINA

INDIVIDUAL PROGRAM PROFILES

GAIN (GREATER ACHIEVEMENT THROUGH INVOLVEMENT NOW)
South Carolina Division of Rural Development & Special Economic Assistance
205 Pendleton Street
Columbia, SC 29201
TEL: 803-758-7804
Purpose: To increase participation of rural residents in community affairs and economic ventures.
Sponsor: Federal agency US/ACTION; state of South Carolina
Contact: Karen Ross Grant
Description: Since 1977 the Governor's Office of Rural Development has sponsored VISTA Volunteers to "extend its arms" into unserved rural areas of the state. These volunteers are responsible for mobilizing community residents and resources to sponsor self-help projects which develop skills (manual, intellectual) among low-income residents. Examples of projects include tutorial centers, craft cooperatives, reupholstery businesses, emergency centers, food banks, sewing clubs and community organizations focusing on rural concerns. Once a project has been initiated through the help of a VISTA, that VISTA trains other community residents to manage and develop the projects. VISTAs

create many volunteer opportunities for the residents; in some, permanent jobs are created.

The Federal Agency, ACTION, provides a subsistance allowance and monthly stipend to VISTAs, while the Governor's Rural Development Office provides transportation reimbursement and long-distance telephone cards. Currently there are eight VISTAs in the project with a staff VISTA Supervisor in charge. Quarterly meetings are held to discuss field activities and make plans. Special workshops are held when needed.

For many rural areas, volunteerism and self-help is "the way to go" due to inadequate or ineffective government programs. Rural churches are a big resource. The desire to see community improvements and work toward them are ever present in rural areas; the challenge is finding and developing good leadership and coordination.

Founded: 1977

GOVERNORS' OFFICES ON VOLUNTEERISM: SOUTH DAKOTA

TRAINING PROGRAMS

VOLUNTEER LEADERSHIP CONFERENCE
South Dakota Governor's Office
State Capitol
500 East Capitol
Pierre, SD 57501
TEL: 605-773-3661
Credit: CEUs
Sponsor: South Dakota Governor's Office
Contact: Nancy Abbott
Description: A statewide annual conference providing 23 to 25 workshops targeted to volunteer leaders and administrators. The workshops have three levels of training: open, advance, and basic so as to meet the needs of all participants:
- Team Building
- Coping with Stress and Conflict
- Creative Use of Volunteers
- Developing Non-Paid Volunteer Leaders
- Selling Yourself and Your Cause
- Job Descriptions and Volunteer Placement
- Legislative and Lobbying Techniques

South Dakota also has statewide regional training workshops throughout the year - meeting the needs of communities and programs. Trainers are drawn from all areas and are known across the state, regionally and nationally.

GOVERNORS' OFFICES ON VOLUNTEERISM: TENNESSEE

INDIVIDUAL PROGRAM PROFILES

FREE THE CHILDREN (FTC)
SEE FUNDING/FUND-RAISING/RELATED SERVICES: FAMILIES

GOVERNORS' OFFICES ON VOLUNTEERISM: TEXAS

NATIONAL/STATE ORGANIZATIONS

RUNAWAY HOTLINE
SEE INFORMATION & REFERRAL: CHILDREN/YOUTH

TRAINING PROGRAMS

TEXAS VOLUNTEER CONFERENCE
Governor's Office for Volunteer Services/TX
104 Sam Houston Building
Austin, TX 78711
TEL: 512-475-4441
Credit: AVA Certification (partial fulfillment)
Sponsor: Governor's Office for Volunteer Services in cooperation with 15 state and local agencies and organizations.
Contact: Deputy Director, Governor's Office for Volunteer Services
Description: Areas of focus vary year to year as needs of volunteers and volunteer administrations are identified by participating agencies.

A typical conference includes a number of workshops and discussions designed to develop skills, to describe how volunteers work in different settings, and to discuss pertinent issues in volunteerism as they relate to volunteers and volunteer administrators. Examples of areas of focus:

Skill building in...
- How to Interview and Screen Interviews
- Your Volunteer Career
- Communication and Feedback Systems
- Monitoring Programs and Evaluating Performance
- Documentation and Reporting

Issues in...
- Professional Development
- Liability and Confidentiality
- Measuring the Impact
- Internship Programs
- Working with Advisory Committees

Volunteers in...
- Religious Settings
- Political Settings
- Health Settings
- Youth Serving Settings
- Criminal Justice Settings
- Senior Citizen Settings
- Cultural Settings

Governor's Awards for Outstanding Volunteer Service are presented during the Conference. Five categories are used:
1. the volunteer who has provided broad and exceptional leadership to a cause, program, or project which ministers to human needs and has advanced the whole realm of voluntarism;
2. the volunteer who has excelled in length, quality and spirit of service to others;
3. the group of volunteers which has been instrumental in designing or creating an innovative project or program to benefit or meet community needs, and in doing so, has demonstrated extraordinary initiative and originality;
4. the paid staff person within a public or private organization who has contributed in a substantial way to the encouragement and nurturing of voluntarism; and
5. the corporation which has demonstrated commitment to the community through an active program of volunteer service.

GOVERNORS' OFFICES ON VOLUNTEERISM: UTAH

TRAINING PROGRAMS

INTER-AGENCY VOLUNTEER QUARTERLY FORUMS
Utah Department of Social Services
Personnel Department
PO Box 255
Salt Lake City, UT 84110
TEL: 801-533-6038
Credit: Inquire
Sponsor: Utah Department of Social Services
Contact: Jeano Campanaro, Utah Department of Social Services Personnel Department
Description: The Utah Department of Social Services conducts training forums for volunteer managers and coordinators on a quarterly basis. Although the six-hour programs are targeted to the Department's agencies and providers, other agencies are admitted on request. Emphasis in the forums is placed upon audience participation to enhance learning.

The Volunteer Training Plan is a series of outlines dealing with most aspects of volunteer programs. The outlines were conceived in order to have written material on hand to assist the trainer with any requests for information assistance from Volunteer Coordinators, or as the need arises in the course of the forums or other training programs. All outlines in the series are listed below, with those in process so noted:

- Philosophical Overview and Departmental Perspectives
- Organizational Climate
- Developing a Job Description
- Recruitment of Volunteers
- The Linking Function
- Supervision and On-The-Job Training
- Record Keeping and Reporting
- Rewards and Recognition of Volunteers
- Evaluations (pending)
- Continuing Incentives (pending)
- Introduction into the Organization (pending)

Outlines are updated as needed, and the series design facilitates the addition of new topics as community and program needs change and grow.

INDIVIDUAL PROGRAM PROFILES

NEIGHBORHOOD PROBATION UNIT
SEE VOLUNTEERS: TEAMS

GOVERNORS' OFFICES ON VOLUNTEERISM: VERMONT

NATIONAL/STATE ORGANIZATIONS

CENTER FOR PREVENTION AND TREATMENT OF SEXUAL ABUSE
State of Vermont
State Capitol
Montpelier, VT 05602
TEL: 802-828-1110

Objectives: To provide a treatment program and aftercare support system to help prevent recidivism in sexual abuse crimes; to operate a statewide education program to prevent sexual abuse crimes.
Services: Developed by the State of Vermont in 1972, this treatment and prevention program has among the lowest recidivism rates ever achieved. While national and statewide statistics are alarming, 80 percent of child molesters across the country repeat the offense, while the Vermont estimate is 60% - only two percent of those who have gone through Vermont's Center for the Prevention and Treatment of Sexual Abuse have been charged with new offenses. Since its beginning, 247 pedophiles have received treatment at the Center.

The *key* to the program is what its director calls "relapse prevention." A mental health professional works closely with a parole officer in treating the offenders both in jail and after they are out. They are shown that it is not something beyond their control. By providing them with greater power over themselves, the need to feel power by controlling others decreases. They are sensitized to the harm they cause their victims and educated about the process they follow in getting to the point where they choose to abuse someone. Since this process is not an impulse but a well-thought out plan, there is a chance to intervene during that process.

Parole is closely supervised, with the added benefit of volunteer assistance by family, friends, employers and colleagues. The volunteers are given the "script" the offender would follow if he were in the process of choosing to offend again. A requirement of the treatment program is that the offender provide this information to all parties concerned. The helpers are taught to watch for signs such as emotional changes which may indicate that the offender is beginning to cycle back towards abuse. Loneliness and fantasy are two examples, and sometimes signs are visible in these cases.

In summary, the director points out that, like alcoholism, there is no cure for the "power of choice." Despite the success rate at the Center, there is no guarantee that the sex offender will not choose to offend again. They do not allow any delusions by the offenders, either, advising them that "the only certificate of graduation is your death certificate. Then you know that you are cured."
Sponsor: State of Vermont
Contact: William D. Pithers, Director

GOVERNORS' OFFICES ON VOLUNTEERISM: VIRGINIA

NATIONAL/STATE ORGANIZATIONS

CHILD ABUSE HOTLINE
SEE INFORMATION & REFERRAL: DOMESTIC ABUSE

COMMISSION ON SELF-SUFFICIENCY
SEE LEADERSHIP DEVELOPMENT/BOARDS: HANDICAPPED

VIRGINIA DIVISION OF VOLUNTEERISM (*formerly Governor's Office on Volunteerism*)
223 Governor Street
Richmond, VA 23219
TEL: 804-786-1431
Objectives: To assist leaders of volunteers through training, technical assistance, networking, information services, recognition and advocacy.

Services: Begun as an adjunct to the Governor's Office, Virginia's volunteer leader support function is now a full-fledged Department of the State. Fiscal year 1988 produced over one-and-a-half million volunteer hours valued at over fifteen million dollars. Among services provided by the Department are:

- **Training and Conferences:** The Department offers a variety of training programs to leaders of volunteers, providing opportunities to improve skills and exchange ideas:
- **Public Workshops:** Events are offered each fall and spring in various locales around the state.
- **Statewide Conference:** The Department sponsors an annual conference on volunteerism which features high quality training as well as a celebration of Virginia's volunteer spirit.
- **Training on Request:** The Department provides individually designed training for local government agencies, state agencies and nonprofit organizations upon request on a wide range of topics.
- **Technical Assistance and Networking:** Agencies may request assistance on specific issues related to volunteerism. The Department then responds with an individualized consultation by phone, letter, or site visit. The Department also facilitates the creation of support systems around the state:
- **Individual Consultation:** These are the one-on-one consultations which seek to solve problems or improve program effectiveness.
- **Community Volunteer Centers:** The Department lends support to the periodic statewide meetings of Volunteer Center directors. This network increases the strength of individual Centers and enhances the volunteer presence in Virginia.
- **Association for Volunteer Administration (AVA):** AVA is the international professional organization for managers of volunteer programs. The Department is supportive of AVA efforts in Virginia, the region, and nationally.
- **Information Services:** The Department acts as a clearinghouse on volunteerism and an important source of information for the Department's constituents. It is an active link of communication among volunteer program managers in Virginia, keeping them in touch with each other and with the larger field:
- **Resource Center:** A comprehensive library of materials constantly updated and catalogued in order to be easily accessible to both Department staff and the volunteer community at large.
- **Research:** Individualized searches on specific questions or problems are conducted upon request.
- **Newsletter:** A quarterly publication is mailed to over 6000 programs and individuals, serving as a mechanism for sharing resource information, building professional skills, and keeping readers aware of national and state issues affecting volunteerism.
- **Materials Development:** Because the Department is part of the national volunteerism network, it is able to identify gaps in literature and other professional needs. Monographs, journal articles and training materials are developed as needed in order to contribute to the knowledge base of volunteerism.
- **State Government Initiatives:** The Department provides intensive ongoing support in volunteer programming to specific state agencies through interagency agreements. Services may include coordination of statewide program planning and policy development; on-site technical assistance to local agencies/institutions wishing to develop and implement volunteer programs; training for local and regional staff; and materials development pertinent to social services and correctional settings.
- **Recognition and Advocacy:** The Department promotes increased public awareness of volunteer contributions to the Commonwealth:
- **Recognition:** The Department annually arranges for the Governor to proclaim "Volunteer Week in Virginia" in conjunction with National Volunteer Week activities. The Department also sponsors an annual statewide recognition program, the Governor's Awards for Volunteering Excellence (GAVE). Developed in accordance with legislative mandate, the GAVE program honors the outstanding efforts of approximatgely 60 individuals and groups from both the public and private sectors. GAVE is totally funded by private contributions.
- **Advocacy:** The Department encourages public support for legislation favorable to volunteers and works within state government to find administrative remedies to barriers to volunteering.

In addition, the Department continually analyzes and works to fill gaps in services to volunteer leaders, often through joint efforts with other public agencies and departments and private organizations.

Contact: Beth Hayes, Director
Publications: Volunteering Virginia; VA Dept. of Volunteerism/Overview of Services; GAVE (Governor's Awards for Volunteering Excellence); VA Dept. of Volunteerism/Training Series; Volunteer Involvement in Virginia State Government

TRAINING PROGRAMS

BASICS OF VOLUNTEER PROGRAM MANAGEMENT*
Virginia Division of Volunteerism
223 Governor Street
Richmond, VA 23219
TEL: 804-786-1431
Credit: Inquire
Sponsor: Virginia Division of Volunteerism; Voluntary Action Center of Lynchburg; Danville Volunteer Council
Contact: Beth Hayes, Director
Description: This workshop is designed for people who are in the beginning stages of developing a volunteer program, or who are experiencing basic problems with their current program. Topics covered include:

- The State of the Art
- Philosophy for Volunteer Programs
- A Management Perspective for Volunteer Programs
- Pre-Planning Considerations and Policy Development
- Program Planning Activities: needs assessment; budgeting; job descriptions; recruitment; staff support
- Program Operation: screening, placement and contracting; orientation and training; supervision and dealing with problems; recordkeeping; motivation, recognition and rewards; evaluation
- Building Effective Volunteer-Staff Relations
- Benefits of Involving Volunteers
- A Wrap-up Problem-Solving Season

The two-day workshop is held in two locations to enable maximum participation. Local volunteer organizations share sponsorship with the Virginia Division on Volunteerism.

CELEBRATION OF VOLUNTEERISM: ANNUAL STATEWIDE CONFERENCE
Virginia Division of Volunteerism
223 Governor Street
Richmond, VA 23219
TEL: 804-786-1431
Credit: Inquire
Sponsor: Virginia Department of Volunteerism
Contact: Beth Hayes, Director
Description: Convened annually, this Conference focuses on a specific theme each year. A typical Conference is described below (1983):
Workshops Sessions I
- Coping Effectively with Stress

- The Legislative Process in Virginia
- Turning Staff Resistance into Staff Support
- The Future of Volunteering
- Presenting Yourself for Success
- Successful Fundraising Approaches from the Funder's Viewpoint
- Volunteer Programs and Computers

Workshops Sessions II
- Professional Development
- Building an Endowment Fund
- Legal Liability of Volunteer Programs
- Personal Selling: The Art of Getting People to Say Yes
- Church Volunteers
- Volunteer Motivation
- A Schematic for Developing a School Volunteer Program

Workshop Sessions III
- The Interview: Don't Call Us, We'll Call You
- Money Talks: A Guide to Establishing the True Value of Volunteer Time
- Special Events for Fun and Profit
- Promoting Your Volunteer Program
- Legal Liability for Nonprofit Board Members
- Evaluating Volunteer Programs
- Management Styles and Motivation

Special features of the Conference include a presentation by a member of the Virginia House of Delegates, who is also Chair of the Select Joint Subcommittee to Study Volunteer Incentives. This is presented in a "public hearing" format, with open microphones to elicit suggestions for the Subcommittee on tax credits and other methods for rewarding volunteer service. Also, a banquet, Celebration of Volunteering, is held at the close of the Conference.

COMPLETE VOLUNTEER LEGAL LIABILITY WORKSHOP
Virginia Division of Volunteerism
223 Governor Street
Richmond, VA 23219
TEL: 804-786-1431
Credit: VCU Workshop, one CEU; inquire about others
Sponsor: Virginia Department of Volunteerism
Contact: Beth Hayes, Director
Description: This workshop is a non-technical practitioner's guide to the legal problems of volunteers, volunteer-using agencies, and non-profit board members. It addresses the following issues:
- Legal Liability of Volunteers
- Legal Liabilities of Volunteer-Involving Agencies
- Legal Liabilities of Non-Profit Board Members
- Practical Strategies for Avoiding Legal Liability Problems
- Practical Strategies for Solving Legal Liability Problems
- Volunteer Insurance
- Workers Compensation and Volunteers

The one-day workshop is held in two locations on consecutive days for maximum participation (1983: Annandale in Northern Virginia, and Hampton in Southeast Virginia). Local volunteer organizations in each location share sponsorship with the Virginia Division on Volunteerism. Other sponsors include the Voluntary Action Centers of Fairfax County, Virginia Peninsula, and Norfolk, and the Volunteer Coordinators' Roundtable of Fairfax County.

The major presenter is an attorney and an executive in a national organization on volunteerism, bringing together the combination of expertise needed for leadership in a workshop on legal aspects of voluntary action.

Due to the scarcity of training in this area, this series always reaches its registration capacity well in advance of each event. Inquiries early each year are advised. Registrations are taken on a first-received, first-served basis.

EFFECTIVE BOARDSMANSHIP
Virginia Division of Volunteerism
223 Governor Street
Richmond, VA 23219
TEL: 804-786-1431
Credit: Inquire
Sponsor: Virginia Department of Volunteerism
Contact: Reenie Marshall
Description: This workshop addresses the need for Boards, Councils or Commissions, and related staff to communicate continually as they work to improve the effectiveness of both the governing bodies and the line staff and volunteers. Topics include:
- the functions and organization of boards;
- legal liability of board members;
- membership and recruitment strategies;
- appropriate roles for board members and staff; and
- how to conduct meetings.

The presenter is Beth Hays, Director of the Virginia Department of Volunteerism. Participation is limited to facilitate interaction and allow maximum attention to concerns of participants.

NORTH CAROLINA/VIRGINIA EXCHANGE: PART ONE
SEE GOVERNORS' OFFICES ON VOLUNTEERISM: NORTH CAROLINA

THE QUEST FOR COMMUNITY
Virginia Division of Volunteerism
233 Governor Street
Richmond, VA 23219
TEL: 804-786-1431
Credit: Inquire
Sponsor: Virginia Department of Volunteerism; Voluntary Action Center/Lynchburg
Contact: Reenie Marshall
Description: This workshops provides participants with an opportunity to explore the concept of community in organizations, neighborhoods and towns. Content focuses on the following points:
- how to foster inclusion and connection rather than exclusiveness and alienation;
- how leaders of volunteers, causes, and coalitions can enable people to help one another while helping themselves;
- how to facilitate the recognition and acceptance of every person's ability to contribute;

This workshop is a mixture of theory and application, along with practical steps to use in capturing and sustaining a sense of community.

Participants have the opportunity for individualized follow-up discussion with the presenter, Dr. Ivan H. Scheier, who is Director of The Center for Creative Community in Albuquerque, New Mexico. Dr. Scheier bases the workshops on two of his books and his experience with countless groups and networks.

The Department's training programs are always limited to facilitate interaction and allow maximum attention to individual concerns.

Publications: Meanwhile Back at the Neighborhood; The New People Approach Handbook

TEAM-BUILDING
Virginia Division of Volunteerism
223 Governor Street
Richmond, VA 23219
TEL: 804-786-1431
Credit: Inquire
Sponsor: Virginia Department of Volunteerism; Voluntary Center of the United Way of Greater Richmond
Contact: Reenie Marshall
Description: This workshop addresses the need for improving leadership skills within groups designated to provide direction for the overall program. A condensed version at the Statewide

Conference on Volunteerism was extremely successful and pointed up the need for the expanded workshop on request across the State. It includes:
- an experiential "bag of tricks" for building a strong team that can get the job done;
- teambuilding exercises designed to improve group effectiveness by establishing trust, cooperation, commitment, and loyalty; and
- ways to provide your team with problem-solving expertise.

The presenter is Winnie Peele of the Loudoun County Extension Service.

Participation in this workshop is limited to allow maximum attention to each participant's concerns.

VIRGINIA ECUMENICAL INFANT MORTALITY PREVENTION PROJECT CONFERENCE
March of Dimes
1505 Staples Mill Road
Richmond, VA 23232
TEL: 804-353-9108
Sponsor: State of Virginia
Contact: Rev. Cessar L. Scott, Executive Minister
Description: This conference, held at the Virginia Governor's mansion in 1989, called on religious leaders for "sheep to keep the wolf from Virginia's nursery door." The Governor challenged leaders of 17 Virginia denominations and religious groups to produce volunteers and projects to preach the importance of maternal prenatal care in preventing deaths of babies before their first birthdays.

The conference was called to "kick off" the *Virginia Ecumenical Infant Mortality Prevention Project,* sponsored by the *March of Dimes* and the *Southern Regional Task Force on Infant Mortality,* whose mission is to increase public awareness of the high incidence of infant mortality in the southern part of the state and promote steps to diminish it. Topics discussed at the conference included:

Statistics - In Virginia in 1987, one of every 98 babies born died before his or her first birthday - those weighing 5 pounds, 8 ounces, or less often in the first 28 days. In 1986, a baby's chance of survival was better in 34 other states than in Virginia.

Causes - Low birth weight is related to 70 percent of infant deaths nationwide. The slight decline in infant mortality is due largely to new technology and neonatal care, not to prevention of low birth weight.

Prenatal Care - This is considered the most significant factor in reducing low birth weight and enhancing a newborn's health. More than 20% of Virginia's mothers receive no prenatal care in their first trimesters, and there is evidence that newborns requiring intensive care are born to these mothers.

Identify the Doers - Invite the doers to regional workshops that are held around the state. Energize them with ideas and inspire them.

Religious Institutions - Highlight in workshops ways in which religious organizations can become involved in preventing infant mortality, such as:
- hot lines for teenagers,
- transportation to services for pregnant women,
- child care for pregnant women during prenatal checkups,
- programs that emphasize male responsibility,
- layette incentive programs to encourage pregnant women to seek prenatal care,
- parenting seminars,
- guest speakers and forums,
- literature racks,
- advocacy.

A religious leader who also leads the infant mortality movement pointed out to the attendees that infant mortality is something that crosses racial and community barriers and something for which there is a solution - "Get expectant mothers to have the proper diet and care. Give of yourselves...this is a problem we can do

something about." The Governor suggested that leaders educate their congregations, initiate direct services or special projects where feasible, and encourage volunteers.

VIRGINIA VOLUNTEERS - HEALTH OF THE COMMONWEALTH
Virginia Division of Volunteerism
223 Governor Street
Richmond, VA 23219
TEL: 804-786-1431
Credit: Inquire
Sponsor: Virginia Department of Volunteerism
Contact: Katherine Noyes
Description: This is the Department's statewide conference for 1989. The title of the conference is also Virginia's new slogan for volunteerism. Each year the statewide conference expands on the previous year's offering and adds new issues and concerns as they arise in the intervening period between annual conferences. The 1989 conference includes:

Opening Session: "Collaboration vs. Competition" - a presentation designed to help individuals and organizations understand how to foster cooperative relationships.

Institute Session One
- Volunteer-to-Volunteer Relationships
- Surviving in a Difficult Organization
- Fundraising Methods and Approaches
- What Really Turns On Volunteers Today?

Institute Session Two
- Working Effectively with Special Volunteers
- The Complete Interviewer
- Transitioning from the "No Longer" into the "Not Yet"
- Designing Effective Workshops
- The Tough Interview: Screening Out Potential Sexual Offenders

Workshop Session One
- Developing Effective Corporate Volunteer Councils (CVC's)
- A Teambuilding Bag of Tricks
- Connecting with the Community
- Be an "Equal Opportunity Employer:" Involve Disabled Volunteers
- Basics of Parliamentary Procedure

Workshop Session Two
- Maximizing the Volunteer Program's Position in Your Organization
- Everything You Want to Know About the Future But Are Afraid to Ask
- The "Type E" Woman
- Dollars and Sense for Volunteer Managers
- Plugging Into the System

Workshop Session Three
- How to "Learn" Those Volunteers
- Promoting Your Program by Publicizing Your Volunteers
- Managing the Money for a Special Event
- An Untapped Resource - the Military Community

Workshop Session Four
- Ensuring the Continuity of Board Leadership
- Overview of Professional Certification
- Hotel Events: Little Things Mean a Lot
- "Projecting" Your Department's Message...On Screen

Presenters for Institutes and Workshops included Susan Ellis and John Paul Dalsimer of ENERGIZE, Eva Schindler-Rainman, Anita Bradshaw, Barry Nickelsberg of The Funding Center, Jeanne King of C&P Telephone Community Relations, Judy Helein of American Association of Retired Persons, Winnie Peele of Loudoun County Extension Service, Richard Starrett of Northampton Department of Social Services, Joy Peters, Montgomery County Department of Recreation, Virginia Dalton, Reenie Marshall, Debbie Russell of Hampton Department of Social Services, Susan Herbert of Fairfax County Area Agency on

Aging, Virginia Gwathmey Yount of the Virginia League of Women Voters, Angie Carerra of the Voluntary Action Center of Fairfax County, Michael Newman, Minnesota Department of Human Services, Sue Ann Morgan, Virginia Department of Corrections, Kathleen McCleskey of KM Consulting and Training Connection, Marcia Penn, Emily Harkins of Lee's Friends/Oncology Patients, Richard Wilburn of Sheraton Beach Inn, and Jerry Williams of Fitzwilly Productions.

For a special closing event, the conference moved to the steps of the State Capitol to demonstrate tangibly the contributions volunteers and volunteering make to the "wealth of our Commonwealth" by presenting a "check" to the Governor's Office. The oversized "check" reflected a dollar figure equal to the annual value of volunteer services of the programs represented at the conference. Members of the news media and key government officials attended the closing ceremony.

VOLUNTEER MANAGEMENT SERIES
Virginia Division of Volunteerism
223 Governor Street
Richmond, VA 23219
TEL: 804-786-1431
Credit: Inquire
Sponsor: Virginia Department of Volunteerism
Contact: Reenie Marshall
Description: This annual series of training programs is scheduled throughout the year at various locations across the state (1990: March, May, and June; Petersburg, Manassas, Richmond and Charlottesville). Themes and topics are based on input and feedback from the field. Although the series varies from year to year, all address the needs of volunteer managers. Following is the 1990 series in summary:

Volunteer Program Management - This session combines sound theory with practical application to equip participants to design, implement and operate a volunteer program. Specific topics include:
- assessing organizational readiness;
- integrating volunteer program goals into over planning;
- gaining support inside and outside the organization;
- designing volunteer jobs;
- formulating policies that prevent problems;
- how to target recruitment and practice appropriate screening and placement procedures;
- orientation and training;
- supervising, motivating and appraising volunteer performance; recordkeeping and program evaluation.

Supervision and Retention: Leading and Keeping Volunteers - This session places emphasis on the fact that supervising and keeping volunteers isn't so very different from directing the work of paid staff. It is designed for managers of volunteer programs, line staff, leaders of volunteer organizations - anyone who supervises the work of volunteers. In addition to learning techniques of supervision, participants consider various motivational theories, how to recognize volunteers, and evaluating performance.

Up to Your Eyebrows in Alligators: Managing External Forces - This session addresses the affect on volunteer programs of decisions, controversies, and events in government, the community and groups within the agency structure. It is designed for veteran volunteer program administrators to help them develop a process for managing these external forces. Participants also develop a plan to minimize the negative impact of these external forces. They use problem-solving exercises along with other practical techniques and interacive processes to identify and begin to manage the forces that previously may have seemed beyond their control.

A New Look at Volunteer Recruitment - This sessions addresses the frustration of trying to use old recruitment approaches and tools, and volunteer burnout, shortages, and dissatisfaction. It enables volunteer managers to diversify their sources and update their plans. Drawing on proven methods, including the use of

problem-solving techniques, participants develop ways to involve new groups and develop a whole new recruitment strategy. Each training session is sponsored by the host community's Voluntary Action Center, for example, Greater Richmond, and the Prince William and Thomas Jefferson areas. Faculty is drawn from business and academe as well as the volunteer community.

VOLUNTEER PROGRAM MANAGEMENT
Virginia Division of Volunteerism
223 Governor Street
Richmond, VA 23219
TEL: 804-786-1431
Credit: Inquire
Sponsor: Virginia Department of Volunteerism
Contact: Reenie Marshall
Description: This session combines sound theory with practical application to equip participants to design, implement and operate a volunteer program. Specific topics include:
- assessing organizational readiness;
- integrating volunteer program goals into overall planning;
- gaining support inside and outside the organization;
- designing volunteer jobs;
- formulating policies that prevent problems;
- targeting recruitment and practicing appropriate screening and placement procedures;
- orientation and training;
- supervising, motivating and appraising volunteer performance;
- recordkeeping and program evaluation.

Presenters are Katherine H. Noyes, Director for Program Services, and Reenie Marshall, Director for State Initiatives, Virginia Department of Volunteerism.

Participation is limited to facilitate maximum problem-solving activities for all participants.

Additional participants include the Alexandria Volunteer Bureau, the Voluntary Action Center of Fairfax County, and Arlington Volunteer Services.

VOLUNTEERING: A CELEBRATION OF COMMUNITY
Virginia Division of Volunteerism
223 Governor Street
Richmond, VA 23219
TEL: 804-786-1431
Credit: Inquire
Sponsor: Virginia Department of Volunteerism
Contact: Betty Biehn
Description: This conference is convened each year to find out how much the state has done in the field of volunteerism, how much more can be done, and to celebrate achievements in the overall field of volunteers as well as to toast volunteer efforts big and small. The format considers the volunteer, the volunteer manager, and the community in the two-day training event:
Especially for Volunteers:
- **Time Management** - to help busy volunteers make better use of that priceless commodity - time.
- **Values Clarification** - to help participants gain insight into their values and the relationship to motivation for volunteer work.
- **Coping Effectively with Stress** - to help participants improve their coping skills through mastering of several stress reduction techniques.
- **The Legislative Process: Arena For All Volunteers** - to familiarize participants with the legislative process in Virginia.
- **Personal Selling: The Art of Getting People to Say Yes** - to help volunteers and voluntary organizations employ personal selling techniques to increase support.
- **Tax Benefits and Personal Liability** - to inform volunteers of the benefits and liabilities of volunteering, and how to minimize risk.
- **Feeling Good About Yourself and What You Do** - to enable

participants to discuss their own creativity and self-worth with fellow participants.

- **Leadership Skills** - to examine the characteristics of leadership and help participants examine their own leadership skills.
- **Transitioning: Volunteering to Paid Work and Paid Work to Volunteering** - to examine the value of skills gained in volunteering for paid employment, and the potential of volunteering as part of retirement planning.

Managing Volunteer Programs:

- **Fund Development** - to assess fund development needs, identify funding sources and plan and implement a fund development campaign.
- **Meetings, Bloody Meetings** - to help participants improve the effectiveness of meetings for which they are responsible; examines five basic elements.
- **Justifying the Effectiveness of Volunteer Programs** - to explore the maintenance and even expansion of volunteer programs in a time of tight budgets; to demonstrate strategies for documenting cost effectiveness to top decision makers.
- **Developing Community Resources** to examine the interrelationship among and between agency image, publicity, and community resources - human, financial, and material.
- **Where Do I Start?** - to discuss planning, needs assessment, involvement of staff and volunteer job design to help new program managers get off to a good start.
- **Confronting Changing Attitudes and Values** - to help volunteer managers understand the implications of changing priorities on their volunteers and their volunteer programs.
- **Board Frustration: An Overview of the Roles and Responsibilities of Board and Staff** - to discuss the functions, organization, and basic workings of a board for the benefit of both board members and staff.
- **New Management Concepts: Quality Circles** - to introduce the concept of worker participation to the volunteer community for possible application to the management of volunteer programs.
- **Turning Staff Resistance to Staff Support** - to help participants begin to empathize with the concerns of staff and offer concrete strategies for improving volunteer-staff relations.

Volunteering in Our Communities

- **Coming Together to Solve a Community Need** - to examine a process for mobilizing a community to action - identification of need, decision to act, achievement of consensus, planning for action, and generating community support.
- **Resource Banks, Skill Banks, and Board Banks** - to present three types of community talent pools: "people banks" - available for community service.
- **Getting Communities Involved** - to examine strategies for involving residents in improving community life, with three different perspectives on neighborhood organization presented to participants.
- **Corporate Volunteerism** - to present an overview of several models of corporate volunteerism and how voluntary organizations can interface with them.
- **Involving Youth as Volunteers** - to examine a frequently overlooked and under-utilized volunteer resource - young people.
- **Partnership with Local Government** - to examine how one city (Virginia Beach) has organized a full-scale volunteer effort to serve local government.
- **Community Cooperatives** - to discuss buying clubs to babysitting co-ops as an old idea that has resurfaced as a community response to today's economy.
- **International Year of Disabled Persons (IYD)** - to examine Virginia's efforts to focus attention on IYD, and the role of volunteers in this effort.

The workshop schedule enables the participant to choose three in-depth workshops during the conference, and arrangements for special meetings for specific groups before and after the conference allows members of national organizations to review together their conference objectives and/or impressions.

INDIVIDUAL PROGRAM PROFILES

GOVERNOR'S ADVISORY COMMITTEE ON CHILD ABUSE AND NEGLECT/VA
Virginia Department of Social Services
Child Protective Services
8007 Discovery Drive
Richmond, VA 23229-8699
TEL: 804-662-9204 (office)
TOLL FREE: 800-552-7096 (hotline)
Purpose: To assist the Governor in coordinating child abuse and neglect matters among all agencies of Virginia state government.
Description: In 1975, when the Virginia Assembly enacted major amendments to the *Virginia Child Abuse and Neglect Law of 1966,* it also created the *Governor's Advisory Committee on Child Abuse and Neglect.* This Committee meets four times a year, and is active in creating policy, making recommendations to the State Department of Social Services, and acting as a coordinator between the Department of Social Services and other major state agencies. Additionally, this Committee has subcommittees taking a very active role in areas such as multidisciplinary teams, legislation, prevention, and treatment.
With the assistance of the Committee, the impact of the amendments to the Act, the Hotline's immediate response on a 24-hour basis, and cooperative efforts with volunteer organizations such as *Parents Anonymous, Parents United,* and *Virginia Chapter of the National Committee for Prevention of Child Abuse,* over 40,000 incidents are reported each year as compared to only 400 prior to these changes and additions.

LITERACY INCENTIVE PROGRAM (NO READ, NO RELEASE)
SEE VOLUNTEERS: PRISONERS/EX-OFFENDERS

GOVERNORS' OFFICES ON VOLUNTEERISM: WASHINGTON

TRAINING PROGRAMS

GOVERNORS' SCHOOL
Seattle University
310 Campion Tower
914 East Jefferson
Seattle, WA 98122
TEL: 206-626-6386
FAX: 206-296-5440
Contact: Stephen Boyd
Description: The *Governors' School* is a one-month intensive training course at *Seattle University* designed for high school juniors and using community service to help develop leadership skills. It is divided into two parts:

- **Summer Institute** - In this month-long session, 100 high school juniors from across the state design individual service projects to address a community problem. The session deals with local, national, and international issues. It encourages students to examine their ideas and ideals and to explore the meanings of leadership. Part of this portion of the program challenges the students physically in outdoor training where they learn wilderness skills and survival tactics.
- **Community Leadership Projects** - In this part of the training, students can apply and test skills learned in the summer institute. The *Governors' School* has informal networks across the state to contact leaders in the students' communities to

serve as project mentors. Coordinators follow the progress of the students and offer aid when it appears necessary.

The projects mounted by the students are diverse and innovative and cover many areas of need not being met by the wider community. Some projects:

- **Food Bank** - One student opened and ran a food bank in a town suffering the effects of a factory shut-down.
- **Rape Crises** - One student worked with the *Seattle Rape Relief,* designing a widely-circulated brochure on teenage rape in the Asian community.
- **Literacy** - One student worked with "at-risk" middle school students to help them develop literacy skills, initiative and motivation.

The *Governors' School* emphasizes the course as a "year-long" commitment, not just a one-month training session. Students may receive credit for their projects from their individual school districts.

Students are chosen for the program by a Statewide Advisory Board on the basis of essays describing the development of their personal values and their solutions to major global problems. Students come from diverse racial and cultural backgrounds, and from every social, economic, and academic level. Leadership ability or potential is an essential qualification.

Although called the *Governors' School,* Washington Governors' roles have been limited to public relations efforts. Major underwriters include business/industry, foundations, and the University.

VOLUNTEERISM: A BRIDGE TO THE FUTURE
Washington State Center for Voluntary Action
PCAA
9th & Columbia Building, GH-51
Olympia, WA 98504
TEL: 206-753-0548
TOLL FREE: 800-562-5677
Credit: Inquire
Sponsor: Council on Voluntary Action; Center for Voluntary Action
Contact: Jane McCurdy
Description: This conference is designed for volunteers, program directors and board members, volunteer coordinators, service club and community organization leaders, and anyone interested in volunteerism. It has four objectives:

- To present new ideas and resources for collaborative efforts in the future.
- To develop linkages of volunteer resources and programs across the state.
- To learn practical skills for future volunteer work.
- To provide an opportunity to exchange information with other volunteer organizations.

The keynote speech (by a member of the corporate community) covers views on how the characteristics of Washington State's present and future population relate to voluntary service needs, what the future holds for volunteerism and how the volunteer program at the local bank is meeting human service needs.

Panel members, representing volunteers, administrators, government officials, consumer clients, business persons and educators, relate ideas presented by the keynote speaker to their individual areas of volunteer involvement.

Simultaneous training workshops address a variety of subjects related to volunteerism and to specific areas of participants' concerns. These include:

- Marketing Your Program
- Volunteers of the Future: Volunteering and Unemployment; Community Service Volunteer
- Volunteer Enhancement: Job Awareness; Your Attitudes
- Strategies for Making a Volunteer Program Work
- Volunteers of the Future: Youth; Families; Elderly
- Volunteer Enhancement: Communications; Human Relations
- Dialogue on Volunteer/Union Relations
- Volunteers of the Future: Corporate; Employee; Retiree
- Volunteers of the Future: Special Populations
- Impact of Computers on Non-profits
- Creative-Collaborative Efforts on Volunteerism

Regional Clinics, Regional Clinic Reports, and a Conference Evaluation conclude the program.

Trainers are experts in the fields of marketing, legal issues, computer technology, personnel management, and human services delivery.

Also request a copy of the State legislation that created the Center, and information about other training programs across the state, with sponsorship by other organizations as well as the State Center; e.g.:

- **Volunteerism,** a class on volunteerism using films and lectures and sponsored by Wenatchee World.
- **How to Choose, Use, Amuse, and Not Lose Them,** a conference on volunteers sponsored by the Interagency Council of Skagit County.

INDIVIDUAL PROGRAM PROFILES

RURAL VOLUNTEER SERVICES NETWORK
Washington Office of Volunteerism
Dept. of Social & Health Services
Mailstop OB-44R
Olympia, WA 98506
TEL: 206-753-4215
Purpose: To prove that, despite great distances, services can be made more accessible - and energy conserved - through a well-organized network of volunteers.
Sponsor: US/ACTION
Contact: Sandra Laney, Chief
Description: The Rural Volunteer Services Network (RVSN) operates through Lead Volunteers located in a number of small towns in eastern Washington. Lead Volunteers then recruit support volunteers as needed.

Volunteers are trained to help rural residents use mail and telephone for many service contacts which, in the past, involved long trips to central locations. When personal contact is necessary, volunteers help clients avoid wasted trips by making sure essential paperwork is in order, with applications and eligibility forms accurately completed.

Through advance planning and scheduling, volunteers make up groups of clients for each trip to the city. When possible, connections are made with other transportation services, like vans provided by the local Area Agency on Aging.

Lead Volunteers provide other services such as informational meetings on the Energy Assistance program, or distribution of surplus foods. With rural isolation a major problem, RVSN provides the needed connecting linking between rural communities and service centers. When federal funding ended (March 1982), the project was connected with the Department's Community Service Offices (CSOs) in the two regions covered by RVSN.

WASHINGTON OFFICE OF VOLUNTEERISM
Washington Department of Social & Health Services
Mail Stop OBB-44R
Olympia, WA 98506
TEL: 206-753-4215
Purpose: To coordinate and promote community involvement activities statewide (both volunteer programs and citizen advisory bodies).
Sponsor: Washington Department of Social & Health Services
Contact: Sandra Laney, Chief
Description: The Office of Volunteerism has been responsible for the overall coordination and promotion of community involvement activities (both volunteer programs and citizen advisory groups) in

the Department of Social and Health Services since 1973. Nearly 40 advisory bodies with over 500 members serve departmental programs, providing community input to decision makers, interpreting department policy and programs back to their communities and offering recommendations regarding service delivery. Each month several thousand volunteers contribute their time and talents to work in nearly every area of the department. The Office of Volunteerism provides consultation and technical assistance to these program efforts, coordinates data collection, and monitors advisory group and volunteer service activities within the department.

Each year volunteers contribute between 700,000 and 800,000 hours of service and over $600,000 in cash and in-kind resources for the benefit of our clients.

The Office of Volunteerism recently completed an ACTION demonstration project to develop a rural network of volunteers to make health and health-related services more accessible to low-income residents. The network project was a recent feature in the media.

The Office has published a volunteer handbook and a handbook for Advisory Body members.

Publications: Volunteer Handbook; Advisory Body Member Handbook
Founded: 1973

GOVERNORS' OFFICES ON VOLUNTEERISM: WEST VIRGINIA

TRAINING PROGRAMS

WEST VIRGINIA CONFERENCE ON VOLUNTEERISM
West Virginia Office on Volunteerism
State Capitol
1800 Washington Street East
Charleston, WV 25305
TEL: 304-348-2000
Credit: Inquire
Sponsor: Volunteers for Volunteers
Contact: Susan Beard
Description: In 1979, West Virginia held its first statewide conference on volunteerism, and the format has been used since that time. More than 50 members of the Coordinating Committee and the Advisory Committee designed and developed the program using the Track system - each of three Tracks led by a nationally-recognized expert in the field, and each designed for a different student body (volunteers, managers, organizations):

TRACK I - Workshop for Volunteers
- Communications Techniques
- Motivation: Who Volunteers and Why
- Community Needs Assessment
- Time Management
- Beginning Course in Advocacy
- Decision Making Skills
- Group Dynamics

TRACK II - Workshops for Managers
- Administration and Staff/Volunteer Relationships
- Improving Effectiveness of Boards and Committees
- Marketing Your Program
- Community Needs Assessment
- Recognizing Overload in Volunteer Organizations
- Recruitment and Job Design
- Responsibility and Management of Other People's Money

TRACK III - Workshops for Organization
- Improving Effectiveness of Boards and Committees

- Long Range Planning Using MBO
- Motivation and Retention of Volunteers
- The Responsibility and Management of Other People's Money
- Community Needs Assessment
- Influencing and Changing the System: Lobbying
- Volunteer Training: Why and How

An opening session included an Orientation for Workshop Leaders, a video cassette presentation, and informal use of a resource center developed for the conference.

The final half day of the conference included Track wrap-up sessions at separate locations, a plenary session, and an evaluation period.

Logistical assistance, including the video cassette presentation, came from some 26 sources including business/industry (18), state government departments (3), a federal regional Commission, the media (radio, TV, newspapers), and three area chapters of the Junior League.

Similar conferences, with changing formats to meet current needs, are convened annually.

INDIVIDUAL PROGRAM PROFILES

WEST VIRGINIA DEPARTMENT OF WELFARE VOLUNTEER PROGRAM
1900 Washington Street, East
Charleston, WV 25305
TEL: 304-348-7980
Purpose: To involve volunteers in meaningful opportunities to extend, enrich and supplement the totality of services provided through the Department of Welfare
Sponsor: West Virginia Department of Welfare
Contact: M. Susan Beard, Director
Description: As mandated by the 1967 Amendments to the Social Security Act, the West Virginia Department of Welfare has initiated volunteer service programs in 27 Administrative Areas. Beginning on a small project basis in May 1970 with five areas participating, the program became statewide in July 1971 with the appointments of area volunteer coordinators and the assignment of a full-time consultant at the state level.

Each month over 900 volunteers contribute 7,000 plus hours of service through the program statewide. Each Administrative Area designs projects in response to identified needs and interests. Agency staff persons receive training and technical assistance in volunteer management on request.

Types of volunteer service provided by volunteers affiliated with the Department include:
- Waiting Room Volunteers
- Clinic Aides
- Friendly and Family Visiting
- Homemakers
- Transportation
- Tutoring
- Family Planning
- Volunteers in Courts
- Clerical
- Day Care
- Big Brothers and Big Sisters
- Home Repair
- Telephone Reassurance
- Case Aides

In addition, Volunteer Coordinators assist local groups in providing seasonal activities, such as Christmas parties and picnics for foster children, Summer Day Camps for senior citizens and for children, ongoing programs of clothing distribution, and others.

Volunteers are recognized in a number of ways. One that was especially well-received and appreciated was a special supplement to *Accent,* the Department's newsletter, saluting West Virginia Volunteers and entitled, *Thank You for Being a Friend.*
Founded: 1970

INFORMATION & REFERRAL

NATIONAL/STATE ORGANIZATIONS

ALLIANCE OF INFORMATION AND REFERRAL SYSTEMS
47 South Pennsylvania Street, #405
Indianapolis, IN 46204
TEL: 317-637-6101
Objectives: To improve information giving, referral and follow-up; to assist people with problems who do not know how to obtain the help they need.
Services: Serves the information and referral community - in concert with libraries, United Way agencies, government, and nonprofit corporations - in the following ways:
- establishes guidelines and standards to improve the delivery of I&R services, including the study of accreditation.
- maintains a clearinghouse for exchange of technical, operational, and research ideas and information.
- assists in the formation of statewide or regional I&R groups.
- sponsors national and regional workshops.
- consults with policy makers, and serves as a "voice" for all I&R agencies.
- publishes a newsletter, a national directory of I&R services, and position papers on key issues affecting human services/resources with recommendations for action.
- provides consultation in specific I&R areas (free to members);
- convenes annual I&R Roundtable for the field (reduced registration fees to members).
Publications: AIRS Newsletter; Journal of the AIRS; AIRS Directory
Founded: 1972

CALL FOR ACTION
575 Lexington Avenue
Seventh Floor
New York, NY 10022
TEL: 212-355-5965
Objectives: To provide troubled citizens with information on and referral to community services and private non-profit agencies which exist to solve their problems.
Services: Provides telephone service staffed by volunteers who direct callers to appropriate agencies; assures confidentiality of calls and anonymity of volunteers; broadcasts editorials to focus public attention on lack of services or unresponsive government; publishes a newsletter and guidelines for the volunteer professional

in the program.
Call For Action functions independently in 25 cities under the direction of a volunteer director and co-director in cooperation with a local broadcast station, which holds the right to the project; it is staffed entirely by volunteers.
The national office employs a small staff to coordinate the work of local affiliates and spearhead national projects.
Publications: Call For Action Network News; CFA Report; The Volunteer Professional
Founded: 1963

CITIZENS COMMUNICATION CENTER
SEE COMMUNICATIONS & PUBLIC RELATIONS

CITIZENS INFORMATION SERVICE*
SEE COMMUNITY SERVICES

CONTACT USA
Pouch A
Harrisburg, PA 17105
TEL: 717-232-3501
Objectives: To establish a national network of telephone counseling ministries and related services.
Services: Promotes, assists in development and accredits telephone counseling centers based on 24-hour a day access; provides supportive and consultative services to accredited centers, including training of volunteers; sponsors annual conferences; publishes handbooks, manuals, and paperbacks as well as audio and visual resources; operates teleministry centers in more than 100 locations in 28 states nationwide.
Publications: Contact Helplines; Contact Paper; Directory of Centers/Services
Founded: 1968

INFORMATION AND REFERRAL RESOURCE AND TRAINING COURSE
National Academy for Volunteerism
United Way of America
701 North Fairfax Street
Alexandria, VA 22314-2045
TEL: 703-836-7100
FAX: 703-683-7840
Objectives: To assist community groups in one or more of the following ways:

- setting up a new I&R service
- evaluating an existing I&R service
- upgrading individual components of an I&R service
- developing new I&R-related programs, such as the Referral Agent program
- training newly-hired staff
- renewing basic knowledge of I&R

Services: Provides consultation in instituting the course, which is designed to be administered by the local I&R Director; makes the Services Outreach Staff available throughout the period of training and for follow-up service.

Course materials include four audio cassettes which involve participants in a series of learning activities, and a looseleaf workbook which includes problems, case studies, check lists and reviews. The completed workbook becomes a reference after the course is completed.

Publications: National Standards for I&R; UW Referral Agent Program; Challenge to United Way: I&R; Programmed Training Course

PROJECT SHARE
SEE ADMINISTRATION

TOLL FREE HOTLINE INFORMATION - A PROGRAM OF RALPH NADER
Public Citizen
PO Box 19404
Washington, DC 20036
TEL: 202-546-4996
FAX: 202-547-7392

Objectives: To assist citizens by providing information on national toll-free hotlines in consumer areas.

Services: Compiles a comprehensive listing of toll-free hotlines to help the consumer gain access to free government and private services; publishes them in an annotated directory, which includes those listed below, are provided here for quick-reference and showing only the nationwide *800 number:*

- *AIDS Hotline* - 800-342-AIDS
- *Asthma-Lung Disease Hotline* - 800-222-LUNG
- *Cancer Information Service* - 800-4-CANCER
- *Child Find* - 800-431-5005
- *Civil Rights Hotline* - 800-368-1019
- *Diabetes Hotline* - 800-227-6776
- *Fair Housing & Equal Opportunity Hotline* - 800-424-8590
- *Federal Crime Insurance Hotline* - 800-638-8780
- *GAY 800* - 800-223-7030
- *Hearing Aid Helpline* - 800-521-5247
- *Heartlife* - 800-241-6993
- *Missing Children Network Hotline* - 800-235-3535
- *National Child Abuse Hotline* - 800-422-4453
- *National Cocaine Hotline* - 800-COC-AINE
- *National Flood Insurance Hotline* - 800-638-6620
- *National Gay Task Force Crisisline* - 800-221-7044
- *National Response Center of the Department of Transportation* (toxic/oil spills) - 800-424-8802
- *National Runaway Switchboard* - 800-621-4000
- *Petfinders* - 800-223-4747
- *Pride Action* (drug abuse) - 800-241-7946
- *RCRA/Superfund Hotline* - (hazardous waste) - 800-424-9346
- *Runaway Hotline* - 800-221-4792
- *Second Opinion Hotline for Non-Emergency Surgery* - 800-638-6833
- *V.D. Hotline* - 800-227-8922
- *Volunteer Hotline* - 800-424-8580

More than a hundred in all are described in the *Toll Free Hotline Directory* with in-state and collect numbers in addition to 800 numbers for some of the above and others, and more.

TRAINING PROGRAMS

FEDERAL INFORMATION POLICIES: ACCESS IS THE KEY
SEE TRAINING/CONFERENCES/TEACHING: I&R

GRASSROOTS CRISIS INTERVENTION CENTER TRAINING PROGRAM
SEE TRAINING/CONFERENCES/TEACHING: I&R

INFORMATION RESOURCES TRAINING PROGRAM
SEE TRAINING/CONFERENCES/TEACHING: I&R

INSTITUTE ON FEDERAL LIBRARY RESOURCES
Catholic University of America
School of Library and Information Science
Marist Hall, Room 230
Washington, DC 20064
TEL: 202-635-5085
Credit: By application (if not a CU student)
Sponsor: US/Federal Library Committee
Contact: Institute Coordinator
Description: This training course, conducted in July and August of 1990, is an outgrowth of growing concern that the government's libraries and information centers are seriously underused. The program examines the scope of the vast federal library collections and specialized services, and the problems of their underutilization. The objectives of the curriculum are:

- Identify the role of the federal libraries, information centers, and data banks in the general and military federal library community;
- Discuss the implication of the *National Commission of Libraries and Information Science's* posture as related to federal libraries;
- Identify resources, publications, and specialized services provided by federal libraries;
- Identify resources available through major government clearinghouses, such as NTIS, ERIC and DTIC;
- Identify the place of the military library and information center in the federal environment;
- Compare the in-operation or the in-process development of the major federal library information services;
- Discuss the implications for information transfer of the existing satellite technology; and
- Identify and articulate performed by the *Federal Library Committee.*

Lectures, panel discussions, and information clinics featuring library leaders, information scientists, government officials, and others prominent in federal library activities, and instructional visits to major federal libraries, information centers, and data banks, give participants the benefit of the experience of the presenters, and the observation and use of the resources. The agenda begins with an on-site presentation at the Pentagon Library, then moves to the University for the following presentations (presenting agency or organization in parenthesis):

- *Introduction to the Federal Library Community* (Federal Library Committee)
- *Introduction to the Federal Agency Library* (U.S. Naval Academy)
- *The Pentagon Library: An Overview* (The Pentagon Library)
- *Standards in Report Processing* (National Information Standards Organization)
- *Library of Congress* (Library of Congress staff)
- *ALA and Federal Libraries* (American Library Association)
- *ASIS and Federal Libraries* (American Society for Information Science)
- *SLA and Federal Libraries* (Special Libraries Association)
- *Federal Research Libraries* (National Institutes of Education)

- *Information Resource Management* (National Oceanic and Atmospheric Agency)
- *Federal Library Service: An Open Discussion of Management and Program Operation* (individual)
- *Smithsonian Institution Libraries* (National Museum of Natural History)
- *National Rehabilitation Information Center* (Director)
- *National Library for the Blind and Physically Handicapped* (individual)
- *Private Sector Organizations and the Federal Information Community* (Herner & Company)
- *Creating Consulting in the Federal Library Milieu with an Emphasis upon Military Uses* (Costabile Associates, Inc.)
- *National Library of Medicine* (NLM Staff)
- *National Agricultural Library* (NAL Staff)
- *Veterans Administration: The Library Network* (Veterans Administration)
- *Defense Technical Information Center* (Deputy Administrator)
- *National Technical Information Service* (Director)
- United States Geological Survey Library (Chief Librarian)
- *National Commission on Libraries and Information Science* (individual)
- *Federally Supported Library and Information Science Programs: A Perspective* (U.S. Department of Education)

On the final day, an overview and summary was presented, followed by an informal discussion and conclusion.
Publications: IFLR Conference Proceedings

MORE THAN MEETS THE EAR - A LISTENING SKILLS SEMINAR
SEE TRAINING/CONFERENCES/TEACHING: I&R

INDIVIDUAL PROGRAM PROFILES

BETHESDA HELP
7115 Plantation Lane
Rockville, MD 20852
TEL: 301-650-8313
Purpose: To offer short-term emergency aid on a 24-hour basis and to assist with information about and referral to professional agencies.
Sponsor: Thirty-two Catholic, Protestant, and Jewish congregations in the Bethesda, Chevy Chase and Kensington area
Contact: Betsy Smoley, Bethesda Help Coordinator
Description: Since its inception in 1968, Bethesda Help has continually served upwards of 1,000 clients annually. To meet this demand, the program needs about 150 volunteers at any one time. Volunteer men and women from the member congregations and from the HELP community serve as:

- **Officers of the Day** - giving one 24-hour period each month to receive calls at home from the HELP answering service; night calls are very rare.
- **Drivers** - giving one day each month to take people of all ages to medical, social services and other important appointments.
- **Operations Workers** - performing a variety of tasks to keep the organization running smoothly.

All volunteers are trained. A handbook is available listing local, county and area-wide agencies and describing their services. Training involves learning the procedures for both Officers of the Day and Drivers. Chairmen coordinate each service and are available for consultation.
Officers of the Day stay in contact with the HELP answering service. The telephone operator furnishes name and number of each person needing HELP. The Officer of the Day calls each client for details of the requested service. Arrangements for financial aid, emergency food, or transportation are then made with respective HELP volunteers. When necessary, a client is referred to an appropriate professional agency.
Founded: 1968

CHAMBER OF COMMERCE LITERACY COUNCIL
SEE BUSINESS/INDUSTRY INVOLVEMENT: LITERACY

COMMUNICATION-HELP CENTER
Kean College
Kean, NJ 07083
TEL: 201-289-2100
Purpose: To provide crisis intervention, information and referral, peer counseling, and other services to students at the college and to people in the community.
Sponsor: Student Organization, Inc.
Contact: Terri Cote, Executive Director
Description: The Communication-Help Center is a student service organization that is funded by Student Organization, Inc. Although the Center is affiliated with Kean College, it is actually independent from the overall college structure. Its main function lies in helping students from the college as well as people from surrounding communities. Student Organization, Inc., the student governing body on campus, is a non-profit organization with a budget of approximately $6,000 per year. Staffing is by 46 student volunteers and two paid professionals.
The Communication-Help Center began in October 1971 as a Hotline staffed by 30 volunteers. Early in 1972, an information service known as Rumor Control became the second division of the Center. This portion was developed during campus and national unrest and kept administrators and students aware of the facts concerning the issues.
During the following academic year, the Walk-In Center was established with a peer-counseling setting in which staff and volunteers met in person with those in need of help. Following years witnessed the development of the Community Outreach Program (which involved a collaboration with community agencies and increased the number of people reached), a child-abuse Parent Line, and the sponsoring of a number of activities designed to help underprivileged children and senior citizens.
All volunteers take part in an ongoing training program. Training sessions cover a variety of topics. For example, types of calls encountered include: sexual, manipulative, depression, suicide, parental, dating, loneliness, etc. Various methods of training are implemented, including audiovisual aids, role playing and discussion.
Volunteers are supervised by the Director and Assistant, who are readily available to deal with any problems that may arise. Feedback is given on both the written reports about each counseling session (Walk-In and Hotline) and the way actual calls are handled. In addition, there is an informal mutual evaluation between volunteers and staff.
In reaching out to disadvantaged community members to inform them of resources open to them, the Center attempts, simultaneously, to educate the community members being reached as well as the volunteer staff - in this way, to build leadership that will enable people to help themselves. As of November 1981, the Center has received and acted upon some 80,000 calls. The Center's efforts have been given national recognition by the American Institute of Family Relations.
Founded: 1972

COMMUNITY INFO LINE
317 Oak Street
Room 402
Chattanooga, TN 37403
TEL: 615-265-8000
Purpose: To provide information and link persons with the most appropriate community resource to meet a need.
Sponsor: Direct service of United Way of Greater Chattanooga; churches; service agencies

Contact: Billy W. Murphy
Description: Community Info Line is an Information and Referral Service for the community. The range of services would include the simple phone call to identify the phone number of a service agency to many calls and contacts that would follow a client through the process of finding a resource to meet a human need. Service agencies are responsive and churches are organized to help on a one-on-one basis within their immediate community. Many indiividual legitimate needs are met and abuse of systems is reduced.

Volunteer Coordinators are named from churches and a three-hour training orientation is offered to coordinators. These coordinators serve as contact points for their community. Other volunteers provide support by helping with mailings and office duties during periods of absence of regular staff.

Staff includes a director, secretary, and master level social worker. All staff members take calls and manage cases. Follow up is an important key to see if the need was met.

COMMUNITY RESOURCE CENTER
SEE LEADERSHIP DEVELOPMENT/BOARDS

COUNTY INFORMATION CENTER
818 County Office Building
White Plains, NY 10601
TEL: 914-682-2222
Purpose: To better serve citizens requesting information concerning assistance programs as well as other County services.
Sponsor: Westchester County
Contact: Janet Mayer
Description: The County Information Center was created in 1974 by the Westchester County Executive as a public service. This action was taken to help improve the accuracy of references given to citizens requesting assistance, and the relevance of the referrals to the inquiries.

Other than the Director and Volunteer Supervisor, the information and referral service is run solely by volunteers. Beginning with 15 volunteers in 1974 (all are still with the Center), the program currently operates with 50 trained volunteers. They enjoy the commitment and service, plus the atmosphere which is nonpressured and pleasant.

Volunteers are given a comprehensive overview of the department and orientation and training for the specific role of information-giver. Following training, the volunteers are placed on probation for a limited time, with the Volunteer Supervisor providing backup support until the volunteer displays enough confidence and efficiency to operate alone.

Some volunteers have been "fired," which has been difficult, but in dealing with the public, accuracy, and a congenial and pleasant atmosphere, are crucial elements that must be maintained.

Information volunteers work in two shifts through an uninterrupted six-hour period (either 10 a.m. to 1 p.m. or 1 p.m. to 4 p.m.). The shifts were set up this way when it was learned that many people could call only on the lunch hour to avoid job conflict.

As well as providing information, the program serves as an initial screening service, since volunteers not only answer questions and make referrals, but they also send out applications to people who may be eligible for public assistance. They have proven to be excellent public relations people, correcting many erroneous impressions of the work of county agencies.
Founded: 1974

CRISIS LINE INFORMATION & REFERRALS
PO Box 3588
Lantana, FL 33462-3588
TEL: 407-243-1000
Purpose: To provide "someone to talk to" for people in crisis.

Contact: Laura McLeod, Volunteer Coordinator, or Anna Stelter, Training Director
Description: The *Crisis Line Information & Referrals* was started in 1971 by a West Palm Beach psychologist as a drug abuse hotline. When hotline operators began receiving calls from people who were getting divorced or couldn't find a place to live, it expanded to its present crisis line operation, receiving 3,000 calls a month from every age group. The average call lasts 20 to 30 minutes, with the longest on record lasting seven hours.

The counseling service operates on the theory that no matter what the problem, callers can find the answer. The function of the volunteers is to help the caller explore the options to solve the problems and to give referrals for ongoing assistance. There are 180 volunteers who work in four-hour shifts.

The volunteers are not professional psychologists or therapists, but people who undergo an intensive 100-hour course in which they are trained to be active listeners. Training programs are conducted at Palm Beach Community College. A typical class includes about fifteen men and women and past classes have included interior designers, stage managers, secretaries, college students, and many other professions.
Other programs include:
- *Teen Hotline,* operated by our youth crisis director
- *Rape Line,* for which we serve as an answering service
- *Sunshine Calls,* which is a daily contact program for the elderly
- *Youth In Crisis,* which includes school visits and is currently preparing a publication on youth services to be distributed communitywide
- *Geriatrics in Crisis,* which involves one registered nurse and four volunteer caregivers to meet needs of the homebound elderly - especially in providing psychosocial support services and referrals to appropriate service agencies
- *Homeless Assistance Program,* which provides case management and follow-up, helping in cases of pending eviction as well as homelessness, and arranging for rental/mortgage help, shelter programs, etc.

The most current venture is a literacy program, still in the planning stages. The program continues to expand and expects to meet new needs as they arise.
Founded: 1971

FIRST CALL FOR HELP/FORT WORTH
United Way of Tarrant County
210 East Ninth Street
Fort Worth, TX 76102
TEL: 817-878-0100
Purpose: To direct callers in need of shelter, counseling, day care, food, etc., to the appropriate agency or organization.
Sponsor: United Way of Tarrant County
Contact: Volunteer Coordinator
Description: First Call for Help is a United Way-sponsored information and referral service involving volunteers who respond to phone calls from citizens needing assistance. In 1988, the helpline handled more than 335,000 phone calls and interviews ranging from requests for help with groceries and utilities, to counseling, day care services or shelter information. Volunteers are trained before being assigned to the helpline.

Each year the *Directory of Tarrant County Services for Older Persons* is updated and distributed free to the area's senior citizens. The directory provides the seniors and their families with information about the resources and services available in Tarrant County for older persons.

FIRST CALL FOR HELP/WICHITA
United Way of the Plains
212 North Market Street
Suite 200
Wichita, KS 67202-2021
TEL: 316-267-1321

Purpose: To provide a link for people in need of social services to appropriate resources.
Sponsor: United Way of Wichita/Sedgwick County
Contact: Arthur Binford
Description: Information & Referral provides I&R to all persons in the city and county who are in need of help. It is a linking of clients to resources that can help them in time of crisis and need. I&R also publishes directories, brochures, and handouts about community services in the area. It also points out unmet needs in the community and tries to see that in some way these needs are addressed.
Volunteer Staff - There is always an opening for volunteers: telephone volunteers, directory up-date volunteers, file and typing volunteers.
Volunteer Duties:
- Telephone - Take incoming calls from clients, and make referrals to agencies.
- Directory - Keep the directory up-to-date and, every other year, get it ready for printing; also, any other smaller or related directories.
- File and Typing - Keep all incoming brochures, etc., filed according to agency; type brochures and directory for printing.

Volunteer Training - Each volunteer has a preliminary interview at which the program is explained. If the volunteer is accepted, training is given, half reading and testing, and half on the job. Experience is nice, but not necessary. It is helpful if volunteers have some knowledge of the community. All volunteers are treated as staff.
Publications: Areawide Community Resource Directory; Aging Resource Directory; One Page Resource Page; Billfold Card with 24-Hour Numbers

FREE HOTLINE
8911 West Ridgewood Drive
Parma, OH 44130
TEL: 216-659-4650
Purpose: To provide counseling, information and referral on all problems, or just to be a friend to the lonely.
Sponsor: All Saints Episcopal Church
Contact: Donna May
Description: With their only support coming from the All Saints Episcopal Church in the form of space, telephone, and other operating expenses, three volunteers have succeeded in keeping open an all-volunteer switchboard linking citizens with needed help. Formerly an emergency service for youth, FREE Hotline now caters to people of all ages in the greater Cleveland area. Recruitment of volunteer switchboard operators is done through Cleveland placement agencies and radio public service announcements. One of the three management volunteers provides four hours of training, and another follows with six weeks of on-the-job training (one four-hour shift per week), or until both feel that the volunteer is able to work alone.
FREE Hotline evolved from a 1970 community project initiated by the church to provide a drop-in center and crash pad for youth, with parent-peer counseling. The smaller emergency telephone service of the Parma Red Cross provided similar services, and the Red Cross felt that the community would be better served if the two services merged. Funds previously provided to the Red Cross were fielded to the church over the next two years. In 1974, the major funding organization, the Citizen's Action Committee on the Prevention of Drug Abuse, disbanded - providing the church with a final $2,000. By 1979, all funding sources withdrew, and the three volunteers have coordinated the program successfully since that time.
The volunteer managers have transformed the former youth emergency service into one that serves the entire community. In spite of the lack of outside funding, FREE Hotline is in the process of developing and printing a training manual for the volunteer switchboard operators.
Founded: 1970

INGRAHAM VOLUNTEERS*
142 High Street
Portland, ME 04101
TEL: 207-773-4830
Purpose: To provide 24-hour all purpose emergency HOTLINE services.
Sponsor: Federal/State/County/Local Governments, private donations; United Way; churches
Contact: Neva S. Gram, ASW, Executive Director
Description: Ingraham Volunteers, Inc. is a private, non-profit social service agency, providing twenty-four hour all-purpose emergency HOTLINE services. Funds are received from state and local governments, as well as the United Way, private foundations and churches.
Volunteer counselors are trained in telephone crisis intervention counseling, information and referral on human service systems, advocacy, and can provide emergency financial aid. The HOTLINE counselors also provide screening for entry to the battered women's shelter.
Telephone-typewriter (TTY) HOTLINE services for vocal relay for the deaf are also provided twenty-four hours a day. The Dial-KIDS (teenage) HOTLINE provides peer counseling to teenagers from 2 - 5 p.m. on week days.
There are specific qualifications, training requirements, time commitments and responsibilities inherent in the HOTLINE positions. An applicant goes through a screening process. A detailed description of requirements is available upon request. Volunteers are supervised by four case management staff persons, one of whom is on call twenty-four hours a day. There is an executive Director, and an office business staff consisting of an Office Manager, Administrative Secretary and Receptionist. Volunteers have additional opportunities for involvement with the agency through work on committees and the Board of Directors.

NORTHERN VIRGINIA HOTLINE
PO Box 187
Arlington, VA 22210
TEL: 703-522-4460
Purpose: To provide a confidential listening, referral, and crisis intervention telephone service.
Sponsor: Local counties and private donations
Contact: Nancy B. Berk
Description: The Northern Virginia Hotline provides a 24-hour, seven-day confidential telephone listening, referral and crisis intervention service. The organization began 20 years ago, growing out of the results of a church study of community needs.
Originally, it was a teen hotline in operation six hours a day, but it soon became a 24-hour service, serving the entire metropolitan Washington population.
The program has approximately 150 volunteers, all of whom complete a 40-hour training program in listening skills. This training program has been conducted by Hotline staff for local, state and national organizations.
Volunteers must commit to "listen" for three to four hours each week, must be over 18 years of age, and must be willing to give a minimum one-year commitment before they begin training.
Volunteer listeners represent a broad spectrum of the community including college students, retired persons, military personnel, professionals, and teachers.
The Hotline lists over 1300 different referrals to agencies in the DC metropolitan area which offer help with problems such as lonliness, depression, coping, crisis, self-help groups, family problems, divorce/separation, child/spouse abuse, sexuality, health, transportation, housing, employment, consumer problems, legal matters, and others. These problems fall into four categories:
- **Mental Health** - This category includes calls related to

depression, anxiety, and other types of adjustment problems.

- **Special Concern** - These calls concern employment needs, and also requests to volunteer.
- **Individual Life** - Calls in this group include those relating to social relationships (especially dating), aging, and personal growth.
- **Sensitivity** - This group includes calls about pregnancy, birth control, homosexuality, etc.
- **Family Life** - This category includes matters relating to marriage, parent-child relationships, divorce, and runaways.

About 2.3% of all *Hotline* calls concern suicide. Special TV programs dealing with suicide bring on a flood of calls from troubled people seeking assistance. Another 2.8% of the calls deal with crime such as battered spouses and child abuse.

Hotline answers after-hours calls for other services (Arlington CA&I, Pro child, Arlington Mental Health, and Fairfax I&R). Volunteers and staff are available through its Speakers Bureau to talk to civic, service, school or church groups, sometimes using a five-minute audio-visual presentation. *Hotline* is accredited by the American Association of Suicidology. Funding comes from the two primary counties served, matching state funds, and private donations.

Since 1970, ACCA (Annandale Christian Community for Action) has participated in the Northern Virginia Hotline.

Publications: Troubled? Let's Talk.

Founded: 1969

INFORMATION & REFERRAL: AIDS

NATIONAL/STATE ORGANIZATIONS

AIDS HOTLINE
US/HHS - National AIDS Information Clearinghouse
PO Box 6003
Rockville, MD 20850
TEL: 800-342-AIDS; 800-344-SIDA (Spanish)
TOLL FREE: 800-AIDS-TTY (deaf)
Objectives: To respond to any questions children, youth, or adults may have about HIV infection and AIDS.
Services: Provides a 24-hour, seven-day service with Public Health Service employees answering a toll-free hotline number to answer questions about HIV infection and AIDS, or refer the caller to other sources; provides specialized service to refer callers to state and local health departments and other groups in his or her immediate area for local counseling and testing; keeps all responses confidential, and callers need not give name; operates a number of AIDS projects to combat this condition, which affects the body's ability to fight off disease; provides a comprehensive guide, a bimonthly bulletin, a pamphlet and other materials on the subject, as well as referrals to sources of additional publications and materials; maintains hotline access for Spanish-speaking and hearing-impaired persons.
Publications: AIDS Information Bulletin; Facts on AIDS

FDA EXPERIMENTAL AIDS TREATMENT HOTLINE
US/HHS - Food and Drug Administration
5600 Fishers Lane
Rockville, MD 20852
TEL: 301-443-3170
TOLL FREE: 800-TRIALS-A
Objectives: To keep the public informed of experimental treatment for AIDS.
Services: Maintains a computerized listing of every experimental AIDS and AIDS-related treatment undergoing clinical testing in FDA-sanctioned trials; provides this information to make it easier for AIDS patients to participate more widely.

Sponsor: US/HHS - Department of Health & Human Services

US/HHS - NATIONAL AIDS INFORMATION CLEARINGHOUSE
PO Box 6003
Rockville , MD 20850
TOLL FREE: 800-458-5231
Objectives: To provide information, referral, publications and other materials and services in response to questions about HIV infection and AIDS.
Services: Conducts extensive AIDS research designed to provide the public with information, referrals, publications, and other materials to foster a better understanding of the AIDS epidemic; designs and publishes separate information kits specific to expressed needs for teachers, parents, health care workers, youth and children, etc.; includes reproduceable handout materials for children and youth, question/answer guides; publishes periodic Surgeon General's reports, and intermittent specific guides such as *Protection Against Occupational Exposure to HBV and HIV* and others as needs arise; oversees the *National AIDS Hotline*.
Sponsor: US/HHS - Department of Health & Human Services
Publications: AIDS Prevention Guide; AIDS Pamphlet Series; Surgeon General's Report; Understanding AIDS; Information Packet Series

INDIVIDUAL PROGRAM PROFILES

DISTRICT OF COLUMBIA AIDS INFORMATION LINE
Whitman-Walker Clinic
1407 S Street, NW
Washington, DC 20009
TEL: 202-797-3568 (Office); 202-332 AIDS (VT/TTY)
Purpose: To answer questions and make referrals on issues involving AIDS and HIV infection.
Sponsor: Whitman-Walker Clinic
Contact: Amelie Zurn
Description: The *DC AIDS Information Line* is a division of Whitman-Walker Clinic, a volunteer-based (1,500 overall) effort, enhanced and supported by professional staff. The Line operates seven days a week (10:00 a.m. - 9:00 p.m. weekdays; 10:00 a.m. - 6:00 weekends), and averages over 500 calls each month.
Information Line volunteers go through extensive training and are equipped to handle calls from persons who have HIV+ or AIDS, or significant others; i.e., people needing someone to talk with as opposed to needing questions answered. Therefore, according to a volunteer, "We are a 'hotline' *as well as* an information line."
Two part-time staff members have been diagnosed with AIDS for several years and are available should someone wish to talk with someone with AIDS (very helpful for the newly-diagnosed).
As with all Clinic programs, Information Line staff work closely with other organizations and the community-at-large to avoid duplication of effort, share effort, etc. For example, the Lesbian and Gay Hotline and the Peer Counseling Group help with stress associated with AIDS and work in cooperation with the Information Line.

EDUCATION & PREVENTION SERVICES: AIDS PROGRAM
SEE COMMUNICATIONS & PUBLIC RELATIONS: AIDS

PROJECT NOVA - AIDS PROGRAM
Whitman-Walker Clinic
1407 S Street, NW
Washington, DC 20009
TEL: 202-358-2839; 202-328-0697

Purpose: To provide/coordinate support and education services in Northern Virginia.
Sponsor: Whitman-Walker Clinic
Contact: Peter Provost
Description: Project NOVA's case management system coordinates the services of the Whitman-Walker Clinic in Northern Virginia. Whitman-Walker Clinic is a volunteer-based (1,500 overall) effort, enhanced and supported by professional staff. NOVA works with other public- and private-sector agencies to insure that Northern Virginians connect with the services they need. The *NOVA Education Resource Center* is housed in Project NOVA, which also conducts educational outreach programs to gay/bisexual men. Project NOVA works with other agencies through the *Northern Virginia HIV Consortium* to build a unified regional response to the epidemic.
Services are provided to all people in need. Objectives are to improve the overall health and well-being of the community. All volunteers in the program receive orientation and extensive training.

INFORMATION & REFERRAL: ARTS

NATIONAL/STATE ORGANIZATIONS

INFORMATION CENTER ON CHILDREN'S CULTURES*
U.S. Committee for United Nations Children's Fund
331 East 38th Street
New York, NY 10016
TEL: 212-686-5522
Objectives: To provide educational and cultural materials to children from preschool to 14 years of age; to answer questions from the public regarding the world's children.
Services: Works with volunteers, parents, librarians, editors, teachers, the media, and the children themselves regarding the various, yet interrelated customs and activities of the children of the world; recommends books and other materials based on specific requests (a free service); covers intercultural topics including arts, crafts, music, holidays, games, family life, problems, customs; offers children's programs at the Center; develops new techniques to satisfy children's natural curiosity about other nations; maintains collection of toys, games, musical instruments, films, filmstrips, slide sets, descriptions of its children's programs, and other materials (free and for sale).
Contact: Librarian/Historian
Publications: News of the World's Children
Founded: 1967

INFORMATION & REFERRAL: CANCER

NATIONAL/STATE ORGANIZATIONS

US/HHS - CANCER INFORMATION CLEARINGHOUSE
US/HHS - National Cancer Institute
Building 31, Room 10A18
Bethesda, MD 20205
TEL: 301-496-4070
Objectives: To provide a central source of information on cancer for patients and the public.
Services: Performs reference searches for health professionals and educators of its collection of about 6000 materials; makes referrals to other information sources when necessary; acts as a medium of

exchange among the Comprehensive Cancer Centers; publishes an accessions list of most recent acquisitions.
Sponsor: US/HHS - Department of Health & Human Services

INDIVIDUAL PROGRAM PROFILES

WOMAN-TO-WOMAN HOTLINE
Adelphi University
School of Social Work
Social Services Center
Garden City, NY 11530
TEL: 516-560-8060
Purpose: To provide emotional support to women who have discovered a breast lump, or have pre-mastectomy or post-mastectomy concerns.
Sponsor: Adelphi University, School of Social Work, Social Services Center
Contact: Lois Lopez, Hotline Project Coordinator
Description: The Woman-to-Woman Hotline began in May, 1982. It is operated within the Social Services Center and is funded by Adelphi University, School of Social Work.
The goals of the Hotline are to provide emotional support to women who have discovered a breast lump, or have pre-mastectomy or post-mastectomy concerns. The hotline has offered a needed service to the community in providing this service.
At the present time, the Hotline Committee consists of five active volunteers who are supervised by a graduate student interning at the Social Services Center. The volunteers have each dealt with the physical and emotional trauma of mastectomy and therefore can provide peer support. Each volunteer is trained for Hotline work and receives group supervision on a weekly basis.
The volunteers provide each caller with time to talk; each call varies and the volunteers must remain sensitive and flexible to each caller's needs. Medical advice is not provided by this Hotline. If a second opinion is sought by the caller, the volunteer refers the caller to the American Cancer Society in Melville for appropriate referral.
If the call has come due to discovery of a breast lump, the important work of the volunteer is to help the caller to visit her doctor in order to be examined and get a medical diagnosis.
Founded: 1982

INFORMATION & REFERRAL: CHILDREN/YOUTH

NATIONAL/STATE ORGANIZATIONS

NATIONAL RUNAWAY SWITCHBOARD
3080 North Lincoln Avenue
Chicago, IL 60657
TOLL FREE: 800-621-4000 (nationwide)
Objectives: To provide information, crisis intervention, and assistance, and referral to runaways, and messages to their families.
Services: Maintains a 24-hour, toll-free national switchboard; provides names and addresses for shelter and counseling services across the country, including counseling centers, referral lines, drug treatment facilities, and other services; offers to relay messages between young people and their families or, if desired, set up conferences between youths and parents or agencies; maintains caller's confidentiality (funded in part by the Office of Youth Development, U.S. Department of Health and Human Services).

RUNAWAY HOTLINE
Governor's Office
PO Box 12428
Austin, TX 78711
TEL: 512-463-1980; 800-392-3352 (TX)
TOLL FREE: 800-231-6946 (nationwide)
Objectives: To enable young people to contact parents or others without divulging location.
Services: Operates 24-hour, seven-day, national toll-free hotline for runaways and potential runaways with the help of a bank of more than 100 volunteers; respects confidentiality of caller; serves as a personal and confidential message relay between runaways and their parents; maintains referral service for callers in need of service (runaway houses, shelters, food, medical services, drug crisis centers, health clinics, counseling centers, etc.)
Founded: 1973

YOUTH DEVELOPMENT
4575 Ruffner Street
San Diego, CA 92111
TEL: 619-292-5683; 800-HIT-HOME (California)
TOLL FREE: 800-MISS-YOU (nationwide)
Objectives: To provide both outreach programs and services for abandoned, neglected, or abused youngsters.
Services: Conducts Christmas outreach program which provides clothing, food, and letters of encouragement to children in local shelters and detention centers; provides opportunities for these youngsters to experience productive living within the community and family environment; maintains listings of shelters throughout the country; operates a telephone hotline which provides counseling and referrals to shelters for runaways nationwide; works with the *National Network of Runaway and Youth Services;* publishes a newsletter and other materials.
Sponsor: National Network of Runaway and Youth Services
Publications: Home Run Quarterly Review
Founded: 1959

INDIVIDUAL PROGRAM PROFILES

CHICAGO RUNAWAY SWITCHBOARD
Metro-HELP
3080 North Lincoln Avenue
Chicago, IL 60613
TEL: 312-880-9860; 312-929-5150
TOLL FREE: 800-621-3230
Purpose: To provide direct support to the estimated 10,000 homeless teens in the Chicago Metropolitan area.
Sponsor: Metro-HELP
Contact: Volunteer Coordinator
Description: Although the National Runaway Switchboard, which was founded in 1974, is located in Chicago, another program to provide more direct service to runaway youth in metropolitan Chicago was established in 1989. Both switchboards are operated by Metro-HELP.
The latter service concentrates on the social service providers in the metropolitan Chicago area and links them to homeless teens or teens who are thinking about running away from home. In much the same way as the national operation, volunteers gather facts about the caller's situation, help focus the caller on the primary issue to be addressed, examine options that are available and then, with the caller, develop a plan of action. There are an estimated 10,000 homeless teens in the Chicago area, and some 21,000 across the state.
Many calls end in referrals to other agencies for ongoing sources of support, and often set up conference (three-way) calls with the youth, the hotline, and the appropriate social service as a way of "introducing" a reticent youth to the social worker, thereby having a greater chance of fruition of the connection.

According to the director, "Our volunteers will listen to callers, believe and support the kids, and work with them to access the supports that can truly make a difference in the life of each of our callers." The program has a continual training program and is always in need of volunteers who would like such an opportunity.

CHILD SECURITY NETWORK OF CONNECTICUT
PO Box 2143
Meriden, CT 06450
TEL: 203-783-3036
TOLL FREE: 800-6-KIDS-ID
Southwest Regional Division
PO Box 3382
Milford, CT 06460
Affiliate:
Child Security Network
Long Beach, California
Purpose: To provide an effective and complete form of identification for children.
Sponsor: Child Security Network
Contact: Clifford Ives
Description: Totally volunteer-operated, the *Child Security Network* has developed an identification program for children that stores pertinent data in a computer file to expedite treatment in a crisis situation. The data include blood type, allergies, pre-existing conditions, and family physician, and it is relayed instantly to emergency personnel to aid in treatment. The file also contains insurance information and contact information for parents, both at home and at work, and three alternate contacts.
The goal of the program is to reach every parent or guardian of every infant, child and youth in Connecticut. One method used by CSN is working through youth groups, schools, unions, churches, corporations, businesses, foundations, politicians, charities, and others with the cooperation of parents and guardians.
The cost of registration, $20, keeps a child on file for a year, including an updating process for any changes in medical, residence, or other situations. The registration fee is the only income for the volunteer group.
As of late 1989, the CSN program had been initiated in all states of the US.
Publications: My Child in a Crisis? ... Never!!!

FIRST (FACTUAL INFORMATION REGARDING SEX AND TEENS)
PO Box 57
Sanford, NC 27330
TEL: 919-774-9515
Purpose: To provide youth answers to their questions on human sexuality.
Sponsor: Lee County Youth Services
Contact: Maureen Farrington
Description: FIRST (Factual Information Regarding Sex and Teens) is a teens helping teens phone line geared towards helping the young people of Lee County better understand the dynamics and consequences of teen sex and pregnancy.
The phone line began operation in March '83 with grant money from the North Carolina Youth Council. The line is in operation four hours weekly. The program is sponsored by Lee County Youth Services (LCYS) a non-profit organization providing services for the youth and families of the county.
At present, 16 high school volunteers work as peer phone helpers. Initially, a core group of five high school students assisted LCYS with the planning of the phone line.
The volunteers receive training prior to becoming peer phone helpers on topics such as: male/female physiology, contraception, pregnancy, V.D., abortion, human sexuality, communication, listening and decision-making skills, awareness of community resources and knowing when to refer a call. In addition, there are monthly volunteer training sessions.

The peer helpers volunteer one hour of their time each week. They provide answers to questions for young callers ranging from simple boy/girlfriend relationships to information on birth control and abortion clinics. They make referrals to community and surrounding area resources when necessary, but the real value of the peer counselor is to provide a listening ear and be an effective helper. Also, they are responsible for assisting LCYS in evaluating the program and making any recommendations for change.

They provide teens with a significant program in which they have the opportunity and responsibility of helping their peers. The volunteers become more effective helpers by obtaining a better understanding of human sexuality, enabling them to answer teens' questions.

With the high incidence rate of teenage pregnancy in Lee County and elsewhere there is a need for this type of service. It gives the youth of the community the opportunity to help their peers by answering their questions or helping them make positive decisions regarding their own sexuality.
Founded: 1983

SOUTHEAST RESOURCE CENTER FOR CHILDREN AND YOUTH SERVICES
Knox County Child and Family Services
114 Dameron Avenue
Knoxville, TN 37917
TEL: 615-524-7483
Purpose: To provide information, training and the exchange of assistance in child welfare to the eight states which comprise Region IV of the Department of Health and Human Services.
Sponsor: US/HHS - Children's Bureau
Contact: Christine P. Holmes
Description: In October of 1983, the University of Tennessee, School of Social Work, through its Office of Continuing Social Work Education (OCSWE) was awarded a Department of Health and Human Services (DHHS) grant to operate the Southeast Resource Center for Children and Youth Services. The purpose of the Center is to provide information, training and the exchange of technical assistance in child welfare to the eight Southeastern states which comprise DHHS Region IV.

The Southeast Resource Center is uniquely organized in that it brings together the technical expertise of OCSWE with the practical experience of Child and Family Services of Knox County. In a subcontract with OCSWE, Child and Family Services provides staffing and technical assistance in order to strengthen intrastate and regional networks among public and voluntary child welfare agencies.

Specifically, the agency is responsible for two program areas: volunteerism and employee assistance programs. Child and Family Services' role is to assist the state to:
● discover the current volunteer networks;
● develop means to improve the systems; and
● disseminate information and resources about innovative volunteer programs in the area of children and youth services.

Also, the agency is interested in the promotion of nonpublic child welfare and family services through employee benefits in business and industry. Both volunteerism and employee assistance are means of tapping those resources in the private sector which are now so urgently needed.

Child and Family Services and the Southeast Resource Center are working to build resource exchange networks, increase the availability to non-public-funded services and maximize joint private/public planning for child welfare services. To accomplish these objectives, the Resource Center provides services to state child welfare agencies; voluntary children's services agencies; parent, child and minority advocacy groups; social work educators; and business and industry.

Information services are available through a computer network; publications of the Center; a lending library of audio-visual and written materials; and newsletters. Training, technical assistance

and information are provided on special topics such as child abuse and neglect, special needs adoption, foster care, permanency planning, volunteerism, employee assistance programs and youth services.
Founded: 1983

TEENLINE
Oklahoma University Health Sciences Center
1100 North Lindsey
Oklahoma City, OK 73107
TEL: 405-271-4000
Information is also available from co-sponsors:
Children's Memorial Hospital of Oklahoma
940 NE Thirteenth Street
Oklahoma City, OK 73104 (405-271-4371)
Oklahoma Department of Mental Health
1200 NE Thirteenth Street
Oklahoma City, OK 73117 (405-271-7474)
Purpose: To serve as a crisis intervention hot line for adolescents.
Sponsor: Oklahoma University Health Sciences Center
Contact: Dr. Robert Hill, Professor of Pediatrics
Description: Sponsored by a university, a children's hospital and the state mental health office, the mission of the *Teenline* is to provide counseling and referrals to youth who are in acute trouble or just in need of a listening ear. The program offers confidential and anonymous services by specially-trained volunteers, including referral to local programs appropriate to their needs.

In its first years of operation, the hot line answered more than 13,000 calls from troubled teens. The service has grown from four hours of operation a day by a group of 15 volunteers to operation by 80 volunteers 12 hours a day. It is staffed from noon to midnight seven days a week. It also has grown from serving only the Oklahoma City area to serving the entire state.
Founded: 1985

INFORMATION & REFERRAL: CONSUMER/LEGAL RIGHTS

NATIONAL/STATE ORGANIZATIONS

FTC VACATION TRAVEL HOTLINE
US/FTC - Federal Trade Commission
Division of Credit Practices
Washington, DC 20580
TEL: 202-326-3237; 202-326-3212
Objectives: To respond to consumers' questions on vacation brokers with an unusually large number of complaints from consumers.
Services: Provides consumers with a point of referral when it has been established that vacation travel companies have not met advertised commitments to consumers; operates hotline on a company-by-company basis (1989 - BankCard Travel Club and World Travel Vacation Brokers) usually regarding companies that are being sued by FTC; provides telephone message tape enabling consumer to describe problem and leave contact information, or responds to written complaints.
Sponsor: US/FTC - Federal Trade Commission

NATIONAL INJURY INFORMATION CENTER
US/Consumer Product Safety Commission
5401 Westbard Avenue
Washington, DC 20207
TEL: 301-492-6424

Objectives: To regulate consumer products which present hazards to users.
Services: Answers about 6,000 requests each year; assesses the scope of consumer product safety problems; makes personal contact with accident victims to compile information on the product and the victim's injuries; prepares reports on investigations, documents on various hazards, and other materials for consumer information; provides most information and services free of charge.

NATIONAL RESOURCE CENTER FOR CONSUMERS OF LEGAL SERVICES*
124-D East Broad Street
Falls Church, VA 22046
TEL: 202-536-8700
Objectives: To keep individuals and groups informed on legal services delivery systems.
Services: Acts as a clearinghouse for information and advice on the performance of legal services delivery systems; holds seminars; provides limited technical assistance; conducts research; maintains library; publishes biweekly newsletter, *Legal Plan Letter,* surveys and other materials.
Publications: Legal Plan Letter; Planforms
Founded: 1977

NHTSA HOTLINE
US/DoT - National Highway Traffic Safety Administration
400 Seventh Street, SW
Washington, DC 20590
TEL: 202-426-0123
TOLL FREE: 800-424-9393
Objectives: To promote and enforce safety as a prime consideration in the manufacture of vehicles.
Services: Dispenses safety information; takes some safety complaints; refers other safety complaints to the appropriate government agencies; provides facts on past or pending recalls; publishes *The Car Book,* which lists points to consider before buying a car (available from U.S. Consumer Information Center; see bibliography), and other tools to help consumers obtain automobiles based on individual needs; maintains special numbers for people with hearing problems (inquire).

INDIVIDUAL PROGRAM PROFILES

CONSUMER INFORMATION SERVICE
Madison House
170 Rugby Road
Charlottesville, VA 22903
TEL: 804-977-7051
Purpose: To educate the community by providing consumer information to the public; to settle disputes between local consumers and business.
Sponsor: Madison House
Contact: Jane Parker
Description: Consumer Information Service (CIS) originated as part of the Madison House Professional Services Center in 1970. It was little more than a consumer column in the local newspaper until 1972, when it separated from the Center and became its own program.
There is no "Better Business Bureau" in the Charlottesville area. In an attempt to fill this void, CIS began Action Line, providing volunteers to act as impartial third party mediators to resolve consumer-merchant disputes. Later, two departments were added to the program: the Trouble$hooter, a monthly newsletter, and the Information Division. The divisions are now referred to as (1) Action Line; (2) The Publications Division; and (3) the Public Relations Division. Approximately 50 CIS volunteers are

organized into the three branches. Volunteer commitment is very flexible within this program, ranging from a two-hours-per-week shift on Action Line to extensive involvement in all three divisions. Action Line attracts the majority of the CIS volunteers and forms the heart of the program. Action Line is a telephone service to which consumers call in complaints and requests for information. Action Line volunteers, acting in the capacity of third-party mediators, record individual complaints and, through a series of phone calls, letters, and personal visits, seek a resolution satisfactory to the parties in disagreement. The Action Line operates from 9 to 5, five days a week. Volunteers are organized in shifts that range from one to three hours so that the telephones are adequately manned at all times.
The Publications Division is responsible for the dissemination of consumer information to the community. Its goal is to educate the consumers and make them aware of the services available in the community. This division publishes a monthly newsletter, the Trouble$hooter, provided free of charge to inform the public of the latest consumer news and helpful hints. It discusses issues of local concern and details recent complaints and their resolutions as well as commendations to local merchants. Publications volunteers also are involved in long term research projects such as price surveys.
The Public Relations Division provides presentations on consumer-related topics to interested groups. This division maintains a library and has a consumer education program. The division also periodically publishes consumer price surveys and, in 1975, published the Charlottesville Banking Survey. Additionally, the Coordinator produces shows on local radio stations and contributes consumer columns and advertisements to local newspapers. Volunteers may write or research for this division.
CIS deals with both minor and serious consumer problems. In its work the program aims to meet the highest of professional standards. Volunteers need no specific background to become involved, but they must be able to learn tact and responsibility in dealing with frequently irate and upset citizens, and possess a firm commitment to providing good, reliable service.
In the beginning, CIS was very similar in design to Madison House's other volunteer programs. However, rapid development and the nature of its activities necessitated incorporating the program as a "Madison House Subsidiary" in January 1976. It now occupies a special position within Madison House as a highly-developed and sophisticated volunteer program.
Founded: 1970

DIRECT LINE
WBBM Newsradio
630 North McClurg Court
Room 268
Chicago, IL 60611
TEL: 312-664-2936
Purpose: To provide assistance to citizens having disagreements with retailers, utilities, small companies, corporations, government agencies, and other entities.
Sponsor: WBBM Newsradio
Contact: Naomi Hood, Director
Description: Direct Line recently celebrated its twentieth anniversary at WBBM Newsradio. In 1988, the 47 volunteers monitoring telephones answered more than 19,000 calls from 21 different states from callers seeking assistance for many types of problems.
Volunteers are trained to respond to people having problems with local retailers, utilities, small companies, corporations and government agencies. Some volunteers are assigned to the investigative work after the call has been answered by another volunteer, and the problem has been fully described in writing on the "problem report." One volunteer - 89 years of age - has developed an uncanny knack for negotiating an agreement between two disputing parties. He has been with the program since 1982. Now others are learning from him. Hours donated by volunteers

average 500-600 per volunteer each year.

The director has been with the program since its inception in the summer of 1969, providing a continuous practice of arriving at WBBM at 6:30 a.m. Monday through Friday to make necessary preparations for the volunteers who arrive at 9:30, and staying two hours after the volunteers leave to finish the follow-up work from the estimated 80 calls each day.

Many calls do not represent problems, per se, but are requests for information about the community or a planned event. Callers often send thank you notes with small donations.

Volunteers - especially the senior volunteers - receive something from the program in return - a meaningful structure in their daily lives. As one older volunteer stated, "I don't know what I would do without *Direct Line*. We always try our best for each caller. There is always something that we can do when a person has a problem. I would be lost without this." The director, although carrying an excessive workload, says, "I can honestly say that I just absolutely love what I do for a living."

Direct Line is sponsored by WBBM in cooperation with United Way/Crusade for Mercy.

Publications: Direct Line Information Packet
Founded: 1969

INFORMATION & REFERRAL: DOMESTIC ABUSE

NATIONAL/STATE ORGANIZATIONS

CHILD ABUSE HOTLINE
Virginia Department of Social Services
Child Protective Services
8007 Discovery Drive
Richmond, VA 23229-8699
TOLL FREE: 800-552-7096
Objectives: To receive reports of child abuse and refer them for action by appropriate authorities.
Services: The Child Abuse Hotline of the Child Protective Services division of the Virginia Department of Social Services is a 24-hour, seven-day service to enable concerned citizens to report cases of child abuse anonymously. The Hotline fills the gap created when local social service agencies close at the end of the business day. It provides for the receipt, identification and immediate referral for investigation of complaints and reports of child abuse and neglect for children under the age of eighteen. The majority of complaints are received by the Hotline after normal working hours, on weekends, and on holidays. When the Hotline operator completes the call, the information is forwarded immediately to a local child protective services worker since often the cases are too critical to wait until the next day. A social worker is available in each city and county throughout the State to receive reports from the Hotline. This assures immediate investigation.

To facilitate citizen action when a child appears to be in jeopardy, Protective Services distributes information on the most common types of child abuse and the signs indicating abuse. Also, copies of the 1974 Virginia Child Abuse and Neglect Act outlining incidences that are considered abusive (lack of supervision, or inadequate food, clothing or shelter, as well as the more obvious sexual abuse) are widely distributed. Such communication has dramatically increased the number of Hotline calls (400 a year before amendments to the law, now almost 40,000 each year) and in some cases has provided life saving assistance to the additional children and their families.

Another important function of the Hotline is the maintenance of the *Child Protective Services Information System (Central*

Registry). The *Registry* receives all reports of abuse and neglect referred to local agencies, helping authorities to determine if prior reports exist on the same child or the same alleged offender anywhere in Virginia. This identification of repeated incidents and repeating offenders is an effective aid in preventing abuse and neglect. Also, the statistical data made possible by the *Registry* is an effective tool to improve overall planning of protective service programs.
Sponsor: Governor's Advisory Committee on Child Abuse & Neglect
Contact: Volunteer Coordinator

CHILD ABUSE LISTENING MEDIATION
CALM
PO Box 718
Santa Barbara, CA 93102
TEL: 805-682-1366 (offices); 805-569-2255 (hotline)
Objectives: To prevent child abuse by providing a listening service for parents "who feel that they cannot cope with their problems and may be on the verge of taking it out on the children."
Services: Provides a 24-hour Hotline, staffed with volunteers (with one bilingual listener available); trains volunteers to go into the homes as Family Aides to help in special situations of crisis; offers emergency child care for parents in stress; refers to other organizations and other resource services; maintains speakers bureau and a resource library; conducts public information/education program; conducts a Pre-Parenting Awareness Program, weekly Parental Support Groups (one bilingual); publishes quarterly newsletter, reports, bibliographies, and other materials.
Publications: CALMWORD
Founded: 1970

NATIONAL DOMESTIC VIOLENCE HOTLINE
Michigan Coalition Against Domestic Violence
PO Box 7032
Huntington Woods, MI 48070
TOLL FREE: 800-333-SAFE/873-6363-TTY
Objectives: To assist women facing domestic violence.
Services: The National Domestic Violence Hotline is one of the programs funded and maintained by a coalition of brand name companies in a program called "Shelter Aid." It was established in 1987 and plans are to continue the process as long as the problem exists. Donations to $450,000 are made each year to benefit the Hotline and local shelters. Special Shelter Aid displays are distributed to stores carrying the products of participating brand name companies.

The National Domestic Violence Hotline is staffed 24 hours a day, seven days a week, and its phones ring an average of 5,000 times a month. Statistics show that domestic violence is the single largest cause of injury to women, occurs every 15 seconds, involves children 50% of the time, affects the lives of 3-4 million women every year, and cuts across race, class, religion and socio-economic status.

Hotline staff and volunteers respond to confidential requests for information, discuss options or provide shelter referrals for women facing domestic violence. It is operated by the Michigan Coalition Against Domestic Violence.

INDIVIDUAL PROGRAM PROFILES

COMMITTEE TO AID ABUSED WOMEN
680 Greenbrae Drive
Suite 270
Sparks, NV 89431
TEL: 702-358-4150

Purpose: To help women and children of domestic violence through the period of crisis and afterward according to individual needs.

Sponsor: City of Sparks, including a tax surcharge; private donations

Contact: Maryanne Aaronson

Description: Recognizing the problem of domestic violence in the Sparks, Nevada area, a group of citizens gathered information on programs around the country designed to aid abused women and children. They found that these programs not only supported the victims through the crisis, but also worked toward elimination of the problem in their communities. In 1977, the Committee to Aid Abused Women was founded in Sparks to serve the city and its surroundings rural area.

The Committee successfully influenced the city to levy a $5.00 surcharge on marriage licenses to help fund the program. Other funding comes from other city channels, and private donations. The Committee receives no federal or state funding.

To develop the program, the Committee extracted selected practices from other programs that would best serve the Sparks population. The organization runs a temporary shelter, housing up to twelve women and children. In addition, it provides crisis counseling - both face-to-face and over the telephone. It serves as a resource and referral clearinghouse to help victims find continuing help in appropriate existing agencies, and advocates for the rights of the victims of domestic violence. Also, the organization provides food, transportation and emotional support as needed.

Volunteers in the program must undergo a seven-week training class twice each year that covers crisis counseling, legal and psychological needs of abused women, children's programs, and the philosophy and practices of CAAW. Inservice training is held bimonthly for the continuing education of all staff and volunteers. As of December 1981, 60 volunteers were involved in CAAW. They work in the following areas: direct client work; work with children, speakers bureau, fundraising, transportation, and office support. A City Development Block Grant in July 1981 made it possible to add three staff persons and expand the volunteer program.

DOMESTIC ABUSE PROJECT OF DELAWARE COUNTY
PO Box 174
Media, PA 19063
TEL: 215-565-6272

Purpose: To work against violence in the home by providing supportive services to victims and their families.

Sponsor: Federal/State/County governments; corporate and private donations.

Contact: Maxine Bailey, Executive Director

Description: The Domestic Abuse Project is a non-profit, community-based, volunteer organization committed to preventing and working against violence in the home by providing advocacy, emergency, supportive service and information to victims and their families; and by educating and involving the community in this process.

Volunteers are the backbone of the Project. There are presently 98 volunteers to answer the 24-hour hotline, counsel victims, plan events and policies, and give 1500-1800 hours per month to training and service.

Services include a 24-hour hotline with calls answered by counselors trained to respond to emergencies; counseling services for victims, and children; court accompaniment to help victims deal with the intricacies of the justice system; screening and referral services; emergency shelter, court and police advocacy; community outreach and education.

FAMILY CRISIS CENTER
PO Box 207
Keyser, WV 26726
TEL: 304-788-6061

Purpose: To provide services to victims of family violence; services include 24-hour hotline, short-term crisis intervention, advocacy, limited emergency shelter, support group, and information and referral.

Sponsor: West Virginia Government; private contributions

Contact: Vanessa Brooks, Executive Director

Description: The Family Crisis Center is a nonprofit agency whose purpose is to provide immediate support for victims of family violence and to develop community awareness and response to the problem of family violence.

The Family Crisis Center was organized through a VISTA grant secured by the Potomac Highlands Mental Health Guild in October, 1980. This grant was initiated in reply to the expressed need of the Mineral County Mental Health Association.

Funding for the program is provided in part by the West Virginia Department of Human Services, Governor's Committee on Crime, Delinquency, and Corrections and donations from groups, organizations and private individuals.

Volunteer Staff and Duties - At present, the Family Crisis Center has 25 volunteers who staff our 24-hour crisis hotline, help with fundraising events, and provide services to victims of family violence. Volunteers cover the phone from their homes changing shifts three times per day.

Currently volunteer training consists of two two-hour training sessions, but this is being developed into a more extensive training program. Monthly volunteer meetings are also held.

Publications: FCC Training Manual
Founded: 1980

PARENTAL STRESS CENTER
1700 East Carson Street
Pittsburgh, PA 15203
TEL: 412-381-4800

Purpose: To provide comprehensive services for abused, neglected, or high-risk infants and toddlers and their families.

Sponsor: Federal, state, county and private foundation sources.

Contact: Barbara S. Schultz, ACSW, Executive Director

Description: The Parental Stress Center is an independent non-profit social service agency providing comprehensive services for abused, neglected, or high-risk infants and toddlers and their families. Participation in Stress Center's direct service programs may be by referral from Allegheny County Children and Youth Services and may be mandated by Juvenile Court. Since its inception in 1975, the Center has been funded by a variety of federal, state, county and private foundation sources. Direct Service Programs include:

Families & Children Together I & II (FACT I & II) are the Parental Stress Center's therapeutic day programs for distressed parents and infants and toddlers with less acute needs than the babies in out-of-home care. The purpose of FACT is to establish a creative learning environment, demonstrating effective ways of caring for infants and toddlers which can be transferred to the home setting.

Begin Again I is a parent training program, designed for birth parents whose infants and toddlers are in foster care, and for the foster parents of these children. The focus of the parent training component is to increase the parenting skills of the birth parents. Foster parents gain additional understanding of the special needs of these children.

Begin Again II (Assessment Program) is an innovative approach to the provision of in-depth assessment of infants and toddlers who are currently in foster care. The objective of the program is to design an individual treatment plan for each child and family. This plan could include referral to other Parental Stress Center Direct Service Programs or other appropriate community resources.

Community Education Programs include:

Bright Beginnings is a program sponsored by the Parental Stress Center to address the non-medical concerns of Allegheny County parents of infants and toddlers, thus helping to reduce the incidence of infant and child abuse. The basic component of Bright Beginnings is a free telephone consultation, Warmline, staffed by professional volunteers with child development knowledge and family relations skills. Parents are invited to call with their everyday worries about their child's development - i.e., sleep disruptions, toilet trainings, etc. All Allegheny County area parents may use this service.

Suspected Child Abuse and Neglect (SCAN) program is a means of interdisciplinary case consultation for any member of the professional community regarding a particular case of abuse, neglect or high risk. Coordination for SCAN is provided by the Parental Stress Center. The SCAN core team includes the coordinator, a child psychiatrist, a pediatrician, a social worker, a legal consultant, a Children and Youth Services supervisor and a community mental health professional. The team also plans a series of large educational SCAN meetings several times a year. These are open to the professional and general community as a means of public education regarding child abuse and neglect. Presentations related to broad child abuse and neglect interests are made by nationally known experts in the field.

Staff/Volunteers/Interns - The professional staff of the Parental Stress Center is multidisciplinary in nature. Regular volunteer consultants to staff include psychiatrists, pediatricians, psychologists, lawyers, nurses, and child development specialists. Qualified students from related fields apply for student volunteer placement and internship.
Founded: 1975

RAPE AND DOMESTIC VIOLENCE INFORMATION CENTER
SEE INFORMATION & REFERRAL: SEXUAL ABUSE

24-HOUR CHILD ABUSE/NEGLECT TELEPHONE REPORT LINE
Delaware State Hospital
Gawthrop Building
1901 North DuPont Highway
New Castle, DE 19720
TEL: 302-421-6786
Purpose: To provide 24-hour telephone answering for the reporting of child abuse and neglect and supportive services for agency clients.
Sponsor: Division of Child Protective Services, Delaware Department of Health and Social Services, Junior League, Inc.
Contact: Mary W. Lewis
Description: The Division of Child Protective Services' Report Line has been operating for 12 years. The Report Line is a 24-hour crisis and referral service which provides help to families and children in crises and information and referral services. The Volunteer receives and screens calls between 4:30 p.m. and 10:30 p.m. After rudimentary screening, the calls indicating a child abuse/neglect problem are referred to the social worker on Emergency Duty assignment. The Report Line is staffed by specially selected, trained community Volunteers and coordinated by an experienced Volunteer.
The Volunteers are trained yearly. Training consists of: an overview of child welfare services, the ideology of child abuse and neglect, communication skills, agency policy and practice, community resources and empathetic and reflective listening. The training also includes an apprenticeship period with supervision being provided by more experienced volunteers.
The Volunteer program has been jointly sponsored by the local chapter of the Junior League. Individual Volunteers have also been accepted.
Also, the Volunteers have participated in a twice-a-year Clothes Closet drive and the Adopt-A-Family program. Clerical work, transportation services, and tutoring services are other service needs filled by Volunteers.
Founded: 1978

WOMEN'S CENTER OF EAST TEXAS (*formerly East Texas Association for Abused Families*)
PO Box 347
Longview, TX 75606
TEL: 214-757-9308
TOLL FREE: 800-441-5555
Purpose: To provide emergency services, temporary shelter to abused families, victims of physical/emotional abuse, and victims of sexual assault.
Sponsor: Texas Department of Human Resources Grant, County and City governments, local service organizations, churches, corporate and private donations
Contact: Judy Baker, Executive Director
Description: The *Women's Center of East Texas (WCET)* is a non-profit non-discriminatory, tax-exempt, social service agency which provides emergency services for abused families; an independent agency designed to fill the gap for shelter, counseling, health and social services coordinated with community agency efforts; and a complete sexual assault program. WCET's primary goals are:

- To break the cycle of violence by providing a safe alternative to a violent home, by providing education, counseling and support services to clients and their children, and by providing family counseling, if desired, for all family members.
- To provide full sexual assault accompaniment services to victims of sexual assault to promote recovery from the assault and prosecution of perpetrators.
- To provide education and awareness to the community concerning family violence and sexual assault.
- To provide priority programs and services to women and their families.
- To assist women - especially those in crisis and transition - in solving problems, seeking opportunities and meeting the challenges of a changing society.
- To inform the community about the needs and concerns of women.

At present 80-100 volunteers work on the crisis hotline, serve as sexual assault escorts and client advocates, assist in fund raising, and child guidance programs. Many are involved in community education and outreach.
Following over thirty hours of extensive training, volunteers perform many duties: answering the crisis hotline, giving referrals to callers, assessing need for shelter, etc. Sexual assault escort services provide support for victims of sexual assault from the time of the incident through court accompaniment. Other volunteer involvement areas are one-to-one counseling with shelter residents, parenting education, and alternatives to physical discipline.
Volunteers also assist in fund raising events, community awareness programs and education.
Volunteers are able to work at WCET with varying levels of experience. In-service training is provided for continuing education, which enables the volunteer to keep abreast of current events, legislation, etc., concerning family violence and sexual assault. The thirty-hour preliminary training session is required for all volunteers wishing to have direct client contact; i.e., hotline, sexual assault escort, counseling.
Volunteer involvement in the delivery of services is one of the main strengths of the family violence and sexual assault programs. Dedicated volunteers keep the cost down and improve the quality of service while participating in public education and outreach into diverse segments of society. Through training, volunteers are made aware of basic communication skills, community resources available and the process for utilizing those. One central focus of training is to develop the volunteer's capacity to be empathetic and understanding to victims of violence.

INFORMATION & REFERRAL: DRUGS/ALCOHOL

NATIONAL/STATE ORGANIZATIONS

DRUG ABUSE INFORMATION HOTLINE*
US/White House
Office of the First Lady
Washington, DC 20500
TEL: 202-456-1414
Objectives: To contact people who have asked for help with
concerns in the area of drug abuse.
Services: Enlists volunteers from the National Federation of
Parents for Drug-Free Youth to operate a pilot phone bank in the
White House; screens mail to select the most urgent questions that
can be answered by phone; responds to other mail-in comments
and questions with informative materials; plans to evaluate this
service to determine the feasibility for an ongoing phone bank of
this type in relation to questions on drug abuse that come to the
White House.
Founded: 1982

PRIDE
Parents' Resource Institute on Drug Education
Parent Resources and Information on Drug Abuse (PRIDE)
50 Hurt Plaza
Room 210
Atlanta, GA 30303
TOLL FREE: 800-67-PRIDE
Objectives: To utilize the parents' instinct to protect their children
to fight drug abuse.
Services: Provides technical assistance to parent groups wishing to
mount drug prevention programs for the benefit of the youth of
their communities; works with youth who are interested in seeing
the parent movement grow, can create peer leadership, and thus
can be an invaluable asset to the parent movement; designs
programs to reach parents and youth at home, school and work;
advocates a community approach, fostering a coming together of
government, business, schools and parents; uses a system of testing
that determines the scope of adolescent drug usage by students in
grades four through twelve; administers an intensive training
workshop for and by young people; teaches positive life skills, such
as how to reverse negative peer pressure; prepares parents to deal
with today's complex drug environment, and to conduct the
PRIDE program themselves after training; conducts the *PRIDE
World Drug Conference* (March 1991; May 1992); administers
government contracts; publishes various materials on drug abuse
prevention.
Publications: PRIDE: Devoted to Drug Abuse Prevention
Through Education

**US/HHS - NATIONAL CLEARINGHOUSE FOR ALCOHOL
AND DRUG INFORMATION**
PO Box 2345
Rockville, MD 20852
TEL: 301-468-2600
TOLL FREE: 800-SAY-NO-TO (Drugs)
FAX: 301-468-6433
Objectives: To serve as a national resource system for alcohol and
drug information.
Services: Serves as a centralized source for information on what is
currently known about alcohol and other drugs; works with and
through the *RADAR (Regional Alcohol and Drug Awareness
Resource) Network Centers* located in almost every state; provides
information on the latest research results, popular press and
scholarly journal articles, videos, prevention curricula, print

materials, and program descriptions; specifically, the *National
Clearinghouse for Alcohol and Drug Information (NCADI)*
provides the following services:
- **RADAR Network** - The *Regional Alcohol and Drug
  Awareness Resource (RADAR) Network* comprises resource
  centers in almost every state, which serve as information
  resource centers close to home. Each RADAR Network
  Center works cooperatively with NCADI, which sends them
  print materials and other resources so they can perform many
  of the same services with an extra advantage - they know the
  uniqueness of their own states. A list of RADAR Network
  offices is available on request.
- **Prevention Pipeline: An Alcohol and Drug Awareness Service**
  - This is a bimonthly news service available to anyone for a
  $15 annual handling fee. It is a forum, a news bulletin, and a
  research alert that allows both professionals and volunteers to
  keep on top of the latest information and events.
- **Technical Support** - NCADI offers support to organizations in
  the field whenever possible through a wide range of resource
  lists, direct mail, editorial support, exhibits, and dissemination
  of materials for conferences, and has an active outreach
  department that works with groups and individuals to
  maximize their efforts.
- **Print Materials** - NCADI creates new materials and offers
  limited quantities free-of-charge through the RADAR
  Network and other channels, including negatives (that you can
  take to your local printer); adapts the best of local efforts so
  the rest of the nation can share information on successful
  programs; distributes materials created by other U.S.
  Departments (e.g., Education, Transportation, and Justice),
  and prepares computerized lists that describe the wide array of
  materials available from both public and private sector groups.
NCADI was mandated by Congress to serve as *the* Federal
resource center for alcohol and other drug information because
lawmakers recognized the need for an unbiased, state-of-the-art
resource center that would be readily accessible to all citizens. The
partnership formed with state governments to create the RADAR
Network makes the program more responsive to the people. With
Federal and state dollars supporting NCADI and the RADAR
network, most of the materials are provided free. There are
minimum handling fees for only a few items. A number of the
items are listed in the Bibliography section of this publication. For
a complete list, request catalog.
Sponsor: US/HHS - Department of Health & Human Services
Contact: John F. Fay
Publications: Alcohol Health/Research World

INFORMATION & REFERRAL: EMPLOYEES

NATIONAL/STATE ORGANIZATIONS

EMPLOYEE ASSISTANCE PROGRAM CONSORTIUM
SEE BUSINESS/INDUSTRY INVOLVEMENT: EMPLOYEE
SUPPORT

INFORMATION & REFERRAL: FAMILIES

NATIONAL/STATE ORGANIZATIONS

FAMILY RESOURCE AND REFERRAL CENTER*
National Council on Family Relations
3989 Central Avenue, NE
Suite 550
Minneapolis, MN 55421-3921
TEL: 612-633-6933
Objectives: To provide current information on family-related topics.
Services: Maintains a clearinghouse on family-related topics in nearly 100 categories, including Day Care, Community Groups and the Family, Military Families, Education and the Family, Religion and the Family, and Employment and the Family; holds approximately 35,000 records, many annotated, and all coded by subject and classified by type and reader audience, including human service organizations, the clergy, media, students, and others; makes information accessible through university and college libraries, state libraries, major medical centers or schools and large hospitals (contact FR&RC for custom searches); keeps fees at a minimum due to a grant from the Charles Stewart Mott Foundation.
Publications: Family Relations; Marriage and the Family
Founded: 1938

NATIONAL COUNCIL ON FAMILY RELATIONS
3989 Central Avenue, NE
Suite 550
Minneapolis, MN 55421-3921
TEL: 612-781-9331
FAX: 612-781-9348
Objectives: To enable professional practitioners, academicians, and interested laypersons to work together to improve the quality of life for the family.
Services: Provides information on community services for families; works to stimulate sound government policies pertaining to family issues; encourages research about the family; maintains a reference service for training centers; coordinates and promotes educational efforts; publishes guides, handbooks and other materials on the family; maintains a major information source which is described below:
The Family Resources Data Base - a core collection of information covering the literature, programs and services of the family and allied fields; includes over 130 subject areas relevant to the family, including *Organizations and Services to Families,* which may be of particular interest to local volunteer groups, which includes subtopics of: day care, working mothers, employment, consumerism, career education, religion, community groups, and others (accessible on-line through BRS, Dialog and HRIN).
Publications: Family Relations; Marriage and the Family; NCFR Directory; NCFR Newsletter
Founded: 1938

INDIVIDUAL PROGRAM PROFILES

CAPE MAY COUNTY VOLUNTEERS AND RESOURCES
PO Box 222
Rio Grande, NJ 08242
TEL: 609-729-9200/Ext. 245; 609-729-2255 (helpline)
Purpose: To enhance existing Social Services to low-income persons; to provide emergency help in the form of food, clothing, shelter; to develop a team of Volunteers matched to specific tasks of community services.

Sponsor: Cape May County Welfare Board
Contact: Marianne Sheik
Description: Volunteers and Resources of Cape May County was developed in July 1982 to reach the needy of the County who neither qualify for existing assistance programs nor have the income and resources to adequately cover an emergency. The program is three-fold consisting of volunteers, resources, and information and referral phone answering service. The program is supported by volunteers, donations, and community interest and support.
Recruitment for volunteers is made through speaking engagements, news releases, and distribution of brochures. The Volunteer Bank contains 88 names of groups and individuals interested in service in various tasks such as transportation; one-to-one to teens, the blind, the elderly; helpers at community food distributions; office work; publicity; recruitment.
Cash donations are deposited in a checking account which is kept on reserve for emergency needs to supply food, clothing and/or shelter. A Food Bank is maintained for which non-perishable food items are accepted. Clothing Bank arrangements are made through a community Thrift Shop which benefits Retarded Citizens. Hand made articles for babies and the elderly are filtered through groups serving those special needs. Eye glasses are donated to the Lions Clubs. A special grant is used to develop and maintain an Infant Formula Bank at the County Child Health Conference.
The phone answering service supplements a 24-hour service provided by United Way of Cape May County during business hours to direct callers to the proper source for solving a particular problem or for getting appropriate help. (First Call For Help 609-729-2255.)
Periodic distribution is made of Surplus Commodities such as cheese and butter; surplus vegetable crops such as sweet potatoes, and vegetable seedlings raised and donated by Volunteers. Other activities include:
- shopping for shut-ins;
- medical transportation for pregnant teens;
- reassurance calling to shut-ins;
- child attending for parents attending interviews and training sessions;
- grounds, building and agency car pool maintenance;
- transportation aides;
- home-aides to shut-ins;
- reception;
- soliciting; and
- public relations.
Founded: 1982

F.A.C.T. HOTLINE (FAMILIES AND CHILDREN IN TROUBLE)
Family Stress Services of DC
1690 36th Street, NW
Washington, DC 20007
TEL: 202-965-1900 (office); 202-628-FACT (hotline)
Purpose: To provide families, individuals and other agencies with help around family stress, child abuse/neglect concerns, or almost any crisis or problem.
Sponsor: Family Stress Services of DC
Contact: Joan Cox Danzansky, Director
Description: This Hotline is a a project of F.A.C.T. (Families and Children in Trouble) which has been operating for over twelve years. The Hotline is a 24-hour crisis and referral helpline, providing families, individuals, and other helping agencies with assistance in matters of family stress, child abuse/neglect, and other types of crises and problems including suicide, depression and spouse abuse. The Hotline is staffed primarily by specially selected, trained and supervised community volunteers.
The comprehensive training and reliance upon committed community volunteers is an integral part of the FACT Program. The Hotline trains volunteer telephone counselors through a

course held three times a year, and is constantly in need of additional volunteers. After a special screening process, volunteers complete the sixty-hour course in empathetic and reflective listening/counseling skills and basic problem-solving processes. The training includes an apprenticeship on the lines and also covers family dynamics, etiology of child abuse, the law and resources, as well as information to aid with other types of calls such as spouse abuse, runaways, suicides, depression, etc.

The hotline, which opened on February 2, 1976, is supported through individual donations, private foundations, a grant from the National Parents Anonymous Organization, and receives funding through a contract with the Family Services Administration of the District of Columbia Department of Human Services.

FACT helps in a variety of ways, depending upon the needs of the caller. It acts as a crisis-intervention, listening, counseling, information and referral service which functions therapeutically when the hotline listener provides immediate understanding and support in times of crisis. It functions in a preventive manner when it allows parents or other caretakers to release their frustrations through talking with a concerned listener, rather than taking them out on children or other family members. When a caller appears to need help other than can be provided over the phone, FACT's information and referral component is used to find assistance for the caller through other community resources, agencies or self-help groups such as Parents Anonymous. The hotline also provides third-party callers with counseling and assistance for the reporting of cases to the proper authorities when necessary.

In addition to the FACT Hotline, Family Stress Services/FACT operates two other components: community education to raise public awareness; advocacy on both an individual and a case basis. Also, it serves as the information and referral line for Parents Anonymous, a self-help organization for parents experiencing child abuse/neglect problems.

Founded: 1976

TACTS VOLUNTEER PROGRAM
The Arlington County Temporary Shelter (TACTS)
PO Box 1285
Arlington, VA 22210
TEL: 703-522-3182
Purpose: To provide temporary shelter to persons in crises.
Sponsor: County governments, churches, community organizations and individuals
Contact: Nancy Dehncke
Description: TACTS is a United Way agency. Its Board of Directors and supporting committees are all composed of volunteers. Other volunteers are recruited, trained, placed and supervised by the Coordinator of Volunteer Services. In addition, many church and civic groups volunteer time in support of the Food Program and other projects.

TACTS has been in operation since November 1979. The basic function of TACTS is to provide temporary shelter to persons in crises. These may be women, women and their children, or intact families. The crises may be due to a natural catastrophe (such as fire or floods), eviction because of condo-conversion, inability to pay rent because of loss of job or health, break-up of living arrangements, or other problems. TACTS is intended for Arlington residents; others are accepted on a space-available basis. Staff is on duty 24 hours daily, seven days a week. Individualized information, referral services and supervision are provided by staff to clients. All clients admitted to TACTS must agree to comply with the house rules which specify: no drugs or alcohol, curfew by 10:30 p.m., children always under supervision, and clients out of the house during weekdays working on plans to resolve their problems.

TACTS works closely with other helping organizations, such as the Department of Human Resources, Red Cross, etc. Counseling

is provided by agencies within the DHR. Clients must have the capacity and willingness to make plans and implement them with assistance from DHR personnel and TACTS staff.

County government, churches, community organizations and individuals all have been supportive of TACTS. Funding has been approximately one-third County and one-third foundations (including United Way); the remaining one-third comes from the private sector and includes donations from individuals, organizations.

Founded: 1979

INFORMATION & REFERRAL: HANDICAPPED

NATIONAL/STATE ORGANIZATIONS

CEC SPECIAL PROJECT: ERIC CLEARINGHOUSE ON HANDICAPPED AND GIFTED CHILDREN
Council for Exceptional Children
1920 Association Drive
Reston, VA 22091-1589
TEL: 703-264-9474 (project); 703-620-3660 (office)
Objectives: To provide information and referral assistance to individuals and agencies working with exceptional children.
Services: Collects and abstracts special education documents for the ERIC database, which contains over 700,000 items; provides database searches, printed literature, and referral assistance to agencies and individuals needing information on children with handicaps or gifted learners.

CLEARINGHOUSE ON DISABILITY INFORMATION
US/DEd - Office of Special Education and Rehabilitative Services
Switzer Building
Room 3132
Washington, DC 20202-2524
TEL: 202-732-1241; 202-732-1245
Objectives: To respond to inquiries on a wide number of topics affecting disabled persons.
Services: Conducts research and provides information on operations serving the handicapped field on national, state and local levels; maintains extensive information in areas of Federal funding for programs serving disabled people, Federal legislation affecting the handicapped community, and Federal programs benefiting people with handicapping conditions; refers inquirers to appropriate sources; publishes a newsletter, legislation summaries, reports, and guides to benefits and services for qualified individuals.
Sponsor: US/DEd - Department of Education
Publications: OSERS News in Print; Summary of Existing Legislation Affecting Disabled Persons; Educating Students with Learning Problems: Shared Responsibility; Pocket Guide to Federal Help for Individuals with Disabilities
Founded: 1973

CLEARINGHOUSE ON THE HANDICAPPED*
US/DEd - Division for the Handicapped
Switzer Building
Washington, DC 20202-2524
TEL: 202-245-0080
Objectives: To provide a central source of information on policies, programs, procedures and activities relevant to the handicapped.
Services: Responds to inquiries on a wide range of topics concerning handicapping conditions and related services;

researches and monitors information operations on national, state and local levels; provides technical assistance; maintains comprehensive, current information on federal funding for programs serving the handicapped, federal programs and federal legislation; produces publications primarily for information providers, such as *Directory of National Information Sources on Handicapping Conditions and Related Services*; publishes a bimonthly newsletter, *Programs for the Handicapped,* which announces new clearinghouses, and other publications, and monitors activities of federal agencies.
Sponsor: US/DEd - Department of Education
Founded: 1975

INFORMATION CENTER FOR INDIVIDUALS WITH DISABILITIES
20 Park Plaza
Room 330
Boston, MA 02116
TEL: 617-727-5540 (voice); 617-727-5236
TOLL FREE: 800-462-5015 (statewide)
Objectives: To help disabled persons lead independent, productive and satisfying lives through access to relevant information.
Services: Operates three separate programs to ensure that the goals of the Information Center are met, described below:
- **Information and Referral** - the largest program within The Center; involves information specialists who take incoming requests and attempt to answer immediately - initiating a search of the resource files or in-house computer system if the answers are not readily available; generates "fact sheets" through this program when the frequency of inquiries suggests the need for one (e.g., "How do I apply for a handicapped license plate?")
- **Resource Development and Training** - a program made possible with a three-year grant from the Massachusetts Commission for the Blind; develops resources for the visually impaired, multi-handicapped person; produces a comprehensive resource manual, which is expanded on a quarterly basis; develops training material in areas such as equipment, housing, transportation, and sexuality (involving qualified professionals and members of the disabled community in this work); provides input on new resources to the I&R component.
- **Together: News for the Rehabilitation Community** - a monthly newsletter supported in part by the Massachusetts Rehabilitation Commission; provides features, resource lists, and other information on current subjects and events of interest to the disabled population; disseminates the newsletter free of charge to individuals in all 50 states, five U.S. territories, and six foreign countries.

Provides access to express concerns and ask questions during the workday with response by the specialists, and after hours through a tape answering machine; welcomes visitors who wish to do their own research through the Center's resource files or in-house computer system.
[Services of the MBTA and The Ride (the MBTA's paratransit system for the disabled) are available within one block of the Information Center]
Publications: Together
Founded: 1977

NATIONAL CENTER FOR HEARING DOG INFORMATION
American Humane Association
9725 East Hampden Avenue
Denver, CO 80231
TEL: 303-695-0811; 303-695-4531 (TTY)
TOLL FREE: 800-842-4637
Objectives: To provide a national hearing dog information and referral service.

Services: Promotes the legal access rights of hearing dogs; works to increase public awareness of the benefits of hearing dogs to deaf citizens; publishes manuals, guides, booklets, a directory and other materials.
Publications: Hearing Dog Recipient Manual; Legal Rights of Dog Guides for the Deaf; Hearing Dog Program Directory
Founded: 1976

NATIONAL INFORMATION CENTER FOR CHILDREN AND YOUTH WITH HANDICAPS
PO Box 1492
Washington, DC 20013
TEL: 703-893-6061; 703-893-8614 (TDD)
TOLL FREE: 800-999-5599 (recording)
Objectives: To assist parents, educators, caregivers, advocates and others in helping children and youth with disabilities to become participating members of the community.
Services: Provides personal responses to specific questions, referrals to other organizations/sources of help, and prepared information packets for frequently-asked questions (lists of state agencies and local parent groups, referral to specific sources, information on legal rights and parent advocacy, and other information and materials as available); requires inquiry by letter due to volume of information available; publishes biennial newsletter, state resources sheets, fact sheets, parent guides and other materials; offers technical assistance to parent, professional, advocate, caregiving and other groups working with handicapped children.
Contact: Information Specialist
Publications: News Digest
Founded: 1970

INFORMATION & REFERRAL: HEALTH

INDIVIDUAL PROGRAM PROFILES

ASK THE DOCTOR
SEE VOLUNTEERS: PROFESSIONALS

CHILD SECURITY NETWORK OF CONNECTICUT
SEE INFORMATION & REFERRAL: CHILDREN/YOUTH

INFORMATION & REFERRAL: HEALTH/EMERGENCIES

NATIONAL/STATE ORGANIZATIONS

NATIONAL CLEARINGHOUSE FOR POISON CONTROL CENTERS
US/HHS - Food and Drug Administration
5401 Westbard Avenue
Bethesda, MD 20014
TEL: 301-496-7691
Objectives: To prevent accidental poisonings, particularly of young children.
Services: Sponsors "National Poison Prevention Week" and other prevention and education programs; sponsors research in treatments and antidotes; provides an information exchange for some 600 poison control centers around the country; maintains a data base of case reports; publishes the *Handbook of Common*

Poisonings in Children, a bulletin for those involved in poison control, and numerous brochures, booklets, fliers, and radio/TV spot announcements.
Sponsor: US/HHS - Department of Health & Human Services
Publications: Common Poisonings in Children

NATIONAL EYE CARE PROJECT
American Academy of Ophthalmology Foundation
PO Box 6988
San Francisco, CA 94101-6988
TOLL FREE: 800-222-EYES (3937)
Objectives: To extend medical eye care to disadvantaged citizens over the age of sixty-five.
Services: Operates a toll-free HELPLINE for citizens or legal residents over the age of 65 who need medical eye care but have no physician; makes referrals to local volunteer opthalmalogists who are participating in the project; provides service to those who are needy, with qualified callers receiving treatment at no out-of-pocket expense for the doctor's services (each caller meeting eligibility requirements is mailed the name of an ophthalmologist participating near his or her home within one week after the call); provides free information to any senior calling the HELPLINE. [The project is funded by corporations and independent ophthalmologists as well as the Academy's Foundation.]
Contact: Anna Zammataro or B. Thomas Hutchinson, MD
Founded: 1896

NATIONAL HOMECARING COUNCIL
Foundation for Hospice and Homecare
519 C Street, NE
Washington, DC 20002
TEL: 202-547-6586
Objectives: To promote, develop and ensure provision of responsible homemaker-home health aide and related services of high quality for all families and individuals in need of such services.
Services: Promotes quality assurance for home care; administers a voluntary accreditation program (developed in 1965), which is based on the basic national standards and, in a number of states, is a requirement for state funds; provides curriculum materials to the federal government for the instruction of the homemaker-home health aide, and as a basis for a number of specialized training materials on subjects such as cancer, Alzheimer's Disease, and high-tech home care; works with the support of the *U.S. Administration on Aging* to develop a national certification program for homemaker-home health aides; produces additional training manuals, pamphlets and audiovisual materials to instruct and inform the field as well as the consumer.
Publications: Model Curriculum & Teaching Guide: Homemaker-Home Health Aide

ODPHP NATIONAL HEALTH INFORMATION CENTER
PO Box 1133
Washington, DC 20013
TEL: 301-565-4167
TOLL FREE: 800-336-4797
Objectives: To assist consumers in locating the health resources they need; to initiate liaison activities among health information providers.
Services: Provides referral information to resource organizations such as educational institutions, voluntary organizations, libraries, hospitals, other clearinghouses, and government agencies at all levels; responds to inquiries from lay persons and professionals; publishes subject-oriented bibliographies and brochures. (The Clearinghouse is a project of the Office of Health Information, Health Promotion, and Physical Fitness and Sports Medicine of HHS.)
Publications: Health Resources in Government
Founded: 1979

PROGRAM EXCHANGE PROCESS (PEP)
American Red Cross
National Headquarters
17th and D Streets
Washington, DC 20006
TEL: 202-639-3535
Objectives: To serve as a method for chapters, blood centers, and all other Red Cross field units to exchange information on successful and innovative programs, activities and products.
Services: Begun in 1972, the Program Exchange Process (PEP) collects, processes and prepares for distribution information on programs at the local level to share with chapters, blood centers and field units across the country. By August 1988, the data bank had more than 1,850 programs available, and information is received every day. PEP is staffed by volunteers and coordinated by a paid staff member. It is located with the Administrative Resources unit of the Programs and Services Department at national headquarters. Programs are forwarded upon request and are structured to help save both time and money for managers wishing to improve or mount similar efforts.
How to Deposit Your Ideas in PEP - A reporting form (#5752) is completed and returned to PEP for review by an intraservice panel. When approved, the program is assigned a number and entered into the computer and the PEP catalog.
How to Withdraw Ideas from PEP - The *Program Exchange Catalog* (ARC 3311) is published twice a year, with supplements as warranted and is available through the General Supply Division. After a review of the catalog, a written request or a telephone call indicating the desired program by number activates the PEP system and the information is forwarded to the requestor. For those who have a computer, the information is designed for *User Access by Modem* directly to PEP national headquarters. Full instructions for accessing the information by computer are available on request.
Materials received include the program's name, purpose, and description, along with facts about the target population, funding sources, cooperating agencies, staffing, and support materials. PEP operates with an ongoing evaluation and updating system that enables users to receive information on current issues. For example, new programs in 1988-89 include:
- Special Concerns of Youth (substance abuse, suicide, teenage pregnancy, and AIDS)
- Latchkey Children
- AIDS Education and Caregiving
- Disaster Education for Children
- Services by and for the Elderly
- Health in the Workplace
- The Homeless in Your Community
- Innovative Donor Recruitment

According to the program's Chairman, "In addition to the value of the experience of others, it is hoped that PEP will strengthen the bond among chapters and help them serve their communities better."
Publications: Program Exchange Process Catalog; Plans and Programs for Community Service

TECHNICAL INFORMATION CENTER OF THE OFFICE ON SMOKING AND HEALTH
US/HHS - Office on Smoking & Health
Parklawn Building
5600 Fishers Lane
Rockville, MD 20857
TEL: 301-443-1690
Objectives: To keep the public informed on the effects of smoking on health.
Services: Issues special reports - both general and technical; operates mail/phone inquiry service, as well as personal service at the Center; maintains over 26,000 files of information on smoking and health; runs computer searches on request (must submit

Search Request Form available from Center); publishes *Smoking and Health Bulletin, The Health Consequences of Smoking*, bibliographies and other materials.
Publications: Smoking and Health Bulletin; Health Consequences of Smoking

WELLNESS AND HEALTH ACTIVATION NETWORKS
PO Box 923
Vienna, VA 22180
TEL: 703-281-3830
Objectives: To teach individuals to more effectively utilize the health resources of the community.
Services: Provides on-site program planning and development assistance in areas of stress management, nutrition, physical awareness and self-responsibility; operates Health Activation Training Institutes; provides technical assistance in proposal writing and other management areas; maintains clearinghouse of health program designs; distributes trainer's guides, planning guides, and other materials.
Publications: Wellness Associates Journal; Members' Directory
Founded: 1980

INFORMATION & REFERRAL: HOMELESS

NATIONAL/STATE ORGANIZATIONS

HOT LINE FOR THE HOMELESS*
Findlay Area Native American Indian Center
Findlay, OH 45840
TOLL FREE: 800-526-5414
Objectives: To provide information for homeless callers on shelters and other services in every state in the union.
Services: A toll-free hot line began operating in January 1990 at the *Findlay Area Native American Center* in Ohio. Referrals are made to shelters, soup kitchens, different social service agencies, and other resources to help people in need in every state of the union.
The center, composed of a house, barn and craft shop on two acres in Findlay, was created to promote American Indian culture. But the center's owner, who is a Cherokee Indian, and an associate who is an Abenaki Indian felt that the resource could be put to better use and converted part of the complex to help the needy. Although several months before the hot line was launched, the center provided food and clothing and emergency shelter to hundreds of people in the Findlay area, the founders are proudest of the hot line, which required research on every state and can help an individual calling from any part of the country in need of food, clothing or shelter.
Contact: Michael Michaud, Spokesman
Founded: 1990

INDIVIDUAL PROGRAM PROFILES

BETHEL LOVE KITCHEN
Bethel AME Church
2460 Parkview Avenue
Knoxville, TN 37917
TEL: 615-522-6396
Purpose: To provide hot meals, and refer people to organizations that provide jobs and shelter.
Contact: Helen Ashe or Ellen Turner, co-founders

Description: Since 1986, the *Bethel Love Kitchen* in East Knoxville has provided meals to hungry men, women and children. On the first day, 22 people came to the Kitchen. By 1989, 62,000 people had been fed.
The Kitchen relies on the federal surplus food program, donations and private supporters, including the wife of a Congressional Representative from Tennessee. The Congressman's office helps work on possible grants for the Kitchen.
The founders of the Kitchen, twin sisters, were nurses at the University of Tennessee Medical Center before their retirement. They find that this health background serves them well in dealing with their clientele. They hope to move to larger quarters with showers and enough land to grow food for meals.
Currently, the Kitchen serves meals every Thursday. Preparation is begun Wednesday, but the actual cooking done Thursday morning. Most of it is done by the founding sisters, with occasional help from volunteers. The food is substantial - fried chicken, potatoes, liver and onions, ham, meatloaf, spaghetti, green beans, corn muffins and cake.
A portion of the meals are packaged and taken by volunteers to elderly people who can't travel. The Kitchen also refers people to organizations that provide jobs and shelter, and fixes emergency food boxes for those in need who miss the meal hour.
The twins, although in poor health with back problems, arthritis and - for one sister, cancer which she says is "under control" - continue the service since, according to one of them, "What am I doing feeling sorry for myself when there are people out there who are much worse?"
Founded: 1986

GIVE THEM A HAND, NOT A HANDOUT
Capitol Hill Association of Merchants and Professionals
CHAMPS
PO Box 15486
Washington, DC 20003
TEL: 202-547-7788
Purpose: To provide information for people in the street to lead them to job counseling and other social services.
Contact: Joan Schindel
Description: This program is an attempt by the *Capital Hill Association of Merchants and Professionals (CHAMPS)* to help the truly needy who may not be aware of services available to them - often just a few steps away. The assistance is in the form of a wallet-sized card providing names, addresses, and phones of organizations which are available immediately, and standing ready to be of assistance. The quick-reference card is provided to citizens on request, and is designed as a substitute for giving cash.
In addition to a desire to help the truly needy, CHAMPS sees the program as a way of eliminating the "professional panhandlers" who stake out the southeast area each day. Since there are no vagrancy laws, and a foot patrol officer does not seem to be enough to discourage the practice, nothing much could be done. In addition to causing problems for the truly needy, the panhandlers - some very aggressive - turn business away from the merchants in the area.
The CHAMPS card lists a church and a social services center in the area, giving name, address, phone, and the services provided. To help provide for an increase in clients, CHAMPS has installed collection containers next to the stacks of cards in member-merchants stores for contributions to the two groups listed. Patrons are encouraged to take a stack of cards, and make a contribution. This has appealed to people who want to help, but are not sure that the money they give directly to the street person will go for a sandwich. In many instances, the money is used for drugs and alcohol. Giving directly to the service providers through the CHAMPS program is reassuring to many citizens. According to the founder of a similar program in California, "We were starting to see a trend, a backlash against those people living on the street," since it was difficult to discern between "economic

victims and criminal vagrants."

Other neighborhoods in the District of Columbia, including Adams-Morgan, Dupont Circle and Georgetown, have experienced similar complaints about panhandlers, and are considering similar programs. In the meantime, one of the recipients of the card on Capitol Hill brightened when he read it and said, "I didn't know there was job counseling available. I've been out here too long!"

INFORMATION & REFERRAL: HOUSING

INDIVIDUAL PROGRAM PROFILES

CHISS (CONSUMER HOUSING INFORMATION SERVICE FOR SENIORS)
Fairfax Area Agency on Aging
11242 Waples Mill Road
Suite 100
Fairfax , VA 22030-6036
TEL: 703-246-5411
Purpose: To help the elderly find housing services in the Fairfax area.
Contact: Volunteer Coordinator
Description: CHISS is a consumer housing information program of the American Association of Retired Persons (AARP), sponsored in Fairfax County by the *Area Agency on Aging*. The *Agency* distributes quick-reference, easy-to-read flyers to libraries and other public places in the area, and makes special efforts to distribute them to areas that emphasize service to the elderly. Through the program, the elderly renter or homeowner looking for information about ways to maintain or improve his or her housing situation can contact CHISS.
Housing Information Volunteers provide information on
- issues to consider when deciding to remain in or move away from home;
- ways to improve liveabliity of the home as one grows older;
- local home repair, maintenance, and weatherization programs;
- local in-home assistance programs;
- ways to increase income or decrease the cost of living; and
- the location of safe, affordable, and comfortable housing if an elderly person decides to move.

After locating housing services for an inquirer, CHISS volunteers help the older person evaluate them *before* making a decision as to which options will best serve the individual's needs. CHISS also provides materials that describe the advantages and disadvantages of various housing options, as well as guidelines for evaluating each option.
The history of the program indicates that the unbiased, "arms length" information provided by CHISS is a good safeguard for the older person seeking housing.
Publications: CHISS Information Packet

INFORMATION & REFERRAL: LAW ENFORCEMENT

NATIONAL/STATE ORGANIZATIONS

US/DOJ - NATIONAL CRIMINAL JUSTICE REFERENCE SERVICE
National Institutes of Justice
1600 Research Blvd, Box 6000
Rockville , MD 20850
TEL: 301-251-5500
Objectives: To further the exchange of information with the goal of improving law enforcement and criminal justice.
Services: Identifies and screens publications and audiovisual materials that will meet the criteria of the service - "to increase the understanding of causes and effects of crime, prevention of crime, and operations of the criminal justice system;" responds to individual reference queries by conducting computer searches of its data base; publishes *Selected Notification of Information (SNI)* announcements to subscribers listing new acquisitions and providing an order form; publishes a series of bibliographies on specific subjects; operates a document loan program with a loan period of four weeks (interlibrary loan system through any library in the U.S. or Canada); provides free microfiche copies of out-of-print or one-of-a-kind documents; maintains a Share Package Program which loans materials prepared by other organizations in the form of newsletters, brochures, posters, etc.
Publications: Selected Notification of Information

INFORMATION & REFERRAL: MENTAL HEALTH

NATIONAL/STATE ORGANIZATIONS

AMERICAN ACADEMY OF CRISIS INTERVENERS
c/o Dr. Edward S. Rosenbluh
218 Breckenridge Lane, Suite 102
Louisville, KY 40207
TEL: 502-896-0200
Objectives: To increase knowledge in all areas of crisis intervention.
Services: Provides a forum for those whose work causes them to deal with crises and emergencies to share research, current information and educational ideas, thus improving skill levels and increasing knowledge (includes fields of mental health, education, law enforcement, religion and medicine); provides instructors and speakers in all areas of crisis intervention; publishes a training manual, and other materials.
Publications: Crisis Counseling: Emotional First Aid; Journal of Crisis Intervention
Founded: 1977

INFORMATION SERVICE*
American Psychiatric Association
1400 K Street, NW
Washington, DC 20005
TEL: 202-682-6000
Objectives: To develop practical information on behalf of the mentally ill.
Services: Identifies outstanding mental health programs (for the aged, for preschoolers, halfway houses, in-community

rehabilitation, etc.); visits the programs to observe and conduct interviews; develops publications using the case study approach - including complete information on how volunteers are involved - to assist practitioners wishing to begin or improve programs; works with both public and private agencies in cooperative ventures that will broaden the base of beneficial services to the mentally ill and, therefore, increase the effectiveness of the entire mental health field.

Publications: Psychiatric News; Community Psychiatry
Founded: 1844

US/HHS - NATIONAL CLEARINGHOUSE FOR MENTAL HEALTH INFORMATION
5600 Fishers Lane
Rockville, MD 20857
TEL: 301-443-4513
Objectives: To respond to the need for centralizing all sources of mental health information.
Services: Makes referrals to other agencies and organizations when appropriate; refers individuals seeking treatment to community mental health centers and state hospitals; provides free single copies of all Clearinghouse publications except periodicals, which must be ordered from the Superintendent of Documents, U.S. Government Printing Office, Washington, DC 20402.
Sponsor: US/HHS - Department of Health & Human Services

TRAINING PROGRAMS

EMPLOYEE ASSISTANCE PROGRAMS
SEE BUSINESS/INDUSTRY INVOLVEMENT: EMPLOYEE SUPPORT

INDIVIDUAL PROGRAM PROFILES

GRASSROOTS CRISIS INTERVENTION & PEER COUNSELING CENTER
Harriet Tubman Center
6700 Freetown Rd.
Columbia, MD 21044
TEL: 301-531-6006
Purpose: To provide alternative mental health services on an individual and group basis, to provide education to the community with a preventative focus, and to provide training to groups and agencies within our community.
Sponsor: Howard County Grant-in-Aid
Contact: Volunteer Coordinator
Description: Grassroots Crisis Intervention and Peer Counseling Center was first opened in 1970 as an alternative to traditional mental health services and with a focus toward reaching youth with drug problems. At the present time Grassroots remains an alternative in its emphasis on providing a friendly, informal response to human needs.
The center provides peer counseling by way of a telephone hotline and walk-in service, emergency shelter facilities, outreach to the scene of a crisis, and there are no appointments necessary or fees required. The objectives of the organization have expanded to include problems with families, sexuality, school, abuse, loneliness, and other concerns.
Grassroots also provides TTY services to the deaf community, advocacy, information and referral, a speaker's bureau, after hours back-up for the Bureau of Mental Health, and acts as a primary resource to the Police Department and Howard County Department of Social Services.
The staff at Grassroots is comprised of people from a variety of backgrounds who have all successfully participated in in-house experiential training in crisis and client-centered counseling skills.

Grassroots' counseling model is based on the belief that the person who is experiencing stress is working through a problem which can be facilitated by a caring, honest relationship, with its elements of support, feedback and reality testing. The hope is that both the client and counselor may benefit from the interaction. Grassroots is committed to protecting the clients' confidentiality.
There are no educational or experience requirements to apply for a volunteer counselor position. Counselor selection is oriented toward open, genuine individuals who are capable of establishing a helping relationship with a client. Some of the opportunities for volunteer involvement include:

- Learning skills in areas such as communication, counseling, group leadership, training, supervision, etc.
- Providing peer counseling, crisis intervention, advocacy, information and referral services to the community.
- Joining the speaker's bureau to talk to community groups about various mental health topics.
- Representing the volunteer counseling staff on the Board of Directors of Grassroots.
- Acquiring practicum credit from area colleges.
- Involvement in fundraising and other committees and groups.

Volunteer counselors are expected to provide 18 counseling hours each month as well as attend one staff meeting each month for information sharing, in-service training, supervision, and team building. There is an expectation that all members of the staff will share in the commitment that Grassroots has made to the community. This occurs not only through time volunteered for counseling but through involvement and input into the operational activities of the organization. Grassroots asks six months commitment for support of the agency from each volunteer counselor. Quote from the Director: "Grassroots values the support and commitment of its volunteer staff."
The United Way of Central Maryland is a sponsor.
Founded: 1970

INFORMATION & REFERRAL: MINORITIES/WOMEN

INDIVIDUAL PROGRAM PROFILES

THE S.O.A.P.S.
Social Services of Akron Project
ACCESS, Inc.
245 South High Street
Akron, OH 44308
TEL: 216-535-2999
Purpose: To disseminate information about health and social services available to Akron-area women.
Sponsor: United Way
Contact: Volunteer Coordinator
Description: In 1987, a program was designed to reach women in need of health and social services. Soap opera plot lines were used to show women that they need not suffer alone. Called *The S.O.A.P.S.,* the project produced 50,000 copies of a 12-page tabloid it created with the help of the local syndicated columnist who synopsizes network soaps for more than 200 papers nationwide. The columnist met with coalition members to determine which problems are most troublesome for women, then chose appropriate soap opera plots and wrote condensed versions of them. For each plot line, a coalition member wrote a follow-up article that explained the kinds of services available to Akron women in similar circumstances. For example, when the "soap opera plot" told the story of "Jo Johnson," an abused spouse, Akron's *Battered Women's Shelter* produced a companion piece that

described the shelter's services and explained what a woman should do if she or her family become victims of abuse. Four nonprofit agencies are among the project's creators - the *YWCA, ACCESS* (a shelter), *Battered Women's Shelter,* and *Planned Parenthood of Summit, Portage, and Medina Counties.* Funding comes from various sources, including corporations, a community foundation, and the *Junior League.*

INFORMATION & REFERRAL: NUTRITION

NATIONAL/STATE ORGANIZATIONS

FOOD SAFETY HOTLINE
US/DoA - Food and Nutrition Service
Independence Avenue, SW
(Between 12th & 14th Sts.)
Washington, DC 20250
TOLL FREE: 800-535-4555
Objectives: To answer questions on safe preparation of food.
Services: Provides five home economists to answer consumer questions regarding the proper handling, preparation and storage of meat and poultry products.

NUTRITION EDUCATION AND INFORMATION
Nutrition Foundation
1126 Sixteenth Street, NW
Suite 111
Washington, DC 20036
TEL: 202-659-0074
Objectives: To advance nutrition knowledge and assure its effective application in improving the health and welfare of mankind.
Services: Responds to requests from the media, industry, government and Congress, organizations and private citizens; sponsors a group of nutrition educators to select materials and guides for distribution; publishes monthly journal, *Nutrition Reviews,* a source book, *The Index of Nutrition Education Materials,* popular booklet entitled *Nutrition Misinformation* and *Food Faddism,* and a series of booklets for the general public on some of the most frequently posed questions about food and nutrition.
Publications: Nutrition Reviews; Present Knowledge in Nutrition; Food Faddism; Nutrition Misinformation
Founded: 1985

INFORMATION & REFERRAL: OLDER PERSON

INDIVIDUAL PROGRAM PROFILES

CHISS (CONSUMER HOUSING INFORMATION SERVICE FOR SENIORS)
SEE INFORMATION & REFERRAL: HOUSING

CORPORATE RETIREES INFORMATION AND ASSISTANCE PROGRAM
RSVP of Morris County
Box 372
West Hanover Avenue
Morris Plains, NJ 07950
TEL: 201-538-7947
Purpose: To provide a service that will help older persons to become more effective consumers.
Sponsor: Junior League
Contact: Martie Wickers
Description: When the need to educate and counsel older citizens to be more effective consumers was identified, it suggested an answer to another identified need - to provide more innovative projects with management opportunities for corporate retiree volunteers in the RSVP program. In 1979 the Fixed-Income Consumer Counseling Project (FICC) was created with ACTION funding. An FICC Coordinator was hired, and an Advisory Committee named. It has become an ongoing project of the RSVP program staffed by corporate retirees.
A natural outgrowth of FICC was the Information and Referral (I&R) program with desks in offices all over the county manned by corporate retirees. I&R services are funded by ACTION, Title III-B and the United Way. Information and assistance is provided in areas of taxes, energy rebate, food stamp eligibility and other forms, and other identified service needs of older persons.
To create public awareness of the above projects and other RSVP projects meeting community needs, the corporate retirees plan, arrange and review a weekly radio show, RSVP Speakout Project. In conjunction with the program, the volunteers operate a Speakers Bureau and speak to various groups on I&R and consumer issues and are on call for college and corporate pre-retirement courses. The radio show was made possible with a two-year Junior League mini-grant.
Both staff and volunteers deliberately operate this program on an open-ended level to enable it to grow and change as new information and assistance needs emerge, and others cease to exist. Written materials on the various components of the program are available to those interested in mounting one or more of the projects.
Founded: 1979

SENIOR CONNECTION
Community Service Council of Broward County
1300 South Andrews Avenue
PO Box 22877
Fort Lauderdale , FL 33335-2877
TEL: 305-524-8371
Purpose: To provide information on everything from health care to social services for seniors.
Sponsor: Area Agency on Aging
Contact: Arthur J. Ellick, Executive Director
Description: In just one month after it began in November 1987, *Senior Connection* had received over 400 calls from people seeking information on services for seniors. One-fourth of the county's population is over 65 (270,000 individuals). The information line is operated by the *Community Service Council of Broward County.* Although the United Way had a general crisis line and I&R service, needs were increasingly focusing on the elderly, and the Council's proposal was welcomed by *United Way* and *Area Agency on Aging* officials. The United Way provided computer support and other nonfinancial help, and the local Area Agency on Aging provided the funding.
A very effective aspect of the program is the follow-up capability. *Senior Connection* staff, via a three-way call, can ensure the individual is put in touch with an appropriate agency. Then, staff can follow up to see if the requested help was received by the individual.
A side benefit, according to the director, is the "much-needed

data" that the program provides for use in planning future services.

SENIOR REPORT
WUST Radio
815 V Street, NW
Washington, DC 20001
TEL: 202-462-0011
Purpose: To keep senior citizens apprised of programs and services designed for them.
Contact: Newton Smith, Jr., or Concha Johnson
Description: Located in Ward 8, which has the poorest and least educated elderly population in Washington, DC, *WUST Radio* presents a daily, 15-minute broadcast, *Senior Report,* that delivers a stream of conversation aimed at providing an estimated 50,000 listeners with the latest news on senior citizen issues, benefits and programs.
Although the "voices" behind *Senior Report* belong to people experienced in the aging field, the program features guests who donate their time to discuss a specific issue and respond to questions from listeners. When the specialist is finished, program staff are ready and waiting with information on local volunteer and free government projects so that the senior citizen can follow up on the advice given by the guest. An example is the visit by an oncologist who talked about the importance of mammograms, and the followup information about a demonstration project offering free mammograms.
On the lighter side, the program's facilitators try to keep seniors current on low-cost entertainment and activities - local theatres that offer senior discounts, or package rates on cruises. Also, they try to stay on top of the news and current events to help develop an informed senior citizenry. In early 1990, the thrust was on the 1990 Census begun in April. Recognizing the uncertainty of many seniors about providing information about themselves, the station assured them that there was nothing to worry about, unless they *didn't* give requested information, since their benefits might be cut or, in matters of "head count," the city might lose money if everyone isn't counted.
The show's hosts are involved in many senior programs, including *Gray Panthers, Senior Citizens Counseling and Delivery Service, St. Teresa of Avila Parish Senior Outreach,* and the city's *Foster Grandparents Program* among others.

INFORMATION & REFERRAL: RECREATION/SPORTS

NATIONAL/STATE ORGANIZATIONS

FTC VACATION TRAVEL HOTLINE
SEE INFORMATION & REFERRAL: CONSUMER/LEGAL RIGHTS

INFORMATION EXCHANGE*
US/DoI - National Park Service
Washington, DC 20240
TEL: 202-343-4747
Objectives: To assist practitioners, government agencies, nonprofit organizations, and individuals involved in recreation.
Services: Serves the above objective by responding to requests from any individual or group for information on all aspects of recreation; provides assistance by phone, mail and personal visit; distributes studies, handbooks, audiovisuals and films, surveys, training manuals and other materials of a practical nature.
(Regional Offices in Seattle, San Francisco, Albuquerque, Denver,

Atlanta, Ann Arbor, Philadelphia and Anchorage; request address list)
Sponsor: US/DoI - Department of the Interior

LEISURE INFORMATION SERVICE
801 D Street, NE
Washington, DC 20002
TEL: 202-547-6696
Objectives: To improve the quality and quantity of leisure time activities.
Services: Reports on legislation, funding, resource organizations, publications, etc., in all aspects of leisure time activities; provides technical assistance; publishes *Fund Development* and *Revenue Resources Report.* [Additional office: 700 Orange Street, PO Box 1992, Wilmington, DE 19899]

INFORMATION & REFERRAL: SEXUAL ABUSE

NATIONAL/STATE ORGANIZATIONS

RAPE CRISIS CENTER
PO Box 21005
Washington, DC 20009
TEL: 202-333-7273
Objectives: To assist/counsel victims through the trauma of rape.
Services: Provides information and counseling to rape victims; provides specialized counseling for victims of incest; develops community education programs and materials; offers consulting services to other groups concerned with rape; provides self-defense referral information for others dealing with rape victims; provides children's services; conducts community education programs for elementary and older students about issues relating to sexual assault and its prevention; publishes *How to Start a Rape Crisis Center* (book), manuals, guidelines, pamphlets, flyers and other materials.
Publications: Rape Prevention ; Shaw Outreach Team; How to Start a Rape Crisis Center

INDIVIDUAL PROGRAM PROFILES

RAPE AND DOMESTIC VIOLENCE INFORMATION CENTER
PO Box 4228
Morgantown, WV 26505
TEL: 304-588-6800
Purpose: To provide shelter, counseling advocacy and referral for victims of domestic violence, sexual assault and incest.
Sponsor: Federal/State/City/County governments; private donations
Contact: Kim van Rijn, Volunteer Coordinator
Description: RDVIC runs a 24-hour hotline for domestic violence, sexual assault and incest victims and temporary emergency shelter for victims.
Staff and volunteers work with victims and their families providing crisis intervention, advocacy, self-help and support groups, individual long-term counseling and information and referral. The shelter provides a safe, supportive and cooperative environment for abused women and their children, where they can work out their problems, explore their options and make decisions about their lives. Volunteers are a crucial part of the RDVIC helping system. At the present time, 24 volunteers work as

"counselor/companions" providing 24-hour hotline services, advocacy and transportation. In addition, 29 volunteers work as shelter workers, providing counseling and support to the victims residing at the shelter. During 1982, volunteers gave a total of 15,032 hours of service to victims.

Volunteers begin their experience at RDVIC by undergoing extensive training. They must attend approximately 18 hours of training on sexual assault, domestic violence and incest issues and procedures and counseling skills. Following training volunteers attend either counselor/companion or shelter worker orientation and are scheduled to begin working. Counselor/companions run the hotline after 5 p.m. on weekdays and all day Saturday and Sunday. Their duties include offering crisis counseling and support over the phone or in person. Counselor/companions accompany victims to the hospital emergency room, the police, the Magistrates Court and the shelter, operating as victim advocates. Shelter workers oversee the shelter operations during evenings and weekends, offering emotional support to the women.

RAPE CRISIS CENTER
423 West Ocondaga Street
Syracuse, NY 11320
TEL: 315-422-7273
Purpose: To provide counseling, medical and legal advocacy, and support to victims of sexual assault via a 24-hour hotline.
Sponsor: Rape Crisis Center (RCC)
Contact: Rosemary Sloane
Description: The Rape Crisis Center is a non-profit organization which helps victims of all types of sexual assault - rape, incest, sodomy and sexual abuse - whether they report it or not. All victim services are free and confidential. Services include:

- a 24-hour telephone hotline for information and crisis counseling;
- support counseling for victims, their families and friends;
- advocacy through medical and legal systems if the victim chooses to report the crime;
- a Public Speakers Bureau to educate the public about the dangers and myths about rape as well as about preventive measures and precautions.

Two specialized programs are: The Incest Treatment Program, which offers counseling, support and advocacy to victims and their families; The Youth Advocate Program, which offers both counseling and education to youth, their families and teachers. The volunteers at the Rape Crisis Center are an integral part of the agency's operations. A large percent of the RCC's activities depend on these dedicated workers who are active in all aspects of our organization. In 1982, the volunteers gave over 10,000 hours or an equivalent of 5.1 full-time staff. Volunteer activities at the RCC include:

- crisis intervention
- short-term counseling
- medical/legal advocate
- working in the office
- taking on-call shifts
- public speaking
- sitting on a committee
- sitting on the Board of Directors

The volunteers are permitted to participate in two programs at the RCC - Volunteer Counseling and Community Service.

RAPE CRISIS SERVICE OF CENTRAL CONTRA COSTA COUNTY
1950 Parkside Drive
Concord, CA 94519
TEL: 415-671-3381
Purpose: To aid victims of sexual assault to make the successful transition from victim to survivor; to provide community education about sexual assault.
Sponsor: State/County/City governments; private donations

Contact: Katharine Wilson
Description: Rape Crisis Service of Central Contra Costa County (RCS/CCCC) was formed in July of 1981 when a merger took place between Diablo Valley RCS and RCS of Concord, both of which had formed in 1976. Funding sources are State/County/City governments and private donations. RCS/CCCC has a Board of Directors, and four paid staff members. At present, we have approximately 20 active volunteers, who provide the majority of direct services to our clients. Our services are as follows: 24-hour crisis line; accompaniment and advocacy services (to hospitals, police, etc.); individual and follow-up counseling for victims and families/friends of victims; court advocacy; support groups; community education.
Volunteers can work in any one (or more than one) of four areas, performing duties related to the services listed above. The four basic areas are: crisis line and accompaniment/advocacy; court advocacy; speaker's bureau; office work.
Volunteers need not have any previous experience to perform any of the above duties. They receive approximately 35 hours of training, with continual in-service training. Supervision is given through regular one-to-one contact, as well as at two monthly meetings. All volunteers go through a screening process before beginning work at RCS. Volunteers are needed in all areas. RCS/CCCC also accepts students who would like to be involved in internship or field placement programs with the agency. Supervision includes that of staff and/or certified therapists.
Founded: 1981

INFORMATION & REFERRAL: STD

NATIONAL/STATE ORGANIZATIONS

STD NATIONAL HOTLINE
American Social Health Association
260 Sheridan Avenue
Palo Alto, CA 94306
TEL: 415-321-5234
TOLL FREE: 800-227-8922
Objectives: To provide information and referral service for people in need of low-cost testing and treatment for sexually-transmitted diseases.
Services: Works with more than 5,000 local facilities to assure quick, accurate, and localized service for testing and treatment of socially-transmitted diseases; maintains 24-hour confidential telephone service on a nationwide basis with highly-trained volunteers; develops and distributes numerous quick-reference brochures on socially-transmitted diseases (available at nominal cost).
Publications: U.S. Crisis Lines; Public Clinics in the U.S.
Founded: 1979

VD NATIONAL HOTLINE
American Social Health Association
PO Box 13827
Research Triangle Pk , NC 27709
TEL: 919-361-2742
TOLL FREE: 800-342-AIDS
Objectives: To provide information and referral service for people in need of low-cost testing and treatment for venereal disease (VD).
Services: Works with more than 5,000 local VD facilities to assure quick, accurate, and localized service; maintains 24-hour confidential telephone service on a nationwide basis; develops and distributes numerous quick-reference brochures on VD and related diseases, available at nominal cost.

Publications: Helper
Founded: 1912

INFORMATION & REFERRAL: SUICIDE PREVENTION

NATIONAL/STATE ORGANIZATIONS

INTERNATIONAL ASSOCIATION FOR SUICIDE PREVENTION
Suicide Prevention & Crisis Center
ATT: C. Ross, 1811 Trousdale Drive
Burlingame, CA 94010
TEL: 415-877-5604
Objectives: To continually upgrade the skills of suicide prevention workers.
Services: Develops specialized training in suicide prevention for professionals, paraprofessionals and volunteers; conducts and encourages research; provides individuals and agencies with a forum for exchanging experience, ideas, literature and other aids for the profession; develops and makes available information on the fundamentals of suicide prevention; holds an annual General Assembly, and a biannual International Congress.
Publications: Crisis
Founded: 1960

THE SAMARITANS USA
c/o Samaritans Hotline
PO Box 9814
Washington, DC 20016
TEL: 202-362-8100
Samaritans Branches:
- Boston, MA - 617-247-0220
- Cape Cod, MA - 508-548-8900
- Rhode Island - 401-272-4044
- Merrimack Valley, MA - 508-688-6607
- Keene, NH - 603-357-5505
- South Middlesex, MA - 508-875-4500
- Fall River/New Bedford, MA - 508-636-6111
- New York, NY - 212-673-3000
- Hartford, CT (Capital Region) - 203-232-2121
- Albany, NY (Capital District) - 518-463-2323
- Washington, DC - 202-362-8100
- North Central NH - 603-644-2525

Objectives: To befriend the suicidal, lonely, and despairing.
Services: Serves as the national council to oversee Samaritans branches across the U.S.; assists all U.S. branches in their 24-hour suicide prevention hotline service; provides training and supervision assistance through materials and on-site visits; helps to set up new branches; affiliated with *Befrienders International Samaritans Worldwide;* works with the *International Association of Suicide Prevention;* publishes quarterly newsletter, and other materials. [*Befrienders International Samaritans Worldwide* is an international volunteer suicide prevention service founded in England in 1953. There are Samaritan branches in 33 countries around the world.]
Sponsor: Befrienders International Samaritans Worldwide
Contact: Ellen Kennedy
Publications: The Samaritans: Suicide Prevention Hotline; Answers to Suicide
Founded: 1974

INDIVIDUAL PROGRAM PROFILES

THE SAMARITANS
Suicide Prevention Hotline
PO Box 9814
Washington, DC 20016
TEL: 202-362-8100
Purpose: To befriend the suicidal, lonely, and despairing.
Sponsor: Samaritans USA; Befrienders International Samaritans Worldwide
Contact: Ellen Kennedy
Description: The Samaritans is a 24-hour, seven-day suicide prevention hotline staffed by carefully-selected and trained nonprofessional volunteers. Professional consultants assist the volunteers. The Samaritans offer *befriending* rather than counseling. This concept is based on the premise that, except in medical emergencies, the most urgent need for most people in a suicidal crisis is for someone to talk to. The Samaritan volunteer, by listening with understanding and concern, seeks to establish an equal-level relationship that can help restore self-esteem and hope. Referrals to professional help are made as necessary.
Volunteers are of all ages, from age 19, and all backgrounds. No special experience or special education is required. A volunteer must be able to listen without making judgements or giving unwanted advice to establish equal-level relationships, and to show caring.
Training classes are held often, either on Saturdays or weeknights (with weekday classes held only when enough trainees are available). Eighteen hours of training prepares volunteers to respond to calls involving suicide, depression, grief and loss, sexual problems, alcoholism, drug abuse, and medical emergencies. Maximum time is one five-hour shift per week, and one overnight (11:00p.m. to 8:00a.m.) each month, and a commitment of at least six months.
In-service education is offered throughout the year. Supervision is by the Director and experienced Samaritan volunteers, with help and back-up from professional consultants. Following training, volunteers may engage in other activities of the Center, such as the speakers' bureau, fund raising, updating referrals, and publicity.
Although the Samaritans respond to any kind of problem, the primary purpose is to respond to those desperate enough to consider suicide. About 35% of the callers mention suicide at the first contact. However, the call itself, and even a suicide threat or attempt are considered a cry for help. The volunteer can help give the suicidal person strength to survive the crisis. As one caller stated, "I still think about suicide, but as long as I can keep calling you when I get to feeling overwhelmed, I think I can keep going." Another caller said, "Now that I understand better, I have some ideas to try."
The service is free and completely confidential. Samaritans do not trace calls, nor take action without the caller's permission.
As a suicide prevention service, *The Samaritans* serve as a resource for professional students and community groups, providing talks and workshops on request.
Publications: Samaritans: Suicide Prevention Hotline

SAMARITANS
500 Commonwealth Avenue
Kenmore Square
Boston, MA 02215
TEL: 617-247-0220
Purpose: To befriend the suicidal, the despairing and the lonely.
Sponsor: Samaritans USA
Contact: Shirley Karnovsky, Executive Director
Description: The Samaritans of Boston is one of seven 24-hour suicide-prevention hotlines in the northeast region of the U.S. Along with hotlines in other regions, it receives technical and other assistance from *The Samaritans USA* and on a wider scale from *Befrienders International Samaritans Worldwide,* the

international organization.
The program consists solely of volunteers who give their time to befriend the suicidal, the despairing and the lonely. The 24-hour hotline provides walk-in service for suicidal and depressed people. An offshoot of the program is *Lifeline,* a suicide intervention program, in Boston area jails. *The Samaritans* develops a team of trained inmates to spot and befriend potential suicides in jails. To involve and work with the community, the program provides an average of 100 talks and training workshops each year for professionals and lay people on suicide prevention, and provides materials on the subject on request.
Founded: 1974

INFORMATION & REFERRAL: WOMEN

INDIVIDUAL PROGRAM PROFILES

WOMAN-TO-WOMAN HOTLINE
SEE INFORMATION & REFERRAL: CANCER

INFORMATION & REFERRAL: 120/80

NATIONAL/STATE ORGANIZATIONS

US/HHS - HIGH BLOOD PRESSURE INFORMATION CENTER
US/HHS - National Institutes of Health
4733 Bethesda Avenue
Suite 530
Bethesda, MD 20814
TEL: 301-558-4880
Objectives: To reduce illness and death from hypertension.
Services: Serves as a national clearinghouse for the collection, evaluation, and dissemination of information on hypertension provides technical assistance to national and local agencies and organizations, groups and individuals; works with health care providers to improve the standards of patient care; publishes fact sheets, reports, bibliographies, catalogs, educational and other materials.
Sponsor: US/HHS - Department of Health & Human Services
Publications: 120/80 Fact Sheet

LEADERSHIP DEVELOPMENT/BOARDS

NATIONAL/STATE ORGANIZATIONS

AMERICAN VALUES: THE COMMUNITY ACTION NETWORK
SEE COMMUNITY SERVICES

COMMUNITY ACTION TRAINING*
128 West State Street
Trenton, NJ 08608
TEL: 609-393-3746
Objectives: To consult with and train community groups to increase organizational effectiveness and human resource development.
Services: Specializes in the training and development of community agency staff and boards; uses no pre-packaged programs; all work is especially designed for the group based upon needs assessments and organizational diagnosis.

COMMUNITY LEADER TRAINING ASSOCIATES
511 Monte Vista Drive, SW
Blacksburg, VA 24060
TEL: 703-552-4838
Objectives: To develop the understanding and skills required to muster broad community support for the decisions that have to be made for effective change at the community level.
Services: Provides on-site training in areas of logical problem solving and effective group techniques for voluntary organizations, government agencies and denominational bodies; maintains training library, including a six-volume set of manuals covering all steps of the problem solving process.
Publications: Volunteer Training Library

COMMUNITY REGENERATION (*formerly Regenerative Agriculture Association***)**
Rodale Institute
222 Main Street
Emmaus, PA 18098
TEL: 215-967-5171
Objectives: To promote community revitalization through individual action and practical, proven procedures.
Services: Motivates and trains public and private individuals to renew and revitalize their communities; applies successful capacity-building techniques to community systems such as housing, food, schools, energy and waste management; helps people, through these techniques, to take advantage of and improve upon available strengths and resources; maintains an extensive database and network of individuals, experts, and successful case histories of community revitalization; provides public speaking, workshops, and consulting services; publishes a bimonthly newsletter, action kits and educational materials; works through membership with individuals and groups through its *Regeneration Network.*
Contact: Ellen Paul, Network Coordinator
Publications: Yes I Can!; Greenfield, Iowa; Hopeful Living; New Visions; Regenerating America: Opportunities to Build On; Community Options: Projects You Can Do; Regeneration: You and Your Environment
Founded: 1947

COMMUNITY TRAINING AND DEVELOPMENT
41 South Main Street
Fond Du Lac, WI 54935
TEL: 414-921-0225
Objectives: To train community advocates and community workers in skills which will aid them in the "war on poverty."
Services: Conducts training seminars for management, paraprofessional, secretarial and community workers; maintains clearinghouse on human resources, and speakers bureau; publishes newsletter, program manuals, project reports, and monographs; grants scholarships for training seminars.
Publications: CTD Newsletter

NATIONAL ACADEMY FOR VOLUNTARISM
United Way of America
701 North Fairfax Street
Alexandria, VA 22314-2045
TEL: 703-836-7100
FAX: 703-683-7840
Objectives: To train/educate/develop health and welfare agency professionals, community leaders, volunteer administrators, and United Way professionals.
Services: Conducts separate courses for specific segments of the agency/organization staff, including:
- Communications Staff
- Fund Raising Staff
- Planning and Allocations Staff
- Agency Executive
- Volunteers (Policy and Direct/Service Adminstrative)

Includes three phases in each program: 1. Self-study Courses; 2. Instructed Courses; and 3. Skill Development Seminars; continually updates course content.
Provides NAV staff for consultation regarding concerns or questions about the appropriateness of a training program for specific organizations or staff; primarily offers program to United Way agencies, and affiliates of the United Way of America (includes Volunteer Centers/Voluntary Action Centers, Boys' Clubs, Salvation Army, etc.); publishes course information booklet, National Academy of Voluntarism: Courses and Seminars, annually to provide details to interested organizations (request free copy).

POINTS OF LIGHT INITIATIVE
SEE NATIONAL SERVICE/POINTS OF LIGHT INITIATIVE

SCHINDLER-RAINMAN INSTITUTES
4267 South Rafael Avenue
Los Angeles, CA 90042
TEL: 213-257-8962
Objectives: To improve the skills of community organizers and volunteer program leaders through group dynamics.
Services: Conducts training seminars through professional organizations for volunteer and community groups, private organizations, governmental units, industry, and others involved in citizen action and/or volunteer programs; convenes meetings, conferences, and other training activities - helping participants to work with each other to develop and enhance skills needed "back at the office;" develops materials for use in training programs such as The Volunteer Community: Creative Use of Human Resources, and Building the Collaborative Community.
Publications: The Volunteer Community; The Collaborative Community; Creative Use/Human Resources

VOLUNTEER DEVELOPMENT INSTITUTE*
1700 North Moore Street, Suite 1622
Arlington, VA 22209
TEL: 703-525-7331
Objectives: To provide services to individuals, public agencies and community service organizations concerned with the personal, social, educational and professional development of volunteers and staff.
Services: Designs accountability systems which include collecting information, analyzing data, and compiling evaluation studies; designs and conducts training sessions, workshops, seminars and conferences; researches and writes reports that assist in policy formation; designs, develops and implements community development programs; drafts proposals for submission to funding sources; researches and compiles information for community service volunteers and others searching for educational and professional recognition for services provided; advocates for the expanded role of voluntary citizen participation in planning evaluation and delivery of public service programs; creates, designs, develops, writes and edits manuals, journals, case studies, newsletters and magazines in the field of volunteer personnel development; publishes newsletter.
Publications: Options
Founded: 1971

VOLUNTEER LEADERSHIP DEVELOPMENT PROGRAM
United Way of America
701 North Fairfax Street
Alexandria, VA 22314-2045
TEL: 703-836-7100
FAX: 703-683-7840
Objectives: To effect citizen board improvement through a comprehensive program that will:
1. assist community leaders to better assume responsibilities of board membership;
2. clarify volunteer/staff roles to effect a more productive partnership; and
3. enhance board members' understanding of their community, enabling them to impact decision-making in both the public and private sectors.
Services: Enlists certified volunteer trainers to conduct eight separate workshops, each ranging from three to four hours in length, for board members and key staff of non-profit organizations (must include at least one board member for every staff member - executives, volunteers, executive committee members, administrators); the workshops:
- Organizing and Governing the Agency
- Board/Staff Relations
- Financial Management
- Agency Self-Help Evaluation
- Decision-making/Problem-solving
- Resource Development
- Your Agency and the Community: The Crucial Relationship
- Planning and Goal Setting
Precedes workshops with a special program, Organizational Training Needs Survey, designed to help participants analyze the needs of their organizations and decide which workshops would be most appropriate in designing a board development plan.
Delivers workshops through Regional Training Centers of selected local United Ways on a regional basis (typically within a radius of 200-500 miles); provides training packages and staff assistance directly to communities not within areas secured by Regional Training Centers (the self-contained training packages can be purchased by United Ways for delivery to any nonprofit agency); selects a maximum of 30 new volunteers interested in board placement in a participating city for an adjunct to the main program, Community Leadership Development Program.
[This program is sponsored by participating United Ways and United Way of America, and is open to any nonprofit organization; contact local United Way offices for details or request the brochure, *Workshops for Voluntary Agencies,* from national headquarters].

VOLUNTEER LEADERSHIP PROGRAM
Federation of Protestant Welfare Agencies
281 Park Avenue South
New York, NY 10010
TEL: 212-777-4800
Objectives: To provide strong support in its program for leadership by volunteers.
Services: Utilizes experience gained since 1946 (when a Board Member Education Department was established in the Federation) to support volunteer leadership by:
- Referrals to Boards of Directors for individuals demonstrating the necessary management skills and seeking such placement.
- Ongoing Workshops at Federation for program leaders wishing to strengthen management skills; provides an opportunity to share trends, ideas and creative problem-solving techniques.
- Sharing of information gathered at workshops with interested groups and individuals wishing to develop more diversified, representative boards and volunteer programs.
Publications: Federation News
Founded: 1922

TRAINING PROGRAMS

ADMINISTRATION OF VOLUNTEER PROGRAMS AND OPERATION OF SOCIAL AGENCIES
Springfield College
Box 1723
Springfield, MA 01109
TEL: 413-787-2100
Credit: M.A. Community Leadership & Development (partial fulfillment)
Sponsor: Springfield College
Contact: Margaret Dreger
Description: This component of a Master's Degree program in Community Leadership and Development was created to meet an expanded need for the type of administrative leadership that could create optimum growth conditions and remove classic limits on volunteers and paraprofessional potential for service. The rising increase in the number of new openings for volunteers and paraprofessionals, and the increasing resistance to traditional assumptions about their training and supervision, were considered in designing the component for volunteer administration. Program core courses include:
- The Community Development process
- Advanced Community Organization
- Principles and Practices of Group Work, Advanced Group Work, and Supervision in Group Work
- Government Programs in Social Welfare
- Operation and Management of Social Agencies
- Theories of Personality
- Psychology of Exceptional Youths and Adults
- Foundations and Methods of Research
- Case Work
- Field Work
- Electives (could included several hours of individual guided study in the student's area of interest)
- One other course selected by student from list of nine core courses

Individual field work arrangements could run concurrent with classes for three terms or full time block placement for one term. In either case, conferences with advisors, a field seminar, and regular reports are required.

BOARD DEVELOPMENT CONSULTATION SERVICE
National Center for Nonprofit Boards
1225 Nineteenth Street, NW
Suite 340
Washington, DC 20036
TEL: 202-452-6262
FAX: 202-452-6299
Credit: Inquire
Contact: Training Coordinator
Description: The *National Center for Nonprofit Boards* administers a variety of workshops, all tailored toward education for board members and chief executives of numerous types of nonprofit organizations. Topics covered in such programs include:
- The Roles and Responsibilities of Board Members;
- The Chief Executive's Role in Developing the Board;
- The Board's Role in Fundraising;
- The Board's Role in Strategic Planning; and
- The Relationship Between the Board and Staff.

In many instances the *Center* provides speakers for other organizations which include board training in a larger conference agenda.

BOARD LEADERSHIP AND DEVELOPMENT
Organizational Dynamics
43434 SE Tapp Road
Sandy, OR 97055
TEL: 503-668-7979

Credit: Inquire
Sponsor: Organizational Dynamics
Contact: Arty Trost, MSW
Description: Programs dealing with the effective development and management of boards of directors and advisory councils are offered nationwide. All training is carefully designed to meet the sponsoring group's needs; some of the program topics are listed below. New ones are continually being developed based on client requests.

Programs can be tailored for new and/or experienced board and council members in public agencies, non-profit organizations, community service groups, civic organizations, schools, hospitals, churches and synagogues. By working closely with the sponsor beforehand, all training is specific to the particular group. Programs blend practice and principle using training methods which actively involve the participants, emphasize skill building as well as knowledge acquisition, and are immediately applicable. Arty Trost is a recognized expert in the area of board development and is co-author of the book *Gaining Momentum For Board Action*.
- Role, Tasks and Responsibilities of the Board
- Board Leadership Training
- Team Building for Boards
- Effective Board Meetings
- Developing and Maintaining Effective Committees
- Board and Staff Teambuilding
- Developing a Board Structure That Works
- Board Planning and Goal Setting
- The Board Recruitment Process
- Organizational Renewal

BOARD MANAGEMENT TRAINING WORKSHOP
Volunteer Center of Topeka
4125 Gage Center Drive
Suite 214
Topeka, KS 66604
TEL: 913-272-8890
Credit: Inquire
Sponsor: Voluntary Action Center of Topeka; Junior League of Topeka; United Way of Greater Topeka; Topeka Public Library
Contact: Nancy Shaughnessy, Director
Description: Recognizing the impact of volunteer boards in a community the size of Topeka, the above sponsors conduct annual workshops specifically for board members. A typical workshop theme is Making a Difference: Board Management in the Eighties. Emphasis is on the need for volunteer programs to improve and expand services in times of inflation and decreasing charitable donors. The purpose of the seminar is to acquaint board members with the concepts, terms, and skills necessary for effective board participation. Content is designed to encompass concerns of both new and experienced board members. Topics include:
- Staff/Board Relationships
- Volunteer Recruitment
- Fund Raising
- Budget Preparation

As a result of the seminar, participants are expected to:
- be able to identify the various types of boards, and functions relevant to each.
- participate in the planning process and relate it to organizational aims.
- utilize the good management techniques necessary for an effective board/program relationship.

This annual event has proven very successful, according to the contact person above
- so successful that some discussion of refocusing this annual workshop met with an overwhelming response in favor of maintaining the focus on board training permanently for this event.

BOARDSMANSHIP SEMINAR*
Voluntary Action Center of Tuscaloosa
United Way of Tuscaloosa County
108 Cotton States Building
PO Box 2291
Tuscaloosa, AL 35403-2291
TEL: 205-345-6440
Credit: CEUs
Sponsor: University of Alabama
Contact: Janice Watkins
Description: Convened by the Junior League of Tuscaloosa, the Continuing Education Division of the University of Alabama, and the local Voluntary Action Center, this forum is designed for Board members, potential Board members, and others involved in agency and group endeavors. Program goals, based on expressed needs from the field, are aimed at helpingparticipants to:
- Develop an understanding of goal setting and establishing objectives.
- Understand benefits of good group dynamics.
- Improve knowledge of parliamentary procedures.
- Clarify the role responsibilities and legal liabilities of Board members.
- Understand the budget planning and presentation process.
- Relate to funding trends and opportunities.
Faculty is drawn from the University, business/industry, social service organizations, and the legal profession. During two sessions and a panel discussion, program goals are addressed by experts in each of the above needs areas, with topics including:
- Setting Goals and Objectives
- Group Dynamics
- Parliamentary Procedure
- Budget Planning and Presentation
- Funding Trends and Opportunities
- Personal Responsibilities and Accountability of Board Members
- Legal Responsibilities and Accountability of Board Members
Faculty includes Board members from the United Way, PARA, Metropolitan YMCA, Mental Health Association, the Junior League of Tuscaloosa, and the local Voluntary Action Center, as well as experts in several areas of Management.

BUILDING AN EFFECTIVE BOARD
Voluntary Action Center of United Way
United Way of Minneapolis Area
404 South Eighth Street
Minneapolis, MN 55404
TEL: 612-340-7532
Credit: CEUs
Contact: Dr. Lorna Michelson
Description: Addressing board members of agencies and organizations, this workshop also suggests attendance by Executive Directors, volunteer Directors, agency staff, and other volunteer leaders and individuals who work with boards. Topics covered in the 12-hour session (six hours on each of two successive days) are:
- Responsibilities of board membership;
- Effective board/staff relations;
- Policy-making versus administration decision-making;
- Lines of authority;
- Committee responsibilities;
- Characteristics of good board members; and
- Evaluating board performance.
Faculty is drawn from national organizations and associations as well as the sponsoring agency, the United Way, which maintains a centralized resource for recruiting and placing volunteers, the Voluntary Action Center for the Minneapolis area.

BUILDING BETTER BOARDS
United Way of South Carolina
1800 Main Street
Suite 1-C
Columbia, SC 29201
TEL: 803-765-2375
Credit: CEUs
Sponsor: Kellogg Foundation, Piedmont TEC, Trident TEC, United Way of America, Voluntary Action Center of the Midlands, Foundations and Technical Colleges in South Carolina
Contact: Carol Taylor
Description: The purpose of this three-part series is to effect citizen board improvement. Objectives are:
- to train community leaders to better assume responsibilities of board membership;
- to clarify the roles of volunteers and staff in voluntary organizations in effecting a more productive partnership; and
- to enhance volunteers' understanding of community environments, systems and resources, enabling them to impact decision-making in both the public and the private sectors.
Workshops address five primary board responsibility areas: Policy Administration, Evaluations, Public and Community Relations, Personnel, and Finance. Three of the courses are available to any agency board; these include:
Organizing and Governing the Agency: This workshop explores the basic functions, responsibilities and activities of boards. During the workshop, many learning aids are introduced, such as a board manual outline, a suggested board member job description, a tool for board composition analysis, a model for a board calendar, and many other planning tools.
Problem Solving/Decision Making: This workshop is designed to assist agency boards in improving their decision-making process, and to help board members make effective decisions about ongoing activities of agencies, new conditions or efforts, and problem situations.
Long Range Planning/Goal Setting: Board members and key staff who participate in this workshop have the opportunity to see how long range planning can be used to improve organizational effectiveness. They are to develop a list of issues which organizations should consider in developing a long range plan, and to learn steps in a long range planning process through setting objectives, organizing to achieve objectives, and assessing performance in relation to the long range plan.
These are separate workshops which may be taken individually. They are scheduled upon request for area Boards of Directors across the state. New Workshops are being developed continually to fulfill needs in all five areas mentioned above to improve Board development.

BUILDING BETTER BOARDS: LEGAL LIABILITY AND RESPONSIBILITIES
Volunteer Center of Central Florida
1900 North Mills Avenue
Suite I
Orlando, FL 32803
TEL: 305-896-0945
Credit: Inquire
Contact: Julie Washburn
Description: This seminar is designed for board members of nonprofit organizations, prospective board members, executive directors of nonprofit organizations, and interested individuals. It covers an area which is just coming to the attention of most nonprofit organizations and their board members - Legal Liabilities and Responsibilities. The workshop takes into consideration the increasing professionalization of nonprofits, resulting in heightened scrutiny by both governments and the courts.
The seminar topics cover areas of legal responsibility common to all board members; topics include:

- Board responsibilities
- Standard of conduct for board members
- Action which show good faith
- Liability insurance
- Indemnification of directors
- Reliance on information and reports of others

This seminar is one of the Building Better Boards Series presented intermittently by the Volunteer Service Center.

BUILDING CREATIVE ORGANIZATIONS*
Voluntary Action Center of the St. Paul Area
251 Starkey Street
Suite 127
St. Paul, MN 55107
TEL: 612-227-3938
Credit: 1.6 CEUs
Sponsor: United Way's Voluntary Action Center of the Minnesota Area; Voluntary Action Center of the St. Paul Area; Community Volunteer Service of the St. Croix Valley Area
Contact: Mary Krueger
Description: Addressing Administrators of public, non-profit, and corporate volunteer programs, this seventh annual conference focuses on advanced concepts and skills to build for the future, "directing today's challenges into tomorrow's opportunities." Participants explore models for building creative organizations with the opportunity to develop personal plans for on-the-job activities, share knowledge and experiences with peers and presenters, and take a creative look at planning for personal growth and organizational development. The conference covers broad areas of:

- **Leadership** - cultivating the art of empowering others;
- **Collaboration** - building personal and organizational partnerships;
- **Power** - discovering our ability to bring about change;
- **Planning** - designing maps to get from "here" to "there;" and
- **Technology** - examining new ways of thinking and doing (featuring a Technology Exhibit, with an opportunity for hands-on experience).

Participants are encouraged to share program information and other materials in the space provided for this purpose.
Faculty is drawn from universities, community groups, schools, and other areas of expertise in organizational development. A limited number of partial scholarships are provided.

CAREER DEVELOPMENT FOR VOLUNTEER LEADERSHIP
SEE TRAINING/CONFERENCES/TEACHING: BOARDS

CHATHAM MANAGEMENT SEMINAR
SEE TRAINING/CONFERENCES/TEACHING

COMMUNITY BOARD TRAINING DAY
Pennsylvania State University
Berks Campus
Tulpehocken Road, PO Box 7009
Reading, PA 19610
TEL: 215-320-4800
Credit: Inquire
Sponsor: Junior League of Reading; United Way of Berks County; Pennsylvania State University
Contact: Elaine Berish
Description: This program was designed to include agency executive directors and staff members as well as the community board members for whom the training was developed. For the first two delegates from a single organization, registration was covered, in part, by a Community Trust Fund Allocation of the local Junior League.
The intent of the program was to provide an experience in various

aspects of community board training. Training was conducted by the Mid-Atlantic Association for Training and Consulting. Participants were asked to select three workshops from the following schedule:
Basic Board Skills
- How to delegate authority
- How to share leadership
- How to get a task done effectively by a "Team" membership
Managerial Skills
- Looking at the total picture: Financial, Legal, Social, Political, Personal
Conflict Management
- How to resolve and handle disagreements in a win-win manner
- Problem-solving techniques workable in a board meeting atmosphere
Assertiveness Training
- The difference betweenassertive and aggressive behavior
- Being comfortable expressing opinion and able to handle criticism
Future Planning
- Setting goals and objectives in a workable manner
- Learning to plan for tomorrow, today
A special visual aids workshop demonstrated a technique in program presentation possible on a manageable budget. Two addresses,"The Volunteer" and "National Trends inVolunteerism," were presented by experts in the volunteerism field. A "Creative Wrap-Up and Evaluation" session concluded the proceedings.

CONFERENCE ON NONPROFIT LEADERSHIP AND MANAGEMENT
SEE TRAINING/CONFERENCES/TEACHING: BOARDS

FINDING AND PREPARING NEW BOARD MEMBERS FOR SERVICE
Volunteers In Action
229 Waterman Street
Providence, RI 02906
TEL: 401-421-6547; 401-421-7472
Credit: AVA Certification (partial fulfillment)
Sponsor: United Way
Contact: Betsy A. Garland
Description: This seminar is designed for Nominating Committees and other recruiting leaders for non-profit organizations. It offers insight into the role and significance of the nominating process in an organization and offers suggestions to improve its effectiveness. Topics covered include:

- The nature of board service today
- Board development issues
- the function of the Nominating Committee and its relationship to the board
- Identifying and recruiting the people your organization needs
- Orienting new board members

In addition to Nominating Committees, this seminar has proven helpful to agency directors, board members, and other community leaders. The session is limited to 15 participants.
Volunteers In Action (VIA) is a statewide voluntary action center accredited by the Association of Volunteer Centers. Its training programs are accepted as partial fulfillment for professional certification by the Association for Volunteer Administration. VIA satellite centers are located in Woonsocket (401-762-0679), and Wakefield (401-789-9149), with others planned (inquire).

THE HOW-TO OF WORKING WITH VOLUNTEERS - TLC (TEACHING/LEARNING/CARING)
SEE TRAINING/CONFERENCES/TEACHING: BOARDS

**HUMAN SERVICE PROGRAMS: VOLUNTEER
LEADERSHIP EMPHASIS AREA**
SEE GOVERNORS' OFFICES ON VOLUNTEERISM:
MINNESOTA

LEADERSHIP FOR THE NINETIES*
Eastern Iowa Community College District
2804 Eastern Avenue
Davenport, IA 52803
TEL: 319-322-1361
Credit: CEUs (20 hours)
Sponsor: Eastern Iowa Community College District; Scott
Community College; Women's Community Leadership Institute
Project Board
Contact: Gale Roeder
Description: This course was developed to provide a vehicle for
women who want to explore new roles and improve their
leadership and boardsmanship skills. It was developed by the
Womens' Community Leadership Institute Project Board
(WCLIP) and presented to the Eastern Iowa Community College
District as a possible course at one of the community colleges.
Placed at Scott Community College, the program was adopted as
an eight-week course to provide Quad City women with a learning
experience that will advance their knowlege of and capabilities in
leadership. The class seeks women from all social and economic
backgrounds, and from all levels of volunteer and educational
experiences. It is expected that the widespread involvement of
women in this course will be reflected in increased board and
leadership activity across the area covered by the District.

**LIVE '89 (LEADERSHIP IN VOLUNTEERISM
EXPERIENCE)**
SEE GOVERNORS' OFFICES ON VOLUNTEERISM:
ILLINOIS

**NATIONAL CONFERENCE FOR VOLUNTEER
LEADERSHIP***
SEE GOVERNORS' OFFICES ON VOLUNTEERISM:
MISSISSIPPI

**ON-SITE PROGRAMS FOR VOLUNTEER
ORGANIZATIONS**
SEE TRAINING/CONFERENCES/TEACHING: BOARDS

**PROFESSIONAL DEVELOPMENT FOR COMMUNITY
TRAINERS**
SEE TRAINING/CONFERENCES/TEACHING: BOARDS

STRATEGIES OF VOLUNTEER LEADERSHIP
SEE TRAINING/CONFERENCES/TEACHING: BOARDS

**SUMMER MASTER'S DEGREE PROGRAM IN
COMMUNITY LEADERSHIP AND DEVELOPMENT**
SEE TRAINING/CONFERENCES/TEACHING: BOARDS

TEAM-BUILDING
SEE GOVERNORS' OFFICES ON VOLUNTEERISM:
VIRGINIA

TOWARD THE YEAR 2000 - THE CHALLENGE
SEE TRAINING/CONFERENCES/TEACHING

VAC BOARD EDUCATION PROGRAM
Voluntary Action Center of Morris County
36 South Street
Morristown, NJ 07960
TEL: 201-538-7200

Credit: Inquire
Contact: Laurie Becker, Education Coordinator
Description: This *Voluntary Action Center (VAC)* program offers
a series of comprehensive training sessions for board members of
nonprofit organizations. The purpose is to help boards improve
their effectiveness and performance.
An updated curriculum, divided into five separate one-hour
modules, is designed to examine the processes essential to the
creation and growth of an effective board. Each interactive
module, described below, can be presented during a board meeting:
- *Roles, Relationships and Responsibilities* introduces the basics
  of board participation emphasizing the relationship of the
  board to the organization, the community, the executive
  director and the staff.
- *Legal Considerations* - provides, through the services of a
  consulting attorney, an analysis of board liability and legal
  requirements and updates New Jersey laws affecting nonprofit
  organizations.
- *The Nominating Process* explores the role of the nominating
  committee and develops an approach for the identification of
  potential members as well as their selection and orientation.
- *Motivation: Preventative Maintenance* evaluates the
  effectiveness of the board, stressing strategies for involving
  new members quickly and avoiding burnout.
- *Board Orientation* - guides the executive director and board
  president through the preparation and presentation of what
  each new board member should know about the organization.
Trained facilitators, including many volunteers from the corporate
community, can adapt any of the programs to suit the particular
concerns and problems of their organization.

VAC WORKSHOPS*
SEE TRAINING/CONFERENCES/TEACHING: BOARDS

VOLUNTEER LEADERSHIP DEVELOPMENT PROGRAM
SEE TRAINING/CONFERENCES/TEACHING: BOARDS

**WORKING EFFECTIVELY WITH BOARDS AND
COMMITTEES**
Allegheny County Community College
Center-North, 111 Pines Plaza
1130 Perry Highway
Pittsburgh, PA 15237
TEL: 412-366-7000
Credit: Inquire
Sponsor: Community College of Allegheny County
Contact: Dr. Grassinger, Chairman, General Studies
Description: This two-part program considers 1) staff-board
relationships, and 2) the Board responsibility for agency
accountability. Basic formats:
Staff Effectiveness with Boards or Committees - This one-day
seminar focuses on principles and factors in successful
committee/Board activity with special emphasis on the staff
person, paid or volunteer, in facilitating such activity. Seminar
content includes:
- mechanics, dynamics, and orchestration of the committee
  process
- role of the staff person before, during, and after the committee
  meeting, with special emphasis on: committee purpose;
  agenda; minute and report preparation; relationship between
  chairperson and staff person; committee participation and
  morale; committee movement.
Activities include lecturettes, discussion groups, videotapes and
role-play presentations, with time allotted to discussion of
problems in committee management experienced by the
participant.
The Art of Chairing a Board or Committee - This two-session
seminar focuses on the Chairman - "a nice title and a lot of
responsibility" - and the various aspects of what the staff expects,

and what the board or committee expects in terms of agency accountability and leadership. The goal of the seminar is to help the Chairman manage the responsibility and balance the communication which compose effective chairmanship. The sessions:

- The first session looks at skills in planning, delegation, communication and personal leadership as components of individual style.
- The second session features a panel of experienced chairpersons from organizations and agencies dealing with human services, community services, and the arts.

Faculties for both sessions are drawn from the health and welfare and volunteer communities.

YOU ARE THE BOARD*
Volunteer Center of the United Way
United Way of Buffalo/Erie County
742 Delaware Avenue
Buffalo, NY 14209
TEL: 716-887-2692
Credit: College credit; inquire
Sponsor: D'Youville College
Contact: Gretchen E. Stringer
Description: Each session in this three-credit course (except the introductory one) begins with an actual Board meeting, handling the business of the group (class). Each session also includes one structure experience during which some tenet of Board Effeciveness is taught. An outside speaker is included in four or five of the sessions. Speakers are experienced volunteers whose topics are pertinent to the subject. Although each class is highly structured, the experiential nature of the structure allows for the changes in format that often develop within the class. Topics included in class sessions, and homework:

- Board Communications
- By-laws
- Conflict Resoulution
- Constitutions
- Decision-making Process
- Financial Responsibilities
- Group Dynamic Skills
- Group Process including Agendas, Budgets, Reports, Committees, Meeting, Evaluation
- Human Relations Skills
- Legal Responsibilities
- Organizational Responsibilities Beyond Community Borders
- Resource Development
- Volunteer-Staff Organizational Characteristics

An evaluation and/or feedback exercise completes the session. At the end of each seminar, participants receive a "mailing." The mailing packet is the assignment for the next week. A board manual, *You Are The Board*, and a workbook, *On Board*, are used with an accompanying film throughout the eight-session course.

INDIVIDUAL PROGRAM PROFILES

CHAIRMAN OF VOLUNTEERS GALLERY
SEE ADMINISTRATION: RECOGNITION

COMMUNITY RESOURCE CENTER
1300 Fifth Avenue
Wenatchee, WA 98801
TEL: 509-662-7992
Purpose: To provide a central clearinghouse for information and to be a catalyst for community dialogue.
Sponsor: Wenatchee Valley College, Community Volunteers
Contact: Marlene Curtis, Coordinator,

Description: The CRC began in December 1978, with funding for three years from the W.K. Kellogg Foundation, and in-kind funding from Wenatchee Valley College. Following conclusion of Kellogg grant, CRC funding is derived from user fees, fund raising activities and in-kind support from WVC.
Staff consists of one half-time coordinator and a quarter-time secretary with other people in the Instruction Department of WVC lending a hand when needed.
Volunteers actually determine the program, carry out projects, and *are* the CRC. These volunteers are members of the CRC Board, which is a working board. They represent fourteen segments of the community and strive to bring their area needs to the CRC to be addressed. They recruit additional people in the community to work on short-term task forces and have developed a skills bank of over 450 skills in the community which can be shared in a variety of ways.
The board of volunteers meet monthly and select a chairman and vice chairman from their ranks. The volunteers have engaged in such activities as:

- town hall meetings
- candidate forums
- brochures and guides which share information
- assistance to new groups trying to organize (divorce and separation network, Widow Information Consultant Service, Community Education Coordinating Council)

Training for these volunteers is really quite informal. The first need is for them to understand the goals of the center and especially to remember that it is a neutral organization and not an advocate for a specific cause. They work together well and recruit from the community as task forces are needed or board positions open up.
Founded: 1978

ENVIRONMENTAL SCAN TASK FORCE
United Way of Greater Los Angeles
621 South Virgil Avenue
Los Angeles, CA 90005-4046
TEL: 213-736-1300
Purpose: Beginning in 1988, 15 volunteer experts from a variety of social-research and public-policy fields formed a Task Force and worked with *United Way of America's Management and Community Studies Institute (MACSI)* to compile an "environmental scan," a study of the critical trends and issues shaping the Los Angeles environment, and an analysis of their impact on human-service providers and the United Way. A policy-making *Strategic Planning Committee* of volunteers, headed by a local businessman, directed and managed the scan. In addition to the task force, the effort required hundreds of individuals from United Way's 4,300 square-mile service area and input from United Way-supported agencies serving the area's population of 9 million.
As the fastest-growing metropolitan region in the United States - both in population and economy - greater Los Angeles is one of the first cities to show evidence of new social trends. The environmental scan, or strategic planning process, is designed to help the United Way to reassess its organizational structure and community role for the decade of the nineties and beyond.
In a little more than a year the Task Force had conducted meetings and interviews with agencies and community organizations, surveyed thousands of local residents, and compiled key research from existing local, regional, state and national data.
The resulting environmental scan, released in November 1989, reveals 17 trends likely to have a significant impact, including:

- *Ethnic diversity,* which will increase throughout the growing population.
- *Elderly population,* which will continue to remain smaller in number as compared with other parts of the country.
- *Poverty problem,* which is mounting with the gap widening between the "haves" and the "have-nots."

Now that the United Way has a "true picture of where dramatic change is taking place in our community" (Committee Chairman), the next step is to formulate an action plan which will direct the organization's structure and operation for the next three to five years. Community feedback and recommendations from nine additional volunteer task forces will play a major role in this plan.
Sponsor: United Way of America
Contact: Leo P. Cornelius, President
Publications: Environmental Scan

HAWAII STATE YOUTH VOLUNTEER BOARD*
SEE GOVERNORS' OFFICES ON VOLUNTEERISM: HAWAII

INDEPENDENCE NEIGHBORHOOD COUNCILS
SEE COMMUNITY SERVICES

INTERNATIONAL AVA LEADERSHIP BANK
Association for Volunteer Administration
PO Box 4584
Boulder, CO 80306
TEL: 303-497-0238
Purpose: To develop effective leadership in the field of volunteer administration.
Sponsor: Association for Volunteer Administration
Contact: Martha Martin
Description: Given AVA's role as perceived by the volunteer community as an international promoter of volunteerism as a profession, it was felt by the AVA Board of Directors that the Association should address the leadership potential and availability of its members as it relates to this international role. Since the large majority of members are directly involved in leadership roles, the task at hand was to learn about special skills and capabilities available to assist with the leadership of the Association. Thus, the Board of AVA has chartered a new international bank - the "AVA Leadership Bank." Specifically, the "Bank" is a vehicle for:

- drawing on the experience, commitment, competency and talent of volunteer managers and administrators in AVA;
- expanding the process by which leaders can be nominated and appointed at *all* levels; capturing information about leaders in a central location and making it accessible throughout the organization when needed; and
- securing the succession of strong leadership in all areas of AVA's activity.

The "Bank" is *not:*
- a bureaucratic system that never gets used; or
- a guarantee that an individual will immediately be asked to serve.

In inviting members to become or suggest "depositors" in the new Bank, it was suggested that each individual ask himself or herself the following questions:
- When you think of your association with AVA, do you wish you could be more involved as a leader, but don't exactly know where to lend your resources?
- Do you have skill and initiative, and seek additional responsibility, but haven't found the opportunity to invest your treasures?
- Have you wondered why an accomplished colleague or recognized champion of the field from your community, state, province or region has never been tapped for a leadership role in the work of AVA?

An answer of "yes" to any of these questions indicates a potential satisfying leadership role for the member who becomes a "depositor" in the Bank.
Affiliates, regional chairs, past and present Board members, and other key leaders involved with AVA are invited to send leadership profiles to the Bank. The profile form may be used also to suggest others - members or potential members - for contact by AVA's Board members.

Leadership is needed at local, regional, national and international levels to maintain a source for referral as needs arise. Areas of special strength or skill are limited only by the many and varied needs of the field and include: public speaking, computer expertise, training skills, political advocacy, contract negotiation, links to business or national organization, group process, resource development, organizational ability, etc.
The data is stored by computer in Boulder (AVA headquarters). The profile form will be inserted in the newsletter, *Update,* once a year, but is available on request at any time.
Founded: 1989

VOLUNTEER VOLUNTEER COORDINATORS*
SEE ADMINISTRATION

LEADERSHIP DEVELOPMENT/BOARDS: ARTS

NATIONAL/STATE ORGANIZATIONS

AMERICAN CRAFT COUNCIL
40 West 53rd Street
New York, NY 10019
TEL: 212-956-3535
Objectives: To stimulate public awareness and appreciation of the work of American craftsmen.
Services: Provides consultation services in craft areas including ceramic, glass, metal, textiles and wood; presents museum exhibitions in regional programs; maintains American Craft Museum and a 3700-volume library on American crafts, which includes biographical information on some craftsmen; develops visual aids; publishes bimonthly magazine, museum exhibit catalogs, bibliographies, directories and manuals.
Publications: American Craft
Founded: 1943

INDIAN ARTS AND CRAFTS BOARD
SEE VOLUNTEERS: ETHNIC GROUPS

NATIONAL COMMITTEE ON ART EDUCATION FOR THE ELDERLY
Culver Stockton College
Canton, MO 63435
TEL: 314-288-5221
Objectives: To promote better art education opportunities for the elderly.
Services: Encourages the establishment of quality art education programs; canvasses those programs serving the elderly in other areas and encourages the addition of art programs; promotes research and development to improve art programs for the elderly; maintains a Clearinghouse of information on the subject; publishes irregular newsletter.
Publications: Switchboard

INDIVIDUAL PROGRAM PROFILES

VOLUNTEER COUNCIL
American Symphony Orchestra League
777 Fourteenth Street, NW
Suite 500
Washington, DC 20005
TEL: 202-628-0099
FAX: 202-783-7228
Purpose: To strengthen and enrich symphony orchestras through the expertise and leadership of orchestra volunteers.
Sponsor: American Symphony Orchestra League
Contact: Phyllis J. Mills, President
Description: Founded in 1964, the *Volunteer Council* has served over 25 years as a resource and ambassador for the *American Symphony Orchestra League.* It is not a guild, but a 32-member board representing orchestras of all sizes and from all over the country. The Council functions within a set of bylaws and is composed of volunteer leaders from orchestras across the country. Since its inception, the Council has served one of the League's most important constituents, the orchestra volunteers. Its purpose is to strengthen and enrich symphony orchestras through the expertise and leadership of the nation's orchestra volunteers.
In 1987 the League created a *Department of Volunteer Services* to strenghen services to volunteers. The League staff is an extension of the *Volunteer Council,* gathering information and implementing programs.
Today, the *Volunteer Council* assists in the following services to League member volunteer associations:
● Plans and presents sessions for volunteers at League seminars and the national conference.
● Cultivates a national arts advocacy network of orchestra volunteers.
● Publishes a quarterly newsletter specifically for orchestra volunteers.
● Provides on-site consultation through the *Volunteer Consultants Program* on a number of subjects, including fundraising, season ticket sales, education projects, effective leadership, and motivational techniques.
● Publishes annually the *Gold Book,* a directory of hundreds of fundraising projects, education programs, and ticket sales campaigns produced by orchestra volunteer associations across the country (in 1989 adding a new section called *Service Projects* pinpointing projects that keep track of volunteer hours).
The *Volunteer Council* strives to help orchestras strengthen and increase their educational outreach activities to fill the gap left by declining arts programs in public schools - to better promote the arts, American artists, and American music. In addition, even with a slight increase in the number of volunteers, the Council recognizes the decrease in hours committed volunteers can give due to part-time or full-time employment. To help counteract this loss of hours, the Council has made recommendations to orchestras to keep administrative offices open some evenings and weekends to make the best use of volunteer power. Volunteers are the backbone of American orchestras, and concessions must be made to accommodate them and guide the League's development of services for orchestra volunteers.
Publications: Recorder (newsletter); The Gold Book: Directory of Successful Projects for Volunteers

LEADERSHIP DEVELOPMENT/BOARDS: CHILDREN/YOUTH

NATIONAL/STATE ORGANIZATIONS

JACKIE ROBINSON FOUNDATION
80-90 Eighth Avenue
New York, NY 10011
TEL: 212-675-1511
Objectives: To development the leadership potential of minority and inner-city youth.
Services: Conducts the *Leadership Development Program* for high school students to address specific needs of urban youth, and to help prepare them to help improve their communities; trains minority and poor youths for sports management and office careers in organized sports; provides counseling and support services for youth; awards full college scholarships and music scholarships to promising minority performers; administers the *Robie Award for Humanitarianism* program; publishes a newsletter, journal, and student handbook on scholarships.
Publications: JRF Newsletter; Awards Dinner Journal; Scholarship Student Handbook
Founded: 1973

NATIONAL ASSOCIATION OF CONSERVATION DISTRICTS
509 Capital Court, NE
Washington, DC 20002
TEL: 202-547-6223
Objectives: To direct and coordinate conservation through districts organized by citizens; the conservation and development of soil, water and related natural resources.
Services: Assists some 3,000 local (usually county) conservation districts and their volunteer directors (approximately 18,000) in achieving soil and water conservation and resource development goals with a maximum of voluntary action and local involvement; encourages districts to form youth boards to aid projects; publishes a monthly newsletter, *The Tuesday Letter,* directories, proceedings, annual reports, guides, etc.
Contact: Ellen Dougherty
Publications: Tuesday Letter; NACD Conference Proceedings; NACD Directory
Founded: 1947

NATIONAL COLLABORATION FOR YOUTH
SEE COMMUNICATIONS & PUBLIC RELATIONS: CHILDREN/YOUTH

NATIONAL NETWORK OF YOUTH ADVISORY BOARDS
PO Box 402036
Ocean View Branch
Miami Beach, FL 33140
TEL: 305-532-2607
Objectives: To increase input by youth in the planning and implementing of programs for youth.
Services: Provides young people with opportunities to help plan, operate, monitor and evaluate programs that are intended to serve them; helps the youth identify community resources, write project proposals, secure grants, learn about federally-funded projects, determine needs, survey problems, set priorities and, generally, to help plan their own future; publishes a set of two handbooks, *Follow-Up Report,* to help community leaders establish youth participation, and a list of supplementary resources and publications on the subject.
Founded: 1975

PROJECT LEAD
Quest International
537 Jones Road
PO Box 566
Granville, OH 43023-0566
TEL: 614-522-6400 (AK, HI); 800-233-7900 (OH)
TOLL FREE: 800-446-2700 (Rest USA)
FAX: 800-247-0500 (Canada)
Purpose: To offer leadership training to a broad range of adolescents.
Sponsor: Quest International; Association of Junior Leagues; W.K. Kellogg Foundation
Contact: Program Director
Description: On September 1, 1982, The Association of Junior Leagues and Quest International initiated Project LEAD for teenaged men and women. During its first four years the project trained more than 1,300 students and involved more than 25,000 youth in projects completed throughout the United States and Canada. LEAD offers leadership training to a broad range of adolescents, from the natural joiners and achievers to those who traditionally have had fewer opportunities to discover their potential in this area.

Students work closely with adults in setting goals and discovering how to achieve them. They undertake hands-on community service, while building personal skills. There are also long-range dividends: caring about the well-being of others, taking responsibility, collaborating on finding solutions, and enjoying the good feeling of making one's community a better place to live. The program involves four steps:

Step 1. Building a Team - To initiate local participation in Project LEAD, a sponsor and a team must be identified. Schools, churches, service or professional organizations, youth centers, park districts, etc., sponsor LEAD teams, each composed of six individuals: an adult volunteer, a teacher or youth leader, and four young people.

- The volunteer acts as a mentor, providing guidance, experience and a network of contacts with the community.
- The teacher or youth leader supports the program within his or her institution.
- Young teammates are chosen in a selection process by their peers.

In a special orientation session, the adults learn how the program works - how to help the teenagers increase their abilities at problem solving, personal communication, and group interaction. This relationship also assists adolescents in making the transition from thinking of adults as authority figures to considering them as friends and partners.

The team, with other young volunteers, conducts a preliminary needs assessment in their city or town - working directly with public officials, administrators, prominent leaders, and media professionals - to determine what can be done to improve the quality of life in their community. This enables them to effect project control right from the start.

Step 2. Learning to LEAD - Teams participate in a week-long leadership conference with trainers presenting resources and practice situations to teach action planning. In this step, less assertive youth gain more confidence - learning to think ahead, cope with hurdles, trust, and direct cooperative action. Bonds form between teens and adults, changing a collection of individuals into a team. Following the conference, the young leaders return home to recruit additional student volunteers for the chosen local project, and to plan for reaching their goals.

Step 3. Ready, Aim, Act! - The teenaged leaders have devised a plan of action, recruited volunteers, evolved budgets and publicized their efforts. Now it is time to implement the chosen project. These projects have included substance abuse, adolescent pregnancy, and domestic violence among many others. A group in Michigan constructed a playground for a shelter for battered women and children. Teens in Nevada set up a latchkey program for school-age children. In Massachusetts, it was a hotline to address teenage suicide. In Mexico City teens built an adobe house for a homeless man. This flexibility makes LEAD adaptive to any community.

Step 4. Wrapping It Up - "Finishing" a project can take as much time as the project itself, since the final step includes an evaluation of accomplishments, hurdles that were overcome, and ideas on how to do it better next time. Also, the "finish" is usually the "start" of bigger and better things.

Project LEAD's Ripple Effect - Attention received by the first project almost always results in more ambitious undertakings that involve larger numbers of volunteers. Other consequences of the program include bridging the generation gap, opening channels of communication, providing opportunities for adults and teens to work together with mutual responsibility and respect, personal planning, setting goals - academic, social, domestic - and achieving them, etc. In addition, volunteering has many rewards besides enhancement of self-image - from simply having the confidence to "raise one's hand" to the satisfaction of having helped to transform a community problem into a shared success. To help communities start the process, Quest International provides leadership training for teams of two adult mentors and four students in areas of needs assessment, student recruitment, project implementation; course materials; and technical assistance and follow-up such as toll-free numbers, networking, and newsletters. According to program leaders, "The underlying concept is service. While details are different in every community, the ultimate goal is the same: Learning to work together to improve communities today, and to build leaders for tomorrow."
Publications: Project LEAD Adult Mentor Manual; Project LEAD Student Volunteer Handbook; Project LEAD Newsletter; Project LEAD (brochure)

TEEN-AGE ASSEMBLY OF AMERICA*
998 Ala Kapua Street
Honolulu, HI 96818
TEL: 808-833-2422
Objectives: To involve young people in overcoming juvenile delinquency through their own efforts in constructive community activities.
Services: Conducts a number of community activities involving its high school, intermediate and elementary school members including drug panels, conferences, police-teenage relations conferences, the *Little White House Conference on Children and Youth,* etc.; publishes *Teen-Age Assembly Comes of Age;.*
Publications: Teen-Age Assembly Comes of Age
Founded: 1959

YOUTH AS RESOURCES
SEE FUNDING/FUND-RAISING/RELATED SERVICES

TRAINING PROGRAMS

COMMUNICATIONS SKILLS FOR THE COLLEGE BOUND
New Brunswick High School
1125 Livingston Avenue
New Brunswick, NJ 08902
TEL: 201-745-5336
Credit: Course credit
Sponsor: New Brunswick Board of Education
Contact: Janet Obrzut, Teacher
Description: This course includes a requirement for students to analyze current trends and act upon their findings. In 1989 this culminated in addressing the deterioration of the environment and working at the local level to help bring about improvement. They had to go no further than their own school yard, where litter was a constant problem. The students began to organize an anti-litter campaign, including a plan to have students pick up litter around

the school for a half-hour after school each day for three days. What sounded so simple at first - get kids to volunteer to go out and pick up all of the trash - proved complex, causing them to postpone the event and regroup. Starting from "square one," the students learned the "nuts and bolts" of publicizing the event, recruiting volunteers, holding meetings, scheduling and other aspects of community organizing. Two critical issues faced by the students this time were:

- Why the project might succeed or fail; and
- What to do if no one shows up at a meeting.

Having learned from the initial effort, the students decided they would "network" - ask friends to come and bring other students, as well as post meeting notices around the school. While doing this, they are required to put their efforts in context - learn more about the subject themselves. In response they checked out beautification and anti-litter programs in New Brunswick, where a lot is being done. They learned from these contacts that it is a good public relations ploy to take before-and-after pictures around the school and make an oral report to the student body. In the outset, enlisting volunteers was not a problem. This time around they had no trouble enlisting volunteers. According to one student, "We didn't realize how many people feel the way we do about our school."

In addition to the group who developed and managed the anti-litter project itself, a second group of students made a television documentary of the anti-litter efforts, showing the "ups and downs and ins and outs" of organizing a community environmental project. A local cable channel is considering showing the video. A third group in the class chose to dramatize the effects of environmental disasters by creating a play in which students enact roles of animals and people whose lives have been changed or lost in events such as the oil spill in Alaska and the escape of lethal gas in India.

The teacher said she is amazed at the effectiveness of the student groups in the course who benefited from the experience while improving the community. She felt that the greatest lesson learned was that organizing a "simple community project" is not as simple as it seems - a lesson that is as valuable in paid careers as it is in volunteer service.

CROSS-CULTURAL COMMUNITY WORKSHOP
Brown University
25 George Street
PO Box 1973
Providence, RI 02912
TEL: 401-863-3555
Sponsor: National Association of Foreign Student Affairs
Contact: Workshop Coordinator
Description: This workshop provides an opportunity to combine foreign study and community service. It is cosponsored by the *Office of International Programs* and the *Center for Public Service.* It features students who have studied abroad who share their unique cross-cultural perspective to integrate international and local experiences by exploring the responsibilities of the individual to the community in a cross-cultural context. The program has three components:

- **Discussion** - a bi-weekly evening discussion that focuses on definitions of *community* and *self.* Through writing and discussion, the group explores issues related to international study and community work, such as cultural biases, social issues, political systems and adaptation to environment.
- **Community Service** - Through a regular volunteer commitment, participants rediscover Providence. Students create an individual service project with a community agency, addressing an issue they studied or observed while abroad (e.g. housing, domestic violence, the rights of children).
- **Journal** - At the end of the program, writing and art that represent each participant's cross-cultural experience is bound and distributed as a journal to *Brown* and *Providence.*

Students receive neither college credit nor payment for participating in this course. The Workshop is supported by funds from the *National Association for Foreign Student Affairs* and *Brown University.*

FIRST ANNUAL SOVIET-AMERICAN YOUTH SUMMIT
SEE TRAINING/CONFERENCES/TEACHING: CHILDREN/YOUTH

THE NAME OF THE GAME IS CARING
SEE VOLUNTEERS: STUDENTS

SEVENTH GRADE SOCIAL PROBLEMS COURSE
United Way of Stamford
62 Palmer's Hill Road
Stamford, CT 06902-2113
TEL: 203-348-7711
Sponsor: Stamford Emergency Shelter
Contact: Jayne Mazur
Description: This course uses a two-month curriculum developed by *United Way of Stamford* and the *Turn of River Middle School.* It is offered to seventh graders *in addition to* their regular classes. The 47 seventh graders in the course learned about the United Way movement, its mission and goals, and the human service needs of the Stamford community. The students were asked to study the area's social needs and make recommendations to a simulated allocations panel.

Assigned in groups, each team chose one agency to study in depth. They visited the agencies, and interviewed staff about the agency's mission, services and budget, then developed their own allocations presentations on a modified United Way budget form, along with the dollar amount received by the agency the previous year. The groups used United Way's standard requirements and developed and submitted their budgets.

Another portion of the course taught community problem solving, and gave the youngsters an opportunity to work with a case study that documented homelessness in Stamford. Working again in small groups, they developed a strategy to help meet the needs of the homeless population.

The case study involved the *Emergency Shelter of Stamford* and its problems such as overcrowding, the loss of the building to redevelopment, etc. Key players were listed as the *Stamford Union of Churches and Synagogues, City of Stamford, Salvation Army* and *United Way.* Among other questions, the youngsters were asked to determine who is responsible for these problems.

The goal of this problem-solving exercise was not to find *the* correct answer but, to encourage students to think independently, creatively, and clearly.

Another part of the course was conducted by the United Way, which taught the seventh-graders the technical side of communications and marketing - relationships with the press and media, and ways to write press releases, brochures, and newsletters. They took their roles as volunteers very seriously and combined this new-found PR knowledge with a fund-raiser at their school, *Turn of River Middle School,* for United Way. They presented a check for $340.52 to the president of the United Way as a result of their efforts.

In spite of the extra work involved, the seventh-graders enjoyed the course, and helped verify the creators' belief that this age group had legitimate concerns and should not be left out of the process of exploring their community's human services needs.

STUDENT CARE DAY
SEE FUNDING/FUND-RAISING/RELATED SERVICES: CHILDREN

YOUNG LEADERS CONFERENCE
SEE TRAINING/CONFERENCES/TEACHING: CHILDREN/YOUTH

INDIVIDUAL PROGRAM PROFILES

BROWN PROGRAM IN LEADERSHIP
Brown University
25 George Street
PO Box 1960
Providence, RI 02912
TEL: 401-863-1954
Purpose: To offer students a variety of experiences aimed at increasing their understanding of the leadership process, particularly in the context of public service.
Contact: Kacy Cuddy, Coordinator
Description: The *Brown Program in Leadership* is jointly run by the *Center for Public Service* and *Psychological Services*. The components of the program are:

- **Public Service Summer Internship Program** - An intensive summer internship in which students do service work in Providence.
- **Effecting Change: The Process of Empowerment** - An interdisciplinary seminar course that focuses on theories of leadership and their application to accounts of leaders, past and present, in a variety of cultures and constituencies.
- **Public Leadership Speakers Series** - A series in which a diverse group of both community leaders and nationally-recognized leaders speak of their experience and ideas on leadership issues.
- **Brown Outdoor Leadership Trip (BOLT)** - A four-day backpacking trip to provide students with opportunities to share confidence-building experiences while learning about group dynamics and leadership.
- **Brown Adventure Program (BAP)** - A group initiatives, low ropes course at *Camp Alder's Gate* in which participants are involved in situations in which they must learn to collaborate in order to accomplish tasks and solve problems.

Enrollment is limited in some cases. Applications for most programs are available in March each year.

MAKING THE GRADE: A REPORT CARD ON AMERICAN YOUTH
United Way of the Plains
212 North Market
Suite 200
Wichita, KS 67202-2021
TEL: 316-267-1321
Purpose: To bring youth issues to the forefront of public awareness.
Contact: Patrick J. Hanrahan, President
Description: In September 1989, a diverse volunteer committee was formed to develop and operate an issue-oriented project. It was co-sponsored by the *United Way of the Plains* and the *National Collaboration for Youth* (a coalition of national youth-serving organizations). The committee included people from some 40 local agencies - many of them youth-service providers, adult representatives from the *Wichita Chamber of Commerce* and city and state governments, business and labor leaders, news media professionals from *KAKE-TV* (the local *ABC Network* affiliate), and high school youth who are service recipients and members of honor societies and student councils.
The issues were problems facing youth, and the *National Collaboration for Youth* provided national statistics for eight major youth problems: functional illiteracy, juvenile crime, school dropouts, substance abuse, teen pregnancy, youth unemployment, and mental and physical health care. The committee determined how best to give a local focus to these problems.
As a result, *KAKE-TV* featured each of the problems in an eight-part news mini-series. Each segment of the series concluded by airing *United Way's First Call for Help* phone number. The series aired immediately preceding the national ABC telecast, *Growing Up, Down and Out,* hosted by Barbara Walters.

Following the national program, *KAKE-TV* aired a live call-in show as a forum for local youth to express their reactions to the program and their concerns about specific youth problems.
About two weeks later, United Way held a town meeting to obtain feedback about the TV broadcasts, and to develop plans for improving local services to youth. More than 100 people came to the meeting and "drew up a report card" on how well the community was dealing with the youth problems.
With the help of two school principals who are United Way board members, plans are being implemented to maintain a dialogue about youth services through monthly meetings with local students - encouraging their input and volunteer participation to gradually improve existing services and fill gaps in service needs.
Founded: 1989

MINDSTRETCHERS
Grissom Middle School
13881 Kern Road
Mishawaka, IN 46544
TEL: 219-633-4061
Purpose: To challenge highly-motivated students to apply their skills for the betterment of school and community.
Sponsor: Grissom Middle School; Lilly Foundation
Contact: Dennis Bottorff
Description: Initiated in 1984, Mindstretchers fully involves students in the decision-making process. The program involves 25 students selected from recommendations by teachers and challenges them to apply their skills to benefit the community. A candidate profile is developed using specific criteria - leadership potential, level of commitment, etc. The director of Mindstretchers makes the final selection after consultation with the teachers.
Mindstretchers has four goals:

- to stretch their minds in school through academic games and "quiz bowls;"
- to stretch their minds outside school through field trips suggested and arranged by students;
- to serve the school through the promotion of esteem-building activities; and
- to serve the community through projects selected by the group.

Community activities have included such activities as "adopting" an elderly handicapped woman, helping the local public television station raise funds, and helping at the Humane Society. Members receive no academic credit for their work.
Students are involved in periodic meetings to discuss current service projects and plan new ones. The director believes that service to the community raises self-esteem dramatically.
Mindstretchers was chosen as one of 20 outstanding programs for youth of Indiana. It was awarded a $3,000 grant from the Lilly Endowment, which provided outside leadership training for the students. Prior to receiving the Lilly grant, Mindstretchers depended on minimal funds donated by the director, the participants themselves and the student council.
Mindstretchers members have developed a motto for the program: "Dedicated to lighting up those dark corners in our minds and brightening up our corner of the world."
Founded: 1984

PREVENTION THROUGH ACTION
SEE VOLUNTEERS: STUDENTS

SPECIAL STUDENT ADVISORY BOARD
Theodore Roosevelt National Bank
1201 New York Avenue
Washington, DC 20006
TEL: 202-371-1201; 202-546-3400
FAX: 202-371-8233
Purpose: To make youth more aware of finances and accountability.

Description: The mission statement of this new bank (grand opening, Fall 1989) calls for a "new standard for community involvement by contributing to a better way of life." The bank promises to "continually reach beyond the norm," and the *Special Student Advisory Board* is one of its efforts in this direction. While the program was on the drawing at the beginning of the planning stages for the bank, it is in its beginning stages as a reality. Members come from junior and senior high schools in the metropolitan area. A 16-year-old high school sophomore is Chairman of the Committee.

As meetings are held, and strategy is formed, the bank will begin to offer targeted services such as:

- Savings accounts with scaled increases in interest rates based on the students' grades.
- Special entrepreneurial seminars.
- Student volunteer community involvement programs sponsored by the Bank.

With the cooperation of school leaders, community resource persons, business and industry, and the youth themselves, it is hoped that this emphasis on self-help will set a standard and serve as a model for other banking institutions, while producing better citizens for the community.

STUDENT VOLUNTEERS
Hudson High School
77 North Oniatt Street
Hudson, OH 44236
TEL: 216-653-3371
Purpose: To provide an opportunity for students to design, develop, and take charge of every aspect of a community volunteer program.
Sponsor: Carnegie Foundation
Contact: Dee Phillips
Description: Each year at Hudson High School a student board is elected from the student body to oversee the *Student Volunteers* program. Begun in 1983, five students and a teacher organized and coordinated the program. It is operated out of the "Volunteer Office" where students receive requests for volunteers throughout the school day. An adult volunteer from the community offers assistance and advice when requested by the students.

The program is voluntary, with no minimum commitment of time. Students receive a quarter-credit per 30 hours served. Recruitment is done during two days in the fall, but there is no deadline for joining the program.

Due to the number of requests, the student board handles the approval and priority process. Requests are filled on the basis of need - a task that cannot be performed by an individual, for example, because of age or ability, or a teacher's plea for a volunteer to work with a student who cannot progress without individual attention. The assistance of the young volunteers is felt across the county, with a favorite accomplishment being the establishment of an entertainment program for the elderly.

The board has a monthly meeting where interaction among volunteers produces shared ideas and meaningful suggestions for improvement of services. In addition, the Volunteer Office is open throughout the day for "walk-in" advice or just conversation. Where specialized training is needed, such as in a nursing home or in a hospital, the training is done on-site. Otherwise, training is provided to new volunteers by experienced student volunteers.

In 1988 the program became computerized due to a Carnegie Foundation grant. This facilitates filling requests from the community. The grant included administrative funds, and the school adds funds as needed to help with supplies.

The program's ownership passes from student board to student board year after year. Because of the unique system of student ownership of the program, students feel a greater need to see it succeed, learning and doing for others as much as time allows. The young volunteers have developed a motto for their program: "Satisfaction through Service."

TEENS AS COMMUNITY RESOURCES*
Crime Justice Foundation
95 Berkeley Street
Boston, MA 02116-6203
TEL: 617-426-9800
Purpose: To involve teenagers - both students and dropouts - in volunteer efforts that will help them grow, learn and become assets to the community.
Sponsor: National Crime Prevention Council
Contact: Tim Cross
Description: Young people in Boston are designing, developing and implementing volunteer resource programs for the community that meet real local needs. With technical assistance and support from the *National Crime Prevention Council*, and funding from the *Boston Foundation*, the community formed a board composed of adult community leaders and youth from across the community. This group advertised for proposals and then voted to determine those that would receive funding from the foundation. The board places the funds with the host agencies, including schools, monitors the grantees' projects, and provides recognition to project participants.

No teenager is turned away from the program. Dropouts are involved on a par with Honor Society members, and all have to contribute to the success of the project.

With funding ranging from $100 to $5,000, the youth set out on a round of projects to increase the funding base - ultimately being responsible themselves for 80% of the program's operating budget. The initial project mounted by the group was building a playground for the children at a Boston women's shelter. Other projects include cleaning up one of Boston's harbor island parks. New projects are based on community needs as they surface and come to the attention of the youth and the board.

YOUTH ALLOCATIONS COMMITTEE
United Way of the Capital Area (Jackson)
414 North Street
Jackson, MS 39225-3169
TEL: 601-948-4725
Purpose: To evaluate and make decisions to fund youth programs in the community.
Sponsor: United Way
Contact: Doris Bridgeman, Youth Programs Coordinator
Description: High school and college students in Jackson, Mississippi, are making decisions on which youth programs receive funding in their community. Started in 1986 as an expansion of the United Way Volunteer Center's *Youth in Action Program*, the *Youth Allocations Committee* is composed of students from 14 high schools and colleges in the Jackson area.

Committee members learn how to make a limited amount of funds benefit the greatest number of people. They attend three orientation sessions to learn about the role and responsibility of volunteers in the community, and about community health and human-care agencies, as well as a basic overview of the allocations process.

The Committee is provided with $5,000 in venture grant funds to distribute. Each September they evaluate how effectively funds allocated the previous year were used. Then, the following March, they review new applications for funding and attend agency presentations. In April decisions are made, and funds are distributed in May. In May 1989, seven youth programs were funded, including a teen center for troubled youth, church youth groups, and programs in local chapters of the *Boys and Girls Clubs*.
Founded: 1986

YOUTH AS RESOURCES
I.U. Natatorium
901 West New York Street
Indianapolis, IN 46202
TEL: 317-274-8605

Purpose: To support teenagers in projects of their own design to improve their community.
Sponsor: National Crime Prevention Council
Contact: Paula Allen
Description: A board composed of adult community leaders and youth has set up a grant program that requires teenagers to design, develop and implement volunteer projects in the community that address local needs and problems.

The Lilly Foundation grants themselves can be as low as $100, and do not surpass $5,000, which indicates that the teenagers are motivated by other factors. The money is placed with the host agency and used for operating expenses.

The program is deliberately based in the community itself rather than a school setting, since the aim is to attract dropouts as well as honor students. Although the students may consult adults, they must take charge of the project development and management. The board does monitor the projects, and provides recognition and awards for the teenagers involved.

Projects implemented by the Indianapolis youth include teaching younger children about drug abuse and prevention, assisting senior citizens with chores, errands, minor maintenance, cleanup, etc., and helping inner-city youth with reading skills.

Leadership skills developed among the young people are considered an important asset to the community and its future.

YOUTH AS RESOURCES/YMCA
226 East Washington
Fort Wayne, IN 46802
TEL: 219-420-0700
Purpose: To support teenagers willing to spend volunteer time to improve their communities.
Sponsor: National Crime Prevention Council; Lilly Foundation
Contact: Donna Koehlinger
Description: Teenagers in Fort Wayne met the challenge offered by the Lilly Foundation through the National Crime Prevention Council (NCPC) - to design and implement projects that would benefit the community. The progress began with the support of a required board composed of adult community leaders and teenagers. This board was charged with the task of advertising in the community for proposals designed to improve the community in any area where there was an expressed need. After selecting the projects to receive the Lilly Foundation grants and technical assistance from NCPC, the board monitors the projects from the beginning, and designs awards and recognition events for the teenagers operating the projects.

The project is based in the community, and draws youth from area high schools and the community itself - with youth ranging from dropouts to school leaders.

The grants ($500 to $5,000) are placed with the host agencies for use by the teenaged volunteers for operating expenses. When additional funds are needed, the students design creative fund-raising events to meet the need.

The projects address needs as seen by the community, and have included the building of a playground for a day care center and an education project that researched colleges and provided briefings for interested students.

Besides the physical and psychosocial benefits to the community, leadership skills are being developed that will benefit the youth throughout his/her life.

YOUTH COMMUNITY SERVICE
SEE COMMUNITY SERVICES

YOUTH-IN-ACTION AUCTION
SEE FUNDING/FUND-RAISING/RELATED SERVICES: AUCTIONS

YOUTH-IN-GOVERNMENT DAY
Youth Advisory Commission
170 Santa Maria Avenue
Pacifica, CA 94044
TEL: 415-877-8631
Purpose: To give teenaged Youth Advisory Commission members an opportunity to discover first-hand how separate city government functions can contribute to the resolution of critical community issues.
Sponsor: Youth Advisory Commission
Contact: John W. Deuel
Description: The Youth Advisory Commission of Pacifica was created by a City Council Ordinance in 1970 to provide young people with a greater voice and more effective representation in the running of their city. It is similar to the other city commissions and operates under the same provisions, except that its members must be between the ages of 14 and 18 years.

One of the Commission's annual projects is Youth-in-Government Day. Through this exercise, the Commission becomes better able to identify and resolve important city issues and also to involve more students in the running of City Government.

Two months prior to the actual Youth-in-Government Day, students from the two local high schools are asked to present a list of topics which they feel are current and important to the city's youth. From this list, the Youth Advisory Commission selects five topics that are to be the focus on Youth-in-Government Day.

During the morning session of Youth-in-Government Day, four groups of six students each discuss separate issues with an objective of developing a resolution which will be presented at the Youth Convention during the afternoon. These meetings are held in the City Council chambers with representatives of each department of City government present to participate in the discussions until noon.

Lunch is hosted at a local restaurant by the Rotary Club and a guest speaker is invited (e.g., Pacifica's City Manager). After lunch, each of the five resolutions is presented and voted on by the entire group of students. Later in the afternoon, the youth participants are brought to City Hall for a brief orientation to departments.

The proposals that result from Youth-in-Government Day are reviewed by the Youth Advisory Commission and presented to the City Council for action recommendations.

YOUTH LEADERSHIP VENTURE FUNDING PROGRAM
United Way of the Capital Area (Hartford)
99 Woodland Street
Hartford, CT 06105-1207
TEL: 203-249-2300
Purpose: To enable youth to make decisions about funding for youth-oriented programs in the community.
Sponsor: United Way Youth Leadership Advisors
Contact: Nancy Roberts, Youth Leadership Advisors Chairman
Description: Youth allocation leaders in Hartford have taken an issue-oriented approach to funding for youth programs. For 1989 funding, 15 students from Hartford area high schools identified youth substance abuse as the target issue of the youth community. Before proceeding, the student volunteers interviewed elected officials and human-service agency directors about priority concerns for youth. The *Connecticut Alcohol and Drug Abuse Commission* confirmed information about local teen substance abuse programs needing funding.

Students on the allocations committee were selected based on applications that had been distributed to public and private schools in the United Way's 30-town coverage area. The students make the funding decisions, while United Way staff keep them informed about the funding process. In addition to receiving training in basic allocations procedures, the students gained a thorough understanding of the substance abuse problem.

Provided with $10,000 in venture funds from the United Way, the

students funded 11 local programs addressing substance abuse. These included *Students Against Drunk Driving (SADD),* a student-produced video on anti-substance abuse peer counseling, and a positive self-development program incorporating anti-substance abuse education for elementary school children. The United Way's board of directors unanimously approved the programs selected by the students.
Publications: Students Against Drunk Driving (video)
Founded: 1988

YOUTH RESOURCES OF SOUTHWESTERN INDIANA
405 Carpenter Street
Evansville, IN 47708
TEL: 812-428-7593
Purpose: To support teenagers in projects of their own design to help the community.
Sponsor: National Crime Prevention Council; Lilly Foundation
Contact: Phyllis Kincaid
Description: The Lilly Foundation, through the National Crime Prevention Council (NCPC), has provided funding, technical assistance and guidance to teenagers in Evansville willing to design, develop and implement volunteer projects that meet a real community need. To obtain this support, the youth submitted proposals to a board composed of their peers and adult community leaders. The board reviewed all proposals, and voted for those which would receive grants from the foundation through NCPC. Project headquarters is in the central community, although teenagers come from a number of high schools as well as the community itself. Dropouts as well as school leaders are made part of the youth teams. In addition to selecting projects for grants ($100 to $5,000), which are placed with the host agencies, the board monitors the projects, and provides recognition to project participants.
The Evansville teenagers mounted a project in an area that has proven difficult for adult volunteer groups - building housing for the elderly. Another badly needed project was a "big brother/big sister" project for children residing in a shelter for battered spouses. As projects are completed, or more students enter the program, additional needs are addressed and the cycle begins again.

LEADERSHIP DEVELOPMENT/BOARDS: CIVIC AFFAIRS

NATIONAL/STATE ORGANIZATIONS

FRIENDS COMMITTEE ON NATIONAL LEGISLATION
Religious Society of Friends
245 Second Street, NE
Washington, DC 20002
TEL: 202-547-6000
Objectives: To determine statements, actions and voting records of senators and representatives.
Services: Researches and analyzes information on legislation and voting records; encourages expression of individual views through letters and calls to members of Congress and other government officials; develops testimony programs for hearings before Congress; conducts interviews with key people in government, including Senators and Representatives; publicizes findings for the general public and makes them available at nominal cost in the form of how-to pamphlets, papers and booklets.
Publications: Washington Newsletter; Action Bulletin; Indian News; Visions of a Warless World
Founded: 1943

INDIVIDUAL PROGRAM PROFILES

COMMUNITY ADVISEMENT BOARD
SEE BUSINESS/INDUSTRY INVOLVEMENT: CIVIC AFFAIRS

LEADERSHIP DEVELOPMENT/BOARDS: COMMUNICATIONS/PR

NATIONAL/STATE ORGANIZATIONS

COMMUNITY ADVISORY BOARDS
Corporation for Public Broadcasting
1111 Sixteenth Street, NW
Washington, DC 20036
TEL: 202-955-5100
Objectives: To make the advisory board experience effective and rewarding: to open dialogue between local stations and the community.
Services: Provides information and assistance to community groups on establishing and maintaining advisory boards; publishes specific CAB manual which details organizational steps, including board makeup based on demographics, how a chairperson can interrupt a long-winded member tactfully, and other details transferable to any citizen board.
Publications: CPB Report
Founded: 1968

INDIVIDUAL PROGRAM PROFILES

UNITED WAY EDITORIAL BOARD
SEE COMMUNICATIONS & PUBLIC RELATIONS

LEADERSHIP DEVELOPMENT/BOARDS: CRIME PREVENTION

NATIONAL/STATE ORGANIZATIONS

NATIONAL ASSOCIATION OF CITIZENS' CRIME COMMISSIONS
Wichita Crime Commission
c/o Bobby Stout
460 Broadway Plaza Building
Wichita, KS 67202
TEL: 316-267-1236
Objectives: To form a network of commissions for sharing of ideas and experiences.
Services: Works with crime commissions not affiliated with local, state, or federal governments; facilitates exchanges of mutually helpful information between member commissions; informs the public on dangers of crime, including organized crime, and offers suggested methods of controlling it; strives to arouse public interest in the issue of clean government, and to encourage formation of citizens' crime commissions where needed; publishes a manual for citizens interested in forming commissions.
Publications: How to Organize and Operate a Citizens' Crime Commission
Founded: 1952

NATIONAL CRIME PREVENTION COUNCIL
735 Fifteenth Street, NW
Washington, DC 20005
TEL: 202-393-7141
Objectives: To enable people to prevent crime and build safer, more caring communities.
Services: Provides training and information services, including a data base of community crime prevention-related programs; conducts demonstration programs to highlight ways to work effectively in crime and drug abuse prevention, especially in developing the community's ability to rely on young people as assets to help meet local needs; coordinates the Crime Prevention Coalition (125 organizations which support community-based crime prevention); publishes books, brochures, kits of camera-ready masters, posters and other items. [Funding for NCPC comes from the Bureau of Justice Assistance (Office of Justice Programs, US Dept. of Justice), and a wide range of private and public foundations, corporations, and individual donors.]
Publications: National Crime Prevention Council Information Packet; Reaching Out: School-Based Community Service Programs; Making a Difference: Young People in Community Crime Prevention

INDIVIDUAL PROGRAM PROFILES

DISTRICT OF COLUMBIA WOMEN'S COMMISSION FOR CRIME PREVENTION
945 G Street, NW
Washington, DC 20001
TEL: 202-347-2695
Purpose: To provide motivation for constructive life styles among young people who might otherwise turn to crime.
Sponsor: Women's organization in the metropolitan area; private donations
Contact: Ettyce H. Moore, President
Description: In 1968, some 125 women's organizations in the Washington, DC, metropolitan area participated in establishing the DC Women's Commission for Crime Prevention. The creation of this private, nonprofit, volunteer organization grew out of a deep concern about rising youth crime in the area. Initial and continuing encouragement and backing has come from the Board of Education, the Metropolitan Police Department, the White House, the DC government, the Department of Justice, and the District committees of both Houses of Congress.
The Commission is managed and operated by volunteers, ranging from its Board with members from the court system, city government, women's commissions and clubs, the local Bar association, and leaders in local crime reduction and prevention programs, to the file clerks in the Commission's office at a local church. The aims of the Commission include:

- The Commission recruits volunteers and channels them to existing programs for high-risk youth in the metropolitan area, such as: Big Sister (providing a successful role model for a young girl); Clothe-A-Thon (providing the necessary clothing to help a young person maintain self-respect and remain in school; Crime Stoppers (providing healthy activities for the very young child to counteract some of the negative influences around him/her), and many other programs designed to divert juveniles from areas of crime.
- The Commission initiates additional programs. For example, it was felt that an easy-reference booklet outlining for teenagers the local laws that could affect them would provide a measure of crime prevention. The *Women's Bar Association of DC* agreed to provide volunteers to write the booklet, and teenaged volunteers were enlisted to illustrate it so that the Commission could publish it and provide free distribution to the schools. The colorful booklet explains the laws so often

broken unknowingly by juveniles, and the penalties, including those for drug and truancy offenses. The booklet has been updated and reprinted a number of times over the years.
- The Commission responds to special requests in cases where no public funds are available to meet the need. For example, the Commission helped with furnishings to make more homelike rooms at the Women's Detention Center; provided books, a typewriter, home decorations and other family necessities for a girls' rehabilitation home; provided circus tickets and assistance for other outings for children, etc.
- As cosponsor with the Hands Up Crime Prevention of the DC Federation of Women's Clubs, the Commission assists in a community education event, the Good Neighbor Fair, an annual event in Washington, DC. The main purpose of the Fair is to generate public awareness, participation, and cooperation in crime prevention and related activities by community groups and government agencies. This event has stimulated outlying areas to hold similar fairs, one example being the 6C's Neighborhood Watch Awareness Fair in Southeast Washington, which attracted considerable media attention.
The Commission maintains a speaker service to inform other groups about the work of the Commission, and develops informative materials about its programs. The booklet for teenagers mentioned above, *Youth and the Law in the District of Columbia,* is available intermittently.
Founded: 1968

LEADERSHIP DEVELOPMENT/BOARDS: DISASTER

NATIONAL/STATE ORGANIZATIONS

BUILDING SEISMIC SAFETY COUNCIL
SEE VOLUNTEERS: PROFESSIONALS

LEADERSHIP DEVELOPMENT/BOARDS: DOMESTIC ABUSE

INDIVIDUAL PROGRAM PROFILES

COMMITTEE TO AID ABUSED WOMEN
SEE INFORMATION & REFERRAL: DOMESTIC ABUSE

GOVERNOR'S ADVISORY COMMITTEE ON CHILD ABUSE AND NEGLECT/VA
SEE GOVERNORS' OFFICES ON VOLUNTEERISM: VIRGINIA

LEADERSHIP DEVELOPMENT/BOARDS: DRUGS/ALCOHOL

NATIONAL/STATE ORGANIZATIONS

PANEL ON DRUG ABUSE/PANEL ON ALCOHOLISM
American Medical Association
Council of Scientific Affairs
535 North Dearborn Street
Chicago, IL 60610
TEL: 312-751-6577
Objectives: To increase educational efforts with the profession and the public regarding the diagnosis, treatment and prevention of drug abuse and alcoholism.
Services: Reviews evidence obtained from scientific research on the causes and effects of non-medical use of drugs and of alcoholism; proposes expanded educational programs to all segments of the population, including members of the medical and legal professions and law-enforcement agencies; develops informative materials on drug abuse and alcoholism and makes them available to the professions and the public at nominal cost.

TRAINING PROGRAMS

SHAVING CREAM LESSON - DRUG PREVENTION SEMINAR
Knox County Schools Drug Prevention Office
PO Box 2188
Knoxville, TN 37901
TEL: 615-544-3666
Credit: Inquire
Sponsor: Governor's Alliance for a Drug-Free Tennessee
Contact: Marty Iroff
Description: This drug prevention seminar had an unusual twist to show parents how easy it is to get into drugs, but how hard it is to stop until an authoritative voice comes forth. A national drug prevention specialist, director of the Atlanta-based *Parent's Resource Institute for Drug Education,* used shaving cream and peer pressure to make a point.
The training session was conducted for 45 representatives from throughout East Tennessee who are part of the *Governor's Alliance for a Drug-Free Tennessee.*
Choosing six volunteers, the specialist playfully suggested they begin sculpturing with the cream. Adults agreed to have mustaches and other "sculptures" painted on their faces and went along with the activity with increased enthusiasm - until a school official rose and ordered the group to stop. The childlike behavior immediately ceased. The primary reason for the exercise was to show parents how easy it is to get into drugs, but how hard it is to stop until an authoritative voice comes forth.
The specialist explained how he had gained the trust of the volunteers to get their cooperation, and then they "crossed the line for mature, dignified adults." He compared the shaving cream experiment to drug use among teens. He listed some of the reasons people do "dumb things" - *acceptance, survival, safety, intimacy and recognition.*
The meeting ended in a serious tone with questions and topics such as:
- "Are we serious about the war on drugs?" The drug dealers are saying we are not.
- Parents are in the biggest fight of their lives in trying to stop their children from using drugs.
A follow-up seminar was convened a month later. This one was designed to prepare parents and drug educators to train others. The two-day seminars are free.

STATEWIDE DRUG TASK FORCE CONFERENCE
SEE TRAINING/CONFERENCES/TEACHING: DRUGS/ALCOHOL

LEADERSHIP DEVELOPMENT/BOARDS: EDUCATION

NATIONAL/STATE ORGANIZATIONS

COUNCIL OF NATIONAL ORGANIZATIONS FOR ADULT EDUCATION
Association of Junior Leagues
660 First Avenue
New York, NY 10016
TEL: 212-683-1515
Objectives: To provide an opportunity for adult education organizations to work together and avoid duplication in services to programs; to assure that life experience is considered in education areas.
Services: Sponsors "I Can" program, a self-administered test which lists the competencies an individual has acquired through experience; currently expanding the "I Can" program; holds periodic task force and board meetings.

INDIVIDUAL PROGRAM PROFILES

BUSINESS/INDUSTRY ADVISORY COUNCIL (BIAC)
SEE BUSINESS/INDUSTRY INVOLVEMENT: EDUCATION

JAMES MADISON NATIONAL COUNCIL
US/Library of Congress
10 First Street, SE
Washington, DC 20540
TEL: 202-707-5093
FAX: 202-707-9898
Purpose: To attract new readers and new supporters to the Library of Congress.
Sponsor: Neutrogena, Inc.
Contact: John Kluge, Chairman
Description: On January 25, 1990, the Library of Congress launched a Council of some of the country's wealthiest people and revealed new efforts to reach a national audience. Members of the new *James Madison National Council* were given a grand tour of the Library's facilities, including a sampling of the almost 100 million books and objects on its shelves. In turn, the 30 new members each gave the Library from $10,000 to $100,000 with promises of annual contributions to come. The founder of the Council, the Librarian of the Congress, emphasized that supplements from the private sector other than money - such as their entrepreneural expertise and spirit - are needed.
The task of the Council is to find ways of breaking the mold of the Library's use mostly by Congress and scholars, and exploring the many ways it can help the whole country. They will examine why, with Americans' unlimited and free access to the greatest store of knowledge in the history of the country, its use is so one-dimensional. One focus will be on youth, many of whom feel that our culture grants no fame and our economy gives few rewards to knowledge. To accomplish these goals, a number of innovations were discussed, including:
- A monthly magazine about culture and libraries similar to that of the *Smithsonian Magazine,* with costs absorbed by a publisher for the privilege of using the Library's name and

cooperation (with the Library having veto power over content).

- An experimental video program, *American Memory,* to put specific subjects on optical laser discs.

A $1 million donation from the *Glenn Jones Cable Company* is to be used to tape and broadcast *The Global Library,* a weekly program on the Library aimed at librarians, teachers and students. The *International Cultural Society of Korea* gave $1 million to expand the Library's Korean collections. In addition, an unnamed New York businessman gave $1 million to fund a traveling exhibition from the Library.

The Council works under a Congressional oversight committee on all matters pertaining to the Library.

The *James Madison National Council* was deliberately named for the man who bought Thomas Jefferson's library and established the Library of Congress. Members include the top officials of Metromedia, Neutrogena, American Society of Composers, The Washington Post Company, American Stock Exchange, Encyclopaedia Britannica, and Murphy Oil Company as well as industrialists, a Texas oilman, and others.

To add to the celebration of Madison's accomplishment, the menu was prepared from Dolley Madison's own recipes developed when she was the town's busiest hostess.

LOCAL VOLUNTEER SCHOOL COUNCILS
Design for Change
222 South State
Chicago, IL 60604
TEL: 312-922-0317
Purpose: To train and develop parents, teachers and neighbors to accept responsibility for, and control of, the schools of Chicago.
Sponsor: City of Chicago
Contact: Don Moore
Description: This massive training effort is a result of a reform plan that puts each separate school in Chicago's school system under the direct control of its parents, teachers and neighbors. With an estimated immediate need of 6,000 volunteers from the community to sit on 11-person councils (17,000 applied for the 540 councils), training became the greatest challenge. It is considered a test by reformers - not of the education theory, per se, but of the whole ethic of community volunteerism - not that parents know best, but that parents care most.

The challenge was met by the community, however, as training took place in schools, in churches, in the halls of 50 major employers, and in other available space around the city.

Training is expected to help the 11-person volunteer councils draw up "school improvement plans" that the principals must implement. Some of the discussion points:

- **Testing** - The consensus is that they are needed for measurement, but must be improved and/or changed.
- **Lack of Experience of Volunteer Councils** - The consensus is that parents and others will learn by training and getting involved.
- **Bigger Role for Principal** - The consensus is that giving the principal more power at the school is offset by the Council's control of his contract.
- **An 80% dropout rate** - The consensus is that it can't get any worse. With employers giving release time to employees to serve, the PTA's enthusiastic involvement, and other factors, this problem will be vigorously attacked.

The head of *Design for Change,* who designed the reform program, lobbied for it, and is responsible for all of the training, said he was jubilant when the candidate numbers came in. "Nobody believed us, but we proved parents can care and get involved," he said.

SCHOOL COUNCIL VOLUNTEERS
SEE BUSINESS/INDUSTRY INVOLVEMENT: EDUCATION

YOUTH AFFAIRS TASK FORCE
United Way of Greater Manchester
20 Merrimack Street
Manchester, NH 03101
TEL: 603-625-6939
Purpose: To respond to the critical dropout problem in Manchester.
Sponsor: Manchester Board of Mayor & Aldermen
Contact: Anne Page, Director
Description: Twenty-seven percent of Manchester's young people never graduate from high school. In response to this critical problem, the *United Way of Greater Manchester* formed the *Youth Affairs Task Force* to assess the current situation and recommend various ways of dealing with it. The Task Force is comprised of people from all over the community who deal with the dropout problem - *Board of Aldermen, School Committee,* youth-serving agencies, law enforcement officers, guidance counselors, and a local TV news anchorman.

To begin its program, the Task Force interviewed students to learn how they perceived dropping out, and how they felt about problems facing today's students. Forty-four percent said the biggest problem was drugs and alcohol; others saw the problems either as family-related or school-related. The conclusion was that drug and alcohol abuse contributes to the problem, along with an extreme shortage of community-based services equipped to deal with the dropout problem. The Task Force also found that the punishment for absenteeism is external suspension and, based on observations, the Task Force concluded that such suspensions may actually encourage students to drop out.

Another discovery was that many students find hands-on experience in a particular field more rewarding than book learning. With students allowed entry into vocational training only after entering the junior year, teachers reported countless students recommitting themselves to learning after they arrived there.

Based on its findings, especially the gaps in community services, the Task Force made recommendations to the *United Way Board, Manchester Board of Mayor and Aldermen, Manchester School Committee,* and local community agencies, including an alternative education center, identifying family problems, developing citywide committees, and exploring existing services in drug and alcohol abuse.

The *Youth Affairs Task Force* meets periodically to monitor progress on its recommendations, also meeting with student representatives from three area high schools on how to reach potential dropouts. One area being explored is the legal issue regarding suspension of students.

As an added measure in the overall program, the school board has formed a subcommittee called the *Drop-Out Prevention Committee* to follow up on the recommendations and to identify future at-risk dropouts at a very early grade level. According to the Task Force director, "There is a lot we can do if we work together."

LEADERSHIP DEVELOPMENT/BOARDS: ETHNIC GROUPS

NATIONAL/STATE ORGANIZATIONS

NATIONAL INDIAN YOUTH COUNCIL
318 Elm Street, SE
Albuquerque, NM 87102
TEL: 505-247-2251
Objectives: To provide young Indian people with a working knowledge of service to their communities.

Services: Provides training and planning assistance on local, regional and national levels; addresses educational resources, preservation of the Indian family unit and community, protection of Indian natural resources, Indian health and education, civil liberties, working relationship with the federal government, and other concerns; develops programs in these areas; sponsors action research projects and direct action programs; conducts research as a basis for planning and disseminating information; publishes bimonthly newsletter.
Publications: Americans Before Columbus
Founded: 1961

INDIVIDUAL PROGRAM PROFILES

PROJECT BLUEPRINT
United Way of America
701 North Fairfax Street
Alexandria, VA 22314-2045
TEL: 703-836-7100
Purpose: To help United Ways recruit minority volunteers for leadership positions on boards and committees.
Sponsor: W.K. Kellogg Foundation
Contact: William Aramony, President, United Way of America
Description: In 1987, the *W.K. Kellogg Foundation* awarded the *United Way of America* a three-year grant of $1,387,064 to accelerate minority volunteer involvement and to provide greater support for minority organizations. A major thrust of the project is to help United Ways recruit minority volunteers for leadership positions on boards and committees.
With the United Way history of funding many comprehensive services to minorities, and involving minorities in the decisions, *Project Blueprint* serves to amplify those efforts.
As part of the project, special services to Native American Indians have been enhanced. The project also has established a computerized information system to better track programs and services available for minorities and the community. The project provides technical assistance to national minority organizations, and makes matching venture grants to local United Ways.
Project Blueprint is part of the *Second Century Initiative* effort to double United Way's volunteer capacity.
Founded: 1987

LEADERSHIP DEVELOPMENT/BOARDS: HANDICAPPED

NATIONAL/STATE ORGANIZATIONS

CO-ORDINATING COUNCIL FOR HANDICAPPED CHILDREN
220 South State Street, Room 412
Chicago, IL 60604
TEL: 312-939-3513
Objectives: To assist parents in advocating for the rights of handicapped children.
Services: Helps parents to organize parent groups and coalitions; trains parents to advocate for the rights of their handicapped children in Individualized Education Program (IEP) meetings, due process hearings, and other special education meetings; works with local and state administrators to obtain more funds for special education services, mental health services, and other programs which have been identified by parents; addresses and acts upon the Education of all Handicapped Children Act (Law 94-142) and

other laws affecting these children; publishes *How to Organize an Effective Parent/Advocacy Group and Move Bureaucracies, The Rights Booklet, How to Get Services by Being Assertive,* and other materials.
Publications: Parent Advocacy Groups; The Rights Booklet; Being Assertive

COMMISSION ON SELF-SUFFICIENCY
Virginia Department for Rights of the Disabled
James Monroe Building, 27th Floor
101 North 14th Street
Richmond, VA 23219
TEL: 804-225-2042
TOLL FREE: 800-552-3962 (Voice/TDD)
Objectives: To coordinate the delivery of services to facilitate the self-sufficiency and support for people with physical and sensory disabilities.
Services: Provides a long-awaited opportunity in the State of Virginia (passage of HJR 45 in *1990 General Assembly)* to develop a coordinated service system that is responsive to the full range of needs being experienced by people with physical and sensory disabilities; includes in its membership legislators, representatives of business and health industries, an educator and a practicing physician, with leadership by the Lieutenant Governor; considers recommendations from previous legislative studies addressing:
  ● accountability and support for coordinated services;
  ● strategies for the use of public, private and insurance funds;
  ● gaps in services;
  ● models for case management;
  ● the need for research and long-term rehabilitation;
  ● service delivery models, and
  ● ways to promote coordination and cost sharing.
Requires an interim report for the 1991 Session of the General Assembly, with the final report due by October 31, 1991 to provide data for the preparation of the Governor's 1992-94 budget recommendations; looks to public, private, voluntary and business sectors to maintain support while these steps are taken to finalization of the *Commission.*

NATIONAL DOWN SYNDROME CONGRESS
1800 Dempster Street
Park Ridge, IL 60068
TEL: 312-823-7550
Objectives: To provide parent support, advocacy, and public awareness programs for Down Syndrome.
Services: Operates through a committee structure which includes committees on adoption, awards, citizens, fundraising, education, media production and review, parent groups, awards, siblings, research and text-editing, and convention; advises and aids parents in the solutions of their special needs; coordinates efforts and activities of parents and others; operates a clearinghouse to gather and disseminate information for parents, other interested individuals and groups; mounts public awareness programs that are designed to promote a better understanding of Down Syndrome; maintains an all-volunteer board of directors consisting of educators, medical professionals, business men and women, housewives, government employees, adult Down Syndrome citizens and others; publishes the monthly *Down Syndrome News,* a bibliography, public awareness booklets, and other materials.
Publications: Down Syndrome News; Down Syndrome (booklet)
Founded: 1974

INDIVIDUAL PROGRAM PROFILES

GALLAUDET BOARD OF TRUSTEES
Gallaudet University
800 Florida Avenue, NE
Washington, DC 20002
TEL: 202-651-5488
FAX: 202-651-5489
Purpose: To better represent the student body of a major school for deaf students by appointing deaf members to the Board of Trustees.
Sponsor: Gallaudet University
Contact: Glen B. Anderson or Carol Padden
Description: In 1988, students with the *Deaf President Now Committee* won three of four demands through a massive student demonstration. They had called for resignations from the newly-appointed President, who was not deaf and did not know sign language, and the Board Chairman. They asked that they be replaced with deaf persons. Both resignations were tendered and accepted, and deaf persons have been placed in those positions. The fourth demand called for the board to have a majority of deaf members. In May 1989, the Board of Trustees for the federally-funded, federally-chartered institution named two deaf members to the 21-member board bringing the total number of deaf persons on the board to six. One of the new members is an associate professor in the Department of Communications at the University of California. The other is an author of several books, including the co-authored *Deaf in America: Voices from a Culture.* Since then the Board has adopted a resolution stating that it should be made up of individuals "of whom the majority should be deaf." As vacancies open, the Board seeks to replace members who have no hearing impairment with members who are deaf.

GRAFTON SCHOOL VOLUNTEER BOARD
Grafton School
P.O. Box 112
Berryville, VA 22601
TEL: 703-955-2400
Purpose: To respond to a child's need for special help.
Contact: Patricia Hockman
Description: Grafton School was founded thirty-one years ago by Ruth Birch, a native of Clarke County, Virginia, in response to a need across the community - assistance for children who need special help. At the time the public school systems were unable to address the needs of children who were having difficulty learning in the usual classroom setting. Grafton School's purpose was to "catch children up" and return them to their public schools.
Though Grafton has outgrown Mrs. Birch's kitchen, the goals for each of the children remains the same ... to provide them with the skills they need to participate in public school programs and, more importantly, to help them return home.
Today, Grafton serves 150 children annually in three program areas: Autism, Emotionally Disturbed/Learning Disabled, and Mentally Retarded/Emotionally Disturbed.
The main campus, located on Virginia Route 7 two miles east of Berryville, serves as Grafton's headquarters and home to 92 students. Grafton also operates four group homes for young adults in the Autism and Emotionally Disturbed/Learning Disabled Programs. Currently, the School has undergone a major expansion project that moved the Autism programs serving children ages 3 to 14 to a second major campus in Winchester. The expansion was completed in late fall of 1989.
Grafton is a private, nonprofit facility serving children from ages three to fifteen at admission. It is governed by a volunteer Board of Directors. Committees of the Board meet monthly.

LEADERSHIP DEVELOPMENT/BOARDS: HEALTH

NATIONAL/STATE ORGANIZATIONS

NATIONAL HEALTH SCREENING COUNCIL FOR VOLUNTEER ORGANIZATIONS*
9411 Connecticut Avenue, NW
Kensington, MD 20895
TEL: 301-942-6601
Objectives: To help communities who wish to provide comprehensive, low-cost Health Fairs to promote health and prevent disease.
Services: Assists communities throughout the United States, and in Puerto Rico, and the Virgin Islands in mounting a Health Fair based on the NHSCVO model, which:
- promotes health awareness and self-assessment through activities, demonstrations, and information;
- encourages participants to assume responsibility for health choices;
- provides free screening to promote health and prevent disease at one convenient time and place;
- detects potential disease at an early, treatable stage;
- reinforces need for continued adherence to prescribed treatments;
- refers participants to health care source for reevaluation if necessary;
- reassures and encourages participants to continue good health behaviors; and
- promotes effective use of community resources by encouraging cooperation among private, voluntary, and government sectors.

Designs its model program to include four components of equal importance to achieve the above objectives:
Learning Centers for Health which serve to motivate participants to become actively involved in learning more about health and how their life style choices relate to health; covers ten topics, which are addressed in the *Learning Center Manual,* and publishes a series of three booklets on health education needs (*Where? Regional Profile of Minorities, What? Outline of Minority Health Needs,* and *How? Addressing Minority Health Needs*).
Screening Tests which do not replace an examination by a physician, but provide information for intelligent referrals.
Summary and Referrals by volunteer health professionals who review test results, provide counseling, information and referrals, answer questions about the tests, and assist the individual in determining personal health goals.
Follow-Up in two parts: Part I: provide the participant with copies of test results within six weeks after the fair; Part II: call the participants with significant abnormalities to inquire about follow-up activity or the need for additional assistance or referral.
Tailors the basic model to different target populations when appropriate; receives "saturation promotion" through major media sponsors (radio, television and newspaper) as well as news coverage during the event, and health education programming to increase health awareness and participation in Health Fair Week Programs.
Receives funding entirely by the private sector, including major national sponsors in specific areas, such as:
- Health Education (Ciba-Geigy Corporation)
- Older Americans Health Fair Program (The Prudential Foundation)
- Minorities and Disability Health Fair Programs (Chevron USA)
- Student Health Fair Program (Atlantic Richfield Foundation)
- Health Fair Week Programs (Blue Cross/Blue Shield, Chevron USA, Gannett Company, and many others)

Enlists volunteer community groups and local media sponsors to organize and promote the local programs; publishes *Everybody Benefits* and other informative materials on the Health Fair program.

INDIVIDUAL PROGRAM PROFILES

SOUTHWEST VIRGINIA BLACK LUNG TASK FORCE
Virginia Department for Rights of the Disabled
James Monroe Building, 17th Floor
101 North 14th Street
Richmond, VA 23219
TEL: 804-225-2042
TOLL FREE: 800-552-3962 (Voice/TDD)
Purpose: To advocate for the rights of victims of black lung.
Description: This *Task Force* is charged with enhancing and improving services and protecting the rights of victims of black lung in southwestern Virginia. Its latest effort has been to locate a *Department of Labor Black Lung Processing Office* in the coalfields of Virginia. County, city and town governments in the area have passed resolutions supporting such an office.
The *Task Force* and the Ninth District Congressman are working together with the Congressman taking a key leadership role in the effort. An accumulated file of letters, petitions, and resolutions of support is kept current and used in meetings with area legislators and the Congressman to help develop additional strategies to bring the *Labor Department* office to the area.
Other areas addressed by the *Task Force* include a monitoring of case precedents such as a recent case that made it easier for miners to receive benefits. The *Task Force* moves quickly to get the word out to the miners after such favorable decisions have been made in the courts.

LEADERSHIP DEVELOPMENT/BOARDS: HOMELESS

NATIONAL/STATE ORGANIZATIONS

NATIONAL COALITION FOR THE HOMELESS
1439 Rhode Island Avenue, NW
Washington, DC 20005
TEL: 202-659-3310
New York office:
105 East 22nd Street
New York, NY 10010
212-460-8110
Objectives: To assure the fundamental rights of decent shelter and housing and adequate food for all.
Services: Works with a federation of individuals, agencies and organizations to secure the rights of the homeless to decent shelter and adequate food; operates under a board of directors with representation from some 50 cities and regions throughout the U.S.; provides legal counsel from professionals experienced in representing the rights of the homeless to assist local counsel in developing and enforcing the rights of the homeless; produces detailed reports on homelessness in targeted cities or states in an effort to increase public awareness and official response to the needs of the homeless; works with churches, synagogues, community and student groups, and city agencies as they organize local shelters and soup kitchens and come together to seek innovative ways to provide support for the homeless; organizes rallies in cities and other areas to bring together concerned

citizens, service providers and homeless people; devises plans for the future to prevent homelessness from growing, and to help homeless Americans find jobs, health care and homes; drafts legislation such as the *Homeless Persons' Survival Act,* which was introduced in Congress in 1986 (parts of the Act have been passed, but most remain in Committees); attacks problems in three distinct areas - emergency relief, preventive measures and long-term solutions; publishes a newsletter, special reports, news on homeless legislation, flyers, brochures, information packets and other materials.
Sponsor: Federation of individuals, agencies and organizations
Contact: Adraine Bennett (Washington, DC)
Publications: Not since the Great Depression...; Homelessness in America: A Summary; Housing Now!; Pending Homeless Legislation; Safety Network

NATIONAL COMMUNITY ORGANIZING PROJECT (NCOP)
National Coalition for the Homeless
1439 Rhode Island Avenue, NW
Washington, DC 20005
TEL: 202-659-3310
Objectives: To build new state homeless coalitions and strengthen existing state organizations.
Services: A National Community Organizing Project (NCOP) has been launched by the National Coalition for the Homeless. NCOP is sending trained community organizers to localities to work with local advocates and homeless people in the development of advocacy-oriented coalitions in their area. The goal is to build new state homeless coalitions where they do not exist, and to strengthen organizations already in place.
By early 1989, organizers were working in Florida and New England. After consulting with local advocates and homeless people, the Coalition targets additional areas and sends organizers to assist at the local level.
Also from the national level, services include volunteer recruitment, development and distribution of community organizing training materials, and fundraising for the NCOP. Initial kits and progress reports are made available to interested localities.
Sponsor: National Coalition for the Homeless
Contact: NCOP Coordinator
Publications: NCOP Information Packet

LEADERSHIP DEVELOPMENT/BOARDS: HOUSING

NATIONAL/STATE ORGANIZATIONS

NATIONAL HOUSING CONFERENCE
1126 Sixteenth Street, NW
Suite 211
Washington, DC 20036
TEL: 202-223-4844
Objectives: To bring together policy-makers (government officials, local housing officials, bankers), service "voices" (unions, builders), and consumers (senior citizens, minorities, church groups, and other consumers) on "decent shelter for all Americans."
Services: Mobilizes support for effective programs in housing and community development; publishes monthly newsletter and other periodicals, legislative bulletins and other materials; convenes monthly forums and annual meeting.
Publications: NHC Newsletter; Policy and Resolutions
Founded: 1931

INDIVIDUAL PROGRAM PROFILES

COMMUNITY HOUSING RESOURCES BOARD
Greater Hartford Association of Realtors
65 Kane Street
West Hartford, CT 06119
TEL: 203-236-2561
Purpose: To help real estate agents meet the objectives of an affirmative marketing agreement.
Contact: Brendan B. Grady, Board Member
Description: The *Community Housing Resources Board* - composed of Realtors, government officials and fair housing advocates - was established to monitor implementation of the *Voluntary Affirmative Marketing Agreement* developed and signed by Hartford-area Realtors in 1979. The agreement requires signers to institute office procedures to ensure that all prospective home buyers are treated equally regardless of race. It is a product of a 1975 agreement between the *U.S. Department of Housing and Urban Development (HUD)* and the *National Association of Realtors.*
Although it has an advisory rather than an enforcement role, the eight-member volunteer Board monitors the effectiveness of the fair housing agreement. When a May 1989 story in *The Courant,* the local newspaper, revealed that reporters posing as prospective home buyers had found discrimination at eight of 15 agencies in the Hartford area, the Board met and developed a five-step program addressing the article and other issues. Steps approved included (1) Urge the Realtors association to investigate the findings by *The Courant's* testers and report the results to the Board; and (2) Begin having quarterly meetings of Board members, Realtors and HUD officials to review the effectiveness of the voluntary agreement.
In a special vote, members voted 5-3 to request a list of the original signers of the agreement. Assenters hope that going back to the innovators who drew up such a lasting agreement may help as they try to determine why the reporters encountered discrimination in more than half of their test cases.
Founded: 1979

LEADERSHIP DEVELOPMENT/BOARDS: LAW ENFORCEMENT

NATIONAL/STATE ORGANIZATIONS

NATIONAL TOWN WATCH ASSOCIATION (*formerly National Association of Town Watch*)
PO Box 303
Wynnewood, PA 19096
TEL: 215-649-7055
Objectives: To improve the crime watch capabilities in local communities.
Services: Promotes, assists and encourages participation in community crime prevention by providing crime prevention groups with the opportunity to pool their resources, develop liaisons, and share crime prevention tips and information on programs in their areas; offers assistance through referrals, fundraising programs, promotional materials, regional affiliates, and training guides; sponsors annual *National Night Out,* a symbolic demonstration in which neighborhood residents across the country spend time in front of their homes to highlight crime prevention programs; presents award to the community with the best *National Night Out* program, as well as other awards for outstanding achievement in crime watch efforts; works with local, state and regional crime watch organizations and individuals working in cooperation with local law enforcement agencies and crime prevention officers; maintains an advisory council composed of law enforcement officers and citizen leaders from across the country; publishes and distributes a quarterly newsletter.
Sponsor: Crime Prevention Coalition
Publications: New Spirit
Founded: 1981

LEADERSHIP DEVELOPMENT/BOARDS: LITERACY

NATIONAL/STATE ORGANIZATIONS

COALITION FOR LITERACY
50 East Huron Street
Chicago, IL 60611
TEL: 312-944-6780
Objectives: To work toward the eradication of illiteracy by teaming volunteers with groups working in the field.
Services: Links existing groups working to eradicate illiteracy with new partners to the cause on local, state, and national levels; operates a three-year campaign to provide opportunity for service, support, and involvement; enlists assistance from television, radio and print public service advertising to alert the public to the magnitude of the issue and recruit volunteers from business, church, professional circles and other sources as help for local programs; appeals directly to local community leaders to provide volunteer tutors, financial help, committed professionals, and other services and assistance as needed; coalition members are:
● American Association of Adult and Continuing Education
● American Association of Advertising Agencies
● American Library Association
● B. Dalton Bookseller
● CONTACT Incorporated
● International Reading Association
● Laubach Literacy International
● Literacy Volunteers of America
● National Advisory Council on Adult Education
● National Commission on Libraries and Information Centers
● National Council of State Directors of Adult Education
Publishes information materials on illiteracy issues, and on its programs (request list).

INDIVIDUAL PROGRAM PROFILES

CHAMBER OF COMMERCE LITERACY COUNCIL
SEE BUSINESS/INDUSTRY INVOLVEMENT: LITERACY

OKLAHOMA CITY LITERACY COUNCIL
131 Dean A. McGee Avenue
Oklahoma City, OK 73102
TEL: 405-232-3780
Purpose: To teach functional illiterates to read and write.
Sponsor: Private donations only
Contact: President
Description: The Oklahoma City Literacy Council (OCLC) is an organization of men and women who have seen the need for teaching functional illiterates to read and write. A functional illiterate is one who cannot read well enough to fill out forms, read street signs, read want ads, or directions for cooking found on packages.
OCLC is a member of Laubach Literacy Action, Syracuse, New

York, and uses the Frank Laubach method of "each one teach one." OCLC is the source for the Skill Books, and Teacher Manuals published by the Laubach press. These are sold to the teachers and students for cost. Volunteers are the only staff and teachers at OCLC.

OCLC staff is composed of those men and women who have taken 10 hours of training to teach basic English and 15 hours of training to teach English to Speakers of Other Languages. They devote at least two hours a week to teaching a student, or students, how to read and write. The preferred time is two hours twice a week. Most of the Tutors hold twice-a-week sessions, and many have more than one student. Also there are a number of tutors who hold group sessions. The workshops are a vital part of the program. This is planned, set up and taught by the Tutor training committee. Many hours of dedication are required to prepare the materials, lesson plans, and to secure the place for the sessions. Also, five to eight of these tutors donate a day a week to staff the office. There is no paid staff.

Tutors can be anyone who is truly interested in his/her fellow man. No teaching experience is required. They are thoroughly trained in the workshops. Experienced tutors are always available for consultation. Tutors are recruited for TV spot announcements, news releases, and talks to civic clubs and church groups. The students are people "who have heard about you," or referrals from the Welfare Department, churches and schools. These students are screened, and their reading level, if they do read, is tested. OCLC is not equipped to handle mentally retarded persons or those with severe learning disabilities.

LEADERSHIP DEVELOPMENT/BOARDS: MILITARY

INDIVIDUAL PROGRAM PROFILES

VA VOLUNTARY SERVICES BOARD
SEE VOLUNTEERS: ARMED FORCES MEMBERS -
VETERANS

LEADERSHIP DEVELOPMENT/BOARDS: NATIONAL SERVICE

NATIONAL/STATE ORGANIZATIONS

PRESIDENT'S ADVISORY COMMITTEE ON POINTS OF LIGHT INITIATIVES FOUNDATION
SEE NATIONAL SERVICE/POINTS OF LIGHT INITIATIVE

LEADERSHIP DEVELOPMENT/BOARDS: OLDER PERSON

NATIONAL/STATE ORGANIZATIONS

NATIONAL COUNCIL ON THE AGING
600 Maryland Avenue, SW
West Wing 100
Washington, DC 20024
TEL: 202-479-1200
Objectives: To develop methods and resources for meeting the needs of the elderly through the efforts of both professionals and volunteers.
Services: Speaks on behalf of elderly before Congress, the Executive Branch, and other pertinent federal agencies; sponsors institutes and embarks on programs and projects including:

● **National Institute on Age, Work and Retirement** - provides training and technical assistance to industry, local groups, colleges and universities, and others to develop comprehensive retirement planning programs.
● **Senior Center Humanities Program** - involves older persons in discussion sessions designed to provide a forum for sharing interests and ideas.
● **National Center on Arts and the Aging** - acts as a clearinghouse for ideas and information among leaders in both the arts and the field of aging.
● **Housing Corporation** - fosters independent living arrangements in a positive environment for older people.
● **National Center on Rural Aging** - directs attention to and advocates the needs of the low-income elderly living in rural America; operates clearinghouse.
● **National Institute on Adult Day Care** - works with voluntary organizations and government agencies at all levels to improve day care services for aging persons who are disabled.

Also, NCOA maintains an extensive library, and produces numerous publications (some of which are annotated in the bibliography preceding the index in this book; write for complete list).
Publications: Perspectives on Aging; Literature on Aging
Founded: 1950

INDIVIDUAL PROGRAM PROFILES

VOLUNTEER SENIOR LEADERS
Retired Senior Volunteer Program
118 North Broadway
Suite 440
San Antonio, TX 78205
TEL: 512-222-0301
Purpose: To provide meaningful opportunities for senior citizens to take leadership roles in their communities through volunteer work.
Sponsor: Senior Community Services, Inc.
Contact: Nancy E. Cunningham
Description: In 1974, program leaders recognized that the program's limited funding would not allow the program to reach its potential growth level because of the expense of daily supervision of volunteer groups. Leaders decided to look to the groups themselves for volunteer supervisory assistance.
Today, all independent volunteer groups are operated under the supervision of a Volunteer Senior Leader. Groups are not started without a commitment from an individual to assume the leadership role.
After the commitment to supervise on a volunteer basis is made by the group member, staff work individually with the volunteer leader to help sharpen and provide a focus for his/her leadership

skills. When the volunteer leader is ready to take over his/her responsibilities, responsibility for a specific group of volunteers is transferred to the new leader. From that time on, the paid staff considers the volunteer leader a liaison to the volunteer group and deals primarily with the leader.

The Senior Volunteer Leaders have greatly enhanced and improved the management and supervision of the 2,500 volunteers in the program, and have enabled the nine professional staff members to extend their efforts and advance the program. Volunteer areas have been expanded and now include home repair, nutrition and recreation as well as the previous mailing, sewing and self-help projects. Another benefit to the program is that some of the projects are partially participant-funded.

It is expected that, with the Senior Volunteer Leaders effort so successful, the program will be able to meet new community needs in a more timely, efficient and thereby effective manner.
Founded: 1974

LEADERSHIP DEVELOPMENT/BOARDS: PARENTS

NATIONAL/STATE ORGANIZATIONS

CENTER FOR THE STUDY OF PARENT INVOLVEMENT
303 Van Buren Avenue
Oakland, CA 94610
TEL: 415-465-3507
Objectives: To bring together parent leaders and community workers to increase the leadership base for the community.
Services: Works with communities in planning, training, and evaluating parents as decisionmakers, volunteers, and advocates for their children and others; brings parents and community leaders together; offers workshops for teachers and human service workers on working with parents; collects and disseminates information on the role of parents as leaders in the community; publishes quarterly newsletter, a handbook, and other materials.
Publications: Apple Pie
Founded: 1981

PAR LEADERSHIP TRAINING FOUNDATION
464 Central Avenue
Northfield, IL 60093
TEL: 312-441-5617
Objectives: To include in its program the development of parent leaders in the inner city to help give them a voice in their communities.
Services: Sponsors workshop training sessions for parent leadership training in local communities on request of interested groups; produces television shows describing this and other programs of the Foundation; publishes *Workshops Procedures* and other materials.
Publications: Workshops Procedures

LEADERSHIP DEVELOPMENT/BOARDS: TENANTS/RESIDENTS

NATIONAL/STATE ORGANIZATIONS

CENTER FOR COMMUNITY CHANGE
1000 Wisconsin Avenue, NW
Washington, DC 20007
TEL: 202-342-0519
Objectives: To provide information and technical assistance to low income and minority community-based organizations to increase program effectiveness; to work with these groups in addressing national issues which have a direct impact on them and their constituencies.
Services: Works to make government more responsive to the needs of the poor; focuses on national issues dealing with poverty; helps community groups of urban and rural poor in developing plans, proposals, and strategies for obtaining federal funds; aids in tapping foundations and church sources for support; helps groups address management and organizational development questions such as board-staff relations, staff training, and fiscal management; assists in specialized areas such as redlining, crime prevention, job development, health care; publishes journal, newsletter, reports, guides, research papers and other materials; sponsors workshops and maintains a National Issues Committee.
Publications: Friday Report; Monitor; CD Citizen; Citizen Action Guide; Special Projects Report
Founded: 1968

CENTER FOR ORGANIZATIONAL AND COMMUNITY DEVELOPMENT
SEE COMMUNITY SERVICES: TENANTS/RESIDENTS

NATIONAL ASSOCIATION OF COMMUNITY LEADERSHIP ORGANIZATIONS
1454 Duke Street
Alexandria, VA 22314
TEL: 703-836-7904
Objectives: To improve the effectiveness of community leadership programs.
Services: Provides a forum for exchange of creative ideas concerning community leadership; promotes exciting community leadership programs; helps to establish new programs nationwide; provides training, publications, and volunteer experts to community leadership organizations; maintains information on relevant statistics; presents awards for outstanding achievements; publishes a newsletter, a brochure, and a book on how to develop a community leadership organization.
Sponsor: American Chamber of Commerce Executives
Publications: NACLO Newsletter; How to Develop a Community Leadership Organization
Founded: 1979

NEIGHBORHOODS USA (*formerly National Conference on Neighborhood Concerns*)
4643 Amesborough
Dayton, OH 45420
TEL: 513-222-2889
Objectives: To build and strengthen the nation's neighborhoods through working partnerships.
Services: Works with neighborhood representatives, local government staff, elected officials, technical assistance providers, and practitioners in the public and private sectors to form working partnerships with the purpose of building and strengthening the nation's neighborhoods; conducts conferences on neighborhood

concerns and related programs that promote educational, social, and cultural objectives for neighborhood residents; maintains a speakers' bureau and a *National Neighborhood of the Year* Committee, which bestows an annual award; publishes a newsletter and annual conference proceedings; enables comprehensive exhibits and presentations by neighborhood representatives from across the country at its annual conference in May of each year.
Publications: NUSA Newsletter; NUSA Conference Proceedings
Founded: 1975

TRAINING PROGRAMS

VISION, PLANNING & PARTNERSHIP IN NEIGHBORHOOD ORGANIZING
SEE TRAINING/CONFERENCES/TEACHING: CIVIC AFFAIRS

INDIVIDUAL PROGRAM PROFILES

LOUDOUN HOUSE
SEE VOLUNTEERS: SELF-HELP

LEADERSHIP DEVELOPMENT/BOARDS: TRANSPORTATION

NATIONAL/STATE ORGANIZATIONS

NATIONAL ASSOCIATION OF WOMEN HIGHWAY SAFETY LEADERS
3008 North 16th Drive
Phoenix, AZ 85015
TEL: 602-264-9327
Objectives: To work with communities to help improve safety on highways, roads and streets.
Services: Supports and implements the National Highway Safety Standards in communities, states and the nation; encourages each political subdivision to assume its responsibility for highway safety; aims at more uniformity in traffic safety programs and regulations within the 50 states, the District of Columbia, and Puerto Rico; maintains regional offices in a number of states (request list); publishes quarterly newsletters for national, regional and state levels, and other materials
Publications: President's Newsletter; Regional Newsletter; NAWHSL Directory; Tempest
Founded: 1967

LEADERSHIP DEVELOPMENT/BOARDS: WELFARE REFORM

NATIONAL/STATE ORGANIZATIONS

ASSOCIATION OF COMMUNITY ORGANIZATIONS FOR REFORM NOW (ACORN)
SEE VOLUNTEERS: SELF-HELP

PROJECT VOLUNTEER
SEE VOLUNTEERS: SELF-HELP

NATIONAL SERVICE/POINTS OF LIGHT INITIATIVE

NATIONAL/STATE ORGANIZATIONS

POINTS OF LIGHT INITIATIVE
US/White House - Office of National Service
Old Executive Office Building
Room 100
Washington, DC 20500
TEL: 456-6266
FAX: 202-456-2461
Objectives: To engage all individuals, groups and organizations in America in direct and consequential action to solve community problems.
Services: Seeks to make community service central to the life and work of every individual, group and organization in America; issues a challenge to individuals and groups across the country to "take action, not only because it is morally right, but because America's continued economic, political and military strength and global competitiveness demand it;" maintains that there are natural leaders in every community, and they must be identified and developed, assisted and rewarded for leading successful community problem-solving initiatives; presents a mission statement that addresses *solving* the nation's most critical social problems; calls on each individual, group and organization to begin to play a direct and consequential role in community problem solving; proposes ways capabilities of communities can be pooled and channeled to attack comprehensively the multiple problems of individuals in need.
Administers the *Points of Light Initiative Foundation,* which will seek $25 million annually in Congressional funding and an equal or higher amount from private sources; recognizes a daily *Point of Light,* which is an initiative, group, organization or individual across the country who shares the President's commitment; works through the White House Office of National Service to keep abreast of community service policy and strategy, and communicate the mission of the *Points of Light Initiative.*
Maintains that every American individual, group and organization has an innate desire to be a point of light, and that the multiplication and magnification of *points of light* across the nation must be America's mission; publishes briefing papers describing in detail the *Points of Light Initiative.*
On November 22, 1989, the President recognized the first *Point of Light* (Memphis Commercial Appeal, a Tennessee newspaper), and on March 26, 1990, the 100 mark was reached when he recognized Barbara Tomblinson of Missouri. Listed below are *The First One Hundred Points of Light* and their areas of service (listed

alphabetically, not chronologically, by organization and individual):
ORGANIZATIONS/GROUPS/BUSINESS/INDUSTRY:
Acres Home War on Drugs, TX (substance abuse)
ActionAIDS, PA (AIDS)
Adopt-A-School, FL (education)
Anchorage Neighborhood Housing Services, AK (housing)
Black Hills Regional Ski for Light (handicapped)
Building & Construction Trades Council of Alameda County, CA (housing)
Cheyenne Botanic Gardens, WY (handicapped/elderly/offenders)
Cincinnati Youth Collaborative, OH (education)
Drop-A-Dime, MA (crime prevention)
Duke Power Company, NC (education)
Foster Care Youth Independence Project, NY (life skills)
Friends, ND (psychosocial support)
G.D. Searle & Company, IL (health)
Gallia Academy High School Key Club, OH (community service)
Get Involved Before Your Kids Do, WI (substance abuse)
Glaxo, Inc., NC (community service)
GlenCastle Project, GA (housing)
Green, Phyllis Lydia and her 6th Graders, IA (community service)
Higher Achievement Program, DC (education)
Holy Rosary Family Center, OH (homeless)
Jefferson County Community Center, CO (handicapped)
Lawrence Eagle Tribute, MA (volunteer recognition)
Little Vikings Program, TX (education)
Mary's House, MD (elderly)
Memphis Commercial Appeal, TN (volunteer recognition)
Men on the Move's ESTEEM, GA (role models)
(MOVE) Mobilization of Volunteer Effort, VT (community service)
Neil J. Houston House, MD (offenders)
Orangeburg School District Five, SC (education)
Page Attacks Trash, AZ (beautification)
PALS (Principle of the Alphabet Literacy System) Energy Corporation, LA (literacy)
Pioneer Human Services, WA (substance abuse/nutrition)
Project Aware, MS (substance abuse)
Project Chesed (community service)
Project Good Turn, MT (beautification)
REACH, Inc., MI (substance abuse/housing)
St. Vincent De Paul-Joan Kroc Center, CA (homeless)
Salvation Army Hope Center, MO (child abuse)
Save The Bay, RI (environment)

Self Enhancement, Inc, OR (substance abuse)
Senior Center Foster Grandparents Program, VA (education)
Senior Health & Peer Counseling Center, CA (health/mental health)
Seniors Serving Schools Program, KS (education)
The Shoulder, TX (substance abuse)
South San Jose Neighborhood Association, NM (crime prevention)
South Seattle Crime Prevention Council, WA (crime prevention)
Stop The Violence Movement, WI (crime prevention)
Third Grade Class of Diane Wurst, NE (elderly)
Town of Hope, NM (community services)
Town of Yoncalla, OR (community services)
The Volunteer Project, CA (volunteer recruitment)
VYTAL (Volunteer Youth Training and Ledership), PA (community service)
WMOR-TV, NJ (education)
Youth Aware, CA (substance abuse)
INDIVIDUALS:
Toni Allee, VA (families)
Jesse Sanchez Berain, ID (migrant workers)
Pamela Calhoun, NV (energy)
Edward Castor, IN (literacy)
Herbert John Chamberlain, NY (handicapped)
Tero Mauldin Coleman, DC (elderly)
Daniel Emanuel Conrad, MN (community services)
Robert & Jacquelyn Corrigan, NH (education)
Katherine Donihi, FL (handicapped)
Kelley Renee Edwards, GA (substance abuse)
Sheila Fitzpatrick, PA (health)
Joseph A.A. Fournier, GA (psychosocial support)
Stephanie Ann Fox, DE (community services)
Julius Glass, NY (handicapped)
Julia Goldstein, MO (education)
Daniel James Greene, KY (education)
William & Sandra Hale, OK (health)
Aja Dyani Henderson, LA (literacy)
Daisy Patricia Hitchcock, KY (community services)
Pauline Hord, TN (literacy)
Carolyn Lantz Jackson, DE (handicapped)
Sophia Jeffery (housing/crime prevention)
Marsha Goggans Johnson, OH (psychosocial support)
William Warner Johnson, DC (youth entrepreneurship)
Ewing Marion Kauffman, MO (education/substance abuse)
Beth, Kerry & Megan Kerry, MI (handicapped)
Eugene Lang, NY (education)
Edith Lewis, TX (homeless youth)
The Reverend Michael Wayne Lewis, FL (boarder babies)
Robert Low, HI (homeless youth)
Richard Andrew McDonough, AZ (homeless)
Marilyn Millard Murphy, CT (volunteer recruitment)
Michael Carlton Noyes, ME (psychosocial support)
Helen VerDuin Palit, NY (nutrition)
Jack L. Powell, MD (families)
Stacy Lynn Priest, AR (children/youth)
George Simmons, UT (arts/cultural enrichment)
Jonathan Soderstrom, TN (psychosocial support)
Joan Stairs & Juanita Suggs, IN (homeless)
Lou & Lola Stouffer, WV (psychosocial support)
Barbara Tomblinson, MO (homeless)
Antonio Valle, Jr., CA (community services)
Alan Waters, AL (community services)
Shahid Samad Watson, NJ (substance abuse)
Zenobia White, IA (psychosocial support)
Joseph Ziskovski, MN (environment).
Provides additional information on projects and services of honorees on request.
Contact: Clark Kent Ervin
Publications: Points of Light Initiative: Community Service/National Policy; President's New Leadership Structures/Points of Light; A Thousand Points of Light: The First One Hundred

PRESIDENT'S ADVISORY COMMITTEE ON POINTS OF LIGHT INITIATIVES FOUNDATION
US/White House - Office of National Service
Old Executive Office Building
Room 100
Washington, DC 20500
TEL: 202-456-6266
FAX: 202-456-2461
Objectives: To make recommendations to the President on the *Points of Light Initiative Foundation.*
Services: Advises the President on the *Points of Light Initiative Foundation,* which was created to support the *Points of Light Initiative* program; recommends both initial and long-term procedures to allow the President sufficient flexibility to pursue his plans for the *Foundation,* including:
- Initially incorporate the *Foundation* as a nonprofit entity so as to begin as soon as possible, pending enactment of authorizing legislation;
- Ultimately structure the *Foundation* and a government/nonprofit corporation to maximize the engagement of all individuals and institutions in voluntary and community service;
- Develop a Board of Directors for the *Foundation* of 19-25 members;
- Encourage the *Foundation* to use loaned staff, with any permanent staff made exempt from civil service requirements;
- Make *Foundation* subject to Congressional and Executive oversight procedures once bills have been enacted and federal funds are received;
- Maintain an active relationship with the Executive Branch with the President serving as Honorary Chairman;
- Authorize the Board to make expenditures to accomplish stated purposes;
- Encourage the *Foundation* to seek resources from private as well as public sources.

Supports *ServNet,* a peer-to-peer action group network to aid new community initiatives, and *ServLink,* a national database and electronic bulletin board to permit people nationwide to learn of volunteer opportunities or successful program approaches; encourages the *Foundation's* proposed recognition and awards program for outstanding community service leaders, participants and initiatives; supports planned workshops and symposia for national and local participation, and the publication of written materials and production of video tapes for distribution by the *Foundation.*
Contact: Committee Chairperson
Founded: 1989

US/WHITE HOUSE - OFFICE OF NATIONAL SERVICE
Old Executive Office Building
Room 100
Washington, DC 20500
TEL: 202-456-6266
FAX: 202-456-2461
Objectives: To solve our most critical social ills through the engagement of each individual and institution in America in community problem solving.
Services: Provides talking points and speech material on community service to leaders in public and private sectors; identifies sites for visits to promote community service by leaders in the public and private sectors; identifies people, institutions and initiatives that are worthy of recognition for their outstanding work in the field of community service; proposes policy reforms to complement and strengthen a nationwide community service movement; identifies key sector leaders, determines their unique institutional resources and asks in the name of the President that those resources be devoted to the community service movement; develops and refines criteria by which to evaluate exemplary community services initiatives. Performs specific functions for the

President, including:
- Advising the President on community service policy and strategy;
- Communicating the President's community service strategy and the role that every individual, group and organization in America can play in the evolving community service movement;
- Proposing ways for the President and other government officials to highlight outstanding community service leaders and initiatives, so as to honor them and to encourage others to follow their example (*Daily Points of Light,* speeches, statements, and site -visits);
- Participating in the solution of problems like drug abuse, education reform and others whose solution is largely dependent on community action; and
- Recommending government policy reforms in such areas as tort law and the tax code in order to remove impediments to community service.

Through the *Points of Light Initiative Foundation,* encourages each individual and institution in America to assume responsibiliity for solving social problems in their own community; through the *Foundation,* links potential servers with community needs; through the *Foundation,* discovers and encourages new leaders in the field of community service; publishes briefing papers and other materials describing in greater detail the objectives and plans of the *Office of National Service* and the *Points of Light Initiative Foundation.*
Sponsor: US/White House
Contact: Clark Kent Ervin
Publications: National Service Briefing Paper
Founded: 1989

INDIVIDUAL PROGRAM PROFILES

C.V. STARR NATIONAL SERVICE FELLOWSHIP PROGRAM
Brown University
25 George Street
PO Box 1974
Providence, RI 02912
TEL: 401-863-2338
Purpose: To provide special fellowships encouraging student participation in voluntary public service.
Contact: Peter Hocking
Description: To foster a sense of community obligation, *Brown University,* with a gift from the *C.V. Starr Foundation,* has established a program of special fellowships encouraging student participation in voluntary public service. The presence of students who have devoted themselves to a period of service will enrich the Brown community and awaken a deeper awareness of the moral relationship between university education and societal obligation. *Starr Fellows* receive $1,000 toward their educational expenses at *Brown.* Entering first year students, including deferred matriculants, are encouraged to apply if they have participated in community service work full time for a year, or its equivalent, for little or no pay during their high school years, or during the year in which admission was deferred.

The service may take place in theU.S. or a foreign country; it must normally have occurred within three years of application for the award. Candidates must submit with their applications an essay that reflects evidence of initiative, personal growth, and a deepended understanding of an identified social issue, and a letter of recommendation. Applications are individually reviewed by the *Starr Fellowship Committee* which consists of faculty, students and staff.

All applicants to Brown University are eligible for the Starr Award. Awardees in the classes of 1990, 1991 and 1993 include a student who worked for a year with mentally handicapped adults in Innisfree, a student who spent a summer with the *Community for Creative Non-Violence,* a student who co-chaired a community service program at *Phillips Academy* in Massachusetts which involved over 200 student volunteers, and a student who spent a year with a Catholic missionary society on the north coast of Peru.

NATIONAL YOUTH SERVICE DAY 1990
Youth Service America
1310 F Street, NW
Suite 900
Washington, DC 20004
TEL: 202-783-8855
Purpose: To document and publicize youth volunteer activities in a national celebration.
Contact: Ann Maura Connelly, Special Projects Coordinator
Description: The first *National Youth Service Day* is a cooperative effort of Youth Service America, COOL (College Outreach Opportunity League), United States Conference of Mayors, The Jefferson Awards, and *Weekly Reader.* Its purpose is to celebrate youth service that goes on across the country every day.

Activities on *National Youth Service Day* (April 27, 1990 was the first) were documented and publicized through photography, newspapers, radio, television and other media. This special day gives the people of the nation a chance to recognize the commitment of young people who are active and involved in addressing the issues of hunger, homelessness, health, drug and alcohol education, the environment, literacy and community development.

The *Day* presented a snapshot of the programs, the people and the support systems that enable thousands of young people to participate in the community every day. Today's young people often are accused of being apathetic or uncaring. This documentation of the promise, commitment and contribution of a generation will help to explode that myth.

Given the enthusiasm and support for the first *National Youth Service Day,* it is expected that this event will continue as an annual activity.

PRIVATE SECTOR INITIATIVES OFFICES

NATIONAL/STATE ORGANIZATIONS

GOVERNOR'S ADVISORY COMMITTEE ON PRIVATE/PUBLIC VOLUNTEER PARTNERSHIPS/NJ
New Jersey Office of Volunteerism
101 South Broad Street
Fourth Floor, CN 800
Trenton, NJ 08625-0800
TEL: 609-292-9069
Objectives: To represent the public, private and independent sectors' concerns in volunteerism.
Services: Operates as a Committee from the community appointed by the Governor to support and advise the New Jersey Office of Volunteerism in its programming and assure that the Office's performance reflects the needs of the state. It is charged with representing concerns of all sectors - public, private, and independent - in matters pertaining to volunteerism and public/private partnerships. Advisory Committee Goals are:
- To advise and prioritize the most important community needs and to identify the resources to meet those needs through volunteerism and public/private support.
- To recognize and rewqrd successful examples of private initiatives and community partnerships and to provide those models to other communities facing similar challenges.
- To identify regulatory and statutory impediments to volunteer activity and to explore and suggest legislative solutions to incrase volunteerism.
- To encourage involvement of the private sector through partnerships and the contribution of resources (time, funds and efforts); strengthening and meeting the needs of New Jersey's communities.

Members come from the State's departments of Labor; Law & Public Safety; Commerce, Energy and Economic Development; Community Affairs; Human Services, and others, and from the American Cancer Society, Community Accountants for the Public Interest; Center for Non-Profits; Focus on Literacy; A.T.&T.; Black United Fund, Voluntary Action Center of Monmouth County; New Jersey Association of Directors of Volunteer Services; corporations, universities, and others. A complete list of the 36 members is available from the *Governor's Office on Volunteerism.*

US/ADMINISTRATION: THE PRESIDENT'S PRIVATE SECTOR INITIATIVES PROGRAM
US/White House
1600 Pennsylvania Avenue, NW
Washington, DC 20500
TEL: 202-456-6266
Objectives: To create cooperative approaches between public and private sectors to meet community needs - *public/private partnerships.*
Services: Operates as a dual program with an initial year-long phase being a *Task Force on Private Sector Initiatives* and a permanent office, the *White House Office on Private Sector Initiatives,* mandated to carry out the recommendations of the *Task Force.*
Task Force on Private Sector Initiatives - consisted of 44 members representing corporations, organizations, agencies and other groups in both public and private sectors (led by the President of *Armco, Inc.)* and served for one year (1982) as a catalytic agent to help chart direction, provide impetus, and pass its recommendations on to the President to help guide further *Private Sector Initiatives (PSI)* activity; included in its work before disbanding:
- Gathering of program information on some 2500 local community and corporate volunteer efforts in cooperation with *DATA/NET* databases, and the *Partnership Data Line.*
- Communication and dialogue with Congress on PSI concept.
- Coverage of PSI highlights by the President in State-of-the-Union messages, and in several speeches to public and private groups.
- Meeting with *National Governors Association* to encourage statewide PSI Task Forces.
- Establishment of 11 Task Force subcommittees; meeting on subcommittee reports, combined with a press conference; distribution of over 2,000 press kits.
- Presentations to the full *Cabinet* by the Chairman of the Task Force.
- Development of White House/ACTION Voluntarism Workshop series (San Francisco, New Orleans, Chicago, and Philadelphia).
- Provided briefings for: agency heads, 120 religious leaders, 150 national service groups, Congressional staff, Cabinet wives, and State, local, and county executives.
- Development of the *U.S. Conference of Mayors/ARCO Partnership Conference,* the *President's Volunteer Awards Program,* and the *National Volunteer Week Proclamation.*

- Arrangment with the *Advertising Council* to announce the Council's 1982 theme: *Volunteerism.*
- Administration of an *International Conference on Public/Private Partnerships,* and a *Workshop on Corporate Community Involvement* with 130 corporate executives.
- Creation of *Statewide Private Sector Initiatives Task Forces* in most states.

Worked with numerous other national groups such as the *National Health Care Screening Council for Voluntary Organizations,* corporations such as *Jones & Laughlin Steel Corporation,* and *Time, Incorporated,* media centers such as *KGAN-TV* in Iowa, small businesses such as the *Wallpaper Factory Outlet* in Baltimore, local programs such as the *Boys' Club of St. Louis,* and many other groups representing various aspects of business and nonprofit communities, and all levels of government; presented its recommendations to the President in March 1983 based on its year of operation, which are reflected below in the work of the *White House Office on Private Sector Initiatives.*

The **Office of Private Sector Initiatives** - serves as government's focal point for promoting increased private sector activity; works toward the following objectives:

- Increase public awareness of the importance of public/private partnerships by drawing attention to successful private sector initiatives.
- Develop communications networks that will provide a market for social services that will connect new service organizations with those in need.
- Remove barriers to the development of effective social service programs that are administered by private organizations and individuals.
- Strengthen the professional resources of the private sector.

Concentrates efforts of the Office on areas of critical national importance in the post-recession economy by giving priority to:

- achieving full employment and improving economic productivity;
- building an educational resource; and
- conserving our family and community resources.

Works with a 39-member *Advisory Council on Private Sector Initiatives* composed of:

- Nine members from the public sector, including the Secretaries of Agriculture, Commerce, Housing and Urban Development, Health and Human Services, Labor, Education, and Transportation, the Director of ACTION, and the White House Deputy Chief of Staff; and
- Thirty members from private life.

Maintains the 39-member, all-volunteer Council to advise the President with respect to the objectives and conduct of private sector initiative policies, including methods of increasing public awareness of the importance of public/private partnerships; removing barriers to development of effective social service programs which are administered by private organizations; and strengthening the professional resources of the private social service sector, and thus influencing the challenges of the future, such as the priority social and economic themes of the Office. As shown in the outline above, these themes are concerned with the nation's families and communities in relation to preservation of existing resources, the need to identify and address the problem of the nation's education system, and the urgency of unemployment and other economic conditions.

Operates a *Video Dataline.* which is a collection of examples of community service efforts on videotape that can be used as models for television stations, associations, corporations and schools; continually seeks copies of videotapes of community service programs which have been aired by television stations at all levels, and from corporate and other sources.

Provide fact sheets on program concerns of the Administration, including:

- Child Care: Employer Options to Support Working Families - an Overview
- Adopt-A-School

- Job-A-Thons
- Summer Youth Employment
- Job Search Assistance

Publishes a portfolio, *The White House Office of Private Sector Initiatives,* which contains a list of members of the *President's Advisory Council on Private Sector Initiatives,* press releases on progress, reprints of clippings which report on its work, an overall mission statement of the Office, a handbook for policymakers, *Volunteers: A Valuable Resource* (see publications section), and other information.
Publications: Volunteers: A Valuable Resource

TRAINING PROGRAMS

STATEWIDE LEADERSHIP SYMPOSIUM: WORKING TOGETHER TO MAKE VISIONS REALITIES
Governor's Office of Voluntary Action/IL
100 West Randolph
16th Floor
Chicago, IL 60601
TEL: 312-814-2789 (GOV); 312-727-9411 (IL Bell)
FAX: 312-781-7260 (IL Bell)
Contact: Richard H. Brown, Illinois Bell, Co-Chairman
Description: This symposium was developed to discuss and explore ways in which the public and private sectors can work together to ensure a productive future for all Illinois young people, particulary those graduating from high school in the 1990s. The focus of the symposium is a panel discussion featuring leaders of business, government and not-for-profit organizations. A highlight is the presentatin by a distinguished scholar in the field of youth education and motivation from the Yale University Department of Psychiatry.
The theme and challenge of the event is found in a quote by the Governor, "How can we make our endeavors more cohesive... spur public and private action to meet unmet needs and broaden public/private cooperation in combatting the dangers threatening our children?" Content includes:

- "The Class of '99: The Challenges Ahead" (a presentation by the Governor);
- A Reactor Panel to the Governor's message;
- Small group discussions, led by business, government and not-for-profit leaders;
- Presentation by a member of the Yale University faculty; and
- Reports from the small group discussion leaders.

Throughout the day, symposium participants are given the opportunity to gather in small groups to share ideas and strategies. Facilitators and sponsors include the *United Way of Illinois, Illinois Bell, Illinois Chamber of Commerce, Pittway Corporation, Bethel New Life, McKinley Educational Services, Jackson Communications Management,* and others. The symposium was developed in cooperation with the *State Educational Policy Seminar.*

PRIVATE SECTOR INITIATIVES OFFICES: COMMERCE

NATIONAL/STATE ORGANIZATIONS

US/DOC - PRIVATE SECTOR INITIATIVES PROGRAM
Office of the Secretary
14th St. between E & Constitution
Washington, DC 20230
TEL: 202-337-2000

Objectives: To identify and pursue incentive programs, partnerships, and services that might best be performed by the private sector.

Services: Provides direct administrative and financial support for private sector initiatives through offices including those listed below:

Bureau of the Census which participates in a joint Census/locality effort to provide social, demographic and economic data that cannot be obtained from other census data products, but is needed as backup for support activities such as grant and loan requests to solve community problems; develops monographs with funding from three foundations (Ford, Russell Sage and Alfred A. Sloan); operates Federal-State cooperative *State Data Centres* in most states.

Patent and Trademark Office which is pursuing the possibility of private sector funding for training courses and field trips to afford patent examiners a better understanding of the practical consequences of their work, to help encourage greater participation by the private sector in the patent and trademark systems.

National Technical Information Service which is the central source for sale to the public of government information needed by business for innovation and decision-making (cost-recovery comes from sales income, not the taxpayer).

National Telecommunications and Information Administration which conducts analyses of the issue of government competition with the private sector in this field, and works on options and alternatives to solve problems in this area.

Minority Business Development Agency which operates Business Development Centers and maintains a *Presidential Initiative on Minority Enterprise* program to provide assistance and information and make recommendations on minority participation in the free enterprise system.

National Oceanic & Atmospheric Administration which relies heavily on volunteers in various aspects of its program such as tornado spotters, river gauge readers in flood-prone areas, and other types of observation tasks critical to its weather forecasting services; mounts objectives for *privatization* in areas of the *Landset* earth satellite program and selected weather forecast programs such as fruit frost prediction (also studying user fee and private sector takeover options for the *National Weather Service).*

Sponsor: US/DoC - Department of Commerce

PRIVATE SECTOR INITIATIVES OFFICES: DEFENSE

NATIONAL/STATE ORGANIZATIONS

US/DOD - PRIVATE SECTOR INITIATIVES PROGRAM
ASD (MRA&L) EA
The Pentagon, 3D968
Washington, DC 20301
TEL: 202-695-1800

Objectives: To help create cooperative public-private partnerships to meet community needs.

Services: Designates a principal Private Sector Initiatives (PSI) contact, with a support staff including the Assistant Secretary of Defense for *Manpower Reserve Affairs and Logistics (MRA&L)* and a Director for *Economic Adjustment (EA)* who also serves as an alternate; mainains an intra-departmental working group, chaired by EA, to coordinate PSI activities among the Office of the Secretary of Defense and the three military departments. Convenes meetings of the group to coordinate preparation of reports to the *White House Office of Private Sector Initiatives;* involves other DoD components on an ad hoc basis; conducts

special briefings for all MRA&L components due to their wide-ranging relationships with communities, and all other participating DoD components, to increase understanding of the PSI program and DoD's role in it, and to stimulate wide participation.

Works with the *Office of the Chairman of the Joint Chiefs of Staff (JCS)* to assure a high level of participation by military commanders, joining with them in weekly *Armed Forces Policy Council* meetings (meetings of top OSD officials and the Chiefs and JCS Chairman); provides staff support through EA, augmented through coordination with staff in all participating organizational components; works toward the objectives listed below:

Increasing Private Sector Participation - to provide profit incentives and remove impediments through programs such as the *A-76 Commercial Activities Program* (promoting greater reliance on the private sector for defense goods/services) and technical assistance for private sector participation in DoD procurement (promoting an increase in business participation and competition in DoD contracting activities).

Forming Public-Private Partnerships - to play a major role in all kinds of community activities through direct linkages to organizations in both the public and private sectors, finding ways to increase the contributions that DoD resources are already making to communities, such as:

- joint military-civilian use of defense installations;
- support of the development of American Indian-owned enterprises and expansion of job opportunities for Indians;
- cooperative efforts with business/industry to find ways to expand job opportunities at the local level;
- sponsorship of a national health fair program;
- sponsorship of a partnerships in education program; and
- sponsorship of a *National Year of Volunteerism* program.

Increasing Employee Volunteer Activity - to develop a headquarters program to increase volunteer involvement by both civilian and military DoD personnel, working with the military command structure across the country, and to promote the *National Year of Volunteerism.*

Promoting the Program - to devise a comprehensive formal promotional program to reach audiences internal and external to DoD by:

- using a full range of media
- disseminating printed information about the PSI program
- using models of private initiatives and public-private partnerships
- using models of individual and organizational achievements
- providing opportunities for participation

Involves a loaned executive for one year from the *President's Executive Interchange Program* (a public-private program itself), *OSD Public Affairs,* and the *Defense Audiovisual Agency* to develop a proposed program for presentation to the *Intra-Departmental PSI Working Group* and the Chiefs of the military departments for review (see publications section on *DoD Action Plan for Increased Voluntarism* and *Volunteerism,* two reports addressing DoD's current and projected activities).

Sponsor: US/DoD - Department of Defense

PRIVATE SECTOR INITIATIVES OFFICES: EDUCATION

NATIONAL/STATE ORGANIZATIONS

PRIVATE SECTOR INITIATIVES PROGRAM
US/DEd - Office of the Secretary
Room 4132
Washington, DC 20202
TEL: 202-732-3860
Objectives: To promote business and community involvement in the schools through private sector initiatives and volunteerism.
Services: Operates through a Staff Director in the Secretary's Office, who is assigned to work with the *White House Office of National Service,* and representatives of education and business. Among its activities, the *Office:*
- Instructs regional offices to play a major role in dealing with the private sector
- Establishes liaisons with other federal agencies including *ACTION, HUD, HHS, Justice, Commerce, Labor, Defense, and Veterans' Administration* to avoid duplication through overlapping interests in areas that affect private sector initiatives.
- Involves external advisors from the profitmaking sector, the non-profit private sector, and from public and non-profit educational systems at elementary, secondary, and postsecondary levels.
Maintains other activities, including the dual-purpose one of informal data gathering to:
- develop some understanding of the breadth of private sector involvement with education; and
- raise awareness of Department of Education staff members relative to the subject.
Mounts projects to address the above goals such as Volunteer Week activities, briefings and in-service activities to increase the competence of key staff to deal with problems of private sector relations, solicitation of information about exemplary programs throughout the country, attendance at meetings around the country (such as *National Association of Partners in Education, PLUS,* business groups).
Conducts briefings on volunteerism for visiting groups such as women's groups, school administrator organizations, chamber of commerce groups, and school headmaster groups from Germany and England.
Plans to expand the above activities to provide a bank of support for the Education community in private sector initiatives; includes in the top priorities:
- Data Gathering
- Conferences
- Development of Existing Exemplary Programs
- Privatization
- Impediments and Incentives
Considers the above activities "the beginning of our efforts" noting that Education is the number one beneficiary of corporate philanthropy and foundation philanthropy, and that more people do volunteer work in education than in any other field except religion; plans to redirect the activities of the federal education staff to justify this type of support from the volunteer and voluntary community.
Sponsor: US/DEd - Department of Education
Contact: Dave Frengel
Founded: 1981

PRIVATE SECTOR INITIATIVES OFFICES: GSA

NATIONAL/STATE ORGANIZATIONS

US/GSA - PRIVATE SECTOR INITIATIVES
F Street between 18th & 19th, NW
Washington, DC 20405
TEL: 202-566-1212
Objectives: To utilize private sector assistance to expose key management officials in GSA to the *entrepreneural can-do spirit* with the goal of upgrading the business practices of GSA.
Services: Works with the private sector on a number of cooperative programs, four of which are highlighted below:
GSA Advisory Board composed of top executives of the nation's corporations and organizations, which provides assistance through the following objectives:
- To review and recommend major policy proposals.
- To advise and counsel on GSA priorities.
- To provide technical review.
- To provide external support.
- To provide Executive Loan Program resources.
Patterns the *GSA Advisory Board* after boards of directors in the private sector; convenes the Board six to eight times a year; provides briefing papers and formal proposals for the Board's recommendation prior to testimony on the papers and proposals before Congressional committees; asks Board members to testify at their options.
Future plans for the Advisory Board include the review of GSA construction and space utilization practices, and further development of the *GSA Executive Loan Program* and *Industry Resources Program,* both described below.
GSA Executive Loan Program formed to provide technical support and private sector perspective on specific GSA problems; includes private sector participants from companies of the Advisory Board members and other organizations who spend substantial amounts of time at GSA, joining GSA employees on project teams led by GSA's *Management Improvement Office.* Future plans include a number of prospective projects with short-term impact (60 to 120 days) covering telecommunications, employee travel, traffic management, and other areas (a joint *Telecommunications Task Force* is in place).
Industry Resources Program provides full-time and part-time assignments for up to two years in GSA; involves full-time designees, who are private sector executives, to supplement staff by giving technical and managerial expertise not presently available within the agency; involves part-time designees from a bank of retirees whose experience can relieve the agency in areas where temporary workload requirements exceed the availability of trained internal resources.
GSA Business Day is a one-day seminar with a series of workshops to enable GSA and the private sector to share innovative business practices, to motivate GSA staff to become more active in their day-to-day responsibilities by making *business* decisions, and to develop within GSA a spirit of *entrepreneurship.*
Other Initiatives include outleasing, Federal supply service with customer-agency interface (based on *American Express Company* support), and warehousing, with other initiatives considered as situations dictate.
Sponsor: US/GSA - General Services Administration

PRIVATE SECTOR INITIATIVES OFFICES: HOUSING

NATIONAL/STATE ORGANIZATIONS

US/HUD - PRIVATE SECTOR INITIATIVE ACTIVITIES IN HUD
US/HUD - Office of the Secretary
Seventh and D Streets, SW
Washington, DC 20410
TEL: 202-755-6417
Objectives: To focus attention on and provide technical support for local problem-solving initiatives.
Services: Organizes private sector initiatives program around three major themes: Community Partnership Initiatives, Strategies for Cities, and Privatization; involves several offices of HUD in each theme, described below:

- **Community Partnership Initiatives** concerns efforts to strengthen the public sector's capacity to solve the widest variety of community problems by working with the private sector and involves several offices of HUD; provides tools, techniques, and programs for communities to develop cooperative relationships among public, private, neighborhood, and voluntary sector organizations to solve local problems; involves the following HUD initiatives:
- **Working Group on Voluntarism,** to bring public and private sectors together both through an interagency working group of the Cabinet Council on Human Resources, and through a nationwide network of Federal Regional Councils; includes interaction with the American Foundation on Volunteerism (which stimulates local community voluntary programs), and the U.S. Jaycees Local Foundation Project (which has committed the full resources of 7500 local clubs) in a joint effort with the American Foundation on Volunteerism to establish a local public foundation in each community where there is a Jaycee Club.
- **Management Work Plan/Strategy,** with assistance from HUD's Office of Community Planning and Development to foster public/private partnership in two major areas: program and legislative changes, and activities to promote partnerships; increases Area and Regional field staff activity, develops continued dialogue with field staff in support of this activity, and promotes speeches and articles by principal staff in areas relevant to the activities.
- **Community Development Block Grants,** as they relate to 1981 legislation which allows local governments to use block grant funds in conjunction with private sector capital investment to strengthen local economies.
- **Enterprise Zones,** to attract new business investments in inner city areas which will provide jobs for residents.
- **Urban Development Action Grants,** to encourage private sector economic development activity to aid distressed communities in their economic recovery through new private capital investments designed to produce jobs and to increase the local tax base.
- **Community Partnerships Resources Center,** to gather and display a body of knowledge, experiences, and practicum related to community partnership initiative activities taking place in local communities.
- **Guided Capacity-Building and Partnership Development,** to identify and support the role of community-based organizations working with the private sector in revitalizing urban neighborhoods; publishes *Partnerships for Community Self-Reliance,* which contains over 100 examples of successful neighborhood projects.
- **State Relationship/Strategy,** to establish Small Business Economic Revitalization Corporations, develop self-sustaining financial delivery systems, mobilize resources of the private sector financial community, and market tax incentives to stimulate capital investment, job creation, and development of small business opportunities.
- **Affordable Housing Demonstration,** to find ways to produce affordable housing for home buyers without direct Federal assistance.
- **National Community Energy Management Center,** to provide a one-stop common source of technical assistance to communities through a consortium of three Federal agencies, seven national associations and six major corporations.
- **Operation Build,** to provide opportunities for improving the lives of pre-teen youths who reside in public housing or HUD-subsidized projects.
- **Federal Procurement Pilot Project,** to enable New York City to link small and minority business activity to Federal procurement contracts (sponsored by New York City Chamber of Commerce and the Rockefeller Foundation).
- **Strategies for Cities,** to strengthen community capacities and processes for developing strategy that enables cities and regions to adapt to change, and to develop information that enables local cities to formulate public/private sector approaches to local problems; involves the following initiatives in this theme: strategies for cities project, to develop a nationwide state-of-the-art report which includes case studies on ways that local communities have applied a strategic process to solving local problems; rehabilitation technical assistance, to offer technical assistance to local governments in carrying out Community Development Block Grant-funded rehabilitation programs and stimulating increased participation by private lenders.
- **Privatization,** to strengthen the public sector capacity to select and implement alternatives to the delivery of public services through: the collection, assessment, and display of information such as a major catalog of *Alternatives for Service Delivery* to identify feasible alternatives through use of the private sector; outreach projects in the form of regional conferences, workshops, and technical assistance efforts to disseminate the information gathered on the theme of privatization; neighborhood service delivery to illustrate that neighborhood organizations can deliver services in a responsive and cost-effective manner to the mutual benefit of local governments and neighborhood residents; housing initiatives to provide greater delegation of responsibility to private lenders in processing single-family FHA insurance applications, conduct an experimental program in privatization of debt collection for defaulted Title I Home Improvement loans, contract out accounting and servicing of HUD-held mortgages, complete an evaluative study of private sector management of public housing, and turn over to the private sector the "Housing Counseling Program" and the "Congregate Housing Services" program for the elderly; a White House Conference on Community Partnership Initiatives to include a privatization component.

[Not a complete list; request information on other initiatives mounted by HUD to increase private sector involvement.]
Sponsor: US/HUD - Department of Housing & Urban Development
Publications: Partnerships for Self-Reliance

PRIVATE SECTOR INITIATIVES OFFICES: HUMAN SERVICES

NATIONAL/STATE ORGANIZATIONS

US/HHS - WORKING GROUP ON PRIVATE SECTOR INITIATIVES
US/HHS - Office of the Secretary
PO Box 1182
Washington, DC 20201
TEL: 202-619-7000

Objectives: To inventory existing HHS/private sector relationships; to develop new approaches to expand public/private partnerships that address health and human service needs.

Services: Operates under a mandate to report on the following tasks:

- Review procedures and regulations to recommend modifications to eliminate barriers to private sector involvement;
- Identify and recommend incentives for private sector involvement, including innovative approaches to public/private partnership in delivery of health and human services;
- Examine existing programs to identify current voluntary efforts and potential for expansion and to recommend those activities which could be carried out more productively in the private sector; and
- Recommend ways in which the dissemination of technical knowledge and other information can enhance private incentives.

Categorizes existing HHS/private sector partnerships (utilize volunteers or involve other types of cooperative interaction with the private sector) into four areas:

HHS programs which utilize volunteers directly
Public Health Service:

- Student Volunteer Program
- NIH Volunteer Program
- Normal Volunteer Program
- Indian Health Services
- National Health Service Corps Clinics
- National Hansen's Disease Center
- Childhood Immunization
- National Institute for Occupational Safety and Health

Social Security Administration:

- Volunteers in all Trust Fund Programs

Health Care Financing Administration:

- Medicare
- Medicare Peer Counseling
- Medigap Training Program

Department-Wide:

- Student Volunteer Program (interns)

Human Development Services:

- Office of Policy Development (over 700 volunteers nationwide serve as field readers in the preapplication selection process for certain HDS grants)

HHS-funded programs, carried out within the private sector
Public Health Service:

- Health Careers Opportunity Program
- National VD Hotline
- Rehabilitation Grant Support
- Bureau of Community Health Services/Family Planning
- Community Health Centers, Migrant Health Projects

Human Development Services:

- Parents Anonymous
- Parent Aide Child Protective Services
- Runaway Youth Programs
- Indian Child Welfare Programs
- Partnership for Permanence Project
- Project Head Start
- Guardian Ad Litem Projects
- Group Live-In Experience
- Toll Free National Communications Network
- Financial Assistance Grants
- Title III (over 250,000 volunteers)
- Title IV (discretionary funds)
- Financial and Life Planning
- Minority/Professional Resource Center

HHS-supported programs partially funded and/or administered by states and localities
Public Health Service:

- Bureau of Community Health Services/Family Planning
- Community Health Centers, Migrant Health Projects
- Maternal and Child Health

Office of Community Services:

- Program Support (block grants)

Health Care Financing Administration:

- Medicaid
- Early Periodic, Screening, Diagnostic and Treatment Program under Medicaid
- Transportation Services under Medicaid

Human Development Services:

- Child Welfare Services
- Project Head Start
- Administration of Developmental Disabilities
- Title III
- Social Security Block Grants
- WIN Program

HHS partnerships with national, regional, state, or local consortia of public/private organizations
Public Health Service:

- Health Promotion Training Program
- Community Based Programs
- National Alliance for Energy Contingency Planning for Health Resources
- Guidelines for Construction and Equipment
- Diabetic Retinopathy Information Campaign
- National Industrial Council for HMO Development
- Comprehensive Cancer Center Communications Network
- Community Health Centers, Migrant Health Projects
- Pregnancy and Infant Health Project
- Hospital Transport Project
- Indian Diabetes Care
- Sodium and Hypertension
- Joint Commission on Patient Education

[Not a complete list; over 1,000 HHS programs involve the private sector and volunteers; ask about criteria used in above selection.]

Works toward completion of potential inducements for increasing public/private partnerships for the delivery of health services in four areas:

- One, promotion of volunteer activity among federal employees.
- Two, expansion of volunteer services and volunteer contributions to federal programs.
- Three, utilization of Federal facilities to assist private sector volunteers initiatives and public/private partnerships.
- Four, use of Federal seed money.

Plans other initiatives such as volunteer fairs, recognition to outstanding volunteer activities at the regional level, service delivery assessments, better coordination of specific programs such as employment of the handicapped, the identification of regulatory and administrative barriers to publicizing successful projects in the private sector, and targeting of discretionary funds to stimulate increased voluntarism and public/private collaboration.

Provides weekly reports to the White House listing private sector initiatives across the country as a result of the Working Group's efforts:

- a new Voluntary Action Center in New Jersey;
- an HHS employee volunteer program in Seattle;
- a day care conference in Philadelphia;

- hunger research in Massachusetts;
- senior housing in unused schools in Colorado;
- food drives in Washington and Missouri;
- chore services in Washington;
- development of volunteer recruitment materials in Oregon;
- youth serving the elderly in California;
- corporate grants for day care in Washington;
- food distribution in New York;
- senior citizen fitness awards in New England;
- meals program in Connecticut;
- donation of outdoor equipment in Massachusetts;
- emergency food and shelter program in Dallas; and
- a task force on food and hunger in Kansas City.

[Many of these and other programs are sponsored or co-sponsored by HHS Regional Offices in concert with the corporate community, local government, community groups, etc.; additional information provided on request.]

In addition to reports on individual partnership efforts, the Working Group provides an overview on reports from the region in specific areas, such as the *Communications Industry Project Update,* which describes efforts in each region by the various media.

Sponsor: US/HHS - Department of Health & Human Services
Publications: Project Update

PRIVATE SECTOR INITIATIVES OFFICES: INTERIOR

NATIONAL/STATE ORGANIZATIONS

PRIVATE SECTOR EFFORTS PROGRAM
US/DoI - Office of the Secretary
Office of the Secretary
18th and C Streets
Washington, DC 20240
TEL: 202-343-7351

Objectives: To develop and mount initiatives that increase involvement of the private sector in the Department's programs.
Services: Operates through three distinct functions toward the above objective, which are outlined below:
Voluntary Efforts Now Underway in Support of Public Goals
Park, Recreation, and Wildlife Protection:
- more than 400 volunteers at 65 field stations of National Wildlife Refuges, National Fish Hatcheries, and research stations, including a national Volunteer Coordinator in the Fish and Wildlife Service.
- private, non-profit land trusts across the country protecting natural, scenic, recreational, scientific, historic, and cultural lands.
- new guidebook on the National Park system by the Travel Industry Association of America; a new map of the system by the National Tour Brokers Association, a new film about the system by the Walter J. Klein Company, and an item not produced before - an information piece by the International Snowmobile Manufacturers Association on winter time activities in the National Parks.
- a "foster plant project" (Adopt-A- Plant) by the Garden Club of America with most of its 180 member clubs opting to select a vulnerable plant as a conservation concern; surveys on endangered species by the Nature Conservancy's Heritage Programs; a network of plant societies in more than a dozen states to address the Endangered Species Act.
- employee volunteer programs working with the Rare and Endangered Native Plant Exchange (50 employees in the

Brooklyn Union Gas Company, for example), which mounts projects and raises funds.
Public Lands Management:
- a nationwide program to recruit/involve volunteers to help manage its 327 million acres of public lands.

Joint Public-Private Enterprises
Park, Recreation, and Wildlife Protection:
- an assessment of national recreation and policy.
- plans for creation of a National Park Corps to coordinate volunteer efforts supporting the National Park system.
- coordination with groups volunteering to rehabilitate the Statue of Liberty, raise funds for reconstruction at Wolf Trap Farm Park, create new parks where a need emerges (such as in Alton Park, Illinois, with $150,000 worth of donated labor and $100,000 worth of donated equipment), mount public awareness campaigns on specific endangered species, purchase and distribute the Service's films, donate wetlands habitats to protect migratory birds, maintain relevant bookstores in visitor centers, etc.
- various Memoranda of Agreement with corporations and local governments to refrain from developing certain lands to protect endangered species, or to provide direct funding to protect this wildlife.
Public Lands and Water Resource Management:
- work with private firms to operate range management programs, find range lands to ease overpopulated refuges of wild animals, dispose of surplus federal property, enter into joint private federal construction projects, etc.
Energy and Minerals:
- operation of joint private-public enterprises within the data systems of the U.S. Geological Survey.
- exercise of cost-sharing research and other projects with academic institutions, private industrial firms, and others.

Programs that Could/Should Involve Greater Private Sector Efforts
Park and Wildlife Protection:
- purchasing of fish to meet stocking requirements (evaluating possibility of purchasing from private sector).
- use of concessionaires for tours, food services, sales outlets, guides, maintenance services, etc. (expanding use of private concessionaires).
- operation of campgrounds and provision of visitor services (exploring increased private sector support).
Water Resource Development:
- mounts cost-sharing arrangements for water resource projects in partnership with the private sector.
- transferral of the operation of completed facilities to local water users.
- voluntary labor for the construction and maintenance of recreation facilities at Bureau water projects.
Energy and Minerals:
- privatizing of large-scale mapping now done by the U.S. Geological Survey, which develops Large Scale Mapping Guidelines that would permit capable and experienced firms in the private sector to collect data and produce the maps.

[Above summarizes a much larger bank of programs aimed at increased private sector involvement; inquire.]
Sponsor: US/DoI - Department of the Interior

PRIVATE SECTOR INITIATIVES OFFICES: JUSTICE

NATIONAL/STATE ORGANIZATIONS

US/DOJ - PRIVATE SECTOR INITIATIVES
10th and Constitution Ave., NW
Office of the Attorney General
Washington, DC 20530
TEL: 202-633-2000
Objectives: To stimulate opportunities to involve private sector groups and volunteers in criminal justice-related activities and in the provision of legal services.
Services: Undertakes numerous programs through the Office of Justice Assistance which encourage a more active role at the community level, including:

- National Citizens' Crime Prevention Campaign, which involves the Advertising Council, corporate America, non-profit organizations and federal agencies in the major theme: "Crime prevention is not solely the job of law enforcement."
- Sting Program, which establishes working relationships with insurance companies to attack the problem of property crime.
- Security Project, which takes advantage of the phenomenon that the property repair records of IBM had a very distinct relationship with the location of stolen property (works with IBM and the Batelle Institute).
- School Enhancement Project, which attempts to discourage delinquency by providing recognized experts to assist in establishing more effective teaching methods, increasing participation by students, and viewing basic subjects in terms of relevance to the world of work (works with the Westinghouse Corporation).
- Older Persons Volunteer Programs, which provide companionship and guidance to juvenile offenders and non-offenders (transferred funds to ACTION's Foster Grandparents Program and Retired Senior Volunteer Program).
- Act Together, which serves as an intermediary between the private sector, the state and local sector and the federal government in efforts to improve services to high risk youth.
- Juvenile Offender Restitution Programs, which administer all aspects of the restitution requirements, including community service placement (funds more than 40 projects, some through private-not-for-profit agencies such as United Way, Youth Service Bureaus, etc.)
- Prison Industries, which involve offenders as employees to produce goods or services for sale within correctional institutions.
- Boys Clubs of America, which sponsors the National Project on Juvenile Justice, a special initiative to prevent and reduce juvenile crime by promoting law-abiding behavior among teenaged residents of communities with high rates of juvenile crime (with the goal of instilling self esteem).
- Victim Assistance, which involves funding of community-based programs to ensure that victims are treated with decency, and to be of service to programs of victim and witness assistance in both the public and the private sectors (funded programs include the National Organization for Victim Assistance and the Center for Women Policy Studies).
- FBI Activities, which include volunteers in all programs, and assists in organizing private sector efforts in this regard, including the National Crime Prevention Coalition, which has hundreds of civic groups as members, the Crime Stoppers USA program, which has several hundred chapters, and Law Enforcement Explorers of the Boy Scouts of America which has 40,000 members.

- Federal Prison System, which has about 4,000 volunteers who assist and augment Department programs as direct service volunteers, and in an advisory capacity to assist prisons in improving programs such as the Prison Industries Program.

Includes efforts other than specific programs in its work to increase private sector involvement, such as encouraging voluntary attorney services, working with "volags" (voluntary immigration counseling agencies; more than 1200 volunteers) and mounting special projects as needs arise.
Maintains an Outreach Program to motivate the voluntary agencies and community organizations to become more involved in volunteering their time through training conferences, technical assistance and specialized information.
Operates a Community Relations Service to identify areas of racial tension and to assist local mediation and conciliation activities to ameliorate those tensions and avoid unnecessary confrontation (works with over 1,000 private groups in hundreds of cases; request list of groups).
Instructs all components of the Department to reassess their activities in the area of maximum participation by private sector groups and make recommendations where improvements appear to be needed.
Sponsor: US/DoJ - Department of Justice
Publications: DoJ/PSI Information Packet

PRIVATE SECTOR INITIATIVES OFFICES: LABOR

NATIONAL/STATE ORGANIZATIONS

US/DOL - PRIVATE SECTOR INVOLVEMENT PROGRAM
Office of the Secretary
Washington, DC 20210
TEL: 202-523-6666
Objectives: To promote greater private sector involvement in resolution of community problems.
Services: Takes actions to reduce and eliminate government activities that have proven to be economically counterproductive and to strengthen programs and policies which enhance the private sector role; includes key components in this effort of:

- A vigilant review of rules and regulations, which includes a cutback on paperwork requirements that burden business but do not contribute to the well-being of the American worker.
- Efforts to improve labor-management cooperation, which include projects with the goal of providing greater protection of workers through greater private sector involvement.
- A strengthening of education and communication activities, which includes efforts by Labor-Management, the Women's Bureau, the Office of the Assistant Secretary on Veterans' Employment, and the Employment and Training Administration - all placing heavy emphasis on community involvement.

Includes in its initiatives on private sector involvement the following actions which have proven successful:
Occupational Safety and Health Administration

- develops a series of voluntary protection programs which rely on private initiatives to maintain safe and healthful working conditions.
- investigates voluntary protection options which could supplement the agency's enforcement program.
- mounts agreements with individual associations to commit the agency to help design job safety and health programs to benefit workers.

Mine Safety and Health

- encourages mine management and labor to assume their fair share of responsibility for safe and healthful operations.
- sponsors and encourages safety associations such as the Joseph A. Holmes Association which grants awards to individuals, officials and groups for achievements in safety, and the Holmes Safety Program which develops and distributes materials for use in safety meetings at mines.
- sponsors "Sentinals of Safety Competition," which is an annual awards program, and the "National Mine Rescue and First-Aid Contest," which is a biannual skill development event.

Employment and Training
- designs major roles for private business in new efforts for training of unemployed groups.
- cooperates with "Job Training Councils" which are established by Governors and consist of private business managers who work with local "Private Industry Councils" toward making the private sector a full partner in managing new training programs.

Small and Disadvantaged Business Utilization
- promotes minority businesses through support of the Commerce Department's Interagency Council for Minority Business Enterprise.
- suggests criteria for the selection of Private Sector Symposium sites to assist above Council.

Women's Employment Opportunities
- mounts actions concerning child care, job fair programs, apprenticeship and construction, and improved conditions for women entering business and on corporation boards.
- plans initiatives that seek to establish at least one employer-sponsored child care system in each region, offering workshops to public and private sector staff with responsibilities in this regard.
- provides information and technical assistance to the private sector on child care, and tax incentives for employer involvement.
- conducts training which focuses on recruiting and preparing women for skilled trade jobs and retaining them in these jobs.
- mounts job fairs which bring together women who are unemployed and employment resources (counselors, personnel specialists, interviewers, etc.) to facilitate job placement.
- assists agencies such as the "Door Opener" agency in Iowa, which conducts training programs for women wishing to enter the small business market.
- helps to establish a network among women who are well-established in business to create mentoring relationships, and to involve board and management level women in improving mobility for women workers in their corporations.

Labor-Management Services Administration
- encourages voluntary settlements between employers and veterans and reservists returning to their pre-service jobs.
- takes steps to reduce unnecessary paperwork and make it easier for employers, unions, and others to comply with Administration laws and regulations.

Veterans Employment
- initiates projects aimed at linking veterans in business with veterans seeking employment in coordination with the Department's Office of Small and Disadvantaged Business Utilization.
- utilizes information on known veteran-owned businesses to locate other veteran-owned businesses, and to promulgate information concerning veterans' employment programs such as "Targeted Tax Credit," a project of veterans helping veterans.

Works continually on new programs that increase private sector involvement in the Department's programs.
Sponsor: US/DoL - Department of Labor

PRIVATE SECTOR INITIATIVES OFFICES: NCUA

NATIONAL/STATE ORGANIZATIONS

US/NCUA - PRIVATE SECTOR INITIATIVES AND VOLUNTEERISM
US/NCUA - Administration Board
1776 G Street, NW
Washington, DC 20456
TEL: 202-356-1000
Objectives: To emphasize activities having a particularly strong focus on involvement of the private sector.
Services: Involves the private sector in all credit union activities, having from five to eleven volunteers typically serving on a board of directors, three to five volunteers on the supervisory committee, and three to five volunteers on the credit committee, with other volunteers serving in organizing and other capacities; includes the following among its overall activities involving the private sector:
New Chartering which involves mobilization of private sector resources to increase the number of volunteers acting as organizers, officials and committee members.
Community-Development Credit Unions which serve to stimulate private sector initiative through the provision of seed money in low-income areas, not only as a means of providing necessary financial services, but also as a means of economically developing the community (provides an incentive to reach into the private sector to obtain funding to supplement the seed money).
Education to promote compliance to consumer laws and regulations and create *self-regulation* to replace former *compliance examinations* and free staff for other duties.
Use of Certified Public Accountants to respond to suggestion on *privatization* of functions when possible (exploring this possibility on the basis of credit union safety and soundness).
Institutes initiatives in other areas such as deregulation, records preservation, legislation, and others; monitors continuously its standard activities to increase, when possible, their potential for private sector initiatives, and continuously studies other programs for maximum relevance to additional involvement in public/private partnerships.
Sponsor: US/NCUA - National Credit Union Administration

PRIVATE SECTOR INITIATIVES OFFICES: PERSONNEL

NATIONAL/STATE ORGANIZATIONS

US/OPM - PRIVATE SECTOR INITIATIVES IN OPM
Office of the Director
1900 E Street, NW
Washington, DC 20415
TEL: 202-632-6106
Objectives: To emphasize programs that bear on the private sector and indicate initiative in the area of public/private partnerships.
Services: Deals primarily with other agencies of the federal government, but maintains contact to some extent with the private sector through programs such as the following:
Outpatient Program for federal employees who have been displaced by reductions in force; includes a *Job Information Exchange* and other programs at the regional level.
Federal Executive Associations in local areas to oversee programs

that benefit employees (also, this group monitors the *Combined Federal Campaign* local efforts).

Mobility Programs which involve the temporary assignment of employees between federal agencies and state, local, and Indian tribal governments, institutions of higher education, and other public and private organizations (assignments can last up to four years); involves three programs:
- *IPA Mobility Program* (initiated by OPM)
- *President's Commission Executive Exchange*
- *White House Fellows Program*

Health Benefits Program which enables federal employees and annuitants to insure themselves through two private health insurance plans, union health plans, and through membership in various local *Health Maintenance Organizations,* commonly called *HMOs* (a system that could serve as a model for large private employers as well).
Sponsor: US/OPM - Office of Personnel Management

PRIVATE SECTOR INITIATIVES OFFICES: SBA

NATIONAL/STATE ORGANIZATIONS

US/SBA - PRIVATE SECTOR INITIATIVES ACTIVITIES
Office of the Director
1441 L Street, NW
Washington, DC 20416
TEL: 202-653-6365
Objectives: To utilize the private sector to obtain maximum leverage from all programs in achievement of goals and meeting small business community needs.
Services: Addresses program priorities with support and compliance from each operational unit and each regional administrator; involves several areas in its private sector initiatives program, as follows:
Current Private Sector Initiatives Programs involve a large number of partnerships with the private sector (over 50% of overall programs), including:
- *SBA Advisory Councils* located in each district and at the national level involve more than 1,100 business owners who channel information from the business community, evaluate current SBA programs, and recommend new programs.
- *Disaster Program* utilizes private sector participation in evaluating disaster damage to home or business, identifying victims, assisting victims in preparing forms, etc. (involves volunteer organizations and lenders, volunteer organizations directly related to SBA, state and local governments, and local businesses).
- *Partnerships with private sector financial institutions* produce guarantees to enable SBA to access private sector lending resources to benefit small businesses which otherwise could not secure private sector financing.
- *Partnerships with local and state development companies* create increased employment, productivity and urban enterprise development with 50% of the financing coming from private participation.
- *SBICs and MESBICs* are small business investment companies and minority enterprise small business investment companies which must meet private capital investment criteria before receiving government money.
- *Management Assistance* identifies management problems that are primary reasons for business failures, and uses experienced professionals in the private sector to assist small business managers in overcoming these problems; calls on sources such

as the following to assist in this area: Chamber of Commerce Resource Center Program, Professional and Trade Associations, SCORE and ACE (see separate entries), Small Business Institute (uses business resources and expertise of 500 colleges and universities), Small Business Development Center (in most states, Centers match funds 50-50 with SBA, employ short-term volunteer professionals, and require involvement of private resources).
Procurement Assistance which places a fair share of government dollars with small business through the SBA-operated PASS (Procurement Automated Source System) and other means of assuring private sector involvement while meeting government needs for goods and services.
Women Business Ownership includes a number of private sector-oriented programs such as the roster of 1,900 private sector corporations who have been solicited by SBA to cooperate in providing subcontracting opportunities for women contractors, and sponsored regional procurement conferences involving local women's groups who provide expertise and advice to businesswomen (such as 12 pilot workshops sponsored by the *National Association of Bank Women* and the *Donner Foundation,* and the *American Women's Economic Development Corporation* sponsored by SBA).
Minority Enterprise receives SBA assistance under three programs:
- *Corporate Market Development Program* (SBA works with Fortune 500 corporations)
- *Trade Association Participation Program* (SBA recruits private sector trade association members to help resolve problems)
- *Presidential Advisory Committee on Small and Minority Business Ownership* (committee of private-sector experts to encourage major firms to place subcontracts with small and minority-owned firms)

Proposed incentive programs include: *Entrepreneur Network; SBA Client Network; Public Library Entrepreneur's Collection; Large Business Partnerships;* and *Small Business and Industry Associations and the Academic Community.*
Proposed administrative, legislative or policy initiatives include adoption of private sector performance standards by all departments and agencies for all of their operational units, working closely with local communities to accomplish partnership goals, fostering legislation that encourages the matching grant concept, and development of cosponsored training and private sector assistance in portfolio management.
Sponsor: US/SBA - Small Business Administration

PRIVATE SECTOR INITIATIVES OFFICES: TRANSPORTATION

NATIONAL/STATE ORGANIZATIONS

US/DOT - PRIVATE SECTOR INITIATIVES PROGRAMS
Office of the Secretary
400 Seventh Street, SW
Washington, DC 20590
TEL: 202-426-4000
Objectives: To promote public/private partnerships and encourage the private sector to decrease dependence on government.
Services: Operates under the premise that the nation's best guarantee of sound transportation systems lies in the private sector; applies the fundamental objective to all of the department's activities to *increase reliance on the private sector,* to improve the system of transportation user charges, and to return transportation

function to private operation; institutes policy guidelines including:

- The provision of transport services should be left to private enterprise as far as feasible.
- Private transport services should function in a competitive market, rather than under regulatory regime.
- Regulations imposed on the private sector should be reevaluated to modify or rescind nonessential requirements.
- When the national interest indicates that certain transportation facilities should be built, operated, and maintained by the government, and are used by private carriers, equitable cost recovery should take place.
- Federal subsidies for publicly owned/operated modes should not undermine and take business from competing modes (private bus, taxi, etc.).

Operates current programs and proposes new ones to encourage private sector initiative, such as those summarized below:

Aviation - makes use of expertise from the private sector, rather than government staffing, to perform many functions; e.g., periodic examination of airmen conducted by physicians who are in private practice.

Proposes production and dissemination of audiovisual training materials by the private sector, additional certification authority to large aircraft manufacturers, removal of documentation and procedural requirements for noise abatement and aircraft emissions that prove costly and do not degrade air quality, and *regulation by objective,* a new concept in compliance.

Highways and Safety - relies heavily on the private sector for program delivery, both the private contractor and the highway associations and societies.

Proposes an awards program for private sector organizations and individuals who provide outstanding support for the seat belt and drunk driving campaigns, bonus payments to highway design and construction contractors as rewards for suggesting time-saving techniques, greater private sector financial participation in the capital costs of highway projects, operation of park-and-ride lots by private industry, and increased assistance to small motor carriers who have entered business since truck deregulation.

Urban Mass Transportation - encourages the growth of *paratransit* (a variety of forms of transportation such as shared-ride, taxi services, van pooling, employer-sponsored car pooling, and subscription buses), monitors local funding to public systems to avoid undermining local private service providers, and funds many research and development projects for transit equipment.

Proposes issuing investment strategy guidelines for transit capital projects as coventures with the private sector, and working with the *Labor Department* to amend labor protection legislation that levy undue constraints on paratransit activity.

Maritime, Coast Guard, and Inland Waterways - relies heavily on the private sector for boating safety activities (through the *Volunteer Coast Guard Auxiliary),* works through non-federal organizations to provide radar training, defrays cost for navigation aids by charging user fees to private boat owners, with legislation pending for full cost recovery.

Proposes to involve the private sector in an expansion of the present agreement on ship inspection, to terminate its *Vessel Traffic Service* as soon as an alternative is found, and to contract out the operation and maintenance of its LORAN-C stations and aids to navigation.

DoT Administration - schedules air travel through a private ticket agency, contracts for printing and graphics work with private contractors, places responsibility for a portion of the department's data-processing workload with the private sector, and contracts with CPAs in all ten regions to audit contracts and grants.

Proposes studying the cost-effectiveness of additional contracts for computer services, analyzing th shuttle bus service for possible transfer to the private sector, and using the services of a private collection agency in certain areas of debt collection.

Works continuously to increase reliance on the private sector and on marketplace mechanisms through establishment and carrying out of policy guidelines through program changes, regulatory reforms, legislative activities, administrative actions, and reductions in budget and personnel.

Sponsor: US/DoT - Department of Transportation

PRIVATE SECTOR INITIATIVES OFFICES: TREASURY

NATIONAL/STATE ORGANIZATIONS

US/DTREAS - TREASURY'S INVOLVEMENT IN PRIVATE SECTOR INITIATIVES
US/DTreas - Office of the Secretary
15th & Pennsylvania Avenue, NW
Washington, DC 20220
TEL: 202-566-2000
Objectives: To apply its programs when possible to the private sector initiatives concept.
Services: Works with volunteers and private businesses, and becomes directly involved with the functions of the private sector in a support role, a public-private partnership in a particular effort, a procurement role or informational role; includes active and proposed programs such as the following:
Internal Revenue Service
- *Volunteer Income Tax Assistance (VITA)* and *Tax Counseling for the Elderly (TCE)* in which IRS recruits, trains, and supports volunteers who prepare income tax returns free for low-income taxpayers, non-English-speaking taxpayers and military taxpayers (37,000 volunteers in a typical year prepared 293,000 federal tax returns).
- *Understanding Taxes Program* and *Fundamentals of Tax Preparation Program,* in which classroom course materials (texts, instructor guides, etc.) are provided free to high school and college teachers who use the materials to teach students at the high school level how to prepare their own returns, and students at the college level how to prepare returns for others.
- Informing taxpayers through free airtime (approximately $5.5 million in a typical year) by television networks and local broadcasters providing public service announcements.
U.S. Savings Bonds Division
- Involves about 50 top executives in a *U.S. Industrial Payroll Savings Committee* which conducts savings bonds campaigns.
- Involves a top business executive from each state and the District of Columbia in the *Volunteer State Chairman's Council* who recruit and appoint a business or banking leader in each county to serve as the grassroots volunteer for savings bonds (saves cost for Treasury while helping Americans save for the future).
- Provides technical assistance to *Take Stock in America Campaigns* which are led by business and banking leaders appointed by members of the *Council of U.S. Savings Bonds Volunteers.*
Bureau of Alcohol, Tobacco and Firearms
- Works with the *Beverage Alcohol Information Council (BAIC)* which is the outgrowth of a joint report to Congress by the *Department of Health and Human Services* and the *Department of the Treasury* on the need for banker-to-banker spokesmen (consists of leading bankers from each state and the District of Columbia, and members of the *American Bankers Association).*
Comptroller of the Currency
- Sponsors a *Community Development Division* to assist national banks in developing community investment programs, and serve as speakers, resource persons, and participants at forums on this subject.

● Oversees the *Community Development Corporation* which enables national banks to invest in and contribute to community development corporations within certain guidelines.

Proposed Areas of Activity

● Voluntary contributions to reduce the national debt on IRS Tax Form 1040.
● Sales area operations of the *U.S. Mint* in Philadelphia.
● Grape Variety Advisory Committee.

Strives continually to encourage the private sector to take a more active role in solving community problems, in establishing community partnerships between the private sector and local government to meet community needs, and in related areas of public/private interaction.

Sponsor: US/DTreas - Department of the Treasury

PRIVATE SECTOR INITIATIVES OFFICES: VETERANS

NATIONAL/STATE ORGANIZATIONS

US/VA - PRIVATE SECTOR INITIATIVES PROGRAM
Office of the Administrator
810 Vermont Avenue, NW
Washington, DC 20420
TEL: 202-393-4120

Objectives: To increase participation of staff at the local level to enhance the public/private initiatives concept.

Services: Involves the private sector though volunteer services, and assists the private sector by disseminating staff knowledge and experience to the community; promotes collaboration between the *Veterans Administration* and the private sector; provides information on how the agency involves and assists the private sector, which includes the following:

How the VA Utilizes the Private Sector

● *Department of Medicine and Surgery* (more than 75,000 volunteers who donate over 100,000,000 hours of service each year).
● *Department of Veterans Benefits* (involves volunteers through public/private collaboration on services for unemployed veterans resulting in *Job Fairs, Veteran Employment Seminars, Opportunity Days* and *Vet-A-Thons).*
● *Department of Memorial Affairs* (involves volunteers in national cemeteries, and in work with veterans and families on benefits and other memorial issues.)

How the VA Assists the Private Sector

Department of Medicine and Surgery

● health fairs, boards of volunteer directors' groups, instructors in volunteer workshops, instructors for special workshops for nursing home staff and volunteers
● supportive services for terminally ill
● *Volunteer for Course Credit* program for high school students
● *Geriatric Motivation Program* involving sixth grade students in nursing homes
● Field internships at medical centers
● Volunteers recruited from runaway and problem teenagers
● Former mental patients as volunteers
● Handicapped persons as volunteers
● Volunteer experience for high school students with mental and emotional disabilities
● *Handyman Program* involving domiciled residents
● *Toys for Tots* involving volunteers and patients as builders and fixers
● Volunteer placements for first-time minor offenders

(alternative sentencing)

Department of Veterans Benefits

● *Interagency Task Force on Information and Referral* (programs for the elderly: retirement planning, funding of programs, counseling/emergency services); Task Force includes *Equitable Life, Red Cross, National Council of Churches, United Way, Salvation Army, Catholic Charities, Peoples Drug,* and others in addition to the VA.
● Regional office/private sector activities on behalf of older veterans (question/answer column on veteran benefits; *Silver and Gold,* a newsletter; 18 mobile assistance programs for seniors; two-day resource seminars; *Veterans Benefits Information,* a cable TV series; visits to high residences for elderly; linkages with relevant U.S. departments).

Department of Memorial Affairs

● Contracting with private firms to operate national cemeteries
● Exploring with national industries for severely handicapped the possibility of contractual services at VA facilities
● Receiving donations of land for expansion
● Working with corporations and states to halt vandalism
● Working with military bases to develop and erect new cemetery signs
● Procuring 83% of materials from private sector

Hindrances to Private Sector Initiatives

● The cost of being a volunteer (should consider increasing tax-deductible mileage).
● The increasing difficulty in securing or affording transportation to and from work site.
● The need to establish a system or network of referral and exchange through which capable volunteers leaving one program or agency could be referred to others.
● The professionalism of volunteers to attract new people by publicizing interesting, creative volunteer positions.

VA Action Plan

● Encourage employees to continue building partnerships with local communities, to involve themselves with local task forces organized to seek solutions to community problems.
● Request staff to offer technical assistance and training services wherever possible, and sharing VA space.
● Urge VA public relations representatives to issue press releases which highlight VA's private sector initiatives program.
● Provide *Project Bank* forms to each VA facility and 350 private organizations which provide volunteers to document their programs.
● Encourage VA staff to increase their involvement with community volunteer programs, and to include community groups in VA-sponsored seminars, training sessions, and recreation activities.

Sponsor: US/VA - Veterans Administration

SELF-HELP

NATIONAL/STATE ORGANIZATIONS

NATIONAL SELF-HELP CLEARINGHOUSE
City University of New York
Graduate School & University Center
25 West 43rd Street, Room 620
New York, NY 10036
TEL: 212-642-2944
Objectives: To provide a central source of information on self-help activities.
Services: Provides information on self-help groups across the country; provides referral service to assist in sharing information and ideas more directly; maintains speakers bureau to inform community groups considering a self-help program; conducts and shares research on self-help program experience; operates training program; maintains a library of over 200 publications on self-help issues; publishes a newsletter four times a year, and numerous other reports, training manuals, brochures, and books.
Publications: Self-Help Reporter
Founded: 1976

NEIGHBORHOODS USA
SEE LEADERSHIP DEVELOPMENT/BOARDS:
TENANTS/RESIDENTS

SELF-HELP CENTER (*formerly Self-Help Development Institute*)
1600 Dodge Avenue
Suite S-122
Evanston , IL 60201
TEL: 312-328-0470
TOLL FREE: 800-322-MASH
Objectives: To provide information on all types of self-help groups.
Services: Serves as a clearinghouse for the collection and dissemination of information on all types of self-help groups; brings laymen and professionals together with self-help group representatives in mutual organization workshops; conducts research in all areas of self-help; conducts training and educational programs; publishes directories, workbooks, pamphlets, articles, and other materials on self-help and mutual aid.
Publications: Directory of Self-Help/Mutual Aid Groups in Illinois; National Directory of Self-Help Groups

TRAINING PROGRAMS

HANDICAPPED VOLUNTEER/VOLUNTEERING FOR THE HANDICAPPED
Adelphi University
Center on Volunteerism
Garden City, NY 11530
TEL: 516-294-8700
Credit: Inquire
Sponsor: Adelphi University
Contact: Rhoda White
Description: The Council of Agencies to Coordinate Homebound Services (CACHS) is a coalition of public and private agencies which assists community groups in mobilizing resources for shut-ins of all ages. It is guided by a volunteer board whose members work for agencies which service the homebound. Initially composed of a half-dozen agencies serving the elderly, CACHS currently includes 40 agencies collectively assisting all ages of handicapped citizens.
In response to a concern of the handicapped - "What can we do for others while others are doing for us?" - the Adelphi University Center on Volunteerism cosponsored with CACHS a conference that brought together for the first time on Long Island the resources of higher education, the expertise of human service agencies, and the personal involvement of the homebound/handicapped themselves.
Services to the handicapped as well as by the handicapped are included in the conference format, led by a panel of professional people working in the field - some of whom are handicapped themselves. In addition to volunteering by the handicapped, the conference dealt with:
- volunteer visiting and sharing;
- making a difference through advocacy;
- educational resources for the homebound; and
- the linking of local resources.

Among the "unanswered questions" that remained at the close of a recent convening of the conference:
- Is there transportation available now to enable the physically handicapped to get to volunteer placements?
- Are there any models in New York State or elsewhere for referring discharged disabled persons to community-based groups for rehabilitative follow-up?
- How does one get transportation for the physically handicapped to sheltered workshops? Isn't it discriminating to have transportation to special schools for children and none

for adults to sheltered workshops?
- During the International Year of Disabled Persons, are any new legislative initiatives being considered at the national and/or state levels to fund projects to help "mainstream" the homebound?
- A disabled person who wants to work will lose the government disability check if he/she does, but can't earn enough to subsist without it. What can be done?

To bolster the workshop discussions, the lunch hour is utilized for an informal exchange of ideas and experiences. In addition, the Human Resources Center and the Northport Veterans' Hospital are linked to the program by a telephone conference line. The questions are printed in Commentary, the Center's newsletter, for additional feedback from subscribers.

THE SELF-HELP MOVEMENT: NEW FORM OF VOLUNTEERISM AND A RESOURCE FOR PROFESSIONALS*
New Jersey Self-Help Clearinghouse
St. Clare's Mental Health Center
Denville, NJ 07834
TOLL FREE: 800-452-9790
Credit: Inquire
Sponsor: New Jersey Self-Help Clearinghouse
Contact: Barrie Alan Peterson, CAVS
Description: Designed for a broad student body (experienced directors of volunteers, executive directors and other staff, volunteer center directors, volunteers, social workers, clergy, etc.), the goal of this workshop is to explore the connection between self-help efforts and volunteerism. Specifically, the purposes are:
- To acquaint participants with the definition of self-help, history and range of the movement, forms of services offered, and basic literature in field.
- To propose to discuss the connection with traditional volunteerism, and to illustrate three models of Director of Volunteer Services Self-Help Group Interaction.
- To sensitize professionals to touchy issues of control, initiation, sponsorship, referrals, anonymity in work with self-help groups.

Each of the above objectives are treated separately with general and group discussions, question and answer sessions, and a wrap-up exercise to discuss what was learned and how it applies to each individual work situation at home.
Handouts include a bibliography, journal reprints, guidelines for starting a self-help group, a list of self-help clearinghouses in the United States, and others specific to the individual objectives.
The instructor is a project director in the Self-Help Clearinghouse of New Jersey, and a former volunteer coordinator and trainer.

VISION, PLANNING & PARTNERSHIP IN NEIGHBORHOOD ORGANIZING
SEE TRAINING/CONFERENCES/TEACHING: CIVIC AFFAIRS

SELF-HELP: AIDS

NATIONAL/STATE ORGANIZATIONS

NATIONAL ASSOCIATION OF PEOPLE WITH AIDS
SEE VOLUNTEERS: PERSONS WITH AIDS

PEOPLE WITH AIDS COALITION
SEE VOLUNTEERS: PERSONS WITH AIDS

INDIVIDUAL PROGRAM PROFILES

AIDS CHRONIC CARE UNIT VOLUNTEER PROGRAM
SEE VOLUNTEERS: TEAMS

SELF-HELP: CHILDREN/YOUTH

INDIVIDUAL PROGRAM PROFILES

DONCASTER YOUTH CHALLENGE, A.K.A. SNEAKER CAMP
Maryland Department of Juvenile Services
1623 Forest Drive
Annapolis, MD 21403
TEL: 301-974-3460
Purpose: To help teenaged boys with criminal records to work through their problems through peer interaction.
Sponsor: Eckerd Foundation
Contact: Mike Ziebell, Program Director; Claire Orologas, Education Coordinator
Description: In this unique program for youth-in-trouble, the youth themselves volunteer at the end of each day to "confront each other" by airing gripes and accepting constructive criticism from each other. In this way they learn how to approach confrontation peacefully instead of fighting, and they are providing "peer feedback" to each other - a valuable service that even the highest paid counselor in the state could not offer. The word "resocialization" is heard often. With names like *Explorers, Challengers, Potomacs,* and *Yukons,* the therapy groups at *Doncaster Youth Challenge* share frank discussions of "who did what to whom" and everyone has a chance to express feelings about the problems aired. This interaction has proven to be a valuable part of the overall program.
The program is referred to as a "sneaker camp" to differentiate it from the adult "boot camp" that the state is planning for older criminals. Although officials describe the youth program as "military style," it is really based more on psychological concepts. The primary concept of the youth program is "Make the teenagers feel good about themselves."
Youth at the Doncaster program are serving their sentences for first-time drug possessions, auto theft or vandalism. Officials don't have figures to prove whether the camp, which opened in 1987, is more successful at reforming juveniles with problems than other forms of treatment, but the evidence at hand has helped the Department make the decision to open another *Challenge* program elsewhere in the state, this time with a special emphasis on drug offenders.
The *Eckerd Foundation* operates the Doncaster program and will operate the planned program for drug offenders as well. The latter will be operated on the same principle - serving in self-help therapy groups to provide peer support for each other.
According to a director, "Although the teenagers frequently grumble about their routine, they acknowledge that they have it comparatively easy - they could be in one of the more traditional programs, such as the rough and rigorous state training school in Baltimore County. The boys who come here wanting to learn something are the ones who will succeed here. Our philosophy is much more growth-oriented than punitive."
Founded: 1987

PROJECT OPPORTUNITY
SEE VOLUNTEERS: SELF-HELP

PROJECT RIGHT START
Teen Parents Self-Sufficiency Programs
Boys & Girls Clubs of Greater Washington
1320 Fenwick Lane
Suite 800
Silver Spring, MD 20910
TEL: 301-543-3887; 301-587-4315
FAX: 301-587-8120
Purpose: To provide assistance to teenage parents.
Sponsor: Boys & Girls Clubs of Greater Washington
Contact: Zelda Fields, Executive Director
Description: Project Right Start is a program for teenage mothers
and fathers in the Washington, DC community. The project is
operated by the *Boys & Girls Clubs of Greater Washington* in
conjunction with the residential *Teen Mothers Support Program.*
Project Right Start offers support to young parents - both mothers
and fathers - so that they can:
 • complete their high school education
 • prepare for college
 • acquire job and career skills
 • retain a good job
Most importantly, *Project Right Start* offers young parents a
chance to learn how to handle all of the pressures of being a
parent. It gives them the opportunity to develop positive parenting
skills and child care techniques, and to prepare for independent
living.
Any teenage parent is eligible for the program, whether or not
they plan to keep the baby. Young fathers who participate most
often do not have the child living with them, but want to
strengthen the father-child relationship and talk to someone about
it.
There is no charge for being a participant in the five-day-a-week,
36-week program. It is a flexible program that is designed to meet
the individual needs of each participant, including extensions
beyond the 36-week period when necessary. Every attempt is made
to adapt the program to the schedules of the young parents. After
an initial consultation, an agreement on required hours and needed
services is signed by the participant. Although day care is not
provided at this time, counselors assist in finding this service when
it is necessary for parent participation.
Workshops and discussion sessions are led by health and human
services professionals in both education and job training. All
parties join in the planning of cultural and recreational activities.
An important aspect of the program is the requirement for all
participants to become actively involved in community service
programs.
Project Right Start is a joint initiative of Boys & Girls Clubs of
Greater Washington and the *Milton Eisenhower Foundation.*
Space for classes and other activities is provided by the *Teen
Mothers Support Program,* a residential program.
Publications: Project Right Start Information Packet

SELF-HELP: COMMUNICATIONS & PR

INDIVIDUAL PROGRAM PROFILES

LOS ANGELES POVERTY DEPARTMENT (LAPD)
SEE COMMUNICATIONS & PUBLIC RELATIONS: IMAGE

SELF-HELP: CRIME PREVENTION

INDIVIDUAL PROGRAM PROFILES

CITIZENS' CRIME WATCH OF DADE COUNTY
SEE VOLUNTEERS: SELF-HELP

SECURITY ALERT GROUP - THREE LINK TOWERS (SAG)
SEE VOLUNTEERS: OLDER PERSONS

SELF-HELP: DRIVERS

NATIONAL/STATE ORGANIZATIONS

**AUTOMOTIVE CONSUMER ACTION PROGRAM
(AUTOCAP)**
SEE VOLUNTEERS: SELF-HELP

INDIVIDUAL PROGRAM PROFILES

MOTOR VOTERS
SEE VOLUNTEERS: SELF-HELP

SELF-HELP: DRUGS/ALCOHOL

INDIVIDUAL PROGRAM PROFILES

KIDS HELPING KIDS
Tri-State Drug Rehabilitation and Counseling Program
c/o Village of Hebron
Municipal Building
Hebron, OH 43025
TEL: 614-928-2261
Purpose: To offer a self-help program for young drug-abusers
based on the self-help concept of Alcoholics Anonymous.
Sponsor: Tri-State Drug Rehabilitation and Counseling Program
Contact: Bonnie Clarkston or Scott Stacy, Counselors
Description: In this program, the kids themselves are the
volunteers. The self-help program, *Kids Helping Kids,* is based on
the premise that kids do not want to hear what adults say, but will
pay attention to their peers. The program is modeled after
Alcoholics Anonymous (AA) and stresses self-help and peer
counseling. Young clients also offer each other support and
guidance in regular rap sessions, which are led by peer counselors,
some of whom are former clients. The peer counselors are trained
to prod teens to be honest with themselves as well as with their
parents, their peers, and the program's staff. In the sometimes
emotional rap sessions, the teens express their fears, concerns and
frustrations. It is emphasized to the teens that the program only
helps them begin the steps they must take to stay drug-free - a
lifetime commitment.
The counselors also decide when clients move up to a higher phase
in the treatment program, and when they should be discharged.
On average, the teens stay in the program for a year. During this
time families receive counseling also to prepare for their children's
return to their homes and schools. According to one expert, "If
you don't change the environment at home, you're really setting

up the child for defeat."

During the early phases of treatment, teens do not go to school, but they meet regularly with academic tutors and stay with families of clients who are nearing the end of their treatment. From its inception in 1981 through spring of 1989, the program has treated 500 youths from Southwestern Ohio, Northern Kentucky and Indiana - from all social and economic levels of society. Currently, 40 youths are in the program.

A 1987 independent survey showed that more than 80% of the teens who complete the program abstain from all drugs. *Kids Helping Kids* is operated by the *Tri-State Drug Rehabilitation and Counseling Program,* a non-profit corporation. It works with other drug prevention and treatment groups, such as *Citizens Against Substance Abuse,* in the Cincinnati area.

Founded: 1981

SUBSTANCE ABUSE TREATMENT CENTER AND SHELTER
SEE VOLUNTEERS: SELF-HELP

SELF-HELP: FAMILIES

NATIONAL/STATE ORGANIZATIONS

CITIZENS FOR SAFE DRIVERS AGAINST DRUNK DRIVERS/CHRONIC OFFENDERS
SEE VOLUNTEERS: SELF-HELP

INDIVIDUAL PROGRAM PROFILES

FAMILY SUPPORT GROUP
SEE VOLUNTEERS: SELF-HELP

PUBLIC ASSISTANCE CLIENTS VOLUNTEER
SEE VOLUNTEERS: SELF-HELP

SELF-HELP: FORMER MENTAL PATIENTS

NATIONAL/STATE ORGANIZATIONS

RECOVERY, INC.
SEE VOLUNTEERS: SELF-HELP

SELF-HELP: HANDICAPPED

NATIONAL/STATE ORGANIZATIONS

NATIONAL ASSOCIATION FOR THE PHYSICALLY HANDICAPPED*
SEE VOLUNTEERS: SELF-HELP

SELF-HELP FOR HARD OF HEARING PEOPLE SHHH
7800 Wisconsin Avenue
Bethesda, MD 20814
TEL: 301-657-2248
Objectives: To create a volunteer network of hearing-impaired individuals in a self-help environment.
Services: Brings together hearing-impaired persons and their relatives and friends, and professionals working with hearing-impaired persons, to educate members of the public on the nature, causes and complications of hearing loss; instructs the public on early detection, management, and possible prevention of hearing loss; works for public acceptance of the hearing-impaired, and use of alternative communication skills by the public in working with the hearing-impaired; maintains a reference library, a speakers bureau, and several committees, including one on parent involvement and one on concerns of the elderly; publishes a journal six times a year, a quarterly newsletter, special reports, manuals, books and other materials.
Publications: SHHH - A Journal about Hearing Loss; Your Eyes Hear for You: A Self-Help Course in Speechreading; SHHH Newsletter
Founded: 1979

TRAINING PROGRAMS

VOLUNTEERS WITH SPECIAL NEEDS
SEE TRAINING/CONFERENCES/TEACHING: HANDICAPPED

INDIVIDUAL PROGRAM PROFILES

GLEANING*
SEE VOLUNTEERS: SELF-HELP

MULTIPLE SCLEROSIS SOCIETY OF ORANGE COUNTY
SEE VOLUNTEERS: HANDICAPPED

SELF-HELP: HOMELESS

INDIVIDUAL PROGRAM PROFILES

SUBSTANCE ABUSE TREATMENT CENTER AND SHELTER
SEE VOLUNTEERS: SELF-HELP

SELF-HELP: HOUSING

INDIVIDUAL PROGRAM PROFILES

GIFT TO THE CITY
SEE VOLUNTEERS: CHURCH/SYNAGOGUE MEMBERS

HABITAT FOR HUMANITY OF RHODE ISLAND
SEE VOLUNTEERS: CHURCH/SYNAGOGUE MEMBERS

PATERSON HABITAT FOR HUMANITY
SEE VOLUNTEERS: CHURCH/SYNAGOGUE MEMBERS

STUDENT HABITAT FOR HUMANITY
SEE VOLUNTEERS: STUDENTS

SELF-HELP: INTERGENERATIONAL

NATIONAL/STATE ORGANIZATIONS

GRAY PANTHERS
1424 Sixteenth Street, NW
Suite L1
Washington, DC 20036
TEL: 202-783-6226
Objectives: To bring youth and the aged together in a concerted effort to improve the status of both groups.
Services: Assists local groups in organization of youth-elderly projects, focusing on the belief that ageism affects both groups adversely, and that working together will achieve more for each than either group working alone; helps all age groups mount and implement projects of their choosing in the goal areas; conducts studies on the role of volunteer/advocacy groups, communal living, alternatives to institutionalization, and other mutual interest areas and publishes findings; writes courses for universities; maintains national speakers bureau; develops publications and films; publishes bimonthly newspaper and a series of organizing manuals books, and other materials; convenes periodic health conferences and biennial meetings.
Publications: Network Newsletter
Founded: 1971

INTERGENERATIONAL SERVICE-LEARNING PROJECT
National Council on the Aging
600 Maryland Avenue, NW
West Wing 100
Washington, DC 20024
TEL: 202-479-1200
Objectives: To bring together two isolated groups - college students and older persons - to form friendships, share knowledge, and engage in mutually-beneficial projects.
Services: Works with volunteer groups, community agencies and campus departments to organize and operate programs and identify needs; emphasizes advocacy, improving access to health care, and delivering health services to economically disadvantaged, homebound and isolated older persons; publishes a handbook for establishing service-learning programs and projects plus a series of technical assistance guides for the community on recruitment, orientation, supervision, and other program management areas, and a national clearinghouse for service-learning projects.
Publications: Perspectives on Aging; Current Literature on Aging; Collage - Cultural Enrichment
Founded: 1950

INDIVIDUAL PROGRAM PROFILES

SENIOR PROGRAM
Joint Educational Project
801 West 34th Street
Los Angeles, CA 90089-0471
TEL: 213-743-7698
Purpose: To foster better communication between generations and to implement a volunteer program which utilizes students and elders as activity leaders and community service providers.
Sponsor: The Public Welfare Foundation; University of Southern California

Contact: Maria Calderon
Description: In January 1981, the *Senior Program,* operated by the *Joint Educational Project (JEP),* created a link between the University and its neighboring community by forming a cooperative bond with a nearby senior citizens center. The project aims at enhancing the services of the site while providing students the experience of working with senior citizens.
Each semester approximately 40 students participate in some of the following activities:
- outreach services, where students pair up to visit homebound elderly, bringing information and referral services and companionship;
- autobiographies, in which students write their senior partner's life history;
- arts and crafts or health classes, in which students research topics and present them to the seniors in classes.
Student volunteers are under the supervision of the Program Assistants, part-time staff employed by either JEP who plan with professors, recruit and train students for assignments or by senior center staff.
The *Senior Program* offers two distinct groups: university students and senior citizens, the opportunity to work together for mutual benefits. This project fosters communication among these groups and has brought about numerous friendships. It has also enhanced the quality of college education, introducing a "real life" experience to classroom learning.
Founded: 1981

SELF-HELP: OLDER PERSONS

INDIVIDUAL PROGRAM PROFILES

AD SUPPORT GROUP OF GREATER ALABAMA
SEE VOLUNTEERS: SELF-HELP

GLEANING*
SEE VOLUNTEERS: SELF-HELP

SELF-HELP: PARENTS

NATIONAL/STATE ORGANIZATIONS

NATIONAL ASSOCIATION FOR PARENTS OF THE VISUALLY IMPAIRED
PO Box 180806
Austin, TX 78718
TEL: 512-323-5710
TOLL FREE: 800-225-0227
Objectives: To provide support for family members, and to promote public understanding of the needs and rights of blind and visually handicapped children.
Services: Addresses needs for emotional support of family members of blind and visually impaired children; provides information about care, education, and treatment of the children; establishes networking capabilities among parents and service agencies at local, state and national levels; conducts intermittent workshops for parents; offers computerized lists of camps and agencies serving blind and visually handicapped children, and bibliographies of resources available; publishes quarterly newsletter, a journal, resource guides and other materials.
Publications: Awareness; Take Charge! Resource Guide for

Parents; How to Pack 'Em In: Resource Guide for Planning Workshops; Your Child's Information Journal
Founded: 1980

PARENTS ANONYMOUS
SEE VOLUNTEERS: PARENTS

TRAINING PROGRAMS

PARENTS EDUCATING PARENTS: TRAINING PROGRAM
SEE VOLUNTEERS: SELF-HELP

INDIVIDUAL PROGRAM PROFILES

FOCUS (FAMILIES OF CHILDREN UNITED FOR SAFETY)
SEE VOLUNTEERS: PARENTS

MOTHERS OF PWAS (PERSONS WITH AIDS)
Shrine of the Immaculate Conception
Michigan Avenue & 4th Street, NE
Washington, DC 20017
TEL: 202-526-8300
Purpose: To help women - especially mothers - deal with the AIDS epidemic.
Sponsor: Shrine of the Immaculate Conception
Contact: Cecelia Bonner, Founder
Description: Since AIDS always has been thought of as a man's disease, efforts to help women deal with the epidemic have been slow in developing. Self-help groups in recent years have been formed with family members, friends and lovers in mind. To address this situation, in May 1989 a support and advocacy group was founded at the *Shrine of the Immaculate Conception* exclusively for women. The founder had lost a son to AIDS. While being careful not to discount men's feelings toward their sons and other close relatives with AIDS, the new support group was set up specifically to address female grief. One issue that surfaces frequently is the loss of a sense of closeness once felt with female friends, when normally a sickness in the family would bring them closer - with frequent visitors carrying covered dishes and offering plenty of hugs. But, contrary to what might be expected, it is the women in the AIDS-affected families who cut off the friendships with former friends as often as it is the other way around. Partly, this is because they prefer to keep the pain to themselves, and partly because confiding in friends too often leads to a rebuke. Remarks like, "You touched them? You hugged them?" are too often heard.
Although discussion centers on how the epidemic has weakened female bonds and forced women inward, it eventually gets around to men. The women agree that men have greater difficulty accepting that their sons might be homosexual and are not confronting the tragedy of AIDS. They are more likely to hold out hope for a cure than deal directly with their sons' mortality. Women, on the other hand, get through denial much quicker and begin the healthy process of grieving. *Mothers of PWAs* is a combination of support, self-help and advocacy and has provided an outlet for emotions that the women have had to keep under wraps in their everyday lives.
Founded: 1989

PARENTS EDUCATING PARENTS
SEE VOLUNTEERS: SELF-HELP

PERSON TO PERSON*
SEE VOLUNTEERS: PARENTS

SELF-HELP: PRISONERS/EX-OFFENDERS

NATIONAL/STATE ORGANIZATIONS

GOOD NEWS JAIL AND PRISON MINISTRIES INTERNATIONAL
1036 South Highland Street
Arlington, VA 22204
TEL: 703-979-2200
Objectives: To provide counseling, education, information and referral and other services to prisoners, ex-offenders and their families.
Services: Places Chaplains at the local level in correctional facilities to provide both spiritual and social services to prisoners and their families both in prison and after their release; oversees other volunteers in the program who provide counseling, crisis intervention, family contact, G.E.D. assistance, and other services on request of prisoners and prison officials, as well as pastoral counseling; assists ex-offenders in readjustment to the community (After Care program); maintains separate programs for jails (average incarceration only four to six months) and prisons (which includes "lifers"); provides training for ex-offenders wishing to become Chaplains in the program; publishes a newsletter, brochures, reports, and other materials.
Publications: Full Pardon; Update; Regeneration THEN... Rehabilitation; Jail Ministry Is Good Business?; Why Bother
Founded: 1961

INDIVIDUAL PROGRAM PROFILES

SUMMIT SHOCK INCARCERATION FACILITY
SEE VOLUNTEERS: PRISONERS/EX-OFFENDERS

SELF-HELP: TENANTS/RESIDENTS

NATIONAL/STATE ORGANIZATIONS

CAMPAIGN FOR HUMAN DEVELOPMENT
U.S. Catholic Conference
1312 Massachusetts Avenue, NW
Washington, DC 20005
TEL: 202-659-6650
Objectives: To raise money for self-help programs.
Services: A program of the *US Catholic Conference* with the specific goal of raising money through collections in Catholic churches for poor and low-income persons; allocates the funds to self-help projects sponsored by the needy themselves; mounts education programs to help the nonpoor community understand the causes of poverty and injustice; publishes a newsletter and a catalog of materials and resources.
Publications: Thirsting for Justice

HABITAT FOR HUMANITY INTERNATIONAL
SEE VOLUNTEERS: CHURCH/SYNAGOGUE MEMBERS

NATIONAL ASSOCIATION OF TOWN WATCH
SEE VOLUNTEERS: SELF-HELP

INDIVIDUAL PROGRAM PROFILES

CABRILLO VILLAGE
SEE VOLUNTEERS: SELF-HELP

SUNDIAL VOLUNTEERS
SEE VOLUNTEERS: CHURCH/SYNAGOGUE MEMBERS

TRAINING/CONFERENCES/TEACHING

NATIONAL/STATE ORGANIZATIONS

CENTER FOR CREATIVE COMMUNITY
SEE ADMINISTRATION

TRAINING PROGRAMS

ADMINISTRATION OF VOLUNTEER SERVICES
California State University
Education and Leisure Studies
Long Beach , CA 90840
TEL: 213-498-4071
Credit: Certification and 25 units
Sponsor: California State University
Contact: Randy Anderson
Description: The Certificate Program in Administration of
Volunteer Services is designed to accommodate several groups of
students; for example:
  - The Certificate may be earned through Continuing Education
    by students who possess a baccalaureate degree but are not
    regularly enrolled at the University. These persons might
    already be working as Coordinators of Volunteer Services, or
    may come from a background in volunteer service and are
    interested in new career possibilities.
  - Students pursuing an approved degree at the University may,
    after receiving their baccalaureate degree, go on to complete
    the Certificate program. Courses taken to meet the
    requirements of the Certificate also may be used
    simultaneously, where appropriate, to meet the General
    Education requirements of cooperating departments.
Required Courses:
  - Working with Boards and Commissions
  - Management of Volunteer Programs
  - Internship in Administration of Volunteer Services
    [Prerequisite: 1,500 hours of paid or unpaid experience in a
    recognized volunteer program OR a special course]
  - Independent Study [Individual research project in the area of
    administration of volunteer services]
Required courses provide ten of the required 25 units needed for
Certification. The remaining 15 units are acquired through elective
courses.
Elective Courses: Each student chooses at least one course from
each of the following areas of study:

  - Special Topics
  - Administrative Skills: Elementary Accounting; Human
    Resources Management: Behavioral Sciences and
    Management; Human Resources Management: Organizational
    Creativity; Interpersonal Skills in Human Resources
    Development; Management and Society.
  - Communication Skills: Elements of Group Discussion;
    Conference Management; Theory and Techniques of
    Interviewing; Introduction to Public Relations (prerequisite to
    following two courses); Publicity Techniques and Procedures;
    Publications for Public Relations.
  - Related Learning: Cultural Ecology; Police and Community
    Relations; Law and Social Change; Social Policies; Social
    Services for Families; and Children.

ADVANCED SEMINARS IN VOLUNTEER
ADMINISTRATION
University of Delaware
Wilcastle Center
2800 Pennsylvania Avenue
Wilmington, DE 19806
TEL: 302-738-8155
Credit: Inquire
Sponsor: University of Delaware
Contact: Jacob Haber
Description: Designed for volunteer coordinators who either have
completed the Certificate Program or have a wide volunteer
administration experience, this series of one-day advanced seminars
addresses tasks that require a high degree of expertise.
Contracting for Volunteer Services - CED 2-03-20-21-320JH
The contract is a basic management tool for defining both internal
and external relationships. It defines the role of the volunteer
within the organization. This workshop provides an arena for
discussion of uses of contracts in volunteer program
administration. Specific components of a contract as well as the
negotiation process are presented. Participants have opportunities
to write and critique different types of contracts.
Writing Volunteer Job Descriptions - CED 1-03-20-21-321JH
A job description is the basic tool for structuring work roles
within a volunteer program. It also becomes the basis for the
evaluation of performance. This workshop focuses on writing and
negotiating job descriptions and examines the description as it
relates to performance evaluation. Additionally, the description is
analyzed as a tool for examining recruiting/training/supervising
volunteers.

Reporting Writing Techniques - CED 1-03-20-21-322JH
All program administrators must be able to write clear, concise and accurate reports. This workshop examines numerous types of reports, the difference and similarity among the types, and the specific skills involved in report writing. Participants also have an opportunity to critique several categories of reports and to improve upon them.

Faculty is drawn from the field of volunteer administration with instructors from the American Red Cross and volunteer consulting organizations as well as the University.

The University of Delaware presents on-site volunteer coordinator seminars as an area package or for individual organizations or agencies.

AFFORDABLE MEETINGS
Hotel Sales & Marketing Association International
c/o Century Exposition Management
150 Broadway, Suite 600
New York, NY 10038
TEL: 212-513-7878
FAX: 212-227-1854
Credit: N/A
Contact: Conference Coordinator
Description: This is the first educational conference offered by the hotel industry focusing on the needs of budgetwise meeting planners. It addresses both full-time, part-time and volunteer meeting planners in organizations of all types and sizes who are responsible for producing successful yet cost-effective meetings.

The objective of the conference is to help planners put on meetings that are productive but well within budget. It was developed in response to the projection of increasingly tighter budgets in the decade ahead. The theme of the conference is *practical advice on how to save money on every aspect of a meeting,* and includes the following topics:

- **The Frugal Planner's Guide to Hotel Selection** - a look at the more than twenty types of hotels available and the advantages of each.
- **More Flash Than Cash** - tips on creative scripting, lighting, audiovisuals, and props.
- **Negotiations with Hotels: Keys to the Best Value for Your Meeting Dollar** - how to prepare for a negotiating session and make the most of your leverage.
- **The Art of Budgeting the Affordable Meeting** - how to anticipate and avoid hidden expenses that can be "budget busters."
- **Make the Most of Your Food and Beverage Dollars** - how to select menus that are healthful and relatively expensive as well as attractive and delicious.
- **101 Ways to Save Money on Your Next Meeting** - how to save meeting dollars without sacrificing quality.
- **The Win Way to Negotiating Transportation and Other Meeting Services** - how to get your money's worth when dealing with airlines, ground transportation operators, and other suppliers.
- **How to Work Behind the Scenes with Your Hotel Team** - what meeting planners, hotel executives and other team members need from each other.
- **Cost-Effective Steps in Successfully Promoting Your Meeting or Convention** - how to capture that "element of magic" in drawing attendees to your meetings.
- **Don't Make a Costly Mistake: How to Give Yourself Legal Protection When Planning Meetings** - overview of rights and potential areas of liability in the meeting planning process.
- **How to Fit 10 Lbs. of Creativity into a 5-Lb. Bag** - how to stretch dollars by taking a unique approach to every stage of the event.
- **How to Evaluate and Price Function Room Space for Meetings and Social Events** - how to evaluate the worth of your business to a hotel so that you can determine what

concessions you can and connot realistically expect.
- **Keeping Costs Down: New Options for Meeting Planners** - cost-conscious coverage of scheduling the meeting, economy lodging, meeting packages, computerization, destination selection, and airfare negotiations.
- **Avoid the Landmines: Don't Let Hidden Costs Demolish Your Meeting Budget** - how to ask the right questions, negotiate alternatives, and execute contracts that cover all bases, plus a "baker's dozen" ideas to generate additional meeting revenue.

Presenters are industry experts from hotels, tour services, airlines, the media, the legal profession, and managing and marketing groups, among others. Admission to this hallmark meeting is free through reservation (by August 24, 1990) for the three-day September 1990 meeting, with special hotel and travel rates available. Ample opportunity for networking with other planners and talking with executives from more than 300 hotels, convention bureaus, airlines and other providers is scheduled throughout the conference.
Publications: Conference Proceedings; Meetings and Conventions; Association Meetings; Official Meeting Facilities Guide; Successful Meetings
Founded: 1910

ASPECTS OF ADMINISTRATIVE FUNCTIONS FOR MANAGERS OF VOLUNTEER PROGRAMS
Volunteers In Action
229 Waterman Street
Providence, RI 02906
TEL: 401-421-6547; 401-421-7472
Credit: AVA Certification (partial fulfillment)
Sponsor: United Way
Contact: Betsy A. Garland
Description: This series is based on the premise that directors of volunteers need management skills to be effective. Six areas have been identified as pertinent to the career development of a volunteer administrator. These areas are over and above those covered in VIA's basic series on volunteer program development. The sessions are designed with an approach both to concepts and to practical applications, with three offered in the spring and three in the fall, as follows:
SPRING SESSIONS:
Program Monitoring Development
- Analyzing the organization as a system
- Identifying the organization's critical information needs
- Developing forms to monitor a program's progress towards achieving its goals

Board Development
- Understanding the roles and responsibilities of a board of directors
- Acquiring tools to improve board effectiveness
- Board-executive relationships
- Recruiting and orienting new board members
- Maximizing individual participation

Leadership Development
- Definition of leadership functions and styles
- Identification of power aspects of leadership

FALL SESSIONS (inquire about details):
Funding for Volunteer Programs
Public Speaking
Public Relations
It is recommended that the volunteer administrator complete the series, but a limited number of registrations for single sessions are taken on a space-available basis.

AVA CERTIFICATION PROGRAM
Association for Volunteer Administration
PO Box 4585
Boulder, CO 80306
TEL: 303-497-0238

Credit: Certification
Sponsor: Association for Volunteer Administration
Contact: Christine G. Franklin, CVA
Description: The AVA CVA (Certified in Volunteer Administration) program is designed to increase professional credibility, expand knowledge, and enhance recognition of leadership potential. Applicants who meet AVA professional standard and certification criteria are awarded CVA status. The performance-based program is open to experienced professionals, salaried and non-salaried, in volunteer administration. Each candidate must have a minimum of two years of administrative experience in volunteer management.

Portfolio development is the essential element in the program. Through a process of self-assessment and portfolio development, each applicant moves at his/her individual pace toward completion of the program. An Independent Assessment Review Panel composed of practitioners, educators, trainers and certified volunteer administrators reviews the application and portfolio, assesses qualifications according to AVA performance criteria, and awards the CVA credential upon successful completion of the program. There is a three-year period in which to complete the process after acceptance into the program.

To assist applicants, workshops are offered in the United States and Canada. These half-day training sessions are sponsored by AVA regions, affiliates, state conferences, local organizations and interested individuals. Following is an overview of the steps in the certification process:

Step 1: Order a Certification Packet from AVA
The *Certification Packet* contains a full description of the certification process and all materials required to complete the self-assessment, application and portfolio.

Step 2: Attend a Certification Workshop
While not mandatory, attendance at a Certification Workshop is strongly recommended. Workshops are scheduled at various locations throughout the year and at the International Conference on Volunteer Administration, sponsored by AVA each October.

Step 3: Make a Formal Application - The following materials must accompany the application form:
● The Self-Assessment Score Sheet
● The Self-Assessment Sheet
● A Performance Narrative (essay) of 1000 words
● A 200-word Statement of Philosophy
● The Application Fee

If the application is not accepted by the Application Review Panel, it will be returned with application fee and a letter outlining the reasons for non-acceptance and detailing the procedure for resubmission.

Step 4: Submit the Portfolio
Candidates for Certification have three years after the acceptance of their application in which to complete the program. Many candidates complete the process in a much shorter time. The portfolio must include:
● Title Page
● Table of Contents
● Autobiographical Outline
● Philosophy of Volunteerism Statement (not to exceed 1000 words)
● Two management Performance Narratives (not to exceed 1000 words each)
● One Behavioral Performance Narrative (not to exceed 1000 words)
● Three Grounding in the Profession Narratives (not to exceed 500 words each)
● A Career Development Plan

The Certification Assessment Review Panel notifies candidates of the results of the review. Candidates who successfully complete the portfolio process are notified in writing and are given the right to use the designation CVA after their names. A certificate is forwarded and, if requested, a letter is sent to an employer. If materials do not meet the required standards, candidates are notified and the reasons for the decision outlined. A candidate may be requested to rewrite narratives that do not clearly demonstrate performance.

Re-Certification Process
During the fifth year after certification, all Certified Volunteer Administrators may apply for Re-Certification.

Re-Certification is a process of analyzing and recording the professional experiences and professional self-developoment activities which have occurred during one's previous five years and reflecting one's original philosophy statement. Candidates for Re-Certification must exhibit evidence of:
● continuing contribution to the profession by writing a 250-500-word essay
● updated reflection on the original philosophy statement by writing a 500-1000-word essay
● professional self-development by writing a 500-1000-word essay

The AVA Re-Certification Review Panel assesses the evidence contained in the essays. The Panel Chair notifies applicants of the results of the review.

Applicants who successfully complete this process are notified in writing and are given the privilege of continuing the use of the designation "CVA" after their names.

This information is a summary of the pertinent steps of the Certification and Re-Certification process. Interested individuals should request the *Certification Packet.*

AVAS ANNUAL CONFERENCE
Association of Voluntary Action Scholars
Lincoln Filene Center
Tufts University
Medford, MA 02155
TEL: 617-628-5000
Credit: Inquire
Sponsor: Association of Voluntary Action Scholars
Contact: Richard Walker, Executive Officer
Description: This conference emphasizes leadership and management issues that affect nonprofit organizations, and other topics related to citizen participation and voluntary action. It includes plenary sessions by major national figures, workshops on practice skills, and paper panels on research and scholarly issues. Specific topics include:
● The Changing Role of the Nonprofit Sector
● Problems in Diverse Nonprofit Arenas
● Factors that May Affect Nonprofit Organizations in the Future
● Skills to Include Strategic Planning and Management
● Assessing Community Needs
● Recruiting and Training Volunteers
● Improving Representation on Boards and Committees
● Building Constitutency Support and Coalitions
● Conducting Media and Fundraising Campaigns
● Providing Advocacy and Lobbying
● Evaluating Programs
● Mobilizing Resources for Action
● Mediating Mechanisms

Ample time for consultation with faculty and peers is allotted throughout the Conference. The annual meeting of the Association of Voluntary Action Scholars is held in conjunction with the Conference.

AVENUES TO AWARENESS: A PROGRAM FOR THE VOLUNTEER
John Carroll University
University Heights, OH 44118
TEL: 216-491-4316
Credit: .5 hours CEUs
Sponsor: John Carroll University
Contact: Cynthia Schubert, Director

Description: this series of workshops is aimed at helping the volunteer become more effective. It is designed for both the seasoned volunteer and the new volunteer, as well as those considering entry into volunteer work for the first time. Volunteers on Boards and Committees as well as direct service volunteers have been considered in the planning of this series. It was conceived by the University in cooperation with local volunteer directors to assure its relevance to the everyday situations an problems faced by the volunteer.

The workshops were conceived in 1975 to professionalize the Junior League volunteer. Today this Volunteer Career Development Program assists all individuals in the community. It is designed to stimulate introspection and foster creative life planning. Through a process of personal assessment, participants are encouraged to conduct their volunteer or career oriented activities on a professional level which stresses both utilization and appreciation of the individual's specific skills and abilities. Volunteer directors and organizers are encouraged to attend with their volunteers. A typical workshop includes such topics as:

- The Creative Use of Leisure Time
- Values Survey
- The Balanced Lifestyle
- Setting Priorities
- Learning How to "Pack Your Own Chute"

Audio-Visual Personnel from the Junior League of Cleveland supplement the presentations of the facilitators. Certificates awarding .5 hours of CEU credit are issued to requesting participants. Credits are approved by the Cleveland Area Association of Directors of Volunteer Services.

AYE SHARE
Washington State University
Adult and Youth Education
323 Hulbert Hall
Pullman, WA 99164-6236
TEL: 509-335-2911
Credit: Certificate
Sponsor: Washington State University; Association of Voluntary Action Scholars; Association for Volunteer Administration
Contact: Ardis Young, James Long or Jan Hiller
Description: At Washington State University the study of volunteerism and the management of volunteer services is an important part of the Department of Adult and Youth Education's (AYE's) statewide outreach programs and its Master's degree program. Graduate courses in volunteerism include:

- CVE 412 Management of Volunteer Programs
- CVE 413 Voluntary Boards of Directors and Advisory Committees
- CVE 510 Program and Curriculum Development and Evaluation
- CVE 516 Research Methods
- CVE 600, 700 Special Projects and Master's Thesis

During 1989-90 the University established a certification program for volunteer service managers in the state. The program is cosponsored by the AYE Department and the State Center for Voluntary Action. Participants begin by going through an assessment center, planning a learning program with a departmental advisor, then becoming part of a "distance-learning cluster" and receiving lessons and course offerings via satellite and video taped presentation. Another assessment takes place after 12 months of study. It is managed at a central site to determine each student's certification readiness.

Plans through 1994 include:

- an option in the Master's program for those with goals in volunteer leadership, and
- supervised internships and directed student interaction with effective organizations that depend on volunteer service.

The University has three branch campuses, so these new program options will be available statewide.

Other activities of the AYE program during the 1989-90 academic year include:

- Train-the-Trainer Workshop, cosponsored with the Washington State Center for Voluntary Action and Region X of the Association for Volunteer Administration.
- Cosponsorship of the Association of Voluntary Action Scholars National Meeting.
- Co-editing a special edition of the *Nonprofit and Voluntary Sector Quarterly.*
- Management of Statewide volunteer-intensive programs/organizations: 4-H Leaders Council, Family Community Leadership, state Program of Local Government Education.
- Conducting research. Students and faculty completed three theses focused on questions of volunteerism.

Faculty has always included representatives from public, private and academic sectors.

BASIC MANAGEMENT OF VOLUNTEER PROGRAMS
United Way of Chicago
104 South Michigan Avenue
Chicago, IL 60603-5901
TEL: 312-580-2800
Credit: Certificate; CEUs on request
Sponsor: United Way of Chicago
Contact: Joe Agnello
Description: This three-day training program is designed to help human service organizations acquire the benefits of organizational growth and base of support that can be derived by training a designated volunteer administrator in the fundamentals of volunteer program management. It is based on the premise that volunteer administrators with managerial competence are likely to have successful volunteer programs. The program is intended for new volunteer administrators, but benefits can be derived by anyone who works with volunteers. Participants must attend all six sessions, described below:

Session I - The dynamics of Volunteer Motivation: helps the volunteer administrator to create opportunities in which there is a genuine need for volunteer help through:

- examination of why people volunteer
- examination of why organizations need volunteers
- application of motivation theory to volunteer programs.

Session II - Designing Volunteer Programs: helps participants to design programs that produce cooperation, thus maximizing human energy through:

- examination of the difference between volunteer and paid staff programs.
- examination of the forces that build and block effectiveness.
- application of systems theory to volunteer programs.

Session III - Professionalization of VolunteerAdministration: helps participants to examine the variety of tasks they are expected to perform, and to learn this role.

Session IV - The Art of Consultation: helps the volunteer administrator to assess staffing needs in consultation with other department managers, and provides volunteers to meet those needs, through:

- examination of coordination problems.
- study of the consultation process.
- application of the process in a simulated exercise.

Session V - The Art of Participative Management: helps volunteer coordinators to understand the participatory nature of the problem-solving process, and the fact that the act of the volunteer in offering help is indicative of the need for participatory management, through:

- identifying when participative management is appropriate.
- identifying the major functions of management.
- applying the principles of participative management to organization problems.

Session VI - The Quality of Volunteer Worklife: helps to acquaint the volunteer coordinator with quality in a volunteer program, and how it is rooted in the volunteer's satisfaction and productivity, as well as how to avoid the alternatives of apathy, burnout, turnover, or poor morale, through:

- assessing the quality of a volunteer program.
- examining the value of recognition.
- applying the skills of performance appraisal.

The presenter utilizes an experiential style, with an emphasis on the practical application of theory to the real experience of volunteer administration. The sessions are deliberately designed in an informal setting with casual attire recommended to facilitate maximum comfort in the application process.

BASIC MANAGERIAL SKILLS FOR DIRECTORS OF VOLUNTEERS
Voluntary Action Center of Morris County
36 South Street
Morristown, NJ 07960
TEL: 201-538-7200
Credit: Inquire
Sponsor: Geraldine R. Dodge Foundation
Contact: Education Coordinator
Description: This seminar covers the creative techniques needed to manage volunteers effectively. It introduces survival skills that are a must to keep an established program healthy and growing, and helps to meet the challenges of the nineties.
The program is intended for directors and coordinators of volunteer services, executives of community organizations, school personnel, managers of political campaigns and other special interest volunteer groups.
Faculty comes from the field of volunteer/staff management, education, and personnel administration.

BASICS OF VOLUNTEER PROGRAM MANAGEMENT*
SEE GOVERNORS' OFFICES ON VOLUNTEERISM: VIRGINIA

THE BRIDGE
United Way of Weld County
PO Box 1944
Greeley, CO 80632
TEL: 303-353-4300
Credit: Inquire
Sponsor: Colorado Office of Volunteerism
Contact: Director
Description: Volunteers, volunteer coordinators, and agency representatives in two counties are convened to explore, through a participatory workshop, the establishment of a peer support system or network (The Bridge) in the volunteer or nonprofit community.
The Bridge is based on the following assumptions:

- That volunteer leaders and human service agency directors need far more individual attention than they are getting for information, consultation, technical assistance, learning and support.
- That all volunteer leaders and agency directors have some area of expertise to give and are more than happy to share their particular talents with their peers.
- Volunteering of peers to one another - peer support systems or networks - was explored in relation to: scarce dollars - "outside expert" help is becoming less affordable and convenient; how can peer support systems relieve this problem? The bridging process - a central networking pool is needed; how can this be accomplished most effectively?

The workshop sponsors - the Colorado Office on Volunteerism, and the Volunteer Resource Center of the United Way of Weld County - present the workshop at a very affordable rate to assure maximum exposure to this relatively new concept in volunteerism. As a result of the workshop, the Volunteer Resource Center is establishing a central networking pool to continue the bridging process.

BRIDGING VOLUNTEER RESOURCES
American Red Cross
Tulsa Area Chapter
3345 South Harvard, PO Box 45726
Tulsa, OK 74145
TEL: 918-743-9741
Credit: Inquire
Sponsor: Tulsa Association of Volunteer Administrators (TAVA); Oklahoma Department of Economic and Community Affairs; Community Service Council of Greater Tulsa
Contact: Dee Oldaker
Description: Designed to help volunteer administrators avoid duplication and get the maximum benefit from efforts and resources, this two-day workshop addresses the need to plan activities so that they will complement and serve each other rather than work against each other. Workshop topics include:

- **Boardsmanship** - better understanding of leadership skills and the responsibilities of serving on a Board or Committee.
- **How to Publicize Your Program On a Shoestring Budget** - making the best use of the various media.
- **Evaluating Your Volunteer Program** - a way to measure the effectiveness of your program to guide you in planning for the future.
- **How to Make $$$!** - panel presentation of fund raising ideas.
- **Volunteerism in the Church** - the increase in organized programs in churches.
- **Stress Management** - how to relax and enjoy the job.
- **How to Start a Volunteer Program** - video tape from State OVCP.
- **Coming of Age** - nursing home volunteer program.
- **Parliamentary Procedure** - tips on how to expedite meetings correctly.
- **Meet the Experts** - panel of experienced Volunteer Administrators focusing on recruitment, interviewing, placement, supervision, motivation, and training.

Although formats change with the needs of participants, training events are conducted on a continuing basis by TAVA.

THE CARE AND NOURISHMENT OF VOLUNTEERS*
Community Coordinating Council of Lee County
2517 Second Street
Fort Myers, FL 33901
TEL: 813-334-7135; 813-334-0405
Credit: Inquire
Sponsor: United Way; Voluntary Action Center
Contact: Gladys Hosch or Carol Sausaman
Description: Following an expressed need from volunteer coordinators, the Community Coordinating Council (a division of the local United Way) joined with the local Voluntary Action Center to enlist assistance to help the coordinators understand the needs of volunteers. Involving a human systems development expert, the sponsors convened a one-day program which included the following topics:

- Crisis in Human Services: Enter the VOLUNTEERS: Who and Where are they?
- Contemporary Volunteerism: Recruitment and Development
- Organization Goal-Setting: Facilitating "togetherness" - Working toward common goals - Interaction.
- Techniques for Utilizing Volunteers: Job Descriptions
- Techniques for Screening, Orientation and Training
- Preparing Staff for Volunteers: How to "pay" volunteers

The workshop is designed for all persons who coordinate the services of volunteers in any setting, paid or unpaid. The final session convenes an Idea Roundtable, which is a forum for "common sense solutions" and suggestions to take back to the office.

CELEBRATION OF VOLUNTEERISM: ANNUAL STATEWIDE CONFERENCE
SEE GOVERNORS' OFFICES ON VOLUNTEERISM: VIRGINIA

CERTIFICATE IN VOLUNTEER MANAGEMENT
Rutgers University
Graduate School of Social Work
Tillet Hall, Livingston Campus
New Brunswick, NJ 08903
TEL: 201-932-2688
Credit: CEUs; AVA Endorsement; Certificate (for each course); Certificate in Volunteer Management (all eight courses)
Sponsor: Rutgers University
Contact: Patricia C. Dunn
Description: The intent of this course is to help participants meet the challenge of the growing volunteer movement by offering a Certificate in Volunteer Management to develop and improve the knowledge and skill of those coordinators, and leaders of volunteers from:
- Human service organizations
- Health and hospitals
- Religious and civic organizations
- Community associations
- Business and private industry
- Federal, state and local government agencies
- Public schools and other educational settings
- Volunteer service programs
- Those wishing to prepare for a career in volunteer management

The Certificate program consists of seven required learning activities and a number of electives from which one is chosen to complete the program:
Required:
- An Overview of Voluntarism: A Forum for Volunteers and Those Who Manage Volunteers
- Developing a Volunteer Program: Basics for the Volunteer Administrator
- Personnel Management: Volunteer/Staff Relations
- Fiscal Management: A Workshop for Human Service Managers
- General Organization Theory
- Program Development and Evaluation (for experienced managers who have completed "Developing a Volunteer Program: Basics for the Volunteer Administrator")

Electives:
- Fund Raising
- Role and Function of Committees
- Basic Training for Trainers
- Interpersonal Style

Five of the courses are described in detail below; other descriptions are available on request:
An Overview of Voluntarism: A Forum for Volunteers and Those Who Manage Volunteers (.6 CEUs) - provides a foundation of background information vital to all individuals involved in the community; involves a six-hour seminar with a panel of experienced practitioners and scholars sharing specialized data and insights about the independent third sector; includes group activities, audiovisual presentations, and exchanges between group leaders, giving the participants the opportunity to:
- Track the history of citizen participation in American from which our current modern volunteer community has evolved;
- Examine the profile of American voluntarism, analyzing who does what to whom, where, when, and why;
- Become acquainted with the names and purposes of major organizations and individual leaders in the field; unscramble specific vocabulary and acronyms;
- Investigate the increasing number and nature of ethical and moral issues facing administrators working in the controversial

environment and volunteer programs in the nineties;
- Diagnose your personal professional skills and match them against the unique administrative and human relations skills required of managers of volunteer programs and agencies.

Developing a Volunteer Program: Basics for the Volunteer Administrator (2.2 CEUs) - provides, in a four-session course, a focus on the role and function of persons who manage volunteer programs; includes exercises such as:
- developing policies and procedures:
- writing job descriptions; and
- designing new approaches for recruiting and retaining volunteers in the eighties.

In addition, participants learn about how training programs for volunteers are developed (i.e., assessing needs, writing instructional goals and objectives, designing, implementing, budgeting, and evaluation). Program evaluation and recordkeeping receive special attention with emphasis on ways to measure and improve the value of volunteer services.

Fiscal Management: A Workshop for Human Service Managers (1.1 CEUs) - covers the current social and political climate and its current pressing demands for an understaning of budgeting, auditing, and other financial management processes; sets a goal, during the two-day workshop, of improving the performance of participants in various areas of fiscal management, including:
- Accounting terminology
- Financial statements
- Budgets
- Cash flow accounts
- Reporting to your board
- Independent audits
- Third party report requests
- Fund accounting
- Program expenditure reporting
- Employment legislation and the human service organization

The learning format for this workshop consists of lectures and guided group discussion.

Interpersonal Style: A Workshop for Managers, Trainers, and Consultants (1.1 CEUs) - addresses the premise that "one of the most important tools that managers, trainers, and consultants possess is use of self" has the general goal of helping participants identify their own individual styles; enables participants to examine several leadership models and theories, and to analyze various types and approaches to management, training and consultation; expects each student to use the conceptual framework presented, and the results of self-assessment and feedback from others in the program, to develop a self-improvement program.

Basic Training for Trainers (4.4 CEUs) - provides participants with the basic analytical, interactional, and technical skills necessary to be a trainer, such as:
- Analytical Skills, which depend on the ability to assess, distinguish, conceptualize and formulate, including: analyzing performance problems; determining training needs; analyzing goals; setting objectives; and writing training designs and evaluation formats.
- Interactional Skills, which are necessary to work successfully with people, including: the ability to create environments which maximize learning experiences; and the ability to elicit cooperation in gathering cognitive and effective data to analyze systems, determine needs, and provide alternatives for problem solving.
- Technical Skills, which refer to the ability to use knowledge, methods, techniques, and equipment necessary for the performance of such tasks as simulations, structured exercises, training cost analysis, video taping, etc.

The goals of this course correspond with the above skill areas:
- Understanding the role of the trainer in an organization.
- Analyzing training needs for organizations and individuals.
- Setting performance objectives.
- Designing training programs.
- Implementing training programs.

● Evaluating the effectiveness of training programs.

Instructors (trainers) employ a variety of training designs and methods and, in so doing, serve as models for participants. The instruction format includes demonstrations, mini-lectures, group exercises, video taping, and playback of each participant's skill practice sessions. Outside preparation is an important part of the learning experience, and attendance at all sessions is essential. Only those who have the total period (8 sessions) cleared by employers should apply for this course.

This is an ongoing program of the Graduate School of Social Work, Continuing Education Program. Printed materials are available.

CERTIFICATE PROGRAM IN VOLUNTEER ADMINISTRATION
University of Delaware
Wilcastle Center
2800 Pennsylvania Avenue
Wilmington, DE 19806
TEL: 302-738-8155
Credit: University of Delaware Certificate in Volunteer Administration
Sponsor: University of Delaware
Contact: Jacob Haber
Description: Developed for volunteer coordinators who work in social service agencies, community agencies, hospitals and other such settings, this program is designed to increase the coordinator's competence in major skill areas as related to his/her job.

Volunteer Training - CED-1-03-20-21-127JH
Discussion of the training planning process and its implementation. Topics include:
● Training as a field of practice
● The actual process of training
● Training techniques and materials
● Practical conceptual framework and applications of training
● Logistics and group composition within the training scheme
● Measurement of training in relation to work performance

Supervision of Volunteers - CED 1-03-20-21-128JH
Exploration of the various models which can be used to supervise volunteers. The volunteer supervisor will be presented in the role of:
● Motivator
● Coordinator
● Objective Setter
● Planner
● Evaluator
● Leader and Teacher

Evaluation of Volunteer Programs - CED 1-03-20-21-129JH
A focus on important aspects of program evaluation as they relate to volunteer services. Topics include:
● The place of program evaluation in the cycle of organizational events
● Various models or program evaluation
● Organizational resistance and support to program evaluation
● Planning and implementing evaluation

Improving Staff-Volunteer Relations - CED 1-03-20-21-130JH
A workshop designed to assist the participant to understand how the volunteer and paid staff employee interact and how and why these relationships can be either positive or negative. Topics include:
● How to determine your organization's receptivity for volunteers
● Some fears and expectations of paid staff toward volunteers
● How using volunteers will affect your paid staff at all levels within the organization
● How to work toward the achievement of optimum conditions between paid and volunteer staff

Volunteer Retention and Recognition - CED 1-03-20-21-131JH

Consideration of the importance of volunteer recognition and its influence on retention of volunteers. Topics include:
● Individual volunteer and agency needs for volunteer recognition and retention
● Specific problems regarding volunteer recognition and retention
● Techniques for volunteer recognition

Recognition of Volunteers - CED 2-03-20-21-126JH
Consideration of volunteer recruitment as part of the coordinator's job responsibility. Topics include:
● What is recruiting?
● Sources of potential volunteers
● How to tell your agency's "story" to potential volunteers
● Pitfalls in recruiting
● Working with the volunteer prior to his/her commencing work

Public Relations - CED 1-03-20-21-298JH
A focus on public relations techniques and methods that can be used by coordinators to enhance and increase public awareness of their programs. Topics include:
● The four components of a public relations program
● Different types of public relations activities available to the volunteer coordinator
● How to identify and solve problems relating to individual public relations

Office Management - CED 2-03-20-21-133JH
A focus on how the coordinator can increase efficiency within the office setting. Topics include:
● Planning and layout of physical facilities
● Organizing and staffing an office
● Administrative management
● Forms control
● Basic record keeping
● Measurement of work performance

Persons completing six of the eight seminars are awarded a University of Delaware Certificate in Volunteer Administration. [Advanced Seminars are available to those completing the Certificate Program.]

CERTIFIED VOLUNTEER MANAGER PROGRAM
Arkansas Public Administration Consortium
UALR Library Room 539-A
2801 South University
Little Rock, AR 72204
TEL: 501-569-8469
Credit: Inquire
Sponsor: Arkansas Office of Volunteerism
Contact: Melissa Hawkins
Description: The Certified Volunteer Manager (CVM) Program is sponsored by the Arkansas Public Administration Consortium and the Arkansas Office of Volunteerism. It is a management training program that provides the opportunity for managers in volunteer organizations to attain a professional designation. It is designed to meet the training needs of managers of volunteers and/or volunteer programs. There are six courses required for the CVM designation as well as a final project. Each course lasts two full days with the six courses completed over a period of about nine months. The final project fulfills necessary requirements of application for international certification with the Association for Volunteer Administration (AVA). The Arkansas CVM program is a designated model of volunteer management training by AVA. The six courses are:
● **The Management Assessment Seminar** - allows the manager to self-assess the management skills already possessed and explains the project step of the certification process.
● **The Leadership Seminar** - focuses on the individual manager's leadership and communication styles and the organizational ideology or climate in which the manager operates.
● **Planning and Program Evaluation** - focuses on the manager's

role in building a model of excellence and mapping strategic directions, then outlining procedures for policy and program assessment based on expectations, and analyzing costs and benefits.

- **The Political Process** - offers an overview of the political process as it relates to volunteer agency managers. Specifically, it helps the manager assess his or her role in the political environment and explore ways that managers can use the political arena to become more effective.
- **Managing Personnel** - is designed to help the manager identify and understand work behavior patterns. Also covered are personnel laws and techniques for improving personnel policies in the participant's organization.
- **Effective Management Communication** - allows the manager to identify the characteristics of interpersonal communication that contribute to communication breakdowns and understand how to use an effective overall communication style.

Applicants to the CVM program must have two years of experience in managing volunteers or volunteer programs. Limited scholarships are available for participants who are not funded by their agency.

The 1990 class is the fourth group of managers to participate in the program. CVM certificates are presented to the graduates at the annual Volunteer Directions Conference.

Additional sponsors are Arkansas State University, University of Arkansas at Little Rock, and University of Arkansas, Fayetteville.

CHATHAM MANAGEMENT SEMINAR
Chatham College
Woodland Road
Pittsburgh, PA 15232
TEL: 412-441-8200
Credit: Non-credit; a certificate is awarded
Sponsor: Chatham College
Contact: Peggy Donaldson
Description: One of several educational programs offered by Chatham College to enhance the effective leadership of volunteer organizations, this two-week course is designed to assist women who have recently achieved management positions, or who are perceived to have the potential for such achievement. The emphasis and objective of this certificate program are:

- To develop effective managerial skills, both analytical and behavioral.
- To offer instruction in Management Principles, Organizational Communication, Organizational Behavior and Problem Solving.
- To prepare participants to address practical and functional issues including motivation, delegation, managerial style, stress management, career management and office organization and technology.
- To provide elective instruction in Economics, Data Management and Information Science, and Marketing to enable each participant to acquire knowledge in areas of particular need.

Seminar faculty is drawn from the Chatham College faculty, outside consultants, and instructors from nearby graduate schools of business.

CONFERENCE ON VOLUNTEERISM
American Red Cross
Greater Buffalo Chapter
786 Delaware Avenue
Buffalo, NY 14209
TEL: 716-886-7500
Credit: AVA Certification (partial fulfillment), CEUs (State University College at Buffalo)
Sponsor: AAUW Group Effectiveness Team
Contact: Peter Von Berg

Description: Developed by a Steering Committee with members coming from a number of human service areas, this two-day workshop covers 20 areas of concern in the management of volunteer programs. Workshops include:

Winning with Staff - A New Look at Enriching Relations Between Volunteers and Staff (seven principles for the development of a stronger staff/volunteer team)

Long Range Planning - Why Long Range/Strategic Planning (managing rather than reacting to change)

Futurology - The Impact of the Future on the Volunteer Agency (the future; today, tomorrow and years hence)

Quality Circles - The Key to Progress and Growth of Human Resources (theory and techniques in applying the concept of Quality Circles to problem flagging, fixing and evaluation). This concept improves the growth of human resources by developing a meaningful relationship with and commitment among staff and volunteers.

Networking/Collaborating: Expanding Horizons on How to Work with Others to Get the Job Done

Lobbying: Action and Reaction (views on how to show support, enlist volunteers and educate legislators to insure a successful outcome)

There's More Than One Way to Fund Programs (five fund raising methods; advantages and disadvantages of each; choosing the best mix; raising the dollars)

Building Partnerships with Corporations: The Tools to Work Effectively with Corporations ("state of the art" corporate volunteer programs, practical techniques and benefits of corporate involvement to the agency and community)

"Board Enrichment" Leadership Development and Beyond... ("hands on" workshop designed to maximize the productivity of volunteer boards)

Organized Labor and Agencies (perspective of involvement of organized labor in the voluntary sector: Union Counselor Program, Board Involvement, Volunteer Recruitment and Model Programs)

Communication Skills (practical methods of organizing and presenting communication messages)

Social Marketing: Implementing the Approved Plan (plan that coordinates people, skills, systems and tactics)

Needs Assessment - Efficacy of Needs Assessment of a Planned vs. Ad Hoc Decision Approach (community planning in an era of economic revitalization?)

Grantsmanship: From the Foundation's Point of View (presentations by local Foundation Directors regarding management of their Foundations)

Volunteer Recruitment - Values, Motivations and Needs: Innovative Tools

Techniques for More Creative Volunteerism: Getting the Most Mileage out of Creative Ideas on Volunteerism (learning and using creative thinking skills to generate ideas and tools for judgment)

Presenting the Agency to the Public (a sharing of knowledge between the radio, television and other media and nonprofit organizations)

Fund Raising: Special Events and Direct Mail (evaluating the potential of the organization and its ability to run successful special events and learning how to operate the direct mail process). Faculty for the conference was drawn from fields of education, fund raising, corporations, public relations, labor medicine, local government, elected officials, federal government, employment, and nonprofit organizations at every level. A special session, AVA Certification in Volunteer Administration, was held in conjunction with the conference to provide an overview of the Association's Certification Program.

Local offices of the American Lung Association, the Buffalo Department of Human Resources, Junior League, Jewish Federation, and the Girl Scout Council also participated in the program.

CONNECTICUT LEADERSHIP CONFERENCE
SEE GOVERNORS' OFFICES ON VOLUNTEERISM:
CONNECTICUT

CORE CURRICULUM - THE VOLUNTEER
Volunteer and Information Agency
United Way of New Orleans
4747 Earhart Boulevard
Suite 105
New Orleans, LA 70125
TEL: 504-488-4636
Credit: Inquire
Sponsor: Volunteer and Information Agency (VIA), a United Way
Agency
Contact: Joan Renton
Description: Based on the core curriculum below, VIA offers
training and technical assistance to non-profit agencies who wish
to establish or expand their volunteer programs. This training
offers Directors of Volunteers opportunities to sharpen their skills
in order to effectively manage a volunteer program and increase
their understanding in organizational behavior and human
relations within a human service delivery setting.
Core Curriculum

- **Trends in Volunteerism** - the issues, challenges, possibilities
  and dreams.
- **Motivation and Organizational Climate** - learn to diagnose
  and create a positive and supportive climate within the
  organization. Learn group process skills that will enhance
  team functioning and staff-volunteer relations; learn what
  motivates both paid and unpaid staff members.
- **Building a Comprehensive Volunteer Program** - learn practical
  skills to plan a program through the MBO method.
- **Designing Training Programs for Volunteers** - learn the
  characteristics of the adult learner; explore various training
  methods and learn when to utilize each and how to translate
  learning objectives into productive learning activities.
- **Writing Volunteer Job Descriptions** - learn key components in
  writing a clear/specific, challenging job design; learn how to
  involve staff and volunteers in the process of designing a
  volunteer position.
- **Recruiting Volunteers** - analyze problems and explore
  methods for effective volunteer recruitment; learn when, how,
  what and where to use the media for recruiting.
- **Interviewing** - learn the theory and practice behind Initial,
  Corrective and Terminal Interviews.
- **Supervising Volunteers** - learn various styles of supervision
  and when to use each.
- **Recognition** - when, what, who and how.
- **Evaluating Programs and People: Record Keeping** - examine
  evaluation models, interpret results and translate evaluation
  data into new program planning cycles; learn the what and
  how of record keeping on programs and people.
- **Growing and Going as a Director of Volunteers** - how to
  enable self and others to grow and avoid burn-out within the
  volunteer program; how to manage your time without your
  time managing you.
- **Communication Skills** - how to problem-solve, deal with
  conflict and make decisions in a healthy, caring manner.

The Volunteer Center of VIA offers this training through three
major service packages:

- VIA sponsors six city-wide training sessions on topics related
  to managing a volunteer program (core curriculum). These
  sessions are three to six hours in length and can be designed
  for inexperienced or experienced directors.
- VIA offers a concentrated 14-hour training session twice a
  year based on topics in the core curriculum. The purpose of
  this training is to offer immediate and comprehensive
  assistance to inexperienced Directors of Volunteers.
- VIA offers in-house training and consultation assistance to

individual agencies. These sessions are individually designed to
meet the unique needs of that agency contracting with VIA.
VIA sponsors an annual conference on volunteerism. Currently,
VIA is the only agency in the state to develop and offer training
for Directors of Volunteers. Plans are to expand these services as
the need arises.

CREDIT AND DEGREE PROGRAMS IN VOLUNTARY
ASSOCIATION ADMINISTRATION IN COLLEGES AND
UNIVERSITIES
Texas A&M
806 Rudder Tower
College Station, TX 77843
TEL: 713-845-5460 (also below)
Credit: Inquire
Sponsor: Texas A&M; Virginia Tech; Association of Voluntary
Action Scholars (AVAS)
Contact: Barbara Stone (Texas A&M); V. Milton Boyce (4-H)
202-447-5853; Delwyn Dyer (VA Tech) 703-961-7966
Description: This conference is designed for persons dedicated to
development or improvement of curriculum and credit courses in
colleges and universities. It is a sharing and development effort
addressing six major topics:
- curriculum and competencies;
- knowledge base and relevant disciplines;
- research base and taxonomy;
- professional degrees and higher education;
- delivery modes and student access; and
- agency and organization support.

The Conference grew out of four mini-conferences convened to
identify the issues and survey the current field. Conference time is
devoted to exploring the dynamics of developing a curriculum,
getting it accepted with a college or university, attracting students
on a career development track, and designing curriculum delivery
modes acceptable to the student and the college or university.
Specific presentations include:

- Curriculum Development, Knowledge Base, Research, and the
  Competency Lists.
- Let Me Tell You About Our Program (small groups learning
  in detail from each other about programs in progress or in
  place).
- Adding a Professional Degree or Program Concentrate in a
  College or University.
- Organization and Delivery Models for Professional Programs
  within Higher Education.
- Professional Education and Voluntary Association/Agency
  Support.
- Small Group Work: Strategies for Influencing Institutions of
  Higher Education and Volunteer Agency Improvements in
  Curriculum and Credentialing.
- The Work that Remains... (based on results of above
  presentations).
- Informal Networking and Coalition Building.

Participants are experts who come from the fields of education,
government, business, and the voluntary sector. The Conference is
limited to 75 participants, each of whom receive copies of the
foundation papers used in the presentations.

CURRICULUM DEVELOPMENT FOR VOLUNTEER
ADMINISTRATORS
Virginia Polytechnic Institute and State University
College of Education
Blacksburg, VA 24061
TEL: 703-961-5706
Credit: Inquire
Sponsor: Virginia Polytechnic Institute and State University; Texas
A&M
Contact: Harold Stubblefield

Description: An outreach of two previous meetings, this conference explores ways to develop professional preparation programs for volunteer administrators. The conference builds on factors recognized at the two previous meetings, including:

- Considerable attention is being directed toward the professionalism of volunteer administration.
- Several competency studies have been conducted.
- A Certification Program has been developed in a major volunteer organization.
- Several colleges and universities offer degree programs in volunteer administration.

Thus, the present conference examines more systematically the present status of professional preparation programs and what specific actions are needed by colleges and universities or other appropriate agencies. Conference activities are divided into three categories:

1. Concerns about Volunteer Administrators and their Professional Preparation.
2. Reports from Participants on Professional Preparation Programs in which they were/are Participants.
3. Several Issues:
   - Needed Research
   - Curriculum Development and Competency Identification
   - Levels of Training Needed at Various Stages of Experience/Practice
   - Conditions Necessary for Anchoring a Volunteer Curriculum in a College or University Setting

Several of the thirty-seven attendees had participated in the previous conferences, providing an additional dimension in that more detail was available than could be presented in the conference proceedings of the earlier meetings.

Results of the conference are the products of two task groups and the summary or integrative statements of several individuals about aspects of curriculum development, as follows:

1. Categories of Research
2. Curriculum Development Issues
3. Voluntary Organization Issues
4. Institution of Higher Education Issues
5. Anchoring a Volunteer Curriculum
6. Need for a National Conference
7. Long-Range Planning Model
8. An Integrated Model for Planning

A full report of the conference, Report of Conference on Curriculum Development for Volunteer Administrators, is available.

DEVELOPING YOUR PERSPECTIVE: A SEMINAR IN VOLUNTEER ADMINISTRATION TODAY
Volunteers In Action
229 Waterman Street
Providence, RI 02906
TEL: 401-421-6547; 401-421-7472
Credit: AVA Certification (partial fulfillment)
Sponsor: United Way
Contact: Betsy A. Garland
Description: The purpose of this seminar is to provide a framework for Volunteer Administrators to focus on the volunteer program. It is designed to help participants identify areas that can be strengthened in individual programs, and offers resources with which to do so. Sessions include:

- Current Trends that Add Dimensions to Your Program
- Overview of the field of volunteerism
- Specific guides for framing your program
- Community resources available to you
- The Opportunity to clarify specific problems

The perspective of this seminar has proven helpful to Agency Directors, Volunteer Administrators, Volunteers, Board Members, Members of Service Clubs, Church and other community organizations. The session is limited to 10 participants.

Volunteers In Action (VIA) is a statewide voluntary action center accredited by the Association of Volunteer Centers. Its training programs are accepted as partial fulfillment for professional certification by the Association for Volunteer Administration. VIA satellite centers are located in Woonsocket (401-762-0679), and Wakefield (401-789-9149), with others planned (inquire).

DOVIA MEETINGS FOR VOLUNTEER ADMINISTRATORS
Directors of Volunteers in Agencies
c/o Voluntary Action Center
36 South Street
Morristown, NJ 07960
TEL: 201-538-7200
Credit: Inquire
Sponsor: DOVIA
Contact: Education Coordinator
Description: The meetings of DOVIA (Directors of Volunteers in Agencies) cover all aspects of volunteer administration, addressing a single topic in each meeting. Typical topics include:

- Marketing Your Program
- Critical Issues Facing Voluntarism Today
- Temporary Assignments for Volunteers and Volunteer Groups
- Keys to Success: Job Descriptions and Interviews
- Recognition
- Volunteer/Staff Relations
- Special Populations: Youth, Elderly, Disabled

These are only a few of the many topics covered by the DOVIA organization. This group develops programs based on expressed needs, enlisting experts in specific areas as presenters.

DOVIA SKILL DEVELOPMENT WORKSHOPS*
United Way of San Diego County
Volunteer Center Division
4699 Murphy Canyon Road
PO Box 23543
San Diego, CA 92111
TEL: 619-492-2000
Credit: AVA Certification (partial fulfillment)
Sponsor: Directors of Volunteers in Agencies
Contact: Workshop Coordinator
Description: This series of workshops provides opportunities for supervisors of volunteers to learn more about important topics related to their work and share their opinions of them. The training is designed to assure a beneficial learning experience for both the new and the experienced volunteer supervisor. Examples of workshop topics are:

- How to Involve Volunteers in Program Development and Management
- Experiential Exercises and Techniques for Training
- Marketing Plans for Recruitment
- Ideas for Retention
- Workshop of Power
- Training Staff to Work with Volunteers

In addition, DOVIA, a statewide organization, invites participants to become part of its planning committee to help assure relevance in the organization's workshops.
[DOVIA, and similar statewide organizations for directors of volunteers, exist in many of the states. For information about such activities in your state, contact Ivan Scheier, *Center for Creative Community,* PO Box 2427, Santa Fe, NM 87504, who has developed the first directory of such organizations on a nationwide basis]

DOVIA TRAINING PROGRAMS
Directors of Volunteers in Agencies
c/o United Way's VAC
404 South Eighth Street
Minneapolis, MN 55404
TEL: 612-340-7532

Credit: Varies; Inquire
Sponsor: Voluntary Action Center of United Way
Contact: Rich Wheaton, Chair, DOVIA
Description: Serving as a support group for Volunteer Directors and Coordinators, DOVIA conducts bimonthly workshops in areas of concern expressed by its member volunteer leaders, such as:

- **Selling Your Volunteer Program - Inside and Out:** public relations as it relates to the general public and to internal communications within the agency.
- **Long Range Planning: Stretching Dollars and Services:** involving volunteers in the agency - when it is best for client services and for budgeting to do so.
- **Position Cuts and Volunteer Involvement:** dealing with the issue of paid position cuts and staff involvement.
- **The Volunteer Perspectives: Partners in the Process:** examining satisfactions and concerns of volunteers and supervisors.
- **Certification: What Does it Mean to Me?** over-view of Association for Volunteer Administration (AVA) competency-based creditation plan.
- **The Effects of Alternative Sentencing on Volunteer Programs:** examining issues concerning sentenced offenders as volunteers, goals, needs, and confidentiality.

DOVIA training is available in many states with series similar to the above for all paid and unpaid Volunteer Directors/Coordinators or other staff responsible for volunteers in an agency or organization. Subject areas of workshops change as needs emerge.

DVC WORKSHOPS AND CONFERENCES
Delaware Volunteer Coordinators
PO Box 7565
Newark, DE 19714-7565
TEL: 302-656-6620
Credit: Inquire
Sponsor: Delaware Volunteer Coordinators (DVC)
Contact: Mary Christine Byrd
Description: As the professional association for volunteer administrators in Delaware, the Delaware Volunteer Coordinators' purpose is to promote volunteerism and assist the volunteer coordinators, supervisors, etc., in developing their professional skills. This is achieved in a number of ways, one of which is a series of workshops and conferences based on expressed needs from the field. Workshops are held six times a year (September through June).
Faculty for the programs is drawn from the universities, churches, business/industry, and individual resource persons. Previous meetings have included topics such as Public Speaking, Listening Skills and Interviewing, Creative Problem Solving, Media in Promoting Volunteer Programs, Designing Innovative Projects for School Volunteers, Serving the Needs of Your Volunteers, and others.
In addition to the periodic workshops and conferences, DVC encourages student internships, and keeps abreast of non-DVC activities that would enhance the development of its members, and pools resources with the *Coalition on Volunteerism* for activities better served through cooperative effort.

THE DYNAMICS OF A SUCCESSFUL VOLUNTEER PROGRAM
Pennsylvania State University
209 J. Orvis Keller Building
University Park, PA 16802
TEL: 814-863-0201
Credit: CEUs; AVA Endorsement; Nursing Home Administrators Certification
Sponsor: Pennsylvania State University
Contact: Charles Meck, Regional CE Director

Description: Developed in 1976 and expanding ever since, this workshop series covers a wide variety of topics relating both to volunteer management and to the administration of nonprofit organizations. The workshops are designed for anyone who directs and leads volunteers, including both religious and civic organizations, public agencies or programs utilizing volunteers, community volunteer programs, and voluntary and nonprofit organizations who work with or are supported by volunteers. The workshops are designed for full- or part-time, paid or unpaid staff or volunteers, and include:
Foundations of Effective Volunteer Programming
- Launching a Volunteer Program: Why, What, and How
- Sustaining a Volunteer Program
- Motivation, Supervision, and Recognition of Volunteers
- Recruiting and Interviewing Volunteers
- Evaluation, Record Keeping, and Accountability of Volunteer Programs
- Developing a Training Program for Volunteers
- Effective Staff/Volunteer Relationships
- Board of Directors
- Recruiting, Training, and Legal Responsibilities
- Working with Committees and Advisory Groups

Management Skills and Functions in Voluntary Nonprofit Organizations and Public Agencies
- Fund Raising
- Proposal and Grant Writing
- Public Relations and Communications
- Management by Objectives
- Time Management
- Coping with Stress

Special Programs in Volunteer Development and Training
- Senior Citizens and Volunteerism
- The Untapped Resource
- Disabled Persons as Volunteers
- Second Statewide Symposium on Volunteerism and Education in Pennsylvania

One CEU per ten contact hours, six hours of credit toward a nursing home administrator's license, and partial fulfillment of requirements for professional certification or recertification by the Association for Volunteer Administration (AVA) are available through this workshop. Faculty was drawn from the University with Advisory Committee members coming from hospitals, VACs, Associations, Corporations. A correspondence course is available.

THE DYNAMICS OF A SUCCESSFUL VOLUNTEER PROGRAM: CORRESPONDENCE COURSE
Pennsylvania State University
Independent Study by Correspondence
3-V Shields Building
University Park, PA 16802
TEL: 800-252-3592 (PA)
TOLL FREE: 800-458-3617 (nationwide)
Credit: 2.5 CEUs
Sponsor: The Pennsylvania State University
Contact: Larry Gamm
Description: This correspondence course addresses Volunteer Program Management and Voluntary Organization Management. It is a Community Development Program in the College of Human Development. It consists of selected portions of basic workshops in the regular curriculum (see above training program description). The course offers an inner view of the role voluntary organizations play in society. It stresses the significance of volunteer activity in the community setting and provides the practical information and conceptual framework necessary to recruit, train, and manage volunteers successfully.
Also, the course introduces the student to regulatory issues, organizational dynamics, and the social effects of this expanding segment of the national economy.
Faculty comes from the University's Community Development

staff, who also offer a training course, Improving Productivity in the Use of Volunteers, and a credit course, Strategies of Volunteer Leadership, and from the Association of Voluntary Action Scholars, the Community Development Society, the American Medical Association, and Boards of national organizations.

DYNAMITE PLANNING... EXPLODE INTO ACTION!
Community Volunteer Service
Minnesota Association of Volunteer Directors
115 South Union Street
Stillwater, MN 55082
TEL: 612-439-7434
Sponsor: Minnesota Association of Volunteer Directors
Contact: Vi Russell
Description: The conferences of the *Minnesota Association of Volunteer Directors (MAVD)* and the *Minnesota Association of Volunteer Centers (MNAVC)* are always combined with the *Lake Sylvia Conferences.*
The purpose of the conference is to introduce participants to *Storyboarding,* a planning and problem-solving process invented by *Leonardo daVinci* and further developed by *Walt Disney.* *Storyboarding* is a technique which brings people together around an issue to develop individual action plans to deal with the issue. A major focus of the conference is its *Planning Groups* format, in which small groups choose *one* issue on which to concentrate, using the storyboarding process. The 1990 conferences offered six choices:
- Diversity and Cultural Awareness
- Positioning Within Your Agency
- Youth Community Service
- Expanding and Declining Resources
- Transition Issues
- Ethical Challenges

Facilitators for the *Focused Planning Groups* are trained at a day-long session before the conference by an experienced trainer and former director of volunteers who has trained facilitators for government, nonprofit organizations, the religious community, and military installations, among others.
To help develop the skills needed to implement the action plans the storyboarding process produces, *Skill Building Workshops* are administered in the following areas:
Marketing
- Dealing with Difficult People
- Preparing for Crisis

External Forces
- Working with the Media
- When the Legislature Throws You a Curve

Technical Skills
- Supervision Basics
- Reading the Scene: Knowing Your Internal Politics

Marketing
- The Changing Face of Volunteers
- Expanding Your Program Through Creative Partnerships

Communications
- Capturing Your Audiences with Dynamic Verbal Skills
- Video Nitty-Gritty

Wednesday Early Bird Sessions - Internships, Mentoring, Old Guard Roundtable
Faculty for the conference was drawn from the media, the nonprofit community, the business community, and the private consulting field.
Publications: Conference Proceedings

EFFECTIVE MANAGEMENT OF VOLUNTEER PROGRAMS
Des Moines Area Community College
2006 South Ankeny Boulevard
Ankeny , IA 50021
TEL: 515-964-6365

Credit: SERV:312, 2 credits, 24 hours; SERV:512; 2.4 CEU, 24 hours
Sponsor: Des Moines Area Community College
Contact: Peggy Cutlip, Coordinator
Description: This program is one of a series designed to provide a comprehensive learning experience for individuals in the development, coordination and supervision of volunteers and volunteer programs. Successful completion of the series leads to a Volunteer Management Specialist Certificate.
Course SERV:312 is a two-credit course which covers the following subject areas over a four-day period:
First Day
- Course overview, expectations, informal discussion
- Volunteerism: definitions; types of volunteers
- Volunteers in perspective of the total organization: volunteer roles; staff roles (coordinator; staff relations; administrator)

Second Day
- Fiscal requirements
- Relations with other organizations (national/state/local)
- Cooperation with other organizations
- Trends in volunteerism
- Burn out - how to avoid it

Third Day
- The administrative volunteer: boards and their functions; working with the board; auxiliary or guild boards; advisory boards, committees; the board in action as an influencer; involving the volunteer in planning meetings and workshops
- The fundraising volunteer: how-to alternatives; public relations; staff role
- Grants and other funding sources

Fourth Day
- Program Management involved in management theory; goal setting
- Communication (channels; organizational styles)
- Conflict resolution
- Review and wrap-up

Ample time was available throughout the conference for networking and exchanging materials.

THE EFFECTIVE VOLUNTEER
Greenville Technical College
PO Box 5616, Station B
Greenville, SC 29606
TEL: 803-242-3170
Credit: CEUs
Sponsor: Greenville Technical College
Contact: Phil McGee
Description: This course is designed for those who would like to become more effective and efficient in their volunteer activities. It is recommended for the general public and for those presently engaged in volunteer activities. Sessions include:
- **Session I** - Self-Assessment as a Volunteer; Volunteer Opportunities; Volunteer Responsibilities and Rights
- **Session II** - Personal Goal Setting and Planning; Time Management
- **Session III** - Communications Skills; Human Relations Skills
- **Session IV** - Crisis Intervention Skills; Stress Management and Burnout

This is an eight-hour course conducted through weekly sessions during the fall session.

EFFECTIVE VOLUNTEER ADMINISTRATION
Fairleigh Dickinson University
Madison, NJ 07940
TEL: 201-377-4700
Credit: 1.2 CEUs
Sponsor: Fairleigh Dickinson University
Contact: Nishan J. Najarian

Description: This workshop is designed to provide leadership for self-help, community, religious and service groups. In the course, participants learn:
- volunteer recruiting techniques
- goal setting
- motivation and guidance of volunteers
- financial management
- effective board-staff relationships
- training techniques and programs
- analysis of recruitment, retention and recognition systems in the organization

The eight-session course is led by faculty drawn from the field of volunteer administration, and addresses new and potential volunteer coordinators.

ENERGIZE VOLUNTEER MANAGEMENT TRAINING PROGRAM
Energize
5450 Wissahickon Avenue, Lobby A
Philadelphia, PA 19144
TEL: 215-438-8342
TOLL FREE: 800-395-9800
Credit: Inquire
Sponsor: Energize
Contact: Susan J. Ellis, Director
Description: Energize Volunteer Management Training Programs are designed to assist volunteer managers in a wide variety of fields - from human services to cultural arts. The programs can be tailored to meet the needs of specific organizations, and have been conducted in justice programs, school and tutoring programs, information and referral programs, youth programs, cultural programs, and others in the human services areas. Among the subjects covered in Energize workshops are:
- Recordkeeping and Accountability
- Volunteer/Salaried Staff Relations
- The Role of the Executive Director in Supporting Volunteers
- Creative Collaborative Ideas
- New Approaches to Volunteer Recruitment
- Children and Teens as Volunteers

Training programs can vary from a half-day to several days, and can be designed for groups of 15 to 100 participants. Both newcomers to the field and those who have reached the saturation point with general training receive individualized technical assistance enabling them to focus on problems of immediate concern to them, but not general enough for a group session. The Energize training programs can be conducted on-site anywhere in the United States. Several smaller area agencies are encouraged to cooperate in arranging training sessions - pooling resources as much as possible.

In addition to training and consulting, Energize publishes books and other materials for use in the workshops and as an ongoing tool within the organization. Since its establishment in 1977, Energize has conducted training programs in 30 states (all regions of the country). The primary trainer is assisted by a corps of Associates covering many specialized fields.

EXPLORING NEW FRONTIERS IN VOLUNTEERISM
Virginia Division of Volunteerism
805 East Broad Street
Sixth Floor
Richmond, VA 23219
TEL: 804-786-1431
Description: This statewide conference on volunteerism includes a preconference orientation session for newcomers so that they can begin the networking process as opportunities arise throughout the program. Following an opening address, *Volunteerism Comes of Age,* topics addressed include:
Institute Sessions
- Promoting Your Own Potential

- Volunteers Make Successful Fundraisers
- How to Get Your Membership to Help with the Work
- Volunteering and Personality
- Health and the Mind
- How to Play the Media Game
- Empowering People You Supervise
- Volunteers as Guardians
- Conflict Management

Workshop Session One
- Putting Compassion Into Action
- Overview of Professional Certification
- Have Camera... Will Conquer
- Encouraging Legendary Performance
- Connecting with the College
- Practical Needs Assessment
- Effective Communication Skills for Managers
- Technology of Enthusiasm
- The *Type E* Woman ("everything to everybody and running on empty")

Workshop Session Two
- How-To's of Special Events
- Broadening Our Participant Base
- Let's Propose
- Youth Volunteers
- Legal Liability for Volunteer Programs
- Corporate/Community Partnerships
- Video Viewings
- How to Hire a Consultant Trainer

The closing luncheon included a presentation on the lighter side of volunteerism, *The Laughing Volunteer Administrator: Terminal Seriousness & Other Management Myths.* Faculty for the 1990 conference was drawn from public, private and volunteer sectors.

4-H GENERAL FORUMS: ADULT VOLUNTEER TRAINING
US/DoA - 4-H Youth/Extension Service
Independence Avenue
(Between 12th & 14th Sts.)
Washington, DC 20250
TEL: 202-447-6527
Credit: Certificate
Sponsor: US/DoA - Department of Agriculture
Description: Conducted an average of five times each year, the 4-H general forum deals with the overall 4-H program: local clubs, leader recruitment and training, parent involvement, awards and recognition programs, training for middle management roles, designing 4-H with people, fund raising and proposal information, translating volunteer experiences into saleable skills, and other areas of general interest to adult volunteer leaders of the 4-H youth programs. Workshops are designed to help the adult volunteer to:
- Become more effective in working with 4-H members and other 4-H leaders;
- Experience new approaches to leadership development;
- Increase understanding of the legislative process;
- Prepare a plan of action for working with other community and/or 4-H leaders;
- Develop skills into building citizenship and careers into 4-H projects;
- Exchange ideas with 4-H leaders from other states; and
- Identify and use community resources.

The major theme for General Forums is "Designing 4-H with People," with sub-themes of Getting, Training, Retaining Leaders, Developing Leadership in Youth, Motivating Members and Keeping Kids, and Roles and Relationship. Each forum includes idea sharing opportunities and exhibits from each state. Held at the National 4-H Training Center in Maryland, options for extra activities include A Day on Capitol Hill, which provides the volunteers with a first-hand look at the legislative process, as well as other planned leadership development tours and sessions based on the Center's proximity to Washington, DC.

FROM ME TO WE: A FUNNY REASON TO HAVE A CONFERENCE
Central Wisconsin Association of Volunteer Administrators
c/o Norwood Health Center
1600 North Chestnut
Marshfield, WI 54449
TEL: 751-344-4052
Credit: Certificate
Sponsor: CWAVA
Contact: Barbara Mozingo, American Red Cross
Description: This workshop for Volunteer Administrators is divided into two tracks:
- **Track I:** for those persons who have recently entered the field of volunteerism, or who manage volunteers as a smaller part of their jobs. This track enables participants to critique their programs.
- **Track II:** for those persons who have critiqued their programs and are confident in their skills.

Track I participants learn all of the components of a well-managed program, with techniques presented in a general nature. Track II participants find out ways to broaden their base of support in recruitment and funding, providing clearly-defined techniques.
Track I Workshops:
- Getting Started
- Selecting and Recruiting the Right Volunteers

Track II Workshops:
- Mapping the Volunteer Community: The Road to Resources
- The Involvement of the Power Structure in Volunteerism

The conference closed with an experiential wrap-up on the conference theme, From Me to We: A Funny Reason to Have a Conference. A Certificate of Training is issued to those attending the conference for the entire day.

FUNDAMENTALS OF VOLUNTEER PROGRAM MANAGEMENT
University of Akron
Community and Technical College
Schrank Hall
Akron, OH 44325
TEL: 216-375-7768
Credit: 9.0 - 13.0 credits
Sponsor: University of Akron, Community Services Program
Contact: John Mumper, MSSW, JD
Description: This ongoing three-credit course has been offered for several years by the University of Akron. Although considered a basic course, the curriculum is flexible and is adapted as necessary to the level(s) of development of students. This flexibility makes the course of equal value for:
- persons interested in pursuing a career in volunteer administration; and
- persons working in the field and wishing to improve their professional skills.

The topics listed below are deliberately broad to allow for the variation and degrees of depth needed for the two groups cited above:
- Setting Goals, Objectives and Priorities for Volunteer Programs
- Developing Work Plans
- Creating and Writing Job Descriptions for Volunteers
- Interviewing Principles and Techniques
- Evaluating Volunteer Performance
- Developing Records
- Evaluating the Volunteer Program
- Publicizing the Volunteer Program

The course instructor, Hope M. Bair, is a Certified Administrator of Volunteer Services (CAVS) with more than twenty years of experience in both volunteer administration and teaching of adults.

THE FUTURE OF VOLUNTEERISM: SHAPES AND SCENARIOS
SEE ADMINISTRATION: PHILOSOPHY OF VOLUNTEERISM

GOING WITH THE CURRENT: VOLUNTEER MANAGEMENT WORKSHOP
Volunteer Center of Central Florida
1900 North Mills Avenue
Suite I
Orlando, FL 32803
TEL: 305-896-0945
Credit: Certificate
Sponsor: Volunteer Service Center
Contact: Julie Washburn
Description: Using a nautical theme, this workshop likens the successful management of a volunteer program with the successful piloting of a ship. It includes sessions that assist the new volunteer coordinator while providing the experienced volunteer coordinator with relevant checkpoints. Sessions include:
Launching the Boat
- Planning a volunteer program.
- Assessing the needs of your agency.
- Recognizing the right individuals for your program.
- Designing meaningful volunteer jobs.
- Writing job descriptions.

Are You in a Glass Bottom Boat?
- Public image of your program.
- Your agency's perception of you and your program.
- Tools for public relations.
- Resources.

Equip Yourself to Catch the "Biggest and Best" Fish
- Who volunteers?
- Where to find volunteers.
- Recruiting.
- Interviewing.
- Training and placing volunteers.

Overcoming Stormy Weather
- How to overcome unique problems of supervising unpaid staff.
- Reducing conflict between staff and volunteers.
- Benefits for the volunteer.

Testing the Water
- Evaluating the success of your program.
- Implementing necessary changes.
- Measuring volunteer results.

Staying at the Helm of Your Ship
- Professional Assertion
- Differentiating passive-aggressive and assertive behavior.
- Examining non-assertive behavior.
- Strategies to use in dealing with conflict.

Faculty for the workshop was drawn from the local university, the medical profession, the public relations field, and local volunteer programs, among others.

GOVERNOR'S CONFERENCE ON VOLUNTEERISM
SEE GOVERNORS' OFFICES ON VOLUNTEERISM: KENTUCKY

GRADUATE CERTIFICATE PROGRAM FOR MANAGEMENT OF VOLUNTEER SERVICES
Adelphi University
Garden City, NY 11530
TEL: 516-294-8700/Ext. 7550
Credit: Certification and 24 to 26 graduate credits
Sponsor: Adelphi University
Contact: Dr. Jay Smith, Coordinator
Description: This New York State-approved program is sponsored by the Department of Education of Adelphi University, and the

Adelphi University Center on Volunteerism. The program is open to:

- persons who are currently serving as paid administrators of volunteer service programs.
- non-paid leaders of volunteer service programs.
- recent college graduates interested in preparing for a career in volunteer services management.
- men and women interested in re-entering the job market or in making a mid-life career change.
- human services professionals who would like to develop their expertise in volunteer services.
- adults with volunteer experience who wish to enhance their knowledge and effectiveness.

This program is designed to help meet the needs of volunteer managers in hospitals, schools, social agencies, religious institutions, nursing homes, youth facilities, and the new movement within corporations to hire professionals to develop and operate corporate volunteer programs. The Adelphi program was developed with the assistance of national leaders in the field, and is composed of a five-course specialization in volunteer services management and four related courses from such fields as social work, business, sociology, psychology, and education. The program outline:

VOL 510 - Foundations of Voluntarism, 3 credits
VOL 610 - Issues in Volunteer Services Management I, 1/2 credit
SWK 508 - Small Group Dynamics and Institutional Perspectives on Behavior, 3 credits
or
SOC 633 - Group Relations, 3 credits
BUS 560 - The Process of Management, 3 credits
VOL 650 - Applied Management of Volunteer Services Programs, 3 credits
VOL 651 - Practicum in the Management of Volunteer Services Programs 2, 3, or 4 credits
BUS 561 - Organizational Behavior, 3 credits
VOL 720 - Volunteer Services Administration in Action, 3 credits
VOL 611 - Issues in Volunteer Services Management II, 1/2 credit
Elective Course, 3 credits
Total Credits, 24-26
Specialized courses in volunteer management are taught by qualified leaders in the field of volunteerism. The related courses are taught by Adelphi University faculty members from the Graduate School of Arts and Sciences, the School of Business, and the School of Social Work.

Standard academic requirements for admission to the Graduate School of Arts and Sciences apply to applicants for the Certificate Program. An additional prerequisite for admission is a minimum of 30 undergraduate credits in the humanities or social sciences, including business administration or education (a requirement that may be waived in cases of extensive field experience in social service). Candidates for the Program must have had prior experience in volunteerism - paid or unpaid. Individual interviews are held with each candidate, with the final decision on admission made by a Graduate Admissions Committee.

HELP FOR YOU!
4155 East Jewell
Suite 405
Denver, CO 80222
TEL: 303-861-1336
Credit: Inquire
Sponsor: Lifework Associates
Contact: Evelyn K. Hottenstein
Description: HELP FOR YOU! Workshops and seminars are designed to assist in the successful management of volunteer programs, and include topics such as:

- Is your program for recruiting and retaining volunteers keeping up with the changing times?
- Is your career development program for volunteers and for

staff challenging and internally productive?
- Are you and your people successfully selling the achievements and value of your program to those you must influence?
- Do you know all the options professionals like yourself have when they feel stuck, frustrated, ineffective, bored - burned out on the job?
- Would you like to learn techniques that can lead to better funding for an under-funded program?
- Do your boards and committees function smoothly and efficiently?
- Is your speaker's bureau as effective as it could be in presenting your program to the public?

Each of these questions is keyed to a workshop or seminar which assists staff and volunteers in formulating creative solutions to the problems of managing volunteer programs.

Each seminar and workshop is tailored to the specific group sponsoring the program and is available at local, state, regional or national levels.

Lecture and group participation exercises are combined to create a dynamic learning experience.

Related courses include: How to Get It All Done and Still Be Human - An Integrated Approach to Time Management, Public Speaking for the Professional, Avoiding Burn-Out, Selling Yourself and Your Program.

HOW TO WORK EFFECTIVELY WITH VOLUNTEERS
North Carolina Justice Academy
Department of Justice
PO Drawer 99
Salemburg, NC 28385
TEL: 919-525-4151
Credit: Certificate
Sponsor: North Carolina Department of Justice
Contact: Eloise E. Melvin, Instructor/Coordinator
Description: The North Carolina Justice Academy conducts two ongoing workshops for volunteer administrators - one a basic program and the other at the advanced level. The dual program is designed to provide an avenue for development of skills through the basic workshop, and for exchanging ideas at the advanced level.

Basics in Volunteers Adminstration - ways to integrate techniques to mutually benefit the agency and the volunteer; topics include:

- Advantages and disadvantages of working with volunteers - expectations/needs
- Planning for volunteers - before they arrive; volunteer-staff relations; job descriptions
- Recruiting, interviewing, placement - one-person offices
- Volunteer training - planning of orientation, training
- Supervision - how to begin; problems encountered
- How to work with an advisory board - recruiting, orienting, training, maintaining attendance/interest
- Evaluation and recognition - current problems, workshop effectiveness, future

Advanced Volunteer Management - Designed for volunteers and volunteer administrators, this workshop presents advanced techniques of volunteer program administration. Instructional content includes: Techniques and Methods of Instruction, A Review of the Systems Approach to Management, Program Planning, Working with the Problem Volunteer.

Inquire about the Academy's Child Abuse and Neglect and other workshops.

HUMAN RELATIONS SKILLS FOR VOLUNTEERS
Volunteer Center of Marion County
520 SE Fort King
Suite C-1
Ocala, FL 32671
TEL: 904-372-4771
Credit: Inquire

Contact: Karen W. May, Director
Description: The basic purpose of this workshop is to help volunteers make decisions about how they will use their time and efforts, and assist them in understanding and affirming their personal identities, or, as the keynote speaker put it, "to help people get the most out of themselves." With the current thrust toward curricula for courses to improve skills of volunteer administrators, the Volunteer Service Center offers this countywide program to assure that volunteers are not being neglected in the broader training areas. Topics in the 1981 program include:

- **Personal Development** - to help people identify their goals before entering into a volunteer commitment.
- **Beginning Interviewing Skills** - how to listen and converse with a purpose
- **Tutoring the Elementary School Child** - how to "lend a hand" to tomorrow's leaders.
- **Early Childhood** - how to understand and have an impact on tots/toddlers.
- **Rape/Spouse Abuse Counseling** - how to give support in this sensitive area.
- **Homosexuality** - how to increase understanding of this social issue.
- **Relating to Seniors** - how to help seniors "cash in" on "golden years."
- **Grief Counseling** - how to help in this unavoidable reality.
- **Volunteers in County Government** - new opportunities to help the volunteer "make a difference" in local government.

Faculty was drawn from youth center staff, state government, education, day care programs, the church, the health field, countywide volunteer organizations, and individuals with experience in the field. Volunteers and other participants selected two of the hour-long sessions.
Other training for volunteers includes: Training for One-to-One Volunteers; Teen Corp Training for Teenagers; Laubach Volunteer Tutor Training; Pastoral Counseling. New programs are developed as needed and announced in a widely distributed "Calendar of Events."

INSTITUTE FOR THE ADVANCED STUDY OF VOLUNTEERISM
Center for Creative Community
PO Box 2427
Santa Fe, NM 87504-2427
TEL: 505-983-8414
Description: This Institute is designed as a "think tank" to bring together experts in the field to examine, explore and discuss issues and developments that can enhance volunteerism. The expectations resulting from this coming together of distinguished leaders in volunteerism include:

- Substantial help with at least one primary challenge/issue of immediate concern to individual volunteer leaders;
- Substantial help with at least one major challenge of concern to volunteerism in general;
- Learning of the "think tank process" well enough to apply the process "back home;" and
- Contribution to a continuing evolution in understanding the potential of such Institutes.

Participants are expected to experience renewal, raised awareness, redirection, visualization, and a feeling of being able to be more effective in problem-solving and long-range planning, so that those who look to them for leadership in volunteerism within their organizations will benefit from the "think tank" experience.

INSTITUTE ON VOLUNTEER ADMINISTRATION: A PROPOSAL
Association for Volunteer Administration
PO Box 4584
Boulder, CO 80306
TEL: 303-497-0238
FAX: 303-497-0291

Credit: None
Sponsor: VOLUNTEER - The National Center
Contact: Valeria Ogden, President, or David Tobin, Executive Director
Description: This brainstorming session was held during the 1989 AVA Conference to consider the establishment of a national institute to train volunteer administrators and provide more opportunities to do research in the field. Organizers of the session have targeted mid-1991 for start-up of the institute. Conclusions drawn at the meeting included:

- Existing training does not meet the needs of the volunteer community.
- Training needs assessment must to be done in a more systematic way than has been done in the past.
- Training should go into substantially more depth and be offered five days a week.
- Annual conferences are not sufficient to meet training needs.
- Much of existing training is targeted to the newcomer.
- University courses tend to take an academic approach to the subject.
- Several large nonprofits such as the Girl Scouts have developed their own programs, and should be consulted.
- No one has ever set any standards to measure the quality of training programs that are offered.
- Ways to offer accreditation to college and university courses on volunteerism should be developed.
- Other individuals, groups and organizations should be encouraged to bring ideas to the proposal.

To date, besides AVA, initial development of the plan has involved VOLUNTEER/The National Center, Arkansas Office of Volunteerism, and VM Systems, a private volunteer training firm, but involvement across the volunteer sector is expected to be as inclusive as possible. Other existing and planned national programs will be studied, such as the in-house training program of the Girl Scouts and Voluntas, an effort spearheaded by the Center for Creative Community to develop a total "university" on volunteerism, along with collections of nationwide training events.
In June 1990, AVA mailed survey packets to volunteer organizations across the country and in some other countries to assist with the development of this concept.
Publications: Educational Needs in Volunteer Administration: A Survey

INSTITUTE ON VOLUNTEERISM
Ball State University
Muncie, IN 47306
TEL: 317-285-8300
Credit: Credit: Graduate, Undergraduate, and CEUs
Sponsor: Ball State University
Description: Presented once a month over a four-month period in four cities, this program sets four goals in areas determined to be underserved in Indiana's volunteer community:

- To provide information, training and resources for volunteers throughout the state.
- To provide an opportunity for volunteers, volunteer coordinators and agency staff working with volunteers to exchange ideas.
- To give statewide visibility and recognition to volunteers, volunteer coordinators and volunteerism in general.
- To offer credibility, support and technical assistance to volunteers, volunteer coordinators and agency staff working with volunteers.

The one-day program was hosted by Voluntary Action Centers in the four cities selected (Evansville, Fort Wayne, Jeffersonville, Hammond) in both college and community settings, with five simultaneous in-depth sessions presented once in the morning and once in the afternoon. The sessions:
Volunteer Program Planning and Development; Strategies and Alternates - Volunteer administrators often face an unnecessary

problem with program planning and development. This in-depth session emphasizes a creative and facilitative approach to program planning and development. Participants become involved in planning a new program from beginning to end with constructive feedback from both the facilitator and participants.

Time Management: New Perspectives in Productivity - Mismanagement of time can often directly account for the personal frustration and anxiety which sometimes accompanies the missing of deadlines and feeling of overextension. This session provides participants with strategies toward increased personal productivity. Individuals develop a personal productivity plan based upon their work situation.

Conflict Management: Creative Methods for Problem Solving - Individuals can choose to handle conflict in volunteer efforts either productively or destructively. Instructors explore creative and growth facilitating approaches to conflict managementcultivating "win-win" situations. Participants practice new strategies and discuss sources of conflict.

Interpersonal Skills and Development: Communications and Human Relations - Not a single more important skill than the ability to effectively relate to people exists in volunteerism. Participants practice new approaches to interpersonal communication and human relations training as a basis for enhancing the effectiveness of volunteer programs. The class explores their own techniques for interpersonal relations work with both individuals and groups.

Funding for Volunteer Programs: Skills, Techniques and Sources - Volunteer program administrators, staff and volunteers are always concerned about funding. This in-depth course provides information on available sources of funding - both public and private - as well as proven strategies for securing a stable funding base. Participants develop a long-range funding plan and/or a specific funding proposal.

A credit workshop follows the evaluation and closing of the institute for those who arrange in advance for one of the three types of credit offered (see citation in heading above).

INTER-AGENCY VOLUNTEER QUARTERLY FORUMS
SEE GOVERNORS' OFFICES ON VOLUNTEERISM: UTAH

INTERCONNECTIONS
Association for Volunteer Administration, Region X
South King County Volunteer Center
305 South 43rd
Renton, WA 98055
TEL: 206-226-0210; 503-649-0480
Credit: AVA Certification (partial fulfillment)
Sponsor: Association for Volunteer Administration; Association of Volunteer Centers
Contact: Pat O'Dell or Sharon Tarlow
Description: Regional conferences with changing formats are convened each year in AVA regions, often with joint sponsorship (see above). The curriculum is designed to assist participants in determining the appropriate times to wear the many, varied hats that represent their various responsibilities. Although developed by and for volunteer administrators, this training program has proven beneficial to educators, researchers, students, agency/organization administrators, and others. Curriculum includes:
- Leadership (for the entire assembly)
- Small Group Workshops: Computers in Your Volunteer Program; Public Speaking; Professional Development; Training Techniques; Marketing Your Volunteer Program

Based on a review of this program's purpose, goals, and instructional plan, attendance is accepted by AVA in partial fulfillment of the criteria defined for professional certification.

INTERFAITH VOLUNTEER CAREGIVING WORKSHOP
SEE VOLUNTEERS: CHURCH/SYNAGOGUE MEMBERS

INTRODUCTION TO VOLUNTEERING, ETC.
North Shore Community College Volunteer Office
Center for Alternative Studies
3 Essex Street
Beverly, MA 01915
TEL: 617-927-4850
Credit: One Credit (Introduction to Volunteering); Inquire about others
Contact: North Shore Community College
Description: The college operates a comprehensive volunteer program, including a Clearinghouse on volunteer opportunities, counseling to assist prospective volunteers in deciding the nature of volunteer work for which they are most suited, and to discuss with them the issues and concerns that are associated with volunteer work.

To reinforce this type of assistance, a one-credit course, Introduction to Volunteering, is offered through the Center. In implementing the Course, the college works with the North Shore Association of Volunteers and others.

As an adjunct to the Course, the Skills Assessment and Portfolio Preparation Program of the Center assists volunteers in evaluating their knowledge and skills gained through volunteering and in the creation of their portfolios. These portfolios are developed for later review by academic departments of the College for award of course credit, and as a documentation of skills for those seeking employment.

In addition, students may earn academic credit for knowledge learned through volunteering under the Center's Contract Learning Program. Some volunteers work directly at the Center, serving as tutors to prepare adults for High School Equivalency Examinations.

In cooperation with the North Shore Association of Volunteers, the Center celebrates achievement of outstanding volunteers and volunteer programs through the LINK Awards Program in areas which LINK learning and personal growth with volunteer contributions.

The Center, involved in volunteerism for more than six years, is totally funded by the state.

LAKE SYLVIA V.I.P. (VERY IMPORTANT PERSON) CONFERENCE*
Community Volunteer Service
115 South Union Street
Stillwater, MN 55082
TEL: 612-439-7434
Credit: Inquire
Sponsor: VAC of the St. Paul Area; VAC of the Minneapolis Area; Community Volunteer Service of the St. Croix Valley Area
Contact: Vi Russell
Description: This advanced-level conference brings together administrators of volunteers from several volunteer-serving regions to "take a breather" from the day-to-day routine to come together and share ideas and experiences. The V.I.P. theme was used creatively to describe faculty (Very Informative People and Very Insightful Persons), the attendees (Very Interesting Participants), and the "promise" of the conference - "to maximize your return from Volunteers' Investment in People." Even a V.I.P. limerick contest was announced! The intent was to provide a relaxed and congenial atmosphere, removing the stiff formalities that often cloud abilities to reach full potential in the learning environment. Topics covered by the V.I.P. faculty included:
- **Trends in Volunteerism** - family and changing life styles; implications for the future.
- **Psychology of Volunteering** - needs that volunteers act on; capitalizing on your resources.
- **Advocacy** - where and how to use it in volunteerism; one-to-one group advocacy.
- **Your Program Is Worth More Than You Think** - program accountability; cost/benefit analysis.

- **Granstmanship** - finding a funding source and marketing your program; proposal design.
- **Boards That Are Effective** - utilizing the skills and expertise of your board; developing the needed resources.
- **Career Planning** - for volunteers in long standing and large agency setting; for volunteers in small agency and new program settings.

Other issues addressed in these annual conferences include: Volunteer and Staff Training; Creativity-Risk Taking; Conflict Management; Management-by-Objective; Volunteer/Staff Relationships; Supervision; Impression Management; Quality Programming; Interpersonal Skills, and others as indicated. Rap groups follow the presentations in topics chosen by participants; i.e., recruitment, training, PR, program evaluation, etc.

LAKES REGION CONFERENCE ON VOLUNTEERISM - VOLUNTEERS: A CARING RESOURCE; A PRACTICAL PERSPECTIVE
SEE GOVERNORS' OFFICES ON VOLUNTEERISM: NEW HAMPSHIRE

LEADERSHIP: A CAPITAL INVESTMENT
Association for Volunteer Administration
PO Box 4584
Boulder, CO 80306
TEL: 303-497-0238
Credit: Inquire
Sponsor: Association for Volunteer Administration
Contact: Martha Martin
Description: This conference includes workshops, institutes, and paper sessions in areas related to volunteer management. The sessions cluster into three tracks:
- Investing in Ourselves
- Investing in Our Programs
- Investing in Our Profession

It offers a wide selection of topics at both the introductory and experienced levels. It is based on the philosophy that competent leadership in volunteer management will provide enhanced human and social service delivery systems. It strives to strengthen and promote the profession of volunteer services management through learning opportunities including:
Preconference Workshops
Volunteerism and the Military - panel of members from each of the military services, including the DoD Family Policy Office, National Military Family Association, and others.
Increasing Board Effectiveness - discussion of board roles regarding the agency, size and composition, recruitment of members, committees, fundraising, and board/staff relations.
Your Leadership Style and Its Influence on Others - overview of leadership styles, how to identify your own personal style, and how to communicate with those whose style is different from yours.
Screening Volunteers for Sexual Abuse - exploration of risk management for programs that work with children and youth, and how to develop an effective screening process to eliminate child molestors.
All-Day Seminars
Educational Horizons in Volunteer Management - a showcase of existing learning opportunities and educational modules.
Conflict Management - assistance for supervisors and managers to identify sources of conflict and explore alternative approaches to manage that conflict.
Conference Workshops
- Devious Resource Raising
- AVA Certification Overview
- Volunteers Speak Out
- Media Partnerships
- Mainstreaming Minorities

- The Welfare Reform Act
- The Role of Paid Staff in A Voluntary Organization
- Stages of Change: How Adults Adopt New Ideas
- Seeing the Heroes Within: A Look at Ourselves
- Convincing Decision Makers: A Presentation Model
- Are You Where You Want to Be?
- Sharpening Your Speaking Skills
- Volunteers and the Challenge of AIDS: Working with an Open Heart
- National Youth Service. What Will It Be, and Will We Be Ready?
- Effective Corporate Volunteer Council Partnership
- Designing Volunteer Leadership Blueprints
- Volunteer 2000: The Future Is You
- Termination Techniques: Ending the Volunteer/Client Relations
- Climate Control: The Pulse of an Organization
- Compeer: A National Model Program Serving the Mentally Ill
- Creative Management: Making it Happen
- The Guiding Light: Developing Volunteer Program Policy
- How to Take Care of You
- Vision Planning: How to Create Consensus
- Introducing and Implementing Change Without Resistance
- When Generations Meet: A Model for Intergenerational Training
- Cranking Your Own Starter
- Targeting Recruiting
- Legislative Trends and Issues
- Legal Issues Clinic
- How to Market Marketing in Your Organization
- How to Be an Artful as Well as Skillful Consultant
- Increasing the Impact of Fundraising Volunteers
- People with Disadvantages: A Source for Innovative Recruitment
- Preventing Burn Out: Taking the Stress Out of the Job
- A "Naturalistic" Approach to Assessing Value to Volunteer Efforts
- A Study Linking Communication, Satisfaction and Organizational Commitment
- Volunteer Research Project
- So You Want to be a Trainer
- The Key to Volunteer Retention
- I'm in Charge Here: Balancing Your Personal and Professional Lives
- Mobilizing Resources for the 90's
- Fire Me and I'll Slue
- Ethical Tools for Personal and Organizational Empowerment
- The Three R's of Training: Rites, Responsibilities and Requirements
- Visioning: Cornerstone of Strategic Planning
- Transparencies: Taming the Technology
- Team Leadership: The Art of Building Cooperation
- Getting Optimum Participation from Members of Boards and Committees
- Volunteering Encounters of the Intercultural Kind
- Weaving the Fabric of Community
- Growing through Loss
- Disadvantages? Sensitivity Leads to Creativity
- Up to Your Eyebrows in Alligators: Strategies for Managing External Forces
- Volunteer Centers: Community Organizing in Rural Communities
- How to Be an Outstanding Speaker
- Sharing the Throne Without Losing the Kingdom
- So You Want to Be an Author
- The No-Time, No-Talent, No-Money Newsletter
- The Card-carrying Volunteer: Is a Bank Card Program for You?
- Winning Volunteers Through Simple Graphic Presentations
- Making That Corporate Connection

- How to Effectively Manage Persons with AIDS
- Youth Volunteers: Putting Them to Good Use
- Volunteer Perks
- Project LEAD: Leadership Experience and Development for Youth
- Evaluating Difficult Programs
- A Study of Volunteer Motivation

Throughout the conference period, individual consultations were made available by appointment with experts from Red Cross Volunteer Services, United Way, Bell Atlantic, Arkansas Office of Volunteerism, U.S. Army Family Support Division, and others. These individual consultation sessions were brought back by popular demand. Small Group Consultations for 15 people or less are included in the conference agenda on very specific areas, some as offshoots of the workshops. Also requested again was the Resource Marketplace, where a comprehensive assortment of books, video tapes, training and recognition items are available for browsing and/or purchase. Also, an interactive theatre allowed participants to arrange for their own videos to be presented to the group.

A Certification Workshop is always included in this annual conference, and is considered a prerequisite for those planning to apply for the professional certification program.

LEADERSHIP AND MANAGEMENT OF VOLUNTEER PROGRAMS*
Volunteer Center of Chicago
United Way Crusade of Mercy
125 South Clark Street
Chicago, IL 60603-4012
TEL: 312-580-2723
Credit: 3 Credits
Sponsor: Northern Illinois University
Contact: Joe Agnello
Description: Northern Illinois University (NIU), in cooperation with the Voluntary Action Center (VAC) of Comprehensive Community Services of Metropolitan Chicago, designed this course to be of special interest to volunteer coordinators and/or people otherwise engaged in a variety of volunteer settings. Course planners also recognized the need for training for administrators and managers planning to begin volunteer programs and developed the program to be useful to this group as well.
Leadership and Management of Volunteer Programs provides practical opportunities in such topic areas as:

- program planning
- assessing program needs
- establishing a climate for volunteer participation
- selection, recruitment, application, and interview approaches
- identifying training needs; conducting pre- and in-service training
- motivating and managing volunteers
- evaluating volunteer programs
- examining the role of the volunteer coordinator
- PR, budgeting, preparing reports

Emphasis is placed on the literature, research and associations which have accompanied the growing national voluntary and adult education movements. Faculty is drawn from the University and includes Paul Isley, author of *Recruiting and Training Volunteers*. Graduate or undergraduate credit is available to those requesting it prior to beginning the course.

LOOKING AHEAD: MANAGING TOMORROW'S VOLUNTEERS
Association for Volunteer Administration, Region I
c/o Univ. of RI Cooperative Ext.
Woodward Hall
Kingston, RI 02879
TEL: 401-792-2959
Credit: AVA Certification, partial fulfillment

Sponsor: AVA Region I; University of Rhode Island
Contact: Whitney Bancroft, 4-H Program Coordinator
Description: AVA conferences are designed to promote certification of volunteer professionals as a major step toward recognition of volunteer administration in its proper perspective - as a viable profession. Beginning with a keynote address by the author of *At the Heart: The New Volunteer Challenge to Community Agencies,* the conference addresses issues for leaders based on expressed needs. Current meeting topics include:

- AVA Certification Overview
- The Cutting Edge: A Report
- Middle Management: Empowering Key Volunteers
- Writing for Publication
- Corporate Volunteer Councils: What they can do for you
- Essential Steps for a Successful Volunteer Program
- Volunteer Issues Before Congress: How they affect you
- Future Directions

The closing session featured the President of AVA, who presented an address entitled, "Looking Ahead: Region I's Part in the International Picture."
A special "AVA Certification Workshop" is held the day before the conference (in 1989 by John D. Mason, AVA International Board Member, Professional Development Chair).
Opportunities are made available for sharing of resources, meeting the author, and networking. Presenters came from Beverly Hospital, University of Rhode Island Extension, Journal of Volunteer Administration, Boston College, United Way of Massachusetts Bay, Marnie Holbrook Roberson Consultant Services, and the Association for Volunteer Administration.

M.A. IN VOLUNTEER ADMINISTRATION: THE GODDARD GRADUATE PROGRAM
Vermont College
Montpelier, VT 05602
TEL: 802-828-8832
Credit: M.A. Degree
Sponsor: Vermont College of Norwich University
Contact: Marguerite Jones
Description: Volunteer Administration is one of a number of study areas pursued by students seeking an M.A. Degree through the Goddard Graduate Program. Potential students are expected to present a clearly-written preliminary study plan. The plan is reviewed by core faculty who make decisions on admissions, and become student advisors after admission. A complementary field faculty guides the student, evaluates his/her work, and recommends graduation to the core faculty. In addition, each student works with a committee consisting of core and field faculty and one or two other persons acceptable to the student and knowledgeable in the student's study area.
One type of study plan that has proven workable is based on phases allowing explicitly for exploration; for example:

- **Phase I** - concentration on reading the literature and building a theoretical base.
- **Phase II** - building on that base and writing a plan for an action project.
- **Phase III** - carrying out the project.
- **Phase IV** - focusing on evaluation.
- **Phase V** - developing an in-depth paper extrapolating from the whole experience and recommending a course of action to others.

Regular regional meetings are organized involving committees and students to supplement and support the individual resources of the student. In some regions clusters of students meet weekly for specialized and inter-disciplinary workshops, seminars, and other discussions groups. Other students meet in small groups to work collectively on joint projects or to pursue overlapping interests. Topical seminars on themes of vital interest to a number of students are held both in the regionsand on campus as needed. A handbook which includes Study Plan Guidelines is available on request.

MAJOR CERTIFICATE PROGRAM FOR VOLUNTEER MANAGERS

University of Connecticut
Extended and Continuing Education
Storrs, CT 06268
TEL: 203-486-3235
Credit: Certificate and 2.4 CEUs
Sponsor: University of Connecticut; Governor's Council on Voluntary Action/CT
Contact: Robert C. Baldwin
Description: This program provides volunteer program managers with a structured review of the basics of recruiting, training, and supervising volunteers, and a professional approach to modern management techniques, advocacy, program fund-raising and lobbying. The program offers two courses:
Volunteer Program Management I includes topics such as:
- Program Planning
- Program Development by the Manager
- Volunteer-Staff Relations
- Evaluation

Volunteer Program Management II explores the Advisory Board development process and offers a more task-oriented approach to some of the topics discussed in Course I, including:
- Management by Objectives
- Cost-Benefit Analysis
- Designing Program Evaluations
- Developing an Annual Report

The University of Connecticut awards a certificate and 2.4 Continuing Education Units to each person who successfully completes a course by attending at least seven of the eight sessions and completing appropriate course projects. The Major Certificate in Volunteer Program Management is awarded to those students who successfully complete both courses.

MANAGEMENT DEVELOPMENT SEMINAR FOR DIRECTORS OF VOLUNTEER SERVICES

Massachusetts General Hospital
Volunteer Services Department
Boston, MA 02114
TEL: 617-726-8540
Credit: .5 CEUs for each full day's attendance
Sponsor: Massachusetts Association Directors Hospital Volunteer Services; Massachusetts Hospital Association
Contact: Maeve Blackman
Description: Each year, usually in April, the Massachusetts Association Directors Hospital Volunteer Services (MADHVS) develops a seminar that reflects current concerns of its members - often covering crucial topics previously unexplored in events of this type. The goal is to provide participants with practical information which can be immediately applied to their institutions.
- "Hear Your Peers" - The Role of DVS During a Strike
- Office Politics: Mixing Machiavelli with Horatio Alger
- Multiple Roles of the Woman Manager
- What Can the Computer Do for You
- The Volunteer in Therapeutic Recreation
- You May Be Hazardous to Your Health - Stress; Burnout
- Evaluating the Effectiveness of Your Volunteer Program
- Is Anybody Listening? - Communication
- Volunteerism Today

A Resource Room and time for informal discussion is provided throughout the seminar for exchange of ideas and materials. Other programs on the schedule include:
- Reaching the Corporate Community;
- Confidentiality in Volunteer/Patient/Staff Relationships;
- Communications: An Advanced Workshop.

For the information of members, the schedule also includes national and regional meetings of major associations in the field.

MANAGEMENT OF VOLUNTEER PROGRAMS/SINCLAIR

Sinclair Community College
Extended Learning & Human Services
Dayton, OH 45402
TEL: 513-226-2702
Credit: 45.5-57 credit hours
Sponsor: Sinclair Community College
Contact: Madelyn Buran
Description: Begun in the fall of 1981, this certificate is designed to provide educational opportunities for those persons whose primary responsibility is to manage and/or coordinate Volunteer Services. Interested persons can elect to take single courses without completing the certificate. The entire certificate can be applied to an Associate Degree in several areas. Certificate courses include:
First Quarter
- ENG 111 - English Composition I, 3 credits
- PSY 121 - General Psychology I, 3 credits
- MAN 205 - Principles of Management, 3 credits
- VOL 205 - Managing a Volunteer Program, 3 credits
- COM 211 - Effective Speaking, 3 credits

Total First Quarter - 15 credits
Second Quarter
- VOL 105 - Volunteer's Role in Community Organizations, 3 credits
- COM 225 - Group Dynamics, 3 credits
- MAN 225, Human Relations in Supervision, 3 credits
- SOC 111 - General Sociology I, 3 credits
- General Education Electives, 3 credits

Total Second Quarter - 15 credits
Third Quarter
- VOL 270 - Volunteer Internship, 3-12 credits
- MAN 245 - Office Management, 3 credits
- COM 235 - Principles of Interviewing, 3 credits
- VOL 190 - Volunteer Seminars, .5-3 credits
- General Education Electives, 6 credits

Total Third Quarter - 15.5-27 credits
Managing a Volunteer Program, one of the required courses above, is designed to assist with organizing and administering a volunteer program. Problems and responsibilities faced by the director are considered, explored and discussed in detail. In addition to prerequisites above, three credit hours of volunteer internship are required. The course outline:
Development of Volunteer Programs
- Why Volunteers? (flexibility, career exploration, resources, support)
- Needs assessment of agency
- Budget
- Job descriptions
- Setting volunteer program goals
- Recruitment and placement
- Orientation and training
- Lines of supervision
- Evaluation
- Recognition
- Involving the staff in planning for volunteers

Directing the Volunteer Program (Guidelines to action)
- Records of volunteer service
- Forms (time sheets, etc.)
- Organizing the work
- Evaluating the volunteers' work by staff and volunteer performance review
- Recognition of volunteers
- Supervision Attitudes Volunteers' expectations

Recruiting Volunteers
- Needs of program
- Time of year to recruit
- Types of advertisement application

Interviewing - Selecting - Placement
- Screening of volunteers
- Notifying volunteer; letter of agreement

- Job descriptions
- Matching needs
- Exit interviews

Training Volunteers (Volunteer Development)
- Orientation to agency
- Job induction
- In-service training
- Workshops
- Volunteer recognition

Special Concerns
- Academic credit
- Time constraints
- Ineffective volunteers
- Transportation
- Liability
- Volunteer costs

Through the Volunteer Internship required course, adult learners with extensive learning from prior experience may receive acknowledgment of that learning with internship credit upon submission of a portfolio to an evaluation committee.

Persons with limited experience will participate in selected off-campus experiences with relationship to their volunteer management needs.

Students already volunteering full- or part-time may apply to use that experience in fulfillment of the internship requirement with approval from his or her advisor.

Students must volunteer a minimum of 20 hours per quarter in an approved placement site to receive one credit of internship.

Among other objectives, students are expected to demonstrate through reports and/or projects the relationship between theoretical learning and practical application.

The courses and certificate were developed by a committee composed of persons who are currently involved in volunteer training and management in the Miami Valley area.

MANAGEMENT OF VOLUNTEER SERVICES
Federation of Protestant Welfare Agencies
Volunteer Program Services
281 Park Avenue South
New York, NY 10010
TEL: 212-777-4800, Ext. 253
Credit: Inquire
Sponsor: Federation of Protestant Welfare Agencies, Inc.
Contact: Jana Smith, Program Associate, Volunteer Services
Description: The Friday Workshop Series (Management of Volunteer Services) is attended by Executive Directors, Program and Project Directors, Coordinators of Volunteers and Board members. The program's primary focus is on strengthening management and human relations skills.

This workshop series is a continuation of the training workshops initiated at New York University in 1970-1972 and subsequently held at the New School for Social Research from 1972-1976 under the title Volunteers and Professionals - Partners for a Better Society.

Program content varies from year to year and is designed to involve participants in acquiring and strengthening skills in the administration of volunteer services. An opportunity is provided to share trends, ideas, innovative programs and creative problem-solving. Partial content includes:
- Using Marketing/Advertising to Promote Voluntarism
- Analyzing Your Agency's Climate
- Communication - Listening and Feedback
- Where Does Your Day Go? Time Management
- Interviewing - Principles, Methods, Goals
- Management Styles - Making Yours Work for You
- Implementing Record-Keeping Systems
- Developing Staff-Volunteer Teamwork
- Evaluating Your Volunteer Program

These workshops are under the leadership of Rita Lambek,

Director of the Department of Volunteer Program Services at the Federation of Protestant Welfare Agencies, and include as faculty outstanding leaders in the field and management trainers from industry.

MANAGEMENT SKILLS FOR VOLUNTEER LEADERS
Volunteer Service Bureau
520 SE Fort King
Suite C-1
Ocala, FL 32671
TEL: 904-732-4771
Credit: Partial Credit for Certification
Sponsor: Ocala Volunteer Service Center
Contact: Karen W. May
Description: This workshop for beginning and advanced volunteer leaders was designed to meet the needs of Volunteer Coordinators, staff who work with volunteers, church leaders, nonprofit agency Boards of Directors, nonprofit agency administrators, civic club leaders, and others in the field. Following a keynote address, "Volunteering in the '80's: Issues and Challenges," by the past President of the Association of Volunteer Centers, Julie Washburn, the following workshops were included in the September 1981 program:
- **Planning for Volunteers** - how to determine suitable jobs for volunteers and develop job descriptions.
- **Boards of Directors** - functions and legal responsibilities of nonprofit Boards.
- **Basic Graphics** - "tricks of the trade" to help beginners prepare camera-ready copy for newsletters and brochures.
- **Goal Setting** - how to determine and accomplish organizational goals.
- **Meeting Dynamics** - how to assure effective participation by all attendees.
- **Insurance and Liability** - effects of state law, where/what kind to buy.
- **Recruitment of Volunteers** - proven strategies for locating/involving people.
- **Record Keeping** - What records to keep, why and how; implications for recording and determining value of volunteer time.
- **Organizational Problem Solving and Decision Making** - causes and solutions.
- **Understanding Volunteer Motivation** - how to apply to interviewing, retention.
- **Orientation and Training of Volunteers** - content, format, how adults learn.
- **Audio-Visual Equipment** - what it is, how to operate it, where to find it.
- **Volunteer-Staff Relations** - building effective staff-volunteer partnerships.

Several workshops run concurrently within three major sessions. Students choose one workshop from each section. This program is one of two that are required for the countywide Volunteer Management Certification program. See separate listing for details on the overall Certification program.

MANAGEMENT WORKSHOPS FOR NONPROFIT ORGANIZATIONS
Support Center of Washington
Public Training Program
1410 Q Street, NW
Washington, DC 20009-3808
TEL: 202-232-1234
Satellite Centers: Boston 617-227-5514; Chicago 312-606-1530; Houston 713-739-1211; Newark 201-643-5774; New York City 212-302-6940; Oklahoma City 405-236-8133; Palo Alto 415-493-5171; Providence 401-521-0710; San Diego 619-272-7720; San Francisco 415-552-7584; Tulsa 918-586-5112; Washington, DC 202-462-2000

Credit: CEUs (.3 to .5, inquire)
Sponsor: Local Host Organization
Contact: Victoria Leonard, Executive Director
Description: This series of one-day workshops is offered in the spring and in the fall and is designed to increase the competency of those who work in the nonprofit sector. Usually spread out over a two-month period, the series addresses a wide range of nonprofit management topics, including:

100: Fundamentals of Management - covers general management theory and practice and explores management functions of planning, organizing, staffing, and controlling.

500: Fundamentals of Marketing - features group discussion exercises covering marketing concepts and techniques as they apply to nonprofit organizations.

502: Marketing Plans - helps to structure a marketing plan that moves from the idea stage to the implementation stage.

276: Writing that Works - discusses ways to solve troublesome writing problems by translating useful information into plain English.

380: Seeking Public Funds - addresses areas of identifying, locating, and approaching government agencies to request funding.

360: Capital/Endowment Campaigns - offers a step-by-step plan for mounting a campaign, getting important "lead" gifts, opening and closing the campaign, and understanding the legal issues involved.

430: Nonprofit Budgeting - introduces a variety of budgets and methods of budget preparation that are suited to different problems and situations in nonprofits.

154: Legal Issues for Existing Nonprofits - presents an overview of many common legal issues faced by nonprofits; helps in planning activities to avoid potential legal problems.

350: Special Events - helps in planning for large and small events, identify and manage volunteer resources, and maximizing visibility, financial gain and fun.

300: Fundamentals of Fundraising - guides participants through the process of designing and organizing a successful fundraising program and plan.

114: Strategic Planning, I - helps in monitoring the environment, selecting the right programs, and organizing strategies for a long-range plan.

303: Asking in Person with Confidence - a look at research data that can lead to successful solicitation.

604: Computers: A Management Tool - reviews all aspects of computer use in the nonprofit sector (hardware, software functions, printers, desktop publishing, maintenance, training, and staff costs).

332: Major Gifts/Planned Giving - discusses the basics of planned giving, tax benefits for donors, ways donors can maximize their gifts, and ways of educating donors to these giving opportunities.

401: Basic Bookkeeping - assists those with no background in accounting covering the fundamentals of nonprofit bookkeeping.

340: Foundation Fundraising - presents overview of family foundations, national general purpose foundations, special purpose foundations, community foundations, and corporate foundations, and how to establish and maintain foundation relationships.

280: Management Skills for Support Staff - concentrates on management skills already in use, and how to make work time more satisfying and productive.

330: Corporate Fundraising - explores ways to make corporate fundraising less mysterious and more successful.

132: Organization Culture - focuses on the importance of uncovering "who we are" and the connection of that activity to maximum success in every aspect of the nonprofit.

142: Boards and Fundraising - focuses on the board's critical responsibility in resource development.

262: Stress in the Workplace - helps to control the negative effects of stress by understanding causes and coping skills.

200: Fundamentals of Supervision - discusses the attributes of effective people management and identifies strengths and weaknesses in the Supervisor.

450: Cash Flow Management - introduces basic techniques for cash flow forecasting and techniques for short-term cash management.

332: Proposal Writing - helps to turn organizational needs into fundable ideas and represents them in competitive proposals for foundations and corporations.

410: Practical Financial Management - blends computerized concepts with discussions and sample financial reports.

140: Developing Effective Boards - describes board structures and relationships and strategies for board members and executive directors to work together effectively.

203: Team Building - provides experiential training in building and maintaining group relationships.

441: Preparing for the Audit - stresses that the audit should be seen as an interesting opportunity to improve accounting and financial information systems for the coming year, not as a trauma.

152: Starting a Nonprofit - provides step-by-step guidance for organizing and incorporating a nonprofit organization.

395: Funders Forum - brings together corporate grantmakers and grantseekers to discuss ways to seek corporate contributions.

The Support Center, itself, is a 501(c)(3) nonprofit organization. Workshops provide, on a limited basis, sign language interpreters (in 1989 in DC, from Gallaudet University) and other translation needs if requested in advance. Grants and equipment are provided for the workshops from individuals, foundations and corporations usually within the presentation area (in 1989 in DC, from C&P Telephone Company, PEPCO, and Washington Gas Company), which help keep costs for participants to a minimum. Space is usually in donated quarters (in 1989 in DC, from the YWCA). Books and CEU certification require a small additional fee. Enrollment is limited in some workshops to 25 participants, on a first come, first served basis. Faculty in addition to support staff is drawn from the public, for-profit, and nonprofit sectors who volunteer their services.
Publications: Practical Financial Management; Nonprofit Budgets and the Budget Process

MANAGING VOLUNTEERS FOR RESULTS
University of Detroit
Continuing Education
4001 McNichols Road
Detroit, MI 48221
TEL: 313-927-1027
Credit: One CEU per ten contact hours
Sponsor: University of Detroit
Contact: Audrey Richards
Description: Designed for Volunteer coordinators, executive directors, Board members, staff, auxiliary and volunteer leaders, and others working with volunteers, the goal of this two-day seminar is to improve the ability of participants to assure that volunteers in their programs are productive members of the organization teams. Specifically, seminar techniques are aimed at helping attendees to:

- improve ability to recruit, interview and place volunteers.
- develop skills in designing challenging and rewarding jobs for volunteers.
- increase ability to use volunteers most effectively.
- design and implement a simple volunteer management system.
- use proven techniques to solve day-to-day volunteer management problems.

Emphasis of the seminar was on practical methods and resources that could be used long after the seminar ended. Areas covered were:

How to Get More Results from Volunteers
- Understanding why people volunteer.
- Discovering what your volunteers want - then giving it to them.
- How to increase volunteer commitment.
- Proven techniques for improving volunteer performance.
- The nine types of volunteers, and how to motivate them.

How to Make Your Organization a Better Place for Volunteers
- How to create an effective, positive climate for volunteers in your organization.
- Reducing conflict between staff and volunteers.
- Improving the communication process in your organization.

Recruiting, Interviewing, and Placing Volunteers
- Where to find the best volunteers.
- How to master the skill of effective interviewing: Listening, asking non-directive questions, and interpreting data.
- Key questions to ask in every volunteer interview.
- How to place volunteers in the most satisfying jobs.
- How to make recruitment, interviewing, and placement of volunteers easier for your staff.

How to Design More Exciting Volunteer Jobs
- How interesting jobs can increase results from volunteers.
- How to make your volunteer jobs more challenging.
- Fitting volunteer jobs into your organizations's long range plan.
- How to involve volunteers in the planning and evaluation of their jobs.
- Designing jobs for women, students, and the elderly.

Maximizing Volunteer Performance Through Good Training
- How to set up a volunteer training program that gets results.
- The key elements of a successful volunteer training program.
- Creating a productive work atmosphere through systematic team building.
- Helping your volunteers develop their skills on the job.

How to Improve Your Volunteer Management Skills
- How to delegate to volunteers and improve their output.
- How to give orders to volunteers that get results.
- Proven techniques for overseeing volunteer work.
- How to overcome the unique problems of supervising unpaid help.

Evaluating the Performance of Your Volunteers
- Planning for volunteer success.
- How to establish standards of performance for your volunteers.
- How to measure volunteer results.
- How to solve volunteer performance problems.

Volunteers and Fund Raising
- How to get your volunteers excited about fund raising.
- Getting your Board of Directors to help you develop more support.
- Training volunteers to solicit.
- How to get volunteers to help you get appointments with foundations, corporations, and individual philanthropists.

Continuing Education Units (CEUs) are accumulated on a permanent record for each individual. One CEU for each ten contact hours is awarded.

METAMORPHOSIS: GROWTH AND CHANGE IN THE ADMINISTRATION OF VOLUNTEER SERVICES
North Dakota Association of Coordinators of Volunteer Services
Box 104
Grand Forks, ND 58201
TEL: 701-773-2455 (Grnd Forks); 701-857-0824 (Minot)
Credit: Inquire
Sponsor: NDACOV
Contact: Nancy Moen (Grand Forks); Maurine Hill (Minot)
Description: This annual conference is designed for coordinators, administrators, managers and leaders of volunteer and citizen participation programs. Content focuses on the growth and development of both individual skills and the field of volunteerism in general. It addresses a variety of topics that apply to both experienced and new volunteer coordinators, such as:
- establishing goals and objectives;
- the future of volunteerism;
- public relations efforts;
- goal setting (establishing priorities; evaluation)

- creativity (free time; maverick groups); and
- power (how to get it; how to use it).

The three sponsoring organizations - Fargo-Morehead Directors of Volunteer Services, Volunteers for Community Sevices, and NDACOVS - design and implement the annual conference. They feel that the combined efforts benefit all concerned - especially since the COVS annual conference has always been "co-sponsored" by these groups, but without the designation. In addition, sharing of time in planning, organizing and hosting the conference results in a more efficiently organized event, and a structured program of assistance assures an educational event on a regular basis. A noticeable increase in community support is apparent, also, as a result of the co-sponsoring policy.

The program's faculty is drawn from leading consultant/trainers in the volunteer field, Governor's Offices on Volunteerism,United Way, public agencies such as the local Housing and Redevelopment Authority, and others.

The sponsoring organizations hold their own annualmeetings at the site to discuss accreditation, legislative issues, and other matters pertaining to the advancement of their members.

The above is a typical annual meeting, Each year formats and topics change to meet the expressed needs of the volunteer community across the state.

NATIONAL CONFERENCE FOR VOLUNTEER LEADERSHIP*
SEE GOVERNORS' OFFICES ON VOLUNTEERISM: MISSISSIPPI

NATIONAL CONFERENCE ON VOLUNTEERISM
Association for Volunteer Administration
PO Box 4584
Boulder, CO 80306
TEL: 303-497-0238
Sponsor: Association for Volunteer Administration (AVA)
Contact: Martha Martin
Description: This annual conference is co-sponsored by AVA, AVC, and AVAS. Participants include volunteer administrators, educators and scholars, and volunteer leaders involved in citizen participation efforts in the U.S., Canada, and abroad. The purpose and goals of the conference include:
- Providing a forum for action on the issues in volunteerism.
- Increasing the understanding of primary issues related to contemporary volunteerism.
- Increasing the skill level of conference participants, and providing the opportunity to share experiences and techniques.
- Focusing attention on the future of volunteerism.
- Annual meetings of the three sponsoring organizations.

A typical Conference theme is Facing a Decade of Decision. Workshops address numerous specific areas of volunteerism, including:
- Role of Various Institutions in Volunteerism
- Working Effectively with Boards and Committees
- Training Staff to Work with Volunteers
- Skills Building
- Building an Expertise in Volunteer Program Management
- Volunteer Involvement from Corporations
- Utilization of Youth Volunteers
- Citizen Participation in Energy Conservation
- Refugee Settlement
- Others in Legal Liabilities; Marketing; Program Development Tools, Evaluation, etc.

Participants completing the four-day program are expected to have gained a better understanding of the social, economic, cultural and civic conditions affecting volunteerism now and for the future.
A second theme is Challenges, Choices and Connections. Conferees at this four-day event have the chance to participate in a full schedule of events, including:
- **Workshops** - two-hour participatory sessions designed for

skill-building in subjects as diverse as board development, maintaining records, and grass-roots fundraising.

- **Challenge Sessions** - one-hour sessions, each meeting three times during the Conference, in which conferees will examine influential issues affecting volunteerism in 1981, including Reaganomics, the New Gallup Poll on Volunteer involvement, and Changing Motivations of Volunteers.
- **Strategy Exchange** - A unique, structured general session allowing conferees to collaborate on specific questions and concerns, and making sure that people who should meet each other, do.
- **Paper Sessions** - wide variety of panel presentations and research findings on subjects of both and practical interest to volunteer programs.
- **Exhibit Area** - Exhibits ranging from model programs to resource materials, and the chance to get individual questions answered.
- **Plenary Sessions** - with national level speakers and resource people.

Presenters are selected following an RFP (Request For Proposal) process, in which people from all over the country submit workshop ideas. This process will be repeated and persons interested in offering workshops or papers at the next *National Conference on Volunteerism* should contact AVA National Office. Based on attendance at the conferences, conference developers plan for 1,000 attendees at each meeting.

NATIONAL WORKSHOP ON VOLUNTARISM
US/ACTION - The Federal Volunteer Agency
1100 Vermont Avenue, NW
Suite 1100
Washington, DC 20525
TEL: 202-634-9108
TOLL FREE: 800-424-8580
Credit: Certificate
Sponsor: Certificate Sponsors: The White House; US/ACTION
Contact: Nancy E. Yde, Public Information Officer
Description: One of four workshops held each year in different parts of the country to address the development and management of volunteer programs. They are designed to help meet the need for expanded volunteer effort to seek solutions to social and human problems in the communities. Workshop sessions include:
Who Are Volunteers?
- What is volunteerism?
- Who volunteers?
- Why do people volunteer?
- Will the volunteer expect a job?
- Will volunteers embarrass the organization?
- Are volunteers insured?
- What level of expertise should the volunteer have?
- How do we retain volunteers
- What fringe benefits do volunteers expect?
How to Utilize Volunteers
- Do volunteer programs cost money?
- Why should a corporation start or support a volunteer program?
- How do we select a project focus?
- Will employees see volunteers as a threat?
- Who supervises and trains volunteers?
- For whom does the volunteer work?
- Can volunteers see confidential information?
Social Services and Volunteers
Refugee Programs and Volunteers
Education Programs and Volunteers
Federal Government and Volunteerism
In addition to the above workshops, participants have an opportunity to hear from representatives from the State Offices on Volunteerism and the President's Task Force on Private Sector Initiatives. Also, information on legislation as it relates to

volunteerism, and resources and references that might help them "back home."
White House/ACTION-sponsored workshops such as the above are held in cities that afford the best possible access by volunteer leaders in specific regions (including, in the past, New Orleans, San Francisco, Atlanta, and Philadelphia).

NEW VOLUNTEER COORDINATOR'S TRAINING
Voluntary Action Center of Boston
United Way of Massachusetts Bay
Two Liberty Square
Boston, MA 02109
TEL: 617-482-8370
Credit: None
Contact: Merle Jones Lindsay
Description: This program was developed to meet the needs of a rapidly changing group of volunteer coordinators, new to the field of volunteer management and often new to program development and personnel supervision as well. The two-and-one-half-hour program provides an overview of a well-managed volunteer program and covers 14 points to be considered:
Essential Steps in a Volunteer Program
- Obtain administrative approval.
- Assess agency needs for volunteers.
- Develop appropriate job descriptions and guidelines for volunteers.
- Develop adequate record-keeping systems.
- Recruit for these jobs.
- Interview and assign volunteers (placement).
- Orient volunteers.
- Ensure that appropriate work is available.
- Establish and maintain good volunteer/staff relations.
- See that volunteers are adequately supervised.
- Provide for continued training.
- Evaluate both volunteer's work and volunteer administration.
- Provide for recognition, promotion and job rotation.
- Make necessary changes in volunteer assignments and/or volunteer program.

These points are provided in a packet with ample space between each point for notes by the participant. The program emphasizes that, although all of the 14 steps are necessary, they are not solely the responsibility of the volunteer coordinator, since the best volunteer programs result from cooperation by the whole staff. The program is conducted by Voluntary Action Center staff and volunteer trainers, with the same format used in each session. Volunteer trainers are recruited from among local coordinators of volunteers. Materials are developed by the trainers and, in addition to their use at the sessions, serve as models for development back at the participant's agency. The packet of materials includes information on Developing a Volunteer Program, Volunteer Job Descriptions, Recruitment, Interviewing, Maintaining a Volunteer Program, and Recognition, as well as sample forms, college contacts book, and brochures on the Voluntary Action Center, the Skillsbank, and the Voluntary Action Center Standards Program. A modest fee is charged for the course materials.

NH STATE CONFERENCE ON VOLUNTEERISM
SEE GOVERNORS' OFFICES ON VOLUNTEERISM: NEW HAMPSHIRE

NORTH CAROLINA/VIRGINIA EXCHANGE: PART ONE
SEE GOVERNORS' OFFICES ON VOLUNTEERISM: NORTH CAROLINA

PERFORMANCE BASED ASSESSMENT PROGRAM FOR CERTIFICATION IN VOLUNTEER ADMINISTRATION

Association for Volunteer Administration
PO Box 4584
Boulder, CO 80306
TEL: 303-497-0238
Credit: CVA (Certified in Volunteer Administration)
Sponsor: AVA
Contact: Martha Martin
Description: This program follows a field test in 1981 by an affiliate organization of AVA, Volunteer Administrators of Southwestern Pennsylvania (VASP), from which the findings were utilized to refine and revise the assessment program. From November 1, 1982, to October 31, 1983, only AVA members or members of AVA voting affiliate organizations or provisional voting affiliate organizations were included for certification. After October 31, 1983, any qualified volunteer administrator, regardless of AVA member status, is eligible for AVA certification. Prospective participants are encouraged to complete the equivalent of two years' full-time experience in volunteer administration as a background for application. An eight-stage process is involved in the certification program, as shown below:

- **Stage 1:** Prospective applicants attend a one-day workshop on certification, receive a detailed self-assessment questionnaire for completion and *I CAN* materials for personal career exploration.
- **Stage 2:** Persons with continued interest in certification complete the application form, which is reviewed by the Certification Assessment Committee. Upon acceptance, academic and field advisors are assigned to the candidate.
- **Stage 3:** Each candidate attends a half-day workshop on portfolio development, a written process through which experiences are translated into stated competency.
- **Stage 4:** Participants work in concert with the portfolio and their academic field advisors, receiving a form evaluation of their progress midway through the stage from two advisors.
- **Stage 5:** The completed portfolio receives a final written evaluation from academic and field advisors, and is then forwarded to the Board of Assessment.
- **Stage 6:** Applicants receive from the Board of Assessment a case study for analysis and response, which is completed and returned to the Board.
- **Stage 7:** The Board of Assessment reviews submitted materials and may request additional information or supporting documents, subsequently notifying applicants as to whether or not they have received certification.
- **Stage 8:** Applicants attaining certification receive an analysis of their portfolio which, along with their personal career development plan, serves as a tool to guide future professional development effort. Applicants denied certification receive a written explanation and instructions pertaining to eligibility for subsequent review (with the right to contest the decision of the Board through AVA's Ethics and Standards Committee).

Recertification review is made every five years to renew CVA credentials. AVA members previously using CAVS (Certified Administrator of Volunteer Services) are advised to seek CVA status, since it is an upgrading of the certification status, and represents the full value of the certification program to the whole field of volunteer administration.

PLANNING TODAY FOR TOMORROW'S VOLUNTEERS*

Community Volunteer Service
115 South Union Street
Stillwater, MN 55082
TEL: 612-439-7434
Credit: Inquire
Sponsor: Minnesota Association of Volunteer Directors
Contact: Vi Russell

Description: Every year directors of volunteers across Minnesota come together to compare notes, exchange ideas, and generally update their techniques in their responsibilities to their volunteer programs. As it developed into an advanced-level educational event, it became apparent that new directors were at a disadvantage. Consequently a *New Directors Workshop* was added to the existing format. Later, *Leadership for Volunteers* was included as a major component to examine more closely the leadership development issues pertinent to volunteer programs. Topics covered in the three areas include:

Advanced-Level Areas:
- **Personnel Management Skills** - documenting volunteer experience.
- **How Well Do You Run a Meeting?** - planning successful meetings.
- **Volunteerism: Exploitation or Opportunity?** - exploring history/trends.
- **Professional Writing: Publications and Formal Papers** - getting articles and papers published.
- **Teaching the Adult Learner** - utilizing effective educational materials.
- **Skills in Providing Consultation** - assisting colleagues.
- **Motivational Techniques Adapted from Business** - using proven techniques.

New Directors Workshop Topics:
- Program Development and Ethics;
- Recruitment and Public Relations;
- Training and Orientation;
- Record-Keeping;
- Staff-Volunteer Team;
- Recognition;
- Program Evaluation;
- Time Management, and others as indicated.

Leadership for Volunteers Areas:
- Board and Committee Planning (Status Analysis; Long Range Goals; Action Plan; Monitoring and Evaluation).
- Program and Project planning (Design Assistance; Management Plans; Monitoring and Evaluation).
- Organization and Leadership Development (Training Design, Implementation and Evaluation; Team Building; Decision-making).
- Organizational Support Materials (Workbooks; Program Manuals; Descriptive Materials).

The programs are always combined with the Lake Sylvia conferences.

PRACTICE EXCELLENCE: NATIONAL CONFERENCE ON VOLUNTEERISM

Association for Volunteer Administration
PO Box 4584
Boulder, CO 80306
TEL: 303-407-0238
Credit: AVA Certification (partial fulfillment)
Contact: Martha Martin
Description: This conference has been planned with ten tracks: Corporate Volunteerism, Ethics and Issues, Health, Fundamental Administration, Experienced Administration, Religion, Special Interest Groups, Education, Personal Growth, and General Interest. Outlines of each track are shown below:

Corporate Volunteerism
- Current Perspectives in Corporate Social Responsibility
- United Way's "Person to Person" Program
- How to Turn Your Local Business School into a Resource - for Free
- More Than Money
- Fraternalism in the Eighties

Fundamentals of Volunteer Administration
- Grantsmanship
- Basic Financial Management

- Measuring Your Volunteer Program: Statistics and Record Keeping
- Writing to Clarify, Present or Persuade
- Special Events and Fundraising
- Planning Productive Meetings
- ABC's of Influencing Public Policy
- Firm Foundation
- Evaluating Volunteer Programs
- Use of Mass Media for Volunteer Recruitment
- Consultation Session: Interviewing Skills
- Starting and Managing Membership Organizations
- Basics of Recruitment and Retention

Experienced Volunteer Administration
- Managing Change in Organization
- Consultation Session: Liability, Legal Issues and Accountability in Volunteerism
- Money-Talks: A Guide to Establishing the True Dollar Value of Volunteer Time
- Quality Circles (new management techniques)
- Consultant Session: Career Satisfaction for the Directors of Volunteers
- Relationship Between Boards of Directors and Executive Directors
- New Directions in Assessing the Volunteer's Motivation
- Capital Fund Drives and Other Big Bucks
- Direct Service on Advocacy
- My Name in Print
- Utilizing Power: How to Make Dreams Come True
- The Volunteer as a Customer?

Education and Volunteerism
- Lessons from the Field: Evaluation of Service Learning Programs
- Benefits of Service Learning: Observations from the Field
- Implementation of Service Learning
- Transferring Volunteer Experience to a Paid Position

Health and Volunteerism
- Hospice Volunteers
- Volunteers in Community Health
- Showcase: Volunteers in Mental Health

Religion and Volunteerism
- Volunteer Development and Management for Clergy and Lay Leaders
- How to Access Human Resources within the Congregation

Special Interest
- Public Relations for Non-Profits
- AVA Certification Session: Application Workshop
- AVA Certification: General Orientation
- Docents

General Interest
- Neighborhood Enablers and Volunteer Networks
- Meet the Experts in a Conference Overview
- Strategy Exchange

Ethics and Issues
- The Effect of Public Policy on Volunteerism
- National Public Policy Issues Which Affect You as a Leader of Volunteers
- Employment, Unemployment and Volunteerism
- Providing the Basic Needs of Food, Shelter and Safety
- Ethics of Volunteer Leadership
- Career as a Public Service Director

Personal Growth
- Career Entry through Volunteerism
- Avoiding Time Traps Set for/by Leaders
- Wellness and Self-Care
- Are You Psychologically Wired to Be a Change Agent?

Faculty for the Conference is drawn from major areas of the field of volunteerism involving experienced, well-known presenters. Conferences are held in various parts of the country each year. The Association's National Conference Informer is published several months in advance of each conference with full details on all aspects of the program.

PROFESSIONAL CERTIFICATION IN VOLUNTEER MANAGEMENT
American University
Division of Continuing Education
McKinley Building
Washington, DC 20016
TEL: 202-686-5150
Credit: 7 CEUs and Certificate
Sponsor: American University
Contact: Elizabeth Pawlson
Description: First offered in Fall 1983, this course is intended for three specific groups: experienced Volunteer Coordinators; newly-appointed Volunteer Managers who need a broad perspective and some specific training; volunteers and Volunteer Managers who need specialized courses. Completion of the Certificate requires successful completion of five out of six core seminars:
- Organization Theory and Behavior for Volunteer Managers;
- Marketing, Promotion, and Public Relations;
- Training Your Volunteers;
- Supervisory Skills;
- Recruiting, Interviewing, Placing Volunteers; and
- Program Planning and Evaluation.

An additional 12 hours of instruction must be satisfied by either:
- Completing the sixth core seminar; or
- Completing 12 hours of workshop instruction from designated workshops.

Certificate requirements may be satisfied by other Professional Development offerings at the University, such as: A "How-to Course for Newsletters," and "Writing and Placing Your Own Publicity." Additional planned seminars include Fund Raising, Volunteer/Staff/Board Relations, Running an Effective Meeting, and Developing Corporate/Community Resources.

REGIONAL VOLUNTEER WORKSHOPS
SEE GOVERNORS' OFFICES ON VOLUNTEERISM: MINNESOTA

RESOURCE DEVELOPMENT SEMINARS
VM Systems
1807 Prairie Avenue
Downers Grove, IL 60515
TEL: 708-964-1194
Credit: Inquire
Sponsor: Local sponsors across USA & Canada. (Past sponsors include: Jr. League; Red Cross; Arthritis Fund; YMCA; YWCA; American Cancer; VACs; State offices on Volunteerism; Lutheran Cuurch; Army; US/ACTION)
Contact: Sue Vineyard or Steve McCurly
Description: Workshops are designed to improve the techniques of the organization as a whole, as well as the effectiveness of individual staff/volunteers. Dozens of seminars are offered, with 14 trainers available:
Effective Management of the Volunteer Resource
Target Audience: Public and private non-profit groups who utilize or provide volunteers.
Training Offered: How To:
- Plan
- Organize
- Staff/Recruit/Retain
- Train
- Supervise/Motivate
- Evaluate/Recognize & Assess
- Trends to discover, develop and deploy the Volunteer Resource

Goal: Practical skill development for participants
Marketing for Non-Profit
Target Audience: Private non-profit agencies & organizations who depend (for survival) on community support.

Training Offered: How to: Identify, generate & maintain people and resources necessary to achieve organization goals.
Goal: Knowledge of marketing principles for groups and beginning of a marketing plan

Grassroots Fundraising (Workshops)
Target Audience: Non-profit community agencies & organizations who depend on community support for funds and resources.
Training Offered: How To:
- Market
- Manage
- Motivate
- Plan for effective development of resources

Goal: One-day workshop: Master concepts of fundraising; 2-day workshop: Master concepts; plan one event

Doing More with Less
Target Audience: Non-profit groups who depend on community support for all or part of funding resources Directors of development & fundraising, event chairs, recruitment chairmen, etc.
Training Offered: How To:
- Plan
- Market
- Motivate
- Manage
- Ask
- Barter
- Develop PR and assess trends to acquire resources of people, goods, money, and services

Goals:
- Create one-year plan for total fundraising
- Plan/timeline one event
- Master skills of effective fundraising
- Develop local resource directory.

Balancing: You and Your World
Target Audience: Corporations, professional organizations, service clubs, non-profit groups. etc.
Training Offered: How to make effective trade-offs between personal, volunteer and professional demands; how to get and give support; assess priorities, etc.
Goal: Maximize personal and professional growth through balance and communication skills.

The above and other seminars are tailored to the specific needs of the host organization through pre-seminar consultation and planning.

SCAVA WORKSHOPS FOR VOLUNTEER ADMINISTRATORS*
Community Service Planning Council of Greenville County
Volunteer Greenville
824 East Washington Street
Columbia, SC 29602
TEL: 803-232-6444
Credit: Inquire
Sponsor: South Carolina Association for Volunteer Administration (SCAVA)
Contact: Elaine Huff-Lowe
Description: When a lack of funding forced closure of the South Carolina State Office of Volunteer Services in 1977, a small group of concerned volunteer directors organized SCAVA (South Carolina Association for Volunteer Administration). The goals, in addition to the primary purpose of creating a community of those involved in volunteerism, include providing an avenue for exerting appropriate legislative leverage to affect public policy, and to develop training opportunities for volunteer administrators. In 1980 a SCAVA study indicated that 307,882 persons (one-fourth of the state's population) volunteered their time - 122,470,190 hours worth $600,000,000. Workshops were developed not only to help volunteer administrators develop and maintain the skills needed to maintain this high level of citizen participation, but also

for moral support.
Each year SCAVA sponsors a two-day fall conference and a one-day spring workshop. Since 1977 more than 700 persons have participated in this training, which includes topics such as:
- Accountability
- Basic Volunteer Management
- Creative Fund Raising
- Legislation
- Publicity
- Volunteer Recruitment
- Staff Resistance
- Urban and Rural Volunteerism

In 1979 SCAVA co-sponsored the first South Eastern Regional Volunteer Conference with a national organization. However, increasingly trainers for the ongoing workshops and conferences are being drawn from within SCAVA. In addition to SCAVA's training program, local Voluntary Action Centers conduct community-wide training in local areas.

SEACOAST CONFERENCE ON VOLUNTEERISM: A TIME FOR GROWTH; A TIME FOR CHANGE
Governor's Office on Volunteerism/NH
State House Annex
Concord , NH 03301
TEL: 603-271-3771
Credit: Inquire
Sponsor: Governor's Office on Volunteerism; New Hampshire Vocational Technical College
Contact: Linda Darling, Executive Director
Description: This one-day training event is one of five regional conferences sponsored each year by the Governor's Office on Volunteerism. It is designed to assist managers and leaders of volunteers in developing skills and resources which can make them more effective. Workshops and presenters have been selected in response to the particular needs of the Seacoast Area. Conference agenda includes:
Keynote Address: "Growth and a New Hampshire Dream," Cathy Burnham, News Anchor, WMUR-TV
- **Communications and Motivational Speaking** - This workshop guides you in using your communication skills to motivate and inspire volunteers.
- **Improving Visibility in a Media Storm** - This panel presents two sides of a story: yours and the media's. It explores your needs for visibility in a storm of media requests. Each panel member provides you with tools for positive media relationships, further understanding and better use of each medium.
- **Back to the Future: Planning for Growth and Change** - This is a presentation of demographics for the Seacoast for the next five years. It includes small and large group discussion of how this will impact you, your work and your volunteers.
- **Middle Management: Empowering Key Volunteers** - Through middle management, key volunteers accept major leadership responsibility, enhancing programs and volunteers. Using the 4-H program as a model, participants will learn how to design and implement an effective, dynamic middle management system for their organizations.
- **Creative Recognition** - This is a panel discussion of volunteer recognition: what it is, what it means to volunteers, and innovative ways to recognize volunteers, focusing on the inexpensive.

The current conference includes presenters from WMUR-TV, WERZ-Radio, Foster's Daily Democrat, N.E. Continental Cable, Riverside Rest Home, Rockingham Planning Commission, Seacoast United Way, Strafford County Cooperative Extension, University of New Hampshire, Salute to Excellence, Muscular Dystrophy Association, Sea Grant Cooperative Extension, New Hampshire Jaycees, Rockingham County Nursing Home, Rockingham County Retired Senior Volunteer Program, and the Governor's Office on Volunteerism.

SELECTING AND TRAINING VOLUNTEERS
University of Washington
Business & Women's Placement Pgms
Seattle, WA 98195
TEL: 206-543-0535
Credit: CEUs
Sponsor: University of Washington
Contact: Phyllis Needy, Program Coordinator
Description: This workshop is one of a series of seven workshops designed to "help participants help their organizations." Although it was developed primarily for Volunteer Coordinators, this program is designed to assist others with some degree of responsibility for volunteers in their programs (board members, trainers, staff supervisors, etc.) as well.

Topics are identified based on the experience of faculty members in human services organizations involving volunteers in their programs (United Way, Camp Fire, Community Council, among others). The curriculum is designed on broad terms to allow the concerns unique to each participant's program to shape the direction of the workshop. The general topics are:

- Defining Volunteer Roles, Needs
- Advertising for Volunteers
- Interviewing Potential Volunteers
- Placement and Orientation
- Providing Functioning, Constructive Evalua tions
- Training, Maintaining, Rewarding Volunteers

In addition to the workshop described above - *The How-To of Working with Volunteers/TLC (Teaching/Learning/Caring),* the six-workshop series includes several on the logistical aspects of operating a nonprofit organization:

- Newsletter and Brochure Writing
- Designing Effective Slide Presentations
- Marketing and Promotion for Non-Profit and Public Organizations
- Fund Raising Basics
- Lobbying Strategies

Faculty for the series is drawn from organizations and agencies from the surrounding area as well as from the University.
Publications: Selecting/Training Volunteers
Founded: 1976

SHORT COURSES AND SEMINARS FOR ADMINISTRATORS OF VOLUNTEERS
Allegheny County Community College
Center-North, 111 Pines Plaza
1130 Perry Highway
Pittsburgh, PA 15237
TEL: 412-931-8500
Credit: AVA Certification (partial fulfillment)
Sponsor: The Community College of Allegheny County; Information and Volunteer Services of Allegheny County
Contact: Marty Angelone, Planning Committee
Description: This series is part of a continuing effort by the College's Institute for Volunteerism to provide programs in volunteer services administration and management to membership of volunteer organizations and agencies staffed primarily with volunteers. Each course/seminar is complete in itself, enabling participants to select according to their needs. Topics include:
Basic Skills in Planning and Administering a Volunteer Services Program - a six-week course for volunteer administrators withminimal experience in the field. Participants examine the role of being a manager of other persons with special emphasis on 1) planning, developing and evaluating a volunteer program; 2) volunteer assignments; 3) recruiting volunteers; 4) supervising volunteers; 5) techniques for record-keeping; 6) effective volunteer/staff relations; and 7) local resource identification.
Seminar for New Directors - one-day seminar to orient new directors to the Voluntary Action Center's recruitment system, technical assistance, information services, and DOVIA (Director of

Volunteers in Agencies) meetings.
Training Trainers in Workshop Development - one-day seminar for professionals who need to utilize effective volunteer training programs presented in the form of an experiential workshop designed to cover the different types of volunteer training; e.g., needs assessment, learning objectives, group learning goals, climate setting for learning, learning models and techniques, and evaluation.
Interviewing and Placement of the Special Volunteer - a six-week course to focus on interviewing skills and techniques geared specifically to the special volunteer - people who are at a point of rehabilitation and transition in their lives and/or who are handicapped; provides opportunity for discussion with persons representing 1) physically and psychologically handicapped; 2) the mentally retarded; and 3) the older adult regarding understanding and creative placement of these persons; covers the special volunteer's needs and their relationship to the goals of the organization.
Working Effectively with Boards and Committees - a one-day seminar centered on the skills and knowledge staff people need to provide support to their boards and committees, and how to develop and maintain this relationship through cooperative effort; covers staff relationships separately from relationship of staff to advisory committees with areas of concern for each including: organization, role and function, membership process, types of boards, committees, training and evaluation.
Recruitment: A New Look - a one-day workshop examining 1) why people volunteer; 2) job descriptions conducive to retaining volunteers; 3) sources of prospective volunteers; 4) techniques for the recruitment of volunteers, with special attention given to matching techniques; concludes with a clinic on special problems in recruitment.
Introduction to Budget Development and Accounting for Managers in Nonprofit Agencies - a short course to provide participants with a basic understanding of budget development and monitoring expenditures for nonprofit programs; geared to persons with minimal knowledge of financial management, with emphasis on providing small nonprofit agencies with insight into 1) financial management; 2) cost effectiveness of programs; 3) basic accounting terminology.
The Volunteer Experience - a one-day workshop to enhance the administrator's understanding of the role of volunteering in the lives of active volunteers, with particular attention given to the 30-50 age group of both administrators and volunteers.

S/OVCP WINTER CONFERENCE
US/ACTION - The Federal Volunteer Agency
1100 Vermont Avenue, NW
Suite 1100
Washington, DC 20525
TEL: 202-634-9108
Credit: Inquire
Sponsor: US/ACTION
Contact: Nancy E. Yde, Public Information Officer
Description: The State Offices of Voluntary Citizen Participation (S/OVCP) Winter Conference is designed to bring together policy makers and implementors to discuss the future of volunteerism in this country and to explore ways in which public and private sector policies will support future needs and initiatives. Participants are Directors of S/OVCPs, Governor's Representatives, Public and Private Policy Makers on Volunteerism, and other volunteer leaders. Topics covered in the four-day program:

- **New Director's Orientation** - for all new S/OVCP Directors and potential S/OVCP sponsors; focuses on issues relating to the day-to-day operation of an S/OVCP, including program development, fiscal management, planning, public relations and setting goals for long-term funding.
- **In-House Sharing** - sharing of S/OVCP program initiatives,

activities, and plans by Directors; presentation of ACTION initiatives; discussion of cooperative programming opportunities between S/OVCPs and ACTION.

- **Strategizing** - introduction to "Day Three" session; preparation of questions and determination of specific issues to be addressed.
- **Prospectus for the Future** - roundtable discussion of national policy on volunteerism as defined by the White House, the Congress and ACTION; national goals on volunteerism; how national policy will affect the states, particularly the S/OVCPs; pending legislation; local pressures.
- **Private Sector Initiatives** - round table discussion of private sector goals on volunteerism vis-a-vis the new public initiatives; what the private sector can be expected and encouraged to provide; future public-private relationships; the degree to which new public sector initiatives will be in lead of or in response to private sector initiatives.
- **Legislative Support** - how to develop legislative support for an S/OVCP; a discussion of back room tactics; a sharing of experiences.
- **Making It Work** - discussion of and planning for the promotion of S/OVCP offices as primary vehicles through which national and state volunteerism goals can be accomplished.

Time and space are provided for informal discussions throughout the day, and for display of individual S/OVCP materials.

THE SPIRIT THAT SUPPORTS ALABAMA - VOLUNTEERS
Governor's Office on Volunteerism/AL
64 North Union Street
Rooms 13-15
Montgomery, AL 36130
TEL: 205-261-2030
Contact: Joyce St. John-Marcus
Description: In developing this conference, planners considered the many facets of volunteerism today, and divided topics into five program tracts - Skillsbuilding, Resource Development, Special Interest, Model Programs, Trends and Issues. Participants are invited to either concentrate on one tract, or sample from the different topical areas offered:
Skillsbuilding
- **Creatively Managing Volunteers in the Stress Age** - A discussion on time management and how to avoid burnout in an age of mounting stress.
- **Effective Delegation and Utilization of Volunteers** - An experimental session on the art and science of effective delegation of tasks; includes a discussion on volunteer assignments delegating.
- **Be Prepared to Speak** - This workshop will prepare the participant for persuasive public speaking at all levels.
- **Management Skills for the Volunteer Administrator** - The Magic of Effective Communication is YOU! - Learn to increase your personal impact through proven communication methods.

Resource Development
- **Community Resource Mobilization** - Learn proven methods of mobilizing resources even in the highly competitive world of fund raising (two parts).
- **Senior Volunteer Resource** - A panel discussion of the powerful potential of older Americans and senior citizens as volunteers.
- **Beyond Promises** - This workshop deals with rural volunteers program development.

Special Interest
- **Volunteers in Criminal Justice** - A panel presentation representative of criminal justice volunteer programs and prison ministries.
- **Special Volunteers** - Presented by a panel representing volunteer programs for disabled persons.

- **Volunteer Friendship Programs for Youth** - A three-member panel will speak on various approaches to adult and youth volunteering in friendship programs for youth.
- **Preparing Your Crew for the Journey** - Learn to mobilize church volunteers, and to use their special gifts and talents.

Model Programs
- **Corporate Sponsorships** - A presentation of a nationally recognized Corporate Good Neighbor Program in Huntsville.
- **Trailblazing Volunteers** - A presention of various projects of the Telephone Pioneers, a group of South Central Bell employee volunteers.
- **Volunteers in Literacy** - A discussion on the efforts of a multi-county group to provide education to all shifts of workers at a factory, and to the general public.
- **Volunteers in the Arts and Humanities** - A panel presentation dealing with volunteers in museums, libraries, and theaters.

Trends and Issues
- **Legal Liability for Volunteer Programs** - A practitioner's guide to liability and practical means for protecting both the volunteer and the agency.
- **AIDS** - A panel discussion on the AIDS issue offering insights from the public, volunteer, and individual perspective.
- **Drug Abuse and Prevention** - A discussion of the Governor's Drug Abuse Policy Board and a breakdown of the implementation of the Drug Free School and Community Act.

In addition to the workshops, a networking luncheon was held with facilitators in 36 topical areas including Aging, Homelessness, AIDS, Drug Abuse, Latch Key Children, Corporate Involvement, Literacy, Farm Crises, and Volunteer Protection Legislation. Facilitators, presenters, committee members, and sponsors represented hundreds of public, private and corporate entities, including ACTION, Alabama Prison Project, Toastmasters International, Voluntary Action Center, Lions Club, Alabama AIDS Outreach, Bell Telephone Pioneers, Alabama Department of Public Health, and the Alabama Assembly on Voluntarism. This was the Governor's third annual conference.
Publications: GOV Conference Report

STATEWIDE CONFERENCE ON VOLUNTEERISM
SEE GOVERNORS' OFFICES ON VOLUNTEERISM: MISSOURI

STATEWIDE LEADERSHIP SYMPOSIUM: WORKING TOGETHER TO MAKE VISIONS REALITIES
SEE PRIVATE SECTOR INITIATIVES OFFICES

STATEWIDE VOLUNTEER MANAGEMENT TRAINING PROGRAM
SEE GOVERNORS' OFFICES ON VOLUNTEERISM: IDAHO

SUPERVISING VOLUNTEERS*
Volunteer Center of Chicago
United Way Crusade of Mercy
125 South Clark Street
Chicago, IL 60603-4012
TEL: 312-580-2723
Credit: Certificate; CEUs on request
Sponsor: United Way of Chicago
Contact: Joe Agnello
Description: This workshop is designed to help participants improve their skills in supervising volunteers. It is intended for the volunteer coordinator as well as anyone else responsible for supervising volunteers, and introduces a process in which participants:
- identify major factors affecting organization behavior in volunteer programs.
- identify patterns of leadership and roles for volunteer coordinators.

• study ways to reinforce the motivation of volunteers.
• practice effective communications and problem solving skills.
An Optional Follow-Up Clinic is held one week after the session to help participants diagnose related organizational and professional problems, and to develop an action plan using new concepts and techniques.

SUPERVISION SKILL SERIES/MAP (MANAGEMENT ASSISTANCE PROGRAM)
United Way of San Diego County
Volunteer Center Division
4699 Murphy Canyon Road
PO Box 23543
San Diego, CA 92123-0543
TEL: 619-492-2000
Credit: CEUs
Sponsor: United Way of San Diego County
Contact: Volunteer Center Director
Description: The Supervision Skill Series is composed of three one-day workshops designed to build on each other or to be taken individually. The series specializes in human relations and communications programs and includes:

Workshop I: Understanding and Supervising Others
Objectives:
• To examine effective and ineffective styles of supervision
• To increase participants' understanding of their work styles and the work styles of others
• To present options for increasing effectiveness as supervisors based on understanding of mutual style needs and preferences
• To examine methods through which supervisors can create a climate which fosters employee self-motivation

Content:
• Effective and ineffective methods of supervision
• Presentation of a work styles model
• Identification by participants of their own work styles
• Options for increasing effectiveness
• Self-scoring FIRO-B questionnaire taken by participants
• Interpretation of questionnaire
• Motivation

Method:
• Lecturette
• Small Group Discussion
• Feedback Sessions

Workshop II: Communications Techniques for Supervisors
Objectives:
• To increase participants' understanding of the communications process, including one-way, two-way, and communications organizations
• To increase participants' skills in giving and receiving feedback, active listening, and reading non-verbal cues
• To increase participants' effectiveness in written communications
• To give participants an opportunity to practice the communications skills presented in the workshop

Content:
• Overview of the communications process
• Communicating in organizations
• Listening
• Non-verbal communications
• Training exercise to practice skills learned
• Hints for written communications
• Effective staff meetings

Method:
• Lecturette
• Small Group Practice Exercise
• Feedback

Workshop III: Delegating and Evaluating Work
Objectives:
• To increase participants' understanding of how and when to delegate
• To give participants techniques for setting work-related objectives for themselves and subordinates
• To give participants techniques for results

Content:
• Presentation of tell, sell, consult and join model
• When and how to delegate
• Why set objectives
• Characteristics of good objectives
• Getting commitment to objectives
• Evaluating results

Method:
• Combination of lecturette
• Practice
• Participant feedback

In addition to the above series of workshops, the Management Assistance Program (MAP) designs workshops according to the needs of requesting organizations. Past requests include board development, personnel policies, planning systems, communications, budgeting, evaluation, time management, assertiveness, public relations and other areas.

THE SUPERVISORY CYCLE
Voluntary Action Center of United Way
United Way of Minneapolis Area
404 South Eighth Street
Minneapolis, MN 55404
TEL: 612-340-7532
Credit: CEUs; partial fulfillment for AVA Certification
Contact: Dr. Lorna Michelson
Description: One of a series of management-level workshops for volunteer program leaders in agencies and organizations, this session not only addresses Volunteer Directors/Coordinators, but is designed to benefit supervisory staff, volunteer supervisors, and volunteer trainers as well. Specific learning segments include:
• Elements of effective supervision of volunteers;
• Making the best use of supervisory time; and
• Dealing with problems.
The workshops represent one phase of a total advocacy process offered by the Center in areas of consultation, recruitment and referral, and information resources on volunteerism. Faculty is drawn from Association for Volunteer Administration membership.

THE SYSTEMATIC INVOLVEMENT OF VOLUNTEERS IN HUMAN SERVICES
National Council of Jewish Women
15 East 26th Street
New York, NY 10010
TEL: 212-532-1740
Credit: Inquire
Sponsor: The National Council of Jewish Women; Adelphi University; Teachers College, Columbia University
Contact: Roberta Stim, Voluntarism Coordinator
Description: This seminar was developed to address college/university teachers on the subject of preparing their students to work with volunteers. The invitation to participate in the seminar includes a section on a few of the areas in which volunteers are involved today, and their relationship to college courses that will be producing the professionals who will work with the volunteers. These include:
• **Social Work** - day care aides, foster parents, runaway counselors, I&R personnel, senior companions, food distributors, etc.
• **Education** - school board trustees, classroom aides, tutors, parent-teacher association members, career counselors, etc.
• **Health** - advocates for patients' rights, workers with the handicapped, nutrition program aides, anti-addiction counselors, etc.

- **Justice** - court monitors, probation/parole aides, civilian review board members, prisoners' rights advocates, role models for delinquents, etc.
- **Nursing** - friendly visitors, occupational therapy aides, fund raisers, behavior modification assistants, etc.
- **Library Science** - Library Board trustees, storytellers, PR display artists, Friends of the Library, etc.
- **Political Science** - citizen watchdogs, campaigners, lobbyists, consumer advocates, human rights activists, etc.

Participants from the above and other divisions of area colleges/universities were provided with general information on volunteers upon their arrival and, on their departure, with materials and data designed to help their students learn the skills they will need to work with volunteers. With faculty drawn from university staff and practitioners in programs involving volunteers, participants were provided with an initial overview on arrival, followed by three presentations - the final two specific to the school curriculum:

- Staff/Volunteer Relations (panel of three)
- Information on voluntarism which could be included in curriculum
- How can we get information on voluntarism into the curriculum?

A general discussion period follows each presentation, and a "wrap-up" session involving faculty and participants concludes the seminar.

TEXAS VOLUNTEER CONFERENCE
SEE GOVERNORS' OFFICES ON VOLUNTEERISM: TEXAS

A TOTAL PROCESS
Voluntary Action Center of United Way
United Way of Minneapolis
404 South Eighth Street
Minneapolis, MN 55404
TEL: 612-340-7532
Credit: One College Credit
Sponsor: Minneapolis Community College
Contact: Dr. Lorna Michelson
Description: Developed on request from the field, this workshop deals with the entire process of establishing and maintaining an effective volunteer program in an agency or as a separate community organization. Co-sponsorship by an education institution and a local Center on volunteerism assures a balance of theory and practice for Volunteer Directors/Coordinators, Executive Directors of voluntary agencies, individuals who work with volunteers, volunteer leaders, and leaders of church-based volunteer programs. Topics covered include:

- Volunteer Program Management
- Trends in Volunteerism
- Recruitment Ideas
- Interviewing Skills
- Evaluation Process

New features in this workshop include in-depth sessions and more time allotted to the sharing of experiences.
Faculty is drawn from the Volunteer Leadership and Management of Non-Profit Agencies program of the College's Human Services Division, and the staff of the Voluntary Action Center, as well as guest presenters.

TOWARD THE YEAR 2000 - THE CHALLENGE
Association for Volunteer Administration
PO Box 4584
Boulder, CO 80306
TEL: 303-497-0238
Description: This annual conference addresses the twenty-first century and aims to enable participants to positively influence their organizations and their communities to meet the challenges ahead. It offers a wide selection of learning opportunities - both at the introductory and the experienced levels, in a variety of formats, including workshops, institutes and paper presentations. Sessions are clustered into three tracks focusing on personal, programmatic and professional aspects of leadership:

- **Track #1: The Challenge to Ourselves** - topics related to growing in our own competencies; negotiation skills; preventing burnout; advocating within our organization; networking; value clarification; delegating; matching oneself to the organizational climate; career advancement strategies; conflict management; personal performance; appraisals; self-development; problem solving; giving and getting recognition, etc.
- **Track #2: The Challenge to Our Programs** - topics related to maximizing the potential impact of volunteers; new models for citizen involvement; management assistance programs; networking; creative utilization of short-term projects; re-channeling long-term volunteers; overcoming staff resistance; career ladders for volunteers; models of cooperative training programs, etc.
- **Track #3: The Challenge to Our Profession** - topics related to exercising our professional clout to determine our future; vision planning; ethical issues; networking; coalition-building; working effectively with elected officials; planning for the impact of demographic trends; intergenerational issues; mobilizing for change; current and developing volunteer administration courses and training; etc.

Conference participants include program directors and other staff from non-profit, for-profit and governmental settings, membership organization leaders, board members, trainers, educators, researchers, consultants and students.

TRAINING FOR THE MUNICIPAL VOLUNTEER COORDINATOR*
New England Municipal Center
Pettee Brook Offices
PO Box L
Durham, NH 03824
TEL: 603-868-5000
Credit: Inquire
Sponsor: New England Municipal Center; The Mott Foundation
Contact: Susan Casey, Staff Associate
Description: The New England Municipal Center (NEMC) is sponsored by: Connecticut Conference of Municipalities, Maine Municipal Association, Massachusetts Municipal Association, New Hampshire Municipal Association, Rhode Island League of Cities and Towns, Vermont League of Cities and Towns.
NEMC conducts monthly seminars for volunteer coordinators in local government volunteer programs to help them deal with a variety of volunteer management issues, including:

- Program Development
- Public Relations
- Recruitment
- Training
- Volunteer/Paid Employee Relations
- "Education" of Municipal Managers and Department Heads
- Handling the Press

These monthly meetings also act as a support and resource base for coordinators who are out there, on their own, breaking new ground. A significant portion of each group meeting involves group consultation and problem solving around specific issues that need to be dealt with by one of the coordinators.
The assistant town/city managers are invited and encouraged to attend and do so occasionally. Their participation is helpful in building a support base and a mutual understanding of the complex issues involved in municipal volunteer management.
Actual training of volunteers occurs on the local level, with each community designing its own training program to meet specific needs. In addition, specific training for individual jobs occurs. Training sessions for volunteers include police station and library volunteers, crossing guards, etc.

UNIVERSITY PROGRAMS FOR VOLUNTEERS AND ADMINISTRATORS OF VOLUNTEERS
SEE GOVERNORS' OFFICES ON VOLUNTEERISM: MINNESOTA

VAC TRAINING
Voluntary Action Center of the Fairfax County Area
10530 Page Avenue
Fairfax, VA 22030
TEL: 703-246-3460
Credit: Inquire
Sponsor: Voluntary Action Center
Contact: Angie Carrera
Description: The Voluntary Action Center develops and conducts workshops based on expressed needs from volunteer program leaders in Fairfax County. Typical workshops include:
Effective Management of Volunteers: for agencies, organizations, religious groups, etc.
Orientation and Board Training: for agencies, organizations, community groups, and others.
Effective Boardsmanship Training and Advanced Management of Volunteer Coordinators
Other training programs are held as needs are expressed from the volunteer community, often in cooperation with other groups.

VIRGINIA VOLUNTEERS - HEALTH OF THE COMMONWEALTH
SEE GOVERNORS' OFFICES ON VOLUNTEERISM: VIRGINIA

VOLUNTARY ACTION ASSOCIATION ADMINISTRATION PROGRAM
Lindenwood Colleges
College for Individual Education
St. Charles, MO 63301
TEL: 314-723-7152
Credit: M.A. or B.S.
Sponsor: The Lindenwood Colleges
Contact: Dr. Arlene Taich
Description: The degree program is designed to provide both the working professional and the acting volunteer with the opportunity to gain expertise and new skill in the specific management and policy concerns of volunteerism. Students focus studies on any aspect of the voluntary sector - from citizen advocacy to institutional change to program administration. Some choose to expand their studies in order to gain expertise in such areas as community organization, environmental protection, youth services, health care administration, etc. The basic program format includes:
Staff Development and Volunteer Administration
- Group Process
- Decision Making and Leadership
- Administration
- The Individual and the Organization
- Organizational Behavior
- Dynamics and Change
Financial Aspects of Non-Profit Management
- Fiscal Management and Accounting in Non-Profit Organizations
- Funding and Grantsmanship
- Governmental and Corporate Interaction with Non-Profit Organizations
- Legal Aspects of Fiscal Management
Organizational Administration
- Resource Assessment and Research
- Program Planning and Development
- Program Evaluation
- Management Issues in Non-Profit organizations

- Public Relations and the Mass Media
- Information Systems
Policies and Strategies in Volunteerism
- Community Development and Community Organization
- Advocacy Through Voluntary Organizations
- Impact of Volunteerism on Public Policy
- Strategies in Community Outreach
- Emergence and Implementation of Grass Roots Program
Politics of the Voluntary Sector
- Interaction of Profit Making, Governmental and Voluntary Agencies
- Voluntary Associations, Pluralism and Democracy
- Citizen Participation and Voluntary Associations
- Values and Issues of Discrimination in Volunteerism
Students do not work alone, but meet in "cluster groups" with other students in their field and with their Faculty Sponsor and Faculty Administrator. This type of structure differentiates the program from a "class" or course setting. The central process in the cluster is dialogue - mutual learning and interaction. Each cluster is limited to eight students and a Faculty Sponsor with expertise in the specific area of study undertaken by the group. Individual projects, papers, and readings are required, as well as objectives identified by and for the group as a whole. Clusters meet 3-5 hours weekly in the evening or on the weekend. Individual plans of study must meet general graduation requirements, which are covered in the Student Handbook provided.
The minimum length of study for a Masters in Voluntary Association Administration is four trimesters, 14 weeks each. The undergraduate program leading to a Bachelor of Science degree in Administration with a specialization in Voluntary Association Administration is based on a liberal arts curriculum designed by the student and requiring a minimum of two trimesters of work in the five core areas of the specialization (see above).
A number of variations and formats are available, but all students must submit a practicum proposal for field placement in a supervised voluntary association setting that allows for application of the conceptual aspects of the student's learning.

VOLUNTARY ACTION CENTER TRAINING (BLACKSBURG)*
Voluntary Action Center of Montgomery County
Corner Roanoke & Otey Streets
PO Box 565
Blacksburg, VA 24060-0565
TEL: 703-552-4909
Credit: Inquire
Sponsor: Roanoke Valley Council of Community Services; Voluntary Action Centers of Blacksburg and Roanoke
Contact: Elaine J. Higgs, Executive Director
Description: The Voluntary Action Center designs a series of workshops each year, some offered statewide. Typical workshops include:
- Basics of Volunteer Program Management
- Legal Liability and Insurance Considerations for Agencies and Boards
- Training for Trainers
- Restoring Your Energy Level: A Mini-Workshop for the Continuing Education of Volunteer Managers
The Voluntary Action Centers and the Council participate also in other statewide offerings by the Virginia Division on Volunteerism and the Center on Volunteerism at the Virginia Polytechnic Institute. Sponsors shown above are not involved in all of the above-listed workshops. Inquire about sponsorships and details on curriculum and faculty for individual workshops.

VOLUNTARY ACTION CENTER TRAINING (MANASSAS)*
Voluntary Action Center of the Prince William Area
9300 Peabody Street
Suite 104
Manassas, VA 22110
TEL: 703-369-5292
Credit: Inquire
Sponsor: Voluntary Action Center; Juvenile Detention Home; Cooperative Extension Service; Mental Health Center; United Way; and others
Contact: Don Poe
Description: The Voluntary Action Center holds bimonthly workshops throughout the year to assist volunteer leaders in starting, improving, or expanding programs. Recent offerings include:
- Volunteers: Needs Assessment/Screening Skills
- Volunteer Coordinators' Roundtable
- Time Management: A Key to Supervision
- Computers and How They Relate to Volunteers and Human Services
- Training for Volunteer Financial Counselors

Sponsors shown above are not involved in all workshops listed. Inquire about sponsorship and details on curriculum and faculty for these and other workshops.

VOLUNTEER ADMINISTRATION SPECIALIZATION
Michigan State University
Center for Urban Affairs
158 West Owen Hall
East Lansing, MI 48824
TEL: 517-353-9035
Credit: Total Program 29-34 credits
Sponsor: College of Urban Development
Contact: Dr. Maxie C. Jackson
Description: Responding to the need for administrators with capabilities essential to developing an effective volunteer program, as well as to aid prospective professionals in working effectively with volunteers in the future, a program has been established at Michigan State University - Volunteer Administration Specialization. This program has been offered to regular students and non-traditional students since the fall term of 1968.
This multi-disciplinary program includes courses from the Departments of Communication; Health, Physical Education and Recreation; Public Affairs Management; and Urban and Metropolitan Studies. This program is a concentration of courses designed to provide an understanding of the principles and skills regarding volunteer program administration. Students, for example, in Social Work, Community Services, Education, Criminal Justice, HPR, Communications, Social Sciences, Public Affairs Management, and Urban Development most likely will work with volunteers and will find that the skills learned in the course are important to this relationship.
To complete the program, students must take the required courses and the field experience for 16-19 credits. Students must then complete 12-15 credits from the identified electives. The required courses are:
- **Communication 100 - Introduction to Human Communication I** (3 credits) offered every term, including Summer. This course provides an understanding of the process and functions of communication as well as principles of underlying communication behavior.
- **Urban and Metropolitan Studies 221** - The Role of the Helping Professions and Organizations in Community Services (4 credits) can be taken in Fall, Winter, or Spring.
- **UMS 325 - Fundamentals of Volunteer Administration** (3 credits) Fall and Winter terms. This course is designed to provide an understanding of basic principles and to develop and improve problem solving, management, use of community resources and evaluation skills regarding the administration of volunteer organizations. UMS 221 is a prerequisite for this course, which must be taken prior to the field experience.
- **Urban Development 499** - Field Experience (3-6 credits). UMS 325 must be taken prior to UD 499. Students may utilize their own departmental field experience course or others that are available.
- **UMS 425 - Advanced Principles of Volunteer Administration** (3 credits) offered Winter and Spring terms. This course is designed to provide an understanding of advanced principles and improve skills in creative programming, supervision, finance and budgeting, and working with organizations in the context of the larger community regarding volunteer program administration. UMS 325 and UD 499 are prerequisites for this course.

Students must select one elective from each of the following groupings:
- COM 101. Human Communication II, 3 credits
- COM 115. Oral Communication, 3 credits
- COM 210. Leadership, 4
- COM 315. Organizational Communication, 4 credits
- UMS 321. Urban Community Self-Development, 4 credits
- UMS 400. Community Financial Resource Development, 3 credits
- HPR 303. Recreation and Youth Organization Programs, 4 credits
- HPR 370. Playground and Day Camp Administration, 3 credits
- HPR 401. Organization and Administration of Community Recreation, 3 credits
- PAM 404. Social Accounts and Community Choice, 3 credits
- PAM 453. Women and Work: Issues and Policy Analysis, 3 credits
- PAM 473. Introduction to Systems Analysis, 3 credits

Students who successfully complete the program will have this noted on their permanent records and their transcripts will contain the notation:
"Undergraduate Specialization in Volunteer Administration completed (date)."

VOLUNTEER ADMINISTRATOR'S CONFERENCE
United Ministries in Higher Education
2133 Clark Street
Stevens Point, WI 54481
TEL: 715-341-0266
Credit: Certificate
Sponsor: Central Wisconsin Association of Volunteer Administrators
Contact: Nancy Moffatt, CAVS
Description: Recognizing the need for sharing of ideas and concerns among volunteer administrators, and given the rural character of the central Wisconsin area, the above contact person and two colleagues initiated an effort to meet this education need. A recruitment effort produced a six-member task force to work on a one-day conference. When 57 people attended that first conference, the task force was increased to 18, and a second workshop attracted 50 additional people. With this high degree of interest and encouragement, CWAVA was born. Current efforts include all-day workshops at the University of Wisconsin at Stevens Point in the spring and fall. Workshops titles to date have included:
- Basic Elements of a Good Volunteer Program
- Leadership Training
- Legal Responsibilities of a Volunteer Board
- Interviewing Volunteers
- Conflict Management

The conference and organization is open to anyone in Central Wisconsin who works with volunteers in either paid or unpaid positions. Although the initial intent was to rotate meetings and responsibilities with four communities in this rural area located 35 miles from each other, interest from small towns outside of that area led to the concept of area chapters. Each local community is committed to developing its own support system and education, but with help from CWAVA. Area Chapters (areas having ten or more members) meet four times a year between the two conferences.

Faculty is drawn from CWAVA, the University, and experts in the field located in the surrounding area. In addition to training events, CWAVA is moving ahead to assist in the formation of regional associations in other non-metropolitan areas of the state (the latter resulting from disbanding of the Wisconsin Task Force on Volunteers which, it was hoped, would fill this need).

VOLUNTEER AND PAID STAFF WORKING TOGETHER
American Red Cross
Wrangler Division
1300 28th Street South, PO Box 2406
Great Falls, MT 59403
TEL: 406-727-2212
Credit: Inquire
Sponsor: American Red Cross Division Office
Contact: Marshall J. Johnson, Director
Description: The purpose of this three- to four-day module in the Basic Administrative Skills Series is to assist volunteer and paid staff to increase knowledge and skills in building and working with specific systems, tools, and guidelines for more effective personnel administration. The point of view for learning is that of a supervisor, manager, or chairman who has responsibility for paid or volunteer staff. Although developed for Red Cross staff and volunteer chairpersons, the course is basic to the field and is shared with the general volunteer community. Learning objectives include:
- developing definitive job descriptions, and effectively recruiting to fill vacancies.
- engaging in productive interviews.
- learning to obtain and provide needed information to assure usable records.
- developing and maintaining an effective training and development program.
- handling relationships with staff effectively.
- conducting a meaningful work performance review.
- handling various types of personnel terminations (including nonvoluntary).
- understanding how to call on the administration for assistance with planning or problems.

Supervisors are asked to counsel participants prior to training as follows:
- Explain purposes and focus of training.
- Establish an expectation of extensive reading followed by class discussion.
- Free prospective participants of work responsibilities for course period.
- Urge participants to consider their own volunteer/paid staff personnel practices and be prepared with questions, examples, experiences to share.
- Encourage participants to complete the "Pre-Workshop Information..." form.
- Indicate interest in follow-up with participant after the course, and your intention to support application of learning to home situation.

The course is taught by persons who have completed national instructor training with authorization to teach the course. The course covers 22-1/3 hours and is usually spread over four days. The course is offered periodically throughout the state of Montana.

VOLUNTEER COORDINATION
Des Moines Area Community College
2006 South Ankeny Boulevard
Ankeny , IA 50021
TEL: 515-964-6365
Credit: 2 credits, 24 hours
Sponsor: Des Moines Area Community College
Contact: Peggy Cutlip
Description: Volunteer Coordination is one of a series of courses that lead to a Volunteer Management Specialist Certificate. Goals are to advance ability to implement and develop methods for maintaining an effective volunteer program, addressing the issues of communication, coordination of staff and board, public relations, and effective boards and meetings. Specific workshops are:
- Training volunteers, staff to work with volunteers, methods and approaches.
- Process of communication - how-to on reward and recognition, handling grievances, dealing with marginal volunteers.
- Coordination of client/staff and volunteer board.
- Public Relations - use of different media, maximizing public exposure, telephone techniques and practices.
- Administrative boards and meetings, rotation and representation of members, committees, manuals, making meetings work.
- Effective Community Change - social action process, volunteers and community development.
- Where to get assistance - associations, services, and sources of information.

Course number for this program is SERV:311; other courses in the Certificate series are SERV:312 and SERV:512 (Effective Management of Volunteer Programs); SERV:310 (Volunteers In Action, a required course). All are detailed elsewhere in this publication.

VOLUNTEER EXPERIENCE: CHANGE, CHALLENGE, CHOICES
Allegheny County Community College
Center-North, 111 Pines Plaza
1130 Perry Highway
Pittsburgh, PA 15237
TEL: 412-931-8500/Ext. 43
Credit: Inquire
Sponsor: Community College of Allegheny County; Voluntary Action Center of the I&R Services of Allegheny County; Junior League of Pittsburgh; Title I of the Higher Education Act
Contact: Sarah Jane Rehnborg, CCAC-North Coordinator
Description: This workshop was designed for persons interested in identifying the skills and interests they have acquired through life experiences and volunteer work. Attention was given to developing life goals and career goals based on individual experiences. Workshops were designed specifically for the New Volunteer, the Experienced Volunteer, and the Administrator of Volunteer Programs and Voluntary Organizations.

An expert in the area of identifying skills and competencies acquired through volunteer work, Winifred L. Brown, presented the keynote address, and led one of the workshops. A publication on the subject, I Can, resulted from her work in this area of volunteerism. The three workshop sessions were:

The New Lifestyle as a Volunteer - how to assess present skills, interests and values; how to search for a meaningful volunteer job - one which will develop skills as well as help others; understanding the rights and responsibilities of volunteering.

The Experienced Volunteer - how to assess present skills; how to develop areas of interest and set goals; how to explore values, analyze and document skills, write resumes, identify roadblocks, learn career development steps and set individual goals. (This session was based on Junior League Volunteer Development

Course.)

The Administrator of a Volunteer Services Program or Organization - how to identify skills acquired in leadership positions; how to develop personal career goals; how to analyze the workshop process so that participants can assist volunteers in their own programs to identify skills and personal life goals (special attention to the latter).

A one-hour mid-day panel program enabled participants to explore volunteerism from many perspectives, including tips about selecting volunteer settings, documenting skills, translating volunteer experiences into employer language, using volunteer credentials when applying for college, and ways to develop volunteer careers. Panel members came from the Museum of Art, the League of Women Voters, the National Council of Jewish Women, RSVP field staff, the local I&R program, and business. A wrap-up session brought together faculty, students, panel members, and workshop facilitators for an informal discussion of the workshop, and individual volunteer programs. Take-home resource packets were provided for future use by participants.

VOLUNTEER LEADERSHIP: CHALLENGES FOR THE NINETIES
SEE GOVERNORS' OFFICES ON VOLUNTEERISM: ILLINOIS

VOLUNTEER LEADERSHIP CONFERENCE
SEE GOVERNORS' OFFICES ON VOLUNTEERISM: SOUTH DAKOTA

VOLUNTEER LEADERSHIP WORKSHOP
Junior League of Fort Smith
PO Box 3266
Fort Smith, AR 72901
TEL: 501-782-0103
Credit: CEUs
Sponsor: Junior League of Fort Smith; Westark Community College
Contact: Linda Schmidt
Description: This workship is the result of a cooperative effort between the Junior League and the Community Services Division of Westark Community College. Its goals are: to create a greater awareness/understanding of volunteerism; and, to offer volunteer leaders skills and tools to meet the social and economic challenges of the nineties. Session topics include:
- Recruitment
- How to Increase Volunteer Rewards
- Professionals as Volunteers
- Public Relations
- Parliamentary Procedure
- Fundraising
- Making Meetings Work
- Boardsmanship
- Communications
- Evaluation

Features of the program include the provision of handout materials at each mini-workshop which can serve as resources long after the conference is over, and taping of the three major sessions for the reference and use of organizations and agencies participating in the meeting as well as those who were unable to attend. Another useful feature of the meeting was a display of books and other materials on volunteerism that had been donated to the local library by the Junior League to increase the library's ability to serve volunteer leaders.

VOLUNTEER MANAGEMENT CERTIFICATION
Volunteer Service Bureau
520 SE Fort King
Suite C-1
Ocala, FL 32671
TEL: 904-732-4771
Credit: Certification
Sponsor: Ocala Volunteer Center; Gainesville Voluntary Action Center
Contact: Karen W. May
Description: Facing increased demand for volunteers to continue the services that are being lost because of tax cuts, the Volunteer Service Center of Marion County recognized another fact that would now have to be taken more seriously: "Good volunteer programs require good managers." Realizing that very few people come to the field of volunteer management with the assortment of skills that the job requires, the Center initiated the Volunteer Management Certification program. To achieve Volunteer Management Certification, an individual must:
Attend the following two workshops as required training:
- Management Skills for Volunteer Leaders - a comprehensive seminar for beginning and advanced leaders of volunteer programs.
- Survival Skills for Managers - a Marlene Wilson seminar.

Participate in nine additional hours of approved training between September and May (Elective Training), including:
- Public Relations Seminar (sponsor: Volunteer Jacksonville)
- Communications Skills (sponsor: West Central Florida Human Resource Center)
- Boardsmanship (sponsor: Gainesville VAC)
- Accounting for Non-Profit Agencies (sponsor: Florida Institute of Certified Public Accountants)

Registration for required and elective courses above is not limited to Volunteer Management Certification program candidates. Certificates are awarded at a social event to which board members and supervisors of graduates' organizations are invited. In addition, a letter giving facts of certification and specifying courses completed will be sent to appropriate supervisory personnel for permanent personnel records.

VOLUNTEER MANAGEMENT FOR THE NON-PROFIT PROFESSIONAL*
University of North Florida
c/o Voluntary Action Center
626 May Street
Jacksonville, FL 32204
TEL: 904-356-9471
Credit: CEUs
Sponsor: University of North Florida
Contact: Pepi Dunay
Description: Offered for a full semester, this program conducts 26 sessions on the following topics (some topics are repeated):
- Board Orientation
- Board Retreat Planning
- Management Assistance
- Long Range Planning
- Board Responsibilities
- Computer
- Staff/Board Relations
- Educational Opportunity
- Time Management
- Board Leadership
- Corporate Seminar
- Volunteer Career Development
- Board Orientation
- Motivating Boards
- Crisis Management
- Board Training
- Personnel Policies

- Corporate Workshop
- Community Team Building
- Public Speaking
- Time Management and Record Keeping

Faculty is drawn from the local volunteer center, Campfire, Willing Hands (volunteer program), Suwanee Presbyterian Church, Housing and Urban Development agency, a home day care center, corporations, a mental health association, Southeast Bank, and other sources.

VOLUNTEER MANAGEMENT: LEVEL I AND LEVEL II
Greenville Technical College
PO Box 5616, Station B
Greenville, SC 29606
TEL: 803-242-3170
Credit: CEUs
Sponsor: Greenville Technical College
Contact: Phil McGee
Description: This is a two-part program: one offering entry-level skills for those volunteers who have managerial and supervisory responsibilities (Level I), and one to assist volunteer managers with an opportunity to gain specialized skills in a number of areas of concern.

Volunteer Management Level I
- **Session I** - Goal setting and planning; Recruiting: Interviewing
- **Session II** - Orienting new volunteers; Training Placement
- **Session III** - Communications; Human Relations
- **Session IV** - Records; Budgets; Fund Raising; Utilizing Community Resources
- **Session V** - Time Management; Delegation
- **Session VI** - Motivating the Volunteer; Avoiding and Dealing with Burnout

Volunteer Management Level II
- Working with the media
- Purchasing specialized services
- Tax/legal/insurance issues and volunteers
- Conflict management
- Advanced communications skills
- Advanced human relations skills
- Topical discussion and problem solving groups

Level I is an eight-hour course and is conducted during the spring semester. Level II is a 12-hour course conducted in the fall.

VOLUNTEER MANAGEMENT PROGRAM: FIRST LEVEL WORKSHOP (1990)
University of Colorado
Office of Conference Services
Campus Box 454
Boulder, CO 80309-0454
TEL: 303-492-5151
Credit: 2.5 CEUs
Contact: Conference Coordinator
Description: The 44th national workshop is designed for individuals relatively new to the profession. It involves administrators of volunteer programs in learning experiences led by national leaders in the field, private consultants, and professionals currently administering successful volunteer programs. The leaders have experience with a variety of problem-solving styles in many different settings.

The workshop is part of the Volunteer Management Program of the University of Colorado at Boulder. Certification under this program consists of completing any combination of three workshops, spread out over a four-month period in the 1990 (July 1990 to February 1991). The curriculum of this first-level workshop includes:
- "The Changing World of Volunteerism" (keynote address);
- Meet Your Counterports;
- Communication: How to Make It Work for You;

- The Volunteer Manager as Enabler of Others;
- UC Volunteer Management Program, CEU and AVA Certification Program Overview;
- Motivation and Organizational Climate;
- Recruiting and Retaining Volunteers;
- The Management of You; and
- How to Make Dreams Happen.

In addition, mini-workshops on many diverse topics are administeredon two days of the six-day event. Throughout the workshop, participants have opportunity to share ideas and materials through networking.

The Association for Volunteer Administration endorses this first level workshop as contributing to the professional development of volunteer adminstrators based on a review of the program's purpose, goals, and instructional plan.

VOLUNTEER MANAGEMENT PROGRAM: SECOND LEVEL WORKSHOP
University of Colorado
Office of Conference Services
Campus Box 454
Boulder, CO 80309-0454
TEL: 303-492-5151
FAX: 303-497-0291 (AVA)
Credit: Certification; 2.5 CEUs
Description: This 1990 workshop is the 43rd annual nationwide program presented by the Office of Conference Services of the University of Colorado at Boulder. Part of a series for participants with varying degrees of experience in the field, this workshop concentrates on the broader challenges of volunteer program management rather than on basic skills. In order to receive maximum benefit, participants should have attended a previous *Volunteer Management Program First Level Workshop* or have at least three years of experience in the field. Each series of three workshops - first, second and third levels - is offered each year, not necessarily in sequence, since each has its own self-contained agenda for a specific group of participants. The *Association for Volunteer Administration* endorses the *Second Level Workshop* as contributing to the professional development of volunteer administrators, based on a review of the program's purpose, goals, and instructional plan. The program includes:
- Planning: Program, Meetings, Time
- Tools for the Trainer
- Personal and Organizational Power
- How to Manage Conflict Instead of *It* Managing *You*
- Balance vs. Chaos: Which Will We Choose?
- What Is - What If?: Present Realities and Future Trends
- Marketing Your Cause
- Personal Profile: Understanding Yourself and Those You Lead
- "As We See It:" Volunteerism's Issues, Challenges and Dreams
- University of Colorado, Volunteer Management Program, *AVA* Certification Program Overview.

Ample time throughout the five-day workshop is provided for networking and sharing materials. Faculty comes from local, state and national organizations, a bank of consultants and authors, and academe, including the United Way, University of Illinois, Special Olympics (state), and the University of Colorado.

Persons taking the workshop for certification are required to submit a paper on an assigned topic, and to attend all workshop sessions. Participants desiring CEUs (2.5 continuing education units) must register separately for them and must attend all sessions. There is a small fee for certification grading ($6.00) and for CEU registration ($5.00).
Publications: Conference Proceedings

VOLUNTEER MANAGEMENT PROGRAM: THIRD LEVEL WORKSHOP
University of Colorado
Office of Conference Services
Campus Box 454
Boulder, CO 80309-0454
TEL: 303-492-5151

This 42nd national workshop for volunteer administrators is the Third Level and is designed for participants who have attended the First and Second Level workshops, or for those who have been in the field of volunteer administration for at least three years.

Three days of intensive small-group work follow a plenary session by presenters about their topics. The program is divided into four tracks, as follows:

Track I - Creative Problem Solving: Beyond Coping: skills to help become innovative problem-solvers:
- The art of problem finding
- The creative roles of explorer, artist, judge, and warior
- Tapping into the wisdom of the team
- Exploring multiple options
- Creating corporate cultures tht motivate
- Learning to strategize to make dreams happen

Track II - Managing Conflict: skills to manage conflict productively
- Personal and organizational barriers to managing conflict
- Recognition and response to unspoken issues in problem situations
- Fine-tuning communication skills to productive conflict management
- Developing multiple styles for managing conflict and choosing a style to match different situations
- Empowering self and others in the conflict
- Separating people from problems
- Reaching do-able and lasting agreements

Track III - Marketing Magic for Volunteer Programs: skills of planning, recruiting, fundraising, bartering, asaking, motivating, and publicizing

Track IV - Training of Trainers: skills to conduct effective training sessions
- The adult as learner
- Presentation Techniques
- Training design and sequencing based on learning objectives
- Group process and dynamics
- Training materials design, production and equipment

Ample time is provided throughout the workshop for sharing of ideas and materials among participants. An exhibit center is provided for this purpose.

Certification is available to participants who attend all sessions of the workshop and submit a four-page paper on an assigned topic within two months after the workshop. CEUs (continuing education credits) are available also for those who attend all sessions (3.5 CEUs). CEUs are not academic credit, per se, but are sometimes accepted in place of academic credit.

The Association of Volunteer Administration endorses this Third Level workshop as contributing to the professional development of volunteer administrators.

VOLUNTEER MANAGEMENT SEMINARS
American University
Division of Continuing Education
McKinley Building
Washington, DC 20016
TEL: 202-686-6150
Credit: CEUs; Volunteer Manager Certification (partial fulfillment)
Sponsor: American University
Contact: See individual seminars for contact persons
Description: These seminars can be taken individually, or selected as part of the 12 hours of instruction required to complete the Volunteer Management Certification program (see above). Topics covered in Fall 1983:

Organizational Theory and Behavior for Volunteer Managers: a six-part seminar (Course 760) that serves as an introduction to nonprofit organizations, their method of governance, their organizational structure, and processes, this program examines the relationships of the Volunteer Manager and the program staff. [Contact: Jillian Poole]

Training Your Volunteers: a six-part seminar (Course 761) designed to supply information on the adult learner, and ways to use that knowledge in designing successful training events, this program teaches techniques for implementing needs assessment, group exercises, and evaluation tools. [Contact: Jean Berg and Judith Helein]

Marketing, Promotion, and Public Relations: a six-part seminar (Course 741) designed to provide an opportunity for Volunteer Managers to focus on how to do marketing, promotion, and public relations for a low-budget organization, this program teaches how ideas are marketed and advertised through traditional and non-traditional channels. Participants examine market opportunities, discuss direct mail testing and analysis, and look at the conception and execution of successful promotional campaigns. This seminar is in the regular Professional Development Program. [Contact: Ann Gilbert]

Additional Volunteer Management Seminars are planned through 1984; preference is given to those taking a seminar for certification. CEUs are available for individual seminars; inquire.

VOLUNTEER MANAGEMENT SERIES
SEE GOVERNORS' OFFICES ON VOLUNTEERISM: VIRGINIA

VOLUNTEER MANAGEMENT SYSTEMS COURSE
Volunteer Action Center
360 South Third Street
Columbus, OH 43215
TEL: 614-224-3535
Credit: Inquire
Sponsor: Volunteer Action Center
Contact: Glenn Esh
Description: This course utilizes a volunteer management system to approach the subjects of organizing a program to attract, involve, and retain qualified, competent volunteer staff members. It enables participants to examine the principles that must be applied in planning and operating a successful volunteer program. The course includes:

Planning/Decisions
- Needs Assessment
- Goals
- Resources

Preparation/Getting Ready
- Policies and Procedures
- Program Components and Materials
- Orientation

Operation/Making It Happen
- Recruitment and Placement
- Management
- Evaluation

Although enrollment in all sessions is recommended, individual sessions can be arranged. Those who complete the course have an opportunity to attend a bonus follow-up session to examine and evaluate the course activities.

VOLUNTEER PROGRAM ADMINISTRATION AND VOLUNTARY ORGANIZATION MANAGEMENT
Pennsylvania State University
Division of Continuing Education
209 J. Orvis Keller Building
University Park, PA 16802
TEL: 814-863-0201

Credit: CEUs; AVA Certification (partial fulfillment); six hours toward Nursing Home Administrator's License
Sponsor: Pennsylvania State University
Contact: Larry D. Gamm
Description: Designed for anyone who manages voluntary organizations or directs or leads volunteers, this series is composed of two types of programs:
Section A covers basic elements in the development and administration of volunteer programs; and
Section B offers workshops dealing with general management skills and program responsibilities that are of concern to management of voluntary organizations and public agencies. Each section convenes a number of workshops relevant to its theme, including:

Section A: Foundations of Effective Volunteer Programming
- Recruiting and Interviewing Volunteers
- Developing a Training Program for Volunteers
- Senior Citizens and Volunteerism
- Effective Staff/Volunteer Relationships
- Evaluation, Recordkeeping, Accountability
- Improving Productivity in the Use of Volunteers
- Organizing for Change
- Advocating for Clients

Section B: Management Skills in Voluntary and Nonprofit Organizations
- Funding Diversification and the Law in the 80s
- Fund Raising for Voluntary and Nonprofit Organizations
- Proposal and Grant Writing
- Basic Public Relations and Communications
- Advanced Public Relations Techniques for Volunteer Nonprofit Organizations
- Working with Committees and Advisory Groups
- Board of Directors
- Recruiting, Training, and Legal Reponsibilities
- Board Dynamics: Competing Claims and Common Needs
- Marketing for Voluntary and Nonprofit Organizations
- Resource Exchange Networks: Nonbureaucratic Responses to Human Needs
- Resource Management Strategies in a Cutback Era
- Interorganizational Coordination
- Time Management

In addition to the campus program above, the University conducts similar on-site programs tailored to the needs of the requesting group.

VOLUNTEER PROGRAM MANAGEMENT
Boston University
Office of Continuing Education
755 Commonwealth Avenue, B4
Boston, MA 02215
TEL: 617-353-4137
Credit: Certification and one CEU per ten hours of instruction
Sponsor: Boston University; Association for Volunteer Administration
Contact: Rebecca Alssid
Description: The purpose of this program is to provide experienced administrators of volunteer programs with the opportunity to increase their knowledge and understanding of the new demands placed on volunteer programs for the 1980s, to develop further their management skills, to explore internal and external communications issues, and to interact and learn from the experiences of other administrators participating in the program. The six courses will run for three six-week semesters - two each semester.
Course I - Voluntary Action - covers the history of voluntary action and its future development in the United States; includesareas of current legislative activity, value systems of volunteers, and how volunteer organizations and their administrators can become directly involved in these issues.
Course II - Human Resources Management - Covers the skills

needed to work with volunteers: interviewing, placement, training, supervision, recognition, people management and group processes, and designing programs to develop volunteer skills; also includes: understanding the relationship between evaluation and program planning, volunteer accountability, and career development for volunteers.
Course III - Financial Management Skills - covers budget preparation, accounting procedures and monitoring methods; enables the administrator to understand his/her volunteer program budget as well as the financial picture of the larger organization of which the volunteer program is a part; includes grantsmanship techniques on identifying funding sources and writing proposals.
Course IV - Internal and Community Relations - explores inter- and intra-agency dynamics including collaboration, recruitment, public relations, marketing and office communications; also included; community organization; understanding networks to facilitate goals.
Course V - Systems for Measuring Volunteer and Program Effectiveness - covers the broad range of systems for evaluation and how to utilize those systems; includes methods for evaluation, documentation of accomplishments, feedback systems and information processing.
Course VI - Volunteer Program Management - deals with the organization and running of the volunteer program including: program planning and evaluation, goal setting, assessing both quantitatively and qualitatively the agency's purpose and its relationship with its volunteer program, program development, problem solving, needs assessment and decision-making.
Each course is designed so that participants can develop competencies needed for Association for Volunteer Administration (AVA) certification; however, AVA membership is not necessary. Continuing Education Units (CEUs) from Boston University is granted upon completion of each course. CEUs are awarded as apermanent record with the University for participation in continuing education activities. Each CEU represents 10 hours of instruction.

VOLUNTEER PROGRAM MANAGEMENT
SEE GOVERNORS' OFFICES ON VOLUNTEERISM: MINNESOTA

VOLUNTEER PROGRAM MANAGEMENT
Organizational Dynamics
43434 SE Tapp Road
Sandy, OR 97055
TEL: 503-668-7979
Credit: Inquire
Sponsor: Organizational Dynamics
Contact: Arty Trost, MSW
Description: Workshops dealing with the effective development and management of volunteer programs are offered nationwide. All programs are especially designed to meet the sponsoring group's needs; some of the program topics are listed below. New ones are continually being developed based on client requests. Programs can be tailored for new and/or experienced volunteer program managers in public agencies, non-profit organizations, community service groups, civic organizations, schools, hospitals, churches and synagogues. By working closely with the sponsor beforehand, all training is specific to the particular group. Programs blend practice and principle using training methods which actively involve the participants, emphasize skill building as well as knowledge acquisition, and are immediately applicable.
- Survival Skills for Volunteer Program Managers
- Developing a Volunteer Program
- Marketing Your Volunteer Program
- Training Volunteers
- Increasing Your Training Skills
- Interviewing and Placement
- Supervision and Retention

- Program Evaluation
- Volunteer-Staff Relations
- Building Administrative Support
- Performance Appraisals for Volunteers
- Volunteer Career Development
- Professional Development for Volunteer Managers
- Preventing Burnout
- Leading Effective Meetings
- Management Communication
- Dealing with Difficult People

VOLUNTEER PROGRAM MANAGEMENT
SEE GOVERNORS' OFFICES ON VOLUNTEERISM:
VIRGINIA

**VOLUNTEER PROGRAM MANAGEMENT CERTIFICATE
PROGRAM**
Portland Community College
PO Box 19000
Portland, OR 97219
TEL: 503-244-6111
Credit: 18 Credit Units (see individual courses below)
Sponsor: Portland Community College; Volunteer Bureau of
Greater Portland
Contact: Mary Lou Webb
Description: As needs in the volunteer community are identified,
Portland Community College and the Volunteer Bureau of
Portland jointly develop courses to meet these needs. Course
numbers are assigned, and credit units are offered. Students
include individuals who are currently administering volunteer
programs - on a paid or unpaid basis - and those people interested
in entering the field of volunteer management. Course
requirements for a Basic Certificate include 18 credit hours, as
follows:
6 Credits/Required 3 Credit Courses:
- *SDP 101* Principles of Management and Supervision
- *SDP 111* Corresponding Effectively at Work
6 Credits/Optional 3 Credit Courses (choose 2):
- *SDP 105* Interpersonal Communication
- *SDP 107* Organizations and People
- *SDP 121* Leadership Skill Development
- *SDP 130* Creative Problem Solving
- *SDP 202* Training the Employee
- *SDP 210* Public Relations
- *SDP 222* Human Resource Management: Personnel (or)
- *SDP 224* Personnel Management.
3 Credits/Required 1 Credit Courses:
- *SDP 299* Planning, Managing, and Evaluating Volunteer
  Programs (proposed)
- *SDP 299* Recruiting, Interviewing, Placing Volunteers
  (proposed)
- *SDP 299* Training, Supervision, and Retention of Volunteers
  (proposed)
- *SDP 299DG* Volunteer Management
3 Credits/Optional 1 Credit Courses (Elective):
- Any 3 one-credit courses offered through the Institute for
  Management and Professional Development or Business
  Department.
This 18-credit course was approved in 1990 for certificate status by
Portland Community College.

VOLUNTEER SERVICES CURRICULUM
Rock Valley Community College
3301 North Mulford
Loves Park, IL 61111
TEL: 815-654-4250
Credit: A.A.S. Degree (60 hours)
Sponsor: Rock Valley Community College
Contact: Hal Norris

Description: This course is designed to prepare those persons
seeking positions in volunteer administration and coordination,
volunteers in those positions wishing to increase their knowledge,
and persons supervising volunteer administrators and coordinators.
It provides an Associate in Applied Science Degree after two years
(60 credit hours) of full-time study. The curriculum:
FIRST YEAR:
Fall Semester (15 credits total):
ENGL 101 - Composition 3
VOLS 101 - Intro to Volunteer Services 3
VOLS 120 - Accounting & Bookkeeping in Volunteer Services 3
VOLS 201 - Community & Public Relations Techniques 3
VOLS 103 - Volunteer Recruitment Techniques 3
Spring Semester (14 credits total):
SPCH 131 - Fundamentals of Speech 3
PSYCH 170 - General Psychology 3
SOCIO 190 - Intro to Sociology 3
VOLS 220 - Volunteer Orientation and In-Service Training 3
VOLS 203 - Field Placement and Seminar 2
SECOND YEAR
Fall Semester (14 credits total):
VOLS 205 - Fundamentals of Volunteer Management 3
HUMS 110 - Survey of Counseling Theories 3
VOLS 110 - Volunteer Placement and Work Assignments 3
VOLS 203 - Field Placement and Seminar 2
VOLS 121 - The Administrative Volunteer 3
Spring Semester (17 credits total):
HUMS 111 - Interviewing Techniques 3
SOCIO 290 - Social Problems 3
VOLS 270 - Volunteer/Staff Relations 3
VOLS 203 - Field Placement and Seminar 2
General Education Requirement 6
Course Descriptions:
VOLS 101 - Introduction to Volunteer Services: familiarizes
students with all volunteer service programs in the college district.
Discusses the pros and cons of volunteerism and the strengths and
weaknesses of present volunteer programs. Students will be
interviewed for field placement.
VOLS 103 - Volunteer Recruitment Techniques: overview of
recruitment methods centering around retention of volunteers.
VOLS 110 - Volunteer Placement and Work Assignments:
introduction to the induction process and the delegation of duties.
Also covered are underplacement and overplacement and the
values of volunteer placement review.
VOLS 120 - Accounting and Bookkeeping in Volunteer Services: a
beginning course in accounting and bookkeping for volunteer
administrator. Topics include timekeeping, budgeting, providing
statistics, and analysis of volunteer duties in statistical form.
VOLS 121 - The Administrative Volunteer: centers around those
volunteers at the policy-making level. The relationships between
administrative volunteers, paid administrative staff, paid staff, and
operational volunteers is discussed.
VOLS 201 - Community and Public Relations Techniques: relating
the volunteer program to the general public. Practical methods of
working with newspapers, radio, and TV are covered.
VOLS 203 - Field Placement and Seminar: students will be placed
on a part-time basis in a supervised experience in a cooperating
agency selected by the student and instructor; 150 hours per
semester for 3 semesters is expected of all students in the program.
No more than 150 hours of credit can be given for experience
accumulated prior to entrance to the program.
VOLS 205 - Fundamentals of Volunteer Management: course
applies modern management techniques to motivating and
supervising volunteers. Various personnel techniques are discussed
with a direction toward problems unique to volunteer supervision.
VOLS 220 - Volunteer Orientation and In-Service Training: the
process of orienting and introducing volunteer staff to a volunteer
setting. Course covers initial job training, advanced training, and
evaluation of training.
VOLS 270 - Volunteer/Staff Relations: bringing volunteer and

paid staff together to work constructively and harmoniously. Graduate requirements are the same as any other Associate in Applied Science Degree Program: completion of one occupational curriculum (60 semester hours of credit); minimum GPA of 2.0; successful completion of U.S. and Illinois Constitution tests (previous testing accepted); successful completion of a core of general education courses; successful completion of the seven standard courses (21 semester hours) included in the program. Faculty is drawn from the College, with outside lecturers invited on an intermittent basis.
[Arrangements can be made for the convenience of part-time students for classes in late afternoon or evening based on number of students involved.]

VOLUNTEER TRAINING
Hawkeye Institute of Technology
PO Box 8015
1501 East Orange Road
Waterloo, IA 50704
TEL: 319-296-1030
Credit: CEUs awarded based on length of specific course
Sponsor: Hawkeye Institute of Technology; Black Hawk County Retired Senior Volunteer Program; Area VII Senior Companion Program; Jesse Cosby Neighborhood Center; Black Hawk County Extension; American Red Cross
Contact: George v. Bennett
Description: Volunteer training is accomplished at the Institute through a series of short courses and seminars in cooperation with the agencies listed above as co-sponsors. Each agency shares sponsorship with the Institute, helping to design courses to meet a specific volunteer need that has been identified by one of the agencies. Past training has included courses, seminars, workshops, and other events in areas such as:
- peer counseling
- working with volunteers
- volunteer supervision
- preventive health care for the elderly
- self-defense and property protection

In addition, the college assists in regularly-scheduled in-service training programs for senior companions and VISTAs that are sponsored by the Adult Continuing Education and Community Services Divisions.

VOLUNTEER TRAINING PROGRAM
Goucher College
Center for Educational Resources
Towson, MD 21204
TEL: 301-825-3300
Credit: .5 CEUs per course (2.5 total)
Sponsor: Goucher College
Contact: Sylvia Eggleston
Description: Drawing faculty from community, civic, cultural, and religious organizations, private business and industry, and the college itself, this program for volunteers and volunteer administrators is part of the college's continuing efforts to meet community educational needs. Although course titles and content may vary from year to year, all training is designed to enable the mounting or improvement of volunteer programs. Courses include:
Advocacy in Action: Effective Lobbying Techniques - Can citizens and volunteers be effective in influencing legislation and in altering systems and institutions? The focus of this one-day seminar is on specifictechniques of legislative and administrative lobbying and advocacy.
Leadership Seminar - Designed to improve leadership skills of volunteer chairmen, presidents or boards, organizations or committees, this course covers time management, setting goals and objectives, delegating responsibility, conducting effective meetings, board orientation, assuming the leadership role.
Time Management Process - Based on the premise that an

effective organization is well-managed and well-led, the focus here is on setting objectives and organizing resources to achieve goals of voluntary/nonprofit organizations.
ABC's of Fund Raising - This basic course helps volunteers acquire skills in planning fund-raising events, investigating funding sources and getting community support.
Grantsmanship - Recognizing the competition for grants, this workshop shows how to write effective proposals to public sources and private foundations, how to look for grant sources, budgeting for grant proposals, etc.
Representatives of the Citizen's Coalition for Maryland's Children, Junior League of Baltimore, the Voluntary Action Center of Central Maryland, and Goucher College were included in the faculty.

VOLUNTEER WORKSHOPS IN MAINE
Area Agency on Aging
143 High Street
Suite 401
Portland, ME 04101
TEL: 207-776-6503
Credit: Inquire
Sponsor: Listed separately below
Contact: Elizabeth S. Gibson
Description: The following workshops and college-level course groundwork represent efforts in the state of Maine to meet the needs of volunteer administrators and volunteers. The first six items are two-day, one-day, and half-day workshops that have been conducted recently; item seven provides information on a a course in the development stages being offered to the University of Southern Maine for implementation.
The Care and Support of Volunteers (one day)
Sponsor: York Adult Learning Cooperative, York Village Maine
Contact: Lib Gibson (see above)
Content:
- Volunteer Needs Assessment
- Development of Volunteer Services
- Volunteers and Careers

Managing Volunteer Resources (two days)
Sponsor: University of Southern Maine, Portland (Susan Ellis, Instructor)
Contact: Joanne Spears, Director of Special Programs, Dept. of Conferences and Special Programs, 96 Falmouth Street, Portland, ME 04103 207-780-4045 or Lib Gibson (see above)
Content: One of five one- to three-day courses as part of package entitled: "Non-Profit Management Services":
- Overview of Volunteerism in America
- Recruiting, Motivation, Interview Skills, Placement, Training
- Record Keeping
- Developing a Volunteer Program
- Exploring Education Needs
- Self-Concept
- Professionalism/Credentialing
- Common Causes of Friction Between Volunteers and Staff
CEU accredited
AVA accredited
The Care and Support of Volunteers (one day)
Sponsor: Aroostook Regional Task Force of Older Citizens, Presque Isle, Maine
Contact: Lib Gibson (see above)
Content: See above
RSVP Basic Training (one day)
Sponsor: Southern Maine Senior Citizens, The Area Agency on Aging, Portland
Contact: Lib Gibson (see above)
Content:
- RSVP Staff Responsibilites
- Volunteer Job Descriptions
- Recruiting, Orientation and Placing Volunteers

- Station Development
- The Paper Trail

Volunteer Recruitment (one-half day)
Sponsor: ACTION and Maine RSVP Directors' Association, Portland
Contact: Sally Ward, Field Office, ACTION, District 5, 66 Pearl Street, Room 210, Portland, ME 04101 207-780-3414 **Content:** Recruiting Process, Techniques Facilitating

RSVP and the 80's! New Directions! New Challenges!
Sponsor: District 5 ACTION and Maine RSVP Directors' Association
Contact: Thomas Endres, Director, ACTION, District 5 (see above)
Content:
- Job Feelings
- Cause and Effect of Changes as it Relates to RSVP
- Creative and Meaningful Use of Volunteer Resources in Community Services

Professional Management and Operation of Volunteer Programs
Offered to: University of Southern Maine, 96 Falmouth Street, Portland, ME 04103
Prepared by: Lib Gibson (see above), reviewed/edited by Winifred Brown, Administrative Director of Mayor's Voluntary Action Center, 61 Chamber, New York, NY 10007 212-566-5950.
Contacts: Thomas Endres, Director, ACTION (see above); Donald W. Sharland, Executive Director, Southern Maine Senior Citizens, 207-657-3615.
Content: College-level course consisting of eight in-depth modules; adaptable to include in social studies course or evening course.

VOLUNTEERING: A CELEBRATION OF COMMUNITY
SEE GOVERNORS' OFFICES ON VOLUNTEERISM: VIRGINIA

VOLUNTEERISM
Chemeketa Community College
Community Education
PO Box 14007
Salem, OR 97309
TEL: 503-399-5181
Credit: Inquire
Sponsor: Chemeketa Community College
Contact: Alvin M. Leach
Description: This course is designed to help social service agency representatives, volunteer coordinators and directors to achieve the following objectives:
- create and develop volunteer programs to meet agency's needs
- improve ability to recruit, train and plan recognition for volunteers
- learn practical skills in management techniques, budgeting and financing of volunteer programs.
- improve the efficiency and scope of their existing volunteer program.

The course has ten components, which are followed by a review and class evaluation. The components are:
Volunteer Programs: an overview of the history, philosophy, and background of volunteerism.
Social and Economic Trends and How They Affect Volunteerism
- increased emphasis on human services
- change in attitudes toward work and leisure
- mandatory retirement and early retirement
- technical complexity
- changes in family structure
- breakdown of natural care systems

Organization of Volunteer Services
- assessing the program's volunteer needs
- assessing the volunteer's needs
- what your agency must be able to offer to establish a good volunteer program

Recruitment, Volunteer Possibilities
- community resources
- Voluntary Action Center
- variety and range of volunteer positions
- Older Americans as a resource population

Interview and Placement
- interview techniques
- interview "do's and dont's"
- matching people with tasks
- special considerations in working with elderly and handicapped volunteers

Designing Meaningful and Productive Orientation Sessions
- checklists for organization

Volunteer Training and Recognition
- supervision and training as an ongoing process
- new ideas for giving recognition
- utilizing the expertise of volunteers

Motivational Dynamics of Volunteerism
- why people volunteer - a look at inside forces and situational forces
- working with volunteer boards.

Record Keeping and Program Evaluation
- everybody's thorn - how to make the most of it and learn from it

Budgeting and Finance Management
- how to schedule your time
- how to decide priorities
- management by objectives
- insurance issues

VOLUNTEERS: EMPOWERMENT TODAY AND TOMORROW
Governor's Office of Voluntary Action/IL
100 West Randolph
16th Floor
Chicago, IL 60601
TEL: 312-917-2789
Credit: Inquire
Sponsor: GOVA, AVA Region VII, AAUW, Chicago Public Library, DuPage County Health Department, Illinois Department on Aging, Illinois Literacy Council, Operation Able
Contact: Jeanne Bradner, Director
Description: This two-day conference is designed for those involved in health and human service organizations, religious organizations, community groups, local and state government, and any other organizations that depend on volunteers to make policy and deliver service. The annual meetings were begun in 1985 and are tailored each year to expressed needs of the volunteer community. Conference schedule includes:
- **Keynote Address:** "Keeping in Touch - With our Clients, our Staff and Each Other."
- **Exploring Oneself; Understanding Others** - character reading exercises to improve managing and caring.
- **Advance Your Career; Don't Be Afraid of Numbers** - Budgeting and reading financial statements from an expert to help put you in control.
- **I Make A Difference!** - Recognizing and appreciating your skills and talent.
- **Beyond Recruitment: Interviewing, Screening and Placing Volunteers** - After you've recruited volunteers, how do you select them for specific jobs and match their needs, skills and interests within the organization? (Two-session Workshop)
- **Gender, Class and Career in the Lives of Volunteer Women** - Presenter is author of *Invisible Women*.
- **Risk Management** - Answers to those questions you've been afraid to ask regarding how to protect your volunteers and your organization.
- **Therapeutic Clowning - The Ultimate Tool for Volunteers** - The Value and joy of clowning as a tool you can create

yourself. (Two-session Workshop)

- **Special Caucus: AVA Certification** - What is it? What will it do for you?
- **Group Dynamics** - Modules in active listening, direction giving, assertive behavior, conflict resolution.
- **Goal: Attainment Scaling As A Means to Value Volunteer Efforts** - Participants will reexamine methods to value voluntgeer services and will receive an overview of a new method based on goal attainment scaling.
- **Volunteer and Volunteer Coordinator: Working Together and Liking It** - The good things and bad things about working with volunteers; with practical methods for overcoming the "bads."
- **COOL and VISTA: Programs of Today for Tomorrow** - With all of the talk about national service, hear about two model approaches.
- **How Can Volunteers Raise Money for an Organization?** - Find out the many ways volunteers can help raise operating funds and feel more a part of the organization.
- **Volunteer Interviewing: Wholistic Screening for Sexual Offenders** - An all-day session for those involved in programs where screening is of great importance.
- **Personal and Organizational Power** - Understanding personal power; getting back what you project. (Two-Session Workshop)
- **Ethical Challenges in Volunteer Programs** - Dialogue on challenges which face the volunteer manager in contemporary society.
- **The Volunteer Skills Portfolio** - How to help your volunteers and yourself evaluate, record and market the skills hones through volunteerism.
- **Take My Volunteer, Please** - How and when to fire a volunteer.
- **Living Up to Commitments: A Two-Way Street** - A marketing approach for staff and volunteers, to avoid burnout from increased or unclear expectations.
- **Marketing Your Program in Government** - Special session for those in local, state or federal government.
- **Special Presentation** - "The Volunteer: Are You Part of an Endangered Species?"

The AVA Certification Session follows the meeting. It is the only professional certification program in the field of volunteer management. It introduces you to the application process and assists you in preparing your application for certification. Personal consultations with well-known Chicago-area Trainers can be arranged before or during the Conference. Opportunity is provided for participants to share resources.

Faculty is drawn from the Association for Volunteer Administration, Blackhawk College, Peat Marwick Mitchell, Chicago Public Library, Girl Scouts of DuPage County, Northwestern University, Corporate Insurance Management Association, American Association of University Women, Family Services of Milwaukee, ACTION, COOL (Campus Outreach Opportunity League), Minnesota Department of Human Services, Civic Center Volunteers, Mayor's Voluntary Action Center, Junior League of Evanston, Community Nutrition Network, ELC Marketing, CNY Enterprises, and Mothers and Daughters Working Together.

VOLUNTEERS: HEROES OF THE 80'S*
Volunteer Center of Maricopa County
1515 East Osborn Road
Phoenix, AZ 85014
TEL: 602-263-9736
Credit: Inquire
Sponsor: Volunteer Bureau of Maricopa County
Contact: Librarian/Historian
Description: The goal of this forum is to bring together a representative group of volunteers and directors of volunteers to discuss how to be a volunteer and how to involve the volunteer, thus helping the "valley of the sun" to meet an ever-increasing number of community problems with all available resources. It is based on the premise that: "To develop an efficient and effective community program of social services, voluntary participation by citizens, organizations and social agencies in the planning and coordination process is a must."

Topics for the forum are based on expressed needs from the volunteer community and include:

- A Historical Overview of Voluntarism in America (keynote address)
- Recruitment of Volunteers
- Commitment and Training
- Incentives/Retention of Volunteers
- Federal and State Legislation Affecting the Volunteer
- Corporate Involvement in the Voluntary Sector

Faculty is drawn from the State of Arizona, the local Red Cross chapter, St. Luke's Hospital, the local Junior League, First National Bank of Arizona, and the field of journalism - all with experience in the volunteer community.

This forum includes the annual volunteer awards program. Previous sessions have addressed specific social service areas; e.g., elderly, handicapped, youth.

VOLUNTEERS IN ACTION
Des Moines Area Community College
2006 South Ankeny Boulevard
Ankeny , IA 50021
TEL: 515-964-6365
Credit: 2 Credits, 24 hours
Sponsor: Des Moines Area Community College
Contact: Peggy Cutlip
Description: Volunteers In Action (Course SERV:310) is a required course in a series that leads to a Volunteer Management Specialist Certificate. Goals are to provide information and enhance skills needed to develop and organize an effective volunteer program. The course addresses the volunteer coordinator's role, guidelines for operation, recruitment, placement, supervision, and evaluation through the following workshops:

- **A look at volunteerism** - history and philosophy, attitudes and necessity of training and skill development, areas of volunteer activity, and elements of a volunteer program.
- **Why people volunteer** and how it relates to successful placement and retention of volunteers.
- **Organization climate** - effect of an organization, assessing climate, implementing change, problem solving process.
- **Role of an administrator** - in planning, organizing, staffing, directing, and controlling volunteers. Leadership in relation to management, supervisory techniques, and awareness of training techniques.
- **Volunteer jobs and recruitment** - creative job design, recruiting techniques and approaches.
- **Planning and Evaluation** - goal setting process, evaluation - a part of planning.
- **Interviewing and placing volunteers** - getting the right person for the right job, procedures, needs of volunteers vs. needs of agency.

VOLUNTEERS IN GREAT BRITAIN: A STUDY TOUR
University of Nebraska
Dept. of Conferences & Institutes
205 Nebraska Center
Lincoln, NE 68583
TEL: 402-472-2844
Credit: CEUs
Sponsor: University of Nebraska; Nebraska Organization of Volunteer Leaders; Association for Volunteer Administration
Contact: Marion Kaple, Program Coordinator

Description: Volunteers in Great Britain is part of the Volunteer Development Certificate Program, which is designed to provide volunteer leaders, paid or unpaid, with both professional growth and training in management skills. This fourteen-day study-tour is designed to afford administrators and leaders of volunteer services and programs the opportunity to learn about the utilization and management of volunteers in Great Britain, to encourage the exchange of information, and to promote personal contact. Participants are given the opportunity to look at the role of volunteers from a broad perspective as well as to focus on programs involving volunteers in the planning and delivery of specialized services. Focus areas:

- Health and Social Services;
- Mental Health and Retardation Services;
- Courts and Correctional Programs;
- Youth and Education Programs.

The first week includes meetings with British counterparts to talk about common concerns, to gain an overview of the British health, social service and educational systems, and to examine the impact of volunteers on contemporary British society. Included is a visit to the national Volunteer Centre, and social activities for informal sharing of concerns. Travel to both cities and rural areas will enable a first-hand look at the use of volunteers outside metropolitan London.

Groups formed in the four focus areas above will visit related institutions, community programs, youth organizations, self-help and advocacy groups, etc., organized by the Information Officer of Great Britain's Volunteer Centre. The tour is limited to 28 persons and based on a preference for participants with three or more years demonstrated experience and current activity in the volunteer sector, and the need to balance participants among the focus areas to enable the most complete exchange of information possible.

Continuing Education Units (CEUs) are available to participants who are enrolled in the Volunteer Leadership Development Certificate Program.

VOLUNTEERS OF AMERICA ANNUAL MEETING
Volunteers of America
3813 North Causeway
Metairie, LA 70002-1784
TEL: 504-837-2652
Sponsor: Volunteers of America
Contact: Raymond C. Tremont, President
Description: Although some of the Christian traditions of Volunteers of America will never change, but the changes that have taken place in recent years caused moments of anxiety for many in the organization. Among these changes were elimination of the use of military rank, and a change in governance to a national corporate structure, which introduced a national board of directors, and mmandated boards of directors for local units as they are chartered. This conference addresses some of these anxieties and is intended to create an atmosphere of openness for discussion and change. The agenda included:

- Plenary Sessions, which began with a video entitled, *The Movement and the Mission,* a history of VOA.
- Keynote Addresses: *The Process of Change; Ministry in the New Testament;* and *That Mystery Called the Church.*
- Ideal Statements of Purpose - presentations by small discussion groups, led by ten VOA ministers.
- Tradition, Identity and Change: We are VOA, a panel discussion by three VOA ministers.
- Showcase of VOA Service Programs.

Participants were asked to evaluate each session. The overall rating from the evaluations was positive. Rated especially high were the use of VOA ministers as speakers, and the Showcase of VOA Programs.

VOLUNTEERS... OUR CARING ALABAMA
Governor's Office on Volunteerism/AL
64 North Union Street
Rooms 13-15
Montgomery, AL 36130
TEL: 205-261-3020
Sponsor: Governor's Office on Volunteerism; US/ACTION
Contact: Joyce St. John-Marcus
Description: With a 17-member Steering Committee, and nine other committees to areas including resource development, awards, program and evaluation, the Fourth Annual Governor's Conference on Volunteerism was designed to reflect expressed needs of volunteer managers across the state. Workshop topics include:

- **Marketing Strategies** - The latest and most up-to-date marketing techniques for non-profits.
- **The Many Faces of Leadership** - How to examine one's self and others as leaders; and, how to recognize and tap the "leader" in self and in others.
- **Corporate Volunteer Programs** - What a corporate volunteer effort can do for the community. How to design a program. How to measure its success.
- **The Trouble with Talking is Words** - Importance of good communication and tricks for overcoming common barriers. How to fine-tune messages.
- **AIDS Update: What to Expect Next** - A panel of knowledgeable people, including AIDS researchers, volunteer caregivers, and PWA's.
- **The Boardsmanship Hook** - Boardsmanship logistics of effective board structure and content. Tenure, training, fund raising, by-laws.
- **Fitness Five Fun** - Physical fitness for volunteer manager, staff, volunteers, and clients. Why physical fitness is important.
- **Delegation: The Art of the Possible** - Skills necessary for successful delegation.
- **Advocating for Volunteerism** - Moving from Lobby to Law - Discussion of legislative process. "How-To's" described in textbooks versus how it *really* functions.
- **The Art of Conducting Effective Business Meetings** - Dealing with irritants that become BIG problems. Theories of communication, business, and philosophy.
- **Survival Skills and Effective Volunteer Management** - Survival skills and volunteer management from top leaders in the field.
- **Public Relations is a Four-Letter Word - E-A-S-Y** - Dealing effectively with the news media. Tips on ways to get material aired or printed.
- **Grantwriting: How to Get the Money You Need Without Robbing a Bank** - Step-by-step instruction on the art of grantwriting. How to write proposals to fit agency needs.
- **WOW: Workshop on Workshops** - A step-by-step approach to workshops after you said, "Yes, I'll be in charge of the workshop."
- **Newsletters: Friend or Foe** - Types of newsletters, how to determine best style, type, and format for your organization; mechancis of production, methods, layout, make-up and content.
- **How to Tell Your Story** - How to better understand the dynamics of effective public speaking to garner greater support for your programs.
- **Operation MOP (Management, Organization & Planning)** - A way to rethink the Management/Organization/Planning process by concentrating onc ase studies, especially as they concern fund raising and distribution.
- **Give Five Alabama** - What is "Give Five Alabama?" Plus creative and innovative ideas for local program implementation. Secrets for generating interest.
- **Challenge of the Homeless** - Inter-Agency Panel to discuss ways to care for the homeless and hungry in our society.

- **Volunteers with Disabilities: An Untapped Resource** - Panel of experts to discuss the placement of volunteers with disabilities.
- **Putting Your Best Foot Forward without Tripping Over It** - Understanding individual self image; becoming aware of image-enhancing and image-damaging behaviors.
- **Substance Abuse and Prevention** - Description of disease concept of chemical dependency, tratment needs, and prevention activities in Alabama.

In addition to the workshops, a networking luncheon provided facilitators for 33 topics including mental health, teen pregnancy, emergency management, church volunteering, corporate volunteering, food banks, environmental issues, and alternative sentencing.

The conference also included the annual recognition and awards program and a tribute to the hundreds of organizations and individuals who cooperated and assisted with the conference.

Publications: GOV Conference Report

VOLUNTEERS: THE RENEWABLE RESOURCE
Hunter College School of Scoial Work
The City University of New York
129 East 79th Street
New York, NY 10021
TEL: 212-570-5179

Description: This Institute begins with a panel discussing the experience of being or working with volunteers from the perspective of the volunteer, the private agency, the governmental agency and the volunteer coordinator. The keynote address, "Changing Trends in the Use of Volunteers in Social Agencies," and the panel discussions are followed by a series of eight workshops grouped under four categories:

Organization
- Management of a Volunteer Program
- Volunteer-Staff Relationships

Recruitment and Training
- Motivation and Recruitment of Volunteers
- Training and Supervision of the Volunteer

Placement and Staffing
- Volunteers in a Treatment Team
- The Older Adult Volunteer

Advocacy and Policy Making
- The Board Member as Volunteer
- The Volunteer as Advocate

Workshops are structured to allow for discussion and exchange of ideas. Whenever possible, specific agency case examples are utilized to illustrate the particular approach or problem being examined. Participants may select any two of the eight workshops. Although the Institute is geared to volunteer managers, board members and other volunteers can gain a broad perspective of the roles they play in social agencies by participating.

The Institute concludes with an informal discussion and reception where participants meet their colleagues, as well as further discuss their particular concerns with workshop leaders.

WEST VIRGINIA CONFERENCE ON VOLUNTEERISM
SEE GOVERNORS' OFFICES ON VOLUNTEERISM: WEST VIRGINIA

WHERE DO WE GO FROM HERE?
Association for Volunteer Administration
Region X
Route 5, Box 474
Vashon, WA 98070
TEL: 206-463-9831
Credit: Partial fulfillment for AVA Certification
Sponsor: Association for Volunteer Administration
Contact: Dorothy Johnson, Chair, Region X
Description: This conference is convened each year to help volunteer administrators adequately and effectively meet the new

and different challenges continually surfacing throughout the field of volunteerism. In addition, educators, researchers, students, and agency/organization administrators benefit from this trainiing event. Workshops include:
- Creativity: Making People and Programs Come Alive
- Working with Administration to Increase Support for Your Program
- Developing Yourself as a Trainer
- Evaluating Your Volunteer Program
- Working with the Physically Disabled Volunteer
- Marketing Your Volunteer Program
- Volunteers in Religious Setting
- Recruiting Volunteers
- Developing Training Programs
- Interviewing Skills
- Supervision and Retention of Volunteers
- Beyond the Basics - for people with knowledge and experience in topics of the workshops and want to explore them in more depth.

In addition to the three-hour workshops above, the curriculum included a series of one-hour "Mini Sessions," including:
- The Involuntary Volunteer: A Look at Court Referral Volunteers
- Preventing Burnout
- Dealing with Job Stress
- Corporate Volunteers
- EEO As It Applies to Volunteers
- Legal Considerations for Volunteer Programs
- The Volunteer Career Portfolio
- Networking with Other Agencies
- How to Develop a Volunteer Manual
- How to Develop and Write a Good Newsletter
- Ideas for Volunteer Recognition
- How to Write a Public Service Announcement
- How to Develop a Policy Manual for the Volunteer Department
- Record Keeping Tips: Why, What, How
- Graphic Design for the Non-Artist (Brochures, Layouts, Camera Ready Art...)
- How to Put Together a Slide/Tape Presentation
- Displaying Statistics: Methods and Trade Tricks for Charts, Pies, Bar Graphs
- Volunteer Job Applications: What They Should Look Like
- How to Effectively Lead Meetings
- How to Involve Handicapped Volunteers
- How to Operate AV Equipment (Slide Projector, Cassette Recorder, Overhead Projector, etc.)
- How to Develop In-Kind Donations
- Training Paid Staff to Work with Volunteers
- Developing Short-Term Volunteer Jobs
- When Is Helping Hurting? Can A Volunteer Be Too Helpful?
- Volunteerism and Politics
- Considerations in Budgeting for Volunteer Programs
- Volunteers and Labor Unions
- The Role of Government in Volunteerism
- Working with the Unsatisfactory Volunteer
- How to Involve Senior Volunteers as Legal Advocates
- Management Training Films (Titles to be Announced)

Based on a review of this program's purpose, goals, and instructional plan, attendance is accepted by AVA in partial fulfillment of the criteria defined for professional certification.

WORKING PARTNERS
Republican National Committee
310 First Street, SE
Washington, DC 20003
TEL: 202-484-6569
Credit: Inquire
Sponsor: Republican National Committee

Contact: Betty Heitman or Lee Edwards
Description: To complement President Reagan's Private Sector Initiative Program, the Republican National Committee convened a discussion group to explore the power and the obstacles of volunteerism. The group consisted of representatives of the voluntary sector who have been actively involved in the field of volunteerism who shared, through informal discussion, their experiences, ideas, and recommendations on topics such as:

- Services provided today by volunteers.
- Both the "good" (positive experiences and procedures), and the "bad" (problems and obstacles) of their day-to-day efforts.
- Issues and concerns within the communities.
- Ways of addressing and meeting needs in the communities.
- General/overall perspectives of participants in this discussion group.
- Activities in other fields that affect the volunteer community.

In addition to sharing ideas, advice and concerns, a major goal of the seminar was to help redirect people resources to effect the maximum benefit to the volunteer community.

Following the scheduled half-day program, participants were invited to use the conference area for continued dialogue in areas requiring more depth than the limited meeting time allows.

WORKSHOP FOR VOLUNTEER MANAGERS*
California Hospital Association
Volunteer Services Division
925 L Street
Sacramento, CA 95814
TEL: 916-443-7401
Credit: AVA credit
Sponsor: California Hospital Association
Contact: Connie Murphy, Director
Description: Designed for directors of volunteer services and those responsible for volunteer program management, the objective of this workshop is to meet developing needs and enhance existing skills for directors as participating members of the management team. To enable maximum participation across the state, the program is conducted in three locations in as many days.

The curriculum is developed around only two major issues to allow participants to explore thoroughly these areas, rather than experience only superficial coverage of a large number of topics. The two topics are:

The Effective Use of Power:
- a definition in both professional and personal contexts.
- identifying and recognizing sources of power from within and external sources.
- examining the positive and negative aspects of power.
- the utilization of power as an acceptable leadership skill.

Assessing Volunteer Productivity:
- the need for active productivity assessment.
- the benchmark: investment in volunteer recruitment, training and administration.
- criteria for personal and organizational productivity assessment.
- measurement tools: worksheets, reporting documents, self-reporting.
- the creative context for reinforcing productivity, organizational development.

Faculty was drawn from the academic and consultant fields. The Association for Volunteer Administration accepts attendance at this workshop for credit toward requirements for AVA certification.

WORKSHOP FOR VOLUNTEERS
Volunteer Center of Central Florida
1900 North Mills Avenue
Suite I
Orlando, FL 32803
TEL: 305-896-0945

Credit: Certificate
Sponsor: Southeast Bank
Contact: Julie Washburn
Description: This workshop is designed to help the volunteer explore personal goals in light of skills and interests, and determine the best volunteer job in relation to those skills and interests, or evaluate a current volunteer commitment. It takes into consideration the varied areas of volunteer involvement and conducts sessions in six of those areas, as well as several management areas. Sessions include:

Information and Referral Skills for Volunteers
- How to ask the right questions to understand a person's need.
- When you can make the referral that will get the individual's needs met.
- Understanding the Information and Referral Service in the Community.

Volunteering with the Refugee
- Insight into the life of the refugee who has settled in the community.
- Understanding who they are and how they got here.
- Discussion with a volunteer who has helped a refugee family.
- Ways volunteers can help.

Volunteering with the Terminally Ill
- Understanding the special needs of the terminally ill and their families.
- Learning about ways that volunteers can help.
- Considering ways in which the information given can help the volunteer also.

Volunteering in the Schools
- Finding out how to become a volunteer in the local schools.
- Learning about a successful local program (ADDitions Program)

Volunteering with the Elderly
- Becoming aware of the needs of the elderly in the community.
- Thinking about ways that volunteers might want to become involved in meeting needs of the elderly.

Volunteering with Troubled Youth
- Exploring ways to be of assistance to troubled youth in the community.
- Identifying their problems.
- Considering ways volunteers might help them become productive adults.

Time Management for Volunteers
- Learning the basics of time management.
- Developing ways to manage volunteer time creatively.
- Establishing volunteer priorities.

An Overview: A Volunteer's Bill of Rights and Responsibilities
- Recognizing that volunteers have rights as well as responsibilities to themselves as well as the groups they serve.
- Discussing, with an experienced volunteer, tips for developing a successful volunteer career.

Your Goals, Skills and Interests and the Right Volunteer Job!
- Exploring personal goals.
- Determining the best volunteer job for this stage of your life.
- Your present commitment, is it right for you?

In addition to the above sessions, a new film, To Care, from Independent Sector was shown to give examples of the many ways volunteers serve. Open discussion periods, and opportunities to consult the presenters, were provided intermittently throughout the program. The program was sponsored by the local bank.

WORKSHOP SERIES ON VOLUNTEERISM
Pennsylvania State University
Division of Continuing Education
J. Orvis Keller Building
University Park, PA 16802
TEL: 814-863-0201
Credit: CEUs; six hours toward a Nursing Home Administrator's license; partial fulfillment for AVA Certification

Sponsor: Pennsylvania State University
Contact: Larry Gamm
Description: Developed in 1976, this workshop series covers a variety of topics relating both to volunteer management and to the administration of nonprofit organizations. The workshops are designed for organizations, public agencies or programs utilizing volunteers, community volunteer programs, and voluntary and nonprofit organizations which work with orare supported by volunteers. The workshops are designed for full- or part-time, paid or unpaid staff or volunteers, and include:

Foundations of Effective Volunteer Programming
- Recruiting and Interviewing Volunteers
- Developing a Training Program for Volunteers
- Senior Citizens and Volunteerism
- Effective Staff/Volunteer Relationships
- Evaluation, Recordkeeping, and Accountability
- Improving Productivity in Use of Volunteers
- Organizing for Change
- Advocating for Clients

Management Skills in Voluntary and Nonprofit Organizations
- Funding Diversification and the Law in the 80s
- Fund Raising for Voluntary and Nonprofit Organizations
- Proposal and Grant Writing
- Basic Public Relations and Communications
- Advanced Public Relations Techniques for Volunteer Nonprofit Organizations
- Working with Committees and Advisory Groups
- Board of Directors: Recruiting, Training and Legal Responsibilities
- Board Dynamics: Competing Claims and Common Needs
- Marketing for Voluntary and Nonprofit Organizations
- Resource Exchange Networks: Nonbureaucratic Responses to Human Needs
- Resource Management Strategies in a Cutback Era
- Interorganizational Coordination
- Time Management

Faculty is drawn from the University with Advisory Committee members coming from hospitals, VACs, associations and corporations.

WORKSHOPS FOR VOLUNTEER MANAGERS
The Voluntary Action Center
2125 East South Boulevard
PO Box 11044
Montgomery, AL 36116-0044
TEL: 205-262-3596
Credit: CEUs from Auburn University at Montgomery
Contact: Alabama Office on Volunteerism
Description: With faculty drawn from the local university, a federal agency, a state office, and the media, this workshop explores several aspects of volunteer programming, including:
- **Workshop #1: Creative Management of Volunteer Programs**
- **Workshop #2: Valuable Communication Skills**
- **Workshop #3: Networking**
- **Workshop #4: Marketing Your Program**

All workshops are based on feedback from the field, and are conducted in participatory style to maximize involvement and enable a sharing of ideas and experiences to become an integral part of the program. Faculty is carefully chosen to reflect the needs indicated by the field.

WORKSHOPS IN EFFECTIVE VOLUNTEER UTILIZATION
Georgia State University
Public and Urban Affairs
University Plaza
Atlanta, GA 30303
TEL: 404-658-3504
Credit: CEUs
Sponsor: College of Public and Urban Affairs, GSU

Contact: Dr. Geraldine A. Corbin
Description: Now in their eighth year, these one-day seminars for volunteer and staff administrators are designed in response to surveys of past workshop participants and volunteer administrators conducted each summer. Their intent is to help the participants develop management skills to be used in the overall agency setting as well as with volunteers. The following is a typical curriculum for these one-day workshops:

Marketing the Non-Profit Organization
- What Is Marketing?
- The Need for Marketing the Non-profit Organization
- The Marketing Process
- What is your Program/Service/Product?
- Who is your Client/Consumer?
- How Do You Make Your Service Available to Your Client?
- Who is Involved in the Marketing Process?
- The Marketing Plan
- Development
- Implementation
- Communication (Organizational; Personal)
- Evaluation and Summary

Speakeasy
The Speakeasy technique includes lectures followed by individual participation. The intent is for participants to gain self-awareness with video-taping and playback, and to benefit from role-playing and group activities which provide additional feedback. The expected results: an effective and authentic speaking style that works whether talking to a friend, two business associates, or an auditorium filled with people.

Other subjects in the series include leadership training, how to motivate volunteers, how to avoid burnout, and how to recruit and work with volunteers from the corporate sector. One continui ng education unit is offered for each 10 contact hours of participation. CEUs are cumulative, with transcripts available on request. Workshops are held four times a year in different cities around the state for maximum participation.

YOUNG VOLUNTEERS IN ACTION: TRAINING FOR PROJECT DIRECTORS
US/ACTION - The Federal Volunteer Agency
1100 Vermont Avenue, NW
Suite 1100
Washington, DC 20525
TEL: 202-634-9108
TOLL FREE: 800-424-8580
Credit: None
Sponsor: US/ACTION - The Federal Volunteer Agency
Contact: Nancy Yde, Public Information Officer
Description: This program enables directors of Young Volunteers in Action (YVA) programs to meet and share ideas with others who are working with young volunteers in other communities. The content of the two-day session includes:

General data on sponsoring a Young Volunteers in Action Program: Roles and Responsibilities of:
- Project Director
- Work-Site Coordinator
- Advisory Council Role
- The Community
- The Volunteers
- ACTION Field Staff

Administrative Details:
- Finances, budget
- Insurance, Transportation
- In-Kind Contributions

Small Group Work:
- Recruitment Techniques
- Activities of Interest to Volunteers
- Community Support and Public Relations
- Selection of Work Assignments and Cooperating Agencies

- Matching Volunteer with Work Assignment

Training:
- Characteristics of Developing a Training Program for Volunteers
- Orientating Work Site Coordinators

General Management:
- Leadership
- Personnel Techniques
- Time Management
- Problem Solving
- Simulations

Closing sessions included Volunteer Recognition and Incentives and Where to go from Here, as well as an open session to enable participants and presenters to discuss the session and address specific problems encountered by the sponsors in local programs.

TRAINING/CONFERENCES/TEACHING: ACCOUNTABILITY

TRAINING PROGRAMS

COMPLETE VOLUNTEER LEGAL LIABILITY WORKSHOP
SEE GOVERNORS' OFFICES ON VOLUNTEERISM: VIRGINIA

MANAGING YOUR FISCAL RESPONSIBILITIES AS A NONPROFIT: HOW TO AVOID FINANCIAL PITFALLS
Virginia Society of Certified Public Accountants
Suite 1010
700 East Main Building
Richmond, VA 23210
TEL: 804-270-5344; 804-786-1431
Credit: Inquire
Sponsor: Virginia Society of Certified Public Accountants; Virginia Department of Volunteerism
Contact: Beth Jacobson, Virginia Society of CPAs; or VA Department of Volunteerism
Description: Based on the most frequent problems referred to the Society of CPAs, this three-and-a-half-hour workshop asks the following questions to potential participants:
- Do you have income that is tax-exempt?
- Do you wish you had a more efficient way to track your cash flow?
- Are you unsure of which IRS regulations apply to you?
- Do you wish you knew more about management to protect your group?

Those who answer YES to any of the questions are expected to benefit from the workshop, which is jointly sponsored by the Virginia CPA Society and the State Department of Volunteerism. Participants at past workshops have included: Board members, directors or treasurers of nonprofit organizations of any size - chambers of commerce, professional associations, civic groups, neighborhood associations, sports leagues, recreation associations and others.

TRAINING/CONFERENCES/TEACHING: AIDS

TRAINING PROGRAMS

HOW TO EFFECTIVELY MANAGE PEOPLE WHO HAVE AIDS AS VOLUNTEERS
Association for Volunteer Administration
PO Box 4584
Boulder, CO 80306
TEL: 303-497-0328
Credit: Inquire
Sponsor: Association for Volunteer Administration
Contact: Irene K. Wysocki
Description: This workshop addresses the benefits of involving volunteers who have HIV infection in agency programs. It addresses the fact that one and a half million people in the United States are living with HIV infection, many of them in the prime of their lives and careers, frequently professionals, and often displaying enthusiasm and energy that can help them as individuals as well as the volunteer program manager. Workshop question/answer sessions and topics include:

As volunteer administrators, what is our obligation to this population? - As volunteer managers we see the many contributions that volunteers provide. These contributions become even more important to infected persons because for them, helping others is very important. As volunteer managers, we have the rare opportunity to channel their energy into focused volunteer work. By using HIV-positive volunteers, you can:
- expand your horizons as a volunteer manager
- set a public example for compassion during a time of widespread misunderstanding about the AIDS epidemic
- support volunteer managers' needs to make changes in their programs which match societal changes around AIDS and AIDS-related discrimination
- use your leadership skills to change community responses to the needs of those with HIV infection

How can managers best learn to support this volunteer base? - The ability to look at our fears about HIV infection and what this means to us personally is to educate ourselves so that we overcome our fears. As effective volunteer managers, we must:
- sensitize ourselves to HIV infection
- reduce homophobia
- reduce irrational fears of HIV infection
- sensitize our staffs and other volunteers to the needs of people with HIV infection
- educate ourselves and our staffs about the issues surrounding a life-threatening illness, such as HIV-infection
- support the will to live in all persons with life-threatening illnesses

Benefits to volunteer administrators and their organizations when they work with people with HIV infection - People living with AIDS or HIV infection will expand our volunteer bases, providing flexible schedules, enormous talent, and extraordinary motivation to help others. Other benefits are:
- Their contributions to AIDS prevention education; they can speak to those issues first hand.
- They offer volunteer managers the opportunity to learn about AIDS and HIV infection in a way that can lessen irrational fears.
- They can provide volunteer managers the personal enjoyment of getting to know and support individuals with AIDS or HIV infection.
- They offer volunteer managers the opportunity to learn special supervision skills.
- Their individual skills increase an organization's talent pool.
- They provide an organization a way to make a direct

contribution to fighting AIDS and to make a statement to other agencies about their leadership in the AIDS/HIV epidemic.

- They can help your agency play a role in changing your community's response to AIDS.
- Their desires to help others are furthered by providing them meaningful work in the organization of their choice.

This program demonstrates support for the AVA Board of Directors' recent resolution which discourages discrimination against volunteers who have HIV infection. It is intended as a challenge to agencies of every type to seriously examine this issue as it affects their volunteer programs.

PARENT-TEEN AIDS EDUCATION PROJECT
San Francisco AIDS Foundation
333 Valencia Street
PO Box 6182
San Francisco, CA 94101-6182
TEL: 415-861-3397
Credit: CEUs or Certificate
Sponsor: Local groups
Contact: Parent-Teen Program Coordinator
Description: The Parent-Teen AIDS Education Project offers several approaches to AIDS education. Each component can be implemented by itself or can be part of the total program. The implementation component provides detailed information on how to choose an appropriate program for your community, present AIDS information, and develop AIDS policies. It includes materials in English and Spanish to help with communication skills and strategies. Topics include:
Implementation
- Parent-teen communication
- Parent meeting guidance
- Community leadership
- Parent-Teen AIDS forums
- Cultural and ethnic concerns
- Working with the media
- Writing AIDS policies

Talking with Teens with Jane Curtin (video) - a presentation to provide parents with a review of basic AIDS information and examples of effective parent-teen communication.
Talking with Your Teen about AIDS - a handout designed to provide parents with basic facts about AIDS, and communication tips for talking with teens.
This program is designed for adult organizations and civic groups such as PTA and the Lions Club, schools, religious organizations, youth-serving agencies such as Big Brothers, Big Sisters, and the YMCA, the workplace, Departments of Health and other government agencies. It is contained in a kit of materials (implementation manual, video and brochures for all participants). It is acquired by the local group presenting the program. Local groups can work with their colleges and universities to qualify the Parent-Teen AIDS Education project as a CEU credit program, or a certificate may be issued. Inquire about program cost to the sponsoring community group.
Publications: Parent-Teen AIDS Education Implementation Manual ; Parent-Teen AIDS Education Video; Talking with Your Teen About AIDS

INDIVIDUAL PROGRAM PROFILES

FAMILY AIDS EDUCATION PROJECT
SEE VOLUNTEERS: CHURCH/SYNAGOGUE MEMBERS

TRAINING/CONFERENCES/TEACHING: ARMED FORCES

TRAINING PROGRAMS

ARMY COMMUNITY SERVICE VOLUNTEER TRAINING
US/DoD - Army Community Service
HQ, Major Command & Installation
DAAG-PSC
Alexandria, VA 22331
TEL: Comm: 202-325-9390 ; AUTOVON: 221-9390
Credit: Inquire
Sponsor: US/DoD - Department of the Army
Contact: Marilyn Keel
Description: The many varied services and programs that involve Army Community Service (ACS) volunteers necessitate the presence of a continuing education program if required levels of excellence are to be retained. Therefore, training occurs on all ACS organization levels - Headquarters, Department of the Army, Major Command and Installation.
Headquarters, Department of the Army, Army Community Service sponsors:
1. ACS Course - offered four times a year and open to both paid and non-paid staff. The one week course covers all aspects of ACS programs, with four hours concentrated solely on volunteer management issues. The volunteer management section covers the following areas:
- The role of the volunteer in ACS
- Volunteer/paid staff relations
- Designing job descriptions
- Recruitment
- Interviewing and Placement
- Training
- Supervision and Evaluation

2. ACS Course - Europe and Hawaii - the course, as described above, is offered twice a year in Europe, and annually in the Pacific for ACS paid and non-paid staff in Hawaii and Korea.
3. ACS Management Course - offered twice a year for ACS Officers/Directors and administrative personnel responsible for resource management. Focus is on:
- The role of the volunteer
- Staff relationships
- Factors necessary for efficient and effective paid and non-paid relationships to achieve agency goals.

4. Annual ACS Training Workshop - approximately two hundred paid and volunteer staff attend this workshop from all ACS centers worldwide. Topics cover all aspects of the ACS program to include specific volunteer management issues.
Major Commands (MACOM) sponsor:
1. Program specific training workshops for paid and non-paid staff; and
2. Volunteer management workshops for key volunteer management personnel.
Local Installations provide:
1. Initial and refresher orientations
2. On-the-job training
3. Continuing in-service training
4. Progressive senior management training
Training is encouraged at the lowest possible level so as to enhance the relevance of the presentations and to minimize cost. All training is a combination of theory and practical application.

US/VA - VAVS WORKSHOPS
US/VA - Voluntary Service Division
VA Voluntary Service (VAVS)
Veterans Administration
Washington, DC 20420
TEL: 202-389-2953
Credit: Certificate
Sponsor: US/VA - Veterans Administration
Contact: Karen Draper
Description: Presenting four workshops, this annual conference combines volunteer roles with needs of the patients, with participants given the option to select two of them. The four workshops:
Selling the Volunteer Program: Based on the fact that recruitment of new volunteers is vital to the success of the VAVS program, this workshop emphasizes "what happens to volunteers after they are recruited." With studies showing that programs excelling in recruiting techniques often fall short of orientation, placement and follow-up of new volunteers, this workshop addresses the elements of retention of volunteers in relation to the recruitment and ongoing supervision. The goal is to reduce the number of volunteers who become dissatisfied and limit or stop their involvement.
Meeting the Needs of the Older Patient... and the Older Volunteer: With the older veteran population growing, and older volunteers who, because of age, have become ineffective in their present assignments, a solution that might meet both needs is explored in this workshop. Based on evidence that the veteran population is growing, and that many faithful volunteers, because of age, can no longer work effectively in demanding volunteer assignments, workshop planners provide a forum for the idea of bringing together these two groups. Results could include improved understanding of the problems of the aging through development of volunteer assignments that meet the needs of both the older patient and the older volunteer, and an improvement of the quality of life for the older person both in the medical center and in the community.
New and Innovative VA Volunteer Assignments: To keep participants abreast of new and challenging volunteer assignments being developed throughout the VA, this workshop discusses these new assignments, how they are developed, and how to document a few "new ideas" to take back to the participant's local organization and local VA Medical Center.
The Volunteer's Role in VA Security and Safety: Although volunteers traditionally play a role in security and safety, this workshop keeps them informed of the most common security and safety hazards, what is being done to combat these problems, appropriate training for volunteers, and precautions for avoiding or correcting security and safety hazards (including hostage-taking by patients, theft of government property, volunteer injuries, etc.).
This meeting also serves as the meeting place for the Annual Meeting of the VAVS Advisory Committee.

TRAINING/CONFERENCES/TEACHING: ARTS

TRAINING PROGRAMS

THE DEAF WAY
SEE VOLUNTEERS: HANDICAPPED

DOCENT EDUCATION WORKSHOP
Philadelphia Zoo
Docent Council of Philadelphia
34th Street and Girard Avenue
Philadelphia, PA 19104
TEL: 215-243-1100/Ext. 317
Credit: Inquire
Sponsor: Docent Council of the Zoological Society of Philadelphia
Contact: Mickey Magid, President
Description: Recognizing the growing need for docent organizations to function better not only within their institutions, but within the volunteer world in general, the Docent Council of the Philadelphia Zoo developed a workshop to help meet this need.
Leaders of docent-type organizations in zoos, aquaria, nature centers, museums, and historical societies in the Mid-Atlantic states were invited, and 45 participants from five states (representing all of the types mentioned above) came together to share experiences and concerns. The principal trainer came from the volunteer training field in general (Susan J. Ellis) rather than the specific docent field to maximize the opportunity to develop the skills and attitudes needed to interface with the broad volunteer community.
In this first workshop, the facilitator focused on two key issues:
 ● Volunteer Burn-Out
 ● Volunteer/Salaried Staff Relations
Both topics led to further discussion of related issues, including retaining volunteers, career ladders for volunteers, management and recognition problems, and others.
Workshop designers requested that the docent organizations send two participants including the staff person most closely involved with the organization (Coordinator of Volunteer Services, Curator of Education, etc.) to increase implementation of ideas "back at the farm." In addition to the ideas resulting from the sessions, training materials were provided for use at the workshop and later at home sites.
In the course of the workshop, participants organized an informal network in order to exchange newsletters, program information, sample forms, etc. Future workshops were discussed for presentation in other cities in the region.

IMPROVING MUSEUM VOLUNTEER PERFORMANCE
University of Delaware
Wilcastle Center
2800 Pennsylvania Avenue
Wilmington, DE 19899
TEL: 302-738-8155
Credit: CEUs
Sponsor: University of Delaware
Contact: Jacob Haber
Description: Designed to extend and enhance job skills related to the volunteer coordinator and/or volunteer supervisor, this two-day program provides opportunities for participant discussion in both large and small groups. Panel discussions and workshops as well as informal discussions provide variety in exploring the following topics:
 ● **Volunteers in the Museum: Integration or Segregation** - An examination of the role of volunteers and their responsibilities in the long-range planning process. Addresses the question of whether volunteers are a segregated audience for the museum or an integrated form of staff assistance.
 ● **Volunteers Wanted: Recruiting for the 80's** - A panel discussion considering cost factors, methodology, image projection, advertising, promotion, and how recruiting of museum volunteers parallels methodology used in industry.
 ● **Skills Analysis Techniques for Improved Volunteer Training** - A workshop on how to assess training and follow through by establishing and agreeing on learning goals; conducting learning events through lectures, demonstrations, films, guest

speakers and field trips; determining if learning has taken place.

- **Potentials and Limitations in Volunteer Supervision** - A workshop on the importance of a strong supervision program: orienting volunteers to museum program/goals; understanding expectations/needs of volunteers; legal aspects; volunteer accountability; performance reviews; dismissals; rewards/recognition.
- **Volunteers and Staff: Working Toward a Harmonious Relationship** - A workshop to assist in understanding volunteer/staff interaction: how to determine receptivity to volunteers; how to anticipate/respond to tears/expectations of staff toward volunteers; how volunteers affect paid staff; how to achieve harmony.
- **Evaluating Your Volunteers and Your Volunteer Program** - A workshop to assist in translation of goals into action by a step-by-step process - beginning with recruiting, ending when volunteer leaves; both individual and program evaluation.
- **Some Perspectives on the Innovative Use of Volunteers within Museum Settings** - A session exploring the ways traditional uses of museum volunteers are changing; ways previously untapped skills of volunteers are being utilized in museums.

This program is approved by the U.S. Association of Museum Volunteers.

ORCHESTRA MANAGEMENT SEMINAR
American Symphony Orchestra League
777 Fourteenth Street, NW
Suite 500
Washington, DC 20005
TEL: 202-628-0099
FAX: 202-783-7228
Credit: Inquire
Sponsor: Alcoa Foundation
Contact: Meeting Coordinator
Description: This six-day comprehensive seminar is in its 38th year. It strives to help people learn from practical wisdom of effective administrators how to begin managing nonprofit organizations. It includes case studies and other formats designed for maximum benefit in areas including:

- **Being an Orchestra Manager** - roles and responsibilities of volunteers, trustees, administrators, and artistic personnel; the basic structure of a symphony orchestra; the qualities and characteristics of an effective manager.
- **Success Through Volunteers** - how to recruit, motivate, and organize volunteers for orchestras; ways to support their efforts at raising money, selling tickets, and promoting the orchestra.
- **Building an Effective Board** - how to find community leaders, put them to work for your orchestra, and support them in their efforts; the responsibilities of board committees; special importance of the nominating committee.
- **Fundraising** - how the psychology of giving relates to your efforts; organizing volunteers for an annual fund drive; ways to identify prospects, solicit gifts, write proposals, secure corporate sponsorships, and thank donors.
- **Public Relations** - defining your public image; creating and executing plans to promote your orchestra and music director; strengths and weaknesses of specific publicity tools.
- **Economic Realities and Artistic Growth** - controlling the growth of your orchestra in conjunction with the community's desire and ability to support it; the manager as a monitor of administrative and artistic expansion.
- **Managing Orchestra Financing** - generating financial plans, nonprofit arts budgets, and financial reports; understanding legal issues; how to monitor your income and expenses more efficiently.
- **Long-Range Planning** - a hands-on exercise in planning; specifics of mission statements, goals, objectives, and

strategies; how to incorporate planning components into day-to-day operations.

In addition to the above sessions that are transferable to any volunteer program, numerous other sessions very specific to orchestras are convened at the seminar. Faculty for all programs is composed of directors, managers, and specialists from symphonies across the country.

All participants receive individualized career attention, a free copy of the textbook, an opportunity for networking and exchanging materials, and specific seminar reading and writing assignments to be used in conjunction with the workshops both in the sessions and during free time. These assignments are prepared with the premise that, in order to get the maximum value out of such a six-day experience, participants must invest their own time. Assignments begin immediately following registration and continue throughout the seminar.

Seminar participants attend concerts and receive tours of cultural institutions sponsored by US/National Endowment for the Arts and US/National Gallery of Art. Seminars are held in various parts of the country (August 1990, Tanglewood, MA; January 1991, San Francisco, CA).

Publications: The Gold Book: Directory of Successful Projects by Volunteers; Principles of Orchestra Management; Training Handbook Series; Youth Orchestra Handbook; How to Organize and Produce a Radiothon; More Dialing, More Dollars

TRAINING/CONFERENCES/TEACHING: BOARDS

TRAINING PROGRAMS

ADMINISTRATION OF VOLUNTEER PROGRAMS AND OPERATION OF SOCIAL AGENCIES
SEE LEADERSHIP DEVELOPMENT/BOARDS

BOARD DEVELOPMENT CONSULTATION SERVICE
SEE LEADERSHIP DEVELOPMENT/BOARDS

BOARD LEADERSHIP AND DEVELOPMENT
SEE LEADERSHIP DEVELOPMENT/BOARDS

BOARD MANAGEMENT TRAINING WORKSHOP
SEE LEADERSHIP DEVELOPMENT/BOARDS

BOARDSMANSHIP SEMINAR*
SEE LEADERSHIP DEVELOPMENT/BOARDS

BUILDING BETTER BOARDS
SEE LEADERSHIP DEVELOPMENT/BOARDS

BUILDING BETTER BOARDS: LEGAL LIABILITY AND RESPONSIBILITIES
SEE LEADERSHIP DEVELOPMENT/BOARDS

CAREER DEVELOPMENT FOR VOLUNTEER LEADERSHIP
Energize
5540 Wissahickon Avenue
Philadelphia, PA 19144
TEL: 215-438-8342
TOLL FREE: 800-395-9800
Credit: Inquire

Sponsor: ENERGIZE; Yellowfire Press (Ivan H. Scheier)
Contact: Susan J. Ellis
Description: This is a workshop offered jointly by the above principals to address the needs of volunteerism practitioners who wish to explore their personal career mobility in the field. Designed mainly for advanced managers, the national-level workshop has an innovative format. It can be scheduled for either two, three or five days, with a varying number of group sessions and individual consultations. The two trainers will present the options for career growth, but will work one-to-onewith participants in charting personal career plans. Relevant topics to be presented include:
- Upward Mobility Pathway Analysis
- Possible/Probable Career Opportunities in Volunteerism
- Developing Personal and Professional Support Networks
- The Role of Executive
- Lateral Advancement
- Changing Fields (in Mid-Stream)
- Getting Published
- Teaching
- On Being a Trainer/Consultant - local and national options
- Growing in Your Present Setting
- Becoming an Association Officer
- Report Writing: Documenting Success; Resume Writing; Documenting Yourself
- Going Out on Your Own
- Resources Available: Professional and Other Associations
- Sexism, Ageism, and Any Other Isms
- Scoping Your Future
- Assessing Your Upward Mobility Potential

The Design Concept considers two kinds of time: class time for structured training; and open time for common-interest groups, individual consultation, feedback and idea-sharing. Alternative Time Frameworks allow a Two-Day Model, a Three-Day Model, and a Five-Day Model.

Additional sponsors are the Center for Creative Community and Yellowfire Press, chaired by Ivan H. Scheier.

COMMUNITY BOARD TRAINING DAY
SEE LEADERSHIP DEVELOPMENT/BOARDS

CONFERENCE ON NONPROFIT LEADERSHIP AND MANAGEMENT
Lincoln Filene Center for Citizenship & Public Affairs
Tufts University
Civic Education Foundation
Medford, MA 02155
TEL: 617-628-5000
Credit: Inquire
Sponsor: Association of Voluntary Action Scholars; Junior League of Boston; United Way of Massachusetts Bay; United Way of Southeastern New England; American Association of Retired Persons; Lincoln Filene Ce
Contact: Conference Coordinator
Description: This conference is designed to help staff members and volunteers of nonprofit organizations such as social agencies, hospitals, educational and advocacy groups, religious institutions, and service organizations to increase their skills in leadership and management. It grew out of a concern about the new skills volunteers need that were not necessary a decade ago in order to survive in the face cutbacks and other problems related to recession and inflation. The program features 49 Skills Workshops in volunteer management, grassroots organizing, board development, and others including the following:
Session I Skills Workshops
- Volunteer Leadership in Environmental Organizations
- Class, Gender and Race in Volunteering: Myths and Realities
- Marketing and Recruiting Volunteers
- Planning for Nonprofits

- Preventing Burnouts
- Stress Management
- Financial Development: $1, $2, $3 ... Fund
- Improving Representation and Performance on Nonprofit Boards
- Values and Nonprofit Leadership
- Planning for Nonprofits

Session II Skills Workshops
- Supervision of Volunteer Programs
- Motivating Volunteers
- Developing Volunteers in Social Agencies
- The College and University Role in Volunteerism: A Model Approach
- Board Development
- Coalition Building
- Leadership in Grassroots Organizing

Session III Skills Workshops
- Elders as Volunteers
- New Perspectives on Volunteers
- Voluntary Leadership in the Arts
- Voluntary Agency Response to Cutbacks
- Increasing Funds: The Donor Option
- Fundraising Essentials: Donor Perspective
- Setting Up a Fee-Based Structure
- Strategic Management

Session IV Skills Workshops
- University Curricula and Voluntary Leadership
- Neighborhoods and Voluntary Action
- Charismatic Leadership - An Appropriate Style for Voluntary Enterprises
- Board-Staff Relations
- Volunteers in Community Access Cable Television Stations
- Partnerships: What They Mean and How They Work
- Government Contracts and Grants
- Program Evaluation

Ample time for idea exchange and consultation with faculty is provided. In addition, an annual award has been established by the Lincoln Filene Center for Citizenship and Public Affairs honoring an outstanding civic leader. Also, the Conference serves as a time for the annual meetings of all six sponsors.

EFFECTIVE BOARDSMANSHIP
SEE GOVERNORS' OFFICES ON VOLUNTEERISM: VIRGINIA

FINDING AND PREPARING NEW BOARD MEMBERS FOR SERVICE
SEE LEADERSHIP DEVELOPMENT/BOARDS

THE HOW-TO OF WORKING WITH VOLUNTEERS - TLC (TEACHING/LEARNING/CARING)
Lakeside School
14050 First Avenue, NE
Seattle, WA 98125
TEL: 206-367-1688
Credit: CEUs
Sponsor: University of Washington
Contact: Edward C. Schumacher
Description: Developed for Board Members, Volunteer Coordinators, staff supervisors, trainers and otherswho lead volunteers in both public agencies and non-profit organizations, this workshop is concerned with the success of the volunteers in their assignments. Its goals are to help volunteer leaders learn new ideas, new insights, skills and evaluation procedures in order to work more effectively and more efficiently with volunteers. Although workshop topics are predetermined for planning purposes, active participation is required by all of those involved. Participants are asked to plan for some changes in their own and

their agency's behavior and current practices. Techniques included lecture, small group discussion, case study, and experience exercises, enabling flexibility in the curriculum. The foundation topics are deliberately broad to allow the input from participants to develop the program in a way that would serve them best upon their return to their home bases. The overall topics are:

- **Volunteerism:** History, traditions, motivations, expectations, roles, current directions.
- **Comprehensive Systems of Support for Volunteers:** Training, advising, recognition, authority and responsibility.
- **The Human Factor in Volunteerism:** working for and working with power: ego... status... burn out... failure.

The goal of the workshop is to combine useful concepts and tools with principles and techniques that the participants can use in their daily work with volunteers.

HUMAN SERVICE PROGRAMS: VOLUNTEER LEADERSHIP EMPHASIS AREA
SEE GOVERNORS' OFFICES ON VOLUNTEERISM: MINNESOTA

LEADERSHIP FOR THE NINETIES*
SEE LEADERSHIP DEVELOPMENT/BOARDS

ON-SITE PROGRAMS FOR VOLUNTEER ORGANIZATIONS
Allegheny County Community College
111 Pines Plaza
1130 Perry Highway
Pittsburgh, PA 15237
TEL: 412-931-8500
Credit: Inquire
Sponsor: Allegheny County Community College
Contact: Dr. Grassinger
Description: Three courses designed to consider the need of individual organizations are presented at a meeting location arranged by the requesting organization, providing that twelve or more participants are registered for the course (may be from more than one organization). The organization staff consults with course facilitators in advance of the presentation to discuss the basic courses and make adjustments if necessary to tailor them to the needs of the specific organization. The basic formats:
Developing Leadership Skills - a fifteen-hour seminar for leaders and active members of volunteer or nonprofit agencies placing special emphasis on:

- How to run a meeting
- Building an agenda
- Encouraging task orientation
- Decision-making in a group situation
- How to delegate, assign work, and work effectively with others
- Understanding your own management and leadership style
- How to work effectively with membership
- How to recognize and recruit people
- How to monitor an organization's financial records

Creative Problem Solving - a ten-hour seminar providing a special approach to solving problems encountered in meeting thegoals and objectives of the organization, with emphasis placed on building upon and sharing ideas generatedin working sessions within the organization; the seminar is designed to adapt to any group size, and builds an effective working relationship in its team building exercises.

Effective Boardsmanship - a ten-hour seminar experience based on the premise that working effectively as a member of a board of directors or on an advisory committee is essential to the efficient and productive volunteer organization: emphasis is placed on 1) understanding the role of board member; 2) working as a member of a group; 3) running board meetings; 4) legal implications of board participation; 5) receiving and writing reports; 6)

communication to membership.
Funding arrangements from public and private sources has enabled the college to offer these courses at minimal or no cost.

PROFESSIONAL DEVELOPMENT FOR COMMUNITY TRAINERS
Organizational Dynamics
43434 SE Tapp Road
Sandy, OR 97055
TEL: 503-668-7979
Credit: Inquire
Sponsor: Organizational Dynamics
Contact: Arty Trost, MSW
Description: This one-day workshop is especially designed for experienced trainers of direct service and board volunteers. Program content is based on training experiences of volunteer trainers which has made them aware of a need for fine-tuning their skills and techniques. Attendees come from community service programs, volunteer programs, social service organizations, civic organizations, service clubs, churches and synagogues. Although topics may be included to meet specific need of an individual group, basic topics covered are:

- training design and sequencing
- presentation skills and techniques
- training group process and dynamics
- self as trainer: exploration
- training evaluation

The program is experiential and utilizes a variety of methodologies, including simulations, structured exercises, small group work and visual aids. The goal of the session is to leave attendees with:

- Increased Skills in areas that the attendee has identified for himself/herself.
- Greater Confidence in himself/herself as a trainer.
- In-depth Awareness of his/her role as trainer.

Enrollment is limited to allow maximum participation. When indicated, the workshop is repeated on a second day to accommodate special local situations.
This course has been accepted by AVA as satisfying partial fulfillment towards Certification.

STRATEGIES OF VOLUNTEER LEADERSHIP
Pennsylvania State University
Delaware County Campus
25 Yearsley Mill Road
Media, PA 19063
TEL: 215-565-8272
Credit: Three credits (graduate course)
Sponsor: Pennsylvania State University
Contact: Waverly Coleman
Description: Designed specifically for Volunteer Administrators, this academic credit course has been offered for several years since its inception into the curriculum in 1976. It is presently scheduled for the fall semester in both Philadelphia and Pittsburgh. Plans are to offer it regularly each year. Objectives of the course are:

- To develop distinctive administrative competencies in volunteer and nonprofit organizations.
- To broaden the students' understanding and knowledge of voluntary organizations, their dynamics, functions and memberships.
- To help practitioners develop an understanding of the values of volunteerism in today's society.
- To teach the students specific skills in order to help them become successful volunteer leaders (in recruiting volunteers, interviewing, placing volunteers, trainng, supervision, program planning, evaluation and recordkeeping, working effectively with boards of directors and advisory committees, fund-raising, proposal writing, etc.).
- To introduce students to the specific issues and problems

facing volunteerism in today's society.
Strategies of Volunteer Leadership is an evening course - three hours one evening each week for the duration of the Fall Semester. Instructors are national consultants on volunteerism.

SUMMER MASTER'S DEGREE PROGRAM IN COMMUNITY LEADERSHIP AND DEVELOPMENT
Springfield College
Community Leadership/Development
Box 1723
Springfield, MA 01109
TEL: 413-787-2100
Credit: M.A. in Community Leadership and Development
Sponsor: Springfield College
Contact: Margaret Dreger
Description: Designed for community social agency professionals, this program enables the student to earn a Master's Degree through a combination of minimal time on campus and a period of time fulfilling field experience contracts while on the job. Candidates, who must have a minimum of five years' work experience, are required to attend a special three-day pre-summer school intensive workshops, which includes an individualized life planning goals component, and educational contract negotiation for the back home field work and research component.
Based on an educational audit upon receipt of application, graduation can vary from the subsequent Spring to the maximum time allowed for completion-five years. Candidates can accelerate their program by taking courses in both summer sessions. Program segments are:
- Special workshops and meetings, with special emphasis on Urbanology
- Field work and research learning contracts
- Graduate all-college core courses
- Summer Session courses plus audit value
Thirty-six semester hours are required for a degree. It is a limited enrollment program which is administered by the Division of Graduate Studies.

VAC BOARD EDUCATION PROGRAM
SEE LEADERSHIP DEVELOPMENT/BOARDS

VAC WORKSHOPS*
Voluntary Action Center of Morris County
36 South Street
Morristown, NJ 07960
TEL: 201-538-7200
Credit: Inquire
Sponsor: Voluntary Action Center (VAC); VAC Board of Directors
Contact: Education Coordinator
Description: One of the functions of the Voluntary Action Center is to provide a forum for volunteer administrators. To accomplish this, the Center conducts training program periodically, or on topics such as:
Training the Trainer: This workshop considers the reasons for training volunteers and determining how these reasons affect the training design and presentation. Different training techniques are explored and the factors which result in the selection of the most appropriate methods are considered. Participants analyze the adult as a member of the training group and learn how to use the strengths of maturity and experience to maximize learning.
Local Fund Development: This is a working meeting aimed primarily at the board members and staff person responsible for fund resource development for voluntary organizations. Content includes planning, strategies and specific techniques.
Starting Off on the Right Foot; A Sound Approach in the Orientation of New Board Members: This is one of a series of workshops on how to design Board orientation. It is based on the premise that adequate orientation and indoctrination to an organization's purpose, goals and history is one of the most important ingredients of a sound board.
Legal Responsibilities of Board Members: This workshop addresses the importance of assuring that directors know exactly what their duties and responsibilities are, and theextent to which they may be held liable for actions of nonprofit organizations. The VAC continually listens for feedback to determine topics and approaches for workshops to assist local volunteer organizations.
Publications: vol-un-teer con-nec-tion

VOLUNTEER LEADERSHIP DEVELOPMENT PROGRAM
United Way of America
701 North Fairfax Street
Alexandria, VA 22314-2045
TEL: 703-836-7100
FAX: 703-683-7840
Credit: One CEU for each 10 contact hours
Sponsor: United Way of America
Contact: Anne Frey or Kathleen Tighe
Description: The Volunteer Leadership Development Program is one of a multitude of courses and seminars provided by the National Academy for Voluntarism (NAV) for education, training and development of volunteers, board members, and agency professionals. The purposes of this program are:
- to train community leaders to better assume responsibilities of voluntary board membership;
- to clarify the roles of volunteers and staff to promote a more effective partnership;
- to enhance volunteers' understanding of community environment systems and resources, enabling them to impact decision making in both the public and the private sectors.
Volunteer Board Development consists of three different training programs for boards of voluntary organizations:
1. Community Leadership Development Program - This program provides new volunteers with experience in a time-limited community project. The basic curriculum is spread over a period of six to twelve weeks. After completion they obtain a volunteer appointment on a board or committee of a local sponsoring community seeking new leadership, or the United Way.
2. Self-Contained Board Member Training Packages - Two four-hour units of instruction provide information on the responsibilities of board membership. Each training unit consists of an Instructor Kit, and a designated number of Participant Kits. The Instructor Kit includes audio cassettes, lecture materials and films; the Participant Kit includes a workbook and reference readings.
3. Regional Workshops - A series of eight separate half-day training workshops are administered through sixteen Regional Training Centers, all sponsored by Local United Way agencies. Working titles are: Organizing and Governing the Agency, Board/Staff Relations, Your Agency and the Community, Financial Management, Agency Self-Evaluation, Decision-Making/Problem Solving, Resource Development, and Planning and Goal Setting.

WORKING EFFECTIVELY WITH BOARDS AND COMMITTEES
SEE LEADERSHIP DEVELOPMENT/BOARDS

YOU ARE THE BOARD*
SEE LEADERSHIP DEVELOPMENT/BOARDS

TRAINING/CONFERENCES/TEACHING: BUSINESS/INDUSTRY

TRAINING PROGRAMS

BUILDING PARTNERSHIPS WITH CORPORATIONS
SEE BUSINESS/INDUSTRY INVOLVEMENT

CREATIVE INVOLVEMENT FOR PRODUCTIVE COMMUNITIES
VOLUNTEER - The National Center
1111 North 19th Street, Suite 500
Arlington, VA 22209
TEL: 703-276-0542; 703-528-6021
Credit: Inquire
Sponsor: VOLUNTEER: The National Center
Contact: Kay Drake, Public Information Officer
Description: This conference exposes participants to new strategies, techniques, and ideas, and offers opportunities for development of new skills, direct contact with volunteer communities of government, corporate and voluntary sectors, discussions with peers, and specific sessions to address unique needs. Workshops include:
Workshop Session I
- Creative Resource Raising from Corporations
- Getting the Most Out of Being a Volunteer
- Personal Public Relations: Tooting Your Own Horn
- Effective Recruitment of Volunteers
- Getting Future VAC Funding from United Way
- Perspectives on International Volunteering
- Creating Community Partnerships
- Volunteers for State Government: Loaned Executive Program
- Meet the Speaker (open discussion)
Workshop Session II
- Corporate Retiree Involvement Programs
- Preventing Volunteer Burnout
- Utilizing Cable TV
- Dealing with Staff Resistance to Volunteers
- Impact of Computers on VAC Operations
- Community Organizing
- Working with Youth Volunteers
- Volunteer Programs for Local Government
- Meet the Speaker (open discussion)
Workshop Session III
- Creating Recruitment Networks Inside Corporations
- Legal Liability of Volunteer Programs
- Transitioning from Volunteer to Paid Work
- Screening and Interviewing Volunteers
- Charging Fees for VAC Services
- Recruiting the Young Professional
- Working with Senior Volunteers
- Setting Up a Volunteer Skillsbank
- Proposal Writing from the Funder's Viewpoint
Workshop Session IV
- Setting Up a Corporate Volunteer Skillsbank
- Volunteers in the Arts and Humanities
- Sources of Technical Assistance
- How to Fire a Volunteer
- Recruiting Families as Volunteers
- Church/Labor Partnerships
- Alternate Sentencing Programs
- How to Run a Special Event
- Fundraising for People Who Hate Fundraising
Workshop Session V
- Models for VAC/Corporate Partnerships
- Insurance for Volunteer Programs

- Accounting for Non-Accountants
- Effective Recruitment of Volunteers
- Improving Board/Staff Relations
- Volunteer Legislation in the 98th Congress
- The Handicapped as Volunteers
- Introduction to Community Computers
- Meet the Speaker (open discussion)
Workshop Session VI
- How to Tap Organized Labor
- Calculating the True Value of Volunteer Time
- Ethics in Volunteer Administration
- Dealing with Agency Resistance to Volunteers
- Legal Liability of Volunteer Board Members
- The Federal Government and Volunteering
- Fund Raising from Churches
- Volunteers for State Government: The Minnesota Project
- Proposal Writing from the Funder's Viewpoint
Workshop Session VII
- Linking Employee Involvement and Corporate Contributions
- Designing Programs to Train Volunteers
- Conflict Management
- Designing Volunteer Jobs for Results
- How VACs Can Be Leaders in the Community
- The Shape of Things to Come
- Planning
- How Small Nonprofits Can Run Businesses
- Meet the Speaker (open discussion)
Workshop Session VIII
- Management and Technical Assistance from Corporations
- How to Be a Consultant
- Communication Skills
- Designing Volunteer Jobs for Results
- VAC/Agency Relationships
- Volunteering and Unemployment
- Volunteers in Educational Settings
- Improving Volunteer/Union Relations
- Hard-Core Fundraising
The Conference addresses corporations, Voluntary Action Centers, local and state governments, arts and humanities groups, educational institutions, neighborhood and community groups, and volunteer administrators.

TRAINING/CONFERENCES/TEACHING: CAREER EXPLORATION

TRAINING PROGRAMS

MAKING THE VOLUNTEER EXPERIENCE COUNT
University of Nebraska
Dept. of Conferences & Institutions
205 Nebraska Center
Lincoln, NE 68583
TEL: 402-472-2844
Credit: CEUs
Sponsor: University of Nebraska; Volunteer Bureau; Junior League; Department of Public Welfare
Contact: Marion Kaple, Program Coordinator
Description: This conference looks at the volunteer movement from a historical perspective, and examines current trends and changes that are affecting volunteerism today and shaping its direction for the future. Topics include:
- the historical roots of volunteerism
- the philosophical, religious, cultural values that have shaped the volunteer movement

- volunteerism as a mode of citizen participation
- societal value changes and their impact on volunteerism
- how changes in volunteerism affect all segments of the community

The conference design encompasses many facets of the volunteer community, and provides information and assistance for:

- volunteer leaders who want to keep abreast of the changing role of volunteerism today
- volunteers seeking to have their experience recognized for academic credit or paid employment
- educators wishing to know more about the impact of volunteerism on student development
- community leaders who want to examine the pros and cons of voluntary citizen participation
- personnel directors and employers who are being urged to recognize volunteer experience in job applications
- agency personnel who work with volunteers
- legislators and government officials interested in the role of local/state/federal government in volunteerism

Workshops titles include: Volunteerism as an Academic Experience; Personal Growth, Values and the Volunteer Experience: The Volunteer Experience and Community Leadership; Employment Credit for Volunteer Experience; The Art of Turning Volunteer Work into Paid Experience; Government and the Volunteer Experience. To enable wider participation, child care is provided.

NCSL JOB SKILLS DEVELOPMENT SEMINARS
US/ACTION - The Federal Volunteer Agency
1100 Vermont Avenue, NW
Suite 1100
Washington, DC 20525
TEL: 202-634-9108
TOLL FREE: 800-424-8480
Credit: Inquire
Sponsor: US/ACTION
Contact: Nancy Yde, Public Information Officer
Description: The National Center for Service Learning (NCSL) offers free job skills development seminars for educators who run programs that involve students in community service. Seven seminars are scheduled across the country each school year. Three types of seminars are conducted: High School Seminars, College Seminars, and Community Impact Seminars.
In addition to building skills for coordinators of service-learning, experiential education, or volunteer programs, the seminars provide a forum for a sharing of ideas and resources. Potential coordinators are encouraged to attend and explore the purposes and functions of such a program.
All seminars are led by teams of trainers with extensive experience in service-learning. An NCSL staff member attends each seminar to provide information about the activities and resources of the national program. The two formats are:
High School and College Seminars - designed to help service-learning program leaders to strengthen existing programs by addressing management issues. These issues include:

- developing volunteer job
- facilitating learning
- cultivating agency relationships
- promoting service-learning in the school or college

Community Impact Seminars - for high school and college coordinators who direct established programs and who want an intensive seminar focused on strategies for developing more effective interaction between the service-learning program and the community. Sessions in this seminar address:

- identification of community needs
- cooperation with community agencies
- involvement of those being served in the planning of services

Seminars are tuition-free; participants cover their own room, board and travel. Information on dates and locations is available in July of each year.

VOLUNTEERING YOUR WAY TO A SUCCESSFUL CAREER
Southeastern University
501 Eye Street, SW
Washington, DC 20024
TEL: 202-488-8162
Credit: 0.6 CEUs
Sponsor: Southeastern University
Contact: John Chase, Dean
Description: Recognizing that both public and private sectors today are acknowledging the value of volunteer work and community service work as a legitimate form of experience on job applications, vitas and resumes, Southeastern University designed a seminar to explore the essential elements of career development as it relates to volunteerism. The three-pronged program, over a three-day period, covers the following topics:

- **first day:** self-assessment, skills determination, how to use self-knowledge to achieve goals.
- **second day:** ways to narrow the gap between past experience and desired or needed experience.
- **third day:** opportunities for paid and non-paid work in the public and private sectors and how to achieve chosen objectives.

Specific areas of instruction include:

- choosing a volunteer career
- volunteer skills transferable to paid work
- using volunteer job contacts for paid work
- volunteer work versus paid employment
- the value of volunteer work on the resume

Faculty includes persons involved in studies of volunteerism and the transition from volunteer to paid employment, and faculty from Southeastern's Cooperative Education, Graduate Studies, and Student Activities Divisions, as well as from other area colleges.

TRAINING/CONFERENCES/TEACHING: CENTER/AGENCY

TRAINING PROGRAMS

TRAINING FOR VOLUNTEERS AND VOLUNTEER AGENCIES
Georgia State University
Division of Continuing Education
University Plaza
Atlanta, GA 30303
TEL: 404-658-3460
Credit: CEUs (one per 10 contact hours)
Sponsor: Division of Continuing Education, GSU
Contact: Eva K. Trussell
Description: In addition to involvement in the Effective Volunteer Utilization Workshops above, the Division of Continuing Education sponsors the following continuing education programs for volunteers and volunteer administrators:
Collaborative Efforts in Volunteers
Target Audience: Volunteer Administrators in Georgia
Description: Participants learn of opportunities for volunteer leadership, and discuss issues for private initiative with the business sector.
Agency Expectations
Target Audience: Youth Agency Personnel
Description: Participants are informed of opportunities available for volunteer effort and learn of expectations of volunteer agencies (such as NW Georgia Girl Scouts, Junior Achievement, United Way and Red Cross) have of their staff and volunteers.

COVA Forum (Council of Volunteer Administrators)
Target Audience: Volunteers and staff from Metro Atlanta area
Description: Participants are exposed to program instruction focused on time management, leadership training, career development for volunteers to assist them in job performance.

United Way Loaned Executives
Target Audience: Executives loaned from 30 to 40 large companies in the metro Atlanta area
Description: Loaned executives are instructed in:
- planning the mobilization of 10,000 volunteers
- recruiting, organizing and supervising volunteers
- managing, directing and implementing the United Way fund-raising campaign

Fund Raising
Target Audience: Future Youth Leaders
Description: participants are advised of future employment opportunities as youth agency professionals and explore what professionals do in the area of fund raising, as well as some marketing discussion.

Group Counseling Workshop
Target Audience: Volunteers who work with cancer patient groups
Description: Participants learn of effective ways to work with cancer patients in the support group. Topics include: psychosocial aspects of cancer (grieving, coping, changes in family relationships), leadership styles, role play, group processes, and individual vs. group focus.

Support Workshop for Group Facilitation Skills
Target Audience: Volunteers, Nurses, and Group Leaders who work with Cancer patients and families.
Description: This workshop enables participants who work with cancer patients and their families to develop group facilitation skills. The focus is on aspects of group dynamics.

Helping Girls Grow
Target Audience: Girl Scout Leaders throughout the state of Georgia
Description: This series of statewide programs for girl scout leaders enables volunteers to learn how to assess group developmental growth, techniques for generating ideas with the groups (Driekurs method of encouragement), and basic group management skills pertaining to adolescents.

Sports for the Cerebral Palsied
Target Audience: Therapeutic recreators, Adaptive Physical Educators, physical therapists and volunteers
Description: Participants learn to design and implement sports programs for the cerebral palsied. Instruction includes identification of needs, selection of equipment, and development of progressions of activities and programs which involves the cerebral palsied in sporting activities with therapeutic value.
Programs differ each year based on expressed needs from the field of volunteerism and from the specific professions in relation to the involvement of volunteers. Continuing Education Credits are offered based on contact hours.

USING VOLUNTEERS IN YOUR AGENCY
US/HHS - National Clearinghouse for Health Information
PO Box 2345
Rockville, MD 20852
TEL: 301-443-2403
Credit: Certificate
Sponsor: US/HHS - Department of Health & Human Services
Contact: Host Agency Training Coordinator
Description: This eight-hour training program was developed by the National Clearinghouse for Alcohol Information to assist the service professional who is currently or will be the volunteer coordinator in his/her agency, or the staff person who is responsible for determining the feasibility of establishing a volunteer program. It is designed to increase the number of volunteer programs in alcohol service delivery agencies and to upgrade those which already exist. The program:

- Explores the pros and cons of volunteer utilization in alcohol service agencies, principles of effective program development, and a systematic process for planning, implementing, and maintaining a program.
- Provides an opportunity for participant analysis of agency readiness to begin program planning, and identification of initiation of initial program developmental tasks.
- Relies on group discussion and problem solving, sound filmstrip presentations, individual paper-and-pencil task assignments.
- Requires a trainer with experience in planning and management of volunteer programs and expertise in group dynamics, management of training events, and use of audiovisual equipment (if such a person is not available in the agency, a resource person with that experience should be employed).
- Includes the Volunteer Program Development Guide, a participant take-home book and primary trainer resource; a Trainer Manual, which includes masters for handouts, overhead transparencies, and evaluation instruments; trainer Session Outline Cards; and two filmstrips.

The training program is designed in four sessions ranging from two-and-a-half hours in length. The content can be modified or adapted to meet local training needs.

TRAINING/CONFERENCES/TEACHING: CHILDREN/YOUTH

NATIONAL/STATE ORGANIZATIONS

CENTER FOR EARLY ADOLESCENCE
University of North Carolina
Suite 228
Carr Mill Mall
Chapel Hill, NC 27510
TEL: 919-966-1148
Objectives: To provide information, training and consultation to agencies and individuals who have an impact on the lives of 10- to 15-year-olds; to build a network of professionals and volunteers who work with this age group.
Services: Provides a variety of services for educators, health professionals, program planners, youth workers, the clergy, and others who work with this age group and their families; fields over 200 requests for information per month and publishes over 40 books, training materials, and other resources, including the *Middle Grades Assessment Program* designed to help school systems assess the effectiveness of their schools for this early adolescent age group; produces for families *Living with 10- to 15-year-olds: A Parent Education Curriculum* and for youth-service organizations and training staff, *Planning Programs for Young Adolescents* to assist in conducting self-assessment and planning new or improving existing programs; continually updates and develops new curricula to help schools and community agencies improve literacy skills of young adolescents; conducts training-for-trainers workshops in these curricula throughout the year.
[The Center for Early Adolescence of the University of North Carolina at Chapel Hill is the first and only center in the nation dedicated exclusively to improving the healthy growth and development of 10- to 15-year-olds.]
Contact: Peter C. Scales, Ph.D.
Publications: Understanding Adolescence; Adolescent Literacy/What Works
Founded: 1979

TRAINING PROGRAMS

COMMUNITY SERVICE
Shoreham-Wading Middle School
Randall Road
Shoreham, NY 11786
TEL: 516-929-8500
Sponsor: Shoreham-Wading School District
Contact: Winifred Pardo
Description: About 200 middle school volunteers in Shoreham, New York, exercise the option offered by their school to learn about volunteerism and perform community service as part of their curriculum. Some of the young adolescents are mainstreamed handicapped students. The course, Community Service, was initiated in 1973 by the principal and backed by the district. It is a ten-week unit of study in the school's social studies curriculum, which includes:
- an advisory technique which sets aside the first period of every school day for small groups of students to meet with one adult advisor. After logistical business is discussed, there is a reading period, and than an opportunity to discuss personal thoughts and feelings. The advisor serves as a friend, counselor and advocate. The school uses this technique to bridge the transition by the young adolescents from the need for adult supervision and counsel to a sense of personal responsibility for their actions;
- one hour of work each week at a field site;
- classroom work revolving around each project;
- orientation sessions which include speakers, films, and discussions; reading; journals and other writing;
- planning for work at the field sites; and
- evaluation.

The primary focus in the classroom is learning the "caring" functions, learning about the groups and ages served, learning cross-age teaching, how to plan, and how to take on responsibililty. Depending on class size, one or two classes participate at a time. Several groups are served on a regular basis:
- children in neighboring day care centers;
- nursery schools;
- Head Starts
- district kindergartens;
- Story Hours at the public library;
- handicapped children at nearby hospitals and special education sites;
- elderly residents of the community;
- elementary schools where volunteers team up with younger students to lead a variety of learning activities.

Many other service opportunites are offered during the term of the course, including: hosting young or handicapped children and the elderly at the Middle School and its farm; taking puppet shows, the band, or the chorus into the community; running a Thanksgiving Food Drive for migrant farm workers, etc.
The school has found that the mainstreamed handicapped volunteers participate very successfully in the course and that the experience enhances their self-esteem. In a study about these students, the researcher noted, "The similarities between the handicapped and the rest of the student population are emphasized while the differences are minimized."
Although young adolescents usually prefer short-term commitments, they are very enthusiastic about the Community Service course. Comments range from, "It's better going out and getting a real life experience" to "It makes me feel good all over."
Founded: 1973

FIRST ANNUAL SOVIET-AMERICAN YOUTH SUMMIT
Youth Ambassadors of America
c/o St. Stephens School
1000 St. Stephens Road
Alexandria, VA 22304
TEL: 703-751-2700

Credit: Inquire
Sponsor: St. Stephens School
Contact: Monica McGoldrick
Description: For three days in June 1989, 30 Soviet and 45 U.S. students between 13 and 18 years old debated the greenhouse effect, air pollution, free speech, crack cocaine and a myriad of other topics looking for ways to "make the world a safer and healthier place."
Sponsored by Youth Ambassadors of America, a nonprofit organization, and hosted by St. Stephens School in Alexandria, the summit is the third of its kind and the first in the United States. Both earlier youth summits were held in Moscow.
Faced at first with a language barrier, the youth soon made use of the resources available to them to overcome this problem. Between finding words in the cross-language dictionary, using hand gestures, drawing pictures and speaking through interpreters, the students overcame the communication obstacles and went on to tackle global issues.
Preliminary proposals were presented to Senator Claiborne Pell, Chairman of the Senate Foreign Relations Committee, Senator Mark Hatfield and Senator Dennis DeConcini and included ways to organize a student grassroots movement. Among the suggestions presented by the youth were:
- Enlist students from around the world to write letters to world leaders and the media "so they understand what needs to be done."
- Develop and operate a youth radio show on human rights to be transmitted in the United States and the Soviet Union.
- Address global warming, air pollution and management of resources as the main problems.
- Encourage environmental education by setting up billboards, distributing pamphlets and demanding ecology classes in schools.
- Bring the problems to all of the people - not just one country.
- Realize that the summit is "just in time" - the relations between our countries are becoming better, and this can make them even better.

For several days the students listened to and interviewed speakers from the Environmental Protection Agency, Greenpeace, homeless shelters and drug abuse centers, and a Chinese student to help them formulate their action plans.
The final day was reserved for meeting with congressional leaders to present their "Plan of Action" resolution. Unlike the Soviet students who had to compete in essay contests to participate in the summit, American youth had only to "show interest in the program."
Parents of some students were involved in organizations relative to the summit, and this background often surfaced. One student whose father was involved with EarthSave, an environmental organization, pointed out that "growing grain to make clean-burning alcohol fuels to run cars" would be great, "but it's very impractical for us." The youth emphasized that although "the things we can do may be smaller than we would like, it's a start." One youth found agreement among the others when he said, "[The Summit] makes me feel 'responsible.'" Immediately following this third summit, plans for number four were underway.
Founded: 1985

GET AWAY CLEAN
Carkhuff Institute of Human Technology
1376 Kirby Road
McLean, VA 22101
TEL: 301-899-6564 (MD)
Credit: College Credit
Sponsor: Carkhuff Institute of Human Technology
Contact: George Logan-El
Description: Get Away Clean is a course at the Alexandria campus of Northern Virginia Community College. This training program is designed to help teens and pre-teens deal with negative

peer pressure, and go on to serve as a support group for others affected by such pressure. In addition, students in the class are trained to be trainers of other teens and younger students in the skills that they have learned at the college. In spite of the young ages of students, they are given college credit for participating in the class.

The course was developed by the *Carkhuff Institute of Human Technology* in response to a group of students who identified peer pressure as the number one problem facing them. Training is divided into three levels:

- **Survival** - At the survival level, students explore different responses to negative peer pressure and compare the consequences of responding positively as opposed to negatively.
- **Relating** - At the relating level, students practice communication skills and different ways to relate to adults, children and peers.
- **Growth** - At the growth level, students learn the nurturing of moral skills so that they can facilitate other students' self-exploration.

The junior and senior high students work with elementary students to teach them the survival and helping skills necessary to turn negative peer pressure into positive. The older students also help school counselors run workshops for younger students four times a week at different recreation centers. Students enact real-life situations involving peer pressure to use drugs, shoplift, skip school, etc.

Students who have experienced the results of negative peer pressure themselves - drug abuse, poor academic or discipline records - are not excluded from the program. The results hoped for in these cases became a reality when the troubled students related how much the course had helped them. One stated, "Before I got involved, I was out of touch with people... when we interact with others, we learn so much from each other."

GOVERNORS' SCHOOL
SEE GOVERNORS' OFFICES ON VOLUNTEERISM: WASHINGTON

SEVENTH GRADE SOCIAL PROBLEMS COURSE
SEE LEADERSHIP DEVELOPMENT/BOARDS: CHILDREN/YOUTH

TENNESSEE VOLUNTEERS FOR CHILDREN CONFERENCE
Metropolitan Council of Directors of Volunteers
PO Box 120471
Nashville, TN 37212
TEL: 615-373-4599
Credit: Inquire
Sponsor: Tennessee Children's Services Commission
Contact: Lannie Richardson
Description: This special project of the Tennessee Children's Services Commission is designed to provide a forum for those who work with and for the children of Tennessee. National and local experts are enlisted to serve as presenters and workshop leaders. Following a keynote address by Ivan Scheier, numerous workshops are conducted with the variety ranging from management areas such as budgets and fundraising to areas that consider special groups such as the handicapped and juvenile probationers.
Workshop topics include:
- Basic Overview of Volunteer Services
- Volunteering in Juvenile Justice Systems
- Using Volunteers in Childcare Programs
- Community Service: An Alternative for Youth
- Children in Adult Jails: The Impact of Voluntary Action
- Assessment of Needs and Resources for Children in the Communities
- Fundraising From the Private Sector

- Advocacy Skill Building on Behalf of Handicapped Children
- Youth Services in the 80s: An Overview
- Understanding Family Systems: The Key to the Child
- Juvenile Court Probation Volunteer Program
- Role of the Budget in Children's Services
- Developing an Interfaith Coalition for Children
- Preparing Excellent Parents: Practical Ways to Help

Time and space for informal discussion with the presenters, idea exchange among participants, and roundtable sessions provide additional benefits to all.

VOLUNTARISM: CONFRONTATION AND OPPORTUNITY*
National Board of YMCAs
291 Broadway
New York, NY 10007
TEL: 212-374-2000
Credit: Inquire
Sponsor: National Board of YMCAs
Contact: Dr. Clifford M. Carey or Dr. James M. Hardy
Description: Three years after adopting a five-year operating goal calling for "mobilizing and utilizing greater numbers of volunteers," the National Board found that very little had been done toward reaching that goal. Thus, an intensive one-day seminar was developed to bring together key leaders and volunteers in the volunteer field for a "knowledge-pooling, action-deriving" session to help the YMCA assess and develop their volunteer efforts. The underlying strategy is to combine the resources of local, regional and national operating experience with:

- an analysis of the historical experience of the Y with volunteers and professional-volunteer relations;
- a review of the futurists' analysis of social trends relevant to volunteerism; and
- a reviewing of innovative approaches to volunteerism in other sectors of the community.

The overall purpose of the seminar is to analyze the dynamics of volunteerism in the society today and in the future with the hope that from this examination will flow derivations and implications for the YMCA nationally, regionally and locally. The model seminar, which has provided stimulus and a working resource for similar meetings around the country, includes the following topics:

Perspectives from Organizational History - A probe into an organization's history as it relates to volunteerism can provide a rationale for change, and objectivity in coping with the present, considering alternatives, and future planning. Such a study may include: 1) approach to community needs; 2) program operations; 3) long-range planning; 4) current financial operations; 5) community and public relations; 6) corporate and legal issues; 7) social action, and other areas pertinent to a particular organization.

Some Current Voluntarism Issues and Confrontations - Challenges continually emerge that reflect growing pressures for change from within and from outside of an organization. In the Y, these were found to be:

- The Interest in Management brought about by increase in the organization's size and scope focuses training activities on managerial functions, resulting in unresolved tensions among lay leaders and staff.
- The Pressure for Improved Staff Work from volunteers so that they can become more responsive and influential in their programs.
- The Leadership Squeeze brought about by the increasing demands on the time of key volunteers by their occupations, and the growing competition for volunteer leadership among organizations.
- Outmoded Structures geared to problems that no longer exist, thereby placing an additional burden on the lay reader.
- Changing Identification and Loyalty based on the Association's potential for continuity in disciplines central to

an individual's training.
- Increased Complexity in Program Methods requiring highly skilled leadership and the application of relatively new methods.

Societal Trends and Organizational Potentials - This session is based on the premise that elements of any projection for the future are already happening in some form somewhere in the USA, and that such futuristic practices may emerge in discussions within the seminar group.

Strategies and Action Steps - In this final session of the seminar, participants are asked to formulate recommendations for the National Board, and suggested the following:
- Formulate proposals for the National Board.
- Retrieve information on the present use of volunteers.
- Improve the reporting procedures and accuracy of statistics for volunteers.
- Strengthen the training resources for volunteerism.
- Prepare a written report of this seminar on volunteerism.
- Test the feasibility of other suggested actions.

VOLUNTEER & COMMUNITY PARTNERSHIPS INSTITUTE
US/HHS - Administration for Children, Youth and Families
200 Independence Avenue, SW
Washington, DC 20201
TEL: 202-245-0572
Sponsor: US/HHS - Department of Health & Human Services
Description: This national conference focused on volunteer management to demonstrate the increasingly important role of the community volunteer in Head Start programs across the country. It also launched a partnership between the *Head Start Bureau* of the *U.S. Department of Health & Human Services* and the *Association for Volunteer Administration (AVA)*, a national organization that provides *Certification and Volunteer Management Training* nationwide. Participants interested in Certification were required to:
- Participate in a Certification Workshop;
- Attend an overview of the Certification process;
- Consult individually with AVA to provide confirmation of both interest and experience.

Forty participants were selected to attend a special volunteer management training event.

A challenge to the AVA Certification Process was presented by eight Head Start staff from Puerto Rico who attended the training and asked if they could submit their portfolios in Spanish. Bilingual members were called upon to assess these portfolios. The experience took AVA one step closer to translating all of its materials into Spanish - and meeting its goal of attaining cultural diversity in training.

YOUNG LEADERS CONFERENCE
United Way of America
701 North Fairfax Street
Alexandria, VA 22314-2045
TEL: 703-836-7100
Credit: Inquire
Contact: Youth Programs Coordinator
Description: This annual workshop provides a challenge to hundreds of young people from around the country who pride themselves in taking an active role in the future of their communities. The 1987 meeting produced a challenge by 400 conferees to themselves and other youth to address and work to solve the many complex issues facing society.

The document called for proper leadership, structure, and challenge to young people, who will respond with "vigor, force, determination, and success." Commitment was made not only to immediate needs, but also to helping to "create a society where human dignity, mutual respect, justice, and equality belong to everyone." Goals listed to support the challenge include:

- Design and support effective, creative, and lasting youth-service programs;
- Develop, recognize, and respect youth leadership and involvement;
- Tap and channel the energy, creativity, and idealism of youth; and
- Meet the needs of all people and the challenge of United Way's Second Century.

A goal is to quadruple youth participation in working to meet community needs over the next five years.

INDIVIDUAL PROGRAM PROFILES

YOUTH SERVICES
SEE VOLUNTEERS: STUDENTS

TRAINING/CONFERENCES/TEACHING: CIVIC AFFAIRS

TRAINING PROGRAMS

ADVOCACY FOR ACTION: A NEW ROLE FOR VOLUNTEERS
Allegheny County Community College
1130 Perry Highway
Pittsburgh, PA 15237
TEL: 412-931-8500
Credit: Inquire
Sponsor: Allegheny County Community College
Contact: Sarah Jane Rehnborg
Description: This program, made possible by a grant from Title I of the Higher Education Act, provides a foundation for individuals or groups involved in volunteer advocacy activities. Beginning with a keynote address, "Yes, You Can Fight City Hall," presented by a City Council member, the program offers the following workshops:

Lobby for Change - This workshop addresses concerns which are of interest to advocates in general, with attention focused on techniques for effective lobbying, and the reading and interpretation of legislation.

The Citizen's Right to Information and Access to Records - This workshop reviews some of the legislation acts providing citizen access to information and records and explores the psychological barriers to asserting oneself as a citizen advocate; techniques for becoming more assertive are examined.

The Task Force: A Tool for Change - This workshop focuses on the many different functions of the task force - a vital tool for the citizen advocate - and explores ways to develop and work with a task force.

Lobbying and Legislation in Developmental Disabilities - In this session a panel presents effective methods and procedures for obtaining legislation to benefit the needs of the developmentally disabled - exploring both the professional and the volunteer perspective for the lobbying process and legislative change.

Structures of Government and Bureaucracy - This workshop focuses on the overall process of policy development from legislation to implementation with particular attention on how a law is translated into a government program; special emphasis is placed on the effects of citizen involvement on all stages of the policy development process.

In the course of the program a United States Representative provides insight through a presentation, "Advocates and

Legislators in Partnership," into the cooperative possibilities between citizen groups and government.

The half-day workshops are repeated in the afternoon session followed by a wrap-up allowing participants to informally gather and share ideas.

BUILDING MOMENTUM FOR A RESPONSIVE AMERICA
Volunteer Leaders Conference
United Way of America
701 North Fairfax Street
Alexandria, VA 22314-2045
TEL: 703-836-7100
Credit: Inquire
Sponsor: United Way of America
Contact: Conference Coordinator
Description: This conference continues the theme, Second Century Initiatives, launched by the 1987 conference. In that first conference of the United Way's second century, goals were to double volunteers and financial resources. Having reached those goals, the United Way has set the theme for this conference as expanding formulas for success. Its purpose is to find out what works, how it works, and why.

In a special full-day symposium, volunteers are matched with other volunteers from similar communities - similar in size, demographics, and economic makeup. They share ideas, examine approaches to problems, and explore critical issues.

Another full day is devoted to how-to workshops that span a wide range of topics, including:
- Resource Development
- Fund Distribution
- Year-Round Communications
- Community Problem-Solving
- Marketing
- Volunteers
- Government Relations
- Workplace Presence
- Strategic Planning
- Youth Involvement
- Gifts in Kind
- United Way State Organizations
- Inclusiveness

The conference works throughout the year to develop a theme for the annual conference that will provide the most benefit for the dedicated volunteer leaders.

CIVIC PARTNERSHIP: INITIATIVE, INNOVATION*
Citizens Forum on Self-Government
National Municipal League
55 West 44th Street
New York, NY 10036
TEL: 212-730-7930
TOLL FREE: 800-223-6004
Credit: Inquire
Sponsor: Citizens Forum on Self-Government
Contact: William G. Anderson, Jr.
Description: Sponsored each year by the Citizens Forum on Self-Government of the National Municipal League, this is the 89th National Conference on public/private partnership efforts. The Conference addresses the issues of its theme by holding sessions covering the following topics:
- An Examination of the Issues of Public/Private Partnerships
- A Close Inspection of the Problems and Opportunities That Local Public/Private Partnerships Face
- The Revitalization of a Community
- Strengthening Institutions of Self-Government
- A Presentation on a Successful Revitalization Effort Involving Leaders from Across the Nation

The Conference includes guided tours of a city's more notable public/private partnership undertakings (in November 1983, a

Baltimore tour). Ample time for open discussion and consultation with faculty is provided throughout the conference.

48 HOURS ON CAPITOL HILL
Nonprofit Mailers Federation
125 Michigan Avenue, NE
PO Box 239
Washington, DC 20017-1094
TEL: 202-944-4188
Credit: Inquire
Contact: Briefings Coordinator
Description: This program consists of issue briefings by legislative experts, followed by a planned visit to Capitol Hill. Highlights include a "get acquainted" reception, comprehensive briefings on a variety of issues, a congressional reception, a training session, a mass visitation to Capitol Hill, a debriefing session following Capitol Hill visits, and advice on how to prepare material to deliver to members of Congress. Preconference informational material, and invitations for participants to send to their Congress people inviting them to the reception, are provided.

GRADUATE PROGRAM IN PUBLIC POLICY AND CITIZEN PARTICIPATION
Tufts University
Department of Political Science
Medford, MA 02155
TEL: 617-628-5000
Credit: Master of Arts (M.A.)
Sponsor: Tufts University
Contact: Professor Jeffrey M. Berry
Description: Developed around the explosion in the number of citizen advocacy groups, and the countless federal, state and local programs that mandate citizen participation, this program hopes to provide a solid background in areas of public policy formulation, analysis and evaluation. In addition to learning general skills in administration and citizen advocacy, a specialization in one or more policy areas is developed. Curriculum for the two-year program is composed of required core courses, electives, a summer internship, a major research project. Electives can be taken in policy areas such as these:
- Housing and Community Development
- Nutrition Planning
- Environment and Energy
- Urban Justice
- Science and Technology
- Welfare
- Health Care
- Education

Core courses include citizen participation, public policy analysis, interest group theory, and research methods. In the summer between the first and second years, a full-time internship is required, which may be continued on a part-time basis during the second year. Writing of the M.A. thesis is done during the final semester, and may be the result of a group project under faculty supervision, or individual work.

Jointly sponsored by the Department of Political Science and the Graduate Department of Urban, Social and Environmental Policy, some of the program's courses are taken in existing graduate classes in the Departments of Sociology, Education, Nutrition, Education, etc. This provides opportunities for interaction with many others in these areas than would be possible in an isolated program.

Also on campus is the Lincoln Filene Center for Citizenship and Public Affairs, which conducts many activities and projects of interest to program students, such as conferences, workshops, training seminars, and continuing education in areas of citizen participation and public policy. The Center also publishes Citizen Participation newsmagazine. Many state and federal offices are in close proximity for contact with practitioners and for placement in summer internships.

Although no previous training in the area is required, a bachelor's degree and some evidence that the applicant is likely to achieve success are required for admission. Graduates are qualified for jobs in voluntary associations, interest groups, community development organizations, research institutions, business and industry, government, etc. Job placement in the program has been excellent.

PEACE CONFERENCE
Interfaith Justice and Peace Center
Lourdes College
6832 Convent Boulevard
Toledo, OH 43560
TEL: 419-885-3211
Sponsor: Lourdes College
Contact: Conference Coordinator
Description: Recognizing that there were no models to study or places to learn new techniques on peace promotion, the Interfaith Justice and Peace Center of Lourdes College in Toledo established a Peace Conference and other activities in 1980 to bring awareness to the community. Among the concerns addressed are hunger, juvenile violence, apartheid, refugees, racism, and nuclear weapon freezes.

One activity encourages the sponsoring of peace clubs in area high schools where students can study communication, national and global issues and begin to take some volunteer action. The Center maintains a roster of volunteer speakers both for the conferences and to work with the high schools.

One emphasis in this community awareness effort is on exploding the myth that the individual has little or no influence. Although the program does not advocate massive protests, per se, through volunteer speakers, printed materials, conferences, and small group interaction (clubs), it works to help people explore ways in which personal responsibility and action can resolve future conflict.
Founded: 1980

STUDY WAR NO MORE
Institute for Creative Conflict Management
Syracuse University
Syracuse, NY 13244
TEL: 315-443-1870
Sponsor: Syracuse University
Contact: Institute Director
Description: This summer course is part of a program at Syracuse University, created in 1970, that is dedicated to human dignity based on values of nonviolence, social justice, trust, and participative decision making. The course is open for credit and non-credit.

The umbrella course, which also includes the Campus Ministry Center, is an undergraduate major designed to study creative, peaceful ways of dealing with conflict. Trained volunteers are available throughout the program to help students find new and peaceful resolutions to problems.

The University also offers graduate degrees in the same field, along with three other higher education institutions across the country - University of Colorado, George Mason University in Virginia, and Notre Dame University. The assistance of volunteers is woven into each of the courses.

VISION, PLANNING & PARTNERSHIP IN NEIGHBORHOOD ORGANIZING
Neighborhoods USA
4643 Amesborough
Dayton, OH 45420
TEL: 513-222-2889
Credit: Inquire
Sponsor: Neighborhoods USA
Contact: William Littlejohn, President

Description: This conference brought together 440 people from across the U.S. to talk about organizing and revitalizing neighborhoods. Attendees included citizen activists, government officials, university professors, police officials and politicians. The keynote speaker set the tone of the meeting by addressing the dormant period from the late 1970s through the early 1980s and appealing to the group to develop a strategy to avoid such a gap in neighborhod activism in the future. Other areas discussed include:

- **Smaller Communities,** which have become part of a major "ripple effect" with problems happening years ago in major metropolitan areas cropping up due to residents' belief that they couldn't happen in small towns.
- **Involvement,** pointing up the frustration that can come from neighborhood organizing, but emphasizing that the price of not getting involved is "too high to pay."
- **Contradiction or "Mixed Signals" from Government,** discussing the neighborhood platforms of politicians which are contradicted when budgets for community programs are cut after elections.
- **Real Solutions (Beyond Federal Support),** emphasizing that neighborhoods must look to themselves and form working partnerships such as the relationship between local churches, neighborhoods, and police in a citizen coalition, Oakland Community Organizations, that brought together 2,000 people in 1988 to develop ways to deal with a crack cocaine epidemic.
- **Changing Laws,** as was accomplished by the Oakland group when more money for jails, and stiffer sentencing guidelines were needed, as well as a task force of police officers (40 were hired for this purpose) to shut down crack houses.
- **Leaning on Local Politicians,** which emphasizes the need to work with officials, outline and detail the critical issues, and involve them in the issue itself by asking them to offer their own recommendations, since they are more accustomed to dealing with physical problems (e.g., potholes) than the kind of investment needed to address families and social problems.
- **Leaving Things to the "Experts,"** which points out that there is no room for complaints when things go wrong if the individual doesn't take responsibility for the governance of his/her own community.
- **What You Represent Besides Your Neighborhood,** which asks attendees to look beyond the neighborhood to the differences that can be made in gaining political power, and making major differences in "everything from City Council elections to the planning process."
- **After Getting the Power,** which emphasizes the danger of simply becoming "naysayers" without acting on the vision that was developed at the outset, and points out the many instances where citizens greatly affected development through halting projects or forcing concessions from developers.

Some dramatic cases were described, such as Seattle's recent history of neighborhood successes, ranging from the fight to save Lake Union in the 1960s to preserving Pike Place Market in the 1970s and the passage in 1989 of the Citizens' Alternative Plan to control downtown growth. According to the presenter, the trick in getting community support is to describe the activity according to the interests of the majority. The "vision" in Seattle's effort was changed from "evicting houseboat owners" (of no interest) to "saving Lake Union for all residents and the city" (which was the same vision, but worked better in garnering support).

The message of the conference, Vision, Planning and Partnership, was evident throughout the sessions. According to one attendee, "This conference has removed a lot of the isolation you feel as a volunteer in the neighborhoods."
Publications: NUSA Conference Report

TRAINING/CONFERENCES/TEACHING: COMMUNICATIONS & PR

TRAINING PROGRAMS

COMMUNICATIONS WORKSHOP/PERSPECTIVES FOR VOLUNTEERS
Phoenix Memorial Hospital
1201 South Seventh Avenue
Phoenix, AZ 85007
TEL: 602-258-5111/Ext. 212
Credit: Inquire
Sponsor: Phoenix Memorial Hospital Auxiliary
Contact: Patricia Drake
Description: Recognizing a need for specific communications training for the hospital's volunteers, the Director of Volunteer Services presented a proposal to the Crisis Communications Class at Arizona State University for assistance. The objectives of the proposal were:
- To assess needs for specific communication skills involving volunteers in a hospital setting.
- To provide appropriate training in necessary skills for volunteers: assertiveness and sensitivity training; listening techniques; body language; human relations; crisis and special needs situations.
- To evaluate success of training procedures through on-the-job observation and the use of an evaluation form.

Of the students who volunteered to make this their communications project in the community, five are chosen to work with the Director of Volunteer Services on methodology and implementation of the project.

For step one, the needs assessment, students determine which volunteer areas each will observe, aiming for each area - but not each volunteer - to be observed at least twice. The workshop content is geared to the areas of greatest need. The needs assessment lasts five weeks. The actual workshop covers various areas of communications and understanding of people, including:
- team-building exercises
- non-verbal communication
- revealing body behavior
- self-esteem and person-non-person treatment
- Sheldon Types (classifying various types of personalities)

Several teaching methods are employed from pencil and paper exercises and role-playing to general discussions and lectures. Handouts are provided for use in the workshops and later on the job. Another auxiliary and its Volunteer Department's paid staff participates in the workshop - increasing benefits to all concerned, due to the broader base for sharing and learning.

Post-Conference Evaluation: The positive attitude and concern for volunteers generated by the students during the observation phase provided, in itself, an enriching experience for volunteers in that it emphasized the importance of their positions, and allowed them the opportunity to "teach" someone about their work. With such a base, the success that was realized by the workshop was expected and enjoyed.

GROWING WITH PUBLIC RELATIONS*
Volunteer Jacksonville
1600 Prudential Drive
Jacksonville, FL 32207
TEL: 904-398-7777
Credit: Inquire
Sponsor: Florida Public Relations Association/Jacksonville; Volunteer Jacksonville
Contact: Pepi Dunay

Description: With cosponsorship including a public relations association, this one-day workshop is designed to help leaders of nonprofit organizations sharpen their communication skills in their efforts to build and improve their organizations. It asks unspoken questions to the president, publicity chairperson, or other individual responsible for public relations such as "What is your public relations IQ?" "Can you target your audience, write a proposal, plan a total public relations program?" "Can you put on a special event?" "Need to produce a newsletter for your group?" "Where do you start?" Following a keynote session led by a leader in the public relations field, workshops are conducted on the following specific topics:
- **Basics of Newsletter Production:** design, concept, composition, layout.
- **Targeting Public Relations:** identifying audiences, advance planning, careful budgeting, marketing tools.
- **Special Events:** planning, timetables, general techniques.
- **Writing Proposals:** putting down in writing what you have to "sell," learning effective techniques for preparing proposals, when to use the telephone versus personal appearance presentations.
- **Planning a Total PR Program:** setting objectives consistent with the organization's mission, timetables, knowing the audience and public relations media.
- **Promoting a Consistent Image:** discussing image, what it is, and why it is important to your organization, the kinds of support you need from inside and outside your organization, problem sharing.
- **Getting to Know Your Local Media:** the press - its relationship to public relations.

In addition, a panel for questions consists of managing editors of two local newspapers, public service directors from two television channels, and a community planning official from the area cablevision network. A general session involving all participants for an overview concludes the program.

MARKETING FOR VOLUNTARY SERVICE ORGANIZATIONS
Virginia Division of Volunteerism
825 East Broad Street
Richmond, VA 23219
TEL: 804-786-1431
Credit: One CEU
Sponsor: Virginia Commonwealth University; Virginia Division of Volunteerism
Contact: Neil Karn
Description: This workshop is designed for those who want to improve, change, or present for the first time the agency or organization's image within the community. Primary topics are:
- Marketing in Voluntary Service Organizations (VSOs)
- Identification of Volunteers
- Marketing Audit for VSOs
- Techniques of Image Development
- Promoting the VSO

Subtopics include:
1. the utilization of marketing to stimulate desired transactions between the VSOs and their public;
2. target market analysis to develop market strategies for VSO;
3. marketing research approaches to develop better decision-making by the VSO staffs;
4. the role of image and techniques for developing a VSO image;
5. developing marketing objectives for the VSO; and
6. how to get the most out of the VSO image.

Most VCU-sponsored workshops are limited to 30 participants.

MEDIA RELATIONS FOR NONPROFIT AND VOLUNTEER ORGANIZATIONS
Chicago City-Wide College
Adult/Continuing Education
30 East Lake Street
Chicago, IL 60601
TEL: 312-782-6830 (College); 217-782-6830 (Gov. Off.)
Credit: CEUs
Sponsor: Governor's Office on Volunteerism/IL; Public Service Institute; Chicago City-Wide College
Contact: Workshop Coordinator (College); Julia Schopick (Governor's Office)
Description: With a presenter who has initiated several media campaigns, this event focuses on helping groups obtain media coverage. It is designed for individuals wanting to learn new techniques for gaining media coverage for nonprofit volunteer and community organizations. Participants learn how to create a media campaign "from start to finish," with emphasis on the following skills:
- How to get your group's representatives on talk shows.
- How to get stories about your organization in print.
- How to create and place public service announcements that the stations will want to air.
- How to get your point across in the media using innovative methods.

Participants have an opportunity to talk with radio and television professionals (both on-air and behind-the-scenes) and an associate editor for a leading Chicago-area newspaper chain.
The sessions are held over a period of five weeks at the College.

PUBLIC RELATIONS ON A SHOESTRING*
Public Relations Society of America
1258 North Highland Avenue
Suite 102
Los Angeles, CA 90038
TEL: 213-469-9490
Credit: Inquire
Sponsor: Occidental Life Insurance Companies
Contact: Laura Tondreault, Chair, Community Service Committee
Description: This program is designed for civic and community groups or persons new to the public relations field. Using the RACE formula for public relations (Research, Action, Communication, and Evaluation), the program takes a close look at the practice of public relations and provides information needed to conduct an organization's public relations program. It is designed to be flexible so that new publicity persons for volunteer organizations can benefit as well as the seasoned public relations professional. The program covers:
- How to insure your success through research.
- Tips on how to beat the high cost of printing.
- How to tell your organization's story to the media.
- How to find sources for just about anything.
- Evaluating and determining your program's success.

Specific subjects by presenters:
- "Building Blocks to Success"
- "You Can Do It Inexpensively"
- "Getting the Message Out"
- "How Do You Know You've Hit the Target"

A question/answer wrap-up and informal idea-sharing opportunities through the session round out the program.
"Public Relations on a Shoestring" is provided as a public service by the Los Angeles Chapter of the Public Relations Society of America.
Assistance was provided by Sears Roebuck and Company, Blue Cross of Southern California, General Communication Company of America, Hospital Council of Southern California, Pomona Valley Hospital, Occidental Life Insurance Company, Goodwill Industries of Southern California, St. Joseph Medical Center, Macdonald Media Services, Monterey Park Progress, KNX-AM

Radio, Tellem Communications, Whitman College Center of Mexican Affairs, St. Francis Hospital, and others.

PUBLICITY WORKSHOP
SEE COMMUNICATIONS & PUBLIC RELATIONS

TRAINING/CONFERENCES/TEACHING: COMMUNITY SERVICES

TRAINING PROGRAMS

CITIZEN INVOLVEMENT TRAINING PROJECT (CITP)
University of Massachusetts
Amherst, MA 01003
TEL: 413-545-0111
Credit: CEUs
Sponsor: University of Massachusetts
Contact: Dr. David Magnani
Description: Drawing on faculty from people who have worked for social change from the grassroots level to federal and state agencies, this program is designed to adapt to fit the specific needs of the individual. Areas represented by faculty experience include neighborhood organizing, direct action groups, Governor's commissions, education activities, etc. Participants represent diverse groups, including those dealing with consumer advocacy, environmental issues, housing, health promotion/education, political advocacy, advocacy for the handicapped, women's issues, and Native American rights, ranging from citizen boards to grassroots organizations. Help is provided in basic issues such as: where the money is and how too get it, how to win issues, how to hold elected officials accountable, who and what the average citizen is up against, internal group problems and conflicts among members, how to deal with the press, planning, etc. Some specifics:
- **Organizing** - The various stages or organizing (defining the problem, building membership and resources, developing a structure, determining strategy, building a coalition, taking action, winning victories); the various approaches to and methods of organizing; consciousness raising for platforms and promises; the organizer as a person; personal and political agendas.
- **Fund-Raising** - How to apply for grants; writing proposals; interviewing strategies for dealing with funding sources and ways to approach specific foundations; how to find out where the funds are; how to prepare a budget; alternative methods of fund raising; dividing responsibilities and tasks among group members; budget monitoring, and preparing financial statements.
- **Using the Media** - Writing press releases; producing public service announcements; public rights to access and traditional methods of using the press; alternative ways of getting information to the public; design, production, and layout of printed materials; using video for social change.
- **Program Planning** - Assessing community needs and member interests; goal-setting, developing program options, defining and prioritizing objectives, and contingency planning; setting tasks and responsibilities; timelining and evaluation.
- **Training of Trainers** - How adults learn; how to identify training and organizational needs; how and when to design workshops; when to and when not to bring in outside trainers; how to develop training materials; how to use training as an organizing strategy; how to get members to take responsibility; how to encourage self-directed learning; how to develop a plan for building group effectiveness.
- **Internal Group Processes** - Resolving conflicts,

decision-making methods, collaborative versus hierarchical structure (problems and alternatives); intergroup communication, building versus blocking, board/staff interaction; using all group members effectively; dealing with staff burn-out; empowering individuals and collective responsibility of group members.

● **Bilingual Training** - The staff includes two bilingual trainers who are available to work with non-English-speaking groups in workshops and consultation on any of the above topics.

Prior to assisting any organization, a two-hour consultation/diagnostic session is held with CITP staff and members of the individual group. In some cases CITP assists the group in developing a workshop which the group itself administers; in other cases CITP refers the group to other training resources which are closer to the group's needs. Such resources are drawn from CITP's extensive library, which can be used by group members themselves before or after consultation.

In all cases, the primary concern of CITP is to effect the best possible training program from all resources on hand for the inquiring group.

COMMON GROUND, COMMON GOOD
Campus Outreach Opportunity League (COOL)
386 McNeal Hall
University of Minnesota
St. Paul, MN 55108-1011
TEL: 612-624-3018 (UM) ; 213-206-5523 (UCLA)
Joint sponsor for this conference is the Community Resource Center of the University of California at Los Angeles (UCLA), Los Angeles, CA 90024-1377 (phone number above)
Credit: Inquire
Sponsor: COOL
Contact: Conference Coordinator at either University
Description: COOL conferences work in the host community (Into the Streets) as much as possible (1990, Los Angeles). Participants go into the streets visiting and working with public schools, meals programs, drug prevention centers, AIDS clinics, environmental sites and other agencies throughout the host area.

On campus at the host University, participants attend workshops on a range of issues, including such nuts and bolts topics as recruiting volunteers and developing effective training methods and evaluation; current topics such as service and the curriculum and racism; and discussion groups on the motivations for service and the challenges of diversity. Specifically, Into the Streets topics available for exploration include:

● AIDS
● Children and Youth
● Criminal Justice
● Disabled Persons
● Domestic Violence
● Education
● Environment
● Health Care
● Homelessness
● Hunger
● Literacy
● Mental Health
● Race Relations
● Refugees/Immigrants
● Senior Citizens
● Substance Abuse

In the Workshops session, a variety of issue, program and "nuts and bolts" workshops and discussions are designed to help strengthen community service on campuses. A Diversity Dialogue session enables participants to discuss diversity and community involvement with a panel of local and national speakers.

To enable networking, a session called Building the Movement brings together campus leaders from home regions and other areas to share ideas and program information. An Opportunities Fair presents exhibits from hundreds of campus, local and national organizations offering information on issues, summer jobs and service programs, internships, careers, etc. Conference papers as well as posters, T-shirts and other COOL items are made available at the Fair.

Benefit programs for COOL, such as the Listen to the Words 1990 concert in Los Angeles in 1990, are planned and presented by the host university. COOL is a national, nonprofit organization promoting student volunteerism which reaches 550 campuses across the country.

COMMUNITY ACTION TRAINING (CAT)
Georgetown University
PO Box 2297
Hoya Station
Washington, DC 20057
TEL: 202-625-4318
Credit: None
Sponsor: Office of Student Affairs
Contact: Georgetown University
Description: Begun more than ten years ago, the CAT seminars are conducted each semester to prepare students for interpersonal and intercultural barriers that they will face in the community. CAT seminars are organized by the District Action Coordinator, who is full-time advisor and trainer to the student-run volunteer organizations at Georgetown University.

Specific skills are learned in areas such as tutoring, listening, and counseling. Over 600 students participate annually in fifteen areas of service, including a crisis intervention hotline, tutoring, work in soup kitchens and free medical clinics with the homeless, as probation aides, and with the elderly, refugees, and D.C.'s Hispanic community. All volunteer service is without remuneration and not-for-credit.

All CAT activities are sponsored by the Office of Student Affairs. Trainers from various academic departments, as well as outside consultants, are utilized in the program. Further support comes from the university's Consultant Center, Campus Ministries, the athletic department and field house, the library, the office of Career Planning and Placement (which cosponsors a biannual seminar on possible social service careers for interested volunteers), and others.

Evaluation, both written and oral, is conducted continually by the District Action Coordinator.

COMMUNITY DEVELOPMENT, NEIGHBORHOOD SELF-SUFFICIENCY AND VOLUNTEERISM/VOLUNTEER PROGRAM MANAGEMENT
University of Oregon
Planning, Public Policy, Management
Eugene, OR 97403
TEL: 503-686-3817
Credit: Inquire
Sponsor: University of Oregon, Department of Planning, Public Policy and Management
Contact: Dr. Bryan T. Downes
Description: Courses in Community Development, Resources for Nonprofits, Community Economic Development, Volunteerism and Volunteer Program Management are offered on a regular basis by the Department of Planning, Public Policy and Management, University of Oregon. Technical assistance and consultation are available in conjunction with the courses or as a separate activity through the faculty and student interns. Although course formats change from year to year, examples of past courses include:
Volunteerism - a course emphasizing the practical aspects of developing and maintaining effective volunteer programs for those wishing to explore career opportunities in volunteerism, and for those interested in increasing understanding and skill in their own volunteer activities. Topics covered:
● Roles of volunteers and volunteer settings

- Recruiting, publicity and public relations
- Screening, placement and termination
- Orientation and training
- Staff-volunteer relationships
- Motivation, incentive and support
- Organization and administration
- Supervision, finance, record keeping
- Boards and committees
- Evaluation

Orientation Workshop for Volunteers to Aging Residents - a course designed to answer citizens' questions on volunteering in nursing homes, how much is expected of the volunteer, what opportunities and changes have arisen in recent years, and what new skills and knowledge the volunteer can acquire while performing this community service. Topics covered include:

- Exploring the volunteer role
- The context of volunteering: the volunteer/resident/staff
- Volunteer skills
- Volunteers/administrators: share expectations; combine skills
- Group activities: Volunteer Orientation Aide

HOME TOWN AWARDS
SEE GOVERNORS' OFFICES ON VOLUNTEERISM:
ILLINOIS

TRAINING/CONFERENCES/TEACHING: CRIME PREVENTION

TRAINING PROGRAMS

FORGING PARTNERSHIPS*
National Association of Volunteers in Criminal Justice
PO Box 6365
University, AL 35486-6365
TEL: 205-348-6738
Credit: CEUs; AVA Certification (partial fulfillment); academic credit through University of Alabama; Alabama Board of Social Work Seminars CEUs; and/or Alabama Department of Youth In-service Credit
Sponsor: National Association of Volunteers in Criminal Justice
Contact: David Gooch
Description: Designed as a working conference, the program features workshops, discussions, idea exchanges, speeches and informal gatherings for volunteer managers, volunteer administrators, agency administrators and judges, line staff who work with volunteers, and others interested in crime prevention. Specific topics include:
Workshop Session I:
- Cost and Payoffs for Agencies Using Volunteers
- What's It Like in Prison?
- Victim/Witness Assistance
- Volunteers: To Support or Supplant?
Workshop Session II:
- Private Sector Involvement
- Mobilizing and Maintaining Christian Church Volunteer Resources for In-Prison and After Care Ministry
- Working Effectively with Boards
Workshop Session III:
- Volunteers: Have You Had Your Check-Up Lately?
- Certification: Who Needs It? Who Owns It?
- The Line Staff as a Supervisor of Volunteers
Workshop Session IV:
- Grant-Writing I
- Marketing Your Volunteer Program

- Getting Along with Agency Personnel
- Alternatives to Secure Detention
- Volunteer Responses to Rural Crime
- Volunteers and Cops
Workshop Session V:
- Public Speaking/Platform Skills
- Grant-Writing II
- Working with Today's Adolescent
- Is Theology Important to a Christian Volunteer Counselor?
This conference aims through the above sessions to lead participants to new ways of forging partnerships between the private sector and public agencies, neighborhoods and law enforcers, citizen volunteers and paid professionals, voluntary organizations and criminal justice systems, and other potential teams that can accomplish more by working together than separately; publishes conference proceedings for wider exposure to the ideas generated at the conference.

FORUM 90: BACKWARD GLANCES... FORWARD VISIONS
Volunteers in Prevention, Probation, Prisons
527 North Main Street
Royal Oak, MI 48067
TEL: 313-398-8550
Credit: Inquire
Sponsor: International Association of Justice Volunteerism
Contact: Judge Keith J. Leenhouts, President
Description: To begin the Forum, participants were given a backward glance at the histories of its two sponsors, the International Association of Justice Volunteerism (IAJV) and Volunteers in Prevention, Probation, and Prisons (VIP), which took them over a span of twenty years of the justice volunteer movement with the presidents of the two organizations as presenters. This was followed by a presentation by Kids on the Block, a nonprofit group that addresses social issues through puppetry.
The keynote presentation, Looking Ahead Together, provided conferees with an opportunity to participate in specially designed Table Topic Groups, which include leaders from adult community programs, juvenile community programs, probation/parole offices, law enforcement divisions, courts, jails, prisons, and juvenile institutions. The networking that takes place through Table Topic Groups is considered one of the most important aspects of the Forum. The forum workshops were divided into five series:
Workshop Series I
- *101 - Volunteers in Law Enforcement* - builds on the English theme that contends "people are the police and the police are the people," which emphasizes that police cannot do it alone; challenges participants to offer suggestions on where citizens fit into modern law enforcement - from serving as policy-makers to serving in a non-sworn capacity.
- *102 - Networking & the Religious Volunteer* - presents a participatory workshop in which members practice networking and examine ways to access community religious resources; features small working groups for developing case studies, and presents a church networking model.
- *103 - Fun & Games for Changing Lives* - discusses therapeutic recreational programs in prisons for severely handicapped inmates in mental health programs, where volunteers provide programs in drama, art, etc.; reports on results that have been termed "life-changing," citing award-winning programs such as the one in the Georgia prison system.
- *104 - So You Want to Become an Author? or Public Speaker? or Become a Certified Volunteer Manager?* - invites conferees to plan to participate in three upcoming IAJV projects: a series of "How To" manuals to be written by and for practitioners in the justice volunteer field; a centrally held listing of individuals willing to become part of the IAJV Resource Bank of public speakers, workshop presenters and technical assistance providers; and a certification program for

justice volunteer managers.

- *105 - Together We Can Make It Work: Developing a Partnership Between the Public and Private Sectors* - helps participants gain a new appreciation for the role of government working in cooperation with private sector agencies; suggests techniques and strategies to facilitate communications, information exchange and networking; helps perpetuate a direct liaison between organizations and agencies within the criminal justice system.

Workshop Series II - Special Focus Workshops - provides an in-depth look at each of three topics crucial to all areas of the justice system: drugs, disease, and troubled youth. The two-session, all day workshops include:

- *201 - Alcohol, Illegal Street Drugs and Legal Drugs*
- *202 - Communicable Diseases ... AIDS, Hepatitis, and Tuberculosis*

[Both of these sessions dealt with the same two topics: "National/State Trends, Education and Issues," and "Local Treatment/Prevention, Legal Trends, and Developing Local Agency Networks."]

- *203 - Youth Subcultures ... Trends, Identification, Prevention and Intervention,* which covers "Gangs and Cults" and "Satanism."

Workshop Series III

- *When You Speak, Do People Listen?* - teaches how to create a personal connection with listeners and other communication skills.
- *Using Ex-Prostitutes as Volunteers* - presents an overview of Project Hope, a program which recruits and trains former prostitutes to help others in jail to recover and leave the lifestyle; includes a discussion of problems associated with prostitution and how to start a recovery group.
- *Administration & Management of Court Volunteer Programs* - trains in the "How To's" of a successful court program, including relating to the judge, accountability, screening and supervision; basics provided by the founder of VIP.
- *Separation, Loss and Grief* - provides understanding of the suffering of a family when a member is incarcerated, the various kinds of loss, the stages of the grief process, and how to facilitate healing and growth.
- *Screening Volunteers for Child Sexual Abuse Prior to Agency Assignment* - focus on interviewing techniques that can be used to screen volunteers who may be sexually abusive to children and youth.

Workshop Series IV: Issues & Perspectives

- *401 - A Backward Glance: Ex-Offenders Now Serving as Volunteers* - offers insights into the lives of ex-offenders who are now volunteers serving others; draws on personal experience of ex-offenders who answer questions like: Who made a difference in your life? How did you change? Why are you volunteering to help others?
- *402 - A Forward Vision: Are Volunteers a Valuable Alternative to Building More Prisons and Juvenile Institutions?* - examines whether volunteers can be viable alternatives in helping to reduce institutional populations; includes panelists who examine current justice policy on building more prisons and juvenile institutions, how citizens can affect political change, and how citizen volunteers can become involved in newly-emerging community programs.
- *403 - A Nostalgic View or Futuristic Vision: Are Justice Volunteers Worth It?* - reviews justice volunteers in terms of where we have been, what problems still remain, and what the future is for justice volunteer efforts; includes a special focus on the philosophy of volunteer services, integration into larger justice programs, stumbling blocks in volunteer/staff relationships, and "electronic monitoring" as an alternative to supervision by volunteers.

Workshop Series V

- *501 - Leadership of Staff and Volunteers* - discusses the dynamics of leadership using a model that defines roles,

responsibility and accountability, balanced with human relationship needs.

- *502 - How to Work with Angry Clients: A Focus on Offenders* - presents a counseling model to help clients who anger easily; based on Rational Behavior Theory, which has been used successfully with offenders and school dropouts.
- *503 - Potpourri: Two Mini-Workshops on Maxi-Topics:* 1) Recruiting and Using 12-Step Volunteers; 2) The Prison-Ashram Project: We're All Doing Time.
- *National Issues Forum* examines a new theory of democracy that involves citizens working through an issue rather than just talking about it; presents a description of the National Issues Forum Program, which is in over 1300 cities.

The Forum celebrates the 20th anniversary of the modern justice volunteer movement. IAJV and VIP worked together for the first time in 1990 in a movement that hopes to rally the volunteer community to combine efforts in a networking system that will benefit all concerned.

FOUNDATION FOR SUCCESS*
National Association of Volunteers in Criminal Justice
PO Box 6365
University, AL 35486
TEL: 205-348-6738
Credit: CEUs; AVA Certification (partial fulfillment); inquire about others
Contact: David Gooch
Description: This Forum focuses on building a foundation for the successful continuation of services through "more effective use of people, dollars and power." The Forum brings together professionals and volunteers who are committed to improvement of the criminal justice system through citizen involvement. The Conference features workshops, speeches, discussions, idea exchanges, and informal gatherings. Many workshops are tailored to specific groups, such as volunteer managers, volunteer administrators, agency administrators and judges, line staff who work with volunteers and others. Speakers address current topics. Presenters, selected for relevance to volunteerism in the criminal justice field, lead workshops such as:

- Advanced volunteer management workshops;
- Service Skills Improvement for Volunteers;
- Workshops for agency administrators and judges;
- Workshops focusing on crime prevention and law enforcement;
- Concentrated workshops on the basics of volunteer management;
- Workshops designed for professional line staff; and
- Workshop sessions dealing with important issues facing justice volunteerism.

In addition to topics such as criminal justice program models, organizing and working within the political process, volunteer management skills, and fundraising, the Forum features a networking laboratory to give participants the maximum opportunity to meet with other persons from around the country to share information and ideas. A limited number of scholarships are awarded.

PRE-FORUM 90 TRAINING INSTITUTES
Volunteers in Prevention, Probation, Prisons
527 North Main Street
Royal Oak, MI 48067
TEL: 313-398-8550
Credit: Inquire
Sponsor: International Association of Justice Volunteerism
Contact: Judge Keith J. Leenhouts, President
Description: These pre-forum workshops represent a cooperative effort between the *International Association of Justice Volunteerism (IAJV), Volunteers in Prevention, Probation and Prisons (VIP),* and the *University of Wisconsin-Milwaukee*

Criminal Justice Institute. They are offered immediately prior to the national conference, *Forum 90: Backward Glances... Forward Visions.* Two pre-forum workshops are conducted - one for administrators, and one for volunteers, as follows:

Pre-Forum 90 Justice Volunteer Management Training Institute: How to Recruit and Utilize Volunteers Effectively - Designed for new justice volunteer managers, this workshop provides an overview of sound volunteer management techniques, including pre-planning needs assessment, recruitment, screening placement, supervision, motivation, record-keeping, evaluation and networking. Instructors represent both public and private sectors and have provided training for both sectors, including religious and university settings.

Pre-Forum 90: Religious Volunteer Institute - Designed for both volunteers and religious program leaders, this workshop examines the changing role and expectations for those who provide religious services in the courts and correctional settings. Emphasis is placed on appropriate training and management behaviors which cultivate partnerships between the religious community and the justice system. Two sessions are conducted during the one-day workshop:

Morning Session - Participants are assisted in focusing on:
- Understanding the changing face of the justice system and how this impacts on religious volunteers.
- Understanding the conflicts between the justice system and the religious community and what the basis of a partnership might be.

Afternoon Session - Participants are involved in presentations and hands-on experience, including:
- Hearing about specific volunteer programs across the nation which have been effective over the past 30 years.
- Examining, in depth, a new program in the Michigan courts; considering possible future volunteer efforts.

Instructors include a former prison chaplain, the president of a chaplaincy school, an ex-offender who is now executive director of a major volunteer organization.

The pre-forum workshops enable early arrivals and others to take part in intensive and productive activity, network, and become acquainted with some of the instructors who are involved also in the national forum.

INDIVIDUAL PROGRAM PROFILES

CORRECTIONAL MINI-COURSES
Connecticut Department of Corrections
Volunteer Services
90 Brainard Road
Hartford, CT 06104
TEL: 203-566-3685; 203-566-2503
FAX: 203-566-2195
Purpose: To provide programming training for pre-trial inmates.
Sponsor: Connecticut Department of Corrections
Contact: Doug Kulmacz, Director
Description: Recognizing the fact that pre-trial people are considered innocent until proven guilty, the Connecticut Department of Corrections developed a program that is not "rehabilitative" in nature, but provides a school experience for men held in pre-trial detention at the Bridgeport Community Correctional Center.

Planners of the training program were faced with a unique set of circumstances with this group of inmates. Many are in and out within a few hours, most are adjudicated within a few weeks, and all but a handful are gone within 120 days of their admission. The Center had become a place to wait and look for diversion. With the options of providing only passive, time-passing diversions like television and games, or offering constructive outlets that stimulate the individual, rechannel some of his thinking, and open new vistas for him, the Center chose the latter. This option was used as the foundation for a series of mini-courses designed expressly for the individual in short-term confinement.

To enlist volunteers and others as teachers, the planners based their recruitment efforts on the premise that almost anyone holds some kind of occupational or avocational knowledge that others do not have, and can offer a unique teaching experience. They placed more importance on the desire to share what one knows than on the holding of a college degree. The spirit should be interesting, but a final quiz is not mandatory. In many cases, the presentation is an introduction to the subject rather than a course in the mastery of it. Given the short space of time, this serves well to stimulate participants, since more detailed courses cannot be completed in most cases, and therefore tends to cause frustration. Guidelines set by the planners include:
- Can the subject be introduced in four to six sessions?
- Can one make the topic alive and interesting to a group of 10-15 men whose average age is 21-23?
- Can the mini-course be designed so that no equipment for the learner is needed?
- Can one make a mini-course interesting to the most reluctant learner?

In relation to the above guidelines, cassette recorders are often provided to facilitate learning, but not as an indication of equipment that might be needed after the student has left the facility. Also, the range of possible topics is very broad. In addition to the 35 volunteers involved, resident teachers help plan and schedule courses, announce the courses, describe them to newly admitted persons, enroll interested participants, have equipment ready when instructors and students arrive, etc. Planners emphasize that the challenge of teaching in a correctional setting is the same as in any school or community setting. Due to the nature of the setting, however, classrooms are within close observational range of correctional officer posts, with officers immediately available to deal with any difficult classroom situation. No such problems have been encountered to date in the program.

TRAINING/CONFERENCES/TEACHING: DOMESTIC ABUSE

TRAINING PROGRAMS

PARENT AIDE TRAINING
Montgomery County Department of Social Services
5630 Fishers Lane
Rockville, MD 20852
TEL: 301-468-4345
Credit: Inquire
Sponsor: Montgomery County Government
Contact: Peggy Nelson
Description: In this training program, volunteers concerned with child abuse problems receive a basic orientation to the Department of Social Services by staff, and on-the-job training by supervisors of specific units. In addition, they are briefed in the following major areas:
- The Philosophy of the Parent Aide Program
- The Structure and Policy of the Protective Services Division
- The Facts and Dynamics of Child Abuse and Neglect

Following the orientation session, participants are involved around the following specific issues:
- Attitudes and Values: Assessment and Clarification
- Parent Aide Experience: The Team Approach
- Role Playing (Rehearsing for Reality)

Ample time for discussion is provided throughout the eight-hour program. Small-group role-playing and a wrap-up with the full student body conclude the course. The emphasis is on a team approach.

TRAINING/CONFERENCES/TEACHING: DRUGS/ALCOHOL

TRAINING PROGRAMS

MONTGOMERY ANTI-DRUG CONFERENCE
Montgomery County Panel on Drug Problems
Montgomery County Executive Office
100 Monroe Street
Rockville, MD 20850
TEL: 301-217-2500
Sponsor: Montgomery County
Contact: Sidney Kramer, County Executive
Description: This conference, convened in June 1989, was composed of 32 business, government and community leaders appointed by the County Executive to devise ways to reach parents of school-age children and neighborhoods victimized by drug-related crime with comprehensive drug-education programs. The conference culminated a year of work by the panel and resulted in six goals for implementation by the county over a two-year period, as follows:
- Various departments of county government should promote anti-drug campaigns by neighborhood organizations, school groups, religious congregations and businesses.
- The county should provide community outreach services, including technical help for groups trying to create their own anti-drug programs and training for young people and others who want to serve as voluntary peer counselors.
- Besides promoting anti-drug campaigns by private groups, the county should conduct its own "broad public education and awareness campaign for substance-abuse prevention."
- County officials ought to push for tougher drug laws, study ways to speed the court system's handling of drug cases, and "review and assess on an ongoing basis the treatment services available" to drug users.
- The county should develop a system for the "monitoring and evaluation" of its anti-drug efforts, especially those outlined in the conference report.
- The county should seek "creative funding" for further prevention efforts; e.g., assign a team of employees to work full time on anti-drug grant applications.

To sum up the conference, the panel member from the Potomac Electric Power Company said, "To reverse the adverse trends of the last decade, every segment of our community must focus on education, prevention and treatment of substance abuse."
Publications: Montgomery County Anti-Drug Study

NATIONAL CONFERENCE ON DRUG ABUSE AND PARENTING*
National Association of Perinatal Addiction Research and Education
11 East Hubbard Street
Suite 200
Chicago, IL 60611-3536
TEL: 312-329-2512
Contact: Conference Coordinator
Description: This conference is concerned with substance abuse during pregnancy and was convened after a study of 715 women revealed some surprising results. Both public health clinics that serve a largely indigent population and private practices which cater to upper-income patients in Pinellas County, Florida, were surveyed for the study. The conference convened to deal with study findings that contradicted accepted beliefs that determined the concept - and thereby funding and related matters - of dealing with substance abuse during pregnancy. These findings included:
- People have always assumed that drug abuse during pregancy is only a problem in urban minority populations.
- A lot more women are using drugs during pregnancy than is widely believed, due in part to the fact that wealthy patients do not show up in in the figures.
- Minority women who use drugs or alcohol during pregnancy are 10 times more likely to be reported to child abuse authorities than white women, because public clinics are required by law to report suspected perinatal substance abuse.

Conference recommendations include encouraging state officials and health care providers to study laws for uniform drug testing and less formal procedures such as lifestyle evaluations to ensure early detection of drug abuse during pregnancy in all populations. Pinellas County was chosen for the study because it includes rural stretches and larger cities such as St. Petersburg and Clearwater. Presenters included staff from the Pinellas County Juvenile Welfare Board.

PREVENTION MAKERS
Cook County Sheriff's Office
Youth Services Department
1401 Maybrook Drive
Maywood, IL 60153
TEL: 312-865-2900
Credit: Inquire
Sponsor: Cook County Sheriff's Office; InTouch Program
Contact: James E. O'Grady, Sheriff
Description: Prevention Makers involves adult role models who have demonstrated personal achievement, and who are willing to share their "secrets of success" with children and youth. The 1989 seminar presenters included a professional basketball star, an Olympics Gold Medal winner (both natives of the area), and a member of the U.S. Olympic Committee Task Force. The goal of the seminar program is to give young people a strong message about drugs.
Advice offered by the speakers included:
- Set goals, and don't let drugs keep you from reaching them.
- Believe in yourself and your abilities when you strive for goals.
- Remember that drug abuse effects not only the user but family, friends and society at large.
- Continue the seminars and find ways that they can help in substance abuse prevention activities in your schools.

Ninety students from 20 schools in three districts, and 30 adult representatives, attended the seminar. Two representatives from the local school for exceptional children also attended. Participant evaluations agreed that the seminar was highly motivating, with adult attendees encouraged by the responsiveness of the youth. At the closing of the seminar, the youth were assured that contact would be maintained by the InTouch coordinators and the Sheriff's Youth Department to provide follow-up seminars, and technical assistance from the two programs for local substance abuse prevention activities.

STATEWIDE DRUG TASK FORCE CONFERENCE
Drug Trafficking Study Task Force
Virginia Department of Volunteerism
223 Governor Street
Richmond, VA 23219
TEL: 804-786-1431
Description: This is the conference of the newly-appointed Drug Trafficking Study Task Force, authorized during the 1988-89 winter general assembly as part of the State Crime Commission. It will culminate in a legislative report to the governor and the 1991 General Assembly. The "first order of business" at the conference, according to the 21 Task Force members, is to "learn the nature of

the beast." More than two dozen speakers ranged from families that had been "torn apart" because of substance abuse to State PTA Substance Abuse Committee members and State Senators and officials from the private sector. Some points made in their presentations:

- Develop a thorough understanding of the problem - how it arises, why it occurs.
- Form a statewide strategy for dealing with drug abuse and related crime.
- Learn from successful efforts in personal struggles as well as legislative enforcement.
- Coordinate the state's educational, medical and law enforcement resources.
- Enact tougher drug laws.
- Execute major drug figures.
- Use "shock incarceration" for small-time social users.
- Levy mandatory sentences for anyone convicted of selling narcotics to a child.
- Increase drug enforcement resources.
- Cut or scale down selected programs so that funds can be reallocated to fight against drugs.
- Act now!

The Task Force has a two-year mandate to examine all facets of the drug problem and seek possible remedies.

INDIVIDUAL PROGRAM PROFILES

INTOUCH
Cook County Sheriff's Office
Youth Services Department
1401 Maybrook Drive
Maywood, IL 60153
TEL: 312-865-2900
Purpose: To develop and enhance substance abuse prevention activities.
Sponsor: Cook County Sheriff's Office; Illinois Department of Alcohol and Substance
Contact: Mary L. Feerick, Director
Description: InTouch is a communication link to community and faculty, students and agencies concerned with prevention of alcohol and drug abuse. It is funded by a grant from the Illinois Department of Alcoholism and Substance Abuse and sponsored by the Cook County Sheriff's Youth Services Department.
A major activity of the program is developing, organizing, and implementing seminars, largely for students, but including family and community meetings. When possible, the seminars include role models who were raised in or near the local area involved in the seminar.
Other activities include needs surveys, technical assistance, and specific projects such as:

- **Project Decide,** which addresses self-esteem building as a key component.
- **Home Is Where the Start Is,** which develops and distributes materials for parents to help them instill self-esteem in their children and provide them and their children with information on substance abuse prevention.

A major role played by InTouch is setting up planning meetings in local schools to help with each year's schedule of technical assistance and other activities to help prevent substance abuse.
Publications: InTouch (newsletter); InTouch Needs Assessment Survey

TRAINING/CONFERENCES/TEACHING: EDUCATION

TRAINING PROGRAMS

AFRICAN-AMERICAN FESTIVAL OF ACADEMIC EXCELLENCE
NAACP
PO Box 2165
Rockville, MD 20852
TEL: 301-468-7744; 301-946-1334
Contact: Robert R. Nix
Description: This conference was convened in response to the trend for black youngsters to avoid achievement because of peer pressures. The purpose was to discuss this problem while recognizing 242 high achievers in the Washington metropolitan area (one with a 4.7 grade point average). Initiated by the Montgomery County Chapter of the NAACP, organizers tried to counteract the negative peer pressure among some of today's black youths, who equate academic success with selling out to the white world.
The theme of the day also included self-help. There were workshops for parents on building self-esteem in children, countering negative peer pressure and preparing for college.
Youths talked about the pressure of drugs and dating, but it was the message of promoting achievement that seemed to sink in. Although teenagers were the target, one adult brought 31 students from a local middle school, and the students were quite verbal about the problems of avoiding peers involved in drugs and petty crimes in their neighborhoods.
The students who were honored represent 13% of the school system's black high school juniors and seniors who, according to the event's sponsors, defied media stereotypes, particularly of young black men.
Faculty came from all sectors, including Howard University. Participants who heard a statement by one of the middle school students agreed that it summed up the objectives of the meeting: "Work hard, stay in school, get good grades, go to college."

BASIC LEADER TRAINING COURSE
Linden School
141 West Main Road
Middletown, RI 02840
TEL: 401-849-2122
Credit: Inquire
Sponsor: Great Books Foundation
Contact: Joseph Krupowicz
Description: This program, sponsored by the Great Books Foundation prepares volunteers, teachers, librarians and school administrators to lead Junior Great Books reading and discussion groups.
Although Chicago-based, the Foundation holds registration session around the country. The Middletown session received widespread interest from volunteers across the state.
The Junior Great Books program, available to students in grades 2-12, is designed to teach children how to interpret what they read. Students learn how to think independently about literature, to articulate ideas about its meaning, and to enrich their ideas through discussion.
A course for those preferring to lead Adult Great Books classes is offered also. Printed materials are offered to those unfamiliar with the program who wish to consider one or both training events for their communities.

FIRST STATE CONFERENCE ON SCHOOL VOLUNTEERS
Fairfax County Public Schools
Masonville Instructional Center
3705 Crest Drive
Annandale, VA 22003
TEL: 703-698-7500
Credit: Inquire
Sponsor: Virginia Department of Education
Contact: Sarah Lahr
Description: In summer 1980, an exploratory meeting was held by the State Department of Education to find ways to encourage and support school volunteerism across the state. One of the conclusions of the meeting was that financing should be sought to hold conferences about school volunteerism in different parts of the state. After the grant was obtained by the Department of Education, a planning committee was formed to determine how the grant would be used.

It was decided that the grant would be used to make the conferences available without cost to attendees. Also, the group considered both the positive and negative aspects of volunteer programs, and possible activities to be undertaken which would enhance the use of volunteers in Virginia's schools.

A subcommittee was named to develop a brief set of objectives and possible strategies for accomplishing objectives. The subcommittee met at the Virginia Division of Volunteerism offices and among their recommendations was the convening of two training seminars.

The statement of purpose for the two seminars, planned by the subcommittee, is as follows:
- To encourage and assist volunteerism by making participants more aware of the potential for volunteering in public schools.
- To develop the skills of participants for involving volunteers in their own school systems.
- To enhance support for volunteer programs by sharing of resources among seminar participants.

The Department of Education issues invitations to all schools in the state to send a "team" consisting of a principal, a teacher, a layperson or volunteer and a central office representative or volunteer coordinator, with one member designated as the team leader. The first sessions were held in Richmond and Roanoke.

In addition to school systems, "all those organizations which have a natural concern about school volunteerism" are invited to participate, including: Virginia Congress of Parents and Teachers; Virginia Education Association; National School Volunteer Program; State Division on Volunteerism, Virginia School Boards Association, Virginia Association of School Administrators, Virginia Association of Elementary School Principals, Virginia State Chamber of Commerce, Mid-Atlantic Center for Community Education, and individuals who are considered leaders in the field. Each is asked to participate in some way, e.g., bring exhibits or volunteer as Table Topics facilitators. Workshop topics include:

Morning Session
- The PTA and the School Volunteer
- In the Beginning
- Students as Volunteers in Schools
- The Effective Management of a Volunteer Program
- Community Resources
- An Unbeatable Combination
- Involved Retired Senior Volunteers
- Viable Volunteer Assistance in the Classroom

Afternoon Session
- Research on the Effectiveness of the School Volunteer Program
- Recruiting Volunteers - and Keeping Them
- Using Volunteers to Improve Writing
- Good Management in Volunteer Programs
- In the Beginning

Evaluation forms are sent out after the conference, and the planning committee convenes to discuss those that are returned. Most respondents feel that they gain much information that can be used to enhance their volunteer programs, and request follow-up conferences. The next most frequent request is for continuing information on training workshop opportunities.

In addition to continuing conferences, two other findings of the subcommittee were reported to the full planning committee after the initial workshops:
- Establishment of a clearinghouse for resource materials and guidelines.
- Seeking support of the State Board of Education by way of a resolution endorsing school volunteerism.

The latter was passed unanimously by the Board of Education, to wit:

"The State Board of Education recognizes and endorses volunteerism in Virginia public schools as a means of assisting faculties in providing varied educational experiences for students and to further good school-community relations."

NATIONAL ACADEMY FOR VOLUNTEERS IN EDUCATION
National Association for Partners in Education
601 Wythe Street
Suite 200
Alexandria, VA 22314
TEL: 703-836-4880
Credit: Certification as NAPE Special Education Volunteer
Sponsor: National Association for Partners in Education
Contact: C.J. Reid, Projects and Membership Services
Description: Currently, NAVIE is a federally-funded event to provide for the training of trainers of volunteers who will be working with mildly handicapped students. The National Student Volunteer Program is committed to work toward making NAVIE an annual event that will include other programs in education as well as those for handicapped.

The program requires each school district's volunteer coordinator to be the team leader, with the school district selecting the other two members of the team. Ideally, the other two members should be an administrator in special education, and someone involved in the education of mildly-handicapped students. For best results, limitations were placed on numbers of participating districts, with the following NAPE selection criteria:
- the presence in the district of a strong, well-established school volunteer program;
- demonstrated support for the program by the school board, administration, and community;
- willingness of the school district to commit itself to carry out project goals;
- demonstrated ability of the school volunteer coordinator to conduct and plan conferences and training sessions.

NAVIE training was conducted on the campus of Dominican College in San Rafael, California. The week-long training program covered:
- volunteer program management;
- delivery of volunteer services to mildly handicapped students;
- in-service training for the effective involvement of volunteers;
- how to set up, administer and provide training for three programs: kindergarten screening, the listener program, and reinforcement of academic skills;
- conference and workshop management;
- skills in group dynamics;
- the function and role of change agents; and
- public policy related to school volunteer programs and the education of handicapped students.

Commitments of participating school districts are: to give release time to the three-person team; to enable the returning team to conduct a conference to train local school volunteers and to involve/assist neighboring school districts; to allow teams to provide technical assistance to other districts (at expense of other districts); to provide evaluation data to NAPE on the local conference, technical assistance given, and other projects resulting from NAVIE training. In addition to expenses, NAPE offers Certification and ongoing assistance.

REFUGEE VOLUNTEER TUTOR TRAINING
SEE TRAINING/CONFERENCES/TEACHING: ETHNIC GROUPS

SECONDARY SCHOOL VOLUNTEERS
Lamar University
4815 Dellwood Lane
Beaumont, TX 77706
TEL: 409-838-8673; 409-892-0595
Credit: Inquire
Sponsor: School Districts; State Education Agencies; School Volunteer Organizations
Contact: Dr. Jerry Wood Tierce
Description: This training program is designed to "answer the puzzle of starting, securing, and strengthening volunteer programs in secondary schools." It is based on the premise that every school can be enriched by volunteers, and that every child can be helped. Materials used in the course come from accepted resources in the field of school volunteerism, covering topics that include the following:
- Needs and objectives of school volunteer programs
- Identifying resources
- Designing the program
- Recruiting volunteers
- Selecting and matching volunteers
- Assigning the volunteer
- Role definition of the secondary school volunteer
- Profile of the volunteer coordinator
- Characteristics of school volunteer programs
- Questions teachers might ask
- Laws concerning volunteers
- Teacher training and volunteer training
- Volunteer dedication and volunteer expertise
- Meeting the needs of adolescents; increased academic achievement

Discussions of the strengths and weaknesses of school volunteer programs, recommendations for improving and/or expanding programs, an overview of curricular specialization in volunteer administration, and evaluation of secondary school volunteer programs are topics that are introduced into the course as appropriate.

SHOW-ME SEMINARS
SEE GOVERNORS' OFFICES ON VOLUNTEERISM: MISSOURI

SKILLS EXPANSION THROUGH RESOURCE VOLUNTEERS IN EDUCATION (SERVE)
Chapel Hill Training Outreach Project
Lincoln Center, Merritt Mill Road
Chapel Hill, NC 27514
TEL: 919-967-8295
Credit: None
Sponsor: Chapel Hill Training Outreach Project
Contact: Jeanne C. James
Description: This training for volunteers and volunteer coordinators is conducted once each month at each site. The series totals five sessions, which are:
- New Friends which examines attitudes toward the disabled and introduces an innovative approach to mainstreaming that uses peer-sized dolls to teach children about disabilities.
- Role of Volunteer Coordinator/Role of Volunteer which clarifies these roles in the center staffing design
- Assessment which explores the purpose of assessment and how to apply assessment results in developing specific remedial

activities.
- Curriculum which focuses on teacher-made materials and the correlated day approach to curriculum development for the young child.
- Accentuate the Positive which addresses the use of positive attitudes and techniques for effective teaching.

Participants in the training program include volunteers and the coordinators with whom they would be working. The training is designed to promote a cooperative relationship between the agency staff and the volunteer, a respect for the services which a volunteer can provide, and a positive attitude towards staff, volunteers and, especially, handicapped children.

In addition to the training, the Project provides participating agencies with publicity aids such as brochures, posters, radio and television PSAs (public service announcements), and newspaper articles. This material is designed to aid the agency in recruiting.

VOLUNTEER TRAINING - SCHOOL DESEGREGATION MONITORING*
Desegregation Monitoring and Advisory Committee
721 Olive
Eleventh Floor
St. Louis, MO 63101
TEL: 314-231-4669
Credit: Inquire
Sponsor: US/DoJ - District Court
Contact: Loverne Cameron, Associate Director
Description: This training program is designed to develop a bank of assistants to assist the Desegregation Monitoring and Advisory Committee (DMAC). This court-appointed Committee is charged with monitoring implementation of the Intra-District Desegregation Plan. Volunteers are recruited to assist in making visits to 217 schools.

Monitoring periods vary, but are always scheduled several months apart. Monitoring is expected to take about two weeks, with reports due about a week after completion of the school visits. An average school visit involves one to three hours.

Following the training, volunteers are expected to be able to handle the following tasks within the framework of the Committee's mandated guidelines:
- Administer questionnaires to school administrators, teachers, staff, and/or students and parents.
- Make personal observations of the conditions in schools which might impact on the desegregation plan.
- Provide data in a form that provides DMAC with an opportunity to observe, independently and "first hand," the extent to which the plan is being implemented.
- Provide data in a form that is conducive to the formulation of reports to the United States District Court.

Actual training is completed in one day, with the Advisory Committee on call for questions that may arise due to unexpected circumstances and have not been covered in the one-day training session. Reimbursement is made available for all Committee-related transportation expenses.

VOLUNTEERS: A CAPITAL IDEA*
National Association of Partners in Education
601 Wythe Street
Suite 200
Alexandria, VA 22314
TEL: 703-636-4880
Credit: Inquire
Sponsor: National Association of Partners in Education
Contact: Carol Pierce
Description: In addition to its training program, the National School Volunteer Program's tenth annual conference will include two very important "firsts" in the ongoing development of the school volunteer movement. One, a panel discussion will highlight the newly-established National Coalition for Parent Involvement in

Education (NCPIE) convened by NAPE. Two, NAPE will charter its first State Affiliates.

Special conference features in addition to the two "firsts" above will be the nationally-prominent faculty from the field of education and volunteerism, seminar leaders recruited by popular demand, regional and state meetings aimed at strengthening school volunteer programs at the state level, and NAPE Awards presentations.

Workshops are scheduled that cover a wide variety of topics based on feedback from the field over the past year, and including:

1-1/2 hour Workshops:
- Small Rural Programs
- Intergenerational Programs
- Career Development for Parents and Children
- Mentor Program for Gifted and Talented Children
- 2A Tutoring (Peer/Cross-Age)
- Adopt-A-School
- Basic Skills
- ESL
- Special Needs
- Student Trades

Panels:
- Volunteers and Desegregation (tentative)
- Older Volunteers

Short Workshops:
- Developing a Volunteer Program
- Teacher Training
- PR/Communications

3-hour Session:
- Business/Community Education

Forum:
- Parents/Community Involvement/Effective Schools

WHOLEFFECTS EDUCATION: NATIONAL CONFERENCE
Wholeffects Institute
IRM Corporation
4 Terrace Drive
PO Box 650
Nyack, NY 10960
TOLL FREE: 800-845-8402
Sponsor: IRM Corporation
Contact: Director of Conference Services
Description: This conference was developed by the *Wholeffects Institute* as a joint training event with the *University of Texas at Austin's* fifth annual *Conference for Educational Excellence.* It is designed as a systematic approach which involves the total community in the education of all children and adults.

Participants in *Wholeffects Education* workshops - both paid and volunteer - include educators of gifted and talented people, substance abuse specialists, staff development specialists, migrant education specialists, compensatory education specialists, assessment specialists, special education personnel, school board members, vocational educators, at-risk coordinators, administrators, counselors, teachers, parents, business leaders, and others. Presentations include:
- Implementing Wholeffects In Your Community: Law Enforcement and Other Agencies;
- Community Involvement in Sex Education;
- A Magnet School and Its Whole Effect: Miracle in Miami; and
- Site-Based Leadership and Its Role in Wholeffects Education.

Presenters for the above topics come from universities, government, the art community, schools, and independent consulting firms. In addition, special presentations are provided by leaders from across the country.

The event is composed of five general sessions and 30 breakout sessions. Ample time is provided for participants to share ideas and materials.

WORKSHOPS FOR VOLUNTEER COORDINATORS AND VOLUNTEERS IN EDUCATION*
ADDitions School Volunteers
Orange County Public Schools
6200 Chancellor Drive #500
Orlando, FL 32809-5697
TEL: 305-422-5817
Credit: Inquire
Sponsor: ADDitions
Contact: Eleanor Y. Fisher
Description: A series of workshops is held annually September through mid-November for school volunteers, prospective volunteers, retired citizens, and persons interested in education, with two of the workshops addressing school-based volunteer coordinators. Topics include:

Volunteer Coordinators: These workshops include techniques of recruiting, record-keeping, inter-personal skills, recognition, etc., broken down into sessions of interest to new coordinators and those that will benefit the experienced coordinator. These are tailored to meet current needs, with programs added as the need indicates (e.g., Circle of Motivation was added in 1983 when coordinators expressed an interest in this subject).

Volunteers: These workshops address specific areas in which the volunteer is the person who is responsible for managing the program. Workshops include Math Superstars, Arty-Facts, Creative Writing, Learning Disabilities, Science, Un Poquito de Espanol (a Little Bit of Spanish), Community Resource Volunteers, Listening to Children/New Students, Reading Support, Art * Art * Art, Speak for Yourself (Speaking in Public), Winning Relationships - Communications Skills, Storytelling, Signing for the Deaf, ESL (English-As-A-Second Language), Listening, and others.

All workshops include manuals, guides and other relevant materials (e.g., Holiday Art, a guide for the Arts program, Fountain Valley, a reading support system, Color Slide Program of the Great Masters for the artifacts program, and What's Right With Our Schools for coordinators' programs).

Two or three additional workshops often are conducted in early fall and spring. Some of these are supplementary, others on subjects that have not been covered in previous workshops. These are based on expressed needs. The series of workshops is in its twelfth year.

TRAINING/CONFERENCES/TEACHING: ENTREPRENEURSHIP

TRAINING PROGRAMS

WASHINGTON FOR MINORITY YOUTH AWARENESS DAY
US/DoC - Office of Minority Business Enterprise
14th Street at E & Constitution
Washington, DC 20230
TEL: 202-377-2000
Information also available from: US/SBA - Minority Business
1441 L Street NW, Washington, DC 20416 (202-653-6365)
Sponsor: US/DoC - Department of Commerce
Contact: Minority Business Coordinator (Commerce) or Anita Holland (SBA)
Description: A faculty of volunteer role models, convened at the request of the *US Small Business Administration* and the *US Department of Commerce,* spearheaded a program involving 200 minority youth from across the country who are interested in becoming entrepreneurs. Now in its third year, the conference

targets promising minority students, and offers them successful role models and government programs. The youth program is part of the agencies' annual *Minority Enterprise Development Week Conference.*

Since Asians and Hispanics have the highest percentage of minority-owned businesses, the meeting was especially important for black youth. Many minorities other than black have been successful in their own countries before coming to America, according to the program's organizers, while blacks have not had the opportunity of starting a business in a nondiscriminatory environment. Most black entrepreneurs are first-generation business owners.

A major concern of the youth themselves was the difficult choices that challenge their work ethic. For this reason, enlisting role models for the youth is the strength of the program, with celebrities and athletes discussing the risk of considering a professional athletic or other high visibility, but short-term, career as the only one. Also discussed with the role models was an issue raised by a 17-year-old participant - the lure of drugs and fast money in inner-city neighborhoods "as a way of getting things your parents can't get you." Although many youth try to avoid the drug scene, the youth participants agreed that it is "hard to get away from" - especially with the obstacles facing them in trying to start businesses. According to presenters, these obstacles can be softened or eliminated as the issues - such as acquiring capital to get started - are addressed and positive solutions found for them. Other presenters talked about financial planning, stress control and self-awareness. The bottom line - with both presenters and young participants in agreement - was stated by a former football player for the *Green Bay Packers* - "It is possible to have it all, but someone must be willing to work hard and do the little extra things you have to do to get ahead."

TRAINING/CONFERENCES/TEACHING: ENVIRONMENT

TRAINING PROGRAMS

GOVERNOR'S CONFERENCE ON VOLUNTEERS IN ENERGY*
SEE GOVERNORS' OFFICES ON VOLUNTEERISM: CONNECTICUT

TRAINING/CONFERENCES/TEACHING: ETHNIC GROUPS

TRAINING PROGRAMS

AMERICAN INDIAN PARTNERSHIPS WITH UNITED WAYS*
United Way of Anchorage
341 West Tudor Road
Suite 106
Anchorage, AK 99502-6639
TEL: 907-272-7531
Information available also from:
United Way of America
701 N. Fairfax Street
Alexandria, VA 22314-2045 (703-836-7100)

Sponsor: United Way of America Project Blueprint
Contact: Diane Kaplan, Board Member
Description: In October 1989 the first national-level roundtable conducted to explore *American Indian Partnerships with United Ways.* Representatives from American Indian communities, national organizations, and United Ways attended. The roundtable took place in Anchorage, Alaska, and was sponsored by *Project Blueprint,* United Way of America's minority-inclusiveness program. The meeting drew upon the experiences of Native American groups which have developed a relationship with local United Ways during the past few years. Presentations included representatives from two Native American organizations - *Navajo United Way* and *Cherokee United Way.*

The Keynote Speaker, *Project Blueprint's* director, described outreach, networking, and community organization in American Indian communities in his state of Michigan, where the northern rural area includes several smaller United Ways in its partnership - all supported by the United Way of Michigan in Lansing.

The cultural barriers which United Ways and American Indians must overcome in order to create effective partnerships were outlined. The conclusion here was that the values of giving, caring, and sharing are very similar among American Indian cultures and the United Way system. According to the director, "Those values need to be community in terms of personal effort - or volunteering - and not just in terms of financial giving."

Roundtable members heard a "trade-off" described which recognized that while Native American communities need to have a better understanding of United Ways link with local business, government, labor, and other community groups, United Ways need to familiarize themselves with the extended families, tribes, spiritual leaders and other components of American Indian communities.

One myth was exploded in the course of the meeting - the widely-held perception that federal funding makes private philanthropy unnecessary. Native Americans were urged not to depend on the federal government for funding, since that type of funding has not generated enough programs oriented toward self-sufficiency in the way that United Way support has done over the years.

At the close of the meeting, the consensus was that the main challenge identified was the need for two-way communication, and for United Ways to initiate that communication by reaching out to American Indian communities.

Project Blueprint, the program's sponsor, is administered by United Way, with major funding from W.K. Kellogg Foundation. *Project Blueprint's* goals are to increase the number of Asian, Black, Hispanic, and Native American volunteers on United Way and agency boards and committees, and to increase local United Way allocations to health and human-service agencies operated by minorities.

REFUGEE VOLUNTEER TUTOR TRAINING
Oregon State University
Adult Education Division
Corvallis, OR 97331
TEL: 503-754-4318
Credit: CEUs
Sponsor: Oregon State University
Contact: Wayne Haverson
Description: This course was designed to meet a need for organizational, management, and maintenance of a professional program to provide volunteer tutors to adult refugees.

Four community college refugee programs are involved in the course, which teaches volunteers to instruct refugees in English as a Second Language. Training and on-site assistance is provided by the Adult Education department of Oregon State University through a special grant from the Oregon Department of Education.

VOLUNTEER TRAINING - SCHOOL DESEGREGATION MONITORING*
SEE TRAINING/CONFERENCES/TEACHING: EDUCATION

TRAINING/CONFERENCES/TEACHING: FAMILIES

TRAINING PROGRAMS

IN-SERVICE TRAINING/STATEWIDE VOLUNTEER DEVELOPMENT
SEE GOVERNORS' OFFICES ON VOLUNTEERISM: MICHIGAN

PROGRAM DEVELOPMENT ASSISTANCE PACKAGE
Michigan Department of Social Services
300 South Capitol Avenue
Suite 704
Lansing, MI 48909
TEL: 517-373-8534
Credit: Inquire
Sponsor: Michigan Department of Social Services
Contact: Barbara Conrad
Description: In a climate of shrinking resources, social agencies may need to look increasingly to volunteers to supplement services to clients and to provide administrative support to the agency. In a well designed volunteer program, staff will be intimately involved in defining roles for volunteers and in assuming responsibility for supervision and evaluation of volunteer involvement.
Description of Content: In a three hour workshop participants examine their personal attitudes toward volunteers, gain knowledge of the components necessary to a well-designed volunteer program, and learn to design volunteer jobs to provide services to children and families and to meet the administrative needs of the agencies. Each participant develops an actual job description for a volunteer which can be taken back to use in the home agency. Several topics are covered, including:
- Attitudes Towards and Expectations of Volunteers - Large group discussion and small group brainstorming.
- 'Components of a Well Designed Volunteer Program - Mini lecture, large group discussion.
- Development of Volunteer Jobs; participant analysis of individual job responsibilities, principles of job enrichment - mini lecture, large group discussion, individual written exercise.
- Job Description Exercise and Application - role playing, group discussion, written exercise.

VOLUNTEERISM AND SOCIAL WORK PRACTICE
Hunter College
School of Social Work
129 East 79th Street
New York, NY 10021
TEL: 212-570-5605
Credit: 3 credits
Sponsor: Hunter College of the City University of New York
Contact: Elizabeth Landing
Description: Volunteerism and Social Work Practice is an elective course open to all School of Social Work students, as well as nonmatriculated students. It is directed to social workers who are considering the use of volunteers; social workers who work with volunteers; and persons who recruit, assign, train, or supervise

volunteers. Objectives of the course are:
- To create understanding of the significance of volunteerism/voluntarism in the field of social work.
- To identify the role of the social worker in providing access for use of volunteers in social agencies.
- To develop skill in the development and management of volunteer programs.
- To provide an opportunity to explore current issues in volunteerism.

Staff of agencies serving as field instruction centers for Hunter College School of Social Work are eligible in some instances for 1/2 tuition wavers. Course content includes:
- The value of volunteerism in the American Democratic Society.
- The different functions performed by volunteers.
- Problems of developing and administering volunteer programs.
- Staff development and training programs.
- Supervision and retention of volunteers.
- Relationship between professional staff and volunteers.
- The constituencies of the volunteer administrator.
- The law and volunteers.
- Current issues.

The principal instructor of the course, Dr. Florence S. Schwartz, is Associate Professor in the Hunter College School of Social Work, member of the Board of Directors of the Association of Voluntary Action Scholars, and an Associate Editor of Volunteer Administration.

TRAINING/CONFERENCES/TEACHING: FUNDING

TRAINING PROGRAMS

CHANGING WAYS WE DO BUSINESS: NEW ROLES AND RESPONSIBILITIES
Independent Sector
1828 L Street, NW
Washington, DC 20036
TEL: 202-223-8100
Credit: Inquire
Sponsor: Independent Sector
Contact: Beverly With
Description: This workshop was developed around the issue of change, and its impact in recent years on the way nonprofit organizations conduct business. It focuses on the reductions in government funding and the accompanying increased expectations regarding the role of philanthropic and voluntary organizations. One goal is to rethink relationships both within the sector and between the sector and the public and commercial sectors. Under the general heading, New Roles and Responsibilities, participants have an opportunity to discuss such topics as:
- Advertising Council campaign on giving and volunteering.
- New opportunities to expand personal giving and volunteering.
- Strengthening the operation and performance of nonprofits.
- How can foundations and corporations cope with increased expectations?
- How can independent sector organizations have the most influence on public policy?
- Who will do what? Who will pay for it?
- How are we going to do our public business in the future?
- Redefining the roles of government and the independent sector.
- Planning the IS Effective Sector Management agenda.
- A global view of philanthropy.

- A world in need.
- Making the most of the public's heightened awareness of the sector and its contributions.
- Profit-making ventures for nonprofits.
- Viable alternatives to government funding.
- Changing roles and responsibilities; models from specific areas of voluntary activity.
- Making the Charitable Contributions Legislation a permanent part of tax policy.
- Increased competition for private contributions and grants - Who's winning? Who's losing?
- Competing for available government funding - Established versus emerging organizations.
- New Technology.
- The wave of the future.

In addition to the training opportunity at the workshop, participants are given the opportunity to attend a reception to hear brief presentations by key members of Congress, and other decision-makers from both the public and the private sectors.

FUND-RAISING SUCCESS SEMINAR
SEE FUNDING/FUND-RAISING/RELATED SERVICES

GRANTSMANSHIP TRAINING PROGRAM
Grantsmanship Center
650 South Spring Street
Suite 507
Los Angeles, CA 90014
TEL: 213-689-9222
TOLL FREE: 800-421-9512
FAX: 213-623-5667
Credit: Varies; inquire
Sponsor: Host Organization (more than 100 across the country)
Contact: Laurel Bartlett
Description: These two three-day workshops, conducted during a single six-day period in host cities around the country, are designed to lead participants through two major steps in seeking foundation and corporate funding: learning about sources and strategies of funding, and hands-on practice in writing proposals. Following is an outline of each program's content:
Foundation and Corporate Funding - a program designed to utilize specific information from each participant's agency or organization as the basis for the highly participatory workshops. Specifically, the program covers:
- the best information sources on foundation and corporate funding
- how to search for funding specifically for your agency
- the best strategies to use in approaching foundations and corporations
- how to find little-known foundations
- how foundations make loans for business ventures and for emergencies
- corporate grants and giving programs
- corporate contributions of goods and services
- the basic elements of proposal writing for private funds
- proposals for general support, project grants and capital needs

Current funding research publications from other sources are used in conjunction with materials developed specifically for the program. This workshop can be taken separately, but provides a solid foundation for the proposal-writing course below.
Grant Proposal Writing - This workshop is an intensive laboratory in writing proposals for private funds. Participants work with a format that is basic to proposal writing, applying the needs of their own agencies and organizations. Topics include:
- writing proposals for projects, general support and capital needs
- generating organizational credibility
- developing problem statements
- conducting needs assessment

- defining program objectives selecting and justifying your approach
- designing a program evaluation
- preparing a budget for foundation and corporate grants
- matching your needs with those of the funding source
- practice on writing proposal components
- review of prior work of your agency
- writing a complete private funding proposal
- how foundations review proposals

This workshop produces an actual proposal that is based on each participant's organization's or agency's needs and can be submitted to funding sources. In addition, actual proposals brought to the workshop are reviewed on request. This course may be taken separately, but the above basic workshop is considered a useful foundation for the course.

GRANTSMANSHIP TRAINING PROGRAM (SHORT COURSE)
SEE FUNDING/FUND-RAISING/RELATED SERVICES

MASTER OF PROFESSIONAL STUDIES DEGREE: FUND RAISING MANAGEMENT
New School for Social Research
66 Fifth Avenue
New York, NY 10011
TEL: 212-741-8664
Credit: 48 credits (leading to MPS degree)
Sponsor: New School for Social Research
Contact: Lois Blume or Lilly Cohen
Description: This part-time graduate program for working professionals leads to the Master of Professional Studies MPS degree. It was developed in 1978 based on an expressed need from the field (fund raisers, development officers, directors of nonprofit agencies, foundation executives and representatives from national professional organizations in the industry). The program incorporates courses including:
- working with boards and volunteers
- market research
- strategic planning
- grantsmanship
- direct mail
- public relations
- corporate giving
- foundations
- the annual campaign
- deferred giving
- philanthropic law

Student body includes volunteer professionals with administrative and leadership experience, managers and staff of nonprofit organizations, and professionals in other fields who need expertise in fund raising and nonprofit management. Two years of professional experience in fund raising, nonprofit management or community leadership, baccalaureate degree (or at least two years of college) are required for admission. Also required are a personal interview, a writing sample, official transcripts and references. Special program features include:
- part-time study (classes meet once a week)
- combined BA/MPS program
- transfer credit and acceleration options
- loan program

Faculty includes both the full-time Management faculty of the Graduate School and a strong adjunct faculty drawn from top leadership of the profession.

PROPOSAL WRITING INSTITUTE*
Virginia Polytechnic Institute and State University
Donaldson Brown Center
Continuing Education
Blacksburg, VA 24061
TEL: 703-961-4848
Credit: 2.1 CEUs
Sponsor: Virginia Tech
Contact: Linda G. Leffel
Description: This sixth annual Institute is designed with the purpose in mind: To help participants write proposals which will be approved and funded. Topics include:

Welcome to the World of Funding
- A look at the big picture
- The key actors involved
- Lets come to terms: what they mean
- Federal, state & local contacts
- The eternal triangle: you, your agency, and your funding source

Developing Project Ideas
- Where do you begin
- What techniques work for you
- Problem solving techniques revisited
- Using your idea to develop a project

Money: Where It's At
- Funding sources and where to find them
- Who can help you get the funds
- Where to go for information
- Alphabet soup and other federal sources

Understanding Federal Regulations
- Knowing where to look
- Knowing what to look for
- Knowing when you've found it

The Anatomy of a Proposal
- Identifying key components
- How proposals fit together
- Examining sample proposals

Developing the Needs Statement
- Communicating the need
- Whose needs are they
- Prove it; building your case
- Matching needs to funding sources

Goals and Objectives
- The heart of the proposal
- Where the action is
- Personalize goals
- The importance of clarity
- A foundation for the rest of the proposal
- Building the proposal around goals and objectives

Budgeting: Learning by Doing
- Taking the mystery out of budgeting
- Building your budgets
- A case study of budgeting
- Relating your budget to your goals

Evaluation Plans/Planning for Evaluation
- The value of evaluations
- Building it into your proposal
- Developing your own evaluation plan

Managing Your Project
- How do you do what you said you'd do
- Developing a management plan
- Expectations of the grantor
- Responsibility of the grantee
- Importance of good records

Post-Writing Phase
- Reviewing your freshly written proposal
- Have you met all terms and conditions
- Your proposal checklist

Congratulations! Your Proposal Is Accepted
- Do you want the money
- Reading the fine print
- Who are your friends now
- Getting organized

Dos and Don'ts of Proposal Writing
- A list of helpful hints for every proposal writer

In addition, the Institute offers special features such as step-by-step instruction, a copy of *Proposal Writers Handbook*, individual attention, and an opportunity for each participant to work on a proposal idea or concept for further development. It provides a foundation for beginners, and broader expertise for the seasoned veteran.

Faculty for this Institute is drawn from the grant and contract development and management field. The primary presenter is editor of Attracting External Funds for Continuing Education and the subject of a major article in the magazine, Funding Review.

RESOURCE DEVELOPMENT CONFERENCE*
Lutheran Resources Commission/Washington
1346 Connecticut Avenue, NW
Suite 823
Washington, DC 20036
TEL: 202-872-0110
Credit: None
Sponsor: Lutheran Resources Commission/Washington
Contact: R. Dix Griesemer
Description: Developed by the Grants Consultation Assistance Division of the Lutheran Resources Commission in Washington, this conference offers community leaders the opportunity to learn the "how-to" of grantsmanship. Participants include staff, volunteers and board members of church-related and community human service delivery agencies. Topics include:
- how to write a proposal;
- how to identify potential funding sources;
- how to approach government, foundation and corporate funders; and
- how to write a case statement.

Presenters are experts in the field of grantsmanship and include LRC-W staff, and officials from government, foundations and corporations. Lutheran Resources Commission/Washington is a grants consultation agency serving units of the American Lutheran Church, The Lutheran Church in America, the Lutheran Church-Missouri Synod, the Roman Catholic Archdiocese of Washington, DC, the United Methodist Church, and Presbyterian Church USA.

TRAINING/CONFERENCES/TEACHING: HANDICAPPED

TRAINING PROGRAMS

HANDICAPPED VOLUNTEER/VOLUNTEERING FOR THE HANDICAPPED
SEE SELF-HELP

PARENTS EDUCATING PARENTS: TRAINING PROGRAM
SEE VOLUNTEERS: SELF-HELP

THE UNTAPPED RESOURCE: DISABLED PERSONS AS VOLUNTEERS
Easter Seal Society of Pennsylvania
1500 Fulling Mill Road
Middletown, PA 17057
TEL: 717-939-7801

Credit: 7 CEUs (Pennsylvania State University)
Sponsor: Pennsylvania Easter Seal Society
Contact: Patricia McGrath, Conference Coordinator
Description: The Pennsylvania Easter Seal Society convened a
general training seminar and three regional workshops for
volunteer coordinators to:

- Familiarize volunteer coordinators with the competencies and
  abilities of disabled persons.
- Update skills on recruiting, interviewing, placement and
  program planning to meet needs of disabled volunteers.
- Identify community resources for recruiting and information
  on accommodation techniques.
- Orient participants to a comprehensive approach to volunteer
  program planning, recruitment, placement and goal setting.

All topics covered new material with practical and sensitive
techniques discussed and practiced to help volunteer directors
more effectively involve this important segment of the volunteer
community. Specific topics covered by the faculty of leaders in
both the volunteer and rehabilitation fields included:
Appropriate Goals for Disabled Volunteers - a discussion of
competencies and capabilities.
Creating the Climate - staff and volunteer preparation.
Program Review: Maximizing Potential - translating skills into
resumes and future career opportunities.
Expectations and Realities - accommodations for special
disabilities; reasonable performance demands.
New Approaches for a New Market - recruiting, interviewing and
placement; discussion and practice of approaches for involving this
segment of the volunteer community.
**Opportunities for the Nontraditional Volunteer: The Federal
Government's Role**
An opportunity was provided for informal discussion with faculty,
consultants, and disabled volunteers during the luncheon period,
and later at a wine and cheese mixer where films, literature, and
posters were reviewed.
The Pennsylvania State University, the Community College of
Allegheny County, and the Pennsylvania Developmental
Disabilities Planning Council are additional sponsors.

VOLUNTEERS WITH SPECIAL NEEDS
Volunteers In Action
229 Waterman Street
Providence, RI 02906
TEL: 401-421-6547; 401-421-7472
Credit: AVA Certification (partial fulfillment)
Sponsor: United Way, Mental Health Association of Rhode Island
Contact: Betsy A. Garland
Description: Cosponsored by a statewide mental health association
and a central volunteer service, this workshop combines the
missions of both and addresses the involvement of the handicapped
as volunteers. An opening session, Why This Conference? is shared
between the two organizations to elicit input from the assembly of
participants. Other sessions include:

- Creative Use of Time for the Chronically Disabled, which is
  led by faculty drawn from the field of rehabilitation
  alternatives.
- Practically Speaking: Referring and Receiving Agency
  Perspectives, which is led by faculty drawn from the field of
  rehabilitation alternatives.
- Practically Speaking: Referring and Receiving Agency
  Perspectives, which is led by faculty from Volunteer in
  Action's "Volunteers with Special Needs" program, with
  assistance from the fields of health, aging, vocational training,
  and occupational therapy.
- Alternatives to Traditional Volunteer Assignments (or "What
  can we do when it doesn't work...?"), which is led by faculty
  from the mental health association, with assistance from staff
  of the local Retired Senior Volunteer Program (RSVP).

Time for a wrap-up and question/answer session was allotted to

permit an idea exchange among participants.
Both sponsoring organizations are statewide, with satellite offices
in areas of greatest need across the state.

TRAINING/CONFERENCES/TEACHING: HEALTH

TRAINING PROGRAMS

ARHA/COUNCIL ON VOLUNTEER TRAINING EVENTS
Arizona Hospital Association
Council on Volunteers
6319 North Mockingbird Lane
Paradise Valley, AZ 85253
TEL: 602-948-0262
Credit: Inquire
Sponsor: Arizona Hospital Association (ArHA)
Contact: Winifred Bolton (or individual contacts listed below)
Description: ArHA and the Council co-sponsor a number of
training events each year. Typical events are:
ArHA Statewide Auxiliary Conference - This gathering addresses
the wide spectrum of successful endeavors and conflicts existing
within hospital auxiliaries, with solutions and achievements
explored during roundtable discussions. Following the keynote
presentation, a panel discussion format is used to air issues of
concern as communicated by participants, including:

- Relationship between Administration, Director of Volunteer
  Services, and Auxiliary.
- Communication within the Auxiliary.
- Retention and Recruitment.

Following the panel discussions, the group of 500 participants
divided for round-table discussion of the following topics:

- Go Get 'em (membership recruitment)
- The Young and the Restless (Junior recruitment)
- Where Are the Bucks? (fund raising)
- Talk It All Out (in-hospital relationships)
- What's Up Doc (communication within auxiliaries)
- Keeping Them Happy (retention and recognition)
- Buying the Best (gift shop)

Junior Volunteer Convention Phoenix/Northern Arizona - This
convention is convened to raise issues on health and health care as
they relate to the Junior Volunteer in the hospital. Approximately
175 young volunteers usually attend and participate in workshops
including:

- Introduction to the Burn Unit
- Esperanca - Hope from Phoenix
- Non-Invasive Medical Procedures

[Specific contact: Sylvia Bandler, Junior Coordinator, St. Luke's
Hospital Medical Center, 525 North 18th Street, Phoenix 85006
(602-251-8476)]
**The Burnout Syndrome and Breakthroughs in Human
Performance** - This workshop is of interest to all levels and
classifications of personnel - volunteers as well as paid staff, and
administrative, managerial, and supervisory as well as support
personnel. Participants learn to recognize the causes and effects of
the burnout syndrome. The workshop focuses on many proven
high performance activities and ten organizational programs to
prevent "burnout" and influence "breakthrough" performances.
Emphasis is on individuals, as well as small work groups, in
conjunction with self-assessment exercises.
This workshop is convened because of declining productivity and
its identification by numerous authorities as one of the major
factors influencing today's economy. Factors attributed to this
decline are several - one of the most important in human terms

being the burnout syndrome (physical, intellectual, psychological, social or spiritual). Faculty was drawn from a research and training institute specializing in human performance and productivity.
[Specific contact: Joan E. Kloos, Director of Public Information, Arizona Hospital Association, 4202 East Raymond Street, Phoenix 85040 (602-246-8901)]
Leadership/Legislature Conference - This conference was held in concert with the ArHA Council on Volunteers Statewide Conference to assist boards and auxiliary/volunteer leaders in these vital, interrelated areas of concern.
The conference provided an opportunity for leaders to learn about the legislative process. Faculty includes legislators who inform participants on how to take an active part in government. Each participant meets with a legislator from his/her district to exchange ideas on pertinent issues and to learn of possible areas of future involvement.
[Specific contact: Fran Cohen, St. Luke's Service League, 4619 E. Calle Redonda, Phoenix 85018 (602-959-5344)]

HOSPICE VOLUNTEER TRAINING PROGRAM*
Divine Redeemer Memorial Hospital
724 Nineteenth Avenue, North
South St. Paul, MN 55075
TEL: 612-450-4500
Credit: Certification
Sponsor: Divine Redeemer Memorial Hospital
Contact: Arnie Hanson
Description: Offered to any individual with an interest in serving hospice patients and their families, this training program has two basic components: five two-hour sessions in a classroom setting; ten hours of supervised clinical practicum involving direct patient care. Spanning a five-week period, study areas are:
- **Overview:** covers the hospice model of care for the terminally ill patient and how it is implemented by the Divine Redeemer Memorial Hospital, as well as course requirements.
- **Dealing with Terminal Illness:** examines the stages of death and dying, the various types of pain and the interventions that a volunteer may initiate to relieve these pains.
- **Communication:** involves a series of role-playing situations in which volunteers are introduced to the communication process, and examines and utilizes good communication techniques.
- **Legal Concerns:** addresses legal and financial questions surrounding terminal illness and death.
- **Loss and Grief:** focuses on the process of grieving and bereavement following the death of a patient, and the role of the volunteer in supporting the family during this period.
- **Family and Social Concerns:** discusses the social-psychological aspects of the family and how the family system is affected by terminal illness and death.
- **Funeral Arrangements:** includes topics such as preparing for death, unfinished business, funeral arrangements, burial rites and privacy of information.

At the completion of the above two-hour sessions and the ten-hour practicum, volunteers receive certification as hospice volunteers qualified to serve terminally-ill patients and families of patients. A monthly hospice volunteer support group provides further education, and gives volunteers a time to share their frustrations, joys, concerns and experiences (not a requirement for certification).

HOSPICE VOLUNTEER TRAINING PROGRAM*
Ocean County College
Department of Community Education
CN 2001
Toms River, NJ 08753
TEL: 609-255-4000
Credit: 1.6 CEU

Sponsor: Ocean County College
Contact: Librarian/Historian
Description: This program was developed in response to a need created by the development of several hospice programs in the Monmouth-Ocean County area. It is a 16-hour, eight-session course designed to teach participants:
- The Hospice Concept
- The role of the volunteer within the hospice program
- the special skills and knowledge necessary to help meet the emotional, psychological, social, spiritual and physical needs of the terminally ill and their families.

Offered for the first time in 1982, this course is intended for nurses, allied health professionals, and lay people interested in learning more about being a hospice volunteer. It depends on evaluation by the participants themselves for relevance of course content, and recommendations for additions, deletions, or changes in the format.

PARKINSON'S INSTITUTE FOR CAREGIVERS
Citadel Retirement Community
Volunteers of America of Mesa
5121 East Broadway
Mesa, AZ 85206
TEL: 602-832-5555
Credit: Institute Coordinator
Description: VOA's Parkinson's Institute is located at the Citadel Retirement Community in Mesa, Arizona. It is the only location in the nation which is offering a program of treatment and education for Parkinson's in a residential setting.
The goal of the personally-tailored health improvement program for persons with Parkinson's is to improve the lifestyles for many with this disease.
The training is designed to allow a caregiver or spouse to form a team with a resident in the program, accompany the resident through all steps in the program, and take an active part in the health education for the resident, and preparation for the resident's return home. Composed of 21-day sessions, the program features:
- health and nutrition;
- exercise;
- speech communication; and
- stress management.

Approximately 15 apartments of the retirement community are used for the resident-caregiver teams enrolled in the program. Other apartments are set up as offices, treatment rooms, a fully-equipped exercise room, and an outpatient clinic for the duration of the session. The exercise facilities are open to residents not in the program, and they are encouraged to attend the medical lectures and use the available medical facilities.

SEASIDE HEALTH PROMOTION CONFERENCE
Centennial School District Wellness Committee
18135 SE Brooklyn
Portland, OR 97236
TEL: 503-760-7990
Sponsor: Centennial School District
Contact: Barbara Velander
Description: This week-long conference brings together volunteers who are school employees from around the state for a concentrated week of sharing and spirit-building about fitness. Most participants have some background in nutrition or fitness - most often coaches of gymnastics, swimming, track or other sports. Although instructors are enlisted to conduct workshops, it is an informal conference, more concerned with networking and finding the methods that have worked best for attendees in the various areas of wellness and fitness.
Another intent of the conference is to "fire up" attendees to return to their districts and promote nutrition and fitness to employees in the schools, who are then expected to use the information to enhance their work with the children.

At least one annual event in the area is an outgrowth of a volunteer's suggestion at the conference - the *Eaglefest Run,* which is a district race that goes past each school - giving all students a feeling of being part of the event. Other less visible projects have resulted in a measurable improvement in wellness and fitness programs at the schools, winning for the District one of a handful of $5,000 *Metropolitan Life Insurance* grants for excellence.

INDIVIDUAL PROGRAM PROFILES

BE ALIVE IN 2005: PROMOTING WELLNESS INTO THE 21ST CENTURY
SEE VOLUNTEERS: ARMED FORCES MEMBERS - ARMY

HEALTH FAIR
SEE VOLUNTEERS: ARMED FORCES MEMBERS - NAVY

TRAINING/CONFERENCES/TEACHING: HOMELESS

TRAINING PROGRAMS

GIVE ME SHELTER: DESIGNS FOR URBAN SURVIVAL
Washington Post
Washington Home Division
1150 Fifteenth Street, NW
Washington, DC 20071
TEL: 202-334-7654
Credit: None
Sponsor: Washington Post
Contact: Panel Coordinator
Description: This forum arose out of the accelerating statistics of the homeless population - including entire families - in the Washington, DC, area. *Washington Post's Washington Home* division brought together a volunteer panel of architects, designers, shelter providers, and others concerned with housing for the homeless to explore ways *design* can help alleviate a social problem. Questions posed and responses offered included:
How do architects get involved in housing and shelters for the homeless?
- A program like *Search for Shelter* inherits a building that may or may not be worth refurbishing, or a program may be thinking about buying a building but doesn't know if it's worth the price. That's where the architects come in.
How do you feel the homeless perceive "home"?
- Emotional security, an emotional environment.
- Where they're loved or esteemed.
- Not in the "throw-away" buildings we throw at them.
- City shelters are depressing places - nothing like home.
- Private shelters are wonderful.
- A home-like atmosphere is needed for people looking for a way back into the mainstream.
- Emergency housing should not be provided without support services to help in a transition to affordable housing.
- It could be as simple as putting partitions between beds for privacy.
If people in need of shelter are in varying stages of development toward independence, requiring different kinds of temporary and transitional environments, what burden does this place upon architects? How do you factor these needs into a design solution, and is there evidence that design helps?
- *Housing Opportunities for Women (HOW)* is transitional

housing with three apartments that have 13 bedrooms, and women there must have jobs, support themselves, pay rent, etc., to the best of their ability.
- Another HOW project involves a broken-down shelter for women which was refurbished by HOW, and women who lived there in despair suddenly went out and got jobs. Providing a nice home raises self-esteem and helps people who have gone through the trauma of homelessness face society again.
- "Dignity" and "Security" is what we want these transitional housing projects to convey. You are telling people who have come to question their worth that they are "worthy to live in a nice place."
- Each project has its own requirements. You address homeless families, homeless single mothers with children, homeless children all by themselves, the elderly, etc.
- We have to promote "ownership" whether it is in the shelter space, a small apartment, or whatever. People know they're in a temporary situation, but can be made to take pride in their surroundings and keep making advancements.
Is there a way that designers and architects can translate dignity and security into design concepts?
- At CCNV we did not economize on lighting ("downlighting" is considered economical, but is not dignified), we partitioned areas containing six cots each (not the privacy we would like to give, but some), and made sure everyone had a locker so that they would feel secure about their belongings. We even put the names - Mr.... Mrs... - on the locker to help take away the feeling of "living in a waiting room." Beyond that, we were budget restricted.
- The government feels that the only way to assure personal safety is with large open spaces.
Is the large open space concept derived from the military? And is that why they always use government green and gray?
- Yes, that approach is very militaristic.
Has anyone experimented with colors and their impact on the human psyche?
- We did the drop-in center for women in peach and white, and most remarked on the warm and feminine look - and that's what we wanted. In one of the dormitories we dropped the ceiling and put sconces on the walls instead of overhead lighting.
Did you have to overcome objections that this would be impractical and hard to clean?
- The only objection was that it was more expensive - but the fact that it would get dirty sooner never came up.
- The nicer the condition of the shelter, the more likely people will try to keep it nice. On a visit to the *House of Ruth,* I heard an argument among the women on whose room was cleaner.
We're talking about a female environment. Was the same true for men?
- The one I worked with was very well kept - shiny floors, nice drapes on the windows, very clean spreads, - and much better order came out of that. Definitely, when you provide a good environment, people respond to it.
What are some of the architectural problems?
- The most difficult problem is to take an old turn-of-the-century home and make it structurally sound. Then we have to design to the DC building code constraints, fire department regulations, etc. It gets to be a question of what you can squeeze out of that budget.
- A standing building and adapting it to particular needs is really the challenge.
Other points were made on using color for signage when illiteracy is a problem, climates in different parts of the country and their influence on housing, designing large shelters, the ideal shelter (five residents in a homelike atmosphere), the issue posed by some of making the shelter "too comfortable," the emotional damage of a shelter that says, "Boy, I can't wait to get you out of here," and

the happy medium of a well-kept shelter combined with case management and staffing to help people move back into the mainstream.

The volunteer panel members came from the architectural firms of *Weihe Partnership, Richard Adams Architects, Duvall/Hendricks, Bruner, Middleton & Associates,* nonprofit organizations *House of Ruth* and *Search for Shelter,* the law firm of *Howrey & Simon,* and *The Washington Post.*

TACTS VOLUNTEER SHELTER MANAGER TRAINING
The Arlington County Temporary Shelter (TACTS)
PO Box 1285
Arlington, VA 22210
TEL: 703-237-0881
Credit: Inquire
Sponsor: The Arlington County Temporary Shelter (TACTS)
Contact: Judy Wallace
Description: This workshop aims to provide volunteers with additional skills in communication, and to help them learn procedures used in a shelter so that the volunteer can feel comfortable in roles as *Shelter Manager Volunteers.* Participants have the benefit of being trained by staff of a dual-purpose shelter, *TACTS (The Arlington Community Temporary Shelters),* which serves as a safe house for battered women and children, and an emergency shelter for homeless women and families. By the end of the training, volunteers are expected to be:
- familiar with TACTS in-house procedures and policies.
- able to screen clients on the telephone.
- able to make appropriate referrals.
- able to communicate more effectively with clients.
- able to complete TACTS forms with staff assistance.

Volunteers serve as *Shelter Manager Substitutes* as well as *Shelter Managers,* and as administrative aides, food committee members, children's aides, transportation aides, special projects managers, and computer program aides. All receive appropriate additional training. The program is open also to those considering volunteer involvement to give them additional insight into shelter programs.

TOWN MEETING FOR THE HOMELESS
Volunteers of America of Delaware Valley
Church & Evergreen Avenue
Thorofare, NJ 08086
TEL: 609-853-0350
Sponsor: Volunteers of America/Delaware Valley
Contact: Pal Shelly, Director/Communications, or Sheila Allen, Social Worker
Description: This community education meeting was born of what volunteers of VOA Delaware Valley considered to be an injustice. The local zoning board had denied a request for a variance to secure a facility to be used for a new shelter for homeless women and children - even though no opposing testimony was forthcoming from neighbors of the facility.

The selected facility is on 26 acres in Elk Township, Gloucester County, and has nine bedrooms and a gymnasium. Gloucester County is a part of New Jersey that has farms, residential suburban areas, industrial parks, and an array of individuals of various races, nationalities and walks of life.

With the crucial zoning meeting for reconsideration near at hand, VOA staff decided to move quickly and mount an education program for the community about the problem of homelessness and the need for a shelter. This could reach any opposition that might surface. A meeting which included both clergy and laity was held just a few days before a final decision on the site was to be rendered. Presenters made the following points, among others:
- Homelessness is a rural and suburban problem - not just an urban problem in the cities.
- Homelessness in Gloucester County cannot be prevented.
- Those who have to leave their homes also leave friends, neighbors, and churches - familiar resources that could help

them get back on their feet.

Following the presentations, an informal question-and-answer session addressed and satisfied any remaining concerns of participants. As a result of the community education meeting and other efforts of VOA, the volunteer presenters, and the homeless themselves, the zoning board decision was overturned on May 19, 1989. The residents moved into the large house in the fall of the same year.

VOA SYMPOSIUM ON HOMELESSNESS
Volunteers of America
3813 North Causeway
Metairie, LA 70002-1784
TEL: 504-837-2652
Sponsor: Volunteers of America
Contact: Volunteer Coordinator
Description: This symposium is based on the work of *Volunteers of America* over many years of helping the homeless. It is designed to give the benefit of this long experience to those just beginning to provide services in this field. The substance of the symposium is drawn from programs in its 170 local groups across the country - all of whom have had continuous programs since VOA's inception in 1896 to assist the alcoholics, drug abusers, disabled persons, families, youth and the elderly - many of them needing shelter. The symposium is the result of considerable research into these programs to provide a distillation that will be of maximum benefit to participants.

TRAINING/CONFERENCES/TEACHING: HOUSING

TRAINING PROGRAMS

ADOPT-A-FAMILY
SEE FUNDING/FUND-RAISING/RELATED SERVICES: HOUSING

TRAINING/CONFERENCES/TEACHING: I&R

NATIONAL/STATE ORGANIZATIONS

INFORMATION AND REFERRAL RESOURCE AND TRAINING COURSE
SEE INFORMATION & REFERRAL

TRAINING PROGRAMS

FEDERAL INFORMATION POLICIES: ACCESS IS THE KEY (*formerly Federal Library Committee*)
US/Federal Library & Information Center Committee
US/Library of Congress
Washington, DC 20540
TEL: 202-707-6400
Credit: Inquire
Sponsor: US/Library of Congress
Contact: Conference Coordinator

Description: This conference addresses the resolution to be brought to the *White House Conference on Library and Information Services* in July 1991: Citizen access to federal information resources through federal agency information organizations. The conference was designed with two parts:

Part I: Government Information Issues
- Access to Government Information: The Canadian Perspective
- The Future of the Depository Library Program
- Future Trends in Government Information Issues

Part II: Views of the Community
- Public Needs for Federal Information
- The States' Views of Access Issues
- The Medical Community's Views on Open Access
- What Industry Expects from Federal Information Providers
- Information Science and Changing Needs

Related questions posed at the forum included:
- With the emergence of *perestroika,* will policy shift from greater controls to one of open access?
- What impact does federal information policy have on states' and citizen access?
- Should the system of depository libraries be rethought in view of new information technologies?
- What impact does federal information policy have on our economy?

This forum celebrates the 25th anniversary of FLICC, established in 1965 to provide leadership when policy issues affecting the provision of information to government employees and the general public arise. Since 1984, the forums have been held to provide an annual *status report* on information access and dissemination policy. Faculty comes from public and private sectors, including the U.S. Congress, state officials, free libraries, and major universities.

GRASSROOTS CRISIS INTERVENTION CENTER TRAINING PROGRAM
6700 Freetown Road
Columbia, MD 21044
TEL: 301-531-6006
Credit: Inquire
Contact: Harriet Bachman
Description: These periodic training programs are offered in *Crisis Intervention Counseling* by a training team that also operates a crisis intervention program. Training programs combine didactic and experiential approaches in small groups at the Center, led by a trainer who has many years of experience both as a counselor and as a trainer in the field of crisis intervention. Special arrangements are made when an organization or agency prefers to have the training administered on-site.

INFORMATION RESOURCES TRAINING PROGRAM
Volunteers in Technical Assistance
1815 North Lynn Street
Arlington, VA 22209
TEL: 703-276-1800
Credit: None
Sponsor: Volunteers in Technical Assistance
Contact: Brij Mathur
Description: This training program is convened by an international voluntary organization which assists leaders in developing countries as well as the volunteer community in the United States. The purpose of the training is to teach participants how to establish and operate a documentation center or specialized library specific to their programs. Participants learn how to:
- process information;
- set up a skills bank of experts; and
- use microcomputer-based systems.

The course has trained participants in more than 18 countries, and is offered in English, French, and Spanish.

MORE THAN MEETS THE EAR - A LISTENING SKILLS SEMINAR
Volunteer Center of Central Florida
1900 North Mills Avenue
Suite I
Orlando, FL 32803
TEL: 305-896-0945
Credit: CEUs
Sponsor: Volunteer Service Center
Contact: Julie Washburn
Description: Based on the premise that the art of listening depends upon "more than a good pair of ears," this seminar is designed to help participants gain an understanding of the listening process. It encourages the participant to answer the questions:
- What kind of listener are you?
- How can you enhance your ability to communicate on the job or in personal relationships?

The sessions discuss the need to develop different types of listening skills to fit different types of situations, the time and energy required to listen, and knowing HOW to listen. Objectives of the seminar are to:
- Learn six different listening attitudes.
- Identify your favorite listening attitude.
- Learn five non-verbal and five verbal ways to improve listening.
- Write a Personal Action Plan for flexible listening.

Goals of the seminar include a sharpening of skills needed for more positive interactions with others, and the development of more flexible listening to serve as a way to build good relationships with clients and co-workers. The day includes maximum group participation, with each participant completing the *Performax* instrument to learn more about his or her personal listening habits. Another sponsor is the Central Florida Association of Health and Social Services.

TRAINING/CONFERENCES/TEACHING: INTERFAITH

TRAINING PROGRAMS

CHURCH VOLUNTEER ADMINISTRATION
76 Heron Road
Holland, PA 18966
TEL: 215-357-7959
Credit: Inquire
Sponsor: Independent organization
Contact: Janet R. Richards, Consultant
Description: Churches and synagogues depend heavily on the volunteer contribution of time and talent for operation of their programs. Oftentimes the responsibility of maintaining the volunteer component of the church/synagogue operation is in the hands of the same few dedicated members. Consequently, "burnout" is a continuing problem. To compound the problem, many of these well-meaning persons are inexperienced and frequently inadvertent "mismanagement" is the result.

Although the unique aspects of volunteer administration in a church setting need to be addressed, first the basic principles of good volunteer management must be translated to the internal programs of the church to provide better utilization of the wealth of human resources available. The church volunteer administration training program is conducted in the consumer's locale for individual churches and for groups of churches. Workshops are designed to cover three important areas of church volunteer administration:

- Introduction of the concept to groups of pastors.
- Introduction of the concept to key leaders within a congregation.
- Provision of training for congregational volunteer coordinating persons or teams ready to start.

Topics covered in the workshops can include "tailored" areas to meet special needs of a particular group, but always include the following basic topics:

- The unique features of church volunteer administration.
- The motivations of the church's volunteers.
- The reasons for introducing good management principles to the Church's programs.
- How to begin and to develop a volunteer administration program in a church.

VOLUNTEERING IN THE RELIGIOUS SETTING
Interfaith Council of Jacksonville
2250 Oak Street
Jacksonville, FL 32204
TEL: 904-388-2233; 904-356-9471
Credit: Certificate
Sponsor: Interfaith Council of Jacksonville; Volunteer Jacksonville
Contact: Workshop Coordinator (Council), Pepi Dunay (Volunteer Jacksonville)
Description: Addressing the Clergy, Board Chairpersons, Sunday School Superintendents, Youth Directors, Auxiliary Presidents, Ministry Coordinators, Education Directors, Administrators, Ministry Coordinators and others in the Church who work with volunteers, this seminar covers the following topics:

- What is happening in our religious institutions today?
- What kind of leadership do we need?
- What makes people volunteer?
- Why are people sometimes hesitant to volunteer?
- How can you find the right person for the right job?
- How can we communicate to volunteers that their work is important?
- How do you provide work satisfaction for volunteers?

Faculty is drawn from a resource development organization, with the major presenter having held volunteer management positions in churches, schools, and civic groups, and an editor and author of two major references on volunteerism.

TRAINING/CONFERENCES/TEACHING: INTERNSHIPS

NATIONAL/STATE ORGANIZATIONS

CENTER FOR PUBLIC SERVICE
Brown University
25 George Street
PO Box 1974
Providence, RI 02912
TEL: 401-863-2338
Objectives: To encourage participation in public service as a central part of a Brown education.
Services: Since 1986, the Center for Public Service (CPS) at Brown University has provided contact information and printed materials to help students, faculty and administrators interested in public service. Its resource library includes information about summer programs, internships, fellowships, and careers in public service. CPS is also affiliated with Brown Community Outreach which maintains a cleringouse of local volunteer opportunities.
In addition, forums, workshops, and events relating to public service are sponsored by the Center throughout the year. Annual

events include:
Taste of Service - a hands-on introduction to the Providence community for first-year and transfer students - a day of small group service projects designed for students to interact with the larger community.
Public Service Career Day - an annual program of discussions and workshops with alumni and guests who have made a commitment to a career in public service. This event is co-sponsored by the Work Learning and Community Concerns Committee.
Volunteer Opportunity Night - an event sponsored each semester by *Brown Community Outreach* to highlight volunteer opportunities in the local community. (In Spring 1988, 75 community agencies and 500 students participated in the event.)
National and Brown fellowships are made available to students who are planning specific service projects after graduation, have had extensive experience in public service (incoming/returning students), and are interested in designing a student-initiated project that addresses specific community needs, or would like to become involved in a leadership development project in the area of public service.
There are several special programs operating through the Center that provide opportunities for community service:

- **The Mayor's A-Team** - a mentoring program designed to reduce substance-abuse and school dropouts, which pairs Brown students with middle school students who live in public housing projects.
- **The Adult Literacy Program** - an adult literacy tutoring program, which maintains an extensive literacy library for volunteers with information and teaching resources.

The Brown ESL Student Tutoring (BEST) - a program placing students at schools, senior centers, libraries, and other facilities as needed, as well as with individual homebound people; includes opportunity to assist immigrants and refugees in adjusting to their new surroundings.
Other groups are operated totally by students, including:

- **Brown Community Outreach** - a volunteer clearinghouse which placed over 1200 students in 104 agencies during 1988.
- **Student Homeless Action Campaign** - a national organization with a chapter at Brown designed to implement creative solutions to the homeless crisis.
- **Brown South Bronx Summer Project** - student-organized land-reclamation projects in the Hunts Point section of the South Bronx, including development of a city farm and related community services.

The students also are involved in international programs such as Oxfam and the Peace Corps and the Council on International Education Exchange.
Publications: Public Works; Help In Providence; Working with Providence Immigrant and Refugee Communities; Center for Public Service; Community Matters
Founded: 1986

COMMON CAUSE
2030 M Street, NW
Washington, DC 20036
TEL: 202-833-1200
Objectives: To make government more responsive to the needs and demands of citizens.
Services: Examines laws and works to replace "rusty ones" that either are no longer effective or only serve powerful organizations; promotes a "sunset" program calling for review of government programs after a stated period to determine effectiveness and end those serving no purpose; researches and offers recommendations in areas of energy, inflation, government spending, and others; speaks to groups such as colleges, high schools, churches, business groups, as well as foreign groups wishing to review American lobbying techniques and see volunteerism at work on a large scale; conducts comprehensive training program for its volunteers - which include college interns and retired persons; publishes a

bimonthly newsletter, a journal, a report from Washington, and numerous other pamphlets and flyers in areas of government performance.
Publications: Common Cause Magazine; In Common; Frontline
Founded: 1970

INTERGENERATIONAL PROJECT FOR SERVICE LEARNING
SEE VOLUNTEERS: STUDENTS

INTERGENERATIONAL SERVICE-LEARNING PROJECT
SEE SELF-HELP: INTERGENERATIONAL

KENNEDY INTERNS IN RECREATION*
SEE VOLUNTEERS: HANDICAPPED

PUBLIC INTEREST RESEARCH GROUP
PIRG
215 Pennsylvania Avenue, SE
Washington, DC 20003
TEL: 202-547-9707
Objectives: To create public awareness on legal aspects of consumer issues and energy.
Services: Supports laws to protect citizens from unsafe products and unfair banking and telephone practices; supports laws to clean up toxic chemicals and deal with other environmental and energy problems; provides opportunities for students to receive academic credit for various efforts on behalf of consumers; has an internship program for college students; develops and disseminates publications and other materials on public policy, banking and energy issues. (PIRG is sponsored by Ralph Nader.)
Publications: Citizen Agenda
Founded: 1983

TRAINING PROGRAMS

CHANGING VALUES IN EXPERIENTIAL EDUCATION*
National Society for Internships & Experiential Education
124 St. Mary's Street
Raleigh, NC 27605
TEL: 919-834-7536
Credit: Inquire
Sponsor: National Society for Internships and Experiential Education
Contact: Jane C. Kendall
Description: This conference, with changing formats, is held annually by NSIEE, a service organization that acts as a clearinghouse on all types of programs for experiential education, including service-learning, internships, and community service. Sessions are designed to involve participants fully and appropriately in the conference program. After a keynote session, a series of five workshops assist participants in exploring the educational and social traditions of experiential education, and the conflicts that face it today. Basic sessions include:
Theme Workshops:
- Honest Internship Programs
- The Role of the Experiential Educator
- The Politics of Accounting for Experiential Learning
- Inside or Outside the Ivory Tower?
- Experiential Education's Relationship to the Private Sector.
Professional Development Workshops:
- Assessing and Addressing the Learning Needs of Students
- Computerizing Experiential Education Programs
- Using Media to Enhance Your Program Priorities and Directions for Research in Experiential Education
- Evaluation of Experiential Education Programs

Sharing Program Information Workshops:
- University Year for Action: An Evaluation of Community Impact
- Fostering Higher Level Thinking Through Service Learning
- Joint Educational Project House: Making Connections with the City/State Work/Study Program
- Small Colleges and Internship Programs
- Family System/Work System: An Innovative Approach to Student Learning
- How Students Can Lead the Way

An opportunity to meet with representatives of a number of disciplines that involve students in experiential learning (small colleges, secondary schools, cooperation education, private/public internship, service-learning, career education, etc.), become involved in networking activities, and view displays on various programs and techniques which include:
- How Students Themselves Can Open Private Sector Doors
- Locating Experiential Education Programs in Academic Institutions
- Hands-On Experience with Computer Relevant Hardware and Software
- Applying Media/Marketing Techniques to Your Program

Pre-conference sessions and clinics are a feature of the conference. Also, the conference provides a meeting place for the Executive High School Internship Association.

DEMYSTIFYING THE INTERNSHIP EXPERIENCE
Voluntary Action Center of United Way
United Way of Minneapolis Area
404 South Eighth Street
Minneapolis, MN 55404
TEL: 612-340-7532
Credit: CEUs
Sponsor: Minnesota Association for Field Experience Learning
Contact: Dr. Lorna Michelson
Description: Designed to help participants see through the problems and issues to a clearer understanding of the internship experience, this workshop suggests attendance by agency Volunteer Directors, agency site supervisors, internship brokers, college internship coordinators, and faculty sponsors. Workshop areas include:
- **Simplifying Internship Programs** - Learning contracts, job descriptions, evaluation methods, benefits, etc.
- **Spotlight: Two Successful Internship Programs** - Creative ways to involve interns; two examples.
- **Attracting Interns in a Competitive Market** - Promoting the program to increase the chances of presenting an image that will interest interns.
- **Communications Strategies for Internship Supervisors** - Adapting supervisory approaches to the diversity of students to consider the differences in work and learning styles.
- **The Student's View** - Looking at the potential learning experience from the point of view of the student (including dialogue with students).
- **The Faculty Sponsor's View** - Determining what faculty is seeking for the student in an internship setting, and expecting from the intern and from the supervisor (covers techniques for working with faculty sponsors).

Case studies are provided to be viewed at the leisure of the participants for comparison and to extract problem-solving techniques through a "resource table" method of sharing following the lunch period.
The program also includes an Internship Market-place/Network Hour in which internship programs at the colleges are discussed by representatives who answer questions for participants, and in which participants have an opportunity to share information and ideas with other agency and organization staff and volunteer leaders.
Additional sponsors: Twin City Urban Corps and Voluntary Action Center of the St. Paul Area.

ENTERING THE COMMUNITY: SUMMER VOLUNTEER SERVICE AND CAREER OPPORTUNITIES FOR STUDENTS
Young Volunteers in Action
2600 Wells Street
Milwaukee, WI 53233
TEL: 414-933-4224
Credit: Inquire
Sponsor: Volunteer Services Unlimited/UWM; Young Volunteers in Action
Contact: Cheri Farnsworth
Description: This workshop provides basic orientation and training for volunteer service for high school and college students in a number of areas of concern to the community, covering benefits, challenges, and special requirements in individual volunteer settings. Special emphasis is placed on volunteer opportunities that are immediately available as well as summer volunteer projects. Curriculum includes:
Concurrent Workshops:
- Working with the Elderly
- Community Organizing and Advocacy
- Working with Children
- Peer Counseling and Tutoring

Volunteer Fair: a gathering of representatives from over 25 agencies prepared to provide information and materials about volunteer opportunities in their organizations available to students, with special emphasis on summer volunteer projects.
A media representative closed the workshop sessions with an overview on Volunteer Service and Career Opportunities for Students.
The conference is open to all secondary and post-secondary students, educators and administrators, especially those involved in community service or service learning.

SOCIAL LAB
Wissahickon High School
Houston Road
Ambler, PA 19002
TEL: 215-628-1690
Credit: 5 credits
Sponsor: Wissahickon School District
Contact: George McNeil
Description: Specific internships selected by students of *Social Lab* are a major part of this year-long academic program. Students are recruited to join the program in the spring prior to their senior year. Begun in 1971, the program spans two class periods per day in the classroom, and two periods each day at the service site. Classwork incorporates community service, sociology, political science, economics, energy, marriage and the family, and human identity. Placements include health programs, police departments, and day care centers, among numerous other service-related organizations.
The course is team-taught, allowing small-group discussion. A new theme is adopted every four weeks, and the class studies related topics. For each theme, the students are required to write a research paper. Class structure is flexible, with themes chosen to respond to students' needs. Students earn one credit in English and one in Social Studies, as well as three credits for the internship. The grade and credit for the service component are based upon the community sponsor's written evaluation.
Students select their own internships in consultation with the Social Lab Coordinator. The Coordinator locates possible sites, and each student usually visits four or five of them before final placements are made. About half work at two different service organizations during the year; the others remain in the same placement for the year. Students ae responsible for their own transportation to and from the placement sites.
One Social Lab student chose to tutor deaf children, but did not know sign language. The student quickly learned this useful skill,

and takes pride in the progress that her students have made with her help.
Founded: 1971

THE SPICE PROGRAM AND INTRODUCTION
University of Nevada
College of Liberal Arts
4505 Maryland Parkway
Las Vegas, NV 89154
TEL: 702-739-3011
Credit: 3 credits
Sponsor: University of Nevada, Las Vegas; local human service agencies
Contact: Shirley Cox, DSW, Field Practice
Description: The Social Work Department of the University of Nevada at Las Vegas works with some 25 local social sevice agencies to provide students with a volunteer lab experience that is relevant to, and will enhance, classroom instructions:
SWK 100 - The Spice Program: An Introduction to Human Service: Instead of attending classes three times per week, students have two class sessions and a two-hour per week volunteer lab experience in a human service agency. The purpose of the course is to enable the student to develop and utilize communication skills, problem-solving techniques, and actual experience in social service agencies. In addition, the course is expected to stimulate and contribute to the social growth of the student, and help him/her determine the degree of interest in human services as a career.
SWK 101 - Experience in Human Service Agencies: Each student is required to spend three hours per week for 15 weeks as a volunteer in an agency where he or she has the opportunity to integrate the material being presented in the classroom **(SWK 102).** The major goal of this course is to insure the development of effective human service graduates to serve the people of the community. It is also an important community contact for those students who will remain in the Las Vegas area after graduation. Since a portion of classroom instruction is geared to providing students with the skills and techniques needed to be successful volunteer workers, the cooperating agencies, too, have benefited from these courses. The programs have become the key resource for volunteers in these agencies, and many students remain as volunteers in the placement agency long after the courses are completed - even those whose major career goals are not in the areas of professional human services provision.

TEACHING SENIOR CENTER
Wichita State University
University Gerontology Center
Box 121
Wichita, KS 67208
TEL: 316-689-3456
Credit: Course Credit (can be adjunct to one of several courses; inquire)
Sponsor: Administration on Aging (training grant)
Contact: Jan Gold
Description: The Teaching Senior Center is a learning opportunity for faculty and students who have an interest in multipurpose senior centers. Students may intern with any of the service providers operating out of Wichita's new downtown senior center. These services include:
- meals on wheels
- roving pantry
- information and referral
- neighborhood senior centers
- transportation program
- YES (Youth Extending Service)
- senior employment program
- regional long term care ombudsman
- senior health screening
- Kansas Alzheimer's and Similar Diseases Association

Participants have an opportunity to develop service and research projects which improve the quantity, quality, or efficiency of service delivery. Two specific programs are described below:

Internship in Volunteer Administration

The Downtown Senior Center administers an internship in volunteer administration. The intern:

- analyzes the need for and use of additional volunteers in the center;
- studies other volunteer systems as the foundation for recommendations to implementing a Downtown Senior Center volunteer system; and
- sets up a volunteer system to include methods of recruitment, job descriptions, training and evaluation.

University Gerontology Center

The Wichita State University Gerontology Center offers undergraduate and graduate degrees in gerontology, requiring internships such as volunteer transportation coordinators, hospice volunteers, and as assistants in the RSVP (Retired Senior Volunteer Program) and the Foster Grandparents programs (both of which involve older volunteers).

Participants - both faculty and students - are asked to describe the proposed project, the academic course and credit that applies, the academic benefit to be derived by the student from the project, and how the project will improve the lives of older persons.

INDIVIDUAL PROGRAM PROFILES

ALTERNATIVE HOUSE
Juvenile Assistance, McLean, Ltd (JAM)
PO Box 637
McLean, VA 22101
TEL: 703-356-2045

Purpose: To provide a safe, secure environment and/or counseling situation where young people and their families can begin to improve their life situations and resolve the issues that led to their seeking counseling.

Sponsor: Federal/State/County governments; corporate and private donations

Contact: Dana DeVor, Volunteer/Internship Coordinator

Description: Alternative House is a crisis intervention center that offers emergency shelter and counseling to troubled teenagers - primarily runaway, throwaway, or abused kids. The runaway incident is both a signal for help and an opportunity for constructive change. It is important to have an environment which supports development of a positive self-image and competence in skills and abilities. *Alternative House* helps young people gain independence of thought, self understanding, self acceptance, and confidence to confront challenges and make decisions.

Alternative House is the oldest program in Northern Virginia offering residential and counseling services for runaway, homeless, and abused teenagers. Since 1972, when a group of concerned community people incorporated the agency, *Alternative House* has served thousands of teenagers and their families. Our goal is to reunite families whenever possible, increase communication between family members, and resolve the crisis that brought the teenager to *Alternative House.*

Alternative House is best known in the community for our crisis shelter for troubled teens. During their two-week stay, residents have individual, group, and family counseling. Many of them return home. If home is not an option, they may go into custody with the *Department of Human Development,* and then to a foster home or group home.

The family counseling program at *Alternative House* recently has been granted full licensure by the State as an outpatient mental health program, attesting to the high level of quality of its professional counseling services. Other programs include a 24-hour toll-free hotline, walk-in counseling, and free workshops on parenting, adolescence, and other family issues.

Volunteer Program - Volunteers are an integral part of *Alternative House,* and are needed to help provide positive experiences for the residents while serving as appropriate role models. Applicants for volunteer positions go through a screening process and attend 8-10 hours of preliminary training before actual shift work begins. Monthly volunteer meetings and in-service training events are held to provide volunteers with ongoing training. Examples of volunteer job opportunities follow:

- *Direct Service Volunteers:* Work directly with individuals and groups (up to 32 hours/month); ongoing need.
- *Project Safe Place Volunteers:* Distribute promotional material, recruit *Safe Place* participants, help with training and follow-up (5-10 hours/month); ongoing need.
- *Drug Prevention Project Evaluation Volunteers:* Help to develop effective ways of evaluating the effectiveness of our *Drug Prevention Grant* and to help prepare our quarterly reports to D-HHS (5 hours/month); ongoing need.
- *Newsletter Volunteers:* Help us write, edit, and publish our quarterly newsletter (5-10 hours/month); ongoing need.
- *Pocket Card Development Volunteers:* Help develop and distribute *Substance Abuse Prevention Resource & Referral Cards* (5-10 hours/month); four-month project.
- *Youth Council Coordinator Volunteers:* Contact local high schools and acquire recommendations of one or two students per school to help create and maintain a *Youth Council* which meets at *Alternative House* once a month with our Director and Program Director in order to give youth input to our program; help facilitate the meetings (4-5 hours/month); ongoing need.
- *Peer Counseling Program Development Volunteers:* Help develop a sound peer counseling program at *Alternative House,* beginning with *Ala-teen, Teen AA,* and *Teen NA* meetings (5-10 hours/month); ongoing need.
- *Administrative Volunteers:* Help send letters of thanks, update the mailing list, etc.; training provided (5-10 hours/month); ongoing need.
- *Special Project Volunteers:* Needed on an ad-hoc basis for various events and temporary projects throughout the year.

Internship Program - We accept student interns as part of the regular volunteer program at *Alternative House.* These interns become involved with the hotline, walk-in, and residential counseling services that we offer to teenagers and their families. This is a crisis intervention setting, which offers a wide range of clinical experience. The time commitment can be individually negotiated for student interns.

Our long-term family counseling program also accepts interns, usually graduate students in counseling or social work programs. This internship offers intensive training in family therapy, and requires a minimum six-month commitment of 16-40 hours per week.

Alternative House has four levels of internship available to students who are seeking experience and clinical training in work with adolescents and their families. Placement depends on the student's level of education, the time commitment of the internship, and the range of responsibilities which the student is seeking and the agency is able to provide.

Students who wish to receive school credit for their work at *Alternative House* must arrange this through their college or university. We are happy to cooperate with school requirements in terms of hours, supervision, or special evaluations. In addition, we require a personal interview for acceptance into the internship program.

Each intern must go through an initial training period before starting to work in the shelter. All interns receive a supervisor and meet weekly, individually or as a group. Interns are required to attend all in-service training events.

Volunteer and Internship Job Descriptions - Job descriptions for both programs are available on request, and include the four levels for intern positions for students ranging from undergraduate to second year graduate levels. A resume must be submitted with an application for either program to the *Volunteer Coordinator* at the above address. An interview with the *Volunteer Coordinator* is required. Application deadlines for interns are December 15th for the Spring Semester, April 20th for the Summer Semester, and August 20th for the Fall Semester. Both volunteers and interns enjoy free meals when they are here during mealtime periods.

CIPED (COMMUNITY INVOLVEMENT PERSONAL EDUCATION DEVELOPMENT)
SEE VOLUNTEERS: STUDENTS

COMMUNITY FIELD WORK
SEE VOLUNTEERS: STUDENTS

COMMUNITY LEARNING PROGRAM
SEE VOLUNTEERS: STUDENTS

EDUCATIONAL PARTICIPATION IN COMMUNITIES
SEE VOLUNTEERS: STUDENTS

FIELD EDUCATION PROGRAM
SEE VOLUNTEERS: CHURCH/SYNAGOGUE MEMBERS

FIELD EXPERIENCE EDUCATION
SEE VOLUNTEERS: STUDENTS

HEALTHHOUSE VOLUNTEER PROGRAM
555 North County Road
St. James, NY 11786
TEL: 516-862-6743
Purpose: To provide health counseling to women.
Sponsor: Women's Health, Information and Resource Center; Women's Health Alliance of Long Island
Contact: Susan Schiff, Coordinator
Description: Healthhouse is a resource, education and short-term counseling center for women seeking information, help and support on health-related issues. Healthhouse is presently co-directed with directors, both certified social workers, who donate their professional expertise supervising student interns, training volunteers, planning programs, maintaining the information and referral files and seeking funds to keep Healthhouse open. Healthhouse runs workshops and support and discussion groups where they ask a $5.00 donation. Healthhouse also offers patient advocacy service (where a staff person will physically accompany a person to the doctor if he or she needs support, to ask questions, interpret information and listen carefully) and walk-in crisis counseling.
Since the only staff are student interns studying for their MSW at nearby SUNY at Stony Brook, they could not provide all of the services adequately. A volunteer program was initiated and fourteen community women have been trained to staff Healthhouse. The volunteers answer inquiries and provide information. Their only limitations are in the counseling services; otherwise they work along with the students.

THE LEARNING WEB
Center for Religion, Ethics and Social Policy
318 Anabel Taylor Hall
Ithaca, NY 14853
TEL: 607-256-6486
Purpose: To place young people in one-on-one, "hands on" learning experiences outside the classroom.
Sponsor: Center for Religion, Ethics and Social Policy; United Way of Tompkins County; Ithaca City School District; Town and Village of Groton; New York State Division for Youth; Tompkins County Youth Bureau
Contact: Philip Snyder, CRESP

Description: The Learning Web is a community organization which places young people in one-on-one, "hands on" learning experiences outside the classroom. These experiences allow the students to explore any area of interest or to develop skills and interests they already possess. In the past, young people have had Learning Web placements in everything from auto mechanics to medicine and plumbing to music, weaving and dance.
Although the skills a young person learns through his or her placement may well become the foundation for future occupations, the Learning Web does not aim to be a career-education program or a youth-employment service. Instead the Learning Web emphasizes the one-to-one relationship as the process whereby the young person can freely explore the world outside the classroom, try on different identities and find his or her place in the adult world. The program also serves to bridge the gap between the young and the older, the classroom and the community.
These goals are accomplished by matching the young person who has expressed an interest in learning a skill or hobby with a community person who is knowledgeable and willing to share his or her expertise with the student. The two then enter into a "apprentice-mentor" relationship of reciprocal learning and sharing. The "apprentice-mentor" relationship is the heart of the program. Neither the apprentice or mentor are paid for this experience. In setting up the placement, the following procedure is generally used:

- **Referral:** The young person is referred to the Learning Web by a guidance counselor, a case worker, a friend, parent or through "word of mouth."
- **Initial Interview:** A staff member interviews the young person to determine his or her special area of interest or need. This interview includes a discussion of the various learning situations related to his or her field of interest that are available.
- **Placement Procedures:** Once the Learning Web staff and the young person have agreed upon the broad outlines of a program, the Learning Web begins to canvass the community to determine who would be best matched up with the student. Each placement is custom-made to promote, as much as possible, a successful experience for all concerned. When a prospective mentor is located, an initial meeting between the apprentice and mentor is arranged. If, after this session, the two feel that they are able to work well together, a two week trial match is set up. If all continues to go well, the relationship is formalized and allowed to run its course. If the match does not survive the trial period, another more suitable apprenticeship is sought. Apprentices are encouraged to take on as much responsibility as they can in setting up the match so they can set up their own learning situations.
- **Evaluation and Supervision:** after a match is formally established, a weekly check is made with all parties during the first three to four weeks. If things continue to run smoothly, contact drops down to about twice a month. The Learning Web is also committed to involving each program participant in a dialogue between action and reflection, between his or her experience in the community and the implications of that experience for his or her own life. This is done through periodic interviews with Learning Web staff members, with other "apprentices," and an extensive final evaluation of the learning experience that involves input from "mentor," "apprentice," parents, schools, and Web staff, all of which is discussed thoroughly with each program participant.

Most people who participate in the Learning Web are between the ages of 14 and 21. However, the Learning Web is a service open to anyone who has a desire to "learn-by-doing" in the Ithaca area. There are no fees involved for the apprentice or the mentor.
Written parental permission is required of all participants under 18 years of age. Parental involvement early in the process is crucial in order to elicit input that might affect the nature of the match, to insure against the young person's efforts being undermined by parental misunderstandings, and to further extend the network of human resources which is the cornerstone of the program.

SENIOR CITIZEN INTERNSHIP PROGRAM
US/Senate
Office of Sen. William Roth
Washington, DC 20510
TEL: 202-224-2441
Purpose: To give senior community leaders a first-hand view of the federal government and how it operates with regard to their community efforts for the elderly.
Sponsor: US/Senate
Contact: Hon. William Roth
Description: For five days in May of each year, older Americans, usually sponsored by their Congressmen, converge on Washington to work daily hours in their sponsors' offices and attend an exhaustive schedule of discussions. The Senior Citizen Internship Program was created by a Congressman in 1972 with nine interns. Since then (through the 1980 program), 730 seniors have participated. In 1980, the largest group so far, 230 older Americans represented 43 states, with 150 Congressmen volunteering to sponsor persons from their home states and districts.
The senior volunteers (who receive expenses only) view the five-day period as an opportunity for "the elderly and Congress to eyeball each other at close range." They come to learn some shortcuts in dealing with the federal government to use back home in their roles as community activists. The first reaction is surprise in learning about programs for the aged that exist but are not now in their communities.
While in Washington, the interns stay at the same hotel to get to know each other and share ideas and experiences. They also develop a rapport with their Congressional sponsors, "planting the seeds of a communication network that will serve as a continuing link between the community and Congress." They make contacts, jot down names and phone numbers of people in aging programs, and generally make themselves visible and their presence felt.
Federal agencies, private organizations, and Congressional leaders schedule discussions, workshops, and other get-togethers for the "armchair advocates." Although usually sedate, some of the workshops have exploded in heated confrontation when straight answers are not forthcoming. Many officials have been stunned by a circle of irate interns - all probably twice his/her age - questioning a policy or statement.
Once back in their home towns, they are expected to become liaisons with their Congressional offices, keeping "the Hill" informed of needs and problems of the aged, while gaining up-to-date legislation. Among activities by returning interns:
- Ohio - senior transportation services
- Georgia - senior fitness center
- Florida - statewide syndicated column on aging
- Iowa - political grass-roots movement
- Maryland - increase of senior housing; solutions to nursing home problems
- Louisiana - health care services

In addition, a 66-year-old man from the 1980 program decided to run for Congress in 1982, and a couple, both 63, were invited to represent the United States and the elderly in a foreign country. To participate in future programs, senior citizens must contact their representatives in Congress.
Founded: 1972

SERVICE-LEARNING CENTER
SEE VOLUNTEERS: STUDENTS

VERMONT INTERNSHIP PROGRAM
University of Vermont
Center for Service-Learning
41 South Prospect Street
Burlington, VA 05405
TEL: 802-656-2062

Purpose: To provide internship, volunteer and community service opportunities wherein students can impact on problems, issues and projects in connection with their academic, personal and career interests.
Sponsor: University of Vermont
Contact: Hal Woods
Description: The Vermont Internship Program provides both short term, medium term and long term opportunities for students to participate in community service projects in connection with their learning process at the University of Vermont. Students from other colleges in the United States often participate, particularly in the year long University Year for Action program which offers a VISTA type experience with academic credit and stipend. The credit is awarded via a Core Seminar which helps students integrate the service experience in primarily public service oriented institutions and projects. Some internships in business and economic development organizations are available.
The Center for Service-Learning staff coordinates all of the various program opportunities of the Vermont Internship Program. The staff is made up of core professional educators and administrative support staff, graduate assistants, interns, work-study students and volunteers, especially in the student operated University of Vermont Volunteers in Action Program.
Interns and volunteers work in many varied Vermont organizations including state and local government, mental health organizations, education, youth centers, family, alcoholic, and health resource programs, museums, Vermont League of Cities and Towns, businesses, advocacy organizations, counseling centers and other similar organizations.
Opportunities are available for the young volunteer exploring possibilities, the developing volunteer or intern developing skills related to a core discipline or career and to the pre-professional, skilled student who needs experience practicing in the field or organization of career choice, as well as to the citizen advocate who wants to develop academic potential related to an issue or project area.
There is a continuing need for interns and volunteers in the Vermont Internship Program. There is a structured process to support the integration of personal, organizational, academic, financial and community objectives for maximum benefit to all participants.

TRAINING/CONFERENCES/TEACHING: JUSTICE SYSTEM

TRAINING PROGRAMS

CRIME, LAW AND COMMUNITY: A STUDENT SERVICE CURRICULUM
John F. Kennedy High School
Kennedy Drive
Plainview, NY 11803
TEL: 516-931-7280
Sponsor: New York State School System; National Crime Prevention Council
Contact: Dr. Richard Koubeck
Description: This course places community service in the political science curriculum. Students examine crime as a social phenomenon and study its impact on themselves and their classmates, combining this activity with the design of a project to improve community safety. This course fulfills the new *Participation in Government* requirement for graduating from New York State High Schools. The course includes:
Three-week Introduction - this period is used to introduce

participants on how crime affects teens and their communities. The text, *Teens, Crime and the Community,* is used during this period.

Practical Application - These applications include four lessons which students can teach to elementary classes:

- *Latchkey Kids Alert* is taught to third graders with the help of *McGruff, the Crime Dog,* suggesting how nine- and ten-year-olds should act when they are at home without adult supervision.
- *Vandalism* is taught to fourth graders and shows how the consequences ripple throughout the community. It links with an existing fourth grade local studies syllabus.
- *Peer Pressure* is taught to fourth graders also, teaching positive peer pressure and effective ways to reject alcohol and other drugs.
- *Stoplift* is taught to sixth graders to show how shoplifting undermines a community.

The balance of the course for the high school volunteers includes an examination of crime in America as a public policy problem. Students are encouraged to apply their studies to real action projects such as are mounted by the school's *Project Outreach.* The four applications in the course described above came from *Project Outreach,* a program in which JFK students work in the community to start neighborhood watch programs, teach crime prevention to elementary schoolers, and design and manage annual community *Discovery and Celebration Days,* a town meeting format and a street festival. Over 200 JFK students are active every year in this effort.

The process of using crime as a theme through three areas of learning - personal consequences, teaching others, and community and public policy - has resulted in instruction which meets the state's requirements as well as the students' needs to be part of their community's political process.

FAIRFAX ALTERNATIVE SERVICES WORKSHOP
Voluntary Action Center of the Fairfax County Area
10530 Page Avenue
Fairfax, VA 22030
TEL: 703-691-3460
Credit: Inquire
Sponsor: Voluntary Action Center
Contact: Volunteer Coordinator
Description: Offered to volunteer coordinators across the state, this workshop is designed to facilitate sharing of resources to avoid duplication of effort. Questions posed are:

- How does a volunteer coordinator deal with the court referred volunteer?
- What policy guidelines should each agency set before these referrals are accepted?

An open session includes presenters who describe court procedures and timetables, and explain the various classes of crimes. This session is followed by a panel discussion which includes administrators of various court referral programs who describe their programs and provide a profile of the offender/volunteer. Open discussion with the panel enables participants to express their concerns about issues such as:

- the time element when involving alternative service volunteers (usually 50 hours), as it relates to the time needed to train the volunteers;
- confidentially required by the court concerning the court referral;
- the alternative service volunteer relationship with staff and regular volunteers; and
- the category of court referrals (are they volunteers or not?).

Workshop sessions focus on Alternative Service participants through the following issues:

- Agency's willingness to participate in an Alternative Service Program;
- Criteria and procedures for acceptance of Alternative Service

Participants;
- Confidentiality;
- Communication with source of referral of Alternative Service Participants; and
- Relationship of Alternative Service Program to regular program.

These workshop issues are taken from a set of policy guidelines developed through the experience of coordinators in the Fairfax area, but are fully adaptable for guidelines or a similar workshop in any locality. In Fairfax County, they have been used in consultation with the Fairfax County Park/Conservation Division, the Alexandria Hospital, and Culpeper Community Services to help form written policy for these agencies in their Alternative Services Programs, and in consultation with the U.S. District Court during the review and revision of the Court's policy for placing offenders in community service.

FORUM ON SCHOOL VANDALISM
Newark City Council
920 Broad Street
Newark, NJ 07102
TEL: 201-733-3788
Sponsor: Newark City Council
Contact: Henry Martinez, President
Description: This Forum was called as a special meeting of school principals, law enforcement officials and city council officials to grapple with the increasing problems of vandalism in Newark schools. In some cases, windows are smashed and vandals enter the building and spray graffiti inside the school. With hundreds of volunteers spending thousands of hours each year painting over graffiti, the group feels that this type of vandalism is costing volunteer hours that could be put to better use. Solutions suggested included:

- Put a tax on spray paint for a dedicated fund for graffiti removal (Los Angeles gets $2.5 million a year from such a tax).
- Form a *Parental Truancy Task Force* in which parents volunteer to assist the existing board of education task force on this issue, bringing youth vandals before the Board, etc..
- Increase police presence around schools, or have the Board hire its own police.
- Keep parents better informed on this matter; enforce parent accountability laws; pick up kids after curfew and fine their parents.
- Provide recreation or other activity to counter boredom among children with low self-esteem who want to feel bigger.
- Develop a consistent policy and enforce it.
- Work more directly with the children, who are in the schools' hands several hours a day.
- Form volunteer student patrols among the youngsters themselves, giving them the side benefit of self-esteem in performing a civic duty.

The overriding purpose of the Forum was to draw a comprehensive policy on vandalism, graffiti, drug use and other problems in the schools. All suggestions were taken under advisement for further study, with a promise of early action on those selected to address the problems.

INTRODUCTION TO VOLUNTEERISM IN THE JUVENILE JUSTICE SYSTEM (SOCIOLOGY 195: WX AND WX2)
Old Dominion University
Arts and Letters 234
5201 Hampton Boulevard
Norfolk, VA 23508
TEL: 703-489-6546
Credit: 3 hours
Sponsor: Old Dominion University
Contact: Laurie Di Padova

Description: This full-semester course uses four textbooks: *A Handbook for Volunteers in Juvenile Court, The Crime of Punishment, The Throwaway Children*, and *Children as Victims of Institutionalization* and, for the introductory session, the film, *Children in Trouble,* with numerous cassettes and other audiovisuals throughout the course. Weekly course topics include:

- Introduction to Volunteerism in America
- An Overview of the Criminal Justice System
- A Child Goes Through the System
- Problems Juveniles Face (three weekly parts)
- Involvement of Volunteers and Their Impact
- The Volunteer-Client Relationship
- Counseling Techniques
- The Community and the Juvenile Justice System

All sessions use audiovisuals and guest instructors to supplement course content. Field trips are used frequently also as a supplement for advanced students, including destinations such as:

- Hampton House
- Tidewater Detention Home
- Regional Girls' Home
- Pendleton Project
- Richmond Diagnostic Center
- Stanhope House
- Juvenile Crisis Center
- Youth Bureau
- Norfolk Detention Home
- Norfolk Juvenile and Domestic Relations Court (Volunteer Office)
- Probation Field Unit (Arranged by Court Volunteer Office)
- A facility dealing with juveniles selected by the student

A mid-term test and a take-home final exam determine the semester grade. The course may be taken by volunteers who are not full-time Old Dominion students with approval from course instructors.

NATIONAL EDUCATION-TRAINING PROGRAM: VOLUNTEER COURT-CORRECTIONS MOVEMENT
Volunteers in Prevention, Probation, Prisons
527 North Main Street
Royal Oak, MI 48067
TEL: 313-398-8550
Credit: Varies with host college/university or organization
Sponsor: Host college/university or organization and support groups
Contact: Keith J. Leenhouts
Description: This course is intended to assist professors of criminal justice and practitioners of the volunteer court-corrections movement (judges, probation officers, parole officers, coordinators of volunteer programs in criminal justice, etc.) in two ways:

- to insure the future of the volunteer court-corrections movement by presenting courses on criminal justice to citizens while they are college students.
- to improve the present status and "state of the art" of the volunteer court-corrections movement by providing tools and techniques to professors and practitioners to enable them to recruit and train volunteers and professionals to work together in volunteer programs in courts, jails, prisons and juvenile institutions.

The course features 34 hours of high quality audiovisual material on all phases of volunteerism in criminal justice, including such subjects as:

- The dynamics of the one-to-one volunteer.
- The many uses of volunteers.
- Volunteers in Pre-sentence and intake investigations.
- Volunteers in Group Counseling.
- Volunteer-Staff Relations.
- Mechanics of Volunteer Programs in criminal justice.
- Volunteers and minorities.
- Management, administration and funding of volunteer

programs in criminal justice.
- Volunteers in Alcoholic and Drug Programs.
- Retirees and Student Volunteers.
- Research and Evaluation of Volunteer Programs.
- Outstanding films and slide presentations utilized with structured interviews.
- Resources for all phases of volunteerism in criminal justice (programs for the delinquent-prone; alternatives to juvenile institutions; juvenile courts; adult misdemeanants; felons; prisons and parole, and others).

The course involves noted practitioners of the volunteer court-corrections movement, who were involved also in the development of the 100+ page manual designed for the course. The manual suggests additional training and educational materials, field trips, additional resources. Although the course is designed for instruction of college students, it can be beneficial to any group involved in the volunteer court-corrections movement.

NEIGHBORHOOD ANTI-CRIME RALLY/COMMUNITY FORUM
SEE VOLUNTEERS: EMPLOYEES

PROBLEMS FACING VOLUNTEER LEADERS TODAY*
National Association of Volunteers in Criminal Justice
PO Box 6365
University, AL 35486
TEL: 205-348-6738
Credit: Inquire
Contact: David Gooch
Description: This Forum addresses problems facing volunteer leaders today, such as:

- a diminishing tax base from which to operate;
- an ever-increasing need for service from the local community.

The conference is structured so that concerned citizens, paid professionals, and offenders can work together to seek solutions to these problems as they relate to volunteerism and criminal justice. Forum Workshops progress from a person-to-person format to group discussion sessions, as follows:

Person-to-Person Skill Building
- Games Clients Play
- Fulfilling Your Obligations
- Dealing with Significant Others in the Life of a Client
- Introduction to Reality Therapy
- Introduction to Rational Emotive Training
- Crisis Intervention Counseling
- Group Leadership Skills
- Volunteers Working with Sexual Offenders
- The Client Speaks on Volunteerism
- Volunteer-Client: Dealing with Differences in Sex, Age, Role, Race and Goals
- Ex-Offender's Perspective on Corrections Volunteer Ministry

Adapting Programs
- Advocacy for Change - Developing a Win/Win Relationship
- Volunteer Directors: Managers or Doers?
- Presentence Investigation Volunteers
- Building Staff Support for Volunteers
- Time Management
- Surviving the Bureaucracy
- The Volunteer Orientation Manual - How to write it - How to use it
- Rural Volunteerism

Skills for Managers
- Basic Training in the Administration of Volunteer Services
- Training Tools of the Trade
- Matching and Assigning Volunteers
- Planned Recognition of Paid Staff Working with Volunteers
- Developing and Maintaining Effective Advisory Boards
- Performance Plans in a Volunteer Program
- Advanced Training in the Administration of Volunteer

Services
- Where Do You Begin? Starting a Volunteer Program
- Dealing with Burnout
- Recruiting from the Church Community

Current Issues
- Survival and Growth for Volunteer Agencies
- Child Abuse: Ramifications and Manifestations
- How to Make Your Program Integral Rather Than Ancillary
- How to Set Up a State Association on Criminal Justice Volunteerism
- Does Sharing Your Faith Fit Into Criminal Justice Volunteerism?

Justice Volunteerism Discussion Sessions
- Adult Diversion
- Adult Courts and Probation
- Adult Institutions
- Adult Parole
- Juvenile Diversion
- Juvenile Courts and Probation
- Juvenile Institutions
- Juvenile Parole

Mid-conference, The National Coalition of Christian Volunteers in Criminal Justice (NCCVCJ) hosted a prayer breakfast for criminal justice professionals and volunteers. At the close of the conference, the Coalition hosted a two-day post-conference retreat for interested participants.

Presenters for both NAVCJ and NCCVCJ include experts in the corrections field, a former governor and other nationally-known authorities with an interest in the relationship between the criminal justice field and the volunteer community.

VOLUNTEER PROGRAM EFFICIENCY IN A DOWN-SIDED ECONOMY*
National Association of Volunteers in Criminal Justice
PO Box 6365
University, AL 35486
TEL: 205-348-6738
Credit: Inquire
Contact: David Gooch
Description: This workshop is based on the premise that programs utilizing citizen input and services are just too valuable to cut, and - if well managed - can remain an integral part of the organization in the years ahead. It hopes to demonstrate to individuals who are developing and maintaining volunteer efforts that the challenge of the decade and its down-sided economy is not to make decisions as to which program to cut... which to keep... which to give priority... which to simply maintain... but to learn to cope with new challenges while continuing to reach for set goals and agency success.

In this workshop, two factors are explored which are considered of ongoing importance in any effort, but crucial in a down-sided economy if the manager is to maximize program efficiency and effectiveness. These are the factors, as described by workshop leaders:
- **First,** it becomes very critical that dynamic techniques and methods which influence program results be understood by the manager. This will equip the manager for stronger leadership, enhancing the methods and quality of services rendered through unpaid staff.
- **Second,** it is important that volunteer administrators understand their own individual management STYLE, and how that style directly affects program results and people. Research tells us that decisive leadership is the most critical variable in achieving overall organizational success.

Repeated in three strategically selected cities, the locations and dates were carefully chosen to facilitate maximum convenience for participants. Workshop faculty includes Ivan Scheier, international consultant on volunteerism, and John Stoeckel, Executive Director of the National Association of Volunteers in Criminal Justice.

TRAINING/CONFERENCES/TEACHING: LEADERSHIP

TRAINING PROGRAMS

4-H SPECIFIC FORUMS: ADULT VOLUNTEER TRAINING
US/DoA - 4-H Youth/Extension Service
Independence Avenue
(Between 12th & 14th Sts.)
Washington, DC 20250
TEL: 202-447-6527
Credit: Certificate
Sponsor: US/DoA - Department of Agriculture
Contact: Dr. V. Milton Boyce
Description: A Specific Forum in the 4-H training series for adult volunteers addresses one project area (e.g., horses, nutrition, the disabled), with up to five topics covered in as many forums each year. Some of these special interest forums enjoy the funding and personal involvement of a donor company - such as the Campbell Soup Company's involvement in the nutrition forum. With these forums, the primary goal is to teach leadership skills using the particular subject matter area as the vehicle. Examples of specific training programs and topics covered are:

Reaching Out to Disabled Youth, which is designed to help adult leaders to:
- Become more aware of the role of youth serving organizations in the personal development of all youth.
- Gain skills in planning, carrying out and evaluating programs involving youth with disabilities.
- Increase a sense of awareness and competency in working with a mainstreamed population.
- Prepare a plan of approach to work with others to make programs more accessible and meaningful to all youth regardless of disability.

Participation in this forum expands continually as interest in and commitment to the disabled audience around the country deepens. Seven hours of workshops, an idea exchange period and several field trips form the nucleus of the program.

Expanding the 4-H Youth Employment Economics Job and Career Education Model, a program designed to:
- Acquaint Extension staff and Volunteer 4-H Leaders with the 4-H Youth Employment, Economic, Job and Career Education Model.
- Develop the skills of volunteer leaders and Extension Staff to teach young people, train volunteer leaders, and identify and utilize community resources.
- Increase 4-H member participation in youth employment, economic job and career projects and activities.
- Develop a team approach to 4-H programs with teens, adult volunteer leaders, donors, community resources, and Extension Staff working together.
- Review successful youth employment, economics job and career education programs offered by 4-H and other organizations, and determine how they may be adapted to meet the needs of other communities.
- Provide a bibliography of teaching materials available in the area of youth employment, economics, jobs and careers.
- Develop a Leader Training Model which can be incorporated into leader development at the state, area and county levels.

Planning for this program each year is done via Telephonic Conference Calls. Ten hours of workshops and general sessions deal with such topics as Developmental Needs of Youth and Curriculum; Strengthening the Economic, Job and Career Emphasis in 4-H Projects; Developing a Family Approach to Career Education; Developing Programs with a Career Focus. The sessions are supplemented with field trips, panel discussions, a resource center, a Trade Fair, and a session on Designing 4-H

With People. Plans of Action were developed to serve as a guide for back home application.

Nutrition Leader Training, which is designed to help volunteer 4-H leaders to:

- Learn more effective teaching methods.
- Make learning fun for youth and adults.
- Identify and use community resources.
- Build careers into nutrition programs.
- Help 4-H leaders and members set learning goals and assess programs.

Donors such as the Campbell Soup Company (inquire about others) sponsor these Forums. A typical forum was attended by 102 adult volunteers and 4-H staff from 34 states. The purpose was to develop a "teamwork" method of bringing together volunteer 4-H leaders and the Extension staff to help 4-H Food and Nutrition Leaders.

Planning sessions are conducted by Telephonic Conference Calls. Participants were involved in nine hours of workshops dealing with such topics as Practical Ideas and Tools to Promote Nutrition Education, Fitness and Food, Expanding Your Leadership Role, Resources - Material and Community, and Managing 4-H Foods and Nutrition Programs. In the forum sponsored by Campbell Soup Company participants spent a day at the company's headquarters, for which Campbell developed six special leader and member guides dealing with nutrition and fitness information. A follow-up survey is conducted nine months after each forum to determine ways in which participants use the learning experience.

Planning committees for the specific forums consist of volunteer leaders, salaried staff, representatives of National 4-H Council and USDA, and the donor company, who develop and conduct the program for each forum. Most specific forums are fully or partially funded by donors.

General forums change to meet the needs expressed by the planning committees and participating states.

In addition to 4-H groups, adult volunteers who attend the forums work with schools, church groups, senior citizens groups, Extension Homemakers Clubs, civic organizations and the general public.

TRAINING/CONFERENCES/TEACHING: LITERACY

INDIVIDUAL PROGRAM PROFILES

CHILDREN'S LITERACY INITIATIVE
1207 Chestnut
Philadelphia, PA 19107
TEL: 215-561-7323
Purpose: To train day care workers, teachers and parents in improving reading skills of young children at risk of illiteracy.
Sponsor: Ragan Henry Law Firm
Contact: Marcia Moon or Linda Katz, Founders
Description: Working since 1988 out of donated space in a local attorney's office, *Children's Literacy Initiative* promotes literacy training and offers literacy workshops to day care centers serving low-income families. Some of the books and other materials used in the training become part of an annual event, *Children's Expo*, which is sponsored by the group and trains day care workers, teachers and parents to develop reading interests and skills in young children, especially poor, inner-city children most at risk of illiteracy. The 1989 *Expo* attracted 14,000 people from the Philadelphia area.

Given the success of the organization's efforts, the founders have

created concepts for seven radio shows and tapped a number of children's entertainers to host them. Called *Kidwaves*, the shows are geared to help children enrich their imaginations, expand their vocabularies and lengthen their attentions spans. They are also aimed at parents - hoping they will be encouraged to read to their children. Programming includes *In Concert*, which features a performance by and an interview with an artist; *Story Stew*, which features stories read and told live by guest tale-tellers, and other enrichment segments.

It is hoped that the volunteer effort and interest shown by the community for the umbrella organization, *Childrens's Literacy Initiative*, and the annual *Children's Expo* will continue for *Kidwaves*. The schools got behind them, distributed handbills, hung posters, etc. Libraries, day care, clergy associations, Head Start programs, and others with an interest in children also got involved in spreading the word.

Unlike the others, *Kidwaves* is necessarily a profit-making venture, but the quality of the programming and types of products in the advertisements are closely monitored. Types of products *not* accepted include video games, pro-wrestling tie-ins or violent toys. Since radio audiences under 12 years of age are not tracked for audience size, attracting advertisers to finance the program is expected to be difficult.

One example that shines like a beacon for the group is KPAL-AM in Little Rock, Arkansas, which began in 1986 to broadcast an all-children's format from 6 a.m. to 9 p.m. each day. It not only was financed long enough to stay in the black, but won the coveted *George Foster Peabody Award* and several other awards. KPAL officials attribute much of its success to quality programming and working closely with city schools, day care facilities and parents/kids groups to continually evalutate the program. Some 8,000 children joined the free KPAL Clubhouse, and 15,000 visited the studios each year.

In mid-1990, *Children's Literacy Initiative* founders began fanning out across the country to talk with AM station owners. In the meantime, the *Initiative* and the *Expo* continue to involve families in inspiring children in the Philadelphia area to read.
Founded: 1988

TRAINING/CONFERENCES/TEACHING: MENTAL HEALTH

TRAINING PROGRAMS

BEFRIENDER TRAINING
Amherst Wilder Foundation
919 Lafond
St. Paul, MN 55104
TEL: 612-457-2420
Credit: Inquire
Sponsor: Amherst Wilder Foundation
Contact: Juanita Geisz
Description: The Foundation provides periodic training for volunteers who are interested in providing supportive friendships to those in stressful situations or times of crisis through mutual concern, mutual contact, and a mutual sense of contribution. Training is designed to increase skills in the following areas:
Communication Skills
How to listen
How to encourage feeling messages
How to communicate without being threatening
Crisis Intervention
How to recognize the need for intervention
How to refer someone if it seems advisable

How to help the person get help through referral
To realize that referral is not a sign of weakness
Grief
How to deal with grief in effective ways
To understand that death is not the only loss we suffer
Depression
How to recognize the signs of depression
How to help the person live through the process
Self-Care
To understand the importance of self-care
in order to be able to be a friend to others
To recognize one's own needs in caring for others

Upon completion of training, volunteers are placed in one of a number of areas of Befriender experience, including:
Experiencing loss
Unemployed or economically disadvantaged
Terminally ill
Parent-child problems
Marriage problems
Chemically dependent
Victim of family violence
Abusive person
Divorced (or going through divorce)
Spiritual crisis
Faculty is drawn from the fields represented by the above areas of concern, and the Foundation itself. Befriender Coordinators participate in the training as instructors and observors to provide a stronger link in the Coordinator/Volunteer relationship.

TRAINING/CONFERENCES/TEACHING: MILITARY

TRAINING PROGRAMS

MANAGEMENT OF VOLUNTEER PROGRAMS IN THE ARMED FORCES
SEE VOLUNTEERS: ARMED FORCES MEMBERS

TRAINING/CONFERENCES/TEACHING: OLDER PERSON

NATIONAL/STATE ORGANIZATIONS

WESTERN GERONTOLOGICAL SOCIETY*
SEE VOLUNTEERS: OLDER PERSONS

TRAINING PROGRAMS

VOLUNTARISM: A KEY TO THE FUTURE*
US/HHS - Administration on Aging
Region V
Chicago, IL 60603
TEL: 312-353-3141
Credit: Certificate
Sponsor: US/HHS - Department of Health & Human Services
Contact: Eli Lipschultz

Description: This seminar is one of an ongoing series entitled Commissioner's Forum on Aging. The purpose of this series is to bring together a cross-section of leaders from both the public and the private sectors to discuss issues and perspectives in the field of aging. Nationally-known presenters work with participants on major aspects of the theme: *Older Americans: Our Keys to the Future.* Presentations focus on voluntarism as a major thread through the fabric of society and addresses questions such as:
- What kind of voluntary programs have evolved in various segments of society, especially in areas of the private sector such as corporations, unions and churches?
- What difference have volunteers made in the quality of life of older persons?
- What barriers in voluntarism, if any, exist and how do we eliminate them?

The ultimate purpose of the workshop is to record comments and recommendations by participants for presentation to the Commissioner on Aging. Recommendations resulting from the Forum often are used to redirect policy and/or to establish new initiatives for the Administration on Aging.

TRAINING/CONFERENCES/TEACHING: OLDER VOLUNTEER

TRAINING PROGRAMS

ELDERS AND VOLUNTARISM*
Western Gerontological Society*
785 Market Street
Suite 1114
San Francisco, CA 94103
TEL: 415-543-2617
Credit: CEUs; AVA Certification (partial fulfillment)
Sponsor: Workshop Coordinator
Contact: ACTION; Western Gerontological Society
Description: Part of a series, this workshop addresses current issues and administrative concerns of people involved with senior volunteers. It provides an opportunity for both project staff and volunteers to consider future directions in senior voluntarism from the perspectives of leaders in the field. Programs schedule includes:
- Voluntarism and Older Adults
- Advocacy: New Forms of Citizen Participation
- Growing Older Bolder
- Creative Programming by Older Volunteers in Institutions of Higher Learning
- Golden Era Handicrafts
- Involving the Homebound in Volunteer Roles
- Spotlight on Older Americans Volunteer Demonstration Projects
- The Use of Deaf Sign Language by Senior Volunteers
- Creative Volunteering for Seniors
- Self-Supporting Senior Services
- Imaginative Volunteer Opportunities in Rural Areas
- Involving Non-Traditional Volunteers
- Ethical Considerations in Voluntarism
- A Look at Older Americans Programs and the Indian Reservations
- Volunteer Transportation Alternatives: Coping with High Cost and Short Supply
- When Health Declines - Phasing out the Older Volunteer
- Senior Voluntarism in the Eighties
- Helping Agencies Utilize Older Volunteers Creatively
- Senior Volunteer Support for High-Risk Pregnant Teenagers
- Spotlight on Three Special Projects

- Creative Assignments for Chemically Dependent Volunteers
- Getting the Most Out of Your Paid and Non-Paid Management Team
- Rural Voluntarism Strategies, Problems and Resources for Involving People
- Working with Committees and Advisory Councils
- Retired Senior Volunteers Living in Nursing Homes
- Volunteers as Fixed Income Consumer Counselors in Rural Areas
- Purposeful Living Through Volunteer Activity
- Voluntarism in a New Decade: The Veterans Administration in a New Frontier
- Developing a Permanent Funding Base
- ACTION's Older Americans Volunteer Programs

In addition to the above workshops, two sessions for the entire assembly address overall issues:

Intensive - Voluntarism and Older Adults - to identify frequent blocks to senior involvement and suggest strategies to remove these obstacles.

Major Symposium - Senior Voluntarism in the Eighties - a projection on voluntarism in this decade, with a faculty of experts in the field of voluntarism.

Peer Group Workshops, Idea Exchanges, Roundtable Discussion Groups, and Lectures are additional features of the five-day program.

OLDER AMERICANS AS A GROWING NATIONAL RESOURCE*
DOVIA (Directors of Volunteers in Agencies)
1017 North Third Street
Suite 20
Phoenix, AZ 85004
TEL: 602-253-6951
Credit: 14 hours/AVA endorsed
Sponsor: DOVIA (Directors of Volunteers in Agencies); US/ACTION
Contact: Nydia Martinez, Director, RSVP
Description: With a $2,000 mini-grant from ACTION, DOVIA developed a mini-conference to formulate specific recommendations for Arizona's delegation to present to the White House Conference related to Older Americans as a Growing National Resource.
Issues identified and scheduled for exploration and discussion at the mini-conference include:
- What should be done to expand the role of Senior Volunteers and enhance the quality of community life?
- What incentives should be developed as to what advocacy is needed to make volunteerism more desirable?
- What form of training is needed for volunteers and volunteer coordinators to participate in and effectively direct volunteer programs (from the perspective of both volunteers and volunteer coordinators)?
- What should the future hold regarding: (1) volunteer recruitment, placement and retention and (2) the philosophy of volunteerism?

Post-Conference Evaluation: Over seventy-five volunteers, volunteer administrators, and other professionals attended the mini-conference. Follow-up with these participants indicated that the meeting did meet its goal with useful recommendations for Arizona's delegation on the White House Conference on Older Americans as a Growing National Resource.
Facilitator for the conference was Dr. Eva Schindler-Rainman, Consultant on Community and Organizational Development.

TRAINING/CONFERENCES/TEACHING: PARENTING

TRAINING PROGRAMS

NATIONAL CONFERENCE ON DRUG ABUSE AND PARENTING*
SEE TRAINING/CONFERENCES/TEACHING: DRUGS/ALCOHOL

TRAINING/CONFERENCES/TEACHING: PHILOSOPHY

TRAINING PROGRAMS

ARROWHEAD 22: FUTURE CHALLENGES: A UNIVERSAL PERSPECTIVE
Lake Arrowhead Conference for Volunteer Program Administrators
University of California
Conference Center
Lake Arrowhead, CA 92352
TEL: 714-337-2478
Credit: Two Units of University Credit
Sponsor: Lake Arrowhead Conferences; University of California
Contact: Eva Schindler-Rainman, DSW, Dean
Description: The Arrowhead conference draws faculty from major leaders in the voluntary and nonprofit fields. The conference is participative, with opportunities to share experiences, learn from experts, study recent literature in the field, and enjoy individual and group consultations with each other and staff.
The conference focus is on creative thinking, skills building, and enlarging perspectives. General topics are set well in advance, with a built-in flexibility to allow for additional participant concerns and/or contributions. Topics on the schedule:
- Making Change Happen
- Conflict Resolution
- Stress Management
- Management Skills
- Creative Funding
- Corporate Involvement
- The Volunteer Workplace

Staffing, in addition to the Dean above, comes from city government, the school system, national and international associations, the mental health field, academe and other fields.

CONFERENCE ON PHILOSOPHICAL ISSUES IN VOLUNTEERISM
Virginia Polytechnic Institute and State University
Department of Political Science
Blacksburg, VA 24061
TEL: 703-961-5268; 703-961-5491
Credit: Inquire
Sponsor: Virginia Polytechnic Institute and State University; Virginia Foundation for Humanities and Public Policy
Contact: Dr. John Harmon or Dr. Richard C. Rich
Description: This conference explores the ethical, legal, strategic and tactical issues confronting the volunteer community, and the importance of the ways these issues are resolved. It provides an opportunity for members and leaders of the volunteer community to meet with scholars who have studied the issues to seek and

share new insights into common problems and possible solutions. Organized around eleven broad issues, the conference presents a panel on each issue led by an authority on the subject who discusses central aspects of the issue and alternative approaches to its resolution. Half of the panel session provides for reaction for panel members from their own experience, and half is reserved for audience discussion, producing an informal working session. The eleven issues are:
- Social Problems and Voluntary Action
- Altruism and Voluntary Action
- Volunteerism, Self-Government, and Democratic Theory
- Professionalism of Voluntary Organizations
- Social Responsibility of Business and Voluntary Organizations
- Rights of Recipients
- Government Sponsorship of Voluntary Action
- Professionals and Volunteers
- Bureaucracy and Voluntary Organizations
- Rights of Volunteers

Three closing workshops represent the three general areas of concern into which the eleven issues can be divided:
1. Environmental Factors and Voluntary Organizations;
2. Internal Aspects of Voluntary Organizations; and
3. Government and Voluntary Organizations.
These workshops strive to produce recommendations on the issues, and a code of ethics for the volunteer community.

NATIONAL FORUM ON A COMMISSION ON VOLUNTEERISM: THE FEDERAL GOVERNMENT AND FUTURE OF VOLUNTEERISM*
SEE ADMINISTRATION: PHILOSOPHY OF VOLUNTEERISM

THE QUEST FOR COMMUNITY
SEE GOVERNORS' OFFICES ON VOLUNTEERISM: VIRGINIA

VOLUNTEERISM: A BRIDGE TO THE FUTURE
SEE GOVERNORS' OFFICES ON VOLUNTEERISM: WASHINGTON

VOLUNTEERS DO MAKE A DIFFERENCE!
SEE GOVERNORS' OFFICES ON VOLUNTEERISM: DELAWARE

VOLUNTEERS: FACTS AND FICTION
Pennsylvania Statewide Symposium on Voluntarism & Education
Pennsylvania State University
410 Keller Conference Center
University Park, PA 16802
TEL: 814-865-4591; 215-357-7959
Credit: 1.4 CEUs; AVA Certification (partial fulfillment)
Sponsor: Pennsylvania State University
Contact: Mary Ann Solic or Janet S. Richards
Description: This symposium looks at "what volunteers are and are not, can and cannot do, will and will not do." It affords an opportunity for information sharing among colleagues and fellow citizens to:
- identify critical issues and opportunities in volunteerism.
- advance the skills and understanding needed to address these issues.
- assess the current and potential role of educational institutions in supporting volunteerism.
- build a stronger statewide network for cooperation among volunteer leaders and administrators.
Following a Strategy Exchange, an open session is convened to bring together people who can benefit most from each other's expertise; specific workshops include:
- The Art and Craft of Training: a seven-step process of:

designing training; diagnosing needs for training; deciding when to train and when to manage; producing a lesson plan; implementing a training program; and evaluating results.
- Managing Human Resources: a job description is not forever; supervision means growth; volunteers move - onward, upward, outward; for whom do you manage: agency or volunteers?
- A Group Is Not a Mob
- Group Dynamics: leadership styles; team building; problem-solving; communication barriers; resistance to change; positive use of conflict; motivation and developmental stages; how the democratic leader makes things happen.
- There's a New Wind A-Blowing: a fresh look at volunteering in the church; why the church is the oldest voluntary organization; the lay ministry: what it is and isn't; does the church exploit its volunteers?
- Making Yourself Felt on the Political Scene: A Panel: The Skills of the Lobbyist; the citizen as activist; life on the "Hill."
- Marketing Volunteering to Management - The New Climate: what volunteer administrators need to do in their own agencies to sell the idea of volunteering and to demonstrate its potential and importance; an update of trends that affect volunteers and voluntary organizations.

The symposium is directed to professional administrators or volunteer community leaders, persons who serve a public agency or a voluntary organization, those who have a primary concern with health and human services, cultural and religious institutions, or community organizations. Faculty is drawn from the volunteer community, the health field, the field of education, professional associations, civic and community groups, and others.

TRAINING/CONFERENCES/TEACHING: RECRUITMENT

TRAINING PROGRAMS

DEVELOPING YOUR PERSPECTIVE: RECRUITING VOLUNTEERS
Volunteers In Action
229 Waterman Street
Providence, RI 02906
TEL: 401-421-6547; 401-421-7472
Credit: AVA Certification (partial fulfillment)
Sponsor: United Way
Contact: Betsy A. Garland
Description: This seminar is designed for anyone who runs a volunteer program. It presents both concepts and methods for recruiting volunteers. The seminar includes:
- Volunteers today: implications for recruitment
- Principles for effective recruitment
- Identification of various recruitment strategies
- Development of a recruitment plan
The seminar is designed for service clubs, community organizations, church groups, volunteer administrators, alumnae groups, committee chairpersons, board members, youth groups, and any other group or individual who wants to recruit volunteers. The seminar is limited to 15 participants.
Volunteers In Action (VIA) is a statewide voluntary action center accredited by the Association of Volunteer Centers. Its training programs are accepted as partial fulfillment for professional certification by the Association for Volunteer Administration. VIA satellite centers are located in Woonsocket (401-762-0679), and Wakefield (401-789-9149), with others planned (inquire).

RECRUITING TECHNIQUES FOR VOLUNTEER ORGANIZATIONS
Chesapeake College
Office of Public Relations
PO Box 8
Wye Mills, MD 21679
TEL: 301-822-5400
Credit: CEUs
Sponsor: Chesapeake College
Contact: Patti K. Willis
Description: This course is designed for the person who is a volunteer worker for a health, social, or other volunteer organization. It is directed primarily to the volunteer or the paid worker responsible for recruiting volunteers.
Course content is designed to increase volunteers' effectiveness and their motivation for doing volunteer work. Course format includes lecture and group discussion, and lasts for 6-1/2 hours in a one-day session. Upon completion of the course, the volunteer recruiter is expected to be familiar with:
- The history of volunteerism in this country.
- The role of volunteers in an organization, and the future hopes for a volunteer market.
- Marketing the organization to recruit volunteers.
- Meeting volunteer needs AND organizational needs.

The course is sponsored and funded by the Chesapeake College Center for Continuing Education. It is a non-credit course. There is a large response to the course each time it is offered, and the college will continue to offer it as long as there is a need. The course may be offered on special request at times other than those scheduled to groups representing specific volunteer efforts.
The faculty is drawn from the college's public relations division, including a volunteer whose interests lie in this area. The college is considering a companion course to this one - a non-credit course on fund raising for volunteer organizations.
Another sponsor is Maryland Nursing Home Ombudsmen.

RECRUITING, TRAINING AND RETENTION OF VOLUNTEERS
People Helping People/Cheyenne
406 Seventeenth Street
PO Box 404
Cheyenne, WY 82001
TEL: 307-632-4132
Credit: Inquire
Sponsor: Laramie County Voluntary Action Center; Laramie County United Way (space provided by Warren Air Force Base)
Contact: Marie Baptiste
Description: This workshop was developed when two related issues became apparent regarding delivery of services to citizens of Laramie County:
- The need to incorporate volunteers effectively into the county's schools and service agencies was increasing daily in urgency.
- Most people in helping professions in the county, who find themselves responsible for volunteers, have little or no training in the management skills necessary to plan, implement and evaluate effective volunteer programs.

The County's VAC and United Way addressed this issue by scheduling a workshop to focus on how to recruit, train and retain volunteers. They enlisted the help of Marlene Wilson for a full day program. Topics include:
- Challenges and Trends in the Volunteer World
- Why do you need to recruit volunteers? - how to plan for volunteer involvement, how to design jobs that attract and keep volunteers
- How and where do you find volunteers today? - how creative recruiting helps you find those you really need, "target" vs "shot-gun" methods of recruiting
- How do you keep volunteers once you have them? -

staff/volunteer relationships, recognition, support/training, evaluation
In addition to the above, the Laramie County Community College and local social service groups address specific concerns of local volunteer leaders.

VOLUNTEER INTERVENING FOR EQUITY (VIE)*
Association of Junior Leagues
Department of Programs
825 Third Avenue
New York, NY 10022
TEL: 212-355-4380
Credit: Inquire
Sponsor: Association of Junior Leagues
Contact: Director, Project V.I.E.
Description: V.I.E. is an advocacy project requiring two kinds of training:
- Pre-project training to equip the participant with a broader community education as well as a general knowledge of the issues in the focus area;
- In-service training to sharpen or build skills needed for specific tasks (to insure quality training and offer a reward for volunteers).

Pre-service training is designed to be accomplished in a relatively short time - three to six weeks - and includes:
- Explanation of the project
- Ground rules for project management (number of meetings to be held, number of hours volunteers will be required to work, etc.)
- A discussion of advocacy
- Introduction to the focus area
- Preliminary discussions of how specific issues within the focus area will be defined and selected

The "laboratory training" component is not extended despite the inevitable timidity of some volunteers.
The in-service training component is based on a design by volunteers and members of a steering committee. It begins as soon as the volunteer advocate begins an assignment, and is flexible to the point that it evolves as volunteers become aware of what more they need to know in order to identify specific issues and plan strategies. For example, in one League site, foster care was the program focus, and volunteers requested that foster parents be brought together to discuss concerns as part of the advocates' in-service training program. Volunteers also hear talks such as "Foster Children and the Juvenile Justice System" by a Juvenile Court Judge, participate in concept sessions with a panel of professors from major universities, host visits from related federal agencies, etc.
Informal support sessions where volunteers learn from each other are important components of the training program. In addition, the agenda includes practice sessions (conducting an interview, counseling a client, etc.), questionnaires, field trips, reading lists, visual aids, being interviewed by others, and other activities based on emerging issues not previously covered, and expressed needs of the volunteer advocates themselves.
This national program expects leaders in each community training site to develop and draw from a local volunteer pool for trainers, including those within the organization itself, community leaders and specialists, and volunteers with special skills from the group to be trained. Experience has shown that excellent resources for training exist in most communities. Some examples: those with marketing backgrounds conduct sessions on questionnaire design and analysis; economists train groups in data analysis, newspaper editors give courses on how to start a newsletter, nurses talk about record keeping, clerics lead workshops in sensitivity training and conflict management.
A final word of advice from V.I.E. people: "Recruit carefully so that chances are good that the group will embody most of the basic skills that will be needed during the lifetime of the project."

This principle, followed by careful training, is the guiding philosophy behind the V.I.E. program.

VOLUNTEER STAFFING WORKSHOPS*
Volunteer Center of Chicago
United Way Crusade of Mercy
125 South Clark Street
Chicago, IL 60603-4012
TEL: 312-580-2723
Credit: Certificate; CEUs on request
Sponsor: United Way of Chicago
Contact: Joe Agnello
Description: This series of workshops (previously offered by the Voluntary Action Center) is intended to help human service organizations develop an effective staffing program. It is based on the premise that when an organization effectively recruits, selects and trains its volunteers, the organization is likely to have a well managed volunteer program. Primarily intended for new volunteer administrators in human service organizations, it can be useful to anyone who works with volunteers. The three one-day workshops are:
Recruiting Volunteers - This workshop is based on the need for human service organizations to cope with rapidly changing conditions through increased involvement of volunteers. It teaches them to choose specific volunteers for specific jobs so that they increase the system's energy, rather than have no effect on it, or even drain it. The workshop is intended to help participants develop an effective system for recruiting volunteers through:
  ● Understanding why people join volunteer organizations.
  ● Learning how to do human resource planning (find the right volunteer for the right job) in a volunteer program.
  ● Understanding the basic elements of the recruitment process.
  ● Dealing with common volunteer recruitment problems.
Selecting Volunteers - This workshop works with the issue of the volunteer's freedom to choose specific volunteer jobs, and helps volunteer administrators develop an effective selection strategy to assure needs and skills are matched to the best advantage of the agency. Development of an exchange relationship in which both the organization's and the volunteer's needs are met is the fundamental goal sought in this workshop through:
  ● Understanding the basic elements of the selection process.
  ● Developing interviewing skills for the selection, placement, performance appraisal and termination of volunteers.
  ● Learning how to match the volunteer's needs, interests and skills with organization jobs.
  ● Dealing with common volunteer selection problems.
Training Volunteers - Recognizing that volunteers bring a wide range of skills and interests with them when they join organizations, this workshop hopes to fill a gap that often exists between what volunteers know and what they need to know. It is based on the premise that experiential education in which action, reflection, theory and testing are integrated is fundamental to an effective training and development strategy. The workshop is intended to help participants develop a system for training volunteers both on the job and in the classroom through:
  ● examining personal learning styles.
  ● understanding the basic elements of effective training.
  ● practicing skills in developing, conducting and evaluating training programs.
  ● dealing with common volunteer training problems.
One of the workshops is scheduled each month for three months. They can be taken individually or as a series. Although primarily intended for new volunteer administrators, they can be beneficial to anyone who works with volunteers.

VOLUNTEER TRAINING AND RECRUITMENT CONFERENCE
Metropolitan Council for Community Services
Box 4029
Chattanooga, TN 37405
TEL: 615-265-0514
Credit: 1.1 CEU
Sponsor: Volunteer Center; Junior League of Chattanooga
Contact: Anne Henniss
Description: This conference is designed to assist Volunteer Coordinators in two tasks that are crucial to any volunteer program - recruitment and training. After opening with a skit on volunteering, two keynote speeches were presented: *On Volunteering* and *Overview of Volunteer Opportunities* (the first day). The second day opened with a panel program entitled *How Safe is the Safety Net?* (on the impact of budget cuts on human services programs). Twenty workshops were conducted over the two-day period, shown below:
  ● Time Management
  ● Working with the Aging
  ● Working with Special Needs Children
  ● Working with Troubled Teenagers
  ● Health Care Services Delivery
  ● Drugs and Alcohol
  ● Assertiveness Training
  ● Working with Staff
  ● The Arts and the Volunteer
  ● Volunteering in a Mental Health Setting
  ● How to Avoid Burnout
  ● Advocacy Volunteering
  ● Community Resources
  ● Being a Board Member
  ● Personal Skills Development as a Volunteer
  ● Volunteer Opportunities for Teens
  ● Communication Skills for Adults and Teens
  ● Lay Ministry in Social Service Delivery
  ● Crisis Management and Conflict Resolution
  ● Working with the Physically Handicapped
Participants select four of these half-day workshops for the conference period. A general session on Legal Liability Aspects of Volunteering concluded the program.

TRAINING/CONFERENCES/TEACHING: SELF-HELP

TRAINING PROGRAMS

THE SELF-HELP MOVEMENT: NEW FORM OF VOLUNTEERISM AND A RESOURCE FOR PROFESSIONALS*
SEE SELF-HELP

TRAINING/CONFERENCES/TEACHING: STUDENTS

TRAINING PROGRAMS

COMMUNITY INVOLVEMENT PROGRAM
Hopkins High School
2400 Lindbergh Drive
Minnetonka, MN 55343
TEL: 612-541-7100
Sponsor: Hopkins High School
Contact: Dan Conrad
Description: The Community Involvement Program of Hopkins High School is an 18-week course which includes eight class periods in the community and a two-hour in-class session each week. It enables students to explore careers, gain skills, learn about the community in particular and society in general, and gain overall personal satisfaction.

The course is designed in modules including:
- **Leadership and Human Service** - This series of workshops covers the first three weeks of the course. They are designed to develop students' skills in working with people and allow them to gain insight into themselves, examine various options for service, and determine where they will begin their community assignments. Agency representatives visit the class early in the semester to discuss placement opportunities. Students may choose from these or develop individualized projects.
- **Community Involvement Seminar** - This seminar takes place each Friday during two regular class periods. Students share their volunteer experiences and listen to and support others.
- **Classes** - Class topics include specific subjects as well as issue-oriented training: sociology, applied psychology, critical thinking, helping skills, issues in understanding people, and working effectively with people
- **Volunteer Agreement** - This results from interviews by prospective agencies enabling both student and site supervisor to decide on an appropriate placement. If both agree that placement will be mutually beneficial, the Volunteer Agreement is signed by both parties. This agreement includes a clear description of the student's tasks and responsibilities, as well as the overall purposes and goals of the effort.

About 100 students of the 500-member senior class can be found on any given day in community volunteer programs. These have included day care centers, nursing homes, schools, drug abuse treatment centers (often as counselors), and political groups.

All students check in with the school's program coordinator before leaving for their volunteer sites. Perfect attendance and performance excellence are expected. Evaluation by both student and supervisor marks the end of the course.
Founded: 1975

COMMUNITY SERVICES
Parkersburg High School
2101 Dudley Avenue
Parkersburg, WV 26101-3492
TEL: 304-420-9595
Credit: One-half credit
Sponsor: Parkersburg School District
Contact: Andre Brown
Description: Students receive one-half social studies credit for participation in the *Community Services* training course. They learn first-hand the various aspects of social work and volunteerism in the community. Each year, about 200 students participate. The curriculum covers five class periods each week - one in the classroom or on field trips, and four in the community

at service sites. Course work is geared to meet any needs that may arise from the field work, and to instill an understanding of social work and volunteerism. The curriculum includes:
- The history of volunteerism in the West and its status today, with an emphasis on the local community
- Seminar on Volunteerism in the Future
- Outside lectures and presentations
- A forum for students to share accomplishments and discuss solutions to problems
- Familiarizing students with placement opportunities (spread over the first two weeks of the course)
- Small-group Action Projects (such as the plan developed by the students for making structural changes in the high school to allow handicapped persons access to the building)

Students have chosen work in hospitals, day care centers, schools (tutoring), the Red Cross, the YMCA, public libraries, mental health institutions, and residential care facilities, among others. Each student is responsible for transportation, but those without cars are placed, when possible, at participating agencies within walking distance.

COOL NATIONAL CONFERENCE
Campus Outreach Opportunity League (COOL)
University of Minnesota
386 McNeal Hall
St. Paul, MN 55108-1011
TEL: 612-624-3018
Credit: Inquire
Sponsor: The eight colleges in New Orleans
Contact: National Meetings Director
Description: This is the seventh annual conference in an established series developed as an outgrowth of a growing movement on campuses across the country to involve college students in community services activities. Different campuses in New Orleans bid to host the annual COOL conference. The 1991 (March 7-10) conference reflects the growth of the organization, involving nationally-known speakers and addressing many of the most crucial, current issues. Over 1,500 participants are expected. More than 100 workshops are carefully planned to help students become involved in building stronger service organizations. They include:
- Service and the Curriculum
- Reflection
- Fundraising
- Recruiting
- Regional Development
- Cultural Diversity
- Publicity
- Training and Evaluation

The specific issues addressed are based on actual involvement - called *Into The Streets* - by students across the country, and include presentations on service projects in New Orleans, including:
- Children and Youth
- Environment
- AIDS
- Substance Abuse
- Literacy
- Hunger
- Racism
- Homelessness
- Senior Citizens
- Refugees and Immigrants
- Domestic Violence
- Disabled
- Criminal Justice
- Health
- Educational Access

There is an *Opportunities Fair* with booths and information on

internships and careers designed to foster networking among student groups, share experiences, and trade materials.
Publications: Conference Proceedings

EDUCATION AND HUMAN SERVICES COURSE
Riverside University High School
1615 East Locust Street
Milwaukee, WI 53211-3298
TEL: 414-964-5900
Credit: Two credits
Sponsor: Riverside University School District
Contact: Judy E. Skurnick
Description: Designed for tenth grade students interested in careers in service, this *Education and Human Services* track has a specific curriculum, and is combined with on site community volunteer efforts. Curriculum requirements include:
- Introduction to Education and Human Services (during tenth grade)
- Psychology (during eleventh grade)
- *Careers in Human Services* (a seminar for twelfth graders)
- On-site training as a continuation of the course

As part of the seminar program for twelfth graders, the students must spend two and a half hours each week in the community, either after school or on weekends. Orientation and training at the site generally include:
- an introduction to the organization
- suggested readings
- participation in staff development sessions. Students receive one credit for the combined course and service work, and one credit for their seminar work.

The field supervisor seeks feedback form the students on their projects, and varies the activities accordingly. Students are required to keep daily journals, and write essays and final evaluations.

Training continues throughout the duration of the project, with students being given specific reading and observational assignments relating to their experiences for class discussion. Through phone calls, visits and evaluations, teachers and service agencies maintain close contact. Public bus transportation is provided for the volunteers.

Although it is a "mandatory" part of the curriculum, it is very popular with students and is considered a strong part of the curriculum at Riverside.

EXPERIENTIAL LEARNING - WORKING WITH STUDENT VOLUNTEERS
SEE VOLUNTEERS: STUDENTS

FAMILY LIFE/COMMUNITY AND GOVERNMENT
Papillion/La Vista High School
7821 Terry Drive
Papillion, NE 68128
TEL: 402-339-0405
Purpose: To demonstrate connections among family, government, and community.
Credit: Two high school credits
Sponsor: Papillion Board of Education
Contact: Doris Harder
Description: A one-semester course developed in 1975 enables students at the school to compare family, government and community issues and analyze their relations to each other. The course is team-taught. Orientation consists of basic dos and don'ts of volunteering, leadership training, communication-building exercises, and role playing. There are two units of study:
- **Community and Government** - an examination of what a community is, the services it provides, and its relationship to government.
- **Family Life and the Community** - a study of issues such as crisis and stress, domestic violence and its relation to crime,

and chemical dependence.

The course requires 1-1/2 hours a day for nine weeks on site. Students are not limited to the school's resource guide listing current placement sites. They can create projects based on their own interests.

To facilitate the program and keep students in the field, half of the students complete community work first while the other half does the classroom work first. One social studies credit is given for class work, and one general elective credit for field work.

In addition to the academic requirements, students complete major projects based on their volunteer assignments. For example, a group of students working with delinquent youths in the court system created a directory of community agencies where youth could meet their alternative sentencing/community service obligations. Another student produced a pictorial study of the homeless in conjunction with her work with them. Other students have worked in hospitals, day care centers, police stations and shelters.

Students keep daily journals, which are graded weekly. The last journal entry is expected to be a wrap-up and evaluation of the volunteer experience in the field.

Roll is taken at school before the students go to their volunteer assignments, and each student must sign in and out at the sites. Two evaluations come from the site supervisor - one at mid-term and another at the end of the quarter. Creativity is strongly encouraged throughout the program.
Founded: 1975

GOVERNOR'S YOUTH ACTION CONFERENCE
SEE GOVERNORS' OFFICES ON VOLUNTEERISM: CONNECTICUT

ISSUES ON VOLUNTEERISM: SERVICE LEARNING IN THE COMMUNITY
University of Wisconsin-Stevens Point
Department of Sociology
Stevens Point, WI 54481
TEL: 715-346-3060
Credit: One credit for each section; pass or fail
Sponsor: University of Wisconsin-Stevens Point
Contact: John E. Moffat, Ph.D.
Description: This two-section course is designed to improve skills in volunteer administration and effectiveness in volunteering. Section One is an evening course; Section Two combines instruction with field placement.
Section 1 - Issues On Volunteerism: A minimum of 15 classroom hours of lecture and discussion. This course meets from the second through the ninth week of the semester, one evening per week. In addition to the course instructor, guest lecturers from the community deal with issues concerning volunteerism in such settings as scouting, political parties, recycling, community corrections (VIP and court-ordered volunteer services for probationers), and natural disasters.

Volunteer service by professionals, the managerial roles in volunteerism such as the United Way Organization and campaign, professional volunteer administration, the phenomenon of the "new volunteer," corporate volunteerism, and volunteerism in an age of austerity also are incorporated. Volunteer service as an aid to career choice/skills development is given special attention. Students are required to submit at least five written reports on these class presentations. This course may not be repeated with the same title.

Section 2 - Service Learning in the Community: Offered from the second through 15th week of the semester. Students must obtain a placement through the ACT (Association for Community Tasks) program at the University. A service/learning contract specifying service objectives and learning objectives must be developed by students in consultation with the student coordinator for a particular project/program and the site supervisor for the host agency.

Students must participate in the interview, training and evaluation administered by ACT. Students must perform a minimum of 20 hours of service which is certified by ACT to the course instructor. Students are required to maintain a current field journal on their voluntary service. The edited journal must be submitted to the instructor by the end of the course.

Attendance at initial orientation, mid-course, and close-out class sessions is required. Class sessions are team-taught by the course instructor, the student head of the ACT program and the staff advisors of ACT.

The objectives of the course are to facilitate experiential learning for the student and to stimulate the motivation of citizen participation in the community as an opportunity/obligation for educated persons.

THE MARSHALL SERVICE UNIT AND VOLUNTEER OUTREACH

Marshall School
1215 Ricelake Road
Duluth, MN 55811
TEL: 218-727-7266
Sponsor: Marshall School; local foundations
Contact: Gerry Ouellette
Description: The Marshall School operates a dual program to help students learn the value - and enjoyment - of helping to make one's community a better place to live. *Volunteer Outreach* is a specific course for upperclass students. *The Marshall Service Unit* is a requirement for all students. Specifically:
Volunteer Outreach is a one-semester elective course open to grades 11 and 12. Students earn one-half credit. The course consists of:

- Five periods per week for 18 weeks or the equivalent (about 80 hours) volunteering on site.
- Daily journals and time sheets.
- Major research related to the placement and essays reflecting on learning and growth.

Student/teacher/supervisor conferences are held at the placements and at the school. Course objectives allow for individual flexibility and unique learning. Before and after students begin at their placements, they are oriented to the course expectations. They are supervised while on site and given direction by the course instructor and the site supervisor.

All students show significant gains through their activities of providing useful, interactive service.

The Marshall Service Unit is an extra-curricular service requirement for all students attending *The Marshall School.* Each student must complete a minimum of ten hours of community service for each year in attendance prior to graduation. Service beyond the minimum may count up to one year ahead. The objective is to recognize, initiate and ultimately involve every student in active, ongoing service to the community.

Service is defined as work without pay, or helping others. Students have chosen to work in hospitals, nursing homes, the soup kitchens, and a host of other options. Students may work in their neighborhoods, or even within the school through many programs, such as our technical crew, sports boosters, student service, *Key Club* and some of the *Student Council* projects.

Both *Volunteer Outreach* and *The Marshall Service Unit* have received widespread recognition and enjoy popularity with the students and the community.

Founded: 1988

SENIOR COURSE ON VOLUNTEERISM

Parish Hill High School
Chaplin, CT 06235
TEL: 203-455-9584
Credit: 1/2 to four credits (high school)
Sponsor: Chaplin Education System

Contact: Georgia J. Turvey
Description: This course of study is a 28-week program which includes a weekly seminar and from three to five hours each week in the field per student. Begun in 1978, the program involves local organizations in field placements (day care centers, hospitals, homes for the elderly, the local chapter of the Cancer Society, and others); also, placements are made in the school special education department, and several junior school classes. Course objectives:

- to bring students and the community into a mutual working relationship based on students' interests and talents.
- to give students a better opportunity to understand social problems and deal with human needs.
- to give students an opportunity to see the need for using knowledge they have acquired in school.
- to provide students with situations that foster the development of responsibility, commitment, and leadership.
- to foster a sense of self-assurance, self-acceptance, self-control, independence, and tolerance of others.

Attendance at the 28 weekly seminars is mandatory to give the student volunteers every possible advantage to effect a successful placement. The basic purpose of these seminars is to provide:

- background knowledge needed to understand the services to the community
- a learning experience that centers on the facilitation of the development of skills and awareness needed in student service situations

The degree and quality of execution of program requirements listed below provide a measurement for awarding credit:

- a minimum of three periods or equivalent time in the community
- maintenance of a weekly log sheet in which they can keep a record of their observations and experience
- written goals and objectives that clearly define the responsibilities they will assume and the task they perform

In brief, the course presents learning within the context of a total human experience rather than merely an intake of knowledge and skills. The course is based on the idea that experience (community input) helps students to develop a positive outlook of self, and a view of self as a social being and a participating member of society.

The course is open to juniors and seniors, who choose the kind of placement they want within the limits of the program. Student evaluation is based on completion of goals, evaluation from placement supervisor, the program director, and the student.

SOCIAL WORK PROGRAM: 60-HOUR VOLUNTEER WORK REQUIREMENT

University of South Dakota
Social Work Program
Department of Social Behavior
Vermillion, SD 57069
TEL: 605-677-5401
Credit: Inquire
Sponsor: University of South Dakota
Contact: Charles L. Schwartz
Description: To help students establish an experiential foundation based on the realities of the social services field, a 60-hour volunteer social service experience is a required component of the Social Work Program. Working with his/her assigned faculty advisor and the Coordinator of the Student Volunteer Program, each student is required to initiate action regarding a suitable volunteer assignment. With a minimum requirement of two hours per week, students usually complete the requirement within two academic years.

No grade is assigned, or academic credit offered for the volunteer experience. However, all students must complete a volunteer social service experience before enrolling in field placement. Therefore, each student is required to submit, as part of his/her permanent file, a statement about performance outlining and highlighting his/her volunteer experience. The statement must include the signature of the agency supervisor and any comments this supervisor deems relevant regarding the volunteer's work performance.

As much as possible, the special interests and needs of individual students are considered in volunteer assignments. This may be limited to some extent by the services offered by participating agencies. Faculty advisors, the Student Volunteer Program Coordinator, and the student identify additional potential participating agencies - the final decision for inclusion resting with the Coordinator. Agencies providing volunteer placements include the Dakota Hospital, Department of Social Services, Southeastern Dakota Nursing Home, USD Hot Line, and Center for the Developmentally Disabled.

Usually volunteer placements are limited to the Vermillion area during the academic year. In certain unique circumstances, volunteer placement is made in the summer - sometimes expanding the geographic area to include any area where the student resides. This occurs only when it is in the best interest of the student and meets his/her special needs, and has the approval of both the faculty advisor and the Student Volunteer Program Coordinator. The volunteer experience may be waived based upon prior volunteer or related experience.

STUDENT VOLUNTEER PROGRAMS: A NEW RESOURCE FOR COMMUNITY AGENCIES*

Young Volunteers in Action
2600 Wells Street
Milwaukee, WI 53233
TEL: 414-933-4224
Credit: Inquire
Sponsor: Greater Milwaukee Voluntary Action Center
Contact: Cheri Farnsworth
Description: This workshop is designed to meet a need for experience on the part of agency staff working with young volunteers. Training topics include:
- How to work with student volunteers in your agency
- Models of successful local student volunteer programs
- Building effective working relationships among educators and agency staff
- The Young Volunteers in Action program; how to begin one

An overview of volunteer management principles, and a panel on Working Effectively with Youth Volunteers are integral parts of the overall training program. Discussions of high school and college volunteers as an important resource are approached in a combination of panel presentations, small groups, skill-building workshops and resource sharing/networking sessions.

TAKING A TRIP TO FRIENDSHIP

HOST (Hands Of Shared Time)
Montgomery General Hospital
3438 Olney-Laytonsville Road
Olney, MD 20832
TEL: 301-774-6114
Credit: Inquire
Sponsor: Montgomery General Hospital
Contact: Kelly M. Ring, Service Coordinator
Description: This program is designed to train volunteers age 15 or older to serve as companions and all-round helpers to older persons in their homes and in nursing homes. It consists of a five-part introductory session, and eleven training modules. Each module includes the step-by-step process for implementation, including background information, specific notes to the instructor, activities/exercises, and handouts. More specifically:

Part One: Overview
- **Introduction to the HOST program** - This is a brief overview of the HOST program, including research results from the training process.
- **Rationale for volunteer training** - Preparing volunteers is often

an unstructured process. This discussion includes the benefits of training for the volunteers, agencies, and community involved.
- **Goals for HOST Training** - Although training is obviously a time for volunteers to learn new skills and acquire knowledge, it is much more than that. This section reviews the training goals and objectives and discusses the role training plays in securing, screening, and supporting volunteers.
- **Tips and techniques for implementation** - This section includes information about group dynamics, intergenerational teaching methods, and training logistics.
- **Notes to the instructor** - This section includes guidelines specific to the manual and training program to enhance the trainer's understanding and facilitation.

Part Two: Training Models
- **Detour to Facts and Attitudes** - This session is designed to help volunteers explore their own attitudes about aging and gain a better understanding of the myths versus realities of growing old.
- **Follow the Road to Normal Aging** - This module promotes healthy living for volunteers while teaching volunteers about normal changes in aging. Volunteers are also taught to identify danger signs in the health of their older friends.
- **Cross a Bridge to Communication** - Volunteers who can communicate effectively feel more comfortable in their volunteer role and make better friends to the older adults. This session focuses on developing those communication skills.
- **Walk a Mile in My Shoes** - It's difficult to imagine what sensory loss and disability are like when one is in good health. This session gives volunteers an opportunity to simulate some age changes by using props and performing simple tasks.
- **Clear Your Path to a Healthy Mind** - This session increases volunteers' knowlege about the causes of dementia and how to communicate with cognitively impaired older adults.
- **Reach for the Stars** - In a supportive group session, volunteers can explore their own coping skills and those necessary for dealing with losses associated with late life. The role spirituality plays in the coping process is also discussed.
- **Better Safe Than Sorry** - Volunteers get "hands on" experience using mobility assistive devices and practicing wheelchair transfer techniques. Emphasis is placed on home safety, independence, and dignity.
- **Share the Experience** - Trained volunteers speaking to the recruits is the highlight of the training. No one can explain the value and joys of volunteering better than a volunteer. The recruits have the opportunity to learn about "real" older friends, ask questions, and meet other volunteers at the same time.
- **Make Friends Along the Way - What to do if?** - *The best surprise is no surprise.* Addressing potential problems enhances volunteers' confidence and security and adds to older adults' safety. This is also a time to reinforce the agency's policies and procedures.
- **I'm On My Way** - Supporting volunteers from the start will encourage volunteer commitment later on. This is a time to review material taught throughout training, reward and congratulate volunteers for their efforts, and provide closure between the volunteers and staff.

All participants are provided with sample agendas, handouts and worksheets, suggested wall charts to help follow the training process, and volunteer forms demonstrating the necessary application, release, follow-up and test procedures. For added incentive, a certificate of award is included.
Publications: Taking a Trip to Friendship: Training Program

TRAINING/CONFERENCES/TEACHING: TENANTS/RESIDENTS

NATIONAL/STATE ORGANIZATIONS

NATIONAL TRAINING AND INFORMATION CENTER*
954 West Washington Boulevard
Chicago, IL 60607
TEL: 312-243-3035
Objectives: To provide training for leaders interested in improving their neighborhoods.
Services: Offers community leaders and organizers "how to" courses dealing with areas such as housing, neighborhood reinvestment, block club organizing, issue development, and media usage; provides on-site consultation services and technical assistance to local groups on organizing campaigns and revitalization efforts; maintains an information clearinghouse; researches areas such as mortgage and lending practices, utility rate increases, and community development funding; keeps legislative bodies and the public informed of its findings; sponsors long- and short-term training sessions; publishes a newsletter and a number of manuals and guides.
Publications: Disclosure; A Challenge for Change; Controlling Neighborhood Development; Basics of Organizing; Organizing to Win; Pass the Buck... Back!; Who, Me A Researcher? Yes, You!
Founded: 1972

TRAINING PROGRAMS

COMMUNITY FORUM ON THE PROPOSED *HARLEM ON THE HUDSON* PROJECT
West Harlem Coalition
PO Box 660
Manhattanville Station
New York, NY 10027
TEL: 212-234-4661
Credit: None
Contact: Forum Coordinator
Description: This Forum was called by West Harlem community leaders to address the proposed development of the pier area near the community. The consultants hired by the city to conduct a feasibility study attended the forum. Residents, community groups, and urban planners have rejected the luxury development plans citing the following factors, among others:
- displacement of longtime residents
- disruption of traffic
- environmental concerns
- the need to develop on a community-wide basis, not a luxury enclave on the outskirts of the community, which will "wall off" the people
- lack of space allocated for the typical CB9 household
- a violation of the basic right to affordable housing
- a threat to the diverse character of the neighborhood

The group has operated a number of forums since 1986, when the plan was first announced, as well as enlisting support in editorials in several media, confronting managers of the plan, and developing and enlisting support for petitions to the city. In all cases, the major thrust is the improvement of all of Harlem, not just Harlem-on-the-Hudson.

VOLUNTEERS

NATIONAL/STATE ORGANIZATIONS

VOLUNTEER LAWYERS FOR THE ARTS
1285 Avenue of the Americas
Third Floor
New York, NY 10019
TEL: 212-977-9270
Objectives: To increase the arts community's awareness and understanding of the legal problems that affect their creative endeavors.
Services: Provides free legal services to art organizations and artists (art-related matters only); conducts educational programs and workshops to familiarize both the legal profession and the arts community with legal problems confronting artists and work with them toward solutions; maintains library and speakers bureau; offers specialized education; publishes a journal, a manual, monographs and pamphlets. (Volunteer Lawyers for the Arts is funded, in part, by the National Endowment for the Arts.)
Publications: Art and the Law; Artists Small Claims Guide; Enterprise and the Arts; Fear of Filing; Not-For-Profit Manual; Artist's Housing Manual; The Buck Starts Here
Founded: 1968

VOLUNTEERS: ADVOCATES

NATIONAL/STATE ORGANIZATIONS

AMERICAN COUNCIL OF THE BLIND
1010 Vermont Avenue, NW
Suite 1100
Washington, DC 20005
TEL: 202-393-3666
Objectives: To advocate legislation for the blind and other handicapped persons; to promote independent and effective participation in society.
Services: Holds periodic workshops for the blind on advocacy and legal rights; provides information about agencies and schools for the blind, national health insurance proposals, how to establish a credit union for the blind, electronic aids, legislation and legal rights; gives advice about specific legal problems over the phone when possible; provides referrals when indicated to other possible sources; publishes a monthly magazine, which is available in large print, braille, disc, or cassette; awards scholarships to blind post secondary students; convenes conference annually.

AMERICAN PARENTS COMMITTEE
SEE VOLUNTEERS: PARENTS

BREAKTHROUGH FOUNDATION
SEE COMMUNITY SERVICES: TENANTS/RESIDENTS

CENTER FOR AUTO SAFETY
2001 S Street, NW
Suite 410
Washington, DC 20009
TEL: 202-328-7700
Objectives: To provide advocacy in matters of auto and highway safety.
Services: Monitors government agencies charged with regulation of the automobile industry; participates in the rule-making procedures of the National Highway Traffic Safety Administration, the Federal Highway Administration and occasionally institutes legal action; maintains extensive library which includes thousands of complaint letters as well as relevant publications and other materials; supports safety standards; analyzes automobile and highway safety developments in the field; publishes *The Lemon Book* by Ralph Nader and others, *The Car Book,* a bimonthly journal, *Impact,* and other materials (Center founded by Ralph Nader and Consumers Union; now independent).
Publications: The Lemon Book; Impact; The Yellow Book Road; Automobile Design Liability; Information on Auto Defects; The Car Book
Founded: 1970

CHILD WELFARE LEAGUE OF AMERICA
440 First Street, NW
Suite 310
Washington, DC 20001
TEL: 202-638-2952
FAX: 202-638-4004
Objectives: To improve care and services for deprived, neglected and dependent children, youth and their families.
Services: Assists agencies in the area of child welfare whose programs are relevant to community needs; provides specialists in various aspects of child welfare based on a study of the local program, structure, administration and policies; assists teenage parents through the League's *Florence Crittenton* division by providing medical care, education, counseling, health and family life education, and parent-reparation programs; gives professional leadership to agencies providing services to troubled families and children; handles especially difficult problems of a requesting agency with surveys; develops standards and guidelines for the child welfare field and makes them available in various publications; maintains a library/information service; works closely with the mass media to properly present the need for good child welfare services; establishes special projects; publishes a journal and over 100 monographs and books; convenes annual regional training conferences.
Publications: Child Welfare; Children's Campaign News; Washington Social Legislation Bulletin; Children's Monitor; CWLA Directory; CWLA Newsletter; CWLA Catalog
Founded: 1920

CHILDREN'S DEFENSE FUND
122 C Street, NW
Washington, DC 20001
TEL: 202-628-8787
Objectives: To make the needs of children an important matter of public policy.

Services: Monitors federal agencies; comments formally on proposed guidelines and regulations affecting children, especially those aged six to sixteen who live on the streets; testifies before Congress; develops specific principles and recommendations for laws affecting children; seeks redress in courts when other negotiations fail; supports local student and volunteer advocates and groups, especially street health care workers; encourages media to make children's issues an important part of programming; publicizes findings and recommendations in several forms - reports and books, articles, handbooks, speeches, news articles, testimony, etc.
Publications: CDF Reports; Adolescent Pregnancy
Founded: 1973

CO-ORDINATING COUNCIL FOR HANDICAPPED CHILDREN
SEE LEADERSHIP DEVELOPMENT/BOARDS: HANDICAPPED

EPILEPSY FOUNDATION OF AMERICA
4351 Garden City Drive
Landover, MD 20781
TEL: 301-459-3700
Objectives: To provide advocacy and a wide variety of services and programs for persons with epilepsy.
Services: Sponsors a number of special projects such as School Alert, Community Alert, Self-Help, Training and Placement Service, and others; provides information on epilepsy for the patient, his family and friends, educators, employment specialists, etc., on a wide range of topics; publishes a directory, pamphlets, reprints, books, cassettes, films, slides, and a monthly newsletter.

FOOD RESEARCH AND ACTION CENTER
1319 F Street, NW
Suite 500
Washington, DC 20004
TEL: 202-393-5060
Objectives: To assist impoverished people and communities in efforts to obtain relief from conditions of hunger and malnutrition.
Services: Offers legal and nonlegal assistance to poor people; provides advocacy to make the public food assistance programs more responsive; identifies and publishes specific reasons for the failure of some of these programs; trains in strategies for local and state-wide antihunger activities; maintains law library; publishes a number of educational pamphlets and guides for the general public; publishes monthly newsletter, and publications related to hunger and food assistance programs in the U.S.
Publications: Foodlines; Guide to Food Stamp Program
Founded: 1970

JOINT ADVOCACY COALITION FOR THE MENTALLY DISABLED
100 North Washington Boulevard
Falls Church, VA 22046
TEL: 703-532-3303
Objectives: To address problems that exist within the service systems and the needs of the mentally disabled (in areas of mental health and mental retardation).
Services: Provides individual representation to mentally disabled persons in administrative and court proceedings; conducts training about Federal and State laws that affect disabled persons; provides information and assistance to consumers, attorneys, advocates, and others working with disabled persons; comments on proposed regulations and legislation; monitors services used by mentally disabled persons; maintains a community education program for public awareness; works toward a mental health/mental retardation institution serving needs including employment, Federal benefits (SSI, Medicaid, Food Stamps), licensing,

guardianship, housing, marital and family rights, rights in institutions, receiving or refusing treatment, special education, sterilization, training, vocational rehabilitation, and zoning. [The Coalition is an undertaking of the Mental Health Association of Northern Virginia, Legal Services of Northern Virginia, and the Northern Virginia Association for Retarded Citizens.]

MATURE OUTLOOK
PO Box 96
Arlington Heights, IL 60006
TOLL FREE: 800-336-6330
Objectives: To provide advocacy on behalf of older persons before state and federal government bodies; to provide practical services for everyday living.
Services: Provides services to older persons including financial guidance and counseling; arranges discount buying; develops and implements education programs; provides free arrest bond certificate; operates travel and recreation programs; offers prescription drug service; offers a motor club plan; publishes bimonthly newsletter, retirement planning guide, and various booklets.
Publications: Best Years; Mature Outlook Magazine; Mature Outlook Newsletter
Founded: 1984

MINORITIES CAUCUS OF FAMILY SERVICE AMERICA
34-1/2 Beacon Street
Boston, MA 02108
TEL: 617-523-6400
Objectives: To make Family Service America (FSA) more relevant to the needs of minority families.
Services: Works with any minority group that is involved with a family service agency or organization; conducts negotiations with, and participates in policy-making groups; supports task forces on institutional racism and related areas; publishes newsletter; convenes periodic meetings.

NATIONAL CLIENTS COUNCIL
2617 Martha Street
Philadelphia, PA 19125
TEL: 215-686-2913
Objectives: To advocate clients' interests and concerns in legal services programs.
Services: Trains clients to participate in the planning and execution of legal services programs; provides a vehicle for communication and clarification between clients and attorneys; publishes monthly Community Notes, annual Conference Proceedings, *The Why's and How's of National Clients Council,* and other materials; convenes annual meeting. (Affiliated with American Bar Association)
Publications: Why's and How's of NCC
Founded: 1968

NATIONAL COMMITTEE ON ART EDUCATION FOR THE ELDERLY
SEE LEADERSHIP DEVELOPMENT/BOARDS: ARTS

NATIONAL COURT APPOINTED SPECIAL ADVOCATE ASSOCIATION
CASA
2722 Eastlake Avenue, East
Suite 220
Seattle, WA 98102
TEL: 206-328-8588
Objectives: To advocate for the best interests of abused and neglected children.
Services: Supports the development, growth and continuation of programs which recruit and train volunteers to serve as court

appointed special advocates for abused and neglected children in juvenile dependency proceedings; provides training and professional development, consultation, public education, resource development, and government relations; advocates for the rights of children; encourages CASA programs and volunteers across the U.S. to join together as a united voice for all children; works toward the goal that every child who needs a CASA volunteer will have one by the year 2000; draws attention to critical issues affecting abused and neglected children; conducts nationwide surveys of CASA programs and publishes results.

Offers training and consultation to CASA programs; sets national standards for CASA programs and volunteers; provides education and training through the first *National Training Curriculum for CASA/GAL Volunteers,* a 40-hour course prepared by the Minnesota Task Force on Permanency Planning and funded by the Edna McConnell Clark Foundation; presents a *Juvenile Court Judge of the Year Award;* recognizes the work of CASA programs through its *Program Excellence Awards* program; arranges for volunteers to speak with attorneys for abused and neglected children in juvenile court; enjoys being the "national philanthropy" of a major fraternity, receiving grants from organizations such as the *American Legion Child Welfare Foundation,* and receiving recognition for its work through awards to the organization; maintains a speaker's bureau for conferences and community groups; publishes a newsletter, an information packet, directories and other materials.

Publications: Speak Up For A Child; A Guide to Member Services; CASA: A Child's Voice in Court; Children: The Time is NOW

NATIONAL DOWN SYNDROME CONGRESS
SEE LEADERSHIP DEVELOPMENT/BOARDS: HANDICAPPED

NATIONAL LEGAL RESOURCE CENTER FOR CHILD ADVOCACY AND PROTECTION
American Bar Association
1800 M Street, NW
Washington, DC 20036
TEL: 202-331-2250
Objectives: To increase professional awareness and competency of the legal community in child welfare issues; to respond to requests for information from laypersons and groups.
Services: Conducts research and development activities to keep both the legal profession and community project leaders informed on legal issues of child maltreatment; addresses specific concerns such as methods of sensitive intervention, an area based on years of research to find the most effective approaches; publishes general directories and bibliographies of interest to both professionals and community groups, such as *National Directory of Programs Providing Court Representation to Abused and Neglected Children* and *Special Education Advocacy for the Abused Child.*
Publications: Special Education Advocacy; Directory of Programs

NATIONAL MENTAL HEALTH ASSOCIATION
SEE COMMUNICATIONS & PUBLIC RELATIONS: MENTAL HEALTH

NATIONAL MILITARY FAMILY ASSOCIATION
6000 Stevenson Avenue
Suite 304
Alexandria, VA 22304-3526
TEL: 703-823-6632
Objectives: To serve as advocates for military families by influencing the development and implementation of policies that affect their lives.
Services: Operates as a membership organization; involves volunteer staff in identifying, addressing, and resolving issues of

concern to military families, including child care, housing, health and dental care, retiree benefits, spousal employment, survivor benefits, voting rights, dependent schools, etc.; works with *Army, Marine Corps, Navy, Air Force, Coast Guard, Public Health Service, National Oceanic and Atmospheric Administration,* including those on active duty, the *National Guard, Reserves,* and retired family members; finances programs through tax-deductible dues and donations as an independent nonprofit organization; maintains programs in research, education, legislation and public information; has a board of advisors of more than 60 members from military, public and private sectors (headed by Anna Chennault, Founder); publishes a newsletter for members.
Publications: Military Family

NATIONAL ORGANIZATION ON DISABILITY (NOD)
SEE COMMUNICATIONS & PUBLIC RELATIONS: HANDICAPPED

NATIONAL SUPPORT CENTER FOR FAMILIES OF THE AGING
SEE VOLUNTEERS: SELF-HELP

PUBLIC CITIZEN
PO Box 19404
Washington, DC 20036
TEL: 202-293-9142
Objectives: To help tourists from across the country (and local residents) become issue-oriented and citizen-conscious while visiting Washington, DC; to provide information to any local group planning a visit.
Services: Provides citizen advocacy in areas including a healthful environment, consumer rights, corporate and government accountability, and citizen empowerment; provides an informational and recreational schedule of alternatives designed to enable the visitor to return to his/her community with a broader knowledge of government than the usual tourist route allows, e.g., assists tour group or individual in attending congressional and regulatory agency hearings, and any one of a number of high-interest attractions such as the Environmental Protection Agency's Center; administers monthly public citizens forum (open discussion between government, citizens, and the news media); publishes detailed biweekly calendar, free to anyone, *Inside the Capitol, Guide to the U.S. Capitol,* and others. (The Center evolved from one of Ralph Nader's ideas.)
Publications: Public Citizen; Buyers Up News; Critical Mass Bulletin; Health Letter; Inside the Capitol; Guide to the U.S. Capitol
Founded: 1971

URBAN ELDERLY COALITION
National Council on the Aging
600 Maryland Avenue, SW
West Wing 100
Washington, DC 20024
TEL: 202-479-1200
Objectives: To resolve such problems as poverty, inner-city housing, crimes against the elderly, limited employment, inadequate health care, and transportation for the mobility-impaired.
Services: Analyzes and informs about legislation affecting the elderly; exchanges technical information among urban aging programs; fosters support of government at all levels; seeks urban leaders with strong goals for the elderly and works closely with them; provides technical assistance, program development and management support services; holds training meetings, and offers personalized training assistance; publishes *Legislative Update,* quarterly, and position papers; convenes annual training conference.

Publications: Legislative Update
Founded: 1950

WESTERN GERONTOLOGICAL SOCIETY*
SEE VOLUNTEERS: OLDER PERSONS

TRAINING PROGRAMS

CHILDREN: THE TIME IS NOW
National CASA Association
2722 Eastlake Avenue, East
Seattle, WA 98102
TEL: 206-328-8588
Credit: Continuing Legal Education Credits
Contact: Amy Duncan-Little
Description: The annual *National CASA (Court Appointed Special Advocates) Conference* is the only official meeting of CASA programs and volunteers. The 1990 session, *Children: The Time Is Now,* is the ninth annual program, again bringing together volunteers, program managers, judges, social workers, attorneys and others who work with abused children in court. Like past conferences, *Children: The Time Is Now* continues to offer the nuts and bolts of professional and volunteer training - the how-to of CASA work, such as interviewing techniques, report writing, an inside look at foster care, the dynamics of child abuse, etc. The 1990 meeting added a special 'advocacy' track to focus on change - how we can make a lasting difference in the lives of the children we serve. Following are selected topics from the schedule:
First Day - General Session: *Child Advocacy on the National level: How CASA Fits In*

- Federal Legislation for Children: What's Next on the Horizon
- Amendments to P.L. 96-272 and What They Mean for CASA Programs
- The Drug Culture's Legacy: Children Born Into Addiction
- Cult and Ritualistic Abuse
- Conflict Management and Negotiation Skills
- Aboguemos Por Los Ninos: Serving the Needs of Hispanic Families
- "I Don't Understand a Word You Said": Communication Skills for CASA
- Screening and Interview Techniques for Use with Volunteers
- Making a Difference for Children at the State Level: The Young Americans Act
- Ten Dimensions of Child Advocacy
- Breaking Down Barriers: Examples of Community Advocacy
- AIDS and Children
- Adolescent Depression and Suicide
- Collaborative Advocacy: Effective Partnerships Between CASA and the Child's Attorney
- How Long is Too Long? Improving Service Delivery in Foster Care
- It Doesn't Have to Be This Way: Examples of How Child Advocates Have Successfully Changed the System
- Working Together: Implementing a Multi-disciplinary Approach to Child Abuse
- How CASA Programs and Volunteers Can Make An Impact for Children in State Legislatures
- Using the Media to Promote Children's Issues
- Challenging the System - What Changes Do We Need to Make?
- Kinship Foster Care: The Double-edged Dilemma
- Children Before the Court Puppet Program
- An Exercise in Futility
- Training Innovations for Attorneys Who Work With CASA Programs
- Supervision and Evaluation of Volunteers

Second Day - General Session: *The Time is NOW for Children*
- Why Am I Doing This When My Friends Work Half as Long

and Earn Twice As Much!
- Expanding to Fill the Need: One Program's Role in Community Advocacy
- Representing the Best Interests of the Family
- What's Best for Children with Fetal Alcohol Syndrome
- Report Writing Skills for CASA Volunteers
- Cross Cultural Awareness
- CASA Volunteer Rap Session

Through these conferences, the National CASA Association is bringing together some of the country's most aggressive and successful child advocates to teach us how CASA - all 15,000 volunteers and 393 programs - can not only be the fastest growing child advocacy movement in the country, but the strongest and most influential. Faculty for *Children: The Time Is Now* was drawn from children's organizations, health services, the legal profession, court systems, child abuse advocacy groups, the federal government, state CASA associations, and others.

VOLUNTEER TRAINING PROGRAM FOR VOLUNTEER ADVOCATES
SEE GOVERNORS' OFFICES ON VOLUNTEERISM: HAWAII

INDIVIDUAL PROGRAM PROFILES

ABUSED ADULT RESOURCE CENTER (AARC)
PO Box 167
Bismarck, ND 58502
TEL: 701-222-8370
Purpose: To provide crisis intervention, emergency shelter, advocacy, referrals and emotional support to victims of adult domestic violence.
Contact: Diane Zainhofsky, Project Director
Description: The Abused Adult Resource Center is one of 18 spouse abuse projects in North Dakota. AARC primarily serves Burleigh and Morton counties and surrounding rural areas.
Services include: safe shelter; emotional support; advocacy with social and legal services; referrals to medical, mental health, social and employment services; and weekly peer support groups. When desired, appropriate referrals are offered (often to mental health or alcoholism treatment) for the abuser.
The lifeline of our organization is a 24-hour hotline and the volunteers who are on call when our office is closed. The hotline averages approximately 35 volunteer advocates at any given time. In addition to our on-call advocates, we generally have a like number of "safe homes" which provide temporary shelter for the victim of adult domestic violence and his or her children.
While use of safe shelter is limited to victims of physical abuse, other services are extended to any abused adult. We define an abused adult as any person who has suffered one or more of the following types of abuse: sexual, verbal, physical, or emotional.
Training of volunteers includes an initial one-on-one interview with either the project director or project advocate. This is supplemented by monthly training sessions and a yearly day-long training seminar. In addition, office staff is always available to answer questions and deal with problems as they arise. While previous experience is desirable in volunteers, it is in no way a prerequisite. "On the job" experience is the best teacher. It is in answering crisis calls, meeting the client (usually at the police department or hospital) and transporting her to safe shelter that our advocates best learn the realities of spouse abuse and put their verbal instructions to the test.
Funding sources are United Way; North Dakota Department of Health; grants; and private donations.

CASA (COURT APPOINTED SPECIAL ADVOCATES)
CASA of Travis County
510 West Tenth
Austin, TX 78701
TEL: 512-478-6627
Purpose: To break the cycle of abuse and neglect of children.
Sponsor: Austin Family Court
Contact: Lila Coughran, Executive Director
Description: The *Court Appointed Special Advocates (CASA)*
program provides family court-appointed volunteers to serve as "a
voice in court" for abused and neglected children. The goal of
CASA is to break the cycle of abuse and neglect through
"permanent placement" for every child who enters the
court/welfare system. Children are reunited with the family, if
possible, or placed with relatives, a foster home or adoptive family.
CASAs undergo an extensive screening process, commit
themselves for at least a year, complete 20 hours of intense
training and devote three to four hours a week to a child. In the
end, the volunteer must tell the court what she believes is best for
the child.
To meet this heavy responsibility, CASAs have access to files,
families, and CASA professional staff as they work to become "a
friend to the child" and in many cases a listener to the pleadings
of a mother or family who wants the child back. Sometimes this
involves regular visitations to jails and prisons to determine
whether or not a child might be reunited with a parent or other
family member. They are trained to respect the family and not
make judgments about different lifestyles. Their work also takes
them at times to some notoriously drug-riddled, dangerous
neighborhoods. They understand that the only way to be sure of
making a good recommndation is to know the lifestyle. As one
volunteer said, "When you want to help someone so much, you
don't let much get in your way."
In one Austin case, a mother in prison, who was a former
prostitute, is now planning to go back to school and "lead a simple
life with a dog, a car, a house and an education for my child." The
inmate credits her new goals to the CASA volunteer who visited
regularly with the inmate's three-year-old son and brought
messages of hope and encouragement. According to the volunteer,
who recommended that the mother and son be given a chance to
make it after the mother's release, "Both of us know that the rest
is up to her. You can only give people choices, tell them about the
programs aimed at helping them, but you can't do it for them."
In spite of the commitment required, there is no dearth of
volunteers for the program. The satisfaction of knowing that you
are "changing the world child-by-child and making a difference" is
a strong motivator, according to CASA's Director.

CASA PROJECT (COURT APPOINTED SPECIAL ADVOCATES)
625 East 26th Street
Kansas City, MO 64108
TEL: 816-435-4814
Purpose: To ensure that the best interests of abused and neglected
children are served.
Sponsor: Greater Kansas City Section
Contact: Mitzi McFatrich, Executive Director
Description: The CASA Project is a community effort to advocate
on behalf of abused and neglected children, and ensure that these
children have the opportunity to have a permanent home without
unnecessary delays.
CASAs - Very Special Volunteers: The CASAs (Court Appointed
Special Advocates) are volunteers who are appointed by juvenile
court as guardians ad litem (legal representatives) for children who
have been referred to the court as abused and/or neglected. The
CASAs investigate the facts of the case through interviews with
the child, parents, professionals, and others; advocate for the child
in all court proceedings; recommend a course of action to the
court; and monitor progress toward the goals established in the
court order.
Currently, the Jackson County project has 22 CASAs serving a
total of 27 children. However, the project is only six months old,
and plans are to expand as rapidly as possible.
CASAs participate in a pre-service training which includes 20
hours of presentations by professionals and other activities; trips to
two agencies serving abused/neglected children; and several visits
to court to observe hearings. The professional trainers are a judge,
an attorney, a child therapist, an expert in child abuse, a
supervisor from the Division of Family Services, and others as
needed. CASAs continue their training as long as they are active
on a case through in-service sessions which are scheduled
frequently.
An important element in volunteer supervision and mutual support
are the CASA Group Meetings, which are held every two weeks.
The Project Coordinator is present to facilitate, but the CASAs
mainly share ideas, suggestions, encouragement, etc., with each
other. In addition, the CASA is expected to report directly to the
Project Coordinator whenever he/she has questions or concerns.
Consultants such as attorneys, child psychologists, physicians, and
others are available to the CASA as needed.
Other Very Important Volunteers: With the exception of the
Project Coordinator, the project is administered entirely by
volunteers. The Project Chairperson is in charge of all aspects of
the project, and working closely with her are two
vice-chairpersons. All three of the chairpersons and all of the
Steering Committee are members of the National Council of
Jewish Women, Greater Kansas City Section. Their duties include
public relations, long-range planning, recruitment, evaluation,
Speakers' Bureau, and fund-raising.
The CASA Advisory Board consists of a broad spectrum of
professionals from throughout the Kansas City community. They
meet quarterly to review progress and advise the project, and are
also available for frequent consultation as needed.
Currently, 45-50 volunteers are active on the Advisory Board,
Steering Committee, and in other activities. Together with the
CASAs, they form a formidable group of dedicated and tireless
volunteers advocating for abused/neglected children in Jackson
County.

CHILD ABUSE SERVICES TEAM (CAST)
SEE VOLUNTEERS: POLICE OFFICERS

CITIZEN ADVOCACY
100 North Washington Street
Falls Church, VA 22046
TEL: 703-532-7279
Purpose: Advocacy for persons with mental retardation.
Sponsor: Association for Retarded Citizens of Northern Virginia;
United Way; private donations
Contact: Debbie Ekimoff, Association for Retarded Citizens of
Northern Virginia
Description: Citizen Advocacy is a one-to-one sustaining
relationship between a capable volunteer called a Citizen Advocate
and a mentally retarded person called a Protege. The Citizen
Advocacy program began as a model program in 1975 under the
auspices of the Association for Retarded Citizens of Northern
Virginia. The program has grown and expanded to the extent that
today there are 45 volunteers in the Northern Virginia area
(Alexandria, Arlington and Fairfax County). There are 27
advocates working with proteges living in the community either in
group homes, supervised apartments, or at home with their
parents. The other 18 advocates work with the residents at the
Northern Virginia Training Center.
Citizen Advocates are volunteers (responsible, stable men and
women 18 years or older) living in Northern Virginia who have an
interest in developing a friendship with a mentally retarded person.
Citizen advocates need no prior experience; training along with
individual support is provided by professional staff. Citizen

Advocates are needed mainly in the evening hours and weekends, a minimum of two hours per week for one year.

Citizen Advocates and their proteges enjoy sharing activities that are a part of community living, like having a birthday party or taking a walk in the park. Advocates often spend time teaching their proteges useful skills along with giving them practical advice and emotional support.

The Citizen Advocacy program is funded by United Way and private donations.

Founded: 1975

CITIZEN ADVOCATES FOR JUSTICE

241 East 116th Street
New York, NY 10029
TEL: 212-534-0600

Purpose: To assist women involved in the New York City Courts and Corrections Department.

Sponsor: Corporations; New York City; ecumenical and private donations; foundations

Contact: Constance M. Baugh, Executive Director

Description: Founded in 1978, Citizen Advocates for Justice (CAFJ) is supported through a combination of foundation grants, corporate funds, city tax dollars, ecumenical donations and private contributions. Four major programs, designed primarily to assist women offenders, are operated by the organization with the assistance of 70 community volunteers. There are four full-time paid staff members, three JTPA and one VISTA volunteer working with the volunteers. The programs are:

- **Revolving Bail Fund Project:** For the pre-trial offender, CAFJ maintains a fund which lends up to $250 to a woman with community roots. This allows her to remain outside of prison at a saving of $30,000 per year per inmate, retain ties to family and custody of children, and begin to build a more productive life with the help of a volunteer caseworker.
- **Inside-Out Program:** Inside-Out matches the offender with a volunteer caseworker who helps and counsels the sentenced female offender during incarceration and at least three months following release from jail. In addition to one-to-one weekly sessions, the caseworker may assist by providing referrals for housing, education, training, employment, child care, drug and alcohol addiction services, welfare, legal and children's advocacy services.
- **Community Work Service Project:** This project provides judges with an alternative to incarcerating female misdemeanants who have been convicted of committing a non-violent criminal offense. Participants in the programs are sentenced by the court to provide a specified number of hours of work (from 80-250 hours) to a not-for-profit organization as a means of restitution for their crimes against society. Optimally, this alternative sentence is rehabilitative for the offender, providing her with needed work experience and increasing her self-esteem through participation in socially-positive activities under supervision by CAFJ and work-site staff. Minimally, it consistently proves to be a cost-effective means of sentencing offenders, and also helps in alleviating overcrowding in the city's overtaxed corrections facilities.
- **Community Resource Center:** The Resource Center is a clearinghouse for employment, cultural, recreational, housing and financial resources upon which the newly-released woman can draw.
- **Volunteer Training:** Community volunteers are provided with an intensive 25-hour training program prior to participating in the work of CAFJ. The training includes an introduction to the New York City Court and Corrections systems, a look at the nature of problems faced by female criminal offenders in these systems and in the community, an examination of sex, race, and class issues as these infringe upon the women's lives, and a rigorous self-inventory which enables the volunteers to

identify their own attitudes and biases and how these will affect their capacities to assist in the work of CAFJ.

Following the completion of training, volunteers identify resources that they are prepared to offer to the organization: time, skills, experience, funds, contacts, etc. They also express the type of volunteer activities they would prefer. CAFJ's staff then proceeds to match these resources and interests with the agency's and the women's needs.

Typical volunteer activities, supervised by Executive and Program Directors, have included:

- one-to-one casework relationships with women in the Community Work Service, Inside-Out, and Bail Fund Projects;
- fundraising activities such as bazaars, mailings, membership drives;
- clothing and food donations;
- building rehab; and
- sharing holidays with women who have no homes or families.

Beyond this, volunteers have had a "ripple effect" in the form of a growing "sense of community" among themselves, the women served, and the neighborhoods in which they concentrate their efforts.

Founded: 1978

COMPANIONSHIP/THERAPY PROGRAM
SEE VOLUNTEERS: STUDENTS

COURT APPOINTED SPECIAL ADVOCATES (CASA)

301 The City Drive
Orange, CA 92668
TEL: 714-834-6460

Purpose: To provide volunteers who act as special friends and advocates of children from group or foster homes.

Sponsor: Orange County (CA)

Contact: Susan Leibel, Director

Description: There is a growing concern among private citizens and professionals that many children in the child welfare system are not receiving the care they need. To help solve that problem, the CASA (Court Appointed Special Advocates) program has revolutionized part of the judicial system by allowing private citizens to participate in previously closed juvenile courts. In a system where social workers carry heavy caseloads, the child advocates have come to be relied on to provide the kind of loving one-to-one contact that caseworkers cannot. The children in the program have no one outside of the system who cares about them and often are moved constantly from foster home to group home to emergency shelter. The CASA program provides some stability for them - a continuing presence that they can count on. With a national office in Seattle, and 393 CASA programs nationwide, thousands of children are being represented who might not have been brought before the courts at all. California alone has 17 CASA programs, and in one state, at least (Florida), counties are required by law to have CASA programs.

The Orange County CASA program is an independent nonprofit organization with offices supplied by the county. Currently the program has 106 active volunteers. With about 2,000 children in the system, this group of volunteers can handle only a small percentage. Volunteers go through a 20-hour course in which they learn about courtroom procedures from judges, lawyers and other court personnel and attend seminars on topics ranging from sexual abuse of children to early childhood development and adolescent behavior.

After the training, they are sworn in by a juvenile court judge as officers of the court and take an oath of confidentiality to gain access to juvenile court files. They are matched with a child and see that child on a weekly basis and provide consistency.

Each time there is a hearing concerning the child, the CASA submits a written report that becomes part of a child's court file. To prepare these court reports, CASA volunteers also talk to the child, parents, other relatives, social workers, school officials, doctors and anyone else knowledgeable about the child's history to determine if it would be better for the child to remain with parents or guardians, be placed in foster care, or be freed for permanent adoption. Unfortunately, there are not nearly enough foster homes to take them. So they must go to group homes, emergency shelter homes or to Orangewood.

One of the aspects that proves an interesting challenge is the fact that the court and caseworkers are obligated by law to work to reunite children with their families, while the volunteers often see the family as unworthy of getting the child back. CASA supporters liken this concept to lay people on a jury and argue that they can apply common sense and community standards to sometimes impersonal judicial proceedings that determine the fates of families. Many judges see them as the *common denominator* in the system. Where caseworkers often work with 60 to 70 children at a time, CASA volunteers work with only one or two. Thus, the volunteer can examine each case more thoroughly and provide emotional and practical support. In addition, volunteers often take kids to the hospital and medical appointments when a social worker finds it impossible to go. In some cases it is possible to assign a medically-knowledgeable volunteer who can ask questions of the doctor, read blood tests, etc.

The volunteers come from all over the county, ranging from 21-year-old students to retired seniors. The majority hold full-time jobs and see children on weekends, evenings, or after school. All make a one-year commitment. According to one volunteer, "The important thing is that they have somebody there for them. And it's important that they have some idea of family life. They need to know that they are special and have a future."
Founded: 1984

COURT REFERRAL PROGRAM
SEE VOLUNTEERS: ALTERNATIVE SENTENCING OFFENDERS

COURT REFERRED VOLUNTEER PROGRAM OF RENSSELAER COUNTY
SEE VOLUNTEERS: ALTERNATIVE SENTENCING OFFENDERS

FRIENDS OF THE SUPERIOR COURT
SEE VOLUNTEERS: PROFESSIONALS

GUARDIAN AD LITEM PROGRAM
King County Superior Court
1211 East Alder Street
Mail Stop 2-L
Seattle, WA 98122
TEL: 206-296-1120
FAX: 206-343-2432
Purpose: To provide volunteer advocates for abused and neglected children who are involved in *King County Superior Court* dependency proceedings.
Contact: Nancy Broaders
Description: The *Guardian ad Litem (GAL) Program* was conceptualized in 1976 by the presiding judge of *King County Superior Court* in Seattle, and began operating in 1977. A *Guardian ad Litem* is a court-appointed special advocate for children involved in a court case. The phrase means "guardian for the term of the litigation." A GAL is a trained community volunteer who acts as an advocate for the best interests of abused and neglected children who are the subject of court proceedings. GALs are appointed to cases in which children are alleged to have been neglected, physically abused, sexually abused, emotionally abused and/or if a parent or guardian is unable or unwilling to care for the child. The GAL talks with the child, parents, family members, caseworker, school personnel, health providers, foster

parents and others who know about the child's situation. The GAL also reviews records pertinent to the child. By closely monitoring the child's status, the GAL can make timely recommendations as to whether the child should be returned home or be freed for adoption. The amount of time required depends on many factors, such as the complexity of the case and the experience of the GAL.

The GAL continues to be involved until the case is permanently solved. This might be when the child is returned home or when the child is freed for adoption. One of the primary benefits of the GAL Program is that, unlike other court principals who often rotate cases, the GAL is a consistent figure in the proceedings and provides continuity for the child.

The GAL provides the judge, who ultimately must decide what is best for the child, with a source of mature, sensitive concern from someone who has no interest but that of the child. The volunteer has brought light, warmth, and hope into court proceedings that had been grim and poorly informed.

The Seattle court-appointed special advocate program resulted in court jurisdictions throughout the country implementing the Seattle model. Currently, there are 341 *GAL/CASA (Court Appointed Special Advocates)* programs operating in 45 states. New CASA programs start at an average of four per month. The *Guardian ad Litem Program* is one of three volunteer programs operating within *Juvenile Court Operations of King County Superior Court.* Superior Court programs operate within the judicial branch of King County government. The GAL program is served by an Advisory Board with representatives from the local community.

The many years of experience with the GAL Program in Seattle has resulted in this definition of a GAL:
The *Guardian ad Litem* is:
- committed to children
- able to maintain objectivity
- a creative problem solver
- skilled in interpersonal relationships
- sensitive to cultural values
- blessed with common sense
- open to personal growth

Fact sheets, brochures and other materials have been developed about the *King County Guardian ad Litem Program* for sharing with other communities.
Publications: Who Speaks for the Child; King County GAL/CASA Program: Questions & Answers; King County Guardian ad Litem/CASA Program: Fact Sheet

JUVENILE ARBITRATION PROGRAM OF SOUTH CAROLINA
PO Box 2327
Aiken, SC 29802
TEL: 803-642-1569
Purpose: To allow first-time offenders to avoid a family court record.
Sponsor: Second Judicial Circuit Court
Contact: Patricia A. Reynolds
Description: The Juvenile Arbitration Program of South Carolina is administered by the Solicitor's office for the Second Judicial Circuit and was initially funded for three years by a grant from the Governor's office which later received permanent continuation by Aiken County after its proven success.

The Program allows first-time offenders to prevent a family court record by successfully completing a tailor-made outline determined by a trained volunteer Arbitrator in the community.

This program not only gives the opportunity for a child to prevent a Family Court record, but invites the victim to be an active participant throughout the Arbitration proceedings by suggesting possible sanctions.

The Arbitration Program affects positively every aspect of the Juvenile Justice System in this Circuit by relieving the caseload on

Law Enforcement, Department of Youth Services, Solicitor's office, Clerk of the Court and the Family Court Judges, thus allowing them to concentrate on more serious offenders.

A success in this program also acts as a crime prevention tool because it removes a juvenile from the crime cycle which all too often leads to his/her becoming a habitual offender.

A first-time offender should not be followed by a criminal record which would possibly hinder his or her future, nor should he/she be allowed to "get away" with the offense.

Through the Juvenile Arbitration Program, the child is given positive learning alternatives such as community service, jail tours, observing films, and General Sessions Court as well as monetary restitution.

Since implementation in 1985, the program has processed over 600 juvenile cases with a less than five percent recidivism rate and a success rate of 88 percent.

Also, the Juvenile Arbitration Program has collected over $17,000 for victims of the Second Judicial Circuit in juvenile crimes which aids in meeting one of the major objectives, which is to satisfy all parties concerned.

The Juvenile Arbitration Program is cost-effective due to the extensive utilization of trained volunteers from the community. The program has demonstrated that it is effective.
Founded: 1985

MANNA, INC.*
SEE VOLUNTEERS: CHURCH/SYNAGOGUE MEMBERS

OMBUDSMAN PROGRAM
Northern Virginia Long-Term Care
Office of Volunteers
11242 Waples Mill Road #100
Fairfax, VA 22030
TEL: 703-246-5411
TOLL FREE: 800-468-1133
Purpose: To provide advocacy for residents of long-term care facilities.
Contact: Sharon K. Lynn, Volunteer Coordinator
Description: The Long-Term Care Ombudsman Program was created by an amendment in 1978 to the Older Americans Act of 1965. This action was taken largely as a result of issues raised at the White House Conference on Aging in 1971, when the Department of Health, Education and Welfare (now Health and Human Services) was charged with developing programs to improve the quality of care for the nation's nursing home residents. Each state is mandated to have an ombudsman, or citizen representative, to investigate and resolve complaints made by or on behalf of individual residents of long-term care facilities, to monitor legislation, to provide public information, and to train volunteers.

The Northern Virginia Long-Term Care Ombudsman Program was planned and developed by the Area Agencies on Aging in Arlington, Fairfax, Loudoun, and Prince William counties, and the City of Alexandria. The Virginia Department for the Aging designated the program to assist the more than 4,500 men and women who live in Northern Virginia nursing homes and homes for adults. The program is funded by both state and local jurisdictions.

The volunteer component of the program consists of approximately 30 volunteers. The volunteers participate in three days of training which provides a thorough orientation to the aging process, homes for adults, and advocacy skills. If certified, volunteers are assigned to a local nursing home or home for adults where they visit residents for approximately four hours each week. The volunteers provide friendly concern, attempt to empower residents to solve their own problems, and advocate for them when necessary. In addition, they provide residents and their families with information about patients' rights, government benefits, and other agencies which can be of assistance.

The volunteers are supervised and supported by weekly phone calls and occasional on-site visits by the Coordinator of Volunteers. Also, volunteers are asked to attend two-hour in-service training sessions held monthly.
Publications: Ombudsman Program Information Packet; Ombudsman Program Volunteer Opportunities; Ombudsman Program (for patients)
Founded: 1978

VIRGINIA CITIZENS CONSUMER COUNCIL
c/o Jean Ann Fox
517 Waters Edge Road
Newport News, VA 23607
TEL: 804-596-6028
Purpose: To examine the state's consumer issues and work toward changes in legislation when indicated.
Sponsor: Virginia Office of the Attorney General
Contact: Jean Ann Fox, President
Description: Consumer credit and insurance bills have been the main thrust of the *Virginia Citizens Consumer Council.* The 400 individual volunteer members, and a few organizational members, take on the big business interests in spite of the stark differences in resources. One example is the "luxury" of having volunteers come in from around the state for *one day* to assist with the tracking of bills, while business interests have lobbyists present on a daily basis. One recent bill which easily passed the state Senate on mandatory disclosure by automobile manufacturers was affected by this difference when it was killed following the increase of the manufacturers' lobbyists before it got to Committee.

Still, the advocates have seen considerable progress over the last few years. For example, the volunteers have successfully enlisted the *Attorney General's Office* and the *Bureau of Insurance* in pushing a legislative agenda, resulting in several key gains for the consumer group, and thus for the citizens of the state. Some of the bills tracked during 1990 concern:
- policy cancellation;
- antitrust violations by insurance companies;
- contractors' poor work;
- more affordable banking services;
- health spa closings; and
- small claims courts.

A major victory has been a compromise on the front-loading of interest on car loans, second mortgages, and home improvement loans. All members of the Council are unpaid volunteers. One legislator suggested that a full-time paid Executive Director is needed to be present during the entire session. However, according to the President, "We have come from being the last state in the country to consider things to being one of the first. This is an amazing amount of consumer legislation for Virginia. Consumers are being more demanding of their rights."

VOLUNTEERS: ALTERNATIVE SENTENCING OFFENDERS

TRAINING PROGRAMS

FAIRFAX ALTERNATIVE SERVICES WORKSHOP
SEE TRAINING/CONFERENCES/TEACHING: JUSTICE SYSTEM

INDIVIDUAL PROGRAM PROFILES

COURT EMPLOYMENT PROJECT (*formerly Manhattan Court Employment Project*)
346 Broadway
New York, NY 10013
TEL: 212-732-0076
Purpose: To provide alternative sentencing and employment opportunities to young offenders (14-21).
Contact: Maximo Blake, Executive Director
Description: This program of the *New York City Criminal and Supreme Courts* offers services to young offenders (14-21) designed to decrease or eliminate recidivism, and return them to their community with a better future. One part of the program provides alternative sentencing to social welfare programs for pre-trial detainees and defendants facing 90-day sentences or felony convictions. In addition, individual, family, group, health, and vocational counseling are offered, followed by career development and job training or academic placement. Courses in preparation for the GED certificate are conducted, and referral to community social service agencies for additional assistance is made as needed. The program also offers paid work experience and training in light building renovation, including painting and carpentry through a general contracting business operated by the program.
Founded: 1967

COURT REFERRAL PROGRAM
PO Box 451
Owensboro, KY 42302
TEL: 502-684-9238
Purpose: The Court Referral Program places adult and juvenile offenders in community service agencies to do a set number of volunteer hours instead of paying a fine or serving a jail sentence.
Sponsor: Voluntary Action Center
Contact: Pamela J. Warwick, Executive Director
Description: The Court Referral Program began in 1975 with a grant from the Kentucky Crime Commission. It is a cooperative effort between the Voluntary Action Center, Davies District Court system, and community service agencies. When grant money ended, city and county funds were secured to continue operating the program.
The program has provided volunteer job placements for adult and juvenile offenders in the community for six years. Offenders are referred to the program by district court judges and placed in community service agencies to complete an assigned number of hours of volunteer work in lieu of paying a fine or serving a jail sentence. The program has become particularly helpful to the courts for those cases where a fine or jail sentence is inappropriate as the program provides a "working alternative." For offenders, the program provides an opportunity to pay back the community while gaining valuable job experience. As a result of working on the program, some volunteers secure jobs with the agencies upon completion of volunteer hours or receive recommendations for securing other employment. Also, the program is helpful in providing community service agencies with court referral volunteers to assist in such areas as programming, office work, and maintenance.
Since the program began, the number of court-referred volunteers has increased steadily. In a typical year, about 600 offenders are referred by the courts to the program. Each year, the Court Referral Program has a success rate of approximately 96% (persons who successfully complete the program). It is a well-liked, valuable, and respected program. As the budget for the program is quite low, continuing the program is necessary when considering the costs to the community if the program were ended.
Founded: 1975

COURT REFERRED VOLUNTEER PROGRAM OF RENSSELAER COUNTY
502 Broadway
Troy, NY 12180
TEL: 518-274-7234
Purpose: To provide community service to minor offenders, as mandated by the Courts.
Sponsor: Volunteer Center of Rensselaer County
Contact: Jacqueline Mulligan
Description: The *Court Referred Volunteer Program* was instituted by the *Volunteer Center of Rensselaer County* in February 1981 after the concept of alternative sentencing was studied by the *Rensselaer County Criminal Justice Coordinating Committee.* The first of its kind in the county and the Capital District, the program provides community service, as mandated by the courts, to persons (primarily youthful offenders), in order to prevent or decrease their incarceration, probation, and re-entry into the criminal justice system.
Under the program, appropriate offenders are sentenced by the courts to complete a designated amount of volunteer service as an alternative to a jail term or fine, or as a condition of probation. Our office interviews, refers and places such offenders in a non-profit agency or government department. Assignments are monitored and the courts are notified when the offenders have completed the service. Our clients have ranged in age from 10-49 years, with the average age being 19. Whenever necessary, clients are referred informally to other service that they may need.
Since its inception, nearly 1,800 CRVs have been assigned to community service. The benefits to the community are many:
- Provides judges with an alternative sentencing tool;
- Enables the offender to have an opportunity to earn a favorable disposition; and
- Increases the pool of volunteer help to nonprofit community organizations.
Funding Sources are *New York State Division for Youth, Rensselaer County Department for Youth,* and *United Way.*
Founded: 1981

CURB IT!
Keep Perrysburg Beautiful
Fraternal Order of Police Lodge 182
900 West Poe Road
Perrysburg, OH 43551
TEL: 419-352-9370
Purpose: To enlist individuals, corporations and others in the community to mount a pilot recycling project to help plan for a future areawide project.
Sponsor: Keep Perrysburg Beautiful
Contact: Mary Cowles, Program Coordinator
Description: A pilot program, *Curb It!* was tried in August 1989 in two neighborhoods totaling 233 houses - Pheasant Run and Perry Commons. Volunteer manpower, recycled buckets, and a recycled truck make up the program's components. *Master Chemical Company* donated the buckets. The *Curb It Committee* of about 20 citizens visit the involved households once a month and survey them about progress and ideas for the ongoing test. Volunteers distribute *Curb It Kits* about the program, and the plastic buckets, door-to-door. The kits include a magnet for differentiating between aluminum and steel cans and a brown paper bag to hold newspapers.
The program requires residents in the pilot areas to tote five-gallon buckets filled with aluminum cans and glass bottles out to the curb with their stacked newspapers. The recycleable materials are then picked up and tossed into a former soft drink truck, separated on the truck during the pickup route, and hauled off for sale.
The three-month pilot program had a $2,425 budget, including $800 for insurance, and $500 for each of the other three items: vehicle expense, printing and production, and awards and promotion costs. The city litter control agency, *Keep Perrysburg*

Beautiful, financed the experimental project, in part, with a $33,876 grant from the *Ohio Department of Natural Resources* along with a 20 percent share from the city.

The test area amounts to about 6 percent of Perrysburg's 3,500 homes, not including apartments. The Saturday morning pickups are aimed at giving city officials some idea of what they could expect from a larger area. Since recycling programs average about 30 percent participation, city officials will consider involvement of 40% of residents in the test area as a successful effort.

Benefits to the community in a successful effort include:
- conservation of landfill space;
- conservation of material resources;
- reducing the number of the city's deposits in landfills ($200 for each refuse truckful dumped in a landfill)

According to officials, a 10 percent reduction in landfill usage would mean a savings of about $10,000. Landfill costs in 1988 were $81,787. Budget for 1989 was $93,000.

Four or five volunteers are assigned each Saturday, and the proceeds from the sale of recycleables are given to organizations who provide the volunteers. One of the first groups to provide volunteers in 1989 was *Perrysburg Fraternal Order of Police Lodge 182.* The citywide program will have far greater manpower demands, but the pilot program may shed some light on possible solutions to those demands. Officials have been encouraged as some neighboring communities institute their own recycling pickup as part of their regular refuse collection.

Founded: 1989

DIVERSION TO COMMUNITY SERVICE*
Volunteer Center, Inc.
115 East Jefferson Street
Suite 300
Syracuse, NY 13202
TEL: 315-474-7011

Purpose: To provide a positive alternative to the criminal justice system for young offenders and other misdemeanants.

Sponsor: State Division for Youth; County of Onondaga

Contact: Jean J. Greene

Description: The Volunteer Center began the Diversion to Community Service in 1978 as a very small pilot program. Today the program receives funds from the New York State Division for Youth via the City-County Youth Board, and matching funds from the County of Onondaga. The underlying philosophy of the program remains the same: to give non-violent first-time offenders an opportunity to perform community service in lieu of a fine or jail sentence, hoping to:
- channel them away from the criminal justice system;
- prevent recidivism; and
- provide a realistic sentence that is positive and not punitive.

The program began in response to a need expressed by City Court judges locally looking for some kind of positive alternative to traditional criminal sentences for the young offenders. Now suitable offenders - with agreement among judge, district attorney, defense lawyer and the offender himself - can be referred to the Volunteer Center for placement as volunteers with community agencies. The judge stipulates the number of hours to be provided, and the Volunteer Center keeps track and notifies the court when the hours are complete. Often, the case is dismissed and no record remains for the young person.

Clients are interviewed in the same way as any other volunteer, and placements are arranged to utilize their skills and interests. Care is taken also to arrange hours outside of work and school time. Volunteer openings include recreation aides; child care; maintenance and repair; clerical work; tutoring; park cleanup; and many more.

After a slow start in the pilot year (placing under 100 clients), the program expects to place over 1,000 in this third year of operation, with over 20,000 hours of community service as a byproduct. City court judges and local town justices in every city and suburban court in the area now use the program.

The Center does not limit its role in this program to that of a placement service and record-keeper. If the clients seem to be in need of other services, such as education or counseling, they are referred to the Information and Referral Service of the Volunteer Center where staff helps them find services needed.

The success rate for the Diversion to Community Service program is 98% in terms of completion of hours. Also, many young people have obtained paid jobs with the agencies for which they were volunteering. Many others have remained as volunteers long after the stipulated hours were completed. The emphasis is on making volunteering a rewarding experience.

Founded: 1978

HITS (HIGH INTENSITY TREATMENT SUPERVISION)
District of Columbia Superior Court
Social Services, Juvenile Branch
500 Indiana Avenue, NW, Room 302
Washington, DC 20001
TEL: 202-879-4332; 202-879-4330
FAX: 202-879-1965

Purpose: To rehabilitate hard core juvenile offenders and remove them from the cycle of crime.

Sponsor: District of Columbia Department of Corrections

Contact: Carroll Boswell, Supervisor

Description: Begun in 1988 as a unique probation program to relieve the crowding in juvenile detention facilities, HITS has become a successful rehabilitation system with a rigid structure. It holds youths, most of them repeat offenders, to more stringent standards than regular probation. It is a system of counseling groups, self-esteem workshops, parent involvement, curfews, urine tests, community service work, jobs and school. It is, according to its supervisor, "confinement without incarceration."

A favorite aspect of the program is the community services arm which sends youth to soup kitchens, housing projects, or recreation centers around the city to do about 10 hours of community service or cleanup work each week. In addition, curfew is 9:00 seven nights a week, with counselors calling at curfew time, and/or appearing at the door unannounced ("night riders") as late as 3:00 a.m.

Although youth placed in HITS have committed crimes for which they would usually be jailed, youths charged with violence are generally not placed in the program. Violation of HITS probation means two years in jail.

Although officials refuse to draw firm conclusions after only one year, recidivism among the youth in the program (5%) compares very favorably with that of youths on regular probation (30%). Success stories include the former leader of a crew of drug dealers, now 18, who is working in construction.

Part of HITS's philosophy is to attack the youths' warped values, records of failure, and low sense of self-worth. One example of this is allowing reporters access to the HITS program on the condition that the youths on probation not be named. This is true in media access to related court proceedings also. The media have honored this condition and the stories have been positive and helpful to the overall program.

For reasons ranging from severe truancy to poor academic performance, most of the youth in the program failed in school. On the streets, where the police kept arresting them, they failed as thugs. And many of them feel that they have failed their parents. The youths typically score in the lower range on standard intelligence tests. One of the program leaders is certain that the reasons behind such poor showings are mostly environmental. However, as pointed out by one of the counselors, every one of them wants to go to school.

Special rap sessions are held for youth facing drug charges. Youth who are not charged, but admit to having used drugs, are invited to participate in the rap sessions.

The involvement of parents is essential to the program, according to a supervisor. Although sessions for parents are mandatory, and some parents attend reluctantly, as time is spent in the program, they become more relaxed and helpful to their children and the program. Some parents attend support groups of their peers - parents who are "at their wit's end, their bag of disciplinary tricks empty." Although too soon to tell, there are signs that this parent involvement has a positive effect after the youths leave the program.

Many HITS youth come from families with existing problems - many of them severe. Some of the parents, mostly single mothers, were teenagers when they had children. Some parents just don't want to know the truth. At the other extreme, some work so hard, have so many mouths to feed, that there is little time for nurturing. Often they are glad to have HITS as an option for assistance, since they have not been able to make a difference. The parents of some youth are dead or not around.

HITS case workers have smaller case loads than other probation officers - about 15 youths each - and can spend more time with each one. HITS also requires involvement of a parent or guardian, whereas in regular probation, parents are often peripheral.

With 6,499 juveniles arrested in 1988, and only 200 slots in the HITS program, the impact is only a fraction of what it could be, according to staff members.

IN-HOME DETENTION PROGRAM
428 Western Avenue
Davenport, IA 52801
TEL: 319-326-8612
Purpose: To provide an alternative to secure detention for juvenile offenders.
Sponsor: Iowa Crime Commission/Scott County
Contact: Kathleen Gillman, Diversion Coordinator
Description: Beginning full operation in August 1981, the In-Home Detention Program is one of many Diversion Programs of the Scott County Juvenile Court. The program has received two years' funding from the Iowa Crime Commission. Scott County picked up the program in 1982.

The In-Home Detention Program was designed to provide an alternative form of detention which allows juveniles to be detained in their own homes. In-home detention is ordered by the juvenile judge when the Court determines that a youth requires some form of detention, but does not require a "secure" detention setting.

A youth on home detention is placed under the supervision of a Home Detention Worker (volunteer) for the duration of the detention period, not to exceed 30 days. The volunteer visits the youth and his/her parents on a daily basis, seven days a week, makes telephone contacts, and is available for consultation at the conclusion of the detention period.

An In-Home Detention Contract and a Detention Order are prepared when a home detention is ordered. The conditions in the contract must be agreed to and signed by the child, his attorney and his parents. The goals of the In-Home Detention Program include:

- to demonstrate the successful supervision of youths outside of a secure detention facility;
- to provide parents with supportive services to enable youths to be maintained in their homes;
- to help keep participating youths trouble-free while they are awaiting court hearings; and
- to keep youths available for their court appearances.

The program is functioning at the present time with eight volunteers. All are under the direct supervision of the Diversion Coordinator. A new volunteer undergoes a personal orientation with the Diversion Coordinator. Volunteers are provided with a Volunteer Manual and are required to attend Volunteer meetings every two months. Experience has shown that the best training is "on-the-job training." One purpose of the volunteer meetings is to discuss both pleasurable and difficult encounters while working with the young people.

During the first full year of operation, 39 youths were placed on In-Home Detention. Only eight of these youths were detained for violations. These youths met the criteria for secure detention and, if the In-Home Detention Program did not exist, would have been placed in the Detention Center.
Founded: 1981

JOB SEARCH
SEE VOLUNTEERS: CHURCH/SYNAGOGUE MEMBERS

JOB THERAPY, INC. (EX-OFFENDER PROGRAM: PROJECT START)*
3927 Aurora Avenue North
Suite 201
Seattle, WA 98103
TEL: 206-447-3650
Purpose: To provide employment services to ex-offenders and to juveniles who are involved or are in danger of becoming involved in prostitution.
Sponsor: Private contributions; CETA; DSHS; State Employment Security
Contact: David Seidel, Executive Director
Description: Job Therapy is a private, nonprofit organization. Under contract to the State of Washington, it has been providing job-finding services to ex-offenders since 1963. In recent years, several foundations have provided grants to enable the program to expand to include youths. Among the job-finding aids provided are:

- Job Orientation
- Job Placement
- Job Development
- Follow-up Services
- Job Counseling
- Supportive Services

The program's target populations are ex-offenders, and youths who are, or who are about to become involved in juvenile prostitution. The Ex-Offender Program continues to be effective in reintegrating the ex-offender into the community. The State of Washington funds the program through the performance-based contracting method.

Project Start is a newer phase of Job Therapy and was created to help reduce the incidence of juvenile prostitution. It is funded primarily by a grant from the Washington Law and Justice Planning Division. Foundations also have provided funding for this youth program. United Way is providing a large percentage of the total funding for the program.

Volunteers generally do counseling tasks and professional, technical duties such as budget forecasting for the entire organization. Since most of the volunteer work is done by individuals who have been ordered by the court to perform a certain number of hours of community service, the program uses less volunteers from the general community - from three to five at any given time.
Founded: 1963

LEE COUNTY RESTITUTION PROGRAM
PO Box 57
Sanford, NC 27330
TEL: 919-774-9515
Purpose: To provide victims of juvenile crime with restitution for damage, either property or physical.
Sponsor: State/County Governments
Contact: Ronnie Martin, Director
Description: The Lee County Restitution program is designed to provide victims of juvenile crime, restitution for either property or physical damage suffered by them.

It began April 1, 1983 and provides services for children ages 10 to 17. The children work one day weekly in stacking, loading and unloading firewood. Any monies earned by the children are given to the Clerk of Court for payment to the victim. The child is terminated from the program after payment is made.

The program operates under Community Based alternative (state) and county funds as well as grants from corporate sources.

The goal of the program is to instill responsibility in the youth and hopefully reduce repeat offenders.

Volunteer Staff: The volunteers act as supervisors at the job site. They are there to see that the work is carried out as well as providing support for the children. Due to the recent implementation of the program, we have only two volunteers but hope to increase this number considerably.

Volunteer Training: Training consists of 6 hours. The volunteers are trained in the techniques of counseling and also how to be an effective job site supervisor. Patience is stressed. The volunteers are screened thoroughly with supervision of the volunteers provided by the Director of Lee County Youth Services.

Founded: 1983

PUBLIC SERVICE VOLUNTEERS
Augusta Mental Health Institute
Box 724
Augusta, ME 04330
TEL: 207-622-3751/Ext. 431
Purpose: To provide a meaningful way for persons convicted of misdemeanor offenses to repay society through public service work.
Sponsor: Augusta Mental Health Institute, Departments of Mental Health & Corrections
Contact: Peter E. Swartz, Chief of Volunteer Services
Description: Public Service Volunteers may be any person over 14 years of age convicted of a misdemeanor offense (e.g., traffic violations, operating under the influence, and petty thefts). Volunteers may be placed in any non-profit agency. In practice, the Augusta Mental Health Institute has utilized most of the individuals due to insurance liability concerns.

Public Service Volunteers utilizes from 75 to 100 individuals a year working from four to several hundred hours on a full or part time basis.

Work assignments include: Houskeeping, Warehouse, Grounds Maintenance, Office Work, and occasionally other areas of special need, usually in non-patient contact areas.

The program benefits the individual and the agency. Persons working over 40 hours are eligible for a job reference. The goal there is a long range deterrent effect.

VOLUNTEERS: ALUMNI

INDIVIDUAL PROGRAM PROFILES

PHI MU SORORITY COMMUNITY SERVICE CHAPTER
SEE VOLUNTEERS: FRATERNAL ORGANIZATIONS

TAU KAPPA EPSILON (TKE) COMMUNITY PROJECTS
SEE VOLUNTEERS: FRATERNAL ORGANIZATIONS

VOLUNTEERS: ARMED FORCES MEMBERS

NATIONAL/STATE ORGANIZATIONS

US/DOD - PRIVATE SECTOR INITIATIVES PROGRAM
SEE PRIVATE SECTOR INITIATIVES OFFICES: DEFENSE

TRAINING PROGRAMS

MANAGEMENT OF VOLUNTEER PROGRAMS IN THE ARMED FORCES
VOLUNTEER - The National Center
1111 North 19th Street, Suite 500
Arlington, VA 22209
TEL: 703-276-0542
FAX: 703-528-6021
Sponsor: VOLUNTEER - The National Center
Contact: Kay Drake
Description: A Department of Defense Volunteer Management Track was made part of an annual VOLUNTEER's national training conference for volunteer managers.

Military people were able to focus on successful volunteer programs being conducted throughout the Services and exchange ideas on program management in this area. Speakers from each of the Armed Services, including Reserve Components, discussed various aspects of volunteerism in their branches of the Service, including successful approaches to volunteer recruitment and management. Opportunities were available throughout the conference for networking with other professionals, both within and outside of the Service, and to exchange examples of volunteer program materials.

Service representatives had an opportunity to participate in the general sessions as well as those related to military volunteer programs.

INDIVIDUAL PROGRAM PROFILES

JANGO (JUNIOR ARMY NAVY GUILD ORGANIZATION)*
Henderson Hall
Arlington, VA 22214
TEL: 703-979-1492
Purpose: To train young volunteers to assist medical personnel in military and civilian hospitals.
Sponsor: US/DoD - JANGO
Contact: Linda S. Mundy, Executive Secretary
Description: JANGO was established at the beginning of World War II to assist the war effort and deal with the manpower shortage. Wives and daughters were invited to join in service in the wider community. They were asked to assist in hospitals on and off the military bases. Although the actual name of the organization has not been changed, membership (since the end of World War II) includes all military services and Department of Defense appointees. The Guild is divided into two sections:

- **Junior Jango,** which involves young men and women (ages 14-19) in training as volunteers in military and civilian hospitals. Junior Jangos are dependents of active, retired, or deceased military persons and Defense Department appointees. They are given 100 hours of study as nurses' aides through both classroom instruction and on-the-job training under nursing supervision. Their duties include patient care and comfort; daily routines such as making beds, taking vital signs, and passing out food trays and water; other responsibilities that may be assigned by the charge nurse; and, as important as the others, giving the individual attention to the patient that cannot be provided by professional staff. Junior Jangos wear a uniform, participate in a capping ceremony at the completion of training, and receive awards based on hours and quality of service. They are expected to make good use of the opportunities provided through this program: (1) learning skills and proficiency in a helping profession; (2) developing responsibility regarding the needs of the community; (3) making an important contribution where it is most needed. Also, many qualify for merit awards and scholarships.

- **Senior Jangos** are dues paying members who may serve on the Senior Board and/or participate in Guild activities.

In addition to the two active divisions, JANGO maintains a roster of Honorary Members, usually distinguished women such as the wives of Presidents of the United States, Secretaries and Chiefs of Staffs. Guilds exist in several cities across the country. Location lists are available.

Founded: 1941

SERVICE TO MILITARY FAMILIES/SERVICE TO VETERANS (OHIO)

American Red Cross
1830 North Limestone Street
Springfield, OH 45503
TEL: 513-399-3875
Purpose: (1) To assist Armed Forces personnel and their families against the strain of separation, and to assist families in meeting problems that arise when a member is in the service; (2) To assist veterans in applying for Veterans Administration benefits.
Sponsor: American Red Cross
Contact: Dorothy LaVelle
Description: The American Red Cross offers a number of services to both active duty and veteran military personnel, including those shown below:
Service to Military Families: The principal Red Cross services to military personnel and their families are counseling, emergency communications, and financial assistance. The Red Cross assists military personnel in utilizing appropriate military and community resources to help resolve problems.
Messages are sent by Chapters to AmCross in Washington, DC, asking for emergency services such as locator information for military personnel in transit, and emergency messages to be sent to service members aboard ships at sea or at small isolated bases in remote parts of the world. These crucial messages receive high priority in handling.
Volunteers, some in leadership positions, assist the paid staff in carrying out the above and other services to military personnel and their families.
Service to Veterans: The American Red Cross recognizes Red Cross responsibility to former service members as a logical extension of service to the Armed Forces.
The Red Cross helps veterans with applications for government benefits, such as:

- Education
- Disability Compensation
- Pensions
- Medical and Dental Care
- Home Loans
- Discharge Reviews and Correction of Military Records

Red Cross also represents the veteran before the Veterans Administration and Military Review Boards. In addition, Clark County has generated $280,000 in benefits for veterans in this area. Volunteers, some in leadership positions, assist paid staff in their efforts to assure maximum benefits to veterans of the Armed Forces.

VOLUNTEERS: ARMED FORCES MEMBERS - AIR FORCE

INDIVIDUAL PROGRAM PROFILES

AIR FORCE MEMBERS AS VOLUNTEERS*
US/DoD - Air Force Office of Public Affairs
1221 South Fern Street
#D-159
Arlington, VA 22202
TEL: 703-695-5331; 703-695-5392
Purpose: To help close the gap that often exists between a community and the nearby military installation.
Sponsor: US/DoD - Department of the Air Force
Contact: Lieutenant Peter S. Meltzer, Jr.
Description: The Magazines and Books Division of the Air Force Office of Public Affairs receives ideas for stories about Air Force personnel activities almost daily. Many of the suggestions address volunteer activities on the base and in the community. They range from linking with scouting and other traditional organizations to seeing a need and independently finding a solution. Some examples follow:
Holloman AFB Volunteer Program - Service members at this New Mexico Base donated more than 95,000 hours and $136,883 to various community and Base organizations (e.g., Boy and Girl Scouts, local churches, youth and fraternal organizations, Older American Centers, children's homes and day care centers, Crime Stoppers and foster parent programs, community disaster response, medical and health assistance and various sports, education and training programs). In addition, the Base's Enlisted Advisory Council works with blind athletes, while other Base volunteers work with the handicapped and provide chauffeur service for the elderly.
Playground for Handicapped Children - More than 100 volunteers from Bolling Air Force Base (AFB) in Washington, DC, assisted with construction of a specially designed playground at Key Center, a public school serving 200 handicapped children in Springfield, Virginia.
Bikes for Laotian Hmong Refugee Children - Members of the Air National Guard's 141st Air Refueling Wing at Fairchild AFB collected repairable cycles and parts to produce 33 bicycles for Laotian Hmong children living in Spokane, Washington (also used by their parents as a modest means of transportation).
Underwater Posse - A Luke AFB technical sergeant is a member of the Maricopa County, California, Sheriff's divers posse, helping to find lost swimmers - or their bodies, and helping recreational divers who panic (the divers posse must be ready to respond within an hour).
Community Exchange Program - Ellsworth AFB personnel and Rapid City, South Dakota, community members host residents of the Fine Ridge Indian Reservation to enable all parties to become better acquainted with each other's lifestyles.
Lips, Inc. - A production company of 25 performers from Fairchild AFB in Washington donate their time and talent raising money for the Red Cross, Muscular Dystrophy Association, and many other welfare agencies.
MAST (Military Assistance to Safety and Traffic) - Aircrews from Detachment 10, 37th Aerospace Rescue and Recovery Squadron at F.E. Warren AFB in Wyoming have logged over 5,000 hours in rescue situations where ground ambulances would be too late.
Base Library for the Hearing Impaired - Through the efforts of one Bolling AFB member (mother of a hearing-impaired child), Air Force Bases throughout the world have library sections for the hearing impaired, including Talking Books from the Library of Congress, amplified headphones, sign classes, TTY telephone and microprinter, and more (all based on Bolling's model in

Washington, DC).

Mini-Open House for the Elderly and Handicapped - Each year (the second Saturday in May) Andrews AFB in Washington, DC, features a day for those who cannot cope with the large crowds of over 500,000 who appear at the annual Department of Defense Joint Services Open House. Entertainment includes performances by the aerial demonstration teams (including the British Royal Air Force aerial team), and flights of vintage aircraft. Funds are donated from base wives' clubs. Interpreters are available for the hearing impaired.

Washoe Jeep Squadron - This Squadron of the Nevada Wing Civil Air Patrol uses four-wheel drive vehicles on search and rescue missions in the canyons and desert in and around Reno.

Camp Willie '90 - For the fifteenth consecutive year, the men and women assigned to Williams AFB, Arizona, hosted and sponsored a summer camp for youth, ages 10 to 12, from the Chandler and Mesa communities. The community has been friendly and helpful toward military members, and this annual activity is one way of showing appreciation, according to the volunteers.

Grandparent-Child Program - Child Care Center officials at Sheppard AFB, Texas, sponsor an activity in which residents from area nursing homes visit children at the Center and, in turn, children visit the residents to share companionship.

Career Day for Campfire and Scouting Organizations - Mountain Home AFB in the Idaho/Oregon area hosts an annual career day for youth stressing vocational careers as they apply to both military and civilian sectors.

Adopt-A-Veteran - A number of Robins AFB members have "adopted" veterans in the nursing care section of the Veterans Administration Center at Dublin, Georgia, by "extending their families" to include a hospitalized veteran through a special visitation program.

Training Dogs for the Deaf - This is an effort to help members of the Epee Deaf Center in Gulfport, Mississippi, by training dogs to hear door bells, baby's cries, alarm clocks and food boiling on the stove. The program was initiated by a Senior Airman at the 2052nd Communications Squadron at the nearby AFB.

Day Camp for Underprivileged Children - Columbus AFB holds an annual day camp for underprivileged children from the surrounding area (five days).

Malmstrom Historical Foundation - This is a cooperative effort between Malmstrom AFB and Great Falls, Montana, convened for the purpose of preserving the 40-year history of cooperation between the two groups ("preserving history for the future"). Artifacts are donated by retirees and others with some knowledge of the region.

Civilian Spotters - With the wide variety of road surfaces and the bad winter weather at Grand Forks, North Dakota, this joint project of the Grand Forks AFB and the surrounding community can mean the difference between life and death for some Air Force people. Some 80 families along the route to and from the missile sites serve as spotters, provide a telephone and shelter, and help in other ways as needed.

Firefighting: Job and Hobby - Airmen from Hancock Field, New York, 4789th Air Base Group, serve as firemen in the Air Force, and as volunteer firemen for the community, thus bringing skills from the job to a crucial community service.

Air Force Big Brothers/Big Sisters - Men and women at Fairchild AFB, Washington, volunteer their time to help children without a mother or father through the Spokane Big Brothers and Big Sisters Program.

Air Force members are involved in numerous other activities, some described elsewhere in this Directory. Additional descriptions, photographs for publication, and other materials are available through the above source.

MCCLELLAN AFB HEALTH FAIR
US/DoD - McClellan Air Force Base
Sacramento, CA 95652
TEL: 916-643-3354

Purpose: To provide a consumer health education program for the surrounding community using base personnel as volunteers.
Sponsor: US/DoD - McClellan Air Force Base
Contact: Pat Thompson
Description: In the fall of 1982 the HEP Committee (Military Consumer Health Education Program) agreed to take responsibility for the planning of the 1983 Health Fair. The Committee's first step was to study the critique of the 1982 Fair. Based on the lessons learned in 1982, the Committee outlined a pre-planning schedule with deadlines assigned. After several additional meetings, the consensus of the Committee was that Health Education should be emphasized in the 1983 Fair.

The Committee Chairperson was designated as the Committee's representative on the Health Fair Advisory Committee, which included representatives from the co-sponsoring organization, NHSCVO (National Health Screening Council for Volunteer Organizations). Total planning time was five months, with key workers doing final checks just hours before the doors opened in March 1983. Some of the screenings offered, and an example of results, follow:

- Height/Weight - out of 244 persons checked, 168 were abnormal.
- Blood Pressures - out of 242 persons checked, 76 were abnormal.
- Vision including Glaucoma check - out of 155 persons checked, 38 were abnormal for vision, and two of 128 checked out for glaucoma were abnormal.
- Dental Soft Tissue Exam - out of 114 persons checked, 38 were abnormal.
- Hearing - of 152 persons checked, 17 were abnormal.
- Pulmonary Function - of 54 persons checked, 16 were abnormal.

When the participant finishes the above and/or other tests, he or she reports to the Review and Referral section. This section is staffed with medical professionals. Those showing no abnormalities are asked to complete an evaluation form for the fair, and are given a *What Happens Next?* fact sheet. All of those with abnormal findings talk with counselors in the medical field, who make referrals and, a few weeks later, followup calls.

All tests are free except the 25 Chem-Panel providing blood workups. This service is contracted by the 3M Company and requires an $8.00 fee. There were 160 participants who chose to have this blood work done. About four weeks after the blood is drawn, test results are received by the site coordinator, and a copy with an explanation sheet is mailed to the participant.

Other activities at the Fair include Happy Tooth, constructed from wire and paper by the McClellan dental personnel. It is large enough for someone to get inside and walk around among the crowd discussing preventive dentistry and answering questions.

Also, a Pharmacy Display featured a self-participating educational format, with someone standing by at the display to answer questions that are not readily answered in the materials.

A food section for volunteers is stocked as a public service by community organizations, or purchased with donated funds. This section is utilized also as a volunteer break area.

[This Health Fair was planned, coordinated and conducted solely by 100 volunteers from McClellan Air Force Base, Mather Air Force Base, and the community. It was the second Health Fair and its success assures additional such programs in the future.]
Founded: 1982

VOLUNTEERS: ARMED FORCES MEMBERS - ARMY

TRAINING PROGRAMS

ARMY COMMUNITY SERVICE VOLUNTEER TRAINING
SEE TRAINING/CONFERENCES/TEACHING: ARMED FORCES

INDIVIDUAL PROGRAM PROFILES

ARMY COMMUNITY SERVICE
US/DoD - Army Community Service
Office of the Adjutant General
Alexandria, VA 22331
TEL: 202-325-9390
Purpose: To provide a resource for identifying and meeting the needs of soldiers and families, including the need to interact with the wider community.
Sponsor: US/DoD - Department of the Army
Contact: Lt. Col. James R. David, Chief
Description: Begun in 1965, Army Community Service (ACS) offers assistance, information, service, and guidance to service members and their families in areas cited in its initial proposal. However, it has evolved into a full service agency by developing programs as needs arise. Programs meet needs of the individual, families, and/or the total community. Many are cooperative ventures with the civilian community surrounding the base. These programs include:

- **Relocation** - help in getting situated in new surroundings.
- **Exceptional Family Member** - identifies military and civilian services for the handicapped.
- **Family Advocacy** - services to strengthen the Army family, including child and spouse abuse counseling.
- **Child Development Services** - full-day, hourly, and part-time child care services for children six to twelve years of age.
- **Foster Care Services** - substitute care for children on a 24-hour basis to meet emergency needs.
- **Consumer Affairs/Financial Management** - training in money management, consumer rights and obligations, shopping strategies, etc.
- **Information Referral and Follow-Up** - help in finding appropriate assistance for emotional, legal, financial, parental, personal and other problems.

Volunteers, working with paid staff, are trained to assist in a variety of programs other than those listed above. These include: Hi Neighbor, Lending Closet, publicity, newsletter, services to waiting families, education and employment assistance, services to foreign-born spouses, etc. Volunteers receive awards and recognition for the time they donate, as well as the benefits of training in program areas. Recruitment of volunteers is a continuous process as ACS strives to provide assistance, information, service, and guidance to service members and their families, as well as to design programs designed to meet the needs of the entire community.
Founded: 1965

BE ALIVE IN 2005: PROMOTING WELLNESS INTO THE 21ST CENTURY
US/DoD - Army Preventive Medicine Activity
Fort Ord, CA 93941
TEL: 408-242-4814
Purpose: To create the awareness that health is important, and that people need to take charge of their own health.
Sponsor: US/DoD - Department of the Army

Contact: David J. Fletcher or Major David Ellington
Description: Be Alive in 2005 is a joint effort of Fort Ord and the local Health Screening Council. It is designed to improve health at the Fort and in the communities of Monterey County. Activities are structured to make participants more aware of their current health status and give them some idea on how to improve their health. They emphasize the need to take the major responsibility of an individual's care away from the doctor.
There is no admission fee to the Be Alive Health Fair. There are seventeen stations where people can have height, weight, blood pressure, vision, hearing and many other physical functions checked. Other stations explain how people can maintain physical fitness through exercise, diet, and breaking bad habits such as smoking and drinking alcohol. A few of the booths are closed to the general public for legal and financial reasons, with a valid military ID required for admittance.
The booth for cancer screening, the family practice clinic, and several others were visited frequently, but one test that proved to be interesting to many people is the health hazard appraisal test. This test shows how old a person is physiologically (statistically shows life expectancy by analyzing risk factors and health habits). Volunteer activities supporting the Fair ranged from those in the medical profession on the base and in the community, to those who maintained a finger-painting station for very young children. In addition, resource volunteers from the Fort and the Community provided referral information for military personnel and civilians. The Health Fair is part of an effort to bring private citizens and the military together to have fun while improving health habits. Youth Activities, which organized adults' and kids' Fun Runs, the Army Community Service volunteers, and the NCO Club staff, which hosted the program, are examples of Fort organizations that participated.

EDUCATION AND EMPLOYMENT RESOURCE CENTER
US/DoD - Army Community Service
1169 Middletown Road
Fort Belvoir, VA 22060
TEL: 703-354-3912; 703-354-6664
Purpose: To provide a variety of resources directly related to education and employment available in the area.
Sponsor: US/DoD - Department of the Army
Contact: Lynn Armstrong
Description: Begun in the fall of 1982, the Education and Employment Resource Center exists to provide a service to the families of active duty and retired military personnel, and family members recently separated by death or divorce from an active duty or retired military member. The range of use is:

- support, assistance, and preparation for first-time employed and new arrivals in area;
- jobs to balance economic need;
- family members in transition - career re-entry;
- employment continuity and upwardly mobile job changing;
- personal development and life planning - goal setting, education, and volunteer opportunities.

Volunteers collect resource materials, do employment/employer research and educational opportunities research, maintain a skills bank (client file), provide program outreach, serve as counselors and counselor trainers, perform clerical services, and research volunteer opportunities for clients.
In addition to a design and planning staff and the volunteers, a consultant from the Bolling Air Force Base Military Spouse Skills and Resource Center is involved in the Center's work. In addition, a seven-point Basic Philosophy has been developed, as well as a 21-point Organizational Task List. The former lists the goals of the service, and the latter outlines the activities to be performed to reach the goals. Tasks range from recruiting volunteers to making the Center inviting to clients.
Steps in working with EERC clients include nine activities in the relationship between the client and the Center, ranging from the

initial interview to the client as an employee. A report with details is available.

Publications: Steps in Working with Clients
Founded: 1982

FEST (FORT EUSTIS SOLDIERS THEATRE)
US/DoD - Fort Eustis
Morale Support Activities Division
Fort Eustis, VA 23604
TEL: 804-878-2283
Purpose: To entertain Fort Eustis personnel, and to train volunteers in theatre skills.
Sponsor: US/DoD - Fort Eustis
Contact: Ann Morgan, Theatre Director
Description: During a ten-month period, the Fort Eustis Soldiers Theatre (FEST) produced three major productions, eight short plays, four skits, stage set-ups for six concerts, conducted ticket sales, ushered, handled lighting, costumes, face painting and other support for post events. This was accomplished with one paid staff member, the director, and from 30 to 50 volunteers. Over 9,000 hours were logged by volunteers during this period. This represents more than $35,000 in value (using GS1, Step 1) to provide entertainment for post personnel and their families, and skills training that is transferrable to the job market for the volunteers.

To be sure that all volunteers are involved immediately, the director maintains a "grief sheet" (task list) ranging from sound and lighting to refinishing or upholstering furniture. Many volunteers choose to move around in the type of tasks assigned to get a broader knowledge of "behind the scenes" work.

The majority of volunteers are active duty military or their family members (33 out of 35 in a recent production) with others coming from the community. All who want an opportunity to get "on the stage" are given the opportunity, switching "from hammer to script" as needed.

In addition to mainstage productions and one-act plays, the group produces brief thematic children's presentations and operates special events indoors and outdoors, such as haunted houses and concerts. Often facing shortages of time, money, experience, personnel or materials, FEST volunteers find a way to meet schedules and fulfill their mission. According to the program's director, "Without the volunteers, FEST would not exist at Fort Eustis."

FORT DIX VOLUNTEERS
US/DoD - Fort Dix
DPCA/ATTN: ATZDGA-S
Army Training Center
Fort Dix, NJ 08640
TEL: 609-562-4045
Purpose: To help the program leaders on the post and in the surrounding local communities to increase their services to families, youth, children, and the elderly.
Sponsor: US/DoD - Department of the Army
Contact: Captain Craig Gilbert
Description: Recognizing a need for additional services to families, youth, children and the elderly, both on the post and in surrounding communities, 550 volunteers are trying to narrow the gap by offering their time to assist in increasing these services, and improving existing ones.

On the post, volunteers assist Army Community Services, and work with the Divisions of Youth Activities and Moral Support, as well as in a number of sports programs. In addition to their help in providing basic needs, they are looked upon as friends with whom to discuss private or domestic matters on a confidential basis. Some volunteers teach English as a second language. Others offer advice on financial matters such as checking accounts, budgets, heavy debts, and bill consolidation. Volunteers with Army Community Service receive free child care services while they

work, provided by other volunteers.

Several programs reach into post housing areas and the surrounding communities. New arrivals are greeted with a house plant and help in learning about available community services. Foreign-born students are assisted in preparing for U.S. citizenship.

Other groups that involve Fort Dix volunteers in their programs include scout organizations, libraries, the post chapel, and the American Red Cross. Those volunteers working with the Red Cross assist in helping active duty persons who need help, work at the Walson Army Community Hospital, and perform other tasks as needed. Much of the Red Cross scheduling of Fort Dix volunteers is done by a board of volunteers, many of whom are wives of retired servicemen. They travel to the post from many parts of the state to serve on the board. On the post, volunteers assist in verifying emergencies for service members when a family member is seriously ill or has died, advance an interest-free loan, and help with emergency travel. They assist in providing emergency services in cases of house fires, and receive training in first aid, CPR and water safety.

At the hospital, volunteers chaperone patients, take vital signs, and perform secretarial duties. They assist at the information desk, in the pharmacy, and in the laboratory. They work at the central appointments desk, and assist volunteer retired doctors and volunteer case workers who work one-on-one with active duty personnel and their families. Personal service volunteers visit in-patients, assisting them with minor shopping and errands. Volunteers with the required education serve in the wards as nurses and aides. Others serve as a liaison for the hospital with groups such a the VFW, American Legion, and various garden clubs.

Potential volunteers are asked to complete an application showing their educational background, experience, and interests. If accepted, their assignments are based on this information. Volunteers who would like to help, but feel unqualified, are given the opportunity to attend classes to learn necessary skills for specific assignments. Work experience gained as a volunteer is recognized by employers, and many volunteers develop specific skills in many areas of office work, health services, and leadership that are transferable to the job market.

The benefits to the post and the community derived from Fort Dix Volunteers have been documented through public recognition programs and the media. There is never a waiting list, and all volunteers are placed in positions that are consistent with their interests and abilities. There are no age restrictions to volunteer in the program. Volunteers as young as 13 have coached sports.

FORT GORDON VOLUNTEER PROGRAM
US/DoD - Fort Gordon
Army Signal Center
Fort Gordon, GA 30905
TEL: 404-791-6001; 404-791-7003
Purpose: To work with the community and volunteers to provide services to service families that might not otherwise be possible.
Sponsor: US/DoD - Fort Gordon
Contact: Robert E. DiMichele
Description: More than two dozen on-post programs are operated by volunteers at Fort Gordon. The programs, collectively, average approximately 640 active volunteers per year, who provide an average of 17,648 volunteer hours per month on the post. Many of the volunteer programs require coordination with and cooperation from the wider community. They include:

- **Information, Referral and Followup Program:** Army Community Service is the primary resource agency for providing information and referral services to military agencies and civilian agencies in the community. They link services between the service members and their families and the appropriate agency or services, on or off post, that can best assist them with their problems.

- **Consumer Affairs and Financial Assistance Program:** This program insures that service members and their families are taught basic financial skills, provides financial assistance, offers specific information on local products and services, and makes the military consumers aware of consumer issues. The issues include debt liquidation, budget development, consumer complaint program, public information and outreach program on consumer education. Emergency funds are made available through AER. Other agencies can be used to supplement Army Community Service programs, such as American Red Cross and veterans' organizations.
- **Relocation Program:** This program provides information, guidance, and assistance to support unit deployments and to support service members and their families as they move from one military community to another. This includes assistance in settling into a new community, installation library services (information on the new installation), use of the Lending Closet, services to waiting families and foreign-born spouses, educational and employment services to family members.
- **Family Advocacy Program:** This is a specialized program to prevent child or spouse maltreatment and its attendant problems. This includes programs that contribute to a healthy family life. The advocacy program insures command and staff personnel awareness of their responsibilities for preventing child or spouse maltreatment. They identify, report, manage and follow up cases of child and spouse abuse; prevent and control child or spouse abuse by educating and training personnel; provide and support health programs such as parenting, child growth and development, family living and family enrichment classes.
- **Foster Care Program:** Foster care is either a voluntary step on the part of the family, or a court mandate. It provides foster family or group care for children whose parents or relatives cannot maintain a home for them, placing the children who need this service in stable, permanent arrangements as soon as possible.
- **Exceptional Family Member Program:** This program assures that the records of a family member with special needs are properly transmitted to assignment authorities reassigning service members with exceptional family members. Army Community Service, which intervenes in this program, insures when possible that service members receive the information and assistance needed to involve family members in specialized programs and services designed to meet their needs at their new location.

To recognize the efforts of all volunteers in the above and other programs, several volunteers are singled out to represent the volunteer program. These selectees showed exceptional leadership ability and motivation in developing and implementing programs such as the Swap and Assist Shop (now implemented on many posts), the Theater Crew (twenty volunteers offering makeup, lighting and sound, costuming, carpentry and other skills for theater groups), and an 18-year-old Christmas program to help military families during the holiday season.
Founded: 1964

FORT SILL VOLUNTEERS
US/DoD - Fort Sill
Commander, USFACFS
DPCA/ATTN: ATZR-P
Fort Sill, OK 73503
TEL: 405-351-3113
Purpose: To prevent having services reduced by developing and maintaining a volunteer program on the post.
Sponsor: US/DoD - Fort Sill
Contact: Director, Personnel and Community Activities
Description: More than 100,000 hours were logged by volunteers at Fort Sill during 1982. Consequently, many services that would have been reduced were maintained at the same level. While the

monetary value of this volunteer effort is significant, the most direct contribution is the service and help given to soldiers and their families.
Volunteer programs operating at Fort Sill are numerous. A summary of the major volunteer activities includes the following programs:

- **Army Community Service:** More than 14,500 hours were logged by volunteers during 1982. These volunteers help new arrivals get settled by distributing welcome packets, lending household goods through the loan closet, and giving tips about locations on the post, and the most effective use of the post's resources. They offer financial counseling and budgeting advice, and advise buyers through the Consumer Affairs Office. At the Child Development Center, volunteers supervise preschool children and help with paperwork.
- **Moral Support Activities Division:** About 1,000 volunteers worked throughout the year for this Division, providing services that would have required the full time of 343 civil service workers. Most of the volunteers are involved in the music and theatre programs, working in plays and musical productions. Also, the Division has volunteers working as coaches for sports activities, as chaperones for field trips, and as swimming instructors for children. In addition, they maintain library story-telling programs and other activities.
- **American Red Cross:** At Reynolds Army Community Hospital, Red Cross Volunteers help in many areas, including greeting patients and helping them through the "system." Also, they do paperwork that medical specialists may not have time to do. In addition, Red Cross volunteers give first aid classes and teach adults and children water safety.
- **Scouting:** During the year, 88 scouting program volunteers put more than 18,000 hours into the 16 scouting units on the post. Volunteers provide a sense of leadership to the youth, and develop friendship through scouting.
- **Thrift Shop:** Proceeds collected by the Thrift Shop are generated back into the Fort Sill community. The money fully funds the Toys for Tots program. Also, it is used for the Food Locker program at Army Community Service, the Volunteer Nursery Fund, layettes for the new mothers at the hospital, the handicapped school, the Armed Forces YMCA, and Mobile Meals at Lawton among others.
- **The Fort Sill Museum:** Tour guides at the Fort Sill Museum are volunteers. They work also behind the scenes researching, cataloging and restoring artifacts.

Many of the volunteers at Fort Sill are busy people who manage households and work full time at other jobs. Recognition events are scheduled periodically to call attention to their volunteer efforts.

FRIENDS OF THE ROUGE
SEE VOLUNTEERS: PRISONERS/EX-OFFENDERS

SPECIAL OLYMPICS TIME
US/DoD - Fort Sill
212 Field Artillery Brigade
Second Bttn, 37th Field Artillery
Fort Sill, OK 73503
TEL: 405-351-3505
Purpose: To give mentally retarded children an opportunity to show their families and communities how much they can accomplish.
Sponsor: Public Service Company of Oklahoma
Contact: Sandra Jones, SW Area Coordinator, or John Patrick, 2nd/37th Spokesman
Description: Special Olympics Time is a two-day sports competition for some 300 mentally retarded youngsters from 13 area towns surrounding the Fort. The youngsters vie for the opportunity to advance to the International Special Olympics Games. Winners at the Fort are eligible to attend the State meet,

with State winners moving on to the final Games.

The numerous athletic events include track and field, swimming, gymnastics, basketball, volleyball, and wheelchair races. The entire community becomes involved in the planning, with meets held at the schools, the YMCA, and the Fort, depending on the event and the field best suited for it. Olympians include those who return year after year and know the procedure, and those who are entering the competition for the first time and need reassurance as well as orientation to the process. It is a year-round program involving countless volunteers.

Volunteers include those who teach trainable mentally retarded, and those who have no knowledge in this area, but have a desire to help. All are trained to emphasize that the goal of Special Olympics is not to win, but to try. The courage, determination, and sportsmanship involved are important parts of the program's philosophy.

On a smaller scale, the pageantry and excitement of the International Games are built into the program. A "parade of stars," opening and closing ceremonies, and award presentations are patterned after the larger event. Fort Sill Units turn out in force, and individuals and businesses across the community become deeply involved every year. The co-sponsorship of the Second Battalion and the local power company is a partnership that has a side benefit of bringing the Fort and the wider community closer together.

Each community is responsible for its local Special Olympics program, and no community could sponsor one without the coaches, guides, chaperones, sports officials, publicists, entertainers and other volunteers.

VOLUNTEER PROGRAM - FORT BENJAMIN HARRISON
US/DoD - Fort Benjamin Harrison
Building 32
Fort Benj. Harrison, IN 46216
TEL: 317-543-6534
Purpose: To improve the quality of life on the post and in the community by increasing services through the involvement of volunteers.
Sponsor: US/DoD - Department of the Army
Contact: Joseph T. Brown, Installation Volunteer Coordinator
Description: The volunteer program at Fort Benjamin Harrison serves the Army Community Service, American Red Cross, and other programs. Volunteers include family members of servicemen and servicewomen, retirees, civilian employees and people from the surrounding communities. They donate their time to various post programs and numerous community activities.

Army Community Service averages two volunteers each month who put in an average of 150 hours during that period. They perform a variety of tasks to make life easier for the military family from the time they arrive at Fort Harrison. Volunteers prepare and distribute welcome packets, set up and assist with the presentation of newcomers' orientations, operate a lending closet and a food locker, compile and maintain a talent lists file, a resource file and a consumer reference library, and provide many other "people" services. At Christmas time, volunteers assist the Fort Harrison Chapter of Federally Employed Women (FEW) in collecting, packing and distributing boxes of food and toys to needy families, for which FEW members also are volunteers.

The Red Cross program provides an average of 50 volunteers each month, who spend about 1,200 hours a month working in Hawley Army Community Hospital, the Dental and Vet Clinics, and the Child Care Center. In the hospital, volunteers help out in Records, Pharmacy, Family Practice, the Laboratory, Library, Eye Clinic and Pediatrics. An Outstanding Red Cross Volunteer of the Year is selected and recognized in October of each year.

Many other programs are staffed by volunteers both on the post and in the wider community. These include:

- **Libraries:** Volunteers supplement the paid staff in the three libraries on the post in order to maintain library hours to better serve post personnel.
- **Thrift Shop/Fund Raising:** The Post Thrift Shop is operated by volunteers from the Officers' Wives Club and the NCO/EM Wives Club. Proceeds go to scholarships for military family members.
- **Carnival/Fund Raising:** A yearly Carnival is held in cooperation with the neighboring community of Lawrence. Volunteers from local organizations man booths at the six-day event to raise money for their own organizations and the local Morale Support Fund.
- **Cultural Enrichment:** The new USA Center at the Indianapolis International Airport is staffed by volunteers, many furnished by Fort Harrison.
- **Youth Camping Experience:** Volunteers help with Camp Elm in the summer. Camp Elm is a local Salvation Army day camp for inner-city youths.
- **Crisis Center:** A recently-formed Harrison Sertoma club sponsors the Family Support Center in Indianapolis, a crisis center for battered, abused and neglected children. Members volunteer their time at the Center, and raise money for the project through fund-raising events.
- **Christmas Activity:** Soldiers from the Second Battalion entertain children from the Knightstown Soldiers and Sailors Home each Christmas, taking them to movies and bowling and sports events.

Other programs and activities are developed as needs arise. Teenagers as well as adults, from the post and the community, are part of the work force, offering a youth perspective which, in many cases, is more effective in the volunteer effort.

VOLUNTEER RESOURCE CENTER
US/DoD - Volunteer Fort Benning
Fort Benning, GA 31905
TEL: 404-545-5602
Purpose: To encourage and promote volunteerism; to organize and improve volunteer services at Fort Benning.
Sponsor: US/DoD - Fort Benning
Contact: Donna L. Ray
Description: The Volunteer Resouce Center is an appropriated-fund agency established to encourage and promote volunteer participation in social services, health, welfare, educational, cultural, and civic programs and to coordinate and help organize and improve volunteer services at the Fort. In order to accomplish this mission, the following goals have been identified:

- to help recruit and refer volunteers;
- to maintain a comprehensive file on specific requests;
- to conduct training or cooperate with organizations giving training for volunteers and for staff working with volunteers;
- to encourage community recognition of volunteers;
- to offer research, training, public relations, and other forms of consultation to agencies initiating, developing or strengthening volunteer programs;
- to initiate new volunteer services to meet changing community needs, and encourage creative utilization of volunteers;
- to keep abreast of changing attitudes involving volunteerism in order to be prepared to respond effectively;
- to educate and advocate for the ongoing appropriate utilization of volunteers.

The public relations staff of the Center maintains and publicizes a calendar of training and other events, and publishes articles on volunteer activities in local papers. Volunteers are referred for training to courses at Columbus College, as well as that provided by the Center. A resource library includes a resource list for training of volunteers. Other training activities include identifying training experts, developing a list of training needs, identifying funds for training, and providing training that leads to college credit by developing specific training leadership development, supervisor training, resume writing, etc.

The development of an efficient and effective standard operating procedure, the establishment and publishing of standards for utilization of volunteers, and a workable recordkeeping system are projects of the administrative staff. Other projects include:

- the development of a comprehensive chart of ideas for recruitment of volunteers. This chart, Recruitment of Volunteers: Who, Where, What, When and How, lists types of volunteers (high school students, retirees, employed persons, etc.), contacts (school counselors, unions, service clubs, etc.), the best print or sound media, and incentives for emphasis.
- the establishment of criteria for the Volunteer of the Year award, the nominating procedure, and sample forms.
- the publishing of a newsletter, VOLUNTEER: You Can Make a Difference, containing eight pages of items and articles on family volunteerism, activities on the post, suggested reading list, and special one-time features such as Bill of Rights of Volunteers and Teaching Kids to Do a Good Job.

The Center develops posters, bibliographies and other materials on an intermittent, as-needed basis.

VOLUNTEERS AT FORT LEAVENWORTH
US/DoD - Fort Leavenworth Combined Arms Center
Public Affairs Office
Fort Leavenworth, KS 66027
TEL: 913-552-4051
Purpose: To enrich the lives of the area's youth, children, families, and the elderly through volunteer efforts.
Sponsor: US/DoD - Fort Leavenworth
Contact: Public Affairs Office
Description: Fort Leavenworth volunteers are involved with Army Community Service, the Red Cross, youth programs, the post museum, the thrift shop, chapel activities, Scouting and Explorer programs, clubs, schools, Toys for Tots, a speakers' bureau, historical and museum societies, and many other volunteer efforts. The programs involve dependents as well as the servicemen and servicewomen, and often require coordination with communities in the area surrounding Fort Leavenworth.
Two programs that appear to be unique to Fort Leavenworth are Musettes, and the Girl Scout Adopt-A-Grandparent program. Following are brief descriptions of these volunteer efforts:

- **Musettes:** The Musettes are volunteers in service to the Fort Leavenworth museum. Beyond the tours normally provided by volunteers in museums, the Musettes get involved in cataloging displays, doing historical research, recataloging books, presenting story hours, and putting on puppet shows about pioneer life for children. In addition, the volunteers raise money for the museum by holding a bazaar each Christmas to sell handcrafted items that they have made.
- **Girl Scout Adopt-A-Grandparent:** The Girl Scouts of Fort Leavenworth have a program wherein they "adopt" senior citizens in the Leavenworth community who are alone. The girls visit, bring goodies and small gifts and, in general, try to make the older folks' lives less lonely.

The above are two examples of programs that are developed by volunteers based on an expressed need that has come to their attention.

VOLUNTEERS: ARMED FORCES MEMBERS - NAVAL RESERVE

NATIONAL/STATE ORGANIZATIONS

CAMPAIGN DRUG FREE
US/DoD - Naval Reserve Force
Office of the Secretary
The Pentagon
Washington, DC 20350
TEL: 202-697-7506
Objectives: To provide Naval Reservists on a volunteer basis to work with fifth- and sixth-grade students in drug abuse prevention.
Services: Involves Naval Reservists as volunteers using their own time in drug prevention programs in upper grade-levels (fifth- and sixth-graders) of elementary schools (working on the "demand" side of drug use); operates under a portion of the *Defense Authorization Bill,* in which Congress gave the Department of Defense an expanded role in drug interdiction (stemming the flow of drugs into the US); consults with federal officials, school boards, educators and principals; utilizes a standardized teaching package on drug abuse prevention with specific points to be covered by the volunteers as a basis for adapting to their own backgrounds and audiences; presents a theme of the military "protecting the country from all enemies, including drugs" to stress to children that fighting illegal drugs is really a "war;" includes Reservists from the Marine Corps and Coast Guard in addition to the Navy; works with the *Navy League of the United States,* which helps with arrangements for Reservists' appearances in local schools and administers the campaign plan; cites pre-campaign volunteer activity by Reservists in drug abuse prevention, many of whom have received awards; publishes administrative packets for Reserve commanding officers and Navy League Presidents; administers recognition program to recognize the individual Reservists who donate their time and energy to this effort.
Sponsor: US/DoD - Department of the Navy
Contact: Captain Ronnie Baker
Publications: Campaign Drug Free Teaching Module; Campaign Drug Free Administrative Package

VOLUNTEERS: ARMED FORCES MEMBERS - NAVY

NATIONAL/STATE ORGANIZATIONS

US/DOD - NAVY FAMILY SERVICE CENTER
Building 42
Great Lakes, IL 60088
TEL: 312-688-3603
Objectives: To enhance and enrich the quality of life of Naval servicemen and servicewomen and their families.
Services: As a result of the *1978 Navy Family Awareness Conference* at Norfolk, Virginia, the Chief of Naval Operations established a network of support centers to enhance and enrich the quality of life of Naval servicemen and servicewomen and their families. Named *Family Service Centers (FSCs),* they assist both single and married personnel with problem-solving and working through the red tape that is normally associated with any large organization. The FSC also helps them obtain assistance and lists the resources that are available to them in both the military and

civilian community. The FSC began operating and providing services at Great Lakes in March 1982.

The FSC serves active duty, reserve and retired personnel of the Navy and Marine Corps, and their families. Other military personnel and civilian employees may also be assisted on a case-by-case basis.

The FSC operates a number of specific programs in addition to individual assistance, including

- **Parent-to-Parent Program** - offers support to families with young children through weekly visits by a volunteer, who is trained to answer parents' questions about child development and to provide other information as needed.

- **Welcome Baby Program** - provides information and support to families of newborns. Volunteers contact new parents and arrangements are made for a visit. Information is shared on child care, infant development, community resources and other topics that relate to the early weeks of a baby's life.

- **Spouse Employment Assistance Program (SEAP)** - enables military spouses to find employment more easily after relocation. Volunteers contact businesses to locate job opportunities, personally interview job seekers and match them with available jobs. Volunteers also give counseling on educational and job-related topics.

- **Spouses of Students (SOS)** - serves as a support group for spouses of military personnel in Corps School, Service School Command or ROTC. Volunteers help plan and organize weekly meetings and serve as a source of information and guidance.

- **Women's Program Planners** - plan and/or coordinate a wide variety of programs for women which promote personal growth, happier families and career information. *The Women's Day Out,* day-long conferences, University of Illinois Cooperative Extension Home Economics Programs, and Spouse Employment Assistant Program workshops are examples of these programs.

- **Gingerbread House** - is a volunteer-operated consignment shop which provides members of the military community the opportunity to increase their income by selling handcrafted items. A small fee is charged, with the money going to various base charities.

- **Volunteer Income Tax Assistance (VITA)** - is a cooperative program with the IRS. After a training program taught by the IRS covering both basic and advanced income tax forms, free tax preparation is offered to all military personnel.

In addition to the many and varied volunteer opportunities in the above program, FSC has administrative needs for volunteers to serve as receptionists, intake clerks, class registration recorders, I&R workers, and general clerical aides.

Sponsor: US/DoD - Department of the Navy
Contact: Phyllis Utley, Volunteer Coordinator
Publications: Volunteers Make a Difference

INDIVIDUAL PROGRAM PROFILES

ASSISTANCE TO EARTHQUAKE VICTIMS
US/DoD - Department of the Navy
Assistant Secretary of Defense
The Pentagon
Washington, DC 28350
TEL: 202-545-6700
Purpose: To respond to a call for immediate assistance to earthquake victims.
Sponsor: US/DoD - Department of the Navy
Contact: LCDR Dave Kennedy
Description: Seventy-three Navy Department social workers who had done work with people who have gone through the trauma of disaster found themselves in a unique "training" situation in Northern California in October 1989. The social workers were attending military conferences in conjunction with the four-day annual meeting of the *National Association of Social Workers,* with six days of training behind them, when the earthquake hit the San Francisco area.

An earlier meeting of professionals from all of the military services had ended and, following a brief Navy meeting, they were to depart in many directions for their home areas. During the Navy meeting, the Bay Area experienced what was later described as the strongest earthquake to hit the area since 1906.

The call for volunteers - especially those experienced in working with disaster victims - was apparent, if not expressed, and the 73 volunteers were quickly briefed by a disaster expert, who is a senior social worker in the Office of the Assistant Secretary of Defense, Family Policy and Support. After the briefing, the expert organized the group to effectively help earthquake victims who were streaming into the hotel from homes in the area that had been damaged or declared unsafe. Besides the logistical needs of setting up sleeping arrangements in areas of the hotel with the least glass, the social workers provided counseling and other assistance to help the victims through the traumatic experience. Usually being in the position of "supervising" volunteers, the social workers enjoyed the experience of "being" volunteers who met an urgent need. From one Navy participant, "Talk about 'hands-on' experience... this was a bit scary, but our presence was needed, and we are glad we were there to help."

HEALTH FAIR
US/DoD - Naval Regional Medical Clinic
Regional Medical Clinic
United States Navy
Key West, FL 33040
TEL: 305-296-2461/Ext. 206
Purpose: To provide health screening and health education services to members of the local community.
Sponsor: US/DoD - Department of the Navy
Contact: R.W. Adams, MSC USN
Description: When requested by the community, Naval Regional Medical Clinic hosts Health Fairs for residents of the City of Key West and residents of the lower Keys. The Clinic makes available two large open wards in the main clinic building which are not used very much. To provide convenient accessibility to all, a weekday (Friday) is usually chosen to attract the elderly and indigent population, and a weekend day (Saturday) for the younger working population. As expected, this breakdown is evident on those days at the Fair.

Almost all of the Naval Clinic's staff volunteer to assist with Health Fairs (in a typical fair, 17 officers, 56 enlisted men, and 21 civilians reported for duty). The staff possesses the expertise to man all areas, particularly the stations requiring specialized training. Having a readily available pool of professionals is a definite advantage, and a significant factor in the success of the Fairs. Since at least 160 volunteers are needed to staff the fair adequately both days, an active drive to recruit volunteers from the community is held. Medical professionals, nursing students, and dependent wives are among the community volunteers involved.

Station Captains, all Navy personnel, receive information on the background of each volunteer who completes an application (medical/non-medical qualifications), and also recruits for additional slots that did not emerge in the applications.

Non-medical volunteers are placed in registration and other areas. To maximize participation for screening, transportation is provided to and from prearranged points in the lower Keys. The Monroe County Social Services Department has arranged transportation in the past. Such interaction between the civilian and Naval communities in pursuit of a common goal helps to avoid costly duplication of services, facilities and equipment.
Founded: 1983

NAVY VOLUNTEERS AT GUANTANAMO BAY
US/DoD - Department of the Navy
Box 25
FPO New York, NY 09593
TEL: Correspondence only
Purpose: To bring the Naval base and the community closer together through volunteering.
Sponsor: American Red Cross
Contact: J.D. Van Sickle, Lieutenant Commander, USNR, Public Affairs Officer, or specific contact below
Description: Navy personnel at Guantanamo Bay, Cuba, are involved in numerous volunteer activities. Among them are:

- **Water Safety/Safety Services** - Red Cross classes in first aid, CPR and swimming are some of the courses offered to the general military community on a regular basis. These courses enable an individual to become proficient at swimming or have knowledge to treat almost any type of injury (until a physician or medical personnel arrive), or even be able to save the life of a victim of a heart attack or near drowning through CPR.

There are 15 military personnel teaching various courses in first aid and water safety. All military personnel are used exclusively for teaching Red Cross courses.

There are 23 different first aid and water safety courses. Each course has a mandated curriculum which specifically gives the required instruction and training each pupil and teacher must receive for each course. Instructors are closely monitored to assure that they are meeting the high Red Cross standard.
Contact: Theodore E. Joyner, Station Director, Box 45, FPO New York, NY 09593

- **Combined Federal Campaign (CFC)** - This program aims to raise funds for various organizations which are designated by the chairman of the U.S. Civil Service Commission. The goal of the program is to provide financial, medical, and counseling assistance to the needy. There are 37 project officers, with approximately one or more "key persons," who solicit funds through personal donations.

There is no training, per se. The project officer supervises key persons, and there is an overall base chairman for CFC.
Contact: CWO4 Jim O'Neal, U.S. Naval Station, Box 15, FBPO Norfolk, VA 23593

- **Guantanamo Bay Youth Athletic Association (GBYAA)** - Although no firm commencement date is available, this program has been ongoing for a great number of years. A group of military families saw an ever-growing need for a program to provide sports activities for the youth of the community. A set of by-laws and a constitution were developed and the association was formed and given final approval by the base commander.

Approximately 75 military personnel from the community participate in the GBYAA on a yearly basis. In addition, the association has an elected director, assistant director, secretary, treasurer, equipment manager and public relations officer.
There is no professional training, as such. The various sports commissioners and team coaches rely on training received elsewhere and self-study of sports rules. The children of the community are highly motivated in the sporting events. They are taught good sportsmanship, trustworthiness, obedience and respect among other traits.
Contact: CWO4 Jim O'Neal, U.S. Naval Station, Box 15, FBPO Norfolk, VA 23593

- **Boy Scouts of America** - Boys Scouts prepares young men for adult life, and teaches them responsibility. There are 16 military scout leaders, who are involved in leading troops, planning activities, and teaching education skills to the scouts. The reason so many military are involved is that scouting has 100 merit badges, and the expertise the military has aids them (scouts) in earning these badges. The Fleet Reserve Association provides the meeting place for the scouts, and additionally donates the scouts' registration funds. GTMO scouts also are involved in an international Boy Scout exchange.

A troop committee is organized to handle finances, and to oversee the quality of training leaders are providing the scouts. Basically, the scouting in Guatanamo Bay is the same as that found in the USA.
Contact: CWO4 Jim O'Neal, U.S. Naval Station, Box 15, FBPO Norfolk, VA 23593

PARENT-TO-PARENT PROGRAM
US/DoD - Navy Family Service Center
Naval Training Center
Building 42
Great Lakes, IL 60088-5123
TEL: 312-688-3603
Purpose: To offer support to families in the armed forces with very young children through weekly home visits.
Sponsor: US/DoD - Navy Family Service Center
Contact: Thia Lester
Description: The Parent-to-Parent Program takes place in the home at the convenience of family and home visitor. The purpose is to give the parents support as they share ideas with the home visitor about enjoyable ways of playing with and caring for young children.
Who is a home visitor?
The home visitor is a volunteer from the community who enjoys working with adults and young children. Training is administered by the Parent-to-Parent Program staff at the Family Service Center. Through weekly visits to the home, the volunteer becomes an important link in a network of community services.
What happens in a home visit?
- The volunteer arrives at the home prepared to share ideas, toys and activities with the parent and child. If it is not the first visit, plans are based on activities and feedback of the previous visit.
- Upon arrival, the visitor talks with the parent about parent-child interaction during the previous week - What has the parent observed the child doing? What has the parent done with the child?
- Using the toys brought by the volunteer, parent and volunteer try activities with the child.
- The volunteer answers the parent's questions about child development and provides information when it is needed, including information about agencies in the community.
- Parent and volunteer plan what activities they will do during the next home visit and discuss what the child will probably be doing during the week.

What training do home visitors receive?
- *Child Development* - Learning about how children grow and what they are like at different stages of development.
- *The Role of the Home Visitor* - Understanding what it means to be a home visitor, including learning how to establish relationships with families, supporting parents in discoveries about their children, sharing child development information, learning how to put parents in contact with a variety of community resources.
- *How Adults Can Support Early Learning* - Learning about the ways in which adults can provide support and create activities which help children learn.

What can a home visitor expect to gain from participating?
- A new awareness of the community, its resources and how to use them.
- Experience with sharing knowledge and skills as well as developing new skills.
- Work experience that can provide a base for future employment.
- An opportunity to meet new people.

What can the family gain from being in the program?
- An understanding of how important the parent is to the child's growth and development.

● Observation of the many exciting ways that learning takes place as the infant's progress is shared with the volunteer.
● Discovery of new ways to provide activities and materials to enhance learning.
● Knowledge of the community and the agencies which can provide services for the family.
● The opportunity to meet new people through "Parent Meetings."

Through this program, the Family Service Center encourages and supports a stable environment for the child, and increased parent/child interaction.

Publications: A chance to contribute to your community...; For you, for your children

PARMA-HILTON PLAYGROUND PROJECT
SEE VOLUNTEERS: TENANTS/RESIDENTS

PARTNERSHIPS *(formerly Adopt-A-School)*
US/DoD - Commander Naval Base San Diego
937 North Harbor Drive
San Diego, CA 92103-5100
TEL: 619-532-1514

Purpose: To address growing concern for the unmet needs of the local education system.

Sponsor: US/DoD - Commander Naval Base San Diego

Contact: Personal Excellence Coordinator

Description: The Adopt-A-School concept had its beginnings in Memphis, Tennessee, when a group of businessmen became concerned about the quality of the local education system. Working with education leaders, they devised a program in which individual businesses formally "adopted" a local elementary school, high school, or community college. The adoptive business provided its resources on a voluntary basis to enrich the school's curriculum. Sometimes the resources were financial, but most of the time they were human. The program has been duplicated in other large cities across the country.

In San Diego, California, school partnerships by the *United States Navy* provided large scale military support for the first time. During the year ending in May 1983, local Navy commands adopted nine schools. There are now over 60 Navy-school partnerships.

Activities - Although the group and the school spokespersons may decide on unique projects based on special needs in a specific situation, all provide the following basic services in some form:
● tutoring and counseling of students;
● presenting mini-courses in specialty areas such as science, electronics, computer technology and athletics;
● conducting tours of their places of business to bring students and teachers closer to vocational opportunities and the work environment;
● helping students in developing extracurricular skills such as photography and woodworking;
● supporting and participating in school events such a field trips, dances, concerts, athletic events and graduation exercises;
● developing special school projects and displays;
● establishing pen pal relationships in order to expand students' awareness of life at sea and in foreign lands.

Benefits to the Navy partner are numerous, and very similar to benefits to a business. The morals and self-esteem of the volunteer tutors are increased, as well as their sense of community involvement and the satisfaction that comes from making a contribution. Also, such a program helps to assure the development of the future technical and leadership skills needed for defense industries and military services. In addition, it strengthens basic interpersonal and technical skills of the Navy volunteer. Other benefits include:
● highlighting the contributions made to communities through routine defense activities, in this case, pointing out the potential for assistance to communities by the nation's largest employer and educational organization - the *Department of Defense.*
● enhancing attractiveness of defense occupations, thereby supporting recruitment objectives.
● helping to relieve boredom and dependency on drugs and alcohol by defense personnel by providing constructive free time activity; for ship personnel, increasing human support network in homeport, making travel and return more enjoyable.
● creating good community relations through better understanding and appreciation of the defense program by students, educators and business people.

Benefits to the school partner are numerous, and include providing positive role models for students who increasingly come from single family homes; fostering a better understanding of, and support for, the school system leading to increased participation by all members of the community; improving education quality by tapping non-traditional resources and bringing textbook learning closer to real vocational applications; and replacing student boredom, apathy and drug/alcohol use with participatory career development activities.

Overall benefits include evidence that money is not the only solution (human resources can make the difference) during this era of scarce resources; the fact that defense installation personnel are taking responsibility as members of the wider community; the meeting of a need to address the deficiencies of the education system, and the move toward strengthening the education system, on which the economic and military security of the country depend.

Founded: 1983

SATURDAY SCHOLARS
Chicago Board of Education
1819 West Pershing Road
Chicago, IL 60609
TEL: 312-890-8435

Purpose: To offer tutoring in mathematics to fourth-, fifth- and sixth-graders in the Chicago Public School System.

Sponsor: Chicago Board of Education

Contact: Francis R. Holliday

Description: In the fall of 1982, the *Chicago Education Corps* (the school system's volunteer organization) addressed the need for remedial help in "the basics" for students in fourth, fifth and sixth grades. Encouraged by a newspaper story regarding tutors from the Marine Corps volunteering in Washington, DC, public schools, the group approached the nearby *Naval Service School Command Post* and, after a favorable response, developed and submitted a proposal. On May 7, 1983 (Saturday), the first *Saturday Scholars* tutors arrived at *Gillespie Elementary School* for the program's initial session.

About 90 Service School Command students from Great Lakes participated as volunteer tutors. The response to the request for volunteers was overwhelming, and many volunteers were placed on a waiting list. Since the pilot program calls for expansion, it is expected that such a waiting list will not exist in the future.

To prepare for the program, the volunteers attend an orientation session at Chicago State University, where they are briefed on the Monterey Learning System, a tutorial math program in operation at Gillespie Elementary School. By using this System, which is a series of books based on step-by-step development in math basics, the student's progress can be easily measured at the end of the program.

Highly motivated by their uniformed tutors (who just happened to have extra sailor hats and medals with them), the children improved their learning both quantitatively and qualitatively. Side benefits are the positive examples set by the volunteers, and the enhancement to the education process provided by the Saturday Scholars program.

Founded: 1983

USS KITTY HAWK/WASHINGTON SQUARE PARTNERSHIP
Washington Square Association
202 South Twelfth
Philadelphia, PA 19107
TEL: 215-545-6092
Purpose: To bring together sailors in port for ship repairs and a civic association in the community to restore the beauty of a central city park.
Sponsor: US/DoD - USS Kitty Hawk
Contact: Anna Marie Marshall, Washington Square Association
Description: The *USS Kitty Hawk* is an aircraft carrier docked at the Navy Yard in Philadelphia to undergo a $717 million overhaul. While there, the Lieutenant Commander was to begin a search for a location for the Kitty Hawk to hold a constitutional celebration in three months hence. When it came to the attention of the officers and crew of the Kitty Hawk that Fairmount Park, where 2,000 Revolutionary War dead are buried in unmarked graves, was in need of volunteers, they decided to clean up the park and hold the celebration there. This began a partnership beyond the sprucing up of the park.
More than two dozen volunteers from the ship spent several Saturdays raking leaves, painting light standards, picking up trash, clipping hedges, using a chemical wash on the statue of George Washington, and helping nearby residents purchase flags representing the original 13 colonies and a large American flag. The sailors then began a ceremony of raising and lowering the American flag every day at the park, and they tended to the eternal flame that burns in front of the tomb of the unknown soldier. When they saw a need for music during the flag ceremonies, they installed a $200 sound system, bought with funds from the ship's welfare and recreation fund, on the roof of a tool shed in the park.
In the fall, the sailors held their anniversary celebration of the signing of the Constitution, but the unique partnership between the Navy and the community didn't end there. At Christmas time they bought and trimmed a Christmas tree, and red bows for the square's antique light poles, and they sang carols.
In the spring of 1989, they planted $10,000 worth of purple petunias and other plants, and when the organizers of the annual *Fair in the Square* in May needed materials for booths, the sailors loaned and delivered 48 tables and 200 chairs. They also sold balloons and served as guides for the house tours.
The work of the sailors - especially the flag ceremony - has made a big difference in the spirit of the community. Citizens are seen stopping and standing at attention during the flag ceremony. In addition to the neighborhood pride that the sailors' work has instilled, the volunteer project has also improved the sailors' morale. With the long-term repair project on the USS Kitty Hawk, it is expected that residents will enjoy the presence of the sailors in the park for some time to come.

WELCOME BABY
US/DoD - Charleston Naval Base
Navy Family Service Center
Charleston, SC 29401
TEL: 803-743-2121/6250
Purpose: To provide support to new parents at Charleston Naval Regional Medical Center, to share educational materials, and to work with hospital personnel in helping new mothers and fathers as they learn to be parents.
Sponsor: US/DoD - Department of the Navy
Contact: Tommie Provost, Coordinator
Description: Welcome Baby is a volunteer program sponsored by the Charleston Navy Family Service Center. While it was modeled after civilian programs, Welcome Baby has particular relevance for the Navy Community where it is not unusual for very young women to give birth without the support of family. The husbands are often deployed and young mothers find themselves in an unfamiliar community with a new baby and new responsibilities. Beginning with hospital visitations, trained volunteers offer support and encouragement to new mothers. In addition the volunteer is an educational resource providing information on child care and community resources. The contact is maintained by the volunteer following discharge from the hospital.
Supportive contacts continue as long as the need exists. Mail-outs are sent monthly for one year, which include information on child growth and development. Through this early contact with mother and child, the trained volunteers are able to detect indicators of abuse and neglect or symptoms of potential problems. If the volunteer identifies a need, referral is made to appropriate services. Training of volunteers over a three-day period covers topics such as communication skills, child abuse and neglect, community and military resources, and Welcome Baby procedure. New volunteers are teamed with experienced volunteers during their initial visits with new mothers. Following the initial visits, volunteers always have access to a support system of team leaders (experienced volunteers) and program co-ordinator.
In addition to hospital volunteers, other volunteers offer secretarial skills and provide support to mothers prenatally. Some volunteers, who have specific experience in special areas, i.e. premature infants, death of infant, offer support to parents in those areas. This program has been very successful at the Charleston Naval Base and it is recommended as an effective method of supporting new mothers in their new roles.
Publications: Welcome Baby Packet

WRITECONNECTION PROGRAM: LOVE A CHILD BY MAIL
Positive Parenting
2635 East Indian School Road
Suite 400
Phoenix, AZ 85016
TEL: 602-956-0070
TOLL FREE: 800-334-3143
Purpose: To maintain writing programs with one's own children, or a little brother or sister.
Sponsor: US/DoD - Office of the Navy Chaplain
Contact: Program Coordinator
Description: A nonprofit program in Phoenix, Arizona, *Positive Parenting,* has developed a program for married and single sailors to begin and maintain a weekly writing program with his or her own children and/or a little brother or sister.
Several Navy chaplains have worked with *Positive Parenting* in achieving effective results when encouraging and training sailors to communicate with family members on a frequent and regular basis. In the *WriteConnection Program,* the sailor is offered a starter kit at a specially-set price for the military, with refills made available when needed. The kit includes:
- colorful stationery for letters;
- monthly calendars to mark special dates;
- return mailers for the child to send back;
- "quick mailers" to show the child you're thinking of him or her;
- activity projects to share with the child through the mail;
- correspondence chart to track what has been sent, and when it was sent; and
- a binder to help organize and store all materials.

Several aircraft carriers have begun stocking the kits in their ship stores. To help reduce costs, *Positive Parenting* encourages joint purchases by the sailors through the ship's or other officers. The packages are offered in conjunction with continuous encouragement and training programs developed with the assistance of the Navy Chaplain's Office, and they have proven to be especially successful in the primary goal of the program - to brighten the lives of children. In doing so, they have also given pleasure and meaning to the sailors involved.
Founded: 1990

VOLUNTEERS: ARMED FORCES MEMBERS - VETERANS

NATIONAL/STATE ORGANIZATIONS

VETERANS FOR PEACE
PO Box 3881
Portland, ME 04104
TEL: 207-797-2770
Objectives: To educate the public on the need to abolish war.
Services: Works through its members, veterans and others who served in the military under combat conditions and their families; strives to educate the public on the cost of war, nuclear and foreign policy issues, and the abolishment of war; sends delegations to other countries; maintains small library and speakers' bureau; publishes a quarterly newsletter and a special report.
Publications: Veterans for Peace; Special Report on Delegations
Founded: 1985

INDIVIDUAL PROGRAM PROFILES

POLISH LEGION OF AMERICAN VETERANS AUXILIARY
Pulaski Auxiliary Post No. 8
Pulaski Hall
1401 South Grant
Pulaski, MI 48505
TEL: 517-893-1465
Purpose: To provide entertainment and assistance to Veterans Hospital patients.
Sponsor: Polish Legion of American Veterans
Contact: Genevieve Smela, President
Description: The *Pulaski Auxiliary Post No. 8* of the *Polish Legion of American Veterans* coordinates groups of volunteers for monthly visits to the *Saginaw Veterans Hospital* and *Chateau Gardens,* a satellite hospital. The purpose is to help and entertain hospital patients.
The auxiliary is responsible for the coffee and donuts served in the outpatient area, operating bingo games for the patients, providing afternoon snacks of cookies and punch, and performing services such as letter-writing, phone calls, etc., in addition to just lending an ear when a patient wants to talk to someone.
To raise funds for these activities, the auxiliary mounts two culturally-oriented picnics each year - the Polish Festival in July, and the Harvest Festival in August. Dancing and the music of two bands are featured at the festivals, which are held on post grounds. A Memorial Day mass on the grounds involves the *Powers High School Choir.* An additional, familiar nationwide fund-raiser is the sale of poppies each year.
The auxiliary has 130 members who are wives, daughters, sisters or granddaughters of Polish veterans. World War II members dominate, but the group includes family members of veterans from the Korean and Vietnam conflicts, mostly of Polish descent. Recently chartered by the government, the organization now accepts non-Polish members.
A side benefit to the senior citizens who are members of the auxiliary is the travel program and bowling tournaments within the auxiliary designed for them.

SECOND AIR DIVISION ASSOCIATION OF THE EIGHTH AIR FORCE
c/o Hathy Veynar
4915 Bristow Drive
Annandale, VA 22003
TEL: 703-256-6482

Purpose: To maintain a *living memorial* to the members of the *Division;* to establish an organization for sons and daughters of members to continue its traditions.
Description: Chartered in the late 1940s, the *Second Air Division Association of the Eighth Air Force* works to maintain the history of the *Division* as a memorial to the group of World War II veterans, and as a heritage to future generations studying the World War II era. A major project of the *Association* is maintenance and monitoring of the *Memorial Room* at the *Norwich Central Library* in Norwich, England. Started by an offhand remark by a member of the *Division* in 1945, the actual dedication of the room by the Queen Mother was in 1963. The young officer in 1945 had said, "Why don't we give just *one paycheck* to a fund to set up a memorial of some kind here (in England) for our *Division?*" The result is a living memorial supported by the proceeds from the original fund and stocks and bonds sold in England. The funds are placed in a Trust which is monitored by the *British Board of Governors' Charities Commission.*
The *Fulbright Commission* originally provided a grant for one year for an American librarian to be stationed at the memorial, but has now extended it for an additional year since the Commission considers the project to be an important one. Since it is important to have an American librarian there to answer specific questions about the U.S., the *Association* has begun a fundraiser to establish and ensure the position. The Association Trust pays for an assistant to the librarian, who is British and has been with the memorial since its inception in 1963.
Close to the site of *East Anglia University,* the memorial is a popular rallying point for students there who are studying Anglo-American relations. The *University* has expressed its appreciation a number of times for the professionalism and extent of the collection. The *Cultural Attache* has shown considerable interest in the Memorial Room, attending meetings and being very supportive in a number of ways. He has stated that the Division is responsible for all of the good Anglo-American relations in East Anglia. Features of the memorial include:
- A pool in the front of the building containing a stone from each of the fifty United States. As stones deteriorate, Association members replace them (seven in 1990).
- An *Honor Roll,* with a page turned each day in honor of the 6,800 members of the *Division* who died in World War II.
- Flags of the United States, the Eighth Air Force, and the Second Airborne Division.
- A book-dedication program in which a book is dedicated periodically to one of the deceased members of the *Division* with a book plate inserted bearing his or her name.

The 1990 meeting in England carries a theme that honors the villages in the area where airfields for the Division were located. In the U.S., the Association holds annual meetings, and participates in projects that will continue its efforts to memorialize the Division. One project is the establishment of the *Heritage League,* which will enable sons and daughters of the veterans to carry on its traditions. Educational projects include involvement in an exhibit program in which a B-24 (the airplane used by the Division during World War II) is flown to various airports around the country for school and community groups to visit, as well as to provide a nostalgic place for the veterans themselves to gather and reminisce. An exhibit schedule is available from the Association.

VA VOLUNTARY SERVICES BOARD
US/VA - Veterans Administration Medical Center
Newington, CT 06111
TEL: 203-666-6951
Purpose: To provide a vehicle enabling members of veterans' groups to make decisions for the veterans' hospital.
Contact: William Sysman, Chief of Voluntary Services
Description: Volunteers who develop and conduct fund-raisers for veterans hospitals, or recreation programs for the residents there,

must go before the *VA Voluntary Services Board*. The all-volunteer Board is composed of members of veterans groups who help determine the scope and types of volunteer programs provided for patients. It often includes widows and/or children of veterans to help maintain the connection that would otherwise be lost when the veteran dies. One Board member at the Hartford hospital has served in that position for 43 years. Her husband died 31 years ago. The same widow served 18 years on the National VA Voluntary Services Board, 15 of them as President. The national board has representatives from throughout the country who determine how voluntary services are operated at all 172 medical centers. This board, also, makes an effort to include survivors of veterans.

Many in-house volunteer activities approved by the Hartford board are in the hospital's medical administration services, where packets of admission forms for patients and other logistical tasks are performed. Volunteers also work in the ambulatory care division, serve as translators for non-English-speaking veterans, and work with outside groups coming into the hospital with approved fund-raising events or entertainment programs.

The hospital awards a *Superior Performance Award* each year to an outstanding volunteer. One volunteer Board member - the widow of a veteran - at the Hartford hospital has been recognized for her work by the past eight presidents, including President Bush, as well as other dignitaries. She was asked why she worked so hard, and said that she remembers watching young men, including relatives, go off to war, and appreciates the contribution they made.

VOLUNTEERS: CELEBRITIES

NATIONAL/STATE ORGANIZATIONS

ACTORS AND OTHERS FOR ANIMALS
5510 Cahuenga Boulevard
North Hollywood, CA 91601
TEL: 818-985-6263
Objectives: To alleviate animal suffering.
Services: Promotes wildlife conservation, and protection of endangered species; provides direct emergency aid and pet adoption program; educates the public on "zero pet population" growth, humane treatment of pets, and other areas to help alleviate suffering of both wild and domesticated animals; conducts biennial *Celebrity Fair* to benefit these causes; publishes annual newsletter.
Publications: Actors and Others Newsletter
Founded: 1971

ENTERTAINMENT INDUSTRIES COUNCIL
1760 Reston Avenue
Suite 101
Reston, VA 22090
TEL: 703-481-1414
Objectives: To combat and deglamorize drug abuse, especially among young people.
Services: Works with corporations and representatives of the entertainment industry, including actors, agents, publicists, producers, directors, and writers, in a national campaign against substance abuse; seeks to identify and provide celebrity role models for young people; hopes to increase youth awareness through television, radio, music, and motion pictures; conducts radio interviews, television specials, meetings and workshops, outreach programs, and employee assistance and fundraising programs; tracks the progress and results of celebrity involvement and compiles statistics; maintains a celebrity speakers' bureau on drug

prevention, seat belt awareness, and intravenous drug use/AIDS; has recognition program to honor celebrities who are leaders in contributing to drug abuse awareness; publishes a quarterly newsletter, annual report, and research papers.
Publications: EIC Newsletter
Founded: 1983

INDIVIDUAL PROGRAM PROFILES

"COOL SCHOOL VIDEO" CONTEST
District of Columbia Public Schools
415 Twelfth Street, NW
Washington, DC 20024
TEL: 202-724-4201
Purpose: To help stem the rising school dropout rate.
Description: With a "stay in school" theme the only rigid requirement, students in District of Columbia Schools have been challenged to create videos for the *Cool School Video* contest. Co-sponsored by the school system and a nationwide athletic shoe retailer, the top prize is a pair of athletic shoes for every student in the school that produces the best video.
Encouraged by the appearance of celebrity role models, more than 13,000 students from the District's 27 junior high schools participated.

FAMILY ASSISTANCE PROJECT OF HOLLYWOOD (FAP)
SEE VOLUNTEERS: FAMILIES

SPARE CHANGE PROJECT
SEE FUNDING/FUND-RAISING/RELATED SERVICES: HOMELESS

VOLUNTEERS: CHURCH/SYNAGOGUE MEMBERS

NATIONAL/STATE ORGANIZATIONS

ASSOCIATION OF LADIES OF CHARITY OF THE US
c/o Romilda Berling
4424 Kemper Avenue
Cincinnati, OH 45217
TEL: 513-641-3053
Objectives: To volunteer services to help the less fortunate.
Services: Serves as an umbrella organization for local autonomous volunteer organizations operating under the auspices of the Roman Catholic church; gives service and pastoral care to the poor, the sick, the elderly, and youth wherever and whenever necessary; maintains committees to monitor and serve Indian missions, immigrants and refugees, the aging, and youth; conducts regional seminars to supplement its national conference and encourage higher participation levels; publishes a newsletter, a directory, manuals and promotional brochures.
Sponsor: National Council of Catholic Women
Publications: Servicette; Directory of Affiliates; ALCUS News Bulletin
Founded: 1960

BUSINESS/INDUSTRY PROGRAM
SEE BUSINESS/INDUSTRY INVOLVEMENT

CAMPAIGN FOR HUMAN DEVELOPMENT
SEE SELF-HELP: TENANTS/RESIDENTS

CATHOLIC CHARITIES USA
SEE FUNDING/FUND-RAISING/RELATED SERVICES

CATHOLIC COMMITTEE OF APPALACHIA
115 Main Street
Box 953
Whitesburg, KY 41858
TEL: 606-633-8440
Objectives: To secure social services and justice for Appalachian poor.
Services: Works to improve and increase social services for the rural poor in Appalachia; fosters and initiates welfare rights, housing, flood prevention, land ownership, health care programs, improved schools, and poor people's coalitions, among others; sponsors "teach-ins" on priority issues concerning land, energy, employment, and housing; advocates collective bargaining for workers; networks with *Common Cause, Council of the Southern Mountains, National Catholic Rural Life Conference, Network,* and *Rural American Women;* publishes a newsletter, a bulletin, books and other materials.
Sponsor: Common Cause
Publications: Patchquilt; CCA Bulletin; Dream of the Mountains' Struggle
Founded: 1972

FRIENDS COMMITTEE ON NATIONAL LEGISLATION
SEE LEADERSHIP DEVELOPMENT/BOARDS: CIVIC AFFAIRS

FRIENDS PEACE COMMITTEE
Religious Society of Friends
1515 Cherry Street
Philadelphia, PA 19102
TEL: 215-241-7230
Objectives: To promote international and individual peace.
Services: Works through the 45-member committee appointed at the yearly meeting of the *Society* to promote both international and individual peace; includes programs on disarmament, draft and enlistment alternatives, and foreign policy issues; maintains a speakers' bureau; works with other committees that address Quaker concerns (taxes, criminal justice, race relations, and others); provides counseling to members of the armed forces and others; publishes bulletins on legislation and government initiatives, and other materials.
Founded: 1892

GOOD NEWS JAIL AND PRISON MINISTRIES INTERNATIONAL
SEE SELF-HELP: PRISONERS/EX-OFFENDERS

HABITAT FOR HUMANITY INTERNATIONAL (*formerly Habitat for Humanity***)**
Habitat and Church Streets
Americus, GA 31709
TEL: 912-924-6935
Objectives: To provide low-cost, nonprofit housing to low-income people throughout the world.
Services: Distributes funds received through contributions from individuals and churches to low-income areas in the U.S. and overseas, where housing is built by volunteers and local people; manages the program through an Ecumenical Christian organization, which helps families to return the cost of the dwelling through a locally-managed *Fund For Humanity* over a period of 25 years; recycles *Fund* money to build more houses; sponsors projects in 25 countries; offers training to volunteers both for U.S. and overseas projects; makes its library holdings available to local project staff and volunteers.

Contact: Millard Fuller, Executive Director
Publications: Habitat World (newspaper); Community Self-Help Housing Manual; Kingdom Building; Love in the Mortar Joints; No More Shacks!
Founded: 1976

INTERFAITH CENTER ON CORPORATE RESPONSIBILITY
SEE BUSINESS/INDUSTRY INVOLVEMENT

JESUIT VOLUNTEER CORPS: NORTHWEST
SEE COMMUNITY SERVICES

JEWISH BRAILLE INSTITUTE OF AMERICA
110 East 30th Street
New York, NY 10016
TEL: 212-889-2525
Objectives: To assist Jewish blind, visually impaired, and reading disabled persons, and other blind individuals.
Services: Distributes materials in large print; develops mechanisms through which the elderly blind and visually impaired can participate in community life; compiles information on programs geared to the social integration of the blind; maintains a lending library of thousands of Braille volumes in English and Hebrew, and films and cassettes in these and other languages; provides speakers to community groups; publishes a newsletter, journal and other materials, some of which are available on sound-scriber discs and cassettes as well as in Braille.
Publications: JBI Voice ; Jewish Braille Review

JEWISH GUILD FOR THE BLIND
15 West 65th Street
New York, NY 10023
TEL: 212-595-2000
Objectives: To assist blind, handicapped and multihandicapped people through a variety of services.
Services: Provides volunteer services for blind and other handicapped people of all ages, races, and creeds; offers casework, counseling, job development, placement and training, sheltered workshops, high school equivalency training, recreational programs, transcription typing, daily living programs, and others; operates a school for multihandicapped children, a psychiatric clinic for emotionally disturbed and mentally retarded blind persons and their families, and a day treatment center and residence for multihandicapped blind young adults, a home for the aging blind, an independent living apartment house, and other programs; maintains a cassette library providing free materials to blind, visually impaired, and reading disabled persons; publishes a quarterly newsletter.
Publications: JGB Newsletter
Founded: 1914

LOW-INCOME APARTMENTS PROGRAM
Volunteers of America
3813 North Causeway Boulevard
Metairie, LA 70002
TEL: 504-837-2652
Objectives: To increase the nation's low-income housing stock.
Services: Works to increase available apartments across the country for low-income families and the elderly; operates a low- and moderate-income housing division that manages 46 low-income apartment projects it built plus another 19 that it developed and syndicated to investors; acquires apartment buildings in depressed markets for half or less of the original value, including some once owned by failed savings and loan associations and made available through the *Resolution Trust Corporation (RTC),* the federal agency handling the disposition of assets from the failed thrifts (under the thrift bailout law, nonprofits are

entitled to a 90-day right-of-first-refusal to buy these properties); implements long-range plans to keep the properties on the market for the target group.
Sponsor: US/RTC - Resolution Trust Corporation
Contact: John Hood, Vice President

MIGRATION AND REFUGEE SERVICE
U.S. Catholic Charities
1312 Massachusetts Avenue, NW
Washington, DC 20005
TEL: 202-659-6630
Objectives: To assist arriving refugees in finding employment and becoming self-sufficient.
Services: Provides pre-arrival orientation for sponsors and refugees, training courses, employment and housing assistance, and aid in obtaining care from local public health organizations; secures sponsors when needed for the refugee prior to his/her arrival, finds living quarters, provides first month's rent and food allowance, and meets refugee at the airport; conducts orientation, employment counseling, health screening, social security and school registration and other services upon arrival; publishes newsletter, resettlement directory, and in-house information on legislative issues and policy development.
Publications: Update; MRS Annual Review; MRS Resettlement and Immigration Directory; Enriched by Their Presence
Founded: 1920

NATIONAL CATHOLIC DISASTER RELIEF COMMITTEE
1319 F Street, NW
Fourth Floor
Washington, DC 20004
TEL: 202-639-8400
Objectives: To marshal Catholic church resources in times of disaster.
Services: Works to give greater visibility and recognition to the work of the Catholic church in times of major natural disasters; represents Catholic organizations that may be able to render assistance in such times; maintains a membership of approximately twenty people on the Committee; develops a network to make expedient contact with local church officials to learn of the extent of damage caused by a natural disaster, and the resulting immediate and urgent needs; coordinates Catholic church resources, and provides consultation for those working in the rehabilitation of disaster-affected areas; operates under the aegis of *Catholic Charities USA* (see separate entry) and through appointment by the *National Conference of Catholic Bishops.*

NATIONAL FEDERATION OF INTERFAITH VOLUNTEER CAREGIVERS
105 Mary's Avenue
PO Box 1939
Kingston, NY 12401
TEL: 914-331-1358
Objectives: To help meet the growing need of the isolated, frail elderly and disabled people.
Services: The National Federation of Interfaith Volunteer Caregivers (IVC) was founded in 1987 with start-up financial support from the Robert Wood Johnson Foundation and the Pew Charitable Trusts. Its purposes are to support the development of new IVC projects around the country and to encourage the growing movement and networking of Interfaith Volunteer Caregivers projects. The Federation's roots are in 1983 when the Foundation, recognizing that the nation's population of frail elderly and disabled people is growing rapidly, with many living alone with few resources, announced a three-year national program to try to strengthen the the role family, friends and neighbors play - often unrecognized - in caring for disabled people of all ages. The plan was to see whether interfaith coalitions could be formed successfully for this purpose. The coalitions would recruit, train,

and match volunteers with frail elderly and disabled people, thereby enabling them to continue living independently in the community and avoiding as long as possible placement in a nursing home.
In funding the Interfaith Volunteer Caregivers Program, the Foundation both acknowledged the importance of nonprofessional caregivers and recognized the tradition among religious congregations of serving the needs of others. The overwhelming response to the Foundation's 1983 call for proposals reflected a high level of awareness and a willingness of congregations to work together. The Foundation had a goal of 15 interfaith coalitions with funding level of $150,000 each. Approximately 1,000 requests were received from 48 states. Consequently the Foundation increased the number of grantees to 25 with a three-year award of $150,000 to each grantee.
The twenty-five IVC grantees were chosen from across the country, and the interfaith coalitions they had organized served densely urban, suburban, and rural communities alike. Volunteers were recruited from churches, synagogues, and other religious institutions reflective of the community.
Requirements for funding include the interfaith coalition representing a community's religious congregations to be responsible for the project, a minimum community population of 25,000 and a full-time director. The funded projects were located in 17 states, the District of Columbia, and the territory of Guam. Within the first year of operation, each project recruited an average of 140 volunteers and served 380 people. Within the three-year grant period, more than 26,000 persons were served, many on an ongoing basis, and more than 11,000 volunteers were recruited, trained, and matched with people in need.
The many different services provided by volunteers include: transportation, shopping, advocacy and referral, friendly visiting, and telephone reassurance, with some providing home care such as assistance in meal preparation, and respite for family caregivers.
Based on the experiences of the grantee programs, the ideal approach to implementing a successful project includes:
- Committed members who feel strong ownership of the project.
- Advisory board with balanced representation from clergy, agencies and community members.
- Director with networking abilities within the community, an understanding of religious institutions and how to work with volunteers.
- Strong well-trained coordinators within congregations.
- System for locating those most in need and introducing volunteers into the home situations.
- Chain of support from coalition to board, to director, to coordinators, to volunteers, to those being served.
- Introduction into the overall community support system for mutual support, referral, and networking.
- A community-wide commitment to ongoing project funding.
Among the benefits volunteers cited when asked about their participation were: companionship, work experience, good use of time, good feeling from helping others, making friends, fulfilling a sense of obligation to the community, religion, or society.
One of the project directors credited the success of the concept this way: "Volunteers are most effective when they are part of a balanced mix of public and private initiatives - with each learning from and supporting the others in their work. When agencies and professional caregivers do their part, volunteers can do theirs better."
Two studies of the coalitions have been completed - one by the National Program Office at Benedictine Hospital, Kingston, New York, and the other by Fordham University's Third Age Center (the latter funded by the Foundation to assess the program).
Sponsor: Robert Wood Johnson Foundation
Publications: Interfaith Volunteer Caregivers: A Special Report; Caregivers Quarterly (newsletter); Benedictine Hospital Study; Fordham University Evaluation
Founded: 1987

OFFICE FOR CHURCH IN SOCIETY
United Church of Christ
105 Madison Avenue
New York, NY 10016
TEL: 212-683-5656
Objectives: To research and study legislation and budget priorities as they affect social issues.
Services: Analyzes findings of research on legislation, publishes resultant conclusions; garners resources of the church for social action projects, and works to increase the number and frequency of such projects; designs and implements legislative and action programs within the church; provides local program suggestions in the area of political responsibility; supports internal committees on public advocacy, church empowerment, and information/publication; publishes monthly newsletter, *UCC Network,* social policy statements, issue packets, listings of resources for research, and other materials.
Publications: Courage in the Struggle
Founded: 1976

ORPHAN FOUNDATION OF AMERICA
1500 Massachusetts Avenue, NW, #448
PO Box 14261
Washington, DC 20044
TEL: 202-861-0762
Objectives: To show support and provide assistance for youth in foster care reaching age 18 and soon to be released as adults.
Services: Offers independent living courses and volunteer counseling services for youth in foster care who are reaching adulthood; offers emergency help, recreation programs, and friendship to children raised outside of the traditional family setting; sponsors *Project Bridge Program,* a community-based volunteer support network that assists youth in foster care in their transition from the child welfare system to independent adulthood; provides training to adult volunteers to assist youth in goal planning, independent living, life skills, career development, job search, maintaining employment, and recreation; sponsors annual Christmas parties and summer picnics; offers speakers to community groups on request; offers scholarships to youth interested in college educations; publishes a newsletter and other materials.
Contact: Reverend Joseph Rivers, Founder

PRISON FELLOWSHIP MINISTRIES
PO Box 17500
Washington, DC 20041
TEL: 703-478-0100
Objectives: To work for a just and effective criminal justice system by involving volunteers and the resources of the church.
Services: Builds volunteer community Care Committees by working with local churches; mobilizes resources for prisoners, ex-offenders and their families; offers proposals for the improvement of the criminal justice system; consults with local, state and political leaders, judges and correctional officials regarding these proposals, which advocate a more just system that would better control crime, save taxes, and aid victims, while employing punishments which minimize destructive long-term imprisonment and promote positive change; publishes *Is There a Better Way: A Perspective on American Prisons* and other materials.
Publications: Jubilee; Justice Report; Is There A Better Way?
Founded: 1976

SALVATION ARMY
799 Bloomfield Avenue
Verona, NJ 07044
TEL: 201-239-0606
Objectives: To meet the physical, spiritual and emotional needs of mankind.

Services: Works through about 10,500 local centers in areas of adult rehabilitation, hospitals, clinics, homes for unwed mothers, recreation centers, camping programs for children and adults, and emergency feeding and shelter stations; cooperates with other community programs in emergencies, more than 6,000 of them operating one or more *Salvation Army* programs; has ordained ministers in leadership roles who spend full time in religious and social welfare activities; maintains library and archives and a speakers' bureau; publishes biweekly, monthly, semiannual and annual publications describing and reporting on the work of the organization.
Publications: The War Cry; The Musician; Young Salvationist; Program Aids; People Helping People; Annual Report; Edward H. McKinney

SUPERIOR COUNCIL
SEE COMMUNITY SERVICES

VOLUNTEER LEADERSHIP PROGRAM
SEE LEADERSHIP DEVELOPMENT/BOARDS

VOLUNTEER READING AIDES PROGRAM
Lutheran Church Women of America
2900 Queen Lane
Philadelphia, PA 19129
TEL: 215-438-2200
Objectives: To give the non-reader individual attention to gain the skills and confidence that is needed for classroom work.
Services: Assists groups, agencies and communities in evaluating needs for an organization of volunteer adult literacy programs; refers groups to already-existing literacy efforts, in cooperation with National Affiliation for Literacy Advance, Literacy Volunteers of America and other literacy groups; trains volunteers in tutoring and leadership skills; provides consultant services; publishes *Handbook for Volunteer Reading Aides* and other books, teaching aids, etc.

VOLUNTEERS OF AMERICA
SEE COMMUNITY SERVICES

YOUNG MEN'S CHRISTIAN ASSOCIATION OF THE U.S.
SEE COMMUNITY SERVICES

YOUNG WOMEN'S CHRISTIAN ASSOCIATION OF THE U.S.
SEE COMMUNITY SERVICES

TRAINING PROGRAMS

CHURCH VOLUNTEER ADMINISTRATION
SEE TRAINING/CONFERENCES/TEACHING: INTERFAITH

INTERFAITH VOLUNTEER CAREGIVING WORKSHOP
National Federation of Interfaith Volunteer Caregivers
105 Mary's Avenue
PO Box 1939
Kingston, NY 12401-1939
TEL: 914-331-1358
Credit: Inquire
Sponsor: National Federation of Interfaith Volunteer Caregivers
Contact: Workshop Coordinator
Description: This series of intensive workshops in interfaith caregiving is offered in five regions of the United States: California, Connecticut, Illinois, Colorado and Georgia. The workshops offer in-depth experience and knowledge of persons

who have first-hand experience in developing and sustaining Caregivers projects and will address the issues of:
- Building an effective interfaith coalition
- Recruiting, training and matching volunteers
- Funding an interfaith caregivers project

The Workshop schedule:

Day One
- Scope and Purpose of Workshop

Day Two
- Board Development;
- Organization of Staff;
- Management Tasks;
- Volunteer Recruitment, Training, Recognition and Support;
- Gaining Community Visibility and Support;
- Informal Group Discussion.

Day Three
- Post-Workshop Networking

Time is set aside during the course of the program to enable participants to develop contact with a national network of over 350 individuals and groups engaged in interfaith caregiving. Handicapped-accessible accommodations are made available on request.

PARKINSON'S INSTITUTE FOR CAREGIVERS
SEE TRAINING/CONFERENCES/TEACHING: HEALTH

PRE-FORUM 90 TRAINING INSTITUTES
SEE TRAINING/CONFERENCES/TEACHING: CRIME PREVENTION

TAKING A TRIP TO FRIENDSHIP
SEE TRAINING/CONFERENCES/TEACHING: STUDENTS

TOWN MEETING FOR THE HOMELESS
SEE TRAINING/CONFERENCES/TEACHING: HOMELESS

VIRGINIA ECUMENICAL INFANT MORTALITY PREVENTION PROJECT CONFERENCE
SEE GOVERNORS' OFFICES ON VOLUNTEERISM: VIRGINIA

VOA SYMPOSIUM ON HOMELESSNESS
SEE TRAINING/CONFERENCES/TEACHING: HOMELESS

VOLUNTEERING IN THE RELIGIOUS SETTING
SEE TRAINING/CONFERENCES/TEACHING: INTERFAITH

VOLUNTEERS OF AMERICA ANNUAL MEETING
SEE TRAINING/CONFERENCES/TEACHING

INDIVIDUAL PROGRAM PROFILES

AFFORDABLE HOUSING PROJECT
Unitarian Universalist Housing Foundation
9601 Cedar Lane
Bethesda, MD 20814
TEL: 301-493-4008; 20014
Purpose: To rehabilitate existing apartment units and create affordable housing for low-income residents and the homeless.
Contact: Anne Thorward, Volunteer
Description: With home prices tripling in the Washington, DC, area over the past decade, the gentrification of older neighborhoods, and a diminished commitment of the federal government to fund affordable housing, churches have added

housing to their long list of social services. The *Unitarian Universalist Affordable Housing Project* is one of those efforts. In 1990, the Project rehabilitated a 60-year old building in the heart of the District's Shaw neighborhood.

Volunteers include entire families who not only work in the construction and rehabilitation of housing, but also participate in raising funds for the projects - $225,000 for the 1990 effort, which includes low-interest and no-interest loans as well as donations. To ensure that the building will stay in the pool of affordable housing if occupants leave, it is structured as a limited-equity cooperative. Under this plan, tenants have management control of the building and act as their own landlords. The group considers the new thrust to housing by churches as a natural extension of services for the homeless. According to one volunteer, "We've worked in soup kitchens and shelters, and it does not take a genius to see that people never get out of those places unless there are solid alternatives."
Founded: 1988

ANNANDALE CHRISTIAN COMMUNITY FOR ACTION (ACCA)
7200 Columbia Pike
Annandale, VA 22003
TEL: 703-256-1378
Purpose: To respond to critical needs of youth, children and families in the area.
Sponsor: Local churches (24 in 1989)
Contact: Gilmer B. Weatherly, Jr.
Description: The Annandale Christian Community for Action (ACCA) was established in 1967 in response to an urgent need for child care. A small group of children were being cared for in the Mount Pleasant Baptist Church under a government program that provided funds for the service. Suddenly the guidelines for the program were changed, and the families could no longer be helped. These were low-income working parents whose meager salaries could not cover the cost of child care in addition to their other expenses. The families had no alternatives. They would have to give up their jobs and seek welfare assistance unless they could have help with the child care expense. A group of concerned Christians met at Peace Lutheran Church and decided that they would dedicate their efforts to the solution of this problem. They established the Annandale Christian Community for Action by starting the first ACCA Day Care Center in the John Calvin Presbyterian Church. With only $1,000 of donated funds, and with no real knowledge of child care, the ACCA Center began as an expression of Christian concern.

As the church sponsors became acquainted with the families of the day care children, and with their neighbors as well, knowledge of the nature and extent of poverty in the community grew. It was learned that many people were indeed hungry in the area, that many families lacked clothing, furniture, and money for essentials such as rent, medical and utility payments. Committees were established to cope with the problems.

From this humble beginning, ACCA has seen amazing growth through the years with 24 churches participating in 1989, with thousands of volunteers involved.

An important point is that ACCA is not a separate or umbrella organization - it is "all of the members of all of the ACCA churches." Programs include: Family Emergency Committee, Child Development Centers, Furniture Committee, Housing Program, Meals on Wheels Program, Transportation Committee, and Scholarship Program (all described separately).
Publications: ACCA Annual Report
Founded: 1967

ARC COVENANT
Lomond Hotel
2510 Washington Boulevard
Ogden, UT 84401
TEL: 801-399-5627; 801-392-8168

Purpose: To sponsor jointly an action project to benefit the Community of Ogden.
Sponsor: Ogden Department of Aging and Volunteer Services
Contact: Father Kaiser or Father Winder
Description: The ARC Covenant is a union of Episcopal Church of the Good Shepherd, St. Joseph Roman Catholic Church and recently Elim Lutheran Church. Based on an ecumenical directive to reunite, these organizations have combined services within their congregations and the Ogden community. Their pledge to benefit Ogden has resulted in the Soup Kitchen and St. Theresa's Shelter.
Community Need - A humanitarian concern existed because of the increased need for food and shelter for the indigent and transient population. Ogden encounters more homeless because of the railway system.
Recipient's Need - Indigents had limited access to social services. Transients had non-existent resources to serve their basic need for food and shelter. Due to the recession, employment was increasingly unavailable resulting in life threatening situations. Persons were forced to scavenge, sometimes resulting in criminal acts. The onset of inclement weather accelerated their urgent need.
Challenge - On December 8, 1982, volunteers began establishing a shelter. Warehouse space was donated, 65 cots were borrowed from the Red Cross, bedding was donated and electricity, water and heat were secured. Within 5 days, 18 indigents were sheltered. A week later the shelter was operating at full capacity. This was accomplished through the cooperative efforts of ARC Covenant and Ogden citizens.
Method - A needs assessment determined that the populace required sustenance beyond the evening meals provided by other organizations. ARC Covenant utilized the St. Anne's Church Center and set up a late morning soup kitchen utilizing donations and government commodities. A portion of St. Anne's bingo proceeds were utilized.
The second shelter concern materialized through word of mouth within the churches and community resulting in the necessary material and monetary donations. A local newspaper provided initial information. Volunteer commitment accomplished the housing objectives.
Scope - The combined efforts of ARC Covenant and the community accomplished the serving of 3,923 meals at the Soup Kitchen during December. This has been achieved through continual donations of volunteer time, money and goods. A growing awareness of the needy has resulted in sheltering 65 to 90 persons nightly since the establishment of St. Theresa's Shelter.
Achievement - The community has generously responded with food, blankets, washer, dryer and funds without active fund raising. Donations have exceeded expectations. As a result, the $26,000 church grant received almost two years ago is not financially drained. Direct requests for aid from the indigent have noticeably declined. The police have noticed a noteworthy decrease in area crime.
Innovation - Nationally, out of 117 established covenants, the ARC Covenant has been recognized as 1 of 3 highly successful unions. This organization in turn has impacted on the community's awareness of the needy. Ogden has overwhelmingly responded without a formal request for assistance. Schools, citizens and other religious groups continue to donate materials and time. ARC Covenant's purpose is to feed the hungry and house the homeless without regard to religious, racial or social restriction. They and the Ogden community are achieving this goal.

BAILEY'S CROSSROADS COMMUNITY SHELTER
3525 Moncure Avenue
Falls Church, VA 22041
TEL: 703-820-7621 (Shelter); 703-256-1378 (ACCA)
Purpose: To help homeless persons overcome the conditions that created their homelessness.
Sponsor: Annandale Christian Community for Action (ACCA)

Contact: Marilyn Morrison, Director; Peter Woolly, Assistant Director; Whitey Rowell, ACCA Liaison
Description: After 20 months of service in temporary trailers and cramped office space, the Bailey's Crossroads Community Shelter was opened on September 22, 1987. It is operated under contract with the County of Fairfax by the Salvation Army with facilities for men and women.
A variety of services are provided by volunteers, who are recruited from ACCA churches and the community. Their activities include, but are not limited to, food preparation, serving meals, monitoring shelter activities and security, serving as receptionists, assisting with office work and, perhaps most important of all, being a friend to residents and helping them to develop social skills and locate jobs.
In 1988, 720 individuals provided a total of about 4,200 hours of service to residents who filled the shelter, frequently to overflowing, almost every night. These volunteers served over 1,480 individual, unduplicated residents during 1988.
Other services provided to the residents are supplied by professional staff from the Salvation Army, Department of Social Services, Substance Abuse Service, Department of Public Health, and Woodburn Mental Health Center. Such services include health screening, employment guidance and referral, mental health counseling, educational and self help training.
Contributions from the community in the form of cash and materials have been a major factor in the operation of the Shelter. Much of the cost of providing the programs and services required by the residents to successfully readjust to being a contributing member of the community must come from such donations. In preparing the contract for operation of the Shelter, the County accepted the assurances from the community that the Shelter would be a joint operation between the County staff and the citizens of the community and its churches.
As experience in operating the Shelter is gained, the need for contributions from citizens continues to increase as more is learned about the residents, their needs and their special problems. The most significant knowledge gained so far seems to be that the homeless problem is growing in the County even though shelter capacity has increased in the Northern Virginia area.
The Annandale Christian Community for Action (ACCA) program has made the Shelter one of its outreach programs and keeps all member churches informed, urging them to continue providing volunteers, materials, and financial help to maintain the growing effectiveness of the Shelter program.
Publications: ACCA Annual Report

BETHESDA HELP
SEE INFORMATION & REFERRAL

BLACK GEORGETOWN REUNION GROUP
Mount Zion United Methodist Church
1334 29th Street, NW
Washington, DC 20007
TEL: 202-234-0248
Purpose: To share common memories and strengthen a growing reunion project.
Sponsor: Georgetown University
Contact: Rev. Kirk D. Monroe
Description: Mount Zion United Methodist Church, founded in 1816, is the oldest of five historic black congregations still in Georgetown in Washington, DC, and is considered the oldest black church in the District. In Spring 1990, a small group of volunteers from the church launched what it hopes will be an annual interfaith event - a union of people who can come together and reminisce about their childhood when the playground, Rose Park in Georgetown, was the first desegregated in the District, their high school days, the former division of Georgetown into two sections, and the period from the early 1800s to about 1950, when the Georgetown population was predominantly black.

The reminiscence program is a spinoff from an annual reunion dinner started by a senior Georgetown resident in 1982. To be sure that the tradition continued, a group of volunteers founded the *Black Georgetown Reunion Group.* The interfaith group meets every six months at a different church.

About two-thirds of the nearly 300 in attendance were from other churches, including the Epiphany Roman Catholic Church and the Alexandria Memorial Baptist Church. Seventeen persons at least 90 years old - many of whom provided stories rich in the history of the area - were honored at the event. The reunion events, along with a *Georgetown University* film, *Black Georgetown Remembered,* are heightening the sense of local history, according to an official of the *Washington Historical Society.*
Publications: Black Georgetown Remembered

BLUE RIDGE AREA FOOD BANK*
SEE BUSINESS/INDUSTRY INVOLVEMENT: NUTRITION

CAMPUS MINISTRY
Fairfield University
1073 North Benson Road
Fairfield, CT 06430
TEL: 203-254-4000
Purpose: To encourage community service as an important part of a complete education.
Sponsor: Fairfield University
Contact: Laura Keenan, Co-Chairman
Description: Fairfield University, the second youngest Jesuit college in the country, considers community service an integral part of its learning curricula for its 2,800 students. Its *Campus Ministry* provides volunteer opportunities for students, including:

- **Appalachian Club** - a spring break trip to the Appalachians each year for students interested in helping with road repairs, house cleaning and other service projects.
- **Tutoring** - a project that addresses learning needs of elementary school students in first to sixth grades in neighboring Bridgeport, considered one of the poorest sections in the country.
- **Homeless Assistance** - an opportunity to help in the various food programs of a nearby soup kitchen.

These and many other community projects are credited as some of the reasons student enrollment is rapidly increasing. The *Campus Ministries* program also sponsors a minor studies course, *Faith, Peace and Justice Studies,* which encourages volunteer involvement.
Founded: 1942

CAUSE (COMMUNITY AND UNIVERSITY SERVICES IN EDUCATION)
SEE VOLUNTEERS: STUDENTS

CENTRAL SUMMER SCHOOL
Central Lutheran Church
333 South 12th Street
Minneapolis, MN 55404
TEL: 612-870-4416
Purpose: To provide a full summer school session in an area where the public school system is not offering this service.
Contact: Barbara Bruneau, Director
Description: When members of the Central Lutheran Church learned that the Minneapolis Public Schools did not plan to offer a summer session in 1989, the church took action to set up the needed service. The six-week summer session is staffed by volunteer teachers and teaches 100 children ages seven to fourteen. The sessions operate four hours each day, five days a week, and include a hot lunch. A nominal tuition of $10 per child pays 10% of the $10,000 cost of the program, with the Church paying the rest.

Central Summer School is not a religious school. It offers instruction in English and math plus a variety of vocational subjects such as baking, carpentry and drug education. Most of the students are blacks, Indians and Southeast Asians, and most come from low-income families.

The school will use ten classrooms plus a couple of activity rooms and large group rooms as available in the church. Students are accepted in the order they enroll, without regard to religion or any other factor. Ten teachers, some of them certified, each take a classroom of about ten students for the entire six weeks. Some 200 volunteers come in for a morning or two mornings each to present programs relating to their professions, countries of origin or cultures where they have lived or traveled, hobbies or crafts, or other skills. Volunteers are intentionally recruited from a variety of religious and cultural backgrounds to provide children with volunteers with whom they can identify and who can provide role models. Conversely, all of the children are exposed to people from cultures and backgrounds they might otherwise not get to know. High interest comes from suburbia, from people who want to have first-hand experience working where there is a need.

A side benefit that grew out of parents' concern was the supervision aspect. Many of the children would have been unsupervised without the summer school option. Since the program was announced, the City of Minneapolis has offered money to help the public schools operate a summer session. Since the 100 children in Central Summer School represent a very small part of the need, the City's offer allows many more children to get the supervision they need, while upgrading their learning skills.
Founded: 1989

CHILD DEVELOPMENT CENTERS OF ACCA
Annandale Christian Community for Action (ACCA)
7200 Columbia Pike
Annandale, VA 22003
TEL: 703-256-1378
Purpose: To respond to a critical need for child care.
Sponsor: ACCA
Contact: Mildred Gunnarson, Chairman
Description: In 1967 a small group of children were being cared for in the Mount Pleasant Baptist Church under a government program that provided funds for the service. Suddenly the guidelines for the program were changed, and the families could no longer be helped. As a result, a group of concerned Christians met at John Calvin Presbyterian Church and, with only $1,000 of donated funds and no real knowledge of child care, began the first ACCA day care center for children of the working poor.

Through the years, the mission of the ACCA Day Care Program has remained the same, but the size of the program and the services offered have been greatly extended. The families helped demonstrate that they are trying to help themselves, but most cannot afford the high cost of day care. ACCA offers a subsidy, and another is offered through Fairfax County. In 1988, the average annual income of the families served by the ACCA Centers was just over $18,000. Since the cost per child is about $4,500 per year, it is obvious that this cost is prohibitive for these families. The churches and individuals in the community who have provided funds have made it possible to help these families.

ACCA operates two child care centers. The initial center (ACCA) - located at a former elementary school - was expanded in 1985 in response to the great demand and, at the present time, serves 138 preschool children. ACCA II is located in Culmore United Methodist Church and enrolls 70 children aged four to six. During the academic year, ACCA II serves as a *Before and After School Center* for 60 Kindergarten youngsters who attend Baileys and Glen Forest Elementary Schools and St. Anthony's Catholic School. ACCA II also serves as a full-time center for 10 preschoolers. During the summer, the 70 children remain at the Center from 7:00 a.m. until 5:45 p.m. The Centers operate 50 weeks a year and close only on major national holidays.

Active participation by the community has enabled the Centers to provide many services for the children and their families as well, including transportation, meals, and an educational program designed to enable children to succeed in school. A paid administrator counsels parents and coordinates assistance through other ACCA programs for families with special needs.

The Centers were honored by a visit in 1987 by the Governor of Virginia, and were featured among 19 centers in the country in *The National Governors' Association Handbook of Promising Prevention Programs for Children Zero to Five Years of Age.* Strengths of the program include its subsidy assistance, educational techniques, and support services.

Publications: ACCA Annual Report
Founded: 1967

CHIP-IN

c/o Family Assistance Program
6605 Hollywood Boulevard
Los Angeles, CA 90028
TEL: 213-461-9632

Purpose: To help solve some of the problems of the homeless and hungry.

Sponsor: Family Assistance Program; Hollywood Mental Health Service; Los Angeles Free Clinic; Hollywood Temple Beth El; Hope Lutheran Church; St. Thomas Episcopal Church; Blessed Sacrament Catholic Church

Contact: M. Patricia Shelhamer

Description: In the fall of 1984 a group of representatives from Hollywood area churches, temples and social service agencies met and joined together to help solve some of the problems of the homeless and hungry. Out of this initial meeting grew the idea of forming a coalition of the like-minded groups and individuals to provide humane and cost-effective solutions for Hollywood's growing homeless population and to preserve and perpetuate the renowned and glamorous image of Hollywood as an ideal place to live and do business, a caring community. Thus CHIP-IN (Community of Hollywood Investing In People In Need) was formed and incorporated as a nonprofit public benefit organization in July of 1985. CHIP-IN is comprised of approximately forty local religious groups and social service agencies, such as:

- Blessed Sacrament Catholic Church
- Centrum of Hollywood
- Family Assistance Program of Hollywood
- First Presbyterian Church of Hollywood
- Gay and Lesbian Community Service Center
- Hollywood Mental Health Service
- Hollywood Temple Beth El
- Hope Lutheran Church
- Immaculate Heart Community
- Jewish Family Services
- Los Angeles Free Clinic
- St. Thomas Episcopal Church
- Senior Multi-Purpose Center
- Temple Israel of Hollywood
- Traveler's Aid/Teen Canteen
- Volunteers of America/Hollywood Shelter Program
- West Hollywood Food Coalition

CHIP-IN was instrumental, in a joint venture with *Volunteers of America,* in establishing a new shelter for the homeless in Hollywood. The *Hollywood Homeless Shelter* opened October 19, 1986. The facility provides shelter for individuals and families through referrals from the Department of Social Services or participating coalition member agencies.

CHIP-IN has been providing approximately 250 meals for the homeless every evening since its inception, first in cooperation with the Salvation Army at its Hollywood facility, and now with the *West Hollywood Food Coalition.*

The *Los Angeles Free Clinic,* with the help of CHIP-IN, is very close to opening a subsidiary of their Beverly Boulevard Facility in the Hollywood area, making medical services available in the central Hollywood area.

CHIP-IN is quartered in the *Family Assistance Program* offices and meets monthly to discuss needs, introduce public officials, and share other information.

Founded: 1984

CHRISTIAN INVOLVEMENT
St. Mary's High School
5648 North El Dorado Street
Stockton, CA 95207
TEL: 209-957-3340

Purpose: To provide service to parishes, to public and private agencies in the Stockton area.

Sponsor: St. Mary's High School

Contact: Sister Benet Molini, O.P.

Description: Christian Involvement is a religion elective offered at St. Mary's High School. For one semester, juniors and seniors perform service during the school day (St. Mary's has a seven period day) in place of classroom religion. The school encourages service to the larger Stockton community in imitation of Christ - "I am in your midst as one who serves."

This religion elective operates as a regular class. The students work four days a week, averaging one and a half hours of work a day. Students must be on time for their work and must call their agencies when they are absent. Each day, students complete tasks assigned to them by their agency supervisors. During evaluation seminars held at St. Mary's, students relate their work to Scripture and Church documents. Much of the data of the program were processed by the school computer.

The class has a workbook that the students purchase at the beginning of the school year. The workbook is published by St. Mary's High School. Funds from the sale of the workbook are used to help run the program.

Through the course, the students become responsive to the needs of others, develop a community conscience, and experience the rewards of giving. The agencies receive enhancement for their programs from a human resource that provides intellectual help, understanding, and friendship for people of differing ages, life styles, and problems. A by-product of the class is career awareness and training. The end product is that the students, through volunteerism, experience a professional life style.

The students do volunteer work in parishes, educational institutions, day care centers, convalescent hospitals, agencies for the hungry, needy, and handicapped. They work as receptionists, tutors, teacher's aides, secretaries, nurses, cooks, counselors, and parish assistants.

During an orientation session with the school moderator, the students review the rules that will effect Christian behavior. The agency supervisor is responsible for giving the students in-service training for their jobs.

CHRISTIAN SERVICE DEPARTMENT
Northeastern Bible College
12 Oak Lane
Essex Fells, NJ 07021
TEL: 201-226-1074

Purpose: To provide NBC students with service-learning opportunities in the New York/New Jersey metropolitan area.

Sponsor: Northeastern Bible College

Contact: Michael E. Marrapodi

Description: The *Christian Service Department* coordinates the field service experience of each student at *Northeastern Bible College.* Students are required to participate in the program for the normal matriculation period of their degree. Opportunities most closely resemble a volunteer program in other colleges and universities in their scope, sequence and development.

The Department is administered by a paid director. This involves 50% of his full-time employment at the College. He is assisted by two student volunteers each semester. In addition, he has access to 7-8 hours of paid secretarial help each week.

Students at NBC come from a wide cross section of the population. Over two-thirds are commuters and many are part-time. Student programs are developed in conjunction with their curriculum area and follow a sequential development process. Students are expected to commit at least three hours per week to their project under the direct supervision of an on-site field supervisor.

Supervision for each student is provided by the agency requesting volunteer assistance. An oral evaluation is given mid-semester and a written report submitted at the conclusion of each semester. Supervisors' evaluations account for one-third of the students' credit/no credit evaluation.

Students are involved in many different services to the church and community. These include: prison, nursing home, rescue mission, school, community and individual projects.

CHRISTIAN SERVICE PROGRAM
Ursuline High School
750 Wick Avenue
Youngstown, OH 44505
TEL: 216-744-4563
Purpose: To provide high school students with supervised in-service volunteer programs.
Sponsor: Ursuline High School; private donations
Contact: Ursuline High School Christian Service Program
Description: The Ursuline High School Christian Service Program is a religious education course open to seniors in high school. It is an elective program offered each semester. Students are provided with an opportunity to work in 40 different agencies, schools, nursing homes, day care centers, etc. Students earn four Ursuline High School religious education credits for having completed the course.

Students entering the program work with three high school staff members to research the available volunteer programs in the Youngstown area. Students then schedule themselves for four different locations in any week. The fifth day is spent at the high school with in-service programs, and reflection about their work experiences.

Each student has both a high school director and an individual location supervisor assigned to direct their volunteer work on each location, and evaluate their performance. Final written evaluations by the supervisors and directors are shared both with the students, and with their parents. Students work in a variety of local volunteer agencies, local nursing homes, local private and public schools, day care centers, etc.

The purpose of the program is to train young people in volunteerism, its responsibilities and its place in their lives as Christian adults. The program also provides young people with a wide range of experiences in community projects.

The students are given in-service training in skills to tutor younger children, to visit nursing homes, work with various handicapped groups, and perform clerical duties. Each student is required to keep a journal of volunteer activities, difficulties, and lists of learning experiences. The Ursuline High School staff directors organize the program, provide in-service experiences, keep contact with individual location supervisors, interview monthly each student participant, and evaluate each student. The program was established in 1975, and has been offered each semester since that time.
Founded: 1975

DOVE, INC.
SEE COMMUNITY SERVICES

FAMILY AIDS EDUCATION PROJECT
Jewish Family Services
1790 SW 27th Avenue
Miami, FL 33145
TEL: 305-445-0555
Purpose: To design an AIDS education program adaptable to all audiences.
Sponsor: Jewish Family Services
Description: Adapts an extensive AIDS education program to any audience, using four volunteer presenters. The project, developed by Jewish Family Services (JFS), Catholic Family Services, Family Counseling Services of Greater Miami, and the Center for Family and Child Enrichment, is coordinated by JFS. The agencies jointly designed a general brochure to accompany the educational presentation and have spoken to audiences ranging from catechism students to Nicaraguan immigrants.

To make conservative religious groups receptive to the presentations, they are scheduled with the approval of rabbis or priests. The brochure was carefully designed with input from each of the agencies involved as well as the community at large as to what words were or were not acceptable. The presentations are not "public meetings," per se, but rather meetings for specific groups already formed. This is necessary to properly adapt the presentation.

The Family AIDS Education Project has received $40,000 from United Way of Dade County to cover six months of the program (January to June 1989). The project's four speakers address hundreds of groups, with the intent of integrating AIDS education into existing orientation and education curriculums.
Founded: 1988

FAMILY EMERGENCY COMMITTEE OF ACCA
Annandale Christian Community for Action (ACCA)
7200 Columbia Pike
Annandale, VA 22003
TEL: 703-256-1378
Purpose: To help families in crisis.
Sponsor: Annandale Christian Community for Action
Contact: Ann Marie Hicks, Chairman; Joan Parnell, Food Pantry Chairman
Description: With scores of volunteers in assistance, the Family Emergency Committee is able to reach out to hundreds of families each year with food, financial aid, and the assurance that someone cares. The Committee itself consists of about 16 *Telephone Captains,* who are on duty in pairs for a week at a time to receive emergency calls from Hotline, Social Services, ministers, the ACCA Day Care Centers, and other volunteer and community agencies. They rotate duty about every six to eight weeks.

The Food Captain receives calls for food requests. After a need is established, one of over fifty volunteers on file is called. The volunteer goes to the food pantry, collects a week's worth of food, and delivers it to the needy family. The Food Pantry is stocked with canned goods and paper products donated by members of ACCA churches. Meat and dairy products are purchased with money from a state grant. A group of volunteers shops for the pantry and keeps it well stocked and well organized, enabling ACCA to provide an average of 3,000 meals per month to approximately 145 people. During 1988, an average of 45 volunteers participated in this effort each month.

The Money Captain collects messages from ACCA's answering machine and handles requests for financial assistance. She takes information and together with the coordinator decides what help ACCA can offer. In addition to immediate financial aid, the program tries to be sure the recipient is in touch with long range help - whether that be social assistance, applying for subsidized housing, pastoral counseling, fuel assistance, credit counseling or other uses of the numerous community services available.

Requests for rental assistance continue to take up the largest part of Family Emergency expenses. Families often must spend more than 60% of their income for rent. Low income housing as well as moderately-priced housing are becoming scarce as more and more apartments convert to condominiums and/or raise their rents yearly. This is a major problem, particularly with the high number of single parents, refugees and people on fixed incomes. We try to keep people in their housing by helping with rent, giving food in order to free up income for rental expenses, and suggesting roommates or other cost-cutting ideas.

Increased support from ACCA churches made possible a good level of assistance in 1988. Financial outreach has climbed steadily each year - from $49,214 in 1984 to $59,506 in 1987 to $65,460 in 1988. Over $52,000 of that total in 1988 went to assist 328 families with rent. Forty-eight families received help with utility bills, and 100 families were assisted with medical bills and other necessary living expenses such as baby formula and supplies, transportation, and shoes. The team effort is what makes the program a success - from those who donate food, to those who deliver weekly food and Thanksgiving and Christmas baskets, to those who answer phone calls.

Publications: Family Emergency Committee Overview

FAR NORTHWEST CAREGIVERS

10633 Lake Creek Parkway
Austin, TX 78750
TEL: 512-250-5021
Purpose: To keep the elderly in their homes by providing services by volunteers.
Sponsor: Pond Springs Baptist Church
Contact: Dee Bruer, Director
Description: The *Far Northwest Caregivers* recognizes the need by many older persons to remain independent and not become burdens to their families. The organization is operated by a group of volunteers who seek to keep the elderly in their homes by providing transportation, visitation, telephone reassurance and short-term meal delivery.

Volunteers in the program have enlisted the help of various community groups not only to donate but also to serve the food needed for special outings. "This gets them involved," according to one volunteer.

Volunteers also stand by to drive seniors on errands, to the doctor, hairdresser or shopping mall. They make corsages, boutonniers and wreaths for special occasions such as birthdays, anniversaries and holidays.

A major activity for the seniors is the organization's *Seniors Day Out* at *Pond Springs Baptist Church* twice each month. About 50 seniors regularly attend, eating a lunch or snacks, and participating in activities such as bridge, dominoes and card games.

The *Far Northwest Caregivers* has been operating since late 1986 and each year more and more seniors call for services that will help keep them in their homes.
Founded: 1986

FIELD EDUCATION PROGRAM

Holy Redeemer College
Department of Field Education
1701 Sharp Road
Waterford, WI 53185
TEL: 414-534-3191
Purpose: To offer the students an opportunity for a guided experience in service to others in the wider community.
Sponsor: Holy Redeemer College
Contact: Rev. Richard Thibodeau, C.Ss.R.
Description: This program has been in operation since the College began in 1968. It is totally funded by the college. It is seen as a vital part of the discernment process for young men considering the Catholic priesthood as a Redemptorist priest or brother.
The program is coordinated by a director at the college and enlists local supervisors wherever the students assist. Presently all

full-time students are involved in some project in the department. Training for a particular area is conducted jointly by the director of the college program in conjunction with the local supervisor. Workshops, seminars and speakers are utilized when possible to give a broader introduction and assistance. Evaluation sheets are used both by the students and their local supervisors. Goals for each student are required in his particular area and the director meets periodically with each student to review these. Meetings with each team of a particular work group are also held to see how the team is functioning and to air any problems or reinforce the positive.

Areas of work have included social justice ministry, Spanish work, youth retreats, work with juvenile delinquents, hospital visitation, work with the mentally handicapped, religious education, nursing homes, underground switchboard (crisis "hot-line"), and deaf work among others.
Founded: 1968

FRED RUFFING MEMORIAL SCHOLARSHIP
SEE FUNDING/FUND-RAISING/RELATED SERVICES: HANDICAPPED

FREE HOTLINE
SEE INFORMATION & REFERRAL

FRIEND TO FRIEND PROGRAM*
Jewish Social Service Agency
6127 Montrose Road
Rockville, MD 20852
TEL: 301-881-3700
Purpose: To provide teenage friends for retarded teenagers.
Sponsor: Jewish Social Service Agency
Contact: Erika Engelman, Volunteer
Description: Fifty volunteers in the Friend to Friend Program spend several hours a week with their handicapped friends. The volunteers have been impressed with the responsibility to which they are committing themselves - entering into a year's contract to develop a friendship with a retarded teenager.

Each handicapped person in the program is matched with a volunteer of about the same age and sex (median age of volunteers is 17 years). The time they spend together is utilized in a variety of ways - learning to bake, going to a museum or to the movies, having a slumber party, playing baseball. In some cases, the handicapped person has been taking his/her first outing without parents.

Both the prospective volunteer and the family of the retarded child are interviewed carefully in order to achieve the best matching. In many instances, it is necessary to guard against a family's unrealistic expectations of the program, while helping them to key themselves to its real benefits.

The Volunteer Services Coordinator has found that the young volunteers need continuing support and supervision if the relationships are to work out successfully. She maintains telephone contact with the volunteers and the parents of the handicapped young people. At least once a month, she meets or talks by phone at length with individual volunteers.

In addition, group meetings for the volunteers are held bi-monthly, and an educational program is offered; for example, a field trip to a diagnostic clinic of the National Institute of Mental Health was arranged.

The most effective recruitment of volunteers is by word of mouth. Talking to groups of high school students was found to be unsuccessful. It is more difficult to recruit male volunteers, and attempts are being made to interest groups of boys in taking on one handicapped youngster per group. The boys seem to feel more comfortable if the responsibility is shared.

The volunteers look at this opportunity as a serious experience and understand that the time commitment is a necessity. Some of the volunteers continue in the program for a number of years. They see their efforts helping the handicapped young person to improve his/her self-image and make progress toward a more fulfilling life. Many volunteers have expressed interest in majoring in special education or social work after their experiences in the Friend to Friend Program.

FURNITURE COMMITTEE OF ACCA
Annandale Christian Community for Action (ACCA)
7200 Columbia Pike
Annandale, VA 22003
TEL: 703-256-1378
Purpose: To meet the basic need of families for adequate furniture.
Sponsor: ACCA
Contact: Betty Jane and George Davis, Co-Chairmen
Description: The number of families needing furniture in ACCA's service area is growing rapidly. Many are coming out of shelters. Through responses to requests of ACCA churches and others in the community for good used furniture, apartments and houses are being completely furnished by the program.
In addition, the number of people from other countries has been growing yearly since 1975. They are in need, also, of complete households of furnishings. The Hispanics are the largest group, with people coming from Brazil, Bolivia, Colombia, El Salvador, Nicaragua, Chile, Honduras, Mexico, Venezuela, Peru and other countries.
In 1988 ACCA volunteers worked on 41 Saturdays. Eighteen of the ACCA churches participated. Each church is asked to provide a truck, trailor or van, and five volunteers. Fairfax County provides a truck and driver each week. The Falls Church Community Council shares the work with ACCA.
Among the volunteers are five Saturday Supervisors and three women taking donation calls.
During 1988 the Furniture Committee made 463 pickups and gave furniture to 245 households.
Publications: ACCA Annual Report
Founded: 1988

GIFT TO THE CITY
Habitat for Humanity/Philadelphia
4211 Chestnut Street
Philadelphia, PA 19104
TEL: 215-387-7592
Purpose: To enable families without an opportunity to buy a house at low cost and receive supportive services to maintain it.
Sponsor: Presbyterian Church USA
Contact: Marshall McBride, Supervisor
Description: Presbyterians from about 30 local congregations are rehabilitating housing for low-income people as their *Gift to the City.* About 200 volunteers are working with *Habitat for Humanity,* the ecumenical Christian housing ministry. Habitat relies on volunteers to restore urban shells into homes for low-income families. The homes, financed by Habitat, are sold at an average price of $30,000.
Although the project was initiated during a Presbyterian USA Assembly marking its 200th anniversary, volunteers come from all denominations, as well as non-churchgoers from all walks of life. Salesman, plumbers, doctors, lawyers, carpenters, Quakers, Episcopalians, Methodists and Catholics can be found among the volunteers. They are helping with Habitat projects in North Philadelphia, West Philadelphia and Coatesville, Chester County, and at a South Philadelphia site sponsored by another organization. While most volunteers are from suburban churches, West Philadelphia volunteers are from center city churches. Area Presbyterians also are contributing $105,000 to the cause.
Habitat plans to build five new homes at the North Philadelphia location this year, with 12 others scheduled to be built in the future. Future homeowners, some of whom are selected before the work begins, will get no-intereest mortgages over 20-25 years, with monthly $125-$150 payments. Also, they must donate 500 hours

of "sweat equity" working on the project. They are chosen on the basis of their income, need, and attitude. The initial down payment for the no-interest loans is about $500.
The real goal is rebuilding the neighborhoods. The volunteers, many of them white, met with hesitation, caution and suspicion at first, but more local involvement - especially in West Philadelphia - is stressed now, and this brings the people in the community together with volunteers from outside the area where they can get to know each other while working together. Put in the words of a supervisor at one of the sites, who called the volunteers *terrific workers,* "They're giving people who wouldn't have any chance of doing so a chance to buy a nice house."

GONZAGA ACTION PROGRAM (GAP)
Gonzaga University
Campus Ministry
Spokane, WA 99258
TEL: 509-328-4220/Ext. 4242
Purpose: To coordinate University students with various relief agencies and private needs throughout the Spokane community.
Sponsor: Gonzaga University and the Associated Students of Gonzaga University
Contact: Linda Bacci, Coordinator
Description: Gonzaga Action Program (GAP) is a student-run organization which coordinates student volunteers with numerous relief organizations as well as with private requests from the community. GAP is a non-profit organization which is funded through the Associated Students of Gonzaga University.
The GAP office is composed of a student director and student staff members - all elected to their positions. Students may either volunteer their time or be paid through *Government Work Study,* depending on financial status. The overall GAP coordinator is a member of the University Campus Ministry team, and his/her job is to help make decisions and maintain GAP's standard of professionalism. The individual GAP programs are coordinated by student volunteers who work with the student and staff director, and volunteers serve in these programs.
An average of 299 students participate in such relief programs as Big Brothers and Big Sisters, Excelsior Youth Home, Senior Contact Service Visitation, House of Charity, Cerebral Palsy Bowling, Hospice, and Shriners' Hospital. Volunteers also do tutoring, hospital work, and Campus Outreach - a program designed to meet the immediate needs of the community.
Volunteer duties vary depending upon the different programs. Volunteers for House of Charity work with the organization's staff members to provide meals and sleeping facilities for transient men, while volunteers in the Cerebral Palsy Bowling program spend one Saturday a month assisting CP patients as they bowl. In the visitation programs, volunteers spend a few hours a week as a companion offering friendship and a listening ear on a one-to-one basis, and volunteers have the choice of working with the elderly, the terminally ill, or troubled teenagers.

GOOD SAMARITAN RECOGNITION CEREMONY
SEE ADMINISTRATION: RECOGNITION

GREEK FESTIVAL
Sts. Constantine & Helen Greek Orthodox Cathedral
30 Malvern Avenue
Richmond, VA 23221
TEL: 804-355-3687
Purpose: To introduce area residents to authentic Greek food and other cultural experiences.
Contact: John G. Halages, Festival Chairman
Description: Volunteer cooks work for months making desserts and organizing preparations to feed some 65,000 people who come to the *Greek Festival* to learn about Greek culture. The four-day event provides the flavor and old-world culture of Greece in a seemingly endless spread of Greek specialties. With today's

cholesterol consciousness, cooks introduced foods that were authentic, yet healthful, according to one of the volunteer cooks. Repeat attendees often seek out their favorite choices from years past, and first-time festivalgoers are given a briefing on the preparation and ingredients of the Greek dishes. Proceeds from the festival benefit the *Virginia Head Injury Foundation, Virginia Health Center,* and the *Emergency Shelter.*

In addition to food, the festival features Greek music, costumed folk dancers, cathedral tours, and film lectures. Also available is a Greek boutique with Oriental rugs, imported jewelry, arts, crafts and icons. For those who enjoyed a specific authentic Greek food item, a cookbook, *Cherished Greek Recipes,* is made available at the festival or, if copies are depleted, by mail after the event.

All proceeds go to the three targeted charities, and all expenditures by visitors are tax-deductible.

HABITAT FOR HUMANITY OF RHODE ISLAND
c/o David Addink
23 Ashton
Narragansett, RI 02882
TEL: 401-783-0769
Purpose: To involve volunteer labor in building and refurbishing affordable housing.
Sponsor: Habitat for Humanity International
Contact: David Addink, Volunteer
Description: Low-income families hoping to buy houses from the nonprofit *Habitat for Humanity* are asked to invest at least 300 hours of sweat equity - or 500 hours if they want to avoid a second mortgage - in the building or refurbishing of the homes. In Providence, these volunteer potential home-buyers are joined by volunteers from churches and others from across the community. Volunteers do everything from filling foundation cavities with rock to stacking and oiling foundation boards to painting the final product. Volunteers uncomfortable with or unable to perform construction work participate instead in selecting eligible families, acquiring lands or raising funds.

Construction experience is not needed for the project, since experienced workers are available at every site to help the uninitiated put their volunteer hours to good use. One volunteer summed up his involvement this way: "I grew up on a farm and it was quite customary for me as a boy to help out a neighbor. I think if you grow up with that background then it's easy to do it later on."

Costs are kept as low as possible for potential buyers. An example is a townhouse in Providence that would list in the open market for $100,000. A family selected by *Habitat for Humanity* volunteers will pay $39,900.

Although volunteers work year-round in the program, one week every year is declared a "special worldwide work week," during which time it is hoped that all local projects will make a special effort to show their full cadres of volunteers during the entire special week.

HELP-ON-WHEELS
Lutheran Metropolitan Ministry
Cancer Task Force
3800 Bridge Avenue
Cleveland, OH 44113
TEL: 216-696-2715
Purpose: To provide transportation for those people who need radiation therapy.
Sponsor: Lutheran Metropolitan Ministry
Contact: Reverend David R. Beese
Description: The Cancer Task Force began meeting in March 1978 with representatives of the medical profession, social services, clergy, and lay members of congregations which have special interest in cancer problems. About a dozen persons attended the first meeting.

For a full year the Task Force studied, talked about, and checked

on the most urgent needs and the best available help for terminal cancer patients. Agencies presently serving their needs in some ways were listed, their services summarized, and a mailing to all congregations was prepared which reported the findings. Gradually, the study and discussions of the Task Force revealed that, though there were areas of need such as home care, spiritual visitation, financial help, job problems, family counseling and others, the area that could be most readily served was transportation for radiation treatment for those patients who had no other means to travel.

Further study revealed that it would be best to start small, since other agencies had foundered by attempting too much. With the cooperation of the Lutheran Medical Center in the summer of 1979, such a program was begun. Mt. Calvary Lutheran Church was the original congregation to supply a twelve-person team of volunteers, and coordinate the scheduling of passengers and drivers. Trips reached 200 per month.

A year later, the Cleveland Foundation granted funds ($78,000) for a three-year period to the Task Force. A full-time staff person is in place, and the transportation program has expanded to all eight hospitals in the Cleveland area which offer radiation therapy. With continuing expansion a necessity, volunteer recruitment is an ongoing activity of the Task Force.

The Task Force also is active in establishing Make Today Count groups for persons who are facing terminal illness and their families, and is involved in an examination of the hospice movement. In addition to serving on Boards of hospice organizing groups, the Task Force holds clergy seminars at Lutheran Medical Center on the work of the clergy with those who are terminally ill.
Founded: 1978

HOST (HANDS OF SHARED TIME)
SEE VOLUNTEERS: STUDENTS

HOUSING PROGRAM OF ACCA
Annandale Christian Community for Action (ACCA)
7200 Columbia Pike
Annandale, VA 22003
TEL: 703-256-1378
Purpose: To help alleviate the pressure within the County for affordable housing.
Sponsor: ACCA
Contact: Marie Monsen, Housing Chair
Description: For ACCA's Housing Program, 1988 marked a year of change. With the growth in the number of homeless people and the tremendous pressure in Fairfax County to provide more affordable housing, we decided it was time to expand in this area. After examining ACCA's involvement, it was decided to divest the program of the two houses owned by ACCA and the mortgages being held on other properties, and to look for new avenues of service in the housing area. (The houses, which were rented to low-income families, were sold to their occupants at cost.) In keeping with ACCA's philosophy of putting ACCA money to work in the community, all current programs were reviewed. The Housing Committee explored a number of options. As of January 1989, ACCA membership approved the following:

- $18,000 to *Shelter House* to launch a Transitional Housing Program. This helps families move from emergency housing to permanent housing by providing help for rent, deposits, and living expenses as well as job training and counseling.
- $4,500 to the Bailey's Crossroads Shelter for a Transitional Housing Program which assists single adults in moving into permanent housing.

Other housing programs under consideration for ACCA support included the County-sponsored *Project Homes,* where families are "sponsored" by a church or family for 4-6 months, and the *Habitat for Humanity* program, which raises money and volunteers to build new homes and rehabilitate older homes. In addition, because of the escalating demand for furniture, membership voted to give $10,000 of the money generated by the sales of old properties to the Furniture Warehouse to purchase items in great demand and to reduce the backlog of requests. Another $20,000 was given to the Day Care Center to help launch a new *Day Care Center for Infants* - a growing need for many working mothers. Completed in 1990, it is housed on the grounds of ACCA I in Annandale.

ACCA expects coming years to present many challenges in the area of housing and invites interested individuals and groups to come forward and assist with ideas and volunteer time and support.

Publications: ACCA Annual Report

INFORME SIDA
SEE VOLUNTEERS: ETHNIC GROUPS

INTERFAITH SHELTER NETWORK
San Diego County Ecumenical Conference
c/o METRO
861 Sixth Avenue, Suite 810
San Diego, CA 92101
TEL: 619-234-3158
Purpose: To fight homelessness throughout San Diego county.
Sponsor: County of San Diego
Contact: Mary Niez, Network Coordinator; Rev. Dennis Mikulanis, Conference President
Description: On July 1, 1989, the *San Diego County Ecumenical Conference* was awarded a joint City and County contract and became the administrator of the *Interfaith Shelter Network.* The network involves more than 100 congregations throughout the county that work to fight homelessness. The Regional Task Force on the Homeless, which directed the program since its inception in 1987, is a planning and coordinating agency and not set up to run long-term programs.

About half of the 100 congregations in the network house up to 12 guests for two or four weeks a year and are called "host congregations." The other half assist the hosts by providing meals, overnight volunteers and transportation. There is only one paid staff member, the Network Coordinator, with an office at METRO, the United Methodist social service agency.

Clusters of congregations, called branches, operated this year in La Jolla-Pacific Beach, South Bay, East County, Point Loma-Ocean Beach, North County Coastal, North County Inland, North Park-Hillcrest and College Heights.

A pilot program was operated in Southeast San Diego in the spring of 1989, with plans set for work in the Clairemont-Kearny Mesa and San Dieguito areas. Recruiting of volunteers takes place each year in June and July to assure adequate resources for the fall-winter-spring shelter season. Training is conducted in August and September.

Founded: 1987

ISAIAH HOUSE
Corpus Christi Catholic Church
71 Prince Street
Rochester, NY 14605
TEL: 716-325-2424
Purpose: To provide an alternative for people for whom it is impossible to remain at home.
Sponsor: Corpus Christi Catholic Church
Contact: Kathie Quinlan, Director
Description: We are a small, two-bed facility called *Isaiah House,* and we hold the philosophy that terminally ill people should be able to die at home, since care focuses on providing comfort, not on prolonging life. When remaining at home becomes impossible because there are no family members to care for a patient, or when a person is homeless or has no insurance to cover the cost of a private nurse, small hospices like *Isaiah House* provide an environment like home. A ministry of *Corpus Christi Catholic*

Church, Isaiah House is located in a blue, three-story, wood-sided home with a large front porch with colorful flower boxes, and an English Garden in the back.

On the waiting list, *Isaiah House* has homeless people and AIDS patients, elderly people and those with families far away. Though limited in the number of people it can serve, the hospice reaches a group of people who often fall through the cracks of the health care system.

Volunteers are the backbone of the facility, and come from numerous creeds, professions and backgrounds. Some volunteers are nurses who have worked with the dying.

Care ranges from arranging medicine schedules to assigning nurses and aides to help a patient's family provide care at home.

Although *Isaiah House* maintains only two beds within the facility so they won't have to go through the licensing process with the state, it acts more like a surrogate family than certified hospice programs do, according to its director. Staff and volunteers spend quiet vigils at bedsides of terminally-ill patients who spend anywhere from weeks to mere hours there.

The hospice also generates interest in other local areas. After learning about *Isaiah House,* a Bible study class at *Bethlehem Lutheran Church* in Fairfield has made the development of its own hospice, *Advent House,* its ministry. Also, the hospices become outreach programs for a number of area churches.

Founded: 1987

JESUIT SERVICE PROJECT
SEE VOLUNTEERS: STUDENTS

JEWISH VOLUNTEER ASSOCIATION
SEE ADMINISTRATION: LOCAL CENTER

JOB SEARCH
Catholic Charities
1231 Prytania Street
New Orleans, LA 70130
TEL: 504-523-3755
Purpose: To serve as a communication link between job searchers and employers.
Sponsor: Catholic Charities
Contact: James Livingston, Director
Description: Job Search is a program of *Catholic Charities* designed to provide employment assistance for clients - most of them desperately in need of work. The service provides job search training and orientation, placement, referral and follow-up. Volunteers also make referrals to other resources clients may need. One volunteer came to the program through an alternative sentencing requirement of 50 hours of community service after a traffic violation, and never left.

The program begins when a volunteer enters the office and "pushes the button on the answering machine." Word of mouth has served to make the service an easy one to approach. Phone messages are answered promptly, showing the program's concern for the individual's distress. Each caller has a different problem, according to one volunteer. They are asked to sign up for job training, and a job search is immediately begun. While the placement is being sought, volunteers give job-seekers words of hope and encouragement, someone to talk to while the problem is addressed.

JUVENILE RECEPTION AND DIAGNOSTIC CENTER (JRDC)
PO Box 116
Baker, CA 70704-0116
TEL: 504-774-7720
Purpose: To provide academic testing, psychological evaluation, and therapeutic treatment to residents committed to the LA Department of Corrections.

Sponsor: Los Angeles Department of Corrections
Contact: Martin B. Patton, Director
Description: The Center is a division of the Los Angeles Department of Corrections, and is the receiving unit for both male and female juvenile offenders committed by the Los Angeles Courts. Personnel consists of diagnostic, custodial and treatment staff. The Center services three kinds of offenders: those who will transfer to a schooling campus within two weeks, those in residences at the maximum security unit, and thirty, sixty, and ninety day evaluation-only commitments.

Staff provides psychological, medical, social and educational evaluations of each resident before he/she is assigned to an institution or returning to court for a hearing. Personnel at the Juvenile Adjustment Center, a maximum security unit, are involved in a treatment program consisting of academics, living skills, G.E.D. preparation, work, counseling, and art classes.

Volunteer Staff: At present, approximately thirty (30) volunteers work in a number of positions. Volunteers provide all religious services, work in arts and crafts and aerobic dance classes and provide parties.

Volunteer Duties: Volunteers perform a number and variety of duties at different times of day - church services on the weekends and bible study in the evenings to instructing art classes and arranging exhibits, providing tutoring, conducting aerobic dance classes, participating in recreation, assisting residents with letter writing, hosting parties, performing concerts and puppet shows and making donations.

Volunteer Experience: Volunteers are able to work at JRDC with varying levels of skills and experience. Expertise is matched with job descriptions, special training is sometimes provided.

Orientation and agreement contracts are required for all incoming volunteers. One-to-one supervision is often given.

LOAVES & FISHES

401 Missouri Avenue
Fort Worth, TX 76104
TEL: 817-334-0903
Purpose: To provide meals, employment counseling, and other services to homeless persons and others in need.
Sponsor: Charity Sports
Contact: Volunteer Coordinator
Description: Founded in 1982, *Loaves & Fishes* has become a distributor of donated food to various charitable, nonprofit agencies serving the needy, sick and elderly - in addition to its many other services. The agencies receiving food include church groups, direct-aid programs, rehabilitation centers, residential treatment facilities and senior citizen centers. At any given time, the *Loaves & Fishes Food Bank* serves between 50 and 100 of these organizatgions on a regular weekly basis. *Loaves & Fishes* depends solely on the donations and volunteer labor.

In addition, the *Loaves & Fishes Soup Kitchen* serves between 150 and 300 homeless and hungry people daily. Other services include employment counseling and job placement, birth certificates and ID replacement, transportation to job sites, a mail center, and hair cuts for job seekers.

Nutritional but unsellable food is donated regularly to the *Loaves & Fishes Food Bank* by various agents such as supermarkets, food brokers, food manufacturers, individuals and groups. *Loaves & Fishes* inspects all food donations before preparing them for delivery. Donors can make use of the *1978 Tax Reform Act* and are covered for liability under the *Good Faith Donor Act*.

Community support for the program is excellent, with more and more innovative ways to raise funds being implemented by individuals, groups, and businesses. A 1989 program called *Help the Homeless Million Dollar Shootout* held at four driving ranges was termed by its local business sponsors as "a fun way to benefit a favorite Fort Worth charity."
Founded: 1982

LOUISIANA TRAINING INSTITUTE*

PO Box 1631
Monroe, LA 71210
TEL: 318-323-4406
Purpose: To provide long-term custody and rehabilitative education to youth offenders.
Sponsor: State of Louisiana
Contact: W. A. Massey, Prot. Chaplain, Director, or Volunteer Coordinator
Description: Louisiana Training Institute-Monroe is a long-term state residential correctional institution charged with custody of the state's adjudicated delinquents. The population is made up of 300 youths between the ages of 14-21. The program is composed of both academic and vocational education. It also maintains a full religion program.

The volunteer program was begun over 60 years ago (1930) with an emphasis on religious activity. It is still basically a religious program, but does include other areas of concern. The basic objective is the enrichment of the experiences of the youth committed to the school.

Organizational structure of the Institute includes volunteers who are recruited because of their management abilities, in addition to other qualities. These volunteers become volunteer coordinators for the various volunteer programs of the institution. One volunteer coordinator coordinates volunteers from 40 churches where, among other activities, the volunteers provide monthly birthday parties for nine cottages. Other coordinators coordinate crafts instructors in our Boys' Club, Bible study instructors, and Chapel program participants.

In this way, about 250 volunteers (mostly occasional) become involved in activities for our students. Presently, four volunteers are volunteer coordinators for various programs. They are supervised by the director of volunteer services. Volunteers who are primarily counselors are supervised by the counseling staff.
Founded: 1930

LUTHER PLACE WOMEN'S SHELTER

Luther Place Memorial Church
1226 Vermont Avenue, NW
Washington, DC 20005
TEL: 202-386-5464 (Shelter); 202-667-1377 (church)
Purpose: To provide shelter for women in need of a place to stay.
Description: Since the city opens emergency sleeping areas in government buildings only when the temperature drops below 25 degrees at night, the unusually warm winter of 1989-90 found few nights that met the city's emergency plan. This did not alleviate the need for shelter, and the *Luther Place Women's Shelter,* in the words of the minister directing the program, was "in turmoil."

The shelter, which opened in 1975 as one of the first church shelters in the city, limits the 100 beds to women, since city shelters offer beds for men.

The 280-member congregation of the *Luther Place Memorial Church* fully supports the shelter program. Members cook and serve meals, work overnight in the shelter, work on related committees and contribute money. The shelter turns no one away. If men show up at the door, church volunteers find them spaces in the city-run shelters. All women are accommodated, even if it means putting mattresses on the floor. The church offers a full dinner each night and a breakfast in the morning.

While most women in the past who sought shelter had mental problems, today there are drug addicts and those with medical problems so serious that they cannot leave the church during the day. In one case, church members transported a homeless woman back and forth to the hospital for dialysis.

The director and the church members see the homeless shelter as an obvious response by a church to the homeless. "Jesus was born a homeless person. There was no space at the Inn."

LUTHERAN SOCIAL SERVICES VOLUNTEER PROGRAM
Lutheran Social Services of Colorado
2695 Alcott
Suite 3385
Denver, CO 80211
TEL: 303-433-6371
Purpose: To plan and carry out volunteer projects that will benefit the community.
Sponsor: Lutheran Church in America; The American Lutheran Church; Association of Evangelical Lutheran Churches; Lutheran Church/Missouri Synod
Contact: Lori Houchen
Description: Lutheran Social Services of Colorado was incorporated in the Spring of 1979. In April 1980, the position of Director of Volunteer Ministries was created to plan volunteer services for all of the programs in which Lutheran Social Services of Colorado (LSSC) is involved. Since LSSC was formed when three services came together, programs spanned age groups with activities for infants as well as elderly, and covered numerous areas ranging from alcohol intervention to institutional visitation. Volunteer projects in operation today are:
- **Hospital and Nursing Home Volunteers** - The hospital volunteer program involves a congregation in "adoption" of a specific hospital where they provide regular weekly visits. When the volunteer sees a patient need that can be filled by the Chaplain, he/she completes and leaves in a designated place in the room a coded sheet informing the Chaplain of specific concerns regarding the patient. The volunteer also provides or arranges for other needs, such as housing and transportation for visiting family members, and after-hospital care for some patients. Fourteen hospitals are being served, involving 13 churches and 50 volunteers. Nursing home volunteers operated in a similar fashion, although the focus here is on elderly people only. Thirty-seven volunteers serve area nursing homes.
- **Refugee Resettlement Volunteers** - Volunteers serve as sponsors for refugees being resettled in this country. In most cases, sponsorship means that the congregation accepts full responsibility for a family and provides financial and personal support for the family until it is self-sufficient. In cases where a congregation is not available for sponsorship, a group of volunteers may coordinate a sponsorship. Volunteers provide transportation, tutoring in English as a Second Language, assistance with employment, and airport transfer for refugees passing through the city. Including congregational volunteers, approximately 200 persons are involved in refugee resettlement.
- **Problem Pregnancy Volunteers** - Approximately 25 volunteers are working with unwed mothers, providing birth education and support for the pregnant young girls.
- **Family to Family Volunteers** - This program involves volunteer families who work to support neighbors who are experiencing stress. Currently, 35 families are involved in this program.
- **Other Volunteer Projects** - In other efforts, 45 volunteers are cooperating with the Denver Public School system in a tutoring program. A Skills Bank has been created and currently lists 25 volunteers who have offered skills ranging from transportation for pregnant girls, to reading to elderly persons and taking senior citizens shopping, to providing office help.
- **Training** - At present, training is provided for hospital and nursing home volunteers, refugee resettlement volunteers and family-to-family volunteers.
Founded: 1979

M.O.M.S. (MOTHERS ON THE MOVE SPIRITUALLY)
SEE VOLUNTEERS: PARENTS

MANNA BOWL
First Lutheran Church
1244 South Utica
Tulsa, OK 74104
TEL: 918-582-0917; 918-492-7874
Purpose: To feed the unemployed of the city.
Sponsor: First Lutheran Church - other churches & private donations
Contact: Esther Endres, Volunteer Coordinator
Description: Manna Bowl was started to offer a hot meal two days each week. Those who attend are mostly men who, because of the economy, are unemployed. Women and children are welcome. The program operates under the leadership of First Lutheran Church, but donations of food, money and clothing come from other churches, markets, bakeries, and private sources. The entire staff is volunteer.
Volunteer Staff: At this time, 40 volunteers work varying times and days. The cook, coordinator, and all others who work are giving their time and expertise to the project. There have been over 400 donors to the program. Manna Bowl has been serving since September 13, 1982, and averages serving 150 persons each day.
Volunteer Duties: The Coordinator is in charge of the feeding process, the scheduling of workers, and the picking up of food products which are not delivered. He provides leadership to those who set up the eating area, serve the food, and the clean-up. He oversees the dining room during the meal and takes care of any problems arising during the meal - before and after. All donations are filed and volunteers send thank you notes and letters for taxable donations requested.
The Cook is in total charge of the kitchen, the preparation, cooking, and storing of foods and directing the volunteers who work in the kitchen. She works very closely with the coordinator. Other volunteer duties include - preparing the meat, vegetables, fruit, etc., to be used by the cook in making soup and other things. When sandwiches are served they are made by volunteers who have procured a food permit from the public health department. The kitchen is set up for assembly line serving. Tables and chairs are put into place, cleaned after the meal, tables and chairs removed, floors cleaned, all equipment cleaned, dishes washed and placed in cabinets, trash removed to proper containers, refrigerators and freezers cleaned, cupboards kept clean and neat, the laundry of towels, aprons, other linen is done.
Volunteer Experience: The Coordinator is a retired public relations man who understands the needs of the guests at the meals. He is capable of meeting the many needs which arise every day and dealing firmly with them.
The cook was with the Tulsa Public School cafeterias for years, so comes with much knowledge of cooking for large numbers as well as heading up a kitchen and its workers. She is a good organizer. Other volunteers need only to be willing workers, and not mind menial tasks - some not too pleasant. They need to be uncomplaining, non-judgmental, and compassionate. A word from the Volunteer Coordinator: "There is always a need for more volunteers."
Founded: 1982

MANNA, INC.*
1711 Fourteenth Street, NW
Washington , DC 20009
TEL: 202-462-8686
Purpose: To make it possible for low- and moderate-income residents to become homeowners.
Sponsor: Local Initiatives Support Corporation
Contact: Jim Dickerson, Executive Director
Description: Established in 1972, Manna, Inc. has a long history of programs that enable low-income people to own homes. It was founded by a minister on the premise that everyone deserves a decent and affordable place to live. Its basic philosophy is

"housing for people, not profit."

Manna focuses on acquisition, rehabilitation and new construction. By fall 1989, working through often confusing, often complicated bureaucratic and financial systems, Manna had completed nearly 2,000 new or rehabilitated housing units in the city for low- and moderate-income residents. In spite of these impressive numbers, however, Manna has a waiting list averaging 500 families.

The DC government, private industry, and foundations fund the current $1.6 million project. Some insured homeowner loans come from the *US/HUD Federal National Mortgage Association,* with others provided by the city's *Department of Housing and Community Development's Home Purchase Assistance Program.*

A recent project, *Victory Lane,* is composed of five single-family, 10 condominium, and two duplex houses. Five of the condominiums were completed and the subject of a celebration on April 4, 1990. The land for the project was reduced in price by the city to make the project possible. In addition to local banks the nonprofit financing organization, *Local Initiative Support Corporation,* provides construction funds.

To minimize what is considered one of the greatest risks in the city, Manna volunteer advocates follow up with homeowners until it is certain that the individual housing situation is stable. Working in neighborhoods where traditional developers are reluctant to work, Manna has gained a reputation among housing advocates as one of the most successful nonprofit housing developers in the area.

MEALS ON WHEELS OF BIRMINGHAM

2718 19th Place South
Birmingham, AL 35209
TEL: 205-870-5042
Purpose: To deliver warm meals to homebound residents over 60 years old who cannot prepare their own meals.
Contact: Linda Hayes, Director
Description: Meals on Wheels started in England after World War II and evolved into a non-profit organization that has spread across the United States. The organization opened a Birmingham branch 13 years ago. The branch relies heavily on more than 800 volunteers in Jefferson County, who cover 44 routes and deliver 525 meals daily. Most of the volunteers are recruited through churches. "Without the cooperation of churches," according to the director, "the Meals on Wheels program would run out of gas."

The program buys food from Bessemer Carraway Medical Center and St. Vincent's Hospital. Vans pick up the food from the hospital kitchens and take it to drop-off points around the county - usually community churches. Volunteers pick up the food and deliver it to the recipients. Most volunteers give two days a week and have a route of nine or ten people. Usually, an individual church manages a designated route.

Meals on Wheels is funded mostly by federal grants and private contributions. Recipients are asked to contribute $1.50 toward the $2.60 cost of each meal, but many recipients can't afford even that and are matched up with sponsors who pay for their meals.

The common response to a request for volunteers is immediate volunteerism from people of all ages. It isn't unusual to get 50-60 volunteers from one presentation. In unusual situations in which a community does not respond, most often paid Meals on Wheels staff members must deliver food to clients in that community. A favorite story of the director's is of a women who received meals after surgery and volunteered to deliver meals when she recovered. The program has a waiting list of more than 700 people needing its services, and it continuously seeks volunteers. Plans to expand into the South East Lake, Bessemer and Cahaba Heights communities must wait until the cadre of volunteers increases to adequately cover these areas.
Founded: 1976

MEALS ON WHEELS PROGRAM OF ACCA
Annandale Christian Community for Action (ACCA)
7200 Columbia Pike
Annandale, VA 22003
TEL: 703-256-1378
Purpose: To serve nutritious meals to people who are ill, handicapped, elderly, or convalescent.
Sponsor: ACCA, Hope Lutheran Church
Contact: Esther Bradsher, Chairperson
Description: Meals for ACCA's Meals on Wheels (MOW) program originate from Fairfax Hospital and Jefferson Memorial Hospital. They are delivered to the ill, handicapped, elderly and convalescent who are unable to shop for or prepare meals to meet their nutritional needs. The Fairfax Hospital meals consist of a hot noon-time meal and a sandwich supper. The Jefferson Hospital meals consist of a hot evening meal and a sandwich noon-time meal for the next day. Volunteers from ACCA Churches are joined by many others from the community to deliver the meals each weekday. Referrals come from personal friendships and the County Council on Aging. Volunteer services are a free gift, as are the meals for those unable to pay the small request of $21.25 per week. Financial assistance is available to help offset the cost, and is utilized by two-thirds of those served. Clients are all ages, but most are over 60 years old.

In 1987 ACCA meals routes were increased from three to five. In 1988 it again became apparent that expansion was necessary. A new route called "Annandale West" was opened, followed by others, making a total of seven routes by 1989. The number of clients fluctuates, but averages between 85 and 90 daily along the seven routes.

The goal is for each route to be manned with a driver and an assistant, but this is a luxury that is not always possible to achieve. With a team on each route expending about two-and-half hours per day, or 9,100 hours per year, and coordinators averaging 500 hours per year, ACCA's meals program would require 3,500 hours per route, or 12,600 hours per year. In 1988, 2,072 meals were delivered on 107 days, using 935 hours of driver time plus many hours of coordinator time for a total of at least 1,500 hours. There were 34 Thanksgiving meals and 36 Christmas meals served.

The five-day-a-week program involves 55-60 volunteers. A small weekend program is maintained serving between 10 and 15 clients. Drivers for the routes claim 22.5 cents per mile reimbursement, and then set it aside to be used to purchase food and supplies for Thanksgiving and Christmas dinners for those without family nearby, or who would not have a holiday meal.

Using the minimum wage figure of $3.50 per hour and mileage reimbursement of 22.5 cents per mile, the program's efforts are equivalent to over $50,000 for the seven week-day routes. All of this, including driver mileage reimbursement, is donated as a gift to assist those in need of the service. A more practical figure of $8.50 per hour for drivers, coordinators, administrative personnel to process payrolls and benefits, vehicle operation and maintenance costs, etc., would bring the program's value to $200,000.

In 1990, a *Meals on Wheels Friendly Telephone Line* was established. Although many homebound persons have telephones, they do not ring often. While meeting the nutritional needs of clients, the program would like to let them know, also, that someone cares enough to call - and perhaps offer an invitation to lunch, a visit, an errand, or just share a cup of coffee. Many genuine and lasting friendships have originated between volunteers and clients.
Publications: ACCA Annual Report; Meals on Wheels Information Packet
Founded: 1986

MIDAS TOUCH
SEE FUNDING/FUND-RAISING/RELATED SERVICES: BUSINESSES

MIRACLE WEEK
Habitat for Humanity of San Antonio
404 North Alamo
San Antonio, TX 78205
TEL: 512-223-5203
Purpose: To help families living in inadequate dwellings to build simple, but decent and affordable, homes.
Sponsor: Habitat for Humanity
Contact: Volunteer Coordinator
Description: In mid-summer 1989, during what has been dubbed *Miracle Week,* hundreds of volunteers built a frame for a four-bedroom house, attached the electrical and plumbing components, completed the interior and exterior trim, put up doors and cabinets, attached the lighting fixtures, arranged for inspection and cleaned up, touched up and hooked up the electric and gas appliances. The object was to raise a house in a week for a family in need. The new 1,000-square-foot home was sold to a low-income family of seven, who worked with the volunteers to build the home, for about $25,000 on a 20-year, no-interest, no-profit mortgage. The home was the 17th since *Habitat for Humanity of San Antonio* began twelve years ago.
Each plot is 50 by 100 feet. The homes are small, but efficiently planned, with three or four bedrooms and one bath. Each house has a sturdy barnlike shed in the back for yard tools. Currently, the houses are surrounded by rolling hills with an old brick convent on the top hill. Habitat officials hope to acquire more land in the same area.
Volunteers come from all walks of life, in some cases in teams from corporations such as the *H.B. Zachry Company,* which provided an entire construction crew, since only licensed, bonded contractors can do the kind of work they volunteered to do. A long list of plumbing, electrical and other local contractors also provided volunteers, as well as work crews from more than a dozen area churches, students from *Trinity University,* and individual volunteers from the community just "showing up to hammer, lift and fetch." In addition, from the Project Director on down, members of *Habitat for Humanity* join the construction teams. This mix of professional and lay craftsman has given the homes a warm, hand-made quality.
Habitat officials feel that house raising, like barn raising, is a great American solution to the dramatic low-income housing shortage. They feel that the recipient families could teach others a lot about frugality because, in spite of the assistance, they still must work very hard and live on a very limited budget. Families who qualify for the small but sturdy homes must have an income from employment, but be unable to "even think about" buying a home in today's market. "*Miracle Week* is designed as a dramatically visual reminder that there is an answer to poverty housing on a much larger scale."
Founded: 1977

MORRIS COUNTY CHAPLAINCY COUNCIL
95 Mount Kemble Avenue
Morristown, NJ 07960
TEL: 201-540-1602
Purpose: To provide supportive services to incarcerated adult offenders, and to adults and juveniles on active probation.
Sponsor: The United Way; local business/industry; churches
Contact: Judy Blackadar
Description: The present Morris County Chaplaincy Council grew out of a desire of local ministers to provide a program for inmates in the County Jail. The Council was incorporated as a non-profit corporation in 1971. Its earliest years were spent in advocating a better physical plant, better-trained personnel, and a substantive rehabilitation program for inmates.
With an LEAA grant in 1972, the Council expanded its staff, developed a well-organized program to train volunteers to work in the jail, and became recognized in the community. Because of the number of people - almost 2,200 a year - passing through the jail,

the Council chose to hire a staff that would coordinate and train a volunteer effort in the jail.
In 1975 United Way joined local churches and Morris County to support the Council, allowing the development of the Post Release Program. The Self-Development of People Program of the United Presbyterian Church provided a substantial grant to make financial assistance possible to released clients, and the Wilks Fund of St. Peter's Episcopal Church gave a one-time grant to enable the Coordinator of Volunteer Services to move from part-time to full-time. In 1977 the Sisters of Charity provided funds for a professionally coordinated and managed Education Program in the jail, and Iona College selected the Council as a field site for pastoral counseling graduate students. Also during this year the Council expanded its volunteer programming to juvenile offenders, working closely with the Morris County Probation Department, the Youth Center, the Youth Shelter, and the Juvenile Court. Today, in addition to support from local Protestant and Catholic Churches and the United Way, support comes from local industry, including Allied Chemical, Exxon, Mennen, Warner-Lambert Pharmaceutical, Beneficial and others. Approximately 100 volunteers lend assistance to the program, but more are needed. Training and orientation is provided by skilled professionals, who also provide counseling, guidance and in-service instruction. One-to-one volunteers are required to participate in a specialized training program held quarterly. Additionally, monthly team meetings are required for all volunteers to share individual learning experiences. Periodic in-service training events are held also throughout the year. Volunteer programs include:

- **One-to-One Adult in Jail:** This is a voluntary program offered sentenced inmates during their last month of incarceration in Morris County Jail. Inmates are screened by the Jail staff and by the Council staff, and paired with a trained volunteer. Volunteers assist clients upon reentry into the community.
- **One-to-One Adult and Juvenile Probation:** This program, in cooperation with the County Probation Department, matches individuals on probation with volunteers for a period not to exceed the length of probation. The volunteer serves as a role model, friend, and counsel during crisis.
- **Women on the Wing:** In this program, volunteers provide visitation, counseling and follow-up to women inmates in jail and following release - establishing contact with families, helping with budgeting, setting goals, etc.
- **Educational Programs:** The Council offers a GED Program for completion of the High School Equivalency Program. Examinations are held quarterly; classes three times weekly. Volunteers assist with remedial tutoring and literacy training.
- **Guided Group Interaction:** Trained by the Administrative Office of the Courts, two volunteers from the Council lead groups of juvenile offenders on a weekly basis for the term of their probation. Youths are referred by County Juvenile Judges.
- **Bed, Breakfast and Supper:** Juveniles in "crisis" may be placed in a Volunteer Host Home by the professional worker involved in the crisis. The juvenile may stay for a period of up to ten days at no cost.

The Morris County Chaplaincy Council is sustained through its Board of Trustees, which meets monthly to establish policies and raise funds. The Board is divided into various program committees and bears the ultimate responsibility for the affairs of the organization.
Founded: 1971

MOVE (MOBILIZATION OF VOLUNTEERS)
SEE VOLUNTEERS: STUDENTS

MT. ADAMS MINISTERIAL ASSOCIATION FOOD BANK
Grace Baptist Church
Route 2, Box 31
White Salmon, WA 98672
TEL: 509-493-3403

Purpose: To provide emergency supplies of food to people in need.
Sponsor: Mt. Adams Ministerial Association; private gifts from area churches
Contact: Gary K. Cowden, President
Description: The Mt. Adams Ministerial Association Food Bank is a locally operated private food bank designed to meet emergency needs of foodstuffs before an applicant can be picked up on one of the welfare programs. Therefore, the Food Bank authorizes the Director to provide three days' supply of food for any one family in any one 30-day period. Referrals to the food bank may come from any of the member churches, the Department of Social and Health Services or the Police Department.
The Food Bank is managed by an all-volunteer staff consisting of one Director, one Assistant Director, and Representatives from each of the participating churches. The Director is responsible to the Association at all times, and the Association makes policy for the food bank. Gifts of money designated for the food bank are processed through the treasury of the Association and used to purchase food when needed to restock the food bank.
The Mt. Adams Ministerial Association is solely responsible for the organization, maintenance and disposition of the food bank. No help from any governmental agency is solicited or desired.

NORFOLK CATHOLIC CHRISTIAN SERVICE PROGRAM
SEE VOLUNTEERS: STUDENTS

OPERATION CLEAN SWEEP
First Presbyterian Church
125 Garden Street
Mount Holly, NJ 08060
TEL: 609-267-0330
Information available also from Rev. Mark A. Medina, Village Church, Prairie Village, Kansas
Purpose: To help clean up, repair and in other ways improve neighborhoods, waterways, playgrounds, parks, and other neglected areas.
Sponsor: First Presbyterian Church
Contact: Donna Kirk, Group Leader
Description: In June 1989, with the help of 65 teenagers from Kansas who were attending a church gathering in Philadelphia, teenagers from churches in the Mount Holly area worked to clean up the Mount Holly Gardens housing development. The effort is part of the church-related nationwide *Operation Clean Sweep.* The young volunteers from Kansas, who paid all of the expenses of their week-long stay, worked with the local teens to clean the streets, the nearby creek, and the buildings - some of which will be painted and repaired, others torn down, with the help of *Habitat for Humanity* and *Homes of Hope.* In addition, they helped the township install playground equipment in the development.
The Kansas youth - members of the *Village Church* in Prairie Village, Kansas - were in the area attending the 201st General Assembly of the *Presbyterian Church of Philadelphia.* "They wanted to make a contribution while attending the Assembly," according to a trip leader. They were housed at the *First Presbyterian Church* in Mount Holly. "Operation Clean Sweep" T-shirts, provided by the *H.W. Fry Realty Corporation,* helped to call attention to their work. As one student put it, "East met midwest, and it was a great cooperative effort!"

OUR COMMUNITY KITCHEN
921 Pleasant
Des Moines, IA 50309
TEL: 515-283-2100
Purpose: "To provide nutrition for the body with dignity for the spirit."
Sponsor: Churches, local community groups and concerned individuals
Contact: Marycecil Dummit (coordinator)

Description: Since January 4, 1983, Our Community Kitchen has been serving free evening meals four nights each week to those in need in the city. The goal is to provide a nutritious meal without stigmatizing the participants in the program. Efforts are made to avoid the soupline image and to promote a friendly atmosphere. The program was started by the Des Moines Urban Mission Council with a $7,000 grant from the United Methodist Hunger Task Force. It is sponsored and funded by churches, community groups, and concerned individuals. It is presently serving over 200 meals each Monday through Thursday at three sites in the city. Each meal consists of a soup or casserole, fruit, sandwiches or freshly-baked bread, and milk or punch.
All work except administration is done by some 50 volunteers under the guidance of a program coordinator. Teams of volunteers prepare the meals in a central kitchen. Another team of volunteers delivers the food to the three serving sites and a third team serves the meals.
The volunteer cooks work a three-week cycle, with each team taking one day in the cycle. They prepare and cook the meal, package the food in containers for delivery and clean up the kitchen and store areas. The volunteer drivers deliver the hot meals to the serving sites on a weekly schedule. The servers, also on a weekly schedule, unpack the food and set up a buffet-style dinner. They help to serve the meals to the elderly, handicapped and small children. They are also in charge of cleaning the facilities and storing the utensils and equipment for the next day.
Founded: 1983

PATERSON HABITAT FOR HUMANITY
511 22nd Street, East
Paterson, NJ 07514
TEL: 201-278-4280
Purpose: To provide safe, affordable housing for low-income families.
Sponsor: Habitat for Humanity International
Contact: The Reverend John Algera
Description: The City of Paterson has a severe housing crisis. Rental units and safe, affordable housing for low-income families are scarce. A group of volunteers, under the leadership of a local pastor, recognized this crisis and focused their efforts on a solution. As a result of their efforts, the ownership of a safe affordable home has become a reality for many and neighborhoods have become revitalized.
Paterson Habitat for Humanity was formed as a nonprofit volunteer organization in 1984. It is an affiliate of the international organization, Habitat for Humanity, whose purpose is to provide affordable housing for the poor and to help them attain home ownership.
The City of Paterson sells city-owned land to Habitat for $1.00. Then, fueled by a primarily volunteer labor force and donated materials, Habitat gets down to the business of building or rehabilitating housing. During 1988, over 500 individuals came to help transform undersized vacant lots into 11 affordable homes. Before 1988, Habitat had constructed 11 new homes and rehabilitated a two-family home.
Habitat families are pre-selected and must contribute 300 hours of "sweat equity" towards the construction of their home. They receive a 10-year interest-free mortgage. The money received from mortgage payments is used to build additional housing. Habitat housing may only be sold to other low-income families.
Since its inception, Habitat has sparked an intense interest in solving the housing crisis in the City of Paterson. Not only has it attracted a large pool of volunteers, Habitat has also built a large community following which includes business and community leaders, local church groups, potential Habitat families and interested citizens.
Paterson's Mayor says, "I cannot think of another group that has provided such an impact on the housing crisis. Their work has sparked other owners to fix up, and ignited private investment.

This program builds responsible citizenship, builds partnerships in the community, and revitalizes a once blighted area."
Publications: Paterson Habitat for Humanity Packet
Founded: 1984

PROJECT GRADUATION
SEE VOLUNTEERS: PARENTS

RE-ENTRY MINISTRIES
PO Box 100461
Birmingham, AL 35210
TEL: 205-322-7966
Purpose: To assist ex-offenders in reestablishing themselves in the community; to provide an interdenominational church for ex-offenders.
Sponsor: St. Mark's Episcopal Church
Contact: Re-Entry Coordinator
Description: Re-Entry Ministries of Birmingham, Alabama, provides comprehensive services to ex-offenders to assist them in regaining a place in the community and becoming productive citizens. Among the services provided are:

- **Re-Entry Ministries Church** - an interdenominational church for ex-offenders with services the first Sunday of each month.
- **Dismas Fellowship** - a support group for ex-offenders, which meets one evening each week.
- **Ruth Fellowship** - a support group for wives, girlfriends, parents or anyone who has a loved one in prison, or recently released from prison, with meetings once each week.
- **AA (Alcoholics Anonymous)** - a sanctioned AA meeting for ex-offenders held one evening each week.
- **Social Activities** - a variety of leisure time activities such as a trip to the zoo, a picnic, concert or football game designed to provide wholesome activities for those who formerly lived on the streets, or in bars or crack houses.
- **One-on-One Counseling** - short-term, family/marital, substance abuse, personal counseling or crisis counseling, providing people to talk to who understand, care and can emotionally support the man or woman during the crucial time of the return to society.
- **In-Prison Services and Ministries** - Pen Pal (ongoing correspondence with inmates); Pre-release talk (information about "life after prison" during the last 90 days of incarceration); Prison visits (assistance with parole plans, special help, ministry to inmates in four prisons each month).
- **Job Assistance** - referrals to employers known to be open to hiring ex-offenders; other personalized assistance as needed (clothes, emergency food, bus passes, help with identification, agency referrals, etc.).
- **Christian Literature** - Bibles and other Christian literature on request.

For ex-offenders with few positive people in their lives to turn to, this re-entry program is an important aspect of their lives.

REHAB PROJECT: NEIGHBORHOOD REVITALIZATION THROUGH HOME OWNERSHIP
Church People for Change and Reconciliation
676 S. Elizabeth Street
Lima, OH 45804-1297
TEL: 419-223-9439
Purpose: To bring about "neighborhood revitalization through home ownership."
Sponsor: Church People for Change and Reconciliation; neighborhood churches
Contact: Public Affairs Officer
Description: Rehab Project is a private nonprofit community development corporation in Lima, Ohio, that was founded in 1977 by four neighborhood churches and *Church People for Change and Reconciliation.* It is an outgrowth of concern for this city of 50,000 people that was caught up in the recent decline in the

midwestern industrial base. With new industry moving into the area, the Project has set a goal of *Neighborhood Revitalization Through Home Ownership.* This is being achieved by the physical rehabilitation of homes and the placement of responsible homeowners in the neighborhoods. More specifically:
Neighborhood - The focus is on neighborhoods. By definition, the focus is broad but discriminating, for it is wider than a mere concern for individuals yet narrower than a citywide agenda. Individual projects are evaluated in the context of neighborhood needs and benefits. Resources are managed with a primary consideration for concentration of effort and the cumulative effect of those efforts.
Revitalization - The revitalization of neighborhoods assumes a previous vitality and an investment of resources, public and private. It further assumes a decline in that vitality, and a corresponding disinvestment of resources. *Revitalization* states an intention to live again where life once flourished.
Through Home Ownership - The self-interest of individuals can best be harnessed for neighborhood benefit through home ownership. Long-term neighborhood stability and self-maintaining investment will result by fostering practical and attractive home ownership opportunities and by conspicuously aggregating those opportunities.
Maximizing Private Sector Participation - Current trends in the public sector appear to indicate a growing scarcity of resources and ever-changing policies and programming. The task of neighborhood revitalization, however, demands a more stable environment. The private sector - by definition, diverse and flexible - holds the best opportunity to build the necessary long-term resources. Neighborhood revitalization shall be achieved through maximizing the support of the private sector and the utilization of all available public resources.
The project strives for affordable and quality housing. Affordability is emphasized on two levels: sales prices and operating costs. The operating costs are minimized through quality construction; the sales prices are kept low through the development and employment of *in-kind* (volunteer) labor resources, including:

- **Churches** - Members devote time and labor.
- **School System** - Vocational Education students are provided the site and construction materials for annual construction of a new home.
- **Correctional Facilities** - *Honor inmates* are trained in carpentry to work on renovating housing.
- **Public Assistance** - individuals in the *work relief* program are trained on carpentry crews.
- **Green Thumb Program** - persons 55 years of age and older work on crews (through *Ohio Farmers Union* and the federal *Older Americans Act*).

All work required - except the licensed plumbing and electrical work - is performed by unskilled, but supervised, volunteer carpentry crews. The result of this process is a quality, energy-efficient home that anyone would be proud to own, but that is priced to be affordable to persons who previously could only dream of owning such a home.
In 1985 project leaders developed a ten-year plan, hoping to rehabilitate more than 700 homes by 1995. To achieve this ambitious goal, the Project expects to institute extensive homeownership education programs, instigate a climate for increased neighborhood and community pride, maximize private sector participation, and broadly market the concept of the neighborhoods as "good places to live."
The Project solicits a wide mix of purchasing clientele: lower-income households seeking the often impossible dream of home ownership; youthful, moderate income households desiring their "first" home; and present homeowners, seeking improved housing, but unable to afford newly-built units. Completed homes are marketed under the product name of *Heart Homes: Homes with a History and a Future.*
Publications: Rehab Project: Neighborhood Revitalization Through

Home Ownership
Founded: 1977

RESPITE FOR AIDS VOLUNTEERS
SEE ADMINISTRATION: VOLUNTEER/CENTER/AGENCY RELATIONS

SAN FERNANDO VALLEY INTERFAITH COUNCIL
SEE COMMUNITY SERVICES

SHARE SELF-HELP AND RESOURCE EXCHANGE
Roman Catholic Diocese of San Diego
San Diego, CA 92199
TEL: 619-574-6300
Purpose: To distribute low-cost food packages to families in need in exchange for community service.
Sponsor: Roman Catholic Diocese of San Diego
Contact: Exchange Coordinator
Description: The concept of the *Share Self-Help and Resource Exchange* is to enable people to maintain their dignity by contributing something to the help they receive. In the exchange program, low-income participants receive about 30 pounds of food for $12 and two hours of community service each month.
The first distribution in 1983 reached 7,000 families, who picked up food packages at the San Diego Stadium. In mid-1989, the number of families served was 17,625, all of whom provided two hours of community service. Areas covered were San Diego, Imperial, Riverside and San Bernardino counties.
Share affiliates modeled after the San Diego program are in 16 cities across the country. The program was initiated through the *Roman Catholic Diocese of San Diego* and has served a quarter of a million families coast-to-coast without any government assistance.
Founded: 1983

SHELTER HOUSE
3080 Patrick Henry Drive
PO Box 4081
Falls Church, VA 22044
TEL: 703-536-2155 (Shelter); 703-256-1378 (ACCA)
Purpose: To meet the critical need for temporary housing for County residents.
Sponsor: Churches, synagogues, ecumenical groups, philanthropic organizations, local and federal government and individuals
Contact: Mary Garwood, President and ACCA Liaison, or Michelle Palmer, Director
Description: Located in the Seven Corners area, Shelter House is one of two facilities in Fairfax County established to assist families in crisis. Shelter House consists of seven apartments with two bedrooms each; administration and counseling offices; a classroom/conference area; and a food service center. The present 36-bed facility opened in 1986 and more than doubled the original housing capacity.
Residents are referred from the Fairfax County Department of Social Services, American Red Cross, and other approved referral agencies. They stay an average of 57 days and do their own cooking, cleaning, and laundry. Special attention is given the children to create the sense of a caring, loving home.
Residents receive 24-hour comprehensive care, professional support, and guidance which enables many to make an expeditious return to the community. In addition to social services support, residences receive three balanced meals a day; housing and career counseling; employment assistance; job referral; and Life Skills Training. Several new programs have been developed including one for single expectant women. It is also anticipated that Shelter House will begin transitional housing in an attempt to move participants once and for all from emergency to permanent housing. ACCA (Annandale Christian Community for Action) has

been instrumental in launching this program, having given an $18,000 grant in December 1988.
Various churches, synagogues, ecumenical groups, philanthropic organizations, local and federal government and individuals provide financial, in-kind and program support to Shelter House. A unique program, *Adopt a Shelter House Family,* enlists churches and groups to become linked with a particular family, helping them in friendship and support. Help is always needed in locating jobs, apartments, and usable cars.
Shelter House is governed by a volunteer Board of Directors, with representation from seven ecumenical groups that were fundamental to its formation. These include ACCA, CHO, ECHO, Falls Church Community Service Council, FISH, FOCUS, and SHARE. A dedicated team of social service professionals work in concert with the Board to provide a safe and supportive environment for the homeless.
Founded: 1986

ST. JOSEPH'S HOUSE OF HOSPITALITY
402 South Avenue
Rochester, NY 14620
TEL: 716-232-3262
Purpose: To provide meals for the homeless and hungry.
Contact: Volunteer Coordinator
Description: The staff of *St. Joseph's House of Hospitality* live in poverty themselves, and devote their lives to the work of the House. All of its services are supported by contributions from area businesses and local individuals. The services are made available to everyone, no questions asked. Clientele is almost exclusively male. The dining room contains six tables which seat 48 people. No one seems to mind the mismatched silverware and dishes, or the flowers in the center of the table that are slightly wilted.
The motto on the kitchen wall, "Work Is Love Made Manifest," is taken seriously, and volunteers find themselves at work within five minutes of their arrival at the House - preparing large, deep pans full of turkey, carrots, peas, gravy, and large quantities of bread, setting tables, replacing flowers, etc. They are encouraged to converse with the clients and most often find them animated and intelligent rather than matching their preconceptions of silent figures with downcast eyes. After the meal is over, and the cleanup is done, the staff invites the volunteers to join them in a circle for a prayer asking for continued ability to offer aid to those in need. One volunteer summed up his work at the House by saying his experiences there leave him "feeling more optimistic about the basic goodness of people. The world is not really all cold and uncaring."

STAR CITY SOCIAL CLUB
Christ Episcopal Church
Franklin Road and Washington, SW
Roanoke, VA 24016
TEL: 703-342-8024
Purpose: To provide caring adults who assist with crafts, dinners, singing, games, field trips, etc., for ex-mental patients.
Sponsor: Christ Episcopal Church; local mental health organizations
Contact: Reverend David D. Stanford
Description: In May 1982, a mental health worker approached the Christ Episcopal Church to present the concept of a social club in the church for ex-mental patients. About ten people expressed interest in such a program. This request for assistance immediately followed a pastoral appeal by letter urging local congregations to assess local needs and then seek out means of addressing these needs.
Initially, anxiety about mental patients, and a "we and they" atmosphere delayed the project in spite of the good intentions of members of the congregation. Planners designed training and other programs with the help of local mental health organizations and agencies.

Training is in two phases: an overview of mental health to deal with myths about the mentally ill, and specific training when needed in the specific areas of involvement (crafts, games, etc.). In the process, volunteers were surprised to discover that some potential social club members were established church members, and close friends of many of those with initial anxieties. The walls between "we" and "they" quickly eroded, and the program now serves as a vital link between former mental patients and the community.

The program is operated by volunteers, with one half of them in leadership/management positions and the other half in direct service delivery. One third of the budget is provided by the church, with the other two thirds coming from foundations and in-kind contributions. Although addressing ex-mental patients, the program has proven helpful and enjoyable to others in the community.

Founded: 1982

SUNDIAL VOLUNTEERS
29 Merriam Parkway
Fitchburg, MA 01420
TEL: 617-345-1559
Purpose: To provide services for senior citizens in a low/moderate income apartment building.
Sponsor: First Parish Church (Universalist-Unitarian)
Contact: George J. Bailey, Manager
Description: In commemoration of its 200th anniversary, the First Parish Church sponsored a 168-unit apartment building for senior citizens. A non-profit corporation was formed by volunteers from the church. Passbooks of church members were hypothecated as security for a loan to obtain options on land, secure a consultant for the project and obtain preliminary drawings from an architect. The building, known as "Sundial," was completed on April 1, 1970, and has been operating at full capacity since October 1970. Sundial is non-sectarian and integrated. Residents represent all geographical areas of the United States.

The first floor of Sundial houses a social and recreation area called the Sundial Lounge. The Lounge hosts planned activities from 10:00 a.m. to 9:00 p.m. Monday through Friday.

Since the opening of Sundial, approximately 125 tenant volunteers have served as guides, lobby hosts or hostesses, receptionists and newspaper distributors. Volunteers are on duty at the lobby desk from 9 to 9 each day, working in one-hour shifts.

In addition, each of the ten floors has a monitor or "Ambassador" who helps new tenants, tries to involve tenants in activities, and is on the lookout for problems or emergencies. The monitors comprise the Tenant Council (also called the "Ambassadors of Goodwill") and are elected each January by all of the residents. They are honored by management each April with a dinner. In general, the duties of the Ambassador of Goodwill are;

- to welcome new tenants to The Sundial.
- to acquaint new tenants with procedures and programs available.
- to make regular contacts with tenants regarding illness, duration of absences, etc.
- to know what to do in case of emergency (training is provided).
- to answer the emergency cord when it rings (cord located in bathroom of each tenant).

To alleviate concerns of elected Ambassadors, meetings with the Manager are held weekly. The greatest concern of these volunteers is lack of experience, and the major purpose of the meetings is to discuss responsibilities of the tenants to the Ambassadors, as well as the other way around.

College student volunteers are very helpful as instructors of arts and crafts, physical fitness programs, music and choral groups, office assistance, etc. A number of Human Services majors complete their college internships at Sundial.

Founded: 1970

TRANSPORTATION COMMITTEE OF ACCA
Annandale Christian Community for Action (ACCA)
7200 Columbia Pike
Annandale, VA 22003
TEL: 703-256-1378
Purpose: To meet the needs of those who are unable to keep essential medical appointments, physical or mental health therapy, cancer treatment sessions, etc.
Sponsor: ACCA
Contact: Ruth Schably, Chairman
Description: The ACCA Transportation Committee endeavors to meet emergency or essential physical or mental health transportation needs through a network of volunteer drivers. Each participating church appoints a Transportation Coordinator, and accepts responsibiliity for the program on a rotating basis for periods of one week at a time. Typically, during a week, about 20 rides are provided by volunteers in the church congregations. The ACCA volunteer receives the name, telephone number and address of the person in need, contacts the person and sets forth on his or her mission.

ACCA with the help of County agencies tries to screen requests to be sure of real need. The majority of requests are valid. They range from a 19-year-old who was brain damaged in an accident and needed treatments twice a week, to a medical check-up for an elderly person. Within a year the 19-year-old was well enough to use the public buses and informed the Committee that he no longer needed its services. This is an example of the way in which this work rewards the volunteer.

During 1988 ACCA's Transportation Committee provided a total of 894 rides - an average of more than 80 rides per month. A Fairfax County-initiated service, FASTRAN, initiated in 1986, has relieved some of the demand. FASTRAN is a transportation system for the elderly, disabled, and persons of limited income. ACCA's greatest need now is by persons who cannot go out to the curb to wait for the FASTRAN bus. Sixteen ACCA churches participate in the transportation program.

Publications: ACCA Annual Report

TUTORIAL PROGRAM
SEE VOLUNTEERS: PROFESSIONALS

VAN MINISTRY
Community Family Life Services
First Trinity Lutheran Church
309 E Street, NW
Washington, DC 20001
TEL: 703-256-5776 (ACCA)
Purpose: To take people to visit prisoners who otherwise might have no visitors.
Sponsor: First Trinity Lutheran Church; Annandale Christian Community for Action
Contact: Ted Gleiter, ACCA Liaison
Description: The Van Ministry began in 1979 with the purchase of a 15-passenger van for use in taking people to visit in prisons. Nearly 100 women from the metropolitan area are incarcerated 300 miles away in the federal prison at Alderson, West Virginia. Most of them rarely, if ever, get a visitor. Donations were requested from individuals and groups to obtain the $8,000 needed for the first van purchase.

As the program progressed it became apparent that there was a need to transport visitors to Virginia State prisons also - Southampton, Goochland, Powhatan, Richmond, and Buckingham. In August 1980 a second van was purchased, and weekend trips to the Virginia prisons were scheduled. Also the two vans were utilized on weekdays by senior citizen groups and by the ACCA churches as well.

Due to difficulty in obtaining liability insurance, it was decided to relinquish ownership of the two vans after July 1, 1985. One van was transferred to First Trinity Lutheran Church in Washington,

DC, with their agreement to continue the prison visitation trips. The second van was sold.

While ACCA no longer conducts the Van Ministry, it continues to contribute funds for the service that is now being carried on by the Community Family Life Services outreach program. Also, ACCA supplies drivers for the prison trips. The following services are currently being offered:

- **Alderson (WV) Federal Women's Prison** - A six-hour trip, with visitors departing Saturday morning and returning Sunday evening.
- **Lewisburg Federal Prison for Men at Lewisburg, Pennsylvania** - A 3-1/2-hour trip, departing Saturday morning and returning the same day.

Riders donate $15.00 each, but this covers only a fraction of the cost.

Founded: 1979

VOLUNTEER SERVICES
SEE VOLUNTEERS: CIVIC GROUPS

VOLUNTEERS FOR YOUTH
SEE VOLUNTEERS: ROLE MODELS

WASHINGTON HEIGHTS ECUMENICAL FOOD PANTRY
801 West 181st Street
Suite 21
New York, NY 10033
TEL: 212-927-8738
Purpose: To provide emergency three-day supply of food to the hungry.
Sponsor: Catholic, Protestant and Jewish congregations in Washington Heights Neighborhood of Manhattan
Contact: Margaret Chen
Description: The Pantry provides a three-day emergency food supply to people referred to them by churches or community agencies.
Funds are supplied by private donations, collections by school and community and church groups.
The Food Pantry is located in the basement of the Broadway Temple Methodist Church.
Volunteer workers are supplied from churches, who are trained and scheduled to work once or twice a month. Some of the volunteers are bi-lingual.
Some advocacy counseling is provided on problems other than food.

WE CARE
Southwest Church of Christ
1601 James Street
Jonesboro, AR 72401
TEL: 501-932-9254
Purpose: To expand the church's role in the community.
Sponsor: Southwest Church of Christ
Contact: Richard L. Akins, Involvement Minister
Description: To meet the goal of becoming known in the community as a caring church, the Southwest Church of Christ developed its "We Care" ministry. Although the program is overseen ultimately by the eldership of the church, a committee made up from the church's membership meets to establish budgets and guidelines.
Most of the program's volunteers come from the large group of older members of the church. Leaders see two reasons for this: (1) older persons have greater time resources, and (2) they have an accumulation of wisdom of years that makes them better suited to really getting at the heart of what a program of this sort should be and do.
Volunteers collect, clean, sort, and store clothing. Food is collected from the entire congregation on periodic "Pack the Pantry"

Sundays and appropriately stored. In addition to distribution of food, a sizable amount of the program's budget is given to those in need of utility payments, housing, transportation, medicine, and help with doctor bills. Volunteers conduct face-to-face interviews with those requesting assistance to be in a better position to assess needs beyond their requests.
Leaders emphasize that it isn't always easy to be a volunteer in such a program. There are so many different kinds of needs. Some situations are heart-rending. According to one volunteer, "You never walk away without wishing you could do much, much more." And, "not having the wisdom of Solomon," volunteers wonder if decisions to help or not to help were correct.
Consequently, the program has adopted a philosophy to help alleviate some of this uncertainty: "We had much rather err in helping someone who is undeserving than in failing to help someone who is deserving." This sustains the volunteers and they feel certain that the majority who come have real needs. Nothing is expected or asked from the people requesting help.
Both program leadership and direct-service volunteers realize that, although the kinds of help provided are essential, they are of the "band-aid" variety - dealing with the symptoms and not the disease. Consequently, Southwest hopes to expand the help offered to include areas such as financial planning, job training, seminars on interviewing skills, etc. Also, a referral bank is planned for situations where "We Care" cannot be of assistance.

WEST ST. JOHN MINISTRY OF CARE
Second African Baptist Church
Edgard, LA 70049
TEL: 504-497-3498; 504-497-8523
Purpose: To help the people in the community in need of services.
Sponsor: Second African Baptist Church
Contact: Merita Johnson
Description: Operated for a year out of the home of one of the volunteers, the *West St. John Ministry of Care* held a grand opening in June 1989 in its new location in the *Second African Baptist Church* in Edgard. The program was formed by an alliance of clergymen in 1985 to help provide emergency assistance to people in need of help with utility bills, food, clothing, shelter and medical assistance. The program also aids transients who may need a meal or gasoline for returning home.
The *Ministry* depends on public and private donations and fundraisers. These have included a motorcycle rally and food and clothing drives.
No referrals are needed to obtain help from the program, but proof of income is required to determine eligibility. The service is confidential, and a special effort is made to reach people who need some help but are reluctant to ask for it.
Several churches support the program including New St. Peter Baptist Church and St. John the Baptist Church. The present location is serving as a temporary headquarters until a permanent site can be found.
Founded: 1988

WRITECONNECTION PROGRAM: LOVE A CHILD BY MAIL
SEE VOLUNTEERS: ARMED FORCES MEMBERS - NAVY

VOLUNTEERS: CIVIC GROUPS

INDIVIDUAL PROGRAM PROFILES

A, B, AND C ON BURGLARY
SEE VOLUNTEERS: POLICE OFFICERS

CHRISTMAS BASKET PROGRAM
SEE VOLUNTEERS: FAMILIES

JUNIOR LEAGUE OF DETROIT
SEE COMMUNITY SERVICES

LAFRENIERE PARK SPECIAL RECREATION
PROGRAMMING DIVISION
2320 Judith Street
Metairie, LA 70003
TEL: 504-454-6687
Purpose: To provide leisure opportunities for both disabled and normal citizens in Jefferson Parish and the Greater New Orleans region.
Sponsor: Federal/State/Parish Government
Contact: Sherry Hunter, Special Recreation Supervisor
Description: The Special Recreation Programming Division was established in the summer of 1983 in conjunction with the completion of the Playground for Special Children in Lafreniere Park. Initial funding for the Programming Division resulted from the sponsorship by Independence Isle, Inc., a non-profit corporation, promoting leisure opportunities for the disabled. The Programming Division is currently involved not only in the provision of recreation opportunities for the disabled, but is seeking active involvement from other public and private agencies in the community in an attempt to promote mainstreamed leisure activities where feasible.
The eventual goal of the Special Program Division is to become the focal point of all area special populations leisure activities. Through its outreach project, the Division hopes to broaden its service delivery through the cooperative use of schools, hospitals, residential homes and other agencies.
Volunteer Staff - At present, the services of a full-time volunteer coordinator are not economically feasible so the Programming Division is primarily dependent on the recruitment of volunteers through the *Friends of Lafreniere,* an auxiliary branch of the fund-raising Lafreniere Park Foundation. "Friends" members are already strong supporters of park activities, and with their help, along with volunteers from Independence Isle, Inc., and the Delta Lions Club members, the volunteer corp is off to a good start.
Volunteer Training - Before a volunteer is allowed to participate in an organized program, he must complete the *Disability Awareness Seminar* offered by the Recreation Programming Staff. This seminar is an in-depth training program that familiarizes the volunteer with the many disability groups and makes him aware of what to expect from any given special participant. A careful screening process is a requisite to assure that even our volunteer corp understands the goal of providing a rewarding leisure opportunity for all individuals. Periodic in-house refresher courses are also required to maintain active volunteer status.
Volunteer Duties - Many phases of volunteerism are used by the Programming Staff. Most of our volunteers assist the therapeutic recreation specialist or instructor by offering personalized care. The low staff participant ratio is vital to insure that each participant receives the best possible instruction and positive reinforcement. However, other facets of volunteer work may involve manning telephones, assisting with decorating for a special event, car-pooling participants or staff, and even lobbying local citizens and politicians to stress the importance and need for continued special recreation programs.
Founded: 1983

RAMAPO KEY CLUB*
SEE VOLUNTEERS: STUDENTS

ROBERTS PARK AND PLAYGROUND/LANTRIP SCHOOL
PARK*
SEE BUSINESS/INDUSTRY INVOLVEMENT:
RECREATION/SPORTS

STS (SHARING TALENTS AND SKILLS)
302 Elm Street
Westfield, NJ 07090
TEL: 201-789-4432
Purpose: To involve citizens in their schools; to tap the wealth of knowledge within the community; to supplement the curriculum in the schools.
Sponsor: Westfield Public Schools
Contact: Mary Ann Brugger, STS Coordinator
Description: STS is a volunteer project in which residents share their talents and skills with students in the classrooom K-12. STS began in 1976 when the Westfield Parent-Teacher Council decided to update an old community resource file compiled in 1973. The Junior League of Elizabeth/Plainfield provided volunteers for the project which was under the aegis of the P-TC. Volunteers from the Junior League and each school set up and staffed an office to coordinate speakers with classroom studies. STS flourished and in August 1981 the Board of Education hired a part-time staff member to coordinate the program.
At the beginning of each school year, teachers receive an up-dated STS Directory of all resource persons, subjects and grade levels available. As the school year progresses, teachers request a resource person and the Coordinator confirms presentation for a time mutually convenient. These presentations are held in the classroom and range from 30-60 minutes. Sample presentations include:
- a local investment broker talks on workings of Wall Street
- a retired banker and amateur astronomer shows slides of solar system
- a local resident shows slides of trip to Russia
- a local amateur trombonist gives history of instrument and performs
- a local dentist gives program on preventative dentistry
- a member of local historical society gives program on colonial times
- a local attorney talks on career in law

As of May 1990, STS had over 300 volunteer resource persons on file (1988-89 school year - 546 programs). The students can only benefit from the generosity of these volunteers who so willingly share their talents and skills.
Founded: 1976

TWENTY-FIRST CENTURY DISCUSSION GROUP
League of Women Voters Education Fund
1730 M Street, NW
Washington, DC 20036
TEL: 202-296-1770
Purpose: To raise questions which citizens must consider if they are to help shape the future of their government.
Sponsor: League of Women Voters Education Fund
Contact: Nan Waterman, Chairperson, Project Committee
Description: In 1973 the League of Women Voters (LWV) tested a new idea for community groups - the 21st Century Discussion Group. National and local LWV members volunteered their time to play the role of the general public, while eleven volunteer experts from as many disciplines led the discussion. Since then, the discussions have been convened with diverse groups such as a welfare mothers' self-help group, political party leaders, church groups, high school classes, union leaders, civic clubs, women's groups, book discussion groups, neighborhood preservation groups, and new careers classes, as well as countless local LWV groups.
Two obstacles emerged in the San Juan meeting and have persisted in subsequent meetings:
1. It is difficult for people to think about the future in any organized or systematic way; and
2. The ideal group is comprised of a cross-section of people, but they are not used to talking to each other, so the process bogs down.
The goals of the San Juan meeting presented flexible guidelines for

future meetings by local LWVs or other groups. Following the obvious first step of deciding what the specific goals of the discussion group will be and with which groups in the community, the basic format could include the following goals:

- **Education:** the presentation of alternative futures through films, role-playing, written material or other devices followed by the discussion. The purpose is to help people become aware of what the future might be like, so that they will be better able to cope with it.
- **Learning About Yourself and Others:** joining with groups in the community with which little contact has been made in the past. Only through collaboration with other groups will meaningful discussion emerge.
- **Community Communication:** assuring representation from all segments of the community's population. These discussions will have the biggest pay-off, since each group will bring different value systems, concerns, and assumptions to the discussion table.
- **One Lesson Learned** - the suggested two-hour duration for the discussions did not allow sufficient time to hear from all participants.

Founded: 1973

VOLUNTEER SERVICES
Stockley Center
Route 1, Box 1000
Georgetown, DE 19947
TEL: 302-934-8031/Ext. 275
Purpose: To provide additional supportive services to both the Center and Clients through dedicated volunteers.
Sponsor: Stockley Center; Delaware Division of Mental Retardation
Contact: Josephine Y. Patterson, Coordinator
Description: Volunteer programs for the mentally retarded residents have played an important role at *Stockley* since 1965 providing approximately 700 volunteer hours monthly. Tasks which the volunteers perform vary tremendously, each offering a special talent in its own way. Volunteer opportunities for individuals include music, art, ceramics and other craftwork, letter writing, reading and assisting with various recreational activities including escort services and maintaining individual gardens during the growing season.
Civic organizations, clubs, schools, youth and church groups participate in all areas at this facility and often provide financial assistance for special projects. The Center receives great rewards from good volunteers and they gain valuable knowledge in the field of Mental Retardation. His/her services can be a stimulating experience with the many new concepts being developed practically daily.
Volunteers are sought through the news media, Stockley Center Newsletter, speaking engagements, friends, relatives, personal contact, tours and by enthusiastic active volunteers.
A short orientation program is provided for all volunteers including the teens who serve during the summer.
In addition to the client volunteer program many individuals choose to be Friendly Visitors sharing several hours weekly being a special friend, taking the client off-campus to lunch or shopping.
A donation room is provided and maintained in the Coordinator's office for the benefit of the clients and staff. The supplies are made possible through clubs, civic organizations and private contributions.
Perhaps one of the greatest benefits from the use of Volunteers is one of attitude and understanding; as the community becomes more aware of the worth of each individual, the community is more tolerant of all individuals.
Founded: 1965

WHITE CANE DRIVE
Wallington Lions Club
c/o VFW Hall
125 Main Avenue
Wallington, NJ 07057
TEL: 201-779-9373
Purpose: To raise money to purchase glasses and supplies needed by those with sight impairments.
Contact: G. Jack Natale
Description: The *Wallington Lions Club* provides support to a number of organizations through its fund-raising efforts. One effort is reserved specifically for the purchase of glasses and supplies needed by those with sight impairments. The *White Cane Drive* provides glasses for people who need them but can't afford them. This fund also offers transportation to people in need of eye checkups, and helps tape-record books for the blind and visually impaired. Volunteers literally "take to the streets" during this campaign, and use the opportunity to talk about the Lions sight conservation programs and other help the Club provides for people who have impaired vision. Although these are primary projects of the service organization, the Club helps in other areas also. Among the organizations receiving Lions Club support are St. Joseph's Home for the Blind in Jersey City, the Mount Carmel Guild in Newark, the New Jersey Special Olympics, and the Delaware Valley Eye Bank in Philadelphia.
Lions Club members also serve as community educators on behalf of the visually-impaired, especially during the *White Cane Drive.* This symbol has become recognized worldwide, and the positive response to volunteers in the street has enabled the Club to reach thousands of people who might not otherwise have had glasses, talking books, or other materials needed because of the visual handicap.

YOUTH VOLUNTEER SERVICES
SEE VOLUNTEERS: STUDENTS

VOLUNTEERS: COUNSELORS

NATIONAL/STATE ORGANIZATIONS

MILITARY EDUCATORS AND COUNSELORS ASSOCIATION
c/o Roger G. Goldberg
2675 Tambridge Circle
Pensacola, FL 32503
TEL: 904-438-7057
Objectives: To provide counseling and guidance to both active and veteran members and employees of the armed forces and their dependents.
Services: Works with professional counselors who work in and for the U.S. Department of Defense; encourages and provides guidance to individuals in the service and their dependents, veterans, and civilians employed by the military; provides services similar to those of employers in their employee assistance programs (EAPs), with a goal of enhancing individual growth and development; conducts research on the subject and shares its findings with counselors; publishes a newsletter and a directory of members.
Sponsor: American Association of Counseling & Development
Publications: MECA Newsletter; Directory of Members
Founded: 1978

INDIVIDUAL PROGRAM PROFILES

BLUEGRASS MEDICARE-MEDICAID ASSISTANCE PROGRAM
SEE VOLUNTEERS: OLDER PERSONS

VETERANS COUNSELING AND GUIDANCE CENTER
California Council for Veterans Affairs
3943 South Western
Los Angeles, CA 90062
TEL: 213-299-6330
Purpose: To assist veterans in obtaining jobs and any military benefits due them.
Contact: Kenneth L. Brooks
Description: The Veterans Counseling and Guidance Center is a multi-faceted program designed originally for assistance to the veterans. Circumstances in the community have necessitated the inclusion of certain non-veterans as well. The Center was established in 1971 and is a federally-funded program.
The Center provides direct referrals for veterans and certain non-veterans to community resources. Proper forms are always on hand for application for benefits, including:
- GI Bill
- Educational and Rehabilitation Programs
- Discharge Upgrading
- Medical and Dental Assistance
- Housing and Loans
In addition, the Center is a member of the *College Entrance Examination Board.* In this regard, forms and assistance are provided for educational benefits such as grants, loans, scholarships, work study and others.
Job developers assist veterans and others who need employment. The program is operated for the community and is located in the community and is responsive to the community. Although it is located in the inner city, it is reaching clientele far beyond the immediate offices. This has necessitated planning for new offices to fulfill the needs of that clientele.
Volunteers and neighborhood groups assist the small staff in carrying out the above tasks and meeting its objectives.
Founded: 1971

VOLUNTEER COUNSELING SERVICE OF ROCKLAND COUNTY
151 South Main Street
New City, NY 10956
TEL: 914-634-5729
Purpose: To assist individuals and families with behavioral problems and emotional distress on a non-profit basis.
Sponsor: State and County governments; corporate and private donations
Contact: Stephen Shapiro, Ph.D., Executive Director
Description: Volunteer Counseling Service, established 13 years ago, is an innovative agency which trains lay volunteers from the community to provide a variety of counseling services to individuals and families in trouble. VCS programs include Individual, Couple and Family Counseling, Parent/Adolescent Center, Post-Divorce Parenting Program, Domestic Violence Project and the Volunteer Mediation Center. Funds are received from State and County governments, corporate and private donations, and fees from clients, which are based on sliding scale. In a typical year more than 4,500 people are served through counseling, educational workshops, mediation and community education.
Volunteers are selected through a system of three separate screening interviews, and are chosen on the basis of maturity, intelligence, flexibility, emotional health and ability to tolerate stress. There are no particular educational criteria, but nearly all the volunteers have a college degree, are attending college or are actively planning to pursue their education.
Applicants who pass the first two screening interviews attend a twelve-session, 24-hour basic training cycle which introduces the basic counseling model, group process, domestic violence philosophy and community resources. Training is conducted by the VCS program staff and other community professionals.
Volunteers who complete the training are given a third screening interview to evaluate their readiness to begin working with clients. If they are deemed suitable, they are asked to sign a contract committing themselves to give six to eight hours of service per week to the agency for a period of eighteen months. Upon signing the contract, they are assigned to work with a supervisor and cases are given to them.
Their hours of service may be given in various ways. Some volunteers do individual, couple or family counseling. Other volunteers are group leaders, mediators or community educators. Some combine several of these tasks. All counselors are also required to attend individual supervision and ongoing training, each for one hour weekly, and must do so for as long as they remain with the agency. VCS currently has 125 volunteer counselors, group leaders. mediators and community educators. Another group of volunteers is the supervisors. More than 60 mental health professionals from the community (psychiatrists, psychologists, social workers) donate an hour a week to VCS for the supervision of counselors.
VCS also has about five office volunteers who help with public relations, the newsletters, answering phones, gathering statistics and general office work.
Founded: 1967

VOLUNTEERS: DOCENTS

TRAINING PROGRAMS

DOCENT EDUCATION WORKSHOP
SEE TRAINING/CONFERENCES/TEACHING: ARTS

IMPROVING MUSEUM VOLUNTEER PERFORMANCE
SEE TRAINING/CONFERENCES/TEACHING: ARTS

INDIVIDUAL PROGRAM PROFILES

ORANGE EMPIRE RAILWAY MUSEUM
2201 A Street
Perris, CA 92370
TEL: 714-657-2605
Purpose: To bring back a bygone era of electric and steam railroading.
Contact: Sheldon Liss, Public Relations
Description: The *Orange Empire Railway Museum* is an all-volunteer organization. Volunteers refurbish, restore and wash the trolleys and steam trains that make up the Museum's collection. They also garden, lay track, take tickets, sell hot dogs and cold drinks on weekends, and do a host of other things that maintain the Museum.
About half of some 2,000 members volunteer regularly to keep things going. Some prefer to use tools and keep things repaired. Others go through a complete course on how to operate the equipment, its safety and technology. They become motormen and conductors. Those not active at the Museum itself donate the money needed to pay for the projects. At least forty or fifty volunteers appear on any weekend.
Considered the largest rail historical museum in the western

United States, Orange Empire's more than 140 steam locomotives, passenger coaches, freight and maintenance and construction cars, trams and trolleys bring back a bygone era covering a period of more than half a century - both here and abroad. One locomotive operated during 1941 and 1942 on the Trans-Iranian Railway supplying Russia with war materials from the Persian Gulf area. At the museum, this same locomotive was pulling cars from the Atchison, Topeka & Santa Fe. A train from Japan had been made in the United States about 1898 and shipped overseas in "kit" form. Many other historic rail vehicles dot the landscape, some in use and some just for viewing. In addition, a "railway post office" demonstrates how mail was moved across the country in years past. And part of the Main Line track actually is part of the original Santa Fe route to San Diego.

As one volunteer said, "Adults like to make you believe that they are here for the children, but everyone out here has a liking for either the trains or the trolleys. There is no question that this is a rare cultural experience for everyone."

VOLUNTEERS: DRIVERS

INDIVIDUAL PROGRAM PROFILES

BAY RIDGE NUTRITION AND HOME CARE PROGRAMS
411 Ovington Avenue
Brooklyn, NY 11209
TEL: 212-748-0873
Purpose: To help older persons avoid unnecessary institutionalization.
Sponsor: Federal/State governments; private donations
Contact: Rosemary Carney, Executive Director
Description: In order to maintain older persons in their own communities and avoid premature and unnecessary institutionalization, the Bay Ridge Nutrition and Home Care Programs were organized in 1976.
The nutrition center provides socialization and meals, Monday thru Saturday for anyone 60 years and older. It serves the mobile elderly and provides them with paid and unpaid work.
The home care program services the homebound frail elderly with transportation, meals on wheels, housekeeping, friendly visiting and telephone reassurance.
Volunteer Staff: ten volunteers serve as receptionists at the nutrition center; five help package the meals on wheels; two teach arts and crafts classes; five do friendly visiting and two write and publish the center's newsletter.
Volunteer Experience: currently, the center is recruiting volunteers to attend a creative movement class. Once they have learned some basic techniques, they will share them with their homebound counterparts under the supervision of the movement specialist.
Founded: 1976

COUNTRY GATHERING
SEE VOLUNTEERS: OLDER PERSONS

EASY RIDERS VOLUNTEER PROGRAM*
Easy Riders Medical Transportation
5886 Bayberry Drive
Cincinnati, OH 45242-8020
TEL: 513-651-2871
Purpose: To utilize volunteer drivers in their own cars to provide medical transportation for physically and financially limited clients.
Sponsor: Easy Riders Medical Transportation
Contact: Margaret E. Carey

Description: More than 100 volunteers are involved in the Easy Riders program, with another 80 serving in management and fund-raising capacities. The program began as an entirely volunteer transportation service in 1970. As the agency has grown, paid drivers have been employed, but volunteer drivers remain the foundation of the service.
The program was started after it was determined that often many people must be institutionalized simply because they are not physically able to use a bus or financially able to afford a taxi. In addition, many people in Greater Cincinnati are unable to get urgently needed medical care because they have no means of transportation. Easy Riders allows these people to lead relatively independent lives in their own homes, maintaining neighborhood activities and friends and, most importantly, their own self-respect and sense of personal worth.
The need for specialized transportation in Cincinnati is constant and ongoing. No matter how much service Easy Riders can provide, there is always a need for more. Thus, the project is constantly recruiting volunteers and seeking funding. The Director's assessment: "To date, the program's efforts have been very successful, and reflect the positive attitude of community residents when asked to rally around a community need."
Founded: 1970

GOD'S LOVE WE DELIVER (GLWD)
PO Box 1776
Old Chelsea Station
New York, NY 10113
TEL: 212-874-1193
Purpose: To deliver free hot meals to persons homebound with AIDS.
Sponsor: God's Love We Deliver
Contact: Michael Bertish, Business Manager
Description: GLWD delivers hot, five-course meals, free of charge, to clients who are homebound with AIDS. The service operates five days a week, Monday through Friday. Volunteers work in the kitchen, in the delivery vans, and in the business office. Without volunteers, the program could not operate.
In addition to recruiting volunteers, GLWD approached the church community. After two years, GLWD was able to create a relationship with the Catholic Archdiocese of New York in which the church operates hospice centers and GLWD is responsible for providing food for the clients. The church provides volunteers.
AIDS education is a constant presence. For example, a food supplier stopped making deliveries when he learned that GLWD is an AIDS program. After receiving AIDS information from the GLWD, not only did delivery resume, but a few people from the company offered to volunteer. Other volunteers have come in unexpected ways, also. One excellent volunteer saw a donation canister in a grocery store and called GLWD to volunteer.
GLWD's problem in recruiting volunteers is its hours - nine to five. Many volunteers offer evening or weekend hours, so GLWD created a Wednesday evening program where volunteers come right from work and perform administrative tasks, party preparation, advanced preparation of some foods, etc. It is a very popular evening for the employed volunteer.
In talking with the media, GLWD makes certain that the person being interviewed is well versed on the AIDS crisis and the role of the program. Media articles are the best sources of volunteers for GLWD, since people see that something is being done and want to be part of it. In addition, people who are HIV positive - unless they are visibly ill - often volunteer 100% of their time. They cook meals, and many deliver them also.
GLWD also attributes much of its success to its total and equal involvement of volunteers in meetings and other activities of the program. They are kept well-informed and often become the program's best spokespersons and fundraisers. Also, training is a factor in the program. Sending a volunteer whose family member is ill with AIDS to deliver a meal to a gravely ill client is not done

until the volunteer offers to do so, or until he or she has been strengthened by involvement in the program for an adequate period of time. A premature visit could be traumatic for both volunteer and client.
Founded: 1986

HELP-ON-WHEELS
SEE VOLUNTEERS: CHURCH/SYNAGOGUE MEMBERS

INSIDE/OUT*
SEE VOLUNTEERS: HANDICAPPED

MEALS ON WHEELS OF BIRMINGHAM
SEE VOLUNTEERS: CHURCH/SYNAGOGUE MEMBERS

MEALS ON WHEELS OF BUFFALO AND ERIE COUNTY
775 Main Street
Suite 510
Buffalo, NY 14203
TEL: 716-852-2626
Purpose: To provide nutritional meals to homebound, elderly and severely handicapped persons in a manner which also enhances the quality of their lives.
Sponsor: Erie County Department of Senior Services
Contact: Richard J. Gehring, Executive Director
Description: Meals on Wheels of Buffalo and Erie County, Inc. (MoW) is a nutrition program that is also rehabilitative and preventative in nature, designed to enhance the quality of life of participants as well as meet their nutritional needs.
MoW provides meal service for the homebound aged person over sixty years of age, and a limited number of severely handicapped persons under sixty years of age who are unable to obtain or prepare adequate meals for themselves. A hot and a cold meal are delivered daily (Monday through Friday) and comprises two-thirds of the Recommended Daily Allowance.
At present, 74 delivery routes are being serviced, reaching some 850 persons. The service includes two Kosher routes (24 clients) and four short-term service routes which provide meals to those who need brief intervention (maximum four months). The short-term routes reach some 200 people annually.
On a monthly basis approximately 500-600 trained volunteers and 33 senior aides provide this food service in a manner which ameliorates loneliness and social isolation, and furnishes a daily check on the well-being of the participant. The volunteers and aides observe and record daily the condition and circumstances in addition to delivering the meal. These observations are reviewed by MoW professional staff on a continuous basis for problem resolution. Identification of unmet needs other than nutrition is an integral part of the program.
Social services are provided for the purpose of conducting initial and reevaluation assessments. In addition, social services staff attempt to identify other problems and link the participant to appropriate resources within the community.
Nutrition staff enhance the nutritional well-being of the participant not only through quality food service, but also through supportive nutrition counseling and nutrition education.
The MoW nutrition program for the elderly and the handicapped is made possible by the Department of Senior Services of Erie County, and the dedication of the program's volunteers and senior aides.
The program considers special diets (35-40% of clients), emergency plans in case of inclement weather, special birthday and holiday meals, and other health and morale-building activities.
Crucial to the entire MoW operation and concept is the use of volunteers to carry out the routine daily service. In addition to delivering the meals and making a daily check and report on the client's well-being, volunteers are trained in protection of the food, and handling emergencies. In MoW's first year, 1,000 volunteers

served in the program. This success is attributed to the recruiting efforts of ten site managers, each drawn from his/her community, and the emphasis by the Field Supervisor on volunteer education and training.

MEALS ON WHEELS PROGRAM OF ACCA
SEE VOLUNTEERS: CHURCH/SYNAGOGUE MEMBERS

OUR COMMUNITY KITCHEN
SEE VOLUNTEERS: CHURCH/SYNAGOGUE MEMBERS

SENIORS: SPECIAL DELIVERY
SEE VOLUNTEERS: OLDER PERSONS

SERVICE DELIVERY FOR THE ELDERLY*
PO Box 304
229 East Cedar Street
Standish, MI 48658
TEL: 517-846-9451
Purpose: To provide transportation to all low-income people over 60 years of age.
Sponsor: Region VII Area Agency on Aging
Contact: Jeanne Anderson
Description: Going to the doctor, check cashing, grocery shopping, and other errands that most people do automatically have always created difficult problems for the many rural elderly people in Arenac County. To try to find a solution to the transportation problem, the Region VII Area Agency on Aging sponsors Service Delivery for the Elderly, a program served by volunteer drivers. Nine volunteer drivers donate their time to provide this service, and receive reimbursement for mileage only. They enjoy the opportunity to assist these elderly people, and even take courses on CPR training and defensive driving techniques offered by the program. Currently, First Aid Training Courses are being organized through the Red Cross also, and the drivers are looking forward to adding this expertise to the knowledge gained from the other two courses.
Although there is no charge, per se, for the transportation service, donations are encouraged in order to allow the elderly to retain their dignity and sense of self worth. Any amount is courteously accepted, no matter how small.
Special trips are arranged also to cultural events, shopping malls, and other places of interest. The use of a van enables a volunteer driver to take groups to these places and many others which, normally, they would not have an opportunity to visit. A side benefit is the opportunity to socialize with other elderly people en route during these special trips.
Although the trips are limited to Arenac County, out-of-county appointments are honored when a physician's medical verification and statement of necessity is presented by the client. Except for emergencies, clients are asked to plan ahead so that grocery and pharmacy trips can be limited to one trip every two weeks for an individual client.
One client's trip is to the Service Delivery program office to volunteer one day per week - or more, when requested. Part of volunteer assistance is in the form of artwork to go along with the articles in the monthly newsletter.
In addition to the transportation service, this program arranges home visits to acquaint the elderly with available services in the county, and specific information in response to unique problems in areas such as fuel assistance, home repair, social security, widowhood, spiritual concerns - and even pet care!
Part of the philosophy of the program in relation to the elderly is that they are entitled to freedom, independence, and the free exercise of individual initiative in planning and managing their own lives. With the help of volunteers, Service Delivery for the Elderly strives to reflect that philosophy.

TRANSPORTATION COMMITTEE OF ACCA
SEE VOLUNTEERS: CHURCH/SYNAGOGUE MEMBERS

TULARE COUNTY FOOD RESOURCES
PO Box 1544
Visalia, CA 93279
TEL: 209-798-0963
Purpose: To collect surplus foods for distribution to non-profit groups with feed-the-needy programs in Tulare County.
Sponsor: Originally conceived through "Inter Church"; has a Community Action Program (CAP) grant, also some funding through Tulare Co. Revenue Sharing
Contact: Ruby Fife
Description: Tulare County Food Resources has been in existence since 1977, incorporated since 1978, occupant of a warehouse since 1979, and intermittent supplier of donated food to local agencies since 1980.
In 1980 donations of approximately $50,000 worth of food were procured and distributed to local agencies. In 1981 distributions were increased to over $100,000; 1982 to over $200,000 plus the USDA commodities of over 450,000 lbs.
In 1981 the program received a CAP grant to purchase a used pick-up truck, fork-lift and a walk-in freezer. For years 1983-84, $13,500 was received to be used to hire an Executive Director to help organize the volunteers, do the PR work, etc. Over 3,500 hours of volunteer time were logged last year. Volunteers include lawyers, accountants, typists, truck drivers, etc. According to the program manager, "Mistakes have been made but, by trial and error, positive progress has been made also."
Founded: 1977

VAN MINISTRY
SEE VOLUNTEERS: CHURCH/SYNAGOGUE MEMBERS

VISITOR HOSPITALITY CENTER*
308 Read Street
Santa Fe, NM 87501
TEL: 505-827-8235
Purpose: To facilitate visitation among inmates at the state penitentiary and their families and friends by assisting the visitors.
Sponsor: United Way
Contact: Pat Powel
Description: Research shows that visitation and continued contact with friends/family are the most important factors contributing to the reduction in recidivism rates for individuals in penal institutions. The Visitor Hospitality Center was established to encourage more frequent visiting by making visits easier for families.
The Center provides a place to relax in a home-like atmosphere for the periods before or after entering the penitentiary to visit. Volunteers lend a shoulder to cry on or listen to problems, and give visitors an outlet to vent emotion. Childcare is available while adults relax, and children can be left at the Center if adults prefer visiting alone. Staff work with visitors helping them understand penitentiary rules, or intercede with prison personnel when various problems arise.
Volunteer Staff - Approximately 15 volunteers donate from three to five hours per week at the Center. One paid staff person is available during operating hours. Volunteers talk to visitors and make them feel welcome, give them a light refreshment, listen to problems. If a problem does arise, volunteers try to find solutions that are workable both with the visitor and the prison staff. Volunteers provide child care throughout the day.
Volunteer Duties - In addition to the above, volunteers answer the phones and sometimes try to get messages from family members to inmates. An accurate list of service agencies is maintained, and volunteers often try to put family members in touch with someone who can assist them with a variety of needs. When visitors are having transportation problems, volunteers try to obtain rides for

them. Volunteers are also responsible for maintaining the Center - keeping it clean and pleasant.
Volunteer Experience - Volunteers are accepted from all types of background. One of the main characteristics looked for in the screening process, however, is that volunteers be accepting and non-judgmental. Volunteers at VHC must be calm and be able to maintain their poise under pressure. Many times situations arise that call for a controlled ability to make decisions and function in spite of the fact that other people have become overly agitated and excited.
Approximately 175 adults and children utilize the facilities of VHC each week. Volunteers must arrive at the Center ready to accept whatever occurs.
Other sponsors include US/ACTION and the Governor's Office of Volunteer Services.

VOLUNTEER TRANSPORTATION
317 South Eighth Street
Griffin, GA 30223
TEL: 404-228-1386
Purpose: To provide transportation for clients to community resources.
Sponsor: Spalding County Department of Children and Family Services
Contact: Linda A. Nixon
Description: In 1967, the Spalding County Department of Family and Children Services initiated a Volunteer Transportation program and had no difficulty finding volunteer drivers willing to participate. Today, the volunteer drivers continue to provide this much-needed service, and most are reimbursed at the current state mileage rate. Insurance is offered at a nominal fee.
Volunteers are recruited by newspaper articles, speeches, personal contact with interested individuals, word-of-mouth, and recruitment by the program's staff and volunteers. Individuals who are retired, and housewives with no children, stay with the program longer than those with more personal responsibility. Volunteer drivers take clients to medical facilities, educational resources, grocery shopping, and - in the case of foster children - visiting relatives. Requests for transportation come into the agency through the client's caseworker and must be received at least two days prior to the date of the needed service. Volunteers are contacted at that time by the Volunteer Coordinator. There is an advantage to having only one person contact the volunteer drivers; that person is able to develop a relationship with the volunteer, know the driver's limitations, what age client he/she relates to best, and other aspects of the volunteer/client relationship that may be unique to an individual volunteer.
Founded: 1967

VOLUNTEER TRANSPORTATION PROGRAM
PO Box 528
Reidsville, GA 30453
TEL: 912-557-4721
Purpose: To provide transportation for medical care for welfare recipients.
Sponsor: Georgia Department of Human Resources
Contact: Debra D. Webster, Volunteer Coordinator
Description: There are 493 square miles in Tattnall County with a population of 18,014, according to the 1980 census report. The county has five doctors, one hospital, two dental offices and two nursing homes. Several specialists are on staff at Tattnall County Memorial Hospital and have office hours on part time basis. Many clients of the Tattnall County Department of Family and Children Services must travel approximately seventy miles to Savannah to receive most types of specialized medical treatment.
The medical aspect of the Volunteer Transportation Program initiated in 1969 by the Department is now funded through the Medical Program. Reimbursed at the rate of 20 cents per mile, volunteer drivers transport Medicaid recipients to medical facilities

for medical care.

Volunteers have come from all walks of life - businessmen, housewives, mothers of small children, retired people with low income and public assistance recipients themselves. They help to create a new image of welfare as they involve other members of the community and help them become aware of the needs of others.

Unfortunately, it is difficult today to recruit and maintain volunteers due to the high cost of fuel, the low reimbursement allowance, and the current economic impact on families.

Volunteers must have a dedication to the needs of others and feel a part of the agency's program in order to continue to be volunteers. The Department makes every effort through orientation, training, and day-to-day contact to accomplish the latter.

VOLUNTEERS: EMPLOYEES

NATIONAL/STATE ORGANIZATIONS

ASSOCIATION OF CERTIFIED SERVERS
600 New Hampshire Avenue, NW
Washington, DC 20037
TEL: 202-337-4583
Objectives: To provide training to bartenders for intervening in cases of excessive alcohol consumption.
Services: Provides *TIPS (Training for Intervening Procedures by Servers of Alcohol)* to bartenders, vendors, and professional alcohol servers to teach them techniques for regulating alcohol consumption in public places; serves as a forum for the exchange of information on the prevention of alcohol abuse; provides referral information and an insurance program; publishes a newsletter for members to report on the application and results of the program in communities across the country.
Publications: Association of Certified Servers Newsletter
Founded: 1985

BUSINESS ISSUES IN THE CLASSROOM
SEE BUSINESS/INDUSTRY INVOLVEMENT: EDUCATION

CENTER FOR PREVENTION AND TREATMENT OF SEXUAL ABUSE
SEE GOVERNORS' OFFICES ON VOLUNTEERISM: VERMONT

INVOLVEMENT, INC.
SEE BUSINESS/INDUSTRY INVOLVEMENT

LEAVE BANK
SEE BUSINESS/INDUSTRY INVOLVEMENT: HEALTH

TRAINING PROGRAMS

NEIGHBORHOOD ANTI-CRIME RALLY/COMMUNITY FORUM
District of Columbia Police Department
300 Indiana Avenue, NW
Washington, DC 20001
TEL: 202-727-4283
Description: After twenty years of working together as good neighbors, residents of one Capitol Hill neighborhood became incensed when a young man on their street was murdered in a robbery attempt. Their concern resulted in a dual

training/discussion event - one in the neighborhood and the other at the Police Department. Bringing together City Council members and DC Police spokespersons, this combination of meetings was attended by over 200 residents of a Capitol Hill neighborhood tired of the day-to-day crime. The neighborhood rally was organized with the help of a resident who is a former school admissions director. Four Council members attended and spoke to the group about actions that could be taken to combat the crime in the neighborhood. The decision that came out of the rally was to form a Neighborhood Watch program.

Five days later the group was invited to a community forum offered by the DC Police Department and facilitated by the Police Chief. The same resident helped to bring about the forum, which again attracted 200 people from his neighborhood as well as people from other neighborhoods. Some of the points made by the Police Chief and other presenters:

- "You've got to get angry."
- Help police to solve murders. Open a dialogue with the Police Department.
- Don't wait for the murders to happen; take steps to protect your neighborhood.
- Discipline your children.
- Don't wait for white neighbors to make that call to the police.
- Get involved, and *stay* involved. Your experience counts for half the battle.

In citing the unwillingness of many city residents to help police solve murders, the Police Chief cited the Capitol Hill neighborhood as an exception. Other groups came forward to discuss how they had watched the crime in their neighborhoods escalate from stolen bikes to armed robberies and now killings. The goal of this and other meetings like it is to establish Neighborhood Watch programs in every neighborhood, with "Reserve Officers" on every block. Reserve Officers are citizens who are trained to do police work but do not carry guns. According to the resident who initiated the meetings, "All this new interest in being a good neighbor is what we have been practicing for more than 20 years. Just think how things would change if we had a reserve officer on every block. That is volunteerism to the max!"

INDIVIDUAL PROGRAM PROFILES

BERKS SCHOOLCASTING*
SEE COMMUNICATIONS & PUBLIC RELATIONS

CARRIER ALERT
US/PS - Office of News and Public Affairs
475 L'Enfant Plaza, SW
Washington, DC 20260
TEL: 202-636-1400
Purpose: To help meet the security needs of homebound, elderly and handicapped persons.
Sponsor: US/PS - Postal Service
Contact: Jeanne O'Neill, Media Relations Officer
Description: The U.S. Postal Service and the National Association of Letter Carriers, recognizing the unique presence of letter carriers in America's neighborhoods and further recognizing the needs of a special segment of postal customers - the homebound, the elderly, and the handicapped - resolved to encourage joint support to local community social service agencies for local Carrier Alert programs.

Under Carrier Alert, the local sponsoring social service agency notifies the local Post Office of customers who wish to participate in the program. The customer's letter carrier, in performing his or her daily rounds, will be alert to an accumulation of mail which might signify a sudden illness or accident. Through locally-developed procedures, the accumulation of mail will be reported to the social service agency for appropriate follow-up.

Carrier Alert, an all volunteer program, is a natural extension of the care which individual letter carriers traditionally have exhibited for their customers - not just in the delivery of their mail - but in a genuine concern for their well-being. It has been customary for letter carriers to show particular consideration for customers on their routes whose health or advanced age requires a little extra special attention.

It is essential for a sponsoring agency to handle the administrative functions of a Carrier Alert program. In some small communities where there is no local social service agency, sometimes the police or fire department will assume the administrative functions, on a voluntary basis.

Local leaders of the National Association of Letter Carriers and local Postmasters are encouraged to work together in developing a plan of action to support Carrier Alert efforts.

JAIL 'N BAIL ON CAPITOL HILL
SEE FUNDING/FUND-RAISING/RELATED SERVICES: HANDICAPPED

MARYLAND HUNTER EDUCATION PROGRAM
SEE GOVERNORS' OFFICES ON VOLUNTEERISM: MARYLAND

PET THERAPY
Little Rock Animal Control
3800 South Chester
Little Rock, AR 72206
TEL: 501-376-3067
Purpose: To help provide a familiar environment to residents who are sick, lonely, or handicapped; to boost the emotions of those depressed and withdrawn.
Sponsor: Little Rock Animal Control
Contact: Anne C. Thompson
Description: Pet Therapy is the study and practice of using animals with the elderly, sick, lonely, or handicapped in nursing homes, day care centers, and other institutions.
Little Rock Animal Control began it's Pet Therapy program April 1982. The agency utilizes stray or owner-surrendered pets. All animals are conditioned for 30 days before going to the nursing home. Volunteers meet Animal Control Officers at the nursing home to visit residents for one hour each week. All animals are prepared and kept at the shelter.
There are currently 24 Pet Therapy puppies in the program. The program is operated with tax revenues.
The major goals of Pet Therapy are to provide residents with a sense of self esteem, physical exercise, an outlet for emotions and a feeling of being needed and wanted, and to see withdrawn and depressed residents communicate with the volunteers. According to a recent survey of nursing home administrators, these goals have been accomplished.
The volunteers encourage conversation with residents as well as show pets. There are currently 43 active volunteers and about 20 temporary inactive volunteers. The volunteers from the community currently visit eight nursing homes once a week and a Child Study Center. These volunteers are supervised by a trained Animal Control officer.
The program requires no special training. However, volunteers must be able to communicate well, have a good attitude toward working with animals and be sensitive to the needs of the elderly.
Founded: 1982

SCHOOL COUNCIL VOLUNTEERS
SEE BUSINESS/INDUSTRY INVOLVEMENT: EDUCATION

SOCIETY BANK/WOLF CREEK ASSOCIATION PARTNERSHIP
SEE BUSINESS/INDUSTRY INVOLVEMENT: ENVIRONMENT

TIME TO READ
SEE BUSINESS/INDUSTRY INVOLVEMENT: LITERACY

VOLUNTEERS: ETHNIC GROUPS

NATIONAL/STATE ORGANIZATIONS

HOT LINE FOR THE HOMELESS*
SEE INFORMATION & REFERRAL: HOMELESS

INDIAN ARTS AND CRAFTS BOARD
US/DoI - Bureau of Indian Affairs
Main Interior Building
Room 4004
Washington, DC 20240
TEL: 202-208-3773
Objectives: To promote the development of American Indian and Alaska Native arts and crafts.
Services: Provides business and personal professional advice, information, fundraising assistance, and promotion to Indian artists and craftsmen and their cultural organizations; operates a coordinated system of three regional museums located in reservation areas; annually answers over 10,000 written and telephone inquiries from the public.
Sponsor: US/DoI - Department of the Interior
Publications: Indian/Eskimo/Aleut Businesses; General Information on IACB

INDOCHINA RESOURCE ACTION CENTER
1628 Sixteenth Street, NW
Third Floor
Washington, DC 20009
TEL: 202-667-4690
Objectives: To help Indochinese refugees become self-sufficient in American society.
Services: Works with local mutual-assistance associations (MAAs) in the southeast Asian communities of cities to speed up the adjustment process for refugees; helps refugees initiate self-help projects; offers one-to-one technical assistance to refugee community organizations throughout the country; conducts forums in conjunction with United Ways sponsored, in part, by funds from the *W.K. Kellogg Foundation,* and provides information on how to organize a board, how to develop and define a mission and objectives, how to write effective grant proposals, and how to develop a networking system and learn more about the American nonprofit system; promotes community development and economic advancement among Southeast Asian refugees; maintains a resource bank of 800 refugee organizations in the U.S.; produces reports and studies in areas of health, employment, information & referral, social adjustment, and outreach, among others; provides the *CAI Lettering System* for computer use; publishes a bimonthly newsletter, a directory, and a bibliography of Asian periodicals and newspapers.
Founded: 1979

NATIONAL CONFERENCE OF BLACK LAWYERS
SEE VOLUNTEERS: PROFESSIONALS

NATIONAL COUNCIL OF PUERTO RICAN VOLUNTEERS
SEE ADMINISTRATION

TRAINING PROGRAMS

MINORITY VOLUNTEERS: PLURALISM IN THE VOLUNTEER ARENA
Hunter College School of Social Work
City University of New York
129 East 79th Street
New York, NY 10021
TEL: 212-570-5179
Credit: Inquire
Sponsor: Center for the Study of Social Administration; Association of Junior Leagues; Federation of Protestant Welfare Agencies; New York City Human Resources Administration
Contact: Florence S. Schwartz or Joel Walker
Description: This one-day Institute explores the needs and opportunities for minority volunteers in some of today's critical social problem areas. From acknowledged experts, participants learn about training, supervising, recruitment and retention of volunteers for more extensive participation in social welfare institutions. Panelists discuss:
- the special talents that minority volunteers can bring to social agencies
- the rewards of volunteering such as: developing skills in dealing with institutions, exploring new job opportunities, developing empowerment skills, and expanding social horizons.

Participants have an opportunity to select one of four workshops in the morning and in the afternoon. Workshops are geared to:
- expanding their knowledge of how to recruit, train and work with minority volunteers; and
- expanding their understanding of current trends in volunteering.

Workshop topics are:
- Keynote Address: Pluralism in the Volunteer Arena
- Invisible Volunteers: Historical Tradition
- Structural Changes in Agencies
- Collaborations in Partnership
- Volunteers in Self Help
- Recruiting Minority Volunteers
- Incentives and Rewards
- Retention: Organization, Attitude and Atmosphere
- Model Programs
- Volunteers in Leadership Roles
- Volunteers and Youth
- Raising Funds to Support Programs

The Institute concludes with a social hour in which participants have an opportunity to network with others currently involved in the volunteer arena.

Faculty is drawn from the community, including for this seminar the Association of Junior Leagues, Federation of Protestant Welfare Agencies, Big Brothers, United Way of PA, Greater New York United Way, Self Help Clearing House, NYC Department of Aging, NYC Human Resources Administration, New York State Voluntary Service Corps, Mutual Benefit Life Insurance Company, Mayor's Voluntary Action Center, New York State Governor's Office, South Bronx AIDS Project, Westchester County LINKS, Hacer Hispanic Women's Center, IMPACT, South Bronx Human Development, and J.C. Geever, Inc.

INDIVIDUAL PROGRAM PROFILES

BROOKLYN AIDS TASK FORCE
SEE VOLUNTEERS: STUDENTS

GREEK FESTIVAL
SEE VOLUNTEERS: CHURCH/SYNAGOGUE MEMBERS

INFORME SIDA
ALLGO
Santa Julia Church
3010 Lyons Road
Austin, TX 78702
TEL: 512-472-2001
Purpose: To provide bilingual AIDS information to the Latino community.
Sponsor: Santa Julia Church
Contact: Volunteer Coordinator
Description: Informe SIDA is a bilingual AIDS education project conducted by ALLGO. It periodically holds door-to-door neighborhood walks to distribute AIDS literature. Volunteers meet at Santa Julia Church and receive route assignments.
The distribution of bilingual literature is concentrated in eastern Travis County and suburban southeast Austin.
Informe SIDA is the only bilingual AIDS education project in Austin. The literature is designed to make information on AIDS available throughout the Latino community. The literature informs people on the methods of AID transmission and on safe practices. It also describes ALLGO and its other programs for the Latino community.

NOCHE CUBANA (CUBAN NIGHT)
Cuban American Association of Austin
PO Box 1603
Austin, TX 78767
TEL: 512-442-0511
Purpose: To promote the history and culture of Cuban Americans.
Contact: Dr. Maria de J. Paez de Ruiz, President
Description: Noche Cubana is a celebration to recognize the beginning of Cuba's fight for independence from Spain and the beginning of the Cuban Republic on May 20, 1902. It is developed and hosted by the *Cuban American Association of Austin.* A proclamation from the Governor recognized the anniversary during the celebration and made it an official state event. More than 50 members of the all-volunteer group helped to make it as traditional as possible with special Cuban delicacies and a piano recital by a Cuban artist, who is also the treasurer of the Association, among other Cuban presentations and performances. Another activity of the Association is a regular tribute to *Our Lady of Charity,* the patroness of Cuba, with a Mass at *Our Lady of Guadalupe Church.*
The organization, which was formed as the *Cuban Committee* following an exodus of Cubans during the Mariel Boatlift in 1980, also assists Hispanics with educational and other problems.
Founded: 1980

NURSING HOME PROJECT
SEE VOLUNTEERS: OLDER PERSONS

POLISH LEGION OF AMERICAN VETERANS AUXILIARY
SEE VOLUNTEERS: ARMED FORCES MEMBERS - VETERANS

RSVP - NURSING HOME PROJECT*
SEE VOLUNTEERS: OLDER PERSONS

U.S.-BASED JAPANESE CORPORATIONS AND THE UNITED WAY
SEE FUNDING/FUND-RAISING/RELATED SERVICES

YOUNG BLACK SCHOLARS PROGRAM (YBS)
One Hundred Black Men of Los Angeles
1950 Sawtelle Boulevard
West Los Angeles, CA 90025
TEL: 213-206-1362

Purpose: To improve the college eligibility of African-American high school students in Los Angeles County.
Sponsor: One Hundred Black Men of Los Angeles
Contact: Warren Valdry, President
Description: Statistics in 1983 indicated that only 800 of the 21,000 African-American students in Los Angeles County high schools met the minimum standards at graduation for admission to the University of California system. This alarming statistic deteriorated in each subsequent year, with fewer graduates and fewer who were able to meet the UC standard, until 1986, when members of *100 Black Men of Los Angeles* were called to action and established the *Young Black Scholars Program (YBS)*, an educational program to address the problem.
To get the program off the ground, YBS planned to work with 2,000 ninth-grade students who had achieved B averages or better in four basic eighth-grade subjects: math, science, history and English. The goal was to have 1,000 of them graduate from high school and be eligible for entrance to the UC system by June 1990. By 1989, the pilot program was beginning to show results. YBS provides counseling and academic support to the 1,250 students remaining in the program out of the 2,000 originally recruited from public, private and parochial high schools in the Los Angeles area. YBS provides a variety of services to the students, all paid for with donations.
Saturday Academic Support classes are staffed by college professors and other professional teachers. Scholastic Aptitude Test preparation classes are scheduled at regular intervals and career seminars assist the young scholars in making viable choices for their futures.
An Academic Math Hotline is housed in space donated by *Kappa Alpha Psi* fraternity and is staffed by volunteer members of the *National Society of Black Engineering Students.* Any math textbook used in area school systems is at the fingertips of the volunteers, who help callers with their homework.
An integral part of the YBS operation is the mentor program. Each student is assigned an adult mentor who maintains regular contact with the pupil and makes sure he or she is enrolled in the proper classes. In addition, YBS clubs are formed in schools where a teacher can be found to volunteer as sponsor - so far about 50% of the area schools.
One weakness in the program pinpointed by sponsors is the poor participation by African-American males - two-thirds of the participants are females. Another serious concern is that there are indications that ninth grade might be too late to begin the YBS program. An evaluation meeting will determine which age groups will be best for the future.
In the meantime, an outpouring of volunteer energy is being expended to reach the goal of 1,000 African-American high school graduates prepared for college admission in 1990.

VOLUNTEERS: FAMILIES

NATIONAL/STATE ORGANIZATIONS

CENTER FOR PREVENTION AND TREATMENT OF SEXUAL ABUSE
SEE GOVERNORS' OFFICES ON VOLUNTEERISM: VERMONT

NATIONAL SUPPORT CENTER FOR FAMILIES OF THE AGING
SEE VOLUNTEERS: SELF-HELP

PATHWAYS TO INDEPENDENCE
PO Box 651
McLean, VA 22101
TEL: 703-671-9619
Objectives: To foster an improved mental health system based on experience of families of patients.
Services: Enlists families of persons recovering from mental illness and members of support groups for families to participate in mental health seminars, workshops and conferences; supports committees on job opportunities, legislation, residential services and education; maintains speakers' bureau; publishes newsletter; convenes monthly conference.

INDIVIDUAL PROGRAM PROFILES

ADOPT-A-FAMILY
Delaware Division of State Service Centers
Hudson State Service Center
Newark, DE 19711
TEL: 302-368-6701
Purpose: To provide substantive help to the neediest families and elderly persons at Christmas; to facilitate personal involvement of donors; to educate the community concerning unmet needs.
Sponsor: Delaware Department of Health and Social Services
Contact: Marjorie Meyermann, Director of Volunteer Services
Description: For eight years the Adopt-a-Family project has been most successful in Delaware. Social workers select families and elderly persons to be anonymously "adopted" or sponsored for Christmas. A brief family profile is given with details of particular needs of family members. Code numbers are assigned to maintain anonymity of recipients and sponsors. By early fall a publicity program is launched (flyer designed by a volunteer), letters are sent to former sponsors, the public media are called into play, and speaking engagements are arranged. During November and December volunteers occupy rent-free Collection Centers, usually empty stores or schools. Phones are installed and volunteers staff the Centers, supervised by a Volunteer Director.
Volunteers recruit sponsors, describe clients' needs, match clients and sponsors, coordinate giving and delivery, receive gifts at the Collection Centers. Coded orders are checked for appropriateness and delivered to clients. Volume and value of gifts range from a $25 purchased gift for an institutionalized elderly person to food, clothing and furniture valued at many hundreds of dollars for a large family.
A unique feature of the project is the individualization of the giving. Sponsors are told of particular needs but are encouraged to personalize their giving to convey their caring. All recipients are experiencing special problems and their psychological needs may be as great as their physical needs.
The appeal of the program is so great that it has become the primary source of recruitment for volunteers for the year-round volunteer program. Participation both as a volunteer and a donor often is described as addictive. Adopt-a-Family has become a giving tradition for many families and groups.
Costs for the state agency: salary of Volunteer Director, six telephones, printing and postage for publicity. In one year, 549 families and 139 single persons were served, and 895 thank you/tax letters were written for goods valued conservatively at $150,000 to $200,000.

ADULT FOSTER CARE
Senior Citizens United Community Services
Black Horse Pike
Camden, NJ 08101
TEL: 609-546-2666
Purpose: To provide a temporary, home-like environment for recuperating senior citizens.
Contact: Suzanne Watson

Description: Adult Foster Care helps seniors who live alone when they are faced with a recuperative period after hospitalization or a serious illness. The risk of being home alone is too great, and a nursing home is not always the right choice for an individual. The program seeks volunteers willing to provide a home-like environment for the seniors facing this problem.

Funded by the Robert Wood Johnson Foundation, the program is designed to meet temporary support needs of seniors who are expected to regain their independence and return to their own homes within six to eight weeks. Program clients are provided with supervision, meals, laundry and other assistance by the program while they recuperate. Volunteer families willing to share their homes are offered a monthly stipend of $400 to $600 to cover the support services. Potential providers and their homes are carefully screened, and those accepted are provided with an extensive training program.

The *Adult Foster Care* concept was developed to fill two gaps in service for county seniors - a critical shortage of home health aides, and a lack of affordable 24-hour in-home care. In addition, hospitals are discharging patients earlier than ever before - often before the patient has had time to regain strength and physical abilities necessary for independent living. The program's philosophy is that temporary support in times of need in a home setting is financially and psychologically a better alternative to institutionalization or the dangers of being alone. The volunteer effort is designed to reflect that philosophy.

AFFORDABLE HOUSING PROJECT
SEE VOLUNTEERS: CHURCH/SYNAGOGUE MEMBERS

BOARDER BABY PROJECT
SEE BUSINESS/INDUSTRY INVOLVEMENT:
CHILDREN/YOUTH

CHRISTMAS BASKET PROGRAM
The Voluntary Action Center of Muscatine
501 Sunset Drive
Muscatine, IA 52761
TEL: 319-263-0959
Purpose: To give "Christmas" to those who otherwise might not have it.
Sponsor: Individuals, families, churches, organizations and clubs
Contact: Katrina Wisniewski, Director
Description: The project began in 1974 with seven families; 1982 served 113 families. Families are recommended by qualified individuals or agencies. They are provided with food for Christmas Day, clothing and toys for children under age 18. All funds are matched with in-kind services.

Volunteers in the Christmas Basket Program are individuals, families, organizations and service groups adopting needy families for the Holidays. After they are "paired" the adopter does the shopping and delivering to the adoptee. In some cases, Churches and organizations give a lump sum of money which volunteer shoppers take to purchase the needed items, which other volunteers deliver. Volunteer shoppers handled almost $3,000.00 last year, and delivered "Christmas" to 32 families.

Information is available on how to set up a Christmas Basket Program and/or avoid the pit-falls often encountered in organizing such an effort.
Founded: 1974

FAMILY ASSISTANCE PROJECT OF HOLLYWOOD (FAP)
6605 Hollywood Boulevard
Suite 300
Hollywood , CA 90028
TEL: 213-461-9632
Purpose: To serve homeless and needy families with dependent children.

Sponsor: Family Assistance Program
Contact: M. Patricia Shelhamer, Executive Director
Description: The Family Assistance Program (FAP) was established in 1984 as a nonprofit California corporation. The mission of FAP is to aid families who, for a variety of reasons, have become unemployed, homeless, or at risk of being removed from their surroundings. During its first three years, with support from individual donors, and with the aid of committed volunteers, FAP helped more than 400 homeless and destitute families in the Hollywood area. It was the first agency in the area to put up deposits for permanent housing. The primary services include assistance in finding and securing:

- adequate housing
- jobs
- job training
- educational opportunities
- child care
- temporary financial assistance with rent and security deposits

Each year, FAP works with hundreds of homeless and destitute families in the Hollywood area, providing counseling, day care, housing, clothing, bus passes for those without any resources, use of office telephones, and a non-cost answering service to help those trying to secure employment. FAP operates under the premise that people must play an active role in changing their own lives. Clients must commit to establishing independent economic stability and enriching the quality of life for their families. Parents must make and demonstrate a conscious decision to actively participate in gaining a measure of independence.

FAP's services are adjusted to fit each individual family's requirements. Family crises are caused by varied circumstances. Therefore, the agency's mission is to provide eclectic guidance geared to long-term solutions - empowering families, returning them to the economic mainstream, and breaking the cycles of recurrent dependence and hopelessness.

Physical needs - housing, food, income and employment - are not the only drawbacks for these families. The strain of being homeless triggers dysfunctional responses such as child abuse, alcohol or drug abuse, lack of self-esteem and stress (both physical and psychosocial). To satisfy these latter needs, FAP has initiated the *Life Planning Services Program*. This program includes individual meetings with counselors, personal growth exercises, leadership development, and group support systems. One-to-one therapy is the most costly and most traditional approach, but there are countless models for group work. Whichever is used, life planning aims to help develop in children and adults alike an awareness of and confidence in their own goals and actions, and the realization that these actions will effect an outcome. The underlying theme of all of the sessions is an emphasis on self-esteem and conscious decision-making.

To augment and expand services provided by the FAP professional staff, an active volunteer group of about 35 people provide approximately 90 hours per week of free time for:

- private and/or group counseling sessions
- tutoring and remedial reading - adults and children
- child care in the Drop-in Center
- English as a Second Language
- a study-hall type situation for teenagers and youth after school for tutoring and recreation
- social activities and outings for young people
- structured play/learning situations with younger children.

In addition, a group of volunteers has organized a Career Development session that meets once a week. Using improvisational acting techniques, they simulate job interview sessions and employer/employee confrontations to teach the client new techniques in approaching employment opportunities.

The volunteer segment of the program is perhaps the most important, somewhat unique, element. The interplay between the volunteers, who can be seen as the *community-at-large*, and the client is particularly healing, usually for both parties, and provides the necessary bonding for real development.

The small, highly-skilled professional staff consists of an executive director, a social worker, two case-workers, and a job developer. In addition to the above basic program elements, parenting education and support groups meet weekly to socialize, discuss things of importance to them, and network with others on social services, legal rights and other concerns. In addition, outside groups such as Alcoholics Anonymous, Narcotics Anonymous and Overeaters Anonymous are brought on-site to foster better attendance. Where in-patient care is necessary, FAP helps with fees, or pays them, and supports the family emotionally and financially as indicated.

One of the most recent programs of FAP is the *Adopt-A-Family* program, which operates along the same line as the Big Brothers Program. A family from the community adopts a homeless or at-risk family and the two families spend time doing things together once a month (trips to the beach, museums, amusement parks, etc.). It serves as an opportunity to share, to reassure, and to build self-esteem.

In addition to the in-house volunteers, a *Volunteer Fund Raising Committee (The Spare Change Project)* puts together fundraising events. It is comprised of six publicists and marketing experts, several advertising executives, writers, casting directors, a professional celebrity recruiter and public speakers. The events attract many celebrities and have included *Rock 'n Bowl, Art Auction,* and others.

FAP does not operate autonomously, but rather has developed solid working relationships with a variety of other service providers. It has built a comprehensive networking system to insure that a family in need is able to access all agencies and the services they provide. The groups in this network include Chip-In (Community of Hollywood Investing in People in Need), Salvation Army, Los Angeles Free Clinic, and West Hollywood Food Coalition.

Publications: FAP (Family Assistance Program); Some Facts You Should Know
Founded: 1984

FARE SHARE
SEE VOLUNTEERS: SELF-HELP

FESTIVAL
Arts Council of Greater Grand Rapids
161 Ottawa Avenue, NW
Grand Rapids, MI 49503
TEL: 616-459-2787
Purpose: To celebrate art through exhibits of artists' works, preparation of ethnic foods, and other cultural experiences.
Sponsor: Arts Council of Greater Grand Rapids
Contact: David T. Mix, President
Description: In 1969 a few volunteers from the *Arts Council of Greater Grand Rapids* established downtown Grand Rapids' first all-arts festival. Initially it was planned as a single event to celebrate the completion of Alexander Calder's *La Grande Vitesse* and to focus attention on the arts. Simply called *Festival 1970,* the 15 volunteers appointed co-chairmen, enlisted performers, arranged for visual arts and set in motion a tradition now in its twentieth year. For that first event the impromptu committee even researched weather for the previous 12 years to assure good Festival sunshine. And, alongside of the fine arts, the youth symphony orchestra and other classical events, was a long-haired pop group.

The 1989 Festival boasted a 200-member volunteer Festival Committee and a total of 15,000 volunteers. Exhibitors and performers numbering in the hundreds in the early years now number in the thousands. Volunteers did everything from managing to handling production and performing to the final clean-up. They worked as individuals, as teams, and in groups. Although hot dogs and other usual fare was offered, the Committee was determined to take advantage of the many

different ethnic groups in the area to provide various ethnic foods. One group of 50 church volunteers prepared 2,000 pork shish kebabs, and almost immediately had to embark on the preparation of 4,000 more. A Greek Orthodox church introduced the Greek specialty, souvlaki, previously unknown to most residents. Many cultural groups introduced the dances of their countries of origin, and other activities of cross-cultural interest. It was a celebration of the community itself as well as the works of the artists.

Crowds were expected to top 500,000 in 1989, to continue the constant growth since the 1970 hallmark festival with an attendance of 7,000. In 1970, 11 artists in three basic categories won awards. In 1989 dozens won cash awards in at least 16 categories. The five food booths in 1970 reached 35 in 1989. Performers have reached the hundreds in areas of visual arts ranging from sculpture to video. And, as noted above, the first festival committee of 15 has reached 200, with a total of 15,000 volunteers.

Funds earned from the festival have a direct impact on the Art Council's *Combined Arts Campaign,* which started in 1972. Not every year's festival makes a profit, but the vast majority of net income always went to the campaign. The 1983 contribution of $60,000 to the campaign was the highest, but with the festival growing each year, the committee saw a need for a reserve fund after that and now contributions to the campaign and the fund are roughly equal each year. Some years, contributions need to be used to balance the books. However, organizers say the festival's success cannot be judged by a bottom line.

A side benefit of the festival is that entire families volunteer, in some cases producing second- and third-generation participants. One 24-year-old volunteer considers himself a "festival brat," since he has volunteered with his family since junior high days. He said, "At first they find you hanging around and say 'come on, you can work on this, too.' After a while it just gets to be a lot of fun."
Founded: 1970

JVS VOLUNTEER TUTORIAL PROGRAM
Jewish Vocational Service
One South Franklin Street
Chicago, IL 60606
TEL: 312-408-2047; 312-346-6700
Purpose: To help make the experience of adjusting to a new culture less trying for Soviet emigres.
Contact: Cara Madansky
Description: In anticipation of an unprecedented influx of Soviet emigres, the *Chicago Jewish Vocational Service's (JVS)* volunteer tutorial program has recently undergone dramatic expansion. In 1989, 200 volunteers saved the community more than $100,000 by providing tutorial services to these new Americans. The volunteers help the immigrants become integrated and self-sustaining much more quickly than they might otherwise.

Each tutor makes a commitment to meet with an individual or family at least once a week for two hours for eight weeks or longer. Most volunteers spend at least four months with their assigned families, and many develop ongoing relationships. Some volunteers involve their entire families.

Upon entering the program, all tutors are given information on JVS's role in the resettlement process, suggested topics and activities to facilitate the acculturation process and a volunteer manual. Twice a year group training sessions are held. Tutors and JVS staff "network" once a month, and these sessions are limited in size so that participants are able to benefit from an informal exchange of ideas and experiences, successes and failures.

Volunteers often ask immigrants to visit the local schools for an exchange with the students. In one case a young Soviet guitar player entranced the students so that the music teacher invited him back.

Volunteers are helping to make the process of being absorbed by, and adjusting to a new culture less difficult. In addition, they are filling a critical need in the absorption process as well as easing the financial burden on the agencies involved in that process. While the emigres benefit from the assistance received, the volunteer tutors thoroughly enjoy the experience. As one volunteer put it, "I'm getting more than I'm giving."

SPECIAL POPULATIONS PROGRAM
Raleigh Parks and Recreation Division
PO Box 590
Raleigh, NC 27602
TEL: 919-755-6832
Purpose: To provide a recreational program for the mentally and physically handicapped residents of Wake County that actively involves their families.
Sponsor: Raleigh Parks and Recreation Division; Wake Area Mental Health Agency
Contact: Debra D. Webster, Volunteer Coordinator
Description: This program serves mentally and physically handicapped residents of Wake County who have the need and desire for supervised recreational activities. The philosophy is to provide wholesome leisure opportunities "emphasizing the ability rather than the disability." In addition, the program strives to involve the family in the program.
The program had its beginnings in 1970 when a group of concerned citizens formed to determine the needs of the handicapped in Wake County. Friendly Day Camp became a reality in June of 1971, and by January of 1972 the Raleigh City Council approved the funding of a full-time program supervisor. This program does not replace the regular schedule of programs for senior citizens and visually impaired.
Due to a positive demand for growth of the program, three full-time staff, part-time instructors or drivers, and volunteers currently are involved in the program. In one year, over 1,700 participants (representing over 40 groups) received the services of the program. With the program's emphasis on family involvement, attendance exceeded 8,000, and the two wheelchair lift-equipped buses had over 4,800 riders.
The program offers assistance to persons with any disability, but emphasis is placed on serving lower-skilled individuals. During the summer and fall, the Special Populations Program offers options which promote leisure education and outdoor recreation to those 16 years of age and older. Friendly Day Camp continues to provide a well-rounded camping experience to those from age five to age sixteen. A six week summer swim program is offered with primary emphasis on enjoyment and basic water safety. A developmental swim program that follows American Red Cross guidelines is available to interested individuals. A Family Swim Program is offered depending on interest, with a nominal fee charged to each non-handicapped member of the family.
Founded: 1970

VOLUNTEERS: FORMER DRUG ADDICTS

INDIVIDUAL PROGRAM PROFILES

PROJECT BRAVO
Bronx AIDS Volunteer Organization
Montefiore Medical Center
3320 Rochambeau Avenue
Bronx, NY 10467
TEL: 212-920-4301
Purpose: To serve and support persons with AIDS.
Sponsor: Montefiore Medical Center
Contact: Bridget Poust, Project Director

Description: The Bronx is the northern borough of the City of New York. It has a population of about 1.1 million people, with a variety of ethnic communities and peoples. The South Bronx, with about 50 percent of the borough's population, is notorious for its poverty and its massive housing destruction. Demographically, the South Bronx is predominantly black and Hispanic and has a high prevalence of HIV-positive persons and persons with AIDS-related conditions and AIDS itself.
Project BRAVO was created to establish support networks for Bronx AIDS patients, many of whom came from impoverished and isolated home situations, or may be homeless. Until Project BRAVO, the Bronx had no support system for persons with AIDS (PWAs).
Initially, the project trained and supervised four methadone maintenance clients as buddies for AIDS patients. The "buddies" would vist PWAs, run errands for them, baby-sit for those with children, act as patient advocates, and perform other services. Several months later, the program was expanded to admit people from all walks of life and all backgrounds - anyone with the willingness to serve as a volunteer.
BRAVO is a cooperative effort of four hospitals - *Montefiore Medical Center, Bronx Lebanon, St. Barnabas,* and *Bronx Municipal.* Today the program, although still small, has grown to 80 active volunteers who have direct contact with patients both in the hospital and at home. The number of people "on call" and in telephone contact, recreation, party-planning, community outreach and volunteer recruitment segments of the program is growing steadily. This bank of volunteers, although not in contact with patients on a regular basis, serves as friendly visitors, escorts PWAs to support groups, assists with arts and crafts and recreation, brings home-cooked meals, etc. Through the telephone contact volunteer activity, assessments of living situations and physical health can be made, in addition to the comfort of the phone conversation.
Volunteers make up a diverse community group, including methadone maintenance clients, gay men and lesbians, working people, and people on public assistance. They are black, Hispanic, and white. Generally, they reflect the population served.
Major administrative components are like those in any other volunteer program - recruitment, screening, training, support and supervision, referral, and assignment. It does not escape the presence of problems, however, which include funding, recruitment, burnout, institutional setting, and others that have cost the program volunteers. The bottom line is that the AIDS volunteer is very different from more traditional volunteers, and demands a new look at the rule book for volunteers and for the utilization of volunteers.
Founded: 1986

VOLUNTEERS: FORMER MENTAL PATIENTS

NATIONAL/STATE ORGANIZATIONS

RECOVERY, INC.
SEE VOLUNTEERS: SELF-HELP

INDIVIDUAL PROGRAM PROFILES

PUBLIC ASSISTANCE CLIENTS VOLUNTEER
SEE VOLUNTEERS: SELF-HELP

TRANSITIONAL VOLUNTEER PROGRAM
United Way Volunteer Center
630 Janet Avenue
Lancaster, PA 17601
TEL: 717-299-3743
Purpose: To place outpatient mental health clients in volunteer positions for rehabilitation purposes.
Sponsor: Lancaster Information and Referral, United Way
Contact: Marilyn G. Sanko
Description: The Transitional Volunteer Program was launched in February 1981 as a pilot project, sponsored jointly by the Lancaster Information Center and the Mental Health Association in Lancaster County. The Volunteer Service Center placed the first transitional volunteer in March 1981.
The program is now funded in part by the Lancaster Mental Health/Mental Retardation Program, which receives a monthly statistical report on placements and volunteer hours.
The challenge of mental health clients makes for a certain instability in volunteering; i.e. hours are not always regular. The program's value, however, has been well established and its credibility is high. Rapport between the Volunteer Service Center, mental health agencies and private physicians is excellent.
Approximately 50-70 client volunteers are introduced to the program annually. When the program originated, 16 agencies were utilizing transitional volunteers. There are currently only a few agencies who are not able or willing to place mental health clients as volunteers. These volunteers provide local agencies with 3,000 to 4,000 hours of community service annually.
Transitional volunteers perform the same services as traditional volunteers. However, additional support and supervision is provided, especially in the beginning of the assignment. Special care is taken to place client volunteers in non-stressful environments.
Founded: 1981

TRANSITIONAL VOLUNTEERS ARE...
Volunteer Resources Division
United Way of Central Massachusetts
484 Main Street
Suite 300
Worcester, MA 01608
TEL: 617-757-3985
Purpose: To help clients at the point of rehabilitation toward taking full responsibility for their own actions; to help human service agencies expand and improve their services.
Sponsor: United Way/Voluntary Action Center
Contact: Barbara M. Stewart, Assistant Director
Description: Recognizing trends in the direction of deinstitutionalization and a slightly more enlightened attitude from some agencies toward involving Transitional Volunteers (persons at the point of rehabilitation), the Voluntary Action Center (VAC) of the United Way of Central Massachusetts, in the mid 1970's, formalized a Transitional Volunteer Program. To stem the flow of the repetitive question from agencies: "Transitional Volunteers! Who are they?" the VAC convened a workshop in 1976 to bring together leaders in the field of volunteer administration who may not understand, or be committed to, this group of volunteers. One of the results of the workshop included the following definition:
"Transitional Volunteers are...
...people at a point of rehabilitation in their lives, on the way toward taking full responsibility for their own actions. This step, from a sheltered environment to a non-stressful working situation, is a part of the therapeutic process."
Since it was crucial to create a climate where the most cooperation and the least resistance could take place, the VAC recruited a volunteer with knowledge and skills in working with a rehabilitation program. Goals and objectives for the program, and a line of communication with referral agencies, were established. The more sophisticated agencies (usually staffed by a professional

Director of Volunteers) were the most receptive, but sometimes pleasant surprises came from staff or agencies from which resistance was expected. A procedure to orient agencies to the goals and objectives of the program was set in motion, and included a line of communication for information and feedback. In the placement process, the Transitional Volunteer is totally involved, taking much of the initiative in dealing with the agency, and making the final decision from available opportunities. However, the VAC interviewer must work closely with referring counselors.
Agencies are asked to make suggestions that they feel might improve the process, and to work with the VAC as problems arise. It has been found that problems can be worked out and can be a step in the right direction. The volunteer is assured that problems do not represent failure. A brochure on the program has been developed by the VAC and is widely distributed to human service agencies.
In 1979, three years after the first workshop, it was felt that enough time had elapsed to generate new leaders who may not be familiar with the program and/or aware of the commitment needed in working with this group of volunteers. The VAC enlisted the help of professionals in the human service field and offered another workshop. Such brainstorming sessions are held periodically as needs arise.
Publications: Transitional Volunteers Are...
Founded: 1975

VOLUNTEER DEPARTMENT
Delaware State Hospital
New Castle, DE 19720
TEL: 302-421-6535
Purpose: To provide volunteer opportunities for community members and ex-clients in a psychiatric setting. Volunteers are used to augment services provided by staff in both the therapeutic and support areas of the hospital.
Sponsor: Delaware State Hospital
Contact: Mrs. Laure N. Unkart, Volunteer Coordinator
Description: The volunteer program at Delaware State Hospital is divided into three sections- adult, student, and group. The use of volunteers is restricted only by the interests and needs of the volunteers. In both the adult and student programs the volunteers are allowed to choose from work assignments in both direct patient care and supportive services. Examples:
Direct Patient Care - Nursing, Occupational Therapy, Recreation, Creative Arts, Release Services, Dental Clinic, Medical Clinic, Homemaking, Dietary, and Beauty Shop.
Support Services - Housekeeping, Maintenance, Garage, Laboratory, Pharmacy, Canteen, Medical Library, Grounds, Greenhouse; Clerks in the following Departments: Business Department, Nursing, Personnel, Research and Education, Medical Records, Dietary, and Hospital Director's Office.
The Adult Section includes programs for both men and women who are either going back into the job market or considering a job change, i.e. short-term commitment, job investigation, and job training.
The Student Section is primarily used for career investigation by both high school and college students. Students from technical/vocational high schools affiliate with the hospital for their senior year in their related area.
Another section of the student program deals with students from local high schools who are underachieving in school or have dropped out and are returning to school. In either case, students are referred to the hospital for job training in goal-oriented programs. Many of these students are employed upon graduation by either the hospital, other agencies, or private industry.
Adults and students also run the Blue Hen Shop (clothing shop) and the Patient Library.
Groups of adults provide social activities for patients, i.e. day and evening parties, dances, luncheons away from the hospital, and the

Annual Carnival. Groups of adults and/or students also wrap all Christmas gifts given to the patients.

The Volunteer Department is responsible also for all donations to the hospital. The Volunteer Department averages approximately 180 volunteers a month giving approximately 2,000-2,500 hours a month.

Volunteers receive orientation from the Coordinator, on-the-job training from their staff supervisors, and In-service Education when appropriate to the position. Volunteers are supervised by their staff supervisors except for the Blue Hen Shop and the Patient Library. Both of these sections are supervised by the Volunteer Coordinator.

The Volunteer Program has been part of the Hospital Program from the early 1900's. It is funded as part of the overall hospital budget each year.

The goals of the department include providing comprehensive programs that are beneficial to patients, volunteers, and staff, improving the image of both the patients and hospital through good public relations, and a volunteer program.

"The accomplishment has been that volunteers are considered staff members and that the Volunteer Department is a vital part of the overall Hospital Program," according to the program's Coordinator.
Founded: 1900

VOLUNTEER PROGRAM OF PRAIRIE VIEW
Prairie View Mental Health Center
1901 East First Street
Box 467
Newton, KS 67114
TEL: 316-283-2400
Purpose: To be responsive to the emotional and mental health needs of both the immediate and the larger community.
Sponsor: Prairie View Inc.
Contact: Nancy Hedrick
Description: The use of volunteers at Prairie View Mental Health Center is designed to increase community involvement in the treatment of the mentally ill and to increase patient contact with the outside community. Mentally ill persons have a need to be accepted by the community and to continue to relate to persons from everyday walks of life. Understanding and concerned volunteers are useful in providing support to the mentally ill both while in the hospital and on their return to everyday life.

Prairie View, established in 1954 as a private psychiatric hospital, today is a non-profit 60-bed psychiatric hospital and a comprehensive mental health center serving three counties on a contractual basis. It is sponsored by the Mennonite churches but aims at close cooperation with the community and seeks to blend these two dynamics with the concern and skills of the staff and volunteers.

Since its inception, Prairie View has utilized volunteers but it was not until 1968 that the Board decided to mobilize this talent in an organized program. Volunteers are considered human resources just as paid staff; the Volunteer Program is under the leadership of the Director of Personnel. The organizaton corresponds to the personnel program and includes job planning, recruiting, application, placement, orientation, training, supervision, evaluation, policies and record keeping and recognition.

Volunteer roles include forming a one-to-one relationship with the patient, assisting in the psychiatric day hospital, participating in psychodrama, involvement in substance abuse groups, providing a monthly tea for inpatients, relating to the elderly, socializing with patients, providing music for patient worship services, giving private piano lessons to patients, serving as librarians in the staff library. On a regular basis, 107 volunteers participate in the program. Since 1969, 812 volunteers have given 169,839 hours of service.

Community support is sought by means of a Volunteer Services Committee made up of community representatives. Patients are invited to have input into the program and can request volunteer services. In the words of the Director: "This creative interaction of volunteers, staff, patients, and community has led to a Volunteer Program that has both been effective locally and received national attention as a model for other programs."
Founded: 1954

VOLUNTEERS: FRATERNAL ORGANIZATIONS

INDIVIDUAL PROGRAM PROFILES

ANNANDALE LIONS CLUB
c/o Colonel Ken Blood
5004 Bradford Drive
Annandale, VA 22003
TEL: 703-256-1591
Purpose: To conduct sight and hearing conservation programs and other health and welfare programs in the local community.
Contact: Colonel Ken Blood
Description: The *Annandale Lions Club* held its 42nd Charter Night in 1990, having begun operations in 1948. With 54 members, it is considered large for a local Club, but an effort at dividing it into smaller groups was unsuccessful.

The *Club* is a member of *Lions Clubs International,* the largest service organization in the world that is dedicated to service only. It has 39,479 local clubs in 166 countries representing 1,363,368 members as of May 1990.

The *Club* provides health and human services assistance to citizens of the Annandale community. Working through a Board of Directors consisting of a president, three vice presidents, and four directors, it administers a budget each year of about $18,000.

Although sight and hearing conservation are its primary concerns, these are not the only areas of assistance. The *Club's* fund-raising efforts serve the following programs:

Sight and Hearing Conservation: In 1925, *International Lions* worked with the *Helen Keller Foundation* and agreed to assist the *Foundation* in its work to help make blind and hearing impaired persons productive citizens. This remains the primary goal of all *Clubs.* In Annandale, programs include:

Sight and Hearing Van: This converted and modified Winnebago travels to schools, health fairs, businesses (e.g., IBM, which contributed to the expenses involved), and other entities to provide free sight, glaucoma and hearing screening, and information on conserving these senses. The van is owned by *Lions Club District 24A,* which covers the area north of Fredericksburg in Northern Virginia. Its facilities can be removed for use inside of a building when necessary (such as in large indoor health fairs). The Annandale Club donates approximately $2,000 to the upkeep and operation of the van.

Eye Bank: The Club provides donation cards for individuals to carry on their person which provides for donation of their eyes upon their deaths. The Eye Bank facilitates corneal transplants and other medical procedures, which are financed by the local as well as the other clubs in the area.

White Cane Drive: This is an annual fundraiser in which the business community cooperates with *Lions* members, providing space for "stations" at businesses with a lot of activity to collect funds for *Lions* sight conservation programs. The 1990 drive raised about $1,500.

Leader Dog Program: This project is often shared by several local Clubs due to the cost (about $25,000 per training course), in which a dog and a blind person are trained at a special facility near Detroit, Michigan, to provide the blind person with better access to his or her community. Area Clubs try to do two or three of these training courses each year.

Eye Care Clinic: The Lions Clubs sponsor an eye care clinic at *Fairfax Hospital,* offering free examinations to the indigent, and works through Lions Club members who are opticians to provide free glasses. The Club averages about four pairs of glasses each month to needy persons through this program.

Eyeglasses Recycling: Contrary to the belief of most citizens, the eyeglasses collected by the Lions Club are not used intact (it is illegal in the U.S. to do so). Rather, at a recycling center in Illinois, the precious metal is melted down and funds from the sale of the metal are used to further sight conservation projects. Since the use law does not exist in other countries, eyeglasses in mint condition, without scratches or other damage, are often sent to other countries where the prescriptions are determined and then matched with diagnosed prescriptions of citizens.

Blind Bowling League: The Club helps a league both financially, and in providing assistance in scorekeeping, etc.

Braille Interpretation Program: The Clubs sponsor a program to translate books into Braille. The books are offered to various programs for the blind.

Other Programs: Although primarily concerned with conservation of sight and hearing, the *Annandale Lions Club* has reached out to other groups with unmet needs in the community, resulting in the following programs, among others:

Pancake Breakfast to Benefit ACCA: ACCA (Annandale Christian Community for Action) always has been a recipient of Lions Club funds, but in recent years ACCA has helped in the raising of these funds. All proceeds from the annual *Pancake Breakfast* held at the local community college go to ACCA, an ecumenical service organization involving 28 churches in the Annandale area. ACCA sells tickets to the breakfast and helps in advertising.

Memorial Fund: Often widows of Lions Club members request that sympathizers planning to send flowers send donations to the Lions Club instead. These funds may be used locally, or they may be forwarded to the *International Memorial Fund* where they might be used to build a school in Sri Lanka or a well in Kenya. There are no set guidelines, and decisions are made on an ad hoc basis.

Northern Virginia Youth Camp: This is a camping and recreation facility in the Shenandoah Valley housing a permanent caretaker and made available to *Boy Scouts, Girl Scouts, 4-H,* etc. The camp is a joint venture of a number of Clubs.

Veterans Stamp Collecting Program (Project Outreach): When it was learned that many veterans remained depressed and withdrawn in spite of the efforts of veterans hospitals, the Lions Club suggested helping them develop a hobby. The stamp collecting program was begun by a club in Tuscon, Arizona, and is now a significant program across the country. The area clubs in Pennsylvania, Maryland, Delaware, the District of Columbia, and Northern Virginia have contributed 784,000 stamps, 69 albums, and 180 packets in an eleven month period during 1989 and 1990. Feedback is very positive regarding the effect this hobby development program has had on veterans.

Leo Clubs, Lady Lions, and Lioness Clubs: The Leo Clubs are composed of youth of high school age, with the Lions Club and a designated counselor or teacher at the school administering the program. The Lady Lions are female members of the Lions Club itself (women accepted as members since 1986). Lioness Clubs remain primarily composed of women (although men are welcome) who act as parallel organizations serving the same needs as do the Lions Clubs.

Melvin Jones Fellowship Award: This award is given to outstanding Lions Club members. Each Club handles the award in its own way. The Annandale Club holds an election to honor an *Annandale Lion of the Year.* To this date there have been two awards based on the following criteria: (1) Must have been an active lion with at least seven years longevity. (2) Must have made significant contributions to all projects - both fund-raising and civic - and always acted in a manner to bring credit to the Club

and *Lions International.* Also, there have been three posthumous awards made by the Annandale Club. There are now 22,000 Fellows worldwide, with a goal of 65,000 by the 75th International Convention in 1992. Each fellowship award costs $1,000. It consists of a plaque from the *International Lions Club,* a lapel pin and a certificate.

Bland Music Contest: This contest honors the black musician James A. Bland, who composed Virginia's song, *Carry Me Back to Old Virginny,* contrary to the belief of many that it was written by Stephen Foster. The contest has two parts - instrumental and vocal. The local winner receives a cash award and a chance to compete on a regional level, where the award is higher, and - if a winner there - a chance to compete at the State Convention. These awards are designated for a music education, and the amount for an individual can reach a significant amount.

Health and Welfare Budget: About $1,000 is set aside each year for emergency services such as covering gas and light bills for the needy. This fund does not require special approval and is operated under broad guidelines so immediate decisions can be made when necessary.

Youth Activities: The Club is involved in many youth activities, including scouts, *Little League, Boys State, Girls' Camp,* etc. The budget for these activities is about $1,500.

Quest Program (Drug Prevention): About $1,300 each year is devoted to training elementary teachers on drug awareness techniques with children who might be getting close to involvement with drugs.

Miscellaneous Fundraisers: The Lions Club has been a steady provider of Christmas trees and fresh fruit in campaigns each year to raise funds for their programs. These funds are not designated for any particular program.

The *Annandale Lions Club* is an individual organization with its own by-laws. It is not necessary to use the standard by-laws of the *International Lions Club.* However, the local by-laws must be submitted for approval if programs are included that differ from the international agenda. Budgetwise, two separate accountability measures are taken to keep specified funds separate from general funds. An administrative account takes care of dues and other administrative functions. An activity account contains funds for sight and hearing conservation and other specific programs. Every dollar over actual expenses in the activity account is returned to the public.

Founded: 1948

PHI MU SORORITY COMMUNITY SERVICE CHAPTER
Gamma Omicron Chapter/Phi Mu
c/o Kenan Neese
6524 Robin Road
Springfield, VA 22150
TEL: 703-451-0677

Purpose: To participate in projects that benefit both campus and community.

Sponsor: Phi Mu Sorority, Gamma Omicron Chapter

Contact: Kenan Neese, President

Description: The Gamma Omicron Chapter of Phi Mu Sorority is located on the campus of George Mason University in Fairfax, Virginia. The Chapter maintains communication with numerous social service projects and provides volunteer services as requested. Projects include:

Children's Miracle Network - Members of the Chapter work very closely with this organization to help raise funds for its program.

Project Hope - This is a nationally-sponsored project of Phi Mu Sorority. The Chapter operates fundraisers for the Project through twice-yearly walks in which sponsors "pay by the mile" as the walkers circle the area, and special projects such as the sale of "pumpkin pops" on Halloween. Funds are sent to Phi Mu national headquarters for presentation.

Childrens Hospital - The Chapter sponsors various events to raise funds to assist in the work of this facility for children.

In addition to the above ongoing projects, the Chapter responds to the community and campus on an as-needed basis to serve in programs designed to address and help find solutions to problems in all areas of the human services and the physical environment.

ST. MATTHIAS OF SOMERSET COUNCIL NO. 9925
Knights of Columbus
PO Box 5183
Somerset, NJ 08875
TEL: 201-560-3589
Purpose: To create, direct and operate projects and programs that will benefit our fellowman.
Contact: William H. Cullen, Grand Knight, or Richard J. Vetter
Description: The St. Matthias Council No. 9925 of the Knights of Columbus in Somerset, New Jersey, is a new Council, a little more than a year old as of Spring 1990. However, in that period of time, the Council has assessed the needs of the community and developed several projects that are helping to improve the quality of life in Somerset.
Based at the *St. Matthias Catholic Church,* the group is working on the following one-time, short-term, long-term and ongoing efforts:

Health Programs
- *Blood Drive:* In May 1990, registration for the Spring blood drive in June was held, with recruitment volunteers signing up for each Mass for the two weekends preceding the drive, and registration volunteers to assist donors on the day of the drive. A Council committee oversees the project each year.
- *Help for Unwed Mothers:* This program recognizes the prenatal care, education, job training and other needs of unwed mothers. The Council provides assistance based on expressed needs from organizations directly serving these young people.

Programs for the Handicapped
- *Retarded Citizens Drive:* In this program, Council members are seen in shopping areas and other stations armed with canisters and winning smiles to encourage people in the community to donate to the Council's drive created to assist the *Association of Retarded Citizens* and the *Raritan Valley Sheltered Workshop.* The May 1990 effort netted $1810 for the two organizations.
- *Assistance with Church Programs*
- *St. Matthias Carnival:* Volunteers for the Spring carnival held by the Church each year sell tickets, park cars, keep the grounds clean, prepare and serve food, operate games, and serve on the hospitality committee. The proceeds are used by *St. Matthias Church* to benefit the community as a whole.

Programs for School-Aged Children
- *Grammar School Spelling Bee:* This program for young children is designed to help inspire them to reach for academic excellence. It is a popular program in which various incentives are offered by the Council.
- *Grammar School Essay Contest:* This contest enables young children to use the words they learn in the spelling bee to write an essay that will convince the Council judges that they are aware of their responsibilities as citizens in their communities.
- *Seminar Meetings on Child Safety and Fire:* This seminar addresses the need to teach children as well as parents, guardians, and concerned citizens the basic rules of child safety. With more and more families requiring a second income, the number of children who spend several hours alone at home after school is growing. This seminar deals with safety precautions, especially as they relate to children's curiosity about fire.

Other Community Programs
- *Flag Donations:* The Council has a special flag program in which American flags are donated to community projects which request them.

St. Matthias of Somerset Council No. 9925 continually listens to the community and responds to as many needs as time allows. Its work is done in the spirit of the original *Knights of Columbus* charter in 1882 in Connecticut - *knightly ideals of spirituality and service to Church, country and fellowman.*Today, the *St. Matthias of Somerset Council No. 9925* is part of an organization of more than 1.45 million Catholic men in some 8,500 councils who have dedicated themselves to these ideals. According to one St. Matthias Council member, "As long as there are unfulfilled needs in our community, we will do what we can to create projects and programs to help."
Publications: The K of C Roundtable

TAU KAPPA EPSILON (TKE) COMMUNITY PROJECTS
Mu Omega Chapter/TKE
c/o Todd Ketch
6050 Burke Center Parkway
Burke, VA 22015
TEL: 703-250-0767
Purpose: To participate in a variety of events to benefit both the campus and community.
Sponsor: Tau Kappa Epsilon, Mu Omega Chapter
Contact: Todd Ketch, Pylortes
Description: The Mu Omega Chapter of Tau Kappa Epsilon Fraternity was founded at George Mason University in Fairfax, Virginia, in 1970. The Chapter, from the beginning, has been active in the Northern Virginia community. Some projects that have proven successful over the years are:
TKE Trek - a fundraiser set up like the "Walk for Mankind," except that it is a run between two colleges sponsored per mile by area businesses. Between 35 and 45 members participate in this event.
Keg Roll for St. Jude's Hospital - a fundraiser much like the TKE (pronounced "teke") Trek, except that a specially-designed beer keg is used. The Keg Roll covers 1,900 miles from Chicago to New Orleans.
Dance Marathon - a fundraiser where couples are sponsored by area businesses per hour danced.
Playgrounds for the Handicapped - a project (funded by McDonald's) in which TKE members join other volunteers in constructing specially-designed playgrounds at area elementary schools.
Blood Drive - a fundraiser in which TKE mounts a blood drive and sells the blood to area hospitals.
"Slave" Day or Rent a Teke or Little Sister for a Day - an auction of TKE members and little sisters in which the "slaves" are "purchased" for eight hours.
Profits from the fundraisers outlined above are donated to charitable organizations. In addition to specific projects, TKE operates a 365-day-a-year Open Community Effort policy. Whenever the community needs 25 or more members for a service, TKEs at George Mason respond. If the request results in a time conflict, TKE sends as many representatives as possible.
TKE advocates friendship, leadership, and scholarship. TKEs have found that all three of these qualities are represented in volunteer services to the community.
Founded: 1970

VOLUNTEERS: HANDICAPPED

NATIONAL/STATE ORGANIZATIONS

CHALLENGE INTERNATIONAL
SEE COMMUNICATIONS & PUBLIC RELATIONS:
HANDICAPPED

KENNEDY INTERNS IN RECREATION*
Ruby M. Gebauer, Coordinator
Route 3, Box 165P
Hammond, LA 70401
TEL: 504-567-3111
Objectives: To expand job training and opportunities in the leisure industry for in-school mentally retarded youth.
Services: Arranges for on-the-job experience depending on intern's interest and qualifications (pre-school teacher aide; recreation assistant, arts/crafts counselor aide, music store clerk, librarian aide, grounds maintenance person, lifeguard, cashier, etc.); pays client/intern's salary up to a year; requires employer to continue for at least one additional year. (This program is co-sponsored by the Department of Labor, Youthwork, Inc., and Special Olympics, Inc.); age requirement for intern is 16 to 21.

NATIONAL ALLIANCE OF BLIND STUDENTS
c/o Marjie Donovan
763 Silver Avenue
San Francisco, CA 94134
TEL: 415-239-2577
TOLL FREE: 800-424-8666
Objectives: To provide advocacy regarding rights and interests of blind students.
Services: Works to educate government, institutions, agencies, and the public on the rights, interests, and needs of blind students - especially in the area of accredited postsecondary education in academic, vocational, trade and professional and related programs; represents blind students at the annual meeting of the American Council for the Blind by mounting a National Student Seminar with other student groups; publishes a quarterly journal (also available in cassette form) and a networking directory.
Publications: Student Advocate; Student Networking Directory
Founded: 1974

SELF-HELP FOR HARD OF HEARING PEOPLE
SEE SELF-HELP: HANDICAPPED

TRAINING PROGRAMS

COMMUNITY SERVICE
SEE TRAINING/CONFERENCES/TEACHING: CHILDREN/YOUTH

THE DEAF WAY
Gallaudet College
800 Florida Avenue, NE
Washington, DC 20002
TEL: 202-651-5488
FAX: 202-651-5489
Credit: Inquire
Sponsor: Gallaudet College
Contact: Jane Norman, Chairman
Description: Called "the international celebration of deaf culture," a 1989 festival/forum sponsored by Gallaudet University and held on its campuses, attracted both deaf and non-deaf volunteers, citizen and organizational advocates, and others from around the world. Gallaudet is the only liberal arts college for the deaf in the world, and is considered by many to be the "world leader in all aspects of deafness." *The Deaf Way* is both a showcase for deaf talent and a forum for the exchange of ideas among deaf people. It is also a celebration of the pride that enabled students at the university to bring a deaf President to Gallaudet in 1988.
An estimated 600 deaf entertainers participated in more than 40 festival performances. They included the Japan Theatre of the Deaf, the International Visual Theatre of France, the London Deaf Comedians, the National Theatre of the Deaf of the US, the

American Dance Theatre of the Deaf, the Greek Theatre of the Deaf, the Moscow Theater of Mime, and the deaf actress who received an Academy Award for her role in "Children of a Lesser God."
The festival features artwork by deaf artists, and unveiled a 30-foot mural containing bright figures representing the many moods of deaf people and their culture. The mural will be permanently housed at the university. The other notable piece of art is the sculpture of hands, indicating that "Our hands are our whole life," according to the festival chairman.
The serious side of the gathering focused on a range of research areas and issues, such as:
  ● the human rights of deaf people
  ● the special challenges of adults who become deaf late in life
  ● the role of sign language in deaf culture
  ● the oppression of deaf people
  ● deafness as a political issue
One controversial issue was the use of sign language in the education of deaf children, with leading advocates preferring that deaf children learn sign language first, and then use the signs to learn English. Although gaining support in recent years, this method is still being vigorously opposed by some educators.
More than 225 sign language interpreters who can use both American Sign Language and Gestuno, an international group of signs, volunteered to help interpret the more than 500 events that are part of *The Deaf Way*. An additional 50 voice interpreters worked in Spanish, French and English.
One purpose of the forum/festival was to provide a sharp contrast with other deaf programs which emphasize "the disability of deafness, or how to fix the hearing loss." The Gallaudet event has a special significance for deaf people, since it is designed to show their accomplishments, and not "what to do to help the poor deaf people." According to the university's first deaf president, "It's a new era for deaf people."

THE UNTAPPED RESOURCE: DISABLED PERSONS AS VOLUNTEERS
SEE TRAINING/CONFERENCES/TEACHING: HANDICAPPED

VOLUNTEERS WITH SPECIAL NEEDS
SEE TRAINING/CONFERENCES/TEACHING: HANDICAPPED

INDIVIDUAL PROGRAM PROFILES

ADVOCACY BY AND FOR THE BLIND
AFB Mid-Atlantic Regional Center
1615 M Street, NW
Washington, DC 20036
TEL: 202-457-1487
Purpose: To improve safety of walkways and other areas used by the blind by advocating for specific legislation.
Sponsor: AFB
Contact: Edward T. Ruch, Regional Director
Description: In early 1989, Virginia organizations of and for blind people, and both blind and sighted individuals, demonstrated their concern for the unsafe practice of trucks and other large vehicles - without "beepers" - backing up at too slow a pace for a blind person to tell which way it is going. Among those actively involved in this advocacy effort was a blind counselor at Northern Virginia Community College, whose wife, also blind, was fatally crushed under the rear wheels of a beeperless trash truck in 1988. In addition to letter-writing and telephone campaigns, the advocates testified before the Virginia General Assembly in support of legislation to require all refuse trucks with limited rear visibility to use audible signals when traveling in reverse. The

legislation went into effect July 1, 1989.

But the advocates did not feel that they had won a full victory. They intend to work to require the warning signals on delivery and public utility trucks as well as the refuse collection and road maintenance vehicles. Many such vehicles often travel in areas where pedestrians normally have the right of way, blocking sidewalks and driveways.

A blind attorney who is legislative chairman for *Old Dominion Council of the Blind and Visually Impaired*, played a major role in guiding the advocates through this early success, and continues to seek ways to approach the system in an effective manner regarding legislation that would improve the quality of life for the blind. This advocacy effort is only one of many mounted by blind individuals and organizations across the state. In fall 1989 they began a campaign to update Virginia's outdated "white cane" laws. Many other issues await their attention. According to one of the leaders, "The list is endless."

CPSS FASHION SHOW
Cerebral Palsy of the South Shore
105 Adams Street
Quincy, MA 02169
TEL: 617-479-7443
Purpose: To raise funds to benefit victims of Cerebral Palsy.
Sponsor: Cerebral Palsy of the South Shore
Contact: Arthur Ciampa, Executive Director
Description: The tenth annual fashion show sponsored by *Cerebral Palsy of the South Shore (CPSS)* showed the newest spring fashions. A fashion expert from *Bernie's Modern Formal Shop* was fashion commentator, with handicapped clients (some in wheelchairs), staff members and parents as models. The show was attended by 265 clients, parents, and friends of the rehabilitation organization.

For the fashion event, 30 South Shore businesses donated raffle prizes, materials and services. More than $5,000 was raised after expenses. Following the show, participants were surprised with a full-course Chinese dinner, served at the Masonic Hall. Following the dinner, an award was given to an outstanding volunteer, also the mother of a young client, for her support and services to CPSS.

CPSS was established in 1952 and serves 47 clients through age eight and 50 adults.

DUO
SEE VOLUNTEERS: STUDENTS

GALLAUDET BOARD OF TRUSTEES
SEE LEADERSHIP DEVELOPMENT/BOARDS: HANDICAPPED

INSIDE/OUT*
Volunteers of Cape Cod
PO Box 717
Hyannis, MA 02601
TEL: 617-771-7925
Purpose: To assist persons who are homebound/handicapped or isolated due to transportation difficulties in becoming providers of services through volunteering.
Sponsor: Volunteers of Cape Cod (A non-profit placement bureau)
Contact: Margie Murphy, Recruitment Coordinator
Description: The Inside/Out program was initiated in 1979. The goal of the program is to provide volunteer opportunities to individuals who are homebound due to physical, social or emotional handicaps or transportation difficulties.

Volunteer projects or assignments are transported to the home of the volunteer by the agency who wishes to utilize that volunteer. The agency introduces the assignment, supervises and maintains contacts with the volunteer. This provides a social contact for the isolated volunteer and assists the individual to become a provider of services rather than a recipient, which increases self-esteem. The program also allows agencies to have a pool of individuals available to assist as volunteers with task-oriented or "portable" volunteer assignments.

Inside/Out volunteers range in age from 16 to 100. Some typical assignments include: telephone reassurance, bulkmailing, collating, mending/sewing, clerical duties, research, information/referral. Any opportunity which can be modified to be transported to a volunteer's home is eligible for a referral of an Inside/Out volunteer.

Inside/Out assignments can be modified so those volunteers who are experiencing decreasing capabilities can remain useful by performing tasks according to their skills.

Inside/Out assignments are also utilized for those individuals who are in transition and are not ready for a traditional assignment. Said individuals can utilize an Inside/Out assignment to prepare them for a traditional structured assignment while maintaining the protective environment of their home or institution. At present this program has worked with over 150 Inside/Out volunteers.

The VOCC representative registers new Inside/Out volunteers in their home. In many cases this interviewer may be a volunteer, rather than staff.

The VOCC staff coordinates the requests for Inside/Out volunteers and matches appropriate referrals. On an annual basis VOCC instructs agencies on the use of Inside/Out volunteers including, as needed, personal instruction or inservices.
Founded: 1979

INTERNATIONAL VERY SPECIAL ARTS FESTIVAL
Very Special Arts
John F. Kennedy Center
Education Office
Washington, DC 20566
TEL: 202-662-8899
Purpose: To bring together disabled artists from every state in the U.S. and other countries to display and celebrate their work.
Sponsor: Very Special Arts
Contact: Ron Miziker
Description: More than 1,000 disabled artists representing every state in the U.S. and some 40 foreign countries attended workshops and receptions in Washington, DC, for what one artist described as "one big artistic party." The five-day *International Very Special Arts Festival* began with a processional including two representatives from each state and foreign country. In addition to sharing their creative talents in two-hour sessions, they attended *Very Special Arts* workshops designed to encourage greater participation in the mainstream of the art profession, and recognize the value of their work. Also, participants were honored at a dinner at the Washington Harbor, and attended numerous receptions, including one on the White House lawn, and a networking opportunity with fellow artists from around the world. At the White House reception, celebrity artists met with the participants and discussed their shared interests.

MAPLEWOOD MANOR RSVP PROGRAM
SEE VOLUNTEERS: OLDER PERSONS

MULTIPLE SCLEROSIS SOCIETY OF ORANGE COUNTY
2500 Michelson Drive
Irvine, CA 92715
TEL: 714-752-1680
Purpose: To provide a wide range of services to people in the county with multiple sclerosis.
Sponsor: National Multiple Sclerosis Society
Contact: Deborah Ballard, Director
Description: The Orange County, California, chapter of the National Multiple Sclerosis Society provides services to 2,000 people in the county known to have multiple sclerosis, and to their

friends and families. Multiple sclerosis is a disease of the central nervous system that usually strikes people between the ages of 20 and 40.

One of the greatest strengths of the program is the self-help component, which includes 12 support groups, divided among those with special needs (such as people whose disease has been diagnosed recently), people with more severe cases, and spouses. More personal attention is given by volunteer peer supporters, each of whom has had the disease for at least two years and has been trained to help people understand the disorder.

Patients and their families are referred to any services they might require, including doctors, exercise programs, transportation and equipment such as wheelchairs, canes and walkers. The chapter also has a library and provides educational seminars.

Founded: 1974

PROJECT PASSAGE
Columbus Developmental Center
Ohio State Hospital
1601 West Broad Street
Columbus, OH 43223·
TEL: 614-272-0509
Purpose: To pair bright but troubled students with mentally retarded adults for mutual benefit.
Sponsor: Columbus Developmental Center
Contact: Joy Rogers, President
Description: Since 1982, students from Columbus schools have been volunteering at the *Columbus Developmental Center,* a facility for mentally retarded adults. Sponsored by *Project Passage,* the program pairs bright but troubled students with residents of the Center. The goal is a mutually beneficial relationship that will help raise the student's self-esteem, while providing a friend for the retarded adult.

The 278 residents at the Center function at the 6-month to 18-month age level. Not only do the young volunteers deal with that very well, but many have seen their grades raised significantly during the 16-week or longer experience. The young volunteers play ball with the residents, feed them dinner, or just chat with them and be a friend. In this way they are taking responsibility for another person's leisure time, and this feeling of helpfulness carries over into the classroom.

Besides feeling needed and learning to care about others, the students are taught skills in working with the mentally retarded. They are shown by occupational therapists how to help the patients identify things around them - placing a patient's hand in a bucket of sand and moving it in circles, or rubbing baby powder on a patient's neck, with the therapist suggesting the added help of letting the patient smell the powder. As one 13-year-old volunteer put it, "My grades are better, and I'm acting better. I really like to work with the residents. They need our help and we need theirs, too."
Founded: 1982

SCHOOLMATE HANDICRAFT VOLUNTEERS
SEE VOLUNTEERS: OLDER PERSONS

WMNR RADIO - ACCESS BROADCASTING COMPANY*
SEE COMMUNICATIONS & PUBLIC RELATIONS

VOLUNTEERS: HOMELESS

INDIVIDUAL PROGRAM PROFILES

SUBSTANCE ABUSE TREATMENT CENTER AND SHELTER
SEE VOLUNTEERS: SELF-HELP

VOLUNTEERS: INTERGENERATIONAL

NATIONAL/STATE ORGANIZATIONS

GRAY PANTHERS
SEE SELF-HELP: INTERGENERATIONAL

INTERGENERATIONAL SERVICE-LEARNING PROJECT
SEE SELF-HELP: INTERGENERATIONAL

INDIVIDUAL PROGRAM PROFILES

SENIOR PROGRAM
SEE SELF-HELP: INTERGENERATIONAL

VOLUNTEERS: LOW-INCOME

NATIONAL/STATE ORGANIZATIONS

OPPORTUNITIES INDUSTRIALIZATION CENTERS OF AMERICA
SEE VOLUNTEERS: SELF-HELP

INDIVIDUAL PROGRAM PROFILES

LINCOLN COUNTY SENIOR COMPANION PROGRAM
169 SW Coast Highway
Newport , OR 97365
TEL: 503-265-3160
Purpose: To provide meaningful volunteer experience to low-income persons over age 60 to serve in one-to-one relationships with adults who are frail elderly.
Sponsor: Lincoln County Council on Aging
Contact: Wilma Earles
Description: The Senior Companion Program in Lincoln County receives a major portion of funding from ACTION. Local funds match on a 90/10 basis. The sponsor has been active in providing services to seniors in the county for 10 years.

The director is half-time. Office staff is volunteer and 11% are full time. The Senior Companions receive a stipend of $2.00 an hour, transportation reimbursement, and meal allowance.

They work in the homes of the elderly to provide services that mean the older client can avoid premature institutionalization.

They provide a variety of services, from letter writing to light meal preparation to medical escort or transportation.

Volunteers receive 40 hours of pre-service training which includes information about social services in the community, how to act as advocates, and agency policies.

Senior Companions must be low-income, over 60 and desire to have a challenging volunteer experience. They work 20 hours a week.
Founded: 1982

NEW HAMPSHIRE FOSTER GRANDPARENT PROGRAM
SEE VOLUNTEERS: OLDER PERSONS

NURSING HOME PROJECT
SEE VOLUNTEERS: OLDER PERSONS

RSVP - NURSING HOME PROJECT*
SEE VOLUNTEERS: OLDER PERSONS

WOMEN OFF WELFARE (WOW)
Mesa United Way
7 South Hibbert, #360
Mesa, AZ 85210-1414
TEL: 602-969-8601
Purpose: To put single mothers on the road to self-sufficiency; to break the cycle of welfare dependency.
Sponsor: Welfare Reform Task Force
Contact: Sue Kathe, Volunteer Chairperson
Description: Started in summer 1988, *Women Off Welfare (WOW)* in Mesa, Arizona, is an outgrowth of the federal Family Support Act of 1988, which legislates welfare reform. WOW is a long-term program designed to help single mothers become self-sufficient. The program was developed under the auspices of a public/private partnership which includes the *Maricopa County Private Industry Council (PIC), Arizona Department of Economic Security (DES), Mesa Chamber of Commerce, City of Mesa, Mesa Ecumenical Council,* and *Mesa Community Council.*
Before the program began, a *Welfare Reform Task Force* was established by the *United Way of America's Public Policy Advisory Committee* to identify the kinds of obstacles there had been to welfare reform in the past, and find solutions to them. A major problem was the discontinuation of federally-funded health-care benefits for welfare recipients who became employed - benefits which were not immediately carried over by the employer. Often, women had to quit their jobs and go back on welfare to get them through costly health problems. The solution to avoid this pitfall was 20 local physicians who agreed to volunteer their services to welfare families in the WOW program. This spirit prevailed across the community and enabled other components of the program to work smoothly as well (day care, job training/placement, transportation, etc.).
All of the women enrolled in the program go through an intensive three-week session to build self-motivation and self-confidence. The session is led by loaned personnel managers from area companies who conduct training in job-interview techniques and discuss what employers expect in the way of on-the-job conduct and appearance. Through *Gifts In Kind, Inc.,* an independent organization, the women were provided with clothing from *Montgomery Ward* and hair care products from *Redken.*
The Maricopa County Skills Center and Mesa Community College offer ongoing job training at no cost for program clients. In addition to office skills, the women are encouraged to take courses in specific career fields, or to learn trades. Education to acquire high school-equivalency diplomas and English-language proficiency is also provided.
Within the first year, WOW helped about 100 women find employment, and another 300 begin job training programs. The second year saw the program expand into five other townships.
Founded: 1988

VOLUNTEERS: OLDER PERSONS

NATIONAL/STATE ORGANIZATIONS

AMERICAN ASSOCIATION OF RETIRED PERSONS
1909 K Street, NW
Washington, DC 20049
TEL: 202-872-4700
Objectives: To help older Americans achieve lives of independence, dignity and purpose.
Services: Sponsors community service programs such as consumer information, crime prevention, driver improvement, health education, housing information, continuing education, tax assistance, pre-retirement planning; arranges for reduced costs in many day-to-day living areas for older persons, such as medicine, transportation; sponsors mail order pharmacy; operates AGELINE, a computerized database which includes an on-line bibliography; maintains programs in areas of pre-retirement planning, defensive driving, crime prevention, tax aid and others; has regional offices in several states; makes consultant and other services available to retired teachers through its National Retired Teachers Association division; publishes monthly bulletin, bimonthly magazine, and other materials.
Publications: Modern Maturity; AARP News Bulletin
Founded: 1958

COMMON CAUSE
SEE TRAINING/CONFERENCES/TEACHING:
INTERNSHIPS

COPE RETIREE PROGRAM
AFL-CIO
815 Sixteenth Street, NW
Sixth Floor
Washington, DC 20006
TEL: 202-637-5000
Objectives: To offer retired union members the opportunity to use their new leisure, combined with their experience, to mount an awareness program regarding government performance.
Services: Conducts political education; designs activities aimed at registering and getting out the vote; provides information to interested groups and individuals on procedures and progress of efforts; publishes a political action handbook for senior citizens and other materials.
Publications: Senior Power
Founded: 1970

FLYING SENIOR CITIZENS OF THE USA*
96 Tamarack Street
Buffalo, NY 14220
TEL: 716-824-3432
Objectives: To petition airlines for half-fare standby privileges for senior citizens.
Services: Assists older persons in expressing themselves to the airlines on a regular basis; acts as a voice for older persons, maintaining that increased travel by the elderly would justify half-fare at off-peak times (Monday through Thursday); publishes semimonthly newsletter and directory.

FOSTER GRANDPARENT PROGRAM (FGP)
US/ACTION - The Federal Volunteer Agency
1100 Vermont Avenue, NW
Suite 1100
Washington, DC 20525
TEL: 202-634-9108
TOLL FREE: 800-424-8580

Objectives: To provide part-time volunteer service opportunities for low-income persons aged 60 or over; to render supportive person-to-person services to children having special or exceptional needs.

Services: Provides grants to public agencies and private nonprofit organizations to develop and manage local projects to provide foster grandparents to children in health, education, welfare and related settings. Grant applicants must demonstrate:
- ability to operate the grant effectively;
- availability of eligible volunteers;
- transportation plan for volunteers;
- community support

Publishes a handbook and a number of recruitment flyers and other materials.

Contact: Roy Tejada

Publications: FGP Operations Handbook; Where Love Grows

HEARTLINE*
SEE COMMUNICATIONS & PUBLIC RELATIONS: IMAGE

INTERGENERATIONAL PROJECT FOR SERVICE LEARNING
SEE VOLUNTEERS: STUDENTS

NATIONAL ALLIANCE OF SENIOR CITIZENS
2525 Wilson Boulevard
Arlington, VA 22201
TEL: 703-528-4380

Objectives: To advocate the advancement of senior citizens through sound fiscal policy; to inform the public of programs and policies being carried out by public and private sectors to meet the needs of older persons.

Services: Presents views of senior citizens before Congress and state legislatures; actively supports numerous Advisory Council Chairs, including one on volunteerism (others include employment, health, adult education, environmental protection, housing, rural transportation); keeps public informed of programs being carried out by the federal government and other groups; maintains the Golden Age Hall of Fame honoring individuals for outstanding service to the senior community; Advisory Council areas include volunteerism, consumerism, adult education, crime, employment security, health care, housing, farm and rural life, retirement, rural transportation and several others; publishes monthly newsletter and a bimonthly tabloid.

Publications: Senior Guardian; Our Age

Founded: 1974

NATIONAL ASSOCIATION OF OLDER AMERICANS*
12 Electric Street
West Alexandria, OH 45381
TEL: 614-775-7634

Objectives: To provide assistance and vital information to older persons.

Services: Acts as advocate for older persons in dealing with government agencies at all levels; provides pharmaceutical, travel and other services at reduced cost; publishes monthly newsletter.

Publications: Heartline/NADA

NATIONAL COUNCIL OF SENIOR CITIZENS
925 Fifteenth Street, NW
Washington, DC 20005
TEL: 202-347-8800
FAX: 202-624-9595

Objectives: To provide advocacy and encourage participation in social and political action on behalf of senior citizens.

Services: Provides assistance in areas ranging from federal and state legislation to community action; works currently in areas of health care, housing, employment, Social Security, crime

prevention, nursing home reforms, and Congressional evaluation; sponsors mass rallies, educational workshops and leadership training institutes; maintains speakers bureau; helps develop and organize programs for local and state groups; maintains library; publishes monthly newsletter and other materials.

Publications: Senior Citizens News; Retirement Newsletter

Founded: 1961

NATIONAL LIBRARY SERVICE FOR THE BLIND
US/Library of Congress
1291 Taylor Street, NW
Washington, DC 20542
TEL: 202-707-5100

Objectives: To enable individuals who cannot hold, handle, or read conventional printed matter to enjoy reading materials through talking books and magazines.

Services: Trains and certifies volunteers in tape narration, braille transcribing, and in braille proofreading; publishes Volunteers Who Produce Books: Braille, Tape, Large Type, a directory that lists by state the names of volunteer groups and individuals who transcribe and record books and other reading materials; distributes materials through a national network of 152 locally-funded cooperating libraries and agencies; operates automated bibliographic service for quick identification and location of materials for network libraries; provides playback equipment which is maintained by the Telephone Pioneers of America (senior or retired telephone industry workers); maintains a children's collection with special features such as combined print/braille materials; publishes bimonthly magazines, Talking Book Topics and Braille Book Review, which are available in braille, recorded, and large type versions; operates two additional services:
- *NLS Reference Section* - a comprehensive collection of materials on various aspects of blindness and physical handicaps; a referral service to additional sources, organizations, and agencies.
- *NLS Music Section* - a large collection of music books and periodicals in braille, large print, and/or recorded music scores, instructional cassettes; a referral service to volunteers who produce appropriate music items; a bibliographic search service; a general inquiry service.

[All materials are loaned free, with postage-free mail provided to and from the borrower.]

RETIRED SENIOR VOLUNTEER PROGRAM
US/ACTION - The Federal Volunteer Agency
1100 Vermont Avenue, NW
Suite 1100
Washington, DC 20525
TEL: 202-684-9108
TOLL FREE: 800-424-8580

Objectives: To provide a variety of opportunities for retired persons aged 60 or over to participate more fully in the life of their community through significant volunteer service.

Services: Provides grants to established community service organizations to conduct such activities as:
- assisting in the development and/or operation of locally organized senior volunteer projects;
- developing a wide variety of volunteer service opportunities throughout the community (hospitals, schools, courts, libraries, day care centers, etc.);
- arranging transportation for retired volunteers as needed;
- enlisting community support for the senior volunteer program, RSVP;

Publishes handbook and recruitment flyers. All materials are provided free on request.

Contact: Suzanne Fahy

Publications: RSVP Operations Handbook; The Most Productive People; Share an Experience; The RSVP Program

SENIOR COMPANION PROGRAM (SCP)
US/ACTION - The Federal Volunteer Agency
1100 Vermont Avenue, NW
Suite 1100
Washington, DC 20525
TEL: 202-634-9208
TOLL FREE: 800-424-8580
Objectives: To render supportive person-to-person services to adults - especially older persons with special or exceptional needs; to provide part-time volunteer service opportunities for low-income older persons.
Services: Provides grants to public agencies and nonprofit organizations to develop and manage a program to provide companions to adults with physical and mental health limitations, adhering to the same guidelines as the Foster Grandparent Program (separate entry); publishes *Senior Companion Program Operations Handbook,* recruitment flyers and other materials.
Contact: Rey Tejada
Publications: SCP Operations Handbook
Founded: 1971

SENIOR OPPORTUNITIES AND SERVICES
US/HHS - Office of Community Services
Office of the Secretary
Washington, DC 20201
TEL: 202-632-2010
Objectives: To meet the needs of the older poor through volunteer opportunities, employment and other services.
Services: Approaches these objectives by taking steps to assure:
- greater involvement in public service by the older poor;
- development of recreation and service centers controlled by older persons;
- provision of volunteer opportunities and new employment for the elderly poor;
- referral services to existing health, housing, legal, transportation, education and other services;
- other activities and services to meet the needs of the older poor and assure them greater self-sufficiency.

CSA provides financial assistance for this program to state and local governments, public agencies, and private nonprofit organizations; also, local Community Action Agencies may delegate individual projects by contract to other agencies.
Sponsor: US/HHS - Department of Health & Human Services

US/SBA - SERVICE CORPS OF RETIRED EXECUTIVES/ACTIVE CORPS OF EXECUTIVES
US/SBA - SCORE/ACE
1441 L Street, NW
Washington, DC 20416
TEL: 202-653-6570
Objectives: To utilize the management experience of retired business executives for the benefit of new and existing small businesses.
Services: Provides volunteer experts to assist the small business entrepreneur with any management problem; operates service through Small Business Administration field offices; places SCORE volunteers in Chamber of Commerce Offices in some areas; reimburses volunteers for out-of-pocket expenses; extends assistance to community organizations; publishes counselor guidebooks and brochures.
Sponsor: US/SBA - Small Business Administration
Publications: SCORE Guidebook

VOLUNTEER SERVICE CORPS COMMITTEE
American Health Care Association
1200 Fifteenth Street, NW
Washington, DC 20005
TEL: 202-833-2050

Objectives: To provide services that otherwise would not be possible; to maintain continuity with the community; to give residents an unpaid concerned friend - often giving them a new outlook on life.
Services: Develops volunteer programs for nursing homes; provides technical assistance on administration and day-to-day operation; publishes *Establishing and Maintaining a Volunteer Program: A Handbook for Long Term Care Facilities* and other materials for program managers; participates in AHCA annual meeting.
Publications: Notes; Handbook for Long Term Care Facilities
Founded: 1949

WESTERN GERONTOLOGICAL SOCIETY*
785 Market Street
Suite 1114
San Francisco, CA 94103
Objectives: To improve the lives of older persons.
Services: Participates in national-level decision-making in the field of aging through such groups as the Leadership Council of Aging Organizations and the Knowledge in Practice in Aging Group sponsored by the Administration on Aging; undertakes special research, conference and training projects such as:
- **Elders in Voluntarism** which incorporates activities by senior volunteers as discussed at a special session of the WGS annual meeting and published in a comprehensive notebook with sections on program profiles, suggested readings and audiovisual resources (designed for local senior volunteer program managers).
- **Mobilizing Resources for Underserved Elders** which is a National Aging Organization project including a taxonomy describing types and degrees of underservice among subgroups of elders, develops profiles of non-aging network resources in the corporate, labor and philanthropic sectors, and establishes strategies for matching resources with needs of elders who are underserved.
- **Advocacy Development Program** which presents testimony and initiates legislative efforts; promotes national, state and local advocacy activities (a previous activity highlighted the California Senior Legislature and events related to the White House Conference on Aging).

Organizes other training events and conferences such as White House Conference on Aging Mini-Conferences and Fall Training Institutes on specific topics; publishes a bimonthly newsletter, a quarterly journal, a monthly bulletin, and other materials; maintains "WGS Answers," an information clearinghouse and library.
Publications: WGS Connection; Generations; WGS Job Alert

YARNS OF YESTERYEAR PROJECT
University of Wisconsin
Extension Service
610 Langdon Street, Room 722
Madison, WI 53706
TEL: 608-263-2954; 608-263-6320
Objectives: To involve older citizens in a leisure time activity that enables them to make a cultural contribution.
Services: Enlists older citizens to write reminiscences of their early lives; publishes annual historical/cultural collections of these writings; involves families, senior centers, nursing homes, retirement centers, radio stations, and interested individuals; publishes the collection *We Were Children Then,* and a booklet, *How to Organize and Promote a Reminiscence Writing Contest;* has home study course in reminiscence writing.
Publications: We Were Children Then; Reminiscence Writing Contest
Founded: 1974

TRAINING PROGRAMS

ELDERS AND VOLUNTARISM*
SEE TRAINING/CONFERENCES/TEACHING: OLDER
VOLUNTEER

**OLDER AMERICANS AS A GROWING NATIONAL
RESOURCE***
SEE TRAINING/CONFERENCES/TEACHING: OLDER
VOLUNTEER

INDIVIDUAL PROGRAM PROFILES

THE BEST YEARS
SEE COMMUNICATIONS & PUBLIC RELATIONS: IMAGE

BETHEL LOVE KITCHEN
SEE INFORMATION & REFERRAL: HOMELESS

**BLUEGRASS MEDICARE-MEDICAID ASSISTANCE
PROGRAM**
Lexington Senior Citizens Center
1530 Nicholasville Road
Lexington, KY 40503
TEL: 606-278-6072
Purpose: To help senior citizens understand and complete forms
for Medicare and Medicaid programs.
Sponsor: American Association of Retired Persons
Contact: Volunteer Coordinator
Description: The *American Association of Retired Persons
(AARP)* and the *Lexington Senior Citizens Center* are jointly
sponsoring a program designed to assist people who have trouble
understanding their Medicare and Medicaid forms. Called the
Bluegrass Medicare-Medicaid Assistance Program, the effort offers
three days of training to volunteer counselors. When training is
completed, volunteers are placed at senior centers in their own
communities.
Volunteers are recruited in eight counties and required to commit
to at least eight hours of service each month, or two hours a week,
for six months. Informal meetings are held periodically to describe
the program and give potential volunteers an opportunity to decide
whether or not to join the project.
Founded: 1989

BROOKDALE-SCORE PROGRAM
Brookdale Community College
SCORE/ACE Chapter #36
Lincroft, NJ 07738
TEL: 201-842-1900/Ext. 568
Purpose: To utilize business expertise of retired executive and
working professionals for the benefit of others in business who
need help.
Sponsor: Brookdale Community College
Contact: Dayton Jones, Chairman
Description: Between 1970 and 1972, two local retired
businessmen worked to develop a SCORE (Service Corps of
Retired Executives) Chapter in the Lincroft area. Efforts were
made to enlist members, develop a working organization, and build
a reputation in the local business community. Monthly planning
meetings were held, but it was the involvement of the Brookdale
Community College and its offer of space and services that was
instrumental in getting SCORE Chapter #36 started. Between
1972 and 1979 membership grew to 33 volunteers, and the group
gained national recognition.
Volunteers are persons who have managerial experience and
include capacities of presidents, vice presidents, and business

owners. Membership is divided into two classifications: SCORE,
whose members are retired, and ACE (Active Corps of Executives)
composed of persons still actively engaged in business. The main
job of the SCORE/ACE volunteer is to counsel people who are
considering starting a new business and business owners who
encounter problems. The counseling is done on a one-to-one
confidential basis, and there is no charge for services provided by
volunteers. Three of the retired volunteers are women; the
remaining thirty of the SCORE/ACE volunteers are men.
In addition to the Chapter officers, Committees are appointed to
handle all operations of the group. At monthly meetings,
volunteers discuss the results of the previous month's efforts,
policy changes, correspondence received, and current and future
developments and projections. Committee meetings are held
separately.
The publicity committee develops tapes and scripts for radio;
reports success stories, events, etc., to newspapers; maintains a
speakers bureau; and operates a poster program in supermarkets,
post offices, bus stations, etc., to fulfill its task of making the local
business community aware of the Chapter's free counseling
services.
Counseling is conducted daily by appointment at the College and,
one evening each week, at the Monmouth County Library. Over
400 clients are counseled each year and the number of hours spent
by counselors exceeds 600. There are about 60 ongoing counseling
cases.
In addition to the counseling sessions, SCORE volunteers work
cooperatively with College representatives in a number of
business-related endeavors, including:
- **Business Seminars:** conducted twice each year in the spring
  and fall; consist of six lectures each day with daily attendance
  ranging from 60 to 100 persons.
- **Small Business Institute Program:** implemented as a pilot
  program sponsored by the US Small Business Administration
  (the first community college to provide such a program).
- **University Business Development Center Program:** patterned
  after above Institute in a working arrangement with Rutgers
  University.
- **Monmouth Employment Research Center Program:**
  established through a grant to audit the CETA program
  throughout Monmouth County.
- **SCORE Addresses Classes:** developed in response to requests
  that SCORE volunteers conduct workshops for students.
Chapter #36 members have over 1100 years of cumulative
experience in dealing with business problems, and they counsel all
types of entrepreneurs - from the small "Mom and Pop" retailer to
the owner or manager of a business with a million-dollar
operation. Volunteers actively participate on college committees,
and have reduced the workload of the Career Services Personnel.
Expansion of the program includes workshop seminars at two
other area colleges, and increased speaking engagements at local
service clubs and other organizations.
Founded: 1972

CALIFORNIA HOUSE
SEE COMMUNITY SERVICES

**CENTRAL NAUGATUCK VALLEY RETIRED SENIOR
VOLUNTEER PROGRAM**
232 North Elm Street
Waterbury, CT 06702
TEL: 203-575-9799
Purpose: To help meet the personal needs of older Americans to
perform satisfying roles and have meaningful lives within their
own community.
Sponsor: New Opportunities for Waterbury
Contact: Doris T. Niedzielski, Director,
Description: This program was established in 1972 under the
Older Americans Act. It operates on a grant from ACTION,

federal funds, sponsored by a CAP Agency, NOW, Inc. It covers seniors age 60 and over and was originated to use the expertise of the older American in non-profit agencies to both help the agency in question and the senior who had finished working economically but still had the skills to give and the time to give them. Support systems are given, such as transportation and meals, so that volunteering does not cost the volunteer anything. Recognition lunches once a year, pins, certificates, etc., are given.

Volunteers are placed in approximately 56 stations which are non-profit agencies: hospitals, nursing homes, schools, Red Cross, Cancer Society, nutrition centers, senior centers, information and referral centers, retarded facilities, energy assistance agencies, libraries, and calling the elderly who live alone. RSVP boasts 550 volunteers.

Duties are diversified and training is given primarily by the station: answering phones, clerical work, teaching classes, selling crafts, making crafts, reading to confined persons in nursing homes, collating newsletters, working in gift shops, serving meals, helping put books on shelves, etc. Some more sophisticated volunteers teach in the high school in a rural area, teach English, or work in the court.

Staff of the RSVP includes a director and a coordinator. They are responsible for running the program, interviewing volunteers, placing volunteers, follow-ups, and all budget materials needed to keep the program running. Transportation for volunteers is coordinated.

RSVP has an advisory board made up of 15 people from the various agencies and stations, some volunteers, and some people from the community at large.

Its purpose is to advise the director on how to provide the services needed, or to raise funds if necessary. They make some policies and have by-laws.
Founded: 1972

CHILDREN'S QUILT PROJECT
1478 University Avenue
Suite 186
Berkeley, CA 94702
TEL: 415-548-3843
Purpose: To make quilts for children suffering from AIDS and other children "born under the shadow of misfortune."
Contact: Diane Dehler, Founder
Description: The Center for Disease Control in Atlanta reports that by March 1989, 1,708 children had been diagnosed with AIDS - 1,130 of them under five years of age. More than 93 percent of these children are children of adult carriers, often drug users. In Miami, one out of 57 newborns tests positive for the HIV virus; in New York, it's one of 61. In the Bay Area, figures are lower, but AIDS workers are worried.

In an attempt to help make children with AIDS feel special, a group of four volunteers from the Bay Area started the *Children's Quilt Project.* This program provides hand-made quilts to children with AIDS and others who can benefit from the gift. By June, the quilting session volunteers increased from the initial four to 60 quilters - including school children and amateur quilters - and over 400 quilts had been distributed to children who are victims of AIDS or other misfortunes.

The program relies entirely on donations and volunteers. At the end of the school year in 1989, 2,000 school children in Alameda, Oakland and Berkeley created panels for quilts. Senior citizens donate their time and skills several hours each week.

Although the project was begun to demonstrate concern and caring, the response by the children themselves was unexpected. In some cases, it represented the first possession that belonged "only to the child."

Within 15 months of its inception, the program had gone nationwide - almost totally by word of mouth. Women in Florida, Ohio, and Colorado formed quilting programs, and word was received that a woman in Switzerland was stitching a quilt. To make the nationwide status official, the founder is seeking volunteer administrative help to organize files and maintain accountability, and funding to pay for more brochures about AIDS which the program has developed for school children. Also, the organization as it expands hopes to become an advocate for AIDS children. Currently, volunteers from the Quilt project visit elementary schools to talk about AIDS.

A social worker working with AIDS children observed, "Children often carry their quilts around with them everywhere. They become a special part of their lives. It makes a tremendous difference." A foster mother who cares for AIDS children adds, "Blankets are very special to small children. I have one little 2-1/2-year old whose quilt is in tatters; he drags it around everywhere. They've offered to make him another, but he refuses."
Founded: 1988

CHIP-IN
SEE VOLUNTEERS: CHURCH/SYNAGOGUE MEMBERS

CONEJO VALLEY RETIRED SENIOR VOLUNTEER PROGRAM
110 South Conejo School Road
Thousand Oaks, CA 91362
TEL: 203-575-9799
Purpose: To provide meaningful volunteer opportunities for persons over the age of 60.
Sponsor: Federal/Conejo Recreation and Park District
Contact: Juanita Barnum
Description: The Retired Senior Volunteer Program (RSVP) is a national program whose primary purpose is to provide volunteer opportunities for persons 60 years of age and older. The Conejo Recreation and Park District has been sponsoring the Conejo Valley based program since its inception in October 1972. Since the beginning, more than 60 non-profit public and private agencies have benefitted from the contribution of over 290,000 hours of volunteer time donated by Conejo Valley seniors.

RSVP is located at the Goebel Senior Center, is staffed by a director, and an assistant director, who are responsible for the operation of the program and volunteer recruitment. Through their efforts, volunteers are interviewed and placed at volunteer stations to perform a specific function within a local agency. Further, RSVP staff provides support services for volunteers which include transportation, volunteer recognition, meals and participant insurance. In addition to stations throughout the community such as the hospitals, schools, Red Cross, American Cancer Society, etc., a number of workshops are held at the center. The handmade items and craft projects that are produced by these talented and dedicated seniors are sold, with proceeds going to support the Meals on Wheels Program and the Fitzgerald Day Care Center and local hospitals and convalariums. Currently, 300 Conejo Valley seniors are active members of RSVP with a lifetime total of 695 senior volunteers.
Founded: 1972

CORPORATE RETIREES INFORMATION AND ASSISTANCE PROGRAM
SEE INFORMATION & REFERRAL: OLDER PERSON

COUNTRY GATHERING
Northeast Kentucky Area Development Council
PO Box U
Olive Hill, KY 41164
TEL: 606-286-4443
Purpose: To provide a well-balanced meal in a social setting to older persons; to provide other services to the elderly as needed.
Sponsor: Kentucky Dept. of Human Resources (through FIVCO); AOA/HHS
Contact: Regina Fannin, Project Director

Description: Country Gathering began as a federally-funded nutrition demonstration project in June 1968 under Title IV (Research and Demonstration Grants) from the Administration on Aging. It now operates five multi-purpose senior centers and seven satellite nutrition sites in the FIVCO (five-county) area covering Lawrence, Greenup, Elliott, Carter and Boyd Counties.

The multi-purpose centers provide meals plus services; the satellite nutrition sites provide meals with a limited number of services. Approximately 500 congregate meals and one hundred homebound meals are served daily Monday through Friday.

The program is administered by twenty-nine full-time employees, five part-time employees, and approximately 200 volunteers. Ninety-five percent of the volunteers are over 65 years of age.

All meals are prepared at a central kitchen and packaged in insulated containers. The food is transported by vans and the travel time varies from five minutes to two hours. The bulk trays maintain safe temperatures for a maximum of four hours. Homebound meals are packaged in individual insulated trays. Meals served at multi-purpose centers and nutrition sites are served free, with a suggested donation of $.75 per person (age 60 or older). This has been done to help maintain the dignity of the elderly participants. A rural transportation system provides transportation at a reduced rate for senior citizens, but the program buys a limited number of free tickets for participants who need them.

Initially, the focus of Country Gathering was on nutrition only. Today services such as legal services, shopping assistance, art and crafts, information and referrals, counseling, chore service, crisis intervention, winterization, discount cards, visiting reassurance in the home, and many others are provided through the five multi-purpose centers, with limited services of this type available at the nutrition sites also. Some of the services are provided by the Community Action Agency, which administers the Aging Program and provides additional employees such as transporters, kitchen aides, and site managers. The Aging Program operates a Home Care Program which provides homemaker services, chore service, home repair, respite, medical transportation and escort, to those vulnerable elderly who would be institutionalized without the service.

Founded: 1968

FAMILY FRIENDS PROJECT
Project Any Baby Can
400 Labor St.
San Antonio, TX 78210
TEL: 512-227-3146

Purpose: To improve life for families with children who need special care through involvement of older volunteers.

Sponsor: National Council on the Aging

Contact: Volunteer Coordinator

Description: The *Family Friends Project* is an outgrowth of a model project developed in 1984 by the *National Council on Aging* to demonstrate how older volunteers can improve life for families with children who need special care. The San Antonio program began in 1986 and is sponsored by *Project Any Baby Can* and *Senior Community Services. Family Friends* matches volunteers age 55 and older with families who have a chronically-ill or handicapped child. The volunteers spend at least four hours a week with the child. By mid-1989, the project's 50 local volunteers had contributed more than 12,000 hours of service.

The volunteers complete a comprehensive training session covering handicaps and serious illnesses, such as leukemia, that they will encounter in their assignments. In cases of handicapped children, they learn some of the techniques of helping the children reach their greatest potential. One three-year-old blind child could not walk when the volunteer arrived. With the extra time that could be spent with the the little girl through the involvement of the older volunteer, she soon was walking, talking, going to school and

learning how to play. Although working with terminally-ill children is the most difficult, the training helps the volunteers "direct the families' love toward the child(ren) they still have," as they learn to accept their losses.

In addition to teaching and playing with the children, the service of the volunteer allows a needed respite for the family. Often they will take full responsibility and enable the family to spend an evening or a weekend away from home.

As one community leader pointed out, "The handicapped or chronically-ill child loves more powerfully than a healthy child." The volunteers find every experience fulfilling, and feel a "sense of satisfaction of having done something really worthwhile a few hours a day." Four of the older volunteers in the project received awards in 1989 for their many hours of dedicated service to the children and their families.

Founded: 1986

GRAND PEOPLE'S RETIRED SENIOR VOLUNTEER PROGRAM
Grand People, Inc.
103 West Nebraska Street
Bonifay, FL 32425
TEL: 904-547-4263

Purpose: To provide volunteer opportunities for senior citizens sixty years of age and over.

Sponsor: Tri-County Community Council

Contact: Julie Prevatt, RSVP Director

Description: The *Grand People's RSVP (Retired Senior Volunteer Program)* covers Holmes, Walton, Washington and Jackson Counties. The goal of *RSVP* is to facilitate the productive involvement of persons sixty and over in community life through volunteer service. Senior Citizens are a rich resource of information, skills, knowledge, and experiences. *RSVP* attempts to provide all senior citizens, regardless of education or income, with the opportunity to use these capabilities to help others in a way that is meaningful to them. Local agencies in need of volunteers may request *RSVP* Volunteers to be placed with their agencies in varied positions. The volunteer experience should provide a chance for the volunteer to develop new interests and skills, as well as form new friendships and social contacts.

At present, 323 volunteers have been placed with agencies such as the *Council on Aging, Health and Rehabilitative Services,* public libraries, hospitals, nursing homes, public schools, and private non-profit agencies. These volunteers have varying levels of experience and education, therefore placement is made by matching volunteers with positions duties and qualifications. Placements have been made in positions such as school class aides, librarians, hospital auxiliary, clerk typists, file clerks, carpenters, crafts coordinator and fund raising coordinators, to name a few. Other sponsors and participants in the program include the South Carolina Department of Corrections, Dutchman Correctional Institute School, South Carolina Literacy Association, Laubach Literacy Action, and United Way.

GRATERFRIENDS
Graterford State Correctional Institution
Bridge Street
Graterford, PA 19426
TEL: 215-489-4151

Purpose: To bring together senior citizens from the community and older offenders about to be released from prison.

Sponsor: Graterford Prison

Contact: Joan Gauker

Description: Graterford Prison's Concerned Senior Group and members of the North Penn Senior Center in the community meet regularly to socialize and prepare for the day that the older offenders will become neighbors of the volunteer seniors from the community. The two groups of seniors sit across from one another in a dismal prison meeting room. Their common bonds of age and humanity quickly bring them through awkward beginnings into easy conversation and laughter.

For the alloted hour and a half, the talk between older folks in brown prison uniforms and folks in street clothing zigzagged through serious concerns for senior citizen safety, spontaneous humor, remembrances of past days, future hopes, hobbies and interests.

Through the many meetings that take place at Graterford Prison, incarcerated seniors and the older volunteers formulate new strategies to help communities to reduce crime against seniors on the street.

According to one observor, "If nothing else emerges from these gatherings, one thing is clear - these folks will be good neighbors - as if there were no concrete wall between them."

HOME LEAGUE
Salvation Army
200 Jefferson Highway
New Orleans, LA 70119
TEL: 504-835-1781
Purpose: To provide volunteer opportunities in a social setting for retirees, widows and others who feel a need for companionship.
Sponsor: Salvation Army
Contact: Mrs. Capt. Linda Adair, Coordinator
Description: Two nights a week different groups of retirees, widows and others come together to socialize and to make gifts for shut-ins and children's homes. The program, *Home League,* was started to fill the need for companionship among this group, but soon became a busy activity for volunteer work. They begin in midsummer to dress dolls for the children's home, and begin preparation for other Christmas projects. In the meantime, most participate also in the *League of Mercy* when time permits. This is a visitation project, offering companionship and home-made gifts to residents of hospitals, nursing homes and other institutions on a monthly basis. On holidays, the group visits the Veteran's Hospital, and takes gifts to prison inmates.

The best part of the program, according to the director, is the reciprocal nature of it. The volunteers get as much as they give, since many of them would be isolated themselves except for the Salvation Army programs. One widow, distraught and lonely, accompanied a friend to the *Home League* several years ago, and has volunteered with the group ever since. "This place saved my life... and these people saved my sanity," she said.

HOME REPAIRS PROJECT
Big Country Retired Senior Volunteer Program
PO Box 5648
Abilene, TX 79608
TEL: 915-691-7225
Purpose: To organize volunteers and make small home repairs in the homes of the elderly.
Sponsor: Senior Community Services, Inc.
Contact: Nancy E. Cummingham
Description: The home repair program for the elderly began after the Regional Agency on Aging made a needs assessment which indicated this service was not available to older adults in this area and was a priority need. An allotment of $1,500 dollars was made the first year to buy necessary tools and supplies and to reimburse the volunteers for mileage and out-of-pocket expenses.

The purpose of this innovative program is to help the elderly remain in their homes and be independent as long as their health allows them to be. Three or four volunteers, with at least one volunteering four or more days a week, can make small home repairs in over 300 homes during the year.

The majority of the volunteers are over 60 years of age, and are members of the Retired Senior Volunteer Program - a part of ACTION. However, since the program began the grantee of RSVP covers all volunteers with insurance. Several younger volunteers have given many hours of service.

The results have been so satisfying that volunteers remain in the program until disabilities force them to curtail the more strenuous assignments. As high as 80 air conditioners are serviced in a two month period in late spring and then winterized in the fall. Because the program can pay for professional plumbing services many older adults do not not have to move from their homes. Many agencies (i.e., Information and Referral, Community Action, etc.) refer clients to the program. RSVP cooperates with other agencies, pooling money and services for expensive repairs, such as a new sewer line. Many goods and services are donated and when recycled, the dollars are stretched to assist even more clients. Program publicity was sent to the Meals on Wheels Plus Program, senior centers, churches, the media, the Community Action Program, the welfare agencies, and all agencies who use volunteers. Six volunteers formed the first Advisory Committee who set the guidelines.

A grant from the State Department on Aging, serving a city of 100,000 and one rural county, has been renewed each year since 1978 for $7,500. The local Rotary Clubs contribute the 10% match.
Founded: 1978

LIFESTORY THEATER
Autumn Stages
Upper Montclair, NJ 07042
TEL: 201-746-7710
Purpose: To stimulate memory and reawaken self-esteem and motivation among the elderly.
Contact: Troupe Director
Description: Depression, isolation and a sense of uselessness are often feelings the elderly experience. Autumn Stages takes an innovative approach to coping with these feelings through a first-of-its-kind improvisational *Lifestory Theater* performed by and for older adults.

The troupe never uses a script. All of their *lifestory* scenes are improvised, which allows them to get audience members into the act and, better yet, to spontaneously share their own life experiences. The creativity and enthusiasm of the troupe is reflected in those who view the plays.

The volunteer troupe of Autumn Stages consists of more than 20 retired individuals, ages 50 to 83, who serve as role models for senior citizens through their active audience participation in *Lifestory Theater.* They come from all walks of life, and only a few have ever acted before. The others have found their latent talents and learned new acting skills in training workshops led by skilled artistic leaders. The workshops cover improvisational drama, mime, storytelling, old dances and song, and, most important, ways to encourage involvement from the audience.

The troupe tours in large vans to nursing homes, nutritional sites, churches and synagogues, geriatric wings of hospitals, libraries, senior centers, festivals and other sites for older adults. Last year, Autumn Stages reached over 12,000 older adults throughout the state.

Autumn Stages received a 1989 *Governor's Volunteer Award* for its volunteer work. According to the nominator, "They exemplify the highest form of giving. It's incredible to watch them take a life story and, after barely a moment, get into its character and enact it."
Publications: Autumn Stages: Information Packet
Founded: 1988

LINCOLN COUNTY SENIOR COMPANION PROGRAM
SEE VOLUNTEERS: LOW-INCOME

LIVINGSTON COUNTY RSVP PROGRAM
Box 445
Chillicothe, MO 64601
TEL: 816-646-0010

Purpose: To provide volunteer opportunities for senior citizens in meaningful public service.
Sponsor: Concerned Christians of Livingston County
Contact: Ruth Seiberling, Director
Description: The program began in September, 1973. Seventy percent of the funding for the program comes from a grant from ACTION (Federal agency); 30% is raised locally by the program and sponsoring organization. The goals are to provide volunteer opportunities for senior citizens in meaningful public service. Volunteers perform a wide variety of tasks, such as:

- drug and alcohol abuse program
- teaching *Laubach Literacy* to adults and older youth
- school volunteering
- tutoring
- working with youthful court offenders
- working with retarded youth and adults
- working with mental patients
- working in the Senior Center
- sponsoring *Just Say No* clubs for elementary students
- working with the *Congregate Meal Program*
- delivering mobile meals
- working in the county library
- assisting in the health center
- visiting in hospitals and in nursing homes
- maintaining a marionette theater for school children
- working as volunteers in the women's prison
- assisting with used clothing distribution centers
- assisting with income tax and tax refund programs
- maintaining a senior citizen gift shop
- working as volunteers in the hospital
- working with the Extension Service in youth projects
- assisting with Family Service and welfare projects
- helping with the Blood Bank
- doing in-home service for shut-ins

There are currently 485 volunteers, all over age 60. Volunteers receive on-the-job training at the start of their job and other training sessions throughout the year. Volunteers are supervised by Volunteer Station personnel who keep a record of their hours and turn them in to the RSVP office. An Advisory Council made up of RSVP volunteers and other citizens from the community acts as a planning council for the program. Approximately 70,000 volunteer hours are involved in a year's time.

The RSVP staff produces a monthly newsletter which informs the volunteers and volunteer stations about new developments in the program, new volunteer opportunities and a report on the various activities being carried on by the program. Recognition parties for volunteers are held three times yearly and volunteers receive certificates, dinners, and other awards at this time. All volunteers are insured for accident, and excess liability is carried on drivers of privately-owned vehicles.

All Retired Senior Volunteers are entitled to furnished meals and transportation on the days that they do volunteer work.
Founded: 1973

MANTENO VETERANS HOME VOLUNTEER PROGRAM
Manteno Veterans Home
One Veterans Drive
Manteno, IL 60950
TEL: 815-468-6581
Purpose: To involve volunteers of all ages in service to veterans at Manteno Veterans Home.
Sponsor: State of Illinois
Contact: Patricia Essington, Director of Volunteers
Description: In 1989, the senior volunteer component of the Manteno Veterans Home was awarded first prize in the Governor's Home Town Award program. Its student component and overall program each won honorable mentions. In addition, the Home was given a street sign to be placed at its entrance, reading *1989 Governor's Home Town Award Winner - Building*

Illinois with Volunteers.
Volunteers come from all over the county, and as far north as the north side of Chicago.

Along with being on call for any need that comes along, volunteers have specific assignments such as escorting the aged and infirm veterans to physical therapy, the barber shop, the commissary, the bank, the x-ray facilities, and the pharmacy. They assist with parties and help members of the home play bingo. Part of their duties includes assisting with meals - both serving them and helping some of the infirm to eat.

Involvement by many volunteers means a long weekly drive - including some volunteers in their mid-70s. Many are members of the area *Veterans of Foreign Wars* and *American Legion* posts as well as various ladies' auxiliaries.

The hours of service run into the thousands for some individuals. As for the reward for the senior volunteers, according to the director, the seniors "understand the needs of these older veterans and they handle them with care and understanding." But she quickly adds that it is the entire volunteer force that is the backbone of the winning program.

MAPLEWOOD MANOR RSVP PROGRAM
American Red Cross
Saratoga County Chapter
368 Broadway
Saratoga, NY 12020
TEL: 518-584-2510
Purpose: To provide services for the blind and visually handicapped, while creating volunteer opportunities for residents of a nursing home.
Sponsor: American Red Cross/Saratoga County
Contact: Denise Smith, RSVP Director
Description: When ACTION's Retired Senior Volunteer Program (RSVP) was first introduced in Maplewood Manor in 1984, the response was negligible. Less than 10 residents became involved, mainly because the workload was infrequent and small in volume. Maplewood Manor is a nursing home with 39 resident men and women with an average age of 80. But when the coordinator of volunteers services for the *New York State Library for the Blind and Visually Handicapped* showed an interest in the volunteer program there, the response more than tripled.

All 39 volunteers are in wheelchairs, and many are debilitated with difficult and limited use of their hands and arms. Working to benefit people with sight limitations is especially meaningful because so many of the residents themselves have a variety of disabilities to overcome.

Residents have prepared bulk mailings and placed address labels with the organization's new address on obsolete posters and pamphlets, making them usable again. The materials are sent to community groups, which place them throughout the town. More than 5,000 of the posters and 32 cases of other materials were put up statewide, giving vital information about the state Library for the Blind and Visually Handicapped. For instance, in spite of the library's name, many do not understand that people who wish to use the library need not be blind. Even people with 20-20 vision can use the facility if they are unable to hold a book or turn pages. A simple matter of changing the address enabled thousands of additional people to use this important facility.

The library coordinator found the library suffering from a shortage of volunteers, since many women who looked for volunteer work while their children were in school are now in the workforce. With more and more agencies seeking volunteer help, the logical step was to look at populations that have not been asked to volunteer before. With the Maplewood experience so positive, the coordinator feels that agencies need to look into how they can accommodate these older groups of volunteers.

The effect of the project on the residents themselves has been very positive and extremely beneficial to their morale and sense of self worth. "They yell at me when I don't bring more work for them," he said.

As a result of their volunteer efforts, the Maplewood Manor volunteers were nominated for a state award.

MATCHING FUNDS PROJECT
SEE FUNDING/FUND-RAISING/RELATED SERVICES

MILTON CARES TELEPHONE REASSURANCE
Retired Senior Volunteer Program
3 Cathedral Square
Burlington, VT 05401
TEL: 802-862-6444
Purpose: To provide daily contact with homebound elderly, and to provide a social contact for people who are essentially alone.
Sponsor: US/ACTION
Contact: Judith R. Dunlop
Description: Milton Cares is a program of telephone reassurance to the shut-in elderly in the rural town of Milton, Vermont. It was developed following two incidents involving elderly shut-in women who were terrorized in their homes and not discovered for several days.

Townspeople responded to these incidents by developing a telephone reassurance program. A door-to-door survey was conducted by senior residents of Milton, with staff from the Area Agency on Aging, the local Community Action Agency, the Milton Police Department, VISTA Volunteers, and RSVP staff. Seniors living alone were identified and matched with a senior volunteer caller from Milton.

The program operates on a continual basis, identifying seniors needing contact who may be newcomers to the area or for some other reason have not been identified previously. Milton Cares proceeds through several steps to provide the most appropriate response to each situation, including:

- Each day the caller places a call at the agreed time.
- If there is no answer, the volunteer calls again a short time later.
- If no answer on the second try, a call is placed to a designated friend or relative in an attempt to determine the whereabouts of the client.
- If the volunteer is unable to obtain assurance of the client's wellbeing, the police are notified.

The Police Department maintains an up-to-date list of clients and callers, and makes an immediate check of the house when notified. In addition, each caller receives a set of instructions, background about the client, monthly reporting form, and reminder card. Results to date include:

- updated list of seniors living alone and in need of daily phone contact;
- thirty seniors are being contacted daily by senior volunteers from their community;
- a waiting list of prospective clients is being matched daily with callers;
- training for callers has been developed and is provided to all volunteers;
- a volunteer coordinator has been designated to keep track of the callers' efforts, process new requests, and place two volunteer coordinators to do home visits prior to enrollment.

The Milton Cares program has served as an example of neighbor helping neighbor. It has allowed citizens to help themselves to remain in their homes alone, to form new friendships, and to have the opportunity to be drawn into senior activities through their volunteer callers.

MULTI-PHASIC HEALTH SCREENING
Retired Senior Volunteer Program
200 North Vineyard Boulevard
Room 603
Honolulu, HI 96817
TEL: 808-536-643

Purpose: To provide free health screening to senior citizens, and provide an opportunity for retired nurses and other senior citizens to serve the community.
Sponsor: State of Hawaii
Contact: Francis S. Dunning, Program Coordinator
Description: In the early 1970's, the Moiliili Community Center, a Retired Senior Volunteer Program (RSVP) volunteer station, developed and set up a model free multi-phasic health screening program for senior citizens residing in the general area around the volunteer station.

Over thirty senior volunteers, some of whom were retired nurses, were responsible for implementation of the program. Once a month the volunteers performed tests and guided participants to the various screening sites. For tasks that required special knowledge, volunteers were given training by public health nurses. When all tests were completed, the results were forwarded to a public health nurse for review and analysis of the results. After the nurse returned them to the screening program with her comments, follow-up letters were written to each of the older persons' physicians.

Screening was conducted in the recreation room of a public housing facility for senior citizens. Many of the volunteers lived in the housing complex and were recruited by the senior citizens' recreation specialist, whose office is in the building.

Recognizing the diversity of backgrounds among senior citizens in the area, bilingual volunteers were recruited to work with older persons who needed this type of assistance to participate. Hot lunches were prepared and served by RSVP after the screening process was completed.

Initially sponsored by the Community Center and ACTION, the model proved to be a complete success. It has become a statewide program now sponsored solely by the State of Hawaii.
Founded: 1972

NEIGHBORHOOD TREE CORPS
SEE VOLUNTEERS: STUDENTS

NEW HAMPSHIRE FOSTER GRANDPARENT PROGRAM
New England Center for Continuing Education
University of New Hampshire
15 Garrison Avenue
Durham, NH 03824
TEL: 603-862-1721
Purpose: To provide meaningful part-time volunteer opportunities for low-income older persons and to render supportive, person-to-person services to children with special or exceptional needs.
Sponsor: New England Center for Continuing Education
Contact: Alfred Goldenburg, Director
Description: The New Hampshire Foster Grandparents Program is one of the federally funded ACTION programs. Its purpose is to provide additional income and meaningful part-time volunteer opportunities for low-income older persons and to render supportive, person-to-person services to children with special or exceptional needs in the areas of health, education and welfare.

The program focuses primarily on a person-to-person continuing relationship between an older person and a child with special needs. Although the primary purpose is to provide for the needs of low-income elderly people, the end result is a mutually beneficial relationship. The program provides low-income men and women age 60 and older an opportunity for meaningful service to children 21 years of age and under who have exceptional needs and are often deprived of normal relationships with adults.

At the present time the New Hampshire Foster Grandparent Program, under the sponsorship of the New England Center for Continuing Education at the University of New Hampshire, is funded for 60 foster grandparents to be used in volunteer stations throughout the state. The foster grandparents serve on a regular schedule: four hours a day, five days a week. They are assigned two children, whom they usually serve individually, each day. The foster grandparents receive a stipend of $2.00/hour, a hot meal daily, transportation to and from their volunteer stations (or reimbursement for driving themselves), training, and a yearly physical.

Currently there is a waiting list for older persons wanting to be foster grandparents and for agencies who would like to be volunteer stations. However, until additional funds are raised to support an expansion, the program is limited to the ACTION funds which now support it at a level of 60 foster grandparents. In addition to helping the elderly in terms of supplemental income, the program fulfills their need for a sense of usefulness and self-worth and adds a new social dimension to their lives.

NURSING HOME PROJECT
Retired Senior Volunteer Program
311 Pine Avenue
PO Box 3149
Albany, GA 31706
TEL: 912-435-9779
Purpose: To provide companionship for nursing home residents, and volunteer opportunities for low-income minority elderly.
Sponsor: SOWEGA Council on Aging; US/ACTION
Contact: Anne Bragg, Director
Description: A nursing home visitation project was begun in Albany several years ago, and it has become a permanent part of the RSVP program. Its focus is twofold in that it benefits both the nursing home residents and the volunteers.

The 25 senior volunteers are predominantly low-income minority without transportation. They are active participants in the Title III nutrition program, attending two sites in Albany. The volunteers are divided into three groups, each visiting the nursing home one day a week. The RSVP van takes the volunteers from their homes to the nursing home, where they spend one to two hours as "friendly visitors." Then the van takes them to the senior nutrition site for their noon meal.

The volunteer support (van service, meals, recognition, and insurance) provided by this program enables the volunteers to serve their community in a meaningful way. The nursing home residents look forward to the companionship of their RSVP "friends," and the volunteers are rewarded with a very real sense of being needed and appreciated. Another older volunteer group, the Georgia Peach Singers, presents musical programs each month at two local nursing homes - delightful old songs, dances, skits, and readings. Transportation is furnished to this group, also, and the nursing homes entertain both volunteers and residents with party refreshments.

The total RSVP project includes 300 volunteers who serve in 35 local agencies. It began in 1972 with a federal ACTION grant. Local funding is provided by the United Way plus in-kind donations, and the sponsor is the Southwest Georgia Council on Aging. The program goal is to serve this community with 42,000 hours of volunteer service per year, and to provide the senior volunteers with opportunities for meaningful involvement.
Founded: 1972

OPERATION COVER UP
Portland General Electric Company
38250 Pioneer Boulevard
Sandy, OR 97055
TEL: 503-668-4158
Purpose: To take seriously what appears on the surface to be a simple winter need - warm head covering for the elderly, migrant workers, low-income people, the homeless and others.
Sponsor: Portland General Electric Company
Contact: Hilda Walker, Customer Service Representative
Description: Since the business of electric companies is providing the means for warmth in the winter home, staff members of the Sandy office of the *Portland General Electric Company* mounted a

related project. Grappling for an idea for a useful community service project, a number of employees said they noticed people without warm head coverings, and after a discussion of the logistics such as volunteer manpower, community awareness materials, etc., *Operation Cover Up* was born. A logo, depicting a knit cap, was designed to help draw attention to the effort. The project collects donations of yarn and coordinates volunteer knitters who make the hand-knitted caps for senior citizens, migrant workers, low-income people and the homeless.

The utility company is working with the Clackamas and Multnomah County units of the *Retired Senior Volunteer Program (RSVP)* to collect yarn and make the caps. Both sides of the partnership contribute to both the knitting and the administrative function of the project.

PEER COUNSELOR PROGRAM*
Dakota Area Referral and Transportation for Seniors
DARTS
125 Sixth Avenue, North
South St. Paul, MN 55075
TEL: 612-455-1560
Purpose: To involve older volunteers in providing peers with companionship, and assisting them in working through difficulties.
Sponsor: DARTS
Contact: Percy Olson, Lillian Olson
Description: Combining a lifetime of experience with formal training the older volunteers in the Peer Counselor Program visit older persons needing companionship and assistance with problems in a wide area (South St. Paul, West St. Paul, Inger Grove Heights, Hastings). Most visits are made in the client's home. Volunteers completing the training are given the title of Certified Peer Counselor. A major thrust of the training is "learning to listen and not give advice." The philosophy is that, many times, a client can solve his or her own problem just by talking it through with someone who will listen.

Counselors are 60 years of age and older and, in addition to participation in the training program, are required to have compassion, a willingness to listen, and the ability to keep pace with a busy program.

Volunteers also have knowledge of available resources and services in the local area as well as the larger community. They are able to match specific problems with appropriate services for a client. Several of the volunteers visit area senior centers to explain, promote, and seek additional volunteers for the program.

Volunteer counselors receive mileage reimbursement, and DARTS provides additional car insurance.

A PERFECT MATCH
Ebensburg Center
Old Main
Ebensburg, PA 15931
TEL: 814-472-7350/Ext. 592-3
Purpose: To provide reciprocal social contact and personal attention for the mentally and physically handicapped residents of the Ebensburg Center and the older patients of Laurel Crest Manor (County Home).
Sponsor: Ebensburg Center and Laurel Crest Manor
Contact: Richard Nikolishen
Description: The program deals with the severely and profoundly mentally and physically handicapped residents of the Ebensburg Center who needs lots of love and training, and the older patients of Laurel Crest Manor who have lots of love and affection. In addition, they have the time and experience to share.

The patients of Laurel Crest Manor are escorted by their staff to the Ebensburg Center one day a week for two hours. Under the supervision of the Ebensburg Center's staff, each patient is assigned one resident and they either reinforce a training program or just provide company for each other.

Laurel Crest Manor and the Ebensburg Center are located in

Cambria County approximately four miles apart. This closeness has ensured fewer cancellations of the program because of bad weather.

The program started in October 1981 and is still working.

Founded: 1981

PHONE PAL
SEE BUSINESS/INDUSTRY INVOLVEMENT: CHILDREN/YOUTH

RETIRED SENIOR VOLUNTEER PROGRAM
Baltimore City Health Department
620 North Caroline Street
Room 9
Baltimore, MD 21205
TEL: 301-396-8146

Purpose: To establish a positive, recognizable role in the community and develop sources of satisfaction and meaning in life for persons 60 and older through volunteer service of genuine value to the community.

Sponsor: Federal/local governments

Contact: Ernestine D. Anderson

Description: Retired Senior Volunteer Program (RSVP) is designed to provide meaningful opportunities to those persons 60 years of age or older to give of their time and energies in community service. The program operates under the auspices of the Baltimore City Health Department - Health Services for the Aging, receiving funds from the federal government's ACTION program.

At present, over 800 volunteers contribute more than 16,000 hours per month to various non-profit agencies throughout the City of Baltimore. Volunteers are always needed and welcome. Volunteers duties include:

- friendly visiting to nursing homes and hospitals to read to patients and write letters for patients;
- make dolls and puppets for day care centers;
- act as librarian in local community colleges and hospitals;
- foodservice and recordkeeping in local nutrition programs;
- serve on various committees;
- mailings for non-profit organizations;
- tutors in schools;
- receptionists for court programs; and
- answering phones.

Volunteers work at RSVP with varying levels of experience. There are no restrictions based on education, income, experience or physical handicap. Prior to placement in an assignment, volunteers do receive orientation from RSVP. After they begin the assignment, they are given extensive training by the facility to which they are assigned. In-service training is then provided on an on-going basis along with supervision.

Founded: 1976

RETIRED SENIOR VOLUNTEER PROGRAM
626 Tucker Street
Room 13
Raleigh, NC 27602
TEL: 919-755-6295

Purpose: To provide older persons with an opportunity for volunteer service; to meet needs in the community.

Sponsor: City of Raleigh

Contact: Rebekah Wolff

Description: The Retired Senior Volunteer Program was established to provide a variety of opportunities for persons of retirement age to participate more fully in the life of their community through significant volunteer service. RSVP was authorized in 1969 under Title VI, Part A, of the Older Americans Act of 1965. RSVP is one of several federal volunteer services programs (Volunteers in Service to America, Foster Grandparent Program and the Senior Companion Program). ACTION's role is to encourage and stimulate broad areas of community volunteer service and to involve many more Americans in the complex poverty-related and social problems of the nation.

RSVP focuses on providing an opportunity to persons of retirement age to make constructive use of their time, talents and lifetime of experiences through volunteer activities, thereby giving them a renewed sense of satisfaction and purpose in life. In addition, it is hoped that the constructive use of this tremendous untapped manpower resource will help meet the many volunteer needs of community agencies and organizations.

RSVP is inherently a local program. In Raleigh/Wake County, North Carolina, the federal government provides 44% of the financial support through a grant awarded to the City of Raleigh. The City assumes the responsibility for administration and contributes 43% of the operating cash cost. An additional 13% comes from non-cash (in-kind) support from the community. This includes office space, transportation, meals and recognition of volunteers.

The major goal of the Raleigh/Wake County RSVP is to enable people to "retire to life rather than from life." This goal was accomplished in February 1982 by placing 636 volunteers in over sixty non-profit and health care facilities throughout Wake County. These volunteers generated 88,833 hours of volunteer service. This represented a dollar value of $266,920 to the community. Research has shown that older adults who remain active by doing volunteer work are healthier both physically and mentally than those who do not. RSVP assisted the volunteers by helping them find suitable placements, arranging for transportation if necessary, providing insurance coverage (accident, liability and excess automobile) during their volunteer assignments, and recognizing them throughout the year for their volunteer efforts. The cost per volunteer hour was $1.06.

Raleigh/Wake County RSVP placements are as varied as the individual volunteers. They impact on basic human needs areas within their own community. Placements include hospitals, mental health, craft co-ops, consumer protection, sewing groups, adult day care, child abuse and neglect, alcohol/drug abuse, literacy, nutrition, state museums and choral and band groups. The number of volunteers participating is 530.

RSVP ensures that senior volunteers receive adequate in-service instruction through the volunteer stations and/or other community resources by providing technical assistance to the volunteer coordinators at each agency.

Individual stations are responsible for the day-to-day supervision of the senior volunteers placed within that agency. RSVP staff is not allowed to supervise volunteers at volunteer stations. Other senior volunteers may be selected for supervision of other volunteers. RSVP ensures that local programs have arranged for adequate supervision through on-site visits.

Maggie Kuhn has stated "Elders need four things to thrive: A goal that transcends one's self, pride in one's personal history, meaningful new roles and a loving supportive community." Through successful volunteer placements, RSVP volunteers have been able to meet this goal.

Founded: 1969

RETIRED SENIOR VOLUNTEER PROGRAM
1721 South University Drive
Fargo, ND 58103
TEL: 701-235-6433

Purpose: To create meaningful opportunities for Retired Senior Citizens to remain active in their communities through volunteer service.

Sponsor: The Village Family Service Center

Contact: Sharon Maier, Director

Description: RSVP, Retired Senior Volunteer Program, was authorized by Congress in 1969 and became nationally operational under ACTION in 1971. The local program in Fargo was started in 1973. The program is funded by 70% Federal grant and 30%

local support.

The purpose of RSVP is to place retired persons 60 years of age and older into meaningful volunteer jobs in their community. Many times after retirement people find themselves feeling useless, and unneeded with nothing but time and lonely hours on their hands. It is the goal of RSVP to get the senior citizen out of his home and back into the community. The elderly are the nation's largest resource of skills, knowledge and experience and just because they reach retirement age doesn't suddenly change that. Therefore, why not have these people get out and share their talents?

This is done by finding volunteer positions for them in non-profit organizations within the community. The volunteers:

- read to the visually handicapped
- conduct crafts for the mentally handicapped
- visit shut-ins
- help care for children in day care centers
- do sewing in nursing homes
- tutor children in schools
- deliver meals to shut-ins
- volunteer in hospital gift shops and information desks.

These are only a few of the places and types of volunteer services. Their services are invaluable to these organizations, not to mention that it once again gives the senior citizen a feeling of worth - a reason to live.

The program currently has 420 volunteers, volunteering at 45 non-profit organizatons. Transportation is provided to volunteers who no longer can drive their own cars and also volunteers who do use their own cars to get to their volunteer station are reimbursed. The volunteers are covered by insurance, paid for by RSVP, in order to enable the senior citizen to volunteer at no cost to himself.

Volunteers are trained and supervised by volunteer coordinators at each volunteer station. The RSVP Director is in constant contact with the Volunteer Coordinators and the volunteers so that the best possible placement is made and so that they do receive proper training. Volunteers report their hours on a quarterly basis. An annual recognition luncheon is held for all of the volunteers in which the Governor, City Mayors and other honored guests take part.

To be an RSVP volunteer, senior citizens simply have to be 60 years of age or older and have an interest in volunteering their time and talents.

Founded: 1973

RETIRED SENIOR VOLUNTEER PROGRAM

470 North State Route 741
Lebanon, OH 45036
TEL: 513-932-6301

Purpose: To provide meaningful volunteer opportunities for persons over the age of 60.

Sponsor: Council on Aging of Warren County, Inc.

Contact: Lois Freeze, Director

Description: The Warren County Senior Volunteer Program began in 1974. Each year the program has increased its number of seniors and agencies served. The program currently has over 650 senior volunteers enrolled, who serve over 60,000 service hours in a fiscal year. This total enrollment ranks the Warren County RSVP project 7th largest in the state and the largest rural program.

Volunteers serve local non-profit agencies such as:

- county and city offices (i.e., Health/Welfare Department)
- Board of Education
- Food Stamp Program
- Human Service Board
- four (soon to be six) elderly nutrition sites
- nursing homes (active at seven institutions)
- charity associations, schools, libraries and many others.

The purpose of RSVP is twofold: while completing volunteer assignments for non-profit agencies is important, a major emphasis is placed on the mental well-being of seniors. By providing meaningful, rewarding volunteer tasks, the program is filling a void in many lives. For many seniors, their volunteer roles, the feeling of being needed and appreciated, is all that keeps them active.

Criteria for becoming an RSVP volunteer in Warren County are: be at least 60 years of age, either live in or volunteer in Warren County, and have the desire to help in the community. Although there are no other volunteer programs in Warren County serving senior citizens, the sponsoring agency also operates the Voluntary Action Center and the Young Volunteers in Action program, thus serving all ages.

There are many benefits to being a RSVP volunteer. Some of these are: covered by insurance while volunteering; learning new skills; meeting new friends; affiliation with a national organization; recognition; and, best of all, there is no charge of any kind to be part of this program. Transportation is provided (at no cost) to and from work stations for those volunteers who need it.

The project is federally funded through ACTION (70%) and locally by the Council on Aging. The 30% local funds are received from: Warren County Commissioners, United Way, in-kind contributions (rent, telephone, meals) and local fund raisers.

Founded: 1974

RETIRED SENIOR VOLUNTEER PROGRAM
Mid-Cumberland Community Action Agency (CAA)
Building 323, G Street
Smyrna, TN 37167
TEL: 615-459-4118/Ext. 24

Purpose: To provide senior citizens the opportunity to remain active and useful by volunteering their services to the community in which they live.

Sponsor: Mid-Cumberland Community Action Agency

Contact: Marjorie Bass, Director RSVP

Description: The Retired Senior Volunteer Program began in Rutherford/Sumner Counties in 1975. It is designed for persons 60 years and older, regardless of race, creed, religious affiliations, or educational background. RSVP is operated by a paid staff of four: Director, Coordinator, Bookkeeper, Clerk/Driver. Also there are one student intern and four Green Thumb workers.

This program is sponsored by Mid-Cumberland Community Action Agency, a non-profit organization that receives funds from federal, state, and local private organizations.

Presently there are over 300 volunteers enrolled in the program. The volunteers work in many phases of the community: nursing homes, hospitals, schools, tutoring adults, sewing classes, and looking after homebound senior citizens. Volunteer hours vary from week to week.

The goal of the Retired Senior Volunteer Program is to reach as many senior citizens as possible to assist them in staying active and to be and feel useful.

An hour of orientation is provided to volunteer stations and two hours of orientation to prospective volunteers before they are placed.

Founded: 1975

RETIRED SENIOR VOLUNTEER PROGRAM

Third and Walnut Streets
PO Box 2711
Texarkana, AR 75504
TEL: 501-774-3161/Ext. 321

Purpose: To provide a recognized role in the community and a meaningful life in retirement for persons 60 years old and older through significant volunteer service - in doing so, not only keeping these volunteers active, but also providing the community with a wealth of knowledge and experience.

Sponsor: The Twin City of Texarkana, Arkansas-Texas

Contact: Lillie Jackson, Director

Description: The *RSVP of Texarkana USA* was established in 1974, and funded by ACTION (a federal volunteer agency). Today, the *Texarkana RSVP* boasts 713 retired senior volunteers, and 30 associate volunteers 55-59 years old serving as community advocates on behalf of RSVP. RSVP provides service throughout eight counties, contributing over 221,571 hours per year.

After adequate training, RSVP volunteers are assigned to perform a variety of community services, listed in part below. The volunteer trend has and is continuously moving from the traditional toward the non-traditional form of volunteerism which means that volunteers' management is being challenged to meet the volunteer interests of the nineties. RSVP programs, in part:

- Adult literacy tutors.
- Intergenerational Library Assistance Program: Bridging generations through education, assisting youth after school with specific classroom assignments.
- Volunteer counselors and youth trainers for youth-against-drugs presentations.
- Computer operators for the *Criminal Investigation Department of Public Safety and Information Clerks.*
- Long-term care for the homebound, frail and handicapped elderly, especially transportation, accessibility ramps, etc.
- *Friendly Listen Intergenerational Program (FLIP):* Telephone pals for latch-key kids.
- Presenters of *We Help Ourselves (WHO),* an anti-victimizational program for youth through the public school system.
- Assist the *Crime Prevention Division of the Police Department* with video simulation of the re-enactment of various crimes.
- *Volunteer Income Tax Assistance (VITA)* and *Tax Counseling for the Elderly (TCE).*

The director notes, "It is evident that volunteerism, with the fast approaching aging America, is becoming a noted need within our society. Therefore, RSVP is one of the many established programs designed to address issues with an impact on the lives of this special population group."

Founded: 1973

ROVERS (RETIRED AND OLDER VOLUNTEERS: AN EDUCATIONAL RESOURCE SERVICE)

1420 Athens Drive
Raleigh, NC 27606
TEL: 919-851-7710

Purpose: To enhance learning and promote intergenerational communication through the interaction of older adults and students in the classroom setting.

Sponsor: Wake County Public School System

Contact: Sharon Hackney, Community Education Coordinator

Description: ROVERS is a program in which older adult volunteers, according to their own areas of interest and expertise, function as resource people in the classroom setting. The volunteer is plugged into the curriculum so that his/her own area of expertise will fit into a particular unit of study.

The ROVERS program began in October of 1981, made possible by a two year grant from National Community Education funds. There has since been a full time staff person assigned to both coordinate and expand this program throughout the Wake County School System. This coordinating position is funded by the local school system.

- **Volunteer Staff** - Initially ROVERS had a total of twenty senior adult volunteers working with the ROVERS program at Athens Drive High School alone. In the fall of 1983, the program expanded into two additional schools in the county. Local organizations such as the American Association of Retired Persons and the Association of Retired Faculty at N.C. State University have "adopted" the program. These two groups will place volunteers from their organizations into the ROVERS program at various school sites.

- **Volunteer Duties And Experience** - Based upon their specific areas of interest or expertise, volunteers share their knowledge and experience with students in the classroom setting. No formal training is necessary in order to be involved in the ROVERS program. However, it is specified that the volunteers should have a strong interest or concern for young people. The program coordinator conducts orientation sessions for the volunteers in order to familiarize them with the faculty, school site, curriculum plans, etc.

The majority of the volunteers come to the school site one hour a day, one day a week, for up to eight or nine weeks. However, the length of commitment is ultimately left up to the volunteer and corresponding teacher to arrange. They are left to work out a schedule that is most appropriate and convenient for both of them. Potential volunteers are both recruited and screened by the program coordinator. Volunteers are matched as closely as possible with the appropriate subject area teacher.

Volunteers sixty and over are eligible for accident, personal liability, and excess automobile liability insurance. This insurance coverage, as well as mileage reimbursement funds, is provided by the city of Raleigh's Retired Senior Volunteer Program.

Founded: 1981

RSVP - NURSING HOME PROJECT*
Retired Senior Volunteer Program

311 Pine Avenue
PO Box 3149
Albany, GA 31706
TEL: 912-435-9779

Purpose: To provide companionship for nursing home residents, and volunteer opportunities for low-income minority elderly.

Sponsor: SOWEGA Council on Aging; US/ACTION

Contact: Anne Bragg, Director

Description: A nursing home visitation project was begun in Albany several years ago, and it has become a permanent part of the RSVP program. Its focus is twofold in that it benefits both the nursing home residents and the volunteers.

The 25 senior volunteers are predominantly low-income minority without transportation. They are active participants in the Title III nutrition program, attending two sites in Albany. The volunteers are divided into three groups, each visiting the nursing home one day a week. The RSVP van takes the volunteers from their homes to the nursing home, where they spend one to two hours as "friendly visitors." Then the van takes them to the senior nutrition site for their noon meal.

The volunteer support (van service, meals, recognition, and insurance) provided by this program enables the volunteers to serve their community in a meaningful way. The nursing home residents look forward to the companionship of their RSVP "friends," and the volunteers are rewarded with a very real sense of being needed and appreciated. Another older volunteer group, the Georgia Peach Singers, presents musical programs each month at two local nursing homes - delightful old songs, dances, skits, and readings.

Transportation is furnished to this group, also, and the nursing homes entertain both volunteers and residents with party refreshments.

The total RSVP project includes 300 volunteers who serve in 35 local agencies. It began in 1972 with a federal ACTION grant. Local funding is provided by the United Way plus in-kind donations, and the sponsor is the Southwest Georgia Council on Aging. The program goal is to serve this community with 42,000 hours of volunteer service per year, and to provide the senior volunteers with opportunities for meaningful involvement.

Founded: 1972

RSVP OF MORRIS COUNTY

Box 372
West Hanover Avenue
Morris Plains, NJ 07950
TEL: 201-538-7947
Purpose: To develop a recognized role in the community and a meaningful life in retirement for older adults through significant volunteer service.
Sponsor: RSVP of Morris County
Contact: Donna V. Earner
Description: The Retired Senior Volunteer Program of Morris County, Inc. was established in 1973 (funded by the federal agency, ACTION) for the purpose of developing a recognized role in the community and a meaningful life in retirement for older adults through significant volunteer service. Program elements include:

- Recruiting, placing, and supporting volunteers, 60 years of age and older.
- Developing meaningful volunteer placements within community non-profit agencies.
- Promoting intellectual and para-professional growth through volunteerism and training, thus enabling senior volunteers to recognize existing skills, channel these skills and develop new ones.
- Establishing seven outreach offices strategically located throughout Morris County providing information and referral, telephone reassurance and a friendly visiting service to isolated, low-income elderly.
- Operation Medication Awareness which provides medication education and drug interaction information to combat medication misuse among the elderly.
- RSVP Speakers Bureau which promotes community awareness of the program.

Public response to the RSVP Program has been enthusiastic and continues to grow. Community support in the form of donated resources and time has been very strong. From its inception in 1973 with a core group of 200 volunteers involved in then-accepted modes of volunteerism (i.e., mailings, sewing groups, etc.), the RSVP program grew to a strength of 550 volunteers involved in a wide spectrum of activities donating 102,000 hours per year to the citizens of Morris County. Recently, the number of requests from community agencies for RSVP volunteers to fill high-expertise volunteer positions has increased dramatically, thus indicating the confidence the community has in the program. The growth in terms of the number of volunteers in the program serves to highlight the volunteers' satisfaction with RSVP, and, as one volunteer recently stated, "RSVP gives me a reason to get up in the morning; I'm growing and learning; I feel alive!"
Founded: 1973

RSVP OF NEW CASTLE COUNTY

SEE GOVERNORS' OFFICES ON VOLUNTEERISM: DELAWARE

RSVP OF RAMSEY COUNTY (*formerly RSVP of Lake Region Community College*)

Sports Center
Devils Lake, ND 58301
TEL: 701-662-7502
Purpose: To assist persons over the age of 60 to continue serving their communities through voluntary efforts after retirement.
Sponsor: Ramsey County
Contact: Trudy A. Ertmann, RSVP Director
Description: The Retired Senior Volunteer Program (RSVP) of Ramsey County had its beginnings in the fall of 1971. By December 1989, volunteers in the program had clocked 573,153-1/2 hours, with 46,643 of them being given in the last year of the first eighteen-year period. Volunteers are persons over the age of 60 who wish to continue serving their communities by linking up, through the RSVP program, with nonprofit organizations needing volunteer assistance.

Presently, 332 senior volunteers serve in Ramsey County. Volunteer activities include services to the handicapped, other senior citizens, the library, schools, day care centers, hospitals, nursing homes, welfare departments, health programs, the United Way and UND-Lake Region.

Volunteer training is handled for the most part by the station utilizing the volunteers in cooperation with RSVP staff. When possible, direct supervision is handled by a staff person within the station; when necessary, it is done by the RSVP staff.

RSVP covers enrolled volunteers with supplemental accident and liability insurance while they are on duty, and can cover out-of-pocket expenses incurred by the volunteer when necessary, such as transportation to their assignments, meals, etc. The program receives 54% of its funding from ACTION, the federal volunteer agency, and 46% from local sources such as the *United Way,* senior citizen clubs, private donations, in-kind donations from stations where the older volunteers serve, etc.
Founded: 1971

RSVP THRIFT SHOP*

SEE FUNDING/FUND-RAISING/RELATED SERVICES

SCHOOLMATE HANDICRAFT VOLUNTEERS

Schoolmate Program
304 Bay Shore Avenue
Mobile, AL 36607
TEL: 205-478-RSVP (7787)
Purpose: To provide arts and crafts instruction to children in an after-school care program.
Sponsor: Retired Senior Volunteer Program
Contact: Volunteer Coordinator
Description: Recognizing that today's youngsters fail to learn many skills their grandparents took for granted, RSVP (Retired Senior Volunteer Program) volunteers teamed up with the *Young Women's Christian Association of Mobile* to arrange for seniors to share their talents with youngsters in the after-school *Schoolmate Program.* Some of the older volunteers are handicapped, giving them an opportunity to provide more than just craft skills to the children. One handicapped volunteer is quick to tell them, "Handicaps don't hold you back. You just learn to do things differently."

The Schoolmate program bridges the gap between the end of the school day and the end of parents' or guardians' business day. The children have access to all of the school's sports equipment, and the library facilities. Although games are coached and all activities supervised, the children make their own decisions as to which activity to choose for participation. Outside programs such as the arts and crafts programs provided by senior volunteers are scheduled to help maintain the interest of the more active children who run the gamut of available regular activities and need something new and different.

Since participation in the program is voluntary, it is a challenge to keep the children interested enough so that they will not become "latchkey children," according to one director of the program. One fact not considered in setting up the crafts program was the benefit to the volunteers themselves, often widows who use handicrafts as a way to stay active and helpful to the rest of the world. One volunteer who is an amputee said, "I won't tell you it was easy. For a while, I was very depressed." The widow first became a volunteer with the *Rotary Club* and then got involved in volunteering to share her craft skills. "It made me feel good. The children are so responsive ... they really get excited about learning. And it's fun to share what you know."

Although the program was begun as a part of *Older Americans Volunteer Month* in June 1989, it has become a regular part of the *Schoolmate* schedule.

SEATTLE-KING COUNTY RSVP (RETIRED SENIOR VOLUNTEER PROGRAM)
American Red Cross
Seattle-King County Chapter
1900 25th Avenue, South
Seattle, WA 90144
TEL: 206-323-2345; 206-883-6709
Purpose: To provide volunteer jobs to ease retirees' transition into retirement while providing needed services to the community.
Sponsor: American Red Cross
Contact: Carolyn Pantier or Chris Marx
Description: Nearly 2,000 seniors each year volunteer to help make the Seattle-King County area a better place to live. They work with the *Police Department, Pacific Science Center, Volunteers of America Foodbank in Greenwood, Seattle Children's Museum, Seattle Public Library, Museum of History and Industry* and other agencies from a list of 140 across the area. The volunteers are part of *RSVP (The Retired Senior Volunteer Program) of Seattle-King County,* which is sponsored by the local chapter of the *American Red Cross.*
All volunteers are over 60 in the dual program, which includes:
- *RSVP (Retired Senior Volunteer Program)* - in which most volunteers seek a position that is different from jobs they performed in their paid careers. Volunteer assignments include driving police cars from point-to-point, making crime-prevention presentations (for which they must attend a training course), running exhibition and demonstration booths at a museum, preparing food for delivery to the needy, etc.
- *REV (Retired Executive Volunteers)* in which volunteers like to stay with what they know best: business. They contribute their marketing, planning, accounting, employee benefits, insurance, public relations and managerial skills to nonprofit agencies around the area.

For the volunteers, there is a social aspect, with many congregating for lunch, and most host agencies holding receptions a few times a year. For the agencies, it means filling positions that would have to remain vacant due to budget restraints. According to one agency's coordinator, "Everybody's looking for these people." Many of the volunteers are retirees from "high-powered" positions, according to the RSVP director, who gets more requests than the program can handle. One retired Boeing electrician has logged more than 7,500 hours with the Police Department since he started there in 1983. He began volunteering four hours a day and eventually attended a police academy crime-prevention course, which qualified him to assist officers in crime-prevention presentations. Today he clocks about 40 hours a week. For those who can work just a few hours a week, there are plenty of requests that are filled.
RSVP was established in 1971 by the Nixon administration's *White House Conference on Aging,* and the Seattle RSVP developed within a year. An existing retirement program, *Retired Executive Volunteers (REV),* begun in 1973, was merged with RSVP in 1978 to form the Seattle-King County RSVP, sponsored by the American Red Cross.
Founded: 1971

SECURITY ALERT GROUP - THREE LINK TOWERS (SAG)
2427 Jefferson
Ogden, UT 84401
TEL: 801-399-4841
Purpose: To provide a secure, safe, crime free environment for 150 elderly residents at Three Link Towers, a low-income senior highrise located in downtown Ogden.
Sponsor: Three Link Towers
Contact: Frank Sturdevant
Description: The aging process is often accompanied by a lessening of abilities and opportunities. Many seniors experience limitations not only in physical capacity but social as well. Loneliness, limited finances, declining health, and restricted resources all contribute to

deterioration among older people.
The reality of increasing crime is evident in our society. For the older American, this reality is coupled with fear and a sense of helplessness. Often older persons are victims of theft, harassment, vandalism and assault. The senior residents at Three Link Towers confronted the issue of crime and responded with vigor, ingenuity and tenacity. The inception of the SAG in March 1981 is a statement of self-help and commitment to minimizing criminal activity and delinquency in their neighborhood. This was the intent of the program, and subsequently has been the successful result of their efforts.
Although the participants of the SAG are low-income, many without family support, some with failing health, and all within the 64-81 age range, their energy and determination is remarkable. They have overcome age barriers and stereotypes and created an opportunity for themselves to contribute their human resources as well as provide a useful community service of crime deterrent and prevention.
The 26 volunteers in SAG serve as night watch-persons in two hour shifts beginning at 8:00 p.m. seven days a week. They patrol the parking lot, streets, and grounds surrounding their complex by observing unusual or suspicious activities from their balconies and windows. Criminals are scared away by shining flashlights on them. If property has been damaged or a crime has occurred, then the local police are summoned. However, this has happened only once since SAG was organized. Through the efforts of the SAG volunteers, crime has virtually been reduced to none.
The contribution to the community by the Security Alert Group has been seen as quite beneficial by the Ogden City Police Department. Due to the location of the highrise, Three Link Towers, in a downtown urban area, crime is a very real problem, and the volunteer effort of the SAG has succeeded in reducing the neighborhood crime rate. The 30 senior volunteers who are active in the SAG program have a sense of self-fulfillment in knowing they are significantly contributing their time and energy for improving the quality of life for themselves and fellow residents. The impact of the SAG activities specifically has diminished the residents' fear of crime and vandalism that so many seniors harbor, and the project positively affects the surrounding neighborhood in downtown Ogden. Accomplishments of the SAG have been in close alignment with the stated objectives of the project as initially outlined.
Founded: 1981

SENIOR ACTING PROGRAM OF THE BARN PLAYERS*
SEE COMMUNICATIONS & PUBLIC RELATIONS: ARTS

SENIOR CITIZEN INTERNSHIP PROGRAM
SEE TRAINING/CONFERENCES/TEACHING: INTERNSHIPS

SENIOR CRAFTSMAN SHOWCASE*
2647 Connecticut Avenue, NW
Washington, DC 20008
TEL: 202-265-3611
Purpose: To put senior citizens back to work through crafts.
Sponsor: District of Columbia Office on Aging; District of Columbia Department of Recreation
Contact: Dorayne Lyons, Project Director
Description: Created in 1970 as a joint project of two DC Offices (Aging and Recreation), the Senior Craftsman Showcase was the first project of its kind in the country. Its primary purpose was to provide an income for senior citizens using talents and skills they already possessed, but also it offers the public a place to purchase handmade items seldom found in the city.
The salespeople in the shop are volunteers, mainly senior citizens. The items, taken on consignment, are priced on the basis of what the craftsman expects to receive, plus 35 percent for the store's overhead. Though they have admittedly taken on some items to

prevent bruised feelings, nothing is lost because of the consignment agreement. In addition to expected items such as nylon net cleanser covers and handpainted toothbrush holders, some of the unique handmade treasures are crewel and bargello pillows, Easter bunnies and chickens in wool and other fabrics, little-girl jumpers, finely-stitched quilts, holiday decorations of all kinds, and hand-made baby blankets and dolls.

The craftspeople in the shop sometimes are not as interested in their financial gain as in the creative process. The oldest craftsman is 101 and makes quilts from whatever fabrics are available to her. A 62-year-old retired government employee stocks the shop with her handmade dolls. A few consignors who have moved away still send in their crafts for extra pocket money. The shop is stocked with crafts from over 700 consignors over age 60.

Many talents are examples of dying arts - skills sometimes brought over from other countries. Organizations working with the aging encourage senior craftsmen to use their own special skills and channel them into highly marketable merchandise by working with the Showcase. The significant side benefit from this venture is the good feeling the senior craftsman gets when someone puts out money for his/her work. For some it was a welcome change from sitting in a chair doing nothing to creating something that others enjoy. Some were plying their craft for their own amusement, but finding that storage in the home was a problem.
Founded: 1970

SENIOR VICTIM ASSISTANCE TEAM
SEE VOLUNTEERS: TEAMS

SENIORS AND CHILDREN TOGETHER
United Way of Great Salt Lake Area
455 East 400 South
Suite 410
Salt Lake City, UT 84111-3000
TEL: 716-366-5424
Purpose: To enable seniors and children to get more out of life by interacting with each other.
Sponsor: United Way of Great Salt Lake Area
Contact: Charles Johnson
Description: Neighborhood House has provided services to children since 1894. In 1984, the agency began offering senior day care as well. The National Council on Aging helped the agency begin to plan a program through which children could learn about seniors in a way that was mutually beneficial for both groups. The result is a program of cooking, crafts, singing, dancing and other activities involving low-income senior citizens over age 60, and low-income children ages 2-12.

The most critical component of the program was orienting the children to being around older people, since many of them don't have grandparents or older people in their lives. A wheelchair was brought into the center, and the children were given rides in it. They were told how some people need a little help walking or need to go a little slower, and what it is like to get older. They explained that yelling and running indoors might upset older people.

According to the program's director, the older men became role models, since 73% of the children at the center do not live with their fathers. The older people tell the children stories, and teach them songs. There are cookie-baking contests and intergenerational teams baking bread (something the children had never had before). When kids become curious about canes and other items needed by the elderly, the staff helps them to ask about them in a sensitive way. All of the 213 children at the center have regular contact with the seniors.

Older persons too feeble to participate enjoy watching the activities and seem to garner energy from the experience.

Intergenerational day care is helping agencies more and more to pool their resources. The new movement to bring the old and the young together enables both groups to get more out of life. "As each day goes by," according to the director, "we find more and more things that the seniors and kids can do together."

SENIORS: SPECIAL DELIVERY
New York Avenue Meals on Wheels
1313 New York Avenue, NW
Washington, DC 20005
TEL: 202-393-3949
Purpose: To provide hot meals to homebound elderly and handicapped persons to help keep them in their homes.
Sponsor: New York Avenue Presbyterian Church
Contact: Sarah Turlington, Director/Founder
Description: Founded 19 years ago, the New York Avenue Meals on Wheels Program (MOW) delivers meals to the homebound across a 14-block area of Washington, DC. The program reaches up to 65 people each day with about 60 older volunteers making the deliveries. In addition, volunteers located near the church devote some of their lunch hour time to deliveries. However, the success of the program is in the number of retired persons who are willing to mount this task, since their time is more flexible.

The service area is divided into four routes, each with two volunteers covering it. One volunteer drives his or her own car, while a "jumper" or visitor delivers the meals. Volunteers give two hours a day, with the same volunteers serving each route to help establish a bond with the homebound resident.

The food is prepared in the church kitchen in conjunction with a federally-funded meals program that serves lunch to 60-80 people at the church each day.

Volunteer packers prepare the meals each day. The hot lunch always includes soup, two vegetables and an entree such as chicken, fish or meatloaf. A salad, sandwich, milk, fruit and packets of coffee and tea are provided for the evening meal. Low-salt meals are offered for diabetics. Participants pay $17.00 per week to help defray costs.
Founded: 1971

SERVICE CORPS OF RETIRED EXECUTIVES (SCORE)
US/SBA - SCORE/ACE
969 Madison Avenue
Memphis, TN 38104
TEL: 901-544-3588
Purpose: To counsel and advise small business owners.
Sponsor: US/SBA - Small Business Administration
Contact: Irving Nathanson, Counselor
Description: About three dozen retirees with lifetimes of experience in the business world volunteer their time to offer free, confidential counseling from the SCORE (Service Corps of Retired Executives) office in Memphis.

The office, staffed during the morning on weekdays, receives an average of 25 calls a day from those who own businesses or want to start them. Half of the prospective entrepreneurs who call for advice have not reached the point where they can be helped, according to the director. They only have a vague idea that they want to go into business for themselves, with no thought of what business, no experience, and no money. When this happens, the inquirer is given the hard realities of needing a financial base, a solid plan, etc., and sent "back to the drawing board."

Those with an existing business, or a good idea, some experience and some source of financing can benefit from the counseling SCORE has to offer. The caller is sent a form to request a counselor, and one with experience related to the caller's needs is assigned.

The U.S. Small Business Administration created SCORE in 1964 and pays the rent and travel expenses for 390 chapters nationwide. The labor is provided by volunteers such as those in the Memphis chapter.

SILVER HAIRED LEGISLATIVE SESSION
SEE GOVERNORS' OFFICES ON VOLUNTEERISM: ARKANSAS

60 KARATS
Culpeper Senior Center
Culpeper Garden
4415 North Pershing Drive
Arlington, VA 22203
TEL: 703-971-5144 (60 Karats); 703-528-0162 (Center)
Purpose: Performing free at local and civic events, *60 Karats* is a dancing troupe with all participants over 60 years of age. It began in 1987 when seven women joined the only dance course in the Arlington County program offered to seniors - tap dancing. Since then, in addition to appearing at senior centers and charitable functions, the troupe has performed three times at the Kennedy Center, and have been featured on CNN (Cable News Network), where their show brought in calls from around the country, including one from Johnny Carson.
To maintain the precision and coordination that has brought them national attention, *60 Karats* practices twice a week in a room at *Culpeper Garden,* with additional time spent when the date for one of their shows is approaching. Although the volunteer troupe does not charge a fee for its performances, donations are accepted to defray expenses.
Contact: Jane Letsche, Choreographer

TIP NEIGHBORHOOD HOUSE/OLDER ADULT
VOLUNTEERS
1028 East 179th Street
Bronx, NY 10460
TEL: 212-893-1224
Purpose: To utilize the skills, resources and experiences of older persons through neighborhood volunteer programs.
Sponsor: TIP Neighborhood House
Contact: Marie A. Brown, Program Director
Description: The TIP Neighborhood House provides social services to an area encompassing 27 blocks in the Bronx Park South section. This area is marked by abandoned, burnt-out buildings, streets crowded with unemployed youth and adults, and a high incidence of crime toward the elderly. In the midst of these streets are eight federally-subsidized, well-designed developments, housing more than one thousand older persons (55 and over) who are predominantly Black and Hispanic. The older residents of these developments feel isolated and few attend the programs that do exist in the area. In an effort to reverse this situation, TIP Neighborhood House mounted a two-pronged Older Adult Volunteer Program. The components, both designed to encourage older persons to share experience, skills and resources with all age groups, are:
Self Help by Older Persons Project (SHOPP)
Beginning in six developments, TIP workers encouraged groups of older residents to identify skills that could be taught to other residents and thereby improve community life. It was suggested that they choose activities in which they themselves had expertise, and for which they could take an increasingly independent role. TIP offered contractual relationships with clearly-defined responsibilities, and mini-matching starter grants.
In response, older persons with professional, paraprofessional, and volunteer experience in painting, designing, sewing, cooking, farming, health care, historical research, political action, and fundraising came forward, identified their skills, attended advanced training workshops, and thus enhanced their abilities to demonstrate and teach.
By the end of 1981, support groups had been formed in six housing developments with a block association, an indoor community gardening work shop, a park volunteer project, a bank volunteer-sponsored group, and a Civil War Memorial Committee. To coordinate the six self-help projects, an advisory committee of leader-representatives has been drawn from the groups. Members advise and assist each other in developing new programs, coordinating special and fundraising events, acting as a sounding board for new proposals, meeting representatives of funding

sources, and representing the committee at hearings, conferences, and planning board meetings.
The older volunteers are involved in teaching and learning gardening, taking courses and instructing each other in seven types of needlecrafts, conducting three clean-up campaigns, organizing a project to give recognition to a Black woman whose Civil War contribution has gone unnoticed, sponsoring ten outdoor gardens, and other activities.
Groups are given $300 in mini-grants to help defray project costs, and have succeeded in raising more than $3,000 through cake sales, luncheons, craft sales, special events, and six Citizens' Committee Awards. In addition, two recent grants have made possible projects in intergenerational gardening and nutrition education involving the homebound elderly.
To help the groups gain visibility, TIP has sponsored two Autumn Festival Caravan Tours of the gardens, two Annual Fashion Shows, four awards ceremonies, and two ceremonies honoring Mary Elizabeth Bowser, the Black woman cited above.
In a relatively short time, SHOPP has moved from an exercise to identify the skills of older residents, to a substantial community and social service to people of all ages.
The Older Adult Service Loop
In cooperation with RSVP of the Community Service Society, and the School Volunteer Program, older volunteers in the area have helped to demonstrate the degree of cooperation that can be engendered among organizations and agencies at the local level. Using TIP's minibus along with other forms of transportation, area agencies and the older residents have developed a "service loop."
In this program, groups of older adults are transported to hospitals, nursing homes, the botanical gardens, and schools to provide volunteer services. In the first few months, eighteen groups visited three hospitals, ten nursing homes, the botanical gardens, and three schools. The older volunteers perform in choral groups, act as health aides, counselors, clerks, and tutors in the classroom.

UNION RETIREES RESOURCES
SEE VOLUNTEERS: UNION MEMBERS

US/SBA - SERVICE CORPS OF RETIRED
EXECUTIVES/ACTIVE CORPS OF EXECUTIVES
US/SBA - SCORE/ACE
Louisville , KY 40202
TEL: 502-582-5976
Purpose: To share business and professional experience with persons interested in starting or improving a business.
Sponsor: US/SBA - Small Business Administration
Contact: William Federhofer, SBA Kentucky District Director
Description: About 61 Louisville retirees are score counselors. They have varied backgrounds - financial, wholesale and retail, import-export, construction, food services and engineering. They range in age from 55 to 85. During 1988, Louisville SCORE Chapter 75 handled 1,908 cases, an average of 31 cases per member. This does not include inquiries by phone or walk-in business that requires no counseling.
To become SCORE volunteers, retirees must complete about 60 hours of training and agree to work three hours a week in the office handling phone calls or walk-in inquiries. Counselors are matched with clients need help in their specialty. When more than one area of expertise is involved, counseling teams are formed. Once the client and counselor or team are matched, they meet as often as needed, ususally about once a month. Counselors must keep detailed records on each session. Counseling continues as long as the client requires it, but most cases are closed after about a year.
Most clients are just "thinking" of starting a small business. Usually they lack two important elements - capital and knowledge. Workshops are designed to address these problems - a total of 70 conducted during 1989. Scheduled sessions include starting an

at-home business, forecasting profits and cash flow, business taxes, and owning a mail-order business. Workshops are open to the general public for a small fee, and are presented and the University of Louisville in Shelby.

Louisville also has a companion program called ACE (Active Corps of Executives), which is composed of volunteers who are still working, but who also want to help business people. The primary difference is the scheduling which must accommodate ACE volunteers' working hours.

VISCAP (VOLUNTEER INCENTIVE SERVICE CREDIT ACCOUNT PROGRAM)
Kirtland Community College
Roscommon, MI 48653
TEL: 517-275-5121
TOLL FREE: 800-433-2517/ext. 264
Purpose: To provide respite services for family caregivers.
Contact: Stuart E. Lawrence, Director Emeritus, Library
Description: VISCAP works to create an awareness of the needs of the primary caregiver of an aging relative, and provide volunteer support services to give the caregiver relief. This role is played by family, friends and relatives of the older person, and - without intervention - often leads to burnout. VISCAP volunteers evaluate each individual situation and provide respite services until the primary caregiver appears to be ready to return to the often-demanding roles.
Publications: VISCAP: Help When Needed
Founded: 1989

VIVA (VERY IMPORTANT VOLUNTEERS IN ACTION)
Scurry County Senior Center
2603 Avenue M
Snyder, TX 79549
TEL: 915-573-4035
Purpose: To provide volunteer work within the community to non-profit organizations, and to the elderly of the community.
Sponsor: Scurry County Senior Citizens Center and Western Texas College; federal/county governments; corporate and private donations
Contact: Susan Thomas, VIVA Coordinator
Description: VIVA is an organization of senior citizens who offer non-profit clubs and organizations their volunteer services. VIVA also provides a lot of volunteer service to the elderly residents of the area. The program operates under the umbrella of the Scurry County Senior Citizens Center. VIVA is a non-profit organization receiving funds from federal and county governments as well as from corporate and private donations. Senior citizen volunteers are the very heart of this program. VIVA volunteers do a variety of things:

- help the local public schools by providing tutor-type programs where a volunteer works on a one-to-one basis with students who need extra help;
- aid in a swimming program for handicapped children;
- man a continual garage sale where all the profits go to the Scurry County Work Center where retarded citizens work;
- provide entertainment and extra help at the Snyder Child Day Care Center, at two local retirement homes, and at the Scurry County Library.

VIVA volunteers are also involved in the community blood drives every six weeks, and also aid the community on an emergency need basis. Volunteers also visit the sick, elderly, and shut-ins. The Senior Center has a Home Delivered Meal Program, and volunteers provide all of the driving needs for that program. VIVA has a volunteer force of 197 senior citizens, serving a community of 12,500 people. Out of the total population approximately 1,200 are over 60 years of age. With the volunteer force nearly 1,000 individuals over 60 are reached, as well as countless numbers under 60 years of age. The 197 volunteers put in an average of 6,000 hours per month in volunteer service to the community.

VOLUNTEER VOLUNTEER COORDINATORS*
SEE ADMINISTRATION

VOLUNTEERS: PARENTS

NATIONAL/STATE ORGANIZATIONS

AMERICAN PARENTS COMMITTEE
1346 Connecticut Avenue, NW
Washington, DC 20036
TEL: 202-785-3169
Objectives: To work for federal legislation on behalf of the nation's children and youth.
Services: Monitors any welfare legislation that emerges, closely examining its impact on children; supports increased efforts to facilitate services recognizing the right of every child to a permanent family; opposes Administration or Congressional attempts to seek relief for the federal Treasury by reducing expenditures for programs for children and youth; reports through its *Washington Report on Federal Legislation for Children* on such matters as day care, homemaker services, Headstart, child health, education, family planning, juvenile justice, etc.; also publishes an annual *Voting Report on Federal Legislation for Children* and other materials.

CENTER FOR THE STUDY OF PARENT INVOLVEMENT
SEE LEADERSHIP DEVELOPMENT/BOARDS: PARENTS

CO-ORDINATING COUNCIL FOR HANDICAPPED CHILDREN
SEE LEADERSHIP DEVELOPMENT/BOARDS: HANDICAPPED

FAMILIES IN ACTION NATIONAL DRUG INFORMATION CENTER
3845 North Druid Hills Road
Suite 300
Decatur, GA 30033
TEL: 404-325-5799
Objectives: To halt the rising use of drugs in the community.
Services: Seeks to educate parents, children and community leaders on the increase of drug use in the communities; works to counteract the societal pressures that condone and promote drug use; collects and disseminates all relevant information about young people and the health effects of drugs; helps to enact laws that will lead to the goal of eradicating drug use in the communities; trains parent group leaders to organize in their communities; conducts speakers' education and training program; provides telephone reference service; maintains a drug information center which contains more than 350,000 documents, studies, books, brochures, and films and videos relating to drug abuse; publishes a quarterly newsletter, a guide to forming family action groups, and other materials.
Publications: Crack Update; Drug Abuse Update; How to Form a Families Action Group in Your Community
Founded: 1977

MOTHERS AGAINST DRUNK DRIVING
MADD
PO Box 1217
Hurst, TX 76053
TEL: 817-268-6233
Objectives: To assist people victimized by the crime of drunk driving, to change public attitudes which find drinking and driving

acceptable behavior, and to change the laws which do not treat drunk and drugged driving seriously.

Services: Involves local volunteer groups who complete a prescribed process in order to become a chartered MADD chapter; includes in its chapter programs *Victim Services, Court Monitoring, Speakers Bureau, Special Programs (Candlelight Vigil, Victim Rights Week, Red Ribbon, Keep It A Safe Summer [K.I.S.S.], Drive for Life, Poster-Essay Contest, Youth Education);* utilizes volunteers in all programs and in all phases of chapter operations, from professional help with support groups to monthly chapter mailings; adds new programs as needs indicate, most recently including *Victim Impact Panels,* which are held nationwide for DWI offenders who have not yet killed or injured anyone.

Publications: MADD In Action; MADDvocate; No Time for Goodbyes; Beyond Sympathy

Founded: 1980

NATIONAL ASSOCIATION FOR PARENTS OF THE VISUALLY IMPAIRED
SEE SELF-HELP: PARENTS

NATIONAL CONFERENCE ON PARENT INVOLVEMENT
579 West Iroquois
Pontiac, MI 48053
TEL: 313-334-5887

Objectives: To build skills, share information, and bring people together who are advocates of parent involvement in the schools.

Services: Identifies, utilizes and provides information on resources available; conducts leadership training; compiles and distributes data on federal legislation and its relationship to parent involvement; works to strengthen communication among school, home and community.

PAR LEADERSHIP TRAINING FOUNDATION
SEE LEADERSHIP DEVELOPMENT/BOARDS: PARENTS

PARENTS ANONYMOUS
6733 South Sepulveda
Suite 270
Los Angeles, CA 90045
TEL: 213-410-9732

Objectives: To provide a self-help setting for parents with problems related to all types of child abuse and neglect.

Services: Helps parents gain insight into their problems through weekly meetings in group settings by sharing fears and experiences with others - exchanging names and phone numbers to provide crisis contacts 24 hours a day (some chapters maintain a 24-hour hotline for this purpose); structures chapters to consist of a Chairperson, who is a parent and a member of the group, a sponsor (such as a social worker, psychologist or psychiatrist who serves as a nondirective support for the Chairperson), and a varying number of members (usually between four and ten); supports 24-hour hotlines when chapters install them to serve as information and referral points for information about chapters in a given metropolitan or rural area, and to give crisis counseling over the telephone to abusive and potentially abusive parents (members or non-members); convenes regional and national meetings.

Founded: 1970

PUBLIC AWARENESS ABOUT CHILD CARE (PAACC)
Denise Reich Real Estate
1400 South Colorado Boulevard
Denver, CO 80222
TEL: 303-757-7474

Objectives: To make the public aware, and the justice system more responsive, to crimes against children.

Services: Addresses barriers in the legal system to bringing child care workers who harm children to justice; works with mothers of victimized children and others to produce information for the media about children killed or hurt by those licensed or hired to care for them; works with legislators on investigations to identify felons employed in day-care centers, and more stringent background checks of child care providers, as well as including *all* child care workers in the checking process; addresses the need for better tracing methods to locate suspected workers who have left the area of the crime; publishes stories and other information on the subject.

Contact: Denise Reich, Founder
Founded: 1989

TRAINING PROGRAMS

GET INVOLVED BEFORE YOUR KIDS DO
AAL Drug and Alcohol Use Prevention Program
Fraternal Benefits & Financial Services for Lutherans
4321 North Ballard Road
Appleton, WI 54919-0001
TEL: 414-734-5721

Purpose: To help parents communicate effectively with their children about drugs and alcohol.

Credit: Inquire

Contact: Phyllis Rusch

Description: This workshop program - designed by a national organization to reach parents *before* their children get involved with drugs - pulls together volunteer programs in local areas across the country to present the workshops in their communities. There is no cost to participants in the workshops. AAL provides all materials, including a videotape featuring well-known actors role-playing family situations, group discussions and a parent guidebook to be completed by families at home. The workshop strives to help parents develop such skills as talking with their children about alcohol and drugs, setting family rules about alcohol and drugs, assessing their own behaviors concerning alcohol and drugs, and networking with other parents to help children through the high-risk years.

The local program is considered a model for the nation to follow in helping to fight drug abuse. AAL groups (called branches) have conducted workshops for parent/teacher associations, hospitals, optimist clubs, counseling centers, school boards and Junior Leagues.

Over 148,000 people in more than 2,550 communities have attended *Get Involved* parent workshops since the program was introduced. Another 229,000 people have been reached through nearly 3,600 community outreach projects that focus on awareness and prevention of alcohol and other drug abuse.

In 1988, *AAL's Get Involved Before Your Kids Do* drug prevention program was selected as one of 16 model programs by the *White House Conference for A Drug Free America.* On January 14, 1990, President Bush named *Get Involved* his 49th *point of light.* Bush's *Points of Light Initiative* recognizes local efforts to combat social problems (see separate entry).

The *Get Involved* program is available free of charge through AAL's 7,100 volunteer branches across the country. AAL continually improves and maintains the program.

PARENT AIDE TRAINING
SEE TRAINING/CONFERENCES/TEACHING: DOMESTIC ABUSE

PARENT-TEEN AIDS EDUCATION PROJECT
SEE TRAINING/CONFERENCES/TEACHING: AIDS

PARENTS EDUCATING PARENTS: TRAINING PROGRAM
SEE VOLUNTEERS: SELF-HELP

SHAVING CREAM LESSON - DRUG PREVENTION SEMINAR
SEE LEADERSHIP DEVELOPMENT/BOARDS: DRUGS/ALCOHOL

INDIVIDUAL PROGRAM PROFILES

ADAMS' EXPRESS: A MINI-GRANT PROGRAM
SEE FUNDING/FUND-RAISING/RELATED SERVICES: EDUCATION

ALEXANDER HUMAN DEVELOPMENT CENTER VOLUNTEER COUNCIL
PO Box 320
Alexander, AR 72002
TEL: 501-847-3506
Purpose: To conduct community awareness/public relations campaign; to secure the services of interested volunteers to provide companionship for residents; to conduct fund-raising drives to help finance programs for Arkansas residents.
Sponsor: Alexander Parents Organization; Arkansas Elks Association
Contact: Patsy Wagner, Volunteer Services Coordinator
Description: The Alexander Volunteer Council was formed in January 1981. During the early formation stages of the Council three goals were established:
● Greenhouse;
● Canteen for residents; and
● Beautification/normalization of living units.
Through the support of the State Elks Association and the Alexander Parents Organization we now have a commercial greenhouse, size 22' by 40' on the campus. Residents are using this for training purposes, the Volunteer Council supplies the needed supplies; volunteers donate plants, etc. Plants from the greenhouse are used to help decorate the living areas, are sold to employees, volunteers, etc. These funds are reinvested in the greenhouse.
Various "sponsors" have helped in beautification/normalization of living units. They provide bedspreads, area rugs, pictures for the walls, etc.
A canteen renovation project is underway at the present time. A style show was held to raise funds for this project. An area has been paneled, wallpapered and tables have been constructed. The next phase of the project will include chairs and a music system. Volunteers are recruited, trained and supervised by the Volunteer Coordinator, with on the site supervision by the Cottage Supervisor.

ALTERNATIVE EDUCATION AND WORK CENTER
SEE VOLUNTEERS: PRISONERS/EX-OFFENDERS

CATCH PROGRAM
Chamber of Commerce
114 West Chatham Street
Cary, NC 27511
TEL: 919-467-1016
Purpose: To follow through on the theme of CATCH: "The love of learning is first established in the home."
Sponsor: Cary High School PTSA
Contact: Ricki Grantmyre, Committee Member
Description: The CATCH (Community Action Through Cooperative Homework) program was developed through the Cary Chamber of Commerce, which targeted homework since it applies to all students. One facet of the CATCH program is the *MegaSkills Workshop,* which teaches parents simple, daily activities to use at home with their children to nurture a love of learning. The skills, also called "little recipes" are designed to enhance children's learning - not only in academics, but also in

everyday living. There is no expenditure of money, since the program makes use of tools already in the home, or consists of activities that do not require any tools at all - making the program feasible for anyone. For example, one "recipe" calls for a "fire brigade" to pick up toys - a chore that usually meets with resistance. According to one volunteer, "It makes it fun, and it teaches the children teamwork - which is one of the *MegaSkills.* Leaders of the workshops are volunteers from the community. In each community, prior to the workshop, a series of training sessions readies local citizens to lead *MegaSkills* workshops. The training of trainers is provided by the *Home and School Institute,* an educational foundation based in Washington, DC, which developed *MegaSkills.* In Cary, an April 1990 workshop was led by 16 business people, educators, and parents from the Cary area who completed the training program. One trainee, an employee from *Union Carbide,* volunteered for the training because of the corporation's emphasis on education, and as a parent. The 16 trained volunteers present workshops throughout the community - in day care centers, businesses, churches, etc. Many of those who volunteer are parents, and find the skills useful in their own homes as well - often trying them out on their own children first.
In the Cary program, in addition to *Union Carbide,* volunteer trainers came from the *Bespak Corporation,* the *PTA, Capital Associates, Cary Elementary School, Cary High School, Buehler Products, Smith & Associates, Board of Education, Chamber of Commerce,* and attorneys and other individuals from the community.

COMMUNITY RESOURCE VOLUNTEERS
SEE VOLUNTEERS: PROFESSIONALS

CRY, INC. (CITIZENS REDIRECTING YOUTH)
4262 Massachusetts Avenue, SE
Washington, DC 20019
TEL: 202-583-7426; 202-783-0030
Purpose: To provide supportive services for parents and others who have been victimized by crime.
Contact: Johnnie Scott Rice, Executive Director
Description: Citizens Redirecting Youth (CRY) was founded in 1988 by a mother who lost a son to violence. CRY is based on a deep need by the founder to talk to others who went through such an experience. There is evidence that survivors of murder victims who do not talk to anyone for several months after the tragedy often develop various psychological problems.
The program offers psychosocial support to parents and others traumatized by crime. During its first year, 400 families were assisted by the program. At any given time, there are 40 families working with CRY's five volunteer counselors.
Recognizing that siblings are not always considered in "grief sessions," CRY tries to give special consideration to a murder victim's sisters and brothers while counseling their parents.
Referrals to CRY are made by other agencies, primarily victim/witness units of local law enforcement departments.
In its comparatively brief existence, it seems to have met a long-time need, since *CRY* has responded to requests for appearances on dozens of national and local radio and television programs, including *Geraldo Show, Nightline* with Ted Koppel, *Sally Jessy Raphael, Voice of America, CBN News, UDC Campus Forum, 700 Club, WPFW Talk Show* with Jolyne Brooks, *Talk at American University, Channel 7 (Beat-Up the Beat), Channel 9 (Crime and Drugs), WDJY Talk Show* with Jerry Phillips, *WRC Talk-Forum, Capital City Magazine* (WTTG 5 Fox TV), *WRC Talk Show* with Joe Spivack, *Workshop for Female Inmates* (DC Jail), *Ballou Senior High School* (Super Team Leaders), *Galilee Baptist Church* (Forum with Bruce Johnson), an all-area-stations presentation on *March of Life,* and others.
Founded: 1988

FOCUS (FAMILIES OF CHILDREN UNITED FOR SAFETY)
California Department of Education
Sacramento, CA 95814
TEL: 916-445-4688
Information also available from founders: Pam Danaher and
Danielle Brock; request contact information from above source.
Purpose: To bolster parents' ability to control their children.
Sponsor: California Board of Education
Contact: Assistant Superintendent/Public Education, Pam
Danaher or Danielle Bock, Founders
Description: About 30 parents and a State Assemblyman attended
an organizational meeting in June 1989 to start a new program
designed to assist parents in controlling rebellious children. The
group elected board members in July and expects to grow into a
statewide organization.

The two founders are mothers of teenaged girls who were
murdered in the area, in part because the parents were unable to
enforce rules designed to keep their children safe. Both of the
victims were chronic truants and drug abusers who knew the
system and used it to their advantage. When confronting the
teenagers and those who had an influence on them, usually adults,
brought no results, one of the parents developed the idea for
FOCUS. Her daughter was murdered before she could continue
the process. By participating now, she hopes to help other parents
avoid such a tragedy.

A major activity of FOCUS is to push for legislation and urge
enforcement of laws to restore the ability of parents to control
their children.

A survey in June found widespread truancy in Sacramento area
schools, and much of the development meeting for FOCUS
centered on truancy problems. Another issue addressed was the
need for stiffer penalties for adults who prey on truants, runaways
and troubled kids. A local lobbyist volunteered to lobby for the
group, and the assistant superintendent of public instruction in the
California Department of Education joined FOCUS and will act as
an official liaison between the department and the group. The
group will urge parents to attend school board meetings and ask
questions - demanding answers about their children's education.
The school superintendent agreed, and said, "Parents think that
when they slow down to 10 miles per hour and let their kid slide
out the car door in front of the school, that's the end of their
responsibility. That's absolutely wrong!"
Founded: 1989

GRADS PROGRAM
South High School
1160 Ann Street
Columbus, OH 43206
TEL: 614-365-5541
Purpose: To encourage pregnant teens to finish school; to involve
fathers voluntarily in the program.
Contact: Barbara Neely, Teacher
Description: GRADS (Graduating Reality and Dual-Role Skills)
was started in 1984 by a high school teacher concerned about
pregnant teens dropping out of school. It caused uneasiness among
city school officials, since some felt it would send a mixed message
to teens (becoming pregnant is not so bad). But now GRADS is
considered a shining example of how the school can help to solve
community problems.

In addition to academics, GRADS tries to reach the young
mothers in a personal way. A picnic day allows them to bring
their babies to school, and invites the fathers to attend. Although
only a few fathers volunteer to come, those who do demonstrate
more interest in their young families with each visit. In addition, a
few grandparents (some only 30 years of age) drop by and show
approval.

An example of the success of the program is a young teen who
needed extra tutoring or classwork to graduate. She rose at 5 a.m.,
took her baby to the sitter, went to school, came home and did her

homework, put the baby to bed, and then boarded a bus for night
classes on the other side of town - all to make sure she graduated,
and in spite of the fact that she was forced out of her home when
she became pregnant.

Although the founder feels that most of the success of GRADS
can be attributed to its nonjudgmental approach and the emphasis
on building a future for the baby, personal touches like inducing
fathers to volunteer time and take some of the responsibility have
proven to be very significant factors in motivating the students. In
1989, of the 250 graduates of South High School, 53 were from
GRADS.
Founded: 1985

GROWING UP WITH NATURE
Louisiana Nature and Science Center
Joe Brown Park
New Orleans, LA 70127
TEL: 504-246-5672
Purpose: To stress the care and safety of animals in their natural
environment.
Contact: Francine Fogelman, Volunteer
Description: Children ages two to five are given an opportunity to
develop a good attitude about wildlife, and to learn how to respect
animals in their natural habitat. Volunteers in the *Growing Up
With Nature Program* of the *Louisiana Nature and Science Center*
work with parents to stress the care and safety of animals in terms
simple enough for young minds. Children are given a chance to
touch the animals, but care is taken to emphasize that the best
place for animals in their natural environment where they are not
bothered by humans.

The program gives parents the opportunity to support the center
while interacting with their children. Often, it is parental presence
and encouragement that assures success in programs for children
in this age group.

Volunteers develop the monthly topics through brainstorming
meetings. They create a lesson based on the most interesting
aspects of the plant or animal, focusing on the life-cycle. An
appropriate lesson for this parent-child activity is one on mammals
that highlights the mother/child relationship.

When parents and children arrive for the program, they work on a
craft that reflects the lesson and involves both parent and child. It
has been found that making crafts puts young children at ease and
gives them something to remember of the program, as well as a
sense of the topic.

The program also includes a story time in which books about
nature are read, and presentations are made at three other stations
that last about ten minutes each dealing with the animals in the
day's lesson.

In 1988 the program was awarded a grant to go into the New
Orleans public schools to present a modified program for a year in
kindergartens and first grades. Just as at the Center, the program
in the school is designed to encourage parents to assist the
volunteers by lending support and encouragement while the
children learn to hold animals without fearing them. According to
school authorities, the program fills a void in the curriculum.
Founded: 1981

HITS (HIGH INTENSITY TREATMENT SUPERVISION)
SEE VOLUNTEERS: ALTERNATIVE SENTENCING
OFFENDERS

HOMEWORK HOTLINE
Trans*Parent* School Model Program
Canton Middle School
801 South Highland Avenue
Baltimore, MD 21224
TEL: 301-396-9172
Purpose: To spur interaction between school and home.
Sponsor: Canton Middle School

Contact: Arthur P. Chenoweth, Assistant Principal
Description: With a $44,000 grant from the Abell Foundation, a homework hotline was added to the Trans*Parent* School Model, which among other things automatically notifies parents by telephone recording when their children are absent. The system was developed in 1987 by educational research staff at Vanderbilt University and - as of mid-1990 - is used in 21 schools from New Jersey to Colorado.

The pilot program was initiated during the 1989-90 school year in the 640-pupil Canton Middle School and two smaller elementary schools, all in lower-income areas of the city, where parental involvement with schools traditionally has been spotty. The schools average about 300 calls per day through the system, which compares with about 60 parent-teacher contacts a day prior to the call-in system. Parents, teachers, and (grudgingly) students all agree that the program works. Teachers, especially, can measure its success through the dramatically-increased homework completions each day.

In addition to homework assignments, the hotline is used for reminders of field trips, play rehearsals, and community service projects. About a third to half of the parents call in every day, according to a school official, compared to an average of two calls per day per teacher.

Teams of teachers assemble each day by grade to list their messages by dictating into the telephone recording system. The system is controlled by a pair of desktop computers at Canton School. A small problem is the requirement for touch-tone telephones. A few parents have rotary phones or no phones at all, but some of those parents have been using neighbors' phones.

In the words of some of the students, "My mom calls the line to see if I did everything." "There's no excuse for not having your work done now." According to officials when asked whether or not the system ultimately boosts the children's performance and grades through greater parental involvement, "The jury is out, but the telephone lines are ringing." Evaluation reports will be prepared when officials feel enough time has elapsed for a meaningful study.

LOCAL VOLUNTEER SCHOOL COUNCILS
SEE LEADERSHIP DEVELOPMENT/BOARDS:
EDUCATION

M.O.M.S. (MOTHERS ON THE MOVE SPIRITUALLY)
St. Teresa of Avila Catholic Church
1244 V Street, SE
Washington, DC 20020
TEL: 202-678-9068
Purpose: To help people with parenting skills *before* there is a problem.
Sponsor: St. Teresa of Avila Catholic Church
Contact: Jean Campbell, Founder
Description: When a member of a Washington, DC, Roman Catholic Church - a licensed practical nurse - lost a son to violence, the church steered her toward community outreach. By redesigning an existing program called *Brothers Keepers,* and renaming it M.O.M.S. (Mothers on the Move Spiritually), a "small army" of volunteer mothers formed in 1987 and began waging what it calls "spiritual warfare."

Much of the work of M.O.M.S. is in counseling juvenile delinquents at the *Oak Hill Correctional Center.* This focus grew out of the frustration of the founder in trying to find a rehabilitation center for a second son who turned to drugs after his brother's death. Upon finding only Centers designed for *after* the problem, M.O.M.S. was directed toward prevention.

The goal of the program is to establish two residential facilities for the incarcerated youth counseled by M.O.M.S. and a community center. To counteract the fact that the youth will return to the same neighborhood, the same friends, and eventually the same way of life, M.O.M.S. hopes to provide the alternative that will work,

involving divinity students to help man the residential centers, and volunteer psychiatrists from the District of Columbia government.
Founded: 1987

MOTHERS OF PWAS (PERSONS WITH AIDS)
SEE SELF-HELP: PARENTS

PARENT-CHILD HOME PROGRAM
10 Campbell Street
New Hyde Park, NY 11040
TEL: 516-482-8650/Ext. 610
Purpose: To prevent educational disadvantage in children from poor families and to help the parent in his/her role as the child's first teacher.
Sponsor: Great Neck & Manhasset Public Schools, BOCES of Nassau County
Contact: Doris Kertzner, Program Coordinator
Description: Operating Scope: The program, begun in 1972, serves about 60 low-income families living in the Manhasset and Great Neck School Districts. Children enter the program between the ages of 18 to 36 months and remain for two years. The families are visited in the home once or twice a week by trained staff (paid and volunteer).

Since 1978, The Parent-Child Home Program (PCHP), has offered a play group for the children one morning a week. Parents attend with their children and are thus able to have dialogue among themselves, arts and crafts sessions, and discussions led by professional psychologists, nutritionists, etc.

- **Time Span:** The program runs concurrently with the school year starting with training in late September, early October, and ending in late May. The office is staffed 9 a.m. to 4 p.m. on school days.
- **Purpose:** The program's purpose is to prevent educational disadvantage in children from poor families and to help the parent in his/her role as the child's first teacher. By encouraging parents to play with and speak to their young children we hope to give the child an enrichment taken for granted in middle-class culture - and to assure that these children do not enter school and face a catch-up situation.
- **Volunteer's Role:** The volunteer is the backbone of the program; in a typical year we have 20 volunteers. After training (described below) she is assigned one or more families whom she visits for a half hour once a week. The volunteer teacher-demonstrator (or TD) takes to the home carefully chosen books and toys and, in playing and reading to the child, she models behavior that the parent observes and imitates.
- **Volunteer's Training:** In late September the director gives a three-day training institute for new volunteers. They hear talks, see films, and become well acquainted with the program's content, purpose and techniques. Training continues throughout the year with weekly hour and a half seminars. The TD's come together at this time and discuss with the director any problems that have come up.
- **Time Commitment:** Volunteers should allow for a time commitment of about four hours a week. A car is a necessity.
- **Background:** No special training or background is necessary. We look for persons of warmth and openness who enjoy young children and are committed to the goals of the program.
Founded: 1972

PARENT-CHILD PROGRAM*
St. Luke's-Roosevelt Hospital Center
Child Psychiatry Clinic
Amsterdam Avenue at 114th Street
New York, NY 10025
TEL: 212-870-1867

Purpose: To help teenage mothers continue their own development toward adulthood, evaluate the development of the baby, and enhance the essential bonding process between mother and child.

Sponsor: St. Luke's-Roosevelt Hospital Center

Contact: Gloria Zicht, Child Psychiatry

Description: Recognizing that the average pregnant adolescent is poorly nourished and does not receive adequate care, the Child Psychiatry Clinic developed a program geared toward helping the young mother through the formative years with her baby. Most often, the teenager is a victim of poor housing, poor nutrition, anemia, toxemia, and other problems of deprivation. Motherhood represents a crisis which often will color her ability to attain a later adult level of adequate personality functioning. Professionals and volunteers lead groups, make home visits, provide in-clinic information services, and conduct research. Examples of these efforts are:

Parent-Child Interaction Group - led by a psychiatrist and a social worker with assistance from psychologists and volunteers; covers mother's relationship to own mother, their babies, impulses to abuse, etc.; activities include cooking, baking, knitting, making baby toys, birthday celebrations, etc.

Babies' Group - led by developmental psychologists to help understimulated babies; mothers are given the option of staying voluntarily and learning techniques, or leaving babies without participating in session.

Mothers' Luncheon Group - led by mental health worker with graduate student assistance; helps mothers learn to plan, organize, socialize, and share in a simple common experience (making lunch together).

Home Visiting - provided by undergraduate students under supervision of a social worker; involves regular visits to mothers to provide supportive help and liaison with hospital and city services.

Pediatric Outreach - performed by volunteers from the Parent-Child Program who sit in the outpatient clinic and talk to mothers with babies about their experiences in raising the child, encouraging them to take advantage of all services of the program. In addition, mental health professionals from the program conduct Assessment Home Visiting to follow-up young mothers who have left the hospital and offer services if the home assessment warrants them.

Also, continuing research is aimed at further developing the Maternal Attitudes and Adaptation Scale, a rating instrument which can be used to assess a woman's adjustment to motherhood and effect prediction and early detection of related problems.

The Parent-Child Program currently is being funded by privately donated funds. The hospital provides the program with an apartment for group sessions and petty cash for group expenses. Other funding sources are being sought to enable the program to expand and continue.

PARENT TO PARENT
Virginia Institute for Developmental Disabilities
Virginia Commonwealth University
910 West Franklin Street
Richmond, VA 23220
TEL: 804-225-3875 (TDD Access); 804-367-1200
TOLL FREE: 800-344-0012 (TDD Access)
FAX: 804-367-0102

Purpose: To put parents of people with disabilities in touch with each other to work together toward the independence of their children.

Sponsor: Virginia Commonwealth University

Contact: Bonnie Atwood, Coordinator

Description: Parent to Parent is one of the 50 university-affiliated programs in the country that work toward the independence, productivity and community integration of people with disabilities. It is a project of the *Virginia Institute for Developmental Disabilities*, which is affiliated with Virginia Commonwealth University.

The Richmond area chapter is housed at the university along with the statewide chapter. Since its inception in 1985, the Richmond chapter has served 200 families. The disabilities range from heart defects, cerebral palsy, vision problems and mental retardation to behavior disorders, autism and diabetes.

A major service of the program is putting volunteer *Parent Partners* in touch with other parents. Requests for matches are continuous, and begin with the staff, who bring together people who are most likely to be helpful to each other. To qualify as a *Parent Partner*, volunteers must attend a 1-1/2-day training seminar.

A side benefit of the program is the library designed to help educate parents about their children's diseases. Another educational tool is a 15-minute videotape of parents expressing their experiences with their special needs children and the organization. Both books and videotape are available on loan to parents.

One parent on the tape summed it up this way, "You're hit so hard in the very beginning..."The program places no limits on the diagnoses they will try to serve. b

Publications: Parent to Parent (videotape)

Founded: 1985

PARENT TO PARENT, ATTENTION ON ATTENDANCE
District of Columbia Public Schools
Volunteer Services/Training Branch
415 Twelfth Street, NW
Washington, DC 20004
TEL: 202-724-4400

Purpose: To expand the effective use of parent-volunteers in secondary schools while improving attendance through a system-wide notification process.

Sponsor: DC Public Schools

Contact: C. Vanessa Spinner/Claryce Nelson

Description: Parent to Parent, Attention on Attendance is a volunteer program that began in 1981 in response to a need to provide parents with timely notification of secondary student absence.

The project, which is totally volunteer, is coordinated by the DC Public Schools and offers parents of secondary school students a meaningful opportunity for involvement.

The unique element of this project is the *Community Awareness Committee,* a group of local business and organization volunteers, who promote the concept of better attendance and work toward rewarding the schools with most-improved attendance.

Volunteer parents are given guidelines and orientation and are governed by the rules of the DC Board of Education on volunteers. The goal of the project is to assist in the improvement of secondary student attendance.

Founded: 1981

PARENT-TO-PARENT PROGRAM
SEE VOLUNTEERS: ARMED FORCES MEMBERS - NAVY

PARENTING AND SCHOOL VOLUNTEER PROGRAM
Orangeburg Public Schools
578 Ellis Street
Orangeburg, SC 29117
TEL: 803-534-5454

Purpose: To break the cycle of apathetic parents in the low-income community by offering parenting classes and volunteer opportunities to parents and guardians.

Sponsor: Orangeburg School System

Contact: Dr. James Wilford, School Superintendent

Description: Although most of Orangeburg's 6,500 students are descendents of slaves and still live in poverty, more than half of its high school graduates are entering college. Parents who once appeared apathetic have become directly involved not only with their own children, but as tutors and other support figures to others. This "cross-parent" tutoring is encouraged, as it appears to have a positive effect on the children, who learn that the community can be an extension of the family.

A large number of parents together volunteer an average 1,000 hours a year as office and library assistants and teachers' aides, and in after-school programs such as the Boys Club, Girl Scouts and anti-drug programs. The parents recognize these programs as keeping their children off the streets and away from harmful influences.

The program began when an inner-city high school principal learned that, although parents may never initiate a phone call to say they are worried about their children, they usually respond when called. Now, with *early childhood parenting classes* in every elementary school, and teachers and counselors keeping in close contact with parents in the middle and high schools as well, parents have become a major force in the jump in grades above the national average. For example, the fourth grade of 1974 had only 14% of the students above the national average. Today, the same grade level boasts 59% above the national average.

Another factor in the dramatic turnaround was South Carolina's 1984 Education Improvement Act, which provided funding for innovative remedial programs to improve literacy and math skills, as well as enrichment programs for gifted students. Adding a penny to the sales tax and earmarking it for education increased the state's 1989-90 school budget by $283 million. Pay raises and incentives have boosted teacher morale, and computer technology has been introduced into the classrooms. This affects parent/volunteers also, since they see that their children have the best learning tools.

An aggressive absenteeism-prevention program directly involves parents, also. A computerized device calls parents, and is backed up by calls from teachers and counselors if necessary. Repeated unexcused absences land child and parent in family court. While rewarded for good behavior with ice cream or popcorn, repeated class disruptions by a student often results in the child being taken to the parent at his or her job. With parents present and showing an interest, this type of discipline has all but disappeared, and absenteeism is at an all-time low.

The visibility of parents throughout the school, whether or not with their own children, has helped to develop a positive attitude toward learning for the child, and a new sense of purpose and control for the parent.

Publications: Involving Parents
Founded: 1989

PARENTS EDUCATING PARENTS
SEE VOLUNTEERS: SELF-HELP

PARENTS FOR THE ENVIRONMENT
c/o James Mulloy
3509 Woodman Drive
Haymarket, VA 22069
TEL: 703-754-9381
Purpose: To challenge the schools on practices that both threaten the environment, and give mixed messages to students.
Sponsor: Prince William County Public Works Department
Contact: James Mulloy, Parent
Description: Since parents of the nineties were children during the major thrust on "saving the environment" in the sixties and seventies, the rallying of parents of children in Gainesville Elementary School around an environmental issue was a natural evolution. The center of the issue during the 1989-90 school year was a pilot program in two schools that replaces trays and dishes in the cafeterias with plastic trays and utensils to eliminate the need for dishwashing each day. According to a parent's spokesperson, this is giving mixed signals to children who are taught about the problem of solid waste and the need for recycling in their daily classes.

The schools say the new practice saves $27,000 a year by cutting

back on expensive dishwashing. As one principal pointed out, a recent hike of 10 cents was "as popular with students as steamed spinach." Parents say that plastic utensils and trays are unhealthful because some residue from the chemicals used can find its way into the food, that they are a threat to the environment, and are a bad influence on children's table manners. The *Prince William County Public Works Department,* which manages the county landfill, feels the move is "not based on sound environmental principles. On one hand, we're badgering the kids to recycle; on the other, we're giving them lunch on a Styrofoam tray."

And the children are not "silent partners" in this issue. As one third-grader said, "If they keep dumping it, they'll have to put it in people's yards. There won't be any more room left." In addition, about a third of the children at Gainesville are boycotting cafeteria lunches in an effort to persuade the school system to scrap its use of plastics.

One practice is beginning to take hold in schools which have used plastic utensils for years. They have begun recycling them through a program with *Amoco*. At its New York City plant, *Amoco* transforms used lunch trays, salad bowls, soup cups and plates into pellets used in insulation, packing material, and VCR tape. In the meantime, Gainesville parents, and a parents' group forming at Stonewall Middle School near the historic Manassas area in the county, continue to spend many volunteer hours seeking ways to impress on the schools that the use of plastics is unacceptable, and that it is in the best interest of all concerned for them to return to the former system of washable plates and trays.

PERSON TO PERSON*
Saginaw County Department of Social Services
411 East Genesee
PO Box 5070
Saginaw, MI 48605
TEL: 517-771-1614
Purpose: To help recipients of Public Assistance reach a pre-determined goal with the help of community volunteers.
Sponsor: Saginaw County Department of Social Services
Contact: Librarian/Historian
Description: The Person to Person program originated in 1971 at a time when a strike situation in Saginaw resulted in high unemployment. Through the Department of Social Services, self supporting male volunteers were matched with unemployed fathers receiving public assistance. The volunteer acted as the client's friend, helping the client find job opportunities, evaluating the client's skills, and assisting the client in applying for jobs. In the course of eight different matches, six clients obtained jobs.

Gradually the program has expanded. Matching on a one-to-one basis has proved beneficial to clients with diverse problems. Along with other problems, many clients have no friends. The supportive friendship of a volunteer is an important contribution to clients entering the mainstream of the community.

One volunteer calls weekly on a disabled woman who needs help in lifting bolts of material so she can cut and sew felt bean bags. She has become nearly self supporting. AFDC mothers have been helped through the rigors of enrolling in college. Elderly people and emotionally disturbed people have also profited from volunteer friendships. Parents who are high risk prospects for neglectful behavior are provided with volunteer friends who encourage appropriate child rearing. Volunteers act as payees for clients unable to handle their own money.

Most volunteers are recruited by word of mouth. Volunteers are recruited through churches, community groups and through the media. About twenty percent of the person to person volunteers are clients themselves and were recruited by referral from casework staff and posters in the office reception areas. Recruiting services purchased from the Voluntary Action Center of Saginaw County provide many capable volunteers for this program.

PROJECT GRADUATION
Connexion
310 East Third Street
Flint, MI 48502
TEL: 313-767-3750
Purpose: To ensure a drug- and alcohol-free graduation season.
Sponsor: Genesee County Commission on Substance Abuse Services
Contact: Deborah K. Medlin, Executive Director
Description: While still meeting with some student resistance, *Project Graduation* is becoming an expected part of high school plans during the graduation period. While some students join parents and educators in supporting the concept of not drinking while driving, they are not readily accepting that of being drug- and alcohol-free. According to one official, there is some progress. "There used to be no awareness at all," he said.
A meeting in early spring each year begins the program. In 1989, 100 schools participated in the project. The theme was "The best of life is yet to be. Make '89 drug and alcohol free."
One awareness project offers an award to the school getting the most high school juniors and seniors and parents to sign alcohol- and drug-free pledge cards. The winning school retains a traveling trophy for a year. New in 1989 was an activity called "Wanna Party." In this project, area businesses and organizations set up booths in the mall and distributed information on things students can do to have fun without alcohol or drugs. In part of this project, students and parents can learn tips for having alcohol-free parties, and participants win door prizes.
At the party, schools again participated in activities such as graduation night lock-ins at schools, halls and gyms, and Las Vegas Nights with students using play money. Parents, school staff, and students at the various schools volunteered to work on events for the parties, which included illusionists, massage therapists, hypnotists, prizes and all-night dancing.
Project Graduation is highlighted from March to June to involve the students themselves in the campaign. Students at four high schools have announced that their common goal at their individual parties is "bringing their graduating class together for a safe, fun-filled evening."
Connexion, a substance abuse prevention agency serving Genesee County, spearheads the area's nine-county coalition, which also includes *Channel 12 (WJRT), Channel 28 (WFUM), Channel 19/35 (WUCM), Genesee County Commission on Substance Abuse Services, Human Development Commission, AAA Michigan, Michigan State Police, the Sterling Area Health Project, Prevention and Youth Services, Christian Family Services of Lapeer County,* and *Top of the Park.*

RECREATION PROGRAMS FOR LEARNING DISABLED TEENS & ADULTS
YWCA of the National Capital Area
8101 Wolftrap Road
Dunn Loring, VA 22027
TEL: 703-560-1111 (VA); 301-460-3900 (MD)
Purpose: To enable participants to build self-esteem, develop social skills, and form friendships.
Contact: Program Coordinator
Description: Two recreational groups for individuals with learning disabilities - one for teens and another for young adults - are offered in several locations in the Washington, DC, metropolitan area. Organized by parents and volunteers, the programs include bike rides, bowling, concerts, dancing, dinner theatre shows, game nights, ice skating, movies, pot luck suppers, sporting events, swimming, and field trips.
The program uses recreational activities in a structured, supportive setting to help participants gain confidence while forming friendships and developing social skills. Each group meets approximately twice a month, with about half of the activities held at YWCA locations. Each registered participant receives advance

schedules of events by mail. Although there is a small fee for participation, scholarships are available for those who cannot afford to pay.

ROSIE'S PATROL
PO Box 306
Burke, VA 22015-0306
TEL: 703-978-5243
FAX: 703-451-9164
Purpose: To help stop the abduction of children; to help prevent offenses which make children victims; to promote child safety in the home.
Contact: Larry Stevens
Description: Rosie's Patrol is a community-based volunteer organization founded by the parents of a ten-year-old, *Rosie,* who was abducted from her neighborhood and later murdered in July 1989. Rosie's parents created *Rosie's Patrol,* a nonprofit corporation, to help prevent the recurrence of this hideous crime. The organization was named for *Rosie,* who was a very active member of her school's *Traffic Safety Patrol.* The members of *Rosie's Patrol* dedicate their efforts and accomplishments to the memory of *Rosie.* Their pledge is to initiate programs and activities that make neighborhoods and homes fun and safe for children. *Rosie's Patrol* has been officially endorsed by the *Fairfax County Board of Supervisors* and the *Fairfax County School Board* by separate resolutions.
Volunteer members work at the community level to promote and support activities and programs relating to children's safety. Organizationally, *Rosie's Patrol* operates at three levels: Board of Directors, action committees, and community chapters. At the present time there are three Chapters, all in Virginia: Burke, Stafford, and Prince William County.
Implementation Target Areas - The objectives of *Rosie's Patrol* are being accomplished by focusing on six implementation target areas, as follows:
- **Education:** Sponsor and support programs that teach child lures to neighborhood kids. Support the Fairfax County School Board *Ready Set Go for Good Health* program. Obtain and distribute child safety training materials. Review the product *Kids and Company* developed by the *National Center for Missing and Exploited Children.* Work with local *PTAs* to promote child safety training in the schools.
- **Community Programs:** Support and participate in established programs that promote child safety, including *Fairfax County Police Department* sponsored *Neighborhood Watch Program;* school sponsored *Block Parent Program;* local community *Block Rep Program, School Bus Stop Safety Program,* and *Safe Walk Program.*
- **Safety Awareness Activities:** Sponsor and support children's safety day programs such as local safety fairs, *Halloween Safety Day,* etc. Include guest appearances, media coverage, safety lectures, fingerprinting, videotaping, educational programs, distribution of safety literature, entertainment and snacks. Thus far, *Rosie's Patrol* has sponsored safety fairs, *Halloween Safety Day,* and community picnics.
- **Communication:** Establish rapport with the media (radio and TV). Export written *How To* literature. Establish a *Rosie's Patrol Computer Bulletin Board* (in process). Publish a *Rosie's Patrol* newsletter. Establish working relationships with outside resources and organizations with similar goals such as the *National Center for Missing and Exploited Children.* Encourage the establishment of neighborhood telephone trees.
- **Legislation:** Monitor child abuse trials and seek tougher penalties for repeat offenders of child abuse laws. Research current laws, policies and procedures regarding child safety and take action to strengthen the weak areas. (Recently, two pieces of Virginia legislation were strengthened with the assistance of a Virginia Delegate who is a member of the *Rosie's Patrol* Board of Directors.) Work closely with the

legal department of the *National Center for Missing and Exploited Children* to target legislation that needs to be strengthened.

- **Outreach:** Compile lists of child safety programs in Fairfax and surrounding counties and share the lists. Gather and disseminate child safety information. Document and export ideas and programs used by *Rosie's Patrol.* Speak to local organizations about *Rosie's Patrol* and child safety. Organize local chapters of *Rosie's Patrol.*

Operational Plan - The operational plan is to organize volunteers in the community to implement the programs, plans, and activities considered appropriate by the members in the community. Residents realize an immediate return on their investment of time because they are protecting their children and those of their neighbors. The program's motto, *Every adult is every child's guardian,* is a key to the concept of *Rosie's Patrol.* We believe that the community chapters of *Rosie's Patrol* are links that are closest to the children and therefore most effective. We also believe that the organizations and special interest groups concerned with the safety of children are also links. The *Rosie's Patrol* concept connects these links to form a strong chain.

Action Committees support the efforts of the community chapters. They also provide guidance and direction when appropriate. Additionally, *Rosie's Patrol* maintains contact with many community and national organizations that do much to deter the abduction and abuse of children. These organizations provide support and information to our cause.

Funding Sources - As of May 1990, *Rosie's Patrol* is operating with contributions received from community members at the time of *Rosie's* death. The organization only requires funds when it can't obtain materials and commodities for safety fairs from donations. Current plans call for the sale of T-shirts to increase available operating funds. This organization needs people's time, not their money.

Volunteer Participation - The *Rosie's Patrol* Board of Directors consists of twelve volunteers, who are the nucleus of the organization. The Board of Directors meets monthly.

The volunteer base consists of approximately 150 local citizens. However, no formal membership lists are maintained. *Rosie's Patrol* volunteers are parents, clergy members, teachers, teenagers, community leaders, and local business people giving their time and energy to the community. Many of them are also active in their *PTA, Block Mother* programs, community watch programs, scouting, school safety patrol, and church groups. The volunteers work with existing groups in their community to satisfy child safety needs. The activities of the volunteers are both formal and informal.

Informally, the volunteers practice child safety in their daily lives. This includes being observant of the needs of other children with whom they come in contact. *Formally,* volunteers participate in the six implementation target areas described above.

Summary - *Rosie's Patrol* volunteers believe there are many community and national organizations in existence that do much to deter the abduction and abuse of children and promote child safety. We view these organizations as links. However, we believe that the links need to be connected together to form a strong chain. We don't want to change or hinder the links; we only want to work with them so they can become a more unified force.

We believe awareness and community action are the best protection we can give our children. We further believe that an active, organized community is a deterrent to criminals who prey on innocent children and will help to create a safe and enjoyable environment for our children.

Our motto, *Every adult is every child's guardian,* was created by *Rosie's* mother. It clearly summarizes our operating philosophy. There are many threats to child safety. If adults will modify their behavior slightly to include being more observant of children and their safety, we believe our objectives will be accomplished.

Publications: Rosie's Patrol Newsletter

SCHOOL FIRE SAFETY MONITORING PROGRAM
Parents United
c/o Rice-Thurston
2135 Newport Place
Washington, DC 20037
TEL: 202-293-7009
Purpose: To monitor schools citywide for compliance with Washington, DC's fire laws.
Sponsor: District of Columbia City Council
Contact: Delabian L. Rice-Thurston, Executive Director
Description: Parents United, a citywide group of parents in Washington, DC, exists to assure adequate education and safety for their children in the public schools. In the Spring of 1990, *Parents United* commissioned a study to determine the safety of the City's schools in the area of fire prevention and response. Through the study the parents' group learned that there were more than 4,000 fire code violations in District of Columbia public schools - including missing or deficient fire doors, falling plaster, leaky roofs, and no heat.

The group's Executive Director contacted both the Mayor and the school system to discuss the immediate development of an effective repair schedule, now lacking in the system, and the financing of needed repairs - in the face of diminishing funds. Information provided by the school system indicated that $10 million requested for fiscal 1991 by school officials for building repair was wiped out when the budget was cut from $100 million to $43 million.

When research by the group showed no inspections for the past year, the parents contacted the *District of Columbia Department of Consumer and Regulatory Affairs (DCRA)* and the fire department's building inspections division. They determined that inspections by DCRA were done on elevators, cafeterias and boilers only, "so the roof could be falling in and that would not routinely be inspected," according to a spokesperson for the parents' group.

In researching fire codes, the group found that adequate precautions were taken against intruders, since they are expected, but no one believes that fires are a serious threat. Although they learned that the schools asked for a moratorium on fire regulation enforcement, Fire Department officials said no exceptions to the law are made.

The study has been presented to all officials and departments concerned, with the parents' group prepared to file suit if appropriate action is not taken to protect the city's school children against fire. With promised cooperation and roundtable discussions, *Parents United* expects to work with authorities to help bring about full compliance to fire codes of the District.

SENECA FALLS CONCERNED PARENTS
Seneca Falls Central School District
Mynderse Academy
105 Troy Street
Seneca Falls, NY 13148
TEL: 315-568-9826
Purpose: To enable youth, ages 11 to 15, either on the fringe of breaking the law or involved with the law, to discover meaningful alternatives and programs to their present lifestyles through the efforts of their concerned parents.
Sponsor: Mynderse Academy
Contact: Gerald Macaluso
Description: This program began in September of 1983 through a group of concerned parents of children of Mynderse Academy. At this particular moment the cost is nothing, in that present social service agencies are providing the bulk of program-related activities to the clients. The Academy serves as the facilitator of the program. The following is of the essence:
Target Population:
- Seneca County Youth - 11 to 15 years of age.
- Youth on the fringe of breaking the law or involved with the law.

● Participation must be voluntary - students as well as parents.

Agencies Involved:

● Religious, Educational, Police, and Social Service

Program includes:

● Youth Assistance Program at Auburn Correctional Institute
● Alternatives to drugs and alcohol
● Post-Counseling and Monitoring

Role of the Academy:

● Coordinating force of the effort.

The strong support and activities of parents is vital to the program.

Founded: 1983

A SHOULDER TO CRY ON
William Beaumont Hospital
3601 West 13-Mile Road
Royal Oak, MI 48072
TEL: 313-551-5000

Purpose: To help first-time parents to develop a routine with their infants upon their return home from the hospital.

Contact: Beth Frydlewicz, Coordinator

Description: Volunteers in the nine-year-old parenting program of *William Beaumont Hospital* are mothers interested in helping new mothers get off on the right foot in caring for their newborn infants. The program started as a Michigan State University research project. The volunteer mothers go through intensive training in eight three-hour classes. They learn about listening to new parents, feeding, sleeping and crying habits of newborns, and how to comfort them.

Many expectant parents take classes on delivering the baby, but at home there was usually a mother, aunt, or someone else from the family to help out the new mother. Today's family setup has changed all of that, and new mothers are finding out how little they know about taking care of an infant.

The volunteer spends time in the home passing on a combination of her own knowledge as a mother, and the techniques learned in the training course. They find that not all new mothers need the same type of help. Some panic, and could reach a dangerous point of frustration, especially with colicky babies. Others simply have very little skill or common sense. Then there are mothers who need to have the volunteer show an interest in them as well as the baby. Some could manage without the program. One of the volunteer's first considerations is to try to determine which of the above applies.

The program is available to first-time parents who deliver at Beaumont or whose pediatrician works out of the hospital. It is believed to be the only program of its kind in the state.

SO SAD (SAVE OUR SONS AND DAUGHTERS)
543 Martin Luther King Blvd
Detroit, MI 48201
TEL: 313-833-3030

Purpose: To help end teen violence.

Contact: Clementine Barfield, Founder

Description: When a mother sought counseling to help her through the grief of losing a son to violence, she found none. She did find more than 100 Detroit parents whose children had been killed, and together they formed their own counseling service, *Save Our Sons and Daughters (SO SAD)*. Part of the motivation for developing SO SAD was to show remaining children in families of victims that revenge is not the way. Doing something positive helps survivors feel that they did not "just lose a valuable human being for nothing."

The all-volunteer counseling service is working with limited funds, but plans for expansion and a major fund-raising drive are underway.

Founded: 1987

STOP! THE MADNESS FOUNDATION
SEE COMMUNICATIONS & PUBLIC RELATIONS: JUSTICE

TEEN CENTER
McLean Community Center
1234 Ingleside Avenue
McLean, VA 22101
TEL: 703-790-0123

Purpose: To offer teenagers a place to drop in for games, snacks, talk, television, dances or just hanging out.

Sponsor: Fairfax County

Contact: Eugene Burman, Chairman

Description: Still disappointed over the closing of *Freedom House,* a teen center resulting from parent efforts in the early 70's, the parents again put forth the effort to fill this need in McLean. Since the earlier effort failed due to lack of funds and volunteers, those two considerations are foremost in the organizers' minds for the current effort. At the beginning of summer 1989, the group received word that they could use an old firehouse for the teen center for $1.00 a year in a two-year experiment. On June 30, ten high school student leaders, and representatives of a local architectural firm held a brainstorming session to work out plans for the new center. The center opened in early 1990.

An important part of the philosophy to make sure this second effort succeeds is placing more decision-making responsibilities in the hands of students. Among their initial decisions in the meeting with the architect:

● Keep the fire station ambience by including memorabilia such as the front end of a firetruck
● Include plenty of air hockey tables.
● Let the kids themselves decide what kind of food should be in the snack bar and vending machines.
● Set aside areas for video games, table tennis or pool, television watching, snacking, quiet study and other activities.
● Stress a casual and laid-back atmosphere.

For organizers, getting the firehouse was not an easy victory. The firehouse occupies a prime half acre in the middle of downtown McLean. About 30 organizations were interested in the property, and the amount the county might have realized was estimated at $2 million. The complainers found a dozen reasons for eliminating the teen center, including its proximity to local businesses, lack of parking space, traffic flow, the mid-town location, etc. But a "town meeting" held earlier showed overwhelming support from the 30 to 40 speakers, who represented neighborhoods and other groups.

Youth and adults alike are aware of the problems. The 18 parking spaces are not ample, and off-site parking is being sought. And the students are aware that they must continue to be "good neighbors," or the "two-year experiment" could be very short-lived, and no doubt the developers would move in again to push for that office building.

Although conditions attached to the lease require that the center be open to *all* Fairfax County teenagers, most youth are from McLean. Although youth, parents and other organizers are volunteers, two paid persons help to monitor youth, trying to screen out what one organizer called "bully-type kids." One night each week is reserved for seventh- and eighth-graders, who are not allowed in at other times. Teenagers are issued identification cards for a nominal fee. The facility is the only publicly-sponsored, full-service teen center in Northern Virginia.

TENAFLY-ALPINE SAFE RIDES PROGRAM AND OTHERS
Boy Scouts of America
Explorer Division
State Highway 9 West
Alpine, NJ 07620
TEL: 201-768-1910

Purpose: To provide a safe ride home for teenagers who have been drinking.

Sponsor: Boy Scouts of America Explorer Division

Contact: Gerald Burstein, Safe Rides Coordinator, Tenafly-Alpine

Description: Operating out of the Tenafly Senior Center since 1984, the *Tenafly-Alpine Safe Rides Program,* sponsored by the *Explorer Division of the Boy Scouts of America,* is thriving while other safe rides programs across the state have stopped operating. The program operates a hot line phone on Friday and Saturday nights during the school year from 10 p.m. to 2 a.m. One or two parents supervise three to five students who answer the phones. The students drive to pick up their fellow teenagers and keep in touch with the home base by citizens band radio. Students who use the service are given anonymity.

The program requires a great deal of student participation. To ensure the number of students required, the program maintains a pool of about 50 student volunteers. This is a challenge, since many students who would be willing to help do not drive. The lack of parent volunteers - which caused the demise of several programs - is no problem in the Tenafly-Alpine effort.

Although some parents and educators are concerned that safe rides programs condone teenage drinking, an active parent in the Tenafly-Alpine program sees it as "offering an immediate solution to a specific problem." He feels that it is useful while teenage drinking still exists and is needed to bridge the gap and save lives while programs are continually mounted to discourage drinking among young people. The vice principal of the Rotary Club-sponsored Northern Valley High School Safe Rides program in Demarest agrees. He sees the program as an interim activity needed to save lives, coupled with the goal of a substance-free school. And the student council president, who helped get Northern Valley's program started, also concurs, saying, "We're not condoning drinking; we're just trying to prevent drunk driving." She feels that thinking that teens won't drink is "too idealistic." A representative of the Boy Scouts Explorer Division adds that safe rides create an awareness through the example of sober teenage volunteers that teens shouldn't drink.

The Department of Education, while remaining somewhat neutral on the issue, recommends considering the *Safe Homes* program, which calls for parents to pledge not to allow alcohol to be served at parties, and to call other parents to make sure they are home at students' parties.

A side benefit is that teens working beside parents enter into a dialogue about the program, discuss it with school and other officials, and work with the adults toward improvements that will lead more directly to the goal of substance-free schools.

The safe rides concept was originated by Darien (Connecticut) High School in 1981 and picked up the following year by the Boy Scouts' Explorer Division. The Boy Scouts sponsor at least 500 safe rides programs nationwide. In New Jersey, 21 programs operated by schools, community groups, businesses, and other organizations are sponsored by the Boy Scouts, up from eight in 1986. The Boy Scouts provide insurance for the groups they sponsor.

VALENTINE SCHOOL ART SHOW
San Marino Schools
1665 West Drive
San Marino, CA 91108
TEL: 818-289-3691
Purpose: To assure that children are not "shortchanged" in the area of arts and cultural enrichment.
Sponsor: Parent-Teachers Association (PTA)
Contact: Cindy Roe, PTA
Description: With the rallying slogan, *Art Is Not Caught, It Must Be Taught,* 50 parents of children in public schools in San Marino embarked on a program to help children learn more about art. Because of school budget cuts that came from Sacramento, things thought of as frill courses had been eliminated. With one of the parents an art history major, and 49 others from the PTA ready for assignments, a year-long program was approved by the school board and conducted in the schools. Grade-by-grade, the program included:

- **Kindergarten** - studied line, looking at pictures by Klee, Picasso, Miro and Mondrian. Then they painted their own pictures.
- **First Grade** - studied shapes, real and abstract, illustrated by the works of Rousseau, Cezanne and Matisse.
- **Second Grade** - studied color, and how it changes the way we feel about a picture, using works of Reynolds, Cassatt, Rothko, Seurat and Gainsborough.
- **Third Grade** - studied texture, both visual and tactile, using knobby pictures and satin smooth ones inspired by Van Gogh, Pollock, Monet, Rembrandt and the Cluny tapestries.
- **Fourth Grade** - studied form in sculpture and architecture - held on the lawn with the "biggest exercise in mud pie making in the land" using Rodin and Michelangelo as inspiration.
- **Fifth Grade** - combined all of the elements in their work and learned about Stuart, Wyeth, Hopper and Roesen.

The windup of the year's work was the *Valentine School Art Show.* Every child in school had at least one picture in the exhibition. Volunteers took the works home and mounted them on bright construction paper, and mounted corkboard for the displays. They designed and decorated the entrance to the exhibit like a Grecian portico to give the kids a sense of a real art museum.

Fundraising for the exhibit consisted of the sale of packets of note paper printed with pictures made by the young artists. Three pictures were chosen for this honor. Also used for fundraising was an apron wildly speckled and sprayed a la some of Pollock's work. Across the top it says, "You've got to have art."

Support from the principal of the school included miraculously managing all year to keep the art display room off limits, even on rainy days when the children are confined inside and find ways to roam around. The excitement level of the children remained at the "explosion point" all year, waiting for class every week on the door sill, and having to be "scooted out" when class was over.

The same group of parents painted the entire outside of the school in 1987. In their words, "We are determined that our children will not be shortchanged!"

WIPING OUT DRUG ABUSE DRUG FREE TEEN CENTER
Codman Square
595 Washington Street
Dorchester, MA 02174
TEL: 617-288-4430
Purpose: To provide a place that will attract at-risk teenagers and keep them off the streets.
Contact: Mattie DeLoach, Director
Description: Parents and leaders of the all-volunteer *Wiping Out Drug Abuse Drug Free Teen Center* firmly believe that youth on drugs are the exception, not the rule. "The rule" is represented by young people who have found a direction and are working hard and reaching for a goal. Programs at the Center are planned so that young people who stay out of trouble participate with at-risk and in-trouble youth. Not only do the at-risk youth see alternatives to gang violence in this way, but the ones who are doing well realize that this is a way of giving them recognition for their accomplishments. The latter - who need acceptance also - are often forgotten in the deep concern for at-risk youth.

Volunteers - some are parents - attempt to counteract what are seen as drastic changes in "trouble-spot" neighborhoods where children once would play together and adults would socialize in a family atmosphere. This is evident as the potential of each child is explored, and singers, artists and poets are found among both those doing well and those doing poorly in school. The Center provides an attractive, relaxed atmosphere where these talents can be expressed and can grow. A safe and secure place to study, do homework, and play is no longer available to youth in many neighborhood areas. One youth, walking near his house, was approached by a gang of youth who simply took his leather jacket - proudly earned with his own money - and walked off.

Officials, parents and volunteers in the program are aware of the effect on teenagers of stories constantly in the media about shootings and stabbings, drugs and crime, and the slow erosion of teenage society. Of deeper concern, however, are the many youths at the Center who have witnessed such crimes in their neighborhoods. The raw talent discovered among the at-risk youth indicates that appropriate opportunities have not been provided for this group.

Without being judgmental or domineering, the volunteers work to demonstrate alternatives designed to "keep kids away from the war zone" (gangs and drugs). By building on latent talents of the youths, and giving them room to explore their potential, the program builds self-esteem - a crucial element in building character and confidence - and the ability to reject drugs and violence as a way of life.

YOUNG AUTHORS' FAIRE
Guadalupe Elementary School
6044 Vera Cruz Drive
San Jose, CA 95120
TEL: 408-268-1030
Purpose: To acknowledge children's writing and creativity.
Sponsor: Guadalupe School
Contact: Karen Mullaly, Principal
Description: Recognizing that writing is the basis for everything pupils do in school, a group of volunteer parents, the school Principal, and several teachers stage a *Young Author's Faire* each year for children from kindergarten through fifth grade.

The children write both individually and as a class, and both compositions and stories that rhyme. They illustrate their works and bind them with Batik book covers and construction paper, some creatively cut into the shape of the animal star of the story. The fourth graders created, on a computer, their own newspapers, and reported on the California Gold Rush. The children are encouraged to acknowledge and appreciate their classmates' work. The *Faire* has served as an excellent forerunner for a new literature-based language arts program incorporated into the school system shortly after the 1989 *Faire.* According to the principal, "It's a new way of using language arts; a whole-language approach in which reading, writing, listening and speaking are all integrated, with lots more reading and greater listening and vocabulary."

Also at the *Faire* was a display of the children's art, put together by the *Art Vistas Docents,* a group of volunteer parents who go into the classroom to give the students an appreciation, understanding and love of art. These works included painting, paper collages, wood burning, "bottle people" creations, and mixed media. There was also a "blacklight" room that highlighted the kindergartners' use of flourescent paints.

A side benefit from the writing, according to a volunteer, is the fact that the children reveal sides of themselves that do not surface otherwise, making it easier to get to know them and serve their best interests. "But the bottom line," she adds, "is that the children love to write and create, and a portion of this enjoyment carries over to the other more serious subjects."

YOUTH TRAIN
2741 Welton
Denver, CO 80205
TEL: 303-295-7912
Purpose: To get at-risk youth back on the right track.
Contact: June Jackson or Nancy Johnson, parent volunteers
Description: Youth Train was founded by two mothers who saw a connection between a parents' movement and a neighborhood watch organization. Gang violence and other crime - and gang involvement by a daughter of one of the parents - spurred them to action as they helped found the organization, which is for parents and children five to nineteen years of age. A parent acts as block captain in every neighborhood in the metro area, similar to *Crime*

Watch programs. Residents put yellow light bulbs in their porch lamps and turn them on as a sign that "they are going to be involved, know where their children are, and take responsibility for their children's actions." The lights are used also to demonstrate the first sign of trouble, then call police and neighbors, who in turn switch on their lights.

Part of the program involves peer groups - taking teens who have positive activities and mixing them with teens who are involved in negative activities. The philosophy behind this mix is that youth are influenced more by their peers than their parents. But it works the other way too, according to volunteers in the program. Gang members, for example, develop a "sign language" of their own that they use to communicate between members - a skill that demands accuracy for street survival. These same youth can teach sign language to deaf children - an accomplishment that, in turn, builds self-esteem in the young teachers. In the process they learn some of the frustrations of teaching, which carries over to the classroom and results in more respect for the teacher.

Thus, the secret of *Youth Train* is to build on existing talents among youth that were often discounted as blanket labels of "throwaways" and "in-trouble youth" placing the youth at a disadvantage, and combine this with parent interest and involvement. All participants in the program are volunteers.

VOLUNTEERS: PEERS

NATIONAL/STATE ORGANIZATIONS

NATIONAL PEER HELPERS ASSOCIATION
SEE VOLUNTEERS: SELF-HELP

VOLUNTEERS: PERSONS WITH AIDS

NATIONAL/STATE ORGANIZATIONS

THE NAMES PROJECT/AIDS MEMORIAL QUILT
SEE COMMUNICATIONS & PUBLIC RELATIONS: AIDS

NATIONAL ASSOCIATION OF PEOPLE WITH AIDS
2025 Eye Street, NW
Suite 415
Washington, DC 20006
TEL: 202-429-2856
Objectives: To create a national system of self-empowering programs.
Services: Promotes participation of local organizations in the provision of AIDS-related health care and social services; works to develop, implement, and maintain a national system of self-empowering programs adminstered by and for people with AIDS (acquired immune deficiency syndrome) and ARC (AIDS-Related Complex); participates in educational programs; provides traveling and other assistance; administers the *Amy Sloan Memorial Fund;* works with other organizations with similar goals; administers a computer bulletin board system (installed May 1990) for nationwide networking; publishes a bimonthly newsletter and other materials.
Publications: NAPWA News

PEOPLE WITH AIDS COALITION (*formerly People With AIDS*)
263A West 19th Street
No. 125
New York, NY 10011
TEL: 212-627-1810
Objectives: To provide a local support network for persons with AIDS.
Services: Operates as a local support group for persons afflicted with AIDS; conducts public forums; maintains a drop-in lounge; works with social service agencies; operates a meal program and an apartment referral service; conducts medical research through the *Community Research Initiative;* operates a speakers bureau; publishes a monthly newsletter, a book on surviving with AIDS, and other materials.
Publications: PWA Coalition Newsline; Surviving with AIDS: Hints for the Newly Diagnosed

TRAINING PROGRAMS

HOW TO EFFECTIVELY MANAGE PEOPLE WHO HAVE AIDS AS VOLUNTEERS
SEE TRAINING/CONFERENCES/TEACHING: AIDS

INDIVIDUAL PROGRAM PROFILES

DISTRICT OF COLUMBIA AIDS INFORMATION LINE
SEE INFORMATION & REFERRAL: AIDS

HOWARD BROWN MEMORIAL CLINIC
945 West George
Chicago, IL 60657
TEL: 312-871-5777
Purpose: To provide low-cost, confidential, community-based health care for sexually transmitted diseases, including AIDS.
Sponsor: Government contracts; grants; corporate and private donations
Contact: Theresa Harper, Volunteer Coordinator
Description: Howard Brown Memorial Clinic (HBMC), founded in 1974, provides low-cost, non-discriminatory confidential diagnostic and treatment services for sexually-transmitted diseases (STDs). HBMC has become one of the largest clinics of its type in the United States.
Since the early 1980s, HBMC has taken a leading role in the fight against Acquired Immune Deficiency Syndrome (AIDS). Today Howard Brown is the largest provider of AIDS services in Chicago and one of the leading AIDS research facilities in the nation.
HBMC's programs and services are administered by health care professionals, including physicians, nurses, laboratory technicians, case management workers, mental health practitioners, health educators and administrative personnel. The expertise provided by these professionals is augmented by more than 400 volunteers. Without volunteers, HBMC could not meet the community's needs or new challenges. Volunteers are essential to the very existence of all HBMC programs and services.
The clinic is organized in three major service divisions: Administrative, Medical Services and Social Services. The Social Services division features special components to serve AIDS clients and to provide AIDS education.
The services provided to AIDS clients encompass many areas, but a particular area where volunteers become foremost providers is the Support Manager (Buddy) program.
This program trains volunteers to work one-on-one with a PWA (person with AIDS) providing emotional support, companionship and practical support.
In this particular program, there are presently 60 volunteers who

have an assigned client who is diagnosed with AIDS. These volunteers have all completed a 25-hour intensive training seminar and also attend a bi-weekly support group.
Sometimes nobody understands better than another person with AIDS. PWAs are trained to share experiences, information and provide short-term support for the client dealing with the initial impact of diagnosis.
Over 300 volunteers provide services throughout the Clinic's other departments, including Medical and Administrative divisions. Our volunteers come from varied backgrounds and age groups and are able to work with varying levels of experience. The need for caring and interested volunteers continues as we strive to conquer AIDS.
Publications: Volunteer Opportunities; Meeting the Challenge; Social Service Programs; HBMC Annual Report
Founded: 1974

VOLUNTEERS: POLICE OFFICERS

NATIONAL/STATE ORGANIZATIONS

NATIONAL ASSOCIATION OF POLICE ATHLETIC LEAGUES
200 Castlewood Drive
North Palm Beach , FL 33408
TEL: 305-844-1823
Objectives: To create a bond between police officers and community youths through athletics to help prevent youth crime.
Services: Works to prevent juvenile delinquency by fostering a strong, positive attitude toward police officers; focuses on the problems of crime and delinquency and on ways to reduce juvenile restlessness; relies on athletics and recreational activities to promote friendship between young people and police officers; fosters a network of local leagues; develops new programs and materials; creates partnerships between state, regional, and national levels and civic and other sports organizations; conducts national tournaments in basketball, baseball, boxing, ice hockey, and girls' softball; offers insurance coverage and a group purchasing program; conducts workshops, training seminars, and research and development programs; produces public service announcements, films, and training aids; publishes a newspaper and a membership directory.
Sponsor: National PAL
Publications: UP-DATE; National PAL Membership Directory
Founded: 1944

TRAINING PROGRAMS

DRUNK-DRIVING SIMULATOR PROGRAM AND FORUM
O'Connell High School
6600 Little Falls Road
Arlington, VA 22213
TEL: 703-237-1400
Credit: Inquire
Sponsor: Mothers Against Drunk Driving
Contact: Principal
Description: This forum was co-sponsored by *Dodge Cars* and *Mothers Against Drunk Driving*. It featured a car whose braking and steering mechanisms are specially rigged to simulate the lethargic reaction time of an intoxicated driver. More than 1300 students attended from Bishop O'Connell High - the host school in Arlington, Virginia, along with students from Yorktown High, St. Mary's Academy, George Mason High, Madison High, and others from throughout Arlington, Fairfax, and Alexandria. Most had

been driving only a few months, and all were under 21, the legal drinking age in Virginia. Speakers came from the Virginia Department of Education Driver Safety Program, WAVA-FM Radio (the local disc jockey), Mothers Against Drunk Driving, and Dodge Motor Company.

The car contains a computer in which is entered the driver's weight and the number of consumed drinks to be simulated (between one and 12). The computer calculates the timing delay on the car's braking and steering based on the number of drinks needed to intoxicate drivers of varying weights. The driver attempts to complete a course in a 150- by 200-foot area without hitting cones or pop-up silhouettes. The car cannot be operated without an instructor, who can shut it down automatically when necessary.

Police officers volunteered for the program and came from all jurisdictions of Northern Virginia. The regional representative from *Mothers Against Drunk Driving* told the students, "This allows you to drive the car, which simulates some level of impairment, and get the experience from that, rather than making the dumb mistake of really drinking and driving." One speaker, who had lost a daughter when a drunk driver collided with her car, gave the students some insight not only into his family's grief, but the toll the experience had taken on the young drunk driver who killed her. The most frequent comment by students at the end of the day summed up the goals of the program: "I'll never drink and drive."

The forum followed a national public awareness campaign held at high schools in the metropolitan area, which carried the slogan, "Think... Don't drive and drink," which was exhorted throughout the program. Under the co-sponsors' program, two professional drivers zigzag across the county with the car during the school year. The car program succeeds an earlier method used by Fairfax County Police in which they had adults actually get legally drunk. The problem was that many of them didn't remember the experience afterward. One student in the forum provided a personal message from the experience which indicated that the young people will not soon forget it. "I could hear all the little cones crunching under the tires. At least they were little cones, and not little people."

FORUM ON SCHOOL VANDALISM
SEE TRAINING/CONFERENCES/TEACHING: JUSTICE SYSTEM

INDIVIDUAL PROGRAM PROFILES

A, B, AND C ON BURGLARY
Franconia District Citizens Advisory Committee
c/o William Urick, Chairman
9453 Park Hunt Court
Springfield, VA 22153
TEL: 703-455-1567
Purpose: To educate the public about precautions against burglary through panel presentations by convicted burglars.
Sponsor: Franconia Police Department; Franconia District Citizens Advisory Committee
Contact: William Urick
Description: Three convicted burglars awaiting sentencing volunteered to make a presentation to a citizens group on "burglary through the eyes of the pros." They called themselves "A, B and C" and together were responsible for 150 to 160 burglaries in the Washington, DC area. During the questioning that followed the 90-minute, hard-hitting, mocking presentation, not one of the 250 citizens questioned the volunteers' credentials. Concerned about Fairfax County's latest burglary statistics, the Advisory Committee put the program together with the help of police officials. From January to April of the current year, 2,446 burglaries (759 more than in the same period of the previous year)

were reported countywide.

Most of the audience consisted of older residents who listened intently and took notes as A, B and C spun their tales of criminal intrigue and gave tips on how to deter burglars like themselves. The panelists did offer some surprises that had an ironic twist - two of them said that their own homes were burglarized while they were in jail. Basic information and advice offered included:

- Be wary of servicemen who make repairs at home. Forty percent of the time service people can give their friends information, or unbolt windows themselves and send someone else back to make the pickup.
- Many non-service people (burglars) dress in dark blue service uniforms and move freely among homes in the daytime.
- Take special precautions when leaving home on winter evenings between five and nine. This period is considered "prime time" because it gets dark at five in winter, and no one sits home with all the lights out.
- Limit open windows and curtains. Burglars "window shop" in neighborhoods looking for valuables. Many are experienced enough to see the "dollar signs" at a single quick glance, and the house goes on a list of prospects.
- Burglars now seek gold and silver items rather than the televisions and stereos previously sought.

The above is a sampling of tips provided by the volunteer burglars. Others are available through the sponsors above.

Citizens in the audience expressed appreciation for the program, many having note pads with several pages of notes. The information most frequently mentioned in a discussion after the program was the description of how burglars obtained tips from - and actually collaborated with - some repairmen.

The only dissenting note on this unique volunteer program was tendered by the local Deputy Sheriff. Since two of the three volunteer inmates were black, he felt that a stereotype could develop among citizens. However, he told the group, "Your idea is a good one and, with more advanced planning - especially to reach more people - this one program could go a long way to eliminate the burglary problem in the county."
Founded: 1981

ALTERNATIVE EDUCATION AND WORK CENTER
SEE VOLUNTEERS: PRISONERS/EX-OFFENDERS

CHAMP BAKERY
District of Columbia Police Department
Office of the Chief of Police
300 Indiana Avenue, NW
Washington, DC 20001
TEL: 202-727-1000
Purpose: To occupy youth in a productive enterprise as a deterrent to drug abuse and other unlawful activities.
Sponsor: District of Columbia Police Department
Contact: Tom Blackburn, Advisor
Description: This effort is an outgrowth of the concern of a former District of Columbia school counselor and an advisor to the city's Chief of Police. They saw the economic problem facing the city's youth as a potentially explosive situation that could involve drug use, drug dealing, and other unlawful activities.

The Champ Bakery received a positive response from all who became aware of it. This encouraged the youth to put forth even greater effort. Another incident that increased their interest in their little business was the death of one of their peers, age 13, who had been killed in a crack house. They are stepping up efforts to expand the cookie business and view it as a way of trying to save lives.

The bakery's recruiter of new salesmen says it is difficult when the $70 over four days that sales can bring pales by comparison to the $10 per minute that can be made from the sale of one crumb of crack cocaine. The youngsters, ranging in age from 11 to 15, realized that drastic action had to be taken to provide larger ovens, a computer, a couple of vans and a downtown location, so they could "give any street-level dope dealer a run for the money." According to one of the young entrepreneurs, a straight-A elementary school student, "If we had the right equipment, I could easily triple my weekly earnings selling cookies. I sell out my inventory every day and I feel bad when people ask for more, and I can't deliver."

A story in the paper about the bakery in March 1989 brought help from many quarters. Assistance by the advocates who responded to the article included:

- Republican National Committee chairman sending a bag of cookies to President Bush, which resulted in a meeting at the White House with the President;
- Radio station WOL-AM promoting the bakery on its morning show;
- Kenilworth-Parkside housing complex directing young recruits to the bakery program;
- Negril Bakery owner allowing the use of space in his downtown store;
- National Strategy in Marketing donating T-shirts;
- Freddie Mac, the Federal Home Loan Mortgage Corporation, donating $500;
- American University asking Marriott corporation to contract with the youths to sell cookies on campus;
- United Black Fund and Washington Informer newspaper donating more than $5,000, and
- Maxima Corporation meeting with the youth to talk about computers.

Champ continues to make progress and receive advice and support from the above advocates plus others who learn about and offer to help the youth program.

Publications: Champ Information Packet

CHILD ABUSE SERVICES TEAM (CAST)
Orangewood Children's Home
401 The City Drive South
Orange, CA 92668
TEL: 714-834-7584; 714-834-7105
Purpose: To provide citizen advocates for sexually abused children.
Sponsor: Orangewood Children's Home
Description: The *Child Abuse Services Team (CAST)* is designed to reduce the trauma for child victims of sexual abuse by reducing the number of interviews and investigations. CAST volunteers serve as advocates as the children undergo interviews and examinations.

CAST provides a single "child-friendly" location to avoid the overwhelming government structures. Crisis intervention and long-term therapy are provided by CAST also on an as-needed basis. The *Team* involves police agencies, medical personnel, child-welfare services and the District Attorney's Office. A day and a half of training is provided for all volunteers prior to assignments with the children. CAST is operated at Orangewood Children's Home.

CONNER-HARRIS MINI MALL
District of Columbia Police Department
Community Relations Department
300 Indiana Avenue, NW
Washington, DC 20001
TEL: 202-727-1000
Purpose: To involve youth in providing a service and making money for themselves.
Sponsor: District of Columbia Police Department
Contact: Officer W.W. Johnson
Description: Assigned to Woodson Junior High School in Northeast Washington, a police officer from the department's Community Relations Division searched for a way to keep the youth interested in productive activities, and too busy to think about drugs and alcohol. His first goal was to install a

weight-lifting room to teach the youth discipline and respect for their bodies. To accomplish this he found an unused room at the school's recreation center, begged mirrors from a hotel that was going out of business, and donated $8,000 worth of weight-lifting equipment.

His concern continued, however, as he observed students leaving school to buy candy, school supplies, jogging shoes and other items. He thought, "Why can't they sell these things to themselves? That way they could provide a service, learn about business, and make some money for themselves."

As a result of his efforts, in the fall of 1989, the *Conner-Harris Mini Mall* was dedicated. The mall was named for two victims of the District's drug war - a 13-year-old youth and a 17-year-old youth. A packed room that included the Chief of Police, neighborhood residents, ministers, a cadre of volunteers and the proud officer's family attended the dedication.

In the youth-run mall there are stalls for candy, T-shirts, woodcraft and athletic shoes. Four youngsters with an interest in photography are working with the National Center for Neighborhood Enterprise (NCNE) to acquire equipment to produce personalized buttons and badges for conventions. Mega Foods has agreed to hire some of the students and train them in food service.

Much of the city-provided space at the rear of the school continues to be renovated. Officer Johnson does much of the carpentry under the direction of an architect he saw on television and promptly recruited.

The mall goes far beyond just giving youngsters a chance to earn a few dollars, according to the officer. He sees it as a chance to reinforce in the children the importance of math and English, to introduce them to such notions as self-respect and cooperation and, above all, to harness and enhance their "entrepreneurial yearnings." The NCNE president is encouraging architects and volunteers to make the mall as attractive as they they can make it - "second only to Union Station." He feels that this demonstrates to the youth why business people have nice offices - because it makes a statement both about the quality of their service and about the people they serve. He visualizes the mall as "an island of excellence in a sea of drugs." To back up his demand for excellence, he presented a $10,000 check to the program representing $200 each from 50 of his associates.

Officer Johnson, who works an eight-hour police shift at the school and then puts in an equal amount of volunteer time each day, marvels at the business ideas coming from the children. He feels that to keep saying legitimate jobs can't compete with the lure of the money to be made in drugs is not a fair statement unless the youngsters are given the option. His message to skeptics: "These kids aren't dumb. They know they've never seen a retired drug dealer. Given a choice, do you think they would choose jail and the cemetery?"

Upon receiving the $10,000 check, he turned to the young entrepreneurs and said, "Boys and girls, we're in business." Renovation by the volunteers is expected to continue through 1990, but the mall has been planned so that operation of existing stalls - and stalls as they are completed - can continue throughout the renovation period.

CRIME PREVENTION COMMITTEE OF CONTRA COSTA COUNTY
2280 Diamond Boulevard
Suite 360
Concord, CA 94520
TEL: 415-798-2572
Purpose: To promote crime prevention and organize community volunteers through organizing neighborhoods in our county of 650,000.
Sponsor: State/County/Corporate and private donations
Contact: Lorraine L. Rivers

Description: The Crime Prevention Committee was organized by citizens in 1973. The committee works with 15 law enforcement agencies and sheriff's departments. A three year grant from LEAA in 1976-1979 helped organize more communities. The largest committee, in Concord, has 36 volunteers; the smallest, in Hercules, has eight volunteers.

Over the years, 400 volunteers have organized neighborhoods, run meetings (with or without an officer), handled media promotion, organized student programs, given public speeches, and assisted victims of crime. Some 4,000 (estimate) have hosted neighborhood meetings throughout the county.

All support for CPC has been through individual, corporate and business donations. (LEAA and state grants have been short term funded projects of the CPC.)

Volunteers have prepared a CPC manual, a written and illustrated "how to" book, *Alternative to Fear,* and have written numerous pamphlets. They have trained trainers and participated in local and Bay Area conferences. A State grant from the Office of Criminal Justice Planning is in progress.

The Committee focuses on the county high crime/high fear areas. San Pablo (18th highest crime rate in the state; $13,000 median income) now has 28 volunteers organizing by area. Training includes: how to organize, how to run an effective meeting, how to be an effective neighborhood leader, speakers bureau training.

The 16-member Board of Directors serves on a volunteer basis. Beginning next year at least one-third will be directly representing local committees, while others will be from the county at large and three agencies. According to the Police Department, "Crime has already been displaced 25% in organized areas."

Founded: 1973

CURB IT!
SEE VOLUNTEERS: ALTERNATIVE SENTENCING OFFENDERS

FAMILY SUPPORT GROUP
SEE VOLUNTEERS: SELF-HELP

FLAME OF HOPE
Rochester Institute of Technology
Henrietta Campus
Lomb Memorial Drive
Rochester, NY 14623
TEL: 716-475-6631

Purpose: To call attention around the state to the 20th state Special Olympics Summer Games.

Sponsor: New York Law Enforcement Division

Contact: Frank Vito, Volunteer Director

Description: Various law enforcement agencies around New York State volunteer to help bring attention to the state's *Special Olympics Summer Games* with its own torch, the *Flame of Hope.* The torch is carried from the previous year's site to the current year's location. The volunteer relay runners are police officers from across the state.

For the 1989 games in Rochester, the torch came from the 1988 Buffalo location - but not by a direct route. The police officers took the opportunity to spread the word about the game by making a relay journey around the state. The 19-day activity started when the torch was sent from Buffalo to Montauk Point on Long Island before heading back west toward Rochester. The torch is taken by runners from one police facility to another, sometimes "resting" in one of them until police officers can be freed to continue the relay process. Target was arrival of the torch at noon in downtown Rochester on the first day of the games. The climax of the journey came at 7:30 on opening day of the state games in the Dome area of the campus of the Rochester Institute of Technology (RIT) when two Special Olympics athletes helped light the flame. Athletes were chosen based on their academic and "real world" efforts, such as employment.

The 1989 state games featured 1,600 winning athletes from local games around the state. The theme reflected its long dedication to the program: *Twenty Years of Special Moments.* Over 4,000 volunteers participated.

FLORIDA SHERIFFS YOUTH VILLA
SEE VOLUNTEERS: TEAMS

INTOUCH
SEE TRAINING/CONFERENCES/TEACHING: DRUGS/ALCOHOL

MAKE IT HOME FOR THE HOLIDAYS
SEE BUSINESS/INDUSTRY INVOLVEMENT: DRUGS/ALCOHOL

OPERATION COVERUP
Safe Streets
1720 South 72nd Street
Tacoma, WA 98408
TEL: 206-272-6824; 206-475-2434

Purpose: To remove and work to eliminate gang graffiti throughout Tacoma.

Sponsor: Tacoma Police Department

Contact: Mark Mann, Police Spokesman

Description: In Tacoma, gangs use graffiti to mark their territories and challenge rival gangs. *Operation Coverup* is a graffiti-removal campaign sponsored by *Safe Streets,* a nonprofit organization, and the *Tacoma Police Department* to remove the graffiti from buildings and homes around the city, and work toward elimination of this practice in the future. The removal process is a Saturday program operating with 80 volunteers and 500 gallons of donated paint.

Volunteers work in teams which are dispatched for four hours each to some twenty-six locations across the city.

Long-term efforts to eliminate the graffiti problem permanently include media efforts to educate the public and reach the gangs, and an ongoing program to monitor progress.

PARKING POSSE
Handicapped Parking Enforcement Team
Flint Police Department
1101 South Saginaw Street
Flint, MI 48502
TEL: 313-232-7111

Purpose: To police handicapped parking spaces.

Sponsor: City of Flint

Contact: Chief of Police

Description: The only handicapped parking patrol in Michigan is the result of a Flint ordinance adopted in summer 1988 setting up the city's *Handicapped Parking Enforcement Team.* A year later results showed that the team (sometimes called the "parking posse") has significantly improved handicapped parking enforcement - averaging more than 180 parking violations a month compared with 34 a month handed out by Flint police before the citizen force was formed. Volunteers, ranging in age from 19 to 78, are trained by police officers "to teach healthy-but-lazy people not to park in spaces reserved for the handicapped."

This use of deputized volunteers has caught the attention of the state legislature, with a proposed law offered by a state Senator. The bill is modeled after the Flint ordinance enabling authorization for trained volunteers to ticket those illegally parked in zones for the handicapped. The Secretary of State has endorsed the proposal for statewide participation.

Founded: 1988

PROJECT GRADUATION
SEE VOLUNTEERS: PARENTS

VSPA FUND-RAISING PROGRAMS
SEE FUNDING/FUND-RAISING/RELATED SERVICES:
DRUGS

VOLUNTEERS: PRISONERS/EX-OFFENDERS

NATIONAL/STATE ORGANIZATIONS

CONFLICT RESOLUTION/ALTERNATIVES TO VIOLENCE CENTER
SEE VOLUNTEERS: SELF-HELP

INDIVIDUAL PROGRAM PROFILES

A, B, AND C ON BURGLARY
SEE VOLUNTEERS: POLICE OFFICERS

ALTERNATIVE EDUCATION AND WORK CENTER
Los Angeles Unified School District
2011 North Soto
Los Angeles, CA 90033
TEL: 213-225-0375
Purpose: To assure that as many children as possible have access to quiet, safe classrooms where learning can occur.
Sponsor: Community Youth Gang Services
Contact: Wendy Reddish, Consultant
Description: In Los Angeles, *Alternative Education and Work Centers (AEWC)* are operated in difficult neighborhoods and run by the adult-education division of the city's Unified School District. The alternative schools attempt to recover school dropouts - many of them gang members from 14 to 19 years old who admit to arrests ranging from selling drugs to grand theft auto. The results from 1988 to 1989 showed a four percent decline in the dropout rate, but the schools hope to do better. As of the 1990-91 school year, the District has 21 AEWC sites, representing an expenditure of $3.6 million. Grants received during the period amounted to $1.7 million.
The schools are entered voluntarily by the youth - many having been in and out of custody of juvenile hall, often running from the police or living in a boys' placement center. The individual lesson plans at AEWC enable students to make up credits and return to high school or prepare for a high school equivalency examination. Although often troublesome, the school finds AEWC the only way to provide such youth with the free, public education they are entitled to just like everyone else.
Bimonthly meetings find former gang members offering firsthand information on how to handle kids in gangs. Gang names like *Crips, Bloods, Big Hazard,* and *Imperial Courts* are commonly-used terms in the presentations - usually followed by the word "territory." Youth joining the gangs are as young as ten in many instances, according to the volunteer panelists.
The all-volunteer *School Safety and Security Task Force* has called for mandatory explusion of students committing serious offenses or possessing firearms, denying them the right to enroll in another district school. It recommends that the violators be transferred to a special school, proposed but not yet funded. Only a small percentage - three percent - were expelled during the 1989-90 school year. The *Task Force* is composed of 65 parents, educators and law-enforcement officials.
The Unified School District works with independent groups such as *Community Youth Gang Services (CYGS),* which focuses on reducing gang violence in Los Angeles through job development, crisis intervention, graffiti removal and gang awareness. One former gang member, now 47, who was shot twice and served two prison terms for gang-related homicide, is now a consultant with CYGS. Amazed to have reached the age of 47, he said "Dealing with gangs to me is a luxury. To a lot of people, it is a nuisance." Signs of the youth "turning around" come from a 15-year-old Hispanic youth who had been a member of the *Big Hazard* gang since the age of ten. "I wanted to get my credits straight so I could get on my level in school."

THE CHOICE IS YOURS
Mecklenburg Correctional Center
c/o Roger K. Coleman 128287
PO Box 500
Boydon, VA 23917
TEL: 804-738-6114
Purpose: To allow prisoners to communicate with young people about the heavy price of breaking the law.
Sponsor: Mecklenburg Correctional Center
Contact: Roger K. Coleman 128287
Description: In 1982, a 23-year-old death-row prisoner wondered why so many young people were in prison. He wrote to circuit court judges asking for suggestions as to how he could help young people understand the heavy price they must pay if they break the law. One Judge suggested that he write an open letter to middle school counselors. His letter, *The Choice is Yours,* went out to juvenile judges, and junior and senior high school counseling departments in Virginia. The letter describes an average day on death row and warns against crime.
From his first efforts, more than 500 young people wrote to him, many to thank him for helping them. Some continue to write regularly. Also, the program has been picked up by death row prisoners in several other states. It has grown into a full-scale program with a how-to packet, a videotape, and a scholarship fund for disadvantaged youth. All materials are made available to inmates wishing to begin a program.
The program literally tries to "scare the daylights" out of kids by telling them the heavy price of breaking the law. The videotape takes the viewer inside of a cell and describes in detail the grinding daily routine of a death row inmate. It was produced, and is made available through the Catholic Communication Center.
The founder, still on death row, has appeared on television (Good Morning America) and radio, and in newspaper stories and as a contributing author for youth magazines. Proof that his program is working is supported by letters he receives from kids exposed to the program.
Rapidly growing across the country, according to the founder, *"The Choice is Yours* could never have gotten off the ground without the support of the warden, the Regional Administrator, the Deputy Director of Corrections in Virginia, and the many Judges who responded with suggestions. And the kids... the letters from the kids make it all worthwhile."
Publications: The Choice is Yours (video); The Choice is Yours Information Packet

FRIENDS OF THE ROUGE
City of Southfield
Evergreen Road
Southfield, MI 48076
TEL: 313-427-1234 (Project); 313-427-6843 (Foundation)
Purpose: To improve the water quality and make the river more accessible to canoes along the nature trails.
Sponsor: Wildlife Habitat Foundation
Contact: James E. Murry, President FOTR; Patrick Rusz, WHF
Description: Friends of the Rouge (FOTR) was formed to help keep the Rouge River clean. One weekend each spring some 4,000 volunteers turn out at 21 locations along the Rouge River banks to help clear debris from the polluted waterway. The goal is to

improve the water quality and increase the recreational potential of the waterway and its adjacent trails. More than half of the 125 miles of the river's main branch and tributaries are cleared through this effort.

A number of the volunteers are county offenders given work assignments instead of jail terms. Others come from local groups such as the *Western Wayne County Conservation Club,* a sportsmen's group. Volunteers from the *U.S. Army Corps of Engineers* helped students and others clear logs and trash from the paved sections of the Rouge by driving heavy-duty vehicles into the water. Volunteers work to get ahead of the log jams by stabilizing the river banks with sediment traps to protect against erosion and remove dead trees before they fall into the river.

The rejuvenation effort began in 1986, when the *Wildlife Habitat Foundation (WHF)* installed six dikes of broken concrete that channeled the Rouge so it cleaned itself to some extent - scouring two feet of polluted sediment from the river bottom. This effort demonstrated what can be done cheaply - costing a total of $8,000 - $5,000 from the Foundation and $3,000 from the city of Southfield. In the past three years, volunteers have dragged out 10,000 cubic yards of debris - including a complete car - which is hauled free of charge to a landfill operated by *Waste Management Inc.* of Southfield. For the first time in two decades, the seven-mile stretch passing by Southfield is navigable.

Communities along the Rouge's banks assign public works crews to assist the volunteers, and companies such as *Michigan Tractor and City Management of Detroit* supply heavy-duty equipment to help "break" up log jams. *Ford Motor Company* has contributed $50,000 to help finance the cleanup work, while *Gannett Outdoors* and *Channel 2* provide instructional material for volunteers. *Friends of the Rouge* have asked the public to help track down illegal dumpers by getting license plate numbers and phoning them into the group's office. The group, in turn, passes the information on to law enforcement agencies. Although the lower reaches of the Rouge are still off limits to canoeing, plans call for the contamination there to be under control by the year 2005 - through both volunteer effort and local taxes.

For its cleanup efforts, *Friends of the Rouge* has twice received the *Keep Michigan Beautiful Award,* and has been cited by the *Michigan Department of Natural Resources* for environmental improvements.
Founded: 1986

INMATE SPRUCE-UP TEAMS
Massachusetts Department of Public Works
One City Hall Square
Boston, MA 08060
TEL: 617-482-5300
Purpose: To involve nonviolent inmates in state beautification projects.
Sponsor: Massachusetts Department of Public Works
Contact: Sheriff Peter Y. Flynn, Plymouth County
Description: Some 116 inmates across the state have volunteered to work eight hours a day, five days a week, picking up litter and cleaning up land, saving the state an estimated $684,000 in labor costs. In exchange, the inmates have their sentences cut by five days for each month they work.

The inmate-volunteers are not violent criminals. They are serving time for failure to pay child support or driving under the influence of alcohol.

The Department of Public Works picks up a crew in the morning, provides them with needed equipment and drops them off at a site where they are supervised by a corrections officer, who remains with them during the workday. State officials find the clean-up project well done in all areas served by the inmates.

A side benefit is the positive attitude of the inmates in providing the service, and the possibility of the volunteer experience influencing them to help their communities on their release.

LITERACY INCENTIVE PROGRAM (NO READ, NO RELEASE)
Virginia Governor's Office
State Capitol Building
Richmond, VA 23219
TEL: 804-786-2211
FAX: 804-786-3985
Purpose: To institute a "no read, no release" literacy program in the state's prisons and work camps.
Sponsor: Virginia Governor's Office
Contact: Osa Coffey, Director of Correctional Education
Description: In January 1986, one month after taking office, the Governor of Virginia installed a literacy program in each of the state's 18 major adult prisons and 10 of its 25 work camps. The goal was to improve the 50 to 75 percent illiteracy rate among prisoners. Titled the *Literacy Incentive Program,* it has earned enthusiastic attention from members of Congress and officials in other states. Although dubbed by the Governor "no read, no release," no inmate is denied parole because he cannot read. A few are denied parole because they would not participate in literacy classes.

By 1989, 981 inmates across Virginia had learned to read after enrolling in the literacy program. Inmates attend classes for one-and-one-half hours a day, five days a week. The learning is self-paced with a supervisory teacher and volunteer inmate-tutors providing individual instruction. The focus is on practical skills, such as being able to read a newspaper's employment ads and fill out job applications.

The program includes a formal tracking system that monitors an eligible inmate's participation in literacy classes and reports back to the Parole Board when an inmate comes up for review. Participation in the program is viewed by the board as an indicator of the inmate's desire and effort to reform himself. Enrollment is voluntary, and one problem is persuading illiterate inmates to take advantage of the program. Prisoners are tested when they enter the state system and are eligible if they read below the eighth-grade level.

In 1988, about half of the eligible inmates enrolled for at least a year; 20 percent refused to participate, 13 percent dropped out and another 27 percent were on waiting lists. New sites are planned in each year's budget with the goal of including all facilities in the program as soon as possible.

MID-VALLEY ADOLESCENT CENTER*
SEE BUSINESS/INDUSTRY INVOLVEMENT: CRIME PREVENTION

PARMA-HILTON PLAYGROUND PROJECT
SEE VOLUNTEERS: TENANTS/RESIDENTS

REHAB PROJECT: NEIGHBORHOOD REVITALIZATION THROUGH HOME OWNERSHIP
SEE VOLUNTEERS: CHURCH/SYNAGOGUE MEMBERS

SUMMIT SHOCK INCARCERATION FACILITY
New York State Department of Corrections
Building Number Two
State Campus
Albany, NY 12226
TEL: 518-457-8182; 518-457-8134
FAX: 518-457-7070
Purpose: To provide intensive schooling, drug counseling, jobs and other services to young offenders in a regimented setting to combat recidivism.
Sponsor: New York State Department of Corrections
Contact: Thomas A. Coughlin, Commissioner; Alan Strong, Counselor

Description: One of four such facilities in a program that originated in 1987, the Summit Shock Incarceration Facility finds many of the young offenders serving as volunteer tutors to bunkmates seeking GED certificates. With the original purpose of helping with the overcrowding problem, according to the Commissioner of the Department of Corrections, this has turned out to be the "best six months these inmates will spend."

By mid-1989, 700 youth graduated from the state's shock program. Only 17% were repeat offenders compared to 25% in the general prison population. Youth are screened to determine whether or not they will benefit from the program. Like other self-help programs, the individual must want to help him/herself.

The program consists of a rigid calisthenics program each morning followed by assignment to work crews to clean and maintain nearby state-owned campsites and ski trails, plant fruit trees for the deer, clear brush and logs, and cut lumber at the sawmill. For some, it is the first time they have been that close to nature, away from life in crowded housing projects.

The cornerstone of the shock program is the "network session," during which inmates are encouraged to engage in self-criticism as well as give constructive critiques of others. According to the head of the drill instructor corps, "The network is what keeps them out of jail, not the military stuff." For two hours each day the youth are expected to discuss their weaknesses and vulnerabilities - an exercise even more difficult than the push-ups for the streetwise group. For each session, one youth is selected to be critiqued by the others, and they reach conclusions such as "He still has a chip on his shoulder," or "He just doesn't want to change," or "He thinks he's too smart for this program." The Counselor in charge sees the progress developing in a youth's admonition of his peer, "This is supposed to be a caring community, but you aren't taking part in it." When the criticized youth later commented, "People get on your back because you need it," the Counselor is further encouraged.

Many inmates eagerly pursue their high school diplomas through the GED program, with computer programs the most popular. These youth, who are high school dropouts, spend three hours a day in math and English classes. Other inmates serve as tutors, staying with their partners until the end. Of the 48 youth who completed shock camp in the summer of 1989, nine sought and won GED certificates. They are quick to thank their volunteer tutors/bunkmates.

All graduates are given state jobs until they can find something on their own. One youth who said he earned $3,000 a day as a drug distributor in the Bronx will be earning $32 a day in his state job. Visitors are allowed every other Sunday, and a graduation ceremony is held at the end of the six-month program. As the graduates leave the grounds with families and friends, as though to spur them on to their new jobs and lives, a sign posted along the country road reads, "Only the best reach the Summit."

Publications: Shock Camp Annual Report; Shock Camp Information Packet

VOLUNTEERS: PROFESSIONALS

NATIONAL/STATE ORGANIZATIONS

AAUW EDUCATIONAL FOUNDATION
American Association of University Women
1111 Sixteenth Street, NW
Washington, DC 20036
TEL: 202-785-7700
FAX: 212-785-7797
Objectives: To award fellowships for completion of doctoral dissertation; to provide grants to women for course work leading to reentry into work force.

Services: Provides sabbaticals for public school teachers to learn how to teach girls, especially at-risk girls, more effectively in math and sciences; supports research and community projects to foster equal educational opportunities from early childhood through high school; awards fellowships for completion of doctoral dissertation, post-doctoral research, or final year in selected professions where female participation has traditionally been low.

Provides *Project Renew* grants to women to pursue course work for reentry into workforce, career change, or career advancement; provides these services through funds by members who contribute to the *AAUW Eleanor Roosevelt Fund for Women and Girls*.
Contact: Mary Boyette

AAUW LEGAL ADVOCACY FUND
American Association of University Women
1111 Sixteenth Street, NW
Washington, DC 20036
TEL: 202-785-7700
FAX: 202-785-7797
Objectives: To provide funding and a support system for women seeking judicial redress for sex discrimination.
Services: Operates under a three-part strategy that provides ammunition in the fight for equality: support, information and visibility:
- Extends financial support to all involved in higher education - students, faculty, and administrators; requests are reviewed by a committee of attorneys and higher education administrators to determine need for financial aid, case's probability of success, and potential for a landmark ruling.
- Provides a network of volunteer attorneys and social scientists to serve as consultants to attorneys, plaintiffs, and potential plaintiffs on litigation, strategies and potential witnesses; alternatives to litigation; and case research.
- Recognizes institutions that have successfully battled inequity by providing annual *Progress in Equity Award.*

As the only legal fund for women focused on higher education, the *Legal Advocacy Fund* plays a pivotal role in guaranteeing equal access and opportunities in academe.
Contact: Mary Boyette
Publications: Leader in Action; Action Alert; Graduate Woman; On Campus with Women
Founded: 1881

AMERICAN ASSOCIATION OF UNIVERSITY WOMEN
1111 Sixteenth Street, NW
Washington, DC 20036
TEL: 202-785-7700
FAX: 202-785-7797
Objectives: To promote education and equity for women and girls.
Services: Works with 1800 local branches in every state to achieve goals through program (Issues), public policy, *AAUW Legal Advocacy Fund,* and the *AAUW Educational Foundation.*
Mounts current program issues, developed by national Task Forces of members, including
- *Promoting Individual Liberties* and *Choices for Tomorrow's Women:* publishes materials to implement these issues and provides them to branch/state leaders.
- *Public Policy:* supports legislation and initiatives that advance AAUW goals through member involvement and action with school board, city councils, state legislatures as well as Congress and the Executive Branch; works with *Lobby Corps* of members at Federal level and in several states to promote bills supported by AAUW.

Publishes *AAUW Outlook* five times a year, informing/updating members on issues supported, and new developments; also publishes *Action Alert,* monthly report on current Congressional Activity on AAUW-supported bills, which indicates action required to achieve success and to help members and leaders to be effective in public policy process.

Operates two services funded by members who contribute to the *AAUW Eleanor Roosevelt Fund for Women and Girls:*
- **AAUW Legal Advocacy Fund** supports women in higher education seeking legal redress for gender-based discrimination and recognizes innovative efforts by institutions to achieve progress for women.
- **AAUW Educational Foundation** awards fellowships for completion of doctoral dissertation, post-doctoral research, or final year in selected professions where female participation has traditionally been low; also provides *Project Renew* grants to women to pursue course work for reentry into work force, career change, or career advancement.

Also provides sabbaticals for public school teachers to learn how to teach girls, especially at-risk girls, more effectively in math and sciences; will also support research and community projects to foster equal educational opportunities from early childhood education through high school.
Contact: Mary Boyette
Publications: AAUW Outlook; Action Alert

BUILDING SEISMIC SAFETY COUNCIL
1201 L Street, NW
Fourth Floor
Washington, DC 20005
TEL: 202-289-7800
Objectives: To focus public attention on earthquake hazards.
Services: Operates under the aegis of a volunteer Board of Directors to propose seismic safety standards and urge their use in local and national building codes; mounts campaigns to make the public aware of the hazards and unpredictability of earthquakes - especially in the east where apathy persists; works with the *Federal Emergency Management Agency (FEMA),* which has provided funding to the Council since 1981; includes in its membership - all volunteers - geologists, engineers and others versed on the subject of earthquakes; emphasizes the need for the public to give more serious attention to this hazard, even in low-risk areas such as Washington, DC; addresses opposition from the real estate and construction industries, whose concerns center on the added costs of making buildings earthquake resistant (estimated at adding five to six percent in costs); cites studies that indicate that added cost is much less than first anticipated (one to two percent); encourages new code provisions such as those proposed in 1986 in New York City, from which a bill was developed for submission to New York's City Council in late 1990; develops earthquake regulations for insertion into model codes developed by local governments; publishes data on the highest risk sections of each area of the country, and other reports and materials.
Sponsor: US/FEMA - Federal Emergency Management Agency
Contact: James Smith, Executive Director
Founded: 1980

COMMITTEE ON COOPERATION WITH THE PROFESSIONAL COMMUNITY
Alcoholics Anonymous (AA)
PO Box 459
Grand Central Station
New York, NY 10163
TEL: 212-686-1100
Objectives: To bring about more communication, understanding, respect and cooperation between AA and the professional community working with alcoholics.
Services: Provides continuing two-way communication at every level, local to national, to share its 55 years of trial-and-error experience with more than two million alcoholics in exchange for information, advice and services that AA can or cannot provide; publishes *About AA,* a newsletter issued specifically to supplement personal communication with professionals in the alcoholism field.
Founded: 1935

LEGAL SERVICES FOR CHILDREN*
149 Ninth Street
Fourth Floor
San Francisco, CA 94103
TEL: 415-863-3762
Objectives: To provide free and comprehensive legal representation and casework services to minors in San Francisco and the Bay Area.
Services: Offers free and comprehensive legal services for minors (from infants to age 17) in all kinds of cases in the Juvenile Court (delinquency, status offense, child abuse or neglect) and in other non-fee-generating civil or administrative matters affecting minors' rights and welfare, including school discipline, special education, guardianships, emancipation, etc.; clients receive the teamed services of an attorney and a caseworker from initial contact through final resolution of the case; caseworkers provide an essential link with other resources to help meet the whole needs of the child (e.g., counseling, job training, placements, etc.).
Publications: Parents' Guide; California Law
Founded: 1975

LEGAL SERVICES FOR THE ELDERLY
132 West 43rd Street
Third Floor
New York, NY 10036
TEL: 212-595-1340
Objectives: To advise on legal problems and areas indigenous to the elderly.
Services: Offers advice and in some cases litigates on behalf of the elderly; maintains library of information on various aspects of legal services on behalf of the elderly; conducts research, litigation and educational programs; publishes a progress report (quarterly) and other materials.
Publications: Progress Report
Founded: 1969

NATIONAL ASSOCIATION OF EXTENSION HOME ECONOMISTS
c/o Dr. B.G. Eichner, Suite 240
2221 East Northern Lights Boulevard
Anchorage, AK 99508
TEL: 907-279-5582
Objectives: To improve and strengthen professional standards for members who help families find solutions to problems concerning family life.
Services: Trains volunteer leaders to work with families and individual family members; offers family education programs in areas of child care and development, nutrition, energy conservation, budgeting, family recreation; sponsors volunteer recruitment and public relations committees; publishes quarterly newsletter, *The Reporter.*

NATIONAL CONFERENCE OF BLACK LAWYERS
126 West 119th Street
New York, NY 10026
TEL: 212-864-4000
Objectives: To use legal skills in the service of black and poor communities through the U.S.
Services: Conducts education programs on legal issues affecting black and poor communities; covers specific areas such as prisoners' rights, juvenile law, and women's rights; operates lawyer referral and placement service; provides speakers on specific issues such as criminal justice, human rights, and civil rights law, maintains charitable program; publishes quarterly newsletter.
Publications: NCBL Notes
Founded: 1968

NATIONAL PRISON PROJECT
American Civil Liberties Union
1616 P Street, NW
Suite 340
Washington , DC 20036
TEL: 202-331-0500
Objectives: To strengthen and protect the rights of adult and juvenile offenders; to improve overall conditions in correctional facilities; to develop alternatives to incarceration.
Services: Handles and assists others in handling litigation; drafts model legislation on rights of offenders; provides information to legislative bodies on request; develops self-help materials for incarcerated persons; coordinates activities of other organizations in the field; serves as a resource center and clearinghouse; develops model institution and regulations, and model pleadings and other legal papers; trains law students and other attorneys; develops materials to keep the public informed; conducts periodic conferences.
Publications: Prison Project Journal; Prisoners Assistance Directory
Founded: 1972

PHARMACISTS AGAINST DRUG ABUSE
SEE BUSINESS/INDUSTRY INVOLVEMENT: DRUGS/ALCOHOL

PUBLIC INTEREST RESEARCH GROUP
SEE TRAINING/CONFERENCES/TEACHING: INTERNSHIPS

PUBLIC SERVICE ACTIVITIES DIVISION
American Bar Association
750 North Lake Shore Drive
Chicago, IL 60611
TEL: 312-988-5000
Objectives: To apply the knowledge and experience of the legal profession to promotion of the public good through volunteer efforts.
Services: Works with non-lawyer professionals and leaders to deal with pressing social problems through:
- Commission on the Mentally Disabled
- Commission on Legal Problems of the Elderly
- Section of Individual Rights and Responsibilities (includes "Pro Bono Project" of volunteer lawyers)
- Special Committee on Housing and Urban Development Law
- Special Committee on Energy Law
- Young Lawyers Division Resource Center for Child Advocacy and Protection

In addition, this ABA Division maintains clearinghouse; mounts demonstration projects; holds working conferences; develops profiles, case studies, and other accounts of its work to keep the public informed.
Founded: 1878

SHARE OUR STRENGTH (SOS)
733 Fifteenth Street, NW
Suite 700
Washington, DC 20005
TEL: 202-393-2925
TOLL FREE: 800-222-ISOS
Objectives: To raise money for national and international hunger relief programs.
Services: Enlists membership through restaurants, currently in over 75 cities; works to maintain the public's awareness about the problem of escalating hunger and homelessness here in America and overseas; raises and donates funds to established relief and development organizations; provides information on community hunger groups in an effort to encourage local volunteerism; coordinates *Schools Against Hunger* program; maintains several boards including a *Hunger Advisory Board* and a *Restaurant Advisory Board;* maintains a speakers' bureau and placement service; publishes a newsletter, brochure and other materials.
Contact: Debbie Shore, Fund Raising Director
Publications: News from S.O.S.
Founded: 1984

SMALL BUSINESS DEVELOPMENT PROGRAM
Volunteers in Technical Assistance
1815 North Lynn Street
Suite 200
Arlington, VA 22209
TEL: 703-276-1800; Cable: VITAINC
TOLL FREE: Telex: 440192 VITAUI
Objectives: To provide experienced volunteers to any community, group or individual involved in a small or medium-size business needing professional and technical assistance in any phase of its operation.
Services: Provides information, expertise and services to anyone interested in developing small and medium industries, particularly in the developing world; offers technical information on numerous technologies, consultants from an international roster of 4,400 experts, technical reports, indentification of potential business collaborators, trade services, bibliographic retrieval, document delivery and data management; works internationally to expand markets, reduce production costs, improve industrial processes, and introduce new technologies.
Publications: VITA News; Technical Paper Series
Founded: 1960

SOCIETY OF CONSUMER AFFAIRS PROFESSIONALS IN BUSINESS
4900 Leesburg Pike, Suite 400
Alexandria, VA 22302
TEL: 703-998-7371
Objectives: To promote harmonious relationships between business, government and consumers.
Services: Maintains continuing communication with business/industry to compare successes and failures in community relations; provides information to any group or individual interested in corporate efforts to demonstrate responsibility to the community; has an awards program and ongoing seminar schedule; provides speakers to the community on request.
Publications: Update; Mobius Journal
Founded: 1973

TRIAL LAWYERS FOR PUBLIC JUSTICE
2000 P Street, NW
Suite 611
Washington, DC 20036
TEL: 202-463-8600
Objectives: To utilize trial litigation as an effective instrument of social change and for vindication of individual rights.
Services: Combines the theories and remedies of a plaintiff's damage litigation with the issues and goals of the public interest movement; enables trial lawyers to focus and enhance their public interest commitment through litigation with a potentially broad impact on corporate or government policy; deals with cases where the novelty of the issues involved or the demands of the litigation make the cases inappropriate for the private practice trial lawyer; chooses cases for their potential impact on the public good; operates with volunteer assistance of hundreds of lawyers across the country; publishes *Trial Lawyers Doing Public Justice.*
Publications: TLPJ Newsletter; TLPJ Membership Directory; Trial Lawyers Doing Public Justice
Founded: 1982

VOLUNTEER INCOME TAX ASSISTANCE (VITA)
US/DTreas - Internal Revenue Service
1111 Constitution Avenue, NW
Washington, DC 20224
TEL: 202-566-2000
Objectives: To provide low-income people with tax preparation counseling services.
Services: Serves low-income, elderly, and disadvantaged taxpayers, and those for whom English is a second language; supports more than 5,500 local VITA programs across the country, utilizing about 30,000 part-time volunteers at sites ranging from community centers to shopping malls; trains volunteers between December and February every year on tax-form problem areas for clients (with some training on state and local returns); monitors program while it is in progress; makes publicity materials available.
Sponsor: US/DTreas - Department of the Treasury

VOLUNTEERS IN TECHNICAL ASSISTANCE
SEE COMMUNITY SERVICES

TRAINING PROGRAMS

ADOPT-A-FAMILY
SEE FUNDING/FUND-RAISING/RELATED SERVICES: HOUSING

FORUM ON SCHOOL VANDALISM
SEE TRAINING/CONFERENCES/TEACHING: JUSTICE SYSTEM

INDIVIDUAL PROGRAM PROFILES

ADVOCACY BY AND FOR THE BLIND
SEE VOLUNTEERS: HANDICAPPED

AIR CRASH DRILL
Greater Rochester International Airport
1200 Brooks Ave
Rochester, NY 14619
TEL: 716-464-6000
Purpose: To test the County's system of emergency management.
Sponsor: Monroe County Government
Contact: John G. Huntoon, Chief, Fire-Rescue Service
Description: The *Greater Rochester International Airport* is required every three years to host an air crash drill in order to keep its Federal Aviation Administration certification. Since the new ruling was not imposed until 1989, the Airport had not had a drill since 1983. Drills are designed to test the county's incident command system, a widely-used concept of emergency management in which police, fire, medical and airport authorities cooperate.
In a mid-1989 drill, more than 600 rescuers battled fake smoke to rescue 125 volunteers posing as passengers and crew aboard the 727 jet (a C-130 on loan from the National Guard). The crew faced a problem in which the plane had lost its landing gear and slid off the runway, bursting into flames in a freight building. The scenario included a little bit of everything - radioactive waste and injured firefighters. Twenty-five percent of the passengers and crew were to die, 50 percent were to be critically injured, and the remainder to suffer lesser injuries.
Reflecting the long period since the last drill, many problems arose that helped rescue teams realize the value of the drills. Equipment and supplies needed to transport and treat patients arrived after the drill was completed; the entire process halted when a firefighter suffered a real case of heat exhaustion; some of the

"injured" waited almost two hours to be transported to hospitals; one area's ambulance driver was unable to contact the medical command post as he approached the airport; oxygen supplies ran out; some people were confused about their roles, etc. As one volunteer put it, "That's what drills are for. You're always going to have pitfalls." He felt that the drill was positive in many respects, including the fact that it strongly indicated that teams should work together on a redesign of equipment kits so that they are coordinated and therefore easier to use among departments when necessary.
The chief of the airport's crash fire-rescue service felt that it worked out pretty well, since one of the objectives was to give rescuers from all over Monroe County a shot at working together. "It used to be they'd sit in their corners and swear at each other. Now they work together," he said.

ALTERNATIVE EDUCATION AND WORK CENTER
SEE VOLUNTEERS: PRISONERS/EX-OFFENDERS

ART AGAINST AIDS EXHIBIT
SEE FUNDING/FUND-RAISING/RELATED SERVICES: AIDS

ART FOR KIDS' SAKE
Child Welfare League of America
440 First Street, NW
Suite 310
Washington, DC 20001-2085
TEL: 202-638-2952
Purpose: To remind the public of children's needs.
Sponsor: American Academy of Pediatrics
Contact: Mark K. Riley, Children's Campaign
Description: The best-known cartoonists in America have created an original collection of cartoon art to remind the public of children's needs. Each cartoon conveys a message, such as "Try a Little Tenderness." The collection includes a poster called "Voice for Children," which was illustrated by 69 cartoonists and traveled 170,766 miles on its way to completion.
The project, known as *Art for Kids' Sake,* is a collaborative effort of Child Welfare League of America (CWLA), American Academy of Pediatrics, Group W Westinghouse Broadcasting, American Greeting Card Company, Federal Express, CWLA member agencies, and local TV stations. Originally available only in print form (posters, note cards, and signed limited editions), the artwork has been incorporated into public service announcements and promotional spots in more than 100 cities across the U.S. Sales from the poster and other artwork benefit agencies serving children across the country. CWLA members benefit by collecting donations for the collector-quality art.
Cartoonists volunteering for the program include Gary Trudeau, Johnny Hart, Jim Davis, Bill Keane, and others.
Founded: 1987

ASK THE DOCTOR
The Wellness Center
Alexandria Hospital
4320 Seminary Road
Alexandria , VA 22304
TEL: 703-379-3494
Purpose: To provide an educational program on health as a community service.
Sponsor: Alexandria Hospital; Individual Doctors
Contact: Wellness Center Director
Description: Ask the Doctor is an educational program offered by *The Wellness Center* at Alexandria Hospital as a free community service. It gives up-to-date information and the opportunity to ask physicians about pertinent health topics. Registration is required for the free lectures, which are offered three times each month.

Volunteer physicians include psychiatrists, podiatrists, internists, plastic surgeons, pulmonary medicine specialists, obstetricians/gynecologists, and others. Requests made for special topics are considered and every attempt is made to provide lectures relating to all requests.

Also, *The Wellness Center* holds regular classes in a variety of health areas. Many are free, but some classes carry minimal fees ($8-$25), with discount tickets for senior citizens. Students are required to wear comfortable clothing and bring their own towels and mats.

The diverse areas include weight control, heart, stress, CPR, high blood pressure and cholesterol, self-esteem/self-image, psychosocial support, massage therapy, smoking cessation, post-natal care, aerobics, senior exercise, investment planning, numerous family-centered classes (Lamaze, grandparenting, etc.), and many others.

Instructors for sessions and classes are selected based on their qualifications and areas of expertise. All exercise/fitness instructors are CPR-certified and trained in anatomy, physiology and injury prevention. To ensure the highest quality for Wellness Community Programs, a *Physician Advisory Board* (seven physicians) provides professional advice and consultation.

Classes are held in five locations in the area to facilitate maximum participation.

Publications: The Way to Wellness

ASSISTANCE TO EARTHQUAKE VICTIMS
SEE VOLUNTEERS: ARMED FORCES MEMBERS - NAVY

BAILEY'S CROSSROADS COMMUNITY SHELTER
SEE VOLUNTEERS: CHURCH/SYNAGOGUE MEMBERS

BAY AREA SCORE PROGRAM
Fremont Chamber of Commerce
39650 Liberty
Fremont, CA 94538
TEL: 415-794-0599 (volunteers); 415-657-1355 (clients)
Purpose: To share business expertise with potential entrepreneurs to help them get started.
Sponsor: Fremont Chamber of Commerce
Contact: Dan Kauffman, SCORE Volunteer
Description: Sixty-five volunteers in the Bay Area chapter of the *Service Corps of Retired Executives (SCORE)* share their expertise with those who would like to go into business for themselves but aren't sure just where to start. Offices are provided by the Fremont Chamber of Commerce each Wednesday. Volunteers are either people who have themselves owned a business or have been an executive in a large company. The skills are diverse, and a volunteer who cannot answer a question has access to information about the skills of the volunteers and can request assistance.

Requests range from local businesses such as a machine shop to those of international currency exchange and imports. The initial volunteer advises on things that are common to any new business - legal matters, licenses, fictitious name statements, taxes and setting up books - before making the referral to another SCORE volunteer for specific technical expertise.

SCORE volunteers primarily see clients before they have launched their business, but after they have a specific idea of what they want to do and have done some research. Those who do not have a clear idea of what they want are asked to come back at a later time when their goals are set. Occasionally, a client has begun a business only to find unexpected pitfalls, for which expert advise is needed. Often it is just an ordinary business problem that simply requires encouragement.

SCORE sponsors monthly workshops, usually "general business types," but the San Francisco-Oakland location has brought about the institution of a workshop specifically about import-export businesses on a less-frequent basis.

SCORE is funded by the *U.S. Small Business Administration* and has been around for about 25 years with chapters nationwide.

CATCH PROGRAM
SEE VOLUNTEERS: PARENTS

CHARITY PLANE RIDE FOR ORANGE GROVE
SEE FUNDING/FUND-RAISING/RELATED SERVICES

A CLASS ACT
SEE COMMUNITY SERVICES

CLASS ACTION SUIT
SEE FUNDING/FUND-RAISING/RELATED SERVICES

COMMUNITY RESOURCE VOLUNTEERS
Minneapolis Public Schools
807 NE Broadway
Minneapolis, MN 55413
TEL: 612-348-6152
Purpose: To enrich the elementary school curriculum by using human resources in the community.
Sponsor: Minneapolis Public Schools
Contact: Betty Jane Reed, Teacher/Coordinator
Description: In operation since 1965, today the Community Resource Volunteers program has over 1,000 active volunteers who go into the Minneapolis classrooms on request to help enrich the curriculum for elementary and secondary school children. This number does not include those functioning in other volunteer programs, such as teachers' aides and tutors.

These citizens - parents and non-parents - offer enrichment in all areas of the curriculum. Every school has catalogs housing information on every available volunteer. The areas represented are: Art, Assemblies, Enrichment for Gifted Children, Health and Safety, Hobbies and Leisure Time Activities, Holidays and special Occasions, Language Arts, Mathematics, Music, Science, and Social Studies - with special emphasis at the secondary level on careers and business-related subjects.

The volunteers are poets, physical fitness experts, accomplished musicians, high school and college students, accomplished professors, experts in agriculture or computers, dentists, government officials, local, country or world-wide travelers, and many others. They share their expertise and experiences, which enlarge on a teacher's efforts to provide information that would be difficult or even impossible to obtain in any other way.

The Community Resource Volunteers program also has made video tapes of volunteers who have been requested more often than they are available. Tapes were made of volunteers leaving the city or withdrawing from the program because of increased work responsibilities, and of those who were in great demand during Black History Week, American Indian Week, or other special occasions. Visiting authors, diplomats and political figures also have volunteered to tape these 15-minute programs. Four or more of the 205 tapes were viewed over educational television each week in the schools until budget reductions and rising costs caused the school district to relinquish the contract with the educational television station. Kinescopes and half-inch tapes were made of some of the most popular programs. Volunteers whose presentations do not require visual materials are taping radio broadcasts now for use on the school district radio station.

On a weekly average, there are more than 100 class visits scheduled. There are more requests for the volunteers than the program's administration is able to fill because of the time-consuming process of recruiting and scheduling each new applicant. The Coordinator points out, "This program indicates the power of community involvement."

Founded: 1965

DISASTER PROFESSIONAL VOLUNTEER NETWORK
American Red Cross
Mid-America Chapter
43 East Ohio
Chicago, IL 60611
TEL: 312-440-2000
Purpose: To provide a mental health response for victims of a major disaster.
Sponsor: American Red Cross, Mid-America Chapter
Contact: Director, Disaster and Family Services
Description: The American Red Cross in its effort to provide a comprehensive service to victims of major disasters is developing a cadre of professionally trained staff from other agencies who will assist Red Cross in addressing the mental health needs of victims. These volunteers will be trained to utilize their knowledge and skill in special ways to address the reactions to disaster, loss and trauma. Crisis intervention will be the method of treatment. High risk groups will be identified as soon as possible and both an individual and group approach implemented as the need indicates. A volunteer advisory committee has been formed which has the responsibility of both short and long-range planning for this undertaking. They will be addressing their attention to areas such as public education, levels of intervention, roles of government, assessment of the network planning and implementation, and access to disaster victims. The Chairman of the committee will be a member of the Board of Directors of the Mid-America Chapter of the American Red Cross and a member of the Service to Military Families and Veterans Committee. For the present, our efforts are being directed to the city of Chicago but future plans will be developed to include the six county area served by Mid-America Chapter.
In addition, a committee of representatives from participating agencies will continue to meet to design and develop intervention modes, assess training, critique operations, address the problem of maintaining a state of readiness and determine further needs. These meetings will be held on a quarterly basis.
Agencies will be asked to make a commitment to participate in this joint venture should a major catastrophe affect a large portion of the people of the community which we all serve.
There are two levels of participation that will be needed. Conceivably, some agencies may not be able to participate on both levels. However, it is critical to the success of the plan that there be sufficient participation at the first level, i.e. on site and/or shelter intervention. The second level would involve providing service in the victims' home site.
Recruitment and/or selection of professionally trained staff who will become members of the cadre is internal and unique to the individual agency. Some features to be considered in personnel selection are:
- They must be interested in volunteer activity within their own profession.
- They must be able to tolerate uncertainty and lack of structure in a work situation.
- They must have the ability to work cooperatively with staff from other agencies on a team with its designated leader.
- The ability to accept direction.
- The ability to prioritize in a chaotic situation.
- The ability to work cooperatively with other disciplines such as emergency medical, fire and police personnel.
- The ability for self-management under stress.

There are a few specific knowledge and skill considerations that are relevant in this process of personnel selection:
- A good working knowledge and skill in crisis intervention theory and technique.
- The ability to make a diagnosis quickly in order to facilitate treatment consideration (situational vs. chronic).
- A good working knowledge of community resources.
- A demonstrated ability to apply knowledge creatively.
- The ability to identify and mobilize strengths within the affected population for achieving stabilization goals.
- The ability to work with all socioeconomic, racial, ethnic, and religious groups.

The American Red Cross will assume responsibility for the specialized training (nine hours) required to heighten the awareness of the cadre members and to orient them to the Red Cross Disaster Service.
Trained cadre members may elect to serve in a variety of ways, i.e., individuals or groups, at disaster site or post-disaster shelter. The following operational plan would become effective when needed and in conjunction and cooperation with the overall plan of the city of Chicago and the American Red Cross Disaster Service. It would function in the following manner:
- Information regarding a disaster would come through the usual radio and telephone communications system of Red Cross which operates on a 24 hour basis.
- Such information will provide an ongoing reading of the nature and extent of the tragedy relative to casualties, injuries, numbers of people undomiciled, involvement of Fire and Police Departments, and the services being provided by the disaster emergency program.

DISCOUNT MART SHOPPING CENTER II
Bruce-Monroe Elementary School
3012 Georgia Avenue, NW
Washington, DC 20001
TEL: 202-576-6215
Purpose: To teach children the different aspects of the business world, while demonstrating the role math and communication will play in their daily lives.
Contact: Evelyn S. Roberson, Teacher
Description: Created by a math teacher for her 48 students.
Discount Mart Shopping Center II is the second shopping center launched at the *Bruce-Monroe Elementary School.* The three-day event each year was designed initially to help students - especially minority youngsters - learn the important role math will play in their daily lives. The shopping center introduces the fifth- and sixth-graders to the business world and helps them communicate with others, while accomplishing the initial goal of creating more enthusiasm about and interest in math.
The project has grown from a classroom event with seven stores to the three-day extravaganza of 17 stores, including an art gallery, a toy store and a gift shop.
The items for purchase are donated by businesses on the Georgia Avenue corridor, *Union Station,* and *Safeway.* Student participants are given play money to operate the stores and purchase the donated items. They are not allowed to keep the items, which are sold at a later date at a flea market to benefit the school.
Students complete ten training courses taught by faculty members who volunteer the extra time - some who owned their own businesses. The subjects include financing, recordkeeping and human relations. Students learn how to fill out loan contracts, inventory slips, receipts and lease applications. They learn to count money, subtract percentages for sales, and browse around the store to spot shoplifters. A license to operate one of the stores costs 30 play dollars.
One student - the owner of the *Impulse Jewelry Store* - summed it up: "This is not an easy job, and there are a lot of things you have to know about running a business if you want to be a success."
Founded: 1990

EAST TENNESSEE COMMUNITY DESIGN CENTER
1522 Highland Avenue
Knoxville, TN 37916
TEL: 615-525-9945; 615-525-9946
[The second number is the Center's Office for Appropriate Technology.]
Purpose: To provide architectural and planning services to community groups unable to pay private, professional fees.
Sponsor: University of Tennessee

Contact: Annette Anderson

Description: The East Tennessee Community Design Center is a private, non-profit organization which serves a sixteen county area of East Tennessee. The Design Center was created in 1970 by design and planning professionals who identified a need for a program through which design and planning services could be provided to community groups which could not otherwise obtain these services. The Design Center serves a variety of clients including day care centers, urban and rural community centers, neighborhood organizations, art groups, and social service programs. The work includes problem definition, design programming, schematic design, cost estimates, and resource development assistance.

The Design Center consists primarily of volunteers - architects, landscape architects, graphic designers, planners, engineers - who contribute their time to work on community projects. During the past twelve years more than 75,000 hours have been donated for Design Center projects. During the past year alone more than 400 people contributed 9,452 hours to projects, a contribution conservatively worth $60,500. Thirty-four projects were completed last year. Twenty-three community projects are "on the boards" now.

The Design Center's volunteer Board of Directors is made up of one-third design professionals, one-third client representatives, and one-third from the community at large. The Board sets policy and selects projects based on the criteria that the client cannot otherwise obtain professional design assistance, that the work benefits a community rather than a single individual, and that there is likelihood that the project will be implemented if design assistance is provided.

The Design Center staff consists of the Coordinator who handles communication and administration, the Resource Developer who finds resources to implement projects, the Staff Architect who works primarily with appropriate technology projects, and the Administrative Assistant.

Volunteers In Service To America (VISTA) serve as liaison between community clients and volunteer task force leaders, doing much of the daily project work. VISTAs are usually recent graduates in architecture or planning who commit one or two years to serving low income communities while they gain experience in the field.

The Coordinator conducts a University of Tennessee School of Architecture studio at the Design Center called "Architecture In Service To Communities" in which fourth and fifth year students work intensively on Design Center projects on a quarterly basis. The offices and studios of the Design Center are located in the historic Fort Sanders neighborhood in a converted residential building owned and occupied entirely by the Design Center.

The Design Center provides an opportunity for people of varying backgrounds and interests to work together to improve the quality of their surroundings. One very valuable aspect of the Design Center is its ability to bring people together to accomplish community goals. For example, during the past three years the Design Center has completed two participatory design projects sponsored by the National Endowment for the Arts. One was designed to improve livability and energy efficiency in Knoxville's inner city. Another, the *Fort Sanders Neighborhood Design Plan* called *Old Town In Town,* duplicated that process to produce development guidelines for that affected neighborhood.

In addition, the Design Center has extensive experience in managing public events. In 1976 it organized a series of Bicentennial Neighborhood Fairs. Later, the Design Center coordinated preparation and management of an Appropriate Community Technology exhibit (ACT '82) on the site of the 1982 World's Fair. About seventy groups participated in the ACT '82 exhibit which provided information about appropriate technologies to more than 250,000 people.

A typical year's records document $3.40 worth of services provided for every dollar spent on staff, space, supplies and other support. In the same year, $632,825 in community improvements were generated by the combination of staff volunteers and budgeted expenditures, making a total return on investment of $7.75 for each Design Center dollar spent.

Founded: 1970

FRIENDS OF THE SUPERIOR COURT

409 E Street, NW
Suite 301
Washington, DC 20001
TEL: 202-727-1788

Purpose: To recruit and train volunteers to provide services to clients of the Superior Court of DC; educate the community on the work of the court; provide funds for special programs to serve court clients.

Sponsor: District of Columbia Superior Court

Contact: Frank McGuire

Description: Friends of the Superior Court of the District of Columbia (Friends) began in 1964 as one of the pioneer groups which set out to demonstrate the value of volunteers working in a court setting. Today, 70% of the courts throughout the nation have volunteer programs. Initially, Friends served only the juvenile court. In 1971, the *Court Reorganization Act* expanded the jurisdiction of the court to include three branches: Intra-family, Adult, and Juvenile. The Chief Judge charged Friends with recruiting and coordinating all volunteers and volunteer groups working in the court.

The Friends organization has a board - a cross-section of the community - which formulates policies and supervises operations. Funds for Friends programs are raised by an annual appeal, and gifts from individuals and foundations. The administrator of volunteers is employed by the court but under the direction of the board of Friends. Volunteer programs include:

Probation Aides - Volunteers choose to work in either an adult or juvenile program. After a training period, each is assigned to a probation officer. Under his/her direct supervision, the volunteer works with the client and his/her family.

Educational and Probational Aides Program - While the program is similar to the probation-aide program, this program addresses itself specifically to school adjustment problems. The goal of the program is to provide (a) tutoring; (b) supportive counseling; (c) communication link between child, parent, school and probation staff.

Volunteer Attorney Program - The law demands that children in "beyond control," neglect, and child abuse cases be represented by their own attorney. However, in these cases, no provisions have been made to compensate lawyers for their work. Friends enlists the aid of volunteer attorneys who represent the children without charge. In a single quarter, the volunteer lawyers gave 876 hours of service. The daily case loads vary between six and eight each day. Estimated saving to taxpayers each quarter: $21,900.

One-to-One Program - In the One-to-One program, a volunteer is assigned to work intensively with a single client, adult or juvenile. The program is based on the premise that one person can have a therapeutic effect upon another. The volunteer can grow through the relationship as well as the client. Basic elements which make the volunteer effective in this program are: (1) empathy and respect for the client; (2) ability to listen effectively and communicate; (3) commitment of time (3-4 hours per week over a six-month period); (4) tolerance for other life styles.

Child Care Center - This center for the Superior Court was developed to provide free childcare by a qualified staff and trained volunteers for clients of the court, allowing court business to proceed without distractions. The Center is located in the basement of a local church and is licensed to care for children from 18 months to 15 years of age.

Summer Programs - Summer programs are divided into two areas:
- **Summer Camp Program** - The Friends arrange for camps in the area to provide services for 100 probationers for six to twelve days without charge. Volunteers contact parents for

permission slips and arrange for physical examinations and transportation. Agencies supplying camp slots include the DC Recreation Department, Family and Child Service, Council of Churches, Salvation Army, and the Police Boys Club.
- **Summer Jobs** - The volunteer office, working in conjunction with the Mayor's office and the Department of Recreation, locates and develops summer jobs for older juveniles.

Community Resource Development - A small group of retired social workers contact community agencies whose services can be enlisted for probationers, circulating information alerting the Social Services Division of changes in organizational policy, standards of personnel, etc., in these agencies.

Clerical Support - Individuals who wish to help but prefer not to serve clients through direct support make a contribution of time for typing reports, filing, telephoning to check data, etc.

Recent expansion of some of the programs include a unique One-to-One arm at Georgetown University, and the new Guardian Ad Litem Program for the Volunteer Attorneys Office. Volunteer applicants for all programs are screened by the Court's Social Service Division and Friends to ensure that they meet all the requirements of the job. The volunteer administrator contacts the volunteers periodically to discuss ways in which their services can be made more effective. Descriptive materials are available upon request.

GOOD NEIGHBOR EXCHANGE PROGRAM
Alexandria Public Schools
Administration Building
3801 West Braddock Road
Alexandria, VA 22302
TEL: 703-824-6660
Purpose: To help parents provide clothing for their growing children through a clothing exchange program.
Sponsor: Alexandria Parent-Teachers Association
Contact: Carol Lisi, Coordinator, or Mary Kehoe, PTA
Description: When band or scout uniforms are outgrown, the expense for replacement is a hardship for some families. Solving this problem is one purpose of the *Good Neighbor Exchange Program.* The other is to provide a means to exchange outgrown clothing for large sizes to address the problem of "fast-growing children," a problem for all income levels.

A teacher in the Alexandria, Virginia, school system organized the program in late 1989, and finds its growth and acceptance to be very rewarding. She also finds the tolerance of the school system - when twice a week its Howard administration building turns into a sort of shopping center - to be exemplary, and in tune with the needs of the families of its pupils.

Volunteers from the Parent-Teacher Association of the city's schools are helping to expand the program through volunteer recruitment and publicity. One unusual aspect of the program is that it is not restricted to Alexandria schools. Anyone in the nearby Northern Virginia communities who needs clothing or who wants to donate clothing is welcome. Items are available for infants through teenagers.

The "community clothing cooperative" has found that other programs receiving gifts of clothing are willing to share their excess, also. One example is *Christ House,* a homeless shelter in the city, which received such an abundance of clothing that it donated some of it to *Good Neighbor.* Conversely, the Alexandria Health Department requested clothing from the exchange for low-income families who had just found housing in the city. The cooperation among groups, parents, and the school system demonstrates the benefits to all concerned of a joint rather than isolated effort, according to the founder.

GRASSROOTS CRISIS INTERVENTION & PEER COUNSELING CENTER
SEE INFORMATION & REFERRAL: MENTAL HEALTH

HAWAII YOUTH AT RISK
810 North Vineyard Boulevard
Honolulu, HI 96817
TEL: 808-842-7078
Purpose: To help former gang members and other youth at risk to "break the cycle" and return to the mainstream.
Contact: Stanley Suyat, Director
Description: With assistance from similar programs in Los Angeles, Boston, New York, Philadelphia, Chicago and Dallas, a volunteer group in Honolulu, Hawaii, tries to turn youth away from street gangs in a program called *Youth At Risk.* When independent research offered by the director of the Los Angeles program showed reductions in felony crime (50%) and truancy (75%), and a *550% increase* in hours worked among youth a year after the program was instituted, the Honolulu group organized and installed the program. Additional statistics from Los Angeles showed a 33% reduction in drug use, and better relationships with parents and teachers.

To begin the program, volunteers explain its operation in correctional facilities, and the youth must commit to it. It is a tough program with set standards of right and wrong, not unlike the discipline they are used to in the gang. A gang member's life is kept within a strict mold. What *Youth At Risk* does, through a program developed by San Francisco's *Breakthrough Foundation,* is teach gang members how to break through the mold.

The two-year involvement period for the youth - many already under sentence or alienated from their parents - begins with several months of preliminary meetings, but the emphasis is on a 10-day residential course that combines classroom discussions and physical activity. The latter is designed purposely to put the youth in a position where they must depend on each other - something they did not have to consider in the gangs. Many feel sick for most of the ten days, suffering withdrawal symptoms either from drugs or liquor or both, but they are still expected to run a mile a day. At the end of the course, all are required to declare their plans - to quit drugs, to get a job, join the Army, finish high school, etc. Some follow through, some don't, but almost all do better than they did before getting involved with *Youth At Risk.* For the next year, each is assigned a committed partner, a trained adult volunteer.

Both volunteers and funds come through fund-raising dinners and auctions. Merchants donate items that have included a 1969 red Chrysler LeBaron convertible, travel packages, restaurant meals and art works. The organization's motto is the ancient Chinese proverb, "If you do not change your direction, you are likely to end up where you are headed."

HOWARD BROWN MEMORIAL CLINIC
SEE VOLUNTEERS: PERSONS WITH AIDS

INDEPENDENT LIVING/HOMELESS YOUTH
SEE BUSINESS/INDUSTRY INVOLVEMENT:
CHILDREN/YOUTH

JOBS FOR OLDER WOMEN*
College of the Emeriti
Emeriti Women's Council
1400 Park Boulevard
San Diego, CA 92101
TEL: 714-230-2445
Purpose: To help older women attain their career potential and meet their earning needs.
Sponsor: Emeriti Women's Council
Contact: Frances Lee Smith, Administrator
Description: A one-to-one mentor relationship is the concept on which Jobs for Older Women is based. It is a project of the Emeriti Women's Council of San Diego's College of the Emeriti, and draws heavily on the expertise of its 30 members. Begun with an Older Americans Program mini-award grant, the Council set

the following objectives for the project:

- Survey existing career needs of older women in the community.
- Develop a recruitment plan in cooperation with local agencies.
- Develop a peer counseling process using experienced business and professional women as mentors.
- Make available to participants a full range of college career and educational planning resources.
- Make available to participants and to mentors a college career counselor to test, advise, and assist in placement.
- Evaluate the mentor process with input from participants, mentors, and college staff.

Volunteer mentors selected the applicants they felt most capable of assisting. A special effort was made to recruit minority and middle-income women, who had been identified as being underserved. Recruitment was done through contact with senior centers and agencies, media announcements, and recruitment aides. Mentors contacted their assigned clients and established meetings on an individual basis. Twenty women were selected for participation in the initial effort.

Participants in the program are offered a nine-session credit or no credit class on job counseling for the mature woman, and personal counseling by volunteer mentors who have received orientation to career counseling resources. Of the first group of older women, eight were successfully placed in jobs following the training program, and twelve other openings were identified within a short time.

One of the unanticipated difficulties of the program was - in the case of minority women - the need for immediate employment, forestalling participation in a lengthy career education program. But, foremost among the problems is a need to clarify beforehand the commitment and expectations of all concerned - participants, volunteers, mentors, and project staff. Also, matching procedures should be tightened, and applicants and mentors need to be more carefully screened and trained.

The first year's project surfaced a number of enlightening facts:

- Placement of older women is very difficult.
- Job sharing and flextime opportunities are crucial.
- The need to draw on outside resources is vital.
- Existing college counseling and placement services provide an excellent headstart for such a project.

On the plus side, certain benefits of the program were unanticipated also, such as the degree of friendship that developed among the older women attending the job counseling class. Also, the mentor system proved to be a rich and varied resource and an excellent way to gain support and involvement from the community. Finally, this volunteer effort could not be duplicated otherwise without prohibitive cost.

LEGAL COUNSEL FOR THE ELDERLY

1331 H Street, NW
Lower Level, Room 120
Washington, DC 20005
TEL: 202-234-0970

Purpose: To deliver free, quality legal services to elderly citizens of the District of Columbia, 60 years of age and older.

Sponsor: American Association of Retired Persons

Contact: Elsie R. Shamwell

Description: Legal Counsel for the Elderly was organized in 1975. It is sponsored by AARP (The American Association of Retired Persons) and receives funding from the D.C. Office on Aging, the Administration on Aging, the U.S. Department of Health and Human Services, the Legal Services Corporation, the D.C. Bar Foundation, and private contributions. The agency is both a law office for the elderly and a national support center that specializes in advocacy systems.

LCE is operated by a small paid staff comprised of attorneys, paralegals and support staff. Approximately 60 in-house volunteer paralegals and volunteer attorneys handle client cases under the supervision of staff attorneys. In addition to these volunteers, approximately 346 practitioners comprise the Volunteer Lawyers Project. They are individual attorneys or representatives of 47 major law firms who take cases on a pro bono (without charge) basis. Volunteer typists, secretaries, interns and other support persons render invaluable services.

In one month 1,208 new clients received legal assistance involving over 1,600 individual legal problems. Typical problems included welfare benefits, housing issues, consumer problems, medical care, and utility bills. Sixty percent of the clients received monetary values of public benefits due them to the extent of $483,000.

Volunteers receive initial training and also periodically scheduled training that keeps them current on updates and changes in rules and regulations that affect their services. Not only volunteers are trained, but many other agencies and persons who serve the elderly avail themselves of this opportunity.

LCE spoke about the legal needs of the elderly to an average of 180 community persons each month. The staff and volunteers also appear on radio and television.

Materials developed by LCE staff include: law manuals, training books, management information, the Legal Rights Calendar, and a local Information and Referral Manual.

In April 1982, LCE received one of the ten Annual Volunteer Activist Awards in the Washington Metropolitan Area for its volunteer program. In 1983, one of LCE's volunteer attorneys received honorable mention for his services to the community.

LCE's most recent project is the Model Volunteer Protective Services Project (MVPSP). The purpose of the project is to provide help for the elderly person who is unable to handle his/her financial affairs. A "representative payee" is appointed to act on the elderly person's behalf. This is achieved through a system of volunteers who are thoroughly trained and prepared to participate in the program. A long range goal is to replicate the project in other sections of the country, both rural and urban.

Founded: 1975

LEGAL PROGRAMS FOR THE HOMELESS
American Bar Association
750 North Lake Shore Drive
Chicago, IL 60611
TEL: 312-968-5000
FAX: 312-968-4684

Purpose: To promote legal programs for the homeless.

Contact: Paul L. Friedman, Co-Chairman

Description: In 1988, the *American Bar Association (ABA)* started a project to promote local legal programs for the homeless, hoping to establish 25 within the year. The goal was exceeded in the first four months. According to an ABA official, "Nothing has been as successful in attracting lawyers as homeless problems throughout the country." Activities resulting from ABA efforts have included:

- **Washington Legal Clinic for the Homeless** - One of the pioneers of the field, this program started with about 20 volunteers and now has more than 200, with many turned away because the DC Bar's training room could not accommodate them.
- **Rachel Women's Center Program** - A lawyer sets up shop one Friday a month to help homeless women cope with government bureaucracies, seek custody of children, deal with rape, and seek visas to remain in the U.S. The clinic also collects information on broader problems and tries to get major firms involved.
- **Washington, DC** - A team of lawyers headed for heating grates, a fire barrel, and other spots where homeless people gather for warmth to interview the homeless about crowding and poor conditions at the city's shelter. A notary public traveled from site to site, certifying the witnesses' statements. With ten assigned lawyers, and about 5,000 hours of free time (worth hundreds of thousands of dollars), their work resulted in a major victory for the homeless - a court settlement

requiring the city to vastly improve conditions and provide more shelters.

These and other efforts have sparked the legal profession across the country to get involved. This tremendous interest by the legal profession caused one project coordinator to pose the question, "Can you imagine the phenomenon of having law firms demanding to volunteer?" In other instances, activities have included:

- **Boston** - A program matches lawyers in private practice with nonprofit groups that want to build housing for the homeless, attracting lawyers who do not usually get involved with the poor.
- **Los Angeles** - Law firms are "signing up in droves" for a program in which law students with summer jobs volunteer to help homeless people seeking benefits at county welfare offices.
- **University of Maryland** - The Law School offers a course in policy and law affecting the homeless.
- **Yale University** - Law students participate in a seminar in which they work to develop low-income housing.

The court action in the District has led to the establishment of major rights for the homeless. Legal battles helped ensure a place on the ballot for *Initiative 17,* which established the city's obligation to give overnight shelter to those who request it.

In the words of one of the DC lawyers involved, "All the negative stuff you hear about lawyers, it can poison your mind against your own profession. But a case like this can make you feel that what you do is important to people... that you can really make a difference in people's lives."
Founded: 1988

LOUISIANA TRAINING INSTITUTE*
SEE VOLUNTEERS: CHURCH/SYNAGOGUE MEMBERS

MAKING THE GRADE: A REPORT CARD ON AMERICAN YOUTH
SEE LEADERSHIP DEVELOPMENT/BOARDS: CHILDREN/YOUTH

MASTER BUILDER GAME
Bechtel Group, Inc.
50 Beale Street
San Francisco, CA 94105
TEL: 415-768-1234
FAX: 415-768-9038
Purpose: To introduce more than 600,000 children nationwide to career opportunities in technical fields.
Sponsor: Bechtel Group
Contact: Stephen D. Bechtel, Jr., Chairman
Description: The *Master Builder Game* is part of a nationwide outreach program called *Discover E* (for *engineering*) - the first ever "teach-in" sponsored by the engineering profession. The *Game* teaches students some of the basic skills of engineering as they apply to city planning. The sponsors hope to introduce more than 600,000 students nationwide to career opportunities in technical fields. More than 10 major national societies, 30 organizations and local engineering councils throughout the country are participating in the program.

A typical class design a city over several class periods and send their plans to the *Bechtel Corporation,* the world's largest international engineering company. Engineers critique the plans and return them to the students. In a Washington, DC, Jefferson Junior High School classroom in early 1990, the Chairman of the Board of Bechtel was the substitute teacher there to answer questions and offer suggestions to the students in designing their project. The school, serving 757 students in grades 7 to 9, is noted for consistently doing well in national and city academic competitions. In 1990 COMSAT, the U.S. representative of a global consortium for satellite users, adopted Jefferson Junior High School and donated $1.1 million to improve its science and math programs.

The *Discover E* program was initiated by the company in response to alarming statistics on students bypassing math- and science-oriented careers. A *National Science Foundation* report said that - unless the present trend changes - by 1996 the demand for science and engineering graduates will outnumber the supply by 45,000 - within the next 20 years the shortfall will be 700,000. Representatives from NASA, a New York Giants placekicker who is an engineer during football's off season, and other volunteers join the corporate leaders in visiting classrooms to encourage young people to pursue careers in engineering.

The engineering program is part of the 40th annual *National Engineers Week,* held each February during the week of President George Washington's birthday. Washington was an engineer and the founder of the country's first engineering school at Valley Forge, Pennsylvania.

MISSION HOUSE
Jefferson County Medical Society
101 West Chestnut Street
Louisville, KY 40202
TEL: 502-589-2001
Purpose: To provide medical care for the homeless.
Sponsor: Jefferson County Medical Society
Contact: Volunteer Coordinator
Description: The members of the *Jefferson County Medical Society* have gone beyond the traditional methods of providing medical care to work with Mission House, the city's oldest and largest shelter for the homeless. In cooperation with the Roman Catholic priest who founded the center nearly twenty years ago, the society has formed a nonprofit corporation to take over its entire operation - from seeing that 500 meals are served daily to meeting the $95,000 annual budget to maintaining the level of volunteer assistance. Discussions began in late 1988. The transfer of ownership of the 200-bed shelter for men took place late in 1989. The Society expects to expand and improve medical services at the shelter house. A few volunteer doctors have been staffing weekly clinics there, but help has been offered by the *Greater Louisville Organization for Health (GLOH),* a group of University of Louisville medical students, who will staff additional clinics at the mission under supervision of volunteer doctors. The students now run a weekly clinic for indigent patients in the Iroquois area. In addition to the student organization, the Society expects to become more active in working with other groups, an avenue not actively pursued by Mission House in the past. Also, the Society will look more closely at federal grants such as the one for $40,000 turned down by the founder in 1988 due to conditions attached by a local screening board. A first step for the new administration was to contact the *Louisville Coalition for the Homeless* as it prepares to work with other service providers. As this goal unfolds, providers such as the *Jefferson County Board of Health* are coming forward. The Board has volunteered the agency to help in diet and nutrition planning for Mission House's kitchen. The effort arose from a growing sense among local doctors that their organization needs to become a more responsible corporate citizen.

This major step is an outgrowth of the long tradition of medical professionals to donate services on a case-by-case basis to those who cannot pay for them. The formal commitment to join forces against a broader, community-wide problem has been applauded by the community and the state.

In part, the move is a response to a challenge laid down a year ago by the new president of the American Medical Association. His mandate to members was "to tithe your time for the benefit of the American people."

Plans for the future include employment and education programs for the men at Mission House. The success of the program is dependent on involvement of Society members. An official pointed out, however, that doctors have always been involved in community service programs, and that their participation in Mission House should not be a problem. It is expected that the project will become a national model.

Facilities for women and children will continue to operate in Old Louisville by original Mission House administrators.

NET RESULT TENNIS FOUNDATION
20 Bayberry Lane
Middletown, NJ 07748
TEL: 201-671-0927
Purpose: To provide free tennis lessons to children who cannot afford private lessons.
Sponsor: United States Tennis Association
Contact: Else Helme or Rosemary Darben
Description: The *Net Result Tennis Foundation* provides free clinics for youngsters two days a week for tennis instruction. Clinics are operated in Red Bank, Holmdel, and Atlantic Highlands. Since its founding in 1987, the Foundation has grown from 25 children at one location to over 150 in 1989 at three locations. With the 14 volunteers of 1989 no longer adequate now that the third location has been added, and the program growing daily, a recruitment drive has become part of the everyday routine. Volunteer instructors range from experts to those who only know the basics of tennis. Since the children are all beginners, experts are not a requirement, although their expertise has helped the program tremendously - partly by showing an interest in helping to hone the skills of the less experienced volunteer instructors. Volunteers include high school tennis players and parents who play.

Recognizing that tennis talent was coming only through country clubs, the founders mounted the program to reach those who could not participate in these clubs or afford private lessons. As a result, much talent is surfacing that would not have been forthcoming without the program. Acknowledgement of the program's philosophy came in the form of a *United States Tennis Association* seed grant to assist the Foundation with the program. One promising participant was selected to attend the U.S. Tennis Association Junior Tennis League Invitational Camp in Indiana.

In the winter of 1990, *Net Result* offered a combination tennis/educational program at a local community center three afternoons and evenings a week. Short court tennis was taught to beginner and advanced players, and students received tutoring in math, English and science. In addition, advanced players received tennis instruction once a week at an indoor facility. Also, a mentorship program has been mounted to enable youngsters to receive individual advice and guidance from professionals in their chosen fields.

In addition to the ongoing tennis instruction program, tutoring will remain a part of the overall operation. According to the founders, "We want the children in our program to be well-prepared when they apply for college scholarships or jobs."
Founded: 1987

OUT OF WORK: WHAT NOW? AN UNEMPLOYMENT CLINIC
Triton College
2000 Fifth Avenue
River Grove, IL 60171
TEL: 312-456-0300
Purpose: To conduct a one-day clinic to provide opportunities for the unemployed to learn basic job search skills, learn how to cope financially and emotionally with unemployment and to become aware of public and private resources available to them.
Sponsor: Triton College
Contact: Ms. Lynn Parker, Associate Dean - Career Education
Description: The Triton College President and Board of Trustees are aware that unemployment is higher now than it has been since World War II. The new unemployed and their families are struggling with a variety of emotional, financial and job search concerns.

As a community service, the College has organized a one-day clinic to assist the unemployed of the district.

The event, titled *Out of Work: What Now? An Unemployment Clinic,* is held on a Saturday, and is staffed completely by volunteer teachers, typists, maintenance staff, organizers, demonstrators and others. The intent is not to offer job placement, but job-search skills and life-coping skills. The program has been developed with consideration for the needs of the unemployed and their families.

Workshops, information booths, demonstrations, and a goods and services exchange are featured. Highlights are listed below:

Workshops: 1-2 hour sessions. Selected topics:
- Unemployment: A Family Issue
- Financial Planning During Job Transition
- Leisure Activities on a Limited Budget
- Retraining: A Matter of Survival
- Make an Application Work for You
- Coping With Stress

Demonstrations: 15-20 minute presentations. Selected topics:
- Buying Smart
- Reassessing Job Goals
- The Job Interview: An Employer's Perspective
- After the Interview: What Now?

Information Booths: Approximately 120 community agencies and organizations staff booths to distribute information and answer questions about their services. Seven broad categories are covered:
- employment and training;
- job search skills;
- financial affairs;
- community services;
- health, leisure and recreation;
- consumer education; and
- job search services.

Goods and Services Exchange: Clinic participants may post information about goods or services they need or are willing to exchange. Exchange participants are mailed a booklet (after the Clinic) containing all listings. The idea is to provide an opportunity for the unemployed to get things they may need without having to exchange money.

The effort is impressive, since assisting in this area of concern, unemployment, is a great challenge for volunteers in today's economy.

PARENTAL STRESS CENTER
SEE INFORMATION & REFERRAL: DOMESTIC ABUSE

PRINCIPAL ON THE ROOF*
Page Traditional Elementary School
1501 North Lincoln Street
Arlington, VA 22201
TEL: 703-358-6290
Purpose: To recognize the *National Year of the Young Reader* (1989) and *National Young Readers Day* (November 15th) with a "special" activity.
Sponsor: Arlington County Public Schools
Contact: Frank Miller, Principal
Description: Page Traditional Elementary School takes pride in its back-to-basics approach to education, including high standards of behavior and appearance. Therefore, a notably "untraditional" challenge by the school's principal offered a distinct contrast. He was not willing to settle for *second highest* reading scores in the county.

Children whose parents opt for *Page* instead of one of Arlington's 17 neighborhood schools are enrolled on a first-come, first-served basis. Individualized instruction and team teaching are given up in favor of a single teacher for each class of about 25 students. The school also has a policy of at least four nights of homework each week. Therefore, if the principal was to see an increase in reading by these busy youngsters, the motivation would have to be something special.

The principal's challenge was offered to the 351 students - from kindergarten to seventh grade - after learning about an elementary school that challenged the children to read 1,500 books in six weeks. *Page's* principal "upped the ante" to 2,500 books, over a period of six weeks culminating on *National Young Readers Day*. He promised to spend a full day on the roof of the school if the pupils met the challenge successfully. He emphasized that monitoring of the reading challenge by parents and teachers would reflect and maintain the school's philosophy of "not just teaching reading skills, but also teaching children that they can get pleasure from reading and learn interesting things."

Parents were enlisted to certify that the reading was done, understood, and enjoyed. Teachers spent extra time keeping tallies. Staff members were issued walkie talkies to keep in touch with their leader when the day arrived. The children, themselves, gave up their play time, movie time, TV time, etc., to meet the challenge, even though most did not take the principal seriously on the "roof-sitting." When the day arrived, the children had averaged eight books each in the six week period - or over 2,700 books.

Upon arrival at school, the pupils were surprised to find the principal, carrying his briefcase, climbing to the roof. Wearing a black tail coat, he entertained the class by donning first a bowler hat, then a baseball cap and top hat. Then he unfolded a chair, pulled out a book, and sat down. He proudly announced that the two books he would read during his day on the roof were recommended by a third grader. When the children recovered from the initial reaction of mostly disbelief, they shouted a delighted "Good morning!" with some heard mumbling "wishes for rain." The most surprised student of all appeared to be a girl who arrived after everyone was inside and heard a voice booming her name from above, followed by "You're late!"

The bottom line of the challenge came from the librarian weeks later when she announced that the momentum continued, and more books were being taken out than ever before. This is what was hoped for in initiating the unusual challenge, which will take various other forms from time-to-time to maintain interest in reading, according to the principal. "What we do here is important," he said, "but it doesn't have to be serious all the time. We also want school to be pleasurable and fun."

PROJECT HELP (HELP EXPEDITE LEGAL PROBLEMS FOR THE HOMELESS)
Lillick & McHose
433 Brookes Avenue
San Diego, CA 92103
TEL: 619-298-5834
Purpose: To give free legal advice to the homeless.
Sponsor: Lillick & McHose
Contact: Dan Stanford
Description: The goal of *Project HELP* is to have lawyers in private industry volunteer to provide legal services to the homeless, so that government money is not spent in this area. This concept goes hand-in-hand with the fact that all lawyers have been encouraged for a long time to give some of their time back to society in the form of "pro bono," or free, legal work as a way of returning the privileges a license to practice law gives them.

The founder of the program was inspired when he saw homeless people appearing whenever and wherever jobs were offered, and asking for legal advice at various offices. He sees this as an effort on the part of the homeless to reverse their situations.

There are an estimated 6,000 homeless people in San Diego, and the number increases each year. Conversely, the number of *Summer Associates* (students who work as clerks in law firms) has increased, also. An estimated 225 *Associates* worked for San Diego law firms in the summer of 1989.

The program involves at least 100 of the students in a three-hour training program in exchange for one day, or eight hours, of volunteer service at the *Legal Aid Society's* storefront facility.

Tasks include interviewing the clients, helping fill out applications, appearing before hearing officers of the Department of Social Services, and obtaining evidence to support eligibility.

Letters are sent each Spring to 60 law firms asking them to encourage their *Summer Associates* to participate. At first a part-time service, 100 *Associates* enable Project HELP to stay open all day everyday during the summer months.

Project HELP's intent is to augment efforts of the *Legal Aid Society* and *Homeless Advocacy Program,* not to displace them.

Founded: 1989

RECORD DEBATE CLASSIC
Ramapo College
Mahwah, NJ 07430
TEL: 201-529-7500
Purpose: To help high school students hone their skills in debating.
Sponsor: Ramapo College
Contact: Dr. Helen Burchell, Coordinator
Description: A volunteer judge's panel of Bergen County attorneys refereed a debate competition among 22 teams from 21 public and private high schools in Bergen County, who faced off for the 11th annual *Record Debate Classic* at Ramapo College. The topic was *Social Security and the Elderly.* The all-day contest involved four rounds of competition to reach the point of two top teams for a final round.

The lawyers became involved when they learned that most of the students said they want to be lawyers. To emphasize that point, students gripped yellow legal pads and paced like prosecutors while grilling opponents. Dressed in suits and ties, they cited magazine and newspaper articles, books, and legal opinions to make their cases and to punch holes in their opponents' arguments. The volunteer judges took notes as the two top teams debated for an hour before about 80 fellow high school debaters, teachers, and friends.

The winning school received a silver cup and $1,000 in scholarship funds from the *Record*, and the runner-up received $500 in scholarship funds. A hard choice for the volunteer judges, the final vote was 3-2 for Frisch Yeshiva High School from Paramus. After the debate, the team members talked with the judges and made notes on suggestions offered. The college helps coordinate the debate competition each year.

REFUGE FOR INJURED WILDLIFE
Davis Nursery
9400 McIntosh Road
Dover, FL 33527
TEL: 813-986-3233
Purpose: To provide a refuge for injured animals until they are well enough to return to their natural habitats.
Sponsor: Florida Freshwater Fish and Game Commission
Contact: Steve or Vivian Davis
Description: Working with the *Companion Animal Hospital* in Thonotosassa, and licensed by the *Florida Freshwater Fish and Game Commission,* a family in Dover saw a need and started a volunteer program to provide food, shelter and care to injured animals brought to them. Residents in the entire community and surrounding area make special efforts to report sightings of injured animals. Although the program works mostly with birds, it has included deer, bobcats and foxes, often babies. There are five holding cages and two flight cages - large enclosures where the birds have an opportunity to move about, the largest made from a converted greenhouse.

The animals go through three or four stages before they are ready to be released, and birds must be moved to larger cages as their ability to fly improves.

The *Companion Animal Hospital* provides volunteer professional services when needed, taking care of wounds that cannot be healed simply by rest and nourishment. The work is not without danger.

Volunteers often must wear heavy-duty gloves to bring an immature horned owl out of a case. The 16-week-old owl was found on the ground by a resident who was unable to locate its nest. Residents are told through numerous media that the most important part of the rehabilitation process is to bring in injured animals, or call, as quickly as possible, since they dehydrate quickly. Residents finding animals and volunteers working in the refuge also are warned to use care in approaching the animals, since they can be mean and aggressive, with one incident reported in which the owl chased the volunteer out of the cage. All parties involved are told that they must have as little contact as possible with the charges, because once the animals become too familiar with people, they no longer fear people, which can be dangerous. A supplemental volunteer program has grown out of the refuge. Birds that are permanently injured and not candidates for release are kept and used in visits to schools and churches to teach children about nature.

SCHOOL ECOLOGY PROJECT
Audubon Naturalist Society
Woodend
8940 Jones Mill Road
Chevy Chase, MD 20815
TEL: 301-652-5924 (Education); 301-652-9188 (HQ)
Purpose: To provide elementary-age children with a course on ecology taught both on-site and in the community.
Sponsor: American Plant Food Company
Contact: Jane D. Winer
Description: The *Audubon Naturalist Society* draws on its professional members for a volunteer project that introduces children to ecology and their relationship to it. Volunteers include biologists, entomologists, National Zoo staff, and others who simply have an interest in children, education, and nature.
The course works under the small group concept, breaking up classrooms of 30 or more students into up to five groups. Children are given name tags cut in the shape of animals and a chance to know group members before volunteers begin. Areas covered include the school's relation to the sun, using a map, points of the compass, tree identification, the function of terrariums, insect life, photosynthesis and flowers, bird surveys, and wild animals.
The course culminates with visits to areas of the Smithsonian Institution that coincide with class subjects. By making these visits last, students are able to understand and enjoy much more than they would have seven weeks before when the course began. At the museum, children and volunteers join hands, make a great circle, and talk about what has been learned. The children then board the waiting bus, and the volunteers return to their offices.
Among Corporate Associates of the Society are: American Plant Food Company, Wild Bird Centers of America, Hechinger Foundation, Crisis Psychiatric Services, Marriott Corporation, Maryland Natural Gas, Northern Counties Lumber, PEPCO, Salt River Project, Clyde Restaurants, Snow Goose Gallery, and 22 other area firms.

SENIOR EMPLOYMENT RESOURCES
4201 John Marr Drive
Suite 236
Annandale, VA 22003
TEL: 703-750-1936
Purpose: To provide a complete, no-fee employment service for older persons.
Sponsor: Fairfax County; foundations; corporations; individuals
Contact: Dr. Robert B. Revere, Executive Director
Description: Senior Employment Resources (SER) is a nonprofit agency founded in 1983 to provide full employment services to persons fifty-five years of age and older - translated by the program's staff and volunteers to "...a little older...A LOT BETTER." SER is funded by Title III of the Older Americans Act and other funding from federal, state and local governments.

Also, contributions come from the clients themselves and other charitable organizations.
SER maintains an active *Talent Bank* of individuals 55 years of age or older who are seeking full- or part-time employment. All applicants go through an interview process that enables referral only to jobs for which they are qualified and for which they meet the specifications of the potential employer. Specializations of experienced job-seekers in SER's *Talent Bank* include:
- accounting, auditing, and bookkeeping
- computer operation, programming, management, photography, commercial art, and publication
- management, administration, and consulting
- property management and real estate
- driving, courier service
- editing and writing research
- secretarial, and administrative assistance
- interpreters and translators
- legal and paralegal
- engineering and scientific
- education and teaching
- sales and retail
- medical and health services
- public relations and public affairs
- ...and many others

There is no fee for either party to the transaction, and no obligation by the employer to hire the individual, or by the individual to accept the job.
Volunteers play a major role in SER both as professionals in counseling and placement, and as support services for the clerical staff. They receive orientation and training when necessary, but efforts are made to match the volunteers' existing skills with the needs of SER. Often, while awaiting placement, clients themselves offer to volunteer. According to the director, "Purely and simply, without the volunteers, we wouldn't be operating this service."
Publications: Ability Is Ageless
Founded: 1983

SENIOR REPORT
SEE INFORMATION & REFERRAL: OLDER PERSON

SERVICE TO MILITARY FAMILIES/SERVICE TO VETERANS (OHIO)
American Red Cross
1830 North Limestone Street
Springfield, OH 45503
TEL: 513-399-3875
Purpose: (1) To assist Armed Forces personnel and their families cope with the strain of separation, and to assist families in meeting problems that arise when a member is in the service; (2) To assist veterans in applying for Veterans Administration benefits.
Sponsor: American Red Cross
Contact: Dorothy LaVelle
Description: The American Red Cross offers a number of services to both active duty and veteran military personnel, including those shown below:
- **Service to Military Families:** The principal Red Cross services to military personnel and their families are counseling, emergency communications, and financial assistance. The Red Cross assists military personnel in utilizing appropriate military and community resources to help resolve problems. Messages are sent by Chapters to AmCross in Washington, DC, asking for emergency services such as locator information for military personnel in transit, and emergency messages to be sent to service members aboard ships at sea or at small isolated bases in remote parts of the world. These crucial messages receive high priority in handling.

Volunteers, some in leadership positions, assist the paid staff in carrying out the above and other services to military personnel and their families.

● **Service to Veterans:** The American Red Cross recognizes Red Cross responsibility to former service members as a logical extension of service to the Armed Forces. The Red Cross helps veterans with applications for government benefits, such as education, disability compensation, pensions, medical and dental care, home loans, discharge reviews and correction of military records. Red Cross also represents the veteran before the Veterans Administration and Military Review Boards. In addition, Clark County has generated $280,000 in benefits for veterans in this area.

Volunteers, some in leadership positions, assist paid staff in their efforts to assure maximum benefits to veterans of the Armed Forces.

THE SHED PROJECT*
R.F.D. #1
Box 359
Sandown, NH 03873
TEL: 603-352-1909
Purpose: To offer handicapped students an opportunity to learn about careers in construction, and to participate in construction jobs.
Sponsor: New Hampshire Public School District; New Hampshire State Department; CETA
Contact: Laurent Cormier
Description: Recognizing that the emotionally disturbed students did not adapt to integration into mainstream classes as other handicapped students did, a special three-phase off-campus program was developed for these students. A behavior specialist and an industrial arts instructor designed the program, which includes:
Phase I - The Shed Project: The class is organized into a crew, alternating various management and labor positions. During the course of the year the crew builds three or four large sheds on job sites in the community.
Phase II - Summer Environmental Education Construction Program for Disadvantaged Youth: Shed Project students qualify for CETA funds and participate in a variety of construction projects along with non-handicapped youngsters.
Phase III - Solar Horticultural Prevocational Program for Students with Special Needs: This project expands the skills learned in the construction cluster by introducing horticultural occupations. The phase includes the construction of a solar greenhouse together with necessary equipment and horticultural operations.
Voluntary action by the community comes in many forms - from serving as resource people, to providing construction materials, to helping evaluate the quality of student work.
Although CETA and Title IV funds are used for this program, costs can be modest. Shed construction is financed from profits realized and a $5,000 grant from members of the community, which helps finance the greenhouse. There is a variety of projects students can undertake if there is no demand for sheds within the community; i.e., building boathouses, maintaining school buses, and urban renewal projects. The following are key factors which every program should preserve.
Make it "Real" - The project should result in a product of genuine usefulness for the school, company, or community.
Provide Options - Provide a variety of activities which will sustain interest and enable all students to experience success.
Assure Diversity and Responsibility in Student Roles - Students should share the responsibility for making rules, setting procedure, monitoring performances and assuming a variety of roles.
Capitalize on Opportunities to Learn about a Variety of Careers - Students need a chance to meet builders, engineers, architects, and workers in the skilled trades as well as managerial and professional workers.
Keep Careful Track of Progress - Careful monitoring of student progress will help not only in determining who is entitled to what

rewards, it also will allow for the early identification of problems and facilitate discussion and resolution.
Involve the Off-Campus World - There are a variety of involvements - employers at whose construction sites students work, persons skilled in trades or professions related to the work students are doing, other students, retired persons, and others. This adds to the realism of the enterprise, and perhaps more importantly, prepares the student for the mainstream of the world.
Involve School Staff with a Variety of Skills - Teachers in special, academic, and vocational fields, and other staff can accomplish more working together than alone. In each phase of the program in Derry, staff combined their skills very effectively.

SNAP (STUDENTS NEED A PAT)
Starrett Elementary School
Fort Worth School District
2675 Fairmont Drive
Fort Worth, TX 76148
TEL: 214-660-7111
Purpose: To provide a little extra one-on-one attention to children who need it.
Sponsor: Fort Worth School District
Contact: Bob Windham, Principal, or Sharon Whitt, Counselor
Description: The *SNAP* program began in September 1988 when an elementary school principal and the school's counselor recognized that some children need a little extra attention mostly because of low self-esteem. The program was launched by inviting teachers to volunteer. Each grade level team submitted a prioritized list of youngsters who would benefit most from the mentor program. Then the principal and counselor carefully matched 36 students and 36 teachers. To get away from the image of teacher-as-an-authority figure, students were teamed with educators outside of their grade levels.
Each child was made to feel important because he or she was chosen as a SNAP. Soon they began snapping their fingers, the SNAP trademark. After the selections were complete, parents of SNAP participants received letters from the principal outlining the program. The same week, SNAP teachers personally delivered invitations to lunch to their students. Some teachers went all out and brought tablecloths and centerpieces, some took pictures, and most are keeping scrapbooks.
Each SNAP relationship is unique, and teacher and student make decisions about activities. The teachers check on their SNAPs each week during their conference periods, and youngsters visit their SNAP teachers before or after school.
The teachers make a special effort to surprise their SNAPs with little treats and notes of encouragement. Some SNAPs review their tougher assignments - like science lessons - with their SNAP teachers. In other cases, the SNAPs become volunteers for their volunteer teachers. For example, one student tutors younger children for his teacher. This also benefits the younger children, who wait eagerly for the SNAP to visit the classroom.
The SNAP teachers give a lot of encouragement, do lots of cheerleading and give lots of pep talks so their SNAPs feel very special. SNAP teachers even intercede when their SNAPs get in trouble with their teachers or find themselves in the principal's office. The volunteer teacher and the SNAP sit down and talk over what led up to the problem, with the teacher in the role of a friend, not an authority figure. Then she helps the SNAP devise some strategies for coping with similar situations. The close relationships have resulted in SNAP students trying extra hard to make their teachers - both volunteer and classroom - proud of them. Classroom teachers constantly report on the positive changes in the pupils who are involved in the SNAP program. Sixth graders and the counselor helped SNAP students compose thank you letters for their SNAP teachers. When the SNAP students move to another school in the district, the volunteer teachers continue to maintain contact - some even visiting the former SNAPs in their new schools.

According to the counselor, the program was started because "We wanted to let these kids know that shool is a neat place to be. We wanted them to know we're real people who do care." She said the principal wants to make Starrett a place where teachers and staff and children feel good about themselves.

SPARE CHANGE PROJECT
SEE FUNDING/FUND-RAISING/RELATED SERVICES: HOMELESS

SPIRIT AND BREATH VOLUNTEER PROGRAM
SEE VOLUNTEERS: SELF-HELP

STUDENT VOLUNTEER/WORK PROJECT (SV/WP)
SEE BUSINESS/INDUSTRY INVOLVEMENT: EMPLOYMENT

TASTE OF THE NATION
Share Our Strength (SOS)
733 Fifteenth Street, NW
Suite 700
Washington, DC 20005
TEL: 202-393-2925
TOLL FREE: 800-222-ISOS
Purpose: To raise funds to help support hunger relief programs.
Sponsor: Watergate Restaurant
Contact: Debbie Shore, Fund Raising Director
Description: As part of a national goal to raise $1,000,000 through the network of 75 cities in which *Share Our Strength (S.O.S.)* chapters exist, 25 of the most outstanding restaurants in the Washington, DC, area held their third annual public awareness and fund-raising forum.
During a pre-forum sampling session, visitors tasted dishes that were the local restaurants' best-held secrets, and had an opportunity to talk informally to the chefs about S.O.S., hunger, and nutrition. S.O.S. is a national nonprofit organization with 500 member restaurants in 75 cities as of 1989. The purpose of the organization is to maintain the public's awareness about hunger, and raise funds for hunger relief organizations.
The speakers for the forum were chefs from four local restaurants: Tila's, New Heights, 21 Federal, and La Brasserie. They talked about nutrition, the goals and activities of S.O.S., and how Taste of the Nation "benefits the community of which we are all a part." One hundred percent of the funds raised at the event (admission is $65.00) is donated to the Capital Area Food Bank, D.C. Central Kitchen, House of Ruth, Food and Friends (a food project for AIDS victims), OXFAM and Save the Children. Honorary chairpersons for the event included Linda Robb, J.C. Hayward of WUSA-TV, and Darrell Green of the Washington Redskins.
Among restaurants contributing sample food dishes were Watergate, Galileo, Germaine's, The Occidental, River Club, and I. Ricchi.
Brochures and other materials about S.O.S. and hunger around the world were distributed at the forum.

TUTORIAL PROGRAM
1050 South Foster Drive
Baton Rouge, LA 70806
TEL: 504-922-5400
Purpose: To provide low-cost after-school tutoring to pupils in the Baton Rouge area.
Contact: Donald Hunter, Director
Description: The church-based *Tutorial Program* gives individual attention to about 3,000 students at 71 sites in 10 parishes. Most of the volunteer tutors are school teachers, with half of them holding advanced degrees. Operated after school in church meeting halls, the program works with students who have fallen behind in class, missed a lot of school, or lack social skills.

Two outside evaluators in 1989 found the average $33 expense for each student served one of the most cost-effective operations in public education, with a high potential for addressing other educational problems as well. Many view it as a dropout prevention program, even though most of the students are still in grade school.
Teachers and facilities for the program are free, but a budget is required for travel to training sessions, supplies, and some paid staff. A serious need for staff (or qualified volunteers) is in the area of evaluation and collection of data. This lack of a measurement tool is causing a problem for the program, since the state Board of Education is requiring a quantitative measurement of its effectiveness in terms of the impact on grades or academic standards. Project leaders are working to correct this problem, planning to measure students' progress by checking improvement in their grades and their teachers' view of their classroom performance. Structured evaluation is difficult with a small paid staff, but progress is being made. In the meantime, intervention by the *Legislative Black Caucus* was necessary to assure that the school's $100,000 budget for the year ending June 1990 was authorized based on the project's efforts to meet the evaluation requirement.
Founded: 1985

VISITING FRIENDS*
Visiting Nurse Association of Milwaukee
1540 North Jefferson
Milwaukee, WI 53202
TEL: 414-327-2295
Purpose: To provide companionship to the homebound.
Sponsor: Visiting Nurse Association of Milwaukee
Contact: Mary P. Gilbert - Volunteer Supervisor
Description: The *Visiting Friends Program* is designed to provide companionship to homebound and isolated patients of the *Visiting Nurse Association (VNA)*. Volunteer visitors make a weekly visit and help patients do small errands and activities as well as providing emotional support and conversation.
Careful screening is done, and a training program is completed prior to placement. Ongoing in-service and support is provided by the Volunteer Supervisor and Volunteer Nurse Association staff.

VOGEL ALCOVE
Dallas Jewish Coalition for the Homeless
1110 Browder Street
Dallas, TX 75215
TEL: 214-565-7824
Purpose: To provide quality day care for homeless children.
Contact: Pat Peiser
Description: In June 1989, *Vogel Alcove* opened the doors of its new center to Dallas' homeless children. This move from its first "alcove" in 1987 enables it to go from serving 20 infants and 35 school-age children to as many as 100 infants, toddlers, and school-age children. One purpose of the center is to help break the cycle of homelessness, since it gives the parents time to look for jobs, get job training, and get "back on track."
Almost immediately after its founding in 1986, the *Dallas Jewish Coalition for the Homeless* began working with other agencies to offer child care for the homeless at different sites throughout the city. The children being cared for at those sites now attend *Vogel Alcove*, which accepts children from six weeks old to teenage. The Center opens at 7:30 a.m. to accommodate working parents, and includes after-school care. It also funds a child-care staff at the family shelter at night so homeless parents can attend classes and counseling, and maintains committees who provide access to food, clothing and other needed items for the entire homeless family.
The big break came in January 1989, when an anonymous Dallas businessman who heard about the group's mission gave it a single-story, 4,500-square-foot office building. In six months, volunteers transformed the building into a professional day care

center capable of handling 100 children. The Coalition spent about $35,000 renovating the building, with the money coming from private donations and from three foundation grants.

A Dallas architect donated his time to ensure that the center meets building code standards, and the Coalition's Vice President coordinated the core of volunteers who transformed the building. The curriculum for homeless children is especially challenging, since they have lost everything - toys, rooms, pets, even clothes - and are more reluctant than other children to see their parents leave. It is found that many children who did well at school before becoming homeless regress at the shelters, and need special attention to be brought back to their levels. In addition to children from the family shelter, *Vogel Alcove* also cares for children from RESTART, Trinity Ministry to the Poor, Genesis, Family Place, the Interfaith Housing Coalition, and Oasis Housing Corporation. There is no longer a waiting list.

Although most staff members are paid child care workers from the YWCA, volunteers are involved in every phase of the operation.

VOLUNTEER COUNCIL
SEE LEADERSHIP DEVELOPMENT/BOARDS: ARTS

VOLUNTEER LAWYERS PROJECT
Erie County Bar Association
290 Main Street
Buffalo, NY 14202
TEL: 716-847-0662
Purpose: To provide legal services for the poor.
Contact: Executive Director
Description: The *Volunteer Lawyers Project* is a project developed to provide legal services to people who cannot afford their own legal services. It is sponsored by the *Erie County Bar Association.* Members of the Association devote time to the Project as available, and as space in Project offices permits.

In mid-1989 the space problem was alleviated as the Project moved to new offices in the Niagara Frontier Building on Main Street. Local attorneys feel that this increased space will enable them to spend more time on cases for the poor, since more attorneys can work simultaneously.

Local businesses assist the Project by donating funds and materials. *Barrister Information Systems* donated more than $12,000 in computer equipment and training when the Project relocated. Another business donated a telephone system and office furniture.

In addition to local business and industry, the project receives encouragement and support from judges and other individuals and organizations across the community. A reception at the new offices was attended by about 80 people, and several businesses were honored for their assistance to the Project.

WOMEN OFF WELFARE (WOW)
SEE VOLUNTEERS: LOW-INCOME

WYANDOTTE HOUSE/NEUTRAL GROUND
Wyandotte House, Inc.
632 Tauromee
Kansas City, KS 66101
TEL: 913-342-9332
Purpose: To provide long and short-term crisis intervention, temporary shelter for teenage runaways, and emergency and residential shelter for children of abused, deprived, and neglected family situations.
Sponsor: Federal/state governments; public and private donations
Contact: Clarence Small, Program Director, Neutral Ground
Description: Neutral Ground is a short-term crisis intervention center offering emergency shelter and counseling to young people, ages 11 through 17, who have run away from home. The program operates under the auspices of Wyandotte House, a non-profit

organization receiving funds from federal and state governments as well as from public and private sources.

At the present time, the program utilizes the services of ten active volunteers and maintains a list of ten volunteers who remain "on-call" in case of emergencies. Six volunteers are assigned by the VISTA volunteer program. They perform various duties including: resident supervision, houseparent aides, youth workers, intake officers, public relations, and general maintenance. Neutral Ground also utilizes volunteers assigned through the Foster Grandparent Program. These individuals give "that extra love and attention" that becomes so vital in service delivery. The other volunteers come from recruiting efforts in the community. They help in general supervision, recreation, and generating interest and support. Their occupational backgrounds include a lawyer, a radio and TV personality, an insurance executive, and a retired civic leader.

Many of the volunteers perform valuable services to Neutral Ground and the community. Without their contribution of time, the program would suffer tremendously because they fill in positions that present funding sources cannot, and they perform and provide quality services. The program also offers internship training to senior college students in the areas of social work, sociology, and psychology.

There is a continuing need for volunteers and interns at Wyandotte House/Neutral Ground. Plans call for expansion of the volunteer program throughout the agency, performing a variety of services to youths and family. Recruiting efforts have been upgraded, and plans to implement on-going training for present volunteers are underway.

YOUNG WINGS USA*
Flight Attendant Volunteer Corps
122 East 42nd Street
Room 1725
New York, NY 10017
TEL: 212-869-8837
Purpose: To provide cultural enrichment for students at elementary, middle, and secondary school levels, and hospitalized and institutionalized children.
Sponsor: Major airlines; business/industry; government; the media
Contact: Gerri Rafferty
Description: Young Wings USA is a project of the Flight Attendant Volunteer Corps, a nonprofit organization founded in 1976. Its basic purpose is to provide for Flight Attendants of all U.S. airlines structured opportunities under professional guidance to utilize available time, education, talents and skills in special volunteer work with institutionalized children. A new development is a program for school children at all levels which highlights the Young Wings Air and Space Academy Program.

Presently there are 1,700 volunteers and 2,400 new applicants. Membership is open to all U.S. airlines whether the individuals are active or inactive (on leave, etc.). All volunteer work is scheduled to avoid interference with airline assignments or requirements. Most assignments involve a minimum of two hours on one day per month. Special degrees or diplomas are not required except for limited, specialized activities. The only requirement is attendance at one complete (two-hour) orientation session offered periodically in each of the flight bases involved.

Because flight schedules and other commitments do not permit most flight attendants to participate more than once or twice per month, the volunteers operate as a team. The teams create a relationship with the children and assure the continuity of the relationship through a team concept over a significant period of time. Example: If 100 Flight Attendants are team members in any given city, each is asked to participate at least one time per month in a weekly session.

Presently, there are close to 750 children involved in the program in 12 cities (12 major children's institutions), and an estimated 4,000 children have participated since the inception of the program in 1976.

Following are brief descriptions of Young Wings activities, which are explained thoroughly with a slide show at the volunteers' Orientation Sessions:

- **Simulated Flights:** A fun and popular monthly event with a "mock airplane," slide shows of various parts of the world, uniformed teams, and artifacts.
- **Weekly Arts and Crafts Projects:** A variety of games and projects with the children based on the ratio of volunteers to children, the needs and wishes of both children and staff, and available supplies. This activity includes Project Postcard, a geography-based game b ased on postcards sent in by Flight Attendants for the children.
- **Special Events:** Periodic parties, and trips. Special events include activities for Halloween, Thanksgiving, Christmas, Valentine's Day, and Easter, as well as occasional trips out of the hospital to movies, airports, zoos, and many other places.
- **Young Wings Magazine:** A 16-page magazine issued every other month and written, edited, illustrated, etc., by Flight Attendants, covering a wide variety of subjects and filled with games, contests with prizes, aviation subjects, and other creative topics for the children's enjoyment and education.
- **Young Wings Air and Space Academy Project:** A new program for school children and institutionalized youngsters staffed by both Flight Attendants and Pilots, and featuring a Mini-Course Air and Space Booklet program, a Flight Learning Center with films, tutoring programs, and Graduations with Wings, Diplomas, Scholarships, Medals and special prize trips.

The Flight Attendant Volunteer Corps plans to develop "Young Wings International" in a format similar to the USA program. Major sponsors to date: Pan Am World Airways, Eastern Airlines, United Air Lines, Trans World Airlines, American Airlines, Delta Air Lines, Western Airlines, The Boeing Company, the National Aeronautics and Space Administration, the US Office of Special Education, the Walt Disney Media Company, and ABC Television Network.
Founded: 1976

YOUTH OCEAN EXPLORER PROGRAM
Cousteau Society
930 West 21st Street
Norfolk, VA 23517
TEL: 804-627-1144
Purpose: To unite the children of the world through an exciting adventure.
Contact: Sandy Bond, Supervisor
Description: In January 1990, six elementary school children accompanied Jean-Michael Cousteau, son of the famed explorer, on a voyage to explore Antartica. The *Cousteau Society* launched the program to "unite the children of the world" through an exploring adventure. Each child came from a country on a different continent - United States, France, Chile, Australia, Japan and Tanzania.

The nominations for the cultural adventure were sent to the Society after a media campaign, with each nominator giving specific information about the youngster and why they felt he or she would benefit from the experience. The representative from the United States was a sixth-grader.

The mission lasted two-and-a-half weeks and included a demonstration of igloo-building and a chance to see the rare wingless fly, found only in Antartica - but, most importantly, an opportunity for six youth from diverse cultures to interact in an educational and exciting setting.

VOLUNTEERS: ROLE MODELS

NATIONAL/STATE ORGANIZATIONS

BIG BROTHERS/BIG SISTERS OF AMERICA
230 North Thirteenth Street
Philadelphia, PA 19107
TEL: 215-567-7000
Objectives: To help children grow into responsible and happy adult members of society and their communities.
Services: Combines the friendship of a mature, stable volunteer with the skill of a professionally trained staff to create a personalized friendship on a one-to-one basis; sets goals to meet the needs of the boy or girl by working as a team with volunteer, parent, staff professional, and child (usually from a one-parent family); provides volunteers with the opportunity to help children and the community through this activity; provides technical assistance to communities to help form Big Brother and/or Big Sister Agencies (evaluation, volunteer development, public relations, etc.); approves standards and practices, taking into consideration the needs of each local community; places recruitment of volunteers as its number one priority due to the long waiting list (some 60,000 children); publicizes the difference between the cost of a Big/Little Brother or Big/Little Sister match ($650/annually) with the cost of maintaining a child in an institution ($18,000 to $65,000); publishes triannual newsletters, and a number of organizational manuals.
Publications: Agency-in-Formation Manual; The Correspondent; Citizen Board Development; Program Management Guide
Founded: 1977

TRAINING PROGRAMS

PREVENTION MAKERS
SEE TRAINING/CONFERENCES/TEACHING:
DRUGS/ALCOHOL

WASHINGTON FOR MINORITY YOUTH AWARENESS DAY
SEE TRAINING/CONFERENCES/TEACHING:
ENTREPRENEURSHIP

INDIVIDUAL PROGRAM PROFILES

BIG BROTHERS/BIG SISTERS OF NASSAU COUNTY*
240 Clinton Street
Hempstead, NY 11413
TEL: 516-489-7440
Purpose: To service single parents, at-risk children between the ages of 7 and 17 by matching them on a one-to-one basis with responsible adult and young adult volunteers.
Sponsor: Nassau County Youth Board, US/ACTION, New York State Division for Youth.
Contact: William G. Tymann, Executive Director
Description: Big Brothers/Big Sisters of Nassau began as a project of Mobilized Community Resources, Inc. in the spring of 1975. Initial funding was provided by the Nassau County Youth Board and the New York State Division for Youth. In 1977, the agency was spun off and incorporated on its own. At the present time, it is a Full Member Agency in Good Standing with Big Brothers/Big Sisters of America.

The volunteers in the program number approximately 300 and their primary function is to work one-to-one with a youngster who is experiencing developmental, emotional, psychosocial or educational difficulty. The volunteers are oriented, trained, screened and matched and supervised by a professional staff. These are goal oriented matches formed to prevent the youngster from getting into more serious difficulties.

The service is delivered by one of three methods: 1) The Core program, which is centrally located in the county, supports the bulk of the casework and match-making functions, 2) the Chapter program, which is an affiliate agency system of delivery. Agencies in eight Nassau communities are involved in providing the service to youth in their areas. This system is developed and managed by the Core program, 3) a High School program in which high school juniors and seniors are matched with children between the ages of 7 and 12 who live in the same school district.

Funding for this program is provided by ACTION. In the first eight years, Big Brothers/Big Sisters of Nassau serviced over 600 children and recruited over 4000 volunteer applicants. In addition, the agency has a vigorous and increasingly successful fund raising program.
Founded: 1975

BIG BROTHERS/BIG SISTERS PROGRAM
Madison House
170 Rugby Road
Charlottesville, VA 22903
TEL: 804-977-7051
Purpose: To create an ongoing, positive adult relationship with a local child who lacks consistent adult attention.
Sponsor: Madison House
Contact: Jane Parker
Description: The Big Brothers/Big Sisters Program is one of Madison House's original volunteer efforts. The Program centers around the one-to-one relationship between the volunteer and the child. The children - due to any number of circumstances - lack the adult attention needed by every child. Many of the children are from low-income, unstable family situations - the parents may be divorced, one parent may be deceased, or the family may be very large.

Most children are referred to the program through counselors in the public school system and through the welfare departments. Referrals also come from churches, the Baptist Student Union of the University of Virginia, Hope House, HELP, and the Probation Department.

Basic information about each child and his/her family situation is provided to the program to assist in the matching of volunteers and children. The children usually are between the ages of five and 15 with varied interests, problems, and backgrounds.

Volunteers in this program attend an orientation and an interview before being matched with a little brother or sister. Once matched, they spend a minimum of five hours a week with the child throughout the school year. It is emphasized to the volunteer that only a consistent, long-term relationship is of any benefit to the child, since an inconsistent, short-term relationship creates additional problems and difficulties in the child's development. Volunteers are asked to make a written commitment that they will spend at least the minimum time with the child, and will attend all monthly program meetings.

Although most of the volunteer's time is spent independently with the little brother or sister, the program also sponsors a series of group activities to supplement the individual volunteer/child relationship. These activities not only provide the child with experience in participating with a group, but they afford the volunteers the opportunity to compare notes and perhaps benefit from the experiences of others. Activities include picnics, holiday parties, skating trips, zoo trips, and University athletic events.

The "bottom line" is that, although a few ups and downs can be expected in the volunteer/child relationship, in the long run the volunteer and child should feel comfortable with each other. The volunteer should be prepared to put a good deal of time and effort into establishing a trusting friendship with the little sister or

brother, since the relationship will have an enormous influence on the young person's life.

Big Brothers/Big Sisters places 150-200 volunteers annually. Because of the growing need for more volunteers, and the time restrictions on student volunteers, the program has expanded to include more community volunteers.

BIG BROTHERS/BIG SISTERS PROGRAM-CHILD PSYCHIATRY*
St. Luke's-Roosevelt Hospital Center
Amsterdam Avenue at 114th Street
New York, NY 10025
TEL: 212-870-1867
Purpose: To meet the needs of children from the clinic who are having difficulty with adult and/or peer relationships; to give college students an opportunity to work within their fields.
Sponsor: St. Luke's-Roosevelt Hospital Center
Contact: Gloria Zicht, Child Psychiatry Center
Description: Students from City College and Manhattan Community College have served for years as Big Sisters and Big Brothers to children undergoing psychiatric treatment at the Child Psychiatry Clinic. This year the Clinic has begun working with students from Columbia University also. The program attempts to help the children develop self-esteem, increase their capacity to verbalize, tolerate frustrations, establish controls, share, empathize, and cooperate. In a few cases, the Big Brothers/Big Sisters Program is the sole treatment.

Student volunteers are required to spend one afternoon per week with the child assigned, write a brief summary of each contact with the child, and attend weekly meetings with supervising members of the social work staff. Most of their work with the children necessarily takes place outside of the home (in parks, zoos, museums, or other places in the city's recreational framework).

In the current academic year, fifty-four students are taking part in the program, logging nearly 3,000 hours by midyear. The students have been active in enlarging the children's horizons as well as helping them to develop new skills (ball playing, bike riding, etc.). Students who demonstrate exceptional capability are given the opportunity for supervised liaison work with the family and with the school.

Student volunteers are involved in sociology, psychology, or social work courses and receive some credit for their volunteer work. In addition they are reimbursed by the hospital for carfare and incidental expenses.

Evaluation of the program has shown it to have great merit within the clinic setting. The gains made within the total group of children in the program have been substantial, with great satisfaction expressed from parents, children, and the students themselves.

COMPANIONS OF ALAMEDA COUNTY
PO Box 3493
Hayward, CA 94544
TEL: 415-785-6690
Purpose: To alleviate some of the problems of low-income single-parent families by providing a one-to-one friendship match for children in this target group.
Sponsor: Municipal funds, corporations, foundations, and own fundraising events.
Contact: Betty DeForest, Executive Director
Description: Companions was formed in 1970 to alleviate some of the problems faced by boys and girls 6-16, from low-income, single-parent homes; to provide positive alternatives, role models, and reinforcement for children from an "at risk" population by providing a one-to-one relationship with a consistent, caring adult volunteer. This service is extended to deaf and physically disabled children.

All direct service to children is delivered by volunteers who are recruited, screened, and oriented by program staff. Volunteer recruitment and support is an integral part of the program. A volunteer must:

- make a minimum six-month commitment to a child with regular visits amounting to at least 12 hours per month;
- attend at least two volunteer support group meetings after the match has been made;
- make at least one contact by phone, mail, or in person with the office each month.

Volunteers come to the program with a variety of skills and experiences. Previous experience with children is not necessary; a sense of responsibility and commitment is most important. The program requires two references (written), car insurance as required by state law, a minimum of two interviews with staff, and fingerprinting before an individual can be matched.

Companions program provides:

- supervisory guidance and support for volunteers
- monthly newsletter sent to volunteers' homes
- monthly group activities for matched pairs
- free passes to local activities
- credit available through local colleges
- in service training through periodic workshops.

INTOUCH
SEE TRAINING/CONFERENCES/TEACHING: DRUGS/ALCOHOL

NEW YORK GIANTS SCHOOL SPEAKERS PROGRAM
Fairleigh Dickinson University
Giants Degree Completion Program
3 University Plaza Drive
Hackensack, NJ 07601
TEL: 201-692-9696
Purpose: To utilize the high-visibility of national athletes to reach elementary, middle and high school youth in areas of educational goals and drug and alcohol abuse.
Sponsor: New York Giants
Contact: George Martin
Description: In 1985 George Martin of the New York Giants, concerned about the "future after football" of his fellow athletes, established a *Degree Completion Program* at Fairleigh Dickinson University to encourage them to complete their academic degrees. The program includes a requirement of weekly visits to elementary, middle and high schools to speak about the importance of setting educational goals and the need to avoid drug and alcohol abuse. As a result, over 20,000 students have heard the athletes speak.

In cooperation with the University, George Martin coordinates the school program, assisting the other athletes in their presentations, and it is said making the most visits per semester himself.
Publications: Degree Completion Program
Founded: 1985

SPECIAL SATURDAY
SEE VOLUNTEERS: STUDENTS

SURRY COUNTY FRIENDS OF YOUTH/BEST FRIENDS PROGRAM
150 North Main Street
Mt. Airy, NC 27030
TEL: 919-789-9064; 919-835-5433
Purpose: To advocate the needs of young people and network services for young people through various services and volunteer programs.
Sponsor: Federal/State/County governments; corporate and private donations
Contact: Selbert M. Wood, Jr., Executive Director

Description: Surry County Friends of Youth (SFOY) is a private, non-profit agency which began in 1976. The purpose of this organization is to network services and advocate the needs of young people in Surry County. Toward that end, various programs and services have been offered since incorporation. At the present time, *SFOY* provides outpatient family, individual and group therapy, the *Best Friends Program,* a *First Offenders Restitution Program,* crisis intervention, and telephone referrals for Surry County.

The *Best Friends Program* is funded through local county and Community-Based Alternative money from the state. The program follows the Big Brother/Big Sister type format and matches a young person exhibiting delinquent, or pre-delinquent behavior with an adult volunteer.

- **Best Friends Staff** - A full-time Best Friends Coordinator is responsible for the *Best Friends Program* and all aspects of it. He/she is responsible for accepting referrals from various community agencies and recruiting adult volunteers. The coordinator also trains the adult volunteers and closely supports each match.
- **Volunteer Duties** - Each volunteer in the *Best Friends Program* is expected to spend a minimum of three hours each week for one year with the young friend. The volunteer is given various optional outings and free activities each month and the volunteer may escort the young friend to various activities sponsored by merchants and business people in Surry County. Although the match is for one year, it is tentatively made for six weeks until all parties agree to continue the match.

Volunteers are recruited from area churches, high schools and community colleges. The volunteers are recruited also through mass media involving local television, radio and newspapers.

THANKS (THOUGHTFUL, HELPING ADULTS N' KIDS SHARING)
Lee County Youth Services
PO Box 57
112 Hillcrest Drive
Sanford, NC 27330
TEL: 919-774-9515
Purpose: To provide appropriate role models for children experiencing difficulty in the community.
Sponsor: State/County government; corporate and private donations
Contact: Nancy Cashion/THANKS Coordinator
Description: THANKS (Thoughtful, Helping Adults N' Kids Sharing) is a one-on-one program designed to provide appropriate role models for children experiencing difficulty at home, school or in the community. The kids who share are boys and girls between the ages of 8 and 15, who want and need a one-to-one relationship with an adult friend. The program operates under the auspices of Lee County Youth Services, which currently has eight programs to serve the families and children of Lee County.

The THANKS Coordinator works closely with both the volunteer and the youth through weekly contact and monthly group activities.

The THANKS program has a goal of matching 30 volunteers each year. In addition to the one-on-one volunteers, THANKS also has volunteers who serve on the Board and provide a variety of other services such as group activities and legal advice.

THANKS volunteers are expected to spend four hours per week for at least a year with their youth. The volunteer and child schedule their own time together doing things they enjoy the most. However, they are also expected to attend group activities and in-service training sessions. The real purpose is for the adult to establish the most meaningful relationship possible with the child. Like the kids, the volunteers come from a wide variety of backgrounds and experiences. They are 18 years of age or older, single or married, or perhaps have families of their own. Each adult is carefully screened to insure the presence of sincere motivation and emotional stability. THANKS asks that each volunteer complete an application form listing four references and participate in an interview. The volunteer then completes a six hour training course.

VOLUNTEERS FOR YOUTH
Gettysburg College
Box 427
Christ Chapel
Gettysburg, PA 17325
TEL: 717-334-3131
Purpose: To meet the needs of youth who lack opportunities for meaningful interaction with adults.
Sponsor: United Way of Adams County; Gettysburg College
Contact: Edward F. McManness
Description: In May 1974, a group of people representing a number of youth and family service organizations began meeting to discuss the problems of youth in Adams County. A common concern of those persons was the absence of a comprehensive volunteer program oriented toward the needs of youth. As a result of that realization, the *Volunteers for Youth* program was organized.
Volunteers for Youth is a "Best Friend" type of organization. In one-parent families and in other situations where a child could benefit from additional guidance and companionship, a Youth Volunteer can be a helpful human resource.
Referrals of children are accepted from community agencies, churches, civic groups, individuals or directly from parents. Volunteers are sought from the community and various organizations within it, including the Lutheran Seminary and Gettysburg College. Children and volunteers are matched with consideration to mutual interest and abilities. Supervision of the volunteers is usually by the program director or in certain cases, is arranged with the cooperation of social service professionals in the area.
Anyone over the age of 18 who is interested in becoming a volunteer will be interviewed and considered. References are required as part of the application as well as an agreement to receive supervision and attend workshops. Monthly activity reports are required. In addition, group activities are arranged on a regular basis, with attendance requested.
Volunteers who wish to be involved with a particular type of child are encouraged to apply and their requests will be considered on the basis of current needs and referrals.
Any child residing in Adams County or the Hanover area who is between the ages of six and 17 will be considered for the program. Acceptance of children into the program will be dependent upon the current family situation and the interest and desire of the child to have a "best friend."
Besides volunteers, the program needs financial assistance in order to provide for insurance, program and administrative costs. VFY also invites comment and discussion from the community.
Founded: 1974

WRITECONNECTION PROGRAM: LOVE A CHILD BY MAIL
SEE VOLUNTEERS: ARMED FORCES MEMBERS - NAVY

VOLUNTEERS: ROLE-PLAYERS

NATIONAL/STATE ORGANIZATIONS

BREAD AND ROSES
SEE FUNDING/FUND-RAISING/RELATED SERVICES: ARTS

INDIVIDUAL PROGRAM PROFILES

HOGAN'S ALLEY, VIRGINIA
FBI Academy
Practical Applications Unit
Quantico Marine Base
Quantico , VA 22134
TEL: 703-640-6131
Purpose: To use role-players to simulate crime situations that FBI Academy students will face some day in the real world.
Contact: John Gray, Instructor
Description: Although it is difficult to "arrest your roommate," students at the FBI Academy do it everyday. The Academy uses role-playing in which students not ready for the training - and wives and family members of students - play roles of kidnappers, extortionists, bank robbers, cop-killers, accomplices, witnesses, bystanders, etc. for those who are ready.
The fictional, but three-dimensional town is called *Hogan's Alley, Virginia,* and was built by the Academy, one of the nation's largest law enforcement schools.
Although the role-players receive carefully-crafted scripts, they are given some latitude to "mouth off, resist arrest or shoot it out" in the confrontations with the Academy trainees. They are encouraged to exploit students' mistakes. Their mission is to rattle, to distract, and to get trainees upset enough to lose their exposure and "blow an arrest." Role-players learn to read trainees' body language, look for nervousness, and exploit any openings they see. They have learned to give only "lip service," however, since - in the heat of the situation - struggling or fighting causes the trainees to fight back.
A pool of about 70 additional role-players - coordinated by a "casting director," supplements the student volunteers and includes police officers, firefighters, park rangers, homemakers, bartenders, college students, computer programmers, people between jobs, etc. Although some role-players are given a subsistance wage, most come just to "play cops and robbers for a good cause." One corrections officer/role-player has no qualms about "making students pay for their mistakes." *Hogan's Alley* is an "open air town," built on the grounds of the Quantico Marine Base in full view of citizen observers passing by the facility. This adds to the trainees' discomfort when they are "shot" by a role-player after making a fatal error. The Academy sees this as a plus, since it impresses the mistake on the trainee the way no classroom can. As one instructor points out, "If students are going to make mistakes, this is the best place to do it."

LIFESTORY THEATER
SEE VOLUNTEERS: OLDER PERSONS

LOS ANGELES POVERTY DEPARTMENT (LAPD)
SEE COMMUNICATIONS & PUBLIC RELATIONS: IMAGE

MENTAL HEALTH PLAYERS
SEE COMMUNICATIONS & PUBLIC RELATIONS: MENTAL HEALTH

MODEL MUGGING
All Souls Church
16th and Harvard Streets, NW
Washington, DC 20009
TEL: 202-332-5266
Purpose: To teach women to ward off attack while on the ground.
Sponsor: All Souls Church
Contact: Carol Middleton
Description: Begun in 1972, Model Mugging is a form of self-defense that teaches women to fight back after they have been thrown to the ground by their attackers. The class primarily addresses rape prevention, where women often are thrown to the

ground. The director terms it a "knockout defense," since that results in less trauma on both sides.

Model Mugging is a two-week course, with a fee, but it provides scholarships as available to those who cannot afford the fee. The course uses volunteer "stand-in muggers" who are versed in martial arts, wearing padding, and playing realistic, hardcore roles of attackers. Most of the volunteer stand-in muggers have family members who went through the trauma of such attacks.

Unlike other martial arts training, where practice sessions stop just short of physically harming an opponent, Model Mugging teaches women to fight with "full force." Although the vicious realism of the classroom attacks disturb some spectators, it is based on the fact that only realism will help a woman learn to fight back adequately.

The course has a psychological side - hardening women to overcome their squeamishness at attacking men's most vulnerable spots - heads and groins.

More than 8,000 women across the country have been trained in Model Mugging courses. Most of the concern is an outgrowth of statistics which show that at least 50% of all rapes occur in the victim's home or a friend's home, and it has happened to females as young as two months and as old as 97.

According to the director, the bottom line is that "the power women acquire is the freedom of choice." If the attacker(s) pose too much of a threat, then it is the woman's choice to fight or not to fight - but it's "always a choice."
Founded: 1972

SENIOR ACTING PROGRAM OF THE BARN PLAYERS*
SEE COMMUNICATIONS & PUBLIC RELATIONS: ARTS

STAY THE NIGHT ON MY STREET
SEE COMMUNICATIONS & PUBLIC RELATIONS: HOMELESS

VOLUNTEERS: SELF-HELP

NATIONAL/STATE ORGANIZATIONS

ASSOCIATION OF COMMUNITY ORGANIZATIONS FOR REFORM NOW (ACORN)
401 Howard Avenue
New Orleans, LA 70130
TEL: 504-523-1691
Objectives: To enable low-income families to have a stronger voice in decisions affecting their future.
Services: Advocates the concept of a "major constituency" which ACORN describes as individuals of low or moderate income who are shut out of the power structure; promotes action on issues including fighting utility rate increases, challenging blockbusting practices, and promoting major reform in legislation regulating prescription drug prices; has adopted a nine-point *People's Platform* which calls for fair taxes, jobs for all, national health insurance, subsidized utility rates for the elderly, saving of family farms, adequate housing, controlled community development, and full representation of low- and moderate-income people in matters that affect their lives; sponsors fund-raising activities, internships, and training events; publishes a newsletter, a manual, and other materials.
Publications: USA (United States of ACORN); The Organizer, Vamanos!
Founded: 1970

AUTOMOTIVE CONSUMER ACTION PROGRAM (AUTOCAP)
National Automobile Dealers Association
8400 Westpark Drive
McLean, VA 22102
TEL: 703-821-7144
Objectives: To provide dealers and their customers with consumer dispute resolution assistance.
Services: Sponsors panels of volunteers (usually three dealers and three consumer representatives) who act as "mini-juries" in cases of customer dissatisfaction with dealers, when direct contact between the two parties fails to resolve the problem; provides this form of conflict resolution opportunity as a public service to address dealer/consumer disputes; works with new car dealers' associations and automobile importers who comply with the standards of the National Automobile Dealers Association; provides research findings on request; publishes a newsletter and a directory.
Publications: AUTOCAP Report; Automotive Customer Relations Directory
Founded: 1973

CAMPAIGN FOR HUMAN DEVELOPMENT
SEE SELF-HELP: TENANTS/RESIDENTS

CHALLENGE INTERNATIONAL
SEE COMMUNICATIONS & PUBLIC RELATIONS: HANDICAPPED

CITIZENS FOR SAFE DRIVERS AGAINST DRUNK DRIVERS/CHRONIC OFFENDERS
7401 McKenzie Court
Bethesda, MD 20817
TEL: 301-469-6282
Objectives: To prevent highway death and injury caused by problem drivers.
Services: Acts as a national information clearinghouse and communications network on state and federal legislation and research data; also acts as a self-help group for families and friends of highway crash victims.
Publications: UPDATE
Founded: 1976

CONFLICT RESOLUTION/ALTERNATIVES TO VIOLENCE CENTER
PO Box 256
Ricker House
Cherryfield, MD 20715
TEL: 301-262-0223
Objectives: To develop and sustain prisoner support groups in the United States and Canada.
Services: Develops and assists prisoner training and support groups in all aspects of criminal justice and prison environment, including conflict resolution and alternatives to violence; provides trained mediators for conflicts and conflict resolution training for prison staff; maintains referral service for resources available on alternatives to prison; conducts nonviolent workshops for prisons.
Founded: 1976

GOOD NEWS JAIL AND PRISON MINISTRIES INTERNATIONAL
SEE SELF-HELP: PRISONERS/EX-OFFENDERS

GRAY PANTHERS
SEE SELF-HELP: INTERGENERATIONAL

HABITAT FOR HUMANITY INTERNATIONAL
SEE VOLUNTEERS: CHURCH/SYNAGOGUE MEMBERS

NATIONAL ASSOCIATION FOR THE PHYSICALLY HANDICAPPED*

440 Lafayette Avenue
Suite 17
Cincinnati, OH 45220-1000
TEL: 614-852-1664
Objectives: To advance the social, economic, and physical welfare of the physically handicapped in the U.S.
Services: Serves as a self-help action group; operates through a committee structure with activities ranging from social to legislative to encouragement of employment of the handicapped and including housing, transportation and barrier-free design; supports chapters which provide services (especially recreation) not provided or minimally provided at the national level (bowling, wheelchair games, etc.); collects and studies data and information of special concern to the physically handicapped and publishes findings; proposes and supports legislation to provide more educational and rehabilitation opportunities, employment, tax relief and other benefits; provides programs which are not readily available otherwise, such as physical fitness and sports; promotes National Employ the Handicapped Week and, during that week, highlights the achievements of the successfully employed physically handicapped person (working to make it a year-round project); works to eliminate all architectural barriers to the handicapped. Cooperates with government agencies, civic groups, and organizations of the physically handicapped to develop programs; publishes *Bill of Rights for the Physically Handicapped* to encourage the handicapped to make full use of their rights, a newsletter, and other materials; convenes area meetings and area and national conventions to enable an information exchange to take place for the benefit of all concerned.
Publications: National Newsletter
Founded: 1958

NATIONAL ASSOCIATION FOR THE SOUTHERN POOR

(*formerly Virginia Community Development Organization*)
749B Delaware Avenue, SW
Washington, DC 20024
TEL: 202-554-3265
Objectives: To involve black, low-income individuals in decision-making that affects their lives.
Services: Creates local organizations, known as *Assemblies,* through which low-income people can gather and become involved in local decision-making regarding community services and opportunities; concentrates on organizing Southern blacks in an effort toward raising levels of health, education, and income; provides information on a number of issues; presents awards for outstanding participation; holds monthly meetings; publishes a monthly newsletter.
Publications: The Epistle
Founded: 1968

NATIONAL ASSOCIATION OF NEIGHBORHOODS
SEE COMMUNITY SERVICES

NATIONAL ASSOCIATION OF PEOPLE WITH AIDS
SEE VOLUNTEERS: PERSONS WITH AIDS

NATIONAL ASSOCIATION OF TOWN WATCH (*formerly National Town Watch Association*)

PO Box 303
Wynnewood, PA 19096
TEL: 215-649-7055
Objectives: To provide a nationwide community crime prevention network for groups and individuals participating in organized, police-affiliated volunteer crime watch programs.
Services: Enables members to communicate with volunteers outside of their own immediate areas, sharing ideas and programs, and other crime prevention ideas; works with law enforcement agencies and local leaders to compile and distribute materials; helps newly-formed Neighborhood Watch, Block Watch, Town Watch, Community Watch, Victim-Witness Programs, etc., to get started and to develop programs in crime prevention according to specific community needs; serves as an active member of the Crime Prevention Coalition in Washington, DC; addresses specific issues when appropriate (drunk driving, vandalism, etc.); sponsors annual *National Night Out* crime/drug prevention event; publishes a quarterly newsletter, a packet of information about the Association, and other materials.
Publications: New Spirit
Founded: 1981

NATIONAL COMMUNITY ORGANIZING PROJECT (NCOP)
SEE LEADERSHIP DEVELOPMENT/BOARDS: HOMELESS

NATIONAL PEER HELPERS ASSOCIATION

2370 Market Street #120
San Francisco, CA 94114
TEL: 415-626-1942
Objectives: To address the success of "peer pressure" and turn it to the benefit of individuals with problems through peer counseling.
Services: Encourages the establishment of peer-counseling programs in schools, universities, and community-based organizations; works to establish a standard of ethics for the field; conducts community education programs; provides information, support, and training to peer counselors; conducts research and compiles statistics for distribution; publishes a quarterly journal.
Publications: Peer Facilitator's Quarterly
Founded: 1986

NATIONAL SELF-HELP CLEARINGHOUSE
SEE SELF-HELP

NATIONAL SUPPORT CENTER FOR FAMILIES OF THE AGING

PO Box 245
Swarthmore, PA 19081
TEL: 215-544-3605
Objectives: To provide support and assistance for family members responsible for older persons.
Services: Seeks to educate the public about the realities of providing care for the aged; encourages formation of support groups to create a self-help network; assists families with decision-making in difficult situations; provides training for leaders in the field of aging; provides support, encouragement, and assistance to family members responsible for the care of an elderly person; provides speakers on request to community groups.
Founded: 1981

NEIGHBORHOODS USA
SEE LEADERSHIP DEVELOPMENT/BOARDS: TENANTS/RESIDENTS

OPPORTUNITIES INDUSTRIALIZATION CENTERS OF AMERICA

100 West Coulter Street
Philadelphia, PA 19144
TEL: 215-951-2200
Objectives: To apply the self-help philosophy in using job training and placement to improve the lives of the hard core unemployed and underemployed, as well as the community.
Services: Trains people in 110 different vocational categories to fill job openings of local employers; provides counseling, remediation, skills training and placement; works with the entire family of the

participant to strengthen family members' ties with each other and with the community; operates National Industrial Advisory Council, which is composed of top executives of 37 major business corporations; sponsors projects for minority high school students; maintains extensive library; publishes quarterly newsletter and annual journal.

PARENTS ANONYMOUS
SEE VOLUNTEERS: PARENTS

PEOPLE WITH AIDS COALITION
SEE VOLUNTEERS: PERSONS WITH AIDS

PROJECT VOLUNTEER
880 Eighty-first Street
Oakland, CA 94621
TEL: 415-562-0290
Objectives: To establish a viable alternative to the welfare system through participation of the disadvantaged being served.
Services: Promotes cooperative activities that identify and utilize existing materials and human resources for social benefit; works with community service, religious, and educational organizations, senior citizens projects, community self-help programs, churches and ministers' associations, community-minded citizens, drug rehabilitation centers, and volunteers; seeks to establish a viable alternative to the welfare system through the participation of those being served and through a network of cooperating private sector churches and community organizations; conducts food redistribution programs, providing nonprofit organizations with three million pounds of food annually; sponsors environmental research and conferences, and awards commendations for outstanding contributions to the goals of the organization.
Founded: 1978

RECOVERY, INC.
Association of Nervous & Former Mental Patients
802 North Dearborn Street
Chicago, IL 60610
TEL: 312-337-5661
Objectives: To help prevent relapses in former mental patients and to forestall chronicity in nervous patients.
Services: Conducts weekly meetings throughout the country to bring together patients for a self-help recovery program; functions as a lay group (although program was developed by a professional); publishes *Directory of Group Meeting Information* for referral purposes by programs in the field; holds semi-annual meetings.
Publications: Recovery Reporter
Founded: 1937

STUDENTS AGAINST DRIVING DRUNK (SADD)
SEE VOLUNTEERS: STUDENTS

TRAINING PROGRAMS

HANDICAPPED VOLUNTEER/VOLUNTEERING FOR THE HANDICAPPED
SEE SELF-HELP

PARENTS EDUCATING PARENTS: TRAINING PROGRAM
Association for Retarded Citizens of Georgia
1851 Ram Runway
Suite 104
College Park, GA 30337
TEL: 404-761-2745

Description: This training program is designed for parents of handicapped children who need help and information in working with teachers and other professionals to educate their handicapped children. The program includes formal workshops, individual apprenticeships, and demonstration activities. Workshops include:
- **Basic Workshop** - Trains parents and professionals on P.L. 94-142, Section 504 and Educational Programming, and *How to Better Communicate with School Personnel.*
- **Parent Leader Workshop** - Trains parents to set up and carry out a *Basic PEP Workshop,* and assists parents in their community.
- **Communication** - Focuses on parent-professional communication with emphasis on techniques for effective participation in the IEP process. Listening, negotiation, assertiveness and letter writing skills are taught in this workshop.
- **Awareness and Sensitivity Presentations** - Trains children, adults, professionals, and lay persons how to improve attitudes toward persons with handicapping conditions.
- **Coalition Building Workshop** - Focuses on problem solving, advocacy, parent support and networking techniques.
- **Transition** - Assists parents in long-term planning, how to undertand the IWRP plans, and how to familiarize the service systems beyond that of education.
- **Preschool** - Addresses the needs of parents of young children in regard to P.L. 99-457.
- **Least Reflective Environment** - Trains parents on different strategies for successful integration of students with handicaps.
- **Strategies** - Focuses on methods for effectively accessing services through the IEP process, communication techniques in the IEP setting, letter writing, and due process procedures.
- **Mediation** - How to use mediation as a means to avoid due process hearings.
- **Related Services** - Explains Related Services in Georgia as defined in P.L. 94-142, and specifically addresses assessment, eligibility, and the development of appropriate IEP goals.
- **IEP Clinic** - Assists parents by helping them develop a better understanding of their children with special needs' school records, evaluations, and other pertinent documents.
- **Metro/Area Mini Series** - Provides additional support to parents and professionals. The series provides ongoing topical information sharing on a monthly basis.

All trainees receive training manuals and other workshop materials for use during the session and as a continuing reference. Some materials are available in other languages, including Spanish, Khmer, and Lao.
Individuals who have completed the training join in a statewide network of parents and professionals working together toward a common goal for children with special needs. Networking groups include parent contacts, local ARC units, key support groups, consumer groups and service providers. PEP is primarily a parent information center and is a part of a parent support network throughout the United States.
Publications: PEP Training Manuals; PEP Talk

THE SELF-HELP MOVEMENT: NEW FORM OF VOLUNTEERISM AND A RESOURCE FOR PROFESSIONALS*
SEE SELF-HELP

INDIVIDUAL PROGRAM PROFILES

AD SUPPORT GROUP OF GREATER ALABAMA
Alzheimer's Disease & Related Disorders Association
Greater Mobile Chapter
1700 Center Street
Mobile, AL 36604
TEL: 205-438-4551

Purpose: To help family members of a victim of Alzheimer's Disease to cope.
Sponsor: Alzheimer's Disease and Related Disorders Association (national)
Contact: Clifton Vernon Weldy
Description: There are an estimated 2,000 AD (Alzheimer's Disease) patients in Mobile County, and about 1,000 cases in Baldwin County. Neither cause nor cure is known for this progressive disease. Opinions vary from a slow-growing virus, to accelerated aging, to immune system breakdown or hereditary or environmental causes. The only thing scientists know for certain is that it is characterized by chemical changes in the brain. AD is characterized by loss of memory, personality changes, and loss of speech and understanding, culminating in loss of control of body functions. It has been diagnosed in patients as young as 28, and statistics show that 5-8 percent of the nation's over-65 population have the disease. Over 80, statistics reach 20 percent.
County records show that primary caregivers in the family sometimes disappear under the strains of caring for an AD patient. As one caregiver said, "The doctor didn't tell us how bad it was going to get." To try to counteract this burnout syndrome, a local chapter of the *Alzheimer's Disease and Related Disorders Association (ADRDA)* helped volunteers organize a support group for caregivers in the Greater Mobile area.
It is not known how many caregivers have been kept with their AD family member because of the program, but many have stated that the support group made the difference. Many of the members become volunteers - with one retired man becoming a 40-hour volunteer treasurer and bookkeeper. He said he felt he had to do more for the group, since "The group has kept me alive." He is also one of the key players in establishing other support groups in Washington, Clarke, Conecuh, Wilcox, Escambia, Covington and Monroe Counties.
The self-help group meets regularly and provides the opportunity to share information, solutions, experiences, and other aspects of the patient-caregiver relationship. Services from the national ADRDA include chapter development and a toll-free hotline for information and consultation.
Founded: 1983

AIDS CHRONIC CARE UNIT VOLUNTEER PROGRAM
SEE VOLUNTEERS: TEAMS

CABRILLO VILLAGE
Cabrillo Improvement Association
PO Box 4216
1515 South Saticoy Avenue
Saticoy, CA 93003
TEL: 805-659-3791
Purpose: To increase the capacity of local farmworkers to own, maintain, and take pride in the housing in their community.
Sponsor: Church and business organizations; Farmworkers Union; Government Agencies; Cabrillo Cooperative Housing Corporation
Contact: Rodney Fernandez
Description: Faced with eviction from their camp due to substandard housing, a small group of farmworkers organized to seek alternatives. Most families had lived in the community for many years, working in the nearby citrus groves. The owner decided to evict the residents rather than rehabilitate the housing. Groups concerned with farmworkers' housing had long existed in the area (church groups, business organizations, the Farmworkers Union, government agencies, etc.), and offered to help the farmworkers form their own nonprofit organization. Cabrillo Improvement Association was born, and the land was purchased from the owner.
The next step was to "revitalize" the community, and it was determined that this would have to include new housing. The Cabrillo Cooperative Housing Corporation (CCHC) was formed to pursue this goal, and successfully applied for financing to build

thirty-five multi-family dwellings. Applying this loan and grant money to a farmworkers' cooperative housing project was a "first" for FmHA's Multi-Family Housing Division.
As the project evolved, Cabrillo developed a list of "firsts" for such a venture:
- passive solar design and solar hot water systems for new farmworker housing.
- rehabilitating the existing houses through special training programs.
- operating a ceramic tile factory, a cabinet shop, and a co-op food store.
- developing a contracting business for housing rehab in other communities.

This massive volunteer effort has had an exciting side effect. With the skills and knowledge developed, Cabrillo residents are reaching out to help others. With the assistance of the Rural Community Assistance Corporation in Sacramento, California, they have developed a training workshop where resource people provide information on self-help housing, mobile homes, manufactured homes and multi-family units. Trainers help participants explore pros and cons of home ownership, cooperatives and rental housing options. By helping farmworker communities with roots much like their own, Cabrillo is contributing to a better quality of life for the general farmworker population.

CITIZENS' CRIME WATCH OF DADE COUNTY
5220 Biscayne Boulevard
Room 200
Miami, FL 33137
TEL: 305-756-0582
Purpose: To educate the community in crime prevention, bring neighbors closer together and improve communication between police and citizens.
Sponsor: Citizens' Crime Watch of Dade County Inc. (CCWDCI)
Contact: Nancy Burdelsky
Description: Citizens' Crime Watch of Dade County, Inc. (CCWDCI) is a Neighborhood Watch Program with the concept of "People to People Protection." The basic goals of CCWDCI are twofold. First, to educate people about crime prevention - home security, in particular; and secondly, to implement a telephone chain in the neighborhood - a means of communication whereby neighbors can alert each other to criminal or suspicious activity in the area and also whereby they can receive information from the police on a periodic basis.
Volunteer Staff - The Program Executive Committee oversees the day-to-day operation of CCWDCI and makes policy decisions, but the key people are the District (unincorporated Dade County is divided into six districts by the Metro Dade Police Department) and City Chairmen.
Volunteer Duties - These Chairmen are responsible for arranging for speakers and setting up presentations in neighborhoods desiring to start a Citizens' Crime Watch. These Chairmen are also responsible for maintaining records and insuring neighborhood telephone chains remain active.
Under these District and City Chairmen are Neighborhood Chairmen who are responsible for anywhere from two to ten or more blocks.
If a Citizens' Crime Watcher spots a criminal or suspicious action, person, vehicle, etc., they immediately contact their local police department. They then contact their Block Captain who passes the information to the other Citizens' Crime Watchers on the block. Once a telephone chain is established, information can flow in either direction, up or down the chain.
In addition, various groups of citizens volunteer to work on committees such as Youth Crime Watch, Sexual Assault, Speakers Bureau, Safe Homes and Assaults on Police Officers.
Cooperation with different police departments is vital and the cooperation is very good. They see citizen involvement as an integral part of crime prevention as the population continues to

rapidly expand and police departments are unable to increase their manpower accordingly. Each district or city has one or two Crime Prevention Officers (CPO) who work with the district or city chairman.

When a presentation for a neighborhood is arranged, a Citizens' Crime Watch Speaker is sent and, whenever possible, a CPO. A nine minute film is shown to introduce people to CCWDCI. The Crime Prevention Officer speaks to the people about home security - proper lighting, proper locks and other items on a security survey checklist to try to make a home as burglar-proof as possible. The speaker from Citizens' Crime Watch talks about the history of the program and explains the actual implementation of the telephone chain and stresses the importance of participation.

Speakers make sure the citizens understand that participation is not that of becoming physically involved with a suspect, but participation through observing and reporting.

CCWDCI relies on donations of services and financial contributions from the private sector for its funding.

CITIZENS ORGANIZED PATROL EFFORTS (COPE)
Shaw Neighborhood Advisory Committee
1726 Seventh Street, NW
Washington, DC 20001
TEL: 202-332-4800
Purpose: To create a drug-free neighborhood.
Contact: Project Coordinator
Description: On June 2, 1989, a group of eight citizens with white and red uniforms, walkie-talkies "and opening night jitters" hit the streets of the Shaw neighborhood of Washington, DC, to begin a new daily patrol. The patrol, meant to dispel drug traffickers, discourage buyers and reassure law-abiding residents, was founded by the neighborhood advisory commissioner, who had sponsored anti-drug marches in the neighborhood for the previous six months. During those rallies, residents trailed suspected drug dealers and stood in front of houses chanting, "This is a crack house!" The patrol was devised to make this effort more visible and intensify what the marchers had accomplished.

Although several dozen residents were expected to sign up for the patrol, only eight enlisted. Undaunted, they donned their uniforms and began the patrol, passing out literature and admonishing drug and alcohol abusers along the way. Most people accept the literature, while others turn away. One former drug dealer just returning from prison cited the effort as well-intentioned, but too dangerous. He said the dealers won't pay attention unless the patrol member says the wrong thing, then they will "just blow him away." The patrol continues without major confrontation and feels that their small effort should mak· a difference in the long run. Uniforms and walkie-talkies were provided by a local contractor who plans to build a shopping center in the neighborhood.
Founded: 1989

DONCASTER YOUTH CHALLENGE, A.K.A. SNEAKER CAMP
SEE SELF-HELP: CHILDREN/YOUTH

FAMILY SUPPORT GROUP
Los Angeles Police Department
Central Office
251 East Sixth Street
Los Angeles, CA 90014
TEL: 213-485-6586
Purpose: To keep communication open between the Police Department and the widows of slain officers.
Sponsor: Los Angeles Police Department
Contact: Chief Daryl Gates
Description: In the mid 1980s, the Los Angeles Police Department realized that, in spite of various efforts, they were losing touch with widows and families of slain police officers. The Department felt it was very important that the survivors were kept constantly aware of the Department's continuing concern for their welfare. It was decided that a support group sponsored by the Department would bring together those of similar circumstances who understand the pain and grief. The Chief appointed a female detective to begin getting the support group organized. Currently there are 35 members, 20 of whom are very active. The group is essentially a "sisterhood" that helps sustain women's nurturing, caretaking roles. The understanding friendship between the women is a unique relationship.

Over the years the group has evolved into a sophisticated organization with specific goals. Speakers and guests are brought in to meetings to discuss topics on various subjects such as recovery, family dysfunction, etc. The basic approach is to guide and assist in whatever the needs of the widow are, but the general coverage is at the common emotion of grief.

Support meetings are held once a month, and have succeeded in the initial goal of keeping families of slain officers in the "Police Department family."

FARE SHARE
807 Hampden Avenue
St. Paul, MN 55114
TEL: 612-644-6003
Purpose: To provide food for the needy through a central effort that distributes prepared bags of food to sites in several adjoining states.
Sponsor: SHARE-USA
Contact: Mimi Sands, Director
Description: Once each month, for one week, part of a total of 275 volunteers count, sort and stack food. The work culminates in thousands of identical grocery bags to be shipped to 312 host sites in 89 counties in Minnesota, Iowa, Wisconsin and the Dakotas, to be picked up from there by 42,000 individual participants. The food, worth $28 to $35 at retail, costs participants $12 and two hours of community service. The $12 contribution pays all expenses; no public money is involved.

When the Fare SHARE was launched in 1986, the program distributed some 2,000 food packages. By contrast, the 1988 total was 21.4 million pounds and 1,223,162 hours of donated service. Service can take almost any form. Although warehouse volunteers are a key to keeping costs down, most volunteering takes place in the wider community. Participants earn credit working with scouts, at-risk students and elderly neighbors. They clean parks, shelve library books and register voters, paint curbs, coach Little Leagues and counsel battered women. One volunteer designed her own community service - clipping 2,000 grocery coupons, sorting them and bringing them to the warehouse for others at each month's marathon food bagging - another form of self-help and resource exchange, which is the heart of the program.

A side benefit is the family involvement that takes place. In one instance, a five-year-old helps her mother fill measuring cups to put together ingredients for recipes. A young man going to chef's school helps maintain recipe integrity with his expertise. Girl Scouts of eight and nine earn merit badges, and members of a church singles group participates as a team.

Fare SHARE is the largest in a network of 16 SHARE-USA programs in the country. According to the director, "A sense of community builds among the strangers who work at Fare SHARE tables or loading Fare SHARE trucks."
Founded: 1986

GIFT TO THE CITY
SEE VOLUNTEERS: CHURCH/SYNAGOGUE MEMBERS

GLEANING*
Idaho Hunger Action Council
621 North Eighth Street
Boise, ID 83702-5518
TEL: 208-336-7010

Purpose: To harvest the left-overs in Idaho fields.
Sponsor: Titcomb President Bishop's Fund
Contact: Peter Benedict
Description: This program organizes groups of low income people into gleaning crews. The crews consist of gleaners and partners. Gleaners do the work and partners are either disabled, senior citizens, or provide child care for the gleaners. Each gleaning team has a partner organization. The organization may be a church or other group which provides free lunches, soup kitchens, or other free food services. The food is divided by the gleaners for the partners and partners' organizations.
The gleaning project started in 1979. Today, there are 22 local gleaner coordinators in the state which harvested 91 tons of food last year. The program goal is to top 100 tons this year with 1,000 gleaners.
Other sponsors include the Presbyterian Hunger Project and the Community Service Block Grant.
Founded: 1979

GREEN COUNTRIE TOWNE PROGRAM
SEE VOLUNTEERS: TENANTS/RESIDENTS

GREEN LINE ACTION ASSOCIATION
SEE BUSINESS/INDUSTRY INVOLVEMENT: ENTREPRENEURSHIP

HABITAT FOR HUMANITY OF RHODE ISLAND
SEE VOLUNTEERS: CHURCH/SYNAGOGUE MEMBERS

KIDS HELPING KIDS
SEE SELF-HELP: DRUGS/ALCOHOL

LOS ANGELES POVERTY DEPARTMENT (LAPD)
SEE COMMUNICATIONS & PUBLIC RELATIONS: IMAGE

LOUDOUN HOUSE
715-16 Edwards Ferry Road
Leesburg, VA 22075
TEL: 703-777-7303
Purpose: To develop and implement outreach programs, and to improve security and maintenance at the facility.
Sponsor: National Housing Partnership; Loudoun House Tenant Organization
Contact: Georgia Coates
Description: Loudoun House has 248 apartment units and more than 620 residents. It stands amidst million-dollar estates, horse farms and historic battlefields. It is owned by the *National Housing Partnership,* a Washington, DC, firm that manages and owns low- and moderate-income housing around the country. In recent years it has become a haven for drug trafficking, attracting buyers and sellers from around the region. It has been the scene of occasional brawls, and has continuous maintenance problems.
In early 1989, however, a number of the residents have begun a concerted effort to change life at Loudoun House. They are actively working with the owner, with the complex's resident manager meeting with the vice president of the *Partnership* and the tenant organization's president. The outcome of the meetings led to the first community projects:

- **Loudoun House Reading Center** - a community library. Within a few weeks the Center had acquired over 500 donated books on subjects ranging from religion to romance as well as back issues of Ebony and National Geographic magazines. Donations have come from county residents, libraries and other local groups. Within the first week, 60 residents signed registration forms to check out books.
- **Positive Youth Works** - a tutorial program. Two nights a week a group operated by several Loudoun House and county residents help children learn to read and do their homework.

- **Other programs** - a crime watch program, job counseling workshops, drug awareness seminars and cardiopulmonary resuscitation classes.

In addition, residents are appealing to the town Parks and Recreation department to provide activities for the project's numerous children, particularly since the complex's swimming pool has been closed down for five years (with estimated repair costs of $100,000). One alternative came from the supervisor of the county's *Big Friends* program, who arranged for transportation to local and Washington area parks and zoos for the children. He has also been instrumental in registering children for summer camp and scholarship programs.
At the top of the list is getting rid of the project's drug problems, which have resulted in numerous arrests and several drug raids in recent years according to Loudoun County police. To supplement the residents' crime watch efforts, the owners are paying a private security force $10,000 a month to patrol the property's ground and report on drug dealers and trespassers. The local police captain and the deputy sheriff both feel that the security force has stopped some of the drug trade, but find it is still an active area. The company has set a 10:00 p.m. curfew for residents and is planning to lease the Plaza Street Park from the town - a small playground adjacent to the complex which is filled with children during the day and drug activities at night. It is expected that the leasing of the park will bring about better control and subsequent elimination of the night-time activity.
The tenant organization has 35 very active residents who attend every meeting and are helping to assure that the volunteer efforts already begun are maintained, and that new projects are mounted as the need surfaces and time and resources permit. Much of this enthusiasm and progress is related to the spirit of cooperation between the residents, owners, police, and the town, according to a tenant organization spokesperson.

MENDED HEARTS
Chapter #36
18 North Grant Street
Westmont, IL 60559
TEL: 312-968-3313
Purpose: To enlist the help of persons who have undergone heart surgery to help other heart surgery patients and their spouses.
Sponsor: Mended Hearts, Chapter #36
Contact: Mrs. Rita V. Zimmer, President
Description: This is an all-volunteer effort whose objective is to visit and encourage, with the approval of a physician, persons anticipating or recovering from heart surgery; to distribute information of specific educational value to members of Mended Hearts, Inc., and to potential heart surgery patients; to counsel and provide advice and services, where possible, to families of patients undergoing heart surgery; to establish a program of assistance to surgeons, physicians and hospitals in their work with heart patients; to cooperate with other organizations in educational and research activities pertaining to heart illness; to establish and to assist in established rehabilitation programs for Mended Hearts and their families; to plan and conduct suitable programs of social and educational events.
There are approximately 125 chapters throughout the United States with the National headquarters being in Dallas, Texas. Persons interested in founding a chapter, particularly those residing in areas where heart surgery is performed, can receive information from the program.

MID-VALLEY ADOLESCENT CENTER*
SEE BUSINESS/INDUSTRY INVOLVEMENT: CRIME PREVENTION

MOTHERS OF PWAS (PERSONS WITH AIDS)
SEE SELF-HELP: PARENTS

MOTOR VOTERS
1350 Beverly Rd
Suite 115-240
McLean, VA 22101
TEL: 703-448-0002
Purpose: To educate the public on car quality and safety.
Contact: Rosemary Dunlap
Description: Motor Voters was formed after one dissatisfied car owner picketed a dealership for six months in an attempt to get her car repaired properly. Although the dealer finally "did the right thing," the car owner saw a need for a support group to help avoid similar ordeals for others. Today, the organization's volunteers lobby the Virginia General Assembly on consumer issues, negotiate with interest groups including auto manufacturers, banks and the insurance industry.

A major goal of the volunteer group is to achieve enactment of consumer disclosure legislation that would require that manufacturers of vans, minivans, light trucks and pickups to tell potential buyers that these vehicles are not required to meet a number of federal safety standards mandated for personal cars - especially important since some of these vehicles are becoming increasingly popular for family use. For example, vans may not provide as much protection if struck broadside or if they roll over, and they may not have automatic seat belts or air bags.

Pro-consumer legislators and advocates came very close in the 1989-90 session to enacting such legislation. It would have been the first state law of its kind in the country. It easily passed the state Senate, but car manufacturers rushed in their lobbyists before it reached the House Roads and Navigation Committee where it was defeated.

Consumer advocates, however, feel that much progress has been made - against long odds - through their volunteer efforts, especially in a number of consumer credit and insurance bills, which they feel certain will be approved in the 1990-91 session. In the President's words, "We don't always win. You have to keep coming back over and over again... persistence counts for a lot on consumer issues."
Founded: 1985

MULTIPLE SCLEROSIS SOCIETY OF ORANGE COUNTY
SEE VOLUNTEERS: HANDICAPPED

OIC NATIONAL SHELTER PROGRAM
Opportunities Industrialization Centers of America
100 West Coulter Street
Philadelphia, PA 19144
TEL: 215-951-2200
Purpose: To build 100 shelters in troubled inner cities to provide housing, clothing, remedial education, job training and counseling programs.
Sponsor: OIC of America
Contact: The Rev. Leon H. Sullivan, Founder, or Elton Jolly, President
Description: A nationwide program announced in May 1989 by OIC (Opportunities Industrialization Centers of America) involves working with its 70 national centers to build 100 shelters in inner cities. In addition to the homeless, target groups include drug addicts, ex-convicts and gang members.

To encourage response, OIC offers $20,000 in seed money to each of the first five cities to participate in the project, requesting that shelters be completed in six months. The city of Philadelphia was among the first to volunteer. By mid-1989, other affiliates who volunteered to build shelters were Delaware County, Pennsylvania; Flint, Michigan; Montgomery, Alabama; Detroit, Milwaukee and Minneapolis. Labor unions assist by volunteering to build the centers in vacant storefronts and abandoned buildings.

All shelters are staffed by volunteers, including doctors and psychiatrists who commit to 24-hour medical and counseling services. Recruitment areas include the business community,

colleges, churches, and OIC training centers. Funding comes from philanthropic foundations, local and federal government, churches and private donors.

The inspiration for the program came from recent reports that 25% of the U.S. population were drug or alcohol abusers and that perhaps as many as two million people were homeless. In addition to beds, the shelters provide counseling for drug addicts, food for the hungry, and reading and writing instruction, with heavy emphasis on self-help.

OIC was started 25 years ago by a Zion Baptist Church pastor in an abandoned jail in North Philadelphia as a self-help job training program. To date it has trained over a million people, and is in place in 13 foreign countries. The same pastor contributed the first $1,000 to the current shelter program.
Founded: 1974

PARENTS EDUCATING PARENTS
1851 Ram Runway
Suite 104
College Park, GA 30337
TEL: 404-761-3150; 404-761-2745
Purpose: To provide parents with necessary information to insure their participation in planning, provision, monitoring of special education for handicapped children in Georgia through Public Law 94-142 and other laws.
Sponsor: Georgia Association for Retarded Citizens
Contact: Cheryl D. Knight
Description: Parents Educating Parents (PEP) began June 1, 1980, after receiving a grant from the Office of Special Education sponsored by the *Georgia Association for Retarded Citizens.* The statewide project's goal is to provide parents with necessary information and training on *P.L. 94-142* to insure their meaningful participation in the planning, provision, and monitoring of special education to handicapped children in Georgia.

Currently, the PEP Project is operating as the parent training component of the *University Affiliated Facility (UAF)* at the *University of Georgia.* Funding comes from the *U.S. Department of Education* through its *Handicapped Personnel Preparation Program.*

PEP believes that receiving an education is every child's right. Handicapped children are no exception. Public Law 94-142 mandates that all handicapped children must have available to them, "a free appropriate public education designed to meet their unique needs and that handicapped children must be educated in a least restrictive environment."

The philosophy of PEP is that parents can educate parents. PEP believes parents can make an important contribution to the education of their children since they possess unique information about their child's development, nature and needs. Therefore, parents can become effective partners with teachers in reinforcing activities and skills acquisition which occur during the school day.
Project goals are:
- To set up an educational advocacy network throughout Georgia, composed of parents and contact people in local areas, to assist parents of handicapped children.
- To establish a viable partnership between local education agencies (LEA), state education agencies (SEA), and parent advocacy organizations.
- To assist parents in exercising their rights under P.L. 94-142 by providing them with specific competencies gained in terms of negotiation and assertiveness skills.
- To foster more meaningful parent participation in individualized education plans (IEP) development to insure that each child's educational program is based on needs rather than available resources.
- To teach parents the special education and legal vocabulary in order to insure true and accurate communication between parent and teacher.
- To promote understanding and awareness concerning the

specific sections of P.L. 94-142 that relate to parent participation.
- To prepare and disseminate to parents and others the *Education Update* six times per year as a continuing education tool (circulation currently 3,700).

The PEP Project has conducted workshops and training for parents (see separate entry); maintains a resource library accessible by phone or mail; provides printed information through its *Education Update, PEP Notebooks,* training manuals, copies of laws, etc.; and provides technical assistance to parents throughout the state as well as to educators and to advocates.
Publications: The Education Update; PEP Information Packet; PEP Training Manuals; PEP Talk; Awareness Coloring Book (Spanish); Avanzando (Spanish)
Founded: 1980

PATERSON HABITAT FOR HUMANITY
SEE VOLUNTEERS: CHURCH/SYNAGOGUE MEMBERS

PERSON TO PERSON*
SEE VOLUNTEERS: PARENTS

PROJECT OPPORTUNITY
Bryant Adult Community Education Center
2709 Popkins Lane
Mount Vernon, VA 22121
TEL: 703-768-0526
Purpose: To help pregnant girls or parenting girls complete high school.
Contact: Elizabeth Link, Program Coordinator
Description: During the 1989-90 school year, a state-funded program in Fairfax County requiring voluntary participation attracted 37 pregnant teenagers and young mothers - ages 13 to 21 - who had given up hope of completing their high school educations. They come from all social and economic backgrounds. Most had dropped out of school and the rest were considering doing so due to pressures of pregnancy and motherhood.
The basic objective of the program is to help pregnant or parenting girls complete high school. The program offers adult education credits, which can be accumulated faster than regular high school credits, for the courses needed to graduate. The program also requires that the students take life skills development classes, which include child development, family living and management skills. In addition, they are required to take career development classes, such as computer training.
In response to detractors who feel that the program encourages pregnancy, officials refer to the hardships endured by participants to complete the program. "Just getting to school is their biggest problem." They must first "feed the baby, get the baby to day care, then catch the bus to school." As other youngsters see the young girls struggle, program leaders feel that, although offering an alternative, the program discourages rather than encourages pregnancy.
The voluntary entry policy, and the fact that the students complete the course in spite of the pressure, is encouraging to school officials. It is a self-help program, with no one being forced to complete the course. The young women say its most positive aspect is the supportive environment from the other participants as well as the part-time staff that runs the program.
Part of the program's support comes in the form of flexibility if a student must stay home with a sick baby, or if she is ill or has a doctor's appointment during the pregnancy. However, according to officials, what the young women need most is an adult with whom they can ask questions and talk about their problems without being judged. A big problem with them is that - in 80% of the cases - the baby's father is not interested and makes himself scarce. "They talk about that a lot," one leader said.
Project Opportunity, in its third year, is one of nine such programs in Virginia. It is financed by a $35,000 grant from the *Virginia*

Department of Education's Vocational Gender Equity Office.
Program leaders must reapply each year for the money.
One example of the effect of the program on the youth is the 17-year-old who has a 2-1/2-year-old son and had felt that this would "hold her back from everything." She is on her way to college with the goal of becoming an Air Force officer. Another student is heading for Catholic University with a full four-year scholarship.
The "bottom line" surfaced in a "rap session" among five students and three staff members. The participants said they want to be called "young adults because of their experience as mothers."
Project Opportunity is fulfilling its goals as a growth experience.

PUBLIC ASSISTANCE CLIENTS VOLUNTEER
Broome County Department of Social Services
36-38 Main Street
Binghamton, NY 13905
TEL: 607-772-2681
Purpose: To provide an opportunity for ego building, an interim step to seeking employment, a chance to give service.
Sponsor: Broome County Department of Social Services
Contact: Alice Manter, Director of Volunteers
Description: All clients interested in volunteering are interviewed. Some take the initiative themselves; others are referred by case workers, examiners, or community workers. Many clients have developed skills and self-confidence and some have become gainfully employed as a result of volunteering. Money for bus transportation, coffee and soda as well as lunch - if the volunteer works through the lunch hour - is provided.
All Food Stamps Authorization to Purchase Cards are put into envelopes monthly by volunteers who may receive Food Stamps, Medicaid or Supplemental Security Income. Thousands of notices, letters, and informational pieces are folded and stuffed. A rehabilitation group of former psychiatric patients work on large mailings at their meeting place and senior citizens also work on large jobs at their housing complexes.
When it is determined that specific skills or interests of the volunteer would be best served elsewhere in the community, an appointment is set up with the appropriate nursing home, general hospital, Blind Workshop, Voluntary Action Center, Meals on Wheels, the YWCA, etc.
Broome County Social Services uses over 500 volunteers a year to assist any worker who requests supplemental help. The program is in its eleventh year under a Director of Volunteers and is an integral part of the Department's overall service structure.
Big Brothers and Sisters share several hours weekly with children who need a friend. A Saturday Afternoon Recreation Program is operated jointly with University students and provides sports and enrichment to 80 children. Other services include Friendly Visiting, tutoring, language interpreting, Polaroid identification cards, parties and picnics, Case Aides, Interns, receptionists, Camperships, clerk and sorting of mail into zip code areas.

REHAB PROJECT: NEIGHBORHOOD REVITALIZATION THROUGH HOME OWNERSHIP
SEE VOLUNTEERS: CHURCH/SYNAGOGUE MEMBERS

ROBERTS PARK AND PLAYGROUND/LANTRIP SCHOOL PARK*
SEE BUSINESS/INDUSTRY INVOLVEMENT: RECREATION/SPORTS

SECURITY ALERT GROUP - THREE LINK TOWERS (SAG)
SEE VOLUNTEERS: OLDER PERSONS

SHARE SELF-HELP AND RESOURCE EXCHANGE
SEE VOLUNTEERS: CHURCH/SYNAGOGUE MEMBERS

SO SAD (SAVE OUR SONS AND DAUGHTERS)
SEE VOLUNTEERS: PARENTS

SPIRIT AND BREATH VOLUNTEER PROGRAM
Spirit and Breath Association
8210 Elmwood Avenue
Suite 209
Skokie, IL 60077
TEL: 708-673-1384
Purpose: To provide mutual support, rehabilitation, emotional and physical support to people who have had lung cancer.
Sponsor: Grants, private sector and private donations
Contact: Morton J. Liebling, Director and Founder
Description: Spirit and Breath was conceived in early 1978. Presently there is a hospital volunteer/patient visiting program at Lutheran General Hospital in Park Ridge Illinois where the patient is introduced to the Spirit and Breath program. This program is sponsored by the American Cancer Society.
There are presently twelve volunteer visitors. Coordinators and volunteers must have had lung cancer and be in good physical shape. Their surgery must have been done a minimum of three years prior to their application to become a volunteer.
The Spirit and Breath Lung Cancer Program was conceived and developed by Morton Liebling in 1979, after he lost his left lung to cancer in 1978. In the absence of any rehabilitation procedure, he found it necessary to build a program to help himself.
The exercises he developed were put into booklet form, which is published and distributed by the Illinois American Cancer Society. Mr. Liebling also conducts group meetings with people with lung cancer.
The goals of Spirit and Breath are to obtain volunteers who are professionals to conduct both land and pool exercise programs.
In summary, this organization is dedicated to creating a positive atmosphere of well-being for people with lung cancer so that they might lead normal productive lives.
Founded: 1978

ST. JOSEPH'S HOUSE OF HOSPITALITY
SEE VOLUNTEERS: CHURCH/SYNAGOGUE MEMBERS

STUDENT HABITAT FOR HUMANITY
SEE VOLUNTEERS: STUDENTS

SUBSTANCE ABUSE TREATMENT CENTER AND SHELTER
Alexandria Mental Health and Substance Abuse Board
Alexandria Community Shelter
2355 Mill Road
Alexandria, VA 22314
TEL: 703-329-2000
Purpose: To combine temporary housing for the homeless with a treatment facility for substance abuse.
Sponsor: Salvation Army
Contact: Captain Steve Smith
Description: The grand plan of including temporary housing for the homeless with a treatment facility has worked well for the Alexandria, Virginia, area. The Alexandria Community Shelter with 65 beds for homeless persons has included a facility in its operation which provides 35 beds for homeless persons suffering from substance abuse. Opening in February 1989, the facility was filled immediately, demonstrating the urgent need for this service. Eleven weeks later 268 persons had been admitted to its residential detoxification program, with 423 active outpatients.
The shelter's comprehensive treatment program consolidated services that were previously scattered throughout the city. Included in the treatment are
• individual and group counseling
• frequent meetings by Alcoholics Anonymous, Narcotics

Anonymous, and other support groups
The convenience of the dual effort has prompted more patients who once sought only medication also to participate in support therapy. According to the director, "Clients go both ways." If someone appears at the shelter who is drunk or high, he or she is sent to the detox program. Those completing the detox program are sent to the shelter for interim housing.
Monitored by Alexandria's mental health and substance abuse board, the program received City funding of $593,000 for its first full fiscal year beginning July 1, 1989. The Salvation Army operates the program.
Founded: 1989

SUMMIT SHOCK INCARCERATION FACILITY
SEE VOLUNTEERS: PRISONERS/EX-OFFENDERS

SUNDIAL VOLUNTEERS
SEE VOLUNTEERS: CHURCH/SYNAGOGUE MEMBERS

TENANT OWNERSHIP/MANAGEMENT PROGRAM
SEE VOLUNTEERS: TENANTS/RESIDENTS

VOLUNTEERS: STAFF SUPPORT

INDIVIDUAL PROGRAM PROFILES

POLICE DEPARTMENT VOLUNTEER PROGRAM
Costa Mesa Police Department
99 Fair Drive
Costa Mesa, CA 92626
TEL: 714-953-5757
Purpose: To relieve police officers of tasks that can be done by others so they can give full attention to tasks needing trained officers.
Sponsor: Costa Mesa Police Department
Contact: Lynn Spear Merles
Description: Sixteen volunteers logged 313 hours in one month at the Costa Mesa Police Department helping police aides write citations on street-sweeping runs, assisting officers with clerical duties, and supporting Neighborhood Watch Programs. The majority of the volunteers come from the *Retired Senior Volunteer Program,* a program sponsored by the *Volunteer Center of Orange County.*
Once it was decided to install the volunteer program, two months of planning was spent deciding where volunteers could best serve the department. Many tasks surfaced that could be done by anyone and did not require a trained officer's time. These included purging records, since most records are destroyed after five years, putting citations on vehicles blocking city street sweepers, helping in the library, and a host of other tasks. Some jobs carry more responsibility than others. For example, records relating to robbery and murder are kept longer than five years, so the volunteers are trained to be very careful in the purging of files. Also, volunteers are briefed on the importance of confidentiality in handling information.
Volunteers come from as far away as El Toro to the south and Long Beach to the north to help the officers. But the officers are not the only beneficiaries of the program. According to one volunteer, "I was so bored when I was not working. I love it here."
Founded: 1988

PROBATION VOLUNTEERS
Hartford Superior Court
95 Washington Street
Hartford, CT 06106
TEL: 203-566-3170
Purpose: To assist the adult probation office of the Connecticut Judicial Department.
Sponsor: Hartford Superior Court
Contact: Clair Collins, Volunteer Services Coordinator
Description: Since the early 1970s, in small adult probation offices across Connecticut, some 450 volunteers have enabled full-time probation officers to give more time to field work, phone calls, and other matters that only they can handle in their heavy caseloads - average 260 cases per officer. In addition to helping the system improve its services, volunteers save the state needed funds - $650,000 in 1987 alone.
Volunteers take information from shoplifters, drunken drivers, and others granted probation by the courts. Many of these offenders receive accelerated rehabilitation, with any record of their arrests erased if they stay out of trouble. Therefore, the volunteers must use extreme care in updating the records following required periodic interviews. Other duties of volunteers range from answering the phones to monitoring cases of neglected children. Most volunteers are from the suburbs, many with postgraduate degrees. Senior citizens and college and law students frequently volunteer for course credit and satisfaction. Also, people considering a switch to a law-oriented career find the experience helpful in making their final decisions. A number of the volunteers have been with the program for more than a dozen years. One volunteer maintains three other volunteer jobs simultaneously - in agricultural, historical, and nutrition programs.
A side benefit for all concerned is that the volunteers are valued as much by the offenders as by those who work for the legal system. Realizing that the offenders are tense, volunteers who interview them try to make it a nonthreatening experience - warmly admonishing the younger ones for not finishing school, and laughing with the older ones who answer "not much" to the question, "Hair?" According to one volunteer, "These people come to you, and you help them."
The statewide program began in early 1971. The Hartford County Bar Association recently recognized 32 adult probation volunteers - three in their eighties - as part of Law Day, a holiday that celebrates the importance of laws in American society.

RESERVE POLICE OFFICER CORPS
Washington Metropolitan Police Department
300 Indiana Avenue, NW
Washington, DC 20001
TEL: 292-727-1000
Purpose: To provide assistance to police officers both in administrative capacities and "on the street."
Contact: Captain Ross E. Swope, Supervisor
Description: The District of Columbia's Police Reserve Corps numbers 166 volunteers. They are lawyers, government employees, and other professionals as well as layman who want to help protect their neighborhoods.
Although some volunteer officers choose to work "on the street," others help in areas of data processing, communications, property division, vehicle management, administrative jobs, and other posts throughout the department. Since Reserve Police Officers cannot, by law, carry a gun, the help on the street is becoming less and less attractive to volunteers who join the Corps. However, the department is recruiting volunteers in an effort to triple the number of Reserve Officers, since they are needed throughout the department.
Reserve Officers receive 108 hours of abbreviated training in traffic enforcement, the DC Code and police procedures. Since many volunteers are older than staff officers, they feel that the training is sufficient, since they are more mature and better able to handle

some police business. In addition to having to meet stiff requirements, the volunteers are required to buy their own bulletproof vests. Legislation is being entered to allow reservists to carry weapons, since many metropolitan cities with populations and crime problems similar to the District's do arm their reserve officers.
Although more and more opportunities are opening up inside the precincts for volunteer officers, most of whom have been working on the street for a time have become familiar with the neighborhoods and opt to stay there. A few request transfers inside after a particularly heavy rash of crime.
During the last six months of 1989, reserve officers volunteered a total of 13,110 hours.

RESERVE POLICE PROGRAM
St. Louis County Police Department
Wellston, MO 63133
TEL: 314-889-2844
Purpose: To provide back up for police officers on regular patrol.
Sponsor: St. Louis County & Municipal Police Academy
Contact: Reserve Coordinator
Description: Volunteer police reserves are involved in all parts of St. Louis County. Both men and women reservists each donate 200 hours of time a year to back up police officers on regular patrol and learn to help in emergencies.
Before assignments are made, volunteers participate in an intensive training program. Classes are held in the St. Louis County and Municipal Police Academy evenings and some Saturdays for the convenience of volunteers who work during the day. Training covers
- law enforcement functions;
- criminal law;
- firearms;
- cardiopulmonary resuscitation; and
- first aid.
The serious nature of these topics requires 180 hours of training over a 13-week period.

VOLUNTEER PROBATION OFFICER PROGRAM
The Volunteer Center
920 Frederica Street
PO Box 123
Owensboro, KY 42302
TEL: 502-683-9161
Purpose: To provide friendship and positive role models to young people having problems at home or in school.
Contact: Pamela J. Warwick, Executive Director
Description: Juveniles, ages 8-17, are referred to the Volunteer Probation Offices program by district court judges, area school officials, and social service agencies.
Volunteers, trained and supervised by salaried staff, are matched with juveniles to provide general counseling and supportive services to the youth and his family. Volunteers may initiate a working relationship by participating in activities of interest to the youth. Local businesses have provided discounts (i.e. bowling, skating, etc.) in an effort to decrease volunteer expense and "burn-out."
Volunteers apply for the position, are interviewed by staff and supply references. Before assignment, volunteers must complete all required orientation and training. Volunteers must agree to complete all cases entered into (averaging six months), maintain personal contact with the youth once a week from one to four hours and be available to the youth and his family in crisis situations. In addition, volunteers agree to attend monthly in-service meetings and submit brief monthly summaries of volunteer work and progress made to staff. Volunteers have 24 hours access to supervision and have the opportunity to discuss goals, treatment plan, and problems with staff on a regular basis.
The program, in operation since February 1981, matches about 32

youths each year with volunteers. Most assignments have worked out well. Although the program is currently quite small, the potential impact is great. The quality attention provided by volunteers may prove to prevent youths from entering the criminal justice system. For truants, the program is particularly helpful and may have a major impact on school attendance and the drop out rate.
Founded: 1981

VOLUNTEERS: STUDENTS

NATIONAL/STATE ORGANIZATIONS

CAMPUS OUTREACH OPPORTUNITY LEAGUE (COOL)
386 McNeal Hall
University of Minnesota
St. Paul, MN 55108-1011
TEL: 612-624-3018
FAX: 612-625-5767
Objectives: To involve undergraduate college students in community improvement projects on a volunteer basis.
Services: COOL, The Campus Outreach Opportunity League, is a national, nonprofit organization which promotes and supports student involvement in community service. COOL is managed by a staff of recent college graduates and represents a network that includes more than 550 campuses and 250 nonprofit service organizations nationwide. COOL is a 1987 recipient of the President's Volunteer Action Award. COOL's mission is to strengthen through service and in an environment of diversity, the capacity of students for thoughtful action, and to create a student voice in the community to address the challenges we face in society.
The *COOL Campus Affiliate Program* is the League's way of forming a partnership with individual campuses to enhance and celebrate the work students are doing in their communities. In addition to agreeing that its work in the community and on campus will be done in the spirit of the *COOL Mission Statement,* the *Affiliate* must appoint one person to serve as the primary campus contact, keep COOL informed through an Annual Report about Community Service on its campus (which is published in the *COOL Affiliate Directory*), and provide samples of any flyers, brochures, newsletters, etc. published by the *Affiliate*. The *Affiliate* receives a monthly phone consultation from COOL Regional Staff Contacts, the *Directory,* a newsletter subscription, first access to information (first class mail), and discounts on all materials published or developed by COOL.
On most campuses, community involvement is coordinated by such offices as *Campus Ministry* or *Student Affairs* and by many student cultural organizations and individual student groups. Collaborating as a COOL Campus Affiliate is a way of bringing these organizations and offices together.
New in 1990 is the *Affiliate Start-Up Plan* for those campuses that would like a one-day on-site consulting visit and one copy of each COOL publication in addition to the regular *Affiliate* benefits. This *Plan* gives the *Affiliate* the chance to work even more closely with the COOL Staff.
The *Affiliate Program* marks an important turning point for COOL, since much of its support will now come from student organizations which are involved in their communities every day. And, because COOL is a part of a larger movement of students in community service, the *League* does not exclude a campus that is not an Affiliate from events or technical assistance.
COOL's annual conference evolves from ideas and information, "dreams and schemes," or innovative projects suggested by people across the country. The 1990 conference, *Common Ground -*

Common Good, instituted a new technique, *In the Streets,* which provided opportunities to work with programs in the community itself during part of the conference. Another innovation that was an outgrowth of the 1990 conference hosted by UCLA was a planned benefit performance for COOL during one evening. Instructors are drawn from *Affiliates* as well as national COOL staff and national nonprofit organizations.
COOL publishes a newsletter five times a year, resource and guide books, program idea collections, etc.
Sponsor: Universities; national nonprofit organizations
Contact: Wayne Meisel, Executive Officer
Publications: Hunger/Homelessness Action: College/University Resource Book; Break Away: A Guide to Organizing an Alternative Spring Break; On Your Mark, GO! Get Set: Campus Ideals to Community Involvement; Literacy Action: College/University Resource Book; Campus Outreach: The COOL Newsletter; Building a Movement: Resource/Students in Community Service; COOL Information Packet
Founded: 1986

CENTER FOR PUBLIC SERVICE
SEE TRAINING/CONFERENCES/TEACHING:
INTERNSHIPS

CHILDREN AS PEACEMAKERS
950 Battery Street
Second Floor
San Francisco, CA 94111
TEL: 415-981-0916
Objectives: To foster world peace through cultural exchange.
Services: Makes arrangements for children to speak to world leaders about peace; operates three major international programs: *Peace Mission,* which brings together children from every continent to meet with world leaders on the subject of peace; *Banner Project,* which coordinates efforts in research and represents children who are victims of war since 1930; *International Children's Peace Prize,* which is presented annually to children from more than 50 countries; operates through membership of individuals interested in fostering world peace through cultural exchange.
Founded: 1982

CITIZENS COMMUNICATION CENTER
SEE COMMUNICATIONS & PUBLIC RELATIONS

COMMISSION ON VOLUNTARY SERVICE AND ACTION
475 Riverside Drive
Room 933
New York, NY 10015
TEL: 212-870-2755 (NY); 316-283-5100 (KS)
Objectives: To serve as a consultative council of private North American organizations which sponsor and/or support voluntary service projects all over the world.
Services: Provides a forum for administrators of voluntary service programs to promote sharing of news or information, engage in collaborative advocacy, cooperate in placement service and re-entry programs, and participate in an international network; holds occasional consultations on issues related to voluntary service programming; publishes a catalog of service opportunities for all ages.
Publications: Volunteer!
Founded: 1946

COMMON CAUSE
SEE TRAINING/CONFERENCES/TEACHING:
INTERNSHIPS

COPRED STUDENTS PEACE NETWORK
Consortium of Peace Research, Education & Development
c/o George Mason University
4400 University Drive
Fairfax, VA 22030
TEL: 703-323-2806
Objectives: To become involved in peace research, peace studies, or peace action in schools and communities.
Services: Brings together students working for disarmament, human rights, economic justice, and ecological balance; acts as a resource and communications channel in developing coordinated efforts toward peace and greater international solidarity among students; sponsors panels and workshops; conducts specialized education; compiles internship, job and fellowship information; maintains network groups that work on peace issues with children.
Publications: COPRED Peace Chronicle
Founded: 1981

GOVERNMENT CONTRACTS CLINIC
George Washington University
Academic Center, Room T412
801 22nd Street, NW
Washington, DC 20052
TEL: 202-676-6815
Objectives: To offer pro bono publico (no fee) services to firms and individuals who are not financially able to afford the services of private legal counsel; to offer third-year students an opportunity to gain experience.
Services: Represents deserving small businesses in federal government contract litigation; offers advice and counsel on specific legal questions; makes decisions on cases to handle based on limited resources of the program and various other considerations, including the merits of the claim involved, the nature of the efforts required, and the size and financial capabilities of the firm.

INTERGENERATIONAL PROJECT FOR SERVICE LEARNING
National Council on the Aging
600 Maryland Avenue, SW
West Wing 100
Washington, DC 20024
TEL: 202-479-1200
Objectives: To bring together two isolated groups - college students and older persons - to form friendships, share knowledge, and engage in mutually-beneficial projects.
Services: Works with volunteer groups, community agencies and campus departments to organize and operate programs and identify needs; emphasizes advocacy, improving access to health care, and delivering health services to economically disadvantaged, homebound and isolated older persons; publishes a handbook for establishing service-learning programs and projects plus a series of technical assistance guides for the community on recruitment, orientation, supervision, and other program management areas (to be developed in 1981), and a national clearinghouse for service-learning projects.
Publications: Service-Learning Programs

NATIONAL ALLIANCE OF BLIND STUDENTS
SEE VOLUNTEERS: HANDICAPPED

NATIONAL COMMISSION ON RESOURCES FOR YOUTH
Institute for Responsive Education
605 Commonwealth Avenue
Boston, MA 02215
TEL: 617-353-3309
Objectives: To provide opportunities for teenagers to assume significant and responsible social roles.

Services: Collects and disseminates information on programs of youth participation in which young people contribute through action projects to improve their communities; assures that youth assume responsible roles that meet real community needs and goals; provides technical assistance, training, and consultation on programs of youth participation; publishes quarterly newsletter describing programs, books, manuals, and other materials on youth tutors, youth counseling youth, and youth in a variety of other community service roles; produces films and videotapes.
Publications: Equity and Choice; Resource Directory
Founded: 1973

NATIONAL INDIAN YOUTH COUNCIL
SEE LEADERSHIP DEVELOPMENT/BOARDS: ETHNIC GROUPS

NATIONAL LISTEN AMERICA CLUB
2686 Townsgate Road
Westlake Village, CA 91359
TEL: 805-497-9457
Objectives: To promote and recognize the positive and constructive things young people are doing.
Services: Administers a variety of community service projects, including an annual national two-hour television special; maintains a membership of junior and senior high school students who have pledged not to smoke, drink alcohol, or use drugs; works with 3,000 local groups; gathers and shares information on projects that demonstrate ways in which youth are making positive contributions to improve the quality of life in their communities, thus improving society as a whole; publishes a biweekly newsletter and a monthly magazine; convenes every summer.
Publications: Tune In; Listen America Magazine
Founded: 1980

NATIONAL NETWORK OF YOUTH ADVISORY BOARDS
SEE LEADERSHIP DEVELOPMENT/BOARDS: CHILDREN/YOUTH

NATIONAL YOUTH COUNCIL ON CIVIC AFFAIRS
2698 Bunnycrest Court
Fremont, CA 94538
TEL: 415-656-8404
Objectives: To assist communities in involving youth in government.
Services: Helps to establish teen juries, youth commissions, and youth boards of governors; conducts research in several areas of teen involvement with an emphasis on teen participation in the decision-making process; publishes a monthly newsletter, a directory and other materials.
Publications: NYCCA Newsletter

PENNSERVE: THE GOVERNOR'S OFFICE OF CITIZEN SERVICE
SEE GOVERNORS' OFFICES ON VOLUNTEERISM: PENNSYLVANIA

PRESIDENTIAL CLASSROOM FOR YOUNG AMERICANS
441 North Lee Street
Alexandria, VA 22314-2346
TEL: 703-683-5400
Objectives: To contribute to leadership training of youth through personal involvement in government functions.
Services: Provides youth with an opportunity for close observation of the U.S. government in Washington, DC; identifies and assists youth who have high leadership potential; works with high school, graduate and undergraduate university students, and teachers; conducts week-long seminars for high school students; leads a one-week program of seminars and workshops for college students

and teachers; maintains extensive library of leadership-oriented materials; publishes a curriculum guide, daily bulletin during the senior high school program, and other materials.
Publications: Presidential Forum; Presidential Daily; Outlook
Founded: 1968

PROJECT CONCERN YOUTH PROGRAM
Project Concern International
3550 Alton Road
San Diego, CA 92123
TEL: 619-279-9690
Objectives: To enable youth to take part in volunteer programs on health and nutrition at the local, state, national and international levels.
Services: Involves youth in segments of its program which provides low-cost health services through a health care training program supported by volunteer assistance; researches and develops volunteer projects such as "Walk for Mankind," a program in which school children, youth and adults raise funds, and nutrition, health education and other programs, which are taught by volunteers in their communities; publishes quarterly Concern News, training manuals, booklets and other materials; convenes semiannual Board meetings.
Publications: Options; Concern News; Field Notes
Founded: 1961

PROJECT LEAD
SEE LEADERSHIP DEVELOPMENT/BOARDS: CHILDREN/YOUTH

PUBLIC RELATIONS STUDENT SOCIETY OF AMERICA
SEE COMMUNICATIONS & PUBLIC RELATIONS: CHILDREN/YOUTH

STUDENT COMMUNITY SERVICE (SCS) PROGRAM
US/ACTION - The Federal Volunteer Agency
1100 Vermont Avenue, NW
Suite 1100
Washington, DC 20525
TEL: 202-634-9108
TOLL FREE: 800-424-8580
Objectives: To support efforts linking the resources of student volunteers with those of the community in resolving human and social problems, emphasizing those that are poverty-related.
Services: Awards Student Community Services grants to provide seed money to organizations that develop projects which involve secondary, vocational, and post-secondary student volunteers in part-time non-stipended activities designed to benefit low-income communities, thus enabling communities to reap immediate benefits from students who serve while in school, and long-term benefits as students leave school and continue to involve themselves in community affairs; involves students in programs such as hunger, homelessness, illiteracy, and unemployment, in a range of volunteer roles such as companions to the elderly, counselors to their peers on drug prevention matters, organizers of home repair projects, and tutors in educational programs.
[Today, more than three-quarters of a million American high school and college students are involved in community service programs dealing with the problems of the poor.]
Contact: Patricia A.E. Rodgers
Publications: Student Community Service

STUDENT CONSERVATION ASSOCIATION
Box 550
Charlestown, NH 03603
TEL: 603-826-4301 (NH); 703-524-2441 (DC)
Objectives: To offer expense-paid educational work experiences and enhance career opportunities for young people; to assist in the accomplishment of important land and resource management of natural resources.
Services: Operates the *Resource Assistant Program* through which college students and other adult volunteers serve as professional assistants in national parks, wildlife refuges, and other areas nationwide for 12-16 weeks in national parks, wilderness areas, and elsewhere (summer only); operates the *Wilderness Workskills Program* providing training in traditional trail construction and wilderness management skills for field personnel; operates the *New Hampshire Conservation Corps;* publishes a monthly conservation employment newsletter and other materials.
Publications: Job Scan (newsletter); SCA Annual Report; Resource Assistant Program Position Listing; High School Program Position Listing
Founded: 1957

STUDENTS AGAINST DRIVING DRUNK (SADD)
PO Box 800
Marlboro, MA 01752
TEL: 617-481-3568
Objectives: To get teenagers and young adults involved in fighting drunk driving.
Services: Works through sponsors in local high schools to recruit teenagers to help attack peer pressure and pave the way for acceptance of the refusal to drink and drive; keeps the community informed by enlisting the help of adults within and outside of the school (such as MADD, above, and local college students) to publicize the program, offer advice, and generally oversee the management and evaluation methods used by the program's teenaged leaders.
Gets the schools involved, especially in the area of combating peer pressure; monitors courts as well as judges, prosecutors, and laws; works with other groups fighting drunk driving; mounts letter-writing campaigns to elected and other government officials; holds school assemblies featuring speakers who are informed about the drunk driving problem; conducts fund-raising events such as bake sales.
Informs school and local newspapers of the work of the club; stages events in regional malls with balloons, bumper stickers, posters, etc., during November, which is Alcohol Awareness Month; enters marching SADD students in Homecoming games at local high schools; holds Walk/Run-a-Thons open to anyone; conducts student and parent surveys; works very closely with state and county drunk driving task forces.
Publishes fact sheets, guidelines, reports, and other informative materials, as well as tools for meetings, fund-raisers, etc., such as bumper stickers, posters and balloons, to assist others planning to mount SADD programs; researches the subject of drunk driving on a continuing basis to keep current on community, education, and legislative developments on the subject.
[This national program was started by a student in W.T. Woodson High School in Fairfax, Virginia]
Publications: SADD Update; SADD in the College; SADD and the Athlete; SADD in the High School; SADD in the Junior High School; SADD Policy and Procedures

SUPER VOLUNTEERS!
Four-One-One (411)
7304 Beverly Street
Annandale, VA 22003
TEL: 703-354-6270
Objectives: To direct the energy, creativity, and enthusiasm of the very young toward improvement of the quality of life in their communities.
Services: Works with teams of young people in traditional youth organizations (ages four to seventeen), who meet with school and community leaders and respond to expressed needs of their communities, sign a volunteer contract, record volunteer hours, and submit program descriptions to *Super Volunteers!* to receive

T-shirts, manuals, and other tools for their projects; has charter teams in Boy Scouts, Boys' and Girls' Clubs, Camp Fire, 4-H Youth, Girl Scouts, Head Start, Red Cross Youth, Special Olympics, Small World News Teams, YMCA, and a number of independent athletic and other groups; holds annual forums to bring together teams from across the country; draws support and sponsorship from business/industry, churches and synagogues, educational institutions, nonprofit organizations, and individuals; administers *Volunteers!,* which is an audiovisual program for schools and youth groups; publishes the *Super Volunteers!/Small World Newsletter* edited by the youth themselves; distributes fictional series on four *Super Volunteers!* and their mascot (17 booklets available on subjects from drug abuse to vandalism), videocassettes, slides, songs, plays, and other tools to enhance volunteer projects mounted by young volunteers; operates several essay and other contests throughout the year.

TEEN-AGE ASSEMBLY OF AMERICA*
SEE LEADERSHIP DEVELOPMENT/BOARDS:
CHILDREN/YOUTH

YOUTH AS RESOURCES
SEE FUNDING/FUND-RAISING/RELATED SERVICES

YOUTH SERVICES TO FRAIL, HOMEBOUND ELDERLY
National Council on the Aging
600 Maryland Avenue, SW
West Wing 100
Washington, DC 20024
TEL: 202-479-1200
Objectives: To conduct a survey to locate successful programs in which young volunteers are working with the frail, homebound elderly.
Services: Operates under a grant from the Wallerstein Foundation for Geriatric Life Improvement; administers nationwide survey to identify and review successful programs in which young volunteers are working with the frail, homebound elderly; reviews programs to determine and describe common elements within the programs that help to ensure success; makes results of survey and individual program descriptions available to individuals and organizations working with the frail, homebound elderly.
Sponsor: Wallerstein Foundation for Geriatric Life Improvement
Contact: Larry Couch, Associate, Intergenerational Programs

TRAINING PROGRAMS

AYE SHARE
SEE TRAINING/CONFERENCES/TEACHING

CHANGING VALUES IN EXPERIENTIAL EDUCATION*
SEE TRAINING/CONFERENCES/TEACHING:
INTERNSHIPS

COMMON GROUND, COMMON GOOD
SEE TRAINING/CONFERENCES/TEACHING:
COMMUNITY SERVICES

COMMUNITY ACTION TRAINING (CAT)
SEE TRAINING/CONFERENCES/TEACHING:
COMMUNITY SERVICES

COMMUNITY INVOLVEMENT PROGRAM
SEE TRAINING/CONFERENCES/TEACHING: STUDENTS

COMMUNITY SERVICE
SEE TRAINING/CONFERENCES/TEACHING:
CHILDREN/YOUTH

COMMUNITY SERVICE PROGRAM
State University of New York at Albany
School of Social Welfare
ULB 66
Albany, NY 12222
TEL: 518-457-8437
Credit: 3 credits (may be taken twice)
Sponsor: State University of New York at Albany
Contact: Hedi McKinley
Description: This course had its beginnings in 1970 when almost 5,000 students spent more than 375,000 hours as volunteers in local agencies. Students are required to spend six hours each week in an agency (under some circumstances, making the selection themselves). The academic requirements are:
  ● a five- to eight-page paper - self-evaluation of performance, self-recognition of attitude and other changes, and finding connections with classwork and reading.
  ● evaluation session - meeting with volunteers from other agencies, obtaining feedback, trouble-shooting
Students may take two semesters of Community Service, remaining whenever possible with the same agency for the second semester. Each agency holds its own orientation and training sessions, and provides a supervisory person for the volunteer program. Students may request a transfer, and agencies are not required to keep a specific student. Transportation and hours are worked out between the student volunteer and the agency. Students cannot receive pay for their volunteer work, nor can they receive credit for this work in more than one course.
Volunteer placements include tutoring of school dropouts, helping patients in emergency rooms, making housing surveys, putting on plays for kids, visiting sick and lonely people, manning emergency switchboards, entertaining with music, designing questionnaires, teaching photography to inner-city children, researching legal problems, preparing tapes for the blind, working in labs, and many others. Students are not expected to possess special skills or knowledge, but agencies expect a person willing to learn, and the school expects a serious commitment to the course assignment.
The Community Service Program is produced by the School of Social Welfare, and administered by the Student Steering Committee. A directory of participating agencies, Student Volunteers, provides a "shopping list" for students with brief descriptions of concern areas for each agency. A backup file containing additional information about each agency is available to the students.

COMMUNITY SERVICES
SEE TRAINING/CONFERENCES/TEACHING: STUDENTS

COOL NATIONAL CONFERENCE
SEE TRAINING/CONFERENCES/TEACHING: STUDENTS

CRIME, LAW AND COMMUNITY: A STUDENT SERVICE CURRICULUM
SEE TRAINING/CONFERENCES/TEACHING: JUSTICE
SYSTEM

CROSS-CULTURAL COMMUNITY WORKSHOP
SEE LEADERSHIP DEVELOPMENT/BOARDS:
CHILDREN/YOUTH

DEMYSTIFYING THE INTERNSHIP EXPERIENCE
SEE TRAINING/CONFERENCES/TEACHING:
INTERNSHIPS

DRUNK-DRIVING SIMULATOR PROGRAM AND FORUM
SEE VOLUNTEERS: POLICE OFFICERS

EDUCATION AND HUMAN SERVICES COURSE
SEE TRAINING/CONFERENCES/TEACHING: STUDENTS

ENTERING THE COMMUNITY: SUMMER VOLUNTEER SERVICE AND CAREER OPPORTUNITIES FOR STUDENTS
SEE TRAINING/CONFERENCES/TEACHING: INTERNSHIPS

EXPERIENTIAL LEARNING - WORKING WITH STUDENT VOLUNTEERS
Westchester Community College
Department of Human Services
Valhalla, NY 10595
TEL: 914-285-6600
Credit: Inquire
Sponsor: Westchester Community College; Volunteer Service Center/United Way
Contact: Pauline Herman
Description: This conference addresses student volunteering at both high school and college levels. It is a dual program with a session of panel presentations, and a series of five workshops. Panel topics include:
- Student Volunteerism, What Is It?
- High School Students' Transition to the Working/Academic World
- A College Field Internship Program
- Working with Students - An Agency Perspective
The panel sessions are followed by an informal meeting with school program representatives in preparation for five workshops designed to provide a natural sequence from one aspect of student volunteer programming to the next. These workshops are:
- Starting to Involve Students in a Volunteer Program
- Staff/Student Relations
- Contracts
- Evaluations
- Expanding Possibilities for Involving Students
Faculty for both panels and workshops was drawn from school volunteer programs, the college, nonprofit organizations, and other areas. The conference includes a "wrap-up" with the representatives from school volunteer programs.

FAMILY LIFE/COMMUNITY AND GOVERNMENT
SEE TRAINING/CONFERENCES/TEACHING: STUDENTS

GET AWAY CLEAN
SEE TRAINING/CONFERENCES/TEACHING: CHILDREN/YOUTH

GOVERNOR'S YOUTH ACTION CONFERENCE
SEE GOVERNORS' OFFICES ON VOLUNTEERISM: CONNECTICUT

ISSUES ON VOLUNTEERISM: SERVICE LEARNING IN THE COMMUNITY
SEE TRAINING/CONFERENCES/TEACHING: STUDENTS

LIVE '89 (LEADERSHIP IN VOLUNTEERISM EXPERIENCE)
SEE GOVERNORS' OFFICES ON VOLUNTEERISM: ILLINOIS

THE MARSHALL SERVICE UNIT AND VOLUNTEER OUTREACH
SEE TRAINING/CONFERENCES/TEACHING: STUDENTS

THE NAME OF THE GAME IS CARING
American Red Cross
17th and D Streets, NW
Washington, DC 20006
TEL: 202-737-8300
FAX: 202-639-3791
Purpose: To help young students in grades 7-12 become recreation leaders.
Description: This model program was developed by the national office of the American Red Cross for use at the local level. It addresses the importance of leisure-time pursuits in today's fast-paced life, and the need to find meaningful volunteer activities for youth. The program defines an effective recreational leader as: a humanitarian, a group worker, a dreamer, an organizer, a performing arts enthusiast, a sports fan, an actor or actress, a media expert, and an innovator. "The Name of the Game is Caring" helps young people in grades 7 through 12 acquire the skills necessary to become effective volunteer recreation leaders. The course prepares these youth to work with children, teenagers, the elderly, the disabled, the ill, or the convalescent in a variety of settings. The course includes:
- Twenty-four activity sheets that enable young people to perform leadership skills while learning about them.
- A 16-page facilitator's guide that includes complete instructions for implementing course activities, suggestions for additional optional activities, and complete background material for the instructor.
- Four two-sided posters that highlight major points covered in each session and serve as transition devices between sessions.
After completing "The Name of the Game is Caring," young people will have the necessary background to:
- Understand what recreation is and why it is important for all ages.
- Evaluate their own leadership abilities.
- Recognize important considerations for different age and ability groups when planning recreational activities.
- Adapt specific recreational activities for various age and ability groups.
- Implement the elements of effective leadership in the planning and executing of recreation activities.
The American Red Cross provides other programs for young people in areas of self-awareness, health and safety, first aid, preparation for employment, consumer knowledge, and alcohol education.

NCSL JOB SKILLS DEVELOPMENT SEMINARS
SEE TRAINING/CONFERENCES/TEACHING: CAREER EXPLORATION

SENIOR COURSE ON VOLUNTEERISM
SEE TRAINING/CONFERENCES/TEACHING: STUDENTS

SEVENTH GRADE SOCIAL PROBLEMS COURSE
SEE LEADERSHIP DEVELOPMENT/BOARDS: CHILDREN/YOUTH

SOCIAL LAB
SEE TRAINING/CONFERENCES/TEACHING: INTERNSHIPS

SOCIAL WORK PROGRAM: 60-HOUR VOLUNTEER WORK REQUIREMENT
SEE TRAINING/CONFERENCES/TEACHING: STUDENTS

THE SPICE PROGRAM AND INTRODUCTION
SEE TRAINING/CONFERENCES/TEACHING:
INTERNSHIPS

STUDENT CARE DAY
SEE FUNDING/FUND-RAISING/RELATED SERVICES:
CHILDREN

STUDENT VOLUNTEER PROGRAMS: A NEW RESOURCE FOR COMMUNITY AGENCIES*
SEE TRAINING/CONFERENCES/TEACHING: STUDENTS

TAKING A TRIP TO FRIENDSHIP
SEE TRAINING/CONFERENCES/TEACHING: STUDENTS

TEACHING SENIOR CENTER
SEE TRAINING/CONFERENCES/TEACHING:
INTERNSHIPS

YOUNG LEADERS CONFERENCE
SEE TRAINING/CONFERENCES/TEACHING:
CHILDREN/YOUTH

YOUNG VOLUNTEERS IN ACTION: TRAINING FOR PROJECT DIRECTORS
SEE TRAINING/CONFERENCES/TEACHING

YOUTH COMMUNITY SERVICE
VOLUNTEER - The National Center
1111 North 19th Street
Suite 500
Arlington, VA 22209
TEL: 703-276-0542
FAX: 703-528-6021
Credit: Inquire
Sponsor: VOLUNTEER - The National Center
Contact: Kay Drake
Description: This three-hour workshop is broadcast across the country via satellite, designed for volunteer program leaders interested in learning more about the youth community service movement. It is based on the premise that youth community service benefits everyone. Highlights of the workshop content are:
Benefits for youth who participate:
- better understanding of their responsibilities as citizens;
- increased self-esteem;
- application of practical skills;
- multi-cultural and intergenerational experiences;
- positive attitude toward learning; and
- better understanding of the job market;
- opportunities to reflect on what they have learned from other service activities.
Benefits for communities and the nation:
- more volunteers to meet community needs; and
- youth who continue to volunteer as adults.
Benefits for schools, organizations and agencies:
- fresh perspectives and creativity;
- idealism and optimism;
- energy; and
- opportunities for organizational change.
The three "R"s for managing young volunteers are:
- Role (clear, specific, manageable);
- Respect (honest and sincere, not lip service); and
- Recognition (immediate, relevant, tangible).
We need to re-think the role of youth in our society and begin focusing on "youth at strength" rather than "youth at risk." We must dare to empower our young citizens in order to begin tapping them as a national resource. This can be depicted as a shift along a

continuum.
Youth as: consumers, objects, victims
Youth as: producers, subjects, heroes
The key messages to send to young people if we want to get them involved in volunteering are:
- We need you!
- The work you will do is important!
- This is a chance to problem-solve!
- You can be included in leadership and decision-making roles!
- This is a way to find meaning and purpose in your life!
As volunteer program managers, we must position ourselves to take advantage of youth involvement. This means:
- educating ourselves and our organizations about youth issues, attitudes and needs;
- building effective collaborations with others in the community (educational institutions, youth-serving programs, youth leadership organizations, state and local government agencies, etc.); and
- creating an organizational philosophy that includes youth involvement.
As managers interested in youth and community service, we should be aware of changes and innovations in the youth community service movement:
- **Virginia Campus Outreach Opportunity League (VA COOL)** has a new initiative to promote and network students in volunteerism (see separate entry).
- **National Association of Partners in Education** is the new name for the former National School Volunteer Program (see separate entry).

INDIVIDUAL PROGRAM PROFILES

AMHERST Y.E.S. (YOUTH ENGAGED IN SERVICE)
Amherst Youth Board
72 South Cayuga Road
Williamsville, NY 14221
TEL: 716-631-7129
Purpose: To provide the opportunity for Amherst's youth and young adults to be participating and contributing members of the community.
Sponsor: Amherst Youth Board; Youth Department-Diocese of Buffalo; the New York State Division for Youth
Contact: Kathleen Mobarek
Description: The Amherst Y.E.S. program began in 1976. The purpose of the program is to provide the opportunity for Amherst's youth and young adults to be participating and contributing members of the community. Community service is the focus of the program, and that service takes the form of directly assisting senior citizens, children, and persons who have a physical handicap or are mentally retarded. The Amherst Y.E.S. is an alternative to volunteering in an agency or institution.
All youth and young adults, between the ages of 12-21, who are residents of the Town of Amherst are welcome to be involved in the Amherst Y.E.S. Thus, the program has a rich mixture of persons representing a variety of faiths, ethnic backgrounds, and socio-economic status.
The youth for the Amherst Y.E.S. are recruited by the Director through the public and private schools, youth groups, churches, and temples. An important part of the program is the motivation of youth to be involved in giving service to others, and the guiding of them in activities that encourage positive self growth. The best recruiters of the Amherst Y.E.S. are the youth and young adults already involved in the program.
In the Amherst Y.E.S. the volunteers are given the choice as to which activity they want to do, and the duration of their involvement. They are sent activity sheets once every two months. On the activity sheet is listed each activity, who is to be helped, what would be the volunteer's responsibility, and where and when

the activity will take place. It is then up to the participant to decide what he/she desires to do, and to send the return sheet back.

Almost all that the program does has the participants interacting directly with people. The agencies and organizations to be helped are carefully selected, as are the activities. The majority of fund raising activities for the various charities are generally avoided, for, many times, the youth and young adults participating only learn to raise monies and nothing else. Also, the gifts and talents of the youth and young adults go beyond their abilities to raise money. They have valuable skills and knowledge and a sensitivity to others that the program tries to develop.

The Amherst Y.E.S. is a flexible program, and it is directly influenced by the youth and young adults in the program. Amherst Y.E.S. members have planned activities, have referred individuals to the program who need assistance, and have represented the program at various workshops, seminars, and functions. The Amherst Y.E.S. allows every participant to be involved in the community, in any manner that is comfortable, enjoyable, or challenging to that individual.

The Amherst Y.E.S. exists for the youth and young adults of the community as well as for those they help. Each year approximately 1,000 children and 500 adults receive benefit from the work of the Amherst Y.E.S. members, but the Amherst Y.E.S. members still are those who are truly being serviced in terms of self-growth, positive direction, and a chance to explore the world around them. The reward for being involved in the Amherst Y.E.S. is not tangible as in class credit, or a guarantee of a job, but it is rooted in feeling good about oneself, increased self-confidence, and caring about others.

Finally, the goals of the Amherst Y.E.S. are:
- Have Amherst youth and young adults involved in community service activities.
- Give benefit to Amherst youth and young adults who are involved in the work of the Amherst Y.E.S.
- To publicize the positive actions of Amherst youth and young adults, initiate contact with local community sources and media.

Facts:
- Each year between 400 and 450 youth and young adults are involved as Amherst Y.E.S. members.
- Each activity is supervised by the Amherst Y.E.S. director, her assistant, or a member of the Amherst Y.E.S. Advisory Board.
- An orientation and training is given if the particular Y.E.S. activity requires it.

Founded: 1976

BASKET OF JOY CAMPAIGN
Volunteers of America
1550 Yates Street
Denver, CO 80204
TEL: 303-623-8052
Purpose: To provide a basket of fresh fruit and a personal visit to a homebound senior citizen during the holiday season.
Sponsor: Volunteers of America
Contact: Linda Dee
Description: The *Basket of Joy Campaign* provides baskets of fresh fruit to elderly, homebound seniors who may otherwise be forgotten during the holiday season. The project is a collaboration between a newspaper columnist, a grocery store produce buyer and a volunteer coordinator. Each player provides the needed component to make the community effort successful. The columnist raises the cash and awareness for the campaign, and the produce manager orders the fruit and basket materials and arranges for use of a large warehouse in which to assemble and pick up baskets. Tables, chairs, a forklift, refreshments and trash collection all are provided by the produce manager. The volunteer coordinator organizes the volunteer corps, deposits the cash

donations, and logs the names of elderly recipients into the computer. Donors' names are faxed to the newspaper and thank you letters are written.

At the end of October each year a column is run in the *Denver Post* newspaper announcing that people may donate cash, offer to volunteer or submit the names of deserving seniors who should receive a holiday fruit basket. The names of all donors are printed in the *Post* on a bi-weekly basis, providing both recognition for the donor, and visibility for the project.

The 470 volunteers include people of all ages (teenagers and older) who choose to either assemble or deliver baskets, or both. Three weeks prior to the event, all volunteers are sent their assignments - five to ten names of seniors in like zip code areas. All volunteers sign an indemnity waiver and a duplicate copy of the seniors' names is stapled to the waiver. Volunteers are encouraged to spend time visiting with the seniors on the lists.

This community effort includes over 700 school children who make greeting cards for the baskets. By 1990, the event had become regionally known and seniors from throughout Colorado request and receive baskets.

Funds are obtained exclusively from donors who respond to newspaper articles. Goals for 1988 were $25,000 to provide 5,000 baskets. Both goals were exceeded as $34,000 was raised and 6,000 baskets made and delivered. Goals for 1989 were $40,000 and 10,000 baskets. Again, the goals were exceeded.

The project could easily be replicated elsewhere. Additional information is available on request.
Publications: Basket of Joy Information Packet
Founded: 1988

BEACHFRONT VOLUNTEERS
Interact Club
Southern Regional High School
Route 9
Manahawkin, NJ 08050
TEL: 609-597-9481
Purpose: To help clean up New Jersey beaches for beautification and recreation.
Sponsor: Long Beach Township Department of Public Works
Contact: Mary Tantillo, Vice President, Interact
Description: Three hundred students from 15 New Jersey high schools in seven counties gathered at Long Beach Island to help clean up the beaches. All are members of *Interact,* a high school organization developed by Rotary International.

The volunteers gathered five truckloads of trash along an eight-mile stretch of beachfront, and kept individual logs of the trash they collected. The logs are sent to the *Center for Environmental Education* in Washington, which is conducting a study on floatables and beach litter.

The *Long Beach Township Department of Public Works* disposes of the trash, which usually consists of bottles, cans, plastic items and cigarette butts - things likely to be left on the beach by visitors or dropped into coastal waters by recreational boaters. Much of it comes from under the sand, where tourists bury their litter rather than carry it to trash barrels.

The *Ocean County Tourism Advisory Council* provided a $750 grant for the project, which provided souvenir T-shirts for participants and the rental of toilet facilities. The *Alliance for a Living Ocean,* an environmental-awareness group based on Long Beach Island, gave each participating club a *Steward of the Earth* award. The consensus of the young volunteers is that the beaches can be kept clean if everyone will do their part.

THE B.E.S.T. PROJECT
Brown University
25 George Street
PO Box 1974
Providence, RI 02912
TEL: 401-863-2338

Purpose: To give *Brown* students the opportunity to teach ESL to immigrants and refugees.
Description: B.E.S.T. *(Brown English as a Second Language Student Tutors)* provides tutors with an opportunity to teach English to immigrants and refugees from all over the world. *Brown University* students are recruited, trained, and given a choice of program options, including:
- *Teach an ESL Class* at *Smith Hill Community Center* on some weekday evenings.
- *Tutor an adult at home* in the *Home Tutoring Program*, the *Senior Citizens Center*, or at a library at times worked out between the parties.
- *Tutor in the Providence Public School System* at *Perry Middle School* or *Central High School* on weekday mornings.

Training is provided by *B.E.S.T.* staff at the *Center for Public Service*. Staff members also offer ongoing support. During the school year, the *Education Department, Portuguese and Brazilian Studies,* and the *Center for Public Service* offer a full-credit course in ESL: P/B 172. Also, students can request an opportunity to observe ESL teachers in a classroom setting.
Transportation for the tutors is organized by coordinators using BCO cars and volunteer car-pooling.
Publications: The B.E.S.T. Project

BIG BROTHERS/BIG SISTERS PROGRAM
SEE VOLUNTEERS: ROLE MODELS

BIG BROTHERS/BIG SISTERS PROGRAM-CHILD PSYCHIATRY*
SEE VOLUNTEERS: ROLE MODELS

BLOODMOBILE
Tully Central School
Route 80
Syracuse, NY 13159
TEL: 315-696-6242
Purpose: To educate teenagers regarding blood donation; to provide them with an opportunity for community service; to create better community relations and enhance the student image.
Sponsor: Tully Central School
Contact: Lorraine Spaulding, Health Careers Club
Description: For the past ten years, the Health Careers Club of the Tully Central School has sponsored a Red Cross Bloodmobile. Each year, 35 to 40 student volunteers begin preparations about one month in advance of the scheduled Bloodmobile. Through trial and error, they have found that the following activity sequence works best:
1. Call Red Cross to schedule date.
2. Get a Red Cross printout sheet of all former donors.
3. Assign student volunteers a list of people to call (former community donors); assign volunteers to personally contact teachers, school personnel; assign volunteers to contact all students who are age 17 or over (but do not coerce or beg students - merely ask). "Peer asking" works well, though.
4. Obtain and/or design posters (many available ones are so cleverly worded).
5. Seek publicity (local radio spots, newspaper, pictures).
6. Bake cookies to be used for donors.
7. Fly Red Cross flag, taking up and down each day for a week before Bloodmobile.
8. Make a large thermometer and display in prominent place; write names of givers on thermometer so students can watch it "rise" throughout the day.
9. Encourage students to give during study hall, not class time.
10. Emphasize the volunteer slots available for students who are squeamish about working with blood.
11. Assign clean-up crew to clean and load trucks after Bloodmobile program.
The Health Club sponsor, and the students themselves, had many

doubts and misgivings when they first undertook the program. Now it has become a yearly project which has grown far beyond expectations. Immediately following one Bloodmobile, students begin planning to make the next one bigger than ever. All concerned feel that the Bloodmobile serves many purposes, among which are:
Education - that donating blood is helping someone else to live; that donating blood is not that painful; that donating blood is a grown-up thing to do; that donating blood is a good habit to start while young.
Service - provides many different ways for teenagers to become involved; enables large numbers of students to participate.
Community Relations - creates good community relations; outside people are asked to give; community people are pleased to see students involved in the effort.
Seventeen-year-old students can give blood in New York State without parental consent. Laws differ, and those considering such a program in another state should check state law well in advance of the program.
Founded: 1980

BROOKLYN AIDS TASK FORCE
22 Chapel Street
Brooklyn, NY 11201
TEL: 718-596-4781
Purpose: To bring AIDS information to a difficult-to-reach population.
Contact: Eugene McGovern, Volunteer Coordinator
Description: The Brooklyn AIDS Task Force (BATF) is faced with a multicultural, multiethnic borough population. Brooklyn is also the borough with the second largest number of AIDS cases in New York City, following Manhattan.
The most obvious problem in trying to get BATF underway was the existing AIDS education materials, which were designed for white, middle-class, educated Americans, but do not necessarily work for other groups.
The breakthrough came in an unusual way for BATF. The Education Director began an outreach project in her own neighborhood, distributing pamphlets in the supermarket, the laundromat and other public places. An 11-year-old child asked why she was carrying around those heavy boxes of pamphlets. When told it was AIDS education materials, the child's interest and curiosity were obvious, and she told of her friends' questions, also. At a later meeting with the young group - five children, black, white and Hispanic - the very serious youngsters had long lists of questions to ask, and wrote down the answers.
Now, those children are BATF's most active, most concerned, and most effective volunteers. They are workers; they are speakers. Throughout the community, it is obvious that people are relating to them. All the statistics and studies in the world could not have attained such results.
The children created drawings to show people that they understand what AIDS is about and the ways in which it is transmitted.
In addition, a videotape, *Children Speak About AIDS,* was produced with the same children telling people, in their own words, all about the disease. It has been done in English, Spanish, French and Creole. It has been a useful tool in reaching the hard-to-reach parts of the community with AIDS information. It opens doors and provides a basis for initiating discussions about topics, such as sexuality and condoms, that people otherwise have trouble talking about. In this and other ways, the Task Force is adjusting its AIDS information and its approach to fit the different cultures of Brooklyn.
In addition to the drawings and the video, the children created an AIDS-related coloring book to be used in our work in the schools. It is the first of a series that will explain the different processes of the infection, virus transmission, etc. The coloring book also comes in four languages.

During a community outreach effort, "AIDS Information Day," the young volunteers spoke, and entertainment, food, and gifts were provided for visitors. There was a children's workshop, and baby-sitting so mothers could attend. People with AIDS, those who have lost a loved one to AIDS, and those who have dealt with AIDS spoke, also, to try to help people come to terms with the disease and understand what AIDS means to those who are sick and their families. One is a volunteer with the Task Force - a mother whose son died of AIDS in 1987.

The chance encounter with the young volunteers and the direction it has taken to help educate the community, and the willingness of AIDS sufferers and their families to share their experiences, have made an enormous difference in the Task Force's ability to present AIDS education information, and to be heard. And a lesson that surfaced is that - in enlisting volunteers - children should be included as a viable resource.

BROWN PROGRAM IN LEADERSHIP
SEE LEADERSHIP DEVELOPMENT/BOARDS: CHILDREN/YOUTH

BUT I'M DIFFERENT...
SEE COMMUNICATIONS & PUBLIC RELATIONS: CHILDREN/YOUTH

C.V. STARR NATIONAL SERVICE FELLOWSHIP PROGRAM
SEE NATIONAL SERVICE/POINTS OF LIGHT INITIATIVE

CAMP GOOD DAYS AND SPECIAL TIMES
American Cancer Society
1400 North Winton Road
Rochester, NY 14609
TEL: 716-288-1950
Purpose: To provide a residential camp for children with cancer.
Contact: Volunteer Coordinator
Description: Camp Good Days and Special Times is a residential camp for children with cancer. It has served children with this illness since 1979. Volunteers at the camp include high school and college students, each assigned to a number of children. The young volunteers are charged with seeing that the young residents enjoy themselves through softball, volleyball, swimming, fishing, riding, painting, singing, dancing or, according to one young volunteer, simply "celebrating life - the real purpose of the camp."
Although the volunteers receive training before being given assignments, many find it difficult to be cheerful at first, since they are constantly aware that the children they are working with are terminally ill. However, soon somewhat of a role reversal happens, and the campers teach the volunteers "how to appreciate things that they have, how to laugh when it hurts, and how to face the unknown with a smile." This inspires the young volunteers to find ways to give the children a reason to fight their illness. When the camp period is over, volunteers return to schools and colleges knowing that one person really can make a difference, and that problems can be faced head on and overcome. Writing of her work with the children for a local newspaper, one volunteer said she got "as much, or more, from the experience as those that I helped."
Founded: 1979

CAMPUS LITERACY AWARENESS MONTH PROGRAM
Student Coalition for Action in Literacy Education (SCALE)
University of North Carolina
Chapel Hill, NC 27514
TEL: 919-962-2333
Purpose: To raise awareness about the problems of illiteracy.
Contact: SCALE Coordinator
Description: March of each year is *Campus Literacy Awareness Month* for COOL (Campus Outreach Opportunity League)

chapters on campuses across the country. On the Chapel Hill campus of the University of North Carolina, SCALE (Student Coalition for Action in Literacy Education) is very active in literacy programs during the entire academic year, but that special month gives the group an opportunity to create special projects to promote literacy.
A popular program is the brainstorming session that the group pulls together every year. SCALE recruits campus volunteers to come together and share ideas about ways in which students can help improve education in the United States. One conclusion was to help other campus groups mount intensive programs during *Campus Literacy Awareness Month.* They decided to develop a package that would help other groups organize literacy projects during this special month.
The Campus Literacy Awareness Month Packet was designed by SCALE and has been distributed nationwide. The packet includes examples of awareness week activities, a listing of national literacy contacts, and advice on how to organize a month of awareness. Many programs that had their roots in *Campus Literacy Awareness Month* have become permanent programs with various sponsors from the community.
Publications: Campus Literacy Awareness Month Packet

CAMPUS MINISTRY
SEE VOLUNTEERS: CHURCH/SYNAGOGUE MEMBERS

CAUSE (COMMUNITY AND UNIVERSITY SERVICES IN EDUCATION)
St. John's University
Student Development
Grand Central & Utopia Parkway
Jamaica, NY 11439
TEL: 212-990-6256
Purpose: To involve students in various volunteer programs enabling them to develop their intellectual, social, and personal qualities by participating in community services.
Sponsor: St. John's University
Contact: Ms. Eileen Devine
Description: CAUSE (Community and University Services in Education) was established in 1965 and until 1981 was primarily a tutoring and workshop program for students in attendance at schools in the Jamaica area. In fall 1981, due to a desire to expand its scope of volunteer involvement, *CAUSE* was reorganized to be, essentially, a student volunteer-administered volunteer placement program. This is accomplished through three separate programs:
- *The Education Program* provides volunteers to tutor grammar school children or to volunteer in the area of special education.
- *VITA (Volunteer Income Tax Program)* trains volunteers, through the IRS, to assist students, senior citizens and others in preparing their income tax returns.
- *The Volunteer Placement Program* acts as a clearinghouse to bring prospective volunteers into contact with agencies which utilize volunteers in the areas of health, social services, business law and special projects.
Founded: 1965

CHAMPIONS RUN FOR LIFE TORCH RELAY
SEE FUNDING/FUND-RAISING/RELATED SERVICES: WALKS/RACES

CHIP/AHIP (CHARLOTTESVILLE HOUSING IMPROVEMENT PROGRAM/ALBEMARLE HOUSING IMPROVEMENT PROGRAM)
Madison House
170 Rugby Road
Charlottesville, VA 22903
TEL: 703-977-7051

Purpose: To assist low-income residents in the area in their efforts to obtain safe and decent housing.
Sponsor: City of Charlottesville; County of Albemarle; Madison House
Contact: Wanda J. Birckhead-Jennings
Description: A group of university students banded together in 1969 to help repair some of the housing damage left by Hurricane Camille. After the initial clean-up work, the students decided to stay together and formed "Students Concerned with Rural and Urban Betterment (SCRUB)." The program focused its attention on the application of volunteer power and expertise to answer the critical housing needs of the area by repairing, renovating, and rehabilitating homes occupied by "low-income" families. The program quickly gained the respect of the entire Charlottesville community.

As the program developed, it quickly outgrew its Madison House program status. On February 20, 1974, the program incorporated as CHIP (Charlottesville Housing Improvement Program), a subsidiary of the Charlottesville Housing Foundation. CHIP concentrates its efforts on renovation of substandard, owner-occupied housing in the City of Charlottesville. AHIP (Albemarle Housing Improvement Program), in Albemarle county, was formed soon after CHIP, and strives toward the same goal in the County of Albemarle. Madison House helps recruit volunteers for both of the programs.

The volunteer possibilities with CHIP and AHIP can completely renovate a home for one-third to one-half the standard commercial cost. This low operating standard is accomplished through the use of student and community volunteers in the labor force. Materials are paid for by the homeowners through their own resources, government grants, or bank loans.
Founded: 1969

CHIP-IN
SEE VOLUNTEERS: CHURCH/SYNAGOGUE MEMBERS

CHRISTIAN INVOLVEMENT
SEE VOLUNTEERS: CHURCH/SYNAGOGUE MEMBERS

CHRISTIAN SERVICE DEPARTMENT
SEE VOLUNTEERS: CHURCH/SYNAGOGUE MEMBERS

CHRISTIAN SERVICE PROGRAM
SEE VOLUNTEERS: CHURCH/SYNAGOGUE MEMBERS

CIPED (COMMUNITY INVOLVEMENT PERSONAL EDUCATION DEVELOPMENT)
South Brunswick High School
Major Road
Monmouth Junction, NJ 08852
TEL: 201-329-4567
Purpose: To provide an experiential learning program for high school students at field sites in the community.
Sponsor: South Brunswick High School
Contact: Mary Ann Stein-Horenstein, Chairperson
Description: The CIPED program began as a solution to overcrowding in South Brunswick High School. There was not enough room to house all the students five days a week; an experiential program, placing one fifth of the student body at field sites each day, was established. The program, now more than ten years old, has continued because it provides valuable learning experiences.

As it is now set up each junior and senior in South Brunswick High School spends one day a week all year out of the school in a helping-learning situation while the sophomores participate for only one quarter of the school year. Most placements are career-oriented, but some are service-oriented and some are involved with the development of leisure-time activities. Students

are placed almost everywhere that adults work: in elementary schools, day care centers, hospitals, nursing homes, government agencies, large corporations such as IBM and Sperry Univac, small businesses ranging from clothing stores to gas stations, theatres, museums, farms, college science labs and computer centers, and artists' studios.

Approximately 500 students have been placed this year; they work for high school credit, not pay. School buses transport them to field sites early in the day and bring them back to school at the end of the day so they can participate in extra-curricular activities or go to work. There is a staff of four professionals, with the support of one secretary, who work full-time in the program: supervising students in the field, counseling and evaluating them and running reflective sessions in school. The program is completely funded locally.

CITY VOLUNTEER CORPS
SEE COMMUNITY SERVICES: URBAN

CITY YEAR
SEE COMMUNITY SERVICES: STUDENTS

CLASS ACTION SUIT
SEE FUNDING/FUND-RAISING/RELATED SERVICES

COLLEGE-IN-RESIDENCE VOLUNTEERS (CIRV)
Washington Department of Social & Health Services
Box 200
Medical Lake, WA 99022
TEL: 509-299-5087
Purpose: To assist developmentally disabled residents in their daily lives.
Sponsor: Department of Social and Health Services, State of Washington
Contact: Diane White
Description: Called the College-in-Residence Volunteers program (CIRV), this program furnishes free room and board to college students in return for 15 hours of volunteer service per week. Students must be taking a minimum of 10 credits per quarter and maintain a C average to continue in the program.

The program has 30 positions at this time. The students live in bachelor apartments with a private bath or two to one double-bedroom apartment. The program is designed for single students, unless both the husband and wife are enrolled in college, then they both must work 15 hours per week.

The students perform a variety of duties. Some of their job assignments are in psychology, social work, clerical, recreation, pre-vocational/vocational training of developmentally disabled residents.

The students involved in the program must be willing to work, have strong initiative, and be interested in helping developmentally disabled residents.

There is a packet of rules and regulations that the student must abide by or be terminated from the program.

Lakeland Village is a state residential facility serving developmentally disabled residents, from the ages of 12-78 years old, male and female. Over 90% of the population is severely to profoundly retarded.

The CIRV Program has been ongoing for the last thirteen years.
Publications: Service from the Heart; CIRV Rules and Regulations
Founded: 1969

COMMUNICATING HUMAN NEEDS
SEE COMMUNICATIONS & PUBLIC RELATIONS: CHILDREN/YOUTH

COMMUNITY FIELD WORK
Beaver County Day School
Hammond Street
Chestnut Hill, MA 02167
TEL: 617-734-6950
Purpose: To provide experience in community welfare and social programs for students.
Sponsor: Beaver County Day School
Contact: Mrs. Kirk, Mrs. Kleppner
Description: The Community Field Work course consists of field work within the community under the supervision of Beaver County Day School faculty and an on-site supervisor. Field work places students in responsible roles in the adult world and provides students with opportunities to learn some of the skills required and problems encountered in the human services field. Field work placements are arranged on an individual basis; the course instructors are available for help in finding a placement.
In addition, there is a weekly class meeting for all students taking community field work. This time is used to learn more about the human services field through readings, outside speakers, trips to other sites, and discussion/supervision on the students' placements. Credit for this course is individually arranged. The number of credits depends both on the amount of time worked outside of class and the amount of academic readings and/or papers the student contracts to do.
Course Requirements
- All students should obtain a field placement as soon as possible. That placement must be okayed by the instructors. A field supervisor should be selected; this is someone who will agree to oversee your work on the job and to write a quarterly report about your progress.
- A field work contract must be written up and signed by the student, the field supervisor, and the instructors. If the student is planning to leave school early in order to participate at her/his placement, the contract must also be signed by the student's parents (and a note allowing the student to drive on and off campus must be presented). The contract should include the following: student's name, location of the placement, the dates and times the student will be there, expected duties, supervisor (and that the supervisor agrees to write reports about the student), and some statement of what the student expects to receive from the placement. A first draft should be checked by one of the instructors before the final draft is written up and signed.
- Each student should make an appointment to speak with the instructors to negotiate the number of credits to be received for this course and what will be done to gain the credits. This should also be included in the contract.
- Each student will be expected to keep a weekly journal, detailing on-site experience. This journal will be checked periodically by the instructor.
- There will be readings assigned for the class meeting. Students are expected to attend the class and to keep up with the assigned work.
- A final project for each semester will be due on the last day of class for the semester. For most students this will entail putting together an annotated bibliography having to do with a subject of interest that also enhances the contribution to the placement. Other possible projects are individually negotiable.

COMMUNITY LABORATORY PROJECT
Benjamin Banneker High School
800 Euclid Street, NW
Washington, DC 20001
TEL: 202-673-7322
Purpose: To enable youth to explore personal and career goals beyond the classroom.
Sponsor: District of Columbia School System
Contact: Vernita L. Jefferson

Description: It is an established fact that the students at Banneker High School are highly motivated, since it is a model school. At the time of its founding in 1981, community service was immediately made part of the curriculum. The "Lab Project" is built into the lesson plan for grades nine through twelve. Both students and the community have reaped benefits, as the students explore personal and career goals through their interaction with the community.
Students receive a general orientation to Community Lab when they arrive at Banneker for the first time. Directors of placement sites are invited to the school for a training program, also. Students receive additional training at the volunteer worksites. Funds for the program are provided from the general school funds, with the Guidance Department in charge of the administration of the program.
During the freshman and sophomore years, students are usually placed in schools, day care centers, hospitals, or libraries - with an attempt to locate positions within walking distance of home or school. Junior and Senior students are not held to this practice and assume primary responsibility for choosing placements and meeting the requirements.
In some cases, Community Lab has altered the direction of career goals. Summer jobs have been offered to the interns in fields in which many of them plan careers. Credit is given for lab participation (one-quarter credit for 45 hours for freshmen and sophomores; one-half credit for 90 hours for juniors and seniors). Each student requires 1.5 community lab credits to graduate. Students have appreciated the opportunity with comments ranging from, "Tutoring taught me to have patience," to "My supervisor taught me many things that I would never have learned in the classroom." One insightful statement was, "I have learned to do without favors."
Founded: 1981

COMMUNITY LEARNING PROGRAM
Fort Campbell High School
South Carolina and Chaffee Road
Fort Campbell, KY 42223
TEL: 502-435-1781
Purpose: To provide students with alternative learning experiences which can be best provided by agencies outside the regular school program.
Sponsor: Fort Campbell High School
Contact: Stan Lane, Coordinator
Description: In order to meet the important goal of developing a student's ability to recognize and to assume the duties and responsibilities of society, the curriculum for Fort Campbell High School should reach beyond the classroom activities and provide students with alternative learning experiences which can be best provided by agencies outside the regular school program.
To accomplish this goal, the Community Learning Program has been developed. In general, this experience can be defined as planned activities organized through the school which provide an opportunity to learn by doing. It draws upon the community resources of business and industry, government, and service organizations to expand student learning beyond the classroom boundary. The Community Learning Program provides students with opportunities to put theory into practice and to bridge the gap from school to career. Program goals and objectives are:
- To provide a more realistic transition from school life to adulthood through constructive student-community interaction.
- To provide for the expansion and maturation of intellectual abilities and skills through the application of classroom knowledge in solving practical problems.
- To encourage the formation and practice of behavioral patterns which are essential for adjustment into society.
- To provide students with the opportunity to explore a variety of career interests.

● To increase the student's understanding and awareness of the nature of various careers.

Community Learning allows the student to work with or without pay in a community business or organization. The student's experience will be supervised by both an on-the-job sponsor and a school coordinator. While the duration of most experiences will, in general, be a minimum of nine weeks, both the length, hours per week, and the nature of the assignment will be agreed upon, in advance, by the student, the sponsor, and the school coordinator. In addition to the off-campus experience, attendance at weekly seminars is required. The student can earn a maximum of two credits per school year for 15 hours of work per week in an approved program. Placement may be accomplished by two methods:

● students desiring to find their own training site or, if presently employed, may petition the school coordinator to determine whether the site meets the requirements for receiving credit; and

● the coordinator, after the interested student has applied and been accepted, assists in locating and selecting a suitable training station.

In all cases, the training experience must conform to Kentucky child labor laws. Participating students must be at least 16 years of age and if below 18, they must secure a work permit. Students above 18 years of age must have a birth certificate on file. The student will be eligible for placement only after successfully:

● receiving positive recommendations from teachers and other school personnel;

● completing a pre-placement interview with the program coordinator or other school official;

● completing an employment interview with the potential training station supervisor.

Evaluation of each student's progress will be ongoing. Because of the subjective and intangible nature of the areas being evaluated, a pass/fail method of grade marking is used which does influence the student's grade point average. Records of periodic observations and evaluations by the training sponsor and the school coordinators are kept on file to verify grades as well as to show student progress.

COMMUNITY RESOURCE VOLUNTEERS
SEE VOLUNTEERS: PROFESSIONALS

COMMUNITY SERVICE/AWARENESS ACTION
Sidwell Friends
3825 Wisconsin Avenue, NW
Washington, DC 20016
TEL: 202-537-8180
Purpose: To introduce students to societal problems that they might encounter in their community service.
Description: All students at Sidwell Friends High School must complete a minimum of 30 hours of service work, which must involve direct contact with the disadvantaged, or they will not graduate. And they must complete this work before the beginning of the senior year.
The school has a three-pronged program for service to the community:
● The Community Service requirement;
● A Freshman Studio Course, a component of which deals with problems of society; and
● The *Community Action Committee (CAC).*
The CAC is one of the largest groups in the school. Training for this committee is done by the site supervisor. CAC completes at least one special project a month and operates long-term projects such as the *Sandwiches Program,* in which members make over 200 sandwiches each week to go to soup kitchens. CAC also works with the elderly, the handicapped, and the infirm, tutors young children in the basic skills, and works in many projects side-by-side with the poor.

The Administrator for Community Service is always available to the students, offering guidance in all areas of the program. When the projects are completed, students are expected to write an evaluation of their community service work experience.
The budget of the Community Service Program is $1,500, with supplemental funds comng from the students' own activities, such as weekly bake sales.

COMMUNITY SERVICE REQUIREMENT
SEE COMMUNITY SERVICES: STUDENTS

COMMUNITY SERVICES PROJECT
SEE COMMUNITY SERVICES: STUDENTS

COMPANIONSHIP/THERAPY PROGRAM
Madison House
170 Rugby Road
Charlottesville, VA 22903
TEL: 804-977-7051
Purpose: To provide assistance for agencies dealing with mental, physical, or emotional problems.
Sponsor: Madison House
Contact: Jane Parker, Director
Description: Begun in 1969 as the "Mental Health/Companionship Program," this program quickly became the "catch-all" for all programs dealing remotely with "companionship." Volunteers worked at Western State Hospital (the Adoptive Grandparents Program), at the Children's Rehabilitation Center, in the operating room at University Hospital, for the Recording for the Blind service, at the Bloomfield School, and for the Association for Retarded Citizens.
As the program became more and more diverse, separate programs began to emerge. The current program, Companionship/Therapy, recruits volunteers for those agencies dealing with physical, mental and emotional problems only. This program places volunteers in many different settings. They work with a variety of age groups and encounter many different emotional, mental, or physical problems. Recently the program expanded to include citizen advocacy and work with troubled youth in the Community Attention Homes.
Long-term assignments are available at Charlottesville-Albemarle Association for Retarded Citizens, Bloomfield School, Mental Health Activities Center, and others. Agencies needing short-term assistance for a special situation contact the Companion/Therapy Program, and every effort is made to assign a volunteer to the agency. These short-term assignments might include campaigning for the March of Dimes or the Walk for Hunger Program, for example.
All assignments - both short- and long-term - demand volunteers who are willing and enthusiastic about working with people who are frequently unable to initiate social interchange. Volunteers must be independent, willing to work with minimal supervision, and willing to strive to be innovative and committed.
Leaders of the Special Olympics program have found Companion/Therapy volunteers to be especially effective in encouraging handicapped children to compete in the Olympics, helping them get to the events, and waiting for them at the finish line with big smiles and warm hugs.
Founded: 1969

COOL IT!
National Wildlife Federation
1400 Sixteenth Street, NW
Washington, DC 20036-2266
TEL: 202-797-6858
Purpose: To bring the reaffirmation of the first *Earth Day* of 1970 to campuses throughout the country.
Contact: Campus Coordinator

Description: Students on campuses across the country began a process in April 1990 that they have termed *COOL IT!* and subtitled *Earth Century: Earth Day - Every Day.* The student-supported campaign is sponsored by the *National Wildlife Federation* and is concerned with recycling, solid waste disposal, public transportation, energy efficiency, and bicycle paths and walkways. Campus leaders expect the programs launched in April 1990 to develop and grow to provide a meaningful agenda for college campuses now and in the future.

DENISON COMMUNITY ASSOCIATION
Denison University
Granville, OH 43023
TEL: 614-587-6639
Purpose: To provide linkage between student volunteers and agencies which use them.
Sponsor: Denison University
Contact: Irene Kennedy, DCA Coordinator
Description: The Denison Community Association is a student-led volunteer organization that allows its members to develop awareness of social conditions existing in the world beyond the college campus. DCA programs serve people who, because of physical or mental disabilities, financial hardships, or loneliness, need companionship or assistance.
At the present time there are well over 300 student volunteers who are participating in one of the committees sponsored by DCA. The students attend an orientation program in the fall which gives a brief introduction as to what their committee does, and then students sign up to work on various committees which work with a specific agency or health care unit. Some of the committees are: *Battered Women's Shelter, Newark Community Hospital, Nursing Home Companions,* and *School Tutoring Programs.*
Each of the various committees has two co-chairpersons who are responsible for their committee. They take care of determining a specific date to travel to their agency and are responsible for contacting their members to make sure they remember their commitment to the program. The co-chairs report to the DCA Cabinet which is a nine-member student group responsible for over-sight of the entire DCA program. The cabinet meets weekly with the DCA Coordinator (a part-time paid university staff member) and the faculty advisor. The Cabinet is responsible for all policy decisions. The cabinet is chaired by two co-presidents who serve as the student leaders of DCA.
DCA receives 50% of its funding directly from the University's general operating budget. This includes the salary of the DCA Coordinator. The other 50% of the operating budget of DCA is funded from the student government budget. DCA leases a car from the University to provide transportation for students to and from their agencies.

DUO
Champlain Valley Union High School
RR2, Box 160
Hinesburg, VT 05461
TEL: 802-482-2101
Purpose: To help students improve their writing through experiences in the community as volunteers.
Credit: one quarter credit/45 hours
Sponsor: Champlain Valley School District
Contact: Joan M. Braun
Description: DUO (Do Unto Others) is a youth community service program with an education component - improving writing skills. It enjoys a high level of commitment on the parts of administration, teachers, parents, students, and the community. It was started in 1971 when an English teacher at the school found that her students were having a difficult time in their creative writing. She felt that community service experience would prod them to improve their writing.
With a proposal to the state in the works for a community service

project called DUO (Do Unto Others), the program, with state funding, became part of the school's curriculum.
Originally, the program was strictly one of community service, but was expanded to include credit for career-oriented volunteer work - one quarter credit for every 45 hours of service.
Students may begin projects at any time during the school year. They may be in-school projects, such as peer counseling or tutoring during their free periods, or work in the community - Big Brothers/Sisters, nursing home and hospital aides, court diversion programs, etc. Students may use only one class period during the school day for the volunteer project, or work on projects after school, on weekends, or during the summer.
Students are bussed from five rural towns, many during the school day to take advantage of the school bus transportation provided. Students range from the handicapped to the gifted, with no exceptions made.
A *Directions Office* keeps staff available at all times to help design community projects after discussing interests, goals, etc. DUO's director is the contact person for agencies and sets up interviews for students. Agency staff and student discuss the position, and tasks are outlined and goals set. All training is done by the agency, on site. After 3-4 weeks at the site, a DUO staff member calls the agency to check the progress of the volunteer and, in some cases, visits the site.
Students keep daily journals, and both volunteer and agency complete evaluations at the end of the project. A DUO workshop is held at the school to enable volunteers to discuss the experience with peers and staff members. If the student is judged successful in all evaluations and the journal entries, credit is awarded.
Each spring, DUO holds a reception for all DUO students, parents, and supervisors. For many parents, this is the first time they have been invited into school for any reason other than to settle a discipline problem. According to one supervisor, "For the first time, many of these students are able to see themselves as the givers." She sees the pride they have in themselves, and the pride that the parents show, as a powerful, positive force.
Founded: 1971

DUTIES TO THE COMMUNITY
Atlanta Public Schools
Planning and Expanded Services
2960 Forrest Hill Drive, SW
Atlanta, GA 30315
TEL: 404-766-0551
Purpose: To enhance student understanding of the responsibility of good citizens to help others.
Sponsor: Atlanta Public Schools
Contact: Barbara I. Whitaker
Description: Duties to the Community is a requisite for graduation in Atlanta high schools. The Board of Education approved this requirement of 75 hours of volunteer work to help the students acquire coping skills, to see how their community works, and to learn that they can make a difference.
Required of students in grades 9-12, the program is operated under the supervision of school staff. Students may volunteer at any "character-building" nonprofit organization approved by the school. These include hospitals, churches, child care centers, and schools. The agencies are considered "learning labs" where people come into contact with people of all ages and backgrounds with needs that they can help to fill.
Orientation to the program is provided for ninth graders as part of a larger program, PECE (Program of Education and Career Exploration). PECE was designed by staff members of the Division, who also have oversight responsiblity. A liaison from the Division visits all school areas, contacts service agencies, and conducts continuing evaluation of the program through interviews with both students and host agencies.
Each local school handles the daily operation and tracks the 75 hours through a system by student, agency staff and school

advisor. Before graduation, students must submit an essay or journal of their experience. This essay is evaluated by the advisor and the school's English Department, who judges its acceptability. One-half unit (7-1/2 hours of credit) is given to each student upon successful completion of the program.

An earlier program of the school system, Youth Challenge, was operated for ten years. Although students received academic credit in that course, also, it was not a required course. Officials feel that many students missed the opportunity to improve basic skills, prepare for meaningful employment, and become better all-around citizens. The required course turns even the most reluctant students into believers.

Founded: 1988

DWIGHT-ENGLEWOOD SCHOOL VOLUNTEER PROGRAM
SEE COMMUNITY SERVICES

EARLY HOME EDUCATION
Madison House
170 Rugby Road
Charlottesville, VA 22903
TEL: 703-977-7051
Purpose: To lay the foundation for learning skills in young children; to stimulate at-home reinforcement by involving parents.
Sponsor: Madison House
Contact: Jane Parker
Description: In 1973, a student in the University Year for Action Program determined that once the Head Start children left the program and its special help to begin Kindergarten, it was often difficult for them to keep up. In 1975 the Head Start Home Based Project resulted from his study and efforts.

This project was designed to send volunteer tutors into the child's home to work with the parent(s) and create a learning environment at home. By having the families more involved in the child's education, it was hoped that their learning ability would increase. When the Head Start office had to discontinue this successful program in 1976, Madison House picked it up as the Early Home Education project and began operating on a limited basis the following year. The major change in the program is that it now deals with children already enrolled in Kindergarten.

Early Home Education is an in-the-home tutoring project in which volunteers tutor parents as well as their kindergarten-aged children. The rationale behind the program is that it is not true that parents have no concern for their children's education. What is true is that many parents do not know how to tutor or how to enhance their child's educational experience on a daily basis in the home.

This program requires no previous experience in tutoring, but it does demand an ability to communicate with both parent and child. Volunteers receive support from the Early Home Education Program Director, who has been in the field, and can offer advice. Information and advice are available also from the child's Kindergarten teacher.

Volunteers have found that getting to know the family is not always easy, but is usually a rewarding task. Families involved in the program often have entirely different outlooks on life than does the average volunteer. However this challenging program has proven to be one of the favorites of the volunteers.

Founded: 1975

EDUCATIONAL PARTICIPATION IN COMMUNITIES
California State University
Experiential Learning Center
1250 Bellflower Blvd, Room 110
Long Beach, CA 90840
TEL: 213-498-5395
Purpose: To place students in volunteer and paid internships.
Sponsor: Federal/state/student government

Contact: Ruby Leavell
Description: EPIC (Educational Participation in Communities) provides volunteer work for student interns in community projects and agencies, where students can gain valuable vocational experience while filling the needs of the community.

Students volunteer three to nine hours a week for at least one semester, and may work during the day, after school, or on weekends.

The EPIC program has valuable field experience positions available for credit, as well as noncredit. Classes for credit are offered on a credit/no credit basis. Students may receive one to three units while gaining experience. Three hours of volunteer work per week per unit of credit are required. All students must either apply for volunteer placement through the EPIC program or develop their own placement with approval from the EPIC program. Meetings with faculty advisors are to be arranged.

Any undergraduate or graduate student in good academic standing who wishes to gain insight into their career, themselves and others, may participate in EPIC. Ways in which students benefit include:

- EPIC provides important on-the-job experience not always available in an academic setting. Students can work with professionals and effectively relate classroom theory with practical application.
- EPIC can help students - especially undergraduates - select their careers and career goals, as they observe and participate in work experiences related to their major.
- EPIC can aid in personal growth, improving students' abilities to work with people, developing self-confidence and social awareness, and giving them a greater understanding of their abilities.
- EPIC enables students to establish contacts with prospective employers, and to evaluate possible job opportunities firsthand.

EMERGENCY INFANT NUTRITION PROGRAM: FREE BREAKFAST PROJECT
Marillac Social Center
2822 West Jackson Boulevard
Chicago, IL 60612
TEL: 312-722-7440
Purpose: To provide supplemental food to infants from very low income families, and free breakfasts in the summer to children under 18 from the school year free breakfast program.
Sponsor: Marillac Agency, private donations, USDA, CSA, JTPA
Contact: Mrs. Kay Hallagan
Description: The death rate for infants in the black ghettos of Chicago is five times as high as for infants living in suburban Chicago. They succumb to many ailments, but often the basis is the poor nutrition of the mother while carrying the child or of the child as an infant. Many of these infants are born to very young mothers, or to mothers with vary large families and very low income. The inflationary rise in food prices has made the gap even higher between what these families can pay for food and what good infant nourishment costs. Marillac is helping to alleviate this infant mortality rate by providing for needy infants who are not being helped in other programs.

Voluntary efforts in providing baby food, donations, and other services helped the program to get started in 1970, enabling the Marillac Agency to give supplemental packages of formula, baby food and sometimes Pampers and baby clothes to needy infants - about 70 per week. Since 1977, CSA funding has funded the program and now about 1,200 infants per year are assisted with food and formula. Community interest continues, i.e., the Chicago Community Trust has given some additional funds to be used for purchasing Pampers, bottles, shirts, etc., for the infants. Space and staff assistance is provided by the Marillac Agency.

The infants are located by outreach social workers or have been located by medical social workers, Chicago Board of Health nurses, or Public Aid workers. The child's name and birth date are recorded on a card, which is presented by a family member once a week to receive the food. Food packages have been assembled by teenaged Neighborhood Youth Corps workers and others.

For the past ten years, the Agency also has sponsored a free summer breakfast program. This year, a total of 65,000 free breakfasts were served to children from eight neighborhood sites, ranging from storefront churches to a motorcycle club room. Initially, about 40 mothers volunteered to distribute the packages for about eight weeks each summer. Today community mothers are assisted by JTPA youngsters in the distribution process. Funds for the food and paper goods are furnished by the U.S. Department of Agriculture.

Founded: 1970

FARE SHARE
SEE VOLUNTEERS: SELF-HELP

FIELD EDUCATION PROGRAM
SEE VOLUNTEERS: CHURCH/SYNAGOGUE MEMBERS

FIELD EXPERIENCE EDUCATION
Sonoma State University
1801 East Cotati Avenue
Rohnert Park, CA 94928
TEL: 707-664-2547
Purpose: To help university students gain valuable "on-the-job" experience in the community to complement and enhance their academic programs.
Sponsor: The State of California and the California State University
Contact: Linda Lipps, Field Experience Coordinator
Description: The Field Experience Program began in 1968 as a tribute to Dr. Martin Luther King and as a vehicle for university students to become active in providing community service to the local community. Since then it has expanded to be a clearinghouse for not only volunteer positions but for internships and cooperative education placements as well.

Field Experience Education refers to various types of field-based or off-campus learning experiences designed to augment classroom theory.

At Sonoma State University the student can choose from a variety of credit-bearing "field experience" opportunities. The Community Inolvement Program is geared toward the undergraduate and is offered in 20 departments. Internships, field experience classes, and practicums are offered through many departments for the upper division and graduate students. Special studies include research projects for the upper division, and graduate level students, and cooperative education (alternating periods of work and school) is now being developed with various agencies and corporations. Field Experience Education is a mechanism to provide career related experiences within the context of a College truly committed to the value of a liberal arts education.

Community Involvement Program
Many undergraduates find the Community Involvement Program (CIP) the most appropriate means to gain valuable work experience and to "reality test" potential career goals while simultaneously accruing college credit.

CIP is a community service program based on the idea that the total value of a college education is not available solely within the confines of a classroom. It is strictly a volunteer program where students work directly with people in the community for an average of six to eight hours a week in roles such as teacher aides, recreation supervisors, hospital aides, peer counselors, and ecology center volunteers.

Each semester over 200 students receive one to four units of credit through 20 different departments for their volunteer work; a total of six units may be applied toward graduation. The student must locate a placement during the first three weeks of the semester and sign a Volunteer Agreement in conjunction with the agency supervisor, the faculty sponsor, and the Field Experience Office to assist the student in the selection of placements.

The student is required to volunteer a minimum of 30 hours per unit of credit each semester and submit a time log with a summary paper to the faculty sponsor at the end of the semester. Students get on-the-job exposure to a variety of settings and then return to classroom seminars where they discuss their work experiences with other students and faculty. The faculty advisor is ultimately responsible for the student evaluation and the granting of academic credit on a Credit/No Credit basis.

Internships
An internship is a supervised program of work and study which involves a student working in a business, governmental or organizational setting for the primary purpose of promoting the student's intellectual, professional and personal growth. An internship usually involves advanced undergraduate students working as pre-professionals or para-professionals in fields that relate directly to their career or academic interests.

Internships engender a crucial three-way relationship between student, faculty sponsor and on-the-job supervisor where supervision and evaluation are key concepts. Many internships involve regularly scheduled classroom meetings that expand upon the supervised work experiences. Internships can be both paid and non-paid, and they may extend a semester, a year, or a summer. Paid internships are particularly valuable for the many students who must work for subsistence because their employment can be integrated with their academic concerns.

Students intern in a great variety of settings including: personnel departments, planning departments, probation offices, juvenile halls, police departments, recreation departments, mental health clinics, corporations, and small businesses.

Regional, state and nationwide opportunities are available for advanced students through programs such as WCLA (Washington Center for Learning Alternatives) in Washington, DC, or WICHE (Western Interstate Commission for Higher Education).

Many students begin as volunteers through CIP and then develop a more responsible and structured placement as an internship. This continuum of experiences often provides the skills and background necessary to gain meaningful employment upon graduation.

Who benefits from Field Experience Education?
The Students:
- Gain a better understanding of the subject matter in their academic fields;
- Expand their understanding, in the broadest sense, of themselves and their environment;
- Explore potential vocations and test interests in a particular vocation;
- Develop basic work skills and professional competencies;
- Clarify personal and educational goals and values.

The Employer/Community:
- Human service enterprises gain needed volunteer assistance;
- Agencies, organizations, businesses, and industries secure the services of able students who are highly motivated and eager to learn;
- Employers are provided with creative personnel familiar with modern concepts;
- Recruitment of experienced and tested personnel by employers is facilitated.

The Campus:
- Improves the educational program by offering students direct experience to broaden their appreciation of theoretical learning;
- Faculty members are provided the opportunity to gain additional information about current and relevant applications of their subject matter;
- Placement of graduates improves;
- A closer relationship between campus and its surrounding communities is fostered.

Founded: 1968

FRESH FORCE
Minneapolis Public Schools
404 South Eighth Street
Minneapolis, MN 55404
TEL: 612-340-7670
Purpose: To invite young teens to develop and participate in community service projects.
Sponsor: Minneapolis Public Schools
Contact: Tim Gusk
Description: Fresh Force is a three-way partnership involving public, private and business sectors. It is operated in junior high schools, reaching seventh and eighth graders in the Minneapolis area. Management is shared among the sponsors and a Board of Directors made up of 35 seventh and eighth graders drawn from each junior high school. Students are chosen for the board based on leadership potential and level of involvement in the projects. They are selected either by the Fresh Force director or the school Fresh Force liaisons.
Internal youth leadership is the key to the success of each school's program. Adult advisors assist the youth when needed. Ten junior high schools are involved in the program. Classes are available in three of the schools for uninvolved students wishing to join the Fresh Force program. These classes provide training in communication, interviewing, and other leadership skills. They require one hour each week for eight weeks. After the sixth week, the students create their projects. Teachers and Fresh Force staff follow up on all projects.
Recruitment of the junior high students is the same as for adult volunteers. Posters, brochures and videos are used in an extensive marketing campaign funded in part with contributions from public relations firms and printers. The video is designed to attract this age group - a popular local band performed the group's theme song, and the Minnesota Twins and the Mayor danced.
A team concept is used in Fresh Force projects, involving at least three teens. They are sponsored by local service organizations, and require completion within a specified amount of time. The youth themselves join with adult advisors in planning and implementing training. Up to $500 in costs are provided for selected projects by Fresh Force.
One reason given for utilizing young teens is because early adolescents are easily excited about the issues involved in community service and are eager to volunteer. Also, project leaders find that younger teens are especially isolated, and the project plays a role in providing constructive interaction with their peers and the community.
Founded: 1984

FRIENDS OF THE ROUGE
SEE VOLUNTEERS: PRISONERS/EX-OFFENDERS

GARDEN OF YOUNG HEARTS
Special Populations Division
Chesterfield Parks and Recreation
Richmond, VA 23832
TEL: 804-748-1623
Purpose: To provide a place where mentally retarded youths could enjoy a prom of their own.
Sponsor: Knights of Columbus
Contact: Sharon Entsminger, Special Populations Manager
Description: A parent, concerned about her mentally retarded child feeling uncomfortable at regular high school proms, began the process of a special prom for these young people. *Chesterfield Parks and Recreation,* the *Knights of Columbus,* and the *Adult Career Center for Exceptional Persons* cosponsored the first prom in 1986, and have held the event each year since then. The theme for the 1989 prom was *A Garden of Young Hearts.*
Volunteers from *Acteen Activators,* a youth group from Baptist churches in the Richmond area, helped out as part of their training for a mission trip later in the year. One parent proudly pointed out that her mentally retarded son had two volunteer jobs - one at a hospital and the other with the Catholic Diocese. The teen volunteers decorated the ballroom with streamers and balloons, served refreshments, led games, and got the students dancing. The *Rubber Biscuit Band* volunteered to provide music as in previous years, stating, "We love to play for these kids because they are so appreciative." The parents were pleased to note that the band members treated the kids like normal teenagers, responding to their song requests and generally chatting with them when they approached the bandstand.
The enthusiasm of the handicapped youth soon spread to the teen volunteers and parents, who danced with and among the youths throughout the evening. According to the project director, "The kids really look forward to it, and each year it gets a little better."

THE GATEHOUSE: THE COOK/DOUGLASS PEER COUNSELING CENTER
Douglass College
DPO J
New Brunswick, NJ 08903
TEL: 201-846-3579 (Gatehouse); 201-932-9069 (Psych Svcs)
Purpose: To provide a one-to-one peer counseling relationship for the students on campus.
Sponsor: Psychological Services and Student Life
Contact: Director
Description: The Gatehouse is a student-run peer counseling organization which serves the Cook/Douglass community. The program began in 1976 when the students on campus, along with Psychological Services, decided that a peer counseling service was needed. Since then, the program has grown into a large organization with approximately 75 student volunteers, open five nights a week, and providing a 1:1 peer relationship for those who need the services.
Most business decisions are decided upon by the Executive Committee, composed of four members. Many of these decisions also are discussed at monthly general meetings with the total membership. There are many other levels of involvement which require different forms of training.
To become a peer counselor at the Gatehouse, volunteers must complete 30 hours of training. The training program is facilitated by previously trained students with the help of two trained professionals. Training is based on Rogerian psychology. During training sessions, topics such as the following are discussed:
- values clarification
- paraphrasing
- reflection of feelings
- listening skills
- crisis intervention
- referrals

After training is completed, students are required to attend one two-and-a-half-hour shift a week. The shifts are led by a supervisor who helps to establish group cohesiveness. Members who want to become shift supervisors are required to complete a two-day training session.
Shifts serve a double purpose. They are also an extension of the original training program. When "shiftees" are not counseling either on the phone or with a "drop-in," they are participating in exercises which help them to develop their skills.
The organization also runs programs for the college population. They include:
- a nutrition and weight control workshop
- a stress workshop
- a program for freshmen on how to adjust to college life

In addition, the organization is involved in various other community activities. Other ways that volunteers get involved in the organization is through a publicity committee, a communications committee, and a committee on workshops.
Funding comes from both Douglass and Cook Colleges as well as fundraisers held by the organization itself.
Founded: 1976

GONZAGA ACTION PROGRAM (GAP)
SEE VOLUNTEERS: CHURCH/SYNAGOGUE MEMBERS

THE GREATER CLEVELAND CONNECTION
Cleveland State University
East 24th and Euclid
Cleveland, OH 44115
TEL: 216-687-2059
Purpose: To help meet community social service needs while involving student volunteers in experiential learning.
Sponsor: The Cleveland Foundation (initially); Cuyahoga Community College; Ursuline College; Cleveland State University
Contact: Paul B. Klein, Director
Description: Founded in 1977 by a group of college students, the Greater Cleveland Connection extends social service and community outreach to the people of Cleveland, while offering an experiential learning program for college students.
During the growth stages of rendering personal care and service to a multitude of social atmospheres and ethnic cultures, the pioneer student volunteers also perceived the opportunity to enhance their educational experiences and explore a variety of careers. With the guidance and support of key community activists, a proposal for grant funds was submitted to The Cleveland Foundation. Shortly thereafter, the concept of the Greater Cleveland Connection became a reality.
Students from Cleveland State University and the Eastern and Western Campuses of Cuyahoga Community College were soon volunteering their time and effort in community settings. Two years later, the Metropolitan Campus of Cuyahoga Community College became a member of the Greater Cleveland Connection. An additional grant award facilitated the incorporation of Ursuline College in 1981. Recently, Cleveland State University and Cuyahoga Community College became independent of grant monies and are presently self-funded entities.
Professionally-trained campus coordinators provide guidance, supervision and support to every volunteer. Prior to referral, they screen all students so that each one will be placed in the best agency or organization in accordance with individual interests, academic backgrounds and personal capabilities.
Over a five-year period, more than 3,000 students actively participated in the Greater Cleveland Connection, and nearly 200 social service agencies sought their assistance.
In 1983, the Greater Cleveland Connection fulfilled another goal - the awarding of volunteer internships. Creative and challenging positions became available in a variety of academic fields, including public relations, urban studies, social sciences, business administration, liberal arts and health sciences. For students not faced with the financial strain of the economy, internships such as these provide the opportunity to discover career options.
Today, student volunteers are helping to meet the needs of people through the development, coordination and implementation of human resource programs in areas such as medical and health care facilities, government offices, children's agencies and business and industrial concerns.
Given the amount of progress and accomplishments achieved during the first five years of community involvement, the Board of Directors, staff and student volunteer/interns continue to seek ways of further developing and expanding the program.
Founded: 1977

GREEN COUNTRIE TOWNE PROGRAM
SEE VOLUNTEERS: TENANTS/RESIDENTS

HAWAII STATE YOUTH VOLUNTEER BOARD*
SEE GOVERNORS' OFFICES ON VOLUNTEERISM:
HAWAII

HEALTH AND SAFETY CIRCUS
American Red Cross
Greater Toledo Area Chapter
2275 Collingwood Boulevard
Toledo, OH 43620
TEL: 419-248-3331
Purpose: To enrich the health and safety curricula of the local schools through the resources of health agencies.
Sponsor: American Red Cross; Northwest Ohio School District; community health agencies
Contact: Sharon A. DeVaughn
Description: Thirty-five volunteers assist nurses in the School Health Education Experiences Program (SHEEP) in planning the Health and Safety Circus each fall. SHEEP is comprised of consultants from various school districts.
During the first phase of the program, community health agencies are contacted and asked to bring samples of educational resources in the form of handouts such as posters and pamphlets, and audiovisuals to an organizational meeting. The support provided by school officials and the assistance offered by the agencies are combined to mount the needed project.
Public relations support is provided by the Red Cross, representatives from the health agencies, and the schools. A brochure, which maintains the circus theme, is printed by a local vocational school. The brochures are distributed to principals in over 600 schools in the Northwest Ohio Division, with two representatives from each school invited to attend the Health Fair. Volunteers are involved in all aspects of the program, including supervisory, project management and public relations capacities, as well as in direct delivery of services. Financial support of the program includes a 10% operating budget, and 90% coming from in-kind contributions of goods and services.
Youth volunteers, with adult volunteer supervision, are involved extensively in the program. They are active in registration and evaluation booths, and in the refreshment area. Clown suits are donated for the youth in order to promote the circus theme.
In addition to the benefits to the general public, the Health Fair enabled teachers and nurses to view the latest health and safety films at the Film Fair and collect massive amounts of resources for future classes on health and safety.
In critiquing the Fair based on evaluations received and other criteria, SHEEP Committee members determined that Fairs should be held every two years. The demonstrated cost effectiveness, and the cooperation received from all segments of the community, were major factors in the decision to continue the program.

HOST (HANDS OF SHARED TIME)
Montgomery General Hospital
3438 Olney-Laytonsville Road
Olney, MD 20832
TEL: 301-774-6114
Purpose: To provide friends and helpers to older individuals either in their homes or in nursing homes.
Sponsor: Montgomery General Hospital
Contact: Kelly M. Ring, Service Coordinator
Description: With this interfaith, intergenerational program, a major hospital reaches out to the community and helps to administer a volunteer program that will provide friendship in the way of companionship and services to older persons in their homes and in nursing homes. Montgomery General Hospital in Maryland sponsors the HOST (Hands Of Shared Time) program, which serves the elderly in the entire county.
The program began in 1987 when the Hospital received a four-year grant from the W.K. Kellogg Foundation of Battle Creek, Michigan. A HOST volunteer is a member of the *HOST Community,* and has many options for providing assistance to an older individual. According to the coordinator, "All of these options involve friendship." They include:
 ● **Companionship** - be a friend, listen and talk, write letters, play

games, read (once a week for one hour at the convenience of the volunteer and the HOST friend).

- **Shopping** - either shopping for the older person, or taking him or her shopping once a week.
- **Medical Transportation** - taking a person to the doctor or for treatments on an as-needed basis.
- **Light Housekeeping** - providing some assistance with caring for the home such as light dusting and vacuuming, light snack preparation, emptying trash, etc. Some grooming assistance may be given, also (one or more times per week one hour at a time).
- **Respite Care** - providing relief for a family who cares for a homebound older adult so that the family may leave for home for several hours (weekly or biweekly).
- **Telephone Reassurance** - call an isolated individual on the phone to check on their wellbeing (several times a week at a schedule designed by the volunteer and HOST friend).

Other services that a HOST volunteer can provide are: in-office support to greet drop-in members of the community; assisting with fundraising and membership programs; developing recreational and educational activities; helping with the newsletter; and supporting clerical staff.

Any person 15 years old or older who lives, works, goes to school, or attends a religious congregation in the HOST area may apply to be a volunteer through the HOST office.

All volunteers must participate in the 14-hour training program which is conducted by the Assistant Project Director, HOST staff, and/or other contracted educators. The training is designed to give volunteers a chance to learn about the aging process, develop communication and safety skills, and gain insight into their own attitudes about aging. On-the-job training is included so that volunteers can practice newly-learned skills and feel prepared before entering into their volunteer relationships. Training is also a fun and informal way to get to know other HOST volunteers. Additional training is offered in the form of rap groups, seminars and workshops.

After training, a volunteer is matched with a HOST friend for a specific service. By 1990, almost 200 volunteers completed sixteen training sessions. Supervision is coordinated between HOST and the *Centralized Friendly Visitor Program*. Cooperative assistance also comes from the Retired Senior Volunteer Program (RSVP) and the MGH Home Health Program.

Commitment of one year is requested, beginning with the first training session. The one-year commitment allows the isolated individuals the opportunity to become friends with their volunteers.

In addition to identifying isolated older adults and recruiting volunteers in the community, HOST offers presentations on pertinent topics of interest for the older adult, monthly seminars and a self-help group for caregivers, and forums to inform local clergy and congregants about aging issues. Maintains a lending library of resource materials about aging issues for families, professionals, and others interested in this issue.

Grant monies are alloted in decreasing increments to encourage the community to develop methods to support HOST and keep it self-sufficient. No fees are charged for services received by older persons. Intensive efforts for financial support are continually explored to keep a much-needed service in the community.

One way community members and businesses support the HOST program is through the membership campaign and other donations. Donations also come from individuals in honor of a special person, such as a volunteer, older friend, or family member. Members of HOST receive the *HOST Post* newsletter and other reports and materials as progress warrants.

Publications: Hands of Shared Time (video); HOST Post (newsletter); HOST: Creating an Intergenerational Volunteer Program; Taking a Trip to Friendship: Training Program; HOST Recruitment Brochure; HOST Training Packet
Founded: 1987

JANGO (JUNIOR ARMY NAVY GUILD ORGANIZATION)*
SEE VOLUNTEERS: ARMED FORCES MEMBERS

JESUIT SERVICE PROJECT
Jesuit High School
4133 Banks Street
New Orleans, LA 70119-6683
TEL: 504-483-3872
Purpose: To bring students in direct contact with disadvantaged people in required community service projects.
Sponsor: Jesuit High School
Contact: Sal Anselmo, Director of Service Projects
Description: The oldest high school service project in New Orleans, the Jesuit Service Project has two specific phases:

- **The required course** which begins in January of the student's junior year and mandates 100 hours over the course of a calendar in the community; and
- **Extraordinary Projects** which enable the student to serve more than the required hours.

To complete the required course, every student must fulfill a contract with the Director of Service Projects, which includes a research paper on a specific current problem or on the history of a problem in the service area where the student is working. The student must also write progress papers and reflection papers. Every project must bring the student into direct contact with the disadvantaged.

This program also calls for parent involvement including project evaluations. The student is expected to prepare an evaluation report, also. If the student is involved in an overnight situation, he must also keep a daily journal. Finally, the Director of Service Projects conducts an "exit interview."

Many areas of concern have received the attention of the Jesuit High School students. These include care for the elderly, health care, services for the poor, tutoring, child care and assistance to handicapped persons.

The "extraordinary projects" program is available for students wishing to perform more than the normal allotment of hours. These projects often include working side by side with counselors who handle troubled youth, tutoring adults, or joining the poor in one of their self-help projects.

JFK LIBRARY CORPS
John F. Kennedy Library Foundation
Columbia Point
Boston, MA 02125
TEL: 617-929-4500; 617-436-9986
Purpose: To demonstrate the Kennedy ideal - that one person can make a difference, and every person should try.
Sponsor: John F. Kennedy Library Foundation
Contact: Ronald E. Whelan, Librarian
Description: In spite of its name, JFK Library Corps, this youth project is not a library program, but a community services program with involvement in all areas of need sponsored by the library that houses records and exhibits of President Kennedy's career and papers of Senator Robert Kennedy.

Volunteers in the Corps decide for themselves what kind of projects are worthwhile, and how they should be done. Open to youth ages 11 to 18, over 150 young volunteers from four area schools were involved the first year. Parents, teachers, school administrators, government officials, business and community leaders as well as Library staff lend guidance and resources.

Through their projects, Corps members learn about public service and the role of government in their daily lives. And they see how public policy is made and changed. In the end, they develop interests in their community, exercise real-life leadership, and make a difference in the lives of people in their city.

Volunteer choices include computer teaching, serving meals to the homeless, helping to organize food banks, working at arts festivals, running recreational programs for the handicapped, and working in a group of 20 on a special project. The groups devote an entire weekend to a single project - the most recent being the renovation of a drug rehabilitation center. Another team works on developing dialogue between police and teens, and high school student volunteers assist at free political forums for the public at the Kennedy Library. Others organize school or community clean-up and improvement projects - not only in their own neighborhoods, but wherever the need arises across the city. The program's goal is to keep alive the spirit of idealism and leadership inspired by John and Robert Kennedy.

Publications: JFK Library Corps
Founded: 1985

KIDS HELPING KIDS
SEE SELF-HELP: DRUGS/ALCOHOL

THE LEARNING WEB
SEE TRAINING/CONFERENCES/TEACHING: INTERNSHIPS

LOUISVILLE YOUTH INVOLVEMENT COMMITTEE
SEE ADMINISTRATION: RECRUITMENT/ORIENTATION

MAKING THE GRADE: A REPORT CARD ON AMERICAN YOUTH
SEE LEADERSHIP DEVELOPMENT/BOARDS: CHILDREN/YOUTH

MANTENO VETERANS HOME VOLUNTEER PROGRAM
SEE VOLUNTEERS: OLDER PERSONS

MEDICAL SERVICES PROGRAM
Madison House
170 Rugby Road
Charlottesville, VA 22903
TEL: 804-977-7051
Purpose: To provide necessary support services to both the hospital staff and the patients.
Sponsor: Madison House
Contact: Jane Parker
Description: The Madison House medical volunteer program is one of the most popular programs with the student volunteers. Also, it has become an important component of the University Hospital. Each year more than 200 volunteers from Madison House devote time to the hospital. In the performance of their duties, they provide the important support services crucial to both hospital staff and patients.
The Medical Services Program separated from the larger Companionship Therapy Program in 1972 and initially offered placements in two wards of the hospital. The only medical volunteer programs previously offered were the University-wide Blood Drive (taken over by Omega Psi Phi and still operating), and a referral program providing information on area doctors and dentists.
Volunteers in the program have the opportunity to gain some realistic insights into the roles of hospital staff, as well as provide a needed service. The program appeals particularly to students in the pre-med and pre-nursing programs, but has proven enriching to all who participate.
Each medical services volunteer fills a regular 1-1/2 to 3-hour time period in one of seven hospital departments including Pediatrics, Burn Unit, Intensive Care Unit, and Neuropsychiatry.
Tasks which the volunteers perform vary tremendously from one department to another and from one shift to another. The Emergency Room and the Operating Room generally afford limited patient contact. Volunteers usually are assigned to perform staff support tasks such as moving equipment and lab specimens and disabled patients. The Pediatrics Department and the Towers

Psychiatric Unit, on the other hand, allow frequent individual contact with many patients.
The Medical Services volunteer by no means practices medicine, but volunteer work does provide the opportunity, especially to pre-med and pre-nursing students, to get a closer look at the medical profession as a career. Other students find satisfaction in providing supportive services and attaining a working knowledge of the day-to-day, around-the-clock functioning of a large hospital. Two staff members of the Hospital Services Division of the hospital work closely with the Medical Services volunteers.

MICHIGAN SPECIAL OLYMPICS STATE GAMES
Special Olympics - Michigan
6010 Cadieux Road
Detroit, MI 48230
TEL: 313-886-5440
Purpose: To give mentally retarded athletes an opportunity to compete at the state level.
Sponsor: Central Michigan University
Contact: Lois Arnold, Games Director, or Karen Lucas, Volunteer
Description: Held in Michigan since 1972, the state *Special Olympics* in Michigan are as much a carnival as a competition. In between events, athletes can visit the petting zoo, attend exercise and power-lifting clinics, or go on a hayride or canoeing. This variety of experiences is scheduled since, for many of the athletes, this is their only oppotunity to spend a night away from home, eat in a restaurant and have fun with friends that they see only once each year.
More than 3,200 mentally-impaired athletes compete on the Central Michigan University campus in about 80 events, including softball, track and field, swimming, gymnastics, bowling, volleyball, weight lifting and tennis.
The games have been held in Michigan since 1972. More than 2,400 volunteers assisted in the 1989 session.
Celebrity volunteers included champions from several professional sports teams (Detroit Lions), Miss Michigan, and others. Besides helping alongside of the other volunteers, the celebrity volunteers held autograph sessions throughout the program.

MIGRANT RECREATION PROGRAM
Madison House
170 Rugby Road
Charlottesville, VA 22903
TEL: 804-977-7051
Purpose: To provide children of migrant workers with organized recreational activities.
Sponsor: Madison House
Contact: Jane Parker
Description: In 1972, Madison House received requests for tutors for the childen of migrant farm workers who reside in Albemarle County from August through October each year during apple-picking season. Volunteers were recruited, but a severe winter resulted in crop failure and the migrants did not come.
The program got started the following year with 20 volunteers visiting the children at their camp on a farm 16 miles from Charlottesville. At about the same time, the Albemarle County School System began operating a more formal tutoring program which included the migrant families, and the Madison House program developed into a recreation program.
Each afternoon in September and October, a car pool of 20 to 30 volunteers visits the camp - organizing softball, badminton, soccer, and kickball, as well as an arts and crafts session.
Most of the childen in the camp have had little formal education and little exposure to organized games and recreation. Spanish is their language, and much of their time is spent helping with the work in the orchards. As an adjunct to the program, volunteers are involved in helping the children receive necessary medical attention at the Children and Youth Clinic of University Hospital. Many of the students have volunteered for more than one year and

have come to know the children. This helps the children each year, since it eliminates much of the trauma of starting new relationships. Thus, both the volunteers and the kids look forward to some reunions each year.
Founded: 1972

MILWAUKEE AND THE SINGLE GIRL*
Girl Scouts of the Milwaukee Area
2500 West Mayfair Road
Milwaukee, WI 53222
TEL: 414-476-1050
Purpose: To generate the support of an entire city in an urban environment education program for members of a young girls' organization.
Sponsor: US/HHS - Department of Health & Human Services
Contact: Pat Pollworth
Description: As a foundation for a major thrust to develop pride in the city among its nearly a quarter of a million residents, the local Girl Scouts office developed a citywide conference on the urban environment. A consultant on conference planning helped create an overview, list tasks for volunteers, and construct a timetable. The first step was to form an all-volunteer Task Force to handle the logistics of the conference, and to recruit other volunteers as needed.
In recruiting volunteers, the Girl Scout network was unbeatable. Each staff person works with half a dozen of the city's 39 neighborhoods. For each neighborhood, a Chairperson coordinates activities of from 16 to 40 troops in operation. The Chairperson is helped by a volunteer service group in each neighborhood for program ideas, technical assistance, etc. Every adult volunteer receives a newsletter each month from central staff.
The built-in communication network served the Task Force well, bringing 325 people to the conference. Twenty-four youth-serving agencies, ten local businesses, six citizens' groups, nine educational institutions, and twelve government agencies were represented. Numerous ideas and suggestions emerged toward the conference goal - to excite young people about Milwaukee to the extent that they would participate in volunteer environmental projects. Workshop categories included experimental land use, public art, waste disposal, mass transit, bikes, the Milwaukee River, human spatial environment, the lakefront, housing and zoning, expressways, and architectural preservation. Awards were offered for the best projects in these categories. As a result, six troops won awards of $50.00 each during the following months.
The effects of the conference continued over the next year as materials on the city were developed: children's books, slide shows and film strips, a roster of speakers and trip planners, an idea book for urban awareness, museum exhibits, library bibliographies, new school curricula, etc. Months after the conference, senior Girl Scouts held their spring conference with the theme, Urban Upswing, and honored the city.
Although the conference and its aftermath have had a major impact on the young people of Milwaukee, the Girl Scouts organization considers it just a beginning in their efforts to instill the desire in young people to care about and participate in their neighborhoods.

MINDSTRETCHERS
SEE LEADERSHIP DEVELOPMENT/BOARDS:
CHILDREN/YOUTH

MOVE (MOBILIZATION OF VOLUNTEERS)
Southern Methodist University
Human Resources/Women's Center
Box 172
Dallas, TX 75275
TEL: 214-692-4403
FAX: 214-692-4127

Purpose: To provide SMU students a meaningful volunteer experience while benefitting the Dallas community.
Sponsor: Southern Methodist University
Contact: Jannae Tunnell
Description: MOVE is a student organization at *Southern Methodist University* which was created in 1972 to encourage students to participate in service to the Dallas community. Student project coordinators plan, recruit and train other students for weekly programs and special events. The weekly programs include:
● Asian refugee tutoring
● After school tutoring
● Adopt-A-Grandparent Program
● Crippled Children Visitation
● Meals-on Wheels
● Soup Kitchen Servers
Special projects planned by MOVE include *Community Service Day* where over 500 students spend a Saturday in March in the community; *Alternate Spring Break Trips* where students volunteer in places such as Belize, Mexico, New Orleans, New Mexico, and the East Texas wilderness; and special events such as a Christmas hayride, a *Careers in the Non-Profit Fair,* and a *Volunteer Fair.*
Founded: 1972

NATIONAL YOUTH SERVICE DAY 1990
SEE NATIONAL SERVICE/POINTS OF LIGHT INITIATIVE

NEIGHBORHOOD PROBATION UNIT
SEE VOLUNTEERS: TEAMS

NEIGHBORHOOD TREE CORPS
Magnolia Tree Earth Center
678 Lafayette Avenue
Brooklyn, NY 11216
TEL: 718-387-2116
Purpose: To involve the entire community in an effort to turn around the rapid decline of the neighborhood.
Contact: Hattie Carthan
Description: The Neighborhood Tree Corps is an outgrowth of the efforts of one woman who was determined to do something about her once tree-lined street, which "progress" had rendered bare. This elderly black woman began by forming a block association to raise money for the purchase of replacement trees. She planted thousands of trees, and came to the attention of the Mayor, the State Council on the Arts, and others. Through this recognition, the Neighborhood Tree Corps surfaced with support of over $11,000 from the Brooklyn Arts Council. In 1975, an umbrella organization, the Magnolia Tree Earth Center, was set up to seek grants and develop new projects like the Corps.
The Neighborhood Tree Corps is a year-round program. During the winter months, thirty students, ages nine to sixteen, take courses at the community center two afternoons a week. In addition to the two-hour classes on trees, occasional weekend field trips to gardens and conservation centers are arranged.
Community volunteers lead the classes and trips under the supervision of an instructor who is trained in this specialty.
When school closes, the program shifts to a summer schedule. Three days a week the youngsters meet at ten in the morning to practice what they have learned in the winter classes. They carry brooms, rakes, pails, and trowels to a specific block and begin sweeping, tilling and watering everything outside the area's home fences. The youngsters make it a point to knock on doors to borrow hoses so that they can talk to residents and get them involved. In two hours, a block can be totally transformed. Volunteers oversee the youngsters, who are paid from three to five dollars a week depending on their ages. This expense and others are covered by a $20 fee paid by block associations for this service. Many of the youngsters stay in the program year after year, until they are too old to participate - most giving their reason as "pride

in taking care of your own neighborhood trees."
The Neighborhood Tree Corps has served as a model for cities nationwide, and has generated numerous other opportunities for volunteer involvement, youth employment, and increased conservation of urban areas.
Founded: 1975

NEW BREED DRILL TEAM
Trenton Board of Education
Clinton and Monmouth
Trenton, NJ 08609
TEL: 609-989-2406
Purpose: To provide a unifying vehicle through which young people can give of themselves to their communities.
Contact: Lena Meekins, Founder
Description: In the socially-turbulent late 1960s, an observant citizen recognized a need for an activity for disadvantaged youth of the Trenton area to constructively apply their energy. The *New Breed Drill Team* was created for junior high and high school students, who soon became a frequent sight with their precision marching routines. In its early years it served as a vehicle for building racial understanding by entertaining and socializing with teen audiences of different backgrounds. Team members have remained goodwill ambassadors but, after more than two decades, the team has evolved into a community service project as well as a precision marching team.
Membership in the *New Breed Drill Team* requires more than just the ability to perform skilled marching routines. All of the members must demonstrate individual excellence, character development, leadership skills and academic success. But the main purpose is to serve the community. Former community service projects adopted by the team include the beautification of Martin Luther King Park, assisting The Needy Children's Christmas Fund and the Cadwalader Public Library, and serving at the Martin Luther King Day community breakfast.
According to its founder, the combination of instilling pride in an accomplishment such as the precision drill team, and creating self-esteem through service to the community is an undisputed and unbeatable success in which everyone shares.
Publications: New Breed Drill Team
Founded: 1968

NORFOLK CATHOLIC CHRISTIAN SERVICE PROGRAM
Norfolk Catholic High School
6401 Granby Street
Norfolk, VA 23509
TEL: 804-423-2553
Purpose: To implement the service aspect of the Gospel Message; to expose the students to the needs of the community and the reward of volunteering; to enhance the image of the school in the community.
Sponsor: Norfolk Catholic High School
Contact: Mary Ellen Minershiem, Coordinator
Description: While attempts of student volunteerism had been made earlier, the service program with a paid coordinator began during the school year 1979-80. Since that time each student who attends Norfolk Catholic must volunteer a minimum of 20 hours in the community. The students work with children in day care programs, with the aged, as teacher aides, with many agencies and Catholic parishes. The student enrollment is approximately 67% per year. In developing the program, the coordinator worked closely with the Voluntary Action Center. VAC continues to support the programs' efforts and helps in the evaluation and direction of the program. During National Volunteer Week, the school has a volunteer recognition assembly and a program in which representatives for the community speak to the students about summer volunteer positions.
The Student Key Club (youth arm of Kiwanis) has funded the program in the past.
Founded: 1979

NORTH HIGH COMMUNITY SERVICE PROGRAM
SEE COMMUNITY SERVICES: STUDENTS

NOXZEMA EXTRAORDINARY TEEN CONTEST
SEE BUSINESS/INDUSTRY INVOLVEMENT

OPERATION CLEAN SWEEP
SEE VOLUNTEERS: CHURCH/SYNAGOGUE MEMBERS

THE OWL (OUTREACH-WORKING-LEARNING) PROGRAM
Northern Virginia Community College
Student Activities Office
8333 Little River Turnpike
Annandale, VA 22003
TEL: 703-323-3455
Purpose: To involve students in community agencies and projects which will benefit both.
Sponsor: Northern Virginia Community College
Contact: Ann Shelton, Volunteerism Coordinator
Description: The Northern Virginia Community College OWL (Outreach-Working-Learning) Volunteerism Program operates locally on each campus under the overall supervision of the Dean for Student Services. Each campus has a volunteer coordinator who is responsible for assisting students interested in volunteer service in reaching community organizations with volunteer needs. Interested community organizations representatives are asked to make contact with the coordinators for information about volunteers on that respective campus. Organizations with continuing volunteer needs may list opportunities with any coordinator.
Community organizations are also encouraged to use the media available on each campus. Materials for publicity about volunteer openings may be directed through the campus volunteer coordinator with a request that they be placed in any of the campus newspapers or newsletters.
Announcements of volunteer openings which might be of interest to the faculty, administration, and staff may be directed to the campus volunteer coordinator with a request to place them in the college-wide newsletter Intercom, if desired.
If a community organization wishes to have a press release prepared which highlights an innovative or unusual volunteer program of interest to the campus community, a request may be made through the coordinator, who will in turn work with the campus information officer to prepare the release for local media.

PARMA-HILTON PLAYGROUND PROJECT
SEE VOLUNTEERS: TENANTS/RESIDENTS

PEER COUNSELING/CROSS-AGE TUTORING PROGRAM
Hastings High School
Hastings, FL 32045
TEL: 904-692-1515
Purpose: To help students grow in their understanding of the learning process and to improve the basic skills of all students.
Sponsor: Mrs. Carole Dulaney
Contact: Mrs. Ethel McNeil, Principal
Description: The peer counseling/cross age tutoring program at Hastings High School is part of the social studies curriculum. Students in the 11th and 12th grades who have a C average and a good behavior record are eligible to apply for the course. Students may receive up to one social studies credit toward graduation representing one year's enrollment.
At the beginning of the course students attend class for a two-week orientation in human relations skills, personality development, child development and learning styles. After this orientation period, one day per week is spent with the peer counseling instructor continuing this training. Tutors are assigned

to classes either at Hastings Elementary School or the 7th and 8th grade classes at Hastings High. Tutors spend four days a week under the direction of a classroom teacher tutoring individual students or small groups.

Acceptance into the Peer Counseling/Cross-Age Tutoring Program is considered an honor and each year more students apply than can be accepted. As one student says, "I like tutoring because I like to help others and I learn more about myself."

PHI MU SORORITY COMMUNITY SERVICE CHAPTER
SEE VOLUNTEERS: FRATERNAL ORGANIZATIONS

POLLUTION CONTROL CENTER
Oak Park and River Forest High School
201 North Scoville Avenue
Oak Park, IL 60302
TEL: 312-383-0700/Ext. 2174
Purpose: To meet a need for continuing environmental education for youth.
Sponsor: Oak Park and River Forest High School
Contact: Ed Radatz
Description: In 1970, it became apparent to both students and faculty at Oak Park and River Forest High school that environmental education was needed. Two students worked with administrators at the school to plan a Conservation Workshop for the first *Earth Day* that year. When experts came forward to educate 4,000 students and citizens, it became further apparent that the environmental education program should be a continuing process.

Initially, the Board of Education instituted environmental science and field biology courses, Earth science, physical science, biology, and other courses, which continue to stress environmental topics. But students and faculty went a step further to create the Pollution Control Center (PCC), a facility staffed by student volunteers. The students answer requests for information on environmental subjects, provide speakers for schools or clubs, and offer other services provided by the Center.

Teams from PCC visit elementary schools that lack environmental programs and speak to students from kindergarten to eighth grade. The aim is to increase the environmental awareness of the younger students with basic ecological concepts that can be followed both at school and at home. Elementary teachers are given related materials for later use, and can request additional information from PCC at any time.

PCC volunteers also give anti-smoking workshops, and often are asked to speak at local organizations.

A special scholarship fund has been developed through donations from community groups, and from school fund-raisers. Students use these funds to attend environmental workshops, and must provide a report to the Biology Club at the school as well as the community groups from which the scholarship funds were received.

A permanent recycling program has been developed by PCC in cooperation with the community's Environmental Advisory Committee.

To avoid duplication of effort, other youth groups at the school - *Student Council* and *Tau Gamma* - work with PCC to promote environmental awareness and youth involvement in the community for *Earth Day 1990.*
Founded: 1970

PREVENTION THROUGH ACTION
Catholic Youth Organization
305 Michigan Avenue
Detroit , MI 48226
TEL: 313-963-7172
Purpose: To educate Hispanic youth about substance-abuse prevention, community values, and leadership responsibilities.
Sponsor: Archdiocese of Detroit

Contact: Ray Hillen, Director
Description: Prevention through Action combines training seminars with recreational activities to teach Hispanic youth the consequences of drug abuse or fighting, and offer positive and enjoyable alternatives. In addition, the youth are taught community values and leadership roles.

In the initial effort, 47 Hispanic youths, ages 14 to 18, were trained at annual four-day *Youth Options* seminars. Participants are taught to lead groups of younger children, ages 6 to 14, in recreational activities which are prefaced by brief, mandatory workshops on coping with youth problems. By early 1989, 500 youths benefitted from the program.

Groups providing support and facilities for the program include other Detroit-based Catholic organizations such as the *Hispanic Affairs Office of the Archdiocese of Detroit,* the *Renaissance Youth Center, Latino Outreach,* and *Detroit Health Department.* Among the positive program elements are a dance group, a basketball league, and the *Urban Link,* a male responsibility program that arranges for community professionals to talk to male youth audiences. Also, the older youth have made a success of the program, and the younger kids look up to the older ones, so the program is making a very real difference, according to the director.
Founded: 1988

PRINCIPAL ON THE ROOF*
SEE VOLUNTEERS: PROFESSIONALS

PROJECT HELP (HELP EXPEDITE LEGAL PROBLEMS FOR THE HOMELESS)
SEE VOLUNTEERS: PROFESSIONALS

PROJECT OASES
Pittsburgh Middle Schools
Boggs C&S Center-OVT
850 Boggs Avenue
Pittsburgh, PA 15211
TEL: 412-488-2531
Purpose: To motivate at-risk eighth grade students who have not responded well to traditional education programs.
Sponsor: Chapter II Block Grant (federal government); foundations; business/industry
Contact: Al Markowski
Description: OASES is considered both a classroom and a community-centered program. It begins with the seventh grade teaching staff, who recommend students who show a lack of self-esteem, poor attitude, and disinterest in school and school work, per se. Recommended students are thoroughly screened by a school dean and counselor so that those who will benefit most are given this opportunity. The two pronged program combines vocational training and volunteer work, requiring three of the seven class periods of the school day.

Most of the students selected for OASES believe strongly that the service-centered program holds the students' interest and deters misbehavior. At the same time the students are motivated to learn and provided a context in which self-esteem and a sense of achievement and competence can grow.

After completing an orientation period and eight weeks of occupational training, the students move on to volunteer in the community. Their volunteer assignments are not "make-work" jobs by any means. OASES volunteers have restored substandard dwellings for nonprofit organizations, built a playhouse for mentally retarded children, constructed an entrance ramp for a double amputee, painted for the Salvation Army, and repaired and built a number of other structures throughout the community. In addition, they have worked for the City of Pittsburgh and Pittsburgh Public Schools as well as other community entities in a number of meaningful capacities. They have built a sound reputation for quality work and reliability and are considered an extremely valuable resource for the community.

The academic side of the student's work has benefited also. From a near-dropout status, 40% of the OASES students were on the honor roll at the end of the first year. Behavioral and discipline problems are almost nonexistent.

Funding for the program was provided initially by private foundations, a Chapter II Block grant, and donations from local merchants and corporations. As of late 1989, the Pittsburgh School District provides 100% funding for all four OASES centers - Allegheny, Frick, Knoxville, and Milliones Middle Schools. Students receive small awards, ranging from T-shirts to trophies, for their successes measured by good attendance, overall improvement, honor roll status, and other standards. They continue to display pride in workmanship, a cooperative attitude, and a willingness to take tasks to completion.

PROJECT PASSAGE
SEE VOLUNTEERS: HANDICAPPED

PROJECTS IN THE COMMUNITY
LeMoyne College
Syracuse, NY 13214
TEL: 315-446-2882/Ext. 526
Purpose: To provide the structure for almost 200 college students to participate in Christian social action, volunteering their services as tutors, recreational aides, etc.
Sponsor: LeMoyne College
Contact: Mrs. Frances E. Campion
Description: Projects In The Community (P.I.C.) was founded in 1969 at LeMoyne College. A student-requested, student-run organization, LeMoyne College's Projects In The Community program was established as a way of sending LeMoyne students into the Syracuse community on a volunteer basis. At this point a relevant question would be, Why send LeMoyne students into the Syracuse community?

P.I.C. believes that the College experience can provide a wealth of intellectual information about society and its problems. Courses, library materials, multi-media and seminars are among the ways in which students can gain knowledge within the college environment. However, the protected atmosphere of the college alone does not provide sufficient preparation for dealing with the harsh reality of many social problems. P.I.C. attempts to match the interests, abilities, and needs of the student volunteer with the interests, needs, and program goals of the agency, school or hospital. A good match between the volunteer and program ensures that the community's needs are met. P.I.C. takes the college student away from the theories in his text and into the heart of life's problems where theories can be used to achieve results. P.I.C. volunteers help solve problems where they happen. The insecurity of a young orphan, the impatience of a young girl who likes school but cannot read because she cannot concentrate, the disappointment of a young man with big dreams and limited resources, the frustrations of a disabled elderly person - these are the problems of the real world a textbook cannot relate.

Projects In the Community provides the structure for over 200 college students to participate in Christian social action, volunteering their services as tutors and recreational aides for children, some of them mentally retarded and emotionally disturbed. The relationships that develop between students and children go beyond a formal schedule, and it is not unusual to see a LeMoyne student with several children in tow during the weekend. Many times, the children students meet through P.I.C. come from troubled families, and P.I.C. volunteers provide some of the love that these children miss at home.

Projects In The Community volunteers, with the help of other student organizations on campus, entertain approximately 100 senior citizens four times a year. The senior citizen groups are offered a wine and cheese party, dinner with the students and entertainment provided by the students. Each year there is a waiting list of senior citizen groups wanting to come on campus for the dinners.

One question might be "How do you get the students at LeMoyne College to sign up for their volunteer work?" Each year, on or about August 1st, letters and brochures are sent to all transfer students and incoming freshmen students explaining what P.I.C. is all about. Brochures are also put into the orientation packets that are given out to students during Orientation Week. About September 15th the P.I.C. office is opened with a bang. One year, ping pong balls were dropped from a helicopter at noon announcing a dessert and coffee that evening in the dining hall. Another year, 1,000 balloons were let loose in the air, and yet another year, the campus was showered with tiny orchids dropped by helicopter.

Representatives from the agencies, hospitals, schools and nursing homes are invited on campus for the evening to explain their needs. The interested volunteers are offered the opportunity to apply their talents, or to develop new ones, when they volunteer their services, and are given the opportunity to choose the kind of work which will be the most rewarding to themselves and the people they serve. LeMoyne volunteers do so without any academic credit. They volunteer and enjoy the rewards that come from helping others, while improving their own skills or talents and many times opening doors for their future employment. Volunteering can be a training ground for a career and, many times, serves that purpose.

Projects In The Community is supported solely by LeMoyne College and is responsible to the Dean of Students. The program is located in the Dean of Students' office complex where many LeMoyne students pass each day. A program director provides centralization for the student organization and acts as a liaison between P.I.C. and the various agencies, hospitals and schools submitting requests for volunteers. The program director interviews students, places them, and provides some training, but in-service training is provided primarily by the agency.

P.I.C. operates with a small budget to transport all of the volunteers to and from their volunteer work, thus providing an added convenience to the volunteer. Obviously, this type of expense would strain P.I.C.'s limited budget, but other campus organizations help in one way or another. Perhaps P.I.C.'s most meaningful resource, therefore, is the LeMoyne student body, and every year since the project's inception, membership has grown.
Founded: 1969

RAMAPO KEY CLUB*
Ramapo High School
465 Viola Road
Spring Valley, NY 10977
TEL: 914-577-6400
Purpose: To participate in volunteer projects in service agencies and organizations in Rockland County.
Sponsor: Kiwanis Club; Ramapo High School
Contact: Bruce Snider
Description: Over 300 volunteers - nearly one-fourth of the student body at Ramapo High School - take part in volunteer programs sponsored by the Ramapo Key Club across the county. The Key Club is the youth arm of Kiwanis International.

A representative from Kiwanis and a faculty member provide orientation to volunteers at the first meeting of the school year. This includes descriptions of volunteer opportunities across the county. Once weekly the Club holds a meeting for discussions and a recap of the week's progress. A guest speaker addresses a project area, and students sign up for new projects. Among volunteer organizations served by the young volunteers are Cystic Fibrosis, the American Heart Association, Muscular Dystrophy, and Multiple Sclerosis. Specific examples include the annual "Super Dance," which raises nearly $15,000 each year to benefit Muscular Dystrophy.

Smaller organizations also receive assistance from the volunteers.

There include Youth Against Cancer (an affiliate of the American Cancer Society), and Rockland County Social Services. A Pet Companionship Program for the Deaf and Geriatric units of the Rockland Psychiatric Center is operated by Club volunteers, as well as a visiting program that covers all eleven nursing homes in the county with visits from both groups and individuals. They are counted on each year for Ramapo High's blood drive, also. Students volunteer both for one-time and long-term service. In addition to direct service, student volunteers raise funds for some organizations. Students may join (or leave) the club at any time. According to the school's Director of Counseling, "the Club's successes breed more success."

RECYCLING FOR RAVI
Knoxville Zoo Tiger Team
Knoxville Zoological Gardens
3333 Woodbine Avenue
Knoxville, TN 37914
TEL: 615-637-5331
Purpose: To raise funds to keep a white tiger at the local zoo; to recycle aluminum to help the environment.
Sponsor: Roddy Coca-Cola Bottling Company
Contact: Jane Creed, Tiger Team Recycling Coordinator
Description: In January 1988, a Florida animal trainer loaned two seven-week-old tigers to *Knoxville Zoological Gardens.* One tiger is a rare white tiger named *Ravi,* and the other is the common orange tiger (*Burma*). Later, the owner offered to sell the white tiger to Knoxville Zoological Gardens for $50,000, with the orange tiger donated.
Hoping to keep the tigers in Knoxville permanently, a volunteer group approached the business community and together they worked out a plan. The program that was considered the most promising for raising money quickly was a recycling program involving the entire Knox County school system. Ten middle schools, representing 5,000 pupils, collected 10,300 pounds of aluminum cans to raise $7,200. The Aluminum Company of America added $3,000, making the initial donation to the Knoxville Zoo Tiger Team $10,200.
By May 1989 the volunteer group had raised $46,100, $3,900 short of Ravi's asking price.
To maintain interest as the pupils worked toward the recycling goal, cash prizes were awarded by *Roddy Coca-Cola Bottling Company:* first place $1,000, second place $500, and third place $250, with a $500 award going to one of the schools for its can sculpture, and another $250 for the second-place can sculpture. *ALCOA, Roddy* and *Waste Management of Knoxville* are sponsors of the project, with volunteer support from the schools and one-time donations from corporations such as the Aluminum Company of America.
The Tiger Team volunteer group met the goal in time to save Ravi and Burma from becoming circus animals.
Publications: Knoxville Zoo Tiger Team Packet

REQUIREMENT: SKIP CLASSES
SEE COMMUNITY SERVICES

RYANS' NURSING HOME VOLUNTEER PROGRAM
Sweet Briar College
Dean of Student Affairs
Sweet Briar, VA 24595
TEL: 804-381-5529
Purpose: To provide an interaction between college students and nursing home residents while filling a need in the community.
Sponsor: Church and Chapel Committee
Contact: Robert H. Barlow
Description: This program began in 1980 with five student volunteers; now approximately 40 volunteers are involved. At least once per week, the volunteer visits for one hour with a particular nursing home resident. Often, the volunteers make additional

visits. The college provides free van transportation to students three times per week in order to expedite student visits. The college has also supported other special programs and services. The volunteers are trained at an initial meeting on the campus before they make at least one supervised visit to the nursing home. The volunteers are supervised by the Dean of Student Affairs. The goals are:
- to provide visitors to the nursing home;
- to develop friendships between students and nursing home residents; and
- to expose students to the aging process and nursing homes.
Founded: 1980

SAN FRANCISCO PEER RESOURCE PROGRAMS
1950 Mission Street, Room 7
San Francisco, CA 94103
TEL: 415-626-1942
Purpose: To meet needs of some students that can be done best through one-to-one peer involvement.
Sponsor: San Francisco Education Fund
Contact: Ira Sachnoff
Description: In 1980, *Galileo High School* initiated its first *Peer Resource Program.* The purpose of the program is to meet a need on a one-to-one basis for attention for some students. Student volunteers are selected to be trained as counselors for their peers. They are trained during regular school hours in decision making and other skills, including self-awareness. Sponsors are the *San Francisco United School District* and the *San Francisco Education Fund.* Some of the specific programs are:
- **Buddy/Friendship Project** - a matching program bringing together upper classmen with new students to help with the transition process. Students help their "buddies" with school work and personal issues, as well as teaching them survival skills. This program is not limited to new students, but is open to any student in the school on request.
- **Peer Tutors** - a program in which students are trained by adults and then do all of the tutoring. Students are selected based on their academic expertise and their willingness to serve in this capacity and to be trained. The tutors help over 7,000 students each year.
- **Peer Counseling Program** - a system designed to keep the schools as crisis-free as possible, with volunteer students working with peers in areas such as drug abuse and alcohol abuse, child abuse, suicide, violence, etc. The student/counselors reach almost 7,000 students each year.
- **Violence Prevention Program** - a program that uses the "peer resource philosophy" as its base: "Everyone has resources to help each other." Activities include the *ESL Rap Group,* which gives immigrant students a comfortable place to practice their English and become accustomed to their new culture. Volunteer students also make classroom presentations, thus serving as educators against violence.
Founded: 1980

SCHOOL AND COMMUNITY SERVICE PROGRAM
East Ramapo Central School District
Spring Valley High School
Route 50
Spring Valley, NY 10977
TEL: 914-356-4100/Ext. 431
Purpose: To involve high school volunteers in service to the community.
Sponsor: East Ramapo Central School District
Contact: Jim Dugan, Advisor
Description: The School and Community Service Program of the East Ramapo Central School District affords students in each of the two high schools in the district the opportunity to become involved in meaningful community work. This work can take the form of tutoring; candy striping; scouting; being a friendly visitor

to the aged, retarded, or physically handicapped in one of the institutions in the county; working as a recreation aide; or helping a teacher in one of the area's twenty elementary schools and three junior high schools meet the needs of the younger child.

Through this program, the student can earn Regents credit for his/her service. Through a specially devised curriculum the student is given a better academic background for his/her service through workshops. These workshops cover the following topics: tutoring, recreation, the aged, the handicapped, and English as a Second Language. As the need arises, the curriculum is revised to include more areas of interest and concern.

In order to earn one-half credit towards graduation, the student is expected to spend a minimum of 40 hours (2-4 hours per week) at his/her place of service, attend seminars to exchange views with other students in the program, and attend individual conferences with an advisor to assess experiences and to discuss any problems which may have arisen. Frequently resource people from the community attend and participate in these workshops and seminars and lend their expertise to them. The students are continuously supervised not only by the personnel in charge at the schools and agencies, but by the SCS advisor as well. All of these people, including the student, participate in ongoing evaluations. This program is open to all students regardless of grade, background or scholastic ability. An observation by the Advisor: "Many students find this program a good avenue for career exploration as well as a way to satisfy their need to help people and gain in their own self-esteem."

SERVICE-LEARNING CENTER
Michigan State University
26 Student Services Building
East Lansing, MI 48824
TEL: 517-353-4400
Purpose: To provide students with oportunities for career exploration, skills development, curriculum enrichment and community services.
Sponsor: State/county government
Contact: Mary I. Edens, Coordinator
Description: Organized volunteering at MSU began over 20 years ago when students began an inner-city tutorial program. In 1967, the MSU Board of Trustees approved the formation of the Office of Volunteer Programs with professional and volunteer staff committed to formally organizing and coordinating volunteer efforts by students in the greater Lansing Area which has a population of 400,000. Each year over 2,500 students invest 4-8 hours a week or more for a 10-week volunteer commitment.

The SLC serves as a liaison between the University, the students, and community agencies, helping to recruit, train, orient, supervise and evaluate student efforts in community opportunities.
Under the supervision of four SLC advisors and 60 student leaders, volunteers have assisted 250 organizations in providing services in such diverse areas as:
- administration
- business
- government
- corrections
- education
- recreation
- environment/science
- human services
- medicine/nutrition
- special education/handicapped services

Working from SLC and agency-developed job descriptions, novice and skilled volunteers can find entry, intermediate, and specialized positions. Positions are also categorized by academic majors and by skill clusters which are meaningful decision-making tools for students.
Volunteers perform tutorial, role-modeling, counseling, research, advocacy, promotional, managerial, care-taking, referral and

recreational duties. Other resources provided by the staff for both agency and volunteer are:
- publicity
- training packets
- needs assessment tools
- workshops
- documentation of volunteer experience along with recommendations
- transportation
- university liability coverage
- evaluation instruments and rewards strategies

Freshmen to older students are selecting volunteer experience for career exploration, supplementary classroom work and for continuing community service.
Founded: 1967

SOS (SERVE OUR SENIORS) STUDENT VOLUNTEER PROGRAM
Highland Park High School
435 Mansfield Street
Highland Park, NJ 08904
TEL: 201-572-2400
FAX: 201-572-5502
Purpose: To provide services and companionship to senior citizens in the Highland Park area.
Contact: John Gallino
Description: During the 1989-90 school year, *Highland Park High School's* student congress discussed needs in the community to determine any gaps that might be filled by the school's teenagers. They learned that many senior citizens in the area would benefit from their assistance not only for chores, but for socialization. To begin the program, contacts were made with a number of people, and some unique relationships were established between the young and the old of our town.

Students in grades nine through twelve are asked to volunteer time to work with senior citizens of the community in the following areas: shopping, house cleaning, running errands, reading to them, or just being a friend. Over 40 of the school's 450 students volunteered their services. The student congress and school officials were pleased that this first effort recruited almost 10% of the student body.

Many of the students who came to know senior citizens on a personal basis said they found it rewarding. Our hope for the future is to expand the program to involve even more teenagers and senior citizens.

SOUTH BRONX SUMMER PROJECT
Brown University
25 George Street
PO Box 1974
Providence, RI 02912
TEL: 401-863-2338
Purpose: To convert previously abandoned property to a community park and garden.
Contact: Susan E. Stroud, Director
Description: The *South Bronx Summer Project* is a student-initiated public service program formed in 1986. Eleven *Brown University* students participated in the project with local assistance from such agencies as the *Bronx Frontier Development Corporation,* the *Council on the Environment, Cornell Cooperative Extension,* the *District Manager's Office,* and the *1325 Lafayette Avenue's Tenants' Association.* The purpose of the project is to convert two-and-one-half acres of previously abandoned property filled with rubble and garbage into *Hunt's Point Farm,* a community park and garden.
With student initiative, local assistance, and private funding, the *South Bronx Summer Project* has become a tradition as each summer eight *Brown University* students return to the South Bronx to expand and maintain development on *Hunt's Point*

Farm. In 1990, the *Center for Public Service* and the *Bronx Frontier Development Corporation* sponsored the fifth *South Bronx Summer Project.*

During the last four summers, Brown undergraduates assisted neighborhood residents in the development of *Hunt's Point Farm.* Construction on the Farm resulted in a playground and an adjoining playing field, picnic tables, an orchard, and a community garden and nursery, with a football field in process across from the Farm.

Student volunteers are housed at *Fordham University, Rosehill Campus,* which is about 15 minutes from the worksite. An eight-passenger van is leased for the twelve weeks of the project to provide transportation for the volunteers. Each student receives a stipend and a food allowance and, in cases of financial need, additional funding.

In addition to park construction and maintenance, the *Project* is responsible for a youth employment and recreation program. The summer of 1990 was the third year of the youth employment program, which employs 20-25 teenaged youth on the *Farm.* The youth recreation program, which was initiated in 1989, allows Brown students to interact with the community's youth. Recreational activities include field trips in the New York area, games, and arts and crafts. Each year the Project expands to include the needs and desires of the community.

The *South Bronx Summer Project* not only provides a fun-filled summer for everyone, but it also gets the community actively involved in the local revitalization of Hunt's Point.

SPARKLE COMMITTEE
Haddon Township Council
Haddon Avenue & Reeve Avenue
Camden, NJ 08103
TEL: 609-854-1176
Purpose: To maintain the "sparkle" of township property by providing the finishing touches.
Sponsor: Haddon Township
Contact: Dennis St. John, Community Activities Coordinator
Description: The *Sparkle Committee* is a special project in Haddon Township, a community which prides itself with having a number of cleanup operations going simultaneously. Besides the satisfaction of having a clean town, the major volunteer cleanup efforts help the township to qualify for $12,000 from the *1987 Clean Communities Act.* The Act's funds, collected as a "tiny tax" on litter-producing businesses such as fast-food restaurants, pay for the "tiny" *Sparkle Committee.*

This Committee is not a cleanup committee, per se, but rather a "finishing touches" group which works all summer to remove piles of dead leaves, prune bushes and spread mulch around trees on public property. The minute summer volunteer group is composed of one adult and five or six teenagers. Its work on the final touches of the area's landscape and enables larger cleanup groups to concentrate on heavier issues such as recycling, tearing down and replacing a deteriorating roof on the community pool bathhouse, etc. Also, the summer group helps increase the high visibility and tangible results that come from state and local cooperation.

SPECIAL SATURDAY
Family Service of Westchester
Big Brothers/Big Sisters
470 Mamaroneck Avenue
White Plains, NY 10605
TEL: 914-948-8004
Purpose: To bridge the waiting time of youngsters waiting for big brothers/sisters; to develop group skills through recreation; to increase the number of adult minority male role models for youngsters in our program.
Sponsor: Special Grant from the United Way of Westchester, community organizations and private donations
Contact: Lawrence R. Murrill, Program Coordinator

Description: Realizing that the number of children waiting for a big brother or sister far exceeds the number of volunteers, the staff of Big Brothers/Big Sisters of Family Service of Westchester, and students from Pace University did something about it. Special Saturday is a weekly recreational and educational activities program for youngsters on the waiting list of the program. It was designed, planned and implemented as a weekly summer program for these children and - because of its success - the summer pilot program has become an established part of the agency.
Volunteer Staff - Staffed primarily by volunteers, Special Saturday could not work without their support, dedication and concern. The core of our volunteers is students - from Pace University, Iona College and New Rochelle High School (all over 18 years of age). Many volunteers also come from community organizations such as the Knights of Columbus and the New York Telephone Company's Future Pioneers.
Volunteer Duties - The duties of the volunteer staff (counselors) include the supervision of the children, weekly training sessions and/or meetings, and the development of activities and programs.
Volunteer Experience - Special Saturday volunteers come with varying levels of experience. It is through the weekly training and meeting sessions that, as a group, attempts are made to tap the resources of our staff and strengthen areas that are weak.
From the Program Coordinator, "We realize and appreciate the fine group of volunteers we have but, because of the limited number of minority adult males, the need for more - many more - continues to be a major problem."
Founded: 1980

STUDENT HABITAT FOR HUMANITY
College of Wooster
Beall Avenue
Wooster, OH 44691
TEL: 216-263-2000
Purpose: To build and rehabilitate houses for the poor in the Wooster area.
Sponsor: Habitat for Humanity
Contact: Chris Alghini, President, Wooster College Chapter
Description: The college chapter of *Habitat for Humanity* finds the project satisfying to students since they see tangible results of their volunteer efforts. *Habitat for Humanity* is an ecumenical Christian housing ministry with 240 chapters in the United States and 50 projects in 25 developing countries. The organization constructs and rehabilitates houses for low-income families. Many student groups have "taken up the call" as a way of contributing to the communities surrounding their colleges.

When the college announced that five houses on its campus were scheduled to be demolished to make way for a new dormitory, the student head of the college chapter of *Habitat for Humanity,* with the advice of the chairman and vice chairman of the Wayne County chapter, approached the college president in an attempt to save the houses for the needy. Working together, the college and Habitat volunteers developed a plan for the school to donate the homes if the volunteers could raise $100,000 by commencement for moving expenses. One day in early June 1989 the moving began.

The Wooster houses represent one of the largest one-time donations ever given to a Habitat chapter. As in all houses offered through the program, low-income families who will occupy the newly-moved homes must donate 500 hours of "sweat equity" to renovate the structures, and will be given counseling regarding their maintenance and upkeep.

A rewarding coincidence in this effort is that - long before the house donation was suggested - the college had selected *Habitat for Humanity* founder, Millard Fuller, to receive a doctorate of humanities at the upcoming commencement.

STUDENT VOLUNTEER SERVICES
University of Texas
Texas Union 4.304
Austin, TX 78712
TEL: 512-471-3065
Purpose: To act as a clearinghouse for volunteers.
Sponsor: The Dean of Students Office, The University of Texas at Austin
Contact: Glenn W. Maloney
Description: The Student Volunteer Services Office is a part of the Dean of Students Office at the University of Texas at Austin. The office maintains information on volunteer positions on campus and in the community and recruits students and refers them to agencies. It provides information, consultation and referral for students who want to volunteer in the Austin community. Services and programs sponsored by the office include:

- Referral of students and student groups interested in doing volunteer work.
- Recruitment of volunteers with special skills and interests to fill volunteer needs in the community.
- Promotion of volunteer activity as a means of acquiring skills, exploring career goals, meeting friends, and helping others.
- Maintaining a file of position descriptions for over 125 community agencies.
- Planning the Volunteer Fair each fall. The fair gives individual agencies an opportunity to set up a booth on campus to recruit volunteers.
- Sponsoring the Students and Community Involvement class, a three-credit upper-division course requiring students to volunteer six hours per week.

STUDENT VOLUNTEERS
SEE LEADERSHIP DEVELOPMENT/BOARDS: CHILDREN/YOUTH

SURROUND*
SEE VOLUNTEERS: TEAMS

TAU KAPPA EPSILON (TKE) COMMUNITY PROJECTS
SEE VOLUNTEERS: FRATERNAL ORGANIZATIONS

TAVS (TEENAGE VOLUNTEERS)
The Voluntary Action Center
2125 East South Boulevard
Montgomery, AL 36116-0044
TEL: 205-284-0006
Purpose: To discover and develop interest in the field of medical science; to acquaint young people with opportunities in the health field and requirements for each position; to share the responsibility of operating and improving the hospital; and to develop leadership talent.
Sponsor: Voluntary Action Center of Montgomery, AL
Contact: Doci Haslam
Description: The TAV program was begun in 1979 with eight very dedicated young people. It was agreed to limit the membership to 35, based on the size of the hospital. By limiting, it was felt a more comprehensive program could be offered and adequate supervision provided. Members are required to be of high moral character, maintain a scholastic average of "C" or above, must be interested in some aspect of the medical field, and have written parental approval.
In one month's time, the membership grew from 8 to 18 and, within that first year, the goal of 35 was reached. Both the president in 1979, and the president in 1980, were named Volunteer of the Year - Youth Category, for outstanding work as TAVS.
The TAVS have given, this past year, close to 10,000 hours of volunteer service to the hospital. In addition, three educational scholarships, totalling $1,950, have been awarded in the past three years to help further the education of deserving TAVS. The TAVS have also donated monies to the hospital for pediatric toys and playroom furniture.
The TAVS must go through three levels of achievement in the program, each level requiring specific training, and at the same time get in required hours of work within the hospital (minimum number of hours required are 28 during the summer months and 10 during school term). With few exceptions, TAVS work far more than the minimum hours required. TAVS are assigned to almost every area of the hospital from patient floors to departments. Assignments are based on their level of achievement, i.e., only Level III TAVS (the highest level of achievement in the program) may work in the Emergency Room or other highly technical areas of the hospital. TAVS must "earn the right" to assist in these specialized areas.
At the present time, this program is well-known and respected in hospital volunteer circles throughout the state and many hospitals have asked for assistance in starting similar programs.
Founded: 1979

TEENAGE VOLUNTEERS WORKING IN ADOLESCENT PROGRAM*
Western State Hospital
301 Greenville Avenue
Staunton, VA 24401
TEL: 703-885-9390; 703-885-9391
Purpose: To provide leisure activities for adolescent patients.
Sponsor: Western State Hospital Volunteer Services Department
Contact: Jane Berry, Director of Volunteer Services
Description: Since 1971, students from the surrounding community have been serving as an integral part of the Western State Hospital Adolescent Program. They come to the hospital once a week (from 9 am to 11 am on Saturdays) to meet with the adolescents in a very unstructured program.
Prospective student volunteers are carefully screened. They receive informal training through meetings with the Special Education Instructor, Director of Training and Research, and Director of Volunteer Services. The meetings emphasize the attitudes toward the young patients that will be most helpful with specific behavioral problems. Training stresses the advantages of including all patients, and the special need for the quiet or withdrawn patient to be included by the volunteer in the group activities. These younger patients need to have activities in a relaxed setting where they can relate to young people in their own peer group from outside of the hospital. During the two-hour sessions, part of the group may just sit and chat, while some of the others listen to records or play chess or cards. Once a month the student volunteers take the patients on a picnic, to someone's house, or to a high school basketball game. There is no direct adult supervision, although someone is always available for consultation and assistance, if needed.
The Director of Volunteer Services has been impressed with the maturity and the dependability of the high school volunteers, who continue their program through the summer months even though the sponsors expected this service to be a school-year project.
Founded: 1971

TEENS AS COMMUNITY RESOURCES*
SEE LEADERSHIP DEVELOPMENT/BOARDS: CHILDREN/YOUTH

THOMAS JEFFERSON FORUM*
SEE ADMINISTRATION: RECRUITMENT/ORIENTATION

THURSDAY AFTERNOON PROGRAM (TAP)
Santa Fe Preparatory School
1101 Camino Cruz Blanca
Santa Fe, NM 87501
TEL: 505-982-1829
Purpose: To give students in grades 7-12 the opportunity for community service.
Sponsor: Volunteer Information Service; Santa Fe Preparatory School
Contact: Gene Harrell
Description: TAP preparation began in the summer of 1988. The Headmaster met with the Executive Director of *Volunteer Involvement Service,* who contacted area nonprofit agencies to see which were ready and willing to use junior high and senior high school students. The Assistant Headmaster was the coordinator for the first school year. For the second year, the science teacher became coordinator, with a portion of his salary designated for his time in the TAP program.
All students go into Santa Fe every Thursday afternoon from 1:30 to 3:30 and are involved in a wide variety of activities from exercising animals at the Animal Shelter to tutoring in a number of area elementary and junior high schools, and working on materials for children at the five State museums, visiting the elderly, keeping nature trails in shape, and acting as receptionists at human service agencies.
The outcome of any particular Thursday can range from sadness or anger resulting from the afternoon's experience to exhilaration at feeling needed and useful. The TAP program has changed the flavor of the Prep School, making it more community-minded, cultivating leadership skills and vision in the students and in the faculty.
Founded: 1988

TOUCH AMERICA PROJECT (TAP)
American Conservation Volunteers
American Forestry Association
1319 Eighteenth Street, NW
Washington, DC 20036
TOLL FREE: 800-368-5748
Purpose: To provide an opportunity for young people to work and learn more about America's natural resources through volunteering.
Sponsor: American Forestry Association
Contact: TAP Coordinator
Description: TAP *(Touch America Project)* is a youth volunteer program through which young people ages 14-17 may work and learn more about America's natural resources. The theme, *Touch America,* refers to volunteer projects on public lands developed cooperatively with private organizations, groups, or individuals. *TAP* volunteers work in national forests, parks, refuges, grasslands, historic preservation areas and other public lands administered by cooperating government agencies. These include *Forest Service, Extension Service, Soil Conservation Service of the Department of Agriculture,* and the *National Park Service, Bureau of Land Management,* and *Fish and Wildlife Service of the Department of Interior. TAP* is a partnership of:
- community groups and nonprofit organizations (which provide supervision and coordination)
- youth, ages 14 through 17 (who volunteer their time and energies)
- Government agencies (which provide supplies, services, or funding needed for the project)

Through *TAP,* business and private contributors have an opportunity to perform a community service, communities can offer meaningful work to local young people, youth obtain work experience, and public lands are improved.
A technical assistance packet is published for organizations or individuals interested in sponsoring or finding a sponsor for a *TAP* project in their community.

Publications: Touch America Project for Youth Volunteers; TAP for TAP

TUTORING VOLUNTEER PROGRAM
Sweet Briar College
Dean of Student Affairs
Sweet Briar, VA 24595
TEL: 804-381-5529
Purpose: To provide remedial and advanced instruction to elementary students.
Sponsor: Church and Chapel Committee, Sweet Briar College
Contact: Robert H. Barlow
Description: This program began in 1982 with twelve students. Approximately fourteen students per term have been involved in the program. Once a week for two hours, the volunteer works with a group or groups of elementary school children. The college provides free van transportation to students in order to expedite their service. The goals are:
- to provide tutors for the elementary schools;
- to develop friendships between college students and local elementary school children; and
- to expose students to the community and the teaching profession.

The volunteers are trained by the school system staff on their initial visit(s). The volunteers are supervised by the Dean of Student Affairs.
Founded: 1982

URBAN INVOLVEMENT
Seattle Pacific University
Office of Campus Ministries
Seattle, WA 98119
TEL: 206-281-2679
Purpose: To match student volunteers with agencies and individuals needing volunteer help.
Sponsor: Seattle Pacific University
Contact: Marta D. Bennett
Description: Urban Involvement is a branch of Campus Ministries at Seattle Pacific University. It provides opportunity for students to serve as volunteers in the local community, to offer their time, energy and skills in service, as well as to gain valuable experience with various types of needs and organizations.
Some students are involved daily or weekly throughout the year; others are involved in only one-time commitments. Opportunities for service are available in working with children, youth, troubled youth, refugees, aging, disabled, and street people. Agencies and needy individuals usually contact the Urban Involvement office requesting volunteers, though students also develop their own projects as well.
Some opportunities provide their own training for the volunteers, while others ask that the Urban Involvement office provide the training. Students may arrange to receive credit or fulfill internship requirements through their volunteer service.

VALUED YOUTH PARTNERSHIP PROGRAM
Intercultural Development Research Association (IDRA)
5835 Gallaghan
Suite 350
San Antonio, TX 78228-1190
TEL: 512-684-8180
Purpose: To prevent students from dropping out of school through cross-age tutoring.
Sponsor: Coca Cola USA
Contact: Alicia Salinas Sosa
Description: When the dropout rate in San Antonio took a dramatic rise, the *Valued Youth Partnership Program* was developed in an attempt to turn this alarming statistic around. It was developed by IDRA and funded by Coca Cola USA.
Cross-age tutoring is the basic concept of the program, but the

tutors in this case are the potential dropouts. In 1988, eight schools were involved in the program.

The process begins when personnel in area school districts identify Hispanic youth at high risk of dropping out of school. They are designated as "valued youth" and are given an opportunity to tutor younger children. As the younger children respond to the teaching of basic skills the older youth reinforce their own knowledge while developing positive perceptions of themselves. They remain in school.

The student tutors must take special classes to reach their greatest competence in communication, reading, and writing skills, as well as to gain a practical awareness of child development procedures. This training continues throughout the partnership relationship. The cross-age tutoring brings the partners together from five to eight hours each week, either during school hours or after school, depending on individual school policy.

Parents are involved in the program as much as possible, beginning with a pre-tutoring understanding of the child's involvement. Parent support is considered an important part of the program.

Field trips bring tutor and tutee together in a social setting, giving them a chance for further interaction.

Adult role models are brought in to talk with the tutors on various topics related to future careers. Often they are graduates of the tutors' school districts.

Coca Cola holds a recognition program for the tutors, as do their teachers.

Statistics demonstrate the success of the program. In 1985-86 an impressive 94 of the 100 high-risk Hispanic youth in the program stayed in school.

Founded: 1988

VERMONT INTERNSHIP PROGRAM

SEE TRAINING/CONFERENCES/TEACHING: INTERNSHIPS

VOLUNTEER PALEONTOLOGY DIG

University of Wisconsin
750 University Avenue
Madison, WI 53706
TEL: 608-262-1234

Purpose: To assist a university museum in locating fossilized bones of prehistoric seagoing animals.

Sponsor: University of Wisconsin

Contact: University Paleontologist

Description: The University of Wisconsin's geological museum is hoping to learn more about seagoing animals that lived 83 million years ago. Volunteers were dispatched to a "digs" in western Kansas in the summer of 1989 where a nearly-intact specimen of a *mosasaur* was found the previous year. The Kansas area was covered by a shallow ocean in prehistoric times when the land was lower and warmer. The site is rich with fossils, many lying exposed on the ground and requiring no digging at all. Others must be extracted from the blue shale and yellow chalk common in washouts. The site is on the banks of a deep gorge cut by rain water flowing toward the Smoky Hill River.

The 1989 effort uncovered pieces from two different species of the mosasaur family, and skull fragments probably from a tylosaurus, a gigantic animal 39 feet in length. What is hoped for is some insight into what may be a pattern - flippers breaking and rehealing before the animal died (true of both the older and more recent flippers found) - and may provide some idea of living habits.

The volunteers are supplied with several small hand tools, including utility knives, paint brushes, dental tools, and super glue. Their training emphasizes extreme care in handling the fossils, with the glue serving the purpose of coating a fossil that appears fragile before removing it from the shale or soil. Aluminum foil is provided for wrapping and plastic bags for transporting.

Although students from the university can do the digging for credit, many other volunteers come forward because they find the experience "fun."

VOLUNTEER SERVICES PROGRAM/UA

University of Alabama
Student Life Office
Box 60 University Station
Birmingham, AL 35294
TEL: 205-934-3827

Purpose: To provide volunteer opportunities for students to gain experience in their chosen field of study.

Sponsor: University of Alabama at Birmingham

Contact: Ray Minor

Description: The Volunteer Services Program (VSP) is primarily offered to University of Alabama at Birmingham students who desire work in a service-learning position without monetary compensation. A variety of opportunities are made available in local hospitals, social service agencies, criminal justice institutions and other such places for students to gain experience in their chosen field of study. Goals of the program are:

● Foster an appreciation of volunteerism among UAB faculty, staff and students.
● Make available to students information about volunteer opportunities in the community
● Provide for the recruitment of student volunteers from the UAB student body.
● Emphasize volunteer work as a complement to classroom learning.
● Work along with instructors who desire to have students engage in volunteer service as a part of the total classroom learning experience.

Service-learning opportunities integrate conscious educational growth with the accomplishment of important tasks. They provide students with opportunities to meet significant public needs while accomplishing such learning objectives as the application of acquired knowledge, the integration of new knowledge with previously acquired learning, and the evaluation of the validity of principles and of the student's skill in applying them.

VOLUNTEER TUTORING PROGRAM

Madison House
170 Rugby Road
Charlottesville, VA 22903
TEL: 804-977-7051

Purpose: To provide elementary, middle and high school students with one-to-one tutoring.

Sponsor: Madison House

Contact: Jane Parker

Description: The Tutoring Program was one of the first volunteer programs sponsored by Madison House. In 1969 a group of interested University students approached the Superintendents of Schools with a proposal for instituting a program in the Charlottesville/Albemarle public school systems - elementary, middle and high schools. Individual principals were contacted and programs were set up in their schools. Tutoring was offered also to first and second year university students and to the children of migrant workers.

Today the Tutoring Program works with ten public schools, placing approximately 150 volunteers. Tutors are assigned also to the Community Attention Homes for troubled youths, and at one private school.

The volunteer's involvement with this program begins with an orientation. This is a three-week series of discussions and presentations with experts in fields of child development, education, and psychology. When the orientation period is completed, volunteers are matched with a younger student according to grade level and subject area specified on the volunteer application.

Tutoring usually takes place in the afternoon after school is dismissed. Carpools are organized to transport tutors to the area schools. The program is flexible and it is possible to arrange other hours. Although numerous subject areas are tutored, the primary emphasis of the Tutoring Program is on the improvement of basic math and reading skills. It is the philosophy of the program that problems in these two basic fields are the root of problems in other fields.

Volunteers are made aware also of the fact that children in need of tutoring often are coping with behavioral and emotional problems as well as with academic weaknesses. Neither profound knowledge in a particular academic field, nor extensive experience in tutoring is required to be an effective tutor, but a genuine interest in helping a young person to learn is an essential quality. Also important in approaching learning difficulties are the qualities of patience and creativity, since tutoring manuals and other structured materials can be only guidelines from which individualized methods are drawn.
Founded: 1969

VOLUNTEERS FOR YOUTH
SEE VOLUNTEERS: ROLE MODELS

WESTERN CAROLINA CENTER VOLUNTEENS
Western Carolina Center
Volunteer Services
Enola Road
Morganton, NC 28655
TEL: 704-433-2614
Purpose: To offer volunteer opportunities for teenagers age 13 and older that will benefit mentally retarded children and adults.
Sponsor: West Carolina Center
Contact: Volunteer Coordinator
Description: This program provides the much-needed opportunity for minor teenagers to become involved in a volunteer activity. It takes into consideration the benefits the energy and enthusiasm of this age group can bring to the mentally retarded. Conversely, this activity is beneficial to the teenagers in providing work experience, career exploration and, in many cases, a first job.
To volunteer at the center, besides the desire to help others, a teenager must be 13 or going into the eighth grade, provide his or her lunch and transportation, be ready to work with people with special needs, and be able to accept supervision - and constructive criticism when necessary - from a professional staff.
Western Carolina Center is a residential center for children and adults in North Carolina who are mentally retarded. Supported by the State Government, its staff and volunteers provide residents with everything from medical care to recreation. Teenagers are involved in the same areas as adult volunteers as appropriate, including:
- **Areas of direct care** - recreation, medical services, psychology, physical therapy, dentistry, special education, infant care, fine arts, and dietary assistance.
- **Areas of indirect care** - maintenance, housekeeping, clerical, and secretarial assistance.

Most importantly for the residents, Volunteens become friends and help to make their summer special, too. As one resident put it, "Volunteens bring SMILES."
Extra activities include fundraisers, picnics, mini-seminars, park activities, swimming, Recognition Day (which selects *Volunteer of the Summer),* *CAROWINDS,* and other programs, often developed by the youth themselves.
Besides the obvious benefits for the teenager - job experience, career exploration, job reference - one volunteer remarked, "The best thing about volunteering is the good feeling you have about yourself."
Publications: Volunteens Are Incredible

WESTTOWN SERVICE NETWORK
Westtown School
Westtown, PA 19395
TEL: 215-399-0123
Purpose: To provide a variety of service opportunities - particularly to help the disabled - for students at Westtown School.
Sponsor: Westtown School District; foundations
Contact: Karen Gallagher
Description: Although *Westtown Service Network* is only a year-long program, 85% of the students at the school volunteer for the entire time that they are there. A quaker school, Westtown has always had a principle of helping the community - especially handicapped persons. Most service opportunites available through the program require a once-a-week commitment (about two hours) for a full trimester. Service work is done outside class - at the end of the school day, either in the late afternoon or early evening, or on weekends. In addition to a 15-passenger van leased from the school, faculty, alumni and parents volunteer to drive. Those who drive small groups in their own cars are reimbursed by Network. Among the volunteer opportunities are group activities, assistance in drama, art, physical therapy, day care, computer instruction, English as a Second Language tutoring, and positions that provide companionship - especially to the elderly and mentally retarded. A popular project is a tutoring program for children awaiting placement in foster homes who are brought to Westtown for this activity.
Students are given credit for journals that they keep regarding their work. These journals often contribute to problem resolution regarding student/agency relations. Also, journals may be used for credit in English, Religion, Spanish or other courses at the discretion of the teacher.
In the ten year period following its inception, *Network* received over $82,000 in foundations grants. A small endowment for operations has been established. The program is run by a full-time dean and teacher. The community served includes Chester, Philadelphia and Wilmington, with an average of 20 agencies participating each trimester.
Besides the obvious benefits to the youth, personal enjoyment is experienced in cases such as the student taking French at Westtown who worked with an elderly former French teacher. With little opportunity to use French in the nursing home, the elderly resident enjoyed helping the young volunteer improve her grades in her French class.
Founded: 1979

WHEELCHAIR WASH
SEE BUSINESS/INDUSTRY INVOLVEMENT

WOMAN-TO-WOMAN HOTLINE
SEE INFORMATION & REFERRAL: CANCER

YES PROGRAM (YOUTH-ELDERLY SERVICES)*
Family Service America
101 Rock Street
Fall River, MA 02720
TEL: 617-678-7542
Purpose: To offer older people companionship, and a chance for both young and old to better understand each other.
Sponsor: Family Service America
Contact: Hank Fairman
Description: The family service association broadened its counseling and group services in the fall of 1970 to include YES - Youth-Elderly Services. Through YES, high school students spend two hours each week with elderly people both in nursing homes and in the community assisting the activities directors in projects which the older men especially enjoy, such as carpentry and photography. Volunteers run simple errands, read and play games, just sit and chat, and in other ways strive to help the shut-in feel a part of the community.

Training takes place monthly in small groups at the high schools immediately after school. Course contents include:

- the social, psychological and physical problems of aging persons, with particular emphasis on the cultural backgrounds of the Fall River area;
- community attitudes toward aging and youth, and a study of community resources for older persons;
- the philosophy of volunteer service and how to promote meaningful relationships between young people and the elderly;
- practical experience in a nursing home, including the appropriate role of the YES volunteer.

The volunteers are assigned reading in the field of aging. Other teaching aids used are audio-visual materials (some of which are developed by the FSA with its own high school volunteers in action in nursing homes), actual case histories, and oral presentations by guest speakers and staff members.

Growing out of the friendship between the young volunteers and older friends is the Living History Program. Since January 1974, the students have been interviewing the elderly about Fall River's cultural and economic past. Trained in interviewing techniques, the students also do research in libraries, schools and the local historical society. They plan to photograph the old and the new and hope to develop a film based on their interviews and photographs.
Founded: 1970

YOU CAN FREE A MIND: ADULT LITERACY PROGRAM
Brown University
25 George Street
PO Box 1974
Providence, RI 02912
TEL: 401-863-2338
Purpose: To provide literacy tutoring for the Providence adult community.
Description: Established in 1987, this program recruits *Brown University* students to provide literacy tutoring to adults in the community. Students are trained by a representative of the *Brown University Adult Academy.*

Training for students is made available at the beginning of each semester and takes about ten hours. After the students have been trained, they are paired with a learner and assigned to a site either on or off campus, depending upon their preference. The on-campus tutoring occurs on Saturday mornings, while the off-campus tutoring takes place at various times during the week. Over the years the volunteers have worked with *Blackstone Valley, Dorcas Place, South Providence Tutorial, Talbot House,* and the *Genesis* program. During the fall of 1989, there were four tutors. The tutors are expected to meet weekly with their learners for one and a half to two hours, and they are urged to stay with one learner for as long as possible to create a stable environment.
Publications: Imagine What It Is Like for Someone Who Cannot Read

YOUNG VOLUNTEERS IN ACTION*
Knoxville Child and Family Services
114 Dameron Avenue
Knoxville, TN 37917
TEL: 615-524-7483
Purpose: To generate young volunteers to assist community agencies and to assist the youth in job preparation and community commitment.
Sponsor: US/ACTION, the national volunteer agency; Head Start, Child and Family Services; community donations and support
Contact: Suzanne Livingood
Description: The Young Volunteers in Action was begun November 1, 1982, co-funded by a grant from ACTION, the national volunteer agency, and Head Start. Child and Family Services is the local sponsor.

The project involves recruiting at least 200 students between the ages 14 and 22, to serve in a minimum of 12 community agencies and contribute a minimum of 10,000 volunteer hours in the grant year.

The Young Volunteers in Action project includes opportunities for long and short term service, assisting local agencies and volunteer groups. Special emphasis is placed on working in the Head Start programs, day care centers, and addressing low income, elderly and handicapped needs. Volunteers are able to choose from many different agencies the type of experience and talents they would like to use.

As a part of Young Volunteers in Action, students will be trained and placed in Volunteer positions in the community. This opportunity will help students develop skills, leadership and experience to be used in future employment as well as the opportunity to explore career choices. The Young Volunteers in Action project assists students by offering them a meaningful and productive use of their free time in community service. Other benefits of the project include on-the-job insurance coverage, development workshops, and participation in recognition activities. Volunteer duties are as varied and creative as the volunteers themselves. All levels of experience, from no experience to budding expertise can be utilized. Training varies according to the duties, agency, and level of experience. Each agency has a volunteer supervisor who will provide the necessary on-the-job training and supervision. Persons interested in the program should complete an application. Applicants are interviewed to determine their interests, qualifications, and availability to facilitate an appropriate referral to a community agency.
Founded: 1982

YOUTH ALLOCATIONS COMMITTEE
SEE FUNDING/FUND-RAISING/RELATED SERVICES

YOUTH ALLOCATIONS COMMITTEE
SEE LEADERSHIP DEVELOPMENT/BOARDS: CHILDREN/YOUTH

YOUTH AS RESOURCES
SEE LEADERSHIP DEVELOPMENT/BOARDS: CHILDREN/YOUTH

YOUTH AS RESOURCES/YMCA
SEE LEADERSHIP DEVELOPMENT/BOARDS: CHILDREN/YOUTH

YOUTH COMMUNITY SERVICE
Oswego County
Personnel Department
Oswego, NY 13126
TEL: 315-342-0025
Purpose: To provide needed community services while offering young people a transition to the adult labor market through voluntary service.
Sponsor: US/ACTION; US/DoL - Department of Labor
Contact: Carolyn Rush, Director
Description: In 1977, Syracuse was one of 44 cities under consideration by ACTION as a site for a project of a national voluntary community service program. Its size, institutions, ethnic and racial mix, varying economic levels, and isolated labor and media markets provide a diverse setting - "a cross-section of urban America." The grant was awarded to Syracuse in 1978 for the pilot project of Youth Community Service (YCS). In addition to the obvious goals - to provide volunteer labor for the community and to help youth prepare for the labor market - the pilot project would provide the base for evaluation of the recruitment of volunteers.

Volunteers are youth ages 16 to 21. In Syracuse, unemployment in this group at the start of YCS exceeded 20%. Low-income youth traditionally do not participate in volunteer service, which offers opportunities to gain marketable experience, increased personal worth, greater responsibility and commitment to the community, increased maturity about the world of work, and less social isolation. Since many community services agencies are understaffed and inadequately funded, they are often incapable of achieving their stated purposes or expanding their scope in new or neglected problem areas. To bring these two problems together in a mutually beneficial "partnership" was not expected to be easy, but unique aspects of the YCS program have made it a desirable affiliation for sponsor and volunteer. These aspects include:

- YCS is open to all economic groups, with special consideration given to handicapped youth and youth referred from the criminal justice system.
- Freedom of Choice, with volunteers studying potential service opportunities, making appointments for interviews. Through the interchange on qualifications, mutual responsibilities, etc., both sponsor and volunteer feel that a choice exists and options are open both ways.
- Nontraditional Nature of Service, which challenges the talents and initiative of the volunteers and allows them to deliver services to the community in a novel and innovative way.
- Health Benefits and Educational Allowance, which is appreciated by the volunteer and includes free health coverage and a $400 educational allowance for a year of service (drawn at $33.33 per month after three months of service).

A variety of services have been provided to the community, including:

- extended day care;
- a thirft shop;
- neighborhood revitalization;
- education of small children on fire emergencies
- a bilingual newspaper;
- investigative consumer services;
- winterization;
- vocational rehabilitation for the handicapped;
- drug awareness;
- recycling;
- playground construction;
- recreation for the retarded;
- adolescent mothers' program; and
- crime prevention for senior citizens.

The rural component of YCS launched a year later mounted similar projects, with some emphasis on education, recreation, and natural resources and beautification. Oswego County was selected by ACTION after all surrounding counties to Onondoga County (site of the Syracuse project) were studied, because it met a variety of criteria as a rural setting. The rural project received its funding in April and 143 projects were developed by December of that year.

About 4200 youth applied to YCS in Syracuse during its initial year of operation. In addition to the YCS office, recruitment staff worked in schools, teen centers, and shopping malls. TV and radio provided air time and brochures and posters were placed in banks, libraries, schools, and nonprofit organizations. In the smaller rural component, almost 500 youth volunteers were involved the first year.

All volunteers of the program are required to attend a Volunteer Orientation Conference. Forty of these were held the first year - some in the field to enable volunteers without transportation to attend. Goals of the conference are:

- Increase volunteers' understanding of YCS.
- Help volunteers identify their skills and potential.
- Help volunteers understand the process of selecting a service opportunity.
- Develop or improve skills necessary to make a match with a project.
- Create a positive attitude in the volunteers toward YCS and the opportunities it offers.

YCS continues to illustrate the fact that youth want to be involved in positive, fulfilling activity. The program has acted as a stimulus for many youth who have returned to school full time, or have left the program and secured employment locally as area employers see program participation as legitimate work experience.

YCS benefits the community in a variety of ways because of its broad citizen involvement. One important aspect often not present in broad community efforts is the fact that smaller agencies can participate, since volunteer expenses are paid directly to the volunteer and not on a reimbursable basis. Even a few grass roots organizations have been able to utilize the services of YCS volunteers.

Founded: 1977

YOUTH COMMUNITY SERVICE
SEE COMMUNITY SERVICES

YOUTH DEVELOPMENT PROGRAM
2202 South Eleventh Street
Lincoln, NE 68502
TEL: 402-472-4515
Purpose: To provide educational assistance to low income youth through an on-going tutoring program; to provide camping experiences for low income children and youth of Lincoln and Lancaster County.
Sponsor: Lincoln Action Program
Contact: Deb Easterly
Description: The Lincoln Action Program tutoring project is designed to help not only the children who are tutored, but also the college students and other volunteers doing the tutoring. The majority of the tutors are students from the colleges in Lincoln, who are using the tutoring experience for credit in psychology, social work and education classes. This provides them with the opportunity to get experience working with children. Volunteers for this program also come from Pre-trial Diversion and the Volunteer Center.

The time spent doing volunteer work in this program is approximately five months, or one college semester. It starts with an orientation at the beginning of each semester and ends at the conclusion of the semester. Throughout this time tutors spend at least two hours a week at the schools. Supervision, which is done by the tutoring coordinator and assistants, is an on-going process throughout the semester. Each tutor writes a journal entry for every visit to chart the progress of the tutoring.

This program is conducted in all Chapter One schools in Lincoln elementary through high school, both public and parochial. Many of these children do not receive the extra scholastic assistance from parents or private tutors that children from an upper income family might receive. Through this program children are given this extra assistance and a chance to use their education to its fullest.

The summer part of the LAP youth services is a camping program. Each year funds are received from the City of Lincoln and Lancaster County to send a limited number of income qualified children to summer camp. This year the seven camps being used include church camps and city parks and recreation camps.

After making an application, the recipients of a camp scholarship are chosen according to several guidelines. Income, number of people in the family, past participation in the LAP Camp Program, single parent families, being a ward of the State and date of application are all used when choosing campers for the Summer Program.

YOUTH IN ACTION
SEE COMMUNITY SERVICES

YOUTH-IN-GOVERNMENT DAY
SEE LEADERSHIP DEVELOPMENT/BOARDS:
CHILDREN/YOUTH

YOUTH LEADERSHIP VENTURE FUNDING PROGRAM
United Way of the Capital Area (Hartford)
99 Woodland Street
Hartford, CT 06105-2476
TEL: 203-247-2580
Purpose: To involve youth in identifying target issues of the youth community for United Way funding.
Sponsor: United Way of the Capital Area
Contact: Shelley Aronson, Youth Leadership Staff
Description: The Youth Leadership Venture Funding Program has taken an issue-oriented approach to funding. During the 1989-90 school year, a group of 15 students from Hartford-area high schools identified youth substance abuse as the target issue of the youth community. Provided with $10,000 in venture funds from United Way of the Capital Area, the students funded 13 local programs addressing that problem.
United Way's Youth Leadership Advisors, a group of adult volunteers, selected students based on applications distributed to public and private schools in the 30-town coverage area. The students make the decisions, and the committee helps keep them informed about the funding process.
In addition to receiving training in basic allocations procedures and education about United Way. the students gained a thorough understanding of the substance problem. The student volunteers also interviewed elected officials and human-service agency directors about priority concerns for youth. In response to students' inquiries, the Connecticut Alcohol and Drug Abuse Commission confirmed information about local teen substance abuse programs needing funding.
Programs funded by the *Youth Leadership Venture Funding Program* included
  ● information directory identifying resources, *Youth Yellow Pages,*
  ● a student-produced video on anti-substance abuse peer counseling, and
  ● a positive self-development program incorporating anti-substance abuse eduction for elementary school children.
The Hartford United Way's board of directors unanimously approved the programs selected by the students. The program's chairman said, "The youth funding program has not only given us input from young people about community needs, but has provided funding for anti-substance abuse programs run by and for students in our schools."
Founded: 1988

YOUTH RECREATION PROGRAM
Madison House
Charlottesville, VA 22903
TEL: 804-977-7051
Purpose: To provide constructive recreational activities for children that they do not receive in school.
Sponsor: Madison House
Contact: Jane Parker
Description: In 1973, Madison House adopted a basketball program sponsored by the University Inter-Fraternity Council and expanded it to include softball, football, and arts and crafts. Today it includes also soccer, dance, gymnastics, tennis, karate, swimming and flag football. These athletic activities are organized for elementary school boys and girls ages eight through eleven. The activities are organized as opposed to the free-for-all recess type games - structured to promote good sportsmanship and a spirit of fun, not competition. The emphasis is on participation, not achievement. Over 300 children from ten area elementary schools participate in the various programs.
Madison House volunteers act as teachers and coaches. Independence and initiative are the primary qualities needed by the volunteer to lead a class or coach a team in an effective manner. If the volunteer can keep the kids interested and develop a rapport with them, the activity is almost always enjoyed by all

participants. Dependability on the part of teachers and coaches is also critical. A football team left coachless one Saturday morning, or a swimming class left teacherless can be a complete frustration for the children.
All Youth Recreation Program activities are conducted in eight-week segments. Volunteers can commit themselves to either one or two semesters and the programs are usually completed well before the exam periods. All activities are scheduled on Saturday or Sunday and usually require two or three hours from the volunteer per weekend. All activities are held at Memorial Gym at the University or on one of the adjacent athletic fields. Consequently, there is no transportation problem for those volunteers living on-grounds without a car.
In addition to its own activities, Youth Recreation refers interested volunteers to area scouting organizations. Another possibility for interested volunteers is to begin a project not already included in the program. Suggestions for new activities are constantly being made and many are implemented and enhance the overall program.
The Youth Recreation Program benefits directly from the Alan Jacobus Memorial Fund, which was started in 1975 by the brothers of the Pi Kappa Phi Fraternity. The fund was started because of Alan Jacobus' role as volunteer program director, and his successful efforts in helping to bring the Youth Recreation Program to its current level of respect in the community.
Founded: 1973

YOUTH RESOURCES OF SOUTHWESTERN INDIANA
SEE LEADERSHIP DEVELOPMENT/BOARDS: CHILDREN/YOUTH

YOUTH SERVICES
American Red Cross
Virginia Capital Chapter
409 East Main Street
Richmond, VA 23219
TEL: 804-780-2266
Purpose: To create and offer training and volunteer opportunities for the young.
Sponsor: American Red Cross/Virginia Capital Chapter
Contact: Joyce Arrington or Linda Bullock
Description: On the National level, Youth Services started in 1917 after President Woodrow Wilson observed a need for children to get involved in the World War I effort. This youth membership provided a channel through which boys and girls in the nation's school systems could alleviate problems related to the war.
Locally, Red Cross Youth Services has been in existence since 1918.
Most of the Youth Service programs are created under National guidelines, but, for the most part, programs are created according to community need.
Chapter budgets include funds allocated for Youth Services which also include a restricted youth fund. Money from the restricted fund is collected in the schools through a Red Cross Enrollment Drive. The expenditure of these funds can be approved only by an interschool council of middle and high school students.
A youth orientation is held every summer to provide training for volunteers who want to work in nursing homes, hospitals, etc. A popular program is an active Clown Corps of youth ranging in age from 11 to 15. The Clown Corps provides entertainment for many community activities throughout the year.
Presently, the Virginia Capital Chapter, Youth Services, has approximately 300 volunteers (including adult supervisors).
Founded: 1917

YOUTH VOLUNTEER SERVICES
Grand Blanc School District
12500 Holly Road
Grand Blanc, MI 48439
TEL: 313-694-8211

Purpose: To help fill a gap in today's society while introducing youth to volunteerism.
Sponsor: Grand Blanc School District
Contact: Lynn Gillespie, Director, or Gary Lipe, Assistant Superintendent
Description: In 1976, while attending a National Conference on Child Advocacy, a *Junior League* member came up with an idea for a youth volunteer community involvement program. In addition to the needed assistance in the community, the intent of the program is to promote citizenshp and leadership within students while also providing them with career guidance. A year later, with the help of another Junior League member, and a professor from the *GMI Engineering & Management Institute, Youth Volunteer Services* was begun in Grand Blanc and Bendle schools. Grand Blanc has continued the program.
About 300 students volunteer their services to businesses, community services organizations and government offices every semester. They have worked with impaired children, at preschool day care centers, in veterinarians' offices, at auto plants, in politicians' offices, and in many others capacities lacking adequate services.
Today, the school district has more requests for youth volunteers than it has youths to fill the posts. Many of the volunteer positions lead to paying jobs. "Generations ago," according to the Assistant Superintendent, "youth worked side-by-side with their parents and learned what work was about and whether their parents' careers were suitable for them." To inject some of this philosophy, the school provides a "real-life laboratory" in which students have an opportunity to interact with adults before beginning their volunteer assignments, which is for most their first workplace experience.
The founder has moved on to become Director of Development for the University of Michigan, but keeps in touch with the youth program, because "Designing that program was one of the most rewarding and special things I have ever done. It causes magic things to happen with these youth."
The state Board of Education honored the program along with 15 *Partners for Education* programs elsewhere in the state. The award-winning *Youth Volunteer Services* effort is funded by the Junior League and the *Mott Foundation.*
Founded: 1976

YOUTH WHO CARE
PO Box 4074
Grand Junction, CO 81502
TEL: 303-245-4160
Purpose: To promote a "high-on-life" substance-free existence among school-age youth.
Sponsor: US/ACTION - VISTA
Contact: YWC Coordinator
Description: Most, but not all, of Youth Who Care's activities are conducted in the schools. The program keeps youth in Mesa County involved in outdoor recreation, with emphasis on education. They hope to provide positive experiences that will counteract the drug problems in the area.
The teenagers who operate the program have a total budget of $57,000 annually. They raise about $8,000 of that, and the rest comes from the Colorado Department of Health, Alcohol and Drug Abuse Division ($14,000) and the VISTA volunteer project ($15,000). Foundations and corporations provide $8,000 and a local business, Mt. Garfield Plumbing and Heating, picks up the $6,000 tab for office space and utilities.
Programs in the schools include YWC clubs (seven schools), YWC 3-D (Don't Drink and Drive) teams, and a speakers' bureau. The outreach arm of this program places teens as volunteers in hospitals, museums, etc. Recreational and other group activities, as well as public relations campaigns, are also implemented by the YWC organizers.
It is estimated that, during 1988-89, the participating teens reached 10,000 people through direct contact, and indirectly over half of

the population, or another 40,000 people in a county that is suffering economic hardships due to the decline of its once booming oil industry. The teens come from both high-risk and low-risk groups, and many choose to continue their involvement in the program beyond their teen years. They work closely on all projects with representatives from all sectors of the community. Communities around the nation as well as in Colorado have requested information and set up similar programs in the hope of making some progress in their drug prevention programs.

VOLUNTEERS: TEAMS

NATIONAL/STATE ORGANIZATIONS

CB RADIO PATROL (*formerly CB Radio Posse*)
American Federation of Police
1100 Northeast 125th Street
North Miami, FL 33161
TEL: 305-891-1700
Objectives: To promote safety and discourage crime.
Services: Works with 30,000 volunteer CB radio operators in 50 states through a "volunteer community radio patrol"; seeks to promote safety and discourage crime by their presence, activities, and immediate access to law enforcement agencies; maintains a library on the subject of community crime and the effectiveness of the radio patrol program nationwide; publishes a newsletter and a manual on civil defense.
Publications: Police Times
Founded: 1976

NATIONAL TOWN WATCH ASSOCIATION
SEE LEADERSHIP DEVELOPMENT/BOARDS: LAW ENFORCEMENT

INDIVIDUAL PROGRAM PROFILES

AIDS CHRONIC CARE UNIT VOLUNTEER PROGRAM
Goldwater Memorial Hospital
Roosevelt Island, NY 10044
TEL: 212-750-6755
Purpose: To provide chronic care to AIDS patients.
Sponsor: Goldwater Memorial Hospital
Contact: Tammy Carlisle, Volunteer Director
Description: Sixty-four beds in Goldwater Memorial Hospital's 944-bed long-term care and rehabilitation facility are in a special unit for patients suffering from AIDS. AIDS patients are referred to Goldwater by other New York City municipal and voluntary hospitals, with some coming from Rikers Island, the city prison. The patient population ranges from the very frail who may need a great deal of care to those who need relatively little help in caring for themselves.
Volunteer recruitment is a continuous process at the Hospital. The volunteer program is set up with a team concept with at least two or more members per team. Volunteers make a commitment of three hours per week to the program.
Training is provided before volunteer service begins, and a very extensive training manual has been developed for the volunteers. Other training resources are provided as they become available to update the AIDS situation and keep them informed about newer approaches to patient care. Volunteers receive public transportation fare and lunch. Not all volunteers take advantage of these perks, however.
With all patients together in a single unit, it is easier to provide a

full range of services and address the patients' needs. Volunteers feed patients, make coffee, and provide recreation programs in and out of the unit. Volunteers act as advocates for family problems and for complaints with Social Security, Medicare, and Medicaid benefits and entitlements. Volunteers also assist with dietary problems, paint, write, sing, hold holiday events, provide clothing when needed, and much more.

Special services are provided as needed for the blind or deaf, for example. Also, special requests are granted when possible - such as holding a memorial service for those from the unit who have died. There is also a support system among the patients themselves. Since they are all in the same unit, they visit, support, and help each other. Patients are not confined to the AIDS unit, but can participate in hospital functions and utilize any service the hospital provides. They are not isolated, and are completely free to visit other parts of the hospital.

AIDS volunteers are expected to address the full range of needs for the entire unit, not just for one individual. They are assigned not to a single patient, but to everyone in the unit. They meet this challenge and offer their services to many people.

Progress notes on each patient are maintained by volunteers as a working tool to assist other volunteers and the hospital staff.

Problems for the program include a shortage of nurses, lack of TV sets for patients, not enough volunteers, and the cultural and social gap often existing between volunteers and patients. The volunteer support system and team concept alleviate many of the problems, often through phone conversations with each other back at home, or meetings on extra days to discuss resolving problems. The volunteer director also calls volunteers from time to time to identify and discuss problems.

A volunteer bulletin is issued by the director to keep everyone informed of changes, social activities, an expected death in the ward, and other issues to assist in preventing burnout and sudden bereavement when a loss occurs.

AIDS Unit volunteers are permitted access to the hospital day or night, have their own identification cards and keys, have a refrigerator and coffee maker and constant access to refreshments, etc. No other unit in the hospital has these amenities, which enable the volunteers to provide unique services for particular patients. Because patients are usually in the last stages of the disease, volunteer training at Goldwater places a special emphasis on preparing for death and dying. On the other hand, a few patients become well enough to be discharged, but have no place to go. They are homeless, abandoned by family and friends. There are few or no visitors for the patients, making the volunteers their only contact with the outside world and their only friends besides hospital staff and patient advocates. The dedicated, loyal volunteers at the Goldwater AIDS Chronic Care Unit make a difference.
Founded: 1987

ALPINE RESCUE TEAM
PO Box 934
Evergreen, CO 80439
TEL: 303-674-5855
Purpose: To respond to emergencies in mountainous and wilderness areas.
Contact: Program Coordinator
Description: The *Alpine Rescue Team* is an organized group of volunteers who are willing to leave their families and holiday picnics on a moment's notice to respond to emergencies in the mountainous and wilderness areas of Colorado. Response is immediate and from their present base they can be at the point of the emergency within 20 minutes. In mountain emergencies, the Team establishes a base camp and organizes small groups to ascend the mountain. Twenty to 30 volunteers assist the ground teams in locating the injured person, and the airlift crew in getting the individual off of the mountain - usually under less-than-ideal flight conditions.

The *Alpine Rescue Team* is the largest rescue team in the state, and the only team that gets no government funding. It performs its services completely free of charge, depending on corporate and individual donations for its continued existence.

Currently, Alpine is trying to build a new headquarters in a location that would greatly decrease its response time to emergencies. Again, the Team looks to individual and corporate donations. If public and community response in the past is any indication, the new headquarters should be a reality in record time, according to a Team volunteer.

CHILD ABUSE SERVICES TEAM (CAST)
SEE VOLUNTEERS: POLICE OFFICERS

CHILD ASSAULT PREVENTION TEAM
Monmouth County
County Office Building
Asbury Park, NJ 07712
TEL: 201-431-7000
Purpose: To teach youngsters how to spot danger and prevent situations that make them vulnerable to abuse or assault.
Sponsor: State of New Jersey
Contact: Carolyn Vacca or Shirley Orlans, Coordinators
Description: In a special program in New Jersey elementary schools, teachers, pupils and parents learn about ways children can defend themselves against assault by other children, strangers and even people they know and trust. The *Monmouth County Child Assault Prevention (CAP) Team* includes two coordinators and 27 female CAP instructors, who visit schools all over the county to train the teachers, parents and children. The program is funded by state grants through the *Division of Youth and Family Services.* There are separate sessions for each group, as follows:

Classroom Session - Before the classroom session begins, any child who feels uncomfortable is given permission to leave. To date, no child has left the session in the more than 40,000 workshops conducted.

The children themselves are asked to volunteer at specific times in the training, rather than be selected for the role playing accompanying the program. During a typical CAP workshop for 11- and 12-year-olds, children arrange their chairs in a semi-circle and a casual conversation begins about rights and privileges. This session is designed to make the children more comfortable before the more active, role-playing part of the session. At first, two CAP instructors play gradeschoolers and act out roles similar to those encountered by the children. As the role-play progresses, pupils from the class are asked to come forward and play some of the roles - like confronting a bully at school, dealing with strangers on the street and in cars, etc. The children are told that they have weapons with which to kick, scratch, bite, butt, etc., and that a special kind of yell - not the squeals they use in playing - is needed to get attention. The *CAP Yell* is demonstrated, and pupils volunteer to help with the demonstration. Other segments of the program include:

● the ability to call the police;
● the ability to give an accurate description;
● what to do when the problem is with the people you know; and
● how to spot danger.

When the classroom session ends, children are invited to meet individually with counselors to discuss personal problems and experiences.

Teacher Workshops - Separate teacher workshops are mainly to help educators prepare for the CAP team's classroom visits.

Parent Workshops - Separate parent workshops explore CAP's history, explain its philosophy on the rights of children and offer parenting skills and statistics on child assault.

The CAP program originated in 1983 through *Women Against Rape,* a Columbus, Ohio, organization, but New Jersey is the only one so far to make it statewide, based upon a recommendation by

the *Governors' Task Force on Child Abuse and Neglect.*
According to a Coordinator, "We have a lot of success stories.
Kids often tell us how they've used CAP strategies. In some cases,
their calls to police have led to arrests. We've made a lot of kids
safe in this county."
Founded: 1989

CITY VOLUNTEER CORPS
SEE COMMUNITY SERVICES: URBAN

FESTIVAL
SEE VOLUNTEERS: FAMILIES

FLORIDA SHERIFFS YOUTH VILLA
Florida Sheriffs Youth Ranches
Boys Ranch, FL 32060
TEL: 904-842-5555
Purpose: To offer a new start to neglected, unsupervised and
troubled girls.
Sponsor: Florida Sheriffs Association
Contact: Ed Freddo, Director of Youth Services
Description: The Florida Sheriffs Youth Villa operates under the
aegis of the nonprofit Florida Sheriffs Youth Ranches, sponsored
by the Florida Sheriffs Association. The Villa emphasizes survival
training to help teenagers cope with the outside world. The
training is offered to neglected, unsupervised and troubled girls to
help them discover that there is a "good life." It is a comfortable,
attractive, secure facility offering many rewarding experiences and
an opportunity to get a fresh start.
Girls at the Youth Villa receive professional counseling and a good
education. They learn to assume responsibility and make good
decisions in an environment that emphasizes positive thinking.
The basic training is enhanced through *Transition Living,* a
program that gives girls who are about to depart the Villa an
opportunity to sample independent living before they go out on
their own.
Tried earlier on a smaller scale, *Transition Living* was expanded
when, in 1988, the program was moved from cramped quarters in
a small cottage to spacious Dorista Villa. This has allowed more
girls to get involved, and has given them the elbow room they
need to simulate true independent living.
Girls at the Villa volunteer for transition living. They have to be at
least 16 years old and high school juniors or above. They must be
recommended by their Youth Villa group parents, and they cannot
get in unless they have demonstrated leadership, maturity and the
ability to assume responsibility.
The Director finds the *Transition Living* program a resounding
success, saying, "The girls are always on time. If they have ever
been late for a curfew, it has been just one time in two years." The
Sheriffs Association also manages Boys Ranch, Youth Ranch, and
Youth Camp in various parts of Florida.
Publications: The Rancher

GLEANING*
SEE VOLUNTEERS: SELF-HELP

GRATERFRIENDS
SEE VOLUNTEERS: OLDER PERSONS

GUARDIAN ANGELS
Alliance of Guardian Angels
982 East 89th Street
Brooklyn, NY 11236
TEL: 212-967-0808
Purpose: To provide a visible, trained patrol to deter crime on the
streets, in subways, and in other inner-city areas.
Sponsor: Individual donors
Contact: Curtis Sliwa, Founder

Description: Founded in 1979 as "The Magnificent 13" to provide
volunteer assistance to the fight against crime in New York City,
the Guardian Angels now have some 3,000 volunteers working in
16 cities across the country. Although most of the volunteers are
average young people from tough neighborhoods, some of the
members are lawyers, teachers, and doctors. The age range is
16-68, with the older members providing services such as manning
walkie-talkies.
Volunteers, who are trained in martial arts, are required to be in
school or working at least part time. They buy their own "colors"
(red berets, white T-shirts) and pay their own subway fares in
cities where they patrol the mass transit systems. All new Chapters
must undergo rigid training. In addition to martial arts the
volunteers are trained in street-patrolling and making citizens'
arrests. Then the Chapter is officially turned over to native youths,
who are committed to run the program according to strict
Guardian Angels guidelines.
The aim of the Guardian Angels is to help deter crime by their
visibility in areas of high crime, and by citizens' arrests. Although
they carry no weapons, the 800 member group in New York City
made 287 citizens' arrests since 1979. The group is a non-profit,
tax-exempt corporation supported entirely by donations, but
refusing to accept funding from the state, local or federal
governments. The group has no salaried members, and
headquarters is in the founder's home.
The main ingredient the Angels rely on is volunteerism. However,
not just anyone can become a Guardian Angel. Applicants have to
be a least 16 years of age with some background in martial arts.
They have to be working or in school, and they are expected to
donate eight hours a week to patrolling. In addition, among the
first 50 recruits in each Chapter, there can be no criminal record
of any kind. (This latter rule may be slightly bent in some cases,
but no convicted murderers, rapists, robbers, or drug-pushers
would be allowed to join.) Also, applicants must go through
various screening processes, both physical and mental. If they pass,
they can attend a rigorous three-month training program, which
includes initiation into the legal ramifications of making citizens'
arrests, cardio-pulmonary resuscitation and first aid, as well as an
upgrading of their martial arts experience. According to the
founder, about half of the recruits are lost during the physical
training program.
Recognizing that the Guardian Angels are brought to the cities
through requests by the people themselves, city officials and police
departments have taken a "wait and see" stance. In New York
City officials feel that the fact that many of the Angels are "very
poor kids" doing something positive makes them "worth taking a
chance with." Among the supporters is a member of the US House
of Representatives who welcomed the group to Washington, and
invited them to set up a chapter in his home city.
Founded: 1979

INMATE SPRUCE-UP TEAMS
SEE VOLUNTEERS: PRISONERS/EX-OFFENDERS

MEALS ON WHEELS PROGRAM OF ACCA
SEE VOLUNTEERS: CHURCH/SYNAGOGUE MEMBERS

NEIGHBORHOOD PROBATION UNIT
Utah Second District Juvenile Court
3522 South 700 West
Salt Lake City, UT 84119
TEL: 801-262-2601
Purpose: To provide close supervision of probationers on a
one-to-one basis.
Sponsor: Utah Second District Juvenile Court
Contact: Carlon J. Cooke, Chief of Probation
Description: The Neighborhood Probation Unit is made up of
teams which work in neighborhood settings accessible to
probationers and their families. Volunteers - most of them college

students - are part of each team. A team is made up of three probation counselors and a supervisor, and a vocational rehabilitation counselor in addition to the volunteers. At present, the Unit has six teams, each using a varied number of volunteers. The student volunteers provide a big brother/big sister program for each of the teams. Every probationer in Salt Lake County is assigned to a Neighborhood Probation Unit.

Volunteers are screened and receive an initial orientation. They receive extensive on-the-job training under the leadership of the unit supervisor and staff once they begin their volunteer assignments. Psychologists are available for consultation if they are needed by the volunteer counselors. Student volunteers from the University of Utah's Departments of Sociology, Psychology, Educational Psychology, and Undergraduate Social Work have been involved in the program, and about 75% of the students receive academic credit for their work.

Following their initial orientation, volunteers willing to commit themselves to one contact a week for six months are assigned to an individual child. Volunteers and probationers take part in shared activity groups. The Unit has learned that careful matching of the volunteer and probationer is essential to the program.

The Units hold parent workshops to involve parents of the probationers in discussions of how to communicate more effectively with their children. They also sponsor therapy groups and high adventure groups for the older juvenile probationers. The high adventure groups go on back-packing expeditions, camp overnight, etc. The groups are formed with a ratio of one volunteer to every two probationers. During the summer, tutoring in reading and math is provided for the probationers.

OUR COMMUNITY KITCHEN
SEE VOLUNTEERS: CHURCH/SYNAGOGUE MEMBERS

PARKING POSSE
SEE VOLUNTEERS: POLICE OFFICERS

PARTNERS IN CARING
SEE BUSINESS/INDUSTRY INVOLVEMENT: OLDER PERSON

SECURITY ALERT GROUP - THREE LINK TOWERS (SAG)
SEE VOLUNTEERS: OLDER PERSONS

SENIOR VICTIM ASSISTANCE TEAM
Colorado Springs Police Department
Office of Volunteer Services
PO Box 2169
Colorado Springs, CO 80901
TEL: 719-578-6113
Purpose: To reduce or reverse the negative effect of being victimized by crime on elderly persons.
Sponsor: Colorado Springs Police Department
Contact: Nancy D. Forgy
Description: Because of time constraints, police officers investigating crimes in Colorado Springs frequently were unable to remain with victims as long as they felt was necessary. More and more the officers approached the department's Volunteer Services Coordinator to request volunteers who could talk to elderly crime victims. As a result, the Senior Victim Assistance Team - a unique group of one-to-one volunteers - was created.
This Team, called SVAT, was designed and developed and is being implemented as a means of serving those often dramatic needs of senior crime victims. By encouraging senior citizens to volunteer, SVAT serves also as a way of utilizing the skills of senior citizens developed over the years. Ages of volunteers range from 30 to 80, with more than half being senior citizens - some former crime victims themselves.
All SVAT volunteers are subjected to a background investigation

and a polygraph examination to verify their credibility and to assure against further trauma being inflicted upon the senior victim. Those accepted then complete a minimum of 35 hours of training, which focuses on counseling skills, familiarization with the criminal justice system, familiarization with local victim-referral resources, and supervised case work by trained SVAT advisors. In concert with team members' training, a briefing is provided to area social service agency staff so that they support and understand the SVAT role as a member of the service community in Colorado Springs.

As a SVAT volunteer, each team member must be committed to four or more hours a week (most average 15 hours each week) in addition to monthly meetings and training sessions. On a rotation basis, a SVAT volunteer visits the police department each morning to review the previous day's police reports and identify those crimes which involve senior citizens. Initial contact is made that same day by a team member to determine what assistance is needed. Concurrently, other SVAT members spend their volunteer time assisting with follow-up support to previously-contacted victims. In addition, a 24-hour on-call paging system for the SVAT makes members available for immediate crisis intervention through the request of law enforcement officers at the scene of the crime.

Costs to the Police Department for SVAT are limited to a portion of the salary of the Volunteer Services Coordinator and the cost of one additional telephone line for use by the SVAT at department headquarters. Office space for the SVAT volunteer reviewing daily reports is provided in a headquarters briefing room and is shared with patrol officers. These costs, however, are more than justified by release time provided to the officer by the SVAT. By freeing the officer for other high priority calls for service, SVAT volunteers facilitate maximum utilization of trained law enforcement professionals.

Since the SVAT's inception, a major thrust of the program has been to increase the reporting rate by the elderly as a result of a diminished fear through increased contact and trust of the law enforcement system, to heighten the sense of personal security among the elderly, and to increase citizen participation as a deterrent to crime.

The Colorado Springs Senior Victim Assistance Team was selected as an exemplary law enforcement project by the Law Enforcement Assistance Administration. In addition, it was chosen by the Colorado Office on Volunteerism as a model program.

SOCIAL ACTION CORPS
11188 Anderson Clinic
Loma Linda, CA 92354
TEL: 714-824-0800/Ext. 2179
Purpose: To provide low-cost primary health care services to medically indigent adults and their families.
Sponsor: United Way of Redlands area, Arrowhead United Way, and private donations
Contact: Janice I. Maynor, M.S.P.H., Associate Director
Description: The Social Action Corps (SAC) is a non-profit organization staffed by volunteer students and professionals from Loma Linda, and local community residents which operates low-cost primary health care clinics in the areas of Bloomington, San Bernardino, and Redlands.
Sources of revenue include the patient fees, funds from Arrowhead United Way, the United Way of Redlands Area, the local SDA University Church, and private donations.
Presently three clinics are operating one time per week. During a one week period 20-25 volunteer medical students, 3-5 volunteer nurses and nursing students, 3 volunteer receptionists, and various translators staff the clinics. One or two licensed physicians supervise at each clinic.
The receptionists register the patients, allowing the medical patients (those who are sick) to register first, and then registering those who need physical examinations. He/she collects the fees,

takes statistics, and puts the charts in proper sequence. After registering with the receptionist, the patient is called to the nurses' station where vitals are taken and recorded. The nurses also assist in the examining rooms. When an examining room is available the patient is called in and the medical student begins consultation for a specific problem or a general physical examination. The students consult the chief physician concerning every patient. Translators contribute a vital service to the clinics, as many Hispanic patients speak a limited amount of English or none at all. One or two student clinic directors provide leadership at each clinic.

The student physicians are primarily second year medical students, although third and fourth year students also participate. The first year medical students are allowed to attend during their second semester of training. Orientation and training of student clinic directors occurs in monthly staff meetings. Each student director (with the aid of a staff person) provides orientation for new students. On-site training for nurses and receptionists is provided by a staff person.

Written guidelines and procedures are provided for each position. No previous experience is necessary, only a strong desire to be part of a team which provides medical services to needy neighbors.

SPECIAL SATURDAY
SEE VOLUNTEERS: STUDENTS

SUPERIOR COURT CONFERENCE COMMITTEE DIVERSION PROGRAM
King County Juvenile Judges Committee
Juvenile Youth Service Center
1211 East Alden Street
Seattle, WA 98122
TEL: 206-296-1133; 206-296-1130
Purpose: To divert juvenile offenders from the formal juvenile justice system.
Contact: Bruce Knutson, Conference Committee Director
Description: The *Superior Court Conference Committee Diversion Program* in King County is a unique community volunteer effort. The program began in 1969, initially sponsored by the Mayor of Renton, Washington's *Youth Guidance Committee.* A handful of administrators and volunteers began diverting youth to community-based citizen groups. Youth were assigned to perform services within their own communities.

By 1972, there were eight *Committees* in King County - two within Seattle and three more in adjacent communities. At first, court staff handled organizational details by taking on extra assignments. In 1973, spurred by the program's growth, the court hired a full-time area manager to expand and maintain the *Committees.* In 1973, referrals increased 70 percent, and committee teams increased from eight to 30. Regular workshops for the committees' volunteers, training workshops and organizational meetings became an integral part of the program. By 1975, there were 14 committees with 60 teams to hear cases. By 1985, the present 25 committees were in place, serving 17 communities within King County and eight neighborhoods within Metropolitan Seattle - handling over 5,900 diverted juveniles.

Today the organization relies on a director of volunteer services, a program manager and four area managers. Goals of the program include:

- To provide an avenue for the community to show its concern for youth; to eliminate alienation and hostility felt by the youth, victim or community; and to establish or restore the youth as a constructive community member.
- To provide prompt, sure and just discipline/punishment which is the minimum needed to facilitate accountability, deterrence and restitution.
- To inform youth and their families about resources available to help them deal with problem situations.
- To alert youth that they will be held accountable to their community for legal violations and unacceptable behavior.

- To ensure the protection of youths' rights as defined by the State of Washington juvenile code.
- To stimulate and maximize citizen participation.

The diversion program is presented as an option to the youth, who must make the decision to participate. Involvement by the youth begins with a meeting with people from the local area, after the committee has reviewed the referral and police report. Private evening conferences, first with the youth, and then with the parents, are held, with all proceedings held in confidence. The record will become public only if the youth commits an additional offense. The *Committee* focuses on four areas: the reason for the referral and details of the offense; how the family functions by examining parent/child relationships, how the incident affected the family unit and how the family handled the incident and past problems; how the youth functions academically, socially and with teachers and students; and finally, the youth's interests and activities outside of school and peer relationships.

The *Committee* can take one of several actions.

- It can conclude that the conferences have resolved the problem and close the case;
- It can recommend further action to deal with the youth's conduct or attitude, resulting in a contract signed by the youth, which may include: community service, restitution, educational sessions, or personal counseling; or
- The *Committee* may opt to provide a disturbed child and/or distraught parent with an opportunity for counseling, and a list of appropriate services within the community.

The final decision is discussed with youth and parents. Community service sites range from senior citizen and convalescent centers to fire departments and libraries. Educational classes include a video series designed to assist youth with developmental tasks. Skill training classes cover subjects such as anger management, substance abuse, making friends and refusal skills.

An interesting aspect of the program is the fact that the youth consider the counseling most helpful, even when the only counseling they attend is the committee conference. The high degree of effectiveness of the program is reflected in the fact that ninety-seven percent of the youth complete their diversion contracts. In 1989 an extensive research project on the program was completed.

SURROUND*
Minnesota Correctional Facility-Red Wing
Red Wing, MN 55066
TEL: 612-388-7154
Purpose: To help rehabilitate delinquents through peer group companionship and support.
Sponsor: State Training School; church youth groups
Contact: The Reverend Ron Hendrickson
Description: The purpose of the Surround program is literally to surround teenagers at the correctional facilities with peers who will help them see themselves in a different light and will provide companionship and support when they are released. Surround volunteers are members of church youth groups from all over the state. They are expected to visit the institution at least monthly. Each Surround group consists of from five to 30 boys and girls and one or more adult advisors. When a group arrives at the school, five to ten members will get together with two or three residents. (Participation by residents is strictly voluntary.) Usually, residents are from the same community as the volunteers. The "surrounding" often takes the form of discussions, but also may include picnics and sports. Frequently the young people are allowed to leave the school grounds together for part of a day. Visits can last a day or an entire weekend. On overnight visits, the volunteers sleep in the school chapel.

When a youth is released from the school and returns to his home community, local Surround members attempt to bring him into active participation in their group. A high percentage of former training school residents return to the school as Surround volunteers.

Before a group may participate in the program, its leader must receive orientation at a workshop held at the training school. He then orients the youth group to the program and its purposes. Surround, which began as a small pilot group in 1965, now includes over 5,000 high school students throughout the state representing 400 church youth groups. The program operates in the 150-resident State Training School at Red Wing, the Minnesota Home School and the Lincoln Boys School in Wisconsin.

Founded: 1965

US/SBA - SERVICE CORPS OF RETIRED EXECUTIVES/ACTIVE CORPS OF EXECUTIVES
SEE VOLUNTEERS: OLDER PERSONS

VOLUNTEERS: TENANTS/RESIDENTS

NATIONAL/STATE ORGANIZATIONS

ANTI-DRUG TEAMS
US/DTreas - Bureau of Alcohol, Tobacco and Firearms
Armed Criminal Enforcement Study
15th & Pennsylvania Avenue, NW
Washington, DC 20220
TEL: 202-366-4570
Objectives: To get armed drug dealers off of the streets.
Services: To help cities which have a high incidence of drug problems, the Bureau of Alcohol, Tobacco and Firearms has developed a highly visible task force program, which sends anti-drug teams into the streets and neighborhoods. This action was an outgrowth of pressure on the agency's leadership to assist Washington, DC, police in what appeared to be a losing battle with drug dealers.
The Washington, DC, team, organized in June 1989, is composed of 40 agents brought to Washington from across the country. D.C. police lent them six detectives, and provided consultation to the Team, as did the U.S. Attorney's Office, before the raids were begun.
While maintaining a tough stance, the Team is also concerned about good public relations with neighborhood residents. They are aware that the voluntary assistance of residents is needed. The tough image is one the agents cultivate through their black pants and shirts and the assault weapons they carry. Arriving on the scene, they immediately order everyone standing nearby to lie down while the entry team hits the door of the suspected crack house. The paramilitary tactics are necessary because the agents go after drug suspects who often have armed guards looking out.
Within the first three months the Team made 155 drug and weapons arrests, and took 105 guns and more than four pounds of crack cocaine off of the streets. The tightness of the organization, and the carefully-scripted raids - along with citizen involvement and assistance - are credited with the success of the Team.
The anti-drug Teams are considered an experiment which, if successful, can be replicated in other cities.
Sponsor: US/DTreas - Department of the Treasury
Contact: Bureau Chief
Founded: 1989

NATIONAL COMMUNITY ACTION FOUNDATION
SEE COMMUNITY SERVICES: COMMUNITY ACTION PROGRAMS

NEIGHBORHOODS USA
SEE LEADERSHIP DEVELOPMENT/BOARDS:
TENANTS/RESIDENTS

TRAINING PROGRAMS

COMMUNITY FORUM ON THE PROPOSED *HARLEM ON THE HUDSON* PROJECT
SEE TRAINING/CONFERENCES/TEACHING:
TENANTS/RESIDENTS

NEIGHBORHOOD ANTI-CRIME RALLY/COMMUNITY FORUM
SEE VOLUNTEERS: EMPLOYEES

VISION, PLANNING & PARTNERSHIP IN NEIGHBORHOOD ORGANIZING
SEE TRAINING/CONFERENCES/TEACHING: CIVIC AFFAIRS

INDIVIDUAL PROGRAM PROFILES

AFFORDABLE HOUSING PROJECT
SEE VOLUNTEERS: CHURCH/SYNAGOGUE MEMBERS

CITIZENS' CRIME WATCH OF DADE COUNTY
SEE VOLUNTEERS: SELF-HELP

CRACKDOWN
City of St. Petersburg
100 Second Avenue South
St. Petersburg, FL 33701
TEL: 813-893-7171
Purpose: To involve the community in the city's efforts to eliminate crack-related crimes.
Sponsor: St. Petersburg Sanitation Department
Contact: Robert Obering, City Manager
Description: St. Petersburg is fighting a tough battle against crack cocaine and its related crimes. Traditional approaches to law enforcement are not working in the fight against crack. What does work is a team effort by the community, working side-by-side with law enforcement, code enforcement and appropriate support personnel to send a clear message to neighborhood drug dealers that their presence will not be tolerated.
In 1988, St. Petersburg introduced CRACKDOWN, a police program that resulted in 100 drug-related arrests. With such success behind them, the City Council appropriated $387,160 for CRACKDOWN 1989, much wider in scope, calling on the services of five city departments: Police, Fire, Code Enforcement, Public Works and Sanitation, as well as residents of the neighborhoods.
The first neighborhood selected, Roser Park, began with a special neighborhood briefing for residents by city officials. The meeting was called by the residents to see what they could do to help. They were told about the "Broken Window Theory" based on crime reports - that unkept homes, littered yards and abandoned cars tell the drug dealer that local homeowners don't care, and that it is an open invitation for the drug dealer and his associates to move in and bring with them the users who rob and burglarize to support their habits. While the CRACKDOWN team went to work, residents began raking their yards, filling their garbage containers and cleaning up. This message tells the drug dealer that this neighborhood cares, watches out for each other and won't welcome drug dealers and their associates.
In the first two months the police made 116 felony arrests, 150

misdemeanor arrests, 163 traffic citations and 1,928 field interrogations, as well as 162 pieces of crack cocaine. Fire Department investigators made 969 new inspections and followed up with 443 reinspections, resulting in 1,802 citations for fire code violations. Codes Enforcement officials identified 82 empty buildings for securing and towed away 100 abandoned cars. Public Works and Sanitation workers boarded up 1,591 windows and began clearing 235 lots of litter and debris. According to city officials, this kind of result can be realized only when neighborhood residents work along with the city CRACKDOWN team.

Every several weeks, the city's special CRACKDOWN team expands to include a new neighborhood. When it expands to a new zone, it does not abandon the previous CRACKDOWN area. The same degree of police service remains, and the same high interest of the residents continues. The CRACKDOWN team appears periodically, unannounced, to ensure that the enforcement pressures are maintained.

In addition to the cooperative effort between city and neighborhood associations to clean up and fix up the area, a very active *Neighborhood Watch Network* is in place in St. Petersburg, with 200 programs and 600 residents volunteering as Crime Watch Coordinators. Each of these coordinators has block captains and volunteers who keep a watchful eye on different areas of this city. According to the City Manager, the crime effort in St. Petersburg relies on the support of the neighborhood associations. To emphasize that the city is getting such support, the City Manager wrote an article in the local paper thanking the neighborhood associations for a job well done.
Founded: 1988

CRIME PREVENTION COMMITTEE OF CONTRA COSTA COUNTY
SEE VOLUNTEERS: POLICE OFFICERS

FIGHTING DIRTY!
SEE BUSINESS/INDUSTRY INVOLVEMENT: ENVIRONMENT

GRAND ISLE EROSION FIGHT
c/o Wateredge Apartments
PO Box 111
Grand Isle, LA 70358
TEL: 504-787-2329
Purpose: To provide a temporary wall of sandbags while waiting for government decisions on disaster relief.
Contact: Henrietta Collins
Description: Residents of Grand Isle have learned to move quickly when the area is threatened by a hurricane. In mid-1989 their efforts saved the state millions of dollars by containing the damage of a severe storm. Grand Isle is a barrier island resort community with a serious erosion problem. For six weeks in the spring of 1989 high tides and southerly winds increased erosion problems still evident from the previous year. When this happens, residents do not wait for official assistance, but address the problem immediately to minimize damage. When government assistance was not immediately forthcoming, volunteers, including the town's mayor, worked night and day in heavy rains building a sandbag wall in an attempt to stop further damage, especially to the area under a beach motel. As they worked, they watched a wooden staircase tear away from the rear of the building. About 30 men, women and children filled more than 2,500 bags with sand to buffer the crumbling shore. The volunteers included crews sent by a local cable television station and a telephone company, owners of two other island motels, friends, relatives, a town alderman and the mayor.

When repeated requests for federal, state or parish help failed, the volunteers worked harder and faster to minimize the effect of the storm. A state representative spoke to the Governor's office requesting a temporary measure until state and federal government can repair the island's sand levee and rebuild the beach. The levee was built and the beach expanded in 1984 as part of a joint project of the state and the U.S. Army Corps of Engineers. Hurricanes have destroyed about half of the levee, and repairs and improvements are estimated to cost $12 million. The state's share of the cost, $5 million, has been approved by the House Ways and Means Committee, but must go to a Senate committee next, and then on to the House and Senate. An additional request by the Mayor of Grand Isle to the state asks for the building of two rock jetties, a rock retaining wall and underwater breakwaters to help stop erosion. Otherwise, according to the mayor, the millions of dollars planned for the levee and beach could result in only temporary solutions.

While awaiting their response, the volunteer team continued their efforts to save the motel. Although the motel, which once sat on the beach, now has a space beneath it over six feet high, the building was saved by the volunteer team. Residents of Grand Isle have learned from experience that a little effort can go a long way.

GREEN COUNTRIE TOWNE PROGRAM
Point Breeze Federation
1248 South 21st
Philadelphia, PA 19146
TEL: 215-334-2666
Purpose: To "go from hopeless to hopeful" in an inner-city community.
Sponsor: Pennsylvania Horticultural Society
Contact: Mamie Nichols, President
Description: Point Breeze is three miles square and has a population of 32,000 people. In the 1970s it was a battlefield for warring gangs of firebomb-toting drug dealers. The gaping holes from the firebombs added to the problems of 900 abandoned homes and thousands of others owned by absentee landlords. Although residents outside the decaying community felt it was not worth saving and should die a natural death, the residents of the North Philadelphia community were not ready to let their community die.

Although drugs, abandoned homes and absentee landlords are still problems for Point Breeze, the determination of the community has brought about highly visible progress, including:
- The first new homes built in 50 years - 34 of them - were built in 1984.
- An after-school tutoring program is operated by volunteers from the *Point Breeze Civic Association.*
- A school for performing arts has been established.
- Anti-drug marches are regular and frequent.
- The community has been called the largest "greened" inner-city neighborhood in the country through its association with the *Pennsylvania Horticultural Society's Philadelphia Green Program.*

Point Breeze is designated as one of Philadelphia's Four *Green Countrie Townes,* and boasts 77 community gardens on vacant lots with direct assistance from the Society, and 95 other projects ranging from trees on otherwise desolate blocks to large sidewalk planters along a whole block of rowhouses with assistance from the Society on request. Many gardens have a mural as a backdrop to replace grafitti-covered walls, or white picket fences to discourage jaywalkers. One has a tall, elegant iron fence donated by a school that didn't want it, and encloses the "wedding garden," so-called because it has become a favorite photo stop for bridal parties. Another has a latticed wood gazebo. The most recent addition is used as a "concert garden," where jazz and gospel music is played.

In addition to those 172 greening projects, residents, businesses and private agencies have planted flower and vegetable gardens on their own. Because the gardens have been so well kept, there is little vandalism or drug dealing in those areas.

Along with the gardening program begun 10 years ago, Point

Breeze has allocated $750,000 in federal community block grants for housing rehabilitation. Since then the neighborhood has also been used as a laboratory for real estate students at the University of Pennsylvania. The students have rehabilitated one home for sale, and are working on others. Many of the hundreds of homes waiting for attention are boarded up, with local artists painting venetian blinds and plants on the boards.

And, according to the Philadelphia 17th Police District, "the tide is turning" against the drug dealers due to the anti-drug marches, the information about illegal activities provided to the police, and the community pride that has resulted from the positive results of residents' efforts. "If you see these nice things springing up, you think, 'Well, someone does care,'" he said.

NOT ON MY BLOCK
District of Columbia City Council
14th and Pennsylvania
Washington, DC 20004
TEL: 202-724-8000
Purpose: To assist residents in "driving drugs from their neighborhoods."
Contact: Sterling Tucker, Councilman
Description: Commissioned with creating innovative ways to prevent and stop drug abuse in Washington, DC, in early 1990 Washington's "Drug Czar" launched a participatory program designed to bond the community and the government in a partnership to maintain the District as being safe, and stop the widespread epidemic of crime and violence. The program, *Not on My Block,* encourages residents to pledge six hours a month to perform specific anti-drug activities on the block where they live. The activities - crime prevention, educational and recreational - are structured to help curb the crime and violence associated with drugs.

The program was formed as a catalyst and in no way diminishes government's role or responsibility in the war on drugs, or established community-based anti-drug programs, according to the Drug Czar.

The request for a six-hour monthly volunteer commitment by residents comes on the heels of a request by citizens in the neighborhoods to have the money seized in drug arrests returned to the communities affected by the crimes. One such request came in the form of a proposal to place parents in schools as paid teachers' aides to monitor their children during and after school, and help deter students prone to skipping school and selling drugs. ACORN (Association of Community Organizations for Reform Now) assisted residents with the proposal, and maintains that such a project would help increase the children's interest in their studies. Since any disposition of seized funds must go through lengthy and complicated procedures, it is hoped that the volunteer effort will "catch on" and play a role in the arduous climb toward drug-free neighborhoods in Washington, DC, according to the Drug Czar.

PARMA-HILTON PLAYGROUND PROJECT
Parma Town Hall Park
c/o Robin Schepler
215 North Avenue
Hilton, NY 14468
TEL: 716-392-3868
Purpose: To provide manpower for a playground for the children of Parma and Hilton.
Sponsor: US/DoD - Navy Civil Engineers Corps
Contact: Robin Schepler, Volunteer Foreman
Description: Ideas from the children themselves were incorporated into a volunteer-built playground for area children. Over 100 volunteers worked in the rain to complete the 93-by-133-foot project, which includes everything from a clock tower to a spaceship. One of the children suggested a PCV-pipe communications system that allows children in the multilevel

structure to help guide friends who get lost in the maze. Another suggested bolting together six tires as a base for a trampoline. Both ideas were incorporated in the playground designed by an architect, which includes a maze, a clock tower with a face that can be changed with a steering wheel, a spiral slide, a tunnel slide, a swinging horse and a spaceship.

Rainy conditions on the day of the project might have delayed most other efforts. But, undaunted, the volunteers ordered several tons of sand and some gravel to build a small road to keep heavy equipment from getting mired in the mud. Next they obtained yellow slickers - soon-to-be mud-spattered - for volunteers. Power was drawn directly from a nearby Rochester Gas and Electric Corporation utility pole, with strict federal safety standards implemented and a knowledgeable volunteer assigned to keep equipment from shorting out. An associate of the architects volunteered to be on hand to offer expert supervision and keep the project on schedule.

Many of the volunteers took vacation time from paying jobs to help with the project. While some worked on the construction of the playground, others ran an on-site day-care center for the workers' children, helped with concessions, or signed up volunteers. Even the children got into the act - the little ones scrubbing tires and those ten and older working alongside their parents. The parents and children also got help from about ten Monroe County inmates on regular work detail and about 40 Seabees from the *Civil Engineer Corps of the U.S. Navy* on regular monthly duty. In addition to the donated labor, most of the tools and other equipment were provided free by local contractors and businesses. To pay for essentials unavailable by donation, the playground committee and the children raised more than $40,000 over an 18-month period prior to the event. About a fourth of the money was spent to make the playground accessible to handicapped youngsters.

The playground was built in Parma because parents had grown weary of having to travel to Spencerport and Brockport to treat their children to a day at one of the special playgrounds.

REHAB PROJECT: NEIGHBORHOOD REVITALIZATION THROUGH HOME OWNERSHIP
SEE VOLUNTEERS: CHURCH/SYNAGOGUE MEMBERS

TENANT OWNERSHIP/MANAGEMENT PROGRAM
Sursum Corda Village
1160 First Place, NW
Washington, DC 20001
TEL: 202-789-0636
Purpose: To own the buildings in which they reside.
Sponsor: US/HUD - Office of Housing & Urban Development
Contact: Sister Diane Roche, Resident Manager
Description: Sursum Corda Village is a 199-unit housing complex that stretches across 4.5 acres near Capital Hill. Over the years, the Village changed from a grassy, golden-bricked place in 1969, where neighbors felt safe strolling at dusk, to a place where crack and cocaine are used and sold openly, and the "killing-of-the-month" is an expected occurrence. Some of the tenants were making efforts to demand better from the owners when, in 1989, the owners announced their intent to sell the Village. Many of the tenants saw an opportunity to try to purchase the buildings, and attempt to restore them to the safe neighborhood of the past.

In the summer of 1989, the tenants embarked on what they hoped would be a year-long process that would end with them, the tenants, owning and managing the complex where they live. It would be the first federally-insured, privately-owned cooperative in the District of Columbia to be owned and managed by tenants. They met with representatives of the owners, Surry, Ltd., in August. With their blessing and the approval of the U.S. Department of Housing and Urban Development, they plotted the steps toward tenant management and ownership. The owners encouraged tenant management and ownership because "they see it as a viable option to meeting housing needs."

One of the first steps taken by the tenants was to recruit a Roman Catholic nun as resident manager. The nun - known and trusted by the tenants - had been a volunteer at the complex, but had no housing management background. Besides, she had relocated to Seattle. However, the tenants were persistent with their letters and phone calls, and the nun worked it out with her superiors at a three-day retreat, and returned to Washington to manage the Village.

There is bustling activity at the Village, with weekly meetings with the police to begin a neighborhood watch program, residents volunteering to plant grass and bushes and repair their neighbors' homes, tenants forming the kinds of clubs that make a community (a football team, a senior citizens group, an adult literacy class), volunteers tutoring in the evenings, senior citizens banding together to make quilts and potholders to raise money, a religious group (Young Life) holding meetings, etc.

When word spread of their efforts, outside groups joined the effort. One Saturday, groups of alumni from Notre Dame University and the University of North Carolina were waiting with clusters of volunteers from five churches and Mount Vernon College and experienced handymen from Habitat for Humanity to begin work. More than 100 people had gathered to volunteer, and by the end of the day seventeen units were cleaned and painted.

However, other problems plagued the Village. The entire maintenance crew quit amid allegations of equipment theft. The vacancy rate was high. The complex owed $341,468 to 42 vendors. The manager could not get needed hardware or electrical items because of unpaid bills. The manager turned to two resident leaders, and together they approached businesses for assistance. Surprisingly, although companies considered it a "very bad risk," small gains were made through this route, and soon Sursum Corda recovered enough to pay its bills.

The success of the business/industry involvement spurred residents on, and fliers were distributed stating, "Let's reclaim our vacant units." The next Saturday, 26 people cleaned 26 units, and the next Saturday more were cleaned, and each Saturday a few more. One resident pointed out that "people are beginning to understand, if you lose here, where else are you going to lose?"

So far, the statistics are promising. Vacancies have been cut in half, to 14. The backlogged requests for repairs have dropped to 60. About 40 of the 200 roofs have been replaced without breaking the budget. Unfortunately, there is still crack dealing and there are still slayings, but the residents are fighting back. The test of management - restoring the physical property, and reestablishing pride - has been passed, according to all parties concerned.

VOLUNTEERS: UNEMPLOYED

INDIVIDUAL PROGRAM PROFILES

SENIOR EMPLOYMENT RESOURCES
SEE VOLUNTEERS: PROFESSIONALS

VOLUNTEERS: UNION MEMBERS

NATIONAL/STATE ORGANIZATIONS

COPE RETIREE PROGRAM
SEE VOLUNTEERS: OLDER PERSONS

ECONET
SEE BUSINESS/INDUSTRY INVOLVEMENT: ENVIRONMENT

INDIVIDUAL PROGRAM PROFILES

CAMP GOOD DAYS AND SPECIAL TIMES REBUILDING PROJECT
AFL-CIO Community Services Committee
c/o United Way of Greater Rochester
55 St. Paul Street
Rochester, NY 14604
TEL: 716-454-2770
Purpose: To provide a camping experience for children affected by cancer.
Contact: Volunteer Coordinator
Description: When *Camp Good Days and Special Times* lost one of its buildings to fire in the winter of 1986, 800 union volunteers set to work to put the summer camp back into action. The camp accommodates more than 200 children affected by cancer at its Keuka Lake setting outside of Rochester, and is a special source of pride to the residents of Rochester.

The rebuilding project involved more than just replacing the lost building, since other facilities were desperately needed, such as a dining hall and recreation center. The union tradespeople designed a new 80' x 46' building that included those facilities plus a kitchen, rest rooms, ramps, low-standing water fountains, and a 10-foot-wide wrap-around porch. The project took 25 weeks and was ready in plenty of time for the camping season.

The union volunteers included painters, carpenters, bricklayers, electricians, floor layers, glaziers, roofers, laborers, plumbers, pipe fitters, and operating engineers. Building materials were donated by *Wilmorite Corporation,* and *Cable-Wiedemer* contributed appliances and fixtures. The improvements represented more than $350,000 in donated materials and labor.

Everyone who works at *Camp Good Days and Special Times,* including the director, is a volunteer. Due to the campers' special needs, the camp has 24-hour on-site medical facilities, as well as ambulance services to local hospitals. The medical teams that staff these facilities also are composed totally of volunteers.

The individual volunteer that rallied the 800 union volunteers, secured donated materials, and coordinated the massive project is president of the *Building and Construction Trades Council of Rochester.* For his efforts, the *AFL-CIO Community Services Committee of Rochester,* and the *United Way of Greater Rochester* honored him at a citywide awards program.

HELPING HAND
SEE BUSINESS/INDUSTRY INVOLVEMENT: EMPLOYMENT

LABOR EDITORS ROUNDTABLE
SEE COMMUNICATIONS & PUBLIC RELATIONS

QUALITY EDUCATION PROGRAM
SEE BUSINESS/INDUSTRY INVOLVEMENT

UNION RETIREES RESOURCES
Labor Temple
2800 First Avenue
Room 218
Seattle, WA 98121
TEL: 206-623-9050
Purpose: To involve retired union craftsmen in volunteer services to older persons.
Sponsor: AFL-CIO Central Labor Council; US/ACTION
Contact: Mary Jane Johnson

Description: The first program of its kind in the country when it started in 1978, the Union Retirees Resources program responds to over 4,000 requests each year. The union affiliation represented a new concept for RSVP and Union Retirees Resources was considered a model with an eye toward replication elsewhere. Volunteers are retired electricians, plumbers, roofers, teamsters, longshoremen, carpenters, sheet metal workers and other union members who work throughout King County and Seattle to assist older persons. They repair leaky plumbing or roofs, handle small electrical problems, build ramps for wheelchair patients, etc.

Several years ago they began picking up donated appliances and televisions, repairing them, and providing them to elderly persons in need of such items. This is now one of the most helpful programs. Since the program has no funding to purchase supplies, any materials needed, such as wiring, are usually donated on a case-by-case basis by suppliers or building contractors.

Also, volunteers offer consumer protection to low-income elderly homeowners by advising them on more extensive home repairs where contractors and purchases are involved, such as buying a new furnace or replacing a roof. In addition, they provide transportation to medical appointments and to shopping facilities for elderly people who would otherwise be confined to their homes.

This volunteer help in minor home repairs, home maintenance, and consumer protection by more than 80 union retirees is helping low-income elderly and handicapped persons to remain in their own homes. Although the volunteers serve without compensation, they are reimbursed for their transportation costs and, if serving more than four hours on a specific assignment, for meals. In addition, the volunteers receive accident and liability coverage for their periods of service.

Initially, only AFL-CIO and ACTION sponsored the program. In 1978 the Community Services Administration provided assistance, and other sponsors are involved in the present program.

Founded: 1978

II.
SUBJECT-SPECIFIC RESOURCES

AIDS

NATIONAL/STATE ORGANIZATIONS

AMERICAN FOUNDATION FOR AIDS RESEARCH
AmFar
5900 Wilshire Boulevard
Second Floor
Los Angeles, CA 90036
TEL: 213-857-5900
Objectives: To raise funds to support research on acquired immune deficiency syndrome (AIDS).
Services: Focuses research on discovering the causes of AIDS, a disease of immune dysfunction, believed to be transmitted through certain body fluids; organizes state and local fundraising and develops educational programs as a preventative to the spread of the disease, for which the cause is unknown and there is no known cure; works with local groups such as *Art Against AIDS* in Washington, DC, and *LAPD (Los Angeles Poverty Department)* in Los Angeles to raise funds, with a share going to the local host group, a share to *AmFar* for research, and the balance distributed among other local groups across the country; provides speakers to groups and organizations; publishes an educational brochure about AIDS for distribution.
Publications: Facts About AIDS
Founded: 1985

GAY MEN'S HEALTH CRISIS
129 West 20th Street
New York, NY 10011-0022
TEL: 212-807-6655 (hotline); 212-645-7470 (TDD)
FAX: 212-337-3656
Objectives: To provide support services to people with AIDS and the people who care for them; to educate the public, individuals at risk and health care professionals; to advocate for fair and effective AIDS public policy.
Services: Serves people with AIDS from all parts of the community - gay men, heterosexuals, hemophiliacs, drug users and children; emphasizes expansion into neighborhoods that are being underserved, poor neighborhoods and minority communities; forms coalitions with other groups providing various services in the AIDS arena.
Involves volunteers in all areas of operation, with client service volunteers being the client's principal link in communicating with various parts of the agency; matches crisis intervention volunteers with clients to provide support in dealing with the disease; trains

Buddies in dealing with medical crises to assist clients with tasks such as shopping, cleaning and cooking; enlists volunteers to assist with the recreational program, cultural events and group meals; utilizes financial advocates to identify problems with city, state and federal entitlement programs, assess clients' eligibility for benefits and provide emergency funds.
Works with 350 volunteer attorneys, who provide a wide range of free services including problems with discrimination, insurance, landlord-tenant and debtor-creditor conflicts, probate and immigration, and who speak to audiences of health care providers, attorneys, workplace managers and professionals in the AIDS service field; maintains a volunteer staff in the ombudsman office who serve as mediators and investigators, helping to solve individual problems in the health care and social service systems. Includes volunteers in every phase of its operation, including:
- 400 volunteers in the education department manning information tables on city streets, at health fairs and at street festivals;
- 87 volunteers staffing the GMHC hotline, the agency's first service, which answered nearly 50,000 calls in 1989; and
- the GMHC volunteer staff who interview, screen and place new volunteers, responding to nearly 200 calls a month.
Has over 1,600 volunteers and a paid staff of 125, which was maintaining a clientele of 2,700 by July 1989 - 8,000 since it began operation; receives its operating budget of $12 million from a variety of sources, with the bulk of it raised in special benefits and events such as AIDS Walk (see separate entry), and approximately 18% coming from government sources.
Contact: Joseph Ripple, Director of Volunteers
Publications: News from GMHC; Volunteer
Founded: 1981

NATIONAL AIDS NETWORK
1012 Fourteenth Street, NW
Suite 601
Washington, DC 20005
TEL: 202-347-0390
Objectives: To provide AIDS information to the community and direct services to AIDS sufferers.
Services: Works through more than 400 community-based member-groups involved in AIDS education and/or services; serves as a resource center and networking agency for the groups; provides funding assistance to AIDS education- or service-providing organizations; coordinates fund-raising activities; provides technical assistance to member groups; holds workshops,

seminars, and conferences; maintains clearinghouse, communications, development, training, minority affairs, and resource development committees; publishes a semimonthly newsletter, a monthly bulletin, a quarterly directory, and other materials.
Publications: NETWORK News; NAN Multicultural Notes; Directory of AIDS Service Providing Organizations; NAN Monitor
Founded: 1986

STATEWIDE HIV/AIDS NETWORK
American Red Cross Office of HIV/AIDS Education
1709 New York Avenue, NW
Washington, DC 20006
TEL: 202-662-1577; 202-662-1580
FAX: 202-662-1555
Objectives: To develop a network of local chapter HIV/AIDS efforts at the state level.
Services: Coordinates local chapter efforts at the state level to strengthen cooperation and communications with organizations providing HIV/AIDS education and services; continues to work with local groups and organizations to help meet the needs of local communities during this networking activity; builds on the successful development of 20 *Statewide HIV/AIDS Networks* in the first year of the *Cooperative Agreement: American Red Cross/Centers for Disease Control;* targets new states each project year for Networks (10 states for 1990).
Sponsor: US/HHS - Centers for Disease Control
Contact: Carole Kauffman
Founded: 1990

WORLD HEALTH ORGANIZATION COLLABORATING CENTER ON AIDS
c/o Centers for Disease Control
1600 Clifton Road, NE
Atlanta, GA 30333
TEL: 404-639-3311
Objectives: To conduct AIDS research and training programs.
Services: Conducts research and training programs dealing with acquired immunodeficiency syndrome (AIDS); provides instruction to public health workers; sponsors laboratory training courses; operates a speakers bureau; publishes statistical reports and training materials.
Sponsor: World Health Organization

TRAINING PROGRAMS

HOW TO EFFECTIVELY MANAGE PEOPLE WHO HAVE AIDS AS VOLUNTEERS
Association for Volunteer Administration
PO Box 4584
Boulder, CO 80306
TEL: 303-497-0328
Credit: Inquire
Sponsor: Association for Volunteer Administration
Contact: Irene K. Wysocki
Description: This workshop addresses the benefits of involving volunteers who have HIV infection in agency programs. It addresses the fact that one and a half million people in the United States are living with HIV infection, many of them in the prime of their lives and careers, frequently professionals, and often displaying enthusiasm and energy that can help them as individuals as well as the volunteer program manager. Workshop question/answer sessions and topics include:
As volunteer administrators, what is our obligation to this population? - As volunteer managers we see the many contributions that volunteers provide. These contributions become

even more important to infected persons because for them, helping others is very important. As volunteer managers, we have the rare opportunity to channel their energy into focused volunteer work. By using HIV-positive volunteers, you can:
- expand your horizons as a volunteer manager
- set a public example for compassion during a time of widespread misunderstanding about the AIDS epidemic
- support volunteer managers' needs to make changes in their programs which match societal changes around AIDS and AIDS-related discrimination
- use your leadership skills to change community responses to the needs of those with HIV infection

How can managers best learn to support this volunteer base? - The ability to look at our fears about HIV infection and what this means to us personally is to educate ourselves so that we overcome our fears. As effective volunteer managers, we must:
- sensitize ourselves to HIV infection
- reduce homophobia
- reduce irrational fears of HIV infection
- sensitize our staffs and other volunteers to the needs of people with HIV infection
- educate ourselves and our staffs about the issues surrounding a life-threatening illness, such as HIV-infection
- support the will to live in all persons with life-threatening illnesses

Benefits to volunteer administrators and their organizations when they work with people with HIV infection - People living with AIDS or HIV infection will expand our volunteer bases, providing flexible schedules, enormous talent, and extraordinary motivation to help others. Other benefits are:
- Their contributions to AIDS prevention education; they can speak to those issues first hand.
- They offer volunteer managers the opportunity to learn about AIDS and HIV infection in a way that can lessen irrational fears.
- They can provide volunteer managers the personal enjoyment of getting to know and support individuals with AIDS or HIV infection.
- They offer volunteer managers the opportunity to learn special supervision skills.
- Their individual skills increase an organization's talent pool.
- They provide an organization a way to make a direct contribution to fighting AIDS and to make a statement to other agencies about their leadership in the AIDS/HIV epidemic.
- They can help your agency play a role in changing your community's response to AIDS.
- Their desires to help others are furthered by providing them meaningful work in the organization of their choice.

This program demonstrates support for the AVA Board of Directors' recent resolution which discourages discrimination against volunteers who have HIV infection. It is intended as a challenge to agencies of every type to seriously examine this issue as it affects their volunteer programs.

INDIVIDUAL PROGRAM PROFILES

AIDS ARMS NETWORK, INC.
2727 Oak Lawn
Suite 222
Dallas, TX 75219
TEL: 214-521-5191 (Voice); 214-521-5266 (TDD)
Purpose: To provide professional and centralized case management for persons with AIDS through a combined volunteer-professional effort.
Sponsor: Government contracts, Foundation grants, contributions, special events
Contact: Warren W. Buckingham, III, Executive Director

Description: AIDS Arms Network was founded as a project of the *Community Council of Greater Dallas* in November 1986. It was incorporated as a Texas non-profit corporation in September of 1989. Start-up funding was provided through a four-year $1.45 million grant from the *Robert Wood Johnson Foundation*.

AIDS Arms acts as the "hub of a wheel" of 40 Dallas County human-service providers by coordinating community resources through case management. This involves assessing needs of each new client, assisting him/her in developing a plan of care for meeting those needs, connecting clients with services of any and all of the affiliated agencies and conducting regular follow-up to ensure that new needs are promptly met. Case management services are provided free of charge by ten professional staff care coordinators who each work with 50-60 seriously debilitated clients; or by highly-trained volunteers who work with clients of lower need levels and reasonably good health.

Some of the services and support the affiliates of the *Network* provide include pastoral, emotional and chemical dependency counseling, adult and child day care, food and clothing banks, emergency shelter and financial assistance, affordable housing, transportation, medical equipment, health and dental care, and volunteer assistance.

AIDS Arms is client-driven and promotes independence for people with AIDS as much as possible. By Spring 1990, the network had provided services for more than 1,300 people with AIDS or ARC, and serves an active caseload of 500+ PWAs (persons with AIDS) at any given time. *AIDS Arms* also provides technical assistance to agencies expanding or implementing programs for persons with AIDS and extends financial support through subcontracts to ten other service providers.

Publications: AIDS Arms Network ...Your Partners in Care
Founded: 1986

JUNIOR LEAGUE OF DETROIT
32 Lake Shore Road
Detroit, MI 48236
TEL: 313-881-0040
Purpose: To reach out to all young women who demonstrate an interest in and a commitment to volunteerism.
Contact: Kathleen Nesi, Trustee
Description: To celebrate its 75th year in 1989, the *Junior League of Detroit* reflected on the changes since its beginnings in 1914.
For years, it appeared to all to be a "private club" with membership only by invitation. African Americans, Jews and other minorities, working women and less-than-affluent women were not invited.
In recent years, a concerted effort has been made to diversify membership. Currently about 25 of the 350 members are minority women. Invitations are no longer required for membership. Interested women simply contact the League themselves. The 1988-89 annual report states that "it reaches out to all young women regardless of race, religion or national origin, who demonstrate an interest in and a commitment to voluntarism." Current projects of the League include:

- **AIDS Volunteer Project** - For this project, the League trains volunteers to work not only with the AIDS patients, but with their families as well. Also, the League maintains a committee for the project to keep abreast of medical and other AIDS issues to find the best way to be helpful to AIDS patients and families as science progresses toward a cure.
- **Barat Human Services** - This special project of the League is an emergency child-care program. Initially, the League raised $60,000 for its operation. They devote untold volunteer hours to taking care of youngsters to keep them from joining the child-abuse statistic.

These are in contrast to its 1914 project of establishing a lunch room for working women in one area of the city. Each member is required to donate at least 75 hours annually to the organization's projects - today, usually in the evening or on weekends to accommodate working women. The League has given some 25,000 volunteer hours and more than $2 million to city projects in its 75-year life.

League volunteers are especially happy to be able to work at all levels of involvement - from a research committee member working 5-10 hours weekly, to a new mother available only 2-3 hours weekly to help with the clerical tasks.

The process of choosing projects begins with the research committee, which conducts surveys to determine the most pressing needs. In 1989, the committee sent proposals to over 100 mental health facilities based on the results of one of the surveys.

A new revelation has surfaced at the League as more and more young women move into the work force. Currently, members over 40 are put on "sustainer" status and are expected to take a less active role. However, research shows that women are more likely to do volunteer work between the ages of 35 and 50, when their children are out of the toddler stage. According to one committee member, "We are losing a whole contingency of volunteers. It would be an improvement to move [the age] up to 50; ideally there would be no age limit at all."
Founded: 1914

VOLUNTEER RESOURCES - AIDS PROGRAM
Whitman-Walker Clinic
1407 S Street, NW
Washington, DC 20009
TEL: 202-797-3576; 202-328-0697 (Spanish)
Purpose: To train, place and provide ongoing support for the Clinic's volunteers.
Sponsor: Whitman-Walker Clinic
Contact: Peter Provost
Description: Volunteer job descriptions in the *Volunteer Resources Department* of the Whitman-Walker Clinic cover 30 distinct positions, providing a wide-range of services within various divisions of the Clinic's AIDS program.
Beginning in 1990 with over 1,500 active volunteers, this department recruits, trains, and places new volunteers and provides ongoing support for them. Orientations for prospective volunteers are held monthly and basic training is held one weekend every other month. Training seminars on a variety of issues, such as death and dying, and grief and healing are held on a regular basis for active volunteers.
Some of the areas in which volunteers are trained to provide care with dignity for persons living with AIDS and HIV infections are: medical services, support services (legal/financial/emotional), housing, education, alcoholism and substance abuse, and others. Volunteer Resources, as in other Clinic programs, coordinates with the community to ensure a unified response to AIDS.
Publications: Volunteer Job Descriptions: AIDS Program

AIDS: CHILDREN/YOUTH

INDIVIDUAL PROGRAM PROFILES

AIDS PREVENTION PROGRAM FOR YOUTH
American Red Cross Office of HIV/AIDS Education
1709 New York Avenue, NW
Washington, DC 20006
TEL: 202-662-1577; 202-662-1580
FAX: 202-662-1555
Purpose: To provide junior and senior high school age youth with the information, educational materials, and training needed to choose behaviors that reduce their risk of contracting the AIDS (HIV) virus.
Contact: Carole Kauffman, Director

Description: The *American Red Cross AIDS Prevention Program for Youth* is a family, school and community based program involving students, parents, teachers, school officials and community leaders. Specific objectives include:

- To increase the educator's acceptance of the need for AIDS education in schools.
- To increase teachers' ability to provide AIDS education.
- To increase parents' ability to discuss AIDS with their children.
- To increase youth's knowledge about AIDS, and encourage behavior that would avoid risk.
- To reach those adolescents who, for various reasons, are not part of the school population.

Materials provided for youth leaders administering the program include three videos, a student workbook, a teacher/leader guide, a brochure for parents, and video discussion guides for each video. One production, *Don't Forget Sherrie,* dramatizes the impact of AIDS and its effect on black and urban youth. In it, a group of black teens are threatened by the news that a former girlfriend (Sherrie) is dying of AIDS, possibly contracted through shared intravenous needles. It explores the personal dilemmas imposed by this news, deals with the range of feelings and concerns these young people undergo and explains how the AIDS epidemic is spread. [All videos are described in the *Annotated Bibliography* at the back of this *Directory.*]

CHILDREN'S QUILT PROJECT

1478 University Avenue
Suite 186
Berkeley, CA 94702
TEL: 415-548-3843
Purpose: To make quilts for children suffering from AIDS and other children "born under the shadow of misfortune."
Contact: Diane Dehler, Founder
Description: The Center for Disease Control in Atlanta reports that by March 1989, 1,708 children had been diagnosed with AIDS - 1,130 of them under five years of age. More than 93 percent of these children are children of adult carriers, often drug users. In Miami, one out of 57 newborns tests positive for the HIV virus; in New York, it's one of 61. In the Bay Area, figures are lower, but AIDS workers are worried.

In an attempt to help make children with AIDS feel special, a group of four volunteers from the Bay Area started the *Children's Quilt Project.* This program provides hand-made quilts to children with AIDS and others who can benefit from the gift. By June, the quilting session volunteers increased from the initial four to 60 quilters - including school children and amateur quilters - and over 400 quilts had been distributed to children who are victims of AIDS or other misfortunes.

The program relies entirely on donations and volunteers. At the end of the school year in 1989, 2,000 school children in Alameda, Oakland and Berkeley created panels for quilts. Senior citizens donate their time and skills several hours each week.

Although the project was begun to demonstrate concern and caring, the response by the children themselves was unexpected. In some cases, it represented the first possession that belonged "only to the child."

Within 15 months of its inception, the program had gone nationwide - almost totally by word of mouth. Women in Florida, Ohio, and Colorado formed quilting programs, and word was received that a woman in Switzerland was stitching a quilt. To make the nationwide status official, the founder is seeking volunteer administrative help to organize files and maintain accountability, and funding to pay for more brochures about AIDS which the program has developed for school children. Also, the organization as it expands hopes to become an advocate for AIDS children. Currently, volunteers from the Quilt project visit elementary schools to talk about AIDS.

A social worker working with AIDS children observed, "Children often carry their quilts around with them everywhere. They become a special part of their lives. It makes a tremendous difference." A foster mother who cares for AIDS children adds, "Blankets are very special to small children. I have one little 2-1/2-year old whose quilt is in tatters; he drags it around everywhere. They've offered to make him another, but he refuses."
Founded: 1988

AIDS: CLINICS/HOSPITALS

INDIVIDUAL PROGRAM PROFILES

AIDS CHRONIC CARE UNIT VOLUNTEER PROGRAM
Goldwater Memorial Hospital
Roosevelt Island, NY 10044
TEL: 212-750-6755
Purpose: To provide chronic care to AIDS patients.
Sponsor: Goldwater Memorial Hospital
Contact: Tammy Carlisle, Volunteer Director
Description: Sixty-four beds in Goldwater Memorial Hospital's 944-bed long-term care and rehabilitation facility are in a special unit for patients suffering from AIDS. AIDS patients are referred to Goldwater by other New York City municipal and voluntary hospitals, with some coming from Rikers Island, the city prison. The patient population ranges from the very frail who may need a great deal of care to those who need relatively little help in caring for themselves.

Volunteer recruitment is a continuous process at the Hospital. The volunteer program is set up with a team concept with at least two or more members per team. Volunteers make a commitment of three hours per week to the program.

Training is provided before volunteer service begins, and a very extensive training manual has been developed for the volunteers. Other training resources are provided as they become available to update the AIDS situation and keep them informed about newer approaches to patient care. Volunteers receive public transportation fare and lunch. Not all volunteers take advantage of these perks, however.

With all patients together in a single unit, it is easier to provide a full range of services and address the patients' needs. Volunteers feed patients, make coffee, and provide recreation programs in and out of the unit. Volunteers act as advocates for family problems and for complaints with Social Security, Medicare, and Medicaid benefits and entitlements. Volunteers also assist with dietary problems, paint, write, sing, hold holiday events, provide clothing when needed, and much more.

Special services are provided as needed for the blind or deaf, for example. Also, special requests are granted when possible - such as holding a memorial service for those from the unit who have died. There is also a support system among the patients themselves. Since they are all in the same unit, they visit, support, and help each other. Patients are not confined to the AIDS unit, but can participate in hospital functions and utilize any service the hospital provides. They are not isolated, and are completely free to visit other parts of the hospital.

AIDS volunteers are expected to address the full range of needs for the entire unit, not just for one individual. They are assigned not to a single patient, but to everyone in the unit. They meet this challenge and offer their services to many people.

Progress notes on each patient are maintained by volunteers as a working tool to assist other volunteers and the hospital staff. Problems for the program include a shortage of nurses, lack of TV sets for patients, not enough volunteers, and the cultural and social gap often existing between volunteers and patients. The volunteer support system and team concept alleviate many of the problems, often through phone conversations with each other back at home, or meetings on extra days to discuss resolving problems. The volunteer director also calls volunteers from time to time to identify and discuss problems.

A volunteer bulletin is issued by the director to keep everyone informed of changes, social activities, an expected death in the ward, and other issues to assist in preventing burnout and sudden bereavement when a loss occurs.

AIDS Unit volunteers are permitted access to the hospital day or night, have their own identification cards and keys, have a refrigerator and coffee maker and constant access to refreshments, etc. No other unit in the hospital has these amenities, which enable the volunteers to provide unique services for particular patients. Because patients are usually in the last stages of the disease, volunteer training at Goldwater places a special emphasis on preparing for death and dying. On the other hand, a few patients become well enough to be discharged, but have no place to go. They are homeless, abandoned by family and friends. There are few or no visitors for the patients, making the volunteers their only contact with the outside world and their only friends besides hospital staff and patient advocates. The dedicated, loyal volunteers at the Goldwater AIDS Chronic Care Unit make a difference.
Founded: 1987

AIDS PROGRAM
Whitman-Walker Clinic
1407 S Street, NW
Washington, DC 20009
TEL: 202-797-3500; 202-328-0697 (Spanish)
See individual descriptions of major divisions of the Clinic.
Purpose: To provide care with dignity for persons living with AIDS and HIV infection.
Sponsor: Commission of Public Health; District of Columbia Department of Human Services; Virginia Department of Health; Montgomery County (MD) Health Department; contributions
Contact: Peter Provost
Description: The AIDS Program of the Whitman-Walker Clinic is the primary community-based AIDS service agency in the Washington, DC, metropolitan area. The AIDS program is a volunteer-based effort, enhanced and supported by professional staff.

There are over 30 distinct volunteer positions providing a wide range of services within the program. The *Volunteer Resources Department* recruits, trains, and places new volunteers and provides ongoing support for the over 1,500 active volunteers. Orientations for prospective volunteers are held monthly and basic training is held one weekend every other month. Training seminars on a variety of issues, such as death and dying, and grief and healing are held on a regular basis for active volunteers.

The program is coordinated with local government services as well as other community-based organizations to ensure a unified response to AIDS. Services are provided to all people in need. The objectives are to improve the overall health and well-being of the community, and provide care with dignity for persons living with AIDS and HIV infection. Program divisions include:
Medical Services - includes HIV Clinic, Pharmacy, Pentamidine Clinic, Dental Clinic, and HIV Antibody Testing.
Support Services - includes Emotional Help, Legal Help, and Financial Help .
Housing Services - includes housing alternatives, a food bank, and other services.
Education and Preventive Services - includes both traditional and nontraditional approaches to community health education.
Project NOVA - includes NOVA Education Resource Center, which provides educational outreach services to gay/bisexual men.
Additional Clinic Services are provided by drawing upon the resources and abilities of other programs at Whitman-Walker Clinic. These include the Gay Men's Venereal Disease Clinic and

Alcoholism and Substance Abuse Services, as well as the Lesbian and Gay Hotline and the Peer Counseling Group.

Sixty percent of the money to support the AIDS program comes from the community it services - much of it in donations of $100 or less. Significant support is received from agencies in the District, Maryland and Virginia.
Publications: AIDS Program; Directory of AIDS Resources

AIDS PROJECT: FRIENDLY VISITORS
SEE AIDS: PSYCHOSOCIAL SUPPORT

DISTRICT OF COLUMBIA AIDS INFORMATION LINE
SEE AIDS: I&R

HOWARD BROWN MEMORIAL CLINIC
945 West George
Chicago, IL 60657
TEL: 312-871-5777
Purpose: To provide low-cost, confidential, community-based health care for sexually transmitted diseases, including AIDS.
Sponsor: Government contracts; grants; corporate and private donations
Contact: Theresa Harper, Volunteer Coordinator
Description: Howard Brown Memorial Clinic (HBMC), founded in 1974, provides low-cost, non-discriminatory confidential diagnostic and treatment services for sexually-transmitted diseases (STDs). HBMC has become one of the largest clinics of its type in the United States.

Since the early 1980s, HBMC has taken a leading role in the fight against Acquired Immune Deficiency Syndrome (AIDS). Today Howard Brown is the largest provider of AIDS services in Chicago and one of the leading AIDS research facilities in the nation.

HBMC's programs and services are administered by health care professionals, including physicians, nurses, laboratory technicians, case management workers, mental health practitioners, health educators and administrative personnel. The expertise provided by these professionals is augmented by more than 400 volunteers. Without volunteers, HBMC could not meet the community's needs or new challenges. Volunteers are essential to the very existence of all HBMC programs and services.

The clinic is organized in three major service divisions: Administrative, Medical Services and Social Services. The Social Services division features special components to serve AIDS clients and to provide AIDS education.

The services provided to AIDS clients encompass many areas, but a particular area where volunteers become foremost providers is the Support Manager (Buddy) program.

This program trains volunteers to work one-on-one with a PWA (person with AIDS) providing emotional support, companionship and practical support.

In this particular program, there are presently 60 volunteers who have an assigned client who is diagnosed with AIDS. These volunteers have all completed a 25-hour intensive training seminar and also attend a bi-weekly support group.

Sometimes nobody understands better than another person with AIDS. PWAs are trained to share experiences, information and provide short-term support for the client dealing with the initial impact of diagnosis.

Over 300 volunteers provide services throughout the Clinic's other departments, including Medical and Administrative divisions.

Our volunteers come from varied backgrounds and age groups and are able to work with varying levels of experience. The need for caring and interested volunteers continues as we strive to conquer AIDS.
Publications: Volunteer Opportunities; Meeting the Challenge; Social Service Programs; HBMC Annual Report
Founded: 1974

MEDICAL SERVICES - AIDS PROGRAM
Whitman-Walker Clinic
1407 S Street, NW
Washington, DC 20009
TEL: 202-797-3533; 212-328-0687 (Spanish)
Purpose: To provide medical services, antibody testing, and confidential counseling for individuals who have tested positive for HIV antibodies and those seeking HIV antibody testing.
Sponsor: Whitman-Walker Clinic
Contact: Peter Provost
Description: Medical Services is part of the Whitman-Walker AIDS Program, which is a volunteer-based (1,500 overall) effort, enhanced and supported by professional staff. The medical program has five components:

- **Pharmacy** - HIV-related medications are available at wholesale cost with a prescription, offering substantial savings to clients.
- **Pentamidine Clinic** - Aerosolized pentamidine treatments help prevent the occurence of *Pneumocystis carinii* pneumonia (PCP), the most common cause of death for people living with AIDS. Bi-weekly treatments open to individuals at risk for PCP have cut the recurrence rate of this often fatal disease by over 90%.
- **Dental Clinic** - Exams, cleanings, extractions, and fillings are offered to HIV antibody-positive individuals who are unable to afford private dental care or were denied treatment elsewhere because of their HIV status.
- **HIV Antibody Testing** - Testing is conducted on a strictly confidential, anonymous basis. No names are collected or recorded. Test results are provided with appropriate counseling and referrals in private individual sessions. Individual counseling for any HIV-related issue is also offered on a weekly basis.

All AIDS services of the clinic are coordinated with local government services as well as other communty-based organizations to ensure a unified response to AIDS.

PROJECT BRAVO
Bronx AIDS Volunteer Organization
Montefiore Medical Center
3320 Rochambeau Avenue
Bronx, NY 10467
TEL: 212-920-4301
Purpose: To serve and support persons with AIDS.
Sponsor: Montefiore Medical Center
Contact: Bridget Poust, Project Director
Description: The Bronx is the northern borough of the City of New York. It has a population of about 1.1 million people, with a variety of ethnic communities and peoples. The South Bronx, with about 50 percent of the borough's population, is notorious for its poverty and its massive housing destruction. Demographically, the South Bronx is predominantly black and Hispanic and has a high prevalence of HIV-positive persons and persons with AIDS-related conditions and AIDS itself.
Project BRAVO was created to establish support networks for Bronx AIDS patients, many of whom came from impoverished and isolated home situations, or may be homeless. Until Project BRAVO, the Bronx had no support system for persons with AIDS (PWAs).
Initially, the project trained and supervised four methadone maintenance clients as buddies for AIDS patients. The "buddies" would vist PWAs, run errands for them, baby-sit for those with children, act as patient advocates, and perform other services. Several months later, the program was expanded to admit people from all walks of life and all backgrounds - anyone with the willingness to serve as a volunteer.
BRAVO is a cooperative effort of four hospitals - *Montefiore Medical Center, Bronx Lebanon, St. Barnabas,* and *Bronx Municipal.* Today the program, although still small, has grown to 80 active volunteers who have direct contact with patients both in the hospital and at home. The number of people "on call" and in telephone contact, recreation, party-planning, community outreach and volunteer recruitment segments of the program is growing steadily. This bank of volunteers, although not in contact with patients on a regular basis, serves as friendly visitors, escorts PWAs to support groups, assists with arts and crafts and recreation, brings home-cooked meals, etc. Through the telephone contact volunteer activity, assessments of living situations and physical health can be made, in addition to the comfort of the phone conversation.
Volunteers make up a diverse community group, including methadone maintenance clients, gay men and lesbians, working people, and people on public assistance. They are black, Hispanic, and white. Generally, they reflect the population served.
Major administrative components are like those in any other volunteer program - recruitment, screening, training, support and supervision, referral, and assignment. It does not escape the presence of problems, however, which include funding, recruitment, burnout, institutional setting, and others that have cost the program volunteers. The bottom line is that the AIDS volunteer is very different from more traditional volunteers, and demands a new look at the rule book for volunteers and for the utilization of volunteers.
Founded: 1986

AIDS: COMMUNICATIONS & PR

NATIONAL/STATE ORGANIZATIONS

AMERICA RESPONDS TO AIDS
National AIDS Information Campaign
Centers for Disease Control
1600 Clifton Road, NE #B-68
Atlanta, GA 30333
TEL: 404-329-2384
Objectives: To keep the public informed on the latest information on AIDS.
Services: Provides technical assistance to *Scholastics, Inc.,* the world's largest publisher of supplementary, English-language educational materials, to assist in age-appropriate coverage of AIDS in classroom magazines; coordinates a variety of events with state medical associations on AIDS prevention and AIDS-related resources; distributes public-service announcements (PSAs) to 7,000 radio stations around the country; prepares national satellite news feeds for television and radio broadcasting of basic information on transmission and prevention of AIDS featuring recognized medical professionals; publishes free AIDS brochures in its *What You Should Know About AIDS* series with segments tailored to different audiences (general public, low-income women, parents of teens, inner-city blacks, employees, inner-city Hispanics, and families); works with various state and local groups - including businesses - to plan activities that will coincide with the themes of CDC campaigns.
Contact: AIDS Information Coordinator

THE NAMES PROJECT/AIDS MEMORIAL QUILT
The NAMES Project Foundation
PO Box 14573
San Francisco, CA 94114
TEL: 415-863-5511
Objectives: To confront individuals and governments with the urgency and enormity of the AIDS epidemic and the need for an immediate and compassionate response by revealing the names and the lives behind the global statics.
To build a powerful, positive, creative symbol of remembrance and

hope, linking diverse peoples worldwide in the shared expression of our common grief, pain and rage in response to AIDS.

To encourage donations in every community where the *Quilt* is displayed, thereby raising the desperately needed funds for people living with AIDS and their caregivers.

Services: The *NAMES Project* is an international AIDS memorial taking the shape of a huge quilt made up of thousands of individual 3'x6' panels. Each panel remembers the life of someone who has died of AIDS.

The *Project* started as a volunteer organization in 1987, a year and a half after the idea of a quilt as an AIDS memorial was posed by an individual (Cleve Jones) in response to a candlelight memorial service. Jones teamed up with several others to organize the *NAMES Project Foundation.*

The response to the *Quilt* was immediate. People from each of the major cities most affected by the epidemic - New York, Los Angeles and San Francisco - sent panels in memory of their friends and loved ones. Lesbians, gay men and their friends in San Francisco were especially generous, responding to wish lists in the *NAMES Project* workshop's storefront window asking for sewing machines, office supplies, and volunteers.

As awareness of the *Quilt* grew, so did participation. Thousands of individuals and groups from all over the U.S. and from many foreign countries began to send the memorial panels to the San Francisco workshop, to be included in the *Quilt.*

On October 11, 1987, the *NAMES Project* displayed the *AIDS Memorial Quilt* on the Capital Mall in Washington, DC during the *National March on Washington for Lesbian and Gay Rights.* The *Quilt* covered a space larger than two football fields, and included 1,920 panels. A half million people saw the *Quilt* that weekend.

The overwhelming response to the *Quilt* during this inaugural display led to a four-month, 20-city, national tour in the Spring of 1988. The tour raised nearly $500,000 for AIDS direct care services. These funds remained in their communities and were distributed through local organizations. The tour also generated community spirit, as more than 9,000 volunteers nationwide helped the seven-person road crew move and display the *Quilt.* Local panels were added in each city, doubling the size of the *Quilt* to more than 6,000 panels by the end of the tour.

The *Quilt* returned to Washington, DC in October 1988 to be displayed once again in its entirely. Having grown to include 8,288 memorial panels, it was displayed on the Ellipse behind the *White House,* and the reading of the names of the dead continued throughout the entire day.

A second tour through North America brought a large section of the *Quilt* to 19 more cities in the U.S. and Canada in 1989. It was displayed once more - for the final time - on Columbus Day weekend, October 1989. However, smaller displays of the *Quilt* will continue to take place in cities all over the U.S. and around the world. The *Quilt,* which presently contains almost 11,000 panels, has been nominated for the *Nobel Peace Prize.*

The *Quilt* is an ongoing memorial and educational tool; panels continue to be added as the AIDS epidemic continues. As the toll of AIDS deaths globally continues to rise, the *Quilt* is offered as one example of an appropriate, compassionate response to the epidemic. The *Foundation* has a commitment to continue for the duration of the epidemic.

Although springing from an idea of one man, who garnered a handful of volunteers in San Francisco in 1987, the organization has grown to include 22 paid staff members. The staff relies on hundreds of volunteers in the San Francisco area, and hundreds of thousands across the country. Over 30 *NAMES Project Chapters* have sprung up in cities all over the U.S., and these volunteers are the ones who "make it happen" whenever there is a display of the *Quilt* anywhere.

An aspect of the program that gives the *NAMES Project* staff and volunteers a feeling of great pride is the fact that, after seeing a display of the *Quilt,* many people are moved to become involved in their own communities' responses to the epidemic. This often

includes volunteering at local AIDS service organizations in their cities. In this way, we foster and encourage volunteerism for AIDS across the country.

Contact: Sue Martin, Director of Development
Publications: Quilt Facts
Founded: 1987

INDIVIDUAL PROGRAM PROFILES

HEART STRINGS - MEMPHIS STOP
SEE AIDS: FUNDING

LOS ANGELES POVERTY DEPARTMENT (LAPD)
SEE ARTS/CULTURAL ENRICHMENT: MUSIC/DANCE/THEATRE

PROJECT NOVA - AIDS PROGRAM
SEE AIDS: I&R

AIDS: EDUCATION

NATIONAL/STATE ORGANIZATIONS

AMERICAN RED CROSS OFFICE OF HIV/AIDS EDUCATION
1709 New York Avenue, NW
Washington, DC 20006
TEL: 202-662-1577; 202-662-1580
FAX: 202-662-1555
Objectives: To increase the capacity of communities to deliver or integrate HIV/AIDS education in the community; to design and deliver targeted HIV/AIDS education programs; to contribute to the global strategy on AIDS; and to evaluate programs, services, and strategies.
Services: Delivers a wide variety of HIV/AIDS educational programs, services and materials through Red Cross Units throughout the United States, which include the implementation of nationally developed programs as well as the development and delivery of programs and services designed to meet the unique needs of the community; includes in national HIV/AIDS programs:
- an HIV/AIDS instructor course;
- targeted education programs for the workplace and youth;
- an HIV/AIDS education program targeted to African-American youth; and
- a program, conceptualized in Spanish, directed to Hispanic youth and families.

Publishes brochures, student materials, teacher/leader guides and a range of videos.
Sponsor: American Red Cross
Contact: Carole Kauffman
Publications: AIDS Prevention Program for Youth; Children, Parents and AIDS; Drugs, Sex and AIDS ; Giving and Receiving Blood; HIV Infection and AIDS; HIV/AIDS in the Workplace; Living with HIV Infection

TRAINING PROGRAMS

PARENT-TEEN AIDS EDUCATION PROJECT
San Francisco AIDS Foundation
333 Valencia Street
PO Box 6182
San Francisco, CA 94101-6182
TEL: 415-861-3397
Credit: CEUs or Certificate
Sponsor: Local groups
Contact: Parent-Teen Program Coordinator
Description: The Parent-Teen AIDS Education Project offers several approaches to AIDS education. Each component can be implemented by itself or can be part of the total program. The implementation component provides detailed information on how to choose an appropriate program for your community, present AIDS information, and develop AIDS policies. It includes materials in English and Spanish to help with communication skills and strategies. Topics include:
Implementation
- Parent-teen communication
- Parent meeting guidance
- Community leadership
- Parent-Teen AIDS forums
- Cultural and ethnic concerns
- Working with the media
- Writing AIDS policies

Talking with Teens with Jane Curtin (video) - a presentation to provide parents with a review of basic AIDS information and examples of effective parent-teen communication.
Talking with Your Teen about AIDS - a handout designed to provide parents with basic facts about AIDS, and communication tips for talking with teens.
This program is designed for adult organizations and civic groups such as PTA and the Lions Club, schools, religious organizations, youth-serving agencies such as Big Brothers, Big Sisters, and the YMCA, the workplace, Departments of Health and other government agencies. It is contained in a kit of materials (implementation manual, video and brochures for all participants). It is acquired by the local group presenting the program. Local groups can work with their colleges and universities to qualify the Parent-Teen AIDS Education project as a CEU credit program, or a certificate may be issued. Inquire about program cost to the sponsoring community group.
Publications: Parent-Teen AIDS Education Implementation Manual ; Parent-Teen AIDS Education Video; Talking with Your Teen About AIDS

THE QUILT AND AIDS EDUCATION
The NAMES Project Foundation
PO Box 14573
San Francisco, CA 94114
TEL: 415-863-5511
FAX: 415-863-0708
Credit: None
Contact: Sue Baelen or Dan Sauro
Description: Although the *Quilt* began as a memorial, it has become one of the nation's most valuable resources for promoting a compassionate and educational dialogue about AIDS. The *Quilt's* non-threatening nature allows people from all walks of life to view and learn about the AIDS epidemic from its human side. It's artistic and creative approach enables accessibility to all, regardless of literacy.
The NAMES Project is now undertaking a more education-oriented stance, and a more aggressive approach toward bringing the *Quilt* to new audiences. Displays and dialogue are targeted specifically at those communities hardest hit by the second wave of the AIDS epidemic: school-age youth, ethnic and racial minorities, and IV drug abusers. Continuing to reach new

audiences slowly affects change in how people view AIDS and its effect on their lives.
The *Quilt* provides a very clear and pure message: *human beings die of AIDS.* It is impossible for visitors to see the personal messages on the panels and not be touched. It is difficult for them to feel immune to the disease when viewing a panel that memorializes someone with a name similar to their own, or someone born the same year, or who enjoyed the same hobbies and interests. It is an emotional and educational experience to understand the value of those lost lives.
The *Quilt* will tour continuously throughout 1990 and beyond, being displayed in airports, schools, universities, drug rehabilitation clinics, shopping malls - anywhere its impact of humanizing the statistics of the AIDS epidemic can be felt. Because the *Quilt's* power lies in the direct experience of it, *The NAMES Project* is committed to displaying it as much as possible. While the *Quilt* has now grown too large to continue to be displayed in its entirety, *The NAMES Project* is an ongoing foundation with a commitment to continue its efforts to educate the public for the duration of the epidemic. New panels will continue to be added, and sections of the *Quilt* will continue to be displayed across the country and around the world, as a visible symbol of the unabated growth of AIDS globally.
Founded: 1987

INDIVIDUAL PROGRAM PROFILES

AIDS PUBLIC EDUCATION PROGRAM
American Red Cross Office of HIV/AIDS Education
1709 New York Avenue, NW
Washington, DC 20006
TEL: 202-662-1577; 202-639-3223
FAX: 202-662-1555
Purpose: To provide reliable, factual information to help prevent the spread of the virus that causes AIDS - the human immunodeficiency virus (HIV).
Sponsor: National Urban League
Contact: Carole Kauffman, Director
Description: Beginning in 1985, the training and community outreach effort of the *American Red Cross AIDS Public Education Program* was formalized and set in operation at the community level nationwide. *Beyond Fear,* a one-hour television documentary, was produced by Red Cross and broadcast to over eight million viewers. A series of brochures was also developed in partnership with the U.S. Department of Health and Human Services with millions of copies distributed. Following the initial effort, the American Red Cross began to develop outreach efforts designed to reach specific segments of the general public. Targeted prevention education programs include:
- **AIDS Prevention Program for Youth** - endorsed by the U.S. Department of Education, the main elements of the program include videos, student workbooks, teaching guides, a brochure for parents, and a video discussion guide. Videos include *Letter From Brian, Don't Forget Sherrie* (directed toward African-American and urban youth), and *Answers About AIDS.* An HIV/AIDS education program for Hispanic youth and families, conceptualized in Spanish, is also in development.
- **AIDS Education for the Workplace** - a program customized to the employees' work setting created to engage workers actively in HIV/AIDS education and conducted by a Red Cross facilitator. Video case studies which portray actual workplace situations involving HIV/AIDS are incorporated into the program.
- **AIDS Minority Outreach** - targeted outreach to the Black, Hispanic, and Native American Indian communities. Red Cross collaboration with organizations representing minorities such as the *National Urban League,* the *National Coalition of*

Hispanic Health and Human Services Organizations (COSSMHO), and the *Bureau of Indian Affairs* is intended to increase the effectiveness of AIDS education programs designed to reach these audiences.

Through a cooperative agreement with the U.S. Centers for Disease Control, these model programs are being broadened to reach more people through new materials, through expanded and improved training programs, and through evaluations and increased cooperation at the state and local levels.

EDUCATION & PREVENTION SERVICES: AIDS PROGRAM
Whitman-Walker Clinic
1407 S Street, NW
Washington, DC 20009
TEL: 202-797-3560; 202-328-0697 (Spanish)
Purpose: To provide HIV-related education and prevention information to targeted communities.
Sponsor: Whitman-Walker Clinic
Contact: Peter Provost
Description: Sunnye Sherman AIDS Education Services is a division of the Whitman-Walker Clinic, a volunteer-based effort enhanced by professional staff. The education program is a multifaceted and multilevel approach to community health education. The program uses both traditional and nontraditional teaching and counseling methods to provide HIV-related eduation and prevention information. While the focus of all education is on risk behaviors, messages are targeted at specific communities. The service has individual emphasis programs such as:
Project HEART (Healthy Relationship Training) - conducts seminars and workshops where gay/bisexual men examine social and sexual lifestyle issues in the context of HIV and AIDS. The project emphasizes skill building and behavior modification leading to risk reduction and healthy practices.
Street Outreach Teams - delivers HIV/AIDS education on the streets to I.V. drug users and sex industry workers.
The Speakers Bureau - addresses general and specialized audiences in the workplace, community centers, classrooms, and health care settings.
The DC AIDS Information Line - operates four lines functioning seven days a week and answers over 500 calls a month.
The Latino AIDS Services Access Network - operates in conjunction with community outreach, HIV counseling and training, and traditional education as part of a project aimed at serving Spanish-speaking communities.
Education services is named in memory of Sunnye Sherman, who was diligent in her efforts to educate the public about the realities of AIDS through speaking out as a person living with AIDS. She died in 1986.
Volunteers in all Clinic programs receive orientation, training, seminars and workshops. All programs are coordinated with local government and community-based organizations.

FAMILY AIDS EDUCATION PROJECT
Jewish Family Services
1790 SW 27th Avenue
Miami, FL 33145
TEL: 305-445-0555
Purpose: To design an AIDS education program adaptable to all audiences.
Sponsor: Jewish Family Services
Description: Adapts an extensive AIDS education program to any audience, using four volunteer presenters. The project, developed by Jewish Family Services (JFS), Catholic Family Services, Family Counseling Services of Greater Miami, and the Center for Family and Child Enrichment, is coordinated by JFS. The agencies jointly designed a general brochure to accompany the educational presentation and have spoken to audiences ranging from catechism students to Nicaraguan immigrants.

To make conservative religious groups receptive to the presentations, they are scheduled with the approval of rabbis or priests. The brochure was carefully designed with input from each of the agencies involved as well as the community at large as to what words were or were not acceptable. The presentations are not "public meetings," per se, but rather meetings for specific groups already formed. This is necessary to properly adapt the presentation.
The Family AIDS Education Project has received $40,000 from United Way of Dade County to cover six months of the program (January to June 1989). The project's four speakers address hundreds of groups, with the intent of integrating AIDS education into existing orientation and education curriculums.
Founded: 1988

FAMILY LIFE AND AIDS INSTRUCTION PROGRAM
Los Gatos Union School District
Los Gatos, CA 95032
TEL: 408-395-5570 (school); 408-356-4111 (hospital)
Purpose: To introduce students to the business world, and provide volunteer opportunities for company employees.
Sponsor: Los Gatos Union School District
Contact: Bob Lowry, Principal, Fisher Middle School
Description: In the fall of 1988, after discussing the Adopt-A-School program with school personnel in the San Jose Unified School District, the Los Gatos School District started a program at Fisher Middle School. The school was "adopted" by Los Gatos Mission Oaks Hospital in October 1988.
School and hospital officials discussed the needs of students in the areas of health. The school sought assistance with its family life and AIDS instruction programs for eighth-graders.
Volunteer pediatricians and other trained staff members from the hospital selected sections of the family life course on human development and birth control and developed courses of instruction. In addition, the hospital provides literature geared to young people on acquired immune deficiency syndrome (AIDS). In turn, the hospital uses the Fisher campus for large meetings, and the Fisher choir sings at hospital events.
Apart from the health resources, the hospital provides costumes for the school's spring musical, and hospital employees are alert for other needs as they communicate with school personnel and work with students. As a result of the program, a number of students have expressed interest in health careers - a definite plus for the hospital as it looks to the future.

AIDS: EMPLOYMENT

TRAINING PROGRAMS

AIDS IN THE WORKPLACE
San Francisco AIDS Foundation
333 Valencia Street
PO Box 6182
San Francisco, CA 94101-6182
TEL: 415-861-3397
Sponsor: Local groups
Contact: Education Coordinator
Description: This multi-media education program was developed with the assistance of top business leaders; provides assistance in employment situations at any level, as well as health programs by educators employed in the workplace; consists of:
1. An Epidemic of Fear: Aids in the Workplace - a video tape using real-life situations to educate managers and employees about AIDS; includes interviews with medical experts, corporate managers, employees with AIDS and their coworkers.

2. An Educational Guide for Managers - provides decisionmakers with information about AIDS and includes a model for educating employees, and using educational resources effectively.

3. Strategy Manual and Appendix - provides hands-on suggestions for the development of policies and guidelines for responding to AIDS in the work environment, and draws on the experience of companies which have successfully dealt with AIDS in the workplace.

4. AIDS in the Workplace - a pamphlet developed for distribution to employees consisting of questions and answers about AIDS. This program was developed in cooperation with the Business Leadership Task Force of the San Francisco Bay Area. Members of the Task Force include Levi Strauss & Co., Pacific Bell, Mervyn's, Bank of America, Wells Fargo Bank, AT&T and Chevron Corporation. These businesses and their associated foundations also funded the development and production of *AIDS in the Workplace* materials.

This education program is designed as a self-contained training program for the business community.

A more advanced program, *The Next Step: HIV in the 90s,* begins where *AIDS in the Workplace* ends. It addresses issues that arise *after* policies are in place and AIDS education is underway. These issues include reasonable accommodation, confidentiality, benefits, fitness for duty, legal issues, and grief and loss. Inquire about cost to local businesses of both segments of the training program.

Publications: An Epidemic of Fear: AIDS in the Workplace; An Educational Guide for Managers; Strategy Manual and Appendix; Aids in the Workplace

INDIVIDUAL PROGRAM PROFILES

AIDS IN THE WORKPLACE
United Way of Central Maryland
22 Light Street
PO Box 1576
Baltimore, MD 21203-1576
TEL: 301-547-8000
Purpose: To encourage the business sector to focus on the AIDS issue.
Sponsor: United Way of Central Maryland
Contact: Dana Struke, Director of Workplace Services
Description: In 1988, the United Way brought together representatives from business and specialists from human resources, medical and legal fields to form a volunteer task force on the AIDS issue. From discussions of the kinds of information and assistance area businesses need to address AIDS in the workplace, the task force recommended an in-depth survey. One goal of the survey was to determine how many businesses had policies for employees with AIDS and/or employee AIDS-awareness programs.

Of the 450 businesses which responded to the survey, 84 percent said they did not have an AIDS policy in place and 76 percent said businesses should be involved with the AIDS issue. Half of the respondents said they would like assistance in developing an AIDS policy.

As a result of the survey, the United Way sponsored publication of an AIDS manual designed for businesses wanting practical information. The manual was developed by the Health Education Resource Organization with a $25,000 grant from the United Way. After the manual was published, the United Way held a follow-up conference for the business community.

According to the project's director, "Interacting with businesses about AIDS is a way of providing year-round communications about the disease. In the long run, we hope it will educate employees as well."
Publications: AIDS Manual for Businesses
Founded: 1988

HIV/AIDS WORKPLACE PROGRAM
American Red Cross Office of HIV/AIDS Education
1709 New York Avenue, NW
Washington, DC 20006
TEL: 202-662-1577; 202-662-1580
FAX: 202-662-1555
Purpose: To provide a means of communication on HIV/AIDS between employer and employees.
Contact: Carole Kauffman
Description: The Red Cross workplace HIV/AIDS education program is being used (as of mid-1990) in over 400 local Red Cross chapters. The program provides employers with the opportunity to explain or reinforce their policies regarding HIV infection, including AIDS. The video/discussion portion of the program combines the delivery of facts and information about how HIV can and cannot be transmitted with guided group discussions about employee responses to potential HIV/AIDS-related events in the workplace.

Additional workplace video scenarios continue to be developed, along with new discussion guides, and are released to the field as they become available. Updating is done periodically throughout each project year.

AIDS: ETHNIC GROUPS

INDIVIDUAL PROGRAM PROFILES

BROOKLYN AIDS TASK FORCE
22 Chapel Street
Brooklyn, NY 11201
TEL: 718-596-4781
Purpose: To bring AIDS information to a difficult-to-reach population.
Contact: Eugene McGovern, Volunteer Coordinator
Description: The Brooklyn AIDS Task Force (BATF) is faced with a multicultural, multiethnic borough population. Brooklyn is also the borough with the second largest number of AIDS cases in New York City, following Manhattan.

The most obvious problem in trying to get BATF underway was the existing AIDS education materials, which were designed for white, middle-class, educated Americans, but do not necessarily work for other groups.

The breakthrough came in an unusual way for BATF. The Education Director began an outreach project in her own neighborhood, distributing pamphlets in the supermarket, the laundromat and other public places. An 11-year-old child asked why she was carrying around those heavy boxes of pamphlets. When told it was AIDS education materials, the child's interest and curiosity were obvious, and she told of her friends' questions, also. At a later meeting with the young group - five children, black, white and Hispanic - the very serious youngsters had long lists of questions to ask, and wrote down the answers.

Now, those children are BATF's most active, most concerned, and most effective volunteers. They are workers; they are speakers. Throughout the community, it is obvious that people are relating to them. All the statistics and studies in the world could not have attained such results.

The children created drawings to show people that they understand what AIDS is about and the ways in which it is transmitted.

In addition, a videotape, *Children Speak About AIDS,* was produced with the same children telling people, in their own words, all about the disease. It has been done in English, Spanish, French and Creole. It has been a useful tool in reaching the hard-to-reach parts of the community with AIDS information. It opens doors and provides a basis for initiating discussions about topics, such as sexuality and condoms, that people otherwise have trouble talking about. In this and other ways, the Task Force is adjusting its AIDS information and its approach to fit the different cultures of Brooklyn.

In addition to the drawings and the video, the children created an AIDS-related coloring book to be used in our work in the schools. It is the first of a series that will explain the different processes of the infection, virus transmission, etc. The coloring book also comes in four languages.

During a community outreach effort, "AIDS Information Day," the young volunteers spoke, and entertainment, food, and gifts were provided for visitors. There was a children's workshop, and baby-sitting so mothers could attend. People with AIDS, those who have lost a loved one to AIDS, and those who have dealt with AIDS spoke, also, to try to help people come to terms with the disease and understand what AIDS means to those who are sick and their families. One is a volunteer with the Task Force - a mother whose son died of AIDS in 1987.

The chance encounter with the young volunteers and the direction it has taken to help educate the community, and the willingness of AIDS sufferers and their families to share their experiences, have made an enormous difference in the Task Force's ability to present AIDS education information, and to be heard. And a lesson that surfaced is that - in enlisting volunteers - children should be included as a viable resource.

HIV/AIDS PREVENTION PROGRAM FOR AFRICAN AMERICAN YOUTH AND FAMILIES
American Red Cross Office of HIV/AIDS Education
1709 New York Avenue, NW
Washington, DC 20006
TEL: 202-662-1577; 202-662-1580
FAX: 202-662-1555
Purpose: To provide a targeted prevention/education program for African American youth.
Contact: Carole Kauffman
Description: This is a major outreach program directed to African American youth. The *National Urban League* and other national black organizations work with the Red Cross on wide-scale promotion and delivery of the program. Cities that have a large number of AIDS cases and a large African American population are targeted.
A video, *Don't Forget Sherrie,* and its accompanying educational materials for students and discussion leaders is a major focus of the program, designed for a teenage audience.
Publications: Don't Forget Sherrie (video)

HIV/AIDS PREVENTION PROGRAM FOR HISPANIC YOUTH AND FAMILIES
American Red Cross Office of HIV/AIDS Education
1709 New York Avenue, NW
Washington, DC 20006
TEL: 202-662-1577; 202-662-1580
FAX: 202-662-1555
Purpose: To provide a major HIV/AIDS education/training program in Spanish for Hispanic youth.
Contact: Carole Kauffman
Description: In cooperation with national Hispanic organizations, the American Red Cross developed a model program in Spanish to provide education and training for Hispanic youth at the local level. The first "graduates" of the training completed the program in June 1990. Training is in community outreach and HIV/AIDS education, with individuals from major Hispanic groups in the U.S. conceptualizing, developing, evaluating, and implementing it. The target population is recent Spanish-speaking immigrants with a low level of formal eduction, and/or Spanish-speaking youth and families.
The program includes a 30-minute video, an accompanying fotonovela, a parents magazine, comic books, and posters.

INFORME SIDA
ALLGO
Santa Julia Church
3010 Lyons Road
Austin, TX 78702
TEL: 512-472-2001
Purpose: To provide bilingual AIDS information to the Latino community.
Sponsor: Santa Julia Church
Contact: Volunteer Coordinator
Description: Informe SIDA is a bilingual AIDS education project conducted by ALLGO. It periodically holds door-to-door neighborhood walks to distribute AIDS literature. Volunteers meet at Santa Julia Church and receive route assignments.
The distribution of bilingual literature is concentrated in eastern Travis County and suburban southeast Austin.
Informe SIDA is the only bilingual AIDS education project in Austin. The literature is designed to make information on AIDS available throughout the Latino community. The literature informs people on the methods of AID transmission and on safe practices. It also describes ALLGO and its other programs for the Latino community.

AIDS: FUNDING

NATIONAL/STATE ORGANIZATIONS

CHAPTER GRANTS PROGRAM
American Red Cross Office of HIV/AIDS Education
AIDS Public Education Program
1709 New York Avenue, NW
Washington, DC 20006
TEL: 202-662-1577; 202-662-1580
FAX: 202-662-1555
Objectives: To help local chapters provide HIV/AIDS education to high-risk populations.
Services: Awards grants to Red Cross chapters for creative and new approaches to HIV/AIDS education; places focus on helping chapters provide community HIV/AIDS education to hard-to-reach, high-risk populations; shares successful programs with other chapters so they can be adapted, if necessary, and used as models for local use; funds programs such as peer counseling in homeless shelters, and education efforts in migrant worker camps, prisons, and schools, with two grants going to evaluation programs using local university resources for assessing effectiveness of local chapter programs; provides chapter mini-grants, which act as seed money to small chapters that lack the resources to begin any sort of community HIV/AIDS education program without assistance.
Contact: Carole Kauffman

INDIVIDUAL PROGRAM PROFILES

AIDS-WALK NEW YORK
GMHC Walkathon
Gay Men's Health Crisis
Old Chelsea Station
PO Box 10
New York, NY 10113
TEL: 212-807-6310
Purpose: To raise funds for the programs of the *Gay Men's Health Crisis.*
Contact: Leif Green, Event Manager
Description: AIDS Walk New York is a ten kilometer fundraising walkathon benefiting *Gay Men's Health Crisis (GMHC).* The

funds raised support the many programs and services provided by GMHC, the largest nonprofit AIDS service, education and advocacy organization in the world, and the first organization to confront the AIDS epidemic.

In mid-1990, GMHC was working with 2,800 clients. Services provided include case management, crisis intervention, financial advocacy, legal services, a hot-meal service, and a buddy program, among others.

Most of the work of organizing the *AIDS Walk* each year is performed by volunteers. Each year, hundreds of people donate time to make sure that the Walkathon is a success. Volunteer activities include:

- **Phonebanking (evenings)** - The Walkathon phonebank takes place during the evenings, with fifteen volunteers on duty each telephoning GMHC supporters to ask them to register for the Walk.
- **Tabling on Weekends** - During each weekend in April of each year, volunteers sign up walkers at designated locations.
- **Office Help on Weekdays** - Volunteers are needed on weekdays to send out Walk materials and assist staff with other Walk-related tasks.
- **Walk Day** - In 1990, tasks on the day of the event required 900 volunteers to serve as *Safety Monitors, Registration Volunteers, Checkpoint Workers,* and *Crowd Control Assistants.* Volunteers are credited with completing the full ten kilometers and may raise funds as well.

Corporate and community groups support *AIDS Walk* by forming teams representing them. These groups include fields of advertising, banking, communications, entertainment, fashion, health care, law, public relations, publishing, securities, and transportation, as well as numerous community groups, schools, and government agencies. A lighter side of the team effort comes in the form of "friendly competition." For example, *American Airlines* flight attendants are being challenged by the flight attendants of *TWA* and *PanAm.* Many teams provide T-shirts, breakfasts, and parties for their team members to encourage full participation. Some companies provide each participating employee with a separate corporate donation. Many companies have a "matching grant" policy for employee donations to charity, and often this donation system is used for the Walk.

In addition to assisting GMHC in providing services, Walk funds help in the production and distribution of AIDS prevention and related information, and a portion of the net Walk proceeds - 15% - is used to fund grants to a number of different organizations whose programs assist people affected by HIV-related illnesses. In 1989, more than $3 million was raised for that year's 6.2-mile walk from 125,000 sponsors. Information about participation in *AIDS Walk New York* is available throughout the year.

Publications: Walk Update; AIDS Walk New York Information Package

FROM ALL WALKS OF LIFE
AIDS Action Committee
131 Clarendon Street
Boston, MA 02190
TEL: 617-437-6200
Purpose: To raise funds for AIDS service organizations.
Sponsor: Bank of Boston; Shawmut Bank
Contact: Larry Kessler, Executive Director
Description: From All Walks of Life is a 10 kilometer (6.2 mile) walk for AIDS care and research in Massachusetts. The event has become a major source of funds at a time when adequate funding is not forthcoming from federal, state and city sources. The 1989 walk drew nearly 15,000 participants, including some AIDS patients and parents of AIDS patients.
Since its beginning in 1986, the walk has become the single largest fund-raiser for AIDS service organizations in the Commonwealth. The 1989 walk generated $600,000 in grants to 34 AIDS community centers, coalitions, and hospices. The U.S. Surgeon

General participated in the 1989 event.

Before the walk there was an aerobic stretch to music led by a fitness instructor, followed by opening ceremonies and a low-cost breakfast. Community support was evident throughout the day. Twenty members of Patriots Trail Council of the Girl Scouts of America made stickers with messages, which were handed out to walkers at water stops. *China Educational Tours of Dorchester* donated a 16-day tour of China to be awarded to the walker earning the highest dollar amount of pledge money. Thirty-six music groups performed along the route - one teen-age group performing *Stop the Madness,* its new single about AIDS. *Creative Gourmets Ltd.* enlisted 200 volunteers to prepare 10,000 vegetable sandwiches on pita bread to be served with a piece of fruit and other food items in sandwich boxes and distributed at the end of the walk. Vendors in the area contributed food for the lunches. Fifty radio stations throughout the state simultaneously broadcast Dionne Warwick's *That's What Friends Are For* at the conclusion of the walk.

Sponsors included the *Bank of Boston, Boston Globe Foundation, Bank of New England, Lotus Development Corporation, John Hancock Financial Services, Digital Equipment Corporation, New England Medical Center Hospitals* and *Shawmut Bank.*

HEART STRINGS - MEMPHIS STOP
Aid to End AIDS Committee
689 Melrose
Memphis, TN 38104
TEL: 901-458-2437; 901-272-0855
Purpose: To raise funds to help a broader spectrum of AIDS victims in the Memphis area.
Sponsor: Aid to End AIDS Committee
Contact: Allen Cook, ATEAC Secretary
Description: Heart Strings is a show sponsored by the *Design Industries Foundation for AIDS,* headquartered in New York. The national production raises funds around the country during a 30-city tour beginning in early fall each year. It's purpose is to expand financial support for AIDS into the community-at-large, while helping communities to understand AIDS. AIDS organizations in the host community receive 85% of the profits from the stop. The other 15% is earmarked for AIDS care and education in cities skipped by the tour.
The host community is expected to provide volunteers and an estimated $15,000 to $20,000 for local production expenses. The musical includes a touring company of about 20 performers. Local celebrities and choirs are often added. Just how much the show makes in each city depends upon such factors as ticket prices and corporate sponsorship. Ticket prices are set after the level of financial support from other sources is determined.
In Memphis, the *Aid to End AIDS Committee (ATEAC)* and the *Memphis AIDS Coalition* spearhead local sponsorship of the show. ATEAC's need for more money stems from the group's growing caseload. In 1988, the group paid an average of about $400 per month in direct financial aid to clients. A year later, the tab averaged about $2,000 per month. Financial support can include making rent or utility payments for needy patients or even paying the first month's fee for the AIDS drug AZT.
The group also rents a house in Memphis used as a shelter for homeless AIDS patients. Clients include hemophiliacs who apparently caught the virus through tainted blood or blood products, and women who apparently contracted the virus through heterosexual relations, as well as members of the gay community. For this reason, the community-at-large is included in the effort to supplement the limited amount of money realized from the very targeted (gay) audience.

AIDS: HOME CARE/HOSPICES

INDIVIDUAL PROGRAM PROFILES

ISAIAH HOUSE
Corpus Christi Catholic Church
71 Prince Street
Rochester, NY 14605
TEL: 716-325-2424
Purpose: To provide an alternative for people for whom it is impossible to remain at home.
Sponsor: Corpus Christi Catholic Church
Contact: Kathie Quinlan, Director
Description: We are a small, two-bed facility called *Isaiah House*, and we hold the philosophy that terminally ill people should be able to die at home, since care focuses on providing comfort, not on prolonging life. When remaining at home becomes impossible because there are no family members to care for a patient, or when a person is homeless or has no insurance to cover the cost of a private nurse, small hospices like *Isaiah House* provide an environment like home. A ministry of *Corpus Christi Catholic Church, Isaiah House* is located in a blue, three-story, wood-sided home with a large front porch with colorful flower boxes, and an English Garden in the back.
On the waiting list, *Isaiah House* has homeless people and AIDS patients, elderly people and those with families far away. Though limited in the number of people it can serve, the hospice reaches a group of people who often fall through the cracks of the health care system.
Volunteers are the backbone of the facility, and come from numerous creeds, professions and backgrounds. Some volunteers are nurses who have worked with the dying.
Care ranges from arranging medicine schedules to assigning nurses and aides to help a patient's family provide care at home.
Although *Isaiah House* maintains only two beds within the facility so they won't have to go through the licensing process with the state, it acts more like a surrogate family than certified hospice programs do, according to its director. Staff and volunteers spend quiet vigils at bedsides of terminally-ill patients who spend anywhere from weeks to mere hours there.
The hospice also generates interest in other local areas. After learning about *Isaiah House,* a Bible study class at *Bethlehem Lutheran Church* in Fairfield has made the development of its own hospice, *Advent House,* its ministry. Also, the hospices become outreach programs for a number of area churches.
Founded: 1987

RESPITE FOR AIDS VOLUNTEERS
Kairos House
114 Douglass Street
San Francisco, CA 94114
TEL: 415-861-0877
Purpose: To help volunteers approaching burnout by providing an evening for retreat once a week in a relaxed setting.
Contact: Father John McGrann, Founder
Description: Almost ten years and more than 4,300 deaths into the local AIDS epidemic, people from cities outside of the Bay Area still marvel at the volunteer response that created the network of AIDS services known as the *San Francisco model.* At a Victorian house founded by a Catholic priest it is clear that the model places a high price on its volunteers. Known as *Kairos House,* it is a place where AIDS volunteers approaching overload and others working with AIDS patients can find relief from the suffering. Leaders in AIDS charities say despair is a common product of a system using up its human resources. Volunteers describe the first sign of approaching burnout as "emotional numbness."
Kairos House has taken one step toward caring for the people on the front-line in the epidemic. It is a place where AIDS caregivers can get a free 15-minute Japanese massage, and where a table full of hors d'oeuvres awaits them. Piano music drifts softly through the rooms, and many volunteers come to just sit and listen to the music. *Kairos House* offers one way to hold on to volunteers approaching burnout or exhaustion. With a recent drop in donations and volunteers throughout AIDS charities, this respite is especially important. According to one AIDS volunteer, "There's a point where there's so much pain, you just shut down." *Kairos House* offers one way of providing the support the San Francisco model needs to keep its trained volunteers, and to attract new sources of donations and volunteers. Age groups not well represented as volunteers in AIDS charities are teenagers and the elderly, and recruitment efforts are under way to attract those groups.
Founded: 1988

THE RESPONSE POOL
United Way of Dade County
600 Brickell Avenue, Eighth Floor
PO Box 010790
Miami, FL 33101-0790
TEL: 305-579-2200
Purpose: To fund in-home care for people with AIDS.
Sponsor: Visiting Nurse Association, Hospice, Inc., Health Crisis Network, United Way
Contact: Alexandra Lindsey, Director of Initiatives
Description: The Response Pool supports AIDS services through a community problem-solving fund. In 1985, The Response Pool began funding an in-home care program for people with AIDS - a program jointly operated by the Visiting Nurse Association, Hospice, Inc., and Miami's Health Crisis Network.
Currently, United Way helps fund more than a dozen agencies with AIDS programs ranging from suicide-prevention hotlines to an AIDS education training program for social service professionals.
With approximately 32 percent of Florida AIDS cases occurring in the Miami area - and 12,000 cases of HIV-infection predicted by 1991 - the United Way is prioritizing AIDS in its public-awareness materials as well. Last year, the organization made AIDS a subject in its campaign film, adding to its examples of human-service needs a portrayal of a woman with AIDS.
Founded: 1989

AIDS: HOUSING

INDIVIDUAL PROGRAM PROFILES

HOUSING SERVICES: AIDS PROGRAM
SEE HOUSING: AIDS

AIDS: I&R

NATIONAL/STATE ORGANIZATIONS

AIDS HOTLINE
US/HHS - National AIDS Information Clearinghouse
PO Box 6003
Rockville, MD 20850
TEL: 800-342-AIDS; 800-344-SIDA (Spanish)
TOLL FREE: 800-AIDS-TTY (deaf)

Objectives: To respond to any questions children, youth, or adults may have about HIV infection and AIDS.

Services: Provides a 24-hour, seven-day service with Public Health Service employees answering a toll-free hotline number to answer questions about HIV infection and AIDS, or refer the caller to other sources; provides specialized service to refer callers to state and local health departments and other groups in his or her immediate area for local counseling and testing; keeps all responses confidential, and callers need not give name; operates a number of AIDS projects to combat this condition, which affects the body's ability to fight off disease; provides a comprehensive guide, a bimonthly bulletin, a pamphlet and other materials on the subject, as well as referrals to sources of additional publications and materials; maintains hotline access for Spanish-speaking and hearing-impaired persons.

Publications: AIDS Information Bulletin; Facts on AIDS

FDA EXPERIMENTAL AIDS TREATMENT HOTLINE
US/HHS - Food and Drug Administration
5600 Fishers Lane
Rockville, MD 20852
TEL: 301-443-3170
TOLL FREE: 800-TRIALS-A
Objectives: To keep the public informed of experimental treatment for AIDS.
Services: Maintains a computerized listing of every experimental AIDS and AIDS-related treatment undergoing clinical testing in FDA-sanctioned trials; provides this information to make it easier for AIDS patients to participate more widely.
Sponsor: US/HHS - Department of Health & Human Services

INDIVIDUAL PROGRAM PROFILES

DISTRICT OF COLUMBIA AIDS INFORMATION LINE
Whitman-Walker Clinic
1407 S Street, NW
Washington, DC 20009
TEL: 202-797-3568 (Office); 202-332 AIDS (VT/TTY)
Purpose: To answer questions and make referrals on issues involving AIDS and HIV infection.
Sponsor: Whitman-Walker Clinic
Contact: Amelie Zurn
Description: The *DC AIDS Information Line* is a division of Whitman-Walker Clinic, a volunteer-based (1,500 overall) effort, enhanced and supported by professional staff. The Line operates seven days a week (10:00 a.m. - 9:00 p.m. weekdays; 10:00 a.m. - 6:00 weekends), and averages over 500 calls each month.
Information Line volunteers go through extensive training and are equipped to handle calls from persons who have HIV+ or AIDS, or significant others; i.e., people needing someone to talk with as opposed to needing questions answered. Therefore, according to a volunteer, "We are a 'hotline' *as well as* an information line."
Two part-time staff members have been diagnosed with AIDS for several years and are available should someone wish to talk with someone with AIDS (very helpful for the newly-diagnosed).
As with all Clinic programs, Information Line staff work closely with other organizations and the community-at-large to avoid duplication of effort, share effort, etc. For example, the Lesbian and Gay Hotline and the Peer Counseling Group help with stress associated with AIDS and work in cooperation with the Information Line.

EDUCATION & PREVENTION SERVICES: AIDS PROGRAM
SEE AIDS: EDUCATION

PROJECT NOVA - AIDS PROGRAM
Whitman-Walker Clinic
1407 S Street, NW
Washington, DC 20009
TEL: 202-358-2839; 202-328-0697
Purpose: To provide/coordinate support and education services in Northern Virginia.
Sponsor: Whitman-Walker Clinic
Contact: Peter Provost
Description: Project NOVA's case management system coordinates the services of the Whitman-Walker Clinic in Northern Virginia. Whitman-Walker Clinic is a volunteer-based (1,500 overall) effort, enhanced and supported by professional staff. NOVA works with other public- and private-sector agencies to insure that Northern Virginians connect with the services they need. The *NOVA Education Resource Center* is housed in Project NOVA, which also conducts educational outreach programs to gay/bisexual men. Project NOVA works with other agencies through the *Northern Virginia HIV Consortium* to build a unified regional response to the epidemic.
Services are provided to all people in need. Objectives are to improve the overall health and well-being of the community. All volunteers in the program receive orientation and extensive training.

AIDS: NUTRITION

INDIVIDUAL PROGRAM PROFILES

GOD'S LOVE WE DELIVER (GLWD)
PO Box 1776
Old Chelsea Station
New York, NY 10113
TEL: 212-874-1193
Purpose: To deliver free hot meals to persons homebound with AIDS.
Sponsor: God's Love We Deliver
Contact: Michael Bertish, Business Manager
Description: GLWD delivers hot, five-course meals, free of charge, to clients who are homebound with AIDS. The service operates five days a week, Monday through Friday. Volunteers work in the kitchen, in the delivery vans, and in the business office. Without volunteers, the program could not operate.
In addition to recruiting volunteers, GLWD approached the church community. After two years, GLWD was able to create a relationship with the Catholic Archdiocese of New York in which the church operates hospice centers and GLWD is responsible for providing food for the clients. The church provides volunteers.
AIDS education is a constant presence. For example, a food supplier stopped making deliveries when he learned that GLWD is an AIDS program. After receiving AIDS information from the GLWD, not only did delivery resume, but a few people from the company offered to volunteer. Other volunteers have come in unexpected ways, also. One excellent volunteer saw a donation canister in a grocery store and called GLWD to volunteer.
GLWD's problem in recruiting volunteers is its hours - nine to five. Many volunteers offer evening or weekend hours, so GLWD created a Wednesday evening program where volunteers come right from work and perform administrative tasks, party preparation, advanced preparation of some foods, etc. It is a very popular evening for the employed volunteer.
In talking with the media, GLWD makes certain that the person being interviewed is well versed on the AIDS crisis and the role of the program. Media articles are the best sources of volunteers for GLWD, since people see that something is being done and want to

be part of it. In addition, people who are HIV positive - unless they are visibly ill - often volunteer 100% of their time. They cook meals, and many deliver them also.

GLWD also attributes much of its success to its total and equal involvement of volunteers in meetings and other activities of the program. They are kept well-informed and often become the program's best spokespersons and fundraisers. Also, training is a factor in the program. Sending a volunteer whose family member is ill with AIDS to deliver a meal to a gravely ill client is not done until the volunteer offers to do so, or until he or she has been strengthened by involvement in the program for an adequate period of time. A premature visit could be traumatic for both volunteer and client.

Founded: 1986

AIDS: PSYCHOSOCIAL SUPPORT

INDIVIDUAL PROGRAM PROFILES

AIDS PROJECT: FRIENDLY VISITORS
St. Luke's-Roosevelt Hospital Center
428 West 59th Street
New York, NY 10019
TEL: 212-523-7155

Purpose: To provide friendly visitors to patients with AIDS.
Sponsor: St. Luke's-Roosevelt Hospital Center
Contact: Virginia D. Crosby, Director of Volunteers
Description: In 1985, when *St. Luke's Roosevelt Hospital Center* had an average daily census of 20 to 30 AIDS inpatients at its Roosevelt Division site, the need to develop special programs to meet the psychosocial needs of these patients and their friends and families, so different from those of the ordinary hospital inpatients, became apparent. The improvement of social support systems for PWAs while they are within the institution could, it was felt, reduce psychosocial distress and, to some degree, physical morbidity and mortality.

The AIDS Friendly Visitor program was developed by the Department of Volunteers and the Department of Social Work to recruit, interview, train, and place appropriate volunteers to work with and support patients with AIDS, providing psychosocial support, entitlement information, advocacy routes, and friendship to PWAs in Roosevelt who might not otherwise have any. At the time the program was developed there was no designated AIDS unit and PWAs were distributed throughout the hospital's medical/surgical floors.

After meeting some institutional opposition to the program, fortunately hospital administrators were supportive and approved the undertaking of a demonstration project. It was decided that the project would be called "Friendly Visitors," and not "AIDS Friendly Visitors." An application for support for the project was made to United Hospital Fund's Special Project Fund grant program. Once the grant was approved, recruiting and screening of potential volunteers began.

Initially, volunteers were recruited through newsletters of community organizations, church bulletins and other volunteer and social agency vehicles. Within a short time, recruitment was halted, since volunteers were learning about the program and there was a waiting list. In the screening process, project leaders looked for a special core group of sensitive and intelligent volunteers who were relaxed, had a good sense of humor, and could be a good guest at the bedside of a patient. It was soon learned that AIDS volunteers are very different from the regular hospital volunteers. They tend to be younger, very sophisticated, very highly educated, very stable people. They are very sincere about what they are doing and don't really want to be thanked for it. They are

committed, and they don't complain.

It was soon found that volunteers could support and supplement social workers, who were overburdened and overstressed as a result of the increasing AIDS patient census. Although volunteers' roles are basically being "guests" at the bedside, their orientation and training is necessarily extensive - including psychosocial overviews of AIDS patients and a component on AIDS epidemiology, mythology, and infection control. Patient referrals come to the volunteer office after the patient is interviewed to determine his or her desire for volunteer support. Every effort is made to match volunteers and patients with similar interests. Volunteers document each visit in a log that is kept in the volunteer office. They attend monthly support meetings to network with other volunteers. This is especially important if a patient a volunteer cares about has died.

Problems encountered were not unexpected for the most part. The time involved was underestimated, for example. Interviewing, alone, is a time-consuming activity. Also, regular hospital volunteers have no interest in visiting AIDS patients, and often do not like the AIDS friendly visitors. It is expected that, in time, these attitudes will break down and change.

Generally, the program is a greater success than expected. Acknowledgments and appreciation expressed by staff, patients and families and loved ones supports this conclusion.

Founded: 1985

MOTHERS OF PWAS (PERSONS WITH AIDS)
Shrine of the Immaculate Conception
Michigan Avenue & 4th Street, NE
Washington, DC 20017
TEL: 202-526-8300

Purpose: To help women - especially mothers - deal with the AIDS epidemic.
Sponsor: Shrine of the Immaculate Conception
Contact: Cecelia Bonner, Founder
Description: Since AIDS always has been thought of as a man's disease, efforts to help women deal with the epidemic have been slow in developing. Self-help groups in recent years have been formed with family members, friends and lovers in mind. To address this situation, in May 1989 a support and advocacy group was founded at the *Shrine of the Immaculate Conception* exclusively for women. The founder had lost a son to AIDS. While being careful not to discount men's feelings toward their sons and other close relatives with AIDS, the new support group was set up specifically to address female grief. One issue that surfaces frequently is the loss of a sense of closeness once felt with female friends, when normally a sickness in the family would bring them closer - with frequent visitors carrying covered dishes and offering plenty of hugs. But, contrary to what might be expected, it is the women in the AIDS-affected families who cut off the friendships with former friends as often as it is the other way around. Partly, this is because they prefer to keep the pain to themselves, and partly because confiding in friends too often leads to a rebuke. Remarks like, "You touched them? You hugged them?" are too often heard.

Although discussion centers on how the epidemic has weakened female bonds and forced women inward, it eventually gets around to men. The women agree that men have greater difficulty accepting that their sons might be homosexual and are not confronting the tragedy of AIDS. They are more likely to hold out hope for a cure than deal directly with their sons' mortality. Women, on the other hand, get through denial much quicker and begin the healthy process of grieving. *Mothers of PWAs* is a combination of support, self-help and advocacy and has provided an outlet for emotions that the women have had to keep under wraps in their everyday lives.

Founded: 1989

SHANTI PROJECT
525 Howard
San Francisco, CA 94105
TEL: 415-777-2273
Purpose: To provide emotional support and practical help for people with AIDS.
Contact: Eric Rofes, Executive Director
Description: The *Shanti Project* is one of a group of service providers for AIDS patients which shares funding and volunteer recruitment efforts to help keep San Francisco's AIDS care cost relatively low. About 550 Shanti volunteers provide emotional support and practical help, such as grocery shopping, for people with AIDS. Shanti also operates a housing program for about 53 people with AIDS.
A mid-1989 cut of about a seventh of its staff due to a drop in donations places a refocus on the volunteer services for people with AIDS that originally brought the agency international renown. Cuts in paid staff are evident in many agencies serving AIDS patients. These cuts are direct results of a sharp jump in expenses (especially medical premiums) and a drop in private donations ($791,000 in 1987-88 to $499,000 in 1989-90). The Shanti's staff reduction saved $200,000 out of Shanti's $3.1 million budget without affecting service for AIDS patients. Most of the savings came from a reduction in administrators in the largely volunteer organization.
In a meeting in mid-1989, AIDS agency administrators from across San Francisco discussed and shared challenges, which are increasing as people with AIDS continue to live longer and add to the extensive caseload of all AIDS agencies. Once again, a commitment to recognizing the volunteer as the hallmark of the AIDS service movement is underway. The model of AIDS care was built on volunteers and donations, and the *Shanti Project* and other agencies are renewing those traditions in the best interest of PWAs (people with AIDS).

SUPPORT SERVICES - AIDS PROGRAM
Whitman-Walker Clinic
1407 S Street, NW
Washington, DC 20009
TEL: 202-797-3540; 202-328-0697
Purpose: To provide a variety of support services to persons with AIDS and HIV infection.
Sponsor: Whitman-Walker Clinic
Contact: Peter Provost
Description: Support Services is a division of *Whitman-Walker Clinic AIDS Program,* which is a volunteer-based (1,500 overall) effort, enhanced and supported by professional staff. The Support Services Division includes:
Financial Help - The AIDS Foundation administers over 250 memorial funds established by lovers, other family members, and friends of local persons so that donations contributed in their memory will be of service to others. Over $370,000 has been distributed over the past four years. The foundation provides direct financial assistance to persons living with AIDS. Among other things, funding has been granted for housing, food, transportation, moving, entertainment, and funeral expenses. Ninety percent of foundation money goes to direct assistance; the remainder is used for administrative costs.
Emotional Help - Support services include individual and group counseling for persons with HIV infection and for lovers and other family members; social work case management to insure proper coordination with available services; buddies and home companions for help with day-to-day tasks; and referrals for religious, visiting nurse, and hospice services. Home health care workers are employed with the support of the *DC Long Term Care Administration.*
Legal Help - The *Legal Services Project,* with over 200 volunteer attorneys and two full-time attorneys, provides basic estate planning such as wills, powers of attorney, and living wills. The

project also assists clients with public benefits applications and appeals, and with problems involving discrimination, insurance, and debt collection. Persons with HIV infection are welcome to telephone for general legal consultations.
Volunteers in Support Services receive orientation and basic training, and seminars on a variety of issues. All of the clinic's programs are coordinated with local government and community-based organizations.

AIDS: SELF-HELP

NATIONAL/STATE ORGANIZATIONS

NATIONAL ASSOCIATION OF PEOPLE WITH AIDS
2025 Eye Street, NW
Suite 415
Washington, DC 20006
TEL: 202-429-2856
Objectives: To create a national system of self-empowering programs.
Services: Promotes participation of local organizations in the provision of AIDS-related health care and social services; works to develop, implement, and maintain a national system of self-empowering programs adminstered by and for people with AIDS (acquired immune deficiency syndrome) and ARC (AIDS-Related Complex); participates in educational programs; provides traveling and other assistance; administers the *Amy Sloan Memorial Fund;* works with other organizations with similar goals; administers a computer bulletin board system (installed May 1990) for nationwide networking; publishes a bimonthly newsletter and other materials.
Publications: NAPWA News

PEOPLE WITH AIDS COALITION (*formerly People With AIDS***)**
263A West 19th Street
No. 125
New York, NY 10011
TEL: 212-627-1810
Objectives: To provide a local support network for persons with AIDS.
Services: Operates as a local support group for persons afflicted with AIDS; conducts public forums; maintains a drop-in lounge; works with social service agencies; operates a meal program and an apartment referral service; conducts medical research through the *Community Research Initiative;* operates a speakers bureau; publishes a monthly newsletter, a book on surviving with AIDS, and other materials.
Publications: PWA Coalition Newsline; Surviving with AIDS: Hints for the Newly Diagnosed

ARTS/CULTURAL ENRICHMENT

NATIONAL/STATE ORGANIZATIONS

AMERICAN COMMUNITY CULTURAL CENTER ASSOCIATION
19 Foothills Drive
Pompton Plains, NJ 07444
TEL: 201-835-2661
Objectives: To encourage people in all communities to develop and/or improve cultural centers in their own localities to enhance and service their own developing artists - regardless of economic status or geographic location, and without spending large sums of money.
Services: Offers programs, exhibitions and courses to schools, art galleries, libraries and other institutions that support its contention that cultural programs and activities can be mounted without spending large amounts of money, or requiring a lot of space; presents programs in topic areas such as *Culture Without Pain, Our Natural Earth - Touch and Tell* (an exhibit), *Write Right!,* etc.; maintains a special children's services division, with programs suitable as basic courses for elementary, junior high, and senior high schools, handicapped, juvenile and hobby groups (e.g., a course for 8- to 12-year-olds on stage production especially suited to children); offers a scholarship program; maintains a speakers' bureau, several specific committees (including *Education, International,* and *Theater)* and a training program; conducts programs in health and mental health centers, senior centers, hospitals, agencies, galleries and theaters; operates the *New Theater* in New Jersey; keeps current a basic book, *Culture Without Pain or Money,* which has been translated into several languages.
[The *American Community Cultural Center Association* was initiated by a grant awarded by the *National Endowment for the Arts.*]
Contact: Milli Janz
Publications: Culture Without Pain or Money
Founded: 1978

AMERICAN COUNCIL FOR THE ARTS
1285 Avenue of the Americas
Third Floor, Area M
New York, NY 10019
TEL: 212-245-4510
Objectives: To assure a central source of information for community and state arts councils, individual community leaders, and others interested in the arts.

Services: Provides education and special assistance to community and state arts councils, community leaders, libraries and universities, corporations and individuals; sponsors specialized seminars on topics such as management, arts fundraising, and public attitudes toward the arts; conducts research on all topics presented; maintains extensive library and provides clearinghouse services; publishes monthly reports and various magazines, handbooks, guides, directories and other publications.
Publications: Update; Horizon Magazine (column)
Founded: 1960

CENTER FOR ARTS INFORMATION
1285 Avenue of the Americas
Third Floor
New York, NY 10019
TEL: 212-977-2544
Objectives: To provide a central source of information for the nonprofit arts.
Services: Maintains clearinghouse and referral services for the nonprofit arts; places special emphasis in its materials and referrals on sources for services and funding for the arts; monitors 325 arts periodicals and houses a 6500-volume library; publishes various resource materials for artists and arts organizations, including a computerized catalog of its library; operates a telephone referral service.
Publications: Spaces; FYI Newsletter
Founded: 1976

NATIONAL ASSOCIATION FOR CREATIVE CHILDREN AND ADULTS
8080 Springvalley Drive
Cincinnati, OH 45236
TEL: 513-631-1777
Objectives: To foster appreciation of the arts as a means of nurturing creativity in people; to stimulate constructive means for use of increased leisure time and longer life span.
Services: Works to encourage appreciation of the arts as an avenue to creativity through its In-service Teacher Training Program, annual school visitation program, and workshops and consultation services in both school and the community at large; serves as a clearinghouse for commissioned works of art, music and literature; conducts research on creativity to benefit groups and individuals; sponsors an international library; publishes newsletter and quarterly journal, brochures and monographs, books, conference

proceedings, and other materials; holds workshops annually, always in June.
Publications: The Creative Child and Adult; NACCA Conference Proceedings; NACCA Invites You to Creativity
Founded: 1974

OFFICE FOR SPECIAL CONSTITUENCIES
National Endowment for the Arts
1100 Pennsylvania Avenue, NW
Washington, DC 20506
TEL: 202-682-5332 (Voice); 202-682-5496 (TTY)
Objectives: To conduct an advocacy program to make the arts more accessible to disabled people, older adults, veterans, and people in hospitals, nursing homes, mental institutions, and prisons.
Services: Provides information and technical assistance to artists, arts organizations, and consumers concerning accessible arts programs and other federal programs which support cultural activities; by means of cooperative agreements with other federal agencies, works to educate administrators and professionals who serve special constituencies about the benefits of arts programming for their respective constituents; supports model projects that demonstrate innovative ways to make the arts accessible to special constituencies; gives grantees assistance with federal regulations that concern special constituencies, including the Endowment's 504 Regulations.
Publications: Endowment 504 Regulations

INDIVIDUAL PROGRAM PROFILES

ARCHAEOLOGICAL VOLUNTEER PROGRAM
St. Augustine Historical Preservation Board
PO Box 1987
St. Augustine, FL 32085
TEL: 904-825-5033
For other sites, contact Volunteer Coordinator:
Crystal River State Archaeological Site (north of Tampa)
904-795-3817
San Luis Archaeological and Historic Site (Tallahassee)
904-487-3711
Purpose: To help "uncover" Florida's history through archaeological volunteers.
Sponsor: State of Florida
Contact: Volunteer Coordinator
Description: Observation areas are set up in each of Florida's archaeological sites - with a double purpose. They provide cultural experiences for individuals and families, and it attracts volunteers from the hundreds of observors. Sites include:
- **Crystal River State Archaeological Site** - located north of Tampa boasts discoveries at the site dating from 200 B.C. to 1400 A.D. There are burial grounds, a temple and a museum.
- **St. Augustine Historical Preservation Board** - located about two hours from Orlando is the site of one of the state's most productive archaeological projects. The area where the city is built has been occupied by Indians, Spaniards, British and finally Americans.
- **San Luis Archeological and Historic Site** - in Tallahassee, where there was a 17th-century mission on the site and excavation has produced an Indian council house and a Spanish church and village. The emphasis for volunteers here is public education programs, but some volunteers work on the digging teams.

Volunteers work seven days a week, year-round. According to one of the directors, "The work is hard, but you may uncover a piece of history."

WOODFORD COUNTY BICENTENNIAL CELEBRATION
City of Versailles
196 South Main
Versailles, KY 40383
TEL: 606-873-5436
Purpose: To provide a cultural experience to involve residents in celebrating Woodford County's bicentennial.
Sponsor: City of Versailles
Contact: JoAnn Gormley, Coordinator/producer
Description: Woodford County covers a 47-mile radius, and the 200 actors and at least as many volunteers came from all corners of the county to plan, develop, and execute the area's bicentennial. Over two years was devoted to mobilizing the event. The celebration centered around a pageant depicting the area over 200 years, and the events that resulted in founding it. The two-part program including the *Living Pageant Excursion,* a bus tour of the county with on-site skits and scenes, and the *Main Street Extravaganza,* a street theatre and other entertainment in downtown Versailles. While rewarding, volunteers also found joining the past two centuries to the present was confounding. One victory was finding an 18th century carriage for the event, but it was 10 feet high, where most garages are two feet lower than that. The firehouse came to the rescue there. The coordinator, still amazed at the scope of the celebration, said, "The whole thing started when I suggested a box lunch with everybody just being together for the bicentennial." The records for the first meeting still say, "JoAnn Gormley - box lunch to celebrate the bicentennial."
Founded: 1989

ARTS/CULTURAL ENRICHMENT: ADOPT-A-SCHOOL

INDIVIDUAL PROGRAM PROFILES

ADOPT-A-SCHOOL DANCE PROGRAM
National Dance Institute
599 Broadway
11th Floor
New York, NY 10012
TEL: 212-226-0083
Purpose: To provide dance classes to individual school children in New York City schools.
Sponsor: Corporations, foundations and individuals
Contact: Meryl Salzinger, Communications Director
Description: Founded in 1976 by a former principal dancer in the New York City Ballet, the National Dance Institute sends dance instructors to 28 schools in Manhattan, Brooklyn and Queens for an hour a week throughout the school year. In 1988, the Institute started a sponsorship program to help defray expenses of the program. By Fall 1989, eight of the schools its serves were "adopted" by individuals, corporations, and foundations. The Institute sponsor donates $5,000 a year for five years to a specific school, and the school raises another $4,000 each year from other sources.
In addition to the one-hour classes, donors sponsor dance performances throughout the year, including a final event in which children from all participating schools perform. Over 1,000 children danced in the closing performance of the 1988-89 school year, which was held at the Felt Forum in New York's Madison Square Garden.
To keep sponsors interested and involved with their adoptive schools, the Institute invites them to performances and to classes to observe the enthusiasm of the students. Also, donors and school

principals are included in "class pictures" and, at the end of the school year, the children in the dance classes write thank-you letters to the sponsors.

Although the Institute's Adopt-A-School program is similar to other arrangements in which individuals or businesses have "adopted" schools, it requires a much smaller donation, thus, according to the program's director, "bringing in a whole group of people who could not otherwise afford to help. For some individual donors, this is their first major gift." Also, corporations and foundations formerly donating less than $5,000 have managed to bring their donations up to the $5,000 level.

Founded: 1976

ARTS/CULTURAL ENRICHMENT: BUSINESS/INDUSTRY

NATIONAL/STATE ORGANIZATIONS

ARTS AND BUSINESS COUNCIL
130 East 40th Street
New York, NY 10016
TEL: 212-683-5555
Objectives: To foster corporate involvement with the arts on a local and national basis; to increase effectiveness of arts managements through corporate volunteers; to create working and mutually-beneficial arts-business partnerships.
Services: Establishes and administers arts programs to benefit both business and arts communities; provides services by specially-trained business executives to assist in problem solving for arts organizations; coordinates national network of business volunteer programs to aid arts managers (e.g., Arts Fare, Business Volunteers for the Arts); maintains extensive data bank and library; conducts advisory service in cable and electronic media; sponsors annual awards program for corporate service to the arts and arts service to the community; aids individual artists through part time job programs.
Publications: Winterfare; ABC Newsletter
Founded: 1973

BUSINESS COMMITTEE FOR THE ARTS
1775 Broadway, Suite 510
New York, NY 10019
TEL: 212-664-0600
Objectives: To encourage all businesses throughout the United States to support the arts; to offer advice to businesses that want to begin supporting the arts; to counsel businesses interested in expanding existing art support programs; to assist businesses interested in developing special arts support projects such as corporate art collecting, a matching gifts program for the arts, museum sponsorship and many other partnerships between business and the arts; to provide the business community and the public with information and statistics about business support to the arts; to encourage communication and cooperation between business, government agencies, foundations and private sector groups interested in supporting the arts; to create public awareness of business support to the arts.
Services: Presents conferences, seminars and workshops for business leaders throughout the United States to increase business support to the arts and to stimulate partnerships between business and the arts; compiles information and statistics about business support to the arts in the United States, the specific needs of American arts organizations, trends in business support to the arts and facts about government and private sector support to the arts; conducts a public service advertising compaign to encourage new

and increased business support to the arts; publishes a newsletter, brochures and policy papers to encourage and to assist business support to the arts; honors corporations for their outstanding efforts to support the arts through the annual BCA Business in the Arts Awards jointly sponsored with Forbes Magazine; presents an annual Award to the arts organization that has done the most to stimulate an outstanding partnership between business and the arts; advocates the development of state and community associations to develop business support to the arts; cooperates with government agencies, foundations and private sector groups interested in supporting the arts; invites prominent business leaders to speak at national gatherings and conventions about business support to the arts.
Publications: BCA News; Matching Gift Programs/Arts
Founded: 1967

ARTS/CULTURAL ENRICHMENT: CHILDREN/YOUTH

INDIVIDUAL PROGRAM PROFILES

ART FOR KIDS' SAKE
SEE RECIPIENTS: CHILDREN/YOUTH - ARTS

BUT I'M DIFFERENT...
SEE TEENAGE PREGNANCY/PARENTING

SENIORS AND CHILDREN TOGETHER
SEE DAY CARE/HEAD START: ARTS

ARTS/CULTURAL ENRICHMENT: CRAFTS

NATIONAL/STATE ORGANIZATIONS

AMERICAN CRAFT COUNCIL
40 West 53rd Street
New York, NY 10019
TEL: 212-956-3535
Objectives: To stimulate public awareness and appreciation of the work of American craftsmen.
Services: Provides consultation services in craft areas including ceramic, glass, metal, textiles and wood; presents museum exhibitions in regional programs; maintains American Craft Museum and a 3700-volume library on American crafts, which includes biographical information on some craftsmen; develops visual aids; publishes bimonthly magazine, museum exhibit catalogs, bibliographies, directories and manuals.
Publications: American Craft
Founded: 1943

INDIAN ARTS AND CRAFTS BOARD
SEE ARTS/CULTURAL ENRICHMENT: ETHNIC GROUPS

THE NAMES PROJECT/AIDS MEMORIAL QUILT
SEE AIDS: COMMUNICATIONS & PR

TRAINING PROGRAMS

THE QUILT AND AIDS EDUCATION
SEE AIDS: EDUCATION

INDIVIDUAL PROGRAM PROFILES

BOISE PEACE QUILT PROJECT
SEE CIVIC AFFAIRS: PEACE

SCHOOLMATE HANDICRAFT VOLUNTEERS
Schoolmate Program
304 Bay Shore Avenue
Mobile, AL 36607
TEL: 205-478-RSVP (7787)
Purpose: To provide arts and crafts instruction to children in an after-school care program.
Sponsor: Retired Senior Volunteer Program
Contact: Volunteer Coordinator
Description: Recognizing that today's youngsters fail to learn many skills their grandparents took for granted, RSVP (Retired Senior Volunteer Program) volunteers teamed up with the *Young Women's Christian Association of Mobile* to arrange for seniors to share their talents with youngsters in the after-school *Schoolmate Program.* Some of the older volunteers are handicapped, giving them an opportunity to provide more than just craft skills to the children. One handicapped volunteer is quick to tell them, "Handicaps don't hold you back. You just learn to do things differently."
The Schoolmate program bridges the gap between the end of the school day and the end of parents' or guardians' business day. The children have access to all of the school's sports equipment, and the library facilities. Although games are coached and all activities supervised, the children make their own decisions as to which activity to choose for participation. Outside programs such as the arts and crafts programs provided by senior volunteers are scheduled to help maintain the interest of the more active children who run the gamut of available regular activities and need something new and different.
Since participation in the program is voluntary, it is a challenge to keep the children interested enough so that they will not become "latchkey children," according to one director of the program. One fact not considered in setting up the crafts program was the benefit to the volunteers themselves, often widows who use handicrafts as a way to stay active and helpful to the rest of the world. One volunteer who is an amputee said, "I won't tell you it was easy. For a while, I was very depressed." The widow first became a volunteer with the *Rotary Club* and then got involved in volunteering to share her craft skills. "It made me feel good. The children are so responsive ... they really get excited about learning. And it's fun to share what you know."
Although the program was begun as a part of *Older Americans Volunteer Month* in June 1989, it has become a regular part of the *Schoolmate* schedule.

SENIOR CRAFTSMAN SHOWCASE*
2647 Connecticut Avenue, NW
Washington, DC 20008
TEL: 202-265-3611
Purpose: To put senior citizens back to work through crafts.
Sponsor: District of Columbia Office on Aging; District of Columbia Department of Recreation
Contact: Dorayne Lyons, Project Director
Description: Created in 1970 as a joint project of two DC Offices (Aging and Recreation), the Senior Craftsman Showcase was the first project of its kind in the country. Its primary purpose was to provide an income for senior citizens using talents and skills they already possessed, but also it offers the public a place to purchase handmade items seldom found in the city.
The salespeople in the shop are volunteers, mainly senior citizens. The items, taken on consignment, are priced on the basis of what the craftsman expects to receive, plus 35 percent for the store's overhead. Though they have admittedly taken on some items to prevent bruised feelings, nothing is lost because of the consignment agreement. In addition to expected items such as nylon net cleanser covers and handpainted toothbrush holders, some of the unique handmade treasures are crewel and bargello pillows, Easter bunnies and chickens in wool and other fabrics, little-girl jumpers, finely-stitched quilts, holiday decorations of all kinds, and hand-made baby blankets and dolls.
The craftspeople in the shop sometimes are not as interested in their financial gain as in the creative process. The oldest craftsman is 101 and makes quilts from whatever fabrics are available to her. A 62-year-old retired government employee stocks the shop with her handmade dolls. A few consignors who have moved away still send in their crafts for extra pocket money. The shop is stocked with crafts from over 700 consignors over age 60.
Many talents are examples of dying arts - skills sometimes brought over from other countries. Organizations working with the aging encourage senior craftsmen to use their own special skills and channel them into highly marketable merchandise by working with the Showcase. The significant side benefit from this venture is the good feeling the senior craftsman gets when someone puts out money for his/her work. For some it was a welcome change from sitting in a chair doing nothing to creating something that others enjoy. Some were plying their craft for their own amusement, but finding that storage in the home was a problem.
Founded: 1970

YOUNG WINGS USA*
SEE EDUCATION: CURRICULUM ENRICHMENT

ARTS/CULTURAL ENRICHMENT: ETHNIC GROUPS

NATIONAL/STATE ORGANIZATIONS

INDIAN ARTS AND CRAFTS BOARD
US/DoI - Bureau of Indian Affairs
Main Interior Building
Room 4004
Washington, DC 20240
TEL: 202-208-3773
Objectives: To promote the development of American Indian and Alaska Native arts and crafts.
Services: Provides business and personal professional advice, information, fundraising assistance, and promotion to Indian artists and craftsmen and their cultural organizations; operates a coordinated system of three regional museums located in reservation areas; annually answers over 10,000 written and telephone inquiries from the public.
Sponsor: US/DoI - Department of the Interior
Publications: Indian/Eskimo/Aleut Businesses; General Information on IACB

INFORMATION CENTER ON CHILDREN'S CULTURES*
U.S. Committee for United Nations Children's Fund
331 East 38th Street
New York, NY 10016
TEL: 212-686-5522

Objectives: To provide educational and cultural materials to children from preschool to 14 years of age; to answer questions from the public regarding the world's children.
Services: Works with volunteers, parents, librarians, editors, teachers, the media, and the children themselves regarding the various, yet interrelated customs and activities of the children of the world; recommends books and other materials based on specific requests (a free service); covers intercultural topics including arts, crafts, music, holidays, games, family life, problems, customs; offers children's programs at the Center; develops new techniques to satisfy children's natural curiosity about other nations; maintains collection of toys, games, musical instruments, films, filmstrips, slide sets, descriptions of its children's programs, and other materials (free and for sale).
Contact: Librarian/Historian
Publications: News of the World's Children
Founded: 1967

INTERNATIONAL CULTURAL CENTERS FOR YOUTH
PO Box 20336
Columbus Circle Station
New York, NY 10023
TEL: 212-581-2279
Objectives: To provide opportunities in music and art for young people who would otherwise be deprived of the privilege of study; to provide educational activities related to youth and the arts.
Services: Sponsors conferences for youth, many of whom would otherwise be deprived of the privilege of study in the fields of music and arts; combines its research center with a learning environment to help promote interfaith, global understanding and unity through education in music, dance, literature, art, theatre and films; rents "Visions of Peace in Painting" exhibit containing 67 paintings by children and a filmstrip; honors cultural contributions of youth; maintains International Culture Center for Youth; continually conducts research and produces filmstrips and other materials to provide information on its programs.
Publications: ICCY Newsletter
Founded: 1941

INDIVIDUAL PROGRAM PROFILES

GREEK FESTIVAL
SEE ARTS/CULTURAL ENRICHMENT: FESTIVALS

ARTS/CULTURAL ENRICHMENT: EXHIBITS

NATIONAL/STATE ORGANIZATIONS

AMERICAN CRAFT COUNCIL
SEE ARTS/CULTURAL ENRICHMENT: CRAFTS

AMERICAN FEDERATION OF ARTS
41 East 65th Street
New York, NY 10021
TEL: 212-988-7700
Objectives: To work toward spreading enjoyment of the work of many periods and cultures in areas of painting, sculpture, design, architecture, crafts, etc.
Services: Originates traveling exhibits of art and film programs and makes them available to art centers, university and small rural art galleries, museums and other cultural programs; assists centers in

developing resources; operates the Museum Management Institute; mounts conferences, workshops, and other training events for museum professionals; offers reduced-rate fine arts insurance and air transportation programs; sponsors annual arts competitions; publishes free information on its more than 20 shows.
Publications: AFA Newsletter; Program and Exhibit Catalog
Founded: 1909

NATIONAL GALLERY OF ART EXTENSION PROGRAMS
National Gallery of Art
Washington, DC 20565
TEL: 202-842-6273; 202-842-6263
Objectives: To develop awareness in the visual arts by making the Gallery's collections accessible to everyone, no matter how far away from the Gallery they may live.
Services: Provides broad access to the resources of the National Gallery through free-loan audiovisual programs involving both the permanent collections and the special exhibitions; provides free (except for return postage) color slide programs, motion pictures, videocassettes, and other audiovisual materials to organized groups and clubs as well as education institutions and libraries; publishes free descriptive catalog describing exhibits and audiovisual programs and including order forms.
Contact: Ruth R. Perlin
Publications: Extension Programs

PEACE MUSEUM
SEE CIVIC AFFAIRS: PEACE

SMITHSONIAN INSTITUTION TRAVELING EXHIBITION SERVICE
Smithsonian Institution
Office of Museum Programs
Washington, DC 20560
TEL: 202-357-3168
Objectives: To provide a public service by the circulation of exhibits on a wide range of subjects throughout the U.S. and abroad.
Services: Provides to any group that meets space and care requirements a choice of a number of exhibits, some with supplementary educational materials and publications; offers exhibits for four- or six- week periods, with options for extensions if schedule permits; requires exhibitor to pay outgoing transportation costs and protection insurance, and to provide the Smithsonian Institution with press releases and copies or information about other publicity generated by the exhibits; publishes annual catalog and individual fact sheets and listings on specific exhibits.
Publications: Update

INDIVIDUAL PROGRAM PROFILES

ART AGAINST AIDS EXHIBIT
Art Against AIDS
406 Seventh Street, NW
Third Floor
Washington, DC 20004
TEL: 202-347-1033
Purpose: To raise funds for AIDS research and local AIDS programs.
Contact: Kevin Williams, Assistant Director
Description: In May 1990, a group of prominent contemporary artists provided artwork for a local fundraiser to assist in AIDS research, and local AIDS efforts to provide education materials and programs for the community, and/or care for AIDS patients. In addition to the artists, support comes from First Lady Barbara Bush (honorary chairperson), celebrities including Elizabeth

Taylor, half of the members of the Senate, and Leonard Marx, who donated the space for the exhibit. In addition more than 130 local artists have contributed works.

The exhibition and sale are part of a campaign that involves the national organization, *American Foundation for AIDS Research (AmFar)*, with local AIDS program leaders to benefit the local host organization (50%), continuing *AmFar* research programs, and other local AIDS programs needing assistance across the country. Beneficiaries in the Washington, DC area are *Walt Whitman Clinic, Best Friends, Clinical Trials Expanded Access Project, DC Coalition of Black Gay Men and Women, Grandma's House, Us Helping Us*, and *St. Francis Center.*

This national partnership has proven to be an excellent way to "spread the wealth" and provide opportunities at the local level where resources are scarce or nonexistent. The fundraising effort has proven beneficial to all, and the substance of the programs offered to the community in return for their generosity have been both cultural and educational. Within the first two weeks of the show, sales reached $300,000.

Prices vary widely. One work sold for $100,000, with others a twentieth of that amount. Some are in the $15,000-$35,000 price range, while others are priced at a small fraction of those figures. Combined with a gala fundraising dinner at the *National Building Museum* during the last week of the exhibit, the goal for the program is $800,000.

Among artists who contributed works for the exhibit program are Louise Bourgeois, Jasper Johns, Cindy Sherman and Christo. The work of the local contributing artists has been noted as very impressive. According to one visitor to the exhibit, a *Washington Post* staff writer, "It rarely suggests fury, the despair of the dying or the anger of AIDS activists. Instead, its spirit is compassionate, collegial, inclusive."

ARTS/CULTURAL ENRICHMENT: FESTIVALS

TRAINING PROGRAMS

THE DEAF WAY
Gallaudet College
800 Florida Avenue, NE
Washington, DC 20002
TEL: 202-651-5488
FAX: 202-651-5489
Credit: Inquire
Sponsor: Gallaudet College
Contact: Jane Norman, Chairman
Description: Called "the international celebration of deaf culture," a 1989 festival/forum sponsored by Gallaudet University and held on its campuses, attracted both deaf and non-deaf volunteers, citizen and organizational advocates, and others from around the world. Gallaudet is the only liberal arts college for the deaf in the world, and is considered by many to be the "world leader in all aspects of deafness." *The Deaf Way* is both a showcase for deaf talent and a forum for the exchange of ideas among deaf people. It is also a celebration of the pride that enabled students at the university to bring a deaf President to Gallaudet in 1988.

An estimated 600 deaf entertainers participated in more than 40 festival performances. They included the Japan Theatre of the Deaf, the International Visual Theatre of France, the London Deaf Comedians, the National Theatre of the Deaf of the US, the American Dance Theatre of the Deaf, the Greek Theatre of the Deaf, the Moscow Theater of Mime, and the deaf actress who received an Academy Award for her role in "Children of a Lesser God."

The festival features artwork by deaf artists, and unveiled a 30-foot mural containing bright figures representing the many moods of deaf people and their culture. The mural will be permanently housed at the university. The other notable piece of art is the sculpture of hands, indicating that "Our hands are our whole life," according to the festival chairman.

The serious side of the gathering focused on a range of research areas and issues, such as:

- the human rights of deaf people
- the special challenges of adults who become deaf late in life
- the role of sign language in deaf culture
- the oppression of deaf people
- deafness as a political issue

One controversial issue was the use of sign language in the education of deaf children, with leading advocates preferring that deaf children learn sign language first, and then use the signs to learn English. Although gaining support in recent years, this method is still being vigorously opposed by some educators.

More than 225 sign language interpreters who can use both American Sign Language and Gestuno, an international group of signs, volunteered to help interpret the more than 500 events that are part of *The Deaf Way*. An additional 50 voice interpreters worked in Spanish, French and English.

One purpose of the forum/festival was to provide a sharp contrast with other deaf programs which emphasize "the disability of deafness, or how to fix the hearing loss." The Gallaudet event has a special significance for deaf people, since it is designed to show their accomplishments, and not "what to do to help the poor deaf people." According to the university's first deaf president, "It's a new era for deaf people."

INDIVIDUAL PROGRAM PROFILES

BAROQUE MUSIC FESTIVAL OF CORONA DEL MAR
PO Box 838
Corona del Mar, CA 92625
TEL: 714-549-7175
Purpose: To bring a cultural experience to the community through an orchestra and organ program of antique music.
Contact: Burton Karson, Founder
Description: The *Baroque Music Festival's* administrators, bookkeepers and publicists are volunteers. Ticket-takers and ushers are members of the board of directors. The stage hands are volunteers. Even the conductor - who is also the founder - donates his services. He states, "The fact that the group is run by volunteers is the secret of its success."

Although the festival employs union musicians and paid singers, it has resisted a growing trend toward replacing volunteers with paid, professional staff. Volunteers perform all administrative functions, including fund-raising. This assures that the people involved with the orchestra are there because they enjoy it.

The festival is distinguished by unusual programming. The director spent several sabbaticals in ancient libraries in Europe seeking music that history has overlooked. A typical program includes works that have not been heard for hundreds of years juxtaposed with music by more familiar Baroque composers. Much of the ancient works are written in the composer's hand. The audience is particularly excited when they are told that a piece of music 300 years old will be heard for the first time.

Because of its unique programming and the volunteer nature of the festival, the festival has always ended its seasons in the black. For this reason, the director resists hiring fund-raising or marketing professionals, pointing out that the volunteers have brought the program through nine years. Citing the dedication and success of the volunteers, the director says, "We are all doing this because we love doing it. What other reason is there? I don't like situations were the arts exist in order to serve the superstructure that supports the arts. The arts have to come first."

CITY SPIRIT CULTURAL ARTS FESTIVAL
Cultural Arts Commission
161 Newkirk Avenue
Jersey City, NJ 07302
TEL: 201-714-2193
Purpose: To get the city's ethnic groups together in a nonpolitical way.
Sponsor: Jersey City Government
Contact: Morris Pesin, Chairman
Description: Fifteen nationality groups competed for the public's appetite and attention during the city's annual summer cultural arts festival, subtitled *Jersey City Living Together in Harmony.* Held at spacious Liberty State Park, volunteers from the many groups displayed arts and crafts, danced in colorful costumes, and passed out samples of foods unique to their cultures.
Entertainment was all volunteer, and included puppet shows for children, rock groups for teenagers, as well as weightlifting, photo sittings, swimming, and other activities of interest to adults and families. One activity involved volunteers bicycling across the George Washington Bridge to raise money for the *American Cancer Society.*
It was also a time for groups like the U.S. Immigration and Naturalization Service, various senior citizens programs, and other service providers to distribute literature to remind people of the services available to them.
The festival is deliberately planned a few days before an election to try to soften the hard feelings among groups that always follows an election. Civic leaders feel that the excitement of being "just one big happy family" lingers and helps to bring the city back to normal following "Election Tuesday."
While more than 15,000 people visited the festival at Liberty State Park, other festivals were held simultaneously across the state featuring ethnic groups unique to those areas.

FESTIVAL
Arts Council of Greater Grand Rapids
161 Ottawa Avenue, NW
Grand Rapids, MI 49503
TEL: 616-459-2787
Purpose: To celebrate art through exhibits of artists' works, preparation of ethnic foods, and other cultural experiences.
Sponsor: Arts Council of Greater Grand Rapids
Contact: David T. Mix, President
Description: In 1969 a few volunteers from the *Arts Council of Greater Grand Rapids* established downtown Grand Rapids' first all-arts festival. Initially it was planned as a single event to celebrate the completion of Alexander Calder's *La Grande Vitesse* and to focus attention on the arts. Simply called *Festival 1970,* the 15 volunteers appointed co-chairmen, enlisted performers, arranged for visual arts and set in motion a tradition now in its twentieth year. For that first event the impromptu committee even researched weather for the previous 12 years to assure good Festival sunshine. And, alongside of the fine arts, the youth symphony orchestra and other classical events, was a long-haired pop group.
The 1989 Festival boasted a 200-member volunteer Festival Committee and a total of 15,000 volunteers. Exhibitors and performers numbering in the hundreds in the early years now number in the thousands. Volunteers did everything from managing to handling production and performing to the final clean-up. They worked as individuals, as teams, and in groups. Although hot dogs and other usual fare was offered, the Committee was determined to take advantage of the many different ethnic groups in the area to provide various ethnic foods. One group of 50 church volunteers prepared 2,000 pork shish kebabs, and almost immediately had to embark on the preparation of 4,000 more. A Greek Orthodox church introduced the Greek specialty, souvlaki, previously unknown to most residents. Many cultural groups introduced the dances of their countries of origin,

and other activities of cross-cultural interest. It was a celebration of the community itself as well as the works of the artists.
Crowds were expected to top 500,000 in 1989, to continue the constant growth since the 1970 hallmark festival with an attendance of 7,000. In 1970, 11 artists in three basic categories won awards. In 1989 dozens won cash awards in at least 16 categories. The five food booths in 1970 reached 35 in 1989. Performers have reached the hundreds in areas of visual arts ranging from sculpture to video. And, as noted above, the first festival committee of 15 has reached 200, with a total of 15,000 volunteers.
Funds earned from the festival have a direct impact on the Art Council's *Combined Arts Campaign,* which started in 1972. Not every year's festival makes a profit, but the vast majority of net income always went to the campaign. The 1983 contribution of $60,000 to the campaign was the highest, but with the festival growing each year, the committee saw a need for a reserve fund after that and now contributions to the campaign and the fund are roughly equal each year. Some years, contributions need to be used to balance the books. However, organizers say the festival's success cannot be judged by a bottom line.
A side benefit of the festival is that entire families volunteer, in some cases producing second- and third-generation participants. One 24-year-old volunteer considers himself a "festival brat," since he has volunteered with his family since junior high days. He said, "At first they find you hanging around and say 'come on, you can work on this, too.' After a while it just gets to be a lot of fun."
Founded: 1970

GREEK FESTIVAL
Sts. Constantine & Helen Greek Orthodox Cathedral
30 Malvern Avenue
Richmond, VA 23221
TEL: 804-355-3687
Purpose: To introduce area residents to authentic Greek food and other cultural experiences.
Contact: John G. Halages, Festival Chairman
Description: Volunteer cooks work for months making desserts and organizing preparations to feed some 65,000 people who come to the *Greek Festival* to learn about Greek culture. The four-day event provides the flavor and old-world culture of Greece in a seemingly endless spread of Greek specialties. With today's cholesterol consciousness, cooks introduced foods that were authentic, yet healthful, according to one of the volunteer cooks. Repeat attendees often seek out their favorite choices from years past, and first-time festivalgoers are given a briefing on the preparation and ingredients of the Greek dishes. Proceeds from the festival benefit the *Virginia Head Injury Foundation, Virginia Health Center,* and the *Emergency Shelter.*
In addition to food, the festival features Greek music, costumed folk dancers, cathedral tours, and film lectures. Also available is a Greek boutique with Oriental rugs, imported jewelry, arts, crafts and icons. For those who enjoyed a specific authentic Greek food item, a cookbook, *Cherished Greek Recipes,* is made available at the festival or, if copies are depleted, by mail after the event.
All proceeds go to the three targeted charities, and all expenditures by visitors are tax-deductible.

INTERNATIONAL VERY SPECIAL ARTS FESTIVAL
Very Special Arts
John F. Kennedy Center
Education Office
Washington, DC 20566
TEL: 202-662-8899
Purpose: To bring together disabled artists from every state in the U.S. and other countries to display and celebrate their work.
Sponsor: Very Special Arts
Contact: Ron Miziker

Description: More than 1,000 disabled artists representing every state in the U.S. and some 40 foreign countries attended workshops and receptions in Washington, DC, for what one artist described as "one big artistic party." The five-day *International Very Special Arts Festival* began with a processional including two representatives from each state and foreign country. In addition to sharing their creative talents in two-hour sessions, they attended *Very Special Arts* workshops designed to encourage greater participation in the mainstream of the art profession, and recognize the value of their work. Also, participants were honored at a dinner at the Washington Harbor, and attended numerous receptions, including one on the White House lawn, and a networking opportunity with fellow artists from around the world. At the White House reception, celebrity artists met with the participants and discussed their shared interests.

MORRO BAY HARBOR FESTIVAL
PO Box 1869
Morro Bay, CA 93443
TEL: 805-772-1155
TOLL FREE: 800-231-0592
Purpose: To bring together fishermen, civic and community groups, marine-related enterprises, small business, corporations, artisans, environmental organizations and individual citizens to focus public awareness on the special value of Morro Bay's harbor and environs.
Sponsor: California Park and Recreation Society
Contact: Galen Ricard
Description: The *Morro Bay Harbor Festival* celebrates one of the few natural harbors and active fishing villages on the west coast by showcasing seafood, the fishing industry, and the diversity of Morro Bay marine life and coastal lifestyles. The main event, the *Seafood Faire,* features a bounty of seafood specialties for all ages and lifestyles, plus fresh fish displays, filleting demonstrations and a flotilla of "see-worthy" events and activities.
Through its *Festival Volunteer Program,* Morro Bay Harbor Festival has as its continuing goal the support of community projects, charitable groups and service organizations. The majority of proceeds from the Festival are given to those community groups who have actively participated in the event through a commitment of volunteer time and labor, with awards commensurate with the level of the groups' respective involvement. In 1989, over $11,000 was awarded to 36 nonprofit and community service groups, making the Harbor Festival one of the most successful community fundraising vehicles on the Central Coast.
The Festival also features over 200 exhibits, including a *Farmers' Market,* a Port of Call Expo (commercial exhibitors), an arts and crafts show, community displays, and a variety of live entertainment. Events and activities range from a fishing derby and *Coast Guard* open house to *Cal Poly's* rowing regatta, kayaking demonstrations, and canoeing. The festival draws between 20,000 and 25,000 visitors, representing a cross-section of Californians.
The *California Park and Recreation Society* recognized *Morro Bay Harbor Festival, Inc.* for bring together the community while serving as a major fund raising vehicle for community service clubs, organizations and programs through its *Festival Volunteer Program.* As of spring 1990, almost $30,000 had been contributed to the community programs with proceeds from its three annual events.

NOCHE CUBANA (CUBAN NIGHT)
Cuban American Association of Austin
PO Box 1603
Austin, TX 78767
TEL: 512-442-0511
Purpose: To promote the history and culture of Cuban Americans.
Contact: Dr. Maria de J. Paez de Ruiz, President

Description: Noche Cubana is a celebration to recognize the beginning of Cuba's fight for independence from Spain and the beginning of the Cuban Republic on May 20, 1902. It is developed and hosted by the *Cuban American Association of Austin.* A proclamation from the Governor recognized the anniversary during the celebration and made it an official state event. More than 50 members of the all-volunteer group helped to make it as traditional as possible with special Cuban delicacies and a piano recital by a Cuban artist, who is also the treasurer of the Association, among other Cuban presentations and performances. Another activity of the Association is a regular tribute to *Our Lady of Charity,* the patroness of Cuba, with a Mass at *Our Lady of Guadalupe Church.*
The organization, which was formed as the *Cuban Committee* following an exodus of Cubans during the Mariel Boatlift in 1980, also assists Hispanics with educational and other problems.
Founded: 1980

SUMMERFEST ART FAIRE
SEE RECIPIENTS: OLDER PERSON - HEALTH

VALENTINE SCHOOL ART SHOW
San Marino Schools
1665 West Drive
San Marino, CA 91108
TEL: 818-289-3691
Purpose: To assure that children are not "shortchanged" in the area of arts and cultural enrichment.
Sponsor: Parent-Teachers Association (PTA)
Contact: Cindy Roe, PTA
Description: With the rallying slogan, *Art Is Not Caught, It Must Be Taught,* 50 parents of children in public schools in San Marino embarked on a program to help children learn more about art. Because of school budget cuts that came from Sacramento, things thought of as frill courses had been eliminated. With one of the parents an art history major, and 49 others from the PTA ready for assignments, a year-long program was approved by the school board and conducted in the schools. Grade-by-grade, the program included:
- **Kindergarten** - studied line, looking at pictures by Klee, Picasso, Miro and Mondrian. Then they painted their own pictures.
- **First Grade** - studied shapes, real and abstract, illustrated by the works of Rousseau, Cezanne and Matisse.
- **Second Grade** - studied color, and how it changes the way we feel about a picture, using works of Reynolds, Cassatt, Rothko, Seurat and Gainsborough.
- **Third Grade** - studied texture, both visual and tactile, using knobby pictures and satin smooth ones inspired by Van Gogh, Pollock, Monet, Rembrandt and the Cluny tapestries.
- **Fourth Grade** - studied form in sculpture and architecture - held on the lawn with the "biggest exercise in mud pie making in the land" using Rodin and Michelangelo as inspiration.
- **Fifth Grade** - combined all of the elements in their work and learned about Stuart, Wyeth, Hopper and Roesen.
The windup of the year's work was the *Valentine School Art Show.* Every child in school had at least one picture in the exhibition. Volunteers took the works home and mounted them on bright construction paper, and mounted corkboard for the displays. They designed and decorated the entrance to the exhibit like a Grecian portico to give the kids a sense of a real art museum.
Fundraising for the exhibit consisted of the sale of packets of note paper printed with pictures made by the young artists. Three pictures were chosen for this honor. Also used for fundraising was an apron wildly speckled and sprayed a la some of Pollock's work. Across the top it says, "You've got to have art."
Support from the principal of the school included miraculously managing all year to keep the art display room off limits, even on

rainy days when the children are confined inside and find ways to roam around. The excitement level of the children remained at the "explosion point" all year, waiting for class every week on the door sill, and having to be "scooted out" when class was over. The same group of parents painted the entire outside of the school in 1987. In their words, "We are determined that our children will not be shortchanged!"

YOUNG AUTHORS' FAIRE
Guadalupe Elementary School
6044 Vera Cruz Drive
San Jose, CA 95120
TEL: 408-268-1030
Purpose: To acknowledge children's writing and creativity.
Sponsor: Guadalupe School
Contact: Karen Mullaly, Principal
Description: Recognizing that writing is the basis for everything pupils do in school, a group of volunteer parents, the school Principal, and several teachers stage a *Young Authors'Faire* each year for children from kindergarten through fifth grade.
The children write both individually and as a class, and both compositions and stories that rhyme. They illustrate their works and bind them with Batik book covers and construction paper, some creatively cut into the shape of the animal star of the story. The fourth graders created, on a computer, their own newspapers, and reported on the California Gold Rush. The children are encouraged to acknowledge and appreciate their classmates' work. The *Faire* has served as an excellent forerunner for a new literature-based language arts program incorporated into the school system shortly after the 1989 *Faire.* According to the principal, "It's a new way of using language arts; a whole-language approach in which reading, writing, listening and speaking are all integrated, with lots more reading and greater listening and vocabulary."
Also at the *Faire* was a display of the children's art, put together by the *Art Vistas Docents,* a group of volunteer parents who go into the classroom to give the students an appreciation, understanding and love of art. These works included painting, paper collages, wood burning, "bottle people" creations, and mixed media. There was also a "blacklight" room that highlighted the kindergartners' use of fluorescent paints.
A side benefit from the writing, according to a volunteer, is the fact that the children reveal sides of themselves that do not surface otherwise, making it easier to get to know them and serve their best interests. "But the bottom line," she adds, "is that the children love to write and create, and a portion of this enjoyment carries over to the other more serious subjects."

ARTS/CULTURAL ENRICHMENT: FUNDING

NATIONAL/STATE ORGANIZATIONS

BREAD AND ROSES
SEE ARTS/CULTURAL ENRICHMENT: MUSIC/DANCE/THEATRE

ARTS/CULTURAL ENRICHMENT: HANDICAPPED

INDIVIDUAL PROGRAM PROFILES

INTERNATIONAL VERY SPECIAL ARTS FESTIVAL
SEE ARTS/CULTURAL ENRICHMENT: FESTIVALS

ARTS/CULTURAL ENRICHMENT: HISTORY/MUSEUMS

NATIONAL/STATE ORGANIZATIONS

NATIONAL GALLERY OF ART EXTENSION PROGRAMS
SEE ARTS/CULTURAL ENRICHMENT: EXHIBITS

PEACE MUSEUM
SEE CIVIC AFFAIRS: PEACE

SMITHSONIAN INSTITUTION TRAVELING EXHIBITION SERVICE
SEE ARTS/CULTURAL ENRICHMENT: EXHIBITS

YARNS OF YESTERYEAR PROJECT
University of Wisconsin
Extension Service
610 Langdon Street, Room 722
Madison, WI 53706
TEL: 608-263-2954; 608-263-6320
Objectives: To involve older citizens in a leisure time activity that enables them to make a cultural contribution.
Services: Enlists older citizens to write reminiscences of their early lives; publishes annual historical/cultural collections of these writings; involves families, senior centers, nursing homes, retirement centers, radio stations, and interested individuals; publishes the collection *We Were Children Then,* and a booklet, *How to Organize and Promote a Reminiscence Writing Contest;* has home study course in reminiscence writing.
Publications: We Were Children Then; Reminiscence Writing Contest
Founded: 1974

TRAINING PROGRAMS

DOCENT EDUCATION WORKSHOP
Philadelphia Zoo
Docent Council of Philadelphia
34th Street and Girard Avenue
Philadelphia, PA 19104
TEL: 215-243-1100/Ext. 317
Credit: Inquire
Sponsor: Docent Council of the Zoological Society of Philadelphia
Contact: Mickey Magid, President
Description: Recognizing the growing need for docent organizations to function better not only within their institutions, but within the volunteer world in general, the Docent Council of the Philadelphia Zoo developed a workshop to help meet this need.
Leaders of docent-type organizations in zoos, aquaria, nature

centers, museums, and historical societies in the Mid-Atlantic states were invited, and 45 participants from five states (representing all of the types mentioned above) came together to share experiences and concerns. The principal trainer came from the volunteer training field in general (Susan J. Ellis) rather than the specific docent field to maximize the opportunity to develop the skills and attitudes needed to interface with the broad volunteer community.

In this first workshop, the facilitator focused on two key issues:
- Volunteer Burn-Out
- Volunteer/Salaried Staff Relations

Both topics led to further discussion of related issues, including retaining volunteers, career ladders for volunteers, management and recognition problems, and others.

Workshop designers requested that the docent organizations send two participants including the staff person most closely involved with the organization (Coordinator of Volunteer Services, Curator of Education, etc.) to increase implementation of ideas "back at the farm." In addition to the ideas resulting from the sessions, training materials were provided for use at the workshop and later at home sites.

In the course of the workshop, participants organized an informal network in order to exchange newsletters, program information, sample forms, etc. Future workshops were discussed for presentation in other cities in the region.

IMPROVING MUSEUM VOLUNTEER PERFORMANCE
University of Delaware
Wilcastle Center
2800 Pennsylvania Avenue
Wilmington, DE 19899
TEL: 302-738-8155
Credit: CEUs
Sponsor: University of Delaware
Contact: Jacob Haber
Description: Designed to extend and enhance job skills related to the volunteer coordinator and/or volunteer supervisor, this two-day program provides opportunities for participant discussion in both large and small groups. Panel discussions and workshops as well as informal discussions provide variety in exploring the following topics:

- **Volunteers in the Museum: Integration or Segregation** - An examination of the role of volunteers and their responsibilities in the long-range planning process. Addresses the question of whether volunteers are a segregated audience for the museum or an integrated form of staff assistance.
- **Volunteers Wanted: Recruiting for the 80's** - A panel discussion considering cost factors, methodology, image projection, advertising, promotion, and how recruiting of museum volunteers parallels methodology used in industry.
- **Skills Analysis Techniques for Improved Volunteer Training** - A workshop on how to assess training and follow through by establishing and agreeing on learning goals; conducting learning events through lectures, demonstrations, films, guest speakers and field trips; determining if learning has taken place.
- **Potentials and Limitations in Volunteer Supervision** - A workshop on the importance of a strong supervision program: orienting volunteers to museum program/goals; understanding expectations/needs of volunteers; legal aspects; volunteer accountability; performance reviews; dismissals; rewards/recognition.
- **Volunteers and Staff: Working Toward a Harmonious Relationship** - A workshop to assist in understanding volunteer/staff interaction: how to determine receptivity to volunteers; how to anticipate/respond to tears/expectations of staff toward volunteers; how volunteers affect paid staff; how to achieve harmony.
- **Evaluating Your Volunteers and Your Volunteer Program** - A

workshop to assist in translation of goals into action by a step-by-step process - beginning with recruiting, ending when volunteer leaves; both individual and program evaluation.
- **Some Perspectives on the Innovative Use of Volunteers within Museum Settings** - A session exploring the ways traditional uses of museum volunteers are changing; ways previously untapped skills of volunteers are being utilized in museums.

This program is approved by the U.S. Association of Museum Volunteers.

INDIVIDUAL PROGRAM PROFILES

BLACK GEORGETOWN REUNION GROUP
Mount Zion United Methodist Church
1334 29th Street, NW
Washington, DC 20007
TEL: 202-234-0248
Purpose: To share common memories and strengthen a growing reunion project.
Sponsor: Georgetown University
Contact: Rev. Kirk D. Monroe
Description: Mount Zion United Methodist Church, founded in 1816, is the oldest of five historic black congregations still in Georgetown in Washington, DC, and is considered the oldest black church in the District. In Spring 1990, a small group of volunteers from the church launched what it hopes will be an annual interfaith event - a union of people who can come together and reminisce about their childhood when the playground, Rose Park in Georgetown, was the first desegregated in the District, their high school days, the former division of Georgetown into two sections, and the period from the early 1800s to about 1950, when the Georgetown population was predominantly black.

The reminiscence program is a spinoff from an annual reunion dinner started by a senior Georgetown resident in 1982. To be sure that the tradition continued, a group of volunteers founded the *Black Georgetown Reunion Group.* The interfaith group meets every six months at a different church.

About two-thirds of the nearly 300 in attendance were from other churches, including the Epiphany Roman Catholic Church and the Alexandria Memorial Baptist Church. Seventeen persons at least 90 years old - many of whom provided stories rich in the history of the area - were honored at the event. The reunion events, along with a *Georgetown University* film, *Black Georgetown Remembered,* are heightening the sense of local history, according to an official of the *Washington Historical Society.*
Publications: Black Georgetown Remembered

DISCOVER CENTER OF IDAHO
131 Myrtle Street
PO Box 192
Boise, ID 83701
TEL: 208-343-9895
Purpose: To offer a "hands-on" learning environment where children and adults are encouraged to learn by discovery, experience and exploration.
Contact: Lorette Williams, Director
Description: In 1982, in response to national concerns for educational advancement in the sciences, the *Junior League of Boise (JLB)* researched the feasibility of a permanent science center for Idaho. *SCIENTOYFIC,* a JLB-sponsored exhibit at the *Idaho Historical Museum* in 1984 attracted over 10,000 people. The program featured locally-produced exhibits and displays from the *Denver Children's Museum.* In 1986, JLB sponsored *SCIENTERRIFIC,* an exhibit displayed at *University Quay.* It was supported by local corporations and volunteers who contributed displays and technical expertise. The 15,000 *SCIENTERRIFIC* visitors encouraged the JLB to establish a permanent science center - a project envisioned by JLB since its

involvement in the exhibit programs in 1982.

In 1988, with $400,000 raised for renovations during 1977-88, interior demolition and renovation/construction of a site donated by the City of Boise was begun for the JLB-sponsored *Discovry Center of Idaho (DCI)*.

At the grand opening in 1989, exhibits created by community volunteers were on display, and educational packets were made available for teachers. A *Technical Committee* ensures the scientific accuracy, safety and durability of all exhibits. A volunteer *Speaker's Bureau* builds awareness of the DCI in the community.

The Director of DCI, appointed in 1987, has been with the science center project since 1983. She is a teacher on a leave-of-absence from the *Boise School district*. The target audience of the Discovery Center of Idaho is the extended family. In other words, the science center appeals to and draws interest and participants from all age groups - toddler to senior. The Center deliberately includes "something for everyone" in its collections and activities; e.g., something a toddler can see and touch; something that interests a busy, curious child; something that provides a deeper explanation for the interested adult; and something to encourage participation by seniors. Specific features include:

- Teaching materials directly related to school curricula.
- Workshops for teachers (begun in summer 1989).
- Demonstrations aimed at improving visitor understanding of the scientific exhibits.
- An Outreach Program to bring travelling exhibits and teaching materials to all parts of the state.

The site donated by the City is in close proximity to many of Boise's major cultural attractions, including the *Boise Art Museum, Idaho Historical Museum, Boise Public Library*, and *Boise City Zoo*.

According to its founders, "Helping to establish the science center has created a lasting legacy to residents and corporate citizens of Idaho who have participated in the project."

Founded: 1982

DISCOVER GRAPHICS
Smithsonian Resident Associate Program
Smithsonian Institution
Dillon Ripley Center
1100 Jefferson Drive, SW
Washington, DC 20560
TEL: 202-357-1300
FAX: 202-357-1853

Purpose: To provide a hands-on arts program for selected high school students.

Description: Every year, 150 students and teachers can be found at the *Smithsonian's S. Dillon Ripley Center* in an arts program offered by the *Smithsonian Resident Associate Program*. Students are selected based on their interests and skills for the program, which provides free, comprehensive studio and museum training in basic printmaking. Teachers are invited to take the course along with the students.

The program is designed to strengthen arts curricula and develop graphic arts skills. Classes are taught by a master printer in the *Gene Davis Printmaking Studio*.

The project culminates in a two-month exhibition featuring the students' art that is open to the public In addition to the satisfaction in completing and exhibiting the projects, the program is considered another way of providing career exploration opportunities to the students.

ECHOES OF THE PAST
Daughters of the American Colonists
5909 South 73rd East Avenue
Tulsa, OK 74145
TEL: 918-585-5520

Purpose: To collect information about historic landmarks and memorials placed in Oklahoma by DAC chapters and others.

Sponsor: National Society of the DAC

Contact: Betty Martin, Historian, or Ollie Longacre, Historic Landmarks Chairman

Description: Echoes of the Past is a theme for a two-pronged historical project that has become an ongoing effort for the group. One part of the project researches and collects information about historic landmarks and memorials placed in Oklahoma by members of the *Daughters of American Colonists (DAC)*. The second phase seeks out the same information for landmarks placed in Oklahoma by other groups, individuals or communities. Volunteer committees work with the *Oklahoma Historical Society* and the *Tulsa County Historical Society* as sources for initial information. Before beginning the project, volunteers visited some of the better-known markers, looked at old photographs of dedication ceremonies, and held a meeting at Sharp Chapel, which was a gift to Tulsa University from an early DAC member. In addition, suggestions of important historical places or events are solicited from across the state. According to the Chapter Regent, "Every historic site or event has a unique background and deserves wide recognition."

When a substantial amount of the data-gathering is complete, uniform descriptions are developed and forwarded to Washington, DC, to be added to similar data from other states preserved there in the library of the *National Society of the DAC*. Although the peak of the information came from the initial intensive effort of the volunteer committees, the search for information does not end there. All suggestions and leads will be researched by volunteers as needed.

Founded: 1926

LIFESTORY THEATER
Autumn Stages
Upper Montclair, NJ 07042
TEL: 201-746-7710

Purpose: To stimulate memory and reawaken self-esteem and motivation among the elderly.

Contact: Troupe Director

Description: Depression, isolation and a sense of uselessness are often feelings the elderly experience. Autumn Stages takes an innovative approach to coping with these feelings through a first-of-its-kind improvisational *Lifestory Theater* performed by and for older adults.

The troupe never uses a script. All of their *lifestory* scenes are improvised, which allows them to get audience members into the act and, better yet, to spontaneously share their own life experiences. The creativity and enthusiasm of the troupe is reflected in those who view the plays.

The volunteer troupe of Autumn Stages consists of more than 20 retired individuals, ages 50 to 83, who serve as role models for senior citizens through their active audience participation in *Lifestory Theater*. They come from all walks of life, and only a few have ever acted before. The others have found their latent talents and learned new acting skills in training workshops led by skilled artistic leaders. The workshops cover improvisational drama, mime, storytelling, old dances and song, and, most important, ways to encourage involvement from the audience.

The troupe tours in large vans to nursing homes, nutritional sites, churches and synagogues, geriatric wings of hospitals, libraries, senior centers, festivals and other sites for older adults. Last year, Autumn Stages reached over 12,000 older adults throughout the state.

Autumn Stages received a 1989 *Governor's Volunteer Award* for its volunteer work. According to the nominator, "They exemplify the highest form of giving. It's incredible to watch them take a life story and, after barely a moment, get into its character and enact it."

Publications: Autumn Stages: Information Packet
Founded: 1988

NOCHE CUBANA (CUBAN NIGHT)
SEE ARTS/CULTURAL ENRICHMENT: FESTIVALS

ORANGE EMPIRE RAILWAY MUSEUM
2201 A Street
Perris, CA 92370
TEL: 714-657-2605
Purpose: To bring back a bygone era of electric and steam railroading.
Contact: Sheldon Liss, Public Relations
Description: The *Orange Empire Railway Museum* is an all-volunteer organization. Volunteers refurbish, restore and wash the trolleys and steam trains that make up the Museum's collection. They also garden, lay track, take tickets, sell hot dogs and cold drinks on weekends, and do a host of other things that maintain the Museum.
About half of some 2,000 members volunteer regularly to keep things going. Some prefer to use tools and keep things repaired. Others go through a complete course on how to operate the equipment, its safety and technology. They become motormen and conductors. Those not active at the Museum itself donate the money needed to pay for the projects. At least forty or fifty volunteers appear on any weekend.
Considered the largest rail historical museum in the western United States, Orange Empire's more than 140 steam locomotives, passenger coaches, freight and maintenance and construction cars, trams and trolleys bring back a bygone era covering a period of more than half a century - both here and abroad. One locomotive operated during 1941 and 1942 on the Trans-Iranian Railway supplying Russia with war materials from the Persian Gulf area. At the museum, this same locomotive was pulling cars from the Atchison, Topeka & Santa Fe. A train from Japan had been made in the United States about 1898 and shipped overseas in "kit" form. Many other historic rail vehicles dot the landscape, some in use and some just for viewing. In addition, a "railway post office" demonstrates how mail was moved across the country in years past. And part of the Main Line track actually is part of the original Santa Fe route to San Diego.
As one volunteer said, "Adults like to make you believe that they are here for the children, but everyone out here has a liking for either the trains or the trolleys. There is no question that this is a rare cultural experience for everyone."

RECYCLING FOR RAVI
SEE PHYSICAL ENVIRONMENT: RECYCLING

SECOND AIR DIVISION ASSOCIATION OF THE EIGHTH AIR FORCE
c/o Hathy Veynar
4915 Bristow Drive
Annandale, VA 22003
TEL: 703-256-6482
Purpose: To maintain a *living memorial* to the members of the *Division;* to establish an organization for sons and daughters of members to continue its traditions.
Description: Chartered in the late 1940s, the *Second Air Division Association of the Eighth Air Force* works to maintain the history of the *Division* as a memorial to the group of World War II veterans, and as a heritage to future generations studying the World War II era. A major project of the *Association* is maintenance and monitoring of the *Memorial Room* at the *Norwich Central Library* in Norwich, England. Started by an offhand remark by a member of the *Division* in 1945, the actual dedication of the room by the Queen Mother was in 1963. The young officer in 1945 had said, "Why don't we give just *one paycheck* to a fund to set up a memorial of some kind here (in England) for our *Division*?" The result is a living memorial supported by the proceeds from the original fund and stocks and bonds sold in England. The funds are placed in a Trust which is

monitored by the *British Board of Governors' Charities Commission.*
The *Fulbright Commission* originally provided a grant for one year for an American librarian to be stationed at the memorial, but has now extended it for an additional year since the Commission considers the project to be an important one. Since it is important to have an American librarian there to answer specific questions about the U.S., the *Association* has begun a fundraiser to establish and ensure the position. The Association Trust pays for an assistant to the librarian, who is British and has been with the memorial since its inception in 1963.
Close to the site of *East Anglia University,* the memorial is a popular rallying point for students there who are studying Anglo-American relations. The *University* has expressed its appreciation a number of times for the professionalism and extent of the collection. The *Cultural Attache* has shown considerable interest in the Memorial Room, attending meetings and being very supportive in a number of ways. He has stated that the Division is responsible for all of the good Anglo-American relations in East Anglia. Features of the memorial include:

- A pool in the front of the building containing a stone from each of the fifty United States. As stones deteriorate, Association members replace them (seven in 1990).
- An *Honor Roll,* with a page turned each day in honor of the 6,800 members of the *Division* who died in World War II.
- Flags of the United States, the Eighth Air Force, and the Second Airborne Division.
- A book-dedication program in which a book is dedicated periodically to one of the deceased members of the *Division* with a book plate inserted bearing his or her name.

The 1990 meeting in England carries a theme that honors the villages in the area where airfields for the Division were located. In the U.S., the Association holds annual meetings, and participates in projects that will continue its efforts to memorialize the Division. One project is the establishment of the *Heritage League,* which will enable sons and daughters of the veterans to carry on its traditions. Educational projects include involvement in an exhibit program in which a B-24 (the airplane used by the Division during World War II) is flown to various airports around the country for school and community groups to visit, as well as to provide a nostalgic place for the veterans themselves to gather and reminisce. An exhibit schedule is available from the Association.

TEA AND TREASURES
Friends of Linden Place
PO Box 328
Bristol, RI 02809
TEL: 401-253-0390
Purpose: To raise funds for restoration of a historical property for use as an educational and cultural center.
Sponsor: Rhode Island Historical Preservation Commission
Contact: Patricia A. Kenyon, Executive Director
Description: Volunteer appraisers, many of whom operate auctions for historical pieces worth millions of dollars, provided the base for a fund-raising event at the Governor's mansion. The jewelry appraisal volunteer is from the distinguished Tilden-Thurber. The purpose of the program was to provide the means of restoring a historic building, Linden Place, to serve as an educational and cultural center for the area. The Governor's wife and the chairwoman of the Rhode Island Historical Preservation Commission share the chairmanship of the *Friends of Linden Place* honorary board of directors.
Appraisals of small art works, old photos, jewelry, silver and furniture were made at *Tea and Treasures* for a $5 donation to the restoration fund for each appraisal. A $10 additional donation allows guests to join a reception and have tea poured by the Governor's wife and the Historical Preservation Commission chairwoman.
The need for the educational and cultural center has been well

established, and fundraisers such as *Tea and Treasures* are helping to make it happen, according to the executive director.

TEXAS PROUD VOYAGE
Galveston Historical Foundation
2016 Strand Street
Galveston, TX 77550
TEL: 409-765-7834
Purpose: To maintain a 112-year-old tall ship and share its historical significance through periodic "voyages" to U.S. ports.
Contact: Ellen Stiveson or Captain Richard Shannon
Description: The Elissa is a 112-year-old tall ship docked for over a decade between voyages at the historic Strand District of Galveston, Texas. It is an 1877 iron baroque, a three-masted sailing vessel, launched from a shipyard in Aberdeen, Scotland, and sailing under the British flag as a cargo ship for 20 years. Sugar, coal, rice, lumber and cotton were traded on its voyages around the world. The ship sailed under the flags of Norway, Finland, Sweden and Greece in subsequent years as it was sold and resold. It was acquired in October 1975 by the Galveston Historical Foundation for $40,000. In search of a ship with direct ties to Galveston, the Foundation learned that the Elissa visited Galveston twice - in 1883 and 1886. Restoration cost $4.5 million and was an 11-year project.

Most tall ships belong to the Navy, Coast Guard or Merchant Marine and are not accessible for sailing. The Elissa provides a rare opportunity to "sail into history" and participates whenever possible when the ship's history will enhance an activity. It was in New York Harbor in the 1986 "Parade of Sail" celebrating the Statue of Liberty's Centennial. It is the only ship to have called on New York before the statue was erected, visiting in 1884. Plans are to be involved in the "1992 America 500" to sail from Palos Spain to San Salvador commemorating the 500th anniversary of Christopher Columbus' voyage.

The crew consists of 30 volunteers and 12 hired crew. Its voyage in 1989 took 90 days and stopped at 10 ports in Texas, Louisiana, Mississippi and Florida. Volunteers spend numerous consecutive weekends caring for the Elissa, as well as precious vacation time reserved to take her on voyages. Most come from Texas - professionals who juggle their lives and sometimes permanently rearrange them just to be part of the experience. They polish brass, sand decks, do "rust-busting," memorize the pinrail diagram and learn the names of 162 lines before they are qualified to sail the Elissa. For this privilege when sailing they go on four-hour bow watches in the middle of the night while cold rains pelt them, pull heavy clumsy lines to position and reposition the massive yards, and obey numerous other shouted commands from the Captain. In port, they sand teak, grease cables or make baggie wringles below, and perform exhaustive sail drills. The joy experienced by the volunteers and crew in the hard work involved is surpassed only by the enrichment provided to the children and adults who are exposed to this rare piece of history.
Founded: 1982

TINY TOWN FOUNDATION
Tiny Town
Morrison, CO 80465
TEL: 303-697-6829
Purpose: To maintain a one-sixth-scale miniature town replicating historic buildings and railroads for the cultural enrichment of the area's children.
Sponsor: Tiny Town Foundation
Contact: Bob Kintzele, Volunteer
Description: For five years, volunteers working for the nonprofit *Tiny Town Foundation* maintained a renovation program to restore a miniature city built in 1915 as a playtown for a businessman's daughter. The one-sixth-scale town features miniature replicas of a number of historic buildings in the Denver area - the first fire station, the first telephone office, Mrs.

Murphy's Boarding House, some landmark mansions and some businesses - a total of about 20 buildings. By 1925, Tiny Town had 125 buildings, and a tiny working railroad which wound its way around the town and back and forth across Turkey Creek on miniature trestles and turned around in a miniature "round house." The area across the creek is a replica of an old mining town similar to those still in place around historical mining towns in the area.

Tiny Town survived damaging floods in 1929 and 1932 and a fire in 1935. In 1969 a flood left behind a debris-strewn miniature ghost town. In 1972 it was restored again by volunteers with improvements designed to prevent future floods. When its benefactor was accidentally killed, it fell into disrepair again and was closed to the public in 1983.

In May 1989, the five years of dedicated work by the volunteers culminated in a grand opening, featuring a Colorado Ballet performance and 11,000 visitors. It was opened on selected weekends throughout the summer with increasingly larger crowds. Although the village is thought of as an entertaining way to provide a cultural experience for children, many groups in the crowd were not "accompanied by children."
Founded: 1985

VOLUNTEER PALEONTOLOGY DIG
University of Wisconsin
750 University Avenue
Madison, WI 53706
TEL: 608-262-1234
Purpose: To assist a university museum in locating fossilized bones of prehistoric seagoing animals.
Sponsor: University of Wisconsin
Contact: University Paleontologist
Description: The University of Wisconsin's geological museum is hoping to learn more about seagoing animals that lived 83 million years ago. Volunteers were dispatched to a "digs" in western Kansas in the summer of 1989 where a nearly-intact specimen of a *mosasaur* was found the previous year. The Kansas area was covered by a shallow ocean in prehistoric times when the land was lower and warmer. The site is rich with fossils, many lying exposed on the ground and requiring no digging at all. Others must be extracted from the blue shale and yellow chalk common in washouts. The site is on the banks of a deep gorge cut by rain water flowing toward the Smoky Hill River.

The 1989 effort uncovered pieces from two different species of the mosasaur family, and skull fragments probably from a tylosaurus, a gigantic animal 39 feet in length. What is hoped for is some insight into what may be a pattern - flippers breaking and rehealing before the animal died (true of both the older and more recent flippers found) - and may provide some idea of living habits.

The volunteers are supplied with several small hand tools, including utility knives, paint brushes, dental tools, and super glue. Their training emphasizes extreme care in handling the fossils, with the glue serving the purpose of coating a fossil that appears fragile before removing it from the shale or soil. Aluminum foil is provided for wrapping and plastic bags for transporting.

Although students from the university can do the digging for credit, many other volunteers come forward because they find the experience "fun."

ARTS/CULTURAL ENRICHMENT: INTERCULTURAL

NATIONAL/STATE ORGANIZATIONS

INTERNATIONAL ASSOCIATION OF VOLUNTEER EFFORT
c/o Mary Ripley
10775 Wilkins Avenue
Los Angeles, CA 90024
TEL: 213-470-1867
Objectives: To promote voluntary commitment to human service throughout the world.
Services: Operates through a membership of 350 individuals in 38 nations, including the United States, who are interested in action through voluntary commitment to human service; maintains an international network to encourage volunteer program development and promote understanding through volunteer effort, with a central office that changes location as leadership changes (1990, Bogota, Colombia), and nine regional offices around the world (one in the United States); makes presentations, etc. in French, Spanish and Japanese; corresponds in English; works in cooperation with the *International Council on Social Welfare;* publishes conference proceedings biannually. [Operated initially under the name *International Association for Volunteer Education.*]
Publications: IAVE Conference Proceedings

TRAINING PROGRAMS

CROSS-CULTURAL COMMUNITY WORKSHOP
Brown University
25 George Street
PO Box 1973
Providence, RI 02912
TEL: 401-863-3555
Sponsor: National Association of Foreign Student Affairs
Contact: Workshop Coordinator
Description: This workshop provides an opportunity to combine foreign study and community service. It is cosponsored by the *Office of International Programs* and the *Center for Public Service.* It features students who have studied abroad who share their unique cross-cultural perspective to integrate international and local experiences by exploring the responsibilities of the individual to the community in a cross-cultural context. The program has three components:
- **Discussion** - a bi-weekly evening discussion that focuses on definitions of *community* and *self.* Through writing and discussion, the group explores issues related to international study and community work, such as cultural biases, social issues, political systems and adaptation to environment.
- **Community Service** - Through a regular volunteer commitment, participants rediscover Providence. Students create an individual service project with a community agency, addressing an issue they studied or observed while abroad (e.g. housing, domestic violence, the rights of children).
- **Journal** - At the end of the program, writing and art that represent each participant's cross-cultural experience is bound and distributed as a journal to *Brown* and *Providence.*
Students receive neither college credit nor payment for participating in this course. The Workshop is supported by funds from the *National Association for Foreign Student Affairs* and *Brown University.*

FIRST ANNUAL SOVIET-AMERICAN YOUTH SUMMIT
SEE CIVIC AFFAIRS: PEACE

INDIVIDUAL PROGRAM PROFILES

U.S.-BASED JAPANESE CORPORATIONS AND THE UNITED WAY
United Way of America
701 North Fairfax Street
Alexandria, VA 22314-2045
TEL: 703-836-7100
Purpose: To provide a framework through which local United Way organizations can work on behalf of communities with U.S.-based Japanese companies toward a mutually-beneficial relationship.
Sponsor: United Way of America
Contact: Marty Walsh
Description: Since 1987, *United Way of America* has been working to develop a national strategy and resource materials for involving Japanese companies in United Way. This has included training sessions for United Way volunteers and professionals and has initiated contact with major U.S.-based Japanese corporations around the country and in Japan. Individual United Ways have joined the effort to help Japanese executives better understand how United Way works.
According to the *International Corporations* division of United Way, there are several fundamental cultural differences between the U.S. and Japan in matters of volunteerism. In Japan, the government, private industry, and the family take care of human-care needs. Also, the process in making decisions about philanthropy often takes a very long time, since consultation with the headquarters in Japan is mandated.
However, several local United Ways have reached a point of understanding with local Japanese companies. Examples are:
- **Battle Creek, Michigan** - *Nippondenso,* Battle Creek's largest Japanese-owned company, has led the Japanese business community in giving to United Way. In addition, the company was influential in helping to recruit other Japanese companies to participate in the campaign. In addition, the company's director of personnel is a United Way board member, and serves as a liaison with the company's president. Battle Creek's Chamber of Commerce helped lay the groundwork through its international committee.
- **Santa Clara, California** - In 1989, 26 Japanese-business liaisons from area banks and certified public accounting firms formed a community-relations advisory committee in Santa Clara. The volunteer committee members rely on senior Japanese executives for financial consultation and for help in understanding the American culture. The committee has developed Japanese-language materials and sponsored special United Way events. Also, the *Japanese Chamber of Commerce* has endorsed the campaign. Consequently, United Way contributions from the Japanese community almost doubled in 1990.
- **Los Angeles, California** - The United Way and the *Japanese Business Association* began working together in 1987. Their first joint effort was to develop a Japanese-language United Way brochure that included information about charitable giving in the United States. In 1989, the United Way recruited its first board member from the Japanese business community. According to the senior campaign associate of the United Way, "Japanese executives are very impressed when they look at United Way boards and see key American business leaders as volunteers. They see United Way board membership as a bridge to the community." The Los Angeles United Way plans to encourage Japanese business leaders to assist with planning, marketing, and allocations - "to help increase their understanding of how United Way works."
At United Way of America, it is felt that as more international companies invest in American communities, they challenge United Ways to be marketing-oriented - to listen to and understand different customers. For example, in dealing with the Japanese, it

has been found that it is important to be consistent. Plans are to continue to work to increase United Way involvement of Japanese and other foreign-owned companies in the U.S.

YOUTH OCEAN EXPLORER PROGRAM
Cousteau Society
930 West 21st Street
Norfolk, VA 23517
TEL: 804-627-1144
Purpose: To unite the children of the world through an exciting adventure.
Contact: Sandy Bond, Supervisor
Description: In January 1990, six elementary school children accompanied Jean-Michael Cousteau, son of the famed explorer, on a voyage to explore Antarctica. The *Cousteau Society* launched the program to "unite the children of the world" through an exploring adventure. Each child came from a country on a different continent - United States, France, Chile, Australia, Japan and Tanzania.
The nominations for the cultural adventure were sent to the Society after a media campaign, with each nominator giving specific information about the youngster and why they felt he or she would benefit from the experience. The representative from the United States was a sixth-grader.
The mission lasted two-and-a-half weeks and included a demonstration of igloo-building and a chance to see the rare wingless fly, found only in Antarctica - but, most importantly, an opportunity for six youth from diverse cultures to interact in an educational and exciting setting.

ARTS/CULTURAL ENRICHMENT: LEGAL SERVICES

NATIONAL/STATE ORGANIZATIONS

VOLUNTEER LAWYERS FOR THE ARTS
SEE CONSUMER SERVICES/LEGAL RIGHTS: ARTS

ARTS/CULTURAL ENRICHMENT: MENTAL HEALTH

INDIVIDUAL PROGRAM PROFILES

STAR CITY SOCIAL CLUB
SEE MENTAL HEALTH: RE-ENTRY

ARTS/CULTURAL ENRICHMENT: MUSIC/DANCE/THEATRE

NATIONAL/STATE ORGANIZATIONS

BREAD AND ROSES
78 Throckmorton Avenue
Mill Valley, CA 90048
TEL: 415-381-0320
Objectives: To donate time and talents to people who "desperately need and appreciate the pleasure and human contact that live entertainment can bring."
Services: Takes free live entertainment to institutions such as convalescent homes, correctional facilities, psychiatric centers, work farms, hospitals, children's homes and similar institutions; produces benefit concerts to raise funds for certain nonprofit organizations; holds two seminars per month to educate other groups on producing benefit concerts; provides information to any individual or group, but performs in California only at the present time. (Operating since 1974, Bread and Roses has found that the performers' benefits are two-fold: bringing enjoyment to others, and having a "sympathetic, noncommercial environment in which to perform.")
Publications: Bread & Roses Handbook; Bread & Roses Newsletter
Founded: 1974

SAN JOSE CHILDREN'S MUSICAL THEATRE*
21 East Santa Clara
San Jose, CA 95113
TEL: 408-288-5437
Objectives: To enlist the support of the local community and the city government to maintain a meaningful arts program for teenagers.
Services: Operates a musical theatre involving hundreds of junior and senior high school students; offers guidelines and information to any group with an interest in establishing a musical theatre for young people; provides consultation for existing musical theatres on establishing a semi-self-support system and other technical areas.
Publications: Children's Theater Guidelines

SUGAR RAY ROBINSON YOUTH FOUNDATION*
1060 South Crenshaw
Los Angeles, CA 90019
TEL: 213-936-8202
Objectives: To provide a cross-cultural arts opportunity for youth using volunteer professional actors, dancers, musicians and other artists as teachers.
Services: Operates athletics and crafts programs and a drama cultural workshop program for young people of all races, creeds and colors; enlists volunteers from arts and cultural professions to administer workshops, provide consultation with youth leaders, and help maintain a comprehensive, cross-cultural opportunity for youth; publishes free brochure on history of foundation and other materials.
Publications: Youth Foundation History

YOUNG AUDIENCES
115 East 92nd Street
New York, NY 10028
TEL: 212-831-8110
Objectives: To increase the creative and imaginative capacities of children through listening to and participating in live performing arts experiences.
Services: Presents to school children, grades K-12, live educational programs in music, dance and theatre during school hours to

increase their creative and arts appreciation abilities; enlists and trains professional ensemble groups in educational techniques to serve as volunteer performers, workshop leaders, and resident teachers; develops performing arts resources for communities; trains ensembles in educational techniques; works with National Advisory Committee; publishes annual report, brochure and newsletter.

Publications: Young Audiences Newsletter
Founded: 1952

TRAINING PROGRAMS

ORCHESTRA MANAGEMENT SEMINAR
American Symphony Orchestra League
777 Fourteenth Street, NW
Suite 500
Washington, DC 20005
TEL: 202-628-0099
FAX: 202-783-7228
Credit: Inquire
Sponsor: Alcoa Foundation
Contact: Meeting Coordinator
Description: This six-day comprehensive seminar is in its 38th year. It strives to help people learn from practical wisdom of effective administrators how to begin managing nonprofit organizations. It includes case studies and other formats designed for maximum benefit in areas including:

- **Being an Orchestra Manager** - roles and responsibilities of volunteers, trustees, administrators, and artistic personnel; the basic structure of a symphony orchestra; the qualities and characteristics of an effective manager.
- **Success Through Volunteers** - how to recruit, motivate, and organize volunteers for orchestras; ways to support their efforts at raising money, selling tickets, and promoting the orchestra.
- **Building an Effective Board** - how to find community leaders, put them to work for your orchestra, and support them in their efforts; the responsibilities of board committees; special importance of the nominating committee.
- **Fundraising** - how the psychology of giving relates to your efforts; organizing volunteers for an annual fund drive; ways to identify prospects, solicit gifts, write proposals, secure corporate sponsorships, and thank donors.
- **Public Relations** - defining your public image; creating and executing plans to promote your orchestra and music director; strengths and weaknesses of specific publicity tools.
- **Economic Realities and Artistic Growth** - controlling the growth of your orchestra in conjunction with the community's desire and ability to support it; the manager as a monitor of administrative and artistic expansion.
- **Managing Orchestra Financing** - generating financial plans, nonprofit arts budgets, and financial reports; understanding legal issues; how to monitor your income and expenses more efficiently.
- **Long-Range Planning** - a hands-on exercise in planning; specifics of mission statements, goals, objectives, and strategies; how to incorporate planning components into day-to-day operations.

In addition to the above sessions that are transferable to any volunteer program, numerous other sessions very specific to orchestras are convened at the seminar. Faculty for all programs is composed of directors, managers, and specialists from symphonies across the country.

All participants receive individualized career attention, a free copy of the textbook, an opportunity for networking and exchanging materials, and specific seminar reading and writing assignments to be used in conjunction with the workshops both in the sessions and during free time. These assignments are prepared with the premise that, in order to get the maximum value out of such a six-day experience, participants must invest their own time. Assignments begin immediately following registration and continue throughout the seminar.

Seminar participants attend concerts and receive tours of cultural institutions sponsored by US/National Endowment for the Arts and US/National Gallery of Art. Seminars are held in various parts of the country (August 1990, Tanglewood, MA; January 1991, San Francisco, CA).

Publications: The Gold Book: Directory of Successful Projects by Volunteers; Principles of Orchestra Management; Training Handbook Series; Youth Orchestra Handbook; How to Organize and Produce a Radiothon; More Dialing, More Dollars

INDIVIDUAL PROGRAM PROFILES

ADOPT-A-SCHOOL DANCE PROGRAM
SEE ARTS/CULTURAL ENRICHMENT: ADOPT-A-SCHOOL

BAROQUE MUSIC FESTIVAL OF CORONA DEL MAR
SEE ARTS/CULTURAL ENRICHMENT: FESTIVALS

FEST (FORT EUSTIS SOLDIERS THEATRE)
US/DoD - Fort Eustis
Morale Support Activities Division
Fort Eustis, VA 23604
TEL: 804-878-2283
Purpose: To entertain Fort Eustis personnel, and to train volunteers in theatre skills.
Sponsor: US/DoD - Fort Eustis
Contact: Ann Morgan, Theatre Director
Description: During a ten-month period, the Fort Eustis Soldiers Theatre (FEST) produced three major productions, eight short plays, four skits, stage set-ups for six concerts, conducted ticket sales, ushered, handled lighting, costumes, face painting and other support for post events. This was accomplished with one paid staff member, the director, and from 30 to 50 volunteers. Over 9,000 hours were logged by volunteers during this period. This represents more than $35,000 in value (using GS1, Step 1) to provide entertainment for post personnel and their families, and skills training that is transferrable to the job market for the volunteers.

To be sure that all volunteers are involved immediately, the director maintains a "grief sheet" (task list) ranging from sound and lighting to refinishing or upholstering furniture. Many volunteers choose to move around in the type of tasks assigned to get a broader knowledge of "behind the scenes" work.

The majority of volunteers are active duty military or their family members (33 out of 35 in a recent production) with others coming from the community. All who want an opportunity to get "on the stage" are given the opportunity, switching "from hammer to script" as needed.

In addition to mainstage productions and one-act plays, the group produces brief thematic children's presentations and operates special events indoors and outdoors, such as haunted houses and concerts. Often facing shortages of time, money, experience, personnel or materials, FEST volunteers find a way to meet schedules and fulfill their mission. According to the program's director, "Without the volunteers, FEST would not exist at Fort Eustis."

GRAND RAPIDS SYMPHONY ORCHESTRA
Grand Rapids, MI 49501
TEL: 616-454-9451
Purpose: To raise funds to keep the Grand Rapids Symphony Orchestra operating.
Contact: Patrick O'Neall, Development Director

Description: Halfway through the *Grand Rapids Symphony Orchestra's* 1989 annual fund-raising campaign, some 243 volunteers had received donations from 875 corporate and individual contributors, reaching more than half of their goal of $1 million. For the all-volunteer orchestra, this indicates that the community is pleased with its program of cultural enrichment for all age groups across the city.

Following this major campaign, volunteers begin to look for new donations at the grass-roots level, primarily from subscribers. Orchestra officials feel that these small gifts are as important as the major ones.

With so many other arts programs seeking funds, accountability has become a major factor for enrichment groups, with a large number of donors wanting to know more about where their dollars are going. This has brought the community's arts groups together to discuss the overall arts programs for the area and compare notes on ways of maintaining adequate funding. In addition, arts groups are becoming more sensitive to meeting the needs of the community, with more surveys and more proactive response to public opinion as to cultural pursuits that will benefit all individuals and groups.

HEART STRINGS - MEMPHIS STOP
SEE AIDS: FUNDING

LIFESTORY THEATER
SEE ARTS/CULTURAL ENRICHMENT: HISTORY/MUSEUMS

LOS ANGELES POVERTY DEPARTMENT (LAPD)
Art Against AIDS
406 Seventh Street, NW
Third Floor
Washington, DC 20004
TEL: 202-347-1033
Purpose: To help raise money for AIDS research, the homeless, child abuse, poverty, etc.
Sponsor: Local host theatre
Contact: Kevin Williams, Assistant Director
Description: In the sixties, the poverty program (Community Action Agencies) created "street theatre," in which the poor would literally "climb on stage and ad lib a play about life in the poverty community." Usually the setting was a kitchen or dining room with a family around the table. Today's *street theatre* is actually set in the streets. Although a little more sophisticated - the method starts with a script - a lot of angry ad libbing soon takes over. One group making its mark in this setting is the *LAPD (Los Angeles Poverty Department) Acting Troupe.* The troupe has a base of 20 full-time actors, and as many of them travel to other cities as budget allows. The Troupe is composed of formerly homeless actors and actresses who team up with homeless people - on-site - in skits that reflect the local realism of homelessness. The purpose for their existence is to raise money not only for the homeless, but also for AIDS research (*Art Against AIDS*) and other issues, including child abuse and poverty.

A typical example is a play on the homeless presented at the *Arena Stage* in Washington, DC. Four LAPD performers were sent to Washington, and it was their task to enlist performers from the area - preferably from the population being served. The result - all of the actors were either homeless or had once been homeless. They played their parts the only way they knew how: for real, according to the director, who didn't expect so much violence. The scripted lines often gave way to some angry ad libs.

Before performing in a city, the assigned performers talk with experts on AIDS, homeless, or other area that will be addressed in their performance. The casting of people from the streets has resulted in the kind of performance that the media calls "raw and wonderful," with "no preachy moments to stop the momentum." Many media cited the work as a way for mainstream America to

learn about life on the street and life on the road - subjects most people know little about. They describe the *LAPD Troupe* and their local volunteer performers as creators of "an underground of rich, elemental interaction among people who are facing a reality that most of us have managed to banish from our lives."

MENTAL HEALTH PLAYERS
SEE MENTAL HEALTH: COMMUNICATIONS & PR

SENIOR ACTING PROGRAM OF THE BARN PLAYERS*
Retired Senior Volunteer Program
5165 Merriam Drive
Merriam, KS 66302
TEL: 913-362-3343 (office); 913-341-8834 (home)
Purpose: To provide new challenges and goals to the participants; to enrich the lives of the audience through theatre.
Sponsor: The Barn Players
Contact: Winifred Laas, Secretary-Steering Committee
Description: In September 1978, a group of 25 older persons made up the original production unit of a new offshoot of the *Barn Players Theatre* - the *Senior Acting Program.* The volunteer company organized the Program with a CETA grant and free space provided by Johnson County Community College. Bookings at that time were through the Johnson County Arts Council.

In 1978, the volunteers prepared six 30-minute one-act plays about the process of aging, held rehearsals and began performing for nutrition sites, nursing homes and other senior organizations in the community. Now the plays tour regularly throughout the Greater Kansas City metropolitan area, performing before church, civic and professional groups of mixed ages, Junior College level social studies, as well as senior groups. Over a four-year period, 443 performances were presented to approximately 18,000 people. Plays are designed with touring in mind and require few props and small casts. Originally each play emphasized some aspect of aging - not the condition of being aged. Material of this nature has been more and more difficult to find and recently light comedies have been included in the repertory. Performances are followed by a period of discussion led by a Program member in which the audience participates. Each performance is based on a choice by the booking organization of the play most suited to their needs and runs approximately 20-30 minutes.

The senior volunteers are highly dedicated to the Program and find that much more time is involved in coordinating the activities than was first anticipated. Auditions are held, plays are rehearsed for at least two months, performers must be willing to devote two to three evenings each week for rehearsals, and their schedules must be flexible enough to enable them to perform during the day or evening; discussion leaders must be chosen, plays selected, and publicity released to local radio, TV and newspaper media. One goal of the Program is to be self-sufficient thereby necessitating the requested donation to be increased from the original $10 per performance to $15 and now to $25.
Founded: 1978

STAY THE NIGHT ON MY STREET
SEE RECIPIENTS: HOMELESS - COMMUNICATIONS & PR

TAE KWON DO CHOREOGRAPHIC PERFORMANCES
SEE RECREATION & SPORTS: ARTS

ARTS/CULTURAL ENRICHMENT: OLDER PERSON

NATIONAL/STATE ORGANIZATIONS

NATIONAL COMMITTEE ON ART EDUCATION FOR THE ELDERLY
SEE RECIPIENTS: OLDER PERSON - ARTS

INDIVIDUAL PROGRAM PROFILES

HOME LEAGUE
SEE PSYCHOSOCIAL SUPPORT SERVICES: OLDER PERSON

60 KARATS
Culpeper Senior Center
Culpeper Garden
4415 North Pershing Drive
Arlington, VA 22203
TEL: 703-971-5144 (60 Karats); 703-528-0162 (Center)
Purpose: Performing free at local and civic events, *60 Karats* is a dancing troupe with all participants over 60 years of age. It began in 1987 when seven women joined the only dance course in the Arlington County program offered to seniors - tap dancing. Since then, in addition to appearing at senior centers and charitable functions, the troupe has performed three times at the Kennedy Center, and have been featured on CNN (Cable News Network), where their show brought in calls from around the country, including one from Johnny Carson.
To maintain the precision and coordination that has brought them national attention, *60 Karats* practices twice a week in a room at *Culpeper Garden,* with additional time spent when the date for one of their shows is approaching. Although the volunteer troupe does not charge a fee for its performances, donations are accepted to defray expenses.
Contact: Jane Letsche, Choreographer

YES PROGRAM (YOUTH-ELDERLY SERVICES)*
SEE RECIPIENTS: OLDER PERSON - ARTS

BUSINESS ASSISTANCE

NATIONAL/STATE ORGANIZATIONS

CHAMBER OF COMMERCE OF THE UNITED STATES
1615 H Street, NW
Washington, DC 20062
TEL: 202-659-6000
Objectives: To provide leadership and services to all businesses, large and small.
Services: Analyzes economic and social problems and works to put solutions in effect; informs Congress and the Administration of the views and recommendations of business on legislative proposals and government policies; keeps members informed on matters that impact on business; works in five areas of leadership and service: Research, Policy Making, Opinion Development, Action, and Service.
Operates special projects based on expressed needs from the field such as: BIZ/NET (The American Business Network): a daily 60-minute newscast focusing on news with the greatest business and economic impact; Communicator Work shops: training sessions designed to sharpen speaking skills of business executives; U.S. Chamber Staff Specialist: a bank of experts to provide information, opinion and analysis on legislation, regulations, etc., on specific issues such as transportation, housing, pensions, plant closings, food/agriculture, employment, health, energy, education, consumer issues, paperwork burden, and others; Economics for Young Americans: a program for instructing secondary and junior college students in the basics of economics.
Works with affiliated groups such as the National Chamber Foundation; Citizen's Choice; The National Chamber Litigation Center; National Chamber Alliance for Politics, and others; publishes *Nation's Business,* a monthly magazine, *The Business Advocate,* a weekly tabloid, and other materials.
Publications: Business Action Network; The Business Advocate; Washington Watch; Nation's Business ; Economic Outlook; Employee Benefits; Workers' Compensation Laws
Founded: 1912

MOST INCOMPREHENSIVE GOVERNMENT REGULATION AWARD PROGRAM
Comprehensive Accounting Corporation
2111 Comprehensive Drive
Aurora , IL 60505
TEL: 708-898-1234

Objectives: To call attention to the burden of government regulations on the nation's small business owners.
Services: Presents "awards" to government agencies issuing "abundant and bewildering" regulations that require small businesses to expend fees to consultants for interpretation; makes the annual award based on a nationwide poll of accountants; cites the more than $12 billion spent by 17 million small businesses just to decipher the confusing regulations (averaging $750 a year per owner); provides statistics demonstrating that confusing government regulations are a major factor in small business failures (based on a poll of its 240 franchised offices); emphasizes that small business owners must get assistance or risk violating regulations because of their inability to understand them; rewrites some regulations to assist business owners - most recently (1990) the *Internal Revenue Service's* rule 469-1T(f)(2)(i)(C) from 70 words to 33 words (putting two disruptive parenthetical references into footnotes and deleting repetitions); invites input from small business owners regarding confusing and ambiguous government regulations. [1989 and 1990 awards were "won" by the *Internal Revenue Service.*]

SMALL BUSINESS ASSISTANCE CENTER
554 Main Street
Worcester, MA 01601
TEL: 617-756-3513
Objectives: To assist the person interested in mounting, improving, or expanding a small business.
Services: Offers a wide range of programs including: Preparing a Business Plan, Applying for and Getting an SBA Loan, Bank or Non-Bank Loan Approvals, How to Buy a computer, etc.; publishes manuals, guides, and other materials on numerous aspects of small business operation; involves 14 volunteers in planning programs and implementing programs; maintains speakers' bureau and computerized databank.
Publications: Legislative News; SBSB Bulletin
Founded: 1967

SMALL BUSINESS DEVELOPMENT PROGRAM
Volunteers in Technical Assistance
1815 North Lynn Street
Suite 200
Arlington, VA 22209
TEL: 703-276-1800; Cable: VITAINC
TOLL FREE: Telex: 440192 VITAUI

Objectives: To provide experienced volunteers to any community, group or individual involved in a small or medium-size business needing professional and technical assistance in any phase of its operation.
Services: Provides information, expertise and services to anyone interested in developing small and medium industries, particularly in the developing world; offers technical information on numerous technologies, consultants from an international roster of 4,400 experts, technical reports, indentification of potential business collaborators, trade services, bibliographic retrieval, document delivery and data management; works internationally to expand markets, reduce production costs, improve industrial processes, and introduce new technologies.
Publications: VITA News; Technical Paper Series
Founded: 1960

SMALLER BUSINESS OF AMERICA*
430 Chester 12th Building
Cleveland, OH 44114
TEL: 216-621-9529
Objectives: To preserve the system of small private enterprise.
Services: Provides information on legislation, taxation, and other governmental action; serves as a clearinghouse for small business problems; supports committees on national legislation and taxes, patent and trade mark, and safety; publishes monthly newsletter.
Publications: The Champion

US/DOC - PRIVATE SECTOR INITIATIVES PROGRAM
Office of the Secretary
14th St. between E & Constitution
Washington, DC 20230
TEL: 202-337-2000
Objectives: To identify and pursue incentive programs, partnerships, and services that might best be performed by the private sector.
Services: Provides direct administrative and financial support for private sector initiatives through offices including those listed below:
Bureau of the Census which participates in a joint Census/locality effort to provide social, demographic and economic data that cannot be obtained from other census data products, but is needed as backup for support activities such as grant and loan requests to solve community problems; develops monographs with funding from three foundations (Ford, Russell Sage and Alfred A. Sloan); operates Federal-State cooperative *State Data Centres* in most states.
Patent and Trademark Office which is pursuing the possibility of private sector funding for training courses and field trips to afford patent examiners a better understanding of the practical consequences of their work, to help encourage greater participation by the private sector in the patent and trademark systems.
National Technical Information Service which is the central source for sale to the public of government information needed by business for innovation and decision-making (cost-recovery comes from sales income, not the taxpayer).
National Telecommunications and Information Administration which conducts analyses of the issue of government competition with the private sector in this field, and works on options and alternatives to solve problems in this area.
Minority Business Development Agency which operates Business Development Centers and maintains a *Presidential Initiative on Minority Enterprise* program to provide assistance and information and make recommendations on minority participation in the free enterprise system.
National Oceanic & Atmospheric Administration which relies heavily on volunteers in various aspects of its program such as tornado spotters, river gauge readers in flood-prone areas, and other types of observation tasks critical to its weather forecasting services; mounts objectives for *privatization* in areas of the *Landset*

earth satellite program and selected weather forecast programs such as fruit frost prediction (also studying user fee and private sector takeover options for the *National Weather Service).*
Sponsor: US/DoC - Department of Commerce

US/GSA - PRIVATE SECTOR INITIATIVES
F Street between 18th & 19th, NW
Washington, DC 20405
TEL: 202-566-1212
Objectives: To utilize private sector assistance to expose key management officials in GSA to the *entrepreneural can-do spirit* with the goal of upgrading the business practices of GSA.
Services: Works with the private sector on a number of cooperative programs, four of which are highlighted below:
GSA Advisory Board composed of top executives of the nation's corporations and organizations, which provides assistance through the following objectives:
● To review and recommend major policy proposals.
● To advise and counsel on GSA priorities.
● To provide technical review.
● To provide external support.
● To provide Executive Loan Program resources.
Patterns the *GSA Advisory Board* after boards of directors in the private sector; convenes the Board six to eight times a year; provides briefing papers and formal proposals for the Board's recommendation prior to testimony on the papers and proposals before Congressional committees; asks Board members to testify at their options.
Future plans for the Advisory Board include the review of GSA construction and space utilization practices, and further development of the *GSA Executive Loan Program* and *Industry Resources Program,* both described below.
GSA Executive Loan Program formed to provide technical support and private sector perspective on specific GSA problems; includes private sector participants from companies of the Advisory Board members and other organizations who spend substantial amounts of time at GSA, joining GSA employees on project teams led by GSA's *Management Improvement Office.* Future plans include a number of prospective projects with short-term impact (60 to 120 days) covering telecommunications, employee travel, traffic management, and other areas (a joint *Telecommunications Task Force* is in place).
Industry Resources Program provides full-time and part-time assignments for up to two years in GSA; involves full-time designees, who are private sector executives, to supplement staff by giving technical and managerial expertise not presently available within the agency; involves part-time designees from a bank of retirees whose experience can relieve the agency in areas where temporary workload requirements exceed the availability of trained internal resources.
GSA Business Day is a one-day seminar with a series of workshops to enable GSA and the private sector to share innovative business practices, to motivate GSA staff to become more active in their day-to-day responsibilities by making *business* decisions, and to develop within GSA a spirit of *entrepreneurship.*
Other Initiatives include outleasing, Federal supply service with customer-agency interface (based on *American Express Company* support), and warehousing, with other initiatives considered as situations dictate.
Sponsor: US/GSA - General Services Administration

US/SBA - PRIVATE SECTOR INITIATIVES ACTIVITIES
Office of the Director
1441 L Street, NW
Washington, DC 20416
TEL: 202-653-6365
Objectives: To utilize the private sector to obtain maximum leverage from all programs in achievement of goals and meeting small business community needs.

Services: Addresses program priorities with support and compliance from each operational unit and each regional administrator; involves several areas in its private sector initiatives program, as follows:

Current Private Sector Initiatives Programs involve a large number of partnerships with the private sector (over 50% of overall programs), including:

- *SBA Advisory Councils* located in each district and at the national level involve more than 1,100 business owners who channel information from the business community, evaluate current SBA programs, and recommend new programs.
- *Disaster Program* utilizes private sector participation in evaluating disaster damage to home or business, identifying victims, assisting victims in preparing forms, etc. (involves volunteer organizations and lenders, volunteer organizations directly related to SBA, state and local governments, and local businesses).
- *Partnerships with private sector financial institutions* produce guarantees to enable SBA to access private sector lending resources to benefit small businesses which otherwise could not secure private sector financing.
- *Partnerships with local and state development companies* create increased employment, productivity and urban enterprise development with 50% of the financing coming from private participation.
- *SBICs and MESBICs* are small business investment companies and minority enterprise small business investment companies which must meet private capital investment criteria before receiving government money.
- *Management Assistance* identifies management problems that are primary reasons for business failures, and uses experienced professionals in the private sector to assist small business managers in overcoming these problems; calls on sources such as the following to assist in this area: Chamber of Commerce Resource Center Program, Professional and Trade Associations, SCORE and ACE (see separate entries), Small Business Institute (uses business resources and expertise of 500 colleges and universities), Small Business Development Center (in most states, Centers match funds 50-50 with SBA, employ short-term volunteer professionals, and require involvement of private resources).

Procurement Assistance which places a fair share of government dollars with small business through the SBA-operated PASS (Procurement Automated Source System) and other means of assuring private sector involvement while meeting government needs for goods and services.

Women Business Ownership includes a number of private sector-oriented programs such as the roster of 1,900 private sector corporations who have been solicited by SBA to cooperate in providing subcontracting opportunities for women contractors, and sponsored regional procurement conferences involving local women's groups who provide expertise and advice to businesswomen (such as 12 pilot workshops sponsored by the *National Association of Bank Women* and the *Donner Foundation*, and the *American Women's Economic Development Corporation* sponsored by SBA).

Minority Enterprise receives SBA assistance under three programs:

- *Corporate Market Development Program* (SBA works with Fortune 500 corporations)
- *Trade Association Participation Program* (SBA recruits private sector trade association members to help resolve problems)
- *Presidential Advisory Committee on Small and Minority Business Ownership* (committee of private-sector experts to encourage major firms to place subcontracts with small and minority-owned firms)

Proposed incentive programs include: *Entrepreneur Network; SBA Client Network; Public Library Entrepreneur's Collection; Large Business Partnerships;* and *Small Business and Industry*

Associations and the Academic Community.
Proposed administrative, legislative or policy initiatives include adoption of private sector performance standards by all departments and agencies for all of their operational units, working closely with local communities to accomplish partnership goals, fostering legislation that encourages the matching grant concept, and development of cosponsored training and private sector assistance in portfolio management.
Sponsor: US/SBA - Small Business Administration

US/SBA - SERVICE CORPS OF RETIRED EXECUTIVES/ACTIVE CORPS OF EXECUTIVES
US/SBA - SCORE/ACE
1441 L Street, NW
Washington, DC 20416
TEL: 202-653-6570
Objectives: To utilize the management experience of retired business executives for the benefit of new and existing small businesses.
Services: Provides volunteer experts to assist the small business entrepreneur with any management problem; operates service through Small Business Administration field offices; places SCORE volunteers in Chamber of Commerce Offices in some areas; reimburses volunteers for out-of-pocket expenses; extends assistance to community organizations; publishes counselor guidebooks and brochures.
Sponsor: US/SBA - Small Business Administration
Publications: SCORE Guidebook

INDIVIDUAL PROGRAM PROFILES

BAY AREA SCORE PROGRAM
Fremont Chamber of Commerce
39650 Liberty
Fremont, CA 94538
TEL: 415-794-0599 (volunteers); 415-657-1355 (clients)
Purpose: To share business expertise with potential entrepreneurs to help them get started.
Sponsor: Fremont Chamber of Commerce
Contact: Dan Kauffman, SCORE Volunteer
Description: Sixty-five volunteers in the Bay Area chapter of the *Service Corps of Retired Executives (SCORE)* share their expertise with those who would like to go into business for themselves but aren't sure just where to start. Offices are provided by the Fremont Chamber of Commerce each Wednesday. Volunteers are either people who have themselves owned a business or have been an executive in a large company. The skills are diverse, and a volunteer who cannot answer a question has access to information about the skills of the volunteers and can request assistance.
Requests range from local businesses such as a machine shop to those of international currency exchange and imports. The initial volunteer advises on things that are common to any new business - legal matters, licenses, fictitious name statements, taxes and setting up books - before making the referral to another SCORE volunteer for specific technical expertise.
SCORE volunteers primarily see clients before they have launched their business, but after they have a specific idea of what they want to do and have done some research. Those who do not have a clear idea of what they want are asked to come back at a later time when their goals are set. Occasionally, a client has begun a business only to find unexpected pitfalls, for which expert advise is needed. Often it is just an ordinary business problem that simply requires encouragement.
SCORE sponsors monthly workshops, usually "general business types," but the San Francisco-Oakland location has brought about the institution of a workshop specifically about import-export businesses on a less-frequent basis.

SCORE is funded by the *U.S. Small Business Administration* and has been around for about 25 years with chapters nationwide.

BROOKDALE-SCORE PROGRAM
Brookdale Community College
SCORE/ACE Chapter #36
Lincroft, NJ 07738
TEL: 201-842-1900/Ext. 568
Purpose: To utilize business expertise of retired executive and working professionals for the benefit of others in business who need help.
Sponsor: Brookdale Community College
Contact: Dayton Jones, Chairman
Description: Between 1970 and 1972, two local retired businessmen worked to develop a SCORE (Service Corps of Retired Executives) Chapter in the Lincroft area. Efforts were made to enlist members, develop a working organization, and build a reputation in the local business community. Monthly planning meetings were held, but it was the involvement of the Brookdale Community College and its offer of space and services that was instrumental in getting SCORE Chapter #36 started. Between 1972 and 1979 membership grew to 33 volunteers, and the group gained national recognition.
Volunteers are persons who have managerial experience and include capacities of presidents, vice presidents, and business owners. Membership is divided into two classifications: SCORE, whose members are retired, and ACE (Active Corps of Executives) composed of persons still actively engaged in business. The main job of the SCORE/ACE volunteer is to counsel people who are considering starting a new business and business owners who encounter problems. The counseling is done on a one-to-one confidential basis, and there is no charge for services provided by volunteers. Three of the retired volunteers are women; the remaining thirty of the SCORE/ACE volunteers are men.
In addition to the Chapter officers, Committees are appointed to handle all operations of the group. At monthly meetings, volunteers discuss the results of the previous month's efforts, policy changes, correspondence received, and current and future developments and projections. Committee meetings are held separately.
The publicity committee develops tapes and scripts for radio; reports success stories, events, etc., to newspapers; maintains a speakers bureau; and operates a poster program in supermarkets, post offices, bus stations, etc., to fulfill its task of making the local business community aware of the Chapter's free counseling services.
Counseling is conducted daily by appointment at the College and, one evening each week, at the Monmouth County Library. Over 400 clients are counseled each year and the number of hours spent by counselors exceeds 600. There are about 60 ongoing counseling cases.
In addition to the counseling sessions, SCORE volunteers work cooperatively with College representatives in a number of business-related endeavors, including:
- **Business Seminars:** conducted twice each year in the spring and fall; consist of six lectures each day with daily attendance ranging from 60 to 100 persons.
- **Small Business Institute Program:** implemented as a pilot program sponsored by the US Small Business Administration (the first community college to provide such a program).
- **University Business Development Center Program:** patterned after above Institute in a working arrangement with Rutgers University.
- **Monmouth Employment Research Center Program:** established through a grant to audit the CETA program throughout Monmouth County.
- **SCORE Addresses Classes:** developed in response to requests that SCORE volunteers conduct workshops for students.

Chapter #36 members have over 1100 years of cumulative

experience in dealing with business problems, and they counsel all types of entrepreneurs - from the small "Mom and Pop" retailer to the owner or manager of a business with a million-dollar operation. Volunteers actively participate on college committees, and have reduced the workload of the Career Services Personnel. Expansion of the program includes workshop seminars at two other area colleges, and increased speaking engagements at local service clubs and other organizations.
Founded: 1972

SERVICE CORPS OF RETIRED EXECUTIVES (SCORE)
US/SBA - SCORE/ACE
969 Madison Avenue
Memphis, TN 38104
TEL: 901-544-3588
Purpose: To counsel and advise small business owners.
Sponsor: US/SBA - Small Business Administration
Contact: Irving Nathanson, Counselor
Description: About three dozen retirees with lifetimes of experience in the business world volunteer their time to offer free, confidential counseling from the SCORE (Service Corps of Retired Executives) office in Memphis.
The office, staffed during the morning on weekdays, receives an average of 25 calls a day from those who own businesses or want to start them. Half of the prospective entrepreneurs who call for advice have not reached the point where they can be helped, according to the director. They only have a vague idea that they want to go into business for themselves, with no thought of what business, no experience, and no money. When this happens, the inquirer is given the hard realities of needing a financial base, a solid plan, etc., and sent "back to the drawing board."
Those with an existing business, or a good idea, some experience and some source of financing can benefit from the counseling SCORE has to offer. The caller is sent a form to request a counselor, and one with experience related to the caller's needs is assigned.
The U.S. Small Business Administration created SCORE in 1964 and pays the rent and travel expenses for 390 chapters nationwide. The labor is provided by volunteers such as those in the Memphis chapter.

US/SBA - SERVICE CORPS OF RETIRED EXECUTIVES/ACTIVE CORPS OF EXECUTIVES
US/SBA - SCORE/ACE
Louisville , KY 40202
TEL: 502-582-5976
Purpose: To share business and professional experience with persons interested in starting or improving a business.
Sponsor: US/SBA - Small Business Administration
Contact: William Federhofer, SBA Kentucky District Director
Description: About 61 Louisville retirees are score counselors. They have varied backgrounds - financial, wholesale and retail, import-export, construction, food services and engineering. They range in age from 55 to 85. During 1988, Louisville SCORE Chapter 75 handled 1,908 cases, an average of 31 cases per member. This does not include inquiries by phone or walk-in business that requires no counseling.
To become SCORE volunteers, retirees must complete about 60 hours of training and agree to work three hours a week in the office handling phone calls or walk-in inquiries. Counselors are matched with clients need help in their specialty. When more than one area of expertise is involved, counseling teams are formed. Once the client and counselor or team are matched, they meet as often as needed, ususally about once a month. Counselors must keep detailed records on each session. Counseling continues as long as the client requires it, but most cases are closed after about a year.
Most clients are just "thinking" of starting a small business. Usually they lack two important elements - capital and knowledge.

Workshops are designed to address these problems - a total of 70 conducted during 1989. Scheduled sessions include starting an at-home business, forecasting profits and cash flow, business taxes, and owning a mail-order business. Workshops are open to the general public for a small fee, and are presented and the University of Louisville in Shelby.

Louisville also has a companion program called ACE (Active Corps of Executives), which is composed of volunteers who are still working, but who also want to help business people. The primary difference is the scheduling which must accommodate ACE volunteers' working hours.

BUSINESS ASSISTANCE: CHILDREN/YOUTH

NATIONAL/STATE ORGANIZATIONS

DISTRIBUTIVE EDUCATION CLUBS OF AMERICA
1908 Association Drive
Reston, VA 22091
TEL: 703-860-5000
Objectives: To encourage private enterprise and economic awareness through student activities; to promote understanding and appreciation for the responsibilities of citizenship in a free, competitive enterprise system.
Services: Develops and provides instructional aids and activities, exposure to business leaders and practical experience in business; offers ideas for community betterment projects and support of community activities; maintains a series of State and National Competitions designed to stimulate, motivate and reward student accomplishment, encourage career choices, strengthen occupational commitment; administers a scholarship program to stimulate, assist and encourage students toward higher education; administers student activity areas such as Leadership Development, Civic Participation, Public Information, Program Development, Career Conferences, and Advisor Aids; operates as a "co-curricular" program structured to serve as part of the classroom instructional program through DECA chapters (classes); offers workshops, seminars and publications for development of student competencies; supports state and regional conferences and the National Career Development Conference, which is attended by teachers, and business and industry representatives as well as the students.
Publications: New Dimensions; DECA Newsletter
Founded: 1946

JUNIOR ACHIEVEMENT (JA)
45 Clubhouse Drive
Colorado Springs, CO 80906
TEL: 303-540-8000
Objectives: To teach high school students how the American business system operates; to help them gain practical experience by running a small-scale business of their own.
Services: Enlists adult volunteers from business and industry to implement above objectives; guides 7000 student-run companies through its 254 franchised corporations across the country; publishes bimonthly magazine, annual National Board List, and other materials; convenes annual meeting.
Publications: Partners; Achiever
Founded: 1919

TRAINING PROGRAMS

WASHINGTON FOR MINORITY YOUTH AWARENESS DAY
US/DoC - Office of Minority Business Enterprise
14th Street at E & Constitution
Washington, DC 20230
TEL: 202-377-2000
Information also available from: US/SBA - Minority Business
1441 L Street NW, Washington, DC 20416 (202-653-6365)
Sponsor: US/DoC - Department of Commerce
Contact: Minority Business Coordinator (Commerce) or Anita Holland (SBA)
Description: A faculty of volunteer role models, convened at the request of the *US Small Business Administration* and the *US Department of Commerce,* spearheaded a program involving 200 minority youth from across the country who are interested in becoming entrepreneurs. Now in its third year, the conference targets promising minority students, and offers them successful role models and government programs. The youth program is part of the agencies' annual *Minority Enterprise Development Week Conference.*
Since Asians and Hispanics have the highest percentage of minority-owned businesses, the meeting was especially important for black youth. Many minorities other than black have been successful in their own countries before coming to America, according to the program's organizers, while blacks have not had the opportunity of starting a business in a nondiscriminatory environment. Most black entrepreneurs are first-generation business owners.
A major concern of the youth themselves was the difficult choices that challenge their work ethic. For this reason, enlisting role models for the youth is the strength of the program, with celebrities and athletes discussing the risk of considering a professional athletic or other high visibility, but short-term, career as the only one. Also discussed with the role models was an issue raised by a 17-year-old participant - the lure of drugs and fast money in inner-city neighborhoods "as a way of getting things your parents can't get you." Although many youth try to avoid the drug scene, the youth participants agreed that it is "hard to get away from" - especially with the obstacles facing them in trying to start businesses. According to presenters, these obstacles can be softened or eliminated as the issues - such as acquiring capital to get started - are addressed and positive solutions found for them. Other presenters talked about financial planning, stress control and self-awareness. The bottom line - with both presenters and young participants in agreement - was stated by a former football player for the *Green Bay Packers* - "It is possible to have it all, but someone must be willing to work hard and do the little extra things you have to do to get ahead."

INDIVIDUAL PROGRAM PROFILES

BUSINESS MANAGEMENT/JUNIOR ACHIEVEMENT
Fairfax County Schools
Vocational, Adult & Community Educ.
7423 Camp Alger Avenue
Falls Church, VA 22042
TEL: 703-698-0400
Purpose: To involve volunteers from business/industry in enabling high school students to run small businesses of their own while learning how the American business system operates.
Sponsor: Junior Achievement (JA); local business/industry; Fairfax County Schools
Contact: Beverly S. Dopler
Description: Guided by adult volunteers from business and industry, high school students in Fairfax County will set up

businesses again this fall to produce jewelry, toys, lamps, ash trays, Christmas decorations, etc., or to provide services such as photography, secretarial, advertising and "fix-it." Others will produce newspapers, magazines, radio and TV shows, etc.

Business/Industry volunteers work through the local Junior Achievement Corporation to guide the companies run by students. At the beginning of each semester JA staff members conduct orientation meetings in individual schools or, where practical, on an areawide basis, for participating teachers and school personnel. Participating students receive one-half credit per semester, and are required to spend 75 hours in the program as follows:

- Junior Achievement meeting time - 38
- Management training at sponsoring firms - 6
- Marketing of products and services - 20
- Tours of business establishments - 4
- Selected activities such as elementary program, preparation of written reports - 7

Sponsoring firms provide six hours of management training designed to teach students the principles of free enterprise and help them run their own miniature businesses. This enables the young people to see a place in free enterprise for themselves in the future.

Adult volunteers contact students who have completed application forms by phone and through a special mailing to discuss their interests and to follow-up on JA notification of the first company meeting. To maintain their standing in the class for credit purposes, the students must attend 85% of the company meetings, attend six out of eight Board of Directors' meetings, and be actively involved in a Junior Achievement company.

Fairfax County also hosts Project Business, a JA program geared to eighth or ninth grade students. Central to this program is the Volunteer Business Consultant, who leads one class each week in seven business topics including The Nature of Economics, The U.S. Market System, Money and Banking, and others. Each Project Business class is sponsored by a local business firm. Training for consultants and teachers is conducted by the JA Project Business staff. Materials and operating costs are covered by the sponsor, and are designed to develop student enthusiasm for business and economics, and as a "lead-in" to the primary JA program.

CHAMP BAKERY
SEE RECIPIENTS: CHILDREN/YOUTH - ENTREPRENEURSHIP

CONNER-HARRIS MINI MALL
District of Columbia Police Department
Community Relations Department
300 Indiana Avenue, NW
Washington, DC 20001
TEL: 202-727-1000
Purpose: To involve youth in providing a service and making money for themselves.
Sponsor: District of Columbia Police Department
Contact: Officer W.W. Johnson
Description: Assigned to Woodson Junior High School in Northeast Washington, a police officer from the department's Community Relations Division searched for a way to keep the youth interested in productive activities, and too busy to think about drugs and alcohol. His first goal was to install a weight-lifting room to teach the youth discipline and respect for their bodies. To accomplish this he found an unused room at the school's recreation center, begged mirrors from a hotel that was going out of business, and donated $8,000 worth of weight-lifting equipment.

His concern continued, however, as he observed students leaving school to buy candy, school supplies, jogging shoes and other items. He thought, "Why can't they sell these things to themselves? That way they could provide a service, learn about

business, and make some money for themselves."

As a result of his efforts, in the fall of 1989, the *Conner-Harris Mini Mall* was dedicated. The mall was named for two victims of the District's drug war - a 13-year-old youth and a 17-year-old youth. A packed room that included the Chief of Police, neighborhood residents, ministers, a cadre of volunteers and the proud officer's family attended the dedication.

In the youth-run mall there are stalls for candy, T-shirts, woodcraft and athletic shoes. Four youngsters with an interest in photography are working with the National Center for Neighborhood Enterprise (NCNE) to acquire equipment to produce personalized buttons and badges for conventions. Mega Foods has agreed to hire some of the students and train them in food service.

Much of the city-provided space at the rear of the school continues to be renovated. Officer Johnson does much of the carpentry under the direction of an architect he saw on television and promptly recruited.

The mall goes far beyond just giving youngsters a chance to earn a few dollars, according to the officer. He sees it as a chance to reinforce in the children the importance of math and English, to introduce them to such notions as self-respect and cooperation and, above all, to harness and enhance their "entrepreneurial yearnings." The NCNE president is encouraging architects and volunteers to make the mall as attractive as they they can make it - "second only to Union Station." He feels that this demonstrates to the youth why business people have nice offices - because it makes a statement both about the quality of their service and about the people they serve. He visualizes the mall as "an island of excellence in a sea of drugs." To back up his demand for excellence, he presented a $10,000 check to the program representing $200 each from 50 of his associates.

Officer Johnson, who works an eight-hour police shift at the school and then puts in an equal amount of volunteer time each day, marvels at the business ideas coming from the children. He feels that to keep saying legitimate jobs can't compete with the lure of the money to be made in drugs is not a fair statement unless the youngsters are given the option. His message to skeptics: "These kids aren't dumb. They know they've never seen a retired drug dealer. Given a choice, do you think they would choose jail and the cemetery?"

Upon receiving the $10,000 check, he turned to the young entrepreneurs and said, "Boys and girls, we're in business." Renovation by the volunteers is expected to continue through 1990, but the mall has been planned so that operation of existing stalls - and stalls as they are completed - can continue throughout the renovation period.

DISCOUNT MART SHOPPING CENTER II
Bruce-Monroe Elementary School
3012 Georgia Avenue, NW
Washington, DC 20001
TEL: 202-576-6215
Purpose: To teach children the different aspects of the business world, while demonstrating the role math and communication will play in their daily lives.
Contact: Evelyn S. Roberson, Teacher
Description: Created by a math teacher for her 48 students. *Discount Mart Shopping Center II* is the second shopping center launched at the *Bruce-Monroe Elementary School.* The three-day event each year was designed initially to help students - especially minority youngsters - learn the important role math will play in their daily lives. The shopping center introduces the fifth- and sixth-graders to the business world and helps them communicate with others, while accomplishing the initial goal of creating more enthusiasm about and interest in math.

The project has grown from a classroom event with seven stores to the three-day extravaganza of 17 stores, including an art gallery, a toy store and a gift shop.

The items for purchase are donated by businesses on the Georgia Avenue corridor, *Union Station,* and *Safeway.* Student participants are given play money to operate the stores and purchase the donated items. They are not allowed to keep the items, which are sold at a later date at a flea market to benefit the school. Students complete ten training courses taught by faculty members who volunteer the extra time - some who owned their own businesses. The subjects include financing, recordkeeping and human relations. Students learn how to fill out loan contracts, inventory slips, receipts and lease applications. They learn to count money, subtract percentages for sales, and browse around the store to spot shoplifters. A license to operate one of the stores costs 30 play dollars.

One student - the owner of the *Impulse Jewelry Store* - summed it up: "This is not an easy job, and there are a lot of things you have to know about running a business if you want to be a success."
Founded: 1990

MIDAS TOUCH
SEE BUSINESS ASSISTANCE: FUNDING

BUSINESS ASSISTANCE: FUNDING

NATIONAL/STATE ORGANIZATIONS

NATIONAL ASSOCIATION OF INVESTMENT COMPANIES
915 Fifteenth Street, NW
Washington, DC 20005
TEL: 202-347-8600
Objectives: To keep small minority businesses current on issues that affect their operations.
Services: Assists organizing groups attempting to form or acquire MESBICS (Minority Enterprise Small Business Investment Companies); provides management and technical assistance; monitors regulatory agency actions; conducts periodic professional and management training seminars; collects and disseminates business information; publishes intermittent *Legislative Alerts,* newsletters, bibliographies, and other materials.
Publications: Perspectives-NAIC; NAIC Membership Directory; Legislative Alert
Founded: 1971

INDIVIDUAL PROGRAM PROFILES

MIDAS TOUCH
Volunteers of America of Los Angeles
3600 Wilshire Boulevard
Los Angeles, CA 90010
TEL: 213-389-1500
Purpose: To provide guaranteed small business loans to teens from humble backgrounds.
Sponsor: Volunteers of America of Los Angeles
Contact: Mark Cosman, VP/Corporate Relations
Description: Begun in 1986, MIDAS is a new VOA project which provides guaranteed small business loans to disadvantaged teens who show the potential for business ownership. Partially funded with a $25,000 grant from TRW, MIDAS loans are offered for after-school, weekend and summer businesses which are started by MIDAS graduates.
The first MIDAS TOUCH Seminar was held in August 1986 in Los Angeles, both administered and funded by TRW employees, who led the way for other members of the business community to become involved.
Funded by TRW's Employees Charitable Organization (ECHO), MIDAS '86 had the hands-on participation of TRW employees - from selecting the project's curriculum to recruiting panelists and serving as counselors.
TRW was also a sponsor of the MIDAS program in Huntsville, Alabama, and is still assisting national VOA in its MIDAS program for disadvantaged teens who demonstrate that they can benefit from such career assistance.

BUSINESS ASSISTANCE: LEGAL RIGHTS

NATIONAL/STATE ORGANIZATIONS

GOVERNMENT CONTRACTS CLINIC
George Washington University
Academic Center, Room T412
801 22nd Street, NW
Washington, DC 20052
TEL: 202-676-6815
Objectives: To offer pro bono publico (no fee) services to firms and individuals who are not financially able to afford the services of private legal counsel; to offer third-year students an opportunity to gain experience.
Services: Represents deserving small businesses in federal government contract litigation; offers advice and counsel on specific legal questions; makes decisions on cases to handle based on limited resources of the program and various other considerations, including the merits of the claim involved, the nature of the efforts required, and the size and financial capabilities of the firm.

BUSINESS ASSISTANCE: MINORITIES/WOMEN

NATIONAL/STATE ORGANIZATIONS

INTERRACIAL COUNCIL FOR BUSINESS OPPORTUNITY
800 Second Avenue
Suite 307
New York, NY 10017
TEL: 212-599-0677
Objectives: To assist minorities in developing, owning and managing business ventures.
Services: Offers business feasibility studies; assists with financing; conducts market development activities and other technical assistance to start or expand minority-owned companies; offers free management training courses; publishes semiannual newsletter and annual report.
Publications: ICBO Newsletter
Founded: 1963

NATIONAL ASSOCIATION OF WOMEN BUSINESS OWNERS
600 South Federal Street
Suite 400
Chicago, IL 60605
TEL: 312-922-0465

Objectives: To broaden opportunities for women in business.
Services: Identifies and brings together women business owners; provides center for sharing of experiences and talents; represents women business owners before government bodies; maintains clearinghouse; operates referral service; establishes cooperative association with groups of similar orientation; publishes monthly newsletter and other materials.
Publications: Statement; Women-Owned Businesses
Founded: 1974

NATIONAL BUSINESS LEAGUE
4324 Georgia Avenue, NW
Washington, DC 20011
TEL: 202-829-5900
Objectives: To promote the economic development of minorities, with full minority participation in the free enterprise system.
Services: Encourages minority ownership and management of small businesses; conducts special projects; supports committees on policy review, and issues affecting minorities in business; maintains file of minority vendors and corporate purchasing agents; publishes annual *Corporate Guide for Minority Vendors,* a monthly newsletter, periodic briefs and other materials.
Publications: National Memo; Guide for Minority Vendors; President's Briefs
Founded: 1900

NATIONAL COUNCIL FOR EQUAL BUSINESS OPPORTUNITY
7932 West Beach Drive
Washington, DC 20012
TEL: 202-723-8348
Objectives: To advance minority business and development and urban development.
Services: Provides services to local community groups whose purpose is to help increase representation of minority groups in business owner ship; trains local groups' board members, staff and volunteers; furnishes both legal and financial advice; develops business models; sets up Small Business Investment Company where none exists; develops general business models; works with large national corporations to foster franchises and technical assistance.
Founded: 1968

NAWBO SCHOLARSHIP FUND
National Association of Women Business Owners
600 South Federal Street
Suite 400
Chicago, IL 60605
TEL: 312-922-0465
Objectives: To encourage young women to become entrepreneurs.
Services: Works to accelerate the growth and stability of businesses owned by women through internships for college students; accepts nominations from colleges based on academic success and the students' desire to own their own businesses; places selected students in six-week internships with local entrepreneurs in its 4,000 local membership areas; provides a stipend (usually about $1,500) for the duration of the internship; offers nominees its general services for potential women business owners, including workshops and seminars, an information clearinghouse, and referral services, as well as access to its corporate relations and leadership development programs and its data bank of women business owners; publishes a newsletter and a directory.
Contact: Barbara Madro, Administrative Director
Publications: Statement (newsletter); Directory of Women Business Owners
Founded: 1974

INDIVIDUAL PROGRAM PROFILES

MINORITY ENTREPRENEURSHIP PROGRAM*
Detroit Public Schools
Stevenson Building
10100 Grand River
Detroit, MI 48204
TEL: 313-931-3838
Purpose: To mount an intensive program of curriculum implementation and practical experience to encourage minority students to consider business ownership.
Sponsor: Detroit Public Schools; Development Career Guidance Program
Contact: Felix R. Sloan, Project Director
Description: Recognizing that the plight of minorities in the area of entrepreneurship in business and industry is one deserving attention and positive action, the Detroit Public School System mounted an intensive program to increase the potential of highly-motivated minority students to succeed as business owners. To succeed, voluntary assistance from the business community was crucial, and was quickly obtained through role models, curriculum advice, materials, and the job stations necessary to provide the practical element to the program.
The program design aspired to give minority students some knowledge and understanding of business fundamentals and management and eventually reduce the high incidence of minority business failure. To reach this goal, the curriculum considers the full K-12 program (K-5 Career Awareness; 6-8 Exploration; 9-12 Pursuit of chosen careers in real situations). The 9-12 program includes work study programs, field trips, actual business operation, and counseling to assist senior high students in getting jobs and scholarships to colleges/schools providing a transition to a career in business management and/or ownership.
Each school is responsible for its own program, providing extensive staff training and access to business representatives for curriculum specialists, teachers, and counselors involved in the effort. The Program Director is responsible for orientation of key school personnel and administrators, and outlines each individual's role. The individual school's administrator then assigns staff persons to the project to:
- disseminate information
- help orient other staff
- arrange field trips for students
- notify staff of working dates, etc.
- assist in contacting resource people
- monitor general progress of the program
- serve on the program's task force committee
Students participate in a classroom/work program, usually spending one to two weeks in the classroom and then the same amount of time at the job station.

BUSINESS ASSISTANCE: SELF-HELP

INDIVIDUAL PROGRAM PROFILES

GREEN LINE ACTION ASSOCIATION
Tuxedo Valet
1715 Seventh Street, NW
Washington, DC 20001
TEL: 202-232-5370
Purpose: To organize business owners affected by the developing metro system, and seek disaster relief to cover extensive loss of business.
Contact: Edward Archie, Owner

Description: When one business owner - operating in the Shaw neighborhood of Washington, DC, in a block that was rendered inaccessible by metro construction - saw his business fall by 50%, he began a process to seek fair and equitable treatment by the city of Washington, DC. His first step was to set up a merchants' organization reflecting the root of the problem, the *Green Line Action Association,* which attracted 33 merchants from the inaccessible area. This organization replaced the once thriving 135-member *Shaw Business and Professional Association.* The small self-help group seeks disaster relief "just like after a hurricane or earthquake."

They are fighting in the face of the opinion of the experts - that, even with help, they will not be able to continue. According to the director of the *Center for Washington Studies,* "Few owners of small businesses survive long disruptions and then stay around long enough to prosper from the changes." Rents skyrocket, and taxes for owners increase drastically when a subway line enters the community, he said.

Motivated by the fact that many of the businesses have been in the family for several generations, the *Green Line Action Association* disagrees. "We are seeing new owners come in when former owners have given up and left, and they expect to get back their investment when the Green Line is completed," he said.

To respond, the City has built two parking lots and a sidewalk to the stores. Although the director of Metro Construction regrets the 90-day closing of the street, he maintains that the five-year subway project had reached a point where safety was paramount, since "running sands" were being encountered - shifting soil that jeopardized the stability of the street overhead during tunneling. Although the Association is optimistic, by mid-1990 the question of disaster relief was not resolved. Members feel that the important thing is that they have joined in a volunteer effort to help maintain long-standing businesses in the Shaw community.

CITIZENSHIP

CITIZENSHIP: CHILDREN/YOUTH

INDIVIDUAL PROGRAM PROFILES

GIRL SCOUTING IN THE INNER CITY
Girl Scouts of the USA
Box 9389
Savannah, GA 31412
TEL: 912-236-1571
Purpose: To bring Girl Scouts to the inner city.
Sponsor: United Way of the Coastal Empire
Contact: Dot Mays, Special Services Director
Description: Since it was difficult to get girls from low-income
urban areas to join the Girl Scouts, the *Girl Scouting in the Inner
City* program brings scouting to them. The program operates
within the inner city, bringing education workshops that range
from basic health and hygiene to teen pregnancy and substance
abuse. In discussing the more serious issues, the sharing of
experiences among the girls themselves is crucial to getting
information across.
Although starting slowly, girls who came into the program said
they knew other girls who needed to be there. They were armed
with sign-up paperwork and went out and got the other girls to
join.
Confidence-building is a strong point of the program. This involves
bringing in role models, like female doctors, to get the girls to
realize that they can have careers like that, too. At the same time
they are shown how teen pregnancy or drug abuse can ruin their
chances for such careers. Explanations are very specific, going into
costs of having a baby, or the harmful effects drugs have on
health.
In addition to funding provided, in part, by the United Way of the
Coastal Empire, the program leaders make a *wish list* each month
of speakers or items they need for projects. As a result, businesses
have given equipment or materials for the education workshops,
the *Junior League* chapter has helped distribute the wish lists and
provided staff for the program, and professionals have come
forward to serve as role models.
According to the director, going into the inner city with the
scouting program is necessary for now, but as confidence grows,
and the networking among the girls from all sectors takes a firmer
hold, it "won't matter where the sessions are held."
Founded: 1988

CIVIC AFFAIRS

NATIONAL/STATE ORGANIZATIONS

AUTOMOTIVE CONSUMER ACTION PROGRAM (AUTOCAP)
SEE CONSUMER SERVICES/LEGAL RIGHTS: TRANSPORTATION

CENTER FOR COMMUNITY CHANGE
1000 Wisconsin Avenue, NW
Washington, DC 20007
TEL: 202-342-0519
Objectives: To provide information and technical assistance to low income and minority community-based organizations to increase program effectiveness; to work with these groups in addressing national issues which have a direct impact on them and their constituencies.
Services: Works to make government more responsive to the needs of the poor; focuses on national issues dealing with poverty; helps community groups of urban and rural poor in developing plans, proposals, and strategies for obtaining federal funds; aids in tapping foundations and church sources for support; helps groups address management and organizational development questions such as board-staff relations, staff training, and fiscal management; assists in specialized areas such as redlining, crime prevention, job development, health care; publishes journal, newsletter, reports, guides, research papers and other materials; sponsors workshops and maintains a National Issues Committee.
Publications: Friday Report; Monitor; CD Citizen; Citizen Action Guide; Special Projects Report
Founded: 1968

CITIZENS INFORMATION SERVICE*
67 East Madison Street
Chicago, IL 60603
TEL: 312-236-0315
Objectives: To foster more effective citizen participation in response to community and organizational needs.
Services: Focuses on providing information to citizens - both in print and in educational classes - that will encourage them to become involved in the concerns of their communities; develops library resources and provides information on civic concerns, government performance in relation to these concerns, and other community-oriented issues; operates a telephone information service, a pamphlet shop, workshops and classes (all services and many publications available in Spanish also).

COMMON CAUSE
2030 M Street, NW
Washington, DC 20036
TEL: 202-833-1200
Objectives: To make government more responsive to the needs and demands of citizens.
Services: Examines laws and works to replace "rusty ones" that either are no longer effective or only serve powerful organizations; promotes a "sunset" program calling for review of government programs after a stated period to determine effectiveness and end those serving no purpose; researches and offers recommendations in areas of energy, inflation, government spending, and others; speaks to groups such as colleges, high schools, churches, business groups, as well as foreign groups wishing to review American lobbying techniques and see volunteerism at work on a large scale; conducts comprehensive training program for its volunteers - which include college interns and retired persons; publishes a bimonthly newsletter, a journal, a report from Washington, and numerous other pamphlets and flyers in areas of government performance.
Publications: Common Cause Magazine; In Common; Frontline
Founded: 1970

COMMUNITY REGENERATION (*formerly Regenerative Agriculture Association***)**
Rodale Institute
222 Main Street
Emmaus, PA 18098
TEL: 215-967-5171
Objectives: To promote community revitalization through individual action and practical, proven procedures.
Services: Motivates and trains public and private individuals to renew and revitalize their communities; applies successful capacity-building techniques to community systems such as housing, food, schools, energy and waste management; helps people, through these techniques, to take advantage of and improve upon available strengths and resources; maintains an extensive database and network of individuals, experts, and successful case histories of community revitalization; provides public speaking, workshops, and consulting services; publishes a bimonthly newsletter, action kits and educational materials; works through membership with individuals and groups through its *Regeneration Network.*
Contact: Ellen Paul, Network Coordinator
Publications: Yes I Can!; Greenfield, Iowa; Hopeful Living; New

Visions; Regenerating America: Opportunities to Build On; Community Options: Projects You Can Do; Regeneration: You and Your Environment
Founded: 1947

FRIENDS COMMITTEE ON NATIONAL LEGISLATION
Religious Society of Friends
245 Second Street, NE
Washington, DC 20002
TEL: 202-547-6000
Objectives: To determine statements, actions and voting records of senators and representatives.
Services: Researches and analyzes information on legislation and voting records; encourages expression of individual views through letters and calls to members of Congress and other government officials; develops testimony programs for hearings before Congress; conducts interviews with key people in government, including Senators and Representatives; publicizes findings for the general public and makes them available at nominal cost in the form of how-to pamphlets, papers and booklets.
Publications: Washington Newsletter; Action Bulletin; Indian News; Visions of a Warless World
Founded: 1943

GOVERNMENT INFORMATION SERVICES
1611 North Kent Street, Suite 508
Arlington, VA 22209
TEL: 703-528-1082
Objectives: To provide the public with information about sources of federal funding.
Services: Operates a hotline service; conducts seminars to teach grantsmanship techniques; publishes *Local Government Funding Report,* which provides current coverage of federal aid programs and funding sources, and *Congressional Boxscore,* which describes all major legislation introduced in the Congress involving federal funding to local and state governments.
Publications: Local Government Funding; Congressional Boxscore

LEAGUE OF CONSERVATION VOTERS*
SEE PHYSICAL ENVIRONMENT

MOVEMENT FOR ECONOMIC JUSTICE
Education and Training Center
413 Eighth Street, SE
Washington, DC 20002
TEL: 202-547-9292
Objectives: To build a political movement that will address national issues.
Services: Communicates with community organizations on economic issues; assists, encourages, promotes and initiates local organizing efforts around basic issues; enters into dialogue with grassroots organizations, organizers, low-income people and others regarding their programs; conducts research, provides training, develops and launches major organizing drives throughout the country; publishes and distributes organizing and other materials.

NATIONAL CIVIC LEAGUE*
55 West 44th Street
New York, NY 10036
TEL: 212-730-7930
Objectives: To help concerned citizens make state and local governments and organized citizen efforts more effective, representative and responsive.
Services: Operates a clearinghouse and monitoring service for information on the civic and government scene; gives special emphasis to particular issues as the need arises (reapportionment and representation, election reform and public ethics, neighborhood and regional governance, local charter and state

constitutional revision, intergovernmental relationships, and citizen participation strategies are examples); establishes linkages between individuals and groups with diverse backgrounds, but with similar concerns and needs; operates through an executive committee, governing council and regional vice presidents, comprising over 100 civic leaders nationwide; receives funding from foundations, corporations, and individual memberships; publishes *Citizen's Forum* monthly, and other publications, video documentaries, model laws and systems; convenes conferences; provides consultation and individualized responses to inquiries; serves as the operating name of the National Municipal League.
Publications: Privatization Report; National Civic Review; Citizen's Forum
Founded: 1894

NATIONAL COALITION FOR VOLUNTEER PROTECTION
c/o Capitol Associates
1575 Eye Street, NW
Washington, DC 20005
TEL: 202-544-1880
Objectives: To help congressional sponsors boost support to Congress for the Volunteer Protection Act (HR 911), and to raise the visibility of the issue.
Services: The National Coalition for Volunteer Protection (NCVP) has found that lobbying on the grass-roots level is an effective way to generate support for legislation in Congress. The Volunteer Protection Act (HR911), introduced in 1985, is designed to encourage states to pass laws that limit volunteer liability under certain circumstances. The Act was generated by the American Society of Association Executives and other major volunteer groups including the American Heart Association, the National Parent Teachers Association, and Big Brothers. The initial direct effort was a four-month grass-roots campaign begun in September 1987. A broad range of volunteer-oriented national organizations have become involved, including thoses who have formally agreed to back the bill (Boys Clubs, American Red Cross, and Little League). In spite of the fact that the bill has not yet passed, by 1989 roughly 25 states had enacted some form of volunteer protection law after the bill was introduced, but many of these are still "patchwork" and inadequate. According to the Director, "The enactment of HR911 would assist these 25 states, as well as those planning to institute protection laws after the bill is passed."
Sponsor: Boys and Girls Clubs of America
Contact: Gordon MacDougall, Executive Director
Publications: Broadening Power Bases (reprint); HR 911: Volunteer Protection Act; S 1430: Volunteer Service Bill; S 520: Volunteer Protection Act

NATIONAL PRIORITIES PROJECT
Citizen Involvement Training Program
377 Hills South
Amherst, MA 01003
TEL: 413-545-2038
Objectives: To help local groups understand the federal budget and its effect on their community.
Services: Works with local groups in a program that addresses the federal budget as it relates to communities; shows how to get involved in the federal budget process by doing strategic research and building broad-based community coalitions to influence budget priorities to be more responsive to community needs; offers training, technical assistance, publications, research and analysis, and workshop participation; produces *Action Packets* based on the objectives of the project.
Sponsor: University of Massachusetts
Publications: Action Packets

OFFICE FOR CHURCH IN SOCIETY
United Church of Christ
105 Madison Avenue
New York, NY 10016
TEL: 212-683-5656
Objectives: To research and study legislation and budget priorities as they affect social issues.
Services: Analyzes findings of research on legislation, publishes resultant conclusions; garners resources of the church for social action projects, and works to increase the number and frequency of such projects; designs and implements legislative and action programs within the church; provides local program suggestions in the area of political responsibility; supports internal committees on public advocacy, church empowerment, and information/publication; publishes monthly newsletter, *UCC Network,* social policy statements, issue packets, listings of resources for research, and other materials.
Publications: Courage in the Struggle
Founded: 1976

TRAINING PROGRAMS

ADVOCACY FOR ACTION: A NEW ROLE FOR VOLUNTEERS
Allegheny County Community College
1130 Perry Highway
Pittsburgh, PA 15237
TEL: 412-931-8500
Credit: Inquire
Sponsor: Allegheny County Community College
Contact: Sarah Jane Rehnborg
Description: This program, made possible by a grant from Title I of the Higher Education Act, provides a foundation for individuals or groups involved in volunteer advocacy activities. Beginning with a keynote address, "Yes, You Can Fight City Hall," presented by a City Council member, the program offers the following workshops:
Lobby for Change - This workshop addresses concerns which are of interest to advocates in general, with attention focused on techniques for effective lobbying, and the reading and interpretation of legislation.
The Citizen's Right to Information and Access to Records - This workshop reviews some of the legislation acts providing citizen access to information and records and explores the psychological barriers to asserting oneself as a citizen advocate; techniques for becoming more assertive are examined.
The Task Force: A Tool for Change - This workshop focuses on the many different functions of the task force - a vital tool for the citizen advocate - and explores ways to develop and work with a task force.
Lobbying and Legislation in Developmental Disabilities - In this session a panel presents effective methods and procedures for obtaining legislation to benefit the needs of the developmentally disabled - exploring both the professional and the volunteer perspective for the lobbying process and legislative change.
Structures of Government and Bureaucracy - This workshop focuses on the overall process of policy development from legislation to implementation with particular attention on how a law is translated into a government program; special emphasis is placed on the effects of citizen involvement on all stages of the policy development process.
In the course of the program a United States Representative provides insight through a presentation, "Advocates and Legislators in Partnership," into the cooperative possibilities between citizen groups and government.
The half-day workshops are repeated in the afternoon session followed by a wrap-up allowing participants to informally gather and share ideas.

FEDERAL INFORMATION POLICIES: ACCESS IS THE KEY (*formerly Federal Library Committee*)
US/Federal Library & Information Center Committee
US/Library of Congress
Washington, DC 20540
TEL: 202-707-6400
Credit: Inquire
Sponsor: US/Library of Congress
Contact: Conference Coordinator
Description: This conference addresses the resolution to be brought to the *White House Conference on Library and Information Services* in July 1991: Citizen access to federal information resources through federal agency information organizations. The conference was designed with two parts:
Part I: Government Information Issues
- Access to Government Information: The Canadian Perspective
- The Future of the Depository Library Program
- Future Trends in Government Information Issues
Part II: Views of the Community
- Public Needs for Federal Information
- The States' Views of Access Issues
- The Medical Community's Views on Open Access
- What Industry Expects from Federal Information Providers
- Information Science and Changing Needs
Related questions posed at the forum included:
- With the emergence of *perestroika,* will policy shift from greater controls to one of open access?
- What impact does federal information policy have on states' and citizen access?
- Should the system of depository libraries be rethought in view of new information technologies?
- What impact does federal information policy have on our economy?
This forum celebrates the 25th anniversary of FLICC, established in 1965 to provide leadership when policy issues affecting the provision of information to government employees and the general public arise. Since 1984, the forums have been held to provide an annual *status report* on information access and dissemination policy. Faculty comes from public and private sectors, including the U.S. Congress, state officials, free libraries, and major universities.

48 HOURS ON CAPITOL HILL
Nonprofit Mailers Federation
125 Michigan Avenue, NE
PO Box 239
Washington, DC 20017-1094
TEL: 202-944-4188
Credit: Inquire
Contact: Briefings Coordinator
Description: This program consists of issue briefings by legislative experts, followed by a planned visit to Capitol Hill. Highlights include a "get acquainted" reception, comprehensive briefings on a variety of issues, a congressional reception, a training session, a mass visitation to Capitol Hill, a debriefing session following Capitol Hill visits, and advice on how to prepare material to deliver to members of Congress. Preconference informational material, and invitations for participants to send to their Congress people inviting them to the reception, are provided.

GRADUATE PROGRAM IN PUBLIC POLICY AND CITIZEN PARTICIPATION
Tufts University
Department of Political Science
Medford, MA 02155
TEL: 617-628-5000
Credit: Master of Arts (M.A.)
Sponsor: Tufts University
Contact: Professor Jeffrey M. Berry

Description: Developed around the explosion in the number of citizen advocacy groups, and the countless federal, state and local programs that mandate citizen participation, this program hopes to provide a solid background in areas of public policy formulation, analysis and evaluation. In addition to learning general skills in administration and citizen advocacy, a specialization in one or more policy areas is developed. Curriculum for the two-year program is composed of required core courses, electives, a summer internship, a major research project. Electives can be taken in policy areas such as these:

- Housing and Community Development
- Nutrition Planning
- Environment and Energy
- Urban Justice
- Science and Technology
- Welfare
- Health Care
- Education

Core courses include citizen participation, public policy analysis, interest group theory, and research methods. In the summer between the first and second years, a full-time internship is required, which may be continued on a part-time basis during the second year. Writing of the M.A. thesis is done during the final semester, and may be the result of a group project under faculty supervision, or individual work.

Jointly sponsored by the Department of Political Science and the Graduate Department of Urban, Social and Environmental Policy, some of the program's courses are taken in existing graduate classes in the Departments of Sociology, Education, Nutrition, Education, etc. This provides opportunities for interaction with many others in these areas than would be possible in an isolated program.

Also on campus is the Lincoln Filene Center for Citizenship and Public Affairs, which conducts many activities and projects of interest to program students, such as conferences, workshops, training seminars, and continuing education in areas of citizen participation and public policy. The Center also publishes Citizen Participation newsmagazine. Many state and federal offices are in close proximity for contact with practitioners and for placement in summer internships.

Although no previous training in the area is required, a bachelor's degree and some evidence that the applicant is likely to achieve success are required for admission. Graduates are qualified for jobs in voluntary associations, interest groups, community development organizations, research institutions, business and industry, government, etc. Job placement in the program has been excellent.

NATIONAL FORUM ON A COMMISSION ON VOLUNTEERISM: THE FEDERAL GOVERNMENT AND FUTURE OF VOLUNTEERISM*
Alliance for Volunteerism
3706 Rhode Island Avenue
Mt. Ranier, MD 20822
TEL: 202-347-0340
Credit: Inquire
Sponsor: Alliance for Volunteerism
Contact: Dorothy Height
Description: This conference was convened to bring together leaders in the national volunteering community - Board Chairpersons, staff executives, Washington representatives - to plan together on issues affecting the future of volunteering in the United States. It was not a position-taking conference, but designed to:

- explore the national situation as it relates to volunteerism today.
- examine current legislation and its implications.
- stimulate exchange of information and opinion.
- prepare to provide input to Congress.
- inspire action plans.

Senator Dave Durenberger's revised legislation on a Commission on Volunteerism, and Senator Paul Tsongas' bill to create a Commission on National Service were discussed along with related issues based on a series of "idea papers" provided to participants in advance of the conference, including:

- A Commission on Volunteerism: Pro and Con
- Legislative Update and Analysis
- The Federal Role in Resources for Volunteerism: Current and Future
- Who Speaks for Volunteers and the Voluntary Sector and Who in Government Listens?
- Mapping the Volunteer Sector
- Roles for Citizen Volunteers in the Federal System
- Government Domination/Government Support and Encouragement of Volunteer Programs
- Youth National Service
- Senior National Service

Additional discussion addressed: use of volunteers in federal programs; federal support for private sector volunteerism; citizen participation in federal decision-making, and other matters of interest to Forum participants.

After the first day of presentations by faculty, an opinion-sharing session to provide stimulation, and informal discussions with resource persons, the small group technique was called into play using a four-fold plan: 1) defining the issue; 2) understanding the issue; 3) dealing with the issue; 4) developing recommendations. This was followed by a dialogue with Congressional representatives on recommendations and, finally, the participants' formulation of action plans.

The Forum was co-sponsored by seven national groups, hosted by a State University, and supported by three foundations.

TRAINING FOR THE MUNICIPAL VOLUNTEER COORDINATOR*
New England Municipal Center
Pettee Brook Offices
PO Box L
Durham, NH 03824
TEL: 603-868-5000
Credit: Inquire
Sponsor: New England Municipal Center; The Mott Foundation
Contact: Susan Casey, Staff Associate
Description: The New England Municipal Center (NEMC) is sponsored by: Connecticut Conference of Municipalities, Maine Municipal Association, Massachusetts Municipal Association, New Hampshire Municipal Association, Rhode Island League of Cities and Towns, Vermont League of Cities and Towns.

NEMC conducts monthly seminars for volunteer coordinators in local government volunteer programs to help them deal with a variety of volunteer management issues, including:

- Program Development
- Public Relations
- Recruitment
- Training
- Volunteer/Paid Employee Relations
- "Education" of Municipal Managers and Department Heads
- Handling the Press

These monthly meetings also act as a support and resource base for coordinators who are out there, on their own, breaking new ground. A significant portion of each group meeting involves group consultation and problem solving around specific issues that need to be dealt with by one of the coordinators.

The assistant town/city managers are invited and encouraged to attend and do so occasionally. Their participation is helpful in building a support base and a mutual understanding of the complex issues involved in municipal volunteer management. Actual training of volunteers occurs on the local level, with each community designing its own training program to meet specific needs. In addition, specific training for individual jobs occurs.

Training sessions for volunteers include police station and library volunteers, crossing guards, etc.

INDIVIDUAL PROGRAM PROFILES

NEW ORLEANS VOLUNTEERS
SEE EDUCATION: SCHOOL VOLUNTEERS

US/WHITE HOUSE - COMMENT LINE
Old Executive Office Building
Washington, DC 20500
TEL: 202-456-7639
Purpose: To give ordinary citizens an opportunity to present opinions, requests, complaints and advice to the president.
Contact: Shirley Green, Correspondence Office Director
Description: The 450 volunteers who answer calls to the *Comment Line* at the *White House* must be able to respond to all types of calls - most from ordinary citizens - ranging from high praise for the President to livid anger about such things as a pay raise for Congress. According to one volunteer, "You need to have people say what they want, whether it's derogatory or in praise." Many insist on talking personally to the President, but no one has accomplished that through the *Comment Line* to date. Callers are assured, however, that their messages will get to the President - and they do. One way is through a biweekly report that tallies pros and cons on the issues and may include a few sample quotes. Flash reports are sent when the director senses unusual activity, or when strategists want a count after a speech or televised news conference.
Telephone calls average 940 each business day - but can surge to 3,000, and 60,000 personal letters for the President are received each week. Acknowledgements are sent for him and may include keepsake Christmas cards, condolence messages, and greetings to couples celebrating golden anniversaries, centenarians on their birthdays, and new Eagle Scouts.
The *Comment Line* started in the Nixon administration when operators on the regular White House switchboard became overwhelmed. With the aid of volunteers - mostly retirees - the practice continued through the Carter administration and grew under President Reagan.
Callers usually must wait on hold, and about 95% of them do. According to the automatic equipment, only 127 out of one day's 2,485 callers decided not to wait.
Volunteers are trained in a system that traces calls threatening the President's life, or indicating other potential problems. These rare calls are switched to the Secret Service.
Screening of volunteers, and training, is thorough. The volunteers are made aware of the fact that they are representing the President of the United States, and that the constituents who call the *Comment Line* are very important to him. When one caller appeared skeptical that the President would see his comment, the volunteer emphatically stated, "If I didn't know this would get to the President, I wouldn't spend my time volunteering!"
Tally counts on call-in opinions are available from the White House for one- or two-week periods - usually several months after the calls are received due to the volume of calls and limited staff.

VIRGINIA CITIZENS CONSUMER COUNCIL
SEE CONSUMER SERVICES/LEGAL RIGHTS

VOLUNTEER CONSULTANT SERVICES PROGRAM
Arkansas Department of Human Services
PO Box 1437
Little Rock, AR 72203-1437
TEL: 501-682-7540
TOLL FREE: 800-482-5850

Purpose: To provide professional volunteers to local government on a consultant basis to address the need for specialized expertise.
Sponsor: Arkansas Office of Volunteerism
Contact: Billie Ann Myers, Director
Description: The Volunteer Consultant Services Program (VCSP) is a part of the Arkansas Office of Volunteerism in the Department of Human Services. It was established to provide local governments with professional volunteers for the purpose of assisting officials in matters relevant to city and county needs. With the curtailment of federal funds to city and county governments to accomplish local projects, it was determined that the only way to solve their problems was through the use of volunteer consultants. "Local solutions to local problems." Dwindling city and county funds can no longer be stretched to meet local needs. A volunteer movement across the state is having a positive effect toward filling the gap.
Independently, and through various volunteer agencies, the VCSP has recruited volunteers across the state in professional areas, including planning and management, fiscal management, budgeting, law, land development, architecture, engineering, recordkeeping, and public administration.
Professional services such as these are frequently needed by local officials and are often the areas that are cut back during times of budgetary distress. The VCSP gives local officials an alternative so that primary services can continue. VCSP is responsive in nature, with the initiative resting with the local government needing the services. Basically, it works this way:
- The local government representative needing assistance calls the VCSP Volunteer Coordinator.
- The VCSP Volunteer Coordinator mails a short project overview form to the caller. The form is completed and returned to the VCSP office.
- Upon receipt of the completed project overview, the VCSP Volunteer Coordinator will review the project and make a determination of the suitability of the project for volunteers.
- Volunteers are then recruited and assigned to the project.
Engineering and architectural projects have been the most requested. Water and sewer systems, fire stations, drainage and street paving projects have been designed by VCSP volunteers. Also, it has developed plans for recreational and industrial parks, removal of barriers to the handicapped, municipal purchasing systems, personnel policies and pension plans. In addition, feasibility studies have been done on computerizing operations, land use, and investment pooling.
One of the most unusual requests was to assist a town in renumbering its house numbers and renaming some of its streets. However, all projects have been for the benefit of the local communities with volunteers coming from local resources. It is interesting to note that no project has had to be refused because a volunteer could not be found. According to the Director, "Cooperation from the various retiree and volunteer groups has been outstanding."
Publications: Volunteer Consultant Services Program
Founded: 1981

CIVIC AFFAIRS: ADVOCACY

NATIONAL/STATE ORGANIZATIONS

ADVOCACY INSTITUTE
1730 M Street, NW
Suite 600
Washington, DC 20036
TEL: 202-659-8475

Objectives: To assist individuals and groups in improving public assistance advocacy skills.
Services: Offers advocacy internship program addressing public interest advocacy; provides training and counseling to conservation, consumer, health, and other nonprofit community interest organizations on how to deal effectively with Congress; conducts training sessions and an awards program (Giant Killers Awards) for outstanding public interest advocacy; publishes a newsletter and other publications.
Publications: Giant Killing; Media Advocacy Cookbook
Founded: 1983

CIVIC AFFAIRS: CHILDREN/YOUTH

NATIONAL/STATE ORGANIZATIONS

CHILDREN'S DEFENSE FUND
122 C Street, NW
Washington, DC 20001
TEL: 202-628-8787
Objectives: To make the needs of children an important matter of public policy.
Services: Monitors federal agencies; comments formally on proposed guidelines and regulations affecting children, especially those aged six to sixteen who live on the streets; testifies before Congress; develops specific principles and recommendations for laws affecting children; seeks redress in courts when other negotiations fail; supports local student and volunteer advocates and groups, especially street health care workers; encourages media to make children's issues an important part of programming; publicizes findings and recommendations in several forms - reports and books, articles, handbooks, speeches, news articles, testimony, etc.
Publications: CDF Reports; Adolescent Pregnancy
Founded: 1973

NATIONAL YOUTH COUNCIL ON CIVIC AFFAIRS
2698 Bunnycrest Court
Fremont, CA 94538
TEL: 415-656-8404
Objectives: To assist communities in involving youth in government.
Services: Helps to establish teen juries, youth commissions, and youth boards of governors; conducts research in several areas of teen involvement with an emphasis on teen participation in the decision-making process; publishes a monthly newsletter, a directory and other materials.
Publications: NYCCA Newsletter

PRESIDENTIAL CLASSROOM FOR YOUNG AMERICANS
441 North Lee Street
Alexandria, VA 22314-2346
TEL: 703-683-5400
Objectives: To contribute to leadership training of youth through personal involvement in government functions.
Services: Provides youth with an opportunity for close observation of the U.S. government in Washington, DC; identifies and assists youth who have high leadership potential; works with high school, graduate and undergraduate university students, and teachers; conducts week-long seminars for high school students; leads a one-week program of seminars and workshops for college students and teachers; maintains extensive library of leadership-oriented materials; publishes a curriculum guide, daily bulletin during the senior high school program, and other materials.
Publications: Presidential Forum; Presidential Daily; Outlook
Founded: 1968

TRAINING PROGRAMS

FAMILY LIFE/COMMUNITY AND GOVERNMENT
SEE CIVIC AFFAIRS: EDUCATION

INDIVIDUAL PROGRAM PROFILES

YOUTH-IN-GOVERNMENT DAY
Youth Advisory Commission
170 Santa Maria Avenue
Pacifica, CA 94044
TEL: 415-877-8631
Purpose: To give teenaged Youth Advisory Commission members an opportunity to discover first-hand how separate city government functions can contribute to the resolution of critical community issues.
Sponsor: Youth Advisory Commission
Contact: John W. Deuel
Description: The Youth Advisory Commission of Pacifica was created by a City Council Ordinance in 1970 to provide young people with a greater voice and more effective representation in the running of their city. It is similar to the other city commissions and operates under the same provisions, except that its members must be between the ages of 14 and 18 years.
One of the Commission's annual projects is Youth-in-Government Day. Through this exercise, the Commission becomes better able to identify and resolve important city issues and also to involve more students in the running of City Government.
Two months prior to the actual Youth-in-Government Day, students from the two local high schools are asked to present a list of topics which they feel are current and important to the city's youth. From this list, the Youth Advisory Commission selects five topics that are to be the focus on Youth-in-Government Day.
During the morning session of Youth-in-Government Day, four groups of six students each discuss separate issues with an objective of developing a resolution which will be presented at the Youth Convention during the afternoon. These meetings are held in the City Council chambers with representatives of each department of City government present to participate in the discussions until noon.
Lunch is hosted at a local restaurant by the Rotary Club and a guest speaker is invited (e.g., Pacifica's City Manager). After lunch, each of the five resolutions is presented and voted on by the entire group of students. Later in the afternoon, the youth participants are brought to City Hall for a brief orientation to departments.
The proposals that result from Youth-in-Government Day are reviewed by the Youth Advisory Commission and presented to the City Council for action recommendations.

CIVIC AFFAIRS: CITY/COUNTY GOALS

NATIONAL/STATE ORGANIZATIONS

NATIONAL LEAGUE OF CITIES
1301 Pennsylvania Avenue, NW
Washington, DC 20004
TEL: 202-626-3000
Objectives: To strengthen the role and capacity of municipal governments in bringing about a better urban America; to help cities solve critical problems that they have in common.
Services: Represents municipalities with Congress and federal agencies; sponsors several committees (Community and Economic

Development, Human Development, Intergovernmental Relations, and others); develops and puts into effect national municipal policy, a statement of major municipal goals in the U.S.; represents municipalities before federal agencies and Congress; works to help officials improve the quality of their local governments through training programs, technical assistance, and information; publishes weekly *Nation's Cities* and other materials designed for municipal officials and urban citizens.
Publications: Nation's Cities Weekly; Urban Affairs Abstracts; City Policy Officials; Local Chief Executives; Local Women Elected Officials
Founded: 1924

NATIONAL URBAN COALITION
1120 G Street, NW
Suite 900
Washington, DC 20005
TEL: 202-628-2990
Objectives: To stimulate others to respond to the need for a reordering of national priorities.
Services: Brings together and combines efforts of leaders among minorities, business, labor, local government, women, youth and religion to work toward improvement of life for the disadvantaged in urban areas; conducts research; provides advocacy, technical assistance, training in areas of housing, urban education, neighborhood revitalization, government decisions, basic necessities, taxes, etc.; publishes *Urban Policy Watch* monthly, *Targeting Employment and Training* monthly, a quarterly magazine, *Network,* and numerous other publications on urban issues.
Publications: Urban Exchange; Urban Health Exchange; Urban Education Exchange; Urban Housing Exchange; Urban Policy Watch; Targeting Employment and Training; Network
Founded: 1967

NEIGHBORHOODS USA (*formerly National Conference on Neighborhood Concerns*)
4643 Amesborough
Dayton, OH 45420
TEL: 513-222-2889
Objectives: To build and strengthen the nation's neighborhoods through working partnerships.
Services: Works with neighborhood representatives, local government staff, elected officials, technical assistance providers, and practitioners in the public and private sectors to form working partnerships with the purpose of building and strengthening the nation's neighborhoods; conducts conferences on neighborhood concerns and related programs that promote educational, social, and cultural objectives for neighborhood residents; maintains a speakers' bureau and a *National Neighborhood of the Year* Committee, which bestows an annual award; publishes a newsletter and annual conference proceedings; enables comprehensive exhibits and presentations by neighborhood representatives from across the country at its annual conference in May of each year.
Publications: NUSA Newsletter; NUSA Conference Proceedings
Founded: 1975

U.S. CONFERENCE OF MAYORS
1620 Eye Street, NW
Washington, DC 20006
TEL: 202-293-7330
Objectives: To provide a national forum through which the nation's larger cities (30,000 or more) can share ideas, express ideals and otherwise meet the challenges facing today's urban leadership; to ensure that federal policy meets urban needs in such areas as drugs and crime, housing, transportation, etc.
Services: Designs programs to aid Mayors and to bring them new information for problem solving in areas such as how to involve volunteers, how to finance urban development, how to interest

private firms and funds for a full public-private development partnership, and numerous other issues designed to improve the quality of life in the larger cities.
Co-sponsors, with Xerox Corporation, the annual Mayors' Awards Program in Recognition of Outstanding Leadership in Citizen Volunteerism, which has a different focus each year (e.g., public-private partnership; unemployment); makes continual efforts to find ways that local community groups, city hall and various federal programs can be made to work more cooperatively, with all of these efforts aimed at building the capacity of Mayors to solve problems.
Publications: Mayors of Principal Cities; U.S. Mayor; City Problems; Federal Budget and Cities
Founded: 1932

TRAINING PROGRAMS

BUILDING MOMENTUM FOR A RESPONSIVE AMERICA
Volunteer Leaders Conference
United Way of America
701 North Fairfax Street
Alexandria, VA 22314-2045
TEL: 703-836-7100
Credit: Inquire
Sponsor: United Way of America
Contact: Conference Coordinator
Description: This conference continues the theme, Second Century Initiatives, launched by the 1987 conference. In that first conference of the United Way's second century, goals were to double volunteers and financial resources. Having reached those goals, the United Way has set the theme for this conference as expanding formulas for success. Its purpose is to find out what works, how it works, and why.
In a special full-day symposium, volunteers are matched with other volunteers from similar communities - similar in size, demographics, and economic makeup. They share ideas, examine approaches to problems, and explore critical issues.
Another full day is devoted to how-to workshops that span a wide range of topics, including:
● Resource Development
● Fund Distribution
● Year-Round Communications
● Community Problem-Solving
● Marketing
● Volunteers
● Government Relations
● Workplace Presence
● Strategic Planning
● Youth Involvement
● Gifts in Kind
● United Way State Organizations
● Inclusiveness
The conference works throughout the year to develop a theme for the annual conference that will provide the most benefit for the dedicated volunteer leaders.

VISION, PLANNING & PARTNERSHIP IN NEIGHBORHOOD ORGANIZING
SEE RECIPIENTS: FAMILIES

INDIVIDUAL PROGRAM PROFILES

FAIRFIELD 2000
SEE CIVIC AFFAIRS: 21ST CENTURY

GOALS FOR DALLAS*
2004 Davis Building
1309 Main Street
Dallas, TX 75202
TEL: 214-741-1738
Purpose: To assist citizens in setting goals, developing plans to achieve goals, and monitoring and facilitating goal achievement activities.
Sponsor: Individuals, business/industry, foundations
Contact: John Lewis, Director
Description: Goals for Dallas was founded in 1965. The basic challenge continues to provide an arena in which all the differing ideas about what should happen in Dallas may be resolved into one list of goals representing a consensus of community opinion. Based on these goals, a continual effort works toward the building of a community that satisfies collective and individual needs of its citizens.

Goals for Dallas works through a Planning Committee which lays the groundwork each year for a new *Goals for Dallas* process. Some 500 volunteers on Goals Achievement Committees in 17 areas of community concern meet in the fall of each year to report on each of the 205 citizens' goals set in 1977. The 150-member Planning Committee forms small groups consisting of ten to twelve members each to explore the various approaches and building blocks that form the bases for the new Goals for Dallas process. The work of the 17 Achievement Committees resulted in a series of published reports covering the following 17 areas of concern:
- Citizen Involvement
- Continuing Education
- Cultural Activities
- The Design of the City
- Economy
- Elementary and Secondary Education
- Energy
- Environment
- Government
- Health
- Higher Education
- Housing
- Human Services
- Public Safety
- Quality of the Citizenry
- Recreation and Leisure Time
- Transportation

In the decade of the eighties, the process of Goals for Dallas diverged somewhat from the one that worked so well for 15 years. The increasing rate of change indicates that more is needed than a collective definition of problems and opportunities, and traditional plans to achieve goals. A recognition of the "new" Dallas - the changing nature of its people, politics, resources and organizations - has indicated that future goals must respond to the "new" Dallas as well as the successes of 15 years of work. In the meantime, activities toward goals achievement continue uninterrupted.

In addition to goals achievement activities and planning for the next decade, Goals for Dallas Trustees and Achievement Committee Executives meet to deal with long-range needs. Their Workshop 2000 examined the city in its present state, predicted change to the year 2000, and assessed the positive and negative impacts of that change on the future. In addition, meetings are held by organizations such as the *Dallas Alliance Convocation of Neighborhoods,* with workshops ranging from neighborhood leadership to zoning, and providing the opportunity for direct citizen-public official contact.

The new Planning Committee consists of elected officials, business people, public administrators, media members, civic leaders, educators, students, retirees, local groups, association chapters, long-time Goals workers, newcomers to Dallas, and many other volunteers. This diversity is reflected, also, in the 17 Achievement Committees.
Publications: Goals for Dallas; New Goals for Dallas
Founded: 1965

MORRIS 2000
Regional Plan Association
60 Park Place
Suite 1603
Newark, NJ 07102
TEL: 201-623-1133
Purpose: To create a balanced growth strategy for Morris County.
Sponsor: Newark Star-Ledger
Description: In 1984 and 1985, hundreds of *Morris County* citizens worked for 18 months to examine techniques that have worked in other parts of the country to create a *balanced growth strategy.* In addition, 77,000 citizens received a survey questionnaire published in the *Star Ledger* to enable the widest input base possible. As a result of the work of the many task forces in public forums and debates and a Countywide conference, 70 specific action steps were taken by the State, the County, municipalities and the private sector. Specific areas of action were:
- Land Use Decisionmaking
- Financial Incentives to Support Regional Planning
- Improving Transportation Prospects
- Meeting Housing Needs
- Protecting Land and Water
- Meeting Human Needs

These steps were an outgrowth of four recommendations aimed at the public sector, but with many actions required by the private sector. These included: (1) Using some of the wealth of developers to meet needs like roads, sewers, water systems, etc.; (2) An open and cooperative process for reconciling municipal and County planning on matters of regional concern; (3) Property Tax System reform; and (4) Increase of County powers.

The *Regional Plan Association* published a special edition of its *Regional Plan News,* which described the activities of the citizens in the *Morris 2000* program, and included a survey questionnaire to elicit feedback from the wider community.
Publications: Morris 2000

NEW DIRECTIONS FOR THE BRONX
Regional Plan Association
1040 Avenue of the Americas
New York, NY 10018
TEL: 212-398-1140
Purpose: To "bring The Bronx into the twenty-first century."
Sponsor: Bronx Development Council
Description: In 1988, 300-400 volunteers responded to an invitation from the *Regional Plan Association* to help find "new directions for The Bronx." Four task forces of the *Bronx Development Council* were formed and met throughout 1988 and 1989. Priority recommendations that developed through the work of the citizens included:
- Prepare people to work;
- Make The Bronx beautiful again;
- Increase the population;
- Combat drugs;
- Help newcomers;
- Increase jobs and business opportunities;
- Get people to the jobs;
- Promote Bronx cultural life; and
- Can we do it?

With the help of the *Daily News,* which printed a special supplement after some progress was made by the initial participants, the wider community was involved, and the Council's initial recommendations were expanded and detailed to include other areas such as traffic congestion, outdoor recreation, and the need for major capital investments by combined public and private sectors to achieve these and other stated goals.

Terms like "centers of business excellence" (where firms share services and support each other in relations with government) were coined, and the "Bronx Harlem River Plan" was formulated to help keep people in The Bronx.

Many hearings, conferences and other meetings were held to be sure every citizen had "a chance to have your say."
Publications: New Directions for the Bronx

WESTCHESTER 2000
SEE CIVIC AFFAIRS: 21ST CENTURY

CIVIC AFFAIRS: EDUCATION

NATIONAL/STATE ORGANIZATIONS

CLOSE UP FOUNDATION
1235 Jefferson Davis Highway
Arlington, VA 22202
TEL: 703-979-2070
Objectives: To increase civic involvement, stimulate civic achievement, and create civic awareness among citizens of all ages.
Services: Conducts a week-long government study visit in Washington, DC, for tenth, eleventh or twelfth grade students, their teachers, and senior citizens, with more than 26,000 participants annually; coordinates community-based programs across the nation to help high school students and teachers examine local governments and regional issues; televises seminars about current issues and the political process over the C-SPAN cable network; conducts the "Citizen Bee," a competition on local, state, and national levels in American studies for high school students; publishes supplemental textbooks which provide comprehensive insights into American government, the political process, and contemporary issues; and conducts the "Civic Achievement Award Program" affording fifth- through eighth-grade students the opportunity to strengthen their civic knowledge and skills and become involved in their communities. [The Close Up Foundation is partially funded by the U.S. Congress through the Allen J. Ellender Fellowship Fund.]
Contact: Richard Horton
Publications: Close Up Chronicle; Current Issues; Perspectives; The Washington Notebook; The Source Book; Focus; New Directions
Founded: 1971

PRESIDENTIAL CLASSROOM FOR YOUNG AMERICANS
SEE CIVIC AFFAIRS: CHILDREN/YOUTH

PUBLIC CITIZEN
PO Box 19404
Washington, DC 20036
TEL: 202-293-9142
Objectives: To help tourists from across the country (and local residents) become issue-oriented and citizen-conscious while visiting Washington, DC; to provide information to any local group planning a visit.
Services: Provides citizen advocacy in areas including a healthful environment, consumer rights, corporate and government accountability, and citizen empowerment; provides an informational and recreational schedule of alternatives designed to enable the visitor to return to his/her community with a broader knowledge of government than the usual tourist route allows, e.g., assists tour group or individual in attending congressional and regulatory agency hearings, and any one of a number of high-interest attractions such as the Environmental Protection Agency's Center; administers monthly public citizens forum (open discussion between government, citizens, and the news media); publishes detailed biweekly calendar, free to anyone, *Inside the Capitol, Guide to the U.S. Capitol,* and others. (The Center

evolved from one of Ralph Nader's ideas.)
Publications: Public Citizen; Buyers Up News; Critical Mass Bulletin; Health Letter; Inside the Capitol; Guide to the U.S. Capitol
Founded: 1971

WASHINGTON WORKSHOPS FOUNDATION
SEE CIVIC AFFAIRS: 21ST CENTURY

TRAINING PROGRAMS

COMMUNICATIONS SKILLS FOR THE COLLEGE BOUND
New Brunswick High School
1125 Livingston Avenue
New Brunswick, NJ 08902
TEL: 201-745-5336
Credit: Course credit
Sponsor: New Brunswick Board of Education
Contact: Janet Obrzut, Teacher
Description: This course includes a requirement for students to analyze current trends and act upon their findings. In 1989 this culminated in addressing the deterioration of the environment and working at the local level to help bring about improvement. They had to go no further than their own school yard, where litter was a constant problem. The students began to organize an anti-litter campaign, including a plan to have students pick up litter around the school for a half-hour after school each day for three days. What sounded so simple at first - get kids to volunteer to go out and pick up all of the trash - proved complex, causing them to postpone the event and regroup. Starting from "square one," the students learned the "nuts and bolts" of publicizing the event, recruiting volunteers, holding meetings, scheduling and other aspects of community organizing. Two critical issues faced by the students this time were:
- Why the project might succeed or fail; and
- What to do if no one shows up at a meeting.

Having learned from the initial effort, the students decided they would "network" - ask friends to come and bring other students, as well as post meeting notices around the school. While doing this, they are required to put their efforts in context - learn more about the subject themselves. In response they checked out beautification and anti-litter programs in New Brunswick, where a lot is being done. They learned from these contacts that it is a good public relations ploy to take before-and-after pictures around the school and make an oral report to the student body. In the outset, enlisting volunteers was not a problem. This time around they had no trouble enlisting volunteers. According to one student, "We didn't realize how many people feel the way we do about our school."
In addition to the group who developed and managed the anti-litter project itself, a second group of students made a television documentary of the anti-litter efforts, showing the "ups and downs and ins and outs" of organizing a community environmental project. A local cable channel is considering showing the video. A third group in the class chose to dramatize the effects of environmental disasters by creating a play in which students enact roles of animals and people whose lives have been changed or lost in events such as the oil spill in Alaska and the escape of lethal gas in India.
The teacher said she is amazed at the effectiveness of the student groups in the course who benefited from the experience while improving the community. She felt that the greatest lesson learned was that organizing a "simple community project" is not as simple as it seems - a lesson that is as valuable in paid careers as it is in volunteer service.

FAMILY LIFE/COMMUNITY AND GOVERNMENT
Papillion/La Vista High School
7821 Terry Drive
Papillion, NE 68128
TEL: 402-339-0405
Purpose: To demonstrate connections among family, government, and community.
Credit: Two high school credits
Sponsor: Papillion Board of Education
Contact: Doris Harder
Description: A one-semester course developed in 1975 enables students at the school to compare family, government and community issues and analyze their relations to each other. The course is team-taught. Orientation consists of basic dos and don'ts of volunteering, leadership training, communication-building exercises, and role playing. There are two units of study:
- **Community and Government** - an examination of what a community is, the services it provides, and its relationship to government.
- **Family Life and the Community** - a study of issues such as crisis and stress, domestic violence and its relation to crime, and chemical dependence.

The course requires 1-1/2 hours a day for nine weeks on site. Students are not limited to the school's resource guide listing current placement sites. They can create projects based on their own interests.

To facilitate the program and keep students in the field, half of the students complete community work first while the other half does the classroom work first. One social studies credit is given for class work, and one general elective credit for field work.

In addition to the academic requirements, students complete major projects based on their volunteer assignments. For example, a group of students working with delinquent youths in the court system created a directory of community agencies where youth could meet their alternative sentencing/community service obligations. Another student produced a pictorial study of the homeless in conjunction with her work with them. Other students have worked in hospitals, day care centers, police stations and shelters.

Students keep daily journals, which are graded weekly. The last journal entry is expected to be a wrap-up and evaluation of the volunteer experience in the field.

Roll is taken at school before the students go to their volunteer assignments, and each student must sign in and out at the sites. Two evaluations come from the site supervisor - one at mid-term and another at the end of the quarter. Creativity is strongly encouraged throughout the program.
Founded: 1975

CIVIC AFFAIRS: EVALUATION/SURVEYS/REPORTS

NATIONAL/STATE ORGANIZATIONS

CENTER FOR INFORMATION ON AMERICA
Washington, CT 06793
TEL: 203-868-2602
Objectives: To further the knowledge and understanding of America by Americans.
Services: Researches areas such as the cost of politics, economic growth, energy, social security, youth unemployment, population, group health; analyzes and publishes its findings for the general public through a periodical, *Vital Issues,* with each edition focusing on a single issue, and *Grass Roots Guide on Democracy*

and Practical Politics, and other materials.
Publications: Vital Issues; Grass Roots Guide on Democracy

SOCIAL LEGISLATION INFORMATION SERVICE/CWLA
Child Welfare League of America
440 First Street, NW
Suite 310
Washington, DC 20001
TEL: 202-638-2952
Objectives: To report impartially on federal social legislation.
Services: Serves national, state and local agencies and organizations and libraries interested in social welfare; researches areas of federal social legislation and activities in areas of health, housing, employment, education, etc. and develops materials for distribution that report impartially on findings of the research; provides reporting service only and takes no position for or against legislation; publishes semimonthly bulletin and other documents.
Publications: Social Legislation Bulletin
Founded: 1944

CIVIC AFFAIRS: LAW ENFORCEMENT

TRAINING PROGRAMS

FORUM ON SCHOOL VANDALISM
SEE LAW ENFORCEMENT/CRIME PREVENTION: CHILDREN/YOUTH

CIVIC AFFAIRS: MINORITIES/WOMEN

NATIONAL/STATE ORGANIZATIONS

JOINT CENTER FOR POLITICAL STUDIES
1301 Pennsylvania Avenue, NW
Washington, DC 20004
TEL: 202-626-3500
Objectives: To promote the informed and effective involvement of blacks in the governmental process.
Services: Conducts research on issues of special concern to black and disadvantaged Americans in three interrelated areas: public policy, political participation, and governmental and social institutions; provides an independent, nonpartisan forum for the appraisal of policy alternatives and the shaping of public policies at all levels of government; engages business and labor leaders, scholars, journalists, and public officials - black and white - in discussion of issues vital to the health of the nation; provides information in the form of published research reports, a monthly newsletter, a roster of black elected officials, and other materials. (This program is partially funded by the Ford Foundation.)
Publications: Focus; Black Elected Officials
Founded: 1970

LEAGUE OF WOMEN VOTERS OF THE US
1730 M Street, NW
Washington, DC 20036
TEL: 202-429-1965
Objectives: To foster citizen involvement and develop citizen leaders; to help people understand public issues and how government works; to promote discussion of government policies; to influence public policy; to promote political responsibility.

Services: Keeps citizens informed on national issues; encourages citizens' active participation in government; studies selected issues at national, state and local levels and takes legislative positions on these issues; distributes information on candidates to encourage registration and voting without supporting or opposing candidates or political parties; publishes numerous guides, handbooks, pamphlets, kits, packets, audiovisual items, and other materials in areas of political responsibility.
Publications: National Voter; Report from the Hill
Founded: 1920

NATIONAL COUNCIL ON THE BLACK AGING
Box 51275
Durham, NC 27717
TEL: 919-684-3175
Objectives: To examine legislation affecting older black persons and publish findings.
Services: Identifies policy areas that appear to affect minority elderly people more adversely than the general older population; uses findings to inform interested individuals, groups and institutions; publishes *Journal of Minority Aging.*
Publications: Journal of Minority Aging
Founded: 1975

PEACE LINKS - WOMEN AGAINST NUCLEAR WAR
SEE CIVIC AFFAIRS: PEACE

INDIVIDUAL PROGRAM PROFILES

PEACE LINKS ARKANSAS
SEE CIVIC AFFAIRS: PEACE

VOTER REGISTRATION ASSISTANCE
SEE CIVIC AFFAIRS: VOTING

CIVIC AFFAIRS: OLDER PERSON

INDIVIDUAL PROGRAM PROFILES

SENIOR CITIZEN INTERNSHIP PROGRAM
US/Senate
Office of Sen. William Roth
Washington, DC 20510
TEL: 202-224-2441
Purpose: To give senior community leaders a first-hand view of the federal government and how it operates with regard to their community efforts for the elderly.
Sponsor: US/Senate
Contact: Hon. William Roth
Description: For five days in May of each year, older Americans, usually sponsored by their Congressmen, converge on Washington to work daily hours in their sponsors' offices and attend an exhaustive schedule of discussions. The Senior Citizen Internship Program was created by a Congressman in 1972 with nine interns. Since then (through the 1980 program), 730 seniors have participated. In 1980, the largest group so far, 230 older Americans represented 43 states, with 150 Congressmen volunteering to sponsor persons from their home states and districts.
The senior volunteers (who receive expenses only) view the five-day period as an opportunity for "the elderly and Congress to eyeball each other at close range." They come to learn some shortcuts in dealing with the federal government to use back home

in their roles as community activists. The first reaction is surprise in learning about programs for the aged that exist but are not now in their communities.
While in Washington, the interns stay at the same hotel to get to know each other and share ideas and experiences. They also develop a rapport with their Congressional sponsors, "planting the seeds of a communication network that will serve as a continuing link between the community and Congress." They make contacts, jot down names and phone numbers of people in aging programs, and generally make themselves visible and their presence felt.
Federal agencies, private organizations, and Congressional leaders schedule discussions, workshops, and other get-togethers for the "armchair advocates." Although usually sedate, some of the workshops have exploded in heated confrontation when straight answers are not forthcoming. Many officials have been stunned by a circle of irate interns - all probably twice his/her age - questioning a policy or statement.
Once back in their home towns, they are expected to become liaisons with their Congressional offices, keeping "the Hill" informed of needs and problems of the aged, while gaining up-to-date legislation. Among activities by returning interns:
- Ohio - senior transportation services
- Georgia - senior fitness center
- Florida - statewide syndicated column on aging
- Iowa - political grass-roots movement
- Maryland - increase of senior housing; solutions to nursing home problems
- Louisiana - health care services

In addition, a 66-year-old man from the 1980 program decided to run for Congress in 1982, and a couple, both 63, were invited to represent the United States and the elderly in a foreign country. To participate in future programs, senior citizens must contact their representatives in Congress.
Founded: 1972

SILVER HAIRED LEGISLATIVE SESSION
Arkansas Division of Aging and Adult Services
Department of Human Services
PO Box 1437
Little Rock, AR 72203
TEL: 501-682-8511
Purpose: To bring attention to the needs of senior Arkansans.
Sponsor: Arkansas Division of Aging and Adult Services; eight Area Agencies on Aging
Contact: Bean Hudson, Advocacy Supervisor
Description: The Silver Haired Legislative Session (SHLS) is a one-day mock session with older Arkansans serving as delegates in a very special session at the State Capitol. The 1988 session was the 6th biennial session conducted to bring attention to the needs of older persons in Arkansas.
The senior "delegates" have the opportunity to write bills, work in committees, speak on the floor of the House Chamber, and vote their opinion. The success rate of a Silver Haired bill or resolution is much higher than for legislation during a real General Assembly session. Only two of the 24 bills and one of the 11 resolutions failed to pass.
During the opening ceremonies, state and elected officials welcomed the delegates and let them know how serious their Silver Haired work is to the General Assembly. They assured the delegates that they would be reading the SHLS bills carefully.
Five Silver Haired committees met in the House committee rooms to discuss bills in six important topic areas: (1) health care cost containment; (2) nursing home reform; (3) transportation issues; (4) taxation and retirement income; (5) alternatives to nursing homes, and (6) consumer concerns. Eight of the 24 bills addressed alternatives to nursing homes and indicated great concern about this issue.
At the close of the program the delegates were reminded that "on August 31 you were legislators, but after the session you should

continue to be 'lobbyists' for the interest of the elderly." He added that grassroots support through their group was instrumental in the success of a number of bills, especially in the area of nursing home reform.

The Silver Haired Legislation Session is sponsored by the Arkansas Division on Aging and Adult Services with assistance from the eight Area Agencies on Aging. A complete report of all aspects of the SHLS, including copies of bills that were passed, is available from the Division.

Publications: Silver Haired Legislation Session Report

CIVIC AFFAIRS: PEACE

NATIONAL/STATE ORGANIZATIONS

CHILDREN AS PEACEMAKERS

950 Battery Street
Second Floor
San Francisco, CA 94111
TEL: 415-981-0916
Objectives: To foster world peace through cultural exchange.
Services: Makes arrangements for children to speak to world leaders about peace; operates three major international programs: *Peace Mission,* which brings together children from every continent to meet with world leaders on the subject of peace; *Banner Project,* which coordinates efforts in research and represents children who are victims of war since 1930; *International Children's Peace Prize,* which is presented annually to children from more than 50 countries; operates through membership of individuals interested in fostering world peace through cultural exchange.
Founded: 1982

COPRED STUDENTS PEACE NETWORK

Consortium of Peace Research, Education & Development
c/o George Mason University
4400 University Drive
Fairfax, VA 22030
TEL: 703-323-2806
Objectives: To become involved in peace research, peace studies, or peace action in schools and communities.
Services: Brings together students working for disarmament, human rights, economic justice, and ecological balance; acts as a resource and communications channel in developing coordinated efforts toward peace and greater international solidarity among students; sponsors panels and workshops; conducts specialized education; compiles internship, job and fellowship information; maintains network groups that work on peace issues with children.
Publications: COPRED Peace Chronicle
Founded: 1981

FRIENDS PEACE COMMITTEE

Religious Society of Friends
1515 Cherry Street
Philadelphia, PA 19102
TEL: 215-241-7230
Objectives: To promote international and individual peace.
Services: Works through the 45-member committee appointed at the yearly meeting of the *Society* to promote both international and individual peace; includes programs on disarmament, draft and enlistment alternatives, and foreign policy issues; maintains a speakers' bureau; works with other committees that address Quaker concerns (taxes, criminal justice, race relations, and others); provides counseling to members of the armed forces and others; publishes bulletins on legislation and government

initiatives, and other materials.
Founded: 1892

NATIONAL PEACE INSTITUTE FOUNDATION

110 Maryland Avenue, NE
Suite 409
Washington, DC 20002
TEL: 202-546-9500
TOLL FREE: 800-23-PEACE
Objectives: To advance peace education and conflict resolution; to assist in developing the *U.S. Institute of Peace* established by Congress.
Services: Provides information and education regarding the management and resolution of conflict and its potential for avoiding nuclear war, conventional war, and terrorism; works to bring together individuals, organizations, and educational institutions interested in peacemaking for an effective working relationship; assists in the development of the *U.S. Institute of Peace* established by the U.S. Congress; provides networking and clearinghouse services; develops multi-media educational programs; maintains a speakers' bureau; operates several computerized databanks on peace issues; publishes a quarterly newsletter and other materials.
Publications: Peace Institute Reporter; A Long Step Toward Security & Peacemaking Behavior

NO GREATER LOVE

1750 New York Avenue, NW
Washington, DC 20006
TEL: 202-783-4665
Objectives: To provide friendship and care to children of servicemen missing or killed in action (original goal, now expanded to other isolated groups).
Services: Operates the *Pledge of Peace* program which provides pledge cards to groups and individuals to sign and return as a commitment to peace as a legacy to the children today and in future generations; aids hospitalized veterans, children of servicemen killed or missing in action in Vietnam, families of servicemen killed in Iran, Lebanon, and Grenada, handicapped veterans, and other military-related groups; expands its services to include non-military-related groups such as badly-burned children, children with leukemia, elderly persons living alone or without families, and other neglected or forgotten groups; sponsors and coordinates Memorial Day ceremonies, salutes to hospitalized veterans and children, and an international *Time of Remembrance* program for the victims of terrorism worldwide, and the children of the Americans killed in Lebanon. [*No Greater Love* created and coordinated the *Free the Hostages* yellow ribbon pin campaign during the Iran hostage crisis. In May 1990 the organization sponsored a reunion of the two U.S. hostages released from Lebanon the month before, inviting their families and relatives of other hostages, and members of the U.S. Senate, to begin the healing process through discussions about the ordeal in a supportive atmosphere.]
Publications: Pledge of Peace Information Kit
Founded: 1971

PEACE LINKS - WOMEN AGAINST NUCLEAR WAR

747 Eighth Street, SE
Washington, DC 20003
TEL: 202-544-0805
Objectives: To encourage citizens to lead their families and communities in activities designed to prevent nuclear war.
Services: Helps people learn more about peace issues, express their concern, organize for action, affiliate with related groups, support leaders advocating peace, and educate children toward involvement in the democratic process; works cooperatively with major women's organizations; oversees 41 state groups; maintains speakers bureau which includes peace panels for meetings and

conferences; conducts seminars and workshops; promotes *Peace Day* on the first Sunday in October of each year; publishes and distributes a newsletter, a journal, and relevant packets.
Publications: The Link; The Connection
Founded: 1982

PEACE MUSEUM
430 West Erie Street
Chicago, IL 60610
TEL: 312-440-1860
Objectives: To provide peace education through the visual, literary and performing arts.
Services: Promotes research and study of war, peace, and conflict resolution; encourages public participation in determining policies that build peace; disseminates peace education materials to schools and communities; uses visual, literary and performing arts in its peace education programs; explores and celebrates the cultural heritage of peace and peacemakers through special programs; sponsors several different traveling exhibits (including a collection of drawings by survivors of the Hiroshima and Nagasaki atomic bombings), film showings, poetry readings, theatrical performances and lectures; maintains a museum, gift shop and bookstore.

PRIMARY/SECONDARY PEACE EDUCATION NETWORK
c/o Betty Cole/Westridge School
324 Madeline Drive
Pasadena, CA 91105
TEL: 818-799-1153
Objectives: To implement peace education in the schools.
Services: Develops peace education curricula for primary and secondary school students; works with teachers to implement the curricula, which include topics such as nonviolent social change, conflict resolution, and international understanding; provides teacher training workshops and conducts research to enhance the program and keep materials and activities current; works with the *Consortium on Peace Research, Education and Development* (parent organization), and *Educators for Social Responsibility* in a cooperative effort in developing and implementing the program.

U.S. INSTITUTE OF PEACE
1550 M Street, NW
Suite 700
Washington, DC 20005
TEL: 202-457-1700
Objectives: To facilitate training in negotiation and conflict resolution.
Services: Promotes and supports peace scholarships and research; offers competitive academic grants to nonprofit institutions and individuals; operates a small library; coordinates training in conflict resolution and negotiation; maintains a speakers' bureau and committees in areas of education and training, information services, institutional planning, and research and studies; administers fellowship and grant programs; publishes a quarterly newsletter, a biennial report, an intermittent journal, and a series of monographs and books.
Sponsor: US/Congress
Publications: USIP Newsletter; USIP Journal; USIP Report
Founded: 1984

VETERANS FOR PEACE
PO Box 3881
Portland, ME 04104
TEL: 207-797-2770
Objectives: To educate the public on the need to abolish war.
Services: Works through its members, veterans and others who served in the military under combat conditions and their families; strives to educate the public on the cost of war, nuclear and foreign policy issues, and the abolishment of war; sends delegations to other countries; maintains small library and speakers' bureau; publishes a quarterly newsletter and a special report.
Publications: Veterans for Peace; Special Report on Delegations
Founded: 1985

TRAINING PROGRAMS

FIRST ANNUAL SOVIET-AMERICAN YOUTH SUMMIT
Youth Ambassadors of America
c/o St. Stephens School
1000 St. Stephens Road
Alexandria, VA 22304
TEL: 703-751-2700
Credit: Inquire
Sponsor: St. Stephens School
Contact: Monica McGoldrick
Description: For three days in June 1989, 30 Soviet and 45 U.S. students between 13 and 18 years old debated the greenhouse effect, air pollution, free speech, crack cocaine and a myriad of other topics looking for ways to "make the world a safer and healthier place."
Sponsored by Youth Ambassadors of America, a nonprofit organization, and hosted by St. Stephens School in Alexandria, the summit is the third of its kind and the first in the United States. Both earlier youth summits were held in Moscow.
Faced at first with a language barrier, the youth soon made use of the resources available to them to overcome this problem. Between finding words in the cross-language dictionary, using hand gestures, drawing pictures and speaking through interpreters, the students overcame the communication obstacles and went on to tackle global issues.
Preliminary proposals were presented to Senator Claiborne Pell, Chairman of the Senate Foreign Relations Committee, Senator Mark Hatfield and Senator Dennis DeConcini and included ways to organize a student grassroots movement. Among the suggestions presented by the youth were:
- Enlist students from around the world to write letters to world leaders and the media "so they understand what needs to be done."
- Develop and operate a youth radio show on human rights to be transmitted in the United States and the Soviet Union.
- Address global warming, air pollution and management of resources as the main problems.
- Encourage environmental education by setting up billboards, distributing pamphlets and demanding ecology classes in schools.
- Bring the problems to all of the people - not just one country.
- Realize that the summit is "just in time" - the relations between our countries are becoming better, and this can make them even better.

For several days the students listened to and interviewed speakers from the Environmental Protection Agency, Greenpeace, homeless shelters and drug abuse centers, and a Chinese student to help them formulate their action plans.
The final day was reserved for meeting with congressional leaders to present their "Plan of Action" resolution. Unlike the Soviet students who had to compete in essay contests to participate in the summit, American youth had only to "show interest in the program."
Parents of some students were involved in organizations relative to the summit, and this background often surfaced. One student whose father was involved with EarthSave, an environmental organization, pointed out that "growing grain to make clean-burning alcohol fuels to run cars" would be great, "but it's very impractical for us." The youth emphasized that although "the things we can do may be smaller than we would like, it's a start." One youth found agreement among the others when he said, "[The Summit] makes me feel 'responsible.'" Immediately following this

third summit, plans for number four were underway.
Founded: 1985

PEACE CONFERENCE
Interfaith Justice and Peace Center
Lourdes College
6832 Convent Boulevard
Toledo, OH 43560
TEL: 419-885-3211
Sponsor: Lourdes College
Contact: Conference Coordinator
Description: Recognizing that there were no models to study or places to learn new techniques on peace promotion, the Interfaith Justice and Peace Center of Lourdes College in Toledo established a Peace Conference and other activities in 1980 to bring awareness to the community. Among the concerns addressed are hunger, juvenile violence, apartheid, refugees, racism, and nuclear weapon freezes.
One activity encourages the sponsoring of peace clubs in area high schools where students can study communication, national and global issues and begin to take some volunteer action. The Center maintains a roster of volunteer speakers both for the conferences and to work with the high schools.
One emphasis in this community awareness effort is on exploding the myth that the individual has little or no influence. Although the program does not advocate massive protests, per se, through volunteer speakers, printed materials, conferences, and small group interaction (clubs), it works to help people explore ways in which personal responsibility and action can resolve future conflict.
Founded: 1980

STUDY WAR NO MORE
Institute for Creative Conflict Management
Syracuse University
Syracuse, NY 13244
TEL: 315-443-1870
Sponsor: Syracuse University
Contact: Institute Director
Description: This summer course is part of a program at Syracuse University, created in 1970, that is dedicated to human dignity based on values of nonviolence, social justice, trust, and participative decision making. The course is open for credit and non-credit.
The umbrella course, which also includes the Campus Ministry Center, is an undergraduate major designed to study creative, peaceful ways of dealing with conflict. Trained volunteers are available throughout the program to help students find new and peaceful resolutions to problems.
The University also offers graduate degrees in the same field, along with three other higher education institutions across the country - University of Colorado, George Mason University in Virginia, and Notre Dame University. The assistance of volunteers is woven into each of the courses.

INDIVIDUAL PROGRAM PROFILES

BOISE PEACE QUILT PROJECT
PO Box 6469
Boise, ID 83707
TEL: 208-342-8560
Purpose: To produce lasting symbols of peace as gestures of international goodwill.
Description: This local organization is made up of about 100 individuals who produce *peace quilts* as awards for peacemakers, and as international gestures of goodwill. The program began in 1981, and has produced friendship quilts and sent them to the *Soviet Women's Committee* as a symbol of peace, hope and

goodwill. In addition, a joint *Soviet-American Peace Quilt* was made in cooperation with Soviet women and presented at the bilateral arms talks in Geneva, Switzerland.
A program sponsored by the organization is the *National Peace Quilt Project,* which is a patchwork quilt made with fifty squares (one representing each state) based on children's drawings.
Another program seeks to have each U.S. Senator spend one night under the *National Peace Quilt* and then make a public statement concerning his or her attempt to promote peace.
A "peace bank" records and shares information on peacemakers nominated to receive peace quilts. The group also provides quilting training for other groups wishing to mount such a symbolic program for a good cause. Weekly board meetings and biweekly "quilting meetings" are held to keep pace with policy on the one hand, and quilting expertise on the other. The group publishes a semiannual newsletter.
Publications: Peaceful Pieces

PEACE GARDEN PROJECT
National Peace Garden
806 Fifteenth Street, NW #218
PO Box 27558
Washington, DC 20038-7558
TEL: 202-393-6248
West Coast Office:
National Peace Garden
Box 5282
Berkeley, CA 94705 (415-652-6351)
Contact: Elizabeth Ratcliff
Objectives: To honor the commitment of the people of the United States to world peace.
Services: Works to create a *National Peace Garden* on 12 acres in Washington, DC, set aside by Congress in a bill signed by President Reagan in 1987; operates with private sector funds to reach a goal of full funding by 1992 ($12 million, including in-kind contributions) in keeping with the Congressional mandate for such bills to have full funding within five years after authorization; plans to include a display area for peace documents (a glass pavilion at the gate), a 4,000-seat amphitheatre, raised walkways, and low landscaping molded in the pattern of an olive branch (the result of a design competition); maintains an all-volunteer jury of architects who made the selection from almost 1,000 entries, and continue to monitor the project, and two offices operated by volunteers (Washington, DC, and Berkeley, CA); publishes a newsletter and a press kit.
Sponsor: Business/Industry, Foundations and Individuals
Contact: Tom Chittendon or Rita Eisenberg
Publications: Peace Garden Newsletter; Peace Garden Press Kit
Founded: 1987

PEACE LINKS ARKANSAS
Women Against Nuclear War
4 Shackleford Plaza
Little Rock, AR 72211
TEL: 501-372-4982
Purpose: To encourage citizens to lead their communities in activities that promote peace.
Sponsor: Winthrop Rockefeller Foundation
Contact: Olivia Guggenheim, Director, or Betty Bumpers, Founder
Description: Peace Links Arkansas is an offshoot of a larger office which was founded in Little Rock in 1982 as an affiliate of the national organization. Currently, two paid employees administer the office with the help of from 60 to several hundred volunteers, depending on its activities. Funding for the larger office came from the *Winthrop Rockefeller Foundation* and private contributions.
As the Foundation funds decreased over the years, it was felt that it was an indication that the office had accomplished its goal of changing the way people think to promote world peace.
Funds remaining will be used by *Peace Links Arkansas* in ways

decided by the local board. One possibility being discussed is to teach teachers how to teach the young a new way of resolving conflict.

In the meantime, a decision to scale back the operation to volunteer workers only has been made. The volunteers will continue the work of the organization as indicated - helping people organize for action, sparking debates, supporting leaders committed to peace, and educating children in the democratic process.
Founded: 1982

CIVIC AFFAIRS: PHYSICAL ENVIRONMENT

NATIONAL/STATE ORGANIZATIONS

COMMUNITY ENVIRONMENTAL PROGRAM*
SEE PHYSICAL ENVIRONMENT

CONCERN, INC.
SEE PHYSICAL ENVIRONMENT

ENVIRONMENTAL ACTION
SEE PHYSICAL ENVIRONMENT

ENVIRONMENTAL ACTION FOUNDATION
SEE PHYSICAL ENVIRONMENT

CIVIC AFFAIRS: TENANTS/RESIDENTS

NATIONAL/STATE ORGANIZATIONS

ASSOCIATION OF COMMUNITY ORGANIZATIONS FOR REFORM NOW (ACORN)
SEE CONSUMER SERVICES/LEGAL RIGHTS: TENANTS/RESIDENTS

BREAKTHROUGH FOUNDATION
25 Van Ness Avenue
Suite 320
San Francisco, CA 94102
TEL: 415-863-4141
Objectives: To help people improve the quality of their lives and their communities.
Services: Develops community projects that help people change what they feel are unacceptable situations in the quality and conditions of their lives; focuses on serious and violent young crime offenders, substance abusers, and professionals working with the disabled; offers two-year programs to teach people how to start and maintain community development projects to address their problems and to improve their communities; trains workers to help local community groups set up and administer development projects in the US and some countries abroad; sponsors fundraising projects and operates programs of corporate sponsorship, internships, volunteers, youth at risk, and youth sponsorship.
Founded: 1980

CENTER FOR ORGANIZATIONAL AND COMMUNITY DEVELOPMENT (*formerly Citizen Involvement Training Program*)
University of Massachusetts
School of Education
Room 225
Amherst, MA 01003
TEL: 413-545-2038
Objectives: To help local citizen groups and agencies become more effective.
Services: Organizes sessions tailored to individual groups to aid them in responding effectively to issues that range from human relations to community development to coalition building; strives to make local groups and agencies more effective in reaching their goals; sponsors workshops on topics including: cultural issues, community development, and interorganizational and organizational development; provides consultation services and training materials on organizing, fundraising, the media, and citizen action training; assists groups and organizations in designing, developing and implementing their own conferences; publishes a series of manuals and information packets.
Sponsor: Community Education Resource Center
Publications: Citizen Action Manual Series; COCD Information Packet
Founded: 1985

NATIONAL ASSOCIATION FOR THE SOUTHERN POOR (*formerly Virginia Community Development Organization*)
749B Delaware Avenue, SW
Washington, DC 20024
TEL: 202-554-3265
Objectives: To involve black, low-income individuals in decision-making that affects their lives.
Services: Creates local organizations, known as *Assemblies,* through which low-income people can gather and become involved in local decision-making regarding community services and opportunities; concentrates on organizing Southern blacks in an effort toward raising levels of health, education, and income; provides information on a number of issues; presents awards for outstanding participation; holds monthly meetings; publishes a monthly newsletter.
Publications: The Epistle
Founded: 1968

NATIONAL ASSOCIATION OF COMMUNITY LEADERSHIP ORGANIZATIONS
1454 Duke Street
Alexandria, VA 22314
TEL: 703-836-7904
Objectives: To improve the effectiveness of community leadership programs.
Services: Provides a forum for exchange of creative ideas concerning community leadership; promotes exciting community leadership programs; helps to establish new programs nationwide; provides training, publications, and volunteer experts to community leadership organizations; maintains information on relevant statistics; presents awards for outstanding achievements; publishes a newsletter, a brochure, and a book on how to develop a community leadership organization.
Sponsor: American Chamber of Commerce Executives
Publications: NACLO Newsletter; How to Develop a Community Leadership Organization
Founded: 1979

NATIONAL COMMUNITY ACTION FOUNDATION
SEE RECIPIENTS: FAMILIES

NATIONAL TRAINING AND INFORMATION CENTER*
954 West Washington Boulevard
Chicago, IL 60607
TEL: 312-243-3035
Objectives: To provide training for leaders interested in improving their neighborhoods.
Services: Offers community leaders and organizers "how to" courses dealing with areas such as housing, neighborhood reinvestment, block club organizing, issue development, and media usage; provides on-site consultation services and technical assistance to local groups on organizing campaigns and revitalization efforts; maintains an information clearinghouse; researches areas such as mortgage and lending practices, utility rate increases, and community development funding; keeps legislative bodies and the public informed of its findings; sponsors long- and short-term training sessions; publishes a newsletter and a number of manuals and guides.
Publications: Disclosure; A Challenge for Change; Controlling Neighborhood Development; Basics of Organizing; Organizing to Win; Pass the Buck... Back!; Who, Me A Researcher? Yes, You!
Founded: 1972

CIVIC AFFAIRS: TRAINING

TRAINING PROGRAMS

CIVIC PARTNERSHIP: INITIATIVE, INNOVATION*
Citizens Forum on Self-Government
National Municipal League
55 West 44th Street
New York, NY 10036
TEL: 212-730-7930
TOLL FREE: 800-223-6004
Credit: Inquire
Sponsor: Citizens Forum on Self-Government
Contact: William G. Anderson, Jr.
Description: Sponsored each year by the Citizens Forum on Self-Government of the National Municipal League, this is the 89th National Conference on public/private partnership efforts. The Conference addresses the issues of its theme by holding sessions covering the following topics:
- An Examination of the Issues of Public/Private Partnerships
- A Close Inspection of the Problems and Opportunities That Local Public/Private Partnerships Face
- The Revitalization of a Community
- Strengthening Institutions of Self-Government
- A Presentation on a Successful Revitalization Effort Involving Leaders from Across the Nation

The Conference includes guided tours of a city's more notable public/private partnership undertakings (in November 1983, a Baltimore tour). Ample time for open discussion and consultation with faculty is provided throughout the conference.

CIVIC AFFAIRS: VOTING

NATIONAL/STATE ORGANIZATIONS

LEAGUE OF WOMEN VOTERS OF THE US
SEE CIVIC AFFAIRS: MINORITIES/WOMEN

INDIVIDUAL PROGRAM PROFILES

MOTOR VOTERS
1350 Beverly Rd
Suite 115-240
McLean, VA 22101
TEL: 703-448-0002
Purpose: To educate the public on car quality and safety.
Contact: Rosemary Dunlap
Description: Motor Voters was formed after one dissatisfied car owner picketed a dealership for six months in an attempt to get her car repaired properly. Although the dealer finally "did the right thing," the car owner saw a need for a support group to help avoid similar ordeals for others. Today, the organization's volunteers lobby the Virginia General Assembly on consumer issues, negotiate with interest groups including auto manufacturers, banks and the insurance industry.
A major goal of the volunteer group is to achieve enactment of consumer disclosure legislation that would require that manufacturers of vans, minivans, light trucks and pickups to tell potential buyers that these vehicles are not required to meet a number of federal safety standards mandated for personal cars - especially important since some of these vehicles are becoming increasingly popular for family use. For example, vans may not provide as much protection if struck broadside or if they roll over, and they may not have automatic seat belts or air bags.
Pro-consumer legislators and advocates came very close in the 1989-90 session to enacting such legislation. It would have been the first state law of its kind in the country. It easily passed the state Senate, but car manufacturers rushed in their lobbyists before it reached the House Roads and Navigation Committee where it was defeated.
Consumer advocates, however, feel that much progress has been made - against long odds - through their volunteer efforts, especially in a number of consumer credit and insurance bills, which they feel certain will be approved in the 1990-91 session. In the President's words, "We don't always win. You have to keep coming back over and over again... persistence counts for a lot on consumer issues."
Founded: 1985

VOTER REGISTRATION ASSISTANCE
New Jersey NAACP
Northern Branch NAACP
1028 Broad Street
Newark, NJ 07102
TEL: 201-624-0321
Purpose: To clear up voter registration problems for thousands of people on the area's ineligible voter list.
Contact: Keith Jones, President
Description: When citizens become ineligible to vote for one reason or another, many are unaware of it until they appear at the polls. Most of the problems relate to "proof of residency." The list is published each year in the local daily newspaper. Still there is always a long line of people on election day either at the polls unaware of their status, or before a Superior Court judge trying to get permission to vote.
Volunteers recruited by the *New Jersey NAACP* try to reduce significantly the number who reach those two roadblocks. Many on the list had their addresses challenged in the previous election, but did not respond to letters asking for clarification.
The NAACP feels that its work has helped. The list of 5,844 in spring 1989 was down from the 7,300 of the previous November. However, with the list still showing a substantial number, especially from the inner city where people are more mobile, the volunteers were out in force.
Citing the fight for the right to vote still prevalent in some countries, the Mayor of Newark - in an effort to help the NAACP in its work - urged people to "think registration" when they

change their addresses for the post office or the electric company. NAACP is especially concerned because there are areas of the county affected that have large populations of black and Hispanic people. This organization promotes same day voter registration since, in its view, the present system does not safeguard the right to vote. In the meantime, volunteers will be calling people on the list at each election, urging them to give more priority to notifying election officials of changes of address, and helping them in correcting problems and getting registered without the hassle of court, or the loss of this privilege for a given election.

CIVIC AFFAIRS: 21ST CENTURY

NATIONAL/STATE ORGANIZATIONS

PREPARING FOR AN AGING SOCIETY
SEE RECIPIENTS: OLDER PERSON

WASHINGTON WORKSHOPS FOUNDATION
3222 N Street, NW
Suite 340
Washington, DC 20007
TEL: 202-965-3434
Objectives: To provide a citizenship education program for secondary school students - "The 21st Century Seminar."
Services: Conducts The 21st Century Seminar in which students and their teachers explore the emerging environmental issues of concern and how they will impact on our new century; serves junior high, middle school and secondary school students in the Seminar, which constitutes a week in residence in the Washington, DC, area and participation in the following six programs and a narrated tour of the city:
  ● The Congress
  ● Executive and Judicial
  ● Model Congress
  ● International
  ● Career Orientation
  ● Academic Overview
Conducts "The Wall Street Seminar" for high school and college students in New York City; offers an advanced congressional seminar for those completing the initial seminar; schedules speakers from public and private sectors with many on-site visits to government agencies and departments key to the energy and environmental areas; focuses in the evenings on volunteerism, directions for environmental change, and new directions and possibilities for individual and local involvement in conservation programs.
Contact: Leo S. Tomkin
Publications: Junior High Seminars; Diplomacy and Global Affairs; Wall Street Seminar; 21st Century Seminar
Founded: 1967

TRAINING PROGRAMS

BUILDING MOMENTUM FOR A RESPONSIVE AMERICA
SEE CIVIC AFFAIRS: CITY/COUNTY GOALS

TOWARD THE YEAR 2000 - THE CHALLENGE
Association for Volunteer Administration
PO Box 4584
Boulder, CO 80306
TEL: 303-497-0238

Description: This annual conference addresses the twenty-first century and aims to enable participants to positively influence their organizations and their communities to meet the challenges ahead. It offers a wide selection of learning opportunities - both at the introductory and the experienced levels, in a variety of formats, including workshops, institutes and paper presentations. Sessions are clustered into three tracks focusing on personal, programmatic and professional aspects of leadership:
  ● **Track #1: The Challenge to Ourselves** - topics related to growing in our own competencies; negotiation skills; preventing burnout; advocating within our organization; networking; value clarification; delegating; matching oneself to the organizational climate; career advancement strategies; conflict management; personal performance; appraisals; self-development; problem solving; giving and getting recognition, etc.
  ● **Track #2: The Challenge to Our Programs** - topics related to maximizing the potential impact of volunteers; new models for citizen involvement; management assistance programs; networking; creative utilization of short-term projects; re-channeling long-term volunteers; overcoming staff resistance; career ladders for volunteers; models of cooperative training programs, etc.
  ● **Track #3: The Challenge to Our Profession** - topics related to exercising our professional clout to determine our future; vision planning; ethical issues; networking; coalition-building; working effectively with elected officials; planning for the impact of demographic trends; intergenerational issues; mobilizing for change; current and developing volunteer administration courses and training; etc.
Conference participants include program directors and other staff from non-profit, for-profit and governmental settings, membership organization leaders, board members, trainers, educators, researchers, consultants and students.

INDIVIDUAL PROGRAM PROFILES

FAIRFIELD 2000
Regional Plan Association
Connecticut Committee
500 Summer Street
Stamford, CT 06901
TEL: 203-356-0390
Purpose: To present problems in Fairfield County, anticipate prospective problems, and prepare to avoid them.
Sponsor: Stamford Advocate
Contact: Lynn R. Laltman, Director
Description: Some 800 citizen volunteers joined the Steering Committee of *Fairfield 2000* in late 1986 to help draft a report on the problems facing the County. Assembling officials with civic leaders, business people, and others, *Fairfield 2000* developed recommendations for solutions of the problems posed in the report. With the theme, "Choices not made are choices just the same - decisions by default," the group sought forceful leaders willing to choose positively - political leaders, civic leaders, and business leaders. Recommendations included:
  ● Manage Growth
  ● Build More Low- and Middle-Income Housing
  ● Include Everyone in the Economy (day care, education, industry, libraries, etc.)
  ● Attract More Ridesharing/Commuter Participation (including improvement of bus and rail systems)
  ● Pursue Rail and Water Alternatives to Trucking
  ● Help Those Who Can't Share the Prosperity (good social services)
  ● Improve Zoning
  ● Encourage Farming
  ● Hold a Quarterly Environmental Action Forum

- Mobilize Support for the Arts, and
- Form FAIRCON (Fairfield County Conference of Municipalities) to Foster Quarterly Meetings to Discuss a Prepared Agenda

In all, eight sets of solutions were prepared by the eight task forces, with enough overlapping to reinforce each other. With questionnaires from citizens who receive the *Stamford Advocate, Greenwich Time, Bridgeport Post,* and *Danbury News-Times,* the solutions appeared to be a mandate from the citizenry. However, the solutions depended on Countywide cooperation across municipal borders and between the cities and towns and the state. Information on progress is available.

Publications: Fairfield 2000

A MESSAGE FOR THE FUTURE - THE VOLUNTAS TIME CAPSULE
Center for Creative Community
PO Box 2427
Santa Fe, NM 87504-2427
TEL: 505-983-8414
Purpose: To send a message to the future on today's volunteerism.
Description: The *Time Capsule Project* is monitored and administered by experts in the field of volunteerism, who will make the final selections for messages, books, videos, recognition items, etc. that best reflect contemporary volunteerism, based on the following points:

- Good things you see about volunteering today in your program or organization, and in general.
- Challenges, problems, things that need improving in volunteerism today.
- Your prediction of what 2050 will be like as far as volunteering is concerned.
- Your message to the future; advice, encouragement, cautions, or a greeting.

From 150 to 200 messages of about 500 words each will be selected and transferred to paper designed for preservation. They will come from individuals, associations, or organizations involved in volunteerism, including volunteer coordinators and consultants; clergy and lay leadership in church, temple and synagogue; self-help and service club leaders, etc. Each message-sender selected will be asked to recommend others, and to vote on the actual contents of the capsule. Message providers are asked to contribute $100 to the project, part of which is used for scholarships for those who are deemed to have a meaningful message, but cannot finance their contribution.
The first actual time capsule messages were prepared at the *Challenge III* think tank on volunteerism on November 1-3 at the Center in Santa Fe.
Because of the fast pace of change in volunteerism today, the capsule is set to be opened in 2050, rather than in centuries from now as other capsules have been scheduled. According to the creator of the concept, "Some younger people invited to the 1990 launching may still be alive in 2050 for the opening! The rest of us can visualize our children there, or their children..."
Publications: VOLUNTAS: A Message for the Future

MORRIS 2000
SEE CIVIC AFFAIRS: CITY/COUNTY GOALS

NEW DIRECTIONS FOR THE BRONX
SEE CIVIC AFFAIRS: CITY/COUNTY GOALS

TWENTY-FIRST CENTURY DISCUSSION GROUP
League of Women Voters Education Fund
1730 M Street, NW
Washington, DC 20036
TEL: 202-296-1770

Purpose: To raise questions which citizens must consider if they are to help shape the future of their government.
Sponsor: League of Women Voters Education Fund
Contact: Nan Waterman, Chairperson, Project Committee
Description: In 1973 the League of Women Voters (LWV) tested a new idea for community groups - the 21st Century Discussion Group. National and local LWV members volunteered their time to play the role of the general public, while eleven volunteer experts from as many disciplines led the discussion. Since then, the discussions have been convened with diverse groups such as a welfare mothers' self-help group, political party leaders, church groups, high school classes, union leaders, civic clubs, women's groups, book discussion groups, neighborhood preservation groups, and new careers classes, as well as countless local LWV groups. Two obstacles emerged in the San Juan meeting and have persisted in subsequent meetings:
1. It is difficult for people to think about the future in any organized or systematic way; and
2. The ideal group is comprised of a cross-section of people, but they are not used to talking to each other, so the process bogs down.
The goals of the San Juan meeting presented flexible guidelines for future meetings by local LWVs or other groups. Following the obvious first step of deciding what the specific goals of the discussion group will be and with which groups in the community, the basic format could include the following goals:

- **Education:** the presentation of alternative futures through films, role-playing, written material or other devices followed by the discussion. The purpose is to help people become aware of what the future might be like, so that they will be better able to cope with it.
- **Learning About Yourself and Others:** joining with groups in the community with which little contact has been made in the past. Only through collaboration with other groups will meaningful discussion emerge.
- **Community Communication:** assuring representation from all segments of the community's population. These discussions will have the biggest pay-off, since each group will bring different value systems, concerns, and assumptions to the discussion table.
- **One Lesson Learned** - the suggested two-hour duration for the discussions did not allow sufficient time to hear from all participants.

Founded: 1973

WESTCHESTER 2000
Westchester County Association
235 Mamaroneck Avenue
White Plains, NY 10605
TEL: 914-948-6444
Purpose: To make recommendations for an institutional base to respond to change in Westchester County.
Sponsor: Regional Plan Association
Contact: James L. Ferguson, Leadership Council Chairman
Description: In 1985, over 700 persons participated in eight task forces to set the scene for wider community participation by forming *Westchester 2000* to look ahead and try to avoid problems and grasp opportunities for Westchester County. Special sections in the *Gannett Westchester Newspapers* and the *Peekskill Star,* with a detailed survey questionnaire inserted in the overview of *Westchester 2000,* involved thousands of citizens who may not have been reached otherwise. The initial recommendations synthesized from the task force reports included:

- More Housing?
- Education Quality Slipping?
- Enough Jobs?
- Social Needs
- Rush-Hour 2000?
- Since We Live Both in Our Hometown and the County,

What's Good for Both?
- Local Taxes
- Our Rich Assets: Can We Save the Natural and Historic and Enhance the Cultural?

The detailed reports emphasized the need to include those left out of the buttressing economy ("Spreading and Enhancing the Good Life"), and the broad categories of more housing, traffic congestion, open space, and downtown revitalization.

Publications: Westchester 2000
Founded: 1985

CONSUMER SERVICES/LEGAL RIGHTS

NATIONAL/STATE ORGANIZATIONS

CENTER FOR STUDY OF RESPONSIVE LAW
PO Box 19367
Washington, DC 20036
TEL: 202-387-8030
Objectives: To bring to public attention some of the problematic consumer issues of the times.
Services: Helps to organize consumers locally; monitors Congress and the regulatory agencies; maintains a clearinghouse of information for press, government officials, and concerned individuals and groups; encourages public and private institutions to be more responsive to the needs of the consumer; areas covered include toxic waste, health and safety issues, discrimination against women, and nursing home conditions.
Founded: 1968

COMMISSION FOR THE ADVANCEMENT OF PUBLIC INTEREST ORGANIZATIONS
Community Information Center
1875 Connecticut Avenue, NW
Washington, DC 20009
TEL: 202-462-0505
Objectives: To develop common strategies among groups and individuals for resolving pressing consumer issues.
Services: Conducts workshops on specific issues of consumer interest to develop common strategies among groups and individuals in order to resolve specific public interest problems; identifies common areas for cooperation; explores ways to increase constituency of the public interest movement; maintains information collection of consumer interest materials; publishes *The Federal Advisory System, Assessment: A Citizen's Guide,* workshop proceedings, and other materials. (Supported by Monsour Medical Foundation)
Publications: A Citizen's Guide; Public Interest Resources; Federal Advisory System; CAPIO Conference Proceedings
Founded: 1974

CONSUMER DEPUTY PROGRAM
US/Consumer Product Safety Commission
5401 Westbard Ave.
Bethesda, MD 20814
TEL: 301-492-5788

Objectives: To utilize volunteers to monitor product compliance and conduct an awareness program for consumers and retailers.
Services: Conducts general surveys and checks specific products to determine regulation compliance in areas such as child-resistant packaging of medicines; informs consumers of violations and works with retailers to encourage voluntary removal of non-complying products.
The Commission itself expands on the above volunteer services by conducting research and developing test methods, publishing injury and hazard data, negotiating corrective plans with manufacturers, conducting consumer education programs, enacting mandatory safety standards etc. (Write or call for list of 13 Area Offices)

CONSUMER EDUCATION AND PROTECTIVE ASSOCIATION INTERNATIONAL
6048 Ogontz Avenue
Philadelphia, PA 19141
TEL: 215-424-1441
Objectives: To strengthen the power of the consumer to deal with economic and political problems affecting his or her interests.
Services: Combats fraud and other unscrupulous business activities by strengthening the power of the consumer through education; conducts leadership training classes for consumer organizations; uses strategies such as peaceful picketing to expose consumer grievances by direct consumer action; publishes *Consumer Voice* irregularly (6 issues yearly).
Publications: Consumer Voice
Founded: 1966

CONSUMER FEDERATION OF AMERICA
1424 Sixteenth Street, NW
Suite 604
Washington, DC 20036
TEL: 202-387-6121
Objectives: To promote the rights of all consumers; to encourage and support consumer programs and activities.
Services: Serves as a clearinghouse not only for general information, but also for ideas and experiences from across the country; stimulates and helps to coordinate local projects in areas including insurance, food pricing, guarantees and servicing, medical care, physical environment, taxes and others; provides lecturers on these issues; researches and analyzes consumer issues; publishes results and makes them available at nominal cost to the general public; constantly articulates on behalf of the consumer.

Publications: CFA News; Voting Records of Congress
Founded: 1967

COUNCIL OF BETTER BUSINESS BUREAUS
1515 Wilson Boulevard
Arlington, VA 22209
TEL: 703-276-0100
Objectives: To assist the consuming public; to help maintain
confidence in the private enterprise system.
Services: Provides free binding arbitration of business consumer
disputes using community volunteers as arbitrators; testifies before
Congress on consumer issues; maintains the Philanthropic
Advisory Service (PAS) which checks non-profit corporations to
determine how much of contributions are actually used for cause,
and how much for management; places public service
announcements, a 30-minute radio program (Conversation for
Consumers), and other mini-series, mini-programs, and
announcements on behalf of the consumer, including "Auto-Line,"
a national arbitration capability putting consumer and
manufacturer in direct touch; publishes an extensive series of
consumer information booklets which are offered to the public.
Publications: CBBB Annual Report
Founded: 1970

LEGAL SERVICES CORPORATION*
US/Congress
733 Fifteenth Street, NW
Washington, DC 20005
TEL: 202-272-4030
Objectives: To support local legal services for the poor (set up by
Congress).
Services: Operates approximately 335 neighborhood offices
throughout the country; explores legal aspects of health (including
Medicaid and Medicare), nursing homes, hospital services for the
poor, after-care, services for the mentally retarded, Social Security,
family law and child abuse; conducts seminars and meetings on
topics that affect the law and other services needed by the poor;
conducts and publishes studies such as *The New Clients: Legal
Services for Mentally Retarded Persons,* and an upcoming study
on legal problems and access difficulties of the elderly and
handicapped.
Publications: The New Clients: Legal Services for Mentally
Retarded Persons

NATIONAL CLIENTS COUNCIL
2617 Martha Street
Philadelphia, PA 19125
TEL: 215-686-2913
Objectives: To advocate clients' interests and concerns in legal
services programs.
Services: Trains clients to participate in the planning and execution
of legal services programs; provides a vehicle for communication
and clarification between clients and attorneys; publishes monthly
Community Notes, annual Conference Proceedings, *The Why's
and How's of National Clients Council,* and other materials;
convenes annual meeting. (Affiliated with American Bar
Association)
Publications: Why's and How's of NCC
Founded: 1968

NATIONAL CONSUMERS LEAGUE
815 Fifteenth Street, NW
Suite 516
Washington, DC 20005
TEL: 202-639-8140
Objectives: To voice consumer concerns to government and
industry leaders and to Congress; to enhance consumer
participation in the decision- making process.

Services: Articulates consumer views to Congress, the executive
branch, and corporate leadership on a variety of issues including
health care quality, access, and costs, product safety, the federal
budget, fraud, long-term care, insurance, and other economic and
social justice issues; publishes the bimonthly *Bulletin* which alerts
readers to legislative developments, probes key consumer issues,
and features guest articles and an array of other consumer
education materials; publishes quarterly update about
telemarketing fraud; conducts annual membership meeting to set
policy priorities.
Publications: NCL Bulletin; Consumer Report Card
Founded: 1899

NATIONAL LEGAL AID AND DEFENDER ASSOCIATION
1625 K Street, NW
Eighth Floor
Washington, DC 20006
TEL: 202-452-0620
Objectives: To establish a central point for information on legal
services for the poor.
Services: Acts as clearinghouse on provision of legal aid and
defender services to those who cannot pay for such services;
maintains files on cases, costs, fund sources, and persons served;
publishes a directory of facilities in the U.S. and Canada, reports,
handbooks, etc.
Publications: Capital Report; Cornerstone; Legal Aid/Defender
Offices/US

NATIONAL RESOURCE CENTER FOR CONSUMERS OF
LEGAL SERVICES*
124-D East Broad Street
Falls Church, VA 22046
TEL: 202-536-8700
Objectives: To keep individuals and groups informed on legal
services delivery systems.
Services: Acts as a clearinghouse for information and advice on the
performance of legal services delivery systems; holds seminars;
provides limited technical assistance; conducts research; maintains
library; publishes biweekly newsletter, *Legal Plan Letter,* surveys
and other materials.
Publications: Legal Plan Letter; Planforms
Founded: 1977

PUBLIC CITIZEN LITIGATION GROUP
2000 P Street, NW
Suite 700
Washington, DC 20036
TEL: 202-785-3704
Objectives: To serve the public interest through litigation relating
to areas of concern to consumers.
Services: Files public interest suits in cases dealing with economic
issues, health and safety of consumers and workers, compliance
with laws by federal agencies as they are written, election laws,
campaign practices, etc.; engages in writing and research; provides
testimony and expertise to Congress; publishes *Public Citizen*
(quarterly), and other materials. (Founded by Ralph Nader)
Publications: Public Citizen
Founded: 1972

PUBLIC INTEREST RESEARCH GROUP
PIRG
215 Pennsylvania Avenue, SE
Washington, DC 20003
TEL: 202-547-9707
Objectives: To create public awareness on legal aspects of
consumer issues and energy.
Services: Supports laws to protect citizens from unsafe products
and unfair banking and telephone practices; supports laws to clean

up toxic chemicals and deal with other environmental and energy problems; provides opportunities for students to receive academic credit for various efforts on behalf of consumers; has an internship program for college students; develops and disseminates publications and other materials on public policy, banking and energy issues. (PIRG is sponsored by Ralph Nader.)
Publications: Citizen Agenda
Founded: 1983

PUBLIC SERVICE ACTIVITIES DIVISION
American Bar Association
750 North Lake Shore Drive
Chicago, IL 60611
TEL: 312-988-5000
Objectives: To apply the knowledge and experience of the legal profession to promotion of the public good through volunteer efforts.
Services: Works with non-lawyer professionals and leaders to deal with pressing social problems through:
- Commission on the Mentally Disabled
- Commission on Legal Problems of the Elderly
- Section of Individual Rights and Responsibilities (includes "Pro Bono Project" of volunteer lawyers)
- Special Committee on Housing and Urban Development Law
- Special Committee on Energy Law
- Young Lawyers Division Resource Center for Child Advocacy and Protection

In addition, this ABA Division maintains clearinghouse; mounts demonstration projects; holds working conferences; develops profiles, case studies, and other accounts of its work to keep the public informed.
Founded: 1878

SOCIETY OF CONSUMER AFFAIRS PROFESSIONALS IN BUSINESS
4900 Leesburg Pike, Suite 400
Alexandria, VA 22302
TEL: 703-998-7371
Objectives: To promote harmonious relationships between business, government and consumers.
Services: Maintains continuing communication with business/industry to compare successes and failures in community relations; provides information to any group or individual interested in corporate efforts to demonstrate responsibility to the community; has an awards program and ongoing seminar schedule; provides speakers to the community on request.
Publications: Update; Mobius Journal
Founded: 1973

TRIAL LAWYERS FOR PUBLIC JUSTICE
2000 P Street, NW
Suite 611
Washington, DC 20036
TEL: 202-463-8600
Objectives: To utilize trial litigation as an effective instrument of social change and for vindication of individual rights.
Services: Combines the theories and remedies of a plaintiff's damage litigation with the issues and goals of the public interest movement; enables trial lawyers to focus and enhance their public interest commitment through litigation with a potentially broad impact on corporate or government policy; deals with cases where the novelty of the issues involved or the demands of the litigation make the cases inappropriate for the private practice trial lawyer; chooses cases for their potential impact on the public good; operates with volunteer assistance of hundreds of lawyers across the country; publishes *Trial Lawyers Doing Public Justice.*
Publications: TLPJ Newsletter; TLPJ Membership Directory; Trial Lawyers Doing Public Justice
Founded: 1982

US/DTREAS - TREASURY'S INVOLVEMENT IN PRIVATE SECTOR INITIATIVES
US/DTreas - Office of the Secretary
15th & Pennsylvania Avenue, NW
Washington, DC 20220
TEL: 202-566-2000
Objectives: To apply its programs when possible to the private sector initiatives concept.
Services: Works with volunteers and private businesses, and becomes directly involved with the functions of the private sector in a support role, a public-private partnership in a particular effort, a procurement role or informational role; includes active and proposed programs such as the following:
Internal Revenue Service
- *Volunteer Income Tax Assistance (VITA)* and *Tax Counseling for the Elderly (TCE)* in which IRS recruits, trains, and supports volunteers who prepare income tax returns free for low-income taxpayers, non-English-speaking taxpayers and military taxpayers (37,000 volunteers in a typical year prepared 293,000 federal tax returns).
- *Understanding Taxes Program* and *Fundamentals of Tax Preparation Program,* in which classroom course materials (texts, instructor guides, etc.) are provided free to high school and college teachers who use the materials to teach students at the high school level how to prepare their own returns, and students at the college level how to prepare returns for others.
- Informing taxpayers through free airtime (approximately $5.5 million in a typical year) by television networks and local broadcasters providing public service announcements.

U.S. Savings Bonds Division
- Involves about 50 top executives in a *U.S. Industrial Payroll Savings Committee* which conducts savings bonds campaigns.
- Involves a top business executive from each state and the District of Columbia in the *Volunteer State Chairman's Council* who recruit and appoint a business or banking leader in each county to serve as the grassroots volunteer for savings bonds (saves cost for Treasury while helping Americans save for the future).
- Provides technical assistance to *Take Stock in America Campaigns* which are led by business and banking leaders appointed by members of the *Council of U.S. Savings Bonds Volunteers.*

Bureau of Alcohol, Tobacco and Firearms
- Works with the *Beverage Alcohol Information Council (BAIC)* which is the outgrowth of a joint report to Congress by the *Department of Health and Human Services* and the *Department of the Treasury* on the need for banker-to-banker spokesmen (consists of leading bankers from each state and the District of Columbia, and members of the *American Bankers Association*).

Comptroller of the Currency
- Sponsors a *Community Development Division* to assist national banks in developing community investment programs, and serve as speakers, resource persons, and participants at forums on this subject.
- Oversees the *Community Development Corporation* which enables national banks to invest in and contribute to community development corporations within certain guidelines.

Proposed Areas of Activity
- Voluntary contributions to reduce the national debt on IRS Tax Form 1040.
- Sales area operations of the *U.S. Mint* in Philadelphia.
- Grape Variety Advisory Committee.

Strives continually to encourage the private sector to take a more active role in solving community problems, in establishing community partnerships between the private sector and local government to meet community needs, and in related areas of public/private interaction.

Sponsor: US/DTreas - Department of the Treasury

US/NCUA - PRIVATE SECTOR INITIATIVES AND VOLUNTEERISM
US/NCUA - Administration Board
1776 G Street, NW
Washington, DC 20456
TEL: 202-356-1000
Objectives: To emphasize activities having a particularly strong focus on involvement of the private sector.
Services: Involves the private sector in all credit union activities, having from five to eleven volunteers typically serving on a board of directors, three to five volunteers on the supervisory committee, and three to five volunteers on the credit committee, with other volunteers serving in organizing and other capacities; includes the following among its overall activities involving the private sector:
New Chartering which involves mobilization of private sector resources to increase the number of volunteers acting as organizers, officials and committee members.
Community-Development Credit Unions which serve to stimulate private sector initiative through the provision of seed money in low-income areas, not only as a means of providing necessary financial services, but also as a means of economically developing the community (provides an incentive to reach into the private sector to obtain funding to supplement the seed money).
Education to promote compliance to consumer laws and regulations and create *self-regulation* to replace former *compliance examinations* and free staff for other duties.
Use of Certified Public Accountants to respond to suggestion on *privatization* of functions when possible (exploring this possibility on the basis of credit union safety and soundness).
Institutes initiatives in other areas such as deregulation, records preservation, legislation, and others; monitors continuously its standard activities to increase, when possible, their potential for private sector initiatives, and continuously studies other programs for maximum relevance to additional involvement in public/private partnerships.
Sponsor: US/NCUA - National Credit Union Administration

US/OFFICE OF CONSUMER AFFAIRS
621 Reporters Building
Washington, DC 20201
TEL: 202-755-8830
Objectives: To represent the interest of consumers in proceedings of federal agencies.
Services: Coordinates and advises other federal agencies on issues of interest to consumers; provides support to the Special Assistant to the President on Consumer Affairs; develops consumer information materials; assists other agencies in responding to consumer complaints; provides information to consumers about issues pending before other federal agencies; publishes *Consumer's Resource Handbook* (first issue 12/79).
Publications: Consumer's Resource Book

INDIVIDUAL PROGRAM PROFILES

CONSUMER INFORMATION SERVICE
Madison House
170 Rugby Road
Charlottesville, VA 22903
TEL: 804-977-7051
Purpose: To educate the community by providing consumer information to the public; to settle disputes between local consumers and business.
Sponsor: Madison House
Contact: Jane Parker

Description: Consumer Information Service (CIS) originated as part of the Madison House Professional Services Center in 1970. It was little more than a consumer column in the local newspaper until 1972, when it separated from the Center and became its own program.
There is no "Better Business Bureau" in the Charlottesville area. In an attempt to fill this void, CIS began Action Line, providing volunteers to act as impartial third party mediators to resolve consumer-merchant disputes. Later, two departments were added to the program: the Trouble$hooter, a monthly newsletter, and the Information Division. The divisions are now referred to as (1) Action Line; (2) The Publications Division; and (3) the Public Relations Division. Approximately 50 CIS volunteers are organized into the three branches. Volunteer commitment is very flexible within this program, ranging from a two-hours-per-week shift on Action Line to extensive involvement in all three divisions. Action Line attracts the majority of the CIS volunteers and forms the heart of the program. Action Line is a telephone service to which consumers call in complaints and requests for information. Action Line volunteers, acting in the capacity of third-party mediators, record individual complaints and, through a series of phone calls, letters, and personal visits, seek a resolution satisfactory to the parties in disagreement. The Action Line operates from 9 to 5, five days a week. Volunteers are organized in shifts that range from one to three hours so that the telephones are adequately manned at all times.
The Publications Division is responsible for the dissemination of consumer information to the community. Its goal is to educate the consumers and make them aware of the services available in the community. This division publishes a monthly newsletter, the Trouble$hooter, provided free of charge to inform the public of the latest consumer news and helpful hints. It discusses issues of local concern and details recent complaints and their resolutions as well as commendations to local merchants. Publications volunteers also are involved in long term research projects such as price surveys.
The Public Relations Division provides presentations on consumer-related topics to interested groups. This division maintains a library and has a consumer education program. The division also periodically publishes consumer price surveys and, in 1975, published the Charlottesville Banking Survey. Additionally, the Coordinator produces shows on local radio stations and contributes consumer columns and advertisements to local newspapers. Volunteers may write or research for this division.
CIS deals with both minor and serious consumer problems. In its work the program aims to meet the highest of professional standards. Volunteers need no specific background to become involved, but they must be able to learn tact and responsibility in dealing with frequently irate and upset citizens, and possess a firm commitment to providing good, reliable service.
In the beginning, CIS was very similar in design to Madison House's other volunteer programs. However, rapid development and the nature of its activities necessitated incorporating the program as a "Madison House Subsidiary" in January 1976. It now occupies a special position within Madison House as a highly-developed and sophisticated volunteer program.
Founded: 1970

COURT APPOINTED SPECIAL ADVOCATES (CASA)
SEE RECIPIENTS: CHILDREN/YOUTH - LEGAL RIGHTS

VIRGINIA CITIZENS CONSUMER COUNCIL
c/o Jean Ann Fox
517 Waters Edge Road
Newport News, VA 23607
TEL: 804-596-6028
Purpose: To examine the state's consumer issues and work toward changes in legislation when indicated.
Sponsor: Virginia Office of the Attorney General
Contact: Jean Ann Fox, President

Description: Consumer credit and insurance bills have been the main thrust of the *Virginia Citizens Consumer Council.* The 400 individual volunteer members, and a few organizational members, take on the big business interests in spite of the stark differences in resources. One example is the "luxury" of having volunteers come in from around the state for *one day* to assist with the tracking of bills, while business interests have lobbyists present on a daily basis. One recent bill which easily passed the state Senate on mandatory disclosure by automobile manufacturers was affected by this difference when it was killed following the increase of the manufacturers' lobbyists before it got to Committee.

Still, the advocates have seen considerable progress over the last few years. For example, the volunteers have successfully enlisted the *Attorney General's Office* and the *Bureau of Insurance* in pushing a legislative agenda, resulting in several key gains for the consumer group, and thus for the citizens of the state. Some of the bills tracked during 1990 concern:

- policy cancellation;
- antitrust violations by insurance companies;
- contractors' poor work;
- more affordable banking services;
- health spa closings; and
- small claims courts.

A major victory has been a compromise on the front-loading of interest on car loans, second mortgages, and home improvement loans. All members of the Council are unpaid volunteers. One legislator suggested that a full-time paid Executive Director is needed to be present during the entire session. However, according to the President, "We have come from being the last state in the country to consider things to being one of the first. This is an amazing amount of consumer legislation for Virginia. Consumers are being more demanding of their rights."

CONSUMER SERVICES/LEGAL RIGHTS: AIDS

INDIVIDUAL PROGRAM PROFILES

SUPPORT SERVICES - AIDS PROGRAM
SEE AIDS: PSYCHOSOCIAL SUPPORT

CONSUMER SERVICES/LEGAL RIGHTS: ARTS

NATIONAL/STATE ORGANIZATIONS

VOLUNTEER LAWYERS FOR THE ARTS
1285 Avenue of the Americas
Third Floor
New York, NY 10019
TEL: 212-977-9270
Objectives: To increase the arts community's awareness and understanding of the legal problems that affect their creative endeavors.
Services: Provides free legal services to art organizations and artists (art-related matters only); conducts educational programs and workshops to familiarize both the legal profession and the arts community with legal problems confronting artists and work with them toward solutions; maintains library and speakers bureau;

offers specialized education; publishes a journal, a manual, monographs and pamphlets. (Volunteer Lawyers for the Arts is funded, in part, by the National Endowment for the Arts.)
Publications: Art and the Law; Artists Small Claims Guide; Enterprise and the Arts; Fear of Filing; Not-For-Profit Manual; Artist's Housing Manual; The Buck Starts Here
Founded: 1968

CONSUMER SERVICES/LEGAL RIGHTS: CHILDREN/YOUTH

NATIONAL/STATE ORGANIZATIONS

LEGAL SERVICES FOR CHILDREN*
149 Ninth Street
Fourth Floor
San Francisco, CA 94103
TEL: 415-863-3762
Objectives: To provide free and comprehensive legal representation and casework services to minors in San Francisco and the Bay Area.
Services: Offers free and comprehensive legal services for minors (from infants to age 17) in all kinds of cases in the Juvenile Court (delinquency, status offense, child abuse or neglect) and in other non-fee-generating civil or administrative matters affecting minors' rights and welfare, including school discipline, special education, guardianships, emancipation, etc.; clients receive the teamed services of an attorney and a caseworker from initial contact through final resolution of the case; caseworkers provide an essential link with other resources to help meet the whole needs of the child (e.g., counseling, job training, placements, etc.).
Publications: Parents' Guide; California Law
Founded: 1975

NATIONAL COURT APPOINTED SPECIAL ADVOCATE ASSOCIATION
SEE RECIPIENTS: CHILDREN/YOUTH - LEGAL RIGHTS

NATIONAL LEGAL RESOURCE CENTER FOR CHILD ADVOCACY AND PROTECTION
SEE RECIPIENTS: CHILDREN/YOUTH - PROTECTIVE SERVICES

TRAINING PROGRAMS

CHILDREN: THE TIME IS NOW
SEE RECIPIENTS: CHILDREN/YOUTH - LEGAL RIGHTS

INDIVIDUAL PROGRAM PROFILES

CASA (COURT APPOINTED SPECIAL ADVOCATES)
SEE RECIPIENTS: CHILDREN/YOUTH - ADVOCACY

CASA PROJECT (COURT APPOINTED SPECIAL ADVOCATES)
625 East 26th Street
Kansas City, MO 64108
TEL: 816-435-4814
Purpose: To ensure that the best interests of abused and neglected children are served.

Sponsor: Greater Kansas City Section
Contact: Mitzi McFatrich, Executive Director
Description: The CASA Project is a community effort to advocate on behalf of abused and neglected children, and ensure that these children have the opportunity to have a permanent home without unnecessary delays.

CASAs - Very Special Volunteers: The CASAs (Court Appointed Special Advocates) are volunteers who are appointed by juvenile court as guardians ad litem (legal representatives) for children who have been referred to the court as abused and/or neglected. The CASAs investigate the facts of the case through interviews with the child, parents, professionals, and others; advocate for the child in all court proceedings; recommend a course of action to the court; and monitor progress toward the goals established in the court order.

Currently, the Jackson County project has 22 CASAs serving a total of 27 children. However, the project is only six months old, and plans are to expand as rapidly as possible.

CASAs participate in a pre-service training which includes 20 hours of presentations by professionals and other activities; trips to two agencies serving abused/neglected children; and several visits to court to observe hearings. The professional trainers are a judge, an attorney, a child therapist, an expert in child abuse, a supervisor from the Division of Family Services, and others as needed. CASAs continue their training as long as they are active on a case through in-service sessions which are scheduled frequently.

An important element in volunteer supervision and mutual support are the CASA Group Meetings, which are held every two weeks. The Project Coordinator is present to facilitate, but the CASAs mainly share ideas, suggestions, encouragement, etc., with each other. In addition, the CASA is expected to report directly to the Project Coordinator whenever he/she has questions or concerns. Consultants such as attorneys, child psychologists, physicians, and others are available to the CASA as needed.

Other Very Important Volunteers: With the exception of the Project Coordinator, the project is administered entirely by volunteers. The Project Chairperson is in charge of all aspects of the project, and working closely with her are two vice-chairpersons. All three of the chairpersons and all of the Steering Committee are members of the National Council of Jewish Women, Greater Kansas City Section. Their duties include public relations, long-range planning, recruitment, evaluation, Speakers' Bureau, and fund-raising.

The CASA Advisory Board consists of a broad spectrum of professionals from throughout the Kansas City community. They meet quarterly to review progress and advise the project, and are also available for frequent consultation as needed.

Currently, 45-50 volunteers are active on the Advisory Board, Steering Committee, and in other activities. Together with the CASAs, they form a formidable group of dedicated and tireless volunteers advocating for abused/neglected children in Jackson County.

GUARDIAN AD LITEM PROGRAM
SEE LAW ENFORCEMENT/CRIME PREVENTION:
ADVOCACY

CONSUMER SERVICES/LEGAL RIGHTS: COOPERATIVES

NATIONAL/STATE ORGANIZATIONS

AMERICAN INSTITUTE OF COOPERATION
50 F Street, NW
Suite 900
Washington, DC 20001
TEL: 202-347-1080
Objectives: To provide a national, structured educational organization for farmer cooperatives in a university setting (chartered as a university offering academic credit).
Services: Cosponsors training programs for directors, managers and members of cooperatives; cosponsors workshops for teachers, extension workers, and research workers concerned with cooperatives; sponsors "Foundation for Agricultural Cooperation," which does research and training for cooperatives; works with the Farm Credit Council, and National Council of Farmer Cooperatives; maintains numerous committees, including one for youth education; publishes a monthly newsletter, the annual *American Cooperation,* and various educational leaflets and bulletins.
Publications: AIC Newsletter; Washington Cooperator; American Cooperation; Educational Services Catalog; Annual Resource Guide
Founded: 1925

FEDERATION OF SOUTHERN COOPERATIVES AND LAND ASSISTANCE FUND
100 Edgewood Avenue, NE
Suite 1228
Atlanta, GA 30303
TEL: 404-524-6882
Objectives: To assist people in building community-owned enterprises so that they can control their own livelihood.
Services: Offers technical assistance in areas of accounting, setting up credit unions, consumer education, research in co-op expansion, market and product development, and improvement of production techniques; works to create housing, health care and educational programs to complement economic development; administers the "Forty Acres and a Mule" endowment fund for educational and social programs that do not have the potential to be self supporting; operates the FSC Rural Training and Research Center in Sumter County, Alabama, which:
- provides training to any cooperative association chartered and doing business in the 17 southern states or Washington, DC;
- offers marketing assistance through its network of stores (120 co-ops through out the rural south);
- prepares publications and other materials regarding credit unions and co-ops to inform the general public.
Founded: 1985

NATIONAL COOPERATIVE BUSINESS ASSOCIATION
1401 New York Avenue, NW
Suite 1100
Washington, DC 20005
TEL: 202-638-6222
Objectives: To represent, strengthen, and expand the cooperative form of business, and to link its members with cooperative organizations both in the United States and around the world, working together in a mutually beneficial manner.
Services: Serves as a national membership and trade association in which cooperatives gain strength by working together to form powerful coalitions; supports the development and expansion of cooperatives through lobbying, training programs, publication of a

newspaper for and about cooperative resource materials, and the provision of information and technical assistance; includes in its membership all types of cooperatives as well as businesses, associations, and individuals interested in cooperatives; mounts international activities of promoting trade among the world's cooperatives, providing technical assistance to cooperatives in lesser-developed countries, and representing U.S. cooperatives in the *International Cooperative Alliance.*

Works with a related entity, the *Cooperative Development Foundation,* which aims to develop cooperative enterprises in order to improve the human, social, and economic condition of people throughout the world. [Significant achievements of the *Foundation* include launching *CARE* and assisting in the establishment of the *Wisconsin Cooperative Development Council* and the *California Center for Cooperatives.*]

Information available includes complementary brochures on cooperatives and a publication catalog with more than 80 cooperative publications, gifts, and videos for purchase or rent.

Publications: Cooperative Business Journal
Founded: 1916

RURAL ADVANCEMENT FUND INTERNATIONAL*
PO Box 1029
Pittsboro, NC 27312
TEL: 919-542-5292

Objectives: To improve economic, social and educational conditions among sharecroppers, tenant and other independent farmers, and other rural poor people.

Services: Provides training for co-op managers, small farmers and migrant farm workers in areas of co-op management and organic farming techniques; aims to protect natural resources while providing nutritious food at reasonable cost; operates a confidential hotline in its "Farm Survival" program which offers assistance - financial and otherwise - to farmers affected by unjust agricultural policies; maintains a "Community Empowerment" program which trains rural people in skills and leadership development; works to bring about legislative changes as indicated; publishes annual report on conditions of farm workers and small farmers, and a newsletter which reports on rural legislation; works with Rural Advancement Fund to carry on its programs.

Founded: 1983

TECHNICAL ASSISTANCE TO COOPERATIVES
US/DoA - Division of Cooperative Services
Independence Avenue
(Between 12th & 14th Sts.)
Washington, DC 20250
TEL: 202-447-8870

Objectives: To improve management capabilities of rural and farmer cooperative operators.

Services: Provides advisory services, counseling and technical information on financial, legal, social, organizational, and other aspects of operating a rural or farmers cooperative; requires application in the form of a resolution from cooperative board of directors; publishes informational periodicals and listings.

Sponsor: US/DoA - Department of Agriculture

INDIVIDUAL PROGRAM PROFILES

AFFORDABLE HOUSING PROJECT
SEE HOUSING: LOW-INCOME

BUYERS UP
PO Box 33757
Washington, DC 20033-0757
TEL: 202-328-3800

Purpose: Buyers Up is a cooperative oil-buying group which receives regular delivery services at a group discount price. It is a nonprofit organization dedicated to saving families, organizations and businesses money on their heating oil bills and energy costs. Organized in 1983, *Buyers Up* is a project of *Public Citizen,* founded by Ralph Nader.

Upon becoming members, applications are sent to fuel suppliers in members' areas. Each member arranges delivery and chooses the most convenient payment payment method. In addition to the group cooperative discount, individuals with high volume usage may qualify for a bulk discount.

Oil furnace maintenance agreements and emergency service are available through the cooperative, also. Advance copies of any service agreement are available upon request to provide the cooperative member with an opportunity to read carefully the "fine print."

Through the *Buyers Up* cooperative oil-buying group, full services are received at lower cost, including consumer assistance and information on radon and other home hazards. Also available is the automatic service, in which members' usage is monitored by the supplier and oil is delivered automatically, especially useful for older persons to avoid running out of fuel. Savings of up to $200 per year have been realized by members of the *Buyers Up* cooperative.

Contact: Membership Chairman
Publications: Buyers Up Cooperative Membership Kit

CONSUMER SERVICES/LEGAL RIGHTS: CREDIT/FINANCES

NATIONAL/STATE ORGANIZATIONS

DEBT AND CREDIT COUNSELING SERVICE
Family Service America
11700 West Lake Park Drive
Milwaukee, WI 53224
TEL: 414-359-1040

Objectives: To enable families, overwhelmed by debt, to function adequately again.

Services: Offers financial counseling to family members of all ages; sponsors Home Economics Consultants who prepare budgets; publishes newsletter, *Highlights,* which covers all areas, including debt counseling, a journal, pamphlets, and other materials.

Publications: Newswire; Families in Society; Directory of Member Agencies; Highlights
Founded: 1911

NATIONAL FOUNDATION FOR CONSUMER CREDIT
8701 Georgia Avenue, #507
Silver Spring, MD 20910
TEL: 301-589-5600

Objectives: To educate the public in the intelligent handling of credit.

Services: Sponsors nationwide Consumer Credit Counseling Service program, free to consumers in credit difficulty, and Consumer Education program for low-income families; provides units of materials for teaching in high schools, colleges, universities; sponsors workshops, state and national conferences; maintains library on consumer credit; offers suggestions to local committees; publishes newsletter and other materials.

Publications: NFCC Newsletter; Directory of Services; NFCC Bulletin
Founded: 1951

VOLUNTEER INCOME TAX ASSISTANCE (VITA)
US/DTreas - Internal Revenue Service
1111 Constitution Avenue, NW
Washington, DC 20224
TEL: 202-566-2000
Objectives: To provide low-income people with tax preparation counseling services.
Services: Serves low-income, elderly, and disadvantaged taxpayers, and those for whom English is a second language; supports more than 5,500 local VITA programs across the country, utilizing about 30,000 part-time volunteers at sites ranging from community centers to shopping malls; trains volunteers between December and February every year on tax-form problem areas for clients (with some training on state and local returns); monitors program while it is in progress; makes publicity materials available.
Sponsor: US/DTreas - Department of the Treasury

INDIVIDUAL PROGRAM PROFILES

BALANCED BUDGETS FOR CONSUMERS
Minnesota Extension Service/Anoka County
550 Bunker Lake Boulevard, NW
Anoka, MN 55304
TEL: 612-755-1280
Purpose: To help consumers in Anoka County live within their income.
Contact: Trish Olson
Description: The *Minnesota Extension Service* in Anoka County responds to community needs as it becomes aware of them. Recent feedback indicated that many county residents develop poor credit ratings not because they do not earn enough income to cover their debts, but because of poor planning, unwise credit use and other factors resulting from a lack of budgeting skills.
To counteract this problem, the Extension Service enlists volunteers to help county residents develop budgets that will enable them to live within their incomes, teach wise credit use, and help consumers develop plans to reduce debts to a few necessary ones, and keep them current.
Before beginning their teaching assignments, volunteers participate in an intensive twelve-hour training program to explore and improve their own budgeting skills and learn the teaching methods recommended by the Extension Service.

CONSUMER SERVICES/LEGAL RIGHTS: ENTREPRENEURSHIP

NATIONAL/STATE ORGANIZATIONS

GOVERNMENT CONTRACTS CLINIC
SEE BUSINESS ASSISTANCE: LEGAL RIGHTS

CONSUMER SERVICES/LEGAL RIGHTS: ETHNIC GROUPS

NATIONAL/STATE ORGANIZATIONS

MEXICAN-AMERICAN LEGAL DEFENSE AND EDUCATIONAL FUND
634 South Spring Street
Eleventh Floor
Los Angeles, CA 90014
TEL: 213-629-2512
Objectives: To promote and protect the civil rights of Mexican Americans and other Hispanics living in the United States.
Services: Provides class-action litigation in areas of education, employment, immigration and voting rights; maintains leadership development program, census outreach program, and law school scholarship program; publishes two newsletters.
Contact: Alicia Maldonado
Publications: Leading Hispanics Newsletter; MALDEF
Founded: 1968

US/COMMISSION ON CIVIL RIGHTS*
2120 L Street, NW
Room 510
Washington, DC 20037
TEL: 202-254-6870
Objectives: To address and act upon violations of the Civil Rights Act of 1957 and its amendments of 1960, 1964, 1967, 1970, 1972, and 1978.
Services: Investigates complaints on discrimination based on color, race, religion, sex, age, handicap or national origin, including denial of the right to vote, denial of equal protection of the law, etc.; studies and collects information concerning legal developments constituting discrimination; appraises laws and policies of the Federal government with respect to discrimination; serves as a national clearinghouse for information in respect to discrimination; submits reports to the President and to Congress on its activities, findings, and recommendations; holds hearings; maintains state advisory committees; consults with representatives of federal, state and local governments and private organizations; publishes a handbook, *Getting Uncle Sam to Enforce Your Civil Rights* (free to the public), an overview of the Commission, and a catalog of publications.
Publications: Enforce Your Civil Rights

CONSUMER SERVICES/LEGAL RIGHTS: HANDICAPPED

NATIONAL/STATE ORGANIZATIONS

AMERICAN COALITION OF CITIZENS WITH DISABILITIES*
SEE RECIPIENTS: HANDICAPPED - EMPLOYMENT

CO-ORDINATING COUNCIL FOR HANDICAPPED CHILDREN
SEE RECIPIENTS: HANDICAPPED - CHILDREN/YOUTH

INDIVIDUAL PROGRAM PROFILES

PARKING POSSE
SEE RECIPIENTS: HANDICAPPED - LEGAL RIGHTS

CONSUMER SERVICES/LEGAL RIGHTS: HEALTH

NATIONAL/STATE ORGANIZATIONS

CONSUMER COALITION FOR HEALTH
SEE HEALTH: ADVOCACY

NATIONAL HEALTH COUNCIL*
SEE HEALTH: ADVOCACY

PUBLIC CITIZEN HEALTH RESEARCH GROUP
SEE HEALTH: ADVOCACY

CONSUMER SERVICES/LEGAL RIGHTS: HOMELESS

NATIONAL/STATE ORGANIZATIONS

NATIONAL COALITION FOR THE HOMELESS
SEE RECIPIENTS: HOMELESS - LEGAL RIGHTS

INDIVIDUAL PROGRAM PROFILES

LEGAL PROGRAMS FOR THE HOMELESS
SEE RECIPIENTS: HOMELESS - LEGAL RIGHTS

PROJECT HELP (HELP EXPEDITE LEGAL PROBLEMS FOR THE HOMELESS)
SEE RECIPIENTS: HOMELESS - LEGAL RIGHTS

CONSUMER SERVICES/LEGAL RIGHTS: HOUSING

NATIONAL/STATE ORGANIZATIONS

NATIONAL ASSOCIATION OF HOUSING & REDEVELOPMENT OFFICIALS
SEE HOUSING

NATIONAL COMMITTEE AGAINST DISCRIMINATION IN HOUSING
SEE HOUSING: DISCRIMINATION

INDIVIDUAL PROGRAM PROFILES

CHISS (CONSUMER HOUSING INFORMATION SERVICE FOR SENIORS)
SEE HOUSING: OLDER PERSON

CONSUMER SERVICES/LEGAL RIGHTS: I&R

INDIVIDUAL PROGRAM PROFILES

DIRECT LINE
WBBM Newsradio
630 North McClurg Court
Room 268
Chicago, IL 60611
TEL: 312-664-2936
Purpose: To provide assistance to citizens having disagreements with retailers, utilities, small companies, corporations, government agencies, and other entities.
Sponsor: WBBM Newsradio
Contact: Naomi Hood, Director
Description: Direct Line recently celebrated its twentieth anniversary at WBBM Newsradio. In 1988, the 47 volunteers monitoring telephones answered more than 19,000 calls from 21 different states from callers seeking assistance for many types of problems.
Volunteers are trained to respond to people having problems with local retailers, utilities, small companies, corporations and government agencies. Some volunteers are assigned to the investigative work after the call has been answered by another volunteer, and the problem has been fully described in writing on the "problem report." One volunteer - 89 years of age - has developed an uncanny knack for negotiating an agreement between two disputing parties. He has been with the program since 1982. Now others are learning from him. Hours donated by volunteers average 500-600 per volunteer each year.
The director has been with the program since its inception in the summer of 1969, providing a continuous practice of arriving at WBBM at 6:30 a.m. Monday through Friday to make necessary preparations for the volunteers who arrive at 9:30, and staying two hours after the volunteers leave to finish the follow-up work from the estimated 80 calls each day.
Many calls do not represent problems, per se, but are requests for information about the community or a planned event. Callers often send thank you notes with small donations.
Volunteers - especially the senior volunteers - receive something from the program in return - a meaningful structure in their daily lives. As one older volunteer stated, "I don't know what I would do without *Direct Line.* We always try our best for each caller. There is always something that we can do when a person has a problem. I would be lost without this." The director, although carrying an excessive workload, says, "I can honestly say that I just absolutely love what I do for a living."
Direct Line is sponsored by WBBM in cooperation with United Way/Crusade for Mercy.
Publications: Direct Line Information Packet
Founded: 1969

CONSUMER SERVICES/LEGAL RIGHTS: LOW-INCOME

NATIONAL/STATE ORGANIZATIONS

CATHOLIC COMMITTEE OF APPALACHIA
SEE RECIPIENTS: FAMILIES - LOW-INCOME

INDIVIDUAL PROGRAM PROFILES

VOLUNTEER LAWYERS PROJECT
Erie County Bar Association
290 Main Street
Buffalo, NY 14202
TEL: 716-847-0662
Purpose: To provide legal services for the poor.
Contact: Executive Director
Description: The *Volunteer Lawyers Project* is a project developed to provide legal services to people who cannot afford their own legal services. It is sponsored by the *Erie County Bar Association.* Members of the Association devote time to the Project as available, and as space in Project offices permits.
In mid-1989 the space problem was alleviated as the Project moved to new offices in the Niagara Frontier Building on Main Street. Local attorneys feel that this increased space will enable them to spend more time on cases for the poor, since more attorneys can work simultaneously.
Local businesses assist the Project by donating funds and materials. *Barrister Information Systems* donated more than $12,000 in computer equipment and training when the Project relocated. Another business donated a telephone system and office furniture.
In addition to local business and industry, the project receives encouragement and support from judges and other individuals and organizations across the community. A reception at the new offices was attended by about 80 people, and several businesses were honored for their assistance to the Project.

CONSUMER SERVICES/LEGAL RIGHTS: MINORITIES/WOMEN

NATIONAL/STATE ORGANIZATIONS

AAUW LEGAL ADVOCACY FUND
American Association of University Women
1111 Sixteenth Street, NW
Washington, DC 20036
TEL: 202-785-7700
FAX: 202-785-7797
Objectives: To provide funding and a support system for women seeking judicial redress for sex discrimination.
Services: Operates under a three-part strategy that provides ammunition in the fight for equality: support, information and visibility:
● Extends financial support to all involved in higher education - students, faculty, and administrators; requests are reviewed by a committee of attorneys and higher education administrators to determine need for financial aid, case's probability of success, and potential for a landmark ruling.
● Provides a network of volunteer attorneys and social scientists

to serve as consultants to attorneys, plaintiffs, and potential plaintiffs on litigation, strategies and potential witnesses; alternatives to litigation; and case research.
● Recognizes institutions that have successfully battled inequity by providing annual *Progress in Equity Award.*
As the only legal fund for women focused on higher education, the *Legal Advocacy Fund* plays a pivotal role in guaranteeing equal access and opportunities in academe.
Contact: Mary Boyette
Publications: Leader in Action; Action Alert; Graduate Woman; On Campus with Women
Founded: 1881

NATIONAL CONFERENCE OF BLACK LAWYERS
126 West 119th Street
New York, NY 10026
TEL: 212-864-4000
Objectives: To use legal skills in the service of black and poor communities through the U.S.
Services: Conducts education programs on legal issues affecting black and poor communities; covers specific areas such as prisoners' rights, juvenile law, and women's rights; operates lawyer referral and placement service; provides speakers on specific issues such as criminal justice, human rights, and civil rights law, maintains charitable program; publishes quarterly newsletter.
Publications: NCBL Notes
Founded: 1968

INDIVIDUAL PROGRAM PROFILES

CITIZEN ADVOCATES FOR JUSTICE
SEE LAW ENFORCEMENT/CRIME PREVENTION: ADVOCACY

CONSUMER SERVICES/LEGAL RIGHTS: NUTRITION

NATIONAL/STATE ORGANIZATIONS

FOOD RESEARCH AND ACTION CENTER
SEE NUTRITION: CONSUMER/LEGAL RIGHTS

FOOD SAFETY HOTLINE
US/DoA - Food and Nutrition Service
Independence Avenue, SW
(Between 12th & 14th Sts.)
Washington, DC 20250
TOLL FREE: 800-535-4555
Objectives: To answer questions on safe preparation of food.
Services: Provides five home economists to answer consumer questions regarding the proper handling, preparation and storage of meat and poultry products.

CONSUMER SERVICES/LEGAL RIGHTS: OLDER PERSON

NATIONAL/STATE ORGANIZATIONS

FLYING SENIOR CITIZENS OF THE USA*
SEE TRANSPORTATION & SAFETY: OLDER PERSON

LEGAL SERVICES FOR THE ELDERLY
SEE RECIPIENTS: OLDER PERSON - LEGAL SERVICES

LEGAL SERVICES FOR THE ELDERLY POOR
132 West 43rd Street
Third Floor
New York, NY 10036
TEL: 212-595-1340
Objectives: To advise on legal problems and areas indigenous to the elderly.
Services: Advises on and litigates cases involving elderly persons; maintains library of information on various aspects of legal services on behalf of the elderly; conducts research, litigation and educational programs; publishes a progress report (quarterly), papers, reports, articles and other materials. [Funded by the Legal Services Corporation of New York City, grants, and attorneys' fees.]
Publications: Progress Report
Founded: 1969

TRAINING PROGRAMS

NATIONAL SENIOR CITIZENS LAW CENTER
2025 M Street, NW
Suite 400
Washington, DC 20036
TEL: 202-887-5280
Objectives: To assist low-income, older persons in matters of litigation and legal rights.
Services: Serves as a legal services support center specializing in legal problems of the elderly; provides advocacy services in matters of litigation and other legal issues affecting elderly, poor citizens; conducts workshops and holds conferences to bring together individuals and groups working with the elderly; provides technical assistance in the various areas of nursing home law; maintains a library of materials addressing legal problems of older persons; publishes two newsletters (one on nursing home law), handbooks, guides, and testimonies to keep advocates, volunteers, staff members, administrators and others working with the elderly informed of the most recent events and activities in the area of legal problems of the elderly.
Publications: NSCLC Newsletter; Nursing Home Law Letter
Founded: 1972

INDIVIDUAL PROGRAM PROFILES

CORPORATE RETIREES INFORMATION AND ASSISTANCE PROGRAM
SEE RECIPIENTS: OLDER PERSON - CONSUMER SERVICES

LEGAL COUNSEL FOR THE ELDERLY
1331 H Street, NW
Lower Level, Room 120
Washington, DC 20005
TEL: 202-234-0970
Purpose: To deliver free, quality legal services to elderly citizens of the District of Columbia, 60 years of age and older.
Sponsor: American Association of Retired Persons
Contact: Elsie R. Shamwell
Description: Legal Counsel for the Elderly was organized in 1975. It is sponsored by AARP (The American Association of Retired Persons) and receives funding from the D.C. Office on Aging, the Administration on Aging, the U.S. Department of Health and Human Services, the Legal Services Corporation, the D.C. Bar Foundation, and private contributions. The agency is both a law office for the elderly and a national support center that specializes in advocacy systems.
LCE is operated by a small paid staff comprised of attorneys, paralegals and support staff. Approximately 60 in-house volunteer paralegals and volunteer attorneys handle client cases under the supervision of staff attorneys. In addition to these volunteers, approximately 346 practitioners comprise the Volunteer Lawyers Project. They are individual attorneys or representatives of 47 major law firms who take cases on a pro bono (without charge) basis. Volunteer typists, secretaries, interns and other support persons render invaluable services.
In one month 1,208 new clients received legal assistance involving over 1,600 individual legal problems. Typical problems included welfare benefits, housing issues, consumer problems, medical care, and utility bills. Sixty percent of the clients received monetary values of public benefits due them to the extent of $483,000. Volunteers receive initial training and also periodically scheduled training that keeps them current on updates and changes in rules and regulations that affect their services. Not only volunteers are trained, but many other agencies and persons who serve the elderly avail themselves of this opportunity.
LCE spoke about the legal needs of the elderly to an average of 180 community persons each month. The staff and volunteers also appear on radio and television.
Materials developed by LCE staff include: law manuals, training books, management information, the Legal Rights Calendar, and a local Information and Referral Manual.
In April 1982, LCE received one of the ten Annual Volunteer Activist Awards in the Washington Metropolitan Area for its volunteer program. In 1983, one of LCE's volunteer attorneys received honorable mention for his services to the community. LCE's most recent project is the Model Volunteer Protective Services Project (MVPSP). The purpose of the project is to provide help for the elderly person who is unable to handle his/her financial affairs. A "representative payee" is appointed to act on the elderly person's behalf. This is achieved through a system of volunteers who are thoroughly trained and prepared to participate in the program. A long range goal is to replicate the project in other sections of the country, both rural and urban.
Founded: 1975

CONSUMER SERVICES/LEGAL RIGHTS: PRISONERS

NATIONAL/STATE ORGANIZATIONS

NATIONAL PRISON PROJECT
SEE LAW ENFORCEMENT/CRIME PREVENTION: FACILITY

PRISON FELLOWSHIP MINISTRIES
SEE LAW ENFORCEMENT/CRIME PREVENTION: LEGAL RIGHTS

CONSUMER SERVICES/LEGAL RIGHTS: RECREATION/SPORTS

NATIONAL/STATE ORGANIZATIONS

FTC VACATION TRAVEL HOTLINE
US/FTC - Federal Trade Commission
Division of Credit Practices
Washington, DC 20580
TEL: 202-326-3237; 202-326-3212
Objectives: To respond to consumers' questions on vacation brokers with an unusually large number of complaints from consumers.
Services: Provides consumers with a point of referral when it has been established that vacation travel companies have not met advertised commitments to consumers; operates hotline on a company-by-company basis (1989 - BankCard Travel Club and World Travel Vacation Brokers) usually regarding companies that are being sued by FTC; provides telephone message tape enabling consumer to describe problem and leave contact information, or responds to written complaints.
Sponsor: US/FTC - Federal Trade Commission

CONSUMER SERVICES/LEGAL RIGHTS: TENANTS/RESIDENTS

NATIONAL/STATE ORGANIZATIONS

ASSOCIATION OF COMMUNITY ORGANIZATIONS FOR REFORM NOW (ACORN)
401 Howard Avenue
New Orleans, LA 70130
TEL: 504-523-1691
Objectives: To enable low-income families to have a stronger voice in decisions affecting their future.
Services: Advocates the concept of a "major constituency" which ACORN describes as individuals of low or moderate income who are shut out of the power structure; promotes action on issues including fighting utility rate increases, challenging blockbusting practices, and promoting major reform in legislation regulating prescription drug prices; has adopted a nine-point *People's Platform* which calls for fair taxes, jobs for all, national health insurance, subsidized utility rates for the elderly, saving of family farms, adequate housing, controlled community development, and full representation of low- and moderate-income people in matters that affect their lives; sponsors fund-raising activities, internships, and training events; publishes a newsletter, a manual, and other materials.
Publications: USA (United States of ACORN); The Organizer, Vamanos!
Founded: 1970

CONSUMER SERVICES/LEGAL RIGHTS: TRANSPORTATION

NATIONAL/STATE ORGANIZATIONS

AUTOMOTIVE CONSUMER ACTION PROGRAM (AUTOCAP)
National Automobile Dealers Association
8400 Westpark Drive
McLean, VA 22102
TEL: 703-821-7144
Objectives: To provide dealers and their customers with consumer dispute resolution assistance.
Services: Sponsors panels of volunteers (usually three dealers and three consumer representatives) who act as "mini-juries" in cases of customer dissatisfaction with dealers, when direct contact between the two parties fails to resolve the problem; provides this form of conflict resolution opportunity as a public service to address dealer/consumer disputes; works with new car dealers' associations and automobile importers who comply with the standards of the National Automobile Dealers Association; provides research findings on request; publishes a newsletter and a directory.
Publications: AUTOCAP Report; Automotive Customer Relations Directory
Founded: 1973

CENTER FOR AUTO SAFETY
SEE TRANSPORTATION & SAFETY: CONSUMERS/LEGAL RIGHTS

NHTSA HOTLINE
US/DoT - National Highway Traffic Safety Administration
400 Seventh Street, SW
Washington, DC 20590
TEL: 202-426-0123
TOLL FREE: 800-424-9393
Objectives: To promote and enforce safety as a prime consideration in the manufacture of vehicles.
Services: Dispenses safety information; takes some safety complaints; refers other safety complaints to the appropriate government agencies; provides facts on past or pending recalls; publishes *The Car Book,* which lists points to consider before buying a car (available from U.S. Consumer Information Center; see bibliography), and other tools to help consumers obtain automobiles based on individual needs; maintains special numbers for people with hearing problems (inquire).

INDIVIDUAL PROGRAM PROFILES

MOTOR VOTERS
SEE CIVIC AFFAIRS: VOTING

DAY CARE/HEAD START

NATIONAL/STATE ORGANIZATIONS

DAY CARE COUNCIL OF AMERICA
1602 Seventeenth Street, NW
Washington, DC 20009
TEL: 202-745-0220
Objectives: To generate broader public understanding of and support for quality services for children.
Services: Maintains an information center; provides technical assistance on program planning, fund raising, organizational techniques, etc.; publishes *Voice for Children, Day Care and Early Education Magazine,* directories and other materials.
Publications: Voice for Children; Day Care and Early Education

HEAD START PROGRAM
US/HHS - Office of Human Development
PO Box 1182
Washington, DC 20201
TEL: 202-472-7257
Objectives: To provide health, educational, nutritional, social and other services to preschool disadvantaged children and families; to involve parents in activities with children.
Services: Provides training and technical assistance to Head Start Programs; enables local government agencies and nonprofit organizations to mount Head Start Programs through grants; requires enrollment opportunities for handicapped children; includes special summer program for children entering school in the fall; provides regulations, guidelines, and numerous publications for Head Start Programs.
Sponsor: US/HHS - Department of Health & Human Services

NATIONAL ASSOCIATION FOR CHILD CARE MANAGEMENT
1255 23rd Street, NW
Suite 850
Washington, DC 20037
TEL: 202-659-5955
Objectives: To promote the growth of quality, center-based child care services for America's working families.
Services: Serves private day care centers of all types, including family day care, in its promotion of quality chid care and effective policy and legislation; conducts training sessions in administration and management; monitors federal and state legislative and regulatory issues; maintains library; publishes monthly newsletter,

NACCM News, a directory, and other materials.
Publications: NACCM News; NACCM Roster
Founded: 1972

NATIONAL ASSOCIATION FOR THE EDUCATION OF YOUNG CHILDREN
1834 Connecticut Avenue, NW
Washington, DC 20009
TEL: 202-232-8777
Objectives: To act on behalf of the needs and rights of young children, with primary focus on educational services and resources.
Services: Participates in the development of standards for children's programs; assists individuals and groups in accomplishing legislation related to the total well-being of children; welcomes assistance from anyone interested in serving and acting on behalf of the needs and rights of young children; offers voluntary accreditation for early childhood education schools and centers; disseminates information about pending federal legislation and interprets issues and alternatives involved; publishes books, booklets and other materials; sponsors national Week of the Young Child.
Publications: Young Children; Early Childhood Research
Founded: 1926

NATIONAL HEAD START ASSOCIATION*
1029 31st Street, NW
Washington, DC 20007
TEL: 202-337-6650
Objectives: To upgrade the quality and quantity of Head Start Program services.
Services: Presents policies, positions and statements based on input from National Head Start Parent Association, National Head Start Directors Association, National Head Start Staff Association, National Head Start Friends Association, and others interested in the Head Start Program; works to upgrade both quality and quantity of head start services by combining, analyzing and utlizing the suggestions of the four divisions; maintains speakers bureau and an awards program; conducts seminars and training sessions in early childhood development.
Publications: Tell the Head Start Story; NHSA Newsletter
Founded: 1973

PLAY SCHOOLS ASSOCIATION*
9 East 38th Street
8th Floor
New York, NY 10016
TEL: 212-921-2940
Objectives: To improve capabilities of professionals,
paraprofessionals, parents, volunteers and other child care/day
care workers to utilize play activities as a teaching tool.
Services: Conducts training programs focusing on play activities as
an educational, recreational and therapeutic tool for children;
develops programs for both normal and handicapped children,
including the "Laboratory Play School" for latchkey children and
an in-service Institute for training paraprofessionals, parents and
volunteers in therapeutic recreation for handicapped children; has
on-site programs for juvenile offenders, hospitalized children, and
others with a variety of problems that precludes their traveling to
a program; develops educational test and evaluation equipment;
maintains a networking program for agencies and individuals
working with children; publishes booklets; produces films.
Founded: 1917

TRAINING PROGRAMS

**VOLUNTEER & COMMUNITY PARTNERSHIPS
INSTITUTE**
US/HHS - Administration for Children, Youth and Families
200 Independence Avenue, SW
Washington, DC 20201
TEL: 202-245-0572
Sponsor: US/HHS - Department of Health & Human Services
Description: This national conference focused on volunteer
management to demonstrate the increasingly important role of the
community volunteer in Head Start programs across the country.
It also launched a partnership between the *Head Start Bureau* of
the *U.S. Department of Health & Human Services* and the
Association for Volunteer Administration (AVA), a national
organization that provides *Certification and Volunteer
Management Training* nationwide. Participants interested in
Certification were required to:
● Participate in a Certification Workshop;
● Attend an overview of the Certification process;
● Consult individually with AVA to provide confirmation of
  both interest and experience.
Forty participants were selected to attend a special volunteer
management training event.
A challenge to the AVA Certification Process was presented by
eight Head Start staff from Puerto Rico who attended the training
and asked if they could submit their portfolios in Spanish.
Bilingual members were called upon to assess these portfolios. The
experience took AVA one step closer to translating all of its
materials into Spanish - and meeting its goal of attaining cultural
diversity in training.

INDIVIDUAL PROGRAM PROFILES

CHILD DEVELOPMENT CENTERS OF ACCA
Annandale Christian Community for Action (ACCA)
7200 Columbia Pike
Annandale, VA 22003
TEL: 703-256-1378
Purpose: To respond to a critical need for child care.
Sponsor: ACCA
Contact: Mildred Gunnarson, Chairman
Description: In 1967 a small group of children were being cared
for in the Mount Pleasant Baptist Church under a government
program that provided funds for the service. Suddenly the

guidelines for the program were changed, and the families could
no longer be helped. As a result, a group of concerned Christians
met at John Calvin Presbyterian Church and, with only $1,000 of
donated funds and no real knowledge of child care, began the first
ACCA day care center for children of the working poor.
Through the years, the mission of the ACCA Day Care Program
has remained the same, but the size of the program and the
services offered have been greatly extended. The families helped
demonstrate that they are trying to help themselves, but most
cannot afford the high cost of day care. ACCA offers a subsidy,
and another is offered through Fairfax County. In 1988, the
average annual income of the families served by the ACCA
Centers was just over $18,000. Since the cost per child is about
$4,500 per year, it is obvious that this cost is prohibitive for these
families. The churches and individuals in the community who have
provided funds have made it possible to help these families.
ACCA operates two child care centers. The initial center (ACCA)
- located at a former elementary school - was expanded in 1985 in
response to the great demand and, at the present time, serves 138
preschool children. ACCA II is located in Culmore United
Methodist Church and enrolls 70 children aged four to six. During
the academic year, ACCA II serves as a *Before and After School
Center* for 60 Kindergarten youngsters who attend Baileys and
Glen Forest Elementary Schools and St. Anthony's Catholic
School. ACCA II also serves as a full-time center for 10
preschoolers. During the summer, the 70 children remain at the
Center from 7:00 a.m. until 5:45 p.m. The Centers operate 50
weeks a year and close only on major national holidays.
Active participation by the community has enabled the Centers to
provide many services for the children and their families as well,
including transportation, meals, and an educational program
designed to enable children to succeed in school. A paid
administrator counsels parents and coordinates assistance through
other ACCA programs for families with special needs.
The Centers were honored by a visit in 1987 by the Governor of
Virginia, and were featured among 19 centers in the country in
*The National Governors' Association Handbook of Promising
Prevention Programs for Children Zero to Five Years of Age.*
Strengths of the program include its subsidy assistance, educational
techniques, and support services.
Publications: ACCA Annual Report
Founded: 1967

SAUNDERS B. MOON CHILD DEVELOPMENT CENTER
**Saunders B. Moon School Community Resource Advisory
Program**
8100 Fordson Road
Alexandria, VA 22306
TEL: 703-360-2100
Purpose: To provide child care and instruction to two- to
five-year-olds from low-income families.
Sponsor: Local business/industry; donations
Contact: Charlotte H. Branch, Director
Description: After over 25 years of representing the poor in
Fairfax County, the Saunders B. Moon Child Development Center
was faced with closing in August 1989 after a dispute with Fairfax
County. The county provided major funding for the Center
($400,000 per year). The new County contract, offering no increase
in budget to care for the 150 children enrolled, stipulated that the
Center must increase its staff-pupil ratio before the contract could
be validated. Without an increase in funding, Center staff found
this requirement to be impossible. This latest problem culminated
a two-year dispute with the County in matters of irregular
inspections, budget autonomy, etc. The Contract was denied.
Undaunted, the Center turned to the community and, with
corporate donations and contributions from individuals, six
volunteers continued operations. They felt that interruption of the
service could affect not only the progress and supervision of the
children, but employment of the parents. Although the Center was

officially closed, and the County would place some of the children in school programs, too many families who would not be in those programs would be affected, since many of them could not pay a babysitter. The Center is a full-day, year-round operation that specializes in instruction and development of the child.

STRIDE RITE CHILDREN'S CENTER
Stride Rite Corporation
960 Harrison Avenue
Boston, MA 02118
TEL: 617-427-1100
Purpose: To help provide an answer to the vital question, "Who's minding the kids?"
Sponsor: Stride Rite Corporation
Contact: Miriam Kertzman, Director
Description: In response to a community group's request in 1971, the Stride Rite Corporation's philanthropic foundation helped fund a community child-care center. It occurred to the company that this center could include employee children, too, and the facility opened with 30 children - 15 employees' children and 15 children from the community at large. Presently, 50 children are accommodated. An additional day care center opened in early 1983 in Kendall Square, Cambridge, to accommodate employees' and community children at the new corporate headquarters site. The staffers and several volunteers run the center, with personnel costs reduced somewhat through affiliation with high-school and college-intern projects and teacher-training programs.
The center is open from 7 a.m. to 5 p.m. to allow for variance in parents' shifts. After breakfast, the children's activities include math and reading readiness, cooking, drama and field trips. Interns from local hospitals work as teacher aides during their pediatrics rotations, and children are taken on a rotating basis to the pedodontic department at Boston University's Dental School for dental care.
The center occupies former office space on the first floor of the plant, which employs about 700 people. It cost about $25,000 to renovate and equip the initial area, with total start-up costs amounting to about $40,000. The facility has been enlarged several times, with $46,000 in company funding supplemented by government subsidies and non-financial sources of support. For example, a federal program reimbursed 75% of the cost of installing the kitchen; a contract with the state school lunch and nutrition bureau pays about 70% of food costs.
The cost of running the center is about $60 per week, per child. Employee parents pay 10% of their weekly gross pay, and community parents pay the state on a sliding-scale basis. The center is a separate corporation with its own charter, board of directors and insurance. The company has no legal responsibility for its operation.
The company considers industry-sponsored day care extremely cost-effective since the company is already paying for heat, light, telephones, maintenance and other services. Reduction in absenteeism is another plus for the company, as well as the side benefit of access to the children to "wear-test" new shoe designs. Stride Rite has developed a summary of the operation in a free booklet, *How We Do It,* and the director conducts a monthly two-hour information-sharing session for persons interested in visiting the center.
A footnote worth mentioning here is an observation made by a staff member. "Some of us try to be near the Center around noon to see the sheer delight on the children's faces when their parents join them for lunch."
Publications: How We Do It
Founded: 1971

DAY CARE/HEAD START: ARTS

INDIVIDUAL PROGRAM PROFILES

SENIORS AND CHILDREN TOGETHER
United Way of Great Salt Lake Area
455 East 400 South
Suite 410
Salt Lake City, UT 84111-3000
TEL: 716-366-5424
Purpose: To enable seniors and children to get more out of life by interacting with each other.
Sponsor: United Way of Great Salt Lake Area
Contact: Charles Johnson
Description: Neighborhood House has provided services to children since 1894. In 1984, the agency began offering senior day care as well. The National Council on Aging helped the agency begin to plan a program through which children could learn about seniors in a way that was mutually beneficial for both groups. The result is a program of cooking, crafts, singing, dancing and other activities involving low-income senior citizens over age 60, and low-income children ages 2-12.
The most critical component of the program was orienting the children to being around older people, since many of them don't have grandparents or older people in their lives. A wheelchair was brought into the center, and the children were given rides in it. They were told how some people need a little help walking or need to go a little slower, and what it is like to get older. They explained that yelling and running indoors might upset older people.
According to the program's director, the older men became role models, since 73% of the children at the center do not live with their fathers. The older people tell the children stories, and teach them songs. There are cookie-baking contests and intergenerational teams baking bread (something the children had never had before). When kids become curious about canes and other items needed by the elderly, the staff helps them to ask about them in a sensitive way. All of the 213 children at the center have regular contact with the seniors.
Older persons too feeble to participate enjoy watching the activities and seem to garner energy from the experience.
Intergenerational day care is helping agencies more and more to pool their resources. The new movement to bring the old and the young together enables both groups to get more out of life. "As each day goes by," according to the director, "we find more and more things that the seniors and kids can do together."

DAY CARE/HEAD START: CRISIS

INDIVIDUAL PROGRAM PROFILES

JUNIOR LEAGUE OF DETROIT
SEE AIDS

DAY CARE/HEAD START: CURRICULUM

NATIONAL/STATE ORGANIZATIONS

ASSOCIATION FOR CHILDHOOD EDUCATION INTERNATIONAL
11141 Georgia Avenue
Suite 200
Wheaton, MD 20902
TEL: 301-942-2443
Objectives: To promote good educational practices for children from infancy to early adolescence; to raise the standard of preparation for teachers, teacher educators, teachers-in-training, supervisors, administrators, librarians and other caregivers involved with the development of children.
Services: Provides professional guidance and consultation in all areas of early childhood education from infancy to early adolescence, including day care; informs the public of the needs of children and the ways in which various programs must be adjusted to fit those needs and rights; aims to raise the standards of teachers and others involved with the care and development of children; maintains extensive library; publishes a journal, a newsletter, bulletins, bibliographies, portfolios on kindergarten, and other materials; convenes annual study conference and regional conference.
Publications: Childhood Education; Journal of Research; ACEI Exchange
Founded: 1931

DAY CARE/HEAD START: ETHNIC/BILINGUAL

NATIONAL/STATE ORGANIZATIONS

NATIONAL BLACK CHILD DEVELOPMENT INSTITUTE
1463 Rhode Island Avenue
Washington, DC 20005
TEL: 202-387-1281
Objectives: To advocate for educational, racial and cultural awareness for black youngsters through quality child-centered programs involving the community.
Services: Analyzes policy decisions, legislative and administrative guidelines from black perspective; provides a forum of conferences for black scholars that relates to development of black children, convenes conferences and seminars for black community groups; maintains a volunteer grassroots network system to address concerns that affect black children, and makes policy makers aware of the network's findings; disseminates information on federal and state programs; publishes monthly newsletter, an annual calendar, irregular reports, and monographs.
Publications: Black Child Advocate; Black Flash; Child Health Talk
Founded: 1970

NATIONAL COMMITTEE ON THE EDUCATION OF MIGRANT CHILDREN
National Child Labor Committee
1501 Broadway
Room 1111
New York, NY 10036
TEL: 212-840-1801

Objectives: To promote programs and projects for the health and education of migrant workers' children.
Services: Provides technical assistance, training and other services regarding the health and education of migrant children and youth in public schools; works with day care centers only when assignment in public school is in the same community or area.
Founded: 1963

DAY CARE/HEAD START: EVALUATION

NATIONAL/STATE ORGANIZATIONS

CHILDREN'S FOUNDATION
725 Fifteenth Street, NW
Suite 505
Washington, DC 20005
TEL: 202-347-3300
Objectives: To address the problems created by the feminization of poverty.
Services: Works with more than 600 state and local family day care associations comprised of thousands of low- and moderate-income women who provide child care in their homes for over 80% of the children in full-time care; provides technical assistance to the *National Association for Family Day Care,* an organization established by providers for providers, parents, and other advocates for home-based child care; works with child support enforcement to improve the present system through consumer involvement and coalition work aimed at developing stronger national policies; works toward cooperation among organizations with the same constituency who have never worked closely together; functions as a national forum for concerns of women and their children, especially child nutrition.
Contact: Kay Hollestelle
Publications: Family Day Care Bulletin; Child Support; Family Day Care Directory; Better Baby Care; Better Baby Care Training; Family Day Care Licensing; State/Local Child Support Groups
Founded: 1969

DAY CARE/HEAD START: FAMILY DAY CARE

NATIONAL/STATE ORGANIZATIONS

HEAD START - FAMILY DAY CARE
US/HHS - Administration for Children, Youth and Families
PO Box 1182
Washington, DC 20201
TEL: 202-475-0257
Objectives: To extend the part-time services of *Head Start* to include full-time child care.
Services: With a $1.9 million grant from the US Department of Health and Human Services to the District of Columbia School System, an extension of the long-standing Head Start program was launched in September 1989. The intent of the pilot program is to assist working parents struggling to break away from the welfare rolls who need full time child care, but would like to see their children receive the benefits of the strong educational component of the popular Head Start program as well.

The Department's solution for this model program is to enlist low-income families as full-time day care providers, with a limit of five children in each home compared to 17 in Head Start classes in the schools. All providers receive training through the school system by early childhood specialists to assure that the educational intent of the Head Start program is as fully utilized as possible in the homes. All materials and supplies, from books to musical instruments, are supplied through the Head Start office. Providers are paid $12 per day per child following completion of their training. The providers are closely supervised, with school monitors assigned to visit the homes weekly. School officials require that the providers keep detailed records on each child's progress and submit monthly reports on their activities.

The element that sets the family program apart from the school program is that it provides a natural setting that makes children feel secure and eager to learn in homes within their neighborhoods. Some volunteer community agencies provide full-day child care in Head Start programs on a limited basis. The *National Child Day Care Association* operates centers in churches, housing projects and community centers in the District, providing full-time care in two of its eight Head Start programs and in the home of one child-care provider.

The Bush administration's 1991 fiscal year request for $500 million increase for Head Start (a 36% increase over 1990) is considered a testament to the success of the program, and its bipartisan reputation (it was begun during the poverty program era of the Kennedy administration). According to a leading organization for children, the *Children's Defense Fund,* "It's made an enormous difference to countless children and families. It's enabled many children to enter school healthy and strong."

The District's program is small. Six day-care providers are operating under the model program. Sixteen similar projects are being tested around the country. Since the project includes an employment element for low-income people, the benefits reach adults and families as well as children.

DAY CARE/HEAD START: HANDICAPPED

INDIVIDUAL PROGRAM PROFILES

PRESCHOOL DIAGNOSTIC AND DEVELOPMENTAL EDUCATION NURSERIES

54 South State Street
Dover, DE 19901
TEL: 302-736-6038
Purpose: To serve developmentally delayed children and their families.
Sponsor: Delaware Department of Health and Social Services
Contact: Nancy Reihm
Description: PDDEN I opened in January 1973 and PDDEN II in 1980. They are administered by the Division of Public Health, Office of Speech and Hearing Services with funds allocated by the State Legislature and from the Department of Public Instruction (P.L. 89-313 and EHA, Part B, P.L. 94-142). These nurseries are designed to serve children (1 1/2 to 4 years of age) residing in Kent County and nearby areas of lower New Castle County and upper Sussex County, with developmental delays in speech/language, motor, social and/or cognitive skills.

In PDDEN I diagnostic assessment, individualized education plan, speech therapy, individual, family and group counseling services are provided. Activities are designed to enable the staff to observe and assess the child's strengths and weaknesses in order to determine how best to accelerate development. Special diagnostic

studies and services are arranged through either the Division of Public Health programs or other agencies. Children may attend this nursery for four months.

PDDEN II is a developmental nursery designed to serve those children who have attended PDDEN I and are not eligible or cannot be served by local education agencies, private nurseries or special programs. Here they receive ongoing educational and developmental programming based on PDDEN I evaluation and observation. The objective here is to raise the child to an optimum level of functioning. The length of time a child remains in this program depends upon the individual needs and progress of the child.

Volunteers work one 2-1/2 period each week and at other times if needed. They assist the teachers in most functions and work with children in small groups and individually. Some volunteers attend Delaware State College as well as workshops with the PDDEN staff. The only supervision needed is a briefing on each new child that enters the program.
Founded: 1973

RAINBOW CENTER FOR EXCEPTIONAL CHILDREN

1098 Fifth Avenue
Yuma, AZ 85364
TEL: 602-782-7586
Purpose: To provide educational services for handicapped children.
Sponsor: Government contracts and private donations
Contact: Gail Ross, Supervising Teacher
Description: Rainbow Center is a private, nonprofit organization which offers preschool and day care to handicapped and non-handicapped children as well as a school-aged classroom and group home residence for handicapped children. Supportive services such as occupational, physical and speech therapies are provided as needed. Educational testing and parent education are offered to all children and their families.

During the first 6 months of the 1982-83 school year, Rainbow has received over 2,000 hours of volunteer service. Volunteers come to us in a variety of ways:
- in answer to our newspaper ad;
- students receiving credit in their civics class (8 hours per grading period);
- court-ordered volunteers who have committed minor offenses; and
- service clubs which perform special duties for the Center.

Also, parents whose incomes qualify work as volunteers in lieu of paying tuition (1 hour of service = $3.00 tuition reduction). Volunteers are coordinated by one person and are made to feel a part of the "Rainbow family." Volunteers are taken on a tour of the Center, asked to fill out a form and interviewed by the coordinator. Special skills of volunteers are matched with special jobs or routine duties from building playground equipment to sewing nap sheets to assisting staff in the classroom. Most are placed in one classroom consistently so they get to know the staff and develop attachments to the children. Each volunteer is given direction on how to care for specific children and how to best assist teachers and aides. They are scheduled and asked to call if they will not be able to come. Not only does this help utilize them better, but conveys to them that their help is needed and they will be missed when they are not here. Also, volunteers are invited to school events and are honored with mementos and gifts at Christmas and an end-of-year volunteer recognition event.

DAY CARE/HEAD START: HOME

NATIONAL/STATE ORGANIZATIONS

CHILDREN'S FOUNDATION
SEE DAY CARE/HEAD START: EVALUATION

TRAINING PROGRAMS

FAMILY DAY CARE TECHNICAL ASSISTANCE CONFERENCE
Save the Children/Child Care Support Center
1340 Spring Street
Suite 200
Atlanta, GA 30309
TEL: 404-885-1578
Sponsor: Save the Children
Contact: Joe Perreault
Description: A four-day meeting, this conference is called to assist and encourage day providers to share their experiences in the various activities related to day care.

INDIVIDUAL PROGRAM PROFILES

EARLY HOME EDUCATION
Madison House
170 Rugby Road
Charlottesville, VA 22903
TEL: 703-977-7051
Purpose: To lay the foundation for learning skills in young children; to stimulate at-home reinforcement by involving parents.
Sponsor: Madison House
Contact: Jane Parker
Description: In 1973, a student in the University Year for Action Program determined that once the Head Start children left the program and its special help to begin Kindergarten, it was often difficult for them to keep up. In 1975 the Head Start Home Based Project resulted from his study and efforts.
This project was designed to send volunteer tutors into the child's home to work with the parent(s) and create a learning environment at home. By having the families more involved in the child's education, it was hoped that their learning ability would increase. When the Head Start office had to discontinue this successful program in 1976, Madison House picked it up as the Early Home Education project and began operating on a limited basis the following year. The major change in the program is that it now deals with children already enrolled in Kindergarten.
Early Home Education is an in-the-home tutoring project in which volunteers tutor parents as well as their kindergarten-aged children. The rationale behind the program is that it is not true that parents have no concern for their children's education. What is true is that many parents do not know how to tutor or how to enhance their child's educational experience on a daily basis in the home.
This program requires no previous experience in tutoring, but it does demand an ability to communicate with both parent and child. Volunteers receive support from the Early Home Education Program Director, who has been in the field, and can offer advice. Information and advice are available also from the child's Kindergarten teacher.
Volunteers have found that getting to know the family is not always easy, but is usually a rewarding task. Families involved in the program often have entirely different outlooks on life than does the average volunteer. However this challenging program has

proven to be one of the favorites of the volunteers.
Founded: 1975

HOME-BASED CHILD CARE IN HARTFORD
United Way of the Capital Area (Hartford)
99 Woodland Street
Hartford, CT 06105-1207
TEL: 203-278-2044
Purpose: To stimulate the development of innovative child-care programs.
Sponsor: YWCA
Contact: Lewis J. Robinson, Jr., Chairman, Venture Funding
Description: Inadequate child care is a barrier to employment for many families in the Hartford area. However, two new child care programs in the Hartford area met the criteria of the *United Way's Venture Funding Committee* for innovative child-care programs. One-year grants totaling $124,353 were given to the two programs - the *YWCA Family Child Care Project,* sponsored by the YWCA, and the *Hispanic Family Day Care Network,* sponsored by the *Community Renewal Team* in conjunction with *La Casa de Puerto Rico* and the *Betances School.* Between them they accommodate 180 children.
What makes the programs unique in the Hartford area is that both provide services for *home-based child-care providers.* The sponsoring agencies recruit and train the providers, hire them as salaried employees, and offer them full benefits and ongoing support. The *Hispanic Network* offers its providers bilingual training.
The programs represent a major breakthrough in the day care field, since lack of medical insurance and other basic employee benefits has discouraged potential home day care providers in the past. The chairman of the *United Way Venture Funding Committee* is also an attorney for the *Travelers Companies,* as well as chairman of the Hartford United Way's Board of Directors.
In addition to increasing child care capabilities in the area, the home-based system provides employment as home-based day care providers for women with small children who find it difficult to work away from home.

PARENT-CHILD HOME PROGRAM
10 Campbell Street
New Hyde Park, NY 11040
TEL: 516-482-8650/Ext. 610
Purpose: To prevent educational disadvantage in children from poor families and to help the parent in his/her role as the child's first teacher.
Sponsor: Great Neck & Manhasset Public Schools, BOCES of Nassau County
Contact: Doris Kertzner, Program Coordinator
Description: Operating Scope: The program, begun in 1972, serves about 60 low-income families living in the Manhasset and Great Neck School Districts. Children enter the program between the ages of 18 to 36 months and remain for two years. The families are visited in the home once or twice a week by trained staff (paid and volunteer).
Since 1978, The Parent-Child Home Program (PCHP), has offered a play group for the children one morning a week. Parents attend with their children and are thus able to have dialogue among themselves, arts and crafts sessions, and discussions led by professional psychologists, nutritionists, etc.
- **Time Span:** The program runs concurrently with the school year starting with training in late September, early October, and ending in late May. The office is staffed 9 a.m. to 4 p.m. on school days.
- **Purpose:** The program's purpose is to prevent educational disadvantage in children from poor families and to help the parent in his/her role as the child's first teacher. By encouraging parents to play with and speak to their young children we hope to give the child an enrichment taken for

granted in middle-class culture - and to assure that these children do not enter school and face a catch-up situation.

- **Volunteer's Role:** The volunteer is the backbone of the program; in a typical year we have 20 volunteers. After training (described below) she is assigned one or more families whom she visits for a half hour once a week. The volunteer teacher-demonstrator (or TD) takes to the home carefully chosen books and toys and, in playing and reading to the child, she models behavior that the parent observes and imitates.
- **Volunteer's Training:** In late September the director gives a three-day training institute for new volunteers. They hear talks, see films, and become well acquainted with the program's content, purpose and techniques. Training continues throughout the year with weekly hour and a half seminars. The TD's come together at this time and discuss with the director any problems that have come up.
- **Time Commitment:** Volunteers should allow for a time commitment of about four hours a week. A car is a necessity.
- **Background:** No special training or background is necessary. We look for persons of warmth and openness who enjoy young children and are committed to the goals of the program.

Founded: 1972

DAY CARE/HEAD START: HOMELESS

INDIVIDUAL PROGRAM PROFILES

FAMILY ASSISTANCE PROJECT OF HOLLYWOOD (FAP)
SEE RECIPIENTS: HOMELESS - FAMILIES

VOGEL ALCOVE
SEE RECIPIENTS: HOMELESS - CHILDREN/YOUTH

DAY CARE/HEAD START: LATCHKEY

INDIVIDUAL PROGRAM PROFILES

SCHOOLMATE HANDICRAFT VOLUNTEERS
SEE ARTS/CULTURAL ENRICHMENT: CRAFTS

DAY CARE/HEAD START: MILITARY

TRAINING PROGRAMS

ARMY CHILD CARE TECHNICAL ASSISTANCE CONFERENCE
SEE RECIPIENTS: MILITARY - ACTIVE/VETERANS

DISASTER RESPONSE/EMERGENCY PREPAREDNESS

NATIONAL/STATE ORGANIZATIONS

AMERICAN RED CROSS
National Headquarters
17th between D and E Streets
Washington, DC 20006
TEL: 202-737-8300
Objectives: The mission of the American Red Cross is to improve the quality of human life, to enhance self-reliance and concern for others, and to help people avoid, prepare for, and cope with emergencies. It does this through services that are governed and directed by volunteers and are consistent with its congressional charter and the principles of the *International Red Cross.*
Services: The personal commitment of 1.2 million volunteers in partnership with salaried staff (ratio 50 volunteers to one salaried staff member) enables the *American Red Cross* to complete its mission through the following services:
Nursing and Health Services: helps people to deal with illness and injury, high medical expenses, preparation for parenthood, and other concerns; promotes preventive health measures; conducts health education courses (ranging from prenatal care to assisting the elderly); offers health services to victims of disasters; participates in health fairs, immunization clinics, and hypertension and other screening follow-up programs; emphasizes self-reliance in health matters through its courses and materials.
Safety Services: addresses life-threatening situations through both preventive and life-saving courses including CPR Training and First Aid, Water Safety, and Boating Safety, and operates summer aquatic, small craft, and first aid schools, all of which provide certification on completion.
Blood Services: collects, processes, and distributes blood and blood products; aids hospitals in identifying red-cell antibodies in donor and patient samples and in solving cross-matching problems; maintains a rare donor registry containing information on nearly 9,000 on-call donors; conducts research and development projects, sometimes in collaboration with other organizations.
Disaster Services: responds to emergencies brought about by disaster by providing shelter, first aid, food, clothing, rent, household needs, small home repairs, health needs, and replacement of occupational supplies/equipment; refers disaster victims to resources in government and the private sector, but provides additional recovery aid if these resources are not available or are inadequate; maintains a short wave emergency radio frequency (designed for the Red Cross) with over 582 chapters participating; utilizes the resources of the American Radio Relay League, REACT, and other voluntary groups when normal communications are disrupted or need to be augmented.
Service to the Armed Forces and Veterans: assists servicemen and servicewomen, and veterans of military service, in emergencies and times of family crisis; includes services such as counseling individuals with personal and family problems, maintaining communications between the individual and his or her family on a worldwide basis, assisting families remaining at home in obtaining state and other local benefits or services from other sources, serving on bases throughout Europe and the Far East as well as in the U.S., representing Veterans Administration and the Department of Defense to help with applications for VA Benefits, and to meet the needs of patients in the VA medical facilities across the country.
Youth Services: converts the energy, concern, and creativity of today's youth into service and leadership in the community by involving them in delivery of Red Cross services; maintains youth seats on chapter boards, service committees, and Youth Councils; supports Red Cross Clubs and activities in the schools; provides leadership development training; appoints youth to national advisory committees which advise the chief policy-making body, the Board of Governors of the Red Cross, and management.
International Services: meets needs of U.S. citizens and foreign nationals in matters that involve parts of the world other than the U.S.; works through the International Committee of the Red Cross, the League of Red Cross Societies, and other national societies; assists in seeking reunions between family members separated by war or other events, and locating individuals with whom contact has been lost due to changing world conditions; collaborates with international Red Cross bodies in meeting emergency needs of refugees or disaster victims; operates language banks, home hospitality, and other services to assist new Americans in the community.
Concludes with *You, Too, Can Volunteer* describing the procedure, benefits, and project examples for potential volunteers; includes section entitled "How It's Financed" to inform the public of ways the Red Cross obtains financial (local fund-raising, special gifts, United Way, etc.), human (volunteers), and other resources (no federal appropriations).
Publications: Red Cross News
Founded: 1881

BUILDING SEISMIC SAFETY COUNCIL
1201 L Street, NW
Fourth Floor
Washington, DC 20005
TEL: 202-289-7800
Objectives: To focus public attention on earthquake hazards.
Services: Operates under the aegis of a volunteer Board of
Directors to propose seismic safety standards and urge their use in
local and national building codes; mounts campaigns to make the
public aware of the hazards and unpredictability of earthquakes -
especially in the east where apathy persists; works with the *Federal
Emergency Management Agency (FEMA),* which has provided
funding to the Council since 1981; includes in its membership - all
volunteers - geologists, engineers and others versed on the subject
of earthquakes; emphasizes the need for the public to give more
serious attention to this hazard, even in low-risk areas such as
Washington, DC; addresses opposition from the real estate and
construction industries, whose concerns center on the added costs
of making buildings earthquake resistant (estimated at adding five
to six percent in costs); cites studies that indicate that added cost
is much less than first anticipated (one to two percent); encourages
new code provisions such as those proposed in 1986 in New York
City, from which a bill was developed for submission to New
York's City Council in late 1990; develops earthquake regulations
for insertion into model codes developed by local governments;
publishes data on the highest risk sections of each area of the
country, and other reports and materials.
Sponsor: US/FEMA - Federal Emergency Management Agency
Contact: James Smith, Executive Director
Founded: 1980

NATIONAL CATHOLIC DISASTER RELIEF COMMITTEE
1319 F Street, NW
Fourth Floor
Washington, DC 20004
TEL: 202-639-8400
Objectives: To marshal Catholic church resources in times of
disaster.
Services: Works to give greater visibility and recognition to the
work of the Catholic church in times of major natural disasters;
represents Catholic organizations that may be able to render
assistance in such times; maintains a membership of approximately
twenty people on the Committee; develops a network to make
expedient contact with local church officials to learn of the extent
of damage caused by a natural disaster, and the resulting
immediate and urgent needs; coordinates Catholic church
resources, and provides consultation for those working in the
rehabilitation of disaster-affected areas; operates under the aegis of
Catholic Charities USA (see separate entry) and through
appointment by the *National Conference of Catholic Bishops.*

NATIONAL INJURY INFORMATION CENTER
SEE HEALTH: EMERGENCIES

**NATIONAL VOLUNTARY ORGANIZATIONS ACTIVE IN
DISASTER**
c/o American Red Cross
431 Eighteenth Street, NW
Washington, DC 20006
TEL: 202-639-3397
Objectives: To meet the needs of people affected by disaster.
Services: Coordinates national and local voluntary organizations
active in disaster service to ensure more effective service to people
beset by disaster; provides training programs to increase awareness
and preparedness; coordinates seminars, meetings, regional and
local conferences, and training programs; supports appropriate
legislation; publishes a quarterly newsletter, a national directory,
studies, and other materials.
Publications: NVOAD Newsletter; NVOAD National Directory;
Gaps in Disaster Services

PROGRAM EXCHANGE PROCESS (PEP)
SEE HEALTH: I&R

TRAINING PROGRAMS

WHEELCHAIR RACE COMMUNICATIONS SERVICES
Amateur Radio Emergency Service (ARES)
American Radio Relay League
225 Main Street
Newington, CT 06111
TEL: 203-666-1541
Purpose: To provide radio communications for the "Wheelchair
Race of Champions."
Sponsor: Ford Motor Company; Hardee's Restaurants; American
Radio Relay League (groups from Winchester, Frederick County,
Loudoun County, Fairfax County, and Arlington in Virginia, and
District of Columbia)
Contact: David Sumner, Executive Vice President
Description: Ham radio operators are best known for their
response and assistance in disasters. They are not CBers. Ham
Radio exists primarily for service to the public through emergency
service. Licensed by the FCC, they are called in by local, state and
federal governments to help in communications emergencies. This
makes them a national resource in times of need.
In the annual wheelchair races, HAM operators find that their
communications skills are sharpened by using such events for
practice and exercise. Skills needed to communicate during special
events are similar to those required during an actual emergency.
They communicate using radio frequencies normally useful only
for short distances by talking through "repeaters" or automatic
relay stations, set up, operated, and maintained by the HAMs.
These repeater stations must also be licensed by the FCC.
Amateur Radio Emergency Service (ARES) groups from
Winchester, Frederick County, Loudoun County, Fairfax County,
and Arlington in Virginia, and the District of Columbia provided
communications for this first annual 54-mile Race of Champions.

INDIVIDUAL PROGRAM PROFILES

AIR CRASH DRILL
Greater Rochester International Airport
1200 Brooks Ave
Rochester, NY 14619
TEL: 716-464-6000
Purpose: To test the County's system of emergency management.
Sponsor: Monroe County Government
Contact: John G. Huntoon, Chief, Fire-Rescue Service
Description: The *Greater Rochester International Airport* is
required every three years to host an air crash drill in order to
keep its Federal Aviation Administration certification. Since the
new ruling was not imposed until 1989, the Airport had not had a
drill since 1983. Drills are designed to test the county's incident
command system, a widely-used concept of emergency
management in which police, fire, medical and airport authorities
cooperate.
In a mid-1989 drill, more than 600 rescuers battled fake smoke to
rescue 125 volunteers posing as passengers and crew aboard the
727 jet (a C-130 on loan from the National Guard). The crew
faced a problem in which the plane had lost its landing gear and
slid off the runway, bursting into flames in a freight building. The
scenario included a little bit of everything - radioactive waste and
injured firefighters. Twenty-five percent of the passengers and crew
were to die, 50 percent were to be critically injured, and the
remainder were to suffer lesser injuries.
Reflecting the long period since the last drill, many problems arose
that helped rescue teams realize the value of the drills. Equipment

and supplies needed to transport and treat patients arrived after the drill was completed; the entire process halted when a firefighter suffered a real case of heat exhaustion; some of the "injured" waited almost two hours to be transported to hospitals; one area's ambulance driver was unable to contact the medical command post as he approached the airport; oxygen supplies ran out; some people were confused about their roles, etc. As one volunteer put it, "That's what drills are for. You're always going to have pitfalls." He felt that the drill was positive in many respects, including the fact that it strongly indicated that teams should work together on a redesign of equipment kits so that they are coordinated and therefore easier to use among departments when necessary.

The chief of the airport's crash fire-rescue service felt that it worked out pretty well, since one of the objectives was to give rescuers from all over Monroe County a shot at working together. "It used to be they'd sit in their corners and swear at each other. Now they work together," he said.

ALPINE RESCUE TEAM
PO Box 934
Evergreen, CO 80439
TEL: 303-674-5855
Purpose: To respond to emergencies in mountainous and wilderness areas.
Contact: Program Coordinator
Description: The *Alpine Rescue Team* is an organized group of volunteers who are willing to leave their families and holiday picnics on a moment's notice to respond to emergencies in the mountainous and wilderness areas of Colorado. Response is immediate and from their present base they can be at the point of the emergency within 20 minutes. In mountain emergencies, the Team establishes a base camp and organizes small groups to ascend the mountain. Twenty to 30 volunteers assist the ground teams in locating the injured person, and the airlift crew in getting the individual off of the mountain - usually under less-than-ideal flight conditions.

The *Alpine Rescue Team* is the largest rescue team in the state, and the only team that gets no government funding. It performs its services completely free of charge, depending on corporate and individual donations for its continued existence.

Currently, Alpine is trying to build a new headquarters in a location that would greatly decrease its response time to emergencies. Again, the Team looks to individual and corporate donations. If public and community response in the past is any indication, the new headquarters should be a reality in record time, according to a Team volunteer.

ASSISTANCE TO EARTHQUAKE VICTIMS
US/DoD - Department of the Navy
Assistant Secretary of Defense
The Pentagon
Washington, DC 28350
TEL: 202-545-6700
Purpose: To respond to a call for immediate assistance to earthquake victims.
Sponsor: US/DoD - Department of the Navy
Contact: LCDR Dave Kennedy
Description: Seventy-three Navy Department social workers who had done work with people who have gone through the trauma of disaster found themselves in a unique "training" situation in Northern California in October 1989. The social workers were attending military conferences in conjunction with the four-day annual meeting of the *National Association of Social Workers,* with six days of training behind them, when the earthquake hit the San Francisco area.

An earlier meeting of professionals from all of the military services had ended and, following a brief Navy meeting, they were to depart in many directions for their home areas. During the Navy

meeting, the Bay Area experienced what was later described as the strongest earthquake to hit the area since 1906.

The call for volunteers - especially those experienced in working with disaster victims - was apparent, if not expressed, and the 73 volunteers were quickly briefed by a disaster expert, who is a senior social worker in the Office of the Assistant Secretary of Defense, Family Policy and Support. After the briefing, the expert organized the group to effectively help earthquake victims who were streaming into the hotel from homes in the area that had been damaged or declared unsafe. Besides the logistical needs of setting up sleeping arrangements in areas of the hotel with the least glass, the social workers provided counseling and other assistance to help the victims through the traumatic experience. Usually being in the position of "supervising" volunteers, the social workers enjoyed the experience of "being" volunteers who met an urgent need. From one Navy participant, "Talk about 'hands-on' experience... this was a bit scary, but our presence was needed, and we are glad we were there to help."

DISASTER PROFESSIONAL VOLUNTEER NETWORK
American Red Cross
Mid-America Chapter
43 East Ohio
Chicago, IL 60611
TEL: 312-440-2000
Purpose: To provide a mental health response for victims of a major disaster.
Sponsor: American Red Cross, Mid-America Chapter
Contact: Director, Disaster and Family Services
Description: The American Red Cross in its effort to provide a comprehensive service to victims of major disasters is developing a cadre of professionally trained staff from other agencies who will assist Red Cross in addressing the mental health needs of victims. These volunteers will be trained to utilize their knowledge and skill in special ways to address the reactions to disaster, loss and trauma. Crisis intervention will be the method of treatment. High risk groups will be identified as soon as possible and both an individual and group approach implemented as the need indicates. A volunteer advisory committee has been formed which has the responsibility of both short and long-range planning for this undertaking. They will be addressing their attention to areas such as public education, levels of intervention, roles of government, assessment of the network planning and implementation, and access to disaster victims. The Chairman of the committee will be a member of the Board of Directors of the Mid-America Chapter of the American Red Cross and a member of the Service to Military Families and Veterans Committee. For the present, our efforts are being directed to the city of Chicago but future plans will be developed to include the six county area served by Mid-America Chapter.

In addition, a committee of representatives from participating agencies will continue to meet to design and develop intervention modes, assess training, critique operations, address the problem of maintaining a state of readiness and determine further needs. These meetings will be held on a quarterly basis.

Agencies will be asked to make a commitment to participate in this joint venture should a major catastrophe affect a large portion of the people of the community which we all serve.

There are two levels of participation that will be needed. Conceivably, some agencies may not be able to participate on both levels. However, it is critical to the success of the plan that there be sufficient participation at the first level, i.e. on site and/or shelter intervention. The second level would involve providing service in the victims' home site.

Recruitment and/or selection of professionally trained staff who will become members of the cadre is internal and unique to the individual agency. Some features to be considered in personnel selection are:

• They must be interested in volunteer activity within their own profession.

- They must be able to tolerate uncertainty and lack of structure in a work situation.
- They must have the ability to work cooperatively with staff from other agencies on a team with its designated leader.
- The ability to accept direction.
- The ability to prioritize in a chaotic situation.
- The ability to work cooperatively with other disciplines such as emergency medical, fire and police personnel.
- The ability for self-management under stress.

There are a few specific knowledge and skill considerations that are relevant in this process of personnel selection:

- A good working knowledge and skill in crisis intervention theory and technique.
- The ability to make a diagnosis quickly in order to facilitate treatment consideration (situational vs. chronic).
- A good working knowledge of community resources.
- A demonstrated ability to apply knowledge creatively.
- The ability to identify and mobilize strengths within the affected population for achieving stabilization goals.
- The ability to work with all socioeconomic, racial, ethnic, and religious groups.

The American Red Cross will assume responsibility for the specialized training (nine hours) required to heighten the awareness of the cadre members and to orient them to the Red Cross Disaster Service.

Trained cadre members may elect to serve in a variety of ways, i.e., individuals or groups, at disaster site or post-disaster shelter. The following operational plan would become effective when needed and in conjunction and cooperation with the overall plan of the city of Chicago and the American Red Cross Disaster Service. It would function in the following manner:

- Information regarding a disaster would come through the usual radio and telephone communications system of Red Cross which operates on a 24 hour basis.
- Such information will provide an ongoing reading of the nature and extent of the tragedy relative to casualties, injuries, numbers of people undomiciled, involvement of Fire and Police Departments, and the services being provided by the disaster emergency program.

EMERGENCY SERVICES PROGRAM
American Red Cross
Chapter House
9 East Fifth Street
Stuart, FL 34994
TEL: 407-461-3950 (Martin); 407-562-2549 (Indian Rvr)
Purpose: To maintain evacuation shelters and volunteers to staff them in preparation for natural disasters.
Contact: Mary Sawyer (Martin/St. Lucie); Doug Wright (Indian River County)
Description: Long before the season's first hurricane is even a suggestion, county officials from emergency services divisions along what is known as the *Treasure Coast* of Florida are working with the American Red Cross to try to assure that accommodations for all evacuees needing them will be available in a natural disaster. An analysis in mid-June 1989 provided the following statistics, however:

- St. Lucie County has 10 volunteers and needs 300;
- Indian River County has 75 of the minimum 150 needed;
- Martin County has 150 volunteers and 75 vacancies;
- St. Lucie County has 20 shelters with 25,000 spaces to house a projected 40,000 evacuees;
- Indian River County has had to cut its shelters in half - from 20 in 1988 to 10 in 1989; Vero Beach's primary shelters, schools, have accommodations for about 15,000, about 10% less than the previous year.

Ideally, according to the Red Cross, a shelter should have 20 volunteer staff workers and a shelter manager and assistant

manager. Shelter staff members register evacuees, prepare meals, provide baby-sitting and day-care services, as well as entertainment and, when needed, basic first aid. Nurses are always needed, but are hard to find because most are employed.

Evacuees are encouraged to stay with relatives or friends in safe areas whenever possible to reduce the numbers in the shelters. Those who must come to the shelter are asked to become shelter staff or managers, since they must be there anyway. This method has always brought the needed additional volunteers, according to Red Cross officials, but they have not gone through the three hours of training and must be briefed quickly by trained volunteers and Red Cross personnel - not the ideal situation.

Disaster Training is offered frequently in a number of locations. Each session is three hours long. Recruiting is a continuous process along the *Treasure Coast*.

EVERYDAY HEROES
Disaster Service Volunteers
American Red Cross
23rd and Chestnut Streets
Philadelphia, PA 19103
TEL: 215-229-4000
Purpose: To provide shelter, food, clothing, psychosocial support and other assistance to victims of fires and natural disasters.
Sponsor: American Red Cross
Contact: Volunteer Director
Description: Southeastern Pennsylvania has ten branch offices of the *American Red Cross Disaster Service*. Hundreds of disaster volunteers work out of these offices to provide shelter, food, clothing, and other services to thousands of victims of fires and natural disasters. Among recent disasters covered by the branch offices were:

- December 1988 - apartment house fire displacing 50 families.
- January 1988 - apartment house fire leaving 21 families homeless, all Cambodian and none who spoke English.
- February 1988 - hotel fire displacing 31 families.

A 1985 tornado called on other skills of the volunteers since children, especially, were traumatized by the loss of their homes and possessions in such a violent way. In each instance, the Red Cross dispenses immediate direct assistance, providing meals and beds, and issuing vouchers for clothing, packets containing essentials for infants, bus fare, and filling other physical and emotional needs. Disaster volunteers are trained in areas including:

- CPR
- First Aid/Health Services
- Emergency Services
- AIDS Prevention
- Blood Services

Specific geographic areas often require a specific skill, with training available at the unique sites. Volunteers in the Southeastern Pennsylvania branches range in age from the teens (most of whom are trained at their high schools) and retirees in their seventies, often having lived through disasters themselves. Often, volunteers are nurses and counselors, who not only help at disaster sites, but assist with training of volunteers. The American Red Cross Disaster Services are international, with 2,900 chapters worldwide.

GRAND ISLE EROSION FIGHT
c/o Wateredge Apartments
PO Box 111
Grand Isle, LA 70358
TEL: 504-787-2329
Purpose: To provide a temporary wall of sandbags while waiting for government decisions on disaster relief.
Contact: Henrietta Collins
Description: Residents of Grand Isle have learned to move quickly when the area is threatened by a hurricane. In mid-1989 their efforts saved the state millions of dollars by containing the damage

of a severe storm. Grand Isle is a barrier island resort community with a serious erosion problem. For six weeks in the spring of 1989 high tides and southerly winds increased erosion problems still evident from the previous year. When this happens, residents do not wait for official assistance, but address the problem immediately to minimize damage. When government assistance was not immediately forthcoming, volunteers, including the town's mayor, worked night and day in heavy rains building a sandbag wall in an attempt to stop further damage, especially to the area under a beach motel. As they worked, they watched a wooden staircase tear away from the rear of the building. About 30 men, women and children filled more than 2,500 bags with sand to buffer the crumbling shore. The volunteers included crews sent by a local cable television station and a telephone company, owners of two other island motels, friends, relatives, a town alderman and the mayor.

When repeated requests for federal, state or parish help failed, the volunteers worked harder and faster to minimize the effect of the storm. A state representative spoke to the Governor's office requesting a temporary measure until state and federal government can repair the island's sand levee and rebuild the beach. The levee was built and the beach expanded in 1984 as part of a joint project of the state and the U.S. Army Corps of Engineers. Hurricanes have destroyed about half of the levee, and repairs and improvements are estimated to cost $12 million. The state's share of the cost, $5 million, has been approved by the House Ways and Means Committee, but must go to a Senate committee next, and then on to the House and Senate. An additional request by the Mayor of Grand Isle to the state asks for the building of two rock jetties, a rock retaining wall and underwater breakwaters to help stop erosion. Otherwise, according to the mayor, the millions of dollars planned for the levee and beach could result in only temporary solutions.

While awaiting their response, the volunteer team continued their efforts to save the motel. Although the motel, which once sat on the beach, now has a space beneath it over six feet high, the building was saved by the volunteer team. Residents of Grand Isle have learned from experience that a little effort can go a long way.

HAZARDOUS WASTE VOLUNTEER PROGRAM
Maricopa County Environmental Services
Department of Health
1825 East Roosevelt Street
Phoenix, AZ 85006
TEL: 602-258-6381
Purpose: To identify illegal hazardous waste dumps in the desert.
Contact: Tom Freestone, County Supervisor
Description: In mid-summer 1989, a special task force was created when 50 volunteers offered to help Maricopa County identify illegal dumps in the desert. The volunteers joined state and county environmental and health workers to form the group.
All task force members are required to attend special training in identification of hazardous wastes that can seep down into the water tables, where it can pollute water supplies.
Volunteers and other task force members also learn that besides polluting water supplies, illegal dumping creates other hazards to the public, as shown by the closure of a grade school in Tucson in 1989 because of health problems among students, after reports that the school was built on land where hazardous wastes had been illegally dumped years before.
The county decided to form the task force to locate illegal dumps in the desert following discussions between county and state agencies and representatives from Arizona industries about waste oils from California being burned by asphalt companies in Arizona as a cheaper alternative to natural gas. Publicity from the talks brought forth the volunteers, who will be thoroughly trained in the identification of the hazardous wastes, but will not be involved in removal or other aspects of the project.
Founded: 1989

HELPING HAND
SEE EMPLOYMENT

HIGH-RISE FIRE RESPONSE TRAINING
Steelcase, Inc.
E. Paris Ave. & 60th St., SE
PO Box 1967
Grand Rapids, MI 49501
TEL: 616-247-2710
FAX: 616-246-4890
Purpose: To assist the local fire department in disaster response methods.
Sponsor: Steelcase, Inc.
Contact: Frank Merlotti, President, or Dale Gipe, Dutton Fire Chief
Description: The 20-member volunteer fire department of Dutton, Michigan, has participated in fire inspections every week for more than two years during construction of Steelcase Inc.'s new Corporate Development Center. Described by the fire chief as "very fire-conscious," the corporation requested this intense inspection activity in preparation for a comprehensive training program that the company has developed for responding to high-rise fires.
The 20 volunteers from the Dutton Fire Department will be instructed in the course at Steelcase by officials there. Since the weekly inspections have familiarized them with the internal structure of the building, training time is used to go beyond any primary explanations of building materials, etc. Dutton works in a "mutual aid" fire response situation with other fire departments such as nearby Kentwood and Gaines Township. All departments expect to benefit from the Steelcase training program either directly or indirectly, in some cases with one fire department being trained and, in turn, training others.
Steelcase is the first corporation in the area to make such an effort to prepare fire personnel should a high-rise fire occur. This will benefit the community at large, since there are many high rises in the area, none of which have taken any responsibility in emergency preparedness.

NORTH SHORE CIVIL DEFENSE TEAM
State of Hawaii
3949 Diamond Head Road
Honolulu, HI 96816
TEL: 808-734-2161
Purpose: To prepare for emergencies and respond to disasters.
Sponsor: State of Hawaii
Contact: Linda Fulp, District Two Coordinator
Description: The 45 volunteers who are responsible for responding to natural disasters on the North Shore of Hawaii use their own vehicles and gas, and respond to an island-wide siren warning system. An initial training program enables volunteers to use the equipment provided, and hard hats and badges are assigned.
Fearing that the fact that Hawaii has not experienced a natural disaster in a number of years has created apathy, in mid-1989 the volunteers approached a newly-created, five member *Citizens Advisory Commission* with some concerns they have had for some time about the inadequacy of both equipment and training. The primary concern of North Shore residents is high-wave conditions which can cause extensive damage and loss of life if warnings are not timely.
Citizens from the community joined the volunteers to ask for modernized equipment and a better means of warning people in areas of high risk, since the island-wide siren system cannot be used for this purpose. Currently, residents in high risk areas are warned about high-wave conditions either by police using bullhorns, or a telephone network which is not effective if people are not at home.
Suggestions from both the volunteers and citizens from the community who attended the meeting to support the volunteers

included a stronger public civil defense education program, and a manually-operated secondary siren warning system in areas of high risk on the North Shore. Another concern of all attendees was the lack of emergency drills for students at schools located near beaches. One resident asked for more consistent forecasting - using an existing buoy 250 miles out and an added buoy - to give residents ample time before the warnings to prepare. In the past, residents have had as little as two hours after the warning to evacuate. Both volunteers and residents made the point that, in many areas around the world, it takes a disaster to "loosen the purse strings."

The volunteers were encouraged after the meeting. Besides the benefit of an outlet for their frustrations and an opportunity to connect quickly with a Commission set up to respond, the volunteers were pleased with the backup and support that came from the community. According to one of the volunteers, "We may wind up with the best civil defense program in the country yet!"

PARAMUS HEAVY RESCUE SQUAD

Jockish Square
Paramus, NJ 07510
TEL: 201-265-2100
Purpose: To respond to many types of community emergencies and disasters.
Sponsor: Paramus Fire Department
Contact: William Jerry Schwartz, Chief
Description: The 30-member, all-volunteer *Paramus Heavy Rescue Squad* answers almost 1,000 calls a year. This is an average of about three calls a day, involving car and bus accidents, building collapses and fires, as well as freak accidents of various types. Squad members must care for victims while dealing with the often unexpected and bizarre direction of the accident or disaster. Exploding cars during accidents and collapsing floors during building fires are two examples.

All volunteers have jobs and must answer the call of the siren any time of the day or night. Some are self-employed and lose some business. Others must work with their employers to be sure they are covered when they are called to emergencies or disasters. "Never knowing how your day will end" is one of the fascinations of the job, according to the volunteer chief. Accidents range from a child with his hand stuck in a gum ball machine to eight-car collisions. Intensive training courses are an attempt to cover every emergency, but the rescue worker often encounters one not covered in the books, and must use his best judgment to help a victim.

PORTLAND MOUNTAIN RESCUE

Multnomah County Sheriff's Office
12240 NE Glisson
Portland, OR 97230
TEL: 503-255-3600
Purpose: To rescue mountain climbers and others in emergency situations on Portland area mountains.
Sponsor: US/DoI - Forest Service
Contact: Tom Stringfield, Chief
Description: Portland Mountain Rescue has 40 active volunteers who assist in search and rescue operations. Responsibility is divided between the U.S. Forest Service (weekend patrols) and the sheriff's department (management of rescue efforts). All members must know about climbing before they can belong to the group. Also, to take part in rescues, they must be proficient in climbing and rescue skills. In addition, they must update their training every year.

The volunteers come from all walks of life - from blue collar workers to ministers to utility tower climbers - and range in age from a 19-year-old Reed College student to people in their fifties. Also, the club tries to enlist as many trained medical workers as possible.

Hand-in-hand with the rescue operations is a new program aimed at reducing the number of those needing rescue, launched in April 1989 in cooperation with *Mount Hood National Forest.* Under the program, every weekend four or five club volunteers accompany a *U.S. Forest Service* climbing ranger on a patrol of the slopes of Mount Hood to warn climbers of dangers and check on their safety.

Mount Hood is one of the most climbed mountains in the world, and may have as many as 300 climbers on its slopes on good climbing days. Much of the problem is with climbers who do not sign in at the Forest Service's registry after completing their climb. This results in the volunteers having to check the parking lot for cars or call relatives to make sure the climbers have returned home. Also, fewer people are renting radios that would allow rescuers to locate them if they got lost or didn't return on time. Renters have dropped from 15 percent in 1988 to the current five percent. Also, people who sign out before their climb often do not understand why it is important to list types and colors of clothes they are wearing, equipment they will be using, and other details that would help rescuers in an search and rescue operation. Although volunteers try to discourage people who come to the mountain without proper clothing, especially where children are involved, they are not authorized to stop them from climbing. Knowing what climbers *are* wearing, however, gives vital information on how well they will survive if lost or injured on the mountain. As one volunteer candidly put it, "It can mean the difference between hunting for a body or a live person."

Much effort is put into advice on minimum safety recommendations for clothing, footwear, equipment and supplies, with detailed information readily available. But, according to rescuers, the information is rarely picked up or requested. Until such recommendations become law, the sight of volunteer rescuers heading for the mountain will continue to be a familiar part of the landscape, according to the head of the group.

RED CROSS DISASTER AID

American Red Cross
1523 St. Charles Avenue
New Orleans, LA 70130
TEL: 504-587-1501
Purpose: To respond to natural and other disasters in the New Orleans area.
Contact: Volunteer Coordinator
Description: When a natural or man-made disaster strikes in the New Orleans area, a Red Cross disaster team is immediately dispatched to alleviate suffering and anguish caused by the resulting destruction. Large-scale disasters require lots of emergency relief, so the organization relies heavily on volunteers. Red Cross volunteers are trained to manage shelters, provide mass feedings, and to perform damage assessment to determine the level of loss to individuals. Volunteers also respond to house fires to assess victims' needs. The information obtained through the disaster-assessment team's work is used to issue cleanup kits, disburse orders for items such as clothing, food, necessary household furnishings such as beds and linens, and occupational supplies that were lost in the disaster. Red Cross assistance is provided at no charge to individuals.

Hurricane season in New Orleans begins in June of each year, a time when staff updates its list of trained volunteers ready to respond quickly should disaster strike. Information about volunteer duties are provided on request to help potential volunteers decide whether or not they would like to join the program. Since many residents feel they probably would be in a shelter anyway if disaster struck, the response is always excellent.

SCHOOL FIRE SAFETY MONITORING PROGRAM
Parents United
c/o Rice-Thurston
2135 Newport Place
Washington, DC 20037
TEL: 202-293-7009
Purpose: To monitor schools citywide for compliance with
Washington, DC's fire laws.
Sponsor: District of Columbia City Council
Contact: Delabian L. Rice-Thurston, Executive Director
Description: Parents United, a citywide group of parents in
Washington, DC, exists to assure adequate education and safety
for their children in the public schools. In the Spring of 1990,
Parents United commissioned a study to determine the safety of
the City's schools in the area of fire prevention and response.
Through the study the parents' group learned that there were
more than 4,000 fire code violations in District of Columbia public
schools - including missing or deficient fire doors, falling plaster,
leaky roofs, and no heat.
The group's Executive Director contacted both the Mayor and the
school system to discuss the immediate development of an effective
repair schedule, now lacking in the system, and the financing of
needed repairs - in the face of diminishing funds. Information
provided by the school system indicated that $10 million requested
for fiscal 1991 by school officials for building repair was wiped out
when the budget was cut from $100 million to $43 million.
When research by the group showed no inspections for the past
year, the parents contacted the *District of Columbia Department
of Consumer and Regulatory Affairs (DCRA)* and the fire
department's building inspections division. They determined that
inspections by DCRA were done on elevators, cafeterias and
boilers only, "so the roof could be falling in and that would not
routinely be inspected," according to a spokesperson for the
parents' group.
In researching fire codes, the group found that adequate
precautions were taken against intruders, since they are expected,
but no one believes that fires are a serious threat. Although they
learned that the schools asked for a moratorium on fire regulation
enforcement, Fire Department officials said no exceptions to the
law are made.
The study has been presented to all officials and departments
concerned, with the parents' group prepared to file suit if
appropriate action is not taken to protect the city's school children
against fire. With promised cooperation and roundtable
discussions, *Parents United* expects to work with authorities to
help bring about full compliance to fire codes of the District.

SEWARD RESCUE CENTER
Exxon
Oil Spill Volunteer Response Center
Anchorage, AK 77002
TEL: 907-276-3688 (volunteers); 212-333-1000 (NY)
FAX: 212-333-1348 (NY)
Purpose: To wash and treat otters coated with oil after the Exxon
Valdez oil spill.
Sponsor: Exxon Corporation
Contact: Jim Styers, Marine Mammalogist
Description: One hundred volunteers from across the country (one
from Germany) wash, dry and help treat oil-coated otters in an
Exxon-financed rescue center in Seward, a southern Alaska coastal
town. The disaster occured in March 1989 when the Exxon
Valdez, a super tanker, ran around and dumped 11.2 million
gallons of oil in Prince William Sound, about 125 miles northeast
of Seward, spilling into the environment crude oil that was carried
300 miles to the southwest by wind and current. By June 1989,
over 800 otters and nearly 23,000 waterfowl had died as a result of
the spill.
When rescue centers in Valdez and Homer proved inadequate, the
center in Seward was opened in May 1989. Biologists,

veterinarians and volunteers work to refine and improve
techniques used in the early days of the spill.
Caught in tangle nets off the Kenai Peninsula, otters are flown to
the Seward center in groups of six to 10 a day. Once inside the
center's network of mobile homes, cages and tanks, they are
treated like patients in any hospital. Their progress is charted,
some are sent to intensive care, and pregnant females go to a
maternity ward. For the first 24 hours after their arrival in
Seward, otters are put in cages (they prefer their cages outside),
fed and calmed by giving them ice to chew on. When they are
ready, they are tranquilized and carried to elaborate washing
tables, where one worker holds the head of the 40- to 100-pound
animal and two more wash the oil from its fur. The job takes three
people about 45 minutes. Drying the otter with dryers takes
another 45 minutes. With an hour and a half per otter for the
cleaning process, all volunteers are utilized to the fullest extent.
Hypothermia is a major cause of death since otters have no layer
of fat and need their thick coats to keep warm, so the teams must
work quickly to remove the oil. Also, learned the hard way,
veterinarians discovered the proper doses of tranquilizers to keep
otters from biting their rescuers. Also, by trial and error, they
learned that ordinary dishwashing liquid, highly diluted, is best for
washing the oil from their fur.
As they recover, otters are placed in big tanks, where they can
frolic and eat shrimp, mussels and clams, and need only minimal
supervision. As of late May 1989, volunteers and staff saw one pup
born. Of the 80 otters at the center up to that time, nine had died.
Recovered otters are transferred from Seward to holding pens in a
remote inlet called Little Jokolof Bay. Volunteers there feed them
and monitor their progress until they are finally released. Camps
for volunteers at Little Jokolof are in a remote but spectacular
area of Alaska, and campers endure a lot of rain, but temperatures
average 40-60 degrees.
In Seward, the dedicated volunteers are faced with scarce
accommodations, also. However, many live in a campground near
town, tolerating drunks and transients, and getting a shower
whenever they can at other workers' accommodations. Others
sleep on floors of shared hotel rooms; some live in their cars. At
least one has given up a job and is living on savings to help bring
the history-making disaster to the best conclusion possible.
Another program identified by the *Oil Spill Volunteer Response
Center* involves volunteers who can identify birds to assess damage
to local bird populations. Millions of birds, including eagles, live or
spend their summers in the affected area. By June 1989, the
dead-bird body count had passed 22,000. Volunteers count birds to
compare their numbers with those before the spill, and track
recovery rates in the future. Because of the controversy
surrounding the oil cleanup efforts, per se, volunteers are not used
in those operations.
Founded: 1989

SIX FRIENDS MEMORIAL FUND
First American Bank
Westover Branch
1701 McKinney Road
Arlington, VA 22205
TEL: 703-284-6550
Purpose: To acknowledge the work of volunteer rescue teams, and
to assist in their efforts.
Sponsor: First American Bank
Contact: Rosemary May, Branch Manager
Description: This memorial fund was established in May 1990 by
the families and friends of six young men who died in a plane
crash on the way home from a fishing trip earlier in the month.
During the weeklong vigil until the plane was found, families and
friends waiting at a command center set up at *Manassas Municipal
Airport,* a local airport in northern Virginia, became aware of the
seemingly tireless efforts of volunteer search and rescue teams, the
dedication to their jobs and their concern and compassion for

survivors. Rescue teams were directed by the *Civil Air Patrol, Virginia Emergency Services,* and the *Appalachian Search and Rescue Conference.* Volunteers from both the community, including a family member of one of the crash victims, and nearby *Fort Belvoir* and other military bases joined the teams. It was the family member who first spotted part of the plane wreckage. The *Virginia State Police* were on hand as well, including the State Police Chaplain, throughout the ordeal.

The fund is designated to support search and rescue teams, but is also intended as a tribute to their all-out efforts that are often taken for granted.

SUMMERFEST ART FAIRE
SEE RECIPIENTS: OLDER PERSON - HEALTH

TRIS (TRAILS INFORMATION SYSTEM)
Mount Hood National Forest
US/DoA - Mount Hood National Forest
Gresham, OR 97080
TEL: 503-666-0700
Information also available from co-sponsor:
Portland Park Bureau
Portland, OR
Purpose: To provide detailed, computerized trail information to make camping, climbing, and other activities safer.
Sponsor: Mount Hood National Forest
Contact: Tim Swedberg, Specialist
Description: TRIS (Trails Information Systems) is a free service to the public on the Columbia-Cascade trails network. The system provides the public access via a personal computer to a data base of trail information, including the name and number of a trail, the difficulty rating, elevation, intended use, restrictions, the managing agency, access points and a trail description. It is designed to enhance the efforts of volunteers, who try their best to head off disaster in advising families about the hazards sometimes encountered on the trails.

Designed to provide information without the need for formal instruction on computer operation, a sequential system of commands helps a user decide on an appropriate trail from among the dozens that are available. Current information can be plugged into the network, such as the snow level, trail obstacles and safety hazards that crop up after the initial reports have been entered into the computer. Currently limited to the Mount Hood National Forest and Portland parks, the Columbia-Cascade network is expected to grow to include the Gifford Pinchot, Willamette, Deschutes and Ochoco national forests, as well as other federal, state and county trail systems in Oregon. Other networks exist around the country. The TRIS network itself is expected to unite these networks and spread across the United States, eventually providing a national data base for the country's trails. It can also be expanded to cover other recreation, such as camping and fishing.

The system has been deliberately designed so that it does not resemble a game. "We want people to get their information and move on," according to one volunteer. Volunteer assistance is always close by to make sure that the user understands the instructions and gets the best possible use out of TRIS. The printout is designed to become an important "piece of equipment in the vacationer's rucksack," possibly giving him the crucial information he needs to return safely from the mountain.
Founded: 1989

VOLUNTEER COMMUNITY BETTERMENT PROJECT
Goodner Brothers Aircraft
Intermountain Regional Airport
Mena, AR 71953
TEL: 501-394-4709
Purpose: To make Polk County a safer place to live.
Sponsor: Goodner Brothers Aircraft

Contact: Albert S. Goodner, Jr.
Description: Goodner Brothers Aircraft is an Arkansas corporation employing 35 people. It is know worldwide for its aircraft painting. From the 1970s, the company has been involved in commuty betterment projects - most in the area of emergency preparedness and disaster response.

Many of the company's volunteer efforts are in the area of painting upkeep of fire engines for the local fire company, airplanes, emergency jeeps, power plants, signs and compressed air cylinders for the County's Office of Emergency Preparedness, and other County vehicles. Although Goodner's efforts are primarily in Polk County, the company has not refused communities outside of Polk County. The value of this volunteer effort for the communities was placed at over $8,000 and involved as much as 20% of the paint shop's work force.

Other projects in which Goodner Brothers Aircraft has played a major role included the upgrading of a taxiway at the local airport when the deteriorated runway was being renovated. This enabled the airport to remain open while runway repairs were underway. In addition, corporate-owned aircraft has been made available for various emergencies that have arisen in Polk County, including medical evacuations and search missions, as well as emergencies arising from floods and tornadoes. These volunteer services are innumerable in dollars and cents.

The volunteer efforts of Goodner Brothers Aircraft have enabled Polk County to become one of the best emergency prepared counties in Arkansas.
Publications: Goodner Brothers Aircraft Volunteer Information Packet

DRUG ABUSE/ALCOHOLISM

NATIONAL/STATE ORGANIZATIONS

ALCOHOLICS ANONYMOUS WORLD SERVICES
PO Box 459
Grand Central Station
New York, NY 10163
TEL: 212-686-1100
Objectives: Works through 74,000 local groups representing 1.6 million members to provide fellowship to men and women who share the experience of alcoholism; serves as a support group for helping each other to achieve sobriety and recover from alcoholism through the *Twelve Steps to Sobriety* developed by *Alcoholics Anonymous*; commits members to helping others in the community when help is requested; publishes a newsletter and several publications describing their programs and goals.
Publications: Alcoholics Anonymous; Twelve Steps and Twelve Traditions; AA Comes of Age; As Bill Sees It; Dr. Bob and the Good Oldtimers; Pass It On
Founded: 1935

CHRISTOPHER D. SMITHERS FOUNDATION
Oyster Bay Road
Mill Neck, NY 11765
TEL: 516-676-0067
Objectives: To develop and assist in the funding of alcoholism projects within and outside of its own organization.
Services: Cosponsors training efforts with the National Institute on Alcohol Abuse and Alcoholism; awards grants for specific projects such as Alcoholism Information and Referral Program, Alcoholism Treatment and Training Center, Alcoholism and Advisory Committee, a newsletter on Alcoholism, Institute for Drug Studies, a visiting nurse service; works with government and industry to study their alcoholism programs; makes general grants to organizations such as the National Council on Alcoholism, Crittenden Memorial Hospital, Community Hospital at Glen Cove; provides scholarships to encourage youth to enter the field; develops major publications.

DO IT NOW FOUNDATION
P.O. Box 27568
Tempe, AZ 85285
TEL: 602-491-0393
Objectives: To provide factual information to young people and adults concerning drugs, alcohol and health.

Services: Publishes low-cost print information, including books, booklets, pamphlets, posters and other educational materials; provides community education services, professional consultation, and technical assistance to organizations and individuals.
Publications: Drug Survival News; D.I.N. Prevue
Founded: 1968

NATIONAL ASSOCIATION OF ALCOHOLISM AND DRUG ABUSE COUNSELORS (*formerly National Association of Alcoholism Counselors*)
1717 Columbia Pike
Suite 300
Arlington, VA 22204
TEL: 703-920-4644
Objectives: To gain public recognition of alcoholism as a disease.
Services: Informs the public about chemical dependency and availability of assistance; provides national representation for the education and training of counselors in alcoholism and drug abuse treatment; seeks legislation establishing accreditation standards for counselors; works to gain public recognition of alcoholism as a disease; maintains a peer assistance committee, and legislative and intergovernmental committees; produces exhibits on alcoholism and drug abuse for display at national conferences.
Founded: 1974

NATIONAL COMMITTEE FOR PREVENTION OF ALCOHOLISM AND DRUG DEPENDENCY
R.R. 1, Box 635
Appomattox, VA 24522
TEL: 804-352-8100
Objectives: To further the study of the effects of alcohol and drugs on the individual.
Services: Works to find ways to improve and increase research and study of the effects on alcohol and other drugs not only on the physical and mental health of the individual abuser, but also on the social and economic life of the community; sponsors seminars; organizes forums; operates nationwide educational program through above meetings, publications, films, radio and television programs; hosts annual three-day meetings.
Founded: 1950

NORTH CONWAY INSTITUTE
14 Beacon Street
Boston, MA 02108
TEL: 617-742-0424

Objectives: To advance the capability of church leaders in dealing with problems of alcohol and drug abuse.

Services: Develops and convenes national seminars to provide an educational vehicle for church leaders; helps society to minister more effectively to problem drinkers and those affected by them; develops productive relations with those in the helping professions, government and private agencies, and the churches to improve prevention, education and treatment; cuts through professional, institutional and cultural boundaries to promote unified action on alcohol and drug related problems; publishes bulletins, periodicals and other materials for the meetings and for interim use in church programs.

Founded: 1951

ODYSSEY HOUSE
309-311 East Sixth Street
New York, NY 10003
TEL: 212-677-3200
Objectives: To treat substance abuse and addiction, educational disabilities and other social dysfunctions.
Services: Operates residential communities in several states; maintains substance abuse information and education division (a training program); operates ACCEPT, a program especially designed to train people to treat adolescents who are poly-addicted (drugs and alcohol); conducts other programs as indicated, e.g., for pregnant addicts, for parents with drug-abusing children; publishes quarterly newsletter.
Publications: Odyssey Newsletter

PANEL ON DRUG ABUSE/PANEL ON ALCOHOLISM
American Medical Association
Council of Scientific Affairs
535 North Dearborn Street
Chicago, IL 60610
TEL: 312-751-6577
Objectives: To increase educational efforts with the profession and the public regarding the diagnosis, treatment and prevention of drug abuse and alcoholism.
Services: Reviews evidence obtained from scientific research on the causes and effects of non-medical use of drugs and of alcoholism; proposes expanded educational programs to all segments of the population, including members of the medical and legal professions and law-enforcement agencies; develops informative materials on drug abuse and alcoholism and makes them available to the professions and the public at nominal cost.

PHARMACISTS AGAINST DRUG ABUSE
McNeil Pharmaceutical, Division of McNeilab
Johnson & Johnson Subsidiary
Spring House, PA 19477
TEL: 215-628-5000
Objectives: To utilize the facility of American pharmacies to help in the fight against drug abuse.
Services: Works with ACTION, the National Volunteer Agency, in a nationwide program which enables development and distribution of free printed materials on drug abuse by the nation's pharmacists and a public service awareness campaign; involves spokespersons such as the First Lady, major television personalities, and others who are nationally known; works to expand the pilot project launched in Maine, New Hampshire and Massachusetts in November 1982 to include some 50,000 pharmacies nationwide.

THE RADAR NETWORK
US/HHS - National Clearinghouse for Alcohol and Drug Information
PO Box 2345
Rockville, MD 20852
TEL: 301-468-2600
TOLL FREE: 800-SAY-NO-TO (Drugs)
FAX: 301-468-6433
Objectives: To provide information services in partnership with NCADI on a state-by-state basis.
Services: Working in partnership with NCDAI, the *Regional Alcohol and Drug Awareness Resource (RADAR) Network* consists of *State Clearinghouses,* specialized information centers of national organizations, the Department of Education Regional Training Centers, and others; offers the public a variety of information services; *State Clearinghouse* and *Regional Training Center* locations and phone numbers are shown below:

State Clearinghouses
- Anchorage, AK (907-349-6602); Montgomery, AL (205-271-9258)
- Little Rock, AR (501-682-6653); Pago Pago, AS
- Sacramento, CA (916-324-7262); Denver, CO (303-331-8201)
- Plainville, CT (203-793-9791); Washington, DC (202-682-1716)
- Wilmington, DE (302-571-6975); Tallahassee, FL (904-878-6922)
- Atlanta, GA (404-894-4204); Tamuning, GU (671-646-9261)
- Honolulu, HI (808-536-7234); Cedar Rapids, IA (319-398-5133)
- Boise, ID (208-377-0068); Springfield, IL (217-525-3456)
- Bloomington, IN (812-855-1237); Topeka, KS (913-296-3925)
- Frankfort, KY (502-564-2880); Baton Rouge, LA (504-342-9352)
- Cambridge, MA (617-445-6999); Baltimore, MD (301-225-6543)
- Augusta, ME (207-289-2781); Lansing, MI (517-482-9902)
- Anoka, MN (612-427-5310/800-223-9513); Jackson, MS (601-359-1288)
- Jefferson City, MO (314-751-4942); Helena, MT (406-444-2878)
- Durham, NC (919-286-5118); Bismarck, ND (701-244-3603)
- Lincoln, NE (402-474-0930); Concord, NH (603-271-4638)
- Trenton, NJ (609-292-0729); Trenton, NJ (609-292-4414)
- Santa Fe, NM (505-827-2589); Carson City, NV (702-885-4790)
- Albany, NY (518-473-3460); New York, NY (212-966-8700)
- Columbus, OH (614-466-7893); Oklahoma City, OK (405-271-8755)
- Portland, OR (800-237-7808/503-280-3673); Harrisburg, PA (717-787-2606/9761)
- Cranston, RI (401-464-2140); Rio Piedras, PR (809-763-3133)
- Columbia, SC (803-734-9559); Pierre, SD (605-773-3123)
- Nashville, TN (615-244-7066); Austin, TX (512-463-5510)
- Salt Lake City, UT (801-538-3949); Richmond, VA (804-786-3909)
- St. Croix, VI (809-773-8443); Waterbury, VT (802-241-2178)
- Bellevue, WA (207-747-9111); Madison, WI (608-293-2797)
- Charleston, WV (304-348-2041); Laramie, WY (307-766-4119)

Regional Training Centers
- Atlanta, GA (404-688-9227); Chicago, IL (312-883-8888)
- Sayville, NY (516-589-7022); Norman, OK (405-325-2454)
- Portland, OR (503-275-9500)

Specialty Centers
- Berkeley, CA (415-486-1111); La Jolla, CA (619-534-6331)
- San Rafael, CA (415-456-5692); South Laguna, CA (714-499-3889)
- Berkeley, CA (415-642-5208); San Francisco, CA (415-861-2142)
- Washington, DC (202-371-2100); Washington, DC (202-458-3809)

- Atlanta, GA (404-934-6364); Atlanta, GA (404-752-1530)
- Rockville, MD (800-251-5531); Rockville, MD (301-251-5531)
- Minneapolis, MN (612-871-7878); Hanover, NH (603-646-7540)
- Piscataway, NJ (201-756-3730); New York, NY (212-966-5660)
- New York, NY (212-206-6770); Pittsburgh, PA (412-391-0900)
- San Juan, PR (809-721-5145/721-6981); Arlington, VA (703-522-6272)
- Alexandria, VA (703-756-3730); Seattle, WA (206-543-0937)

Space does not permit designation of specialty in *Specialty Centers,* they include EAPs, AIDS, crime, Hispanic, prevention, research, family, and other issues as they relate to drug abuse and alcoholism, and may be housed in a Governor's office, university, national organization, foundation, etc. Inquire at the nearest *State Clearinghouse, Training Center,* or *Specialty Center,* any of which can direct inquirers to other specialty centers.

TRAINING PROGRAMS

GET INVOLVED BEFORE YOUR KIDS DO
AAL Drug and Alcohol Use Prevention Program
Fraternal Benefits & Financial Services for Lutherans
4321 North Ballard Road
Appleton, WI 54919-0001
TEL: 414-734-5721
Purpose: To help parents communicate effectively with their children about drugs and alcohol.
Credit: Inquire
Contact: Phyllis Rusch
Description: This workshop program - designed by a national organization to reach parents *before* their children get involved with drugs - pulls together volunteer programs in local areas across the country to present the workshops in their communities. There is no cost to participants in the workshops. AAL provides all materials, including a videotape featuring well-known actors role-playing family situations, group discussions and a parent guidebook to be completed by families at home. The workshop strives to help parents develop such skills as talking with their children about alcohol and drugs, setting family rules about alcohol and drugs, assessing their own behaviors concerning alcohol and drugs, and networking with other parents to help children through the high-risk years.

The local program is considered a model for the nation to follow in helping to fight drug abuse. AAL groups (called branches) have conducted workshops for parent/teacher associations, hospitals, optimist clubs, counseling centers, school boards and Junior Leagues.

Over 148,000 people in more than 2,550 communities have attended *Get Involved* parent workshops since the program was introduced. Another 229,000 people have been reached through nearly 3,600 community outreach projects that focus on awareness and prevention of alcohol and other drug abuse.

In 1988, *AAL's Get Involved Before Your Kids Do* drug prevention program was selected as one of 16 model programs by the *White House Conference for A Drug Free America.* On January 14, 1990, President Bush named *Get Involved* his 49th *point of light.* Bush's *Points of Light Initiative* recognizes local efforts to combat social problems (see separate entry).

The *Get Involved* program is available free of charge through AAL's 7,100 volunteer branches across the country. AAL continually improves and maintains the program.

INDIVIDUAL PROGRAM PROFILES

INTOUCH
Cook County Sheriff's Office
Youth Services Department
1401 Maybrook Drive
Maywood, IL 60153
TEL: 312-865-2900
Purpose: To develop and enhance substance abuse prevention activities.
Sponsor: Cook County Sheriff's Office; Illinois Department of Alcohol and Substance
Contact: Mary L. Feerick, Director
Description: InTouch is a communication link to community and faculty, students and agencies concerned with prevention of alcohol and drug abuse. It is funded by a grant from the Illinois Department of Alcoholism and Substance Abuse and sponsored by the Cook County Sheriff's Youth Services Department.

A major activity of the program is developing, organizing, and implementing seminars, largely for students, but including family and community meetings. When possible, the seminars include role models who were raised in or near the local area involved in the seminar.

Other activities include needs surveys, technical assistance, and specific projects such as:

- **Project Decide,** which addresses self-esteem building as a key component.
- **Home Is Where the Start Is,** which develops and distributes materials for parents to help them instill self-esteem in their children and provide them and their children with information on substance abuse prevention.

A major role played by InTouch is setting up planning meetings in local schools to help with each year's schedule of technical assistance and other activities to help prevent substance abuse.
Publications: InTouch (newsletter); InTouch Needs Assessment Survey

NEW YORK GIANTS SCHOOL SPEAKERS PROGRAM
SEE EDUCATION: DROPOUT PREVENTION

OIC NATIONAL SHELTER PROGRAM
SEE RECIPIENTS: HOMELESS - SHELTERS

SHALOM ET BENEDICTUS SUBSTANCE ABUSE PROGRAMS
Shalom Et Benedictus
Box 309
Stephenson, VA 22656
TEL: 703-665-0877
Purpose: To provide help to young people with drug and alcohol problems.
Contact: Becki Porter-Harmon
Description: Shalom et Benedictus is a non-profit, non-denominational corporation currently managing four programs: Shalom, Benedictus House, the Community Assistance Program and the First Step, described below:
Shalom - a long-term residential program designed to serve up to 21 young people, ages 14 to 18, with drug and alcohol as well as other related emotional, behavioral, and family problems. Shalom's broad purpose is to provide a structured, caring drug- and alcohol-free environment in which residents can gain insight into past and present emotional difficulties caused by and resulting in their drug and alcohol dependency, and to provide an opportunity for them to explore and rehearse alternative ways of behaving and coping with life problems.
Benedictus House - a transitional program for young men and women, ages 16 to 19, who have successfully completed a formalized treatment program and are preparing for independent

living. Benedictus House provides a supportive residential environment, counseling services, assistance with job placement and vocational development, and social and task skills development. Benedictine House was opened in 1986.

Community Assistance Program (CAP) - a program developed around the premise that adolescent drug and alcohol dependency is a whole community problem. The program provides a number of services to the community including support groups, pre-assessment, crisis intervention, education, and information and referral services in collaboration with the schools in the Winchester, Clarke and Frederick County area in Virginia as well as Morgan County, West Virginia. The program began in 1985.

First Step - a day treatment program providing service to eighth through twelfth grade students in Frederick and Clarke counties and the city of Winchester, Monday through Friday, year-round. Serving as a locus for a number of substance abuse treatment approaches, this program provides intensive outpatient therapy in the form of individual group and family therapy, aftercare services, recreation therapy, and educational services. It works in conjunction with schools, human services agencies, professionals and treatment programs in order to offer the most complete continuum of services appropriate for each individual. First Step was opened in December 1987. According to the Director, "Drug and alcohol dependency affects the lives of all types of people - people who can, with help, become independent, contributing members of our community. We plan programs as if someone's life depended on it ... it does!"

VSPA FUND-RAISING PROGRAMS
Virginia State Police Association
6944 Forest Hill Avenue
Richmond, VA 23225
TOLL FREE: 800-523-5088
Purpose: To mount fund-raising programs to help provide support for volunteer programs around the Commonwealth.
Sponsor: Virginia Department of State Police
Contact: Kyle L. Miller, President
Description: Founded in 1975, the Virginia State Police Association (VSPA) strives to be mutually helpful to one another in an effort to provide a higher degree of professionalism and morale within the Department, and to provide better police services to the citizens of the Commonwealth of Virginia. These services include numerous fund-raising efforts for citizens who support the efforts of the State Police to make our communities better places to live.

Drug abuse resistance efforts are a primary concern of the Association, and contributions for citizen efforts in this area of concern have included:

- Drug Abuse Resistance Education (DARE), which is sponsored by the Virginia Department of State Police, and which is active in nearly 100 school districts
- Virginia Federation of Parents for Drug-Free Youth
- Greater Richmond Informed Parents (GRIP)
- Drugbusters
- Parents' Association to Neutralize Drug and Alcohol Abuse (PANDAA)
- Amherst County DARE Program

In addition to the many drug abuse prevention programs, VSPA contributes to volunteer programs in other areas of concern, such as:

- Portsmouth Family/Community Task Force
- Virginia Beach Council of PTAs
- Sheltered Homes of Alexandria
- Tough Love of Northern Virginia
- South Augusta Babe Ruth League
- Allegheny County ESCAPE Club
- Virginia Special Olympics
- Make-A-Wish Foundation
- Salvation Army

- VSPA Scholarship and Emergency Relief Fund

According to the Association's President, "All fund-raising programs come with problems, but we feel the positive results far outweigh the negative. We are acutely aware of the positive image of the Department of State Police and are making a good faith effort to maintain that image."
Publications: VSPA Annual Report
Founded: 1975

DRUG ABUSE/ALCOHOLISM: AIDS

INDIVIDUAL PROGRAM PROFILES

ALCOHOLISM AND SUBSTANCE ABUSE - AIDS PROGRAM
Whitman-Walker Clinic
1407 S Street, NW
Washington, DC 20009
TEL: 202-797-3580; 202-328-0697 (Spanish)
Purpose: To help lesbians and gay men overcome substance abuse.
Sponsor: Whitman-Walker Clinic
Contact: Peter Provost
Description: Alcoholism and Substance Abuse Services is a professionally-staffed project of Whitman-Walker Clinic. The service is known for its achievements in helping lesbians and gay men overcome substance abuse. The program also provides important expertise in understanding the link between substance abuse and a weakened immune system. The alcoholism program was instrumental in developing a substance-abuse intervention project for individuals attending the HIV antibody testing unit. As in all Whitman-Walker Clinic programs, coordination with local government services as well as other community-based organizations is an important activity designed to ensure a unified response to the targeted issue. In addition, all Whitman-Walker volunteers receive training, orientation, seminars and workshops periodically.

DRUG ABUSE/ALCOHOLISM: ALCOHOL

NATIONAL/STATE ORGANIZATIONS

ALCOHOL EDUCATION FOR YOUTH AND COMMUNITY*
362 State Street
Albany, NY 12210
TEL: 518-436-9319
Objectives: To provide seminars for professionals, workshops for families, and varied programs with youth.
Services: Brings together all segments of the community in workshops, school presentations and in-service training programs; provides consultants for school/community/church presentations; "Alcohol Awareness" workshops for educators, clergy and other community leaders; specials in communications skills development for youth and adults in programs such as "Youth and Power" retreats; operates comprehensive DWI projects; applies limited legislative pressure; maintains speakers bureau; publishes a newsletter, a journal, an alcohol education resource workbook and other alcoholism information and materials.
Publications: US/ACTION; CATALYST II
Founded: 1905

AMERICAN COUNCIL ON ALCOHOL PROBLEMS
3426 Bridgeland Drive
Bridgeton, MO 63044
TEL: 314-739-5944
Objectives: To seek long-range solutions to the problems posed by alcohol.
Services: Coordinates the work of its state affiliates who carry on programs in areas of research, education and legislative protection for the prevention of alcohol-related problems; promotes legislative reform, especially putting alcohol control largely at state level; publishes quarterly.
Publications: The American Issue
Founded: 1895

ASSOCIATION OF CERTIFIED SERVERS
600 New Hampshire Avenue, NW
Washington, DC 20037
TEL: 202-337-4583
Objectives: To provide training to bartenders for intervening in cases of excessive alcohol consumption.
Services: Provides *TIPS (Training for Intervening Procedures by Servers of Alcohol)* to bartenders, vendors, and professional alcohol servers to teach them techniques for regulating alcohol consumption in public places; serves as a forum for the exchange of information on the prevention of alcohol abuse; provides referral information and an insurance program; publishes a newsletter for members to report on the application and results of the program in communities across the country.
Publications: Association of Certified Servers Newsletter
Founded: 1985

ASSOCIATION OF HALFWAY HOUSE ALCOHOLISM PROGRAMS OF NORTH AMERICA
786 East Seventh Street
St. Paul, MN 55106
TEL: 612-771-0933
Objectives: To educate and serve day-to-day needs of halfway house alcoholism programs.
Services: Provides technical assistance; offers consultant services for specific problems; conducts intermittent workshops and conferences to train and educate staff; maintains information service; conducts specialized education for areas not covered in structured training programs; publishes Optimism (for women), two newsletters, Counselors on Alcoholism and Communications and services, and other materials.
Publications: Communications & Services
Founded: 1966

COMMITTEE ON COOPERATION WITH THE PROFESSIONAL COMMUNITY
Alcoholics Anonymous (AA)
PO Box 459
Grand Central Station
New York, NY 10163
TEL: 212-686-1100
Objectives: To bring about more communication, understanding, respect and cooperation between AA and the professional community working with alcoholics.
Services: Provides continuing two-way communication at every level, local to national, to share its 55 years of trial-and-error experience with more than two million alcoholics in exchange for information, advice and services that AA can or cannot provide; publishes *About AA,* a newsletter issued specifically to supplement personal communication with professionals in the alcoholism field.
Founded: 1935

MOTHERS AGAINST DRUNK DRIVING
MADD
PO Box 1217
Hurst, TX 76053
TEL: 817-268-6233
Objectives: To assist people victimized by the crime of drunk driving, to change public attitudes which find drinking and driving acceptable behavior, and to change the laws which do not treat drunk and drugged driving seriously.
Services: Involves local volunteer groups who complete a prescribed process in order to become a chartered MADD chapter; includes in its chapter programs *Victim Services, Court Monitoring, Speakers Bureau, Special Programs (Candlelight Vigil, Victim Rights Week, Red Ribbon, Keep It A Safe Summer [K.I.S.S.], Drive for Life, Poster-Essay Contest, Youth Education);* utilizes volunteers in all programs and in all phases of chapter operations, from professional help with support groups to monthly chapter mailings; adds new programs as needs indicate, most recently including *Victim Impact Panels,* which are held nationwide for DWI offenders who have not yet killed or injured anyone.
Publications: MADD In Action; MADDvocate; No Time for Goodbyes; Beyond Sympathy
Founded: 1980

NATIONAL COUNCIL ON ALCOHOLISM
12 West 21st Street
New York, NY 10010
TEL: 212-206-6770
Objectives: To use its resources as a national voluntary health agency to combat the disease of alcoholism.
Services: Serves at the local level through its 220 local affiliates - each with its own volunteer Board of Directors; stimulates, promotes reviews, and comments on research and evaluation projects; devises methods to deal with alcoholism in the workplace, initiating employee alcoholism programs in cooperation with business and industry; maintains an information service accessible by telephone, letters, or personal consultation; publishes books, pamphlets, other materials in specific categories (youth, women, labor-management, clergy, courts and the law, the family of the alcoholic, etc.).
Founded: 1944

US/HHS - NATIONAL CLEARINGHOUSE FOR ALCOHOL AND DRUG INFORMATION
PO Box 2345
Rockville, MD 20852
TEL: 301-468-2600
TOLL FREE: 800-SAY-NO-TO (Drugs)
FAX: 301-468-6433
Objectives: To serve as a national resource system for alcohol and drug information.
Services: Serves as a centralized source for information on what is currently known about alcohol and other drugs; works with and through the *RADAR (Regional Alcohol and Drug Awareness Resource) Network Centers* located in almost every state; provides information on the latest research results, popular press and scholarly journal articles, videos, prevention curricula, print materials, and program descriptions; specifically, the *National Clearinghouse for Alcohol and Drug Information (NCADI)* provides the following services:
- **RADAR Network -** The *Regional Alcohol and Drug Awareness Resource (RADAR) Network* comprises resource centers in almost every state, which serve as information resource centers close to home. Each RADAR Network Center works cooperatively with NCADI, which sends them print materials and other resources so they can perform many of the same services with an extra advantage - they know the uniqueness of their own states. A list of RADAR Network

offices is available on request.

- **Prevention Pipeline: An Alcohol and Drug Awareness Service** - This is a bimonthly news service available to anyone for a $15 annual handling fee. It is a forum, a news bulletin, and a research alert that allows both professionals and volunteers to keep on top of the latest information and events.
- **Technical Support** - NCADI offers support to organizations in the field whenever possible through a wide range of resource lists, direct mail, editorial support, exhibits, and dissemination of materials for conferences, and has an active outreach department that works with groups and individuals to maximize their efforts.
- **Print Materials** - NCADI creates new materials and offers limited quantities free-of-charge through the RADAR Network and other channels, including negatives (that you can take to your local printer); adapts the best of local efforts so the rest of the nation can share information on successful programs; distributes materials created by other U.S. Departments (e.g., Education, Transportation, and Justice), and prepares computerized lists that describe the wide array of materials available from both public and private sector groups.

NCADI was mandated by Congress to serve as *the* Federal resource center for alcohol and other drug information because lawmakers recognized the need for an unbiased, state-of-the-art resource center that would be readily accessible to all citizens. The partnership formed with state governments to create the RADAR Network makes the program more responsive to the people. With Federal and state dollars supporting NCADI and the RADAR network, most of the materials are provided free. There are minimum handling fees for only a few items. A number of the items are listed in the Bibliography section of this publication. For a complete list, request catalog.

Sponsor: US/HHS - Department of Health & Human Services
Contact: John F. Fay
Publications: Alcohol Health/Research World

INDIVIDUAL PROGRAM PROFILES

TENAFLY-ALPINE SAFE RIDES PROGRAM AND OTHERS
SEE DRUG ABUSE/ALCOHOLISM: TRANSPORTATION

DRUG ABUSE/ALCOHOLISM: CHILDREN/YOUTH

NATIONAL/STATE ORGANIZATIONS

FAMILIES IN ACTION NATIONAL DRUG INFORMATION CENTER
3345 North Druid Hills Road
Suite 300
Decatur, GA 30033
TEL: 404-325-5799
Objectives: To halt the rising use of drugs in the community.
Services: Seeks to educate parents, children and community leaders on the increase of drug use in the communities; works to counteract the societal pressures that condone and promote drug use; collects and disseminates all relevant information about young people and the health effects of drugs; helps to enact laws that will lead to the goal of eradicating drug use in the communities; trains parent group leaders to organize in their communities; conducts speakers' education and training program; provides telephone reference service; maintains a drug information center which

contains more than 350,000 documents, studies, books, brochures, and films and videos relating to drug abuse; publishes a quarterly newsletter, a guide to forming family action groups, and other materials.
Publications: Crack Update; Drug Abuse Update; How to Form a Families Action Group in Your Community
Founded: 1977

NATIONAL LISTEN AMERICA CLUB
2686 Townsgate Road
Westlake Village, CA 91359
TEL: 805-497-9457
Objectives: To promote and recognize the positive and constructive things young people are doing.
Services: Administers a variety of community service projects, including an annual national two-hour television special; maintains a membership of junior and senior high school students who have pledged not to smoke, drink alcohol, or use drugs; works with 3,000 local groups; gathers and shares information on projects that demonstrate ways in which youth are making positive contributions to improve the quality of life in their communities, thus improving society as a whole; publishes a biweekly newsletter and a monthly magazine; convenes every summer.
Publications: Tune In; Listen America Magazine
Founded: 1980

STUDENTS AGAINST DRIVING DRUNK (SADD)
PO Box 800
Marlboro, MA 01752
TEL: 617-481-3568
Objectives: To get teenagers and young adults involved in fighting drunk driving.
Services: Works through sponsors in local high schools to recruit teenagers to help attack peer pressure and pave the way for acceptance of the refusal to drink and drive; keeps the community informed by enlisting the help of adults within and outside of the school (such as MADD, above, and local college students) to publicize the program, offer advice, and generally oversee the management and evaluation methods used by the program's teenaged leaders.

Gets the schools involved, especially in the area of combating peer pressure; monitors courts as well as judges, prosecutors, and laws; works with other groups fighting drunk driving; mounts letter-writing campaigns to elected and other government officials; holds school assemblies featuring speakers who are informed about the drunk driving problem; conducts fund-raising events such as bake sales.

Informs school and local newspapers of the work of the club; stages events in regional malls with balloons, bumper stickers, posters, etc., during November, which is Alcohol Awareness Month; enters marching SADD students in Homecoming games at local high schools; holds Walk/Run-a-Thons open to anyone; conducts student and parent surveys; works very closely with state and county drunk driving task forces.

Publishes fact sheets, guidelines, reports, and other informative materials, as well as tools for meetings, fund-raisers, etc., such as bumper stickers, posters and balloons, to assist others planning to mount SADD programs; researches the subject of drunk driving on a continuing basis to keep current on community, education, and legislative developments on the subject.

[This national program was started by a student in W.T. Woodson High School in Fairfax, Virginia]
Publications: SADD Update; SADD in the College; SADD and the Athlete; SADD in the High School; SADD in the Junior High School; SADD Policy and Procedures

TARGET - HELPING STUDENTS COPE WITH ALCOHOL AND DRUGS
National Federation of State High School Associations
11724 Plaza Circle
PO Box 20626
Kansas City, MO 64195
TEL: 816-464-5400
TOLL FREE: 800-366-6667
Objectives: To work with students in drug and alcohol abuse prevention programs.
Services: Provides information to members of the *National Federation of State High School Associations* (parent organization) on helping students deal with drugs and alcohol; serves as a resource center for information on substance abuse and prevention from preschool to grade twelve; gives referrals for adolescent treatment facilities, prevention programs, speakers and literature; offers workshops and seminars; publishes a monthly newsletter during the school year, and other materials.
Publications: On Target

WITHIN YOU, INC./JUST SAY NO CLUBS (*formerly Just Say No Clubs*)
3101-A Sacramento
Berkeley, CA 94702
TEL: 415-848-0845
TOLL FREE: 800-258-2766
Objectives: To combat and eventually eliminate drug abuse among children.
Services: Administers a nationwide series of young student clubs dedicated to fighting drug abuse; garners support from parents, educators, polilce officers, local officials, and others; works through the schools to encourage children to "just say no" to drugs; strives to give students a positive social role and serve as a supportive peer group; enables the children to operation their own clubs, in which each *Club*: shares information among student groups; holds classroom discussions; helps develop a "just say no" curriculum for their schools; helps fellow students who have drug problems; works with founders of the first *Just Say No Club* (Oakland Parents in Action), who developed the widely used publication, *How to Start a Just Say No Club.*

INDIVIDUAL PROGRAM PROFILES

CHAMP BAKERY
SEE RECIPIENTS: CHILDREN/YOUTH - ENTREPRENEURSHIP

PREVENTION THROUGH ACTION
Catholic Youth Organization
305 Michigan Avenue
Detroit , MI 48226
TEL: 313-963-7172
Purpose: To educate Hispanic youth about substance-abuse prevention, community values, and leadership responsibilities.
Sponsor: Archdiocese of Detroit
Contact: Ray Hillen, Director
Description: Prevention through Action combines training seminars with recreational activities to teach Hispanic youth the consequences of drug abuse or fighting, and offer positive and enjoyable alternatives. In addition, the youth are taught community values and leadership roles.
In the initial effort, 47 Hispanic youths, ages 14 to 18, were trained at annual four-day *Youth Options* seminars. Participants are taught to lead groups of younger children, ages 6 to 14, in recreational activities which are prefaced by brief, mandatory workshops on coping with youth problems. By early 1989, 500 youths benefitted from the program.

Groups providing support and facilities for the program include other Detroit-based Catholic organizations such as the *Hispanic Affairs Office of the Archdiocese of Detroit,* the *Renaissance Youth Center, Latino Outreach,* and *Detroit Health Department.* Among the positive program elements are a dance group, a basketball league, and the *Urban Link,* a male responsibility program that arranges for community professionals to talk to male youth audiences. Also, the older youth have made a success of the program, and the younger kids look up to the older ones, so the program is making a very real difference, according to the director.
Founded: 1988

PROJECT GRADUATION
Connexion
310 East Third Street
Flint, MI 48502
TEL: 313-767-3750
Purpose: To ensure a drug- and alcohol-free graduation season.
Sponsor: Genesee County Commission on Substance Abuse Services
Contact: Deborah K. Medlin, Executive Director
Description: While still meeting with some student resistance, *Project Graduation* is becoming an expected part of high school plans during the graduation period. While some students join parents and educators in supporting the concept of not drinking while driving, they are not readily accepting that of being drug- and alcohol-free. According to one official, there is some progress. "There used to be no awareness at all," he said.
A meeting in early spring each year begins the program. In 1989, 100 schools participated in the project. The theme was "The best of life is yet to be. Make '89 drug and alcohol free."
One awareness project offers an award to the school getting the most high school juniors and seniors and parents to sign alcohol- and drug-free pledge cards. The winning school retains a traveling trophy for a year. New in 1989 was an activity called "Wanna Party." In this project, area businesses and organizations set up booths in the mall and distributed information on things students can do to have fun without alcohol or drugs. In part of this project, students and parents can learn tips for having alcohol-free parties, and participants win door prizes.
At the party, schools again participated in activities such as graduation night lock-ins at schools, halls and gyms, and Las Vegas Nights with students using play money. Parents, school staff, and students at the various schools volunteered to work on events for the parties, which included illusionists, massage therapists, hypnotists, prizes and all-night dancing.
Project Graduation is highlighted from March to June to involve the students themselves in the campaign. Students at four high schools have announced that their common goal at their individual parties is "bringing their graduating class together for a safe, fun-filled evening."
Connexion, a substance abuse prevention agency serving Genesee County, spearheads the area's nine-county coalition, which also includes *Channel 12 (WJRT), Channel 28 (WFUM), Channel 19/35 (WUCM), Genesee County Commission on Substance Abuse Services, Human Development Commission, AAA Michigan, Michigan State Police, the Sterling Area Health Project, Prevention and Youth Services, Christian Family Services of Lapeer County,* and *Top of the Park.*

DRUG ABUSE/ALCOHOLISM: COMMUNICATIONS & PR

NATIONAL/STATE ORGANIZATIONS

ENTERTAINMENT INDUSTRIES COUNCIL
1760 Reston Avenue
Suite 101
Reston, VA 22090
TEL: 703-481-1414
Objectives: To combat and deglamorize drug abuse, especially among young people.
Services: Works with corporations and representatives of the entertainment industry, including actors, agents, publicists, producers, directors, and writers, in a national campaign against substance abuse; seeks to identify and provide celebrity role models for young people; hopes to increase youth awareness through television, radio, music, and motion pictures; conducts radio interviews, television specials, meetings and workshops, outreach programs, and employee assistance and fundraising programs; tracks the progress and results of celebrity involvement and compiles statistics; maintains a celebrity speakers' bureau on drug prevention, seat belt awareness, and intravenous drug use/AIDS; has recognition program to honor celebrities who are leaders in contributing to drug abuse awareness; publishes a quarterly newsletter, annual report, and research papers.
Publications: EIC Newsletter
Founded: 1983

INDIVIDUAL PROGRAM PROFILES

MAKE IT HOME FOR THE HOLIDAYS
Washington Regional Alcohol Program
8720 Georgia Avenue
Silver Spring, MD 20910
TEL: 301-565-4161
Purpose: To bring together all segments of the metropolitan region in a concerted effort to reduce drunk driving during the holidays.
Contact: Susan Morris, Board Chairman
Description: With statistics showing December second only to June for the highest number of motor vehicle fatalities, the *Washington Regional Alcohol Program (WRAP)* and the *Council of Governments' Police Chiefs Committee* launched the *Make It Home for the Holidays* campaign. They joined forces with local business and media organizations to promote safe driving messages urging people to think twice before taking chances behind the wheel. The essence of the campaign was a reminder to citizens that the best present they can give is their safe return home.
One sponsor, *Coors Brewing Company,* provided a *Sober Ride* service during the entire month of December, the height of office parties. With a few restrictions, *Sober Ride* offers a free, no-questions-asked taxi ride home to wary revelers. During the two weeks *Sober Ride* operated in 1988, over 1,000 people used the service. The program is provided only to people who drove their own cars to parties and bars and who are not able to drive themselves home. They are taken only to their homes and not any other place.
All of the region's 21 law enforcement agencies are alerted during the period to help make the highways safe, conducting sobriety checkpoints, organizing "six pack" patrols and setting up radar stop teams to reduce the number of alcohol-related accidents. Other efforts include 15,000 posters provided by new car dealers and put on display in buildings and businesses throughout the region. In addition, public service announcements produced and aired by WMZQ-radio, and television announcements produced by

Rock Creek Films, are heard and seen throughout the month. The *Corporate Guide to the Holidays,* published by *Greater Washington Board of Trade,* offers responsible party giving tips to its 1,500 members.
The success of the program is attributed, in part, to the combination of a caring theme, *Make It Home for the Holidays,* and the law enforcement presence - two good reasons not to drive drunk, according to one of the business sponsors.
Publications: Corporate Guide to the Holidays

DRUG ABUSE/ALCOHOLISM: DRUGS

NATIONAL/STATE ORGANIZATIONS

DRUG ABUSE INFORMATION HOTLINE*
US/White House
Office of the First Lady
Washington, DC 20500
TEL: 202-456-1414
Objectives: To contact people who have asked for help with concerns in the area of drug abuse.
Services: Enlists volunteers from the National Federation of Parents for Drug-Free Youth to operate a pilot phone bank in the White House; screens mail to select the most urgent questions that can be answered by phone; responds to other mail-in comments and questions with informative materials; plans to evaluate this service to determine the feasibility for an ongoing phone bank of this type in relation to questions on drug abuse that come to the White House.
Founded: 1982

DRUG ALLIANCE
US/ACTION - The Federal Volunteer Agency
1100 Vermont Avenue, NW
Suite 1100
Washington, DC 20525
TEL: 202-634-9108
TOLL FREE: 800-424-8580
Objectives: To mobilize public and private resources to expand illicit drug abuse prevention and education efforts.
Services: Strengthens and expands local volunteer activities through support of community coalitions and seeks to ensure their continuation beyond Federal funding by stimulating private sector involvement; awards grants, promotes contracts and provides technical assistance to support community organizations which are committed to prevention strategies that emphasize volunteerism and increase public education and awareness; seeks to strengthen the family, and promote positive alternatives to drug use; initiates conferences and workshops at the State level, both to alert individuals and organizations to the extent of the problem, and to present and solicit solutions; encourages local Kidsummit Against Drugs projects based on a pilot project in Washington, DC; joins with the U.S. Department of Education to promote the following learning objectives for drug prevention programs:
- **Drug Information** - To value and maintain sound personal health; to understand how drugs affect health;
- **Decision Making** - To respect laws and rules prohibiting drugs;
- **Peer Pressure/Saying No** - To recognize and resist pressures to use drugs;
- **Self-Esteem** - To promote activities that reinforce the positive, drug-free elements of student life.
Publishes handbooks on starting community anti-drug campaigns, KIDSUMMITS, and other activities.

Contact: Calvin Dawson
Publications: Kid Summit Against Drugs; Take Action Against Drug Abuse
Founded: 1971

NATIONAL ASSOCIATION ON DRUG ABUSE PROBLEMS

355 Lexington Avenue, NW
New York, NY 10017
TEL: 212-986-1170
Objectives: To fight drug and substance abuse through furthering of knowledge and work in all of its phases.
Services: Aids in rehabilitation, employment and prevention programs; offers training for individuals with a drug abuse history; operates a job-placement service; conducts work shops to train treatment counselors; promotes results of research which placed former addicts on a par with others in similar job situations; sponsors invitational conference; publishes quarterly newsletter and other materials
Publications: NADP News/Report
Founded: 1972

PRIDE

Parents' Resource Institute on Drug Education
Parent Resources and Information on Drug Abuse (PRIDE)
50 Hurt Plaza
Room 210
Atlanta, GA 30303
TOLL FREE: 800-67-PRIDE
Objectives: To utilize the parents' instinct to protect their children to fight drug abuse.
Services: Provides technical assistance to parent groups wishing to mount drug prevention programs for the benefit of the youth of their communities; works with youth who are interested in seeing the parent movement grow, can create peer leadership, and thus can be an invaluable asset to the parent movement; designs programs to reach parents and youth at home, school and work; advocates a community approach, fostering a coming together of government, business, schools and parents; uses a system of testing that determines the scope of adolescent drug usage by students in grades four through twelve; administers an intensive training workshop for and by young people; teaches positive life skills, such as how to reverse negative peer pressure; prepares parents to deal with today's complex drug environment, and to conduct the PRIDE program themselves after training; conducts the *PRIDE World Drug Conference* (March 1991; May 1992); administers government contracts; publishes various materials on drug abuse prevention.
Publications: PRIDE: Devoted to Drug Abuse Prevention Through Education

TRAINING PROGRAMS

MONTGOMERY ANTI-DRUG CONFERENCE

Montgomery County Panel on Drug Problems
Montgomery County Executive Office
100 Monroe Street
Rockville, MD 20850
TEL: 301-217-2500
Sponsor: Montgomery County
Contact: Sidney Kramer, County Executive
Description: This conference, convened in June 1989, was composed of 32 business, government and community leaders appointed by the County Executive to devise ways to reach parents of school-age children and neighborhoods victimized by drug-related crime with comprehensive drug-education programs. The conference culminated a year of work by the panel and resulted in six goals for implementation by the county over a

two-year period, as follows:
- Various departments of county government should promote anti-drug campaigns by neighborhood organizations, school groups, religious congregations and businesses.
- The county should provide community outreach services, including technical help for groups trying to create their own anti-drug programs and training for young people and others who want to serve as voluntary peer counselors.
- Besides promoting anti-drug campaigns by private groups, the county should conduct its own "broad public education and awareness campaign for substance-abuse prevention."
- County officials ought to push for tougher drug laws, study ways to speed the court system's handling of drug cases, and "review and assess on an ongoing basis the treatment services available" to drug users.
- The county should develop a system for the "monitoring and evaluation" of its anti-drug efforts, especially those outlined in the conference report.
- The county should seek "creative funding" for further prevention efforts; e.g., assign a team of employees to work full time on anti-drug grant applications.

To sum up the conference, the panel member from the Potomac Electric Power Company said, "To reverse the adverse trends of the last decade, every segment of our community must focus on education, prevention and treatment of substance abuse."
Publications: Montgomery County Anti-Drug Study

PREVENTION MAKERS

Cook County Sheriff's Office
Youth Services Department
1401 Maybrook Drive
Maywood, IL 60153
TEL: 312-865-2900
Credit: Inquire
Sponsor: Cook County Sheriff's Office; InTouch Program
Contact: James E. O'Grady, Sheriff
Description: Prevention Makers involves adult role models who have demonstrated personal achievement, and who are willing to share their "secrets of success" with children and youth. The 1989 seminar presenters included a professional basketball star, an Olympics Gold Medal winner (both natives of the area), and a member of the U.S. Olympic Committee Task Force. The goal of the seminar program is to give young people a strong message about drugs.
Advice offered by the speakers included:
- Set goals, and don't let drugs keep you from reaching them.
- Believe in yourself and your abilities when you strive for goals.
- Remember that drug abuse effects not only the user but family, friends and society at large.
- Continue the seminars and find ways that they can help in substance abuse prevention activities in your schools.

Ninety students from 20 schools in three districts, and 30 adult representatives, attended the seminar. Two representatives from the local school for exceptional children also attended. Participant evaluations agreed that the seminar was highly motivating, with adult attendees encouraged by the responsiveness of the youth. At the closing of the seminar, the youth were assured that contact would be maintained by the InTouch coordinators and the Sheriff's Youth Department to provide follow-up seminars, and technical assistance from the two programs for local substance abuse prevention activities.

SHAVING CREAM LESSON - DRUG PREVENTION SEMINAR

Knox County Schools Drug Prevention Office
PO Box 2188
Knoxville, TN 37901
TEL: 615-544-3666
Credit: Inquire

Sponsor: Governor's Alliance for a Drug-Free Tennessee
Contact: Marty Iroff
Description: This drug prevention seminar had an unusual twist to show parents how easy it is to get into drugs, but how hard it is to stop until an authoritative voice comes forth. A national drug prevention specialist, director of the Atlanta-based *Parent's Resource Institute for Drug Education,* used shaving cream and peer pressure to make a point.

The training session was conducted for 45 representatives from throughout East Tennessee who are part of the *Governor's Alliance for a Drug-Free Tennessee.*

Choosing six volunteers, the specialist playfully suggested they begin sculpturing with the cream. Adults agreed to have mustaches and other "sculptures" painted on their faces and went along with the activity with increased enthusiasm - until a school official rose and ordered the group to stop. The childlike behavior immediately ceased. The primary reason for the exercise was to show parents how easy it is to get into drugs, but how hard it is to stop until an authoritative voice comes forth.

The specialist explained how he had gained the trust of the volunteers to get their cooperation, and then they "crossed the line for mature, dignified adults." He compared the shaving cream experiment to drug use among teens. He listed some of the reasons people do "dumb things" - *acceptance, survival, safety, intimacy and recognition.*

The meeting ended in a serious tone with questions and topics such as:
- "Are we serious about the war on drugs?" The drug dealers are saying we are not.
- Parents are in the biggest fight of their lives in trying to stop their children from using drugs.

A follow-up seminar was convened a month later. This one was designed to prepare parents and drug educators to train others. The two-day seminars are free.

STATEWIDE DRUG TASK FORCE CONFERENCE
Drug Trafficking Study Task Force
Virginia Department of Volunteerism
223 Governor Street
Richmond, VA 23219
TEL: 804-786-1431
Description: This is the conference of the newly-appointed Drug Trafficking Study Task Force, authorized during the 1988-89 winter general assembly as part of the State Crime Commission. It will culminate in a legislative report to the governor and the 1991 General Assembly. The "first order of business" at the conference, according to the 21 Task Force members, is to "learn the nature of the beast." More than two dozen speakers ranged from families that had been "torn apart" because of substance abuse to State PTA Substance Abuse Committee members and State Senators and officials from the private sector. Some points made in their presentations:
- Develop a thorough understanding of the problem - how it arises, why it occurs.
- Form a statewide strategy for dealing with drug abuse and related crime.
- Learn from successful efforts in personal struggles as well as legislative enforcement.
- Coordinate the state's educational, medical and law enforcement resources.
- Enact tougher drug laws.
- Execute major drug figures.
- Use "shock incarceration" for small-time social users.
- Levy mandatory sentences for anyone convicted of selling narcotics to a child.
- Increase drug enforcement resources.
- Cut or scale down selected programs so that funds can be reallocated to fight against drugs.
- Act now!

The Task Force has a two-year mandate to examine all facets of the drug problem and seek possible remedies.

INDIVIDUAL PROGRAM PROFILES

BUREAU OF DRUG ABUSE SERVICES GRANTS PROGRAM
Santa Clara County
645 South Bascom Avenue
San Jose, CA 95128
TEL: 408-299-6002
Purpose: To find and fund creative methods among community organizations to get the anti-drug message across.
Sponsor: Santa Clara County
Contact: Lily Alvarez, Assistant Prevention Services Coordinator
Description: A series of $2,000 grants from the Prevention Services Office of the County's Bureau of Drug Abuse Services has enabled social agencies and volunteer groups in Santa Clara County to continue to widen the battle against drug abuse. Tactics range from an *American Indian Youth Sobriety Pow Wow* to a group therapy session for women at Elmwood Rehabilitation Center. Grants have been allotted to organizations in Los Gatos, San Jose, Santa Clara and Mountain View. Funded programs include:
- **American Indian Youth Sobriety Pow Wow** - a program of the *Four Winds Lodge,* an intermediate alcohol recovery residence affiliated with the *Indian Center of San Jose* which includes music, dancing, arts and crafts exhibits in its program designed to appeal to youth never to abuse drugs or alcohol. [This was the second mini-grant to the lodge in 1989. The first paid for a puppet show called *BABES* which is used to educate young children about drug abuse.]
- **Anti-drug Group Therapy** - a series of 15 therapeutic educational sessions by *Lutheran Social Services* for women at *Elmwood Rehabilitation Center.* Topics covered include effect of alcohol on the fetus, ways to reduce drug abuse by children, and community services available to women.
- **Preparing for the Drug-Free Years** - a series of five workshops for parents conducted by Los Gatos Unified School District. Remaining funds were used to develop a brochure listing area organizations that provide information and seminars for parents on drug abuse by children and ways to cope with it.
- **A Clean and Sober Summer** - a rally administered by CASA (Community Against Substance Abuse), a totally-volunteer group, and the Los Gatos *Teen Counseling Center* featuring music, clowns and jugglers, and talks by former drug and alcohol abusers. [Each organization was given a $2,000 mini-grant for its part in the rally.]
- **Drug Abuse and the Foster Child** - two workshops on drug abuse prevention conducted cooperatively by the *Adult and Child Guidance Center* in San Jose and the *Foster Parents Association* in Santa Clara County. [The *Center* also sponsors training sessions in foster parents' homes to help them identify drug abuse in its early stages and learn strategies for managing the resulting problem behavior by the children.]
- **Drug Abuse Prevention: The Asian Way** - a publication for distribution to clients and agencies serving Asian Americans, to be translated in 13 Asian dialects as well as English.
- **Educational materials on drug abuse prevention** - materials developed by Santa Clara County's *Juvenile Hall Medical Clinic* based on group discussions involving input from 30 adolescents in custody working with a clinic consultant and geared toward youth coming into *Juvenile Hall* later.

The grants program was begun by the Bureau when it became evident that standard approaches were not working well enough and "more creative methods are needed to get the anti-drug message across." The Bureau received 28 proposals and gave out 20 grants.

REGIONAL YOUTH SUBSTANCE ABUSE PROJECT
(RYSAP)
United Way of Eastern Fairfield County
75 Washington Avenue
Bridgeport, CT 06604-4001
TEL: 203-334-5106
Purpose: To create a regionwide focus on youth substance abuse; to bring together diverse segments of the community to address the growing drug epidemic.
Sponsor: United Way of Eastern Fairfield County
Contact: John Higgins-Biddle, Director
Description: RYSAP (Regional Youth Substance Abuse Project) resulted from a 1984 needs assessment conducted by volunteers serving on United Way's Community Human Service Planning Council. Needs assessment results revealed that the community lacked information on the incidence of substance abuse among local youth. A United Way task force survey of 2,700 students in grades 7-12 found high levels of drug and alcohol use. After discussing survey results with residents of the six-town area, United Way determined that a consensus existed for building a communitywide campaign against youth substance abuse.
Early in 1985, United Way established RYSAP. Governed by a coordinating committee, RYSAP includes representatives from each of the region's six towns, including the chief municipal official, the school superintendent, the police chief, key business and legislative leaders, CEOs of local hospitals, and key drug and alcohol professionals. At the county level, the chief administrative judge serves on the committee, and at the state level it is the commissioner of the Department of Children and Youth Services (DCYS) and the ex-officio executive director of the Connecticut Alcohol and Drug Abuse Commission (CADAC).
In addition, three advisory committees consist of prevention experts (from each town's substance abuse council), treatment system professionals (from insurance companies, corporations, medical and psychiatric research institutes, CADAC and DCYS), and youth from area high schools. The Chairs and Cochairs from each advisory committee serve on the coordinating committee, and provide input from the grassroots level.
While approximately 150 volunteers serve on RYSAP committees, altogether more than 1,000 volunteers are involved in ongoing RYSAP activities.
In its role as coordinator, RYSAP has succeeded in closing gaps in service and communication. Key areas include:

- **Student Assistance Teams** - Through RYSAP, the police chiefs and school superintendents developed a communitywide school drug policy. The policy led to the establishment of student assistance teams made up of specially-trained school counselors, nurses, and teachers. These teams were formed in all of the junior high and senior high schools in the region.
- **First Statewide Conference on Crack-Cocaine Abuse** - One way RYSAP developed community awareness of youth substance abuse was through a statewide conference - the first of its kind - on crack and cocaine abuse. It was attended by community leaders and state legislators.
- **Anti-substance Video for Parents** - RYSAP has sponsored a number of youth-involvement projects, a notable one being a student-produced anti-substance abuse video targeted to parents.
- **Anti-Substance Abuse Training** - RYSAP has coordinated anti-substance abuse training for youth-service agency staff, teachers, and parent groups.
- **"Dribble Against Drugs"** - An awareness program for inner-city youth and parents featuring professional basketball player John Bagley of the New Jersey Nets. It took place on Bridgeport's Main Street, and drew several hundred youth who tried out their basketball skills. It was part of Substance Abuse Prevention Month and was cosponsored by United Illuminating, Freihofer's Bakery and RYSAP.
- **Printed Materials** - The project has distributed anti-drug brochures and posters to all elementary, junior high, and senior high schools in the region.

RYSAP received its initial funding from United Way - $360,000 for a three-year period. The project has since received additional funds from private foundations and individuals, as well as from municipal, state, and federal governments, including a $671,721 grant from the Robert Wood Johnson Foundation in Princeton, New Jersey, and $200,000 from the state government in 1989. These funds helped to establish the Youth Evaluation Services (Y.E.S.), administered by United Way-funded Family Services-Woodfield, a member agency of Family Service America (see separate entry).
According to the Director, "...youth substance-abuse treatment is part of a much bigger health-care crisis, involving lack of insurance coverage, health services to the poor, and lack of documentation about substance abuse." RYSAP is hoping to develop systems that can be adopted by other program leaders fighting youth substance abuse in their communities.
Publications: It's never too early to talk to your children about DRUGS; RYSAP (Regional Youth Substance Abuse Project); What To Do If Your Child Is In Trouble with Drugs and Alcohol; Here Are the Things You Can Do
Founded: 1985

VALLEY GREEN JUVENILE DRUG ABUSE PREVENTION
FACILITY
Boys & Girls Clubs of Greater Washington
1320 Fenwick Lane
Suite 800
Silver Spring, MD 20910
TEL: 301-587-4315
FAX: 301-587-8120
Purpose: To establish a drug-abuse prevention facility for juveniles in public housing.
Contact: Coordinator, Drug Abuse Prevention Programs
Description: In 1989, the *Valley Green* public housing development had the highest rate of violent crime of any housing development in Washington, DC. In the winter of 1990, the *Boys & Girls Club of Greater Washington* was awarded a $25,000 grant by the *U.S. Department of Housing and Urban Development* in a national competition to establish a new drug prevention facility in *Valley Green*. A total of one hundred such grants were awarded across the nation. The proposal was submitted through the *DC Government.*
Plans for the facility are to emphasize the reduction of juvenile drug-related violence and substance abuse through sports, recreation, educational assistance, vocational training, cultural programs and, most importantly, community involvement and support. The facility was opened in early 1990 in temporary quarters in order to provide services immediately. The *DC Department of Public and Assisted Housing* is committed to providing space, utilities and janitorial services.
Within two years after startup, a major capital campaign will be launched by the *Boys & Girls Clubs of Greater Washington* to build a permanent $3 million structure and ball fields.

YOUTH EVALUATION SERVICES (Y.E.S.)
Family Services-Woodfield
475 Clinton Avenue
Bridgeport, CT 06605
TEL: 203-368-4291
Purpose: To standardize the method of diagnosing addiction.
Sponsor: United Way of Eastern Fairfield County; Family Service America
Contact: YES Coordinator
Description: Youth Evaluation Services (Y.E.S.) is considered a vital link in the war on drugs since it standardizes the method of diagnosing addiction. Using very sophisticated medical and computerized equipment, Y.E.S. can diagnose physical, emotional,

social, and family-oriented factors through one system instead of through many different counselors or case workers. It standardizes which questions are asked to determine levels of addiction. For example, Y.E.S. allows the results of different types of treatment to be measured and evaluated, and defines what is working and what is not. In part, the process includes:

- a series of screening tests administered to the child and to all available family members;
- interviews which focus on the issues of family relationships;
- a treatment plan based on the severity of the problem and emotional support with the family

The primary benefit of the program is the avoidance of coping with many different resources to determine the most effective course of treatment. Y.E.S. not only maintains updated information about in-patient, residential and out-patient treatment availability, but the staff is knowledgeable about the types of treatment that individual insurance plans will support. Also, Y.E.S. monitors a child for a period of up to 18 months. In addition, it has built a resource bank that can make referrals to families in other parts of the country for local treatment.

Between its beginning in April 1989, and September 1989, Y.E.S. served 60 youth from the Bridgeport area.

Y.E.S. was made possible through the United Way with funds received from the Robert Wood Johnson Foundation and the state government.

Publications: What's Working and What Isn't: Evaluating Drug Treatment
Founded: 1989

DRUG ABUSE/ALCOHOLISM: DRUGS - CRIME WATCH

NATIONAL/STATE ORGANIZATIONS

ANTI-DRUG TEAMS
US/DTreas - Bureau of Alcohol, Tobacco and Firearms
Armed Criminal Enforcement Study
15th & Pennsylvania Avenue, NW
Washington, DC 20220
TEL: 202-366-4570
Objectives: To get armed drug dealers off of the streets.
Services: To help cities which have a high incidence of drug problems, the Bureau of Alcohol, Tobacco and Firearms has developed a highly visible task force program, which sends anti-drug teams into the streets and neighborhoods. This action was an outgrowth of pressure on the agency's leadership to assist Washington, DC, police in what appeared to be a losing battle with drug dealers.

The Washington, DC, team, organized in June 1989, is composed of 40 agents brought to Washington from across the country. D.C. police lent them six detectives, and provided consultation to the Team, as did the U.S. Attorney's Office, before the raids were begun.

While maintaining a tough stance, the Team is also concerned about good public relations with neighborhood residents. They are aware that the voluntary assistance of residents is needed. The tough image is one the agents cultivate through their black pants and shirts and the assault weapons they carry. Arriving on the scene, they immediately order everyone standing nearby to lie down while the entry team hits the door of the suspected crack house. The paramilitary tactics are necessary because the agents go after drug suspects who often have armed guards looking out.

Within the first three months the Team made 155 drug and weapons arrests, and took 105 guns and more than four pounds of crack cocaine off of the streets. The tightness of the organization, and the carefully-scripted raids - along with citizen involvement and assistance - are credited with the success of the Team. The anti-drug Teams are considered an experiment which, if successful, can be replicated in other cities.
Sponsor: US/DTreas - Department of the Treasury
Contact: Bureau Chief
Founded: 1989

INDIVIDUAL PROGRAM PROFILES

CITIZENS ORGANIZED PATROL EFFORTS (COPE)
SEE LAW ENFORCEMENT/CRIME PREVENTION: CRIME WATCH

CRACKDOWN
City of St. Petersburg
100 Second Avenue South
St. Petersburg, FL 33701
TEL: 813-893-7171
Purpose: To involve the community in the city's efforts to eliminate crack-related crimes.
Sponsor: St. Petersburg Sanitation Department
Contact: Robert Obering, City Manager
Description: St. Petersburg is fighting a tough battle against crack cocaine and its related crimes. Traditional approaches to law enforcement are not working in the fight against crack. What does work is a team effort by the community, working side-by-side with law enforcement, code enforcement and appropriate support personnel to send a clear message to neighborhood drug dealers that their presence will not be tolerated.

In 1988, St. Petersburg introduced CRACKDOWN, a police program that resulted in 100 drug-related arrests. With such success behind them, the City Council appropriated $387,160 for CRACKDOWN 1989, much wider in scope, calling on the services of five city departments: Police, Fire, Code Enforcement, Public Works and Sanitation, as well as residents of the neighborhoods.

The first neighborhood selected, Roser Park, began with a special neighborhood briefing for residents by city officials. The meeting was called by the residents to see what they could do to help. They were told about the "Broken Window Theory" based on crime reports - that unkept homes, littered yards and abandoned cars tell the drug dealer that local homeowners don't care, and that it is an open invitation for the drug dealer and his associates to move in and bring with them the users who rob and burglarize to support their habits. While the CRACKDOWN team went to work, residents began raking their yards, filling their garbage containers and cleaning up. This message tells the drug dealer that this neighborhood cares, watches out for each other and won't welcome drug dealers and their associates.

In the first two months the police made 116 felony arrests, 150 misdemeanor arrests, 163 traffic citations and 1,928 field interrogations, as well as 162 pieces of crack cocaine. Fire Department investigators made 969 new inspections and followed up with 443 reinspections, resulting in 1,802 citations for fire code violations. Codes Enforcement officials identified 82 empty buildings for securing and towed away 100 abandoned cars. Public Works and Sanitation workers boarded up 1,591 windows and began clearing 235 lots of litter and debris. According to city officials, this kind of result can be realized only when neighborhood residents work along with the city CRACKDOWN team.

Every several weeks, the city's special CRACKDOWN team expands to include a new neighborhood. When it expands to a new zone, it does not abandon the previous CRACKDOWN area. The same degree of police service remains, and the same high interest of the residents continues. The CRACKDOWN team appears periodically, unannounced, to ensure that the enforcement pressures are maintained.

In addition to the cooperative effort between city and neighborhood associations to clean up and fix up the area, a very active *Neighborhood Watch Network* is in place in St. Petersburg, with 200 programs and 600 residents volunteering as Crime Watch Coordinators. Each of these coordinators has block captains and volunteers who keep a watchful eye on different areas of this city. According to the City Manager, the crime effort in St. Petersburg relies on the support of the neighborhood associations. To emphasize that the city is getting such support, the City Manager wrote an article in the local paper thanking the neighborhood associations for a job well done.
Founded: 1988

GREEN COUNTRIE TOWNE PROGRAM
SEE PHYSICAL ENVIRONMENT: BEAUTIFICATION

NOT ON MY BLOCK
District of Columbia City Council
14th and Pennsylvania
Washington, DC 20004
TEL: 202-724-8000
Purpose: To assist residents in "driving drugs from their neighborhoods."
Contact: Sterling Tucker, Councilman
Description: Commissioned with creating innovative ways to prevent and stop drug abuse in Washington, DC, in early 1990 Washington's "Drug Czar" launched a participatory program designed to bond the community and the government in a partnership to maintain the District as being safe, and stop the widespread epidemic of crime and violence. The program, *Not on My Block,* encourages residents to pledge six hours a month to perform specific anti-drug activities on the block where they live. The activities - crime prevention, educational and recreational - are structured to help curb the crime and violence associated with drugs.

The program was formed as a catalyst and in no way diminishes government's role or responsibility in the war on drugs, or established community-based anti-drug programs, according to the Drug Czar.

The request for a six-hour monthly volunteer commitment by residents comes on the heels of a request by citizens in the neighborhoods to have the money seized in drug arrests returned to the communities affected by the crimes. One such request came in the form of a proposal to place parents in schools as paid teachers' aides to monitor their children during and after school, and help deter students prone to skipping school and selling drugs. ACORN (Association of Community Organizations for Reform Now) assisted residents with the proposal, and maintains that such a project would help increase the children's interest in their studies. Since any disposition of seized funds must go through lengthy and complicated procedures, it is hoped that the volunteer effort will "catch on" and play a role in the arduous climb toward drug-free neighborhoods in Washington, DC, according to the Drug Czar.

DRUG ABUSE/ALCOHOLISM: DRUGS - DRUG-FREE ZONES

NATIONAL/STATE ORGANIZATIONS

CAMPAIGN DRUG FREE
US/DoD - Naval Reserve Force
Office of the Secretary
The Pentagon
Washington, DC 20350
TEL: 202-697-7506
Objectives: To provide Naval Reservists on a volunteer basis to work with fifth- and sixth-grade students in drug abuse prevention.
Services: Involves Naval Reservists as volunteers using their own time in drug prevention programs in upper grade-levels (fifth- and sixth-graders) of elementary schools (working on the "demand" side of drug use); operates under a portion of the *Defense Authorization Bill,* in which Congress gave the Department of Defense an expanded role in drug interdiction (stemming the flow of drugs into the US); consults with federal officials, school boards, educators and principals; utilizes a standardized teaching package on drug abuse prevention with specific points to be covered by the volunteers as a basis for adapting to their own backgrounds and audiences; presents a theme of the military "protecting the country from all enemies, including drugs" to stress to children that fighting illegal drugs is really a "war;" includes Reservists from the Marine Corps and Coast Guard in addition to the Navy; works with the *Navy League of the United States,* which helps with arrangements for Reservists' appearances in local schools and administers the campaign plan; cites pre-campaign volunteer activity by Reservists in drug abuse prevention, many of whom have received awards; publishes administrative packets for Reserve commanding officers and Navy League Presidents; administers recognition program to recognize the individual Reservists who donate their time and energy to this effort.
Sponsor: US/DoD - Department of the Navy
Contact: Captain Ronnie Baker
Publications: Campaign Drug Free Teaching Module; Campaign Drug Free Administrative Package

INDIVIDUAL PROGRAM PROFILES

URBAN DRUG-FREE SCHOOLS INITIATIVE
District of Columbia Public Schools
415 Twelfth Street, NW
Washington, DC 20004
TEL: 202-724-4222
Purpose: To begin a drug-free initiative to include all DC public schools.
Sponsor: US/DEd - Department of Education
Contact: Andrew E. Jenkins, Superintendent, DC Public Schools
Description: The U.S. Department of Education and the public school system of the District of Columbia joined forces in the fall of 1989 to begin a drug-free schools initiative that includes students counseling other students and a confidential drug usage survey of all students in grades four through twelve.
The project has features for each school level, including:
- **An early intervention program for the city's elementary schools** - initially, a pilot program of 10 schools to train school staffs to recognize the signs and symptoms of early drug use in young children.
- **A peer counseling program for junior high schools** - special training for 10 student leaders in each of the District's junior high schools, away from the city, in anti-drug counseling.

- **Peer leadership and anti-drug musical performance programs in the senior high schools** - training for student leaders in high schools to help counsel their peers and run workshops for younger students; a program to select other students to perform anti-drug songs and dances at school assemblies.

Technical assistance for the project is provided by the federal government's Southeast Regional Center for Drug-Free Schools and Communities, with about $200,000 in federal funds covering the cost of technical and other assistance and services. Some of the major concerns that prompted the extensive program are:

- Average age of those using drugs for the first time has dropped from 14 to 12.
- Time and money for drug prevention efforts lowers the amount used for tutoring and textbooks.
- Drug use is costing the nation $60 billion a year in lost productivity, accidents and illness.
- Lives are being ruined by drugs in large part because children grow up in areas where drugs are the number one issue.
- Much of the success of any new anti-drug effort depends on the city's students.

The program draws on successful efforts already in place, including Operation SAND (Student Activities, Not Drugs), a successful program of the District's Spingarn high school which has resulted in an improvement in both attendance and test scores. Spingarn was honored recently, along with MacArthur School, a private school in the District, and 45 other schools across the nation at a White House ceremony in June 1989 for being drug-free.

As the pilot program progresses, additional schools will be added to reach the goal of helping school authorities and student leaders conduct an anti-drug program in every school.

Founded: 1989

WIPING OUT DRUG ABUSE DRUG FREE TEEN CENTER
Codman Square
595 Washington Street
Dorchester, MA 02174
TEL: 617-288-4430
Purpose: To provide a place that will attract at-risk teenagers and keep them off the streets.
Contact: Mattie DeLoach, Director
Description: Parents and leaders of the all-volunteer *Wiping Out Drug Abuse Drug Free Teen Center* firmly believe that youth on drugs are the exception, not the rule. "The rule" is represented by young people who have found a direction and are working hard and reaching for a goal. Programs at the Center are planned so that young people who stay out of trouble participate with at-risk and in-trouble youth. Not only do the at-risk youth see alternatives to gang violence in this way, but the ones who are doing well realize that this is a way of giving them recognition for their accomplishments. The latter - who need acceptance also - are often forgotten in the deep concern for at-risk youth.

Volunteers - some are parents - attempt to counteract what are seen as drastic changes in "trouble-spot" neighborhoods where children once would play together and adults would socialize in a family atmosphere. This is evident as the potential of each child is explored, and singers, artists and poets are found among both those doing well and those doing poorly in school. The Center provides an attractive, relaxed atmosphere where these talents can be expressed and can grow. A safe and secure place to study, do homework, and play is no longer available to youth in many neighborhood areas. One youth, walking near his house, was approached by a gang of youth who simply took his leather jacket - proudly earned with his own money - and walked off.

Officials, parents and volunteers in the program are aware of the effect on teenagers of stories constantly in the media about shootings and stabbings, drugs and crime, and the slow erosion of teenage society. Of deeper concern, however, are the many youths at the Center who have witnessed such crimes in their

neighborhoods. The raw talent discovered among the at-risk youth indicates that appropriate opportunities have not been provided for this group.

Without being judgmental or domineering, the volunteers work to demonstrate alternatives designed to "keep kids away from the war zone" (gangs and drugs). By building on latent talents of the youths, and giving them room to explore their potential, the program builds self-esteem - a crucial element in building character and confidence - and the ability to reject drugs and violence as a way of life.

YOUTH WHO CARE
PO Box 4074
Grand Junction, CO 81502
TEL: 303-245-4160
Purpose: To promote a "high-on-life" substance-free existence among school-age youth.
Sponsor: US/ACTION - VISTA
Contact: YWC Coordinator
Description: Most, but not all, of Youth Who Care's activities are conducted in the schools. The program keeps youth in Mesa County involved in outdoor recreation, with emphasis on education. They hope to provide positive experiences that will counteract the drug problems in the area.

The teenagers who operate the program have a total budget of $57,000 annually. They raise about $8,000 of that, and the rest comes from the Colorado Department of Health, Alcohol and Drug Abuse Division ($14,000) and the VISTA volunteer project ($15,000). Foundations and corporations provide $8,000 and a local business, Mt. Garfield Plumbing and Heating, picks up the $6,000 tab for office space and utilities.

Programs in the schools include YWC clubs (seven schools), YWC 3-D (Don't Drink and Drive) teams, and a speakers' bureau. The outreach arm of this program places teens as volunteers in hospitals, museums, etc. Recreational and other group activities, as well as public relations campaigns, are also implemented by the YWC organizers.

It is estimated that, during 1988-89, the participating teens reached 10,000 people through direct contact, and indirectly over half of the population, or another 40,000 people in a county that is suffering economic hardships due to the decline of its once booming oil industry. The teens come from both high-risk and low-risk groups, and many choose to continue their involvement in the program beyond their teen years. They work closely on all projects with representatives from all sectors of the community. Communities around the nation as well as in Colorado have requested information and set up similar programs in the hope of making some progress in their drug prevention programs.

DRUG ABUSE/ALCOHOLISM: FUNDING

INDIVIDUAL PROGRAM PROFILES

YOUTH LEADERSHIP VENTURE FUNDING PROGRAM
United Way of the Capital Area (Hartford)
99 Woodland Street
Hartford, CT 06105-1207
TEL: 203-249-2300
Purpose: To enable youth to make decisions about funding for youth-oriented programs in the community.
Sponsor: United Way Youth Leadership Advisors
Contact: Nancy Roberts, Youth Leadership Advisors Chairman

Description: Youth allocation leaders in Hartford have taken an issue-oriented approach to funding for youth programs. For 1989 funding, 15 students from Hartford area high schools identified youth substance abuse as the target issue of the youth community. Before proceeding, the student volunteers interviewed elected officials and human-service agency directors about priority concerns for youth. The *Connecticut Alcohol and Drug Abuse Commission* confirmed information about local teen substance abuse programs needing funding.

Students on the allocations committee were selected based on applications that had been distributed to public and private schools in the United Way's 30-town coverage area. The students make the funding decisions, while United Way staff keep them informed about the funding process. In addition to receiving training in basic allocations procedures, the students gained a thorough understanding of the substance abuse problem.

Provided with $10,000 in venture funds from the United Way, the students funded 11 local programs addressing substance abuse. These included *Students Against Drunk Driving (SADD)*, a student-produced video on anti-substance abuse peer counseling, and a positive self-development program incorporating anti-substance abuse education for elementary school children. The United Way's board of directors unanimously approved the programs selected by the students.

Publications: Students Against Drunk Driving (video)
Founded: 1988

DRUG ABUSE/ALCOHOLISM: HOMELESS

INDIVIDUAL PROGRAM PROFILES

SUBSTANCE ABUSE TREATMENT CENTER AND SHELTER
SEE RECIPIENTS: HOMELESS - DRUGS/ALCOHOL

DRUG ABUSE/ALCOHOLISM: MINORITIES/WOMEN

INDIVIDUAL PROGRAM PROFILES

CHRYSALIS HOUSE
8148 Jumpers Hole Road
Pasadena, MD 21102
TEL: 301-544-1633
Purpose: To help overcome some of the obstacles women face in trying to overcome drug abuse.
Contact: Ruth Hudacek
Description: Chrysalis House, an all-female halfway house in Anne Arundel County, Maryland, has found that the traditional approach to chemical dependency - to confront, confront, confront, and make you see what a terrible person you are - does not work with most women. Since women are far outnumbered by men in typical treatment clinics, their particular health, sexuality, employment and relationship concerns have gone unaddressed there, according to staff at the halfway house.

The program at Chrysalis House is highly structured. Self-help is a very important aspect of the process. Residents are required to attend daily meetings of self-help fellowships such as *Narcotics*

Anonymous, as well as group therapy sessions five times a week in which they listen to each other's concerns and offer critiques and suggestions. Many of the concerns relate to the guilt of having to place their children in foster homes while the mothers undergo treatment, and the fear that the children may not be returned to them. The sessions provide a place where a woman can heal without the worries or fantasies of how she appears in the eyes of the opposite sex. Some find the transition to an all-female environment rough because most of the women had adapted to a drug culture dominated by men, where women were more competitive than helpful. New residents at Chrysalis often find comfort and comraderie among women for the first time, and soon become believers. Residents stay for up to a year in the self-help program, depending on progress and related external factors. With the proliferation of "boarder babies," it has become evident that crack is devouring men and women in equal numbers. With the success of Chrysalis House, other local governments are scrambling to make their facilities more accessible to women. Also, in July 1990 the state of Maryland opened its first treatment facility for women that allows children to stay with their mothers. It is believed that such an arrangement will facilitate healing among the women in treatment.

DRUG ABUSE/ALCOHOLISM: PRESCRIPTIONS

NATIONAL/STATE ORGANIZATIONS

INFORMAL STEERING COMMITTEE ON PRESCRIPTION DRUG ABUSE
American Medical Association
535 North Dearborn Street
Chicago, IL 60610
TEL: 312-751-6579
Objectives: To promote interdisciplinary cooperation in identifying prescription drug misuse, abuse and diversion, as well as in developing specific programs to reduce inappropriate use of prescription drugs.
Services: Provides a forum for consultation with all interested private sector organizations and government agencies on the nature of the prescription drug abuse problem and the kinds of programs best suited to combat it; develops educational materials and programs for the professions and the public; works with professional organizations, licensing, regulatory and law-enforcement agencies to implement action programs at the national and state level.

DRUG ABUSE/ALCOHOLISM: SELF-HELP

INDIVIDUAL PROGRAM PROFILES

KIDS HELPING KIDS
Tri-State Drug Rehabilitation and Counseling Program
c/o Village of Hebron
Municipal Building
Hebron, OH 43025
TEL: 614-928-2261

Purpose: To offer a self-help program for young drug-abusers based on the self-help concept of Alcoholics Anonymous.
Sponsor: Tri-State Drug Rehabilitation and Counseling Program
Contact: Bonnie Clarkston or Scott Stacy, Counselors
Description: In this program, the kids themselves are the volunteers. The self-help program, *Kids Helping Kids,* is based on the premise that kids do not want to hear what adults say, but will pay attention to their peers. The program is modeled after Alcoholics Anonymous (AA) and stresses self-help and peer counseling. Young clients also offer each other support and guidance in regular rap sessions, which are led by peer counselors, some of whom are former clients. The peer counselors are trained to prod teens to be honest with themselves as well as with their parents, their peers, and the program's staff. In the sometimes emotional rap sessions, the teens express their fears, concerns and frustrations. It is emphasized to the teens that the program only helps them begin the steps they must take to stay drug-free - a lifetime commitment.

The counselors also decide when clients move up to a higher phase in the treatment program, and when they should be discharged. On average, the teens stay in the program for a year. During this time families receive counseling also to prepare for their children's return to their homes and schools. According to one expert, "If you don't change the environment at home, you're really setting up the child for defeat."

During the early phases of treatment, teens do not go to school, but they meet regularly with academic tutors and stay with families of clients who are nearing the end of their treatment.

From its inception in 1981 through spring of 1989, the program has treated 500 youths from Southwestern Ohio, Northern Kentucky and Indiana - from all social and economic levels of society. Currently, 40 youths are in the program.

A 1987 independent survey showed that more than 80% of the teens who complete the program abstain from all drugs. *Kids Helping Kids* is operated by the *Tri-State Drug Rehabilitation and Counseling Program,* a non-profit corporation. It works with other drug prevention and treatment groups, such as *Citizens Against Substance Abuse,* in the Cincinnati area.
Founded: 1981

DRUG ABUSE/ALCOHOLISM: TEEN PREGNANCY/PARENTING

TRAINING PROGRAMS

NATIONAL CONFERENCE ON DRUG ABUSE AND PARENTING*
SEE TEENAGE PREGNANCY/PARENTING

DRUG ABUSE/ALCOHOLISM: TRANSPORTATION

NATIONAL/STATE ORGANIZATIONS

CITIZENS FOR SAFE DRIVERS AGAINST DRUNK DRIVERS/CHRONIC OFFENDERS
SEE TRANSPORTATION & SAFETY: DRUGS/ALCOHOL

TRAINING PROGRAMS

DRUNK-DRIVING SIMULATOR PROGRAM AND FORUM
O'Connell High School
6600 Little Falls Road
Arlington, VA 22213
TEL: 703-237-1400
Credit: Inquire
Sponsor: Mothers Against Drunk Driving
Contact: Principal
Description: This forum was co-sponsored by *Dodge Cars* and *Mothers Against Drunk Driving.* It featured a car whose braking and steering mechanisms are specially rigged to simulate the lethargic reaction time of an intoxicated driver. More than 1300 students attended from Bishop O'Connell High - the host school in Arlington, Virginia, along with students from Yorktown High, St. Mary's Academy, George Mason High, Madison High, and others from throughout Arlington, Fairfax, and Alexandria. Most had been driving only a few months, and all were under 21, the legal drinking age in Virginia. Speakers came from the Virginia Department of Education Driver Safety Program, WAVA-FM Radio (the local disc jockey), Mothers Against Drunk Driving, and Dodge Motor Company.

The car contains a computer in which is entered the driver's weight and the number of consumed drinks to be simulated (between one and 12). The computer calculates the timing delay on the car's braking and steering based on the number of drinks needed to intoxicate drivers of varying weights. The driver attempts to complete a course in a 150- by 200-foot area without hitting cones or pop-up silhouettes. The car cannot be operated without an instructor, who can shut it down automatically when necessary.

Police officers volunteered for the program and came from all jurisdictions of Northern Virginia. The regional representative from *Mothers Against Drunk Driving* told the students, "This allows you to drive the car, which simulates some level of impairment, and get the experience from that, rather than making the dumb mistake of really drinking and driving." One speaker, who had lost a daughter when a drunk driver collided with her car, gave the students some insight not only into his family's grief, but the toll the experience had taken on the young drunk driver who killed her. The most frequent comment by students at the end of the day summed up the goals of the program: "I'll never drink and drive."

The forum followed a national public awareness campaign held at high schools in the metropolitan area, which carried the slogan, "Think... Don't drive and drink," which was exhorted throughout the program. Under the co-sponsors' program, two professional drivers zigzag across the county with the car during the school year. The car program succeeds an earlier method used by Fairfax County Police in which they had adults actually get legally drunk. The problem was that many of them didn't remember the experience afterward. One student in the forum provided a personal message from the experience which indicated that the young people will not soon forget it. "I could hear all the little cones crunching under the tires. At least they were little cones, and not little people."

INDIVIDUAL PROGRAM PROFILES

TENAFLY-ALPINE SAFE RIDES PROGRAM AND OTHERS
Boy Scouts of America
Explorer Division
State Highway 9 West
Alpine, NJ 07620
TEL: 201-768-1910
Purpose: To provide a safe ride home for teenagers who have been drinking.

Sponsor: Boy Scouts of America Explorer Division
Contact: Gerald Burstein, Safe Rides Coordinator, Tenafly-Alpine
Description: Operating out of the Tenafly Senior Center since
1984, the *Tenafly-Alpine Safe Rides Program,* sponsored by the
Explorer Division of the Boy Scouts of America, is thriving while
other safe rides programs across the state have stopped operating.
The program operates a hot line phone on Friday and Saturday
nights during the school year from 10 p.m. to 2 a.m. One or two
parents supervise three to five students who answer the phones.
The students drive to pick up their fellow teenagers and keep in
touch with the home base by citizens band radio. Students who use
the service are given anonymity.

The program requires a great deal of student participation. To
ensure the number of students required, the program maintains a
pool of about 50 student volunteers. This is a challenge, since
many students who would be willing to help do not drive. The
lack of parent volunteers - which caused the demise of several
programs - is no problem in the Tenafly-Alpine effort.

Although some parents and educators are concerned that safe rides
programs condone teenage drinking, an active parent in the
Tenafly-Alpine program sees it as "offering an immediate solution
to a specific problem." He feels that it is useful while teenage
drinking still exists and is needed to bridge the gap and save lives
while programs are continually mounted to discourage drinking
among young people. The vice principal of the Rotary
Club-sponsored Northern Valley High School Safe Rides program
in Demarest agrees. He sees the program as an interim activity
needed to save lives, coupled with the goal of a substance-free
school. And the student council president, who helped get
Northern Valley's program started, also concurs, saying, "We're
not condoning drinking; we're just trying to prevent drunk
driving." She feels that thinking that teens won't drink is "too
idealistic." A representative of the Boy Scouts Explorer Division
adds that safe rides create an awareness through the example of
sober teenage volunteers that teens shouldn't drink.

The Department of Education, while remaining somewhat neutral
on the issue, recommends considering the *Safe Homes* program,
which calls for parents to pledge not to allow alcohol to be served
at parties, and to call other parents to make sure they are home at
students' parties.

A side benefit is that teens working beside parents enter into a
dialogue about the program, discuss it with school and other
officials, and work with the adults toward improvements that will
lead more directly to the goal of substance-free schools.

The safe rides concept was originated by Darien (Connecticut)
High School in 1981 and picked up the following year by the Boy
Scouts' Explorer Division. The Boy Scouts sponsor at least 500
safe rides programs nationwide. In New Jersey, 21 programs
operated by schools, community groups, businesses, and other
organizations are sponsored by the Boy Scouts, up from eight in
1986. The Boy Scouts provide insurance for the groups they
sponsor.

EDUCATION

NATIONAL/STATE ORGANIZATIONS

AAUW EDUCATIONAL FOUNDATION
American Association of University Women
1111 Sixteenth Street, NW
Washington, DC 20036
TEL: 202-785-7700
FAX: 212-785-7797
Objectives: To award fellowships for completion of doctoral dissertation; to provide grants to women for course work leading to reentry into work force.
Services: Provides sabbaticals for public school teachers to learn how to teach girls, especially at-risk girls, more effectively in math and sciences; supports research and community projects to foster equal educational opportunities from early childhood through high school; awards fellowships for completion of doctoral dissertation, post-doctoral research, or final year in selected professions where female participation has traditionally been low.
Provides *Project Renew* grants to women to pursue course work for reentry into workforce, career change, or career advancement; provides these services through funds by members who contribute to the *AAUW Eleanor Roosevelt Fund for Women and Girls.*
Contact: Mary Boyette

AMERICAN ASSOCIATION OF UNIVERSITY WOMEN
1111 Sixteenth Street, NW
Washington, DC 20036
TEL: 202-785-7700
FAX: 202-785-7797
Objectives: To promote education and equity for women and girls.
Services: Works with 1800 local branches in every state to achieve goals through program (Issues), public policy, *AAUW Legal Advocacy Fund,* and the *AAUW Educational Foundation.*
Mounts current program issues, developed by national Task Forces of members, including
- *Promoting Individual Liberties* and *Choices for Tomorrow's Women:* publishes materials to implement these issues and provides them to branch/state leaders.
- *Public Policy:* supports legislation and initiatives that advance AAUW goals through member involvement and action with school board, city councils, state legislatures as well as Congress and the Executive Branch; works with *Lobby Corps* of members at Federal level and in several states to promote bills supported by AAUW.

Publishes *AAUW Outlook* five times a year, informing/updating members on issues supported, and new developments; also publishes *Action Alert,* monthly report on current Congressional Activity on AAUW-supported bills, which indicates action required to achieve success and to help members and leaders to be effective in public policy process.
Operates two services funded by members who contribute to the *AAUW Eleanor Roosevelt Fund for Women and Girls:*
- **AAUW Legal Advocacy Fund** supports women in higher education seeking legal redress for gender-based discrimination and recognizes innovative efforts by institutions to achieve progress for women.
- **AAUW Educational Foundation** awards fellowships for completion of doctoral dissertation, post-doctoral research, or final year in selected professions where female participation has traditionally been low; also provides *Project Renew* grants to women to pursue course work for reentry into work force, career change, or career advancement.
Also provides sabbaticals for public school teachers to learn how to teach girls, especially at-risk girls, more effectively in math and sciences; will also support research and community projects to foster equal educational opportunities from early childhood education through high school.
Contact: Mary Boyette
Publications: AAUW Outlook; Action Alert

ASSOCIATION OF VOLUNTARY ACTION SCHOLARS
Lincoln Filene Center
Tufts University
Medford, MA 02155
TEL: 617-628-5000
Objectives: To provide services to individuals who conduct, make use of, or have a serious interest in research and study of voluntary action - including the nature and characteristics of a voluntary society, voluntary associations, volunteers, and voluntary acts.
Services: Organizes, sponsors and operates conferences, forums, conventions, workshops, symposia to study voluntary action in any form (including consumer action, community development, social movements, religious activities, etc.); sponsors and organizes study panels, research teams, task forces, and other groups of voluntary action scholars; publishes a newsletter, a journal and other periodicals, books, pamphlets, abstracts that may further above-stated objectives.
Publications: Citizen Participation Abstract; Voluntary Action

Abstracts; Voluntary Action Research
Founded: 1971

NATIONAL ASSOCIATION OF SECONDARY SCHOOL PRINCIPALS

1904 Association Drive
Reston, VA 22091-1594
TEL: 703-860-0200
FAX: 703-476-5432
Objectives: To provide opportunities for the examination of issues facing secondary school education; to suggest ways business community groups and parents can provide help to improve the quality of education through volunteer assistance.
Services: Operates program offices in areas such as urban services, student activities and communications; publishes journals, monographs, special reports, program announcements, and public information materials such as *Education: An American Essential,* which informs businesses, community groups and parents of ways that they can provide volunteer assistance in the schools to help improve the quality of education; serves as administrator for the National Honor Society, the National Junior Honor Society, the National Association of Student Councils, and National Association of Student Activities Advisers; works with public and private agencies in an effort to meet the educational, employment, and social needs of today's youth.
Contact: Thomas F. Koerner
Publications: Tips for School Principals; NewsLeader; Leadership Magazine; Schools in the Middle; Education: American Essential; NASSP Bulletin
Founded: 1916

PRIVATE SECTOR INITIATIVES PROGRAM

US/DEd - Office of the Secretary
Room 4132
Washington, DC 20202
TEL: 202-732-3860
Objectives: To promote business and community involvement in the schools through private sector initiatives and volunteerism.
Services: Operates through a Staff Director in the Secretary's Office, who is assigned to work with the *White House Office of National Service,* and representatives of education and business.
Among its activities, the *Office:*
- Instructs regional offices to play a major role in dealing with the private sector
- Establishes liaisons with other federal agencies including *ACTION, HUD, HHS, Justice, Commerce, Labor, Defense, and Veterans' Administration* to avoid duplication through overlapping interests in areas that affect private sector initiatives.
- Involves external advisors from the profitmaking sector, the non-profit private sector, and from public and non-profit educational systems at elementary, secondary, and postsecondary levels.

Maintains other activities, including the dual-purpose one of informal data gathering to:
- develop some understanding of the breadth of private sector involvement with education; and
- raise awareness of Department of Education staff members relative to the subject.

Mounts projects to address the above goals such as Volunteer Week activities, briefings and in-service activities to increase the competence of key staff to deal with problems of private sector relations, solicitation of information about exemplary programs throughout the country, attendance at meetings around the country (such as *National Association of Partners in Education, PLUS,* business groups).
Conducts briefings on volunteerism for visiting groups such as women's groups, school administrator organizations, chamber of commerce groups, and school headmaster groups from Germany and England.
Plans to expand the above activities to provide a bank of support for the Education community in private sector initiatives; includes in the top priorities:
- Data Gathering
- Conferences
- Development of Existing Exemplary Programs
- Privatization
- Impediments and Incentives

Considers the above activities "the beginning of our efforts" noting that Education is the number one beneficiary of corporate philanthropy and foundation philanthropy, and that more people do volunteer work in education than in any other field except religion; plans to redirect the activities of the federal education staff to justify this type of support from the volunteer and voluntary community.
Sponsor: US/DEd - Department of Education
Contact: Dave Frengel
Founded: 1981

TRAINING PROGRAMS

FIRST STATE CONFERENCE ON SCHOOL VOLUNTEERS

Fairfax County Public Schools
Masonville Instructional Center
3705 Crest Drive
Annandale, VA 22003
TEL: 703-698-7500
Credit: Inquire
Sponsor: Virginia Department of Education
Contact: Sarah Lahr
Description: In summer 1980, an exploratory meeting was held by the State Department of Education to find ways to encourage and support school volunteerism across the state. One of the conclusions of the meeting was that financing should be sought to hold conferences about school volunteerism in different parts of the state. After the grant was obtained by the Department of Education, a planning committee was formed to determine how the grant would be used.
It was decided that the grant would be used to make the conferences available without cost to attendees. Also, the group considered both the positive and negative aspects of volunteer programs, and possible activities to be undertaken which would enhance the use of volunteers in Virginia's schools.
A subcommittee was named to develop a brief set of objectives and possible strategies for accomplishing objectives. The subcommittee met at the Virginia Division of Volunteerism offices and among their recommendations was the convening of two training seminars.
The statement of purpose for the two seminars, planned by the subcommittee, is as follows:
- To encourage and assist volunteerism by making participants more aware of the potential for volunteering in public schools.
- To develop the skills of participants for involving volunteers in their own school systems.
- To enhance support for volunteer programs by sharing of resources among seminar participants.

The Department of Education issues invitations to all schools in the state to send a "team" consisting of a principal, a teacher, a layperson or volunteer and a central office representative or volunteer coordinator, with one member designated as the team leader. The first sessions were held in Richmond and Roanoke.
In addition to school systems, "all those organizations which have a natural concern about school volunteerism" are invited to participate, including: Virginia Congress of Parents and Teachers; Virginia Education Association; National School Volunteer Program; State Division on Volunteerism, Virginia School Boards Association, Virginia Association of School Administrators,

Virginia Association of Elementary School Principals, Virginia State Chamber of Commerce, Mid-Atlantic Center for Community Education, and individuals who are considered leaders in the field. Each is asked to participate in some way, e.g., bring exhibits or volunteer as Table Topics facilitators. Workshop topics include:

Morning Session
- The PTA and the School Volunteer
- In the Beginning
- Students as Volunteers in Schools
- The Effective Management of a Volunteer Program
- Community Resources
- An Unbeatable Combination
- Involved Retired Senior Volunteers
- Viable Volunteer Assistance in the Classroom

Afternoon Session
- Research on the Effectiveness of the School Volunteer Program
- Recruiting Volunteers - and Keeping Them
- Using Volunteers to Improve Writing
- Good Management in Volunteer Programs
- In the Beginning

Evaluation forms are sent out after the conference, and the planning committee convenes to discuss those that are returned. Most respondents feel that they gain much information that can be used to enhance their volunteer programs, and request follow-up conferences. The next most frequent request is for continuing information on training workshop opportunities.

In addition to continuing conferences, two other findings of the subcommittee were reported to the full planning committee after the initial workshops:
- Establishment of a clearinghouse for resource materials and guidelines.
- Seeking support of the State Board of Education by way of a resolution endorsing school volunteerism.

The latter was passed unanimously by the Board of Education, to wit:
"The State Board of Education recognizes and endorses volunteerism in Virginia public schools as a means of assisting faculties in providing varied educational experiences for students and to further good school-community relations."

NATIONAL ACADEMY FOR VOLUNTEERS IN EDUCATION
National Association for Partners in Education
601 Wythe Street
Suite 200
Alexandria, VA 22314
TEL: 703-836-4880
Credit: Certification as NAPE Special Education Volunteer
Sponsor: National Association for Partners in Education
Contact: C.J. Reid, Projects and Membership Services
Description: Currently, NAVIE is a federally-funded event to provide for the training of trainers of volunteers who will be working with mildly handicapped students. The National Student Volunteer Program is committed to work toward making NAVIE an annual event that will include other programs in education as well as those for handicapped.

The program requires each school district's volunteer coordinator to be the team leader, with the school district selecting the other two members of the team. Ideally, the other two members should be an administrator in special education, and someone involved in the education of mildly-handicapped students. For best results, limitations were placed on numbers of participating districts, with the following NAPE selection criteria:
- the presence in the district of a strong, well-established school volunteer program;
- demonstrated support for the program by the school board, administration, and community;
- willingness of the school district to commit itself to carry out

project goals;
- demonstrated ability of the school volunteer coordinator to conduct and plan conferences and training sessions.

NAVIE training was conducted on the campus of Dominican College in San Rafael, California. The week-long training program covered:
- volunteer program management;
- delivery of volunteer services to mildly handicapped students;
- in-service training for the effective involvement of volunteers;
- how to set up, administer and provide training for three programs: kindergarten screening, the listener program, and reinforcement of academic skills;
- conference and workshop management;
- skills in group dynamics;
- the function and role of change agents; and
- public policy related to school volunteer programs and the education of handicapped students.

Commitments of participating school districts are: to give release time to the three-person team; to enable the returning team to conduct a conference to train local school volunteers and to involve/assist neighboring school districts; to allow teams to provide technical assistance to other districts (at expense of other districts); to provide evaluation data to NAPE on the local conference, technical assistance given, and other projects resulting from NAVIE training. In addition to expenses, NAPE offers Certification and ongoing assistance.

SECONDARY SCHOOL VOLUNTEERS
Lamar University
4815 Dellwood Lane
Beaumont, TX 77706
TEL: 409-838-8673; 409-892-0595
Credit: Inquire
Sponsor: School Districts; State Education Agencies; School Volunteer Organizations
Contact: Dr. Jerry Wood Tierce
Description: This training program is designed to "answer the puzzle of starting, securing, and strengthening volunteer programs in secondary schools." It is based on the premise that every school can be enriched by volunteers, and that every child can be helped. Materials used in the course come from accepted resources in the field of school volunteerism, covering topics that include the following:
- Needs and objectives of school volunteer programs
- Identifying resources
- Designing the program
- Recruiting volunteers
- Selecting and matching volunteers
- Assigning the volunteer
- Role definition of the secondary school volunteer
- Profile of the volunteer coordinator
- Characteristics of school volunteer programs
- Questions teachers might ask
- Laws concerning volunteers
- Teacher training and volunteer training
- Volunteer dedication and volunteer expertise
- Meeting the needs of adolescents; increased academic achievement

Discussions of the strengths and weaknesses of school volunteer programs, recommendations for improving and/or expanding programs, an overview of curricular specialization in volunteer administration, and evaluation of secondary school volunteer programs are topics that are introduced into the course as appropriate.

SHOW-ME SEMINARS
Missouri Volunteers
PO Box 563
Jefferson City, MO 65102
TEL: 314-751-3222

Credit: Inquire
Sponsor: Missouri Division of Family Services; Missouri School System; Missouri Volunteer Office; National School Volunteer Program
Contact: Lt. Gov. William C. Phelps, Coordinator
Description: The Show-Me Seminars are an outgrowth of the Missouri Volunteer Program's desire to focus on providing training to specific groups, instead of the volunteer community in general. The first two targeted groups were school volunteer coordinators and staff of the Division of Family Services, with plans begun for a variety of other volunteer groups interested in a marketplace for new ideas.

The school volunteer program began in response to a survey by the Missouri Volunteer Program that targeted 39 school districts interested in starting volunteer programs or wanting to increase their program's effectiveness. Regional seminars for this group were held in four locations across the state in late spring. As a follow-up to the smaller meetings, two major school volunteer seminars were held in the fall in Kansas City and St. Louis for volunteers as well as volunteer leaders in Missouri schools.

The day-long school seminars offered six workshops for school volunteers, new volunteer leaders and volunteer leaders with experience. Topics covered were:

- Kindergarten Screening
- Strengthening Your School Volunteer Program
- Volunteers as Tutors
- Setting Up a Volunteer Program for Children with Special Needs
- Starting a New School Volunteer program
- Involving Older School Volunteers

During the summer, workshops for Division of Family Services volunteer leaders were held in five cities to provide in-service training, promote a sharing of ideas about successes and failures, focus on supervision and motivation of volunteers, and offer new insights to enable the Volunteer Division to expand and grow. Overall goals were:

- to expand the number of DFS volunteer programs; and
- to strengthen and promote growth of existing programs.

The nursing home volunteer program was the third target for Show-Me Seminars, with other groups who would benefit from the program being included as time and resources permitted. Publicity about the Seminars resulted in requests from groups needing this type of assistance, thereby eliminating much of the time-consuming groundwork in locating and prioritizing volunteer groups in need of training.

SKILLS EXPANSION THROUGH RESOURCE VOLUNTEERS IN EDUCATION (SERVE)
Chapel Hill Training Outreach Project
Lincoln Center, Merritt Mill Road
Chapel Hill, NC 27514
TEL: 919-967-8295
Credit: None
Sponsor: Chapel Hill Training Outreach Project
Contact: Jeanne C. James
Description: This training for volunteers and volunteer coordinators is conducted once each month at each site. The series totals five sessions, which are:

- New Friends which examines attitudes toward the disabled and introduces an innovative approach to mainstreaming that uses peer-sized dolls to teach children about disabilities.
- Role of Volunteer Coordinator/Role of Volunteer which clarifies these roles in the center staffing design
- Assessment which explores the purpose of assessment and how to apply assessment results in developing specific remedial activities.
- Curriculum which focuses on teacher-made materials and the correlated day approach to curriculum development for the young child.

- Accentuate the Positive which addresses the use of positive attitudes and techniques for effective teaching.

Participants in the training program include volunteers and the coordinators with whom they would be working. The training is designed to promote a cooperative relationship between the agency staff and the volunteer, a respect for the services which a volunteer can provide, and a positive attitude towards staff, volunteers and, especially, handicapped children.

In addition to the training, the Project provides participating agencies with publicity aids such as brochures, posters, radio and television PSAs (public service announcements), and newspaper articles. This material is designed to aid the agency in recruiting.

VOLUNTEERS: A CAPITAL IDEA*
National Association of Partners in Education
601 Wythe Street
Suite 200
Alexandria, VA 22314
TEL: 703-636-4880
Credit: Inquire
Sponsor: National Association of Partners in Education
Contact: Carol Pierce
Description: In addition to its training program, the National School Volunteer Program's tenth annual conference will include two very important "firsts" in the ongoing development of the school volunteer movement. One, a panel discussion will highlight the newly-established National Coalition for Parent Involvement in Education (NCPIE) convened by NAPE. Two, NAPE will charter its first State Affiliates.

Special conference features in addition to the two "firsts" above will be the nationally-prominent faculty from the field of education and volunteerism, seminar leaders recruited by popular demand, regional and state meetings aimed at strengthening school volunteer programs at the state level, and NAPE Awards presentations.

Workshops are scheduled that cover a wide variety of topics based on feedback from the field over the past year, and including:

1-1/2 hour Workshops:
- Small Rural Programs
- Intergenerational Programs
- Career Development for Parents and Children
- Mentor Program for Gifted and Talented Children
- 2A Tutoring (Peer/Cross-Age)
- Adopt-A-School
- Basic Skills
- ESL
- Special Needs
- Student Trades

Panels:
- Volunteers and Desegregation (tentative)
- Older Volunteers

Short Workshops:
- Developing a Volunteer Program
- Teacher Training
- PR/Communications

3-hour Session:
- Business/Community Education

Forum:
- Parents/Community Involvement/Effective Schools

WHOLEFFECTS EDUCATION: NATIONAL CONFERENCE
Wholeffects Institute
IRM Corporation
4 Terrace Drive
PO Box 650
Nyack, NY 10960
TOLL FREE: 800-845-8402
Sponsor: IRM Corporation
Contact: Director of Conference Services

Description: This conference was developed by the *Wholeffects Institute* as a joint training event with the *University of Texas at Austin's* fifth annual *Conference for Educational Excellence.* It is designed as a systematic approach which involves the total community in the education of all children and adults. Participants in *Wholeffects Education* workshops - both paid and volunteer - include educators of gifted and talented people, substance abuse specialists, staff development specialists, migrant education specialists, compensatory education specialists, assessment specialists, special education personnel, school board members, vocational educators, at-risk coordinators, administrators, counselors, teachers, parents, business leaders, and others. Presentations include:

- Implementing Wholeffects In Your Community: Law Enforcement and Other Agencies;
- Community Involvement in Sex Education;
- A Magnet School and Its Whole Effect: Miracle in Miami; and
- Site-Based Leadership and Its Role in Wholeffects Education.

Presenters for the above topics come from universities, government, the art community, schools, and independent consulting firms. In addition, special presentations are provided by leaders from across the country.

The event is composed of five general sessions and 30 breakout sessions. Ample time is provided for participants to share ideas and materials.

WORKSHOPS FOR VOLUNTEER COORDINATORS AND VOLUNTEERS IN EDUCATION*
ADDitions School Volunteers
Orange County Public Schools
6200 Chancellor Drive #500
Orlando, FL 32809-5697
TEL: 305-422-5817
Credit: Inquire
Sponsor: ADDitions
Contact: Eleanor Y. Fisher
Description: A series of workshops is held annually September through mid-November for school volunteers, prospective volunteers, retired citizens, and persons interested in education, with two of the workshops addressing school-based volunteer coordinators. Topics include:
Volunteer Coordinators: These workshops include techniques of recruiting, record-keeping, inter-personal skills, recognition, etc., broken down into sessions of interest to new coordinators and those that will benefit the experienced coordinator. These are tailored to meet current needs, with programs added as the need indicates (e.g., Circle of Motivation was added in 1983 when coordinators expressed an interest in this subject).
Volunteers: These workshops address specific areas in which the volunteer is the person who is responsible for managing the program. Workshops include Math Superstars, Arty-Facts, Creative Writing, Learning Disabilities, Science, Un Poquito de Espanol (a Little Bit of Spanish), Community Resource Volunteers, Listening to Children/New Students, Reading Support, Art * Art * Art, Speak for Yourself (Speaking in Public), Winning Relationships - Communications Skills, Storytelling, Signing for the Deaf, ESL (English-As-A-Second Language), Listening, and others.
All workshops include manuals, guides and other relevant materials (e.g., Holiday Art, a guide for the Arts program, Fountain Valley, a reading support system, Color Slide Program of the Great Masters for the artifacts program, and What's Right With Our Schools for coordinators' programs).
Two or three additional workshops often are conducted in early fall and spring. Some of these are supplementary, others on subjects that have not been covered in previous workshops. These are based on expressed needs. The series of workshops is in its twelfth year.

INDIVIDUAL PROGRAM PROFILES

BERKS SCHOOLCASTING*
Reading and Berks County Chamber of Commerce
541 Court Street
Reading, PA 19601
TEL: 215-376-6766
Purpose: To create a dedicated educational access channel.
Sponsor: Berks County Schools; Berks-Suburban Cable Company; Berks County Chamber of Commerce
Contact: J.F. Horrigan, President
Description: Berks Schoolcasting is an organization of volunteers from local schools, industry and government media personnel who meet monthly during the school year to coordinate the scheduling of locally-produced educational television programs. Membership is open to all public, parochial and private schools and colleges in Berks County as well as to any community group or individual willing to work on a cooperative voluntary basis toward a common goal.
The process began in 1962 when the Chamber of Commerce created the Public School Educational Television Advisory Committee to explore and report on ways in which educational TV involving the local school system might be provided. Although the Committee determined that it was cost-prohibitive, Berks County continued to seek ways to provide the service. The first encouraging move was made by Berks TV Cable Company, who offered to wire two school buildings and interconnect them via the cable system. When Berks County Schools was approached with this offer of free help, officials agreed to purchase the necessary internal equipment for the two schools.
In addition, in 1969, the Superintendent of Schools created the "Berks County Educational Television Subcommittee" to serve as a clearinghouse and monitor of the initial efforts.
As citizen involvement increased, and additional schools began to develop media programs, the Berks Suburban Cable Company continued to assist in wiring buildings. In addition, they provided, and still provide, technical assistance and information on the acquisition and use of television and related equipment. Some of the schools and their programs follow:
Governor Mifflin School District - Sports Program, Cooperation with Community Groups, District Feature Program, In-Service Programs, Seasonal Programs.
Kutztown Area School District - weekly half-hour program transmitted to local community inviting citizens to interact on pre-announced subject with students and an invited volunteer specializing in the week's subject.
Central Catholic High School - oral history project in cooperation with elderly; National/State Political Convention with candidates present.
Several additional school districts, business/industry, and local colleges also develop and present innovative programming through this voluntary effort, thus providing a vehicle for interaction that was created by an unmet need within the community.
Founded: 1962

BUSINESS/INDUSTRY ADVISORY COUNCIL (BIAC)
Fairfax County Public Schools
Burkholder Administration Center
10700 Page Avenue
Fairfax, VA 22030
TEL: 703-246-2502
Purpose: To involve the business community in education through service on an advisory committee to advise school officials on specific matters.
Sponsor: Fairfax County Public Schools; local businesses
Contact: Robert Spillane, Superintendent of Schools
Description: The *Superintendent's Business/Industry Advisory Council* has 33 members who serve on four committees created to study issues and make recommendations to the school system in

the following areas:

- International Education (Arthur Anderson & Co. and SYCOM)
- Teacher Professionalization (Hekiman Laboratories)
- Vocational Education (Dynasty Enterprises of Virginia)
- Outlook 2010 (Bell Atlantic and Squibb Corporation)

A new thrust in 1989 by the Council was students with disabilities, and an additional committee was formed as the year progressed:

- Disabled Workers in the Business Setting (Sovran Bank)

After six years of serving the school system, Council members decided to visit *Thomas Jefferson High School for Science and Technology* to observe the results of the Council's work that started in 1983. The school, which opened its doors in 1985, was supported by the Council with funding through the *Fairfax County Public Schools Education Foundation*. This provided an outstanding example of how cooperation between the public schools and the business community can achieve goals not usually possible for either sector alone. The first class was graduated in June 1989.

The 1990 conference sponsored by the Council is *Outlook 2010* bringing together business and education leaders. It is designed to explore the future - what Fairfax County will look like and what students will need to know in order to be prepared to enter the work force in the year 2010.

The Council grows every year with new businesses stepping forward with ideas and assistance, and an opportunity for young people to reciprocate and learn what cooperation is all about.

PARENT TO PARENT, ATTENTION ON ATTENDANCE
District of Columbia Public Schools
Volunteer Services/Training Branch
415 Twelfth Street, NW
Washington, DC 20004
TEL: 202-724-4400
Purpose: To expand the effective use of parent-volunteers in secondary schools while improving attendance through a system-wide notification process.
Sponsor: DC Public Schools
Contact: C. Vanessa Spinner/Claryce Nelson
Description: Parent to Parent, Attention on Attendance is a volunteer program that began in 1981 in response to a need to provide parents with timely notification of secondary student absence.
The project, which is totally volunteer, is coordinated by the DC Public Schools and offers parents of secondary school students a meaningful opportunity for involvement.
The unique element of this project is the *Community Awareness Committee,* a group of local business and organization volunteers, who promote the concept of better attendance and work toward rewarding the schools with most-improved attendance.
Volunteer parents are given guidelines and orientation and are governed by the rules of the DC Board of Education on volunteers. The goal of the project is to assist in the improvement of secondary student attendance.
Founded: 1981

SCHOOL COUNCIL VOLUNTEERS
Harris Bank
503 North Washington Street
Naperville, IL 60540
TEL: 312-420-3500
FAX: 312-420-6670
Purpose: To encourage employees to volunteer for leadership roles in the community.
Sponsor: Harris Bank
Contact: B. Kenneth West, CEO
Description: School Councils are new vehicles in the Chicago area to encourage citizen involvement in the schools. Harris Bank is encouraging its employees to run for local Chicago school council

elections. In addition to pointing to school reform as "our one best shot at improving education for the young people in this city," Bank officials are interested in school reform because of the need they have for a bank of qualified employees.

Harris Bank encourages its employees in this effort by allowing release time to campaign and, when elected, to attend meetings called during business hours, as well as arranging flexible work hours to allow the volunteer employee to fill obligations that may arise. Those not elected who are parents of school-age children will be allowed these privileges also at times when parents are important to the issue.

In addition, the Bank trains employees for the responsibilities involved in being a local school council member. Nominees are given ample time to campaign, and other employees are encouraged to work with them on their campaigns. Flexible time, and time off with pay, is offered to employee campaign workers also.

Following Harris' announcement, other Chicago area corporations joined the program.

EDUCATION: ADOPT-A-SCHOOL

NATIONAL/STATE ORGANIZATIONS

NATIONAL ASSOCIATION OF PARTNERS IN EDUCATION
601 Wythe Street
Suite 200
Alexandria, VA 22314
TEL: 703-836-4880
Objectives: To improve the quality of education in America through the promotion of effective partnerships and the collaboration of individual citizens, business, public agencies, community organizations and the education community.
Services: Provides technical assistance; operates the NAPE Information Bank (descriptions of successful school volunteer projects); develops training materials for school volunteers, including those who work with the handicapped; publishes two newsletters, *Partners in Education* (monthly) and *School Volunteering* (quarterly); provides over 20 publications focused on the training and support of citizens involved in enriching and enhancing education.
Contact: Carol Pierce

US/WHITE HOUSE - PARTNERSHIPS IN EDUCATION
US/White House - Office of National Service
White House
Room 34
Washington, DC 20500
TEL: 202-56-6676; 212-456-6573
Objectives: To increase private and federal involvement in public schools around the country through volunteer "school adoptions."
Services: Directs heads of various federal departments and agencies to form partnerships with schools to help improve the quality of education; works with the Department of Education to provide seminars around the country at which business leaders, community groups, and other organizations are encouraged to become more involved in their community's schools; sets an example through the October 1983 adoption of the Congress Heights Elementary School by the White House following a requested "needs evaluation" on the best ways to assist the school with volunteer help (not federal dollars), and by making this program a priority (the White House adoption kicked off a nationwide drive to promote private sector involvement in education); provides information on the overall program, Partnerships in Education,

specific information as to roles of the schools and the businesses or community organizations who adopt them, and/or on the White House local adoption program to any individual or group on request.

INDIVIDUAL PROGRAM PROFILES

ADOPT-A-SCHOOL
School Volunteers
440 East First Street
Salt Lake City, UT 84111
TEL: 801-328-7344
Purpose: To encourage established businesses and organizations to help the school system enhance the students' learning experience.
Sponsor: Salt Lake School District; business/industry; community groups
Contact: Gene Berry
Description: School Volunteers, Inc., was organized in 1969 to help supplement and enrich the educational program of the Salt Lake School District. Some 5,000 volunteers each put in over 215,000 hours of service in a number of volunteer projects. One such project is the "Adopt-A-School" program.
The Adopt-A-School program is a partnership between business and community organizations and the schools. Businesses currently involved in the program include Mountain Bell, Mountain Fuel, Kennecott Copper and IBM. Participants also include church groups, civic groups, military units, government groups, service groups, athletic teams and fraternal organizations. Volunteers in the program are given released time by employers to assist in expanding the curriculum of the adopted school. Since volunteers from the business community include executives and middle-management persons as well as on-the-line workers and self-employed men and women, their contributions run the spectrum of student interest. In addition to communicating an understanding of the business world, they provide technical assistance, job-shadowing services, training, tutoring, and materials.
Leaders of the volunteer-providing businesses and organizations who adopted a school because they considered it a worthwhile community service project that would improve their public images have found an unexpected side benefit. Employees reinforce their own skills and feelings of self-worth through this involvement, thereby improving morale and production at the job site.
Schools have discovered that, in addition to teaching students the principles of the free enterprise system and broadening their knowledge of the community, the program builds students' self-esteem, increases their interest in education, and has helped to bring about a marked reduction in dropouts among the seventh to twelfth-grade students it serves. Also, as a project of a model programs being replicated across the state and in other states, many other school districts benefit from its successes.
Other projects of the overall School Volunteers, Inc., program are:
  ● **SMILES** (Senior Motivators in Learning and Education Services) - a project for volunteers 55 years of age and older.
  ● **Basic Skills Program** - a variety of volunteer tutoring programs at the elementary, intermediate and high school levels.
  ● **Public Awareness Committee** - to develop awareness of school volunteer programs (coordinated with an advisory board committee).
  ● **Volunteer Training Program** - to plan and execute a variety of workshops and classes for teachers and volunteers, designed to enhance the involvement of volunteers in the classroom.
Handbooks for principals, volunteers, coordinators, and teachers have been printed. Inquire for further information.
Founded: 1969

ADOPT-A-SCHOOL
Fairfax County Public Schools
The Burkholder Center
10700 Page Avenue
Fairfax, VA 22030
TEL: 703-246-2502
Purpose: To enrich school curiculum through partnerships with local businesses.
Sponsor: Fairfax County Public Schools
Contact: Adopt-A-School Coordinator
Description: Since 1986, more than 50 businesses have entered into Adopt-A-School programs with Fairfax County. This business involvement enriches the students' curriculum in a number of ways. Some of the most recent partnerships include:
Centreville High School and Media General - Media General assists with the school's communication program by supporting student internships in areas such as cable installation, engineering, computer programming, and studio production and by providing speakers. Centerville High provides Media General employees with complimentary tickets to athletic events, plays, and concerts. Media General also has access to the school's facilities.
Falls Church High School and Mobil Oil - Mobil Oil employees serve as role models through a mentor program, tutor students in basic skills, serve as classroom speakers, provide internships for students, and offer career orientations. Falls Church High School provides parenting seminars and workshops on educational issues, entertainment for Mobil events, catering services, and the use of athletic facilities.
Langston Hughes Intermediate School and Tandem Computers - Tandem employees tutor students, judge schoolwide competitions, and lecture students on career opportunities. Additionally, Tandem invites students and faculty to attend selected teleconferences and to tour the company's facilities. In return, Hughes Intermediate provides student choral, band, and string ensemble concerts and student artwork for the company offices. Tandem employees are invited to attend school functions. Students also provide information for Tandem's publication.
Mount Vernon High School and the U.S. Engineering and Housing Support Center - The government agency provides science fair judges, lecturers in numerous classes, mentors for groups of minority students, and information about careers in the military and government for students. In return, students offer to correspond with overseas military personnel, to provide artwork, and to give band and coral performances. The government agency also has access to the school's facilities.
Fair Oaks Hospital and Navy Elementary School - Students take tours of hospital departments to learn about health care, career opportunities in health fields, and hospital services. In return, Navy students make graphics to be used to visually stimulate premature babies, publish books for hospital visitors, and prepare audio- and videotapes for patients.

ADOPT-A-SCHOOL
San Jose Unified School District
1605 Park Avenue
San Jose, CA 95110
TEL: 408-998-6000 (schools); 408-279-7900 (Water Co.)
Purpose: To introduce students to the business world while employees share business talents with students.
Sponsor: San Jose Unified School District
Contact: Gayle Jones (school); Scott Yo (Water Co.); Theresa Johnson (Chamber of Commerce)
Description: In San Jose, businesses share their human resources, expertise, technology, equipment, etc., to expose students to the business world. When appropriate, businesses include written curricula to be incorporated into classroom teaching. In turn, students give back to the businesses by performing skits and musicals or sending pictures and murals.
Every school in the San Jose Unified School District has been

adopted except one, and some have more than one sponsor. The San Jose program was the first in the area and served as a strong pilot for other districts to emulate.

Science magnet *Hacienda Valley View Elementary School* was adopted in 1966 by the *San Jose Water Company.* The school emphasizes science and maintains an outdoor biology lab designed to simulate the Santa Clara Valley, with two ponds connected by a small creek. Aside from maintaining the ecology ponds, the water company provides curriculum and helps with field trips that focus on water conservation. Curricula is available for every grade level.

To emphasize saving and conserving water, the first act of the water company was to install an organic filtering system to avoid wasting water during cleaning of the ecology ponds. The company continually places emphasis on the relation of water to the environment and the importance of conserving it.

Students reciprocate in many ways, including sending pictures, student stories and murals to water company employees.

Sponsoring businesses benefit by developing business-literate students for the future and by raising the morale of employees who volunteer for the program.

ADOPT-A-SCHOOL*
Knoxville Volunteer Coordinating Center
35 Market Square Mall
Knoxville, TN 37902
TEL: 614-525-9964
Purpose: To create a partnership between a business or community organization and a public school for their mutual benefit.
Sponsor: Knoxville Coordinating Center, Knoxville City Schools
Contact: Donna W. Bletner
Description: Members of the sponsoring organizations formed an advisory council of 10 (two from each group). The Junior League provided funds for printing a brochure for prospective business adopters and for postage and incidentals. The League also promised to provide five persons to serve as liaisons between a school and a business after the formal adoption.

The Advisory Council meets about once a month to organize calls on prospective business adopters and discuss potential adoptees (schools). Plans are also made for at least one meeting of all participants each year to facilitate intercommunication and stimulate ideas for new projects by the schools and their adopters. Junior League members serve as liaisons to help school and business coordinators plan activities and carry them out. Each person has two to four adoptions.

Both liaisons and Advisory Council members attend formal adoption ceremonies at the schools. These ceremonies are planned by the school and its adopter. The School Volunteer Coordinator puts out an occasional News from the Adopted Schools to keep participants informed. A Junior League member always chairs the Advisory Council. Funding is provided by the Junior League of Knoxville.
Publications: News from the Adopted Schools

AMERIBANC ADOPT-A-SCHOOL PROGRAM
Ameribanc Savings Bank
7630 Little River Turnpike
Suite 932
Annandale, VA 22003
TEL: 703-658-5555 (No. VA)
TOLL FREE: 800-638-7768 (nationwide)
Purpose: To follow through on its belief that *Tomorrow's Future Rests with Today's Youth.*
Description: To help combat the problems of budget cuts and teacher shortages in schools, *Ameribanc Savings Bank* has adopted six elementary schools in southeastern Virginia (Birdneck, Kingston, Tallwood, Providence, Thoroughgood, and Fairlawn schools). The school/business partnership program in the Virginia Beach area began as a pilot in 1984, involving businesses, military commands and civic organizations. The purpose was to utilize

available resources in the community in order to add a broader dimension of education.

The program is considered a success in many ways. Businesses are able to increase their visibility while providing valuable services. Schools are able to enrich their curriculum. The community receives better-educated citizens.

Participating organizations provide expertise on many topics ranging from banking and computers to firefighting and water safety. Financial assistance through contributions of materials and equipment, along with sponsorships of school activities, and donations of services is also essential to the success of the partnership between schools and businesses.

Ameribanc's involvement has been very beneficial to all involved, including our bank employees. This is very obvious at the *Hilltop Branch* as they proudly wear their *Rough Reader* T-shirts donated by the bank for participants in Birdneck Elementary School's *Reading Rodeo Round-Up* program.

We have provided guest speakers for topics on money, especially highlighting the importance of saving. Many students opened savings accounts at their sponsored branch offices after our presentations. In addition to doing special learning activies, *Ameribanc* sponsors advertisements in school yearbooks and a gifted and improved student award, and displays children's artwork and hosts school choruses for mini-concerts at the branches.

From a spokesman for the bank: "*Ameribanc* is excited to have this opportunity to work with today's youth and looks forward to continuing our successful partnerships with our schools."

BUSINESS/SCHOOL PARTNERSHIP PROGRAM
Community Relations
3830 Richmond Avenue
Houston, TX 77027
TEL: 713-892-6384
Purpose: To involve business in public education.
Sponsor: Houston Independent School District
Contact: Mrs. Terry Chauche, Director
Description: In 1988-89, the *Houston Independent School District (HISD)* had as much real involvement with the business community as any school district in the country. The Houston story differed from other cities, though, in that ours was particularly people-intensive. It also differed in that, along with a number of programs initiated by HISD with the business community, there were a number of organizations outside the HISD that initiated and developed programs. The various programs are not coordinated under any one umbrella.

The *Business/School Partnership Program* was initiated by HISD in 1980 with the support of the *Houston Chamber of Commerce.* It grew progressively from 17 connections in 1980-81 to 682 in 1988-89. In 1986, the chamber started active recruitment efforts to supplement that of the school district.

As to the 1988-89 contributions of the business community to HISD, some were partnerships or adopt-a-school; some were other connections; some were large; some were small; some were HISD-initiated; some were initiated from the outside. All of them involved the business community and HISD schools. Students at risk of dropping out are the target of a majority of the programs. The major thrust continued to be to involve as many business people as possible, as often as possible, directly in the schools. Business people, whatever the activity, serve as motivators, role models, and mentors. They are virtually unanimous in their support of HISD's efforts. There were:
- 682 connections
- 262 businesses and 2,250 business people involved
- 237 schools that had minimal business involvement
- 110 schools that had regular involvement of business people
- 72 substantive partnerships
- $7,000,000 estimated time, fund, and in-kind donations

Not only did 1988-89 see a 15% increase in numbers of businesses and connections, it saw the addition of some very substantive partnerships and significant deepening of several existing partnerships.

Partnerships included Aetna, Allstate Insurance, Altrusa Club, American Airlines, American General Life, American Institute of Architects, American Productivity & Quality Center, and 640 other businesses and organizations.

Founded: 1980

FAMILY LIFE AND AIDS INSTRUCTION PROGRAM
SEE AIDS: EDUCATION

PARTNERSHIPS (*formerly Adopt-A-School*)
US/DoD - Commander Naval Base San Diego
937 North Harbor Drive
San Diego, CA 92103-5100
TEL: 619-532-1514
Purpose: To address growing concern for the unmet needs of the local education system.
Sponsor: US/DoD - Commander Naval Base San Diego
Contact: Personal Excellence Coordinator
Description: The Adopt-A-School concept had its beginnings in Memphis, Tennessee, when a group of businessmen became concerned about the quality of the local education system. Working with education leaders, they devised a program in which individual businesses formally "adopted" a local elementary school, high school, or community college. The adoptive business provided its resources on a voluntary basis to enrich the school's curriculum. Sometimes the resources were financial, but most of the time they were human. The program has been duplicated in other large cities across the country.

In San Diego, California, school partnerships by the *United States Navy* provided large scale military support for the first time. During the year ending in May 1983, local Navy commands adopted nine schools. There are now over 60 Navy-school partnerships.

Activities - Although the group and the school spokespersons may decide on unique projects based on special needs in a specific situation, all provide the following basic services in some form:
- tutoring and counseling of students;
- presenting mini-courses in specialty areas such as science, electronics, computer technology and athletics;
- conducting tours of their places of business to bring students and teachers closer to vocational opportunities and the work environment;
- helping students in developing extracurricular skills such as photography and woodworking;
- supporting and participating in school events such a field trips, dances, concerts, athletic events and graduation exercises;
- developing special school projects and displays;
- establishing pen pal relationships in order to expand students' awareness of life at sea and in foreign lands.

Benefits to the Navy partner are numerous, and very similar to benefits to a business. The morals and self-esteem of the volunteer tutors are increased, as well as their sense of community involvement and the satisfaction that comes from making a contribution. Also, such a program helps to assure the development of the future technical and leadership skills needed for defense industries and military services. In addition, it strengthens basic interpersonal and technical skills of the Navy volunteer. Other benefits include:
- highlighting the contributions made to communities through routine defense activities, in this case, pointing out the potential for assistance to communities by the nation's largest employer and educational organization - the *Department of Defense.*
- enhancing attractiveness of defense occupations, thereby supporting recruitment objectives.
- helping to relieve boredom and dependency on drugs and

alcohol by defense personnel by providing constructive free time activity; for ship personnel, increasing human support network in homeport, making travel and return more enjoyable.
- creating good community relations through better understanding and appreciation of the defense program by students, educators and business people.

Benefits to the school partner are numerous, and include providing positive role models for students who increasingly come from single family homes; fostering a better understanding of, and support for, the school system leading to increased participation by all members of the community; improving education quality by tapping non-traditional resources and bringing textbook learning closer to real vocational applications; and replacing student boredom, apathy and drug/alcohol use with participatory career development activities.

Overall benefits include evidence that money is not the only solution (human resources can make the difference) during this era of scarce resources; the fact that defense installation personnel are taking responsibility as members of the wider community; the meeting of a need to address the deficiencies of the education system, and the move toward strengthening the education system, on which the economic and military security of the country depend.

Founded: 1983

EDUCATION: ADULT

NATIONAL/STATE ORGANIZATIONS

AMERICAN ASSOCIATION FOR ADULT AND CONTINUING EDUCATION
1112 Sixteenth Street, NW
Suite 140
Washington, DC 20036
TEL: 202-463-6333
Objectives: To increase opportunities for lifelong learning for all citizens.
Services: Provides leadership in advancing education as a lifelong learning process by: serving as a central forum for a wide variety of adult and continuing education special interest groups, advocating for the field of adult and continuing education, and encouraging the use of research, and to assist in the development of human resources; publishes *Adult Education, Lifelong Learning: An Omnibus of Practice and Research,* etc.
[Formerly Adult Education Association of the United States of America and National Association for Public Continuing and Adult Education]

COUNCIL OF NATIONAL ORGANIZATIONS FOR ADULT EDUCATION
Association of Junior Leagues
660 First Avenue
New York, NY 10016
TEL: 212-683-1515
Objectives: To provide an opportunity for adult education organizations to work together and avoid duplication in services to programs; to assure that life experience is considered in education areas.
Services: Sponsors "I Can" program, a self-administered test which lists the competencies an individual has acquired through experience; currently expanding the "I Can" program; holds periodic task force and board meetings.

ELDERHOSTEL
SEE RECIPIENTS: OLDER PERSON - EDUCATION

INSTITUTE OF LIFETIME LEARNING
SEE RECIPIENTS: OLDER PERSON - EDUCATION

SYRACUSE UNIVERSITY CONTINUING EDUCATION PROGRAM
Syracuse University
224 Huntington Hall
Syracuse, NY 13210
TEL: 315-443-1870
Objectives: To keep information as current as possible in the field of adult education.
Services: Solicits manuscripts for reproduction and distribution that will help keep adult educators informed of the latest theories and practices in the field; funds the editing, printing and distribution of information.

TRAINING PROGRAMS

REFUGEE VOLUNTEER TUTOR TRAINING
SEE EDUCATION: ETHNIC/BILINGUAL

INDIVIDUAL PROGRAM PROFILES

ADULT TUTORIAL PROGRAM
Keene State College
Cheshire House
67 Winchester Street
Keene, NH 03431
TEL: 603-352-1909/Ext. 298
Purpose: To meet the educational needs of undereducated Cheshire County residents 16 years of age or older.
Sponsor: State Office of Adult Education/Keene School District
Contact: Betty Cox, Coordinator
Description: The Adult Tutorial Program (ATP) began in September 1975. The ATP is sponsored by the State Office of Adult Education and the Keene School District. It is a volunteer-based program, relying on volunteer tutors.
People interested in becoming tutors need no previous experience, as they are trained and supervised by the coordinator. Trained tutors are assigned one student or more; they meet at a time and place of mutual convenience. Hours are flexible but a minimum of two hours per week is suggested. In-service workshops for tutors are offered throughout the year to provide additional training and support. In one typical year the ATP in Cheshire County served 145 clients-adults in more than 25 communities. Thousands of adults in Cheshire County have less than a eighth-grade education, and many more have less than 12 years of formal education. In many cases, such undereducated adults are locked into second-class status because they are unable to cope in our competitive system. Often they are the last hired and the first fired.
The ATP offers free, one-to-one teaching for the adult learner. Working with their own tutors in a non-threatening atmosphere, adult learners can make progress. Their names are kept confidential.
The ATP's main emphasis is on basic reading and writing, but tutoring is also provided for adults who want to learn English as a second language and for those who need help to pass the high school equivalency test (GED). Students may also learn math and life-coping skills (filling out applications, telling time, handling money, reading directions, etc.). Students can study for their drivers' licenses or for U.S. citizenship.
Although most ATP students have no special problems, the tutors have helped many with learning disabilities, hearing or vision impairments, or other difficulties.
The ATP is part of Adult Basic Education in New Hampshire and serves largely the same population. Most adult learners have jobs and some cannot attend evening classes because they work nights. ABE classes are offered from October through April, while ATP tutors are usually year-round. ATP often provides individual help for the profoundly undereducated student, for whom class time is not enough or is too public.
Founded: 1975

VITA (VOLUNTEERS IN TEACHING ADULTS)
Oakton Community College/MONNACEP
7901 North Lincoln
Skokie, IL 60077
TEL: 708-635-1426
Purpose: To involve of volunteers in instructional programs for adults.
Sponsor: Federal, State and County Resources
Contact: Marilyn Antonik
Description: For the past eleven years, *Volunteers in Teaching Adults (VITA)* has utilized community volunteers to respond to the needs of limited English proficiency and basic literacy adult students. Men and women from the community are recruited, screened, oriented, and trained to help students in an English as a Second Language class or *Learn To Read* class offered by Oakton Community College and MONNACEP. Adults from 50 different countries are enrolled in English as a Second Language classes. Segments of the limited English speaking population require individualized tutoring:
- some have had little or no educational experience and are illiterate or semi-literate in their own language
- some are illiterate in English
- some have learning styles which cause them to respond better in smaller group instruction
- some need longer learning time
- some need additional reinforcement
- some need English for special purposes, and
- some need "catch-up" or "make-up" tutoring.

In the *Learn To Read* literacy classes, tutors work on a one-on-one basis with students in a classroom setting under the guidance of a master teacher/facilitator. Tutors work with small groups in the *Bridges to Academic Reading* program for those preparing for GED or college classes. Volunteers are also helping in pre-*GED, Sunshine, High School Completion,* and various other college programs as well as in the *VITA/MONNACEP* Office.
VITA has a structured approach to volunteer utilization. Based on the needs and goals of students, professional staff members identify tasks which the volunteers are trained to perform. Incoming volunteers receive a minimum of eight hours of classroom instruction. Observation of professional instructors and one-to-one supervision is encouraged. A handbook of 56 lessons and activities, developed specifically for the volunteers, is used by the VITA tutors.
The tutors are eager to donate their time and skills to augment and enrich the instructional process by devoting their attention to specific adults who require tutorial reinforcement or special individualized instruction. The volunteers are recognized as an integral and useful part of an innovative approach to learning by providing instructional options and creating a link to a new language, culture, and community.
During the FY 1989 semester, over 425 individuals participated in VITA as volunteers. In addition to making a quantitative contribution, the rich backgrounds of VITA volunteers are a valuable qualitative asset to the *English as a Second Language and Literacy Programs.*
Publications: HELP (Handbook for English Language Paraprofessionals)
Founded: 1978

EDUCATION: AIDS

INDIVIDUAL PROGRAM PROFILES

FAMILY LIFE AND AIDS INSTRUCTION PROGRAM
SEE AIDS: EDUCATION

EDUCATION: CAREER EXPLORATION

NATIONAL/STATE ORGANIZATIONS

COUNCIL ON LEGAL EDUCATION OPPORTUNITY
1800 M Street, NW
Suite 290, North Lobby
Washington, DC 20036
TEL: 202-785-4840
Objectives: To assist students who come from a background of "cyclical poverty" who would otherwise have little opportunity to attend an accredited law school due to financial and admission credential limitations.
Services: Sponsors Regional Summer Institutes at ABA-accredited law schools to prepare disadvantaged students for law school through a six-week intensive course; provides stipends for law school averaging $2,500 per academic year. (The Council is sponsored by the *Association of American Law Schools,* the *American Bar Association, National Bar Association, Law School Admission Council,* and the *Hispanic National Bar Association.)*
Sponsor: Association of American Law Schools
Publications: CLEO: Advancing Legal Education

DISTRIBUTIVE EDUCATION CLUBS OF AMERICA
SEE BUSINESS ASSISTANCE: CHILDREN/YOUTH

INDIVIDUAL PROGRAM PROFILES

BUSINESS MANAGEMENT/JUNIOR ACHIEVEMENT
SEE BUSINESS ASSISTANCE: CHILDREN/YOUTH

CAUSE (COMMUNITY AND UNIVERSITY SERVICES IN EDUCATION)
St. John's University
Student Development
Grand Central & Utopia Parkway
Jamaica, NY 11439
TEL: 212-990-6256
Purpose: To involve students in various volunteer programs enabling them to develop their intellectual, social, and personal qualities by participating in community services.
Sponsor: St. John's University
Contact: Ms. Eileen Devine
Description: CAUSE (Community and University Services in Education) was established in 1965 and until 1981 was primarily a tutoring and workshop program for students in attendance at schools in the Jamaica area. In fall 1981, due to a desire to expand its scope of volunteer involvement, *CAUSE* was reorganized to be, essentially, a student volunteer-administered volunteer placement program. This is accomplished through three separate programs:
- *The Education Program* provides volunteers to tutor grammar school children or to volunteer in the area of special education.
- *VITA (Volunteer Income Tax Program)* trains volunteers,

through the IRS, to assist students, senior citizens and others in preparing their income tax returns.
- *The Volunteer Placement Program* acts as a clearinghouse to bring prospective volunteers into contact with agencies which utilize volunteers in the areas of health, social services, business law and special projects.
Founded: 1965

CE-2
Tigard High School
PO Box 23059
Tigard, OR 97223
TEL: 503-684-2255
Purpose: To enable students to test their career choices by volunteering in organizations and agencies reflecting their interests.
Sponsor: Tigard High School
Contact: Garry J. Wagner
Description: An alternative program, *Career Education* - popularly called CE-2 - enables students of Tigard High School to spend a major portion of their time in the community at job sites. Sites are selected according to the students' career interests. The cooperation of employers across the community makes this program possible.
School time away from job sites is spent in the CE-2 learning center at the school. Rather than working in a group, such as a class, each student works on an individualized study program in keeping with career interests. This includes learning projects, journals, survival skills, and job site requirements.
Involving the community in the educational process has many benefits for all concerned. For the student the on-site exploratory activities develop basic skills, help students develop positive work habits and attitudes, foster students' desire to learn, and involves the students in designing their own educational programs.
Although learning plans for students are individualized, an accountability system continually monitors student behavior. The CE-2 curriculum depends on imaginative use of community resources. Every student project has three facets: basic skills, life skills, and career development.
Upon completion of their site work, students receive credit toward graduation requirements.

CIPED (COMMUNITY INVOLVEMENT PERSONAL EDUCATION DEVELOPMENT)
South Brunswick High School
Major Road
Monmouth Junction, NJ 08852
TEL: 201-329-4567
Purpose: To provide an experiential learning program for high school students at field sites in the community.
Sponsor: South Brunswick High School
Contact: Mary Ann Stein-Horenstein, Chairperson
Description: The CIPED program began as a solution to overcrowding in South Brunswick High School. There was not enough room to house all the students five days a week; an experiential program, placing one fifth of the student body at field sites each day, was established. The program, now more than ten years old, has continued because it provides valuable learning experiences.
As it is now set up each junior and senior in South Brunswick High School spends one day a week all year out of the school in a helping-learning situation while the sophomores participate for only one quarter of the school year. Most placements are career-oriented, but some are service-oriented and some are involved with the development of leisure-time activities. Students are placed almost everywhere that adults work: in elementary schools, day care centers, hospitals, nursing homes, government agencies, large corporations such as IBM and Sperry Univac, small businesses ranging from clothing stores to gas stations, theatres, museums, farms, college science labs and computer centers, and

artists' studios.

Approximately 500 students have been placed this year; they work for high school credit, not pay. School buses transport them to field sites early in the day and bring them back to school at the end of the day so they can participate in extra-curricular activities or go to work. There is a staff of four professionals, with the support of one secretary, who work full-time in the program: supervising students in the field, counseling and evaluating them and running reflective sessions in school. The program is completely funded locally.

MASTER BUILDER GAME
Bechtel Group, Inc.
50 Beale Street
San Francisco, CA 94105
TEL: 415-768-1234
FAX: 415-768-9038
Purpose: To introduce more than 600,000 children nationwide to career opportunities in technical fields.
Sponsor: Bechtel Group
Contact: Stephen D. Bechtel, Jr., Chairman
Description: The *Master Builder Game* is part of a nationwide outreach program called *Discover E* (for *engineering*) - the first ever "teach-in" sponsored by the engineering profession. The *Game* teaches students some of the basic skills of engineering as they apply to city planning. The sponsors hope to introduce more than 600,000 students nationwide to career opportunities in technical fields. More than 10 major national societies, 30 organizations and local engineering councils throughout the country are participating in the program.
A typical class design a city over several class periods and send their plans to the *Bechtel Corporation,* the world's largest international engineering company. Engineers critique the plans and return them to the students. In a Washington, DC, Jefferson Junior High School classroom in early 1990, the Chairman of the Board of Bechtel was the substitute teacher there to answer questions and offer suggestions to the students in designing their project. The school, serving 757 students in grades 7 to 9, is noted for consistently doing well in national and city academic competitions. In 1990 COMSAT, the U.S. representative of a global consortium for satellite users, adopted Jefferson Junior High School and donated $1.1 million to improve its science and math programs.
The *Discover E* program was initiated by the company in response to alarming statistics on students bypassing math- and science-oriented careers. A *National Science Foundation* report said that - unless the present trend changes - by 1996 the demand for science and engineering graduates will outnumber the supply by 45,000 - within the next 20 years the shortfall will be 700,000. Representatives from NASA, a New York Giants placekicker who is an engineer during football's off season, and other volunteers join the corporate leaders in visiting classrooms to encourage young people to pursue careers in engineering.
The engineering program is part of the 40th annual *National Engineers Week,* held each February during the week of President George Washington's birthday. Washington was an engineer and the founder of the country's first engineering school at Valley Forge, Pennsylvania.

EDUCATION: CURRICULUM ENRICHMENT

NATIONAL/STATE ORGANIZATIONS

BUSINESS ISSUES IN THE CLASSROOM
Constitutional Rights Foundation
601 South Kingsley Drive
Los Angeles, CA 90005
TEL: 213-487-5590
Objectives: To involve business in preparing students to confront the business dilemmas that they will encounter in the future; to complement business visitations with a related classroom format.
Services: Recruits business participants for classroom visits; works with Business Advisory Council comprised of senior-level executives; supports the B-I-C Education Council, which conducts field tests, develops lesson plans, and coordinates activities; publishes *Business Issues in the Classroom* lesson plans with *Economic Supplements to Instructors' Guides.*
Publications: Bill of Rights Newsletter; Business Issues Lesson Plan; Business Issues in the Classroom (audiovisual)
Founded: 1963

INSTITUTE FOR DEVELOPMENT OF EDUCATIONAL ACTIVITIES
/I/D/E/A/
259 Regency Ridge
Dayton, OH 45459
TEL: 513-434-6969
Objectives: To design and test new responses to problems in education, and to create arrangements for their widespread application.
Services: Establishes partnership efforts with other foundations and organizations interested in improving education; seeks ways to involve parents and other citizens in school program; conducts training to upgrade skills of education personnel; develops opportunities for learning outside the school; conducts research to generate solutions to persistent and emerging problems; develops new and improved processes, systems, and tools; produces films and publications reflecting its efforts; sponsors seminars and summer institutes.

OLYMPIC DAY IN THE SCHOOLS/OLYMPIC DAY FOR YOUTH
SEE RECREATION & SPORTS: OLYMPICS

PRESIDENTIAL CLASSROOM FOR YOUNG AMERICANS
SEE CIVIC AFFAIRS: CHILDREN/YOUTH

PRIMARY/SECONDARY PEACE EDUCATION NETWORK
SEE CIVIC AFFAIRS: PEACE

USOC EDUCATION COMMITTEE
SEE RECREATION & SPORTS: OLYMPICS

INDIVIDUAL PROGRAM PROFILES

APPLES FOR THE STUDENTS
Giant Food
6300 Sheriff Road
Landover, MD 20785
TEL: 301-341-4100
FAX: 301-341-4582

Purpose: To continue a long-standing commitment to education.
Contact: Odonna Matthews or Barry Scher
Description: Recognizing that many schools have limited dollars for computer equipment, *Giant Food* launched a six-month partnership program to provide free computers to area schools. From October 1989 through April 1990, schools were able to redeem special *Giant Food* register tapes from participating stores for free Apple computers, printers and educational software.
To begin the program, schools were given a checklist providing redemption amounts for each piece of equipment. "Deposits" of register tapes were recorded at *Giant Food,* and "statements" were provided regularly to the schools. Both parties kept the same record of deposits and account balance information.
Many schools worked with their parent-teacher associations to generate community support. Parents spread the word in their jobs to garner tapes from co-workers without children of school-age. Some businesses adopted schools and collected the tapes for the designated school.
The offer was made available to all public, private and parochial schools, grades kindergarten through grade twelve.

CHILDREN'S ROOM
SEE EDUCATION: LIBRARY SERVICES

COMMUNITY RESOURCE VOLUNTEERS
Minneapolis Public Schools
807 NE Broadway
Minneapolis, MN 55413
TEL: 612-348-6152
Purpose: To enrich the elementary school curriculum by using human resources in the community.
Sponsor: Minneapolis Public Schools
Contact: Betty Jane Reed, Teacher/Coordinator
Description: In operation since 1965, today the Community Resource Volunteers program has over 1,000 active volunteers who go into the Minneapolis classrooms on request to help enrich the curriculum for elementary and secondary school children. This number does not include those functioning in other volunteer programs, such as teachers' aides and tutors.
These citizens - parents and non-parents - offer enrichment in all areas of the curriculum. Every school has catalogs housing information on every available volunteer. The areas represented are: Art, Assemblies, Enrichment for Gifted Children, Health and Safety, Hobbies and Leisure Time Activities, Holidays and special Occasions, Language Arts, Mathematics, Music, Science, and Social Studies - with special emphasis at the secondary level on careers and business-related subjects.
The volunteers are poets, physical fitness experts, accomplished musicians, high school and college students, accomplished professors, experts in agriculture or computers, dentists, government officials, local, country or world-wide travelers, and many others. They share their expertise and experiences, which enlarge on a teacher's efforts to provide information that would be difficult or even impossible to obtain in any other way.
The Community Resource Volunteers program also has made video tapes of volunteers who have been requested more often than they are available. Tapes were made of volunteers leaving the city or withdrawing from the program because of increased work responsibilities, and of those who were in great demand during Black History Week, American Indian Week, or other special occasions. Visiting authors, diplomats and political figures also have volunteered to tape these 15-minute programs. Four or more of the 205 tapes were viewed over educational television each week in the schools until budget reductions and rising costs caused the school district to relinquish the contract with the educational television station. Kinescopes and half-inch tapes were made of some of the most popular programs. Volunteers whose presentations do not require visual materials are taping radio broadcasts now for use on the school district radio station.

On a weekly average, there are more than 100 class visits scheduled. There are more requests for the volunteers than the program's administration is able to fill because of the time-consuming process of recruiting and scheduling each new applicant. The Coordinator points out, "This program indicates the power of community involvement."
Founded: 1965

DISCOVER CENTER OF IDAHO
SEE ARTS/CULTURAL ENRICHMENT: HISTORY/MUSEUMS

GROWING UP WITH NATURE
SEE PHYSICAL ENVIRONMENT: WILDLIFE/PETS

HEALTH AND SAFETY CIRCUS
SEE HEALTH: HEALTH FAIRS

MINDSTRETCHERS
Grissom Middle School
13881 Kern Road
Mishawaka, IN 46544
TEL: 219-633-4061
Purpose: To challenge highly-motivated students to apply their skills for the betterment of school and community.
Sponsor: Grissom Middle School; Lilly Foundation
Contact: Dennis Bottorff
Description: Initiated in 1984, Mindstretchers fully involves students in the decision-making process. The program involves 25 students selected from recommendations by teachers and challenges them to apply their skills to benefit the community. A candidate profile is developed using specific criteria - leadership potential, level of commitment, etc. The director of Mindstretchers makes the final selection after consultation with the teachers.
Mindstretchers has four goals:
- to stretch their minds in school through academic games and "quiz bowls;"
- to stretch their minds outside school through field trips suggested and arranged by students;
- to serve the school through the promotion of esteem-building activities; and
- to serve the community through projects selected by the group.

Community activities have included such activities as "adopting" an elderly handicapped woman, helping the local public television station raise funds, and helping at the Humane Society. Members receive no academic credit for their work.
Students are involved in periodic meetings to discuss current service projects and plan new ones. The director believes that service to the community raises self-esteem dramatically.
Mindstretchers was chosen as one of 20 outstanding programs for youth of Indiana. It was awarded a $3,000 grant from the Lilly Endowment, which provided outside leadership training for the students. Prior to receiving the Lilly grant, Mindstretchers depended on minimal funds donated by the director, the participants themselves and the student council.
Mindstretchers members have developed a motto for the program: "Dedicated to lighting up those dark corners in our minds and brightening up our corner of the world."
Founded: 1984

RECORD DEBATE CLASSIC
Ramapo College
Mahwah, NJ 07430
TEL: 201-529-7500
Purpose: To help high school students hone their skills in debating.
Sponsor: Ramapo College

Contact: Dr. Helen Burchell, Coordinator
Description: A volunteer judge's panel of Bergen County attorneys refereed a debate competition among 22 teams from 21 public and private high schools in Bergen County, who faced off for the 11th annual *Record Debate Classic* at Ramapo College. The topic was *Social Security and the Elderly.* The all-day contest involved four rounds of competition to reach the point of two top teams for a final round.

The lawyers became involved when they learned that most of the students said they want to be lawyers. To emphasize that point, students gripped yellow legal pads and paced like prosecutors while grilling opponents. Dressed in suits and ties, they cited magazine and newspaper articles, books, and legal opinions to make their cases and to punch holes in their opponents' arguments. The volunteer judges took notes as the two top teams debated for an hour before about 80 fellow high school debaters, teachers, and friends.

The winning school received a silver cup and $1,000 in scholarship funds from the *Record*, and the runner-up received $500 in scholarship funds. A hard choice for the volunteer judges, the final vote was 3-2 for Frisch Yeshiva High School from Paramus. After the debate, the team members talked with the judges and made notes on suggestions offered. The college helps coordinate the debate competition each year.

ROVERS (RETIRED AND OLDER VOLUNTEERS: AN EDUCATIONAL RESOURCE SERVICE)

1420 Athens Drive
Raleigh, NC 27606
TEL: 919-851-7710
Purpose: To enhance learning and promote intergenerational communication through the interaction of older adults and students in the classroom setting.
Sponsor: Wake County Public School System
Contact: Sharon Hackney, Community Education Coordinator
Description: ROVERS is a program in which older adult volunteers, according to their own areas of interest and expertise, function as resource people in the classroom setting. The volunteer is plugged into the curriculum so that his/her own area of expertise will fit into a particular unit of study.

The ROVERS program began in October of 1981, made possible by a two year grant from National Community Education funds. There has since been a full time staff person assigned to both coordinate and expand this program throughout the Wake County School System. This coordinating position is funded by the local school system.

- **Volunteer Staff** - Initially ROVERS had a total of twenty senior adult volunteers working with the ROVERS program at Athens Drive High School alone. In the fall of 1983, the program expanded into two additional schools in the county. Local organizations such as the American Association of Retired Persons and the Association of Retired Faculty at N.C. State University have "adopted" the program. These two groups will place volunteers from their organizations into the ROVERS program at various school sites.
- **Volunteer Duties And Experience** - Based upon their specific areas of interest or expertise, volunteers share their knowledge and experience with students in the classroom setting. No formal training is necessary in order to be involved in the ROVERS program. However, it is specified that the volunteers should have a strong interest or concern for young people. The program coordinator conducts orientation sessions for the volunteers in order to familiarize them with the faculty, school site, curriculum plans, etc.

The majority of the volunteers come to the school site one hour a day, one day a week, for up to eight or nine weeks. However, the length of commitment is ultimately left up to the volunteer and corresponding teacher to arrange. They are left to work out a schedule that is most appropriate and convenient for both of them.

Potential volunteers are both recruited and screened by the program coordinator. Volunteers are matched as closely as possible with the appropriate subject area teacher.

Volunteers sixty and over are eligible for accident, personal liability, and excess automobile liability insurance. This insurance coverage, as well as mileage reimbursement funds, is provided by the city of Raleigh's Retired Senior Volunteer Program.
Founded: 1981

SNAP (STUDENTS NEED A PAT)
Starrett Elementary School
Fort Worth School District
2675 Fairmont Drive
Fort Worth, TX 76148
TEL: 214-660-7111
Purpose: To provide a little extra one-on-one attention to children who need it.
Sponsor: Fort Worth School District
Contact: Bob Windham, Principal, or Sharon Whitt, Counselor
Description: The *SNAP* program began in September 1988 when an elementary school principal and the school's counselor recognized that some children need a little extra attention mostly because of low self-esteem. The program was launched by inviting teachers to volunteer. Each grade level team submitted a prioritized list of youngsters who would benefit most from the mentor program. Then the principal and counselor carefully matched 36 students and 36 teachers. To get away from the image of teacher-as-an-authority figure, students were teamed with educators outside of their grade levels.

Each child was made to feel important because he or she was chosen as a SNAP. Soon they began snapping their fingers, the SNAP trademark. After the selections were complete, parents of SNAP participants received letters from the principal outlining the program. The same week, SNAP teachers personally delivered invitations to lunch to their students. Some teachers went all out and brought tablecloths and centerpieces, some took pictures, and most are keeping scrapbooks.

Each SNAP relationship is unique, and teacher and student make decisions about activities. The teachers check on their SNAPs each week during their conference periods, and youngsters visit their SNAP teachers before or after school.

The teachers make a special effort to surprise their SNAPs with little treats and notes of encouragement. Some SNAPs review their tougher assignments - like science lessons - with their SNAP teachers. In other cases, the SNAPs become volunteers for their volunteer teachers. For example, one student tutors younger children for his teacher. This also benefits the younger children, who wait eagerly for the SNAP to visit the classroom.

The SNAP teachers give a lot of encouragement, do lots of cheerleading and give lots of pep talks so their SNAPs feel very special. SNAP teachers even intercede when their SNAPs get in trouble with their teachers or find themselves in the principal's office. The volunteer teacher and the SNAP sit down and talk over what led up to the problem, with the teacher in the role of a friend, not an authority figure. Then she helps the SNAP devise some strategies for coping with similar situations. The close relationships have resulted in SNAP students trying extra hard to make their teachers - both volunteer and classroom - proud of them. Classroom teachers constantly report on the positive changes in the pupils who are involved in the SNAP program. Sixth graders and the counselor helped SNAP students compose thank you letters for their SNAP teachers. When the SNAP students move to another school in the district, the volunteer teachers continue to maintain contact - some even visiting the former SNAPs in their new schools.

According to the counselor, the program was started because "We wanted to let these kids know that shool is a neat place to be. We wanted them to know we're real people who do care." She said the principal wants to make Starrett a place where teachers and staff and children feel good about themselves.

STS (SHARING TALENTS AND SKILLS)
302 Elm Street
Westfield, NJ 07090
TEL: 201-789-4432
Purpose: To involve citizens in their schools; to tap the wealth of knowledge within the community; to supplement the curriculum in the schools.
Sponsor: Westfield Public Schools
Contact: Mary Ann Brugger, STS Coordinator
Description: STS is a volunteer project in which residents share their talents and skills with students in the classrooom K-12.
STS began in 1976 when the Westfield Parent-Teacher Council decided to update an old community resource file compiled in 1973. The Junior League of Elizabeth/Plainfield provided volunteers for the project which was under the aegis of the P-TC. Volunteers from the Junior League and each school set up and staffed an office to coordinate speakers with classroom studies. STS flourished and in August 1981 the Board of Education hired a part-time staff member to coordinate the program.
At the beginning of each school year, teachers receive an up-dated STS Directory of all resource persons, subjects and grade levels available. As the school year progresses, teachers request a resource person and the Coordinator confirms presentation for a time mutually convenient. These presentations are held in the classroom and range from 30-60 minutes. Sample presentations include:
- a local investment broker talks on workings of Wall Street
- a retired banker and amateur astronomer shows slides of solar system
- a local resident shows slides of trip to Russia
- a local amateur trombonist gives history of instrument and performs
- a local dentist gives program on preventative dentistry
- a member of local historical society gives program on colonial times
- a local attorney talks on career in law

As of May 1990, STS had over 300 volunteer resource persons on file (1988-89 school year - 546 programs). The students can only benefit from the generosity of these volunteers who so willingly share their talents and skills.
Founded: 1976

YOUNG WINGS USA*
Flight Attendant Volunteer Corps
122 East 42nd Street
Room 1725
New York, NY 10017
TEL: 212-869-8837
Purpose: To provide cultural enrichment for students at elementary, middle, and secondary school levels, and hospitalized and institutionalized children.
Sponsor: Major airlines; business/industry; government; the media
Contact: Gerri Rafferty
Description: Young Wings USA is a project of the Flight Attendant Volunteer Corps, a nonprofit organization founded in 1976. Its basic purpose is to provide for Flight Attendants of all U.S. airlines structured opportunities under professional guidance to utilize available time, education, talents and skills in special volunteer work with institutionalized children. A new development is a program for school children at all levels which highlights the Young Wings Air and Space Academy Program.
Presently there are 1,700 volunteers and 2,400 new applicants. Membership is open to all U.S. airlines whether the individuals are active or inactive (on leave, etc.). All volunteer work is scheduled to avoid interference with airline assignments or requirements. Most assignments involve a minimum of two hours on one day per month. Special degrees or diplomas are not required except for limited, specialized activities. The only requirement is attendance at one complete (two-hour) orientation session offered periodically

in each of the flight bases involved.
Because flight schedules and other commitments do not permit most flight attendants to participate more than once or twice per month, the volunteers operate as a team. The teams create a relationship with the children and assure the continuity of the relationship through a team concept over a significant period of time. Example: If 100 Flight Attendants are team members in any given city, each is asked to participate at least one time per month in a weekly session.
Presently, there are close to 750 children involved in the program in 12 cities (12 major children's institutions), and an estimated 4,000 children have participated since the inception of the program in 1976.
Following are brief descriptions of Young Wings activities, which are explained thoroughly with a slide show at the volunteers' Orientation Sessions:
- **Simulated Flights:** A fun and popular monthly event with a "mock airplane," slide shows of various parts of the world, uniformed teams, and artifacts.
- **Weekly Arts and Crafts Projects:** A variety of games and projects with the children based on the ratio of volunteers to children, the needs and wishes of both children and staff, and available supplies. This activity includes Project Postcard, a geography-based game b ased on postcards sent in by Flight Attendants for the children.
- **Special Events:** Periodic parties, and trips. Special events include activities for Halloween, Thanksgiving, Christmas, Valentine's Day, and Easter, as well as occasional trips out of the hospital to movies, airports, zoos, and many other places.
- **Young Wings Magazine:** A 16-page magazine issued every other month and written, edited, illustrated, etc., by Flight Attendants, covering a wide variety of subjects and filled with games, contests with prizes, aviation subjects, and other creative topics for the children's enjoyment and education.
- **Young Wings Air and Space Academy Project:** A new program for school children and institutionalized youngsters staffed by both Flight Attendants and Pilots, and featuring a Mini-Course Air and Space Booklet program, a Flight Learning Center with films, tutoring programs, and Graduations with Wings, Diplomas, Scholarships, Medals and special prize trips.

The Flight Attendant Volunteer Corps plans to develop "Young Wings International" in a format similar to the USA program.
Major sponsors to date: Pan Am World Airways, Eastern Airlines, United Air Lines, Trans World Airlines, American Airlines, Delta Air Lines, Western Airlines, The Boeing Company, the National Aeronautics and Space Administration, the US Office of Special Education, the Walt Disney Media Company, and ABC Television Network.
Founded: 1976

EDUCATION: DROPOUT PREVENTION

INDIVIDUAL PROGRAM PROFILES

CE-2
SEE EDUCATION: CAREER EXPLORATION

"COOL SCHOOL VIDEO" CONTEST
District of Columbia Public Schools
415 Twelfth Street, NW
Washington, DC 20024
TEL: 202-724-4201
Purpose: To help stem the rising school dropout rate.

Description: With a "stay in school" theme the only rigid requirement, students in District of Columbia Schools have been challenged to create videos for the *Cool School Video* contest. Co-sponsored by the school system and a nationwide athletic shoe retailer, the top prize is a pair of athletic shoes for every student in the school that produces the best video.

Encouraged by the appearance of celebrity role models, more than 13,000 students from the District's 27 junior high schools participated.

GRADS PROGRAM
SEE TEENAGE PREGNANCY/PARENTING

NEW LIVES
SEE TEENAGE PREGNANCY/PARENTING

NEW YORK GIANTS SCHOOL SPEAKERS PROGRAM
Fairleigh Dickinson University
Giants Degree Completion Program
3 University Plaza Drive
Hackensack, NJ 07601
TEL: 201-692-9696
Purpose: To utilize the high-visibility of national athletes to reach elementary, middle and high school youth in areas of educational goals and drug and alcohol abuse.
Sponsor: New York Giants
Contact: George Martin
Description: In 1985 George Martin of the New York Giants, concerned about the "future after football" of his fellow athletes, established a *Degree Completion Program* at Fairleigh Dickinson University to encourage them to complete their academic degrees. The program includes a requirement of weekly visits to elementary, middle and high schools to speak about the importance of setting educational goals and the need to avoid drug and alcohol abuse. As a result, over 20,000 students have heard the athletes speak.

In cooperation with the University, George Martin coordinates the school program, assisting the other athletes in their presentations, and it is said making the most visits per semester himself.
Publications: Degree Completion Program
Founded: 1985

PROJECT BRAVO
United Way of San Diego County
4699 Murphy Canyon Road
PO Box 23543
San Diego, CA 92123-0543
TEL: 619-492-2000
Purpose: To prevent Hispanic youths from dropping out of school.
Sponsor: United Way of San Diego County
Contact: Glen Estell, Volunteer Committee Chairman
Description: When a survey indicated that up to 40% of the San Diego area's Hispanic student body is at risk of dropping out, the United Way conducted a follow-up study. When the alarming statistics were confirmed, United Way authorized a two-year grant of $167,000 to *Project Bravo,* a program designed to prevent Hispanic youths from dropping out of school.

Different from other dropout programs, *Project Bravo* focuses on students from kindergarten through grade three. It is the first program in San Diego to approach the problem through intervention at the earliest grade levels - perhaps one of the first in the country.

A stipulation of the grant was that it be carried out in a school district which has a high percentage of ethnic students. The San Ysidro District was chosen, where 95 percent of the students are of ethnic backgrounds, with 92 percent of them Hispanic. The school district and the project's sponsors work together to track the academic achievement of youth involved in the program.

The project is sponsored jointly by three agencies - *Casa Familiar, YWCA,* and *Metropolitan Area Advisory Committee (MAAC Project).* Each has a specific task:
- *Casa Familiar* provides a range of activities designed to increase the participation of parents, establishing parent support groups at each of three designated schools.
- *YWCA* provides enrichment and tutoring programs for some 300 students - homework assistance, games and sports, creative opportunities, activities with peers/teens/adults, field trips, summer programs, and school visitations by Hispanic adults who can serve as role models.
- *MAAC Project* provides fiscal administration, office and meeting space, a variety of in-kind support services, and referral for participants and their families to additional health and human services indicated.

With United Way's help, as an extension of the program, *Boy Scouts* and *Girl Scouts* organizations are seeking funding to expand in-school scouting programs in conjunction with *Project Bravo.* United Way expects the project to be an ongoing United Way-funded service.

PROJECT OPPORTUNITY
SEE TEENAGE PREGNANCY/PARENTING

VALUED YOUTH PARTNERSHIP PROGRAM
Intercultural Development Research Association (IDRA)
5835 Gallaghan
Suite 350
San Antonio, TX 78228-1190
TEL: 512-684-8180
Purpose: To prevent students from dropping out of school through cross-age tutoring.
Sponsor: Coca Cola USA
Contact: Alicia Salinas Sosa
Description: When the dropout rate in San Antonio took a dramatic rise, the *Valued Youth Partnership Program* was developed in an attempt to turn this alarming statistic around. It was developed by IDRA and funded by Coca Cola USA.

Cross-age tutoring is the basic concept of the program, but the tutors in this case are the potential dropouts. In 1988, eight schools were involved in the program.

The process begins when personnel in area school districts identify Hispanic youth at high risk of dropping out of school. They are designated as "valued youth" and are given an opportunity to tutor younger children. As the younger children respond to the teaching of basic skills the older youth reinforce their own knowledge while developing positive perceptions of themselves. They remain in school.

The student tutors must take special classes to reach their greatest competence in communication, reading, and writing skills, as well as to gain a practical awareness of child development procedures. This training continues throughout the partnership relationship.

The cross-age tutoring brings the partners together from five to eight hours each week, either during school hours or after school, depending on individual school policy.

Parents are involved in the program as much as possible, beginning with a pre-tutoring understanding of the child's involvement. Parent support is considered an important part of the program.

Field trips bring tutor and tutee together in a social setting, giving them a chance for further interaction.

Adult role models are brought in to talk with the tutors on various topics related to future careers. Often they are graduates of the tutors' school districts.

Coca Cola holds a recognition program for the tutors, as do their teachers.

Statistics demonstrate the success of the program. In 1985-86 an impressive 94 of the 100 high-risk Hispanic youth in the program stayed in school.
Founded: 1988

YOUTH AFFAIRS TASK FORCE
United Way of Greater Manchester
20 Merrimack Street
Manchester, NH 03101
TEL: 603-625-6939
Purpose: To respond to the critical dropout problem in Manchester.
Sponsor: Manchester Board of Mayor & Aldermen
Contact: Anne Page, Director
Description: Twenty-seven percent of Manchester's young people never graduate from high school. In response to this critical problem, the *United Way of Greater Manchester* formed the *Youth Affairs Task Force* to assess the current situation and recommend various ways of dealing with it. The Task Force is comprised of people from all over the community who deal with the dropout problem - *Board of Aldermen, School Committee,* youth-serving agencies, law enforcement officers, guidance counselors, and a local TV news anchorman.
To begin its program, the Task Force interviewed students to learn how they perceived dropping out, and how they felt about problems facing today's students. Forty-four percent said the biggest problem was drugs and alcohol; others saw the problems either as family-related or school-related. The conclusion was that drug and alcohol abuse contributes to the problem, along with an extreme shortage of community-based services equipped to deal with the dropout problem. The Task Force also found that the punishment for absenteeism is external suspension and, based on observations, the Task Force concluded that such suspensions may actually encourage students to drop out.
Another discovery was that many students find hands-on experience in a particular field more rewarding than book learning. With students allowed entry into vocational training only after entering the junior year, teachers reported countless students recommitting themselves to learning after they arrived there.
Based on its findings, especially the gaps in community services, the Task Force made recommendations to the *United Way Board, Manchester Board of Mayor and Aldermen, Manchester School Committee,* and local community agencies, including an alternative education center, identifying family problems, developing citywide committees, and exploring existing services in drug and alcohol abuse.
The *Youth Affairs Task Force* meets periodically to monitor progress on its recommendations, also meeting with student representatives from three area high schools on how to reach potential dropouts. One area being explored is the legal issue regarding suspension of students.
As an added measure in the overall program, the school board has formed a subcommittee called the *Drop-Out Prevention Committee* to follow up on the recommendations and to identify future at-risk dropouts at a very early grade level. According to the Task Force director, "There is a lot we can do if we work together."

EDUCATION: ETHNIC/BILINGUAL

NATIONAL/STATE ORGANIZATIONS

DISSEMINATION AND ASSESSMENT CENTER FOR BILINGUAL EDUCATION
7703 North Lamar Boulevard
Austin, TX 78752
TEL: 512-458-9131
Objectives: To serve as a national source of information on bilingual bicultural education products and professional services.

Services: Collects and makes available project descriptions of bilingual education efforts across the country; works closely with local, state, and federal groups and agencies to avoid duplication; publishes a newsletter designed to foster communication between its subscribers, a handbook, a guide to projects in the U.S., annotated listings of materials developed within local projects as well as those generally available on the market, and other materials.
Publications: Bilingual Teacher Aide

REGIONAL BILINGUAL TRAINING RESOURCE CENTER*
New York City Board of Education
66 Fourth Street
New York, NY 11211
TEL: 212-596-8038
Objectives: To provide support services to bilingual/multicultural education programs.
Services: Provides in-service training for volunteers, parents, and staff in bilingual/multicultural programs; conducts field tests of curriculum materials developed by Title VII Materials Development Centers and makes results available to local programs; coordinates services and activities with the various local, state and federal agencies and organizations in the field; maintains library, media center, and information service; publishes articles, reports, enrichment materials, and a bimonthly newsletter.
Publications: Bilingual Review

TRAINING PROGRAMS

AFRICAN-AMERICAN FESTIVAL OF ACADEMIC EXCELLENCE
NAACP
PO Box 2165
Rockville, MD 20852
TEL: 301-468-7744; 301-946-1334
Contact: Robert R. Nix
Description: This conference was convened in response to the trend for black youngsters to avoid achievement because of peer pressures. The purpose was to discuss this problem while recognizing 242 high achievers in the Washington metropolitan area (one with a 4.7 grade point average). Initiated by the Montgomery County Chapter of the NAACP, organizers tried to counteract the negative peer pressure among some of today's black youths, who equate academic success with selling out to the white world.
The theme of the day also included self-help. There were workshops for parents on building self-esteem in children, countering negative peer pressure and preparing for college.
Youths talked about the pressure of drugs and dating, but it was the message of promoting achievement that seemed to sink in. Although teenagers were the target, one adult brought 31 students from a local middle school, and the students were quite verbal about the problems of avoiding peers involved in drugs and petty crimes in their neighborhoods.
The students who were honored represent 13% of the school system's black high school juniors and seniors who, according to the event's sponsors, defied media stereotypes, particularly of young black men.
Faculty came from all sectors, including Howard University. Participants who heard a statement by one of the middle school students agreed that it summed up the objectives of the meeting: "Work hard, stay in school, get good grades, go to college."

REFUGEE VOLUNTEER TUTOR TRAINING
Oregon State University
Adult Education Division
Corvallis, OR 97331
TEL: 503-754-4318

Credit: CEUs
Sponsor: Oregon State University
Contact: Wayne Haverson
Description: This course was designed to meet a need for organizational, management, and maintenance of a professional program to provide volunteer tutors to adult refugees.
Four community college refugee programs are involved in the course, which teaches volunteers to instruct refugees in English as a Second Language. Training and on-site assistance is provided by the Adult Education department of Oregon State University through a special grant from the Oregon Department of Education.

VOLUNTEER TRAINING - SCHOOL DESEGREGATION MONITORING*
Desegregation Monitoring and Advisory Committee
721 Olive
Eleventh Floor
St. Louis, MO 63101
TEL: 314-231-4669
Credit: Inquire
Sponsor: US/DoJ - District Court
Contact: Loverne Cameron, Associate Director
Description: This training program is designed to develop a bank of assistants to assist the Desegregation Monitoring and Advisory Committee (DMAC). This court-appointed Committee is charged with monitoring implementation of the Intra-District Desegregation Plan. Volunteers are recruited to assist in making visits to 217 schools.
Monitoring periods vary, but are always scheduled several months apart. Monitoring is expected to take about two weeks, with reports due about a week after completion of the school visits. An average school visit involves one to three hours.
Following the training, volunteers are expected to be able to handle the following tasks within the framework of the Committee's mandated guidelines:
- Administer questionnaires to school administrators, teachers, staff, and/or students and parents.
- Make personal observations of the conditions in schools which might impact on the desegregation plan.
- Provide data in a form that provides DMAC with an opportunity to observe, independently and "first hand," the extent to which the plan is being implemented.
- Provide data in a form that is conducive to the formulation of reports to the United States District Court.

Actual training is completed in one day, with the Advisory Committee on call for questions that may arise due to unexpected circumstances and have not been covered in the one-day training session. Reimbursement is made available for all Committee-related transportation expenses.

INDIVIDUAL PROGRAM PROFILES

THE B.E.S.T. PROJECT
Brown University
25 George Street
PO Box 1974
Providence, RI 02912
TEL: 401-863-2338
Purpose: To give *Brown* students the opportunity to teach ESL to immigrants and refugees.
Description: B.E.S.T. *(Brown English as a Second Language Student Tutors)* provides tutors with an opportunity to teach English to immigrants and refugees from all over the world.
Brown University students are recruited, trained, and given a choice of program options, including:
- *Teach an ESL Class* at *Smith Hill Community Center* on

some weekday evenings.
- *Tutor an adult at home* in the *Home Tutoring Program,* the *Senior Citizens Center,* or at a library at times worked out between the parties.
- *Tutor in the Providence Public School System* at *Perry Middle School* or *Central High School* on weekday mornings.

Training is provided by *B.E.S.T.* staff at the *Center for Public Service.* Staff members also offer ongoing support. During the school year, the *Education Department, Portuguese and Brazilian Studies,* and the *Center for Public Service* offer a full-credit course in ESL: P/B 172. Also, students can request an opportunity to observe ESL teachers in a classroom setting.
Transportation for the tutors is organized by coordinators using BCO cars and volunteer car-pooling.
Publications: The B.E.S.T. Project

CENTRAL SUMMER SCHOOL
Central Lutheran Church
333 South 12th Street
Minneapolis, MN 55404
TEL: 612-870-4416
Purpose: To provide a full summer school session in an area where the public school system is not offering this service.
Contact: Barbara Bruneau, Director
Description: When members of the Central Lutheran Church learned that the Minneapolis Public Schools did not plan to offer a summer session in 1989, the church took action to set up the needed service. The six-week summer session is staffed by volunteer teachers and teaches 100 children ages seven to fourteen. The sessions operate four hours each day, five days a week, and include a hot lunch. A nominal tuition of $10 per child pays 10% of the $10,000 cost of the program, with the Church paying the rest.
Central Summer School is not a religious school. It offers instruction in English and math plus a variety of vocational subjects such as baking, carpentry and drug education. Most of the students are blacks, Indians and Southeast Asians, and most come from low-income families.
The school will use ten classrooms plus a couple of activity rooms and large group rooms as available in the church. Students are accepted in the order they enroll, without regard to religion or any other factor. Ten teachers, some of them certified, each take a classroom of about ten students for the entire six weeks. Some 200 volunteers come in for a morning or two mornings each to present programs relating to their professions, countries of origin or cultures where they have lived or traveled, hobbies or crafts, or other skills. Volunteers are intentionally recruited from a variety of religious and cultural backgrounds to provide children with volunteers with whom they can identify and who can provide role models. Conversely, all of the children are exposed to people from cultures and backgrounds they might otherwise not get to know. High interest comes from suburbia, from people who want to have first-hand experience working where there is a need.
A side benefit that grew out of parents' concern was the supervision aspect. Many of the children would have been unsupervised without the summer school option. Since the program was announced, the City of Minneapolis has offered money to help the public schools operate a summer session. Since the 100 children in Central Summer School represent a very small part of the need, the City's offer allows many more children to get the supervision they need, while upgrading their learning skills.
Founded: 1989

JVS VOLUNTEER TUTORIAL PROGRAM
SEE LITERACY

PROJECT BRAVO
SEE EDUCATION: DROPOUT PREVENTION

VALUED YOUTH PARTNERSHIP PROGRAM
SEE EDUCATION: DROPOUT PREVENTION

YOUNG BLACK SCHOLARS PROGRAM (YBS)
One Hundred Black Men of Los Angeles
1950 Sawtelle Boulevard
West Los Angeles, CA 90025
TEL: 213-206-1362
Purpose: To improve the college eligibility of African-American high school students in Los Angeles County.
Sponsor: One Hundred Black Men of Los Angeles
Contact: Warren Valdry, President
Description: Statistics in 1983 indicated that only 800 of the 21,000 African-American students in Los Angeles County high schools met the minimum standards at graduation for admission to the University of California system. This alarming statistic deteriorated in each subsequent year, with fewer graduates and fewer who were able to meet the UC standard, until 1986, when members of *100 Black Men of Los Angeles* were called to action and established the *Young Black Scholars Program (YBS),* an educational program to address the problem.
To get the program off the ground, YBS planned to work with 2,000 ninth-grade students who had achieved B averages or better in four basic eighth-grade subjects: math, science, history and English. The goal was to have 1,000 of them graduate from high school and be eligible for entrance to the UC system by June 1990. By 1989, the pilot program was beginning to show results. YBS provides counseling and academic support to the 1,250 students remaining in the program out of the 2,000 originally recruited from public, private and parochial high schools in the Los Angeles area. YBS provides a variety of services to the students, all paid for with donations.
Saturday Academic Support classes are staffed by college professors and other professional teachers. Scholastic Aptitude Test preparation classes are scheduled at regular intervals and career seminars assist the young scholars in making viable choices for their futures.
An Academic Math Hotline is housed in space donated by *Kappa Alpha Psi* fraternity and is staffed by volunteer members of the *National Society of Black Engineering Students.* Any math textbook used in area school systems is at the fingertips of the volunteers, who help callers with their homework.
An integral part of the YBS operation is the mentor program. Each student is assigned an adult mentor who maintains regular contact with the pupil and makes sure he or she is enrolled in the proper classes. In addition, YBS clubs are formed in schools where a teacher can be found to volunteer as sponsor - so far about 50% of the area schools.
One weakness in the program pinpointed by sponsors is the poor participation by African-American males - two-thirds of the participants are females. Another serious concern is that there are indications that ninth grade might be too late to begin the YBS program. An evaluation meeting will determine which age groups will be best for the future.
In the meantime, an outpouring of volunteer energy is being expended to reach the goal of 1,000 African-American high school graduates prepared for college admission in 1990.

EDUCATION: FUNDING

INDIVIDUAL PROGRAM PROFILES

EDUCATION SUPPORT PROGRAM
Dollywood Foundation
700 Dollywood Lane
Pigeon Forge, TN 37863-4101
TEL: 615-428-9498
FAX: 703-941-4360
Purpose: To reduce high school dropout rate by working both at the college-entry level and the elementary level of the school system.
Description: In 1988, Dolly Parton launched a campaign to reduce the high school dropout rate in Sevier County by forming buddy teams of two students to help each other stay in school and graduate. In 1989, a follow-up program provided a college scholarship to each of those students who graduated from any of the three high schools in the county.
The scholarship program has been developed in connection with *Hiwassee College,* with the college offering a $500 scholarship to any student graduating from one of the high schools and applying to the college. If admission qualifications are met, inadequate S.A.T. score or grade point average will be disregarded. In addition, the college will provide financial aid above the $500 scholarship when necessary. This financial assistance is in addition to Dollywood scholarships already funded by the *Dollywood Foundation.*
Through the Foundation plan, each high school recieves a $1500 scholarship to be given to a music or arts student, and another $1200 scholarship to be given to a deserving student on the basis of academics. High school administrators make the final selection. Another program by the Foundation is a curriculum enrichment program in a local elementary school. A $10,000 grant, along with assistance from the P.T.A., the local bank, and others, will allow the school's arts and crafts program to meet its $20,000 budget and continue through 1990. A special bonus is an invitation to all students in Sevier county - 9,000 total - to be guests of Dolly Parton free of charge at *Dollywood* during the *National Crafts Festival.*
The philosophy behind the gift, in Dolly Parton's words, is that "Giving kids the opportunity to excel in their own personal skills such as arts, crafts and entertainment is part of what will motivate them to finish school. That's the primary purpose of the *Dollywood Foundation.*"

TOWNWIDE CENSUS
SEE PHYSICAL ENVIRONMENT: DEMOGRAPHICS

VOLUNTEERS IN ACTION
1000 Coconut Creek Boulevard
Coconut Creek, FL 33066
TEL: 305-973-2205
Purpose: To assist the community college in continuing to offer programs and services during a time of decreased budgets.
Sponsor: Broward Community College, North Campus, Community Services
Contact: Judy Fink, Coordinator
Description: Volunteers in Action was created in 1981 to develop and train a corps of volunteers to serve Broward Community College, North Campus, in a wide range of volunteer assignments, thereby reducing the current strain on staffing while improving services to students and community. The program is funded primarily by *Community Services - Community Instructional Services (CIS)* and supplemented by a small grant through the college's *Staff and Program Development (SPD)* grant program. The program has grown from August 1981 when one volunteer

donated twenty-one hours to a current average of forty-four, donating 650 hours. Volunteers serve in various positions throughout North Campus (i.e., Behavioral Science, and Political Science research assistants, Newspaper editor, Tutors, Advisement and Registration assistants).

Volunteer Assignments - Volunteers are interviewed by the volunteer coordinator and a second time by a department supervisor. The job descriptions allow a volunteer to choose a position most suitable to his/her experience and interests. The interview with a supervisor allows volunteers to further explore their prospective duties, and acquaint themselves with work site and supervisor. If both the supervisor and volunteer are satisfied, an orientation time is set with the Volunteer Coordinator.

The volunteer is expected to be available at least four hours a week for one term. The orientation, which covers general college information in one half hour, is followed by on-the-job training. Unique volunteer opportunities are available on college campuses. A man volunteers as the hands for a handicapped student - going to class with him to take notes and tests. Although difficult to refrain from helping, this means writing the test answers down right or WRONG! Another is the "eyes" for a blind instructor. Several work in the Career Placement Center, assisting students and community residents with career exploration. The book store, test monitoring, test grading, typing, reading and writing labs also involve volunteers in positions that challenge their skills, allow them to grow and assist the college programs to operate as efficiently and effectively as possible.

Volunteer Staff Recognition - Volunteer/Staff recognition and appreciation are important aspects of the program at *Broward Community College.* The day-to-day "thank you" a volunteer receives and the climate in which they work are the responsibility of the staff. Recognition and reinforcement of this effort is especially important. The coordinator interviews and places the volunteer. Much of the rest of the relationship and job assignment are the responsibility of the staff person. At *Broward Community College* both receive periodic "thank you" notes from the volunteer coordinator. Both receive periodic "comfort conferences" (our term for an evaluation and growth builder). In the second term of volunteering, both volunteer and staff involved with supporting and supervising volunteers receive Broward Community College Coffee Mugs.

In the second year of volunteering both receive a canvas book bag. Certificates were presented at first Annual Recognition Coffee. Broward Community College tie tacks were presented at the second.

The Recognition coffee is short...one hour. The Provost and Dean make very short "thank you" speeches, pins are presented informally rather than in a formal ceremony. The object is food, fun, fellowship and appreciation. The feedback from staff and volunteers has been positive for each Coffee.

The success of this program lies in its organization. Goals and Objectives are written, every job has a written job description, sign-in sheets are used, evaluations - on-going and exit - are conducted, and statistics are recorded. A monthly statistical report is filed, enabling an annual report to be easily compiled with a narrative, both of which are useful for program justification and refunding.

Broward Community College also offers program assistance to area volunteer programs, libraries, social service agencies and schools.
Founded: 1981

EDUCATION: HANDICAPPED

NATIONAL/STATE ORGANIZATIONS

COUNCIL FOR EXCEPTIONAL CHILDREN
1920 Association Drive
Reston, VA 22091-1589
TEL: 703-620-3660
Objectives: To protect and enhance the right of exceptional children (those needing instructional services different from the average) to receive full and appropriate educational and related services.
Services: Trains advocates to improve their skills to influence governmental action and public awareness; monitors government programs to assure full appropriate participation of exceptional children; analyzes and disseminates information about pending legislation, established laws, government policies and procedures, and court actions; supports specific legislation and court actions, and related strategies for change; serves the educational community through publications and special conferences.
Founded: 1922

FOUNDATION FOR CHILDREN WITH LEARNING DISABILITIES
SEE RECIPIENTS: HANDICAPPED - LEARNING-DISABLED

LEARNING DISABILITIES ASSOCIATION OF AMERICA
SEE RECIPIENTS: HANDICAPPED - LEARNING-DISABLED

NATIONAL LIBRARY SERVICE FOR THE BLIND
SEE RECIPIENTS: HANDICAPPED - BLIND

INDIVIDUAL PROGRAM PROFILES

PROJECT PASSAGE
SEE PSYCHOSOCIAL SUPPORT SERVICES

EDUCATION: HOME

NATIONAL/STATE ORGANIZATIONS

HOME AND SCHOOL INSTITUTE
Special Project Office
1201 Sixteenth Street, NW
Washington, DC 20036
TEL: 202-466-3633
Objectives: To develop family education strategies which are academically effective and cost-effective for use with school-age children.
Services: Develops educational activities that take little time, are cost-free, and can be implemented in the home by parents or other family members; works to increase public awareness that parents are important teachers of their children and that all homes and neighborhoods are important learning places; publishes *Families Learning Together,* and other materials; sponsors the "Home Learning Place" program, and Project HELP; publishes large number of pamphlets, books, study guides; conducts *MegaSkills* workshops nationally.

INDIVIDUAL PROGRAM PROFILES

CATCH PROGRAM
Chamber of Commerce
114 West Chatham Street
Cary, NC 27511
TEL: 919-467-1016
Purpose: To follow through on the theme of CATCH: "The love of learning is first established in the home."
Sponsor: Cary High School PTSA
Contact: Ricki Grantmyre, Committee Member
Description: The CATCH (Community Action Through Cooperative Homework) program was developed through the Cary Chamber of Commerce, which targeted homework since it applies to all students. One facet of the CATCH program is the *MegaSkills Workshop,* which teaches parents simple, daily activities to use at home with their children to nurture a love of learning. The skills, also called "little recipes" are designed to enhance children's learning - not only in academics, but also in everyday living. There is no expenditure of money, since the program makes use of tools already in the home, or consists of activities that do not require any tools at all - making the program feasible for anyone. For example, one "recipe" calls for a "fire brigade" to pick up toys - a chore that usually meets with resistance. According to one volunteer, "It makes it fun, and it teaches the children teamwork" - which is one of the *MegaSkills.* Leaders of the workshops are volunteers from the community. In each community, prior to the workshop, a series of training sessions readies local citizens to lead *MegaSkills* workshops. The training of trainers is provided by the *Home and School Institute,* an educational foundation based in Washington, DC, which developed *MegaSkills.* In Cary, an April 1990 workshop was led by 16 business people, educators, and parents from the Cary area who completed the training program. One trainee, an employee from *Union Carbide,* volunteered for the training because of the corporation's emphasis on education, and as a parent. The 16 trained volunteers present workshops throughout the community - in day care centers, businesses, churches, etc. Many of those who volunteer are parents, and find the skills useful in their own homes as well - often trying them out on their own children first.
In the Cary program, in addition to *Union Carbide,* volunteer trainers came from the *Bespak Corporation,* the *PTA, Capital Associates, Cary Elementary School, Cary High School, Buehler Products, Smith & Associates, Board of Education, Chamber of Commerce,* and attorneys and other individuals from the community.

EDUCATION: HOMELESS

INDIVIDUAL PROGRAM PROFILES

FIRST PLACE
SEE RECIPIENTS: HOMELESS - EDUCATION

RAINBOW SUNSHINE SCHOOL
Shelter for Victims of Domestic Violence
PO Box 336
Albuquerque, NM 87103
TEL: 505-247-4219
Purpose: To bridge the education gap for children who are victims of domestic violence.
Sponsor: Albuquerque Public Schools
Contact: Beverly Wilkins, Director
Description: Staff and volunteers of the *Shelter for Victims of Domestic Violence* in Albuquerque surveyed the shelter population for six months in 1987 and determined that one-third of the 484 children who received shelter there were school-age, and some spent as many as 30 days there.
The survey was an outgrowth of their concern about the gap in education that resulted from their stay at the shelter. Since going to school was risky because of the possibility of the abusing parent picking up the child, the children were not sent to school during these traumatic disruptions of their homes. Since the children were in an unfamiliar and possibly frightening setting, not being able to attend school added to the trauma of being in a shelter.
The goal was to present the results of the survey to Albuquerque school authorities and request an on-site school at the shelter. In meetings with school officials, shelter representatives were able to make a convincing case for the on-site school. Among other things, officials were told that mothers sheltered there needed to heal both physically and mentally, and didn't have the resources to focus on their children's needs, and the on-site school would provide some much-needed normality in the lives of the children. School officials agreed unanimously in favor of the on-site school, and by fall 1987 a teacher, accredited to teach grades K-12, was in place at the shelter. The teacher runs the classes in the "one-room schoolhouse" concept. Also, she maintains contact with the children's former schools to let administrators know the children are keeping pace with the required academic instruction.
The children responded enthusiastically, and named their school the *Rainbow Sunshine School* and selected a unicorn for a mascot. The school operates during the same hours as regular school, and even has field trips, although these must be closely supervised with almost a one-to-one volunteer/child ratio because of the constant threat posed by the abusing parent. Such supervision is done very discreetly to put as little stress on the children as possible.
On a typical day, up to nine children are in class. Most are under high-school age.

EDUCATION: LIBRARY SERVICES

NATIONAL/STATE ORGANIZATIONS

FRIENDS OF LIBRARIES USA*
c/o Sandy Dolnick
9125 Briarwood Court
Milwaukee, WI 53217
TEL: 414-961-2095
Objectives: To help libraries meet the increasing demand for information through volunteer assistance.
Services: Assists in forming local Friends of Library groups; makes the public aware of these groups and the services they perform; insures that local groups have access to information and ideas to help them develop and improve their organizations; publishes quarterly newsletter, *Friends of Libraries National Notebook,* to keep local groups informed of its programs and activities, and to link local groups through the column, "Friends in Action," which features local program ideas, materials to sell or buy and news of other Friends' groups; convenes annual meeting in conjunction with the Annual Conference of the American Library Association.
Publications: National Notebook; Idea Bank; Pamphlet-A Legislative Agenda
Founded: 1979

NATIONAL LIBRARY SERVICE FOR THE BLIND
SEE RECIPIENTS: HANDICAPPED - BLIND

YOUNG ADULT SERVICES
American Library Association
50 East Huron Street
Chicago, IL 60611
TEL: 312-944-6780
Objectives: To advocate, promote, and strengthen services to young adults in all types of libraries - school, public and institutional.
Services: Operates through 24 committees working in areas including Leadership Training, Program Planning Clearinghouse, Library Services for Spanish-Speaking Youth, Library Services for Young Adults with Special Needs, Media Selection and Usage, High Interest/Low Reading Level, Public Relations, and others; convenes specific workshops such as Adolescent Sexuality and the Role of the Youth Librarian and Paperback Power; publishes a quarterly journal, *Top of the News.*
Publications: Top of the News

TRAINING PROGRAMS

INSTITUTE ON FEDERAL LIBRARY RESOURCES
Catholic University of America
School of Library and Information Science
Marist Hall, Room 230
Washington, DC 20064
TEL: 202-635-5085
Credit: By application (if not a CU student)
Sponsor: US/Federal Library Committee
Contact: Institute Coordinator
Description: This training course, conducted in July and August of 1990, is an outgrowth of growing concern that the government's libraries and information centers are seriously underused. The program examines the scope of the vast federal library collections and specialized services, and the problems of their underutilization. The objectives of the curriculum are:
- Identify the role of the federal libraries, information centers, and data banks in the general and military federal library community;
- Discuss the implication of the *National Commission of Libraries and Information Science's* posture as related to federal libraries;
- Identify resources, publications, and specialized services provided by federal libraries;
- Identify resources available through major government clearinghouses, such as NTIS, ERIC and DTIC;
- Identify the place of the military library and information center in the federal environment;
- Compare the in-operation or the in-process development of the major federal library information services;
- Discuss the implications for information transfer of the existing satellite technology; and
- Identify and articulate performed by the *Federal Library Committee.*
Lectures, panel discussions, and information clinics featuring library leaders, information scientists, government officials, and others prominent in federal library activities, and instructional visits to major federal libraries, information centers, and data banks, give participants the benefit of the experience of the presenters, and the observation and use of the resources. The agenda begins with an on-site presentation at the Pentagon Library, then moves to the University for the following presentations (presenting agency or organization in parenthesis):
- *Introduction to the Federal Library Community* (Federal Library Committee)
- *Introduction to the Federal Agency Library* (U.S. Naval Academy)
- *The Pentagon Library: An Overview* (The Pentagon Library)
- *Standards in Report Processing* (National Information

Standards Organization)
- *Library of Congress* (Library of Congress staff)
- *ALA and Federal Libraries* (American Library Association)
- *ASIS and Federal Libraries* (American Society for Information Science)
- *SLA and Federal Libraries* (Special Libraries Association)
- *Federal Research Libraries* (National Institutes of Education)
- *Information Resource Management* (National Oceanic and Atmospheric Agency)
- *Federal Library Service: An Open Discussion of Management and Program Operation* (individual)
- *Smithsonian Institution Libraries* (National Museum of Natural History)
- *National Rehabilitation Information Center* (Director)
- *National Library for the Blind and Physically Handicapped* (individual)
- *Private Sector Organizations and the Federal Information Community* (Herner & Company)
- *Creating Consulting in the Federal Library Milieu with an Emphasis upon Military Uses* (Costabile Associates, Inc.)
- *National Library of Medicine* (NLM Staff)
- *National Agricultural Library* (NAL Staff)
- *Veterans Administration: The Library Network* (Veterans Administration)
- *Defense Technical Information Center* (Deputy Administrator)
- *National Technical Information Service* (Director)
- United States Geological Survey Library (Chief Librarian)
- *National Commission on Libraries and Information Science* (individual)
- *Federally Supported Library and Information Science Programs: A Perspective* (U.S. Department of Education)
On the final day, an overview and summary was presented, followed by an informal discussion and conclusion.
Publications: IFLR Conference Proceedings

INDIVIDUAL PROGRAM PROFILES

ADULT LITERACY PROJECT
SEE LITERACY

CHICAGO PUBLIC LIBRARY VOLUNTEER SERVICES
Chicago Public Library
1224 West Van Buren Street
Chicago, IL 60607
TEL: 312-738-7692
Purpose: To assist the *Chicago Public Library* with providing services to library users.
Description: The *Volunteer Services* unit of the *Chicago Public Library* was started in 1978. Volunteers may be assigned to any of the library's facilities.
Volunteers have the opportunity to acquire job experience, improve skills, and contribute to their communities. They are assigned to work in the following areas: literacy, research, community relations, children's services, clerical assistance, crafts and special projects.
Short- and long-term work assignments are based on the library's needs and the volunteers' skills, preferences and availability. Orientations are held regularly for new volunteers. In-house training is provided when necessary.

CHILDREN'S ROOM
Boulder Public Library
PO Drawer H
Boulder, CO 80306
TEL: 303-444-0556
Purpose: To provide children's programs at the Boulder Public Library.

Sponsor: City of Boulder
Contact: Carol Heepke
Description: Children's programs at the Boulder Public Library are run solely by adult and youth volunteers. Some of the programs that take place in the "Children's Room" are:

- **Sunday Specials** - special events which depend on time donated by area citizens. Artists, dancers, musicians, puppeteers, hobbyists, psychologists, even hot-air balloonists have all volunteered a Sunday afternoon or two on behalf of this program. "Behind the scenes" volunteers donate time to research and organize each event, distribute fliers, and help with crowd control. Two Colorado University students and a teacher served behind the scenes during 1989. Some of the programs:
- **Pets Pets Pets** - a visit from the local pet shop owner with snakes, amphibians, cats and dogs, and other creatures, and other "animal people" with a llama, a bear, etc.
- **Puppet Shows** including *Little Stage Puppet Theater* - with fairy tales and other familiar stories; *Bunraka* - the Japanese version of a puppet show with life-size puppets; and *Shining Mountain Marionettes.*
- **St. Vrain Black Power Club** - with a "return to the west" in their authentic trapper/trader costumes and pelts and artifacts.
- **Story Hours** - with trained story tellers who select their own books and provide the necessary props.
- **Booklook** - a quarterly newspaper for children with the majority of the staff under 15 years of age who review books and conduct interviews with local writers, or make up puzzles and word games.

Many volunteers help with a variety of jobs in the children's room, such as graphics and paste-up for *Booklook* or working with computers, games and shelving or just being a "friendly floater" and doing what is needed. The range of scope of volunteer at the Boulder Public Library Children's Room is limited only by the volunteer's imagination.
Publications: Booklook (newsletter)

FRIENDS OF HANDICAPPED READERS
Mississippi Library Commission
Service for the Handicapped
PO Box 3260
Jackson, MS 39207
TEL: 601-354-7221
Purpose: To improve services and promote utilization of the Talking Book Program; to add recorded books of local interest to collection.
Sponsor: Retired Senior Volunteer Program
Contact: Edna Goldring
Description: Friends of Handicapped Readers began in 1979. At that time, the purpose was to raise money for a recording booth in which to record books of local interest to Mississippians. These books were planned by the Friends board as a supplement to the book provided by the *Library of Congress National Library Service* for the Blind and Physically Handicapped Talking Book Program.
Today the Friends program has two additional major goals: to promote education of the public to the special library needs of handicapped patrons; and to help eligible people receive the special services they require.
Volunteers in the program maintain a recording program to make available to the patrons materials about Mississipi. Volunteers work in teams to assure quality; while one volunteer reads, another is listening for errors. After the local book or other item is completely finished, another volunteer reviews again for errors.
Most of the office volunteers come to the program through the Retired Senior Volunteer Program, although a considerable number come from other sources. The office volunteers help assemble materials and prepare them for mailing to patrons. Also,

they help check all tapes and records before mailing to the patrons to be sure all parts are in the container.
The Telephone Pioneers of America have a contract with the Library of Congress to repair and maintain the equipment issued to patrons of the Talking Book Program for playing of records and tapes. The local Pioneers work three days a week. These retired telephone employees repair record players, cassette players, cassettes, Braillers, and various other items that cause problems in service to the handicapped. The Pioneers provide pick-up and delivery service within the Jackson area, while other Mississippians mail their machines to Jackson, postage free, when repairs by the Pioneers become necessary.
The Talking Book service is heavily used in the Jackson area, with patrons especially appreciative of the addition of locally-oriented materials.
Founded: 1979

JAMES MADISON NATIONAL COUNCIL
US/Library of Congress
10 First Street, SE
Washington, DC 20540
TEL: 202-707-5093
FAX: 202-707-9898
Purpose: To attract new readers and new supporters to the Library of Congress.
Sponsor: Neutrogena, Inc.
Contact: John Kluge, Chairman
Description: On January 25, 1990, the Library of Congress launched a Council of some of the country's wealthiest people and revealed new efforts to reach a national audience. Members of the new *James Madison National Council* were given a grand tour of the Library's facilities, including a sampling of the almost 100 million books and objects on its shelves. In turn, the 30 new members each gave the Library from $10,000 to $100,000 with promises of annual contributions to come. The founder of the Council, the Librarian of the Congress, emphasized that supplements from the private sector other than money - such as their entrepreneural expertise and spirit - are needed.
The task of the Council is to find ways of breaking the mold of the Library's use mostly by Congress and scholars, and exploring the many ways it can help the whole country. They will examine why, with Americans' unlimited and free access to the greatest store of knowledge in the history of the country, its use is so one-dimensional. One focus will be on youth, many of whom feel that our culture grants no fame and our economy gives few rewards to knowledge. To accomplish these goals, a number of innovations were discussed, including:

- A monthly magazine about culture and libraries similar to that of the *Smithsonian Magazine*, with costs absorbed by a publisher for the privilege of using the Library's name and cooperation (with the Library having veto power over content).
- An experimental video program, *American Memory,* to put specific subjects on optical laser discs.

A $1 million donation from the *Glenn Jones Cable Company* is to be used to tape and broadcast *The Global Library,* a weekly program on the Library aimed at librarians, teachers and students.
The *International Cultural Society of Korea* gave $1 million to expand the Library's Korean collections. In addition, an unnamed New York businessman gave $1 million to fund a traveling exhibition from the Library.
The Council works under a Congressional oversight committee on all matters pertaining to the Library.
The *James Madison National Council* was deliberately named for the man who bought Thomas Jefferson's library and established the Library of Congress. Members include the top officials of Metromedia, Neutrogena, American Society of Composers, The Washington Post Company, American Stock Exchange, Encyclopaedia Britannica, and Murphy Oil Company as well as

industrialists, a Texas oilman, and others.

To add to the celebration of Madison's accomplishment, the menu was prepared from Dolley Madison's own recipes developed when she was the town's busiest hostess.

NEWARK LIBRARY LEAGUE SCHOLARSHIP PROGRAM
SEE EDUCATION: SCHOLARSHIPS

EDUCATION: MILITARY - ACTIVE/VETERANS

NATIONAL/STATE ORGANIZATIONS

MILITARY EDUCATORS AND COUNSELORS ASSOCIATION
SEE PSYCHOSOCIAL SUPPORT SERVICES: MILITARY

INDIVIDUAL PROGRAM PROFILES

EDUCATION AND EMPLOYMENT RESOURCE CENTER
SEE RECIPIENTS: MILITARY - ACTIVE/VETERANS

EDUCATION: PARENT INVOLVEMENT

NATIONAL/STATE ORGANIZATIONS

CENTER FOR THE STUDY OF PARENT INVOLVEMENT
303 Van Buren Avenue
Oakland, CA 94610
TEL: 415-465-3507
Objectives: To increase awareness of the value of parents as volunteers, decision-makers, and advocates for children and community.
Services: Offers workshops for teachers to prepare them to work with parent volunteers; brings together parent-leaders and parent/community workers; provides consultation in planning, training, and evaluation of parent involvement; publishes newsletter and issues papers.
Publications: Apple Pie

NATIONAL CONFERENCE ON PARENT INVOLVEMENT
579 West Iroquois
Pontiac, MI 48053
TEL: 313-334-5887
Objectives: To build skills, share information, and bring people together who are advocates of parent involvement in the schools.
Services: Identifies, utilizes and provides information on resources available; conducts leadership training; compiles and distributes data on federal legislation and its relationship to parent involvement; works to strengthen communication among school, home and community.

INDIVIDUAL PROGRAM PROFILES

LOCAL VOLUNTEER SCHOOL COUNCILS
Design for Change
222 South State
Chicago, IL 60604
TEL: 312-922-0317
Purpose: To train and develop parents, teachers and neighbors to accept responsibility for, and control of, the schools of Chicago.
Sponsor: City of Chicago
Contact: Don Moore
Description: This massive training effort is a result of a reform plan that puts each separate school in Chicago's school system under the direct control of its parents, teachers and neighbors. With an estimated immediate need of 6,000 volunteers from the community to sit on 11-person councils (17,000 applied for the 540 councils), training became the greatest challenge. It is considered a test by reformers - not of the education theory, per se, but of the whole ethic of community volunteerism - "not that parents know best, but that parents care most.

The challenge was met by the community, however, as training took place in schools, in churches, in the halls of 50 major employers, and in other available space around the city.

Training is expected to help the 11-person volunteer councils draw up "school improvement plans" that the principals must implement. Some of the discussion points:

- **Testing** - The consensus is that they are needed for measurement, but must be improved and/or changed.
- **Lack of Experience of Volunteer Councils** - The consensus is that parents and others will learn by training and getting involved.
- **Bigger Role for Principal** - The consensus is that giving the principal more power at the school is offset by the Council's control of his contract.
- **An 80% dropout rate** - The consensus is that it can't get any worse. With employers giving release time to employees to serve, the PTA's enthusiastic involvement, and other factors, this problem will be vigorously attacked.

The head of *Design for Change,* who designed the reform program, lobbied for it, and is responsible for all of the training, said he was jubilant when the candidate numbers came in. "Nobody believed us, but we proved parents can care and get involved," he said.

PARENTING AND SCHOOL VOLUNTEER PROGRAM
Orangeburg Public Schools
578 Ellis Street
Orangeburg, SC 29117
TEL: 803-534-5454
Purpose: To break the cycle of apathetic parents in the low-income community by offering parenting classes and volunteer opportunities to parents and guardians.
Sponsor: Orangeburg School System
Contact: Dr. James Wilford, School Superintendent
Description: Although most of Orangeburg's 6,500 students are descendents of slaves and still live in poverty, more than half of its high school graduates are entering college. Parents who once appeared apathetic have become directly involved not only with their own children, but as tutors and other support figures to others. This "cross-parent" tutoring is encouraged, as it appears to have a positive effect on the children, who learn that the community can be an extension of the family.

A large number of parents together volunteer an average 1,000 hours a year as office and library assistants and teachers' aides, and in after-school programs such as the Boys Club, Girl Scouts and anti-drug programs. The parents recognize these programs as keeping their children off the streets and away from harmful influences.

The program began when an inner-city high school principal

learned that, although parents may never initiate a phone call to say they are worried about their children, they usually respond when called. Now, with *early childhood parenting classes* in every elementary school, and teachers and counselors keeping in close contact with parents in the middle and high schools as well, parents have become a major force in the jump in grades above the national average. For example, the fourth grade of 1974 had only 14% of the students above the national average. Today, the same grade level boasts 59% above the national average.

Another factor in the dramatic turnaround was South Carolina's 1984 Education Improvement Act, which provided funding for innovative remedial programs to improve literacy and math skills, as well as enrichment programs for gifted students. Adding a penny to the sales tax and earmarking it for education increased the state's 1989-90 school budget by $283 million. Pay raises and incentives have boosted teacher morale, and computer technology has been introduced into the classrooms. This affects parent/volunteers also, since they see that their children have the best learning tools.

An aggressive absenteeism-prevention program directly involves parents, also. A computerized device calls parents, and is backed up by calls from teachers and counselors if necessary. Repeated unexcused absences land child and parent in family court. While rewarded for good behavior with ice cream or popcorn, repeated class disruptions by a student often results in the child being taken to the parent at his or her job. With parents present and showing an interest, this type of discipline has all but disappeared, and absenteeism is at an all-time low.

The visibility of parents throughout the school, whether or not with their own children, has helped to develop a positive attitude toward learning for the child, and a new sense of purpose and control for the parent.

Publications: Involving Parents
Founded: 1989

EDUCATION: PRISONER/EX-OFFENDER

INDIVIDUAL PROGRAM PROFILES

COURT EMPLOYMENT PROJECT
SEE LAW ENFORCEMENT/CRIME PREVENTION: RE-ENTRY

EDUCATION: READING

NATIONAL/STATE ORGANIZATIONS

AMERICAN READING COUNCIL
45 John Street
Suite 811
New York, NY 10038
TEL: 212-619-6044
Objectives: To make information available on successful reading programs.
Services: Gathers and disseminates information on reading programs which have demonstrated success in motivating people to read; emphasizes children and parents; sponsors demonstration programs; publishes articles, manuals, and other materials.

DARIEN BOOK AID PLAN
1926 Post Road
Darien, CT 06820
TEL: 203-655-2777/2096; 203-327-1512/1079
Objectives: To provide free reading materials to anyone on request through the efforts of a full staff of volunteers.
Services: Collects and disseminates reading material in areas of: text books, fiction, nonfiction, and certain magazines in response to requests on official stationery from schools, libraries, universities, reading clubs, teenage and community centers, correctional centers, Peace Corps Volunteers, VISTA projects, and any other nonprofit organized group.

GREAT BOOKS FOUNDATION
40 East Huron
Chicago, IL 60611
TEL: 312-332-5870
TOLL FREE: 800-222-5870
Objectives: To increase reading and discussion among children and adults.
Services: Offers special course for volunteers and teachers on discussion techniques in relation to its program comprising 16 series of readings; fosters education of children and adults through reading and group discussion of books dealing with issues basic to mankind; publishes paperbound book sets and a handbook on reading and discussion; works with 32,500 local groups, which hold weekly adult meetings and periodic meetings for students (see separate Linden School, Middletown, Rhode Island local group description).
Publications: Great Books (set); Junior Great Books (set)
Founded: 1947

TRAINING PROGRAMS

BASIC LEADER TRAINING COURSE
Linden School
141 West Main Road
Middletown, RI 02840
TEL: 401-849-2122
Credit: Inquire
Sponsor: Great Books Foundation
Contact: Joseph Krupowicz
Description: This program, sponsored by the Great Books Foundation prepares volunteers, teachers, librarians and school administrators to lead Junior Great Books reading and discussion groups.

Although Chicago-based, the Foundation holds registration session around the country. The Middletown session received widespread interest from volunteers across the state.

The Junior Great Books program, available to students in grades 2-12, is designed to teach children how to interpret what they read. Students learn how to think independently about literature, to articulate ideas about its meaning, and to enrich their ideas through discussion.

A course for those preferring to lead Adult Great Books classes is offered also. Printed materials are offered to those unfamiliar with the program who wish to consider one or both training events for their communities.

INDIVIDUAL PROGRAM PROFILES

ADAMS' EXPRESS: A MINI-GRANT PROGRAM
Teaching-for-Excellence Mini-Grant Program
Lynch Elementary School
1901 71st Avenue North
St. Petersburg, FL 33702
TEL: 813-527-7304

Purpose: To develop an innovative solution to the literacy crisis.
Sponsor: Pinellas County School System
Contact: Kay Adams, Second Grade Teacher
Description: After receiving a *Teaching for Excellence* mini-grant from the Pinellas County School System, the second grade class of Lynch Elementary School acquired a camera and a typewriter with a plan to produce a newspaper. The goal was to motivate students who were reluctant readers at the start of the year. According to the teacher, some of the pupils "would rather have gone to the dentist than write a report." At the end of the school year they had become "inquisitive reporters," anxious to write about things they read or experienced.

The metamorphosis is the result of *Adams' Express,* a newspaper that improved with each edition. A month before the end of the year, copies of the third edition were sent to the principal, offices of state and city government officials and the homes of Pinellas County residents.

Subjects tackled by the young reporters ranged from a classmate welcoming his new brother to an assessment of the oil spill in Alaska, and from a reporter's story of a student who was stabbed to a scolding look at parental misconduct at a Little League baseball game.

The mini-grants are made available by the County school system as an incentive for teachers to try innovative teaching approaches. Funds were given to 85 such projects during the 1989 school year at a cost of $115,000 - $50,000 from the school system, and $65,000 from the *Education Foundation,* composed of a group of businesses.

Grants range from $50 to $2,500 and must address a student-based problem.

A pleasant side benefit of the *Adams' Express* newspaper program was that parent involvement increased tremendously after the project began. Pupils' enthusiasm over the paper consumed parents as well. Parents provided much of the production and technical help for the paper. They also served as a "second source" for the young reporters seeking to verify information. When facts get cloudy, according to the young weather reporter, "Ask Mom." Asked what to do when that fails, her answer is "Ask Dad." According to the teacher, "In 19 years of teaching, I have never seen such cooperation from parents."

Over 400 applicants competed for the 85 grants in 1989. Approved programs included improved curriculum for gifted pupils by interaction with Eckerd College and area businesses, swimming and water safety lessons for K-3 pupils; *Project CARES (Children At Risk in Elementary School)* to identify potential dropouts; and a computer lab where volunteers work with "average" students.

FRIENDS OF HANDICAPPED READERS
SEE EDUCATION: LIBRARY SERVICES

PRINCIPAL ON THE ROOF*
Page Traditional Elementary School
1501 North Lincoln Street
Arlington, VA 22201
TEL: 703-358-6290
Purpose: To recognize the *National Year of the Young Reader* (1989) and *National Young Readers Day* (November 15th) with a "special" activity.
Sponsor: Arlington County Public Schools
Contact: Frank Miller, Principal
Description: *Page Traditional Elementary School* takes pride in its back-to-basics approach to education, including high standards of behavior and appearance. Therefore, a notably "untraditional" challenge by the school's principal offered a distinct contrast. He was not willing to settle for *second highest* reading scores in the county.

Children whose parents opt for *Page* instead of one of Arlington's 17 neighborhood schools are enrolled on a first-come, first-served basis. Individualized instruction and team teaching are given up in favor of a single teacher for each class of about 25 students. The school also has a policy of at least four nights of homework each week. Therefore, if the principal was to see an increase in reading by these busy youngsters, the motivation would have to be something special.

The principal's challenge was offered to the 351 students - from kindergarten to seventh grade - after learning about an elementary school that challenged the children to read 1,500 books in six weeks. *Page's* principal "upped the ante" to 2,500 books, over a period of six weeks culminating on *National Young Readers Day.* He promised to spend a full day on the roof of the school if the pupils met the challenge successfully. He emphasized that monitoring of the reading challenge by parents and teachers would reflect and maintain the school's philosophy of "not just teaching reading skills, but also teaching children that they can get pleasure from reading and learn interesting things."

Parents were enlisted to certify that the reading was done, understood, and enjoyed. Teachers spent extra time keeping tallies. Staff members were issued walkie talkies to keep in touch with their leader when the day arrived. The children, themselves, gave up their play time, movie time, TV time, etc., to meet the challenge, even though most did not take the principal seriously on the "roof-sitting." When the day arrived, the children had averaged eight books each in the six week period - or over 2,700 books.

Upon arrival at school, the pupils were surprised to find the principal, carrying his briefcase, climbing to the roof. Wearing a black tail coat, he entertained the class by donning first a bowler hat, then a baseball cap and top hat. Then he unfolded a chair, pulled out a book, and sat down. He proudly announced that the two books he would read during his day on the roof were recommended by a third grader. When the children recovered from the initial reaction of mostly disbelief, they shouted a delighted "Good morning!" with some heard mumbling "wishes for rain." The most surprised student of all appeared to be a girl who arrived after everyone was inside and heard a voice booming her name from above, followed by "You're late!"

The bottom line of the challenge came from the librarian weeks later when she announced that the momentum continued, and more books were being taken out than ever before. This is what was hoped for in initiating the unusual challenge, which will take various other forms from time-to-time to maintain interest in reading, according to the principal. "What we do here is important," he said, "but it doesn't have to be serious all the time. We also want school to be pleasurable and fun."

EDUCATION: SCHOLARSHIPS

NATIONAL/STATE ORGANIZATIONS

I HAVE A DREAM FOUNDATION
31 West 34th Street
New York, NY 10001
TEL: 212-736-1730
Objectives: To motivate disadvantaged grade school students to attend college.
Services: Works to encourage disadvantaged youth to consider college; offers scholarships; oversees local, individually-run *I Have a Dream (IHAD)* projects; provides reading materials, support groups, and counseling services to sponsors of local chapters; provides information and guidance for establishment of local IHAD projects; encourages networking among local project leaders to exchange ideas and experiences; collects and shares information about project ideas; furnishes special funding for program enrichment; provides speakers to local communities; bases program

on the first IHAD project started in 1981 by Eugene Lang, who pledged full college scholarships to all sixth graders in a New York City School who finished high school.
Founded: 1985

INDIVIDUAL PROGRAM PROFILES

DOLLARS FOR SCHOLARS
Citizens' Scholarship Foundation of America
1505 Riverview Road
Box 297
St. Peter, MN 56082
TEL: 507-931-1682
Purpose: To expand access to higher education by involving and assisting the private sector in the support of students and in the encouragement of higher levels of educational achievement.
Contact: John Nadeau, National Director
Description: Dollars for Scholars are volunteer-operated community scholarship programs affiliated with *Citizens' Scholarship Foundation of America (CSFA)*. Over 500 chapters nationwide raise money for local students to continue their education beyond high school.
In addition, 300 higher education institutions have joined *CSFA's Collegiate Partner Program* and provide support, and often matching funds, to students with scholarships from a *Dollars for Scholars* chapter. Information regarding starting a chapter in your community is available on request.

EASTERN HIGH SCHOOL'S 500 CLUB
Washington Post
1150 Fifteenth Street, NW
Washington, DC 20071
TEL: 202-334-6130; 202-334-7969
Purpose: To help students reach their academic potential.
Sponsor: Washington Post
Contact: Community Services Coordinator
Description: In 1986, The Washington Post challenged Eastern High's students to reach their academic potential through its Washington Post/Eastern High School Incentive Program (500 Club). As incentive, The Post promised $500 per semester to any student who made no grade less than a B. A freshman who maintains As or Bs throughout high school can therefore earn $4,000 for post-secondary education. The money is held in a special account and sent to the accredited college, trade school or business school where the graduate has been accepted.
In addition, over 30 colleges across the country in partnership with The Post offer matching funds to any 500 Club member graduate who is admitted to their institutions, bringing to $8,000 the amount he or she can earn for college.
To offer additional support, The Post has a Mentor Program, which matches individual students with volunteer Post employees - positive professional role models. In this way the students experience first-hand in a one-on-one relationship what professional life demands. They discuss academic goals, college choices and career decisions. The student observes the mentor at work, which strengthens the partnership further.
And the Post has involved its employees further. Recognizing that personal growth encompasses much more than academic achievements, each school year the 500 Club visits The Post for informal luncheons, receptions, award ceremonies and to participate in seminars designed for their needs (SAT Instruction, Why It's OK To Be Smart, Selecting a College, etc.).
The Post initiated this program because, with today's pressures on youth, now more than ever, students need assurances that academic achievements can make their dreams come true.
Publications: Washington Post/Eastern High School Incentive Program
Founded: 1986

FRED RUFFING MEMORIAL SCHOLARSHIP
Annandale Christian Community for Action (ACCA)
7200 Columbia Pike
Annandale, VA 22003
TEL: 703-256-1378
Purpose: To provide scholarships to handicapped students.
Sponsor: ACCA
Contact: George Davis, Chairman
Description: ACCA awards a scholarship each year to one or more handicapped graduating high school seniors in the Northern Virginia area. The idea for the scholarship grew out of the interest Fred Ruffing, ACCA's Founder, had in the handicapped. He was spearheading a program for the deaf at his workplace at the time of his death.
The *Fred Ruffing Memorial Scholarship* honors the achievements of young persons who have risen to the special challenges in their lives. It is hoped it will give them the leverage needed for tackling the next rung on their educational ladders. It also gives ACCA volunteers an opportunity to establish a model to demonstrate the commitment of the community to education.
By 1989, ACCA had awarded $19,800. Recipients include students with vision, hearing, learning, muscular and paralytic problems. Among the careers they are pursuing are human services, geology, medical records technology, child development, history, economics and math.
Publications: ACCA Annual Report

NEWARK LIBRARY LEAGUE SCHOLARSHIP PROGRAM
Newark Library League
6300 Cedar Terrace Avenue
Newark, CA 94560
TEL: 415-489-0360
Purpose: To provide scholarships for students interested in the library profession.
Sponsor: Newark Library League
Contact: Susan Johnson, President
Description: A new scholarship program in the San Jose area requires community involvement as one of its stipulations for receiving the funds. For the first time, in 1989, the *Newark Library League* offered $250 scholarships to college-bound Newark Memorial High School seniors interested in a liberal Arts curriculum at a college or university.
A major requirement in addition to academic achievement and extra-curricular activities is community involvement. Also, a 3.0 high school average, a 500 word essay entitled "What the Library Means to Me" and a resume are required.
Awards are made at the end of the school year to enable the student to plan for the college freshman year.

EDUCATION: SCHOOL VOLUNTEERS

INDIVIDUAL PROGRAM PROFILES

ADDITIONS SCHOOL VOLUNTEERS*
410 Woods Avenue
Orlando, FL 32805
TEL: 305-422-5817
Purpose: To build better understanding of schools - their problems and accomplishments - by involving the community in education; to recruit, train, and place volunteers where needed in Orange County District Schools; to assist teachers by providing general and tutorial help; to individualize instruction when possible. To enrich curriculum and experiences of students by providing special programs by volunteers at no expense to schools.
Sponsor: Orange County Public Schools

Contact: Eleanor Y. Fisher
Description: This program began March 1, 1971 and is funded originally by the school system (85%), with the remainder coming from fund-raising by ADDitons Board of Directors - contributions from individuals, corporations, and foundations. The operation has a paid staff of four plus one secretary. The staff recruits, trains, administers volunteers, implement new programs, keeps records, and sponsors recognition jointly with the Board of Directors. ADDitions is an official part of the school system. Some 4,869 volunteers conducted 184,206 hours from September through April. Tutorial, Un Poquito De Espanol (Spanish conversation taught in elementary grades by volunteers); Community Resource Volunteers (special program upon request); Turnabout Tutors (peer tutoring and cross-age); Interest Groups; Living History; Basic Science Experiments; ARTY-FACTS (art appreciation); and others.

ADDitions serve during the school day in Kindergarten through High School and sometimes in the Adult Education Centers. They work in all aspects of education from the gifted to the handicapped, including a Listening to Children program. Each fall about 23 workshops are conducted in as many subjects for parents and volunteers at no charge.

Besides having the largest volunteer program in Orange County, ADDitions has won six $1,000 Community Service Awards from Walt Disney World and one $5,000 special judges award plus four top national awards for excellence given by the NSVP (National School Volunteer Programs) and Tupperware Home Parties, Inc. and other local awards.
Founded: 1971

CECIL COUNTY PUBLIC SCHOOLS VOLUNTEER PROGRAM
Cecil County Public Schools
Booth Street Center
Elkton, MD 21921
TEL: 301-398-0400
Purpose: To supplement classroom instruction through tutors, help teachers make instructional materials and serve as resource speakers.
Sponsor: Board of Education of the Cecil County Public Schools
Contact: Peter L. McCallum, Specialist in Instruction Elementary Education
Description: The Cecil County Volunteer Program began in 1973 and since then has grown steadily. Of the 26 schools in the county, 23 have established and maintained volunteer programs. Although volunteers are more active and utilized with greater frequency at the elementary level, several middle and high schools have developed effective volunteer programs.

Currently, approximately 12,400 students attend the schools in Cecil County. Last year, 4,134 students received a variety of services from 992 volunteers. Of the volunteers working in Cecil County, 265 were students (peer tutors) and 727 were adults. Individual schools are responsible for orienting and training volunteers for tasks particular to their instructional setting. Two general curriculum-oriented inservice training programs are conducted semi-annually at the county level. The county volunteer coordinator is responsible for training principals as how to work with volunteers and each principal is responsible for supervising the volunteers in his/her building.

A pamphlet for teachers has been published. During the 1983-84 school year, one for volunteers will be published. The Cecil County School Volunteer Program is completely supported by local funds.
Founded: 1973

MONTGOMERY COUNTY SCHOOL VOLUNTEER PROGRAM
Montgomery County Public Schools
850 Hungerford Drive
Rockville, MD 20850
TEL: 301-840-5340
Purpose: To provide volunteer support for school instructional and support programs Kindergarten through Adult Education.
Sponsor: Montgomery County Public Schools
Contact: Sally Marchessault, Coordinator of Volunteer & Community Resources
Description: The program began as an organized School Volunteer Program in 1978, providing management training for school volunteer (lay) chairmen who recruit, schedule, and recognize volunteers at the school building level. Training and supervision of volunteers are provided by paid staff. Central administration provides material as follows:

- **Recruitment:** brochures, flyers, bookmarks, slide-tape presentation.
- **Placement:** teacher request forms, volunteer registration forms, central clearinghouse placement, identification badges.
- **Training:** "model" training programs in reading, ESOL, health, special needs, math, adult literacy; handbooks in above-mentioned areas for staff and general volunteers; training for professional staff in use of volunteer service; certificates of completion.
- **Evaluation:** Yearly survey; annual report.
- **Recognition:** certificates for volunteers and volunteer chairmen.

Founded: 1978

NEW ORLEANS VOLUNTEERS
City of New Orleans
1300 Perdido Avenue
New Orleans, LA 70112
TEL: 504-565-6285
Purpose: To supplement maintenance, clerical and other staff during financial crises in the school system.
Sponsor: City of New Orleans
Contact: Volunteer Coordinator
Description: When a financial crunch hit New Orleans city government including the school system, volunteers who normally provide "extras" such as field trips and zoo tours rallied around schools and city offices to do more. They painted buildings, mowed grounds, planted gardens, answered phones, filed papers, cleaned bayous and donated paper, old furniture and money to keep schools and city government functioning. Whole departments of city government such as *Safety and Permits* were adopted by groups and businesses. A member of a law firm visiting a school noted the paint peeling and dropping from the ceiling. He convinced his associates and fellow employees that their help could make a difference. The firm spent $15,000 to get the stairwells and ceilings painted. There is no official total on just how much money volunteers contribute to the city and the schools, but figures from various programs show that more than $4 million a year is a safe estimate. In addition, if the 9,000 citizens who volunteered in 1988 had been paid only minimum wage, the cost to the city would be $3 million for the year.

Although the city could not have survived without the volunteers who stepped out of their roles of providing only "extras" to help meet the financial crisis, city officials were relieved when the crisis came to an end. As the tax increase passed in 1988 began to ease financial restraints, the volunteers went back to providing extras in the schools - field trips, speakers, career days and the like, and city volunteers returned to the popular volunteer assignments in the zoo, the museum, and the science and nature center. Coordinators of both the city and the school partnership programs agreed that the partnerships were never intended to replace the paid work force. "But our volunteers were right on target for us at a crucial period," the school partnership coordinator said.

NEW YORK CITY SCHOOL VOLUNTEER PROGRAM*
20 West 40th Street
New York, NY 10018
TEL: 212-921-5620
Purpose: To supplement the work of teachers by helping individual children and to provide services for which school personnel is not available.
Sponsor: NYC Board of Education, contributions from foundations, corporations, and individuals.
Contact: Mildred E. Jones, Director
Description: The New York City School Volunteer Program, in partnership with the New York City public schools, has been enriching the educational experience for thousands of city children since 1956. The program recruits, professionally trains and supervises volunteers of all ages and backgrounds who serve on a regular basis in the public schools. The NYC program, which launched the school volunteer movement in America, has served as a model for thousands of similar organizations, involving over four million volunteers across the country.

The primary goal of the School Volunteer Program continues to be the strengthening of the public school system by providing services to students. School Volunteers supplement the work of teachers by working one-on-one with children who need extra help to keep up with their classmates. They tutor reading, English as a second language, math and other subjects. Some volunteers also share special skills such as music, dance or photography. While providing individual assistance, volunteers free teachers to give the rest of their class increased attention.

School Volunteers also assist school operations to make the school day more productive for both students and staff. For example, volunteers act as hall monitors, library assistants and playground supervisors. Some help hard pressed teachers in the early grades with routine, non-teaching chores such as paper distribution and lunch money collection. Other volunteers help with kindergarten registration and health screening tests.

Throughout the years the School Volunteer Program has implemented many special projects to provide new and enrichment services for which school personnel is not available. Special programs include: the Early Identification Program, where volunteers give predictive screening tests and follow-up tutorial help to prevent reading failure in grades K through two.

Youngsters receive classroom art appreciation courses and visit museums and concerts with School Volunteers through the Cultural Resources Program.

The Career Education Project provides high school students with volunteer and paid work opportunities and career counseling, guided by trained staff and adult School Volunteers.

FACTS Volunteers help students secure financial aid for college and technical skills.

The Parent and Child program prepares parents and their preschool children for the school experience, while stressing child development concepts and the parents' role in helping their children learn.

Last year, a record 21,000 School Volunteers served in 575 public schools throughout New York City, working with over 500,000 children in grades from kindergarten through high school. More than 50,000 children in 436 schools received direct one-to-one assistance. The program's success is evidenced not only by the student's progress but also by the fact that hundreds of principals request new or expanded programs each year.

The New York City School Volunteer Program is funded by the New York City Board of Education and from contributions made by foundations, corporations and individuals.
Founded: 1956

SALT LAKE CITY SCHOOL VOLUNTEERS
440 East First South
Salt Lake City, UT 84111
TEL: 801-328-7346; 801-328-7345

Purpose: To assist professional personnel in their efforts to provide the optimum in educational opportunity.
Sponsor: Salt Lake City School District
Contact: Daphne Williams
Description: Salt Lake City School Volunteers, a non-profit organization, was organized in 1969 for the purpose of supplementing and enriching the educational program of the Salt Lake City School District. The program is designed not to relieve teachers of their duties, rather to make the school more effective, creative and viable.

The program has steadily increased in numbers and variety of volunteers, hours of service and quality of assistance. Records show more than 7,400 volunteers with over 265,000 hours of service during the school year of 1988-89.

The activities of School Volunteers are directed by a board of approximately thirty-two men and women representatives of the community. All donate their time. Board members participate:
- in guiding the training of coordinators, volunteers and professional staff;
- in evaluating each school's program throughout the year;
- in encouraging community involvement;
- in preparing special materials; and
- in funding special projects which are beyond the budget of the school district.

A full-time coordinator is hired to run the overall program. Previously, the money for the director's salary was obtained from grants from the Travis Fund, the Junior League and Model Cities, with the Salt Lake City School District donating office space and supplies. These innovative funds have now been depleted, but due to the success of the program, the school district has assumed the director's salary and other program expenses.

Volunteers come from all backgrounds and are all ages. They include homemakers, mothers and fathers, retired people and college students as well as professional persons who take time from their regular jobs to help students. Recruits from the business community are increasing in addition to self-employed men and women.

Volunteers do everything! They are involved in every facet of school operations today. While many work as teachers' assistants, or one-to-one tutors, school volunteers can be found throughout the school system. Specific volunteer jobs include, but are not limited to, reading and mathematics tutors, classroom assistants, library assistants, community resource speakers and career education assistants.

The PTA assists in an important way by providing coordinators of volunteers at each of the twenty-seven elementary schools. The district provides staff coordinators of volunteers at each of its nine secondary schools.

The programs listed below are given direction and assistance by the board committees of Salt Lake City School Volunteers. Programs are implemented by the volunteer coordinator of the school district and her staff with much help from many volunteers:
- **SMILES** - Senior Motivators in Learning and Educational Services, a senior volunteer program.
- **Business Partnerships** - a partnership between business and community organizations and the schools.
- **Basic Skills** - one-on-one tutoring in specific subjects.
- **Public Awareness Committee** - a committee to develop public awareness of school volunteer programs.
- **Kids on the Block** - puppet shows using handicapped puppets to heighten awareness of special concerns of handicapped people.
- **Volunteer Training Programs** - the planning and execution of a variety of workshops and classes for teachers and volunteers designed to enhance the involvement of volunteers in the classroom.
- **Salteens** - a student volunteer program.

This program has been used as a model to set up volunteer programs in a number of other school districts of the state and in several other states. Handbooks for principals, volunteers,

coordinators and teachers have been printed and are available as an aid to other districts.
Founded: 1969

SOUTH HUNTINGTON SCHOOL VOLUNTEER PROGRAM

Weston Street
Huntington Station, NY 11746
TEL: 516-673-1641
Purpose: To offer additional help to students needing more than the professional can offer; to enrich the curriculum.
Sponsor: School District
Contact: Rita Siegel, Coordinator
Description: The South Huntington School Volunteer Program (SHSVP) began 24 years ago. It is the only district-wide School Volunteer Program in Suffolk County. Originally, SHSVP was a federally funded program; however, the school district now funds it entirely.
The program was originated in order to utilize volunteers in school to perform non-professional chores for teachers, enabling the teacher to make better use of his or her professional skills.
Also, the program enhances the educational experience of the children through the special talents of the volunteers and through individual attention the children receive by having extra adults available.
There are a total of over 200 volunteers each year. Many of our volunteers have been with us since the program's inception. They receive one training session, and on-the-job training from the teacher for whom they work.
Volunteers work in areas of reading, math, language arts, and English as a Second Language. In the resource areas, volunteers serve in music, art, colonial history, India, Germany, etc.
Volunteers work under the supervision of the professional in the classroom, always reinforcing a skill that has already been taught.
Volunteers are parents, students and senior citizens.
Founded: 1966

VISA - VOLUNTEERS IN SCHOOL ACTION

Springville Griffith Central School
North Street
Springville, NY 14141
TEL: 716-592-3225
Purpose: To involve parents and community in the schools and their programs.
Sponsor: Springville Griffith Central School
Contact: Mary Lou Andrews, Volunteer Coordinator
Description: There are presently 40 volunteers who report weekly to the three elementary schools within the district. Also about 20 student volunteers report from 2 - 3:20 weekly after they finish their school day.
The main goal of VISA is to provide volunteers who will help teachers help children learn.

- VISA will supply trained volunteers who will offer individual help to children in an effort to stimulate their interest, skills and motivation.
- VISA will make available to the educational program (on a short term basis) the talents and resources of the community as resource volunteers.
- VISA will provide services to the school staff to relieve them of non-professional duties.
- VISA will promote better school-community relations by fostering an understanding of school needs.

The volunteer program is designed to offer supplementary and supportive services to the professional staff; to aid teachers in the individualization of instruction and the extension of their professional skills in ways not otherwise possible, but

- Volunteers are not used in the place of substitute teachers.
- Volunteers are not solicited to replace teachers under any circumstances.
- The volunteer program is not used as a strategy for increasing pupil-teacher ratios.
- Volunteers do not assume classroom responsibilities, except under the direct supervision of the classroom teacher.

Volunteers are assigned for service only at the request of the teacher.
Volunteers serve only in an auxiliary capacity under the direction and supervision of professional school personnel.
Relationships between volunteers and professional staff are ones of mutual respect and confidence.
Volunteers will at all times respect the confidence expected of professional staff members in regard to school records, information about students and relationships between staff members and children.
The VISA program operates with the approval of the Board of Education and the School Administration and is guided by the principles and policies of the school district.

VOLUNTEER SERVICES

Minneapolis Public Schools
WISE Resources Volunteers
807 NE Broadway
Minneapolis, MN 55413
TEL: 612-627-2242
Purpose: To provide volunteers who support and enrich the education of students in all Minneapolis Public Schools and all grade levels, pre-kindergarten to grade 12.
Sponsor: Minneapolis Public Schools
Contact: Robyn Cousin, Teacher/Coordinator
Description: WISE Resource Volunteers is a districtwide program that recruits, trains and places community volunteers in the classroom as tutors, resource speakers and classroom aides. Volunteers provide a vital link in the school/community partnership as role models, to build students' self-esteem, to help underachieving students with special needs, to assist with special projects, and to share their expertise.
In operation since 1965, the *Community Resource Volunteer* component of the program has over 600 volunteers listed in the *Speaker Catalog* who go into the Minneapolis classrooms at the request of teachers. Catalogs are located in every Media Center and are updated every two years. Sections are arranged by subject and speaker, color-coded and cross-referenced for easy access. Each speaker listing includes material covered, visual aids, length of presentation and appropriate grades. A grade level curriculum guide to identify appropriate speakers is also available. Some of the areas represented are Art, Assemblies, Enrichment and Mini-Courses, Health and Safety, Hobbies and Leisure Time Activities, Holidays and Special Occasions, Cultural Awareness, Language Arts, Mathematics, Music and the Arts, Science, and Social Studies - with special emphasis at the secondary level on careers and business-related subjects.
Parents, professionals, retirees, community members, skilled workers, high school and college students, etc., help enrich the curriculum and serve as positive role models for elementary and secondary school students. The volunteers may be poets, physical fitness experts, musicians and performers, professors and scientists, experts in agriculture or computers, job and career specialists, dentists, government officials, local, country or worldwide travelers, hobbyists or collectors, and many others. They share their expertise and experiences which enlarge on a teacher's efforts to provide information that would be difficult or even impossible to obtain any other way.
A *Tip Sheet (newsletter)*, identifying newly-recruited speakers and providing information on using volunteers effectively in the classroom, is published several times each year for all teachers in the district. New speakers recruited during the year are evaluated by a curriculum specialist, a teacher or an experienced resource speaker before they can be included in the *Speaker Catalog.*
Another program component provides volunteer tutors to work with students in the schools. Volunteers serve a minimum of two

hours each week in the school and grade level of their choice. They are placed with a teacher who has requested a volunteer to work with the same students each week in 30- to 45-minute sessions. Most volunteer tutors help underachieving students with basic skills, but others work with students who have physical or mental handicaps, learning disabilities, hearing and speech impairments or who do not speak English as their native language. Volunteers may also work as classroom aides with small groups to reinforce skills or help with special projects. College students also volunteer to gain field experience in their chosen major or to test career opportunities in education by working with students in a variety of ways.

Training sessions on educational topics are offered throughout the year to help volunteers in their capacity as tutors. Additional training is suggested, but not mandatory. All volunteers are asked to attend a two-hour orientation and training session prior to placement.

In 25 years, *WISE Resource Volunteers* has grown to a program which places more than 800 tutors and schedules more than 1,800 speaker presentations at 68 elementary and secondary schools. School volunteers give over 35,000 hours of volunteer time each year. In 1979, WISE incorporated as a non-profit organization. It is a public foundation composed of civic organizations which assist the Department of Volunteer Services with recruitment, publicity, and recognition of volunteers, and does fundraising to supplement the monies provided by the school district for this program.
Founded: 1965

VOLUNTEERS IN PROVIDENCE SCHOOLS
Providence School System
25 Dorrance Street
Providence, RI 02903
TEL: 401-456-9100
Purpose: To get people who care about kids to help with their education.
Sponsor: Providence School System
Contact: Dorothy Grannell, Director
Description: Recognizing that many students need individual attention that cannot be provided by a teacher in a crowded class, and is often beyond the capacities of family and friends, *Volunteers in Providence Schools* went to work. They launched a media campaign emphasizing that, although students can fall behind in school for a number of reasons, one very significant one is the lack of assistance outside the classroom. Started in 1988, the efforts of *Volunteers in Providence Schools,* through three major tutoring and reading programs, enabled 7,000 students to receive the external help needed.

The program is a consolidation of two tutorial programs - Lippitt Hill and Mount Pleasant. It has evolved into several different programs - ranging from book distributions (13,000 free books in 1989 to eight schools and a community center) to after-school study centers - made possible by a $153,000 budget provided by the School Department the *United Way,* and the *Rhode Island, Hazzard* and *Hasbro* foundations. In the distribution program, which encourages reading, each student from kindergarten to eighth grade receives three free books, which they swap with other each other when they finish with them. There are nine after-school study centers averaging 200 students each each week.

There is considerable diversity among the volunteers as well as the students, enabling targeted assignments to specific classrooms or programs. Over half of the volunteers are college students, others are upperclassmen in high school helping out their peers, or concerned adults - both working and retired. Although it is not required, some volunteers help their students before school and by phone at home at night.

Benefits to individual students go beyond the instruction aspect, providing motivation and support as well. At least 30 percent of the students are dealing with more than one language, and the volunteers help them to realize that falling behind the others

because of the language barrier does not mean that they are not good students. The volunteers gain, too, whether they are high school seniors learning teaching skills first-hand, or senior citizens gaining satisfaction in imparting their accumulated knowledge to another generation.
Founded: 1988

EDUCATION: TUTORING

TRAINING PROGRAMS

REFUGEE VOLUNTEER TUTOR TRAINING
SEE EDUCATION: ETHNIC/BILINGUAL

INDIVIDUAL PROGRAM PROFILES

ADULT TUTORIAL PROGRAM
SEE EDUCATION: ADULT

HOMEWORK HOTLINE
Trans*Parent* School Model Program
Canton Middle School
801 South Highland Avenue
Baltimore, MD 21224
TEL: 301-396-9172
Purpose: To spur interaction between school and home.
Sponsor: Canton Middle School
Contact: Arthur P. Chenoweth, Assistant Principal
Description: With a $44,000 grant from the Abell Foundation, a homework hotline was added to the Trans*Parent* School Model, which among other things automatically notifies parents by telephone recording when their children are absent. The system was developed in 1987 by educational research staff at Vanderbilt University and - as of mid-1990 - is used in 21 schools from New Jersey to Colorado.

The pilot program was initiated during the 1989-90 school year in the 640-pupil Canton Middle School and two smaller elementary schools, all in lower-income areas of the city, where parental involvement with schools traditionally has been spotty. The schools average about 300 calls per day through the system, which compares with about 60 parent-teacher contacts a day prior to the call-in system. Parents, teachers, and (grudgingly) students all agree that the program works. Teachers, especially, can measure its success through the dramatically-increased homework completions each day.

In addition to homework assignments, the hotline is used for reminders of field trips, play rehearsals, and community service projects. About a third to half of the parents call in every day, according to a school official, compared to an average of two calls per day per teacher.

Teams of teachers assemble each day by grade to list their messages by dictating into the telephone recording system. The system is controlled by a pair of desktop computers at Canton School. A small problem is the requirement for touch-tone telephones. A few parents have rotary phones or no phones at all, but some of those parents have been using neighbors' phones.

In the words of some of the students, "My mom calls the line to see if I did everything." "There's no excuse for not having your work done now." According to officials when asked whether or not the system ultimately boosts the children's performance and grades through greater parental involvement, "The jury is out, but the telephone lines are ringing." Evaluation reports will be prepared when officials feel enough time has elapsed for a meaningful study.

JOHNS HOPKINS TUTORIAL PROJECT
Johns Hopkins University
Office of the Chaplain
Levering Hall
Baltimore, MD 21218
TEL: 301-338-8188; 301-366-0614
Purpose: To provide one-on-one tutorial services for elementary school children in reading and/or math.
Sponsor: Johns Hopkins Office of the Chaplain, Johns Hopkins University, and Urban Services Agency
Contact: Tracey Stambaugh/Maddy Arnstein
Description: The Johns Hopkins Tutorial Project has three semesters (spring, summer, and fall); each semester fifty children come to the University for tutoring on Mondays and Wednesdays and another fifty children on Tuesdays and Thursdays. Thus, one hundred tutors are required each semester. Each tutor is matched up with one child, and works with him/her each session on reading or math, for one and one-half hours.
The children are anywhere from slightly behind grade level to very much behind, and they range from very cooperative and motivated to highly frustrated with learning, with short attention spans, behavior problems, and high levels of activity.
Tutors are matched up according to their experience with children (relevant would be having children of one's own, babysitting, etc.), teaching experience (preferable but not necessary!), and their desire to tackle certain problems. What is required of tutors is a commitment to be present for sessions and a desire to work with a child.
Training is provided for tutors through an orientation program; also, a tutoring manual is produced and workshops, during the course of the semester, and persons are always available to give support, advice and ideas.

JVS VOLUNTEER TUTORIAL PROGRAM
SEE LITERACY

OPERATION OUTREACH
District of Columbia Public Schools
415 Twelfth Street, NW
Room 1001
Washington, DC 20004
TEL: 202-724-4400
Purpose: To expand opportunities for community involvement in tutoring and to offer an after-school tutoring program for secondary students that focuses on basic skill reinforcement.
Sponsor: DC Public Schools/Volunteer Services and Training Branch
Contact: C. Vanessa Spinner, Director, Margaret Jones
Description: Operation Outreach is an after-school tutorial assistance program that is designed to provide basic skills reinforcement services to secondary students. Outreach also offers working community members the opportunity to volunteer in neighborhood Community Schools between the hours of 5:00 p.m. and 8:00 p.m.
Outreach, which is coordinated by the Volunteer Services and Training Branch of the Division of Adult and Continuing Education, provides training and placement services to volunteer tutors. The program, which is housed in community schools and churches, provides services to hundreds of students and places as many volunteers during the each school year. Funding for materials and coordination is provided by the DC Public Schools. The goal of the program is to directly support the system-wide goal of basic skills improvement through the implementation of the competency-based curriculum.
Founded: 1981

OPERATION RESCUE
District of Columbia Board of Education
415 Twelfth Street, NW
Washington, DC 20004
TEL: 202-724-4482
Purpose: To expand community/school partnership by recruiting volunteer tutors to work with students in grades 1-6 in reading and math in support of the DC Public Schools Student Program Plan.
Sponsor: DC Public School System and Washington Urban League
Contact: Betti S. Whaley, Project Director
Description: Operation Rescue is a community-based tutorial assistance program launched in March 1981 by the D. C. Public Schools, in concert with a broad range of community organizations, local businesses and industries, religious institutions, and individuals in support of the newly implemented Student Progress Plan. The program provides direct remedial support to children in fifty-three targeted schools.
Tutorial services are currently being provided to students in grades one through six. Approximately 2000 children are provided with instructional enhancement services in fifty-three elementary schools scattered throughout the city. Tutors can participate in one to three tutorial sessions per year. Each session is twelve weeks in length. Each tutor is responsible for working with three to five pupils. Approximately 1500 volunteers were recruited in the first year.
Co-sponsored by the DC Public Schools and the Washington Urban League, Operation Rescue was designed to continue the mission to strengthen and enlarge community support of the instructional goals of the DC Public Schools. This was achieved through the mobilization and expansion of volunteer services. Media campaigns (electronic and print) were developed and launched, organizational tutor recruitment expanded, government agency recruitment broadened, and tutor training assistance and resource programs enlarged.
Also, recruitment campaigns were mounted in nine Federal agencies. As a result of the expanded effort to secure tutors from these agencies, Operation Rescue "agency" coordinators were designated by the Departments of Agriculture, Commerce, Housing and Urban Development, Justice, Transportation Health and Human Services and Defense. ACTION and the U. S. Marines also designated "agency" coordinators.
In addition to the agencies where recruitment appeals were made, individual tutors applied from other Federal agencies including but not limited to the Library of Congress, the Department of Education, the State Department, Congressional staff offices, the White House, OMB, and the National Archives. A total of two hundred and nine Federal employees were placed during the first year.
Volunteer support for the administration of Operation Rescue continued into the third year. Administrative staff support was rendered by volunteers who were unable to tutor but wanted to participate. Again, four major corporations loaned executives to Operation Rescue. These companies were Washington Gas Light Company, PEPCO, Deloitte, Haskins and Sells and Mark Battle Associates.
The administrative staff team was further expanded in March, 1982 when ACTION approved the Washington Urban League application for nineteen 19 VISTA Volunteers. Several of the VISTA volunteers also tutored in the classroom. Two student interns joined the staff working half days for three months.
Phase III, 1982-83 school year, expanded upon activities begun in Phase II. In preparation for the entree of tutors into the schools, a four-week hour training program was developed and conducted. Sixteen retired educators were recruited to work as program monitors.
Founded: 1981

PEER COUNSELING/CROSS-AGE TUTORING PROGRAM
Hastings High School
Hastings, FL 32045
TEL: 904-692-1515
Purpose: To help students grow in their understanding of the learning process and to improve the basic skills of all students.
Sponsor: Mrs. Carole Dulaney
Contact: Mrs. Ethel McNeil, Principal
Description: The peer counseling/cross age tutoring program at Hastings High School is part of the social studies curriculum. Students in the 11th and 12th grades who have a C average and a good behavior record are eligible to apply for the course. Students may receive up to one social studies credit toward graduation representing one year's enrollment.
At the beginning of the course students attend class for a two-week orientation in human relations skills, personality development, child development and learning styles. After this orientation period, one day per week is spent with the peer counseling instructor continuing this training. Tutors are assigned to classes either at Hastings Elementary School or the 7th and 8th grade classes at Hastings High. Tutors spend four days a week under the direction of a classroom teacher tutoring individual students or small groups.
Acceptance into the Peer Counseling/Cross-Age Tutoring Program is considered an honor and each year more students apply than can be accepted. As one student says, "I like tutoring because I like to help others and I learn more about myself."

SATURDAY SCHOLARS
Chicago Board of Education
1819 West Pershing Road
Chicago, IL 60609
TEL: 312-890-8435
Purpose: To offer tutoring in mathematics to fourth-, fifth- and sixth-graders in the Chicago Public School System.
Sponsor: Chicago Board of Education
Contact: Francis R. Holliday
Description: In the fall of 1982, the *Chicago Education Corps* (the school system's volunteer organization) addressed the need for remedial help in "the basics" for students in fourth, fifth and sixth grades. Encouraged by a newspaper story regarding tutors from the Marine Corps volunteering in Washington, DC, public schools, the group approached the nearby *Naval Service School Command Post* and, after a favorable response, developed and submitted a proposal. On May 7, 1983 (Saturday), the first *Saturday Scholars* tutors arrived at *Gillespie Elementary School* for the program's initial session.
About 90 Service School Command students from Great Lakes participated as volunteer tutors. The response to the request for volunteers was overwhelming, and many volunteers were placed on a waiting list. Since the pilot program calls for expansion, it is expected that such a waiting list will not exist in the future.
To prepare for the program, the volunteers attend an orientation session at Chicago State University, where they are briefed on the Monterey Learning System, a tutorial math program in operation at Gillespie Elementary School. By using this System, which is a series of books based on step-by-step development in math basics, the student's progress can be easily measured at the end of the program.
Highly motivated by their uniformed tutors (who just happened to have extra sailor hats and medals with them), the children improved their learning both quantitatively and qualitatively. Side benefits are the positive examples set by the volunteers, and the enhancement to the education process provided by the Saturday Scholars program.
Founded: 1983

SCHOOL TUTORING PROGRAM
Cardinal Gibbons High School
2401 Western Boulevard
Raleigh, NC 27606
TEL: 919-834-1625
Purpose: To assist students with learning needs.
Sponsor: Cardinal Gibbons High School
Contact: Volunteer Coordinator
Description: The tutoring volunteer program at Cardinal Gibbons began during the 1982-83 school year. The program arose from the need to assist individual students with study skills, remedial help in particular subject areas and hands-on assistance with special projects, such as photography.
Qualified adults offer to come for an hour or more a week to work with a particular student to give direct assistance in a particular subject area and to follow-upon the progress with the respective teacher.
There is no funding involved. Five volunteers are currently active in the program.
Orientation is informal with the individual volunteer depending upon the area and student he/she will be working with. The guidance counselor is responsible for this orientation.
Founded: 1982

SOUTH PROVIDENCE TUTORIAL
One Louisa Street
Providence, RI 02905
TEL: 401-785-2126
Purpose: To provide general tutoring in reading, language arts, math and supportive services for elementary and middle school-aged youngsters on a year-round basis.
Sponsor: Federal, state, city governments; private foundations; local charities; individuals
Contact: Malvene Brice, Executive Director
Description: The agency was organized as a result of Project ENABLE Parent Conferences held in the spring of 1966. Area agents decided that they needed to focus their attention on educational issues and problems that adversely affected their children attending the Providence School System.
The purpose of the program is to respond to the unmet academic and supportive needs of students residing within South Providence and surrounding neighborhoods. The agency provides supplemental remedial educational services and counseling to students who are identified by the Public School Department as performing below grade levels. The goals of the program are to upgrade students' grade levels in reading and math; reengage students in the public school system; engage parents more fully in the child's intellectual, social growth and development; act as the liaison between the school system and the student and enhance positive learning experiences for all participants. The program was incorporated in 1971 and is a non-profit organization.
The agency recruits volunteer tutors from local high schools, colleges and universities. These volunteers provide one-to-one tutoring for students (tutees) who are experiencing difficulties with their school work. Tutors are trained and supervised in the implementation of the Individualized Educational Plan (IEP) on a daily basis. At present, 51 volunteers are engaged in the program. In addition, volunteer education consultants are recruited from colleges and Volunteers In Action (VIA) from their professional skills bank to assist with the training of tutors.
Tutors tutor on a 1:1 ratio following the IEP, file daily activity summaries, assist as chaperones on field trips, plan for tutee special events, and participate in scheduled conferences and workshops. Volunteers are asked to share one three-hour day a week with tutees.
Founded: 1966

TUTORIAL PROGRAM
1050 South Foster Drive
Baton Rouge, LA 70806
TEL: 504-922-5400
Purpose: To provide low-cost after-school tutoring to pupils in the Baton Rouge area.
Contact: Donald Hunter, Director
Description: The church-based *Tutorial Program* gives individual attention to about 3,000 students at 71 sites in 10 parishes. Most of the volunteer tutors are school teachers, with half of them holding advanced degrees. Operated after school in church meeting halls, the program works with students who have fallen behind in class, missed a lot of school, or lack social skills.

Two outside evaluators in 1989 found the average $33 expense for each student served one of the most cost-effective operations in public education, with a high potential for addressing other educational problems as well. Many view it as a dropout prevention program, even though most of the students are still in grade school.

Teachers and facilities for the program are free, but a budget is required for travel to training sessions, supplies, and some paid staff. A serious need for staff (or qualified volunteers) is in the area of evaluation and collection of data. This lack of a measurement tool is causing a problem for the program, since the state Board of Education is requiring a quantitative measurement of its effectiveness in terms of the impact on grades or academic standards. Project leaders are working to correct this problem, planning to measure students' progress by checking improvement in their grades and their teachers' view of their classroom performance. Structured evaluation is difficult with a small paid staff, but progress is being made. In the meantime, intervention by the *Legislative Black Caucus* was necessary to assure that the school's $100,000 budget for the year ending June 1990 was authorized based on the project's efforts to meet the evaluation requirement.
Founded: 1985

TUTORING VOLUNTEER PROGRAM
Sweet Briar College
Dean of Student Affairs
Sweet Briar, VA 24595
TEL: 804-381-5529
Purpose: To provide remedial and advanced instruction to elementary students.
Sponsor: Church and Chapel Committee, Sweet Briar College
Contact: Robert H. Barlow
Description: This program began in 1982 with twelve students. Approximately fourteen students per term have been involved in the program. Once a week for two hours, the volunteer works with a group or groups of elementary school children. The college provides free van transportation to students in order to expedite their service. The goals are:
- to provide tutors for the elementary schools;
- to develop friendships between college students and local elementary school children; and
- to expose students to the community and the teaching profession.

The volunteers are trained by the school system staff on their initial visit(s). The volunteers are supervised by the Dean of Student Affairs.
Founded: 1982

TWO TOGETHER*
345 Madison Avenue
New York , NY 10017
TEL: 212-878-0137; 212-878-0255
Purpose: To provide tutoring in remedial reading to disadvantaged children under 18 years of age.
Sponsor: Jewish Child Care Association of New York

Contact: Suzanne Heller
Description: Two Together was founded in 1970 to provide volunteer services to the Office of Probation and Family Court of New York City Department of Probation, and the Family Court of the State of New York. At the present time, its chief service is to supply reading assistance to disadvantaged children from 6 to 18 years of age. Tutoring is conducted on a one-to-one basis, with each tutor committed to remain with a child for a minimum of one year.

Under the supervision of the Coordinator, a trained reading specialist, volunteer tutors provides individual reading instruction to students referred from schools, courts, hospitals and social agencies. These children function at least two years below grade level in reading. Currently, 50 students can be accommodated in the program and provided tutoring in 90-minute sessions on a once-a-week basis.

Volunteer tutors are recruited primarily from the business community. Their training in Two Together includes a general orientation by the Coordinator, bi-monthly workshops in reading skills, and individual conferences with the Coordinator as need arises. Volunteers tend to remain with the program for many years.

Admission of children to program is determined following a screening interview with the child and the parent(s). Upon admission, the Coordinator completes a diagnostic evaluation of the child's learning needs and develops an individualized program which is implemented by the volunteer tutor. Along with progress in reading skills and attitudes toward learning, testing shows that many students develop heightened feelings of self-confidence. Participation of the child's parents is strongly encouraged. Parent involvement is stimulated through periodic individual conferences with the Coordinator, as well as through social functions. Another dimension aimed at buoying student interest is the program's annual activities which provide recognition and enjoyment as well as another means to sharpen skills. These activities include:
- **Students' Writing Contest** with winners featured in the program's newsletter;
- **Season's Greeting Card Contest** with the winning entry being used as the official Two Together greeting card;
- **Two Together Get-Togethers** in December and June for tutors, students and their families, and friends of the program.

At these events, prizes are awarded for the student contests and tutors are recognized for years of service to the program. In addition, there are Saturday outings scheduled four times a year, when a small group of students and tutors visit someplace educational and enjoyable in New York City.

The program's $30,000 annual budget is funded by contributions from individuals and foundations as well as the general operation funds of the Association. It is sustained by an Advisory Committee, which includes two representatives from the bank of volunteer tutors.
Founded: 1970

VALUED YOUTH PARTNERSHIP PROGRAM
SEE EDUCATION: DROPOUT PREVENTION

VOLUNTEER TUTORING PROGRAM
Madison House
170 Rugby Road
Charlottesville, VA 22903
TEL: 804-977-7051
Purpose: To provide elementary, middle and high school students with one-to-one tutoring.
Sponsor: Madison House
Contact: Jane Parker
Description: The Tutoring Program was one of the first volunteer programs sponsored by Madison House. In 1969 a group of interested University students approached the Superintendents of Schools with a proposal for instituting a program in the

Charlottesville/Albemarle public school systems - elementary, middle and high schools. Individual principals were contacted and programs were set up in their schools. Tutoring was offered also to first and second year university students and to the children of migrant workers.

Today the Tutoring Program works with ten public schools, placing approximately 150 volunteers. Tutors are assigned also to the Community Attention Homes for troubled youths, and at one private school.

The volunteer's involvement with this program begins with an orientation. This is a three-week series of discussions and presentations with experts in fields of child development, education, and psychology. When the orientation period is completed, volunteers are matched with a younger student according to grade level and subject area specified on the volunteer application.

Tutoring usually takes place in the afternoon after school is dismissed. Carpools are organized to transport tutors to the area schools. The program is flexible and it is possible to arrange other hours. Although numerous subject areas are tutored, the primary emphasis of the Tutoring Program is on the improvement of basic math and reading skills. It is the philosophy of the program that problems in these two basic fields are the root of problems in other fields.

Volunteers are made aware also of the fact that children in need of tutoring often are coping with behavioral and emotional problems as well as with academic weaknesses. Neither profound knowledge in a particular academic field, nor extensive experience in tutoring is required to be an effective tutor, but a genuine interest in helping a young person to learn is an essential quality. Also important in approaching learning difficulties are the qualities of patience and creativity, since tutoring manuals and other structured materials can be only guidelines from which individualized methods are drawn.

Founded: 1969

YOUTH DEVELOPMENT PROGRAM

2202 South Eleventh Street
Lincoln, NE 68502
TEL: 402-472-4515
Purpose: To provide educational assistance to low income youth through an on-going tutoring program; to provide camping experiences for low income children and youth of Lincoln and Lancaster County.
Sponsor: Lincoln Action Program
Contact: Deb Easterly
Description: The Lincoln Action Program tutoring project is designed to help not only the children who are tutored, but also the college students and other volunteers doing the tutoring. The majority of the tutors are students from the colleges in Lincoln, who are using the tutoring experience for credit in psychology, social work and education classes. This provides them with the opportunity to get experience working with children. Volunteers for this program also come from Pre-trial Diversion and the Volunteer Center.

The time spent doing volunteer work in this program is approximately five months, or one college semester. It starts with an orientation at the beginning of each semester and ends at the conclusion of the semester. Throughout this time tutors spend at least two hours a week at the schools. Supervision, which is done by the tutoring coordinator and assistants, is an on-going process throughout the semester. Each tutor writes a journal entry for every visit to chart the progress of the tutoring.

This program is conducted in all Chapter One schools in Lincoln elementary through high school, both public and parochial. Many of these children do not receive the extra scholastic assistance from parents or private tutors that children from an upper income family might receive. Through this program children are given this extra assistance and a chance to use their education to its fullest.

The summer part of the LAP youth services is a camping program. Each year funds are received from the City of Lincoln and Lancaster County to send a limited number of income qualified children to summer camp. This year the seven camps being used include church camps and city parks and recreation camps.

After making an application, the recipients of a camp scholarship are chosen according to several guidelines. Income, number of people in the family, past participation in the LAP Camp Program, single parent families, being a ward of the State and date of application are all used when choosing campers for the Summer Program.

EDUCATION: VOCATIONAL/ALTERNATIVE

NATIONAL/STATE ORGANIZATIONS

FLINT COMMUNITY SCHOOLS
923 East Kearsley Street
Flint, MI 48502
TEL: 313-762-1256 (elementary); 313-762-1237 (secondary)
Objectives: To provide leadership in bringing together the community and its resources.
Services: Initiates, promotes, and maintains enrichment programs for children, youth and adults; develops and maintains lines of communication between parents, residents and the school in planning and implementing programs; assists in identifying community concerns and develops strategies to help resolve them; works with a School-Community Advisory Council (SCAC) at each location; provides Home School Counselors to help alleviate family problems that may block participation in community programs; publishes information on all programs in the form of booklets, fact sheets, flyers, etc.

INDIVIDUAL PROGRAM PROFILES

ALTERNATIVE EDUCATION AND WORK CENTER
Los Angeles Unified School District
2011 North Soto
Los Angeles, CA 90033
TEL: 213-225-0375
Purpose: To assure that as many children as possible have access to quiet, safe classrooms where learning can occur.
Sponsor: Community Youth Gang Services
Contact: Wendy Reddish, Consultant
Description: In Los Angeles, *Alternative Education and Work Centers (AEWC)* are operated in difficult neighborhoods and run by the adult-education division of the city's Unified School District. The alternative schools attempt to recover school dropouts - many of them gang members from 14 to 19 years old who admit to arrests ranging from selling drugs to grand theft auto. The results from 1988 to 1989 showed a four percent decline in the dropout rate, but the schools hope to do better. As of the 1990-91 school year, the District has 21 AEWC sites, representing an expenditure of $3.6 million. Grants received during the period amounted to $1.7 million.

The schools are entered voluntarily by the youth - many having been in and out of custody of juvenile hall, often running from the police or living in a boys' placement center. The individual lesson plans at AEWC enable students to make up credits and return to high school or prepare for a high school equivalency examination.

Although often troublesome, the school finds AEWC the only way to provide such youth with the free, public education they are entitled to just like everyone else.

Bimonthly meetings find former gang members offering firsthand information on how to handle kids in gangs. Gang names like *Crips, Bloods, Big Hazard,* and *Imperial Courts* are commonly-used terms in the presentations - usually followed by the word "territory." Youth joining the gangs are as young as ten in many instances, according to the volunteer panelists.

The all-volunteer *School Safety and Security Task Force* has called for mandatory expulsion of students committing serious offenses or possessing firearms, denying them the right to enroll in another district school. It recommends that the violators be transferred to a special school, proposed but not yet funded. Only a small percentage - three percent - were expelled during the 1989-90 school year. The *Task Force* is composed of 65 parents, educators and law-enforcement officials.

The Unified School District works with independent groups such as *Community Youth Gang Services (CYGS),* which focuses on reducing gang violence in Los Angeles through job development, crisis intervention, graffiti removal and gang awareness. One former gang member, now 47, who was shot twice and served two prison terms for gang-related homicide, is now a consultant with CYGS. Amazed to have reached the age of 47, he said "Dealing with gangs to me is a luxury. To a lot of people, it is a nuisance." Signs of the youth "turning around" come from a 15-year-old Hispanic youth who had been a member of the *Big Hazard* gang since the age of ten. "I wanted to get my credits straight so I could get on my level in school."

BOSTROM ALTERNATIVE CENTER FOR EDUCATION*
801 West Woodland
Phoenix, AZ 85007
TEL: 602-253-1175
Purpose: To provide an education program that considers individual student needs, abilities, and learning styles.
Sponsor: Phoenix Union High School District
Contact: Betty Sheeley
Description: Experience-Based Career Education is a fundamentally different type of education for secondary students. While students in traditional programs attend classes all day, EBCE students spend a major portion of their time on learning projects in the community, with businesses, institutions, and other establishments voluntarily setting aside time and staff to assist with the program.

The Bostrom Alternative Center for Education operates an EBCE program. Bostrom has chosen to divide its staff and students into three levels. The level III team is described below:

Level III activities are tailored to individual student needs, abilities, learning styles and goals. Students are guided at their learning/job sites by working adults and Learning Managers who visit their sites. These sites include offices, factories, shops, hospitals, schools - anywhere careers are practiced.

FIRST PLACE
SEE RECIPIENTS: HOMELESS - EDUCATION

MASTER BUILDER GAME
SEE EDUCATION: CAREER EXPLORATION

PROJECT OASES
Pittsburgh Middle Schools
Boggs C&S Center-OVT
850 Boggs Avenue
Pittsburgh, PA 15211
TEL: 412-488-2531
Purpose: To motivate at-risk eighth grade students who have not responded well to traditional education programs.

Sponsor: Chapter II Block Grant (federal government); foundations; business/industry
Contact: Al Markowski
Description: OASES is considered both a classroom and a community-centered program. It begins with the seventh grade teaching staff, who recommend students who show a lack of self-esteem, poor attitude, and disinterest in school and school work, per se. Recommended students are thoroughly screened by a school dean and counselor so that those who will benefit most are given this opportunity. The two pronged program combines vocational training and volunteer work, requiring three of the seven class periods of the school day.

Most of the students selected for OASES believe strongly that the service-centered program holds the students' interest and deters misbehavior. At the same time the students are motivated to learn and provided a context in which self-esteem and a sense of achievement and competence can grow.

After completing an orientation period and eight weeks of occupational training, the students move on to volunteer in the community. Their volunteer assignments are not "make-work" jobs by any means. OASES volunteers have restored substandard dwellings for nonprofit organizations, built a playhouse for mentally retarded children, constructed an entrance ramp for a double amputee, painted for the Salvation Army, and repaired and built a number of other structures throughout the community. In addition, they have worked for the City of Pittsburgh and Pittsburgh Public Schools as well as other community entities in a number of meaningful capacities. They have built a sound reputation for quality work and reliability and are considered an extremely valuable resource for the community.

The academic side of the student's work has benefited also. From a near-dropout status, 40% of the OASES students were on the honor roll at the end of the first year. Behavioral and discipline problems are almost nonexistent.

Funding for the program was provided initially by private foundations, a Chapter II Block grant, and donations from local merchants and corporations. As of late 1989, the Pittsburgh School District provides 100% funding for all four OASES centers - Allegheny, Frick, Knoxville, and Milliones Middle Schools. Students receive small awards, ranging from T-shirts to trophies, for their successes measured by good attendance, overall improvement, honor roll status, and other standards. They continue to display pride in workmanship, a cooperative attitude, and a willingness to take tasks to completion.

QUALITY EDUCATION PROGRAM
SEE EMPLOYMENT: CHILDREN/YOUTH

SCHOOL COMMUNITY RELATIONS PROGRAM (*formerly Concord-Cabarrus Community Schools Program*)
Cabarrus County Schools
PO Box 388
660 Highway 29 North
Concord, NC 28026-0388
TEL: 704-786-6191
Purpose: To promote volunteerism in schools; to provide use of school buildings to the public; to encourage and promote business and industry involvement in schools; to provide up-to-date public information.
Sponsor: varies
Contact: Margaret K. Dabbs
Description: "Together, we can strengthen our schools" is the basic philosophy of the Cabarrus County School Community Relations Program.

The "we" in the previous statement refers to the school community and the non-school community. It is a partnership that links those two communities.

The local school superintendent and board of education have generated an enthusiastic springboard to community involvement

in the twenty local schools. The program works to foster
inter-agency coordination and more accessible use of schools by
members of the community. The Cabarrus County School systems
agreed to participate in the program in 1978.

Funds are provided locally and by the North Carolina General
Assembly. The local program is under the Division of
Communication Services with the Department of Public
Instruction in Raleigh.

The economy is on everyone's mind. So, it is especially important
that education, business/industry and community members form
partnerships to deal with the needs of students and society in the
1990's. This is something the School Community Relations
Program is doing and hopes to expand.

The Cabarrus School Community Relations Program urges
coordination of existing services and cooperation between all to
improve the quality of life for all.

Civic organizations, churches, businesses and industries, senior
citizens groups and institutions of higher learning serve as a wealth
of people for the volunteer program. Volunteers do a myriad of
different jobs from tutoring to storytelling, to teaching art to
providing money or clothes. Everyone has a talent and many are
willing to share this with school children.

Outside of the volunteer component, schools provides a physical
setting for adult education classes, recreation for children and
adults, physical fitness such as aerobics and many activities by the
community at large.

The School Community Relations Program strives to bring the
schools and the community together - because we believe
"Together we can strengthen our schools."

EMPLOYMENT

NATIONAL/STATE ORGANIZATIONS

COMMUNITY CAREERS RESOURCE CENTER
1516 P Street, NW
Washington, DC 20005
TEL: 202-667-0661
Objectives: To help socially-concerned individuals find meaningful work with nonprofit public interest organizations; to help those organizations recruit qualified and dedicated staff.
Services: Maintains an extensive nationwide job listing bank, arranged by region, for community organizers, outreach workers, VISTAs, and other interested citizens; examines major issues of concern to community-betterment groups; profiles organizations that are challenging these issues and interviews the individuals who are leading the efforts; provides how-to information on mounting a community program, or making an existing one more effective; publishes a monthly newspaper with community-oriented columns, readers forum, reviews, announcements, information on resource guides and other materials.
Publications: Community Jobs; Survival Planning; Making the Community a Career
Founded: 1977

NATIONAL EMPLOYMENT AND TRAINING ASSOCIATION
653 Eason Boulevard
Tupelo, MS 38801
TEL: 601-842-5621
Objectives: To monitor development of Vocational Education/Job Training Partnership Act (JTPA) programs to assure quality and nondiscrimination.
Services: Works with public and private sectors, including business/industry and JTPA (Job Training Partnership Act) programs, to recommend standards for JTPA training programs; sponsors educational and leadership development programs; publishes quarterly *Manpower Notes* and other materials

US/DOL - EMPLOYMENT AND TRAINING ADMINISTRATION
601 D Street, NW
Washington, DC 20210
TEL: 202-376-6750
Objectives: To assist people out of work through services and activities designed to meet diverse needs.

Services: Conducts and arranges training programs, placement services, transitional public service jobs, and unemployment compensation; contracts for experimental and demonstration programs to guide its long-term actions; directs the Job Training Partnership Act (JTPA), which gives authority to state and local governments to design and operate their own training programs to meet local needs; directs other national programs including: WIN (Work Incentive Program for welfare recipients); youth employment; special programs for Indians, migrant and seasonal farm workers, older workers, and others with particular job disadvantages. [The Women's Bureau of the Department of Labor is outlined on the next page; for details on other divisions (mostly technical) request 10-page booklet, *The U.S. Department of Labor*]
REGIONAL OFFICES:
I. Boston, 617-223-6439
II. New York, 212-944-3210
III. Philadelphia, 215-596-6336
IV. Atlanta, 404-881-4411
V. Chicago, 312-353-0313
VI. Dallas, 214-767-6877
VII. Kansas City, 816-374-3796
VIII. Denver, 303-837-4477
IX. San Francisco, 415-556-7414
X. Seattle, 206-442-7700
[Write or call for complete address/phone list]
Sponsor: US/DoL - Department of Labor

US/DOL - PRIVATE SECTOR INVOLVEMENT PROGRAM
Office of the Secretary
Washington, DC 20210
TEL: 202-523-6666
Objectives: To promote greater private sector involvement in resolution of community problems.
Services: Takes actions to reduce and eliminate government activities that have proven to be economically counterproductive and to strengthen programs and policies which enhance the private sector role; includes key components in this effort of:
- A vigilant review of rules and regulations, which includes a cutback on paperwork requirements that burden business but do not contribute to the well-being of the American worker.
- Efforts to improve labor-management cooperation, which include projects with the goal of providing greater protection of workers through greater private sector involvement.
- A strengthening of education and communication activities, which includes efforts by Labor-Management, the Women's

Bureau, the Office of the Assistant Secretary on Veterans' Employment, and the Employment and Training Administration - all placing heavy emphasis on community involvement.

Includes in its initiatives on private sector involvement the following actions which have proven successful:

Occupational Safety and Health Administration
- develops a series of voluntary protection programs which rely on private initiatives to maintain safe and healthful working conditions.
- investigates voluntary protection options which could supplement the agency's enforcement program.
- mounts agreements with individual associations to commit the agency to help design job safety and health programs to benefit workers.

Mine Safety and Health
- encourages mine management and labor to assume their fair share of responsibility for safe and healthful operations.
- sponsors and encourages safety associations such as the Joseph A. Holmes Association which grants awards to individuals, officials and groups for achievements in safety, and the Holmes Safety Program which develops and distributes materials for use in safety meetings at mines.
- sponsors "Sentinals of Safety Competition," which is an annual awards program, and the "National Mine Rescue and First-Aid Contest," which is a biannual skill development event.

Employment and Training
- designs major roles for private business in new efforts for training of unemployed groups.
- cooperates with "Job Training Councils" which are established by Governors and consist of private business managers who work with local "Private Industry Councils" toward making the private sector a full partner in managing new training programs.

Small and Disadvantaged Business Utilization
- promotes minority businesses through support of the Commerce Department's Interagency Council for Minority Business Enterprise.
- suggests criteria for the selection of Private Sector Symposium sites to assist above Council.

Women's Employment Opportunities
- mounts actions concerning child care, job fair programs, apprenticeship and construction, and improved conditions for women entering business and on corporation boards.
- plans initiatives that seek to establish at least one employer-sponsored child care system in each region, offering workshops to public and private sector staff with responsibilities in this regard.
- provides information and technical assistance to the private sector on child care, and tax incentives for employer involvement.
- conducts training which focuses on recruiting and preparing women for skilled trade jobs and retaining them in these jobs.
- mounts job fairs which bring together women who are unemployed and employment resources (counselors, personnel specialists, interviewers, etc.) to facilitate job placement.
- assists agencies such as the "Door Opener" agency in Iowa, which conducts training programs for women wishing to enter the small business market.
- helps to establish a network among women who are well-established in business to create mentoring relationships, and to involve board and management level women in improving mobility for women workers in their corporations.

Labor-Management Services Administration
- encourages voluntary settlements between employers and veterans and reservists returning to their pre-service jobs.
- takes steps to reduce unnecessary paperwork and make it easier for employers, unions, and others to comply with Administration laws and regulations.

Veterans Employment
- initiates projects aimed at linking veterans in business with veterans seeking employment in coordination with the Department's Office of Small and Disadvantaged Business Utilization.
- utilizes information on known veteran-owned businesses to locate other veteran-owned businesses, and to promulgate information concerning veterans' employment programs such as "Targeted Tax Credit," a project of veterans helping veterans.

Works continually on new programs that increase private sector involvement in the Department's programs.

Sponsor: US/DoL - Department of Labor

US/OPM - PRIVATE SECTOR INITIATIVES IN OPM
Office of the Director
1900 E Street, NW
Washington, DC 20415
TEL: 202-632-6106
Objectives: To emphasize programs that bear on the private sector and indicate initiative in the area of public/private partnerships.
Services: Deals primarily with other agencies of the federal government, but maintains contact to some extent with the private sector through programs such as the following:

Outpatient Program for federal employees who have been displaced by reductions in force; includes a *Job Information Exchange* and other programs at the regional level.

Federal Executive Associations in local areas to oversee programs that benefit employees (also, this group monitors the *Combined Federal Campaign* local efforts).

Mobility Programs which involve the temporary assignment of employees between federal agencies and state, local, and Indian tribal governments, institutions of higher education, and other public and private organizations (assignments can last up to four years); involves three programs:
- *IPA Mobility Program* (initiated by OPM)
- *President's Commission Executive Exchange*
- *White House Fellows Program*

Health Benefits Program which enables federal employees and annuitants to insure themselves through two private health insurance plans, union health plans, and through membership in various local *Health Maintenance Organizations,* commonly called *HMOs* (a system that could serve as a model for large private employers as well).

Sponsor: US/OPM - Office of Personnel Management

TRAINING PROGRAMS

VOLUNTEERING YOUR WAY TO A SUCCESSFUL CAREER
Southeastern University
501 Eye Street, SW
Washington, DC 20024
TEL: 202-488-8162
Credit: 0.6 CEUs
Sponsor: Southeastern University
Contact: John Chase, Dean
Description: Recognizing that both public and private sectors today are acknowledging the value of volunteer work and community service work as a legitimate form of experience on job applications, vitas and resumes, Southeastern University designed a seminar to explore the essential elements of career development as it relates to volunteerism. The three-pronged program, over a three-day period, covers the following topics:
- **first day:** self-assessment, skills determination, how to use self-knowledge to achieve goals.
- **second day:** ways to narrow the gap between past experience

and desired or needed experience.

- **third day:** opportunities for paid and non-paid work in the public and private sectors and how to achieve chosen objectives.

Specific areas of instruction include:

- choosing a volunteer career
- volunteer skills transferable to paid work
- using volunteer job contacts for paid work
- volunteer work versus paid employment
- the value of volunteer work on the resume

Faculty includes persons involved in studies of volunteerism and the transition from volunteer to paid employment, and faculty from Southeastern's Cooperative Education, Graduate Studies, and Student Activities Divisions, as well as from other area colleges.

INDIVIDUAL PROGRAM PROFILES

HELPING HAND
United Way of Allegheny County & SW PA
200 Ross Street
PO Box 735
Pittsburgh, PA 15230-0735
TEL: 412-261-6010
Purpose: To respond to the needs of the unemployed.
Sponsor: Pittsburgh Steelers Football Club
Contact: L. Stanton Williams, Chief Volunteer Officer
Description: Families who once prospered working in the steel industry in western Pennsylvania are now jobless and struggling to put food on their tables. To respond to the needs of the unemployed, a project called *Helping Hand* was developed by the United Way of Allegheny County. The board president, who is also a director of *PPG Industries,* proposed a plan that would help families and individuals suffering as a result of the area's economic problems.

A *Helping Hand Task Force* was formed to run a one-month fund-raising drive completely separate from the annual United Way campaign. When funds were in hand, the program began distributing vouchers which could be redeemed at various distribution sites for goods and services, with the value of the vouchers depending on the size of the family. Vouchers could be redeemed for food, health care, and help with utility payments. Once the vouchers were redeemed, participating agencies submitted them to *Helping Hand* for reimbursement. At the same time, employment and financial counseling for individuals and families was made available.

A portion of the proceeds was allocated to food banks, health insurance companies, and counseling services, allowing more people to take advantage of the free help. In-kind services also were offered to the program, including an offer from *St. Francis Hospital* to give free medical care to the unemployed. Participants in the program received a catalog detailing the services offered at various social service agencies.

In addition to helping the unemployed, *Helping Hand* has assisted others in need. In response to a string of destructive tornadoes that struck western Pennsylvania, the board voted to allocate $20,000 from the fund to ease the financial crunch on the *Salvation Army* and the *American Red Cross.* To help raise money, collection containers were placed in *McDonald's* restaurants, and WTAE-TV hosted a successful day-long telethon. In addition, *Helping Hand* received grants from foundations and corporations, and individuals gave one-time cash or credit card donations.

Chairman of *Helping Hand* is the president of the *Pittsburgh Steelers Football Club,* and Vice Chairman is the international president of the *United Steelworkers of America.* The body of the Committee included representatives from labor, as well as United Way labor-relations specialists, who knew were help was needed most and how it could be delivered. Overall, the program represents a major community response to problems of people in need, bringing together a broad-based coalition of agencies and individuals dedicated to helping the unemployed.

JOB SEARCH
Catholic Charities
1231 Prytania Street
New Orleans, LA 70130
TEL: 504-523-3755
Purpose: To serve as a communication link between job searchers and employers.
Sponsor: Catholic Charities
Contact: James Livingston, Director
Description: Job Search is a program of *Catholic Charities* designed to provide employment assistance for clients - most of them desperately in need of work. The service provides job search training and orientation, placement, referral and follow-up. Volunteers also make referrals to other resources clients may need. One volunteer came to the program through an alternative sentencing requirement of 50 hours of community service after a traffic violation, and never left.

The program begins when a volunteer enters the office and "pushes the button on the answering machine." Word of mouth has served to make the service an easy one to approach. Phone messages are answered promptly, showing the program's concern for the individual's distress. Each caller has a different problem, according to one volunteer. They are asked to sign up for job training, and a job search is immediately begun. While the placement is being sought, volunteers give job-seekers words of hope and encouragement, someone to talk to while the problem is addressed.

OUT OF WORK: WHAT NOW? AN UNEMPLOYMENT CLINIC
Triton College
2000 Fifth Avenue
River Grove, IL 60171
TEL: 312-456-0300
Purpose: To conduct a one-day clinic to provide opportunities for the unemployed to learn basic job search skills, learn how to cope financially and emotionally with unemployment and to become aware of public and private resources available to them.
Sponsor: Triton College
Contact: Ms. Lynn Parker, Associate Dean - Career Education
Description: The Triton College President and Board of Trustees are aware that unemployment is higher now than it has been since World War II. The new unemployed and their families are struggling with a variety of emotional, financial and job search concerns.

As a community service, the College has organized a one-day clinic to assist the unemployed of the district.

The event, titled *Out of Work: What Now? An Unemployment Clinic,* is held on a Saturday, and is staffed completely by volunteer teachers, typists, maintenance staff, organizers, demonstrators and others. The intent is not to offer job placement, but job-search skills and life-coping skills. The program has been developed with consideration for the needs of the unemployed and their families.

Workshops, information booths, demonstrations, and a goods and services exchange are featured. Highlights are listed below:
Workshops: 1-2 hour sessions. Selected topics:

- Unemployment: A Family Issue
- Financial Planning During Job Transition
- Leisure Activities on a Limited Budget
- Retraining: A Matter of Survival
- Make an Application Work for You
- Coping With Stress

Demonstrations: 15-20 minute presentations. Selected topics:

- Buying Smart
- Reassessing Job Goals

- The Job Interview: An Employer's Perspective
- After the Interview: What Now?

Information Booths: Approximately 120 community agencies and organizations staff booths to distribute information and answer questions about their services. Seven broad categories are covered:

- employment and training;
- job search skills;
- financial affairs;
- community services;
- health, leisure and recreation;
- consumer education; and
- job search services.

Goods and Services Exchange: Clinic participants may post information about goods or services they need or are willing to exchange. Exchange participants are mailed a booklet (after the Clinic) containing all listings. The idea is to provide an opportunity for the unemployed to get things they may need without having to exchange money.

The effort is impressive, since assisting in this area of concern, unemployment, is a great challenge for volunteers in today's economy.

PUBLIC ASSISTANCE CLIENTS VOLUNTEER
SEE RECIPIENTS: FAMILIES - EMPLOYMENT

WORK INCENTIVE DEMONSTRATION PROGRAM/JOB FACTORY
Northeast Service Center
500 Vandeveer Avenue
Wilmington, DE 19802
TEL: 302-571-2938
Purpose: To teach job search techniques to persons unemployed and receiving public assistance.
Sponsor: Division of Economic Services, Delaware Department of Health and Social Services
Contact: Barbara Kaminski or Maurice Beeman
Description: The Job Factory began in May 1982. It is a component of the Work Incentive Program, in which welfare recipients are taught innovative job search techniques. The program goal is placement of participants in unsubsidized employment within 15 days.
The Job Factory program consists of four days of classroom training, in the areas of:

- job applications,
- grooming and dress for the interview,
- answering tough interview questions, and
- contacting employers on the telephone to set up job interviews.

Emphasis is also placed on participants' self-esteem, and several exercises are devoted to increasing self-confidence. The remainder of the 15 day period is spent on the phones, contacting employers and arranging job interviews.
Volunteers working in the Job Factory participate fully in the program, helping with teaching, individual supportive counseling, clerical duties, and providing transportation for participants to and from job interviews.
According to the Director, "The volunteers have become very deeply involved and are crucial to the operation and success of the program."
Founded: 1982

EMPLOYMENT: AIDS

TRAINING PROGRAMS

AIDS IN THE WORKPLACE
SEE AIDS: EMPLOYMENT

EMPLOYMENT: CAREER EXPLORATION

TRAINING PROGRAMS

MAKING THE VOLUNTEER EXPERIENCE COUNT
University of Nebraska
Dept. of Conferences & Institutions
205 Nebraska Center
Lincoln, NE 68583
TEL: 402-472-2844
Credit: CEUs
Sponsor: University of Nebraska; Volunteer Bureau; Junior League; Department of Public Welfare
Contact: Marion Kaple, Program Coordinator
Description: This conference looks at the volunteer movement from a historical perspective, and examines current trends and changes that are affecting volunteerism today and shaping its direction for the future. Topics include:

- the historical roots of volunteerism
- the philosophical, religious, cultural values that have shaped the volunteer movement
- volunteerism as a mode of citizen participation
- societal value changes and their impact on volunteerism
- how changes in volunteerism affect all segments of the community

The conference design encompasses many facets of the volunteer community, and provides information and assistance for:

- volunteer leaders who want to keep abreast of the changing role of volunteerism today
- volunteers seeking to have their experience recognized for academic credit or paid employment
- educators wishing to know more about the impact of volunteerism on student development
- community leaders who want to examine the pros and cons of voluntary citizen participation
- personnel directors and employers who are being urged to recognize volunteer experience in job applications
- agency personnel who work with volunteers
- legislators and government officials interested in the role of local/state/federal government in volunteerism

Workshops titles include: Volunteerism as an Academic Experience; Personal Growth, Values and the Volunteer Experience: The Volunteer Experience and Community Leadership; Employment Credit for Volunteer Experience; The Art of Turning Volunteer Work into Paid Experience; Government and the Volunteer Experience. To enable wider participation, child care is provided.

NCSL JOB SKILLS DEVELOPMENT SEMINARS
US/ACTION - The Federal Volunteer Agency
1100 Vermont Avenue, NW
Suite 1100
Washington, DC 20525
TEL: 202-634-9108
TOLL FREE: 800-424-8480
Credit: Inquire
Sponsor: US/ACTION
Contact: Nancy Yde, Public Information Officer
Description: The National Center for Service Learning (NCSL) offers free job skills development seminars for educators who run programs that involve students in community service. Seven seminars are scheduled across the country each school year. Three types of seminars are conducted: High School Seminars, College Seminars, and Community Impact Seminars.
In addition to building skills for coordinators of service-learning,

experiential education, or volunteer programs, the seminars provide a forum for a sharing of ideas and resources. Potential coordinators are encouraged to attend and explore the purposes and functions of such a program.

All seminars are led by teams of trainers with extensive experience in service-learning. An NCSL staff member attends each seminar to provide information about the activities and resources of the national program. The two formats are:

High School and College Seminars - designed to help service-learning program leaders to strengthen existing programs by addressing management issues. These issues include:
- developing volunteer job
- facilitating learning
- cultivating agency relationships
- promoting service-learning in the school or college

Community Impact Seminars - for high school and college coordinators who direct established programs and who want an intensive seminar focused on strategies for developing more effective interaction between the service-learning program and the community. Sessions in this seminar address:
- identification of community needs
- cooperation with community agencies
- involvement of those being served in the planning of services

Seminars are tuition-free; participants cover their own room, board and travel. Information on dates and locations is available in July of each year.

VOLUNTEER EXPERIENCE: CHANGE, CHALLENGE, CHOICES
Allegheny County Community College
Center-North, 111 Pines Plaza
1130 Perry Highway
Pittsburgh, PA 15237
TEL: 412-931-8500/Ext. 43
Credit: Inquire
Sponsor: Community College of Allegheny County; Voluntary Action Center of the I&R Services of Allegheny County; Junior League of Pittsburgh; Title I of the Higher Education Act
Contact: Sarah Jane Rehnborg, CCAC-North Coordinator
Description: This workshop was designed for persons interested in identifying the skills and interests they have acquired through life experiences and volunteer work. Attention was given to developing life goals and career goals based on individual experiences. Workshops were designed specifically for the New Volunteer, the Experienced Volunteer, and the Administrator of Volunteer Programs and Voluntary Organizations.

An expert in the area of identifying skills and competencies acquired through volunteer work, Winifred L. Brown, presented the keynote address, and led one of the workshops. A publication on the subject, I Can, resulted from her work in this area of volunteerism. The three workshop sessions were:

The New Lifestyle as a Volunteer - how to assess present skills, interests and values; how to search for a meaningful volunteer job - one which will develop skills as well as help others; understanding the rights and responsibilities of volunteering.

The Experienced Volunteer - how to assess present skills; how to develop areas of interest and set goals; how to explore values, analyze and document skills, write resumes, identify roadblocks, learn career development steps and set individual goals. (This session was based on Junior League Volunteer Development Course.)

The Administrator of a Volunteer Services Program or Organization - how to identify skills acquired in leadership positions; how to develop personal career goals; how to analyze the workshop process so that participants can assist volunteers in their own programs to identify skills and personal life goals (special attention to the latter).

A one-hour mid-day panel program enabled participants to explore volunteerism from many perspectives, including tips about selecting volunteer settings, documenting skills, translating volunteer experiences into employer language, using volunteer credentials when applying for college, and ways to develop volunteer careers. Panel members came from the Museum of Art, the League of Women Voters, the National Council of Jewish Women, RSVP field staff, the local I&R program, and business. A wrap-up session brought together faculty, students, panel members, and workshop facilitators for an informal discussion of the workshop, and individual volunteer programs. Take-home resource packets were provided for future use by participants.

EMPLOYMENT: CHILDREN/YOUTH

NATIONAL/STATE ORGANIZATIONS

JOB CORPS
US/DoA - Forest Service
Independence Avenue
(Between 12th & 14th Sts.)
Washington, DC 20250
TEL: 202-545-6700; 202-347-2500
TOLL FREE: 800-424-5111
Objectives: To train disadvantaged American youth in basic educational and vocational skills; to assist the Agency in its charter to preserve our natural resources.
Services: Operates under the Jobs Training Partnership Act of 1982; maintains Job Corps Civilian Conservation Corps (JCCCC) centers primarily in rural areas which provide, in addition to training and assistance, programs of work experience to conserve, develop, or manage public natural resources or public recreation areas; or to develop community projects in the public interest; trains young men and women over 16 and under 22 to become skilled in areas of Center construction and rehabilitation, roads, trails, recreation areas, cattle guards, fireplace grates, gates, timber stand improvement, heavy equipment, auto repair, carpentry, painting, nursing, keypunch operating, clerical work, slash burning, and forest fire-fighting and control; operates Centers in all parts of the United States both in large cities and in national parks.

Provides room, board, clothing, books and supplies, counseling, medical and dental care, and other services as well as a small cash allowance; holds classes in general living skills such as health and grooming, getting along with other people and the boss at work, and how to use leisure time; helps with job search at completion of training.
Sponsor: US/DoA - Department of Agriculture
Contact: Robert Williams
Publications: Forest Service Volunteer; Volunteers in the National Forest; A Parents' Guide to Job Corps; Tell Them About Job Corps; Training Opportunities in Job Corps; Job Corps Civilian Conservation Centers; Job Corps Works - So Does Its Graduates

OPERATION CHILD WATCH
SEE RECIPIENTS: CHILDREN/YOUTH - PROTECTIVE SERVICES

RENT-A-KID REFERRAL SERVICE
Citizens Committee on Youth
2147 Central Avenue
Cincinnati, OH 45214
TEL: 513-632-5200
Objectives: To give very young teenagers the opportunity to gain work experience, acquire references, and earn spending money; to provide homeowners and small businesses a convenient and reasonably-priced source of labor.

Services: Places youths between the ages of 14 and 16 who are enrolled in school; assigns Rent-A-Kids to their own communities to perform odd jobs such as housecleaning, leaf raking, lawn moving, flyer distribution, moving, gardening; allows lower than minimum wage (not less than $2.25/hour) where federal and state minimum provisions do not apply; conducts registration each spring via school counselors and community agencies; provides services in Cincinnati area only, but sends detailed information about the program to any requesting individual or group.

70001 TRAINING AND EMPLOYMENT INSTITUTE
600 Maryland Avenue, SW
West Wing, Suite 300
Washington, DC 20024
TEL: 202-484-0103
Objectives: To help disadvantaged 16- to 22-year-old high school dropouts to find unsubsidized jobs and careers in the private sector.
Services: Provides a two- to five-week program of work-readiness training; conducts workshops, held after work hours, to prepare participants for their high school equivalency diplomas; teaches basic living skills, such as how to find an apartment, how to dress for a job interview, how to balance a checkbook (20% of participants are high school graduates, adults, and ex-offenders); sponsors a youth organization, SEVCA, which is involved in numerous projects; conducts regional and national employment and training seminars for enrollees; convenes annual coordinator training institutes; publishes a quarterly magazine, Going Places!, a monthly newsletter, and other materials.

INDIVIDUAL PROGRAM PROFILES

CE-2
SEE EDUCATION: CAREER EXPLORATION

EMPLOYMENT SKILLS FOR HOMELESS YOUTH
SEE RECIPIENTS: HOMELESS - CHILDREN/YOUTH

FUTURES FOR YOUTH
Teen Complex
2580 Richmond Road
Lexington, KY 40509
TEL: 606-259-2744
Purpose: To assist young people in learning interviewing techniques and job skills.
Contact: Doug Remick, Executive Director
Description: Futures for Youth is a free program designed to take the fear out of job interviews for youth from ages 15 to 22. Just as important as "getting through the interview" is understanding the purpose of it - a means for both parties to decide the suitability of the job from respective points of view. *Futures for Youth* emphasizes the importance of asking specific questions about the job to gain the proper knowledge to decide whether or not to accept the job.
A major aspect of the program is its emphasis on volunteer work experience as an impressive entry on a resume - especially if paid work experience is minimal. Counselors stress the importance of describing volunteer involvement since it tells an employer two things - that the applicant has the ability to work, and that he or she is conscious of the problems of the community.
Training sessions are 90 minutes a day for two weeks. They are held at the local *Teen Center Complex,* which makes the project visible to a substantial portion of the target group, thus resulting in more inquiries than it might otherwise receive, and an increase in the success of the project goal - to help reduce youth employment in the area.

QUALITY EDUCATION PROGRAM
UAW-GM Human Resource Center
Region 1-C
Flint, MI 48501
TEL: 313-257-0440
Purpose: To work with business/industry to help students prepare for careers.
Sponsor: United Auto Workers
Contact: Coordinator of Education Activities
Description: The Flint Quality Education Program is operated by the UAW-GM (United Auto Workers-General Motors) Human Resource Center, region 1-C Office. The Center's program is nationwide.
This program does not provide resource persons to go into the schools, per se, but instead brings teachers to the Centers in Flint and Lansing for summer work experience through which they can gain insight into potential career opportunities for students. It is a "partnership" in the sense that, in exchange for gaining such insight, and introducing their students to math-related skills they may need as General Motors workers, the teachers serve as plant trainers and developers of training modules that can be used in General Motors Plants across the country.
The Quality Education Program was one of 16 that received honors in a 1989 awards program conducted by the Michigan Board of Education.
Publications: Employee Training Modules

ROADRUNNER PROGRAM
SEE TRANSPORTATION & SAFETY: CHILDREN/YOUTH

STUDENT VOLUNTEER/WORK PROJECT (SV/WP)
National Association of Partners in Education
601 Wythe Street
Suite 601
Alexandria, VA 22314
TEL: 703-836-4880
Purpose: To use volunteerism as a vehicle for providing students with the opportunity to develop, test and extend their interests, skills and talents; to apply the skills developed to paid job situations.
Sponsor: National Association of Partners in Education; Citibank; New York State General Accounting Service; National Alliance of Business
Contact: Carol Pierce
Description: Recognizing the problems low-achieving disadvantaged high school students are likely to encounter in seeking to enter the job market, the National School Volunteer Program of New York City developed a special project aimed at helping to offset these expected difficulties. The Student Volunteer/Work Project locates volunteer work placements for the students to help them develop marketable skills, provides career counseling for the volunteers, and exposes them to employment possibilities.
The student volunteers are placed in day care centers, hospitals, nursing homes, schools and museums. They are required to give a minimum of four hours a week. Each volunteer assignment is approached as if it were a paying job. Training is provided to help the student become proficient in the interviewing process, filling out applications, arranging for appointments, applying for working papers, writing resumes, and determining appropriate work behavior.
Adult volunteers from the School Volunteer Program provide basic skills development through one-to-one tutoring. In addition, school volunteers on released time from their companies provide one-to-one counseling in the area of career development - also serving as role models. The Volunteer Coordinator follows up on interviews and placements, contacts agencies for progress reports, makes site visits and requests student volunteer evaluations. References are maintained for each student to be used for future

job applications. Monthly sessions are scheduled for sharing placement experiences for ongoing career awareness.

A challenging assignment for 20 student volunteers was to serve as volunteer job developers for the National Alliance of Business, and approach corporations for summer job pledges for themselves and fellow students. Student volunteers also participated in an employment workshop convened by the School Volunteer Program, the National Alliance of Business, and Citibank. A bank personnel administrator explained how to read want ads, fill out applications, and write resumes. New York State's General Accounting Service led a lecture series on economics to introduce the students to the financial realities of today's society.

Based on the total number of hours given to community service, students receive academic credit.

TEEN OPPORTUNITIES PROMOTE SUCCESS (TOPS)
Birmingham Area Alliance of Business
2027 First Avenue, North
Birmingham, AL 35203
TEL: 205-326-4153
Purpose: To develop jobs for teenaged youth.
Contact: C. Dowd Ritter, AmSouth Bank
Description: For summer 1989, The *Birmingham Area Alliance of Business* completed its most successful job development campaign for the TOPS (Teen Opportunities Promote Success) program in the organization's history. The program involved volunteer efforts of all companies in the *Alliance* as well as cooperation across the community.

To begin the program, a call went out for volunteer executives. A dozen local businesses loaned an executive each. Each executive worked full time for eight weeks. The volunteers developed more than 150 jobs for the youth in some 80 companies.

The success of the program is attributed to the ability of many companies to release an executive for full-time participation in the program. They came from utilities, medical, financial, retail, industry, and church sources, among others.
Founded: 1989

YOUTH-IN-ACTION AUCTION
SEE PHYSICAL ENVIRONMENT: BEAUTIFICATION

EMPLOYMENT: HANDICAPPED

NATIONAL/STATE ORGANIZATIONS

AMERICAN COALITION OF CITIZENS WITH DISABILITIES*
SEE RECIPIENTS: HANDICAPPED - EMPLOYMENT

HUMAN RESOURCES CENTER
SEE RECIPIENTS: HANDICAPPED - EMPLOYMENT

MAINSTREAM
SEE RECIPIENTS: HANDICAPPED - EMPLOYMENT

PRESIDENT'S COMMITTEE ON EMPLOYMENT OF THE HANDICAPPED
1111 Twentieth Street, NW
Washington, DC 20210
TEL: 202-653-5044
Objectives: To provide employment opportunities for all handicapped workers.
Services: Sponsors nationwide program with its focus on the above objective; keeps Governors' and Community Committees informed of new promotional and educational ideas and activities; provides up-to-date general information concerning latest developments in the field of rehabilitation and placement of the disabled; administers special committee on disabled veterans to promote jobs and keep public informed; co-sponsors annual high school "Ability Counts" contest in which students write essays on their views of the handicapped at work.

INDIVIDUAL PROGRAM PROFILES

CENTRAL FAIRFAX SERVICES
SEE RECIPIENTS: HANDICAPPED - EMPLOYMENT

DATA SYSTEMS UNLIMITED
Goodwill Industries of San Francisco
PO Box 548
San Francisco, CA 94101
TEL: 415-362-0778
Purpose: To train disabled adults and offenders and ex-offenders to become qualified computer operators and data entry clerks, and to help them find entry-level career opportunities in this field.
Sponsor: Goodwill Industries of America; IBM
Contact: Judy A. Langley
Description: In 1981, IBM awarded Goodwill the three-year gratis loan of their Computer System 34 for the purpose of providing vocational training to disabled people. It is the second program of its kind in the country, established exclusively for disabled individuals.

In accordance with the agreement with IBM, the program can operate only on a break-even basis, and the equipment cannot be used for money-making ventures or Goodwill business.

The instructor's salary, administrative costs and trainee stipends are funded mostly through student tuitions, which come from the San Francisco Department of Rehabilitation, private rehabilitation, fund-raising sources, and occasionally from students' own resources.

Six staff and 25 volunteers operate the program, with volunteers involved in supervisory and advocacy capacities as well as in direct delivery of services. They have succeeded in involving public, private and corporate sectors in support of the program.

The Industry Advisory Board, made up of personnel and data processing managers from the business community, help in planning and implementing the program.

During the first year, twelve students registered for the class, with eight of them graduating, and three being placed immediately in data processing jobs, and two involved in internships. Based on the success of this size class, the program each year will be limited to twelve students.

To be eligible for the training program, interested disabled individuals must first pass Goodwill's extensive testing to determine their abilities for handling course requirements, their levels of emotional stability, and their motivations to seek and find employment.

In an effort to be of assistance to the wider community also, Goodwill accepts applications from offenders and ex-offenders for the program.
Founded: 1981

PATOWMACK HERBAL FARM: SUMMER EMPLOYMENT FOR THE HANDICAPPED
SEE RECIPIENTS: HANDICAPPED - MENTALLY RETARDED

THE SHED PROJECT*
SEE RECIPIENTS: HANDICAPPED - EMPLOYMENT

TRAINING FOR DISABLED STUDENTS
Roy Rogers Restaurants
Marriott Corporation
1 Marriott Drive
Washington, DC 20058
TEL: 202-380-0000
FAX: 301-897-5181
Purpose: To provide job training and placement for disabled students.
Sponsor: Fairfax County Public Schools
Contact: Robert R. Spillane, Superintendent of Schools
Description: Training personnel from *Roy Rogers Restaurants* are being "loaned" to the *S. John Davis Center of Fairfax County Public Schools* to train disabled students in various aspects of food service. This loan of executives is the result of an agreement between the Restaurant chain and the school system. Students at the Falls Church center are selected for training by Davis Center staff, interviewed by Roy Rogers representatives, and approved for employment by both parties.
Roy Rogers provides equipment, utensils, food products, and training personnel to the Davis Center, while Fairfax County provides seminars to selected management-level employees of Roy Rogers in the day-to-day supervision and instruction of disabled individuals.
Students complete job applications and are interviewed by their prospective managers. Assignments are made as close to students' homes as possible. The training operates on a two- to three-week cycle, with the length of each student's training based on individual performance. Each cycle involves four to six students. After successfully completing the training, each student is assigned to the previously-selected restaurant. Job coaches are provided on-site by the school if necessary. Transportation needs are the responsibility of the Davis Center.
Job development categories addressed by the volunteer trainers include: food preparation worker, salad bar preparation and maintenance worker, deep-fryer cook, and dining room attendant. In the summer of 1989, the program involved about a dozen students who successfully made the transition from training to job. The program was expanded in September of the same year, and continues to grow.

EMPLOYMENT: HOMELESS

INDIVIDUAL PROGRAM PROFILES

LOAVES & FISHES
SEE RECIPIENTS: HOMELESS - NUTRITION

STREET NEWS HOMELESS VENDORS PROGRAM
SEE RECIPIENTS: HOMELESS - EMPLOYMENT

EMPLOYMENT: LOW-INCOME

NATIONAL/STATE ORGANIZATIONS

HEAD START - FAMILY DAY CARE
SEE DAY CARE/HEAD START: FAMILY DAY CARE

INDIVIDUAL PROGRAM PROFILES

PERSON TO PERSON*
SEE RECIPIENTS: FAMILIES - PSYCHOSOCIAL SUPPORT

EMPLOYMENT: MILITARY - ACTIVE/VETERANS

INDIVIDUAL PROGRAM PROFILES

EDUCATION AND EMPLOYMENT RESOURCE CENTER
SEE RECIPIENTS: MILITARY - ACTIVE/VETERANS

EMPLOYMENT: MINORITIES/WOMEN

NATIONAL/STATE ORGANIZATIONS

JOBS FOR OLDER WOMEN ACTION PROJECT
3102 Telegraph Avenue
Berkeley, CA 94705
TEL: 415-849-0332
Objectives: To utilize volunteers to assist older women in finding employment.
Services: Offers vocational counseling; holds seminars; maintains speakers bureau and library; deals with age discrimination; sponsors Community Outreach and other Committees; publishes newsletter.

R-T-P, INC.*
162 Fifth Avenue
New York, NY 10010
TEL: 212-620-7300
Objectives: To assist minority and disadvantaged individuals in qualifying for skilled, semi-skilled, managerial, professional and technical positions in public and private sectors.
Services: Operates a training institute for "outreach techniques;" recruits, screens, tutors, counsels, and follows up enrollees; provides an overview of above services for groups and organizations in its newsletter, *Breakthrough*.

US/DOL - WOMEN'S BUREAU
Washington, DC 20210
TEL: 202-523-6611
Objectives: To assure that the needs of women workers are being met.
Services: Advocates more extensive utilization of women in volunteer services in federal and community programs; establishes direct linkages with women's organizations and women such as minority women, mature women, low-income women, youth, rural women, and women offenders, who are not likely to be reached through the usual communications channels; monitors and works to improve legislation related to equal rights for women, including discrimination based on sex and race, in employment; improves opportunities for training, counseling and guidance, continuing education, expansion of day care; encourages the movement of women into nontraditional jobs, and their advancement to more responsible and skilled jobs in the economy; provides technical and advisory services; maintains clearinghouse which includes extensive

publications on matters relating to women workers (request catalog)

REGIONAL OFFICES:

I. Boston, 617-223-4036
II. New York, 212-944-3445
III. Philadelphia, 215-596-1183
IV. Atlanta, 404-881-4461
V. Chicago, 312-353-6985
VI. Dallas, 214-767-6985
VII. Kansas City, 816-374-6108
VIII. Denver, 303-837-4138
IX. San Francisco, 415-556-2377
X. Seattle, 206-442-1534

Sponsor: US/DoL - Department of Labor

EMPLOYMENT: OLDER PERSON

NATIONAL/STATE ORGANIZATIONS

JOBS FOR OLDER WOMEN ACTION PROJECT
SEE EMPLOYMENT: MINORITIES/WOMEN

NATIONAL ASSOCIATION FOR HISPANIC ELDERLY
SEE RECIPIENTS: OLDER PERSON - ETHNIC GROUPS

INDIVIDUAL PROGRAM PROFILES

ABILITY IS AGELESS
SEE RECIPIENTS: OLDER PERSON - EMPLOYMENT

JOBS FOR OLDER WOMEN*
College of the Emeriti
Emeriti Women's Council
1400 Park Boulevard
San Diego, CA 92101
TEL: 714-230-2445
Purpose: To help older women attain their career potential and meet their earning needs.
Sponsor: Emeriti Women's Council
Contact: Frances Lee Smith, Administrator
Description: A one-to-one mentor relationship is the concept on which Jobs for Older Women is based. It is a project of the Emeriti Women's Council of San Diego's College of the Emeriti, and draws heavily on the expertise of its 30 members. Begun with an Older Americans Program mini-award grant, the Council set the following objectives for the project:
- Survey existing career needs of older women in the community.
- Develop a recruitment plan in cooperation with local agencies.
- Develop a peer counseling process using experienced business and professional women as mentors.
- Make available to participants a full range of college career and educational planning resources.
- Make available to participants and to mentors a college career counselor to test, advise, and assist in placement.
- Evaluate the mentor process with input from participants, mentors, and college staff.

Volunteer mentors selected the applicants they felt most capable of assisting. A special effort was made to recruit minority and middle-income women, who had been identified as being underserved. Recruitment was done through contact with senior centers and agencies, media announcements, and recruitment aides. Mentors contacted their assigned clients and established meetings on an individual basis. Twenty women were selected for

participation in the initial effort.

Participants in the program are offered a nine-session credit or no credit class on job counseling for the mature woman, and personal counseling by volunteer mentors who have received orientation to career counseling resources. Of the first group of older women, eight were successfully placed in jobs following the training program, and twelve other openings were identified within a short time.

One of the unanticipated difficulties of the program was - in the case of minority women - the need for immediate employment, forestalling participation in a lengthy career education program. But, foremost among the problems is a need to clarify beforehand the commitment and expectations of all concerned - participants, volunteers, mentors, and project staff. Also, matching procedures should be tightened, and applicants and mentors need to be more carefully screened and trained.

The first year's project surfaced a number of enlightening facts:
- Placement of older women is very difficult.
- Job sharing and flextime opportunities are crucial.
- The need to draw on outside resources is vital.
- Existing college counseling and placement services provide an excellent headstart for such a project.

On the plus side, certain benefits of the program were unanticipated also, such as the degree of friendship that developed among the older women attending the job counseling class. Also, the mentor system proved to be a rich and varied resource and an excellent way to gain support and involvement from the community. Finally, this volunteer effort could not be duplicated otherwise without prohibitive cost.

SECOND CAREERS PROGRAM
Volunteer Action Center of Los Angeles
621 South Virgil
Los Angeles, CA 90005
TEL: 213-931-8192
Purpose: To provide professional assistance to organizations which desire to develop pre-retirement and retirement programs for their senior personnel.
Sponsor: Voluntary Action Center of Los Angeles
Contact: Director
Description: The need for development of volunteer and paid employment opportunities is of major concern to retirees. Second Careers Consultants help to meet that need through individual and group counseling. It is the goal of the Second Careers Program to develop projects and activities which will benefit and enhance the lives of the senior population and the community. Specific objectives include, but are not limited to:
- To establish pre-retirement and retirement programs which further the goals and give purpose to the lives of senior citizens.
- To establish and strengthen the volunteer information and referral system for employees and retirees.
- To provide a program of paid temporary employment for the retiree who needs and desires work.
- To counsel with the retiree on an individual or a group basis.

Second Careers consults with both business firms and community organizations to implement programs and services beneficial to pre-retirees. Comprehensive programs are planned and implemented. Audits of existing retirement and pre-retirement programs, policies and procedures are performed.

Recommendations are then presented to the organization and assistance on how to implement these recommendations is available.

In addition to the multiple consultant services available, Second Careers maintains a Retiree Relations Representatives Organization which meets bimonthly to discuss, review and mutually share knowledge and information on current retirement issues.

Also, the Second Careers Library of resource materials is made available to interested individuals, groups, and corporations.

SENIOR EMPLOYMENT RESOURCES
4201 John Marr Drive
Suite 236
Annandale, VA 22003
TEL: 703-750-1936
Purpose: To provide a complete, no-fee employment service for older persons.
Sponsor: Fairfax County; foundations; corporations; individuals
Contact: Dr. Robert B. Revere, Executive Director
Description: Senior Employment Resources (SER) is a nonprofit agency founded in 1983 to provide full employment services to persons fifty-five years of age and older - translated by the program's staff and volunteers to "...a little older...A LOT BETTER." SER is funded by Title III of the Older Americans Act and other funding from federal, state and local governments. Also, contributions come from the clients themselves and other charitable organizations.
SER maintains an active *Talent Bank* of individuals 55 years of age or older who are seeking full- or part-time employment. All applicants go through an interview process that enables referral only to jobs for which they are qualified and for which they meet the specifications of the potential employer. Specializations of experienced job-seekers in SER's *Talent Bank* include:
- accounting, auditing, and bookkeeping
- computer operation, programming, management, photography, commercial art, and publication
- management, administration, and consulting
- property management and real estate
- driving, courier service
- editing and writing research
- secretarial, and administrative assistance
- interpreters and translators
- legal and paralegal
- engineering and scientific
- education and teaching
- sales and retail
- medical and health services
- public relations and public affairs
- ...and many others

There is no fee for either party to the transaction, and no obligation by the employer to hire the individual, or by the individual to accept the job.
Volunteers play a major role in SER both as professionals in counseling and placement, and as support services for the clerical staff. They receive orientation and training when necessary, but efforts are made to match the volunteers' existing skills with the needs of SER. Often, while awaiting placement, clients themselves offer to volunteer. According to the director, "Purely and simply, without the volunteers, we wouldn't be operating this service."
Publications: Ability Is Ageless
Founded: 1983

EMPLOYMENT: PRISONER/EX-OFFENDER

NATIONAL/STATE ORGANIZATIONS

OLDER ADULT OFFENDER PROJECT
Alston Wilkes Society
2215 Devine Street
Columbia, SC 29205
TEL: 803-799-2490
Objectives: To assist older inmates, both in prison and on their release.

Services: Operates a visitation program for inmates in prisons involving volunteers who have completed the organization's training program; works with community pre-release centers; develops its programs for inmates 45 years of age or older both in prison and after release in their localities; offers placement services.
Publications: AWS Newsletter
Founded: 1962

INDIVIDUAL PROGRAM PROFILES

COURT EMPLOYMENT PROJECT
SEE LAW ENFORCEMENT/CRIME PREVENTION: RE-ENTRY

FEMALE OFFENDER REHABILITATION PROGRAM
Understanding is Progress
405 North Wabash Avenue
Suite 3609
Chicago, IL 60611
TEL: 312-644-1193
Purpose: To provide the participant with marketable vocational reintegration skills, employment, emotional support, and follow-up to help her live a useful and responsible life when she returns to the community.
Contact: Delores J. Mosier, Executive Director
Description: Understanding is Progress (UPI), begun in 1981 with 60 volunteers and corporate, in-kind and foundation funding, serves as a catalyst in utilizing the resources and capabilities of corrections, business, community and government to rehabilitate the women incarcerated by the State of Illinois. It is one of a handful of programs available to women in the US, and it is the only program that incorporates the best elements of existing programs for male offenders and ex-offenders, as well as the specific recommendations suggested by the Comptroller General of the US.
UPI's program consists of four essential components to reintegrate successfully the female ex-offender into the community. The components include vocation skills (with an emphasis on non-traditional), reintegration skills, employment opportunities, and emotional support.
Vocational Skills, taught through programs jointly instituted at Dwight Correctional Center by UPI and the business community. When this phase is completely implemented, it will include the following vocational training programs: automotive repair; reprographics; data processing; health care; building trades; appliance repair.
Reintegration Skills, taught in workshop sessions, during the last six months at DCC. A participant learns skills that will help her plan her life through effective and realistic goal setting; find and keep a job; and function as a responsible adult, parent, or partner.
Employment Opportunities, identified by UPI's job placement staff, are presented to each ex-offender. UPI arranges interviews between employers and the client. And they provide human relations and communications training to the supervisors and personnel representatives who will work with the female ex-offender.
Emotional Support, provided to the ex-offender by a working woman who volunteers to be her "big sister" for one year. UPI matches the women for compatibility, and provides training to the volunteer to orient her to the client relationship and the role of a volunteer.
Founded: 1981

HOUSTON EX-OFFENDER PROGRAM
SEE LAW ENFORCEMENT/CRIME PREVENTION: RE-ENTRY

JOB THERAPY, INC. (EX-OFFENDER PROGRAM: PROJECT START)*
3927 Aurora Avenue North
Suite 201
Seattle, WA 98103
TEL: 206-447-3650
Purpose: To provide employment services to ex-offenders and to juveniles who are involved or are in danger of becoming involved in prostitution.
Sponsor: Private contributions; CETA; DSHS; State Employment Security
Contact: David Seidel, Executive Director
Description: Job Therapy is a private, nonprofit organization. Under contract to the State of Washington, it has been providing job-finding services to ex-offenders since 1963. In recent years, several foundations have provided grants to enable the program to expand to include youths. Among the job-finding aids provided are:
- Job Orientation
- Job Placement
- Job Development
- Follow-up Services
- Job Counseling
- Supportive Services

The program's target populations are ex-offenders, and youths who are, or who are about to become involved in juvenile prostitution. The Ex-Offender Program continues to be effective in reintegrating the ex-offender into the community. The State of Washington funds the program through the performance-based contracting method.
Project Start is a newer phase of Job Therapy and was created to help reduce the incidence of juvenile prostitution. It is funded primarily by a grant from the Washington Law and Justice Planning Division. Foundations also have provided funding for this youth program. United Way is providing a large percentage of the total funding for the program.
Volunteers generally do counseling tasks and professional, technical duties such as budget forecasting for the entire organization. Since most of the volunteer work is done by individuals who have been ordered by the court to perform a certain number of hours of community service, the program uses less volunteers from the general community - from three to five at any given time.
Founded: 1963

EMPLOYMENT: PSYCHOSOCIAL SUPPORT

NATIONAL/STATE ORGANIZATIONS

EMPLOYEE ASSISTANCE PROGRAM CONSORTIUM
SEE PSYCHOSOCIAL SUPPORT SERVICES: EMPLOYEES

EMPLOYEE ASSISTANCE SOCIETY OF NORTH AMERICA
SEE PSYCHOSOCIAL SUPPORT SERVICES: EMPLOYEES

EMPLOYMENT: SELF-HELP

NATIONAL/STATE ORGANIZATIONS

OPPORTUNITIES INDUSTRIALIZATION CENTERS OF AMERICA
100 West Coulter Street
Philadelphia, PA 19144
TEL: 215-951-2200
Objectives: To apply the self-help philosophy in using job training and placement to improve the lives of the hard core unemployed and underemployed, as well as the community.
Services: Trains people in 110 different vocational categories to fill job openings of local employers; provides counseling, remediation, skills training and placement; works with the entire family of the participant to strengthen family members' ties with each other and with the community; operates National Industrial Advisory Council, which is composed of top executives of 37 major business corporations; sponsors projects for minority high school students; maintains extensive library; publishes quarterly newsletter and annual journal.

HEALTH

NATIONAL/STATE ORGANIZATIONS

AMERICAN RED CROSS
SEE DISASTER RESPONSE/EMERGENCY PREPAREDNESS

AMERICAN SOCIETY OF DIRECTORS OF VOLUNTEER SERVICES
American Hospital Association
840 North Lake Shore Drive
Chicago, IL 60611
TEL: 312-280-6110
Objectives: To provide an organized structure to advance and develop effective volunteer administration in health care institutions.
Services: Provides long-term skills development for both the new and the experienced volunteer services director; convenes conferences, workshops and institutes which cover such subjects as: the role of the director of volunteer services, the needs and functions of the department of volunteer services, the needs and motivations of volunteers, the development of management skills and techniques, humanism in management, effective time management, effective communications, utilizing human resources, attaining organization objectives, selected volunteer programs, current issues affecting health care institutions; publishes a journal and other materials; makes available *American Hospital Association* publications, including *Hospitals;* provides access to extensive library; sponsors special consultants; convenes annual convention.
Publications: Volunteer Service Magazine; Administration Newsletter; Membership Roster
Founded: 1972

COALITION FOR A NATIONAL HEALTH SYSTEM*
Brainard Road
RD 3, PO Box 315-C
Averill Park, NY 12018
TEL: 518-794-9388
Objectives: To educate people about the need for a national health service.
Services: Analyzes legislation relating to community-based health programs; conducts research and operates public education programs; convenes conferences and workshops; publishes quarterly *Health Service Action-Line Newsletter.*
Publications: NHS Newsletter
Founded: 1977

INDIVIDUAL PROGRAM PROFILES

HEALTHOUSE VOLUNTEER PROGRAM
555 North County Road
St. James, NY 11786
TEL: 516-862-6743
Purpose: To provide health counseling to women.
Sponsor: Women's Health, Information and Resource Center; Women's Health Alliance of Long Island
Contact: Susan Schiff, Coordinator
Description: Healthouse is a resource, education and short-term counseling center for women seeking information, help and support on health-related issues. Healthouse is presently co-directed with directors, both certified social workers, who donate their professional expertise supervising student interns, training volunteers, planning programs, maintaining the information and referral files and seeking funds to keep Healthouse open. Healthouse runs workshops and support and discussion groups where they ask a $5.00 donation. Healthouse also offers patient advocacy service (where a staff person will physically accompany a person to the doctor if he or she needs support, to ask questions, interpret information and listen carefully) and walk-in crisis counseling.
Since the only staff are student interns studying for their MSW at nearby SUNY at Stony Brook, they could not provide all of the services adequately. A volunteer program was initiated and fourteen community women have been trained to staff Healthouse. The volunteers answer inquiries and provide information. Their only limitations are in the counseling services; otherwise they work along with the students.

HOPE
Sixteenth Street Community Health Center
1032 South 16th Street
Milwaukee, WI 53204
TEL: 414-672-1353
Purpose: To provide quality, comprehensive health care services to low-income/minority persons
Sponsor: Sixteenth Street Community Health Center
Contact: Mary Jo Baisch, Executive Director, or Jennifer Poulos
Description: Hope, Inc., began in 1969 and has been providing health and health-related services to the inner-city southside of Milwaukee for over 21 years. The area covered has 67,000 potential clients. There are 50 staff members. Funding is a

combination of self-generated revenue, United Way, in-kind contributions foundation grants, and state & federal government monies.

Hope is particularly effective in the areas of project planning and design, creation of coalitions with other organizations and agencies, and demonstrated cost effectiveness.

Through a combination of funding sources and integration of services we provide a full-range of service including prenatal, postpartum, reproductive health care, adult care and care for children. This includes diagnosis, treatment and education.
Founded: 1969

HEALTH: ADVOCACY

NATIONAL/STATE ORGANIZATIONS

CONSUMER COALITION FOR HEALTH
1511 K Street, NW
Washington, DC 20005
TEL: 202-347-8088
Objectives: To provide national advocacy in Congress, the agencies and the courts to promote consumer interests in the area of health.
Services: Gives assistance to consumers who are involved in health programs; provides public education programs to stimulate interest in community health; publishes a bimonthly newsletter.

NATIONAL HEALTH COUNCIL*
350 Fifth Avenue
34th Floor
New York, NY 10018
TEL: 212-972-2700
Objectives: To stimulate its members to work together more effectively in the public interest; to identify health problems of the nation and to work toward their solution; and to improve private and governmental efforts to achieve optimal health for the public.
Services: Sponsors the National Health Forum, which is an annual gathering of America's health leadership to debate and examine emerging health developments and issues; maintains a meeting ground between the private and governmental sectors through its Washington Government Relations office; stimulates awareness of health career opportunities for young people, particularly minorities and women, through its distribution of *200 Ways to Put Your Talent to Work in the Health Field;* promotes public accountability of voluntary health agencies; facilitates problem-solving and mutual efforts among the membership in community health promotion, volunteer initiative and varied issues and concerns which impact on national health policy.
Publications: Health Groups in Washington; In Search of a National Policy
Founded: 1920

PUBLIC CITIZEN HEALTH RESEARCH GROUP
2000 P Street, NW
Washington, DC 20036
TEL: 202-872-0320
Objectives: To protect consumers in matters of health care delivery, occupational health, environmental influences on health, etc.
Services: Petitions (or sues) federal agencies on consumers' behalf; testifies before Congress on health matters; monitors the enforcement of health and safety legislation; publicizes important health findings through the media; distributes consumer action materials to the public (free publications list available).
Publications: Health Letter; Health Research Group
Founded: 1971

HEALTH: BLOOD/ORGAN DONATION

INDIVIDUAL PROGRAM PROFILES

BLOODMOBILE
Tully Central School
Route 80
Syracuse, NY 13159
TEL: 315-696-6242
Purpose: To educate teenagers regarding blood donation; to provide them with an opportunity for community service; to create better community relations and enhance the student image.
Sponsor: Tully Central School
Contact: Lorraine Spaulding, Health Careers Club
Description: For the past ten years, the Health Careers Club of the Tully Central School has sponsored a Red Cross Bloodmobile. Each year, 35 to 40 student volunteers begin preparations about one month in advance of the scheduled Bloodmobile. Through trial and error, they have found that the following activity sequence works best:
1. Call Red Cross to schedule date.
2. Get a Red Cross printout sheet of all former donors.
3. Assign student volunteers a list of people to call (former community donors); assign volunteers to personally contact teachers, school personnel; assign volunteers to contact all students who are age 17 or over (but do not coerce or beg students - merely ask). "Peer asking" works well, though.
4. Obtain and/or design posters (many available ones are so cleverly worded).
5. Seek publicity (local radio spots, newspaper, pictures).
6. Bake cookies to be used for donors.
7. Fly Red Cross flag, taking up and down each day for a week before Bloodmobile.
8. Make a large thermometer and display in prominent place; write names of givers on thermometer so students can watch it "rise" throughout the day.
9. Encourage students to give during study hall, not class time.
10. Emphasize the volunteer slots available for students who are squeamish about working with blood.
11. Assign clean-up crew to clean and load trucks after Bloodmobile program.
The Health Club sponsor, and the students themselves, had many doubts and misgivings when they first undertook the program. Now it has become a yearly project which has grown far beyond expectations. Immediately following one Bloodmobile, students begin planning to make the next one bigger than ever. All concerned feel that the Bloodmobile serves many purposes, among which are:
Education - that donating blood is helping someone else to live; that donating blood is not that painful; that donating blood is a grown-up thing to do; that donating blood is a good habit to start while young.
Service - provides many different ways for teenagers to become involved; enables large numbers of students to participate.
Community Relations - creates good community relations; outside people are asked to give; community people are pleased to see students involved in the effort.
Seventeen-year-old students can give blood in New York State without parental consent. Laws differ, and those considering such a program in another state should check state law well in advance of the program.
Founded: 1980

BUDDIES FOR LIFE
Clara Barton Council
American Red Cross/Tulsa
10151 East Eleventh Street
Tulsa, OK 74128
TEL: 918-431-1100, ext. 413

Purpose: To establish community awareness of the need for organ and tissue donations; to encourage people to sign organ donor cards.
Sponsor: American Red Cross
Contact: Margie Filstrup, President
Description: More than 5,000 people in the U.S. are waiting for a kidney transplant. An estimated 60,000 need bone transplants, and only one-sixth of the skin needed for burn patients is currently available. The Tulsa chapter of the *American Red Cross* has designed a new project, a transplant outreach program called *Buddies for Life,* which was made part of a national campaign in 1990. The goal of the *Buddies for Life* program is to see that every person in need of tissue or organ transplants will receive one. The 1989 pilot, sponsored by the Tulsa chapter of the *American Red Cross,* and managed by the nonprofit *Clara Barton Council,* involves up to 2,000 volunteers, who wear special T-shirts for visibility and walk in "Buddy" teams of two. Carrying pinwheels, the logo of the program, the volunteers participate in fund-raising walks, distribute packets of information to 40,000 area homes, and perform other tasks throughout the year in the public awareness program. The packets ask individuals to take 20 minutes to discuss the organ/tissue transplant question with other family members, so that a donor's wishes can be carried out with minimum family concern. A rally for all volunteers is held prior to the annual walk. The day of the initial walk in 1989 was proclaimed "Buddies for Life Day" by Oklahoma's Governor.
The *Clara Barton Council* was organized in 1985 to assist Red Cross management in carrying out its responsibility, and to provide resources for leadership. While the American National Red Cross works directly with health-care facilities in collecting, storing and providing donated tissue, it serves only as a referral agency for organ transplant donations. The Tulsa chapter was chosen for the project because of its reputation for dedication and commitment. The results of the Tulsa pilot serves as a foundation for the national effort.
Founded: 1989

HEALTH: CANCER

NATIONAL/STATE ORGANIZATIONS

US/HHS - CANCER INFORMATION CLEARINGHOUSE
US/HHS - National Cancer Institute
Building 31, Room 10A18
Bethesda, MD 20205
TEL: 301-496-4070
Objectives: To provide a central source of information on cancer for patients and the public.
Services: Performs reference searches for health professionals and educators of its collection of about 6000 materials; makes referrals to other information sources when necessary; acts as a medium of exchange among the Comprehensive Cancer Centers; publishes an accessions list of most recent acquisitions.
Sponsor: US/HHS - Department of Health & Human Services

INDIVIDUAL PROGRAM PROFILES

CAMP GOOD DAYS AND SPECIAL TIMES
American Cancer Society
1400 North Winton Road
Rochester, NY 14609
TEL: 716-288-1950
Purpose: To provide a residential camp for children with cancer.
Contact: Volunteer Coordinator

Description: Camp Good Days and Special Times is a residential camp for children with cancer. It has served children with this illness since 1979. Volunteers at the camp include high school and college students, each assigned to a number of children. The young volunteers are charged with seeing that the young residents enjoy themselves through softball, volleyball, swimming, fishing, riding, painting, singing, dancing or, according to one young volunteer, simply "celebrating life - the real purpose of the camp."
Although the volunteers receive training before being given assignments, many find it difficult to be cheerful at first, since they are constantly aware that the children they are working with are terminally ill. However, soon somewhat of a role reversal happens, and the campers teach the volunteers "how to appreciate things that they have, how to laugh when it hurts, and how to face the unknown with a smile." This inspires the young volunteers to find ways to give the children a reason to fight their illness. When the camp period is over, volunteers return to schools and colleges knowing that one person really can make a difference, and that problems can be faced head on and overcome. Writing of her work with the children for a local newspaper, one volunteer said she got "as much, or more, from the experience as those that I helped."
Founded: 1979

CAMP GOOD DAYS AND SPECIAL TIMES REBUILDING PROJECT
SEE RECREATION & SPORTS: CHILDREN/YOUTH

CHAMPIONS RUN FOR LIFE TORCH RELAY
Jonathan Jaques Children's Cancer Center
Long Beach Memorial Medical Center
2801 Atlantic Avenue
Long Beach, CA 90806
TEL: 213-595-8592
Purpose: To raise money for the Cancer Center, while giving patients a morale boost.
Sponsor: Local corporations and individuals
Contact: Dr. Jerry Finklestein, Director
Description: Almost 100 young cancer patients trotted and wheeled around the circular sidewalk of *Long Beach Aquatic Park* in a relay race held each year to raise funds for the *Jonathan Jaques Children's Cancer Center* and to give a morale boost to the young patients. The torch relay provides funds for a school reintegration program and psychosocial support services, which were not available before the race program was instituted. Since they were added to the cancer center's agenda, these two programs have made a big difference in the overall treatment of the children. Especially dramatic improvements have been in the social and psychological programs made available by the fundraising effort. The nearly 100 racers from the center - from toddlers to teenagers - carried the torch, which was a gold-painted flashlight adorned with a crown. Hundreds of family members, sponsors, doctors, celebrities (over 40) and volunteers cheered them on.
Each patient ran, walked, rode or wheeled at least an eighth of a mile on the sidewalk around the park's lagoon. The relay's corporate sponsors and benefactors had donated more than $75,000 to set up 13 way stations along the route. Each station had its own rooting section, with all stations cheering in unison as the relay got underway.
The torch relay was followed by a dinner dance and auction. Funds are earmarked for the Cancer Center's endowment fund and its research, education and social programs.

CUYAHOGA FALLS CANCER CLUB
PO Box 3244
Cuyahoga Falls, OH 44223
TEL: 216-929-2796
Purpose: To give cancer patients in Cuyahoga Falls financial and moral support.
Contact: Juanita Wenzel, President

Description: Recognizing the high cost of medical care for a family with a member who is a victim of cancer, the *Cuyahoga Falls Cancer Club* never investigates the financial status of a patient before helping. They provide services to anyone who requests them. The club is run solely by volunteers.

The club has 65 volunteers providing assistance ranging from paying prescription and hospital costs to supplying hospital beds, wheelchairs and other equipment. The volunteers also act as an informal support group for the patients and their families. Volunteers do not give medical advice, but lend a listening ear to let patients know that someone cares. Currently the club is helping 57 Cuyahoga Falls residents. In one instance, three children from the same family were stricken at age two or under with the disease. All were helped by the club, with a contribution over the years of about $10,000 toward the family's medical expenses. All three children are free from the disease now. Some volunteers have been with the club for as long as 20 years.

The club was started by three women from Cuyahoga Falls in 1948. A year later it had more than 60 members and 24 patients. In the early days, none of the purchases for patients could exceed $25. Today the figure is much higher, with more than $10,000 given out by the club in 1989. Funds are raised through bake sales, rummage sales, luncheons and other community projects, as well as individual and group donations.
Founded: 1948

HELP-ON-WHEELS
Lutheran Metropolitan Ministry
Cancer Task Force
3800 Bridge Avenue
Cleveland, OH 44113
TEL: 216-696-2715
Purpose: To provide transportation for those people who need radiation therapy.
Sponsor: Lutheran Metropolitan Ministry
Contact: Reverend David R. Beese
Description: The Cancer Task Force began meeting in March 1978 with representatives of the medical profession, social services, clergy, and lay members of congregations which have special interest in cancer problems. About a dozen persons attended the first meeting.

For a full year the Task Force studied, talked about, and checked on the most urgent needs and the best available help for terminal cancer patients. Agencies presently serving their needs in some ways were listed, their services summarized, and a mailing to all congregations was prepared which reported the findings.

Gradually, the study and discussions of the Task Force revealed that, though there were areas of need such as home care, spiritual visitation, financial help, job problems, family counseling and others, the area that could be most readily served was transportation for radiation treatment for those patients who had no other means to travel.

Further study revealed that it would be best to start small, since other agencies had foundered by attempting too much. With the cooperation of the Lutheran Medical Center in the summer of 1979, such a program was begun. Mt. Calvary Lutheran Church was the original congregation to supply a twelve-person team of volunteers, and coordinate the scheduling of passengers and drivers. Trips reached 200 per month.

A year later, the Cleveland Foundation granted funds ($78,000) for a three-year period to the Task Force. A full-time staff person is in place, and the transportation program has expanded to all eight hospitals in the Cleveland area which offer radiation therapy. With continuing expansion a necessity, volunteer recruitment is an ongoing activity of the Task Force.

The Task Force also is active in establishing Make Today Count groups for persons who are facing terminal illness and their families, and is involved in an examination of the hospice movement. In addition to serving on Boards of hospice organizing

groups, the Task Force holds clergy seminars at Lutheran Medical Center on the work of the clergy with those who are terminally ill.
Founded: 1978

I CAN COPE
American Cancer Society, Ohio Division
3085 West Market
Akron, OH 44303
TEL: 216-867-9445
Purpose: To help cancer patients and their families learn to deal in a positive, hope-filled way with problems related to living with cancer.
Contact: Gayle Wehman
Description: I Can Cope is an educational program for cancer patients and their families administered by the *American Cancer Society (ACS)*. It is based on a pilot course devised by two oncology nurses at the *North Memorial Center* in Robbinsdale, Minnesota. This initial test, with almost 100 cancer patients and family members participating, was so successful that it was decided that a packaged version, complete with teaching guidelines and educational aids, would be offered to health professionals.

Today, *I Can Cope* has become national in scope. Courses have been, and are continuing to be, presented by health professionals in large and small communities across the country. In Ohio, *I Can Cope* courses are now being presented in over sixty hospitals and health care agencies around the state.

Courses are taught by a team, with two designated as co-leaders for a given course. Team members may include an oncologist, a nurse, a social worker, a psychologist, a dietitian, a physical therapist, appropriate community resource people, and volunteers serving on a Unit's *Professional Education* or *Service and Rehabilitation* committees. The subjects of the eight sessions:

- Introduction and basics of anatomy.
- Learning about your disease.
- Coping with daily health problems.
- Learning to express your feelings.
- Learning to like yourself.
- Learning to live with limitations.
- Resources that can help.
- Graduation and evaluation.

The American Cancer Society provides the leader training at no charge. Area training sessions for new leaders are held several times a year. Programs to update current leaders are offered yearly.

Initiating the program is the responsibility of the hospital or other community health care agency. When the decision is made to administer an *I Can Cope* education program, the health care facility appoints a team of individuals who are genuinely interested and meet the criteria mentioned above.

Ohio is divided by the *American Cancer Society* into four areas for this program. Each area has a coordinator who has had experience in leading a minimum of three groups. Scheduling of training, certification of leaders, statewide recertification, documentation of program changes, etc., are accomplished through a cooperative effort between the four area coordinators, and ACS Unit and Division staff. This effort includes developed shared programs with nonhospital-based health care facilities and agencies.

Program leaders and community resource persons are acting as volunteers for the ACS and therefore do not receive payment for their services.
Publications: I Can Cope

WOMAN-TO-WOMAN HOTLINE
Adelphi University
School of Social Work
Social Services Center
Garden City, NY 11530
TEL: 516-560-8060

Purpose: To provide emotional support to women who have discovered a breast lump, or have pre-mastectomy or post-mastectomy concerns.
Sponsor: Adelphi University, School of Social Work, Social Services Center
Contact: Lois Lopez, Hotline Project Coordinator
Description: The Woman-to-Woman Hotline began in May, 1982. It is operated within the Social Services Center and is funded by Adelphi University, School of Social Work.
The goals of the Hotline are to provide emotional support to women who have discovered a breast lump, or have pre-mastectomy or post-mastectomy concerns. The hotline has offered a needed service to the community in providing this service.
At the present time, the Hotline Committee consists of five active volunteers who are supervised by a graduate student interning at the Social Services Center. The volunteers have each dealt with the physical and emotional trauma of mastectomy and therefore can provide peer support. Each volunteer is trained for Hotline work and receives group supervision on a weekly basis.
The volunteers provide each caller with time to talk; each call varies and the volunteers must remain sensitive and flexible to each caller's needs. Medical advice is not provided by this Hotline. If a second opinion is sought by the caller, the volunteer refers the caller to the American Cancer Society in Melville for appropriate referral.
If the call has come due to discovery of a breast lump, the important work of the volunteer is to help the caller to visit her doctor in order to be examined and get a medical diagnosis.
Founded: 1982

HEALTH: CHILDREN/YOUTH

NATIONAL/STATE ORGANIZATIONS

MAKE-A-WISH FOUNDATION OF AMERICA (*formerly Make-A-Wish Foundation*)
PO Box 78236
Phoenix, AZ 85062
TEL: 602-240-6600
TOLL FREE: 800-722-9474
Objectives: To grant the wishes of a terminally-ill child.
Services: Considers the wish of any terminally-ill child to age 18 in the United States; includes the whole family in planning the response to the child's wish; sponsors many trips to Disneyland (the most popular request) but also responds to unusual and unique requests ranging from a simple birthday greeting to making a child a lawyer with a degree or sending a child to the Super Bowl; covers all expenses of the activities involved; holds meetings the first week in October each year.
Founded: 1980

TRAINING PROGRAMS

SEASIDE HEALTH PROMOTION CONFERENCE
Centennial School District Wellness Committee
18135 SE Brooklyn
Portland, OR 97236
TEL: 503-760-7990
Sponsor: Centennial School District
Contact: Barbara Velander
Description: This week-long conference brings together volunteers who are school employees from around the state for a concentrated week of sharing and spirit-building about fitness.

Most participants have some background in nutrition or fitness - most often coaches of gymnastics, swimming, track or other sports. Although instructors are enlisted to conduct workshops, it is an informal conference, more concerned with networking and finding the methods that have worked best for attendees in the various areas of wellness and fitness.
Another intent of the conference is to "fire up" attendees to return to their districts and promote nutrition and fitness to employees in the schools, who are then expected to use the information to enhance their work with the children.
At least one annual event in the area is an outgrowth of a volunteer's suggestion at the conference - the *Eaglefest Run,* which is a district race that goes past each school - giving all students a feeling of being part of the event. Other less visible projects have resulted in a measurable improvement in wellness and fitness programs at the schools, winning for the District one of a handful of $5,000 *Metropolitan Life Insurance* grants for excellence.

VIRGINIA ECUMENICAL INFANT MORTALITY PREVENTION PROJECT CONFERENCE
March of Dimes
1505 Staples Mill Road
Richmond, VA 23232
TEL: 804-353-9108
Sponsor: State of Virginia
Contact: Rev. Cessar L. Scott, Executive Minister
Description: This conference, held at the Virginia Governor's mansion in 1989, called on religious leaders for "sheep to keep the wolf from Virginia's nursery door." The Governor challenged leaders of 17 Virginia denominations and religious groups to produce volunteers and projects to preach the importance of maternal prenatal care in preventing deaths of babies before their first birthdays.
The conference was called to "kick off" the *Virginia Ecumenical Infant Mortality Prevention Project,* sponsored by the *March of Dimes* and the *Southern Regional Task Force on Infant Mortality,* whose mission is to increase public awareness of the high incidence of infant mortality in the southern part of the state and promote steps to diminish it. Topics discussed at the conference included:
Statistics - In Virginia in 1987, one of every 98 babies born died before his or her first birthday - those weighing 5 pounds, 8 ounces, or less often in the first 28 days. In 1986, a baby's chance of survival was better in 34 other states than in Virginia.
Causes - Low birth weight is related to 70 percent of infant deaths nationwide. The slight decline in infant mortality is due largely to new technology and neonatal care, not to prevention of low birth weight.
Prenatal Care - This is considered the most significant factor in reducing low birth weight and enhancing a newborn's health. More than 20% of Virginia's mothers receive no prenatal care in their first trimesters, and there is evidence that newborns requiring intensive care are born to these mothers.
Identify the Doers - Invite the doers to regional workshops that are held around the state. Energize them with ideas and inspire them.
Religious Institutions - Highlight in workshops ways in which religious organizations can become involved in preventing infant mortality, such as:
● hot lines for teenagers,
● transportation to services for pregnant women,
● child care for pregnant women during prenatal checkups,
● programs that emphasize male responsibility,
● layette incentive programs to encourage pregnant women to seek prenatal care,
● parenting seminars,
● guest speakers and forums,
● literature racks,
● advocacy.
A religious leader who also leads the infant mortality movement

pointed out to the attendees that infant mortality is something that crosses racial and community barriers and something for which there is a solution - "Get expectant mothers to have the proper diet and care. Give of yourselves...this is a problem we can do something about." The Governor suggested that leaders educate their congregations, initiate direct services or special projects where feasible, and encourage volunteers.

INDIVIDUAL PROGRAM PROFILES

CAMP GOOD DAYS AND SPECIAL TIMES
SEE HEALTH: CANCER

CHAMPIONS RUN FOR LIFE TORCH RELAY
SEE HEALTH: CANCER

CHILD SECURITY NETWORK OF CONNECTICUT
SEE RECIPIENTS: CHILDREN/YOUTH - PROTECTIVE SERVICES

CHILDREN'S MIRACLE NETWORK TELETHON
SEE RECIPIENTS: CHILDREN/YOUTH - HEALTH

HEALTH: CLINICS

INDIVIDUAL PROGRAM PROFILES

COMMUNITY PARTNERS PROGRAM*
Robert Wood Johnson Foundation
Mid-Atlantic Regional Council
20 West Ninth Street
Kansas City, MO 64105
TEL: 816-474-4240
Purpose: To promote improved health services to the medically underserved through implementation of low cost, largely self-supporting neighborhood health centers.
Sponsor: Robert Wood Johnson Foundation
Contact: Jean G. Bacon
Description: Recognizing that responding to the health care needs of the elderly requires a multi-year strategy based on extensive community collaboration and support, the Mid-Atlantic Regional Council, in collaboration with the Robert Wood Johnson Foundation, initiated the Community Partners Program.
Based on the overall health care strategy for the elderly developed by the Mid-Atlantic Regional Council (MARC), the following assumptions provide the foundation for the strategy of the Community Partners Program design:
● Health service needs vary by level of functional status. Healthy elderly need different forms of health services than the moderately or severely impaired.
● Both preventive and treatment-oriented services must exist for the healthy, declining, and frail population groups.
● Health services must be made available in more flexible settings to encourage accessibility.
● Health services capacities should be based upon projections of future need, rather than documentation of the past problems.
Emphasis for development of improved care for the well elderly is almost exclusively on prevention-oriented services. In the case of the declining elderly, prevention emphasis is maintained, but as a supplement to improvement of non-institutional treatment services. For the frail elderly, the emphasis is on development of effective treatment services in both the institutional and non-institutional settings.

Fifteen volunteers assist the five full-time and five part-time staff members. The volunteers are involved in supervisory and project management roles as well as in the direct service capacity. In addition to individual volunteers, project leaders initiate coalitions with other organizations, corporations, and local government units to effect the widest possible community participation.
All of the project's funding comes from foundation grants.

SOCIAL ACTION CORPS
11188 Anderson Clinic
Loma Linda, CA 92354
TEL: 714-824-0800/Ext. 2179
Purpose: To provide low-cost primary health care services to medically indigent adults and their families.
Sponsor: United Way of Redlands area, Arrowhead United Way, and private donations
Contact: Janice I. Maynor, M.S.P.H., Associate Director
Description: The Social Action Corps (SAC) is a non-profit organization staffed by volunteer students and professionals from Loma Linda, and local community residents which operates low-cost primary health care clinics in the areas of Bloomington, San Bernardino, and Redlands.
Sources of revenue include the patient fees, funds from Arrowhead United Way, the United Way of Redlands Area, the local SDA University Church, and private donations.
Presently three clinics are operating one time per week. During a one week period 20-25 volunteer medical students, 3-5 volunteer nurses and nursing students, 3 volunteer receptionists, and various translators staff the clinics. One or two licensed physicians supervise at each clinic.
The receptionists register the patients, allowing the medical patients (those who are sick) to register first, and then registering those who need physical examinations. He/she collects the fees, takes statistics, and puts the charts in proper sequence. After registering with the receptionist, the patient is called to the nurses' station where vitals are taken and recorded. The nurses also assist in the examining rooms. When an examining room is available the patient is called in and the medical student begins consultation for a specific problem or a general physical examination. The students consult the chief physician concerning every patient. Translators contribute a vital service to the clinics, as many Hispanic patients speak a limited amount of English or none at all. One or two student clinic directors provide leadership at each clinic.
The student physicians are primarily second year medical students, although third and fourth year students also participate. The first year medical students are allowed to attend during their second semester of training. Orientation and training of student clinic directors occurs in monthly staff meetings. Each student director (with the aid of a staff person) provides orientation for new students. On-site training for nurses and receptionists is provided by a staff person.
Written guidelines and procedures are provided for each position. No previous experience is necessary, only a strong desire to be part of a team which provides medical services to needy neighbors.

HEALTH: DIABETES

INDIVIDUAL PROGRAM PROFILES

CLARA BARTON CAMP FOR GIRLS WITH DIABETES
68 Clara Barton Road
PO Box 356
North Oxford, MA 01357
TEL: 508-987-2056 (Camp); 508-987-2002 (Admin.)

Purpose: To provide girls with diabetes with information and education needed for their personal responsibilities to their health; to provide recreation and socialization in a supportive setting.
Sponsor: Unitarian Universalist Women's Federation
Contact: Shelley D. Yeager, Administrator
Description: The *Clara Barton Camp for Girls with Diabetes (CBC)* provides a supportive, recreational and educational setting for girls with diabetes. During the camping experience, girls learn about food exchanges, adjusting insulin scales, treating an insulin reaction, and other activities necessary for them to meet the personal responsibility of their health. In the process, they develop lifetime friendships, and create a supportive network of campers to draw on for comfort, support and advice whenever needed.
In addition to the summer-long camp, CBC hosts *Family Weekends* year-round in cooperation with the *American Diabetes Association.* Staffed by volunteers, these weekends are aimed at supporting families as they work together to live well with the diabetes challenge. Together in group settings, mothers, fathers, sisters and brothers discuss diabetes management, diabetes challenges and life successes. More importantly, families have fun together. For example, meals are planned by the staff, but prepared by families together. Eight family weekends were held over the fall, winter and spring of 1989-90.
In addition to the camp volunteers, support comes to CBC from many sources, including:

- **Friends of the Clara Barton Camp** who "turned over the key" on December 2, 1989, for a newly-constructed staff residence at the Camp. *Friends* raised all but $50,000 of the funds needed, and continue with their campaign to help raise these final dollars.
- **Business/Industry** which includes computer equipment donated by *Aetna Life and Casualty* and *AT&T.*
- **Upkeep Volunteers** including *Project Coffee,* Oxford High School volunteers who put a new railing on the CBC conference center deck, saving the camp over $3,000, and the *Lions Club,* which put new roofs on capins.
- **The Media** including a popular local disc jockey who volunteers his services complete with flashing lights and "monstrous equipment" for camp dances.
- **Miscellaneous Fundraisers** including the first *Ski-a-thon* held at *Brookfield Orchards,* which provided food for participants, and the *Lions Club* scholarship program to sponsor youth attendance at CBC.

In conjunction with the camp, the *Birthplace Museum* is maintained in the house of Clara Barton's birth, with education programs offered to schools and youth groups on a continuing basis. The camp is operated by the *Unitarian Universalist Women's Federation.*

HEALTH: EDUCATION

NATIONAL/STATE ORGANIZATIONS

CENTER FOR SCIENCE IN THE PUBLIC INTEREST
SEE NUTRITION: EDUCATION

NATIONAL RURAL HEALTH ASSOCIATION
301 East Armour Boulevard
Suite 420
Kansas City, MO 64111
TEL: 816-756-3140
Objectives: To bring together organizations, agencies, and citizens to solve rural health problems.
Services: Identifies health problems unique to rural areas, and works to create a better understanding of and more specific health

care for these problems; offers continuing education credit for courses designed for health care providers; operates an awards program; maintains library of information on rural health; convenes conferences; publishes bimonthly newsletter, *Rural Health Communications.*
Publications: Rural Health Care; Journal of Rural Health
Founded: 1987

PROJECT CONCERN YOUTH PROGRAM
Project Concern International
3550 Alton Road
San Diego, CA 92123
TEL: 619-279-9690
Objectives: To enable youth to take part in volunteer programs on health and nutrition at the local, state, national and international levels.
Services: Involves youth in segments of its program which provides low-cost health services through a health care training program supported by volunteer assistance; researches and develops volunteer projects such as "Walk for Mankind," a program in which school children, youth and adults raise funds, and nutrition, health education and other programs, which are taught by volunteers in their communities; publishes quarterly Concern News, training manuals, booklets and other materials; convenes semiannual Board meetings.
Publications: Options; Concern News; Field Notes
Founded: 1961

TRAINING PROGRAMS

SEASIDE HEALTH PROMOTION CONFERENCE
SEE HEALTH: CHILDREN/YOUTH

INDIVIDUAL PROGRAM PROFILES

ASK THE DOCTOR
SEE HEALTH: I&R

HEALTH AND SAFETY CIRCUS
SEE HEALTH: HEALTH FAIRS

TAVS (TEENAGE VOLUNTEERS)
SEE HEALTH: HOSPITALS

HEALTH: EMERGENCIES

NATIONAL/STATE ORGANIZATIONS

LEAVE BANK
US/OPM - Office of Information
1900 E Street, NW
Washington, DC 20006
TEL: 202-632-5582
Objectives: To enable workers to donate and receive annual leave for personal emergencies after their own leave is exhausted.
Services: Offers a leave-sharing program "along the lines of a blood bank;" enables workers to donate and receive annual leave for crisis situations when their own leave is exhausted; operates leave banks in six agencies - Internal Revenue Service, Environmental Protection Agency, Defense Nuclear Agency, Farm Credit Administration, National Gallery of Art, and Occupational

Safety and Health Commission; enables transfer of leave to another employee designated as a needy recipient; operates under the *Employees Leave Act of 1987,* created when an employee contacted his congressman about a friend who did not have enough leave for an emergency situation; plans a review of the program on October 31, 1993, to determine success/continuation.
Sponsor: US/OPM - Office of Personnel Management
Contact: John P. Cahill, Specialist

NATIONAL CLEARINGHOUSE FOR POISON CONTROL CENTERS
US/HHS - Food and Drug Administration
5401 Westbard Avenue
Bethesda, MD 20014
TEL: 301-496-7691
Objectives: To prevent accidental poisonings, particularly of young children.
Services: Sponsors "National Poison Prevention Week" and other prevention and education programs; sponsors research in treatments and antidotes; provides an information exchange for some 600 poison control centers around the country; maintains a data base of case reports; publishes the *Handbook of Common Poisonings in Children*, a bulletin for those involved in poison control, and numerous brochures, booklets, fliers, and radio/TV spot announcements.
Sponsor: US/HHS - Department of Health & Human Services
Publications: Common Poisonings in Children

NATIONAL INJURY INFORMATION CENTER
US/Consumer Product Safety Commission
5401 Westbard Avenue
Washington, DC 20207
TEL: 301-492-6424
Objectives: To regulate consumer products which present hazards to users.
Services: Answers about 6,000 requests each year; assesses the scope of consumer product safety problems; makes personal contact with accident victims to compile information on the product and the victim's injuries; prepares reports on investigations, documents on various hazards, and other materials for consumer information; provides most information a❤️ services free of charge.

INDIVIDUAL PROGRAM PROFILES

LEAD POISONING PREVENTION PROGRAM
District of Columbia Government
1411 K Street, NW
12th Floor
Washington, DC 20005
TEL: 202-727-9850
Purpose: To help counteract the affects of lead poisoning - the "ticking time bomb" - in the District of Columbia.
Contact: Community Affairs Officer
Description: This District of Columbia government program offers free tests for lead poisoning detection to District residents. Most experts agree that the method used by the *Center* - a simple *fingerstick* - is the best way to check to see if a child is being poisoned. In nearby Virginia and Maryland, testing in laboratories or doctors' offices can cost in the neighborhood of $30.00 each. Federal estimates indicate that thousands of houses in the Washington, DC area - including neighborhoods with million-dollar homes - contain some lead-contaminated paint. While most houses have been repainted, wallpapered or paneled, reducing immediate risk, even minor renovations can release dangerous amounts of lead. Older District neighborhoods run the greatest risk, since in some of them more than 40% of the housing

was built before 1940. The *Environmental Defense Fund* estimates a cost of $5,000 per home for lead removal, so program staff does not see the problem going away soon.
According to the chief of the program, it is a cumulative poison in which even small doses build up. "Eating a paint chip the size of a fingernail every day is enough to cause lead poisoning in a child." Since lead is sweet-tasting, it presents a particular problem with very young children. Anyone can get lead poisoning, but children under six and fetuses are most vulnerable because of their immature and developing body systems - sometimes causing permanant damage to nervous systems as well as learning, behaviorial and psychological problems. With pregnant women, lead poisoning can lead to premature or still-born infants.
In 1989, the program reported 17,887 blood-lead screenings. Some 250 children were found to have elevated levels of lead, and in early 1990 some 757 children with elevated levels were being monitored.
Referrals for testing come to the program in many ways, many coming through public service announcements and other media announcements, and from social services, volunteer organizations, parents themselves, or concerned citizens who voluntarily either inform families at risk of the service or call the *DC Lead Poisoning Prevention Program* for follow-up. Like any benefit to a community, for this program to reach its highest potential of assistance, a concerted effort involving the whole community is needed to reach and help as many victims of lead poisoning as possible.
Publications: DC Lead Poisoning Prevention Program Packet

HEALTH: EXERCISE

INDIVIDUAL PROGRAM PROFILES

MALL WALKERS
Alexandria Hospital
Public Relations Department
4320 Seminary Road
Alexandria, VA 22304
TEL: 703-379-3000
Purpose: To organize a walking club to promote exercise and health.
Description: Alexandria Hospital and *Springfield Mall* have joined forces to organize a mall walking club. Mall walking allows you to exercise in a secure and climate-controlled environment. Club members walk a charted course through the mall on weekday mornings at 7:30 (before the mall opens for business). Enrollment as a mall walker is free and includes the following benefits:
- stretching and exercise instruction
- monthly blood pressure screenings by hospital nurses
- information series presented by medical experts on topics including stress management, medications and proper exercising
- membership card
- mileage chart
- prizes

With doctors finding that walking is a good way to stay fit, the mall walk is a popular program. Walking offers many of the same benefits of more strenuous exercises such as biking, jogging or swimming, without the same degree of inconvenience or risk. In the mall setting, while you walk to cardiovascular fitness, you can also meet new people - and even do some window-shopping.

HEALTH: FUNDING

INDIVIDUAL PROGRAM PROFILES

ARLINGTON HOSPITAL FOUNDATION
Arlington Hospital
Development Office
1701 North George Mason Drive
Arlington, VA 22205
TEL: 703-558-6613
Purpose: To keep pace with ever-changing technology, maintain the highest quality service, and work hard to control costs.
Contact: James L. Rieder, President
Description: The *Arlington Hospital Foundation* brings together consumers and providers as partners to help maintain the quality and affordability of healthcare in Northern Virginia. In 1989, nearly 7,000 individuals, corporations, service clubs and foundations contributed toward hospital programs, medical equipment, nursing scholarships and endowments.
Through programs like *Friends of Nursing,* the *Galen Society, Associate Membership,* the *Annual Ball,* and the *Golf and Tennis Tournament,* the community donated $1.44 million to the *Arlington Hospital Foundation.*
Accomplishments of the *Foundation* during 1989 include:
- Continuation of the long-standing teaching affiliation with *Georgetown University;*
- Addition of an open heart surgery program;
- Approval of an ambulatory care center (construction to begin in 1990);
- Opening of the *Women's Health Connection* in Tysons Corner;
- Expanding of the *Arlington Treatment Center* in Harrisonburg (addiction treatment); and
- Continuing work through *Arlington Joint Ventures Group,* which oversees joint ventures with area hospitals and physicians to provide services to local residents, and the *Arlington Health Services Corporation,* which generates revenue for the hospital by operating the parking garage on the hospital campus.
Without the community as a *partner in healthcare,* many of these programs would not reach fruition. With community support, the *Foundation* continues to work toward providing the best possible health services to the residents of Northern Virginia. One way the *Foundation* "gives back" to the community is to offer members special benefits such as one hour free parking, a special discount on mammograms, cafeteria discounts, reduced rates for hospital seminars, and the *Prime Time 55* (formerly *65 plus*) program with special seminars and other benefits for older persons, among others. Full details are available on request.
Publications: Health Reach

BACK ROADS BIKE TREK
SEE HEALTH: LUNG DISEASE

HEALTH: HEALTH FAIRS

NATIONAL/STATE ORGANIZATIONS

NATIONAL HEALTH SCREENING COUNCIL FOR VOLUNTEER ORGANIZATIONS*
9411 Connecticut Avenue, NW
Kensington, MD 20895
TEL: 301-942-6601

Objectives: To help communities who wish to provide comprehensive, low-cost Health Fairs to promote health and prevent disease.
Services: Assists communities throughout the United States, and in Puerto Rico, and the Virgin Islands in mounting a Health Fair based on the NHSCVO model, which:
- promotes health awareness and self-assessment through activities, demonstrations, and information;
- encourages participants to assume responsibility for health choices;
- provides free screening to promote health and prevent disease at one convenient time and place;
- detects potential disease at an early, treatable stage;
- reinforces need for continued adherence to prescribed treatments;
- refers participants to health care source for reevaluation if necessary;
- reassures and encourages participants to continue good health behaviors; and
- promotes effective use of community resources by encouraging cooperation among private, voluntary, and government sectors.
Designs its model program to include four components of equal importance to achieve the above objectives:
Learning Centers for Health which serve to motivate participants to become actively involved in learning more about health and how their life style choices relate to health; covers ten topics, which are addressed in the *Learning Center Manual,* and publishes a series of three booklets on health education needs (*Where? Regional Profile of Minorities, What? Outline of Minority Health Needs,* and *How? Addressing Minority Health Needs*).
Screening Tests which do not replace an examination by a physician, but provide information for intelligent referrals.
Summary and Referrals by volunteer health professionals who review test results, provide counseling, information and referrals, answer questions about the tests, and assist the individual in determining personal health goals.
Follow-Up in two parts: Part I: provide the participant with copies of test results within six weeks after the fair; Part II: call the participants with significant abnormalities to inquire about follow-up activity or the need for additional assistance or referral. Tailors the basic model to different target populations when appropriate; receives "saturation promotion" through major media sponsors (radio, television and newspaper) as well as news coverage during the event, and health education programming to increase health awareness and participation in Health Fair Week Programs.
Receives funding entirely by the private sector, including major national sponsors in specific areas, such as:
- Health Education (Ciba-Geigy Corporation)
- Older Americans Health Fair Program (The Prudential Foundation)
- Minorities and Disability Health Fair Programs (Chevron USA)
- Student Health Fair Program (Atlantic Richfield Foundation)
- Health Fair Week Programs (Blue Cross/Blue Shield, Chevron USA, Gannett Company, and many others)
Enlists volunteer community groups and local media sponsors to organize and promote the local programs; publishes *Everybody Benefits* and other informative materials on the Health Fair program.

INDIVIDUAL PROGRAM PROFILES

BE ALIVE IN 2005: PROMOTING WELLNESS INTO THE 21ST CENTURY
US/DoD - Army Preventive Medicine Activity
Fort Ord, CA 93941
TEL: 408-242-4814

Purpose: To create the awareness that health is important, and that people need to take charge of their own health.
Sponsor: US/DoD - Department of the Army
Contact: David J. Fletcher or Major David Ellington
Description: Be Alive in 2005 is a joint effort of Fort Ord and the local Health Screening Council. It is designed to improve health at the Fort and in the communities of Monterey County. Activities are structured to make participants more aware of their current health status and give them some idea on how to improve their health. They emphasize the need to take the major responsibility of an individual's care away from the doctor.

There is no admission fee to the Be Alive Health Fair. There are seventeen stations where people can have height, weight, blood pressure, vision, hearing and many other physical functions checked. Other stations explain how people can maintain physical fitness through exercise, diet, and breaking bad habits such as smoking and drinking alcohol. A few of the booths are closed to the general public for legal and financial reasons, with a valid military ID required for admittance.

The booth for cancer screening, the family practice clinic, and several others were visited frequently, but one test that proved to be interesting to many people is the health hazard appraisal test. This test shows how old a person is physiologically (statistically shows life expectancy by analyzing risk factors and health habits). Volunteer activities supporting the Fair ranged from those in the medical profession on the base and in the community, to those who maintained a finger-painting station for very young children. In addition, resource volunteers from the Fort and the Community provided referral information for military personnel and civilians. The Health Fair is part of an effort to bring private citizens and the military together to have fun while improving health habits. Youth Activities, which organized adults' and kids' Fun Runs, the Army Community Service volunteers, and the NCO Club staff, which hosted the program, are examples of Fort organizations that participated.

HEALTH AND SAFETY CIRCUS
American Red Cross
Greater Toledo Area Chapter
2275 Collingwood Boulevard
Toledo, OH 43620
TEL: 419-248-3331
Purpose: To enrich the health and safety curricula of the local schools through the resources of health agencies.
Sponsor: American Red Cross; Northwest Ohio School District; community health agencies
Contact: Sharon A. DeVaughn
Description: Thirty-five volunteers assist nurses in the School Health Education Experiences Program (SHEEP) in planning the Health and Safety Circus each fall. SHEEP is comprised of consultants from various school districts.

During the first phase of the program, community health agencies are contacted and asked to bring samples of educational resources in the form of handouts such as posters and pamphlets, and audiovisuals to an organizational meeting. The support provided by school officials and the assistance offered by the agencies are combined to mount the needed project.

Public relations support is provided by the Red Cross, representatives from the health agencies, and the schools. A brochure, which maintains the circus theme, is printed by a local vocational school. The brochures are distributed to principals in over 600 schools in the Northwest Ohio Division, with two representatives from each school invited to attend the Health Fair. Volunteers are involved in all aspects of the program, including supervisory, project management and public relations capacities, as well as in direct delivery of services. Financial support of the program includes a 10% operating budget, and 90% coming from in-kind contributions of goods and services.

Youth volunteers, with adult volunteer supervision, are involved

extensively in the program. They are active in registration and evaluation booths, and in the refreshment area. Clown suits are donated for the youth in order to promote the circus theme.

In addition to the benefits to the general public, the Health Fair enabled teachers and nurses to view the latest health and safety films at the Film Fair and collect massive amounts of resources for future classes on health and safety.

In critiquing the Fair based on evaluations received and other criteria, SHEEP Committee members determined that Fairs should be held every two years. The demonstrated cost effectiveness, and the cooperation received from all segments of the community, were major factors in the decision to continue the program.

HEALTH FAIR
US/DoD - Naval Regional Medical Clinic
Regional Medical Clinic
United States Navy
Key West, FL 33040
TEL: 305-296-2461/Ext. 206
Purpose: To provide health screening and health education services to members of the local community.
Sponsor: US/DoD - Department of the Navy
Contact: R.W. Adams, MSC USN
Description: When requested by the community, Naval Regional Medical Clinic hosts Health Fairs for residents of the City of Key West and residents of the lower Keys. The Clinic makes available two large open wards in the main clinic building which are not used very much. To provide convenient accessibility to all, a weekday (Friday) is usually chosen to attract the elderly and indigent population, and a weekend day (Saturday) for the younger working population. As expected, this breakdown is evident on those days at the Fair.

Almost all of the Naval Clinic's staff volunteer to assist with Health Fairs (in a typical fair, 17 officers, 56 enlisted men, and 21 civilians reported for duty). The staff possesses the expertise to man all areas, particularly the stations requiring specialized training. Having a readily available pool of professionals is a definite advantage, and a significant factor in the success of the Fairs. Since at least 160 volunteers are needed to staff the fair adequately both days, an active drive to recruit volunteers from the community is held. Medical professionals, nursing students, and dependent wives are among the community volunteers involved.

Station Captains, all Navy personnel, receive information on the background of each volunteer who completes an application (medical/non-medical qualifications), and also recruits for additional slots that did not emerge in the applications.

Non-medical volunteers are placed in registration and other areas. To maximize participation for screening, transportation is provided to and from prearranged points in the lower Keys. The Monroe County Social Services Department has arranged transportation in the past. Such interaction between the civilian and Naval communities in pursuit of a common goal helps to avoid costly duplication of services, facilities and equipment.
Founded: 1983

MCCLELLAN AFB HEALTH FAIR
US/DoD - McClellan Air Force Base
Sacramento, CA 95652
TEL: 916-643-3354
Purpose: To provide a consumer health education program for the surrounding community using base personnel as volunteers.
Sponsor: US/DoD - McClellan Air Force Base
Contact: Pat Thompson
Description: In the fall of 1982 the HEP Committee (Military Consumer Health Education Program) agreed to take responsibility for the planning of the 1983 Health Fair. The Committee's first step was to study the critique of the 1982 Fair. Based on the lessons learned in 1982, the Committee outlined a

pre-planning schedule with deadlines assigned. After several additional meetings, the consensus of the Committee was that Health Education should be emphasized in the 1983 Fair. The Committee Chairperson was designated as the Committee's representative on the Health Fair Advisory Committee, which included representatives from the co-sponsoring organization, NHSCVO (National Health Screening Council for Volunteer Organizations). Total planning time was five months, with key workers doing final checks just hours before the doors opened in March 1983. Some of the screenings offered, and an example of results, follow:

- Height/Weight - out of 244 persons checked, 168 were abnormal.
- Blood Pressures - out of 242 persons checked, 76 were abnormal.
- Vision including Glaucoma check - out of 155 persons checked, 38 were abnormal for vision, and two of 128 checked out for glaucoma were abnormal.
- Dental Soft Tissue Exam - out of 114 persons checked, 38 were abnormal.
- Hearing - of 152 persons checked, 17 were abnormal.
- Pulmonary Function - of 54 persons checked, 16 were abnormal.

When the participant finishes the above and/or other tests, he or she reports to the Review and Referral section. This section is staffed with medical professionals. Those showing no abnormalities are asked to complete an evaluation form for the fair, and are given a *What Happens Next?* fact sheet. All of those with abnormal findings talk with counselors in the medical field, who make referrals and, a few weeks later, followup calls.

All tests are free except the 25 Chem-Panel providing blood workups. This service is contracted by the 3M Company and requires an $8.00 fee. There were 160 participants who chose to have this blood work done. About four weeks after the blood is drawn, test results are received by the site coordinator, and a copy with an explanation sheet is mailed to the participant.

Other activities at the Fair include Happy Tooth, constructed from wire and paper by the McClellan dental personnel. It is large enough for someone to get inside and walk around among the crowd discussing preventive dentistry and answering questions. Also, a Pharmacy Display featured a self-participating educational format, with someone standing by at the display to answer questions that are not readily answered in the materials.

A food section for volunteers is stocked as a public service by community organizations, or purchased with donated funds. This section is utilized also as a volunteer break area.

[This Health Fair was planned, coordinated and conducted solely by 100 volunteers from McClellan Air Force Base, Mather Air Force Base, and the community. It was the second Health Fair and its success assures additional such programs in the future.]
Founded: 1982

HEALTH: HEART DISEASE

INDIVIDUAL PROGRAM PROFILES

MENDED HEARTS
Chapter #36
18 North Grant Street
Westmont, IL 60559
TEL: 312-968-3313
Purpose: To enlist the help of persons who have undergone heart surgery to help other heart surgery patients and their spouses.
Sponsor: Mended Hearts, Chapter #36
Contact: Mrs. Rita V. Zimmer, President

Description: This is an all-volunteer effort whose objective is to visit and encourage, with the approval of a physician, persons anticipating or recovering from heart surgery; to distribute information of specific educational value to members of Mended Hearts, Inc., and to potential heart surgery patients; to counsel and provide advice and services, where possible, to families of patients undergoing heart surgery; to establish a program of assistance to surgeons, physicians and hospitals in their work with heart patients; to cooperate with other organizations in educational and research activities pertaining to heart illness; to establish and to assist in established rehabilitation programs for Mended Hearts and their families; to plan and conduct suitable programs of social and educational events.

There are approximately 125 chapters throughout the United States with the National headquarters being in Dallas, Texas. Persons interested in founding a chapter, particularly those residing in areas where heart surgery is performed, can receive information from the program.

HEALTH: HOMEBOUND

INDIVIDUAL PROGRAM PROFILES

VISITING FRIENDS*
Visiting Nurse Association of Milwaukee
1540 North Jefferson
Milwaukee, WI 53202
TEL: 414-327-2295
Purpose: To provide companionship to the homebound.
Sponsor: Visiting Nurse Association of Milwaukee
Contact: Mary P. Gilbert - Volunteer Supervisor
Description: The *Visiting Friends Program* is designed to provide companionship to homebound and isolated patients of the *Visiting Nurse Association (VNA)*. Volunteer visitors make a weekly visit and help patients do small errands and activities as well as providing emotional support and conversation.

Careful screening is done, and a training program is completed prior to placement. Ongoing in-service and support is provided by the Volunteer Supervisor and Volunteer Nurse Association staff.

HEALTH: HOMELESS

INDIVIDUAL PROGRAM PROFILES

HEALTH CARE FOR THE HOMELESS COALITION
SEE RECIPIENTS: HOMELESS - HEALTH

MISSION HOUSE
SEE RECIPIENTS: HOMELESS - HEALTH

HEALTH: HOSPICES

NATIONAL/STATE ORGANIZATIONS

FOUNDATION FOR HOSPICE AND HOMECARE
519 C Street, NE
Stanton Park
Washington, DC 20002
TEL: 202-547-6586
Objectives: To serve the dying, the disabled, and the disadvantaged.
Services: Dedicates itself to the "redefinition of the American health delivery system, shifting its focus from institutionalized and acute care to a true continuum of comprehensive services; emphasizes preventative care and good public health; proposes to balance reliance on technology with concern for humanity, reflected in community services like hospice and home care; reinforces efforts of individuals and organizations which share the *Foundation's* mission and commitment to service; bases its goals on the crisis created by the absence of an effective public policy for meeting the needs of the aging; strives to set the standard of excellence in health care; operates under the aegis of a Board of Trustees, chaired and vice-chaired by U.S. Senators; works toward the goal of bringing the disadvantaged with enormous health problems "out of the shadows and into the mainstream of society."

NATIONAL HOSPICE ORGANIZATION
1901 North Moore Street
Suite 901
Arlington, VA 22209
TEL: 703-243-5900
FAX: 703-525-5762
Objectives: To promote the hospice concept of care, to ensure the quality of that care, and to help make it available for every terminally ill American who needs it.
Services: Promotes the hospice concept and program of care imported from England in the mid-seventies), which makes the entire family the unit of care, centers caring process in the home whenever possible, and makes inpatient facilities available for those unable to be cared for at home, a concept reflected in its logo donated by a prominent artist, which symbolizes hope, life, love (within patients, families, and providers), a continuum of life and whatever comes after, and the psychological, social and spiritual components of hospice given to each hospice patient and family, and which was designed to have an international interpretation; promotes standards of care in program planning and implementation; monitors health care legislation and regulation relevant to the hospice movement, much of which was prompted by the rapid growth of hospices ("We have changed the entire health care system - not just care of the terminally ill. Before anyone told us what we would be, we told them what we are." - NHO President); sponsors professional and peer group networking; encourages medical teaching institutions to provide instruction in hospice care; conducts training programs for both administrators and caregivers; sponsors a competition for media programs; maintains a speakers bureau and a telephone referral service; publishes a monthly newsletter, a quarterly journal, a history of the organization (which includes background for the entire movement in this country), a hospice guide, technical assistance materials, monographs, and other materials.
Publications: The History of the National Hospice Organization; Hospice News; NHO Hospice Team; Hospice Journal; Guide to the Nation's Hospices; NHO Annual Report
Founded: 1978

TRAINING PROGRAMS

HOSPICE VOLUNTEER TRAINING PROGRAM*
Divine Redeemer Memorial Hospital
724 Nineteenth Avenue, North
South St. Paul, MN 55075
TEL: 612-450-4500
Credit: Certification
Sponsor: Divine Redeemer Memorial Hospital
Contact: Arnie Hanson
Description: Offered to any individual with an interest in serving hospice patients and their families, this training program has two basic components: five two-hour sessions in a classroom setting; ten hours of supervised clinical practicum involving direct patient care. Spanning a five-week period, study areas are:
- **Overview:** covers the hospice model of care for the terminally ill patient and how it is implemented by the Divine Redeemer Memorial Hospital, as well as course requirements.
- **Dealing with Terminal Illness:** examines the stages of death and dying, the various types of pain and the interventions that a volunteer may initiate to relieve these pains.
- **Communication:** involves a series of role-playing situations in which volunteers are introduced to the communication process, and examines and utilizes good communication techniques.
- **Legal Concerns:** addresses legal and financial questions surrounding terminal illness and death.
- **Loss and Grief:** focuses on the process of grieving and bereavement following the death of a patient, and the role of the volunteer in supporting the family during this period.
- **Family and Social Concerns:** discusses the social-psychological aspects of the family and how the family system is affected by terminal illness and death.
- **Funeral Arrangements:** includes topics such as preparing for death, unfinished business, funeral arrangements, burial rites and privacy of information.

At the completion of the above two-hour sessions and the ten-hour practicum, volunteers receive certification as hospice volunteers qualified to serve terminally-ill patients and families of patients. A monthly hospice volunteer support group provides further education, and gives volunteers a time to share their frustrations, joys, concerns and experiences (not a requirement for certification).

HOSPICE VOLUNTEER TRAINING PROGRAM*
Ocean County College
Department of Community Education
CN 2001
Toms River, NJ 08753
TEL: 609-255-4000
Credit: 1.6 CEU
Sponsor: Ocean County College
Contact: Librarian/Historian
Description: This program was developed in response to a need created by the development of several hospice programs in the Monmouth-Ocean County area. It is a 16-hour, eight-session course designed to teach participants:
- The Hospice Concept
- The role of the volunteer within the hospice program
- The special skills and knowledge necessary to help meet the emotional, psychological, social, spiritual and physical needs of the terminally ill and their families.

Offered for the first time in 1982, this course is intended for nurses, allied health professionals, and lay people interested in learning more about being a hospice volunteer. It depends on evaluation by the participants themselves for relevance of course content, and recommendations for additions, deletions, or changes in the format.

INDIVIDUAL PROGRAM PROFILES

HOSPICE - DIVINE REDEEMER MEMORIAL HOSPITAL
724 Nineteenth Avenue North
South St. Paul, MN 55075
TEL: 612-450-4500
Purpose: Primary purpose of the program lies in promoting the physical, psychological, social, and spiritual comfort of the patient and the family members during the advanced stages of terminal illness and in the mourning period following the death of the patient. Care may be provided in the settings of home care, and/or hospital care. Hospice care includes as well supportive services for the survivors during the period of bereavement.
Sponsor: Divine Redeemer Memorial Hospital
Contact: Mr. Arnie Hanson, Director
Description: The program was established in 1968, and is presently coordinated by a Hospice Director whose salary is paid for by Divine Redeemer Hospital. A hospice fund was established through private donations (i.e., memorials, etc.) and is utilized for educational purposes for the hospice team and volunteers.
The hospice team, referred to as the inter-disciplinary team, are a physician directed team of professionals providing "holistic" care focusing on the physical, emotional, social, and spiritual needs of the patient/family unit. This team includes the patient's family doctor, Hospice nurses in home and hospital, social workers, dietician, pharmacist, clergymen, therapists, medical doctor. The care is coordinated by the director and volunteers supplement the team. The goals of the Hospice program in offering its services include:
- To provide skilled care, assistance, and comfort for the patient and family members, at home or in the hospital should hospitalization become necessary;
- To manage pain in its physical dimensions, to encourage growth out of psychological, social, and spiritual suffering;
- To maintain the patient's normal activities in his environment as possible;
- To support and assist family members after the death of the patient;
- To be present, to listen, to LOVE...

At present, 13 volunteers are coordinated by a Volunteer Coordinator under the direction of the Hospice Director. The Volunteer Coordinator was a previously paid staff position, but was eliminated due to hospital budget cuts.
Volunteers are required to complete five two-hour sessions and an additional ten-hour supervised clinical practicum involving direct patient care before being certified as a hospice volunteer. A monthly hospice volunteer support group was also established for further education, but most importantly, to give volunteers a time to share their concerns, frustrations, experiences and joys.
Divine Redeemer Hospice Program depends on its volunteers to fill the role of loving, supportive friend. Along with the family and primary nurse, volunteers form a mini-team in caring for the patient. The three areas of hospice care: home care, in-patient (hospital) care, bereavement involve different areas of volunteering. Upon completion of the Volunteer Training Program, the volunteer is required to spend three hours in each phase of hospice care. Thereafter, in assessing the volunteer's talents, interests and availability with the Volunteer Coordinators, they can then choose the area in which they prefer to work.
Founded: 1968

HOSPICE ORGANIZATION
7020 Cass Street
Omaha, NE 68132
TEL: 402-978-8809
Purpose: To provide hospice care at home through the use of volunteers.
Contact: William Ramacciotti, President

Description: In the Omaha area, hospice care is provided at home, and in some hospitals and some nursing homes. The *Hospice Organization* oversees hospices across the area and coordinates training and other universal aspects of the service.
Hospice care is provided when patients accept that they are terminally ill and decide to die without life-sustaining efforts, such as the use of machines. Volunteers are not assigned until they complete 16.5 hours of training in Hospice classes at the *Visiting Nurses Association.* Nurses from the *Visiting Nurses Association* supplement volunteer assistance when necessary, usually coming twice a week, but increasing their visits to five or six times a week as more professional care is needed - such as intravenous feeding as the patient weakens.
Although volunteers are trained to help feed and care for the terminally ill person, it is often the family that needs help. Volunteers run errands, do laundry, stay with the ill person while a relative takes a nap, or do whatever else needs to be done. Volunteers agree that it is easy to walk into your neighbor's house, but tough to walk into a strange place - especially on that first assignment. Some circumstances find the volunteer walking into tense family situations, or he finds that the patient prefers not to see him. These situations are worked out with the families, and most often the experience is rewarding for all concerned. As one volunteer said, "It's not easy to watch a wife or husband die, but through the program you meet wonderful people."

ISAIAH HOUSE
SEE AIDS: HOME CARE/HOSPICES

HEALTH: HOSPITALS

TRAINING PROGRAMS

ARHA/COUNCIL ON VOLUNTEER TRAINING EVENTS
Arizona Hospital Association
Council on Volunteers
6319 North Mockingbird Lane
Paradise Valley, AZ 85253
TEL: 602-948-0262
Credit: Inquire
Sponsor: Arizona Hospital Association (ArHA)
Contact: Winifred Bolton (or individual contacts listed below)
Description: ArHA and the Council co-sponsor a number of training events each year. Typical events are:
ArHA Statewide Auxiliary Conference - This gathering addresses the wide spectrum of successful endeavors and conflicts existing within hospital auxiliaries, with solutions and achievements explored during roundtable discussions. Following the keynote presentation, a panel discussion format is used to air issues of concern as communicated by participants, including:
- Relationship between Administration, Director of Volunteer Services, and Auxiliary.
- Communication within the Auxiliary.
- Retention and Recruitment.

Following the panel discussions, the group of 500 participants divided for round-table discussion of the following topics:
- Go Get 'em (membership recruitment)
- The Young and the Restless (Junior recruitment)
- Where Are the Bucks? (fund raising)
- Talk It All Out (in-hospital relationships)
- What's Up Doc (communication within auxiliaries)
- Keeping Them Happy (retention and recognition)
- Buying the Best (gift shop)

Junior Volunteer Convention Phoenix/Northern Arizona - This convention is convened to raise issues on health and health care as they relate to the Junior Volunteer in the hospital. Approximately 175 young volunteers usually attend and participate in workshops including:

- Introduction to the Burn Unit
- Esperanca - Hope from Phoenix
- Non-Invasive Medical Procedures

[Specific contact: Sylvia Bandler, Junior Coordinator, St. Luke's Hospital Medical Center, 525 North 18th Street, Phoenix 85006 (602-251-8476)]

The Burnout Syndrome and Breakthroughs in Human Performance - This workshop is of interest to all levels and classifications of personnel - volunteers as well as paid staff, and administrative, managerial, and supervisory as well as support personnel. Participants learn to recognize the causes and effects of the burnout syndrome. The workshop focuses on many proven high performance activities and ten organizational programs to prevent "burnout" and influence "breakthrough" performances. Emphasis is on individuals, as well as small work groups, in conjunction with self-assessment exercises.

This workshop is convened because of declining productivity and its identification by numerous authorities as one of the major factors influencing today's economy. Factors attributed to this decline are several - one of the most important in human terms being the burnout syndrome (physical, intellectual, psychological, social or spiritual). Faculty was drawn from a research and training institute specializing in human performance and productivity.

[Specific contact: Joan E. Kloos, Director of Public Information, Arizona Hospital Association, 4202 East Raymond Street, Phoenix 85040 (602-246-8901)]

Leadership/Legislature Conference - This conference was held in concert with the ArHA Council on Volunteers Statewide Conference to assist boards and auxiliary/volunteer leaders in these vital, interrelated areas of concern.

The conference provided an opportunity for leaders to learn about the legislative process. Faculty includes legislators who inform participants on how to take an active part in government. Each participant meets with a legislator from his/her district to exchange ideas on pertinent issues and to learn of possible areas of future involvement.

[Specific contact: Fran Cohen, St. Luke's Service League, 4619 E. Calle Redonda, Phoenix 85018 (602-959-5344)]

INDIVIDUAL PROGRAM PROFILES

JANGO (JUNIOR ARMY NAVY GUILD ORGANIZATION)*
Henderson Hall
Arlington, VA 22214
TEL: 703-979-1492
Purpose: To train young volunteers to assist medical personnel in military and civilian hospitals.
Sponsor: US/DoD - JANGO
Contact: Linda S. Mundy, Executive Secretary
Description: JANGO was established at the beginning of World War II to assist the war effort and deal with the manpower shortage. Wives and daughters were invited to join in service in the wider community. They were asked to assist in hospitals on and off the military bases. Although the actual name of the organization has not been changed, membership (since the end of World War II) includes all military services and Department of Defense appointees. The Guild is divided into two sections:

- **Junior Jango,** which involves young men and women (ages 14-19) in training as volunteers in military and civilian hospitals. Junior Jangos are dependents of active, retired, or deceased military persons and Defense Department appointees. They are given 100 hours of study as nurses' aides through both classroom instruction and on-the-job training under nursing supervision. Their duties include patient care and

comfort; daily routines such as making beds, taking vital signs, and passing out food trays and water; other responsibilities that may be assigned by the charge nurse; and, as important as the others, giving the individual attention to the patient that cannot be provided by professional staff. Junior Jangos wear a uniform, participate in a capping ceremony at the completion of training, and receive awards based on hours and quality of service. They are expected to make good use of the opportunities provided through this program: (1) learning skills and proficiency in a helping profession; (2) developing responsibility regarding the needs of the community; (3) making an important contribution where it is most needed. Also, many qualify for merit awards and scholarships.

- **Senior Jangos** are dues paying members who may serve on the Senior Board and/or participate in Guild activities.

In addition to the two active divisions, JANGO maintains a roster of Honorary Members, usually distinguished women such as the wives of Presidents of the United States, Secretaries and Chiefs of Staffs. Guilds exist in several cities across the country. Location lists are available.
Founded: 1941

MEDICAL SERVICES PROGRAM
Madison House
170 Rugby Road
Charlottesville, VA 22903
TEL: 804-977-7051
Purpose: To provide necessary support services to both the hospital staff and the patients.
Sponsor: Madison House
Contact: Jane Parker
Description: The Madison House medical volunteer program is one of the most popular programs with the student volunteers. Also, it has become an important component of the University Hospital. Each year more than 200 volunteers from Madison House devote time to the hospital. In the performance of their duties, they provide the important support services crucial to both hospital staff and patients.

The Medical Services Program separated from the larger Companionship Therapy Program in 1972 and initially offered placements in two wards of the hospital. The only medical volunteer programs previously offered were the University-wide Blood Drive (taken over by Omega Psi Phi and still operating), and a referral program providing information on area doctors and dentists.

Volunteers in the program have the opportunity to gain some realistic insights into the roles of hospital staff, as well as provide a needed service. The program appeals particularly to students in the pre-med and pre-nursing programs, but has proven enriching to all who participate.

Each medical services volunteer fills a regular 1-1/2 to 3-hour time period in one of seven hospital departments including Pediatrics, Burn Unit, Intensive Care Unit, and Neuropsychiatry.

Tasks which the volunteers perform vary tremendously from one department to another and from one shift to another. The Emergency Room and the Operating Room generally afford limited patient contact. Volunteers usually are assigned to perform staff support tasks such as moving equipment and lab specimens and disabled patients. The Pediatrics Department and the Towers Psychiatric Unit, on the other hand, allow frequent individual contact with many patients.

The Medical Services volunteer by no means practices medicine, but volunteer work does provide the opportunity, especially to pre-med and pre-nursing students, to get a closer look at the medical profession as a career. Other students find satisfaction in providing supportive services and attaining a working knowledge of the day-to-day, around-the-clock functioning of a large hospital.

Two staff members of the Hospital Services Division of the hospital work closely with the Medical Services volunteers.

TAVS (TEENAGE VOLUNTEERS)
The Voluntary Action Center
2125 East South Boulevard
Montgomery, AL 36116-0044
TEL: 205-284-0006
Purpose: To discover and develop interest in the field of medical science; to acquaint young people with opportunities in the health field and requirements for each position; to share the responsibility of operating and improving the hospital; and to develop leadership talent.
Sponsor: Voluntary Action Center of Montgomery, AL
Contact: Doci Haslam
Description: The TAV program was begun in 1979 with eight very dedicated young people. It was agreed to limit the membership to 35, based on the size of the hospital. By limiting, it was felt a more comprehensive program could be offered and adequate supervision provided. Members are required to be of high moral character, maintain a scholastic average of "C" or above, must be interested in some aspect of the medical field, and have written parental approval.
In one month's time, the membership grew from 8 to 18 and, within that first year, the goal of 35 was reached. Both the president in 1979, and the president in 1980, were named Volunteer of the Year - Youth Category, for outstanding work as TAVS.
The TAVS have given, this past year, close to 10,000 hours of volunteer service to the hospital. In addition, three educational scholarships, totalling $1,950, have been awarded in the past three years to help further the education of deserving TAVS. The TAVS have also donated monies to the hospital for pediatric toys and playroom furniture.
The TAVS must go through three levels of achievement in the program, each level requiring specific training, and at the same time get in required hours of work within the hospital (minimum number of hours required are 28 during the summer months and 10 during school term). With few exceptions, TAVS work far more than the minimum hours required. TAVS are assigned to almost every area of the hospital from patient floors to departments. Assignments are based on their level of achievement, i.e., only Level III TAVS (the highest level of achievement in the program) may work in the Emergency Room or other highly technical areas of the hospital. TAVS must "earn the right" to assist in these specialized areas.
At the present time, this program is well-known and respected in hospital volunteer circles throughout the state and many hospitals have asked for assistance in starting similar programs.
Founded: 1979

HEALTH: I&R

NATIONAL/STATE ORGANIZATIONS

NATIONAL CLEARINGHOUSE FOR POISON CONTROL CENTERS
SEE HEALTH: EMERGENCIES

ODPHP NATIONAL HEALTH INFORMATION CENTER
PO Box 1133
Washington, DC 20013
TEL: 301-565-4167
TOLL FREE: 800-336-4797
Objectives: To assist consumers in locating the health resources they need; to initiate liaison activities among health information providers.

Services: Provides referral information to resource organizations such as educational institutions, voluntary organizations, libraries, hospitals, other clearinghouses, and government agencies at all levels; responds to inquiries from lay persons and professionals; publishes subject-oriented bibliographies and brochures. (The Clearinghouse is a project of the Office of Health Information, Health Promotion, and Physical Fitness and Sports Medicine of HHS.)
Publications: Health Resources in Government
Founded: 1979

PROGRAM EXCHANGE PROCESS (PEP)
American Red Cross
National Headquarters
17th and D Streets
Washington, DC 20006
TEL: 202-639-3535
Objectives: To serve as a method for chapters, blood centers, and all other Red Cross field units to exchange information on successful and innovative programs, activities and products.
Services: Begun in 1972, the Program Exchange Process (PEP) collects, processes and prepares for distribution information on programs at the local level to share with chapters, blood centers and field units across the country. By August 1988, the data bank had more than 1,850 programs available, and information is received every day. PEP is staffed by volunteers and coordinated by a paid staff member. It is located with the Administrative Resources unit of the Programs and Services Department at national headquarters. Programs are forwarded upon request and are structured to help save both time and money for managers wishing to improve or mount similar efforts.
How to Deposit Your Ideas in PEP - A reporting form (#5752) is completed and returned to PEP for review by an intraservice panel. When approved, the program is assigned a number and entered into the computer and the PEP catalog.
How to Withdraw Ideas from PEP - The *Program Exchange Catalog* (ARC 3311) is published twice a year, with supplements as warranted and is available through the General Supply Division. After a review of the catalog, a written request or a telephone call indicating the desired program by number activates the PEP system and the information is forwarded to the requestor. For those who have a computer, the information is designed for *User Access by Modem* directly to PEP national headquarters. Full instructions for accessing the information by computer are available on request.
Materials received include the program's name, purpose, and description, along with facts about the target population, funding sources, cooperating agencies, staffing, and support materials. PEP operates with an ongoing evaluation and updating system that enables users to receive information on current issues. For example, new programs in 1988-89 include:
- Special Concerns of Youth (substance abuse, suicide, teenage pregnancy, and AIDS)
- Latchkey Children
- AIDS Education and Caregiving
- Disaster Education for Children
- Services by and for the Elderly
- Health in the Workplace
- The Homeless in Your Community
- Innovative Donor Recruitment

According to the program's Chairman, "In addition to the value of the experience of others, it is hoped that PEP will strengthen the bond among chapters and help them serve their communities better."
Publications: Program Exchange Process Catalog; Plans and Programs for Community Service

TECHNICAL INFORMATION CENTER OF THE OFFICE ON SMOKING AND HEALTH
SEE HEALTH: LUNG DISEASE

US/HHS - CANCER INFORMATION CLEARINGHOUSE
SEE HEALTH: CANCER

US/HHS - HIGH BLOOD PRESSURE INFORMATION CENTER
SEE HEALTH: 120/80

VD NATIONAL HOTLINE
SEE HEALTH: STD

WELLNESS AND HEALTH ACTIVATION NETWORKS
PO Box 923
Vienna, VA 22180
TEL: 703-281-3830
Objectives: To teach individuals to more effectively utilize the health resources of the community.
Services: Provides on-site program planning and development assistance in areas of stress management, nutrition, physical awareness and self-responsibility; operates Health Activation Training Institutes; provides technical assistance in proposal writing and other management areas; maintains clearinghouse of health program designs; distributes trainer's guides, planning guides, and other materials.
Publications: Wellness Associates Journal; Members' Directory
Founded: 1980

INDIVIDUAL PROGRAM PROFILES

ASK THE DOCTOR
The Wellness Center
Alexandria Hospital
4320 Seminary Road
Alexandria , VA 22304
TEL: 703-379-3494
Purpose: To provide an educational program on health as a community service.
Sponsor: Alexandria Hospital; Individual Doctors
Contact: Wellness Center Director
Description: Ask the Doctor is an educational program offered by *The Wellness Center* at Alexandria Hospital as a free community service. It gives up-to-date information and the opportunity to ask physicians about pertinent health topics. Registration is required for the free lectures, which are offered three times each month. Volunteer physicians include psychiatrists, podiatrists, internists, plastic surgeons, pulmonary medicine specialists, obstetricians/gynecologists, and others. Requests made for special topics are considered and every attempt is made to provide lectures relating to all requests.
Also, *The Wellness Center* holds regular classes in a variety of health areas. Many are free, but some classes carry minimal fees ($8-$25), with discount tickets for senior citizens. Students are required to wear comfortable clothing and bring their own towels and mats.
The diverse areas include weight control, heart, stress, CPR, high blood pressure and cholesterol, self-esteem/self-image, psychosocial support, massage therapy, smoking cessation, post-natal care, aerobics, senior exercise, investment planning, numerous family-centered classes (Lamaze, grandparenting, etc.), and many others.
Instructors for sessions and classes are selected based on their qualifications and areas of expertise. All exercise/fitness instructors are CPR-certified and trained in anatomy, physiology and injury prevention. To ensure the highest quality for Wellness Community Programs, a *Physician Advisory Board* (seven physicians) provides professional advice and consultation.
Classes are held in five locations in the area to facilitate maximum participation.
Publications: The Way to Wellness

HEALTH: LUNG DISEASE

NATIONAL/STATE ORGANIZATIONS

AMERICAN LUNG ASSOCIATION
1740 Broadway
New York, NY 10019
TEL: 212-315-8700
Objectives: To work towards the prevention and control of lung disease.
Services: Plans and conducts programs in community services, and mounts public, professional and patient education programs; operates through a medical section (American Thoracic Society) and the National Air Conservation Commission (see description under "Physical Environment" in this book); conducts research into environmental hazards that affect the lungs, and other probable causes of the disease; maintains committees in air conservation, communications, government relations, occupational health, smoking and health, program services, and other areas; publishes a monthly journal, a bulletin (11/year), and other materials.
Publications: Respiratory Diseases
Founded: 1904

TECHNICAL INFORMATION CENTER OF THE OFFICE ON SMOKING AND HEALTH
US/HHS - Office on Smoking & Health
Parklawn Building
5600 Fishers Lane
Rockville, MD 20857
TEL: 301-443-1690
Objectives: To keep the public informed on the effects of smoking on health.
Services: Issues special reports - both general and technical; operates mail/phone inquiry service, as well as personal service at the Center; maintains over 26,000 files of information on smoking and health; runs computer searches on request (must submit Search Request Form available from Center); publishes *Smoking and Health Bulletin, The Health Consequences of Smoking,* bibliographies and other materials.
Publications: Smoking and Health Bulletin; Health Consequences of Smoking

INDIVIDUAL PROGRAM PROFILES

BACK ROADS BIKE TREK
American Lung Association of Northern Virginia
9735 Main Street
Fairfax, VA 22031
TEL: 703-591-4131
Purpose: To raise funds to assist the American Lung Association of Northern Virginia.
Description: The *American Lung Association of Northern Virginia (ALA)* is the beneficiary of a cycling weekend each year in which cyclists raise pledges for each mile of cycling. Called the *Back Roads Bike Trek,* the 1990 event covered 100 miles of the Old Dominion's scenic countryside, from Nokesville to Fredericksburg. Trekkers traveled a mapped route that included lunch on the banks of the Rappahannock, Chancellorsville Battlefield Park, and an overnight stay at the Holiday Inn South's Indoor Recreation Center in Fredericksburg.
Volunteer cyclists are accompanied by trained staff, "sag wagons," mechanical and emergency care, radio support and refreshments. Cyclists must be 18 years of age or older unless accompanied by a parent. They pay a tax-deductible registration fee of $25, which includes all meals, hotel lodging, food along the route, a *Back*

Roads Bike Trek T-shirt, maps, accompanying support, and a one-month free membership to all area *Courts Royal* and *Sport and Health* clubs. In addition, volunteer trekkers are required to raise a minimum of $250 in pledges before the trek.

The 1990 event was the fifth annual trek, and each year volunteer support is greater, according to an ALA official. "The volunteers seem to find this a great way to meet and help others while enjoying a sport and comraderie," he said. "Lung disease is a devastating illness, and we never know when or where it will strike next. The funds raised through the trek are helping to cure, and perhaps eradicate, this disease."

SPIRIT AND BREATH VOLUNTEER PROGRAM
Spirit and Breath Association
8210 Elmwood Avenue
Suite 209
Skokie, IL 60077
TEL: 708-673-1384
Purpose: To provide mutual support, rehabilitation, emotional and physical support to people who have had lung cancer.
Sponsor: Grants, private sector and private donations
Contact: Morton J. Liebling, Director and Founder
Description: Spirit and Breath was conceived in early 1978. Presently there is a hospital volunteer/patient visiting program at Lutheran General Hospital in Park Ridge Illinois where the patient is introduced to the Spirit and Breath program. This program is sponsored by the American Cancer Society.
There are presently twelve volunteer visitors. Coordinators and volunteers must have had lung cancer and be in good physical shape. Their surgery must have been done a minimum of three years prior to their application to become a volunteer.
The Spirit and Breath Lung Cancer Program was conceived and developed by Morton Liebling in 1979, after he lost his left lung to cancer in 1978. In the absence of any rehabilitation procedure, he found it necessary to build a program to help himself.
The exercises he developed were put into booklet form, which is published and distributed by the Illinois American Cancer Society. Mr. Liebling also conducts group meetings with people with lung cancer.
The goals of Spirit and Breath are to obtain volunteers who are professionals to conduct both land and pool exercise programs.
In summary, this organization is dedicated to creating a positive atmosphere of well-being for people with lung cancer so that they might lead normal productive lives.
Founded: 1978

VIRGINIA GROUP TO ALLEVIATE SMOKING IN PUBLIC
GASP
Verona, VA 24482
TEL: 703-795-2006
Purpose: To restrict smoking in public places.
Contact: Anne Morrow Donley
Description: Begun in 1986, the *Virginia Group to Alleviate Smoking in Public (GASP)* has focused a large part of its time trying to get legislation passed that would seriously restrict smoking in public places. Since tobacco is a major cash crop for Virginia, the work of the all-volunteer group, in the words of a member, was "cut out for them."
Although many across the state were surprised to see the General Assembly take steps toward approving a major smoking-restriction bill, it was not a surprise to GASP. Soon after its inception, the group grew to 1,000 members, joining a cadre of some 230,000 members in major health groups across the country. One turning point for the Assemblymen came in the form of surveys presented by volunteer groups showing that two-thirds of voting-age Virginians favor state restrictions of smoking in public places. Many Senators switched and supported the no-smoking bill after receiving "a lot of flak" for voting against it the year before. The fact that many of those contacting the Assembly were doctors also was a factor. The positive results of the group's appeal to the Assembly on the tobacco issues has been termed "a historic first" for Virginia.

Although GASP is one of the smaller anti-smoking groups, it is the most vocal, according to observers. It has developed a number of items such as buttons, cartoons, and histories of legislators' votes on the issues to pass out at hearings. Hardly considered a match for the powerful tobacco industry, the group credits its success to its policy to "take-no-prisoners" in contrast to the more compromising approach of the older, established health groups. Mailings and newspaper ads showing the votes of incumbents on anti-smoking legislation and the position of challengers were used during the November 1989 elections, and letters were written directly to people on the Committees, as well as Congress and gubernatorial candidates. As GASP sees more and more success in its efforts, the founder points out, "This is one of the few organizations that has been formed to put itself out of business."

HEALTH: MILITARY - ACTIVE/VETERANS

TRAINING PROGRAMS

US/VA - VAVS WORKSHOPS
SEE RECIPIENTS: MILITARY - ACTIVE/VETERANS

INDIVIDUAL PROGRAM PROFILES

MANTENO VETERANS HOME VOLUNTEER PROGRAM
SEE RECIPIENTS: MILITARY - ACTIVE/VETERANS

HEALTH: OLDER PERSON

NATIONAL/STATE ORGANIZATIONS

ALZHEIMER'S DISEASE & RELATED DISORDERS ASSOCIATION
SEE RECIPIENTS: OLDER PERSON - HEALTH

NATIONAL ASSOCIATION FOR HUMAN DEVELOPMENT
SEE RECIPIENTS: OLDER PERSON - HEALTH

NATIONAL EYE CARE PROJECT
American Academy of Ophthalmology Foundation
PO Box 6988
San Francisco, CA 94101-6988
TOLL FREE: 800-222-EYES (3937)
Objectives: To extend medical eye care to disadvantaged citizens over the age of sixty-five.
Services: Operates a toll-free HELPLINE for citizens or legal residents over the age of 65 who need medical eye care but have no physician; makes referrals to local volunteer opthalmalogists who are participating in the project; provides service to those who are needy, with qualified callers receiving treatment at no out-of-pocket expense for the doctor's services (each caller meeting eligibility requirements is mailed the name of an ophthalmologist participating near his or her home within one week after the call); provides free information to any senior calling the HELPLINE.

[The project is funded by corporations and independent ophthalmologists as well as the Academy's Foundation.]
Contact: Anna Zammataro or B. Thomas Hutchinson, MD
Founded: 1896

INDIVIDUAL PROGRAM PROFILES

AD SUPPORT GROUP OF GREATER ALABAMA
Alzheimer's Disease & Related Disorders Association
Greater Mobile Chapter
1700 Center Street
Mobile, AL 36604
TEL: 205-438-4551
Purpose: To help family members of a victim of Alzheimer's Disease to cope.
Sponsor: Alzheimer's Disease and Related Disorders Association (national)
Contact: Clifton Vernon Weldy
Description: There are an estimated 2,000 AD (Alzheimer's Disease) patients in Mobile County, and about 1,000 cases in Baldwin County. Neither cause nor cure is known for this progressive disease. Opinions vary from a slow-growing virus, to accelerated aging, to immune system breakdown or hereditary or environmental causes. The only thing scientists know for certain is that it is characterized by chemical changes in the brain. AD is characterized by loss of memory, personality changes, and loss of speech and understanding, culminating in loss of control of body functions. It has been diagnosed in patients as young as 28, and statistics show that 5-8 percent of the nation's over-65 population have the disease. Over 80, statistics reach 20 percent.
County records show that primary caregivers in the family sometimes disappear under the strains of caring for an AD patient. As one caregiver said, "The doctor didn't tell us how bad it was going to get." To try to counteract this burnout syndrome, a local chapter of the *Alzheimer's Disease and Related Disorders Association (ADRDA)* helped volunteers organize a support group for caregivers in the Greater Mobile area.
It is not known how many caregivers have been kept with their AD family member because of the program, but many have stated that the support group made the difference. Many of the members become volunteers - with one retired man becoming a 40-hour volunteer treasurer and bookkeeper. He said he felt he had to do more for the group, since "The group has kept me alive." He is also one of the key players in establishing other support groups in Washington, Clarke, Conecuh, Wilcox, Escambia, Covington and Monroe Counties.
The self-help group meets regularly and provides the opportunity to share information, solutions, experiences, and other aspects of the patient-caregiver relationship. Services from the national ADRDA include chapter development and a toll-free hotline for information and consultation.
Founded: 1983

ADULT FOSTER CARE
SEE RECIPIENTS: OLDER PERSON - HEALTH

MULTI-PHASIC HEALTH SCREENING
Retired Senior Volunteer Program
200 North Vineyard Boulevard
Room 603
Honolulu, HI 96817
TEL: 808-536-643
Purpose: To provide free health screening to senior citizens, and provide an opportunity for retired nurses and other senior citizens to serve the community.
Sponsor: State of Hawaii
Contact: Francis S. Dunning, Program Coordinator

Description: In the early 1970's, the Moiliili Community Center, a Retired Senior Volunteer Program (RSVP) volunteer station, developed and set up a model free multi-phasic health screening program for senior citizens residing in the general area around the volunteer station.
Over thirty senior volunteers, some of whom were retired nurses, were responsible for implementation of the program. Once a month the volunteers performed tests and guided participants to the various screening sites. For tasks that required special knowledge, volunteers were given training by public health nurses. When all tests were completed, the results were forwarded to a public health nurse for review and analysis of the results. After the nurse returned them to the screening program with her comments, follow-up letters were written to each of the older persons' physicians.
Screening was conducted in the recreation room of a public housing facility for senior citizens. Many of the volunteers lived in the housing complex and were recruited by the senior citizens' recreation specialist, whose office is in the building.
Recognizing the diversity of backgrounds among senior citizens in the area, bilingual volunteers were recruited to work with older persons who needed this type of assistance to participate. Hot lunches were prepared and served by RSVP after the screening process was completed.
Initially sponsored by the Community Center and ACTION, the model proved to be a complete success. It has become a statewide program now sponsored solely by the State of Hawaii.
Founded: 1972

HEALTH: SELF-HELP

INDIVIDUAL PROGRAM PROFILES

SPIRIT AND BREATH VOLUNTEER PROGRAM
SEE HEALTH: LUNG DISEASE

HEALTH: STD

NATIONAL/STATE ORGANIZATIONS

STD NATIONAL HOTLINE
American Social Health Association
260 Sheridan Avenue
Palo Alto, CA 94306
TEL: 415-321-5234
TOLL FREE: 800-227-8922
Objectives: To provide information and referral service for people in need of low-cost testing and treatment for sexually-transmitted diseases.
Services: Works with more than 5,000 local facilities to assure quick, accurate, and localized service for testing and treatment of socially-transmitted diseases; maintains 24-hour confidential telephone service on a nationwide basis with highly-trained volunteers; develops and distributes numerous quick-reference brochures on socially-transmitted diseases (available at nominal cost).
Publications: U.S. Crisis Lines; Public Clinics in the U.S.
Founded: 1979

VD NATIONAL HOTLINE
American Social Health Association
PO Box 13827
Research Triangle Pk , NC 27709
TEL: 919-361-2742
TOLL FREE: 800-342-AIDS
Objectives: To provide information and referral service for people in need of low-cost testing and treatment for venereal disease (VD).
Services: Works with more than 5,000 local VD facilities to assure quick, accurate, and localized service; maintains 24-hour confidential telephone service on a nationwide basis; develops and distributes numerous quick-reference brochures on VD and related diseases, available at nominal cost.
Publications: Helper
Founded: 1912

HEALTH: STROKE

INDIVIDUAL PROGRAM PROFILES

ORGANIZATION FOR AFTER-STROKE RESOURCES
804 East Foothill Boulevard
Glendora, CA 91740
TEL: 213-335-0712
Purpose: To help persons who have suffered a stroke find a road back to independence and regain lost skills in a social setting.
Sponsor: Organization for After-Stroke Resources
Contact: Sharon B. Meyer, Director
Description: OASR was incorporated as a non-profit organization in July 1973, after a study conducted by *Casa Colina Hospital* found that one year after being released from their therapy department, stroke patients had regressed and were staying home feeling sorry for themselves.
OASR operates six Activity Centers that meet one day a week for about five hours, headed by a Center Director, assisted by many volunteers. OASR is funded by donations, memberships and fund raisers.
Referrals come from hospitals in the area and from persons within the organization. Volunteers are trained by the Center Directors and at training sessions held about two times a year, where they learn what to expect from a person who has had a stroke, how to handle those who are in wheelchairs, ways to help with their disabilities.
Founded: 1973

HEALTH: TRANSPORTATION

INDIVIDUAL PROGRAM PROFILES

EASY RIDERS VOLUNTEER PROGRAM*
SEE TRANSPORTATION & SAFETY: HEALTH

HELP-ON-WHEELS
SEE HEALTH: CANCER

HEALTH: WOMEN

INDIVIDUAL PROGRAM PROFILES

THE S.O.A.P.S.
SEE RECIPIENTS: WOMEN

WOMAN-TO-WOMAN HOTLINE
SEE HEALTH: CANCER

HEALTH: 120/80

NATIONAL/STATE ORGANIZATIONS

US/HHS - HIGH BLOOD PRESSURE INFORMATION CENTER
US/HHS - National Institutes of Health
4733 Bethesda Avenue
Suite 530
Bethesda, MD 20814
TEL: 301-558-4880
Objectives: To reduce illness and death from hypertension.
Services: Serves as a national clearinghouse for the collection, evaluation, and dissemination of information on hypertension provides technical assistance to national and local agencies and organizations, groups and individuals; works with health care providers to improve the standards of patient care; publishes fact sheets, reports, bibliographies, catalogs, educational and other materials.
Sponsor: US/HHS - Department of Health & Human Services
Publications: 120/80 Fact Sheet

HOUSING

NATIONAL/STATE ORGANIZATIONS

**NATIONAL ASSOCIATION OF HOUSING &
REDEVELOPMENT OFFICIALS**
1320 Eighteenth Street, NW
Washington, DC 20036
TEL: 202-429-2960
FAX: 202-429-9684
Objectives: To meet the need of a close alliance between public
officials and private leaders for successful housing and other
programs.
Services: Provides technical assistance to individual agencies, or to
groups of agencies who face similar issues and problems; maintains
ongoing relationship with HUD and other public agencies to be of
maximum service to programs; provides training for program
staff/volunteers on the practical needs of the housing community;
conducts certification program covering certain tasks in the
housing and community development field; maintains extensive
library and a personalized reference service; publishes *New Alert,
Journal of Housing,* and a variety of technical books and
pamphlets; convenes annual convention and three other national
conferences each year.
Publications: Monitor; Journal of Housing; NAHRO Action
Alerts; Directory of Local Agencies
Founded: 1933

NATIONAL HOUSING CONFERENCE
1126 Sixteenth Street, NW
Suite 211
Washington, DC 20036
TEL: 202-223-4844
Objectives: To bring together policy-makers (government officials,
local housing officials, bankers), service "voices" (unions, builders),
and consumers (senior citizens, minorities, church groups, and
other consumers) on "decent shelter for all Americans."
Services: Mobilizes support for effective programs in housing and
community development; publishes monthly newsletter and other
periodicals, legislative bulletins and other materials; convenes
monthly forums and annual meeting.
Publications: NHC Newsletter; Policy and Resolutions
Founded: 1931

**US/HUD - PRIVATE SECTOR INITIATIVE ACTIVITIES IN
HUD**
US/HUD - Office of the Secretary
Seventh and D Streets, SW
Washington, DC 20410
TEL: 202-755-6417
Objectives: To focus attention on and provide technical support for
local problem-solving initiatives.
Services: Organizes private sector initiatives program around three
major themes: Community Partnership Initiatives, Strategies for
Cities, and Privatization; involves several offices of HUD in each
theme, described below:
  - **Community Partnership Initiatives** concerns efforts to
    strengthen the public sector's capacity to solve the widest
    variety of community problems by working with the private
    sector and involves several offices of HUD; provides tools,
    techniques, and programs for communities to develop
    cooperative relationships among public, private, neighborhood,
    and voluntary sector organizations to solve local problems;
    involves the following HUD initiatives:
  - **Working Group on Voluntarism,** to bring public and private
    sectors together both through an interagency working group of
    the Cabinet Council on Human Resources, and through a
    nationwide network of Federal Regional Councils; includes
    interaction with the American Foundation on Volunteerism
    (which stimulates local community voluntary programs), and
    the U.S. Jaycees Local Foundation Project (which has
    committed the full resources of 7500 local clubs) in a joint
    effort with the American Foundation on Volunteerism to
    establish a local public foundation in each community where
    there is a Jaycee Club.
  - **Management Work Plan/Strategy,** with assistance from
    HUD's Office of Community Planning and Development to
    foster public/private partnership in two major areas: program
    and legislative changes, and activities to promote partnerships;
    increases Area and Regional field staff activity, develops
    continued dialogue with field staff in support of this activity,
    and promotes speeches and articles by principal staff in areas
    relevant to the activities.
  - **Community Development Block Grants,** as they relate to 1981
    legislation which allows local governments to use block grant
    funds in conjunction with private sector capital investment to
    strengthen local economies.
  - **Enterprise Zones,** to attract new business investments in inner
    city areas which will provide jobs for residents.

- **Urban Development Action Grants,** to encourage private sector economic development activity to aid distressed communities in their economic recovery through new private capital investments designed to produce jobs and to increase the local tax base.
- **Community Partnerships Resources Center,** to gather and display a body of knowledge, experiences, and practicum related to community partnership initiative activities taking place in local communities.
- **Guided Capacity-Building and Partnership Development,** to identify and support the role of community-based organizations working with the private sector in revitalizing urban neighborhoods; publishes *Partnerships for Community Self-Reliance*, which contains over 100 examples of successful neighborhood projects.
- **State Relationship/Strategy,** to establish Small Business Economic Revitalization Corporations, develop self-sustaining financial delivery systems, mobilize resources of the private sector financial community, and market tax incentives to stimulate capital investment, job creation, and development of small business opportunities.
- **Affordable Housing Demonstration,** to find ways to produce affordable housing for home buyers without direct Federal assistance.
- **National Community Energy Management Center,** to provide a one-stop common source of technical assistance to communities through a consortium of three Federal agencies, seven national associations and six major corporations.
- **Operation Build,** to provide opportunities for improving the lives of pre-teen youths who reside in public housing or HUD-subsidized projects.
- **Federal Procurement Pilot Project,** to enable New York City to link small and minority business activity to Federal procurement contracts (sponsored by New York City Chamber of Commerce and the Rockefeller Foundation).
- **Strategies for Cities,** to strengthen community capacities and processes for developing strategy that enables cities and regions to adapt to change, and to develop information that enables local cities to formulate public/private sector approaches to local problems; involves the following initiatives in this theme: strategies for cities project, to develop a nationwide state-of-the-art report which includes case studies on ways that local communities have applied a strategic process to solving local problems; rehabilitation technical assistance, to offer technical assistance to local governments in carrying out Community Development Block Grant-funded rehabilitation programs and stimulating increased participation by private lenders.
- **Privatization,** to strengthen the public sector capacity to select and implement alternatives to the delivery of public services through: the collection, assessment, and display of information such as a major catalog of *Alternatives for Service Delivery* to identify feasible alternatives through use of the private sector; outreach projects in the form of regional conferences, workshops, and technical assistance efforts to disseminate the information gathered on the theme of privatization; neighborhood service delivery to illustrate that neighborhood organizations can deliver services in a responsive and cost-effective manner to the mutual benefit of local governments and neighborhood residents; housing initiatives to provide greater delegation of responsibility to private lenders in processing single-family FHA insurance applications, conduct an experimental program in privatization of debt collection for defaulted Title I Home Improvement loans, contract out accounting and servicing of HUD-held mortgages, complete an evaluative study of private sector management of public housing, and turn over to the private sector the "Housing Counseling Program" and the "Congregate Housing Services" program for the elderly; a White House Conference on Community Partnership

Initiatives to include a privatization component.
[Not a complete list; request information on other initiatives mounted by HUD to increase private sector involvement.]
Sponsor: US/HUD - Department of Housing & Urban Development
Publications: Partnerships for Self-Reliance

TRAINING PROGRAMS

ADOPT-A-FAMILY
Columbus Board of Realtors
200 Town Street
Columbus, OH 43230
TEL: 614-221-5353
Sponsor: Columbus Board of Realtors
Contact: Beverley Halterman, Chairperson
Description: To celebrate *American Home Week* in April 1989, the *Columbus Board of Realtors* initiated a new seminar program, *Adopt-A-Family,* designed to help families earning $15,000 to $24,000 per year to buy homes. It started with five seminars held in various parts of the city, where Realtor and lender volunteers met with potential buyers. Seminars attracted as many as 70 families, 75 to 100 Realtor volunteers, and more than a dozen lender volunteers. The highest attendance was at *Beery Middle School,* where the principal took a personal interest and recruited families. Volunteers work with families one-on-one.
Seminars help families look realistically at their income-debt ratio, and work toward paying off debts to help qualify them for purchasing a home. The 1989 seminars produced 40 families with a potential for home purchase, and the goal is to get at least 25 of them into their own homes. Some will be delayed until their financial situations are better, with volunteers staying with them until they qualify. Six families were "in contract" within 30 days of the last seminar. The volunteer project helped some with down payments and closing costs.
Word spread quickly about the program, and the board continually receives calls from families and volunteer Realtors and lenders who want to be involved. The board hopes to hold the seminar program each year, and plans to suggest similar projects to other boards around the country.

INDIVIDUAL PROGRAM PROFILES

MANNA, INC.*
1711 Fourteenth Street, NW
Washington , DC 20009
TEL: 202-462-8686
Purpose: To make it possible for low- and moderate-income residents to become homeowners.
Sponsor: Local Initiatives Support Corporation
Contact: Jim Dickerson, Executive Director
Description: Established in 1972, Manna, Inc. has a long history of programs that enable low-income people to own homes. It was founded by a minister on the premise that everyone deserves a decent and affordable place to live. Its basic philosophy is "housing for people, not profit."
Manna focuses on acquisition, rehabilitation and new construction. By fall 1989, working through often confusing, often complicated bureaucratic and financial systems, Manna had completed nearly 2,000 new or rehabilitated housing units in the city for low- and moderate-income residents. In spite of these impressive numbers, however, Manna has a waiting list averaging 500 families.
The DC government, private industry, and foundations fund the current $1.6 million project. Some insured homeowner loans come from the *US/HUD Federal National Mortgage Association,* with others provided by the city's *Department of Housing and*

Community Development's Home Purchase Assistance Program.
A recent project, *Victory Lane,* is composed of five single-family,
10 condominium, and two duplex houses. Five of the
condominiums were completed and the subject of a celebration on
April 4, 1990. The land for the project was reduced in price by the
city to make the project possible. In addition to local banks the
nonprofit financing organization, *Local Initiative Support
Corporation,* provides construction funds.

To minimize what is considered one of the greatest risks in the
city, Manna volunteer advocates follow up with homeowners until
it is certain that the individual housing situation is stable.

Working in neighborhoods where traditional developers are
reluctant to work, Manna has gained a reputation among housing
advocates as one of the most successful nonprofit housing
developers in the area.

HOUSING: AIDS

INDIVIDUAL PROGRAM PROFILES

HOUSING SERVICES: AIDS PROGRAM
Whitman-Walker Clinic
1407 S Street, NW
Washington, DC 20009
TEL: 202-797-3555; 202-328-0697 (Spanish)
Purpose: To provide low-cost housing alternatives and related
services such as groceries to persons living with AIDS.
Sponsor: Whitman-Walker Clinic
Contact: Peter Provost
Description: Robert N. Schwartz Housing Services is a division of
the Whitman-Walker Clinic, a volunteer-based (1,500 overall)
effort, enhanced and supported by professional staff. Housing
services includes:
Permanent Housing - The service maintains five group homes,
each providing permanent housing for four to five persons capable
of independent living. Each resident has a separate bedroom and
shares common areas, such as a kitchen, living room, and
bathrooms. In addition, the system includes an apartment building
with six units to accommodate couples, children, and those who
are better served by apartment living. There is a capacity of 34
residents.
Short-Term Residence Facility - A community residence facility
provides short-term, non-intensive nursing care for individuals who
do not require hospitalization, but are not well enough to care for
themselves. The facility provides meals, assistance with daily tasks,
and 24-hour supervision in a home-like setting for seven patients.
The locations of the residences are confidential to protect the
privacy of the residents. A variety of outings including trips to the
theater, beach weekends, and holiday celebrations are planned for
the residents through the *Living Spaces Program.*
Food Distribution - A food bank provides non-perishable grocery
items to resident and non-resident persons with AIDS on a regular
basis.
The project is named in memory of Dr. Robert N. Schwartz, a
psychiatrist who organized Whitman-Walker Clinic's AIDS
counseling services in 1983. He died of AIDS in 1984. As new
residences are added, they are named in memory of individuals
who have made significant contributions to the community.
Volunteers in the program receive orientation, basic training, and
seminars on a variety of issues, such as death and dying, and grief
and healing.
All AIDS programs are coordinated with local government
services and community-based organizations.

HOUSING: COOPERATIVES

NATIONAL/STATE ORGANIZATIONS

COMMUNITY ECONOMICS
1904 Franklin Street
Suite 900
Oakland, CA 94612
TEL: 415-832-8300
Objectives: To assist community groups and local public agencies
in matters of nonprofit and cooperatively-owned housing, rural
development, economic development, and alternative investment
funds.
Services: Provides technical assistance for planning and developing
limited-equity cooperative housing, teaches classes in housing and
economic development; conducts research in the area of
development-oriented pension funds to channel this major source
of capital toward areas such as affordable housing and job
creation; works as a partner with local government and
community groups to improve the capital flow for low-income
housing and other revitalization activities; advises on
tenant-initiated cooperative conversions (ask about handbook
prepared for California's Department of Housing and Community
Development); makes presentations at conferences and workshops;
publishes the Community Economics Prospectus, which provides
brief case studies of projects developed with the involvement of
this organization including:
Chico Housing Improvement Program: Chico, California, which
began with a land purchase at half price, with half being donated
by the owner, and added financial assistance from the State's
Urban Predevelopment Loan Fund, the Farm-worker Grant
Program, and National Consumer Cooperative Bank.
Niumalu-Nawiliwili Tenants Association, Kauai, Hawaii, which
evolved from a seven-year fight against eviction from housing that
had been in residents' families for as long as 65 years, and ended
with tenants purchasing the land in order to rehabilitate existing
homes and construct new housing.
Grove/Shafter Freeway Replacement Housing: Oakland, CA,
which was developed to provide community-owned housing for
residents who were displaced by construction of a freeway using
State Highway Funds for basic capital, building writedowns from
the Oakland Redevelopment Agency, and HUD Section 8 rental
subsidies for 200 of the 400 units.
Describes numerous other housing and economic development
projects in prospectus, and develops other materials to inform
communities of programs available to them in housing and related
crises.
Publications: Community Economics Prospectus
Founded: 1973

COOPERATIVE HOUSING FOUNDATION*
2501 M Street, NW
Suite 450
Washington, DC 20037
TEL: 202-887-0700; Telex 440271 CHFUI
Objectives: To encourage cooperative housing; to help improve the
quality of housing for low- and moderate-income people.
Services: Helps organize and develop housing cooperatives -
especially those sponsored by local consumer groups; manages
cooperative housing studies and conducts research on the
effectiveness of specific cooperative housing techniques; publishes
News Briefs and other publications (some in Spanish).
Publications: CHF Newsbriefs
Founded: 1950

NATIONAL ASSOCIATION OF HOUSING COOPERATIVES
2501 M Street, NW
Washington, DC 20037
TEL: 202-887-0706
Objectives: To assist member-owners of housing cooperatives.
Services: Aids individuals and groups in finding resources for technical assistance; develops standards; assists with management problems; conducts workshops on all aspects of cooperative home ownership, including boards, community relations, energy conservation, and taxation; publishes *Cooperative Housing Bulletin, Cooperative Housing Journal,* a directory, a handbook, and other materials.
Publications: Cooperative Housing Bulletin; Cooperative Housing Journal; Directory/Housing Cooperatives
Founded: 1950

INDIVIDUAL PROGRAM PROFILES

BUYERS UP
SEE CONSUMER SERVICES/LEGAL RIGHTS: COOPERATIVES

HOUSING: DISCRIMINATION

NATIONAL/STATE ORGANIZATIONS

NATIONAL COMMITTEE AGAINST DISCRIMINATION IN HOUSING
1425 H Street, NW
Washington, DC 20005
TEL: 202-783-8150
Objectives: To work for the provision of free choice in housing for every American.
Services: Provides technical assistance to requesting local groups; provides legal advice to local fair housing groups and initiates suits in selected cases; distributes free public service television and radio announcements when available; conducts surveys to document degree of discrimination at any given time imposed on minorities and poor; publishes bimonthly newsletter, intermittent bulletin, other materials.
Publications: Trends; Flash

US/HUD - OFFICE OF FAIR HOUSING AND EQUAL OPPORTUNITY
400 Seventh Street, SW
Washington, DC 20410
TEL: 202-755-7252
TOLL FREE: 800-424-8590
Objectives: To assist rural Americans with supervised credit and technical assistance in four primary areas: housing, farming, community programs, and business/industrial development.
Services: Provides loans and grants to rural Americans, including:
- **Homeownership Loans** - money to buy, build, or improve homes, including housing sites; certain housing debts may be refinanced; for low- or moderate-income.
- **Rural Rental Housing** - loans to build, maintain, and operate rental facilities for low- to moderate-income families.
- **Repair and Rehabilitation Housing Loans** - to make repairs to remove health and safety hazards; for very low income.
- **Self-Help Technical Assistance Grants** - to provide technical assistance to families in self-help homebuilding; grants to public agencies or nonprofit corporations who provide assistance.

- **Farm Ownership Loans** - long-term credit to family size farmers to purchase farms or to make major improvements.
- **Emergency Loans** - credit to farmers and ranchers in designated disaster areas for actual losses to property or production.
- **Water and Waste Disposal Loans and Grants** - to install or improve rural community water systems, sewage disposal systems or solid waste disposal systems.
- **"Other" Community Facility Loans** - credit to build or improve public-use facilities, such as hospitals, fire and police departments, community centers, libraries, schools publicly-owned recreation centers, and other essential community facilities.
- **Business and Industry Loan Guarantees** - guarantees assuring up to 90% repayment of funds from commercial lenders to establish a variety of enterprises in rural areas, including towns up to 50,000 population; interest rates and repayment terms negotiated between lender and borrower.

INDIVIDUAL PROGRAM PROFILES

COMMUNITY HOUSING RESOURCES BOARD
Greater Hartford Association of Realtors
65 Kane Street
West Hartford, CT 06119
TEL: 203-236-2561
Purpose: To help real estate agents meet the objectives of an affirmative marketing agreement.
Contact: Brendan B. Grady, Board Member
Description: The *Community Housing Resources Board* - composed of Realtors, government officials and fair housing advocates - was established to monitor implementation of the *Voluntary Affirmative Marketing Agreement* developed and signed by Hartford-area Realtors in 1979. The agreement requires signers to institute office procedures to ensure that all prospective home buyers are treated equally regardless of race. It is a product of a 1975 agreement between the *U.S. Department of Housing and Urban Development (HUD)* and the *National Association of Realtors.*
Although it has an advisory rather than an enforcement role, the eight-member volunteer Board monitors the effectiveness of the fair housing agreement. When a May 1989 story in *The Courant,* the local newspaper, revealed that reporters posing as prospective home buyers had found discrimination at eight of 15 agencies in the Hartford area, the Board met and developed a five-step program addressing the article and other issues. Steps approved included (1) Urge the Realtors association to investigate the findings by *The Courant's* testers and report the results to the Board; and (2) Begin having quarterly meetings of Board members, Realtors and HUD officials to review the effectiveness of the voluntary agreement.
In a special vote, members voted 5-3 to request a list of the original signers of the agreement. Assenters hope that going back to the innovators who drew up such a lasting agreement may help as they try to determine why the reporters encountered discrimination in more than half of their test cases.
Founded: 1979

HOUSING: FUNDING

NATIONAL/STATE ORGANIZATIONS

MORTGAGE BURNING FUND
SEE HOUSING: HOMELESS

NATIONAL HOUSING PARTNERSHIP
1126 Sixteenth Street, NW
Washington, DC 20036
TEL: 202-223-4844
Objectives: To stimulate the production by private industry of low- and moderate-income housing through partnerships with community organizations, developers, builders at the local level.
Services: Provides equity capital and joint venture funds to partnerships it forms; provides working capital to single family home builders through its Small Business Investment Company (licensed by Small Business Administration); functions with staff of specialists provided by the National Corporation for Housing Partnerships, its administrative arm; rehabilitates old, and constructs new, buildings for Section 8 programs; works with FmHA in the development of housing for senior citizens and families in rural areas and small communities; publishes various materials on its rural and urban programs; participates in NCHP annual meetings; manages low- and moderate-income housing nationwide.

VIRGINIA PARTNERSHIP FUND AND OTHER PROGRAMS
Virginia Department of Housing & Community Development
State Office Building
205 North 4th Street
Richmond, VA 23219-1747
TEL: 804-786-1575
Objectives: To provide housing assistance for low-income, handicapped and elderly people.
Services: Oversees a number of housing assistance programs to assist special populations, including:
- **Virginia Partnership Fund** - established in 1988 to increase housing opportunities for low-income households throughout Virginia. Three programs under this fund either directly or indirectly benefit persons with disabilities:
- **Emergency Home Repair Grant** - funds repairs to properties which present an immediate health and safety threat; also funds grants of up to $1,000 per household to be used for accessibility adaptations for people with physical disabilities. [Of the 513 jobs funded by this grant in the past year, 80 of them involved unit adaptations for persons with physical disabilities.]
- **Multifamily Production Loan Program** - provides low-interest loans to developers for the construction of new housing for low and moderate income persons; adheres to Uniform Statewide Building Code which requires that in developments of 21 to 99 units, at least one of those units must be accessible; if more than 100, one unit per 100 or fraction thereof.
- **Congregate Housing Loan Program** - benefits persons who are elderly or disabled, providing up to $250,000 per project to be used to rehabilitate or construct new units for individuals who are not able to function without assistance; includes separate rooms for individuals with a central food preparation area and group dining area.
Works with a federal program available through the Department of Housing and Urban Development (HUD) - *Permanant Housing for the Handicapped Homeless* - which offers funding through states to developers to construct permanent housing for people with disabilities. [When approved, states are required to provide a 50% match and monitor project sponsors.]
Administers Virginia Uniform Statewide Building Code regulations (Section 512.0), which addresses accessibility based on the American National Standard Specifications for making public buildings and facilities accessible to and usable by persons with disabilities.
Brings together representatives of persons with disabilities and the housing industry to discuss changes required by the federal *Fair Housing Amendments Act,* producing proposed amendments agreed to by both groups. Many other activities of the department serve special members of the Commonwealth.

Sponsor: State of Virginia
Contact: Neal J. Barber, Director

INDIVIDUAL PROGRAM PROFILES

HOMELESSNESS PREVENTION PROGRAM
SEE HOUSING: HOMELESS

HOUSING: HANDICAPPED

NATIONAL/STATE ORGANIZATIONS

INDEPENDENT LIVING FOR THE HANDICAPPED
SEE RECIPIENTS: HANDICAPPED - INDEPENDENT LIVING

HOUSING: HOMELESS

NATIONAL/STATE ORGANIZATIONS

MORTGAGE BURNING FUND
PO Box 762
Annandale, VA 22003
TEL: 703-354-6270
Objectives: To provide crisis assistance when older persons are victims of the "fine print" in equity and other housing loans.
Services: Provides crisis intervention assistance and psychosocial support services to older homeowners in financial trouble regarding their homes; addresses financial documents drawn up "within the law," but containing language that create emergency situations regarding imminent loss of the home; works toward changing legislation to preserve a specified portion of an elderly person's home equity from indebtness no matter how long they live in the house; provides emergency funds when legality is in question but cannot be challenged; maintains a bureau of experts to work with the lender to help the elderly person or persons stay in the home; administers donations from private business/industry to provide crisis intervention when appropriate; provides assistance only after all over avenues are exhausted and only to stabilize the situation; provides counseling when the only alternative for the older person has been deemed by expert legal counseling to relocate.

INDIVIDUAL PROGRAM PROFILES

ARC COVENANT
SEE RECIPIENTS: HOMELESS - NUTRITION

HOMELESSNESS PREVENTION PROGRAM
New Jersey Office of the Governor
101 South Broad Street
CN 800
Trenton, NJ 08625
TEL: 609-292-9069
Purpose: To enlist assistance the Red Cross, Salvation Army, and other service agencies to locate and help families at risk of becoming homeless.

Sponsor: American Red Cross
Contact: Helen Seitz, Director (state); Tricia Fagan, Director (Rutgers University)
Description: When New Jersey announced that it would administer and fund a "homelessness prevention project" across the State, volunteer organizations, universities, legal services, and others offered to help by referring families-at-risk that came to their attention. This network of volunteer referral organizations has worked so well that it has helped New Jersey's program to be considered a national model, and several other states are emulating the idea by instituting projects of their own. Maryland, Michigan and Pennsylvania offer emergency mortgage assistance for homeowners. New York and Connecticut offer eviction mediation services for renters, and Virginia has begun a program based on the New Jersey experiment.
Begun in 1984, by 1990 the New Jersey project had assisted 15,000 New Jersey families by paying rents, mortgages and providing the security deposits that often make the difference between shelter and the streets. In one instance, a blind woman with a mentally-handicapped son called an attorney at the *Commission for the Blind* for help, and was put in touch with the state program which paid the back rent and penalties.
According to the initiators, the project was begun to counteract the focus in recent years on opening massive shelters or housing families in dilapidated hotels like the recently-closed Capital City Inn in Washington. Besides, the $4.8 million New Jersey spent on the program last year is cost-effective, since State officials estimate that intervention before a family becomes homeless is three times cheaper than putting the family up in an emergency shelter and 30 times cheaper than a welfare hotel.
The State's program offers one-time assistance for people suffering temporary financial crises but are not eligible for other emergency assistance. For homeowners, the assistance is treated as a loan and a lien is placed on their property. All applicants must demonstrate that they are in imminent danger of eviction or foreclosure and cannot get the money any other way. "The best way to do something about homelessness is to prevent it."
With assistance of *Rutgers, The State University's American Affordable Housing Institute,* which provides studies and statistics, private groups such as the *Elizabeth Coalition to House the Homeless,* which serve thousands of homeless individuals and families, and the volunteer and nonprofit organizations that refer families at risk of becoming homeless, the project is expected to continue.

HOUSING NOW!
Community for Creative Non-Violence
425 Second Street, NW
Washington , DC 20001
TEL: 202-393-1909
Purpose: To demand the "American dream" of affordable housing for all.
Sponsor: Community for Creative Non-Violence
Contact: Mitch Snyder
Description: On October 7, 1989, 250,000 homeless persons and their supporters marched through the streets of Washington, DC. The throng included housing advocates, college students, social workers, shelter residents, and children - the latter in a caravan of red wagons who converged on the Capitol. The youngsters presented the House Speaker with hundreds of letters written by the children, asking Congress to help end homelessness.
Many actors and music stars served as masters of ceremonies, spokespersons, and entertainers. Speakers ranged from Coretta Scott King to homeless men who had walked to Washington from New York and Roanoke, Virginia, in marches called a "New Exodus."
While homeless men and women led the main march, the crowd was dominated by college students, organized-labor delegations and church groups participating as a sign of solidarity with those

less fortunate.
A major emphasis of the housing march was to make sure that, after housing is provided, support services such as job assistance is offered to help the homeless persons get back to reality.
Publications: Housing Now! Information Packet

STREET NEWS HOMELESS VENDORS PROGRAM
SEE RECIPIENTS: HOMELESS - EMPLOYMENT

HOUSING: I&R

INDIVIDUAL PROGRAM PROFILES

CHISS (CONSUMER HOUSING INFORMATION SERVICE FOR SENIORS)
SEE HOUSING: OLDER PERSON

HOUSING: LOW-INCOME

NATIONAL/STATE ORGANIZATIONS

HABITAT FOR HUMANITY INTERNATIONAL (*formerly Habitat for Humanity*)
Habitat and Church Streets
Americus, GA 31709
TEL: 912-924-6935
Objectives: To provide low-cost, nonprofit housing to low-income people throughout the world.
Services: Distributes funds received through contributions from individuals and churches to low-income areas in the U.S. and overseas, where housing is built by volunteers and local people; manages the program through an Ecumenical Christian organization, which helps families to return the cost of the dwelling through a locally-managed *Fund For Humanity* over a period of 25 years; recycles *Fund* money to build more houses; sponsors projects in 25 countries; offers training to volunteers both for U.S. and overseas projects; makes its library holdings available to local project staff and volunteers.
Contact: Millard Fuller, Executive Director
Publications: Habitat World (newspaper); Community Self-Help Housing Manual; Kingdom Building; Love in the Mortar Joints; No More Shacks!
Founded: 1976

INDIVIDUAL PROGRAM PROFILES

AFFORDABLE HOUSING PROJECT
Unitarian Universalist Housing Foundation
9601 Cedar Lane
Bethesda, MD 20814
TEL: 301-493-4008; 20014
Purpose: To rehabilitate existing apartment units and create affordable housing for low-income residents and the homeless.
Contact: Anne Thorward, Volunteer
Description: With home prices tripling in the Washington, DC, area over the past decade, the gentrification of older neighborhoods, and a diminished commitment of the federal government to fund affordable housing, churches have added housing to their long list of social services. The *Unitarian*

Universalist Affordable Housing Project is one of those efforts. In 1990, the Project rehabilitated a 60-year old building in the heart of the District's Shaw neighborhood.

Volunteers include entire families who not only work in the construction and rehabilitation of housing, but also participate in raising funds for the projects - $225,000 for the 1990 effort, which includes low-interest and no-interest loans as well as donations.

To ensure that the building will stay in the pool of affordable housing if occupants leave, it is structured as a limited-equity cooperative. Under this plan, tenants have management control of the building and act as their own landlords. The group considers the new thrust to housing by churches as a natural extension of services for the homeless. According to one volunteer, "We've worked in soup kitchens and shelters, and it does not take a genius to see that people never get out of those places unless there are solid alternatives."

Founded: 1988

CHIP/AHIP (CHARLOTTESVILLE HOUSING IMPROVEMENT PROGRAM/ALBEMARLE HOUSING IMPROVEMENT PROGRAM)
SEE HOUSING: REVITALIZATION

FUTURE GENERATIONS
Dickerson Associates
1059 East Long
Columbus, OH 43203
TEL: 614-258-5761
Purpose: To help alleviate the dearth of low-cost housing for the needy.
Sponsor: Dickerson Associates
Contact: Sarni Dickerson, Founder, or William Davis, President
Description: A new trend to move a house or two and rehabilitate them for low-income families prompted a local businesswomen in the construction field in Columbus to question the demolition of 17 houses to make way for a parking lot at the St. Anthony Medical Center. Enlisting volunteer backup and support from the community, the entrepreneur set up a non-profit low-income housing corporation, *Future Generations,* induced the medical center to donate the houses, and worked out details on moving them to low-income neighborhoods.

By mid-April 1989, all 17 of the 200- to 240-ton homes were on foundations in four locations around the city. The homes are being rehabilitated for sale without profit at affordable prices in the working-class neighborhoods. Six homes awaiting renovation already have been sold, with the city making available rehabilitation loans of $20,000 for each home at a three percent interest rate.

Although much of the rehabilitation is done by paid laborers to expedite completion, board members of *Future Generations* enlist volunteer help in many aspects of the operation - especially in dealings with licensing agencies and other local government officials. The founder, who has a history of community service and involvement, has garnered her entire family as volunteers in the project - including three sons ages 21 to 25.

The new organization continues to seek innovative projects to help support the commercial and residential growth of the community, to bring attention to the plight of the poor, and to foster volunteer involvement by all citizens.

Founded: 1989

HONEYWELL NEIGHBORHOOD IMPROVEMENT PROGRAM
Honeywell Foundation
Honeywell Plaza
Minneapolis, MN 55408
TEL: 612-870-6411

Purpose: To provide housing choices to people whose alternatives are restricted, and to improve the appearance of the neighborhood.
Sponsor: Honeywell Foundation
Contact: Ray Frellsen
Description: With its general offices located in a relatively small geographic area, Honeywell noted that some 500 families in one neighborhood of this area did not have adequate income to keep their homes in good repair. To assist in meeting this need, Honeywell collaborated with local voluntary organizations and local government units to establish the Neighborhood Improvement Program (NIP), which is 100% funded by corporate contributions.

At the outset, the Program was designed as a two-pronged effort - housing improvement and more effective use of open land. Since the Neighborhood Improvement Program began in 1971, Honeywell built or renovated 54 living units in the Minneapolis neighborhood surrounding the Honeywell general offices. The company purchased single-family homes, duplexes and fourplexes, then rehabilitated and resold them primarily to people who live in the neighborhood.

The Foundation, acting as a non-profit sponsor, acquires the buildings at a markdown from the Minneapolis Community Development Agency, then renovates and sells them at prices neighborhood residents are able to pay.

In addition to the rehabilitation and resale program, Honeywell assisted more than 100 owners with exterior improvements to their properties. Owner assistance funds have been used for siding repair, fences, cement work, windows, doors, porch repair, roofing, landscaping and paint.

The combination of renovation and repair has proven to be an ideal method of assuring total neighborhood improvement instead of the disappointing "spotty" effect that is evident when only one or the other is implemented.

In 1978, seven years after the Program began, Honeywell completed the companion phase of the ongoing Program - an eight-acre park. Honeywell Plaza Park is landscaped with trees, flowers, shrubs, pieces of sculpture, a waterfall and reflecting pools. Open during the daylight hours, seven days a week, it was built for the enjoyment of Honeywell employees and neighborhood residents.

A number of activities are held in the park on an ongoing basis. These activities have included free summer concerts by the Minnesota Orchestra, and arts and crafts fairs.

Among the benefits noted by the Foundation in addition to the aesthetic value of the Program are: the rapport developed with other organizations; increased communication with the public; and the Foundation's new understanding of the community through the exchange of information that takes place on a continuing basis.

NIP is part of Honeywell's overall plan to help enhance growth and development in the neighborhood by "making changes that are real and can be seen and felt." The Phillips Neighborhood Improvement Association has presented Honeywell with two awards for its work in the neighborhood: a Special Service Award and the Good Neighbor Award.

MIRACLE WEEK
Habitat for Humanity of San Antonio
404 North Alamo
San Antonio, TX 78205
TEL: 512-223-5203
Purpose: To help families living in inadequate dwellings to build simple, but decent and affordable, homes.
Sponsor: Habitat for Humanity
Contact: Volunteer Coordinator
Description: In mid-summer 1989, during what has been dubbed *Miracle Week,* hundreds of volunteers built a frame for a four-bedroom house, attached the electrical and plumbing components, completed the interior and exterior trim, put up doors and cabinets, attached the lighting fixtures, arranged for

inspection and cleaned up, touched up and hooked up the electric and gas appliances. The object was to raise a house in a week for a family in need. The new 1,000-square-foot home was sold to a low-income family of seven, who worked with the volunteers to build the home, for about $25,000 on a 20-year, no-interest, no-profit mortgage. The home was the 17th since *Habitat for Humanity of San Antonio* began twelve years ago.

Each plot is 50 by 100 feet. The homes are small, but efficiently planned, with three or four bedrooms and one bath. Each house has a sturdy barnlike shed in the back for yard tools. Currently, the houses are surrounded by rolling hills with an old brick convent on the top hill. Habitat officials hope to acquire more land in the same area.

Volunteers come from all walks of life, in some cases in teams from corporations such as the *H.B. Zachry Company,* which provided an entire construction crew, since only licensed, bonded contractors can do the kind of work they volunteered to do. A long list of plumbing, electrical and other local contractors also provided volunteers, as well as work crews from more than a dozen area churches, students from *Trinity University,* and individual volunteers from the community just "showing up to hammer, lift and fetch." In addition, from the Project Director on down, members of *Habitat for Humanity* join the construction teams. This mix of professional and lay craftsman has given the homes a warm, hand-made quality.

Habitat officials feel that house raising, like barn raising, is a great American solution to the dramatic low-income housing shortage. They feel that the recipient families could teach others a lot about frugality because, in spite of the assistance, they still must work very hard and live on a very limited budget. Families who qualify for the small but sturdy homes must have an income from employment, but be unable to "even think about" buying a home in today's market. "*Miracle Week* is designed as a dramatically visual reminder that there is an answer to poverty housing on a much larger scale."

Founded: 1977

SPECIAL MORTGAGE AFFORDABLE HOUSING PROGRAM
Theodore Roosevelt National Bank
1201 New York Avenue, NW
Washington , DC 20005
TEL: 202-371-1201; 202-546-3400
FAX: 202-371-8233
Purpose: To assist the community by providing an affordable housing program.
Description: Only one of two lenders in the Washington area to revive a languishing HUD low-cost housing program (203[k]), *Theodore Roosevelt National Bank* officials see it as a way to help the community. *HUD's Federal Housing Administration* guaranteed mortgage program is designed for moderate- and low-income borrowers. It allows banks to extend acquisition, construction and fixed-rate long-term mortgage financing in one package for borrowers who might not qualify for conventional loans.

Although Roosevelt Bank officials plan to be conservative in the lending program, they feel that, because of the loan limits, they will be making a lot of loans "in the eastern part of town - Northeast, Southeast and Prince George's County" (primarily low-income areas).

With a backlog of repossessed real estate, and a need to accelerate the disposal of it, HUD is pleased with the Bank's expressed plans, and would like to see other area banks follow suit. HUD has made all of its inventory eligible for the three-in-one loans. Nationwide, the program is being used by first-time home buyers to get decent housing at an affordable price. Many are buying two-unit houses, or converting single-family dwellings into two units. In this way, the rental from the second unit often pays a high percentage - sometimes all - of the mortgage. Another benefit of this type of

purchase is that the anticipated income from renting the second unit can be used as a part of the potential buyers' income to help meet qualifications of the mortgage.

Roosevelt Bank officials feel that the benefits of the program outweigh the problems, one of which is the requirement for the low- or moderate-income buyer to retain a knowledgeable contractor to bring the home up to *HUD Minimum Property Standards* - no "home handymen allowed." Contractors with proven track records make the transition less problematic for all concerned, according to HUD officials.

Although Roosevelt Bank considers its initial involvement in HUD's 203(k) program an "experiment," the president says, "We think we can make it work."

With skeptic counterparts describing the Roosevelt Bank as a *boutique bank* (fresh fruit and free umbrellas in its antique-filled lobby, extra interest for kid clients who get good grades, home phone numbers on its employees' business cards, etc.), and cautioning that *TLC* "will only get you so far," the Bank moves on toward its program of "charities on the deposit side, and lower income housing on the loan side," winning praise from all quarters of the community along the way.

HOUSING: OLDER PERSON

NATIONAL/STATE ORGANIZATIONS

MORTGAGE BURNING FUND
SEE HOUSING: HOMELESS

INDIVIDUAL PROGRAM PROFILES

CHISS (CONSUMER HOUSING INFORMATION SERVICE FOR SENIORS)
Fairfax Area Agency on Aging
11242 Waples Mill Road
Suite 100
Fairfax , VA 22030-6036
TEL: 703-246-5411
Purpose: To help the elderly find housing services in the Fairfax area.
Contact: Volunteer Coordinator
Description: CHISS is a consumer housing information program of the American Association of Retired Persons (AARP), sponsored in Fairfax County by the *Area Agency on Aging.* The *Agency* distributes quick-reference, easy-to-read flyers to libraries and other public places in the area, and makes special efforts to distribute them to areas that emphasize service to the elderly. Through the program, the elderly renter or homeowner looking for information about ways to maintain or improve his or her housing situation can contact CHISS.

Housing Information Volunteers provide information on
● issues to consider when deciding to remain in or move away from home;
● ways to improve liveabliity of the home as one grows older;
● local home repair, maintenance, and weatherization programs;
● local in-home assistance programs;
● ways to increase income or decrease the cost of living; and
● the location of safe, affordable, and comfortable housing if an elderly person decides to move.

After locating housing services for an inquirer, CHISS volunteers help the older person evaluate them *before* making a decision as to which options will best serve the individual's needs. CHISS also provides materials that describe the advantages and disadvantages of various housing options, as well as guidelines for evaluating each option.

The history of the program indicates that the unbiased, "arms length" information provided by CHISS is a good safeguard for the older person seeking housing.

Publications: CHISS Information Packet

COMMUNITY BETTERMENT PROGRAM
SEE HOUSING: REVITALIZATION

SUNDIAL VOLUNTEERS
SEE RECIPIENTS: OLDER PERSON - HOUSING

UNION RETIREES RESOURCES
SEE HOUSING: REPAIRS/MAINTENANCE

HOUSING: RENTAL

NATIONAL/STATE ORGANIZATIONS

LOW-INCOME APARTMENTS PROGRAM
Volunteers of America
3813 North Causeway Boulevard
Metairie, LA 70002
TEL: 504-837-2652
Objectives: To increase the nation's low-income housing stock.
Services: Works to increase available apartments across the country for low-income families and the elderly; operates a low- and moderate-income housing division that manages 46 low-income apartment projects it built plus another 19 that it developed and syndicated to investors; acquires apartment buildings in depressed markets for half or less of the original value, including some once owned by failed savings and loan associations and made available through the *Resolution Trust Corporation (RTC),* the federal agency handling the disposition of assets from the failed thrifts (under the thrift bailout law, nonprofits are entitled to a 90-day right-of-first-refusal to buy these properties); implements long-range plans to keep the properties on the market for the target group.
Sponsor: US/RTC - Resolution Trust Corporation
Contact: John Hood, Vice President

INDIVIDUAL PROGRAM PROFILES

LOUDOUN HOUSE
715-16 Edwards Ferry Road
Leesburg, VA 22075
TEL: 703-777-7303
Purpose: To develop and implement outreach programs, and to improve security and maintenance at the facility.
Sponsor: National Housing Partnership; Loudoun House Tenant Organization
Contact: Georgia Coates
Description: Loudoun House has 248 apartment units and more than 620 residents. It stands amidst million-dollar estates, horse farms and historic battlefields. It is owned by the *National Housing Partnership,* a Washington, DC, firm that manages and owns low- and moderate-income housing around the country. In recent years it has become a haven for drug trafficking, attracting buyers and sellers from around the region. It has been the scene of occasional brawls, and has continuous maintenance problems.
In early 1989, however, a number of the residents have begun a concerted effort to change life at Loudoun House. They are actively working with the owner, with the complex's resident

manager meeting with the vice president of the *Partnership* and the tenant organization's president. The outcome of the meetings led to the first community projects:

- **Loudoun House Reading Center** - a community library. Within a few weeks the Center had acquired over 500 donated books on subjects ranging from religion to romance as well as back issues of Ebony and National Geographic magazines. Donations have come from county residents, libraries and other local groups. Within the first week, 60 residents signed registration forms to check out books.
- **Positive Youth Works** - a tutorial program. Two nights a week a group operated by several Loudoun House and county residents help children learn to read and do their homework.
- **Other programs** - a crime watch program, job counseling workshops, drug awareness seminars and cardiopulmonary resuscitation classes.

In addition, residents are appealing to the town Parks and Recreation department to provide activities for the project's numerous children, particularly since the complex's swimming pool has been closed down for five years (with estimated repair costs of $100,000). One alternative came from the supervisor of the county's *Big Friends* program, who arranged for transportation to local and Washington area parks and zoos for the children. He has also been instrumental in registering children for summer camp and scholarship programs.

At the top of the list is getting rid of the project's drug problems, which have resulted in numerous arrests and several drug raids in recent years according to Loudoun County police. To supplement the residents' crime watch efforts, the owners are paying a private security force $10,000 a month to patrol the property's ground and report on drug dealers and trespassers. The local police captain and the deputy sheriff both feel that the security force has stopped some of the drug trade, but find it is still an active area. The company has set a 10:00 p.m. curfew for residents and is planning to lease the Plaza Street Park from the town - a small playground adjacent to the complex which is filled with children during the day and drug activities at night. It is expected that the leasing of the park will bring about better control and subsequent elimination of the night-time activity.

The tenant organization has 35 very active residents who attend every meeting and are helping to assure that the volunteer efforts already begun are maintained, and that new projects are mounted as the need surfaces and time and resources permit. Much of this enthusiasm and progress is related to the spirit of cooperation between the residents, owners, police, and the town, according to a tenant organization spokesperson.

SUNDIAL VOLUNTEERS
SEE RECIPIENTS: OLDER PERSON - HOUSING

TENANT OWNERSHIP/MANAGEMENT PROGRAM
Sursum Corda Village
1160 First Place, NW
Washington, DC 20001
TEL: 202-789-0636
Purpose: To own the buildings in which they reside.
Sponsor: US/HUD - Office of Housing & Urban Development
Contact: Sister Diane Roche, Resident Manager
Description: Sursum Corda Village is a 199-unit housing complex that stretches across 4.5 acres near Capital Hill. Over the years, the Village changed from a grassy, golden-bricked place in 1969, where neighbors felt safe strolling at dusk, to a place where crack and cocaine are used and sold openly, and the "killing-of-the-month" is an expected occurrence. Some of the tenants were making efforts to demand better from the owners when, in 1989, the owners announced their intent to sell the Village. Many of the tenants saw an opportunity to try to purchase the buildings, and attempt to restore them to the safe neighborhood of the past.

In the summer of 1989, the tenants embarked on what they hoped would be a year-long process that would end with them, the tenants, owning and managing the complex where they live. It would be the first federally-insured, privately-owned cooperative in the District of Columbia to be owned and managed by tenants. They met with representatives of the owners, Surry, Ltd., in August. With their blessing and the approval of the U.S. Department of Housing and Urban Development, they plotted the steps toward tenant management and ownership. The owners encouraged tenant management and ownership because "they see it as a viable option to meeting housing needs."

One of the first steps taken by the tenants was to recruit a Roman Catholic nun as resident manager. The nun - known and trusted by the tenants - had been a volunteer at the complex, but had no housing management background. Besides, she had relocated to Seattle. However, the tenants were persistent with their letters and phone calls, and the nun worked it out with her superiors at a three-day retreat, and returned to Washington to manage the Village.

There is bustling activity at the Village, with weekly meetings with the police to begin a neighborhood watch program, residents volunteering to plant grass and bushes and repair their neighbors' homes, tenants forming the kinds of clubs that make a community (a football team, a senior citizens group, an adult literacy class), volunteers tutoring in the evenings, senior citizens banding together to make quilts and potholders to raise money, a religious group (Young Life) holding meetings, etc.

When word spread of their efforts, outside groups joined the effort. One Saturday, groups of alumni from Notre Dame University and the University of North Carolina were waiting with clusters of volunteers from five churches and Mount Vernon College and experienced handymen from Habitat for Humanity to begin work. More than 100 people had gathered to volunteer, and by the end of the day seventeen units were cleaned and painted.

However, other problems plagued the Village. The entire maintenance crew quit amid allegations of equipment theft. The vacancy rate was high. The complex owed $341,468 to 42 vendors. The manager could not get needed hardware or electrical items because of unpaid bills. The manager turned to two resident leaders, and together they approached businesses for assistance. Surprisingly, although companies considered it a "very bad risk," small gains were made through this route, and soon Sursum Corda recovered enough to pay its bills.

The success of the business/industry involvement spurred residents on, and fliers were distributed stating, "Let's reclaim our vacant units." The next Saturday, 26 people cleaned 26 units, and the next Saturday more were cleaned, and each Saturday a few more. One resident pointed out that "people are beginning to understand, if you lose here, where else are you going to lose?"

So far, the statistics are promising. Vacancies have been cut in half, to 14. The backlogged requests for repairs have dropped to 60. About 40 of the 200 roofs have been replaced without breaking the budget. Unfortunately, there is still crack dealing and there are still slayings, but the residents are fighting back. The test of management - restoring the physical property, and reestablishing pride - has been passed, according to all parties concerned.

HOUSING: REPAIRS/MAINTENANCE

INDIVIDUAL PROGRAM PROFILES

HOME REPAIRS PROJECT
Big Country Retired Senior Volunteer Program
PO Box 5648
Abilene, TX 79608
TEL: 915-691-7225

Purpose: To organize volunteers and make small home repairs in the homes of the elderly.
Sponsor: Senior Community Services, Inc.
Contact: Nancy E. Cummingham
Description: The home repair program for the elderly began after the Regional Agency on Aging made a needs assessment which indicated this service was not available to older adults in this area and was a priority need. An allotment of $1,500 dollars was made the first year to buy necessary tools and supplies and to reimburse the volunteers for mileage and out-of-pocket expenses.

The purpose of this innovative program is to help the elderly remain in their homes and be independent as long as their health allows them to be. Three or four volunteers, with at least one volunteering four or more days a week, can make small home repairs in over 300 homes during the year.

The majority of the volunteers are over 60 years of age, and are members of the Retired Senior Volunteer Program - a part of ACTION. However, since the program began the grantee of RSVP covers all volunteers with insurance. Several younger volunteers have given many hours of service.

The results have been so satisfying that volunteers remain in the program until disabilities force them to curtail the more strenuous assignments. As high as 80 air conditioners are serviced in a two month period in late spring and then winterized in the fall. Because the program can pay for professional plumbing services many older adults do not not have to move from their homes. Many agencies (i.e., Information and Referral, Community Action, etc.) refer clients to the program. RSVP cooperates with other agencies, pooling money and services for expensive repairs, such as a new sewer line. Many goods and services are donated and when recycled, the dollars are stretched to assist even more clients. Program publicity was sent to the Meals on Wheels Plus Program, senior centers, churches, the media, the Community Action Program, the welfare agencies, and all agencies who use volunteers. Six volunteers formed the first Advisory Committee who set the guidelines.

A grant from the State Department on Aging, serving a city of 100,000 and one rural county, has been renewed each year since 1978 for $7,500. The local Rotary Clubs contribute the 10% match.
Founded: 1978

UNION RETIREES RESOURCES
Labor Temple
2800 First Avenue
Room 218
Seattle, WA 98121
TEL: 206-623-9050
Purpose: To involve retired union craftsmen in volunteer services to older persons.
Sponsor: AFL-CIO Central Labor Council; US/ACTION
Contact: Mary Jane Johnson
Description: The first program of its kind in the country when it started in 1978, the Union Retirees Resources program responds to over 4,000 requests each year. The union affiliation represented a new concept for RSVP and Union Retirees Resources was considered a model with an eye toward replication elsewhere. Volunteers are retired electricians, plumbers, roofers, teamsters, longshoremen, carpenters, sheet metal workers and other union members who work throughout King County and Seattle to assist older persons. They repair leaky plumbing or roofs, handle small electrical problems, build ramps for wheelchair patients, etc. Several years ago they began picking up donated appliances and televisions, repairing them, and providing them to elderly persons in need of such items. This is now one of the most helpful programs. Since the program has no funding to purchase supplies, any materials needed, such as wiring, are usually donated on a case-by-case basis by suppliers or building contractors. Also, volunteers offer consumer protection to low-income elderly

homeowners by advising them on more extensive home repairs where contractors and purchases are involved, such as buying a new furnace or replacing a roof. In addition, they provide transportation to medical appointments and to shopping facilities for elderly people who would otherwise be confined to their homes.

This volunteer help in minor home repairs, home maintenance, and consumer protection by more than 80 union retirees is helping low-income elderly and handicapped persons to remain in their own homes. Although the volunteers serve without compensation, they are reimbursed for their transportation costs and, if serving more than four hours on a specific assignment, for meals. In addition, the volunteers receive accident and liability coverage for their periods of service.

Initially, only AFL-CIO and ACTION sponsored the program. In 1978 the Community Services Administration provided assistance, and other sponsors are involved in the present program.
Founded: 1978

HOUSING: REVITALIZATION

NATIONAL/STATE ORGANIZATIONS

OFFICE OF COMMUNITY INVESTMENT
US/Federal Home Loan Bank Board
Washington, DC 20552
TEL: 202-377-6211
Objectives: To stimulate and support thrift industry efforts to revitalize and develop communities.
Services: Operates through Community Investment Officers (CIOs) who provide leadership and day-to-day assistance to thrifts, public and private organizations, and community groups; provides information and training in Federal programs and new regulations to help meet community credit needs; conducts an awareness campaign to help thrifts recognize the business opportunities that stem from community investment; develops new regulatory and legislative tools that will stimulate community revitalization (increased authority for mobile homes, home improvement loans, and loans for cooperative units, for example); helps to write legislation to protect consumers and assist examiners in detecting violations, such as the Bank Board's Nondiscrimination Regulations; works with Federal, state and local groups to develop more effective community lending programs, including such activities as:

- training industry and consumer groups in such issues as the Community Reinvestment Act and related Civil Rights legislation, rural lending programs, the secondary mortgage market, and energy conservation;
- working with other government agencies including the White House, the Department of Commerce, the Department of Housing and Urban Development, the other financial regulatory agencies, the Federal Home Loan Mortgage Corporation and the Federal National Mortgage Association to develop programs that stimulate lending in older urban and rural communities;
- preparing videotapes, pamphlets and brochures on issues of revitalization;
- providing speakers on community investment problems and programs; and
- providing clearinghouse and information services on community investment issues.

Administers an overall program combining financial incentives, development of new regulatory framework, continuous efforts to remove road blocks in existing laws, effective enforcement, and education and technical assistance.

Sponsor: US/Federal Home Loan Bank Board

PARTNERS FOR LIVABLE PLACES
1429 21st Street, NW
Washington, DC 20036
TEL: 202-887-5990
Objectives: To pursue strategies to improve the quality of life in towns, cities, and neighborhoods.
Services: Operates the Livability Clearinghouse which is a computerized database containing more than 3500 examples of innovative solutions to local design problems; administers an "Economics of Amenity" program to explore the value of urban amenities (cultural facilities and planning, natural scenic resources, cultural conservation programs, design quality, etc.); strives to avoid duplication of efforts and to share information among members and with the public toward this end; publishes a monthly journal, *Place,* a quarterly review, *Livability Digest,* and books and reports on subjects ranging from economic development strategies for Hispanic-American communities to the economic value of aesthetics in transportation systems; receives funding through dues income, contracts and grants, contributions, and sale of books and services; operates through a board of 27 trustees, who are advised by a council of Partners-members; maintains an office in Oakland, California.
Publications: PLACE; Livability Digest; City as a Stage; Enterprise in Nonprofit Sector; Negotiating for Amenities; Art in Public Places
Founded: 1977

INDIVIDUAL PROGRAM PROFILES

CABRILLO VILLAGE
Cabrillo Improvement Association
PO Box 4216
1515 South Saticoy Avenue
Saticoy, CA 93003
TEL: 805-659-3791
Purpose: To increase the capacity of local farmworkers to own, maintain, and take pride in the housing in their community.
Sponsor: Church and business organizations; Farmworkers Union; Government Agencies; Cabrillo Cooperative Housing Corporation
Contact: Rodney Fernandez
Description: Faced with eviction from their camp due to substandard housing, a small group of farmworkers organized to seek alternatives. Most families had lived in the community for many years, working in the nearby citrus groves. The owner decided to evict the residents rather than rehabilitate the housing. Groups concerned with farmworkers' housing had long existed in the area (church groups, business organizations, the Farmworkers Union, government agencies, etc.), and offered to help the farmworkers form their own nonprofit organization. Cabrillo Improvement Association was born, and the land was purchased from the owner.

The next step was to "revitalize" the community, and it was determined that this would have to include new housing. The Cabrillo Cooperative Housing Corporation (CCHC) was formed to pursue this goal, and successfully applied for financing to build thirty-five multi-family dwellings. Applying this loan and grant money to a farmworkers' cooperative housing project was a "first" for FmHA's Multi-Family Housing Division.

As the project evolved, Cabrillo developed a list of "firsts" for such a venture:

- passive solar design and solar hot water systems for new farmworker housing.
- rehabilitating the existing houses through special training programs.
- operating a ceramic tile factory, a cabinet shop, and a co-op food store.

- developing a contracting business for housing rehab in other communities.

This massive volunteer effort has had an exciting side effect. With the skills and knowledge developed, Cabrillo residents are reaching out to help others. With the assistance of the Rural Community Assistance Corporation in Sacramento, California, they have developed a training workshop where resource people provide information on self-help housing, mobile homes, manufactured homes and multi-family units. Trainers help participants explore pros and cons of home ownership, cooperatives and rental housing options. By helping farmworker communities with roots much like their own, Cabrillo is contributing to a better quality of life for the general farmworker population.

CHIP/AHIP (CHARLOTTESVILLE HOUSING IMPROVEMENT PROGRAM/ALBEMARLE HOUSING IMPROVEMENT PROGRAM)
Madison House
170 Rugby Road
Charlottesville, VA 22903
TEL: 703-977-7051
Purpose: To assist low-income residents in the area in their efforts to obtain safe and decent housing.
Sponsor: City of Charlottesville; County of Albemarle; Madison House
Contact: Wanda J. Birckhead-Jennings
Description: A group of university students banded together in 1969 to help repair some of the housing damage left by Hurricane Camille. After the initial clean-up work, the students decided to stay together and formed "Students Concerned with Rural and Urban Betterment (SCRUB)." The program focused its attention on the application of volunteer power and expertise to answer the critical housing needs of the area by repairing, renovating, and rehabilitating homes occupied by "low-income" families. The program quickly gained the respect of the entire Charlottesville community.

As the program developed, it quickly outgrew its Madison House program status. On February 20, 1974, the program incorporated as CHIP (Charlottesville Housing Improvement Program), a subsidiary of the Charlottesville Housing Foundation. CHIP concentrates its efforts on renovation of substandard, owner-occupied housing in the City of Charlottesville. AHIP (Albemarle Housing Improvement Program), in Albemarle county, was formed soon after CHIP, and strives toward the same goal in the County of Albemarle. Madison House helps recruit volunteers for both of the programs.

The volunteer possibilities with CHIP and AHIP can completely renovate a home for one-third to one-half the standard commercial cost. This low operating standard is accomplished through the use of student and community volunteers in the labor force. Materials are paid for by the homeowners through their own resources, government grants, or bank loans.
Founded: 1969

COMMUNITY BETTERMENT PROGRAM
Carondelet Community Betterment Federation
6408 Michigan Avenue
St. Louis, MO 63111
TEL: 314-752-6339
Purpose: To make Carondelet a better place in which to live, by updating properties and improving the quality of life for those who need assistance.
Sponsor: Carondelet Community Betterment Federation (CCBF)
Contact: Sister Marie Charles Buford
Description: The Carondolet Community Better Foundation (CCBF) operates several programs, the largest being a House Repair Program for Senior Persons living in the service area.
Criteria for participation in the program are:
- at least 60 years of age;

- property owner;
- live in service area; and
- document income level.

With an executive director, a volunteer manager, and a staff of four, CCBF completes a minimum of 130 house repair jobs for senior persons. Such jobs consist of any type of house repairs, including windows, painting, replacement of total porches (front or back), building ramps for handicapped persons, concrete repairs, roof repairs, some small tuckpointing jobs. Interior work includes plastering, painting, wall-papering, panelling, flooring replacement or new, door repairs, plumbing, installation of water heaters, basement waterproofing, replacement of stairs, etc.

Through this program, now in its sixth year, property values have improved; senior persons have been assisted to remain in their homes, upkeep their properties and avoid city citations; and community housing stock has improved.

The program also acts as an incentive program. Annually, from 80 to 190 other property owners have improved their own properties since this program began. This was not happening previously. Older houses are also being purchased by younger families for rehabilitation and improvements. Other programs by CCBF are:
- operates a Senior Center;
- provides social services to homebound elderly;
- publishes a newsletter;
- sponsors a businessmen's group; and
- sponsors youth programs in the summer.

Publications: CCBF Newsletter
Founded: 1976

FUTURE GENERATIONS
SEE HOUSING: LOW-INCOME

REHAB PROJECT: NEIGHBORHOOD REVITALIZATION THROUGH HOME OWNERSHIP
Church People for Change and Reconciliation
676 S. Elizabeth Street
Lima, OH 45804-1297
TEL: 419-223-9439
Purpose: To bring about "neighborhood revitalization through home ownership."
Sponsor: Church People for Change and Reconciliation; neighborhood churches
Contact: Public Affairs Officer
Description: Rehab Project is a private nonprofit community development corporation in Lima, Ohio, that was founded in 1977 by four neighborhood churches and *Church People for Change and Reconciliation.* It is an outgrowth of concern for this city of 50,000 people that was caught up in the recent decline in the midwestern industrial base. With new industry moving into the area, the Project has set a goal of *Neighborhood Revitalization Through Home Ownership.* This is being achieved by the physical rehabilitation of homes and the placement of responsible homeowners in the neighborhoods. More specifically:
Neighborhood - The focus is on neighborhoods. By definition, the focus is broad but discriminating, for it is wider than a mere concern for individuals yet narrower than a citywide agenda. Individual projects are evaluated in the context of neighborhood needs and benefits. Resources are managed with a primary consideration for concentration of effort and the cumulative effect of those efforts.
Revitalization - The revitalization of neighborhoods assumes a previous vitality and an investment of resources, public and private. It further assumes a decline in that vitality, and a corresponding disinvestment of resources. *Revitalization* states an intention to live again where life once flourished.
Through Home Ownership - The self-interest of individuals can best be harnessed for neighborhood benefit through home ownership. Long-term neighborhood stability and self-maintaining investment will result by fostering practical and attractive home

ownership opportunities and by conspicuously aggregating those opportunities.

Maximizing Private Sector Participation - Current trends in the public sector appear to indicate a growing scarcity of resources and ever-changing policies and programming. The task of neighborhood revitalization, however, demands a more stable environment. The private sector - by definition, diverse and flexible - holds the best opportunity to build the necessary long-term resources. Neighborhood revitalization shall be achieved through maximizing the support of the private sector and the utilization of all available public resources.

The project strives for affordable and quality housing. Affordability is emphasized on two levels: sales prices and operating costs. The operating costs are minimized through quality construction; the sales prices are kept low through the development and employment of *in-kind* (volunteer) labor resources, including:

- **Churches** - Members devote time and labor.
- **School System** - Vocational Education students are provided the site and construction materials for annual construction of a new home.
- **Correctional Facilities** - *Honor inmates* are trained in carpentry to work on renovating housing.
- **Public Assistance** - individuals in the *work relief* program are trained on carpentry crews.
- **Green Thumb Program** - persons 55 years of age and older work on crews (through *Ohio Farmers Union* and the federal *Older Americans Act*).

All work required - except the licensed plumbing and electrical work - is performed by unskilled, but supervised, volunteer carpentry crews. The result of this process is a quality, energy-efficient home that anyone would be proud to own, but that is priced to be affordable to persons who previously could only dream of owning such a home.

In 1985 project leaders developed a ten-year plan, hoping to rehabilitate more than 700 homes by 1995. To achieve this ambitious goal, the Project expects to institute extensive homeownership education programs, instigate a climate for increased neighborhood and community pride, maximize private sector participation, and broadly market the concept of the neighborhoods as "good places to live."

The Project solicits a wide mix of purchasing clientele: lower-income households seeking the often impossible dream of home ownership; youthful, moderate income households desiring their "first" home; and present homeowners, seeking improved housing, but unable to afford newly-built units. Completed homes are marketed under the product name of *Heart Homes: Homes with a History and a Future.*

Publications: Rehab Project: Neighborhood Revitalization Through Home Ownership

Founded: 1977

HOUSING: RURAL

NATIONAL/STATE ORGANIZATIONS

RURAL AMERICA
725 Fifteenth Street, NW
Suite 900
Washington, DC 20005
TEL: 202-628-1480
Objectives: To assure rural people equity in the allocation of public resources and services.
Services: Provides technical assistance to community-based organizations that develop housing for farmworkers; provides

specific help to small farmers to strengthen their positions on the land; help individuals and groups who wish to become involved in the legislative process; sponsors "self-help housing" program; publishes *Self-Help Housing Handbook,* monthly newsletter, and over 70 books, papers, and reprints on America.
Publications: Ruralamerica
Founded: 1975

US/DOA - FARMERS HOME ADMINISTRATION
Independence Avenue, SW
(Between 12th & 14th Sts.)
Washington, DC 20250
TEL: 202-447-8732
Objectives: To "build" rural America through supervised credit in four primary areas: housing, farming, community programs, business/industrial development.
Services: Serves housing needs through the following programs, among others:

- **INDIVIDUAL HOMEOWNERSHIP LOANS** - money to buy, build, improve, or relocate homes; to buy building sites; to refinance certain housing debts (for low- to moderate-income).
- **REPAIR AND REHABILITATION HOUSING LOANS** - to make repairs to remove health and safety hazards (for very low income).
- **SELF-HELP TECHNICAL ASSISTANCE GRANTS** - to provide technical assistance to families involved in self-help homebuilding (grants go to public agencies or nonprofit corporations who provide assistance). *This is FmHa,* a brochure, outlines all programs; detailed, specific publications are available on each loan or grant program.

Sponsor: US/DoA - Department of Agriculture

US/HUD - OFFICE OF FAIR HOUSING AND EQUAL OPPORTUNITY
SEE HOUSING: DISCRIMINATION

HOUSING: SELF-HELP

INDIVIDUAL PROGRAM PROFILES

GIFT TO THE CITY
Habitat for Humanity/Philadelphia
4211 Chestnut Street
Philadelphia, PA 19104
TEL: 215-387-7592
Purpose: To enable families without an opportunity to buy a house at low cost and receive supportive services to maintain it.
Sponsor: Presbyterian Church USA
Contact: Marshall McBride, Supervisor
Description: Presbyterians from about 30 local congregations are rehabilitating housing for low-income people as their *Gift to the City.* About 200 volunteers are working with *Habitat for Humanity,* the ecumenical Christian housing ministry. Habitat relies on volunteers to restore urban shells into homes for low-income families. The homes, financed by Habitat, are sold at an average price of $30,000.

Although the project was initiated during a Presbyterian USA Assembly marking its 200th anniversary, volunteers come from all denominations, as well as non-churchgoers from all walks of life. Salesman, plumbers, doctors, lawyers, carpenters, Quakers, Episcopalians, Methodists and Catholics can be found among the volunteers. They are helping with Habitat projects in North Philadelphia, West Philadelphia and Coatesville, Chester County, and at a South Philadelphia site sponsored by another organization. While most volunteers are from suburban churches, West Philadelphia volunteers are from center city churches. Area Presbyterians also are contributing $105,000 to the cause.

Habitat plans to build five new homes at the North Philadelphia location this year, with 12 others scheduled to be built in the future. Future homeowners, some of whom are selected before the work begins, will get no-intereest mortgages over 20-25 years, with monthly $125-$150 payments. Also, they must donate 500 hours of "sweat equity" working on the project. They are chosen on the basis of their income, need, and attitude. The initial down payment for the no-interest loans is about $500.

The real goal is rebuilding the neighborhoods. The volunteers, many of them white, met with hesitation, caution and suspicion at first, but more local involvement - especially in West Philadelphia - is stressed now, and this brings the people in the community together with volunteers from outside the area where they can get to know each other while working together. Put in the words of a supervisor at one of the sites, who called the volunteers *terrific workers,* "They're giving people who wouldn't have any chance of doing so a chance to buy a nice house."

HABITAT FOR HUMANITY OF RHODE ISLAND
c/o David Addink
23 Ashton
Narragansett, RI 02882
TEL: 401-783-0769
Purpose: To involve volunteer labor in building and refurbishing affordable housing.
Sponsor: Habitat for Humanity International
Contact: David Addink, Volunteer
Description: Low-income families hoping to buy houses from the nonprofit *Habitat for Humanity* are asked to invest at least 300 hours of sweat equity - or 500 hours if they want to avoid a second mortgage - in the building or refurbishing of the homes. In Providence, these volunteer potential home-buyers are joined by volunteers from churches and others from across the community. Volunteers do everything from filling foundation cavities with rock to stacking and oiling foundation boards to painting the final product. Volunteers uncomfortable with or unable to perform construction work participate instead in selecting eligible families, acquiring lands or raising funds.

Construction experience is not needed for the project, since experienced workers are available at every site to help the uninitiated put their volunteer hours to good use. One volunteer summed up his involvement this way: "I grew up on a farm and it was quite customary for me as a boy to help out a neighbor. I think if you grow up with that background then it's easy to do it later on."

Costs are kept as low as possible for potential buyers. An example is a townhouse in Providence that would list in the open market for $100,000. A family selected by *Habitat for Humanity* volunteers will pay $39,900.

Although volunteers work year-round in the program, one week every year is declared a "special worldwide work week," during which time it is hoped that all local projects will make a special effort to show their full cadres of volunteers during the entire special week.

PATERSON HABITAT FOR HUMANITY
511 22nd Street, East
Paterson, NJ 07514
TEL: 201-278-4280
Purpose: To provide safe, affordable housing for low-income families.
Sponsor: Habitat for Humanity International
Contact: The Reverend John Algera
Description: The City of Paterson has a severe housing crisis. Rental units and safe, affordable housing for low-income families are scarce. A group of volunteers, under the leadership of a local pastor, recognized this crisis and focused their efforts on a solution. As a result of their efforts, the ownership of a safe affordable home has become a reality for many and neighborhoods have become revitalized.

Paterson Habitat for Humanity was formed as a nonprofit volunteer organization in 1984. It is an affiliate of the international organization, Habitat for Humanity, whose purpose is to provide affordable housing for the poor and to help them attain home ownership.

The City of Paterson sells city-owned land to Habitat for $1.00. Then, fueled by a primarily volunteer labor force and donated materials, Habitat gets down to the business of building or rehabilitating housing. During 1988, over 500 individuals came to help transform undersized vacant lots into 11 affordable homes. Before 1988, Habitat had constructed 11 new homes and rehabilitated a two-family home.

Habitat families are pre-selected and must contribute 300 hours of "sweat equity" towards the construction of their home. They receive a 10-year interest-free mortgage. The money received from mortgage payments is used to build additional housing. Habitat housing may only be sold to other low-income families.

Since its inception, Habitat has sparked an intense interest in solving the housing crisis in the City of Paterson. Not only has it attracted a large pool of volunteers, Habitat has also built a large community following which includes business and community leaders, local church groups, potential Habitat families and interested citizens.

Paterson's Mayor says, "I cannot think of another group that has provided such an impact on the housing crisis. Their work has sparked other owners to fix up, and ignited private investment. This program builds responsible citizenship, builds partnerships in the community, and revitalizes a once blighted area."
Publications: Paterson Habitat for Humanity Packet
Founded: 1984

REHAB PROJECT: NEIGHBORHOOD REVITALIZATION THROUGH HOME OWNERSHIP
SEE HOUSING: REVITALIZATION

STUDENT HABITAT FOR HUMANITY
College of Wooster
Beall Avenue
Wooster, OH 44691
TEL: 216-263-2000
Purpose: To build and rehabilitate houses for the poor in the Wooster area.
Sponsor: Habitat for Humanity
Contact: Chris Alghini, President, Wooster College Chapter
Description: The college chapter of *Habitat for Humanity* finds the project satisfying to students since they see tangible results of their volunteer efforts. *Habitat for Humanity* is an ecumenical Christian housing ministry with 240 chapters in the United States and 50 projects in 25 developing countries. The organization constructs and rehabilitates houses for low-income families. Many student groups have "taken up the call" as a way of contributing to the communities surrounding their colleges.

When the college announced that five houses on its campus were scheduled to be demolished to make way for a new dormitory, the student head of the college chapter of *Habitat for Humanity,* with the advice of the chairman and vice chairman of the Wayne County chapter, approached the college president in an attempt to save the houses for the needy. Working together, the college and Habitat volunteers developed a plan for the school to donate the homes if the volunteers could raise $100,000 by commencement for moving expenses. One day in early June 1989 the moving began.

The Wooster houses represent one of the largest one-time donations ever given to a Habitat chapter. As in all houses offered through the program, low-income families who will occupy the newly-moved homes must donate 500 hours of "sweat equity" to renovate the structures, and will be given counseling regarding their maintenance and upkeep.

A rewarding coincidence in this effort is that - long before the house donation was suggested - the college had selected *Habitat for Humanity* founder, Millard Fuller, to receive a doctorate of humanities at the upcoming commencement.

LAW ENFORCEMENT/CRIME PREVENTION

NATIONAL/STATE ORGANIZATIONS

**INTERNATIONAL ASSOCIATION OF JUSTICE
VOLUNTEERISM (IAJV)** (*formerly National Association of
Volunteers in Criminal Justice*)
University of Wisconsin/Milwaukee
Criminal Justice Institute
Box 786
Milwaukee, WI 53201
TEL: 414-229-6092
Objectives: To improve the juvenile and criminal justice systems
through citizen participation.
Services: Carries out the mission of early pioneers in justice
volunteerism - to bring together localized volunteer efforts
throughout the country in a national movement; seeks to carry out
this mission by working to unify, strengthen and coordinate the
efforts of various local programs and join them with other local
programs across the nation and Canada; sets specific goals
including:
- Establishing guidelines for effective citizen involvement in
  criminal justice.
- Facilitating exchange of information on volunteers in criminal
  justice through an annual national forum, a newsletter, other
  publications, and library services.
- Enhancing the image of volunteerism in criminal justice by
  serving as an advocate for volunteers, developing relationships
  with organizations having similar goals, and building a
  national constituency.
Works to improve technical assistance techniques to volunteer
programs; upgrades education and training for volunteers; provides
a national information clearinghouse; works with other national
organizations with similar goals; provides advocacy; mounts
publicity programs to enhance the image of volunteer efforts;
sponsors seminars and workshops at annual forum.
Operates under the aegis of duly elected volunteer officials
governing eleven regions, each with a two-year elected volunteer
representative; functions under board-determined policy and
programs; provides organizational support for IAJV activities
through its international office located at the University of
Wisconsin-Milwaukee, Division of Outreach and Continuing
Education, Criminal Justice Institute.
Publications: IAJV In Action; Membership Resource Directory
Founded: 1970

LAW ENFORCEMENT ASSISTANCE PROGRAM
US/DoJ - Law Enforcement Assistance Agency
Criminal Justice Assistance Div.
Washington, DC 20531
TEL: 202-476-3611
Objectives: To provide assistance to criminal justice programs
where a need is indicated.
Services: Provides grants, advisory services, counseling, training,
and other services in the major areas of crime control (police,
courts, corrections, etc.); requires a letter expressing need for
service; includes short-term on-site visits and assistance in
evaluation among its services; maintains files on previously-funded
programs such as (1) Corrections Innovations Assistance, (2)
Treatment and Rehabilitation for Addicted Prisoners; publishes
information concerning available consultative services, and
numerous guides, handbooks and other program materials.
Sponsor: US/DoJ - Department of Justice

**NATIONAL ASSOCIATION OF CITIZENS' CRIME
COMMISSIONS**
Wichita Crime Commission
c/o Bobby Stout
460 Broadway Plaza Building
Wichita, KS 67202
TEL: 316-267-1236
Objectives: To form a network of commissions for sharing of ideas
and experiences.
Services: Works with crime commissions not affiliated with local,
state, or federal governments; facilitates exchanges of mutually
helpful information between member commissions; informs the
public on dangers of crime, including organized crime, and offers
suggested methods of controlling it; strives to arouse public
interest in the issue of clean government, and to encourage
formation of citizens' crime commissions where needed; publishes
a manual for citizens interested in forming commissions.
Publications: How to Organize and Operate a Citizens' Crime
Commission
Founded: 1952

NATIONAL CRIME PREVENTION COUNCIL
735 Fifteenth Street, NW
Washington, DC 20005
TEL: 202-393-7141

Objectives: To enable people to prevent crime and build safer, more caring communities.

Services: Provides training and information services, including a data base of community crime prevention-related programs; conducts demonstration programs to highlight ways to work effectively in crime and drug abuse prevention, especially in developing the community's ability to rely on young people as assets to help meet local needs; coordinates the Crime Prevention Coalition (125 organizations which support community-based crime prevention); publishes books, brochures, kits of camera-ready masters, posters and other items. [Funding for NCPC comes from the Bureau of Justice Assistance (Office of Justice Programs, US Dept. of Justice), and a wide range of private and public foundations, corporations, and individual donors.]

Publications: National Crime Prevention Council Information Packet; Reaching Out: School-Based Community Service Programs; Making a Difference: Young People in Community Crime Prevention

TWENTY-FIVE YEAR PRESIDENTIAL AWARD CERTIFICATE PROGRAM FOR VOLUNTEERS IN JUVENILE CRIMINAL JUSTICE
US/Presidential Awards Programs
Office of Public Liaison
Washington, DC 20500
TEL: 202-456-1414

Objectives: To recognize professionals (paid or unpaid) who supervise volunteers, and volunteers in the juvenile and criminal justice systems who meet the criteria of the awards program.

Services: Provides a certificate, signed by the President, to show appreciation for administrative service in the criminal justice volunteer community (supervision of 50 volunteers for at least one year, 10 volunteers for at least five years, etc.), and for the extraordinary volunteer (at least 50 hours a month for a year); represents a tradition involving five Presidents as of 1989 (Presidents Nixon, Carter, Ford, Reagan and Bush); covers service from 1959; distribution is by Volunteers in Prevention, Probation, and Prison (a national organization) or through individuals or offices within a state.

Sponsor: US/White House
Founded: 1968

US/DOJ - PRIVATE SECTOR INITIATIVES
10th and Constitution Ave., NW
Office of the Attorney General
Washington, DC 20530
TEL: 202-633-2000

Objectives: To stimulate opportunities to involve private sector groups and volunteers in criminal justice-related activities and in the provision of legal services.

Services: Undertakes numerous programs through the Office of Justice Assistance which encourage a more active role at the community level, including:

- National Citizens' Crime Prevention Campaign, which involves the Advertising Council, corporate America, non-profit organizations and federal agencies in the major theme: "Crime prevention is not solely the job of law enforcement."
- Sting Program, which establishes working relationships with insurance companies to attack the problem of property crime.
- Security Project, which takes advantage of the phenomenon that the property repair records of IBM had a very distinct relationship with the location of stolen property (works with IBM and the Batelle Institute).
- School Enhancement Project, which attempts to discourage delinquency by providing recognized experts to assist in establishing more effective teaching methods, increasing participation by students, and viewing basic subjects in terms

of relevance to the world of work (works with the Westinghouse Corporation).
- Older Persons Volunteer Programs, which provide companionship and guidance to juvenile offenders and non-offenders (transferred funds to ACTION's Foster Grandparents Program and Retired Senior Volunteer Program).
- Act Together, which serves as an intermediary between the private sector, the state and local sector and the federal government in efforts to improve services to high risk youth.
- Juvenile Offender Restitution Programs, which administer all aspects of the restitution requirements, including community service placement (funds more than 40 projects, some through private-not-for-profit agencies such as United Way, Youth Service Bureaus, etc.)
- Prison Industries, which involve offenders as employees to produce goods or services for sale within correctional institutions.
- Boys Clubs of America, which sponsors the National Project on Juvenile Justice, a special initiative to prevent and reduce juvenile crime by promoting law-abiding behavior among teenaged residents of communities with high rates of juvenile crime (with the goal of instilling self esteem).
- Victim Assistance, which involves funding of community-based programs to ensure that victims are treated with decency, and to be of service to programs of victim and witness assistance in both the public and the private sectors (funded programs include the National Organization for Victim Assistance and the Center for Women Policy Studies).
- FBI Activities, which include volunteers in all programs, and assists in organizing private sector efforts in this regard, including the National Crime Prevention Coalition, which has hundreds of civic groups as members, the Crime Stoppers USA program, which has several hundred chapters, and Law Enforcement Explorers of the Boy Scouts of America which has 40,000 members.
- Federal Prison System, which has about 4,000 volunteers who assist and augment Department programs as direct service volunteers, and in an advisory capacity to assist prisons in improving programs such as the Prison Industries Program.

Includes efforts other than specific programs in its work to increase private sector involvement, such as encouraging voluntary attorney services, working with "volags" (voluntary immigration counseling agencies; more than 1200 volunteers) and mounting special projects as needs arise.

Maintains an Outreach Program to motivate the voluntary agencies and community organizations to become more involved in volunteering their time through training conferences, technical assistance and specialized information.

Operates a Community Relations Service to identify areas of racial tension and to assist local mediation and conciliation activities to ameliorate those tensions and avoid unnecessary confrontation (works with over 1,000 private groups in hundreds of cases; request list of groups).

Instructs all components of the Department to reassess their activities in the area of maximum participation by private sector groups and make recommendations where improvements appear to be needed.

Sponsor: US/DoJ - Department of Justice
Publications: DoJ/PSI Information Packet

VOLUNTEER PRISON LEAGUE
Volunteers of America
3813 Causeway Boulevard
Metairie, LA 70002
TEL: 504-837-2652

Objectives: To aid prisoners in overcoming personal and family problems.

Services: Gives material assistance to inmates' families; provides job placement for discharged prisoners and parolees; operates halfway houses and pre- and post-release centers to help the prisoner resettle in the community.
Publications: National Newsline; Gazette

VOLUNTEERS IN PREVENTION, PROBATION, PRISONS

527 North Main Street
Royal Oak, MI 48067
TEL: 313-398-8550
Objectives: To stimulate citizen participation in court and correction programs; to upgrade existing volunteer programs; to improve the criminal justice system for juveniles and adults and to support the development of state organizations in this area.
Services: Sponsors the National Education Training Program developed for both professionals and nonprofessionals; assists in the development of volunteer programs with courts and correctional institutions by furnishing speakers, consultants, workshops, demonstrations, films, literature, tapes, etc.
Publications: VIP Examiner; A Father, A Son
Founded: 1969

TRAINING PROGRAMS

FORUM 90: BACKWARD GLANCES... FORWARD VISIONS
Volunteers in Prevention, Probation, Prisons
527 North Main Street
Royal Oak, MI 48067
TEL: 313-398-8550
Credit: Inquire
Sponsor: International Association of Justice Volunteerism
Contact: Judge Keith J. Leenhouts, President
Description: To begin the Forum, participants were given a backward glance at the histories of its two sponsors, the International Association of Justice Volunteerism (IAJV) and Volunteers in Prevention, Probation, and Prisons (VIP), which took them over a span of twenty years of the justice volunteer movement with the presidents of the two organizations as presenters. This was followed by a presentation by Kids on the Block, a nonprofit group that addresses social issues through puppetry.
The keynote presentation, Looking Ahead Together, provided conferees with an opportunity to participate in specially designed Table Topic Groups, which include leaders from adult community programs, juvenile community programs, probation/parole offices, law enforcement divisions, courts, jails, prisons, and juvenile institutions. The networking that takes place through Table Topic Groups is considered one of the most important aspects of the Forum. The forum workshops were divided into five series:
Workshop Series I
- *101 - Volunteers in Law Enforcement* - builds on the English theme that contends "people are the police and the police are the people," which emphasizes that police cannot do it alone; challenges participants to offer suggestions on where citizens fit into modern law enforcement - from serving as policy-makers to serving in a non-sworn capacity.
- *102 - Networking & the Religious Volunteer* - presents a participatory workshop in which members practice networking and examine ways to access community religious resources; features small working groups for developing case studies, and presents a church networking model.
- *103 - Fun & Games for Changing Lives* - discusses therapeutic recreational programs in prisons for severely handicapped inmates in mental health programs, where volunteers provide programs in drama, art, etc.; reports on results that have been termed "life-changing," citing award-winning programs such as the one in the Georgia prison system.
- *104 - So You Want to Become an Author? or Public Speaker?*

or Become a Certified Volunteer Manager? - invites conferees to plan to participate in three upcoming IAJV projects: a series of "How To" manuals to be written by and for practitioners in the justice volunteer field; a centrally held listing of individuals willing to become part of the IAJV Resource Bank of public speakers, workshop presenters and technical assistance providers; and a certification program for justice volunteer managers.
- *105 - Together We Can Make It Work: Developing a Partnership Between the Public and Private Sectors* - helps participants gain a new appreciation for the role of government working in cooperation with private sector agencies; suggests techniques and strategies to facilitate communications, information exchange and networking; helps perpetuate a direct liaison between organizations and agencies within the criminal justice system.

Workshop Series II - Special Focus Workshops - provides an in-depth look at each of three topics crucial to all areas of the justice system: drugs, disease, and troubled youth. The two-session, all day workshops include:
- *201 - Alcohol, Illegal Street Drugs and Legal Drugs*
- *202 - Communicable Diseases ... AIDS, Hepatitis, and Tuberculosis*

[Both of these sessions dealt with the same two topics: "National/State Trends, Education and Issues," and "Local Treatment/Prevention, Legal Trends, and Developing Local Agency Networks."]
- *203 - Youth Subcultures ... Trends, Identification, Prevention and Intervention,* which covers "Gangs and Cults" and "Satanism."

Workshop Series III
- *When You Speak, Do People Listen?* - teaches how to create a personal connection with listeners and other communication skills.
- *Using Ex-Prostitutes as Volunteers* - presents an overview of Project Hope, a program which recruits and trains former prostitutes to help others in jail to recover and leave the lifestyle; includes a discussion of problems associated with prostitution and how to start a recovery group.
- *Administration & Management of Court Volunteer Programs* - trains in the "How To's" of a successful court program, including relating to the judge, accountability, screening and supervision; basics provided by the founder of VIP.
- *Separation, Loss and Grief* - provides understanding of the suffering of a family when a member is incarcerated, the various kinds of loss, the stages of the grief process, and how to facilitate healing and growth.
- *Screening Volunteers for Child Sexual Abuse Prior to Agency Assignment* - focus on interviewing techniques that can be used to screen volunteers who may be sexually abusive to children and youth.

Workshop Series IV: Issues & Perspectives
- *401 - A Backward Glance: Ex-Offenders Now Serving as Volunteers* - offers insights into the lives of ex-offenders who are now volunteers serving others; draws on personal experience of ex-offenders who answer questions like: Who made a difference in your life? How did you change? Why are you volunteering to help others?
- *402 - A Forward Vision: Are Volunteers a Valuable Alternative to Building More Prisons and Juvenile Institutions?* - examines whether volunteers can be viable alternatives in helping to reduce institutional populations; includes panelists who examine current justice policy on building more prisons and juvenile institutions, how citizens can affect political change, and how citizen volunteers can become involved in newly-emerging community programs.
- *403 - A Nostalgic View or Futuristic Vision: Are Justice Volunteers Worth It?* - reviews justice volunteers in terms of where we have been, what problems still remain, and what the future is for justice volunteer efforts; includes a special focus

on the philosophy of volunteer services, integration into larger justice programs, stumbling blocks in volunteer/staff relationships, and "electronic monitoring" as an alternative to supervision by volunteers.

Workshop Series V

- *501 - Leadership of Staff and Volunteers* - discusses the dynamics of leadership using a model that defines roles, responsibility and accountability, balanced with human relationship needs.
- *502 - How to Work with Angry Clients: A Focus on Offenders* - presents a counseling model to help clients who anger easily; based on Rational Behavior Theory, which has been used successfully with offenders and school dropouts.
- *503 - Potpourri: Two Mini-Workshops on Maxi-Topics:* 1) Recruiting and Using 12-Step Volunteers; 2) The Prison-Ashram Project: We're All Doing Time.
- *National Issues Forum* examines a new theory of democracy that involves citizens working through an issue rather than just talking about it; presents a description of the National Issues Forum Program, which is in over 1300 cities.

The Forum celebrates the 20th anniversary of the modern justice volunteer movement. IAJV and VIP worked together for the first time in 1990 in a movement that hopes to rally the volunteer community to combine efforts in a networking system that will benefit all concerned.

NATIONAL EDUCATION-TRAINING PROGRAM: VOLUNTEER COURT-CORRECTIONS MOVEMENT
Volunteers in Prevention, Probation, Prisons
527 North Main Street
Royal Oak, MI 48067
TEL: 313-398-8550
Credit: Varies with host college/university or organization
Sponsor: Host college/university or organization and support groups
Contact: Keith J. Leenhouts
Description: This course is intended to assist professors of criminal justice and practitioners of the volunteer court-corrections movement (judges, probation officers, parole officers, coordinators of volunteer programs in criminal justice, etc.) in two ways:

- to insure the future of the volunteer court-corrections movement by presenting courses on criminal justice to citizens while they are college students.
- to improve the present status and "state of the art" of the volunteer court-corrections movement by providing tools and techniques to professors and practitioners to enable them to recruit and train volunteers and professionals to work together in volunteer programs in courts, jails, prisons and juvenile institutions.

The course features 34 hours of high quality audiovisual material on all phases of volunteerism in criminal justice, including such subjects as:

- The dynamics of the one-to-one volunteer.
- The many uses of volunteers.
- Volunteers in Pre-sentence and intake investigations.
- Volunteers in Group Counseling.
- Volunteer-Staff Relations.
- Mechanics of Volunteer Programs in criminal justice.
- Volunteers and minorities.
- Management, administration and funding of volunteer programs in criminal justice.
- Volunteers in Alcoholic and Drug Programs.
- Retirees and Student Volunteers.
- Research and Evaluation of Volunteer Programs.
- Outstanding films and slide presentations utilized with structured interviews.
- Resources for all phases of volunteerism in criminal justice (programs for the delinquent-prone; alternatives to juvenile institutions; juvenile courts; adult misdemeanants; felons;

prisons and parole, and others).

The course involves noted practitioners of the volunteer court-corrections movement, who were involved also in the development of the 100+ page manual designed for the course. The manual suggests additional training and educational materials, field trips, additional resources. Although the course is designed for instruction of college students, it can be beneficial to any group involved in the volunteer court-corrections movement.

PRE-FORUM 90 TRAINING INSTITUTES
Volunteers in Prevention, Probation, Prisons
527 North Main Street
Royal Oak, MI 48067
TEL: 313-398-8550
Credit: Inquire
Sponsor: International Association of Justice Volunteerism
Contact: Judge Keith J. Leenhouts, President
Description: These pre-forum workshops represent a cooperative effort between the *International Association of Justice Volunteerism (IAJV)*, *Volunteers in Prevention, Probation and Prisons (VIP)*, and the *University of Wisconsin-Milwaukee Criminal Justice Institute.* They are offered immediately prior to the national conference, *Forum 90: Backward Glances... Forward Visions.* Two pre-forum workshops are conducted - one for administrators, and one for volunteers, as follows:
Pre-Forum 90 Justice Volunteer Management Training Institute: How to Recruit and Utilize Volunteers Effectively - Designed for new justice volunteer managers, this workshop provides an overview of sound volunteer management techniques, including pre-planning needs assessment, recruitment, screening placement, supervision, motivation, record-keeping, evaluation and networking. Instructors represent both public and private sectors and have provided training for both sectors, including religious and university settings.
Pre-Forum 90: Religious Volunteer Institute - Designed for both volunteers and religious program leaders, this workshop examines the changing role and expectations for those who provide religious services in the courts and correctional settings. Emphasis is placed on appropriate training and management behaviors which cultivate partnerships between the religious community and the justice system. Two sessions are conducted during the one-day workshop:
Morning Session - Participants are assisted in focusing on:
- Understanding the changing face of the justice system and how this impacts on religious volunteers.
- Understanding the conflicts between the justice system and the religious community and what the basis of a partnership might be.

Afternoon Session - Participants are involved in presentations and hands-on experience, including:
- Hearing about specific volunteer programs across the nation which have been effective over the past 30 years.
- Examining, in depth, a new program in the Michigan courts; considering possible future volunteer efforts.

Instructors include a former prison chaplain, the president of a chaplaincy school, an ex-offender who is now executive director of a major volunteer organization.

The pre-forum workshops enable early arrivals and others to take part in intensive and productive activity, network, and become acquainted with some of the instructors who are involved also in the national forum.

INDIVIDUAL PROGRAM PROFILES

HOGAN'S ALLEY, VIRGINIA
FBI Academy
Practical Applications Unit
Quantico Marine Base
Quantico, VA 22134
TEL: 703-640-6131

Purpose: To use role-players to simulate crime situations that FBI Academy students will face some day in the real world.

Contact: John Gray, Instructor

Description: Although it is difficult to "arrest your roommate," students at the FBI Academy do it everyday. The Academy uses role-playing in which students not ready for the training - and wives and family members of students - play roles of kidnappers, extortionists, bank robbers, cop-killers, accomplices, witnesses, bystanders, etc. for those who are ready.

The fictional, but three-dimensional town is called *Hogan's Alley, Virginia,* and was built by the Academy, one of the nation's largest law enforcement schools.

Although the role-players receive carefully-crafted scripts, they are given some latitude to "mouth off, resist arrest or shoot it out" in the confrontations with the Academy trainees. They are encouraged to exploit students' mistakes. Their mission is to rattle, to distract, and to get trainees upset enough to lose their exposure and "blow an arrest." Role-players learn to read trainees' body language, look for nervousness, and exploit any openings they see. They have learned to give only "lip service," however, since - in the heat of the situation - struggling or fighting causes the trainees to fight back.

A pool of about 70 additional role-players - coordinated by a "casting director," supplements the student volunteers and includes police officers, firefighters, park rangers, homemakers, bartenders, college students, computer programmers, people between jobs, etc. Although some role-players are given a subsistance wage, most come just to "play cops and robbers for a good cause." One corrections officer/role-player has no qualms about "making students pay for their mistakes." *Hogan's Alley* is an "open air town," built on the grounds of the Quantico Marine Base in full view of citizen observers passing by the facility. This adds to the trainees' discomfort when they are "shot" by a role-player after making a fatal error. The Academy sees this as a plus, since it impresses the mistake on the trainee the way no classroom can. As one instructor points out, "If students are going to make mistakes, this is the best place to do it."

LAW ENFORCEMENT/CRIME PREVENTION: ADVOCACY

INDIVIDUAL PROGRAM PROFILES

CITIZEN ADVOCATES FOR JUSTICE
241 East 116th Street
New York, NY 10029
TEL: 212-534-0600

Purpose: To assist women involved in the New York City Courts and Corrections Department.

Sponsor: Corporations; New York City; ecumenical and private donations; foundations

Contact: Constance M. Baugh, Executive Director

Description: Founded in 1978, Citizen Advocates for Justice (CAFJ) is supported through a combination of foundation grants, corporate funds, city tax dollars, ecumenical donations and private contributions. Four major programs, designed primarily to assist women offenders, are operated by the organization with the assistance of 70 community volunteers. There are four full-time paid staff members, three JTPA and one VISTA volunteer working with the volunteers. The programs are:

- **Revolving Bail Fund Project:** For the pre-trial offender, CAFJ maintains a fund which lends up to $250 to a woman with community roots. This allows her to remain outside of prison at a saving of $30,000 per year per inmate, retain ties to

family and custody of children, and begin to build a more productive life with the help of a volunteer caseworker.

- **Inside-Out Program:** Inside-Out matches the offender with a volunteer caseworker who helps and counsels the sentenced female offender during incarceration and at least three months following release from jail. In addition to one-to-one weekly sessions, the caseworker may assist by providing referrals for housing, education, training, employment, child care, drug and alcohol addiction services, welfare, legal and children's advocacy services.

- **Community Work Service Project:** This project provides judges with an alternative to incarcerating female misdemeanants who have been convicted of committing a non-violent criminal offense. Participants in the programs are sentenced by the court to provide a specified number of hours of work (from 80-250 hours) to a not-for-profit organization as a means of restitution for their crimes against society. Optimally, this alternative sentence is rehabilitative for the offender, providing her with needed work experience and increasing her self-esteem through participation in socially-positive activities under supervision by CAFJ and work-site staff. Minimally, it consistently proves to be a cost-effective means of sentencing offenders, and also helps in alleviating overcrowding in the city's overtaxed corrections facilities.

- **Community Resource Center:** The Resource Center is a clearinghouse for employment, cultural, recreational, housing and financial resources upon which the newly-released woman can draw.

- **Volunteer Training:** Community volunteers are provided with an intensive 25-hour training program prior to participating in the work of CAFJ. The training includes an introduction to the New York City Court and Corrections systems, a look at the nature of problems faced by female criminal offenders in these systems and in the community, an examination of sex, race, and class issues as these infringe upon the women's lives, and a rigorous self-inventory which enables the volunteers to identify their own attitudes and biases and how these will affect their capacities to assist in the work of CAFJ.

Following the completion of training, volunteers identify resources that they are prepared to offer to the organization: time, skills, experience, funds, contacts, etc. They also express the type of volunteer activities they would prefer. CAFJ's staff then proceeds to match these resources and interests with the agency's and the women's needs.

Typical volunteer activities, supervised by Executive and Program Directors, have included:

- one-to-one casework relationships with women in the Community Work Service, Inside-Out, and Bail Fund Projects;
- fundraising activities such as bazaars, mailings, membership drives;
- clothing and food donations;
- building rehab; and
- sharing holidays with women who have no homes or families.

Beyond this, volunteers have had a "ripple effect" in the form of a growing "sense of community" among themselves, the women served, and the neighborhoods in which they concentrate their efforts.

Founded: 1978

GUARDIAN AD LITEM PROGRAM
King County Superior Court
1211 East Alder Street
Mail Stop 2-L
Seattle, WA 98122
TEL: 206-296-1120
FAX: 206-343-2432

Purpose: To provide volunteer advocates for abused and neglected children who are involved in *King County Superior Court* dependency proceedings.

Contact: Nancy Broaders

Description: The *Guardian ad Litem (GAL) Program* was conceptualized in 1976 by the presiding judge of *King County Superior Court* in Seattle, and began operating in 1977. A *Guardian ad Litem* is a court-appointed special advocate for children involved in a court case. The phrase means "guardian for the term of the litigation." A GAL is a trained community volunteer who acts as an advocate for the best interests of abused and neglected children who are the subject of court proceedings. GALs are appointed to cases in which children are alleged to have been neglected, physically abused, sexually abused, emotionally abused and/or if a parent or guardian is unable or unwilling to care for the child. The GAL talks with the child, parents, family members, caseworker, school personnel, health providers, foster parents and others who know about the child's situation. The GAL also reviews records pertinent to the child. By closely monitoring the child's status, the GAL can make timely recommendations as to whether the child should be returned home or be freed for adoption. The amount of time required depends on many factors, such as the complexity of the case and the experience of the GAL.

The GAL continues to be involved until the case is permanently solved. This might be when the child is returned home or when the child is freed for adoption. One of the primary benefits of the GAL Program is that, unlike other court principals who often rotate cases, the GAL is a consistent figure in the proceedings and provides continuity for the child.

The GAL provides the judge, who ultimately must decide what is best for the child, with a source of mature, sensitive concern from someone who has no interest but that of the child. The volunteer has brought light, warmth, and hope into court proceedings that had been grim and poorly informed.

The Seattle court-appointed special advocate program resulted in court jurisdictions throughout the country implementing the Seattle model. Currently, there are 341 *GAL/CASA (Court Appointed Special Advocates)* programs operating in 45 states. New CASA programs start at an average of four per month. The *Guardian ad Litem Program* is one of three volunteer programs operating within *Juvenile Court Operations of King County Superior Court.* Superior Court programs operate within the judicial branch of King County government. The GAL program is served by an Advisory Board with representatives from the local community.

The many years of experience with the GAL Program in Seattle has resulted in this definition of a GAL:

The *Guardian ad Litem* is:
- committed to children
- able to maintain objectivity
- a creative problem solver
- skilled in interpersonal relationships
- sensitive to cultural values
- blessed with common sense
- open to personal growth

Fact sheets, brochures and other materials have been developed about the *King County Guardian ad Litem Program* for sharing with other communities.

Publications: Who Speaks for the Child; King County GAL/CASA Program: Questions & Answers; King County Guardian ad Litem/CASA Program: Fact Sheet

LAW ENFORCEMENT/CRIME PREVENTION: CHILDREN/YOUTH

NATIONAL/STATE ORGANIZATIONS

CHILD ABUSE LISTENING MEDIATION
SEE RECIPIENTS: CHILDREN/YOUTH - PROTECTIVE SERVICES

COMMUNITY RESEARCH FORUM*
505 East Green Street
Suite 210
Champaign, IL 61820
TEL: 217-333-0443

Objectives: To plan and promote improvement of human services at the community and neighborhood levels (currently directed toward the juvenile justice system).

Services: Provides technical assistance to communities in program management areas, including program development, staff training, citizen involvement, and evaluation; mounts long- and short-term projects, currently directed toward the juvenile justice system; for example:

- *Children in Adult Jails* - assists communities in eliciting citizen participation, identifying issues, developing alternative programs, monitoring the justice system, etc., to separate detained juvenile and adult offenders.
- *Planning Regional Services for Youth* - looks into the cost implications of removing juveniles from adult jails and providing relevant services in the community.

In addition, CRF responds to requests from local organizations faced with a crisis situation involving juvenile offenders, including citizen pressure when residential facilities and/or nonresidential alternatives are deemed inadequate; maintains extensive library collection; works with public or private, urban or rural local programs; publishes *Removing Children from Adult Jails and Lockups: A Citizen's Guide to Action,* and numerous other materials based on past and current projects; conducts workshops and sponsors symposia.

Publications: Removing Children from Jails and Lockups

NATIONAL ASSOCIATION OF POLICE ATHLETIC LEAGUES
SEE RECREATION & SPORTS: CHILDREN/YOUTH

PUBLIC AWARENESS ABOUT CHILD CARE (PAACC)
Denise Reich Real Estate
1400 South Colorado Boulevard
Denver, CO 80222
TEL: 303-757-7474

Objectives: To make the public aware, and the justice system more responsive, to crimes against children.

Services: Addresses barriers in the legal system to bringing child care workers who harm children to justice; works with mothers of victimized children and others to produce information for the media about children killed or hurt by those licensed or hired to care for them; works with legislators on investigations to identify felons employed in day-care centers, and more stringent background checks of child care providers, as well as including *all* child care workers in the checking process; addresses the need for better tracing methods to locate suspected workers who have left the area of the crime; publishes stories and other information on the subject.

Contact: Denise Reich, Founder

Founded: 1989

TIPS PROGRAM
Educational Information and Resource Center
700 Hollydell Court
Sewell, NJ 08080
TEL: 609-582-7000
Objectives: To teach students protective strategies to reduce their vulnerability to crime.
Services: Provides schools with awareness, training, evaluation, and technical assistance in the implementation of the *TIPS Program* in the classroom; assists students in meeting their responsibilities to help ensure the safety and welfare of themselves and others by utilizing protective strategies to reduce their vulnerability to crime; teaches kindergarten through eighth grade students to positively resolve conflict, resist crime, and protect themselves and their property; develops and distributes curricula and teaching strategies; provides personnel to train teachers, administrators and program instructors.
Founded: 1976

TRAINING PROGRAMS

FORUM ON SCHOOL VANDALISM
Newark City Council
920 Broad Street
Newark, NJ 07102
TEL: 201-733-3788
Sponsor: Newark City Council
Contact: Henry Martinez, President
Description: This Forum was called as a special meeting of school principals, law enforcement officials and city council officials to grapple with the increasing problems of vandalism in Newark schools. In some cases, windows are smashed and vandals enter the building and spray graffiti inside the school. With hundreds of volunteers spending thousands of hours each year painting over graffiti, the group feels that this type of vandalism is costing volunteer hours that could be put to better use. Solutions suggested included:

- Put a tax on spray paint for a dedicated fund for graffiti removal (Los Angeles gets $2.5 million a year from such a tax).
- Form a *Parental Truancy Task Force* in which parents volunteer to assist the existing board of education task force on this issue, bringing youth vandals before the Board, etc..
- Increase police presence around schools, or have the Board hire its own police.
- Keep parents better informed on this matter; enforce parent accountability laws; pick up kids after curfew and fine their parents.
- Provide recreation or other activity to counter boredom among children with low self-esteem who want to feel bigger.
- Develop a consistent policy and enforce it.
- Work more directly with the children, who are in the schools' hands several hours a day.
- Form volunteer student patrols among the youngsters themselves, giving them the side benefit of self-esteem in performing a civic duty.

The overriding purpose of the Forum was to draw a comprehensive policy on vandalism, graffiti, drug use and other problems in the schools. All suggestions were taken under advisement for further study, with a promise of early action on those selected to address the problems.

INDIVIDUAL PROGRAM PROFILES

THE CHOICE IS YOURS
Mecklenburg Correctional Center
c/o Roger K. Coleman 128287
PO Box 500
Boydon, VA 23917
TEL: 804-738-6114
Purpose: To allow prisoners to communicate with young people about the heavy price of breaking the law.
Sponsor: Mecklenburg Correctional Center
Contact: Roger K. Coleman 128287
Description: In 1982, a 23-year-old death-row prisoner wondered why so many young people were in prison. He wrote to circuit court judges asking for suggestions as to how he could help young people understand the heavy price they must pay if they break the law. One Judge suggested that he write an open letter to middle school counselors. His letter, *The Choice is Yours,* went out to juvenile judges, and junior and senior high school counseling departments in Virginia. The letter describes an average day on death row and warns against crime.
From his first efforts, more than 500 young people wrote to him, many to thank him for helping them. Some continue to write regularly. Also, the program has been picked up by death row prisoners in several other states. It has grown into a full-scale program with a how-to packet, a videotape, and a scholarship fund for disadvantaged youth. All materials are made available to inmates wishing to begin a program.
The program literally tries to "scare the daylights" out of kids by telling them the heavy price of breaking the law. The videotape takes the viewer inside of a cell and describes in detail the grinding daily routine of a death row inmate. It was produced, and is made available through the Catholic Communication Center.
The founder, still on death row, has appeared on television (Good Morning America) and radio, and in newspaper stories and as a contributing author for youth magazines. Proof that his program is working is supported by letters he receives from kids exposed to the program.
Rapidly growing across the country, according to the founder, *"The Choice is Yours* could never have gotten off the ground without the support of the warden, the Regional Administrator, the Deputy Director of Corrections in Virginia, and the many Judges who responded with suggestions. And the kids... the letters from the kids make it all worthwhile."
Publications: The Choice is Yours (video); The Choice is Yours Information Packet

COMMUNITY BLOCK HOMES
SEE RECIPIENTS: CHILDREN/YOUTH - PROTECTIVE SERVICES

DISTRICT OF COLUMBIA WOMEN'S COMMISSION FOR CRIME PREVENTION
945 G Street, NW
Washington, DC 20001
TEL: 202-347-2695
Purpose: To provide motivation for constructive life styles among young people who might otherwise turn to crime.
Sponsor: Women's organization in the metropolitan area; private donations
Contact: Ettyce H. Moore, President
Description: In 1968, some 125 women's organizations in the Washington, DC, metropolitan area participated in establishing the DC Women's Commission for Crime Prevention. The creation of this private, nonprofit, volunteer organization grew out of a deep concern about rising youth crime in the area. Initial and continuing encouragement and backing has come from the Board of Education, the Metropolitan Police Department, the White House, the DC government, the Department of Justice, and the

District committees of both Houses of Congress.

The Commission is managed and operated by volunteers, ranging from its Board with members from the court system, city government, women's commissions and clubs, the local Bar association, and leaders in local crime reduction and prevention programs, to the file clerks in the Commission's office at a local church. The aims of the Commission include:

- The Commission recruits volunteers and channels them to existing programs for high-risk youth in the metropolitan area, such as: Big Sister (providing a successful role model for a young girl); Clothe-A-Thon (providing the necessary clothing to help a young person maintain self-respect and remain in school; Crime Stoppers (providing healthy activities for the very young child to counteract some of the negative influences around him/her), and many other programs designed to divert juveniles from areas of crime.
- The Commission initiates additional programs. For example, it was felt that an easy-reference booklet outlining for teenagers the local laws that could affect them would provide a measure of crime prevention. The *Women's Bar Association of DC* agreed to provide volunteers to write the booklet, and teenaged volunteers were enlisted to illustrate it so that the Commission could publish it and provide free distribution to the schools. The colorful booklet explains the laws so often broken unknowingly by juveniles, and the penalties, including those for drug and truancy offenses. The booklet has been updated and reprinted a number of times over the years.
- The Commission responds to special requests in cases where no public funds are available to meet the need. For example, the Commission helped with furnishings to make more homelike rooms at the Women's Detention Center; provided books, a typewriter, home decorations and other family necessities for a girls' rehabilitation home; provided circus tickets and assistance for other outings for children, etc.
- As cosponsor with the Hands Up Crime Prevention of the DC Federation of Women's Clubs, the Commission assists in a community education event, the Good Neighbor Fair, an annual event in Washington, DC. The main purpose of the Fair is to generate public awareness, participation, and cooperation in crime prevention and related activities by community groups and government agencies. This event has stimulated outlying areas to hold similar fairs, one example being the 6C's Neighborhood Watch Awareness Fair in Southeast Washington, which attracted considerable media attention.

The Commission maintains a speaker service to inform other groups about the work of the Commission, and develops informative materials about its programs. The booklet for teenagers mentioned above, *Youth and the Law in the District of Columbia,* is available intermittently.
Founded: 1968

DONCASTER YOUTH CHALLENGE, A.K.A. SNEAKER CAMP
Maryland Department of Juvenile Services
1623 Forest Drive
Annapolis, MD 21403
TEL: 301-974-3460
Purpose: To help teenaged boys with criminal records to work through their problems through peer interaction.
Sponsor: Eckerd Foundation
Contact: Mike Ziebell, Program Director; Claire Orologas, Education Coordinator
Description: In this unique program for youth-in-trouble, the youth themselves volunteer at the end of each day to "confront each other" by airing gripes and accepting constructive criticism from each other. In this way they learn how to approach confrontation peacefully instead of fighting, and they are providing "peer feedback" to each other - a valuable service that even the

highest paid counselor in the state could not offer. The word "resocialization" is heard often. With names like *Explorers, Challengers, Potomacs,* and *Yukons,* the therapy groups at *Doncaster Youth Challenge* share frank discussions of "who did what to whom" and everyone has a chance to express feelings about the problems aired. This interaction has proven to be a valuable part of the overall program.

The program is referred to as a "sneaker camp" to differentiate it from the adult "boot camp" that the state is planning for older criminals. Although officials describe the youth program as "military style," it is really based more on psychological concepts. The primary concept of the youth program is "Make the teenagers feel good about themselves."

Youth at the Doncaster program are serving their sentences for first-time drug possessions, auto theft or vandalism. Officials don't have figures to prove whether the camp, which opened in 1987, is more successful at reforming juveniles with problems than other forms of treatment, but the evidence at hand has helped the Department make the decision to open another *Challenge* program elsewhere in the state, this time with a special emphasis on drug offenders.

The *Eckerd Foundation* operates the Doncaster program and will operate the planned program for drug offenders as well. The latter will be operated on the same principle - serving in self-help therapy groups to provide peer support for each other.

According to a director, "Although the teenagers frequently grumble about their routine, they acknowledge that they have it comparatively easy - they could be in one of the more traditional programs, such as the rough and rigorous state training school in Baltimore County. The boys who come here wanting to learn something are the ones who will succeed here. Our philosophy is much more growth-oriented than punitive."
Founded: 1987

FOCUS (FAMILIES OF CHILDREN UNITED FOR SAFETY)
SEE TEENAGE PREGNANCY/PARENTING

HAWAII YOUTH AT RISK
810 North Vineyard Boulevard
Honolulu, HI 96817
TEL: 808-842-7078
Purpose: To help former gang members and other youth at risk to "break the cycle" and return to the mainstream.
Contact: Stanley Suyat, Director
Description: With assistance from similar programs in Los Angeles, Boston, New York, Philadelphia, Chicago and Dallas, a volunteer group in Honolulu, Hawaii, tries to turn youth away from street gangs in a program called *Youth At Risk.* When independent research offered by the director of the Los Angeles program showed reductions in felony crime (50%) and truancy (75%), and a *550% increase* in hours worked among youth a year after the program was instituted, the Honolulu group organized and installed the program. Additional statistics from Los Angeles showed a 33% reduction in drug use, and better relationships with parents and teachers.

To begin the program, volunteers explain its operation in correctional facilities, and the youth must commit to it. It is a tough program with set standards of right and wrong, not unlike the discipline they are used to in the gang. A gang member's life is kept within a strict mold. What *Youth At Risk* does, through a program developed by San Francisco's *Breakthrough Foundation,* is teach gang members how to break through the mold.

The two-year involvement period for the youth - many already under sentence or alienated from their parents - begins with several months of preliminary meetings, but the emphasis is on a 10-day residential course that combines classroom discussions and physical activity. The latter is designed purposely to put the youth in a position where they must depend on each other - something they did not have to consider in the gangs. Many feel sick for most of the ten days, suffering withdrawal symptoms either from drugs or liquor or both, but they are still expected to run a mile a day. At the end of the course, all are required to declare their plans - to quit drugs, to get a job, join the Army, finish high school, etc. Some follow through, some don't, but almost all do better than they did before getting involved with *Youth At Risk.* For the next year, each is assigned a committed partner, a trained adult volunteer.

Both volunteers and funds come through fund-raising dinners and auctions. Merchants donate items that have included a 1969 red Chrysler LeBaron convertible, travel packages, restaurant meals and art works. The organization's motto is the ancient Chinese proverb, "If you do not change your direction, you are likely to end up where you are headed."

JUVENILE ARBITRATION PROGRAM OF SOUTH CAROLINA

PO Box 2327
Aiken, SC 29802
TEL: 803-642-1569
Purpose: To allow first-time offenders to avoid a family court record.
Sponsor: Second Judicial Circuit Court
Contact: Patricia A. Reynolds
Description: The Juvenile Arbitration Program of South Carolina is administered by the Solicitor's office for the Second Judicial Circuit and was initially funded for three years by a grant from the Governor's office which later received permanent continuation by Aiken County after its proven success.

The Program allows first-time offenders to prevent a family court record by successfully completing a tailor-made outline determined by a trained volunteer Arbitrator in the community.

This program not only gives the opportunity for a child to prevent a Family Court record, but invites the victim to be an active participant throughout the Arbitration proceedings by suggesting possible sanctions.

The Arbitration Program affects positively every aspect of the Juvenile Justice System in this Circuit by relieving the caseload on Law Enforcement, Department of Youth Services, Solicitor's office, Clerk of the Court and the Family Court Judges, thus allowing them to concentrate on more serious offenders.

A success in this program also acts as a crime prevention tool because it removes a juvenile from the crime cycle which all too often leads to his/her becoming a habitual offender.

A first-time offender should not be followed by a criminal record which would possibly hinder his or her future, nor should he/she be allowed to "get away" with the offense.

Through the Juvenile Arbitration Program, the child is given positive learning alternatives such as community service, jail tours, observing films, and General Sessions Court as well as monetary restitution.

Since implementation in 1985, the program has processed over 600 juvenile cases with a less than five percent recidivism rate and a success rate of 88 percent.

Also, the Juvenile Arbitration Program has collected over $17,000 for victims of the Second Judicial Circuit in juvenile crimes which aids in meeting one of the major objectives, which is to satisfy all parties concerned.

The Juvenile Arbitration Program is cost-effective due to the extensive utilization of trained volunteers from the community. The program has demonstrated that it is effective.
Founded: 1985

JUVENILE RECEPTION AND DIAGNOSTIC CENTER (JRDC)

PO Box 116
Baker, CA 70704-0116
TEL: 504-774-7720

Purpose: To provide academic testing, psychological evaluation, and therapeutic treatment to residents committed to the LA Department of Corrections.
Sponsor: Los Angeles Department of Corrections
Contact: Martin B. Patton, Director
Description: The Center is a division of the Los Angeles Department of Corrections, and is the receiving unit for both male and female juvenile offenders committed by the Los Angeles Courts. Personnel consists of diagnostic, custodial and treatment staff. The Center services three kinds of offenders: those who will transfer to a schooling campus within two weeks, those in residences at the maximum security unit, and thirty, sixty, and ninety day evaluation-only commitments.

Staff provides psychological, medical, social and educational evaluations of each resident before he/she is assigned to an institution or returning to court for a hearing. Personnel at the Juvenile Adjustment Center, a maximum security unit, are involved in a treatment program consisting of academics, living skills, G.E.D. preparation, work, counseling, and art classes.
Volunteer Staff: At present, approximately thirty (30) volunteers work in a number of positions. Volunteers provide all religious services, work in arts and crafts and aerobic dance classes and provide parties.
Volunteer Duties: Volunteers perform a number and variety of duties at different times of day - church services on the weekends and bible study in the evenings to instructing art classes and arranging exhibits, providing tutoring, conducting aerobic dance classes, participating in recreation, assisting residents with letter writing, hosting parties, performing concerts and puppet shows and making donations.
Volunteer Experience: Volunteers are able to work at JRDC with varying levels of skills and experience. Expertise is matched with job descriptions, special training is sometimes provided. Orientation and agreement contracts are required for all incoming volunteers. One-to-one supervision is often given.

LOUISIANA TRAINING INSTITUTE*

PO Box 1631
Monroe, LA 71210
TEL: 318-323-4406
Purpose: To provide long-term custody and rehabilitative education to youth offenders.
Sponsor: State of Louisiana
Contact: W. A. Massey, Prot. Chaplain, Director, or Volunteer Coordinator
Description: Louisiana Training Institute-Monroe is a long-term state residential correctional institution charged with custody of the state's adjudicated delinquents. The population is made up of 300 youths between the ages of 14-21. The program is composed of both academic and vocational education. It also maintains a full religion program.

The volunteer program was begun over 60 years ago (1930) with an emphasis on religious activity. It is still basically a religious program, but does include other areas of concern. The basic objective is the enrichment of the experiences of the youth committed to the school.

Organizational structure of the Institute includes volunteers who are recruited because of their management abilities, in addition to other qualities. These volunteers become volunteer coordinators for the various volunteer programs of the institution. One volunteer coordinator coordinates volunteers from 40 churches where, among other activities, the volunteers provide monthly birthday parties for nine cottages. Other coordinators coordinate crafts instructors in our Boys' Club, Bible study instructors, and Chapel program participants.

In this way, about 250 volunteers (mostly occasional) become involved in activities for our students. Presently, four volunteers are volunteer coordinators for various programs. They are supervised by the director of volunteer services. Volunteers who

are primarily counselors are supervised by the counseling staff.
Founded: 1930

M.O.M.S. (MOTHERS ON THE MOVE SPIRITUALLY)
St. Teresa of Avila Catholic Church
1244 V Street, SE
Washington, DC 20020
TEL: 202-678-9068
Purpose: To help people with parenting skills *before* there is a problem.
Sponsor: St. Teresa of Avila Catholic Church
Contact: Jean Campbell, Founder
Description: When a member of a Washington, DC, Roman Catholic Church - a licensed practical nurse - lost a son to violence, the church steered her toward community outreach. By redesigning an existing program called *Brothers Keepers,* and renaming it M.O.M.S. (Mothers on the Move Spiritually), a "small army" of volunteer mothers formed in 1987 and began waging what it calls "spiritual warfare."
Much of the work of M.O.M.S. is in counseling juvenile delinquents at the *Oak Hill Correctional Center.* This focus grew out of the frustration of the founder in trying to find a rehabilitation center for a second son who turned to drugs after his brother's death. Upon finding only Centers designed for *after* the problem, M.O.M.S. was directed toward prevention.
The goal of the program is to establish two residential facilities for the incarcerated youth counseled by M.O.M.S. and a community center. To counteract the fact that the youth will return to the same neighborhood, the same friends, and eventually the same way of life, M.O.M.S. hopes to provide the alternative that will work, involving divinity students to help man the residential centers, and volunteer psychiatrists from the District of Columbia government.
Founded: 1987

MID-VALLEY ADOLESCENT CENTER*
1610 Court Street, NE
Salem, OR 97301
TEL: 503-364-9152
Purpose: To provide community-based treatment for delinquent adolescent males as an alternative to institutional care, court-committed youth, and residential treatment.
Sponsor: State contract; Juvenile Justice grants; federal funds for in-program teachers
Contact: Jan Rutschman
Description: Mid-Valley is a residential youth care center for delinquent males, ages 13-18, who have been court-committed. Seventeen youth are involved in the three program components: residential, proctor care, and partial residential. Youth care centers aim at keeping youth out of state institutions and at enabling the youth to grow and change. Funds are obtained primarily by contracting to provide those services for the State of Oregon. Miscellaneous amounts are also obtained from other sources. Volunteers are used as on-line staff, recreational aides, on a volunteer resource board, to add extras on holidays and for special projects, i.e., foster grandparents, a skiing outing, etc. Currently, Mid-Valley has about 20 volunteers.
Volunteers do essentially the same things that on-line (supervision of youth) staff do with the exception of having a caseload and writing reports. Volunteers are especially appreciated for their relationship and fun activities, for which the staff often have difficulty in finding time.
Volunteers of all levels of experience are accepted, including ex-residents and participants in the program. Expansion of the volunteer program is underway and employers are being recruited to help with the Experience-Based Career Education program.

NEIGHBORHOOD PROBATION UNIT
SEE RECIPIENTS: POLICE/COURT OFFICERS - RESPITE

OFFENDER AID AND RESTORATION OF ROANOKE, VIRGINIA*
PO Box 553
Roanoke, VA 24003
TEL: 703-985-0200
Purpose: To help to ensure that high risk youth and minor juvenile offenders are steered away from official court action and therefore not stigmatized or hardened by establishment of a criminal record.
Sponsor: O.A.R. of Roanoke
Contact: Nancy L. Goehring, Volunteer Director
Description: Offender Aid and Restoration endeavors to assist troubled youth up to the age of 17, who find themselves in violation of the law, recognize their problems and eventually correct their delinquent ways. Working through a cadre of dedicated volunteer counselors, assistance has been provided to these youngsters and their parents primarily through listening to their problems, allowing them the opportunity to discover their own shortcomings and eventually guiding them to an acceptable solution. Referrals to the program are from Roanoke City Juvenile Court, Social Services, Police Dept. Youth Bureau, and schools, clergymen and parents.
For many years, O.A.R. was supported through A D.J.C.P. grant and private funding, wherein a paid director and administrative staff managed all aspects of the program. By November 1981, funding ceased, only a small amount of private funds remained, and closure of the program was imminent.
The O.A.R. Board of Directors recognized that the heart of the program, the seasoned staff of volunteer counselors, was still intact, and that this dedicated group had every intention of continuing the rewarding and satisfying work for which it was originally chartered. The key to continuance of the program, therefore, was to establish a staff of part time administrators to perform a full time administrative function. Quickly, managerial, organizational and clerical talent began to surface. Soon the problems heretofore solved by the paid staff were being solved by a group of volunteers who were pledging their time on a "watch" basis. Volunteer burnout seemed to have diminished in the enthusiasm to keep the agency alive.

PARTNERS*
1260 West Baysud
Denver, CO 80223
TEL: 303-777-7000
Purpose: To match volunteers one-to-one with young people who have been referred by courts, schools, police.
Sponsor: 90% private, 10% state funding
Contact: Jeffrey W. Pryor, Executive Director
Description: Partners was founded in 1968 by a Denver businessman and a small group of volunteers who believe that a one-to-one "partnership" with an in-trouble youth would have positive effects on the problem of juvenile delinquency. This concept is the foundation for the Partners program and has resulted in a significant reduction in recidivism and has improved opportunities for youth in the program to lead more successful lives. Partners has nine branches in three states and a Central office. To date, Partners has involved over 15,000 youth and adult volunteers.
Adult volunteers, called Senior Partners, and youth, or Junior Partners, agree to spend a minimum of three hours a week together for one year. During that time the youngsters have an opportunity to strengthen feelings of self-worth, improve academics, decrease delinquent behaviors, and increase abilities to cope with stressful situations.
The relationship formed between the Junior and Senior Partner is aided by Partners' staff which provides supervision and guidance through support groups, counseling and Life Skills, a series of trainings that help the Partnership seek out options and alternatives to situations they encounter. Various activities to aid in the relationship-building are available, such as water sports,

hiking, skiing, and educational classes. The staff also refers the Partnerships to community agencies for legal, educational and mental health services as needed.

Involvement of the community is essential to the success of Partners. Interested, caring adults serve as volunteer Senior Partners, assist in fundraising, provide health services, and help in a myriad of other ways. Foundations and corporations offer business and management expertise to Partners' Board of Directors, committees, and staff, thereby strengthening the Partners organization. Partners receives 90 percent of its financial support from local, private contributors.
Founded: 1968

SENECA FALLS CONCERNED PARENTS
Seneca Falls Central School District
Mynderse Academy
105 Troy Street
Seneca Falls, NY 13148
TEL: 315-568-9826
Purpose: To enable youth, ages 11 to 15, either on the fringe of breaking the law or involved with the law, to discover meaningful alternatives and programs to their present lifestyles through the efforts of their concerned parents.
Sponsor: Mynderse Academy
Contact: Gerald Macaluso
Description: This program began in September of 1983 through a group of concerned parents of children of Mynderse Academy. At this particular moment the cost is nothing, in that present social service agencies are providing the bulk of program-related activities to the clients. The Academy serves as the facilitator of the program. The following is of the essence:
Target Population:
 ● Seneca County Youth - 11 to 15 years of age.
 ● Youth on the fringe of breaking the law or involved with the law.
 ● Participation must be voluntary - students as well as parents.
Agencies Involved:
 ● Religious, Educational, Police, and Social Service
Program includes:
 ● Youth Assistance Program at Auburn Correctional Institute
 ● Alternatives to drugs and alcohol
 ● Post-Counseling and Monitoring
Role of the Academy:
 ● Coordinating force of the effort.
The strong support and activities of parents is vital to the program.
Founded: 1983

SO SAD (SAVE OUR SONS AND DAUGHTERS)
543 Martin Luther King Blvd
Detroit, MI 48201
TEL: 313-833-3030
Purpose: To help end teen violence.
Contact: Clementine Barfield, Founder
Description: When a mother sought counseling to help her through the grief of losing a son to violence, she found none. She did find more than 100 Detroit parents whose children had been killed, and together they formed their own counseling service, *Save Our Sons and Daughters (SO SAD)*. Part of the motivation for developing SO SAD was to show remaining children in families of victims that revenge is not the way. Doing something positive helps survivors feel that they did not "just lose a valuable human being for nothing."
The all-volunteer counseling service is working with limited funds, but plans for expansion and a major fund-raising drive are underway.
Founded: 1987

SUMMIT SHOCK INCARCERATION FACILITY
New York State Department of Corrections
Building Number Two
State Campus
Albany, NY 12226
TEL: 518-457-8182; 518-457-8134
FAX: 518-457-7070
Purpose: To provide intensive schooling, drug counseling, jobs and other services to young offenders in a regimented setting to combat recidivism.
Sponsor: New York State Department of Corrections
Contact: Thomas A. Coughlin, Commissioner; Alan Strong, Counselor
Description: One of four such facilities in a program that originated in 1987, the Summit Shock Incarceration Facility finds many of the young offenders serving as volunteer tutors to bunkmates seeking GED certificates. With the original purpose of helping with the overcrowding problem, according to the Commissioner of the Department of Corrections, this has turned out to be the "best six months these inmates will spend."
By mid-1989, 700 youth graduated from the state's shock program. Only 17% were repeat offenders compared to 25% in the general prison population. Youth are screened to determine whether or not they will benefit from the program. Like other self-help programs, the individual must want to help him/herself.
The program consists of a rigid calisthenics program each morning followed by assignment to work crews to clean and maintain nearby state-owned campsites and ski trails, plant fruit trees for the deer, clear brush and logs, and cut lumber at the sawmill. For some, it is the first time they have been that close to nature, away from life in crowded housing projects.
The cornerstone of the shock program is the "network session," during which inmates are encouraged to engage in self-criticism as well as give constructive critiques of others. According to the head of the drill instructor corps, "The network is what keeps them out of jail, not the military stuff." For two hours each day the youth are expected to discuss their weaknesses and vulnerabilities - an exercise even more difficult than the push-ups for the streetwise group. For each session, one youth is selected to be critiqued by the others, and they reach conclusions such as "He still has a chip on his shoulder," or "He just doesn't want to change," or "He thinks he's too smart for this program." The Counselor in charge sees the progress developing in a youth's admonition of his peer, "This is supposed to be a caring community, but you aren't taking part in it." When the criticized youth later commented, "People get on your back because you need it," the Counselor is further encouraged.
Many inmates eagerly pursue their high school diplomas through the GED program, with computer programs the most popular. These youth, who are high school dropouts, spend three hours a day in math and English classes. Other inmates serve as tutors, staying with their partners until the end. Of the 48 youth who completed shock camp in the summer of 1989, nine sought and won GED certificates. They are quick to thank their volunteer tutors/bunkmates.
All graduates are given state jobs until they can find something on their own. One youth who said he earned $3,000 a day as a drug distributor in the Bronx will be earning $32 a day in his state job. Visitors are allowed every other Sunday, and a graduation ceremony is held at the end of the six-month program. As the graduates leave the grounds with families and friends, as though to spur them on to their new jobs and lives, a sign posted along the country road reads, "Only the best reach the Summit."
Publications: Shock Camp Annual Report; Shock Camp Information Packet

SUPERIOR COURT CONFERENCE COMMITTEE DIVERSION PROGRAM
SEE LAW ENFORCEMENT/CRIME PREVENTION: RE-ENTRY

SURROUND*

Minnesota Correctional Facility-Red Wing
Red Wing, MN 55066
TEL: 612-388-7154
Purpose: To help rehabilitate delinquents through peer group companionship and support.
Sponsor: State Training School; church youth groups
Contact: The Reverend Ron Hendrickson
Description: The purpose of the Surround program is literally to surround teenagers at the correctional facilities with peers who will help them see themselves in a different light and will provide companionship and support when they are released. Surround volunteers are members of church youth groups from all over the state. They are expected to visit the institution at least monthly. Each Surround group consists of from five to 30 boys and girls and one or more adult advisors. When a group arrives at the school, five to ten members will get together with two or three residents. (Participation by residents is strictly voluntary.) Usually, residents are from the same community as the volunteers. The "surrounding" often takes the form of discussions, but also may include picnics and sports. Frequently the young people are allowed to leave the school grounds together for part of a day. Visits can last a day or an entire weekend. On overnight visits, the volunteers sleep in the school chapel.
When a youth is released from the school and returns to his home community, local Surround members attempt to bring him into active participation in their group. A high percentage of former training school residents return to the school as Surround volunteers.
Before a group may participate in the program, its leader must receive orientation at a workshop held at the training school. He then orients the youth group to the program and its purposes. Surround, which began as a small pilot group in 1965, now includes over 5,000 high school students throughout the state representing 400 church youth groups. The program operates in the 150-resident State Training School at Red Wing, the Minnesota Home School and the Lincoln Boys School in Wisconsin.
Founded: 1965

YOUTH TRAIN

SEE RECIPIENTS: CHILDREN/YOUTH

LAW ENFORCEMENT/CRIME PREVENTION: CRIME WATCH

NATIONAL/STATE ORGANIZATIONS

CB RADIO PATROL (*formerly CB Radio Posse*)

American Federation of Police
1100 Northeast 125th Street
North Miami, FL 33161
TEL: 305-891-1700
Objectives: To promote safety and discourage crime.
Services: Works with 30,000 volunteer CB radio operators in 50 states through a "volunteer community radio patrol"; seeks to promote safety and discourage crime by their presence, activities, and immediate access to law enforcement agencies; maintains a library on the subject of community crime and the effectiveness of the radio patrol program nationwide; publishes a newsletter and a manual on civil defense.
Publications: Police Times
Founded: 1976

NATIONAL TOWN WATCH ASSOCIATION (*formerly National Association of Town Watch*)

PO Box 303
Wynnewood, PA 19096
TEL: 215-649-7055
Objectives: To improve the crime watch capabilities in local communities.
Services: Promotes, assists and encourages participation in community crime prevention by providing crime prevention groups with the opportunity to pool their resources, develop liaisons, and share crime prevention tips and information on programs in their areas; offers assistance through referrals, fundraising programs, promotional materials, regional affiliates, and training guides; sponsors annual *National Night Out,* a symbolic demonstration in which neighborhood residents across the country spend time in front of their homes to highlight crime prevention programs; presents award to the community with the best *National Night Out* program, as well as other awards for outstanding achievement in crime watch efforts; works with local, state and regional crime watch organizations and individuals working in cooperation with local law enforcement agencies and crime prevention officers; maintains an advisory council composed of law enforcement officers and citizen leaders from across the country; publishes and distributes a quarterly newsletter.
Sponsor: Crime Prevention Coalition
Publications: New Spirit
Founded: 1981

TRAINING PROGRAMS

NEIGHBORHOOD ANTI-CRIME RALLY/COMMUNITY FORUM

District of Columbia Police Department
300 Indiana Avenue, NW
Washington, DC 20001
TEL: 202-727-4283
Description: After twenty years of working together as good neighbors, residents of one Capitol Hill neighborhood became incensed when a young man on their street was murdered in a robbery attempt. Their concern resulted in a dual training/discussion event - one in the neighborhood and the other at the Police Department. Bringing together City Council members and DC Police spokespersons, this combination of meetings was attended by over 200 residents of a Capitol Hill neighborhood tired of the day-to-day crime. The neighborhood rally was organized with the help of a resident who is a former school admissions director. Four Council members attended and spoke to the group about actions that could be taken to combat the crime in the neighborhood. The decision that came out of the rally was to form a Neighborhood Watch program.
Five days later the group was invited to a community forum offered by the DC Police Department and facilitated by the Police Chief. The same resident helped to bring about the forum, which again attracted 200 people from his neighborhood as well as people from other neighborhoods. Some of the points made by the Police Chief and other presenters:
- "You've got to get angry."
- Help police to solve murders. Open a dialogue with the Police Department.
- Don't wait for the murders to happen; take steps to protect your neighborhood.
- Discipline your children.
- Don't wait for white neighbors to make that call to the police.
- Get involved, and *stay* involved. Your experience counts for half the battle.

In citing the unwillingness of many city residents to help police solve murders, the Police Chief cited the Capitol Hill neighborhood as an exception. Other groups came forward to discuss how they had watched the crime in their neighborhoods escalate from stolen bikes to armed robberies and now killings. The goal of this and other meetings like it is to establish Neighborhood Watch programs in every neighborhood, with "Reserve Officers" on every block. Reserve Officers are citizens who are trained to do police work but do not carry guns. According to the resident who initiated the meetings, "All this new interest in being a good neighbor is what we have been practicing for more than 20 years. Just think how things would change if we had a reserve officer on every block. That is volunteerism to the max!"

INDIVIDUAL PROGRAM PROFILES

CITIZENS' CRIME WATCH OF DADE COUNTY
5220 Biscayne Boulevard
Room 200
Miami, FL 33137
TEL: 305-756-0582
Purpose: To educate the community in crime prevention, bring neighbors closer together and improve communication between police and citizens.
Sponsor: Citizens' Crime Watch of Dade County Inc. (CCWDCI)
Contact: Nancy Burdelsky
Description: Citizens' Crime Watch of Dade County, Inc. *(CCWDCI)* is a Neighborhood Watch Program with the concept of "People to People Protection." The basic goals of CCWDCI are twofold. First, to educate people about crime prevention - home security, in particular; and secondly, to implement a telephone chain in the neighborhood - a means of communication whereby neighbors can alert each other to criminal or suspicious activity in the area and also whereby they can receive information from the police on a periodic basis.
Volunteer Staff - The Program Executive Committee oversees the day-to-day operation of CCWDCI and makes policy decisions, but the key people are the District (unincorporated Dade County is divided into six districts by the Metro Dade Police Department) and City Chairmen.
Volunteer Duties - These Chairmen are responsible for arranging for speakers and setting up presentations in neighborhoods desiring to start a Citizens' Crime Watch. These Chairmen are also responsible for maintaining records and insuring neighborhood telephone chains remain active.
Under these District and City Chairmen are Neighborhood Chairmen who are responsible for anywhere from two to ten or more blocks.
If a Citizens' Crime Watcher spots a criminal or suspicious action, person, vehicle, etc., they immediately contact their local police department. They then contact their Block Captain who passes the information to the other Citizens' Crime Watchers on the block. Once a telephone chain is established, information can flow in either direction, up or down the chain.
In addition, various groups of citizens volunteer to work on committees such as Youth Crime Watch, Sexual Assault, Speakers Bureau, Safe Homes and Assaults on Police Officers.
Cooperation with different police departments is vital and the cooperation is very good. They see citizen involvement as an integral part of crime prevention as the population continues to rapidly expand and police departments are unable to increase their manpower accordingly. Each district or city has one or two Crime Prevention Officers (CPO) who work with the district or city chairman.
When a presentation for a neighborhood is arranged, a Citizens' Crime Watch Speaker is sent and, whenever possible, a CPO. A nine minute film is shown to introduce people to CCWDCI. The Crime Prevention Officer speaks to the people about home security - proper lighting, proper locks and other items on a security survey checklist to try to make a home as burglar-proof as possible. The

speaker from Citizens' Crime Watch talks about the history of the program and explains the actual implementation of the telephone chain and stresses the importance of participation.
Speakers make sure the citizens understand that participation is not that of becoming physically involved with a suspect, but participation through observing and reporting.
CCWDCI relies on donations of services and financial contributions from the private sector for its funding.

CITIZENS ORGANIZED PATROL EFFORTS (COPE)
Shaw Neighborhood Advisory Committee
1726 Seventh Street, NW
Washington, DC 20001
TEL: 202-332-4800
Purpose: To create a drug-free neighborhood.
Contact: Project Coordinator
Description: On June 2, 1989, a group of eight citizens with white and red uniforms, walkie-talkies "and opening night jitters" hit the streets of the Shaw neighborhood of Washington, DC, to begin a new daily patrol. The patrol, meant to dispel drug traffickers, discourage buyers and reassure law-abiding residents, was founded by the neighborhood advisory commissioner, who had sponsored anti-drug marches in the neighborhood for the previous six months. During those rallies, residents trailed suspected drug dealers and stood in front of houses chanting, "This is a crack house!" The patrol was devised to make this effort more visible and intensify what the marchers had accomplished.
Although several dozen residents were expected to sign up for the patrol, only eight enlisted. Undaunted, they donned their uniforms and began the patrol, passing out literature and admonishing drug and alcohol abusers along the way. Most people accept the literature, while others turn away. One former drug dealer just returning from prison cited the effort as well-intentioned, but too dangerous. He said the dealers won't pay attention unless the patrol member says the wrong thing, then they will "just blow him away." The patrol continues without major confrontation and feels that their small effort should make a difference in the long run. Uniforms and walkie-talkies were provided by a local contractor who plans to build a shopping center in the neighborhood.
Founded: 1989

CRIME PREVENTION COMMITTEE OF CONTRA COSTA COUNTY
2280 Diamond Boulevard
Suite 360
Concord, CA 94520
TEL: 415-798-2572
Purpose: To promote crime prevention and organize community volunteers through organizing neighborhoods in our county of 650,000.
Sponsor: State/County/Corporate and private donations
Contact: Lorraine L. Rivers
Description: The Crime Prevention Committee was organized by citizens in 1973. The committee works with 15 law enforcement agencies and sheriff's departments. A three year grant from LEAA in 1976-1979 helped organize more communities. The largest committee, in Concord, has 36 volunteers; the smallest, in Hercules, has eight volunteers.
Over the years, 400 volunteers have organized neighborhoods, run meetings (with or without an officer), handled media promotion, organized student programs, given public speeches, and assisted victims of crime. Some 4,000 (estimate) have hosted neighborhood meetings throughout the county.
All support for CPC has been through individual, corporate and business donations. (LEAA and state grants have been short term funded projects of the CPC.)
Volunteers have prepared a CPC manual, a written and illustrated "how to" book, *Alternative to Fear,* and have written numerous pamphlets. They have trained trainers and participated in local

and Bay Area conferences. A State grant from the Office of Criminal Justice Planning is in progress.

The Committee focuses on the county high crime/high fear areas. San Pablo (18th highest crime rate in the state; $13,000 median income) now has 28 volunteers organizing by area. Training includes: how to organize, how to run an effective meeting, how to be an effective neighborhood leader, speakers bureau training. The 16-member Board of Directors serves on a volunteer basis. Beginning next year at least one-third will be directly representing local committees, while others will be from the county at large and three agencies. According to the Police Department, "Crime has already been displaced 25% in organized areas."
Founded: 1973

GREEN COUNTRIE TOWNE PROGRAM
SEE PHYSICAL ENVIRONMENT: BEAUTIFICATION

GUARDIAN ANGELS
Alliance of Guardian Angels
982 East 89th Street
Brooklyn, NY 11236
TEL: 212-967-0808
Purpose: To provide a visible, trained patrol to deter crime on the streets, in subways, and in other inner-city areas.
Sponsor: Individual donors
Contact: Curtis Sliwa, Founder
Description: Founded in 1979 as "The Magnificent 13" to provide volunteer assistance to the fight against crime in New York City, the Guardian Angels now have some 3,000 volunteers working in 16 cities across the country. Although most of the volunteers are average young people from tough neighborhoods, some of the members are lawyers, teachers, and doctors. The age range is 16-68, with the older members providing services such as manning walkie-talkies.

Volunteers, who are trained in martial arts, are required to be in school or working at least part time. They buy their own "colors" (red berets, white T-shirts) and pay their own subway fares in cities where they patrol the mass transit systems. All new Chapters must undergo rigid training. In addition to martial arts the volunteers are trained in street-patrolling and making citizens' arrests. Then the Chapter is officially turned over to native youths, who are committed to run the program according to strict Guardian Angels guidelines.

The aim of the Guardian Angels is to help deter crime by their visibility in areas of high crime, and by citizens' arrests. Although they carry no weapons, the 800 member group in New York City made 287 citizens' arrests since 1979. The group is a non-profit, tax-exempt corporation supported entirely by donations, but refusing to accept funding from the state, local or federal governments. The group has no salaried members, and headquarters is in the founder's home.

The main ingredient the Angels rely on is volunteerism. However, not just anyone can become a Guardian Angel. Applicants have to be a least 16 years of age with some background in martial arts. They have to be working or in school, and they are expected to donate eight hours a week to patrolling. In addition, among the first 50 recruits in each Chapter, there can be no criminal record of any kind. (This latter rule may be slightly bent in some cases, but no convicted murderers, rapists, robbers, or drug-pushers would be allowed to join.) Also, applicants must go through various screening processes, both physical and mental. If they pass, they can attend a rigorous three-month training program, which includes initiation into the legal ramifications of making citizens' arrests, cardio-pulmonary resuscitation and first aid, as well as an upgrading of their martial arts experience. According to the founder, about half of the recruits are lost during the physical training program.

Recognizing that the Guardian Angels are brought to the cities through requests by the people themselves, city officials and police departments have taken a "wait and see" stance. In New York City officials feel that the fact that many of the Angels are "very poor kids" doing something positive makes them "worth taking a chance with." Among the supporters is a member of the US House of Representatives who welcomed the group to Washington, and invited them to set up a chapter in his home city.
Founded: 1979

NOT ON MY BLOCK
SEE DRUG ABUSE/ALCOHOLISM: DRUGS - CRIME WATCH

ROSIE'S PATROL
PO Box 306
Burke, VA 22015-0306
TEL: 703-978-5243
FAX: 703-451-9164
Purpose: To help stop the abduction of children; to help prevent offenses which make children victims; to promote child safety in the home.
Contact: Larry Stevens
Description: Rosie's Patrol is a community-based volunteer organization founded by the parents of a ten-year-old, *Rosie,* who was abducted from her neighborhood and later murdered in July 1989. Rosie's parents created *Rosie's Patrol,* a nonprofit corporation, to help prevent the recurrence of this hideous crime. The organization was named for *Rosie,* who was a very active member of her school's *Traffic Safety Patrol.* The members of *Rosie's Patrol* dedicate their efforts and accomplishments to the memory of *Rosie.* Their pledge is to initiate programs and activities that make neighborhoods and homes fun and safe for children. *Rosie's Patrol* has been officially endorsed by the *Fairfax County Board of Supervisors* and the *Fairfax County School Board* by separate resolutions.

Volunteer members work at the community level to promote and support activities and programs relating to children's safety. Organizationally, *Rosie's Patrol* operates at three levels: Board of Directors, action committees, and community chapters. At the present time there are three Chapters, all in Virginia: Burke, Stafford, and Prince William County.

Implementation Target Areas - The objectives of *Rosie's Patrol* are being accomplished by focusing on six implementation target areas, as follows:

- **Education:** Sponsor and support programs that teach child lures to neighborhood kids. Support the Fairfax County School Board *Ready Set Go for Good Health* program. Obtain and distribute child safety training materials. Review the product *Kids and Company* developed by the *National Center for Missing and Exploited Children.* Work with local *PTAs* to promote child safety training in the schools.

- **Community Programs:** Support and participate in established programs that promote child safety, including *Fairfax County Police Department* sponsored *Neighborhood Watch Program;* school sponsored *Block Parent Program;* local community *Block Rep Program, School Bus Stop Safety Program,* and *Safe Walk Program.*

- **Safety Awareness Activities:** Sponsor and support children's safety day programs such as local safety fairs, *Halloween Safety Day,* etc. Include guest appearances, media coverage, safety lectures, fingerprinting, videotaping, educational programs, distribution of safety literature, entertainment and snacks. Thus far, *Rosie's Patrol* has sponsored safety fairs, *Halloween Safety Day,* and community picnics.

- **Communication:** Establish rapport with the media (radio and TV). Export written *How To* literature. Establish a *Rosie's Patrol Computer Bulletin Board* (in process). Publish a *Rosie's Patrol* newsletter. Establish working relationships with outside resources and organizations with similar goals such as the *National Center for Missing and Exploited Children.*

Encourage the establishment of neighborhood telephone trees.

- **Legislation:** Monitor child abuse trials and seek tougher penalties for repeat offenders of child abuse laws. Research current laws, policies and procedures regarding child safety and take action to strengthen the weak areas. (Recently, two pieces of Virginia legislation were strengthened with the assistance of a Virginia Delegate who is a member of the *Rosie's Patrol* Board of Directors.) Work closely with the legal department of the *National Center for Missing and Exploited Children* to target legislation that needs to be strengthened.

- **Outreach:** Compile lists of child safety programs in Fairfax and surrounding counties and share the lists. Gather and disseminate child safety information. Document and export ideas and programs used by *Rosie's Patrol*. Speak to local organizations about *Rosie's Patrol* and child safety. Organize local chapters of *Rosie's Patrol*.

Operational Plan - The operational plan is to organize volunteers in the community to implement the programs, plans, and activities considered appropriate by the members in the community. Residents realize an immediate return on their investment of time because they are protecting their children and those of their neighbors. The program's motto, *Every adult is every child's guardian,* is a key to the concept of *Rosie's Patrol*. We believe that the community chapters of *Rosie's Patrol* are links that are closest to the children and therefore most effective. We also believe that the organizations and special interest groups concerned with the safety of children are also links. The *Rosie's Patrol* concept connects these links to form a strong chain.

Action Committees support the efforts of the community chapters. They also provide guidance and direction when appropriate. Additionally, *Rosie's Patrol* maintains contact with many community and national organizations that do much to deter the abduction and abuse of children. These organizations provide support and information to our cause.

Funding Sources - As of May 1990, *Rosie's Patrol* is operating with contributions received from community members at the time of *Rosie's* death. The organization only requires funds when it can't obtain materials and commodities for safety fairs from donations. Current plans call for the sale of T-shirts to increase available operating funds. This organization needs people's time, not their money.

Volunteer Participation - The *Rosie's Patrol* Board of Directors consists of twelve volunteers, who are the nucleus of the organization. The Board of Directors meets monthly.

The volunteer base consists of approximately 150 local citizens. However, no formal membership lists are maintained. *Rosie's Patrol* volunteers are parents, clergy members, teachers, teenagers, community leaders, and local business people giving their time and energy to the community. Many of them are also active in their *PTA, Block Mother* programs, community watch programs, scouting, school safety patrol, and church groups. The volunteers work with existing groups in their community to satisfy child safety needs. The activities of the volunteers are both formal and informal.

Informally, the volunteers practice child safety in their daily lives. This includes being observant of the needs of other children with whom they come in contact. *Formally,* volunteers participate in the six implementation target areas described above.

Summary - *Rosie's Patrol* volunteers believe there are many community and national organizations in existence that do much to deter the abduction and abuse of children and promote child safety. We view these organizations as links. However, we believe that the links need to be connected together to form a strong chain. We don't want to change or hinder the links; we only want to work with them so they can become a more unified force. We believe awareness and community action are the best protection we can give our children. We further believe that an active, organized community is a deterrent to criminals who prey on innocent children and will help to create a safe and enjoyable environment for our children.

Our motto, *Every adult is every child's guardian,* was created by *Rosie's* mother. It clearly summarizes our operating philosophy. There are many threats to child safety. If adults will modify their behavior slightly to include being more observant of children and their safety, we believe our objectives will be accomplished.

Publications: Rosie's Patrol Newsletter

SECURITY ALERT GROUP - THREE LINK TOWERS (SAG)
2427 Jefferson
Ogden, UT 84401
TEL: 801-399-4841

Purpose: To provide a secure, safe, crime free environment for 150 elderly residents at Three Link Towers, a low-income senior highrise located in downtown Ogden.

Sponsor: Three Link Towers

Contact: Frank Sturdevant

Description: The aging process is often accompanied by a lessening of abilities and opportunities. Many seniors experience limitations not only in physical capacity but social as well. Loneliness, limited finances, declining health, and restricted resources all contribute to deterioration among older people.

The reality of increasing crime is evident in our society. For the older American, this reality is coupled with fear and a sense of helplessness. Often older persons are victims of theft, harassment, vandalism and assault. The senior residents at Three Link Towers confronted the issue of crime and responded with vigor, ingenuity and tenacity. The inception of the SAG in March 1981 is a statement of self-help and commitment to minimizing criminal activity and delinquency in their neighborhood. This was the intent of the program, and subsequently has been the successful result of their efforts.

Although the participants of the SAG are low-income, many without family support, some with failing health, and all within the 64-81 age range, their energy and determination is remarkable. They have overcome age barriers and stereotypes and created an opportunity for themselves to contribute their human resources as well as provide a useful community service of crime deterrent and prevention.

The 26 volunteers in SAG serve as night watch-persons in two hour shifts beginning at 8:00 p.m. seven days a week. They patrol the parking lot, streets, and grounds surrounding their complex by observing unusual or suspicious activities from their balconies and windows. Criminals are scared away by shining flashlights on them. If property has been damaged or a crime has occurred, then the local police are summoned. However, this has happened only once since SAG was organized. Through the efforts of the SAG volunteers, crime has virtually been reduced to none.

The contribution to the community by the Security Alert Group has been seen as quite beneficial by the Ogden City Police Department. Due to the location of the highrise, Three Link Towers, in a downtown urban area, crime is a very real problem, and the volunteer effort of the SAG has succeeded in reducing the neighborhood crime rate. The 30 senior volunteers who are active in the SAG program have a sense of self-fulfillment in knowing they are significantly contributing their time and energy for improving the quality of life for themselves and fellow residents. The impact of the SAG activities specifically has diminished the residents' fear of crime and vandalism that so many seniors harbor, and the project positively affects the surrounding neighborhood in downtown Ogden. Accomplishments of the SAG have been in close alignment with the stated objectives of the project as initially outlined.

Founded: 1981

LAW ENFORCEMENT/CRIME PREVENTION: DOMESTIC ABUSE

NATIONAL/STATE ORGANIZATIONS

CHILD ABUSE HOTLINE
SEE RECIPIENTS: CHILDREN/YOUTH - PROTECTIVE SERVICES

NATIONAL CENTER ON CHILD ABUSE AND NEGLECT
SEE RECIPIENTS: CHILDREN/YOUTH - PROTECTIVE SERVICES

NATIONAL COMMITTEE FOR PREVENTION OF CHILD ABUSE
SEE RECIPIENTS: CHILDREN/YOUTH - PROTECTIVE SERVICES

PARENTS ANONYMOUS
6733 South Sepulveda
Suite 270
Los Angeles, CA 90045
TEL: 213-410-9732
Objectives: To provide a self-help setting for parents with problems related to all types of child abuse and neglect.
Services: Helps parents gain insight into their problems through weekly meetings in group settings by sharing fears and experiences with others - exchanging names and phone numbers to provide crisis contacts 24 hours a day (some chapters maintain a 24-hour hotline for this purpose); structures chapters to consist of a Chairperson, who is a parent and a member of the group, a sponsor (such as a social worker, psychologist or psychiatrist who serves as a nondirective support for the Chairperson), and a varying number of members (usually between four and ten); supports 24-hour hotlines when chapters install them to serve as information and referral points for information about chapters in a given metropolitan or rural area, and to give crisis counseling over the telephone to abusive and potentially abusive parents (members or non-members); convenes regional and national meetings.
Founded: 1970

TRAINING PROGRAMS

PARENT AIDE TRAINING
SEE RECIPIENTS: CHILDREN/YOUTH - PROTECTIVE SERVICES

INDIVIDUAL PROGRAM PROFILES

ABUSED ADULT RESOURCE CENTER (AARC)
SEE RECIPIENTS: FAMILIES - DOMESTIC ABUSE

BLOUNT COUNTY CHILDREN'S CENTER
SEE RECIPIENTS: CHILDREN/YOUTH - PROTECTIVE SERVICES

CHILD ABUSE SERVICES TEAM (CAST)
SEE RECIPIENTS: CHILDREN/YOUTH - PROTECTIVE SERVICES

COMMITTEE TO AID ABUSED WOMEN
SEE RECIPIENTS: FAMILIES - CRISIS INTERVENTION

DOMESTIC ABUSE PROJECT OF DELAWARE COUNTY
SEE RECIPIENTS: FAMILIES - CRISIS INTERVENTION

FAMILY CRISIS CENTER
SEE RECIPIENTS: FAMILIES - I&R

GOVERNOR'S ADVISORY COMMITTEE ON CHILD ABUSE AND NEGLECT/VA
SEE RECIPIENTS: CHILDREN/YOUTH - PROTECTIVE SERVICES

PARENT AIDE PROGRAM - CENTRALIZED SERVICE UNIT
SEE RECIPIENTS: FAMILIES - CRISIS INTERVENTION

PARENT-CHILD PROGRAM*
SEE TEENAGE PREGNANCY/PARENTING

PARENTAL STRESS CENTER
SEE TEENAGE PREGNANCY/PARENTING

RAINBOW SUNSHINE SCHOOL
SEE EDUCATION: HOMELESS

RAPE AND DOMESTIC VIOLENCE INFORMATION CENTER
SEE LAW ENFORCEMENT/CRIME PREVENTION: SEXUAL ABUSE

SAFE HOUSE
SEE RECIPIENTS: FAMILIES - CRISIS INTERVENTION

SCAN (SPOKANE CHILD ABUSE AND NEGLECT PREVENTION CENTER)
SEE RECIPIENTS: CHILDREN/YOUTH - PROTECTIVE SERVICES

WOMEN'S CENTER OF EAST TEXAS
SEE RECIPIENTS: FAMILIES - CRISIS INTERVENTION

WYANDOTTE HOUSE/NEUTRAL GROUND
SEE RECIPIENTS: CHILDREN/YOUTH - PROTECTIVE SERVICES

LAW ENFORCEMENT/CRIME PREVENTION: DRUGS/ALCOHOL

NATIONAL/STATE ORGANIZATIONS

ANTI-DRUG TEAMS
SEE DRUG ABUSE/ALCOHOLISM: DRUGS - CRIME WATCH

LAW ENFORCEMENT/CRIME PREVENTION: EDUCATION

NATIONAL/STATE ORGANIZATIONS

NATIONAL CENTER FOR COMMUNITY CRIME PREVENTION
PO Box 37456
Washington, DC 20013
TEL: 202-783-6215
Objectives: To administer a program of public education on community crime prevention.
Services: Works under the premise that crime prevention begins in the community with the responsibility shared by criminal justice practitioners and citizens; provides specialized and general training; develops related educational programs; conducts research and makes its findings available; provides general information and an advisory and technical assistance service to support and supplement community crime prevention programs; uses the resources of criminal justice practitioners, educators, and advisors to plan, develop, and implement community crime prevention programs; assists and encourages state and local governments in evaluating the status of their crime prevention standards; makes recommendations based on the government evaluations; publishes a newsletter, *We CAN Prevent Crime*, and other informative materials.
Publications: We CAN Prevent Crime

TRAINING PROGRAMS

CRIME, LAW AND COMMUNITY: A STUDENT SERVICE CURRICULUM
John F. Kennedy High School
Kennedy Drive
Plainview, NY 11803
TEL: 516-931-7280
Sponsor: New York State School System; National Crime Prevention Council
Contact: Dr. Richard Koubeck
Description: This course places community service in the political science curriculum. Students examine crime as a social phenomenon and study its impact on themselves and their classmates, combining this activity with the design of a project to improve community safety. This course fulfills the new *Participation in Government* requirement for graduating from New York State High Schools. The course includes:
Three-week Introduction - this period is used to introduce participants on how crime affects teens and their communities. The text, *Teens, Crime and the Community,* is used during this period.
Practical Application - These applications include four lessons which students can teach to elementary classes:
- *Latchkey Kids Alert* is taught to third graders with the help of *McGruff, the Crime Dog,* suggesting how nine- and ten-year-olds should act when they are at home without adult supervision.
- *Vandalism* is taught to fourth graders and shows how the consequences ripple throughout the community. It links with an existing fourth grade local studies syllabus.
- *Peer Pressure* is taught to fourth graders also, teaching positive peer pressure and effective ways to reject alcohol and other drugs.
- *Stoplift* is taught to sixth graders to show how shoplifting undermines a community.
The balance of the course for the high school volunteers includes

an examination of crime in America as a public policy problem. Students are encouraged to apply their studies to real action projects such as are mounted by the school's *Project Outreach.* The four applications in the course described above came from *Project Outreach,* a program in which JFK students work in the community to start neighborhood watch programs, teach crime prevention to elementary schoolers, and design and manage annual community *Discovery and Celebration Days,* a town meeting format and a street festival. Over 200 JFK students are active every year in this effort.
The process of using crime as a theme through three areas of learning - personal consequences, teaching others, and community and public policy - has resulted in instruction which meets the state's requirements as well as the students' needs to be part of their community's political process.

FORGING PARTNERSHIPS*
National Association of Volunteers in Criminal Justice
PO Box 6365
University, AL 35486-6365
TEL: 205-348-6738
Credit: CEUs; AVA Certification (partial fulfillment); academic credit through University of Alabama; Alabama Board of Social Work Seminars CEUs; and/or Alabama Department of Youth In-service Credit
Sponsor: National Association of Volunteers in Criminal Justice
Contact: David Gooch
Description: Designed as a working conference, the program features workshops, discussions, idea exchanges, speeches and informal gatherings for volunteer managers, volunteer administrators, agency administrators and judges, line staff who work with volunteers, and others interested in crime prevention. Specific topics include:
Workshop Session I:
- Cost and Payoffs for Agencies Using Volunteers
- What's It Like in Prison?
- Victim/Witness Assistance
- Volunteers: To Support or Supplant?
Workshop Session II:
- Private Sector Involvement
- Mobilizing and Maintaining Christian Church Volunteer Resources for In-Prison and After Care Ministry
- Working Effectively with Boards
Workshop Session III:
- Volunteers: Have You Had Your Check-Up Lately?
- Certification: Who Needs It? Who Owns It?
- The Line Staff as a Supervisor of Volunteers
Workshop Session IV:
- Grant-Writing I
- Marketing Your Volunteer Program
- Getting Along with Agency Personnel
- Alternatives to Secure Detention
- Volunteer Responses to Rural Crime
- Volunteers and Cops
Workshop Session V:
- Public Speaking/Platform Skills
- Grant-Writing II
- Working with Today's Adolescent
- Is Theology Important to a Christian Volunteer Counselor?
This conference aims through the above sessions to lead participants to new ways of forging partnerships between the private sector and public agencies, neighborhoods and law enforcers, citizen volunteers and paid professionals, voluntary organizations and criminal justice systems, and other potential teams that can accomplish more by working together than separately; publishes conference proceedings for wider exposure to the ideas generated at the conference.

FORUM 90: PRE-CONFERENCE AGENDA (TENTATIVE)
Volunteers in Prevention, Probation, Prisons
527 North Main Street
Royal Oak, MI 48067
TEL: 313-398-8550
Credit: Inquire
Sponsor: International Association of Justice Volunteerism
Contact: Conference Coordinator
Description: This is the first conference jointly sponsored by the *International Association of Justice Volunteerism (IAJV)* and *Volunteers in Prevention, Probation and Prisons.* Their combined resources has enabled a diverse slate of workshops drawing on the unique experience of each organization, covering the following and other topics in a series of formal workshops:
- Ex-Prostitutes as Volunteers
- Church Networks as a Source of Volunteers
- Myths and Realities of Criminal Justice Policies
- Dispute Resolution
- Substance Abuse, Communicable Diseases and Youth Subcultures - Education, Treatment and Trends
- Psychology for Success
- When You Speak, Do People Listen?
- Administration of Court Volunteer Programs
- Leadership for Staff and Volunteers
- Pornography
- Teaching Life Management Skills to Criminal Justice Clients

Two pre-conference opportunities were: *I. Pre-Forum 90 Justice Volunteer Management Training Institute* and *II. Pre-Forum 90 Religious Volunteer Institute.* In addition to the issue-oriented workshops above, broader areas were explored, including:

101 Volunteers in Law Enforcement - which builds on the English theme, "people are the police and the police are the people."
102 Networking & the Religious Volunteer - a participatory workshop with small groups developing case studies.
103 Fun & Games for Changing Lives - which describes therapeutic recreational programs in prisons for severely handicapped inmates in mental health programs.
104 So You Want to Be An Author? or a Public Speaker? or Become a Certified Volunteer Manager? - which focuses on writing, public speaking, and certification.
105 Together We Can Make it Work: Developing a Partnership Between the Public and Private Sector - which details the role of government working in cooperation with the private sector.
201 Substance Abuse - Alcohol, Illegal Street Drugs and Legal Drugs - which cites the 45-85 percent of violent and non-violent crimes that were committed by persons under the influence of alcohol or other drugs.
202 Communicable Diseases - AIDS, Hepatitis, and Tuberculosis - which discusses the apprehension of justice personnel, inmates, volunteers, and others about working with people with some communicable diseases.
203 Youth Subcultures - Trends, Identification, Prevention/Intervention - which discusses major trends relating to gangs, skinheads and the satanic occult.
302 Games People Play - which examines the dilemma for the volunteer when juvenile clients don't keep appointments, refuse to communicate, etc.
303 Administration & Management of Court Volunteer Programs - which provides the "How To's" of a successful local court program.
304 Separation, Loss and Grief - which helps participants understand various kinds of loss.
305 Screening Volunteers for Child Sexual Abuse prior to Agency Assignment - which teaches interviewing techniques for screening volunteers for work with children.
401 A Backward Glance: Ex-Offenders/Family Members Now Serving as Volunteers - which offers insights into the lives of those who are now serving others.
402 A Forward Vision: Are Volunteers a Valuable Alternative to Building More Prisons? - which addresses the 30-35 percent of prisoners who may not need incarceration.
403 A Nostalgic View or Futuristic Vision: Are Justice Volunteers Worth It? - which reviews where we have been, what problems remain, and what the future is for justice volunteer efforts.
501 Leadership of Staff and Volunteers - which uses a model to demonstrate the dynamics of leadership.
502 How to Work with Angry Clients: A Focus on Offenders - which addresses *Rational Behavior Therapy* used with offenders and school dropouts.
503/1 Recruiting & Using 12-step Volunteers and **503/2 The Prison-Ashram Project: We're All Doing Time** - which are two mini-workshops on "anonymous" volunteers, and growth skills.
504 National Issues Forum - a presentation describing the *National Issues Forum Program* which is in 1300 cities.

As in past years, three individuals who exemplify the volunteer spirit through their daily contributions to justice volunteerism are honored durng the course of the Forum. These are *Justice Volunteer of the Year, Outstanding Contributor to Justice Volunteerism,* and *Creative Criminal Justice Program.* Guest speakers, various exhibits, time for networking, a silent auction, and other events are included in the program.
Publications: Conference Proceedings

FOUNDATION FOR SUCCESS*
National Association of Volunteers in Criminal Justice
PO Box 6365
University, AL 35486
TEL: 205-348-6738
Credit: CEUs; AVA Certification (partial fulfillment); inquire about others
Contact: David Gooch
Description: This Forum focuses on building a foundation for the successful continuation of services through "more effective use of people, dollars and power." The Forum brings together professionals and volunteers who are committed to improvement of the criminal justice system through citizen involvement. The Conference features workshops, speeches, discussions, idea exchanges, and informal gatherings. Many workshops are tailored to specific groups, such as volunteer managers, volunteer administrators, agency administrators and judges, line staff who work with volunteers and others. Speakers address current topics. Presenters, selected for relevance to volunteerism in the criminal justice field, lead workshops such as:
- Advanced volunteer management workshops;
- Service Skills Improvement for Volunteers;
- Workshops for agency administrators and judges;
- Workshops focusing on crime prevention and law enforcement;
- Concentrated workshops on the basics of volunteer management;
- Workshops designed for professional line staff; and
- Workshop sessions dealing with important issues facing justice volunteerism.

In addition to topics such as criminal justice program models, organizing and working within the political process, volunteer management skills, and fundraising, the Forum features a networking laboratory to give participants the maximum opportunity to meet with other persons from around the country to share information and ideas. A limited number of scholarships are awarded.

INTRODUCTION TO VOLUNTEERISM IN THE JUVENILE JUSTICE SYSTEM (SOCIOLOGY 195: WX AND WX2)
Old Dominion University
Arts and Letters 234
5201 Hampton Boulevard
Norfolk, VA 23508
TEL: 703-489-6546
Credit: 3 hours

Sponsor: Old Dominion University
Contact: Laurie Di Padova
Description: This full-semester course uses four textbooks: *A Handbook for Volunteers in Juvenile Court, The Crime of Punishment, The Throwaway Children,* and *Children as Victims of Institutionalization* and, for the introductory session, the film, *Children in Trouble,* with numerous cassettes and other audiovisuals throughout the course. Weekly course topics include:
- Introduction to Volunteerism in America
- An Overview of the Criminal Justice System
- A Child Goes Through the System
- Problems Juveniles Face (three weekly parts)
- Involvement of Volunteers and Their Impact
- The Volunteer-Client Relationship
- Counseling Techniques
- The Community and the Juvenile Justice System

All sessions use audiovisuals and guest instructors to supplement course content. Field trips are used frequently also as a supplement for advanced students, including destinations such as:
- Hampton House
- Tidewater Detention Home
- Regional Girls' Home
- Pendleton Project
- Richmond Diagnostic Center
- Stanhope House
- Juvenile Crisis Center
- Youth Bureau
- Norfolk Detention Home
- Norfolk Juvenile and Domestic Relations Court (Volunteer Office)
- Probation Field Unit (Arranged by Court Volunteer Office)
- A facility dealing with juveniles selected by the student

A mid-term test and a take-home final exam determine the semester grade. The course may be taken by volunteers who are not full-time Old Dominion students with approval from course instructors.

PROBLEMS FACING VOLUNTEER LEADERS TODAY*

National Association of Volunteers in Criminal Justice
PO Box 6365
University, AL 35486
TEL: 205-348-6738
Credit: Inquire
Contact: David Gooch
Description: This Forum addresses problems facing volunteer leaders today, such as:
- a diminishing tax base from which to operate;
- an ever-increasing need for service from the local community.

The conference is structured so that concerned citizens, paid professionals, and offenders can work together to seek solutions to these problems as they relate to volunteerism and criminal justice. Forum Workshops progress from a person-to-person format to group discussion sessions, as follows:

Person-to-Person Skill Building
- Games Clients Play
- Fulfilling Your Obligations
- Dealing with Significant Others in the Life of a Client
- Introduction to Reality Therapy
- Introduction to Rational Emotive Training
- Crisis Intervention Counseling
- Group Leadership Skills
- Volunteers Working with Sexual Offenders
- The Client Speaks on Volunteerism
- Volunteer-Client: Dealing with Differences in Sex, Age, Role, Race and Goals
- Ex-Offender's Perspective on Corrections Volunteer Ministry

Adapting Programs
- Advocacy for Change - Developing a Win/Win Relationship
- Volunteer Directors: Managers or Doers?

- Presentence Investigation Volunteers
- Building Staff Support for Volunteers
- Time Management
- Surviving the Bureaucracy
- The Volunteer Orientation Manual - How to write it - How to use it
- Rural Volunteerism

Skills for Managers
- Basic Training in the Administration of Volunteer Services
- Training Tools of the Trade
- Matching and Assigning Volunteers
- Planned Recognition of Paid Staff Working with Volunteers
- Developing and Maintaining Effective Advisory Boards
- Performance Plans in a Volunteer Program
- Advanced Training in the Administration of Volunteer Services
- Where Do You Begin? Starting a Volunteer Program
- Dealing with Burnout
- Recruiting from the Church Community

Current Issues
- Survival and Growth for Volunteer Agencies
- Child Abuse: Ramifications and Manifestations
- How to Make Your Program Integral Rather Than Ancillary
- How to Set Up a State Association on Criminal Justice Volunteerism
- Does Sharing Your Faith Fit Into Criminal Justice Volunteerism?

Justice Volunteerism Discussion Sessions
- Adult Diversion
- Adult Courts and Probation
- Adult Institutions
- Adult Parole
- Juvenile Diversion
- Juvenile Courts and Probation
- Juvenile Institutions
- Juvenile Parole

Mid-conference, The National Coalition of Christian Volunteers in Criminal Justice (NCCVCJ) hosted a prayer breakfast for criminal justice professionals and volunteers. At the close of the conference, the Coalition hosted a two-day post-conference retreat for interested participants.
Presenters for both NAVCJ and NCCVCJ include experts in the corrections field, a former governor and other nationally-known authorities with an interest in the relationship between the criminal justice field and the volunteer community.

VOLUNTEER PROGRAM EFFICIENCY IN A DOWN-SIDED ECONOMY*

National Association of Volunteers in Criminal Justice
PO Box 6365
University, AL 35486
TEL: 205-348-6738
Credit: Inquire
Contact: David Gooch
Description: This workshop is based on the premise that programs utilizing citizen input and services are just too valuable to cut, and - if well managed - can remain an integral part of the organization in the years ahead. It hopes to demonstrate to individuals who are developing and maintaining volunteer efforts that the challenge of the decade and its down-sided economy is not to make decisions as to which program to cut... which to keep... which to give priority... which to simply maintain... but to learn to cope with new challenges while continuing to reach for set goals and agency success.
In this workshop, two factors are explored which are considered of ongoing importance in any effort, but crucial in a down-sided economy if the manager is to maximize program efficiency and effectiveness. These are the factors, as described by workshop leaders:

● **First,** it becomes very critical that dynamic techniques and methods which influence program results be understood by the manager. This will equip the manager for stronger leadership, enhancing the methods and quality of services rendered through unpaid staff.

● **Second,** it is important that volunteer administrators understand their own individual management STYLE, and how that style directly affects program results and people. Research tells us that decisive leadership is the most critical variable in achieving overall organizational success.

Repeated in three strategically selected cities, the locations and dates were carefully chosen to facilitate maximum convenience for participants. Workshop faculty includes Ivan Scheier, international consultant on volunteerism, and John Stoeckel, Executive Director of the National Association of Volunteers in Criminal Justice.

INDIVIDUAL PROGRAM PROFILES

A, B, AND C ON BURGLARY
Franconia District Citizens Advisory Committee
c/o William Urick, Chairman
9453 Park Hunt Court
Springfield, VA 22153
TEL: 703-455-1567
Purpose: To educate the public about precautions against burglary through panel presentations by convicted burglars.
Sponsor: Franconia Police Department; Franconia District Citizens Advisory Committee
Contact: William Urick
Description: Three convicted burglars awaiting sentencing volunteered to make a presentation to a citizens group on "burglary through the eyes of the pros." They called themselves "A, B and C" and together were responsible for 150 to 160 burglaries in the Washington, DC area. During the questioning that followed the 90-minute, hard-hitting, mocking presentation, not one of the 250 citizens questioned the volunteers' credentials. Concerned about Fairfax County's latest burglary statistics, the Advisory Committee put the program together with the help of police officials. From January to April of the current year, 2,446 burglaries (759 more than in the same period of the previous year) were reported countywide.
Most of the audience consisted of older residents who listened intently and took notes as A, B and C spun their tales of criminal intrigue and gave tips on how to deter burglars like themselves. The panelists did offer some surprises that had an ironic twist - two of them said that their own homes were burglarized while they were in jail. Basic information and advice offered included:

● Be wary of servicemen who make repairs at home. Forty percent of the time service people can give their friends information, or unbolt windows themselves and send someone else back to make the pickup.

● Many non-service people (burglars) dress in dark blue service uniforms and move freely among homes in the daytime.

● Take special precautions when leaving home on winter evenings between five and nine. This period is considered "prime time" because it gets dark at five in winter, and no one sits home with all the lights out.

● Limit open windows and curtains. Burglars "window shop" in neighborhoods looking for valuables. Many are experienced enough to see the "dollar signs" at a single quick glance, and the house goes on a list of prospects.

● Burglars now seek gold and silver items rather than the televisions and stereos previously sought.

The above is a sampling of tips provided by the volunteer burglars. Others are available through the sponsors above.
Citizens in the audience expressed appreciation for the program, many having note pads with several pages of notes. The information most frequently mentioned in a discussion after the

program was the description of how burglars obtained tips from - and actually collaborated with - some repairmen.
The only dissenting note on this unique volunteer program was tendered by the local Deputy Sheriff. Since two of the three volunteer inmates were black, he felt that a stereotype could develop among citizens. However, he told the group, "Your idea is a good one and, with more advanced planning - especially to reach more people - this one program could go a long way to eliminate the burglary problem in the county."
Founded: 1981

CORRECTIONAL MINI-COURSES
Connecticut Department of Corrections
Volunteer Services
90 Brainard Road
Hartford, CT 06104
TEL: 203-566-3685; 203-566-2503
FAX: 203-566-2195
Purpose: To provide programming training for pre-trial inmates.
Sponsor: Connecticut Department of Corrections
Contact: Doug Kulmacz, Director
Description: Recognizing the fact that pre-trial people are considered innocent until proven guilty, the Connecticut Department of Corrections developed a program that is not "rehabilitative" in nature, but provides a school experience for men held in pre-trial detention at the Bridgeport Community Correctional Center.
Planners of the training program were faced with a unique set of circumstances with this group of inmates. Many are in and out within a few hours, most are adjudicated within a few weeks, and all but a handful are gone within 120 days of their admission. The Center had become a place to wait and look for diversion. With the options of providing only passive, time-passing diversions like television and games, or offering constructive outlets that stimulate the individual, rechannel some of his thinking, and open new vistas for him, the Center chose the latter. This option was used as the foundation for a series of mini-courses designed expressly for the individual in short-term confinement.
To enlist volunteers and others as teachers, the planners based their recruitment efforts on the premise that almost anyone holds some kind of occupational or avocational knowledge that others do not have, and can offer a unique teaching experience. They placed more importance on the desire to share what one knows than on the holding of a college degree. The spirit should be interesting, but a final quiz is not mandatory. In many cases, the presentation is an introduction to the subject rather than a course in the mastery of it. Given the short space of time, this serves well to stimulate participants, since more detailed courses cannot be completed in most cases, and therefore tends to cause frustration.
Guidelines set by the planners include:

● Can the subject be introduced in four to six sessions?

● Can one make the topic alive and interesting to a group of 10-15 men whose average age is 21-23?

● Can the mini-course be designed so that no equipment for the learner is needed?

● Can one make a mini-course interesting to the most reluctant learner?

In relation to the above guidelines, cassette recorders are often provided to facilitate learning, but not as an indication of equipment that might be needed after the student has left the facility. Also, the range of possible topics is very broad. In addition to the 35 volunteers involved, resident teachers help plan and schedule courses, announce the courses, describe them to newly admitted persons, enroll interested participants, have equipment ready when instructors and students arrive, etc.
Planners emphasize that the challenge of teaching in a correctional setting is the same as in any school or community setting. Due to the nature of the setting, however, classrooms are within close observational range of correctional officer posts, with officers

immediately available to deal with any difficult classroom situation. No such problems have been encountered to date in the program.

LITERACY INCENTIVE PROGRAM (NO READ, NO RELEASE)
SEE LITERACY

LAW ENFORCEMENT/CRIME PREVENTION: EMPLOYMENT

NATIONAL/STATE ORGANIZATIONS

OPERATION CHILD WATCH
SEE RECIPIENTS: CHILDREN/YOUTH - PROTECTIVE SERVICES

INDIVIDUAL PROGRAM PROFILES

DATA SYSTEMS UNLIMITED
SEE EMPLOYMENT: HANDICAPPED

JOB THERAPY, INC. (EX-OFFENDER PROGRAM: PROJECT START)*
SEE EMPLOYMENT: PRISONER/EX-OFFENDER

LAW ENFORCEMENT/CRIME PREVENTION: FACILITIES

NATIONAL/STATE ORGANIZATIONS

NATIONAL CLEARINGHOUSE FOR CRIMINAL JUSTICE PLANNING AND ARCHITECTURE
505 East Green Street
Suite 200
Champaign, IL 61820
TEL: 217-333-0312
Objectives: To demonstrate the various ways in which the correctional program is inextricably involved in the design of the physical facility.
Services: Serves as a specialized clearinghouse to provide information based on its research in the area set out in the above objective; publishes *The High Cost of Building Unconstitutional Jails* and other materials to assist concerned citizens in corrections programs.
Publications: High Cost of Building Jails

NATIONAL PRISON PROJECT
American Civil Liberties Union
1616 P Street, NW
Suite 340
Washington , DC 20036
TEL: 202-331-0500
Objectives: To strengthen and protect the rights of adult and juvenile offenders; to improve overall conditions in correctional facilities; to develop alternatives to incarceration.

Services: Handles and assists others in handling litigation; drafts model legislation on rights of offenders; provides information to legislative bodies on request; develops self-help materials for incarcerated persons; coordinates activities of other organizations in the field; serves as a resource center and clearinghouse; develops model institution and regulations, and model pleadings and other legal papers; trains law students and other attorneys; develops materials to keep the public informed; conducts periodic conferences.
Publications: Prison Project Journal; Prisoners Assistance Directory
Founded: 1972

LAW ENFORCEMENT/CRIME PREVENTION: FAMILIES

INDIVIDUAL PROGRAM PROFILES

VAN MINISTRY
Community Family Life Services
First Trinity Lutheran Church
309 E Street, NW
Washington, DC 20001
TEL: 703-256-5776 (ACCA)
Purpose: To take people to visit prisoners who otherwise might have no visitors.
Sponsor: First Trinity Lutheran Church; Annandale Christian Community for Action
Contact: Ted Gleiter, ACCA Liaison
Description: The Van Ministry began in 1979 with the purchase of a 15-passenger van for use in taking people to visit in prisons. Nearly 100 women from the metropolitan area are incarcerated 300 miles away in the federal prison at Alderson, West Virginia. Most of them rarely, if ever, get a visitor. Donations were requested from individuals and groups to obtain the $8,000 needed for the first van purchase.
As the program progressed it became apparent that there was a need to transport visitors to Virginia State prisons also - Southampton, Goochland, Powhatan, Richmond, and Buckingham. In August 1980 a second van was purchased, and weekend trips to the Virginia prisons were scheduled. Also the two vans were utilized on weekdays by senior citizen groups and by the ACCA churches as well.
Due to difficulty in obtaining liability insurance, it was decided to relinquish ownership of the two vans after July 1, 1985. One van was transferred to First Trinity Lutheran Church in Washington, DC, with their agreement to continue the prison visitation trips. The second van was sold.
While ACCA no longer conducts the Van Ministry, it continues to contribute funds for the service that is now being carried on by the Community Family Life Services outreach program. Also, ACCA supplies drivers for the prison trips. The following services are currently being offered:
- **Alderson (WV) Federal Women's Prison** - A six-hour trip, with visitors departing Saturday morning and returning Sunday evening.
- **Lewisburg Federal Prison for Men at Lewisburg, Pennsylvania** - A 3-1/2-hour trip, departing Saturday morning and returning the same day.

Riders donate $15.00 each, but this covers only a fraction of the cost.
Founded: 1979

VISITOR HOSPITALITY CENTER*
308 Read Street
Santa Fe, NM 87501
TEL: 505-827-8235
Purpose: To facilitate visitation among inmates at the state penitentiary and their families and friends by assisting the visitors.
Sponsor: United Way
Contact: Pat Powel
Description: Research shows that visitation and continued contact with friends/family are the most important factors contributing to the reduction in recidivism rates for individuals in penal institutions. The Visitor Hospitality Center was established to encourage more frequent visiting by making visits easier for families.
The Center provides a place to relax in a home-like atmosphere for the periods before or after entering the penitentiary to visit. Volunteers lend a shoulder to cry on or listen to problems, and give visitors an outlet to vent emotion. Childcare is available while adults relax, and children can be left at the Center if adults prefer visiting alone. Staff work with visitors helping them understand penitentiary rules, or intercede with prison personnel when various problems arise.
Volunteer Staff - Approximately 15 volunteers donate from three to five hours per week at the Center. One paid staff person is available during operating hours. Volunteers talk to visitors and make them feel welcome, give them a light refreshment, listen to problems. If a problem does arise, volunteers try to find solutions that are workable both with the visitor and the prison staff. Volunteers provide child care throughout the day.
Volunteer Duties - In addition to the above, volunteers answer the phones and sometimes try to get messages from family members to inmates. An accurate list of service agencies is maintained, and volunteers often try to put family members in touch with someone who can assist them with a variety of needs. When visitors are having transportation problems, volunteers try to obtain rides for them. Volunteers are also responsible for maintaining the Center - keeping it clean and pleasant.
Volunteer Experience - Volunteers are accepted from all types of background. One of the main characteristics looked for in the screening process, however, is that volunteers be accepting and non-judgmental. Volunteers at VHC must be calm and be able to maintain their poise under pressure. Many times situations arise that call for a controlled ability to make decisions and function in spite of the fact that other people have become overly agitated and excited.
Approximately 175 adults and children utilize the facilities of VHC each week. Volunteers must arrive at the Center ready to accept whatever occurs.
Other sponsors include US/ACTION and the Governor's Office of Volunteer Services.

LAW ENFORCEMENT/CRIME PREVENTION: FUNDING

NATIONAL/STATE ORGANIZATIONS

LAW ENFORCEMENT ASSISTANCE PROGRAM
SEE LAW ENFORCEMENT/CRIME PREVENTION

YOUTH AS RESOURCES
National Crime Prevention Council
733 15th Street, NW, Suite 540
Washington, DC 20005
TEL: 202-393-7141
FAX: 202-638-2928

Objectives: To develop young people's stake and role in the community through sponsorship of youth volunteer efforts.
Services: Funding of youth volunteer efforts in school-based programs was generated by the belief of the *National Crime Prevention Council (NCPC)* that the best way to steer youth in the direction of good citizenship is to involve them in meaningful activities that meet the needs of the community. Some of these programs are funded by the *Lilly Foundation* through NCPC. Others receive guidance from NCPC, but find local foundations or other funding sources.
The program is open to any city. The procedure requires a board of community leaders and youth to head up the program, advertise for and screen proposals, vote on the grants (from $100 to $5,000) to be awarded to host agencies including, but not limited to, schools. The board also monitors the grantees' projects and provides recognition to project participants.
One unique strength of the program is that it is based in the community proper with the youth involved ranging from dropouts to Honor Society members, and from nonjoiners to class and school leaders. Although they may work with adults, the grant requires that the youth themselves develop and manage the projects. Each project is based in the community, although it draws from a wide range of secondary schools and the community at large. The project is based on the premise that teen-operated projects will help the young people grow and learn, and become assets to their communities.
Sponsor: Lilly Foundation

LAW ENFORCEMENT/CRIME PREVENTION: I&R

NATIONAL/STATE ORGANIZATIONS

US/DOJ - NATIONAL CRIMINAL JUSTICE REFERENCE SERVICE
National Institutes of Justice
1600 Research Blvd, Box 6000
Rockville , MD 20850
TEL: 301-251-5500
Objectives: To further the exchange of information with the goal of improving law enforcement and criminal justice.
Services: Identifies and screens publications and audiovisual materials that will meet the criteria of the service - "to increase the understanding of causes and effects of crime, prevention of crime, and operations of the criminal justice system;" responds to individual reference queries by conducting computer searches of its data base; publishes *Selected Notification of Information (SNI)* announcements to subscribers listing new acquisitions and providing an order form; publishes a series of bibliographies on specific subjects; operates a document loan program with a loan period of four weeks (interlibrary loan system through any library in the U.S. or Canada); provides free microfiche copies of out-of-print or one-of-a-kind documents; maintains a Share Package Program which loans materials prepared by other organizations in the form of newsletters, brochures, posters, etc.
Publications: Selected Notification of Information

LAW ENFORCEMENT/CRIME PREVENTION: LEGAL RIGHTS

NATIONAL/STATE ORGANIZATIONS

PRISON FELLOWSHIP MINISTRIES
PO Box 17500
Washington, DC 20041
TEL: 703-478-0100
Objectives: To work for a just and effective criminal justice system by involving volunteers and the resources of the church.
Services: Builds volunteer community Care Committees by working with local churches; mobilizes resources for prisoners, ex-offenders and their families; offers proposals for the improvement of the criminal justice system; consults with local, state and political leaders, judges and correctional officials regarding these proposals, which advocate a more just system that would better control crime, save taxes, and aid victims, while employing punishments which minimize destructive long-term imprisonment and promote positive change; publishes *Is There a Better Way: A Perspective on American Prisons* and other materials.
Publications: Jubilee; Justice Report; Is There A Better Way?
Founded: 1976

INDIVIDUAL PROGRAM PROFILES

PARKING POSSE
SEE RECIPIENTS: HANDICAPPED - LEGAL RIGHTS

LAW ENFORCEMENT/CRIME PREVENTION: OFFENDERS

INDIVIDUAL PROGRAM PROFILES

ECO
Energy Committed to Offenders
PO Box 33533
Charlotte, NC 28233
TEL: 704-374-0571
Purpose: To serve inmates, their families and ex-offenders returning from prison.
Sponsor: Private non-profit organization receiving funds from several sources
Contact: James H. Plumley, Director
Description: ECO, Inc. (Energy Committed to Offenders) began as a grass roots effort approximately 10 years ago. It was a direct result of a VISTA project that was sponsored by the N.C. Department of Corrections. It was incorporated in 1974 and since has had, as its main goal, employment of people returning from serving time in the state prison system. ECO is funded by private foundation money, church and membership local support, United Way, and 2 federal grants.
Volunteers work mainly in the family support section of the program, helping with visitation and other projects. These volunteers come from family members themselves and a long range goal is to enable them to gain more control over their situation (i.e. become better acquainted and involved with policies and procedures). In addition volunteers travel to the prisons and work with the half-way house.
Founded: 1974

LAW ENFORCEMENT/CRIME PREVENTION: OLDER PERSON

NATIONAL/STATE ORGANIZATIONS

OLDER ADULT OFFENDER PROJECT
SEE EMPLOYMENT: PRISONER/EX-OFFENDER

INDIVIDUAL PROGRAM PROFILES

MARTIAL ARTS FOR SENIORS
Good Hope Senior Center
1400 Fenwick Lane
Silver Spring , MD 20910
TEL: 301-565-7613
Purpose: To help senior citizens both protect themselves and strengthen their bodies.
Sponsor: Montgomery County Department of Recreation
Contact: Senior Program Coordinator
Description: The *Montgomery County Department of Recreation* and the Montgomery Chapter branch of *World Classic Martial Arts* cosponsor a martial arts program for senior citizens. The purpose of the program is not only to give older persons a means of protecting themselves, but also to encourage physical fitness. Twenty senior citizens signed up for the first session in early 1990. The martial art used is *tae kwon do,* which dates back to 37 B.C. It is one of the martial arts that can be done by anyone, according to the instructor. The purpose of the program was to demonstrate that senior citizens can do it. "If they learn just a small amount of self defense, it would help them feel more comfortable," he said. Initially, two of the simpler moves were taught - how to flex and exercise hand muscles to have enough force to poke out the eyes of an attacker, and how to flex and strengthen back and shoulder muscles to have enough strength to break away from an assailant. Stretching exercises (kibons) were introduced to improve power, balance and timing.
Senior volunteers who are experienced - often black belts - are brought in to demonstrate their proficiency in the art form to the group. They talk about the benefits the art has brought to them including controlling stress. "Aside from the physical, which everyone knows it is, it helps you mentally," according to one of the older volunteer demonstrators.
The program was initiated when officials in the *Department of Recreation* felt that "the elderly residents could use a little help while out on the area's sometimes mean streets." The instructor added, "Tae kwon do, as opposed to aerobics, is never boring." Regular 45-minute classes are scheduled at the Center.

LAW ENFORCEMENT/CRIME PREVENTION: PARENTS

INDIVIDUAL PROGRAM PROFILES

AID TO INCARCERATED MOTHERS
88 Tremont Street
Boston, MA 02108
TEL: 617-523-5856
Purpose: To help incarcerated mothers meet their parental responsibilities.
Contact: Jean Fox, Executive Director

Description: This program matches incarcerated mothers with volunteers in order to provide friendship and advocacy. The goal is to help the mothers meet their parental responsibilities by providing them with the necessary information, resources, and support to do so. Volunteers furnish transportation for family visits, and help mothers learn self-help advocacy skills and their legal rights. Post-release support services are an integral part of the program in helping mothers make the transition back to the community.

Program leaders and volunteers work to make the social services, the prison system, and the public more aware and responsive to incarcerated mothers' needs.

In addition to directly working with the mothers, volunteers speak to community groups, organizations and schools in the community and, occasionally, in other states; maintain a number of programs, including community outreach, family support and advocacy, volunteers, and transportation; information developed by the program is made available on request to groups nationwide; the program publishes a newsletter three times a year.

Publications: Staying Together

LAW ENFORCEMENT/CRIME PREVENTION: RE-ENTRY

NATIONAL/STATE ORGANIZATIONS

OFFENDER AID AND RESTORATION
OAR/USA
918 F Street, NW
Suite 500
Washington, DC 20004
TEL: 202-638-2830
Objectives: To bring volunteers into the lives of prisoners and ex-prisoners in community jails.
Services: Works with prisoners and ex-prisoners who may be experiencing, or have recently experienced, incarceration for the first time, is probably a member of the community where the violation occurred, and who may welcome the opportunity to work with a volunteer to return to the community as a productive citizen; functions through volunteers who make weekly visits to the jail, help ex-prisoners find employment, rise above arrest and poverty, help offenders to identify their skills, provide tutoring services, and offer general support; refers certain offenders to an alternative sentencing program to work out restitution through community service (OAR has seven Community Service Programs for this purpose); works to eliminate money bonds on the premise that it violates the constitutional provision "presumed innocent until proven guilty."
Operates Dispute Mediation Programs at three of the OAR sites; supplies technical assistance to state government on sentencing reform and the overuse of incarceration; convenes national forum each fall to exchange ideas and hear from specialists on subjects such as using senior citizens as volunteers, and counseling the families of offenders; holds an annual OAR congress each spring with two representatives from every site; publishes manuals for volunteers and materials for public information.
Publications: OAR Report
Founded: 1969

INDIVIDUAL PROGRAM PROFILES

COURT EMPLOYMENT PROJECT (*formerly Manhattan Court Employment Project*)
346 Broadway
New York, NY 10013
TEL: 212-732-0076
Purpose: To provide alternative sentencing and employment opportunities to young offenders (14-21).
Contact: Maximo Blake, Executive Director
Description: This program of the *New York City Criminal and Supreme Courts* offers services to young offenders (14-21) designed to decrease or eliminate recidivism, and return them to their community with a better future. One part of the program provides alternative sentencing to social welfare programs for pre-trial detainees and defendants facing 90-day sentences or felony convictions. In addition, individual, family, group, health, and vocational counseling are offered, followed by career development and job training or academic placement. Courses in preparation for the GED certificate are conducted, and referral to community social service agencies for additional assistance is made as needed. The program also offers paid work experience and training in light building renovation, including painting and carpentry through a general contracting business operated by the program.
Founded: 1967

FEMALE OFFENDER REHABILITATION PROGRAM
SEE EMPLOYMENT: PRISONER/EX-OFFENDER

GRATERFRIENDS
Graterford State Correctional Institution
Bridge Street
Graterford, PA 19426
TEL: 215-489-4151
Purpose: To bring together senior citizens from the community and older offenders about to be released from prison.
Sponsor: Graterford Prison
Contact: Joan Gauker
Description: Graterford Prison's Concerned Senior Group and members of the North Penn Senior Center in the community meet regularly to socialize and prepare for the day that the older offenders will become neighbors of the volunteer seniors from the community. The two groups of seniors sit across from one another in a dismal prison meeting room. Their common bonds of age and humanity quickly bring them through awkward beginnings into easy conversation and laughter.
For the alloted hour and a half, the talk between older folks in brown prison uniforms and folks in street clothing zigzagged through serious concerns for senior citizen safety, spontaneous humor, remembrances of past days, future hopes, hobbies and interests.
Through the many meetings that take place at Graterford Prison, incarcerated seniors and the older volunteers formulate new strategies to help communities to reduce crime against seniors on the street.
According to one observer, "If nothing else emerges from these gatherings, one thing is clear - these folks will be good neighbors - as if there were no concrete wall between them."

HOUSTON EX-OFFENDER PROGRAM
National Alliance of Business/Houston
3637 West Alabama
Suite 340
Houston, TX 77027
TEL: 713-627-9600
Purpose: To help ex-offenders obtain immediate employment by preparing them for job-hunting.
Contact: George Trabing

Description: This program is designed to place as much responsibility as possible on the ex-offender himself or herself for future participation as a productive member of the community. Participants are not given jobs, but are provided with skills to find and keep a job.

The one-day workshops offer a five-hour instruction session on how to apply for and interview for a job, followed by a three-hour practice session in which trainees participate in simulated job interviews. Participants are expected to identify job-related skills in their own backgrounds, and set goals for themselves - in this way enhancing their self-confidence and motivation.

More than 100 volunteers assist NAB with the program, many of them making the crucial contacts by telephone with both potential students and potential employers. Others are involved in supervisory and management capacities.

Most participants are referred from individual Parole Board case officers, and by the local Department of Corrections. The majority of the participants come with work skills developed in the vocational, academic, and work experience programs of the correctional facilities.

The instruction is designed to highlight the initial telephone call and the interview itself. Also, instructors emphasize that a prison record is not necessarily a liability which cannot be overcome. Participants are told to re-emphasize their goals in the interview. The key elements to the success of the program are threefold:

- the practical value of the workshop material;
- the dedication and enthusiasm of the staff; and
- the Director's effort to maintain personal relationships with corrections, parole, and probation officials.

The long-term goal is to prepare ex-offenders to find and keep employment. The results of one program show that, of the 719 offenders enrolled, 583 found employment. Much of this success is attributable to the cooperation and direct involvement of local businesses, corporations, and governments. Also, all of the project funding comes from corporate contributions.

MORRIS COUNTY CHAPLAINCY COUNCIL
95 Mount Kemble Avenue
Morristown, NJ 07960
TEL: 201-540-1602
Purpose: To provide supportive services to incarcerated adult offenders, and to adults and juveniles on active probation.
Sponsor: The United Way; local business/industry; churches
Contact: Judy Blackadar
Description: The present Morris County Chaplaincy Council grew out of a desire of local ministers to provide a program for inmates in the County Jail. The Council was incorporated as a non-profit corporation in 1971. Its earliest years were spent in advocating a better physical plant, better-trained personnel, and a substantive rehabilitation program for inmates.

With an LEAA grant in 1972, the Council expanded its staff, developed a well-organized program to train volunteers to work in the jail, and became recognized in the community. Because of the number of people - almost 2,200 a year - passing through the jail, the Council chose to hire a staff that would coordinate and train a volunteer effort in the jail.

In 1975 United Way joined local churches and Morris County to support the Council, allowing the development of the Post Release Program. The Self-Development of People Program of the United Presbyterian Church provided a substantial grant to make financial assistance possible to released clients, and the Wilks Fund of St. Peter's Episcopal Church gave a one-time grant to enable the Coordinator of Volunteer Services to move from part-time to full-time. In 1977 the Sisters of Charity provided funds for a professionally coordinated and managed Education Program in the jail, and Iona College selected the Council as a field site for pastoral counseling graduate students. Also during this year the Council expanded its volunteer programming to juvenile offenders, working closely with the Morris County Probation Department,

the Youth Center, the Youth Shelter, and the Juvenile Court. Today, in addition to support from local Protestant and Catholic Churches and the United Way, support comes from local industry, including Allied Chemical, Exxon, Mennen, Warner-Lambert Pharmaceutical, Beneficial and others. Approximately 100 volunteers lend assistance to the program, but more are needed. Training and orientation is provided by skilled professionals, who also provide counseling, guidance and in-service instruction. One-to-one volunteers are required to participate in a specialized training program held quarterly. Additionally, monthly team meetings are required for all volunteers to share individual learning experiences. Periodic in-service training events are held also throughout the year. Volunteer programs include:

- **One-to-One Adult in Jail:** This is a voluntary program offered sentenced inmates during their last month of incarceration in Morris County Jail. Inmates are screened by the Jail staff and by the Council staff, and paired with a trained volunteer. Volunteers assist clients upon reentry into the community.
- **One-to-One Adult and Juvenile Probation:** This program, in cooperation with the County Probation Department, matches individuals on probation with volunteers for a period not to exceed the length of probation. The volunteer serves as a role model, friend, and counsel during crisis.
- **Women on the Wing:** In this program, volunteers provide visitation, counseling and follow-up to women inmates in jail and following release - establishing contact with families, helping with budgeting, setting goals, etc.
- **Educational Programs:** The Council offers a GED Program for completion of the High School Equivalency Program. Examinations are held quarterly; classes three times weekly. Volunteers assist with remedial tutoring and literacy training.
- **Guided Group Interaction:** Trained by the Administrative Office of the Courts, two volunteers from the Council lead groups of juvenile offenders on a weekly basis for the term of their probation. Youths are referred by County Juvenile Judges.
- **Bed, Breakfast and Supper:** Juveniles in "crisis" may be placed in a Volunteer Host Home by the professional worker involved in the crisis. The juvenile may stay for a period of up to ten days at no cost.

The Morris County Chaplaincy Council is sustained through its Board of Trustees, which meets monthly to establish policies and raise funds. The Board is divided into various program committees and bears the ultimate responsibility for the affairs of the organization.
Founded: 1971

OFFENDER AID AND RESTORATION OF FAIRFAX COUNTY
4153 Chain Bridge Road
Fairfax, VA 22030
TEL: 703-273-7552
Purpose: To counsel and assist inmates, ex-prisoners and their families; to develop other rehabilitative programs for adult and juvenile offenders as needs arise.
Sponsor: OAR/USA
Contact: Cynthia Holley, Deputy Director, or Peter Miro, Executive Director
Description: Offender Aid and Restoration (OAR) of Fairfax is one of the original sites of a program which was founded in Virginia to work with prisoners after a 1968 prison strike in the State Penitentiary. The nonprofit organization was chartered in 1971 and, since that time, the concept has grown into a national program, OAR-USA, Inc., with 11 affiliates in six states.

OAR of Fairfax focuses its attention on offenders in the Fairfax County jail who will be eligible for release in a year or less and their families. Among services provided are:

- one-to-one assignment to an OAR volunteer;
- assistance in finding employment and/or education/training

programs, as well as employability skills training;

- *Preparation for Release* classes;
- emergency financial aid for food, housing, clothing, medical needs, counseling and appropriate referrals.

OAR volunteers commit themselves to visiting assigned inmates and family members for a minimum of one hour per week over the course of a year. Volunteers also provide information services to inmates and families, teach classes at the jail, facilitate inmate and family support groups, and other special projects.

Another program administered by OAR of Fairfax is the Community Service Restitution Program (CSRP). CSRP is a discretionary pre-trial diversion for first offenders charged in the General District Court with shoplifting. The program provides an opportunity for defendants to work fifty hours (volunteer service) in one of 200 participating agencies. Successful completion of the program results in a decision by the Commonwealth Attorney not to prosecute. The value to agencies can be seen in statistics from FY 1989 when 411 persons completed the program and contributed 18,903 hours of community service. This represents more than $190,164 worth of services in a one-year period.

OAR of Fairfax's second alternative program, the *Prescription Sentencing Program (PSP),* is for non-violent offenders. In FY 1989, 10,548 hours of community service were completed at 200 public and nonprofit agencies for a total value of $106,112. In the process, 7,650 jail days were diverted for a saving of $430,050. Participants have a "prescription plan," which may include substance abuse or mental health treatment, restitution, employment or education.

OAR's *Family Assistance Program (FAP)* offers family and inmate support groups, individual counseling and an information handbook.
Publications: Handling the Crisis
Founded: 1971

PROBATION VOLUNTEERS
SEE RECIPIENTS: POLICE/COURT OFFICERS - RESPITE

RE-ENTRY MINISTRIES
PO Box 100461
Birmingham, AL 35210
TEL: 205-322-7966
Purpose: To assist ex-offenders in reestablishing themselves in the community; to provide an interdenominational church for ex-offenders.
Sponsor: St. Mark's Episcopal Church
Contact: Re-Entry Coordinator
Description: Re-Entry Ministries of Birmingham, Alabama, provides comprehensive services to ex-offenders to assist them in regaining a place in the community and becoming productive citizens. Among the services provided are:

- **Re-Entry Ministries Church** - an interdenominational church for ex-offenders with services the first Sunday of each month.
- **Dismas Fellowship** - a support group for ex-offenders, which meets one evening each week.
- **Ruth Fellowship** - a support group for wives, girlfriends, parents or anyone who has a loved one in prison, or recently released from prison, with meetings once each week.
- **AA (Alcoholics Anonymous)** - a sanctioned AA meeting for ex-offenders held one evening each week.
- **Social Activities** - a variety of leisure time activities such as a trip to the zoo, a picnic, concert or football game designed to provide wholesome activities for those who formerly lived on the streets, or in bars or crack houses.
- **One-on-One Counseling** - short-term, family/marital, substance abuse, personal counseling or crisis counseling, providing people to talk to who understand, care and can emotionally support the man or woman during the crucial time of the return to society.
- **In-Prison Services and Ministries** - Pen Pal (ongoing

correspondence with inmates); Pre-release talk (information about "life after prison" during the last 90 days of incarceration); Prison visits (assistance with parole plans, special help, ministry to inmates in four prisons each month).
- **Job Assistance** - referrals to employers known to be open to hiring ex-offenders; other personalized assistance as needed (clothes, emergency food, bus passes, help with identification, agency referrals, etc.).
- **Christian Literature** - Bibles and other Christian literature on request.

For ex-offenders with few positive people in their lives to turn to, this re-entry program is an important aspect of their lives.

SUPERIOR COURT CONFERENCE COMMITTEE DIVERSION PROGRAM
King County Juvenile Judges Committee
Juvenile Youth Service Center
1211 East Alden Street
Seattle, WA 98122
TEL: 206-296-1133; 206-296-1130
Purpose: To divert juvenile offenders from the formal juvenile justice system.
Contact: Bruce Knutson, Conference Committee Director
Description: The *Superior Court Conference Committee Diversion Program* in King County is a unique community volunteer effort. The program began in 1969, initially sponsored by the Mayor of Renton, Washington's *Youth Guidance Committee.* A handful of administrators and volunteers began diverting youth to community-based citizen groups. Youth were assigned to perform services within their own communities.

By 1972, there were eight *Committees* in King County - two within Seattle and three more in adjacent communities. At first, court staff handled organizational details by taking on extra assignments. In 1973, spurred by the program's growth, the court hired a full-time area manager to expand and maintain the *Committees.* In 1973, referrals increased 70 percent, and committee teams increased from eight to 30. Regular workshops for the committees' volunteers, training workshops and organizational meetings became an integral part of the program. By 1975, there were 14 committees with 60 teams to hear cases. By 1985, the present 25 committees were in place, serving 17 communities within King County and eight neighborhoods within Metropolitan Seattle - handling over 5,900 diverted juveniles.

Today the organization relies on a director of volunteer services, a program manager and four area managers. Goals of the program include:

- To provide an avenue for the community to show its concern for youth; to eliminate alienation and hostility felt by the youth, victim or community; and to establish or restore the youth as a constructive community member.
- To provide prompt, sure and just discipline/punishment which is the minimum needed to facilitate accountability, deterrence and restitution.
- To inform youth and their families about resources available to help them deal with problem situations.
- To alert youth that they will be held accountable to their community for legal violations and unacceptable behavior.
- To ensure the protection of youths' rights as defined by the State of Washington juvenile code.
- To stimulate and maximize citizen participation.

The diversion program is presented as an option to the youth, who must make the decision to participate. Involvement by the youth begins with a meeting with people from the local area, after the committee has reviewed the referral and police report. Private evening conferences, first with the youth, and then with the parents, are held, with all proceedings held in confidence. The record will become public only if the youth commits an additional offense. The *Committee* focuses on four areas: the reason for the referral and details of the offense; how the family functions by examining parent/child relationships, how the incident affected the family unit and how the family handled the incident and past problems; how the youth functions academically, socially and with teachers and students; and finally, the youth's interests and activities outside of school and peer relationships.

The *Committee* can take one of several actions.

- It can conclude that the conferences have resolved the problem and close the case;
- It can recommend further action to deal with the youth's conduct or attitude, resulting in a contract signed by the youth, which may include: community service, restitution, educational sessions, or personal counseling; or
- The *Committee* may opt to provide a disturbed child and/or distraught parent with an opportunity for counseling, and a list of appropriate services within the community.

The final decision is discussed with youth and parents. Community service sites range from senior citizen and convalescent centers to fire departments and libraries. Educational classes include a video series designed to assist youth with developmental tasks. Skill training classes cover subjects such as anger management, substance abuse, making friends and refusal skills.

An interesting aspect of the program is the fact that the youth consider the counseling most helpful, even when the only counseling they attend is the committee conference. The high degree of effectiveness of the program is reflected in the fact that ninety-seven percent of the youth complete their diversion contracts. In 1989 an extensive research project on the program was completed.

LAW ENFORCEMENT/CRIME PREVENTION: RECREATION

NATIONAL/STATE ORGANIZATIONS

NATIONAL CORRECTIONAL RECREATIONAL ASSOCIATION
c/o David Montgomery
Blackburn Correctional Complex
Lexington, KY 40511
TEL: 606-254-2791
Objectives: To raise inmate morale by providing healthy activity; to promote correctional recreation as a separate area of corrections concern; to arouse interest in recreation - especially the sports aspect - as a post-release constructive interest.
Services: Develops and implements recreational program designed to initiate or enforce socially acceptable attitudes and conduct; sponsors athletic contests and meets (weight-lifting, track, horseshoes, etc.); conducts national surveys; serves inmates in the United States and Canada; publishes quarterly newsletter.
Publications: Grapevine
Founded: 1966

LAW ENFORCEMENT/CRIME PREVENTION: SELF-HELP

NATIONAL/STATE ORGANIZATIONS

CONFLICT RESOLUTION/ALTERNATIVES TO VIOLENCE CENTER
PO Box 256
Ricker House
Cherryfield, MD 20715
TEL: 301-262-0223
Objectives: To develop and sustain prisoner support groups in the United States and Canada.
Services: Develops and assists prisoner training and support groups in all aspects of criminal justice and prison environment, including conflict resolution and alternatives to violence; provides trained mediators for conflicts and conflict resolution training for prison staff; maintains referral service for resources available on alternatives to prison; conducts nonviolent workshops for prisons.
Founded: 1976

GOOD NEWS JAIL AND PRISON MINISTRIES INTERNATIONAL
1036 South Highland Street
Arlington, VA 22204
TEL: 703-979-2200
Objectives: To provide counseling, education, information and referral and other services to prisoners, ex-offenders and their families.
Services: Places Chaplains at the local level in correctional facilities to provide both spiritual and social services to prisoners and their families both in prison and after their release; oversees other volunteers in the program who provide counseling, crisis intervention, family contact, G.E.D. assistance, and other services on request of prisoners and prison officials, as well as pastoral counseling; assists ex-offenders in readjustment to the community (After Care program); maintains separate programs for jails (average incarceration only four to six months) and prisons (which includes "lifers"); provides training for ex-offenders wishing to become Chaplains in the program; publishes a newsletter, brochures, reports, and other materials.
Publications: Full Pardon; Update; Regeneration THEN... Rehabilation; Jail Ministry Is Good Business?; Why Bother
Founded: 1961

LAW ENFORCEMENT/CRIME PREVENTION: SENTENCING

TRAINING PROGRAMS

CHALLENGES FOR ALTERNATIVE SENTENCING IN OUR COMMUNITIES
National Community Service Sentencing Association
c/o Dale Hancock/County Courthouse
109 Eighth Street, Suite 300
Colorado Springs , CO 81601-3303
TEL: 303-945-1377; 303-625-5571
FAX: 303-945-2379
Credit: Inquire
Contact: Dale Hancock

Description: Subtitled *Substance Abusers and Other Special Needs Offenders,* this conference takes *alternative sentencing* a step further by emphasizing the need to work with the ever-increasing groups of offenders often overlooked in community-based sentencing - offenders with special needs. This group includes drug abusers, compulsive gamblers, domestic abusers, sex offenders, women, minorities, juveniles who are learning disabled or school dropouts, etc.

The Conference is jointly sponsored by the *National Community Service Sentencing Association* and the *Minnesota Association of Restitution Services.* Conference sessions were divided into four parts: *Direct Services Workshops, Training Sessions, Policy Implications Workshops,* and *Administrative Skills Workshops* described below:

Direct Services Workshops
- Program for Juveniles at Risk (learning disabled, school dropouts)
- How to Testify and Communicate in Court (relieving fears of the courtroom, avoiding pitfalls, what is expected)
- Privatizing Community Sentencing: The Minnesota and Wisconsin Experiences (how these programs started, advantages and disadvantages, experience to date)
- Attention to Juvenile Jailing (attention-deficient juveniles; how programs address the issue)
- Alternatives to Juvenile Jailing (community-based agencies' experiences)
- Domestic Violence: Treatment for Male Offenders (experiences of Hackensack, New Jersey agency)
- Victim-Sensitive Sex Offender Therapy (three-stage, victim-sensitive offender therapy model that maximizes victim safety, respect and therapeutic closure)
- Ethical Issues in Defense-Based Sentencing Services (role of the treatment providers, relationships between attorney and treatment provider, special problems)
- Community Sentences and the Media (panel of newspaper and newsletter writers and editors on coverage of community sentencing)
- Women and Community Sentencing (use of community sentencing for women offenders)

Training Sessions
- VORP/Mediation (Victim-Offender Reconciliation Program as a criminal justice intervention)
- National and Statewide Community Service Standards (overview of the few states who have developed standards for alternative service; discussion of developing national standards)
- Relapse Prevention for Substance Abuser and Other Substance Abuse Training Sessions (joint program with American Probation and Parole Association, National Institute of Corrections, National Academy of Corrections, and Drug Policy Foundation)

Policy Implications Workshops
- Community Service for Compulsive Gamblers
- Drug Addiction, What Is It?
- VORP: Implications for Drug Offenders
- Prison Overcrowding and Public Policy
- Packaging Community Service and Restitution Legislation
- Community Sentencing in Minnesota
- Race, Imprisonment and Community Sentencing
- Breaking Chains, Forging Justice (with National Commission on Crime and Justice, a program of the American Friends Service Committee, on African-American offenders)
- Women and Community Corrections
- U.S. Sentencing Commission and Community Sentencing (advisory panel)

Administrative Skills Workshops
- Community Services as a Dumping Ground for Probation
- Developing and Using Statistical Data to Improve Community Sentencing Programs
- Working with the Courts: Turning Judges Into Advocates

- Liability and Community Service
- Linking Community and Sentencing Alternatives
- New Generation of Risk Assessment Instruments for Adolescents and Adults
- Creating Community CSOs for Juveniles (community service organizations)

Numerous other workshops were included as time and space were available in areas ranging from parole and victim services to community sentencing of johns and prostitutes. Faculty was drawn from both public and private sectors, academe, business/industry, and nonprofit organizations. Nineteen additional co-sponsors range from local programs to state colleges to the federal government. Information and details on workshops not listed here, organizations involved and the proceedings will follow the September 1990 conference and be published for distribution.

Publications: Conference Proceedings

FAIRFAX ALTERNATIVE SERVICES WORKSHOP
Voluntary Action Center of the Fairfax County Area
10530 Page Avenue
Fairfax, VA 22030
TEL: 703-691-3460
Credit: Inquire
Sponsor: Voluntary Action Center
Contact: Volunteer Coordinator
Description: Offered to volunteer coordinators across the state, this workshop is designed to facilitate sharing of resources to avoid duplication of effort. Questions posed are:
- How does a volunteer coordinator deal with the court referred volunteer?
- What policy guidelines should each agency set before these referrals are accepted?

An open session includes presenters who describe court procedures and timetables, and explain the various classes of crimes. This session is followed by a panel discussion which includes administrators of various court referral programs who describe their programs and provide a profile of the offender/volunteer. Open discussion with the panel enables participants to express their concerns about issues such as:
- the time element when involving alternative service volunteers (usually 50 hours), as it relates to the time needed to train the volunteers;
- confidentially required by the court concerning the court referral;
- the alternative service volunteer relationship with staff and regular volunteers; and
- the category of court referrals (are they volunteers or not?).

Workshop sessions focus on Alternative Service participants through the following issues:
- Agency's willingness to participate in an Alternative Service Program;
- Criteria and procedures for acceptance of Alternative Service Participants;
- Confidentiality;
- Communication with source of referral of Alternative Service Participants; and
- Relationship of Alternative Service Program to regular program.

These workshop issues are taken from a set of policy guidelines developed through the experience of coordinators in the Fairfax area, but are fully adaptable for guidelines or a similar workshop in any locality. In Fairfax County, they have been used in consultation with the Fairfax County Park/Conservation Division, the Alexandria Hospital, and Culpeper Community Services to help form written policy for these agencies in their Alternative Services Programs, and in consultation with the U.S. District Court during the review and revision of the Court's policy for placing offenders in community service.

INDIVIDUAL PROGRAM PROFILES

COURT REFERRAL PROGRAM
PO Box 451
Owensboro, KY 42302
TEL: 502-684-9238
Purpose: The Court Referral Program places adult and juvenile offenders in community service agencies to do a set number of volunteer hours instead of paying a fine or serving a jail sentence.
Sponsor: Voluntary Action Center
Contact: Pamela J. Warwick, Executive Director
Description: The Court Referral Program began in 1975 with a grant from the Kentucky Crime Commission. It is a cooperative effort between the Voluntary Action Center, Davies District Court system, and community service agencies. When grant money ended, city and county funds were secured to continue operating the program.

The program has provided volunteer job placements for adult and juvenile offenders in the community for six years. Offenders are referred to the program by district court judges and placed in community service agencies to complete an assigned number of hours of volunteer work in lieu of paying a fine or serving a jail sentence. The program has become particularly helpful to the courts for those cases where a fine or jail sentence is inappropriate as the program provides a "working alternative." For offenders, the program provides an opportunity to pay back the community while gaining valuable job experience. As a result of working on the program, some volunteers secure jobs with the agencies upon completion of volunteer hours or receive recommendations for securing other employment. Also, the program is helpful in providing community service agencies with court referral volunteers to assist in such areas as programming, office work, and maintenance.

Since the program began, the number of court-referred volunteers has increased steadily. In a typical year, about 600 offenders are referred by the courts to the program. Each year, the Court Referral Program has a success rate of approximately 96% (persons who successfully complete the program). It is a well-liked, valuable, and respected program. As the budget for the program is quite low, continuing the program is necessary when considering the costs to the community if the program were ended.
Founded: 1975

COURT REFERRED VOLUNTEER PROGRAM OF RENSSELAER COUNTY
502 Broadway
Troy, NY 12180
TEL: 518-274-7234
Purpose: To provide community service to minor offenders, as mandated by the Courts.
Sponsor: Volunteer Center of Rensselaer County
Contact: Jacqueline Mulligan
Description: The *Court Referred Volunteer Program* was instituted by the *Volunteer Center of Rensselaer County* in February 1981 after the concept of alternative sentencing was studied by the *Rensselaer County Criminal Justice Coordinating Committee.* The first of its kind in the county and the Capital District, the program provides community service, as mandated by the courts, to persons (primarily youthful offenders), in order to prevent or decrease their incarceration, probation, and re-entry into the criminal justice system.

Under the program, appropriate offenders are sentenced by the courts to complete a designated amount of volunteer service as an alternative to a jail term or fine, or as a condition of probation. Our office interviews, refers and places such offenders in a non-profit agency or government department. Assignments are monitored and the courts are notified when the offenders have completed the service. Our clients have ranged in age from 10-49 years, with the average age being 19. Whenever necessary, clients are referred informally to other service that they may need.

Since its inception, nearly 1,800 CRVs have been assigned to community service. The benefits to the community are many:
- Provides judges with an alternative sentencing tool;
- Enables the offender to have an opportunity to earn a favorable disposition; and
- Increases the pool of volunteer help to nonprofit community organizations.

Funding Sources are *New York State Division for Youth, Rensselaer County Department for Youth,* and *United Way.*
Founded: 1981

CURB IT!
SEE PHYSICAL ENVIRONMENT: RECYCLING

DIVERSION TO COMMUNITY SERVICE*
Volunteer Center, Inc.
115 East Jefferson Street
Suite 300
Syracuse, NY 13202
TEL: 315-474-7011
Purpose: To provide a positive alternative to the criminal justice system for young offenders and other misdemeanants.
Sponsor: State Division for Youth; County of Onondaga
Contact: Jean J. Greene
Description: The Volunteer Center began the Diversion to Community Service in 1978 as a very small pilot program. Today the program receives funds from the New York State Division for Youth via the City-County Youth Board, and matching funds from the County of Onondaga. The underlying philosophy of the program remains the same: to give non-violent first-time offenders an opportunity to perform community service in lieu of a fine or jail sentence, hoping to:
- channel them away from the criminal justice system;
- prevent recidivism; and
- provide a realistic sentence that is positive and not punitive.

The program began in response to a need expressed by City Court judges locally looking for some kind of positive alternative to traditional criminal sentences for the young offenders. Now suitable offenders - with agreement among judge, district attorney, defense lawyer and the offender himself - can be referred to the Volunteer Center for placement as volunteers with community agencies. The judge stipulates the number of hours to be provided, and the Volunteer Center keeps track and notifies the court when the hours are complete. Often, the case is dismissed and no record remains for the young person.

Clients are interviewed in the same way as any other volunteer, and placements are arranged to utilize their skills and interests. Care is taken also to arrange hours outside of work and school time. Volunteer openings include recreation aides; child care; maintenance and repair; clerical work; tutoring; park cleanup; and many more.

After a slow start in the pilot year (placing under 100 clients), the program expects to place over 1,000 in this third year of operation, with over 20,000 hours of community service as a byproduct. City court judges and local town justices in every city and suburban court in the area now use the program.

The Center does not limit its role in this program to that of a placement service and record-keeper. If the clients seem to be in need of other services, such as education or counseling, they are referred to the Information and Referral Service of the Volunteer Center where staff helps them find services needed.

The success rate for the Diversion to Community Service program is 98% in terms of completion of hours. Also, many young people have obtained paid jobs with the agencies for which they were volunteering. Many others have remained as volunteers long after the stipulated hours were completed. The emphasis is on making volunteering a rewarding experience.
Founded: 1978

HITS (HIGH INTENSITY TREATMENT SUPERVISION)
District of Columbia Superior Court
Social Services, Juvenile Branch
500 Indiana Avenue, NW, Room 302
Washington, DC 20001
TEL: 202-879-4332; 202-879-4330
FAX: 202-879-1965
Purpose: To rehabilitate hard core juvenile offenders and remove them from the cycle of crime.
Sponsor: District of Columbia Department of Corrections
Contact: Carroll Boswell, Supervisor
Description: Begun in 1988 as a unique probation program to relieve the crowding in juvenile detention facilities, HITS has become a successful rehabilitation system with a rigid structure. It holds youths, most of them repeat offenders, to more stringent standards than regular probation. It is a system of counseling groups, self-esteem workshops, parent involvement, curfews, urine tests, community service work, jobs and school. It is, according to its supervisor, "confinement without incarceration."
A favorite aspect of the program is the community services arm which sends youth to soup kitchens, housing projects, or recreation centers around the city to do about 10 hours of community service or cleanup work each week. In addition, curfew is 9:00 seven nights a week, with counselors calling at curfew time, and/or appearing at the door unannounced ("night riders") as late as 3:00 a.m.
Although youth placed in HITS have committed crimes for which they would usually be jailed, youths charged with violence are generally not placed in the program. Violation of HITS probation means two years in jail.
Although officials refuse to draw firm conclusions after only one year, recidivism among the youth in the program (5%) compares very favorably with that of youths on regular probation (30%). Success stories include the former leader of a crew of drug dealers, now 18, who is working in construction.
Part of HITS's philosophy is to attack the youths' warped values, records of failure, and low sense of self-worth. One example of this is allowing reporters access to the HITS program on the condition that the youths on probation not be named. This is true in media access to related court proceedings also. The media have honored this condition and the stories have been positive and helpful to the overall program.
For reasons ranging from severe truancy to poor academic performance, most of the youth in the program failed in school. On the streets, where the police kept arresting them, they failed as thugs. And many of them feel that they have failed their parents. The youths typically score in the lower range on standard intelligence tests. One of the program leaders is certain that the reasons behind such poor showings are mostly environmental. However, as pointed out by one of the counselors, every one of them wants to go to school.
Special rap sessions are held for youth facing drug charges. Youth who are not charged, but admit to having used drugs, are invited to participate in the rap sessions.
The involvement of parents is essential to the program, according to a supervisor. Although sessions for parents are mandatory, and some parents attend reluctantly, as time is spent in the program, they become more relaxed and helpful to their children and the program. Some parents attend support groups of their peers - parents who are "at their wit's end, their bag of disciplinary tricks empty." Although too soon to tell, there are signs that this parent involvement has a positive effect after the youths leave the program.
Many HITS youth come from families with existing problems - many of them severe. Some of the parents, mostly single mothers, were teenagers when they had children. Some parents just don't want to know the truth. At the other extreme, some work so hard, have so many mouths to feed, that there is little time for nurturing. Often they are glad to have HITS as an option for assistance, since they have not been able to make a difference. The

parents of some youth are dead or not around.
HITS case workers have smaller case loads than other probation officers - about 15 youths each - and can spend more time with each one. HITS also requires involvement of a parent or guardian, whereas in regular probation, parents are often peripheral.
With 6,499 juveniles arrested in 1988, and only 200 slots in the HITS program, the impact is only a fraction of what it could be, according to staff members.

IN-HOME DETENTION PROGRAM
SEE RECIPIENTS: POLICE/COURT OFFICERS - RESPITE

LEE COUNTY RESTITUTION PROGRAM
SEE LAW ENFORCEMENT/CRIME PREVENTION: VICTIMS

PUBLIC SERVICE VOLUNTEERS
Augusta Mental Health Institute
Box 724
Augusta, ME 04330
TEL: 207-622-3751/Ext. 431
Purpose: To provide a meaningful way for persons convicted of misdemeanor offenses to repay society through public service work.
Sponsor: Augusta Mental Health Institute, Departments of Mental Health & Corrections
Contact: Peter E. Swartz, Chief of Volunteer Services
Description: Public Service Volunteers may be any person over 14 years of age convicted of a misdemeanor offense (e.g., traffic violations, operating under the influence, and petty thefts). Volunteers may be placed in any non-profit agency. In practice, the Augusta Mental Health Institute has utilized most of the individuals due to insurance liability concerns.
Public Service Volunteers utilizes from 75 to 100 individuals a year working from four to several hundred hours on a full or part time basis.
Work assignments include: Houskeeping, Warehouse, Grounds Maintenance, Office Work, and occasionally other areas of special need, usually in non-patient contact areas.
The program benefits the individual and the agency. Persons working over 40 hours are eligible for a job reference. The goal there is a long range deterrent effect.

LAW ENFORCEMENT/CRIME PREVENTION: SEXUAL ABUSE

NATIONAL/STATE ORGANIZATIONS

CENTER FOR PREVENTION AND TREATMENT OF SEXUAL ABUSE
State of Vermont
State Capitol
Montpelier, VT 05602
TEL: 802-828-1110
Objectives: To provide a treatment program and aftercare support system to help prevent recidivism in sexual abuse crimes; to operate a statewide education program to prevent sexual abuse crimes.
Services: Developed by the State of Vermont in 1972, this treatment and prevention program has among the lowest recidivism rates ever achieved. While national and statewide statistics are alarming, 80 percent of child molesters across the country repeat the offense, while the Vermont estimate is 60% -

only two percent of those who have gone through Vermont's Center for the Prevention and Treatment of Sexual Abuse have been charged with new offenses. Since its beginning, 247 pedophiles have received treatment at the Center.

The *key* to the program is what its director calls "relapse prevention." A mental health professional works closely with a parole officer in treating the offenders both in jail and after they are out. They are shown that it is not something beyond their control. By providing them with greater power over themselves, the need to feel power by controlling others decreases. They are sensitized to the harm they cause their victims and educated about the process they follow in getting to the point where they choose to abuse someone. Since this process is not an impulse but a well-thought out plan, there is a chance to intervene during that process.

Parole is closely supervised, with the added benefit of volunteer assistance by family, friends, employers and colleagues. The volunteers are given the "script" the offender would follow if he were in the process of choosing to offend again. A requirement of the treatment program is that the offender provide this information to all parties concerned. The helpers are taught to watch for signs such as emotional changes which may indicate that the offender is beginning to cycle back towards abuse. Loneliness and fantasy are two examples, and sometimes signs are visible in these cases.

In summary, the director points out that, like alcoholism, there is no cure for the "power of choice." Despite the success rate at the Center, there is no guarantee that the sex offender will not choose to offend again. They do not allow any delusions by the offenders, either, advising them that "the only certificate of graduation is your death certificate. Then you know that you are cured."

Sponsor: State of Vermont
Contact: William D. Pithers, Director

RAPE CRISIS CENTER
PO Box 21005
Washington, DC 20009
TEL: 202-333-7273
Objectives: To assist/counsel victims through the trauma of rape.
Services: Provides information and counseling to rape victims; provides specialized counseling for victims of incest; develops community education programs and materials; offers consulting services to other groups concerned with rape; provides self-defense referral information for others dealing with rape victims; provides children's services; conducts community education programs for elementary and older students about issues relating to sexual assault and its prevention; publishes *How to Start a Rape Crisis Center* (book), manuals, guidelines, pamphlets, flyers and other materials.
Publications: Rape Prevention ; Shaw Outreach Team; How to Start a Rape Crisis Center

INDIVIDUAL PROGRAM PROFILES

MODEL MUGGING
All Souls Church
16th and Harvard Streets, NW
Washington, DC 20009
TEL: 202-332-5266
Purpose: To teach women to ward off attack while on the ground.
Sponsor: All Souls Church
Contact: Carol Middleton
Description: Begun in 1972, Model Mugging is a form of self-defense that teaches women to fight back after they have been thrown to the ground by their attackers. The class primarily addresses rape prevention, where women often are thrown to the ground. The director terms it a "knockout defense," since that results in less trauma on both sides.

Model Mugging is a two-week course, with a fee, but it provides scholarships as available to those who cannot afford the fee. The course uses volunteer "stand-in muggers" who are versed in martial arts, wearing padding, and playing realistic, hardcore roles of attackers. Most of the volunteer stand-in muggers have family members who went through the trauma of such attacks.

Unlike other martial arts training, where practice sessions stop just short of physically harming an opponent, Model Mugging teaches women to fight with "full force." Although the vicious realism of the classroom attacks disturb some spectators, it is based on the fact that only realism will help a woman learn to fight back adequately.

The course has a psychological side - hardening women to overcome their squeamishness at attacking men's most vulnerable spots - heads and groins.

More than 8,000 women across the country have been trained in Model Mugging courses. Most of the concern is an outgrowth of statistics which show that at least 50% of all rapes occur in the victim's home or a friend's home, and it has happened to females as young as two months and as old as 97.

According to the director, the bottom line is that "the power women acquire is the freedom of choice." If the attacker(s) pose too much of a threat, then it is the woman's choice to fight or not to fight - but it's "always a choice."
Founded: 1972

RAPE AND DOMESTIC VIOLENCE INFORMATION CENTER
PO Box 4228
Morgantown, WV 26505
TEL: 304-588-6800
Purpose: To provide shelter, counseling advocacy and referral for victims of domestic violence, sexual assault and incest.
Sponsor: Federal/State/City/County governments; private donations
Contact: Kim van Rijn, Volunteer Coordinator
Description: RDVIC runs a 24-hour hotline for domestic violence, sexual assault and incest victims and temporary emergency shelter for victims.

Staff and volunteers work with victims and their families providing crisis intervention, advocacy, self-help and support groups, individual long-term counseling and information and referral. The shelter provides a safe, supportive and cooperative environment for abused women and their children, where they can work out their problems, explore their options and make decisions about their lives. Volunteers are a crucial part of the RDVIC helping system. At the present time, 24 volunteers work as "counselor/companions" providing 24-hour hotline services, advocacy and transportation. In addition, 29 volunteers work as shelter workers, providing counseling and support to the victims residing at the shelter. During 1982, volunteers gave a total of 15,032 hours of service to victims.

Volunteers begin their experience at RDVIC by undergoing extensive training. They must attend approximately 18 hours of training on sexual assault, domestic violence and incest issues and procedures and counseling skills. Following training volunteers attend either counselor/companion or shelter worker orientation and are scheduled to begin working. Counselor/companions run the hotline after 5 p.m. on weekdays and all day Saturday and Sunday. Their duties include offering crisis counseling and support over the phone or in person. Counselor/companions accompany victims to the hospital emergency room, the police, the Magistrates Court and the shelter, operating as victim advocates. Shelter workers oversee the shelter operations during evenings and weekends, offering emotional support to the women.

RAPE CRISIS CENTER
423 West Ocondaga Street
Syracuse, NY 11320
TEL: 315-422-7273

Purpose: To provide counseling, medical and legal advocacy, and support to victims of sexual assault via a 24-hour hotline.
Sponsor: Rape Crisis Center (RCC)
Contact: Rosemary Sloane
Description: The Rape Crisis Center is a non-profit organization which helps victims of all types of sexual assault - rape, incest, sodomy and sexual abuse - whether they report it or not. All victim services are free and confidential. Services include:
- a 24-hour telephone hotline for information and crisis counseling;
- support counseling for victims, their families and friends;
- advocacy through medical and legal systems if the victim chooses to report the crime;
- a Public Speakers Bureau to educate the public about the dangers and myths about rape as well as about preventive measures and precautions.

Two specialized programs are: The Incest Treatment Program, which offers counseling, support and advocacy to victims and their families; The Youth Advocate Program, which offers both counseling and education to youth, their families and teachers. The volunteers at the Rape Crisis Center are an integral part of the agency's operations. A large percent of the RCC's activities depend on these dedicated workers who are active in all aspects of our organization. In 1982, the volunteers gave over 10,000 hours or an equivalent of 5.1 full-time staff. Volunteer activities at the RCC include:
- crisis intervention
- short-term counseling
- medical/legal advocate
- working in the office
- taking on-call shifts
- public speaking
- sitting on a committee
- sitting on the Board of Directors

The volunteers are permitted to participate in two programs at the RCC - Volunteer Counseling and Community Service.

RAPE CRISIS SERVICE OF CENTRAL CONTRA COSTA COUNTY
1950 Parkside Drive
Concord, CA 94519
TEL: 415-671-3381
Purpose: To aid victims of sexual assault to make the successful transition from victim to survivor; to provide community education about sexual assualt.
Sponsor: State/County/City governments; private donations
Contact: Katharine Wilson
Description: Rape Crisis Service of Central Contra Costa County (RCS/CCCC) was formed in July of 1981 when a merger took place between Diablo Valley RCS and RCS of Concord, both of which had formed in 1976. Funding sources are State/County/City governments and private donations.
RCS/CCCC has a Board of Directors, and four paid staff members. At present, we have approximately 20 active volunteers, who provide the majority of direct services to our clients. Our services are as follows: 24-hour crisis line; accompaniment and advocacy services (to hospitals, police, etc.); individual and follow-up counseling for victims and families/friends of victims; court advocacy; support groups; community education.
Volunteers can work in any one (or more than one) of four areas, performing duties related to the services listed above. The four basic areas are: crisis line and accompaniment/advocacy; court advocacy; speaker's bureau; office work.
Volunteers need not have any previous experience to perform any of the above duties. They receive approximately 35 hours of training, with continual in-service training. Supervision is given through regular one-to-one contact, as well as at two monthly meetings. All volunteers go through a screening process before beginning work at RCS. Volunteers are needed in all areas.

RCS/CCCC also accepts students who would like to be involved in internship or field placement programs with the agency. Supervision includes that of staff and/or certified therapists.
Founded: 1981

LAW ENFORCEMENT/CRIME PREVENTION: STAFF SUPPORT

INDIVIDUAL PROGRAM PROFILES

FRIENDS OF THE SUPERIOR COURT
409 E Street, NW
Suite 301
Washington, DC 20001
TEL: 202-727-1788
Purpose: To recruit and train volunteers to provide services to clients of the Superior Court of DC; educate the community on the work of the court; provide funds for special programs to serve court clients.
Sponsor: District of Columbia Superior Court
Contact: Frank McGuire
Description: Friends of the Superior Court of the District of Columbia (Friends) began in 1964 as one of the pioneer groups which set out to demonstrate the value of volunteers working in a court setting. Today, 70% of the courts throughout the nation have volunteer programs. Initially, Friends served only the juvenile court. In 1971, the *Court Reorganization Act* expanded the jurisdiction of the court to include three branches: Intra-family, Adult, and Juvenile. The Chief Judge charged Friends with recruiting and coordinating all volunteers and volunteer groups working in the court.
The Friends organization has a board - a cross-section of the community - which formulates policies and supervises operations. Funds for Friends programs are raised by an annual appeal, and gifts from individuals and foundations. The administrator of volunteers is employed by the court but under the direction of the board of Friends. Volunteer programs include:
Probation Aides - Volunteers choose to work in either an adult or juvenile program. After a training period, each is assigned to a probation officer. Under his/her direct supervision, the volunteer works with the client and his/her family.
Educational and Probational Aides Program - While the program is similar to the probation-aide program, this program addresses itself specifically to school adjustment problems. The goal of the program is to provide (a) tutoring; (b) supportive counseling; (c) communication link between child, parent, school and probation staff.
Volunteer Attorney Program - The law demands that children in "beyond control," neglect, and child abuse cases be represented by their own attorney. However, in these cases, no provisions have been made to compensate lawyers for their work. Friends enlists the aid of volunteer attorneys who represent the children without charge. In a single quarter, the volunteer lawyers gave 876 hours of service. The daily case loads vary between six and eight each day. Estimated saving to taxpayers each quarter: $21,900.
One-to-One Program - In the One-to-One program, a volunteer is assigned to work intensively with a single client, adult or juvenile. The program is based on the premise that one person can have a therapeutic effect upon another. The volunteer can grow through the relationship as well as the client. Basic elements which make the volunteer effective in this program are: (1) empathy and respect for the client; (2) ability to listen effectively and communicate; (3) commitment of time (3-4 hours per week over a six-month period); (4) tolerance for other life styles.

Child Care Center - This center for the Superior Court was developed to provide free childcare by a qualified staff and trained volunteers for clients of the court, allowing court business to proceed without distractions. The Center is located in the basement of a local church and is licensed to care for children from 18 months to 15 years of age.

Summer Programs - Summer programs are divided into two areas:

- **Summer Camp Program** - The Friends arrange for camps in the area to provide services for 100 probationers for six to twelve days without charge. Volunteers contact parents for permission slips and arrange for physical examinations and transportation. Agencies supplying camp slots include the DC Recreation Department, Family and Child Service, Council of Churches, Salvation Army, and the Police Boys Club.
- **Summer Jobs** - The volunteer office, working in conjunction with the Mayor's office and the Department of Recreation, locates and develops summer jobs for older juveniles.

Community Resource Development - A small group of retired social workers contact community agencies whose services can be enlisted for probationers, circulating information alerting the Social Services Division of changes in organizational policy, standards of personnel, etc., in these agencies.

Clerical Support - Individuals who wish to help but prefer not to serve clients through direct support make a contribution of time for typing reports, filing, telephoning to check data, etc.

Recent expansion of some of the programs include a unique One-to-One arm at Georgetown University, and the new Guardian Ad Litem Program for the Volunteer Attorneys Office. Volunteer applicants for all programs are screened by the Court's Social Service Division and Friends to ensure that they meet all the requirements of the job. The volunteer administrator contacts the volunteers periodically to discuss ways in which their services can be made more effective. Descriptive materials are available upon request.

POLICE DEPARTMENT VOLUNTEER PROGRAM
SEE RECIPIENTS: POLICE/COURT OFFICERS - RESPITE

RESERVE POLICE OFFICER CORPS
Washington Metropolitan Police Department
300 Indiana Avenue, NW
Washington, DC 20001
TEL: 292-727-1000
Purpose: To provide assistance to police officers both in administrative capacities and "on the street."
Contact: Captain Ross E. Swope, Supervisor
Description: The District of Columbia's Police Reserve Corps numbers 166 volunteers. They are lawyers, government employees, and other professionals as well as layman who want to help protect their neighborhoods.

Although some volunteer officers choose to work "on the street," others help in areas of data processing, communications, property division, vehicle management, administrative jobs, and other posts throughout the department. Since Reserve Police Officers cannot, by law, carry a gun, the help on the street is becoming less and less attractive to volunteers who join the Corps. However, the department is recruiting volunteers in an effort to triple the number of Reserve Officers, since they are needed throughout the department.

Reserve Officers receive 108 hours of abbreviated training in traffic enforcement, the DC Code and police procedures. Since many volunteers are older than staff officers, they feel that the training is sufficient, since they are more mature and better able to handle some police business. In addition to having to meet stiff requirements, the volunteers are required to buy their own bulletproof vests. Legislation is being entered to allow reservists to carry weapons, since many metropolitan cities with populations and crime problems similar to the District's do arm their reserve officers.

Although more and more opportunities are opening up inside the precincts for volunteer officers, most of whom have been working on the street for a time have become familiar with the neighborhoods and opt to stay there. A few request transfers inside after a particularly heavy rash of crime.

During the last six months of 1989, reserve officers volunteered a total of 13,110 hours.

RESERVE POLICE PROGRAM
St. Louis County Police Department
Wellston, MO 63133
TEL: 314-889-2844
Purpose: To provide back up for police officers on regular patrol.
Sponsor: St. Louis County & Municipal Police Academy
Contact: Reserve Coordinator
Description: Volunteer police reserves are involved in all parts of St. Louis County. Both men and women reservists each donate 200 hours of time a year to back up police officers on regular patrol and learn to help in emergencies.

Before assignments are made, volunteers participate in an intensive training program. Classes are held in the St. Louis County and Municipal Police Academy evenings and some Saturdays for the convenience of volunteers who work during the day. Training covers

- law enforcement functions;
- criminal law;
- firearms;
- cardiopulmonary resuscitation; and
- first aid.

The serious nature of these topics requires 180 hours of training over a 13-week period.

VOLUNTEER PROBATION OFFICER PROGRAM
SEE RECIPIENTS: POLICE/COURT OFFICERS - RESPITE

LAW ENFORCEMENT/CRIME PREVENTION: VICTIMS

INDIVIDUAL PROGRAM PROFILES

AID TO VICTIMS OF CRIME*
607 North Grand
Suite 705
St. Louis, MO 63103
TEL: 314-531-2597
Purpose: To help stabilize the St. Louis Community and build strong neighborhoods.
Sponsor: Law Enforcement Assistance Administration; private donations
Contact: Volunteer Coordinator
Description: Aid to Victims of Crime is a not-for-profit tax-exempt corporation, incorporated under the laws of the State of Missouri. It provides emergency supportive services to victims of rape, robbery, burglary, assault and homicide. Aid to Victims of Crime is primarily a volunteer organization, with a small paid staff, servicing the City of St. Louis.

The need for volunteers comes from a need for citizens in the City of St. Louis to take control of their lives and face some of the major problems of an urban area. Crime cannot be reduced and victims cannot be served unless there is a genuine positive response on behalf of the citizen. Neighborhood volunteers enable the program to contact and serve many more victims of crime than if only staff were used.

After receiving the name of a victim, the case is assigned to a volunteer living in the victim's neighborhood. The volunteer visits the victim and helps in any way he can. If needed, the volunteer calls the office for aid. Later, the volunteer makes a short, simple report, telling how the case was handled. Volunteers must attend a training session concerned with office procedures and community resources before visiting a victim.

Volunteers are asked to commit a minimum of one hour per month to the job. Volunteers are also asked to act as victim advocates, taking the side of the victims and helping them deal with various community resources. Services offered:

- Helping the victim or family get in touch with public or private agencies, such as the welfare office, food stamp office, hospitals, social security office, etc.
- Helping the victim get credit payments extended when there is loss of money or job.
- Contacting the employers to ask them to hold a victim's position or persuade the employer to allow paid time off for court attendance.
- Arranging for transportation to court, hospital, police station, etc.
- Arranging for child care, home care and grocery shopping.
- Providing emergency food and clothing.
- Helping to arrange funerals.
- Helping with filing insurance claims.
- Helping relocate a victim or family.
- Helping replace stolen items that are essential to the victim, such as eyeglasses, walking canes, locks on doors, keys and window panes.

CRY, INC. (CITIZENS REDIRECTING YOUTH)
SEE PSYCHOSOCIAL SUPPORT SERVICES: VICTIMS

FAMILY SUPPORT GROUP
Los Angeles Police Department
Central Office
251 East Sixth Street
Los Angeles, CA 90014
TEL: 213-485-6586
Purpose: To keep communication open between the Police Department and the widows of slain officers.
Sponsor: Los Angeles Police Department
Contact: Chief Daryl Gates
Description: In the mid 1980s, the Los Angeles Police Department realized that, in spite of various efforts, they were losing touch with widows and families of slain police officers. The Department felt it was very important that the survivors were kept constantly aware of the Department's continuing concern for their welfare.
It was decided that a support group sponsored by the Department would bring together those of similar circumstances who understand the pain and grief. The Chief appointed a female detective to begin getting the support group organized. Currently there are 35 members, 20 of whom are very active. The group is essentially a "sisterhood" that helps sustain women's nurturing, caretaking roles. The understanding friendship between the women is a unique relationship.
Over the years the group has evolved into a sophisticated organization with specific goals. Speakers and guests are brought in to meetings to discuss topics on various subjects such as recovery, family dysfunction, etc. The basic approach is to guide and assist in whatever the needs of the widow are, but the general coverage is at the common emotion of grief.
Support meetings are held once a month, and have succeeded in the initial goal of keeping families of slain officers in the "Police Department family."

LEE COUNTY RESTITUTION PROGRAM
PO Box 57
Sanford, NC 27330
TEL: 919-774-9515

Purpose: To provide victims of juvenile crime with restitution for damage, either property or physical.
Sponsor: State/County Governments
Contact: Ronnie Martin, Director
Description: The Lee County Restitution program is designed to provide victims of juvenile crime, restitution for either property or physical damage suffered by them.
It began April 1, 1983 and provides services for children ages 10 to 17. The children work one day weekly in stacking, loading and unloading firewood. Any monies earned by the children are given to the Clerk of Court for payment to the victim. The child is terminated from the program after payment is made.
The program operates under Community Based alternative (state) and county funds as well as grants from corporate sources.
The goal of the program is to instill responsibility in the youth and hopefully reduce repeat offenders.
Volunteer Staff: The volunteers act as supervisors at the job site. They are there to see that the work is carried out as well as providing support for the children. Due to the recent implementation of the program, we have only two volunteers but hope to increase this number considerably.
Volunteer Training: Training consists of 6 hours. The volunteers are trained in the techniques of counseling and also how to be an effective job site supervisor. Patience is stressed. The volunteers are screened thoroughly with supervision of the volunteers provided by the Director of Lee County Youth Services.
Founded: 1983

SENIOR VICTIM ASSISTANCE TEAM
Colorado Springs Police Department
Office of Volunteer Services
PO Box 2169
Colorado Springs, CO 80901
TEL: 719-578-6113
Purpose: To reduce or reverse the negative effect of being victimized by crime on elderly persons.
Sponsor: Colorado Springs Police Department
Contact: Nancy D. Forgy
Description: Because of time constraints, police officers investigating crimes in Colorado Springs frequently were unable to remain with victims as long as they felt was necessary. More and more the officers approached the department's Volunteer Services Coordinator to request volunteers who could talk to elderly crime victims. As a result, the Senior Victim Assistance Team - a unique group of one-to-one volunteers - was created.
This Team, called SVAT, was designed and developed and is being implemented as a means of serving those often dramatic needs of senior crime victims. By encouraging senior citizens to volunteer, SVAT serves also as a way of utilizing the skills of senior citizens developed over the years. Ages of volunteers range from 30 to 80, with more than half being senior citizens - some former crime victims themselves.
All SVAT volunteers are subjected to a background investigation and a polygraph examination to verify their credibility and to assure against further trauma being inflicted upon the senior victim. Those accepted then complete a minimum of 35 hours of training, which focuses on counseling skills, familiarization with the criminal justice system, familiarization with local victim-referral resources, and supervised case work by trained SVAT advisors. In concert with team members' training, a briefing is provided to area social service agency staff so that they support and understand the SVAT role as a member of the service community in Colorado Springs.
As a SVAT volunteer, each team member must be committed to four or more hours a week (most average 15 hours each week) in addition to monthly meetings and training sessions. On a rotation basis, a SVAT volunteer visits the police department each morning to review the previous day's police reports and identify those crimes which involve senior citizens. Initial contact is made that

same day by a team member to determine what assistance is needed. Concurrently, other SVAT members spend their volunteer time assisting with follow-up support to previously-contacted victims. In addition, a 24-hour on-call paging system for the SVAT makes members available for immediate crisis intervention through the request of law enforcement officers at the scene of the crime.

Costs to the Police Department for SVAT are limited to a portion of the salary of the Volunteer Services Coordinator and the cost of one additional telephone line for use by the SVAT at department headquarters. Office space for the SVAT volunteer reviewing daily reports is provided in a headquarters briefing room and is shared with patrol officers. These costs, however, are more than justified by release time provided to the officer by the SVAT. By freeing the officer for other high priority calls for service, SVAT volunteers facilitate maximum utilization of trained law enforcement professionals.

Since the SVAT's inception, a major thrust of the program has been to increase the reporting rate by the elderly as a result of a diminished fear through increased contact and trust of the law enforcement system, to heighten the sense of personal security among the elderly, and to increase citizen participation as a deterrent to crime.

The Colorado Springs Senior Victim Assistance Team was selected as an exemplary law enforcement project by the Law Enforcement Assistance Administration. In addition, it was chosen by the Colorado Office on Volunteerism as a model program.

STOP! THE MADNESS FOUNDATION
1325 W Street, NW
Washington, DC 20009
TEL: 202-483-2771
Purpose: To help make "the system" more responsive to the needs of survivors of victims of homicide.
Sponsor: Gannett Foundation
Contact: Cynthia Harris, Founder
Description: With a grant from the *Gannett Foundation* and successful recruitment of the Democratic and Republican National Committee Chairmen for the board of directors, *Stop! The Madness Foundation,* a public awareness program, opened its doors in April 1988. The founder is the mother of a young victim of homicide in the District of Columbia.

A major thrust of the program involves speaking to community groups around the country, encouraging them to build up their communities and put pressure on the criminal justice system to see that those responsible for violence are kept out of circulation.

The theme of the public awareness campaign is: "We are all responsible for stopping the killing." It is an effort to make the public more aware of the seriousness of what they are facing - "illegal guns and drugs among young people for starters."

The project has produced a series of posters and printed materials calling for the end of teenage violence and murder, designed to assist volunteer groups across the country - many led by mothers who had experienced the loss of a child through violence.
Publications: Stop! The Madness Information Packet
Founded: 1988

VICTIM-WITNESS ASSISTANCE CENTER*
103 East Water Street
Syracuse, NY 13202
TEL: 315-474-7011
Purpose: To improve services for victims and witnesses of crimes.
Sponsor: Volunteer Center
Contact: Jean J. Greene
Description: The Victim-Witness program began in 1976 as a cooperative effort of the Volunteer Center, the District Attorney's Office of the County of Onondaga, and the Rape Crisis Center. Originally the program received funding from LEAA for a three-year pilot, and now has been picked up by the county.

The program goal is to humanize the criminal justice system and redress the balance in favor of the victim. The Volunteer Center's role is to recruit, train and place interested volunteers and to develop volunteer position. Volunteer duties include:
- accompanying sensitive, elderly, handicapped or injured victims and witness to court appearances.
- assisting victims with filing complaint affidavits in the District Attorney's office.
- contacting crime victims to offer supportive services.
- notifying victims, witnesses and police officers of the final disposition of the cases in which they were involved.
- providing safe, comfortable and informative witness reception areas.

Volunteers provided other supportive services as needed, such as babysitting and transportation. In addition, they communicate with Information and Referral professionals, who give victims and witnesses assistance in securing community services to meet their needs and to help solve problems that they experience as a result of crimes - in some cases, problems that existed before the crimes, also.

About 40 volunteers are involved in the program at any one time. The work is demanding and there is some turnover. Training usually consists of two half days of scheduled, formal lectures and discussion with much information on the criminal justice system, interviewing skills, community services, etc. This is followed by extensive on-the-job training by the two volunteer coordinators. Volunteers are provided with a volunteer training manual for ongoing reference.
Founded: 1976

LITERACY

NATIONAL/STATE ORGANIZATIONS

COALITION FOR LITERACY
50 East Huron Street
Chicago, IL 60611
TEL: 312-944-6780
Objectives: To work toward the eradication of illiteracy by teaming volunteers with groups working in the field.
Services: Links existing groups working to eradicate illiteracy with new partners to the cause on local, state, and national levels; operates a three-year campaign to provide opportunity for service, support, and involvement; enlists assistance from television, radio and print public service advertising to alert the public to the magnitude of the issue and recruit volunteers from business, church, professional circles and other sources as help for local programs; appeals directly to local community leaders to provide volunteer tutors, financial help, committed professionals, and other services and assistance as needed; coalition members are:

- American Association of Adult and Continuing Education
- American Association of Advertising Agencies
- American Library Association
- B. Dalton Bookseller
- CONTACT Incorporated
- International Reading Association
- Laubach Literacy International
- Literacy Volunteers of America
- National Advisory Council on Adult Education
- National Commission on Libraries and Information Centers
- National Council of State Directors of Adult Education

Publishes information materials on illiteracy issues, and on its programs (request list).

LAUBACH LITERACY ACTION
Laubach Literacy International
1320 Jamesville Avenue
Box 131
Syracuse, NY 13210
TEL: 315-422-9121
Objectives: To enable community-based volunteer programs to provide basic literacy instruction to native speakers of English and to speakers of other languages.
Services: Provides materials, technical assistance and information enabling literacy groups to train volunteer tutors, writers for new readers, and program managers; develops and disseminates

materials on effective recruitment and placement of students and tutors, student and tutor support services, promotion and fundraising; promotes adult literacy through the national and local media and through contacts with national and state agencies which serve the nonreader; provides information about current literacy programs, methods and materials; develops new literacy program techniques and services to meet emerging student needs; and convenes biennial conferences, and, on alternate years, regional conferences.

LITERACY VOLUNTEERS OF AMERICA
5795 South Widewaters Parkway
Syracuse, NY 13214
TEL: 315-445-8000
Objectives: To increase the number and capabilities of individuals and organizations tutoring adults in basic reading and conversational English.
Services: Provides training to individuals and adults in tutoring techniques; offers technical assistance and materials to both member and non-member groups interested in organizing or improving tutorial programs; maintains library; publishes handbooks on teaching techniques, diagnostic reading test and a bibliography of suitable reading materials.

NEW READERS PRESS
Laubach Literacy International
1320 Jamesville Avenue
Box 131
Syracuse, NY 13210
TEL: 315-422-9121
Objectives: To publish and disseminate adult literacy materials designed for use in volunteer literacy programs and adult basic education programs.
Services: Demonstrates methods and materials used in teaching literacy skills to native speakers of English and to speakers of other languages; demonstrates methods and materials used in teaching basic math skills; provides sample materials for display at conferences, workshops and seminars.

VOLUNTEER READING AIDES PROGRAM
Lutheran Church Women of America
2900 Queen Lane
Philadelphia, PA 19129
TEL: 215-438-2200

Objectives: To give the non-reader individual attention to gain the skills and confidence that is needed for classroom work.
Services: Assists groups, agencies and communities in evaluating needs for an organization of volunteer adult literacy programs; refers groups to already-existing literacy efforts, in cooperation with National Affiliation for Literacy Advance, Literacy Volunteers of America and other literacy groups; trains volunteers in tutoring and leadership skills; provides consultant services; publishes *Handbook for Volunteer Reading Aides* and other books, teaching aids, etc.

INDIVIDUAL PROGRAM PROFILES

ADULT LITERACY PROJECT
Beaver County Federated Library System
2020 Main Street
Aliquippa, PA 15001
TEL: 412-728-0330
Purpose: To train volunteer tutors to provide one-to-one tutoring for adults requesting help to improve their basic reading, writing, math, or English-as-a-second-language skills.
Sponsor: Federal/State/County governments; foundation grants; contracts; public and private donations.
Contact: Nancy Woods
Description: Since 1978, hundreds of tutors have been certified and thousands of students have been served through this project. Approximately 150 volunteers are actively tutoring at all times. The staff includes a Project Coordinator, a Project secretary, a part-time guidance counselor and two part-time paid teachers to coordinate volunteer efforts. The U.S. Department of Labor Green Thumb program provides three part-time senior citizen workers and the VISTA-ACTION program provides three full-time workers. The Literacy Council executive board assists in coordination of many volunteer activities.
Funding is provided by the Pennsylvania Department of Education 306 grant; MH/MR Contracts; U.S. Department of Labor contracts; B. Dalton Bookseller (Dayton-Hudson Foundation) grant; Beaver County government (Federated Library System); public and private donations; and funding activities.
Founded: 1978

CALIFORNIA LITERACY*
317 West Main Street
Alhambra, CA 91801
TEL: 213-282-2196
Purpose: To help adults become functional in our English-speaking society through the use of the Laubach Method in teaching reading, writing and speaking English.
Sponsor: Private donations, grants from B. Dalton Bookseller, Atlantic Richfield Foundation, Security Pacific Foundation
Contact: Florence Peetz, Public Relations
Description: California Literacy, Inc. started in 1957 when the first class of volunteer tutors was trained in the Laubach Method of teaching through phonics and picture/symbol association. This method was created by Dr. Frank C. Laubach fifty years ago and has been proven successful worldwide.
The California Laubach volunteers are organized into 25 councils with over 170 teaching centers scattered throughout the state, with the greatest concentration being in the southern part of the state. However, great stride in expansion of activities are being made in northern California. The program is affiliated with the national organization, Laubach Literacy Action of Syracuse, New York.
The state headquarters operation is funded by private donations, grants from Security Pacific Foundation, The Atlantic Richfield Foundation and B. Dalton Bookseller. The major source of support, however, is from the sale of New Readers Press books to our tutors, students, schools, prisons, etc.
The aim of the program is to double the number of volunteer

tutors and more than double the number of students helped. Last year 2600 volunteer tutors helped 10,000 Californians toward becoming functional in an English-speaking society.
The volunteer tutors are very carefully trained in the Laubach Method. Trainers are certified by a national board of certification. Workshops of 12-15 hours are given for training in tutoring English-speaking people to read and write, whereas 18 hours are required for training tutors to help non-English-speaking people. Once trained, the volunteer tutors help students on a one-to-one basis once or twice a week for sessions of one to two hours each. There is no charge for the training, since that, too, is a volunteer effort.
Founded: 1957

CAMPUS LITERACY AWARENESS MONTH PROGRAM
Student Coalition for Action in Literacy Education (SCALE)
University of North Carolina
Chapel Hill, NC 27514
TEL: 919-962-2333
Purpose: To raise awareness about the problems of illiteracy.
Contact: SCALE Coordinator
Description: March of each year is *Campus Literacy Awareness Month* for COOL (Campus Outreach Opportunity League) chapters on campuses across the country. On the Chapel Hill campus of the University of North Carolina, SCALE (Student Coalition for Action in Literacy Education) is very active in literacy programs during the entire academic year, but that special month gives the group an opportunity to create special projects to promote literacy.
A popular program is the brainstorming session that the group pulls together every year. SCALE recruits campus volunteers to come together and share ideas about ways in which students can help improve education in the United States. One conclusion was to help other campus groups mount intensive programs during *Campus Literacy Awareness Month.* They decided to develop a package that would help other groups organize literacy projects during this special month.
The Campus Literacy Awareness Month Packet was designed by SCALE and has been distributed nationwide. The packet includes examples of awareness week activities, a listing of national literacy contacts, and advice on how to organize a month of awareness.
Many programs that had their roots in *Campus Literacy Awareness Month* have become permanent programs with various sponsors from the community.
Publications: Campus Literacy Awareness Month Packet

CENTER FOR LITERACY
3723 Center Street
Philadelphia, PA 19104
TEL: 215-382-3700
Purpose: To raise the adult functional illiterate's reading and writing skills.
Sponsor: Federal/state/county governments; corporate and private donations.
Contact: Marlyn DeWitt, Executive Director
Description: The Center for Literacy is a nonprofit agency that has been tackling the problem of adult functional illiteracy since 1968. The Center is a member of both national literacy organizations, Laubach Literacy Action and Literacy Volunteers of America. The Center provides individualized one-on-one instruction. Based on the principle that if one can speak, read and write English, one can share those skills with someone else, the Center for Literacy utilizes an extensive network of trained community volunteers.
In May of 1983, CFL had a total of 283 active tutors participating in the program. CFL's volunteer tutors are Philadelphians of all ages, religions, races and educational backgrounds. Each tutor attends a ten-hour training workshop. Once tutors have received training, they are matched with a student.
Volunteers are asked to make an initial commitment of 50 hours.

In addition, student/tutor pairs meet at least two times a week. Tutors prepare lessons and homework assignments for students. Materials for assignments are provided by the Center. Teachers and counselors are available to volunteers for technical assistance and on-going training.

As noted above, volunteers are from all segments of society. The most important criteria is commitment. The payoff for volunteers is the knowledge that through their persistence and dedication, new opportunities will open for students.

Funding comes from the Pennsylvania Department of Education Federal Adult Education Act monies; corporate sector funds donated for Neighborhood Assistance; membership fees; and private donations. The largest donation is the in-kind source of volunteers (valued at $63,000 in calendar 1983) and rent-free space (valued at $12,000 in 1983) for agency headquarters.
Founded: 1968

CENTER FOR LITERACY
3723 Chestnut Street
Philadelphia, PA 19104-3189
TEL: 215-382-3850
Purpose: To help adult Philadelphians improve their reading, writing and math.
Sponsor: Federal/state/county governments; corporate and private foundations, individuals
Contact: Ashley Husley, Director of Public Affairs
Description: Since 1968, the Center for Literacy has provided adult Philadelphians with instruction in basic reading, writing and math. The oldest and largest adult literacy provider in Pennsylvania, CFL offers both one-to-one instruction with trained volunteer tutors and small classes with professional teachers.

CFL is a community-based organization, with 91 sites throughout Philadelphia, including neighborhood libraries, corporate offices, and community centers. In addition to providing tutor training, CFL works with other nonprofit organizations to provide literacy services to special populations: the homeless, job training participants, parolees and probationers. CFL also provides workplace literacy classes with local employers. CFL publishes a variety of curriculum for adult educators.
Publications: Basic Literacy Tutor Handbook; Plain Talk on Taxes; Read to Me; Tips for Reading to Children; I Don't Speak English... But I Understand You
Founded: 1968

CHAMBER OF COMMERCE LITERACY COUNCIL
Gadsden Chamber of Commerce
One Commerce Square
Gadsden, AL 35904
TEL: 205-543-3472
Purpose: To fight an illiteracy rate estimated at 25 percent among the county's approximately 100,000 residents.
Sponsor: Mid-South Industries
Contact: Dennis Phillips, Council Chairman
Description: The *Gadsden Chamber of Commerce,* enlisted the *United Way,* literacy service providers, and more than 35 other leaders from area businesses, school systems, and industry to form a *Literacy Council* to combat illiteracy in the Gadsden area.

The Chairman of the Council, corporate director of human-resource development of *Mid-South Industries,* and other members oversee individual literacy efforts in the community. The *United Way* provided venture grants to fund information materials to get the word out about available literacy services. Recognizing the difficulty of encouraging people to ask for help, the materials are carefully developed to make it as easy as possible for people to come forward.

The *Gadsden United Way* also has added a *Literacy Hotline* to its regular *Information & Referral Service.* In addition, it has funded production of a videotape that promotes local literacy assistance programs. The video is distributed to stores, restaurants, and other locations with video monitors, all of whom cooperate fully with the program.

CHILDREN'S LITERACY INITIATIVE
1207 Chestnut
Philadelphia, PA 19107
TEL: 215-561-7323
Purpose: To train day care workers, teachers and parents in improving reading skills of young children at risk of illiteracy.
Sponsor: Ragan Henry Law Firm
Contact: Marcia Moon or Linda Katz, Founders
Description: Working since 1988 out of donated space in a local attorney's office, *Children's Literacy Initiative* promotes literacy training and offers literacy workshops to day care centers serving low-income families. Some of the books and other materials used in the training become part of an annual event, *Children's Expo,* which is sponsored by the group and trains day care workers, teachers and parents to develop reading interests and skills in young children, especially poor, inner-city children most at risk of illiteracy. The 1989 *Expo* attracted 14,000 people from the Philadelphia area.

Given the success of the organization's efforts, the founders have created concepts for seven radio shows and tapped a number of children's entertainers to host them. Called *Kidwaves,* the shows are geared to help children enrich their imaginations, expand their vocabularies and lengthen their attentions spans. They are also aimed at parents - hoping they will be encouraged to read to their children. Programming includes *In Concert,* which features a performance by and an interview with an artist; *Story Stew,* which features stories read and told live by guest tale-tellers, and other enrichment segments.

It is hoped that the volunteer effort and interest shown by the community for the umbrella organization, *Childrens's Literacy Initiative,* and the annual *Children's Expo* will continue for *Kidwaves.* The schools got behind them, distributed handbills, hung posters, etc. Libraries, day care, clergy associations, Head Start programs, and others with an interest in children also got involved in spreading the word.

Unlike the others, *Kidwaves* is necessarily a profit-making venture, but the quality of the programming and types of products in the advertisements are closely monitored. Types of products *not* accepted include video games, pro-wrestling tie-ins or violent toys. Since radio audiences under 12 years of age are not tracked for audience size, attracting advertisers to finance the program is expected to be difficult.

One example that shines like a beacon for the group is KPAL-AM in Little Rock, Arkansas, which began in 1986 to broadcast an all-children's format from 6 a.m. to 9 p.m. each day. It not only was financed long enough to stay in the black, but won the coveted *George Foster Peabody Award* and several other awards. KPAL officials attribute much of its success to quality programming and working closely with city schools, day care facilities and parents/kids groups to continually evalutate the program. Some 8,000 children joined the free KPAL Clubhouse, and 15,000 visited the studios each year.

In mid-1990, *Children's Literacy Initiative* founders began fanning out across the country to talk with AM station owners. In the meantime, the *Initiative* and the *Expo* continue to involve families in inspiring children in the Philadelphia area to read.
Founded: 1988

JVS VOLUNTEER TUTORIAL PROGRAM
Jewish Vocational Service
One South Franklin Street
Chicago, IL 60606
TEL: 312-408-2047; 312-346-6700
Purpose: To help make the experience of adjusting to a new culture less trying for Soviet emigres.
Contact: Cara Madansky

Description: In anticipation of an unprecedented influx of Soviet emigres, the *Chicago Jewish Vocational Service's (JVS)* volunteer tutorial program has recently undergone dramatic expansion. In 1989, 200 volunteers saved the community more than $100,000 by providing tutorial services to these new Americans. The volunteers help the immigrants become integrated and self-sustaining much more quickly than they might otherwise.

Each tutor makes a commitment to meet with an individual or family at least once a week for two hours for eight weeks or longer. Most volunteers spend at least four months with their assigned families, and many develop ongoing relationships. Some volunteers involve their entire families.

Upon entering the program, all tutors are given information on JVS's role in the resettlement process, suggested topics and activities to facilitate the acculturation process and a volunteer manual. Twice a year group training sessions are held. Tutors and JVS staff "network" once a month, and these sessions are limited in size so that participants are able to benefit from an informal exchange of ideas and experiences, successes and failures.

Volunteers often ask immigrants to visit the local schools for an exchange with the students. In one case a young Soviet guitar player entranced the students so that the music teacher invited him back.

Volunteers are helping to make the process of being absorbed by, and adjusting to a new culture less difficult. In addition, they are filling a critical need in the absorption process as well as easing the financial burden on the agencies involved in that process. While the emigres benefit from the assistance received, the volunteer tutors thoroughly enjoy the experience. As one volunteer put it, "I'm getting more than I'm giving."

LITERACY AND LIFE SKILLS
Community Education Services of Chinatown
777 Stockton Street
San Francisco, CA 94108
TEL: 415-982-0615; 415-982-0617
Purpose: To teach Asian immigrant students how to adopt to life in the United States.
Sponsor: Community Education Services of Chinatown
Contact: Volunteer Coordinator
Description: Community Education Services of Chinatown recruits volunteers to work with Asian students on language and cultural skills needed for a life in the United States. In spring 1989, seventy-five Asian students successfully completed the long and often difficult process.

Thirty-six adult volunteers worked with the students during the 1988-89 school year to help ease them into the mainstream of American life. Students came from three high schools - Galileo, Mission and Newcomer.

During the graduation ceremonies for the students, the volunteers were recognized for their accomplishments.

LITERACY INCENTIVE PROGRAM (NO READ, NO RELEASE)
Virginia Governor's Office
State Capitol Building
Richmond, VA 23219
TEL: 804-786-2211
FAX: 804-786-3985
Purpose: To institute a "no read, no release" literacy program in the state's prisons and work camps.
Sponsor: Virginia Governor's Office
Contact: Osa Coffey, Director of Correctional Education
Description: In January 1986, one month after taking office, the Governor of Virginia installed a literacy program in each of the state's 18 major adult prisons and 10 of its 25 work camps. The goal was to improve the 50 to 75 percent illiteracy rate among prisoners. Titled the *Literacy Incentive Program,* it has earned enthusiastic attention from members of Congress and officials in

other states. Although dubbed by the Governor "no read, no release," no inmate is denied parole because he cannot read. A few are denied parole because they would not participate in literacy classes.

By 1989, 981 inmates across Virginia had learned to read after enrolling in the literacy program. Inmates attend classes for one-and-one-half hours a day, five days a week. The learning is self-paced with a supervisory teacher and volunteer inmate-tutors providing individual instruction. The focus is on practical skills, such as being able to read a newspaper's employment ads and fill out job applications.

The program includes a formal tracking system that monitors an eligible inmate's participation in literacy classes and reports back to the Parole Board when an inmate comes up for review. Participation in the program is viewed by the board as an indicator of the inmate's desire and effort to reform himself. Enrollment is voluntary, and one problem is persuading illiterate inmates to take advantage of the program. Prisoners are tested when they enter the state system and are eligible if they read below the eighth-grade level.

In 1988, about half of the eligible inmates enrolled for at least a year; 20 percent refused to participate, 13 percent dropped out and another 27 percent were on waiting lists. New sites are planned in each year's budget with the goal of including all facilities in the program as soon as possible.

LITERACY VOLUNTEERS OF CHICAGO
207 South Wabash
Eighth Floor
Chicago, IL 60604
TEL: 312-663-0543
Purpose: To foster increased literacy in the Chicago metropolitan area through the support and organization of trained volunteer tutors.
Sponsor: Federal/State governments; corporate private foundations
Contact: Inez Alexander, Project Referral Coordinator
Description: Literacy Volunteers of Chicago provides free one-to-one small group instruction in Basic Reading or English as a Second Language to adults who have reading problems or do not speak English. The tutoring is conducted by volunteers who work out of a network of 27 decentralized tutor training/reading centers located in predominantly minority communities throughout Chicago. These sites are located in public libraries, churches, YMCA's community centers and Adult Basic Education facilities. Often these sites are staffed with volunteers who work in partnership with existing site staff.

Currently over 250 volunteers provide tutorial services, function as student and tutor recruiters, serve as evaluators and assist the staff as program planners and trainers.

Volunteers are recruited through voluntary agencies, corporations and the media. Each volunteer is interviewed, trained, and supervised. All volunteers must successfully complete an 18 hour pre-service teaching training workshop that prepares him or her to respond professionally to the needs of the student. In addition to learning how to teach reading and language skills, the volunteers are taught how to create lesson plans, motivate students, and provide long and short term goals. After successfully completing the training, each tutor is matched with a student, and asked to commit a minimum of 50 hours to the program. During the volunteers' involvement in the program, periodic in-service workshops are given to help hone and refine the tutor's skills.

As the programs develop, volunteers become involved in all facets of the program from curriculum development to fund raising. In this way, ownership of the program will eventually be turned over to the volunteers and people in the communities that it serves.

LITERACY VOLUNTEERS OF NEW YORK STATE
1479 Kensington Avenue
Buffalo, NY 14215
TEL: 716-835-2677

Purpose: To provide training in Basic Reading and English as a Second Language to volunteers interested in eradicating illiteracy and its attendant problems.
Sponsor: New York State Continuing Education, private foundations, businesses and personal contributions.
Contact: Kevin G. Smith, Executive Director
Description: Literacy Volunteers of New York State (LVNYS) is a non-profit volunteer program. Literacy Volunteers Affiliates are community-based volunteer groups that tutor basic reading and writing or English as a second language to teenagers and adults on an individual basis. There are 48 Literacy Volunteers Affiliates in New York State, in which 3500 volunteers are active and more than 3600 students are being tutored. In FY 1981-82, 115,465 hours were spent in instructional activities involving student/tutor dyads. In addition, LVNYS provides leadership training, Board of Director's development and organizational management to its affiliates upon request.
According to the policies and procedures of Literacy Volunteers of America, dedicated volunteers under the direction of Literacy Volunteers of New York State organize self-governing affiliates that train and supervise volunteers to tutor adults and teenagers in basic reading and writing. Training is also given in the teaching of English as a second language, with emphasis on conversational skills, as well as cultural orientation for foreign born students. The students are found in the community at large, in schools, business, industry, hospitals, social agencies, and even government installations.
All Literacy Volunteers are trained in the Basic Reading Workshop and/or English as a Second Language Workshop as developed by Literacy Volunteers of America, Inc. These workshops are reproduced on slides and tapes and distributed to Literacy Volunteers Affiliates to ensure continuity and quality of training.
Literacy Volunteers are asked to tutor a student twice a week for an hour each time at a location mutually convenient to both tutor and student. An Affiliate generally asks each tutor to commit him/herself to one year of service or one hundred hours of tutoring.
The American Council on Education and the University of the State of New York grants three (3) college credit hours at the undergraduate level or graduate level in Reading Instruction for students who have completed the Literacy Volunteer Basic Reading Training/Tutorial Experience.

MEMPHIS LITERACY COUNCIL
703 South Greer
Memphis, TN 38111
TEL: 901-327-6000 ; 901-327-6001
Purpose: To teach functionally illiterate adults basic reading and writing skills
Sponsor: Independent affiliate of Laubach Literacy Action
Contact: Mrs. Gay M. Johnston
Description: The Memphis Literacy Council was organized in 1974 to teach adults how to read and write through the operation of its "Each One Teach One" program. Last year 650 students were served in this program.
Volunteers are recruited by TV and radio spots, posters, speaking engagements and bookmarks and brochures. Volunteers come from all areas of the city and are of all ages. A job description has been developed for a literacy tutor. Each volunteer has completed a basic 12-hour training course which is conducted by Volunteer Certified Trainers.
Tutors are paired with a non-reading adult and meet this student twice a week at any public place for one to two hour lessons.
Books are provided for both the tutor and the student. Additional training is available during the year for all tutors.
At present, there are over 400 tutors, each working with at least one new reader. In addition, the Council is governed by a volunteer Board of Directors composed of 36 people. It is an

active working Board.
Memphis Literacy Council is a United Way agency and receives 80% of its financial support from this source. The remaining 20% funding is provided by private donations and small local grants.
Founded: 1974

NORTHWEST ALABAMA READING AIDES
PO Box 391
Florence, AL 35631
TEL: 205-766-6952
Purpose: To help adult non-readers improve their reading and writing skills.
Sponsor: United Way, private donations and service clubs
Contact: Mary Fountain, President
Description: Northwest Alabama Reading Aides began in March of 1976 with about 50 original members as a non-denominational organization with the intent of helping the adult non-readers in Lauderdale and Colbert counties improve their reading and writing skills.
The Good Shepherd Lutheran Church sponsored the first tutor training workshops with the help of the Lutheran Church Women. The Lutheran Church Women had qualified trainers in the Laubach each-one-teach-one method of teaching, and were also experienced in organizing literacy groups.
In the course of the next few months officers were elected, a constitution and by-laws provided, and NARA was incorporated as a non-profit corporation. In 1977, NARA sought and received funding from the local United Way agency.
NARA Volunteers and Students - Presently there are 129 members in NARA. To be a member a person must know how to read and attend a ten hour workshop. Dues are $2.00.
A member is not required to take a student, and as the motto each-one-teach-one implies, a person has fulfilled his obligation as a tutor if he has helped, even if only for a short period of time, one person learn to read. Some tutors take another student after they have finished with one student, and some tutor two or more at the same time. Last year 41 volunteers taught 43 students, and approximately 900 hours were spent in tutoring by the group.
There are five books in the Laubach Way to Reading. The students are asked to buy their own books and the tutors pay for their own Teacher's Manuals. There is also a small library for supplementary reading material, and these books can be borrowed at no cost to either student or tutor.
Students are required to be 16 years of age or older and must make the request personally to be tutored.
After a volunteer has finished a training session, the Student/Tutor Coordinator assigns him/her a student. The tutor and student then must make their own arrangements as to when and where they will meet for the lessons.
Volunteer Staff - NARA has seven elected officers: President, two Co-Vice-Presidents, Secretary, Treasurer, Tutor/Student Record Keeper and Tutor/Student Coordinator.
- The two vice-presidents are responsible for all the publicity of the organization, reaching students as well as volunteers.
- The Tutor/Student Record Keeper documents tutors' hours.
- The Tutor/Student Coordinators matches people who want to learn to read with a tutor.
Besides these seven officers there are also two Co-Directors of Student Training. They are certified to run the workshops in which the tutors are trained. There are usually four workshops a year, two in the fall and two in the spring. Last year 20 new tutors were trained.
There is also a Librarian and a Supplies Chairman who orders the textbooks. Other volunteers accept phone calls from people who wish to learn to read and from those wanting to take the tutor training. Other duties performed by members include helping out at the workshops, setting up and manning display booths, making phone contacts with students and tutors, and bringing food and beverages to the three meetings that are held each year.

There are usually three newsletters each year, which are sent out by the secretary, two officers' meetings and the three general meetings.

Funding - Northwest Alabama Reading Aides has an annual budget of approximately $1,800.00. The majority of this money comes from United Way and the rest comes from donations and dues.

The biggest expense is supplies. Money is budgeted also for helping to send one or two members to the national and regional Laubach Literacy Conferences each year. Most of the rest of the money is spent either on postage or printing.

Founded: 1976

OKLAHOMA CITY LITERACY COUNCIL

131 Dean A. McGee Avenue
Oklahoma City, OK 73102
TEL: 405-232-3780
Purpose: To teach functional illiterates to read and write.
Sponsor: Private donations only
Contact: President
Description: The Oklahoma City Literacy Council (OCLC) is an organization of men and women who have seen the need for teaching functional illiterates to read and write. A functional illiterate is one who cannot read well enough to fill out forms, read street signs, read want ads, or directions for cooking found on packages.

OCLC is a member of Laubach Literacy Action, Syracuse, New York, and uses the Frank Laubach method of "each one teach one." OCLC is the source for the Skill Books, and Teacher Manuals published by the Laubach press. These are sold to the teachers and students for cost. Volunteers are the only staff and teachers at OCLC.

OCLC staff is composed of those men and women who have taken 10 hours of training to teach basic English and 15 hours of training to teach English to Speakers of Other Languages. They devote at least two hours a week to teaching a student, or students, how to read and write. The preferred time is two hours twice a week. Most of the Tutors hold twice-a-week sessions, and many have more than one student. Also there are a number of tutors who hold group sessions. The workshops are a vital part of the program. This is planned, set up and taught by the Tutor training committee. Many hours of dedication are required to prepare the materials, lesson plans, and to secure the place for the sessions. Also, five to eight of these tutors donate a day a week to staff the office. There is no paid staff.

Tutors can be anyone who is truly interested in his/her fellow man. No teaching experience is required. They are thoroughly trained in the workshops. Experienced tutors are always available for consultation. Tutors are recruited for TV spot announcements, news releases, and talks to civic clubs and church groups. The students are people "who have heard about you," or referrals from the Welfare Department, churches and schools. These students are screened, and their reading level, if they do read, is tested. OCLC is not equipped to handle mentally retarded persons or those with severe learning disabilities.

PALS PROGRAM
Gulf State Steel
174 South 26th Street
Gadsden, AL 35904
TEL: 205-543-6100
Purpose: To provide literary assistance to employees and the wider community.
Sponsor: Gadsden Board of Education
Contact: Human Resources Director
Description: Recognizing a considerable literacy problem among employees, *Gulf State Steel* purchased the *IBM Corporation's Principles of the Alphabet Literacy System (PALS)* program. The computer package was installed and set up on-site in a facility where employees could have a quiet place to receive literacy assistance. This approach proved very successful, with employees constantly using the resource.

The *Gadsden Board of Education* saw an opportunity in this corporate effort to avoid duplication of an innovative idea. With help from the *United Way,* arrangements were made with *Gulf State Steel* to allow community residents to take advantage of the facility also. According to United Way officials, "Cooperative ventures such as these help to conserve resources in the fight against illiteracy."

READ FOR LITERACY

325 North Michigan
Toledo, OH 43624
TEL: 419-242-7323
Purpose: To teach adults to read or improve reading skills.
Contact: Diana McClellan, Tutor-Student Coordinator
Description: Although *Read for Literacy* has a more-than-adequate cadre of volunteers (500) for most of the year, every summer a gap of 40 volunteer slots opens up due to summer vacation or other plans. In late Spring the popular program begins recruiting to fill those slots and avoid any interruption in tutoring service to people who need it.

Volunteer tutors teach twice a week for an hour to an hour and a half each time. Students and tutors are matched up based on time constraints and convenient meeting places. Volunteers receive a 10-hour training course in the *Laubach Reading Method,* which emphasizes phonetics. This method is used because a lot of people learned to read by sight, memorizing the words and saying them when they see them. They are taught to sound out the words, since memorization often causes confusion.

Students are referred to *Read for Literacy* by more than 30 social agencies throughout the metropolitan area. Most students are between the ages of 25 and 34 and, until recently, mostly male. Many are on welfare, and most didn't graduate from high school. Women begin to request help when their children start school, since they want to be able to read to them.

In early September the program holds a "Rally by the River," which is a volunteer-staffed event designed to provide visibility for the program and information to the community.

SPARTANBURG ADULT WRITING AND READING (AWARE)

PO Box 308
Spartanburg, SC 29304
TEL: 803-583-8141 (Services); 803-573-8541 (Admin.)
Purpose: To offer non-reading and limited-reading adult residents of the County the chance to improve or develop basic skills in reading, and writing.
Sponsor: Corporate and private donations, some government funds
Contact: Beverly C. Campbell, Executive Director
Description: AWARE, Inc., began operation as a grassroots agency in September of 1977 with the appointment of a 16-member volunteer Board of Directors. The present Board stands at 11, by amendment of the by-laws. AWARE was incorporated under the laws of the State of South Carolina as a non-profit, eleemosynary organization. In August of 1980, the literacy group received an offer from the State Department of Education, Office of Adult Education, to receive and manage a 310-Project Demonstration Grant for Education.

AWARE then opened a full-time office on August 15, and the group became affiliated with the Adult Reading Campaign (a joint effort of education and volunteer literacy groups).

AWARE employs a full-time Executive Director, Executive Assistant, and Volunteer Services Coordinator. A *VISTA (Volunteers In Service to America)* worker manages the *Committee on Minority Awareness (CMA).* An appointee of the *Senior Employment Program (SEP)* is the half-time Services Assistant. All tutors, Board members, and other supporters work on a strictly volunteer basis.

Volunteer tutors are required to attend a minimum of 12 hours of training in the Laubach Way to Reading method of teaching reading. AWARE uses strictly Laubach materials, as provided by the by-laws of the corporation. In addition, 18 hours in Writing for New Readers (production of low-level reading materials), is available.

In-service seminars in phonetics and use of specific materials are also offered from time to time. To qualify for training, the volunteer need only be able to read and write English well enough to use the training manuals effectively.

Spartanburg AWARE refers students completing the Laubach program to *The Transitional Class,* a project of AWARE and local Adult Education. The class is open only to AWARE students. This project teaches job search skills as well as supplementing education toward passage of the GED (General Education Development) test.

AWARE also refers students to the GED programs of the seven school districts and to the English teaching classes of Spartanburg Technical College and local churches.

Other sponsors and participants in the program include the South Carolina Department of Corrections, Dutchman Correctional Institute School, South Carolina Literacy Association, Laubach Literacy Action, and United Way.

Founded: 1977

TIME TO READ
Time, Inc.
Corporate Community Relations
Rockefeller Center
New York, NY 10020
TEL: 212-522-1212
Purpose: To combat functional illiteracy through trained volunteer tutors and innovative teaching methods and materials.
Sponsor: Time, Inc.
Contact: TTR Coordinator
Description: Time to Read (TTR) is a model volunteer literacy program that began in 1985 as a Time, Inc. employee volunteer program in New York City. It was launched nationally to address the problem of 27 million Americans who cannot read well enough to fill out a job application, understand a supermarket ad, or read instructions on the job. TTR is not for people who cannot read at all, but for those who lack the skills to read fluently. The program is designed to augment and work in concert with existing literacy programs by providing the needed bridge between basic programs such as *Laubach Literacy* and *Literacy Volunteers of America,* and high school equivalency (GED) programs.

Time To Read works as a community partnership involving local businesses, institutions, and community organizations. Corporate and community volunteers manage the program and provide tutoring. Specially-trained volunteer tutors spend two hours a week for one year with one learner or a group of two to five learners. Learners are recruited through four different settings - schools, prisons, the workplace, and community organizations.

TTR skills are ones that learners "can take home with them" since they work as well with newspapers, magazines, a job application, etc., as they do with school assignments. In addition to instructional materials, each TTR learner and tutor gets a subscription to *Time* magazine and a choice of one other (*People, Sports Illustrated, Life, Money,* or *Southern Living*).

Between 1985 and 1988, TTR grew from five pilot sites to 35 sites in 12 states. Surveys have shown that up to 71% of the learners improved their reading scores, and 82% said they enjoyed reading more. Almost two-thirds of the volunteer tutors repeat the service for a second year due to its high success rate.

Tutor training involves one 6-hour training session, one 3-hour follow-up training session, and a videotape and manual. In addition to the magazine subscriptions for tutor and learner, instructional materials provided to each tutor include 50 lesson

plans with guide, and a loose-leaf manual with activity sheets, and the learner receives an Activity Sheet Pad, a dictionary and a bookbag. Costs are minimal and are borne by the sponsor. Where no sponsor is available, *Time, Inc.* defrays costs through an assistance program.

A special free publication, *The Time to Read Approach to Reading,* details the theory and practice behind TTR.

Publications: The Time to Read Approach to Reading; Time to Read: The Time, Inc. Literacy Program
Founded: 1985

YOU CAN FREE A MIND: ADULT LITERACY PROGRAM
Brown University
25 George Street
PO Box 1974
Providence, RI 02912
TEL: 401-863-2338
Purpose: To provide literacy tutoring for the Providence adult community.
Description: Established in 1987, this program recruits *Brown University* students to provide literacy tutoring to adults in the community. Students are trained by a representative of the *Brown University Adult Academy.*

Training for students is made available at the beginning of each semester and takes about ten hours. After the students have been trained, they are paired with a learner and assigned to a site either on or off campus, depending upon their preference. The on-campus tutoring occurs on Saturday mornings, while the off-campus tutoring takes place at various times during the week. Over the years the volunteers have worked with *Blackstone Valley, Dorcas Place, South Providence Tutorial, Talbot House,* and the *Genesis* program. During the fall of 1989, there were four tutors. The tutors are expected to meet weekly with their learners for one and a half to two hours, and they are urged to stay with one learner for as long as possible to create a stable environment.

Publications: Imagine What It Is Like for Someone Who Cannot Read

MENTAL HEALTH

INDIVIDUAL PROGRAM PROFILES

COMPEER
Mental Health Association
744 McCallie Avenue
Suite 515
Chattanooga, TN 37303
TEL: 615-265-2408
Purpose: To bring together mental health clients ready to function on their own and volunteer peers to provide friendship for the transition period.
Contact: Martha Westbrook or Susan Ewing, Co-Chairpersons
Description: The *Mental Health Association's Compeer Program* started in 1989. "Compeer" literally means "an equal match, a companion or peer." The program pairs community volunteers and mental health clients on a one-to-one basis for the simple purpose of friendship - in much the same way that the *Big Brothers and Big Sisters* program pairs one-parent children with role-model adults.
A survey of area mental health care providers turned up more than 1,000 clients who could benefit from the program's one-on-one friendships. The *Compeer* volunteer fills the gap between tratment services and the absence of adequate support by family, friends and the community.
Compeer clients are referred from local mental health care centers by a therapist who believes they are both ready and capable of functioning on their own. Many of the people referred give no signal that they are mentally ill, some being in remission, and others having learned how to manage the illness. Clients and volunteers are paired according to interests, age and sex. Each has the opportunity to approve or veto the match.
The first training session for Chattanooga's *Compeer* program was conducted in May 1989. Basically, training is designed to dispel prejudice and wrong expectations and to help the volunteers understand that there is no cause for alarm. They learn that dealing with a mentally ill person is much like dealing with a disabled person - that you must look beyond the handicap. Unless you do, according to a program official, "we miss wonderful opportunities for knowing people."
Completing the training does not obligate a volunteer to join the program. Many go through the training, but support the program in ways other than direct contact.
The *Compeer* concept originated in Rochester, New York, in 1973. Since its inception it has served over 10,000 people of all ages who suffer from mental illness. There are now over 100 operational programs in 37 states. The program has received local, state and national recognition, including the 1989 President's Volunteer Action Award. Therapists in cities where the program is established cite over 65 percent improvement in social, communication and living skills of their clients, as well as significant increases in self-esteem based on the intervention of the volunteer.
Founded: 1989

MENTAL HEALTH: ADVOCACY

NATIONAL/STATE ORGANIZATIONS

JOINT ADVOCACY COALITION FOR THE MENTALLY DISABLED
100 North Washington Boulevard
Falls Church, VA 22046
TEL: 703-532-3303
Objectives: To address problems that exist within the service systems and the needs of the mentally disabled (in areas of mental health and mental retardation).
Services: Provides individual representation to mentally disabled persons in administrative and court proceedings; conducts training about Federal and State laws that affect disabled persons; provides information and assistance to consumers, attorneys, advocates, and others working with disabled persons; comments on proposed regulations and legislation; monitors services used by mentally disabled persons; maintains a community education program for public awareness; works toward a mental health/mental retardation institution serving needs including employment, Federal benefits (SSI, Medicaid, Food Stamps), licensing, guardianship, housing, marital and family rights, rights in institutions, receiving or refusing treatment, special education, sterilization, training, vocational rehabilitation and zoning.
[The Coalition is an undertaking of the Mental Health Association of Northern Virginia, Legal Services of Northern Virginia, and the Northern Virginia Association for Retarded Citizens.]

NATIONAL MENTAL HEALTH ASSOCIATION
1021 Prince Street
Alexandria, VA 22314
TEL: 703-684-7722
Objectives: To provide advocacy and public education in areas of mental and emotional disorders.
Services: Conducts public awareness campaigns to effect changes in neighborhood and business community attitudes toward recovered mental patients; works for improved community-based treatment facilities; engages in litigation where a test case seems warranted; handles inquiries through 850 local offices as well as the national office; publishes an extensive list of publications such as *Civil Rights of Patients* and *What Every Child Needs for Good Mental Health, How to Deal with Your Tensions,* and various publications and position statements on services, legislation, rehabilitation, citizen activism, and other areas.
Publications: Civil Rights of Patients; Good Mental Health; How to Deal with Your Tensions; FOCUS
Founded: 1909

NATIONAL ORGANIZATION ON DISABILITY (NOD)
SEE RECIPIENTS: HANDICAPPED

MENTAL HEALTH: CENTERS/HOSPITALS

NATIONAL/STATE ORGANIZATIONS

NATIONAL COUNCIL OF COMMUNITY MENTAL HEALTH CENTERS*
6101 Montrose Road
Suite 360
Rockville, MD 20852
TEL: 301-984-6200
Objectives: To improve the quality and quantity of mental health services through inter-agency/organization cooperation.
Services: Helps to develop standards for community mental health centers; develops state and national legislative issues; works for full health care coverage; creates volunteer task forces for specific problems; publishes *National Council News* monthly, and other materials.
Publications: National Council News; Mental Health Journal; Community Mental Health Services
Founded: 1969

INDIVIDUAL PROGRAM PROFILES

ALEXANDRIA COMMUNITY MENTAL HEALTH CENTER
206 North Washington Street
Alexandria, VA 22314
TEL: 703-836-5751
Purpose: To provide comprehensive mental health services to the community.
Sponsor: City of Alexandria
Contact: Candy Spritz, Community Organizer
Description: The *Alexandria Community Mental Health Center* (ACMHC) was established in 1947 as the City agency responsible for responding to the mental health needs of any citizen living in Alexandria. The main office is centrally located, and there are satellite offices to better serve the total community. The Center's goal is to achieve and maintain good mental health by employing prevention and treatment methods. ACMHC philosophy

endorses the concepts of preventing crises before they occur; the early detection of problem areas; and treating an individual in the community in the least restrictive manner possible. Funding is obtained from Federal and State as well as City monies, client fees and third party reimbursement.

Presently, the Center provides outpatient services in the form of individual, group, family, and play therapies, 24-hour Emergency services for individuals experiencing a crisis, a Therapeutic Nursery for preschoolers with emotional problems, Inpatient services for those people needing intensive treatment, a structured Day Treatment program for adults and adolescents, a Community Living/Apartment Program, a Diagnostic and Evaluation service, a Consultation and Education unit to provide case and program consultation to other agencies, preventative education through workshops, self-help groups and community outreach. The In-Home Counseling program is one aspect of specialized service offered to the elderly. Another group receiving specialized attention is youth. All of these program seek to provide a comprehensive response to the identified needs of Alexandrians. ACMHC seeks to involve community members in many facets of its organization. Thirty volunteers serve on the Center's two policy making boards: The Mental Health, Mental Retardation, and Substance Abuse Services Board; the ACMHC Governing Board. Other volunteers provide direct service to clients through many of the above programs. Currently, over thirty citizens assist in the following activities:

- lead activity groups (occupational therapy, psychodrama, recreation therapy, living skills) in the Partial Hospitalization program
- help in the Social Center
- co-lead groups
- work with preschoolers and their parents in the Therapeutic Nursery School
- lead discussion groups
- provide clerical assistance
- conduct surveys of the community
- keypunch
- provide home visits to clients of the In-Home Counseling program

All volunteers at ACMHC receive an orientation to the Center, general and specific job training, monthly seminars on mental health-related topics, regular supervision by Center staff, a monthly newsletter, and special recognition at a yearly luncheon where awards are presented in appreciation for the many hours served.
Founded: 1947

BLUEPRINT
St. Lawrence Hospital & Healthcare Services
Community Mental Health Center
1210 West Saginaw Street
Lansing, MI 48915
TEL: 517-377-0350
Purpose: To provide better service delivery methods that would bring continuity of care for mental patients.
Sponsor: St. Lawrence Hospital
Contact: Rita Carbuhn
Description: The assignemnt read, simply, "Develop a Volunteer Service for this Center." That was in 1972. The postscript was, "We have never paid for any part of a volunteer program, and assuredly do not want to set any new precedents." In the midwestern community of Lansing, where community volunteering is an accepted way of life for most citizens, the mandate was accepted by administrators of the Hospital's Community Mental Health Center as a challenge to pull together existing resources. They did meet some opposition along the way, but proceeded to groom their representatives in the community to do a good job in selling the philosophy of a volunteer program in the mental health center. Two priorities were:

- identification of leadership;
- coordination of volunteer activities at the Center.

The strong Hospital Auxiliary, in the process of celebrating its fiftieth anniversary, met the first need. An Office of Volunteer Programs at the Center was set up to take care of the second priority. The Auxiliary's Chairperson shared responsibility with the Center's Chairperson, and the Office of Volunteer Programs took all requests for volunteers, originated all programs involving volunteers, made all volunteer assignments, and handled all changes and terminations of volunteers. Chairmen were appointed for each volunteer assignment area, and together they comprised the Volunteer Advisory Board. Monthly contacts were encouraged, but quarterly meetings were required to share progress reports. Annual reports from each Chairperson were submitted to the General Chairperson, who prepared a summary report for distribution.

Due to its general appeal and the possibility of an onrush of volunteers - who would then have to wait to be placed - a more selective method was used. Groups with records of successful volunteer programs (the Auxiliary, Red Cross, Junior League, Urban League, National Secretaries Association, etc.) were invited to a Recruitment Coffee (one in the morning and one in the evening to accommodate varied commitments). A Profile of the potential CMHC Volunteer was provided at the Coffee with an application attached, and a steady response followed.

Each applicant is brought in for a personal interview, using volunteer-experienced interviewers. Because of laws governing confidentiality, etc., the program plan must be an organized, rather than an informal, one. Placements are made on a trial basis to ease the unpleasant task of dismissing a volunteer who may not be suitable for this particular type of volunteer work - a fact not always visible even in a lengthy training process such as is used at the Center.

Volunteer assignments are developed to assure help for the professional staff and choices for the volunteers. They assist in the crisis intervention component, perform a variety of tasks in the inpatient and outpatient divisions, and work in specific programs such as research/evaluation, child/adolescent, extended care, rehabilitation, recreation, addictions, education and community service, fundraising, satellite clinic, administration, and general assignments. Job descriptions are provided in all cases.

Founded: 1972

GRASSROOTS CRISIS INTERVENTION & PEER COUNSELING CENTER

Harriet Tubman Center
6700 Freetown Rd.
Columbia, MD 21044
TEL: 301-531-6006
Purpose: To provide alternative mental health services on an individual and group basis, to provide education to the community with a preventative focus, and to provide training to groups and agencies within our community.
Sponsor: Howard County Grant-in-Aid
Contact: Volunteer Coordinator
Description: Grassroots Crisis Intervention and Peer Counseling Center was first opened in 1970 as an alternative to traditional mental health services and with a focus toward reaching youth with drug problems. At the present time Grassroots remains an alternative in its emphasis on providing a friendly, informal response to human needs.

The center provides peer counseling by way of a telephone hotline and walk-in service, emergency shelter facilities, outreach to the scene of a crisis, and there are no appointments necessary or fees required. The objectives of the organization have expanded to include problems with families, sexuality, school, abuse, loneliness, and other concerns.

Grassroots also provides TTY services to the deaf community, advocacy, information and referral, a speaker's bureau, after hours back-up for the Bureau of Mental Health, and acts as a primary resource to the Police Department and Howard County Department of Social Services.

The staff at Grassroots is comprised of people from a variety of backgrounds who have all successfully participated in in-house experiential training in crisis and client-centered counseling skills. Grassroots' counseling model is based on the belief that the person who is experiencing stress is working through a problem which can be facilitated by a caring, honest relationship, with its elements of support, feedback and reality testing. The hope is that both the client and counselor may benefit from the interaction. Grassroots is committed to protecting the clients' confidentiality.

There are no educational or experience requirements to apply for a volunteer counselor position. Counselor selection is oriented toward open, genuine individuals who are capable of establishing a helping relationship with a client. Some of the opportunities for volunteer involvement include:

- Learning skills in areas such as communication, counseling, group leadership, training, supervision, etc.
- Providing peer counseling, crisis intervention, advocacy, information and referral services to the community.
- Joining the speaker's bureau to talk to community groups about various mental health topics.
- Representing the volunteer counseling staff on the Board of Directors of Grassroots.
- Acquiring practicum credit from area colleges.
- Involvement in fundraising and other committees and groups.

Volunteer counselors are expected to provide 18 counseling hours each month as well as attend one staff meeting each month for information sharing, in-service training, supervision, and team building. There is an expectation that all members of the staff will share in the commitment that Grassroots has made to the community. This occurs not only through time volunteered for counseling but through involvement and input into the operational activities of the organization. Grassroots asks six months commitment for support of the agency from each volunteer counselor. Quote from the Director: "Grassroots values the support and commitment of its volunteer staff."

The United Way of Central Maryland is a sponsor.
Founded: 1970

KENT COUNTY MENTAL HYGIENE CLINIC/DAY HOSPITAL VOLUNTEERS*

805 River Road
PO Box 1401
Dover, DE 19901
TEL: 302-736-4275
Purpose: To provide volunteers to assist in day hospital activities and program.
Sponsor: Kent County Mental Hygiene Clinic (Division of Mental Health, Delaware Department of Health and Social Services)
Contact: Sarah A. McKim, Coordinator of Volunteers
Description: The Day Hospital program has seventeen active volunteers who bring with them various educational backgrounds, talents, interests, and skills. This present program began in 1972 and evolved from the socialization club which met one day a week as a Century Club program.

The goal of the volunteer program is to have skilled and caring people working directly with patients in Day Hospital who are referred by the staff of the KCMHC for evaluation and treatment. The volunteers are supervised by the Day Hospital Staff which consists of two full-time registered nurses and one part-time volunteer coordinator.

The volunteers meet monthly to plan activities which include arts and crafts, all day bus trips, and a variety of daily activities. Two volunteers are scheduled to work each day; also, extra volunteers participate by accompanying special programs and trips. They also plan and prepare picnics and special luncheons. These activities are funded by revenue sharing via the Kent County Levy Court.

When an interested person is referred to the Day Hospital Program, a personal interview is scheduled with the coordinator. At that time the prospective volunteer meets the staff, patients, visit the facility, and is given opportunity to read informative articles about the program. They decide how and when they can be most useful and then they complete a personal skill and volunteer services form. The potential volunteer is given a three-month trial period, working closely with the staff before becoming a permanent volunteer.

The goal of the volunteer program is to work closely with the patients to establish social interaction, caring, and acceptance. "Indirectly," according to the Volunteer coordinator, "the volunteer may serve as a role model and teacher of new skills."
Founded: 1972

VOLUNTEER DEPARTMENT
Delaware State Hospital
New Castle, DE 19720
TEL: 302-421-6535
Purpose: To provide volunteer opportunities for community members and ex-clients in a psychiatric setting. Volunteers are used to augment services provided by staff in both the therapeutic and support areas of the hospital.
Sponsor: Delaware State Hospital
Contact: Mrs. Laure N. Unkart, Volunteer Coordinator
Description: The volunteer program at Delaware State Hospital is divided into three sections- adult, student, and group. The use of volunteers is restricted only by the interests and needs of the volunteers. In both the adult and student programs the volunteers are allowed to choose from work assignments in both direct patient care and supportive services. Examples:
Direct Patient Care - Nursing, Occupational Therapy, Recreation, Creative Arts, Release Services, Dental Clinic, Medical Clinic, Homemaking, Dietary, and Beauty Shop.
Support Services - Housekeeping, Maintenance, Garage, Laboratory, Pharmacy, Canteen, Medical Library, Grounds, Greenhouse; Clerks in the following Departments: Business Department, Nursing, Personnel, Research and Education, Medical Records, Dietary, and Hospital Director's Office.
The Adult Section includes programs for both men and women who are either going back into the job market or considering a job change, i.e. short-term commitment, job investigation, and job training.
The Student Section is primarily used for career investigation by both high school and college students. Students from technical/vocational high schools affiliate with the hospital for their senior year in their related area.
Another section of the student program deals with students from local high schools who are underachieving in school or have dropped out and are returning to school. In either case, students are referred to the hospital for job training in goal-oriented programs. Many of these students are employed upon graduation by either the hospital, other agencies, or private industry.
Adults and students also run the Blue Hen Shop (clothing shop) and the Patient Library.
Groups of adults provide social activities for patients, i.e. day and evening parties, dances, luncheons away from the hospital, and the Annual Carnival. Groups of adults and/or students also wrap all Christmas gifts given to the patients.
The Volunteer Department is responsible also for all donations to the hospital. The Volunteer Department averages approximately 180 volunteers a month giving approximately 2,000-2,500 hours a month.
Volunteers receive orientation from the Coordinator, on-the-job training from their staff supervisors, and In-service Education when appropriate to the position. Volunteers are supervised by their staff supervisors except for the Blue Hen Shop and the Patient Library. Both of these sections are supervised by the Volunteer Coordinator.

The Volunteer Program has been part of the Hospital Program from the early 1900's. It is funded as part of the overall hospital budget each year.
The goals of the department include providing comprehensive programs that are beneficial to patients, volunteers, and staff, improving the image of both the patients and hospital through good public relations, and a volunteer program.
"The accomplishment has been that volunteers are considered staff members and that the Volunteer Department is a vital part of the overall Hospital Program," according to the program's Coordinator.
Founded: 1900

VOLUNTEER PROGRAM OF PRAIRIE VIEW
Prairie View Mental Health Center
1901 East First Street
Box 467
Newton, KS 67114
TEL: 316-283-2400
Purpose: To be responsive to the emotional and mental health needs of both the immediate and the larger community.
Sponsor: Prairie View Inc.
Contact: Nancy Hedrick
Description: The use of volunteers at Prairie View Mental Health Center is designed to increase community involvement in the treatment of the mentally ill and to increase patient contact with the outside community. Mentally ill persons have a need to be accepted by the community and to continue to relate to persons from everyday walks of life. Understanding and concerned volunteers are useful in providing support to the mentally ill both while in the hospital and on their return to everyday life.
Prairie View, established in 1954 as a private psychiatric hospital, today is a non-profit 60-bed psychiatric hospital and a comprehensive mental health center serving three counties on a contractual basis. It is sponsored by the Mennonite churches but aims at close cooperation with the community and seeks to blend these two dynamics with the concern and skills of the staff and volunteers.
Since its inception, Prairie View has utilized volunteers but it was not until 1968 that the Board decided to mobilize this talent in an organized program. Volunteers are considered human resources just as paid staff; the Volunteer Program is under the leadership of the Director of Personnel. The organizaton corresponds to the personnel program and includes job planning, recruiting, application, placement, orientation, training, supervision, evaluation, policies and record keeping and recognition.
Volunteer roles include forming a one-to-one relationship with the patient, assisting in the psychiatric day hospital, participating in psychodrama, involvement in substance abuse groups, providing a monthly tea for inpatients, relating to the elderly, socializing with patients, providing music for patient worship services, giving private piano lessons to patients, serving as librarians in the staff library. On a regular basis, 107 volunteers participate in the program. Since 1969, 812 volunteers have given 169,839 hours of service.
Community support is sought by means of a Volunteer Services Committee made up of community representatives. Patients are invited to have input into the program and can request volunteer services. In the words of the Director: "This creative interaction of volunteers, staff, patients, and community has led to a Volunteer Program that has both been effective locally and received national attention as a model for other programs."
Founded: 1954

MENTAL HEALTH: CHILDREN/YOUTH

INDIVIDUAL PROGRAM PROFILES

BIG BROTHERS/BIG SISTERS PROGRAM-CHILD PSYCHIATRY*
SEE RECIPIENTS: CHILDREN/YOUTH - PSYCHOSOCIAL SUPPORT

GREENHOUSE
Concern of Durham
1804 W. Southern Parkway
Suite 209
Durham, NC 27707
TEL: 919-489-5652
Purpose: To prevent inappropriate institutional placement of emotionally disturbed adolescent girls by providing residential treatment.
Sponsor: Concern of Durham
Contact: Vivian Roberti
Description: Thirteen volunteers assist nine staff persons in operating Greenhouse, a community-based residential treatment facility for emotionally disturbed adolescent girls. The program is designed to assist these youngsters in continuing to be members of the community.
Greenhouse is a highly structured, stable and predictable environment that provides safety, support, clear limits, and expectations. Personal responsibility for behavior is stressed. The program is designed to provide a supportive therapeutic milieu where residents are able to work on their problems in a group setting and receive important feedback on their behavior. In addition, individual, group, and family therapy is provided to enable the girls to work through the problems that they have had and are presently experiencing in their lives.
Volunteers are involved in many phases of the program, including, fund-raising and public relations, as well as direct delivery of services. Also, local and state governments play a role in assuring the success of the program.

TEENAGE VOLUNTEERS WORKING IN ADOLESCENT PROGRAM*
Western State Hospital
301 Greenville Avenue
Staunton, VA 24401
TEL: 703-885-9390; 703-885-9391
Purpose: To provide leisure activities for adolescent patients.
Sponsor: Western State Hospital Volunteer Services Department
Contact: Jane Berry, Director of Volunteer Services
Description: Since 1971, students from the surrounding community have been serving as an integral part of the Western State Hospital Adolescent Program. They come to the hospital once a week (from 9 am to 11 am on Saturdays) to meet with the adolescents in a very unstructured program.
Prospective student volunteers are carefully screened. They receive informal training through meetings with the Special Education Instructor, Director of Training and Research, and Director of Volunteer Services. The meetings emphasize the attitudes toward the young patients that will be most helpful with specific behavioral problems. Training stresses the advantages of including all patients, and the special need for the quiet or withdrawn patient to be included by the volunteer in the group activities. These younger patients need to have activities in a relaxed setting where they can relate to young people in their own peer group from outside of the hospital. During the two-hour sessions, part of the group may just sit and chat, while some of the others listen to records or play chess or cards. Once a month the student volunteers take the patients on a picnic, to someone's house, or to

a high school basketball game. There is no direct adult supervision, although someone is always available for consultation and assistance, if needed.
The Director of Volunteer Services has been impressed with the maturity and the dependability of the high school volunteers, who continue their program through the summer months even though the sponsors expected this service to be a school-year project.
Founded: 1971

MENTAL HEALTH: COMMUNICATIONS & PR

NATIONAL/STATE ORGANIZATIONS

NATIONAL MENTAL HEALTH ASSOCIATION
SEE MENTAL HEALTH: ADVOCACY

INDIVIDUAL PROGRAM PROFILES

MENTAL HEALTH PLAYERS
The Voluntary Action Center
2125 East South Boulevard
Montgomery, AL 36116-0044
TEL: 205-284-0006
Purpose: To raise the consciousness of the community to its role in promoting and fostering the mental health of its citizens.
Contact: Doci Haslam
Description: The Mental Health Players use drama in the form of role-playing to spark the consciousness of the community to its role in promoting and fostering the mental health of its citizens. The intention of the role-played situation is to involve the audience on an emotional level and elicit questions and discussion from the audience regarding their feelings in reaction to the situation.
One, two or three players make up a given skit. They work without scripts. Each skit is role-played spontaneously after a situation is decided on, and with previous input, discussion and direction from the Moderator/Director and the entire troupe of players. Examples of situations that might be role-played are:
- An alcoholic mother in a family.
- A depressed woman and her manic-depressed neighbor.
- A depressed man in the work situation.
- Mid-life crisis between husband and wife.
- A former mental patient's first encounter back with family.
- Teenagers on drugs (their family, their school and their social problems).
- Adult children discussing putting mother in a nursing home.
These experiences lead members of the audience into an awareness usually not recognized before and into some type of action involving the mentally disabled.
Since the formation of the group in 1979, the Players have become increasingly in demand for educational programs for schools, churches, civic and social clubs. They tailor each presentation specifically to meet the needs of each group. There are currently around 15 players and they did about 50 skits during last year. This involved the actual performance time plus travel and practice time. They have also traveled to other parts of the state to conduct training sessions for other organizations who want to start their own players group.
Founded: 1979

MENTAL HEALTH: FOSTER CARE

INDIVIDUAL PROGRAM PROFILES

OPERATION GOOD NEIGHBOR
Huron County Mental Health Services
1108 South VanDyke
Bad Axe, MI 48413
TEL: 517-269-9293
Purpose: To provide visitation and companionship to the mentally ill and mentally retarded in foster homes.
Sponsor: Huron County Mental Health Services
Contact: Richard Jeffries
Description: Operation Good Neighbor began eight years ago and usually has between 40 and 45 volunteers. They are not reimbursed in any way. It is a visitation program whereby volunteers visit the mentally retarded and mentally ill in foster care homes, the elderly and those needing a friend. A number of volunteers visit more than one person each week.
In addition to visiting, a volunteer and his visitee may go for a ride, go shopping or eat out. Training exercises for volunteers include aspects of confidentiality. The group has regular meetings. A volunteer of the month and a volunteer of the year are chosen. An annual banquet is held.
Founded: 1976

MENTAL HEALTH: I&R

NATIONAL/STATE ORGANIZATIONS

AMERICAN ACADEMY OF CRISIS INTERVENERS
c/o Dr. Edward S. Rosenbluh
218 Breckenridge Lane, Suite 102
Louisville, KY 40207
TEL: 502-896-0200
Objectives: To increase knowledge in all areas of crisis intervention.
Services: Provides a forum for those whose work causes them to deal with crises and emergencies to share research, current information and educational ideas, thus improving skill levels and increasing knowledge (includes fields of mental health, education, law enforcement, religion and medicine); provides instructors and speakers in all areas of crisis intervention; publishes a training manual, and other materials.
Publications: Crisis Counseling: Emotional First Aid; Journal of Crisis Intervention
Founded: 1977

INFORMATION SERVICE*
American Psychiatric Association
1400 K Street, NW
Washington, DC 20005
TEL: 202-682-6000
Objectives: To develop practical information on behalf of the mentally ill.
Services: Identifies outstanding mental health programs (for the aged, for preschoolers, halfway houses, in-community rehabilitation, etc.); visits the programs to observe and conduct interviews; develops publications using the case study approach - including complete information on how volunteers are involved - to assist practitioners wishing to begin or improve programs; works with both public and private agencies in cooperative ventures that will broaden the base of beneficial services to the mentally ill and, therefore, increase the effectiveness of the entire mental health field.
Publications: Psychiatric News; Community Psychiatry
Founded: 1844

INTERNATIONAL ASSOCIATION FOR SUICIDE PREVENTION
Suicide Prevention & Crisis Center
ATT: C. Ross, 1811 Trousdale Drive
Burlingame, CA 94010
TEL: 415-877-5604
Objectives: To continually upgrade the skills of suicide prevention workers.
Services: Develops specialized training in suicide prevention for professionals, paraprofessionals and volunteers; conducts and encourages research; provides individuals and agencies with a forum for exchanging experience, ideas, literature and other aids for the profession; develops and makes available information on the fundamentals of suicide prevention; holds an annual General Assembly, and a biannual International Congress.
Publications: Crisis
Founded: 1960

US/HHS - NATIONAL CLEARINGHOUSE FOR MENTAL HEALTH INFORMATION
5600 Fishers Lane
Rockville, MD 20857
TEL: 301-443-4513
Objectives: To respond to the need for centralizing all sources of mental health information.
Services: Makes referrals to other agencies and organizations when appropriate; refers individuals seeking treatment to community mental health centers and state hospitals; provides free single copies of all Clearinghouse publications except periodicals, which must be ordered from the Superintendent of Documents, U.S. Government Printing Office, Washington, DC 20402.
Sponsor: US/HHS - Department of Health & Human Services

INDIVIDUAL PROGRAM PROFILES

GRASSROOTS CRISIS INTERVENTION & PEER COUNSELING CENTER
SEE MENTAL HEALTH: CENTERS/HOSPITALS

MENTAL HEALTH: RE-ENTRY

NATIONAL/STATE ORGANIZATIONS

PATHWAYS TO INDEPENDENCE
PO Box 651
McLean, VA 22101
TEL: 703-671-9619
Objectives: To foster an improved mental health system based on experience of families of patients.
Services: Enlists families of persons recovering from mental illness and members of support groups for families to participate in mental health seminars, workshops and conferences; supports committees on job opportunities, legislation, residential services and education; maintains speakers' bureau; publishes newsletter; convenes monthly conference.

INDIVIDUAL PROGRAM PROFILES

COMMUNITY FRIENDS*
Mental Health Association in Maui
95 Mahalani Street
Wailuku, HI 96793
TEL: 808-242-6461
Purpose: To provide a one-to-one friendship for the chronically mentally ill.
Sponsor: Mental Health Association in Maui
Contact: Al Vierra or Barbara Mickey
Description: Community Friends is a program designed to give support to those persons who are recovering from a chronic mental illness, are lonely or depressed, going through a life crisis, etc. Trained volunteers are brought together with referred clients for a one-to-one relationship for a period of a six month commitment. Matched friendships are reviewed at the end of a six month period and a decision is made on whether to continue the friendship. Staff is available should the volunteer friend need any advice or assistance in providing service to his matched friend.
A part-time co-ordinator is employed by the Mental Health Association in Maui to oversee the program. The co-ordinator's supervisor is the director of the Mental Health Association in Maui.
Volunteers for the Community Friends Program are given training to acquaint them with their responsibilities and situations that may come up while they are being a friend. Volunteers are instructed that they are to be friends and not therapists. Any situation which may arise that requires the intervention of a professional, the volunteer would then refer the client back to the therapist or agency that referred him. The volunteer supplies caring and support, he does not take the place of a therapist or professional. Community Friends was organized in 1979 under the Mental Health Association. It is a statewide program. It is hoped that it will one day be spun off by a separate agency or taken over by a state or federal funding program.
Founded: 1979

STAR CITY SOCIAL CLUB
Christ Episcopal Church
Franklin Road and Washington, SW
Roanoke, VA 24016
TEL: 703-342-8024
Purpose: To provide caring adults who assist with crafts, dinners, singing, games, field trips, etc., for ex-mental patients.
Sponsor: Christ Episcopal Church; local mental health organizations
Contact: Reverend David D. Stanford
Description: In May 1982, a mental health worker approached the Christ Episcopal Church to present the concept of a social club in the church for ex-mental patients. About ten people expressed interest in such a program. This request for assistance immediately followed a pastoral appeal by letter urging local congregations to assess local needs and then seek out means of addressing these needs.
Initially, anxiety about mental patients, and a "we and they" atmosphere delayed the project in spite of the good intentions of members of the congregation. Planners designed training and other programs with the help of local mental health organizations and agencies.
Training is in two phases: an overview of mental health to deal with myths about the mentally ill, and specific training when needed in the specific areas of involvement (crafts, games, etc.). In the process, volunteers were surprised to discover that some potential social club members were established church members, and close friends of many of those with initial anxieties. The walls between "we" and "they" quickly eroded, and the program now serves as a vital link between former mental patients and the community.

The program is operated by volunteers, with one half of them in leadership/management positions and the other half in direct service delivery. One third of the budget is provided by the church, with the other two thirds coming from foundations and in-kind contributions. Although addressing ex-mental patients, the program has proven helpful and enjoyable to others in the community.
Founded: 1982

TRANSITIONAL VOLUNTEER PROGRAM
United Way Volunteer Center
630 Janet Avenue
Lancaster, PA 17601
TEL: 717-299-3743
Purpose: To place outpatient mental health clients in volunteer positions for rehabilitation purposes.
Sponsor: Lancaster Information and Referral, United Way
Contact: Marilyn G. Sanko
Description: The Transitional Volunteer Program was launched in February 1981 as a pilot project, sponsored jointly by the Lancaster Information Center and the Mental Health Association in Lancaster County. The Volunteer Service Center placed the first transitional volunteer in March 1981.
The program is now funded in part by the Lancaster Mental Health/Mental Retardation Program, which receives a monthly statistical report on placements and volunteer hours.
The challenge of mental health clients makes for a certain instability in volunteering; i.e. hours are not always regular. The program's value, however, has been well established and its credibility is high. Rapport between the Volunteer Service Center, mental health agencies and private physicians is excellent.
Approximately 50-70 client volunteers are introduced to the program annually. When the program originated, 16 agencies were utilizing transitional volunteers. There are currently only a few agencies who are not able or willing to place mental health clients as volunteers. These volunteers provide local agencies with 3,000 to 4,000 hours of community service annually.
Transitional volunteers perform the same services as traditional volunteers. However, additional support and supervision is provided, especially in the beginning of the assignment. Special care is taken to place client volunteers in non-stressful environments.
Founded: 1981

VOLUNTEER PROGRAM OF PRAIRIE VIEW
SEE MENTAL HEALTH: CENTERS/HOSPITALS

MENTAL HEALTH: SELF-HELP

NATIONAL/STATE ORGANIZATIONS

RECOVERY, INC.
Association of Nervous & Former Mental Patients
802 North Dearborn Street
Chicago, IL 60610
TEL: 312-337-5661
Objectives: To help prevent relapses in former mental patients and to forestall chronicity in nervous patients.
Services: Conducts weekly meetings throughout the country to bring together patients for a self-help recovery program; functions as a lay group (although program was developed by a professional); publishes *Directory of Group Meeting Information* for referral purposes by programs in the field; holds semi-annual meetings.
Publications: Recovery Reporter
Founded: 1937

NUTRITION

INDIVIDUAL PROGRAM PROFILES

SHARE*
PO Box 9325
Ogden, UT 84409
TEL: 801-399-2553
Purpose: To provide a short-term, nutritionally balanced supply of food to those in need who would not otherwise receive help in Weber County.
Contact: Naomi Bender
Description: What do individuals or families do when, because of personal tragedy, misfortune or relocation problems, they find they are completely without food and aid is not available or is delayed through normal channels? Local churches, government assistance programs and community service outlets in Weber County have not always been prepared to provide this kind of emergency help, especially on a seven-day-a-week, 24-hour-a-day basis. SHARE was born from this critical community need.
SHARE was organized in 1975 by a group of citizens who were concerned about the emergency food needs of the community. SHARE, Inc. provides special dietary items for diabetics and others on restricted diets as well as baby food and special formula for infants. SHARE is the only organization in this community which will supply baby food and formula on an emergency basis. Southeast Asian refugees have often requested aid and yet are not educated or knowledgeable in the American use of canned meats, vegetables and fruits. SHARE meets their very specific need by providing a supply of rice, eggs, fresh vegetables, cooking oil and other items which are familiar and usable to them.
SHARE also delivers the food directly to each recipient. This is an essential and challenging aspect of this program as many individuals in the greatest need do not have any transportation to come get the food. This means that the volunteer drivers often find themselves delivering food to transients right on the banks of the river, to motel rooms, to campsites, and sadly, to just a stationary vehicle in which a family is living. For those who have no cooking facilities, SHARE provides prepared and already cooked foods. The efficient organization and dedicated nature of this group is reflected in the fact that SHARE meets an emergency call for food within two hours and without the usual amount of "red tape" which is involved in filling out forms and requiring authorization. Efforts are made to insure that each recipient is truly needy and not being helped elsewhere. The important thing that can be said about this volunteer effort's method of operation is that it works! Since 1975 SHARE has been able to help almost 7,000 individuals

or families. Some 1,959 deliveries of emergency food have been made to needy people all over Weber County by SHARE volunteers. More than 70,000 meals have been provided from this completely volunteer organization.
More than 300 volunteers contribute time on a regular basis with donations of food and money coming from almost every section of this community of 144,616 persons.
According to the Director, "SHARE has been able to touch those in need and also those who have a need to share."
Founded: 1975

NUTRITION: AIDS

INDIVIDUAL PROGRAM PROFILES

GOD'S LOVE WE DELIVER (GLWD)
SEE AIDS: NUTRITION

HOUSING SERVICES: AIDS PROGRAM
SEE HOUSING: AIDS

NUTRITION: CHILDREN/YOUTH

NATIONAL/STATE ORGANIZATIONS

CHILDREN'S FOUNDATION
SEE DAY CARE/HEAD START: EVALUATION

INDIVIDUAL PROGRAM PROFILES

EMERGENCY INFANT NUTRITION PROGRAM: FREE BREAKFAST PROJECT
Marillac Social Center
2822 West Jackson Boulevard
Chicago, IL 60612
TEL: 312-722-7440
Purpose: To provide supplemental food to infants from very low income families, and free breakfasts in the summer to children under 18 from the school year free breakfast program.
Sponsor: Marillac Agency, private donations, USDA, CSA, JTPA
Contact: Mrs. Kay Hallagan
Description: The death rate for infants in the black ghettos of Chicago is five times as high as for infants living in suburban Chicago. They succumb to many ailments, but often the basis is the poor nutrition of the mother while carrying the child or of the child as an infant. Many of these infants are born to very young mothers, or to mothers with vary large families and very low income. The inflationary rise in food prices has made the gap even higher between what these families can pay for food and what good infant nourishment costs. Marillac is helping to alleviate this infant mortality rate by providing for needy infants who are not being helped in other programs.
Voluntary efforts in providing baby food, donations, and other services helped the program to get started in 1970, enabling the Marillac Agency to give supplemental packages of formula, baby food and sometimes Pampers and baby clothes to needy infants - about 70 per week. Since 1977, CSA funding has funded the program and now about 1,200 infants per year are assisted with food and formula. Community interest continues, i.e., the Chicago Community Trust has given some additional funds to be used for purchasing Pampers, bottles, shirts, etc., for the infants. Space and staff assistance is provided by the Marillac Agency.
The infants are located by outreach social workers or have been located by medical social workers, Chicago Board of Health nurses, or Public Aid workers. The child's name and birth date are recorded on a card, which is presented by a family member once a week to receive the food. Food packages have been assembled by teenaged Neighborhood Youth Corps workers and others.
For the past ten years, the Agency also has sponsored a free summer breakfast program. This year, a total of 65,000 free breakfasts were served to children from eight neighborhood sites, ranging from storefront churches to a motorcycle club room. Initially, about 40 mothers volunteered to distribute the packages for about eight weeks each summer. Today community mothers are assisted by JTPA youngsters in the distribution process. Funds for the food and paper goods are furnished by the U.S. Department of Agriculture.
Founded: 1970

NUTRITION: COMMUNICATIONS & PR

NATIONAL/STATE ORGANIZATIONS

NATIONAL HUNGER COALITION
SEE NUTRITION: HUNGER

SOCIETY FOR NUTRITION EDUCATION*
SEE NUTRITION: EDUCATION

INDIVIDUAL PROGRAM PROFILES

END HUNGER PROJECT
SEE NUTRITION: FOOD BANKS

PRIME TIME TO END HUNGER
SEE RECIPIENTS: HOMELESS - COMMUNICATIONS & PR

NUTRITION: CONSUMER/LEGAL RIGHTS

NATIONAL/STATE ORGANIZATIONS

FOOD RESEARCH AND ACTION CENTER
1319 F Street, NW
Suite 500
Washington, DC 20004
TEL: 202-393-5060
Objectives: To assist impoverished people and communities in efforts to obtain relief from conditions of hunger and malnutrition.
Services: Offers legal and nonlegal assistance to poor people; provides advocacy to make the public food assistance programs more responsive; identifies and publishes specific reasons for the failure of some of these programs; trains in strategies for local and state-wide antihunger activities; maintains law library; publishes a number of educational pamphlets and guides for the general public; publishes monthly newsletter, and publications related to hunger and food assistance programs in the U.S.
Publications: Foodlines; Guide to Food Stamp Program
Founded: 1970

NUTRITION: DELIVERY

INDIVIDUAL PROGRAM PROFILES

BAY RIDGE NUTRITION AND HOME CARE PROGRAMS
SEE NUTRITION: OLDER PERSON

COUNTRY GATHERING
SEE NUTRITION: OLDER PERSON

MEALS ON WHEELS OF BIRMINGHAM
SEE RECIPIENTS: OLDER PERSON - NUTRITION

MEALS ON WHEELS OF BUFFALO AND ERIE COUNTY
775 Main Street
Suite 510
Buffalo, NY 14203
TEL: 716-852-2626
Purpose: To provide nutritional meals to homebound, elderly and severely handicapped persons in a manner which also enhances the quality of their lives.
Sponsor: Erie County Department of Senior Services
Contact: Richard J. Gehring, Executive Director
Description: Meals on Wheels of Buffalo and Erie County, Inc. (MoW) is a nutrition program that is also rehabilitative and preventative in nature, designed to enhance the quality of life of participants as well as meet their nutritional needs.

MoW provides meal service for the homebound aged person over sixty years of age, and a limited number of severely handicapped persons under sixty years of age who are unable to obtain or prepare adequate meals for themselves. A hot and a cold meal are delivered daily (Monday through Friday) and comprises two-thirds of the Recommended Daily Allowance.

At present, 74 delivery routes are being serviced, reaching some 850 persons. The service includes two Kosher routes (24 clients) and four short-term service routes which provide meals to those who need brief intervention (maximum four months). The short-term routes reach some 200 people annually.

On a monthly basis approximately 500-600 trained volunteers and 33 senior aides provide this food service in a manner which ameliorates loneliness and social isolation, and furnishes a daily check on the well-being of the participant. The volunteers and aides observe and record daily the condition and circumstances in addition to delivering the meal. These observations are reviewed by MoW professional staff on a continuous basis for problem resolution. Identification of unmet needs other than nutrition is an integral part of the program.

Social services are provided for the purpose of conducting initial and reevaluation assessments. In addition, social services staff attempt to identify other problems and link the participant to appropriate resources within the community.

Nutrition staff enhance the nutritional well-being of the participant not only through quality food service, but also through supportive nutrition counseling and nutrition education.

The MoW nutrition program for the elderly and the handicapped is made possible by the Department of Senior Services of Erie County, and the dedication of the program's volunteers and senior aides.

The program considers special diets (35-40% of clients), emergency plans in case of inclement weather, special birthday and holiday meals, and other health and morale-building activities. Crucial to the entire MoW operation and concept is the use of volunteers to carry out the routine daily service. In addition to delivering the meals and making a daily check and report on the client's well-being, volunteers are trained in protection of the food, and handling emergencies. In MoW's first year, 1,000 volunteers served in the program. This success is attributed to the recruiting efforts of ten site managers, each drawn from his/her community, and the emphasis by the Field Supervisor on volunteer education and training.

MEALS ON WHEELS PROGRAM OF ACCA
SEE RECIPIENTS: HOMEBOUND

MORRIS COUNTY NUTRITION PROGRAM
SEE NUTRITION: OLDER PERSON

SENIORS: SPECIAL DELIVERY
New York Avenue Meals on Wheels
1313 New York Avenue, NW
Washington, DC 20005
TEL: 202-393-3949
Purpose: To provide hot meals to homebound elderly and handicapped persons to help keep them in their homes.
Sponsor: New York Avenue Presbyterian Church
Contact: Sarah Turlington, Director/Founder
Description: Founded 19 years ago, the New York Avenue Meals on Wheels Program (MOW) delivers meals to the homebound across a 14-block area of Washington, DC. The program reaches up to 65 people each day with about 60 older volunteers making the deliveries. In addition, volunteers located near the church devote some of their lunch hour time to deliveries. However, the success of the program is in the number of retired persons who are willing to mount this task, since their time is more flexible.
The service area is divided into four routes, each with two volunteers covering it. One volunteer drives his or her own car,

while a "jumper" or visitor delivers the meals. Volunteers give two hours a day, with the same volunteers serving each route to help establish a bond with the homebound resident.
The food is prepared in the church kitchen in conjunction with a federally-funded meals program that serves lunch to 60-80 people at the church each day.
Volunteer packers prepare the meals each day. The hot lunch always includes soup, two vegetables and an entree such as chicken, fish or meatloaf. A salad, sandwich, milk, fruit and packets of coffee and tea are provided for the evening meal. Low-salt meals are offered for diabetics. Participants pay $17.00 per week to help defray costs.
Founded: 1971

ST. JOSEPH COMMUNITY SERVICES
Continental Boulevard
PO Box 910
Merrimack, NH 03054
TEL: 603-424-9967
Purpose: To avoid unnecessary and premature institutionalization of the elderly by offering nutritious meals and social support services.
Sponsor: St. Joseph Community Services
Contact: Elaine T. Lyons
Description: St. Joseph Community Services, Inc. began in 1977 and was founded by the Grey Nuns of Montreal, St. Joseph Hospital, Nashua, NH. The agency provides nutritious meals and social support services to senior citizens at 12 Nutrition Sites in Hillsborough County. Meals-on-Wheels are also provided from seven of these sites to the homebound and frail elderly.
The primary funding source is from a grant provided by the Older Americans Act. Local towns and Title XX also provide funding. The agency presently provides approximately 1,000 meals daily. Other services, including outreach, information and referral, health and welfare counseling, nutrition education, recreation and transportation are also offered. These services help to maintain dignity and independence among our senior population.
Volunteers are an important element in the survival of the program. Volunteers serve in many capacities including site coordinator, driver, and food service aides, as well as contributing each day to the operation of the sites as dishwashers, table setters, hostesses, and reservation attendants. There are presently 163 volunteers working throughout the program who are supervised at each site by the site coordinator. Each volunteer is a special and important part of St. Joseph Community Services.
Founded: 1977

NUTRITION: EDUCATION

NATIONAL/STATE ORGANIZATIONS

AMERICAN NUTRITION SOCIETY
405 South Los Robles
Pasadena, CA 91101
TEL: 213-796-1790
Objectives: To help community groups establish educational nutrition programs (in its capacity as the layman arm of the American Academy of Applied Nutrition/AAAN).
Services: Provides technical assistance for setting up idea/discussion groups and study groups on nutrition (information only; no on-site consultants); disseminates to the general public information on good health and nutrition based on AAAN research; designs courses on nutrition for educational institutions; develops information on techniques of organic gardening; maintains library on nutrition.

CENTER FOR SCIENCE IN THE PUBLIC INTEREST
1501 Sixteenth Street, NW
Washington, DC 20036
TEL: 202-332-9110
Objectives: To educate the public on good nutrition in particular, and health in general.
Services: Works to strengthen laws that regulate the use of food additives and other chemicals to be tested for their effects on human behavior and mental health; provides information on National Food Day celebrations and their effect on the Federal Government's national nutrition policy recommending the kind of diet advocated at the celebrations; obtains restrictions on certain food additives; publicizes links between diet and disease; enters litigation when necessary to pursue a result of the Center's research; informs the public through reports, press releases, speeches, and media appearances; continues to seek solutions by:
- strengthening laws that regulate the use of food additives and ingredients;
- requiring that food additives and other chemicals be tested for their effects on human behavior and mental health;
- halting deceptive advertising;
- preventing alcohol abuse and alcoholism; and
- investigating the market practices of the beverage industry.
Publishes a journal of food advocacy, a number of colorful posters on nutrition designed for educational purposes (*Nutrition Scoreboard* and *Chemical Cuisine,* for example), and a free catalog of publications.
Publications: Nutrition Action Healthletter
Founded: 1971

COMMUNITY FOOD AND NUTRITION PROGRAM
US/HHS - Office of the Secretary
PO Box 1182
Washington, DC 20201
TEL: 202-245-7000
Objectives: To help communities counteract the conditions of hunger and malnutrition among the poor.
Services: Provides financial and training assistance to extend and broaden food programs (whether federally-funded or supported by state or local public or private resources); enables local programs to provide services such as emergency foodstuffs to low-income families; emphasizes the design of programs that will stimulate services through other institutions and organizations; suggests that programs include advocacy as an integral part of its program to assure that the views of the poor are heard, involves the poor themselves in planning and operation, and working in one of the following four areas:
- Access - increase participation of the poor in federally-funded programs;
- Self-help - improve the capability of the poor to purchase and produce food efficiently;
- Nutrition and Consumer Education - to improve the understanding of the poor in matters of diet and health;
- Crisis Relief - to improve methods for emergency provision of foodstuffs; publishes detailed instructions regarding this program.

NUTRITION EDUCATION AND INFORMATION
Nutrition Foundation
1126 Sixteenth Street, NW
Suite 111
Washington, DC 20036
TEL: 202-659-0074
Objectives: To advance nutrition knowledge and assure its effective application in improving the health and welfare of mankind.
Services: Responds to requests from the media, industry, government and Congress, organizations and private citizens; sponsors a group of nutrition educators to select materials and guides for distribution; publishes monthly journal, *Nutrition*

Reviews, a source book, *The Index of Nutrition Education Materials,* popular booklet entitled *Nutrition Misinformation* and *Food Faddism,* and a series of booklets for the general public on some of the most frequently posed questions about food and nutrition.
Publications: Nutrition Reviews; Present Knowledge in Nutrition; Food Faddism; Nutrition Misinformation
Founded: 1985

NUTRITION INSTITUTE OF AMERICA
200 West 86th Street
Suite 17A
New York, NY 10024
TEL: 212-799-2234
Objectives: To administer adult education programs on nutrition.
Services: Sponsors original research into areas of nutrition that are not adequately covered; provides special tutoring for persons working in programs that would benefit from better nutrition knowledge; acts as a referral and information center; sponsors lectures, symposia; publishes reports of special investigations that affect nutrition.
Founded: 1974

PROJECT CONCERN YOUTH PROGRAM
SEE HEALTH: EDUCATION

SOCIETY FOR NUTRITION EDUCATION*
1700 Broadway
Suite 300
Oakland, CA 94612
TEL: 415-444-7133
Objectives: To promote nutritional well-being for all people through education and communication.
Services: Sponsors an annual meeting, conducted in part by volunteers, addressing the above objectives; collects, analyzes and provides information regarding nutrition through: films on nutrition (two for professionals; three for laymen); library facilities (open to all; loans to San Francisco area only); reference lists and annotated bibliographies contract services; in addition, the Society for Nutrition Education sponsors a Public Policy Advisory Council and a Legislative Committee, both of which help to design strategies for community action; publishes a quarterly newsletter and bimonthly journal.
Publications: Journal of Nutrition Education; SNE Exchange
Founded: 1967

NUTRITION: FAMILIES

INDIVIDUAL PROGRAM PROFILES

CHRISTMAS BASKET PROGRAM
SEE RECIPIENTS: FAMILIES - GIVEAWAY PROGRAMS

NUTRITION: FOOD BANKS

NATIONAL/STATE ORGANIZATIONS

COMMUNITY FOOD AND NUTRITION PROGRAM
SEE NUTRITION: EDUCATION

INDIVIDUAL PROGRAM PROFILES

ATLANTA COMMUNITY FOOD BANK
970 Jefferson, NW
Atlanta, GA 30318
TEL: 404-892-9822

Purpose: To provide a "supermarket" for nonprofit meal-providing agencies only, to help them expand their programs through savings on food purchases.

Contact: Bill Bolling, Executive Director

Description: In 1979, after consistently rounding up more food for his church's community kitchen, a member of St. Luke's Episcopal Church decided that, rather than discard the food, it would be helpful to store the unused products for other programs and agencies that operated similar meal programs. By 1984, the impromptu food bank had outgrown St. Luke's and moved into a 61,000 square foot warehouse in northwest Atlanta. In 1989, the food bank celebrated its tenth anniversary with bluegrass music, a cook-off and an awards program to honor ten of its original member organizations.

Today the Community Food Bank helps to meet the needs of 423 other nonprofit agencies that provide meals to homeless and low-income people. It is not open to the general public. Cost of the food averages ten cents a pound.

Although the Food Bank's budget (a million dollars), staff, volunteers and list of contributors has grown significantly in the last decade, it is an effort to keep pace with the growth of the number of people in need of food. "At the time of our greatest prosperity, we also have our greatest number of needy people," according to the founder.

BLUE RIDGE AREA FOOD BANK*
818 Richmond Avenue
Staunton, VA 24401
TEL: 703-886-3003

Purpose: To reduce food waste, and feed the needy, through distributing donated food to charities.

Sponsor: Corporate and private donations

Contact: Phil Grasty

Description: Blue Ridge Area Food Bank (BRAFB) is a clearinghouse for surplus and non-marketable (but edible products). These products are distributed to non-profit agencies and churches who feed the needy. These agencies become members of the BRAFB and are requested to contribute $.10 per lb., for food received.

BRAFB is a non-profit public supported corporation, which began operations on November 23, 1981 and is currently distributing more than 100,000 lbs. of food per month. The organization operates a main warehouse in Staunton, Virginia, with branch locations in Charlottesville, and Winchester.

At present more than 100 volunteers are involved in the operation of the Food bank, including VISTA and Green Thumb federally funded volunteers.

Volunteers perform many and varied tasks. Some of these include serving on the Board of Directors, assisting with management of branches, working in the warehouse, clerical duties, etc.

Some volunteers are used in the outreach work, calling on potential member agencies and food donors, financial supporters and arranging public relations.

BRAFB utilizes volunteers with varying levels of experience. Training is provided in various skills, such as:
- Clerical
- Public Relations
- Warehousing Skills

One-to-One supervision is given as needed. There is a continuing need for volunteers, both to work on-site and to work with special projects, such as:
- Gleaning
- Canned Food Drives
- Arranging Media Events
- Repacking Food Products, etc.

BRAFB serves an eighteen-county area. A screening and interviewing process is used in placing volunteers.

Founded: 1981

CAPITAL AREA COMMUNITY FOOD BANK
2266 25th Place, NE
Washington, DC 20018
TEL: 202-526-5344

Purpose: To distribute surplus food to area charities.

Sponsor: United Way; churches, foundations, grocery retailers/wholesalers

Contact: Richard Stack, Executive Director

Description: The food bank concept originated in Phoenix about 15 years ago and has since spread across the country. The 1976 Tax Reform Act made it better for grocery businesses to "donate rather than dump" salvageable surplus foods, and helped to proliferate the establishment of food banks. The Capital Area Community Food Bank (CACFB) began operations in mid-1980. CACFB collects overstocked or slightly damaged food products in large quantities from grocery retailers and wholesalers, including Giant and Safeway. This merchandise is usually discarded by the merchants while it is still edible because of laws regarding dating, etc. Through a network of 130 agencies, CACFB volunteers distribute the food without charge.

With the recent cutbacks, many more individuals and families are expected to need this type of private sector help. With the passing of the District of Columbia's *Good Faith Food Donor and Donee Act of 1981,* CACFB expects to be in a position to increase its distribution of food to area charities for redistribution to the needy. In September 1981, the month prior to the passing of the Act, the Bank distributed 88,196 pounds of food, which included items such as baby food, vegetables and condiments.

To avoid resale for profit, return of the item to the store for refund, etc., volunteers and staff stamp individual products with the word "donated." In the area of liability, CACFB has all agencies sign a waiver of liability, and the legislation itself provides additional protection in this area.

In addition to volunteer staffing, CACFB helps finance its organization by charging member agencies $.12 per pound for the food it dispenses. Other funds come from the United Way, churches and foundations.

EMERGENCY FOOD PROGRAM
Woodland Volunteer Center
509 College Street
Woodland, CA 95695
TEL: 916-662-7020

Purpose: To provide emergency food for three days for those in need.

Sponsor: County Government, United Way, corporate and private donations.

Contact: Suzanne M. Lopez

Description: Woodland Volunteer Center began in 1968 as a result of the Yolo County Grand Jury recommendation that some emergency help be offered in the city of Woodland. The Center is funded through the county and United Way, as well as from corporations and private donations.

The purpose of the organization is to provide food to needy individuals on an emergency basis. Referrals are made to the Volunteer Center by the Yolo County Department of Social Services, area churches, and other community-based organizations. In the calendar year 1982, the Center provided emergency food to 1,330 individuals. In 1981, food was provided to 1,385 individuals. Each person receives a three-day supply of food.

The activities of the center are coordinated by a part-time staff person. Volunteers are on duty on a daily basis to take referral calls and to pack the food packages for pick-up by needy

individuals. Approximately 60 volunteers aid the Center in the distribution of food.
Founded: 1982

END HUNGER PROJECT
United Way of Fresno County
4270 North Blackston Avenue #212
PO Box 5177
Fresno, CA 93755-5177
TEL: 209-224-9202
Purpose: To mount a two-pronged hunger program that collects food for the hungry while educating the public about the root causes of hunger.
Sponsor: Fresno Bee
Contact: Anthony J. Folcarelli, Executive Director
Description: The *End-Hunger Project* took shape when a Fresno newspaper, *Fresno Bee,* decided to sponsor a food drive. The newspaper turned to the United Way of Fresno County for help, requesting the the United Way organize and administer the communitywide effort. The newspaper planned to include in one edition of the paper a grocery bag printed with the words *Share & Care Package.* People would be asked to fill the bags with nonperishable food and drop them off at collection sites throughout the Fresno area for final coordination and distribution by the United Way.
United Way agreed to the newspaper's request for administering the program and, in turn, requested that the paper include with its food-drive coverage additional information about the six major root causes of hunger in the Fresno area based on a survey by Fresno's *Hunger Coalition:*
- Minority, elderly, and seasonal unemployment;
- Insufficient variety of well-paying jobs;
- Educational inadequacies;
- Shift in government priorities;
- Educational barriers to job-skill development; and
- Resource distribution.

United Way saw an excellent opportunity in the *Fresno Bee's* planned coverage of the food drive to publicize and reinforce these root causes.
The newspaper ran a full-page ad promoting the food drive, illustrating the information printed on the grocery bag, and featured a follow-up article, and a front-page photograph of food collected during the drive. To assist the newspaper with expenses of printing the bags, the United Way enlisted KFSN-TV Channel 30 (an ABC affiliate) to share the cost. Thirty-five members of the Grocery Manufacturers Representatives Organization volunteered to pick up the filled bags from the 44 drop-off points and transport them to a warehouse donated for the drive by *Fleming Foods,* a wholesale distributor.
The goal set for the five-day drive was 40 tons of food and $4,000 in contributions. The drive's final tally was 64 tons of food and $7,000. Food was distributed by four organizations to more than 8,000 people, with the remainder and the cash contributions divided among area food banks. The *Fresno Bee* ran a full-page thank you ad after the event, which repeated the area's six causes of hunger and a reminder that work remained to be done to eliminate hunger from the Fresno community. The linking of the food drive *and* the public education effort turned out to be a winning combination.

FARE SHARE
807 Hampden Avenue
St. Paul, MN 55114
TEL: 612-644-6003
Purpose: To provide food for the needy through a central effort that distributes prepared bags of food to sites in several adjoining states.
Sponsor: SHARE-USA
Contact: Mimi Sands, Director

Description: Once each month, for one week, part of a total of 275 volunteers count, sort and stack food. The work culminates in thousands of identical grocery bags to be shipped to 312 host sites in 89 counties in Minnesota, Iowa, Wisconsin and the Dakotas, to be picked up from there by 42,000 individual participants. The food, worth $28 to $35 at retail, costs participants $12 and two hours of community service. The $12 contribution pays all expenses; no public money is involved.
When the Fare SHARE was launched in 1986, the program distributed some 2,000 food packages. By contrast, the 1988 total was 21.4 million pounds and 1,223,162 hours of donated service. Service can take almost any form. Although warehouse volunteers are a key to keeping costs down, most volunteering takes place in the wider community. Participants earn credit working with scouts, at-risk students and elderly neighbors. They clean parks, shelve library books and register voters, paint curbs, coach Little Leagues and counsel battered women. One volunteer designed her own community service - clipping 2,000 grocery coupons, sorting them and bringing them to the warehouse for others at each month's marathon food bagging - another form of self-help and resource exchange, which is the heart of the program.
A side benefit is the family involvement that takes place. In one instance, a five-year-old helps her mother fill measuring cups to put together ingredients for recipes. A young man going to chef's school helps maintain recipe integrity with his expertise. Girl Scouts of eight and nine earn merit badges, and members of a church singles group participates as a team.
Fare SHARE is the largest in a network of 16 SHARE-USA programs in the country. According to the director, "A sense of community builds among the strangers who work at Fare SHARE tables or loading Fare SHARE trucks."
Founded: 1986

GALLATIN VALLEY EMERGENCY FOOD BANK
317 East Mendenhall
Bozeman, MT 59175
TEL: 406-587-4486
Purpose: To provide emergency food assistance to needy persons by salvaging food stuffs that would otherwise be wasted.
Sponsor: Human Resource Development Council District IX, United Way, Gallatin County Council on Aging, Local Wholesalers and Retailers, and Private Individuals.
Contact: Julie Hintz
Description: The Gallatin Valley Emergency Food Bank is an incorporated, non-profit organization which works in cooperation with the food industry to responsibly collect, store, record, and redistribute surplus and salvaged food stuffs. The Food Bank serves the hungry poor, and non-profit organizations serving congregate meals.
The Food Bank, governed by a nine member Board of Directors began operation January 11, 1982. It is sponsored by the Human Resource Development Council District IX, a community action agency serving three rural counties in southwestern Montana.
In order to begin operation, it was necessary to pass legislation allowing wholesalers, retailers, and individuals to donate food items in good faith without being subject to criminal or civil liability. This was accomplished in February 1981 by the former director of the program.
The Food Bank was able to acquire a building for $15.00 a month, two refrigerators and two freezers at no cost, donated repair and construction from refrigeration and electrical contractors, also flooring and office furniture at a minimal expense.
The Food Bank staff has been successful in obtaining funds from VISTA, United Way, and Gallatin County Council on Aging to partially cover expenses of the operation. The staff has also sponsored fundraisers to help offset some of the costs.
The two main purposes for the Gallatin Valley Emergency Food Bank's existence are to eliminate waste and to reduce domestic hunger. By utilizing a seventeen-volunteer staff, the Food Bank

collects, stores, records and redistributes food stuffs donated by local businesses, community groups, and individuals. For the most part this food is either surplus or salvaged. Surplus refers primarily to food companies' surplus products - overruns and discontinued products that cannot be sold before their "pull date." This food is edible but does not meet the company's quality control standards. Salvaged food includes edible but not readily marketable products such as food in dented cans, or damaged cases (where food quality is not affected), and crushed loaves of bread and produce that do not meet supermarket standards of attractiveness.

By providing emergency food assistance to needy persons the Food Bank is helping to reduce domestic hunger in these hard economic times. These people are in need of food due to a crisis situation such as loss of spouse, natural disaster, high living expenses with low incomes, or loss of a job. The Food Bank volunteers prepare nutritional three-day food boxes for those needy individuals and families who are faced with the problem of inadequate food budgets.

Food is also given to other non-profit agencies to aid them in serving the poor and needy. Senior Centers, Meals on Wheels, Day Care Centers, the Salvation Army, and homes for the Developmentally Disabled are some of the agencies who have benefited from Food Bank donations. With Food Banks doing the legwork in obtaining food from donors, agencies have more time and funds to concentrate on other activities.

Industry can benefit because of the 1976 Tax Reform Act which allows it to deduct, as a charitable contribution, its manufacturing cost plus one-half of the difference between cost and fair market value on items it contributes. In addition to solving the problem of what to do with surplus and salvaged food, companies are exhibiting their social consciousness by helping to solve the hunger problem in Gallatin County.

In one typical year, the Gallatin Valley Emergency Food Bank recovered approximately $29,326.00 worth of usable yet unsalable food and received approximately $2,146.00 of canned and boxed food from community groups and individuals totalling $31,472.00 worth of food collected and salvaged in the year.

This enabled the Food Bank to provide 549 families (1,497 individuals) with emergency food assistance. On the average, a three-day food box is worth $9.72.

The Food Bank also contributed $13,759.81 worth of food to non-profit agencies serving congregate meals, which has proven to significantly reduce the cost of their food programs.

With Gallatin County's current unemployment rate at 9.7%, persons living below the federal poverty level at 13%, and cutbacks in federal help programs, the Food Bank is seeing an increased need for emergency food assistance. The Director notes, "By keeping this program alive, the Gallatin Valley Emergency Food Bank, together with the local community's support, will continue to 'care for it's own.'"

Founded: 1982

MT. ADAMS MINISTERIAL ASSOCIATION FOOD BANK
Grace Baptist Church
Route 2, Box 31
White Salmon, WA 98672
TEL: 509-493-3403
Purpose: To provide emergency supplies of food to people in need.
Sponsor: Mt. Adams Ministerial Association; private gifts from area churches
Contact: Gary K. Cowden, President
Description: The Mt. Adams Ministerial Association Food Bank is a locally operated private food bank designed to meet emergency needs of foodstuffs before an applicant can be picked up on one of the welfare programs. Therefore, the Food Bank authorizes the Director to provide three days' supply of food for any one family in any one 30-day period. Referrals to the food bank may come from any of the member churches, the Department of Social and Health Services or the Police Department.

The Food Bank is managed by an all-volunteer staff consisting of one Director, one Assistant Director, and Representatives from each of the participating churches. The Director is responsible to the Association at all times, and the Association makes policy for the food bank. Gifts of money designated for the food bank are processed through the treasury of the Association and used to purchase food when needed to restock the food bank.

The Mt. Adams Ministerial Association is solely responsible for the organization, maintenance and disposition of the food bank. No help from any governmental agency is solicited or desired.

NEIGHBORS HELPING NEIGHBORS
Washington Post
Promotion Department
1150 Fifteenth Street, NW
Washington, DC 20071
TEL: 202-334-4371
FAX: 212-334-4319
Co-sponsors: Giant Food, Inc., PO Box 1804 D-599, Washington, DC 20013 - Barry Scher, Vice President (301-341-4710); Capital Area Community Food Bank, 2266 25th Place, NE, Washington, DC 20018 - Lynn Brantley, Executive Director (202-334-5344)
Purpose: To raise food and money to help feed needy people in the metropolitan area.
Contact: Kathy Soulia
Description: Neighbors Helping Neighbors is a program designed to raise food and money to help feed 160,000 needy people in the Washington, DC metropolitan area. In its second year, this joint project among the *Capital Area Community Food Bank, The Washington Post, Giant Food, Inc.* and the people who live in the metropolitan Washington area was mid-campaign at the time of publication. *Washington Post* columnist Bob Levy served as official spokesperson.

During the campaign's first-year effort in 1989, the organizations collected more than 250,040 pounds of food and more than $100,000 in cash. The food alone provided 83,346 meals for the hungry.

All costs of the *Neighbors Helping Neighbors* campaign are covered by *The Washington Post* and *Giant Food*. Every dollar donated and all of the food goes directly toward feeding the hungry of the Washington area.

1990 Campaign
The Washington Post kicked off the campaign on Sunday, April 8, 1990, by printing and inserting a grocery shopping bag into every issue, reaching 1,200,000 homes. The bags and the two-page ad published that day encouraged people to do one of two things - either fill out a check and mail it to the *Food Bank,* or fill up a bag with non-perishable goods and drop it at the nearest *Giant Food* store.

The *Post* continued to run in-paper advertising to promote awareness of the Washington-area hunger problem during the three-week campaign and provided 10-second radio broadcast support.

Giant Food, Inc., with more than 180 stores in the Washington area, supported the campaign with: in-store displays featuring posters and food products suggested for the drive, in-store point-of-purchase materials at the checkout and on the shelves, and window posters. *Giant* also placed *Neighbors Helping Neighbors* tags in print and radio advertising.

Giant's stores served as collection sites for the food and *Giant* transported food to the *Food Bank.*

The *Capital Area Community Food Bank* sorted the food and processed the cash donations. The *Food Bank* also handled publicity including news releases to local clergy with an informational flyer that was inserted in church bulletins.

The *Capital Area Community Food Bank* is a nonprofit organization that solicits food, sorts and warehouses it, and distributes it to organizations which feed the hungry. More than 5500 people volunteer at the *Food Bank* each year. About 80% of the volunteers sort through dented cans, crushed boxes and other food that is good to eat but cannot be sold in stores.

Nearly 700 organizations - churches, community groups - come to the food bank and "shop" for their clients. They contribute $.12 per pound, which covers approximately 60% of the *Food Bank's* operating expenses. The rest of its expenses are covered by corporate donations. Approximately 160,000 people, half children, are fed each month.

The *Capital Area Community Food Bank* serves the District of Columbia, south and central Maryland and northern Virginia.
Publications: Tis The Season

SHARE SELF-HELP AND RESOURCE EXCHANGE
Roman Catholic Diocese of San Diego
San Diego, CA 92199
TEL: 619-574-6300
Purpose: To distribute low-cost food packages to families in need in exchange for community service.
Sponsor: Roman Catholic Diocese of San Diego
Contact: Exchange Coordinator
Description: The concept of the *Share Self-Help and Resource Exchange* is to enable people to maintain their dignity by contributing something to the help they receive. In the exchange program, low-income participants receive about 30 pounds of food for $12 and two hours of community service each month.
The first distribution in 1983 reached 7,000 families, who picked up food packages at the San Diego Stadium. In mid-1989, the number of families served was 17,625, all of whom provided two hours of community service. Areas covered were San Diego, Imperial, Riverside and San Bernardino counties.
Share affiliates modeled after the San Diego program are in 16 cities across the country. The program was initiated through the *Roman Catholic Diocese of San Diego* and has served a quarter of a million families coast-to-coast without any government assistance.
Founded: 1983

SHARING AND CARING - A FOOD PANTRY
Second and Union Streets
Old Armory Building
Dardanelle, AR 72834
TEL: 501-229-1220
Purpose: To meet emergency food needs of the less fortunate.
Contact: Volunteer Coordinator
Description: An outgrowth of a Christmas Basket program jointly operated by several churches, Sharing and Caring is designed to meet food needs throughout the year. The program, at first a vision of five volunteers, began with letters and meetings involving churches, civic organizations and government agencies. After several meetings, support in the form of food, cash and volunteer help came from this community effort.
In its first month of operation, June 1987, 40 families were served. By September of the same year the program served 70 families. During the first year, 517 families were serviced - a total of 1,820 people receiving food for 10,632 meals - and 1,437 volunteers hours had been donated. During the first four months of the second year, the statistics were close to those for the entire previous year.
Clients are referred by the Department of Human Services from the original area of Dardanelle, and now from Yell and Pope Counties, Russellville Police Departments, County Judge's Office and Arvac, Inc. as well.
Each family receives five to seven days' food, depending on need. Sharing and Caring also assists clients in obtaining food stamps, commodities, housing, shoes, clothing, furniture and bedding, education and learning to read. Referrals are made to other agencies when Sharing and Caring is unable to meet specific needs.
To supplement the support provided by the many organizations and individuals in the community, funds have been raised by

holding bake sales, yard sales and sale of aluminum cans.
Arkansas River Valley United Way also provides support, as does the Arkansas State Baptist Convention World Hunger Program. Although the food pantry maintains specific hours, volunteers in the program are on call 24 hours a day.

TULARE COUNTY FOOD RESOURCES
PO Box 1544
Visalia, CA 93279
TEL: 209-798-0963
Purpose: To collect surplus foods for distribution to non-profit groups with feed-the-needy programs in Tulare County.
Sponsor: Originally conceived through "Inter Church"; has a Community Action Program (CAP) grant, also some funding through Tulare Co. Revenue Sharing
Contact: Ruby Fife
Description: Tulare County Food Resources has been in existence since 1977, incorporated since 1978, occupant of a warehouse since 1979, and intermittent supplier of donated food to local agencies since 1980.
In 1980 donations of approximately $50,000 worth of food were procured and distributed to local agencies. In 1981 distributions were increased to over $100,000; 1982 to over $200,000 plus the USDA commodities of over 450,000 lbs.
In 1981 the program received a CAP grant to purchase a used pick-up truck, fork-lift and a walk-in freezer. For years 1983-84, $13,500 was received to be used to hire an Executive Director to help organize the volunteers, do the PR work, etc. Over 3,500 hours of volunteer time were logged last year. Volunteers include lawyers, accountants, typists, truck drivers, etc. According to the program manager, "Mistakes have been made but, by trial and error, positive progress has been made also."
Founded: 1977

WASHINGTON HEIGHTS ECUMENICAL FOOD PANTRY
801 West 181st Street
Suite 21
New York, NY 10033
TEL: 212-927-8738
Purpose: To provide emergency three-day supply of food to the hungry.
Sponsor: Catholic, Protestant and Jewish congregations in Washington Heights Neighborhood of Manhattan
Contact: Margaret Chen
Description: The Pantry provides a three-day emergency food supply to people referred to them by churches or community agencies.
Funds are supplied by private donations, collections by school and community and church groups.
The Food Pantry is located in the basement of the Broadway Temple Methodist Church.
Volunteer workers are supplied from churches, who are trained and scheduled to work once or twice a month. Some of the volunteers are bi-lingual.
Some advocacy counseling is provided on problems other than food.

NUTRITION: FOOD PRODUCTION

NATIONAL/STATE ORGANIZATIONS

NATIONAL GARDENING ASSOCIATION
SEE RECREATION & SPORTS: GARDENING

INDIVIDUAL PROGRAM PROFILES

CONNECTICUT MASTER GARDENERS
University of Connecticut
Cooperative Exension Service
U-36
Storrs, CT 06268
TEL: 203-486-4126
Purpose: To provide Home Grounds Education.
Sponsor: Cooperative Extension Service - University of Connecticut
Contact: Ronald F. Aronson
Description: The *Cooperative Extension Service* was established by legislative act in 1914 to provide informal education in agriculture, home economics and related subjects. The program is cooperatively funded through the USDA, State Land-Grant Universities and county governments.
The *Extension Master Gardener Program* was started in 1978. It is now in the fifth year of the program.
Each fall, about 135 adult gardeners who have an interest and experience in home fruit or vegetable production are recruited. Volunteers fill out an application form and are selected for the program. Those selected attend twelve 3-hour training programs held at four sites in the state. Training programs emphasize fundamentals of plant growth, use of pesticides, application of fertilizers, diagnostic procedures and available references. A final examination is given at the completion of the training program.
Those who successfully complete the training program receive 60 hours of supervised, practical work in one of the county Extension offices. Practical experience includes responding to questions from the public concerning problems in the home grounds. In many cases they identify insects, weeds, plants and plant diseases. The questions, responses and references cited are recorded for review by the supervising agent.
At the completion of the supervised experience the volunteers are declared to be Extension Master Gardeners. At this point, they not only have greatly expanded their knowledge of plants but have grown in their personal development. Approximately 100 volunteers complete the classroom portion of the program and about 80 complete the total program each year.
Founded: 1978

NUTRITION: HOMELESS

INDIVIDUAL PROGRAM PROFILES

ARC COVENANT
SEE RECIPIENTS: HOMELESS - NUTRITION

BETHEL LOVE KITCHEN
Bethel AME Church
2460 Parkview Avenue
Knoxville, TN 37917
TEL: 615-522-6396
Purpose: To provide hot meals, and refer people to organizations that provide jobs and shelter.
Contact: Helen Ashe or Ellen Turner, co-founders
Description: Since 1986, the *Bethel Love Kitchen* in East Knoxville has provided meals to hungry men, women and children. On the first day, 22 people came to the Kitchen. By 1989, 62,000 people had been fed.
The Kitchen relies on the federal surplus food program, donations and private supporters, including the wife of a Congressional Representative from Tennessee. The Congressman's office helps work on possible grants for the Kitchen.

The founders of the Kitchen, twin sisters, were nurses at the University of Tennessee Medical Center before their retirement. They find that this health background serves them well in dealing with their clientele. They hope to move to larger quarters with showers and enough land to grow food for meals.
Currently, the Kitchen serves meals every Thursday. Preparation is begun Wednesday, but the actual cooking done Thursday morning. Most of it is done by the founding sisters, with occasional help from volunteers. The food is substantial - fried chicken, potatoes, liver and onions, ham, meatloaf, spaghetti, green beans, corn muffins and cake.
A portion of the meals are packaged and taken by volunteers to elderly people who can't travel. The Kitchen also refers people to organizations that provide jobs and shelter, and fixes emergency food boxes for those in need who miss the meal hour.
The twins, although in poor health with back problems, arthritis and - for one sister, cancer which she says is "under control" - continue the service since, according to one of them, "What am I doing feeling sorry for myself when there are people out there who are much worse?"
Founded: 1986

GOOD SAMARITAN RECOGNITION CEREMONY
St. Paul's Episcopal Cathedral
Genessee Street
Chittenango, NY 13037
TEL: 315-687-6304
Purpose: To recognize volunteers from 50 area churches who serve hot meals to the needy at the *Samaritan Center.*
Sponsor: St. Paul's Episcopal Cathedral and other churches
Contact: Dean William Hale, Rector
Description: The board of directors of the *Samaritan Center,* which serves hot meals to the needy, honored the volunteers who serve the meals with - what else - a recognition dinner. More than 200 people representing 50 of the churches involved with the Center attended. Piano selections were played throughout the evening as *Certificates of Outstanding Service* were presented to volunteers from the Center's clothing shop, maintenance department, home bakers group, cleanup crew, carpentry workers, volunteer administrative aides and weekend volunteers.
In addition to the tasks indicated above, volunteers collect clothing, set out reading materials, and provide a multitude of other services as needed to the homeless, people down on their luck, or those simply unable to make the check last for one more meal. As many as 200 people are served every afternoon at the Center.
The rector at St. Paul's Cathedral said, "The dinner is a way of saying thank you to all the volunteers. After all of their baking, stirring, slicing and preparing of food for others, we felt that it was time our 'good Samaritans' got served themselves."

LOAVES & FISHES
SEE RECIPIENTS: HOMELESS - NUTRITION

OUR DAILY BREAD
SEE RECIPIENTS: HOMELESS - NUTRITION

PRIME TIME TO END HUNGER
SEE RECIPIENTS: HOMELESS - NUTRITION

ST. JOSEPH'S HOUSE OF HOSPITALITY
SEE RECIPIENTS: HOMELESS - NUTRITION

NUTRITION: HUNGER

NATIONAL/STATE ORGANIZATIONS

FREEDOM FROM HUNGER FOUNDATION
PO Box 2000
Davis, CA 95617
TEL: 916-758-6200
Objectives: To assist families, communities, organizations and institutions in developing self-help projects which will improve food and nutrition.
Services: Develops programs in response to food and nutrition needs recognized in the field; provides assistance in nutrition education and training, rural nutrition programs, food preservation and storage, loans; maintains a Resource Center on nutrition, food technology and other related subjects; publishes booklets and how-to manuals, quarterly newsletter, and a series of pamphlets.
Publications: NewsBriefs; Connections
Founded: 1979

NATIONAL HUNGER COALITION
Food Research and Action Center
1319 F Street, NW
Washington, DC 20004
TEL: 202-393-5060
Objectives: To speak with one voice on child nutrition, food stamps, and elderly nutrition programs.
Services: Seeks increased involvement of food program participants in the policy decision process; acts as a clearinghouse for food program information; promotes stronger regulatory advocacy; assists in regional training in the area of education on food program issues; strengthens linkages with other groups; works on special projects such as Foodless June, Poor People's Food Platform, full funding for food stamps, and others; operates through 50 State Coordinators (plus Puerto Rico and Virgin Islands), 35 Regional Representatives, and seven national organizations, which involve church members, legal services workers, parents, Community Action Agencies, advocates, and food program participants, as well as interested persons and groups from the general community; works through state-wide networks, local organizations, and locally-based national agencies and organizations; convenes regional and national meetings.
Founded: 1970

SHARE OUR STRENGTH (SOS)
733 Fifteenth Street, NW
Suite 700
Washington, DC 20005
TEL: 202-393-2925
TOLL FREE: 800-222-ISOS
Objectives: To raise money for national and international hunger relief programs.
Services: Enlists membership through restaurants, currently in over 75 cities; works to maintain the public's awareness about the problem of escalating hunger and homelessness here in America and overseas; raises and donates funds to established relief and development organizations; provides information on community hunger groups in an effort to encourage local volunteerism; coordinates *Schools Against Hunger* program; maintains several boards including a *Hunger Advisory Board* and a *Restaurant Advisory Board;* maintains a speakers' bureau and placement service; publishes a newsletter, brochure and other materials.
Contact: Debbie Shore, Fund Raising Director
Publications: News from S.O.S.
Founded: 1984

TRAINING PROGRAMS

END HUNGER NETWORK (*formerly Action Support Center for Ending Hunger*)
7080 Hollywood Boulevard
Suite 1105
Hollywood, CA 90028
TEL: 213-465-1377
Objectives: To end world hunger.
Services: Acts as a catalyst both for individual and combined community action; involves the media and entertainment industry in efforts to end world hunger; educates the public on world hunger issues; creates resources and support for hunger organizations; sponsors *End Hunger Televents* (a series of television specials); produces audiovisual materials; maintains a database of private voluntary organizations working on relief and development; sponsors *Presidential End Hungar Awards;* maintains contact with the entertainment industry for support; publishes a newsletter, handbook, and other materials.
Founded: 1982

INDIVIDUAL PROGRAM PROFILES

TASTE OF THE NATION
Share Our Strength (SOS)
733 Fifteenth Street, NW
Suite 700
Washington, DC 20005
TEL: 202-393-2925
TOLL FREE: 800-222-ISOS
Purpose: To raise funds to help support hunger relief programs.
Sponsor: Watergate Restaurant
Contact: Debbie Shore, Fund Raising Director
Description: As part of a national goal to raise $1,000,000 through the network of 75 cities in which *Share Our Strength (S.O.S.)* chapters exist, 25 of the most outstanding restaurants in the Washington, DC, area held their third annual public awareness and fund-raising forum.
During a pre-forum sampling session, visitors tasted dishes that were the local restaurants' best-held secrets, and had an opportunity to talk informally to the chefs about S.O.S., hunger, and nutrition. S.O.S. is a national nonprofit organization with 500 member restaurants in 75 cities as of 1989. The purpose of the organization is to maintain the public's awareness about hunger, and raise funds for hunger relief organizations.
The speakers for the forum were chefs from four local restaurants: Tila's, New Heights, 21 Federal, and La Brasserie. They talked about nutrition, the goals and activities of S.O.S., and how Taste of the Nation "benefits the community of which we are all a part." One hundred percent of the funds raised at the event (admission is $65.00) is donated to the Capital Area Food Bank, D.C. Central Kitchen, House of Ruth, Food and Friends (a food project for AIDS victims), OXFAM and Save the Children. Honorary chairpersons for the event included Linda Robb, J.C. Hayward of WUSA-TV, and Darrell Green of the Washington Redskins.
Among restaurants contributing sample food dishes were Watergate, Galileo, Germaine's, The Occidental, River Club, and I. Ricchi.
Brochures and other materials about S.O.S. and hunger around the world were distributed at the forum.

NUTRITION: I&R

NATIONAL/STATE ORGANIZATIONS

FOOD SAFETY HOTLINE
SEE CONSUMER SERVICES/LEGAL RIGHTS: NUTRITION

NUTRITION EDUCATION AND INFORMATION
SEE NUTRITION: EDUCATION

NUTRITION: OLDER PERSON

INDIVIDUAL PROGRAM PROFILES

BAY RIDGE NUTRITION AND HOME CARE PROGRAMS
411 Ovington Avenue
Brooklyn, NY 11209
TEL: 212-748-0873
Purpose: To help older persons avoid unnecessary institutionalization.
Sponsor: Federal/State governments; private donations
Contact: Rosemary Carney, Executive Director
Description: In order to maintain older persons in their own communities and avoid premature and unnecessary institutionalization, the Bay Ridge Nutrition and Home Care Programs were organized in 1976.
The nutrition center provides socialization and meals, Monday thru Saturday for anyone 60 years and older. It serves the mobile elderly and provides them with paid and unpaid work.
The home care program services the homebound frail elderly with transportation, meals on wheels, housekeeping, friendly visiting and telephone reassurance.
Volunteer Staff: ten volunteers serve as receptionists at the nutrition center; five help package the meals on wheels; two teach arts and crafts classes; five do friendly visiting and two write and publish the center's newsletter.
Volunteer Experience: currently, the center is recruiting volunteers to attend a creative movement class. Once they have learned some basic techniques, they will share them with their homebound counterparts under the supervision of the movement specialist.
Founded: 1976

COUNTRY GATHERING
Northeast Kentucky Area Development Council
PO Box U
Olive Hill, KY 41164
TEL: 606-286-4443
Purpose: To provide a well-balanced meal in a social setting to older persons; to provide other services to the elderly as needed.
Sponsor: Kentucky Dept. of Human Resources (through FIVCO); AOA/HHS
Contact: Regina Fannin, Project Director
Description: Country Gathering began as a federally-funded nutrition demonstration project in June 1968 under Title IV (Research and Demonstration Grants) from the Administration on Aging. It now operates five multi-purpose senior centers and seven satellite nutrition sites in the FIVCO (five-county) area covering Lawrence, Greenup, Elliott, Carter and Boyd Counties.
The multi-purpose centers provide meals plus services; the satellite nutrition sites provide meals with a limited number of services.
Approximately 500 congregate meals and one hundred homebound meals are served daily Monday through Friday.
The program is administered by twenty-nine full-time employees,

five part-time employees, and approximately 200 volunteers. Ninety-five percent of the volunteers are over 65 years of age.
All meals are prepared at a central kitchen and packaged in insulated containers. The food is transported by vans and the travel time varies from five minutes to two hours. The bulk trays maintain safe temperatures for a maximum of four hours. Homebound meals are packaged in individual insulated trays. Meals served at multi-purpose centers and nutrition sites are served free, with a suggested donation of $.75 per person (age 60 or older). This has been done to help maintain the dignity of the elderly participants. A rural transportation system provides transportation at a reduced rate for senior citizens, but the program buys a limited number of free tickets for participants who need them.
Initially, the focus of Country Gathering was on nutrition only. Today services such as legal services, shopping assistance, art and crafts, information and referrals, counseling, chore service, crisis intervention, winterization, discount cards, visiting reassurance in the home, and many others are provided through the five multi-purpose centers, with limited services of this type available at the nutrition sites also. Some of the services are provided by the Community Action Agency, which administers the Aging Program and provides additional employees such as transporters, kitchen aides, and site managers. The Aging Program operates a Home Care Program which provides homemaker services, chore service, home repair, respite, medical transportation and escort, to those vulnerable elderly who would be institutionalized without the service.
Founded: 1968

MEALS ON WHEELS OF BIRMINGHAM
SEE RECIPIENTS: OLDER PERSON - NUTRITION

MORRIS COUNTY NUTRITION PROGRAM
Morris County Department of Human Services
Morristown, NJ 07961
TEL: 201-285-6868
Purpose: To provide meals to needy seniors both at nutrition sites and in their homes.
Sponsor: Morris County Department of Human Services
Contact: Carol Murphy, Freeholder
Description: The *Morris County Nutrition Program* has a budget of about $889,000 to provide nutritionally-balanced meals to senior citizens. The federal government pays $546,000, the freeholders pay $212,000 and clients contribute $131,000. Volunteers help to stretch these funds so that more people can be served. The average home meal recipient is between the late 70s and the 80s in age, in frail health, with no family or close friends.
Volunteers supplement staff in the nutrition project to pack the meals and deliver them. Volunteers come from churches, senior centers and hospitals. A majority of the meals are provided on weekdays at eight nutrition sites, with the remainder delivered to residences around the county. One meal is provided on weekdays, and two on weekends. In one typical month, 9,271 meals were provided at the sites, while 5,475 (37%) were delivered to residences.
As the county's elderly population continues to increase, the need for home delivery rises. The federal estimate for the county's senior citizen population in 1990 is 65,900, a 27% increase from 1980. Some have termed this the "graying" of the county, which requires more volunteers and staff, and increased financing. Countywide recruiting drives are constant, especially for weekend delivery to "areas where the need is greatest" - Boonton, Dover, Roxbury and Morris Plains. There is some relief in that Morristown has its own seven-day-a-week meals program, and local hospitals have programs for elderly or ill persons recently released from hospitals.

SENIOR NUTRITION PROGRAM
SEE RECIPIENTS: OLDER PERSON - NUTRITION

NUTRITION: ON-SITE

INDIVIDUAL PROGRAM PROFILES

COMMUNITY PROGRAMS
Marillac House
2822 West Jackson Boulevard
Chicago, IL 60612
TEL: 312-722-7440
Purpose: To provide service for the poor of East Garfield Park.
Sponsor: Chicago Community Trust
Contact: Mrs. Kay Hallagan
Description: Marillac House is committed to the community of East Garfield Park. With unemployment at an all-time peak and government assistance slashed, the families of this community are enormously deprived. Homes are without heat due to impossible utility costs. Fires and eviction are forcing people out on the streets. Crime and violence are commonplace. Meager aid checks and food stamp allotments are snatched from homemakers as they struggle to pay their bills.
Frequently a family is without food for a month due to theft. Marillac House maintains a food pantry five days a week for families in emergency need. The *Emergency Infant Nutrition Program* provides needed formula for babies who have not yet been added to the grant or who have not yet qualified for WIC. Over one hundred infants per month are served through this program. The Chicago Community Trust is funding this program. Donations specifically for infant care are used to purchase disposable diapers and layettes for newborns.
A summer feeding program funded by a private donation supplied breakfast to 1,300 children every morning for eight weeks during the summer of 1982. The private funding replaced resources previously supplied by the Department of Agriculture through the Illinois Department of Education, cancelled by the federal government.
The agency operates Day Care for children of mothers employed or in school. The Child Protection units counsel families under the auspices of the Department of Children and Family Services. Elderly Outreach seeks out senior citizens who are without family and resources to help them survive. Alcoholics Anonymous groups meet regularly and a GED program is offered. Neighborhood recreation programs attract children of all ages.
A new program specifically designed for teen mothers has been funded by the Chicago Community Trust. Its goal is to intervene in the constantly recurring cycle of poverty.

COUNTRY GATHERING
SEE NUTRITION: OLDER PERSON

EMERGENCY INFANT NUTRITION PROGRAM: FREE BREAKFAST PROJECT
SEE NUTRITION: CHILDREN/YOUTH

GOOD SAMARITAN RECOGNITION CEREMONY
SEE NUTRITION: HOMELESS

HOUSING SERVICES: AIDS PROGRAM
SEE HOUSING: AIDS

MANNA BOWL
First Lutheran Church
1244 South Utica
Tulsa, OK 74104
TEL: 918-582-0917; 918-492-7874
Purpose: To feed the unemployed of the city.

Sponsor: First Lutheran Church - other churches & private donations
Contact: Esther Endres, Volunteer Coordinator
Description: Manna Bowl was started to offer a hot meal two days each week. Those who attend are mostly men who, because of the economy, are unemployed. Women and children are welcome. The program operates under the leadership of First Lutheran Church, but donations of food, money and clothing come from other churches, markets, bakeries, and private sources. The entire staff is volunteer.
Volunteer Staff: At this time, 40 volunteers work varying times and days. The cook, coordinator, and all others who work are giving their time and expertise to the project. There have been over 400 donors to the program. Manna Bowl has been serving since September 13, 1982, and averages serving 150 persons each day.
Volunteer Duties: The Coordinator is in charge of the feeding process, the scheduling of workers, and the picking up of food products which are not delivered. He provides leadership to those who set up the eating area, serve the food, and the clean-up. He oversees the dining room during the meal and takes care of any problems arising during the meal - before and after. All donations are filed and volunteers send thank you notes and letters for taxable donations requested.
The Cook is in total charge of the kitchen, the preparation, cooking, and storing of foods and directing the volunteers who work in the kitchen. She works very closely with the coordinator. Other volunteer duties include - preparing the meat, vegetables, fruit, etc., to be used by the cook in making soup and other things. When sandwiches are served they are made by volunteers who have procured a food permit from the public health department. The kitchen is set up for assembly line serving. Tables and chairs are put into place, cleaned after the meal, tables and chairs removed, floors cleaned, all equipment cleaned, dishes washed and placed in cabinets, trash removed to proper containers, refrigerators and freezers cleaned, cupboards kept clean and neat, the laundry of towels, aprons, other linen is done.
Volunteer Experience: The Coordinator is a retired public relations man who understands the needs of the guests at the meals. He is capable of meeting the many needs which arise every day and dealing firmly with them.
The cook was with the Tulsa Public School cafeterias for years, so comes with much knowledge of cooking for large numbers as well as heading up a kitchen and its workers. She is a good organizer. Other volunteers need only to be willing workers, and not mind menial tasks - some not too pleasant. They need to be uncomplaining, non-judgmental, and compassionate. A word from the Volunteer Coordinator: "There is always a need for more volunteers."
Founded: 1982

MORRIS COUNTY NUTRITION PROGRAM
SEE NUTRITION: OLDER PERSON

OUR COMMUNITY KITCHEN
921 Pleasant
Des Moines, IA 50309
TEL: 515-283-2100
Purpose: "To provide nutrition for the body with dignity for the spirit."
Sponsor: Churches, local community groups and concerned individuals
Contact: Marycecil Dummit (coordinator)
Description: Since January 4, 1983, Our Community Kitchen has been serving free evening meals four nights each week to those in need in the city. The goal is to provide a nutritious meal without stigmatizing the participants in the program. Efforts are made to avoid the soupline image and to promote a friendly atmosphere. The program was started by the Des Moines Urban Mission

Council with a $7,000 grant from the United Methodist Hunger Task Force. It is sponsored and funded by churches, community groups, and concerned individuals. It is presently serving over 200 meals each Monday through Thursday at three sites in the city. Each meal consists of a soup or casserole, fruit, sandwiches or freshly-baked bread, and milk or punch.

All work except administration is done by some 50 volunteers under the guidance of a program coordinator. Teams of volunteers prepare the meals in a central kitchen. Another team of volunteers delivers the food to the three serving sites and a third team serves the meals.

The volunteer cooks work a three-week cycle, with each team taking one day in the cycle. They prepare and cook the meal, package the food in containers for delivery and clean up the kitchen and store areas. The volunteer drivers deliver the hot meals to the serving sites on a weekly schedule. The servers, also on a weekly schedule, unpack the food and set up a buffet-style dinner. They help to serve the meals to the elderly, handicapped and small children. They are also in charge of cleaning the facilities and storing the utensils and equipment for the next day.
Founded: 1983

OUR DAILY BREAD
SEE RECIPIENTS: HOMELESS - NUTRITION

SENIOR NUTRITION PROGRAM
SEE RECIPIENTS: OLDER PERSON - NUTRITION

ST. JOSEPH'S HOUSE OF HOSPITALITY
SEE RECIPIENTS: HOMELESS - NUTRITION

NUTRITION: SELF-HELP

INDIVIDUAL PROGRAM PROFILES

GLEANING*
Idaho Hunger Action Council
621 North Eighth Street
Boise, ID 83702-5518
TEL: 208-336-7010
Purpose: To harvest the left-overs in Idaho fields.
Sponsor: Titcomb President Bishop's Fund
Contact: Peter Benedict
Description: This program organizes groups of low income people into gleaning crews. The crews consist of gleaners and partners. Gleaners do the work and partners are either disabled, senior citizens, or provide child care for the gleaners. Each gleaning team has a partner organization. The organization may be a church or other group which provides free lunches, soup kitchens, or other free food services. The food is divided by the gleaners for the partners and partners' organizations.

The gleaning project started in 1979. Today, there are 22 local gleaner coordinators in the state which harvested 91 tons of food last year. The program goal is to top 100 tons this year with 1,000 gleaners.

Other sponsors include the Presbyterian Hunger Project and the Community Service Block Grant.
Founded: 1979

PHYSICAL ENVIRONMENT

NATIONAL/STATE ORGANIZATIONS

AMERICA THE BEAUTIFUL FUND
219 Shoreham Building
Washington, DC 20005
TEL: 202-638-1649
Objectives: To initiate new local action projects which improve the quality of the environment.
Services: Gives recognition, technical support, and small seed grants to private citizens and community groups; considers programs that affect the design, land preservation and planning, historical and cultural preservation, arts, or communications of the community; conducts workshops and professional training programs; publishes quarterly newsletter, and other materials.
Publications: Better Times

COMMUNITY ENVIRONMENTAL PROGRAM*
League of Women Voters of the US
1730 M Street, NW
Washington, DC 20036
TEL: 202-429-1965
Objectives: To promote political resposibility through citizen participation in current issue areas' including the environment.
Services: Assists local groups in identifying community environmental problems, monitoring corrective developments, and influencing decision-making; provides services through local leagues (write for directory).
Publications: National Voter

CONCERN, INC.
1794 Columbia Road, NW
Washington, DC 20009
TEL: 202-328-8160
Objectives: To help communities find solutions to environmental problems that threaten public health and the quality of life.
Services: Provides environmental information to community groups, public officials, educational institutions, private individuals, and many others involved in public education and policy development; develops, publishes and distributes community action guides which define major issues, explain relevant legislation, describe successful regional, state, and local initiatives, give resource information, and recommend specific action guidelines.

Contact: Susan Boyd, Executive Director
Publications: Household Waste: Issues and Opportunities; Farmland: A Community Issue; Drinking Water: A Community Action Guide; Groundwater: A Community Action Guide; Pesticides: A Community Action Guide; Waste: Choices for Communities; Concern, Inc.

ENVIRONMENT INFORMATION CENTER
48 West 38th Street
New York, NY 10018
TEL: 212-9400-8500
Objectives: To provide a forum and immediate source of information for those involved in environmental and energy problems.
Services: Locates, abstracts, stores and retrieves information tools on all aspects of environmental quality; includes published contributions from universities, government agencies, conservation groups and interested individuals; maintains film library; publishes several periodicals, handbooks, update binders, and other materials.

ENVIRONMENTAL ACTION
1525 New Hampshire Avenue, NW
Washington, DC 20036
TEL: 202-745-4870
Objectives: To prevent pollution, reduce the use of nonrenewable resources, encourage conservation of energy and materials, eliminate threats to natural cycles, promote a stable population size consistent with available resources, and broaden citizen participation in political and economic decision-making.
Services: Engages in lobbying, demonstrations, educational activities (served as national coordinating office for Earth Day 1970); focuses on legislation that has a direct relationship to environment-oriented efforts of local groups (Clean Air Act, Clean Water Act, Resource Conservation and Recovery Act, and others); publishes monthly magazine, *Environmental Action*, "Filthy Five" (polluting corporations that give local PAC contributions to anti-environmental candidates, making the connection with anti-environmental voting on Capitol Hill), political action alerts, books, pamphlets and other materials.
Publications: Environmental Action; "Filthy Five"

ENVIRONMENTAL ACTION FOUNDATION

1525 New Hampshire Avenue, NW
Washington, DC 20036
TEL: 202-745-4870

Objectives: To provide local activists with the expertise they need to tackle issues of pollution and energy.

Services: Mobilizes grassroots environmental action; promotes environmental protection through research, public education, organizing assistance and legal action; works in the areas of energy conservation, utility polity, toxics pollution, solid waste and recycling, pesticides, and nuclear waste and weapons.

Publications: Environmental Action; Powerline; Waste Lines

ENVIRONMENTAL POLICY INSTITUTE

218 D Street, SE
Washington, DC 20003
TEL: 202-544-2600

Objectives: To provide public interest lobbyists specializing in diverse citizen interests on environmental issues.

Services: Works to influence public policy to assure that necessary energy production will provide payrolls, capital investments and tax revenues while protecting the health and safety of workers and the rights of citizens and their local, state and regional governments; emphasizes the health of miners, the preservation of land and water resources of farmers, the air and water quality in urban and rural areas, and related issues; encourages the balance of energy conservation and energy production that will meet environmental standards and economic needs.

Publications: EPI Alert

LEAGUE OF CONSERVATION VOTERS*

320 Fourth Street, NE
Washington, DC 20002
TEL: 202-547-1196

Objectives: To identify and support environmentalists running for House, Senate and gubernatorial offices.

Services: Provides an information service which enables voters to better interpret campaign rhetoric to determine individual candidate's environmental position; raises campaign funds and provides other means of support for selected candidates who face tough challenges; publishes a support slate with pre-election information and post-election reports analyzing the results; designs and distributes voting charts for quick reference on key environmental issues by House and Senate members.

Publications: How Congress Voted; Presidential Profiles

PRIVATE SECTOR EFFORTS PROGRAM

US/DoI - Office of the Secretary
Office of the Secretary
18th and C Streets
Washington, DC 20240
TEL: 202-343-7351

Objectives: To develop and mount initiatives that increase involvement of the private sector in the Department's programs.

Services: Operates through three distinct functions toward the above objective, which are outlined below:

Voluntary Efforts Now Underway in Support of Public Goals
Park, Recreation, and Wildlife Protection:
- more than 400 volunteers at 65 field stations of National Wildlife Refuges, National Fish Hatcheries, and research stations, including a national Volunteer Coordinator in the Fish and Wildlife Service.
- private, non-profit land trusts across the country protecting natural, scenic, recreational, scientific, historic, and cultural lands.
- new guidebook on the National Park system by the Travel Industry Association of America; a new map of the system by the National Tour Brokers Association, a new film about the system by the Walter J. Klein Company, and an item not

produced before - an information piece by the International Snowmobile Manufacturers Association on winter time activities in the National Parks.
- a "foster plant project" (Adopt-A- Plant) by the Garden Club of America with most of its 180 member clubs opting to select a vulnerable plant as a conservation concern; surveys on endangered species by the Nature Conservancy's Heritage Programs; a network of plant societies in more than a dozen states to address the Endangered Species Act.
- employee volunteer programs working with the Rare and Endangered Native Plant Exchange (50 employees in the Brooklyn Union Gas Company, for example), which mounts projects and raises funds.

Public Lands Management:
- a nationwide program to recruit/involve volunteers to help manage its 327 million acres of public lands.

Joint Public-Private Enterprises
Park, Recreation, and Wildlife Protection:
- an assessment of national recreation and policy.
- plans for creation of a National Park Corps to coordinate volunteer efforts supporting the National Park system.
- coordination with groups volunteering to rehabilitate the Statue of Liberty, raise funds for reconstruction at Wolf Trap Farm Park, create new parks where a need emerges (such as in Alton Park, Illinois, with $150,000 worth of donated labor and $100,000 worth of donated equipment), mount public awareness campaigns on specific endangered species, purchase and distribute the Service's films, donate wetlands habitats to protect migratory birds, maintain relevant bookstores in visitor centers, etc.
- various Memoranda of Agreement with corporations and local governments to refrain from developing certain lands to protect endangered species, or to provide direct funding to protect this wildlife.

Public Lands and Water Resource Management:
- work with private firms to operate range management programs, find range lands to ease overpopulated refuges of wild animals, dispose of surplus federal property, enter into joint private federal construction projects, etc.

Energy and Minerals:
- operation of joint private-public enterprises within the data systems of the U.S. Geological Survey.
- exercise of cost-sharing research and other projects with academic institutions, private industrial firms, and others.

Programs that Could/Should Involve Greater Private Sector Efforts
Park and Wildlife Protection:
- purchasing of fish to meet stocking requirements (evaluating possibility of purchasing from private sector).
- use of concessionaires for tours, food services, sales outlets, guides, maintenance services, etc. (expanding use of private concessionaires).
- operation of campgrounds and provision of visitor services (exploring increased private sector support).

Water Resource Development:
- mounts cost-sharing arrangements for water resource projects in partnership with the private sector.
- transferral of the operation of completed facilities to local water users.
- voluntary labor for the construction and maintenance of recreation facilities at Bureau water projects.

Energy and Minerals:
- privatizing of large-scale mapping now done by the U.S. Geological Survey, which develops Large Scale Mapping Guidelines that would permit capable and experienced firms in the private sector to collect data and produce the maps.

[Above summarizes a much larger bank of programs aimed at increased private sector involvement; inquire.]

Sponsor: US/DoI - Department of the Interior

PHYSICAL ENVIRONMENT: AIR POLLUTION

NATIONAL/STATE ORGANIZATIONS

AIR AND WASTE MANAGEMENT ASSOCIATION
PO Box 2861
Pittsburgh, PA 15230
TEL: 412-232-3444
Objectives: To promote a clean environment through education and exchange of technical information.
Services: Sponsors ongoing education courses for groups and individuals; works with local groups; maintains extensive library; supports numerous committees, including Public Utilities Committee, Community Relations Committee, Hazardous Waste Committee, Cleaner Air Week Committee, Waste Disposal Committee, and Indoor Air Quality Committee; publishes monthly journal, a directory and resource book, educational materials, local group proceedings, and other materials.
Publications: Directory/Resource Book; Journal of A&WMA; Proceedings Digest

NATIONAL AIR CONSERVATION COMMISSION
American Lung Association
1726 M Street, NW
Suite 902
Washington, DC 20036
TEL: 202-785-3355
Objectives: To establish national air conservation activities.
Services: Works with voluntary organizations and public agencies to restore clean air; offers information on preventive and corrective measures; creates public awareness of the causes and harmful effects of air pollution; monitors air pollution legislation; makes policy recommendations regarding air conservation; works with other organizations in planning and conducting programs.
Publications: American Review of Respiratory Disease

NATIONAL CLEAN AIR COALITION
801 Pennsylvania Avenue, SW
Third Floor
Washington, DC 20003
TEL: 202-543-8200
Objectives: To provide a voice for the public in government treatment of air quality matters.
Services: Lobbies for strong national clean air legislation; seeks to insure that legislation is effectively implemented through regulations, state activity, and local air program efforts; conducts workshops for the public on clean air issues.

PHYSICAL ENVIRONMENT: BEAUTIFICATION

TRAINING PROGRAMS

FORUM ON SCHOOL VANDALISM
SEE LAW ENFORCEMENT/CRIME PREVENTION: CHILDREN/YOUTH

INDIVIDUAL PROGRAM PROFILES

BEACHFRONT VOLUNTEERS
Interact Club
Southern Regional High School
Route 9
Manahawkin, NJ 08050
TEL: 609-597-9481
Purpose: To help clean up New Jersey beaches for beautification and recreation.
Sponsor: Long Beach Township Department of Public Works
Contact: Mary Tantillo, Vice President, Interact
Description: Three hundred students from 15 New Jersey high schools in seven counties gathered at Long Beach Island to help clean up the beaches. All are members of *Interact,* a high school organization developed by Rotary International.
The volunteers gathered five truckloads of trash along an eight-mile stretch of beachfront, and kept individual logs of the trash they collected. The logs are sent to the *Center for Environmental Education* in Washington, which is conducting a study on floatables and beach litter.
The *Long Beach Township Department of Public Works* disposes of the trash, which usually consists of bottles, cans, plastic items and cigarette butts - things likely to be left on the beach by visitors or dropped into coastal waters by recreational boaters. Much of it comes from under the sand, where tourists bury their litter rather than carry it to trash barrels.
The *Ocean County Tourism Advisory Council* provided a $750 grant for the project, which provided souvenir T-shirts for participants and the rental of toilet facilities. The *Alliance for a Living Ocean,* an environmental-awareness group based on Long Beach Island, gave each participating club a *Steward of the Earth* award. The consensus of the young volunteers is that the beaches can be kept clean if everyone will do their part.

COMMUNITY ACTIVITIES COUNCIL
Haddon Township Council
Haddon Avenue & Reeve Avenue
Camden, NJ 08103
TEL: 609-854-1176
Purpose: To enlist volunteers from the community to help clean up and improve the appearance of the township.
Contact: Dennis St. John, Community Activity Coordinator
Description: Throughout the year, volunteers from the community join township employees in the common goal of improving their town. Throughout 1989, 44 volunteers assisted more than a dozen township employees, including public works employees, township commissioners and *Community Activities Council* at numerous cleanup sites. A major site was the community pool, which needed major repairs as well as cleaning. In addition to replacing a deteriorating roof on the bathhouse, the team raked together and sorted glass, metal, paper and plastic debris for recycling, pruned trees, cut grass, trimmed bushes, etc.
In four other sites around the city, volunteers and township employees worked together to perform major paint-up, fix-up chores based on a schedule prepared by the *Community Activities Council.* One reward for its work is qualifying for $12,000 from the *1987 Clean Communities Act* to fund a small group of volunteers, the 6-member *Sparkle Committee,* which does no major cleanup tasks, but provides the necessary finishing touches in public areas of the township.

FEAT FOUNDATION
c/o Timothy H. Knecht
5112 Territorial
Grand Blanc, MI 48439
TEL: 313-232-3141 (Found.); 313-694-0190 (Pres.)
Purpose: To operate recycling and beautification programs in the Flint area.

Sponsor: Mott Foundation
Contact: Timothy H. Knecht, Chairman
Description: With the help of community volunteers, the *FEAT Foundation* is recovering from a financial and manpower slump that threatened its existence. Begun in the high-interest period of the 1970s in matters of environmental issues with funding from the *Mott Foundation* and the *City of Flint,* and membership reaching 800, the Foundation's beautification and recycling programs enjoyed a high profile. In the late 1980s, funding was not as readily available, and volunteers became more scarce with the advent of women in the labor force and other factors.

In 1988, the chairmanship changed hands, more volunteers were enlisted, and the beautification and recycling programs are in full swing again.

The recycling program was begun in 1987 with funding from the *Clean Michigan Fund.* Recycling includes glass, paper and some plastics. Some of these materials come from the City of Flint as part of the city's voluntary recycling pilot program.

Proceeds from recycling enables FEAT to supplement donations received for beautification projects. Surveys of traffic triangles and other areas that have deteriorated are being made, and a new membership drive is underway. Periodic weekend open houses help increase public awareness.

Founded: 1976

FIGHTING DIRTY!
PhilaPride
123 South Broad
Philadelphia, PA 19107
TEL: 215-545-5823
Purpose: To rally the community to help restore the reputation of a once clean, historic Philadelphia.
Sponsor: KYW-TV
Contact: Paula Young, Executive Director
Description: With the help of *The Daily News, KYW-TV,* the city *Streets and Licenses & Inspection Departments,* and citizens, *PhilaPride* has launched a campaign that will eliminate the new name some people are giving to Philadelphia - *Philthydelphia.* Using innovative terminology to attract attention, the program calls on neighborhood people, community volunteers, businesses, shop owners, and individuals to join the nonprofit litter-prevention organization in "fighting dirty." Teams are dubbed "MOD (Monarchs of Dirt) Squad" and asked to be on the lookout for *DMZs (Disgusting Mucky Zones)* and report them to the "Top MOD (Marquis of Debris)." This is done by completing a reporting form printed in the daily paper, shooting a videotape of the scene, or taking photographs and mailing the report to *KYW-TV.* Some videos are shown on the TV program.

One victory for a persistent MOD squad was getting the city to clean up a city-owned area that was being used as a dumping ground. After the long battle, "dump watchers" were assigned to stake out the lot and send potential dumpers packing. After chasing away three or four violators, "the word must have spread and they haven't dumped here since."

An outgrowth of the initial neighborhood effort resulted in the volunteers going into other neighborhoods and instructing people on how to conduct dump serveillance and record vital information. The illegal dumping problem is the most troublesome, by far, according to the volunteers. In addition to tires and the usual junk, large appliances, like refrigerators, are dumped at illegal dumping sites. However, with volunteer MOD squads moving across the area from neighborhood to neighborhood, getting license numbers, and turning information over to the police, significant improvement is seen - especially since the word has spread that it is a misdemeanor offense which could result in fines ranging from $2,500 to $10,000.

According to a Streets Department official, "There's nothing so unusual about the approach. It's just a matter of getting organized and spreading the word." *PhilaPride* adds, "Just send in your DMZ reports. The Marquis and his court will do the rest!"

GREEN COUNTRIE TOWNE PROGRAM
Point Breeze Federation
1248 South 21st
Philadelphia, PA 19146
TEL: 215-334-2666
Purpose: To "go from hopeless to hopeful" in an inner-city community.
Sponsor: Pennsylvania Horticultural Society
Contact: Mamie Nichols, President
Description: Point Breeze is three miles square and has a population of 32,000 people. In the 1970s it was a battlefield for warring gangs of firebomb-toting drug dealers. The gaping holes from the firebombs added to the problems of 900 abandoned homes and thousands of others owned by absentee landlords. Although residents outside the decaying community felt it was not worth saving and should die a natural death, the residents of the North Philadelphia community were not ready to let their community die.

Although drugs, abandoned homes and absentee landlords are still problems for Point Breeze, the determination of the community has brought about highly visible progress, including:

- The first new homes built in 50 years - 34 of them - were built in 1984.
- An after-school tutoring program is operated by volunteers from the *Point Breeze Civic Association.*
- A school for performing arts has been established.
- Anti-drug marches are regular and frequent.
- The community has been called the largest "greened" inner-city neighborhood in the country through its association with the *Pennsylvania Horticultural Society's Philadelphia Green Program.*

Point Breeze is designated as one of Philadelphia's Four *Green Countrie Townes,* and boasts 77 community gardens on vacant lots with direct assistance from the Society, and 95 other projects ranging from trees on otherwise desolate blocks to large sidewalk planters along a whole block of rowhouses with assistance from the Society on request. Many gardens have a mural as a backdrop to replace grafitti-covered walls, or white picket fences to discourage jaywalkers. One has a tall, elegant iron fence donated by a school that didn't want it, and encloses the "wedding garden," so-called because it has become a favorite photo stop for bridal parties. Another has a latticed wood gazebo. The most recent addition is used as a "concert garden," where jazz and gospel music is played.

In addition to those 172 greening projects, residents, businesses and private agencies have planted flower and vegetable gardens on their own. Because the gardens have been so well kept, there is little vandalism or drug dealing in those areas.

Along with the gardening program begun 10 years ago, Point Breeze has allocated $750,000 in federal community block grants for housing rehabilitation. Since then the neighborhood has also been used as a laboratory for real estate students at the University of Pennsylvania. The students have rehabilitated one home for sale, and are working on others. Many of the hundreds of homes waiting for attention are boarded up, with local artists painting venetian blinds and plants on the boards.

And, according to the Philadelphia 17th Police District, "the tide is turning" against the drug dealers due to the anti-drug marches, the information about illegal activities provided to the police, and the community pride that has resulted from the positive results of residents' efforts. "If you see these nice things springing up, you think, 'Well, someone does care,'" he said.

INMATE SPRUCE-UP TEAMS
Massachusetts Department of Public Works
One City Hall Square
Boston, MA 08060
TEL: 617-482-5300

Purpose: To involve nonviolent inmates in state beautification projects.
Sponsor: Massachusetts Department of Public Works
Contact: Sheriff Peter Y. Flynn, Plymouth County
Description: Some 116 inmates across the state have volunteered to work eight hours a day, five days a week, picking up litter and cleaning up land, saving the state an estimated $684,000 in labor costs. In exchange, the inmates have their sentences cut by five days for each month they work.
The inmate-volunteers are not violent criminals. They are serving time for failure to pay child support or driving under the influence of alcohol.
The Department of Public Works picks up a crew in the morning, provides them with needed equipment and drops them off at a site where they are supervised by a corrections officer, who remains with them during the workday. State officials find the clean-up project well done in all areas served by the inmates.
A side benefit is the positive attitude of the inmates in providing the service, and the possibility of the volunteer experience influencing them to help their communities on their release.

OPERATION CLEAN SWEEP
First Presbyterian Church
125 Garden Street
Mount Holly, NJ 08060
TEL: 609-267-0330
Information available also from Rev. Mark A. Medina, Village Church, Prairie Village, Kansas
Purpose: To help clean up, repair and in other ways improve neighborhoods, waterways, playgrounds, parks, and other neglected areas.
Sponsor: First Presbyterian Church
Contact: Donna Kirk, Group Leader
Description: In June 1989, with the help of 65 teenagers from Kansas who were attending a church gathering in Philadelphia, teenagers from churches in the Mount Holly area worked to clean up the Mount Holly Gardens housing development. The effort is part of the church-related nationwide *Operation Clean Sweep.* The young volunteers from Kansas, who paid all of the expenses of their week-long stay, worked with the local teens to clean the streets, the nearby creek, and the buildings - some of which will be painted and repaired, others torn down, with the help of *Habitat for Humanity* and *Homes of Hope.* In addition, they helped the township install playground equipment in the development.
The Kansas youth - members of the *Village Church* in Prairie Village, Kansas - were in the area attending the 201st General Assembly of the *Presbyterian Church of Philadelphia.* "They wanted to make a contribution while attending the Assembly," according to a trip leader. They were housed at the *First Presbyterian Church* in Mount Holly. "Operation Clean Sweep" T-shirts, provided by the *H.W. Fry Realty Corporation,* helped to call attention to their work. As one student put it, "East met midwest, and it was a great cooperative effort!"

OPERATION COVERUP
Safe Streets
1720 South 72nd Street
Tacoma, WA 98408
TEL: 206-272-6824; 206-475-2434
Purpose: To remove and work to eliminate gang graffiti throughout Tacoma.
Sponsor: Tacoma Police Department
Contact: Mark Mann, Police Spokesman
Description: In Tacoma, gangs use graffiti to mark their territories and challenge rival gangs. *Operation Coverup* is a graffiti-removal campaign sponsored by *Safe Streets,* a nonprofit organization, and the *Tacoma Police Department* to remove the graffiti from buildings and homes around the city, and work toward elimination of this practice in the future. The removal process is a Saturday

program operating with 80 volunteers and 500 gallons of donated paint.
Volunteers work in teams which are dispatched for four hours each to some twenty-six locations across the city.
Long-term efforts to eliminate the graffiti problem permanently include media efforts to educate the public and reach the gangs, and an ongoing program to monitor progress.

OTTAWA RIVER "FIGHTING BACK" CAMPAIGN
Ottawa River Improvement Association
Ohio State Scenic Rivers Program
1009 West Bancroft
Toledo, OH 43606
TEL: 419-723-7403 (Assn); 419-929-6533 (State)
Information also available from the cosponsor:
Lake Erie Marine Trades Association, Toledo, Ohio
Purpose: To maintain the beauty of the Ottawa River's natural environment.
Sponsor: Ohio Department of Natural Resources
Contact: Rick Knapp
Description: The first major project to be undertaken by the *Ottawa River Improvement Association* is a river cleanup campaign. The group was formed in 1989 by boaters, Point Place property owners, clubs, and others interested in the use and management of the Ottawa River and its waterfront.
Concerned about the "unnatural predators" (timbers and trash) on the river bottom that often destroy motor propellers and boat keels, the group turned to the community.
A wide variety of businesses, clubs, individuals, and government agencies volunteered to assist with the project. About 250 people responded to the call for volunteers, including three Boy Scout troops, four yacht clubs, the *Neighborhood Improvement Foundation,* and some off-duty Coast Guard officers. The *Ohio Department of Natural Resources* and the *Lake Erie Marine Trades Association* cosponsored the event, and supplied coffee and donuts at registration, and refreshments throughout the day, as well as a free T-shirt for each volunteer. Refuse containers, various other equipment, and additional volunteers were provided by *Browning Ferris Industries, Tidy,* and *Ace's Portable Toilets.* Each person was assigned to a shore crew or boat crew, with the latter asked to bring their own life jackets, gloves, and fishnets. Oil drums, tires, and a newspaper vending machine are just a few of the objects pulled from the river. All of it is not careless litter, however, as storms and the resulting high water also pick things up on shore and carry them upstream or downstream, sometimes depositing them back on the shore when the water level goes down. The debris remaining in the river creates a hazard for boats, and is one of the first priorities. The campaign wound up back at the registration point (Point Place Junior High School) with a "trash bash," or appreciation rally, with free hot dogs, soft drinks, and prizes. The Association plans to make the river cleanup an annual event. Other goals include dredging, monitoring construction, crime prevention, and educating people about legislation and waterfront issues.

SOCIETY BANK/WOLF CREEK ASSOCIATION
PARTNERSHIP
Society Bank
Bellbrook, OH 45305
TEL: 513-848-6111
Purpose: To emphasize the bank's commitment to the community through volunteer effort and community partnership.
Sponsor: Society Bank
Contact: Anna Vasilakos, Chairwoman
Description: Society Bank's Community Affairs Department and the Wolf Creek Association have become partners in community service with a commitment to make Wolf Creek a better place in which to live. Wolf Creek is one of the lowest income areas in the

city, according to a bank official, with an average yearly income of $7,000.

The first project involved paint brushes and lawn mowers as volunteers from the bank and the association joined forces to spruce up the neighborhood. In addition to cutting grass and clearing debris from three vacant lots, the bank selected two homes in need of paint owned by senior citizens who could not afford to paint them.

The Society Bank Community Affairs Officer requested two volunteers from each branch office, and received many more - in one instance, all of the employees of a branch. Some Society Bank managers came from as far away as Waynesville, Bellbrook and Fairborn to participate in the Wolf Creek neighborhood cleanup. Nearby Pilgrim Church served lunch for the volunteers.

The cleanup project is just the beginning of the bank's commitment to Wolf Creek, according to a Society officer. A housing development project is also in the works. The bank spent $27,000 to conduct a feasibility study on housing needs in the community. The housing will be in the low- to moderate-income range. Other volunteer projects will be mounted by the partnership as needs arise.

SPARKLE COMMITTEE
Haddon Township Council
Haddon Avenue & Reeve Avenue
Camden, NJ 08103
TEL: 609-854-1176
Purpose: To maintain the "sparkle" of township property by providing the finishing touches.
Sponsor: Haddon Township
Contact: Dennis St. John, Community Activities Coordinator
Description: The *Sparkle Committee* is a special project in Haddon Township, a community which prides itself with having a number of cleanup operations going simultaneously. Besides the satisfaction of having a clean town, the major volunteer cleanup efforts help the township to qualify for $12,000 from the *1987 Clean Communities Act.* The Act's funds, collected as a "tiny tax" on litter-producing businesses such as fast-food restaurants, pay for the "tiny" *Sparkle Committee.*

This Committee is not a cleanup committee, per se, but rather a "finishing touches" group which works all summer to remove piles of dead leaves, prune bushes and spread mulch around trees on public property. The minute summer volunteer group is composed of one adult and five or six teenagers. Its work on the final touches of the area's landscape and enables larger cleanup groups to concentrate on heavier issues such as recycling, tearing down and replacing a deteriorating roof on the community pool bathhouse, etc. Also, the summer group helps increase the high visibility and tangible results that come from state and local cooperation.

TAMPA CAUSEWAY BEAUTIFICATION PROJECT
Tampa Parks Department
315 East Kennedy Boulevard
Tampa, FL 33602
TEL: 813-272-6310
Purpose: To beautify the barren roadsides left by the state in upgrading and widening a parkway to make it safer.
Sponsor: Florida Department of Transportation
Contact: Diana Kyle, Deputy Director, Parks Dept.
Description: There was no doubt that the Courtney Campbell Parkway had to be made safer by the *Florida Department of Transportation (DOT)*, but the barren roadsides left as a result were "a blight on the city landscape." A group of volunteers decided to turn the sand, rock and asphalt into a well-designed landscaped area.

Cooperation and support was immediate from the *Tampa Parks Department,* which won a grant from the state DOT and the *Highway Beautification Council.* With a total budget of $355,000, the Parks Department bought 825 palm trees and 30,000 shrubs for landscaping 17 locations between the bridge and the Memorial Highway interchange.

Hundreds of volunteers rallied to the cause. Even the landscape design for the project was donated (*Odell Associates, Inc.*), which meant that the money spent on the project went almost entirely for truckloads of plants. The design was a challenge to the volunteer architectural designer because many factors had to be taken into account - including the fact that plants could not interfere with the line of vision of drivers either on the causeway or on frontage roads bordering the bay. Also, the causeway has no irrigation system, so the plants had to be able to survive long periods without water, as well as tolerate salt spray and exhaust fumes. All this, and the volunteers stipulated that they wanted to turn the area into a lush tropical garden. Without the expertise of the volunteer designer, according to a Parks Department official, this would not have been possible.

Once the grant money was in hand and the plants obtained by competitive bidding, hundreds of volunteers stepped forward on Saturday mornings until the job was done - more than enough to fill the schedule set for the project. Volunteers came from the landscape firm, the *Westshore Alliance, Cigna, Law Engineering, Boy Scouts, Tampa Electric, Critikon, Palma Ceia Methodist Church, USAA Insurance* (which signed up 100 volunteers), and others. The Parks Department supplies ice water, shovels and a five-person crew to supervise the volunteers. According to the volunteers, passing motorists supply the motivation by honking their horns in approval or stopping to compliment the workers. City officials cite the project as an example of what volunteerism, determination, and plain old enthusiasm can do when a community's pride is at stake.

A drawback to the finished product is that now the Pinellas side of the causeway, once considered attractive with its grass and occasional tree, looks unadorned and unimpressive. The Tampa group has volunteered to share their design with a group from Pinellas to install a similar beautification project on the Pinellas side.

USS KITTY HAWK/WASHINGTON SQUARE PARTNERSHIP
Washington Square Association
202 South Twelfth
Philadelphia, PA 19107
TEL: 215-545-6092
Purpose: To bring together sailors in port for ship repairs and a civic association in the community to restore the beauty of a central city park.
Sponsor: US/DoD - USS Kitty Hawk
Contact: Anna Marie Marshall, Washington Square Association
Description: The *USS Kitty Hawk* is an aircraft carrier docked at the Navy Yard in Philadelphia to undergo a $717 million overhaul. While there, the Lieutenant Commander was to begin a search for a location for the Kitty Hawk to hold a constitutional celebration in three months hence. When it came to the attention of the officers and crew of the Kitty Hawk that Fairmount Park, where 2,000 Revolutionary War dead are buried in unmarked graves, was in need of volunteers, they decided to clean up the park and hold the celebration there. This began a partnership beyond the sprucing up of the park.

More than two dozen volunteers from the ship spent several Saturdays raking leaves, painting light standards, picking up trash, clipping hedges, using a chemical wash on the statue of George Washington, and helping nearby residents purchase flags representing the original 13 colonies and a large American flag. The sailors then began a ceremony of raising and lowering the American flag every day at the park, and they tended to the eternal flame that burns in front of the tomb of the unknown soldier. When they saw a need for music during the flag ceremonies, they installed a $200 sound system, bought with funds from the ship's welfare and recreation fund, on the roof of a tool shed in the park.

In the fall, the sailors held their anniversary celebration of the signing of the Constitution, but the unique partnership between the Navy and the community didn't end there. At Christmas time they bought and trimmed a Christmas tree, and red bows for the square's antique light poles, and they sang carols.

In the spring of 1989, they planted $10,000 worth of purple petunias and other plants, and when the organizers of the annual *Fair in the Square* in May needed materials for booths, the sailors loaned and delivered 48 tables and 200 chairs. They also sold balloons and served as guides for the house tours.

The work of the sailors - especially the flag ceremony - has made a big difference in the spirit of the community. Citizens are seen stopping and standing at attention during the flag ceremony. In addition to the neighborhood pride that the sailors' work has instilled, the volunteer project has also improved the sailors' morale. With the long-term repair project on the USS Kitty Hawk, it is expected that residents will enjoy the presence of the sailors in the park for some time to come.

YOUTH-IN-ACTION AUCTION
Youth Advisory Commission
170 Santa Maria Avenue
Pacifica, CA 94044
TEL: 415-877-8631
Purpose: To raise sufficient funds for a Summer Beach Cleaning Program; to give youth the opportunity to put on a community auction and to provide jobs for youth.
Sponsor: City of Pacifica
Contact: John W. Deuel
Description: An annual fundraising project executed by Youth Advisory Commission is a televised community auction called The Youth-in-Action Auction. The purposes of the auction are:

- to improve the local beaches through a summer beach cleaning program;
- to hire high school age city youth as part-time beach cleaners to staff the beach crews; and
- to give youth volunteers a variety of community experiences in fundraising and producing a televised auction.

Preparation for the auction begins in early September when the Youth Advisory Commission begins to solicit donations from local merchants and community members. The YAC takes on the jobs of publicity, merchandise inventory, scheduling local dignitaries and personalities as auctioneers, and arranging for youth volunteers to staff the auction.

The auction is held during three consecutive evenings at the City Council Chambers. The Community Cable TV station handles the technical production each night and the YAC coordinates all other activities. On the nights of the auction, each donated item or service is auctioned off by a volunteer auctioneer from one of four tables. Each table has from five to eight items at a time and each item is assigned a number which is written on a chalkboard behind each table for identification purposes. Home viewers who want to bid on an item call into a bank of phones manned by youth volunteers. Each new bid is run up to the table where it is written on the board. Bids are taken until it is decided by the floor director to sell the item. When an entire board is sold off, new items are put up on the table by the inventory manager. The high bid is immediately confirmed on a separate phone, to make sure the item wasn't sold to a phony bid.

To pick up items, the high bidders come in to pick up and pay in an area where items have been marked with the high bidder's name.

PHYSICAL ENVIRONMENT: CONSERVATION

NATIONAL/STATE ORGANIZATIONS

CONSERVATION FOUNDATION
1250 24th Street, NW
Washington, DC 20037
TEL: 202-293-4800
Objectives: To improve the quality of the environment and to promote wise use of the earth's natural resources and the built environment.
Services: Develops and applies techniques for citizens training; produces films designed to reach the general public and foster action; sponsors Economics of the Environment, a program to explore ways to deal with the divisive problems of progress versus environment, and programs on land, energy, pollution control, and other current issues; publishes monthly newsletter, and numerous publications on all aspects of conservation; produces films; convenes conferences and workshops.
Publications: Conservation Foundation Letter; Resolve

CONSERVATION TILLAGE INFORMATION CENTER*
1025 Vermont Avenue, NW
Suite 730
Washington, DC 20005
TEL: 202-347-4735
Objectives: To gather and disseminate information that will encourage a better understanding and a more effective use of conservation tillage on American farms.
Services: Provides telephone referral service, research information and status surveys to resource individuals; develops slide sets/films on conservation tillage; publishes a monthly newsletter, *Conservation Tillage News,* and other informational materials.
Publications: Conservation Tillage News

NATIONAL ASSOCIATION OF CONSERVATION DISTRICTS
509 Capital Court, NE
Washington, DC 20002
TEL: 202-547-6223
Objectives: To direct and coordinate conservation through districts organized by citizens; the conservation and development of soil, water and related natural resources.
Services: Assists some 3,000 local (usually county) conservation districts and their volunteer directors (approximately 18,000) in achieving soil and water conservation and resource development goals with a maximum of voluntary action and local involvement; encourages districts to form youth boards to aid projects; publishes a monthly newsletter, *The Tuesday Letter,* directories, proceedings, annual reports, guides, etc.
Contact: Ellen Dougherty
Publications: Tuesday Letter; NACD Conference Proceedings; NACD Directory
Founded: 1947

NATURE CONSERVANCY
1815 North Lynn Street
Arlington, VA 22209
TEL: 703-841-4832
Objectives: To preserve ecologically significant areas (forests, swamps, marshes, prairies, mountains, beaches, etc.), and the diversity of life they support.
Services: Identifies ecologically significant lands; protects lands by acquiring them through purchase with funds raised locally and nationally, through donation by concerned individuals and

organizations, and through cooperative programs with public and other private conservation groups; works with local groups to act quickly and efficiently to save a threatened natural area; formulates and implements a management plan after a preserve is established to insure the endurance of the land's natural quality; publishes bimonthly magazine.
Publications: Nature Conservancy Magazine

STUDENT CONSERVATION ASSOCIATION
PO Box 550
Charlestown, NH 03603
TEL: 603-826-4301 (NH); 703-524-2441 (DC)
Objectives: To offer expense-paid educational work experiences and enhance career opportunities for young people; to assist in the accomplishment of important land and resource management activities; and to foster public participation in the management of natural resources.
Services: Operates the *Resource Assistant Program* through which college students and other adult volunteers serve as professional assistants in national parks, wildlife refuges, and other areas nationwide for 12-16 weeks (year-round); operates the *High School Program* in which students work on trail construction and similar projects for 3-5 weeks in national parks, wilderness areas, and elsewhere (summer only); operates the *Wilderness Workskills Program* providing training in traditional trail construction and wilderness management skills for field personnel; operates the New Hampshire Conservation Corps; publishes a monthly conservation employment newsletter and other materials.
Publications: Job Scan; SCA Annual Report; High School Program Position Listing; Resource Assistant Program Listing
Founded: 1957

STUDENT CONSERVATION ASSOCIATION
SEE RECREATION & SPORTS: PARKS/FORESTS

INDIVIDUAL PROGRAM PROFILES

THE EARTH TEAM
US/DoA - Soil Conservation Service
Independence Avenue
(Between 12th & 14th, SW)
Washington, DC 20250
TEL: 202-382-0430; 202-590-2855
TOLL FREE: 800-THE-SOUL
Purpose: To respond to citizens calling a posted 800 number asking for volunteers to work in soil conservation programs across the country.
Sponsor: US/DoA - Department of Agriculture
Contact: Doug Gahn
Description: The *Earth Team* is a group of concerned citizens and civic-minded volunteers who are interested in learning more about our nation's soil and water resources and how to help conserve them. This nationwide volunteer service group is sponsored by the U.S. Department of Agriculture's *Soil Conservation Service* through more than 3,000 locations across the country.
Volunteers must be 16 years old or older to join the *Earth Team.* All volunteers receive a permanent work record of their service as well as liability protection. Thousands of Americans who have already become *Earth Team* volunteers work to improve the condition of the soil and water resources where they live. They help reduce soil erosion, conserve water, develop conservation plans for farmers and ranchers across the country and build community pride. Some specific ways they help are:
- **On the Land** - with soil conservationists who are working directly with farmers, ranchers, and other land users, studying soils and making maps and conservation plans.
- **In Schools** - elementary schools, high schools, vocational schools, universities and colleges - explaining the importance

of understanding the interrelationships of plants, animals, soil, water and mankind, helping teachers train students for land judging contests, assisting schools in planning outdoor classrooms where students learn about natural resource conservation, or helping students transform an eroded schoolyard into a smooth and more beautiful place to play.
- **With organizations** - youth groups, churches, and garden clubs, and professional and civic groups, presenting information about the interdependence of living things, and putting what they've learned to practical use in outdoor activities, selecting appropriate trees and planting a windbreak, cleaning a trash-filled creek, reclaiming abandoned, eroded land and turning it into a nature center, a playground or a city park, providing support for a local, statewide, or national campaign on a natural resource issue.
- **In offices** - where your conservation district may want to use your talents for clerical assistance, organizing information, preparing newsletters, or talking with other prospective volunteers.

The Department of Agriculture works cooperatively with the *Soil and Water Conservation Society* in a public/private partnership in the *Earth Team* project. The *Society* answers the hotline number and refers volunteers to one of the 3,000 local agencies of the Department. In addition, both the Department and the Society distribute brochures, posters, and other materials to bring the program to the attention of the public.

FOREST SERVICE VOLUNTEER PROGRAM
US/DoA - Forest Service
1375 K Street, NW, #613
PO Box 96090
Washington, DC 20013-5090
TEL: 202-535-0927
Purpose: To enable citizens to assist in the conservation work of the Forest Service.
Sponsor: US/DoA - Department of Agriculture
Description: In 1972, Congress passed special legislation to establish a volunteer program within the Forest Service. As a result, hundreds of interested citizens concerned about the country's natural resources have joined in the Service's conservation work. Volunteers include retirees, professionals, housewives, students, teenagers and youngsters (a volunteer under 18 years of age must have written consent from parent or guardian).
Students have an option to volunteer for work in many different parts of the country to earn college credits, based on agreements between their colleges and the Forest Service. Retired professionals have a wealth of knowledge to share. Youngsters have boundless energy and a thirst for knowledge about the great outdoors. Volunteers are limited only by their willingness to serve. However, such services must also benefit a Forest Service activity. A volunteer may work full time or only a few hours or days each week. A volunteer may also contribute a *one-time* service.
Opportunities are available in *Cooperative Forestry, National Forest Administration,* and *National Forest Research.* Typical volunteer jobs include:
- conducting interpretive natural history walks and auto tours for the *Visitor Information Center.*
- acting in a campfire historical presentation.
- writing or editing interpretive stories in the library.
- assisting in forest fire protection activities.
- building and maintaining trails, constructing campgrounds, and improving wildlife habitats.
- working in a youth program to teach members about our environment.

Although opportunities exist in over 20 states and Puerto Rico, volunteers have the option of working close to home. Volunteers are protected under the *Volunteers in the National Forests Act of 1972* in cases of injury or property damage. However, volunteers

are not classified as Federal employees. Upon completion of service, volunteers are provided with a formal record of their contributions, and Certificates of Appreciation from the Forest Service, U.S. Department of Agriculture.
Publications: Forest Service Volunteer
Founded: 1972

PHYSICAL ENVIRONMENT: DEMOGRAPHICS

NATIONAL/STATE ORGANIZATIONS

ENVIRONMENTAL ACTION
SEE PHYSICAL ENVIRONMENT

PLANNED PARENTHOOD FEDERATION OF AMERICA
SEE TEENAGE PREGNANCY/PARENTING

POPULATION COUNCIL
One Dag Hammarskjold Plaza
New York, NY 10017
TEL: 212-644-1300
Objectives: To further understanding of the relationship between fertility, population growth, and socio-economic development.
Services: Maintains a Program Support and Services division, which offers technical assistance and population information; maintains extensive library; publishes two journals, *Studies in Family Planning* and *Population and Development Review*, books, pamphlets, brochures, and other materials.
Publications: Studies in Family Planning; Population and Development Review

POPULATION CRISIS COMMITTEE
1120 Nineteenth Street, NW
Suite 550
Washington, DC 20036
TEL: 202-659-1833 ; Telex 440450 PCCDF
FAX: 202-202-293-1795
Objectives: To promote public understanding of, and action regarding, global population problems.
Services: Stimulates government and private organizations to adopt or increase population programs; educates the public through media campaigns and publications; works with concerned citizens, leaders in business, religion, government, the professions and science through meetings, discussions, and distribution of policy statements; publishes population briefing sheets and other materials.
Publications: PCC Wall Chart; PCC Policy Information Sheets; PCC Information Kit

POPULATION-ENVIRONMENT BALANCE
1325 G Street, NW
Suite 1003
Washington, DC 20005
TEL: 202-879-3000
Objectives: To maintain a grassroots member organization dedicated to public education of the adverse effects of continued population growth on the environment.
Services: Advocates measures which would encourage population stabilization in the United States; promotes a responsible immigration policy for the U.S., and increased funding for contraceptive research and availability; publishes a quarterly newsletter, a light-hearted quarterly information sheet, and regular

fact sheets.
Publications: Have You Heard?; Balance Report; Balance Data

POPULATION INSTITUTE
110 Maryland Avenue, NE
Suite 207
Washington, DC 20002
TEL: 202-544-3300
Objectives: To create concern among the public for excessive population growth.
Services: Acts as a catalyst with media, youth, educators, groups and organizations in community efforts in matters of population growth; publishes pamphlets and periodical reports.
Publications: Popline

POPULATION REFERENCE BUREAU
777 Fourteenth Street, NW
Suite 800
Washington, DC 20005
TEL: 202-639-8040
Objectives: To gather, interpret and disseminate information on the facts and implications of population change.
Services: Provides reference library services by mail, telephone and personal visit; organizes conferences, seminars, briefings and specialized training; gives awards for outstanding achievements in the field of of demography; has comprehensive publications program.
Publications: Population Today; Population Bulletin; US Population Data Sheet; Population Trends; Population Handbook

PREPARING FOR AN AGING SOCIETY
SEE RECIPIENTS: OLDER PERSON

ZERO POPULATION GROWTH
1601 Connecticut Avenue, NW
Suite 400
Washington, DC 20009
TEL: 202-265-7546
Objectives: To mobilize broad public support for stabilization of the population of the U.S. and worldwide.
Services: Informs the general public of the disadvantages of continued population growth; provides a voice before legislators to foster greater awareness by decision-makers, and legislation favorable to stabilized population goals; publishes National Reporter; convenes annual meeting; trains teachers and publishes curricula materials for population education in the schools.
Publications: Media Targets; ZPG Activist; ZPG Reporter; Teacher's PET Term Paper

INDIVIDUAL PROGRAM PROFILES

TOWNWIDE CENSUS
Lincoln School System
Lincoln, RI 02865
TEL: 401-726-2150
Purpose: To involve volunteers in a townside census to help the school system project its needs.
Contact: Kenneth Grew, School Superintendent
Description: Eighteen volunteers responded to a call for 20 volunteers to assist the Lincoln School System in the townwide census needed to help project education needs and qualify for adequate funding. Since 20 or more volunteers are needed to assure the most accurate census possible, and it must be done before school lets out each year, the school board faced a decision of hiring at least two paid persons (at a cost of up to $29,000) or expand the amount of time to wait for more volunteers. The decision was to tap a $25,000 fund that was never spent for a

special report on the school's computer system. Since the leftover computer funds must be spent before the school year ends to keep the money, the shortage of volunteers was not the problem it might have been. All census volunteer and paid census-takers undergo a training session with the contractor hired (1989, Alpha Research) to administer the door-to-door census. Since the census must be accurate, it must be completed before school closes and families leave town for summer vacations.

Although the Superintendent felt the school committee expected more volunteers just as he did, he felt that the main concern is to have a valid instrument, and the school committee agreed. "The lesson learned that may be of help to other school systems," he said, "is that a campaign for volunteers must have enough lead time to accomplish goals set." The advent of more women in the job market than ever before, rather than a lack of interest, is considered a primary factor in lower volunteer response.

PHYSICAL ENVIRONMENT: EARTH DAY

NATIONAL/STATE ORGANIZATIONS

ECONET
Stanford University
PO Box AA
Stanford University, CA 94305
TEL: 415-321-1990 (CA); 202-347-1990 (DC)
Objectives: To present coordinated themes for *Earth Day 1990* and beyond.
Services: Econet is a system developed by Stanford University to reach out to all parts of the world with ideas for participation in *Earth Day 1990 and Beyond: Launching a Decade of the Environment* at the local, regional, national, and international levels.

Some of the coordinated themes include planting a billion trees; participating in urban parades and public gatherings; coordinating with school and college teach-ins; educating business and government leaders; participating in clean-up and restoration projects; and "wearing something green." All but the latter are expected to have lasting effect and consciousness-raising value into the next century.

To facilitate involvement across the country, the University opened an east coast office in Washington, DC, called *Earth Day 1990,* a part of *Econet,* which will continue beyond 1990 to help monitor progress. The DC office was launched with an all-day rally on the Mall on April 22 and another the next day at the PEPCO plant in the northeast quadrant of the city.

Numerous environmental organizations have joined with the University in this effort, including the Natural Resource Defense Council, National Audubon Society, United Auto Workers, Earth Island Institute, Environmental Action, Friends of the Earth, Sierra Club, Wilderness Society, National Wildlife Federation, Rainforest Action Network, Renew America, Environmental Defense Fund, Izaak Walton League, Rocky Mountain Institute, Better World Society, Trust for Public Land, Earth First, World Resources Institute, and Hewlett Packard.
Sponsor: United Auto Workers
Contact: Denis Hayes (CA); James Day (DC)

NATIONAL CELEBRATION OF THE OUTDOORS
Conservation Foundation
1250 24th Street, NE
Suite 500
Washington, DC 20037
TEL: 202-293-4800

Objectives: To create an awareness of environmental concerns among all age groups.
Services: Sponsors the *National Celebration of the Outdoors,* subtitled *Earth Week;* develops a model program of activities to ensure that all age levels have an opportunity to participate not only during *Earth Day 1990,* but beyond; patterns model program after programs mounted 20 years ago as a reaffirmation of the first *Earth Day* on April 22, 1970.

Involves schools and youth groups as well as adult volunteers in the planning process [youth organizations participating in the planning of the week's programs included *Boy Scouts of America* and *Girl Scouts of the USA*]; involves other organizations including the *US Conference of Mayors, National Geographic Society, Garden Club of America, American Hiking Society,* and *American Farmland Trust;* provides materials describing some of the projects [as supplies last; also request from the organizations cited above].
Sponsor: Boy Scouts of America
Contact: Earth Day Coordinator

INDIVIDUAL PROGRAM PROFILES

ADOPT-A-STREAM
SEE PHYSICAL ENVIRONMENT: WATER POLLUTION

CHESAPEAKE CAMPAIGN
Johns Hopkins University
3400 North Charles Street
Baltimore, MD 21218
TEL: 301-367-7700; 301-338-6000
FAX: 301-338-8099
Purpose: To launch the 1990s as the "international decade of the environment."
Contact: Earth Day Coordinator
Description: The *Chesapeake Campaign* operates out of the Office of the Chaplain at *Johns Hopkins University.* The *Campaign* is a coalition of individuals and groups working for the environmental movement, which implemented numerous events and activities during what has been termed *Earth Week* (April 14-22, 1990) by those groups with multiple days of activities. The programs were planned to help celebrate the 20th anniversary of the first *Earth Day* on April 22, 1970.

In addition to a series of local events throughout the week, the more than 100 environmental groups involved developed publications, and pledged ongoing participation into the next century. Thousands of local volunteers helped launch the 1990s as the *International Decade of the Environment,* with activities ranging from an exposition called *Local Bridges to Global Vision* to a concluding special day event on April 11 - *Earthwalk.* The University provides information on activities during *Earth Week* as materials are made available to share.

COOL IT!
National Wildlife Federation
1400 Sixteenth Street, NW
Washington, DC 20036-2266
TEL: 202-797-6858
Purpose: To bring the reaffirmation of the first *Earth Day* of 1970 to campuses throughout the country.
Contact: Campus Coordinator
Description: Students on campuses across the country began a process in April 1990 that they have termed *COOL IT!* and subtitled *Earth Century: Earth Day - Every Day.* The student-supported campaign is sponsored by the *National Wildlife Federation* and is concerned with recycling, solid waste disposal, public transportation, energy efficiency, and bicycle paths and walkways. Campus leaders expect the programs launched in April

1990 to develop and grow to provide a meaningful agenda for college campuses now and in the future.

EARTH DAY 1990
Audubon Naturalist Society
8940 Jonesville Road
Chevy Chase, MD 20815
TEL: 301-652-5964 (days); 301-933-5623 (eve/wknds)
Purpose: To make the 20th anniversary of *Earth Day* represent only the beginning of plans for *Earth Week, Earth Year,* and *Earth Century.*
Contact: Karyn Molines (days); Margy Mayo (evenings/weekends)
Description: The first *Earth Day,* April 22, 1970, saw more than 20 million people join in organized groups throughout the U.S. to demonstrate their concern for the protection and conservation of the natural resources of "planet earth." One response to its 20th anniversary was the forming of a committee in 1989 by the Audubon Naturalist Society to make *Earth Day 1990* reach far beyond April 22 into the next century by raising the awareness of what each individual can do to practice conservation and protect the environment.
Specific activities included "Plant a tree" or "Clean a stream," with an emphasis on organizing projects with area schools and networking efforts with other environmental groups planning activities during the month of April.
Other organizations used *Earth Day* (April 22, 1990) as a "kick-off" for longer-term programs including *Earth Week, Earth Year,* and even *Earth Century.*
The enthusiasm and commitment during *Earth Day* 20 years ago resulted in enhanced awareness of the environment on the part of citizens, schools, conservation societies, and on a national level in the establishment of the federal *Environment Protection Agency,* the *Clean Air Act* and the *Clean Water Act.* Also, the tremendous success of the call for volunteers for *Earth Day 1990* has been attributed to that first effort in 1970, and its lasting effect. The *Society* provides information on *Earth Day* projects as available.

EARTH DAY 1990/EPA
US/EPA - Earth Day
401 M Street, SW
Washington, DC 20460
TEL: 202-475-7751
Other contacts for *Earth Day* information:
Boston, MA 617-565-3420 (Brooke Chamberlain-Cook)
New York, NY 212-264-2515 (Lisa Peterson)
Philadelphia, PA 215-597-9370 (Janet Viniski)
Atlanta, GA 404-347-3004 (Jan McConathy)
Chicago, IL 312-353-2072 (Jon Grand)
Dallas, TX 214-655-2200 (Phil Charles)
Kansas City, KS 913-236-2803 (Rowena Michaels)
Denver, CO 303-294-7599 (Eric Johnson)
San Francisco, CA 415-974-8083 (Deanna Wieman)
Seattle, WA 206-442-1203 (Jean Baker)
Purpose: To commemorate the twentieth anniversary of the original *Earth Day* with renewed commitment through individual and group effort.
Sponsor: US/EPA - Environmental Protection Agency
Contact: Ann Boren, Director
Description: With the theme, "Think Globally, Act Locally," the *Environmental Protection Agency (EPA)* launched a program to celebrate the 20th anniversary of *Earth Day* (April 22, 1970). In the late 1960s, a series of unacceptable environmental conditions - industrial pollution, raw sewage, automobile emissions, etc. - led to the first *Earth Day.* Soon thereafter the *U.S. Environmental Protection Agency* was formed to address these and other growing problems. By the late 1970s, progress was noted in water quality, automobile emissions, and waste disposal. By *Earth Day's* tenth anniversary (1980), a second wave of environmental challenges surfaced - largely toxic chemicals in food, water, soil and air.

The twentieth anniversary (1990) brought yet a new wave of environmental threats - acid rain, global warming, habitat destruction, and stratospheric ozone depletion. With the earth's climate at stake, and with it the very survival of life as we know it, America responded again.
Just as they did in 1970, towns and cities all over America with their millions of citizens demonstrated their concerns on *Earth Day 1990* (April 22, 1990). *Earth Day's* twentieth anniversary offered a special opportunity for individuals to again make a personal commitment to the protection of the environment. Simple acts such as planting a tree and assuring that it survived or making changes to conserve energy or recycle waste products were just as prevalent as the larger issues of monitoring major waterways and tackling acid rain. In summary:
- **Earth Day was Powerful** - the highest offices of the land gave time and attention to environmental issues.
- **Earth Day was Enduring** - evidence was clear that public commitment has been strengthened down through through the years.
- **Earth Day was Active** - groups, organizations and agencies planned programs, and individuals made record inquiries in efforts to get involved.
Where no program existed, EPA provided information, ideas, program directories and other tools to help an individual or group start a program. As quoted in an early EPA brochure, "Earth Day belongs to everyone; you don't need anyone's permission to take part." As information is gathered, EPA will publish information on innovative, effective *Earth Day* programs for distribution.
Publications: Directory of National Citizen Environmental Monitoring Programs

PHYSICAL ENVIRONMENT: ECOLOGY

NATIONAL/STATE ORGANIZATIONS

NEW LIFE FARM
Bioregional Project
HCR 3, Box 3
Brixey, MO 65618
TEL: 417-679-4773
Objectives: To promote cooperation and regard for all parts of the ecosystem.
Services: Promotes *bioregionalism,* which is based on utilization of ecology to make people more aware of their surrounding natural systems, and to create and maintain a safer environment by adapting to these systems; provides research, education, and technical assistance in areas of community economic development, environmentally responsible practices, water quality, renewable resource development, safe energy, appropriate technology, forest husbandry, sustainable agriculture methods, and family, community and bioregional self-reliance, among others; works toward establishment of societies based on ecological laws and principles; promotes respect for all living and non-living parts of the ecosystem; publishes and shares materials on bioregionalism.
Founded: 1982

PLANET DRUM FOUNDATION
PO Box 31251
San Francisco, CA 94131
TEL: 415-285-6556
Objectives: To make people more appreciative of and involved in the natural systems around them.
Services: Conducts community education programs on bioregionalism, which refers to people and societies being aware of where they live and adapting to the natural systems that exist in

those places; studies the relationship between human culture and natural processes, and publishes and makes available its findings; promotes the concept of bioregionalism through workshops, conferences and lectures as well as a through a national and international network of individuals and groups working in areas involving the planetary biosphere; publishes a newsletter, directories, periodicals, and other materials related to the ecosystem and its potential in developing a safer and healthier environment.

Publications: Raise the States; Planet/Drum Bundles; Reinhabiting a Separate Country; Eco-Decentralist Design; Devolutionary Notes; Backbone: The Rockies

Founded: 1974

PHYSICAL ENVIRONMENT: EDUCATION

INDIVIDUAL PROGRAM PROFILES

CHATTANOOGA NATURE CENTER
Route 4
Garden Road
Chattanooga, TN 37409
TEL: 615-821-1160

Purpose: To promote environmental awareness through education especially for youth.

Sponsor: Privately funded through donations (foundations, corporations and memberships) and program fees.

Contact: Sandra L. Kurtz

Description: The Chattanooga Nature Center was first visualized by the Junior League of Chattanooga after a feasibility study concerned with community needs. After a capital funds drive was launched, the passive solar facility was designed and opened its doors in 1979. Today the Nature Center serves over 12,000 students each year, primarily in school groups, as they explore the outdoors in investigative groups along trails. The primary emphasis is on discovering processes in nature and the interdependencies of people and nature through experiential learning. The Nature Center also features a wildlife diorama, natural history and science exhibits, energy displays and a wildlife rehabilitation laboratory.

About 75 volunteers assist a full-time staff of six to conduct trail experiences, guide the policy making, assist in membership tasks, work in the office, gift shop or resource/exhibit areas. The Friends of the Nature Center also assist in fund raising efforts, especially Earthfest, the arts and crafts fair.

As a very small community organization, the staff works closely with volunteers in comfortable, amiable settings. Field class leaders are put through a rigorous 5-week training course (15 hours) but other volunteers learn "on the job" working along with staff members or experienced volunteers. Some volunteers complete projects while in their own homes.

Founded: 1979

FOREST SERVICE VOLUNTEER PROGRAM
SEE PHYSICAL ENVIRONMENT: CONSERVATION

POLLUTION CONTROL CENTER
Oak Park and River Forest High School
201 North Scoville Avenue
Oak Park, IL 60302
TEL: 312-383-0700/Ext. 2174

Purpose: To meet a need for continuing environmental education for youth.

Sponsor: Oak Park and River Forest High School

Contact: Ed Radatz

Description: In 1970, it became apparent to both students and faculty at Oak Park and River Forest High school that environmental education was needed. Two students worked with administrators at the school to plan a Conservation Workshop for the first *Earth Day* that year. When experts came forward to educate 4,000 students and citizens, it became further apparent that the environmental education program should be a continuing process.

Initially, the Board of Education instituted environmental science and field biology courses, Earth science, physical science, biology, and other courses, which continue to stress environmental topics. But students and faculty went a step further to create the Pollution Control Center (PCC), a facility staffed by student volunteers. The students answer requests for information on environmental subjects, provide speakers for schools or clubs, and offer other services provided by the Center.

Teams from PCC visit elementary schools that lack environmental programs and speak to students from kindergarten to eighth grade. The aim is to increase the environmental awareness of the younger students with basic ecological concepts that can be followed both at school and at home. Elementary teachers are given related materials for later use, and can request additional information from PCC at any time.

PCC volunteers also give anti-smoking workshops, and often are asked to speak at local organizations.

A special scholarship fund has been developed through donations from community groups, and from school fund-raisers. Students use these funds to attend environmental workshops, and must provide a report to the Biology Club at the school as well as the community groups from which the scholarship funds were received.

A permanent recycling program has been developed by PCC in cooperation with the community's Environmental Advisory Committee.

To avoid duplication of effort, other youth groups at the school - *Student Council* and *Tau Gamma* - work with PCC to promote environmental awareness and youth involvement in the community for *Earth Day 1990.*

Founded: 1970

SCHOOL ECOLOGY PROJECT
Audubon Naturalist Society
Woodend
8940 Jones Mill Road
Chevy Chase, MD 20815
TEL: 301-652-5924 (Education); 301-652-9188 (HQ)

Purpose: To provide elementary-age children with a course on ecology taught both on-site and in the community.

Sponsor: American Plant Food Company

Contact: Jane D. Winer

Description: The *Audubon Naturalist Society* draws on its professional members for a volunteer project that introduces children to ecology and their relationship to it. Volunteers include biologists, entomologists, National Zoo staff, and others who simply have an interest in children, education, and nature.

The course works under the small group concept, breaking up classrooms of 30 or more students into up to five groups. Children are given name tags cut in the shape of animals and a chance to know group members before volunteers begin. Areas covered include the school's relation to the sun, using a map, points of the compass, tree identification, the function of terrariums, insect life, photosynthesis and flowers, bird surveys, and wild animals.

The course culminates with visits to areas of the Smithsonian Institution that coincide with class subjects. By making these visits last, students are able to understand and enjoy much more than they would have seven weeks before when the course began. At the museum, children and volunteers join hands, make a great circle, and talk about what has been learned. The children then board the waiting bus, and the volunteers return to their offices. Among Corporate Associates of the Society are: American Plant Food Company, Wild Bird Centers of America, Hechinger Foundation, Crisis Psychiatric Services, Marriott Corporation, Maryland Natural Gas, Northern Counties Lumber, PEPCO, Salt River Project, Clyde Restaurants, Snow Goose Gallery, and 22 other area firms.

PHYSICAL ENVIRONMENT: ENERGY

NATIONAL/STATE ORGANIZATIONS

CITIZEN/LABOR ENERGY COALITION
225 West Ohio
Suite 250
Chicago, IL 60610
TEL: 312-645-6013
Objectives: To educate the public and public officials on issues related to the supply and demand of energy.
Services: Monitors the activities of government and industry in the energy area; maintains contact with members of Congress on energy legislation; urges the public to become active in working for a more effective public energy policy; engages in research; prepares and distributes educational materials; maintains resource library; publishes fact books; sponsors a major project designed to inform and teach the public - Energy Action Education Project of C/LEC (see separate entry).
Publications: Citizen Power
Founded: 1978

CONSUMER ENERGY COUNCIL OF AMERICA
RESEARCH FOUNDATION
2000 L Street, NW
Suite 802
Washington, DC 20036
TEL: 202-659-0404
Objectives: To advocate the consumers' interest in national energy policy.
Services: Presents the consumers' interest before Congress, the Administration, the courts and other public forums; informs consumers on energy policy issues; provides analyses of energy policy issues for distribution to members of Congresss and the public; conducts research on the impacts of energy pricing and supply policies on consumers; publishes fact sheets, legislative analyses and research reports which are available to the general public.
Publications: Economics of Heating & Cooling
Founded: 1973

COUNCIL ON ENVIRONMENTAL ALTERNATIVES*
355 Lexington Avenue
Sixteenth Floor
New York, NY 10017
TEL: 212-566-0990
Objectives: To encourage people to conserve, rather than consume, their environment.
Services: Concentrates on the areas of energy; provides specific recommendations; operates national energy program designed to develop conservation practices and stimulate consumer interest in renewable energy sources, such as solar energy and wind energy; publishes newsletter, guides, a fact book on energy, and other materials.

CRITICAL MASS ENERGY PROJECT
Public Citizen
215 Pennsylvania Avenue, SE
Washington, DC 20003
TEL: 202-546-4996
Objectives: To oppose nuclear power and to promote safer energy alternatives - particularly energy efficiency and renewable energy technologies.
Services: Promotes sound energy options; documents and publicizes the potential of energy conservation, renewable energy systems, and some natural gas technologies to replace coal and oil at lower environmental and economic costs than nuclear power; works with local groups on a targeted campaign which focuses on nuclear plants with the worst safety records; maintains an outreach program for local safe energy groups across the country; plans to expand media outreach program and grassroots networking efforts, and increase its program of published studies, litigation, and a higher profile in Congress; publishes a bimonthly newsletter and other materials.
Contact: Ken Bossong, Director
Publications: Nuclear Power Safety Report; Critical Mass Advocates; Rethinking Tomorrow; Home Energy Ratings; The Six Myths of Electricity; Shutdown Strategies: Citizens; Radon: What You Don't Know
Founded: 1974

ENERGY ACTION EDUCATION PROJECT
Citizen/Labor Energy Coalition
2000 P Street, NW
Suite 310
Washington , DC 20036
TEL: 202-775-0370
Objectives: To educate the public and public officials on issues related to the supply and demand of energy.
Services: Aims to increase the number of people who are active in seeking a more effective public policy on energy; monitors government and industry in matters pertaining to energy policy; maintains a running dialogue with members of Congress; makes available its resource library; develops, publishes and distributes educational materials.
Publications: Natural Gas Factbook; Divestiture Factbook
Founded: 1975

ENVIRONMENT INFORMATION CENTER
SEE PHYSICAL ENVIRONMENT

ENVIRONMENTAL POLICY INSTITUTE
SEE PHYSICAL ENVIRONMENT

NATIONAL CENTER FOR APPROPRIATE TECHNOLOGY
PO Box 3838
Butte, MT 59702
TEL: 406-494-4572
Objectives: To promote the application of conservation and renewable energy technologies that can provide immediate help to individuals, organizations, and communities struggling with escalating energy costs.
Services: Determines, through research and development, technologies that are both workable and accessible at relatively low cost; demonstrates through field testing technologies in actual practical settings; provides useful information through publications, outreach and training programs to all individuals and groups on request; has an extensive library of books and periodicals; publishes booklets for consumers, research reports and monographs.
Founded: 1976

NATIONAL ENERGY FOUNDATION
5160 Wiley Post Way
Suite 200
Salt Lake City, UT 84116
TEL: 801-539-1406
Objectives: To stimulate interest and increase knowledge about the current energy situation for educators.
Services: Provides educational materials on usage, conservation and sources of energy; conducts motivating teacher training programs; publishes catalog providing overview of services, and energy education and other materials produced by the foundation.
Publications: NEF Catalog
Founded: 1976

NATIONAL ENERGY RESOURCES ORGANIZATION
11529 Montgomery Road
Beltsville, MD 20705
TEL: 301-937-2799
Objectives: To provide a forum for discussion of current energy concerns.
Services: Conducts public education program on energy; recognizes individuals and organizations that have contributed to energy conservation and development; encourages interaction between government, industry, education and the general public to seek solutions to energy problems; publishes monthly newsletter.
Founded: 1975

NATIONAL SOLAR HEATING AND COOLING INFORMATION CENTER
PO Box 1607
Rockville, MD 20850
TOLL FREE: 800-523-2929
Objectives: To assist groups and individuals interested in solar energy as a cooling and heating source.
Services: Collects, categorizes, and computerizes data on solar products; maintains a file of over 2,000 products, from absorbers to storage tanks; obtains data from manufacturers' product literature; maintains complementary files of solar professionals, sources of information, and state legislation; serves professionals and consumers alike; retrieves information according to dealer or product, if known, as well as general subject areas; provides most information without charge.

PUBLIC INTEREST RESEARCH GROUP
SEE CONSUMER SERVICES/LEGAL RIGHTS

RENEW AMERICA
1001 Connecticut Avenue, NW
Suite 638
Washington, DC 20036
TEL: 202-466-6880
Objectives: To promote the use of renewable solar energy and conservation.
Services: Assists with grassroots coalition formation; represents consumer interests in obtaining low-cost energy; operates a public education program; works to ensure that renewable energy technologies such as solar, wind, water, biomass and others have an equal chance to compete with traditional forms of energy; monitors legislators, analyzes congressional voting records and testifies before Congress; maintains extensive library on renewable energy resources; operates an awards program.
Publications: State of States; Renew America Catalog
Founded: 1986

TRAINING PROGRAMS

GOVERNOR'S CONFERENCE ON VOLUNTEERS IN ENERGY*
Governor's Council on Voluntary Action/CT*
80 Washington Street
Hartford, CT 06106
TEL: 203-566-8320
Credit: Inquire
Sponsor: US/ACTION
Contact: Karen S. Lee
Description: The statewide forum on energy is convened by the Governor's Council on Voluntary Action to enable participants to learn about volunteer projects, exchange ideas and volunteers and local and state officials, expand volunteer involvement, and plan for the future.
Preceding the workshops are "Swap Shops" - small groups of participants exchanging ideas, techniques and suggestions for new projects for volunteers. Of the three workshops that follow, participants are asked to select two - one for the morning and one for the afternoon session. Workshop topics are:
- *Workshop A* - **Energy and Crisis Intervention** - Information on both private fuel banks and volunteer involvement in government assistance programs, especially outreach to the elderly and the handicapped.
- *Workshop B* - **Energy Conservation and Your Community** - Successful energy conservation projects done by local groups; programs to encourage individuals to change their energy habits.
- *Workshop C* - **Expanding Your Community's Energy Awareness** - Model awareness campaigns; strategies for the 1980s.

Each workshop includes a section on Energy Issues in the Hispanic Community. Between morning and afternoon sessions, a panel presentation is offered by staff from the Massachusetts Office of Citizen Participation on Fitchburg Action to Conserve Energy. The conference wrap-up - Where Do We Go From Here? - is presented by the Connecticut Governor's Council on Voluntary Action.
Although designed to bring together volunteer leaders and local/state officials, the conference is open to all interested citizens.
During the course of the proceedings, community volunteers active in energy conservation throughout the state are recognized.

INDIVIDUAL PROGRAM PROFILES

PERFORMANCE CONTRACTING
United Way of Wyoming Valley
9 East Market Street
Wilkes-Barre, PA 18711-0351
TEL: 717-829-6711
Purpose: To reduce expenses involved in energy consumption.
Sponsor: Exxon
Contact: Charles J. Reynolds, Jr., President
Description: Six volunteer organizations in Wilkes-Barre have pooled their energy-saving potential by *performance contracting*. This is a method that allows agencies to voluntarily come together in order to take advantage of a plan to finance conservation measures with no capital investment.
The agencies jointly enter into a contract with the *National Energy Management Institute (NEMI)* and receive $250,000 worth of energy-saving improvements on their buildings. In return, the agencies use the money they save on energy bills to reimburse NEMI for the energy-conserving improvements ranging from roof insulation to high efficiency boilers and energy-management systems.

Exxon funded the project, which was developed by *United Way of America* and the *Alliance to Save Energy.* According to the Alliance chairman, who is also a U.S. Congressman, "United Way-supported agencies nationwide could save $250 million annually on energy bills through conservation."

PHYSICAL ENVIRONMENT: LAND USE

NATIONAL/STATE ORGANIZATIONS

HOSTED PROGRAMS AND YOUTH CONSERVATION CORPS
US/DoA - Forest Service
1375 K Street, NW, #613
PO Box 96090
Washington, DC 20013-6090
TEL: 202-535-0927
Objectives: To provide volunteer and intern assistance in the management, protection, and use of the Nation's forests and rangelands.
Services: In addition to an extensive volunteer program to assist with its mandate to manage and protect the nation's forests and rangelands, the Forest Service provides a means to employ youth and retirees under the various employment and training Acts. This provides a resource for workers with youth and the elderly who might otherwise be unemployed. These programs include:
- **Job Corps Civilian Conservation Centers** - 18 Centers which provide education and training to 8,000 disadvantaged youths ages 18-22, in cooperation with the U.S. Department of Labor;
- **Senior Community Service Employment Program** - a three-fold program with purposes of (1) community services, (2) part-time employment and supplemental income, and (3) training and transition to the labor market.
- **Cooperative Human Resource Programs** - joint efforts with state and local governments in various programs to host thousands of otherwise unemployed and underemployed persons (*Cooperative Work Study, Work Incentive Program, Vocational Skills Training,* and others).

The Forest Service has a comprehensive "inform and involve" program to update matters on natural resources as a basis for involving them in decisions and programs on both national and state levels. The Agency's *environmental education program* places special emphasis on involving educators, resource professionals, and citizen groups in developing skills and techniques for investigating and teaching others about the environment. The *Woodsy Owl* program creates public awareness of pollution and environmental improvement problems and suggests solutions. Another program addresses privately-owned forest lands and the assistance available for improving these lands. Research reports are available on all of its programs.
Last but not least, the Agency keeps the public informed on how it can use National Forest System lands, resources, and facilities for family, individual, and group recreation.
Sponsor: US/DoA - Department of Agriculture
Contact: Nancy Mjelde, Program Manager
Publications: What the Forest Service Does; Job Corps Information Packet; Senior Conservation Employment Program; Human Resource Programs Hosted by the Forest Service

NATURE CONSERVANCY
SEE PHYSICAL ENVIRONMENT: CONSERVATION

SOIL AND WATER CONSERVATION SOCIETY OF AMERICA
7515 NE Ankeny Road
Ankeny, IA 50021
TEL: 515-289-2331
Objectives: To advance the science and art of good land use.
Services: Sponsors civic projects; conducts conservation field tours; works with schools on environmental education programs; grants scholarships to students and teachers; sponsors local, state and regional workshops on such topics as surface mine reclamation; works through local chapters (write for directory); publishes bimonthly newsletter, bimonthly journal, guides such as *Evironmental Quality and the Citizen* and *Planning and Organizing an Adult Education Program,* a series of educational cartoon books to motivate youngsters in areas of conservation, and other materials.
Publications: Conservogram; Soil/Water Conservation Journal
Founded: 1945

TRAINING PROGRAMS

HAPPY TRAILS TO YOU: A WORKSHOP FOR VOLUNTEERS
Potomac Appalachian Trail Club
1178 N Street, NW
Washington, DC 20036
TEL: 202-638-5306
Credit: Inquire
Contact: Steve Bair, Backcountry Supervisor, or George Walters
Description: At this workshop, experienced volunteers and trail overseers demonstrated the finer points of trail maintenance to attract people interested in adopting a trail. Sponsored by the *Potomac Appalachian Trail Club (PATC),* the workshop attracted 24 people. At the end of the workshop, most of them expressed a desire to join the 250 existing trails volunteers from the Club. Volunteers were told that each individual, family or team adopts a segment of the trail and maintains it. Discussions at the workshop included:
- How to Take Proper Care of a Trail
- What Are the "Tools of the Trade?"
- How Much Time Is Required by the Volunteer?
- The Trails Overseer; Managing the Trails System
- When a Trail Needs Major Repairs
- Volunteer Jobs Other Than Trail Maintenance
- The Shenandoah National Park

The most important aspect, according to one facilitator, is to provide regular attention to "your adopted trail." Volunteers were told that at times a decision would have to be their own, since problems arise on the trail that require a creative solution, when overseers are not available. Training of volunteers helps to prepare them for these isolated incidents.
An overview of the social aspects, "fun" of trail work, and cooperation among volunteers (carpooling, sharing meals, readying cabins for some necessary overnight stays, etc.) concluded the workshop.

INDIVIDUAL PROGRAM PROFILES

GLEANING*
SEE NUTRITION: SELF-HELP

HONEYWELL NEIGHBORHOOD IMPROVEMENT PROGRAM
SEE HOUSING: LOW-INCOME

NEIGHBORHOOD TREE CORPS
Magnolia Tree Earth Center
678 Lafayette Avenue
Brooklyn, NY 11216
TEL: 718-387-2116

Purpose: To involve the entire community in an effort to turn around the rapid decline of the neighborhood.

Contact: Hattie Carthan

Description: The Neighborhood Tree Corps is an outgrowth of the efforts of one woman who was determined to do something about her once tree-lined street, which "progress" had rendered bare. This elderly black woman began by forming a block association to raise money for the purchase of replacement trees. She planted thousands of trees, and came to the attention of the Mayor, the State Council on the Arts, and others. Through this recognition, the Neighborhood Tree Corps surfaced with support of over $11,000 from the Brooklyn Arts Council. In 1975, an umbrella organization, the Magnolia Tree Earth Center, was set up to seek grants and develop new projects like the Corps.

The Neighborhood Tree Corps is a year-round program. During the winter months, thirty students, ages nine to sixteen, take courses at the community center two afternoons a week. In addition to the two-hour classes on trees, occasional weekend field trips to gardens and conservation centers are arranged. Community volunteers lead the classes and trips under the supervision of an instructor who is trained in this specialty.

When school closes, the program shifts to a summer schedule. Three days a week the youngsters meet at ten in the morning to practice what they have learned in the winter classes. They carry brooms, rakes, pails, and trowels to a specific block and begin sweeping, tilling and watering everything outside the area's home fences. The youngsters make it a point to knock on doors to borrow hoses so that they can talk to residents and get them involved. In two hours, a block can be totally transformed. Volunteers oversee the youngsters, who are paid from three to five dollars a week depending on their ages. This expense and others are covered by a $20 fee paid by block associations for this service. Many of the youngsters stay in the program year after year, until they are too old to participate - most giving their reason as "pride in taking care of your own neighborhood trees."

The Neighborhood Tree Corps has served as a model for cities nationwide, and has generated numerous other opportunities for volunteer involvement, youth employment, and increased conservation of urban areas.

Founded: 1975

PATC VOLUNTEERS
Potomac Appalachian Trail Club
1178 N Street, NW
Washington, DC 20036
TEL: 202-638-5306

Purpose: To maintain about 800 miles of Shenandoah trails.

Sponsor: Shenandoah National Park

Contact: Steve Bair, Backcountry Supervisor

Description: Some 250 volunteers from the Washington, DC, area have taken responsibility for one or more Appalachian Trail segments ranging in length from one to six miles, and located in areas as far away as West Virginia, and as close as Rock Creek Park in the city. Most volunteers are members of the *Potomac Appalachian Trail Club (PATC)* and range in age from six to seventy-four. They spend their weekends doing various types of trail maintenance. Through a formal agreement with the Shenandoah Park, the Club maintains the Appalachian Trail and all of the blue-blazed hiking trails in the park.

Keeping a trail in shape requires special tools, training, and regular attention, according to one volunteer, "what with Mother Nature constantly dropping trees across it, trying to wash it away with rain, and obliterating it with vegetation." Each volunteer or volunteer team adopts a trail that is maintained by the same individual or group throughout the year. Maintenance is done at more than one level, with a "blue-blazed trail" requiring about three trips a year by the overseer to keep it in condition, but a major section of the Appalachian Trail requiring an additional two or three trips because the club maintains it to a higher standard. Overseers, who are experienced volunteers, are on hand at all times.

As in many programs, there is always more work than volunteers, and most of the work is done by a dedicated few. When volunteers from the 4,000-member group come out and try it, a large percentage of them stay on and get involved, according to one official. "They just have to take that first step." The PATC tries to make it easy to take that first step, having a variety of volunteer opportunities ranging from trail maintenance to cabin construction to office work. Opportunities exist for all levels of skill and vigor, from moving rocks to cooking for the crew. Volunteers generally carpool, share meals, and stay in a rustic cabin.

Periodically, workshops are held in which experienced volunteers demonstrate the tools needed, then pass them around for hands-on learning by the participants.

The greatest response from members comes when a segment of trail is found to need major repairs. The overseers organize a work trip where many club members not otherwise involved turn out to tackle the job over a weekend. Openings always exist for volunteer trail overseers.

ROBERTS PARK AND PLAYGROUND/LANTRIP SCHOOL PARK*
SEE RECREATION & SPORTS: PARKS/FORESTS

SOUTH BRONX SUMMER PROJECT
Brown University
25 George Street
PO Box 1974
Providence, RI 02912
TEL: 401-863-2338

Purpose: To convert previously abandoned property to a community park and garden.

Contact: Susan E. Stroud, Director

Description: The *South Bronx Summer Project* is a student-initiated public service program formed in 1986. Eleven *Brown University* students participated in the project with local assistance from such agencies as the *Bronx Frontier Development Corporation*, the *Council on the Environment*, *Cornell Cooperative Extension*, the *District Manager's Office*, and the *1325 Lafayette Avenue's Tenants' Association*. The purpose of the project is to convert two-and-one-half acres of previously abandoned property filled with rubble and garbage into *Hunt's Point Farm*, a community park and garden.

With student initiative, local assistance, and private funding, the *South Bronx Summer Project* has become a tradition as each summer eight *Brown University* students return to the South Bronx to expand and maintain development on *Hunt's Point Farm*. In 1990, the *Center for Public Service* and the *Bronx Frontier Development Corporation* sponsored the fifth *South Bronx Summer Project*.

During the last four summers, Brown undergraduates assisted neighborhood residents in the development of *Hunt's Point Farm*. Construction on the Farm resulted in a playground and an adjoining playing field, picnic tables, an orchard, and a community garden and nursery, with a football field in process across from the Farm.

Student volunteers are housed at *Fordham University, Rosehill Campus*, which is about 15 minutes from the worksite. An eight-passenger van is leased for the twelve weeks of the project to provide transportation for the volunteers. Each student receives a stipend and a food allowance and, in cases of financial need, additional funding.

In addition to park construction and maintenance, the *Project* is responsible for a youth employment and recreation program. The summer of 1990 was the third year of the youth employment program, which employs 20-25 teenaged youth on the *Farm*. The youth recreation program, which was initiated in 1989, allows Brown students to interact with the community's youth. Recreational activities include field trips in the New York area, games, and arts and crafts. Each year the Project expands to include the needs and desires of the community.

The *South Bronx Summer Project* not only provides a fun-filled summer for everyone, but it also gets the community actively involved in the local revitalization of Hunt's Point.

TOUCH AMERICA PROJECT (TAP)
American Conservation Volunteers
American Forestry Association
1319 Eighteenth Street, NW
Washington, DC 20036
TOLL FREE: 800-368-5748
Purpose: To provide an opportunity for young people to work and learn more about America's natural resources through volunteering.
Sponsor: American Forestry Association
Contact: TAP Coordinator
Description: TAP (Touch America Project) is a youth volunteer program through which young people ages 14-17 may work and learn more about America's natural resources. The theme, *Touch America,* refers to volunteer projects on public lands developed cooperatively with private organizations, groups, or individuals. *TAP* volunteers work in national forests, parks, refuges, grasslands, historic preservation areas and other public lands administered by cooperating government agencies. These include *Forest Service, Extension Service, Soil Conservation Service of the Department of Agriculture,* and the *National Park Service, Bureau of Land Management,* and *Fish and Wildlife Service of the Department of Interior. TAP* is a partnership of:
- community groups and nonprofit organizations (which provide supervision and coordination)
- youth, ages 14 through 17 (who volunteer their time and energies)
- Government agencies (which provide supplies, services, or funding needed for the project)

Through *TAP,* business and private contributors have an opportunity to perform a community service, communities can offer meaningful work to local young people, youth obtain work experience, and public lands are improved.

A technical assistance packet is published for organizations or individuals interested in sponsoring or finding a sponsor for a *TAP* project in their community.
Publications: Touch America Project for Youth Volunteers; TAP for TAP

USS KITTY HAWK/WASHINGTON SQUARE PARTNERSHIP
SEE PHYSICAL ENVIRONMENT: BEAUTIFICATION

VOLUNTEERS IN PARKS (VIP)
Kansas City Department of Parks and Recreation
3915 East 63rd Street
Kansas City, MO 64130
TEL: 816-561-6630
Purpose: To provide non-skilled and semi-skilled volunteer help in park and boulevard maintenance on a regular, dependable basis.
Sponsor: Kansas City Department of Parks and Recreation; various corporate sponsors
Contact: Phil Thornburg, Volunteer Coordinator
Description: The VIP program is an incentive-based program to encourage ongoing individual and group participation in the non-skilled and semi-skilled routine maintenance of Parks and Recreation properties, facilities, structures, and displays. The program allows for volunteers to work in a location convenient to home or work, the time of day, day(s) of the week, and number of hours available or convenient to them by contacting the manager of the work site.

The VIP program was begun June 21, 1982 and offered as incentives passes to a number of Parks and Recreation facilities/activities as well as passes, discounts, and coupons offered by four local merchants.

Staffing requirements are only the Supervisor of the sections involved such as Park District Managers, Golf Course Supervisors, Florist, etc. The program expenses are minimal and are financed through the Corporate Sponsor Coupon donations and the maintenance budget for paint or other special items. Trash bags, hand tools, etc. are furnished by the volunteer as needed.

Volunteer Duties - VIP's may volunteer for any of a number of projects or suggest an alternative of their own subject to approval. The types of projects listed included weeding of flower beds; litter removal in parks or sections of a boulevard; sweeping and cleaning hard surface walks, courts, and curbs; shrub bed cleaning and leaf removal; painting of restrooms, play equipment, trash containers; glass, trash, and weed removal from playgrounds and sand boxes.

How the Program Operates - The volunteer must schedule the location and time with the appropriate supervisor.

The incentives are cumulative and may be collected as work is completed. Choices of activities are given for some hours to provide maximum appeal to volunteers.

Groups and one-time projects are accommodated by providing the representative the incentives based on the number of hours worked and the number in the group.
Founded: 1982

WOODEND VOLUNTEER PROGRAM
Audubon Naturalist Society
Woodend
8940 Jones Mill Road
Chevy Chase, MD 20815
TEL: 301-652-9188
Purpose: To enlist volunteer help in maintaining a natural resource.
Contact: Darryl Speicher
Description: To provide a volunteer vehicle for people who work Monday through Friday, *Woodend* has changed one coordinator's schedule from those days to Tuesday through Saturday. The high rate of response to that announcement has prompted a published list of projects that require volunteer help at the park. These include:
- *Meadow management* - the removal of encroaching woody plants, and the controlled planting of native wildflowers.
- *Soil erosion control* - the use of logs and stones as rip-rap, and the removal of sediment.
- *Pond cleaning* - cleanup of the pond after the flow slows down; maintaining its effectiveness in sediment control.
- *Wildlife management* - the monitoring and recordkeeping of wildlife, and the repair and/or construction of nesting boxes.
- *Painting* and *fenceline maintenance* - two examples of important maintenance that needs to be performed.

The specific projects are combined with other activities to create a balanced and enjoyable experience for volunteers. Training is provided as indicated. In addition to training sessions, volunteers meet periodically with the coordinator to report their findings, make suggestions, and schedule hours.

PHYSICAL ENVIRONMENT: RECYCLING

INDIVIDUAL PROGRAM PROFILES

CURB IT!
Keep Perrysburg Beautiful
Fraternal Order of Police Lodge 182
900 West Poe Road
Perrysburg, OH 43551
TEL: 419-352-9370
Purpose: To enlist individuals, corporations and others in the community to mount a pilot recycling project to help plan for a future areawide project.
Sponsor: Keep Perrysburg Beautiful
Contact: Mary Cowles, Program Coordinator
Description: A pilot program, *Curb It!* was tried in August 1989 in two neighborhoods totaling 233 houses - Pheasant Run and Perry Commons. Volunteer manpower, recycled buckets, and a recycled truck make up the program's components. *Master Chemical Company* donated the buckets. The *Curb It Committee* of about 20 citizens visit the involved households once a month and survey them about progress and ideas for the ongoing test. Volunteers distribute *Curb It Kits* about the program, and the plastic buckets, door-to-door. The kits include a magnet for differentiating between aluminum and steel cans and a brown paper bag to hold newspapers.
The program requires residents in the pilot areas to tote five-gallon buckets filled with aluminum cans and glass bottles out to the curb with their stacked newspapers. The recycleable materials are then picked up and tossed into a former soft drink truck, separated on the truck during the pickup route, and hauled off for sale.
The three-month pilot program had a $2,425 budget, including $800 for insurance, and $500 for each of the other three items: vehicle expense, printing and production, and awards and promotion costs. The city litter control agency, *Keep Perrysburg Beautiful,* financed the experimental project, in part, with a $33,876 grant from the *Ohio Department of Natural Resources* along with a 20 percent share from the city.
The test area amounts to about 6 percent of Perrysburg's 3,500 homes, not including apartments. The Saturday morning pickups are aimed at giving city officials some idea of what they could expect from a larger area. Since recycling programs average about 30 percent participation, city officials will consider involvement of 40% of residents in the test area as a successful effort.
Benefits to the community in a successful effort include:
- conservation of landfill space;
- conservation of material resources;
- reducing the number of the city's deposits in landfills ($200 for each refuse truckful dumped in a landfill)
According to officials, a 10 percent reduction in landfill usage would mean a savings of about $10,000. Landfill costs in 1988 were $81,787. Budget for 1989 was $93,000.
Four or five volunteers are assigned each Saturday, and the proceeds from the sale of recycleables are given to organizations who provide the volunteers. One of the first groups to provide volunteers in 1989 was *Perrysburg Fraternal Order of Police Lodge 182.* The citywide program will have far greater manpower demands, but the pilot program may shed some light on possible solutions to those demands. Officials have been encouraged as some neighboring communities institute their own recycling pickup as part of their regular refuse collection.
Founded: 1989

FEAT FOUNDATION
SEE PHYSICAL ENVIRONMENT: BEAUTIFICATION

RECYCLING FOR RAVI
Knoxville Zoo Tiger Team
Knoxville Zoological Gardens
3333 Woodbine Avenue
Knoxville, TN 37914
TEL: 615-637-5331
Purpose: To raise funds to keep a white tiger at the local zoo; to recycle aluminum to help the environment.
Sponsor: Roddy Coca-Cola Bottling Company
Contact: Jane Creed, Tiger Team Recycling Coordinator
Description: In January 1988, a Florida animal trainer loaned two seven-week-old tigers to *Knoxville Zoological Gardens.* One tiger is a rare white tiger named *Ravi,* and the other is the common orange tiger (*Burma*). Later, the owner offered to sell the white tiger to Knoxville Zoological Gardens for $50,000, with the orange tiger donated.
Hoping to keep the tigers in Knoxville permanently, a volunteer group approached the business community and together they worked out a plan. The program that was considered the most promising for raising money quickly was a recycling program involving the entire Knox County school system. Ten middle schools, representing 5,000 pupils, collected 10,300 pounds of aluminum cans to raise $7,200. The Aluminum Company of America added $3,000, making the initial donation to the Knoxville Zoo Tiger Team $10,200.
By May 1989 the volunteer group had raised $46,100, $3,900 short of Ravi's asking price.
To maintain interest as the pupils worked toward the recycling goal, cash prizes were awarded by *Roddy Coca-Cola Bottling Company:* first place $1,000, second place $500, and third place $250, with a $500 award going to one of the schools for its can sculpture, and another $250 for the second-place can sculpture. *ALCOA, Roddy* and *Waste Management of Knoxville* are sponsors of the project, with volunteer support from the schools and one-time donations from corporations such as the Aluminum Company of America.
The Tiger Team volunteer group met the goal in time to save Ravi and Burma from becoming circus animals.
Publications: Knoxville Zoo Tiger Team Packet

PHYSICAL ENVIRONMENT: REVITALIZATION

NATIONAL/STATE ORGANIZATIONS

COMMUNITY ECONOMICS
SEE HOUSING: COOPERATIVES

NEIGHBORHOOD DEVELOPMENT SERVICES CENTER
Urban Coalition
1120 G Street, NW, Suite 900
Washington, DC 20005
TEL: 202-628-2990
Objectives: To assist community development corporations in their efforts to improve communities.
Services: Operates through a Ford Foundation grant to assist community development groups in revitalization efforts; provides technical assistance to community development corporations undertaking physical and economic development such as new business start-ups, housing, mixed use development, adaptive reuse projects, etc.; provides technical assistance through mail, phone and on-site visit; conducts workshops on issues vital to communities; publishes a monthly newsletter, neighborhood booklets, and other materials designed to inform and assist

neighborhood groups.
Publications: Housing Exchange; Urban Exchange; Urban
Education Exchange ; Urban Health Exchange; Neighborhood
Exchange
Founded: 1967

TRAINING PROGRAMS

COMMUNITY FORUM ON THE PROPOSED *HARLEM ON THE HUDSON* PROJECT
West Harlem Coalition
PO Box 660
Manhattanville Station
New York, NY 10027
TEL: 212-234-4661
Credit: None
Contact: Forum Coordinator
Description: This Forum was called by West Harlem community
leaders to address the proposed development of the pier area near
the community. The consultants hired by the city to conduct a
feasibility study attended the forum. Residents, community groups,
and urban planners have rejected the luxury development plans
citing the following factors, among others:

- displacement of longtime residents
- disruption of traffic
- environmental concerns
- the need to develop on a community-wide basis, not a luxury
  enclave on the outskirts of the community, which will "wall
  off" the people
- lack of space allocated for the typical CB9 household
- a violation of the basic right to affordable housing
- a threat to the diverse character of the neighborhood

The group has operated a number of forums since 1986, when the
plan was first announced, as well as enlisting support in editorials
in several media, confronting managers of the plan, and developing
and enlisting support for petitions to the city. In all cases, the
major thrust is the improvement of all of Harlem, not just
Harlem-on-the-Hudson.

INDIVIDUAL PROGRAM PROFILES

EAST TENNESSEE COMMUNITY DESIGN CENTER
1522 Highland Avenue
Knoxville, TN 37916
TEL: 615-525-9945; 615-525-9946
[The second number is the Center's Office for Appropriate
Technology.]
Purpose: To provide architectural and planning services to
community groups unable to pay private, professional fees.
Sponsor: University of Tennessee
Contact: Annette Anderson
Description: The East Tennessee Community Design Center is a
private, non-profit organization which serves a sixteen county area
of East Tennessee. The Design Center was created in 1970 by
design and planning professionals who identified a need for a
program through which design and planning services could be
provided to community groups which could not otherwise obtain
these services. The Design Center serves a variety of clients
including day care centers, urban and rural community centers,
neighborhood organizations, art groups, and social service
programs. The work includes problem definition, design
programming, schematic design, cost estimates, and resource
development assistance.
The Design Center consists primarily of volunteers - architects,
landscape architects, graphic designers, planners, engineers - who
contribute their time to work on community projects. During the
past twelve years more than 75,000 hours have been donated for
Design Center projects. During the past year alone more than 400
people contributed 9,452 hours to projects, a contribution
conservatively worth $60,500. Thirty-four projects were completed
last year. Twenty-three community projects are "on the boards"
now.
The Design Center's volunteer Board of Directors is made up of
one-third design professionals, one-third client representatives, and
one-third from the community at large. The Board sets policy and
selects projects based on the criteria that the client cannot
otherwise obtain professional design assistance, that the work
benefits a community rather than a single individual, and that
there is likelihood that the project will be implemented if design
assistance is provided.
The Design Center staff consists of the Coordinator who handles
communication and administration, the Resource Developer who
finds resources to implement projects, the Staff Architect who
works primarily with appropriate technology projects, and the
Administrative Assistant.
Volunteers In Service To America (VISTA) serve as liaison
between community clients and volunteer task force leaders, doing
much of the daily project work. VISTAs are usually recent
graduates in architecture or planning who commit one or two
years to serving low income communities while they gain
experience in the field.
The Coordinator conducts a University of Tennessee School of
Architecture studio at the Design Center called "Architecture In
Service To Communities" in which fourth and fifth year students
work intensively on Design Center projects on a quarterly basis.
The offices and studios of the Design Center are located in the
historic Fort Sanders neighborhood in a converted residential
building owned and occupied entirely by the Design Center.
The Design Center provides an opportunity for people of varying
backgrounds and interests to work together to improve the quality
of their surroundings. One very valuable aspect of the Design
Center is its ability to bring people together to accomplish
community goals. For example, during the past three years the
Design Center has completed two participatory design projects
sponsored by the National Endowment for the Arts. One was
designed to improve livability and energy efficiency in Knoxville's
inner city. Another, the *Fort Sanders Neighborhood Design Plan*
called *Old Town In Town,* duplicated that process to produce
development guidelines for that affected neighborhood.
In addition, the Design Center has extensive experience in
managing public events. In 1976 it organized a series of
Bicentennial Neighborhood Fairs. Later, the Design Center
coordinated preparation and management of an Appropriate
Community Technology exhibit (ACT '82) on the site of the 1982
World's Fair. About seventy groups participated in the ACT '82
exhibit which provided information about appropriate technologies
to more than 250,000 people.
A typical year's records document $3.40 worth of services
provided for every dollar spent on staff, space, supplies and other
support. In the same year, $632,825 in community improvements
were generated by the combination of staff volunteers and
budgeted expenditures, making a total return on investment of
$7.75 for each Design Center dollar spent.
Founded: 1970

MILWAUKEE AND THE SINGLE GIRL*
Girl Scouts of the Milwaukee Area
2500 West Mayfair Road
Milwaukee, WI 53222
TEL: 414-476-1050
Purpose: To generate the support of an entire city in an urban
environment education program for members of a young girls'
organization.
Sponsor: US/HHS - Department of Health & Human Services
Contact: Pat Pollworth

Description: As a foundation for a major thrust to develop pride in the city among its nearly a quarter of a million residents, the local Girl Scouts office developed a citywide conference on the urban environment. A consultant on conference planning helped create an overview, list tasks for volunteers, and construct a timetable. The first step was to form an all-volunteer Task Force to handle the logistics of the conference, and to recruit other volunteers as needed.

In recruiting volunteers, the Girl Scout network was unbeatable. Each staff person works with half a dozen of the city's 39 neighborhoods. For each neighborhood, a Chairperson coordinates activities of from 16 to 40 troops in operation. The Chairperson is helped by a volunteer service group in each neighborhood for program ideas, technical assistance, etc. Every adult volunteer receives a newsletter each month from central staff.

The built-in communication network served the Task Force well, bringing 325 people to the conference. Twenty-four youth-serving agencies, ten local businesses, six citizens' groups, nine educational institutions, and twelve government agencies were represented. Numerous ideas and suggestions emerged toward the conference goal - to excite young people about Milwaukee to the extent that they would participate in volunteer environmental projects. Workshop categories included experimental land use, public art, waste disposal, mass transit, bikes, the Milwaukee River, human spatial environment, the lakefront, housing and zoning, expressways, and architectural preservation. Awards were offered for the best projects in these categories. As a result, six troops won awards of $50.00 each during the following months.

The effects of the conference continued over the next year as materials on the city were developed: children's books, slide shows and film strips, a roster of speakers and trip planners, an idea book for urban awareness, museum exhibits, library bibliographies, new school curricula, etc. Months after the conference, senior Girl Scouts held their spring conference with the theme, Urban Upswing, and honored the city.

Although the conference and its aftermath have had a major impact on the young people of Milwaukee, the Girl Scouts organization considers it just a beginning in their efforts to instill the desire in young people to care about and participate in their neighborhoods.

PHYSICAL ENVIRONMENT: SOLID WASTE

NATIONAL/STATE ORGANIZATIONS

AIR AND WASTE MANAGEMENT ASSOCIATION
SEE PHYSICAL ENVIRONMENT: AIR POLLUTION

CLEAN COMMUNITY SYSTEM
Keep America Beautiful
Mill River Plaza
9 West Broad Street
Stamford, CT 06902
TEL: 203-323-8987
Objectives: To serve as the national resource agency for 270+ cities and counties implementing KAB's Clean Community System, the behavioral approach to changing attitudes about littering and waste handling.
Services: Trains local groups to organize and operate Clean Community System (CCS) program; closely monitors progress and provides certification; provides continued counseling and on-site visits; links CCS programs across the country for exchange of ideas in this system which scientifically changes the way an entire

community thinks and acts regarding the litter problem; keeps CCS leaders informed and continues to provide professional services on request; expands to meet related needs in the community with in-plant, college campus, and military installation programs, and Waste-In-Place, a K-6 program for youngsters (being developed for older students also).
In addition to CCS (through which KAB does most of its work), ongoing programs include: The KAB/Advertising Council National Advertising Campaign, KAB Week and The National Awards Program; publications include the monthly bulletin, guides, transcripts, posters, litter bags, and other items.
Publications: Network; Vision; KAB Review; KAB Bulletin

WASTE ALERT!
US/EPA - Office of Solid Waste Management
401 M Street, NW
Washington, DC 20460
TEL: 202-755-9157
Objectives: To provide opportunities for volunteers to become involved in waste management decisions.
Services: Assists leaders and key activists with development of programs in public participation in seeking solutions to solid waste problems, including hazardous waste; operates on an individual state basis managed by a state coalition (in some states by the League of Women Voters); works closely with six organizations who founded the program and managed it from 1979-1981 through a steering committee (League of Women Voters Educational Fund, American Public Health Association, National Wildlife Federation, Environmental Action Foundation, Izaak Walton League, and Technical Information Project); encourages volunteer citizen participation through a speakers service and regional conferences; publishes *How to Salvage a Wasting Dream* and other public awareness materials.
Sponsor: US/EPA - Environmental Protection Agency
Publications: How to Salvage a Wasting Dream

TRAINING PROGRAMS

COMMUNICATIONS SKILLS FOR THE COLLEGE BOUND
SEE CIVIC AFFAIRS: EDUCATION

INDIVIDUAL PROGRAM PROFILES

FIGHTING DIRTY!
SEE PHYSICAL ENVIRONMENT: BEAUTIFICATION

LITTERTHON
Citizens for a Better Bernardsville (CBB)
c/o Howard Lemberg
56 Mine Mount Road
Bernardsville, NJ 07924
TEL: 201-766-3420
Purpose: To combine forces of community groups to attack the litter problem in Bernardsville.
Sponsor: Bernardsville Business Alliance
Contact: Howard Lemberg, President, CBB
Description: Three Bernardsville groups jointly sponsored *Litterthon,* a project aimed at cleaning up the borough's downtown. About fifty volunteers collected 65 bags of trash in time for the community's Memorial celebration on the following weekend. The *Bernardsville Business Alliance, Citizens for a Better Bernardsville,* and the *Bernardsville Environmental Commission* working together took a major step toward public-private partnership in trying to improve downtown Bernardsville.
Joining together in the *Litterthon* project is only the beginning of a

long-term effort mounted by the groups. A report from a consultant hired by the planning board and business alliance is awaited by the groups. The study is expected to point to ways to boost the declining downtown. The report, according to the consultant, will emphasize that residents, business owners and local government must work together to get the job done.
The groups see the cleanup campaign as a start in strengthening the partnership needed to deal effectively with other challenges facing Bernardsville.

PARENTS FOR THE ENVIRONMENT
c/o James Mulloy
3509 Woodman Drive
Haymarket, VA 22069
TEL: 703-754-9381
Purpose: To challenge the schools on practices that both threaten the environment, and give mixed messages to students.
Sponsor: Prince William County Public Works Department
Contact: James Mulloy, Parent
Description: Since parents of the nineties were children during the major thrust on "saving the environment" in the sixties and seventies, the rallying of parents of children in Gainesville Elementary School around an environmental issue was a natural evolution. The center of the issue during the 1989-90 school year was a pilot program in two schools that replaces trays and dishes in the cafeterias with plastic trays and utensils to eliminate the need for dishwashing each day. According to a parent's spokesperson, this is giving mixed signals to children who are taught about the problem of solid waste and the need for recycling in their daily classes.
The schools say the new practice saves $27,000 a year by cutting back on expensive dishwashing. As one principal pointed out, a recent hike of 10 cents was "as popular with students as steamed spinach." Parents say that plastic utensils and trays are unhealthful because some residue from the chemicals used can find its way into the food, that they are a threat to the environment, and are a bad influence on children's table manners. The *Prince William County Public Works Department,* which manages the county landfill, feels the move is "not based on sound environmental principles. On one hand, we're badgering the kids to recycle; on the other, we're giving them lunch on a Styrofoam tray."
And the children are not "silent partners" in this issue. As one third-grader said, "If they keep dumping it, they'll have to put it in people's yards. There won't be any more room left." In addition, about a third of the children at Gainesville are boycotting cafeteria lunches in an effort to persuade the school system to scrap its use of plastics.
One practice is beginning to take hold in schools which have used plastic utensils for years. They have begun recycling them through a program with *Amoco.* At its New York City plant, *Amoco* transforms used lunch trays, salad bowls, soup cups and plates into pellets used in insulation, packing material, and VCR tape. In the meantime, Gainesville parents, and a parents' group forming at Stonewall Middle School near the historic Manassas area in the county, continue to spend many volunteer hours seeking ways to impress on the schools that the use of plastics is unacceptable, and that it is in the best interest of all concerned for them to return to the former system of washable plates and trays.

PHYSICAL ENVIRONMENT: TOXIC WASTE

INDIVIDUAL PROGRAM PROFILES

HAZARDOUS WASTE VOLUNTEER PROGRAM
SEE DISASTER RESPONSE/EMERGENCY PREPAREDNESS

PHYSICAL ENVIRONMENT: WATER POLLUTION

NATIONAL/STATE ORGANIZATIONS

CLEAN WATER ACTION PROJECT
317 Pennsylvania Avenue, SE
Suite 200
Washington, DC 20003
TEL: 202-547-1196
Objectives: To work for strong water pollution controls and safe drinking water through citizen action.
Services: Monitors and influences legislation such as the 1972 Clean Water Act and the 1974 Safe Drinking Water Act; develops information and activities aimed at preservation of wetlands and promotion of sewage recycling and alternative waste water treatment; responds to citizen inquiries regarding water conservation programs; convenes annual meeting. (This project is an outgrowth of Ralph Nader's task force on water pollution.) [Also maintains an office at 2530 North Calvert Street, Baltimore, MD 21218, 301-235-8808.]
Publications: CWAP Newsletter
Founded: 1971

NATIONAL WATER PROJECT*
1111 North 19th Street, NW
Suite 400
Arlington, VA 22209
TEL: 703-527-2282
Objectives: To assist low-income rural areas in resolving water problems.
Services: Works through locally-based organizations to provide adequate, affordable drinking water; conducts research to develop information for concerned citizens and others; supports ad hoc committees as needed; publishes bimonthly newsletter, directories, manuals, management guides, and other materials; conducts semiannual network meeting.
Publications: Rural Water News; Network Organizations
Founded: 1973

INDIVIDUAL PROGRAM PROFILES

ADOPT-A-SCHOOL
SEE EDUCATION: ADOPT-A-SCHOOL

ADOPT-A-STREAM
Maryland Department of Natural Resources
Brandywine, MD 20613
TEL: 301-372-8128
TOLL FREE: 800-448-5826

Purpose: To involve local organizations in a voluntary effort to protect the state's streams.
Sponsor: Maryland Save Our Streams (SOS)
Contact: Earth Day Coordinator
Description: The state of Maryland has approximately 17,000 miles of streams, 95 percent of which feed the Chesapeake Bay directly. For *Earth Day 1990,* a joint effort has been mounted by *Maryland Save Our Streams (SOS)* and the state *Department of Natural Resources* to involve the public in the state's continuing efforts to maintain the streams. Called *Adopt-A-Stream,* the statewide project encourages local organizations to adopt 5,000 miles of stream for *Earth Day.*
Voluntary activities have included stream clean-ups, water quality monitoring, stream surveys, watershed inventories, tree plantings, and sediment and erosion control monitoring. Other organizations and agencies involved in the project include the *Department of Natural Resources' Tidewater Administration* and *One Million Marylanders for the Bay.*
Earth Day was considered only the "starting date" for this project, which will require monitoring and adjustments by the volunteer groups on a continuing basis.

CLEAN THE BAY DAY
Center for Marine Conservation
Hampton, VA 23670
TEL: 804-851-6734 (Center); 804-427-6066 (volunteer)
Purpose: To protect the Bay area so important to the city.
Sponsor: Center for Marine Conservation
Contact: Kathy O'Hara, Biologist (Center); Robert Dean, Volunteer
Description: The heightened public awareness of marine pollution generated by the Alaskan oil spill brought people in Hampton Roads to a meeting to discuss the Bay so important to the city.
The proposed effort attracted thousands of volunteers, who swept trash from beaches, bays and rivers from the North Carolina line to Hampton in an intensive day's work.
The Hampton Roads beach cleanup was organized by a commodore of the *Lynnhaven Yacht Club* and based on cleanups conducted in 23 states since 1987 by the *Center for Environmental Education,* a conservation group dedicated to protecting marine life. In Texas alone during that time, more than 7,000 people filled more than 17,000 trash bags with 300 tons of debris, according to a report provided to Hampton organizers by the *Center.* Given the benefit derived from the ocean in Hampton Roads, organizers felt it was crucial that such an effort be mounted to improve the Bay area.
Organizations participating in the cleanup included local chapters of the *Sierra Club* and *National Audubon Society,* scout troops, public schools, and the *Army, Navy,* and *Coast Guard.* Corporate sponsors included *Signet Bank* and *Bell Atlantic.* Military and private divers picked up underwater trash.
Several bay, creek and river areas were covered by the volunteers, with the exception of the Elizabeth River. Experts have warned that the Elizabeth River presents a cleanup hazard because of toxic wastes that have long been buried there, along with decomposing meal and other debris. That river, according to organizers, is on the agenda for another year, so that careful planning and analysis will assure that volunteers do not get hurt.
Volunteers were asked to fill out forms to record what was collected to forward to the *Center for Environmental Education* to be used in a national study of marine debris. The study is expected to help policymakers control litter that is not only ugly, but dangerous to marine life.
Founded: 1989

FRIENDS OF THE ROUGE
City of Southfield
Evergreen Road
Southfield, MI 48076
TEL: 313-427-1234 (Project); 313-427-6843 (Foundation)

Purpose: To improve the water quality and make the river more accessible to canoes along the nature trails.
Sponsor: Wildlife Habitat Foundation
Contact: James E. Murry, President FOTR; Patrick Rusz, WHF
Description: Friends of the Rouge (FOTR) was formed to help keep the Rouge River clean. One weekend each spring some 4,000 volunteers turn out at 21 locations along the Rouge River banks to help clear debris from the polluted waterway. The goal is to improve the water quality and increase the recreational potential of the waterway and its adjacent trails. More than half of the 125 miles of the river's main branch and tributaries are cleared through this effort.
A number of the volunteers are county offenders given work assignments instead of jail terms. Others come from local groups such as the *Western Wayne County Conservation Club,* a sportsmen's group. Volunteers from the *U.S. Army Corps of Engineers* helped students and others clear logs and trash from the paved sections of the Rouge by driving heavy-duty vehicles into the water. Volunteers work to get ahead of the log jams by stabilizing the river banks with sediment traps to protect against erosion and remove dead trees before they fall into the river.
The rejuvenation effort began in 1986, when the *Wildlife Habitat Foundation (WHF)* installed six dikes of broken concrete that channeled the Rouge so it cleaned itself to some extent - scouring two feet of polluted sediment from the river bottom. This effort demonstrated what can be done cheaply - costing a total of $8,000 - $5,000 from the Foundation and $3,000 from the city of Southfield. In the past three years, volunteers have dragged out 10,000 cubic yards of debris - including a complete car - which is hauled free of charge to a landfill operated by *Waste Management Inc.* of Southfield. For the first time in two decades, the seven-mile stretch passing by Southfield is navigable.
Communities along the Rouge's banks assign public works crews to assist the volunteers, and companies such as *Michigan Tractor and City Management of Detroit* supply heavy-duty equipment to help "break" up log jams. *Ford Motor Company* has contributed $50,000 to help finance the cleanup work, while *Gannett Outdoors* and *Channel 2* provide instructional material for volunteers. *Friends of the Rouge* have asked the public to help track down illegal dumpers by getting license plate numbers and phoning them into the group's office. The group, in turn, passes the information on to law enforcement agencies. Although the lower reaches of the Rouge are still off limits to canoeing, plans call for the contamination there to be under control by the year 2005 - through both volunteer effort and local taxes.
For its cleanup efforts, *Friends of the Rouge* has twice received the *Keep Michigan Beautiful Award,* and has been cited by the *Michigan Department of Natural Resources* for environmental improvements.
Founded: 1986

MASSACHUSETTS AQUATIC RESOURCE EDUCATION PROGRAM (AREP)
SEE RECREATION & SPORTS: PARKS/FORESTS

SAVE OUR WATER*
308 Read Street
Santa Fe, NM 87501
TEL: 505-827-8235
Purpose: To educate citizens about the benefits of conserving water.
Sponsor: The Governor's Office of Volunteer Services/NM and US/ACTION
Contact: Pat Powell
Description: In the past, most communities have turned to water conservation only as a last resort - as an emergency measure in a crisis situation. This project, however, establishes the fact that water conservation is an effective management tool to be used in both short and long term water supply planning.

Save Our Water is based upon the premise that a locally-designed and orchestrated community-wide campaign which features simple, affordable conservation technologies will motivate large numbers of people to take specific water conservation measures in their daily lives; and that the direct participation of local residents in the community effort is essential to the ultimate success of the program.

Volunteer Staff - Volunteers are recruited in each community to conduct workshops on water conservation, assemble and distribute water conservation kits, handle publicity and promotion, speak to civic and service organizations and a variety of other activities. Volunteers are the essential ingredient for the success of this project because they can approach their neighbors and friends on a equal level, convincing them of the need for conserving water.

Volunteer Experience - There are jobs in this project which can be handled by youth groups, senior citizens - or any other specific group. Volunteers who conduct workshops must have prior experience in this field, or be willing to undergo appropriate training.

PHYSICAL ENVIRONMENT: WILDLIFE/PETS

NATIONAL/STATE ORGANIZATIONS

ACTORS AND OTHERS FOR ANIMALS
5510 Cahuenga Boulevard
North Hollywood, CA 91601
TEL: 818-985-6263
Objectives: To alleviate animal suffering.
Services: Promotes wildlife conservation, and protection of endangered species; provides direct emergency aid and pet adoption program; educates the public on "zero pet population" growth, humane treatment of pets, and other areas to help alleviate suffering of both wild and domesticated animals; conducts biennial *Celebrity Fair* to benefit these causes; publishes annual newsletter.
Publications: Actors and Others Newsletter
Founded: 1971

AMERICAN SOCIETY FOR THE PREVENTION OF CRUELTY TO ANIMALS
441 East 92nd Street
New York, NY 10128
TEL: 212-876-7700
Objectives: To promote appreciation for and humane treatment of animals.
Services: Provides effective means for the prevention of cruelty to animals, enforces all laws for the protection of animals, promote appreciation for and human treatment of animals; maintains shelters for lost, stray, or unwanted animals; operates a veterinary hospital and a major low-cost spay/neuter clinic; operates "pet therapy" program; conducts educational programs and disseminates animal-related information for children and adults; maintains airport shelter to care for airborne animals before, after and between flights; campaigns for federal, state and local legislation to improve animal welfare; offers consulting, educational, and legislative services both in the U.S. and abroad; presents a number of certificates and awards to encourage humane treatment of animals; maintains departments on adoption, ambulance rescue, law enforcement, shelter operations, and library resources; publishes reports and information and educational brochures; holds fund-raising dinner-dance annually.
Publications: ASPCA Report
Founded: 1866

CARE ABOUT THE STRAYS
PO Box 474
New Albany, OH 43054
TEL: 614-855-2494
Objectives: To educate the public on the issue of stray animals.
Services: Conducts workshops designed to educate the public on the feeding, spaying, neutering, and care of stray animals; operates a charitable program to address and support this goal; offers a speakers service, statistics for interested individuals and groups, and related services; maintains a number of Committees, including Farm Animals, Humane Education, Spay/Neuter, and Pet Vendors Investigations; works with regional, state and local groups.
Founded: 1985

DELTA SOCIETY
321 Burnett Avenue, South #303
PO Box 1080
Renton, WA 98057-1080
TEL: 206-226-7357
FAX: 206-235-1076
Objectives: To promote positive interaction among people, animals and the environment.
Services: Serves as a resource for - and helps to establish - pet therapy programs; utilizes the services of volunteers as an integral component of pet therapy and other community service programs designed to involve people, pets and the environment in healthy and positive interaction; examines and assesses the role of animal companions in the mental and physical well-being of people; makes findings available to increase the awareness of these interactions in health and social care settings; has a network of local chapters which are organized and managed by volunteers and function as volunteer programs; has services in community education, people/pet programs, pets in public housing, and other areas requiring special attention; offers consultation to any interested group or individual; works with doctors, nurses, veterinarians, therapists, nursing home personnel, animal trainers and breeders, pet owners, academicians, and students of gerontology, psychology therapeutic recreation and other health fields; maintains a database of speakers active in research and service programs, and article reprints; distributes research grants and presents a number of awards for individuals and programs; publishes a newsletter, a magazine, and a journal.
Publications: People, Animals and the Environment; Anthrozoos; Interactions

DOGS FOR THE DEAF
SEE RECIPIENTS: HANDICAPPED - DEAF

HEARING EAR DOG PROGRAM
SEE RECIPIENTS: HANDICAPPED - DEAF

INTERNATIONAL GUIDING EYES
SEE RECIPIENTS: HANDICAPPED - BLIND

INTERNATIONAL HEARING DOG, INC.
SEE RECIPIENTS: HANDICAPPED - DEAF

LEADER DOGS FOR THE BLIND
SEE RECIPIENTS: HANDICAPPED - BLIND

NATIONAL CENTER FOR HEARING DOG INFORMATION
American Humane Association
9725 East Hampden Avenue
Denver, CO 80231
TEL: 303-695-0811; 303-695-4531 (TTY)
TOLL FREE: 800-842-4637

Objectives: To provide a national hearing dog information and referral service.
Services: Promotes the legal access rights of hearing dogs; works to increase public awareness of the benefits of hearing dogs to deaf citizens; publishes manuals, guides, booklets, a directory and other materials.
Publications: Hearing Dog Recipient Manual; Legal Rights of Dog Guides for the Deaf; Hearing Dog Program Directory
Founded: 1976

NATURE CONSERVANCY
SEE PHYSICAL ENVIRONMENT: CONSERVATION

INDIVIDUAL PROGRAM PROFILES

CHATTANOOGA NATURE CENTER
SEE PHYSICAL ENVIRONMENT: EDUCATION

GROWING UP WITH NATURE
Louisiana Nature and Science Center
Joe Brown Park
New Orleans, LA 70127
TEL: 504-246-5672
Purpose: To stress the care and safety of animals in their natural environment.
Contact: Francine Fogelman, Volunteer
Description: Children ages two to five are given an opportunity to develop a good attitude about wildlife, and to learn how to respect animals in their natural habitat. Volunteers in the *Growing Up With Nature Program* of the *Louisiana Nature and Science Center* work with parents to stress the care and safety of animals in terms simple enough for young minds. Children are given a chance to touch the animals, but care is taken to emphasize that the best place for animals in their natural environment where they are not bothered by humans.
The program gives parents the opportunity to support the center while interacting with their children. Often, it is parental presence and encouragement that assures success in programs for children in this age group.
Volunteers develop the monthly topics through brainstorming meetings. They create a lesson based on the most interesting aspects of the plant or animal, focusing on the life-cycle. An appropriate lesson for this parent-child activity is one on mammals that highlights the mother/child relationship.
When parents and children arrive for the program, they work on a craft that reflects the lesson and involves both parent and child. It has been found that making crafts puts young children at ease and gives them something to remember of the program, as well as a sense of the topic.
The program also includes a story time in which books about nature are read, and presentations are made at three other stations that last about ten minutes each dealing with the animals in the day's lesson.
In 1988 the program was awarded a grant to go into the New Orleans public schools to present a modified program for a year in kindergartens and first grades. Just as at the Center, the program in the school is designed to encourage parents to assist the volunteers by lending support and encouragement while the children learn to hold animals without fearing them. According to school authorities, the program fills a void in the curriculum.
Founded: 1981

MARINE MAMMAL STRANDING CENTER
3625 Atlantic Brigantine Blvd
Brigantine, NJ 08203
TEL: 609-266-0538

Purpose: To assist marine mammals which become stranded on the beach; to remove and test hazardous dead animals from the beach, test for cause of death, and share results with other researchers.
Sponsor: State of New Jersey
Contact: Bob or Sheila Schoelkopf, Directors
Description: The Marine Mammal Stranding Center, formally incorporated as a non-profit public service organization in 1984, is the only facility of its kind in New Jersey committed to assisting whales, dolphins, porpoises, seals, and sea turtles which become stranded on the beach as a result of injury, illness or disorientation.
Mammals and sea turtles found alive are taken to the Center for treatment, medication and eventual release to the New Jersey waters. Potentially hazardous dead animals are removed from the beach and tested for cause of death. Samples are taken and provided to other marine mammal researchers.
Until 1988, the Center was a totally volunteer operation. In 1988, the Center received a one-time grant from the State to help offset operating costs. Today the Center operates with the help of its 200 trained volunteers. Since the Center's inception, they have handled over 500 marine mammals and sea turtles. More than half of those animals were members of an endangered species.
Volunteers are called upon to assist in all aspects of the retrieval and rehabilitation process. The initial retrieval of an animal takes about five hours. When the animal is alive, an extensive period of rehabilitation is required before it is ready to be returned to its natural habitat, especially if the mammal is a dolphin or a whale. Constant surveillance is necessary to maintain the stability of the mammal and to keep it from drowning.
During the 1988 dolphin crisis, volunteers worked 20-hour days and averaged 70-hour work weeks. The Center operates 24 hours a day, seven days a week on the New Jersey coastline.
Publications: Volunteering at the Stranding Center
Founded: 1984

MARYLAND HUNTER EDUCATION PROGRAM
Tawes State Office Building
Annapolis , MD 21401
TEL: 301-269-3188
Purpose: To train young and inexperienced hunters in an effort to reduce hunting accidents and make hunters aware of their responsibility while afield.
Sponsor: Department of Natural Resources
Contact: Lt. Thomas R. Turner
Description: The program began in 1966 with the primary responsibility of firearms safety. As time passed, the need for more education concerning hunter responsibility, knowledge of game laws and conservation practices, and skills in use of different methods of hunting became necessary. To that end the program evolved into the present day Hunter Education Program.
The program is funded 25% by funds received from Hunting License sales and 75% by funds received from an excise tax on firearms and archery equipment sales.
The primary goal of the program is still to reduce hunting accidents but a fast growing concern is to instill an attitude of responsibility in each hunter and improve hunter/landowner relationships.
The program became mandatory for all first time hunters before they purchase a hunter's license in 1977. Since then, hunting accidents decreased by more than 60%.
The program is coordinated by the Maryland Natural Resources Police and the classes are taught by 384 volunteers. Each volunteer must complete the course as a student, attend a seven (7) hour training session, assist with a class for on the job training, and is then assigned to a team for certification. Retraining workshops are given annually and each volunteer must attend one session at least every two (2) years.
The program is divided into four (4) regions with a Regional Coordinator responsible for the activity within that region.

Supervision and evaluations are conducted by the State Coordinator, the Regional Coordinator, team leaders, Senior Instructors, and occasionally by other DNR members.
Founded: 1966

MASSACHUSETTS AQUATIC RESOURCE EDUCATION PROGRAM (AREP)
SEE RECREATION & SPORTS: PARKS/FORESTS

PET THERAPY
SEE PSYCHOSOCIAL SUPPORT SERVICES

PETS FOR PEOPLE
SEE RECIPIENTS: OLDER PERSON - PSYCHOSOCIAL SUPPORT

RECYCLING FOR RAVI
SEE PHYSICAL ENVIRONMENT: RECYCLING

REFUGE FOR INJURED WILDLIFE
Davis Nursery
9400 McIntosh Road
Dover, FL 33527
TEL: 813-986-3233
Purpose: To provide a refuge for injured animals until they are well enough to return to their natural habitats.
Sponsor: Florida Freshwater Fish and Game Commission
Contact: Steve or Vivian Davis
Description: Working with the *Companion Animal Hospital* in Thonotosassa, and licensed by the *Florida Freshwater Fish and Game Commission,* a family in Dover saw a need and started a volunteer program to provide food, shelter and care to injured animals brought to them. Residents in the entire community and surrounding area make special efforts to report sightings of injured animals. Although the program works mostly with birds, it has included deer, bobcats and foxes, often babies. There are five holding cages and two flight cages - large enclosures where the birds have an opportunity to move about, the largest made from a converted greenhouse.
The animals go through three or four stages before they are ready to be released, and birds must be moved to larger cages as their ability to fly improves.
The *Companion Animal Hospital* provides volunteer professional services when needed, taking care of wounds that cannot be healed simply by rest and nourishment. The work is not without danger. Volunteers often must wear heavy-duty gloves to bring an immature horned owl out of a case. The 16-week-old owl was found on the ground by a resident who was unable to locate its nest. Residents are told through numerous media that the most important part of the rehabilitation process is to bring in injured animals, or call, as quickly as possible, since they dehydrate quickly. Residents finding animals and volunteers working in the refuge also are warned to use care in approaching the animals, since they can be mean and aggressive, with one incident reported in which the owl chased the volunteer out of the cage. All parties involved are told that they must have as little contact as possible with the charges, because once the animals become too familiar with people, they no longer fear people, which can be dangerous. A supplemental volunteer program has grown out of the refuge. Birds that are permanently injured and not candidates for release are kept and used in visits to schools and churches to teach children about nature.

SEWARD RESCUE CENTER
SEE DISASTER RESPONSE/EMERGENCY PREPAREDNESS

WILDLIFE VOLUNTEERS
Utah Division of Wildlife Resources
1596 West North Temple
Salt Lake City, UT 84116
TEL: 801-538-4700
Purpose: To help preserve Utah's wildlife.
Sponsor: Utah Division of Wildlife Resources
Contact: Bob Walters, Non-Game Biologist
Description: When the *Utah Division of Wildlife Resources* encounters a situation where the Division does not have enough "hands and eyes" to meet an emergency, volunteers come forward and stand watch, perform rescues, carry birds back to their nests, and monitor special activities to report back to the Division. Some volunteers are specialists, such as the "volunteer falcon watchers" who observed a young peregrine falcon - an endangered species - attempting its first flight in downtown Salt Lake City from its nest on the roof of Hotel Utah, but missing its mark and breaking its wing against the building. They summoned the Division of Wildlife Resources director and, since there was another baby falcon in the nest, the director called on citizen volunteers to come forward and surround the building. The second bird was saved by volunteers after it attempted a flight. The first bird was taken to a veterinarian by a volunteer to have a pin put in its wing. This was the fourth straight year that Salt Lake City's pair of endangered Peregrine falcons produced young on the Hotel Utah.
Since 60 to 70 percent of the endangered peregrines die during their first year, this rescue by the volunteers was especially important, according to the Division director.
Most volunteers are ordinary citizens who follow instructions and provide the manpower so often needed for backup and support when wildlife is found in crucial and life-threatening situations. The volunteers are cautioned about the danger when an animal is injured, and given tasks that are controlled and do not put them in jeopardy.

PSYCHOSOCIAL SUPPORT SERVICES

NATIONAL/STATE ORGANIZATIONS

INSTITUTE OF MARRIAGE AND FAMILY RELATIONS
SEE RECIPIENTS: FAMILIES - PSYCHOSOCIAL SUPPORT

NATIONAL ASSOCIATION FOR PARENTS OF THE VISUALLY IMPAIRED
PO Box 180806
Austin, TX 78718
TEL: 512-323-5710
TOLL FREE: 800-225-0227
Objectives: To provide support for family members, and to promote public understanding of the needs and rights of blind and visually handicapped children.
Services: Addresses needs for emotional support of family members of blind and visually impaired children; provides information about care, education, and treatment of the children; establishes networking capabilities among parents and service agencies at local, state and national levels; conducts intermittent workshops for parents; offers computerized lists of camps and agencies serving blind and visually handicapped children, and bibliographies of resources available; publishes quarterly newsletter, a journal, resource guides and other materials.
Publications: Awareness; Take Charge! Resource Guide for Parents; How to Pack 'Em In: Resource Guide for Planning Workshops; Your Child's Information Journal
Founded: 1980

OLDER ADULT OFFENDER PROJECT
SEE EMPLOYMENT: PRISONER/EX-OFFENDER

TRAINING PROGRAMS

BEFRIENDER TRAINING
Amherst Wilder Foundation
919 Lafond
St. Paul, MN 55104
TEL: 612-457-2420
Credit: Inquire
Sponsor: Amherst Wilder Foundation
Contact: Juanita Geisz

Description: The Foundation provides periodic training for volunteers who are interested in providing supportive friendships to those in stressful situations or times of crisis through mutual concern, mutual contact, and a mutual sense of contribution. Training is designed to increase skills in the following areas:
Communication Skills
How to listen
How to encourage feeling messages
How to communicate without being threatening
Crisis Intervention
How to recognize the need for intervention
How to refer someone if it seems advisable
How to help the person get help through referral
To realize that referral is not a sign of weakness
Grief
How to deal with grief in effective ways
To understand that death is not the only loss we suffer
Depression
How to recognize the signs of depression
How to help the person live through the process
Self-Care
To understand the importance of self-care
in order to be able to be a friend to others
To recognize one's own needs in caring for others
Upon completion of training, volunteers are placed in one of a number of areas of Befriender experience, including:
Experiencing loss
Unemployed or economically disadvantaged
Terminally ill
Parent-child problems
Marriage problems
Chemically dependent
Victim of family violence
Abusive person
Divorced (or going through divorce)
Spiritual crisis
Faculty is drawn from the fields represented by the above areas of concern, and the Foundation itself. Befriender Coordinators participate in the training as instructors and observers to provide a stronger link in the Coordinator/Volunteer relationship.

INDIVIDUAL PROGRAM PROFILES

COMMUNITY FRIENDS*
SEE MENTAL HEALTH: RE-ENTRY

COMPANIONSHIP/THERAPY PROGRAM
Madison House
170 Rugby Road
Charlottesville, VA 22903
TEL: 804-977-7051
Purpose: To provide assistance for agencies dealing with mental, physical, or emotional problems.
Sponsor: Madison House
Contact: Jane Parker, Director
Description: Begun in 1969 as the "Mental Health/Companionship Program," this program quickly became the "catch-all" for all programs dealing remotely with "companionship." Volunteers worked at Western State Hospital (the Adoptive Grandparents Program), at the Children's Rehabilitation Center, in the operating room at University Hospital, for the Recording for the Blind service, at the Bloomfield School, and for the Association for Retarded Citizens.
As the program became more and more diverse, separate programs began to emerge. The current program, Companionship/Therapy, recruits volunteers for those agencies dealing with physical, mental and emotional problems only. This program places volunteers in many different settings. They work with a variety of age groups and encounter many different emotional, mental, or physical problems. Recently the program expanded to include citizen advocacy and work with troubled youth in the Community Attention Homes.
Long-term assignments are available at Charlottesville-Albemarle Association for Retarded Citizens, Bloomfield School, Mental Health Activities Center, and others. Agencies needing short-term assistance for a special situation contact the Companion/Therapy Program, and every effort is made to assign a volunteer to the agency. These short-term assignments might include campaigning for the March of Dimes or the Walk for Hunger Program, for example.
All assignments - both short- and long-term - demand volunteers who are willing and enthusiastic about working with people who are frequently unable to initiate social interchange. Volunteers must be independent, willing to work with minimal supervision, and willing to strive to be innovative and committed.
Leaders of the Special Olympics program have found Companion/Therapy volunteers to be especially effective in encouraging handicapped children to compete in the Olympics, helping them get to the events, and waiting for them at the finish line with big smiles and warm hugs.
Founded: 1969

FRIEND TO FRIEND PROGRAM*
Jewish Social Service Agency
6127 Montrose Road
Rockville, MD 20852
TEL: 301-881-3700
Purpose: To provide teenage friends for retarded teenagers.
Sponsor: Jewish Social Service Agency
Contact: Erika Engelman, Volunteer
Description: Fifty volunteers in the Friend to Friend Program spend several hours a week with their handicapped friends. The volunteers have been impressed with the responsibility to which they are committing themselves - entering into a year's contract to develop a friendship with a retarded teenager.
Each handicapped person in the program is matched with a volunteer of about the same age and sex (median age of volunteers is 17 years). The time they spend together is utilized in a variety of ways - learning to bake, going to a museum or to the movies, having a slumber party, playing baseball. In some cases, the

handicapped person has been taking his/her first outing without parents.
Both the prospective volunteer and the family of the retarded child are interviewed carefully in order to achieve the best matching. In many instances, it is necessary to guard against a family's unrealistic expectations of the program, while helping them to key themselves to its real benefits.
The Volunteer Services Coordinator has found that the young volunteers need continuing support and supervision if the relationships are to work out successfully. She maintains telephone contact with the volunteers and the parents of the handicapped young people. At least once a month, she meets or talks by phone at length with individual volunteers.
In addition, group meetings for the volunteers are held bi-monthly, and an educational program is offered; for example, a field trip to a diagnostic clinic of the National Institute of Mental Health was arranged.
The most effective recruitment of volunteers is by word of mouth. Talking to groups of high school students was found to be unsuccessful. It is more difficult to recruit male volunteers, and attempts are being made to interest groups of boys in taking on one handicapped youngster per group. The boys seem to feel more comfortable if the responsibility is shared.
The volunteers look at this opportunity as a serious experience and understand that the time commitment is a necessity. Some of the volunteers continue in the program for a number of years. They see their efforts helping the handicapped young person to improve his/her self-image and make progress toward a more fulfilling life. Many volunteers have expressed interest in majoring in special education or social work after their experiences in the Friend to Friend Program.

GRATERFRIENDS
SEE LAW ENFORCEMENT/CRIME PREVENTION: RE-ENTRY

MAPLEWOOD MANOR RSVP PROGRAM
American Red Cross
Saratoga County Chapter
368 Broadway
Saratoga, NY 12020
TEL: 518-584-2510
Purpose: To provide services for the blind and visually handicapped, while creating volunteer opportunities for residents of a nursing home.
Sponsor: American Red Cross/Saratoga County
Contact: Denise Smith, RSVP Director
Description: When ACTION's Retired Senior Volunteer Program (RSVP) was first introduced in Maplewood Manor in 1984, the response was negligible. Less than 10 residents became involved, mainly because the workload was infrequent and small in volume. Maplewood Manor is a nursing home with 39 resident men and women with an average age of 80. But when the coordinator of volunteers services for the *New York State Library for the Blind and Visually Handicapped* showed an interest in the volunteer program there, the response more than tripled.
All 39 volunteers are in wheelchairs, and many are debilitated with difficult and limited use of their hands and arms. Working to benefit people with sight limitations is especially meaningful because so many of the residents themselves have a variety of disabilities to overcome.
Residents have prepared bulk mailings and placed address labels with the organization's new address on obsolete posters and pamphlets, making them usable again. The materials are sent to community groups, which place them throughout the town. More than 5,000 of the posters and 32 cases of other materials were put up statewide, giving vital information about the state Library for the Blind and Visually Handicapped. For instance, in spite of the library's name, many do not understand that people who wish to

use the library need not be blind. Even people with 20-20 vision can use the facility if they are unable to hold a book or turn pages. A simple matter of changing the address enabled thousands of additional people to use this important facility.

The library coordinator found the library suffering from a shortage of volunteers, since many women who looked for volunteer work while their children were in school are now in the workforce. With more and more agencies seeking volunteer help, the logical step was to look at populations that have not been asked to volunteer before. With the Maplewood experience so positive, the coordinator feels that agencies need to look into how they can accommodate these older groups of volunteers.

The effect of the project on the residents themselves has been very positive and extremely beneficial to their morale and sense of self worth. "They yell at me when I don't bring more work for them," he said.

As a result of their volunteer efforts, the Maplewood Manor volunteers were nominated for a state award.

MILTON CARES TELEPHONE REASSURANCE
Retired Senior Volunteer Program
3 Cathedral Square
Burlington, VT 05401
TEL: 802-862-6444
Purpose: To provide daily contact with homebound elderly, and to provide a social contact for people who are essentially alone.
Sponsor: US/ACTION
Contact: Judith R. Dunlop
Description: Milton Cares is a program of telephone reassurance to the shut-in elderly in the rural town of Milton, Vermont. It was developed following two incidents involving elderly shut-in women who were terrorized in their homes and not discovered for several days.

Townspeople responded to these incidents by developing a telephone reassurance program. A door-to-door survey was conducted by senior residents of Milton, with staff from the Area Agency on Aging, the local Community Action Agency, the Milton Police Department, VISTA Volunteers, and RSVP staff. Seniors living alone were identified and matched with a senior volunteer caller from Milton.

The program operates on a continual basis, identifying seniors needing contact who may be newcomers to the area or for some other reason have not been identified previously. Milton Cares proceeds through several steps to provide the most appropriate response to each situation, including:
- Each day the caller places a call at the agreed time.
- If there is no answer, the volunteer calls again a short time later.
- If no answer on the second try, a call is placed to a designated friend or relative in an attempt to determine the whereabouts of the client.
- If the volunteer is unable to obtain assurance of the client's wellbeing, the police are notified.

The Police Department maintains an up-to-date list of clients and callers, and makes an immediate check of the house when notified. In addition, each caller receives a set of instructions, background about the client, monthly reporting form, and reminder card. Results to date include:
- updated list of seniors living alone and in need of daily phone contact;
- thirty seniors are being contacted daily by senior volunteers from their community;
- a waiting list of prospective clients is being matched daily with callers;
- training for callers has been developed and is provided to all volunteers;
- a volunteer coordinator has been designated to keep track of the callers' efforts, process new requests, and place two volunteer coordinators to do home visits prior to enrollment.

The Milton Cares program has served as an example of neighbor helping neighbor. It has allowed citizens to help themselves to remain in their homes alone, to form new friendships, and to have the opportunity to be drawn into senior activities through their volunteer callers.

PET THERAPY
Little Rock Animal Control
3800 South Chester
Little Rock, AR 72206
TEL: 501-376-3067
Purpose: To help provide a familiar environment to residents who are sick, lonely, or handicapped; to boost the emotions of those depressed and withdrawn.
Sponsor: Little Rock Animal Control
Contact: Anne C. Thompson
Description: Pet Therapy is the study and practice of using animals with the elderly, sick, lonely, or handicapped in nursing homes, day care centers, and other institutions.

Little Rock Animal Control began it's Pet Therapy program April 1982. The agency utilizes stray or owner-surrendered pets. All animals are conditioned for 30 days before going to the nursing home. Volunteers meet Animal Control Officers at the nursing home to visit residents for one hour each week. All animals are prepared and kept at the shelter.

There are currently 24 Pet Therapy puppies in the program. The program is operated with tax revenues.

The major goals of Pet Therapy are to provide residents with a sense of self esteem, physical exercise, an outlet for emotions and a feeling of being needed and wanted, and to see withdrawn and depressed residents communicate with the volunteers. According to a recent survey of nursing home administrators, these goals have been accomplished.

The volunteers encourage conversation with residents as well as show pets. There are currently 43 active volunteers and about 20 temporary inactive volunteers. The volunteers from the community currently visit eight nursing homes once a week and a Child Study Center. These volunteers are supervised by a trained Animal Control officer.

The program requires no special training. However, volunteers must be able to communicate well, have a good attitude toward working with animals and be sensitive to the needs of the elderly.
Founded: 1982

PROJECT PASSAGE
Columbus Developmental Center
Ohio State Hospital
1601 West Broad Street
Columbus, OH 43223
TEL: 614-272-0509
Purpose: To pair bright but troubled students with mentally retarded adults for mutual benefit.
Sponsor: Columbus Developmental Center
Contact: Joy Rogers, President
Description: Since 1982, students from Columbus schools have been volunteering at the *Columbus Developmental Center,* a facility for mentally retarded adults. Sponsored by *Project Passage,* the program pairs bright but troubled students with residents of the Center. The goal is a mutually beneficial relationship that will help raise the student's self-esteem, while providing a friend for the retarded adult.

The 278 residents at the Center function at the 6-month to 18-month age level. Not only do the young volunteers deal with that very well, but many have seen their grades raised significantly during the 16-week or longer experience. The young volunteers play ball with the residents, feed them dinner, or just chat with them and be a friend. In this way they are taking responsibility for another person's leisure time, and this feeling of helpfulness carries over into the classroom.

Besides feeling needed and learning to care about others, the students are taught skills in working with the mentally retarded. They are shown by occupational therapists how to help the patients identify things around them - placing a patient's hand in a bucket of sand and moving it in circles, or rubbing baby powder on a patient's neck, with the therapist suggesting the added help of letting the patient smell the powder. As one 13-year-old volunteer put it, "My grades are better, and I'm acting better. I really like to work with the residents. They need our help and we need theirs, too."
Founded: 1982

RE-ENTRY MINISTRIES
SEE LAW ENFORCEMENT/CRIME PREVENTION: RE-ENTRY

RSVP OF NEW CASTLE COUNTY
Hudson State Service Center
501 Ogletown Road
Newark, DE 19711
TEL: 302-368-6874
Purpose: To enable people 60 years of age or older to volunteer.
Sponsor: Delaware Department of Community Affairs
Contact: Marion Seibold
Description: RSVP (Retired Senior Volunteer Program) of New Castle County, Delaware, has over 1,000 active members who serve at over 125 different sites, contributing over 240,000 hours of service to the community each year.
RSVP has been a resource in New Castle County since 1973. One of its unique services is transportation - we provide transportation for nearly 70 seniors each week, to and from their volunteer assignments, with the help of paid and volunteer drivers, and provide mileage reimbursements for nearly 400 members.
While the vast majority of our members serve outside their homes at agencies and organizations, we also try to develop opportunities for homebound seniors to volunteer. About 40 volunteers knit all year long: in December, they donate more than 1,500 items to a dozen different agencies for distribution to needy families. Our five mail groups process over 200,000 items each year for about 25 non-profits.
We have also developed some innovative projects for frail elderly residents of nursing homes, linking them with non-profits that need their expertise.

THE SAMARITANS
Suicide Prevention Hotline
PO Box 9814
Washington, DC 20016
TEL: 202-362-8100
Purpose: To befriend the suicidal, lonely, and despairing.
Sponsor: Samaritans USA; Befrienders International Samaritans Worldwide
Contact: Ellen Kennedy
Description: The Samaritans is a 24-hour, seven-day suicide prevention hotline staffed by carefully-selected and trained nonprofessional volunteers. Professional consultants assist the volunteers. The Samaritans offer *befriending* rather than counseling. This concept is based on the premise that, except in medical emergencies, the most urgent need for most people in a suicidal crisis is for someone to talk to. The Samaritan volunteer, by listening with understanding and concern, seeks to establish an equal-level relationship that can help restore self-esteem and hope. Referrals to professional help are made as necessary.
Volunteers are of all ages, from age 19, and all backgrounds. No special experience or special education is required. A volunteer must be able to listen without making judgements or giving unwanted advice to establish equal-level relationships, and to show caring.
Training classes are held often, either on Saturdays or weeknights

(with weekday classes held only when enough trainees are available). Eighteen hours of training prepares volunteers to respond to calls involving suicide, depression, grief and loss, sexual problems, alcoholism, drug abuse, and medical emergencies. Maximum time is one five-hour shift per week, and one overnight (11:00p.m. to 8:00a.m.) each month, and a commitment of at least six months.
In-service education is offered throughout the year. Supervision is by the Director and experienced Samaritan volunteers, with help and back-up from professional consultants. Following training, volunteers may engage in other activities of the Center, such as the speakers' bureau, fund raising, updating referrals, and publicity. Although the Samaritans respond to any kind of problem, the primary purpose is to respond to those desperate enough to consider suicide. About 35% of the callers mention suicide at the first contact. However, the call itself, and even a suicide threat or attempt are considered a cry for help. The volunteer can help give the suicidal person strength to survive the crisis. As one caller stated, "I still think about suicide, but as long as I can keep calling you when I get to feeling overwhelmed, I think I can keep going." Another caller said, "Now that I understand better, I have some ideas to try."
The service is free and completely confidential. Samaritans do not trace calls, nor take action without the caller's permission.
As a suicide prevention service, *The Samaritans* serve as a resource for professional students and community groups, providing talks and workshops on request.
Publications: Samaritans: Suicide Prevention Hotline

SAN FRANCISCO PEER RESOURCE PROGRAMS
1950 Mission Street, Room 7
San Francisco, CA 94103
TEL: 415-626-1942
Purpose: To meet needs of some students that can be done best through one-to-one peer involvement.
Sponsor: San Francisco Education Fund
Contact: Ira Sachnoff
Description: In 1980, *Galileo High School* initiated its first *Peer Resource Program*. The purpose of the program is to meet a need on a one-to-one basis for attention for some students. Student volunteers are selected to be trained as counselors for their peers. They are trained during regular school hours in decision making and other skills, including self-awareness. Sponsors are the *San Francisco United School District* and the *San Francisco Education Fund*. Some of the specific programs are:
- **Buddy/Friendship Project** - a matching program bringing together upper classmen with new students to help with the transition process. Students help their "buddies" with school work and personal issues, as well as teaching them survival skills. This program is not limited to new students, but is open to any student in the school on request.
- **Peer Tutors** - a program in which students are trained by adults and then do all of the tutoring. Students are selected based on their academic expertise and their willingness to serve in this capacity and to be trained. The tutors help over 7,000 students each year.
- **Peer Counseling Program** - a system designed to keep the schools as crisis-free as possible, with volunteer students working with peers in areas such as drug abuse and alcohol abuse, child abuse, suicide, violence, etc. The student/counselors reach almost 7,000 students each year.
- **Violence Prevention Program** - a program that uses the "peer resource philosophy" as its base: "Everyone has resources to help each other." Activities include the *ESL Rap Group*, which gives immigrant students a comfortable place to practice their English and become accustomed to their new culture. Volunteer students also make classroom presentations, thus serving as educators against violence.
Founded: 1980

SPECIAL SATURDAY
SEE RECREATION & SPORTS: CHILDREN/YOUTH

VAN MINISTRY
SEE LAW ENFORCEMENT/CRIME PREVENTION:
FAMILIES

PSYCHOSOCIAL SUPPORT SERVICES: AIDS

INDIVIDUAL PROGRAM PROFILES

AIDS PROJECT: FRIENDLY VISITORS
SEE AIDS: PSYCHOSOCIAL SUPPORT

MOTHERS OF PWAS (PERSONS WITH AIDS)
SEE AIDS: PSYCHOSOCIAL SUPPORT

SHANTI PROJECT
SEE AIDS: PSYCHOSOCIAL SUPPORT

SUPPORT SERVICES - AIDS PROGRAM
SEE AIDS: PSYCHOSOCIAL SUPPORT

PSYCHOSOCIAL SUPPORT SERVICES: CHILDREN/YOUTH

NATIONAL/STATE ORGANIZATIONS

BIG BROTHERS/BIG SISTERS OF AMERICA
SEE RECIPIENTS: CHILDREN/YOUTH - PSYCHOSOCIAL
SUPPORT

MAKE-A-WISH FOUNDATION OF AMERICA
SEE HEALTH: CHILDREN/YOUTH

SKY RANCH FOR BOYS
Sky Ranch, SD 57724
TEL: 605-797-4422
Objectives: To provide a secure setting conducive to improving
self-image and learning skills of boys ages 10 to 18.
Services: Operates a ranch in a home-like setting to facilitate
rehabilitation of boys at risk and in trouble; includes special
education facilities for learning disabled, socially maladjusted, and
behaviorally disordered boys; publishes a newsletter and a
descriptive brochure.
Publications: Sky Ranch Log
Founded: 1960

YOUTH DEVELOPMENT
4575 Ruffner Street
San Diego, CA 92111
TEL: 619-292-5683; 800-HIT-HOME (California)
TOLL FREE: 800-MISS-YOU (nationwide)
Objectives: To provide both outreach programs and services for
abandoned, neglected, or abused youngsters.

Services: Conducts Christmas outreach program which provides
clothing, food, and letters of encouragement to children in local
shelters and detention centers; provides opportunities for these
youngsters to experience productive living within the community
and family environment; maintains listings of shelters throughout
the country; operates a telephone hotline which provides
counseling and referrals to shelters for runaways nationwide;
works with the *National Network of Runaway and Youth
Services;* publishes a newsletter and other materials.
Sponsor: National Network of Runaway and Youth Services
Publications: Home Run Quarterly Review
Founded: 1959

TRAINING PROGRAMS

GET AWAY CLEAN
Carkhuff Institute of Human Technology
1376 Kirby Road
McLean, VA 22101
TEL: 301-899-6564 (MD)
Credit: College Credit
Sponsor: Carkhuff Institute of Human Technology
Contact: George Logan-El
Description: Get Away Clean is a course at the Alexandria
campus of Northern Virginia Community College. This training
program is designed to help teens and pre-teens deal with negative
peer pressure, and go on to serve as a support group for others
affected by such pressure. In addition, students in the class are
trained to be trainers of other teens and younger students in the
skills that they have learned at the college. In spite of the young
ages of students, they are given college credit for participating in
the class.
The course was developed by the *Carkhuff Institute of Human
Technology* in response to a group of students who identified peer
pressure as the number one problem facing them. Training is
divided into three levels:
- **Survival** - At the survival level, students explore different
responses to negative peer pressure and compare the
consequences of responding positively as opposed to
negatively.
- **Relating** - At the relating level, students practice
communication skills and different ways to relate to adults,
children and peers.
- **Growth** - At the growth level, students learn the nurturing of
moral skills so that they can facilitate other students'
self-exploration.
The junior and senior high students work with elementary students
to teach them the survival and helping skills necessary to turn
negative peer pressure into positive. The older students also help
school counselors run workshops for younger students four times a
week at different recreation centers. Students enact real-life
situations involving peer pressure to use drugs, shoplift, skip
school, etc.
Students who have experienced the results of negative peer
pressure themselves - drug abuse, poor academic or discipline
records - are not excluded from the program. The results hoped
for in these cases became a reality when the troubled students
related how much the course had helped them. One stated,
"Before I got involved, I was out of touch with people... when we
interact with others, we learn so much from each other."

INDIVIDUAL PROGRAM PROFILES

BIG BROTHERS/BIG SISTERS OF NASSAU COUNTY*
SEE RECIPIENTS: CHILDREN/YOUTH - PSYCHOSOCIAL
SUPPORT

BIG BROTHERS/BIG SISTERS PROGRAM
SEE RECIPIENTS: CHILDREN/YOUTH - PSYCHOSOCIAL SUPPORT

BIG BROTHERS/BIG SISTERS PROGRAM-CHILD PSYCHIATRY*
SEE RECIPIENTS: CHILDREN/YOUTH - PSYCHOSOCIAL SUPPORT

COMPANIONS OF ALAMEDA COUNTY
SEE RECIPIENTS: CHILDREN/YOUTH - PSYCHOSOCIAL SUPPORT

SNAP (STUDENTS NEED A PAT)
SEE EDUCATION: CURRICULUM ENRICHMENT

SURRY COUNTY FRIENDS OF YOUTH/BEST FRIENDS PROGRAM
SEE RECIPIENTS: CHILDREN/YOUTH - PSYCHOSOCIAL SUPPORT

TEENAGE VOLUNTEERS WORKING IN ADOLESCENT PROGRAM*
SEE MENTAL HEALTH: CHILDREN/YOUTH

THANKS (THOUGHTFUL, HELPING ADULTS N' KIDS SHARING)
SEE RECIPIENTS: CHILDREN/YOUTH - PSYCHOSOCIAL SUPPORT

VOLUNTEERS FOR YOUTH
SEE RECIPIENTS: CHILDREN/YOUTH - PSYCHOSOCIAL SUPPORT

WRITECONNECTION PROGRAM: LOVE A CHILD BY MAIL
Positive Parenting
2635 East Indian School Road
Suite 400
Phoenix, AZ 85016
TEL: 602-956-0070
TOLL FREE: 800-334-3143
Purpose: To maintain writing programs with one's own children, or a little brother or sister.
Sponsor: US/DoD - Office of the Navy Chaplain
Contact: Program Coordinator
Description: A nonprofit program in Phoenix, Arizona, *Positive Parenting,* has developed a program for married and single sailors to begin and maintain a weekly writing program with his or her own children and/or a little brother or sister.
Several Navy chaplains have worked with *Positive Parenting* in achieving effective results when encouraging and training sailors to communicate with family members on a frequent and regular basis. In the *WriteConnection Program,* the sailor is offered a starter kit at a specially-set price for the military, with refills made available when needed. The kit includes:
● colorful stationery for letters;
● monthly calendars to mark special dates;
● return mailers for the child to send back;
● "quick mailers" to show the child you're thinking of him or her;
● activity projects to share with the child through the mail;
● correspondence chart to track what has been sent, and when it was sent; and
● a binder to help organize and store all materials.
Several aircraft carriers have begun stocking the kits in their ship stores. To help reduce costs, *Positive Parenting* encourages joint

purchases by the sailors through the ship's or other officers. The packages are offered in conjunction with continuous encouragement and training programs developed with the assistance of the Navy Chaplain's Office, and they have proven to be especially successful in the primary goal of the program - to brighten the lives of children. In doing so, they have also given pleasure and meaning to the sailors involved.
Founded: 1990

PSYCHOSOCIAL SUPPORT SERVICES: DISASTER

INDIVIDUAL PROGRAM PROFILES

DISASTER PROFESSIONAL VOLUNTEER NETWORK
SEE DISASTER RESPONSE/EMERGENCY PREPAREDNESS

PSYCHOSOCIAL SUPPORT SERVICES: EMPLOYEES

NATIONAL/STATE ORGANIZATIONS

EMPLOYEE ASSISTANCE PROGRAM CONSORTIUM
Lincoln Center Building
Lincoln, NE 68508
TEL: 402-476-0186
Objectives: To provide free professional counseling for troubled workers and their dependents.
Services: Addresses any personal problems that affect job performance; helps employees to help themselves through the use of professional counselors, psychologists, psychiatric social workers, doctors, and attorneys; covers wide range of problems from marital discord to compulsive habits such as gambling, overeating, and drinking; works as coordinating EAP for several companies and a public school system.

EMPLOYEE ASSISTANCE SOCIETY OF NORTH AMERICA
PO Box 3909
Oak Park, IL 60303
TEL: 312-383-6668
Objectives: To assist managers of employee assistance counseling programs.
Services: Serves as a network for employee assistance programs (EAPs) nationwide; works with individuals in the field of employee assistance, including psychiatrists, psychologists, and managers; facilitates communication among these groups; maintains a file of resumes of employee assistance professionals; conducts research and shares its findings among EAPs; maintains committees on credentialing, ethics, regional affairs and research; publishes a newsletter and a membership list; bring EAP leaders together annually to share experiences and ideas.
Publications: The Source; Who's Who Directory
Founded: 1984

TRAINING PROGRAMS

EMPLOYEE ASSISTANCE PROGRAMS
Chamber of Commerce
801 North Fairfax Street
Alexandria, VA 22314
TEL: 703-549-1000
Credit: None
Sponsor: Alexandria Chamber of Commerce
Contact: Brenda Hunt, Chairman, Health Care Committee
Description: This forum focused on services available to
employees, usually through programs that have come to be known
as EAPs (Employee Assistance Programs). It defined an EAP as a
program designed to provide employees with short-term counseling
for problems with family, finances, substance abuse, and jobs.
EAPs also serve as referral services - especially if the problem in
question requires specialized care, connecting employees to
specialists. When this becomes necessary, the company's insurance
usually picks up the tab.
During the course of the forum, the following conclusions,
opinions, and facts surfaced based on the experiences of the
presenters:

- The average company saves five dollars for every dollar they
  invest in an EAP.
- A company's bottom line is affected by the health and
  happiness of its workers.
- Up until a few years ago, most personal problems were
  ignored by employers until performance plunged so low that
  drastic action - usually dismissal - had to be taken.
- Managers are starting to realize that good workers are their
  most important resource.
- With an EAP, employers gain an ally in dealing with
  employees who are often absent or tardy - confidential
  counseling instead of the "pink slip."
- Businesses who subscribe to EAPs find that employees are
  making less use of sick leave and are taking less time off.
- Employers are holding on to valuable workers who otherwise
  might lose their jobs.
- It's a lot cheaper to rehabilitate someone than to hire and
  train a new worker.
- Despite the claimed advantages of EAPs, health experts
  concede that the idea has not yet caught on in the overall
  business community.
- EAPs have been used mostly by big companies, and are just
  now starting to trickle down.
- A drawback of EAPs is that some employees are reluctant to
  divulge personal information to anyone "being paid by the
  boss."
- EAP staff must be sure that any information given to
  employers must first be approved by the employee.

Among attendees was the director of AHEAD (Alexandria Health
Employee Assistance Division), the assistance program of the
Alexandria, Virginia, Community Services Board; a personnel
administration and benefits service manager from a small northern
Virginia community; a spokesman for an Atlanta-based health care
and payroll management firm, and an outpatient coordinator of an
addiction-treatment center in a small city. It was determined that
the cost to the company to provide the program is $10 to $15 per
employee.

PSYCHOSOCIAL SUPPORT SERVICES: FAMILIES

NATIONAL/STATE ORGANIZATIONS

FAMILY SERVICE AMERICA
SEE RECIPIENTS: FAMILIES - PSYCHOSOCIAL SUPPORT

**NATIONAL SUPPORT CENTER FOR FAMILIES OF THE
AGING**
PO Box 245
Swarthmore, PA 19081
TEL: 215-544-3605
Objectives: To provide support and assistance for family members
responsible for older persons.
Services: Seeks to educate the public about the realities of
providing care for the aged; encourages formation of support
groups to create a self-help network; assists families with
decision-making in difficult situations; provides training for leaders
in the field of aging; provides support, encouragement, and
assistance to family members responsible for the care of an elderly
person; provides speakers on request to community groups.
Founded: 1981

INDIVIDUAL PROGRAM PROFILES

ADOPT-A-FAMILY
SEE RECIPIENTS: FAMILIES - PSYCHOSOCIAL SUPPORT

CHILD AND FAMILY SERVICES OF KNOX COUNTY
SEE RECIPIENTS: FAMILIES - PSYCHOSOCIAL SUPPORT

ECO
SEE LAW ENFORCEMENT/CRIME PREVENTION:
OFFENDERS

FAMILY SUPPORT GROUP
SEE LAW ENFORCEMENT/CRIME PREVENTION:
VICTIMS

ROSES FOR FALLEN FATHERS
SEE RECIPIENTS: MILITARY - ACTIVE/VETERANS

**VOLUNTEER COUNSELING SERVICE OF ROCKLAND
COUNTY**
151 South Main Street
New City, NY 10956
TEL: 914-634-5729
Purpose: To assist individuals and families with behavioral
problems and emotional distress on a non-profit basis.
Sponsor: State and County governments; corporate and private
donations
Contact: Stephen Shapiro, Ph.D., Executive Director
Description: Volunteer Counseling Service, established 13 years
ago, is an innovative agency which trains lay volunteers from the
community to provide a variety of counseling services to
individuals and families in trouble. VCS programs include
Individual, Couple and Family Counseling, Parent/Adolescent
Center, Post-Divorce Parenting Program, Domestic Violence
Project and the Volunteer Mediation Center. Funds are received
from State and County governments, corporate and private
donations, and fees from clients, which are based on sliding scale.
In a typical year more than 4,500 people are served through

counseling, educational workshops, mediation and community education.

Volunteers are selected through a system of three separate screening interviews, and are chosen on the basis of maturity, intelligence, flexibility, emotional health and ability to tolerate stress. There are no particular educational criteria, but nearly all the volunteers have a college degree, are attending college or are actively planning to pursue their education.

Applicants who pass the first two screening interviews attend a twelve-session, 24-hour basic training cycle which introduces the basic counseling model, group process, domestic violence philosophy and community resources. Training is conducted by the VCS program staff and other community professionals.

Volunteers who complete the training are given a third screening interview to evaluate their readiness to begin working with clients. If they are deemed suitable, they are asked to sign a contract committing themselves to give six to eight hours of service per week to the agency for a period of eighteen months. Upon signing the contract, they are assigned to work with a supervisor and cases are given to them.

Their hours of service may be given in various ways. Some volunteers do individual, couple or family counseling. Other volunteers are group leaders, mediators or community educators. Some combine several of these tasks. All counselors are also required to attend individual supervision and ongoing training, each for one hour weekly, and must do so for as long as they remain with the agency. VCS currently has 125 volunteer counselors, group leaders. mediators and community educators. Another group of volunteers is the supervisors. More than 60 mental health professionals from the community (psychiatrists, psychologists, social workers) donate an hour a week to VCS for the supervision of counselors.

VCS also has about five office volunteers who help with public relations, the newsletters, answering phones, gathering statistics and general office work.

Founded: 1967

WEDNESDAY MORNING MOTHERS
SEE RECIPIENTS: FAMILIES - PSYCHOSOCIAL SUPPORT

PSYCHOSOCIAL SUPPORT SERVICES: HANDICAPPED

NATIONAL/STATE ORGANIZATIONS

FOSTER GRANDPARENT PROGRAM (FGP)
SEE RECIPIENTS: HANDICAPPED - PSYCHOSOCIAL SUPPORT

INDIVIDUAL PROGRAM PROFILES

OPERATION GOOD NEIGHBOR
SEE MENTAL HEALTH: FOSTER CARE

A PERFECT MATCH
SEE RECIPIENTS: HANDICAPPED - PSYCHOSOCIAL SUPPORT

PET THERAPY
SEE PSYCHOSOCIAL SUPPORT SERVICES

THERAPY ON HORSEBACK*
SEE RECIPIENTS: HANDICAPPED - RECREATION/SPORTS

PSYCHOSOCIAL SUPPORT SERVICES: HEALTH

INDIVIDUAL PROGRAM PROFILES

CUYAHOGA FALLS CANCER CLUB
SEE HEALTH: CANCER

MENDED HEARTS
SEE HEALTH: HEART DISEASE

PSYCHOSOCIAL SUPPORT SERVICES: HOMEBOUND

INDIVIDUAL PROGRAM PROFILES

VISITING FRIENDS*
SEE HEALTH: HOMEBOUND

PSYCHOSOCIAL SUPPORT SERVICES: I&R

NATIONAL/STATE ORGANIZATIONS

THE SAMARITANS USA
c/o Samaritans Hotline
PO Box 9814
Washington, DC 20016
TEL: 202-362-8100
Samaritans Branches:
- Boston, MA - 617-247-0220
- Cape Cod, MA - 508-548-8900
- Rhode Island - 401-272-4044
- Merrimack Valley, MA - 508-688-6607
- Keene, NH - 603-357-5505
- South Middlesex, MA - 508-875-4500
- Fall River/New Bedford, MA - 508-636-6111
- New York, NY - 212-673-3000
- Hartford, CT (Capital Region) - 203-232-2121
- Albany, NY (Capital District) - 518-463-2323
- Washington, DC - 202-362-8100
- North Central NH - 603-644-2525

Objectives: To befriend the suicidal, lonely, and despairing.
Services: Serves as the national council to oversee Samaritans branches across the U.S.; assists all U.S. branches in their 24-hour suicide prevention hotline service; provides training and supervision assistance through materials and on-site visits; helps to set up new branches; affiliated with *Befrienders International Samaritans Worldwide;* works with the *International Association*

of Suicide Prevention; publishes quarterly newsletter, and other materials. [*Befrienders International Samaritans Worldwide* is an international volunteer suicide prevention service founded in England in 1953. There are Samaritan branches in 33 countries around the world.]
Sponsor: Befrienders International Samaritans Worldwide
Contact: Ellen Kennedy
Publications: The Samaritans: Suicide Prevention Hotline; Answers to Suicide
Founded: 1974

INDIVIDUAL PROGRAM PROFILES

SAMARITANS
500 Commonwealth Avenue
Kenmore Square
Boston, MA 02215
TEL: 617-247-0220
Purpose: To befriend the suicidal, the despairing and the lonely.
Sponsor: Samaritans USA
Contact: Shirley Karnovsky, Executive Director
Description: The Samaritans of Boston is one of seven 24-hour suicide-prevention hotlines in the northeast region of the U.S. Along with hotlines in other regions, it receives technical and other assistance from *The Samaritans USA* and on a wider scale from *Befrienders International Samaritans Worldwide,* the international organization.
The program consists solely of volunteers who give their time to befriend the suicidal, the despairing and the lonely. The 24-hour hotline provides walk-in service for suicidal and depressed people. An offshoot of the program is *Lifeline,* a suicide intervention program, in Boston area jails. *The Samaritans* develops a team of trained inmates to spot and befriend potential suicides in jails. To involve and work with the community, the program provides an average of 100 talks and training workshops each year for professionals and lay people on suicide prevention, and provides materials on the subject on request.
Founded: 1974

PSYCHOSOCIAL SUPPORT SERVICES: MILITARY

NATIONAL/STATE ORGANIZATIONS

MILITARY EDUCATORS AND COUNSELORS ASSOCIATION
c/o Roger G. Goldberg
2675 Tambridge Circle
Pensacola, FL 32503
TEL: 904-438-7057
Objectives: To provide counseling and guidance to both active and veteran members and employees of the armed forces and their dependents.
Services: Works with professional counselors who work in and for the U.S. Department of Defense; encourages and provides guidance to individuals in the service and their dependents, veterans, and civilians employed by the military; provides services similar to those of employers in their employee assistance programs (EAPs), with a goal of enhancing individual growth and development; conducts research on the subject and shares its findings with counselors; publishes a newsletter and a directory of members.

Sponsor: American Association of Counseling & Development
Publications: MECA Newsletter; Directory of Members
Founded: 1978

INDIVIDUAL PROGRAM PROFILES

VETERANS COUNSELING AND GUIDANCE CENTER
SEE RECIPIENTS: MILITARY - ACTIVE/VETERANS

PSYCHOSOCIAL SUPPORT SERVICES: OLDER PERSON

NATIONAL/STATE ORGANIZATIONS

SENIOR COMPANION PROGRAM (SCP)
SEE RECIPIENTS: OLDER PERSON - PSYCHOSOCIAL SUPPORT

VOLUNTEER SERVICE CORPS COMMITTEE
SEE RECIPIENTS: OLDER PERSON - NURSING HOMES

TRAINING PROGRAMS

TAKING A TRIP TO FRIENDSHIP
SEE RECIPIENTS: OLDER PERSON - PSYCHOSOCIAL SUPPORT

INDIVIDUAL PROGRAM PROFILES

BASKET OF JOY CAMPAIGN
SEE RECIPIENTS: OLDER PERSON - PSYCHOSOCIAL SUPPORT

HOME LEAGUE
Salvation Army
200 Jefferson Highway
New Orleans, LA 70119
TEL: 504-835-1781
Purpose: To provide volunteer opportunities in a social setting for retirees, widows and others who feel a need for companionship.
Sponsor: Salvation Army
Contact: Mrs. Capt. Linda Adair, Coordinator
Description: Two nights a week different groups of retirees, widows and others come together to socialize and to make gifts for shut-ins and children's homes. The program, *Home League,* was started to fill the need for companionship among this group, but soon became a busy activity for volunteer work. They begin in midsummer to dress dolls for the children's home, and begin preparation for other Christmas projects. In the meantime, most participate also in the *League of Mercy* when time permits. This is a visitation project, offering companionship and home-made gifts to residents of hospitals, nursing homes and other institutions on a monthly basis. On holidays, the group visits the Veteran's Hospital, and takes gifts to prison inmates.
The best part of the program, according to the director, is the reciprocal nature of it. The volunteers get as much as they give, since many of them would be isolated themselves except for the Salvation Army programs. One widow, distraught and lonely,

accompanied a friend to the *Home League* several years ago, and has volunteered with the group ever since. "This place saved my life... and these people saved my sanity," she said.

HOST (HANDS OF SHARED TIME)
SEE RECIPIENTS: OLDER PERSON - NURSING HOMES

LINCOLN COUNTY SENIOR COMPANION PROGRAM
SEE RECIPIENTS: OLDER PERSON - PSYCHOSOCIAL SUPPORT

NEW HAMPSHIRE FOSTER GRANDPARENT PROGRAM
SEE RECIPIENTS: HANDICAPPED - CHILDREN/YOUTH

NURSING HOME PROJECT
SEE RECIPIENTS: OLDER PERSON - NURSING HOMES

PARTNERS IN CARING
SEE RECIPIENTS: OLDER PERSON - NURSING HOMES

A PERFECT MATCH
SEE RECIPIENTS: HANDICAPPED - PSYCHOSOCIAL SUPPORT

PETS FOR PEOPLE
SEE RECIPIENTS: OLDER PERSON - PSYCHOSOCIAL SUPPORT

RYANS' NURSING HOME VOLUNTEER PROGRAM
SEE RECIPIENTS: OLDER PERSON - NURSING HOMES

SOS (SERVE OUR SENIORS) STUDENT VOLUNTEER PROGRAM
Highland Park High School
435 Mansfield Street
Highland Park, NJ 08904
TEL: 201-572-2400
FAX: 201-572-5502
Purpose: To provide services and companionship to senior citizens in the Highland Park area.
Contact: John Gallino
Description: During the 1989-90 school year, *Highland Park High School's* student congress discussed needs in the community to determine any gaps that might be filled by the school's teenagers. They learned that many senior citizens in the area would benefit from their assistance not only for chores, but for socialization. To begin the program, contacts were made with a number of people, and some unique relationships were established between the young and the old of our town.
Students in grades nine through twelve are asked to volunteer time to work with senior citizens of the community in the following areas: shopping, house cleaning, running errands, reading to them, or just being a friend. Over 40 of the school's 450 students volunteered their services. The student congress and school officials were pleased that this first effort recruited almost 10% of the student body.
Many of the students who came to know senior citizens on a personal basis said they found it rewarding. Our hope for the future is to expand the program to involve even more teenagers and senior citizens.

ST. JOSEPH COMMUNITY SERVICES
SEE NUTRITION: DELIVERY

VISITS THROUGH VIDEO
SEE RECIPIENTS: OLDER PERSON - PSYCHOSOCIAL SUPPORT

WILLING WORKERS OF COLLEGE HILL
SEE RECIPIENTS: OLDER PERSON - HOMEBOUND

PSYCHOSOCIAL SUPPORT SERVICES: PARENTS

INDIVIDUAL PROGRAM PROFILES

PARENT-CHILD PROGRAM*
SEE TEENAGE PREGNANCY/PARENTING

PARENTAL STRESS CENTER
SEE TEENAGE PREGNANCY/PARENTING

PSYCHOSOCIAL SUPPORT SERVICES: PEERS

NATIONAL/STATE ORGANIZATIONS

NATIONAL PEER HELPERS ASSOCIATION
2370 Market Street #120
San Francisco, CA 94114
TEL: 415-626-1942
Objectives: To address the success of "peer pressure" and turn it to the benefit of individuals with problems through peer counseling.
Services: Encourages the establishment of peer-counseling programs in schools, universities, and community-based organizations; works to establish a standard of ethics for the field; conducts community education programs; provides information, support, and training to peer counselors; conducts research and compiles statistics for distribution; publishes a quarterly journal.
Publications: Peer Facilitator's Quarterly
Founded: 1986

INDIVIDUAL PROGRAM PROFILES

THE GATEHOUSE: THE COOK/DOUGLASS PEER COUNSELING CENTER
Douglass College
DPO J
New Brunswick, NJ 08903
TEL: 201-846-3579 (Gatehouse); 201-932-9069 (Psych Svcs)
Purpose: To provide a one-to-one peer counseling relationship for the students on campus.
Sponsor: Psychological Services and Student Life
Contact: Director
Description: The Gatehouse is a student-run peer counseling organization which serves the Cook/Douglass community. The program began in 1976 when the students on campus, along with Psychological Services, decided that a peer counseling service was needed. Since then, the program has grown into a large organization with approximately 75 student volunteers, open five nights a week, and providing a 1:1 peer relationship for those who need the services.
Most business decisions are decided upon by the Executive Committee, composed of four members. Many of these decisions also are discussed at monthly general meetings with the total

membership. There are many other levels of involvement which require different forms of training.

To become a peer counselor at the Gatehouse, volunteers must complete 30 hours of training. The training program is facilitated by previously trained students with the help of two trained professionals. Training is based on Rogerian psychology. During training sessions, topics such as the following are discussed:

- values clarification
- paraphrasing
- reflection of feelings
- listening skills
- crisis intervention
- referrals

After training is completed, students are required to attend one two-and-a-half-hour shift a week. The shifts are led by a supervisor who helps to establish group cohesiveness. Members who want to become shift supervisors are required to complete a two-day training session.

Shifts serve a double purpose. They are also an extension of the original training program. When "shiftees" are not counseling either on the phone or with a "drop-in," they are participating in exercises which help them to develop their skills.

The organization also runs programs for the college population. They include:

- a nutrition and weight control workshop
- a stress workshop
- a program for freshmen on how to adjust to college life

In addition, the organization is involved in various other community activities. Other ways that volunteers get involved in the organization is through a publicity committee, a communications committee, and a committee on workshops. Funding comes from both Douglass and Cook Colleges as well as fundraisers held by the organization itself.
Founded: 1976

PEER COUNSELOR PROGRAM*
SEE RECIPIENTS: OLDER PERSON - PSYCHOSOCIAL SUPPORT

PSYCHOSOCIAL SUPPORT SERVICES: PET THERAPY

NATIONAL/STATE ORGANIZATIONS

DELTA SOCIETY
SEE PHYSICAL ENVIRONMENT: WILDLIFE/PETS

PSYCHOSOCIAL SUPPORT SERVICES: PRISONERS

NATIONAL/STATE ORGANIZATIONS

GOOD NEWS JAIL AND PRISON MINISTRIES INTERNATIONAL
SEE LAW ENFORCEMENT/CRIME PREVENTION: SELF-HELP

INDIVIDUAL PROGRAM PROFILES

AID TO INCARCERATED MOTHERS
SEE LAW ENFORCEMENT/CRIME PREVENTION: PARENTS

FEMALE OFFENDER REHABILITATION PROGRAM
SEE EMPLOYMENT: PRISONER/EX-OFFENDER

SURROUND*
SEE LAW ENFORCEMENT/CRIME PREVENTION: CHILDREN/YOUTH

VISITOR HOSPITALITY CENTER*
SEE LAW ENFORCEMENT/CRIME PREVENTION: FAMILIES

PSYCHOSOCIAL SUPPORT SERVICES: VICTIMS

INDIVIDUAL PROGRAM PROFILES

CRY, INC. (CITIZENS REDIRECTING YOUTH)
4262 Massachusetts Avenue, SE
Washington, DC 20019
TEL: 202-583-7426; 202-783-0030
Purpose: To provide supportive services for parents and others who have been victimized by crime.
Contact: Johnnie Scott Rice, Executive Director
Description: Citizens Redirecting Youth (CRY) was founded in 1988 by a mother who lost a son to violence. CRY is based on a deep need by the founder to talk to others who went through such an experience. There is evidence that survivors of murder victims who do not talk to anyone for several months after the tragedy often develop various psychological problems.

The program offers psychosocial support to parents and others traumatized by crime. During its first year, 400 families were assisted by the program. At any given time, there are 40 families working with CRY's five volunteer counselors.

Recognizing that siblings are not always considered in "grief sessions," CRY tries to give special consideration to a murder victim's sisters and brothers while counseling their parents. Referrals to CRY are made by other agencies, primarily victim/witness units of local law enforcement departments.

In its comparatively brief existence, it seems to have met a long-time need, since *CRY* has responded to requests for appearances on dozens of national and local radio and television programs, including *Geraldo Show, Nightline* with Ted Koppel, *Sally Jessy Raphael, Voice of America, CBN News, UDC Campus Forum, 700 Club, WPFW Talk Show* with Jolyne Brooks, *Talk at American University,* Channel 7 *(Beat-Up the Beat),* Channel 9 *(Crime and Drugs), WDJY Talk Show* with Jerry Phillips, *WRC Talk-Forum, Capital City Magazine* (WTTG 5 Fox TV), *WRC Talk Show* with Joe Spivack, *Workshop for Female Inmates* (DC Jail), *Ballou Senior High School* (Super Team Leaders), *Galilee Baptist Church* (Forum with Bruce Johnson), an all-area-stations presentation on *March of Life,* and others.
Founded: 1988

STOP! THE MADNESS FOUNDATION
SEE LAW ENFORCEMENT/CRIME PREVENTION: VICTIMS

RECIPIENTS

RECIPIENTS: CHILDREN/YOUTH

NATIONAL/STATE ORGANIZATIONS

AMERICAN PARENTS COMMITTEE
1346 Connecticut Avenue, NW
Washington, DC 20036
TEL: 202-785-3169
Objectives: To work for federal legislation on behalf of the nation's children and youth.
Services: Monitors any welfare legislation that emerges, closely examining its impact on children; supports increased efforts to facilitate services recognizing the right of every child to a permanent family; opposes Administration or Congressional attempts to seek relief for the federal Treasury by reducing expenditures for programs for children and youth; reports through its *Washington Report on Federal Legislation for Children* on such matters as day care, homemaker services, Headstart, child health, education, family planning, juvenile justice, etc.; also publishes an annual *Voting Report on Federal Legislation for Children* and other materials.

CENTER FOR EARLY ADOLESCENCE
University of North Carolina
Suite 228
Carr Mill Mall
Chapel Hill, NC 27510
TEL: 919-966-1148
Objectives: To provide information, training and consultation to agencies and individuals who have an impact on the lives of 10- to 15-year-olds; to build a network of professionals and volunteers who work with this age group.
Services: Provides a variety of services for educators, health professionals, program planners, youth workers, the clergy, and others who work with this age group and their families; fields over 200 requests for information per month and publishes over 40 books, training materials, and other resources, including the *Middle Grades Assessment Program* designed to help school systems assess the effectiveness of their schools for this early adolescent age group; produces for families *Living with 10- to 15-year-olds: A Parent Education Curriculum* and for youth-service organizations and training staff, *Planning Programs for Young Adolescents* to assist in conducting self-assessment and

planning new or improving existing programs; continually updates and develops new curricula to help schools and community agencies improve literacy skills of young adolescents; conducts training-for-trainers workshops in these curricula throughout the year.
[The Center for Early Adolescence of the University of North Carolina at Chapel Hill is the first and only center in the nation dedicated exclusively to improving the healthy growth and development of 10- to 15-year-olds.]
Contact: Peter C. Scales, Ph.D.
Publications: Understanding Adolescence; Adolescent Literacy/What Works
Founded: 1979

NATIONAL COLLABORATION FOR YOUTH
1319 F Street, NW
Suite 601
Washington, DC 20004
TEL: 202-347-2080
Objectives: To increase public awareness of the needs of youth.
Services: Works to affect public and private policy on the needs of youth; seeks to redirect national resources toward youth development; involves youth in the decision-making processes of programs and institutions affecting their lives; collaborates on areas such as youth employment, education, health, family life, and juvenile justice; works with government and voluntary agencies to improve services for youth; includes in its membership Boy Scouts of America, 4-H Program, Big Brothers/Big Sisters of America, and the national boards of YMCAs and YWCAs, and works with the *National Assembly of National Voluntary Health and Social Welfare Organizations;* publishes a newsletter and other materials.
Sponsor: Boy Scouts of America
Publications: NCY Today
Founded: 1973

NATIONAL NETWORK OF YOUTH ADVISORY BOARDS
PO Box 402036
Ocean View Branch
Miami Beach, FL 33140
TEL: 305-532-2607
Objectives: To increase input by youth in the planning and implementing of programs for youth.

Services: Provides young people with opportunities to help plan, operate, monitor and evaluate programs that are intended to serve them; helps the youth identify community resources, write project proposals, secure grants, learn about federally-funded projects, determine needs, survey problems, set priorities and, generally, to help plan their own future; publishes a set of two handbooks, *Follow-Up Report,* to help community leaders establish youth participation, and a list of supplementary resources and publications on the subject.
Founded: 1975

TRAINING PROGRAMS

FIRST ANNUAL SOVIET-AMERICAN YOUTH SUMMIT
SEE CIVIC AFFAIRS: PEACE

GOVERNORS' SCHOOL
Seattle University
310 Campion Tower
914 East Jefferson
Seattle, WA 98122
TEL: 206-626-6386
FAX: 206-296-5440
Contact: Stephen Boyd
Description: The *Governors' School* is a one-month intensive training course at *Seattle University* designed for high school juniors and using community service to help develop leadership skills. It is divided into two parts:
- **Summer Institute** - In this month-long session, 100 high school juniors from across the state design individual service projects to address a community problem. The session deals with local, national, and international issues. It encourages students to examine their ideas and ideals and to explore the meanings of leadership. Part of this portion of the program challenges the students physically in outdoor training where they learn wilderness skills and survival tactics.
- **Community Leadership Projects** - In this part of the training, students can apply and test skills learned in the summer institute. The *Governors' School* has informal networks across the state to contact leaders in the students' communities to serve as project mentors. Coordinators follow the progress of the students and offer aid when it appears necessary.

The projects mounted by the students are diverse and innovative and cover many areas of need not being met by the wider community. Some projects:
- **Food Bank** - One student opened and ran a food bank in a town suffering the effects of a factory shut-down.
- **Rape Crises** - One student worked with the *Seattle Rape Relief,* designing a widely-circulated brochure on teenage rape in the Asian community.
- **Literacy** - One student worked with "at-risk" middle school students to help them develop literacy skills, initiative and motivation.

The *Governors' School* emphasizes the course as a "year-long" commitment, not just a one-month training session. Students may receive credit for their projects from their individual school districts.
Students are chosen for the program by a Statewide Advisory Board on the basis of essays describing the development of their personal values and their solutions to major global problems. Students come from diverse racial and cultural backgrounds, and from every social, economic, and academic level. Leadership ability or potential is an essential qualification.
Although called the *Governors' School,* Washington Governors' roles have been limited to public relations efforts. Major underwriters include business/industry, foundations, and the University.

PARENT-TEEN AIDS EDUCATION PROJECT
SEE AIDS: EDUCATION

TENNESSEE VOLUNTEERS FOR CHILDREN CONFERENCE
Metropolitan Council of Directors of Volunteers
PO Box 120471
Nashville, TN 37212
TEL: 615-373-4599
Credit: Inquire
Sponsor: Tennessee Children's Services Commission
Contact: Lannie Richardson
Description: This special project of the Tennessee Children's Services Commission is designed to provide a forum for those who work with and for the children of Tennessee. National and local experts are enlisted to serve as presenters and workshop leaders. Following a keynote address by Ivan Scheier, numerous workshops are conducted with the variety ranging from management areas such as budgets and fundraising to areas that consider special groups such as the handicapped and juvenile probationers. Workshop topics include:
- Basic Overview of Volunteer Services
- Volunteering in Juvenile Justice Systems
- Using Volunteers in Childcare Programs
- Community Service: An Alternative for Youth
- Children in Adult Jails: The Impact of Voluntary Action
- Assessment of Needs and Resources for Children in the Communities
- Fundraising From the Private Sector
- Advocacy Skill Building on Behalf of Handicapped Children
- Youth Services in the 80s: An Overview
- Understanding Family Systems: The Key to the Child
- Juvenile Court Probation Volunteer Program
- Role of the Budget in Children's Services
- Developing an Interfaith Coalition for Children
- Preparing Excellent Parents: Practical Ways to Help

Time and space for informal discussion with the presenters, idea exchange among participants, and roundtable sessions provide additional benefits to all.

VOLUNTARISM: CONFRONTATION AND OPPORTUNITY*
National Board of YMCAs
291 Broadway
New York, NY 10007
TEL: 212-374-2000
Credit: Inquire
Sponsor: National Board of YMCAs
Contact: Dr. Clifford M. Carey or Dr. James M. Hardy
Description: Three years after adopting a five-year operating goal calling for "mobilizing and utilizing greater numbers of volunteers," the National Board found that very little had been done toward reaching that goal. Thus, an intensive one-day seminar was developed to bring together key leaders and volunteers in the volunteer field for a "knowledge-pooling, action-deriving" session to help the YMCA assess and develop their volunteer efforts. The underlying strategy is to combine the resources of local, regional and national operating experience with:
- an analysis of the historical experience of the Y with volunteers and professional-volunteer relations;
- a review of the futurists' analysis of social trends relevant to volunteerism; and
- a reviewing of innovative approaches to volunteerism in other sectors of the community.

The overall purpose of the seminar is to analyze the dynamics of volunteerism in the society today and in the future with the hope that from this examination will flow derivations and implications for the YMCA nationally, regionally and locally. The model seminar, which has provided stimulus and a working resource for similar meetings around the country, includes the following topics:

Perspectives from Organizational History - A probe into an organization's history as it relates to volunteerism can provide a rationale for change, and objectivity in coping with the present, considering alternatives, and future planning. Such a study may include: 1) approach to community needs; 2) program operations; 3) long-range planning; 4) current financial operations; 5) community and public relations; 6) corporate and legal issues; 7) social action, and other areas pertinent to a particular organization.

Some Current Voluntarism Issues and Confrontations - Challenges continually emerge that reflect growing pressures for change from within and from outside of an organization. In the Y, these were found to be:

- The Interest in Management brought about by increase in the organization's size and scope focuses training activities on managerial functions, resulting in unresolved tensions among lay leaders and staff.
- The Pressure for Improved Staff Work from volunteers so that they can become more responsive and influential in their programs.
- The Leadership Squeeze brought about by the increasing demands on the time of key volunteers by their occupations, and the growing competition for volunteer leadership among organizations.
- Outmoded Structures geared to problems that no longer exist, thereby placing an additional burden on the lay reader.
- Changing Identification and Loyalty based on the Association's potential for continuity in disciplines central to an individual's training.
- Increased Complexity in Program Methods requiring highly skilled leadership and the application of relatively new methods.

Societal Trends and Organizational Potentials - This session is based on the premise that elements of any projection for the future are already happening in some form somewhere in the USA, and that such futuristic practices may emerge in discussions within the seminar group.

Strategies and Action Steps - In this final session of the seminar, participants are asked to formulate recommendations for the National Board, and suggested the following:

- Formulate proposals for the National Board.
- Retrieve information on the present use of volunteers.
- Improve the reporting procedures and accuracy of statistics for volunteers.
- Strengthen the training resources for volunteerism.
- Prepare a written report of this seminar on volunteerism.
- Test the feasibility of other suggested actions.

INDIVIDUAL PROGRAM PROFILES

BOARDER BABY PROJECT
Gartenhaus Furs
6950 Wisconsin Avenue
Chevy Chase, MD 20015
TEL: 202-656-2800
Purpose: To reduce or eliminate hospital stays of babies abandoned by their drug-addicted mothers.
Contact: Lynne or Patty Gartenhaus
Description: Starting with a fashion show in early 1990, *Gartenhaus Furs* plans to raise $200,000 for a "boarder baby home," which would give priority to the abandoned infants at DC General Hospital. These babies are medically ready to be discharged, but have no place to go. Most were abandoned by drug-addicted mothers.
Although the DC City Council has taken steps to force the city to take custody of such children soon after they are declared ready for discharge, the caseloads of social workers prohibit any hope of

a rapid solution. Since caseload priority is given to abused children who must be removed from their homes, the boarder babies - considered safe as long as they are in the hospital - are not always placed first. During the 1988-90 fiscal years, the child welfare system added only about 30 new foster parents to its rosters. Therefore, *Gartenhaus Furs* is making an effort to "fill in the gap."

According to the founders, however, help is not far away. With the publicity surrounding the babies, many benefits are surfacing. A March 1990 celebrity auction brought out many stars to call attention to the problem - including the world heavyweight boxing champion, who donated his champion's belt. In addition, due to a surge in volunteers in the social services system, by March 1990 more than 230 families either had enrolled in classes, or were awaiting final approval to become foster or adoptive parents for the infants. Unfortunately, this expanded help is accompanied by a dramatic rise in the number of pregnant women using drugs. In one week at a local hospital, 18 of the 29 children born had been exposed to drugs.

The boarder baby home is not expected to be a permanent solution, according to its founders. However, experts warn that the hospital setting during the first year causes children to miss opportunities to bond and they are likely to be developmentally delayed. Plans for the Gartenhaus project are to create a home-like setting and enough volunteers and staff to make each child feel special - in the hope of counteracting the dire prediction of the experts. "Hopefully, foster families will make even that stay a short one," one founder said, "and will create permanent homes and families for the youngsters. The important thing is to remove them from that necessarily sterile setting."

BOYS & GIRLS CLUBS OF GREATER WASHINGTON
1320 Fenwick Lane
Suite 800
Silver Spring, MD 20910
TEL: 301-587-4315
FAX: 301-587-8120
Purpose: To help build self-esteem through instilling a sense of belonging, competence, usefulness and influence; to help young people become productive, civic-minded and responsible adults.
Contact: Program Coordinator
Description: The *Boys & Girls Club of Greater Washington* has been providing services for young boys and girls from all backgrounds for over 100 years. There are eight branch *Clubs* in the District of Columbia, Maryland and Virginia. There are nine shelters and residential facilities for neglected, abused and homeless young people, and special services are pioneered to help youth-at-risk. The organization provides educational assistance, recreational and social opportunities, job training and personalized counseling. Specific programs include:

- *Career Education and Vocational Training Services,* helping young people to complete school and move to college and work with educational and scholarship assistance, computer education, preparation for college, job training and tutoring.
- *Citizenship and Leadership Development Services,* giving youngsters a sense of civic responsibility by becoming involved in the leadership process, with opportunities for planning and decision-making, as well as becoming aware of their heritage, through *Torch and Keystone Clubs,* special interest groups, and an annual awards program for *Youth of the Year.*
- *Cultural Enrichment Services,* encouraging understanding of many cultures through classes and performances to provide skills and experiences in the visual and performing arts.
- *Personal Development Services,* helping young people plan and set goals and helping them to cope with physical, social, academic and emotional problems.
- *Health and Physical Education Services,* developing and maintaining health through physical fitness and education in team and individual sports, and health education including

drug and substance abuse counseling.

- *Social Recreation Services,* teaching youngsters good use of leisure time and helping them get along with peers and make new friends through special co-ed teenage activities, a game room, hobby groups, and outings and special events.
- *Targeting Special Needs,* providing specialized assistance through programs such as the *Teen Parent Self-Sufficiency Program, Targeted Outreach* (youth-at-risk), and *Cities in Schools* (a support team to keep youth in school).
- *Summer Camping,* providing a variety of activities in day camps at eight *Clubs* which include swimming, arts and crafts, building new friendships, learning about careers, etc. *Gift of Summer* scholarship assistance is available when needed.

In addition to volunteer counselors and other direct service individuals and groups, supporters include foundations, businesses and corporations.
Publications: Capital Connection; Project Right Start; Boys & Girls Club Information Packet

CHILDREN'S LITERACY INITIATIVE
SEE LITERACY

FUND FOR NEEDY SCHOOL CHILDREN
1466 Harbert
Memphis, TN 38104
TEL: 901-276-0372
Purpose: To assist in meeting some of the health and welfare needs of economically-disadvantaged elementary school children.
Sponsor: United Way
Contact: Sheryl Bowen
Description: The activities of this volunteer community organization are designed to help meet needs of disadvantaged elementary school children. Working in the public schools with the approval of the elected Board of Education, the superintendent and his staff, the program is directed by a 12-member steering committee, headed by the co-chairman.
As a United Way agency, it receives funds for that part of the program which provides new clothing, shoes, and glasses from United Way. Additional limited foundation and private group donations also contribute to the purchase of glasses. Other phases of its work are supported by funds from the city and county governments and contributions from the general public.
The elimination of hunger in the classroom was one of the main thrusts of the program until the federal program became firmly established. In 1969, Fund volunteers insisted successfully that 40,000 or more school children coming from poverty-income families should be reflected on the free lunch/breakfast roster. Volunteer concern has followed these children as they have been bussed to schools all over the city.
In addition to increasing free lunch participation, the Fund has found the means to meet other needs of some of the children as newborns and later at school. An Infant Formula program supported by funds from city and county governments, and a layette program supported by contributions from the public, are examples. The formula and layette programs are carried out in coordination with the City of Memphis Hospital and the Health Department. The provision of new clothes and shoes is carried out through the Pupil Services Department of the Board of Education.
The Fund for Needy School Children began in 1964 with 12 volunteers in four elementary schools seeking out and enrolling eligible children in the national school lunch program. Volunteer activities expanded into all Title I elementary schools and, by 1971, there were more than 400 volunteers in over 50 city and county schools providing a solid base for continuing interest in the program.
Founded: 1964

GROWING UP WITH NATURE
SEE PHYSICAL ENVIRONMENT: WILDLIFE/PETS

MAKING THE GRADE: A REPORT CARD ON AMERICAN YOUTH
United Way of the Plains
212 North Market
Suite 200
Wichita, KS 67202-2021
TEL: 316-267-1321
Purpose: To bring youth issues to the forefront of public awareness.
Contact: Patrick J. Hanrahan, President
Description: In September 1989, a diverse volunteer committee was formed to develop and operate an issue-oriented project. It was co-sponsored by the *United Way of the Plains* and the *National Collaboration for Youth* (a coalition of national youth-serving organizations). The committee included people from some 40 local agencies - many of them youth-service providers, adult representatives from the *Wichita Chamber of Commerce* and city and state governments, business and labor leaders, news media professionals from *KAKE-TV* (the local *ABC Network* affiliate), and high school youth who are service recipients and members of honor societies and student councils.
The issues were problems facing youth, and the *National Collaboration for Youth* provided national statistics for eight major youth problems: functional illiteracy, juvenile crime, school dropouts, substance abuse, teen pregnancy, youth unemployment, and mental and physical health care. The committee determined how best to give a local focus to these problems.
As a result, *KAKE-TV* featured each of the problems in an eight-part news mini-series. Each segment of the series concluded by airing *United Way's First Call for Help* phone number. The series aired immediately preceding the national ABC telecast, *Growing Up, Down and Out,* hosted by Barbara Walters. Following the national program, *KAKE-TV* aired a live call-in show as a forum for local youth to express their reactions to the program and their concerns about specific youth problems.
About two weeks later, United Way held a town meeting to obtain feedback about the TV broadcasts, and to develop plans for improving local services to youth. More than 100 people came to the meeting and "drew up a report card" on how well the community was dealing with the youth problems.
With the help of two school principals who are United Way board members, plans are being implemented to maintain a dialogue about youth services through monthly meetings with local students - encouraging their input and volunteer participation to gradually improve existing services and fill gaps in service needs.
Founded: 1989

YOUTH TRAIN
2741 Welton
Denver, CO 80205
TEL: 303-295-7912
Purpose: To get at-risk youth back on the right track.
Contact: June Jackson or Nancy Johnson, parent volunteers
Description: Youth Train was founded by two mothers who saw a connection between a parents' movement and a neighborhood watch organization. Gang violence and other crime - and gang involvement by a daughter of one of the parents - spurred them to action as they helped found the organization, which is for parents and children five to nineteen years of age. A parent acts as block captain in every neighborhood in the metro area, similar to *Crime Watch* programs. Residents put yellow light bulbs in their porch lamps and turn them on as a sign that "they are going to be involved, know where their children are, and take responsibility for their children's actions." The lights are used also to demonstrate the first sign of trouble, then call police and neighbors, who in turn switch on their lights.
Part of the program involves peer groups - taking teens who have positive activities and mixing them with teens who are involved in negative activities. The philosophy behind this mix is that youth

are influenced more by their peers than their parents. But it works the other way too, according to volunteers in the program. Gang members, for example, develop a "sign language" of their own that they use to communicate between members - a skill that demands accuracy for street survival. These same youth can teach sign language to deaf children - an accomplishment that, in turn, builds self-esteem in the young teachers. In the process they learn some of the frustrations of teaching, which carries over to the classroom and results in more respect for the teacher.

Thus, the secret of *Youth Train* is to build on existing talents among youth that were often discounted as blanket labels of "throwaways" and "in-trouble youth" placing the youth at a disadvantage, and combine this with parent interest and involvement. All participants in the program are volunteers.

RECIPIENTS: CHILDREN/YOUTH - ADVOCACY

NATIONAL/STATE ORGANIZATIONS

CHILD WELFARE LEAGUE OF AMERICA
440 First Street, NW
Suite 310
Washington, DC 20001
TEL: 202-638-2952
FAX: 202-638-4004
Objectives: To improve care and services for deprived, neglected and dependent children, youth and their families.
Services: Assists agencies in the area of child welfare whose programs are relevant to community needs; provides specialists in various aspects of child welfare based on a study of the local program, structure, administration and policies; assists teenage parents through the League's *Florence Crittenton* division by providing medical care, education, counseling, health and family life education, and parent-reparation programs; gives professional leadership to agencies providing services to troubled families and children; handles especially difficult problems of a requesting agency with surveys; develops standards and guidelines for the child welfare field and makes them available in various publications; maintains a library/information service; works closely with the mass media to properly present the need for good child welfare services; establishes special projects; publishes a journal and over 100 monographs and books; convenes annual regional training conferences.
Publications: Child Welfare; Children's Campaign News; Washington Social Legislation Bulletin; Children's Monitor; CWLA Directory; CWLA Newsletter; CWLA Catalog
Founded: 1920

INDIVIDUAL PROGRAM PROFILES

CASA (COURT APPOINTED SPECIAL ADVOCATES)
CASA of Travis County
510 West Tenth
Austin, TX 78701
TEL: 512-478-6627
Purpose: To break the cycle of abuse and neglect of children.
Sponsor: Austin Family Court
Contact: Lila Coughran, Executive Director
Description: The *Court Appointed Special Advocates (CASA)* program provides family court-appointed volunteers to serve as "a voice in court" for abused and neglected children. The goal of

CASA is to break the cycle of abuse and neglect through "permanent placement" for every child who enters the court/welfare system. Children are reunited with the family, if possible, or placed with relatives, a foster home or adoptive family. CASAs undergo an extensive screening process, commit themselves for at least a year, complete 20 hours of intense training and devote three to four hours a week to a child. In the end, the volunteer must tell the court what she believes is best for the child.

To meet this heavy responsibility, CASAs have access to files, families, and CASA professional staff as they work to become "a friend to the child" and in many cases a listener to the pleadings of a mother or family who wants the child back. Sometimes this involves regular visitations to jails and prisons to determine whether or not a child might be reunited with a parent or other family member. They are trained to respect the family and not make judgments about different lifestyles. Their work also takes them at times to some notoriously drug-riddled, dangerous neighborhoods. They understand that the only way to be sure of making a good recommndation is to know the lifestyle. As one volunteer said, "When you want to help someone so much, you don't let much get in your way."

In one Austin case, a mother in prison, who was a former prostitute, is now planning to go back to school and "lead a simple life with a dog, a car, a house and an education for my child." The inmate credits her new goals to the CASA volunteer who visited regularly with the inmate's three-year-old son and brought messages of hope and encouragement. According to the volunteer, who recommended that the mother and son be given a chance to make it after the mother's release, "Both of us know that the rest is up to her. You can only give people choices, tell them about the programs aimed at helping them, but you can't do it for them." In spite of the commitment required, there is no dearth of volunteers for the program. The satisfaction of knowing that you are "changing the world child-by-child and making a difference" is a strong motivator, according to CASA's Director.

RECIPIENTS: CHILDREN/YOUTH - ARTS

NATIONAL/STATE ORGANIZATIONS

INFORMATION CENTER ON CHILDREN'S CULTURES*
SEE ARTS/CULTURAL ENRICHMENT: ETHNIC GROUPS

INTERNATIONAL CULTURAL CENTERS FOR YOUTH
SEE ARTS/CULTURAL ENRICHMENT: ETHNIC GROUPS

SAN JOSE CHILDREN'S MUSICAL THEATRE*
SEE ARTS/CULTURAL ENRICHMENT:
MUSIC/DANCE/THEATRE

SUGAR RAY ROBINSON YOUTH FOUNDATION*
SEE ARTS/CULTURAL ENRICHMENT:
MUSIC/DANCE/THEATRE

YOUNG AUDIENCES
SEE ARTS/CULTURAL ENRICHMENT:
MUSIC/DANCE/THEATRE

INDIVIDUAL PROGRAM PROFILES

ADOPT-A-SCHOOL DANCE PROGRAM
SEE ARTS/CULTURAL ENRICHMENT: ADOPT-A-SCHOOL

ART FOR KIDS' SAKE
Child Welfare League of America
440 First Street, NW
Suite 310
Washington, DC 20001-2085
TEL: 202-638-2952
Purpose: To remind the public of children's needs.
Sponsor: American Academy of Pediatrics
Contact: Mark K. Riley, Children's Campaign
Description: The best-known cartoonists in America have created an original collection of cartoon art to remind the public of children's needs. Each cartoon conveys a message, such as "Try a Little Tenderness." The collection includes a poster called "Voice for Children," which was illustrated by 69 cartoonists and traveled 170,766 miles on its way to completion.
The project, known as *Art for Kids' Sake,* is a collaborative effort of Child Welfare League of America (CWLA), American Academy of Pediatrics, Group W Westinghouse Broadcasting, American Greeting Card Company, Federal Express, CWLA member agencies, and local TV stations. Originally available only in print form (posters, note cards, and signed limited editions), the artwork has been incorporated into public service announcements and promotional spots in more than 100 cities across the U.S. Sales from the poster and other artwork benefit agencies serving children across the country. CWLA members benefit by collecting donations for the collector-quality art.
Cartoonists volunteering for the program include Gary Trudeau, Johnny Hart, Jim Davis, Bill Keane, and others.
Founded: 1987

RECYCLING FOR RAVI
SEE PHYSICAL ENVIRONMENT: RECYCLING

SCHOOLMATE HANDICRAFT VOLUNTEERS
SEE ARTS/CULTURAL ENRICHMENT: CRAFTS

TINY TOWN FOUNDATION
SEE ARTS/CULTURAL ENRICHMENT: HISTORY/MUSEUMS

VALENTINE SCHOOL ART SHOW
SEE ARTS/CULTURAL ENRICHMENT: FESTIVALS

YOUNG AUTHORS' FAIRE
SEE ARTS/CULTURAL ENRICHMENT: FESTIVALS

YOUTH OCEAN EXPLORER PROGRAM
SEE ARTS/CULTURAL ENRICHMENT: INTERCULTURAL

RECIPIENTS: CHILDREN/YOUTH - CITIZENSHIP

INDIVIDUAL PROGRAM PROFILES

GIRL SCOUTING IN THE INNER CITY
SEE RECREATION & SPORTS: CHILDREN/YOUTH

PREVENTION THROUGH ACTION
SEE DRUG ABUSE/ALCOHOLISM: CHILDREN/YOUTH

TROOP 400 AND TROOP 391
SEE RECIPIENTS: HANDICAPPED - CHILDREN/YOUTH

RECIPIENTS: CHILDREN/YOUTH - CRIME PREVENTION

INDIVIDUAL PROGRAM PROFILES

THE CHOICE IS YOURS
SEE LAW ENFORCEMENT/CRIME PREVENTION: CHILDREN/YOUTH

DONCASTER YOUTH CHALLENGE, A.K.A. SNEAKER CAMP
SEE LAW ENFORCEMENT/CRIME PREVENTION: CHILDREN/YOUTH

HAWAII YOUTH AT RISK
SEE LAW ENFORCEMENT/CRIME PREVENTION: CHILDREN/YOUTH

HITS (HIGH INTENSITY TREATMENT SUPERVISION)
SEE LAW ENFORCEMENT/CRIME PREVENTION: SENTENCING

JUVENILE RECEPTION AND DIAGNOSTIC CENTER (JRDC)
SEE LAW ENFORCEMENT/CRIME PREVENTION: CHILDREN/YOUTH

LEE COUNTY RESTITUTION PROGRAM
SEE LAW ENFORCEMENT/CRIME PREVENTION: VICTIMS

LOUISIANA TRAINING INSTITUTE*
SEE LAW ENFORCEMENT/CRIME PREVENTION: CHILDREN/YOUTH

MID-VALLEY ADOLESCENT CENTER*
SEE LAW ENFORCEMENT/CRIME PREVENTION: CHILDREN/YOUTH

PARTNERS*
SEE LAW ENFORCEMENT/CRIME PREVENTION: CHILDREN/YOUTH

SENECA FALLS CONCERNED PARENTS
SEE LAW ENFORCEMENT/CRIME PREVENTION: CHILDREN/YOUTH

SUMMIT SHOCK INCARCERATION FACILITY
SEE LAW ENFORCEMENT/CRIME PREVENTION: CHILDREN/YOUTH

RECIPIENTS: CHILDREN/YOUTH - DAY CARE

NATIONAL/STATE ORGANIZATIONS

HEAD START - FAMILY DAY CARE
SEE DAY CARE/HEAD START: FAMILY DAY CARE

INDIVIDUAL PROGRAM PROFILES

HOME-BASED CHILD CARE IN HARTFORD
SEE DAY CARE/HEAD START: HOME

JUNIOR LEAGUE OF DETROIT
SEE AIDS

RECIPIENTS: CHILDREN/YOUTH - DRUGS/ALCOHOL

NATIONAL/STATE ORGANIZATIONS

CAMPAIGN DRUG FREE
SEE DRUG ABUSE/ALCOHOLISM: DRUGS - DRUG-FREE ZONES

NATIONAL LISTEN AMERICA CLUB
SEE DRUG ABUSE/ALCOHOLISM: CHILDREN/YOUTH

RECIPIENTS: CHILDREN/YOUTH - EDUCATION

INDIVIDUAL PROGRAM PROFILES

PRINCIPAL ON THE ROOF*
SEE EDUCATION: READING

RECIPIENTS: CHILDREN/YOUTH - EMPLOYMENT

INDIVIDUAL PROGRAM PROFILES

YOUTH-IN-ACTION AUCTION
SEE PHYSICAL ENVIRONMENT: BEAUTIFICATION

RECIPIENTS: CHILDREN/YOUTH - ENTREPRENEURSHIP

TRAINING PROGRAMS

WASHINGTON FOR MINORITY YOUTH AWARENESS DAY
SEE BUSINESS ASSISTANCE: CHILDREN/YOUTH

INDIVIDUAL PROGRAM PROFILES

CHAMP BAKERY
District of Columbia Police Department
Office of the Chief of Police
300 Indiana Avenue, NW
Washington, DC 20001
TEL: 202-727-1000
Purpose: To occupy youth in a productive enterprise as a deterrent to drug abuse and other unlawful activities.
Sponsor: District of Columbia Police Department
Contact: Tom Blackburn, Advisor
Description: This effort is an outgrowth of the concern of a former District of Columbia school counselor and an advisor to the city's Chief of Police. They saw the economic problem facing the city's youth as a potentially explosive situation that could involve drug use, drug dealing, and other unlawful activities.
The Champ Bakery received a positive response from all who became aware of it. This encouraged the youth to put forth even greater effort. Another incident that increased their interest in their little business was the death of one of their peers, age 13, who had been killed in a crack house. They are stepping up efforts to expand the cookie business and view it as a way of trying to save lives.
The bakery's recruiter of new salesmen says it is difficult when the $70 over four days that sales can bring pales by comparison to the $10 per minute that can be made from the sale of one crumb of crack cocaine. The youngsters, ranging in age from 11 to 15, realized that drastic action had to be taken to provide larger ovens, a computer, a couple of vans and a downtown location, so they could "give any street-level dope dealer a run for the money." According to one of the young entrepreneurs, a straight-A elementary school student, "If we had the right equipment, I could easily triple my weekly earnings selling cookies. I sell out my inventory every day and I feel bad when people ask for more, and I can't deliver."
A story in the paper about the bakery in March 1989 brought help from many quarters. Assistance by the advocates who responded to the article included:
- Republican National Committee chairman sending a bag of cookies to President Bush, which resulted in a meeting at the White House with the President;
- Radio station WOL-AM promoting the bakery on its morning show;
- Kenilworth-Parkside housing complex directing young recruits to the bakery program;
- Negril Bakery owner allowing the use of space in his downtown store;
- National Strategy in Marketing donating T-shirts;
- Freddie Mac, the Federal Home Loan Mortgage Corporation, donating $500;
- American University asking Marriott corporation to contract with the youths to sell cookies on campus;
- United Black Fund and Washington Informer newspaper donating more than $5,000, and
- Maxima Corporation meeting with the youth to talk about

computers.

Champ continues to make progress and receive advice and support from the above advocates plus others who learn about and offer to help the youth program.

Publications: Champ Information Packet

RECIPIENTS: CHILDREN/YOUTH - ENVIRONMENT

INDIVIDUAL PROGRAM PROFILES

CHATTANOOGA NATURE CENTER
SEE PHYSICAL ENVIRONMENT: EDUCATION

RECIPIENTS: CHILDREN/YOUTH - ETHNIC GROUPS

NATIONAL/STATE ORGANIZATIONS

JACKIE ROBINSON FOUNDATION
80-90 Eighth Avenue
New York, NY 10011
TEL: 212-675-1511
Objectives: To development the leadership potential of minority and inner-city youth.
Services: Conducts the *Leadership Development Program* for high school students to address specific needs of urban youth, and to help prepare them to help improve their communities; trains minority and poor youths for sports management and office careers in organized sports; provides counseling and support services for youth; awards full college scholarships and music scholarships to promising minority performers; administers the *Robie Award for Humanitarianism* program; publishes a newsletter, journal, and student handbook on scholarships.
Publications: JRF Newsletter; Awards Dinner Journal; Scholarship Student Handbook
Founded: 1973

INDIVIDUAL PROGRAM PROFILES

PREVENTION THROUGH ACTION
SEE DRUG ABUSE/ALCOHOLISM: CHILDREN/YOUTH

RECIPIENTS: CHILDREN/YOUTH - FUNDING

INDIVIDUAL PROGRAM PROFILES

CHAMPIONS RUN FOR LIFE TORCH RELAY
SEE HEALTH: CANCER

YOUTH ALLOCATIONS COMMITTEE
United Way of the Capital Area (Jackson)
843 North President Street
Jackson, MS 39202
TEL: 601-948-4725
Purpose: To evaluate and to make decisions to fund youth programs in their communities.
Sponsor: United Way of the Capital Area
Contact: Mack Mitchell, Chairman
Description: In 1986, the United Way Volunteer Center's *Youth in Action Program* expanded to include a *Youth Allocations Committee.* The students must make a two-year commitment to get the most out of the training provided - making a limited amount of funds benefit the greatest number of people. Students may serve a third year if they desire.
Sixteen senior high schools and eight colleges in the Jackson area endorse and participate in the program. Student allocations committee members attend three orientation sessions to learn about the role and responsibility of volunteers in the community, about United Way and community health and human-care agencies, and acquire a basic overview of the allocation process.
The Chairman is a student, a freshman at Millsaps College. For many students, it is the first time they have volunteered for anything - and the program's process of learning what community services exist and how they work lays a good foundation for future community involvement.
The United Way provides $5,000 in venture grant funds for the committee to distribute. In September of each year students evaluate how effectively funds allocated the previous year were used. Beginning the following March, the students review new applications for funding and attend agency presentations. Final funding decisions are made in April, and United Way funds are distributed by committee members in May.
In 1989-90 the Committee funded eight youth-oriented programs: *Epilepsy Foundation of Mississippi* for its summer camp for children with Epilepsy, *Metro YMCA* for its *Youth Development Program*, *Metro Boys and Girls Clubs* for various projects, *Exchange Club/Parent Child Center* for its *Teen Parent Education Scholarship Program*, *Jackson State University/Division of Continuing Education* for training of GED students, and the *Jackson YWCA* for the development of an educational program.
In 1988-89 the committee funded seven youth programs, including several offered by local chapters of the Boys and Girls Clubs, a teen center for troubled youth, and church youth groups.
Founded: 1986

YOUTH LEADERSHIP VENTURE FUNDING PROGRAM
United Way of the Capital Area (Hartford)
99 Woodland Street
Hartford, CT 06105-2476
TEL: 203-247-2580
Purpose: To involve youth in identifying target issues of the youth community for United Way funding.
Sponsor: United Way of the Capital Area
Contact: Shelley Aronson, Youth Leadership Staff
Description: The Youth Leadership Venture Funding Program has taken an issue-oriented approach to funding. During the 1989-90 school year, a group of 15 students from Hartford-area high schools identified youth substance abuse as the target issue of the youth community. Provided with $10,000 in venture funds from United Way of the Capital Area, the students funded 13 local programs addressing that problem.
United Way's Youth Leadership Advisors, a group of adult volunteers, selected students based on applications distributed to public and private schools in the 30-town coverage area. The students make the decisions, and the committee helps keep them informed about the funding process.
In addition to receiving training in basic allocations procedures and education about United Way. the students gained a thorough

understanding of the substance problem. The student volunteers also interviewed elected officials and human-service agency directors about priority concerns for youth. In response to students' inquiries, the Connecticut Alcohol and Drug Abuse Commission confirmed information about local teen substance abuse programs needing funding.

Programs funded by the *Youth Leadership Venture Funding Program* included

- information directory identifying resources, *Youth Yellow Pages,*
- a student-produced video on anti-substance abuse peer counseling, and
- a positive self-development program incorporating anti-substance abuse eduction for elementary school children.

The Hartford United Way's board of directors unanimously approved the programs selected by the students. The program's chairman said, "The youth funding program has not only given us input from young people about community needs, but has provided funding for anti-substance abuse programs run by and for students in our schools."
Founded: 1988

RECIPIENTS: CHILDREN/YOUTH - HANDICAPPED

NATIONAL/STATE ORGANIZATIONS

FOSTER GRANDPARENT PROGRAM (FGP)
SEE RECIPIENTS: HANDICAPPED - PSYCHOSOCIAL SUPPORT

INDIVIDUAL PROGRAM PROFILES

TROOP 400 AND TROOP 391
SEE RECIPIENTS: HANDICAPPED - CHILDREN/YOUTH

RECIPIENTS: CHILDREN/YOUTH - HEALTH

INDIVIDUAL PROGRAM PROFILES

CHILDREN'S MIRACLE NETWORK TELETHON
KMOL-TV
1031 Navarro
San Antonio, TX 78205
TEL: 512-226-4444
Purpose: To raise money for children's hospitals in the U.S. and other countries.
Contact: Denise F. Barkis, Telethon Coordinator
Description: Six *Marathon Miracle Men* operated phone banks during the entire 22 hours of Austin's 1989 "Children's Miracle Network Telethon" mounted to benefit the *Santa Rosa Children's Hospital* - one of five such hospitals across the state. They anchored a show that involved some 1,000 volunteers of all ages and from all walks of life. The two-day 1989 telethon raised over $900,000 - about $100,000 more than the previous year. The response from individuals was continuous and often accompanied

by encouraging statements. Over $200,000 came from three benefactors - *WalMart, Sam's Wholesale Club,* and *Credit Unions for Kids.*
A variety of performers, group skits, and a visit by a child who was badly injured when his father's car backed over him ("I was squished!") but now totally healed through the Children's Hospital's services were some of the activities used to maintain interest. The *Marathon Miracle Men,* who facilitated the program, came from *Jaycees, Kiwanis Club, Knights of Columbus, Lions Club, Optimist Club* and *Rotary Club.*
An unexpected occurrence increased the poignancy of the Telethon when a co-host left the studio in a rush after receiving a phone call that his 13-year-old son was rushed to Children's Hospital.
The *Children's Miracle Network Telethon* was begun in 1982 by the *Osmond Foundation* and is broadcast nationwide to raise money for more than 170 children's hospitals in five countries. KMOL began airing the local show in 1983.
Founded: 1982

HEALTH AND SAFETY CIRCUS
SEE HEALTH: HEALTH FAIRS

RECIPIENTS: CHILDREN/YOUTH - HOMELESS

NATIONAL/STATE ORGANIZATIONS

YOUTH DEVELOPMENT
SEE PSYCHOSOCIAL SUPPORT SERVICES: CHILDREN/YOUTH

INDIVIDUAL PROGRAM PROFILES

INDEPENDENT LIVING/HOMELESS YOUTH
SEE RECIPIENTS: HOMELESS - CHILDREN/YOUTH

RECIPIENTS: CHILDREN/YOUTH - I&R

NATIONAL/STATE ORGANIZATIONS

NATIONAL RUNAWAY SWITCHBOARD
3080 North Lincoln Avenue
Chicago, IL 60657
TOLL FREE: 800-621-4000 (nationwide)
Objectives: To provide information, crisis intervention, and assistance, and referral to runaways, and messages to their families.
Services: Maintains a 24-hour, toll-free national switchboard; provides names and addresses for shelter and counseling services across the country, including counseling centers, referral lines, drug treatment facilities, and other services; offers to relay messages between young people and their families or, if desired, set up conferences between youths and parents or agencies; maintains caller's confidentiality (funded in part by the Office of Youth Development, U.S. Department of Health and Human Services).

RUNAWAY HOTLINE
Governor's Office
PO Box 12428
Austin, TX 78711
TEL: 512-463-1980; 800-392-3352 (TX)
TOLL FREE: 800-231-6946 (nationwide)
Objectives: To enable young people to contact parents or others without divulging location.
Services: Operates 24-hour, seven-day, national toll-free hotline for runaways and potential runaways with the help of a bank of more than 100 volunteers; respects confidentiality of caller; serves as a personal and confidential message relay between runaways and their parents; maintains referral service for callers in need of service (runaway houses, shelters, food, medical services, drug crisis centers, health clinics, counseling centers, etc.)
Founded: 1973

INDIVIDUAL PROGRAM PROFILES

CHICAGO RUNAWAY SWITCHBOARD
Metro-HELP
3080 North Lincoln Avenue
Chicago, IL 60613
TEL: 312-880-9860; 312-929-5150
TOLL FREE: 800-621-3230
Purpose: To provide direct support to the estimated 10,000 homeless teens in the Chicago Metropolitan area.
Sponsor: Metro-HELP
Contact: Volunteer Coordinator
Description: Although the National Runaway Switchboard, which was founded in 1974, is located in Chicago, another program to provide more direct service to runaway youth in metropolitan Chicago was established in 1989. Both switchboards are operated by Metro-HELP.
The latter service concentrates on the social service providers in the metropolitan Chicago area and links them to homeless teens or teens who are thinking about running away from home. In much the same way as the national operation, volunteers gather facts about the caller's situation, help focus the caller on the primary issue to be addressed, examine options that are available and then, with the caller, develop a plan of action. There are an estimated 10,000 homeless teens in the Chicago area, and some 21,000 across the state.
Many calls end in referrals to other agencies for ongoing sources of support, and often set up conference (three-way) calls with the youth, the hotline, and the appropriate social service as a way of "introducing" a reticent youth to the social worker, thereby having a greater chance of fruition of the connection.
According to the director, "Our volunteers will listen to callers, believe and support the kids, and work with them to access the supports that can truly make a difference in the life of each of our callers." The program has a continual training program and is always in need of volunteers who would like such an opportunity.

FIRST (FACTUAL INFORMATION REGARDING SEX AND TEENS)
PO Box 57
Sanford, NC 27330
TEL: 919-774-9515
Purpose: To provide youth answers to their questions on human sexuality.
Sponsor: Lee County Youth Services
Contact: Maureen Farrington
Description: FIRST (Factual Information Regarding Sex and Teens) is a teens helping teens phone line geared towards helping the young people of Lee County better understand the dynamics and consequences of teen sex and pregnancy.

The phone line began operation in March '83 with grant money from the North Carolina Youth Council. The line is in operation four hours weekly. The program is sponsored by Lee County Youth Services (LCYS) a non-profit organization providing services for the youth and families of the county.
At present, 16 high school volunteers work as peer phone helpers. Initially, a core group of five high school students assisted LCYS with the planning of the phone line.
The volunteers receive training prior to becoming peer phone helpers on topics such as: male/female physiology, contraception, pregnancy, V.D., abortion, human sexuality, communication, listening and decision-making skills, awareness of community resources and knowing when to refer a call. In addition, there are monthly volunteer training sessions.
The peer helpers volunteer one hour of their time each week. They provide answers to questions for young callers ranging from simple boy/girlfriend relationships to information on birth control and abortion clinics. They make referrals to community and surrounding area resources when necessary, but the real value of the peer counselor is to provide a listening ear and be an effective helper. Also, they are responsible for assisting LCYS in evaluating the program and making any recommendations for change.
They provide teens with a significant program in which they have the opportunity and responsibility of helping their peers. The volunteers become more effective helpers by obtaining a better understanding of human sexuality, enabling them to answer teens' questions.
With the high incidence rate of teenage pregnancy in Lee County and elsewhere there is a need for this type of service. It gives the youth of the community the opportunity to help their peers by answering their questions or helping them make positive decisions regarding their own sexuality.
Founded: 1983

SOUTHEAST RESOURCE CENTER FOR CHILDREN AND YOUTH SERVICES
Knox County Child and Family Services
114 Dameron Avenue
Knoxville, TN 37917
TEL: 615-524-7483
Purpose: To provide information, training and the exchange of assistance in child welfare to the eight states which comprise Region IV of the Department of Health and Human Services.
Sponsor: US/HHS - Children's Bureau
Contact: Christine P. Holmes
Description: In October of 1983, the University of Tennessee, School of Social Work, through its Office of Continuing Social Work Education (OCSWE) was awarded a Department of Health and Human Services (DHHS) grant to operate the Southeast Resource Center for Children and Youth Services. The purpose of the Center is to provide information, training and the exchange of technical assistance in child welfare to the eight Southeastern states which comprise DHHS Region IV.
The Southeast Resource Center is uniquely organized in that it brings together the technical expertise of OCSWE with the practical experience of Child and Family Services of Knox County. In a subcontract with OCSWE, Child and Family Services provides staffing and technical assistance in order to strengthen intrastate and regional networks among public and voluntary child welfare agencies.
Specifically, the agency is responsible for two program areas: volunteerism and employee assistance programs. Child and Family Services' role is to assist the state to:
- discover the current volunteer networks;
- develop means to improve the systems; and
- disseminate information and resources about innovative volunteer programs in the area of children and youth services.
Also, the agency is interested in the promotion of nonpublic child welfare and family services through employee benefits in business

and industry. Both volunteerism and employee assistance are means of tapping those resources in the private sector which are now so urgently needed.

Child and Family Services and the Southeast Resource Center are working to build resource exchange networks, increase the availability to non-public-funded services and maximize joint private/public planning for child welfare services. To accomplish these objectives, the Resource Center provides services to state child welfare agencies; voluntary children's services agencies; parent, child and minority advocacy groups; social work educators; and business and industry.

Information services are available through a computer network; publications of the Center; a lending library of audio-visual and written materials; and newsletters. Training, technical assistance and information are provided on special topics such as child abuse and neglect, special needs adoption, foster care, permanency planning, volunteerism, employee assistance programs and youth services.
Founded: 1983

TEENLINE
Oklahoma University Health Sciences Center
1100 North Lindsey
Oklahoma City, OK 73107
TEL: 405-271-4000
Information is also available from co-sponsors:
Children's Memorial Hospital of Oklahoma
940 NE Thirteenth Street
Oklahoma City, OK 73104 (405-271-4371)
Oklahoma Department of Mental Health
1200 NE Thirteenth Street
Oklahoma City, OK 73117 (405-271-7474)
Purpose: To serve as a crisis intervention hot line for adolescents.
Sponsor: Oklahoma University Health Sciences Center
Contact: Dr. Robert Hill, Professor of Pediatrics
Description: Sponsored by a university, a children's hospital and the state mental health office, the mission of the *Teenline* is to provide counseling and referrals to youth who are in acute trouble or just in need of a listening ear. The program offers confidential and anonymous services by specially-trained volunteers, including referral to local programs appropriate to their needs.
In its first years of operation, the hot line answered more than 13,000 calls from troubled teens. The service has grown from four hours of operation a day by a group of 15 volunteers to operation by 80 volunteers 12 hours a day. It is staffed from noon to midnight seven days a week. It also has grown from serving only the Oklahoma City area to serving the entire state.
Founded: 1985

24-HOUR CHILD ABUSE/NEGLECT TELEPHONE REPORT LINE
Delaware State Hospital
Gawthrop Building
1901 North DuPont Highway
New Castle, DE 19720
TEL: 302-421-6786
Purpose: To provide 24-hour telephone answering for the reporting of child abuse and neglect and supportive services for agency clients.
Sponsor: Division of Child Protective Services, Delaware Department of Health and Social Services, Junior League, Inc.
Contact: Mary W. Lewis
Description: The Division of Child Protective Services' Report Line has been operating for 12 years. The Report Line is a 24-hour crisis and referral service which provides help to families and children in crises and information and referral services. The Volunteer receives and screens calls between 4:30 p.m. and 10:30 p.m. After rudimentary screening, the calls indicating a child abuse/neglect problem are referred to the social worker on

Emergency Duty assignment. The Report Line is staffed by specially selected, trained community Volunteers and coordinated by an experienced Volunteer.
The Volunteers are trained yearly. Training consists of: an overview of child welfare services, the ideology of child abuse and neglect, communication skills, agency policy and practice, community resources and empathetic and reflective listening. The training also includes an apprenticeship period with supervision being provided by more experienced volunteers.
The Volunteer program has been jointly sponsored by the local chapter of the Junior League. Individual Volunteers have also been accepted.
Also, the Volunteers have participated in a twice-a-year Clothes Closet drive and the Adopt-A-Family program. Clerical work, transportation services, and tutoring services are other service needs filled by Volunteers.
Founded: 1978

RECIPIENTS: CHILDREN/YOUTH - INDEPENDENT LIVING

NATIONAL/STATE ORGANIZATIONS

ORPHAN FOUNDATION OF AMERICA
1500 Massachusetts Avenue, NW, #448
PO Box 14261
Washington, DC 20044
TEL: 202-861-0762
Objectives: To show support and provide assistance for youth in foster care reaching age 18 and soon to be released as adults.
Services: Offers independent living courses and volunteer counseling services for youth in foster care who are reaching adulthood; offers emergency help, recreation programs, and friendship to children raised outside of the traditional family setting; sponsors *Project Bridge Program,* a community-based volunteer support network that assists youth in foster care in their transition from the child welfare system to independent adulthood; provides training to adult volunteers to assist youth in goal planning, independent living, life skills, career development, job search, maintaining employment, and recreation; sponsors annual Christmas parties and summer picnics; offers speakers to community groups on request; offers scholarships to youth interested in college educations; publishes a newsletter and other materials.
Contact: Reverend Joseph Rivers, Founder

INDIVIDUAL PROGRAM PROFILES

INDEPENDENT LIVING/HOMELESS YOUTH
SEE RECIPIENTS: HOMELESS - CHILDREN/YOUTH

RECIPIENTS: CHILDREN/YOUTH - LEGAL RIGHTS

NATIONAL/STATE ORGANIZATIONS

LEGAL SERVICES FOR CHILDREN*
SEE CONSUMER SERVICES/LEGAL RIGHTS:
CHILDREN/YOUTH

**NATIONAL COURT APPOINTED SPECIAL ADVOCATE
ASSOCIATION**
CASA
2722 Eastlake Avenue, East
Suite 220
Seattle, WA 98102
TEL: 206-328-8588
Objectives: To advocate for the best interests of abused and
neglected children.
Services: Supports the development, growth and continuation of
programs which recruit and train volunteers to serve as court
appointed special advocates for abused and neglected children in
juvenile dependency proceedings; provides training and
professional development, consultation, public education, resource
development, and government relations; advocates for the rights of
children; encourages CASA programs and volunteers across the
U.S. to join together as a united voice for all children; works
toward the goal that every child who needs a CASA volunteer will
have one by the year 2000; draws attention to critical issues
affecting abused and neglected children; conducts nationwide
surveys of CASA programs and publishes results.
Offers training and consultation to CASA programs; sets national
standards for CASA programs and volunteers; provides education
and training through the first *National Training Curriculum for
CASA/GAL Volunteers,* a 40-hour course prepared by the
Minnesota Task Force on Permanency Planning and funded by the
Edna McConnell Clark Foundation; presents a *Juvenile Court
Judge of the Year Award;* recognizes the work of CASA programs
through its *Program Excellence Awards* program; arranges for
volunteers to speak with attorneys for abused and neglected
children in juvenile court; enjoys being the "national philanthropy"
of a major fraternity, receiving grants from organizations such as
the *American Legion Child Welfare Foundation,* and receiving
recognition for its work through awards to the organization;
maintains a speaker's bureau for conferences and community
groups; publishes a newsletter, an information packet, directories
and other materials.
Publications: Speak Up For A Child; A Guide to Member
Services; CASA: A Child's Voice in Court; Children: The Time is
NOW

TRAINING PROGRAMS

CHILDREN: THE TIME IS NOW
National CASA Association
2722 Eastlake Avenue, East
Seattle, WA 98102
TEL: 206-328-8588
Credit: Continuing Legal Education Credits
Contact: Amy Duncan-Little
Description: The annual *National CASA (Court Appointed Special
Advocates) Conference* is the only official meeting of CASA
programs and volunteers. The 1990 session, *Children: The Time Is
Now,* is the ninth annual program, again bringing together
volunteers, program managers, judges, social workers, attorneys
and others who work with abused children in court. Like past

conferences, *Children: The Time Is Now* continues to offer the
nuts and bolts of professional and volunteer training - the how-to
of CASA work, such as interviewing techniques, report writing, an
inside look at foster care, the dynamics of child abuse, etc. The
1990 meeting added a special 'advocacy' track to focus on change -
how we can make a lasting difference in the lives of the children
we serve. Following are selected topics from the schedule:
First Day - General Session: *Child Advocacy on the National
level: How CASA Fits In*
- Federal Legislation for Children: What's Next on the Horizon
- Amendments to P.L. 96-272 and What They Mean for CASA
  Programs
- The Drug Culture's Legacy: Children Born Into Addiction
- Cult and Ritualistic Abuse
- Conflict Management and Negotiation Skills
- Aboguemos Por Los Ninos: Serving the Needs of Hispanic
  Families
- "I Don't Understand a Word You Said": Communication
  Skills for CASA
- Screening and Interview Techniques for Use with Volunteers
- Making a Difference for Children at the State Level: The
  Young Americans Act
- Ten Dimensions of Child Advocacy
- Breaking Down Barriers: Examples of Community Advocacy
- AIDS and Children
- Adolescent Depression and Suicide
- Collaborative Advocacy: Effective Partnerships Between
  CASA and the Child's Attorney
- How Long is Too Long? Improving Service Delivery in Foster
  Care
- It Doesn't Have to Be This Way: Examples of How Child
  Advocates Have Successfully Changed the System
- Working Together: Implementing a Multi-disciplinary
  Approach to Child Abuse
- How CASA Programs and Volunteers Can Make An Impact
  for Children in State Legislatures
- Using the Media to Promote Children's Issues
- Challenging the System - What Changes Do We Need to
  Make?
- Kinship Foster Care: The Double-edged Dilemma
- Children Before the Court Puppet Program
- An Exercise in Futility
- Training Innovations for Attorneys Who Work With CASA
  Programs
- Supervision and Evaluation of Volunteers
Second Day - General Session: *The Time is NOW for Children*
- Why Am I Doing This When My Friends Work Half as Long
  and Earn Twice As Much!
- Expanding to Fill the Need: One Program's Role in
  Community Advocacy
- Representing the Best Interests of the Family
- What's Best for Children with Fetal Alcohol Syndrome
- Report Writing Skills for CASA Volunteers
- Cross Cultural Awareness
- CASA Volunteer Rap Session
Through these conferences, the National CASA Association is
bringing together some of the country's most aggressive and
successful child advocates to teach us how CASA - all 15,000
volunteers and 393 programs - can not only be the fastest growing
child advocacy movement in the country, but the strongest and
most influential. Faculty for *Children: The Time Is Now* was
drawn from children's organizations, health services, the legal
profession, court systems, child abuse advocacy groups, the federal
government, state CASA associations, and others.

INDIVIDUAL PROGRAM PROFILES

CASA PROJECT (COURT APPOINTED SPECIAL ADVOCATES)
SEE CONSUMER SERVICES/LEGAL RIGHTS: CHILDREN/YOUTH

COURT APPOINTED SPECIAL ADVOCATES (CASA)
301 The City Drive
Orange, CA 92668
TEL: 714-834-6460
Purpose: To provide volunteers who act as special friends and advocates of children from group or foster homes.
Sponsor: Orange County (CA)
Contact: Susan Leibel, Director
Description: There is a growing concern among private citizens and professionals that many children in the child welfare system are not receiving the care they need. To help solve that problem, the CASA (Court Appointed Special Advocates) program has revolutionized part of the judicial system by allowing private citizens to participate in previously closed juvenile courts. In a system where social workers carry heavy caseloads, the child advocates have come to be relied on to provide the kind of loving one-to-one contact that caseworkers cannot. The children in the program have no one outside of the system who cares about them and often are moved constantly from foster home to group home to emergency shelter. The CASA program provides some stability for them - a continuing presence that they can count on. With a national office in Seattle, and 393 CASA programs nationwide, thousands of children are being represented who might not have been brought before the courts at all. California alone has 17 CASA programs, and in one state, at least (Florida), counties are required by law to have CASA programs.
The Orange County CASA program is an independent nonprofit organization with offices supplied by the county. Currently the program has 106 active volunteers. With about 2,000 children in the system, this group of volunteers can handle only a small percentage. Volunteers go through a 20-hour course in which they learn about courtroom procedures from judges, lawyers and other court personnel and attend seminars on topics ranging from sexual abuse of children to early childhood development and adolescent behavior.
After the training, they are sworn in by a juvenile court judge as officers of the court and take an oath of confidentiality to gain access to juvenile court files. They are matched with a child and see that child on a weekly basis and provide consistency.
Each time there is a hearing concerning the child, the CASA submits a written report that becomes part of a child's court file. To prepare these court reports, CASA volunteers also talk to the child, parents, other relatives, social workers, school officials, doctors and anyone else knowledgeable about the child's history to determine if it would be better for the child to remain with parents or guardians, be placed in foster care, or be freed for permanent adoption. Unfortunately, there are not nearly enough foster homes to take them. So they must go to group homes, emergency shelter homes or to Orangewood.
One of the aspects that proves an interesting challenge is the fact that the court and caseworkers are obligated by law to work to reunite children with their families, while the volunteers often see the family as unworthy of getting the child back. CASA supporters liken this concept to lay people on a jury and argue that they can apply common sense and community standards to sometimes impersonal judicial proceedings that determine the fates of families. Many judges see them as the *common denominator* in the system. Where caseworkers often work with 60 to 70 children at a time, CASA volunteers work with only one or two. Thus, the volunteer can examine each case more thoroughly and provide emotional and practical support. In addition, volunteers often take kids to the hospital and medical appointments when a social worker finds it impossible to go. In some cases it is possible to assign a medically-knowledgeable volunteer who can ask questions of the doctor, read blood tests, etc.
The volunteers come from all over the county, ranging from 21-year-old students to retired seniors. The majority hold full-time jobs and see children on weekends, evenings, or after school. All make a one-year commitment. According to one volunteer, "The important thing is that they have somebody there for them. And it's important that they have some idea of family life. They need to know that they are special and have a future."
Founded: 1984

RECIPIENTS: CHILDREN/YOUTH - MENTAL HEALTH

INDIVIDUAL PROGRAM PROFILES

GREENHOUSE
SEE MENTAL HEALTH: CHILDREN/YOUTH

PARENT-CHILD PROGRAM*
SEE TEENAGE PREGNANCY/PARENTING

RECIPIENTS: CHILDREN/YOUTH - NUTRITION

NATIONAL/STATE ORGANIZATIONS

CHILDREN'S FOUNDATION
SEE DAY CARE/HEAD START: EVALUATION

INDIVIDUAL PROGRAM PROFILES

COMMUNITY PROGRAMS
SEE NUTRITION: ON-SITE

EMERGENCY INFANT NUTRITION PROGRAM: FREE BREAKFAST PROJECT
SEE NUTRITION: CHILDREN/YOUTH

RECIPIENTS: CHILDREN/YOUTH - OFFENDERS

INDIVIDUAL PROGRAM PROFILES

JUVENILE ARBITRATION PROGRAM OF SOUTH CAROLINA
SEE LAW ENFORCEMENT/CRIME PREVENTION: CHILDREN/YOUTH

MORRIS COUNTY CHAPLAINCY COUNCIL
SEE LAW ENFORCEMENT/CRIME PREVENTION:
RE-ENTRY

NEIGHBORHOOD PROBATION UNIT
SEE RECIPIENTS: POLICE/COURT OFFICERS - RESPITE

**OFFENDER AID AND RESTORATION OF ROANOKE,
VIRGINIA***
SEE LAW ENFORCEMENT/CRIME PREVENTION:
CHILDREN/YOUTH

RECIPIENTS: CHILDREN/YOUTH - PERSONAL GROWTH

NATIONAL/STATE ORGANIZATIONS

BOY SCOUTS OF AMERICA
1325 Walnut Hill Lane
Irving, TX 75038
TEL: 214-580-2000
Objectives: To provide an educational program for boys and young
adults; to build character; to train in the responsibilities of
participating citizenship, and to develop personal fitness.
Services: Issues national charters to community groups who use
the Scouting program as a part of their own youth work, and who
have goals compatible with those of the BSA; includes groups
from religious, educational, civic, fraternal, business, labor,
governmental, corporate, and professional areas, as well as
autonomous groups of citizens; operates programs at several levels
of ability, including:
- **Tiger Scouting,** which has been developed for seven-year-old
  boys.
- **Cub Scouting,** which serves boys eight, nine, and ten years of
  age (at ten, they become Webelos Scouts in preparation for
  Boy Scouting).
- **Boy Scouting,** which is designed for boys aged 11 through 17
  as a vigorous outdoor program and peer group leadership
  program.
- **Exploring,** which is a contemporary program for young men
  and women aged 15 through 20 to provide opportunities to
  learn about adult roles and vocational opportunities in
  association with business and community partners.

(Varies age limits from those stated above when school grade and
other considerations warrant a departure from the general
guidelines.)
Involves volunteer adult leaders at all levels of scouting in 415
local councils, 32 areas, six regions, and nationally with volunteer
executive boards and committees providing guidance; celebrates
Scouting Anniversary Week in February of each year, Scouting
Environment Day in April, and Scouting Energy Day in October;
publishes three magazines: *Boys' Life* for all boys, *Exploring* for
young men and women and Explorer leaders, and *Scouting* for all
registered adults in scouting programs.
Receives most of its support from pack, troop and post fees, the
sale of scouting equipment, bequests and special gifts (local
programs receive United Way support and have a dues structure
for this purpose); fees from local programs help support national
training events for leaders, counseling, camping and outdoor
facilities, program materials, literature, planning tools, etc.
Publications: Boys' Life; Scouting Magazine; Exploring Magazine;
Annual Report to Congress
Founded: 1910

CAMP FIRE
4601 Madison Avenue
Kansas City, MO 64112
TEL: 816-756-1950
TOLL FREE: 800-821-6180
Objectives: To provide an informal education program for young
people to help them become self-directed, responsible, caring
individuals.
Services: Administers program to children in small group settings
in three basic ways:
- **Club Programs** - programs created at the national level and
  offered to groups who meet on a regular basis with a volunteer
  leader.
- **Outdoor Programs** - programs created by the national
  organization and by Camp Fire councils, and including group
  camping, day camping, resident camping, trips, environmental
  projects and outdoor recreation.
- **Response Programs** - programs based on researching the needs
  of young people and creating the content, systems and
  materials responsive to these needs (developed by Camp Fire
  councils and the national organization); includes response
  programs in day care centers, after school recreation
  programs, tutorial reading programs, job training programs,
  drop-in centers, campership projects, delinquency prevention
  projects, in-school enrichment programs, and projects to
  mainstream the handicapped.

Includes both boys and girls as members, from birth to 21 years of
age; divides program into four groupings: Blue Bird (grades 1-3;
largest group); Adventure (grades 4-8); Discovery (grades 7 and 8);
and Horizon (grades 9-12); supplements these groupings in some
Councils with preschool and post-high school programs; delivers
programs directly to youth, as well as through sponsoring
institutions, church bodies, businesses and other organizations;
trains volunteer leaders so that Program Standards are uniform
across the country; exercises social/advocacy responsibility
through programs in juvenile justice, immunization of children,
rape prevention, youth employment, tutoring, tree planting, CPR,
English as a Second Language, and numerous other areas
reflecting social concerns within the community.
Promotes volunteerism by demonstrating volunteer leadership
through its Councils, and by involving volunteers in management
and decision-making.
Publications: Camp Fire Management; Leadership Magazine
Founded: 1910

GIRL SCOUTS OF THE USA
830 Third Avenue
New York, NY 10022
TEL: 212-940-7500
Objectives: To provide an informal education program for girls
and adults to inspire high ideals of character, conduct, patriotism
and service.
Services: Guides and supports approximately 336 Councils and
over 553,000 volunteers; provides assistance through three field
centers (Dallas, New York, and Chicago) with each Center
recruiting, promoting, and retaining its own adult volunteers;
provides opportunity for volunteer activity in areas ranging from
policy making at local and national levels to direct service to girls
in troops (the volunteer program supports the total girl scout
program); involves volunteers as Council board members,
community administrators, committee members, neighborhood
chairpersons, consultants and supervisors at the administrative
level; involves volunteers as troop/camp leaders, learning
consultants, recruiters, trainers, fund raisers, project leaders,
speakers' bureau members, and numerous other areas at the
operational level; maintains salaried staff in the field offices to
provide support and guidance, with actual supervision of local staff
and volunteers being controlled by the respective local Council;
offers financial aid to relevant seminars and courses to qualified

volunteer staff.

Publishes instructional materials for distribution to volunteer staff, including *Leader's Digest: Blue Book of Basic Documents, Tips for the Program Consultant, Mix and Match, Directing the Work of Others,* etc.; provides job descriptions for all volunteer appointments, as well as supervision and career guidance for volunteers through clarification of expectations, performance goals, monitoring, coaching, and ongoing evaluation of performance; convenes regional and national meetings.
Publications: GSUSA News; Girl Scout Leader; Environmental Scanning Report
Founded: 1912

GIRLS CLUBS OF AMERICA
30 East 33rd Street
New York, NY 10016
TEL: 212-689-3700 (New York); 317-634-7546 (Indiana)
Objectives: To focus national attention on the special needs of girls; to enable them to achieve responsible and confident adulthood, economic independence and personal fulfillment.
Services: Serves a quarter of a million girls ages 6-18 through over 200 Clubs and various outreach programs, over half belonging to racial and ethnic minority groups and two-thirds coming from families earning under $15,000 a year; currently operates national programs addressing AIDS education, substance abuse prevention, science, math and technology, adolescent pregnancy, and sports and physical fitness; includes among traditional and nontraditional programs initiated by local Clubs activities in drama, the arts, computer science, humanities and life skills; includes 2500 professional staff members and 8,000 volunteers in Girls Clubs buildings, extensions and branches across the country, including volunteer board members from local communities; through local Clubs offers an average of 30 hours a week of programs and activities in an informal educational environment after school, on weekends and during school vacations; has four regional service centers which provide training, technical and organizational assistance to Clubs' professional staff and volunteers.
[All programs developed by Girls Clubs of America are researched, analyzed and evaluated at the National Resource Center, the nation's first and most extensive clearinghouse of its kind for information about girls. It contains library and research facilities and distributes publications and materials to parents, educators, policymakers, women's groups and others concerned with girls.]
Contact: Susan Ellis (Indiana)
Publications: Voice for Girls; We're On The Move; Girls and Substance Abuse; Sporting Chance
Founded: 1945

SCOUTING FOR THE HANDICAPPED
SEE RECIPIENTS: HANDICAPPED

SKY RANCH FOR BOYS
SEE PSYCHOSOCIAL SUPPORT SERVICES: CHILDREN/YOUTH

US/DOA - 4-H YOUTH/EXTENSION SERVICE
South Building
Third Floor
Washington, DC 20250
TEL: 202-447-5853
Objectives: To involve youth and adults, working together, in learn-by-doing educational activities and real-life experiences.
Services: Involves parents, volunteer leaders, and other adults in organizing and conducting projects for community and family settings; operates in counties, towns, and cities through Cooperative Extension Service agents who guide and supervise nearly 600,000 volunteer leaders and other volunteers; serves

nearly five million members between the ages of nine and 19 both on farms and in big cities, suburbs, small towns and communities; varies planning to reflect the diversity of the clubs, working in the following areas:
- organized community or neighborhood 4-H clubs;
- special interest or short-term groups;
- school enrichment programs;
- 4-H instructional television;
- camping; and
- individual 4-H members.

Operates an international youth exchange program to work with the 82 countries around the globe that have adapted youth programs similar to 4-H; enlists leadership through the combined efforts of federal, state and county Extension staff, existing leaders, support from the National 4-H Council, and other private support donors.
Founded: 1900

TRAINING PROGRAMS

4-H GENERAL FORUMS: ADULT VOLUNTEER TRAINING
US/DoA - 4-H Youth/Extension Service
Independence Avenue
(Between 12th & 14th Sts.)
Washington, DC 20250
TEL: 202-447-6527
Credit: Certificate
Sponsor: US/DoA - Department of Agriculture
Description: Conducted an average of five times each year, the 4-H general forum deals with the overall 4-H program: local clubs, leader recruitment and training, parent involvement, awards and recognition programs, training for middle management roles, designing 4-H with people, fund raising and proposal information, translating volunteer experiences into saleable skills, and other areas of general interest to adult volunteer leaders of the 4-H youth programs. Workshops are designed to help the adult volunteer to:
- Become more effective in working with 4-H members and other 4-H leaders;
- Experience new approaches to leadership development;
- Increase understanding of the legislative process;
- Prepare a plan of action for working with other community and/or 4-H leaders;
- Develop skills into building citizenship and careers into 4-H projects;
- Exchange ideas with 4-H leaders from other states; and
- Identify and use community resources.

The major theme for General Forums is "Designing 4-H with People," with sub-themes of Getting, Training, Retaining Leaders, Developing Leadership in Youth, Motivating Members and Keeping Kids, and Roles and Relationship. Each forum includes idea sharing opportunities and exhibits from each state. Held at the National 4-H Training Center in Maryland, options for extra activities include A Day on Capitol Hill, which provides the volunteers with a first-hand look at the legislative process, as well as other planned leadership development tours and sessions based on the Center's proximity to Washington, DC.

4-H SPECIFIC FORUMS: ADULT VOLUNTEER TRAINING
US/DoA - 4-H Youth/Extension Service
Independence Avenue
(Between 12th & 14th Sts.)
Washington, DC 20250
TEL: 202-447-6527
Credit: Certificate
Sponsor: US/DoA - Department of Agriculture
Contact: Dr. V. Milton Boyce

Description: A Specific Forum in the 4-H training series for adult volunteers addresses one project area (e.g., horses, nutrition, the disabled), with up to five topics covered in as many forums each year. Some of these special interest forums enjoy the funding and personal involvement of a donor company - such as the Campbell Soup Company's involvement in the nutrition forum. With these forums, the primary goal is to teach leadership skills using the particular subject matter area as the vehicle. Examples of specific training programs and topics covered are:

Reaching Out to Disabled Youth, which is designed to help adult leaders to:

- Become more aware of the role of youth serving organizations in the personal development of all youth.
- Gain skills in planning, carrying out and evaluating programs involving youth with disabilities.
- Increase a sense of awareness and competency in working with a mainstreamed population.
- Prepare a plan of approach to work with others to make programs more accessible and meaningful to all youth regardless of disability.

Participation in this forum expands continually as interest in and commitment to the disabled audience around the country deepens. Seven hours of workshops, an idea exchange period and several field trips form the nucleus of the program.

Expanding the 4-H Youth Employment Economics Job and Career Education Model, a program designed to:

- Acquaint Extension staff and Volunteer 4-H Leaders with the 4-H Youth Employment, Economic, Job and Career Education Model.
- Develop the skills of volunteer leaders and Extension Staff to teach young people, train volunteer leaders, and identify and utilize community resources.
- Increase 4-H member participation in youth employment, economic job and career projects and activities.
- Develop a team approach to 4-H programs with teens, adult volunteer leaders, donors, community resources, and Extension Staff working together.
- Review successful youth employment, economics job and career education programs offered by 4-H and other organizations, and determine how they may be adapted to meet the needs of other communities.
- Provide a bibliography of teaching materials available in the area of youth employment, economics, jobs and careers.
- Develop a Leader Training Model which can be incorporated into leader development at the state, area and county levels.

Planning for this program each year is done via Telephonic Conference Calls. Ten hours of workshops and general sessions deal with such topics as Developmental Needs of Youth and Curriculum; Strengthening the Economic, Job and Career Emphasis in 4-H Projects; Developing a Family Approach to Career Education; Developing Programs with a Career Focus. The sessions are supplemented with field trips, panel discussions, a resource center, a Trade Fair, and a session on Designing 4-H With People. Plans of Action were developed to serve as a guide for back home application.

Nutrition Leader Training, which is designed to help volunteer 4-H leaders to:

- Learn more effective teaching methods.
- Make learning fun for youth and adults.
- Identify and use community resources.
- Build careers into nutrition programs.
- Help 4-H leaders and members set learning goals and assess programs.

Donors such as the Campbell Soup Company (inquire about others) sponsor these Forums. A typical forum was attended by 102 adult volunteers and 4-H staff from 34 states. The purpose was to develop a "teamwork" method of bringing together volunteer 4-H leaders and the Extension staff to help 4-H Food and Nutrition Leaders.

Planning sessions are conducted by Telephonic Conference Calls.

Participants were involved in nine hours of workshops dealing with such topics as Practical Ideas and Tools to Promote Nutrition Education, Fitness and Food, Expanding Your Leadership Role, Resources - Material and Community, and Managing 4-H Foods and Nutrition Programs. In the forum sponsored by Campbell Soup Company participants spent a day at the company's headquarters, for which Campbell developed six special leader and member guides dealing with nutrition and fitness information. A follow-up survey is conducted nine months after each forum to determine ways in which participants use the learning experience.

Planning committees for the specific forums consist of volunteer leaders, salaried staff, representatives of National 4-H Council and USDA, and the donor company, who develop and conduct the program for each forum. Most specific forums are fully or partially funded by donors.

General forums change to meet the needs expressed by the planning committees and participating states.

In addition to 4-H groups, adult volunteers who attend the forums work with schools, church groups, senior citizens groups, Extension Homemakers Clubs, civic organizations and the general public.

INDIVIDUAL PROGRAM PROFILES

CENTER FOR YOUTH SERVICE
921 Pennsylvania Avenue, SE
Washington, DC 20003
TEL: 202-543-5707
Purpose: To offer inner city adolescents a new way of expanding their skills and overcoming their obstacles and deficits.
Sponsor: March of Dimes
Contact: Youth Service Coordinator
Description: The Center for Youth Services (CYS) is a nonprofit, private corporation with a goal of helping youth be the best that they can. Youth become members of CYS through a four-step program which begins with an orientation to the center and the signing of a contract agreeing to do his or her best to complete the program as planned. Next the youth are exposed to a series of seminars on issues such as values, environmental influences, decisionmaking, and employment options. Following the seminars, the youth have an interview with a staff member to determine interests, goals and needs. The result of the interview is a program of services designed especially for the youth.

The opportunities at CYS include an extensive employment program, which includes supervised on-the-job experience, building maintenance training, summer youth employment, and direct placement with follow-up services. The educational component is also an important aspect of CYS. It includes classes in Basic Skills I and II, GED preparation, and tutoring. CYS has had a high success rate in helping students to pass the GED.

In the counseling program, the mental health staff of CYS become involved with nearly all of the young people who use the center. They are available to discuss personal problems, strengthen self-esteem, and encourage goal-setting. Also, CYS has a health clinic which provides general health care, treatment of sexually-transmitted diseases, and prenatal care.

CYS offers day care free of charge to young people while they participate in center activities or one of the job components. CYS staff also work to provide a wide range of recreational opportunities for youth, including sports teams, table games, and field trips.

CYS is unique in that it allows each youth to create a program to suit his individual needs, concerns and interests.

Since 1985 the March of Dimes has awarded local grants to CYS totaling $19,996 as of early 1989. An additional grant of $10,000 was awarded to CYS to fund the "Male Health Clinic," which promotes sexual responsibility among adolescents and young males through a combined program of education and medical services.

YOUTH SERVICES
American Red Cross
Princeton Area Chapter
182 North Harrison Street
Princeton, NJ 08540
TEL: 609-924-2404
Purpose: To provide students from grades kindergarten through twelve with the opportunity for leadership development while gaining a greater awareness for people in their community.
Sponsor: Princeton Area Chapter, American Red Cross
Contact: Director, Youth Services
Description: Youth Services at the Princeton Area Chapter seeks to provide area youth with the opportunity for leadership development, personal growth, and career exploration through participation in worthwhile volunteer activities. The program strives to furnish young people with the skills needed to become responsible, self-reliant adults and to stimulate them to be lifetime volunteers in service to the community.

Opportunities for growth and development are mainly provided through high school youth involvement in the Youth Teaching Youth program, in which student volunteers teach children at the elementary and middle school levels. This year, the chapter's youth volunteer instructors taught 195 classes to children on topics such as first aid, safety, drug awareness and abuse, babysitting, and components of blood. Currently, twenty-one youth volunteers are active participants in the program, coming from Stuart County Day School, West Windsor-Plainsboro High School, Princeton Day School, and Princeton High School.

Program growth has been noted in the provision of nine youth volunteers to serve as aides at the chapter office on a periodic basis to perform support functions for blood, safety, youth, and secretarial services. Significant progress has also been evidenced in the recruiting of eligible youth blood donors from local public and private high schools to assist in meeting the growing need for blood at the Princeton Medical Center.

Goals for future expansion of Youth Services include the formation of a Youth Advisory Committee to generate new methods of introducing Red Cross services into the schools. Finally, the chapter is investigating methods of further developing leadership among area youth through participation in a Leadership Development Conference, designed to introduce youth to various Red Cross activities and to inspire them to continued community involvement.

RECIPIENTS: CHILDREN/YOUTH - PROTECTIVE SERVICES

NATIONAL/STATE ORGANIZATIONS

CHILD ABUSE HOTLINE
Virginia Department of Social Services
Child Protective Services
8007 Discovery Drive
Richmond, VA 23229-8699
TOLL FREE: 800-552-7096
Objectives: To receive reports of child abuse and refer them for action by appropriate authorities.
Services: The Child Abuse Hotline of the Child Protective Services division of the Virginia Department of Social Services is a 24-hour, seven-day service to enable concerned citizens to report cases of child abuse anonymously. The Hotline fills the gap created when local social service agencies close at the end of the business day. It provides for the receipt, identification and immediate referral for investigation of complaints and reports of child abuse and neglect

for children under the age of eighteen. The majority of complaints are received by the Hotline after normal working hours, on weekends, and on holidays. When the Hotline operator completes the call, the information is forwarded immediately to a local child protective services worker since often the cases are too critical to wait until the next day. A social worker is available in each city and county throughout the State to receive reports from the Hotline. This assures immediate investigation.

To facilitate citizen action when a child appears to be in jeopardy, Protective Services distributes information on the most common types of child abuse and the signs indicating abuse. Also, copies of the 1974 Virginia Child Abuse and Neglect Act outlining incidences that are considered abusive (lack of supervision, or inadequate food, clothing or shelter, as well as the more obvious sexual abuse) are widely distributed. Such communication has dramatically increased the number of Hotline calls (400 a year before amendments to the law, now almost 40,000 each year) and in some cases has provided life saving assistance to the additional children and their families.

Another important function of the Hotline is the maintenance of the *Child Protective Services Information System (Central Registry).* The *Registry* receives all reports of abuse and neglect referred to local agencies, helping authorities to determine if prior reports exist on the same child or the same alleged offender anywhere in Virginia. This identification of repeated incidents and repeating offenders is an effective aid in preventing abuse and neglect. Also, the statistical data made possible by the *Registry* is an effective tool to improve overall planning of protective service programs.
Sponsor: Governor's Advisory Committee on Child Abuse & Neglect
Contact: Volunteer Coordinator

CHILD ABUSE LISTENING MEDIATION
CALM
PO Box 718
Santa Barbara, CA 93102
TEL: 805-682-1366 (offices); 805-569-2255 (hotline)
Objectives: To prevent child abuse by providing a listening service for parents "who feel that they cannot cope with their problems and may be on the verge of taking it out on the children."
Services: Provides a 24-hour Hotline, staffed with volunteers (with one bilingual listener available); trains volunteers to go into the homes as Family Aides to help in special situations of crisis; offers emergency child care for parents in stress; refers to other organizations and other resource services; maintains speakers bureau and a resource library; conducts public information/education program; conducts a Pre-Parenting Awareness Program, weekly Parental Support Groups (one bilingual); publishes quarterly newsletter, reports, bibliographies, and other materials.
Publications: CALMWORD
Founded: 1970

CHILD FIND OF AMERICA
PO Box 277
New Paltz, NY 12561
TEL: 914-255-1848; 800-A-WAY-OUT
TOLL FREE: 800-I-AM-LOST
Objectives: To establish a known point of contact for parents and children who are searching for each other.
Services: Works with other missing children-related organizations and agencies through information exchange; includes in its membership parents of missing children, local and international social service agencies and organizations; maintains a registry of missing children in the U.S.; works to establish a known point of contact for parents and children seeking each other; sponsors an annual *Missing Children's Day;* maintains toll-free numbers for use by abducted children and individuals identifying missing

children; publishes a newsletter, and a directory providing photographs and physical descriptions of missing children.
Publications: Child Find Newsletter
Founded: 1980

HUG-A-TREE AND SURVIVE
c/o Jacqueline Heet
6465 Lance Way
San Diego, CA 92120
TEL: 619-286-7536
Objectives: To teach children what to do if they are lost.
Services: Provides teaching program for children to help them make the right decisions when lost - *stay put, hug a tree, until help arrives;* produces slide program that is presented by search and rescue or sheriff's reserve personnel, who are trained by Hug-A-Tree in the program that familiarizes children with the type of people who will be searching for them, as well as what they should do to aid searchers and protect themselves until rescued; derives name of the program from its primary message to the child to stay in one place.
Founded: 1981

NATIONAL CENTER FOR MISSING AND EXPLOITED CHILDREN
1835 K Street, NW
Suite 700
Washington, DC 20006
TEL: 202-634-9821; 800-826-7653 (TDD)
TOLL FREE: 800-843-5678
Objectives: To aid parents and law enforcement agencies in preventing child exploitation and in locating missing children.
Services: Serves as a national clearinghouse of information on effective state and federal legislation directed at the protection of children; provides technical assistance to individuals, parents, groups, agencies, and state and local governments involved in locating and returning children in cases of child exploitation; maintains videotapes for staff training and education; publishes materials on effectiving searching techniques; maintains toll-free hotlines (one for the hearing-impaired) to collect and disseminate information on sightings of children; provides technical assistance; works with other organizations with similar concerns.

NATIONAL CENTER ON CHILD ABUSE AND NEGLECT
US/HHS - Administration for Children, Youth and Families
PO Box 1182
Washington, DC 20013
TEL: 703-821-2086
Objectives: To assist state, local and voluntary agencies and organizations in strengthening their capacities in areas of child abuse.
Services: Provides grants for demonstration programs, research into causes, prevention and treatment; funds states for efforts related to child abuse prevention, investigation and treatment; operates the Clearinghouse on Child Abuse and Neglect Information; publishes manuals, available without charge.
Sponsor: US/HHS - Department of Health & Human Services
Founded: 1975

NATIONAL COMMITTEE FOR PREVENTION OF CHILD ABUSE
332 South Michigan Avenue
Suite 1250
Chicago, IL 60604
TEL: 312-663-3520
Objectives: To prevent all forms of child abuse, including: nonaccidental injury, physical and emotional abuse and neglect of children.

Services: Operates ongoing national media campaign to create public awareness of child abuse; conducts research on how to prevent abuse; publishes a wide variety of publications for professionals and the lay public on the issue; and organizes concerned citizens into volunteer-based chapters which develop primary prevention programs in their own communities.
Founded: 1972

NATIONAL LEGAL RESOURCE CENTER FOR CHILD ADVOCACY AND PROTECTION
American Bar Association
1800 M Street, NW
Washington, DC 20036
TEL: 202-331-2250
Objectives: To increase professional awareness and competency of the legal community in child welfare issues; to respond to requests for information from laypersons and groups.
Services: Conducts research and development activities to keep both the legal profession and community project leaders informed on legal issues of child maltreatment; addresses specific concerns such as methods of sensitive intervention, an area based on years of research to find the most effective approaches; publishes general directories and bibliographies of interest to both professionals and community groups, such as *National Directory of Programs Providing Court Representation to Abused and Neglected Children* and *Special Education Advocacy for the Abused Child.*
Publications: Special Education Advocacy; Directory of Programs

OPERATION CHILD WATCH
US/DoL - Women's Bureau
200 Constitution Avenue, NW
Washington, DC 20210
TEL: 202-523-6666
Objectives: To monitor employers of youth to assure compliance with child labor laws.
Services: Operates "surprise sweeps" of fast-food restaurants, pizza delivery services, doughnut shops, grocery stores, dry cleaners, movie theatres, and other youth-employing businesses with regard to child labor laws - primarily age, hours worked, and degree of hazard; levies stiff civil penalties, which increase dramatically for repeat offenders; maintains a "strike force" of 500 investigators throughout the country to monitor youth-hiring practices; makes available to all employers the *Fair Labor Standards Act,* which includes child labor provisions and is enforced by the Department of Labor's Wage and Hour Division; cites statistics such as 1989 violations of 22,508, and the same year's fines of $1.8, to deter future violations; files suits against companies who are flagrant repeaters or have a long history of violations.
Sponsor: US/DoL - Department of Labor
Contact: William Brooks, Assistant Secretary/Employment Standards

PUBLIC AWARENESS ABOUT CHILD CARE (PAACC)
SEE LAW ENFORCEMENT/CRIME PREVENTION: CHILDREN/YOUTH

TIPS PROGRAM
SEE LAW ENFORCEMENT/CRIME PREVENTION: CHILDREN/YOUTH

TRAINING PROGRAMS

PARENT AIDE TRAINING
Montgomery County Department of Social Services
5630 Fishers Lane
Rockville, MD 20852
TEL: 301-468-4345

Credit: Inquire
Sponsor: Montgomery County Government
Contact: Peggy Nelson
Description: In this training program, volunteers concerned with child abuse problems receive a basic orientation to the Department of Social Services by staff, and on-the-job training by supervisors of specific units. In addition, they are briefed in the following major areas:

- The Philosophy of the Parent Aide Program
- The Structure and Policy of the Protective Services Division
- The Facts and Dynamics of Child Abuse and Neglect

Following the orientation session, participants are involved around the following specific issues:

- Attitudes and Values: Assessment and Clarification
- Parent Aide Experience: The Team Approach
- Role Playing (Rehearsing for Reality)

Ample time for discussion is provided throughout the eight-hour program. Small-group role-playing and a wrap-up with the full student body conclude the course. The emphasis is on a team approach.

INDIVIDUAL PROGRAM PROFILES

ALTERNATIVE HOUSE
Juvenile Assistance, McLean, Ltd (JAM)
PO Box 637
McLean, VA 22101
TEL: 703-356-2045
Purpose: To provide a safe, secure environment and/or counseling situation where young people and their families can begin to improve their life situations and resolve the issues that led to their seeking counseling.
Sponsor: Federal/State/County governments; corporate and private donations
Contact: Dana DeVor, Volunteer/Internship Coordinator
Description: Alternative House is a crisis intervention center that offers emergency shelter and counseling to troubled teenagers - primarily runaway, throwaway, or abused kids. The runaway incident is both a signal for help and an opportunity for constructive change. It is important to have an environment which supports development of a positive self-image and competence in skills and abilities. *Alternative House* helps young people gain independence of thought, self understanding, self acceptance, and confidence to confront challenges and make decisions.
Alternative House is the oldest program in Northern Virginia offering residential and counseling services for runaway, homeless, and abused teenagers. Since 1972, when a group of concerned community people incorporated the agency, *Alternative House* has served thousands of teenagers and their families. Our goal is to reunite families whenever possible, increase communication between family members, and resolve the crisis that brought the teenager to *Alternative House.*
Alternative House is best known in the community for our crisis shelter for troubled teens. During their two-week stay, residents have individual, group, and family counseling. Many of them return home. If home is not an option, they may go into custody with the *Department of Human Development,* and then to a foster home or group home.
The family counseling program at *Alternative House* recently has been granted full licensure by the State as an outpatient mental health program, attesting to the high level of quality of its professional counseling services. Other programs include a 24-hour toll-free hotline, walk-in counseling, and free workshops on parenting, adolescence, and other family issues.
Volunteer Program - Volunteers are an integral part of *Alternative House,* and are needed to help provide positive experiences for the residents while serving as appropriate role models. Applicants for volunteer positions go through a screening process and attend 8-10

hours of preliminary training before actual shift work begins. Monthly volunteer meetings and in-service training events are held to provide volunteers with ongoing training. Examples of volunteer job opportunities follow:

- *Direct Service Volunteers:* Work directly with individuals and groups (up to 32 hours/month); ongoing need.
- *Project Safe Place Volunteers:* Distribute promotional material, recruit *Safe Place* participants, help with training and follow-up (5-10 hours/month); ongoing need.
- *Drug Prevention Project Evaluation Volunteers:* Help to develop effective ways of evaluating the effectiveness of our *Drug Prevention Grant* and to help prepare our quarterly reports to D-HHS (5 hours/month); ongoing need.
- *Newsletter Volunteers:* Help us write, edit, and publish our quarterly newsletter (5-10 hours/month); ongoing need.
- *Pocket Card Development Volunteers:* Help develop and distribute *Substance Abuse Prevention Resource & Referral Cards* (5-10 hours/month); four-month project.
- *Youth Council Coordinator Volunteers:* Contact local high schools and acquire recommendations of one or two students per school to help create and maintain a *Youth Council* which meets at *Alternative House* once a month with our Director and Program Director in order to give youth input to our program; help facilitate the meetings (4-5 hours/month); ongoing need.
- *Peer Counseling Program Development Volunteers:* Help develop a sound peer counseling program at *Alternative House,* beginning with *Ala-teen, Teen AA,* and *Teen NA* meetings (5-10 hours/month); ongoing need.
- *Administrative Volunteers:* Help send letters of thanks, update the mailing list, etc.; training provided (5-10 hours/month); ongoing need.
- *Special Project Volunteers:* Needed on an ad-hoc basis for various events and temporary projects throughout the year.

Internship Program - We accept student interns as part of the regular volunteer program at *Alternative House.* These interns become involved with the hotline, walk-in, and residential counseling services that we offer to teenagers and their families. This is a crisis intervention setting, which offers a wide range of clinical experience. The time commitment can be individually negotiated for student interns.
Our long-term family counseling program also accepts interns, usually graduate students in counseling or social work programs. This internship offers intensive training in family therapy, and requires a minimum six-month commitment of 16-40 hours per week.
Alternative House has four levels of internship available to students who are seeking experience and clinical training in work with adolescents and their families. Placement depends on the student's level of education, the time commitment of the internship, and the range of responsibilities which the student is seeking and the agency is able to provide.
Students who wish to receive school credit for their work at *Alternative House* must arrange this through their college or university. We are happy to cooperate with school requirements in terms of hours, supervision, or special evaluations. In addition, we require a personal interview for acceptance into the internship program.
Each intern must go through an initial training period before starting to work in the shelter. All interns receive a supervisor and meet weekly, individually or as a group. Interns are required to attend all in-service training events.
Volunteer and Internship Job Descriptions - Job descriptions for both programs are available on request, and include the four levels for intern positions for students ranging from undergraduate to second year graduate levels. A resume must be submitted with an application for either program to the *Volunteer Coordinator* at the above address. An interview with the *Volunteer Coordinator* is required. Application deadlines for interns are December 15th for the Spring Semester, April 20th for the Summer Semester, and

August 20th for the Fall Semester. Both volunteers and interns enjoy free meals when they are here during mealtime periods.

BLOUNT COUNTY CHILDREN'S CENTER
SCAN (Stop Child Abuse Now)
106 First Avenue, West
Oneonta, AL 35121
TEL: 205-274-7226
Purpose: To help prevent, treat, and raise awareness about child abuse in Blount County.
Sponsor: Private Donations
Contact: Patti Stephens, Executive Director
Description: In 1983, when the state Department of Human Resources mobilized a community effort to prevent child abuse and neglect, two of the Department's officials got the idea for a private sector program to help supplement the state's efforts. Based on their first-hand knowledge that social workers don't have time for prevention or treatment, they formed the *Blount County Children's Center* which, except for the Director, is run entirely by volunteers. Soon, auxiliary programs were formed.
The primary program is *SCAN (Stop Child Abuse Now).* SCAN began to recruit volunteers through public meetings on six consecutive Thursday nights. The meetings were open to the public free of charge. Outgrowths of the SCAN program include:
- **Better Safe Than Sorry** - a school-based program consisting of three films on child sexual abuse produced by *Film Fair Communications.* The three films are geared to kindergarten, primary and high school with the latter film focusing on date-rape and incest.
- **STEP (Systematic Training for Effective Parenting)** - a parenting curriculum used nationwide.
- **Adolescent Pregnancy Prevention Program** - a program featuring an informal discussion, films and "very plain talk" with the county's students.
- **Support Groups** - a program designed to help victims of child abuse, including a full-time therapist for children.

This volunteer effort has made Blount County the leader in the state in the number of reports on child abuse. According to the Director, "Public awareness is such that people are quicker to pick up the phone and report child abuse." An official of the state's *Children's Trust Fund* points out that an increased number of child abuse reports is not a sign the county is going backward. "When the public becomes more aware, the reports go up. That is progress. If it is not reported, it is not going to be stopped." Plans call for submitting a federal grant application to do a full program, hire three people, and set up a toll-free county line to call for help.
Founded: 1983

CHILD ABUSE SERVICES TEAM (CAST)
Orangewood Children's Home
401 The City Drive South
Orange, CA 92668
TEL: 714-834-7584; 714-834-7105
Purpose: To provide citizen advocates for sexually abused children.
Sponsor: Orangewood Children's Home
Description: The *Child Abuse Services Team (CAST)* is designed to reduce the trauma for child victims of sexual abuse by reducing the number of interviews and investigations. CAST volunteers serve as advocates as the children undergo interviews and examinations.
CAST provides a single "child-friendly" location to avoid the overwhelming government structures. Crisis intervention and long-term therapy are provided by CAST also on an as-needed basis. The *Team* involves police agencies, medical personnel, child-welfare services and the District Attorney's Office. A day and a half of training is provided for all volunteers prior to assignments with the children. CAST is operated at Orangewood Children's Home.

CHILD ASSAULT PREVENTION TEAM
Monmouth County
County Office Building
Asbury Park, NJ 07712
TEL: 201-431-7000
Purpose: To teach youngsters how to spot danger and prevent situations that make them vulnerable to abuse or assault.
Sponsor: State of New Jersey
Contact: Carolyn Vacca or Shirley Orlans, Coordinators
Description: In a special program in New Jersey elementary schools, teachers, pupils and parents learn about ways children can defend themselves against assault by other children, strangers and even people they know and trust. The *Monmouth County Child Assault Prevention (CAP) Team* includes two coordinators and 27 female CAP instructors, who visit schools all over the county to train the teachers, parents and children. The program is funded by state grants through the *Division of Youth and Family Services.* There are separate sessions for each group, as follows:
Classroom Session - Before the classroom session begins, any child who feels uncomfortable is given permission to leave. To date, no child has left the session in the more than 40,000 workshops conducted.
The children themselves are asked to volunteer at specific times in the training, rather than be selected for the role playing accompanying the program. During a typical CAP workshop for 11- and 12-year-olds, children arrange their chairs in a semi-circle and a casual conversation begins about rights and privileges. This session is designed to make the children more comfortable before the more active, role-playing part of the session. At first, two CAP instructors play gradeschoolers and act out roles similar to those encountered by the children. As the role-play progresses, pupils from the class are asked to come forward and play some of the roles - like confronting a bully at school, dealing with strangers on the street and in cars, etc. The children are told that they have weapons with which to kick, scratch, bite, butt, etc., and that a special kind of yell - not the squeals they use in playing - is needed to get attention. The *CAP Yell* is demonstrated, and pupils volunteer to help with the demonstration. Other segments of the program include:
- the ability to call the police;
- the ability to give an accurate description;
- what to do when the problem is with the people you know; and
- how to spot danger.

When the classroom session ends, children are invited to meet individually with counselors to discuss personal problems and experiences.
Teacher Workshops - Separate teacher workshops are mainly to help educators prepare for the CAP team's classroom visits.
Parent Workshops - Separate parent workshops explore CAP's history, explain its philosophy on the rights of children and offer parenting skills and statistics on child assault.
The CAP program originated in 1983 through *Women Against Rape,* a Columbus, Ohio, organization, but New Jersey is the only one so far to make it statewide, based upon a recommendation by the *Governors' Task Force on Child Abuse and Neglect.*
According to a Coordinator, "We have a lot of success stories. Kids often tell us how they've used CAP strategies. In some cases, their calls to police have led to arrests. We've made a lot of kids safe in this county."
Founded: 1989

CHILD IDENTIFICATION PROGRAM
Safeway Stores
Little Rock Division
8109 Highway I-30
Little Rock, AR 72202
TEL: 501-562-3583

Purpose: To demonstrate the spirit of volunteerism through community involvement.
Sponsor: Safeway Stores
Contact: Community Relations Officer
Description: As a matter of policy, Safeway has always recognized its responsibility as a corporate citizen and has urged its employees to become involved in community activities where they live and work. In Little Rock, Arkansas, one community service program that received overwhelming participation was the Child Identification Program in which six area Safeway stores participated. This was a joint effort of Safeway, Pepsi Cola and Channel 4 and involved establishing "Child ID Centers" in the six Safeway stores stores.
The program ran for four consecutive weeks in late fall to be sure as many children as possible would be in the area and could participate.
Parents were invited to bring their children 12 years of age and under. An ID card for each child included a photograph and finger prints, along with vital statistical information. Volunteers experienced in the areas needed prepared the cards. They were developed for parents to keep in the event a child should ever be lost or missing.
The response to the Child ID Program was overwhelming. Almost 10,000 children visited the stores with their parents to be photographed and fingerprinted.
Plans are to make the Child Identification Program an ongoing activity on an as-needed basis.
Publications: Safeway Community Involvement Packet

CHILD PROTECTIVE SERVICES
Virginia Department of Social Services
8007 Discovery Drive
Richmond, VA 23229-8699
TEL: 800-552-7096
Purpose: To protect children ages birth to 18 in the State of Virginia.
Sponsor: Parents Anonymous
Description: To fulfill its mission, *Child Protective Services in Virginia* works with volunteer organizations such as *Parents Anonymous, Parents United, the Virginia Chapter of the National Committee for Prevention of Child Abuse (NCPCA),* and *the Governor's Advisory Committee on Child Abuse and Neglect.* These liaisons, coupled with amendments to the Child Abuse laws, have dramatically increased the number of children helped through this Service (from 400 per year to over 40,000 each year). The State of Virginia receives an annual assistance grant from NCPCA to aid in the implementation of the law. Funds from this grant enable the agency to improve children's protective services programs by providing the means for public awareness, training, technical assistance, program development and coordination with the other groups and organizations concerned with child abuse. Examples of these efforts include:
- provision of small grants for community-based prevention and treatment services.
- support for multidisciplinary teams through technical assistance and dissemination of information.
- dissemination of information packets for professionals and the general public.
- support for the *Virginia Child Protection Newsletter.*
Virginia's Child Protective Services Program is designed to involve parents in the prevention and treatment of abused or neglected children - helping the parents to resolve their problems and learn better methods of child care and discipline. It recognizes the need for children to live in a physically and emotionally healthy environment and strives to keep families together. Once a child protective services worker becomes involved with a family, the parents are expected to cooperate fully with the worker in a plan to provide for the child's best interest. It is the experience of workers that most parents who abuse or neglect their children

want what is best for them, but stress prevents them from being the kind of parents they would like to be. Once the treatment begins, parents voluntarily report changes in the family situation and keep in contact with the child protective services worker. Anyone may report a concern about a child's wellbeing, provided the report is made in good faith. Caregivers (doctors, nurses, social workers, teachers, court and police officers, mental health professionals, staff of institutions, etc.) are required by law to report cases of suspected abuse or neglect. They are provided with literature to help them recognize signs of abuse or neglect, and many of them provide new input for this literature. Anonymity is an important factor for the reporter of the incident in most cases, and this is strictly enforced.
With the Child Protective Services unit receiving the support of 124 local offices in seven regions of the State, the annual grant from NCPCA, and the cooperative efforts with several private voluntary organizations, it will continue to provide services to the children and families of the Commonwealth in the best manner possible.
Publications: Child Protective Services in Virginia; Virginia's Child Abuse/Neglect Programs; Child Protective Services Annual Report; Survival Tips for Parents and Kids

CHILD SECURITY NETWORK OF CONNECTICUT
PO Box 2143
Meriden, CT 06450
TEL: 203-783-3036
TOLL FREE: 800-6-KIDS-ID
Southwest Regional Division
PO Box 3382
Milford, CT 06460
Affiliate:
Child Security Network
Long Beach, California
Purpose: To provide an effective and complete form of identification for children.
Sponsor: Child Security Network
Contact: Clifford Ives
Description: Totally volunteer-operated, the *Child Security Network* has developed an identification program for children that stores pertinent data in a computer file to expedite treatment in a crisis situation. The data include blood type, allergies, pre-existing conditions, and family physician, and it is relayed instantly to emergency personnel to aid in treatment. The file also contains insurance information and contact information for parents, both at home and at work, and three alternate contacts.
The goal of the program is to reach every parent or guardian of every infant, child and youth in Connecticut. One method used by CSN is working through youth groups, schools, unions, churches, corporations, businesses, foundations, politicians, charities, and others with the cooperation of parents and guardians.
The cost of registration, $20, keeps a child on file for a year, including an updating process for any changes in medical, residence, or other situations. The registration fee is the only income for the volunteer group.
As of late 1989, the CSN program had been initiated in all states of the US.
Publications: My Child in a Crisis? ... Never!!!

COMMUNITY BLOCK HOMES
Illinois State Board of Education
Instructional Improvement Section
100 North First Street
Springfield, IL 62777
TEL: 217-782-9374
Purpose: To provide help for children in the community should an emergency arise.
Sponsor: McDonald's Restaurants
Contact: Volunteer Coordinator

Description: Community Block Home is a program being sponsored with the cooperation of *McDonald's Restaurants* throughout the State of Illinois. The foundation of the program is a network of homes and businesses that have been approved as safe havens for children in danger. The homes and businesses are recognized by a statewide safety symbol placed in the window. This symbol signals a home where children can find help in an emergency. Block Homes function in cooperation with local elementary schools and law enforcement agencies.

Adults interest in children's wellbeing must qualify to be a Block Home participant, although it is not necessary to be a parent to apply. Some of the volunteers in the program are:
- Adults who are home during the daytime hours
- Small neighborhood businesses that are open during the day
- Senior Citizens

Approved volunteers promise the children in their community that they will provide aid should an emergency arise. The *Block Home Safety Symbol* in the window lets children know they can turn to that home for protection.

FLORIDA SHERIFFS YOUTH VILLA
Florida Sheriffs Youth Ranches
Boys Ranch, FL 32060
TEL: 904-842-5555
Purpose: To offer a new start to neglected, unsupervised and troubled girls.
Sponsor: Florida Sheriffs Association
Contact: Ed Freddo, Director of Youth Services
Description: The Florida Sheriffs Youth Villa operates under the aegis of the nonprofit Florida Sheriffs Youth Ranches, sponsored by the Florida Sheriffs Association. The Villa emphasizes survival training to help teenagers cope with the outside world. The training is offered to neglected, unsupervised and troubled girls to help them discover that there is a "good life." It is a comfortable, attractive, secure facility offering many rewarding experiences and an opportunity to get a fresh start.

Girls at the Youth Villa receive professional counseling and a good education. They learn to assume responsibility and make good decisions in an environment that emphasizes positive thinking. The basic training is enhanced through *Transition Living*, a program that gives girls who are about to depart the Villa an opportunity to sample independent living before they go out on their own.

Tried earlier on a smaller scale, *Transition Living* was expanded when, in 1988, the program was moved from cramped quarters in a small cottage to spacious Dorista Villa. This has allowed more girls to get involved, and has given them the elbow room they need to simulate true independent living.

Girls at the Villa volunteer for transition living. They have to be at least 16 years old and high school juniors or above. They must be recommended by their Youth Villa group parents, and they cannot get in unless they have demonstrated leadership, maturity and the ability to assume responsibility.

The Director finds the *Transition Living* program a resounding success, saying, "The girls are always on time. If they have ever been late for a curfew, it has been just one time in two years." The Sheriffs Association also manages Boys Ranch, Youth Ranch, and Youth Camp in various parts of Florida.
Publications: The Rancher

GOVERNOR'S ADVISORY COMMITTEE ON CHILD ABUSE AND NEGLECT/VA
Virginia Department of Social Services
Child Protective Services
8007 Discovery Drive
Richmond, VA 23229-8699
TEL: 804-662-9204 (office)
TOLL FREE: 800-552-7096 (hotline)

Purpose: To assist the Governor in coordinating child abuse and neglect matters among all agencies of Virginia state government.
Description: In 1975, when the Virginia Assembly enacted major amendments to the *Virginia Child Abuse and Neglect Law of 1966,* it also created the *Governor's Advisory Committee on Child Abuse and Neglect.* This Committee meets four times a year, and is active in creating policy, making recommendations to the State Department of Social Services, and acting as a coordinator between the Department of Social Services and other major state agencies. Additionally, this Committee has subcommittees taking a very active role in areas such as multidisciplinary teams, legislation, prevention, and treatment.

With the assistance of the Committee, the impact of the amendments to the Act, the Hotline's immediate response on a 24-hour basis, and cooperative efforts with volunteer organizations such as *Parents Anonymous, Parents United,* and *Virginia Chapter of the National Committee for Prevention of Child Abuse,* over 40,000 incidents are reported each year as compared to only 400 prior to these changes and additions.

OFFICE OF CHILDREN AND YOUTH (OCY)
Hawaii Office of the Governor
PO Box 3044
Honolulu, HI 96802
TEL: 808-548-7582
Purpose: To improve and promote the coordination of all children and youth services in the State of Hawaii and to assist in the resolution of pressing problems affecting children and youth.
Sponsor: Hawaii State Agency
Contact: Genevieve T. Okinaga, Director
Description: There are about 417,900 children and youth in Hawaii from birth through age 24, almost half of the State's total population. Most are too young to vote or mobilize themselves for public action in their own behalf. The Office of Children and Youth (OCY), therefore, was created by the 1976 Legislature with the intent to promote a high level of public concern to better insure the protection and well-being of our youngest population by assisting agencies who provide direct services to them. Thus, the OCY's scope of operation mandated by legislation includes the entire range of programs and agencies who deliver services to children and youth in education, health, social services, welfare, employment, recreation, and others.

Undergirding the extensive duties of OCY as mandated by law are the wide array of OCY activities via fact finding, analysis and mobilizing existing resources to address the problems. OCY duties and responsibilities are mandated by H.R.S. Chapter 581 as amended by Act 207 and Act 187, Session Laws of Hawaii 1976, and Act 297, Session Laws of Hawaii 1980.

The Office of Children and Youth utilizes volunteers to supplement work performance on an as-needed basis. Program staff managers actively pursue appropriate volunteers for specific needs such as professional expertise, clerical abilities, etc. Program staff managers provide orientation, supervision and support to volunteers. One particular area where volunteers are greatly utilized is in Task Forces created by the Office to advise the Director on matters relating to a particular subject area. Volunteers are called upon for the production of major conferences. For example, in 1979 the International Year of the Child was held in which hundreds of volunteers were involved. The Office also co-sponsored the Governor's Hawaii State White House Conference on Children and Youth Project which included activities within all four counties and culminated at the State Conference.

The basic operational premise of the Office of Children and Youth has been and will continue to be to encourage and foster community involvement (via volunteers) for OCY projects, which are usually multi-agency endeavors involving both public and private sectors of individuals and agencies. The involvement of community representatives from the initial phase of decision

making on project specifications is vital to the educative process leading to the completion of any project. This makes possible use of existing resources from the involved sectors, and even more importantly, the educative process results in a knowledgeable commitment when statewide implementation is sought.
Founded: 1976

PHONE PAL
Southwestern Bell
1010 Pine Street
Room 921
St. Louis, MO 63101
TEL: 314-235-9800
Purpose: To provide "latchkey children" and their parents with an added sense of security.
Sponsor: Southwestern Bell
Contact: Darrell Lauer
Description: When Southwestern Bell in St. Louis started "Phone Pal," a program to pair older adults with "latchkey" children - grade schoolers who are alone at home before or after school, it was picked up almost immediately by the Southwestern Bell office in El Dorado, Arkansas.
Phone Pal, started in 1986 at Yokum Elementary School in El Dorado, matches child and adult according to shared interests. They keep in touch regularly by telephone. Phone Pal children are offered a monthly club meeting at the school. According to the principal of the school, the child devlops a sense of responsibility, since the experience of talking to an older adult enhances courtesy, telephone skills, and communication skills in general. It has been determined that a program like Phone Pal works best with grade schoolchildren.
Both partners of the Phone Pal team represent growing segments of the population. Due to increases in the number of working women and single-parent families, more children are returning to empty homes after school. At the same time, the number of homebound seniors is growing. Phone Pal meets needs in both groups: children who need to be cared for and older adults who need someone to care about.
Publications: Phone Pal Information Packet

ROSIE'S PATROL
SEE LAW ENFORCEMENT/CRIME PREVENTION: CRIME WATCH

SAFE PLACE
Metro Alternative Shelter House (MASH)
536 West Third Street
Lexington, KY 40508
TEL: 606-254-2501
Purpose: To provide a safe place to wait for troubled youths until a trained volunteer arrives from the local center.
Contact: Suzanne Conrad
Description: The *Metro Alternative Shelter House (MASH)* had a problem. When a youth needing help was reported, often they arrived to find the youth gone. In mid-1989 a volunteer in the program suggested *Safe Place,* a project that enlists the help of area businesses to solve the dilemma.
Once designated as a "safe place," a business agrees to provide shelter for troubled youths until a trained volunteer arrives from MASH. Unfortunately, most businesses fail to meet the criteria. The site needs to be:
- a business, not a home;
- highly visible;
- easily accessible;
- open nearly 24 hours a day;
- an appropriate location for a young person to wait; and
- staffed by at least two qualified people at all times.
Summer time is a busy time for the shelter, with schools closed and young people without direction, leading to restlessness.

Children are without adult supervision, or spending the whole day in homes which are abusive. Also, summer is a prime time for 14 to 15-year-old runaways.
Because of these problems, MASH continues to try to increase the number of *Safe Places* - especially in the inner city. Male volunteers are best for inner-city locations, and recruitment efforts are underway to increase their numbers.
Although many more *Safe Places* are needed, the present level of assistance has helped. Each business receives a bright, highly visible, yellow and black *Safe Place* sign for window or door. Word is spread through schools and other youth-serving sources to make this sign a recognizable and acceptable means of help for youth.

SAFETY TOWN (WHERE CHILDREN LEARN TO LIVE)
SEE TRANSPORTATION & SAFETY: CHILDREN/YOUTH

SCAN (SPOKANE CHILD ABUSE AND NEGLECT PREVENTION CENTER)
South 500 Stone
Spokane, WA 99202
TEL: 509-458-7445
Purpose: Primary child abuse and neglect prevention.
Sponsor: United Way, Spokane Community Mental Health Center
Contact: Sue Hiale, Coordinator
Description: The SCAN Center was established in 1973 to provide direct parent aide services to families with the goal of preventing child abuse and neglect and establishing a positive, nurturing home environment for children. As the number of reports of child abuse and neglect have increased SCAN has become a major resource for prevention and treatment for troubled families.
For the past three years SCAN has been a program area of Spokane Community Mental Health Center. SCAN receives in-kind administrative services and consultation skills from the Mental Health Center. This merger has provided stability and quality to the SCAN program. The SCAN budget and physical location remain separate from the Community Mental Health Center.
United Way of Spokane County funds approximately forty percent of the SCAN budget. Local fund raising events provide a little over twenty percent of the total. It is estimated that in 1990 SCAN will need to receive over $14,000 from foundation and grant requests.
The SCAN program consists of five areas of service delivery, each with the major goal of preventing child abuse and neglect.
The public education aspect of SCAN is an essential means of informing citizens about how to report suspected cases of child abuse and neglect. SCAN provides speakers throughout the community to present information on the definitions, identification and causes of child abuse and neglect. These speakers are specially trained and will speak to any group requesting information. These requests come from schools, service clubs, churches, and the corporate community to name a few. Community resources and opportunities for citizen involvement are also discussed at public presentations.
The professional staff at SCAN presents training to medical, legal and educational personnel regarding prevention, identification and treatment of child abuse and neglect.
Community education and awareness are essential ingredients in the prevention of child abuse and neglect. In 1989 SCAN presented over 200 education sessions in response to local requests. In addition to these on-site presentations, SCAN maintains a resource center which includes films and a wide assortment of materials on child abuse and neglect, community agencies, parenting and related topics.
The SCAN parent aide program provides direct one-to-one services for troubled families,with primary focus on the prevention of child abuse and neglect.
Parent aides are volunteers who are trained in a 30-hour initial

training class. The classes emphasize interpersonal relationships, communication skills, problems of parenting and child discipline to prepare volunteers to work individually with a client family. Although this class was previously taught at the local community college, the professional staff at SCAN now presents the training with the assistance of experts throughout the community. After completing the initial training, volunteers are matched on a one-to-one basis with clients. The role of the parent aide is to give nurturing support and model good parenting for clients who are assessed as high risk, or who have already abused or neglected their children. The parent aide is available in times of crisis and commits to three to four hours per week of contact with the client. There are currently 70 volunteers who will serve approximately 175 families during the year.

Clients are referred to SCAN by other community resources such as Child Protective Services, Community Mental Health Center and the Public Health Department. Additionally, approximately forty percent of clients contact SCAN directly for help before any abuse has occurred and volunteers respond to the needs of parents who are seeking help before they hurt their children. SCAN is the only local agency with the stated primary focus of child abuse and neglect prevention.

Client families stay involved with SCAN an average of six months or more. Over half of the clients are single parents. Most clients report an improved relationship with their children as a result of parent aide services. Current research indicates that parent aide programs are the most effective means of preventing child abuse and neglect.

SCAN maintains support groups, two child protection teams, and parent advocates. The SCAN staff includes the program coordinator, a caseworker, secretary and half-time registered nurse. The professional staff provides consultation, motivation, support and training for volunteers. In addition, the staff actively participates in community projects which assess, evaluate or develop resources for the prevention or treatment of child abuse and neglect.

Founded: 1973

SCHOOL FIRE SAFETY MONITORING PROGRAM
SEE DISASTER RESPONSE/EMERGENCY PREPAREDNESS

WYANDOTTE HOUSE/NEUTRAL GROUND
Wyandotte House, Inc.
632 Tauromee
Kansas City, KS 66101
TEL: 913-342-9332
Purpose: To provide long and short-term crisis intervention, temporary shelter for teenage runaways, and emergency and residential shelter for children of abused, deprived, and neglected family situations.
Sponsor: Federal/state governments; public and private donations
Contact: Clarence Small, Program Director, Neutral Ground
Description: Neutral Ground is a short-term crisis intervention center offering emergency shelter and counseling to young people, ages 11 through 17, who have run away from home. The program operates under the auspices of Wyandotte House, a non-profit organization receiving funds from federal and state governments as well as from public and private sources.

At the present time, the program utilizes the services of ten active volunteers and maintains a list of ten volunteers who remain "on-call" in case of emergencies. Six volunteers are assigned by the VISTA volunteer program. They perform various duties including: resident supervision, houseparent aides, youth workers, intake officers, public relations, and general maintenance. Neutral Ground also utilizes volunteers assigned through the Foster Grandparent Program. These individuals give "that extra love and attention" that becomes so vital in service delivery. The other volunteers come from recruiting efforts in the community. They help in general supervision, recreation, and generating interest and

support. Their occupational backgrounds include a lawyer, a radio and TV personality, an insurance executive, and a retired civic leader.

Many of the volunteers perform valuable services to Neutral Ground and the community. Without their contribution of time, the program would suffer tremendously because they fill in positions that present funding sources cannot, and they perform and provide quality services. The program also offers internship training to senior college students in the areas of social work, sociology, and psychology.

There is a continuing need for volunteers and interns at Wyandotte House/Neutral Ground. Plans call for expansion of the volunteer program throughout the agency, performing a variety of services to youths and family. Recruiting efforts have been upgraded, and plans to implement on-going training for present volunteers are underway.

YOUTH HAVEN
PO Box 7007
Naples, FL 33941
TEL: 813-262-3227
Purpose: To provide temporary emergency care to children in crisis birth to 18 years of age; to expand the program for long term care of adolescents who have no hope of a permanent home elsewhere.
Sponsor: Individuals and groups in the community dedicated to children in need.
Contact: E. Bernard Blackburn, ACSW, Executive Director
Description: Youth Haven Children's Home is a private, non-profit home for the abused, neglected and abandoned children of Collier County, Florida. Since 1969 children of all ages, birth to 18 years of age, receive temporary, emergency care until they can be returned to their parents.

Youth Haven is an independent child care agency, working in close cooperation with parents, social agencies (state and local) and professional groups that assist children and parents in crisis. Youth Haven is also licensed to care for homeless adolescents for one year or longer until they reach adulthood.

LUVS (Let Us Volunteer Service) - The Youth Haven Auxiliary, know as LUVS, is the heartbeat of Youth Haven. The volunteers are a group of dedicated, goodwill ambassadors of Youth Haven within the community. They assist Youth Haven in three ways:

- **House Volunteers:** assisting with child care duties, such as providing transportation to medical appointments and recreational activities, assisting with homework, helping with baths and bedtime, etc.;
- **Shop Volunteers:** working regularly in one of the resale shops which provide income for Youth Haven Home;
- **Community Volunteers:** conducting special fund raising events and assisting with administrative functions. This ranges from chairing a dinner dance benefit to helping in the office with typing and filing.

All new volunteers go through an orientation program that provides background information regarding Youth Haven Children's Home and instructions as to their particular volunteer service. Home Volunteers work under close staff supervision. Volunteers are adults of all ages, male and female, who enjoy working with the children and/or sharing their special skills, hobbies and talents to benefit Youth Haven. Presently there are approximately 300 members of LUVS, but there is a continuing need for new volunteers.

Founded: 1969

RECIPIENTS: CHILDREN/YOUTH - PSYCHOSOCIAL SUPPORT

NATIONAL/STATE ORGANIZATIONS

BIG BROTHERS/BIG SISTERS OF AMERICA
230 North Thirteenth Street
Philadelphia, PA 19107
TEL: 215-567-7000
Objectives: To help children grow into responsible and happy adult members of society and their communities.
Services: Combines the friendship of a mature, stable volunteer with the skill of a professionally trained staff to create a personalized friendship on a one-to-one basis; sets goals to meet the needs of the boy or girl by working as a team with volunteer, parent, staff professional, and child (usually from a one-parent family); provides volunteers with the opportunity to help children and the community through this activity; provides technical assistance to communities to help form Big Brother and/or Big Sister Agencies (evaluation, volunteer development, public relations, etc.); approves standards and practices, taking into consideration the needs of each local community; places recruitment of volunteers as its number one priority due to the long waiting list (some 60,000 children); publicizes the difference between the cost of a Big/Little Brother or Big/Little Sister match ($650/annually) with the cost of maintaining a child in an institution ($18,000 to $65,000); publishes triannual newsletters, and a number of organizational manuals.
Publications: Agency-in-Formation Manual; The Correspondent; Citizen Board Development; Program Management Guide
Founded: 1977

MAKE-A-WISH FOUNDATION OF AMERICA
SEE HEALTH: CHILDREN/YOUTH

SKY RANCH FOR BOYS
SEE PSYCHOSOCIAL SUPPORT SERVICES: CHILDREN/YOUTH

TRAINING PROGRAMS

GET AWAY CLEAN
SEE PSYCHOSOCIAL SUPPORT SERVICES: CHILDREN/YOUTH

INDIVIDUAL PROGRAM PROFILES

BIG BROTHERS/BIG SISTERS OF NASSAU COUNTY*
240 Clinton Street
Hempstead, NY 11413
TEL: 516-489-7440
Purpose: To service single parents, at-risk children between the ages of 7 and 17 by matching them on a one-to-one basis with responsible adult and young adult volunteers.
Sponsor: Nassau County Youth Board, US/ACTION, New York State Division for Youth.
Contact: William G. Tymann, Executive Director
Description: Big Brothers/Big Sisters of Nassau began as a project of Mobilized Community Resources, Inc. in the spring of 1975. Initial funding was provided by the Nassau County Youth Board and the New York State Division for Youth. In 1977, the agency was spun off and incorporated on its own. At the present time, it is a Full Member Agency in Good Standing with Big Brothers/Big Sisters of America.

The volunteers in the program number approximately 300 and their primary function is to work one-to-one with a youngster who is experiencing developmental, emotional, psychosocial or educational difficulty. The volunteers are oriented, trained, screened and matched and supervised by a professional staff. These are goal oriented matches formed to prevent the youngster from getting into more serious difficulties.

The service is delivered by one of three methods: 1) The Core program, which is centrally located in the county, supports the bulk of the casework and match-making functions, 2) the Chapter program, which is an affiliate agency system of delivery. Agencies in eight Nassau communities are involved in providing the service to youth in their areas. This system is developed and managed by the Core program, 3) a High School program in which high school juniors and seniors are matched with children between the ages of 7 and 12 who live in the same school district.

Funding for this program is provided by ACTION. In the first eight years, Big Brothers/Big Sisters of Nassau serviced over 600 children and recruited over 4000 volunteer applicants. In addition, the agency has a vigorous and increasingly successful fund raising program.
Founded: 1975

BIG BROTHERS/BIG SISTERS PROGRAM
Madison House
170 Rugby Road
Charlottesville, VA 22903
TEL: 804-977-7051
Purpose: To create an ongoing, positive adult relationship with a local child who lacks consistent adult attention.
Sponsor: Madison House
Contact: Jane Parker
Description: The Big Brothers/Big Sisters Program is one of Madison House's original volunteer efforts. The Program centers around the one-to-one relationship between the volunteer and the child. The children - due to any number of circumstances - lack the adult attention needed by every child. Many of the children are from low-income, unstable family situations - the parents may be divorced, one parent may be deceased, or the family may be very large.

Most children are referred to the program through counselors in the public school system and through the welfare departments. Referrals also come from churches, the Baptist Student Union of the University of Virginia, Hope House, HELP, and the Probation Department.

Basic information about each child and his/her family situation is provided to the program to assist in the matching of volunteers and children. The children usually are between the ages of five and 15 with varied interests, problems, and backgrounds.

Volunteers in this program attend an orientation and an interview before being matched with a little brother or sister. Once matched, they spend a minimum of five hours a week with the child throughout the school year. It is emphasized to the volunteer that only a consistent, long-term relationship is of any benefit to the child, since an inconsistent, short-term relationship creates additional problems and difficulties in the child's development. Volunteers are asked to make a written commitment that they will spend at least the minimum time with the child, and will attend all monthly program meetings.

Although most of the volunteer's time is spent independently with the little brother or sister, the program also sponsors a series of group activities to supplement the individual volunteer/child relationship. These activities not only provide the child with experience in participating with a group, but they afford the volunteers the opportunity to compare notes and perhaps benefit from the experiences of others. Activities include picnics, holiday parties, skating trips, zoo trips, and University athletic events.

The "bottom line" is that, although a few ups and downs can be expected in the volunteer/child relationship, in the long run the volunteer and child should feel comfortable with each other. The volunteer should be prepared to put a good deal of time and effort into establishing a trusting friendship with the little sister or brother, since the relationship will have an enormous influence on the young person's life.

Big Brothers/Big Sisters places 150-200 volunteers annually. Because of the growing need for more volunteers, and the time restrictions on student volunteers, the program has expanded to include more community volunteers.

BIG BROTHERS/BIG SISTERS PROGRAM-CHILD PSYCHIATRY*
St. Luke's-Roosevelt Hospital Center
Amsterdam Avenue at 114th Street
New York, NY 10025
TEL: 212-870-1867
Purpose: To meet the needs of children from the clinic who are having difficulty with adult and/or peer relationships; to give college students an opportunity to work within their fields.
Sponsor: St. Luke's-Roosevelt Hospital Center
Contact: Gloria Zicht, Child Psychiatry Center
Description: Students from City College and Manhattan Community College have served for years as Big Sisters and Big Brothers to children undergoing psychiatric treatment at the Child Psychiatry Clinic. This year the Clinic has begun working with students from Columbia University also. The program attempts to help the children develop self-esteem, increase their capacity to verbalize, tolerate frustrations, establish controls, share, empathize, and cooperate. In a few cases, the Big Brothers/Big Sisters Program is the sole treatment.
Student volunteers are required to spend one afternoon per week with the child assigned, write a brief summary of each contact with the child, and attend weekly meetings with supervising members of the social work staff. Most of their work with the children necessarily takes place outside of the home (in parks, zoos, museums, or other places in the city's recreational framework).
In the current academic year, fifty-four students are taking part in the program, logging nearly 3,000 hours by midyear. The students have been active in enlarging the children's horizons as well as helping them to develop new skills (ball playing, bike riding, etc.). Students who demonstrate exceptional capability are given the opportunity for supervised liaison work with the family and with the school.
Student volunteers are involved in sociology, psychology, or social work courses and receive some credit for their volunteer work. In addition they are reimbursed by the hospital for carfare and incidental expenses.
Evaluation of the program has shown it to have great merit within the clinic setting. The gains made within the total group of children in the program have been substantial, with great satisfaction expressed from parents, children, and the students themselves.

COMPANIONS OF ALAMEDA COUNTY
PO Box 3493
Hayward, CA 94544
TEL: 415-785-6690
Purpose: To alleviate some of the problems of low-income single-parent families by providing a one-to-one friendship match for children in this target group.
Sponsor: Municipal funds, corporations, foundations, and own fundraising events.
Contact: Betty DeForest, Executive Director
Description: Companions was formed in 1970 to alleviate some of the problems faced by boys and girls 6-16, from low-income, single-parent homes; to provide positive alternatives, role models, and reinforcement for children from an "at risk" population by

providing a one-to-one relationship with a consistent, caring adult volunteer. This service is extended to deaf and physically disabled children.
All direct service to children is delivered by volunteers who are recruited, screened, and oriented by program staff. Volunteer recruitment and support is an integral part of the program. A volunteer must:
- make a minimum six-month commitment to a child with regular visits amounting to at least 12 hours per month;
- attend at least two volunteer support group meetings after the match has been made;
- make at least one contact by phone, mail, or in person with the office each month.
Volunteers come to the program with a variety of skills and experiences. Previous experience with children is not necessary; a sense of responsibility and commitment is most important. The program requires two references (written), car insurance as required by state law, a minimum of two interviews with staff, and fingerprinting before an individual can be matched.
Companions program provides:
- supervisory guidance and support for volunteers
- monthly newsletter sent to volunteers' homes
- monthly group activities for matched pairs
- free passes to local activities
- credit available through local colleges
- in service training through periodic workshops.

SPECIAL SATURDAY
SEE RECREATION & SPORTS: CHILDREN/YOUTH

SURRY COUNTY FRIENDS OF YOUTH/BEST FRIENDS PROGRAM
150 North Main Street
Mt. Airy, NC 27030
TEL: 919-789-9064; 919-835-5433
Purpose: To advocate the needs of young people and network services for young people through various services and volunteer programs.
Sponsor: Federal/State/County governments; corporate and private donations
Contact: Selbert M. Wood, Jr., Executive Director
Description: Surry County Friends of Youth (SFOY) is a private, non-profit agency which began in 1976. The purpose of this organization is to network services and advocate the needs of young people in Surry County. Toward that end, various programs and services have been offered since incorporation. At the present time, *SFOY* provides outpatient family, individual and group therapy, the *Best Friends Program,* a *First Offenders Restitution Program,* crisis intervention, and telephone referrals for Surry County.
The *Best Friends Program* is funded through local county and Community-Based Alternative money from the state. The program follows the Big Brother/Big Sister type format and matches a young person exhibiting delinquent, or pre-delinquent behavior with an adult volunteer.
- **Best Friends Staff** - A full-time Best Friends Coordinator is responsible for the *Best Friends Program* and all aspects of it. He/she is responsible for accepting referrals from various community agencies and recruiting adult volunteers. The coordinator also trains the adult volunteers and closely supports each match.
- **Volunteer Duties** - Each volunteer in the *Best Friends Program* is expected to spend a minimum of three hours each week for one year with the young friend. The volunteer is given various optional outings and free activities each month and the volunteer may escort the young friend to various activities sponsored by merchants and business people in Surry County. Although the match is for one year, it is tentatively made for six weeks until all parties agree to continue the

match.

Volunteers are recruited from area churches, high schools and community colleges. The volunteers are recruited also through mass media involving local television, radio and newspapers.

THANKS (THOUGHTFUL, HELPING ADULTS N' KIDS SHARING)

Lee County Youth Services
PO Box 57
112 Hillcrest Drive
Sanford, NC 27330
TEL: 919-774-9515

Purpose: To provide appropriate role models for children experiencing difficulty in the community.

Sponsor: State/County government; corporate and private donations

Contact: Nancy Cashion/THANKS Coordinator

Description: THANKS (Thoughtful, Helping Adults N' Kids Sharing) is a one-on-one program designed to provide appropriate role models for children experiencing difficulty at home, school or in the community. The kids who share are boys and girls between the ages of 8 and 15, who want and need a one-to-one relationship with an adult friend. The program operates under the auspices of Lee County Youth Services, which currently has eight programs to serve the families and children of Lee County.

The THANKS Coordinator works closely with both the volunteer and the youth through weekly contact and monthly group activities.

The THANKS program has a goal of matching 30 volunteers each year. In addition to the one-on-one volunteers, THANKS also has volunteers who serve on the Board and provide a variety of other services such as group activities and legal advice.

THANKS volunteers are expected to spend four hours per week for at least a year with their youth. The volunteer and child schedule their own time together doing things they enjoy the most. However, they are also expected to attend group activities and in-service training sessions. The real purpose is for the adult to establish the most meaningful relationship possible with the child. Like the kids, the volunteers come from a wide variety of backgrounds and experiences. They are 18 years of age or older, single or married, or perhaps have families of their own. Each adult is carefully screened to insure the presence of sincere motivation and emotional stability. THANKS asks that each volunteer complete an application form listing four references and participate in an interview. The volunteer then completes a six hour training course.

VOLUNTEERS FOR YOUTH

Gettysburg College
Box 427
Christ Chapel
Gettysburg, PA 17325
TEL: 717-334-3131

Purpose: To meet the needs of youth who lack opportunities for meaningful interaction with adults.

Sponsor: United Way of Adams County; Gettysburg College

Contact: Edward F. McManness

Description: In May 1974, a group of people representing a number of youth and family service organizations began meeting to discuss the problems of youth in Adams County. A common concern of those persons was the absence of a comprehensive volunteer program oriented toward the needs of youth. As a result of that realization, the *Volunteers for Youth* program was organized.

Volunteers for Youth is a "Best Friend" type of organization. In one-parent families and in other situations where a child could benefit from additional guidance and companionship, a Youth Volunteer can be a helpful human resource.

Referrals of children are accepted from community agencies,

churches, civic groups, individuals or directly from parents. Volunteers are sought from the community and various organizations within it, including the Lutheran Seminary and Gettysburg College. Children and volunteers are matched with consideration to mutual interest and abilities. Supervision of the volunteers is usually by the program director or in certain cases, is arranged with the cooperation of social service professionals in the area.

Anyone over the age of 18 who is interested in becoming a volunteer will be interviewed and considered. References are required as part of the application as well as an agreement to receive supervision and attend workshops. Monthly activity reports are required. In addition, group activities are arranged on a regular basis, with attendance requested.

Volunteers who wish to be involved with a particular type of child are encouraged to apply and their requests will be considered on the basis of current needs and referrals.

Any child residing in Adams County or the Hanover area who is between the ages of six and 17 will be considered for the program. Acceptance of children into the program will be dependent upon the current family situation and the interest and desire of the child to have a "best friend."

Besides volunteers, the program needs financial assistance in order to provide for insurance, program and administrative costs. VFY also invites comment and discussion from the community.

Founded: 1974

WRITECONNECTION PROGRAM: LOVE A CHILD BY MAIL
SEE PSYCHOSOCIAL SUPPORT SERVICES: CHILDREN/YOUTH

RECIPIENTS: CHILDREN/YOUTH - RECREATION/SPORTS

NATIONAL/STATE ORGANIZATIONS

FUND FOR ADVANCEMENT OF CAMPING
SEE RECREATION & SPORTS: FUNDING

NATIONAL ASSOCIATION OF POLICE ATHLETIC LEAGUES
SEE RECREATION & SPORTS: CHILDREN/YOUTH

INDIVIDUAL PROGRAM PROFILES

CAMP GOOD DAYS AND SPECIAL TIMES REBUILDING PROJECT
SEE RECREATION & SPORTS: CHILDREN/YOUTH

CHRISTMAS TOY SHOP
SEE RECREATION & SPORTS: CHILDREN/YOUTH

OUTINGS FOR HOMELESS CHILDREN
SEE RECIPIENTS: HOMELESS - RECREATION/SPORTS

SPECIAL SATURDAY
SEE RECREATION & SPORTS: CHILDREN/YOUTH

TEEN CENTER
McLean Community Center
1234 Ingleside Avenue
McLean, VA 22101
TEL: 703-790-0123
Purpose: To offer teenagers a place to drop in for games, snacks, talk, television, dances or just hanging out.
Sponsor: Fairfax County
Contact: Eugene Burman, Chairman
Description: Still disappointed over the closing of *Freedom House,* a teen center resulting from parent efforts in the early 70's, the parents again put forth the effort to fill this need in McLean. Since the earlier effort failed due to lack of funds and volunteers, those two considerations are foremost in the organizers' minds for the current effort. At the beginning of summer 1989, the group received word that they could use an old firehouse for the teen center for $1.00 a year in a two-year experiment. On June 30, ten high school student leaders, and representatives of a local architectural firm held a brainstorming session to work out plans for the new center. The center opened in early 1990.
An important part of the philosophy to make sure this second effort succeeds is placing more decision-making responsibilities in the hands of students. Among their initial decisions in the meeting with the architect:
- Keep the fire station ambience by including memorabilia such as the front end of a firetruck
- Include plenty of air hockey tables.
- Let the kids themselves decide what kind of food should be in the snack bar and vending machines.
- Set aside areas for video games, table tennis or pool, television watching, snacking, quiet study and other activities.
- Stress a casual and laid-back atmosphere.

For organizers, getting the firehouse was not an easy victory. The firehouse occupies a prime half acre in the middle of downtown McLean. About 30 organizations were interested in the property, and the amount the county might have realized was estimated at $2 million. The complainers found a dozen reasons for eliminating the teen center, including its proximity to local businesses, lack of parking space, traffic flow, the mid-town location, etc. But a "town meeting" held earlier showed overwhelming support from the 30 to 40 speakers, who represented neighborhoods and other groups.
Youth and adults alike are aware of the problems. The 18 parking spaces are not ample, and off-site parking is being sought. And the students are aware that they must continue to be "good neighbors," or the "two-year experiment" could be very short-lived, and no doubt the developers would move in again to push for that office building.
Although conditions attached to the lease require that the center be open to *all* Fairfax County teenagers, most youth are from McLean. Although youth, parents and other organizers are volunteers, two paid persons help to monitor youth, trying to screen out what one organizer called "bully-type kids." One night each week is reserved for seventh- and eighth-graders, who are not allowed in at other times. Teenagers are issued identification cards for a nominal fee. The facility is the only publicly-sponsored, full-service teen center in Northern Virginia.

YOUTH RECREATION PROGRAM
SEE RECREATION & SPORTS: CHILDREN/YOUTH

RECIPIENTS: CHILDREN/YOUTH - ROLE MODELS

INDIVIDUAL PROGRAM PROFILES

REGIONAL YOUTH SUBSTANCE ABUSE PROJECT (RYSAP)
SEE DRUG ABUSE/ALCOHOLISM: DRUGS

RECIPIENTS: CHILDREN/YOUTH - TRANSPORTATION

INDIVIDUAL PROGRAM PROFILES

ROADRUNNER PROGRAM
SEE TRANSPORTATION & SAFETY: CHILDREN/YOUTH

RECIPIENTS: ETHNIC GROUPS

NATIONAL/STATE ORGANIZATIONS

NATIONAL COUNCIL ON THE BLACK AGING
SEE CIVIC AFFAIRS: MINORITIES/WOMEN

INDIVIDUAL PROGRAM PROFILES

CLASS OF 2000: THE PREJUDICE PUZZLE
National Public Radio
2025 M Street, NW
Washington, DC 20036
TEL: 202-822-2000
FAX: 202-822-2329
Purpose: To explore how young people with a variety of backgrounds deal with prejudices and stereotyping.
Contact: Sallie Bodie, Special Project Outreach Coordinator
Description: In 1989, *National Public Radio (NPR)* commissioned *Significance, Inc.* to survey teenage attitudes. This was the first step toward a new ongoing series, *Special Projects* (see separate entry), which will examine national issues which affect our communities. From a series of focus groups formed by the survey team and conducted in four cities across the U.S., NPR learned that "Although most panelists try to draw a rosy picture of race relations, they seemed naive and euphemistic when discussing race relations. Several teens did acknowledge race problems, although they frequently ascribed these race-motivated problems to others." The 1990 project on prejudice features young people telling in their own words how they feel about prejudice. They will talk about issues such as job barriers, the importance of belonging to groups, and the impact of stereotypes and racial incidents. The stories in this series will raise the question of how youth are being prepared to live in the demographically different society of the 21st century. The program finale is a two-hour "national call-in" with a panel to respond live to queries. The finale is designed so that either hour can be aired separately, or delayed for rebroadcast. Segments in the series range from five to 22 minutes.

Although the groundwork is done, planning for the initial, week-long series, *Class of 2000: The Prejudice Puzzle,* is in process. *The Prejudice Puzzle* is designed to learn the feelings and attitudes of young people from many walks of life in the area of prejudice. The program is building a strong *Outreach Partnership* of public radio and national organizations with some interest and service in the area of the special issue being explored. With the appeal for *Outreach Partners* barely begun, three organizations are in place - *Very Special Arts,* the *American Library Association,* and *Four-One-One (National Clearinghouse on Volunteerism)* - with an anticipation of hundreds of nonprofits joining the effort. *Outreach Partners* lend their names, state and local contacts, and services in promotion, program support, community involvement, etc., to a major resource directory being compiled by NPR for distribution to member stations. The stations will be invited to contact these local resources for follow-up local programming on youth and prejudice, and for mounting jointly-sponsored community activities.

Organizations participating as *Outreach Partners* will become part of a nationwide network of community resources available to NPR's 375-plus members. A benefit to the *Outreach Partners* is an increase in visibility in a collaborative effort that will establish new links with public radio and other nonprofits.

One of the responsibilities of the *Outreach Partners* is to "spread the word" by publicizing the *Special* in their communications vehicles, contacting the closest station periodically to find out when *Prejudice Puzzle* programs will air, and the agenda for each program. Through this and other issue specials, NPR members hope to make their communities better places in which to live.

HOME-BASED CHILD CARE IN HARTFORD
SEE DAY CARE/HEAD START: HOME

OUTREACH PLAN: FOCUS ON THE HISPANIC COMMUNITY
United Way of the Capital Area (Hartford)
99 Woodland Street
Hartford, CT 06105-1207
TEL: 203-249-2300
Purpose: To increase United Way involvement among specific ethnic and other groups in its community.
Sponsor: United Way of the Capital Area
Contact: Marilyn Cruz-Aponte, Chair, United Way's Special Constituencies Committee, and Administrative Aide to the Governor, or Dale Gray, United Way
Description: Launched in 1989, the United Way's five-year effort to increase United Way involvement among specific ethnic and other groups begins with an outreach to the Hispanic community. The effort began with a visit by a popular musician to appear in two United Way public-service announcements (PSAs) and a videotape to be used for the first full year's campaign. Songs by the singer, Ruben Blades, encourage positive social action among Hispanic people.

The videotape is in Spanish and features Blades talking about United Way, with students at a Hartford elementary school in the background. The video, partially-funded by Aetna Life Insurance, began showing in the spring of 1990.

The PSAs and videotape are part of a larger agenda of United Way's Special Constituencies Committee. This Committee was created to concentrate communications and community outreach among specific groups. The Hispanic population is one of the largest ethnic groups, and many companies do special marketing to that group.

Other phases of this effort include translation of Health Appeal Drive brochures into Spanish and Polish, which were printed at a Hispanic-owned printshop, then sent with letters to 2,000 Hispanic residents, and the *Plant Together, Harvest Together* theme, which was developed specifically for the Hispanic community, and will continue for the next few years. To facilitate the latter, area elementary schools having a large Hispanic population mounted a poster contest sponsored by the United Way, with a prize and media exposure for the winning poster.

The *Plant Together, Harvest Together* theme was launched in the community with a kickoff luncheon attended by 130 Hispanic professionals from business and human service fields. The keynote speaker at the luncheon praised Hispanics for their history of informal generosity towards those in need, and urged them to make the transition from "generosity to philanthropy."

The Special Constituencies Committee plans similar outreach efforts tailored to other groups, such as the Polish community, during the next few years.
Founded: 1989

PREVENTION THROUGH ACTION
SEE DRUG ABUSE/ALCOHOLISM: CHILDREN/YOUTH

VOLUNTEER AWARDS PROGRAM
Oregon Human Development Corporation
835 NE Twentieth
Portland, OR 97232
TEL: 503-236-9670
Purpose: To recognize volunteers who have assisted the OHD in meeting its goals to improve the lives of low-income groups and farm workers.
Sponsor: Human Development Corporation
Contact: Volunteer Coordinator
Description: This awards program reached across the state to honor individuals and organizations who have volunteered to assist the needy. The *Oregon Human Development Corporation (OHD)* is a private, nonprofit organization that assists low-income groups and farm workers. The awards given included recognition for:
- lifetime volunteer work with low-income groups and farm workers;
- efforts to ease the state's 1988 crisis among farm workers;
- home-school counseling for the needy;
- advocacy for farm workers;
- representation for the Hispanic and the elderly;
- health clinic services for target population; and
- education and job training for farm workers.

Award recipients came from the *Governor's Office,* social service agencies, Hispanic groups, the education field, organizations for the aging, advocacy groups, journalism, labor agencies, church groups, and health clinics, and included the former Governor of Oregon who raised $500,000 through the state to help alleviate the 1988 farmworker crisis.

The *Oregon Human Development Corporation* is based in Portland and has offices in Hermiston, Hillsboro, Klamath Falls, Ontario, Salem and Woodburn. It is part of a network operating in four states - California (parent corporation), Washington, and Hawaii in addition to Oregon.

RECIPIENTS: ETHNIC GROUPS - IMMIGRANTS/REFUGEES

NATIONAL/STATE ORGANIZATIONS

ASSOCIATION OF LADIES OF CHARITY OF THE US
c/o Romilda Berling
4424 Kemper Avenue
Cincinnati, OH 45217
TEL: 513-641-3053
Objectives: To volunteer services to help the less fortunate.

Services: Serves as an umbrella organization for local autonomous volunteer organizations operating under the auspices of the Roman Catholic church; gives service and pastoral care to the poor, the sick, the elderly, and youth wherever and whenever necessary; maintains committees to monitor and serve Indian missions, immigrants and refugees, the aging, and youth; conducts regional seminars to supplement its national conference and encourage higher participation levels; publishes a newsletter, a directory, manuals and promotional brochures.
Sponsor: National Council of Catholic Women
Publications: Servicette; Directory of Affiliates; ALCUS News Bulletin
Founded: 1960

INDOCHINA RESOURCE ACTION CENTER
1628 Sixteenth Street, NW
Third Floor
Washington, DC 20009
TEL: 202-667-4690
Objectives: To help Indochinese refugees become self-sufficient in American society.
Services: Works with local mutual-assistance associations (MAAs) in the southeast Asian communities of cities to speed up the adjustment process for refugees; helps refugees initiate self-help projects; offers one-to-one technical assistance to refugee community organizations throughout the country; conducts forums in conjunction with United Ways sponsored, in part, by funds from the *W.K. Kellogg Foundation,* and provides information on how to organize a board, how to develop and define a mission and objectives, how to write effective grant proposals, and how to develop a networking system and learn more about the American nonprofit system; promotes community development and economic advancement among Southeast Asian refugees; maintains a resource bank of 800 refugee organizations in the U.S.; produces reports and studies in areas of health, employment, information & referral, social adjustment, and outreach, among others; provides the *CAI Lettering System* for computer use; publishes a bimonthly newsletter, a directory, and a bibliography of Asian periodicals and newspapers.
Founded: 1979

MIGRATION AND REFUGEE SERVICE
U.S. Catholic Charities
1312 Massachusetts Avenue, NW
Washington, DC 20005
TEL: 202-659-6630
Objectives: To assist arriving refugees in finding employment and becoming self-sufficient.
Services: Provides pre-arrival orientation for sponsors and refugees, training courses, employment and housing assistance, and aid in obtaining care from local public health organizations; secures sponsors when needed for the refugee prior to his/her arrival, finds living quarters, provides first month's rent and food allowance, and meets refugee at the airport; conducts orientation, employment counseling, health screening, social security and school registration and other services upon arrival; publishes newsletter, resettlement directory, and in-house information on legislative issues and policy development.
Publications: Update; MRS Annual Review; MRS Resettlement and Immigration Directory; Enriched by Their Presence
Founded: 1920

RECIPIENTS: FAMILIES

NATIONAL/STATE ORGANIZATIONS

NATIONAL ASSOCIATION OF EXTENSION HOME ECONOMISTS
c/o Dr. B.G. Eichner, Suite 240
2221 East Northern Lights Boulevard
Anchorage, AK 99508
TEL: 907-279-5582
Objectives: To improve and strengthen professional standards for members who help families find solutions to problems concerning family life.
Services: Trains volunteer leaders to work with families and individual family members; offers family education programs in areas of child care and development, nutrition, energy conservation, budgeting, family recreation; sponsors volunteer recruitment and public relations committees; publishes quarterly newsletter, *The Reporter.*

NATIONAL COMMUNITY ACTION FOUNDATION
2100 M Street, NW
Suite 604A
Washington, DC 20037
TEL: 202-775-0223
Objectives: To assist low-income families in becoming self-sufficient.
Services: Serves as the umbrella organization for community action agencies that provide services at the local level, such as Head Start, Meals on Wheels, low-income energy assistance, weatherization services, emergency food and shelter, and job training and placement; assists low-income families in becoming self sufficient and obtaining employment and decent housing; helps to improve communities by developing local solutions to problems and stimulating economic development; lobbies for federal programs that serve the poor, including employment and training, energy assistance, nutrition, and services to children and senior citizens; provides information on energy programs for low-income people, and neighborhood block grants; conducts a program for communities entitled *How Congress Works;* publishes a newsletter and periodic research reports.
Publications: How Congress Works Information Packet; NCAF Newsletter
Founded: 1981

NATIONAL EXTENSION HOMEMAKERS COUNCIL (
formerly National Home Demonstration Council)
4089 Snake Island Road
Sturgeon Bay, WI 54235
TEL: 414-743-9783
Objectives: To assist individuals and family members in identifying and solving family and community problems in cooperation with local resources.
Services: Works in cooperation with local resources, state land-grant universities, and the United States Department of Agriculture to assist individuals and family members in identifying and solving family and community problems; includes on its agenda programs of citizenship, arts/cultural enrichment, disaster response and emergency preparedness, certified volunteer units, international affairs, community outreach, safety, family relationships/child development, health, resource management, nutrition, housing, physical environment, and others; presents awards for outstanding accomplishments in each of the program areas; maintains a committee to advise young homemakers; sponsors special projects; works in affiliatiation with *Country Women of the World;* publishes a newsletter and a handbook.
Publications: Update (newsletter); NEHC Handbook
Founded: 1936

NEIGHBORHOODS USA
SEE CIVIC AFFAIRS: CITY/COUNTY GOALS

SALVATION ARMY
799 Bloomfield Avenue
Verona, NJ 07044
TEL: 201-239-0606
Objectives: To meet the physical, spiritual and emotional needs of mankind.
Services: Works through about 10,500 local centers in areas of adult rehabilitation, hospitals, clinics, homes for unwed mothers, recreation centers, camping programs for children and adults, and emergency feeding and shelter stations; cooperates with other community programs in emergencies, more than 6,000 of them operating one or more *Salvation Army* programs; has ordained ministers in leadership roles who spend full time in religious and social welfare activities; maintains library and archives and a speakers' bureau; publishes biweekly, monthly, semiannual and annual publications describing and reporting on the work of the organization.
Publications: The War Cry; The Musician; Young Salvationist; Program Aids; People Helping People; Annual Report; Edward H. McKinney

STATE VOLUNTEER PROGRAM
Iowa Department of Social Services
Hoover Building
Des Moines, IA 50319
TEL: 515-281-8269
Objectives: To enhance the services provided to the Iowa Department of Social Services through the involvement of volunteers.
Services: The original manual of the Department of Social Services Volunteer Program was written in 1976. At that time volunteers worked only in the Mental Health Institutions. Today volunteers are working in all 99 counties plus juvenile and adult correctional institutions.
The State of Iowa is divided into eight Districts. Each District has from one to five volunteer coordinators who recruit volunteers on the basis of need for the county offices where they are assigned. The need for a volunteer is identified by a staff member, who sends a written request for a volunteer to the coordinator. The coordinator uses this request to develop a volunteer job description and as a tool to recruit the volunteer. Orientation is provided to the volunteer by the volunteer coordinator and any specialized training needed is provided by the staff who made the request for the volunteer. During National Volunteer week, the Department of Social Services hosts a statewide recognition in the Capitol Complex. At this time outstanding volunteers are recognized in Social Services from all over the state.
The volunteer program is funded through federal and state funds. There are 4,000 volunteers, registered with the Department of Social Services, who work an average of 30,000 hours a month. In the Central Office, volunteers work in the Bureau of Communications answering the phone, filing, and as a graphic artist. There is also a team of volunteers in the Community Service Division which operates the adoption exchange program and answers mail from people inquiring about parents and children. In the field, volunteers handle the distribution of cheese and butter commodities. They also operate many food pantries and clothes closet. Other volunteers work to prevent child abuse and, in the case of proven child abuse, to stop it. The training for all of these programs is provided by staff, experienced volunteers and professionals from related fields who volunteer their time.
Sponsor: Iowa Department of Social Services
Contact: J.D. Hall
Founded: 1976

US/HHS - WORKING GROUP ON PRIVATE SECTOR INITIATIVES
US/HHS - Office of the Secretary
PO Box 1182
Washington, DC 20201
TEL: 202-619-7000
Objectives: To inventory existing HHS/private sector relationships; to develop new approaches to expand public/private partnerships that address health and human service needs.
Services: Operates under a mandate to report on the following tasks:
- Review procedures and regulations to recommend modifications to eliminate barriers to private sector involvement;
- Identify and recommend incentives for private sector involvement, including innovative approaches to public/private partnership in delivery of health and human services;
- Examine existing programs to identify current voluntary efforts and potential for expansion and to recommend those activities which could be carried out more productively in the private sector; and
- Recommend ways in which the dissemination of technical knowledge and other information can enhance private incentives.

Categorizes existing HHS/private sector partnerships (utilize volunteers or involve other types of cooperative interaction with the private sector) into four areas:
HHS programs which utilize volunteers directly
Public Health Service:
- Student Volunteer Program
- NIH Volunteer Program
- Normal Volunteer Program
- Indian Health Services
- National Health Service Corps Clinics
- National Hansen's Disease Center
- Childhood Immunization
- National Institute for Occupational Safety and Health

Social Security Administration:
- Volunteers in all Trust Fund Programs

Health Care Financing Administration:
- Medicare
- Medicare Peer Counseling
- Medigap Training Program

Department-Wide:
- Student Volunteer Program (interns)

Human Development Services:
- Office of Policy Development (over 700 volunteers nationwide serve as field readers in the preapplication selection process for certain HDS grants)

HHS-funded programs, carried out within the private sector
Public Health Service:
- Health Careers Opportunity Program
- National VD Hotline
- Rehabilitation Grant Support
- Bureau of Community Health Services/Family Planning
- Community Health Centers, Migrant Health Projects

Human Development Services:
- Parents Anonymous
- Parent Aide Child Protective Services
- Runaway Youth Programs
- Indian Child Welfare Programs
- Partnership for Permanence Project
- Project Head Start
- Guardian Ad Litem Projects
- Group Live-In Experience
- Toll Free National Communications Network
- Financial Assistance Grants
- Title III (over 250,000 volunteers)
- Title IV (discretionary funds)

- Financial and Life Planning
- Minority/Professional Resource Center

HHS-supported programs partially funded and/or administered by states and localities

Public Health Service:
- Bureau of Community Health Services/Family Planning
- Community Health Centers, Migrant Health Projects
- Maternal and Child Health

Office of Community Services:
- Program Support (block grants)

Health Care Financing Administration:
- Medicaid
- Early Periodic, Screening, Diagnostic and Treatment Program under Medicaid
- Transportation Services under Medicaid

Human Development Services:
- Child Welfare Services
- Project Head Start
- Administration of Developmental Disabilities
- Title III
- Social Security Block Grants
- WIN Program

HHS partnerships with national, regional, state, or local consortia of public/private organizations

Public Health Service:
- Health Promotion Training Program
- Community Based Programs
- National Alliance for Energy Contingency Planning for Health Resources
- Guidelines for Construction and Equipment
- Diabetic Retinopathy Information Campaign
- National Industrial Council for HMO Development
- Comprehensive Cancer Center Communications Network
- Community Health Centers, Migrant Health Projects
- Pregnancy and Infant Health Project
- Hospital Transport Project
- Indian Diabetes Care
- Sodium and Hypertension
- Joint Commission on Patient Education

[Not a complete list; over 1,000 HHS programs involve the private sector and volunteers; ask about criteria used in above selection.]
Works toward completion of potential inducements for increasing public/private partnerships for the delivery of health services in four areas:
- One, promotion of volunteer activity among federal employees.
- Two, expansion of volunteer services and volunteer contributions to federal programs.
- Three, utilization of Federal facilities to assist private sector volunteers initiatives and public/private partnerships.
- Four, use of Federal seed money.

Plans other initiatives such as volunteer fairs, recognition to outstanding volunteer activities at the regional level, service delivery assessments, better coordination of specific programs such as employment of the handicapped, the identification of regulatory and administrative barriers to publicizing successful projects in the private sector, and targeting of discretionary funds to stimulate increased voluntarism and public/private collaboration.
Provides weekly reports to the White House listing private sector initiatives across the country as a result of the Working Group's efforts:
- a new Voluntary Action Center in New Jersey;
- an HHS employee volunteer program in Seattle;
- a day care conference in Philadelphia;
- hunger research in Massachusetts;
- senior housing in unused schools in Colorado;
- food drives in Washington and Missouri;
- chore services in Washington;
- development of volunteer recruitment materials in Oregon;
- youth serving the elderly in California;
- corporate grants for day care in Washington;

- food distribution in New York;
- senior citizen fitness awards in New England;
- meals program in Connecticut;
- donation of outdoor equipment in Massachusetts;
- emergency food and shelter program in Dallas; and
- a task force on food and hunger in Kansas City.

[Many of these and other programs are sponsored or co-sponsored by HHS Regional Offices in concert with the corporate community, local government, community groups, etc.; additional information provided on request.]
In addition to reports on individual partnership efforts, the Working Group provides an overview on reports from the region in specific areas, such as the *Communications Industry Project Update,* which describes efforts in each region by the various media.
Sponsor: US/HHS - Department of Health & Human Services
Publications: Project Update

YOUNG MEN'S CHRISTIAN ASSOCIATION OF THE U.S.
(*formerly National Council of the YMCAs*)
YMCA
101 North Wacker Drive
Chicago, IL 60606
TEL: 312-977-0031
Objectives: To offer a flexible program approach designed to meet the developing needs of people of all ages, races, religions, and incomes.
Services: Works through 2,048 local groups representing almost 13.5 million members to strengthen families, increase international understanding, promote healthy lifestyles, and develop communities, youth leadership, and adult health enhancement programs; offers group and club activities, facilities for physical and health education and training, youth sports activities, aquatics instruction, camping, parent-child programs, child care, world service work, and counseling; operates the *International Camp Counselor Program* which recruits counselors from other countries to work with youth in the U.S.; maintains a library and database of its activities; publishes a journal, a newsletter, a yearbook/Roster, a directory, and several bulletins, manuals, books and pamphlets.
Publications: Discovery YMCA; YMCA Newsletter; YMCA Yearbook and Official Roster; YMCA Directory; Executive Notes; Program Notes
Founded: 1851

YOUNG WOMEN'S CHRISTIAN ASSOCIATION OF THE U.S.
726 Broadway
New York, NY 10003
TEL: 212-614-2700
Objectives: To provide service programs for women and girls over 12 years of age.
Services: Works through its 4,000 local groups representing two million members to provide programs in health education, recreation, clubs and classes, and counseling and assistance to girls and women in the areas of employment, education, human sexuality, self-improvement, volunteerism, community citizenship, emotional and physical health, and juvenile justice; seeks to make contributions to peace, justice, freedom and dignity for all people; works toward elimination of racism; maintains national advocacy programs on the *Equal Rights Amendment,* sex-based discrimination against women, national policy of full employment, pay for work of comparable value, prevention of teenage pregnancy, protection against violence for all individuals, and child care services; includes men and boys in programs as associates; maintains 44 camps for children; publishes a journal, a newsletter, an annual report, a directory, and several bulletins and other materials.
Publications: YWCA Interchange; Communicator's Exchange; The

Print Out; YWCA Directory; Annual Report
Founded: 1858

TRAINING PROGRAMS

IN-SERVICE TRAINING/STATEWIDE VOLUNTEER DEVELOPMENT
Michigan Statewide Volunteer Development
Department of Social Services
PO Box 30037
Lansing, MI 48909
TEL: 517-373-0920
Credit: Inquire
Sponsor: Michigan Department of Social Services
Contact: Elizabeth Albee Frier
Description: Periodically, as needed, one-day training sessions are offered to volunteer coordinators, directors, and service staff of the Department of Social Services, with guests from other state departments included.
Faculty consists of state DSS office directors with visiting lecturers from other public and private agencies. Topics covered in the program include:
- Overturning Turnover
- Overcoming Staff Hostility
- Recruiting Volunteers
- Training Volunteers
- Stretching Dollars
- Organizing Food Co-ops
- Making Toys out of Trash
- Family-to-Family Program
- Third Party Payees
- Youth Companions
- Cashing in on Cash-off Coupons and Refunds
- Poverty
- Transportation
- Insurance and Liability
- Michigan's Cooperative Volunteer Program
- Fund-raising - Thrift Shops, Used Book Sales
- Parent Aides

Curriculum changes from year to year to respond to emerging needs and delete topics that cease to be relevant.

PROGRAM DEVELOPMENT ASSISTANCE PACKAGE
Michigan Department of Social Services
300 South Capitol Avenue
Suite 704
Lansing, MI 48909
TEL: 517-373-8534
Credit: Inquire
Sponsor: Michigan Department of Social Services
Contact: Barbara Conrad
Description: In a climate of shrinking resources, social agencies may need to look increasingly to volunteers to supplement services to clients and to provide administrative support to the agency. In a well designed volunteer program, staff will be intimately involved in defining roles for volunteers and in assuming responsibility for supervision and evaluation of volunteer involvement.
Description of Content: In a three hour workshop participants examine their personal attitudes toward volunteers, gain knowledge of the components necessary to a well-designed volunteer program, and learn to design volunteer jobs to provide services to children and families and to meet the administrative needs of the agencies. Each participant develops an actual job description for a volunteer which can be taken back to use in the home agency. Several topics are covered, including:
- Attitudes Towards and Expectations of Volunteers - Large group discussion and small group brainstorming.

- Components of a Well Designed Volunteer Program - Mini lecture, large group discussion.
- Development of Volunteer Jobs; participant analysis of individual job responsibilities, principles of job enrichment - mini lecture, large group discussion, individual written exercise.
- Job Description Exercise and Application - role playing, group discussion, written exercise.

VISION, PLANNING & PARTNERSHIP IN NEIGHBORHOOD ORGANIZING
Neighborhoods USA
4643 Amesborough
Dayton, OH 45420
TEL: 513-222-2889
Credit: Inquire
Sponsor: Neighborhoods USA
Contact: William Littlejohn, President
Description: This conference brought together 440 people from across the U.S. to talk about organizing and revitalizing neighborhoods. Attendees included citizen activists, government officials, university professors, police officials and politicians. The keynote speaker set the tone of the meeting by addressing the dormant period from the late 1970s through the early 1980s and appealing to the group to develop a strategy to avoid such a gap in neighborhod activism in the future. Other areas discussed include:
- **Smaller Communities,** which have become part of a major "ripple effect" with problems happening years ago in major metropolitan areas cropping up due to residents' belief that they couldn't happen in small towns.
- **Involvement,** pointing up the frustration that can come from neighborhood organizing, but emphasizing that the price of not getting involved is "too high to pay."
- **Contradiction or "Mixed Signals" from Government,** discussing the neighborhood platforms of politicians which are contradicted when budgets for community programs are cut after elections.
- **Real Solutions (Beyond Federal Support),** emphasizing that neighborhoods must look to themselves and form working partnerships such as the relationship between local churches, neighborhoods, and police in a citizen coalition, Oakland Community Organizations, that brought together 2,000 people in 1988 to develop ways to deal with a crack cocaine epidemic.
- **Changing Laws,** as was accomplished by the Oakland group when more money for jails, and stiffer sentencing guidelines were needed, as well as a task force of police officers (40 were hired for this purpose) to shut down crack houses.
- **Leaning on Local Politicians,** which emphasizes the need to work with officials, outline and detail the critical issues, and involve them in the issue itself by asking them to offer their own recommendations, since they are more accustomed to dealing with physical problems (e.g., potholes) than the kind of investment needed to address families and social problems.
- **Leaving Things to the "Experts,"** which points out that there is no room for complaints when things go wrong if the individual doesn't take responsibility for the governance of his/her own community.
- **What You Represent Besides Your Neighborhood,** which asks attendees to look beyond the neighborhood to the differences that can be made in gaining political power, and making major differences in "everything from City Council elections to the planning process."
- **After Getting the Power,** which emphasizes the danger of simply becoming "naysayers" without acting on the vision that was developed at the outset, and points out the many instances where citizens greatly affected development through halting projects or forcing concessions from developers.

Some dramatic cases were described, such as Seattle's recent history of neighborhood successes, ranging from the fight to save Lake Union in the 1960s to preserving Pike Place Market in the 1970s and the passage in 1989 of the Citizens' Alternative Plan to control downtown growth. According to the presenter, the trick in getting community support is to describe the activity according to the interests of the majority. The "vision" in Seattle's effort was changed from "evicting houseboat owners" (of no interest) to "saving Lake Union for all residents and the city" (which was the same vision, but worked better in garnering support).

The message of the conference, Vision, Planning and Partnership, was evident throughout the sessions. According to one attendee, "This conference has removed a lot of the isolation you feel as a volunteer in the neighborhoods."

Publications: NUSA Conference Report

VOLUNTEERISM AND SOCIAL WORK PRACTICE
Hunter College
School of Social Work
129 East 79th Street
New York, NY 10021
TEL: 212-570-5605
Credit: 3 credits
Sponsor: Hunter College of the City University of New York
Contact: Elizabeth Landing
Description: Volunteerism and Social Work Practice is an elective course open to all School of Social Work students, as well as nonmatriculated students. It is directed to social workers who are considering the use of volunteers; social workers who work with volunteers; and persons who recruit, assign, train, or supervise volunteers. Objectives of the course are:
- To create understanding of the significance of volunteerism/voluntarism in the field of social work.
- To identify the role of the social worker in providing access for use of volunteers in social agencies.
- To develop skill in the development and management of volunteer programs.
- To provide an opportunity to explore current issues in volunteerism.

Staff of agencies serving as field instruction centers for Hunter College School of Social Work are eligible in some instances for 1/2 tuition wavers. Course content includes:
- The value of volunteerism in the American Democratic Society.
- The different functions performed by volunteers.
- Problems of developing and administering volunteer programs.
- Staff development and training programs.
- Supervision and retention of volunteers.
- Relationship between professional staff and volunteers.
- The constituencies of the volunteer administrator.
- The law and volunteers.
- Current issues.

The principal instructor of the course, Dr. Florence S. Schwartz, is Associate Professor in the Hunter College School of Social Work, member of the Board of Directors of the Association of Voluntary Action Scholars, and an Associate Editor of Volunteer Administration.

INDIVIDUAL PROGRAM PROFILES

DSS VOLUNTEER SERVICES PROGRAM
Saginaw County Department of Social Services
310 Johnson Street
PO Box 5070
Saginaw, MI 48605
TEL: 817-771-1615
Purpose: To supplement services to public assistance clients of the *Saginaw County Department of Social Services.*
Contact: Susan L. Topliff

Description: The focus of our *Volunteer Services Program* is on distributing donated goods and services to those in need through the use of volunteers. We have a large *Christmas Wish* program and a *Coats for Kids* program at Christmas (see separate entry), which is run in conjunction with the *Saginaw Voluntary Action Center.*

Volunteers coordinate and provide medical transportation for those who are otherwise unable to obtain such. Volunteers serve as representative payees as well as providing food stamp outreach services. *Volunteer Services* recently became involved in facilitating a *Client Advisory Committee.*

The entire program is gradually expanding with many new programs and services currently being examined.

FREE THE CHILDREN (FTC)
SEE WELFARE REFORM

GOOD NEIGHBOR EXCHANGE PROGRAM
Alexandria Public Schools
Administration Building
3801 West Braddock Road
Alexandria, VA 22302
TEL: 703-824-6660
Purpose: To help parents provide clothing for their growing children through a clothing exchange program.
Sponsor: Alexandria Parent-Teachers Association
Contact: Carol Lisi, Coordinator, or Mary Kehoe, PTA
Description: When band or scout uniforms are outgrown, the expense for replacement is a hardship for some families. Solving this problem is one purpose of the *Good Neighbor Exchange Program.* The other is to provide a means to exchange outgrown clothing for large sizes to address the problem of "fast-growing children," a problem for all income levels.

A teacher in the Alexandria, Virginia, school system organized the program in late 1989, and finds its growth and acceptance to be very rewarding. She also finds the tolerance of the school system - when twice a week its Howard administration building turns into a sort of shopping center - to be exemplary, and in tune with the needs of the families of its pupils.

Volunteers from the Parent-Teacher Association of the city's schools are helping to expand the program through volunteer recruitment and publicity. One unusual aspect of the program is that it is not restricted to Alexandria schools. Anyone in the nearby Northern Virginia communities who needs clothing or who wants to donate clothing is welcome. Items are available for infants through teenagers.

The "community clothing cooperative" has found that other programs receiving gifts of clothing are willing to share their excess, also. One example is *Christ House,* a homeless shelter in the city, which received such an abundance of clothing that it donated some of it to *Good Neighbor.* Conversely, the Alexandria Health Department requested clothing from the exchange for low-income families who had just found housing in the city. The cooperation among groups, parents, and the school system demonstrates the benefits to all concerned of a joint rather than isolated effort, according to the founder.

HOMELESSNESS PREVENTION PROGRAM
SEE HOUSING: HOMELESS

INTERDIVISIONAL VOLUNTEER PROGRAM
Oregon Department of Human Resources
Post Office Box 628
Hillsboro, OR 97123
TEL: 503-648-0711
Purpose: To incorporate local citizen involvement in many areas of social service delivery with the clientele of the Adult and Family Services, Children's Services, Senior Services and Mental Health Division of the State of Oregon, Department of Human Resources.

Sponsor: State of Oregon, Department of Human Resources, private donations

Contact: Guy Hornbeck, Volunteer Services Supervisor

Description: The Interdivisional Volunteer Program has its origin in the 1967 Harris Amendments to the Social Security Act of 1935. These amendments mandated the use of volunteers in the delivery of services by all public assistance and service programs. The goals of the interdivisional Volunteer Program are:

- To extend, supplement and enrich services to clients.
- To provide the personalized help and interest of a sincere friend.
- To provide opportunity for persons with different life styles and varied socio-economic levels, including clients themselves, to help agency clients.
- To provide first hand information to the public on the nature of the services and problems of the agencies.
- To assist in developing community awareness of social problems and the need for finding appropriate solutions.

The Interdivisional Volunteer Program is funded through Title XIX of the Social Security Act of 1935, State of Oregon General Fund monies, and through private donations.

Volunteers in Washington County participate in activities that range from serving as a "big sister" to a sexually abused girl, to advocating for the needs of nursing home patients, to soliciting and delivering donated food and furniture items to destitute families, to befriending a mentally handicapped adult.

Volunteers in these programs are considered "Agents of the State" and as such are covered by certain Tort Liability immunity and Workman's Compensation Insurance...just like any other "Agent of the State."

Founded: 1967

VOLUNTEER SERVICES PROGRAM/SOCIAL SERVICES
Washtenaw County Department of Social Services
2350 West Stadium Boulevard
Ann Arbor, MI 48103
TEL: 313-994-1810

Purpose: To provide services enabling self-sufficiency, protection, and community-based care to the elderly and disabled, adults and children served by the Department of Social Services.

Sponsor: Washtenaw County Department of Social Services

Contact: Linda King, Volunteer Services Supervisor

Description: Washtenaw County has operated a Volunteer Services Program for many years, with volunteers filling important slots in five areas of service - Companionship, Agency Aides, Transportation, Special Services, and Community Services. An overview of the Department structure, and orientation and training to the specific volunteer assignment are provided, hours are flexible to enable more people to volunteer, and mileage and other expenses are reimbursable. Examples of volunteer opportunities in the various areas are:

Companionship
- Friendly Visitors - providing concern and friendship to elderly or disabled adults who live in their communities.
- Adult Foster Care Friends - helping elderly long-term residents become more involved in daily living and community activities.
- Youth Companion - working with children who need enriched adult attention.

Transportation
- Transporters - providing rides for clients with no other means of transportation (includes foster children as well as other clients).
- Shopping Aides - assisting elderly and disabled clients with shopping and transportation (usually one-to-one weekly or semi-monthly service).

Agency Aides
- Application Assistance - helping clients fill in applications to facilitate prompt service by staff.

- Clerical Aides - assisting with clerical work.
- Food Stamp Outreach - helping in coordinated public awareness effort.

Special Services
- Furniture Delivery - picking up, delivering usable donated furniture.
- Emergency Food Bank - soliciting food contributions for emergency use.
- Special Resources - assisting with material needs on referral of caseworker.
- Tutors - aiding both adults and children academically.
- Representative Payees - handling client budget/money management problems.
- Holiday Gifts - groups/families/individuals providing food/gifts to families.
- Task and Advisory Service Committee - assisting a member to oversee program.

Community Services
- Home Repairs - helping elderly and disabled with small home repairs.
- Safe House - helping women in domestic violence shelter.
- Refugee Assistance - helping to settle refugee families.

WEST ST. JOHN MINISTRY OF CARE
Second African Baptist Church
Edgard, LA 70049
TEL: 504-497-3498; 504-497-8523

Purpose: To help the people in the community in need of services.

Sponsor: Second African Baptist Church

Contact: Merita Johnson

Description: Operated for a year out of the home of one of the volunteers, the *West St. John Ministry of Care* held a grand opening in June 1989 in its new location in the *Second African Baptist Church* in Edgard. The program was formed by an alliance of clergymen in 1985 to help provide emergency assistance to people in need of help with utility bills, food, clothing, shelter and medical assistance. The program also aids transients who may need a meal or gasoline for returning home.

The *Ministry* depends on public and private donations and fundraisers. These have included a motorcycle rally and food and clothing drives.

No referrals are needed to obtain help from the program, but proof of income is required to determine eligibility. The service is confidential, and a special effort is made to reach people who need some help but are reluctant to ask for it.

Several churches support the program including New St. Peter Baptist Church and St. John the Baptist Church. The present location is serving as a temporary headquarters until a permanent site can be found.

Founded: 1988

WEST VIRGINIA DEPARTMENT OF WELFARE VOLUNTEER PROGRAM
1900 Washington Street, East
Charleston, WV 25305
TEL: 304-348-7980

Purpose: To involve volunteers in meaningful opportunities to extend, enrich and supplement the totality of services provided through the Department of Welfare

Sponsor: West Virginia Department of Welfare

Contact: M. Susan Beard, Director

Description: As mandated by the 1967 Amendments to the Social Security Act, the West Virginia Department of Welfare has initiated volunteer service programs in 27 Administrative Areas. Beginning on a small project basis in May 1970 with five areas participating, the program became statewide in July 1971 with the appointments of area volunteer coordinators and the assignment of a full-time consultant at the state level.

Each month over 900 volunteers contribute 7,000 plus hours of service through the program statewide. Each Administrative Area designs projects in response to identified needs and interests. Agency staff persons receive training and technical assistance in volunteer management on request.

Types of volunteer service provided by volunteers affiliated with the Department include:

- Waiting Room Volunteers
- Clinic Aides
- Friendly and Family Visiting
- Homemakers
- Transportation
- Tutoring
- Family Planning
- Volunteers in Courts
- Clerical
- Day Care
- Big Brothers and Big Sisters
- Home Repair
- Telephone Reassurance
- Case Aides

In addition, Volunteer Coordinators assist local groups in providing seasonal activities, such as Christmas parties and picnics for foster children, Summer Day Camps for senior citizens and for children, ongoing programs of clothing distribution, and others. Volunteers are recognized in a number of ways. One that was especially well-received and appreciated was a special supplement to *Accent,* the Department's newsletter, saluting West Virginia Volunteers and entitled, *Thank You for Being a Friend.*
Founded: 1970

WOMEN OFF WELFARE (WOW)
SEE WELFARE REFORM

RECIPIENTS: FAMILIES - CRISIS INTERVENTION

INDIVIDUAL PROGRAM PROFILES

ANNANDALE CHRISTIAN COMMUNITY FOR ACTION (ACCA)
7200 Columbia Pike
Annandale, VA 22003
TEL: 703-256-1378
Purpose: To respond to critical needs of youth, children and families in the area.
Sponsor: Local churches (24 in 1989)
Contact: Gilmer B. Weatherly, Jr.
Description: The Annandale Christian Community for Action (ACCA) was established in 1967 in response to an urgent need for child care. A small group of children were being cared for in the Mount Pleasant Baptist Church under a government program that provided funds for the service. Suddenly the guidelines for the program were changed, and the families could no longer be helped. These were low-income working parents whose meager salaries could not cover the cost of child care in addition to their other expenses. The families had no alternatives. They would have to give up their jobs and seek welfare assistance unless they could have help with the child care expense. A group of concerned Christians met at Peace Lutheran Church and decided that they would dedicate their efforts to the solution of this problem. They established the Annandale Christian Community for Action by starting the first ACCA Day Care Center in the John Calvin Presbyterian Church. With only $1,000 of donated funds, and with no real knowledge of child care, the ACCA Center began as an

expression of Christian concern.
As the church sponsors became acquainted with the families of the day care children, and with their neighbors as well, knowledge of the nature and extent of poverty in the community grew. It was learned that many people were indeed hungry in the area, that many families lacked clothing, furniture, and money for essentials such as rent, medical and utility payments. Committees were established to cope with the problems.
From this humble beginning, ACCA has seen amazing growth through the years with 24 churches participating in 1989, with thousands of volunteers involved.
An important point is that ACCA is not a separate or umbrella organization - it is "all of the members of all of the ACCA churches." Programs include: Family Emergency Committee, Child Development Centers, Furniture Committee, Housing Program, Meals on Wheels Program, Transportation Committee, and Scholarship Program (all described separately).
Publications: ACCA Annual Report
Founded: 1967

COMMITTEE TO AID ABUSED WOMEN
680 Greenbrae Drive
Suite 270
Sparks, NV 89431
TEL: 702-358-4150
Purpose: To help women and children of domestic violence through the period of crisis and afterward according to individual needs.
Sponsor: City of Sparks, including a tax surcharge; private donations
Contact: Maryanne Aaronson
Description: Recognizing the problem of domestic violence in the Sparks, Nevada area, a group of citizens gathered information on programs around the country designed to aid abused women and children. They found that these programs not only supported the victims through the crisis, but also worked toward elimination of the problem in their communities. In 1977, the Committee to Aid Abused Women was founded in Sparks to serve the city and its surroundings rural area.
The Committee successfully influenced the city to levy a $5.00 surcharge on marriage licenses to help fund the program. Other funding comes from other city channels, and private donations. The Committee receives no federal or state funding.
To develop the program, the Committee extracted selected practices from other programs that would best serve the Sparks population. The organization runs a temporary shelter, housing up to twelve women and children. In addition, it provides crisis counseling - both face-to-face and over the telephone. It serves as a resource and referral clearinghouse to help victims find continuing help in appropriate existing agencies, and advocates for the rights of the victims of domestic violence. Also, the organization provides food, transportation and emotional support as needed.
Volunteers in the program must undergo a seven-week training class twice each year that covers crisis counseling, legal and psychological needs of abused women, children's programs, and the philosophy and practices of CAAW. Inservice training is held bimonthly for the continuing education of all staff and volunteers. As of December 1981, 60 volunteers were involved in CAAW. They work in the following areas: direct client work; work with children, speakers bureau, fundraising, transportation, and office support. A City Development Block Grant in July 1981 made it possible to add three staff persons and expand the volunteer program.

DOMESTIC ABUSE PROJECT OF DELAWARE COUNTY
PO Box 174
Media, PA 19063
TEL: 215-565-6272

Purpose: To work against violence in the home by providing supportive services to victims and their families.
Sponsor: Federal/State/County governments; corporate and private donations.
Contact: Maxine Bailey, Executive Director
Description: The Domestic Abuse Project is a non-profit, community-based, volunteer organization committed to preventing and working against violence in the home by providing advocacy, emergency, supportive service and information to victims and their families; and by educating and involving the community in this process.
Volunteers are the backbone of the Project. There are presently 98 volunteers to answer the 24-hour hotline, counsel victims, plan events and policies, and give 1500-1800 hours per month to training and service.
Services include a 24-hour hotline with calls answered by counselors trained to respond to emergencies; counseling services for victims, and children; court accompaniment to help victims deal with the intricacies of the justice system; screening and referral services; emergency shelter, court and police advocacy; community outreach and education.

F.A.C.T. HOTLINE (FAMILIES AND CHILDREN IN TROUBLE)
Family Stress Services of DC
1690 36th Street, NW
Washington, DC 20007
TEL: 202-965-1900 (office); 202-628-FACT (hotline)
Purpose: To provide families, individuals and other agencies with help around family stress, child abuse/neglect concerns, or almost any crisis or problem.
Sponsor: Family Stress Services of DC
Contact: Joan Cox Danzansky, Director
Description: This Hotline is a a project of F.A.C.T. (Families and Children in Trouble) which has been operating for over twelve years. The Hotline is a 24-hour crisis and referral helpline, providing families, individuals, and other helping agencies with assistance in matters of family stress, child abuse/neglect, and other types of crises and problems including suicide, depression and spouse abuse. The Hotline is staffed primarily by specially selected, trained and supervised community volunteers.
The comprehensive training and reliance upon committed community volunteers is an integral part of the FACT Program. The Hotline trains volunteer telephone counselors through a course held three times a year, and is constantly in need of additional volunteers. After a special screening process, volunteers complete the sixty-hour course in empathetic and reflective listening/counseling skills and basic problem-solving processes. The training includes an apprenticeship on the lines and also covers family dynamics, etiology of child abuse, the law and resources, as well as information to aid with other types of calls such as spouse abuse, runaways, suicides, depression, etc.
The hotline, which opened on February 2, 1976, is supported through individual donations, private foundations, a grant from the National Parents Anonymous Organization, and receives funding through a contract with the Family Services Administration of the District of Columbia Department of Human Services.
FACT helps in a variety of ways, depending upon the needs of the caller. It acts as a crisis-intervention, listening, counseling, information and referral service which functions therapeutically when the hotline listener provides immediate understanding and support in times of crisis. It functions in a preventive manner when it allows parents or other caretakers to release their frustrations through talking with a concerned listener, rather than taking them out on children or other family members. When a caller appears to need help other than can be provided over the phone, FACT's information and referral component is used to find assistance for the caller through other community resources,

agencies or self-help groups such as Parents Anonymous. The hotline also provides third-party callers with counseling and assistance for the reporting of cases to the proper authorities when necessary.
In addition to the FACT Hotline, Family Stress Services/FACT operates two other components: community education to raise public awareness; advocacy on both an individual and a case basis. Also, it serves as the information and referral line for Parents Anonymous, a self-help organization for parents experiencing child abuse/neglect problems.
Founded: 1976

FAMILY EMERGENCY COMMITTEE OF ACCA
Annandale Christian Community for Action (ACCA)
7200 Columbia Pike
Annandale, VA 22003
TEL: 703-256-1378
Purpose: To help families in crisis.
Sponsor: Annandale Christian Community for Action
Contact: Ann Marie Hicks, Chairman; Joan Parnell, Food Pantry Chairman
Description: With scores of volunteers in assistance, the Family Emergency Committee is able to reach out to hundreds of families each year with food, financial aid, and the assurance that someone cares. The Committee itself consists of about 16 *Telephone Captains,* who are on duty in pairs for a week at a time to receive emergency calls from Hotline, Social Services, ministers, the ACCA Day Care Centers, and other volunteer and community agencies. They rotate duty about every six to eight weeks.
The Food Captain receives calls for food requests. After a need is established, one of over fifty volunteers on file is called. The volunteer goes to the food pantry, collects a week's worth of food, and delivers it to the needy family. The Food Pantry is stocked with canned goods and paper products donated by members of ACCA churches. Meat and dairy products are purchased with money from a state grant. A group of volunteers shops for the pantry and keeps it well stocked and well organized, enabling ACCA to provide an average of 3,000 meals per month to approximately 145 people. During 1988, an average of 45 volunteers participated in this effort each month.
The Money Captain collects messages from ACCA's answering machine and handles requests for financial assistance. She takes information and together with the coordinator decides what help ACCA can offer. In addition to immediate financial aid, the program tries to be sure the recipient is in touch with long range help - whether that be social assistance, applying for subsidized housing, pastoral counseling, fuel assistance, credit counseling or other uses of the numerous community services available.
Requests for rental assistance continue to take up the largest part of Family Emergency expenses. Families often must spend more than 60% of their income for rent. Low income housing as well as moderately-priced housing are becoming scarce as more and more apartments convert to condominiums and/or raise their rents yearly. This is a major problem, particularly with the high number of single parents, refugees and people on fixed incomes. We try to keep people in their housing by helping with rent, giving food in order to free up income for rental expenses, and suggesting roommates or other cost-cutting ideas.
Increased support from ACCA churches made possible a good level of assistance in 1988. Financial outreach has climbed steadily each year - from $49,214 in 1984 to $59,506 in 1987 to $65,460 in 1988. Over $52,000 of that total in 1988 went to assist 328 families with rent. Forty-eight families received help with utility bills, and 100 families were assisted with medical bills and other necessary living expenses such as baby formula and supplies, transportation, and shoes. The team effort is what makes the program a success - from those who donate food, to those who deliver weekly food and Thanksgiving and Christmas baskets, to those who answer phone calls.
Publications: Family Emergency Committee Overview

PARENT AIDE PROGRAM - CENTRALIZED SERVICE UNIT

2809 26th Avenue South
Seattle, WA 98144
TEL: 206-721-4243; 206-721-4191
Purpose: To provide emotional support to parents who have abused or neglected their children or who are at risk of doing so by pairing with a volunteer parent aide. The goal is to reduce or prevent abuse of the children in these families.
Sponsor: State Department of Social and Health Services
Contact: Dinah Martin or Helen Eyssen
Description: The Parent Aide Program began operation March 1980 with 33 volunteers. The average number of volunteers today is 35 with approximately 20 active matches at any one time. The Parent Aide Program helps prevent child abuse and neglect by working with "high risk" parents. Parent Aide volunteers offer these parents warmth, friendship and support. Having a "friend who really cares" helps break down the social isolation of the parent and improve his/her self-esteem, while improving the parent-child relationship and reducing the likelihood of further child abuse and neglect.
Abusive parents are often socially isolated individuals, many of whom were abused themselves as children. The goal of the Parent Aide is to help break down that isolation and help the parent learn to cope more effectively with his/her problems. The long-term goal of the relationship is to decrease the likelihood of further abuse, thereby protecting the child and breaking the child abuse cycle.
Volunteers are men or women, age 21 or older, who have enjoyed parenting or child care experience and are familiar with normal child development. They commit 4-6 hours a week for a minimum of one year. They are warm, tolerant, open and patient. They listen rather than give advice. Volunteers are reimbursed for their travel expenses by the Department of Social and Health Services (DSHS), which coordinates the program.
Parents are referred to the program by DSHS Child Protective Services (CPS) caseworkers, who are responsible for investigating child abuse and neglect. The caseworkers give the parents information about the program, but all parent participation is voluntary.
Parent Aide Program coordinators recruit volunteers and train them in areas such as child abuse and neglect, communication skills, child development, networking and locating community resources. CPS caseworkers refer the parent participants to the coordinators, who then interview the parents and match them with Parent Aide volunteers. The match then provides support to the parent through a long-term relationship.
The Seattle Parent Aide program began in 1980 and serves the greater Seattle area, as well as north and west King County. Other Parent Aide programs in the county include the Kent Parent Aide program, the East King County program in Bellevue, and a small Parent Aide program operated by Children's Orthopedic Hospital. New Parent Aides are always needed. Currently, there are not enough volunteers to match the number of abusive and neglectful parents in need of support. Individuals who are unable to volunteer as Parent Aides can support the program by providing services such as occasional babysitting and transportation assistance.
Founded: 1980

SAFE HOUSE

PO Box 3426
Kingsport, TN 37664
TEL: 615-246-1619
Purpose: To provide emergency shelter for battered women and their children.
Sponsor: Corporate and private donations
Contact: Gail Myers, Executive Director
Description: SAFE House opened in December 1982 as a twenty-four-hour, short-term shelter for battered women and their

children. Services include comfort, food, counseling and guidance through the helping system (food stamp, legal aid, medical attention, mental health counseling, etc.). SAFE House is a non-profit, state chartered corporation governed by a board of directors of thirty men and women representatives of the community. Presently, funding is through private and corporate contributions. The goal: to become an agency of Kingsport Area Community Chest plus other area Chests.
Professional staff discusses options with each batterd woman - all decisions being left to the guests - with hope that battering victims will discover their right to live without violence. Paid staff consists of an Executive Director and a House Manager.
- **Area Served** - SAFE House is a regional service and has provided shelter for women and children from Kentucky, West Virginia, and Tennessee since December 1982.
- **Volunteer Staff** - At present, fifteen volunteers provide assistance as Client Advocates, Child Nurturers, Transporters, Office Assistants and Menu Planners/Shoppers. Additional volunteers are being recruited.
- **Volunteer Experience** - Each volunteer receives training and ongoing orientation plus group discussions at will.

TACTS VOLUNTEER PROGRAM

The Arlington County Temporary Shelter (TACTS)
PO Box 1285
Arlington, VA 22210
TEL: 703-522-3182
Purpose: To provide temporary shelter to persons in crises.
Sponsor: County governments, churches, community organizations and individuals
Contact: Nancy Dehncke
Description: TACTS is a United Way agency. Its Board of Directors and supporting committees are all composed of volunteers. Other volunteers are recruited, trained, placed and supervised by the Coordinator of Volunteer Services. In addition, many church and civic groups volunteer time in support of the Food Program and other projects.
TACTS has been in operation since November 1979. The basic function of TACTS is to provide temporary shelter to persons in crises. These may be women, women and their children, or intact families. The crises may be due to a natural catastrophe (such as fire or floods), eviction because of condo-conversion, inability to pay rent because of loss of job or health, break-up of living arrangements, or other problems. TACTS is intended for Arlington residents; others are accepted on a space-available basis. Staff is on duty 24 hours daily, seven days a week. Individualized information, referral services and supervision are provided by staff to clients. All clients admitted to TACTS must agree to comply with the house rules which specify: no drugs or alcohol, curfew by 10:30 p.m., children always under supervision, and clients out of the house during weekdays working on plans to resolve their problems.
TACTS works closely with other helping organizations, such as the Department of Human Resources, Red Cross, etc. Counseling is provided by agencies within the DHR. Clients must have the capacity and willingness to make plans and implement them with assistance from DHR personnel and TACTS staff.
County government, churches, community organizations and individuals all have been supportive of TACTS. Funding has been approximately one-third County and one-third foundations (including United Way); the remaining one-third comes from the private sector and includes donations from individuals, organizations.
Founded: 1979

WOMEN'S CENTER OF EAST TEXAS (*formerly East Texas Association for Abused Families*)
PO Box 347
Longview, TX 75606
TEL: 214-757-9308
TOLL FREE: 800-441-5555
Purpose: To provide emergency services, temporary shelter to abused families, victims of physical/emotional abuse, and victims of sexual assault.
Sponsor: Texas Department of Human Resources Grant, County and City governments, local service organizations, churches, corporate and private donations
Contact: Judy Baker, Executive Director
Description: The *Women's Center of East Texas (WCET)* is a non-profit non-discriminatory, tax-exempt, social service agency which provides emergency services for abused families; an independent agency designed to fill the gap for shelter, counseling, health and social services coordinated with community agency efforts; and a complete sexual assault program. WCET's primary goals are:

- To break the cycle of violence by providing a safe alternative to a violent home, by providing education, counseling and support services to clients and their children, and by providing family counseling, if desired, for all family members.
- To provide full sexual assault accompaniment services to victims of sexual assault to promote recovery from the assault and prosecution of perpetrators.
- To provide education and awareness to the community concerning family violence and sexual assault.
- To provide priority programs and services to women and their families.
- To assist women - especially those in crisis and transition - in solving problems, seeking opportunities and meeting the challenges of a changing society.
- To inform the community about the needs and concerns of women.

At present 80-100 volunteers work on the crisis hotline, serve as sexual assault escorts and client advocates, assist in fund raising, and child guidance programs. Many are involved in community education and outreach.
Following over thirty hours of extensive training, volunteers perform many duties: answering the crisis hotline, giving referrals to callers, assessing need for shelter, etc. Sexual assault escort services provide support for victims of sexual assault from the time of the incident through court accompaniment. Other volunteer involvement areas are one-to-one counseling with shelter residents, parenting education, and alternatives to physical discipline.
Volunteers also assist in fund raising events, community awareness programs and education.
Volunteers are able to work at WCET with varying levels of experience. In-service training is provided for continuing education, which enables the volunteer to keep abreast of current events, legislation, etc., concerning family violence and sexual assault. The thirty-hour preliminary training session is required for all volunteers wishing to have direct client contact; i.e., hotline, sexual assault escort, counseling.
Volunteer involvement in the delivery of services is one of the main strengths of the family violence and sexual assault programs. Dedicated volunteers keep the cost down and improve the quality of service while participating in public education and outreach into diverse segments of society. Through training, volunteers are made aware of basic communication skills, community resources available and the process for utilizing those. One central focus of training is to develop the volunteer's capacity to be empathetic and understanding to victims of violence.

RECIPIENTS: FAMILIES - DOMESTIC ABUSE

INDIVIDUAL PROGRAM PROFILES

ABUSED ADULT RESOURCE CENTER (AARC)
PO Box 167
Bismarck, ND 58502
TEL: 701-222-8370
Purpose: To provide crisis intervention, emergency shelter, advocacy, referrals and emotional support to victims of adult domestic violence.
Contact: Diane Zainhofsky, Project Director
Description: The Abused Adult Resource Center is one of 18 spouse abuse projects in North Dakota. AARC primarily serves Burleigh and Morton counties and surrounding rural areas. Services include: safe shelter; emotional support; advocacy with social and legal services; referrals to medical, mental health, social and employment services; and weekly peer support groups. When desired, appropriate referrals are offered (often to mental health or alcoholism treatment) for the abuser.
The lifeline of our organization is a 24-hour hotline and the volunteers who are on call when our office is closed. The hotline averages approximately 35 volunteer advocates at any given time. In addition to our on-call advocates, we generally have a like number of "safe homes" which provide temporary shelter for the victim of adult domestic violence and his or her children.
While use of safe shelter is limited to victims of physical abuse, other services are extended to any abused adult. We define an abused adult as any person who has suffered one or more of the following types of abuse: sexual, verbal, physical, or emotional. Training of volunteers includes an initial one-on-one interview with either the project director or project advocate. This is supplemented by monthly training sessions and a yearly day-long training seminar. In addition, office staff is always available to answer questions and deal with problems as they arise. While previous experience is desirable in volunteers, it is in no way a prerequisite. "On the job" experience is the best teacher. It is in answering crisis calls, meeting the client (usually at the police department or hospital) and transporting her to safe shelter that our advocates best learn the realities of spouse abuse and put their verbal instructions to the test.
Funding sources are United Way; North Dakota Department of Health; grants; and private donations.

RECIPIENTS: FAMILIES - EMPLOYMENT

NATIONAL/STATE ORGANIZATIONS

HEAD START - FAMILY DAY CARE
SEE DAY CARE/HEAD START: FAMILY DAY CARE

INDIVIDUAL PROGRAM PROFILES

PUBLIC ASSISTANCE CLIENTS VOLUNTEER
Broome County Department of Social Services
36-38 Main Street
Binghamton, NY 13905
TEL: 607-772-2681

Purpose: To provide an opportunity for ego building, an interim step to seeking employment, a chance to give service.

Sponsor: Broome County Department of Social Services

Contact: Alice Manter, Director of Volunteers

Description: All clients interested in volunteering are interviewed. Some take the initiative themselves; others are referred by case workers, examiners, or community workers. Many clients have developed skills and self-confidence and some have become gainfully employed as a result of volunteering. Money for bus transportation, coffee and soda as well as lunch - if the volunteer works through the lunch hour - is provided.

All Food Stamps Authorization to Purchase Cards are put into envelopes monthly by volunteers who may receive Food Stamps, Medicaid or Supplemental Security Income. Thousands of notices, letters, and informational pieces are folded and stuffed. A rehabilitation group of former psychiatric patients work on large mailings at their meeting place and senior citizens also work on large jobs at their housing complexes.

When it is determined that specific skills or interests of the volunteer would be best served elsewhere in the community, an appointment is set up with the appropriate nursing home, general hospital, Blind Workshop, Voluntary Action Center, Meals on Wheels, the YWCA, etc.

Broome County Social Services uses over 500 volunteers a year to assist any worker who requests supplemental help. The program is in its eleventh year under a Director of Volunteers and is an integral part of the Department's overall service structure.

Big Brothers and Sisters share several hours weekly with children who need a friend. A Saturday Afternoon Recreation Program is operated jointly with University students and provides sports and enrichment to 80 children. Other services include Friendly Visiting, tutoring, language interpreting, Polaroid identification cards, parties and picnics, Case Aides, Interns, receptionists, Camperships, clerk and sorting of mail into zip code areas.

RECIPIENTS: FAMILIES - ETHNIC GROUPS

NATIONAL/STATE ORGANIZATIONS

MINORITIES CAUCUS OF FAMILY SERVICE AMERICA
34-1/2 Beacon Street
Boston, MA 02108
TEL: 617-523-6400

Objectives: To make Family Service America (FSA) more relevant to the needs of minority families.

Services: Works with any minority group that is involved with a family service agency or organization; conducts negotiations with, and participates in policy-making groups; supports task forces on institutional racism and related areas; publishes newsletter; convenes periodic meetings.

NATIONAL ASSOCIATION FOR THE SOUTHERN POOR
SEE CIVIC AFFAIRS: TENANTS/RESIDENTS

RECIPIENTS: FAMILIES - GIVEAWAY PROGRAMS

INDIVIDUAL PROGRAM PROFILES

ABUSED ADULT RESOURCE CENTER (AARC)
SEE RECIPIENTS: FAMILIES - DOMESTIC ABUSE

CHRISTMAS BASKET PROGRAM
The Voluntary Action Center of Muscatine
501 Sunset Drive
Muscatine, IA 52761
TEL: 319-263-0959

Purpose: To give "Christmas" to those who otherwise might not have it.

Sponsor: Individuals, families, churches, organizations and clubs

Contact: Katrina Wisniewski, Director

Description: The project began in 1974 with seven families; 1982 served 113 families. Families are recommended by qualified individuals or agencies. They are provided with food for Christmas Day, clothing and toys for children under age 18. All funds are matched with in-kind services.

Volunteers in the Christmas Basket Program are individuals, families, organizations and service groups adopting needy families for the Holidays. After they are "paired" the adopter does the shopping and delivering to the adoptee. In some cases, Churches and organizations give a lump sum of money which volunteer shoppers take to purchase the needed items, which other volunteers deliver. Volunteer shoppers handled almost $3,000.00 last year, and delivered "Christmas" to 32 families.

Information is available on how to set up a Christmas Basket Program and/or avoid the pit-falls often encountered in organizing such an effort.

Founded: 1974

CHRISTMAS CLEARING HOUSE
The Voluntary Action Center
2125 East South Boulevard
PO Box 11044
Montgomery, AL 36116-0044
TEL: 205-285-0006

Purpose: To provide gifts, food and clothing to indigent families at Christmas time.

Contact: Doci Haslam

Description: The Christmas Clearing House was established in Montgomery, Alabama in 1980. The Clearing House is a central file of families in need who are not able to provide the traditional gifts, food and clothing for their loved ones at Christmas time. These names are placed in the files by the large service providers such as Salvation Army, Pensions and Security and Catholic Social Services.

To be included in the Clearing House, each family must file an application and must be willing to document income, expenses, etc. When the families are registered, the VAC starts a blitz of publicity and asks the clubs, churches, businesses, organizations and individuals to help these families.

In 1980 more than 12,000 people were served and more than 5,000 volunteers participated. In 1981 again more than 12,000 were served and more than 6,000 volunteers gave 53,360 hours. In 1982, 18,000 people were served and approximately 7,000 volunteers were involved.

The Clearing House was established with two goals in mind:
- That more needy people could be served at Christmas.
- That duplication of giving be eliminated.

These goals have been accomplished each year.

Funding for operating the Clearing House has been furnished by the Presidents Council of Montgomery and the Junior League of Montgomery. In 1983 it was funded by the Kiwanis Club of Montgomery. A part-time employee will be added this year. The Clearing House funds are totally separate from the VAC operating budget.

A very important part of the Clearing House is the Christmas Clearing House Fund. A local radio station sponsors this and arrangements are made with a local bank for direct deposits to be made to the fund. It is most successful. In 1981, $8,249 was raised; in 1982, $10,480 was raised.

The Clearing House serves as an example of bringing a community together for a common cause. It spreads the spirit of cooperation.
Founded: 1980

CHRISTMAS WISHES
Saginaw County Department of Social Services
411 East Genesee
PO Box 5070
Saginaw, MI 48605
TEL: 517-771-1614
Purpose: To fill as many "Christmas Wishes" submitted by clients as possible.
Contact: Evelyn L. Palmer
Description: This program is a coordinated effort with *Saginaw Voluntary Action Center, Saginaw News,* and *The Altrusa Club.* It solicits "Christmas wishes" from Saginaw County Department of Social Services (DSS) families. The first year over 16,000 letters were mailed to the families. Of these, 6,000 were returned and approximately 3,000 wishes were filled. Because of the enormous response, problems arose on a daily basis. This year, three volunteers will coordinate the program under the supervision of the Volunteer Services Supervisor and the Voluntary Action Center Director. These volunteers will be the Wishbook Volunteer Coordinator and Project Chairperson, the WishBook Public Relations Coordinator and the WishBook Public Publisher and Systems Developer. Volunteers have a variety of tasks, including:
- Develop and supervise overall program.
- Contact and work with media.
- Develop workable system.
- Categorize and code wishes.
- Answer telephone to coordinate donor with wish.
- Send thank you notes.

Referrals in this program come from the clients themselves by filling out and returning the form mailed to them. Sample groups of wishes are coded and published in the local daily newspaper. The donor calls the *Christmas Hotline* to fill the wish; if published wish is filled, donor is referred to a similar wish according to code. The three volunteers spearheading the project this year meet periodically with the DSS Volunteer Services Supervisor and the Voluntary Action Center Director to give progress reports and feedback. Problems are dealt with as they arise.

Recruitment of donors is by newspaper, word of mouth, college social work classes, and service groups. Orientation and training is through the Volunteer Service Supervisor and the Voluntary Action Center Director, who train the three volunteers who then, in turn, train the project volunteers.

The entire community becomes caught up in the project. Positive feedback is always received for weeks after the holiday. Because of this, the program is being repeated each year.
Publications: Christmas Wish Information Packet

FURNITURE COMMITTEE OF ACCA
Annandale Christian Community for Action (ACCA)
7200 Columbia Pike
Annandale, VA 22003
TEL: 703-256-1378
Purpose: To meet the basic need of families for adequate furniture.
Sponsor: ACCA
Contact: Betty Jane and George Davis, Co-Chairmen

Description: The number of families needing furniture in ACCA's service area is growing rapidly. Many are coming out of shelters. Through responses to requests of ACCA churches and others in the community for good used furniture, apartments and houses are being completely furnished by the program.

In addition, the number of people from other countries has been growing yearly since 1975. They are in need, also, of complete households of furnishings. The Hispanics are the largest group, with people coming from Brazil, Bolivia, Colombia, El Salvador, Nicaragua, Chile, Honduras, Mexico, Venezuela, Peru and other countries.

In 1988 ACCA volunteers worked on 41 Saturdays. Eighteen of the ACCA churches participated. Each church is asked to provide a truck, trailor or van, and five volunteers. Fairfax County provides a truck and driver each week. The Falls Church Community Council shares the work with ACCA.

Among the volunteers are five Saturday Supervisors and three women taking donation calls.

During 1988 the Furniture Committee made 463 pickups and gave furniture to 245 households.
Publications: ACCA Annual Report
Founded: 1988

RSVP THRIFT SHOP*
605 East Main Street
East Prairie, MO 63845
TEL: 314-649-5243
Purpose: To provide monies for the volunteer program while providing low-cost items to needy people in the community.
Sponsor: US/ACTION; Chamber of Commerce
Contact: Betty Johnson
Description: Initiated in 1975 with a rent-free building and donated racks, tables and other necessities, the RSVP thrift shop has met a community as well as a program need. It is a favorite project of the volunteers because they know it is really needed in the community, and also have the satisfaction of raising funds for their own volunteer program.

Twelve volunteers man the shop five days a week. Donated items for resale are solicited through newspaper, radio and other media advertising. Duties of the volunteer salespersons include mending and repairing the usable household items and clothing received. Items are sold at a very low cost from the downtown location, which is convenient to low-income neighborhoods.

All income from the thrift shop is used for volunteer insurance, special recognition and awards events, volunteer transportation, and other program costs. The Chamber of Commerce pays for utilities and volunteer meals.

Descriptive printed materials have been prepared describing the development and operation of the program, and are available to individuals and groups interested in starting a thrift shop to raise funds for their volunteer programs.
Founded: 1975

RECIPIENTS: FAMILIES - HEALTH

NATIONAL/STATE ORGANIZATIONS

NATIONAL HOMECARING COUNCIL
Foundation for Hospice and Homecare
519 C Street, NE
Washington, DC 20002
TEL: 202-547-6586
Objectives: To promote, develop and ensure provision of responsible homemaker-home health aide and related services of high quality for all families and individuals in need of such services.

Services: Promotes quality assurance for home care; administers a voluntary accreditation program (developed in 1965), which is based on the basic national standards and, in a number of states, is a requirement for state funds; provides curriculum materials to the federal government for the instruction of the homemaker-home health aide, and as a basis for a number of specialized training materials on subjects such as cancer, Alzheimer's Disease, and high-tech home care; works with the support of the *U.S. Administration on Aging* to develop a national certification program for homemaker-home health aides; produces additional training manuals, pamphlets and audiovisual materials to instruct and inform the field as well as the consumer.
Publications: Model Curriculum & Teaching Guide: Homemaker-Home Health Aide

RECIPIENTS: FAMILIES - HOMELESS

TRAINING PROGRAMS

TACTS VOLUNTEER SHELTER MANAGER TRAINING
SEE RECIPIENTS: HOMELESS - SHELTERS

RECIPIENTS: FAMILIES - HOUSING

TRAINING PROGRAMS

ADOPT-A-FAMILY
SEE HOUSING

RECIPIENTS: FAMILIES - I&R

NATIONAL/STATE ORGANIZATIONS

FAMILY RESOURCE AND REFERRAL CENTER*
National Council on Family Relations
3989 Central Avenue, NE
Suite 550
Minneapolis, MN 55421-3921
TEL: 612-633-6933
Objectives: To provide current information on family-related topics.
Services: Maintains a clearinghouse on family-related topics in nearly 100 categories, including Day Care, Community Groups and the Family, Military Families, Education and the Family, Religion and the Family, and Employment and the Family; holds approximately 35,000 records, many annotated, and all coded by subject and classified by type and reader audience, including human service organizations, the clergy, media, students, and others; makes information accessible through university and college libraries, state libraries, major medical centers or schools and large hospitals (contact FR&RC for custom searches); keeps fees at a minimum due to a grant from the Charles Stewart Mott Foundation.
Publications: Family Relations; Marriage and the Family
Founded: 1938

NATIONAL COUNCIL ON FAMILY RELATIONS
3989 Central Avenue, NE
Suite 550
Minneapolis, MN 55421-3921
TEL: 612-781-9331
FAX: 612-781-9348
Objectives: To enable professional practitioners, academicians, and interested laypersons to work together to improve the quality of life for the family.
Services: Provides information on community services for families; works to stimulate sound government policies pertaining to family issues; encourages research about the family; maintains a reference service for training centers; coordinates and promotes educational efforts; publishes guides, handbooks and other materials on the family; maintains a major information source which is described below:
The Family Resources Data Base - a core collection of information covering the literature, programs and services of the family and allied fields; includes over 130 subject areas relevant to the family, including *Organizations and Services to Families,* which may be of particular interest to local volunteer groups, which includes subtopics of: day care, working mothers, employment, consumerism, career education, religion, community groups, and others (accessible on-line through BRS, Dialog and HRIN).
Publications: Family Relations; Marriage and the Family; NCFR Directory; NCFR Newsletter
Founded: 1938

NATIONAL DOMESTIC VIOLENCE HOTLINE
Michigan Coalition Against Domestic Violence
PO Box 7032
Huntington Woods, MI 48070
TOLL FREE: 800-333-SAFE/873-6363-TTY
Objectives: To assist women facing domestic violence.
Services: The National Domestic Violence Hotline is one of the programs funded and maintained by a coalition of brand name companies in a program called "Shelter Aid." It was established in 1987 and plans are to continue the process as long as the problem exists. Donations to $450,000 are made each year to benefit the Hotline and local shelters. Special Shelter Aid displays are distributed to stores carrying the products of participating brand name companies.
The National Domestic Violence Hotline is staffed 24 hours a day, seven days a week, and its phones ring an average of 5,000 times a month. Statistics show that domestic violence is the single largest cause of injury to women, occurs every 15 seconds, involves children 50% of the time, affects the lives of 3-4 million women every year, and cuts across race, class, religion and socio-economic status.
Hotline staff and volunteers respond to confidential requests for information, discuss options or provide shelter referrals for women facing domestic violence. It is operated by the Michigan Coalition Against Domestic Violence.

INDIVIDUAL PROGRAM PROFILES

CAPE MAY COUNTY VOLUNTEERS AND RESOURCES
PO Box 222
Rio Grande, NJ 08242
TEL: 609-729-9200/Ext. 245; 609-729-2255 (helpline)
Purpose: To enhance existing Social Services to low-income persons; to provide emergency help in the form of food, clothing, shelter; to develop a team of Volunteers matched to specific tasks of community services.
Sponsor: Cape May County Welfare Board
Contact: Marianne Sheik
Description: Volunteers and Resources of Cape May County was developed in July 1982 to reach the needy of the County who

neither qualify for existing assistance programs nor have the income and resources to adequately cover an emergency. The program is three-fold consisting of volunteers, resources, and information and referral phone answering service. The program is supported by volunteers, donations, and community interest and support.

Recruitment for volunteers is made through speaking engagements, news releases, and distribution of brochures. The Volunteer Bank contains 88 names of groups and individuals interested in service in various tasks such as transportation; one-to-one to teens, the blind, the elderly; helpers at community food distributions; office work; publicity; recruitment.

Cash donations are deposited in a checking account which is kept on reserve for emergency needs to supply food, clothing and/or shelter. A Food Bank is maintained for which non-perishable food items are accepted. Clothing Bank arrangements are made through a community Thrift Shop which benefits Retarded Citizens. Hand made articles for babies and the elderly are filtered through groups serving those special needs. Eye glasses are donated to the Lions Clubs. A special grant is used to develop and maintain an Infant Formula Bank at the County Child Health Conference.

The phone answering service supplements a 24-hour service provided by United Way of Cape May County during business hours to direct callers to the proper source for solving a particular problem or for getting appropriate help. (First Call For Help 609-729-2255.)

Periodic distribution is made of Surplus Commodities such as cheese and butter; surplus vegetable crops such as sweet potatoes, and vegetable seedlings raised and donated by Volunteers. Other activities include:
- shopping for shut-ins;
- medical transportation for pregnant teens;
- reassurance calling to shut-ins;
- child attending for parents attending interviews and training sessions;
- grounds, building and agency car pool maintenance;
- transportation aides;
- home-aides to shut-ins;
- reception;
- soliciting; and
- public relations.

Founded: 1982

F.A.C.T. HOTLINE (FAMILIES AND CHILDREN IN TROUBLE)
SEE RECIPIENTS: FAMILIES - CRISIS INTERVENTION

FAMILY CRISIS CENTER
PO Box 207
Keyser, WV 26726
TEL: 304-788-6061
Purpose: To provide services to victims of family violence; services include 24-hour hotline, short-term crisis intervention, advocacy, limited emergency shelter, support group, and information and referral.
Sponsor: West Virginia Government; private contributions
Contact: Vanessa Brooks, Executive Director
Description: The Family Crisis Center is a nonprofit agency whose purpose is to provide immediate support for victims of family violence and to develop community awareness and response to the problem of family violence.

The Family Crisis Center was organized through a VISTA grant secured by the Potomac Highlands Mental Health Guild in October, 1980. This grant was initiated in reply to the expressed need of the Mineral County Mental Health Association.

Funding for the program is provided in part by the West Virginia Department of Human Services, Governor's Committee on Crime, Delinquency, and Corrections and donations from groups, organizations and private individuals.

Volunteer Staff and Duties - At present, the Family Crisis Center has 25 volunteers who staff our 24-hour crisis hotline, help with fundraising events, and provide services to victims of family violence. Volunteers cover the phone from their homes changing shifts three times per day.

Currently volunteer training consists of two two-hour training sessions, but this is being developed into a more extensive training program. Monthly volunteer meetings are also held.
Publications: FCC Training Manual
Founded: 1980

RECIPIENTS: FAMILIES - LOW-INCOME

NATIONAL/STATE ORGANIZATIONS

CATHOLIC COMMITTEE OF APPALACHIA
115 Main Street
Box 953
Whitesburg, KY 41858
TEL: 606-633-8440
Objectives: To secure social services and justice for Appalachian poor.
Services: Works to improve and increase social services for the rural poor in Appalachia; fosters and initiates welfare rights, housing, flood prevention, land ownership, health care programs, improved schools, and poor people's coalitions, among others; sponsors "teach-ins" on priority issues concerning land, energy, employment, and housing; advocates collective bargaining for workers; networks with *Common Cause, Council of the Southern Mountains, National Catholic Rural Life Conference, Network,* and *Rural American Women;* publishes a newsletter, a bulletin, books and other materials.
Sponsor: Common Cause
Publications: Patchquilt; CCA Bulletin; Dream of the Mountains' Struggle
Founded: 1972

RECIPIENTS: FAMILIES - MILITARY

NATIONAL/STATE ORGANIZATIONS

NATIONAL MILITARY FAMILY ASSOCIATION
6000 Stevenson Avenue
Suite 304
Alexandria, VA 22304-3526
TEL: 703-823-6632
Objectives: To serve as advocates for military families by influencing the development and implementation of policies that affect their lives.
Services: Operates as a membership organization; involves volunteer staff in identifying, addressing, and resolving issues of concern to military families, including child care, housing, health and dental care, retiree benefits, spousal employment, survivor benefits, voting rights, dependent schools, etc.; works with *Army, Marine Corps, Navy, Air Force, Coast Guard, Public Health Service, National Oceanic and Atmospheric Administration,* including those on active duty, the *National Guard, Reserves,* and retired family members; finances programs through tax-deductible dues and donations as an independent nonprofit organization;

maintains programs in research, education, legislation and public information; has a board of advisors of more than 60 members from military, public and private sectors (headed by Anna Chennault, Founder); publishes a newsletter for members.
Publications: Military Family

US/DOD - NAVY FAMILY SERVICE CENTER
Building 42
Great Lakes, IL 60088
TEL: 312-688-3603
Objectives: To enhance and enrich the quality of life of Naval servicemen and servicewomen and their families.
Services: As a result of the *1978 Navy Family Awareness Conference* at Norfolk, Virginia, the Chief of Naval Operations established a network of support centers to enhance and enrich the quality of life of Naval servicemen and servicewomen and their families. Named *Family Service Centers (FSCs),* they assist both single and married personnel with problem-solving and working through the red tape that is normally associated with any large organization. The FSC also helps them obtain assistance and lists the resources that are available to them in both the military and civilian community. The FSC began operating and providing services at Great Lakes in March 1982.
The FSC serves active duty, reserve and retired personnel of the Navy and Marine Corps, and their families. Other military personnel and civilian employees may also be assisted on a case-by-case basis.
The FSC operates a number of specific programs in addition to individual assistance, including

- **Parent-to-Parent Program** - offers support to families with young children through weekly visits by a volunteer, who is trained to answer parents' questions about child development and to provide other information as needed.
- **Welcome Baby Program** - provides information and support to families of newborns. Volunteers contact new parents and arrangements are made for a visit. Information is shared on child care, infant development, community resources and other topics that relate to the early weeks of a baby's life.
- **Spouse Employment Assistance Program (SEAP)** - enables military spouses to find employment more easily after relocation. Volunteers contact businesses to locate job opportunities, personally interview job seekers and match them with available jobs. Volunteers also give counseling on educational and job-related topics.
- **Spouses of Students (SOS)** - serves as a support group for spouses of military personnel in Corps School, Service School Command or ROTC. Volunteers help plan and organize weekly meetings and serve as a source of information and guidance.
- **Women's Program Planners** - plan and/or coordinate a wide variety of programs for women which promote personal growth, happier families and career information. *The Women's Day Out,* day-long conferences, University of Illinois Cooperative Extension Home Economics Programs, and Spouse Employment Assistant Program workshops are examples of these programs.
- **Gingerbread House** - is a volunteer-operated consignment shop which provides members of the military community the opportunity to increase their income by selling handcrafted items. A small fee is charged, with the money going to various base charities.
- **Volunteer Income Tax Assistance (VITA)** - is a cooperative program with the IRS. After a training program taught by the IRS covering both basic and advanced income tax forms, free tax preparation is offered to all military personnel.

In addition to the many and varied volunteer opportunities in the above program, FSC has administrative needs for volunteers to serve as receptionists, intake clerks, class registration recorders, I&R workers, and general clerical aides.

Sponsor: US/DoD - Department of the Navy
Contact: Phyllis Utley, Volunteer Coordinator
Publications: Volunteers Make a Difference

INDIVIDUAL PROGRAM PROFILES

FORT DIX VOLUNTEERS
SEE RECIPIENTS: MILITARY - ACTIVE/VETERANS

PARENT-TO-PARENT PROGRAM
US/DoD - Navy Family Service Center
Naval Training Center
Building 42
Great Lakes, IL 60088-5123
TEL: 312-688-3603
Purpose: To offer support to families in the armed forces with very young children through weekly home visits.
Sponsor: US/DoD - Navy Family Service Center
Contact: Thia Lester
Description: The Parent-to-Parent Program takes place in the home at the convenience of family and home visitor. The purpose is to give the parents support as they share ideas with the home visitor about enjoyable ways of playing with and caring for young children.
Who is a home visitor?
The home visitor is a volunteer from the community who enjoys working with adults and young children. Training is administered by the Parent-to-Parent Program staff at the Family Service Center. Through weekly visits to the home, the volunteer becomes an important link in a network of community services.
What happens in a home visit?
- The volunteer arrives at the home prepared to share ideas, toys and activities with the parent and child. If it is not the first visit, plans are based on activities and feedback of the previous visit.
- Upon arrival, the visitor talks with the parent about parent-child interaction during the previous week - What has the parent observed the child doing? What has the parent done with the child?
- Using the toys brought by the volunteer, parent and volunteer try activities with the child.
- The volunteer answers the parent's questions about child development and provides information when it is needed, including information about agencies in the community.
- Parent and volunteer plan what activities they will do during the next home visit and discuss what the child will probably be doing during the week.
What training do home visitors receive?
- *Child Development* - Learning about how children grow and what they are like at different stages of development.
- *The Role of the Home Visitor* - Understanding what it means to be a home visitor, including learning how to establish relationships with families, supporting parents in discoveries about their children, sharing child development information, learning how to put parents in contact with a variety of community resources.
- *How Adults Can Support Early Learning* - Learning about the ways in which adults can provide support and create activities which help children learn.
What can a home visitor expect to gain from participating?
- A new awareness of the community, its resources and how to use them.
- Experience with sharing knowledge and skills as well as developing new skills.
- Work experience that can provide a base for future employment.
- An opportunity to meet new people.
What can the family gain from being in the program?

- An understanding of how important the parent is to the child's growth and development.
- Observation of the many exciting ways that learning takes place as the infant's progress is shared with the volunteer.
- Discovery of new ways to provide activities and materials to enhance learning.
- Knowledge of the community and the agencies which can provide services for the family.
- The opportunity to meet new people through "Parent Meetings."

Through this program, the Family Service Center encourages and supports a stable environment for the child, and increased parent/child interaction.

Publications: A chance to contribute to your community...; For you, for your children

WELCOME BABY
US/DoD - Charleston Naval Base
Navy Family Service Center
Charleston, SC 29401
TEL: 803-743-2121/6250
Purpose: To provide support to new parents at Charleston Naval Regional Medical Center, to share educational materials, and to work with hospital personnel in helping new mothers and fathers as they learn to be parents.
Sponsor: US/DoD - Department of the Navy
Contact: Tommie Provost, Coordinator
Description: Welcome Baby is a volunteer program sponsored by the Charleston Navy Family Service Center. While it was modeled after civilian programs, Welcome Baby has particular relevance for the Navy Community where it is not unusual for very young women to give birth without the support of family. The husbands are often deployed and young mothers find themselves in an unfamiliar community with a new baby and new responsibilities. Beginning with hospital visitations, trained volunteers offer support and encouragement to new mothers. In addition the volunteer is an educational resource providing information on child care and community resources. The contact is maintained by the volunteer following discharge from the hospital.
Supportive contacts continue as long as the need exists. Mail-outs are sent monthly for one year, which include information on child growth and development. Through this early contact with mother and child, the trained volunteers are able to detect indicators of abuse and neglect or symptoms of potential problems. If the volunteer identifies a need, referral is made to appropriate services. Training of volunteers over a three-day period covers topics such as communication skills, child abuse and neglect, community and military resources, and Welcome Baby procedure. New volunteers are teamed with experienced volunteers during their initial visits with new mothers. Following the initial visits, volunteers always have access to a support system of team leaders (experienced volunteers) and program co-ordinator.
In addition to hospital volunteers, other volunteers offer secretarial skills and provide support to mothers prenatally. Some volunteers, who have specific experience in special areas, i.e. premature infants, death of infant, offer support to parents in those areas. This program has been very successful at the Charleston Naval Base and it is recommended as an effective method of supporting new mothers in their new roles.
Publications: Welcome Baby Packet

RECIPIENTS: FAMILIES - NUTRITION

INDIVIDUAL PROGRAM PROFILES

MANNA BOWL
SEE NUTRITION: ON-SITE

OUR COMMUNITY KITCHEN
SEE NUTRITION: ON-SITE

RECIPIENTS: FAMILIES - PSYCHOSOCIAL SUPPORT

NATIONAL/STATE ORGANIZATIONS

FAMILY SERVICE AMERICA
11700 West Lake Park Drive
Milwaukee, WI 53224
TEL: 414-359-1040
Objectives: To improve the quality of family life; to improve services to families.
Services: Provides family counseling in all areas of family living (parent-child, mental health, credit, etc.); develops new methods and raises standards to help agencies provide more effective family service; activates committees on advocacy, minorities resources, plays for living, public policy and the family, etc.; publishes a newsletter, *Newswire,* a journal, a book, *Families in Society,* and other materials.
Publications: Newswire; Families in Society
Founded: 1911

INSTITUTE OF MARRIAGE AND FAMILY RELATIONS
6116 Rolling Road
Suite 316
Springfield, VA 22152
TEL: 703-569-2400
Objectives: To assist families in understanding, coping with, and working through problems in everyday living.
Services: Operates family service centers to diagnose and treat family problems through counseling of family members, and education and training in family relationships; develops community programs; convenes and publishes reports on workshops/conferences.

NATIONAL ASSOCIATION FOR PARENTS OF THE VISUALLY IMPAIRED
SEE PSYCHOSOCIAL SUPPORT SERVICES

INDIVIDUAL PROGRAM PROFILES

ADOPT-A-FAMILY
Delaware Division of State Service Centers
Hudson State Service Center
Newark, DE 19711
TEL: 302-368-6701
Purpose: To provide substantive help to the neediest families and elderly persons at Christmas; to facilitate personal involvement of donors; to educate the community concerning unmet needs.
Sponsor: Delaware Department of Health and Social Services
Contact: Marjorie Meyermann, Director of Volunteer Services

Description: For eight years the Adopt-a-Family project has been most successful in Delaware. Social workers select families and elderly persons to be anonymously "adopted" or sponsored for Christmas. A brief family profile is given with details of particular needs of family members. Code numbers are assigned to maintain anonymity of recipients and sponsors. By early fall a publicity program is launched (flyer designed by a volunteer), letters are sent to former sponsors, the public media are called into play, and speaking engagements are arranged. During November and December volunteers occupy rent-free Collection Centers, usually empty stores or schools. Phones are installed and volunteers staff the Centers, supervised by a Volunteer Director.

Volunteers recruit sponsors, describe clients' needs, match clients and sponsors, coordinate giving and delivery, receive gifts at the Collection Centers. Coded orders are checked for appropriateness and delivered to clients. Volume and value of gifts range from a $25 purchased gift for an institutionalized elderly person to food, clothing and furniture valued at many hundreds of dollars for a large family.

A unique feature of the project is the individualization of the giving. Sponsors are told of particular needs but are encouraged to personalize their giving to convey their caring. All recipients are experiencing special problems and their psychological needs may be as great as their physical needs.

The appeal of the program is so great that it has become the primary source of recruitment for volunteers for the year-round volunteer program. Participation both as a volunteer and a donor often is described as addictive. Adopt-a-Family has become a giving tradition for many families and groups.

Costs for the state agency: salary of Volunteer Director, six telephones, printing and postage for publicity. In one year, 549 families and 139 single persons were served, and 895 thank you/tax letters were written for goods valued conservatively at $150,000 to $200,000.

AID TO INCARCERATED MOTHERS
SEE LAW ENFORCEMENT/CRIME PREVENTION: PARENTS

CHILD AND FAMILY SERVICES OF KNOX COUNTY
114 Dameron Avenue
Knoxville, TN 37917
TEL: 615-524-7483
Purpose: To preserve and strengthen family life to prevent individual and family breakdown and waste.
Sponsor: United Way
Contact: Teresa Jackson
Description: For over 50 years, Child and Family Services of Knox County, Inc. has been providing a variety of social services to residents of Knox, Blount, Roane, Jefferson, and Cocke Counties. Child and Family Services is a United Way agency and a member of the Child Welfare League of America and the Family Services Association of America and is accredited by the Council on Accreditation of Services for Families and Children. Funding is from a wide variety of sources: United Way, Tennessee Department of Human Services, city and county and federal governments, numerous foundations and private donations and client fees.

Services offered include family and individual counseling, family life enrichment, other training and consultation, intake and referral, advocacy, private and "special needs" adoptions, problem pregnancy counseling, foster care and research. Residential services include three group homes for troubled teenagers, a Runaway Shelter and Family Crisis Center.

Volunteers are an essential and welcome part of the agency, providing personal, individualized, one-to-one work with clients and sharing with the agency special skills such as secretarial, electrical, commercial design, renovation and repair, publicity, etc. Volunteers establish friendly, supportive relationships with counseling clients, answer the Sex Abuse Helpline, tutor, provide in-house activities as well as outings for the residential clients, assist with record keeping and transportation, provide play therapy for children, lead discussion groups, prepare for meetings, help with fund-raising, teach skills, etc.

Volunteers are generally recruited, interviewed, given an orientation, screened and placed in one of the various programs by the agency Director of Volunteers. Volunteer supervision and on-the-job training are provided by the counselors, house parents or house supervisors at each of the facilities that use volunteers. Child and Family Services has over 10,000 volunteer service hours donated by some 250 volunteers each year, including the Board of Directors and Advisory Committees.
Founded: 1930

ECO
SEE LAW ENFORCEMENT/CRIME PREVENTION: OFFENDERS

PERSON TO PERSON*
Saginaw County Department of Social Services
411 East Genesee
PO Box 5070
Saginaw, MI 48605
TEL: 517-771-1614
Purpose: To help recipients of Public Assistance reach a pre-determined goal with the help of community volunteers.
Sponsor: Saginaw County Department of Social Services
Contact: Librarian/Historian
Description: The Person to Person program originated in 1971 at a time when a strike situation in Saginaw resulted in high unemployment. Through the Department of Social Services, self supporting male volunteers were matched with unemployed fathers receiving public assistance. The volunteer acted as the client's friend, helping the client find job opportunities, evaluating the client's skills, and assisting the client in applying for jobs. In the course of eight different matches, six clients obtained jobs.

Gradually the program has expanded. Matching on a one-to-one basis has proved beneficial to clients with diverse problems. Along with other problems, many clients have no friends. The supportive friendship of a volunteer is an important contribution to clients entering the mainstream of the community.

One volunteer calls weekly on a disabled woman who needs help in lifting bolts of material so she can cut and sew felt bean bags. She has become nearly self supporting. AFDC mothers have been helped through the rigors of enrolling in college. Elderly people and emotionally disturbed people have also profited from volunteer friendships. Parents who are high risk prospects for neglectful behavior are provided with volunteer friends who encourage appropriate child rearing. Volunteers act as payees for clients unable to handle their own money.

Most volunteers are recruited by word of mouth. Volunteers are recruited through churches, community groups and through the media. About twenty percent of the person to person volunteers are clients themselves and were recruited by referral from casework staff and posters in the office reception areas. Recruiting services purchased from the Voluntary Action Center of Saginaw County provide many capable volunteers for this program.

ROSES FOR FALLEN FATHERS
SEE RECIPIENTS: MILITARY - ACTIVE/VETERANS

RSVP OF NEW CASTLE COUNTY
SEE PSYCHOSOCIAL SUPPORT SERVICES

VOLUNTEER COUNSELING SERVICE OF ROCKLAND COUNTY
SEE PSYCHOSOCIAL SUPPORT SERVICES: FAMILIES

WEDNESDAY MORNING MOTHERS
Miami County Cooperative Extension Service
Court House
Troy, OH 45373
TEL: 513-335-8341/Ext. 2241
Purpose: To help low-income homemakers improve their way of life, improve homemaking skills, and increase their self-confidence and self-respect.
Sponsor: Miami County Extension Service and Health Department
Contact: Patricia J. Long
Description: Wednesday Morning Mothers (WMM) reaches homemakers living within a limited income. The programs presented include homemaking skills, health topics, field trips, self-improvement and such. They are held in the Extension meeting room in the Court House twice monthly.
WMM operates on donations (mainly from church groups). The only person receiving any pay is the person in charge of the nursery. All others volunteer on a transportation committee, a child care committee, a hospitality committee, and a Board of Directors. The Board of Directors includes six of the homemakers, who plan and evaluate the programs.
There are nine full-time volunteers plus those volunteering to help with programs and other parts of meetings. Attendance at meetings is consistently around 30 homemakers.
The local high school also cooperates and helps with child care volunteers. The local J.V.S. provides grooming programs. Other programs include: cooking, sewing, beauty care, health talks, mental health, first aid, adult education, field trips and one picnic each year.
The mothers' class has helped to give new dimensions to the lives of many, as well as improved skills. Increased self confidence and self respect are natural by-products of this experience. There is no cost to the mothers. The class is supported by donations.

RECIPIENTS: FAMILIES - RESPITE

NATIONAL/STATE ORGANIZATIONS

NATIONAL SUPPORT CENTER FOR FAMILIES OF THE AGING
SEE PSYCHOSOCIAL SUPPORT SERVICES: FAMILIES

INDIVIDUAL PROGRAM PROFILES

FAMILY FRIENDS PROJECT
SEE RECIPIENTS: HANDICAPPED - CHILDREN/YOUTH

RECIPIENTS: HANDICAPPED

NATIONAL/STATE ORGANIZATIONS

CHALLENGE INTERNATIONAL (formerly National Challenge Committee on Disability)
6719 Lowell Avenue
McLean, VA 22101
TEL: 703-790-1616
Objectives: To make disability a familiar and comfortable issue by closing the communication gap between the public and disabled community.

Services: Mounts a media awareness campaign to change the way in which Americans perceive disabled individuals; promotes positive images of disabled persons in the media through newspaper articles, radio and television news reports, television shows, motion pictures, and advertisements; educates the public about disability issues; serves as a clearinghouse on the needs of the disabled; works with and assists organizations which represent the disabled; maintains a *National Media Council on Disability;* provides internships for disabled persons in media-related fields; offers speakers to community groups; designs school programs and educational materials; publishes printed and video promotional materials; oversees a national network of education, information, and entertainment services for the disabled; awards outstanding accomplishments by and for the disabled; produces public service announcements on disability issues.
Contact: Mary Nemec Doremus, Founder
Founded: 1983

COMMISSION ON SELF-SUFFICIENCY
Virginia Department for Rights of the Disabled
James Monroe Building, 27th Floor
101 North 14th Street
Richmond, VA 23219
TEL: 804-225-2042
TOLL FREE: 800-552-3962 (Voice/TDD)
Objectives: To coordinate the delivery of services to facilitate the self-sufficiency and support for people with physical and sensory disabilities.
Services: Provides a long-awaited opportunity in the State of Virginia (passage of HJR 45 in *1990 General Assembly)* to develop a coordinated service system that is responsive to the full range of needs being experienced by people with physical and sensory disabilities; includes in its membership legislators, representatives of business and health industries, an educator and a practicing physician, with leadership by the Lieutenant Governor; considers recommendations from previous legislative studies addressing:
  ● accountability and support for coordinated services;
  ● strategies for the use of public, private and insurance funds;
  ● gaps in services;
  ● models for case management;
  ● the need for research and long-term rehabilitation;
  ● service delivery models, and
  ● ways to promote coordination and cost sharing.
Requires an interim report for the 1991 Session of the General Assembly, with the final report due by October 31, 1991 to provide data for the preparation of the Governor's 1992-94 budget recommendations; looks to public, private, voluntary and business sectors to maintain support while these steps are taken to finalization of the *Commission.*

NATIONAL ASSOCIATION FOR THE PHYSICALLY HANDICAPPED*
440 Lafayette Avenue
Suite 17
Cincinnati, OH 45220-1000
TEL: 614-852-1664
Objectives: To advance the social, economic, and physical welfare of the physically handicapped in the U.S.
Services: Serves as a self-help action group; operates through a committee structure with activities ranging from social to legislative to encouragement of employment of the handicapped and including housing, transportation and barrier-free design; supports chapters which provide services (especially recreation) not provided or minimally provided at the national level (bowling, wheelchair games, etc.); collects and studies data and information of special concern to the physically handicapped and publishes findings; proposes and supports legislation to provide more educational and rehabilitation opportunities, employment, tax relief and other benefits; provides programs which are not readily

available otherwise, such as physical fitness and sports; promotes National Employ the Handicapped Week and, during that week, highlights the achievements of the successfully employed physically handicapped person (working to make it a year-round project); works to eliminate all architectural barriers to the handicapped. Cooperates with government agencies, civic groups, and organizations of the physically handicapped to develop programs; publishes *Bill of Rights for the Physically Handicapped* to encourage the handicapped to make full use of their rights, a newsletter, and other materials; convenes area meetings and area and national conventions to enable an information exchange to take place for the benefit of all concerned.
Publications: National Newsletter
Founded: 1958

NATIONAL EASTER SEAL SOCIETY
70 East Lake Street
Chicago, IL 60601
TEL: 312-726-6200; 312-726-4258 (TDD)
Objectives: To provide direct rehabilitation services to persons with disabilities.
Services: Draws on its experience as one of the largest and oldest voluntary health agencies in the nation to assist local affiliates with programs that include recreation, housing, transportation, equipment loans, public education, medical or vocational rehabilitation facilities, advocacy and other services; conducts national public awareness and fund raising campaigns; and through its Research Foundation awards grants for relevant research; publishes a catalog which includes publications about attitudes, dental care, independent living and employment, recreation and camping, sexual adjustment, psychological aspects, and on specific conditions such as learning disabilities, strokes, and speech and hearing impairment.
Publications: Easter Seal Society Catalog
Founded: 1919

NATIONAL ORGANIZATION ON DISABILITY (NOD)
910 Sixteenth Street, NW
Suite 600
Washington, DC 20006
TEL: 202-293-5960
Objectives: To expand opportunity for America's 35 million persons with physical or mental disabilities, thereby enhancing their contribution to society.
Services: Works with the private sector and government to strengthen public understanding of the unmet needs and potential contribution of disabled persons; fosters the partnership of people from all walks of life in furthering the long-term goals of and for citizens with disabilities, described below:
- Expanded educational opportunity;
- Improved access to housing, buildings, transportation;
- Greater opportunity for employment;
- Greater participation in recreational, social, cultural activities;
- Expanded and strengthened rehabilitation programs and facilities;
- Purposeful application of biomedical research aimed at conquering major disabling conditions;
- Reduction in the incidence of disability through accident and disease prevention;
- Increased application of technology to ameliorate the effects of disability; and
- Expanded international exchange of information and experience to benefit all disabled persons.

Operates two programs in response to the proclamation of the UN General Assembly declaring 1983-1992 as the Decade of Disabled Persons:
- **The Community Partnership Program** promotes awareness and disseminates information on disability programs/issues; advocates partnership and private sector self-help initiatives;

supports local committees of disabled and non-disabled volunteers working to improve attitudes toward disabled persons (in more than 1,000 communities); expands access; promotes greater opportunities in education, housing, employment, recreation and transportation; prevents disabling conditions.
- **The Corporate Partnership Program** encourages the business community to expand employment and other opportunities; provides technical assistance and advice to corporations on disability programs.

Supports above programs by providing technical assistance and materials to local groups; acts as a clearinghouse for information; carries out an ongoing public information and awareness program, obtains support from key leaders and groups; sponsors a national Advertising Council campaign; a special $25,000 National Awards Program; and "Friends of the National Organization," a nationwide group of people interested in activities on behalf of the handicapped; publishes a quarterly newsletter, which focuses on program ideas, and *Meeting the Challenge of Disability,* a program manual for local community partnership liaisons and chairpersons; works with 300 national partner organizations; spearheads the U.S. program for the Decade of Disabled Persons; convenes workshops on specific topics and national conferences.
Publications: Community Action Guide; Community Idea Book; NOD Report; Update
Founded: 1982

SCOUTING FOR THE HANDICAPPED
Girl Scouts of the USA
830 Third Avenue
New York, NY 10022
TEL: 212-940-7500
Objectives: To make the troop/camp experience for girls with disabilities as much as possible like that of the nondisabled girl.
Services: Provides training and other services to scout troops without designating "special" or different activities for girls with disabilities; encourages leaders to adapt activities to suit abilities and limitations when necessary; includes information about special needs in most program materials.

TASH: THE ASSOCIATION FOR THE SEVERELY HANDICAPPED
7010 Roosevelt Way, NE
Seattle, WA 98115
TEL: 312-940-9633
Objectives: To respond to the need for diverse services to the severely and profoundly handicapped; to stress the importance of integration in living, working and learning environments for all handicapped persons.
Services: Charters chapters at the local level to facilitate increased involvement in local concerns; works closely with parents, educators, social workers, lawyers, and others interested in this area of concern; publishes a quarterly journal, four volumes of *Teaching the Severely Handicapped,* which reports on current innovations and research, *Methods of Instruction with Severely Handicapped Students,* books, papers, reprints and bibliographies (one of special interest to parents on advocacy, recreation, and self-help skills development); conducts surveys of parent needs and works closely with a parent-to-parent network organized by the Association; makes referrals to direct service providers via letter, phone or personal visit.
Founded: 1973

TRAINING PROGRAMS

THE DEAF WAY
SEE ARTS/CULTURAL ENRICHMENT: FESTIVALS

HANDICAPPED VOLUNTEER/VOLUNTEERING FOR THE HANDICAPPED
SEE RECIPIENTS: HOMEBOUND

RECIPIENTS: HANDICAPPED - ACCESSIBILITY

NATIONAL/STATE ORGANIZATIONS

NATIONAL CENTER FOR A BARRIER FREE ENVIRONMENT
1140 Connecticut Avenue, NW
Washington, DC 20036
TEL: 202-466-6896
Objectives: To provide information and technical assistance to persons working to create an environment that is accessible to handicapped and elderly people.
Services: Serves persons with disabilities, design professionals, rehabilitation professionals, and the business community in providing a clearinghouse on accessibility issues; sponsors a network of design resource persons in each state to consult with local organizations; compiles information on projects, programs, standards, new products, and other pertinent areas; publishes manuals and books including Planning for Accessibility, Opening Doors, and Accessibility Assistance, a bimonthly newsletter, Report, and other materials; develops resource packets for specific problems.

RECIPIENTS: HANDICAPPED - ADVOCACY

NATIONAL/STATE ORGANIZATIONS

AMERICAN COUNCIL OF THE BLIND
SEE RECIPIENTS: HANDICAPPED - BLIND

EPILEPSY FOUNDATION OF AMERICA
SEE RECIPIENTS: HANDICAPPED - EPILEPSY

TRAINING PROGRAMS

VOLUNTEER TRAINING PROGRAM FOR VOLUNTEER ADVOCATES
Hawaii Protection and Advocacy Agency
1580 Makaloa Street
Honolulu, HI 96814
TEL: 808-949-2922
Credit: 3 hours (Leeward Community College)
Sponsor: Hawaii Protection and Advocacy Agency
Contact: Patty Henderson
Description: Hawaii's volunteer advocacy program was started in 1974 by the Hawaii chapter of the Association for Retarded Citizens (ARC). Today it is administered by the Hawaii Protection and Advocacy Agency. Training is an important part of the program, which has two components:

● **Citizen Advocates** - volunteers who enter into a one-to-one

relationship with the developmentally disabled on a long-term basis.
● **Advocacy for Our Community Volunteers** - citizens who are specialists and work on specific problems for the developmentally disabled.

Since assuming responsibility for the Volunteer Advocacy Program, the Protection and Advocacy Agency has offered 115 training sessions and trained 250 private citizens as volunteer advocates.

In addition, Leeward Community College offers a three-hour credit course on advocacy skills, which is attended by disabled as well as non-disabled volunteers. Kapolani Community College offers a course in self-advocacy as part of its community education program on Advocates for the Rights of the Disabled.

Training programs for advocates attempt to give the volunteers "a mind-set which provides the advocates a reason for staying as an advocate." Recently, ten new trainers were initiated statewide, and 4618 media announcements mentioned one or another component of the citizen advocacy program. These efforts are aimed at making the prospect of being a citizen advocate more attractive, more visible and carrying more prestige.

A trainer's manual for the volunteer advocate in a teaching role, and a self-advocacy handbook for the developmentally disabled themselves have been widely distributed nationally. An important part of the self-advocacy training is developing the ability to train others to be self-advocates.

Other sponsors include H-CAP, Hawaii Office on Aging, and US/ACTION.

INDIVIDUAL PROGRAM PROFILES

ADVOCACY BY AND FOR THE BLIND
SEE RECIPIENTS: HANDICAPPED - BLIND

CITIZEN ADVOCACY
100 North Washington Street
Falls Church, VA 22046
TEL: 703-532-7279
Purpose: Advocacy for persons with mental retardation.
Sponsor: Association for Retarded Citizens of Northern Virginia; United Way; private donations
Contact: Debbie Ekimoff, Association for Retarded Citizens of Northern Virginia
Description: Citizen Advocacy is a one-to-one sustaining relationship between a capable volunteer called a Citizen Advocate and a mentally retarded person called a Protege. The Citizen Advocacy program began as a model program in 1975 under the auspices of the Association for Retarded Citizens of Northern Virginia. The program has grown and expanded to the extent that today there are 45 volunteers in the Northern Virginia area (Alexandria, Arlington and Fairfax County). There are 27 advocates working with proteges living in the community either in group homes, supervised apartments, or at home with their parents. The other 18 advocates work with the residents at the Northern Virginia Training Center.

Citizen Advocates are volunteers (responsible, stable men and women 18 years or older) living in Northern Virginia who have an interest in developing a friendship with a mentally retarded person. Citizen advocates need no prior experience; training along with individual support is provided by professional staff. Citizen Advocates are needed mainly in the evening hours and weekends, a minimum of two hours per week for one year.

Citizen Advocates and their proteges enjoy sharing activities that are a part of community living, like having a birthday party or taking a walk in the park. Advocates often spend time teaching their proteges useful skills along with giving them practical advice and emotional support.

The Citizen Advocacy program is funded by United Way and private donations.
Founded: 1975

RECIPIENTS: HANDICAPPED - ARTS

TRAINING PROGRAMS

THE DEAF WAY
SEE ARTS/CULTURAL ENRICHMENT: FESTIVALS

INDIVIDUAL PROGRAM PROFILES

INTERNATIONAL VERY SPECIAL ARTS FESTIVAL
SEE ARTS/CULTURAL ENRICHMENT: FESTIVALS

YOUNG WINGS USA*
SEE EDUCATION: CURRICULUM ENRICHMENT

RECIPIENTS: HANDICAPPED - BLIND

NATIONAL/STATE ORGANIZATIONS

AMERICAN BLIND BOWLING ASSOCIATION
c/o Ron Beverly
67 Barne Avenue
Buffalo, NY 14215
TEL: 716-836-1472
Objectives: To promote bowling as a recreational activity for adult blind persons.
Services: Sponsors competitions in organized ten-pin bowling for legally blind men and women 18 years of age or older; supports an annual championship blind bowling tournament; publishes Blind Bowler three times a year; conducts annual meeting.

AMERICAN COUNCIL OF THE BLIND
1010 Vermont Avenue, NW
Suite 1100
Washington, DC 20005
TEL: 202-393-3666
Objectives: To advocate legislation for the blind and other handicapped persons; to promote independent and effective participation in society.
Services: Holds periodic workshops for the blind on advocacy and legal rights; provides information about agencies and schools for the blind, national health insurance proposals, how to establish a credit union for the blind, electronic aids, legislation and legal rights; gives advice about specific legal problems over the phone when possible; provides referrals when indicated to other possible sources; publishes a monthly magazine, which is available in large print, braille, disc, or cassette; awards scholarships to blind post secondary students; convenes conference annually.

AMERICAN FOUNDATION FOR THE BLIND
15 West Sixteenth Street
New York, NY 10011
TEL: 212-620-2000
Objectives: To help the blind and visually impaired acquire improved rehabilitation services and educational and employment opportunities, as well as assistance in daily living.

Services: Conducts national and local surveys on needs of the blind; mounts research leading to the design of a variety of devices which help the blind person to lead an independent life; manufactures (or adapts) and sells more than 400 different devices, including Braille watches and measuring instruments, shop tools, and games (Braille) for adults and children; records and manufactures about 400 talking books per year for the Library of Congress; maintains library of more than 30,000 books, periodicals, and other publications on blindness; serves both lay and professional people; makes referrals to service facilities, local agencies, and other sources; publishes quarterly newsletter, a professional journal, the *Journal of Visual Impairment and Blindness,* and other materials; convenes annual meeting.

ASSOCIATED SERVICES FOR THE BLIND
919 Walnut Street
Philadelphia, PA 19107
TEL: 215-627-0600
Objectives: To support the independence of blind and visually-impaired people by offering the skills and the tools needed for independent living; to work to build self-reliance by helping visually-impaired persons help themselves.
Services: Offers expanded, varied services following 1984 merger of Volunteer Services for the Blind, Nevil Institute for Rehabilitation and Service, and Radio Information Center for the Blind to form ASB, including:
- **Center for Independent Living:** offers counseling, advocacy, referral, Life Skills education, Electronic Aids training and subsidy, and Mobility Training; evaluates skills of visually impaired and deaf-blind individuals; provides a variety of specific services - such as training handicapped persons to use the Optacon (a tactile scanning device available at cost) to help them achieve independence in home and community;
- **Deaf-Blind services:** increases its capabilities of serving deaf-blind individuals through the combined services made possible by the merger;
- **Radio Information Center (RICB):** provides listeners 19 hours a day, seven days a week of a wide range of vital information such as in-depth reading of newspapers, books and magazines; educational material; shopping and health information; and specific information for blind listeners;
- **Recorded books, magazines and other print materials:** provides Braille, large type, and recordings of a variety of reading materials to blind and partially sighted persons;
- **Volunteer Braille transcription:** transcribes materials for the Library of Congress and other government agencies; offers annual braille transcriber training program for potential volunteers, and arranges certification through the Library of Congress for those who complete the course (ASB is one of only five Braille transcribers in the United States);
- **Job placement services:** assists with job search, resume preparation and the interviewing process; provides on-the-job orientation and support; conducts Employer Awareness Training to prepare firms to hire and manage people with visual impairments;
- **Social services:** maintains a well-trained team of professionals to match service to client (transportation, escort service, errand runners, orientation to senior centers, Diabetes Support Group, etc.);
- **Sens-Sations:** operates a catalogue and retail sales store of specialty items and vision aids (talking clocks, scales and calculators; adapted games; adapted kitchen devices, gift items, etc.); distributes catalogues nationwide to more than 12,000 blind and visually impaired people;
- **Blindness prevention and Community and Corporate Workshops:** works to prevent blindness through informational programs at senior centers; provides speakers and conducts workshops for corporate, community and professional organizations; and distributes information on eye care and

blindness prevention at employer and community health fairs. Assigns its more than 500 volunteers across the country to other specific tasks, such as transcribing textbooks and professional materials, and music and recreational material; fills individual requests for journals and other periodicals not available from other sources; provides materials free, except for those transcribed by a computer (nominal charge); publishes a list of recorded periodicals and other information. According to ASB's Executive Director, "Volunteers are a vital part of ASB's work, with our volunteer corps providing over 50,000 hours in 1988 at a dollar value of over $162,000."
Contact: Peg Hess-Fennell
Publications: ASB Programs; ASB Annual Report
Founded: 1874

INTERNATIONAL GUIDING EYES
13445 Glenoaks Boulevard
Sylmar, CA 91342
TEL: 818-362-5834; 800-528-2552 (CA)
TOLL FREE: 800-824-9726 (nationwide)
Objectives: To train guide dogs and and the blind persons who will use them.
Services: Trains black labradors, golden retrievers, and German shepherds as guide dogs for blind persons; offers residential four-week training program for students and dogs in which a guide dog is "matched" to each student based on many factors; provides training and dogs without charge to blind persons with the help of donations from individuals, companies, organizations and service clubs; provides speakers to communities on request; publishes a quarterly newsletter.
Founded: 1948

JEWISH BRAILLE INSTITUTE OF AMERICA
110 East 30th Street
New York, NY 10016
TEL: 212-889-2525
Objectives: To assist Jewish blind, visually impaired, and reading disabled persons, and other blind individuals.
Services: Distributes materials in large print; develops mechanisms through which the elderly blind and visually impaired can participate in community life; compiles information on programs geared to the social integration of the blind; maintains a lending library of thousands of Braille volumes in English and Hebrew, and films and cassettes in these and other languages; provides speakers to community groups; publishes a newsletter, journal and other materials, some of which are available on sound-scriber discs and cassettes as well as in Braille.
Publications: JBI Voice ; Jewish Braille Review

JEWISH GUILD FOR THE BLIND
15 West 65th Street
New York, NY 10023
TEL: 212-595-2000
Objectives: To assist blind, handicapped and multihandicapped people through a variety of services.
Services: Provides volunteer services for blind and other handicapped people of all ages, races, and creeds; offers casework, counseling, job development, placement and training, sheltered workshops, high school equivalency training, recreational programs, transcription typing, daily living programs, and others; operates a school for multihandicapped children, a psychiatric clinic for emotionally disturbed and mentally retarded blind persons and their families, and a day treatment center and residence for multihandicapped blind young adults, a home for the aging blind, an independent living apartment house, and other programs; maintains a cassette library providing free materials to blind, visually impaired, and reading disabled persons; publishes a quarterly newsletter.
Publications: JGB Newsletter
Founded: 1914

LEADER DOGS FOR THE BLIND
1039 South Rochester Road
Rochester, MI 48063
TEL: 313-651-9011
Objectives: To provide trained guide dogs for blind persons.
Services: Trains dogs to serve as guides for blind persons; conducts a supervised course of training to coordinate blind persons and their leader dogs as operating units; mounts continuous research efforts to determine the best breeds of dog for leader dog purposes; includes residential facilities, kennels, a veterinary hospital, and training centers on its campus; provides all services without charge.

NATIONAL ALLIANCE OF BLIND STUDENTS
c/o Marjie Donovan
763 Silver Avenue
San Francisco, CA 94134
TEL: 415-239-2577
TOLL FREE: 800-424-8666
Objectives: To provide advocacy regarding rights and interests of blind students.
Services: Works to educate government, institutions, agencies, and the public on the rights, interests, and needs of blind students - especially in the area of accredited postsecondary education in academic, vocational, trade and professional and related programs; represents blind students at the annual meeting of the American Council for the Blind by mounting a National Student Seminar with other student groups; publishes a quarterly journal (also available in cassette form) and a networking directory.
Publications: Student Advocate; Student Networking Directory
Founded: 1974

NATIONAL ASSOCIATION FOR PARENTS OF THE VISUALLY IMPAIRED
SEE PSYCHOSOCIAL SUPPORT SERVICES

NATIONAL BRAILLE ASSOCIATION
1290 University Avenue
Rochester, NY 14607
TEL: 716-473-0900
Objectives: To unite volunteers and professional workers for the visually impaired in one national organization to develop, provide and coordinate services in the production and distribution of reading materials in all media: Braille, recording and large type.
Services: Provides assistance on a continuing basis to groups and individuals who prepare reading matter for the print handicapped through seminars, workshops, consultations, and the publication of instruction manuals; maintains a nationwide network of volunteer consultants to respond to individual transcribers seeking answers to transcribing problems; has a merit award and continuing service certificate program for members.
Maintains a depository of Braille materials and offers transcription services; provides braille textbooks, music, career and technical materials at below cost to blind college students and professionals, and helps meet other adult needs of a more general nature; publishes catalogs of the braille collection.
Contact: Angela Coffaro
Publications: NBA BULLETIN; NBA Textbook Catalog; NBA Music Catalog; NBA General Interest Catalog; NBA Technical Tables Catalog
Founded: 1945

NATIONAL LIBRARY SERVICE FOR THE BLIND
US/Library of Congress
1291 Taylor Street, NW
Washington, DC 20542
TEL: 202-707-5100

Objectives: To enable individuals who cannot hold, handle, or read conventional printed matter to enjoy reading materials through talking books and magazines.

Services: Trains and certifies volunteers in tape narration, braille transcribing, and in braille proofreading; publishes Volunteers Who Produce Books: Braille, Tape, Large Type, a directory that lists by state the names of volunteer groups and individuals who transcribe and record books and other reading materials; distributes materials through a national network of 152 locally-funded cooperating libraries and agencies; operates automated bibliographic service for quick identification and location of materials for network libraries; provides playback equipment which is maintained by the Telephone Pioneers of America (senior or retired telephone industry workers); maintains a children's collection with special features such as combined print/braille materials; publishes bimonthly magazines, Talking Book Topics and Braille Book Review, which are available in braille, recorded, and large type versions; operates two additional services:

- *NLS Reference Section* - a comprehensive collection of materials on various aspects of blindness and physical handicaps; a referral service to additional sources, organizations, and agencies.
- *NLS Music Section* - a large collection of music books and periodicals in braille, large print, and/or recorded music scores, instructional cassettes; a referral service to volunteers who produce appropriate music items; a bibliographic search service; a general inquiry service.

[All materials are loaned free, with postage-free mail provided to and from the borrower.]

RECORDING FOR THE BLIND

20 Roszel Road
Princeton, NJ 08540
TEL: 609-452-0606

Objectives: To provide recorded textbooks, library services, and other educational resources to individuals with a visual, physical, or perceptual disability.

Services: Operates through 32 recording studios located in 15 states and the District of Columbia; involves 4,000 volunteer monitors, readers, and recorders of textbooks that are provided in cassette form, available free on loan to registered borrowers; serves print-handicapped students at primary, secondary, undergraduate, graduate, and post-graduate levels in all 50 states and 35 foreign countries; holds a computerized Master Tape Library in Princeton, New Jersey, containing 75,000 texts; fills orders for existing texts in 1-2 days, and the first installment of newly-recorded texts within 10 working days; involves teams of volunteers who come from all walks of life (professionals, business people, retirees, students, etc.); recruits readers with appropriate backgrounds for special subjects (volunteers with backgrounds in science and mathematics are urgently needed at the present time); publishes a newsletter, a catalog, an annual report, brochures and other materials.

Publications: Recording for the Blind News; Catalog of Recorded Books; Volunteers Closing the Science Gap; Volunteers: The Heart of RFB; RFB Annual Report

Founded: 1948

TAPES FOR THE BLIND

7852 Cole Street
Downey, CA 90242
TEL: 213-923-3388

Objectives: To provide a central source of low-cost recording tapes for the blind.

Services: Acquires donated tapes from industry which are no longer usable for their original purpose; uses specially designed machines to slit the tapes to fit home tape recorders; makes the tapes available for about one-fifth of the ordinary cost; sends tapes on request from any state or country, with the U.S. Government providing free postage, and some countries providing customs-free admittance of the tapes. (This organization is the outgrowth of an idea implemented by a VISTA Volunteer.)

INDIVIDUAL PROGRAM PROFILES

ADVOCACY BY AND FOR THE BLIND
AFB Mid-Atlantic Regional Center
1615 M Street, NW
Washington, DC 20036
TEL: 202-457-1487

Purpose: To improve safety of walkways and other areas used by the blind by advocating for specific legislation.

Sponsor: AFB

Contact: Edward T. Ruch, Regional Director

Description: In early 1989, Virginia organizations of and for blind people, and both blind and sighted individuals, demonstrated their concern for the unsafe practice of trucks and other large vehicles - without "beepers" - backing up at too slow a pace for a blind person to tell which way it is going. Among those actively involved in this advocacy effort was a blind counselor at Northern Virginia Community College, whose wife, also blind, was fatally crushed under the rear wheels of a beeperless trash truck in 1988. In addition to letter-writing and telephone campaigns, the advocates testified before the Virginia General Assembly in support of legislation to require all refuse trucks with limited rear visibility to use audible signals when traveling in reverse. The legislation went into effect July 1, 1989.

But the advocates did not feel that they had won a full victory. They intend to work to require the warning signals on delivery and public utility trucks as well as the refuse collection and road maintenance vehicles. Many such vehicles often travel in areas where pedestrians normally have the right of way, blocking sidewalks and driveways.

A blind attorney who is legislative chairman for *Old Dominion Council of the Blind and Visually Impaired*, played a major role in guiding the advocates through this early success, and continues to seek ways to approach the system in an effective manner regarding legislation that would improve the quality of life for the blind. This advocacy effort is only one of many mounted by blind individuals and organizations across the state. In fall 1989 they began a campaign to update Virginia's outdated "white cane" laws. Many other issues await their attention. According to one of the leaders, "The list is endless."

ANNANDALE LIONS CLUB
c/o Colonel Ken Blood
5004 Bradford Drive
Annandale, VA 22003
TEL: 703-256-1591

Purpose: To conduct sight and hearing conservation programs and other health and welfare programs in the local community.

Contact: Colonel Ken Blood

Description: The *Annandale Lions Club* held its 42nd Charter Night in 1990, having begun operations in 1948. With 54 members, it is considered large for a local Club, but an effort at dividing it into smaller groups was unsuccessful.

The *Club* is a member of *Lions Clubs International*, the largest service organization in the world that is dedicated to service only. It has 39,479 local clubs in 166 countries representing 1,363,368 members as of May 1990.

The *Club* provides health and human services assistance to citizens of the Annandale community. Working through a Board of Directors consisting of a president, three vice presidents, and four directors, it administers a budget each year of about $18,000. Although sight and hearing conservation are its primary concerns, these are not the only areas of assistance. The *Club's* fund-raising efforts serve the following programs:

Sight and Hearing Conservation: In 1925, *International Lions* worked with the *Helen Keller Foundation* and agreed to assist the *Foundation* in its work to help make blind and hearing impaired persons productive citizens. This remains the primary goal of all *Clubs.* In Annandale, programs include:

Sight and Hearing Van: This converted and modified Winnebago travels to schools, health fairs, businesses (e.g., IBM, which contributed to the expenses involved), and other entities to provide free sight, glaucoma and hearing screening, and information on conserving these senses. The van is owned by *Lions Club District 24A,* which covers the area north of Fredericksburg in Northern Virginia. Its facilities can be removed for use inside of a building when necessary (such as in large indoor health fairs). The Annandale Club donates approximately $2,000 to the upkeep and operation of the van.

Eye Bank: The Club provides donation cards for individuals to carry on their person which provides for donation of their eyes upon their deaths. The Eye Bank facilitates corneal transplants and other medical procedures, which are financed by the local as well as the other clubs in the area.

White Cane Drive: This is an annual fundraiser in which the business community cooperates with *Lions* members, providing space for "stations" at businesses with a lot of activity to collect funds for *Lions* sight conservation programs. The 1990 drive raised about $1,500.

Leader Dog Program: This project is often shared by several local Clubs due to the cost (about $25,000 per training course), in which a dog and a blind person are trained at a special facility near Detroit, Michigan, to provide the blind person with better access to his or her community. Area Clubs try to do two or three of these training courses each year.

Eye Care Clinic: The Lions Clubs sponsor an eye care clinic at *Fairfax Hospital,* offering free examinations to the indigent, and works through Lions Club members who are opticians to provide free glasses. The Club averages about four pairs of glasses each month to needy persons through this program.

Eyeglasses Recycling: Contrary to the belief of most citizens, the eyeglasses collected by the Lions Club are not used intact (it is illegal in the U.S. to do so). Rather, at a recycling center in Illinois, the precious metal is melted down and funds from the sale of the metal are used to further sight conservation projects. Since the use law does not exist in other countries, eyeglasses in mint condition, without scratches or other damage, are often sent to other countries where the prescriptions are determined and then matched with diagnosed prescriptions of citizens.

Blind Bowling League: The Club helps a league both financially, and in providing assistance in scorekeeping, etc.

Braille Interpretation Program: The Clubs sponsor a program to translate books into Braille. The books are offered to various programs for the blind.

Other Programs: Although primarily concerned with conservation of sight and hearing, the *Annandale Lions Club* has reached out to other groups with unmet needs in the community, resulting in the following programs, among others:

Pancake Breakfast to Benefit ACCA: ACCA (Annandale Christian Community for Action) always has been a recipient of Lions Club funds, but in recent years ACCA has helped in the raising of these funds. All proceeds from the annual *Pancake Breakfast* held at the local community college go to ACCA, an ecumenical service organization involving 28 churches in the Annandale area. ACCA sells tickets to the breakfast and helps in advertising.

Memorial Fund: Often widows of Lions Club members request that sympathizers planning to send flowers send donations to the Lions Club instead. These funds may be used locally, or they may be forwarded to the *International Memorial Fund* where they might be used to build a school in Sri Lanka or a well in Kenya. There are no set guidelines, and decisions are made on an ad hoc basis.

Northern Virginia Youth Camp: This is a camping and recreation facility in the Shenandoah Valley housing a permanent caretaker and made available to *Boy Scouts, Girl Scouts, 4-H,* etc. The camp is a joint venture of a number of Clubs.

Veterans Stamp Collecting Program (Project Outreach): When it was learned that many veterans remained depressed and withdrawn in spite of the efforts of veterans hospitals, the Lions Club suggested helping them develop a hobby. The stamp collecting program was begun by a club in Tuscon, Arizona, and is now a significant program across the country. The area clubs in Pennsylvania, Maryland, Delaware, the District of Columbia, and Northern Virginia have contributed 784,000 stamps, 69 albums, and 180 packets in an eleven month period during 1989 and 1990. Feedback is very positive regarding the effect this hobby development program has had on veterans.

Leo Clubs, Lady Lions, and Lioness Clubs: The Leo Clubs are composed of youth of high school age, with the Lions Club and a designated counselor or teacher at the school administering the program. The Lady Lions are female members of the Lions Club itself (women accepted as members since 1986). Lioness Clubs remain primarily composed of women (although men are welcome) who act as parallel organizations serving the same needs as do the Lions Clubs.

Melvin Jones Fellowship Award: This award is given to outstanding Lions Club members. Each Club handles the award in its own way. The Annandale Club holds an election to honor an *Annandale Lion of the Year.* To this date there have been two awards based on the following criteria: (1) Must have been an active lion with at least seven years longevity. (2) Must have made significant contributions to all projects - both fund-raising and civic - and always acted in a manner to bring credit to the Club and *Lions International.* Also, there have been three posthumous awards made by the Annandale Club. There are now 22,000 Fellows worldwide, with a goal of 65,000 by the 75th International Convention in 1992. Each fellowship award costs $1,000. It consists of a plaque from the *International Lions Club,* a lapel pin and a certificate.

Bland Music Contest: This contest honors the black musician James A. Bland, who composed Virginia's song, *Carry Me Back to Old Virginny,* contrary to the belief of many that it was written by Stephen Foster. The contest has two parts - instrumental and vocal. The local winner receives a cash award and a chance to compete on a regional level, where the award is higher, and - if a winner there - a chance to compete at the State Convention. These awards are designated for a music education, and the amount for an individual can reach a significant amount.

Health and Welfare Budget: About $1,000 is set aside each year for emergency services such as covering gas and light bills for the needy. This fund does not require special approval and is operated under broad guidelines so immediate decisions can be made when necessary.

Youth Activities: The Club is involved in many youth activities, including scouts, *Little League, Boys State, Girls' Camp,* etc. The budget for these activities is about $1,500.

Quest Program (Drug Prevention): About $1,300 each year is devoted to training elementary teachers on drug awareness techniques with children who might be getting close to involvement with drugs.

Miscellaneous Fundraisers: The Lions Club has been a steady provider of Christmas trees and fresh fruit in campaigns each year to raise funds for their programs. These funds are not designated for any particular program.

The *Annandale Lions Club* is an individual organization with its own by-laws. It is not necessary to use the standard by-laws of the *International Lions Club.* However, the local by-laws must be submitted for approval if programs are included that differ from the international agenda. Budgetwise, two separate accountability measures are taken to keep specified funds separate from general funds. An administrative account takes care of dues and other administrative functions. An activity account contains funds for sight and hearing conservation and other specific programs. Every

dollar over actual expenses in the activity account is returned to the public.
Founded: 1948

FRIENDS OF HANDICAPPED READERS
SEE EDUCATION: LIBRARY SERVICES

INDUSTRIAL HOME FOR THE BLIND
57 Willoughby Street
Brooklyn, NY 11201
TEL: 212-522-2122
Purpose: To serve the blind and deaf-blind people of the community.
Sponsor: Public contributions, foundation grants, legacies, and from time to time government grants
Contact: Anne Rose
Description: IHB has on its roster 12,000 blind and deaf-blind people in Brooklyn, Queens, Nassau and Suffolk counties. We offer social service counseling; a low vision clinic including supplying optical aids; a rehabilitation program covering mobility, communications, skills of daily living, etc.; a transcription library (braille, large type, and tape); a sheltered workshop, senior centers and a residence for aging blind and deaf-blind. Volunteers participate in almost all these areas as readers, guides, braille and large type transcribers, arts and crafts aides in our senior centers as well as guides and drivers for all of the above. At present, there are approximately 500 active volunteers serving our clients. They are trained generally on how to work with blind people and specifically for the job they will be doing.
We are funded by public donations foundation grants and endowments plus some government grants for new programs from time to time. Since 1893 the goal of IHB has been to help the blind to help themselves.
Founded: 1893

MAPLEWOOD MANOR RSVP PROGRAM
SEE PSYCHOSOCIAL SUPPORT SERVICES

MASSACHUSETTS ASSOCIATION FOR THE BLIND*
200 Ivy Street
Fitchburg, MA 01420
TEL: 617-345-1100
Purpose: To provide programs and services which enable visually handicapped persons to make maximum use of their abilities and community resources.
Sponsor: United Way of North Central Massachusetts
Contact: Donna Fisher
Description: Any individual in North Worcester County with eye problems, whether or not legally blind, is eligible for MAB's services. Programs include:
Outreach Services: Information and referral, consultation, follow-up and advocacy.
Public Education: Monthly newsletter, consultation with related professionals, training and educational programs on blindness upon request, participation in community programs and exhibitions.
Aids & Appliances: An inventory of special aids for blind persons, as well as other items for persons with significant sight loss, i.e., time pieces, games, sewing and kitchen aids, writing equipment, sunglasses, canes and accessories.
Volunteer Services: Assistance where sight is needed. Help for the blind in order to retain or achieve independence. Volunteers attend a basic training session (two hours long) regarding knowledge of blindness, procedures in working with the blind, and volunteer responsibilities. Volunteers work on a one-to-one basis with clients, serving as: Friendly Visitors, Readers, Clerical Helpers, Drivers, Shoppers, Escorts and Aids for recreational programs.
This satellite office was re-established in October 1980 with a one year federal grant. Fifteen months later, it was accepted as a United Way agency. There are approximately 50 volunteers and another eight who are active members of an Advisory Committee, which is putting together a pamphlet titled Here's Help If You Are Losing Your Sight, listing resources and agencies where help is available.
Volunteers work one-to-one with consumers, not giving much contact between staff and volunteers. Quarterly volunteer meetings are convened to share experiences, problems and give suggestions. Volunteers are requested to report their hours monthly. An assignment sheet, the bottom half of which is a questionnaire, is returned by the volunteer after the first visit.
Publications: MAB Newsletter
Founded: 1980

RADIO INFORMATION SERVICE (RIS)
Golden Triangle Radio Information Center
PO Box 3663
Pittsburgh, PA 15230
TEL: 412-434-6023
Purpose: To provide radio reading service to the blind and print handicapped persons; and to provide programs to other stations and cable systems.
Sponsor: Federal/State grants; corporate underwriting; private donations
Contact: Norman H. Russell, General Manager
Description: Radio Information Service, "Pittsburgh's Most Unusual Radio Station," is a radio reading service for the blind and print handicapped. It is headquartered on the campus of Duquesne University and serves the Southwestern Pennsylvania area. Its goal is to provide current printed material such as the daily newspapers, periodicals like *Time* and *People* magazines, current best selling novels and much more to its listeners. There are currently over 100 such stations across the country and several of the shows that RIS produces are marketed to many of these other stations. RIS is an affiliate of National Public Radio's service for the print handicapped.
Originally, 95% of RIS funds came from Federal and State Title XX monies. However, the budget cuts lowered this proportion considerably and the station is now more reliant on corporate and private donations.
RIS operates as a sub-carrier of WDUQ, 90.5 FM. Because of this sub-carrier status, RIS cannot be heard on AM or FM. Special radio receivers which resemble a small table radio are distributed free of charge to the listeners. It is also available on various cable TV and hospital audio systems.
There is a paid staff of four full time and three part time persons as well as over 300 volunteers who generously donate their time and talents to do the reading and other assignments. The RIS volunteers represent a large cross section in terms of age and background. The majority of them are employed as readers. However, jobs as office personnel, producers, engineers and public relations assistants are also available. Internships with RIS are also available to both high school and college students.
Previous experience in any of the above areas is not a prerequisite. What is stressed is reliability and an aptitude for whatever task the volunteer wishes to do. For example, readers should have a pleasant voice and be able to read fluently. All prospective volunteers are asked to complete an application form and those specifically interested in reading are given a voice test to determine the types of materials they read best and their level of fluency in reading aloud.

VOLUNTEER SERVICE PROGRAM
Delaware Division for the Visually Impaired
305 West 8th Street
Wilmington, DE 19801
TEL: 302-571-6234
Purpose: To provide needed volunteer service for all visually impaired persons in the state of Delaware.

Sponsor: Delaware Department of Health and Social Services
Contact: Marion Levenberg
Description: The volunteer services program for the Division for the Visually Impaired provides needed ancillary volunteer service for all units of the Division dealing directly with clients. In Adult Services and Vocational Rehabilitation, the program attempts to provide readers, drivers for medical appointments, shopping trips, and friendly visiting. In the Educational Department, volunteers assist in the Instructional Resource Materials Center which provides textbooks in various media for visually impaired students. Braillists and tapists transcribe textbooks. Volunteers operate reproduction machinery and maintain the book depository of the Division.

Approximately 35 volunteers have been obtained through recruitment by newspaper solicitation. Others were recruited through presentations before organizations which might provide volunteers. "Word of mouth" has been a very good recruitment source of volunteers also. The program has been operating for nine years.

WHITE CANE DRIVE
Wallington Lions Club
c/o VFW Hall
125 Main Avenue
Wallington, NJ 07057
TEL: 201-779-9373
Purpose: To raise money to purchase glasses and supplies needed by those with sight impairments.
Contact: G. Jack Natale
Description: The *Wallington Lions Club* provides support to a number of organizations through its fund-raising efforts. One effort is reserved specifically for the purchase of glasses and supplies needed by those with sight impairments. The *White Cane Drive* provides glasses for people who need them but can't afford them. This fund also offers transportation to people in need of eye checkups, and helps tape-record books for the blind and visually impaired. Volunteers literally "take to the streets" during this campaign, and use the opportunity to talk about the Lions sight conservation programs and other help the Club provides for people who have impaired vision. Although these are primary projects of the service organization, the Club helps in other areas also. Among the organizations receiving Lions Club support are St. Joseph's Home for the Blind in Jersey City, the Mount Carmel Guild in Newark, the New Jersey Special Olympics, and the Delaware Valley Eye Bank in Philadelphia.
Lions Club members also serve as community educators on behalf of the visually-impaired, especially during the *White Cane Drive.* This symbol has become recognized worldwide, and the positive response to volunteers in the street has enabled the Club to reach thousands of people who might not otherwise have had glasses, talking books, or other materials needed because of the visual handicap.

RECIPIENTS: HANDICAPPED - CEREBRAL PALSY

INDIVIDUAL PROGRAM PROFILES

CEREBRAL PALSY SPORTS PROGRAM
United Cerebral Palsy of Middle Tennessee
2014 Broadway
Nashville, TN 37203
TEL: 615-327-0073

Purpose: To help individuals with Cerebral Palsy develop athletic skills.
Contact: Ian Miller, Coach
Description: United Cerebral Palsy of Middle Tennessee administers a sports program as one of the ways it provides needed services for victims of cerebral palsy and other related disabilities. The sports program helps individuals develop athletic skills and provides them with the opportunity to participate in sports that would otherwise be closed to them.
Coaches are volunteers from the community. They train participants in power lifting, swimming, track and field, team wheelchair handball, soccer, shotputting and boccia ball. They compete in the *Southwest Regional Games* in Dallas, with four of the team members qualifying in 1989 for the national contest held in Minnesota. Another six qualified the same year for the nationals in the Tennessee state tournament held at Vanderbilt University. The sports coordinator on the staff of United Cerebral Palsy recognizes the dedication of the volunteers and the fact that the program could not exist without the hard-working and dependable volunteer coaches and other volunteers in the program.

CPSS FASHION SHOW
Cerebral Palsy of the South Shore
105 Adams Street
Quincy, MA 02169
TEL: 617-479-7443
Purpose: To raise funds to benefit victims of Cerebral Palsy.
Sponsor: Cerebral Palsy of the South Shore
Contact: Arthur Ciampa, Executive Director
Description: The tenth annual fashion show sponsored by *Cerebral Palsy of the South Shore (CPSS)* showed the newest spring fashions. A fashion expert from *Bernie's Modern Formal Shop* was fashion commentator, with handicapped clients (some in wheelchairs), staff members and parents as models. The show was attended by 265 clients, parents, and friends of the rehabilitation organization.
For the fashion event, 30 South Shore businesses donated raffle prizes, materials and services. More than $5,000 was raised after expenses. Following the show, participants were surprised with a full-course Chinese dinner, served at the Masonic Hall. Following the dinner, an award was given to an outstanding volunteer, also the mother of a young client, for her support and services to CPSS.
CPSS was established in 1952 and serves 47 clients through age eight and 50 adults.

UNITED CEREBRAL PALSY/SPASTIC CHILDREN'S FOUNDATION*
7603 Gloria Avenue
Van Nuys, CA 91406
TEL: 213-873-3366
Purpose: To meet the needs of individuals with Developmental Disabilities
Sponsor: Corporate and private donations
Contact: David Myers, Project/Spastic Children's Foundation
Description: United Cerebral Palsy/Spastic Children's Foundation serves over 3,000 individuals and their families with developmental disabilities, through residential programs, counseling and referral programs, and research.
The goal of the Foundation is to help those with developmental disabilities to maximize their potential and to live as independently as their abilities will allow. Volunteers work closely with staff in therapy and training sessions.
The agency currently operates 13 facilities in Los Angeles County with a volunteer network of over 3,000 interested individuals. These volunteers work not only with clients, but also with the extensive fund-raising campaigns which are necessary to support the ongoing work of the Foundation.
Individuals from all walks of life are welcome and encouraged to participate according to their skills and talents.

RECIPIENTS: HANDICAPPED - CHILDREN/YOUTH

NATIONAL/STATE ORGANIZATIONS

CO-ORDINATING COUNCIL FOR HANDICAPPED CHILDREN
220 South State Street, Room 412
Chicago, IL 60604
TEL: 312-939-3513
Objectives: To assist parents in advocating for the rights of handicapped children.
Services: Helps parents to organize parent groups and coalitions; trains parents to advocate for the rights of their handicapped children in Individualized Education Program (IEP) meetings, due process hearings, and other special education meetings; works with local and state administrators to obtain more funds for special education services, mental health services, and other programs which have been identified by parents; addresses and acts upon the Education of all Handicapped Children Act (Law 94-142) and other laws affecting these children; publishes *How to Organize an Effective Parent/Advocacy Group and Move Bureaucracies, The Rights Booklet, How to Get Services by Being Assertive,* and other materials.
Publications: Parent Advocacy Groups; The Rights Booklet; Being Assertive

NATIONAL INFORMATION CENTER FOR CHILDREN AND YOUTH WITH HANDICAPS
SEE RECIPIENTS: HANDICAPPED - I&R

SCOUTING FOR THE HANDICAPPED
Boy Scouts of America
1325 Walnut Hill Lane
Irving, TX 75062
TEL: 214-659-2127
Objectives: To encourage the inclusion of handicapped youngsters in regular packs, troops, and posts.
Services: Assists with job preparation for handicapped scouts; encourages packs, troops, posts at schools and homes for the handicapped when impossible to include them in local programming; includes scouting for the hearing impaired, the visually impaired, the mentally retarded, and the physically handicapped; publishes manuals in each of the handicap areas, plus numerous other pamphlets, brochures, and program suggestion materials; convenes biennial meeting.

INDIVIDUAL PROGRAM PROFILES

FAMILY FRIENDS PROJECT
Project Any Baby Can
400 Labor St.
San Antonio, TX 78210
TEL: 512-227-3146
Purpose: To improve life for families with children who need special care through involvement of older volunteers.
Sponsor: National Council on the Aging
Contact: Volunteer Coordinator
Description: The *Family Friends Project* is an outgrowth of a model project developed in 1984 by the *National Council on Aging* to demonstrate how older volunteers can improve life for families with children who need special care. The San Antonio program began in 1986 and is sponsored by *Project Any Baby Can* and *Senior Community Services. Family Friends* matches volunteers age 55 and older with families who have a chronically-ill or handicapped child. The volunteers spend at least four hours a week with the child. By mid-1989, the project's 50 local volunteers had contributed more than 12,000 hours of service.

The volunteers complete a comprehensive training session covering handicaps and serious illnesses, such as leukemia, that they will encounter in their assignments. In cases of handicapped children, they learn some of the techniques of helping the children reach their greatest potential. One three-year-old blind child could not walk when the volunteer arrived. With the extra time that could be spent with the the the little girl through the involvement of the older volunteer, she soon was walking, talking, going to school and learning how to play. Although working with terminally-ill children is the most difficult, the training helps the volunteers "direct the families' love toward the child(ren) they still have," as they learn to accept their losses.

In addition to teaching and playing with the children, the service of the volunteer allows a needed respite for the family. Often they will take full responsibility and enable the family to spend an evening or a weekend away from home.

As one community leader pointed out, "The handicapped or chronically-ill child loves more powerfully than a healthy child." The volunteers find every experience fulfilling, and feel a "sense of satisfaction of having done something really worthwhile a few hours a day." Four of the older volunteers in the project received awards in 1989 for their many hours of dedicated service to the children and their families.
Founded: 1986

NEW HAMPSHIRE FOSTER GRANDPARENT PROGRAM
New England Center for Continuing Education
University of New Hampshire
15 Garrison Avenue
Durham, NH 03824
TEL: 603-862-1721
Purpose: To provide meaningful part-time volunteer opportunities for low-income older persons and to render supportive, person-to-person services to children with special or exceptional needs.
Sponsor: New England Center for Continuing Education
Contact: Alfred Goldenburg, Director
Description: The New Hampshire Foster Grandparents Program is one of the federally funded ACTION programs. Its purpose is to provide additional income and meaningful part-time volunteer opportunities for low-income older persons and to render supportive, person-to-person services to children with special or exceptional needs in the areas of health, education and welfare.

The program focuses primarily on a person-to-person continuing relationship between an older person and a child with special needs. Although the primary purpose is to provide for the needs of low-income elderly people, the end result is a mutually beneficial relationship. The program provides low-income men and women age 60 and older an opportunity for meaningful service to children 21 years of age and under who have exceptional needs and are often deprived of normal relationships with adults.

At the present time the New Hampshire Foster Grandparent Program, under the sponsorship of the New England Center for Continuing Education at the University of New Hampshire, is funded for 60 foster grandparents to be used in volunteer stations throughout the state. The foster grandparents serve on a regular schedule: four hours a day, five days a week. They are assigned two children, whom they usually serve individually, each day. The foster grandparents receive a stipend of $2.00/hour, a hot meal daily, transportation to and from their volunteer stations (or reimbursement for driving themselves), training, and a yearly physical.

Currently there is a waiting list for older persons wanting to be foster grandparents and for agencies who would like to be volunteer stations. However, until additional funds are raised to support an expansion, the program is limited to the ACTION funds which now support it at a level of 60 foster grandparents. In addition to helping the elderly in terms of supplemental income, the program fulfills their need for a sense of usefulness and self-worth and adds a new social dimension to their lives.

PARENT TO PARENT
Virginia Institute for Developmental Disabilities
Virginia Commonwealth University
910 West Franklin Street
Richmond, VA 23220
TEL: 804-225-3875 (TDD Access); 804-367-1200
TOLL FREE: 800-344-0012 (TDD Access)
FAX: 804-367-0102
Purpose: To put parents of people with disabilities in touch with each other to work together toward the independence of their children.
Sponsor: Virginia Commonwealth University
Contact: Bonnie Atwood, Coordinator
Description: Parent to Parent is one of the 50 university-affiliated programs in the country that work toward the independence, productivity and community integration of people with disabilities. It is a project of the *Virginia Institute for Developmental Disabilities*, which is affiliated with Virginia Commonwealth University.
The Richmond area chapter is housed at the university along with the statewide chapter. Since its inception in 1985, the Richmond chapter has served 200 families. The disabilities range from heart defects, cerebral palsy, vision problems and mental retardation to behavior disorders, autism and diabetes.
A major service of the program is putting volunteer *Parent Partners* in touch with other parents. Requests for matches are continuous, and begin with the staff, who bring together people who are most likely to be helpful to each other. To qualify as a *Parent Partner*, volunteers must attend a 1-1/2-day training seminar.
A side benefit of the program is the library designed to help educate parents about their children's diseases. Another educational tool is a 15-minute videotape of parents expressing their experiences with their special needs children and the organization. Both books and videotape are available on loan to parents.
One parent on the tape summed it up this way, "You're hit so hard in the very beginning..."The program places no limits on the diagnoses they will try to serve. b
Publications: Parent to Parent (videotape)
Founded: 1985

TROOP 400 AND TROOP 391
Boy Scouts of America
National Capital Area Council
Wisconsin Avenue at Cedar Lane
Bethesda, MD 20014
TEL: 301-530-9360
Purpose: To put handicapped scouts into a more competitive and challenging environment through mainstreaming.
Sponsor: Boy Scouts of America
Contact: Stephen Zungali, Program Director; David Henderson, Special Projects Executive for Handicapped Scouting
Description: The National Capital Area Council of the Boy Scouts of America, which covers the Washington, DC, area, has special camps for its 28 troops of disabled scouts. However, until July 1989, an entire troop of disabled scouts had never attended a regular week of camp. At Camp Marriott in Goshen, Virginia, two troops of handicapped scouts joined 200 other campers for a week to "swim, fish and fight off mosquitoes." Troop 400 is from the National Children's Center in northwest Washington, which is a school for autistic and mentally retarded students. Troop 391 is

from Gibbs P.A.C.E., a special education program in northwest Washington.
The disabled scouts followed the same program as other scouts to earn merit badges. With disabled scouts, some of the projects took a little longer, but they learned the skills, according to camp staff. By mainstreaming in this way, the handicapped campers are in a more competitive and challenging environment, and scouts who are not disabled find serving as "buddies" a rewarding experience. Leaders found that the disabled scouts worked harder at Camp Marriott than they did the previous year at a special camp. At the special camp many things were done for the scouts, such as having meals delivered to them. At Camp Marriott they had to "rough it" while learning specific skills to get their merit badges, and other scouts eagerly volunteered to assist them.
Observations from the young volunteers indicated that the non-handicapped scouts received as much growth from the experience as did the disabled scouts. The director was pleased with some of the comments of the young volunteer/scouts, including: "They're just like us!" "They don't laugh at you if you make a mistake." "A lot of people treat handicapped people like they're not normal. They're just like normal people."
According to the camp director, "As the week wore on, the line between teacher and pupil became fuzzy as the paired youths laughed and talked about everything from their favorite comedian (Eddie Murphy) to insects." Plans of the National Capitol Area Council is to increase the number of troops of disabled scouts for the next session of regular camp to three or four - until as many of the 28 troops as possible have merged into the regular program.

RECIPIENTS: HANDICAPPED - COMMUNICATIONS & PR

NATIONAL/STATE ORGANIZATIONS

CHALLENGE INTERNATIONAL
SEE RECIPIENTS: HANDICAPPED

INDIVIDUAL PROGRAM PROFILES

ALEXANDER HUMAN DEVELOPMENT CENTER
VOLUNTEER COUNCIL
PO Box 320
Alexander, AR 72002
TEL: 501-847-3506
Purpose: To conduct community awareness/public relations campaign; to secure the services of interested volunteers to provide companionship for residents; to conduct fund-raising drives to help finance programs for Arkansas residents.
Sponsor: Alexander Parents Organization; Arkansas Elks Association
Contact: Patsy Wagner, Volunteer Services Coordinator
Description: The Alexander Volunteer Council was formed in January 1981. During the early formation stages of the Council three goals were established:
- Greenhouse;
- Canteen for residents; and
- Beautification/normalization of living units.
Through the support of the State Elks Association and the Alexander Parents Organization we now have a commercial greenhouse, size 22' by 40' on the campus. Residents are using this for training purposes, the Volunteer Council supplies the needed supplies; volunteers donate plants, etc. Plants from the greenhouse

are used to help decorate the living areas, are sold to employees, volunteers, etc. These funds are reinvested in the greenhouse. Various "sponsors" have helped in beautification/normalization of living units. They provide bedspreads, area rugs, pictures for the walls, etc.

A canteen renovation project is underway at the present time. A style show was held to raise funds for this project. An area has been paneled, wallpapered and tables have been constructed. The next phase of the project will include chairs and a music system. Volunteers are recruited, trained and supervised by the Volunteer Coordinator, with on the site supervision by the Cottage Supervisor.

GIVEN OPPORTUNITIES...

Little City Foundation
4801 Peterson Avenue
Chicago, IL 60646
TEL: 312-282-2207
Purpose: To highlight the accomplishments and abilities of people with developmental challenges.
Sponsor: Little City Foundation
Contact: Cable TV Coordinator
Description: The Little City Foundation has developed a national public access cable monthly television program to bring to the attention of the general public the abilities and talents of people with disabilities. The program features individuals who have succeeded as a result of being given an opportunity, or people who have achieved beyond the limits and barriers imposed upon them by society, circumstances, or their disabilities.

The success of the program depends on the willingness of people to volunteer their experiences on camera, and the recommendations provided for follow-up by people across the country.

The Foundation also serves as an information source for professionals, advocates and volunteers in areas of educational, residential, vocational and recreational opportunities available. Begun in fall 1989, this program continually seeks exemplary people who have overcome obstacles so that they can provide positive information to the general public about people with developmental challenges.
Publications: Given Opportunities...

HUG IN

Community Workshop and Training Center
3215 North University
Peoria, IL 61604
TEL: 309-686-3314
Purpose: To conduct an awareness event to inform the community of the needs of handicapped people.
Sponsor: Community Workshop and Training Center, Inc.
Contact: Nikki Vulgaris
Description: In May 1982 volunteers and staff of Community Workshop and Training Center (CWTC) felt that public relations efforts regarding the agency needed to be increased to promote employment and independent living for handicapped persons. With this in mind, something new had to be tried.

The Hug-In developed through agency volunteer recognition items. Earlier in the year, a cartoon figure was adopted which appeared on "hug" cards (Thank You notes) and the volunteer newsletter.
In addition, the population (developmentally disabled) is one which requires much positive reinforcement so the Hug-In occurred naturally.

The Hug-In took place in September and was held in downtown Peoria, in an area where people mill during their lunch hour. Buttons were purchased to promote the event, and Hug Coupons were used for advertising time, place, etc.

To establish a crowd, local celebrities, communiity leaders and others were invited to participate as "official" huggers. In addition, since hugging a stranger is uncomfortable for many, we arranged

with other organizations to have costume characters. On hand were: Miss Piggy, Cookie Monster, clowns and many others. Other entertainment included a jazz band and the Community Workshop Chorus.

What were the benefits of the Hug-In? It:
- increased CWTC visibility in the community;
- opened doors for placement opportunities with local employers;
- obtained new work contracts for training;
- increased interest by community volunteers to volunteer in the agency;
- opened doors for fundraising. Two local businesses sponsored fundraising events for CWTC.

Founded: 1982

RADIO INFORMATION SERVICE (RIS)
SEE RECIPIENTS: HANDICAPPED - BLIND

WMNR RADIO - ACCESS BROADCASTING COMPANY*

Masuk High School
Monroe, CT 06468
TEL: 203-268-9667
Purpose: To deliver quality arts programming, and to make the handicapped highly visible in the community.
Sponsor: CETA (initially); private and corporate donations
Contact: Stewart Nazzaro, General Manager
Description: WMNR-FM is the only radio station in the country that is totally managed by the handicapped. WMNR began operating in January 1980 with a rock music format. Since that time it has switched to a classical and big band jazz format, and emphasizes cultural programming. In addition to an interest in an arts format, talk shows will alternate with public service spots on civic events and local jobs for the disabled. A call-in rider service, for example, helps homebound listeners get to appointments, entertainment programs, etc.

The WMNR crew ranges in age from 14 to 65 and includes alcoholics, amputees, the cerebral palsied, stutterers, etc. The station director is a legally blind albino who is determined to use radio to help other handicapped people combat some of the obstacles he faced when growing up. Many disabled listeners visit the studio to see first hand the accomplishments of the crew. These visitors range from very young children to the elderly, and all have come away with renewed hope and satisfaction.

Because of limited funds, only five of the disabled personnel are actually on the payroll. Both handicapped and able-bodied volunteers are recruited to keep the station operating seven days a week from 7 a.m. to midnight. However, the period from 7 a.m. to 2 p.m. every weekday is reserved for operation by only handicapped staff and volunteers. This was done to make one section of the program unique.

Formerly, WMNR was the local high school's radio club. With a degree in radio and TV from Syracuse University in hand, the present station manager convinced the Board of Education that he could transform it into an actual aired station. With a $52,300 CETA grant, the first program went on the air.

Now that the CETA funding has been depleted, the station is planning to raise $100,000 needed to keep WMNR on the air (each year). WMNR has no commercials, and depends solely on grants and contributions.

To accept donations, the station founded Access Broadcasting Company. Several corporations have talked with the station's officers, and are considering funding assistance. Future plans include increasing WMNR's signal from 600 to 10,000 watts to expand coverage to 450 square miles, enlarging the staff, winning affiliation with National Public Radio and sponsorship by the Corporation for Public Broadcasting. There is no locally-based, arts-oriented radio station in the area, and WMNR plans to fill that need.
Founded: 1980

RECIPIENTS: HANDICAPPED - DAY CARE/HEAD START

INDIVIDUAL PROGRAM PROFILES

PRESCHOOL DIAGNOSTIC AND DEVELOPMENTAL EDUCATION NURSERIES
SEE DAY CARE/HEAD START: HANDICAPPED

RAINBOW CENTER FOR EXCEPTIONAL CHILDREN
SEE DAY CARE/HEAD START: HANDICAPPED

RECIPIENTS: HANDICAPPED - DEAF

NATIONAL/STATE ORGANIZATIONS

ALEXANDER GRAHAM BELL ASSOCIATION FOR THE DEAF
3417 Volta Place, NW
Washington, DC 20007
TEL: 202-337-5220 (TDD/Voice)
Objectives: To see that hearing-impaired children and older adults are afforded the opportunity to develop spoken communication.
Services: Operates a nationwide volunteer program where volunteers serve as knowledgeable resources for hearing-impaired children and their families; collaborates in research relating to auditory/verbal communication; promotes detection of hearing loss in early infancy; provides in-service training for teachers of hearing-impaired children; provides college/university scholarships for hearing-impaired students; advocates educational options for deaf children; offers information and printed materials for older, hearing-impaired adults on hearing aids, assistance devices, lipreading, etc.; provides consultant services for families pursuing their legal rights; works with doctors, audiologists, speech/language specialists, educators and others to promote educational, vocational and social opportunities for hearing-impaired people of all ages; publishes a journal, a newsletter, and a variety of books and audiovisual materials regarding the implications of hearing loss, its causes and options for remedial treatment; conducts eight annual workshops to train teachers, parents, professionals and volunteers working with hearing-impaired people (see training section).
Publications: The Volta Review; Newsounds; Our Kids; Listen! Hear! Hearing Alert; Alexander Bell's Dream is Here
Founded: 1890

AMERICAN ATHLETIC ASSOCIATION FOR THE DEAF*
1052 Darling
Ogden, UT 84403
TEL: 816-765-5520 (TTY)
Objectives: To foster athletic competition among the deaf.
Services: Regulates uniform rules governing athletic competition; provides a social outlet for the deaf and their friends; promotes nationwide tournaments in basketball, soft ball, and other sports; publishes a quarterly bulletin.

DOGS FOR THE DEAF
13260 Highway 238
Jacksonville, OR 97530
TEL: 503-899-7177
Objectives: To train hearing ear dogs and deaf persons to work together for the safety and independent living of the hearing-impaired individual.
Services: Trains dogs to recognize and alert hearing-impaired individuals to sounds such as alarm clocks, smoke alarms, doorbells, oven timers, crying babies, telephones, etc., using individuals who have been trained to be *Certified Audio Canine Trainers;* selects dogs from pet adoption centers for four or five months of training; matches dogs with deaf or hearing-impaired persons who are considered mature enough to assume responsibility for the care of the dog; assigns trainers to spend a week in recipient's home to train recipient and dog to work together; covers costs through donations (accepts recipient donations only when recipient is able to make a contribution); appears in various media to discuss the training process, and options for the placement of dogs; publishes a newsletter three times a year.
Publications: Canine Listener
Founded: 1977

HEARING EAR DOG PROGRAM
PO Box 213
West Boylston, MA 01583
TEL: 617-835-3304
Objectives: To train dogs to work with deaf and hearing-impaired persons.
Services: Provides three to five months of training to teach dogs to alert deaf and hearing-impaired individuals to specific sounds of importance to safety and independent living; teaches carefully-screened dogs basic obedience and how to respond to sounds such as car horn, siren, kettle whistle, telephone, doorbell or knock, alarm clark, baby crying, etc.; publishes a quarterly newsletter and other materials.
Publications: HEDP Newsletter; Hearing Ear Dogs: A Sound Relationship
Founded: 1976

INTERNATIONAL HEARING DOG, INC. (*formerly Hearing Dogs, Inc.*)
5901 East 89th Avenue
Henderson, CO 80640
TEL: 303-287-3277
Objectives: To train and place dogs with the deaf.
Services: Trains and places dogs, free of cost, with deaf persons to alert them to important sounds in their environment, such as doorbell or knocking, crying baby, smoke alarm, alarm clock, telephone, security alarm, and other sounds related to safety and independent living; appears in media presentations to raise public awareness of the problems of the deaf; publishes a newsletter three times a year.
Publications: Paws for Silence
Founded: 1979

NATIONAL CENTER FOR HEARING DOG INFORMATION
SEE PHYSICAL ENVIRONMENT: WILDLIFE/PETS

ORGANIZATION FOR THE USE OF THE TELEPHONE (OUT)
PO Box 175
Owings Mill, MD 21117
TEL: 301-655-1827
Objectives: To make the telephone an accessible instrument of communication to those who are "phone deaf."
Services: Persuades telephone companies to convert public, home and business phones to make them electronically compatible with telephone pick-ups in hearing aids, and to amplify public pay phones; advocates for the installation of Induction Loop Amplification (ILA) systems in places of public gatherings;

publishes the OUT-Line on an occasional basis to keep people informed of new developments in this area; publishes various items on the use of the telephone with hearing aids, including *All Telephones Must Work with All Hearing Aids - Everywhere*, which is a guide to action for interested individuals and groups (all materials are free).
Contact: David Saks
Publications: OUT-Line; OUT Annual Report; Telephones and Hearing Aids; All Telephones... Everywhere
Founded: 1973

PHONE-TTY

202 Lexington Avenue
Hackensack, NJ 07601
TEL: 201-489-7889; 201-489-3323 (Bull.Bd.)
Objectives: To develop and promote better communication for the deaf.
Services: Uses an ordinary telephone and current technology to develop better communication for the deaf; installs computerized phone-teletype equipment in the homes of individuals who are deaf which is compatible with that of local police, hospitals, answering services, and news services as well as other members of the deaf community who have a *Phone-TTY* in their homes; continually researches, designs, manufactures, and distributes other communications devices for the deaf; solicits grants and donations to help defray costs; operates an electronic bulletin board.
Founded: 1976

SELF-HELP FOR HARD OF HEARING PEOPLE
SHHH

7800 Wisconsin Avenue
Bethesda, MD 20814
TEL: 301-657-2248
Objectives: To create a volunteer network of hearing-impaired individuals in a self-help environment.
Services: Brings together hearing-impaired persons and their relatives and friends, and professionals working with hearing-impaired persons, to educate members of the public on the nature, causes and complications of hearing loss; instructs the public on early detection, management, and possible prevention of hearing loss; works for public acceptance of the hearing-impaired, and use of alternative communication skills by the public in working with the hearing-impaired; maintains a reference library, a speakers bureau, and several committees, including one on parent involvement and one on concerns of the elderly; publishes a journal six times a year, a quarterly newsletter, special reports, manuals, books and other materials.
Publications: SHHH - A Journal about Hearing Loss; Your Eyes Hear for You: A Self-Help Course in Speechreading; SHHH Newsletter
Founded: 1979

TDD/TTY OPERATOR SERVICES
Bell of Pennsylvania
1631 Arch Street
Philadelphia, PA 19103
TEL: 215-855-1155
TOLL FREE: 800-855-1155
Objectives: To provide information on services available to hearing and speech impaired people who use Telecommunications Devices for the Deaf (known as TDDs or TTYs).
Please Note: This service cannot respond to inquiries by mail; inquirers must use the telephone for service.
Services: Maintains a nationwide information and referral service involving telephone operators; provides assistance to the calling party in making calls from a TDD to a TDD, including:
- Credit Card Calls (for those with a telephone credit card);
- Collect Calls (calls being paid for by the person called);
- Third Number Telephone Calls (calls billed to a number other

than the one being used by the caller);
- Person-to-Person Calls (calls to a specific person);
- Calls from a Hotel or Motel; and
- Calls from a Coin Phone (only credit card, collect, or bill to a third number calls)

Provides additional help when the TDD operator helps the caller to: get the number if the caller has a problem with the call; get assistance for problems with calls; get telephone numbers that the caller cannot find in the telephone book; and report problems with your telephone (but most calls made with operator assistance cost more than a number dialed directly by the caller); makes referrals to the specific local telephone office for the inquirer's location that can install new equipment, check, repair, or adapt existing equipment, and answer questions about the operation of the equipment (TDD operators cannot interpret voice to TDD or TDD to voice).

INDIVIDUAL PROGRAM PROFILES

GALLAUDET BOARD OF TRUSTEES
Gallaudet University
800 Florida Avenue, NE
Washington, DC 20002
TEL: 202-651-5488
FAX: 202-651-5489
Purpose: To better represent the student body of a major school for deaf students by appointing deaf members to the Board of Trustees.
Sponsor: Gallaudet University
Contact: Glen B. Anderson or Carol Padden
Description: In 1988, students with the *Deaf President Now Committee* won three of four demands through a massive student demonstration. They had called for resignations from the newly-appointed President, who was not deaf and did not know sign language, and the Board Chairman. They asked that they be replaced with deaf persons. Both resignations were tendered and accepted, and deaf persons have been placed in those positions. The fourth demand called for the board to have a majority of deaf members. In May 1989, the Board of Trustees for the federally-funded, federally-chartered institution named two deaf members to the 21-member board bringing the total number of deaf persons on the board to six. One of the new members is an associate professor in the Department of Communications at the University of California. The other is an author of several books, including the co-authored *Deaf in America: Voices from a Culture*. Since then the Board has adopted a resolution stating that it should be made up of individuals "of whom the majority should be deaf." As vacancies open, the Board seeks to replace members who have no hearing impairment with members who are deaf.

VOLUNTEER ORIENTATION PROGRAM
National Information Center on Deafness
Gallaudet University
Volunteer Office
800 Florida Avenue, NE
Washington, DC 20002
TEL: 202-651-5606
Purpose: To assist the Information Center on Deafness in all phases of its program
Sponsor: National Information Center on Deafness/Visitors Center
Contact: Cindi Olson
Description: The Volunteer Orientation Program is a one-day orientation to deafness and Gallaudet College for individuals who have been interviewed and screened by the Volunteer Coordinator. All volunteers are required to complete the program which covers such topics as:
- deafness;
- communication;

- functions of Gallaudet University;
- discussion of the role of Alumni Publication Relations;
- the objectives of the National Information Center on Deafness and the Visitors Center; and
- other relevant volunteer placements.

Upon completion, volunteers are assigned to either the Information Center, Visitors Center, or other placement concommittant with their interest and backgrounds. Volunteers have such varied responsibilities as leading tours, responding to inquiries, research for responses or development of new materials; information collection; telephone support, clerical support. Volunteers are given continuing individual attention and guidance by supervisors in all Centers. At the present time, periodic volunteer meetings are scheduled for discussion of topics of concern and as a forum for continued learning related to Gallaudet University and deafness.

RECIPIENTS: HANDICAPPED - EDUCATION

NATIONAL/STATE ORGANIZATIONS

COUNCIL FOR EXCEPTIONAL CHILDREN
SEE EDUCATION: HANDICAPPED

RECORDING FOR THE BLIND
SEE RECIPIENTS: HANDICAPPED - BLIND

SPECIAL MATERIALS PROJECT*
Handicapped Learner Materials
Associations for the Education of the Deaf
624 East Walnut Street
Second Floor
Indianapolis, IN 46204
TEL: 317-636-1902
Objectives: To make information available on loan to individuals or organizations working with the handicapped.
Services: Operates under the aegis of the Associations for Education of the Deaf under contract with the Department of Education; administers a loan service of educational, cultural, and advocacy materials for schools or independent classes for the handicapped, foundations or nonprofit organizations, religious organizations serving the handicapped, teacher training in special needs area, parent groups, adult and continuing education programs, and other organizations with an interest in this area; serves all disabled populations with free loan materials for one to seven days (user pays return postage expenses only).

INDIVIDUAL PROGRAM PROFILES

FRED RUFFING MEMORIAL SCHOLARSHIP
SEE EDUCATION: SCHOLARSHIPS

GRAFTON SCHOOL VOLUNTEER BOARD
Grafton School
P.O. Box 112
Berryville, VA 22601
TEL: 703-955-2400
Purpose: To respond to a child's need for special help.
Contact: Patricia Hockman
Description: Grafton School was founded thirty-one years ago by Ruth Birch, a native of Clarke County, Virginia, in response to a

need across the community - assistance for children who need special help. At the time the public school systems were unable to address the needs of children who were having difficulty learning in the usual classroom setting. Grafton School's purpose was to "catch children up" and return them to their public schools. Though Grafton has outgrown Mrs. Birch's kitchen, the goals for each of the children remains the same ... to provide them with the skills they need to participate in public school programs and, more importantly, to help them return home.

Today, Grafton serves 150 children annually in three program areas: Autism, Emotionally Disturbed/Learning Disabled, and Mentally Retarded/Emotionally Disturbed.

The main campus, located on Virginia Route 7 two miles east of Berryville, serves as Grafton's headquarters and home to 92 students. Grafton also operates four group homes for young adults in the Autism and Emotionally Disturbed/Learning Disabled Programs. Currently, the School has undergone a major expansion project that moved the Autism programs serving children ages 3 to 14 to a second major campus in Winchester. The expansion was completed in late fall of 1989.

Grafton is a private, nonprofit facility serving children from ages three to fifteen at admission. It is governed by a volunteer Board of Directors. Committees of the Board meet monthly.

PARENTS EDUCATING PARENTS
1851 Ram Runway
Suite 104
College Park, GA 30337
TEL: 404-761-3150; 404-761-2745
Purpose: To provide parents with necessary information to insure their participation in planning, provision, monitoring of special education for handicapped children in Georgia through Public Law 94-142 and other laws.
Sponsor: Georgia Association for Retarded Citizens
Contact: Cheryl D. Knight
Description: Parents Educating Parents (PEP) began June 1, 1980, after receiving a grant from the Office of Special Education sponsored by the *Georgia Association for Retarded Citizens*. The statewide project's goal is to provide parents with necessary information and training on *P.L. 94-142* to insure their meaningful participation in the planning, provision, and monitoring of special education to handicapped children in Georgia.

Currently, the PEP Project is operating as the parent training component of the *University Affiliated Facility (UAF)* at the *University of Georgia*. Funding comes from the *U.S. Department of Education* through its *Handicapped Personnel Preparation Program.*

PEP believes that receiving an education is every child's right. Handicapped children are no exception. Public Law 94-142 mandates that all handicapped children must have available to them, "a free appropriate public education designed to meet their unique needs and that handicapped children must be educated in a least restrictive environment."

The philosophy of PEP is that parents can educate parents. PEP believes parents can make an important contribution to the education of their children since they possess unique information about their child's development, nature and needs. Therefore, parents can become effective partners with teachers in reinforcing activities and skills acquisition which occur during the school day.
Project goals are:
- To set up an educational advocacy network throughout Georgia, composed of parents and contact people in local areas, to assist parents of handicapped children.
- To establish a viable partnership between local education agencies (LEA), state education agencies (SEA), and parent advocacy organizations.
- To assist parents in exercising their rights under P.L. 94-142 by providing them with specific competencies gained in terms of negotiation and assertiveness skills.

- To foster more meaningful parent participation in individualized education plans (IEP) development to insure that each child's educational program is based on needs rather than available resources.
- To teach parents the special education and legal vocabulary in order to insure true and accurate communication between parent and teacher.
- To promote understanding and awareness concerning the specific sections of P.L. 94-142 that relate to parent participation.
- To prepare and disseminate to parents and others the *Education Update* six times per year as a continuing education tool (circulation currently 3,700).

The PEP Project has conducted workshops and training for parents (see separate entry); maintains a resource library accessible by phone or mail; provides printed information through its *Education Update, PEP Notebooks,* training manuals, copies of laws, etc.; and provides technical assistance to parents throughout the state as well as to educators and to advocates.
Publications: The Education Update; PEP Information Packet; PEP Training Manuals; PEP Talk; Awareness Coloring Book (Spanish); Avanzando (Spanish)
Founded: 1980

U.S. OPEN VOLUNTEER COMMITTEE
SEE RECIPIENTS: HANDICAPPED - EMPLOYMENT

RECIPIENTS: HANDICAPPED - EMPLOYMENT

NATIONAL/STATE ORGANIZATIONS

AMERICAN COALITION OF CITIZENS WITH DISABILITIES*
1200 Fifteenth Street, NW
Washington, DC 20005
TEL: 202-785-4265 (voice); 202-784-4341 (TDD)
Objectives: Acts as a unified voice to support legislation for the handicapped; to provide job placement services for the handicapped.
Services: Provides information about legislation for the handicapped, especially in areas of transportation and education; holds training seminars in local communities to inform handicapped people about educational opportunities available to them; leads local workshops in advocacy training to teach the handicapped about their legal rights, how to lobby, and how to work with the media; publishes two newsletters, guides and handbooks such as Self-Help Groups in Rehabilitation, Planning Effective Advocacy Programs, and Rehabilitating America.

HUMAN RESOURCES CENTER
201 I.U. Willets Road West
Albertson, NY 11507
TEL: 516-747-5400
Objectives: To create employment opportunities for the physically handicapped.
Services: Brings together industry, labor, education and rehabilitation in a forum to find ways to increase and create job opportunities for the handicapped (more than 70 major companies and labor unions involved); provides workshops, seminars and conferences at the Center and throughout the country; plays key role in a national and somewhat international information exchange network on employment of the handicapped; conducts research on the nature of job placement practices for disabled persons and publishes its findings; maintains coordinated divisions:

- **Human Resources School** is a specially-designed barrier-free facility which offers a tuition-free fully-accredited education program for physically-disabled children from pre-school to senior high.
- **The Research and Training Institute** conducts national demonstration studies in areas such as career education, job placement, independent living, attitudes toward the disabled, and driver training; disseminates information aimed at enhancing the employability and quality of life of persons with disabilities.
- **Vocational Rehabilitation Services** provides vocational evaluation, counseling, skills training, and placement; serves over 600 disabled adults per year between the ages of 17 and 70.
- **Abilities Inc.** is a work center which demonstrates the capabilities of disabled workers (includes fields of banking, data processing, electronics, and other clerical and industrial operations).
- **Industry-Labor Council** is a membership organization of 84 major corporations and unions, including Warner-Lambert Company, Mobil Oil Corporation, General Electric Company, Xerox Corporation, and International Brotherhood of Electrical Workers, which assists industry/labor nationwide to develop employment opportunities for disabled Americans.
- **Independent Living Project** is a program for senior high school students and high school graduates (one of four organizations selected for federal grants to develop and administrate projects).

Publishes numerous guides and manuals for business, industry, and labor, for groups and individuals working with the handicapped, and for the handicapped themselves in areas of education, placement, work independence, recreation and others (request complete catalog).
Founded: 1952

MAINSTREAM
1030 Fifteenth Street, NW
Suite 1010
Washington, DC 20005
TEL: 202-898-1400
Objectives: To encourage increased employment opportunities for handicapped Americans; to provide employers, national handicap organizations, federal regulators and other groups with the information that will help mainstream handicapped individuals into the workplace.
Services: Designs and coordinates national demonstration programs that involve handicap organizations and employers in making the training and placement of more disabled persons a reality in a specific metropolitan area; gives companies training in handicap awareness, interviewing and recruiting, job analysis, information on legal incentives for employing handicapped persons; presents forum for employers to discuss their affirmative action concerns and efforts with representatives of national handicap groups; publishes a bimonthly, subscription newsletter, *In the Mainstream,* that reports on the legal and practical issues of employing disabled persons; also publishes specific issue brochures and reports; maintains a resource center on handicap employment issues and serves as an information source on handicap employment, disabled individuals, disability service providers and governmental officials.
Founded: 1975

PRESIDENT'S COMMITTEE ON EMPLOYMENT OF THE HANDICAPPED
SEE EMPLOYMENT: HANDICAPPED

INDIVIDUAL PROGRAM PROFILES

CENTRAL FAIRFAX SERVICES
5001 Backlick Road
Annandale, VA 22003
TEL: 703-354-0900
Purpose: To provide training, supervision, education and work opportunities for adults who are developmentally disabled.
Sponsor: Chapter Ten Services Board, private donations
Contact: Mary Ann Payne, Executive Director
Description: Central Fairfax Services (CFS) is a private, nonprofit agency that provides training, supervision, education and vocational opportunities for developmentally disabled adults. CFS was started in 1967 as a pilot program by the Northern Virginia Association for Retarded Citizens and became incorporated in 1972. Opening in one church and expanding to three churches, CFS reached the goal of having one main building in August 1979. CFS operates three program components emphasizing different levels of rehabilitation:

- **The Intensive Developmental Center** has 16 severely handicapped clients whose needs are sensorimotor, speech and language, and personal care.
- **Vocational Development** services 45 individuals, stressing pre-vocational, personal adjustment, and communications skills.
- **Work Experience**, serving 47 clients, meets their vocational needs by providing training on work samples and contract jobs.

In addition, work-related behavior and skills in personal adjustment and communication are stressed.
The staffing pattern for each center consists of floor supervisors who provide direct care and training, adaptive skills instructors responsible for individual and group training on specific objectives, and a center supervisor. In addition, the services of REHAB, INC. are available, providing speech, occupational and physical therapies. An art therapist provides consultation and direct intervention with clients on a part-time basis.
Volunteers are utilized in providing direct client supervision, working along with professional staff members in implementing treatment plans for our clients. They are afforded all the training and supervision a salaried employee receives through in-service training, didactic materials and team meetings.
CFS receives funding from the Chapter Ten Services Board and through private donations.
Founded: 1967

DATA SYSTEMS UNLIMITED
SEE EMPLOYMENT: HANDICAPPED

PATOWMACK HERBAL FARM: SUMMER EMPLOYMENT FOR THE HANDICAPPED
SEE RECIPIENTS: HANDICAPPED - MENTALLY RETARDED

THE SHED PROJECT*
R.F.D. #1
Box 359
Sandown, NH 03873
TEL: 603-352-1909
Purpose: To offer handicapped students an opportunity to learn about careers in construction, and to participate in construction jobs.
Sponsor: New Hampshire Public School District; New Hampshire State Department; CETA
Contact: Laurent Cormier
Description: Recognizing that the emotionally disturbed students did not adapt to integration into mainstream classes as other handicapped students did, a special three-phase off-campus program was developed for these students. A behavior specialist and an industrial arts instructor designed the program, which includes:
Phase I - The Shed Project: The class is organized into a crew, alternating various management and labor positions. During the course of the year the crew builds three or four large sheds on job sites in the community.
Phase II - Summer Environmental Education Construction Program for Disadvantaged Youth: Shed Project students qualify for CETA funds and participate in a variety of construction projects along with non-handicapped youngsters.
Phase III - Solar Horticultural Prevocational Program for Students with Special Needs: This project expands the skills learned in the construction cluster by introducing horticultural occupations. The phase includes the construction of a solar greenhouse together with necessary equipment and horticultural operations.
Voluntary action by the community comes in many forms - from serving as resource people, to providing construction materials, to helping evaluate the quality of student work.
Although CETA and Title IV funds are used for this program, costs can be modest. Shed construction is financed from profits realized and a $5,000 grant from members of the community, which helps finance the greenhouse. There is a variety of projects students can undertake if there is no demand for sheds within the community; i.e., building boathouses, maintaining school buses, and urban renewal projects. The following are key factors which every program should preserve.
Make it "Real" - The project should result in a product of genuine usefulness for the school, company, or community.
Provide Options - Provide a variety of activities which will sustain interest and enable all students to experience success.
Assure Diversity and Responsibility in Student Roles - Students should share the responsibility for making rules, setting procedure, monitoring performances and assuming a variety of roles.
Capitalize on Opportunities to Learn about a Variety of Careers - Students need a chance to meet builders, engineers, architects, and workers in the skilled trades as well as managerial and professional workers.
Keep Careful Track of Progress - Careful monitoring of student progress will help not only in determining who is entitled to what rewards, it also will allow for the early identification of problems and facilitate discussion and resolution.
Involve the Off-Campus World - There are a variety of involvements - employers at whose construction sites students work, persons skilled in trades or professions related to the work students are doing, other students, retired persons, and others. This adds to the realism of the enterprise, and perhaps more importantly, prepares the student for the mainstream of the world.
Involve School Staff with a Variety of Skills - Teachers in special, academic, and vocational fields, and other staff can accomplish more working together than alone. In each phase of the program in Derry, staff combined their skills very effectively.

TRAINING FOR DISABLED STUDENTS
SEE EMPLOYMENT: HANDICAPPED

U.S. OPEN VOLUNTEER COMMITTEE
School of the Holy Childhood
1150 Buffalo Road
Rochester, NY 14611
TEL: 716-436-9200
Information also available from:
Twigs Volunteers for the U.S. Open
Norma Horn, Chairwoman, Rochester General Hospital Association
Rochester, NY
Purpose: To raise money for a school for the handicapped (School of the Holy Childhood), and a birthing center (Rochester General Hospital Association).

Sponsor: U.S. Open Golf Tournament
Contact: Lynda Kessler Newman, Chairman
Description: Volunteers at the U.S. Open work for pay at the concession stands - $4.50 an hour. It is a unique way of raising funds for their service programs, since the entire paycheck goes to the volunteer project they represent.
The *School of the Holy Childhood* will use the money it raises either for general education expenses or a planned 20,000-square-foot expansion of its woodworking shop. The workshop helps residents become independent, since they work for a wage there. The final decision comes through a school board vote after the funds are received.
The *Rochester General Hospital Association* set a target of $15,000 from their U.S. Open volunteers to be applied to its $700,000 pledge to the *Twig Birthing Center* at the hospital. The Center is designed to allow a room for mothers and fathers to stay overnight with their newborns to help develop the initial family bond with the infant.
In return for their efforts, the volunteers - some in their seventies - are able to watch the Open when their shifts end.

RECIPIENTS: HANDICAPPED - EPILEPSY

NATIONAL/STATE ORGANIZATIONS

EPILEPSY FOUNDATION OF AMERICA
4351 Garden City Drive
Landover, MD 20781
TEL: 301-459-3700
Objectives: To provide advocacy and a wide variety of services and programs for persons with epilepsy.
Services: Sponsors a number of special projects such as School Alert, Community Alert, Self-Help, Training and Placement Service, and others; provides information on epilepsy for the patient, his family and friends, educators, employment specialists, etc., on a wide range of topics; publishes a directory, pamphlets, reprints, books, cassettes, films, slides, and a monthly newsletter.

RECIPIENTS: HANDICAPPED - FUNDING

INDIVIDUAL PROGRAM PROFILES

DAISY (FRIEND-RAISER) BALL
Kessler Institute for Rehabilitation Auxiliary
1199 Pleasant Valley Way
West Orange, NJ 07052
TEL: 201-731-3600
Purpose: To raise funds for the Kessler Institute for Rehabilitation.
Contact: Shelly Mandel, President
Description: The annual fund-raising ball of the *Kessler Institute Auxiliary* has come to be known the "Friend-Raiser Ball." Organizers have found that making friends for the Institute is more fun than raising funds, and once the friends see the work that is done at the Institute, they provide the funds anyway.
One of the goals of the auxiliary is to help the Institute realize its goal in a $2.5 million building campaign. The Auxiliary's pledge is

$300,000, and it is ahead of schedule. Another $50,000 remains, and there is a full year-and-a-half before the total is due.
Besides money volunteers from the auxiliary and the community assist in all other areas of the physical rehabilitation operation, as they have since its beginning in 1948. Many came through the efforts of the auxiliary's "friend-raiser" activities. They work for both in-patient and out-patient services, which have been expanded into Bergen, Passaic and Union counties. Volunteer board members help decide the allocation of funds among research projects, educational programs, and advanced equipment. Other volunteers continually study and restructure the many activities of the Institute for maximum benefit and growth. One way of returning something to the community is the Institute's policy to open its auditorium to the general public for community activities.

FLINT AIRSHOW
Bishop Airport Authority
3425 West Bristol Road
Flint, MI 48507
TEL: 313-766-8620
Purpose: To raise funds for Area XIII Special Olympics, while providing entertainment for the community.
Sponsor: US/DoD - Air Force
Contact: Michael W. Mills, Director
Description: The *Flint Airshow* has an economic impact each year of more than $1.5 million to the Flint area, and a major impact on the annual budget of *Area III Special Olympics*. Organizers feel that the show, which features the *United States Air Force Thunderbirds* and is geared toward family entertainment, is a way to give something back to the community for their assistance.
The beginnings of the show are in 1984 when, with virtually no money, a handful of volunteers, and very little support, the City of Flint and Bishop Airport approved plans for the event. Since then the Airshow has grown to be Genesee County's single largest weekend event with a budget of more than $250,000. It includes skydivers, wing-walkers, and other athletic feats as well as airplane maneuvers. The show represents a year's planning and organizing, and 500 volunteers throughout the year. In addition to raising funds, volunteers work with scheduling and other logistical aspects of the show. Planning for the subsequent year begins almost immediately following the close of each show.
The majority of volunteers come from *Area III Special Olympics*. Other volunteers include the *Genesee County Sheriff's Department* and its Special Deputies, *125th Combat Support Company of the Michigan Army National Guard, Young Marines, ROTC, Flint Township* and *Flint Police*, Flint businesses, and many others. Beginning with the 1990 show, the future of the *Flint Airshow* is in the hands of the *Bishop Airport Authority*.
The director believes that the fact that the Airshow is financed entirely by corporate sponsorship, advertising, and admission tickets and volunteer staff is a success story of its own.
Founded: 1984

JAIL 'N BAIL ON CAPITOL HILL
March of Dimes
National Capital Area Chapter
2700 South Quincy Street, Ste 220
Arlington, VA 22206
TEL: 703-824-0111
Purpose: To raise funds to help prevent birth defects.
Sponsor: US Congress Staff; March of Dimes
Contact: Leo Schargorodski, Editor
Description: In December 1988, Capitol Hill staffers were "arrested" by the March of Dimes of the National Capital Area - by agreement - to help prevent birth defects; the "Hill Arrest" involved the incarceration of good-natured volunteers at the Tiber Creek Pub in the Bellevue Hotel on Capitol Hill.
The "jailbirds" were sentenced to calling their friends and business associates, seeking donations for the March of Dimes.

Participating offices included those of Congressmen Oberstar, Whittaker, Hunter, Kyl, Chandler and Ackerman, and of Senator Metzenbaum.

Although many staffers claimed they were "framed" in the "Hill Arrest," the only "record" these ex-cons had to beat was a goal of $12,000 to ensure a healthy birth for all of their newborn and future constituents.

Publications: Jail 'N Bail Report

WALKAMERICA
March of Dimes Birth Defects Foundation
National Capital Area Chapter
2700 Quincy Street, Suite 220
Arlington, VA 22206
TEL: 703-824-0111
Purpose: To raise funds to help prevent birth defects.
Sponsor: March of Dimes Birth Defects Foundation (national); local business, industry, and individuals
Contact: S. Ross Hechinger, Honorary Chairman
Description: WalkAmerica is the March of Dimes national walk-a-thon. The national capital area chapter sponsors WalkAmerica annually in April. It is the biggest springtime event in the Washington, DC metropolitan area. Thousands of people come out for a festive day of fun and fellowship, while raising money to fight birth defects.

Whether walkers raise $5 or $5,000 by walking the 30 kilometer event, the money helps to secure a healthier beginning for all of our children.

TeamWalk is people walking together as a team of *WalkAmerica.* It is a very popular volunteer activity with corporations and organizations. Teams adorned in T-shirts and hats show their team pride and take on the competition. Building a team is an organizational activity and is considered a challenge, a way of meeting people with similar concerns and talking about civic involvement, and a way of helping give every baby a healthy start in life. In addition, volunteers say "It is fun!"

In what is called "The Team Recipe," the Teamleader coordinates the team effort, sets team goals, develops strategies to reach goals, and is the "spark" that makes things happen. He or she must first organize a committee to help promote the team, recruit team members, challenge another department or division within the company, and help encourage the registration and fill out cards. This Chapter uses the "Pyramid Method," which asks each person that registers to recruit three other people among family, friends and associates.

Team promotion includes announcements in the Company newsletter, letters from the boss, Company prizes, "Team Barometer" using a wall chart with names of walkers, and close collaboration and cooperation with committees.

Organizational backing is represented by endorsement of top management, a company van to supply refreshments to team along walk route, recognition of walkers by the company after the event, setting a Corporate Challenge in funding goals and challenging another company within the industry classification.

Tips to walkers include: arrive early, dress appropriately, listen to your body, celebrate.

Committee members include U.S. Treasury Department, Virginia Power, DC Public Schools, United Airlines, House of Representatives, Ameritemps, Stouffer Hotels, Hechinger Company, Children's Defense Fund, Sovran Bank, Electrical Workers' Union, and others.

Publications: TeamWalk Team Leader Guide

WHITE CANE DRIVE
SEE RECIPIENTS: HANDICAPPED - BLIND

RECIPIENTS: HANDICAPPED - I&R

NATIONAL/STATE ORGANIZATIONS

CEC SPECIAL PROJECT: ERIC CLEARINGHOUSE ON HANDICAPPED AND GIFTED CHILDREN
Council for Exceptional Children
1920 Association Drive
Reston, VA 22091-1589
TEL: 703-264-9474 (project); 703-620-3660 (office)
Objectives: To provide information and referral assistance to individuals and agencies working with exceptional children.
Services: Collects and abstracts special education documents for the ERIC database, which contains over 700,000 items; provides database searches, printed literature, and referral assistance to agencies and individuals needing information on children with handicaps or gifted learners.

CLEARINGHOUSE ON DISABILITY INFORMATION
US/DEd - Office of Special Education and Rehabilitative Services
Switzer Building
Room 3132
Washington, DC 20202-2524
TEL: 202-732-1241; 202-732-1245
Objectives: To respond to inquiries on a wide number of topics affecting disabled persons.
Services: Conducts research and provides information on operations serving the handicapped field on national, state and local levels; maintains extensive information in areas of Federal funding for programs serving disabled people, Federal legislation affecting the handicapped community, and Federal programs benefiting people with handicapping conditions; refers inquirers to appropriate sources; publishes a newsletter, legislation summaries, reports, and guides to benefits and services for qualified individuals.
Sponsor: US/DEd - Department of Education
Publications: OSERS News in Print; Summary of Existing Legislation Affecting Disabled Persons; Educating Students with Learning Problems: Shared Responsibility; Pocket Guide to Federal Help for Individuals with Disabilities
Founded: 1973

CLEARINGHOUSE ON THE HANDICAPPED*
US/DEd - Division for the Handicapped
Switzer Building
Washington, DC 20202-2524
TEL: 202-245-0080
Objectives: To provide a central source of information on policies, programs, procedures and activities relevant to the handicapped.
Services: Responds to inquiries on a wide range of topics concerning handicapping conditions and related services; researches and monitors information operations on national, state and local levels; provides technical assistance; maintains comprehensive, current information on federal funding for programs serving the handicapped, federal programs and federal legislation; produces publications primarily for information providers, such as *Directory of National Information Sources on Handicapping Conditions and Related Services*; publishes a bimonthly newsletter, *Programs for the Handicapped,* which announces new clearinghouses, and other publications, and monitors activities of federal agencies.
Sponsor: US/DEd - Department of Education
Founded: 1975

NATIONAL CENTER FOR HEARING DOG INFORMATION
SEE PHYSICAL ENVIRONMENT: WILDLIFE/PETS

NATIONAL INFORMATION CENTER FOR CHILDREN AND YOUTH WITH HANDICAPS
PO Box 1492
Washington, DC 20013
TEL: 703-893-6061; 703-893-8614 (TDD)
TOLL FREE: 800-999-5599 (recording)
Objectives: To assist parents, educators, caregivers, advocates and others in helping children and youth with disabilities to become participating members of the community.
Services: Provides personal responses to specific questions, referrals to other organizations/sources of help, and prepared information packets for frequently-asked questions (lists of state agencies and local parent groups, referral to specific sources, information on legal rights and parent advocacy, and other information and materials as available); requires inquiry by letter due to volume of information available; publishes biennial newsletter, state resources sheets, fact sheets, parent guides and other materials; offers technical assistance to parent, professional, advocate, caregiving and other groups working with handicapped children.
Contact: Information Specialist
Publications: News Digest
Founded: 1970

RECIPIENTS: HANDICAPPED - INDEPENDENT LIVING

NATIONAL/STATE ORGANIZATIONS

AMERICAN FOUNDATION FOR THE BLIND
SEE RECIPIENTS: HANDICAPPED - BLIND

ASSOCIATED SERVICES FOR THE BLIND
SEE RECIPIENTS: HANDICAPPED - BLIND

INDEPENDENT LIVING FOR THE HANDICAPPED
800 Third Street, NE
Washington, DC 20002
TEL: 202-547-4644
Objectives: To promote barrier-free housing for handicapped persons; to administer training programs to develop a bank of attendants for those who need such assistance.
Services: Operates through a volunteer board of directors to administer programs to improve the quality of life of the handicapped; conducts the 30-hour ILH Training Program for personal care assistants (PCAs), which is a free course held in two six-week cycles, and covers motion, nutrition, adaptative equipment, etc.; builds barrier-free apartments with funds received from national and local funding sources ($10,000 from Local Initiatives Support Corporation and a no-interest loan from Change-All Souls Housing, for example); operates an information and referral service, an advocacy program, and a public awareness campaign; operates a volunteer driver program seven days a week; involves volunteers in menu-planning, swimming, arts, reading bills and important documents for the blind, "outdoor trippers," gardeners, etc. - all to help keep the handicapped independent in their own homes; publishes the *ILH Newsletter* monthly to report on its programs and individual successes and news items about and by the handicapped persons served.
Publications: ILH Newsletter

NATIONAL FEDERATION OF INTERFAITH VOLUNTEER CAREGIVERS
105 Mary's Avenue
PO Box 1939
Kingston, NY 12401
TEL: 914-331-1358
Objectives: To help meet the growing need of the isolated, frail elderly and disabled people.
Services: The National Federation of Interfaith Volunteer Caregivers (IVC) was founded in 1987 with start-up financial support from the Robert Wood Johnson Foundation and the Pew Charitable Trusts. Its purposes are to support the development of new IVC projects around the country and to encourage the growing movement and networking of Interfaith Volunteer Caregivers projects. The Federation's roots are in 1983 when the Foundation, recognizing that the nation's population of frail elderly and disabled people is growing rapidly, with many living alone with few resources, announced a three-year national program to try to strengthen the the role family, friends and neighbors play - often unrecognized - in caring for disabled people of all ages. The plan was to see whether interfaith coalitions could be formed successfully for this purpose. The coalitions would recruit, train, and match volunteers with frail elderly and disabled people, thereby enabling them to continue living independently in the community and avoiding as long as possible placement in a nursing home.
In funding the Interfaith Volunteer Caregivers Program, the Foundation both acknowledged the importance of nonprofessional caregivers and recognized the tradition among religious congregations of serving the needs of others. The overwhelming response to the Foundation's 1983 call for proposals reflected a high level of awareness and a willingness of congregations to work together. The Foundation had a goal of 15 interfaith coalitions with funding level of $150,000 each. Approximately 1,000 requests were received from 48 states. Consequently the Foundation increased the number of grantees to 25 with a three-year award of $150,000 to each grantee.
The twenty-five IVC grantees were chosen from across the country, and the interfaith coalitions they had organized served densely urban, suburban, and rural communities alike. Volunteers were recruited from churches, synagogues, and other religious institutions reflective of the community.
Requirements for funding include the interfaith coalition representing a community's religious congregations to be responsible for the project, a minimum community population of 25,000 and a full-time director. The funded projects were located in 17 states, the District of Columbia, and the territory of Guam. Within the first year of operation, each project recruited an average of 140 volunteers and served 380 people. Within the three-year grant period, more than 26,000 persons were served, many on an ongoing basis, and more than 11,000 volunteers were recruited, trained, and matched with people in need.
The many different services provided by volunteers include: transportation, shopping, advocacy and referral, friendly visiting, and telephone reassurance, with some providing home care such as assistance in meal preparation, and respite for family caregivers.
Based on the experiences of the grantee programs, the ideal approach to implementing a successful project includes:
● Committed members who feel strong ownership of the project.
● Advisory board with balanced representation from clergy, agencies and community members.
● Director with networking abilities within the community, an understanding of religious institutions and how to work with volunteers.
● Strong well-trained coordinators within congregations.
● System for locating those most in need and introducing volunteers into the home situations.
● Chain of support from coalition to board, to director, to coordinators, to volunteers, to those being served.

● Introduction into the overall community support system for mutual support, referral, and networking.

● A community-wide commitment to ongoing project funding.

Among the benefits volunteers cited when asked about their participation were: companionship, work experience, good use of time, good feeling from helping others, making friends, fulfilling a sense of obligation to the community, religion, or society.

One of the project directors credited the success of the concept this way: "Volunteers are most effective when they are part of a balanced mix of public and private initiatives - with each learning from and supporting the others in their work. When agencies and professional caregivers do their part, volunteers can do theirs better."

Two studies of the coalitions have been completed - one by the National Program Office at Benedictine Hospital, Kingston, New York, and the other by Fordham University's Third Age Center (the latter funded by the Foundation to assess the program).

Sponsor: Robert Wood Johnson Foundation

Publications: Interfaith Volunteer Caregivers: A Special Report; Caregivers Quarterly (newsletter); Benedictine Hospital Study; Fordham University Evaluation

Founded: 1987

INDIVIDUAL PROGRAM PROFILES

COLLEGE-IN-RESIDENCE VOLUNTEERS (CIRV)
Washington Department of Social & Health Services
Box 200
Medical Lake, WA 99022
TEL: 509-299-5087

Purpose: To assist developmentally disabled residents in their daily lives.

Sponsor: Department of Social and Health Services, State of Washington

Contact: Diane White

Description: Called the College-in-Residence Volunteers program (CIRV), this program furnishes free room and board to college students in return for 15 hours of volunteer service per week. Students must be taking a minimum of 10 credits per quarter and maintain a C average to continue in the program.

The program has 30 positions at this time. The students live in bachelor apartments with a private bath or two to one double-bedroom apartment. The program is designed for single students, unless both the husband and wife are enrolled in college, then they both must work 15 hours per week.

The students perform a variety of duties. Some of their job assignments are in psychology, social work, clerical, recreation, pre-vocational/vocational training of developmentally disabled residents.

The students involved in the program must be willing to work, have strong initiative, and be interested in helping developmentally disabled residents.

There is a packet of rules and regulations that the student must abide by or be terminated from the program.

Lakeland Village is a state residential facility serving developmentally disabled residents, from the ages of 12-78 years old, male and female. Over 90% of the population is severely to profoundly retarded.

The CIRV Program has been ongoing for the last thirteen years.

Publications: Service from the Heart; CIRV Rules and Regulations

Founded: 1969

UNE SOIREE PARISIENNE (AN EVENING IN PARIS)
Outreach & Escort
San Jose, CA 95101
TEL: 408-436-2865

Purpose: To raise funds for a program designed to help disabled people lead independent lives.

Sponsor: Outreach & Escort

Contact: Terry Bialas, Event Coordinator

Description: Outreach & Escort is a service that finances the transportation needs and support services that allow disabled people to lead independent lives. Each year, volunteers and staff plan a fund-raiser using a theme that mimics an exotic, distant locale. The 1988 event was a lavish *Far East Fest* featuring Asian food, music and dance.

The theme for 1989 is *Une Soiree Parisienne* or *An Evening in Paris,* chosen for the program's tenth anniversary to coincide with the bicentennial of the French Republic. Much care was taken to assure that people will savor the tastes, sights and sounds of Paris in the evening, with four-star French cuisine, and strolling musicians, singers and can-can dancers providing the entertainment. American and French flags were displayed, with both national anthems played while they were being put into place. The lavish experience costs an individual $89.10, and a group of ten (one table) $891.00. Both types of reservations are quickly depleted after announcements are made of the unique cultural opportunities each year. This event is a major fund-raiser for Outreach & Escort, which annually serves more than 7,000 disabled people.

RECIPIENTS: HANDICAPPED - LEARNING-DISABLED

NATIONAL/STATE ORGANIZATIONS

FOUNDATION FOR CHILDREN WITH LEARNING DISABILITIES
99 Park Avenue
Sixth Floor
New York, NY 10016
TEL: 212-687-7211

Objectives: To address the needs of learning disabled children; to increase public awareness of these needs.

Services: Provides direct financial support to programs which academically and socially aid learning disabled children; sponsors projects and fund-raising benefits; works closely with a professional advisory board on all foundation activities; provides information on programs and progress to any group or individual.

Founded: 1977

LEARNING DISABILITIES ASSOCIATION OF AMERICA
(*formerly Association for Children and Adults with Learning Disabilities*)
4156 Liberty Road
Pittsburgh, PA 15234
TEL: 412-341-1515

Objectives: To advance the education and welfare of children with adequate intelligence who have specific learning disabilities.

Services: Provides technical and other assistance to state and local programs (schools, camps, recreation programs, parent education programs, information services, development and publication of books/pamphlets, etc.); conducts research into the link between juvenile delinquency and learning disabilities; works directly with school systems on early diagnosis and remediation; provides parent-counseling, nursery school, and day camps through some 800 chapters; sponsors many active committees working to create awareness and stimulate activity; publishes bimonthly Newsbriefs, a bibliography of more than 500 publications; intermittent conference proceedings and other materials.

Publications: LDA Journal; LDA Newsbriefs

Founded: 1964

INDIVIDUAL PROGRAM PROFILES

RECREATION PROGRAMS FOR LEARNING DISABLED TEENS & ADULTS
YWCA of the National Capital Area
8101 Wolftrap Road
Dunn Loring, VA 22027
TEL: 703-560-1111 (VA); 301-460-3900 (MD)
Purpose: To enable participants to build self-esteem, develop social skills, and form friendships.
Contact: Program Coordinator
Description: Two recreational groups for individuals with learning disabilities - one for teens and another for young adults - are offered in several locations in the Washington, DC, metropolitan area. Organized by parents and volunteers, the programs include bike rides, bowling, concerts, dancing, dinner theatre shows, game nights, ice skating, movies, pot luck suppers, sporting events, swimming, and field trips.
The program uses recreational activities in a structured, supportive setting to help participants gain confidence while forming friendships and developing social skills. Each group meets approximately twice a month, with about half of the activities held at YWCA locations. Each registered participant receives advance schedules of events by mail. Although there is a small fee for participation, scholarships are available for those who cannot afford to pay.

RECIPIENTS: HANDICAPPED - LEGAL RIGHTS

NATIONAL/STATE ORGANIZATIONS

AMERICAN COALITION OF CITIZENS WITH DISABILITIES*
SEE RECIPIENTS: HANDICAPPED - EMPLOYMENT

CO-ORDINATING COUNCIL FOR HANDICAPPED CHILDREN
SEE RECIPIENTS: HANDICAPPED - CHILDREN/YOUTH

INDIVIDUAL PROGRAM PROFILES

PARKING POSSE
Handicapped Parking Enforcement Team
Flint Police Department
1101 South Saginaw Street
Flint, MI 48502
TEL: 313-232-7111
Purpose: To police handicapped parking spaces.
Sponsor: City of Flint
Contact: Chief of Police
Description: The only handicapped parking patrol in Michigan is the result of a Flint ordinance adopted in summer 1988 setting up the city's *Handicapped Parking Enforcement Team.* A year later results showed that the team (sometimes called the "parking posse") has significantly improved handicapped parking enforcement - averaging more than 180 parking violations a month compared with 34 a month handed out by Flint police before the citizen force was formed. Volunteers, ranging in age from 19 to 78, are trained by police officers "to teach healthy-but-lazy people not to park in spaces reserved for the handicapped."
This use of deputized volunteers has caught the attention of the

state legislature, with a proposed law offered by a state Senator. The bill is modeled after the Flint ordinance enabling authorization for trained volunteers to ticket those illegally parked in zones for the handicapped. The Secretary of State has endorsed the proposal for statewide participation.
Founded: 1988

RECIPIENTS: HANDICAPPED - MENTALLY RETARDED

NATIONAL/STATE ORGANIZATIONS

ASSOCIATION FOR RETARDED CITIZENS
PO Box 6109
2501 Avenue J
Arlington, TX 76006
TEL: 817-640-0204
Objectives: To prevent mental retardation, find its cures, and assist mentally retarded persons in their daily living.
Services: Trains volunteers working with the mentally retarded; develops effective advocacy systems; furthers employment opportunities for the mentally retarded; conducts research studies on prevention and cure; develops demonstration models for educational, training and residential facilities; answers lay and professional inquiries through relevant publications or by letter; publishes an extensive number of publications including pamphlets, monographs, books, handbooks and audiovisuals related to parenting, child development, citizen advocacy, civil rights, education, recreation, etc.; publishes newsletters which report on local ARC projects, research and legislative activities and *The ARC,* a bimonthly publication.

JOINT ADVOCACY COALITION FOR THE MENTALLY DISABLED
SEE MENTAL HEALTH: ADVOCACY

KENNEDY INTERNS IN RECREATION*
Ruby M. Gebauer, Coordinator
Route 3, Box 165P
Hammond, LA 70401
TEL: 504-567-3111
Objectives: To expand job training and opportunities in the leisure industry for in-school mentally retarded youth.
Services: Arranges for on-the-job experience depending on intern's interest and qualifications (pre-school teacher aide; recreation assistant, arts/crafts counselor aide, music store clerk, librarian aide, grounds maintenance person, lifeguard, cashier, etc.); pays client/intern's salary up to a year; requires employer to continue for at least one additional year. (This program is co-sponsored by the Department of Labor, Youthwork, Inc., and Special Olympics, Inc.); age requirement for intern is 16 to 21.

MENTAL RETARDATION ASSOCIATION OF AMERICA
211 East 300 South Street
Suite 212
Salt Lake City, UT 84111
TEL: 801-328-1575
Objectives: To work for the improvement of the quality of life for the mentally retarded.
Services: Provides general advocacy, information and referral and other services in matters of importance to the quality of life for mentally retarded individuals; includes parents, relatives, friends, and professionals as volunteers; works with federal government

agencies on monitoring existing programs and assuring new ones as needed; keeps the public informed on matters pertaining to mental retardation; encourages the development of community-based homes with family-like atmospheres in compliance with accepted standards, recommends similar homes on campuses of institutions; promotes research aimed at preventing mental retardation in the future; assists parents and legal guardians in matters of legal rights and responsibilities.
Founded: 1974

NATIONAL DOWN SYNDROME CONGRESS

1800 Dempster Street
Park Ridge, IL 60068
TEL: 312-823-7550
Objectives: To provide parent support, advocacy, and public awareness programs for Down Syndrome.
Services: Operates through a committee structure which includes committees on adoption, awards, citizens, fundraising, education, media production and review, parent groups, awards, siblings, research and text-editing, and convention; advises and aids parents in the solutions of their special needs; coordinates efforts and activities of parents and others; operates a clearinghouse to gather and disseminate information for parents, other interested individuals and groups; mounts public awareness programs that are designed to promote a better understanding of Down Syndrome; maintains an all-volunteer board of directors consisting of educators, medical professionals, business men and women, housewives, government employees, adult Down Syndrome citizens and others; publishes the monthly *Down Syndrome News,* a bibliography, public awareness booklets, and other materials.
Publications: Down Syndrome News; Down Syndrome (booklet)
Founded: 1974

PRESIDENT'S COMMITTEE ON MENTAL RETARDATION

RO Building
7th & D Streets, SW
Washington, DC 20201
TEL: 202-245-7634
Objectives: To promote public understanding of the mentally retarded; to keep the President informed in this area.
Services: Stimulates individual, group, and media action; fosters cooperation among public and private agencies; recommends federal action where needed; works with the President.

INDIVIDUAL PROGRAM PROFILES

FRIEND TO FRIEND PROGRAM*
SEE PSYCHOSOCIAL SUPPORT SERVICES

PATOWMACK HERBAL FARM: SUMMER EMPLOYMENT FOR THE HANDICAPPED
Association for Retarded Citizens
Loudoun County Chapter
15 East Market Street
Leesburg, VA 22075
TEL: 703-777-1939
Purpose: To provide jobs for the handicapped while helping the small farmer to find affordable workers.
Sponsor: Patowmack Herbal Farm
Contact: Barbara June Appelgren, Director
Description: When a small farmer found the going rate of $6.00 for farm workers to be too high for her budget, she called the Loudoun County Association for Retarded Citizens. She had heard that advocates for the handicapped are always looking for summer work for them. Although the Association had never placed handicapped teenagers in private sector jobs, the Director felt it was time to experiment with a small group. Six mentally- and

physically-handicapped youngsters were sent to Patowmack Herbal Farm to plant, pick and weed garlic crops. The youth were selected because they had demonstrated a high degree of independence. Handicaps ranged from mental retardation and emotional problems to spina bifida and brittle bones. When they first arrived at the farm, much time had to be spent to show them what to do. They were uncertain of themselves and exhibited a low tolerance for teasing, often getting into scraps. They took frequent water breaks, which tended to become times for "goofing off." Some of them had done yard chores, but had only a vague idea of what it means to work regularly - most never having worked a six-hour-long period before. However, with much time and patience freely given by the owners, they were completing assigned tasks, anticipating the next chores and avoiding friction.
For five weeks they worked through muggy days in muddy fields to harvest about 8,000 elephant garlic bulbs - a mild form of garlic prized by chefs which rots if left in the ground too long. In addition to the harvesting, assignments included sorting garlic, weeding sage, mowing lawns, and producing labels on a copying machine and pasting them on vinegar bottles. They were allowed to choose their tasks. At the same time, they reveled in the fresh air, learned about herbs, and "befriending chickens."
Awareness that what they were doing was the way the farm owners made money turned out to be an important concept to the handicapped teens. Also, their own paychecks, at $4.00 an hour, helped them understand what it means to "earn a living." And the parents of the teens, realizing that they will not always be around to support the youngsters, were grateful for the opportunity provided the youngsters to learn an important fact - "if you don't work, you don't get paid."
The Association's coordinator at the job site sees this experience as a major step toward independent living and believes that each of the youngsters in the program will be able to live in a supervised apartment setting - with a couple of them not requiring the supervision at all. She cited a bed and breakfast inn near Winchester, Virginia, that is run entirely by retarded people and feels that people like the owners of Patowmack Herbal Farm help speed the process toward independence for the handicapped.
An added pleasure was to witness the feelings the youth had developed for the Furnace Mountain farm as a special place, and their intentions to return.

SAN FRANCISCO SPECIAL OLYMPICS WINTER GAMES
c/o Shaklee Corporation
444 Market Street
San Francisco, CA 94111
TEL: 415-221-6575
Purpose: To promote physical fitness and provide an experience in skill building and increased confidence for mentally handicapped participants.
Sponsor: Shaklee Corporation
Description: The San Francisco Special Olympics Games began at Soda Springs in 1977 when only five San Francisco athletes could compete. The raw talent and enthusiasm displayed by these five athletes warranted that the winter games program be expanded and become a permanent part of the Special Olympics program. Members of the San Francisco Special Olympics Board approached the Shaklee Corporation for the help needed to expand the program. The Shaklee Corporation agreed to become the corporate sponsor of the Winter Games Program.
In the years following, the Winter Games Program has seen an even more rapid growth pattern. In 1979, 25 athletes and eight chaperones were active in the California State Special Olympics Winter Games at Dodge Ridge. This represented an increase of five times the original number. Since 1982, over 100 athletes participated in winter activities.
The surrounding communities in the Tahoe area became involved, and volunteer ski instructors and other assistance came from local ski hills, ski shops, and nurses from the community hospital.

Equipment was donated by the Boreal Ridge Ski Area, and owners of demonstration vans loaned equipment from various manufacturers.

Besides over ten years of underwriting the costs of this program, Shaklee Corporation has made available many sincere and dedicated personnel to assist as chaperones and to help in the training and supervision of the athletes. These employees volunteer as part of the Shaklee Volunteer Employee Program, SERVE. Also made available to each athlete has been a sports bag or backpack of Shaklee products, including energy bars and skin care products. Official winter games uniforms for the athletes were obtained through Shaklee donations. The official uniform consists of a cap, vest, goggles, after-ski boots, gloves, thermal underwear and gaiters.

The San Francisco Special Olympics is staffed by one paid Executive Director and many volunteers from both the sponsoring corporation and the community. Volunteers are involved in supervisory, management, and public relations activities as well as in training and supervision of the athletes and as chaperones.

The programs are coordinated through the Recreation and Parks Department. Ninety percent of the funding comes from the sponsoring corporation with the remaining 10% received in the form of in-kind contributions, both goods and services.
Founded: 1977

VOLUNTEER SERVICES
Stockley Center
Route 1, Box 1000
Georgetown, DE 19947
TEL: 302-934-8031/Ext. 275
Purpose: To provide additional supportive services to both the Center and Clients through dedicated volunteers.
Sponsor: Stockley Center; Delaware Division of Mental Retardation
Contact: Josephine Y. Patterson, Coordinator
Description: Volunteer programs for the mentally retarded residents have played an important role at *Stockley* since 1965 providing approximately 700 volunteer hours monthly. Tasks which the volunteers perform vary tremendously, each offering a special talent in its own way. Volunteer opportunities for individuals include music, art, ceramics and other craftwork, letter writing, reading and assisting with various recreational activities including escort services and maintaining individual gardens during the growing season.

Civic organizations, clubs, schools, youth and church groups participate in all areas at this facility and often provide financial assistance for special projects. The Center receives great rewards from good volunteers and they gain valuable knowledge in the field of Mental Retardation. His/her services can be a stimulating experience with the many new concepts being developed practically daily.

Volunteers are sought through the news media, Stockley Center Newsletter, speaking engagements, friends, relatives, personal contact, tours and by enthusiastic active volunteers.

A short orientation program is provided for all volunteers including the teens who serve during the summer.

In addition to the client volunteer program many individuals choose to be Friendly Visitors sharing several hours weekly being a special friend, taking the client off-campus to lunch or shopping.

A donation room is provided and maintained in the Coordinator's office for the benefit of the clients and staff. The supplies are made possible through clubs, civic organizations and private contributions.

Perhaps one of the greatest benefits from the use of Volunteers is one of attitude and understanding; as the community becomes more aware of the worth of each individual, the community is more tolerant of all individuals.
Founded: 1965

WESTERN CAROLINA CENTER VOLUNTEERS
Western Carolina Center
Volunteer Services
Enola Road
Morganton, NC 28655
TEL: 704-433-2614
Purpose: To offer volunteer opportunities for teenagers age 13 and older that will benefit mentally retarded children and adults.
Sponsor: West Carolina Center
Contact: Volunteer Coordinator
Description: This program provides the much-needed opportunity for minor teenagers to become involved in a volunteer activity. It takes into consideration the benefits the energy and enthusiasm of this age group can bring to the mentally retarded. Conversely, this activity is beneficial to the teenagers in providing work experience, career exploration and, in many cases, a first job.

To volunteer at the center, besides the desire to help others, a teenager must be 13 or going into the eighth grade, provide his or her lunch and transportation, be ready to work with people with special needs, and be able to accept supervision - and constructive criticism when necessary - from a professional staff.

Western Carolina Center is a residential center for children and adults in North Carolina who are mentally retarded. Supported by the State Government, its staff and volunteers provide residents with everything from medical care to recreation. Teenagers are involved in the same areas as adult volunteers as appropriate, including:

- **Areas of direct care** - recreation, medical services, psychology, physical therapy, dentistry, special education, infant care, fine arts, and dietary assistance.
- **Areas of indirect care** - maintenance, housekeeping, clerical, and secretarial assistance.

Most importantly for the residents, Voluteens become friends and help to make their summer special, too. As one resident put it, "Voluteens bring SMILES."

Extra activities include fundraisers, picnics, mini-seminars, park activities, swimming, Recognition Day (which selects *Volunteer of the Summer)*, *CAROWINDS,* and other programs, often developed by the youth themselves.

Besides the obvious benefits for the teenager - job experience, career exploration, job reference - one volunteer remarked, "The best thing about volunteering is the good feeling you have about yourself."
Publications: Voluteens Are Incredible

YAI ALUMNI CLUB KARATE PROGRAM
SEE RECREATION & SPORTS: CHILDREN/YOUTH

YOUNG ADULT INSTITUTE
460 West 34th Street
New York, NY 10001-2382
TEL: 212-563-7474
FAX: 212-268-1083
Purpose: To help improve the quality of life for children and adults with mental retardation and developmental disabilities and their families.
Contact: Rick Kramer, Director
Description: The *Yount Adult Institute (YAI)* is a nonprofit agency which has served children and adults with mental retardation and developmental disabilities for over three decades in more than 50 programs throughout the New York Metropolitan area. YAI involves mothers, entire families, community groups, and others in committees, fairs, and other activities to help meet its goals. Specifically, programs at YAI include:

In-Home Respite - These programs are designed to provide a desperately-needed break from the demands of raising a disabled child. In 1989, 206 families in Manhattan, Brooklyn, and Queens were served by the program. In addition to the in-home services, the program serves small groups of children during holidays, summer vacations, and special events (in order for parents to attend community camp fairs, family picnics, and conferences). There is an active mothers' group in Queens and a similar group starting up in Brooklyn. In addition to parent involvement, the program receives funding from the borough governments to help YAI assist an additional 30 to 100 families waiting for service.

Drop-Off Respite - This is a center-based respite program provided 48 Saturdays each year to 52 families in Brooklyn and Queens. There is a schedule of trips and events planned, including basketball and baseball games, movies, dinner, social events, etc. Special efforts are made to have enough individuals on hand to keep the program open on holidays.

Extend-A-Family - This program enlists families "who have room in their homes and their hearts" to provide overnight respite care to a guest with a developmental disability. Each family's home is checked to ensure safety features, such as fire extinguishers and smoke detectors. Sixteen hours of training is provided for the host family, and YAI staff visit during the respite for support and supervision.

Independent Living Project - This is a course that involves family involvement as the trainees go through a program geared toward independent living; the graduation ceremony includes family members as "graduates," and continuing follow-up is provided. The first such training event was held in April 1990 with 15 trainees and ten families participating.

Family Training Program - Two six-session events in this program provided 614 hours of training and respite services to 50 families in 1989, and involved 112 families in an early-1990 event. The workshops focus on behavior management, future planning, and teaching skills for parents. Respite is provided on site so that family members can participate. This program has brought in new families who are now on our waiting lists for residential and day services.

Crisis Intervention Program - Advocacy and networking both in-home and community-based crisis services are provided (232 families in Queens and Manhattan in 1989-90), with typical crisis situations including persons who are homeless, abused and in severe stress.

Project Intervene - This program provides specialized training for the family and the disabled child to improve the home situation. (123 families in Brooklyn and Manhattan were served in 1989-90.)

Family Support Committees/Fairs - The *Family Support Commitee* plans and administers areawide family support fairs to help spread the word to families about YAI services. Over 500 families attended the first fair and received information about new services and techniques and heard experts in the field speak on the subject of MR/DD.

Minority Access - YAI works with agencies which serve minorities for referrals, including the *Chinese American Planning Council, Sinergia,* and the *Caribbean Women's Health Association.* A side benefit are the resulting translations of YAI materials into Spanish and Chinese, and the two-hour workshop entirely for Spanish-speaking caregivers.

Task Force for Curriculum Development - A supervising psychologist of the state task force assisted YAI in developing a parent training curriculum.

YAI Recreational Programs - These programs range from the Brooklyn Saturday Recreation Program to the Alumni Club for highly independent adults and from a karate program for the children to the Saturday Evening Drop-Off Center programs. Self-evaluation is continuous in the program with an eye toward streamlining practices and freeing up enough funds to begin some new ideas and increase the levels of service to and participation by families of mentally retarded and developmentally disabled individuals.

RECIPIENTS: HANDICAPPED - MULTIPLE SCLEROSIS

INDIVIDUAL PROGRAM PROFILES

MULTIPLE SCLEROSIS SOCIETY OF ORANGE COUNTY
2500 Michelson Drive
Irvine, CA 92715
TEL: 714-752-1680
Purpose: To provide a wide range of services to people in the county with multiple sclerosis.
Sponsor: National Multiple Sclerosis Society
Contact: Deborah Ballard, Director
Description: The Orange County, California, chapter of the National Multiple Sclerosis Society provides services to 2,000 people in the county known to have multiple sclerosis, and to their friends and families. Multiple sclerosis is a disease of the central nervous system that usually strikes people between the ages of 20 and 40.
One of the greatest strengths of the program is the self-help component, which includes 12 support groups, divided among those with special needs (such as people whose disease has been diagnosed recently), people with more severe cases, and spouses. More personal attention is given by volunteer peer supporters, each of whom has had the disease for at least two years and has been trained to help people understand the disorder.
Patients and their families are referred to any services they might require, including doctors, exercise programs, transportation and equipment such as wheelchairs, canes and walkers. The chapter also has a library and provides educational seminars.
Founded: 1974

RECIPIENTS: HANDICAPPED - NUTRITION

INDIVIDUAL PROGRAM PROFILES

SENIORS: SPECIAL DELIVERY
SEE NUTRITION: DELIVERY

RECIPIENTS: HANDICAPPED - PSYCHOSOCIAL SUPPORT

NATIONAL/STATE ORGANIZATIONS

FOSTER GRANDPARENT PROGRAM (FGP)
US/ACTION - The Federal Volunteer Agency
1100 Vermont Avenue, NW
Suite 1100
Washington, DC 20525
TEL: 202-634-9108
TOLL FREE: 800-424-8580
Objectives: To provide part-time volunteer service opportunities for low-income persons aged 60 or over; to render supportive person-to-person services to children having special or exceptional needs.

Services: Provides grants to public agencies and private nonprofit organizations to develop and manage local projects to provide foster grandparents to children in health, education, welfare and related settings. Grant applicants must demonstrate:
- ability to operate the grant effectively;
- availability of eligible volunteers;
- transportation plan for volunteers;
- community support

Publishes a handbook and a number of recruitment flyers and other materials.
Contact: Roy Tejada
Publications: FGP Operations Handbook; Where Love Grows

INDIVIDUAL PROGRAM PROFILES

COMPANIONSHIP/THERAPY PROGRAM
SEE PSYCHOSOCIAL SUPPORT SERVICES

FRIEND TO FRIEND PROGRAM*
SEE PSYCHOSOCIAL SUPPORT SERVICES

OPERATION GOOD NEIGHBOR
SEE MENTAL HEALTH: FOSTER CARE

A PERFECT MATCH
Ebensburg Center
Old Main
Ebensburg, PA 15931
TEL: 814-472-7350/Ext. 592-3
Purpose: To provide reciprocal social contact and personal attention for the mentally and physically handicapped residents of the Ebensburg Center and the older patients of Laurel Crest Manor (County Home).
Sponsor: Ebensburg Center and Laurel Crest Manor
Contact: Richard Nikolishen
Description: The program deals with the severely and profoundly mentally and physically handicapped residents of the Ebensburg Center who needs lots of love and training, and the older patients of Laurel Crest Manor who have lots of love and affection. In addition, they have the time and experience to share.
The patients of Laurel Crest Manor are escorted by their staff to the Ebensburg Center one day a week for two hours. Under the supervision of the Ebensburg Center's staff, each patient is assigned one resident and they either reinforce a training program or just provide company for each other.
Laurel Crest Manor and the Ebensburg Center are located in Cambria County approximately four miles apart. This closeness has ensured fewer cancellations of the program because of bad weather.
The program started in October 1981 and is still working.
Founded: 1981

PROJECT PASSAGE
SEE PSYCHOSOCIAL SUPPORT SERVICES

THERAPEUTIC RIDING PROGRAM
SEE RECIPIENTS: HANDICAPPED - RECREATION/SPORTS

THERAPY ON HORSEBACK*
SEE RECIPIENTS: HANDICAPPED - RECREATION/SPORTS

RECIPIENTS: HANDICAPPED - READING

NATIONAL/STATE ORGANIZATIONS

NATIONAL BRAILLE ASSOCIATION
SEE RECIPIENTS: HANDICAPPED - BLIND

TAPES FOR THE BLIND
SEE RECIPIENTS: HANDICAPPED - BLIND

INDIVIDUAL PROGRAM PROFILES

FRIENDS OF HANDICAPPED READERS
SEE EDUCATION: LIBRARY SERVICES

RECIPIENTS: HANDICAPPED - RECREATION/SPORTS

NATIONAL/STATE ORGANIZATIONS

AMERICAN ATHLETIC ASSOCIATION FOR THE DEAF*
SEE RECIPIENTS: HANDICAPPED - DEAF

AMERICAN BLIND BOWLING ASSOCIATION
SEE RECIPIENTS: HANDICAPPED - BLIND

KENNEDY INTERNS IN RECREATION*
SEE RECIPIENTS: HANDICAPPED - MENTALLY RETARDED

SPECIAL OLYMPICS INTERNATIONAL
1350 New York Avenue, NW
Suite 500
Washington, DC 20005
TEL: 202-628-3630
Objectives: To provide athletic competition for the mentally retarded.
Services: Tests and adapts activities so that they will provide the maximum of fun and benefit for the mentally retarded (swimming, gymnastics, bowling, ice skating, basketball and others); maintains speakers bureau; sponsors research; provides materials on organization of programs and participation of athletes (age range is from eight to adult); publishes quarterly newsletter and materials; convenes annual meeting.
Founded: 1968

SPECIAL RECREATION
SEE RECREATION & SPORTS: HANDICAPPED

TRAINING PROGRAMS

WHEELCHAIR RACE COMMUNICATIONS SERVICES
SEE DISASTER RESPONSE/EMERGENCY PREPAREDNESS

INDIVIDUAL PROGRAM PROFILES

BLUE RIDGE TO THE WHITE HOUSE: WHEELCHAIR RACE OF CHAMPIONS
National Wheelchair Athletic Association
1604 East Pikes Peak Avenue
Colorado Springs, CO 80909-5619
TEL: 303-697-8330
Purpose: To identify United States Olympic representatives for wheelchair long distance road racing.
Sponsor: Ford Motor Company
Description: The first annual "Race of Champions" for long distance wheelchair racers was held in May 1989 in Virginia and Washington, DC. The ten top wheelchair road racing athletes in the world compete for $20,000 in prizes in a grueling, double marathon (approximately 54 miles) endurance race to identify United States Olympics representatives. The race is organized in cooperation with the Mid Atlantic region of the National Wheelchair Athletic Association.
The 1989 race began at 8:00 a.m. in Purcellville, Virginia, and took the racers along some of Virginia's most scenic countryside, then into Washington, DC, past the national monuments and reflecting pool to the finish line at the Washington Monument. The estimated time of arrival for the winning racer was 12 noon, only four hours later.
Joining many other dignitaries at the finish line was Virginia's Senator Charles Robb and former White House Press Secretary James Brady, as well as members of Congress from each racer's locality and state.
Proceeds from the Blue Ridge to the White House Wheelchair Race of Champions benefits Grafton School (a residential educational facility for seriously handicapped children) and Shalom et Benedictus (a drug and alcohol treatment facility for young adolescents).
The course for the race was laid out by a wheelchair racer - an executive at the Grafton School and the Race of Champions organizer - who tested the course by "running" it himself a month before the event.
Publications: Blue Ridge to the White House Wheelchair Race of Champions

CEREBRAL PALSY SPORTS PROGRAM
SEE RECIPIENTS: HANDICAPPED - CEREBRAL PALSY

FLAME OF HOPE
Rochester Institute of Technology
Henrietta Campus
Lomb Memorial Drive
Rochester, NY 14623
TEL: 716-475-6631
Purpose: To call attention around the state to the 20th state Special Olympics Summer Games.
Sponsor: New York Law Enforcement Division
Contact: Frank Vito, Volunteer Director
Description: Various law enforcement agencies around New York State volunteer to help bring attention to the state's *Special Olympics Summer Games* with its own torch, the *Flame of Hope*. The torch is carried from the previous year's site to the current year's location. The volunteer relay runners are police officers from across the state.
For the 1989 games in Rochester, the torch came from the 1988 Buffalo location - but not by a direct route. The police officers took the opportunity to spread the word about the game by making a relay journey around the state. The 19-day activity started when the torch was sent from Buffalo to Montauk Point on Long Island before heading back west toward Rochester. The torch is taken by runners from one police facility to another, sometimes "resting" in one of them until police officers can be freed to continue the relay process. Target was arrival of the torch

at noon in downtown Rochester on the first day of the games. The climax of the journey came at 7:30 on opening day of the state games in the Dome area of the campus of the Rochester Institute of Technology (RIT) when two Special Olympics athletes helped light the flame. Athletes were chosen based on their academic and "real world" efforts, such as employment.
The 1989 state games featured 1,600 winning athletes from local games around the state. The theme reflected its long dedication to the program: *Twenty Years of Special Moments.* Over 4,000 volunteers participated.

FLINT AIRSHOW
SEE RECIPIENTS: HANDICAPPED - FUNDING

GARDEN OF YOUNG HEARTS
Special Populations Division
Chesterfield Parks and Recreation
Richmond, VA 23832
TEL: 804-748-1623
Purpose: To provide a place where mentally retarded youths could enjoy a prom of their own.
Sponsor: Knights of Columbus
Contact: Sharon Entsminger, Special Populations Manager
Description: A parent, concerned about her mentally retarded child feeling uncomfortable at regular high school proms, began the process of a special prom for these young people. *Chesterfield Parks and Recreation,* the *Knights of Columbus,* and the *Adult Career Center for Exceptional Persons* cosponsored the first prom in 1986, and have held the event each year since then. The theme for the 1989 prom was *A Garden of Young Hearts.*
Volunteers from *Acteen Activators,* a youth group from Baptist churches in the Richmond area, helped out as part of their training for a mission trip later in the year. One parent proudly pointed out that her mentally retarded son had two volunteer jobs - one at a hospital and the other with the Catholic Diocese. The teen volunteers decorated the ballroom with streamers and balloons, served refreshments, led games, and got the students dancing. The *Rubber Biscuit Band* volunteered to provide music as in previous years, stating, "We love to play for these kids because they are so appreciative." The parents were pleased to note that the band members treated the kids like normal teenagers, responding to their song requests and generally chatting with them when they approached the bandstand.
The enthusiasm of the handicapped youth soon spread to the teen volunteers and parents, who danced with and among the youths throughout the evening. According to the project director, "The kids really look forward to it, and each year it gets a little better."

GEORGIA SPECIAL OLYMPICS SUMMER GAMES
Special Olympics
3166 Chestnut Drive
Doraville, GA 30340
TEL: 404-458-3838
Purpose: To demonstrate through sports what mentally handicapped people can do with a little encouragement.
Sponsor: Coca Cola Company
Contact: Volunteer Coordinator
Description: In Georgia, the *Special Olympics* began in 1970 with 4,000 athletes. By the 1989 Summer Games, the number had grown to 11,000. In schools and institutions across the state, mentally retarded people work all year long in the hope of competing in the games. Those who participate are chosen partly on the basis of their performance in county meets, but also as a reward for good behavior. They compete with other people at their skill level in events from track and field to weightlifting. Gold medalists strive to be selected to represent Georgia at the next *International Special Olympics* (every four years).
The Coca Cola Company is the main sponsor for the statewide games, which span the weekend from Friday night to Sunday

afternoon. A highlight for the athletes is Saturday night's "Club Coca-Cola" victory dance. Emory University makes its athletic facilities available each year.

Most of the athletes live in institutions, and only about 500 family members attended the 1989 Summer Games. Some who attended for the first time were surprised and proud of their retarded children or siblings, not only of their athletic prowess, but because they saw them interact with other people, learned they had girlfriends or boyfriends, and realized that they are not really so different. It is hoped that, by word of mouth and reporting of some of the parents' feelings at the games, more parents and family members will attend to cheer on their athletes.

Founded by Eunice Kennedy Shriver in 1961, the *Special Olympics* has since spread to 75 countries, with about a million athletes taking part in more than 15,000 games, meets and tournaments.

Founded: 1970

HORSES AND THE HANDICAPPED OF SOUTH FLORIDA
Tradewinds Park
3600 West Sample Road
Coconut Creek, FL 33063
TEL: 305-974-2007
Purpose: Horses for the Handicapped teaches children and adults - who are blind, deaf, paralyzed, or stricken by strokes, cerebral palsy, autism or spina bifida - coordination and confidence through horseback riding.

Currently, the program has 12 horses and 80 students from Fort Lauderdale to Jupiter. Program goals are to serve 250 students at three locations in Broward and Palm Beach Counties. The waiting list is growing, and program leaders are trying to keep up with this growth by negotiating with Palm Beach County for 20 acres of county-owned land to establish a branch of its program. Also, a fund-raising drive is underway to build a $60,000 barn with 16 stalls at its present location in Tradewinds Park. The site at the northern end of the park is made available without charge by the County Parks and Recreation Division.

Sponsor: Broward County Parks & Recreation Division
Contact: Michael Alexander, Executive Director
Founded: 1982

KAISER ROLL
Lincoln Del/Storer Cable Communications
4401 West South 80th Street
Bloomington, MN 55420
TEL: 612-888-0222
Purpose: To provide a sports activity for the handicapped while raising funds for nonprofit organizations that specialize in physical rehabilitation.
Sponsor: Lincoln Del/Storer Cable Communications
Contact: Daniel Berenberg or George Stanfield
Description: More than 200 volunteers assist the program sponsor of this event in drawing attention to handicapped athletes, and raising funds to support rehabilitation efforts of three nonprofit health organizations. They help to stage five and ten kilometer races for handicapped and other athletes. Competition is held for able-bodied runners and wheelchair racers.

The program is administered through the Kaiser Roll Foundation, with the goal of making it the prime event of its kind in the country. Among support activities obtained by the Foundation is the tape-delayed cable coverage provided by Storer Cable. Through this community-wide public awareness effort, maximum community awareness is attained.

Volunteers do much more than provide direct delivery of service. They are involved in supervisory, management, public relations, fund-raising, advocacy and self-help capacities.

Beneficiary organizations of the first program were Sister Kenny Institute, Vinland National Center and Courage Center. Although more than two-thirds of project funds come from the corporate sponsor, the balance is raised by the volunteers/staff and/or received in goods and services from across the community. Given the success of the initial effort, Kaiser Roll has become an annual event.

LAFRENIERE PARK SPECIAL RECREATION PROGRAMMING DIVISION
SEE RECREATION & SPORTS: HANDICAPPED

LOUISIANA STATE SPECIAL OLYMPICS SUMMER GAMES
Special Olympics - New Orleans
University of New Orleans
Lakefront
New Orleans, LA 70148
TEL: 504-286-6000
Purpose: To enable handicapped athletes to compete at the state level in sporting events.
Sponsor: Louisiana State University
Contact: Pat Carpenter, LSU Training Director
Description: The "Parade of Athletes" opens the Louisiana Special Olympics State Summer Games each year, with dozens of volunteers mobilized to pass out water to the athletes as they complete the march. Competition began shortly thereafter at several locations on and off the campus of Louisiana State University (LSU). They included running events, high jump, running and standing long jump, wheelchair races, shot put, softball throw, gymnastics, soccer and tennis on campus, and roller skating and cycling at other locations.

When temperatures during the 1989 games soared into the nineties, medical volunteers were put on campuswide alert. About 100 people volunteered as medical assistants during the games, including nurses, physicians and emergency medical technicians, since many of the athletes are on medication. The medical technicians treated strained and pulled muscles, heat-generated cramps, and exhaustion under a tent near the track finish line. To assist medical personnel, complete medical information is available to them, and athletes wear identification with a number that matches it with appropriate medical information held by the volunteer. Preparations are made for cardiac problems, sutures, heat stress, etc. Medical assistance is needed for coaches and volunteers also.

In addition to medical volunteers, the games included volunteer huggers, timekeepers, entertainers, etc., to make the experience as meaningful as possible for the 2,000 athletes competing in the three-day event. The 1990 summer games were held at Tulane University in New Orleans after 15 years at LSU. The games have outgrown the LSU facilities and will have a permanent home at Tulane.

MICHIGAN SPECIAL OLYMPICS STATE GAMES
Special Olympics - Michigan
6010 Cadieux Road
Detroit, MI 48230
TEL: 313-886-5440
Purpose: To give mentally retarded athletes an opportunity to compete at the state level.
Sponsor: Central Michigan University
Contact: Lois Arnold, Games Director, or Karen Lucas, Volunteer
Description: Held in Michigan since 1972, the state *Special Olympics* in Michigan are as much a carnival as a competition. In between events, athletes can visit the petting zoo, attend exercise and power-lifting clinics, or go on a hayride or canoeing. This variety of experiences is scheduled since, for many of the athletes, this is their only oppotunity to spend a night away from home, eat in a restaurant and have fun with friends that they see only once each year.

More than 3,200 mentally-impaired athletes compete on the

Central Michigan University campus in about 80 events, including softball, track and field, swimming, gymnastics, bowling, volleyball, weight lifting and tennis.

The games have been held in Michigan since 1972. More than 2,400 volunteers assisted in the 1989 session.

Celebrity volunteers included champions from several professional sports teams (Detroit Lions), Miss Michigan, and others. Besides helping alongside of the other volunteers, the celebrity volunteers held autograph sessions throughout the program.

SAN FRANCISCO SPECIAL OLYMPICS WINTER GAMES
SEE RECIPIENTS: HANDICAPPED - MENTALLY RETARDED

SPECIAL OLYMPICS - LAPEER
City of Lapeer
1996 West Oregon
Lapeer, MI 48446
TEL: 313-664-5917
Purpose: To provide an opportunity at the local level for mentally retarded athletes to compete.
Sponsor: Lapeer Board of Education
Contact: Lane Odalovich, District Coordinator
Description: Special Olympics is an international program with more than one million participants and more than 250,000 volunteers. Athletes compete at the local, area, state and national levels. While the state meets are most often held at universities, local programs involve elementary, junior and senior high schools in many cases. Such is the case with the local competition in Lapeer, Michigan. In addition, according to the area director, Lapeer "grabs anybody who is interested - parents and siblings, staff members, community people, service groups, Vietnam vets, Kiwanians - whoever you can touch."
Students involved in the 1989 competition came from Grove Elementary School, White Junior High School, Lapeer West High School and Lapeer East High School. White Junior High school students became involved as a class community service project. Students serve as timers, ribbon awarders, huggers, practice helpers, etc. One student summed up the experience by saying, "I went to help, but they helped me more."
The Lapeer games are forerunners for the state games in Central Michigan University, in which winning athletes from local and area games compete at the state level in preparation for national-level games.
Founded: 1971

SPECIAL OLYMPICS TIME
US/DoD - Fort Sill
212 Field Artillery Brigade
Second Bttn, 37th Field Artillery
Fort Sill, OK 73503
TEL: 405-351-3505
Purpose: To give mentally retarded children an opportunity to show their families and communities how much they can accomplish.
Sponsor: Public Service Company of Oklahoma
Contact: Sandra Jones, SW Area Coordinator, or John Patrick, 2nd/37th Spokesman
Description: Special Olympics Time is a two-day sports competition for some 300 mentally retarded youngsters from 13 area towns surrounding the Fort. The youngsters vie for the opportunity to advance to the International Special Olympics Games. Winners at the Fort are eligible to attend the State meet, with State winners moving on to the final Games.
The numerous athletic events include track and field, swimming, gymnastics, basketball, volleyball, and wheelchair races. The entire community becomes involved in the planning, with meets held at the schools, the YMCA, and the Fort, depending on the event and the field best suited for it. Olympians include those who return

year after year and know the procedure, and those who are entering the competition for the first time and need reassurance as well as orientation to the process. It is a year-round program involving countless volunteers.

Volunteers include those who teach trainable mentally retarded, and those who have no knowledge in this area, but have a desire to help. All are trained to emphasize that the goal of Special Olympics is not to win, but to try. The courage, determination, and sportsmanship involved are important parts of the program's philosophy.

On a smaller scale, the pageantry and excitement of the International Games are built into the program. A "parade of stars," opening and closing ceremonies, and award presentations are patterned after the larger event. Fort Sill Units turn out in force, and individuals and businesses across the community become deeply involved every year. The co-sponsorship of the Second Battalion and the local power company is a partnership that has a side benefit of bringing the Fort and the wider community closer together.

Each community is responsible for its local Special Olympics program, and no community could sponsor one without the coaches, guides, chaperones, sports officials, publicists, entertainers and other volunteers.

SPECIAL POPULATIONS PROGRAM
SEE RECREATION & SPORTS: HANDICAPPED

THERAPEUTIC RIDING PROGRAM
National Center for Therapeutic Riding
5110 Glover Road, NW
Washington, DC 20015
TEL: 202-966-8004
Purpose: To help handicapped students improve self-confidence, social skills and other areas through horseback riding lessons.
Sponsor: Rock Creek Park Horse Centre
Contact: Volunteer Coordinator
Description: Activities of volunteers in RCP Horse Centre Therapeutic Riding Program, mainly, are as leaders and side-walkers during riding lessons. Student population is drawn from DC Public School children in special education classes, mainly mentally retarded, emotionally disturbed, learning disabled, and multi-handicapped. Some 400 students are served each year, each student requiring help from at least one and up to three volunteers in order to ride in the program.
Students ride once a week for 8 week sessions, in groups of 12 or less. Through evaluation studies, a majority of participating students improve gross and fine motor skills, improve language skills, behavioral and social skills, emotional control, self-confidence, improvement in number work, improvement in eye-hand coordination; the achievement of these improvements use volunteer aid in extending effectiveness of riding instructor upon student skills.
Currently 100 volunteers are participating on a weekly basis in the program. Without volunteer help, the program could not function effectively, as nearly all the student population would not be able to attend riding sessions and ride a horse without a leader and/or sidewalker.
Stipend for volunteers includes riding lessons at half-price, and a certificate for a free trail ride at Rock Creek Park Horse Centre after 25 volunteer hours completed.
Hours of program: Mondays through Fridays, 9:00 am to 2:00 pm during the DC Public School year.

THERAPY ON HORSEBACK*
North American Riding for the Handicapped Association
PO Box 100
Auburn, VA 22011
TEL: 703-777-3540

Purpose: To use riding as a form of recreational therapy for the learning disabled, for physically handicapped, the mentally retarded, the emotionally disturbed, blind, deaf, autistic children.
Sponsor: North American Riding for the Handicapped Association
Contact: Leonard Warner, Executive Director
Description: The North American Riding for the Handicapped Association (NARHA) is an all-volunteer, nonprofit organization dedicated to bringing the benefits and joys of horseback riding to the physically and emotionally handicapped. Even the Executive Director is a volunteer.

The riding program for the handicapped is a new form of recreational therapy and has developed programs in numerous handicapping areas. Doubling in the last two years, there are now 140 centers operating in 37 states and Canada that serve approximately 4,000 participants. All centers are required to have at least one accredited instructor on the staff. Due to the rapid growth of the program, the current concern is training enough accredited instructors to keep up.

The existence of the program virtually depends on volunteers. Currently, some 6,000-8,000 of all ages serve the program nationwide. The success in recruiting volunteers is attributed to the fact that it is one of the few not-for-profit programs where the volunteers actually can see the benefits of their work up close.

At one of the larger centers, Cheff Center in Augusta, Michigan, classes for more than 200 handicapped riders are held each week. Riding instructors are trained at this facility for all centers - not only in horsemanship, but also to be alert to the problems of the various disabilities. Riders include the physically handicapped, the mentally retarded, the learning disabled, blind, deaf, and emotionally disturbed children.

Today, orthopedic surgeons, physiologists, and psychiatrists make referrals to the riding program. It has been found that therapeutic horsemanship stimulates and relaxes muscles that the handicapped person cannot use in a wheelchair or on crutches. This exercise of the muscle system also exercises the mind. An example is found in the case of a 13-year-old girl who rarely spoke, couldn't read, and was imprisoned by her own lonely, private world - despite the traditional efforts to involve her in activities. Now, as a member of the riding center, she is happy and outgoing, and a willing participant in many group activities.

In another rewarding case, an autistic child was found in the barn talking to the pony she had been riding that day. The story told most often by NARHA members, though, is concerning the young woman who planted the seed for such a program in 1952. A woman at the Olympic Games that year in Helsinki, Finland, won a silver medal for horsemanship; she was a polio victim. Shortly thereafter therapeutic riding began in Europe, and by the mid-1960's the first program was established in the U.S. Without volunteers, according to NARHA's President, the program would fall apart. To date, they have always had volunteers in sufficient numbers - partly due to stories told by the volunteers in the program. However, with burgeoning interest, this may not be enough, and a recruitment effort will be needed.
Founded: 1981

RECIPIENTS: HANDICAPPED - REHABILITATION

INDIVIDUAL PROGRAM PROFILES

DAISY (FRIEND-RAISER) BALL
SEE RECIPIENTS: HANDICAPPED - FUNDING

HORSES AND THE HANDICAPPED OF SOUTH FLORIDA
SEE RECIPIENTS: HANDICAPPED - RECREATION/SPORTS

THERAPEUTIC RIDING PROGRAM
SEE RECIPIENTS: HANDICAPPED - RECREATION/SPORTS

RECIPIENTS: HANDICAPPED - SELF-HELP

TRAINING PROGRAMS

VOLUNTEERS WITH SPECIAL NEEDS
Volunteers In Action
229 Waterman Street
Providence, RI 02906
TEL: 401-421-6547; 401-421-7472
Credit: AVA Certification (partial fulfillment)
Sponsor: United Way, Mental Health Association of Rhode Island
Contact: Betsy A. Garland
Description: Cosponsored by a statewide mental health association and a central volunteer service, this workshop combines the missions of both and addresses the involvement of the handicapped as volunteers. An opening session, Why This Conference? is shared between the two organizations to elicit input from the assembly of participants. Other sessions include:

- Creative Use of Time for the Chronically Disabled, which is led by faculty drawn from the field of rehabilitation alternatives.
- Practically Speaking: Referring and Receiving Agency Perspectives, which is led by faculty drawn from the field of rehabilitation alternatives.
- Practically Speaking: Referring and Receiving Agency Perspectives, which is led by faculty from Volunteer in Action's "Volunteers with Special Needs" program, with assistance from the fields of health, aging, vocational training, and occupational therapy.
- Alternatives to Traditional Volunteer Assignments (or "What can we do when it doesn't work...?"), which is led by faculty from the mental health association, with assistance from staff of the local Retired Senior Volunteer Program (RSVP).

Time for a wrap-up and question/answer session was allotted to permit an idea exchange among participants.

Both sponsoring organizations are statewide, with satellite offices in areas of greatest need across the state.

RECIPIENTS: HANDICAPPED - TRANSPORTATION

INDIVIDUAL PROGRAM PROFILES

EASY RIDERS VOLUNTEER PROGRAM*
SEE TRANSPORTATION & SAFETY: HEALTH

WHEELCHAIR WASH
Northside Surgical Supply
1165 Portland Avenue
Rochester, NY 14621
TEL: 716-544-9060
Purpose: To provide a needed service to handicapped persons who use wheelchairs.
Sponsor: Southside Apothecary
Contact: Bernie Huffer
Description: For the sixteenth year, employees of a medical supply company and 23 other businesses and agencies volunteered their labor to clean wheelchairs. After motors and other power components are removed, the chairs are blasted with water, scrubbed by hand with industrial detergent, rinsed, wiped dry by *Boy Scouts,* and then reassembled and checked over for mechanical problems. All labor is free, but owners pay for any parts needed for repair.
Based in the parking lot of *Northside Surgical Supply,* the project took on a carnival air. A tent sheltered some wheelchair owners, while others chose to sit in the sunshine, chatting, sipping pop, nibbling cookies and listening to rock music from the local radio station. Helium balloons decorated the area, and volunteers and wheelchair owners wore bright blue T-shirts commemorating the 16th annual wheelchair wash.
Since owners know that well-functioning wheelchairs often mean the difference between isolation at home and an independent, active life, participation is extensive, with 135 chairs cleaned, checked and/or repaired during the event. According to one owner, "It is very important that we have a chair that is mechanically safe because you can get into some very real problems when you're alone."
Founded: 1973

RECIPIENTS: HOMEBOUND

TRAINING PROGRAMS

HANDICAPPED VOLUNTEER/VOLUNTEERING FOR THE HANDICAPPED
Adelphi University
Center on Volunteerism
Garden City, NY 11530
TEL: 516-294-8700
Credit: Inquire
Sponsor: Adelphi University
Contact: Rhoda White
Description: The Council of Agencies to Coordinate Homebound Services (CACHS) is a coalition of public and private agencies which assists community groups in mobilizing resources for shut-ins of all ages. It is guided by a volunteer board whose members work for agencies which service the homebound. Initially composed of a half-dozen agencies serving the elderly, CACHS currently includes 40 agencies collectively assisting all ages of handicapped citizens.
In response to a concern of the handicapped - "What can we do for others while others are doing for us?" - the Adelphi University Center on Volunteerism cosponsored with CACHS a conference that brought together for the first time on Long Island the resources of higher education, the expertise of human service agencies, and the personal involvement of the homebound/handicapped themselves.
Services to the handicapped as well as by the handicapped are included in the conference format, led by a panel of professional people working in the field - some of whom are handicapped themselves. In addition to volunteering by the handicapped, the

conference dealt with:
- volunteer visiting and sharing;
- making a difference through advocacy;
- educational resources for the homebound; and
- the linking of local resources.

Among the "unanswered questions" that remained at the close of a recent convening of the conference:
- Is there transportation available now to enable the physically handicapped to get to volunteer placements?
- Are there any models in New York State or elsewhere for referring discharged disabled persons to community-based groups for rehabilitative follow-up?
- How does one get transportation for the physically handicapped to sheltered workshops? Isn't it discriminating to have transportation to special schools for children and none for adults to sheltered workshops?
- During the International Year of Disabled Persons, are any new legislative initiatives being considered at the national and/or state levels to fund projects to help "mainstream" the homebound?
- A disabled person who wants to work will lose the government disability check if he/she does, but can't earn enough to subsist without it. What can be done?

To bolster the workshop discussions, the lunch hour is utilized for an informal exchange of ideas and experiences. In addition, the Human Resources Center and the Northport Veterans' Hospital are linked to the program by a telephone conference line. The questions are printed in Commentary, the Center's newsletter, for additional feedback from subscribers.

INDIVIDUAL PROGRAM PROFILES

INSIDE/OUT*
Volunteers of Cape Cod
PO Box 717
Hyannis, MA 02601
TEL: 617-771-7925
Purpose: To assist persons who are homebound/handicapped or isolated due to transportation difficulties in becoming providers of services through volunteering.
Sponsor: Volunteers of Cape Cod (A non-profit placement bureau)
Contact: Margie Murphy, Recruitment Coordinator
Description: The Inside/Out program was initiated in 1979. The goal of the program is to provide volunteer opportunities to individuals who are homebound due to physical, social or emotional handicaps or transportation difficulties.
Volunteer projects or assignments are transported to the home of the volunteer by the agency who wishes to utilize that volunteer. The agency introduces the assignment, supervises and maintains contacts with the volunteer. This provides a social contact for the isolated volunteer and assists the individual to become a provider of services rather than a recipient, which increases self-esteem. The program also allows agencies to have a pool of individuals available to assist as volunteers with task-oriented or "portable" volunteer assignments.
Inside/Out volunteers range in age from 16 to 100. Some typical assignments include: telephone reassurance, bulkmailing, collating, mending/sewing, clerical duties, research, information/referral. Any opportunity which can be modified to be transported to a volunteer's home is eligible for a referral of an Inside/Out volunteer.
Inside/Out assignments can be modified so those volunteers who are experiencing decreasing capabilities can remain useful by performing tasks according to their skills.
Inside/Out assignments are also utilized for those individuals who are in transition and are not ready for a traditional assignment. Said individuals can utilize an Inside/Out assignment to prepare them for a traditional structured assignment while maintaining the

protective environment of their home or institution. At present this program has worked with over 150 Inside/Out volunteers.

The VOCC representative registers new Inside/Out volunteers in their home. In many cases this interviewer may be a volunteer, rather than staff.

The VOCC staff coordinates the requests for Inside/Out volunteers and matches appropriate referrals. On an annual basis VOCC instructs agencies on the use of Inside/Out volunteers including, as needed, personal instruction or inservices.

Founded: 1979

MEALS ON WHEELS PROGRAM OF ACCA
Annandale Christian Community for Action (ACCA)
7200 Columbia Pike
Annandale, VA 22003
TEL: 703-256-1378

Purpose: To serve nutritious meals to people who are ill, handicapped, elderly, or convalescent.

Sponsor: ACCA, Hope Lutheran Church

Contact: Esther Bradsher, Chairperson

Description: Meals for ACCA's Meals on Wheels (MOW) program originate from Fairfax Hospital and Jefferson Memorial Hospital. They are delivered to the ill, handicapped, elderly and convalescent who are unable to shop for or prepare meals to meet their nutritional needs. The Fairfax Hospital meals consist of a hot noon-time meal and a sandwich supper. The Jefferson Hospital meals consist of a hot evening meal and a sandwich noon-time meal for the next day. Volunteers from ACCA Churches are joined by many others from the community to deliver the meals each weekday. Referrals come from personal friendships and the County Council on Aging. Volunteer services are a free gift, as are the meals for those unable to pay the small request of $21.25 per week. Financial assistance is available to help offset the cost, and is utilized by two-thirds of those served. Clients are all ages, but most are over 60 years old.

In 1987 ACCA meals routes were increased from three to five. In 1988 it again became apparent that expansion was necessary. A new route called "Annandale West" was opened, followed by others, making a total of seven routes by 1989. The number of clients fluctuates, but averages between 85 and 90 daily along the seven routes.

The goal is for each route to be manned with a driver and an assistant, but this is a luxury that is not always possible to achieve. With a team on each route expending about two-and-half hours per day, or 9,100 hours per year, and coordinators averaging 500 hours per year, ACCA's meals program would require 3,500 hours per route, or 12,600 hours per year. In 1988, 2,072 meals were delivered on 107 days, using 935 hours of driver time plus many hours of coordinator time for a total of at least 1,500 hours. There were 34 Thanksgiving meals and 36 Christmas meals served.

The five-day-a-week program involves 55-60 volunteers. A small weekend program is maintained serving between 10 and 15 clients. Drivers for the routes claim 22.5 cents per mile reimbursement, and then set it aside to be used to purchase food and supplies for Thanksgiving and Christmas dinners for those without family nearby, or who would not have a holiday meal.

Using the minimum wage figure of $3.50 per hour and mileage reimbursement of 22.5 cents per mile, the program's efforts are equivalent to over $50,000 for the seven week-day routes. All of this, including driver mileage reimbursement, is donated as a gift to assist those in need of the service. A more practical figure of $8.50 per hour for drivers, coordinators, administrative personnel to process payrolls and benefits, vehicle operation and maintenance costs, etc., would bring the program's value to $200,000.

In 1990, a *Meals on Wheels Friendly Telephone Line* was established. Although many homebound persons have telephones, they do not ring often. While meeting the nutritional needs of clients, the program would like to let them know, also, that someone cares enough to call - and perhaps offer an invitation to

lunch, a visit, an errand, or just share a cup of coffee. Many genuine and lasting friendships have originated between volunteers and clients.

Publications: ACCA Annual Report; Meals on Wheels Information Packet

Founded: 1986

RECIPIENTS: HOMELESS

NATIONAL/STATE ORGANIZATIONS

NATIONAL COMMUNITY ORGANIZING PROJECT (NCOP)
National Coalition for the Homeless
1439 Rhode Island Avenue, NW
Washington, DC 20005
TEL: 202-659-3310

Objectives: To build new state homeless coalitions and strengthen existing state organizations.

Services: A National Community Organizing Project (NCOP) has been launched by the National Coalition for the Homeless. NCOP is sending trained community organizers to localities to work with local advocates and homeless people in the development of advocacy-oriented coalitions in their area. The goal is to build new state homeless coalitions where they do not exist, and to strengthen organizations already in place.

By early 1989, organizers were working in Florida and New England. After consulting with local advocates and homeless people, the Coalition targets additional areas and sends organizers to assist at the local level.

Also from the national level, services include volunteer recruitment, development and distribution of community organizing training materials, and fundraising for the NCOP. Initial kits and progress reports are made available to interested localities.

Sponsor: National Coalition for the Homeless

Contact: NCOP Coordinator

Publications: NCOP Information Packet

TRAINING PROGRAMS

VOA SYMPOSIUM ON HOMELESSNESS
Volunteers of America
3813 North Causeway
Metairie, LA 70002-1784
TEL: 504-837-2652

Sponsor: Volunteers of America

Contact: Volunteer Coordinator

Description: This symposium is based on the work of *Volunteers of America* over many years of helping the homeless. It is designed to give the benefit of this long experience to those just beginning to provide services in this field. The substance of the symposium is drawn from programs in its 170 local groups across the country - all of whom have had continuous programs since VOA's inception in 1896 to assist the alcoholics, drug abusers, disabled persons, families, youth and the elderly - many of them needing shelter. The symposium is the result of considerable research into these programs to provide a distillation that will be of maximum benefit to participants.

INDIVIDUAL PROGRAM PROFILES

OPERATION COVER UP
Portland General Electric Company
38250 Pioneer Boulevard
Sandy, OR 97055
TEL: 503-668-4158
Purpose: To take seriously what appears on the surface to be a simple winter need - warm head covering for the elderly, migrant workers, low-income people, the homeless and others.
Sponsor: Portland General Electric Company
Contact: Hilda Walker, Customer Service Representative
Description: Since the business of electric companies is providing the means for warmth in the winter home, staff members of the Sandy office of the *Portland General Electric Company* mounted a related project. Grappling for an idea for a useful community service project, a number of employees said they noticed people without warm head coverings, and after a discussion of the logistics such as volunteer manpower, community awareness materials, etc., *Operation Cover Up* was born. A logo, depicting a knit cap, was designed to help draw attention to the effort. The project collects donations of yarn and coordinates volunteer knitters who make the hand-knitted caps for senior citizens, migrant workers, low-income people and the homeless.
The utility company is working with the Clackamas and Multnomah County units of the *Retired Senior Volunteer Program (RSVP)* to collect yarn and make the caps. Both sides of the partnership contribute to both the knitting and the administrative function of the project.

RECIPIENTS: HOMELESS - CHILDREN/YOUTH

NATIONAL/STATE ORGANIZATIONS

YOUTH DEVELOPMENT
SEE PSYCHOSOCIAL SUPPORT SERVICES: CHILDREN/YOUTH

INDIVIDUAL PROGRAM PROFILES

EMPLOYMENT SKILLS FOR HOMELESS YOUTH
Boys & Girls Clubs of Greater Washington
1320 Fenwick Lane
Suite 800
Silver Spring, MD 20910
TEL: 301-587-4315
FAX: 301-587-8120
Purpose: To provide employment readiness programs for homeless youth.
Contact: Training Coordinator
Description: This project is designed to train youth, ages 16-24, who live in foster care, group homes and emergency shelters throughout the District of Columbia, in skills that will help them live independently. It was made possible through a grant from the *U.S. Department of Labor* in the winter of 1990. The project is administered with the cooperation of the *Mayor's Homeless Coordinator* and the *DC Department of Human Services.*
The $395,250 grant enables *Boys & Girls Clubs of Greater Washington* to initiate the first year of a three-year program providing 70 severely-disadvantaged homeless youth with basic education skills, job readiness, and employment training. The program will use facilities at a *Club* branch which provides existing training programs and has appropriate facilities already in place.
The *District of Columbia Private Industry Council* offered to provide an evaluation of the project.

INDEPENDENT LIVING/HOMELESS YOUTH
The Bridge
1115 Ball, NE
Grand Rapids, MI 49505
TEL: 616-451-3001
Purpose: To offer help to newly-emancipated 16- and 17-year-old youths.
Sponsor: United Way
Contact: Connie Hendershot, Director
Description: In Michigan, *legal emancipation* is the phrase used when a youngster's parents, for whatever reason, ask to be relieved of all legal obligations toward their child and are granted their request. With emancipation, the child suddenly must assume full responsibility for his or her life, no matter how ill-equipped the youngster might be.
In Grand Rapids, the youth can turn to the *Independent Living/Homeless Youth* project sponsored by *The Bridge,* a United Way-sponsored program. The project helps homeless 16- and 17-year-olds find suitable housing, financial assistance, employment, food, clothing, health care, and educational and vocational training.
The youth project was an outgrowth of the concern of staff and volunteers of *The Bridge,* a short-term shelter for homeless individuals. They noticed a disturbing rise in the number of emancipated youths seeking shelter. Most of them appeared to need assistance, and it was felt that hiring a case manager to work one-to-one with individual youths could provide them with the resources they needed, both material and emotional. A three-month period for each youth was considered ample to help them acquire the skills and sense of responsibility needed to survive.
Youths who enter the program agree, in writing, to commit themselves to the program and to follow its rules, including attending school or working 40 hours a week, taking good care of their housing, and maintaining the confidentiality of other program participants.
When the youths leave the program after the three-month period, the case manager meets with each participant once every 30 days for six months to provide follow-up assistance.
To help participants on their way following their stay, *The Bridge* established a pool of funds from which clients can borrow the amount of security deposits for apartments. Funds come from the *Federal Emergency Management Agency (FEMA),* the *State of Michigan,* and other sources. At the same time, staff has been able to negotiate with some local landlords to waive such deposits.
The goal is to assure that each youth, by the end of his or her 90 days, can find housing and employment, and can gain access to appropriate health and human services they might require. In this way, *The Bridge* is enabling teens to accept responsibility for their lives.
Founded: 1987

RAINBOW SUNSHINE SCHOOL
SEE EDUCATION: HOMELESS

VOGEL ALCOVE
Dallas Jewish Coalition for the Homeless
1110 Browder Street
Dallas, TX 75215
TEL: 214-565-7824
Purpose: To provide quality day care for homeless children.
Contact: Pat Peiser

Description: In June 1989, *Vogel Alcove* opened the doors of its new center to Dallas' homeless children. This move from its first "alcove" in 1987 enables it to go from serving 20 infants and 35 school-age children to as many as 100 infants, toddlers, and school-age children. One purpose of the center is to help break the cycle of homelessness, since it gives the parents time to look for jobs, get job training, and get "back on track."

Almost immediately after its founding in 1986, the *Dallas Jewish Coalition for the Homeless* began working with other agencies to offer child care for the homeless at different sites throughout the city. The children being cared for at those sites now attend *Vogel Alcove*, which accepts children from six weeks old to teenage. The Center opens at 7:30 a.m. to accommodate working parents, and includes after-school care. It also funds a child-care staff at the family shelter at night so homeless parents can attend classes and counseling, and maintains committees who provide access to food, clothing and other needed items for the entire homeless family.

The big break came in January 1989, when an anonymous Dallas businessman who heard about the group's mission gave it a single-story, 4,500-square-foot office building. In six months, volunteers transformed the building into a professional day care center capable of handling 100 children. The Coalition spent about $35,000 renovating the building, with the money coming from private donations and from three foundation grants.

A Dallas architect donated his time to ensure that the center meets building code standards, and the Coalition's Vice President coordinated the core of volunteers who transformed the building. The curriculum for homeless children is especially challenging, since they have lost everything - toys, rooms, pets, even clothes - and are more reluctant than other children to see their parents leave. It is found that many children who did well at school before becoming homeless regress at the shelters, and need special attention to be brought back to their levels. In addition to children from the family shelter, *Vogel Alcove* also cares for children from RESTART, Trinity Ministry to the Poor, Genesis, Family Place, the Interfaith Housing Coalition, and Oasis Housing Corporation. There is no longer a waiting list.

Although most staff members are paid child care workers from the YWCA, volunteers are involved in every phase of the operation.

YOUTH HAVEN
SEE RECIPIENTS: CHILDREN/YOUTH - PROTECTIVE SERVICES

RECIPIENTS: HOMELESS - COMMUNICATIONS & PR

INDIVIDUAL PROGRAM PROFILES

LOS ANGELES POVERTY DEPARTMENT (LAPD)
SEE ARTS/CULTURAL ENRICHMENT:
MUSIC/DANCE/THEATRE

PRIME TIME TO END HUNGER
End Hunger Network
7080 Hollywood Boulevard
Suite 105
Hollywood, CA 90028
TEL: 213-465-1377
Information available also from:
Alice Barkus
Volunteer and Outreach Services
United Way of America
701 North Fairfax Street

Alexandria, VA 22314-2045
703-836-7100
Purpose: To focus the power of the communications industry on a current social issue.
Contact: Jerry Michaud, Executive Director
Description: Developed by the *End Hunger Network,* this nationwide recruitment project works with some of television's most popular prime-time shows to motivate millions of viewers nationwide to volunteer their time, talents, and energy to address the country's most serious problems - including hunger, homelessness, and illiteracy.

The project gains commitments from the major television networks to script prime-time shows which will feature episodes about major social concerns, followed by public-service announcements inviting viewers to call a "900" phone number for information on how they can volunteer. Callers hear a recorded message from one of the show's stars and are asked to leave a message stating their name and address. Within two weeks, callers receive a personalized letter and a handbook on volunteering, produced with assistance from the *United Way of America*. The prospective volunteer is first referred to a local *Volunteer Center*. Where none exists, callers are directed to their community's United Way, or to a local Emergency Food and Shelter office for information about volunteer opportunities.

Considered unusual because the project does not solicit funds from TV viewers, it is expected that 290 million viewers throughout the U.S. could collectively watch these episodes during this initial project's run (December 1-20, 1989). *Prime Time to End Hunger* was launched in October 1989 by President Bush at a White House press conference attended by *End Hunger Network* executives, corporate sponsors, and representatives from United Way of America, VOLUNTEER, and the Emergency Food and Shelter Board.

A packet of information is available from local United Ways, Volunteer Centers, and Emergency Food and Shelter Board offices. The packets include fact sheets, a schedule of project-related broadcasts, sample press releases, tips for local participation, project logo slicks, and information to help local organizations collect volunteer data and conduct project evaluations.
Founded: 1982

STAY THE NIGHT ON MY STREET
Emergency Shelter Council
United Way of the Midlands
1800 Main Street, PO Box 152
Columbia, SC 29202-0152
TEL: 803-733-5400
Purpose: To dispel some of the myths and fears about street people.
Sponsor: Columbia Experimental Theatre
Contact: John L. Heins, Jr., Executive Director
Description: Developed by *Columbia Experimental Theatre* and cosponsored by the *United Way of the Midlands, Stay the Night on My Street* is an original play about the problems of the homeless in the Midlands of South Carolina. It was first presented in 1987 in special recognition of that year as the *International Year of Shelter for the Homeless.* Opening performance was at the *University of South Carolina Law School,* with performances moving among the University and six other locations.

The all-volunteer cast uses comedy and rapidly-shifting scenes to depict the lives of both the haves and the have-nots. Although taking a lighthearted approach, the play points out that the growing occurrence of homelessness is indicative of the failure of existing institutions to break the cycle of poverty and oppression, according to the play's director. The performers hope to dispel some of the myths and fears about street people - some of which performers had held themselves before signing on for the performance. The play features original music by a local musician created for the play.

Performances are followed by informal panel discussions involving community leaders, shelter providers, and homeless individuals. Admission is always free.

RECIPIENTS: HOMELESS - DRUGS/ALCOHOL

INDIVIDUAL PROGRAM PROFILES

SUBSTANCE ABUSE TREATMENT CENTER AND SHELTER
Alexandria Mental Health and Substance Abuse Board
Alexandria Community Shelter
2355 Mill Road
Alexandria, VA 22314
TEL: 703-329-2000
Purpose: To combine temporary housing for the homeless with a treatment facility for substance abuse.
Sponsor: Salvation Army
Contact: Captain Steve Smith
Description: The grand plan of including temporary housing for the homeless with a treatment facility has worked well for the Alexandria, Virginia, area. The Alexandria Community Shelter with 65 beds for homeless persons has included a facility in its operation which provides 35 beds for homeless persons suffering from substance abuse. Opening in February 1989, the facility was filled immediately, demonstrating the urgent need for this service. Eleven weeks later 268 persons had been admitted to its residential detoxification program, with 423 active outpatients.
The shelter's comprehensive treatment program consolidated services that were previously scattered throughout the city. Included in the treatment are
- individual and group counseling
- frequent meetings by Alcoholics Anonymous, Narcotics Anonymous, and other support groups
The convenience of the dual effort has prompted more patients who once sought only medication also to participate in support therapy. According to the director, "Clients go both ways." If someone appears at the shelter who is drunk or high, he or she is sent to the detox program. Those completing the detox program are sent to the shelter for interim housing.
Monitored by Alexandria's mental health and substance abuse board, the program received City funding of $593,000 for its first full fiscal year beginning July 1, 1989. The Salvation Army operates the program.
Founded: 1989

RECIPIENTS: HOMELESS - EDUCATION

INDIVIDUAL PROGRAM PROFILES

FIRST PLACE
Department P
PO Box 15112
Seattle, WA 98115-0112
TEL: 206-323-6715
Purpose: To stabilize homeless children who have missed school so that they can reach the appropriate level for return to the regular classroom.

Contact: Carolyn Pringle, Founder
Description: To utilize the waiting time involved in government procedures to enroll homeless children in public school, a Seattle schoolteacher assembled a staff, enlisted volunteers, solicited contributions and incorporated *First Place* as a nonprofit elementary school for these children. Locating classroom space in a local building, the teacher arranged for the Seattle School District to provide buses to pick up children from all over the city. After being uprooted for a while, going to a regular school can be devastating for a homeless child. At *First Place* they do not have to explain their circumstances to the other childen, and if they are without shoes, they are quietly and quickly provided. The school is designed for children from kindergarten to sixth grade. Volunteers assist the two salaried teachers in the "two-room schoolhouse." The school day includes breakfast, academic work, lunch and quiet time for reading. Gifted children are encouraged to explore their potential, with one example being a fourth grader doing sixth grade work, who is also a gifted artist who has illustrated a book. Teachers are planning to try to get his book published. Other children are given the individual attention they need to catch up with the schoolwork they have missed while trying to settle permanently again. Once the children are established and expected to be in one shelter or other residence for a reasonable length of time, they are returned to the public schools.
An adjunct of the school is a supply of sneakers, books, furniture and other items that has been donated to *First Place* for distribution to homeless families.
Understanding the conviction of some educators that such children should not be segregated, *First Place* officials point out that these youngsters often need individual attention and counseling to catch up with the studies they have missed, and to rebuild self-esteem. As quickly as is feasible, the children are enrolled in regular schools. And just as quickly, their places are filled by other homeless children.
Publications: First Place Information Packet
Founded: 1989

RECIPIENTS: HOMELESS - EMPLOYMENT

INDIVIDUAL PROGRAM PROFILES

LOAVES & FISHES
SEE RECIPIENTS: HOMELESS - NUTRITION

STREET NEWS HOMELESS VENDORS PROGRAM
Street Aid
1457 Broadway
Suite 305
New York , NY 10036
TEL: 212-768-7290
Purpose: To provide employment and other services to homeless persons while providing a news service to pedestrians and commuters.
Sponsor: Street Aid
Contact: Hutchinson Persons, Editor-in-Chief
Description: Street News was launched in New York City by a dancer and a musician who conceived it as a way to put homeless people to work. It is backed by an alliance of celebrities, fashion designers, ad executives and major real estate developer. The sales force is recruited from homeless shelters and terminal benches. A homeless person in New York City can average from $200 to $250 a week selling the newspaper.
"Word of mouth" is the recruiting method here. One homeless

jobseeker found that he could not get a job because he did not have an address or telephone, so he gave a street phone number. The potential employer discovered the ruse and refused to hire him. He learned about *Street News* and asked a vender how he could get involved. At the *Street News* office, he was hired immediately, and within three weeks became the top salesman, earning $300.

The vendor receives 50 cents of the 75 cents selling price. Of the 25 cents *Street News* takes for its printing and distribution costs, a nickel is deposited in the vendor's escrow housing account, up to $500. In a little more than three months, 12 vendors received their escrow funds after signing leases or rental agreements. Also, vendors are assisted in opening bank accounts. A top vendor has designated his bank account to go toward his first apartment since he became homeless in January 1989. He also serves as a volunteer mentor to other homeless persons hired as *Street News* vendors. Obviously the sales force of the paper creates public awareness about the homeless, but the editors are quick to point out that it's 26 pages provide current news about timely topics as diverse as rock-'n-roll, Mikhail Gorbachev's visit, and government spending, and includes a pull-out page of job-training listings. Submitted poetry, stories, articles and other writings are included in some issues, both by the homeless and by the general public. One homeless person described the events that led to his losing his moving business, leaving him with $34.00 in his pocket. By early 1990, he was the paper's top salesman with sales of 2,200 papers in one week.

As word spread, *Street News* T-shirts, hats and change aprons (all sales incentives) were seen more and more and, increasingly, paper cups in stretched-out hands disappeared. One factor in this phenomenon is a suggestion to purchasers by *Street News*: "Instead of spare change, give panhandlers the clip-out work-opportunities listing from the paper."

Although not without problems, the idea in general has worked well.

One problem that has arisen is a new policy of the Metropolitan Transit Authority (MTA) - no one can live in subways or stations or sell their products there. Unfortunately, the best market is with the bored subway travelers, and this new ruling is a depressing blow to the homeless salespersons.

Street News has approached MTA and hopes to appeal on the basis of allowing the homeless to earn a living so that they can find housing and help eliminate the problematic issue of homeless people living in subways. The challenge to MTA is: "Provide a solution rather than merely move the homeless from underground back to the streets." With the mood of the country on helping the homeless, and the evidence that the newspaper's job program is working, MTA is expected to approve the vending of *Street News* in the subways.

In the meantime, the homeless continue to sell the papers in subways, and continue to live there, despite difficulty with the police. This police-homeless struggle is preferable to "going back to the paper cup," so they take their chances and wait and see. While dealing with MTA, *Street News* continues to help the homeless open bank accounts and save for the housing they need. The *Street News* effort has received approval and much support in the employment program - donated space by real estate companies (often considered a major cause of the homeless problem), computers from Bell Labs, office machines from Stratocom, and major ads paid for by ad agencies and other corporations. Without this help, the rapid growth to a staff of 14 would not have been possible in so short a time. The premiere issue sold about 30,000 copies; the second, 150,000, and the third (January 1990) may reach 300,000 circulation. The vendor force has climbed to 500 people.

Creators of the program deliberately chose a labor-intensive project requiring little training "so people can go out and work right now and without a telephone, without clean clothes, without a place to live, and start picking themselves up."

The editor adds that sales styles vary greatly among the homeless

vendors. One is aggressive and explains to potential buyers that he is working to earn rent money. Another gently tells potential purchasers that with their support she can be successful again. *Street Aid* does not tamper with these selling styles. They offer the basics in what it takes to be a good vendor and volunteer other help as well - goal-setting, money management, and other constructive training - and rejoice with each milestone the vendors make as they move toward normal lives once again. One official pointed out: "Our original vendor is a college graduate, and some of the others are former doctors - evidence, again, that homelessness can happen to anyone."

According to the newspaper's editor-in-chief, "It's so simple. People know what you're saying. You're selling something; you're working. If you want to pay the rent, this is a decent way to do it."

Convinced that *Street News* can work in other places, especially those with dense populations, creators are expanding to Newark, Philadelphia and Washington, DC. According to Mitch Snyder of the Community for Creative Non-Violence in Washington, DC, any project that helps through voluntary participation by the homeless is welcome.

Publications: Street News

RECIPIENTS: HOMELESS - FAMILIES

INDIVIDUAL PROGRAM PROFILES

FAMILY ASSISTANCE PROJECT OF HOLLYWOOD (FAP)
6605 Hollywood Boulevard
Suite 300
Hollywood , CA 90028
TEL: 213-461-9632
Purpose: To serve homeless and needy families with dependent children.
Sponsor: Family Assistance Program
Contact: M. Patricia Shelhamer, Executive Director
Description: The Family Assistance Program (FAP) was established in 1984 as a nonprofit California corporation. The mission of FAP is to aid families who, for a variety of reasons, have become unemployed, homeless, or at risk of being removed from their surroundings. During its first three years, with support from individual donors, and with the aid of committed volunteers, FAP helped more than 400 homeless and destitute families in the Hollywood area. It was the first agency in the area to put up deposits for permanent housing. The primary services include assistance in finding and securing:
- adequate housing
- jobs
- job training
- educational opportunities
- child care
- temporary financial assistance with rent and security deposits

Each year, FAP works with hundreds of homeless and destitute families in the Hollywood area, providing counseling, day care, housing, clothing, bus passes for those without any resources, use of office telephones, and a non-cost answering service to help those trying to secure employment. FAP operates under the premise that people must play an active role in changing their own lives. Clients must commit to establishing independent economic stability and enriching the quality of life for their families. Parents must make and demonstrate a conscious decision to actively participate in gaining a measure of independence.

FAP's services are adjusted to fit each individual family's requirements. Family crises are caused by varied circumstances. Therefore, the agency's mission is to provide eclectic guidance geared to long-term solutions - empowering families, returning them to the economic mainstream, and breaking the cycles of recurrent dependence and hopelessness.

Physical needs - housing, food, income and employment - are not the only drawbacks for these families. The strain of being homeless triggers dysfunctional responses such as child abuse, alcohol or drug abuse, lack of self-esteem and stress (both physical and psychosocial). To satisfy these latter needs, FAP has initiated the *Life Planning Services Program.* This program includes individual meetings with counselors, personal growth exercises, leadership development, and group support systems. One-to-one therapy is the most costly and most traditional approach, but there are countless models for group work. Whichever is used, life planning aims to help develop in children and adults alike an awareness of and confidence in their own goals and actions, and the realization that these actions will effect an outcome. The underlying theme of all of the sessions is an emphasis on self-esteem and conscious decision-making.

To augment and expand services provided by the FAP professional staff, an active volunteer group of about 35 people provide approximately 90 hours per week of free time for:

- private and/or group counseling sessions
- tutoring and remedial reading - adults and children
- child care in the Drop-in Center
- English as a Second Language
- a study-hall type situation for teenagers and youth after school for tutoring and recreation
- social activities and outings for young people
- structured play/learning situations with younger children.

In addition, a group of volunteers has organized a Career Development session that meets once a week. Using improvisational acting techniques, they simulate job interview sessions and employer/employee confrontations to teach the client new techniques in approaching employment opportunities.

The volunteer segment of the program is perhaps the most important, somewhat unique, element. The interplay between the volunteers, who can be seen as the *community-at-large*, and the client is particularly healing, usually for both parties, and provides the necessary bonding for real development.

The small, highly-skilled professional staff consists of an executive director, a social worker, two case-workers, and a job developer.

In addition to the above basic program elements, parenting education and support groups meet weekly to socialize, discuss things of importance to them, and network with others on social services, legal rights and other concerns. In addition, outside groups such as Alcoholics Anonymous, Narcotics Anonymous and Overeaters Anonymous are brought on-site to foster better attendance. Where in-patient care is necessary, FAP helps with fees, or pays them, and supports the family emotionally and financially as indicated.

One of the most recent programs of FAP is the *Adopt-A-Family* program, which operates along the same line as the Big Brothers Program. A family from the community adopts a homeless or at-risk family and the two families spend time doing things together once a month (trips to the beach, museums, amusement parks, etc.). It serves as an opportunity to share, to reassure, and to build self-esteem.

In addition to the in-house volunteers, a *Volunteer Fund Raising Committee (The Spare Change Project)* puts together fundraising events. It is comprised of six publicists and marketing experts, several advertising executives, writers, casting directors, a professional celebrity recruiter and public speakers. The events attract many celebrities and have included *Rock 'n Bowl, Art Auction,* and others.

FAP does not operate autonomously, but rather has developed solid working relationships with a variety of other service providers. It has built a comprehensive networking system to insure that a family in need is able to access all agencies and the services they provide. The groups in this network include Chip-In (Community of Hollywood Investing in People in Need), Salvation Army, Los Angeles Free Clinic, and West Hollywood Food Coalition.

Publications: FAP (Family Assistance Program); Some Facts You Should Know
Founded: 1984

SPARE CHANGE PROJECT
SEE RECIPIENTS: HOMELESS - FUNDING

RECIPIENTS: HOMELESS - FUNDING

INDIVIDUAL PROGRAM PROFILES

CONTINENTAL HOMELESS ASSISTANCE PROGRAM
Continental Airlines
Western Division
1605 California Street
Denver, CO 80202
TEL: 303-398-3000
Purpose: To provide funds for homeless programs in the Colorado area.
Sponsor: Continental Airlines
Contact: James Bacon, Vice President, Western Division
Description: In summer 1989, through its project to help the homeless and hungry, the western division of Continental Airlines presented $30,000 to a project designed to coordinate homeless programs in Colorado. A portion of the funds ($5,000) is earmarked for a planned Denver mission by Mother Theresa, who indicated in a spring 1989 visit that her *Missionary Sisters of Charity* wants to open a Denver mission.

The program was funded by the airline through coupon sales to business customers over a 60-day period. The airline backed up the ticket sales with numerous full-page newspaper advertisements.

In addition to charting its own public service course, and improving its image, the airline looks for "win-win" situations in which it can both help charities and save money for its business customers.

The presentation ceremonies at *Holy Ghost Church,* where the founder of the coordinated program serves as pastor, drew leaders of ten of the groups in the project - representing thousands of volunteers, including the *Salvation Army, Volunteers of America,* the *Mennonite Urban Ministry* and a number of Catholic charities. According to the founder, many corporations have talked about helping the needy, but Continental is the first to act. He added, "Someone has to bridge the gap between those who have and those who do not. We have to keep trying."

Continental's contribution to the homeless brought to $80,000 the amount funneled by the airline into 26 Colorado charitable agencies through its discounted airline coupon program.

HELP THE HOMELESS MILLION DOLLAR SHOOTOUT
Charity Sports
c/o Grubbs Oldsmobile
I-30 & 183 South
Fort Worth, TX 76119
TEL: 817-560-9000
Purpose: To benefit a Fort Worth charity which helps the homeless in the Fort Worth area.
Sponsor: Grubbs Oldsmobile
Contact: Project Director
Description: In summer 1989, *Charity Sports* mounted a golf project designed to help improve and increase the services of a Fort Worth charity working with homeless people in the area. The charity, *Loaves & Fishes,* was founded in 1982 by Franciscans and includes *The Soup Kitchen,* which feeds between 150 and 300

homeless and hungry people daily, employment counseling, and other services.

Charity Sports brings together the business community in a concerted, eight-day effort to help relieve the financial burden of *Loaves & Fishes* so that services can be expanded as needs among the homeless arise. Some of the merchants provided "free shot coupons" to encourage participation, and four participating car dealers - Grubbs Oldsmobile, Longhorn Dodge, Alan Young Buick, and Hilcher Ford - offered new 1989 cars to winners of the competition. As a further incentive, the dealers put the prize cars on display well in advance of the event - a luxury car, a converted van, a pickup truck, and a convertible.

The games were held at four local driving ranges, with shots costing visitors $1 each. The two top contestants each day move into the final competition.

A *Charity Sports* spokesperson said that the needs of the target volunteer organization keep growing, and "it is our hope that the results of our efforts during this event will fill a big part of these needs."

SPARE CHANGE PROJECT
Volunteer Fund Raising Committee
9255 Sunset Boulevard
Suite 620
Los Angeles, CA 90069
TEL: 213-550-6771
FAX: 213-550-7105
Purpose: To raise funds for the Family Assistance Program of Hollywood.
Sponsor: The Ford Group; Business/Industry
Contact: Judith A. Katz or Linda Ford
Description: In November 1987, a group of professional men and women from the business community created the *Spare Change Project,* a campaign to raise funds for the Family Assistance Program (FAP). The Spare Change Project was founded by a public relations agency with the help of friends and associates in the PR and entertainment fields who volunteer their time and resources to develop and implement fund raising activities for FAP.

FAP is a privately-funded organization that was created in 1984 to counsel and assist those homeless families who are willing to do something to help themselves. FAP works with social service agencies, and the Employment Development Department to find jobs and adequate housing for homeless families.

The Spare Change Project promotes its fundraising efforts via a massive public service campaign with public service announcements by celebrities - most recently Martin Sheen and Gregory Hines. The Project is coordinated by a committee of individuals and organizations including advertising agencies, public relations firms, media specialists, graphic artists, entertainers, musicians, fundraisers, and restauranteurs. Funds raised are directed at efforts to work with homeless families in Los Angeles County in areas of employment, training, counseling, housing, education and transportation - helping families once again to become productive members of society.

The Spare Change Project launched its first massive public service campaign during the Summer of 1988 throughout Los Angeles. It included people in the entertainment industry doing radio and television PSAs using very recognizable names of actors, elected officials, comedians, and related personnel as honorary board members, and highlighting over an extended period the plight and needs of homeless families in Los Angeles. The goal was $500,000 for organizations working in a comprehensive way with homeless families. Since that initial successful campaign, many events have been mounted by the Committee, including: a celebrity-studded concert, an art auction (works by Rembrandt, Picasso and others), a celebrity bowling tournament, a restaurant celebration of the Eiffel Tower Centennial, a photo auction of polaroid pictures taken by celebrities (*A Vision of Home*), etc.

Other plans are in progress with the continued collaboration of public relations and advertising firms to create supportive promotional relationships. One film director said, "Our support of FAP has become an important part of our lives. We hope that, more and more, others will feel that way, too."
Publications: Spare Change Project; Spare Change Summary; Spare Change Press Kit
Founded: 1987

RECIPIENTS: HOMELESS - HEALTH

INDIVIDUAL PROGRAM PROFILES

CHIP-IN
SEE RECIPIENTS: HOMELESS - SHELTERS

HEALTH CARE FOR THE HOMELESS COALITION
United Way of San Antonio and Bexar County
700 South Alamo
PO Box 898
San Antonio, TX 78293-0898
TEL: 512-224-5000
Purpose: To provide a package of services for the homeless in San Diego.
Contact: Richard Alvarado, Director
Description: The *Health Care for the Homeless Coalition* of San Antonio is composed of 28 organizations, including the *United Way of San Antonio & Bexar County, City of San Antonio, Texas Employment Commission,* three universities, nine clinics, four hospitals, and other concerned community organizations.
Formed in 1984, the Coalition's first grant was $1 million from the *Robert Wood Johnson Trust* and *Pew Charitable Trust.* When the Trusts wanted assurance that United Way would continue funding services to the homeless once the grant money was exhausted, United Way gave the assurance. In 1987, the United Way took a more direct role when the Coalition asked that it take over administration of the *Johnson/Pew* grant and the health care project. In 1988, the Coalition received a $275,000 grant under the *Stewart B. McKinney Homeless Assistance Act of 1987,* which enabled expansion of health care services for the homeless.
The project operates clinics at the shelters in which nurse practitioners provide medical care, resolving 85 percent of the medical problems encountered. Problems they cannot handle are referred to county hospitals or two public clinics. In its first two years of operation, the clinics cared for over 5,000 people in 16,000 clinic visits. The largest percentage (43%) are homeless *families,* 32 percent are *females,* and 20 percent are *under the age of 12.* These figures have defied the stereotype of homeless persons: "male, single, and adult."
Outreach teams travel around the city and provide on-the-spot information-and-referral services. The team is equipped with two-way radios and a van filled with clothing, personal hygiene products, sandwiches, and infant formula.
Part of the federal grant is used to identify persons or families at risk of becoming homeless *before* they wind up on the streets - individuals living with family members or friends, more than one family living together in cramped quarters, or families about to be evicted. Staff and volunteers are trained to look for the "not-so-obvious" problems that can cause people to become homeless.

MISSION HOUSE
Jefferson County Medical Society
101 West Chestnut Street
Louisville, KY 40202
TEL: 502-589-2001

Purpose: To provide medical care for the homeless.
Sponsor: Jefferson County Medical Society
Contact: Volunteer Coordinator
Description: The members of the *Jefferson County Medical Society* have gone beyond the traditional methods of providing medical care to work with Mission House, the city's oldest and largest shelter for the homeless. In cooperation with the Roman Catholic priest who founded the center nearly twenty years ago, the society has formed a nonprofit corporation to take over its entire operation - from seeing that 500 meals are served daily to meeting the $95,000 annual budget to maintaining the level of volunteer assistance. Discussions began in late 1988. The transfer of ownership of the 200-bed shelter for men took place late in 1989. The Society expects to expand and improve medical services at the shelter house. A few volunteer doctors have been staffing weekly clinics there, but help has been offered by the *Greater Louisville Organization for Health (GLOH)*, a group of University of Louisville medical students, who will staff additional clinics at the mission under supervision of volunteer doctors. The students now run a weekly clinic for indigent patients in the Iroquois area. In addition to the student organization, the Society expects to become more active in working with other groups, an avenue not actively pursued by Mission House in the past. Also, the Society will look more closely at federal grants such as the one for $40,000 turned down by the founder in 1988 due to conditions attached by a local screening board. A first step for the new administration was to contact the *Louisville Coalition for the Homeless* as it prepares to work with other service providers. As this goal unfolds, providers such as the *Jefferson County Board of Health* are coming forward. The Board has volunteered the agency to help in diet and nutrition planning for Mission House's kitchen. The effort arose from a growing sense among local doctors that their organization needs to become a more responsible corporate citizen.

This major step is an outgrowth of the long tradition of medical professionals to donate services on a case-by-case basis to those who cannot pay for them. The formal commitment to join forces against a broader, community-wide problem has been applauded by the community and the state.

In part, the move is a response to a challenge laid down a year ago by the new president of the American Medical Association. His mandate to members was "to tithe your time for the benefit of the American people."

Plans for the future include employment and education programs for the men at Mission House. The success of the program is dependent on involvement of Society members. An official pointed out, however, that doctors have always been involved in community service programs, and that their participation in Mission House should not be a problem. It is expected that the project will become a national model.

Facilities for women and children will continue to operate in Old Louisville by original Mission House administrators.

RECIPIENTS: HOMELESS - HOUSING

INDIVIDUAL PROGRAM PROFILES

HOUSING NOW!
SEE HOUSING: HOMELESS

STREET NEWS HOMELESS VENDORS PROGRAM
SEE RECIPIENTS: HOMELESS - EMPLOYMENT

RECIPIENTS: HOMELESS - I&R

NATIONAL/STATE ORGANIZATIONS

HOT LINE FOR THE HOMELESS*
Findlay Area Native American Indian Center
Findlay, OH 45840
TOLL FREE: 800-526-5414
Objectives: To provide information for homeless callers on shelters and other services in every state in the union.
Services: A toll-free hot line began operating in January 1990 at the *Findlay Area Native American Center* in Ohio. Referrals are made to shelters, soup kitchens, different social service agencies, and other resources to help people in need in every state of the union.
The center, composed of a house, barn and craft shop on two acres in Findlay, was created to promote American Indian culture. But the center's owner, who is a Cherokee Indian, and an associate who is an Abenaki Indian felt that the resource could be put to better use and converted part of the complex to help the needy. Although several months before the hot line was launched, the center provided food and clothing and emergency shelter to hundreds of people in the Findlay area, the founders are proudest of the hot line, which required research on every state and can help an individual calling from any part of the country in need of food, clothing or shelter.
Contact: Michael Michaud, Spokesman
Founded: 1990

INDIVIDUAL PROGRAM PROFILES

BETHEL LOVE KITCHEN
SEE NUTRITION: HOMELESS

GIVE THEM A HAND, NOT A HANDOUT
Capitol Hill Association of Merchants and Professionals
CHAMPS
PO Box 15486
Washington, DC 20003
TEL: 202-547-7788
Purpose: To provide information for people in the street to lead them to job counseling and other social services.
Contact: Joan Schindel
Description: This program is an attempt by the *Capital Hill Association of Merchants and Professionals (CHAMPS)* to help the truly needy who may not be aware of services available to them - often just a few steps away. The assistance is in the form of a wallet-sized card providing names, addresses, and phones of organizations which are available immediately, and standing ready to be of assistance. The quick-reference card is provided to citizens on request, and is designed as a substitute for giving cash.
In addition to a desire to help the truly needy, CHAMPS sees the program as a way of eliminating the "professional panhandlers" who stake out the southeast area each day. Since there are no vagrancy laws, and a foot patrol officer does not seem to be enough to discourage the practice, nothing much could be done. In addition to causing problems for the truly needy, the panhandlers - some very aggressive - turn business away from the merchants in the area.
The CHAMPS card lists a church and a social services center in the area, giving name, address, phone, and the services provided. To help provide for an increase in clients, CHAMPS has installed collection containers next to the stacks of cards in member-merchants stores for contributions to the two groups listed. Patrons are encouraged to take a stack of cards, and make a contribution. This has appealed to people who want to help, but

are not sure that the money they give directly to the street person will go for a sandwich. In many instances, the money is used for drugs and alcohol. Giving directly to the service providers through the CHAMPS program is reassuring to many citizens. According to the founder of a similar program in California, "We were starting to see a trend, a backlash against those people living on the street," since it was difficult to discern between "economic victims and criminal vagrants."

Other neighborhoods in the District of Columbia, including Adams-Morgan, Dupont Circle and Georgetown, have experienced similar complaints about panhandlers, and are considering similar programs. In the meantime, one of the recipients of the card on Capitol Hill brightened when he read it and said, "I didn't know there was job counseling available. I've been out here too long!"

RECIPIENTS: HOMELESS - LEGAL RIGHTS

NATIONAL/STATE ORGANIZATIONS

NATIONAL COALITION FOR THE HOMELESS
1439 Rhode Island Avenue, NW
Washington, DC 20005
TEL: 202-659-3310
New York office:
105 East 22nd Street
New York, NY 10010
212-460-8110
Objectives: To assure the fundamental rights of decent shelter and housing and adequate food for all.
Services: Works with a federation of individuals, agencies and organizations to secure the rights of the homeless to decent shelter and adequate food; operates under a board of directors with representation from some 50 cities and regions throughout the U.S.; provides legal counsel from professionals experienced in representing the rights of the homeless to assist local counsel in developing and enforcing the rights of the homeless; produces detailed reports on homelessness in targeted cities or states in an effort to increase public awareness and official response to the needs of the homeless; works with churches, synagogues, community and student groups, and city agencies as they organize local shelters and soup kitchens and come together to seek innovative ways to provide support for the homeless; organizes rallies in cities and other areas to bring together concerned citizens, service providers and homeless people; devises plans for the future to prevent homelessness from growing, and to help homeless Americans find jobs, health care and homes; drafts legislation such as the *Homeless Persons' Survival Act,* which was introduced in Congress in 1986 (parts of the Act have been passed, but most remain in Committees); attacks problems in three distinct areas - emergency relief, preventive measures and long-term solutions; publishes a newsletter, special reports, news on homeless legislation, flyers, brochures, information packets and other materials.
Sponsor: Federation of individuals, agencies and organizations
Contact: Adraine Bennett (Washington, DC)
Publications: Not since the Great Depression...; Homelessness in America: A Summary; Housing Now!; Pending Homeless Legislation; Safety Network

INDIVIDUAL PROGRAM PROFILES

LEGAL PROGRAMS FOR THE HOMELESS
American Bar Association
750 North Lake Shore Drive
Chicago, IL 60611
TEL: 312-968-5000
FAX: 312-968-4684
Purpose: To promote legal programs for the homeless.
Contact: Paul L. Friedman, Co-Chairman
Description: In 1988, the *American Bar Association (ABA)* started a project to promote local legal programs for the homeless, hoping to establish 25 within the year. The goal was exceeded in the first four months. According to an ABA official, "Nothing has been as successful in attracting lawyers as homeless problems throughout the country." Activities resulting from ABA efforts have included:

- **Washington Legal Clinic for the Homeless** - One of the pioneers of the field, this program started with about 20 volunteers and now has more than 200, with many turned away because the DC Bar's training room could not accommodate them.
- **Rachel Women's Center Program** - A lawyer sets up shop one Friday a month to help homeless women cope with government bureaucracies, seek custody of children, deal with rape, and seek visas to remain in the U.S. The clinic also collects information on broader problems and tries to get major firms involved.
- **Washington, DC** - A team of lawyers headed for heating grates, a fire barrel, and other spots where homeless people gather for warmth to interview the homeless about crowding and poor conditions at the city's shelter. A notary public traveled from site to site, certifying the witnesses' statements. With ten assigned lawyers, and about 5,000 hours of free time (worth hundreds of thousands of dollars), their work resulted in a major victory for the homeless - a court settlement requiring the city to vastly improve conditions and provide more shelters.

These and other efforts have sparked the legal profession across the country to get involved. This tremendous interest by the legal profession caused one project coordinator to pose the question, "Can you imagine the phenomenon of having law firms demanding to volunteer?" In other instances, activities have included:

- **Boston** - A program matches lawyers in private practice with nonprofit groups that want to build housing for the homeless, attracting lawyers who do not usually get involved with the poor.
- **Los Angeles** - Law firms are "signing up in droves" for a program in which law students with summer jobs volunteer to help homeless people seeking benefits at county welfare offices.
- **University of Maryland** - The Law School offers a course in policy and law affecting the homeless.
- **Yale University** - Law students participate in a seminar in which they work to develop low-income housing.

The court action in the District has led to the establishment of major rights for the homeless. Legal battles helped ensure a place on the ballot for *Initiative 17,* which established the city's obligation to give overnight shelter to those who request it.
In the words of one of the DC lawyers involved, "All the negative stuff you hear about lawyers, it can poison your mind against your own profession. But a case like this can make you feel that what you do is important to people... that you can really make a difference in people's lives."
Founded: 1988

PROJECT HELP (HELP EXPEDITE LEGAL PROBLEMS FOR THE HOMELESS)
Lillick & McHose
433 Brookes Avenue
San Diego, CA 92103
TEL: 619-298-5834

Purpose: To give free legal advice to the homeless.
Sponsor: Lillick & McHose
Contact: Dan Stanford
Description: The goal of *Project HELP* is to have lawyers in private industry volunteer to provide legal services to the homeless, so that government money is not spent in this area. This concept goes hand-in-hand with the fact that all lawyers have been encouraged for a long time to give some of their time back to society in the form of "pro bono," or free, legal work as a way of returning the privileges a license to practice law gives them.
The founder of the program was inspired when he saw homeless people appearing whenever and wherever jobs were offered, and asking for legal advice at various offices. He sees this as an effort on the part of the homeless to reverse their situations.
There are an estimated 6,000 homeless people in San Diego, and the number increases each year. Conversely, the number of *Summer Associates* (students who work as clerks in law firms) has increased, also. An estimated 225 *Associates* worked for San Diego law firms in the summer of 1989.
The program involves at least 100 of the students in a three-hour training program in exchange for one day, or eight hours, of volunteer service at the *Legal Aid Society's* storefront facility. Tasks include interviewing the clients, helping fill out applications, appearing before hearing officers of the Department of Social Services, and obtaining evidence to support eligibility.
Letters are sent each Spring to 60 law firms asking them to encourage their *Summer Associates* to participate. At first a part-time service, 100 *Associates* enable Project HELP to stay open all day everyday during the summer months.
Project HELP's intent is to augment efforts of the *Legal Aid Society* and *Homeless Advocacy Program,* not to displace them.
Founded: 1989

RECIPIENTS: HOMELESS - NUTRITION

INDIVIDUAL PROGRAM PROFILES

ARC COVENANT
Lomond Hotel
2510 Washington Boulevard
Ogden, UT 84401
TEL: 801-399-5627; 801-392-8168
Purpose: To sponsor jointly an action project to benefit the Community of Ogden.
Sponsor: Ogden Department of Aging and Volunteer Services
Contact: Father Kaiser or Father Winder
Description: The ARC Covenant is a union of Episcopal Church of the Good Shepherd, St. Joseph Roman Catholic Church and recently Elim Lutheran Church. Based on an ecumenical directive to reunite, these organizations have combined services within their congregations and the Ogden community. Their pledge to benefit Ogden has resulted in the Soup Kitchen and St. Theresa's Shelter.
Community Need - A humanitarian concern existed because of the increased need for food and shelter for the indigent and transient population. Ogden encounters more homeless because of the railway system.
Recipient's Need - Indigents had limited access to social services. Transients had non-existent resources to serve their basic need for food and shelter. Due to the recession, employment was increasingly unavailable resulting in life threatening situations. Persons were forced to scavenge, sometimes resulting in criminal acts. The onset of inclement weather accelerated their urgent need.
Challenge - On December 8, 1982, volunteers began establishing a shelter. Warehouse space was donated, 65 cots were borrowed from the Red Cross, bedding was donated and electricity, water

and heat were secured. Within 5 days, 18 indigents were sheltered. A week later the shelter was operating at full capacity. This was accomplished through the cooperative efforts of ARC Covenant and Ogden citizens.
Method - A needs assessment determined that the populace required sustenance beyond the evening meals provided by other organizations. ARC Covenant utilized the St. Anne's Church Center and set up a late morning soup kitchen utilizing donations and government commodities. A portion of St. Anne's bingo proceeds were utilized.
The second shelter concern materialized through word of mouth within the churches and community resulting in the necessary material and monetary donations. A local newspaper provided initial information. Volunteer commitment accomplished the housing objectives.
Scope - The combined efforts of ARC Covenant and the community accomplished the serving of 3,923 meals at the Soup Kitchen during December. This has been achieved through continual donations of volunteer time, money and goods. A growing awareness of the needy has resulted in sheltering 65 to 90 persons nightly since the establishment of St. Theresa's Shelter.
Achievement - The community has generously responded with food, blankets, washer, dryer and funds without active fund raising. Donations have exceeded expectations. As a result, the $26,000 church grant received almost two years ago is not financially drained. Direct requests for aid from the indigent have noticeably declined. The police have noticed a noteworthy decrease in area crime.
Innovation - Nationally, out of 117 established covenants, the ARC Covenant has been recognized as 1 of 3 highly successful unions. This organization in turn has impacted on the community's awareness of the needy. Ogden has overwhelmingly responded without a formal request for assistance. Schools, citizens and other religious groups continue to donate materials and time. ARC Covenant's purpose is to feed the hungry and house the homeless without regard to religious, racial or social restriction. They and the Ogden community are achieving this goal.

BETHEL LOVE KITCHEN
SEE NUTRITION: HOMELESS

CHIP-IN
SEE RECIPIENTS: HOMELESS - SHELTERS

GOOD SAMARITAN RECOGNITION CEREMONY
SEE NUTRITION: HOMELESS

LOAVES & FISHES
401 Missouri Avenue
Fort Worth, TX 76104
TEL: 817-334-0903
Purpose: To provide meals, employment counseling, and other services to homeless persons and others in need.
Sponsor: Charity Sports
Contact: Volunteer Coordinator
Description: Founded in 1982, *Loaves & Fishes* has become a distributor of donated food to various charitable, nonprofit agencies serving the needy, sick and elderly - in addition to its many other services. The agencies receiving food include church groups, direct-aid programs, rehabilitation centers, residential treatment facilities and senior citizen centers. At any given time, the *Loaves & Fishes Food Bank* serves between 50 and 100 of these organizatgions on a regular weekly basis. *Loaves & Fishes* depends solely on the donations and volunteer labor.
In addition, the *Loaves & Fishes Soup Kitchen* serves between 150 and 300 homeless and hungry people daily. Other services include employment counseling and job placement, birth certificates and ID replacement, transportation to job sites, a mail center, and hair

cuts for job seekers.

Nutritional but unsellable food is donated regularly to the *Loaves & Fishes Food Bank* by various agents such as supermarkets, food brokers, food manufacturers, individuals and groups. *Loaves & Fishes* inspects all food donations before preparing them for delivery. Donors can make use of the *1978 Tax Reform Act* and are covered for liability under the *Good Faith Donor Act*. Community support for the program is excellent, with more and more innovative ways to raise funds being implemented by individuals, groups, and businesses. A 1989 program called *Help the Homeless Million Dollar Shootout* held at four driving ranges was termed by its local business sponsors as "a fun way to benefit a favorite Fort Worth charity."
Founded: 1982

OUR DAILY BREAD
St. Thomas Episcopal Church
231 South Sunset Avenue
Sunnyvale, CA 94086
TEL: 408-736-4155
Purpose: To provide noontime meals to the needy.
Sponsor: St. Thomas Episcopal Church
Contact: Ed Rogers, Volunteer
Description: Our Daily Bread was founded in 1983 to meet a need for noontime meals for the needy. The *St. Thomas Episcopal Church* opens its doors on Mondays, Wednesdays and Fridays for the food program. *Our Daily Bead* is a nonprofit group that feeds as many as 600 needy Peninsula residents each week.
With an annual budget of $20,000, all from private donations, the program has served more than 100,000 meals since its inception. The program has 100 volunteers, many of whom are charter members, having been there since *Our Daily Bread* began in 1983. One of the volunteers, a 76-year-old retired personnel manager for Lockheed Missiles and Space Company who is a charter member, helps to administer the program, and was chosen by the Sunnyvale Mayor's Awards Committee as Sunnyvale's 1989 *Citizen of the Year.*
Founded: 1983

PRIME TIME TO END HUNGER
VOLUNTEER - The National Center
1111 North 19th Street
Suite 500
Arlington, VA 22209
TEL: 703-276-0542
FAX: 703-528-6052
Purpose: To help volunteering become more visible.
Sponsor: VOLUNTEER - The National Center
Contact: Pamela Warwick
Description: Prime Time to End Hunger is a national initiative to recruit volunteers. It uses the power of prime time television to encourage volunteering. Six prime time shows, representing all three television networks, incorporate themes that reflect today's social issues in the regular programming. Following each show, viewers are encouraged to call a *900* number to obtain information about how they can volunteer.
Callers are mailed a *Consumer's Guide to Community Service,* which includes a personalized letter and the telephone number of the *Volunteer Center, United Way,* or *Emergency Food and Shelter Board* in their communities.
Prime Time to End Hunger receives support from *VOLUNTEER, United Way of America,* and the *National Emergency Food and Shelter Board* program in partnership with *The End Hunger Network.* Other sponsors include Governors' Offices on Volunteerism.
As a result of this and other media campaigns such as *The Volunteer Connection* and *Time to Care,* thousands of new volunteers have come forward to contribute their time and skills.
Publications: Consumer's Guide to Community Service

ST. JOSEPH'S HOUSE OF HOSPITALITY
402 South Avenue
Rochester, NY 14620
TEL: 716-232-3262
Purpose: To provide meals for the homeless and hungry.
Contact: Volunteer Coordinator
Description: The staff of *St. Joseph's House of Hospitality* live in poverty themselves, and devote their lives to the work of the House. All of its services are supported by contributions from area businesses and local individuals. The services are made available to everyone, no questions asked. Clientele is almost exclusively male. The dining room contains six tables which seat 48 people. No one seems to mind the mismatched silverware and dishes, or the flowers in the center of the table that are slightly wilted.
The motto on the kitchen wall, "Work Is Love Made Manifest," is taken seriously, and volunteers find themselves at work within five minutes of their arrival at the House - preparing large, deep pans full of turkey, carrots, peas, gravy, and large quantities of bread, setting tables, replacing flowers, etc. They are encouraged to converse with the clients and most often find them animated and intelligent rather than matching their preconceptions of silent figures with downcast eyes. After the meal is over, and the cleanup is done, the staff invites the volunteers to join them in a circle for a prayer asking for continued ability to offer aid to those in need. One volunteer summed up his work at the House by saying his experiences there leave him "feeling more optimistic about the basic goodness of people. The world is not really all cold and uncaring."

RECIPIENTS: HOMELESS - RECREATION/SPORTS

INDIVIDUAL PROGRAM PROFILES

OUTINGS FOR HOMELESS CHILDREN
Columbus Zoo
990 Riverside Drive
Columbus, OH 43221
TEL: 614-645-3550
Purpose: To provide a cultural experience and "some fun" for children at homeless shelters and their families.
Sponsor: Columbus Zoo
Contact: Barbara Boatwright, Docent
Description: Sponsored by local business/industry, a trip to the Columbus Zoo provided diversion for hundreds of homeless children and their families. The trip included admission to Wyandot Lake, an amusement area, following the zoo tour.
Sponsors arranged for bus pickups at designated stops serving six homeless shelter programs, provided 230 chicken lunches, meat, beverages and salads for a picnic at the zoo, disposable diapers, baby food in jars, toys, coloring books and crayons, and prizes for games the children played while at the picnic, as well as volunteers to serve as escorts and guides.
Since many other volunteer groups are working very hard to meet the basic needs of the residents of the shelters, the sponsors felt someone had to reach out to provide a little fun in the process.
The program is expected to be a periodic, ongoing recreation event for shelter residents in the area.
Founded: 1989

RECIPIENTS: HOMELESS - SHELTERS

TRAINING PROGRAMS

GIVE ME SHELTER: DESIGNS FOR URBAN SURVIVAL
Washington Post
Washington Home Division
1150 Fifteenth Street, NW
Washington, DC 20071
TEL: 202-334-7654
Credit: None
Sponsor: Washington Post
Contact: Panel Coordinator
Description: This forum arose out of the accelerating statistics of the homeless population - including entire families - in the Washington, DC, area. *Washington Post's Washington Home* division brought together a volunteer panel of architects, designers, shelter providers, and others concerned with housing for the homeless to explore ways *design* can help alleviate a social problem. Questions posed and responses offered included:
How do architects get involved in housing and shelters for the homeless?
- A program like *Search for Shelter* inherits a building that may or may not be worth refurbishing, or a program may be thinking about buying a building but doesn't know if it's worth the price. That's where the architects come in.
How do you feel the homeless perceive "home"?
- Emotional security, an emotional environment.
- Where they're loved or esteemed.
- Not in the "throw-away" buildings we throw at them.
- City shelters are depressing places - nothing like home.
- Private shelters are wonderful.
- A home-like atmosphere is needed for people looking for a way back into the mainstream.
- Emergency housing should not be provided without support services to help in a transition to affordable housing.
- It could be as simple as putting partitions between beds for privacy.
If people in need of shelter are in varying stages of development toward independence, requiring different kinds of temporary and transitional environments, what burden does this place upon architects? How do you factor these needs into a design solution, and is there evidence that design helps?
- *Housing Opportunities for Women (HOW)* is transitional housing with three apartments that have 13 bedrooms, and women there must have jobs, support themselves, pay rent, etc., to the best of their ability.
- Another HOW project involves a broken-down shelter for women which was refurbished by HOW, and women who lived there in despair suddenly went out and got jobs. Providing a nice home raises self-esteem and helps people who have gone through the trauma of homelessness face society again.
- "Dignity" and "Security" is what we want these transitional housing projects to convey. You are telling people who have come to question their worth that they are "worthy to live in a nice place."
- Each project has its own requirements. You address homeless families, homeless single mothers with children, homeless children all by themselves, the elderly, etc.
- We have to promote "ownership" whether it is in the shelter space, a small apartment, or whatever. People know they're in a temporary situation, but can be made to take pride in their surroundings and keep making advancements.
Is there a way that designers and architects can translate dignity and security into design concepts?
- At CCNV we did not economize on lighting ("downlighting" is considered economical, but is not dignified), we partitioned

areas containing six cots each (not the privacy we would like to give, but some), and made sure everyone had a locker so that they would feel secure about their belongings. We even put the names - Mr.... Mrs... - on the locker to help take away the feeling of "living in a waiting room." Beyond that, we were budget restricted.
- The government feels that the only way to assure personal safety is with large open spaces.
Is the large open space concept derived from the military? And is that why they always use government green and gray?
- Yes, that approach is very militaristic.
Has anyone experimented with colors and their impact on the human psyche?
- We did the drop-in center for women in peach and white, and most remarked on the warm and feminine look - and that's what we wanted. In one of the dormitories we dropped the ceiling and put sconces on the walls instead of overhead lighting.
Did you have to overcome objections that this would be impractical and hard to clean?
- The only objection was that it was more expensive - but the fact that it would get dirty sooner never came up.
- The nicer the condition of the shelter, the more likely people will try to keep it nice. On a visit to the *House of Ruth,* I heard an argument among the women on whose room was cleaner.
We're talking about a female environment. Was the same true for men?
- The one I worked with was very well kept - shiny floors, nice drapes on the windows, very clean spreads, - and much better order came out of that. Definitely, when you provide a good environment, people respond to it.
What are some of the architectural problems?
- The most difficult problem is to take an old turn-of-the-century home and make it structurally sound. Then we have to design to the DC building code constraints, fire department regulations, etc. It gets to be a question of what you can squeeze out of that budget.
- A standing building and adapting it to particular needs is really the challenge.
Other points were made on using color for signage when illiteracy is a problem, climates in different parts of the country and their influence on housing, designing large shelters, the ideal shelter (five residents in a homelike atmosphere), the issue posed by some of making the shelter "too comfortable," the emotional damage of a shelter that says, "Boy, I can't wait to get you out of here," and the happy medium of a well-kept shelter combined with case management and staffing to help people move back into the mainstream.
The volunteer panel members came from the architectural firms of *Weihe Partnership, Richard Adams Architects, Duvall/Hendricks, Bruner, Middleton & Associates,* nonprofit organizations *House of Ruth* and *Search for Shelter,* the law firm of *Howrey & Simon,* and *The Washington Post.*

TACTS VOLUNTEER SHELTER MANAGER TRAINING
The Arlington County Temporary Shelter (TACTS)
PO Box 1285
Arlington, VA 22210
TEL: 703-237-0881
Credit: Inquire
Sponsor: The Arlington County Temporary Shelter (TACTS)
Contact: Judy Wallace
Description: This workshop aims to provide volunteers with additional skills in communication, and to help them learn procedures used in a shelter so that the volunteer can feel comfortable in roles as *Shelter Manager Volunteers.* Participants have the benefit of being trained by staff of a dual-purpose shelter, *TACTS (The Arlington Community Temporary Shelters),* which

serves as a safe house for battered women and children, and an emergency shelter for homeless women and families. By the end of the training, volunteers are expected to be:

- familiar with TACTS in-house procedures and policies.
- able to screen clients on the telephone.
- able to make appropriate referrals.
- able to communicate more effectively with clients.
- able to complete TACTS forms with staff assistance.

Volunteers serve as *Shelter Manager Substitutes* as well as *Shelter Managers,* and as administrative aides, food committee members, children's aides, transportation aides, special projects managers, and computer program aides. All receive appropriate additional training. The program is open also to those considering volunteer involvement to give them additional insight into shelter programs.

TOWN MEETING FOR THE HOMELESS
Volunteers of America of Delaware Valley
Church & Evergreen Avenue
Thorofare, NJ 08086
TEL: 609-853-0350
Sponsor: Volunteers of America/Delaware Valley
Contact: Pal Shelly, Director/Communications, or Sheila Allen, Social Worker
Description: This community education meeting was born of what volunteers of VOA Delaware Valley considered to be an injustice. The local zoning board had denied a request for a variance to secure a facility to be used for a new shelter for homeless women and children - even though no opposing testimony was forthcoming from neighbors of the facility.
The selected facility is on 26 acres in Elk Township, Gloucester County, and has nine bedrooms and a gymnasium. Gloucester County is a part of New Jersey that has farms, residential suburban areas, industrial parks, and an array of individuals of various races, nationalities and walks of life.
With the crucial zoning meeting for reconsideration near at hand, VOA staff decided to move quickly and mount an education program for the community about the problem of homelessness and the need for a shelter. This could reach any opposition that might surface. A meeting which included both clergy and laity was held just a few days before a final decision on the site was to be rendered. Presenters made the following points, among others:

- Homelessness is a rural and suburban problem - not just an urban problem in the cities.
- Homelessness in Gloucester County cannot be prevented.
- Those who have to leave their homes also leave friends, neighbors, and churches - familiar resources that could help them get back on their feet.

Following the presentations, an informal question-and-answer session addressed and satisfied any remaining concerns of participants. As a result of the community education meeting and other efforts of VOA, the volunteer presenters, and the homeless themselves, the zoning board decision was overturned on May 19, 1989. The residents moved into the large house in the fall of the same year.

INDIVIDUAL PROGRAM PROFILES

ARC COVENANT
SEE RECIPIENTS: HOMELESS - NUTRITION

BAILEY'S CROSSROADS COMMUNITY SHELTER
3525 Moncure Avenue
Falls Church, VA 22041
TEL: 703-820-7621 (Shelter); 703-256-1378 (ACCA)
Purpose: To help homeless persons overcome the conditions that created their homelessness.
Sponsor: Annandale Christian Community for Action (ACCA)

Contact: Marilyn Morrison, Director; Peter Woolly, Assistant Director; Whitey Rowell, ACCA Liaison
Description: After 20 months of service in temporary trailers and cramped office space, the Bailey's Crossroads Community Shelter was opened on September 22, 1987. It is operated under contract with the County of Fairfax by the Salvation Army with facilities for men and women.
A variety of services are provided by volunteers, who are recruited from ACCA churches and the community. Their activities include, but are not limited to, food preparation, serving meals, monitoring shelter activities and security, serving as receptionists, assisting with office work and, perhaps most important of all, being a friend to residents and helping them to develop social skills and locate jobs.
In 1988, 720 individuals provided a total of about 4,200 hours of service to residents who filled the shelter, frequently to overflowing, almost every night. These volunteers served over 1,480 individual, unduplicated residents during 1988.
Other services provided to the residents are supplied by professional staff from the Salvation Army, Department of Social Services, Substance Abuse Service, Department of Public Health, and Woodburn Mental Health Center. Such services include health screening, employment guidance and referral, mental health counseling, educational and self help training.
Contributions from the community in the form of cash and materials have been a major factor in the operation of the Shelter. Much of the cost of providing the programs and services required by the residents to successfully readjust to being a contributing member of the community must come from such donations. In preparing the contract for operation of the Shelter, the County accepted the assurances from the community that the Shelter would be a joint operation between the County staff and the citizens of the community and its churches.
As experience in operating the Shelter is gained, the need for contributions from citizens continues to increase as more is learned about the residents, their needs and their special problems. The most significant knowledge gained so far seems to be that the homeless problem is growing in the County even though shelter capacity has increased in the Northern Virginia area.
The Annandale Christian Community for Action (ACCA) program has made the Shelter one of its outreach programs and keeps all member churches informed, urging them to continue providing volunteers, materials, and financial help to maintain the growing effectiveness of the Shelter program.
Publications: ACCA Annual Report

CHIP-IN
c/o Family Assistance Program
6605 Hollywood Boulevard
Los Angeles, CA 90028
TEL: 213-461-9632
Purpose: To help solve some of the problems of the homeless and hungry.
Sponsor: Family Assistance Program; Hollywood Mental Health Service; Los Angeles Free Clinic; Hollywood Temple Beth El; Hope Lutheran Church; St. Thomas Episcopal Church; Blessed Sacrament Catholic Church
Contact: M. Patricia Shelhamer
Description: In the fall of 1984 a group of representatives from Hollywood area churches, temples and social service agencies met and joined together to help solve some of the problems of the homeless and hungry. Out of this initial meeting grew the idea of forming a coalition of the like-minded groups and individuals to provide humane and cost-effective solutions for Hollywood's growing homeless population and to preserve and perpetuate the renowned and glamorous image of Hollywood as an ideal place to live and do business, a caring community. Thus CHIP-IN (Community of Hollywood Investing In People In Need) was formed and incorporated as a nonprofit public benefit organization

in July of 1985. CHIP-IN is comprised of approximately forty local religious groups and social service agencies, such as:

- Blessed Sacrament Catholic Church
- Centrum of Hollywood
- Family Assistance Program of Hollywood
- First Presbyterian Church of Hollywood
- Gay and Lesbian Community Service Center
- Hollywood Mental Health Service
- Hollywood Temple Beth El
- Hope Lutheran Church
- Immaculate Heart Community
- Jewish Family Services
- Los Angeles Free Clinic
- St. Thomas Episcopal Church
- Senior Multi-Purpose Center
- Temple Israel of Hollywood
- Traveler's Aid/Teen Canteen
- Volunteers of America/Hollywood Shelter Program
- West Hollywood Food Coalition

CHIP-IN was instrumental, in a joint venture with *Volunteers of America,* in establishing a new shelter for the homeless in Hollywood. The *Hollywood Homeless Shelter* opened October 19, 1986. The facility provides shelter for individuals and families through referrals from the Department of Social Services or participating coalition member agencies.

CHIP-IN has been providing approximately 250 meals for the homeless every evening since its inception, first in cooperation with the Salvation Army at its Hollywood facility, and now with the *West Hollywood Food Coalition.*

The *Los Angeles Free Clinic,* with the help of CHIP-IN, is very close to opening a subsidiary of their Beverly Boulevard Facility in the Hollywood area, making medical services available in the central Hollywood area.

CHIP-IN is quartered in the *Family Assistance Program* offices and meets monthly to discuss needs, introduce public officials, and share other information.

Founded: 1984

HOUSING PROGRAM OF ACCA
Annandale Christian Community for Action (ACCA)
7200 Columbia Pike
Annandale, VA 22003
TEL: 703-256-1378
Purpose: To help alleviate the pressure within the County for affordable housing.
Sponsor: ACCA
Contact: Marie Monsen, Housing Chair
Description: For ACCA's Housing Program, 1988 marked a year of change. With the growth in the number of homeless people and the tremendous pressure in Fairfax County to provide more affordable housing, we decided it was time to expand in this area. After examining ACCA's involvement, it was decided to divest the program of the two houses owned by ACCA and the mortgages being held on other properties, and to look for new avenues of service in the housing area. (The houses, which were rented to low-income families, were sold to their occupants at cost.) In keeping with ACCA's philosophy of putting ACCA money to work in the community, all current programs were reviewed. The Housing Committee explored a number of options. As of January 1989, ACCA membership approved the following:

- $18,000 to *Shelter House* to launch a Transitional Housing Program. This helps families move from emergency housing to permanent housing by providing help for rent, deposits, and living expenses as well as job training and counseling.
- $4,500 to the Bailey's Crossroads Shelter for a Transitional Housing Program which assists single adults in moving into permanent housing.

Other housing programs under consideration for ACCA support included the County-sponsored *Project Homes,* where families are "sponsored" by a church or family for 4-6 months, and the *Habitat for Humanity* program, which raises money and volunteers to build new homes and rehabilitate older homes. In addition, because of the escalating demand for furniture, membership voted to give $10,000 of the money generated by the sales of old properties to the Furniture Warehouse to purchase items in great demand and to reduce the backlog of requests. Another $20,000 was given to the Day Care Center to help launch a new *Day Care Center for Infants* - a growing need for many working mothers. Completed in 1990, it is housed on the grounds of ACCA I in Annandale.

ACCA expects coming years to present many challenges in the area of housing and invites interested individuals and groups to come forward and assist with ideas and volunteer time and support.

Publications: ACCA Annual Report

INTERFAITH SHELTER NETWORK
San Diego County Ecumenical Conference
c/o METRO
861 Sixth Avenue, Suite 810
San Diego, CA 92101
TEL: 619-234-3158
Purpose: To fight homelessness throughout San Diego county.
Sponsor: County of San Diego
Contact: Mary Niez, Network Coordinator; Rev. Dennis Mikulanis, Conference President
Description: On July 1, 1989, the *San Diego County Ecumenical Conference* was awarded a joint City and County contract and became the administrator of the *Interfaith Shelter Network.* The network involves more than 100 congregations throughout the county that work to fight homelessness. The Regional Task Force on the Homeless, which directed the program since its inception in 1987, is a planning and coordinating agency and not set up to run long-term programs.

About half of the 100 congregations in the network house up to 12 guests for two or four weeks a year and are called "host congregations." The other half assist the hosts by providing meals, overnight volunteers and transportation. There is only one paid staff member, the Network Coordinator, with an office at METRO, the United Methodist social service agency.

Clusters of congregations, called branches, operated this year in La Jolla-Pacific Beach, South Bay, East County, Point Loma-Ocean Beach, North County Coastal, North County Inland, North Park-Hillcrest and College Heights.

A pilot program was operated in Southeast San Diego in the spring of 1989, with plans set for work in the Clairemont-Kearny Mesa and San Dieguito areas. Recruiting of volunteers takes place each year in June and July to assure adequate resources for the fall-winter-spring shelter season. Training is conducted in August and September.

Founded: 1987

LUTHER PLACE WOMEN'S SHELTER
Luther Place Memorial Church
1226 Vermont Avenue, NW
Washington, DC 20005
TEL: 202-386-5464 (Shelter); 202-667-1377 (church)
Purpose: To provide shelter for women in need of a place to stay.
Description: Since the city opens emergency sleeping areas in government buildings only when the temperature drops below 25 degrees at night, the unusually warm winter of 1989-90 found few nights that met the city's emergency plan. This did not alleviate the need for shelter, and the *Luther Place Women's Shelter,* in the words of the minister directing the program, was "in turmoil." The shelter, which opened in 1975 as one of the first church shelters in the city, limits the 100 beds to women, since city shelters offer beds for men.

The 280-member congregation of the *Luther Place Memorial*

Church fully supports the shelter program. Members cook and serve meals, work overnight in the shelter, work on related committees and contribute money. The shelter turns no one away. If men show up at the door, church volunteers find them spaces in the city-run shelters. All women are accommodated, even if it means putting mattresses on the floor. The church offers a full dinner each night and a breakfast in the morning.

While most women in the past who sought shelter had mental problems, today there are drug addicts and those with medical problems so serious that they cannot leave the church during the day. In one case, church members transported a homeless woman back and forth to the hospital for dialysis.

The director and the church members see the homeless shelter as an obvious response by a church to the homeless. "Jesus was born a homeless person. There was no space at the Inn."

OIC NATIONAL SHELTER PROGRAM
Opportunities Industrialization Centers of America
100 West Coulter Street
Philadelphia, PA 19144
TEL: 215-951-2200
Purpose: To build 100 shelters in troubled inner cities to provide housing, clothing, remedial education, job training and counseling programs.
Sponsor: OIC of America
Contact: The Rev. Leon H. Sullivan, Founder, or Elton Jolly, President
Description: A nationwide program announced in May 1989 by OIC (Opportunities Industrialization Centers of America) involves working with its 70 national centers to build 100 shelters in inner cities. In addition to the homeless, target groups include drug addicts, ex-convicts and gang members.

To encourage response, OIC offers $20,000 in seed money to each of the first five cities to participate in the project, requesting that shelters be completed in six months. The city of Philadelphia was among the first to volunteer. By mid-1989, other affiliates who volunteered to build shelters were Delaware County, Pennsylvania; Flint, Michigan; Montgomery, Alabama; Detroit, Milwaukee and Minneapolis. Labor unions assist by volunteering to build the centers in vacant storefronts and abandoned buildings.

All shelters are staffed by volunteers, including doctors and psychiatrists who commit to 24-hour medical and counseling services. Recruitment areas include the business community, colleges, churches, and OIC training centers. Funding comes from philanthropic foundations, local and federal government, churches and private donors.

The inspiration for the program came from recent reports that 25% of the U.S. population were drug or alcohol abusers and that perhaps as many as two million people were homeless. In addition to beds, the shelters provide counseling for drug addicts, food for the hungry, and reading and writing instruction, with heavy emphasis on self-help.

OIC was started 25 years ago by a Zion Baptist Church pastor in an abandoned jail in North Philadelphia as a self-help job training program. To date it has trained over a million people, and is in place in 13 foreign countries. The same pastor contributed the first $1,000 to the current shelter program.
Founded: 1974

SHELTER HOUSE
3080 Patrick Henry Drive
PO Box 4081
Falls Church, VA 22044
TEL: 703-536-2155 (Shelter); 703-256-1378 (ACCA)
Purpose: To meet the critical need for temporary housing for County residents.
Sponsor: Churches, synagogues, ecumenical groups, philanthropic organizations, local and federal government and individuals

Contact: Mary Garwood, President and ACCA Liaison, or Michelle Palmer, Director
Description: Located in the Seven Corners area, Shelter House is one of two facilities in Fairfax County established to assist families in crisis. Shelter House consists of seven apartments with two bedrooms each; administration and counseling offices; a classroom/conference area; and a food service center. The present 36-bed facility opened in 1986 and more than doubled the original housing capacity.

Residents are referred from the Fairfax County Department of Social Services, American Red Cross, and other approved referral agencies. They stay an average of 57 days and do their own cooking, cleaning, and laundry. Special attention is given the children to create the sense of a caring, loving home.

Residents receive 24-hour comprehensive care, professional support, and guidance which enables many to make an expeditious return to the community. In addition to social services support, residences receive three balanced meals a day; housing and career counseling; employment assistance; job referral; and Life Skills Training. Several new programs have been developed including one for single expectant women. It is also anticipated that Shelter House will begin transitional housing in an attempt to move participants once and for all from emergency to permanent housing. ACCA (Annandale Christian Community for Action) has been instrumental in launching this program, having given an $18,000 grant in December 1988.

Various churches, synagogues, ecumenical groups, philanthropic organizations, local and federal government and individuals provide financial, in-kind and program support to Shelter House. A unique program, *Adopt a Shelter House Family,* enlists churches and groups to become linked with a particular family, helping them in friendship and support. Help is always needed in locating jobs, apartments, and usable cars.

Shelter House is governed by a volunteer Board of Directors, with representation from seven ecumenical groups that were fundamental to its formation. These include ACCA, CHO, ECHO, Falls Church Community Service Council, FISH, FOCUS, and SHARE. A dedicated team of social service professionals work in concert with the Board to provide a safe and supportive environment for the homeless.
Founded: 1986

RECIPIENTS: INTERGENERATIONAL

NATIONAL/STATE ORGANIZATIONS

GRAY PANTHERS
1424 Sixteenth Street, NW
Suite L1
Washington, DC 20036
TEL: 202-783-6226
Objectives: To bring youth and the aged together in a concerted effort to improve the status of both groups.
Services: Assists local groups in organization of youth-elderly projects, focusing on the belief that ageism affects both groups adversely, and that working together will achieve more for each than either group working alone; helps all age groups mount and implement projects of their choosing in the goal areas; conducts studies on the role of volunteer/advocacy groups, communal living, alternatives to institutionalization, and other mutual interest areas and publishes findings; writes courses for universities; maintains national speakers bureau; develops publications and films; publishes bimonthly newspaper and a series of organizing manuals books, and other materials; convenes periodic health conferences and biennial meetings.

Publications: Network Newsletter
Founded: 1971

INTERGENERATIONAL SERVICE-LEARNING PROJECT
National Council on the Aging
600 Maryland Avenue, NW
West Wing 100
Washington, DC 20024
TEL: 202-479-1200
Objectives: To bring together two isolated groups - college students and older persons - to form friendships, share knowledge, and engage in mutually-beneficial projects.
Services: Works with volunteer groups, community agencies and campus departments to organize and operate programs and identify needs; emphasizes advocacy, improving access to health care, and delivering health services to economically disadvantaged, homebound and isolated older persons; publishes a handbook for establishing service-learning programs and projects plus a series of technical assistance guides for the community on recruitment, orientation, supervision, and other program management areas, and a national clearinghouse for service-learning projects.
Publications: Perspectives on Aging; Current Literature on Aging; Collage - Cultural Enrichment
Founded: 1950

INDIVIDUAL PROGRAM PROFILES

SENIOR PROGRAM
Joint Educational Project
801 West 34th Street
Los Angeles, CA 90089-0471
TEL: 213-743-7698
Purpose: To foster better communication between generations and to implement a volunteer program which utilizes students and elders as activity leaders and community service providers.
Sponsor: The Public Welfare Foundation; University of Southern California
Contact: Maria Calderon
Description: In January 1981, the *Senior Program,* operated by the *Joint Educational Project (JEP),* created a link between the University and its neighboring community by forming a cooperative bond with a nearby senior citizens center. The project aims at enhancing the services of the site while providing students the experience of working with senior citizens.
Each semester approximately 40 students participate in some of the following activities:
- outreach services, where students pair up to visit homebound elderly, bringing information and referral services and companionship;
- autobiographies, in which students write their senior partner's life history;
- arts and crafts or health classes, in which students research topics and present them to the seniors in classes.
Student volunteers are under the supervision of the Program Assistants, part-time staff employed by either JEP who plan with professors, recruit and train students for assignments or by senior center staff.
The *Senior Program* offers two distinct groups: university students and senior citizens, the opportunity to work together for mutual benefits. This project fosters communication among these groups and has brought about numerous friendships. It has also enhanced the quality of college education, introducing a "real life" experience to classroom learning.
Founded: 1981

RECIPIENTS: MILITARY - ACTIVE/VETERANS

NATIONAL/STATE ORGANIZATIONS

MILITARY EDUCATORS AND COUNSELORS ASSOCIATION
SEE PSYCHOSOCIAL SUPPORT SERVICES: MILITARY

NATIONAL MILITARY FAMILY ASSOCIATION
SEE RECIPIENTS: FAMILIES - MILITARY

US/DOD - NAVY FAMILY SERVICE CENTER
SEE RECIPIENTS: FAMILIES - MILITARY

US/VA - PRIVATE SECTOR INITIATIVES PROGRAM
Office of the Administrator
810 Vermont Avenue, NW
Washington, DC 20420
TEL: 202-393-4120
Objectives: To increase participation of staff at the local level to enhance the public/private initiatives concept.
Services: Involves the private sector though volunteer services, and assists the private sector by disseminating staff knowledge and experience to the community; promotes collaboration between the *Veterans Administration* and the private sector; provides information on how the agency involves and assists the private sector, which includes the following:
How the VA Utilizes the Private Sector
- *Department of Medicine and Surgery* (more than 75,000 volunteers who donate over 100,000,000 hours of service each year).
- *Department of Veterans Benefits* (involves volunteers through public/private collaboration on services for unemployed veterans resulting in *Job Fairs, Veteran Employment Seminars, Opportunity Days* and *Vet-A-Thons).*
- *Department of Memorial Affairs* (involves volunteers in national cemeteries, and in work with veterans and families on benefits and other memorial issues.)
How the VA Assists the Private Sector
Department of Medicine and Surgery
- health fairs, boards of volunteer directors' groups, instructors in volunteer workshops, instructors for special workshops for nursing home staff and volunteers
- supportive services for terminally ill
- *Volunteer for Course Credit* program for high school students
- *Geriatric Motivation Program* involving sixth grade students in nursing homes
- Field internships at medical centers
- Volunteers recruited from runaway and problem teenagers
- Former mental patients as volunteers
- Handicapped persons as volunteers
- Volunteer experience for high school students with mental and emotional disabilities
- *Handyman Program* involving domiciled residents
- *Toys for Tots* involving volunteers and patients as builders and fixers
- Volunteer placements for first-time minor offenders (alternative sentencing)
Department of Veterans Benefits
- *Interagency Task Force on Information and Referral* (programs for the elderly: retirement planning, funding of programs, counseling/emergency services); Task Force includes *Equitable Life, Red Cross, National Council of Churches, United Way, Salvation Army, Catholic Charities, Peoples Drug,* and others in addition to the VA.

- Regional office/private sector activities on behalf of older veterans (question/answer column on veteran benefits; *Silver and Gold,* a newsletter; 18 mobile assistance programs for seniors; two-day resource seminars; *Veterans Benefits Information,* a cable TV series; visits to high residences for elderly; linkages with relevant U.S. departments).

Department of Memorial Affairs
- Contracting with private firms to operate national cemeteries
- Exploring with national industries for severely handicapped the possibility of contractual services at VA facilities
- Receiving donations of land for expansion
- Working with corporations and states to halt vandalism
- Working with military bases to develop and erect new cemetery signs
- Procuring 83% of materials from private sector

Hindrances to Private Sector Initiatives
- The cost of being a volunteer (should consider increasing tax-deductible mileage).
- The increasing difficulty in securing or affording transportation to and from work site.
- The need to establish a system or network of referral and exchange through which capable volunteers leaving one program or agency could be referred to others.
- The professionalism of volunteers to attract new people by publicizing interesting, creative volunteer positions.

VA Action Plan
- Encourage employees to continue building partnerships with local communities, to involve themselves with local task forces organized to seek solutions to community problems.
- Request staff to offer technical assistance and training services wherever possible, and sharing VA space.
- Urge VA public relations representatives to issue press releases which highlight VA's private sector initiatives program.
- Provide *Project Bank* forms to each VA facility and 350 private organizations which provide volunteers to document their programs.
- Encourage VA staff to increase their involvement with community volunteer programs, and to include community groups in VA-sponsored seminars, training sessions, and recreation activities.

For more detail, see separate entry on *Veterans Administration Voluntary Service (VAVS).*
Sponsor: US/VA - Veterans Administration

TRAINING PROGRAMS

ARMY CHILD CARE TECHNICAL ASSISTANCE CONFERENCE
US/DoD - Army TRADOC, CFSC-FSC
2461 Eisenhower Avenue
Hoffman Bldg 1, #1400
Alexandria, VA 22331-0521
TEL: 202-325-0710
Sponsor: US/DoD - Department of the Army
Contact: Patty Kasold
Description: Every year, following the *Save the Children* annual conference, the Army's child care directors, professional staff, educators, outreach workers and volunteers hold a four-day meeting to review child care technical assistance matters throughout the Army. A recurring problem for mobile military families, this brainstorming session had the goal of finding solutions that would be the least disruptive to the children involved. Proceeds and other materials resulting from the conference are available on request.

MANAGEMENT OF VOLUNTEER PROGRAMS IN THE ARMED FORCES
VOLUNTEER - The National Center
1111 North 19th Street, Suite 500
Arlington, VA 22209
TEL: 703-276-0542
FAX: 703-528-6021
Sponsor: VOLUNTEER - The National Center
Contact: Kay Drake
Description: A Department of Defense Volunteer Management Track was made part of an annual VOLUNTEER's national training conference for volunteer managers.

Military people were able to focus on successful volunteer programs being conducted throughout the Services and exchange ideas on program management in this area. Speakers from each of the Armed Services, including Reserve Components, discussed various aspects of volunteerism in their branches of the Service, including successful approaches to volunteer recruitment and management. Opportunities were available throughout the conference for networking with other professionals, both within and outside of the Service, and to exchange examples of volunteer program materials.

Service representatives had an opportunity to participate in the general sessions as well as those related to military volunteer programs.

US/VA - VAVS WORKSHOPS
US/VA - Voluntary Service Division
VA Voluntary Service (VAVS)
Veterans Administration
Washington, DC 20420
TEL: 202-389-2953
Credit: Certificate
Sponsor: US/VA - Veterans Administration
Contact: Karen Draper
Description: Presenting four workshops, this annual conference combines volunteer roles with needs of the patients, with participants given the option to select two of them. The four workshops:

Selling the Volunteer Program: Based on the fact that recruitment of new volunteers is vital to the success of the VAVS program, this workshop emphasizes "what happens to volunteers after they are recruited." With studies showing that programs excelling in recruiting techniques often fall short of orientation, placement and follow-up of new volunteers, this workshop addresses the elements of retention of volunteers in relation to the recruitment and ongoing supervision. The goal is to reduce the number of volunteers who become dissatisfied and limit or stop their involvement.

Meeting the Needs of the Older Patient... and the Older Volunteer: With the older veteran population growing, and older volunteers who, because of age, have become ineffective in their present assignments, a solution that might meet both needs is explored in this workshop. Based on evidence that the veteran population is growing, and that many faithful volunteers, because of age, can no longer work effectively in demanding volunteer assignments, workshop planners provide a forum for the idea of bringing together these two groups. Results could include improved understanding of the problems of the aging through development of volunteer assignments that meet the needs of both the older patient and the older volunteer, and an improvement of the quality of life for the older person both in the medical center and in the community.

New and Innovative VA Volunteer Assignments: To keep participants abreast of new and challenging volunteer assignments being developed throughout the VA, this workshop discusses these new assignments, how they are developed, and how to document a few "new ideas" to take back to the participant's local organization and local VA Medical Center.

The Volunteer's Role in VA Security and Safety: Although volunteers traditionally play a role in security and safety, this workshop keeps them informed of the most common security and safety hazards, what is being done to combat these problems, appropriate training for volunteers, and precautions for avoiding or correcting security and safety hazards (including hostage-taking by patients, theft of government property, volunteer injuries, etc.). This meeting also serves as the meeting place for the Annual Meeting of the VAVS Advisory Committee.

INDIVIDUAL PROGRAM PROFILES

ARMY COMMUNITY SERVICE
US/DoD - Army Community Service
Office of the Adjutant General
Alexandria, VA 22331
TEL: 202-325-9390
Purpose: To provide a resource for identifying and meeting the needs of soldiers and families, including the need to interact with the wider community.
Sponsor: US/DoD - Department of the Army
Contact: Lt. Col. James R. David, Chief
Description: Begun in 1965, Army Community Service (ACS) offers assistance, information, service, and guidance to service members and their families in areas cited in its initial proposal. However, it has evolved into a full service agency by developing programs as needs arise. Programs meet needs of the individual, families, and/or the total community. Many are cooperative ventures with the civilian community surrounding the base. These programs include:
- **Relocation** - help in getting situated in new surroundings.
- **Exceptional Family Member** - identifies military and civilian services for the handicapped.
- **Family Advocacy** - services to strengthen the Army family, including child and spouse abuse counseling.
- **Child Development Services** - full-day, hourly, and part-time child care services for children six to twelve years of age.
- **Foster Care Services** - substitute care for children on a 24-hour basis to meet emergency needs.
- **Consumer Affairs/Financial Management** - training in money management, consumer rights and obligations, shopping strategies, etc.
- **Information Referral and Follow-Up** - help in finding appropriate assistance for emotional, legal, financial, parental, personal and other problems.

Volunteers, working with paid staff, are trained to assist in a variety of programs other than those listed above. These include: Hi Neighbor, Lending Closet, publicity, newsletter, services to waiting families, education and employment assistance, services to foreign-born spouses, etc. Volunteers receive awards and recognition for the time they donate, as well as the benefits of training in program areas. Recruitment of volunteers is a continuous process as ACS strives to provide assistance, information, service, and guidance to service members and their families, as well as to design programs designed to meet the needs of the entire community.
Founded: 1965

EDUCATION AND EMPLOYMENT RESOURCE CENTER
US/DoD - Army Community Service
1169 Middletown Road
Fort Belvoir, VA 22060
TEL: 703-354-3912; 703-354-6664
Purpose: To provide a variety of resources directly related to education and employment available in the area.
Sponsor: US/DoD - Department of the Army
Contact: Lynn Armstrong

Description: Begun in the fall of 1982, the Education and Employment Resource Center exists to provide a service to the families of active duty and retired military personnel, and family members recently separated by death or divorce from an active duty or retired military member. The range of use is:
- support, assistance, and preparation for first-time employed and new arrivals in area;
- jobs to balance economic need;
- family members in transition - career re-entry;
- employment continuity and upwardly mobile job changing;
- personal development and life planning - goal setting, education, and volunteer opportunities.

Volunteers collect resource materials, do employment/employer research and educational opportunities research, maintain a skills bank (client file), provide program outreach, serve as counselors and counselor trainers, perform clerical services, and research volunteer opportunities for clients.

In addition to a design and planning staff and the volunteers, a consultant from the Bolling Air Force Base Military Spouse Skills and Resource Center is involved in the Center's work. In addition, a seven-point Basic Philosophy has been developed, as well as a 21-point Organizational Task List. The former lists the goals of the service, and the latter outlines the activities to be performed to reach the goals. Tasks range from recruiting volunteers to making the Center inviting to clients.

Steps in working with EERC clients include nine activities in the relationship between the client and the Center, ranging from the initial interview to the client as an employee. A report with details is available.
Publications: Steps in Working with Clients
Founded: 1982

FEST (FORT EUSTIS SOLDIERS THEATRE)
SEE ARTS/CULTURAL ENRICHMENT:
MUSIC/DANCE/THEATRE

FORT DIX VOLUNTEERS
US/DoD - Fort Dix
DPCA/ATTN: ATZDGA-S
Army Training Center
Fort Dix, NJ 08640
TEL: 609-562-4045
Purpose: To help the program leaders on the post and in the surrounding local communities to increase their services to families, youth, children, and the elderly.
Sponsor: US/DoD - Department of the Army
Contact: Captain Craig Gilbert
Description: Recognizing a need for additional services to families, youth, children and the elderly, both on the post and in surrounding communities, 550 volunteers are trying to narrow the gap by offering their time to assist in increasing these services, and improving existing ones.

On the post, volunteers assist Army Community Services, and work with the Divisions of Youth Activities and Moral Support, as well as in a number of sports programs. In addition to their help in providing basic needs, they are looked upon as friends with whom to discuss private or domestic matters on a confidential basis. Some volunteers teach English as a second language. Others offer advice on financial matters such as checking accounts, budgets, heavy debts, and bill consolidation. Volunteers with Army Community Service receive free child care services while they work, provided by other volunteers.

Several programs reach into post housing areas and the surrounding communities. New arrivals are greeted with a house plant and help in learning about available community services. Foreign-born students are assisted in preparing for U.S. citizenship.

Other groups that involve Fort Dix volunteers in their programs include scout organizations, libraries, the post chapel, and the

American Red Cross. Those volunteers working with the Red Cross assist in helping active duty persons who need help, work at the Walson Army Community Hospital, and perform other tasks as needed. Much of the Red Cross scheduling of Fort Dix volunteers is done by a board of volunteers, many of whom are wives of retired servicemen. They travel to the post from many parts of the state to serve on the board. On the post, volunteers assist in verifying emergencies for service members when a family member is seriously ill or has died, advance an interest-free loan, and help with emergency travel. They assist in providing emergency services in cases of house fires, and receive training in first aid, CPR and water safety.

At the hospital, volunteers chaperone patients, take vital signs, and perform secretarial duties. They assist at the information desk, in the pharmacy, and in the laboratory. They work at the central appointments desk, and assist volunteer retired doctors and volunteer case workers who work one-on-one with active duty personnel and their families. Personal service volunteers visit in-patients, assisting them with minor shopping and errands. Volunteers with the required education serve in the wards as nurses and aides. Others serve as a liaison for the hospital with groups such a the VFW, American Legion, and various garden clubs.

Potential volunteers are asked to complete an application showing their educational background, experience, and interests. If accepted, their assignments are based on this information. Volunteers who would like to help, but feel unqualified, are given the opportunity to attend classes to learn necessary skills for specific assignments. Work experience gained as a volunteer is recognized by employers, and many volunteers develop specific skills in many areas of office work, health services, and leadership that are transferable to the job market.

The benefits to the post and the community derived from Fort Dix Volunteers have been documented through public recognition programs and the media. There is never a waiting list, and all volunteers are placed in positions that are consistent with their interests and abilities. There are no age restrictions to volunteer in the program. Volunteers as young as 13 have coached sports.

FORT GORDON VOLUNTEER PROGRAM
US/DoD - Fort Gordon
Army Signal Center
Fort Gordon, GA 30905
TEL: 404-791-6001; 404-791-7003
Purpose: To work with the community and volunteers to provide services to service families that might not otherwise be possible.
Sponsor: US/DoD - Fort Gordon
Contact: Robert E. DiMichele
Description: More than two dozen on-post programs are operated by volunteers at Fort Gordon. The programs, collectively, average approximately 640 active volunteers per year, who provide an average of 17,648 volunteer hours per month on the post. Many of the volunteer programs require coordination with and cooperation from the wider community. They include:

- **Information, Referral and Followup Program:** Army Community Service is the primary resource agency for providing information and referral services to military agencies and civilian agencies in the community. They link services between the service members and their families and the appropriate agency or services, on or off post, that can best assist them with their problems.

- **Consumer Affairs and Financial Assistance Program:** This program insures that service members and their families are taught basic financial skills, provides financial assistance, offers specific information on local products and services, and makes the military consumers aware of consumer issues. The issues include debt liquidation, budget development, consumer complaint program, public information and outreach program on consumer education. Emergency funds are made available

through AER. Other agencies can be used to supplement Army Community Service programs, such as American Red Cross and veterans' organizations.

- **Relocation Program:** This program provides information, guidance, and assistance to support unit deployments and to support service members and their families as they move from one military community to another. This includes assistance in settling into a new community, installation library services (information on the new installation), use of the Lending Closet, services to waiting families and foreign-born spouses, educational and employment services to family members.

- **Family Advocacy Program:** This is a specialized program to prevent child or spouse maltreatment and its attendant problems. This includes programs that contribute to a healthy family life. The advocacy program insures command and staff personnel awareness of their responsibilities for preventing child or spouse maltreatment. They identify, report, manage and follow up cases of child and spouse abuse; prevent and control child or spouse abuse by educating and training personnel; provide and support health programs such as parenting, child growth and development, family living and family enrichment classes.

- **Foster Care Program:** Foster care is either a voluntary step on the part of the family, or a court mandate. It provides foster family or group care for children whose parents or relatives cannot maintain a home for them, placing the children who need this service in stable, permanent arrangements as soon as possible.

- **Exceptional Family Member Program:** This program assures that the records of a family member with special needs are properly transmitted to assignment authorities reassigning service members with exceptional family members. Army Community Service, which intervenes in this program, insures when possible that service members receive the information and assistance needed to involve family members in specialized programs and services designed to meet their needs at their new location.

To recognize the efforts of all volunteers in the above and other programs, several volunteers are singled out to represent the volunteer program. These selectees showed exceptional leadership ability and motivation in developing and implementing programs such as the Swap and Assist Shop (now implemented on many posts), the Theater Crew (twenty volunteers offering makeup, lighting and sound, costuming, carpentry and other skills for theater groups), and an 18-year-old Christmas program to help military families during the holiday season.
Founded: 1964

FORT SILL VOLUNTEERS
US/DoD - Fort Sill
Commander, USFACFS
DPCA/ATTN: ATZR-P
Fort Sill, OK 73503
TEL: 405-351-3113
Purpose: To prevent having services reduced by developing and maintaining a volunteer program on the post.
Sponsor: US/DoD - Fort Sill
Contact: Director, Personnel and Community Activities
Description: More than 100,000 hours were logged by volunteers at Fort Sill during 1982. Consequently, many services that would have been reduced were maintained at the same level. While the monetary value of this volunteer effort is significant, the most direct contribution is the service and help given to soldiers and their families.

Volunteer programs operating at Fort Sill are numerous. A summary of the major volunteer activities includes the following programs:

- **Army Community Service:** More than 14,500 hours were logged by volunteers during 1982. These volunteers help new arrivals get settled by distributing welcome packets, lending household goods through the loan closet, and giving tips about locations on the post, and the most effective use of the post's resources. They offer financial counseling and budgeting advice, and advise buyers through the Consumer Affairs Office. At the Child Development Center, volunteers supervise preschool children and help with paperwork.

- **Moral Support Activities Division:** About 1,000 volunteers worked throughout the year for this Division, providing services that would have required the full time of 343 civil service workers. Most of the volunteers are involved in the music and theatre programs, working in plays and musical productions. Also, the Division has volunteers working as coaches for sports activities, as chaperones for field trips, and as swimming instructors for children. In addition, they maintain library story-telling programs and other activities.
- **American Red Cross:** At Reynolds Army Community Hospital, Red Cross Volunteers help in many areas, including greeting patients and helping them through the "system." Also, they do paperwork that medical specialists may not have time to do. In addition, Red Cross volunteers give first aid classes and teach adults and children water safety.
- **Scouting:** During the year, 88 scouting program volunteers put more than 18,000 hours into the 16 scouting units on the post. Volunteers provide a sense of leadership to the youth, and develop friendship through scouting.
- **Thrift Shop:** Proceeds collected by the Thrift Shop are generated back into the Fort Sill community. The money fully funds the Toys for Tots program. Also, it is used for the Food Locker program at Army Community Service, the Volunteer Nursery Fund, layettes for the new mothers at the hospital, the handicapped school, the Armed Forces YMCA, and Mobile Meals at Lawton among others.
- **The Fort Sill Museum:** Tour guides at the Fort Sill Museum are volunteers. They work also behind the scenes researching, cataloging and restoring artifacts.

Many of the volunteers at Fort Sill are busy people who manage households and work full time at other jobs. Recognition events are scheduled periodically to call attention to their volunteer efforts.

JANGO (JUNIOR ARMY NAVY GUILD ORGANIZATION)*
SEE HEALTH: HOSPITALS

MANTENO VETERANS HOME VOLUNTEER PROGRAM
Manteno Veterans Home
One Veterans Drive
Manteno, IL 60950
TEL: 815-468-6581
Purpose: To involve volunteers of all ages in service to veterans at Manteno Veterans Home.
Sponsor: State of Illinois
Contact: Patricia Essington, Director of Volunteers
Description: In 1989, the senior volunteer component of the Manteno Veterans Home was awarded first prize in the Governor's Home Town Award program. Its student component and overall program each won honorable mentions. In addition, the Home was given a street sign to be placed at its entrance, reading *1989 Governor's Home Town Award Winner - Building Illinois with Volunteers.*
Volunteers come from all over the county, and as far north as the north side of Chicago.
Along with being on call for any need that comes along, volunteers have specific assignments such as escorting the aged and infirm veterans to physical therapy, the barber shop, the commissary, the bank, the x-ray facilities, and the pharmacy. They assist with parties and help members of the home play bingo. Part of their duties includes assisting with meals - both serving them and helping some of the infirm to eat.

Involvement by many volunteers means a long weekly drive - including some volunteers in their mid-70s. Many are members of the area *Veterans of Foreign Wars* and *American Legion* posts as well as various ladies' auxiliaries.
The hours of service run into the thousands for some individuals. As for the reward for the senior volunteers, according to the director, the seniors "understand the needs of these older veterans and they handle them with care and understanding." But she quickly adds that it is the entire volunteer force that is the backbone of the winning program.

NAVY VOLUNTEERS AT GUANTANAMO BAY
US/DoD - Department of the Navy
Box 25
FPO New York, NY 09593
TEL: Correspondence only
Purpose: To bring the Naval base and the community closer together through volunteering.
Sponsor: American Red Cross
Contact: J.D. Van Sickle, Lieutenant Commander, USNR, Public Affairs Officer, or specific contact below
Description: Navy personnel at Guantanamo Bay, Cuba, are involved in numerous volunteer activities. Among them are:

- **Water Safety/Safety Services** - Red Cross classes in first aid, CPR and swimming are some of the courses offered to the general military community on a regular basis. These courses enable an individual to become proficient at swimming or have knowledge to treat almost any type of injury (until a physician or medical personnel arrive), or even be able to save the life of a victim of a heart attack or near drowning through CPR.

There are 15 military personnel teaching various courses in first aid and water safety. All military personnel are used exclusively for teaching Red Cross courses.
There are 23 different first aid and water safety courses. Each course has a mandated curriculum which specifically gives the required instruction and training each pupil and teacher must receive for each course. Instructors are closely monitored to assure that they are meeting the high Red Cross standard.
Contact: Theodore E. Joyner, Station Director, Box 45, FPO New York, NY 09593

- **Combined Federal Campaign (CFC)** - This program aims to raise funds for various organizations which are designated by the chairman of the U.S. Civil Service Commission. The goal of the program is to provide financial, medical, and counseling assistance to the needy. There are 37 project officers, with approximately one or more "key persons," who solicit funds through personal donations.

There is no training, per se. The project officer supervises key persons, and there is an overall base chairman for CFC.
Contact: CWO4 Jim O'Neal, U.S. Naval Station, Box 15, FBPO Norfolk, VA 23593

- **Guantanamo Bay Youth Athletic Association (GBYAA)** - Although no firm commencement date is available, this program has been ongoing for a great number of years. A group of military families saw an ever-growing need for a program to provide sports activities for the youth of the community. A set of by-laws and a constitution were developed and the association was formed and given final approval by the base commander.

Approximately 75 military personnel from the community participate in the GBYAA on a yearly basis. In addition, the association has an elected director, assistant director, secretary, treasurer, equipment manager and public relations officer.
There is no professional training, as such. The various sports commissioners and team coaches rely on training received elsewhere and self-study of sports rules. The children of the community are highly motivated in the sporting events. They are taught good sportsmanship, trustworthiness, obedience and respect among other traits.

Contact: CWO4 Jim O'Neal, U.S. Naval Station, Box 15, FBPO Norfolk, VA 23593

- **Boy Scouts of America** - Boys Scouts prepares young men for adult life, and teaches them responsibility. There are 16 military scout leaders, who are involved in leading troops, planning activities, and teaching education skills to the scouts. The reason so many military are involved is that scouting has 100 merit badges, and the expertise the military has aids them (scouts) in earning these badges. The Fleet Reserve Association provides the meeting place for the scouts, and additionally donates the scouts' registration funds. GTMO scouts also are involved in an international Boy Scout exchange.

A troop committee is organized to handle finances, and to oversee the quality of training leaders are providing the scouts. Basically, the scouting in Guatanamo Bay is the same as that found in the USA.

Contact: CWO4 Jim O'Neal, U.S. Naval Station, Box 15, FBPO Norfolk, VA 23593

PARENT-TO-PARENT PROGRAM
SEE RECIPIENTS: FAMILIES - MILITARY

POLISH LEGION OF AMERICAN VETERANS AUXILIARY
Pulaski Auxiliary Post No. 8
Pulaski Hall
1401 South Grant
Pulaski, MI 48505
TEL: 517-893-1465
Purpose: To provide entertainment and assistance to Veterans Hospital patients.
Sponsor: Polish Legion of American Veterans
Contact: Genevieve Smela, President
Description: The *Pulaski Auxiliary Post No. 8* of the *Polish Legion of American Veterans* coordinates groups of volunteers for monthly visits to the *Saginaw Veterans Hospital* and *Chateau Gardens,* a satellite hospital. The purpose is to help and entertain hospital patients.
The auxiliary is responsible for the coffee and donuts served in the outpatient area, operating bingo games for the patients, providing afternoon snacks of cookies and punch, and performing services such as letter-writing, phone calls, etc., in addition to just lending an ear when a patient wants to talk to someone.
To raise funds for these activities, the auxiliary mounts two culturally-oriented picnics each year - the Polish Festival in July, and the Harvest Festival in August. Dancing and the music of two bands are featured at the festivals, which are held on post grounds. A Memorial Day mass on the grounds involves the *Powers High School Choir.* An additional, familiar nationwide fund-raiser is the sale of poppies each year.
The auxiliary has 130 members who are wives, daughters, sisters or granddaughters of Polish veterans. World War II members dominate, but the group includes family members of veterans from the Korean and Vietnam conflicts, mostly of Polish descent. Recently chartered by the government, the organization now accepts non-Polish members.
A side benefit to the senior citizens who are members of the auxiliary is the travel program and bowling tournaments within the auxiliary designed for them.

ROSES FOR FALLEN FATHERS
Friends of the Vietnam Veterans Memorial
1350 Connecticut Avenue, NW
Suite 300
Washington, DC 20036
TEL: 202-296-1726
Purpose: To offer a long-distance way on Fathers Day to remember a father who lost his life in Vietnam.
Contact: Volunteer Coordinator

Description: The *Friends of the Vietnam Veterans Memorial* is an all-volunteer group which helps to care for and maintain the Memorial, and answers questions about it from families, friends, and others interested in the monument. To assure families that their losses of loved ones are not forgotten, *Friends* offers various programs throughout the year.
The Fathers Day program delivers a red rose to the *Vietnam Veterans Memorial* and places it at the base of the panel of the monument which contains the name of a loved one. *Friends* has found that this and other programs are well worth the effort, since they serve to remove the isolation factor that often embitters families and friends of the serviceman. Although this is a free service as long as funds are available, families sometimes send donations with their requests, which helps to expand this and other programs administered throughout the year.

SERVICE TO MILITARY FAMILIES/SERVICE TO VETERANS (OHIO)
American Red Cross
1830 North Limestone Street
Springfield, OH 45503
TEL: 513-399-3875
Purpose: (1) To assist Armed Forces personnel and their families cope with the strain of separation, and to assist families in meeting problems that arise when a member is in the service; (2) To assist veterans in applying for Veterans Administration benefits.
Sponsor: American Red Cross
Contact: Dorothy LaVelle
Description: The American Red Cross offers a number of services to both active duty and veteran military personnel, including those shown below:

- **Service to Military Families:** The principal Red Cross services to military personnel and their families are counseling, emergency communications, and financial assistance. The Red Cross assists military personnel in utilizing appropriate military and community resources to help resolve problems. Messages are sent by Chapters to AmCross in Washington, DC, asking for emergency services such as locator information for military personnel in transit, and emergency messages to be sent to service members aboard ships at sea or at small isolated bases in remote parts of the world. These crucial messages receive high priority in handling.

Volunteers, some in leadership positions, assist the paid staff in carrying out the above and other services to military personnel and their families.

- **Service to Veterans:** The American Red Cross recognizes Red Cross responsibility to former service members as a logical extension of service to the Armed Forces. The Red Cross helps veterans with applications for government benefits, such as education, disability compensation, pensions, medical and dental care, home loans, discharge reviews and correction of military records. Red Cross also represents the veteran before the Veterans Administration and Military Review Boards. In addition, Clark County has generated $280,000 in benefits for veterans in this area.

Volunteers, some in leadership positions, assist paid staff in their efforts to assure maximum benefits to veterans of the Armed Forces.

VA VOLUNTARY SERVICES BOARD
US/VA - Veterans Administration Medical Center
Newington, CT 06111
TEL: 203-666-6951
Purpose: To provide a vehicle enabling members of veterans' groups to make decisions for the veterans' hospital.
Contact: William Sysman, Chief of Voluntary Services
Description: Volunteers who develop and conduct fund-raisers for veterans hospitals, or recreation programs for the residents there, must go before the *VA Voluntary Services Board.* The

all-volunteer Board is composed of members of veterans groups who help determine the scope and types of volunteer programs provided for patients. It often includes widows and/or children of veterans to help maintain the connection that would otherwise be lost when the veteran dies. One Board member at the Hartford hospital has served in that position for 43 years. Her husband died 31 years ago. The same widow served 18 years on the National VA Voluntary Services Board, 15 of them as President. The national board has representatives from throughout the country who determine how voluntary services are operated at all 172 medical centers. This board, also, makes an effort to include survivors of veterans.

Many in-house volunteer activities approved by the Hartford board are in the hospital's medical administration services, where packets of admission forms for patients and other logistical tasks are performed. Volunteers also work in the ambulatory care division, serve as translators for non-English-speaking veterans, and work with outside groups coming into the hospital with approved fund-raising events or entertainment programs.

The hospital awards a *Superior Performance Award* each year to an outstanding volunteer. One volunteer Board member - the widow of a veteran - at the Hartford hospital has been recognized for her work by the past eight presidents, including President Bush, as well as other dignitaries. She was asked why she worked so hard, and said that she remembers watching young men, including relatives, go off to war, and appreciates the contribution they made.

VETERANS COUNSELING AND GUIDANCE CENTER
California Council for Veterans Affairs
3943 South Western
Los Angeles, CA 90062
TEL: 213-299-6330
Purpose: To assist veterans in obtaining jobs and any military benefits due them.
Contact: Kenneth L. Brooks
Description: The Veterans Counseling and Guidance Center is a multi-faceted program designed originally for assistance to the veterans. Circumstances in the community have necessitated the inclusion of certain non-veterans as well. The Center was established in 1971 and is a federally-funded program.

The Center provides direct referrals for veterans and certain non-veterans to community resources. Proper forms are always on hand for application for benefits, including:
- GI Bill
- Educational and Rehabilitation Programs
- Discharge Upgrading
- Medical and Dental Assistance
- Housing and Loans

In addition, the Center is a member of the *College Entrance Examination Board*. In this regard, forms and assistance are provided for educational benefits such as grants, loans, scholarships, work study and others.

Job developers assist veterans and others who need employment. The program is operated for the community and is located in the community and is responsive to the community. Although it is located in the inner city, it is reaching clientele far beyond the immediate offices. This has necessitated planning for new offices to fulfill the needs of that clientele.

Volunteers and neighborhood groups assist the small staff in carrying out the above tasks and meeting its objectives.
Founded: 1971

VOLUNTEER PROGRAM - FORT BENJAMIN HARRISON
US/DoD - Fort Benjamin Harrison
Building 32
Fort Benj. Harrison, IN 46216
TEL: 317-543-6534

Purpose: To improve the quality of life on the post and in the community by increasing services through the involvement of volunteers.
Sponsor: US/DoD - Department of the Army
Contact: Joseph T. Brown, Installation Volunteer Coordinator
Description: The volunteer program at Fort Benjamin Harrison serves the Army Community Service, American Red Cross, and other programs. Volunteers include family members of servicemen and servicewomen, retirees, civilian employees and people from the surrounding communities. They donate their time to various post programs and numerous community activities.

Army Community Service averages two volunteers each month who put in an average of 150 hours during that period. They perform a variety of tasks to make life easier for the military family from the time they arrive at Fort Harrison. Volunteers prepare and distribute welcome packets, set up and assist with the presentation of newcomers' orientations, operate a lending closet and a food locker, compile and maintain a talent lists file, a resource file and a consumer reference library, and provide many other "people" services. At Christmas time, volunteers assist the Fort Harrison Chapter of Federally Employed Women (FEW) in collecting, packing and distributing boxes of food and toys to needy families, for which FEW members also are volunteers.

The Red Cross program provides an average of 50 volunteers each month, who spend about 1,200 hours a month working in Hawley Army Community Hospital, the Dental and Vet Clinics, and the Child Care Center. In the hospital, volunteers help out in Records, Pharmacy, Family Practice, the Laboratory, Library, Eye Clinic and Pediatrics. An Outstanding Red Cross Volunteer of the Year is selected and recognized in October of each year.

Many other programs are staffed by volunteers both on the post and in the wider community. These include:
- **Libraries:** Volunteers supplement the paid staff in the three libraries on the post in order to maintain library hours to better serve post personnel.
- **Thrift Shop/Fund Raising:** The Post Thrift Shop is operated by volunteers from the Officers' Wives Club and the NCO/EM Wives Club. Proceeds go to scholarships for military family members.
- **Carnival/Fund Raising:** A yearly Carnival is held in cooperation with the neighboring community of Lawrence. Volunteers from local organizations man booths at the six-day event to raise money for their own organizations and the local Morale Support Fund.
- **Cultural Enrichment:** The new USA Center at the Indianapolis International Airport is staffed by volunteers, many furnished by Fort Harrison.
- **Youth Camping Experience:** Volunteers help with Camp Elm in the summer. Camp Elm is a local Salvation Army day camp for inner-city youths.
- **Crisis Center:** A recently-formed Harrison Sertoma club sponsors the Family Support Center in Indianapolis, a crisis center for battered, abused and neglected children. Members volunteer their time at the Center, and raise money for the project through fund-raising events.
- **Christmas Activity:** Soldiers from the Second Battalion entertain children from the Knightstown Soldiers and Sailors Home each Christmas, taking them to movies and bowling and sports events.

Other programs and activities are developed as needs arise. Teenagers as well as adults, from the post and the community, are part of the work force, offering a youth perspective which, in many cases, is more effective in the volunteer effort.

VOLUNTEER RESOURCE CENTER
US/DoD - Volunteer Fort Benning
Fort Benning, GA 31905
TEL: 404-545-5602

Purpose: To encourage and promote volunteerism; to organize and improve volunteer services at Fort Benning.
Sponsor: US/DoD - Fort Benning
Contact: Donna L. Ray
Description: The Volunteer Resouce Center is an appropriated-fund agency established to encourage and promote volunteer participation in social services, health, welfare, educational, cultural, and civic programs and to coordinate and help organize and improve volunteer services at the Fort. In order to accomplish this mission, the following goals have been identified:

- to help recruit and refer volunteers;
- to maintain a comprehensive file on specific requests;
- to conduct training or cooperate with organizations giving training for volunteers and for staff working with volunteers;
- to encourage community recognition of volunteers;
- to offer research, training, public relations, and other forms of consultation to agencies initiating, developing or strengthening volunteer programs;
- to initiate new volunteer services to meet changing community needs, and encourage creative utilization of volunteers;
- to keep abreast of changing attitudes involving volunteerism in order to be prepared to respond effectively;
- to educate and advocate for the ongoing appropriate utilization of volunteers.

The public relations staff of the Center maintains and publicizes a calendar of training and other events, and publishes articles on volunteer activities in local papers. Volunteers are referred for training to courses at Columbus College, as well as that provided by the Center. A resource library includes a resource list for training of volunteers. Other training activities include identifying training experts, developing a list of training needs, identifying funds for training, and providing training that leads to college credit by developing specific training leadership development, supervisor training, resume writing, etc.

The development of an efficient and effective standard operating procedure, the establishment and publishing of standards for utilization of volunteers, and a workable recordkeeping system are projects of the administrative staff. Other projects include:

- the development of a comprehensive chart of ideas for recruitment of volunteers. This chart, Recruitment of Volunteers: Who, Where, What, When and How, lists types of volunteers (high school students, retirees, employed persons, etc.), contacts (school counselors, unions, service clubs, etc.), the best print or sound media, and incentives for emphasis.
- the establishment of criteria for the Volunteer of the Year award, the nominating procedure, and sample forms.
- the publishing of a newsletter, VOLUNTEER: You Can Make a Difference, containing eight pages of items and articles on family volunteerism, activities on the post, suggested reading list, and special one-time features such as Bill of Rights of Volunteers and Teaching Kids to Do a Good Job.

The Center develops posters, bibliographies and other materials on an intermittent, as-needed basis.

RECIPIENTS: MINORITIES/WOMEN

INDIVIDUAL PROGRAM PROFILES

LUTHER PLACE WOMEN'S SHELTER
SEE RECIPIENTS: HOMELESS - SHELTERS

MODEL MUGGING
SEE LAW ENFORCEMENT/CRIME PREVENTION:
SEXUAL ABUSE

MORRIS COUNTY CHAPLAINCY COUNCIL
SEE LAW ENFORCEMENT/CRIME PREVENTION:
RE-ENTRY

RECIPIENTS: OLDER PERSON

NATIONAL/STATE ORGANIZATIONS

AMERICAN ASSOCIATION OF RETIRED PERSONS
1909 K Street, NW
Washington, DC 20049
TEL: 202-872-4700
Objectives: To help older Americans achieve lives of independence, dignity and purpose.
Services: Sponsors community service programs such as consumer information, crime prevention, driver improvement, health education, housing information, continuing education, tax assistance, pre-retirement planning; arranges for reduced costs in many day-to-day living areas for older persons, such as medicine, transportation; sponsors mail order pharmacy; operates AGELINE, a computerized database which includes an on-line bibliography; maintains programs in areas of pre-retirement planning, defensive driving, crime prevention, tax aid and others; has regional offices in several states; makes consultant and other services available to retired teachers through its National Retired Teachers Association division; publishes monthly bulletin, bimonthly magazine, and other materials.
Publications: Modern Maturity; AARP News Bulletin
Founded: 1958

HEARTLINE*
National Association of Older Americans*
12 Electric Street
West Alexandria, OH 45381
TEL: 614-775-7634
Objectives: To reestablish a satisfactory level of comfort and security for older Americans, to restore a well-deserved dignity to the elderly image, and to provide individual assistance and vital information to older Americans.
Services: Conducts specialized education and research programs; assists older Americans in dealing with government agencies; offers an insurance policy program to supplement Medicare; provides a pharmaceutical plan; sponsors a travel program; publishes a monthly newsletter, an almanac, and specialized publications on pre-retirement planning.
Publications: Crime Prevention Guide; Almanac for Retirement

NATIONAL ASSOCIATION OF OLDER AMERICANS*
12 Electric Street
West Alexandria, OH 45381
TEL: 614-775-7634
Objectives: To provide assistance and vital information to older persons.
Services: Acts as advocate for older persons in dealing with government agencies at all levels; provides pharmaceutical, travel and other services at reduced cost; publishes monthly newsletter.
Publications: Heartline/NADA

NATIONAL COUNCIL OF SENIOR CITIZENS
925 Fifteenth Street, NW
Washington, DC 20005
TEL: 202-347-8800
FAX: 202-624-9595

Objectives: To provide advocacy and encourage participation in social and political action on behalf of senior citizens.
Services: Provides assistance in areas ranging from federal and state legislation to community action; works currently in areas of health care, housing, employment, Social Security, crime prevention, nursing home reforms, and Congressional evaluation; sponsors mass rallies, educational workshops and leadership training institutes; maintains speakers bureau; helps develop and organize programs for local and state groups; maintains library; publishes monthly newsletter and other materials.
Publications: Senior Citizens News; Retirement Newsletter
Founded: 1961

NATIONAL COUNCIL ON THE AGING
600 Maryland Avenue, SW
West Wing 100
Washington, DC 20024
TEL: 202-479-1200
Objectives: To develop methods and resources for meeting the needs of the elderly through the efforts of both professionals and volunteers.
Services: Speaks on behalf of elderly before Congress, the Executive Branch, and other pertinent federal agencies; sponsors institutes and embarks on programs and projects including:

- **National Institute on Age, Work and Retirement** - provides training and technical assistance to industry, local groups, colleges and universities, and others to develop comprehensive retirement planning programs.
- **Senior Center Humanities Program** - involves older persons in discussion sessions designed to provide a forum for sharing interests and ideas.
- **National Center on Arts and the Aging** - acts as a clearinghouse for ideas and information among leaders in both the arts and the field of aging.
- **Housing Corporation** - fosters independent living arrangements in a positive environment for older people.
- **National Center on Rural Aging** - directs attention to and advocates the needs of the low-income elderly living in rural America; operates clearinghouse.
- **National Institute on Adult Day Care** - works with voluntary organizations and government agencies at all levels to improve day care services for aging persons who are disabled.

Also, NCOA maintains an extensive library, and produces numerous publications (some of which are annotated in the bibliography preceding the index in this book; write for complete list).
Publications: Perspectives on Aging; Literature on Aging
Founded: 1950

NATIONAL COUNCIL ON THE BLACK AGING
SEE CIVIC AFFAIRS: MINORITIES/WOMEN

OLDER WOMEN'S LEAGUE (OWL)
730 Eleventh Street, NW
Suite 300
Washington, DC 20001
TEL: 202-783-6686
Objectives: To bring together people of all ages to support the cause of the underserved elderly.
Services: Maintains a national office and 120 chapters with over 20,000 participants (both men and women) to address the needs of older persons; supports chapters (a minimum of eight persons) through training, technical assistance, printed materials, etc.; enables local chapters to select projects according to needs at their local level; publishes educational materials in areas such as defense and reform of social security, health care insurance, and equity in pensions for women, as well as a regular series of papers, a bimonthly newsletter, action bulletins, statistical reports, videotapes, books, and occasional papers.

Publications: OWL Observe; Gray Papers; Women Take Care
Founded: 1980

PREPARING FOR AN AGING SOCIETY
Aging Futures Project
United Way of America
701 North Fairfax Street
Alexandria, VA 22314-2045
TEL: 703-836-7100, Ext. 538
Objectives: To help community leaders and service providers construct a detailed picture of the long-term needs of the community's elderly population.
Services: Assists communities in projecting data about the health, financial status, and number of elderly in a given community for as long a period as 70 years, which helps them plan for the human-care needs of future aging populations through a computerized program, *Preparing for an Aging Society* (by 2010, about one-third of America's population will be between 55 and 75 years old); works through a grant from the *U.S. Administration on Aging* to enable 10 cities to pilot the program; links pilot cities' efforts with those of local offices of the federal government's *Area Agencies on Aging* and with those of planning councils and local agencies serving the elderly; serves as a catalyst for public-private partnerships on the issue; incorporates data projected by the program into a new needs assessment planned for late 1990; studies previous projections (a 1987 study called for a 205 percent increase needed for senior day care by 2010) which point to "alternatives to institutionalization for the elderly" such as at-home care, service delivery, and alternative living arrangements; brings together local elder-care agencies and representatives from the *Social Security Administration* among others through the program; maintains a corporate advisory network; issues RFPs (requests for proposal) for elder-care services identified in local needs assessments; provides a demonstration diskette to United Way local offices on request.
Sponsor: United Way of America
Publications: Preparing for an Aging Society

US/HHS - ADMINISTRATION ON AGING
200 C Street, SW
Washington, DC 20201
TEL: 202-619-0724
Objectives: To work with the states and their subdivisions to assist older persons in securing equal opportunity in health and mental health, housing, employment, community services, institutional care, civic/cultural/recreational activities, dignity in retirement (including adequate retirement income), action on beneficial research, and the freedom and independence to make decisions that affect their own lives.
Services: Encourages and assists state and local agencies serving the aging to concentrate resources by working with other providers of social services to the elderly, especially in areas of nutrition services and multi-purpose centers; specifically, to:
- secure and maintain maximum independence and dignity in a home environment for older individuals capable of self care with appropriate supportive services;
- remove individual and social barriers to economic and personal independence for older individuals; and
- to provide a continuum of care for the vulnerable elderly.
Makes grants to States under approved State plans for any of the following social services:
- health, continuing education, welfare, informational, recreational, homemaker, counseling, or referral services;
- transportation services to facilitate access to social services or nutrition services or both;
- services designed to encourage and assist older individuals to use the facilities and services available to them;
- services designed to assist older individuals in obtaining adequate housing, including renovation and repair, or adapting

homes to meet needs of older persons with physical disabilities;
- services designed to assist older individuals in avoiding institutionalization (preinstitution evaluation and screening, shopping services, escort services, home health services, homemaker services, reader services, letter writing services, etc., to help such individuals remain in their own homes);
- services designed to provide legal and other counseling assistance (tax counseling/assistance, financial counseling, etc.);
- services designed to enable older individuals to attain and maintain physical and mental wellbeing through programs of regular physical activity and exercise;
- services designed to provide health screening to detect and/or prevent illness that occurs most frequently in older persons.

Sponsor: US/HHS - Department of Health & Human Services
Publications: Declaration of Objectives; Grants for Programs on Aging; Older Americans Act/Amended

WESTERN GERONTOLOGICAL SOCIETY*
785 Market Street
Suite 1114
San Francisco, CA 94103
Objectives: To improve the lives of older persons.
Services: Participates in national-level decision-making in the field of aging through such groups as the Leadership Council of Aging Organizations and the Knowledge in Practice in Aging Group sponsored by the Administration on Aging; undertakes special research, conference and training projects such as:
- **Elders in Voluntarism** which incorporates activities by senior volunteers as discussed at a special session of the WGS annual meeting and published in a comprehensive notebook with sections on program profiles, suggested readings and audiovisual resources (designed for local senior volunteer program managers).
- **Mobilizing Resources for Underserved Elders** which is a National Aging Organization project including a taxonomy describing types and degrees of underservice among subgroups of elders, develops profiles of non-aging network resources in the corporate, labor and philanthropic sectors, and establishes strategies for matching resources with needs of elders who are underserved.
- **Advocacy Development Program** which presents testimony and initiates legislative efforts; promotes national, state and local advocacy activities (a previous activity highlighted the California Senior Legislature and events related to the White House Conference on Aging).

Organizes other training events and conferences such as White House Conference on Aging Mini-Conferences and Fall Training Institutes on specific topics; publishes a bimonthly newsletter, a quarterly journal, a monthly bulletin, and other materials; maintains "WGS Answers," an information clearinghouse and library.
Publications: WGS Connection; Generations; WGS Job Alert

TRAINING PROGRAMS

VOLUNTARISM: A KEY TO THE FUTURE*
US/HHS - Administration on Aging
Region V
Chicago, IL 60603
TEL: 312-353-3141
Credit: Certificate
Sponsor: US/HHS - Department of Health & Human Services
Contact: Eli Lipschultz
Description: This seminar is one of an ongoing series entitled Commissioner's Forum on Aging. The purpose of this series is to bring together a cross-section of leaders from both the public and

the private sectors to discuss issues and perspectives in the field of aging. Nationally-known presenters work with participants on major aspects of the theme: *Older Americans: Our Keys to the Future.* Presentations focus on voluntarism as a major thread through the fabric of society and addresses questions such as:
- What kind of voluntary programs have evolved in various segments of society, especially in areas of the private sector such as corporations, unions and churches?
- What difference have volunteers made in the quality of life of older persons?
- What barriers in voluntarism, if any, exist and how do we eliminate them?

The ultimate purpose of the workshop is to record comments and recommendations by participants for presentation to the Commissioner on Aging. Recommendations resulting from the Forum often are used to redirect policy and/or to establish new initiatives for the Administration on Aging.

INDIVIDUAL PROGRAM PROFILES

THE BEST YEARS
RSVP of Humboldt County
Humboldt State University
Arcata, CA 95521
TEL: 707-826-3372
Purpose: To utilize the television media to inform and educate the four-county area to services available, political issues, special happenings; to present a positive view of the aging.
Sponsor: KVIQ-TV
Contact: Charlotte Tropp, Director
Description: In May 1975, leaders of the Retired Senior Volunteer Program negotiated with KVIQ-TV officials for public service air time on a regular basis, and conducted an active search for older people who would be assets on a planning committee and in actual production. Through this effort they hoped, through profiles and examples, to present a positive view of aging, to educate older adults in the viewing area about all the services available to them, to inform older adults about current political issues and special happenings important to them, to provide a stimulating and creative volunteer opportunity for older adults. KVIQ viewing area covers Humboldt, Del Norte, Mendocino and Trinity Counties. The resultant biweekly, 30-minute television program shown on Sunday afternoons over the last seven years has covered every conceivable topic, and the program has a very large viewing audience. KVIQ-TV provides all broadcast services including tape, sets, time, audiovisual materials. RSVP, along with nonfederal community resources, provides all out-of-pocket expenses for volunteers.
The television program is generally divided into five segments: News, Focus, Uncommon Knowledge, Upbeat and Mailbag. Volunteers serve as coordinators and hosts, and provide all services including writing, scheduling, visual effects, publicity, guest appearances, producing and directing.
A Best Years committee meets weekly with RSVP and KVIQ staff to plan the shows. The planning committee itself changes frequently and the circle of older guests grows monthly. Appearing on television is a very exciting new growth experience for a lot of people. The shows are taped three days before they are shown to allow for review before airing. KVIQ-TV is a commercial station.
Founded: 1975

FORT DIX VOLUNTEERS
SEE RECIPIENTS: MILITARY - ACTIVE/VETERANS

SENIOR CITIZEN INTERNSHIP PROGRAM
SEE CIVIC AFFAIRS: OLDER PERSON

SILVER HAIRED LEGISLATIVE SESSION
SEE CIVIC AFFAIRS: OLDER PERSON

SOS (SERVE OUR SENIORS) STUDENT VOLUNTEER PROGRAM
SEE PSYCHOSOCIAL SUPPORT SERVICES: OLDER PERSON

VIVA (VERY IMPORTANT VOLUNTEERS IN ACTION)
Scurry County Senior Center
2603 Avenue M
Snyder, TX 79549
TEL: 915-573-4035
Purpose: To provide volunteer work within the community to non-profit organizations, and to the elderly of the community.
Sponsor: Scurry County Senior Citizens Center and Western Texas College; federal/county governments; corporate and private donations
Contact: Susan Thomas, VIVA Coordinator
Description: VIVA is an organization of senior citizens who offer non-profit clubs and organizations their volunteer services. VIVA also provides a lot of volunteer service to the elderly residents of the area. The program operates under the umbrella of the Scurry County Senior Citizens Center. VIVA is a non-profit organization receiving funds from federal and county governments as well as from corporate and private donations. Senior citizen volunteers are the very heart of this program. VIVA volunteers do a variety of things:

- help the local public schools by providing tutor-type programs where a volunteer works on a one-to-one basis with students who need extra help;
- aid in a swimming program for handicapped children;
- man a continual garage sale where all the profits go to the Scurry County Work Center where retarded citizens work;
- provide entertainment and extra help at the Snyder Child Day Care Center, at two local retirement homes, and at the Scurry County Library.

VIVA volunteers are also involved in the community blood drives every six weeks, and also aid the community on an emergency need basis. Volunteers also visit the sick, elderly, and shut-ins. The Senior Center has a Home Delivered Meal Program, and volunteers provide all of the driving needs for that program. VIVA has a volunteer force of 197 senior citizens, serving a community of 12,500 people. Out of the total population approximately 1,200 are over 60 years of age. With the volunteer force nearly 1,000 individuals over 60 are reached, as well as countless numbers under 60 years of age. The 197 volunteers put in an average of 6,000 hours per month in volunteer service to the community.

RECIPIENTS: OLDER PERSON - ACCESSIBILITY

NATIONAL/STATE ORGANIZATIONS

NATIONAL CENTER FOR A BARRIER FREE ENVIRONMENT
SEE RECIPIENTS: HANDICAPPED - ACCESSIBILITY

RECIPIENTS: OLDER PERSON - ADVOCACY

NATIONAL/STATE ORGANIZATIONS

MATURE OUTLOOK
PO Box 96
Arlington Heights, IL 60006
TOLL FREE: 800-336-6330
Objectives: To provide advocacy on behalf of older persons before state and federal government bodies; to provide practical services for everyday living.
Services: Provides services to older persons including financial guidance and counseling; arranges discount buying; develops and implements education programs; provides free arrest bond certificate; operates travel and recreation programs; offers prescription drug service; offers a motor club plan; publishes bimonthly newsletter, retirement planning guide, and various booklets.
Publications: Best Years; Mature Outlook Magazine; Mature Outlook Newsletter
Founded: 1984

NATIONAL ALLIANCE OF SENIOR CITIZENS
2525 Wilson Boulevard
Arlington, VA 22201
TEL: 703-528-4380
Objectives: To advocate the advancement of senior citizens through sound fiscal policy; to inform the public of programs and policies being carried out by public and private sectors to meet the needs of older persons.
Services: Presents views of senior citizens before Congress and state legislatures; actively supports numerous Advisory Council Chairs, including one on volunteerism (others include employment, health, adult education, environmental protection, housing, rural transportation); keeps public informed of programs being carried out by the federal government and other groups; maintains the Golden Age Hall of Fame honoring individuals for outstanding service to the senior community; Advisory Council areas include volunteerism, consumerism, adult education, crime, employment security, health care, housing, farm and rural life, retirement, rural transportation and several others; publishes monthly newsletter and a bimonthly tabloid.
Publications: Senior Guardian; Our Age
Founded: 1974

URBAN ELDERLY COALITION
National Council on the Aging
600 Maryland Avenue, SW
West Wing 100
Washington, DC 20024
TEL: 202-479-1200
Objectives: To resolve such problems as poverty, inner-city housing, crimes against the elderly, limited employment, inadequate health care, and transportation for the mobility-impaired.
Services: Analyzes and informs about legislation affecting the elderly; exchanges technical information among urban aging programs; fosters support of government at all levels; seeks urban leaders with strong goals for the elderly and works closely with them; provides technical assistance, program development and management support services; holds training meetings, and offers personalized training assistance; publishes *Legislative Update*, quarterly, and position papers; convenes annual training conference.
Publications: Legislative Update
Founded: 1950

INDIVIDUAL PROGRAM PROFILES

OMBUDSMAN PROGRAM
Northern Virginia Long-Term Care
Office of Volunteers
11242 Waples Mill Road #100
Fairfax, VA 22030
TEL: 703-246-5411
TOLL FREE: 800-468-1133
Purpose: To provide advocacy for residents of long-term care facilities.
Contact: Sharon K. Lynn, Volunteer Coordinator
Description: The Long-Term Care Ombudsman Program was created by an amendment in 1978 to the Older Americans Act of 1965. This action was taken largely as a result of issues raised at the White House Conference on Aging in 1971, when the Department of Health, Education and Welfare (now Health and Human Services) was charged with developing programs to improve the quality of care for the nation's nursing home residents. Each state is mandated to have an ombudsman, or citizen representative, to investigate and resolve complaints made by or on behalf of individual residents of long-term care facilities, to monitor legislation, to provide public information, and to train volunteers.
The Northern Virginia Long-Term Care Ombudsman Program was planned and developed by the Area Agencies on Aging in Arlington, Fairfax, Loudoun, and Prince William counties, and the City of Alexandria. The Virginia Department for the Aging designated the program to assist the more than 4,500 men and women who live in Northern Virginia nursing homes and homes for adults. The program is funded by both state and local jurisdictions.
The volunteer component of the program consists of approximately 30 volunteers. The volunteers participate in three days of training which provides a thorough orientation to the aging process, homes for adults, and advocacy skills. If certified, volunteers are assigned to a local nursing home or home for adults where they visit residents for approximately four hours each week. The volunteers provide friendly concern, attempt to empower residents to solve their own problems, and advocate for them when necessary. In addition, they provide residents and their families with information about patients' rights, government benefits, and other agencies which can be of assistance.
The volunteers are supervised and supported by weekly phone calls and occasional on-site visits by the Coordinator of Volunteers. Also, volunteers are asked to attend two-hour in-service training sessions held monthly.
Publications: Ombudsman Program Information Packet; Ombudsman Program Volunteer Opportunities; Ombudsman Program (for patients)
Founded: 1978

RECIPIENTS: OLDER PERSON - ARTS

NATIONAL/STATE ORGANIZATIONS

NATIONAL COMMITTEE ON ART EDUCATION FOR THE ELDERLY
Culver Stockton College
Canton, MO 63435
TEL: 314-288-5221
Objectives: To promote better art education opportunities for the elderly.
Services: Encourages the establishment of quality art education programs; canvasses those programs serving the elderly in other areas and encourages the addition of art programs; promotes research and development to improve art programs for the elderly; maintains a Clearinghouse of information on the subject; publishes irregular newsletter.
Publications: Switchboard

YARNS OF YESTERYEAR PROJECT
SEE ARTS/CULTURAL ENRICHMENT:
HISTORY/MUSEUMS

INDIVIDUAL PROGRAM PROFILES

HOME LEAGUE
SEE PSYCHOSOCIAL SUPPORT SERVICES: OLDER PERSON

LIFESTORY THEATER
SEE ARTS/CULTURAL ENRICHMENT:
HISTORY/MUSEUMS

SENIOR CRAFTSMAN SHOWCASE*
SEE ARTS/CULTURAL ENRICHMENT: CRAFTS

60 KARATS
SEE ARTS/CULTURAL ENRICHMENT: OLDER PERSON

YES PROGRAM (YOUTH-ELDERLY SERVICES)*
Family Service America
101 Rock Street
Fall River, MA 02720
TEL: 617-678-7542
Purpose: To offer older people companionship, and a chance for both young and old to better understand each other.
Sponsor: Family Service America
Contact: Hank Fairman
Description: The family service association broadened its counseling and group services in the fall of 1970 to include YES - Youth-Elderly Services. Through YES, high school students spend two hours each week with elderly people both in nursing homes and in the community assisting the activities directors in projects which the older men especially enjoy, such as carpentry and photography. Volunteers run simple errands, read and play games, just sit and chat, and in other ways strive to help the shut-in feel a part of the community.
Training takes place monthly in small groups at the high schools immediately after school. Course contents include:
- the social, psychological and physical problems of aging persons, with particular emphasis on the cultural backgrounds of the Fall River area;
- community attitudes toward aging and youth, and a study of community resources for older persons;
- the philosophy of volunteer service and how to promote meaningful relationships between young people and the elderly;
- practical experience in a nursing home, including the appropriate role of the YES volunteer.
The volunteers are assigned reading in the field of aging. Other teaching aids used are audio-visual materials (some of which are developed by the FSA with its own high school volunteers in action in nursing homes), actual case histories, and oral presentations by guest speakers and staff members.
Growing out of the friendship between the young volunteers and older friends is the Living History Program. Since January 1974, the students have been interviewing the elderly about Fall River's cultural and economic past. Trained in interviewing techniques, the students also do research in libraries, schools and the local

historical society. They plan to photograph the old and the new and hope to develop a film based on their interviews and photographs.
Founded: 1970

RECIPIENTS: OLDER PERSON - COMMUNICATIONS & PR

NATIONAL/STATE ORGANIZATIONS

NATIONAL MEDIA RESOURCE CENTER ON THE AGING
National Council on the Aging
600 Maryland Avenue
West Wing 100
Washington, DC 20024
TEL: 202-479-1200
Objectives: To supply information to editors, writers and producers in the press, film and broadcasting industries to improve the image of the elderly.
Services: Furnishes items for the media's use; serves as resource to program planners; works with existing networks, and creates additional ones; develops educational programs; stimulates consciousness-raising among the elderly themselves; leads briefings and workshops; draws from major 1974 study on attitudes about older persons; has continuous research and survey program; convenes intermittent conferences.
Publications: Perspective on Aging
Founded: 1950

RECIPIENTS: OLDER PERSON - CONSUMER SERVICES

NATIONAL/STATE ORGANIZATIONS

FLYING SENIOR CITIZENS OF THE USA*
SEE TRANSPORTATION & SAFETY: OLDER PERSON

INDIVIDUAL PROGRAM PROFILES

CORPORATE RETIREES INFORMATION AND ASSISTANCE PROGRAM
RSVP of Morris County
Box 372
West Hanover Avenue
Morris Plains, NJ 07950
TEL: 201-538-7947
Purpose: To provide a service that will help older persons to become more effective consumers.
Sponsor: Junior League
Contact: Martie Wickers
Description: When the need to educate and counsel older citizens to be more effective consumers was identified, it suggested an answer to another identified need - to provide more innovative projects with management opportunities for corporate retiree volunteers in the RSVP program. In 1979 the Fixed-Income Consumer Counseling Project (FICC) was created with ACTION funding. An FICC Coordinator was hired, and an Advisory

Committee named. It has become an ongoing project of the RSVP program staffed by corporate retirees.
A natural outgrowth of FICC was the Information and Referral (I&R) program with desks in offices all over the county manned by corporate retirees. I&R services are funded by ACTION, Title III-B and the United Way. Information and assistance is provided in areas of taxes, energy rebate, food stamp eligibility and other forms, and other identified service needs of older persons.
To create public awareness of the above projects and other RSVP projects meeting community needs, the corporate retirees plan, arrange and review a weekly radio show, RSVP Speakout Project. In conjunction with the program, the volunteers operate a Speakers Bureau and speak to various groups on I&R and consumer issues and are on call for college and corporate pre-retirement courses. The radio show was made possible with a two-year Junior League mini-grant.
Both staff and volunteers deliberately operate this program on an open-ended level to enable it to grow and change as new information and assistance needs emerge, and others cease to exist. Written materials on the various components of the program are available to those interested in mounting one or more of the projects.
Founded: 1979

RECIPIENTS: OLDER PERSON - CRIME PREVENTION

INDIVIDUAL PROGRAM PROFILES

MARTIAL ARTS FOR SENIORS
SEE LAW ENFORCEMENT/CRIME PREVENTION: OLDER PERSON

SECURITY ALERT GROUP - THREE LINK TOWERS (SAG)
SEE LAW ENFORCEMENT/CRIME PREVENTION: CRIME WATCH

SENIOR VICTIM ASSISTANCE TEAM
SEE LAW ENFORCEMENT/CRIME PREVENTION: VICTIMS

RECIPIENTS: OLDER PERSON - EDUCATION

NATIONAL/STATE ORGANIZATIONS

ELDERHOSTEL
100 Boylston Street
Suite 400
Boston, MA 02116
TEL: 617-426-7788
Objectives: To serve older adults by responding to their capacity to meet change and intellectual challenge.
Services: Coordinates a nationwide network of short-term, intensive residential educational experiences for individuals 60 years of age or older; works with a variety of colleges and universities, independent schools and specialized study and conference centers to plan and administer the programs; designs

course material to include elders from all walks of life, ranging from high school dropouts to Ph.D.'s and including a broad spectrum of occupational backgrounds (doctors, factory workers, librarians, civil servants, teachers, nurses, homemakers, farmers, businessmen, etc.), and no prerequisites are required; develops courses and logistics through campus directors located at each institution, who combine the Elderhostel program format with the strengths and environment of the institution to create week-long programs; requires all institutions hosting programs to adhere to a single maximum national tuition; administers a centralized registration system; publishes a national catalog.
Publications: Between Classes; Elderhostel Catalog
Founded: 1974

INSTITUTE OF LIFETIME LEARNING
American Association of Retired Persons
1909 K Street, NW
Washington , DC 20049
TEL: 202-662-4895
Objectives: To stimulate and provide opportunities for continuing education for older persons.
Services: Serves as the continuing education service of the *American Association of Retired Persons (AARP)*; helps to ensure that the diverse population of older persons has the opportunity to learn by fostering a wide range of educational opportunites for older persons; coordinates with other national aging and education organizations to carry out its mission; works with other AARP divisions and departments to address the educational needs and interests of older learners and mobilize volunteers to become involved in educational activities and programs.
Produces a number of publications and provides other forums for the exchange of information and technical assistance; includes in current priority areas: older adult learning theory and application, school volunteering, literacy and skills; provides information on college programs designed exclusively for older persons, literacy, and high school equivalency programs.
Publications: Modern Maturity

RECIPIENTS: OLDER PERSON - EMPLOYMENT

NATIONAL/STATE ORGANIZATIONS

JOBS FOR OLDER WOMEN ACTION PROJECT
SEE EMPLOYMENT: MINORITIES/WOMEN

NATIONAL ASSOCIATION FOR HISPANIC ELDERLY
SEE RECIPIENTS: OLDER PERSON - ETHNIC GROUPS

INDIVIDUAL PROGRAM PROFILES

ABILITY IS AGELESS
Long Island Lighting Company
175 East Old Country Road
Hicksville, NY 11801
TEL: 516-933-4590
Purpose: To assist senior citizens in obtaining full or part time employment, and to offer other informational, health, education and ancillary services.
Sponsor: WNBC-TV; Long Island Lighting Company; other cooperating companies
Contact: J. Joseph Crowley

Description: In the spring of 1981, Long Island Lighting Company, in conjunction with WNBC-TV, embarked on a program directed toward the holding of a Senior Citizen Job Fair, with the intended purpose of affording all attendees the opportunity to register for full- or part-time positions with Long Island firms. Some 50 companies joined in the effort as well as representatives of the New York State Department of Labor, Long Island State Park Commission, Nassau and Suffolk County senior citizen agencies, local county Bar associations, local hospitals and universities, news media, U.S. Marine Corps, and the U.S. Social Security Administration.
Approximately 3,000 seniors attended the first fair at Bethpage State Park. Each private sector representative had its own area with large tents to register and/or interview potential job seekers. Approximately 1,500 individuals were registered for jobs, and this registry has been maintained by the major sponsor as an ongoing job bank.
As part of the service, educational, health, legal and other applicable information of interest to our senior population is distributed by appropriate agencies. Also, during the course of the fair, entertainment is presented by professionals, and food is provided by major food chains with no cost to participants.
Job pledges are made by private firms at the fair and later in referring to the job bank created by this activity. More than 65 companies participate, answering questions about possible part-time employment as well as regular job openings.
Also, participating companies assist in staging the job fair by lending personnel to serve as volunteers for the arrangements committee and for interviewing job fair attendees seeking part-time employment. All sponsoring committees are asked to seek employment possibilities within their organizations for Job Fair attendees. The expenses of the Job Fair are shared among the participating companies on an assessment basis.
Other volunteers are involved in supervisory and management capacities, fund-raising and public relations. In addition, educational institutions and local and state governments played major roles in the success of the Fair.
Founded: 1981

JOBS FOR OLDER WOMEN*
SEE EMPLOYMENT: OLDER PERSON

SECOND CAREERS PROGRAM
SEE EMPLOYMENT: OLDER PERSON

SENIOR EMPLOYMENT RESOURCES
SEE EMPLOYMENT: OLDER PERSON

RECIPIENTS: OLDER PERSON - ETHNIC GROUPS

NATIONAL/STATE ORGANIZATIONS

NATIONAL ASSOCIATION FOR HISPANIC ELDERLY
Asociacion Nacional Por Personas Mayores
2727 West Sixth Street
Suite 270
Los Angeles, CA 90057
TEL: 213-487-1922
Objectives: To articulate the needs of the Hispanic and other low-income elderly.
Services: Works to increase representation of Hispanic elderly in social service programs aimed at older Americans; administers the

Senior Community Employment Project, funded by the *Department of Labor,* which provides subsidized employment to Hispanics over 55 years of age, and works to develop their skills to enable employment outside of the program at the end of the program period; conducts research; holds training seminars; maintains a library; publishes *Legislative Bulletin* and *Our Heritage,* both issued quarterly.
Publications: Legislative Bulletin; Our Heritage; Conference Proceedings
Founded: 1975

RECIPIENTS: OLDER PERSON - GIVEAWAY PROGRAMS

INDIVIDUAL PROGRAM PROFILES

BASKET OF JOY CAMPAIGN
SEE RECIPIENTS: OLDER PERSON - PSYCHOSOCIAL SUPPORT

RECIPIENTS: OLDER PERSON - HEALTH

NATIONAL/STATE ORGANIZATIONS

ALZHEIMER'S DISEASE & RELATED DISORDERS ASSOCIATION
70 East Lake Street
Suite 600
Chicago, IL 60601
TEL: 312-853-3060; 800-572-6037 (IL)
TOLL FREE: 800-621-0379 (nationwide)
Objectives: To combat Alzheimer's disease and related disorders; to develop family support systems.
Services: Promotes research to find the cause, treatment and cure for Alzheimer's disease (AD); develops and offers educational programs to the media, health care professionals, and the general public; represents the needs of both victims and caregivers before the federal government; works with the media, local civic groups and others to explode the myth that AD is a natural part of the aging process; assists in the development of self-help groups or family support systems through more than 160 local chapters; provides toll-free information and referral services to groups and individuals across the country; maintains a speakers' bureau and a number of committees on the aspects of the disease and nursing home and patient care management; has a bank of experts available for technical questions; offers research grants; publishes a quarterly newsletter.
Publications: ADRDA Quarterly
Founded: 1980

NATIONAL ASSOCIATION FOR HUMAN DEVELOPMENT
1620 Eye Street, NW
Washington, DC 20006
TEL: 202-331-1737
Objectives: To encourage older people to participate in physical fitness programs.
Services: Operates "Active People Over 60" campaign; conducts several community awareness activities, including multimedia events; develops and manages model demonstration projects; provides training; conducts workshops and nutrition seminars;

offers employment counseling; publishes quarterly digest, a training manual, booklets, evaluation, bibliographical, audiovisual and media-oriented materials.
Publications: Digest
Founded: 1974

TRAINING PROGRAMS

PARKINSON'S INSTITUTE FOR CAREGIVERS
Citadel Retirement Community
Volunteers of America of Mesa
5121 East Broadway
Mesa, AZ 85206
TEL: 602-832-5555
Credit: Institute Coordinator
Description: VOA's Parkinson's Institute is located at the Citadel Retirement Community in Mesa, Arizona. It is the only location in the nation which is offering a program of treatment and education for Parkinson's in a residential setting.
The goal of the personally-tailored health improvement program for persons with Parkinson's is to improve the lifestyles for many with this disease.
The training is designed to allow a caregiver or spouse to form a team with a resident in the program, accompany the resident through all steps in the program, and take an active part in the health education for the resident, and preparation for the resident's return home. Composed of 21-day sessions, the program features:
● health and nutrition;
● exercise;
● speech communication; and
● stress management.
Approximately 15 apartments of the retirement community are used for the resident-caregiver teams enrolled in the program. Other apartments are set up as offices, treatment rooms, a fully-equipped exercise room, and an outpatient clinic for the duration of the session. The exercise facilities are open to residents not in the program, and they are encouraged to attend the medical lectures and use the available medical facilities.

INDIVIDUAL PROGRAM PROFILES

AD SUPPORT GROUP OF GREATER ALABAMA
SEE HEALTH: OLDER PERSON

ADULT FOSTER CARE
Senior Citizens United Community Services
Black Horse Pike
Camden, NJ 08101
TEL: 609-546-2666
Purpose: To provide a temporary, home-like environment for recuperating senior citizens.
Contact: Suzanne Watson
Description: Adult Foster Care helps seniors who live alone when they are faced with a recuperative period after hospitalization or a serious illness. The risk of being home alone is too great, and a nursing home is not always the right choice for an individual. The program seeks volunteers willing to provide a home-like environment for the seniors facing this problem.
Funded by the Robert Wood Johnson Foundation, the program is designed to meet temporary support needs of seniors who are expected to regain their independence and return to their own homes within six to eight weeks. Program clients are provided with supervision, meals, laundry and other assistance by the program while they recuperate. Volunteer families willing to share their homes are offered a monthly stipend of $400 to $600 to cover the support services. Potential providers and their homes are

carefully screened, and those accepted are provided with an extensive training program.

The *Adult Foster Care* concept was developed to fill two gaps in service for county seniors - a critical shortage of home health aides, and a lack of affordable 24-hour in-home care. In addition, hospitals are discharging patients earlier than ever before - often before the patient has had time to regain strength and physical abilities necessary for independent living. The program's philosophy is that temporary support in times of need in a home setting is financially and psychologically a better alternative to institutionalization or the dangers of being alone. The volunteer effort is designed to reflect that philosophy.

BLUEGRASS MEDICARE-MEDICAID ASSISTANCE PROGRAM
Lexington Senior Citizens Center
1530 Nicholasville Road
Lexington, KY 40503
TEL: 606-278-6072
Purpose: To help senior citizens understand and complete forms for Medicare and Medicaid programs.
Sponsor: American Association of Retired Persons
Contact: Volunteer Coordinator
Description: The *American Association of Retired Persons (AARP)* and the *Lexington Senior Citizens Center* are jointly sponsoring a program designed to assist people who have trouble understanding their Medicare and Medicaid forms. Called the *Bluegrass Medicare-Medicaid Assistance Program,* the effort offers three days of training to volunteer counselors. When training is completed, volunteers are placed at senior centers in their own communities.
Volunteers are recruited in eight counties and required to commit to at least eight hours of service each month, or two hours a week, for six months. Informal meetings are held periodically to describe the program and give potential volunteers an opportunity to decide whether or not to join the project.
Founded: 1989

MULTI-PHASIC HEALTH SCREENING
SEE HEALTH: OLDER PERSON

SUMMERFEST ART FAIRE
Logan Regional Hospital
Logan , UT 84321
TEL: 801-752-2050
Purpose: To raise funds for the hospital's 24-hour emergency response system for the elderly and disabled.
Sponsor: Logan Regional Hospital
Contact: Marilyn Sedgwik, Chairwoman
Description: Community artists, musicians, merchants and volunteers come together each year in Logan to create and operate *Summerfest Art Faire,* which draws artists, performers and visitors from across the country. The festival is organized by the volunteer directors of *Logan Regional Hospital* with help in 1989 from the *Utah State University Chamber of Music* and many local merchants.
Entertainers included a saxophonist from the *Tonight Show Band,* who performed a free concert, a production of the musical *Carousel* in the historic Capitol Theatre produced by a nationally-known vocalist, a well-known jazz artist, and other celebrities. Additions in 1989 were an antique carousel merry-go-round brought in from another county, and a new "guest artist" display featuring new artists who created and painted for visitors as well as displaying their work. Local artists continued to display their work as in years past, and local restaurants participated by providing food.
The hospital volunteers have found that by organizing this event they help erase the image of "pink ladies" that some people harbor. The program for which all of the effort is expended is

Lifeline, an electronic system that keeps the hospital in touch with people who may require emergency treatment. Each year the festival attracts more people from out-of-town and out-of-state.

RECIPIENTS: OLDER PERSON - HOMEBOUND

NATIONAL/STATE ORGANIZATIONS

YOUTH SERVICES TO FRAIL, HOMEBOUND ELDERLY
National Council on the Aging
600 Maryland Avenue, SW
West Wing 100
Washington, DC 20024
TEL: 202-479-1200
Objectives: To conduct a survey to locate successful programs in which young volunteers are working with the frail, homebound elderly.
Services: Operates under a grant from the Wallerstein Foundation for Geriatric Life Improvement; administers nationwide survey to identify and review successful programs in which young volunteers are working with the frail, homebound elderly; reviews programs to determine and describe common elements within the programs that help to ensure success; makes results of survey and individual program descriptions available to individuals and organizations working with the frail, homebound elderly.
Sponsor: Wallerstein Foundation for Geriatric Life Improvement
Contact: Larry Couch, Associate, Intergenerational Programs

TRAINING PROGRAMS

TAKING A TRIP TO FRIENDSHIP
SEE RECIPIENTS: OLDER PERSON - PSYCHOSOCIAL SUPPORT

INDIVIDUAL PROGRAM PROFILES

BAY RIDGE NUTRITION AND HOME CARE PROGRAMS
SEE NUTRITION: OLDER PERSON

HOST (HANDS OF SHARED TIME)
SEE RECIPIENTS: OLDER PERSON - NURSING HOMES

VISCAP (VOLUNTEER INCENTIVE SERVICE CREDIT ACCOUNT PROGRAM)
Kirtland Community College
Roscommon, MI 48653
TEL: 517-275-5121
TOLL FREE: 800-433-2517/ext. 264
Purpose: To provide respite services for family caregivers.
Contact: Stuart E. Lawrence, Director Emeritus, Library
Description: VISCAP works to create an awareness of the needs of the primary caregiver of an aging relative, and provide volunteer support services to give the caregiver relief. This role is played by family, friends and relatives of the older person, and - without intervention - often leads to burnout. VISCAP volunteers evaluate each individual situation and provide respite services until the primary caregiver appears to be ready to return to the often-demanding roles.
Publications: VISCAP: Help When Needed
Founded: 1989

WILLING WORKERS OF COLLEGE HILL
Arkansas Convalescent Center
2107 Dudley Avenue
Texarkana, AR 75502
TEL: 501-772-4427
Purpose: To visit shut-ins once a month and on birthdays and holidays, and as services are needed.
Sponsor: Willing Workers of College Hill
Contact: Patty Brown, President
Description: After carefully considering immediate needs in the community, *Willing Workers of College Hill* selected friendly visiting to shut-ins in the area. The regular monthly visits are bolstered with birthday and holiday visits, and - when needs arise unexpectedly - appropriate services are provided.
In the course of their friendly visiting program, volunteers learned of a critical need for a convalescent center for the elderly in the area. *Willing Workers* wrote letters, circulated petitions, went to meetings, and contacted city and state officials. This dedication and hard work by volunteers led to the building of the *Arkansas Convalescent Center.*
To help speed up the process, *Willing Workers* rolled up their sleeves, started making beds, getting the rooms ready, fixing up a library, assisting the Activity Director, and served as hosts and hostesses for the open house of 500 guests who came to see the Center. During this process at the Center, volunteers "never missed a beat" in their friendly visits to their shut-in friends, according to the program's coordinator.

RECIPIENTS: OLDER PERSON - HOUSING

NATIONAL/STATE ORGANIZATIONS

MORTGAGE BURNING FUND
SEE HOUSING: HOMELESS

INDIVIDUAL PROGRAM PROFILES

CHISS (CONSUMER HOUSING INFORMATION SERVICE FOR SENIORS)
SEE HOUSING: OLDER PERSON

COMMUNITY BETTERMENT PROGRAM
SEE HOUSING: REVITALIZATION

HOME REPAIRS PROJECT
SEE HOUSING: REPAIRS/MAINTENANCE

SUNDIAL VOLUNTEERS
29 Merriam Parkway
Fitchburg, MA 01420
TEL: 617-345-1559
Purpose: To provide services for senior citizens in a low/moderate income apartment building.
Sponsor: First Parish Church (Universalist-Unitarian)
Contact: George J. Bailey, Manager
Description: In commemoration of its 200th anniversary, the First Parish Church sponsored a 168-unit apartment building for senior citizens. A non-profit corporation was formed by volunteers from the church. Passbooks of church members were hypothecated as security for a loan to obtain options on land, secure a consultant

for the project and obtain preliminary drawings from an architect. The building, known as "Sundial," was completed on April 1, 1970, and has been operating at full capacity since October 1970. Sundial is non-sectarian and integrated. Residents represent all geographical areas of the United States.
The first floor of Sundial houses a social and recreation area called the Sundial Lounge. The Lounge hosts planned activities from 10:00 a.m. to 9:00 p.m. Monday through Friday.
Since the opening of Sundial, approximately 125 tenant volunteers have served as guides, lobby hosts or hostesses, receptionists and newspaper distributors. Volunteers are on duty at the lobby desk from 9 to 9 each day, working in one-hour shifts.
In addition, each of the ten floors has a monitor or "Ambassador" who helps new tenants, tries to involve tenants in activities, and is on the lookout for problems or emergencies. The monitors comprise the Tenant Council (also called the "Ambassadors of Goodwill") and are elected each January by all of the residents. They are honored by management each April with a dinner. In general, the duties of the Ambassador of Goodwill are;
- to welcome new tenants to The Sundial.
- to acquaint new tenants with procedures and programs available.
- to make regular contacts with tenants regarding illness, duration of absences, etc.
- to know what to do in case of emergency (training is provided).
- to answer the emergency cord when it rings (cord located in bathroom of each tenant).
To alleviate concerns of elected Ambassadors, meetings with the Manager are held weekly. The greatest concern of these volunteers is lack of experience, and the major purpose of the meetings is to discuss responsibilities of the tenants to the Ambassadors, as well as the other way around.
College student volunteers are very helpful as instructors of arts and crafts, physical fitness programs, music and choral groups, office assistance, etc. A number of Human Services majors complete their college internships at Sundial.
Founded: 1970

UNION RETIREES RESOURCES
SEE HOUSING: REPAIRS/MAINTENANCE

RECIPIENTS: OLDER PERSON - I&R

INDIVIDUAL PROGRAM PROFILES

CORPORATE RETIREES INFORMATION AND ASSISTANCE PROGRAM
SEE RECIPIENTS: OLDER PERSON - CONSUMER SERVICES

SENIOR CONNECTION
Community Service Council of Broward County
1300 South Andrews Avenue
PO Box 22877
Fort Lauderdale , FL 33335-2877
TEL: 305-524-8371
Purpose: To provide information on everything from health care to social services for seniors.
Sponsor: Area Agency on Aging
Contact: Arthur J. Ellick, Executive Director
Description: In just one month after it began in November 1987, *Senior Connection* had received over 400 calls from people seeking information on services for seniors. One-fourth of the county's population is over 65 (270,000 individuals). The information line is

operated by the *Community Service Council of Broward County.* Although the United Way had a general crisis line and I&R service, needs were increasingly focusing on the elderly, and the Council's proposal was welcomed by *United Way* and *Area Agency on Aging* officials. The United Way provided computer support and other nonfinancial help, and the local Area Agency on Aging provided the funding.

A very effective aspect of the program is the follow-up capability. *Senior Connection* staff, via a three-way call, can ensure the individual is put in touch with an appropriate agency. Then, staff can follow up to see if the requested help was received by the individual.

A side benefit, according to the director, is the "much-needed data" that the program provides for use in planning future services.

SENIOR REPORT
WUST Radio
815 V Street, NW
Washington, DC 20001
TEL: 202-462-0011
Purpose: To keep senior citizens apprised of programs and services designed for them.
Contact: Newton Smith, Jr., or Concha Johnson
Description: Located in Ward 8, which has the poorest and least educated elderly population in Washington, DC, *WUST Radio* presents a daily, 15-minute broadcast, *Senior Report,* that delivers a stream of conversation aimed at providing an estimated 50,000 listeners with the latest news on senior citizen issues, benefits and programs.

Although the "voices" behind *Senior Report* belong to people experienced in the aging field, the program features guests who donate their time to discuss a specific issue and respond to questions from listeners. When the specialist is finished, program staff are ready and waiting with information on local volunteer and free government projects so that the senior citizen can follow up on the advice given by the guest. An example is the visit by an oncologist who talked about the importance of mammograms, and the followup information about a demonstration project offering free mammograms.

On the lighter side, the program's facilitators try to keep seniors current on low-cost entertainment and activities - local theatres that offer senior discounts, or package rates on cruises. Also, they try to stay on top of the news and current events to help develop an informed senior citizenry. In early 1990, the thrust was on the 1990 Census begun in April. Recognizing the uncertainty of many seniors about providing information about themselves, the station assured them that there was nothing to worry about, unless they *didn't* give requested information, since their benefits might be cut or, in matters of "head count," the city might lose money if everyone isn't counted.

The show's hosts are involved in many senior programs, including *Gray Panthers, Senior Citizens Counseling and Delivery Service, St. Teresa of Avila Parish Senior Outreach,* and the city's *Foster Grandparents Program* among others.

RECIPIENTS: OLDER PERSON - INDEPENDENT LIVING

NATIONAL/STATE ORGANIZATIONS

NATIONAL FEDERATION OF INTERFAITH VOLUNTEER CAREGIVERS
SEE RECIPIENTS: HANDICAPPED - INDEPENDENT LIVING

NATIONAL VOLUNTARY ORGANIZATIONS FOR INDEPENDENT LIVING FOR THE AGED
National Council on the Aging
600 Maryland Avenue, SW
West Wing 100
Washington, DC 20024
TEL: 202-479-1200
Objectives: To promote independent living for vulnerable and frail older persons.
Services: Assists local communities in planning and implementing services and programs to make the environment of the vulnerable and frail elderly safe, enjoyable, and more equitable; works through national voluntary organizations (200) who collaborate in order to strengthen their individual efforts; provides consultation, conferences and publications to any group or individual concerned with the frail elderly; publishes informative materials and useful tools to assist program managers.
Publications: Update for Voluntary Sector; voluntary Organizations
Founded: 1971

INDIVIDUAL PROGRAM PROFILES

FAR NORTHWEST CAREGIVERS
10633 Lake Creek Parkway
Austin, TX 78750
TEL: 512-250-5021
Purpose: To keep the elderly in their homes by providing services by volunteers.
Sponsor: Pond Springs Baptist Church
Contact: Dee Bruer, Director
Description: The *Far Northwest Caregivers* recognizes the need by many older persons to remain independent and not become burdens to their families. The organization is operated by a group of volunteers who seek to keep the elderly in their homes by providing transportation, visitation, telephone reassurance and short-term meal delivery.

Volunteers in the program have enlisted the help of various community groups not only to donate but also to serve the food needed for special outings. "This gets them involved," according to one volunteer.

Volunteers also stand by to drive seniors on errands, to the doctor, hairdresser or shopping mall. They make corsages, boutonniers and wreaths for special occasions such as birthdays, anniversaries and holidays.

A major activity for the seniors is the organization's *Seniors Day Out* at *Pond Springs Baptist Church* twice each month. About 50 seniors regularly attend, eating a lunch or snacks, and participating in activities such as bridge, dominoes and card games.

The *Far Northwest Caregivers* has been operating since late 1986 and each year more and more seniors call for services that will help keep them in their homes.
Founded: 1986

SENIOR CITIZENS HOME ASSISTANCE SERVICES
PO Box 3025
Knoxville, TN 37927
TEL: 615-523-2920
Purpose: To keep the elderly in their homes as long as possible.
Contact: Linda Flynn, Administrative Assistant
Description: The *Senior Citizens Home Assistance Services (SCHAS)* is a four-part program aimed at keeping the elderly in their own homes and out of nursing facilities for as long as possible. The four programs are:
- **RENEW** - uses trained volunteers to provide in-home companionship to the elderly in the absence of relatives with

whom they live.
- **The Bridge Project** - matches workers with the elderly who need inside or outside maintenance work.
- **The Home Hair-Care Plan** - brings a licensed beautician into the homes of the elderly for grooming of their hair, beards, nails, etc.
- **There's no place like home** - offers trained workers to come into the homes of the elderly and help them with whatever chores they need done - from cleaning the floors to preparing meals to grocery shopping.

The program places emphasis on offering paid worker positions to former welfare recipients coming out of the *Job Training Partnership Act* programs to locate jobs that will help to keep them off the welfare rolls.

RECIPIENTS: OLDER PERSON - LEGAL SERVICES

NATIONAL/STATE ORGANIZATIONS

LEGAL SERVICES FOR THE ELDERLY
132 West 43rd Street
Third Floor
New York, NY 10036
TEL: 212-595-1340
Objectives: To advise on legal problems and areas indigenous to the elderly.
Services: Offers advice and in some cases litigates on behalf of the elderly; maintains library of information on various aspects of legal services on behalf of the elderly; conducts research, litigation and educational programs; publishes a progress report (quarterly) and other materials.
Publications: Progress Report
Founded: 1969

LEGAL SERVICES FOR THE ELDERLY POOR
SEE CONSUMER SERVICES/LEGAL RIGHTS: OLDER PERSON

TRAINING PROGRAMS

NATIONAL SENIOR CITIZENS LAW CENTER
SEE CONSUMER SERVICES/LEGAL RIGHTS: OLDER PERSON

INDIVIDUAL PROGRAM PROFILES

LEGAL COUNSEL FOR THE ELDERLY
SEE CONSUMER SERVICES/LEGAL RIGHTS: OLDER PERSON

RECIPIENTS: OLDER PERSON - NURSING HOMES

NATIONAL/STATE ORGANIZATIONS

VOLUNTEER SERVICE CORPS COMMITTEE
American Health Care Association
1200 Fifteenth Street, NW
Washington, DC 20005
TEL: 202-833-2050
Objectives: To provide services that otherwise would not be possible; to maintain continuity with the community; to give residents an unpaid concerned friend - often giving them a new outlook on life.
Services: Develops volunteer programs for nursing homes; provides technical assistance on administration and day-to-day operation; publishes *Establishing and Maintaining a Volunteer Program: A Handbook for Long Term Care Facilities* and other materials for program managers; participates in AHCA annual meeting.
Publications: Notes; Handbook for Long Term Care Facilities
Founded: 1949

TRAINING PROGRAMS

TAKING A TRIP TO FRIENDSHIP
SEE RECIPIENTS: OLDER PERSON - PSYCHOSOCIAL SUPPORT

INDIVIDUAL PROGRAM PROFILES

HOST (HANDS OF SHARED TIME)
Montgomery General Hospital
3438 Olney-Laytonsville Road
Olney, MD 20832
TEL: 301-774-6114
Purpose: To provide friends and helpers to older individuals either in their homes or in nursing homes.
Sponsor: Montgomery General Hospital
Contact: Kelly M. Ring, Service Coordinator
Description: With this interfaith, intergenerational program, a major hospital reaches out to the community and helps to administer a volunteer program that will provide friendship in the way of companionship and services to older persons in their homes and in nursing homes. Montgomery General Hospital in Maryland sponsors the HOST (Hands Of Shared Time) program, which serves the elderly in the entire county.
The program began in 1987 when the Hospital received a four-year grant from the W.K. Kellogg Foundation of Battle Creek, Michigan. A HOST volunteer is a member of the *HOST Community,* and has many options for providing assistance to an older individual. According to the coordinator, "All of these options involve friendship." They include:
- **Companionship** - be a friend, listen and talk, write letters, play games, read (once a week for one hour at the convenience of the volunteer and the HOST friend).
- **Shopping** - either shopping for the older person, or taking him or her shopping once a week.
- **Medical Transportation** - taking a person to the doctor or for treatments on an as-needed basis.
- **Light Housekeeping** - providing some assistance with caring for the home such as light dusting and vacuuming, light snack preparation, emptying trash, etc. Some grooming assistance may be given, also (one or more times per week one hour at a

time).

- **Respite Care** - providing relief for a family who cares for a homebound older adult so that the family may leave for home for several hours (weekly or biweekly).
- **Telephone Reassurance** - call an isolated individual on the phone to check on their wellbeing (several times a week at a schedule designed by the volunteer and HOST friend).

Other services that a HOST volunteer can provide are: in-office support to greet drop-in members of the community; assisting with fundraising and membership programs; developing recreational and educational activities; helping with the newsletter; and supporting clerical staff.

Any person 15 years old or older who lives, works, goes to school, or attends a religious congregation in the HOST area may apply to be a volunteer through the HOST office.

All volunteers must participate in the 14-hour training program which is conducted by the Assistant Project Director, HOST staff, and/or other contracted educators. The training is designed to give volunteers a chance to learn about the aging process, develop communication and safety skills, and gain insight into their own attitudes about aging. On-the-job training is included so that volunteers can practice newly-learned skills and feel prepared before entering into their volunteer relationships. Training is also a fun and informal way to get to know other HOST volunteers. Additional training is offered in the form of rap groups, seminars and workshops.

After training, a volunteer is matched with a HOST friend for a specific service. By 1990, almost 200 volunteers completed sixteen training sessions. Supervision is coordinated between HOST and the *Centralized Friendly Visitor Program*. Cooperative assistance also comes from the Retired Senior Volunteer Program (RSVP) and the MGH Home Health Program.

Commitment of one year is requested, beginning with the first training session. The one-year commitment allows the isolated individuals the opportunity to become friends with their volunteers.

In addition to identifying isolated older adults and recruiting volunteers in the community, HOST offers presentations on pertinent topics of interest for the older adult, monthly seminars and a self-help group for caregivers, and forums to inform local clergy and congregants about aging issues. Maintains a lending library of resource materials about aging issues for families, professionals, and others interested in this issue.

Grant monies are alloted in decreasing increments to encourage the community to develop methods to support HOST and keep it self-sufficient. No fees are charged for services received by older persons. Intensive efforts for financial support are continually explored to keep a much-needed service in the community.

One way community members and businesses support the HOST program is through the membership campaign and other donations. Donations also come from individuals in honor of a special person, such as a volunteer, older friend, or family member. Members of HOST receive the *HOST Post* newsletter and other reports and materials as progress warrants.

Publications: Hands of Shared Time (video); HOST Post (newsletter); HOST: Creating an Intergenerational Volunteer Program; Taking a Trip to Friendship: Training Program; HOST Recruitment Brochure; HOST Training Packet
Founded: 1987

NURSING HOME PROJECT
Retired Senior Volunteer Program
311 Pine Avenue
PO Box 3149
Albany, GA 31706
TEL: 912-435-9779
Purpose: To provide companionship for nursing home residents, and volunteer opportunities for low-income minority elderly.
Sponsor: SOWEGA Council on Aging; US/ACTION

Contact: Anne Bragg, Director
Description: A nursing home visitation project was begun in Albany several years ago, and it has become a permanent part of the RSVP program. Its focus is twofold in that it benefits both the nursing home residents and the volunteers.

The 25 senior volunteers are predominantly low-income minority without transportation. They are active participants in the Title III nutrition program, attending two sites in Albany. The volunteers are divided into three groups, each visiting the nursing home one day a week. The RSVP van takes the volunteers from their homes to the nursing home, where they spend one to two hours as "friendly visitors." Then the van takes them to the senior nutrition site for their noon meal.

The volunteer support (van service, meals, recognition, and insurance) provided by this program enables the volunteers to serve their community in a meaningful way. The nursing home residents look forward to the companionship of their RSVP "friends," and the volunteers are rewarded with a very real sense of being needed and appreciated. Another older volunteer group, the Georgia Peach Singers, presents musical programs each month at two local nursing homes - delightful old songs, dances, skits, and readings. Transportation is furnished to this group, also, and the nursing homes entertain both volunteers and residents with party refreshments.

The total RSVP project includes 300 volunteers who serve in 35 local agencies. It began in 1972 with a federal ACTION grant. Local funding is provided by the United Way plus in-kind donations, and the sponsor is the Southwest Georgia Council on Aging. The program goal is to serve this community with 42,000 hours of volunteer service per year, and to provide the senior volunteers with opportunities for meaningful involvement.
Founded: 1972

OMBUDSMAN PROGRAM
SEE RECIPIENTS: OLDER PERSON - ADVOCACY

PARTNERS IN CARING
Telephone Pioneers of America
3841 Green Hills Village Drive
Nashville, TN 37215
TEL: 615-665-8845
Purpose: To get people in companies interested in nursing home patients and to link them with individual nursing homes.
Sponsor: Telephone Pioneers of America
Contact: Suzanne Petrey
Description: The *Partners in Caring* program was initiated to improve services to older Nashvillians. The main goal is to get people in companies interested in nursing home patients and to link them with individual nursing homes. In the spring of 1989, an initial *pilot* partnership was forged between the patients at *Bordeaux Hospital* and the *Telephone Pioneers,* a volunteer organization of telecommunications employees. Twenty *Pioneers* signed up for the program. Volunteer training is administered before the two sides of the partnership are brought together, and includes:

- how to talk, listen to and look at an older person;
- death and dying concerns;
- the importance of confidentiality; and
- how to handle concerns and suggestions.

Also, the individual nursing homes involved conduct orientations of their own. They provide information about aging issues, and what to expect while volunteering at the nursing home. The volunteers are matched according to their interests and the nursing home's needs, such as staffing the patient information desk, forming a one-on-one family-type relationship with a specific patient, and a wide variety of other jobs. Some volunteers commit to weekly activities, some monthly and some yearly.

According to the director, groups of non-working volunteers of the past are now part of the work force. Without a program like

Partners, which gets corporations involved, the program would be inadequate or nonexistent. Feedback from the volunteers indicate that they, themselves, benefit personally from the experience.
Founded: 1989

RYANS' NURSING HOME VOLUNTEER PROGRAM
Sweet Briar College
Dean of Student Affairs
Sweet Briar, VA 24595
TEL: 804-381-5529
Purpose: To provide an interaction between college students and nursing home residents while filling a need in the community.
Sponsor: Church and Chapel Committee
Contact: Robert H. Barlow
Description: This program began in 1980 with five student volunteers; now approximately 40 volunteers are involved. At least once per week, the volunteer visits for one hour with a particular nursing home resident. Often, the volunteers make additional visits. The college provides free van transportation to students three times per week in order to expedite student visits. The college has also supported other special programs and services. The volunteers are trained at an initial meeting on the campus before they make at least one supervised visit to the nursing home. The volunteers are supervised by the Dean of Student Affairs. The goals are:
- to provide visitors to the nursing home;
- to develop friendships between students and nursing home residents; and
- to expose students to the aging process and nursing homes.
Founded: 1980

WILLING WORKERS OF COLLEGE HILL
SEE RECIPIENTS: OLDER PERSON - HOMEBOUND

YES PROGRAM (YOUTH-ELDERLY SERVICES)*
SEE RECIPIENTS: OLDER PERSON - ARTS

RECIPIENTS: OLDER PERSON - NUTRITION

INDIVIDUAL PROGRAM PROFILES

COUNTRY GATHERING
SEE NUTRITION: OLDER PERSON

MEALS ON WHEELS OF BIRMINGHAM
2718 19th Place South
Birmingham, AL 35209
TEL: 205-870-5042
Purpose: To deliver warm meals to homebound residents over 60 years old who cannot prepare their own meals.
Contact: Linda Hayes, Director
Description: Meals on Wheels started in England after World War II and evolved into a non-profit organization that has spread across the United States. The organization opened a Birmingham branch 13 years ago. The branch relies heavily on more than 800 volunteers in Jefferson County, who cover 44 routes and deliver 525 meals daily. Most of the volunteers are recruited through churches. "Without the cooperation of churches," according to the director, "the Meals on Wheels program would run out of gas." The program buys food from Bessemer Carraway Medical Center and St. Vincent's Hospital. Vans pick up the food from the hospital kitchens and take it to drop-off points around the county -

usually community churches. Volunteers pick up the food and deliver it to the recipients. Most volunteers give two days a week and have a route of nine or ten people. Usually, an individual church manages a designated route.
Meals on Wheels is funded mostly by federal grants and private contributions. Recipients are asked to contribute $1.50 toward the $2.60 cost of each meal, but many recipients can't afford even that and are matched up with sponsors who pay for their meals. The common response to a request for volunteers is immediate volunteerism from people of all ages. It isn't unusual to get 50-60 volunteers from one presentation. In unusual situations in which a community does not respond, most often paid Meals on Wheels staff members must deliver food to clients in that community. A favorite story of the director's is of a women who received meals after surgery and volunteered to deliver meals when she recovered. The program has a waiting list of more than 700 people needing its services, and it continuously seeks volunteers. Plans to expand into the South East Lake, Bessemer and Cahaba Heights communities must wait until the cadre of volunteers increases to adequately cover these areas.
Founded: 1976

MEALS ON WHEELS OF BUFFALO AND ERIE COUNTY
SEE NUTRITION: DELIVERY

MORRIS COUNTY NUTRITION PROGRAM
SEE NUTRITION: OLDER PERSON

SENIOR NUTRITION PROGRAM
Volunteers of America
700 East Broadway
Long Beach, CA 90802
TEL: 213-435-8262
Purpose: To provide hot lunches to seniors in the greater Long Beach area.
Sponsor: Los Angeles County Area Agency on Aging
Contact: Program Coordinator
Description: The *Senior Nutrition Program* offers nutritious hot lunches to seniors over 60 and their spouses six days a week in the greater Long Beach area. The program differs from many meals programs in that the lunches are served on-site in pleasant surroundings. All locations are accessible to the disabled. The program is operated by the *Volunteers of America* with partial funding coming from the Los Angeles County Area Agency on Aging.
Lunches are served Mondays through Fridays at nine locations, and on Saturdays at three of the locations. To sssure that everyone who comes is served, reservations are required at least 24 hours in advance. A $1.35 donation is requested to cover meal costs and to enable the program to be expanded as much as possible. Menus are published in the local paper a week in advance. Entrees include steak, chicken, ham, and turkey. All lunches include milk.
Volunteers of America also delivers meals to home-bound seniors 60 and older. For the home-delivered meals a contribution of $1.50 is suggested. Seniors are not required to make contributions for either on-site or home-delivered meals, and their inability to do so is handled with sensitivity.

SENIORS: SPECIAL DELIVERY
SEE NUTRITION: DELIVERY

ST. JOSEPH COMMUNITY SERVICES
SEE NUTRITION: DELIVERY

RECIPIENTS: OLDER PERSON - PSYCHOSOCIAL SUPPORT

NATIONAL/STATE ORGANIZATIONS

SENIOR COMPANION PROGRAM (SCP)
US/ACTION - The Federal Volunteer Agency
1100 Vermont Avenue, NW
Suite 1100
Washington, DC 20525
TEL: 202-634-9208
TOLL FREE: 800-424-8580
Objectives: To render supportive person-to-person services to adults - especially older persons with special or exceptional needs; to provide part-time volunteer service opportunities for low-income older persons.
Services: Provides grants to public agencies and nonprofit organizations to develop and manage a program to provide companions to adults with physical and mental health limitations, adhering to the same guidelines as the Foster Grandparent Program (separate entry); publishes *Senior Companion Program Operations Handbook,* recruitment flyers and other materials.
Contact: Rey Tejada
Publications: SCP Operations Handbook
Founded: 1971

VOLUNTEER SERVICE CORPS COMMITTEE
SEE RECIPIENTS: OLDER PERSON - NURSING HOMES

TRAINING PROGRAMS

TAKING A TRIP TO FRIENDSHIP
HOST (Hands Of Shared Time)
Montgomery General Hospital
3438 Olney-Laytonsville Road
Olney, MD 20832
TEL: 301-774-6114
Credit: Inquire
Sponsor: Montgomery General Hospital
Contact: Kelly M. Ring, Service Coordinator
Description: This program is designed to train volunteers age 15 or older to serve as companions and all-round helpers to older persons in their homes and in nursing homes. It consists of a five-part introductory session, and eleven training modules. Each module includes the step-by-step process for implementation, including background information, specific notes to the instructor, activities/exercises, and handouts. More specifically:
Part One: Overview
- **Introduction to the HOST program** - This is a brief overview of the HOST program, including research results from the training process.
- **Rationale for volunteer training** - Preparing volunteers is often an unstructured process. This discussion includes the benefits of training for the volunteers, agencies, and community involved.
- **Goals for HOST Training** - Although training is obviously a time for volunteers to learn new skills and acquire knowledge, it is much more than that. This section reviews the training goals and objectives and discusses the role training plays in securing, screening, and supporting volunteers.
- **Tips and techniques for implementation** - This section includes information about group dynamics, intergenerational teaching methods, and training logistics.
- **Notes to the instructor** - This section includes guidelines specific to the manual and training program to enhance the trainer's understanding and facilitation.

Part Two: Training Models
- **Detour to Facts and Attitudes** - This session is designed to help volunteers explore their own attitudes about aging and gain a better understanding of the myths versus realities of growing old.
- **Follow the Road to Normal Aging** - This module promotes healthy living for volunteers while teaching volunteers about normal changes in aging. Volunteers are also taught to identify danger signs in the health of their older friends.
- **Cross a Bridge to Communication** - Volunteers who can communicate effectively feel more comfortable in their volunteer role and make better friends to the older adults. This session focuses on developing those communication skills.
- **Walk a Mile in My Shoes** - It's difficult to imagine what sensory loss and disability are like when one is in good health. This session gives volunteers an opportunity to simulate some age changes by using props and performing simple tasks.
- **Clear Your Path to a Healthy Mind** - This session increases volunteers' knowlege about the causes of dementia and how to communicate with cognitively impaired older adults.
- **Reach for the Stars** - In a supportive group session, volunteers can explore their own coping skills and those necessary for dealing with losses associated with late life. The role spirituality plays in the coping process is also discussed.
- **Better Safe Than Sorry** - Volunteers get "hands on" experience using mobility assistive devices and practicing wheelchair transfer techniques. Emphasis is placed on home safety, independence, and dignity.
- **Share the Experience** - Trained volunteers speaking to the recruits is the highlight of the training. No one can explain the value and joys of volunteering better than a volunteer. The recruits have the opportunity to learn about "real" older friends, ask questions, and meet other volunteers at the same time.
- **Make Friends Along the Way - What to do if?** - *The best surprise is no surprise.* Addressing potential problems enhances volunteers' confidence and security and adds to older adults' safety. This is also a time to reinforce the agency's policies and procedures.
- **I'm On My Way** - Supporting volunteers from the start will encourage volunteer commitment later on. This is a time to review material taught throughout training, reward and congratulate volunteers for their efforts, and provide closure between the volunteers and staff.

All participants are provided with sample agendas, handouts and worksheets, suggested wall charts to help follow the training process, and volunteer forms demonstrating the necessary application, release, follow-up and test procedures. For added incentive, a certificate of award is included.
Publications: Taking a Trip to Friendship: Training Program

INDIVIDUAL PROGRAM PROFILES

BASKET OF JOY CAMPAIGN
Volunteers of America
1550 Yates Street
Denver, CO 80204
TEL: 303-623-8052
Purpose: To provide a basket of fresh fruit and a personal visit to a homebound senior citizen during the holiday season.
Sponsor: Volunteers of America
Contact: Linda Dee
Description: The *Basket of Joy Campaign* provides baskets of fresh fruit to elderly, homebound seniors who may otherwise be forgotten during the holiday season. The project is a collaboration between a newspaper columnist, a grocery store produce buyer and a volunteer coordinator. Each player provides the needed

component to make the community effort successful. The columnist raises the cash and awareness for the campaign, and the produce manager orders the fruit and basket materials and arranges for use of a large warehouse in which to assemble and pick up baskets. Tables, chairs, a forklift, refreshments and trash collection all are provided by the produce manager. The volunteer coordinator organizes the volunteer corps, deposits the cash donations, and logs the names of elderly recipients into the computer. Donors' names are faxed to the newspaper and thank you letters are written.

At the end of October each year a column is run in the *Denver Post* newspaper announcing that people may donate cash, offer to volunteer or submit the names of deserving seniors who should receive a holiday fruit basket. The names of all donors are printed in the *Post* on a bi-weekly basis, providing both recognition for the donor, and visibility for the project.

The 470 volunteers include people of all ages (teenagers and older) who choose to either assemble or deliver baskets, or both. Three weeks prior to the event, all volunteers are sent their assignments - five to ten names of seniors in like zip code areas. All volunteers sign an indemnity waiver and a duplicate copy of the seniors' names is stapled to the waiver. Volunteers are encouraged to spend time visiting with the seniors on the lists.

This community effort includes over 700 school children who make greeting cards for the baskets. By 1990, the event had become regionally known and seniors from throughout Colorado request and receive baskets.

Funds are obtained exclusively from donors who respond to newspaper articles. Goals for 1988 were $25,000 to provide 5,000 baskets. Both goals were exceeded as $34,000 was raised and 6,000 baskets made and delivered. Goals for 1989 were $40,000 and 10,000 baskets. Again, the goals were exceeded.

The project could easily be replicated elsewhere. Additional information is available on request.

Publications: Basket of Joy Information Packet
Founded: 1988

GRATERFRIENDS
SEE LAW ENFORCEMENT/CRIME PREVENTION: RE-ENTRY

HOME LEAGUE
SEE PSYCHOSOCIAL SUPPORT SERVICES: OLDER PERSON

HOST (HANDS OF SHARED TIME)
SEE RECIPIENTS: OLDER PERSON - NURSING HOMES

LINCOLN COUNTY SENIOR COMPANION PROGRAM
169 SW Coast Highway
Newport , OR 97365
TEL: 503-265-3160
Purpose: To provide meaningful volunteer experience to low-income persons over age 60 to serve in one-to-one relationships with adults who are frail elderly.
Sponsor: Lincoln County Council on Aging
Contact: Wilma Earles
Description: The Senior Companion Program in Lincoln County receives a major portion of funding from ACTION. Local funds match on a 90/10 basis. The sponsor has been active in providing services to seniors in the county for 10 years.
The director is half-time. Office staff is volunteer and 11% are full time. The Senior Companions receive a stipend of $2.00 an hour, transportation reimbursement, and meal allowance.
They work in the homes of the elderly to provide services that mean the older client can avoid premature institutionalization.
They provide a variety of services, from letter writing to light meal preparation to medical escort or transportation.

Volunteers receive 40 hours of pre-service training which includes information about social services in the community, how to act as advocates, and agency policies.
Senior Companions must be low-income, over 60 and desire to have a challenging volunteer experience. They work 20 hours a week.
Founded: 1982

MAPLEWOOD MANOR RSVP PROGRAM
SEE PSYCHOSOCIAL SUPPORT SERVICES

MILTON CARES TELEPHONE REASSURANCE
SEE PSYCHOSOCIAL SUPPORT SERVICES

NEW HAMPSHIRE FOSTER GRANDPARENT PROGRAM
SEE RECIPIENTS: HANDICAPPED - CHILDREN/YOUTH

PEER COUNSELOR PROGRAM*
Dakota Area Referral and Transportation for Seniors
DARTS
125 Sixth Avenue, North
South St. Paul, MN 55075
TEL: 612-455-1560
Purpose: To involve older volunteers in providing peers with companionship, and assisting them in working through difficulties.
Sponsor: DARTS
Contact: Percy Olson, Lillian Olson
Description: Combining a lifetime of experience with formal training the older volunteers in the Peer Counselor Program visit older persons needing companionship and assistance with problems in a wide area (South St. Paul, West St. Paul, Inger Grove Heights, Hastings). Most visits are made in the client's home. Volunteers completing the training are given the title of Certified Peer Counselor. A major thrust of the training is "learning to listen and not give advice." The philosophy is that, many times, a client can solve his or her own problem just by talking it through with someone who will listen.
Counselors are 60 years of age and older and, in addition to participation in the training program, are required to have compassion, a willingness to listen, and the ability to keep pace with a busy program.
Volunteers also have knowledge of available resources and services in the local area as well as the larger community. They are able to match specific problems with appropriate services for a client. Several of the volunteers visit area senior centers to explain, promote, and seek additional volunteers for the program.
Volunteer counselors receive mileage reimbursement, and DARTS provides additional car insurance.

A PERFECT MATCH
SEE RECIPIENTS: HANDICAPPED - PSYCHOSOCIAL SUPPORT

PETS FOR PEOPLE
Ralston Purina Company
Checkerboard Square
St. Louis, MO 63164
TEL: 314-982-1000
FAX: 314-982-1211
Purpose: To provide pet therapy and/or pet ownership to senior citizens.
Sponsor: Ralston Purina Company
Description: This program of Ralston Purina Company makes shelter pets available to older persons by working with local participating Humane Societies, which are all-volunteer groups.
Pet therapy volunteer programs have long demonstrated the value of bringing together pets and older people, especially nursing home residents or elderly people living alone.

Ralston Purina Company pays initial pet "adoption" fees (up to $100 per adoption), and includes veterinary fees and pet supplies in the service. The corporation donates up to a total of one million dollars each year to the program.

ST. JOSEPH COMMUNITY SERVICES
SEE NUTRITION: DELIVERY

VISITS THROUGH VIDEO
Greater Southeast Community Center for the Aging
3847 Branch Avenue
Temple Hills, MD 20748
TEL: 301-889-7182
Purpose: To help nursing home residents communicate with relatives and friends.
Contact: Project Director
Description: Visits Through Video was launched by the *Greater Southeast Community Center for the Aging* when it became apparent that visits, of necessity in most cases, were going to be "few and far between" from relatives and friends of patients at the area nursing homes operated by the Center.
The program has grown to include "visits" between patients in separate nursing homes through friendships that have developed during various joint social activities. Every other week patients who wish to create a video message for family, friends, or residents in other homes are brought before the camera and microphone, operated by volunteers, for 15 to 20 minutes. The video messages are then mailed, or picked up by a volunteer and delivered. In some cases the video cassettes are sent by courier to the intended recipient. Incoming tapes are stored at each of the nursing homes so the patients can view them at any time.
In at least one instance, romance has developed between two patients in nursing homes at different locations. A woman with multiple sclerosis, but self-sufficient from her wheelchair, and a man recovering from a stroke, and now ambulatory, have exchanged about two dozen video messages during the year after they met. Although the nursing homes are only 45 minutes apart, they have met in person only five times due to the limited transportation available. According to the man involved, "When I am down and out, I pick the tape up and watch it and come back to life again."

RECIPIENTS: OLDER PERSON - RECREATION/SPORTS

TRAINING PROGRAMS

VACATION AND SENIOR CITIZENS ASSOCIATION
SEE RECREATION & SPORTS: OLDER PERSON

INDIVIDUAL PROGRAM PROFILES

SENIOR GAMES OF INDIANA
SEE RECREATION & SPORTS: OLDER PERSON

U.S. NATIONAL SENIOR OLYMPICS
SEE RECREATION & SPORTS: OLDER PERSON

RECIPIENTS: OLDER PERSON - SENIOR CENTERS

TRAINING PROGRAMS

TEACHING SENIOR CENTER
Wichita State University
University Gerontology Center
Box 121
Wichita, KS 67208
TEL: 316-689-3456
Credit: Course Credit (can be adjunct to one of several courses; inquire)
Sponsor: Administration on Aging (training grant)
Contact: Jan Gold
Description: The Teaching Senior Center is a learning opportunity for faculty and students who have an interest in multipurpose senior centers. Students may intern with any of the service providers operating out of Wichita's new downtown senior center. These services include:
- meals on wheels
- roving pantry
- information and referral
- neighborhood senior centers
- transportation program
- YES (Youth Extending Service)
- senior employment program
- regional long term care ombudsman
- senior health screening
- Kansas Alzheimer's and Similar Diseases Association

Participants have an opportunity to develop service and research projects which improve the quantity, quality, or efficiency of service delivery. Two specific programs are described below:
Internship in Volunteer Administration
The Downtown Senior Center administers an internship in volunteer administration. The intern:
- analyzes the need for and use of additional volunteers in the center;
- studies other volunteer systems as the foundation for recommendations to implementing a Downtown Senior Center volunteer system; and
- sets up a volunteer system to include methods of recruitment, job descriptions, training and evaluation.

University Gerontology Center
The Wichita State University Gerontology Center offers undergraduate and graduate degrees in gerontology, requiring internships such as volunteer transportation coordinators, hospice volunteers, and as assistants in the RSVP (Retired Senior Volunteer Program) and the Foster Grandparents programs (both of which involve older volunteers).
Participants - both faculty and students - are asked to describe the proposed project, the academic course and credit that applies, the academic benefit to be derived by the student from the project, and how the project will improve the lives of older persons.

INDIVIDUAL PROGRAM PROFILES

BLUEGRASS MEDICARE-MEDICAID ASSISTANCE PROGRAM
SEE RECIPIENTS: OLDER PERSON - HEALTH

CALIFORNIA HOUSE
820 East California Boulevard
Pasadena, CA 91106
TEL: 213-449-6950

Purpose: To provide senior adults with opportunities for community service and for social contact.
Sponsor: Assistance League of Pasadena; California House membership
Contact: Marge McIntyre, Director
Description: California House is different from most senior centers, because older people gather there not to receive services, but to give them. Through one of its two major activities, the *Senior Service Volunteer Program,* members of California House donate thousands of hours of volunteer service each year to community agencies.
From 130 to 150 volunteers are involved weekly in the Senior Service Volunteer Program. From 10:00 a.m. to 2:00 p.m., Tuesday through Friday, the sewing and community rooms, the kitchen and the workshop at California House are busy with groups meeting requests from hundreds of different nonprofit agencies. The volunteers help with folding, stuffing, and addressing mailings; make and repair clothing for children; make crafts and educational aids for schools; knit slippers and other articles for hospitals; bake cookies for children and servicemen; create and repair toys, puzzles, teaching aids and other wooden items.
The schedule of activities is announced in a monthly newsletter mailed to each California House member. A steering committee, composed of represenatives of each activity group - sewing, woodworking, knitting, etc. - meets several times a year to develop and guide the Senior Service programs.
California House was built in 1965 by the Assistance League of Pasadena, a nonprofit volunteer service organization that provides continuing support to the facility. Members pay an annual fee of $2.50 to belong to California House. A light luncheon is available daily for a nominal fee. Assistance League members prepare and serve a monthly birthday luncheon, which is followed by a speaker, entertainment, or other program. Monthly tours and other special events, such as an annual volunteer recognition tea, also are held for members.
Founded: 1965

RECIPIENTS: OLDER PERSON - TRANSPORTATION

NATIONAL/STATE ORGANIZATIONS

FLYING SENIOR CITIZENS OF THE USA*
SEE TRANSPORTATION & SAFETY: OLDER PERSON

INDIVIDUAL PROGRAM PROFILES

EASY RIDERS VOLUNTEER PROGRAM*
SEE TRANSPORTATION & SAFETY: HEALTH

SERVICE DELIVERY FOR THE ELDERLY*
PO Box 304
229 East Cedar Street
Standish, MI 48658
TEL: 517-846-9451
Purpose: To provide transportation to all low-income people over 60 years of age.
Sponsor: Region VII Area Agency on Aging
Contact: Jeanne Anderson
Description: Going to the doctor, check cashing, grocery shopping, and other errands that most people do automatically have always created difficult problems for the many rural elderly people in

Arenac County. To try to find a solution to the transportation problem, the Region VII Area Agency on Aging sponsors Service Delivery for the Elderly, a program served by volunteer drivers. Nine volunteer drivers donate their time to provide this service, and receive reimbursement for mileage only. They enjoy the opportunity to assist these elderly people, and even take courses on CPR training and defensive driving techniques offered by the program. Currently, First Aid Training Courses are being organized through the Red Cross also, and the drivers are looking forward to adding this expertise to the knowledge gained from the other two courses.
Although there is no charge, per se, for the transportation service, donations are encouraged in order to allow the elderly to retain their dignity and sense of self worth. Any amount is courteously accepted, no matter how small.
Special trips are arranged also to cultural events, shopping malls, and other places of interest. The use of a van enables a volunteer driver to take groups to these places and many others which, normally, they would not have an opportunity to visit. A side benefit is the opportunity to socialize with other elderly people en route during these special trips.
Although the trips are limited to Arenac County, out-of-county appointments are honored when a physician's medical verification and statement of necessity is presented by the client. Except for emergencies, clients are asked to plan ahead so that grocery and pharmacy trips can be limited to one trip every two weeks for an individual client.
One client's trip is to the Service Delivery program office to volunteer one day per week - or more, when requested. Part of volunteer assistance is in the form of artwork to go along with the articles in the monthly newsletter.
In addition to the transportation service, this program arranges home visits to acquaint the elderly with available services in the county, and specific information in response to unique problems in areas such as fuel assistance, home repair, social security, widowhood, spiritual concerns - and·even pet care!
Part of the philosophy of the program in relation to the elderly is that they are entitled to freedom, independence, and the free exercise of individual initiative in planning and managing their own lives. With the help of volunteers, Service Delivery for the Elderly strives to reflect that philosophy.

RECIPIENTS: PERSONS WITH AIDS

INDIVIDUAL PROGRAM PROFILES

VOLUNTEER RESOURCES - AIDS PROGRAM
SEE AIDS

RECIPIENTS: POLICE/COURT OFFICERS - RESPITE

INDIVIDUAL PROGRAM PROFILES

CASA PROJECT (COURT APPOINTED SPECIAL ADVOCATES)
SEE CONSUMER SERVICES/LEGAL RIGHTS: CHILDREN/YOUTH

FRIENDS OF THE SUPERIOR COURT
SEE LAW ENFORCEMENT/CRIME PREVENTION: STAFF SUPPORT

IN-HOME DETENTION PROGRAM
428 Western Avenue
Davenport, IA 52801
TEL: 319-326-8612
Purpose: To provide an alternative to secure detention for juvenile offenders.
Sponsor: Iowa Crime Commission/Scott County
Contact: Kathleen Gillman, Diversion Coordinator
Description: Beginning full operation in August 1981, the In-Home Detention Program is one of many Diversion Programs of the Scott County Juvenile Court. The program has received two years' funding from the Iowa Crime Commission. Scott County picked up the program in 1982.
The In-Home Detention Program was designed to provide an alternative form of detention which allows juveniles to be detained in their own homes. In-home detention is ordered by the juvenile judge when the Court determines that a youth requires some form of detention, but does not require a "secure" detention setting.
A youth on home detention is placed under the supervision of a Home Detention Worker (volunteer) for the duration of the detention period, not to exceed 30 days. The volunteer visits the youth and his/her parents on a daily basis, seven days a week, makes telephone contacts, and is available for consultation at the conclusion of the detention period.
An In-Home Detention Contract and a Detention Order are prepared when a home detention is ordered. The conditions in the contract must be agreed to and signed by the child, his attorney and his parents. The goals of the In-Home Detention Program include:
- to demonstrate the successful supervision of youths outside of a secure detention facility;
- to provide parents with supportive services to enable youths to be maintained in their homes;
- to help keep participating youths trouble-free while they are awaiting court hearings; and
- to keep youths available for their court appearances.
The program is functioning at the present time with eight volunteers. All are under the direct supervision of the Diversion Coordinator. A new volunteer undergoes a personal orientation with the Diversion Coordinator. Volunteers are provided with a Volunteer Manual and are required to attend Volunteer meetings every two months. Experience has shown that the best training is "on-the-job training." One purpose of the volunteer meetings is to discuss both pleasurable and difficult encounters while working with the young people.
During the first full year of operation, 39 youths were placed on In-Home Detention. Only eight of these youths were detained for violations. These youths met the criteria for secure detention and, if the In-Home Detention Program did not exist, would have been placed in the Detention Center.
Founded: 1981

IN-HOME DETENTION PROGRAM
SEE RECIPIENTS: POLICE/COURT OFFICERS - RESPITE

NEIGHBORHOOD PROBATION UNIT
Utah Second District Juvenile Court
3522 South 700 West
Salt Lake City, UT 84119
TEL: 801-262-2601
Purpose: To provide close supervision of probationers on a one-to-one basis.
Sponsor: Utah Second District Juvenile Court
Contact: Carlon J. Cooke, Chief of Probation

Description: The Neighborhood Probation Unit is made up of teams which work in neighborhood settings accessible to probationers and their families. Volunteers - most of them college students - are part of each team. A team is made up of three probation counselors and a supervisor, and a vocational rehabilitation counselor in addition to the volunteers. At present, the Unit has six teams, each using a varied number of volunteers. The student volunteers provide a big brother/big sister program for each of the teams. Every probationer in Salt Lake County is assigned to a Neighborhood Probation Unit.
Volunteers are screened and receive an initial orientation. They receive extensive on-the-job training under the leadership of the unit supervisor and staff once they begin their volunteer assignments. Psychologists are available for consultation if they are needed by the volunteer counselors. Student volunteers from the University of Utah's Departments of Sociology, Psychology, Educational Psychology, and Undergraduate Social Work have been involved in the program, and about 75% of the students receive academic credit for their work.
Following their initial orientation, volunteers willing to commit themselves to one contact a week for six months are assigned to an individual child. Volunteers and probationers take part in shared activity groups. The Unit has learned that careful matching of the volunteer and probationer is essential to the program.
The Units hold parent workshops to involve parents of the probationers in discussions of how to communicate more effectively with their children. They also sponsor therapy groups and high adventure groups for the older juvenile probationers. The high adventure groups go on back-packing expeditions, camp overnight, etc. The groups are formed with a ratio of one volunteer to every two probationers. During the summer, tutoring in reading and math is provided for the probationers.

POLICE DEPARTMENT VOLUNTEER PROGRAM
Costa Mesa Police Department
99 Fair Drive
Costa Mesa, CA 92626
TEL: 714-953-5757
Purpose: To relieve police officers of tasks that can be done by others so they can give full attention to tasks needing trained officers.
Sponsor: Costa Mesa Police Department
Contact: Lynn Spear Merles
Description: Sixteen volunteers logged 313 hours in one month at the Costa Mesa Police Department helping police aides write citations on street-sweeping runs, assisting officers with clerical duties, and supporting Neighborhood Watch Programs. The majority of the volunteers come from the *Retired Senior Volunteer Program,* a program sponsored by the *Volunteer Center of Orange County.*
Once it was decided to install the volunteer program, two months of planning was spent deciding where volunteers could best serve the department. Many tasks surfaced that could be done by anyone and did not require a trained officer's time. These included purging records, since most records are destroyed after five years, putting citations on vehicles blocking city street sweepers, helping in the library, and a host of other tasks. Some jobs carry more responsibility than others. For example, records relating to robbery and murder are kept longer than five years, so the volunteers are trained to be very careful in the purging of files. Also, volunteers are briefed on the importance of confidentiality in handling information.
Volunteers come from as far away as El Toro to the south and Long Beach to the north to help the officers. But the officers are not the only beneficiaries of the program. According to one volunteer, "I was so bored when I was not working. I love it here."
Founded: 1988

PROBATION VOLUNTEERS
Hartford Superior Court
95 Washington Street
Hartford, CT 06106
TEL: 203-566-3170
Purpose: To assist the adult probation office of the Connecticut Judicial Department.
Sponsor: Hartford Superior Court
Contact: Clair Collins, Volunteer Services Coordinator
Description: Since the early 1970s, in small adult probation offices across Connecticut, some 450 volunteers have enabled full-time probation officers to give more time to field work, phone calls, and other matters that only they can handle in their heavy caseloads - average 260 cases per officer. In addition to helping the system improve its services, volunteers save the state needed funds - $650,000 in 1987 alone.
Volunteers take information from shoplifters, drunken drivers, and others granted probation by the courts. Many of these offenders receive accelerated rehabilitation, with any record of their arrests erased if they stay out of trouble. Therefore, the volunteers must use extreme care in updating the records following required periodic interviews. Other duties of volunteers range from answering the phones to monitoring cases of neglected children. Most volunteers are from the suburbs, many with postgraduate degrees. Senior citizens and college and law students frequently volunteer for course credit and satisfaction. Also, people considering a switch to a law-oriented career find the experience helpful in making their final decisions. A number of the volunteers have been with the program for more than a dozen years. One volunteer maintains three other volunteer jobs simultaneously - in agricultural, historical, and nutrition programs.
A side benefit for all concerned is that the volunteers are valued as much by the offenders as by those who work for the legal system. Realizing that the offenders are tense, volunteers who interview them try to make it a nonthreatening experience - warmly admonishing the younger ones for not finishing school, and laughing with the older ones who answer "not much" to the question, "Hair?" According to one volunteer, "These people come to you, and you help them."
The statewide program began in early 1971. The Hartford County Bar Association recently recognized 32 adult probation volunteers - three in their eighties - as part of Law Day, a holiday that celebrates the importance of laws in American society.

RESERVE POLICE OFFICER CORPS
SEE LAW ENFORCEMENT/CRIME PREVENTION: STAFF SUPPORT

RESERVE POLICE PROGRAM
SEE LAW ENFORCEMENT/CRIME PREVENTION: STAFF SUPPORT

VOLUNTEER PROBATION OFFICER PROGRAM
The Volunteer Center
920 Frederica Street
PO Box 123
Owensboro, KY 42302
TEL: 502-683-9161
Purpose: To provide friendship and positive role models to young people having problems at home or in school.
Contact: Pamela J. Warwick, Executive Director
Description: Juveniles, ages 8-17, are referred to the Volunteer Probation Offices program by district court judges, area school officials, and social service agencies.
Volunteers, trained and supervised by salaried staff, are matched with juveniles to provide general counseling and supportive services to the youth and his family. Volunteers may initiate a working relationship by participating in activities of interest to the youth. Local businesses have provided discounts (i.e. bowling,

skating, etc.) in an effort to decrease volunteer expense and "burn-out."
Volunteers apply for the position, are interviewed by staff and supply references. Before assignment, volunteers must complete all required orientation and training. Volunteers must agree to complete all cases entered into (averaging six months), maintain personal contact with the youth once a week from one to four hours and be available to the youth and his family in crisis situations. In addition, volunteers agree to attend monthly in-service meetings and submit brief monthly summaries of volunteer work and progress made to staff. Volunteers have 24 hours access to supervision and have the opportunity to discuss goals, treatment plan, and problems with staff on a regular basis. The program, in operation since February 1981, matches about 32 youths each year with volunteers. Most assignments have worked out well. Although the program is currently quite small, the potential impact is great. The quality attention provided by volunteers may prove to prevent youths from entering the criminal justice system. For truants, the program is particularly helpful and may have a major impact on school attendance and the drop out rate.
Founded: 1981

RECIPIENTS: PRISONERS/EX-OFFENDERS

NATIONAL/STATE ORGANIZATIONS

GOOD NEWS JAIL AND PRISON MINISTRIES INTERNATIONAL
SEE LAW ENFORCEMENT/CRIME PREVENTION: SELF-HELP

NATIONAL PRISON PROJECT
SEE LAW ENFORCEMENT/CRIME PREVENTION: FACILITY

OLDER ADULT OFFENDER PROJECT
SEE EMPLOYMENT: PRISONER/EX-OFFENDER

PRISON FELLOWSHIP MINISTRIES
SEE LAW ENFORCEMENT/CRIME PREVENTION: LEGAL RIGHTS

VOLUNTEER PRISON LEAGUE
SEE LAW ENFORCEMENT/CRIME PREVENTION

VOLUNTEERS IN PREVENTION, PROBATION, PRISONS
SEE LAW ENFORCEMENT/CRIME PREVENTION

INDIVIDUAL PROGRAM PROFILES

CORRECTIONAL MINI-COURSES
SEE LAW ENFORCEMENT/CRIME PREVENTION: EDUCATION

ECO
SEE LAW ENFORCEMENT/CRIME PREVENTION: OFFENDERS

FEMALE OFFENDER REHABILITATION PROGRAM
SEE EMPLOYMENT: PRISONER/EX-OFFENDER

GRATERFRIENDS
SEE LAW ENFORCEMENT/CRIME PREVENTION:
RE-ENTRY

M.O.M.S. (MOTHERS ON THE MOVE SPIRITUALLY)
SEE LAW ENFORCEMENT/CRIME PREVENTION:
CHILDREN/YOUTH

MORRIS COUNTY CHAPLAINCY COUNCIL
SEE LAW ENFORCEMENT/CRIME PREVENTION:
RE-ENTRY

**OFFENDER AID AND RESTORATION OF FAIRFAX
COUNTY**
SEE LAW ENFORCEMENT/CRIME PREVENTION:
RE-ENTRY

RE-ENTRY MINISTRIES
SEE LAW ENFORCEMENT/CRIME PREVENTION:
RE-ENTRY

SURROUND*
SEE LAW ENFORCEMENT/CRIME PREVENTION:
CHILDREN/YOUTH

RECIPIENTS: PRISONERS/EX-OFFENDERS - EMPLOYMENT

INDIVIDUAL PROGRAM PROFILES

DATA SYSTEMS UNLIMITED
SEE EMPLOYMENT: HANDICAPPED

HOUSTON EX-OFFENDER PROGRAM
SEE LAW ENFORCEMENT/CRIME PREVENTION:
RE-ENTRY

RECIPIENTS: PRISONERS/EX-OFFENDERS - LITERACY

INDIVIDUAL PROGRAM PROFILES

**LITERACY INCENTIVE PROGRAM (NO READ, NO
RELEASE)**
SEE LITERACY

RECIPIENTS: PRISONERS/EX-OFFENDERS - RE-ENTRY

NATIONAL/STATE ORGANIZATIONS

OFFENDER AID AND RESTORATION
SEE LAW ENFORCEMENT/CRIME PREVENTION:
RE-ENTRY

RECIPIENTS: PRISONERS/EX-OFFENDERS - VISITATION

INDIVIDUAL PROGRAM PROFILES

VAN MINISTRY
SEE LAW ENFORCEMENT/CRIME PREVENTION:
FAMILIES

VISITOR HOSPITALITY CENTER*
SEE LAW ENFORCEMENT/CRIME PREVENTION:
FAMILIES

RECIPIENTS: TENANTS/RESIDENTS

NATIONAL/STATE ORGANIZATIONS

**CENTER FOR ORGANIZATIONAL AND COMMUNITY
DEVELOPMENT**
SEE CIVIC AFFAIRS: TENANTS/RESIDENTS

INDIVIDUAL PROGRAM PROFILES

COMMUNITY ADVISEMENT BOARD
Acacia Federal Savings Bank
7023 Little River Turnpike
Annandale, VA 22003
TEL: 703-642-3000
Purpose: To involve citizens in advising the bank on community
needs.
Contact: Community Reinvestment Act Officer
Description: The *Acacia Federal Savings Bank* has been an active
member of the community for many years. Many of its projects
are a direct result of recommendations by its all-volunteer
Community Advisement Board, which is composed of citizens
from the surrounding area. The purpose of the Board is to advise
the bank on credit needs of the community, including the needs of
low- and moderate-income neighborhoods.
The Board is composed of religious, business, educational and
political leaders as well as individuals from the neighborhoods.
When new members are needed, Acacia notifies the community
through various media. All interested persons submit a brief

statement outlining their interest and qualifications to the *Community Reinvestment Division* of the bank. When they are notified of their appointments, members meet with the Division's officials. Meetings are held twice a year.

RECIPIENTS: VICTIMS

INDIVIDUAL PROGRAM PROFILES

CRY, INC. (CITIZENS REDIRECTING YOUTH)
SEE PSYCHOSOCIAL SUPPORT SERVICES: VICTIMS

SO SAD (SAVE OUR SONS AND DAUGHTERS)
SEE LAW ENFORCEMENT/CRIME PREVENTION: CHILDREN/YOUTH

STOP! THE MADNESS FOUNDATION
SEE LAW ENFORCEMENT/CRIME PREVENTION: VICTIMS

RECIPIENTS: WOMEN

INDIVIDUAL PROGRAM PROFILES

THE S.O.A.P.S.
Social Services of Akron Project
ACCESS, Inc.
245 South High Street
Akron, OH 44308
TEL: 216-535-2999
Purpose: To dissemminate information about health and social services available to Akron-area women.
Sponsor: United Way
Contact: Volunteer Coordinator
Description: In 1987, a program was designed to reach women in need of health and social services. Soap opera plot lines were used to show women that they need not suffer alone. Called *The S.O.A.P.S.,* the project produced 50,000 copies of a 12-page tabloid it created with the help of the local syndicated columnist who synopsizes network soaps for more than 200 papers nationwide. The columnist met with coalition members to determine which problems are most troublesome for women, then chose appropriate soap opera plots and wrote condensed versions of them. For each plot line, a coalition member wrote a follow-up article that explained the kinds of services available to Akron women in similar circumstances. For example, when the "soap opera plot" told the story of "Jo Johnson," an abused spouse, Akron's *Battered Women's Shelter* produced a companion piece that described the shelter's services and explained what a woman should do if she or her family become victims of abuse.
Four nonprofit agencies are among the project's creators - the *YWCA, ACCESS* (a shelter), *Battered Women's Shelter,* and *Planned Parenthood of Summit, Portage, and Medina Counties.* Funding comes from various sources, including corporations, a community foundation, and the *Junior League.*

RECREATION & SPORTS

NATIONAL/STATE ORGANIZATIONS

AMERICAN ASSOCIATION FOR LEISURE AND RECREATION
1900 Association Drive
Reston, VA 22091
TEL: 703-476-3472
Objectives: To aid organizations seeking to begin or improve programs of leisure and recreation in the community.
Services: Provides technical assistance; facilitates communication between professionals and lay people, and between the schools and the community around the conceptualization of leisure as an area for growth and development; monitors recreation legislation and consults with legislators; works with other organizations with an interest in leisure and recreation; maintains extensive library; publishes a journal, *Leisure Today,* which comes as an insert in the *Journal of Physical Education, Recreation and Dance,* intermittent newsletters, and other materials; convenes periodic workshops and annual meeting.
Publications: Leisure Today; PE, Recreation and Dance; AALReporter
Founded: 1974

AMERICAN CAMPING ASSOCIATION
5000 State Road 67 North
Martinsville, IN 46151
TEL: 317-342-46151
Objectives: To help make the camping experience an enjoyable, educational, and worthwhile experience for America's citizens.
Services: Works in nearly every capacity of a camp situation, from outdoor living skills to Camp Director certification programs; provides information in areas of camp administration, federal legislation, programs in education, and legal matters; maintains a 5,000 volume library and a mail order bookstore offering hundreds of publications, including the hallmark *Camping Magazine;* has divisions for agency camping, private independent camping, religion-affiliated camping, resident camping, day camping, and travel camping; publishes a magazine seven times a year, and numerous other guides and books listed in its free catalog.
Contact: Grechen Throop
Publications: ACA Catalog; Camping Magazine; Parents Guide to Accredited Camps; Facilities for Conferences, Retreats and Outdoor Education

NATIONAL RECREATION AND PARK ASSOCIATION
3101 Park Center Drive
12th Floor
Alexandria, VA 22302
TEL: 703-820-4940
Objectives: To improve the human environment through improved park, recreation and leisure opportunities.
Services: Operates program for development and upgrading of professional and citizen leaders in the recreation/leisure field; provides technical assistance to local communities, members, and affiliated organizations; provides advocacy on public policy; conducts research; maintains an extensive publications program; publishes several periodicals including *Journal of Leisure Research* and *Therapeutic Recreation Journal,* newsletters, books, pamphlets, management aids, etc.; maintains regional service centers in Decatur, Georgia; Palatine, Illinois; Colorado Springs, Colorado; Rock Hill, Connecticut; and Sacramento, California.
Publications: Dateline; Parks & Recreation Magazine; Therapeutic Recreation Journal; Journal of Leisure Research
Founded: 1965

NATIONAL VOLUNTEER PROJECT*
Appalachian Mountain Club
Regional Office
PO Box 298-V
Gorham, NH 03581
TEL: 603-466-2721
Objectives: To provide cost-effective recreation services by maximizing citizen participation and control in planning, managing and delivery of services in six different geographical areas.
Services: Initiates cooperative relationships between public and private agencies and the Club; coordinates the planning, selection and delivery of recreation services with other non-profit organizations; operates through a volunteer steering committee which meets monthly to direct NSP's services, and which adopted, in May 1982, the major objective shown above, and the supplementary objectives listed below:
  ● to create long-lasting partnerships among voluntary organizations, government land management agencies, the business community, and the public at large;
  ● to support these partnerships in developing creative solutions to current resource management problems;
  ● to broaden the constituency of support for the enjoyment and wise use of America's natural resources;

● to promote a healthier American society.

Delivers services to other volunteer organizations so that they can enter into long-lasting partnerships with official land managers and work toward the following benefits:

● **Volunteer organizations** will be stronger and better able to plan and implement their own solutions to local recreation management issues.

● **Land Managers** will have the opportunity to work more closely and productively with organized user groups in addressing current land management issues.

● **The public** will not only be able to continue to enjoy the outdoors, but will also have new opportunities to participate in the management of their recreational open space by joining stronger, more active volunteer organizations.

Administers demonstration projects including "Volunteers for the Outdoors," Albuquerque, New Mexico; "Volunteers for Outdoor Washington," Seattle, Washington; and "Florida Trail Association Volunteers," Gainesville, Florida; encourages local groups to form coalitions of existing smaller, activity-based outdoor recreation societies, and then carry out volunteer land management "events" to increase capabilities for mutual assistance and stronger interface with federal, state, and city land managers; involves small and large landowners from business, industry, the farming community and others in meeting the recreation goals of communities; operates through a cooperative agreement with the U.S. Forest Service, which includes a detailed work plan; convenes annual meeting, monthly steering committee meetings, and other planning and fact-finding sessions; publishes a bimonthly newsletter, *Volunteer News, National Volunteer Project Annual Report,* books, maps, and other materials.

Contact: Reuben Rajala, Trails Program Director
Publications: Volunteer News; Volunteer Project Report
Founded: 1876

PRESIDENT'S COUNCIL ON PHYSICAL FITNESS
400 Sixth Street, SW
Washington, DC 20201
TEL: 202-755-7478
Objectives: To increase interest in community recreation and its relationship to the physical wellbeing of citizens.
Services: Assists community leadership in mobilizing human and other resources to serve the causes of recreation as an important concern.

PRIVATE SECTOR EFFORTS PROGRAM
SEE PHYSICAL ENVIRONMENT

RECREATION & SPORTS: ARTS

INDIVIDUAL PROGRAM PROFILES

TAE KWON DO CHOREOGRAPHIC PERFORMANCES
Jhoon Rhee Institute of Tae Kwon Do
1258 Wisconsin Avenue, NW
Washington, DC
TEL: 202-USA-1000
Purpose: To demonstrate to youth the discipline and enjoyment of karate.
Contact: Jhoon Rhee
Description: The *Jhoon Rhee Institute of Tae Kwon Do* was the first such group to develop choreographed performances by participants in a karate program. The performers range in age from four to adult, and the performances are offered to schools and nonprofit groups throughout the Washington metropolitan area.

A typical performance is the show provided for the national meeting of *Super Volunteers.* The troupe, in silks, satins and sequins, performed a dance of intricate *Tae Kwon Do* movements with a finale in which the performers took the shape of the American flag. Also, the *Institute* presented a five-year-old *black belt* who, with a seven-year-old partner, performed a dance choreographed by the two youngsters themselves; and had a number of children and teenagers display their talents in the various levels of *Tae Kwon Do.*

Following the performance, the young participants mingled with the audience to answer questions about their involvement in the program, how their school grades had improved, and how much better they felt, physically, because of the exercise involved. This was followed by a presentation by Jhoon Rhee who talked about shy, withdrawn youngsters who "blossom" in the program - one who was failing in school, and now heads the class - and an 84-year-old participant who was rapidly rising in the levels of the program.

In addition to the performing troupe, a speakers program is maintained, and some scholarships are made available to youngsters who cannot otherwise participate in the program. The constant reminder is that the program is one of discipline and self-esteem, not violence.

RECREATION & SPORTS: CHILDREN/YOUTH

NATIONAL/STATE ORGANIZATIONS

FUND FOR ADVANCEMENT OF CAMPING
SEE RECREATION & SPORTS: FUNDING

JACKIE ROBINSON FOUNDATION
SEE RECIPIENTS: CHILDREN/YOUTH - ETHNIC GROUPS

NATIONAL ASSOCIATION OF POLICE ATHLETIC LEAGUES
200 Castlewood Drive
North Palm Beach , FL 33408
TEL: 305-844-1823
Objectives: To create a bond between police officers and community youths through athletics to help prevent youth crime.
Services: Works to prevent juvenile delinquency by fostering a strong, positive attitude toward police officers; focuses on the problems of crime and delinquency and on ways to reduce juvenile restlessness; relies on athletics and recreational activities to promote friendship between young people and police officers; fosters a network of local leagues; develops new programs and materials; creates partnerships between state, regional, and national levels and civic and other sports organizations; conducts national tournaments in basketball, baseball, boxing, ice hockey, and girls' softball; offers insurance coverage and a group purchasing program; conducts workshops, training seminars, and research and development programs; produces public service announcements, films, and training aids; publishes a newspaper and a membership directory.
Sponsor: National PAL
Publications: UP-DATE; National PAL Membership Directory
Founded: 1944

TURRELL FUND
SEE RECREATION & SPORTS: FUNDING

TRAINING PROGRAMS

THE NAME OF THE GAME IS CARING
American Red Cross
17th and D Streets, NW
Washington, DC 20006
TEL: 202-737-8300
FAX: 202-639-3791
Purpose: To help young students in grades 7-12 become recreation leaders.
Description: This model program was developed by the national office of the American Red Cross for use at the local level. It addresses the importance of leisure-time pursuits in today's fast-paced life, and the need to find meaningful volunteer activities for youth. The program defines an effective recreational leader as: a humanitarian, a group worker, a dreamer, an organizer, a performing arts enthusiast, a sports fan, an actor or actress, a media expert, and an innovator. "The Name of the Game is Caring" helps young people in grades 7 through 12 acquire the skills necessary to become effective volunteer recreation leaders. The course prepares these youth to work with children, teenagers, the elderly, the disabled, the ill, or the convalescent in a variety of settings. The course includes:
- Twenty-four activity sheets that enable young people to perform leadership skills while learning about them.
- A 16-page facilitator's guide that includes complete instructions for implementing course activities, suggestions for additional optional activities, and complete background material for the instructor.
- Four two-sided posters that highlight major points covered in each session and serve as transition devices between sessions.

After completing "The Name of the Game is Caring," young people will have the necessary background to:
- Understand what recreation is and why it is important for all ages.
- Evaluate their own leadership abilities.
- Recognize important considerations for different age and ability groups when planning recreational activities.
- Adapt specific recreational activities for various age and ability groups.
- Implement the elements of effective leadership in the planning and executing of recreation activities.

The American Red Cross provides other programs for young people in areas of self-awareness, health and safety, first aid, preparation for employment, consumer knowledge, and alcohol education.

INDIVIDUAL PROGRAM PROFILES

AIR PRODUCTS DEVELOPMENTAL CYCLING PROGRAM
Air Products and Chemicals
PO Box 538
Allentown, PA 18105
TEL: 215-481-8079
Purpose: To teach bicycle safety, maintenance and the fundamentals of riding and racing.
Sponsor: Air Products and Chemicals, Inc.
Contact: Pamela S. Handwerk
Description: The Air Products Developmental Cycling Program is designed to encourage area residents to experience first-hand what the exciting sport of bicycle racing is all about. It continues to be a good example of how industry and recreation work together to provide a worthwhile program for the community.
The program is a corporate-underwritten event, open to people eight years or older who have bicycling interest. Depending on experience, participants are assigned to one of three categories: beginners, intermediate or advanced, where they are taught bicycle safety, maintenance and the fundamentals of riding. All equipment

is provided and the coaches are the top racers in North America. The summer climaxes with Air Products night, where participants in the program have their own night of racing.
Graduates of the Developmental Cycling Program are able to participate at a more advanced level. Novice racers can gain the necessary experience and training from coaches who have been recognized nationally.
All training, coaching and racing is done at Lehigh County Velodrome under close supervision by expert instructors. There is no cost to participants, as the program is financed through corporate contributions.
The program enjoys considerable success and has gained national recognition. A number of other velodromes have indicated their intention of duplicating the program. Two graduates of the program have gone on to become the U.S. Junior National Champions.

CAMP GOOD DAYS AND SPECIAL TIMES
SEE HEALTH: CANCER

CAMP GOOD DAYS AND SPECIAL TIMES REBUILDING PROJECT
AFL-CIO Community Services Committee
c/o United Way of Greater Rochester
55 St. Paul Street
Rochester, NY 14604
TEL: 716-454-2770
Purpose: To provide a camping experience for children affected by cancer.
Contact: Volunteer Coordinator
Description: When *Camp Good Days and Special Times* lost one of its buildings to fire in the winter of 1986, 800 union volunteers set to work to put the summer camp back into action. The camp accommodates more than 200 children affected by cancer at its Keuka Lake setting outside of Rochester, and is a special source of pride to the residents of Rochester.
The rebuilding project involved more than just replacing the lost building, since other facilities were desperately needed, such as a dining hall and recreation center. The union tradespeople designed a new 80' x 46' building that included those facilities plus a kitchen, rest rooms, ramps, low-standing water fountains, and a 10-foot-wide wrap-around porch. The project took 25 weeks and was ready in plenty of time for the camping season.
The union volunteers included painters, carpenters, bricklayers, electricians, floor layers, glaziers, roofers, laborers, plumbers, pipe fitters, and operating engineers. Building materials were donated by *Wilmorite Corporation,* and *Cable-Wiedemer* contributed appliances and fixtures. The improvements represented more than $350,000 in donated materials and labor.
Everyone who works at *Camp Good Days and Special Times,* including the director, is a volunteer. Due to the campers' special needs, the camp has 24-hour on-site medical facilities, as well as ambulance services to local hospitals. The medical teams that staff these facilities also are composed totally of volunteers.
The individual volunteer that rallied the 800 union volunteers, secured donated materials, and coordinated the massive project is president of the *Building and Construction Trades Council of Rochester.* For his efforts, the *AFL-CIO Community Services Committee of Rochester,* and the *United Way of Greater Rochester* honored him at a citywide awards program.

CHRISTMAS TOY SHOP
1655 Sixteenth Street, South
St. Petersburg, FL 33705
TEL: 813-898-3962; 813-895-0057
Purpose: To refurbish donated toys year-round for Christmas giving to poor children.
Contact: Ardith Rutland, Vice President

Description: A child who received a red bicycle for Christmas over 20 years ago now works as a volunteer in the toy shop that gave him the bicycle. *Christmas Toy Shop* is a volunteer project that works all year long repairing and refurbishing donated toys so that no child in the St. Petersburg area is without a toy at Christmas time.

Volunteers complete work on more than 200 bicycles each year. In a given year, volunteers from the toy shop deliver at least two new and one used toy to more than 7,000 children in lower Pinellas County. To accomplish that, volunteers begin working in January at the toy shop. Hours at the shop are based on volunteer hours, with a reduction in the summer due to vacations. Schedules vary from two days to five days each week. No experience is necessary as, in the case of bicycles, anyone who has owned a bicycle knows how, and can easily learn to do the repairs, and many other toys need only painting and minor attention.

Shop owners find that the biggest problem is the conception that help is needed only at Christmas time. When November rolls around, donated toys and volunteers are at their peak. In fact, the project would not be possible without year-round volunteers.
Founded: 1951

GIRL SCOUTING IN THE INNER CITY
Girl Scouts of the USA
Box 9389
Savannah, GA 31412
TEL: 912-236-1571
Purpose: To bring Girl Scouts to the inner city.
Sponsor: United Way of the Coastal Empire
Contact: Dot Mays, Special Services Director
Description: Since it was difficult to get girls from low-income urban areas to join the Girl Scouts, the *Girl Scouting in the Inner City* program brings scouting to them. The program operates within the inner city, bringing education workshops that range from basic health and hygiene to teen pregnancy and substance abuse. In discussing the more serious issues, the sharing of experiences among the girls themselves is crucial to getting information across.

Although starting slowly, girls who came into the program said they knew other girls who needed to be there. They were armed with sign-up paperwork and went out and got the other girls to join.

Confidence-building is a strong point of the program. This involves bringing in role models, like female doctors, to get the girls to realize that they can have careers like that, too. At the same time they are shown how teen pregnancy or drug abuse can ruin their chances for such careers. Explanations are very specific, going into costs of having a baby, or the harmful effects drugs have on health.

In addition to funding provided, in part, by the United Way of the Coastal Empire, the program leaders make a *wish list* each month of speakers or items they need for projects. As a result, businesses have given equipment or materials for the education workshops, the *Junior League* chapter has helped distribute the wish lists and provided staff for the program, and professionals have come forward to serve as role models.

According to the director, going into the inner city with the scouting program is necessary for now, but as confidence grows, and the networking among the girls from all sectors takes a firmer hold, it "won't matter where the sessions are held."
Founded: 1988

JUNIOR NATIONAL TRACK AND FIELD
SEE RECREATION & SPORTS: OLYMPICS

NET RESULT TENNIS FOUNDATION
20 Bayberry Lane
Middletown, NJ 07748
TEL: 201-671-0927

Purpose: To provide free tennis lessons to children who cannot afford private lessons.
Sponsor: United States Tennis Association
Contact: Else Helme or Rosemary Darben
Description: The *Net Result Tennis Foundation* provides free clinics for youngsters two days a week for tennis instruction. Clinics are operated in Red Bank, Holmdel, and Atlantic Highlands. Since its founding in 1987, the Foundation has grown from 25 children at one location to over 150 in 1989 at three locations. With the 14 volunteers of 1989 no longer adequate now that the third location has been added, and the program growing daily, a recruitment drive has become part of the everyday routine. Volunteer instructors range from experts to those who only know the basics of tennis. Since the children are all beginners, experts are not a requirement, although their expertise has helped the program tremendously - partly by showing an interest in helping to hone the skills of the less experienced volunteer instructors. Volunteers include high school tennis players and parents who play.

Recognizing that tennis talent was coming only through country clubs, the founders mounted the program to reach those who could not participate in these clubs or afford private lessons. As a result, much talent is surfacing that would not have been forthcoming without the program. Acknowledgement of the program's philosophy came in the form of a *United States Tennis Association* seed grant to assist the Foundation with the program. One promising participant was selected to attend the U.S. Tennis Association Junior Tennis League Invitational Camp in Indiana.

In the winter of 1990, *Net Result* offered a combination tennis/educational program at a local community center three afternoons and evenings a week. Short court tennis was taught to beginner and advanced players, and students received tutoring in math, English and science. In addition, advanced players received tennis instruction once a week at an indoor facility. Also, a mentorship program has been mounted to enable youngsters to receive individual advice and guidance from professionals in their chosen fields.

In addition to the ongoing tennis instruction program, tutoring will remain a part of the overall operation. According to the founders, "We want the children in our program to be well-prepared when they apply for college scholarships or jobs."
Founded: 1987

NEW BREED DRILL TEAM
Trenton Board of Education
Clinton and Monmouth
Trenton, NJ 08609
TEL: 609-989-2406
Purpose: To provide a unifying vehicle through which young people can give of themselves to their communities.
Contact: Lena Meekins, Founder
Description: In the socially-turbulent late 1960s, an observant citizen recognized a need for an activity for disadvantaged youth of the Trenton area to constructively apply their energy. The *New Breed Drill Team* was created for junior high and high school students, who soon became a frequent sight with their precision marching routines. In its early years it served as a vehicle for building racial understanding by entertaining and socializing with teen audiences of different backgrounds. Team members have remained goodwill ambassadors but, after more than two decades, the team has evolved into a community service project as well as a precision marching team.

Membership in the *New Breed Drill Team* requires more than just the ability to perform skilled marching routines. All of the members must demonstrate individual excellence, character development, leadership skills and academic success. But the main purpose is to serve the community. Former community service projects adopted by the team include the beautification of Martin Luther King Park, assisting The Needy Children's Christmas

Fund and the Cadwalader Public Library, and serving at the Martin Luther King Day community breakfast.
According to its founder, the combination of instilling pride in an accomplishment such as the precision drill team, and creating self-esteem through service to the community is an undisputed and unbeatable success in which everyone shares.
Publications: New Breed Drill Team
Founded: 1968

PARMA-HILTON PLAYGROUND PROJECT
Parma Town Hall Park
c/o Robin Schepler
215 North Avenue
Hilton, NY 14468
TEL: 716-392-3868
Purpose: To provide manpower for a playground for the children of Parma and Hilton.
Sponsor: US/DoD - Navy Civil Engineers Corps
Contact: Robin Schepler, Volunteer Foreman
Description: Ideas from the children themselves were incorporated into a volunteer-built playground for area children. Over 100 volunteers worked in the rain to complete the 93-by-133-foot project, which includes everything from a clock tower to a spaceship. One of the children suggested a PCV-pipe communications system that allows children in the multilevel structure to help guide friends who get lost in the maze. Another suggested bolting together six tires as a base for a trampoline. Both ideas were incorporated in the playground designed by an architect, which includes a maze, a clock tower with a face that can be changed with a steering wheel, a spiral slide, a tunnel slide, a swinging horse and a spaceship.
Rainy conditions on the day of the project might have delayed most other efforts. But, undaunted, the volunteers ordered several tons of sand and some gravel to build a small road to keep heavy equipment from getting mired in the mud. Next they obtained yellow slickers - soon-to-be mud-spattered - for volunteers. Power was drawn directly from a nearby Rochester Gas and Electric Corporation utility pole, with strict federal safety standards implemented and a knowledgeable volunteer assigned to keep equipment from shorting out. An associate of the architects volunteered to be on hand to offer expert supervision and keep the project on schedule.
Many of the volunteers took vacation time from paying jobs to help with the project. While some worked on the construction of the playground, others ran an on-site day-care center for the workers' children, helped with concessions, or signed up volunteers. Even the children got into the act - the little ones scrubbing tires and those ten and older working alongside their parents. The parents and children also got help from about ten Monroe County inmates on regular work detail and about 40 Seabees from the *Civil Engineer Corps of the U.S. Navy* on regular monthly duty. In addition to the donated labor, most of the tools and other equipment were provided free by local contractors and businesses. To pay for essentials unavailable by donation, the playground committee and the children raised more than $40,000 over an 18-month period prior to the event. About a fourth of the money was spent to make the playground accessible to handicapped youngsters.
The playground was built in Parma because parents had grown weary of having to travel to Spencerport and Brockport to treat their children to a day at one of the special playgrounds.

SPECIAL SATURDAY
Family Service of Westchester
Big Brothers/Big Sisters
470 Mamaroneck Avenue
White Plains, NY 10605
TEL: 914-948-8004

Purpose: To bridge the waiting time of youngsters waiting for big brothers/sisters; to develop group skills through recreation; to increase the number of adult minority male role models for youngsters in our program.
Sponsor: Special Grant from the United Way of Westchester, community organizations and private donations
Contact: Lawrence R. Murrill, Program Coordinator
Description: Realizing that the number of children waiting for a big brother or sister far exceeds the number of volunteers, the staff of Big Brothers/Big Sisters of Family Service of Westchester, and students from Pace University did something about it. Special Saturday is a weekly recreational and educational activities program for youngsters on the waiting list of the program. It was designed, planned and implemented as a weekly summer program for these children and - because of its success - the summer pilot program has become an established part of the agency.
Volunteer Staff - Staffed primarily by volunteers, Special Saturday could not work without their support, dedication and concern. The core of our volunteers is students - from Pace University, Iona College and New Rochelle High School (all over 18 years of age). Many volunteers also come from community organizations such as the Knights of Columbus and the New York Telephone Company's Future Pioneers.
Volunteer Duties - The duties of the volunteer staff (counselors) include the supervision of the children, weekly training sessions and/or meetings, and the development of activities and programs.
Volunteer Experience - Special Saturday volunteers come with varying levels of experience. It is through the weekly training and meeting sessions that, as a group, attempts are made to tap the resources of our staff and strengthen areas that are weak.
From the Program Coordinator, "We realize and appreciate the fine group of volunteers we have but, because of the limited number of minority adult males, the need for more - many more - continues to be a major problem."
Founded: 1980

TEEN CENTER
SEE RECIPIENTS: CHILDREN/YOUTH - RECREATION/SPORTS

WIPING OUT DRUG ABUSE DRUG FREE TEEN CENTER
SEE DRUG ABUSE/ALCOHOLISM: DRUGS - DRUG-FREE ZONES

YAI ALUMNI CLUB KARATE PROGRAM
Young Adult Institute
460 West 34th Street
New York, NY 10001-2382
TEL: 212-563-7474
Purpose: To utilize the discipline provided by *Seido-Karate* to help mentally retarded and developmentally disabled young adults develop self-esteem.
Contact: Bill Brennan
Description: The *Young Adult Institute (YAI)* is a nonprofit program in New York City that serves mentally retarded and developmentally disabled individuals in the metropolitan area (see separate entry). About three years ago, YAI began the *Seido-Karate* program for its clients and others wishing to attend. The karate program strives to help mentally retarded and developmentally disabled individuals develop a sense of self-worth. The program is offered as part of YAI's *Evening Program* and *Alumni Club,* but does not turn away other individuals from the metropolitan area who wish to participate.
The group consists of individuals in the high functioning/borderline range, some of whom live with their families, some in apartments with others, and others on their own. The group meets once each week. Instructors stress that teaching participants to defend themselves on the streets is *not* a goal of the program. Rather, it is to help them build self-esteem, concentrate

and become more in control, improve motor movements, etc. Although originally designed for high-functioning youth, recently the program has been offered to youth in other program areas of the *Young Adult Institute.* YAI organizers of the program have found that not only is the program popular with clients, but it is meeting its stated goals in areas of self-esteem and control among participants.

YOUTH RECREATION PROGRAM
Madison House
Charlottesville, VA 22903
TEL: 804-977-7051
Purpose: To provide constructive recreational activities for children that they do not receive in school.
Sponsor: Madison House
Contact: Jane Parker
Description: In 1973, Madison House adopted a basketball program sponsored by the University Inter-Fraternity Council and expanded it to include softball, football, and arts and crafts. Today it includes also soccer, dance, gymnastics, tennis, karate, swimming and flag football. These athletic activities are organized for elementary school boys and girls ages eight through eleven. The activities are organized as opposed to the free-for-all recess type games - structured to promote good sportsmanship and a spirit of fun, not competition. The emphasis is on participation, not achievement. Over 300 children from ten area elementary schools participate in the various programs.
Madison House volunteers act as teachers and coaches. Independence and initiative are the primary qualities needed by the volunteer to lead a class or coach a team in an effective manner. If the volunteer can keep the kids interested and develop a rapport with them, the activity is almost always enjoyed by all participants. Dependability on the part of teachers and coaches is also critical. A football team left coachless one Saturday morning, or a swimming class left teacherless can be a complete frustration for the children.
All Youth Recreation Program activities are conducted in eight-week segments. Volunteers can commit themselves to either one or two semesters and the programs are usually completed well before the exam periods. All activities are scheduled on Saturday or Sunday and usually require two or three hours from the volunteer per weekend. All activities are held at Memorial Gym at the University or on one of the adjacent athletic fields. Consequently, there is no transportation problem for those volunteers living on-grounds without a car.
In addition to its own activities, Youth Recreation refers interested volunteers to area scouting organizations. Another possibility for interested volunteers is to begin a project not already included in the program. Suggestions for new activities are constantly being made and many are implemented and enhance the overall program.
The Youth Recreation Program benefits directly from the Alan Jacobus Memorial Fund, which was started in 1975 by the brothers of the Pi Kappa Phi Fraternity. The fund was started because of Alan Jacobus' role as volunteer program director, and his successful efforts in helping to bring the Youth Recreation Program to its current level of respect in the community.
Founded: 1973

RECREATION & SPORTS: CYCLING

INDIVIDUAL PROGRAM PROFILES

BACK ROADS BIKE TREK
SEE HEALTH: LUNG DISEASE

RECREATION & SPORTS: ETHNIC GROUPS

INDIVIDUAL PROGRAM PROFILES

MIGRANT RECREATION PROGRAM
Madison House
170 Rugby Road
Charlottesville, VA 22903
TEL: 804-977-7051
Purpose: To provide children of migrant workers with organized recreational activities.
Sponsor: Madison House
Contact: Jane Parker
Description: In 1972, Madison House received requests for tutors for the childen of migrant farm workers who reside in Albemarle County from August through October each year during apple-picking season. Volunteers were recruited, but a severe winter resulted in crop failure and the migrants did not come. The program got started the following year with 20 volunteers visiting the children at their camp on a farm 16 miles from Charlottesville. At about the same time, the Albemarle County School System began operating a more formal tutoring program which included the migrant families, and the Madison House program developed into a recreation program.
Each afternoon in September and October, a car pool of 20 to 30 volunteers visits the camp - organizing softball, badminton, soccer, and kickball, as well as an arts and crafts session.
Most of the childen in the camp have had little formal education and little exposure to organized games and recreation. Spanish is their language, and much of their time is spent helping with the work in the orchards. As an adjunct to the program, volunteers are involved in helping the children receive necessary medical attention at the Children and Youth Clinic of University Hospital. Many of the students have volunteered for more than one year and have come to know the children. This helps the children each year, since it eliminates much of the trauma of starting new relationships. Thus, both the volunteers and the kids look forward to some reunions each year.
Founded: 1972

RECREATION & SPORTS: FACILITIES

TRAINING PROGRAMS

COMMUNICATIONS SKILLS FOR THE COLLEGE BOUND
SEE CIVIC AFFAIRS: EDUCATION

HAPPY TRAILS TO YOU: A WORKSHOP FOR VOLUNTEERS
SEE PHYSICAL ENVIRONMENT: LAND USE

INDIVIDUAL PROGRAM PROFILES

BEACHFRONT VOLUNTEERS
SEE PHYSICAL ENVIRONMENT: BEAUTIFICATION

CLEAN THE BAY DAY
SEE PHYSICAL ENVIRONMENT: WATER POLLUTION

FRIENDS OF THE ROUGE
SEE PHYSICAL ENVIRONMENT: WATER POLLUTION

**USS KITTY HAWK/WASHINGTON SQUARE
PARTNERSHIP**
SEE PHYSICAL ENVIRONMENT: BEAUTIFICATION

YOUTH-IN-ACTION AUCTION
SEE PHYSICAL ENVIRONMENT: BEAUTIFICATION

RECREATION & SPORTS: FUNDING

NATIONAL/STATE ORGANIZATIONS

FUND FOR ADVANCEMENT OF CAMPING
PO Box 8
Hatteras, NC 27943
TEL: 919-986-2163
Objectives: To stimulate and fund innovative projects to benefit the organized camping/outdoor activity experience; to increase the scope and effectiveness of camping for children and youth.
Services: Funds pilot projects and research; provides camping scholarships; sponsors Camping Unlimited, which conducts intergroup projects and activities; publishes quarterly newsletter; convenes semiannual trustee meetings.
Publications: Occasional Papers
Founded: 1965

TURRELL FUND
15 South Munn Avenue
Orange, NJ 07018
TEL: 201-678-8580
Objectives: To promote and support recreation programs for children and youth, with special emphasis on the needy youngster.
Services: Aids youth organizations in setting up and maintaining recreational facilities and programs; provides money for inner-city children to take part in camping expeditions and special cultural activities (other thrusts are juvenile rehabilitation, family service and child guidance); publishes the *Turrell Fund Annual Report* which reviews its year's activities on behalf of youth and children (currently gives priority to requests from the states of New Jersey and Vermont).
Publications: Turrell Fund Annual Report

RECREATION & SPORTS: GARDENING

NATIONAL/STATE ORGANIZATIONS

NATIONAL GARDENING ASSOCIATION
180 Flynn Avenue
Burlington, VT 05401
TEL: 802-863-1308
Objectives: To assist communities in developing programs to plant gardens on undeveloped lots owned by others which otherwise present "eye sores"; to provide a means of exercise, fresh air, food production, and conservation.
Services: Conducts teaching programs and broadcasts; maintains contact with more than 2,000 community gardening programs for information-sharing purposes; provides speakers and consultants; develops special programs for schools, business/industry, prisons,

churches, service clubs and others; appears before Congressional Committees (the USDA Extension Service is increasingly involved in urban garden programs); involves other agencies, e.g., the Bureau of Outdoor Recreation classifies gardening as a "leisure pursuit" and qualifies garden sites for federal grants as they qualify parks; publishes quarterly newsletter, a series of guides on specific crops, a program description booklet, *Life begins...the day you start a garden, Your Independence Garden*, and other materials.
Publications: National Gardening Magazine; National Gardening Survey; Gardens for All; Life begins...

INDIVIDUAL PROGRAM PROFILES

CONNECTICUT MASTER GARDENERS
SEE NUTRITION: FOOD PRODUCTION

RECREATION & SPORTS: HANDICAPPED

NATIONAL/STATE ORGANIZATIONS

AMERICAN ATHLETIC ASSOCIATION FOR THE DEAF*
SEE RECIPIENTS: HANDICAPPED - DEAF

AMERICAN BLIND BOWLING ASSOCIATION
SEE RECIPIENTS: HANDICAPPED - BLIND

KENNEDY INTERNS IN RECREATION*
SEE RECIPIENTS: HANDICAPPED - MENTALLY RETARDED

SPECIAL OLYMPICS INTERNATIONAL
SEE RECIPIENTS: HANDICAPPED - RECREATION/SPORTS

SPECIAL RECREATION
362 Koser Avenue
Iowa City, IA 52246-3038
TEL: 319-337-7578
Objectives: To encourage self-determination in recreation for people with disabilities; to promote a national philosophy in support of special recreation.
Services: Assists organizations in the development of special recreation programs; conducts research and training in special recreation; and carries on related activities that serve to advance special recreation for people with disabilities; encourages and works with volunteers, parents, professionals, the public at large, and people with disabilities themselves to form an advocacy network to work toward adequate recreation opportunity for children, youth, adults and seniors with disabilities both in the community and in institutions; assists volunteers in the identification of architectural barriers, transportation barriers, program and service barriers and attitudinal barriers to full recreation access for the handicapped; publishes *Special Recreation Digest,* a quarterly publication, *Information Sources on Special Recreation for Disabled Persons* (a series), *Handicapped Children and Youth* (a series), *Training Materials in Special Recreation for Disabled Persons* (a series), *Program Guides on Special Recreation for Disabled Persons,* and other materials.
Publications: Special Recreation Digest; Special Recreation Catalog; Special Recreation Compendium; Training Guides Series;

Program Guide Series; Information Sources Series
Founded: 1978

TRAINING PROGRAMS

WHEELCHAIR RACE COMMUNICATIONS SERVICES
SEE DISASTER RESPONSE/EMERGENCY PREPAREDNESS

INDIVIDUAL PROGRAM PROFILES

BLUE RIDGE TO THE WHITE HOUSE: WHEELCHAIR RACE OF CHAMPIONS
SEE RECIPIENTS: HANDICAPPED -
RECREATION/SPORTS

CEREBRAL PALSY SPORTS PROGRAM
SEE RECIPIENTS: HANDICAPPED - CEREBRAL PALSY

FLAME OF HOPE
SEE RECIPIENTS: HANDICAPPED -
RECREATION/SPORTS

FLINT AIRSHOW
SEE RECIPIENTS: HANDICAPPED - FUNDING

GARDEN OF YOUNG HEARTS
SEE RECIPIENTS: HANDICAPPED -
RECREATION/SPORTS

GEORGIA SPECIAL OLYMPICS SUMMER GAMES
SEE RECIPIENTS: HANDICAPPED -
RECREATION/SPORTS

HORSES AND THE HANDICAPPED OF SOUTH FLORIDA
SEE RECIPIENTS: HANDICAPPED -
RECREATION/SPORTS

KAISER ROLL
SEE RECIPIENTS: HANDICAPPED -
RECREATION/SPORTS

LAFRENIERE PARK SPECIAL RECREATION PROGRAMMING DIVISION
2320 Judith Street
Metairie, LA 70003
TEL: 504-454-6687
Purpose: To provide leisure opportunities for both disabled and normal citizens in Jefferson Parish and the Greater New Orleans region.
Sponsor: Federal/State/Parish Government
Contact: Sherry Hunter, Special Recreation Supervisor
Description: The Special Recreation Programming Division was established in the summer of 1983 in conjunction with the completion of the Playground for Special Children in Lafreniere Park. Initial funding for the Programming Division resulted from the sponsorship by Independence Isle, Inc., a non-profit corporation, promoting leisure opportunities for the disabled. The Programming Division is currently involved not only in the provision of recreation opportunities for the disabled, but is seeking active involvement from other public and private agencies in the community in an attempt to promote mainstreamed leisure activities where feasible.
The eventual goal of the Special Program Division is to become the focal point of all area special populations leisure activities.

Through its outreach project, the Division hopes to broaden its service delivery through the cooperative use of schools, hospitals, residential homes and other agencies.
Volunteer Staff - At present, the services of a full-time volunteer coordinator are not economically feasible so the Programming Division is primarily dependent on the recruitment of volunteers through the *Friends of Lafreniere,* an auxiliary branch of the fund-raising Lafreniere Park Foundation. "Friends" members are already strong supporters of park activities, and with their help, along with volunteers from Independence Isle, Inc., and the Delta Lions Club members, the volunteer corp is off to a good start.
Volunteer Training - Before a volunteer is allowed to participate in an organized program, he must complete the *Disability Awareness Seminar* offered by the Recreation Programming Staff. This seminar is an in-depth training program that familiarizes the volunteer with the many disability groups and makes him aware of what to expect from any given special participant. A careful screening process is a requisite to assure that even our volunteer corp understands the goal of providing a rewarding leisure opportunity for all individuals. Periodic in-house refresher courses are also required to maintain active volunteer status.
Volunteer Duties - Many phases of volunteerism are used by the Programming Staff. Most of our volunteers assist the therapeutic recreation specialist or instructor by offering personalized care. The low staff participant ratio is vital to insure that each participant receives the best possible instruction and positive reinforcement. However, other facets of volunteer work may involve manning telephones, assisting with decorating for a special event, car-pooling participants or staff, and even lobbying local citizens and politicians to stress the importance and need for continued special recreation programs.
Founded: 1983

LOUISIANA STATE SPECIAL OLYMPICS SUMMER GAMES
SEE RECIPIENTS: HANDICAPPED -
RECREATION/SPORTS

MICHIGAN SPECIAL OLYMPICS STATE GAMES
SEE RECIPIENTS: HANDICAPPED -
RECREATION/SPORTS

RECREATION PROGRAMS FOR LEARNING DISABLED TEENS & ADULTS
SEE RECIPIENTS: HANDICAPPED -
LEARNING-DISABLED

SAN FRANCISCO SPECIAL OLYMPICS WINTER GAMES
SEE RECIPIENTS: HANDICAPPED - MENTALLY RETARDED

SPECIAL OLYMPICS - LAPEER
SEE RECIPIENTS: HANDICAPPED -
RECREATION/SPORTS

SPECIAL OLYMPICS TIME
SEE RECIPIENTS: HANDICAPPED -
RECREATION/SPORTS

SPECIAL POPULATIONS PROGRAM
Raleigh Parks and Recreation Division
PO Box 590
Raleigh, NC 27602
TEL: 919-755-6832
Purpose: To provide a recreational program for the mentally and physically handicapped residents of Wake County that actively involves their families.

Sponsor: Raleigh Parks and Recreation Division; Wake Area Mental Health Agency
Contact: Debra D. Webster, Volunteer Coordinator
Description: This program serves mentally and physically handicapped residents of Wake County who have the need and desire for supervised recreational activities. The philosophy is to provide wholesome leisure opportunities "emphasizing the ability rather than the disability." In addition, the program strives to involve the family in the program.

The program had its beginnings in 1970 when a group of concerned citizens formed to determine the needs of the handicapped in Wake County. Friendly Day Camp became a reality in June of 1971, and by January of 1972 the Raleigh City Council approved the funding of a full-time program supervisor. This program does not replace the regular schedule of programs for senior citizens and visually impaired.

Due to a positive demand for growth of the program, three full-time staff, part-time instructors or drivers, and volunteers currently are involved in the program. In one year, over 1,700 participants (representing over 40 groups) received the services of the program. With the program's emphasis on family involvement, attendance exceeded 8,000, and the two wheelchair lift-equipped buses had over 4,800 riders.

The program offers assistance to persons with any disability, but emphasis is placed on serving lower-skilled individuals. During the summer and fall, the Special Populations Program offers options which promote leisure education and outdoor recreation to those 16 years of age and older. Friendly Day Camp continues to provide a well-rounded camping experience to those from age five to age sixteen. A six week summer swim program is offered with primary emphasis on enjoyment and basic water safety. A developmental swim program that follows American Red Cross guidelines is available to interested individuals. A Family Swim Program is offered depending on interest, with a nominal fee charged to each non-handicapped member of the family.
Founded: 1970

THERAPEUTIC RIDING PROGRAM
SEE RECIPIENTS: HANDICAPPED - RECREATION/SPORTS

THERAPY ON HORSEBACK*
SEE RECIPIENTS: HANDICAPPED - RECREATION/SPORTS

YOUNG WINGS USA*
SEE EDUCATION: CURRICULUM ENRICHMENT

RECREATION & SPORTS: HOMELESS

INDIVIDUAL PROGRAM PROFILES

OUTINGS FOR HOMELESS CHILDREN
SEE RECIPIENTS: HOMELESS - RECREATION/SPORTS

RECREATION & SPORTS: I&R

NATIONAL/STATE ORGANIZATIONS

INFORMATION EXCHANGE*
US/DoI - National Park Service
Washington, DC 20240
TEL: 202-343-4747
Objectives: To assist practitioners, government agencies, nonprofit organizations, and individuals involved in recreation.
Services: Serves the above objective by responding to requests from any individual or group for information on all aspects of recreation; provides assistance by phone, mail and personal visit; distributes studies, handbooks, audiovisuals and films, surveys, training manuals and other materials of a practical nature. (Regional Offices in Seattle, San Francisco, Albuquerque, Denver, Atlanta, Ann Arbor, Philadelphia and Anchorage; request address list)
Sponsor: US/DoI - Department of the Interior

LEISURE INFORMATION SERVICE
801 D Street, NE
Washington, DC 20002
TEL: 202-547-6696
Objectives: To improve the quality and quantity of leisure time activities.
Services: Reports on legislation, funding, resource organizations, publications, etc., in all aspects of leisure time activities; provides technical assistance; publishes *Fund Development* and *Revenue Resources Report.* [Additional office: 700 Orange Street, PO Box 1992, Wilmington, DE 19899]

RECREATION & SPORTS: OLDER PERSON

TRAINING PROGRAMS

VACATION AND SENIOR CITIZENS ASSOCIATION (
formerly Vacations for the Aging)
275 Seventh Avenue, 15th Floor
New York, NY 10001
TEL: 212-645-6590
Objectives: To enhance the quality of life for older persons through leisure and recreational services.
Services: Serves as an umbrella group for senior citizens centers and vacation camps; provides leisure and recreational services to senior citizen groups; organizes training sessions for staff of centers and camps; offers technical assistance to camps and senior centers; participates in public advocacy activities with similar groups on behalf of senior citizens; conducts public relations campaign on senior citizens and recreation; assists vacation centers in scholarship funds by providing grants; provides speakers on request to community groups on the subject of vacations for older persons; publishes a newsletter and an informative brochure.
Publications: Views and News; What is VASCA?
Founded: 1973

INDIVIDUAL PROGRAM PROFILES

SENIOR GAMES OF INDIANA
REAL Services
622 North Michigan
South Bend, IN 46601
TEL: 219-233-8205
Purpose: To provide an opportunity for preliminary championship games for athletes 55 years of age and over in preparation for national competition.
Contact: Marilyn Huber, Executive Director
Description: In the summer each year, volunteers help bring together a statewide program to provide sports competition for Indiana citizens 55 years of age and over. In 1989, 500 volunteers manned the championship games for competitors from 55 to 91 years of age.
One of the volunteers, a ham radio operataor, watched the competition so that he could patch through to a hospital if one of the contestants became ill during the tournament. This was the result of one woman passing out the previous year.
Sixteen sporting events, including shuffleboard which is popular for older seniors, are held throughout five counties during a weekend. Other events include men's and women's tennis, and a men's and women's 5K run. A 91-year-old shuffleboard player has been playing the game for 21 years, and made it to the consolation game after being beaten by what he called "a 61-year-old youngster."
A 100% increase in competitors was seen in 1989 - 800 participants compared to the previous year's 400. Many seniors feel that the exercise alone is worth their many weeks of practice, but also find it a social event. The closing ceremony includes a parade of all of the competing athletes. Those who win medals are given an opportunity to go to the national *Senior Olympics* in St. Louis in 1991. "Whether they win medals or not, one volunteer said, "we cheer them on."
Founded: 1986

U.S. NATIONAL SENIOR OLYMPICS
Washington University
One Brookings Drive
St. Louis, MO 63130
TEL: 314-889-5000
Purpose: To provide a means for older winning athletes to compete at the national level in olympics games.
Sponsor: Post Natural Bran Flakes
Contact: Ken Marshall, President, St. Louis Organizing Committee
Description: More than 3,500 older athletes from 47 states, Puerto Rico and Canada competed in the 1989 *U.S. Senior Olympics* on the Washington University campus in St. Louis. The event is held every two years (1991 in Syracuse, NY). Athletes competed in 14 sports throughout St. Louis, ranging from cycling to shuffleboard. Headquarters was at the Washington University campus, with events scheduled at Forest Park - where the ice rink was transformed into a shuffleboard, Glen Echo Country Club, the Strike 'N Spare Lanes, and at Shaw Park in Clayton. More than 3,500 volunteers - including celebrities - served as hosts for the games. Keynote speakers opened the games on Monday and closed them on Friday.
Volunteers came from the *National Council of Jewish Women, Junior League of St. Louis, Boy Scouts, Girl Scouts, Rotary Club, DeMolay* and the *Women's Club of Washington.* National sponsors are *Post Natural Bran Flakes, Holiday Inn, Digital Equipment Corporation, May Department Stores, Trans World Airlines,* and *Pfizer Pharmaceuticals.* An hour long television special featuring highlights of the games was broadcast about a month after the games were completed.

RECREATION & SPORTS: OLYMPICS

NATIONAL/STATE ORGANIZATIONS

OLYMPIC DAY IN THE SCHOOLS/OLYMPIC DAY FOR YOUTH
U.S. Olympic Committee
1750 East Boulder Street
Colorado Springs, CO 80909
TEL: 719-578-4575
TOLL FREE: Telex: 3730251
FAX: 719-632-5352
Objectives: To educate the nation's youth in the deeper meaning of The Olympic Games - promoting self-development and improvement of the individual.
Services: Develops materials based on "Olympism" (a set of values) to enrich the curriculum in the teaching of Language Arts, Social Studies, Science, Mathematics, Art, Music, Foreign Language Study, Health Education, and Physical Education; tests the materials in practical school situations; provides training for teachers using videotape, films, and other training tools; designs the materials to appeal to the educationally disadvantaged in a way that is readily adaptable to their special needs; considers gifted and talented students in presenting a wide selection of suggested activities; designs materials to work in concert with the day-to-day curriculum, thus eliminating the need for a separate block of time, an additional teacher, or special materials; provides comprehensive materials on its two programs for youth: (1) *Olympic Day in the Schools* and (2) *Olympic Day for Youth,* with detailed instructions for planning, developing, and administering the events; publishes three curriculum units and a resource supplement (see bibliography section for details).
Publications: Corporate Sponsor Newsletter ; USOC Newsletter; The Olympian; Olympic Day in the Schools; Olympic Day for Youth

OLYMPIC ORGANIZING COMMITTEE*
Los Angeles, CA 90084
TEL: 213-305-1984
Objectives: To organize and operate the games of the Olympiad.
Services: Maintains Volunteer Coordinators to assist in all areas of the program - working with volunteers who spend two days each week (45-50 volunteers on any given day) assisting in areas of personnel, finance and planning, "Olympic Villages" (where Olympic Athletes are housed), and other areas of involvement; trains selected volunteers (about 150) for the Host-Hostess Corps which assists with the international meeting when Olympic guests from nearly 150 member nation Committees come together. Involves some 4,000 volunteers in summer sports competition, selected Olympic sports and demonstration sports available each summer preceding the Olympic Games to serve as a dry run for the Committee; recruits volunteers for the Olympic Games (the goal: 25,000 volunteers) to be involved for four months, the Design Center, the Torch Relay (described below), and other volunteer opportunities using varying degrees of skill and/or enthusiasm. Carry the Torch - an Olympic torch relay begun in 1936 at the Berlin Games; offers an opportunity for all Americans to become a part of the Games through a 19,000-kilometer, or 12,000-mile walk, hand-carrrying the torch through every state in the country (beginning in New York City and ending in Los Angeles) and opening the competition for 12,000 athletes from 150 countries; creates a fund for young people through sponsorships of "Youth Legacy Kilometers" along the Torch Relay Route, developing a fund to promote and expand amateur sports training in cities and towns throughout the country; works through youth organizations to implement this legacy (Boys and Girls Clubs of America, Family Ys, and others); fills sponsorship reservations on a

first-come, first-served basis through official application orders only.

SPECIAL OLYMPICS INTERNATIONAL
SEE RECIPIENTS: HANDICAPPED - RECREATION/SPORTS

USOC EDUCATION COMMITTEE
U.S. Olympic Committee
1750 East Boulder Street
Colorado Springs, CO 80909
TEL: 719-578-4575
TOLL FREE: Telex: 3730251
FAX: 719-632-5352
Objectives: To promote the concept of Olympism in the United States.
Services: Works closely with *National Sports Governing Bodies (NGB)* and other national sport, educational and civic organizations to further the objectives and ideals of the Olympic movement; implements a variety of projects which encourage the spirit of Olympism with individuals and groups; nominates and selects U.S. delegates to the *International Olympics Academy* held annually in Greece; sponsors annual *United States Olympic Academies* at colleges and universities; develops, disseminates, and implements appropriate educational programs and materials for use in U.S. schools (grades K-12); implements various other educational programs on behalf of the USOC, including the *USOC Education Center* at Northern Michigan University, development of educational programs and opportunities for athletes at Olympic training centers; selection of the winner of the *Jack Kelly Fair Play Award* each year; selection of the *Olympic Book of the Year;* and conduct of the *Olympic Art Project* among the nation's elementary schools.

INDIVIDUAL PROGRAM PROFILES

CHAMPIONS RUN FOR LIFE TORCH RELAY
SEE HEALTH: CANCER

FLAME OF HOPE
SEE RECIPIENTS: HANDICAPPED - RECREATION/SPORTS

FLINT AIRSHOW
SEE RECIPIENTS: HANDICAPPED - FUNDING

GEORGIA SPECIAL OLYMPICS SUMMER GAMES
SEE RECIPIENTS: HANDICAPPED - RECREATION/SPORTS

JUNIOR NATIONAL TRACK AND FIELD
Ohio State University
Columbus, OH 43216
TEL: 614-292-6446
Information is also available from the co-host:
Columbus Recreation and Parks Department
Columbus, Ohio
Purpose: To produce a successful meet for young athletes aspiring to become members of the U.S. team at the 1992 Olympics in Spain.
Sponsor: Ohio State University
Contact: Volunteer Coordinator
Description: More than 100 volunteers, with the help of donations from businesses and the sponsorship of Ohio State University and Columbus Recreation and Parks Department produced a successful *Junior National Track and Field Championship* meet in

June 1989 for 14- to 19-year-old athletes - some of whom will become future Olympians in the two areas of competition. The winners among the young athletes will become the U.S. team for a number of upcoming international meets. Some may become members on the U.S. team at the 1992 Olympics in Barcelona, Spain.
The *Athletics Congress* approved the city's bid for the track and field events, and also selected Columbus as the site for the 1990 and 1991 National Marathon Championships and the 1992 Olympic Marathon Trials. Columbus had captured the congress' attention with its successful hosting of the *Junior International Summer Games* previously.
Volunteers are evident in every aspect of the event - from initial planning to the closing ceremonies. According to one local executive, "I think you can safely say it is the volunteers who are putting Columbus on the map."

KAISER ROLL
SEE RECIPIENTS: HANDICAPPED - RECREATION/SPORTS

LOUISIANA STATE SPECIAL OLYMPICS SUMMER GAMES
SEE RECIPIENTS: HANDICAPPED - RECREATION/SPORTS

MICHIGAN SPECIAL OLYMPICS STATE GAMES
SEE RECIPIENTS: HANDICAPPED - RECREATION/SPORTS

SAN FRANCISCO SPECIAL OLYMPICS WINTER GAMES
SEE RECIPIENTS: HANDICAPPED - MENTALLY RETARDED

SENIOR GAMES OF INDIANA
SEE RECREATION & SPORTS: OLDER PERSON

SPECIAL OLYMPICS - LAPEER
SEE RECIPIENTS: HANDICAPPED - RECREATION/SPORTS

SPECIAL OLYMPICS TIME
SEE RECIPIENTS: HANDICAPPED - RECREATION/SPORTS

U.S. NATIONAL SENIOR OLYMPICS
SEE RECREATION & SPORTS: OLDER PERSON

RECREATION & SPORTS: PARKS/FORESTS

NATIONAL/STATE ORGANIZATIONS

NATURE CONSERVANCY
SEE PHYSICAL ENVIRONMENT: CONSERVATION

NORTH AMERICAN FAMILY CAMPERS ASSOCIATION
PO Box 117
East Haven, VT 05837
TEL: 802-467-3098
Objectives: To improve camping conditions for family campers.

Services: Provides leadership training through seminars and conferences; promotes good manners in camping, conservation and anti-litter programs; provides advocacy in legislative matters; promotes and guides development of campgrounds; works to improve camping conditions and foster fellowship among family campers; publishes newsletter, fact sheets and other information on family camping; convenes spring regional conventions and fall state conventions. [Responds to mail inquiries only]
Publications: Campfire Chatter
Founded: 1957

STUDENT CONSERVATION ASSOCIATION
SEE PHYSICAL ENVIRONMENT: CONSERVATION

STUDENT CONSERVATION ASSOCIATION
Box 550
Charlestown, NH 03603
TEL: 603-826-4301 (NH); 703-524-2441 (DC)
Objectives: To offer expense-paid educational work experiences and enhance career opportunities for young people; to assist in the accomplishment of important land and resource management of natural resources.
Services: Operates the *Resource Assistant Program* through which college students and other adult volunteers serve as professional assistants in national parks, wildlife refuges, and other areas nationwide for 12-16 weeks in national parks, wilderness areas, and elsewhere (summer only); operates the *Wilderness Workskills Program* providing training in traditional trail construction and wilderness management skills for field personnel; operates the *New Hampshire Conservation Corps;* publishes a monthly conservation employment newsletter and other materials.
Publications: Job Scan (newsletter); SCA Annual Report; Resource Assistant Program Position Listing; High School Program Position Listing
Founded: 1957

VOLUNTEER VACATION PROGRAM
Appalachian Mountain Club
Regional Office
PO Box 298-V
Gorham, NH 03581
TEL: 603-466-2721
Objectives: To provide challenging and rewarding volunteer trail and conservation projects for individuals, families and groups.
Services: Offers a smorgasbord of weekend, weekly and multi-week public service volunteer options in the Northeast and around the U.S.:
- *Weekends:* Trail Days, Adopt-A-Trail and regularly scheduled AMC Chapter and Camp Projects.
- *Weekly:* Three unique volunteer base camps in New Hampshire, New York and Massachusetts with room and board provided.
- *10- to 12-day Trips:* Backcountry Service Trips to Alaska, Wyoming, Maine and elsewhere.

Provides information, which includes application, and other publications, outdoor workshops and facilities for the public and its 37,000 members.
Contact: Reuben Rajala, Trails Program Director
Publications: Appalachia; Appalachia Journal; Volunteer in the Mountains; Guide to AMC Huts and Lodges; AMC Workshops and Seminars; Join the Appalachian Mountain Club

INDIVIDUAL PROGRAM PROFILES

CHATTANOOGA NATURE CENTER
SEE PHYSICAL ENVIRONMENT: EDUCATION

COMMUNITY ACTIVITIES COUNCIL
SEE PHYSICAL ENVIRONMENT: BEAUTIFICATION

FOREST SERVICE VOLUNTEER PROGRAM
SEE PHYSICAL ENVIRONMENT: CONSERVATION

HONEYWELL NEIGHBORHOOD IMPROVEMENT PROGRAM
SEE HOUSING: LOW-INCOME

MASSACHUSETTS AQUATIC RESOURCE EDUCATION PROGRAM (AREP) (*formerly Urban Angler*)
Massachusetts Division of Fisheries and Wildlife
Field Headquarters
Westboro, MA 01581
TEL: 508-366-4479
Purpose: To introduce people to the basics of fishing and the intricate relationship of the water environment and fisheries resource available close to home.
Sponsor: Massachusetts Division of Fisheries & Wildlife - State agency
Contact: Gary Zima, Program Coordinator
Description: Urban Angler was started by one volunteer in 1979. In 1984 it was reclassified into our present format of the *Massachusetts Aquatic Resource Education Program,* and is now operating as a program within the *Division of Fisheries & Wildlife.* Goals and objectives are to:
- teach basic fishing skills to beginners; demonstrate ways to catch, prepare, cook abundant, but underutilized fish species;
- provide residents with a healthy, inexpensive, life-long outdoor recreation which can be done close to home;
- increase people's awareness of the effects of environmental factors on water;
- aid in the emotional, intellectual, and physical development of participants.

Emphasis is on children, women, senior citizens and handicapped. The program has proven its effectiveness and can record the following accomplishments:
- conducted many clinics throughout Massachusetts exposing over 5000 people to the values to be found in learning how to fish;
- designed and implemented four pilot training sessions which have recently produced 75 Master Instructors (all volunteers) who design and implement local learn-to-fish clinics in their local towns.

The programs's *Instructor Training Manual* is available for purchase by interested states/organizations wishing to set up similar clinics. Volunteers provide invaluable cost-effective manpower needs - art, instruction, publicity, water access information gathering, creel census, etc. A Time Sheet has been developed for their use in keeping track of manhours donated and costs involved.
Various materials we have developed, include program descriptions of both the Urban Angler and the Volunteer Training segment, recipes, and artwork showing various techniques of cleaning fish or rigging up for fishing, all mentioned the above training manual.
Expansion of program depends heavily on volunteers and training sessions are presently being planned for all other urban centers in Massachusetts - approximately six other sites will produce approximately 300 new Master Instructors. These instructors will in turn help create Field Instructors and local clinics which have the potential of reaching over 200,000 new people if we use 3% of our total population figures.
Founded: 1979

PATC VOLUNTEERS
SEE PHYSICAL ENVIRONMENT: LAND USE

ROBERTS PARK AND PLAYGROUND/LANTRIP SCHOOL PARK*
Sun Company
6200 Savoy Drive
Houston, TX 77001
TEL: 713-974-9800
Purpose: To transform a barren school ground into an award-winning community park with picnic areas, climbing towers, sand lots and gardens.
Sponsor: The Park People
Contact: Walter Erwin
Description: In 1979, The Park People, Inc., called for proposals for park-related projects from its membership. At the same time, the Eastwood Civic Association was embarking on a campaign to improve its neighborhood by becoming involved and providing opportunities for residents of the area to help themselves. The Civic Association determined that a small park and playground at Lantrip Elementary School would benefit the neighborhood, and pledged to rally its membership to construct the playground if funding became available. Houston Independent School District agreed to the concept of placing the playground at the school.
A proposal for the park/playground was prepared for The Park People. This proposal was a short, two-page document that outlined the need for more play sites in inner-city neighborhoods and stressed the importance of the involvement of the community in the actual construction of the project. A grant of $13,000 was requested for the park project.
The Park People presented the Eastwood-Lantrip proposal along with several others to Sun Company for consideration. After examining all of the proposals, Sun Company selected the Eastwood-Lantrip Proposal for funding. The school district was asked to further support the project by awarding the school a $5,000 grant from a special community projects fund.
In March 1980, the plans for the park were completed and construction began. Sixty volunteers assisted with the construction. The East End Progress Association provided valuable assistance in locating heavy equipment at no charge and locating free or discounted material. Lantrip students assisted neighborhood work crews by moving sand, laying bricks, and planting trees and shrubs.
This project - totally volunteer - provides an example of the results that can be attained when local organizations, agencies, and business/industry work together. One Sun employee said: "A primary consideration in the selection was the community involvement that the project would engender."
Founded: 1979

SOUTH BRONX SUMMER PROJECT
SEE PHYSICAL ENVIRONMENT: LAND USE

TOUCH AMERICA PROJECT (TAP)
SEE PHYSICAL ENVIRONMENT: LAND USE

TRIS (TRAILS INFORMATION SYSTEM)
SEE DISASTER RESPONSE/EMERGENCY PREPAREDNESS

VOLUNTEERS IN PARKS (VIP)
SEE PHYSICAL ENVIRONMENT: LAND USE

WOODEND VOLUNTEER PROGRAM
SEE PHYSICAL ENVIRONMENT: LAND USE

RECREATION & SPORTS: PRISONERS/EX-OFFENDERS

NATIONAL/STATE ORGANIZATIONS

NATIONAL CORRECTIONAL RECREATIONAL ASSOCIATION
SEE LAW ENFORCEMENT/CRIME PREVENTION: RECREATION

RECREATION & SPORTS: SAFETY

INDIVIDUAL PROGRAM PROFILES

VOLUNTEER SAILBOAT NAVIGATORS
US/Coast Guard Auxiliary
c/o Dixon AHL Recreation Ctr
2220 NE 38th Street
Lighthouse Point, FL 33064
TEL: 305-942-4381; 305-979-2999
Purpose: To help boaters stay safe under bad weather conditions.
Sponsor: US/DoT - Coast Guard
Contact: Ralph Reynolds, Acting Education Officer
Description: This team of volunteers represents many years of seamanship experience. Given the number of boat accidents that occur every year, the group felt that training and information to inexperienced boaters might decrease or eliminate that statistic. A course, *Sailing Seamanship,* has been developed and is offered frequently to reach as many boaters in need of this service as possible. Instructors and staff of the program are volunteers. Further information is provided on request.
Publications: Sailing Seamanship

TEENAGE PREGNANCY/PARENTING

NATIONAL/STATE ORGANIZATIONS

AMERICAN PARENTS COMMITTEE
SEE RECIPIENTS: CHILDREN/YOUTH

FATHERHOOD PROJECT
Bank Street College of Education
610 West 112th Street
New York, NY 10025
TEL: 212-663-7200
Objectives: (1989) - a comprehensive overview of programs across the country addressing the problems inherent in cases of pregnancy among adolescent girls; includes descriptions and contact information, 557pp, $29.95
Services: Serves as a national clearinghouse for information on father-participation programs; seeks to encourage the development of new options to involve fathers in raising their children; examines aspects of male parenthood in the areas of employment, law, education, social and supportive services, and health; conducts research on innovative programs supporting men in nurturing roles; publishes a book on the subject and other materials.
Publications: Fatherhood USA

FLORENCE CRITTENTON ASSOCIATION OF AMERICA
Child Welfare League of America
440 First Street, NW
Suite 310
Washington, DC 20006
TEL: 202-638-2952
Objectives: To assist teenage parents.
Services: Works with pregnant teenagers and teenage parents through the *Child Welfare League of America* as the League's division for providing the young parents with medical care, education, counseling, health and family life education, and parent-reparation programs.
Founded: 1920

NATIONAL ORGANIZATION OF ADOLESCENT PREGNANCY AND PARENTING
PO Box 2365
Reston, VA 22090
TEL: 703-435-3948
Objectives: To address problems associated with adolescent pregnancy and parenting.

Services: Works through professionals, policymakers, community and state leaders, and other concerned individuals to promote comprehensive and coordinated services designed for the prevention and resolution of problems associated with adolescent pregnancy and parenthood; supports families in expanding their capability of nurturing children and setting standards that encourage their healthy development through loving, stable relationships; provides advocacy services at local, state and national levels for pregnant adolescents, school-age parents, and their children; shares information and promotes public awareness; conducts conferences and workshops to encourage the establishment of effective programs; offers coalition building assistance; publishes a quarterly newsletter and an intermittent directory.
Publications: Network Newsletter; Directory of Adolescent Pregnancy & Parenting Programs
Founded: 1979

NURTURING NETWORK
910 Main Street
Boise, ID 83702
TEL: 208-344-7200
Objectives: To help single working women and college students get through "crisis pregnancies."
Services: Recruits physicians, counselors, families, employers, colleges and financial contributions to help students and career women unprepared to put career plans aside, but unwilling to end a pregnancy; addresses issues including social stigma, family denial, financial difficulty and employer animosity caused by "crisis pregnancies;" works with a minimal staff and several dozen volunteers to marshal resources of thousands of volunteers across the country to address the dilemma of the women who reluctantly opt for abortion because they do not qualify for "assistance programs which are geared toward helping teenagers and the poor," but do not have adequate resources themselves to pursue the "birth choice" when faced with an unplanned pregnancy (assisting 800 women by January 1990); advocates autonomous choices in a program that has met with approval of people on both sides of the issue; publishes general information packet.
Sponsor: Nurturing Network Members
Contact: Mary Cunningham Agee, Founder
Publications: Nurturing Network Information Packet
Founded: 1986

PLANNED PARENTHOOD FEDERATION OF AMERICA
810 Seventh Avenue
New York, NY 10019
TEL: 212-541-7800
Objectives: To assure that every individual has the fundamental right to make and implement independent decisions about when or whether to have a child.
Services: Provides family planning medical, educational and counseling services to four million Americans each year through 172 affiliates that operate nearly 900 clinics nationwide; serves an additional four million women and men in the developing world through its international division, *Family Planning International Assistance;* promotes national, state and local public policies that enhance reproductive rights, expand access to sexuality education and reproductive health care services, and support research and development into new methods of birth control; maintains an extensive family planning and reproductive rights library; publishes a wide variety of consumer-oriented brochures on family planning and sexuality education issues, published in a free catalog.
Founded: 1916

TRAINING PROGRAMS

NATIONAL CONFERENCE ON DRUG ABUSE AND PARENTING*
National Association of Perinatal Addiction Research and Education
11 East Hubbard Street
Suite 200
Chicago, IL 60611-3536
TEL: 312-329-2512
Contact: Conference Coordinator
Description: This conference is concerned with substance abuse during pregnancy and was convened after a study of 715 women revealed some surprising results. Both public health clinics that serve a largely indigent population and private practices which cater to upper-income patients in Pinellas County, Florida, were surveyed for the study. The conference convened to deal with study findings that contradicted accepted beliefs that determined the concept - and thereby funding and related matters - of dealing with substance abuse during pregnancy. These findings included:

- People have always assumed that drug abuse during pregacy is only a problem in urban minority populations.
- A lot more women are using drugs during pregnancy than is widely believed, due in part to the fact that wealthy patients do not show up in in the figures.
- Minority women who use drugs or alcohol during pregnancy are 10 times more likely to be reported to child abuse authorities than white women, because public clinics are required by law to report suspected perinatal substance abuse.

Conference recommendations include encouraging state officials and health care providers to study laws for uniform drug testing and less formal procedures such as lifestyle evaluations to ensure early detection of drug abuse during pregnancy in all populations. Pinellas County was chosen for the study because it includes rural stretches and larger cities such as St. Petersburg and Clearwater. Presenters included staff from the Pinellas County Juvenile Welfare Board.

VIRGINIA ECUMENICAL INFANT MORTALITY PREVENTION PROJECT CONFERENCE
SEE HEALTH: CHILDREN/YOUTH

INDIVIDUAL PROGRAM PROFILES

BUT I'M DIFFERENT...
Duke Ellington School of the Arts
35th and R streets, NW
Washington, DC 20007
TEL: 202-282-0123
Purpose: To dramatize a somber message: "Teenage pregnancy is a serious problem."
Sponsor: Metropolitan Washington Council of Governments
Contact: Roger Bellamy
Description: Washington, DC teenagers periodically join students from the *Duke Ellington School of the Arts* for workshops designed to enable students to educate each other about pregnancy, unsafe sex, AIDS and substance abuse. In March 1990, the subject was teenage pregnancy.
The Ellington School students also are volunteer counselors at Planned Parenthood of Metropolitan Washington. Before teaching at the workshops, they work to compel their peers to think about the issues. To accomplish this they perform skits. The skit on teenage pregnancy featured two teenagers playing sisters, with the younger sister breaking the news of her pregnancy to her older sister. Although the skit is light so as to amuse as well as teach, the bottom line is the message it hopes will be impressed on the nearly 100 teens usually in the audience - that teen pregnancy is more than just a "cute baby to cuddle."
The workshops are sponsored by the *Metropolitan Washington Council of Governments (COG)*, the *Washington Consortium on HIV Infection in Youth,* and the *District of Columbia Independent Living Program.* According to a COG official, the concern is not only the pregnancy itself, but reports of teenagers with sexually-transmitted diseases is increasing. Through experience with the workshops and skits, COG and the other sponsors have learned first-hand that the best people to teach young people are other young people.
Apart from education, the teen counselors talked about self-esteem, telling their peers that, ultimately, each individual is responsible for his actions, "which sometimes means being the oddball. With self-esteem, if you're pressured, you won't give in." Teen volunteer counselors from several high schools were represented at the workshop - *Terrific Peers* from *Rockville High School,* and *Teen Council* of *Coolidge Senior High School,* for example. Others not involved in counseling groups volunteered to lead sessions and help in other ways. Sponsors stayed in the background, since the students did not appear to need any assistance. The teens ranged from 14 to 19 years of age.
Other workshops cover other issues, including AIDS and substance abuse. One of the volunteer counselors was very direct about the reasons for his participation: "I do this because I may be saving somebody's life."

EMERGENCY INFANT NUTRITION PROGRAM: FREE BREAKFAST PROJECT
SEE NUTRITION: CHILDREN/YOUTH

FIRST (FACTUAL INFORMATION REGARDING SEX AND TEENS)
SEE RECIPIENTS: CHILDREN/YOUTH - I&R

FOCUS (FAMILIES OF CHILDREN UNITED FOR SAFETY)
California Department of Education
Sacramento, CA 95814
TEL: 916-445-4688
Information also available from founders: Pam Danaher and Danielle Brock; request contact information from above source.
Purpose: To bolster parents' ability to control their children.
Sponsor: California Board of Education

Contact: Assistant Superintendent/Public Education, Pam Danaher or Danielle Bock, Founders
Description: About 30 parents and a State Assemblyman attended an organizational meeting in June 1989 to start a new program designed to assist parents in controlling rebellious children. The group elected board members in July and expects to grow into a statewide organization.

The two founders are mothers of teenaged girls who were murdered in the area, in part because the parents were unable to enforce rules designed to keep their children safe. Both of the victims were chronic truants and drug abusers who knew the system and used it to their advantage. When confronting the teenagers and those who had an influence on them, usually adults, brought no results, one of the parents developed the idea for FOCUS. Her daughter was murdered before she could continue the process. By participating now, she hopes to help other parents avoid such a tragedy.

A major activity of FOCUS is to push for legislation and urge enforcement of laws to restore the ability of parents to control their children.

A survey in June found widespread truancy in Sacramento area schools, and much of the development meeting for FOCUS centered on truancy problems. Another issue addressed was the need for stiffer penalties for adults who prey on truants, runaways and troubled kids. A local lobbyist volunteered to lobby for the group, and the assistant superintendent of public instruction in the *California Department of Education* joined FOCUS and will act as an official liaison between the department and the group. The group will urge parents to attend school board meetings and ask questions - demanding answers about their children's education. The school superintendent agreed, and said, "Parents think that when they slow down to 10 miles per hour and let their kid slide out the car door in front of the school, that's the end of their responsibility. That's absolutely wrong!"
Founded: 1989

GRADS PROGRAM
South High School
1160 Ann Street
Columbus, OH 43206
TEL: 614-365-5541
Purpose: To encourage pregnant teens to finish school; to involve fathers voluntarily in the program.
Contact: Barbara Neely, Teacher
Description: GRADS (Graduating Reality and Dual-Role Skills) was started in 1984 by a high school teacher concerned about pregnant teens dropping out of school. It caused uneasiness among city school officials, since some felt it would send a mixed message to teens (becoming pregnant is not so bad). But now GRADS is considered a shining example of how the school can help to solve community problems.

In addition to academics, GRADS tries to reach the young mothers in a personal way. A picnic day allows them to bring their babies to school, and invites the fathers to attend. Although only a few fathers volunteer to come, those who do demonstrate more interest in their young families with each visit. In addition, a few grandparents (some only 30 years of age) drop by and show approval.

An example of the success of the program is a young teen who needed extra tutoring or classwork to graduate. She rose at 5 a.m., took her baby to the sitter, went to school, came home and did her homework, put the baby to bed, and then boarded a bus for night classes on the other side of town - all to make sure she graduated, and in spite of the fact that she was forced out of her home when she became pregnant.

Although the founder feels that most of the success of GRADS can be attributed to its nonjudgmental approach and the emphasis on building a future for the baby, personal touches like inducing fathers to volunteer time and take some of the responsibility have

proven to be very significant factors in motivating the students. In 1989, of the 250 graduates of South High School, 53 were from GRADS.
Founded: 1985

NEW LIVES
Fort Worth Independent School District
3210 West Lancaster Street
Fort Worth, TX 76107
TEL: 817-336-8311
Purpose: To help pregnant teens and new teenaged mothers to stay in school and earn a diploma while learning parenting skills.
Sponsor: Fort Worth Independent School District
Contact: Sandy Dickson or Liz Smith
Description: At *New Lives,* some 200 pregnant and parenting teens study for high school diplomas while learning to care for their babies.

New Lives is supported by the *Fort Worth Independent School District,* and also receives assistance from the *Tarrant County Hospital District* and the *Fort Worth Adolescent Pregnancy Board*. The program is located in an elementary school building where girls from across the area come together to participate.

While fulfilling the district's academic requirements - math, science and language - the teenagers learn how to become good parents. The *New Lives* nursery cares for infants ages two weeks to three months, enabling the girls to take turns learning how to feed, burp, and diaper their babies. After the babies are born, the students have the option of staying at *New Lives* until the end of that school year. They eventually return to their previous schools to complete their education.

Through the program, the girls find help in obtaining transportation to school, medical care, and counseling. Many girls ride the *New Lives* bus to school with their babies. The girls are involved in weekly group-counseling sessions where they explore the issues of priority setting, decision making, life management, and self-esteem. They are also helped to see the use of family planning as an option for their future. During the sessions, many stories are told by girls who thought they were having emotional breakdowns when they were told about *New Lives*. In the program, they openly share their feelings with the group and approach their studies with enthusiasm. They have found that they do not have to make a choice between graduation and quality parenting, since both are within reach through *New Lives*.

PARENT-CHILD PROGRAM*
St. Luke's-Roosevelt Hospital Center
Child Psychiatry Clinic
Amsterdam Avenue at 114th Street
New York, NY 10025
TEL: 212-870-1867
Purpose: To help teenage mothers continue their own development toward adulthood, evaluate the development of the baby, and enhance the essential bonding process between mother and child.
Sponsor: St. Luke's-Roosevelt Hospital Center
Contact: Gloria Zicht, Child Psychiatry
Description: Recognizing that the average pregnant adolescent is poorly nourished and does not receive adequate care, the Child Psychiatry Clinic developed a program geared toward helping the young mother through the formative years with her baby. Most often, the teenager is a victim of poor housing, poor nutrition, anemia, toxemia, and other problems of deprivation. Motherhood represents a crisis which often will color her ability to attain a later adult level of adequate personality functioning. Professionals and volunteers lead groups, make home visits, provide in-clinic information services, and conduct research. Examples of these efforts are:
Parent-Child Interaction Group - led by a psychiatrist and a social worker with assistance from psychologists and volunteers; covers mother's relationship to own mother, their babies, impulses to

abuse, etc.; activities include cooking, baking, knitting, making baby toys, birthday celebrations, etc.

Babies' Group - led by developmental psychologists to help understimulated babies; mothers are given the option of staying voluntarily and learning techniques, or leaving babies without participating in session.

Mothers' Luncheon Group - led by mental health worker with graduate student assistance; helps mothers learn to plan, organize, socialize, and share in a simple common experience (making lunch together).

Home Visiting - provided by undergraduate students under supervision of a social worker; involves regular visits to mothers to provide supportive help and liaison with hospital and city services.

Pediatric Outreach - performed by volunteers from the Parent-Child Program who sit in the outpatient clinic and talk to mothers with babies about their experiences in raising the child, encouraging them to take advantage of all services of the program. In addition, mental health professionals from the program conduct Assessment Home Visiting to follow-up young mothers who have left the hospital and offer services if the home assessment warrants them.

Also, continuing research is aimed at further developing the Maternal Attitudes and Adaptation Scale, a rating instrument which can be used to assess a woman's adjustment to motherhood and effect prediction and early detection of related problems. The Parent-Child Program currently is being funded by privately donated funds. The hospital provides the program with an apartment for group sessions and petty cash for group expenses. Other funding sources are being sought to enable the program to expand and continue.

PARENT-TO-PARENT PROGRAM
SEE RECIPIENTS: FAMILIES - MILITARY

PARENTAL STRESS CENTER
1700 East Carson Street
Pittsburgh, PA 15203
TEL: 412-381-4800
Purpose: To provide comprehensive services for abused, neglected, or high-risk infants and toddlers and their families.
Sponsor: Federal, state, county and private foundation sources.
Contact: Barbara S. Schultz, ACSW, Executive Director
Description: The Parental Stress Center is an independent non-profit social service agency providing comprehensive services for abused, neglected, or high-risk infants and toddlers and their families. Participation in Stress Center's direct service programs may be by referral from Allegheny County Children and Youth Services and may be mandated by Juvenile Court. Since its inception in 1975, the Center has been funded by a variety of federal, state, county and private foundation sources. Direct Service Programs include:

Families & Children Together I & II (FACT I & II) are the Parental Stress Center's therapeutic day programs for distressed parents and infants and toddlers with less acute needs than the babies in out-of-home care. The purpose of FACT is to establish a creative learning environment, demonstrating effective ways of caring for infants and toddlers which can be transferred to the home setting.

Begin Again I is a parent training program, designed for birth parents whose infants and toddlers are in foster care, and for the foster parents of these children. The focus of the parent training component is to increase the parenting skills of the birth parents. Foster parents gain additional understanding of the special needs of these children.

Begin Again II (Assessment Program) is an innovative approach to the provision of in-depth assessment of infants and toddlers who are currently in foster care. The objective of the program is to design an individual treatment plan for each child and family. This plan could include referral to other Parental Stress Center Direct

Service Programs or other appropriate community resources.
Community Education Programs include:
Bright Beginnings is a program sponsored by the Parental Stress Center to address the non-medical concerns of Allegheny County parents of infants and toddlers, thus helping to reduce the incidence of infant and child abuse. The basic component of Bright Beginnings is a free telephone consultation, Warmline, staffed by professional volunteers with child development knowledge and family relations skills. Parents are invited to call with their everyday worries about their child's development - i.e., sleep disruptions, toilet trainings, etc. All Allegheny County area parents may use this service.

Suspected Child Abuse and Neglect (SCAN) program is a means of interdisciplinary case consultation for any member of the professional community regarding a particular case of abuse, neglect or high risk. Coordination for SCAN is provided by the Parental Stress Center. The SCAN core team includes the coordinator, a child psychiatrist, a pediatrician, a social worker, a legal consultant, a Children and Youth Services supervisor and a community mental health professional. The team also plans a series of large educational SCAN meetings several times a year. These are open to the professional and general community as a means of public education regarding child abuse and neglect. Presentations related to broad child abuse and neglect interests are made by nationally known experts in the field.

Staff/Volunteers/Interns - The professional staff of the Parental Stress Center is multidisciplinary in nature. Regular volunteer consultants to staff include psychiatrists, pediatricians, psychologists, lawyers, nurses, and child development specialists. Qualified students from related fields apply for student volunteer placement and internship.
Founded: 1975

PROJECT OPPORTUNITY
Bryant Adult Community Education Center
2709 Popkins Lane
Mount Vernon, VA 22121
TEL: 703-768-0526
Purpose: To help pregnant girls or parenting girls complete high school.
Contact: Elizabeth Link, Program Coordinator
Description: During the 1989-90 school year, a state-funded program in Fairfax County requiring voluntary participation attracted 37 pregnant teenagers and young mothers - ages 13 to 21 - who had given up hope of completing their high school educations. They come from all social and economic backgrounds. Most had dropped out of school and the rest were considering doing so due to pressures of pregnancy and motherhood.

The basic objective of the program is to help pregnant or parenting girls complete high school. The program offers adult education credits, which can be accumulated faster than regular high school credits, for the courses needed to graduate. The program also requires that the students take life skills development classes, which include child development, family living and management skills. In addition, they are required to take career development classes, such as computer training.

In response to detractors who feel that the program encourages pregnancy, officials refer to the hardships endured by participants to complete the program. "Just getting to school is their biggest problem." They must first "feed the baby, get the baby to day care, then catch the bus to school." As other youngsters see the young girls struggle, program leaders feel that, although offering an alternative, the program discourages rather than encourages pregnancy.

The voluntary entry policy, and the fact that the students complete the course in spite of the pressure, is encouraging to school officials. It is a self-help program, with no one being forced to complete the course. The young women say its most positive aspect is the supportive environment from the other participants as well as the part-time staff that runs the program.

Part of the program's support comes in the form of flexibility if a student must stay home with a sick baby, or if she is ill or has a doctor's appointment during the pregnancy. However, according to officials, what the young women need most is an adult with whom they can ask questions and talk about their problems without being judged. A big problem with them is that - in 80% of the cases - the baby's father is not interested and makes himself scarce. "They talk about that a lot," one leader said.

Project Opportunity, in its third year, is one of nine such programs in Virginia. It is financed by a $35,000 grant from the *Virginia Department of Education's Vocational Gender Equity Office.* Program leaders must reapply each year for the money.

One example of the effect of the program on the youth is the 17-year-old who has a 2-1/2-year-old son and had felt that this would "hold her back from everything." She is on her way to college with the goal of becoming an Air Force officer. Another student is heading for Catholic University with a full four-year scholarship.

The "bottom line" surfaced in a "rap session" among five students and three staff members. The participants said they want to be called "young adults because of their experience as mothers."

Project Opportunity is fulfilling its goals as a growth experience.

PROJECT RIGHT START
Teen Parents Self-Sufficiency Programs
Boys & Girls Clubs of Greater Washington
1320 Fenwick Lane
Suite 800
Silver Spring, MD 20910
TEL: 301-543-3887; 301-587-4315
FAX: 301-587-8120
Purpose: To provide assistance to teenage parents.
Sponsor: Boys & Girls Clubs of Greater Washington
Contact: Zelda Fields, Executive Director
Description: Project Right Start is a program for teenage mothers and fathers in the Washington, DC community. The project is operated by the *Boys & Girls Clubs of Greater Washington* in conjunction with the residential *Teen Mothers Support Program.*
Project Right Start offers support to young parents - both mothers and fathers - so that they can:
- complete their high school education
- prepare for college
- acquire job and career skills
- retain a good job

Most importantly, *Project Right Start* offers young parents a chance to learn how to handle all of the pressures of being a parent. It gives them the opportunity to develop positive parenting skills and child care techniques, and to prepare for independent living.

Any teenage parent is eligible for the program, whether or not they plan to keep the baby. Young fathers who participate most often do not have the child living with them, but want to strengthen the father-child relationship and talk to someone about it.

There is no charge for being a participant in the five-day-a-week, 36-week program. It is a flexible program that is designed to meet the individual needs of each participant, including extensions beyond the 36-week period when necessary. Every attempt is made to adapt the program to the schedules of the young parents. After an initial consultation, an agreement on required hours and needed services is signed by the participant. Although day care is not provided at this time, counselors assist in finding this service when it is necessary for parent participation.

Workshops and discussion sessions are led by health and human services professionals in both education and job training. All parties join in the planning of cultural and recreational activities. An important aspect of the program is the requirement for all participants to become actively involved in community service

programs.

Project Right Start is a joint initiative of Boys & Girls Clubs of Greater Washington and the *Milton Eisenhower Foundation.* Space for classes and other activities is provided by the *Teen Mothers Support Program,* a residential program.
Publications: Project Right Start Information Packet

A SHOULDER TO CRY ON
William Beaumont Hospital
3601 West 13-Mile Road
Royal Oak, MI 48072
TEL: 313-551-5000
Purpose: To help first-time parents to develop a routine with their infants upon their return home from the hospital.
Contact: Beth Frydlewicz, Coordinator
Description: Volunteers in the nine-year-old parenting program of *William Beaumont Hospital* are mothers interested in helping new mothers get off on the right foot in caring for their newborn infants. The program started as a Michigan State University research project. The volunteer mothers go through intensive training in eight three-hour classes. They learn about listening to new parents, feeding, sleeping and crying habits of newborns, and how to comfort them.

Many expectant parents take classes on delivering the baby, but at home there was usually a mother, aunt, or someone else from the family to help out the new mother. Today's family setup has changed all of that, and new mothers are finding out how little they know about taking care of an infant.

The volunteer spends time in the home passing on a combination of her own knowledge as a mother, and the techniques learned in the training course. They find that not all new mothers need the same type of help. Some panic, and could reach a dangerous point of frustration, especially with colicky babies. Others simply have very little skill or common sense. Then there are mothers who need to have the volunteer show an interest in them as well as the baby. Some could manage without the program. One of the volunteer's first considerations is to try to determine which of the above applies.

The program is available to first-time parents who deliver at Beaumont or whose pediatrician works out of the hospital. It is believed to be the only program of its kind in the state.

U.S. OPEN VOLUNTEER COMMITTEE
SEE RECIPIENTS: HANDICAPPED - EMPLOYMENT

WEDNESDAY MORNING MOTHERS
SEE RECIPIENTS: FAMILIES - PSYCHOSOCIAL SUPPORT

WELCOME BABY
SEE RECIPIENTS: FAMILIES - MILITARY

TRANSPORTATION & SAFETY

NATIONAL/STATE ORGANIZATIONS

AUTOMOTIVE CONSUMER ACTION PROGRAM (AUTOCAP)
SEE CONSUMER SERVICES/LEGAL RIGHTS: TRANSPORTATION

NATIONAL ASSOCIATION OF WOMEN HIGHWAY SAFETY LEADERS
3008 North 16th Drive
Phoenix, AZ 85015
TEL: 602-264-9327
Objectives: To work with communities to help improve safety on highways, roads and streets.
Services: Supports and implements the National Highway Safety Standards in communities, states and the nation; encourages each political subdivision to assume its responsibility for highway safety; aims at more uniformity in traffic safety programs and regulations within the 50 states, the District of Columbia, and Puerto Rico; maintains regional offices in a number of states (request list); publishes quarterly newsletters for national, regional and state levels, and other materials
Publications: President's Newsletter; Regional Newsletter; NAWHSL Directory; Tempest
Founded: 1967

NATIONAL SAFETY COUNCIL
Traffic Safety Division
444 North Michigan Avenue
Chicago, IL 60611
TEL: 312-527-4800
Objectives: To reduce the number and severity of traffic and motor-fleet related accidents.
Services: Maintains several working committees in its Traffic Safety Division in such areas as alcohol and drugs, winter driving hazards, pedestrian safety, safety belt usage, roadway environment and railroad grade crossing safety, traffic records; publishes *Traffic Safety* and *Safe Driver,* a quarterly journal, posters, numerous booklets, films, and other materials on safety; convenes annual meeting during the National Safety Congress and Exposition each year.
Publications: Safe Driver; Safe Driver; Accident Facts; Journal of Safety Research
Founded: 1913

NHTSA HOTLINE
SEE CONSUMER SERVICES/LEGAL RIGHTS: TRANSPORTATION

US/DOT - PRIVATE SECTOR INITIATIVES PROGRAMS
Office of the Secretary
400 Seventh Street, SW
Washington, DC 20590
TEL: 202-426-4000
Objectives: To promote public/private partnerships and encourage the private sector to decrease dependence on government.
Services: Operates under the premise that the nation's best guarantee of sound transportation systems lies in the private sector; applies the fundamental objective to all of the department's activities to *increase reliance on the private sector,* to improve the system of transportation user charges, and to return transportation function to private operation; institutes policy guidelines including:
- The provision of transport services should be left to private enterprise as far as feasible.
- Private transport services should function in a competitive market, rather than under regulatory regime.
- Regulations imposed on the private sector should be reevaluated to modify or rescind nonessential requirements.
- When the national interest indicates that certain transportation facilities should be built, operated, and maintained by the government, and are used by private carriers, equitable cost recovery should take place.
- Federal subsidies for publicly owned/operated modes should not undermine and take business from competing modes (private bus, taxi, etc.).

Operates current programs and proposes new ones to encourage private sector initiative, such as those summarized below:
Aviation - makes use of expertise from the private sector, rather than government staffing, to perform many functions; e.g., periodic examination of airmen conducted by physicians who are in private practice.
Proposes production and dissemination of audiovisual training materials by the private sector, additional certification authority to large aircraft manufacturers, removal of documentation and procedural requirements for noise abatement and aircraft emissions that prove costly and do not degrade air quality, and *regulation by objective,* a new concept in compliance.
Highways and Safety - relies heavily on the private sector for program delivery, both the private contractor and the highway associations and societies.

Proposes an awards program for private sector organizations and individuals who provide outstanding support for the seat belt and drunk driving campaigns, bonus payments to highway design and construction contractors as rewards for suggesting time-saving techniques, greater private sector financial participation in the capital costs of highway projects, operation of park-and-ride lots by private industry, and increased assistance to small motor carriers who have entered business since truck deregulation.

Urban Mass Transportation - encourages the growth of *paratransit* (a variety of forms of transportation such as shared-ride, taxi services, van pooling, employer-sponsored car pooling, and subscription buses), monitors local funding to public systems to avoid undermining local private service providers, and funds many research and development projects for transit equipment.

Proposes issuing investment strategy guidelines for transit capital projects as coventures with the private sector, and working with the *Labor Department* to amend labor protection legislation that levy undue constraints on paratransit activity.

Maritime, Coast Guard, and Inland Waterways - relies heavily on the private sector for boating safety activities (through the *Volunteer Coast Guard Auxiliary),* works through non-federal organizations to provide radar training, defrays cost for navigation aids by charging user fees to private boat owners, with legislation pending for full cost recovery.

Proposes to involve the private sector in an expansion of the present agreement on ship inspection, to terminate its *Vessel Traffic Service* as soon as an alternative is found, and to contract out the operation and maintenance of its LORAN-C stations and aids to navigation.

DoT Administration - schedules air travel through a private ticket agency, contracts for printing and graphics work with private contractors, places responsibility for a portion of the department's data-processing workload with the private sector, and contracts with CPAs in all ten regions to audit contracts and grants.

Proposes studying the cost-effectiveness of additional contracts for computer services, analyzing th shuttle bus service for possible transfer to the private sector, and using the services of a private collection agency in certain areas of debt collection.

Works continuously to increase reliance on the private sector and on marketplace mechanisms through establishment and carrying out of policy guidelines through program changes, regulatory reforms, legislative activities, administrative actions, and reductions in budget and personnel.
Sponsor: US/DoT - Department of Transportation

INDIVIDUAL PROGRAM PROFILES

BICYCLE SAFETY AND SEAT BELT AWARENESS PROGRAMS
SEE TRANSPORTATION & SAFETY: CYCLING

MOTOR VOTERS
SEE CIVIC AFFAIRS: VOTING

TRANSPORTATION COMMITTEE OF ACCA
Annandale Christian Community for Action (ACCA)
7200 Columbia Pike
Annandale, VA 22003
TEL: 703-256-1378
Purpose: To meet the needs of those who are unable to keep essential medical appointments, physical or mental health therapy, cancer treatment sessions, etc.
Sponsor: ACCA
Contact: Ruth Schably, Chairman
Description: The ACCA Transportation Committee endeavors to meet emergency or essential physical or mental health transportation needs through a network of volunteer drivers. Each

participating church appoints a Transportation Coordinator, and accepts responsibiliity for the program on a rotating basis for periods of one week at a time. Typically, during a week, about 20 rides are provided by volunteers in the church congregations. The ACCA volunteer receives the name, telephone number and address of the person in need, contacts the person and sets forth on his or her mission.

ACCA with the help of County agencies tries to screen requests to be sure of real need. The majority of requests are valid. They range from a 19-year-old who was brain damaged in an accident and needed treatments twice a week, to a medical check-up for an elderly person. Within a year the 19-year-old was well enough to use the public buses and informed the Committee that he no longer needed its services. This is an example of the way in which this work rewards the volunteer.

During 1988 ACCA's Transportation Committee provided a total of 894 rides - an average of more than 80 rides per month. A Fairfax County-initiated service, FASTRAN, initiated in 1986, has relieved some of the demand. FASTRAN is a transportation system for the elderly, disabled, and persons of limited income. ACCA's greatest need now is by persons who cannot go out to the curb to wait for the FASTRAN bus. Sixteen ACCA churches participate in the transportation program.
Publications: ACCA Annual Report

TRANSPORTATION & SAFETY: CHILDREN/YOUTH

INDIVIDUAL PROGRAM PROFILES

ROADRUNNER PROGRAM
Capital Metropolitan Transportation Authority
City of Austin
2910 East Fifth Street
Austin, TX 78702
TEL: 512-474-1200
Purpose: To assist youth with transportation expenses by providing a reduced-fair program and other cost-saving features.
Sponsor: City of Austin
Contact: Youth Coordinator
Description: Recognizing that many youth are hindered from pursuing jobs and services available to them due to transportation expense, the *Capital Metropolitan Transportation Authority* decided to try to help. The agency introduced the *Roadrunner Program* for youth 18 years of age and under, which provides a pass for a considerable saving on transportation, and qualifies participants for discounts on items ranging from food to music to miniature golf from more than 20 area merchants.

Young riders can purchase Roadrunner passes by showing one of a number of IDs - including a school report card - at most of the locations that sell regular Capital Metro passes. It is hoped that the cost-saving feature and the support of area merchants will encourage more youth to seek summer employment and pursue social activities that will counteract the practice of idle youth congregating in the neighborhoods with nothing productive to keep them occupied.

SAFETY TOWN (WHERE CHILDREN LEARN TO LIVE)
Norman Police Department
201-B West Gray
Norman, OK 73069
TEL: 405-321-1444
Purpose: To teach children fundamentals of safety, with emphasis on pedestrian and bicyclist safety, to help prevent accidents.

Sponsor: Norman Police Department; Sooner Fashion Mall Merchants
Contact: Officer Lahoma Nelson
Description: The Grand Opening of Safety Town was June, 1977. Safety Town, the first such project in Oklahoma, is a miniature city designed especially for children five and six years old to learn the basics of traffic safety. The "City" has six streets, a working traffic light, authentic traffic and street signs, stores, and school hours.

Police officers teach the free classes which are one hour for five days, ending with graduation on Friday, complete with diploma. There are two classes held each day from (9:30 to 10:30 a.m. and 11:00 to 12:00 noon). Enrollment for the classes is conducted by the Sooner Fashion Mall office. The entire program is conducted without charge to the public.

Teenage boys and girls volunteer to work one to seven weeks. Sometimes, Boy Scouts volunteer to work two days for a safety merit badge.

The volunteers perform many duties in assisting the police officers. Before each class, they set up and arrange the bicycles and tractors. Each day after the last class, the volunteers put away the vehicles. The volunteers help to teach techniques to those children who do not know how to pedal a bicycle or tractor. They help remind the children to stop at the stop signs and red light, to obey the yield signs, and to stay in the correct lane in the road. The volunteers perform many other duties as needed.

Officer Nelson observed: "While the teenagers are working with the five and six year old children, they are learning more about safety themselves. They make new friends and gain more self esteem."
Founded: 1977

TRANSPORTATION & SAFETY: COMMUTERS

NATIONAL/STATE ORGANIZATIONS

ASSOCIATION FOR COMMUTER TRANSPORTATION
1776 Massachusetts Avenue, NW
Suite 521
Washington, DC 20036-1904
TEL: 202-659-0600
Objectives: To promote the expansion of ride sharing in van, bus and car pools as an alternative commuting mode.
Services: Works with corporations and agencies operating van, car or bus pools, vendors offering ridesharing equipment and services, and others who advocate ridesharing through vehicle pools as a viable alternative for commuters; operates through some 500 members involving an estimated 10,000 vehicles (this does not include the thousands of owner-operator van pool services); takes action to eliminate institutional barriers to vehicle pooling; mounts a public awareness campaign to inform the public of the benefits of this mode of commuting (one 12-passenger van replaces eight cars, conserves 5388 gallons of gasoline per year, and keeps more than two tons of pollutants from the air).

Emphasizes that local, state and federal assistance is available to any person interested in pooling; maintains a speakers bureau for on-site consultation and assistance; publishes a bimonthly newsletter, a membership directory, and other materials; convenes workshops, seminars, quarterly meetings for officers and an annual membership meeting.
Publications: ACT NOW; The Clips; ACT Membership Directory; TMA Directory
Founded: 1976

TRANSPORTATION & SAFETY: CONSUMERS/LEGAL RIGHTS

NATIONAL/STATE ORGANIZATIONS

CENTER FOR AUTO SAFETY
2001 S Street, NW
Suite 410
Washington, DC 20009
TEL: 202-328-7700
Objectives: To provide advocacy in matters of auto and highway safety.
Services: Monitors government agencies charged with regulation of the automobile industry; participates in the rule-making procedures of the National Highway Traffic Safety Administration, the Federal Highway Administration and occasionally institutes legal action; maintains extensive library which includes thousands of complaint letters as well as relevant publications and other materials; supports safety standards; analyzes automobile and highway safety developments in the field; publishes *The Lemon Book* by Ralph Nader and others, *The Car Book,* a bimonthly journal, *Impact,* and other materials (Center founded by Ralph Nader and Consumers Union; now independent).
Publications: The Lemon Book; Impact; The Yellow Book Road; Automobile Design Liability; Information on Auto Defects; The Car Book
Founded: 1970

TRANSPORTATION & SAFETY: CRIME PREVENTION

INDIVIDUAL PROGRAM PROFILES

VAN MINISTRY
SEE LAW ENFORCEMENT/CRIME PREVENTION: FAMILIES

VISITOR HOSPITALITY CENTER*
SEE LAW ENFORCEMENT/CRIME PREVENTION: FAMILIES

TRANSPORTATION & SAFETY: CYCLING

INDIVIDUAL PROGRAM PROFILES

AIR PRODUCTS DEVELOPMENTAL CYCLING PROGRAM
SEE RECREATION & SPORTS: CHILDREN/YOUTH

BICYCLE SAFETY AND SEAT BELT AWARENESS PROGRAMS
McDonald's of Paragould, Arkansas
One Medical Drive
Paragould, AR 77450
TEL: 501-236-3715

Purpose: To emphasize, demonstrate, and help improve bicycle safety practices and seat belt usage in Paragould.
Sponsor: McDonald's of Paragould; Paragould Police Department
Contact: Community Services Officer
Description: In cooperation with the Paragould Police Department, McDonald's of Paragould mounted two programs: a bicycle safety and engraving program, and a "Buckle Up and Make It Click" seat belt program.

The bicycle program began with a bicycle parade down the main street with over 50 children participating. Prizes were given for the best decorated bikes, and a festive and cooperative spirit prevailed afterwards as bicycle safety was discussed and demonstrated, and bicycles were engraved for identification purposes should they be stolen.

The buckle up program involved the police department also, and included the local hospital as well. Volunteers from the hospital and McDonald's visited local elementary schools to show a film on the benefits of buckling up, demonstrated how to buckle up a car seatbelt, and presented each child with a sticker for a free surprise at McDonald's if they buckled up for seven days in a row.

Both programs were considered a great success, making children aware of the responsibility that goes with owning a bicycle, and bringing seat belt restraint to top-of-mind awareness. The programs will be continued on request. According to McDonald's manager, "If we helped make Paragould just a little safer for our children through these programs, our investment of time and resources is well worth the effort."
Publications: Bicycle Program Packet

TRANSPORTATION & SAFETY: DRUGS/ALCOHOL

NATIONAL/STATE ORGANIZATIONS

CITIZENS FOR SAFE DRIVERS AGAINST DRUNK DRIVERS/CHRONIC OFFENDERS
7401 McKenzie Court
Bethesda, MD 20817
TEL: 301-469-6282
Objectives: To prevent highway death and injury caused by problem drivers.
Services: Acts as a national information clearinghouse and communications network on state and federal legislation and research data; also acts as a self-help group for families and friends of highway crash victims.
Publications: UPDATE
Founded: 1976

TRAINING PROGRAMS

DRUNK-DRIVING SIMULATOR PROGRAM AND FORUM
SEE DRUG ABUSE/ALCOHOLISM: TRANSPORTATION

TRANSPORTATION & SAFETY: HANDICAPPED

INDIVIDUAL PROGRAM PROFILES

PARKING POSSE
SEE RECIPIENTS: HANDICAPPED - LEGAL RIGHTS

WHEELCHAIR WASH
SEE RECIPIENTS: HANDICAPPED - TRANSPORTATION

TRANSPORTATION & SAFETY: HEALTH

INDIVIDUAL PROGRAM PROFILES

EASY RIDERS VOLUNTEER PROGRAM*
Easy Riders Medical Transportation
5886 Bayberry Drive
Cincinnati, OH 45242-8020
TEL: 513-651-2871
Purpose: To utilize volunteer drivers in their own cars to provide medical transportation for physically and financially limited clients.
Sponsor: Easy Riders Medical Transportation
Contact: Margaret E. Carey
Description: More than 100 volunteers are involved in the Easy Riders program, with another 80 serving in management and fund-raising capacities. The program began as an entirely volunteer transportation service in 1970. As the agency has grown, paid drivers have been employed, but volunteer drivers remain the foundation of the service.

The program was started after it was determined that often many people must be institutionalized simply because they are not physically able to use a bus or financially able to afford a taxi. In addition, many people in Greater Cincinnati are unable to get urgently needed medical care because they have no means of transportation. Easy Riders allows these people to lead relatively independent lives in their own homes, maintaining neighborhood activities and friends and, most importantly, their own self-respect and sense of personal worth.

The need for specialized transportation in Cincinnati is constant and ongoing. No matter how much service Easy Riders can provide, there is always a need for more. Thus, the project is constantly recruiting volunteers and seeking funding. The Director's assessment: "To date, the program's efforts have been very successful, and reflect the positive attitude of community residents when asked to rally around a community need."
Founded: 1970

HELP-ON-WHEELS
SEE HEALTH: CANCER

VOLUNTEER TRANSPORTATION PROGRAM
PO Box 528
Reidsville, GA 30453
TEL: 912-557-4721
Purpose: To provide transportation for medical care for welfare recipients.
Sponsor: Georgia Department of Human Resources

Contact: Debra D. Webster, Volunteer Coordinator
Description: There are 493 square miles in Tattnall County with a population of 18,014, according to the 1980 census report. The county has five doctors, one hospital, two dental offices and two nursing homes. Several specialists are on staff at Tattnall County Memorial Hospital and have office hours on part time basis. Many clients of the Tattnall County Department of Family and Children Services must travel approximately seventy miles to Savannah to receive most types of specialized medical treatment.

The medical aspect of the Volunteer Transportation Program initiated in 1969 by the Department is now funded through the Medical Program. Reimbursed at the rate of 20 cents per mile, volunteer drivers transport Medicaid recipients to medical facilities for medical care.

Volunteers have come from all walks of life - businessmen, housewives, mothers of small children, retired people with low income and public assistance recipients themselves. They help to create a new image of welfare as they involve other members of the community and help them become aware of the needs of others.

Unfortunately, it is difficult today to recruit and maintain volunteers due to the high cost of fuel, the low reimbursement allowance, and the current economic impact on families.

Volunteers must have a dedication to the needs of others and feel a part of the agency's program in order to continue to be volunteers. The Department makes every effort through orientation, training, and day-to-day contact to accomplish the latter.

TRANSPORTATION & SAFETY: LOW-INCOME

INDIVIDUAL PROGRAM PROFILES

VOLUNTEER TRANSPORTATION
317 South Eighth Street
Griffin, GA 30223
TEL: 404-228-1386
Purpose: To provide transportation for clients to community resources.
Sponsor: Spalding County Department of Children and Family Services
Contact: Linda A. Nixon
Description: In 1967, the Spalding County Department of Family and Children Services initiated a Volunteer Transportation program and had no difficulty finding volunteer drivers willing to participate. Today, the volunteer drivers continue to provide this much-needed service, and most are reimbursed at the current state mileage rate. Insurance is offered at a nominal fee.

Volunteers are recruited by newspaper articles, speeches, personal contact with interested individuals, word-of-mouth, and recruitment by the program's staff and volunteers. Individuals who are retired, and housewives with no children, stay with the program longer than those with more personal responsibility. Volunteer drivers take clients to medical facilities, educational resources, grocery shopping, and - in the case of foster children - visiting relatives. Requests for transportation come into the agency through the client's caseworker and must be received at least two days prior to the date of the needed service. Volunteers are contacted at that time by the Volunteer Coordinator. There is an advantage to having only one person contact the volunteer drivers; that person is able to develop a relationship with the volunteer, know the driver's limitations, what age client he/she relates to best, and other aspects of the volunteer/client relationship that may be unique to an individual volunteer.
Founded: 1967

VOLUNTEER TRANSPORTATION PROGRAM
SEE TRANSPORTATION & SAFETY: HEALTH

TRANSPORTATION & SAFETY: OLDER PERSON

NATIONAL/STATE ORGANIZATIONS

FLYING SENIOR CITIZENS OF THE USA*
96 Tamarack Street
Buffalo, NY 14220
TEL: 716-824-3432
Objectives: To petition airlines for half-fare standby privileges for senior citizens.
Services: Assists older persons in expressing themselves to the airlines on a regular basis; acts as a voice for older persons, maintaining that increased travel by the elderly would justify half-fare at off-peak times (Monday through Thursday); publishes semimonthly newsletter and directory.

INDIVIDUAL PROGRAM PROFILES

SERVICE DELIVERY FOR THE ELDERLY*
SEE RECIPIENTS: OLDER PERSON - TRANSPORTATION

WELFARE REFORM

INDIVIDUAL PROGRAM PROFILES

FREE THE CHILDREN (FTC)
409 Ayers Street
Memphis, TN 38105
TEL: 901-521-8084
Purpose: To reduce county welfare rolls 75 percent by 1997.
Sponsor: State of Tennessee
Contact: Bob Cannon, President
Description: The *Free The Children (FTC)* initiative has set a
target date of 1997 to reduce welfare rolls by 75 percent. Basically,
it operates with a small staff, a $300,000 state grant and other
smaller grants, the generosity of strangers, and hundreds of
volunteer hours and in-kind services from Memphis and Shelby
County governments.
The $300,000 grant received in late January 1989 had generated
$3,627 in interest by June, and had paid for nearly $50,000 in
labor costs, more than $8,000 in office expense, and $15,000 for
rent, office furniture, etc. Other grants and the services they have
made possible include:

- **Case Management Work** - funding of seven CSA case workers
  supervised by a veteran social worker ($174,738 Community
  Service Block Grant).
- **Professional Services by Groups** - funding for groups such as
  the *Volunteer Center,* which organizes volunteers for FTC, the
  Memphis Literacy Foundation, which coordinates
  literacy-related programs, and *Porter Leath Children's Center,*
  which helps form home-based day care programs ($183,174
  Community Service Block Grant).
- **Economic Development and Training Coordinator** -
  administrative support for this position (paid through CSA).
- **Nurses** - funding for two Health Department nurses to assess
  health needs of more than 140 families ($60,000 county grant).
- **Scholarships** - funding for the *Memphis Pre-Science Scholars
  Program* - a program for black junior and senior high school
  students interested in health science careers, and for the
  coordinator of the science project, who also administers an
  evaluation program for the entire FTC concept ($1 million
  Henry J. Kaiser Family Foundation grant).
- **Housing** - funding for homeownership programs for low- or
  moderate-income families ($5 million Shelby County Home
  Buyers Revolving Loan Fund grant).

Smaller funds include the *Cliff Tuck Memorial Scholarship Fund*
($928), the *Recreation Playground Equipment Fund* ($550), and
Book Friends ($1,075), the latter of which also collects children's
books (12,000 in early 1989 campaign).
Donations in early 1989 amounted to $25,000, with $5,900 coming
from individuals and $19,300 from a February fund-raiser, the
Coppertone/Maybelline Ladies Tennis Challenge.
In addition, FTC's operations manager continually seeks new
sources of funds, most recently applying to the *Plough Foundation*
for grants for a teen pregnancy program, computer equipment, and
an anti-arson program. Many other needed programs await the
results of his and other staff persons' efforts in a program that
counties across the state and in other states are observing closely
for relevance to their own areas.

WOMEN OFF WELFARE (WOW)
Mesa United Way
7 South Hibbert, #360
Mesa, AZ 85210-1414
TEL: 602-969-8601
Purpose: To put single mothers on the road to self-sufficiency; to
break the cycle of welfare dependency.
Sponsor: Welfare Reform Task Force
Contact: Sue Kathe, Volunteer Chairperson
Description: Started in summer 1988, *Women Off Welfare (WOW)*
in Mesa, Arizona, is an outgrowth of the federal Family Support
Act of 1988, which legislates welfare reform. WOW is a long-term
program designed to help single mothers become self-sufficient.
The program was developed under the auspices of a public/private
partnership which includes the *Maricopa County Private Industry
Council (PIC), Arizona Department of Economic Security (DES),
Mesa Chamber of Commerce, City of Mesa, Mesa Ecumenical
Council,* and *Mesa Community Council.*
Before the program began, a *Welfare Reform Task Force* was
established by the *United Way of America's Public Policy
Advisory Committee* to identify the kinds of obstacles there had
been to welfare reform in the past, and find solutions to them. A
major problem was the discontinuation of federally-funded
health-care benefits for welfare recipients who became employed -
benefits which were not immediately carried over by the employer.
Often, women had to quit their jobs and go back on welfare to get
them through costly health problems. The solution to avoid this
pitfall was 20 local physicians who agreed to volunteer their
services to welfare families in the WOW program. This spirit
prevailed across the community and enabled other components of
the program to work smoothly as well (day care, job
training/placement, transportation, etc.).
All of the women enrolled in the program go through an intensive

three-week session to build self-motivation and self-confidence. The session is led by loaned personnel managers from area companies who conduct training in job-interview techniques and discuss what employers expect in the way of on-the-job conduct and appearance. Through *Gifts In Kind, Inc.*, an independent organization, the women were provided with clothing from *Montgomery Ward* and hair care products from *Redken.*

The Maricopa County Skills Center and Mesa Community College offer ongoing job training at no cost for program clients. In addition to office skills, the women are encouraged to take courses in specific career fields, or to learn trades. Education to acquire high school-equivalency diplomas and English-language proficiency is also provided.

Within the first year, WOW helped about 100 women find employment, and another 300 begin job training programs. The second year saw the program expand into five other townships.

Founded: 1988

III.
ANNOTATED BIBLIOGRAPHY

ADMINISTRATION

ACTIVE VOLUNTEER
(quarterly) - primary communication of the Governor's Office on Volunteerism covering special events, new resources, legislative update, funding news, calendar of events, opportunity listings, volunteer centers directory, local program activities, etc., 8pp, free subscription **New Jersey Office of Volunteerism** 101 South Broad Street, CN 800, Trenton, NJ 08625-0800 609-292-9069

AGENCY VOLUNTEER REQUEST PACKET
(kept current) - the kit that is given to each agency on its initial contact with the VAC; includes introductory letter, guidelines for effective participation, list of volunteer job titles to coordinate VAC/agency system, VAC services, required forms, and other materials, $1.50/packet **Greater Milwaukee Voluntary Action Center** 161 West Wisconsin Avenue, Milwaukee, WI 53203 414-271-7337

AN AMERICAN EXPERIENCE
(undated) - a film recalling the nation's rich voluntary tradition, and its unique reliance on volunteerism; includes ways in which United Way has contributed, #CF1012, 16mm, 22 minutes, inquire about cost **United Way of America** 701 North Fairfax Street, Alexandria, VA 22314-2045 701-836-7100

AMERICA'S VOLUNTARY SPIRIT: A BOOK OF READINGS
(1983) by Brian O'Connell - a presentation of 45 selections analyzing the voluntary sector's strengths and variety; includes as contributors Thoreau, Erma Bombeck, Vernon Jordan, and others chosen for their quality, representativeness, and long-term relevance; emphasizes several lessons, including: the size and pervasiveness of giving and volunteering in America, the complexity and diversity of the origins of American generosity, the ease and danger of overemphasizing and glorifying this sector, the importance of its independence, and the importance of this participation in terms of the individual's uniqueness; includes an index and a listing of 560 references, 460pp, $14.95 (paperback), $19.95 (hardback) **Independent Sector** 1828 L Street, NW, Washington, DC 20036 202-223-8100

ASSESSING COMMUNITY NEEDS OF WOMEN
(1979) - the purpose of a survey, how it is used, the advantages, and the seven steps that need to be taken to adequately identify needs (transferable to any needs survey); includes sample survey forms geared to women's needs, 10pp, $1.00 **National Council of Jewish Women** 15 East 26th Street, New York, NY 10010 212-532-1740

ASSESSING RURAL NEEDS
(1978) by Jeffrey Ashe, Volunteer - description of a low-cost, rapid system to determine needs and priorities in rural communities and activate policymakers and others to see that they are met; includes copies of all forms necessary to implement the assessment system, 127pp, $5.95 **Volunteers in Technical Assistance** 1815 North Lynn Street, Arlington, VA 22209 703-276-1800

ASSOCIATION DIRECTORS & OFFICERS LIABILITY INSURANCE PLAN
(1989) - information about a liability insurance plan that protects directors, officers, volunteers and employees of nonprofit human service organizations, as well as the organization itself (expansion of a plan that has served United Way-supported agencies since 1983), unpaged packet, free **Partnership Umbrella** 102 South Alfred Street, Alexandria, VA 22314 703-836-1442

AVA IN THE MARKETPLACE
(kept current) - Ed. Cherrie Carpetyan - a national directory of resources for the field of volunteer administration; offers alphabetical, business and geographical listings of trainers, consultants and materials that are useful to all types of volunteer/citizen participation programs, 55pp, $3.00 **Association for Volunteer Administration** PO Box 4584, Boulder, CO 80306 303-497-0238

AVA IV THOUGHT
(monthly) - newsletter of a four-state regional division of the Association for Volunteer Administration; includes message from

the Region Chair, feedback from regional and national meetings, fund raising and membership activities, professional development update, news from each state director, current listings of Council, Task Force, and membership, invitation and guidelines for articles, etc., Av. 8pp, sample copy free **Association for Volunteer Administration, Region IV** c/o Voluntary Action Center, 1520 Aberdeen Road, Hampton, VA 23666 804-838-9770

BASIC FACTS ON VOLUNTEER CENTERS: WHAT THEY DO AND HOW THEY DO IT

(1988) - facts and figures on the operations of volunteer centers that are run as part of a United Way; includes comparative data on how volunteer centers are organized, staffed, budgeted, and operated; analyzes critical issues facing volunteer centers; provides examples of collaborative working arrangements, and shows how centers use automated information systems, #UC10584, 20pp, $2.00 **United Way of America** 701 North Fairfax Street, Alexandria, VA 22314-2045 703-836-7100

BASIC FEEDBACK SYSTEM: A SELF-ASSESSMENT PROCESS FOR VOLUNTEER PROGRAMS

(1977) - a hard look at various components of a volunteer program for evaluation purposes; enables the evaluator to use a step-by-step method with forms, checklists and other aids in areas of client, board, volunteer director, staff, volunteer, administration and community resources, 52pp, $4.50 **VOLUNTEER - The National Center** 1111 North 19th Street, Arlington, VA 22209 703-276-0542

BASIC VOLUNTEER MANAGEMENT: BUILDING A BRIDGE FROM DREAMS TO REALITY

(1989) - an audiovisual including ten segments designed to address concerns of volunteer managers; e.g., stereotypical volunteer, modern trends in volunteerism, setting goals, organizing, staffing/recruiting, training, evaluating, recognizing, and the climate of a program; uses the philosophy, "If you can *dream* it you can *do* it!" 75 minutes, $98.00 plus $4.00 postage **VMS/Heritage Arts** 1807 Prairie Avenue, Downers Grove, IL 60515 708-964-1194

BUILDING INNOVATION INTO PROGRAM REVIEWS: ANALYSIS OF SERVICE DELIVERY ALTERNATIVES

(1989) - guidance on how to resolve the dilemma between constant pressure to improve program efficiency and effectiveness on the one hand, and the risk of wasting money on new ways of doing things on the other; lays out steps of the alternatives analysis approach including how the analysis team should operate, how to collect the data needed to compare alternatives, and how to prepare the report, 126pp, $15.75 (paper); $29.50 (cloth) **Urban Institute Press** 4720 Boston Way, Lanham, MD 20706 301-459-3366

BY THE PEOPLE: A HISTORY OF AMERICANS AS VOLUNTEERS

(Rev. 1990) - a two-part overview of Americans as volunteers: (1) history of volunteering in the U.S.; (2) current and future challenges; includes demonstrations of how volunteers have pioneered community action and social change through three centuries of American history; describes ways in which the actions of individual citizens and volunteer groups have shaped the nation; catalogs a wide variety of voluntary actions now taking place; analyzes recent developments such as volunteer care for people with AIDS and the presidential "thousand points of light" community service initiative; explores prospects of the future of volunteerism, 400 pages, $22.95 (also available from ENERGIZE, 5450 Wissahickon Avenue, Philadelphia, PA 19144 -

215-438-8342, same price) **Jossey Bass, Publishers** 350 Sansome Street, San Francisco, CA 94104 415-433-1767

CAMPUS OUTREACH: THE COOL NEWSLETTER

(5/year) - newsletter about student/community involvement which highlights individual, program, and campus efforts as well as current issues, resources and coming events; includes features such as *Post Cards from Campus, First Person, Interview,* and *Campus Calendar,* $15.00/year **Campus Outreach Opportunity League (COOL)** 386 McNeal Hall, University of Minnesota, St. Paul, MN 55108-1011 612-624-3018

CITIZEN PARTICIPATION CERTIFICATION FOR COMMUNITY DEVELOPMENT: A READER ON THE CITIZEN

(1977) - an overview of current trends in citizen participation, financial resources, good participation programs, and the potential/limitations of citizen participation; examples are provided with comments on structure, functions, and effectiveness; includes resource listings, 204pp, #N583, $9.50 **National Association of Housing & Redevelopment Officials** 1320 Eighteenth Street, NW, Washington, DC 20036 202-429-2960

CITIZEN PARTICIPATION IN AMERICA

(1978) - a discussion of some of the activities that have helped to bring about constructive change - the public interest movement, neighborhood grassroots participation, public involvement programs and the past efforts and challenges of these and other groups, 123pp, $8.95 **Lincoln Filene Center for Citizenship & Public Affairs,** Medford, MA 02155 617-628-5000

COLLEAGUES: THE VOLUNTEER/EMPLOYEE RELATIONSHIP

(1989) - guide for a 6-hour training sequence for preparing paid staff to work effectively with volunteers; includes suggestions for shorter modules, unpaged, $7.00 (designed both as a companion to a videotape of the same name as well as an independent guide; videotape described elsewhere) **ENERGIZE** 5450 Wissahickon Avenue, Philadelphia, PA 19144 215-438-8342

COLLEAGUES: THE VOLUNTEER/EMPLOYEE RELATIONSHIP: A VIDEO

(1990) - a video designed to be used with a workbook of the same name in a six-hour training program addressing volunteer/staff relations; covers the preparation of paid staff before the volunteer arrives, and training on working effectively together, $395 ($699 for both; workbook and companion video/workbook are described elsewhere in this section); preview tape $20 (both preview tapes $25) **ENERGIZE** 5450 Wissahickon Avenue, Philadelphia, PA 19144 215-438-8342

COMMUNITY VOLUNTEER SERVICES ACTION MEMO: TAX DEDUCTIONS

(1980) - facts based on IRS 1978 edition of Income Tax Deduction for Contribution detailing areas relevant to volunteers (uniform, automobile expense, per diem allowance, etc.), 2pp, single copy free **B'nai B'rith International** Community Volunteer Services, 1640 Rhode Island Avenue, NW, Washington, DC 20036 202-857-6580

CONSULTATION REPORT ON OLDER PERSONS AND VOLUNTARY SERVICE

(1973) - report on a meeting of program and other leaders advocating volunteer service for older persons in federal, state, local, church, and other programs to utilize their experience while providing them with opportunities for helping to bring about change, 101pp, $3.00 **Commission on Voluntary Service and Action** 475 Riverside Drive, New York, NY 10027 212-870-2707

CURRICULUM-BASED ASSESSMENT
(1985) - a special issue of *Exceptional Children,* which examines all aspects of curriculum-based assessment as it relates to the education of exceptional children (general, but useful for day care and head start as well as the traditional classroom), 96pp, $7.00 **Council for Exceptional Children** 1920 Association Drive, Reston, VA 22091-1589 703-620-3660

DESIGNING PROGRAMS FOR THE VOLUNTEER SECTOR
(1990) - a five-step process to designing programs that will attract volunteers; includes sections on conducting a program needs assessment, setting program objectives, arranging and planning activities, developing an administrative plan, and evaluating the overall program, 24pp, $5.00 (by mail, $6.00) **Macduff/Bunt Associates** 821 Lincoln Street, Walla Walla, WA 99362 509-529-0244

DEVELOPING AND MANAGING VOLUNTEER PROGRAMS: A GUIDE FOR SOCIAL SERVICE AGENCIES
(1986) - handbook designed to help the volunteer program developer to examine exactly what benefits volunteers can lend to an agency's program; explores the range of volunteer roles that can expand and reinforce the program of an agency citing six volunteer programs as examples; details specifics of obtaining administrative support; addresses the development of a training program for volunteers, supervision, and evaluation; includes 46 references, 190pp, inquire about cost **Charles C. Thomas, Publisher** 2600 South First Street, PO Box 4709, Springfield, IL 62708-4709 217-789-8990

DIMENSIONS OF THE INDEPENDENT SECTOR: A STATISTICAL PROFILE
(Update, Fall 1988) - an update of major national tables covering the size, scope and dimensions of the nonprofit sector through 1986; includes summary tables on giving and volunteering and grants made by foundations and corporations, 40pp, $8.00 **Independent Sector** 1828 L Street, NW, Washington, DC 20036 202-223-8100

DO OR DIE: SURVIVAL FOR NONPROFITS
(1973) - discussion of the "anti-profit" syndrome and how it misleads the not-for-profit organizer; covers other myths, misconceptions, and frequent mistakes; includes overview of how nonprofit organizations should be run to be successful, 102pp, $9.95 **Taft Group** 5130 McArthur Boulevard, NW, Washington, DC 20037 202-966-7086

DONATE ENERGY
(1980) - packet of recruitment materials including brochure, bookmarks (listing 101 volunteer ideas!), mini-posters, "Volunteer Hot line" which lists current volunteer jobs, and a recruitment form created for submission to local newspapers, single packet free (inquire about proceedings of Recruiting - The Ongoing Challenge!, a recent conference) **Volunteer Forum** 50 Prince Street, Rochester, NY 14607 716-275-9800

ECONOMIC IMPACT OF ARKANSAS VOLUNTEERS
(1988) - overview of survey demonstrating how volunteering across the state of Arkansas saved the state almost $67 million dollars; includes sections on methodology and response rate, volunteer categories, and economic impact; appends rosters and charts of responding state agencies, counties, cities and public school districts (study conducted in cooperation with UALR Research and Public Service Division), 48pp, single copy free **Arkansas Office of Volunteers** Department of Human Services, Seventh & Main Streets, Ste 1300, Little Rock, AR 72201 501-682-7540

EFFECTIVE LEADERSHIP IN VOLUNTARY ORGANIZATIONS
(1976) by Brian O'Connell - a detailed handbook on how to get a voluntary association started, with much attention given to identification, motivation and roles of volunteers; includes guidelines on fund raising, staff development, effective meetings, involvement of minorities, evaluation, and long-range goals based, in part, on the experience of two operating voluntary associations, 202pp, $8.95 (hardback) **Association Press** 291 Broadway, New York, NY 10007 212-374-2000

EMPLOYEE VOLUNTEER SURVEY QUESTIONNAIRE
(undated) - a series of 17 questions designed to provide information to *Time's Community Relations Task Force* to help the Task Force explore potential employee volunteer programs; solicits interests, ideas and guidance from employees, 8-panel foldout, questionnaire only, single copy free **Time Incorporated, Community Relations Office** Time and Life Building, Rockefeller Center, New York, NY 10010 212-841-2526

ENVIRONMENTAL SCAN
(1989) - results of an effort by a volunteer task force and planning body to identify and analyze the changing trends that relate to human services, and to assess the United Way's internal structure and capacity to respond to changing needs; covers 4,300-square-mile service area of the United Way of Greater Los Angeles, inquire about cost **United Way of Greater Los Angeles** 621 South Virgil Avenue, Los Angeles, CA 90005-4046 213-736-1300

ESTABLISHING AND MAINTAINING A VOLUNTEER PROGRAM*
(1976) - a manual for establishing a program, selecting staff and volunteers, training, evaluating, etc. Includes sample news release for volunteer recruitment, sample radio/TV announcements, and other aids, 60pp, $10.00 (member $5.00) **American Health Care Association** 1200 Fifteenth Street, NW, Washington , DC 20005 202-833-2050

EVALUATING HEALTH PROMOTION PROGRAMS
(1989) - guidance on designing and conducting evaluation of programs aimed at enhancing individual health - such as drug and alcohol abuse prevention, AIDS education, and cardiac health promotion programs; shows how to overcome common dilemmas encountered - such as assessing community impact; considers a variety of settings including communities, schools and hospitals, and the effectiveness of media campaigns; discusses the influence of public demand for fast solutions, $14.95 (developed by a 4-H Specialist and University of California behavioral science lecturer) **Jossey Bass, Publishers** 350 Sansome Street, San Francisco, CA 94104-1310 415-433-1767

EVALUATION AND CHANGE: A FORUM FOR HUMAN SERVICE DECISION-MAKERS
(irregular) - a journal providing insight into the who/how/what of evaluation and how to base decision-making on its results; makes back issues available, av. 96pp, price per issue varies (av. $4.00) **Evaluation and Change** 501 South Park Avenue, Minneapolis, MN 55415 612-873-8023

EVALUATION: PROMISE AND PERFORMANCE
(1979) by Joseph S. Wholey - a tool for policy-makers to demonstrate how evaluators can help them clarify the intent of a program, and improve efficiency, effectiveness, and responsiveness; discusses the problem in comparing actual performance with expected performance, and other areas of monitoring and measuring programs, 234pp, $9.50 (out-of-print, but loan copies

and/or photocopies are available; inquire about cost) **Urban Institute Press** 2100 M Street, NW, Washington, DC 20037 202-857-8686

EXPLORING VOLUNTEER SPACE: THE RECRUITING OF A NATION

(1980) by Ivan H. Scheier - an analysis of styles of helping participation in terms of ten sets of alternatives; for example:
as individual..........or............with group
continuously...........or..........occasionally
Includes numbers of combinations, variations and gradations of such preferred or natural helping styles to demonstrate the need to engage in a broader range of participatory styles than those in use today, 200pp, $10.95 **VOLUNTEER - The National Center** 1111 North 19th Street, Suite 500, Arlington, VA 22209 703-276-0542

FILTHY RICH & OTHER NONPROFIT FANTASIES: CHANGING THE WAY NONPROFITS DO BUSINESS IN THE 90'S

(1989) - discusses ways in which nonprofits can become successful entrepreneurs while maintaining their ethical standards; contains suggestions for working with corporations and dealing with tax issues; includes case studies, 223pp, $8.95 **Ten Speed Press** PO Box 7123, Berkeley, CA 94707 415-845-8414

FOSTERING VOLUNTEER PROGRAMS IN THE PUBLIC SECTOR

(1990) - practical steps that public agencies can take to foster volunteer involvement in the public sector; describes methods to plan and organize a volunteer program, attract and retain capable volunteers, coordinate the efforts of paid staff and volunteers, assess performance, and improve opportunities for service; details procedures for evaluating and improving the cost-effectiveness of volunteer-based services, 255pp, $26.95 **Jossey Bass, Publishers** 350 Sansome Street, San Francisco, CA 94104 415-433-1767

FROM THE TOP DOWN: THE EXECUTIVE ROLE IN VOLUNTEER PROGRAM SUCCESS

(1986) - a look at volunteer management issues from the executive's perspective; presents volunteers as "non-salaried personnel;" examines the power of the executive to effectively establish policy for and about volunteers, budget funds and other resources, to select volunteer program staff, and to inspire teamwork between volunteers and employees, 1986, $16.75 **ENERGIZE** 5450 Wissahickon Avenue, Philadelphia, PA 19144 215-438-8342

FRONTIERS 1989

(1989) - a compendium of short essays outlining promising fresh perspectives and creative approaches to old issues and problems in the field of volunteerism; draws authors from every area of the field; invites readers to become authors of future editions, 30pp, $6.00 **Center for Creative Community** PO Box 2427, Santa Fe, NM 87504 505-983-8414

THE FUTURE OF THE NONPROFIT SECTOR: CHALLENGES, CHANGES AND POLICY CONSIDERATIONS

(1989) by Virginia A. Hodgkinson, Richard W. Lyman, and Associates - overview of the changing role, scope, and responsibilities of the nonprofit sector; offers in-depth analysis of current trends in the field, and present insights into future challenges and opportunities facing the nonprofit sector; includes sections on volunteering, individual giving, underserved constituencies, commercialization of, and future directions for the nonprofit sector, 546pp, $35.00 **Jossey Bass, Publishers** 350 Sansome Street, San Francisco, CA 94104-1310 415-433-1767

GIRAFFE GAZETTE

(quarterly) - reports of Giraffe's activities across the country and abroad; includes practical advice for effective action, news of meetings, etc., free with membership; others inquire **Giraffe Project** 120 Second Street, PO Box 759, Langley, Whidbey Island, WA 98260 206-221-7989

GIRAFFE INFORMATION PACKET

(undated) - brochures, newspaper articles, nomination information, and other materials describing a program that seeks out and recognizes ordinary people who are "sticking their necks out" to help their communities, unpaged, free **Giraffe Project** 102 Second Street, PO Box 759, Langley, Whidbey Island, WA 98260 206-221-7989

GIRAFFE MEMBERSHIP KIT

(kept current) - packet of information provided to new members describing membership privileges (newsletter subscription, 20% discount on publications and materials, scripts of monthly radio stories, membership card and button, *Giraffe Spotter/Giraffe Sighting* nomination information and forms, etc.), free to new members **Giraffe Project** 120 Second Street, PO Box 759, Langley, Whidbey Island, WA 98260 206-221-7989

GIRAFFE RADIO SCRIPTS

(various dates) - scripts of public service announcements and other appearances and recordings on the various media, unpaged, free to members, others inquire **Giraffe Project** 102 Second Street, PO Box 759, Langley, Whidbey Island, WA 98260 206-221-7989

GIRAFFENALIA CATALOG

(kept current) - illustrated listing of materials available carrying the Giraffe Project logo, including shirts, mugs, T-shirts, etc., free **Giraffe Project** 102 Second Street, PO Box 759, Langley, Whidbey Island, WA 98260 206-221-7989

GIVE FIVE BROCHURE

(1990) - an overview of a campaign that is setting a national standard for individual giving and volunteering, asking Americans to strive for five hours of volunteer time each week and five percent of their annual income to the causes they care about, foldout brochure, free in limited quantities **Independent Sector** 1828 L Street, NW, Washington, DC 20036 202-223-8100

GIVING AND VOLUNTEERING IN THE UNITED STATES: FINDINGS FROM A NATIONAL SURVEY

(1990) - a study by the *Gallup Organization* commissioned by *Independent Sector* detailing the motivations, patterns and satisfactions of giving and volunteering in the U.S.; includes information on who gives and volunteers the most, how much time and money is actually donated, what motivates donors and volunteers, which organizations benefit from this giving, etc., 74pp, $25.00 ($17.50 members) **Independent Sector** 1828 L Street, NW, Washington, DC 20036 202-223-8100

GRAPEVINE

(6/year) - newsletter covering topics of concern to volunteerism such as National Service, interfaith volunteers, "grief-work," college scholarships, communications, relevant books, etc., 8pp, $15/year **VMS/Heritage Arts** 1807 Prairie Avenue, Downers Grove, IL 60515 708-964-1194

GREAT CAREERS: CAREERS/INTERNSHIPS/VOLUNTEER OPPORTUNITIES

(1990) - a career guide written by a team of over 30 college career planning and placement counselors and other staff, with special consideration for those considering service occupations; includes sections on volunteer opportunities, homelessness, hunger, labor unions, legal aid, people with disabilities, media, peace, fundraising, advocacy, education, environment, urban planning, women's issues, and others, 605pp, $35.00 (includes shipping/handling) **Garrett Park Press** PO Box 190, Garrett Park, MD 20896 301-946-2553

GROUP HOMES FOR CHILDREN: TYPES AND CHARACTERISTICS

(1979) - assistance for those with the responsibility of finding the right setting for a particular child who must be placed out of his/her home; discusses group home variables, and how they affect a child in care, 16pp, single copy free **US/HHS - Administration for Children, Youth and Families** PO Box 1182, Washington, DC 20101 202-245-7000

GUIDELINES AND STANDARDS FOR THE FIELD OF VOLUNTEERISM

(1978) Ann Jacobson, Ed. - a handbook, guide and evaluation tool that grew out of a need to bridge the gap between existing practices and desirable goals among those concerned with assisting volunteer efforts; collaboration of over 60 major volunteer organizations has resulted in a blending of common elements that have proven successful in reaching goals; practical areas covered (boards, staff/volunteer work practices, volunteer skill assessment, volunteer retention, etc.) are preceded by an overview of the field and its relationship to public policy, 32pp, $6.00 (postage/handling included; quantity discounts) **Association of Volunteer Centers** 1111 North 19th Street, Suite 500, Arlington, VA 22209 703-276-0542

GUIDELINES AND STANDARDS FOR VOLUNTEER PROGRAMS

(1979) - a compilation of information that includes hard-to-find facts on insurance, minors, laws, public accommodations, accreditation, business/industry, and professional ethics as they relate to volunteers, volunteer administrators, and others in the field; the VAC's mission and policy statements, services and other details of operation are included, 34pp, $4.00 **Volunteer Center of Greater Milwaukee** 600 East Mason Street, Milwaukee, WI 53202 414-273-7887

GUIDELINES FOR INTERVIEWERS

(1979) - a step-by-step outline to help the interviewer find the most effective placement for the volunteer; includes instructions for the receptionist at the arrival and departure of the volunteer, 5pp, $.75 **Mayor's Voluntary Action Center** 61 Chambers Street, New York, NY 10007 212-566-5960

HANDBOOK FOR AGENCY COORDINATORS OF VOLUNTEER PROGRAMS

(1983) - a guide for the agency to clarify the agency/VAC working relationship in areas of security requirements, record-keeping, training, supervision, evaluation, recognition, publicity, agency eligibility, criteria for volunteer jobs, etc.; sample completed forms included, 16pp, $1.00 **Mayor's Voluntary Action Center** 61 Chambers Street, New York, NY 10007 212-566-5950

HANDBOOK OF PROMISING PREVENTION PROGRAMS FOR CHILDREN ZERO TO FIVE YEARS OF AGE

(1987) - overview of nineteen child care centers across the country demonstrating strengths in areas of educational techniques and family support, **National Governors' Association** 444 North Capitol Street, NW, Suite 250, Washington, DC 20001 202-624-5300

HAPPINESS IS...CARING AND SHARING

(1990) - a kit of materials produced in honor of the 40th anniversary of the *Peanuts* cartoon to motivate children in grades four through six to volunteer - a joint project of *United Way of America*, the *American Newspaper Publishers Association (ANPA)*, and *United Media*, syndicator of *Peanuts*; utilizes the resources of the *Newspaper in Education* program of the ANPA Foundation, reaching youth through more than 700 newspapers; includes illustrated guidelines featuring Charlie Brown, Snoopy, and the rest of the gang on how kids can start discussing important social issues and get involved in volunteer activities; suggested activities (in process at press time) include:
- *Help Others Read* - organizing a used-book sale, with proceeds donated to a literacy agency, hospital, nursing home, library, or day-care center; reading to younger children.
- *Make Someone Happy* - collecting and donating used toys to a shelter for homeless families, a children's hospital, or day-care center; making a gift and giving it to someone.
- *Feed the Hungry* - holding a food drive for nonperishable food items and donating them to a food bank or homeless shelter.
- *Make New Friends* - creating a welcome kit for new kids with information about fun places to visit and things to do, school clubs and activities, and after-school activities offered by local agencies such as the *Girl Scouts* and *Boy Scouts*.
- *Make an Old Friend* - doing things for elderly neighbors, like volunteering to shovel their walks after a snowstorm or raking their yards - for free; visiting senior centers.

United Way of America 701 North Fairfax Street, Alexandria, VA 22314-2045 703-836-7850

HEISKELL AWARDS FOR COMMUNITY SERVICE

(undated) - kit of materials describing Time's awards program to honor employees who make "exceptional contributions to equal opportunity and human rights" in their workplace and in the community; includes fact sheet, press releases, profiles of winners, etc. (three winners are involved in areas of boards, organizational leadership, fund-raising, minority recruiting, affirmative action, and other areas), single kit free **Time Incorporated, Community Relations Office** Time and Life Building, Rockefeller Center, New York, NY 10010 212-841-2526

HELPING PEOPLE VOLUNTEER

(undated) - a resource to teach you how to more effectively *help people volunteer*; includes worksheets and an opinion survey to help you determine the specific needs of your volunteer program; provides practical ideas to make the volunteer program manager's job easier, 96pp, $9.95 **YMCA Program Store** PO Box 5077, Champaign, IL 61825-5077 217-351-5077

HORIZONS IN VOLUNTEERISM: THE SERIES

(1989) - a new, annual series built on the theme of volunteerism as a growing phenomenon - one "in which dreams are nurtured and supported, rather than ridiculed or ignored;" includes three books in the 1989 series (described elsewhere): *A Reconstruction of Volunteerism: Exercises for Creative Gadflies; Shapes and Scenarios in the Future of Volunteerism: Forecasting & Creating Your Own;* and *Frontiers 1989* (the final title becoming a standard in each year's series), pages range from 30-35, average cost $6.00 each **Center for Creative Community** PO Box 2427, Santa Fe, NM 87504 505-983-8414

HOW DOES YOUR GARDEN GROW?

(1980) - an overview for the placement agency on the procedures and the mutual benefit to be realized by the placement of volunteers in the agency's overall program (developed by a VISTA Volunteer), 14pp, **Volunteer Center of United Way of Central Iowa** 1111 Ninth Street, Suite 300, Des Moines, IA 50314 515-246-6545

HOW MUCH REALLY IS TAX DEDUCTIBLE? A USER'S GUIDE TO IRS PUBLICATION 1391

(1990) - this publication is designed to help voluntary organizations and foundations and their members in planning for fundraising efforts and preparing materials which solicit contributions; appends a question and answer section and examples, unpaged, $2.00 ($1.40 for IS members), bulk discounts available **Independent Sector** 1828 L Street, NW, Washington, DC 20036 202-223-8100

HOW TO ORGANIZE A MULTI-SERVICE WOMEN'S CENTER

(1976) - a guide to organizing a women's center that is responsive to a wide range of community needs and involves community women in planning and implementing its services, 35pp, $3.50 **Women's Action Alliance** 370 Lexington Avenue, Suite 603, New York, NY 10017 212-779-2846

HOW TO RECEIVE A DELEGATED ASSIGNMENT: SOME USEFUL GUIDELINES

(1989) - tips for employees or volunteers seeking reasons to take on assignments that might become available; offers point-by-point guidelines for accepting such assignments and making them work; includes short self-quiz, 4pp, available in packs of five, $12.00 **ODT, Inc.** PO Box 134, Amherst, MA 01004 413-549-1293

HOW TO START A VAC

(1980) - a composite of the best thinking of members of the Florida VAC Association based on successful techniques and methods in their individual central volunteer operations, inquire about cost **Volunteer Action Center of Broward County** Box 22877, 1300 South Andrews , Fort Lauderdale, FL 33335 305-522-6761

HOW TO VOLUNTEER IN SOCIAL SERVICE AGENCIES

(1982) - guide to roles and relationships of various types of volunteering in several types of agencies; discusses essential traits and qualities necessary in a helping relationship, interviewing, crisis intervention, group work, and theoretical and technical materials used in programs; explores administration from two perspectives: (1) volunteers in administrative positions; and (2) components of the administrative process; includes details regarding definition, techniques, preparation, presentation, evaluation and feedback; appends an index and 28 references, 84pp, inquire about cost **Project SHARE** 7830 Old Georgetown Road, Suite 204, Bethesda, MD 20814 301-231-9539

IAJV IN ACTION

(quarterly) - program profiles, resources, articles, calendar, etc., to keep readers informed of the activities and support services available for volunteer managers and volunteers working in the criminal justice system, 8pp, inquire about cost *[IAJV was formerly the National Association of Volunteers in Criminal Justice.]* **International Association of Justice Volunteerism** Criminal Justice Institute, PO Box 786, Milwaukee, WI 53201 414-229-5630

IMPACT EVALUATION OF THE FOSTER GRANDPARENT PROGRAM ON FOSTER GRANDPARENTS

(1984) - study presenting findings of a three-year evaluation to measure the effects of the Foster Grandparent Program (FGP) on the older volunteers; analyzes effects of participation by comparing them with the Wait-List group on a wide variety of measures; includes findings which indicate that the FGP maintains or improves mental and physical health and social and economic resources of participants (developed by ACTION and D-HHS), 71pp, single copy free **US/ACTION - The Federal Volunteer Agency** 1100 Vermont Avenue, NW, Suite 1100, Washington, DC 20525 202-634-9108

INSTITUTE FOR COMMUNITY SERVICE MANUAL: A PROCESS FOR DEVELOPING AGENCY-BASED VOLUNTEER PROGRAMS

(1973) - outline of a comprehensive plan of volunteer/staff development for agencies wishing to implement their own volunteer staff programs, 122pp, $3.50 **Lutheran Social Service of Minnesota** 2414 Park Avenue, Minneapolis, MN 55404 612-871-0221

INSURANCE PROGRAM: VOLUNTEERS INSURANCE SERVICE

(updated as needed) - general description of the insurance coverages that can be provided to protect volunteers who drive; includes guidelines to pinpoint limitations (e.g., sports clubs, volunteer firemen among those not eligible), includes application form, 8-panel foldout **Volunteers Insurance Service Association/CIMA** 216 South Peyton Street, Alexandria, VA 22314 703-739-9300

INTERFAITH VOLUNTEER CAREGIVERS: A SPECIAL REPORT

(1989) - overview of a program initiated by the Foundation that serves the elderly and disabled through interfaith coalitions; includes summary, background (including information on 25 programs), program implementation, impact, and emerging issues, 18pp, free **Robert Wood Johnson Foundation** PO Box 2316, Princeton, NJ 08543-2316 609-452-8701

JOURNAL OF VOLUNTEER ADMINISTRATION

(quarterly) - professional journal for administrators of volunteer programs, volunteers who lead other volunteers, officers in volunteer organizations, members of volunteer boards, educators or researchers in related fields, and other professionals with an interest in volunteerism; includes articles that cover a wide diversity of program types, settings, and geographical locations, with emphasis on how to apply the experiences of others to your particular setting; topics include program management, model projects, research results, training designs, career development, and a regular abstracts column; articles welcome, 40pp, $24/year ($65/three years; free to members) **Association for Volunteer Administration** PO Box 4584, Boulder, CO 80306 303-497-0238

KEYS TO MAKING A VOLUNTEER PROGRAM WORK

(1982) - guidebook discussing seven key ingredients that make a volunteer program work: (1) good job design; (2) staff commitment; (3) careful screening and selection; (4) appropriate training; (5) good supervision; (6) appropriate surveillance; and (7) systematic evaluation; emphasizes the management area, 82pp, inquire about cost **Arden Publications** 401 Vista Heights Road, Richmond, CA 94805

LEADERSHIP FOR VOLUNTEERING

(1978) - by Harriet H. Naylor - a series of speeches and seminar presentations that appeal for the orderly development of the volunteer potential with emphasis on strong administrative support; includes such topics as volunteer/staff relations, the volunteer as advocate; volunteers in areas of rehabilitation, retirement, welfare, government, etc.; volunteer careers, training, services; the central volunteer operation; and many other relevant subjects in the field, 178pp, $4.50 **Dryden Associates** PO Box 363, Dryden, NY 13053

LET THE SPIRIT FREE

(1983) - a videotape narrated by Earl Holliman, providing an introduction to the vast variety of volunteers representing all age groups and walks of life, filmed on location around the country; includes testimonials by the volunteers, which give insight into the motivation and benefits of being a volunteer, available in several formats, 16mm, Fairchild, Technicolor, MPQ, and a special video cassette copy for those with impaired hearing, any format $150 **United Way of America** 701 North Fairfax Street, Alexandria, VA 22314-2045 703-836-7100

MAKE TIME. MAKE FRIENDS. MAKE A DIFFERENCE. *BE A VOLUNTEER!*

(1990) - overview of the function of the Voluntary Action Center, shopping list of volunteer opportunities, student-oriented volunteer jobs, older person-oriented opportunities, and the procedure following an inquiry by a potential volunteer, 6-panel foldout, free **Prince George's Voluntary Action Center** 6309 Baltimore Avenue, Suite 305, Riverdale, MD 20737 301-779-9444

MAKING A DIFFERENCE

(kept current) - overview of the Center's function, needs, progress, scope, and specific programs such as Long-term Recruitment and Referral; SkillsBank, BoardBank, Corporate Volunteer Project, Group Opportunities, and - at the Longmont satellite office - Dining-Out, a dinner program for nursing home residents, and Icebusters, a sidewalk shoveling program to assist the elderly and handicapped; includes outline of Center-sponsored training events, 8-panel foldout, single copy free **Volunteer Boulder County** 3305 North Broadway, Suite One, Boulder, CO 80304 303-444-4904

MANAGEMENT COMPENSATION REPORT OF VOLUNTARY HEALTH AND HUMAN SERVICE ORGANIZATIONS

(1989) - tracking of 1988 compensation levels, compensation practices and supplemental benefits and perquisites o.. 56 selected management positions (exclusive to nonprofit health and social welfare organizations), unpaged, $25.00 (prepared in collaboration with the National Health Council) **National Assembly of Voluntary Health and Social Welfare Organizations** 1319 F Street, NW, Suite 601, Washington, DC 20004 202-347-2080

MANAGING CHANGE: A GUIDE TO PRODUCING INNOVATION FROM WITHIN

(1989) - a guide addressing the award-winning STEP approach, which stresses the importance of involving employees if significant long-term change is desired, and won a special award from the *Ford Foundation* for the state of Minnesota, 194pp, $14.95 (paper) **Urban Institute Press** 4720 Boston Way, Lanham, MD 20706 301-459-3366

THE METROPOLIS SPEAKS

(undated) - special issue of the *Regional Plan News* giving results of the balloting in the "Choices '76" town meetings, and their implications for the community, 34pp, $2.00 (members $1.40) **Regional Plan Association** 1040 Avenue of the Americas, New York, NY 10018 212-398-1140

MIRROR ON VOLUNTEERISM

(semianually) - a newsletter/journal with invitational articles from both well-known celebrities and "in-the-trenches" executives to provide a twice-yearly reflection on volunteering of the times, Av. 16pp, $15/year **Four-One-One (411)** 7304 Beverly Street, Annandale, VA 22003 703-354-6270

NINE-PART NONPROFIT MANAGEMENT SERIES

(1990) by Brian O'Connell - a management series designed to assist managers in areas of:
- The Role of the Board and Board Members
- Finding, Developing, and Rewarding Good Board Members
- Operating Effective Committees
- Conducting Good Meetings
- The Roles and Relations of the Chief Volunteer and Chief Staff Officers, Board and Staff: Who Does What?
- Recruiting, Encouraging and Evaluating the Chief Staff Officer
- Fund Raising
- Budgeting and Financial Accountability
- Evaluating Results

Arranged in nine separate publications for convenience in use and sharing, 24pp each publication, $5.00 each or $35.00 for nine-part series **Independent Sector** 1828 L Street, NW, Washington, DC 20036 202-223-8100

NO EXCUSES: THE TEAM APPROACH TO VOLUNTEER MANAGEMENT

(1981) - an aid addressed to part-time administrators who manage volunteers without salaried staff; discusses ways to recruit a management team from inside the organization and the surrounding community; defines roles, problems, delegation, and coordination such a team faces; includes detailed job description for the Director of Volunteers, 64pp, $8.75 (this is a *Volunteer Energy Series* publication; others described elsewhere) **ENERGIZE** 5450 Wissahickon Avenue, Philadelphia, PA 19144 215-438-6342

NONPROFIT AND VOLUNTARY SECTOR QUARTERLY

(quarterly) - scholarly journal dedicated to exploring the dynamics, needs, and concerns of today's nonprofit and voluntary organizations; draws together work being done in sociology, psychology, public administration, and management, among others, in areas of national trends, complex organizations, fundraising practices, philanthropy, demographics, management, and interrelationships with for-profit and government organizations, etc., 100+pp, $45/year individual; $75/year institution, agency, or library (sponsored by the Association of Voluntary Action Scholars) **Jossey Bass, Publishers** 350 Sansome Street, San Francisco, CA 94104-1310 415-433-1740

THE NONPROFIT BOARD'S ROLE IN RISK MANAGEMENT: MORE THAN BUYING INSURANCE

(1990) - the pros and cons of insurance; explains and demystifies the fundamentals of risk management, and the board's role in understanding and controlling risks inherent in nonprofit organizations, 20pp, $5.95 **National Center for Nonprofit Boards** 1225 Nineteenth Street, NW, Suite 340, Washington, DC 20036 202-452-6262

THE NONPROFIT ORGANIZATION HANDBOOK

(1980) Ed. in Chief, Tracy B. Connors - a comprehensive practical guide for setting up and managing a nonprofit organization based on numerous real life examples; includes some 40 pages on the volunteer component by Eva Schindler-Rainman, and major sections on fund raising, public relations and other areas; appendix takes samples from an operating organization to outline some of the required record-keeping procedure, 740pp, $44.95 (hardback) **McGraw-Hill Book Store** 1221 Avenue of the Americas, New York, NY 10020 212-997-4100

NONPROFIT TIMES

(monthly) - extensive coverage of issues of concern to nonprofit organizations; includes topics such as volunteers, boards, foundations, churches, National Service, Red Cross, funding for women, direct mail, recognition, liability, surveys, operating funds, fundraising, drugs, housing, dealing with IRS, public relations, management, computerized recordkeeping, relevant books, etc. (management section includes material from *Support Centers of America* and a bi-monthly column titled *On Volunteers* by Susan Ellis), Av. 56pp, free to full-time nonprofit directors in the U.S., Canada, and Europe; others $39.00/year **Davis Information Group** PO Box 870, Wantagh, NY 11793 516-781-7032

NONPROFIT WORLD
(bimonthly) - a journal covering major aspects of the nonprofit community with topics in areas such as fundraising, interns, annual reports, organization finances, postal rates/joint mailing, boards, legal counsel, relevant books, public relations, volunteer management, computerization, recordkeeping, etc., 40pp, $59/year (single copies, $10 each) **Society for Nonprofit Organizations** 6314 Odana Road, Suite One, Madison, WI 53719 608-274-9777

NVAVA NEWSLETTER
(monthly) - news of events and concerns of a regional affiliate of the International Association for Volunteer Administration; includes the President's column, volunteer job descriptions, conference information, member spotlight, committee news, state and local training events, meeting reviews, new member application, etc., 6pp, sample copy free (also request "What is NVAVA?" - a brochure describing this regional association) **Northern Virginia Association for Volunteer Administration** PO Box 2247 , Merrifield, VA 22116-2247 703-534-5700

OBTAINING CITIZEN FEEDBACK
(1973) - description of present feedback devices available; uses of citizen surveys; different ways to undertake surveys, funding sources, survey illustrations, 105pp, $8.75 **Urban Institute Press** 4720 Boston Way, Lanham, MD 20706 301-459-3366

101 IDEAS FOR VOLUNTEER PROGRAMS
(1990) - ideas (949 of them) in 50 categories including planning, recruitment, screening, training, supervision, recognition, public relations, staff relations, marketing, and more to assist the volunteer manager, unpaged, $5.00 **VMS/Heritage Arts** 1807 Prairie Avenue, Downers Grove, IL 60515 312-964-1194

101 TIPS FOR VOLUNTEER RECRUITMENT
(1990) - hundreds of ideas in 45 categories including motivation, options, assessment, factors, overcoming objections, sites, getting youth, low income and macho males, recruiting for difficult jobs, boards, membership groups, etc., to assist the manager in the tough job of recruitment, unpaged, $8.00 **VMS/Heritage Arts** 1807 Prairie Avenue, Downers Grove, IL 60515 312-954-1194

THE 1, 2, 3 OF EVALUATION
(1989) - guide containing three evaluation tools to help nonprofit organization leaders, fundraisers and planners establish better controls, plan more realistically and create a better climate for telling the organization's story and thus attracting more funds (tools were tested by NCIB for 10 years), unpaged, $10.00 **National Charities Information Bureau** 19 Union Square West, New York, NY 10003-3395 212-929-6300

ORGANIZATIONAL NEEDS ASSESSMENT SURVEY PACKET
(undated) - a "tool kit" enabling an organization to mount an ongoing evaluation and needs survey, including:
- Organizational Needs Assessment Survey - survey, answer sheet, and talley sheet, set of 20, #UCR531, $10.00
- *Organizational Needs Assessment Survey - Answer Sheets (Advisory Boards)* - set of 20 sheets, #UCR0531, $4.00
- *Organizational Needs Assessment Survey - Group Tally Sheet Poster* - wall poster for tallying data, #URC3179, $1.75 each

United Way of America 701 North Fairfax Street, Alexandria, VA 22314-2045 703-836-7100

PATTERNS FOR PARTNERSHIP
(1980) - rights and responsibilities of volunteer center, agency and volunteer; agency eligibility policy; sample three-way agreement signed by volunteer center, agency and volunteer, 7pp, $2.00

Volunteer Center of United Way 700 Sixth Avenue, Hawley Building, Des Moines, IA 50309 515-282-5100

PICA NEWSLETTER
(monthly) - a newsletter designed to keep nonprofit organizations informed about effective utilization of microcomputer technology for their organizations; includes information on training, both on-site and in laboratories, and relevant publications, 8pp, single copy free **Public Interest Computer Association** 1025 Connecticut Avenue, NW, Suite 1015, Washington, DC 20036 202-775-1588

PLANNING: AN ORIENTATION FOR SOCIAL AGENCIES
(1989) - overview of the planning process with special emphasis on accreditation and the Code of Ethics; relates the process to Catholic Charities agency planning, including its Cadre Report; reviews resources and appends a bibliography and planning worksheets for nonprofits, 60pp, $7.00 **Catholic Charities USA** Communications Department, 1219 F Street, NW, Washington, DC 20004 202-639-8400

POVERTY IN RURAL AMERICA: A NATIONAL OVERVIEW
(1989) - a report examining the extent of poverty in various segments of the population, and providing a geographical breakdown on rural poverty, 36pp, $7.00 **Center on Budget and Policy Priorities** 236 Massachusetts Avenue, NE, Washington, DC 20002 202-544-0591

PRACTICAL PROGRAM EVALUATION FOR STATE AND LOCAL GOVERNMENT OFFICIALS
(2nd ed., 1981) - an aid for developing program evaluation capabilities; covers identification of program objectives, data collection, program effectiveness, etc., 124pp, $10.50 **Urban Institute Press** 4720 Boston Way, Lanham, MD 20706 301-459-3366

PREPARING FOR AN AGING SOCIETY (DISKETTE)
(1989) - a demonstration diskette on a computer program designed to project information about health, financial status, and number of elderly in a given community for as long a period as 70 years, using data from county, state, and Census Bureau population figures; runs on any IBM or IBM-compatible microcomputer which has 640 RAM and graphic capabilities, free to United Ways, others inquire (also ask about cost of the computer program) **Aging Futures Project** United Way of America, 701 North Fairfax Street, Alexandria, VA 22314-2045 703-836-7100, Ext. 538

PROFESSIONAL BUSINESS SEMINARS
(intermittent) - a booklet describing educational seminars that incorporate lectures, roundtable discussions, videotapes, films, audiovisual presentations, overhead slides, brochures, reference materials, charts, and other materials to help bulk mail users select the most efficient mail program for their specific types of operations; seminars held in 39 locations around the country, 12pp, free **US/PS - Mailer Education Center** PO Box 836, Windsor, CT 06006-0836 203-285-7030

PROFESSIONAL ETHICS IN VOLUNTEER SERVICES ADMINISTRATION
(1975) Carol G. Moore, Ed. - an ethics statement for the field of volunteer administration; sections cover philosophy of volunteerism, human dignity, self-determination, mutuality, privacy, staff relationships, social responsibility, and professional responsibility, $2.00 ($1.50 for AVA members) **Association for Volunteer Administration** PO Box 4584, Boulder, CO 80306 303-497-0238

PROGRAM ANALYSIS FOR STATE AND LOCAL GOVERNMENTS

(2nd ed., 1987) - discussion of three major specific applications common to most governments: considering alternative service delivery approaches such as contracting, analyzing service productivity, and making capital improvement choices; builds also on the first edition of 1976, which explored ways in which better and more useful information can be provided for program and policy decisions (addressed to public officials, but useful for anyone charged with program evaluation), 184pp, $12.95 (paper); $29.25 (cloth) **Urban Institute Press** 4720 Boston Way, Lanham, MD 20706 301-459-3366

PROGRAM PLANNING AND EVALUATION IN COMMUNITY-BASED AGENCIES

(1978) - guide for program managers designed in a workbook format to help them evaluate progress toward goals; includes intermittent instructions and worksheets to create a "learn by doing" atmosphere throughout the proposal, budget, and planning stages before embarking on evaluation procedures, 215pp, $10.00 **Texas Tech Research and Training Center in Mental Retardation** Box 4510 , Texas Tech University, Lubbock, TX 79409 806-742-3131

PROJECT OUTREACH DAY

(1989) - guide for developing a one-day event designed to get the entire campus involved in community service; includes campus profiles, publicity ideas, and planning tips, $5.00 **Campus Outreach Opportunity League (COOL)** 386 McNeal Hall, University of Minnesota, St. Paul, MN 55108-1011 612-624-3018

PROOF POSITIVE: DEVELOPING SIGNIFICANT VOLUNTEER RECORDKEEPING SYSTEMS: 1990 EDITION

(Rev. 1990) - a presentation of the basic elements of a volunteer recordkeeping system, and guidelines for developing forms and procedures to suit the needs of individual programs - with a new chapter on computers in the 1990 update; includes application forms, volunteer fact cards, individual and group volunteer folders, assignment logs, time and activity reports, etc., 68pp, $8.75 (this is a *Volunteer Energy Series* publication; others described elsewhere) **ENERGIZE** 5450 Wissahickon Avenue, Philadelphia, PA 19144 215-438-8342

RECOGNITION PACKET*

(kept current) - materials for a volunteer awards ceremony, including invitation, nomination list, parade poster, etc., $1.50 **Volunteer Center of Lincoln*** 216 Centennial Mall South, Lincoln, NE 68508 402-474-6218

A RECONSIDERATION OF VOLUNTEERISM: EXERCISES FOR CREATIVE GADFLIES

(1989) - nine exercises for the encouragement and support of creative approaches to volunteerism; includes sections based on the CHALLENGE series: *Questioning the Question, The Power of Assumptions, The Freedom to Dream; Getting Out of the Groove: Avoiding Creativity Traps in Pursuit of the Possible*, etc., 35pp, $6.00 **Center for Creative Community** PO Box 2427, Santa Fe, NM 87504 505-98308414

RECONSIDERING LEGAL LIABILITY AND INSURANCE FOR NONPROFIT ORGANIZATIONS

(1989) - a look at all sides of the issue of legal liability and insurance to provide readers with the foundation for reaching their own conclusions and developing their own strategies; appends surveys, laws, and recommendations; includes bibliography, 213pp, paperback, $9.95 (postage/handling $3.50 first copy, $1.00 additional copies) **Society for Nonprofit Organizations** 6314 Odana Road, Suite 1, Madison , WI 53719 608-274-9777

RECRUITING AND TRAINING VOLUNTEERS

(1981) - handbook defining recruitment methods, selection, orientation, placement, and training; examines ways of introducing volunteers to existing programs, planning future programs incorporating volunteers, myths and fears about volunteers, and the six types of working climates that affect volunteer participation: open, autonomous, controlled, familiar, paternalistic, and closed; illustrates discussions throughout with examples, charts, sample forms, diagrams, and case studies; appends index and bibliography, 150pp, inquire about cost **Project SHARE** 7830 Old Georgetown Road, Suite 204, Bethesda, MD 20814 301-231-9539

RECRUITING, TRAINING AND MOTIVATING VOLUNTEER WORKERS

(Rev. 1990) - by Arthur R. Pell - guide for professional staff and volunteer leaders on finding, attracting, interviewing, selecting and placing volunteer workers, as well as rejecting diplomatically those who do not fit in; includes in revised edition orientation and training on small budgets, techniques of motivating and wupervising volunteers to keep enthusiasm high and turnover low, and how volunteers can be of maximum benefit to the organization, 62pp, $4.95 **Pilot Books** 103 Cooper Street, Babylon, NY 11702 516-422-2225

RECRUITING VOLUNTEERS: THE GRIZZLY CREEK SOLUTION

(1989) - award-winning audiovisual presentation for recruiters of volunteers that serves as the centerpiece of a two-and-a-half-hour workshop, but can be used separately or adapted to meet unique needs; offers a simple five-step process designed to make recruitment more effective, presented in the form of a drama that sends the citizens of Grizzly Creek on a search for a new volunteer sheriff; includes comprehensive instructor's manual, reproducible handouts for "take-home" use, and other materials (produced for the Boy Scouts of Canada using a cast of well-known Canadian actors), 16 minutes, $345 first copy, $150 additional copies, preview tape $25, conference planners call for group showings/costs (primary distributor: Haines Elliott Marketing Services, 1020 Southport Road, SW, Calgary, Alberta T2W 4X9) **Heritage Arts/VMS Systems** 1807 Prairie Avenue, Downers Grove, IL 60515 708-964-1194

RISK MANAGEMENT FOR VOLUNTEER PROGRAMS

(1990) - coverage of tort claims, liability management, risk reduction strategies, the importance of by-laws, policies, and procedures, plus *How to Create a Paper Trail;* appends worksheets that can be used by risk management teams, and sample documents for such programs, 132pp, $19.95 (by mail, $23.00) **Macduff/Bunt Associates** 821 Lincoln Street, Walla Walla, WA 99362 509-529-0244

SELF-ASSESSMENT SYSTEM FOR SCHOOL VOLUNTEER PROGRAMS

(1979) Senior Editor, Ivan H. Scheier - systematic assessment process for improving specific management functions for a program which brings community adult volunteers into a high school setting, 190pp, $6.00 **VOLUNTEER - The National Center** Volunteer Readership, 1111 North 19th Street, Suite 500, Arlington, VA 22209 703-276-0542

SELF-HELP ACCOUNTING: A GUIDE FOR THE VOLUNTEER TREASURER

(1989) - how-to guide for the treasurer of a small organization without accounting background; includes sample forms and examples to help in "keeping the books" and handling cash and financial reports, 104pp, $18.75 **ENERGIZE** 5450 Wissahickon Avenue, Philadelphia, PA 19144 215-438-8342

SHAPES AND SCENARIOS IN THE FUTURE OF VOLUNTEERISM: FORECASTING & CREATING YOUR OWN FUTURE

(1989) - an introductory orientation to purposes, paradoxes and pitfalls in the futuring process; includes seven strategies for the do-it-yourself futurist in volunteerism; e.g., *Threat Strategy, Visualizing Volunteer Futures, Seeing Yourself as Somebody's Ancestor,* etc.; presents these topics as practical procedures designed to be easily handled by any practitioner, 35pp, $6.00 **Center for Creative Community** PO Box 2427, Santa Fe, NM 87504 505-983-8414

STANDARDS FOR CENTRAL VOLUNTEER COORDINATING SERVICES

(1975) - guidelines for local communities interested in developing and maintaining organized volunteer recruitment, training and referral services; sections on Organizational Framework (governing body, location in nonprofit organization or government agency, financing, staff, facilities, etc.) and Program Components (recruitment, referral, follow-up, training, evaluation, advocacy, etc.) serve separate purposes when appropriate, but are intended to be interrelated to comprise an effective system, 15pp, $1.50 plus postage/handling (quantity discounts) **United Way of America** 701 North Fairfax Street, Alexandria, VA 22314-2045 703-836-7100

STANDARDS FOR DIRECT SERVICE VOLUNTEER PROGRAMS

(1980) - guidelines based on national standards; includes outline of Self Evaluation/Certification Program, 6-panel foldout, single copy free **United Way of San Diego County** 4699 Murphy Canyon Road, PO Box 23543, San Diego, CA 92123-0543 619-492-2000

SUCCESSFUL VOLUNTEER INVOLVEMENT (TENTATIVE TITLE)

(1991) by Ivan H. Scheier - a combination of revised material developed over the last two decades by this distinguished volunteer leader and author, and new material addressing "cutting-edge" issues; includes practical information on the start-up of organized volunteer programs in agencies, an exploration of the "secret sectors" of volunteerism, including all-volunteer groups and informal volunteering, and creating the best future for leadership of volunteers, in process at press time, approximately 300pp, inquire about cost **ENERGIZE** 5450 Wissahickon Avenue, Philadelphia, PA 19144 215-438-8342

SUPER VOLUNTEERS!/SMALL WORLD NEWSLETTER

(quarterly) - the newsletter of *Super Volunteers!* who are children ages four to seventeen who form teams of 12 or more youth to mount community projects; editors are the youth themselves and stories are both volunteer and issue themes; one guest issue a year features adults who share their ideas and experiences in volunteerism with young subscribers; wordfind, crosswords, and other games are included as space permits; $15/year (request free sample back issue as supply lasts) **Four-One-One (411)** 7304 Beverly Street, Annandale, VA 22003 703-354-6270

SURVEY OF NONPROFIT ASSOCIATIONS

(1990) - a survey commissioned by the *California Association of Nonprofits* in conjunction with *Encouraging Beginnings,* a conference of associations of nonprofits; identifies new structural mechanisms to enhance the resource base of charitable organizations; includes characteristics of the organizations which completed the survey (purpose, age and size, governance, finances, programs/services, rating of state support for nonprofits, etc.) and concerns (insurance plans, purchasing discount programs, etc.) and details on what they have in common (providing a greater variety of services, relying on membership fees, etc.) which would help to profile - and thus meet the needs of - today's nonprofit

organizations, 36+pp, $3.00 postpaid **Center for Public Policy** 1731 Connecticut Avenue, NW, Suite 300, Washington, DC 20009-1146 202-667-1313

THANK YOU VOLUNTEERS

(undated) - special issue of newsletter demonstrating one way a small center can recognize volunteers without added expense, yet in a meaningful and visible way, 4pp, single copy free **Volunteer Center of Memphis** 203 South McLean Boulevard, Memphis, TN 38104 901-276-8655

THE THIRD AMERICA: THE EMERGENCE OF THE NONPROFIT SECTOR IN THE UNITED STATES

(1989) by Michael O'Neill - a guide to understanding the complex and diverse nonprofit sector within the United States; identifies and discusses the major subsectors - religion, private education and research, health care and other areas - and describes concerns as they relate to each (funding, policy, historical development, etc.); offers insights into the direction, growth and role of the third sector during the next 25 years, 215pp, $22.95 **Jossey Bass, Publishers** 350 Sansome Street, San Francisco, CA 94104-1310 415-433-1767

THIS IS HOW WE SERVE

(1980) - brief descriptions of services in three areas: Information and Referral, Advocacy, and Training, 10pp, single copy free **United Way of San Diego County** 4699 Murphy Canyon Road, PO Box 23543, San Diego, CA 92123-0543 619-492-2000

TOGETHER: VOLUNTEER-TO-VOLUNTEER RELATIONSHIPS

(1989) - a guide to 12 different group training designs to be mixed and matched by the volunteer who has taken on leadership responsibilities in his/her work with other volunteers, unpaged, $7.00 (designed both as a companion to a videotape of the same name and as an independent guide) **ENERGIZE** 5450 Wissahickon Avenue, Philadelphia, PA 19144 215-438-8342

TOGETHER: VOLUNTEER-TO-VOLUNTEER RELATIONSHIPS: A VIDEO

(1989) - a video in a series of two designed to be used with a workbook/guide describing 12 different group training styles for mixing and matching at the discretion of the volunteer manager in the total process of working with volunteers, $395 (both $699; workbook and companion video/workbook program are described elsewhere in this section); preview tape, $20 ($25 for both preview tapes) **ENERGIZE** 5450 Wissahickon Avenue, Philadelphia, PA 19144 215-438-8342

USING THE VOLUNTEER EXPECTATIONS SURVEY TOOL (VEST)

(1989) - a survey tool with instructions on the two important components of conducting a survey: administering the survey to get accurate, objective data; and tabulating and analyzing the results to get the information needed; includes two-part questionnaire: (1) for chief professional officers and selected staff; (2) for volunteer leaders, 8pp, inquire about cost **United Way of America** 701 North Fairfax Street, Alexandria, VA 22314-2045 703-836-7100

VAC NEWS

(quarterly) - news of conferences, programs, awards, workshops, activities in both home and satellite offices, and upcoming events (calendar), 4pp w/inserts, free subscription **Prince George's Voluntary Action Center** 6309 Baltimore Avenue, Suite 305, Riverdale, MD 20737 301-779-9444

VIRGINIA LEGISLATION RELATED TO VOLUNTEERISM: 1990

(1990) - listing with annotations of 18 bills passed by the 1990 Virginia General Assembly; covers release time, motor vehicles, donations of food to the needy, parental involvement in school programs, gleaning, etc., one page, free **Virginia Division of Volunteerism** 805 East Broad Street, Sixth Floor, Richmond, VA 23219 804-786-1431

VOLUNTARISM: A NATIONAL OVERVIEW

(1985) - a survey commissioned by *The Rockefeller Brothers Fund* to explore the charitable giving and volunteer behavior of Americans (conducted by an independent survey group and published by *Independent Sector*); includes findings in areas such as time volunteered, dollar value of contributed time, reasons for volunteering, who volunteers, etc., inquire about availability and cost **Independent Sector** 1828 L Street, NW, Washington, DC 20036 202-223-8100

VOLUNTARISM AT THE CROSSROADS

(1976) - Examination of the idea that Voluntarism is at a crossroads, with political, economic and social forces impacting on it - political forces such as the economy, changing relationships with government, the changing status and role of volunteers, and lack of public understanding and societal forces such as the increasing scale of society, expanding acceptance of the concept that all people have a right to participate in decisions affecting them, and the growing interdependence of all persons; provides historical perspective of voluntarism, defines the roots of voluntarism, the scope and extent of voluntary efforts, and roles of volunteers versus professionals; examines the impact of internal and external forces; appends index, 262pp, inquire about cost **Family Service America** 11700 West Lake Park Drive, Milwaukee, WI 53224 414-359-2111

VOLUNTARY ACTION CENTER-AGENCY INTERACTION

(kept current) - a collection of forms, proposed projects to agencies, orientation guidelines, fact sheets on training, news clippings, letters, etc., providing a look at the working arrangements possible between the VAC and the agency, approx. 40pp, single copy free **Voluntary Action Center of Greensboro** 1301 North Elm Street, Greensboro, NC 27401 919-373-1633

VOLUNTARY PARTICIPATION AMONG WOMEN IN THE UNITED STATES

(1976) - overview of volunteer activities from 1950 to 1976 in bibliographic form; covers all areas of volunteerism and provides insight and ideas into the changing roles and increasing involvement of women in communities across the country, and the areas that need more attention by today's volunteer leaders, 35pp, $3.00 (prepaid) **Center for the American Woman and Politics** Wood Lawn, Nielson Campus, New Brunswick, NJ 08901 201-828-2210

VOLUNTARY SECTOR IN BRIEF

(1979) - Assessment of the status of the voluntary sector in 1978 based on a review of the literature, questionnaires, and interviews; provides overview of results which found that the voluntary sector is divided into four parts: (1) organizations enjoying tax-exempt status to which contributions are tax-deductible; (2) activist organizations, some of which enjoy tax-exempt status; (3) human support groups directed toward meeting unique individual needs; and (4) trade associations primarily serving economic or membership interests; emphasizes first two groups to map major issues of the voluntary sector, includes footnotes and bibliography, 42pp, inquire about cost **Academy for Educational Development** 100 Fifth Avenue, New York, NY 10019 212-243-1110

VOLUNTAS: THE PLACE OF VOLUNTEERS...A PLACE OF DREAMS

(1989) - overview of the progress of a participative plan initiated by Dr. Ivan H. Scheier, an internationally-known leader in volunteerism, to enlist the entire volunteer community in erection of the first building entirely dedicated to volunteers and their leaders, and expected to be built largely by volunteers, donated materials, and proceeds from a dedication fund created by contributions; includes in existing blueprints a library dedicated to Harriet H. Naylor (one of the founders of modern volunteerism), a museum, overnight visiting facilities, a time capsule to be sealed in late 1990, and other features to provide a living symbol of volunteering and possibly lead to a University on Volunteerism, packet of materials, including architect's sketch, free **Center for Creative Community** PO Box 2427, Santa Fe, NM 87504 505-983-8414

VOLUNTEER!

(1990) - a kit of motivational materials including an 8-page booklet listing responsibilities and rights of all parties to the volunteer relationship - the volunteer, the center, and the agency; includes a brochure *Have A Heart,* which provides a sampling of the types of volunteer positions available to individuals and groups in areas of education, health, mental health, legal rights, crime prevention, recreation, transportation, psychosocial support, and communictions (a speakers bureau), materials may vary as available, unpaged, single kit free **Volunteer Center/United Way At Work** 12 East Park Street, PO Box 1585, Stockton, CA 95201 209-943-0870

VOLUNTEER CENTER DEVELOPMENT KIT

(1990) - a general introduction to the role and mission of *Volunteer Centers,* the need for their existence, a "how-to" method of getting one started, and guidelines for its development, expansion, and funding [developed in consultation with the *National Volunteer Center Advisory Council*]; includes some 30 items covering bylaws and articles of incorporation, *101 Ways to Fund a Volunteer Center,* guidelines for partnerships with business/industry, sample forms, skillsbank information, profile of the Board of Directors, etc., unpaged kit, $35.00 **VOLUNTEER - The National Center** 1111 N. Nineteenth Street, Suite 500, Arlington, VA 22209 703-276-0542

VOLUNTEER CENTERS: GEARING UP FOR THE 1990'S

(1989) by Susan J. Ellis - a manual outlining the step-by-step process for starting and running a successful Volunteer Center in the community; includes sections on making the Center more than a clearinghouse, the four major constituencies of a Center, the services most commonly offered by Centers, 25 out-of-the-ordinary service ideas, relationships with United Way and other funding sources or sponsors, starting a databank, and recruiting volunteers, 92pp, $20.00 **United Way of America** Volunteer and Outreach Services, 701 North Fairfax Street, Alexandria, VA 22314-2045 703-836-7100

THE VOLUNTEER COMMUNITY: CREATIVE USE OF HUMAN RESOURCES

(2nd ed. 1975) by Eva Schindler-Rainman and Ronald Lippitt - an overview of ways to mobilize and use volunteer energy effectively in the community, social trends, volunteer motivation, recruitment/orientation/training, the training of trainers, functions and role of the volunteer administrator, community leadership, and the future of volunteerism, 176pp, $9.50 **University Associates** 8517 Production Avenue, San Diego, CA 92121 619-578-5900

VOL-UN-TEER CON-NEC-TION

(1990) - a recruitment piece with its cover defining the words *volunteer* and *connection* - and its contents urging community residents to "make the connection" and look into the many volunteer opportunities listed with the Center from over 400 community-service organizations in Morris County, 6-panel foldout, single copy free **Voluntary Action Center of Morris County** 36 South Street, Morristown, NJ 07960 201-538-7200

VOLUNTEER COORDINATORS: OCCUPATIONAL BRIEF
(1990) - one of a series of occupational briefs written to conform to seventh-grade reading index for easy understanding by high school students; enlists professional experts to review the material in each brief to ensure that it is up-to-date and accurate; serves career education offices of schools and colleges, career placement centers, and libraries throughout the country; maintains a bank of more than 600 occupational briefs, including "Volunteer Coordinators" for the first time in 1990, draft only, inquire about availability and cost (in process, being reviewed at press time by *Four-One-One* and other leading organizations in the field of volunteerism), **Chronicle Guidance Publications** Aurora Street, PO Box 1190, Moravia, NY 13116-1190 315-497-0330

VOLUNTEER: EARN GRADUATION CREDIT IN YOUR COMMUNITY
(1990) - an overview for parents of the *X67 Student Volunteer Program* of the *Boulder Valley Schools,* which enables students to earn high school credit by doing a variety of volunteer jobs in the community, with attention to providing practical experience outside the classroom, and self-esteem, 6-panel foldout, free **X67 Student Volunteer Program** 6500 Arapahoe Avenue, PO Box 9011, Boulder, CO 80301 303-447-1010

VOLUNTEER EXPERIENCE: IT COUNTS!
(1980) - overview of the steps one large city has taken to permit documentation of volunteer experience on an equal par with employment background; includes sample volunteer record, letters, and other documentation, 24pp, single copy free **United Way of San Diego** 4699 Murphy Canyon Road, PO Box 23543, San Diego , CA 92123-0543 619-492-2000

VOLUNTEER HANDBOOK
(1978) - a resource guide on the benefits of volunteer services to the agency, the community, and the volunteer; questions and answers on what often stops volunteer programs before they start; basic guidelines for establishing and maintaining a volunteer program; detailed case studies of successful volunteer programs in existence nationwide, and publications and agencies that can help before, during and after setting up a volunteer program, 45pp, single copy free **US/DoI - National Park Service** Information Exchange, 18th and C Streets, NW, Washington, DC 20240 202-343-4747

VOLUNTEER INCENTIVES PROGRAM
(undated) - discussion of the Volunteer Incentives Program (VIP), a demonstration program administered by the Oneida County Office for the Aging in Utica, New York; emphasizes serving the rural elderly; describes the project's three components: (1) business/industry involvement involving employees as volunteers; (2) service organization involvement providing donations of time and money; and (3) public and parochial school involvement making community service a part of the K-12 curriculum; examines the training, program materials, and opportunities for leadership roles offered to potential volunteers; discusses results of all three efforts (developed by Oneida County Office on Aging and the Administration on Aging/D-HHS), 39pp, inquire about cost **US/DoC - National Technical Information Service** 5285 Port Royal Road, Springfield, VA 22151 703-557-4650

VOLUNTEER MANUAL
(updated as needed) - orientation for volunteers providing an

overview of the Association's volunteer services, the Board of Directors, volunteer program policy, job descriptions, categories of services, steering committee function, other organizations volunteer should know about, etc., $4.00 (other materials will be included with manual free of charge as available) **Association for Jewish Children of Philadelphia** 1301 Spencer Street, Philadelphia, PA 19141 215-549-9000

VOLUNTEER OPPORTUNITIES
(1990) - information on eleven of the Society's volunteer assignments, including bookshop, Greenhouse, grounds, tour guide, school ecology project, seminars, Birdathon, speakers' bureau, birdseed sales, holiday fair, and library; gives brief description and contact information; one page, free **Audubon Naturalist Society** 8940 Jones Mill Road, Chevy Chase, MD 20815 301-652-5964

VOLUNTEER PROTECTION ACT PACKET
(1990) - information on H.R. 911 and S.520, both being considered by the federal legislature in Washington, which encourage states to enact laws to protect volunteers from personal financial liability related to their service, unpaged, free **National Coalition for Volunteer Protection** 426 C Street, NE, Washington, DC 20002 202-544-1880

VOLUNTEER RECRUITING AND RETENTION: A MARKETING APPROACH
(1990) - a step-by-step approach to the recruiting and retention of volunteers, with the first seven steps explaining a marketing approach; includes sections on needs assessments, promotion, volunteer recruiting teams, training, etc., 196pp, $24.95 (by mail, $28.00) **Macduff/Bunt Associates** 821 Lincoln Street, Walla Walla, WA 99362 509-529-0244

"VOLUNTEER - THANK YOU" SWEEPSTAKES
(1979) - a recognition program which calls on local merchants to provide gifts for a drawing reserved for the community's volunteers, and provides a special postcard of thanks for all volunteers; includes information on 1978 program (on TV) and 1979 program (in a shopping mall), 5pp, single copy free **ENERGIZE** 5450 Wissahickon Avenue, Philadelphia, PA 19144 215-438-8342

VOLUNTEER! THE COMPREHENSIVE GUIDE TO VOLUNTARY SERVICE IN THE U.S. AND ABROAD
(1988-89) - a joint project of the *Council on International Educational Exchange* and the *Commission on Voluntary Service and Action,* this book is designed to link people who want to serve with those who need their services on a full-time basis; indexed by skills, location, length of service, opportunities for volunteers under 18, and volunteer opportunities for the disabled; includes an overview of voluntary service, suggested readings, and a list of private organizations that sponsor voluntary service projects, $6.95 plus $1.35 shipping cost (5 or more copies, $5.50/each plus $.25 shipping for additional copies) **Commission on Voluntary Service and Action** Volunteer! Distribution, Box 347, Newton, KS 67114 316-283-5100

VOLUNTEER TODAY
(bimonthly) - a national newsletter featuring articles and other information on recruiting, retention, training, communication, and late-breaking news affecting the volunteer community, 8pp, $20.00/year **Macduff/Bunt Associates** 821 Lincoln Street, Walla Walla, WA 99362 509-529-0244

VOLUNTEER 2000 STUDY
(1988-9) - an award-winning study presenting a range of critical

findings and issues in volunteerism and volunteer administration confronting the American Red Cross now and into the next century, and the history of volunteerism in the American Red Cross since its inception; includes three volumes:

- *Volume I* - recommendations based on research to determine ways to enhance volunteer involvement and development within the organization and to assure a leadership role for the Red Cross within the nonprofit sector for the enhancement of volunteerism; bases findings on close to 1,000 structured interviews covering a broad scope of volunteer issues, and a variety of quantitative and qualitative information from internal and external resources.
- *Volume II* - a more complete set of findings and tables than in Volume I, including findings that are over and beyond those that led directly to the recommendations in the previous volume, dealing with the social, economic, demographic, and philosophical trends in the U.S. as a whole, and in the nonprofit sector in particular.
- *Volume III* - the history of voluntarism in the American Red Cross since its inception, providing a context from which to view current developments in the volunteer arena, and the recommendations of the study.

The study addresses the Red Cross, but is relevant for any organization in the field of volunteerism. Inquire about cost and availability. **American Red Cross** National Headquarters, 17th & D Streets, Washington, DC 20006 202-639-3535

VOLUNTEER USA

(1991) by Andrew Carroll - a comprehensive guide to becoming a volunteer; includes 14 chapters on subjects of AIDS, Alcohol and Drugs, Animals, Blood and Organ/Tissue Donations, Children and Young Adults, Crime, Disabilities, Education and Illiteracy, The Elderly, The Environment, Homelessness and Housing, Hunger, Suicide, and Veterans; subchapters provide in-depth information into related issues (e.g., *Child Abuse* and *Runaways* under *Children and Young Adults);* divides chapters into three parts: *Why Help Is Needed, What You Can Do,* and *National Organizations,* estimated 300+pp, $8.95 **Random House, Inc.** 201 East 50th Street, Ninth Floor, New York, NY 10022 212-751-2600

VOLUNTEER WORLD SUBJECT-SPECIFIC PACKETS

(intermittent) - special packets of information in areas of drug abuse, day care, student volunteerism, older volunteers, health, physical environment, etc., based on specific requests and compiled upon receipt of outline of needs from Four-One-One National Clearinghouse on Volunteerism files, unpaged, $3.00 plus $1.50 postage (specify subject, allow three weeks) **Four-One-One (411)** 7304 Beverly Street, Annandale, VA 22003 703-354-6270

VOLUNTEER: X67 COMMUNITY SERVICE

(1990) - a recruitment piece detailing for students volunteer opportunities, benefits, and other details of an off-campus school volunteer program which provides high school credits for participants, 6-panel foldout, free **Boulder Valley Public Schools** 6500 Arapahoe Avenue, PO Box 9011, Boulder, CO 80301 303-447-1010

VOLUNTEERING IS FOR WINNERS: A GUIDE FOR THE HELPER, THE PROGRAM MANAGER, AND THE ORGANIZATION

(1982) - Practical suggestions on managing a volunteer program; covers recruitment, screening, orientation and training, program maintenance, legal concerns, burnout, volunteer rights, and volunteer recognition; highlights various resources available to help maintain a healthy volunteer organization; reviews how the concepts of *pure volunteer* and *gratuitous employee* affect an organization's legal liabilities; appends materials on *Management by Objectives* planning, tax deductions for volunteers, surveys for

evaluation, and over 100 references, 110pp, inquire about cost **Great Plains Volunteer** PO Box 80821, Sioux Falls, SD 57116 605-339-4357

VOLUNTEERISM

(1991) by Harriet Clyde Kipps - a comprehensive guide to volunteer programs and organizations across the country, from broad organizational resources at national and federal levels to local programs in areas such as day care, drug abuse, housing and nutrition; includes training events both in the community and on campus, and a bibliography of over 2,000 books, newsletters, periodicals, audiovisuals, and other tools, 1,000pp, inquire about cost **R. R. Bowker** Box 762, New York, NY 10011

VOLUNTEERISM IN THE EIGHTIES: FUNDAMENTAL ISSUES IN VOLUNTARY ACTION

(1982) - Essays on issues relevant to volunteerism including problems unique to the voluntary sector, flawed public appraisal of the relationship between altruism and volunteerism, the management scientist's perspective, the volunteer's role in democracy and funding concerns, volunteerism as one of the few possibilities for preserving American values in an era of intellectual and social crisis, etc.; provides references and a few illustrations, 281pp, inquire about cost **Joint Action in Community Service** PO Box 1700, 1730 M Street, NW, Washington, DC 20013 202-223-0912

VOLUNTEERS: A VALUABLE RESOURCE

(1983) - a handbook developed by *Committee on Marshalling Human Resources* for the *Office of Private Sector Initiatives* of the Reagan Administration for use of policymakers based on the premises that:

- Elected officials can help increase public awareness of the importance of volunteering.
- Public officials can recognize that volunteering is a legimate area of public policy discussion.
- Public officials can understand the role government has played in supporting volunteering and the structures through which people volunteer.
- Public officials can accept responsibility for helping to maintain and protect the independence of voluntary organizations.

Expands on each of the above premises, and adds a comprehensive question and answer section, a statistical survey on *who volunteers,* selected quotations from American leaders, and two sample speeches written by the Committee's staff but never delivered *(The Hidden Face of Volunteering* and *What...Life Without Volunteers?);* appends contact information for the *Advisory Group to the Committee on Marshalling Human Resources,* 24pp, available only by photocopy or fax, $8.40 prepaid **Ronald Reagan Presidential Materials Staff** 9055 Exposition Drive, Los Angeles, CA 90034 213-215-2125 (library)

VOLUNTEERS IN ACTION

(1989) by Brian O'Connell - stories, citations, and testimonials of ordinary citizens and the scope and effect of their diverse volunteer efforts, $24.95 (hardbound), $19.95 (paperbound) **Foundation Center** 79 Fifth Avenue, New York, NY 10003 212-620-4230

VOLUNTEERS MAKE A DIFFERENCE

(kept current) - a recruitment brochure providing brief profiles of several of the programs of the Navy Family Service Center (spouse employment, parenting, tax preparation, spouses of students, arts, and other programs); hours of operation, location, etc., 6-panel foldout, free **Navy Family Service Center** Building 42, Great Lakes, IL 60088 312-688-3603

VOLUNTEERS, RESOURCE FOR HUMAN SERVICES

(1979) by Harriet H. Naylor - a look at the separate leadership roles of the executive and the professional director of volunteers, and the many ways they complement each other; discusses the volunteer both as advocate and in direct service, the government and volunteering, organizing a volunteer service, and volunteerism in the future; includes extensive bibliography, 49pp, single copy free (summarized from full manuscript for *Occasional Paper Series*) **Project SHARE** PO Box 30666, Bethesda, MD 20814 301-231-9539

VOLUNTEERS! THE BOARD GAME
(1985) - a board game in which players take on the role of community leaders vying for the scarce resources available for their volunteer programs (administrator, board, volunteers, financing, etc.); includes an element of the effects of mismanagement on the community, board, playing pieces, cards, $17.50 plus $2.50 postage/handling (card game of same name, $4.11 plus $.89 postage/handling) **Four-One-One (411)** 7304 Beverly Street, Annandale, VA 22003 703-354-6270

VOLUNTEERS TODAY: FINDING, TRAINING AND WORKING WITH THEM
(1973) by Harriet H. Naylor - handbook for volunteer center managers and potential managers to enable them to mount or improve efforts to assist the community through volunteer involvement; chapters on motivation, clues for assignments, training events, personnel administration of volunteers, and other areas of day-to-day operation are linked with a preface and postscript on new forms of volunteering and volunteers for the future, 195pp, $4.50 **Dryden Associates** PO Box 363, Dryden, NY 13053

VOLUNTEERS! WHO NEEDS THEM?
(1980) - an appeal to the potential user of VAC services to outline its client services and earmark those that could be done by volunteers to free staff time for improvement and expansion of client services, 4-panel foldout, single copy free (send stamped, self-addressed envelope) **Volunteer Service Bureau** 520 SE Ft. King, Ste. C-1, Ocala, FL 32671 904-732-4771

WELCOME TO VOLUNTARISM!
(1980) - orientation piece about the Center, including facts about volunteer rights, tax deductions and other information to inform the volunteer, 12pp, $1.25 **Volunteer Center of the Greater Quad Cities** 1417 Sixth Avenue, Moline, IL 61265 309-764-6804

WELL SPENT TIMES
(1982) - a case for giving interviewing of volunteers the time it deserves; suggests allowing 45 minutes to an hour for the interview, discussing the agency's general operations and philosophy with the recruit, and meeting in comfortable surroundings; provides sample job descriptions, ideas for the volunteer on the job, topics for volunteer orientation, a bill of rights for volunteers, and the actual volunteer handbook used by the Beverly Manor Convalescent Hospital in Laguna Hills, California (developed by Beverly Enterprises), 34pp, single copy free **Project SHARE** 7830 Old Georgetown Road, Suite 204, Bethesda, MD 20814 301-231-9539

WHAT ARE YOUR VOLUNTEER NEEDS?*
(1980) - a look at one VAC's approach to making annual contact in a group approach with active and potential users of the Center's volunteer-providing services; record of steps leading to two of these seminars (1978 and 1979) and accounts of the results, approx. 15pp, single copy free **Voluntary Action Center of Greensboro** 1301 North Elm Street, Greensboro, NC 27401 919-373-1633

WHAT LIES AHEAD: LOOKING TOWARD THE '90S
(biyearly) - continuation of an effort begun in 1980 to alert volunteers and professionals to changes in the environment in which United Way does business; monitors change and identifies points of change important to health- and human-care organizations; includes information drawn from print and broadcast media and other sources to depict the most likely scenario in the years ahead; emphasizes that change is uncertain and the journal is only a view of the future with a high probability of success, 87pp, inquire about cost **United Way of America** Strategic Planning Division, 701 North Fairfax Street, Alexandria, VA 22314-2045 703-836-7100

WINNING WITH STAFF: A NEW LOOK AT STAFF SUPPORT FOR VOLUNTEERS
(1978) by Ivan H. Scheier - seven strategies to foster agency and staff support for volunteers; includes staff rewards, staff participation, volunteers in leadership roles, training, education, job diversification for volunteers, etc., 77pp, $5.75 **VOLUNTEER - The National Center** Volunteer Readership, 1111 North 19th Street, Suite 500, Arlington, VA 22209 703-276-0542

YOUTH INVOLVEMENT HANDBOOK FOR LEADERS
(1989) - a guide for the youth leader in areas of administrative roles and relationships, starting a Red Cross youth involvement program, programs and services for youth, national resources, chapter and station program examples, youth involvement programs, awards and recognition, and the five key commitments and aspects of career development for youth, (although addressed to Red Cross youth leaders, adaptable to any youth-oriented volunteer program), 9pp, single copy free **American Red Cross** Youth Programs, National Headquarters, Washington, DC 20006 202-639-3039

YOUTH SERVICE: A GUIDEBOOK FOR DEVELOPING AND OPERATING EFFECTIVE PROGRAMS
(1990) - a guide for engaging more youth in volunteer activities, and strengthening programs that are already in existence, 70pp, $12.50 (bulk discounts) **Independent Sector** 1828 L Street, NW, Washington, DC 20036 202-223-8100

AIDS

ABOUT TEENAGE PREGNANCY
(1990) - basic information teens need to make responsible
decisions; describes how conception occurs, methods of
contraception, signs of pregnancy, and sources of help; presents
the challenges of teenage parenthood, 16pp, $.79 (minimum 25);
quantity discounts (ask for free catalog with review copy coupon)
Channing L. Bete Company 200 State Road, South Deerfield, MA
01373-0200

AIDS: A GUIDE FOR HISPANIC LEADERSHIP
(1989) - a booklet designed to help Hispanic community leaders
participate in AIDS education, prevention, policy development,
and research efforts in their communities; includes basic facts
about the transmission of AIDS, data on how the disease is
affecting Hispanic communities, information on how to assess the
community response to AIDS, and suggestions for determining,
communicating, and meeting AIDS-related needs among local
Hispanic populations, single copy free **National Coalition of
Hispanic Health & Human Service Organizations** 1030 Fifteenth
Street, NW, Suite 1053, Washington, DC 20005 202-371-2100

AIDS, ALCOHOL AND DRUGS SERIES
(1987-88) - a series of fact sheets and publications addressing
acquired immunodeficiency syndrome (AIDS) and drugs and
alcohol; includes:
- *Alcohol and AIDS: Update* - reading list, 36pp
- *Surgeon General's Report on Acquired Immune Deficiency
  Syndrome (AIDS)* - risks of infection and ways to prevent
  infection, 36pp
- *NIDA's Drug Abuse and AIDS Public Education* - overview
  of program and its materials and radio messages, 2pp
- *AIDS and Drug Abuse* - extent of the problem and methods
  of transmission, 2pp
- *Acquired Immunodeficiency Syndrome and Chemical
  Dependency* - report of a symposium sponsored by the
  *American Medical Society on Alcoholism and Other
  Dependencies* and the *National Council on Alcoholism*, 78pp
- *Psychological, Neuropsychiatric, and Substance Abuse Aspects
  of AIDS* - exploration of areas of AIDS research emphasizing
  traditional and recently-developed research approaches, 261pp
- *Needle Sharing Among Intravenous Drug Abusers* - Research
  Monograph 80 describing a wide variety of programs and
  policies reported at a 1987 meeting of 40 experts convened by
  NIDA, 189pp

- *Posters and Flyers on AIDS* - a series of eight posters on
  needle-sharing, pregnancy and AIDS.
Single copies of all materials are free; request complete catalog.
**US/HHS - National Clearinghouse for Alcohol and Drug
Information** PO Box 2345, Rockville, MD 20852 301-468-2600

AIDS ARMS NETWORK ...YOUR PARTNERS IN CARE
(1990) - a guide to services and support that the *AIDS Arms
Network* provides; includes section on creating a personal plan for
a client, the mission of the *Network* and other details to provide a
quick-reference for those seeking services, 6-panel foldout, free
AIDS Arms Network, Inc. 2727 Oak Lawn, Suite 222, Dallas, TX
75219 214-521-5191

AIDS AUDIOVISUAL SERIES
(1987-89) - a series of videotapes sponsored by *The National
Clearinghouse for Alcohol and Drug Information (NCADI)* and
available through NCADI's free loan program; includes:
- **Alicia** - a dramatic portrayal of a women who learns that she
  and her child test positive for the human immunodeficiency
  virus (HIV); addresses Hispanic men and women at risk for
  AIDS, 20 minutes.
- **Drug Abuse and AIDS: Getting the Message Out** - model
  programs in Baltimore, Maryland, New Jersey, and Brooklyn,
  New York using physicians, educators, and outreach workers;
  addresses high school to adult, 27-1/2 minutes.
- **Olga's Story** - an interview with a woman who has AIDS,
  talking about her youngest child who has AIDS, and her will
  to live for her children, addresses Hispanic men and women at
  risk for AIDS, Spanish and English.
The above videotapes are available for purchase, also; inquire.
**US/HHS - National Clearinghouse for Alcohol and Drug
Information** PO Box 2345, Rockville, MD 20852 301-468-2600

AIDS BOOKLET SERIES
(1989-90) - series of booklets providing information on what AIDS
is, how the AIDS virus is transmitted, activities that put people at
risk, and other information specific to each title, including: *What
Everyone Should Know About AIDS, Why You Should Be
Informed About AIDS, Protecting Yourself from AIDS, About
AIDS and Shooting Drugs, What Young People Should Know
About AIDS, Let's Talk About AIDS (activities book), About
AIDS in the Workplace, Women and AIDS, AIDS and
Emergency Responder, What Gay and Bisexual Men Should*

Know About AIDS, and others in press, Av. 16pp, $.79, minimum 25, most titles available in Spanish (ask for catalog with free review copy coupon) **Channing L. Bete Company** 200 State Road, South Deerfield, MA 01373-0200

AIDS CAREGIVERS HANDBOOK
(1989) - a compilation of materials developed by the AIDS Project of the Oak Lawn Counseling Center in Dallas; covers all aspects of AIDS - scientific, medical, nutritional, psychological, interpersonal and spiritual; appends a checklist of opportunistic infections with symptoms and medications as well as instructions in providing home care for someone seriously ill, 331pp, $10.95 **San Francisco AIDS Foundation** 333 Valencia Street, PO Box 6182, San Francisco, CA 94101-6182 415-861-3397

THE AIDS CHALLENGE: PREVENTION EDUCATION FOR YOUNG PEOPLE
(1988) - facts and strategies essential to creating an effective AIDS education program in school and non-school settings; addresses the needs of children in grades 3-12 in dealing with the controversies surrounding AIDS; includes information on tailoring programs for minority and special populations, working with parents, clergy and other community groups, 526pp, $24.95 **San Francisco AIDS Foundation** 333 Valencia Street, PO Box 6182, San Francisco, CA 94101-6182 415-861-3397

AIDS DIRECTORY OF RESOURCES
(1988) - brief descriptions of national resources available on the subject of AIDS and its prevention; includes publications, directories of services, audiovisual materials, etc.; categorizes by types of organizations, and types of information, 34pp, #UC10581, $7.00 **United Way of America** 701 North Fairfax Street, Alexandria, VA 22314-2045 703-836-7100

AIDS DOES NOT DISCRIMINATE
(1990) - chart suitable for handing out at meetings, posting, etc., listing ten facts everyone needs to know about AIDS, $10.00/100 **Health Education Services** PO Box 7126, Albany, NY 12224 518-474-2121

AIDS EDUCATION: INTERDISCIPLINARY, MULTICULTURAL APPROACHES
(undated) - information about a special project of the *Council for Exceptional Children* that addresses AIDS education curricula potentially suitable for use with handicapped children, free information packet **Council for Exceptional Children** 1920 Association Drive, Reston, VA 22091-1589 703-264-9451

AIDS HOME CARE AND HOSPICE MANUAL
(1988) - a training guide for administrators, staff and volunteers who care for persons diagnosed with AIDS; provides educational guidelines and resources, an overview of AIDS and ARC (epidemiology, infection control, physical and psychosocial interventions, etc.), easy reference tools for field staff as well as local, state and national resources and examples of documentation used for reimbursement (based on the first AIDS Home Care and Hospice Program at the Visiting Nurses Association of San Francisco), 195pp, 3-ring binder, $95.00 **San Francisco AIDS Foundation** 333 Valencia Street, PO Box 6182, San Francisco, CA 94101-6182 415-861-3397

AIDS HOME CARE AND HOSPICE VIDEO
(1989) - help for nurses and other caregivers to recognize the physical and psychosocial complications associated with HIV infection; describes the continuum of disability and necessary interventions through narration and interviews with nurses, social workers and attendants, 30 minutes, VHS, $95.00 **San Francisco**

AIDS Foundation 333 Valencia Street, PO Box 6182, San Francisco, CA 94101-6182 415-861-3397

AIDS HOTLINE TRAINING MANUAL
(1987) - a comprehensive manual providing guidelines for training volunteers on an AIDS hotline; includes:
● an in-depth AIDS education program
● active listening techniques
● appropriate language and phone responses
● how to handle crisis calls
● using TDDs to communicate with deaf callers
● hotline rules and regulations
● an appendix of AIDS reference materials
159pp, $25.00 **San Francisco AIDS Foundation Speakers Bureau** 333 Valencia Street, PO Box 6182, San Francisco, CA 94101-6182 415-861-3397

AIDS: 100 QUESTIONS AND ANSWERS
(1990) - a compilation of information concerning AIDS providing responses to the most frequently asked questions and concerns; includes sections on modes of disease, transmission, risk factors, symptoms, incidence and human rights issues, 20pp, $1.00 ($75.00/100) **Health Education Services** PO Box 7126, Albany, NY 12224 518-474-2121

AIDS PAMPHLET SERIES
(kept current) - a series of pamphlets including: *What About AIDS Testing?, How You WON'T Get AIDS, Caring for the AIDS Patient at Home,* and others (new titles added as available), Av. 6-panel foldout, free **US/HHS - National AIDS Information Clearinghouse** PO Box 6003, Rockville, MD 20850

AIDS PREVENTION GUIDE
(kept current) - a guide for parents and other adults concerned about youth addressing AIDS prevention for young people; encourages open discussions with youth and provides step-by-step assistance through a number of guides, including *What is HIV Infection? And What Is AIDS?* and *Talking With Young People About HIV Infection and AIDS;* includes specific guides for each school level from elementary to high school, and *Common Questions; Accurate Answers,* as well as a discussion on how to join the overall community response to the issue; appends information about the *National AIDS Hotline* and state and local resources, unpaged, free **US/HHS - National AIDS Information Clearinghouse** , PO Box 6003, Rockville, MD 20850

AIDS PREVENTION PROGRAM FOR YOUTH: INFORMATION FOR STUDENTS
(1987) - a manual/workbook for students to be used in conjunction with a 29-minute video (*A Letter From Brian*), a teacher's/leader's guide, a brochure for parents, and other materials to provide junior and senior high school youth with the information and support they need to choose behaviors that reduce their risk of coming into contact with the AIDS virus, 33pp, inquire about availability of the program at local Red Cross Chapter **American Red Cross Office of HIV/AIDS Education** AIDS Public Education Program, 1709 New York Avenue, NW, Washington, DC 20006 202-662-1577

AIDS PROGRAM
(undated) - overview of the many programs of one of the largest AIDS-serving clinics in the country; covers medical, housing, education, legal, financial, drug abuse, nutrition and other services for persons living with AIDS and HIV infection, 10-panel foldout, free **Whitman-Walker Clinic** 1407 S Street, NW, Washington, DC 20009 202-797-3500

AIDS: THE WOMEN

(1988) - a new collection of essays telling the story of women with AIDS and ARC, women who are HIV positive and the women who work in AIDS wards, staff hotlines, and educate other women about HIV, 250pp, $9.95 **San Francisco AIDS Foundation** 333 Valencia Street, PO Box 6182, San Francisco, CA 94101-6182 415-861-3397

AIDS VIDEO SERIES

(1989-90) - two videos delivering messages about how AIDS is - and isn't - transmitted: (1) *About AIDS* (for ages 18 and up); (2) *Young People & AIDS* (award-winning video for ages 11-18); addresses each group in an age-appropriate manner with answers to commonly-asked questions and specific advice on how to avoid high-risk behaviors, inquire about cost, preview tape available for 15 days' free use **Channing L. Bete Company** 200 State Road, South Deerfield, MA 01373-0200

AIDS-WISE, NO LIES (VIDEO)

(1988) - a multi-ethnic video that captures its teen audience by using rap and young performers to talk about safe sex and IV drug use; also presents several people with HIV speaking of their personal experience, 22 minutes, VHS, $250 (rental $50) **San Francisco AIDS Foundation** 333 Valencia Street, PO Box 6182, San Francisco, CA 94101-6182 415-861-3397

ALCOHOL, DRUGS AND AIDS

(1989) - a brochure describing the links between the use of alcohol and drugs, damage to the immune system and increased susceptibility to the AIDS virus; advises reader on how to avoid infection caused by drug use and unsafe sex (English on one side, Spanish on the reverse), 8-panel foldout, $.30 (quantity discounts) **San Francisco AIDS Foundation** 333 Valencia Street, PO Box 6182, San Francisco, CA 94101-6182 415-861-3397

ANSWERS ABOUT AIDS

(1987) - a video in which former U.S. Surgeon General C. Everett Koop addresses students' concerns and misconceptions about AIDS; offers advice about making decisions that will help teenagers protect themselves from getting AIDS, 15 minutes, free loan to community groups, libraries and educators from your local Red Cross Chapter **American Red Cross Office of HIV/AIDS Education** AIDS Public Education Program, 1709 New York Avenue, NW, Washington, DC 20006 202-662-1577

A BABY BORN WITH AIDS IS BORN DYING

(1989) - an overview of the AIDS and pregnancy connection, and how education and assistance can turn the tide of this crisis, 6-panel foldout, free **March of Dimes** National Capital Area Chapter, 2700 South Quincy Street, Suite 220, Arlington, VA 22206 703-824-0111

BEVERLY'S STORY: PREGNANCY AND THE TEST FOR AIDS VIRUS

(1990) - a video designed for viewing by pregnant women and women of childbearing age discussing pregnancy and the AIDS virus "between two 'best friends'" anxious about the baby's father's use of IV drugs, 12.5 minutes, $25.00 (one of a series of five videos on AIDS; entire set available for $100.00; see other descriptions in AIDS section) **Health Education Services** PO Box 7126, Albany, NY 12224 518-474-2121

CHILDREN AND THE AIDS VIRUS

(1989) - an overview on the subject of children and AIDS; cites examples of AIDS situations regarding children; appends bibliography and other tools, 36pp, inquire about cost **Clarion Press** 52 Vanderbilt Avenue, New York, NY 10017 212-972-1190

CHILDREN, PARENTS, AND AIDS

(1989) - a guide to help parents talk to their children about HIV infection/AIDS; answers questions parents may have on why they should talk to their children, how children get HIV infection/AIDS, how safe children are at school, how to protect children, what facts to share with teens and preteens, and more, 12-panel foldout, available free from your local Red Cross chapter **American Red Cross Office of HIV/AIDS Education** AIDS Public Education Program, 1709 New York Avenue, NW, Washington, DC 20006 202-662-1577

DEVELOPING AIDS RESIDENTIAL SETTINGS

(1988) - direction on how to provide residential care for persons with HIV infection when home care is no longer an option; includes topics such as needs assessment, service delivery, public relations, community participation, legal requirements, building design, costs and financing (based on the model of care developed at Coming Home Hospice in San Francisco, a 15-bed residential facility), 105pp, 3-ring binder, $95.00 **San Francisco AIDS Foundation** 333 Valencia Street, PO Box 6182, San Francisco, CA 94101-6182 415-861-3397

DIRECTORY OF AIDS RESOURCES: WASHINGTON, DC, METROPOLITAN AREA

(1990) - almost 70 resource groups, including hotlines, clinics and other AIDS organizations, multipurpose organizations offering to provide legal services (e.g., American Civil Liberties Union), publications/information (e.g., National Library of Medicine), testing (e.g., Montgomery County Health Department) and other services, and national organizations with major AIDS components, 30pp, inquire about cost *[Although geared to the DC area, can serve as an example for any community in developing a directory]* **FOX Television - WTTG** 5151 Wisconsin Avenue, NW, Washington, DC 20016 202-244-5151

DOES AIDS HURT? EDUCATING YOUNG CHILDREN ABOUT AIDS

(1988) - guide for those who spend time with young children under 10 years old for addressing AIDS concerns with this age group; emphasizes the use of age-appropriate responses to children's questions, 149pp, $14.95 **San Francisco AIDS Foundation** 333 Valencia Street, PO Box 6182, San Francisco, CA 94101-6182 415-861-3397

DON'T FORGET SHERRIE

(1988) - a video focusing on a group of urban teenagers who are responding to the spread of the AIDS virus, as well as questioning their own values and behaviors; includes discussion guide and written materials, 30 minutes, free on loan to community groups, libraries, amd educators from your local Red Cross Chapter **American Red Cross Office of HIV/AIDS Education** AIDS Public Education Program, 1706 New York Avenue, NW, Washington, DC 20006 202-662-1577

DOOR'S OPEN!

(1987) - the first in a series of stories recognizing the difficult job of the home teacher, who teaches children and youth who cannot attend school for medical or other reasons - many terminally ill; shows how even the toughest youth in the inner city neighborhoods protect the home teacher; tells the story of a child with AIDS who was denied admittance to his local school, 40pp, $9.00 (proceeds will benefit a homelessness program) **Mortgage Burning Fund** PO Box 762, Annandale, VA 22003 703-354-6270

DRUGS, SEX, AND AIDS

(1988) - an overview on HIV/AIDS as it relates to drugs and alcohol in terms of risky behavior, kissing, sex, pregnancy, protection, partners, blood tests, what to do after becoming infected, helping those who are infected, etc.; appends a list of resources, programs and materials, 12pp foldout, free from your local Red Cross Chapter **American Red Cross Office of HIV/AIDS Education** AIDS Public Education Program, 1709 New York Avenue, NW, Washington, DC 20006 202-662-1577

A DUTY TO RESPOND: EMERGENCY AND PUBLIC SAFETY WORKERS AND HIV/AIDS

(1989) - a look at the duties of law enforcement workers, fire fighters, emergency medical service personnel, lifeguards, and rescue workers at the scene of an accident or crime which frequently involves blood; includes answers to direct questions on bleeding, wearing gloves, precautions, giving CPR, blood spills (including dried blood and blood-stained clothing), body removal, pool and spa safety, occupational exposure, etc., 23pp, free from your local Red Cross Chapter **American Red Cross Office of HIV/AIDS Education** AIDS Public Education Program, 1709 New York Avenue, Washington, DC 20006 202-662-1577

EDDIE'S STORY: HOW TO PROTECT YOURSELF FROM STDS AND AIDS

(1990) - a video featuring a young man who "likes the ladies" and "brushes off" the advice of friends to protect himself from AIDS and other sexually-transmitted diseases, only to become infected, 12 minutes, $25.00 (one of a series of five videos on AIDS; entire set, $100.00; see descriptions of others elsewhere in the AIDS section) **Health Education Services** PO Box 7126, Albany, NY 12224 518-474-2121

EL DESPERTAR DE RAMON (THE AWAKENING OF RAMON)

(1988) - a tabloid for Spanish-speaking adults and teenagers covering the basic facts about AIDS in a format that is familiar to many Latin Americans - a 'fotonovela' that is like a soap opera which tells the dramatic story of a man who denies the existence of AIDS until he learns that his son has the disease, 4pp, $.30 (quantity discounts) **San Francisco AIDS Foundation** 333 Valencia Street, PO Box 6182, San Francisco, CA 94101-6182 415-861-3397

EVALUATION OF THE HIV/AIDS EDUCATION PROJECTS

(1990) - an assessment of the American Red Cross HIV/AIDS programs using formative, process, and outcome evaluation strategies; focuses on useful and measurable evaluation criteria, analysis, and data collection to identify critical evaluation issues during project development, determine the extent and nature of program delivery and assess the effectiveness of selected education programs, in process, inquire **American Red Cross Office of HIV/AIDS Education** AIDS Public Education Program, 1709 New York Avenue, NW, Washington, DC 20006 202-662-1577

FACING AIDS: TEENS ASK A YOUNG MAN WHAT IT'S LIKE

(1990) - a video on AIDS featuring an interview by teenagers with a young man who later died of AIDS, giving a first-hand picture of what living with AIDS is like, 20 minutes, $25.00 (one of a series of five videos on AIDS; entire set, $100.00; see descriptions of others elsewhere in this section on AIDS) **Health Education Services** PO Box 7126, Albany, NY 12224 518-474-1212

FACTS ABOUT AIDS

(1990) - a brochure developed by an organization whose primary purpose is to conduct research on acquired immune deficiency syndrome (AIDS); provides quick-reference question and answer format based on the most recent research information available, foldout brochure, free **American Foundation for AIDS Research** 5900 Wilshire Boulevard, Second Floor, Los Angeles, CA 90036 213-857-5900

FIGHTING BACK

(1989) - a focus on a group of volunteers ("buddies") in New York City which pairs a PWA (person with AIDS) and a volunteer helper to help children (11+) and adults to understand acquired immune deficiency syndrome (AIDS); gives equal space to PWAs and helpers providing detail about both sides of the relationship, 110pp, $13.95 **G.P. Putnam's Sons** 390 Murray Hill Parkway, East Rutherford, NJ 07073 201-933-9292

FIRST IN THE FIGHT AGAINST AIDS: GMHC ANNUAL REPORT

(1988-89) - an overview of the year's operation including sections on *A Day in the Life of GMHC, Client Services, Public Policy, Education, Legal Services, Office of the Ombudsman, Communications, etc., Finances,* etc., 40pp, single copy free while supply lasts **Gay Men's Health Crisis** 129 West 20th Street, New York, NY 10011-0022 212-807-6655 (hotline)

FOR THE FAMILY

(1989) - explanation of transmission, symptoms, and prevention; emphasizes the need for Blacks, Latinos, Asians and Native Americans to educate their communities to prevent the spread of AIDS, in production at press time, $.30 (quantity discounts) **San Francisco AIDS Foundation** 333 Valencia Street, PO Box 6182, San Francisco, CA 94101-6182 415-861-3397

FRIENDS FOR LIFE

(1988) - a story for young readers age 9-12 examining the strong emotions - feelings of loss, anger, love and hope - that surround AIDS; presents facts about AIDS in the personal and social context that children experience, 48pp, hardbound, $12.95 **San Francisco AIDS Foundation** 333 Valencia Street, PO Box 6182, San Francisco, CA 94101-6182 415-861-3397

GIVING AND RECEIVING BLOOD

(1990) - facts about giving and receiving blood which explode many myths that have emerged around this vital activity; includes information on how the nation's blood supply is protected, hemophilia, transfusions, storing one's own blood, treatments, how individuals can help, etc., 10-panel foldout, free from your local Red Cross Chapter **American Red Cross Office of HIV/AIDS Education** AIDS Public Education Program, 1709 New York Avenue, NW, Washington, DC 20006 202-662-1577

HIV/AIDS IN THE WORKPLACE: ARE YOU AND YOUR EMPLOYEES PREPARED?

(1989) - a guide for employers to help them prepare for AIDS among their employees; includes statistics to inform employers on what to expect in the next few years, ways the American Red Cross can help, and how increased knowledge will not only save lives, but will save billions of dollars each year for business/industry, 8-panel foldout, free from your local Red Cross Chapter **American Red Cross Office of HIV/AIDS Education** AIDS Public Education Program, 1709 New York Avenue, NW, Washington, DC 20006 202-662-1577

HIV/AIDS INFORMATION UPDATE

(monthly) - a newsletter distributed to Red Cross HIV/AIDS coordinators in the U.S. and at military stations worldwide, as well as to state public health officials; includes announcements of new materials by Red Cross and other organizations, articles reprinted from current periodicals, updates on scientific and legislative developments, information about funding opportunities, and highlights of chapter HIV/AIDS education activities, unpaged, single copy free (inquire about subscription availability) **American Red Cross Office of HIV/AIDS Education** 1709 New York Avenue, NW, Washington, DC 20006 202-662-1577

HIV INFECTION AND AIDS
(1989) - the basic facts about HIV infection and AIDS, including discussions about the virus that causes AIDS, signs of HIV, how people get HIV or AIDS, degree of AIDS reported by each state, blood donation, protection, etc., 14-panel foldout, free from your local Red Cross Chapter [also available in Spanish] **American Red Cross Office of HIV/AIDS Education** AIDS Public Education Program, 1709 New York Avenue, NW, Washington, DC 20006 202-662-1577

HIV INFECTION AND WORKERS IN HEALTH CARE SETTINGS
(1989) - a discussion of health care workers and HIV, including how workers can protect themselves on the job - in surgical procedures, in dentistry, drawing blood, handling specimens, and other health care activities, 16-panel foldout, free from your local Red Cross Chapter **American Red Cross Office of HIV/AIDS Education** AIDS Public Education Program, 1709 New York Avenue, NW, Washington, DC 20006 202-662-1577

HOW FRAUD ARTISTS EXPLOIT AIDS
(1989) - a paper issued by the Council of Better Business Bureaus and the Food and Drug Administration on how health fraud artists exploit the AIDS situation, and how to guard against being defrauded; warns against accepting testimonials as scientific proof, explains that manufacturers of experimental treatments cannot charge for their products without FDA approval, etc., single copy free **Council of Better Business Bureaus** National Headquarters, 4200 Wilson Boulevard, Arlington, VA 22203 703-276-0100

INFORMATION PACKET SERIES
(kept current) - a series of tailored information packets to assist in specific situations, including *Information Packet for Teachers* and *Information Packet for Health Care Workers* as well as a *General Information Packet;* includes in each packet both general *(Understanding AIDS)* and specific *(Recommendations for Prevention of HIV Transmission in Health-Care Settings)* information, with encouragement to reproduce all or any of the items, unpaged, single packet free (may request additional after review) **US/HHS - National AIDS Information Clearinghouse** PO Box 6003, Rockville, MD 28050

JOAN'S STORY: HOW WOMEN CAN PROTECT THEMSELVES FROM AIDS
(1990) - a video discussing women and AIDS and how to reduce the risk of transmission, featuring two women who act on the issue, 8.2 minutes, $25.00 (one of a series of five videos on AIDS; entire set, $100.00; see descriptions of others elsewhere in the AIDS section) **Health Education Services** PO Box 7126, Albany, NY 12224 518-474-2121

LEARNING AIDS
(1989) - bibliography of over 1,000 current items on AIDS education targeted to a wide variety of audiences, including children and adolescents, health care professionals, IV drug users, gay and bisexual men, Latino and black communities, pastoral counselors, sexually-active adults, and many other groups, 280pp, $24.95 **R. R. Bowker** Box 762, New York, NY 10011

LEARNING BY HEART: AIDS AND SCHOOLCHILDREN IN AMERICA'S COMMUNITIES
(1989) - a collection of dramas on how American communities handled the advent of AIDS in schoolchildren; includes interviews with people across the country - both the most mean-spirited who add to the family's tragedy, and those who do not feel that a schoolchild with AIDS is a danger, 305pp, $22.95 **Rutgers**

University Press 109 Church Street, New Brunswick, NJ 08901 201-932-7764

A LETTER FROM BRIAN
(1990) - a video developed to be used in conjunction with a program on AIDS education for junior and senior high school students; depicts how a letter from an ex-boyfriend started an avalanche of questions, doubts, conflicts, fears, and hard decisions for a young girl and her friends; has accompanying brochure, *AIDS Prevention for Youth,* 29 minutes, available on free loan to community groups, libraries and educators from your local Red Cross Chapter **American Red Cross Office of HIV/AIDS Education** AIDS Public Education Program, 1706 New York Avenue, NW, Washington, DC 20006 202-662-1577

LIVING WITH HIV INFECTION
(1990) - a message to the person who discovers he or she is infected with HIV; answers questions about tests, self-care, emotional support, having children, health insurance, legal rights, telling employers, volunteering, raising funds, etc., 12-panel foldout, free from your local Red Cross Chapter **American Red Cross Office of HIV/AIDS Education** AIDS Public Education Program, 1709 New York Avenue, NW, Washington, DC 20006 202-662-1577

MEETING THE CHALLENGE
(kept current) - background and history of the Howard Brown Memorial Clinic's program of low-cost, confidential, community-based health care for sexually transmitted diseases (STDs), including AIDS; includes information about research, testing, treatment, counseling, screening, referral, and education programs of the Clinic, 8-panel foldout, free **Howard Brown Memorial Clinic** 945 West George Street, Chicago, IL 60657 312-871-5777

MINI-POSTER SERIES
(1989) - ten topics, including AIDS, teen pregnancy, literacy and others illustrated by black-and-white reproduction-quality advertising sheets for use in local communities, set of 10 8-1/2"x11" sheets, $3.00/set (#PR3215) **United Way of America** 701 North Fairfax Street, Alexandria, VA 22314-2045 703-836-7100

NEWS FROM GMHC
(monthly) - to keep clients, donors and volunteers informed of the activities of the organization, Av. 12pp, single copy free, inquire about subscription **Gay Men's Health Crisis** 129 West 20th Street, New York, NY 10011-0022 212-807-6655 (hotline)

NOT-2-NITE
(1989) - an award-winning audiovisual on AIDS and sex produced by high school students from two Seattle-area schools for a contest sponsored by the Seattle public broadcasting TV station; includes suggestions from a young AIDS patient who died shortly before the award was announced, 5 minutes, inquire about availability and cost **KCTS-TV** Public Broadcasting Station, 401 Mercer Street, Seattle, WA 98102 206-728-6463

QUILT FACTS/AIDS MEMORIAL QUILT
(1990) - a fact sheet that is constantly updated to reflect activities of *The NAMES Project,* an international program which coordinates the display of a quilt, of which each patchwork square represents a person who died with AIDS, and contains personalized craftwork by families, friends and/or fans, and the name of the person who died; includes logistics such as weight, number of panels, countries represented, number of visitors, materials used, and AIDS statistics, one page fact sheet and other

materials as available, free **The NAMES Project Foundation** PO Box 14573, San Francisco, CA 94114 415-863-5511

RISKY BUSINESS

(1988) - a comic book designed for teenagers aged 13-17; uses multi-ethnic graphics to provide information about AIDS using humor and real-life situations to appeal to young people; includes a glossary and a list of questions most asked by teens (second to fifth grade reading level), 20pp, $1.00 **San Francisco AIDS Foundation** 333 Valencia Street, PO Box 6182, San Francisco, CA 94101-6182 415-861-3397

SCHOOL SYSTEMS AND AIDS: INFORMATION FOR TEACHERS AND SCHOOL OFFICIALS

(1988) - information for health educators in schools including answers to questions on the spread of AIDS virus, the safety of children from HIV/AIDS at school, how children get HIV/AIDS, students with AIDS in school, who should be informed about a student with the infection, giving first aid in school settings, etc., 14pp, free from your local Red Cross Chapter **American Red Cross Office of HIV/AIDS Education** AIDS Public Education Program, 1709 New York Avenue, NW, Washington, DC 20006 202-662-1577

SIMPLE ACTS OF KINDNESS

(1989) - an overview of the growth of community-based volunteer activities in areas of advocacy, counseling, and support networking on behalf of AIDS victims and their families; includes ten stories by volunteers relating how they have made a difference in the lives of people with AIDS - either by volunteering or by organizing volunteers; describes five model volunteer programs, 128pp, $5.00 **United Hospital Fund** 55 Fifth Avenue, New York, NY 10003-4392 212-645-2500

SPEAKERS' MANUAL

(1988) - sample outlines and strategies for presenting talks on the most important topics confronting the AIDS educator: antibody testing, blood donation and transfusion, condoms, children, drugs and alcohol, minorities, homosexuality, prostitutes, etc.; includes guidelines for addressing specific audiences: college-aged, developmentally disabled, drug users in treatment, ESL classes, health workers, parents, religious groups, teens and senior citizens, 66pp, $20.00 **San Francisco AIDS Foundation Speakers Bureau** 333 Valencia Street, PO Box 6182, San Francisco, CA 94101-6182 415-861-3397

SURGEON GENERAL'S REPORT

(annually) - a report designed to inform the American people about AIDS, how it is transmitted, the relative risks of infection, and how to prevent it; discusses fear and ways in which it can be useful, and ways in which it is as crippling as the disease itself; includes overview of the present situation, signs and symptoms, exposure, prevention/protection, drug users, transfusions, pregnancy, confidentiality, safe and unsafe behavior, etc.; appends list of additional resources, 35 pages, free **US/HHS - National AIDS Information Clearinghouse** PO Box 6003, Rockville, MD 20850

TEACHING AIDS

(1988) - resource guide for use with teenagers, junior college students and community education projects; includes AIDS curriculum in a clear and exact presentation with sample lecture and guidelines, seven teaching plans for soliciting student responses, and a 10-question test on AIDS transmission and prevention, 163pp, $19.95 (quantity discounts) **San Francisco AIDS Foundation** 333 Valencia Street, PO Box 6182, San Francisco, CA 94101-6182 415-861-3397

UNA CUESTION DE VIDA O MUERTA: UNA HISTORIA SOBRE EL SIDA

(1990) - (A Question of Life or Death: A Story About AIDS) a video addressing the Latino community featuring a family who is concerned about the wrong daughter, emphasizing the "secretive nature" often surrounding teenage activities; demonstrates the long-term worry involved when risks are taken, and tests are delayed, 20 minutes, $25.00 (one of a series of five videos on AIDS; entire set, $100.00; see descriptions of others elsewhere in this section on AIDS) **Health Education Services** PO Box 7126, Albany, NY 12224 518-474-2121

UNDERSTANDING AIDS

(1988) - a quick-reference message from the Surgeon General providing direct and hard-hitting answers to questions often asked about AIDS, including *How Do You Get AIDS from Sex?* and *What Behavior Puts You At Risk?*; covers AIDS and pregnancy, kids and AIDS, how to help someone with AIDS, and the problem of drugs and AIDS; appends a quiz of six questions to help determine how much an individual knows about AIDS, 8pp, free **US/HHS - National AIDS Information Clearinghouse** PO Box 6003, Rockville, MD 20850

UNITED WAY ACTIONS ON AIDS

(1989) - a national overview of the AIDS epidemic, summary of United Way actions and funding to support AIDS-related services in specific cities; summary of corporate and labor actions; projected AIDS-related health and human service needs, $3.00 (#UC10632) **United Way of America** 701 North Fairfax Street, Alexandria, VA 22314-2045 703-836-7100

VOLUNTEER: GMHC

(bimonthly) - news from the volunteer department of GMHC keeping interested groups and individuals informed of the activites of the organization's volunteers, Av. 8pp, single copy free **Gay Men's Health Crisis** 129 West 20th Street, New York, NY 10011-0022 212-807-6655 (hotline)

WALK UPDATE

(intermittent) - a newsbrief providing general and specific information about the annual walkathon, *AIDS Walk New York*; includes volunteer job descriptions, information on registration and getting sponsors, vignettes from supporters, overview of corporate and community involvement, etc., 12-panel foldout, free **GMHC Walkathon** Old Chelsea Station, PO Box 10, New York, NY 10113 212-807-6310

WHAT BUSINESSES REALLY NEED TO KNOW ABOUT AIDS

(1989) - a brochure for chief executive officers of small and medium-sized businesses; includes relevant laws and lists additional resources, 3-panel foldout with blank panel for printing local service information, $15/100 (#UC10607) **United Way of America** 701 North Fairfax Street, Alexandria, VA 22314-2045 703-836-7100

WHAT PARENTS NEED TO TELL CHILDEN ABOUT AIDS

(1990) - a guide designed to help parents talk to their preteen and teenage children about AIDS, 6pp, $.50 **Health Education Services** PO Box 7126, Albany, NY 12224 518-474-2121

WOMEN'S CENTERS AND AIDS: A GUIDEBOOK FOR COMMUNITY GROUPS

(1990) - a guide developed to assist groups in the community who are concerned about AIDS as the trend toward centers and shelters for women escalates, in process at press time, inquire **Women's Action Alliance** 370 Lexington Avenue, Suite 603, New York, NY 10017 212-779-2846

YOUR JOB AND AIDS: ARE THERE RISKS?

(1988) - an overview of the facts about HIV infection and AIDS as they relate to the workplace; includes questions: Should I worry about working with someone who has HIV infection or AIDS? When should workers take special precautions? What about giving first aid or CPR on the job? What can I do to help? Includes a list of suggestions, including volunteering, and other sources of information for workers, 12-panel foldout, free from your local Red Cross Chapter **American Red Cross Office of HIV/AIDS Education** AIDS Public Education Program, 1709 New York Avenue, NW, Washington, DC 20006 202-662-1577

ARTS/CULTURAL ENRICHMENT

ADVOCATES FOR THE ARTS RESOURCE KIT
(kept current) - articles, samples, models and other materials for developing advocacy programs in the arts, $6.95/kit **American Council for the Arts** 570 Seventh Avenue, New York, NY 10018 212-354-6655

ARTS AND THE AGING: AN AGENDA FOR ACTION
(1977) - highlights of the first national conference aimed at making the arts accessible to the aging both in the community and in institutions; includes guidelines on initiating or expanding programs, 100pp, $4.30 **National Council on the Aging** 1828 L Street, NW, Washington, DC 20036 202-225-6250

ARTS FESTIVALS
(1979) - proceedings of a "festivals conference" to determine steps in planning, funding, and other steps needed for successful arts festival programs, 24pp, $5.00 **American Council for the Arts** 570 Seventh Avenue, New York, NY 10018 212-354-6655

ARTS IN EDUCATION PARTNERS: SCHOOLS AND THEIR COMMUNITIES
(1977) - a handbook addressed to volunteer service groups, arts organizations and school districts interested in working together to make arts an integral part of the community; includes resource agencies and model projects, 128pp, $6.00 **American Council for the Arts** 570 Seventh Avenue, New York, NY 10018 212-354-6655

THE ARTS MANAGEMENT READER
(1979) - hundreds of verified methods and case histories for managing and promoting arts programs; includes information on obtaining corporate support and volunteer executive assistance; building and strengthening audiences, developing donor audiences, preparing long-range planning, and other ideas and suggestions, 704pp, $27.50 **Audience Arts** 270 Madison Avenue, New York, NY 10016 212-696-9000

ATTRACTING OLDER AMERICANS TO MUSEUMS
(1990) - a booklet designed to help museum professionals to attract and utilize older persons in a variety of ways; lists exemplary programs for older persons in museums around the country *(must be involved with this audience to receive this publication)*, inquire about cost and availability **Institute of Lifetime Learning** 1909 K Street, NW, Washington, DC 20049 202-872-4700

CHILDREN AND INTERCULTURAL EDUCATION
(1973) - kit of three guides for developing appreciation for cultural diversity, designed to sensitize teachers and other workers with children as well as provide curriculum information, 72pp, $1.50 **Association for Childhood Education International** 11141 Georgia Avenue , Suite 200, Wheaton, MD 20902 301-942-2443

CHILDREN AND INTERNATIONAL EDUCATION
(1973) - portfolio of ten leaflets on ways of developing international understanding and fellowship in children and those who work with them; suggests many activities and resources, $1.00/kit **Association for Childhood Education International** 11141 Georgia Avenue , Suite 200, Wheaton, MD 20902 301-942-2443

CHILDREN GIVE COLOR TO THE WORLD
(1983) - free-form sketches of the world's children at work and at play, 32pp, #5040, $2.00 **U.S. Committee on UNICEF** 331 East 38th Street, New York, NY 10016 212-686-5522

CHILDREN'S BOOKS OF INTERNATIONAL INTEREST
(1978) - selection of books categorized by age group and including areas of folklore, history, peoples and places, poetry, etc., to provide depth to children's knowledge on topics that are not immediately around them, 77pp, $5.00 **American Library Association** 50 East Huron Street, Chicago, IL 60611 312-944-6780

CHILDREN'S FACES LOOKING UP
(1979) - techniques for the storyteller to keep children interested, e.g., pursue latent themes in one story by injecting brief related stories; provides sample programs demonstrating the balance, rhythm, pacing and variety that can be used or adapted to help beginners develop effective storytelling programs, 166pp, $15.00 **American Library Association** 50 East Huron Street, Chicago, IL 60611 312-944-6780

CITIES, COUNTIES AND THE ARTS
(1979) - handbook giving models of what some local governments around the country are doing for the arts; includes information on arts, zoning, taxes and outside funding, 44pp, $2.50 **American Council for the Arts** 570 Seventh Avenue, New York, NY 10018 212-354-6655

COMMUNITY ARTS AGENCIES: A HANDBOOK AND GUIDE
(1979) - answers questions facing both established and new community programs in the arts; includes information on fundraising, management, services, etc., and lists arts groups which contributed information, 408pp, $12.50 **American Council for the Arts** 570 Seventh Avenue, New York, NY 10018 212-354-6655

CORPORATE FUND RAISING: A PRACTICAL PLAN OF ACTION
(1979) - a systematic approach to soliciting contributions from business; applicable to any location and any type of nonprofit fundraising, 74pp, $12.50 **American Council for the Arts** 570 Seventh Avenue, New York, NY 10018 212-354-6655

CROSS-CULTURAL EDUCATION: TEACHING TOWARD A PLANETARY PERSPECTIVE
(1977) - the case for polycultural education beginning at an early age to help children value their own and other ethnocultural dimensions; provides step-by-step organization approaches, including involvement of lay citizens, students, parents, and community groups; advocates Polycultural Community Advisory Committee, and tells how to get one started, 64pp, $4.75 **National Education Association** Order Department, The Academic Building, West Haven, CT 06516 203-934-2669

DANCE THERAPY PROGRAM FOR NURSING HOMES
(1978) - manual on establishing the program, policy, basics on psychosocial problems of patients, record-keeping, equipment, dance exercises, etc. (instructor/author, Mabel C. Merritt, is 73 years old), 34pp, $2.75 **Committee on Aging** 25 Beacon Street, Boston, MA 02108 617-742-2100

ETHNIC ART SLIDE LIBRARY CATALOG
(updated as needed) - descriptions of slides available on the works of Mexican-American, Black, and American Indian artists, at minimal cost; catalog free **Ethnic American Art Slide Library** College of Arts and Sciences, Mobile, AL 36688

FESTIVAL VOLUNTEERS
(1980) - details of a service that provides volunteers as information guides, backstage assistants, sign/banner coordinators, printed program coordinators, radio liaison publicists, etc., in the arts field; includes activity calendar, flow chart, evaluation, and other specifics, 12pp, $2.50 **Volunteer Center of Greater Milwaukee** 600 East Mason Street, Milwaukee , WI 53202 414-273-7887

FINANCIAL MANAGEMENT FOR THE ARTS: A GUIDEBOOK FOR ARTS ORGANIZATIONS
(1975) - details for the layman on managing money, developing budgets, and otherwise accomplishing financial planning for arts groups, 52pp, $5.95 **American Council for the Arts** 570 Seventh Avenue, New York, NY 10018 212-354-6655

FINE ARTS PROGRAM FOR DISADVANTAGED CHILDREN
(1979) - overview of a program which involved children of kindergarten age through age 17 and the facilities of college fine arts and music departments; included sessions in art, drama, poetry and music; describes funding arrangement for volunteer transportation, field trips, special cultural events and materials, 8pp, single copy free with stamped self-addressed envelope **Volunteer Center of United Way** PO Drawer 23169, Jackson, MS 39225-3169 601-354-1765

THE GOLD BOOK: DIRECTORY OF SUCCESSFUL PROJECTS BY VOLUNTEERS
(1989) - a look at ways in which more than $16 million was raised by orchestra volunteers during 1988; describes over 450 individual fundraising projects; shares secrets behind successful fundraising projects; features volunteer education projects, ticket sales campaigns, and comparative statistical reports; includes name, address, and phone number for each volunteer project; serves as a fundraising tool for volunteers, board members, managers and others promoting nonprofit organizations; arranged by state and city; appends index keyed to type of project, 180pp, $35.00 (members); $50 (nonmembers) [also available through The Volunteer Council of the League at the same address] **American Symphony Orchestra League** 777 Fourteenth Street, NW, Suite 500, Washington, DC 20005 202-628-0099

I'D LIKE TO TEACH THE WORLD TO SING
(1983) - a coloring book depicting girls and boys in festive attire from 20 countries which illustrates the words of a song of global friendship, the flag of each country, and other educational features; includes a two-page insert with map (designed for ages 7-11), #5092, $3.00 **U.S. Committee on UNICEF** 331 East 38th Street, New York, NY 10016 212-686-5522

KNOXVILLE ZOO TIGER TEAM PACKET
(1989) - information on the way one community brought together the business community, the cultural program and the schools to keep a cultural item for its citizens; describes a massive communitywide campaign involving a recycling program which raised $50,000 to purchase a white tiger loaned to the zoo and scheduled for the circus; includes press clippings and other materials, unpaged, free **Knoxville Zoological Gardens** 333 Woodbine Avenue, Knoxville, TN 37914 615-617-5331

LOCAL GOVERNMENT AND THE ARTS
(1979) - looseleaf guide to civic programs successfully using the arts to gain a place among municipal priorities such as transportation and human resources, 271pp, $15.00 **American Council for the Arts** 570 Seventh Avenue, New York, NY 10018 212-354-6655

MANY FRIENDS COOKING
(1983) - an illustrated cookbook for children ages seven and older; contains 40 easy-to-prepare recipes from 33 countries as well as information on herbs and spices, how to use chopsticks, and other hints for young chefs, #5065, $6.00 **U.S. Committee on UNICEF** 331 East 38th Street, New York, NY 10016 212-686-5522

MILLIONS FOR THE ARTS
(updated as needed) - compendium of facts and information on what is being done by federal and state governments in the areas of the arts and humanities, 64pp, $20.00 (includes update) **Washington International Arts Letter** PO Box 12010, Des Moines, IA 50312 515-243-8691

MUSEUM OPPORTUNITIES FOR OLDER PERSONS
(1990) - a booklet designed to help older persons learn more about the variety of opportunities offered by museums and suggest ways they can serve as volunteers in a museum setting, inquire about availability and cost **Institute of Lifetime Learning** 1909 K Street, NW, Washington, DC 20049 202-872-4700

NACCA INVITES YOU TO CREATIVITY
(1990) - an overview of the NACCA program on creativity; includes answers to questions such as: *Why become more creative?* and *How do we define creativity?* offers hints on nurturing creativity and on the *Three A's of Creativity* (Avoid, Acquire, Adopt), one page, free (packet of information, $1.00 plus SASE) **National Association for Creative Children and Adults** 8080 Springvalley Drive, Cincinnati, OH 45236 513-631-1777

THE PEACE CORPS TODAY

(1986) by M. Fitzgerald - A book written for children providing a brief history of the Peace Corps, created in March 1961 by President Kennedy to send volunteers to help the needy in other countries; how it started; ways individuals - including children - can help the Peace Corps, etc.; includes chapter on the *Peace Corps Partnership Program,* in which groups of children can become *Partners* with people in a school or a community in another country, 128pp, $11.95 **Dodd, Mead & Company** 71 Fifth Avenue, New York, NY 10003

SO YOU WANT TO BE IN THE MOVIES

(1990) - an overview written by an actress based on a survey of well-known actors who rose to stardom from a poverty background (with interviews from some of them); covers preparation, the importance of training and discipline, and roles in the acting profession other than 'the star' that can be very satisfying; uses lively conversational style and a paperback format to attract talented youth who may not relate to structured texts; appends self-tests to determine individual feasibility in pursuing such a career, and *A Word to the Youth Worker* to help maintain reality in counseling youth for this profession, 50pp, $6.50 *[proceeds from this book benefit a homeless-prevention program]* **Mortgage Burning Fund** PO Box 762, Annandale, VA 22003 703-354-6270

STORY-CRAFT SERIES

(1983) - a hardcover book collection of folk tales and crafts from China, Poland, and Sweden; contains two volumes per set (one telling a traditional tale, the other offering instructions on crafts, plays or puppet shows that are unique to each country); designed to be read to younger children, 4-8, while older children try out the crafts, 32pp per book, two-book set $9.00 (specify the country) **U.S. Committee on UNICEF** 331 East 38th Street, New York, NY 10016 212-686-5522

STORYTELLING

(1987) - a guide to selecting, preparing and telling stories to captivate children of all ages and from all backgrounds; includes tips on planning, administering and publicizing a story hour, and utilizing wide-ranging sources from anthologies to cassettes, 182pp, $29.95, also available from book dealers **R. R. Bowker** PO Box 762, New York, NY 10011

STORYTELLING:
READINGS/BIBLIOGRAPHIES/RESOURCES

(1978) - references for the storyteller selected to help build a well-rounded storytelling program in any setting; lists books, articles, recordings, films, videotapes, etc., 16pp, $2.00 **American Library Association** 50 East Huron Street, Chicago, IL 60611 312-944-6780

SUPER VOLUNTEERS!
(ENGLISH/SPANISH/FRENCH/PORTUGUESE)

(1990) - a translated version of the illustrated book of the same name (all four languages each page) depicting four children and a dog who get into and out of trouble but along the way learn about the rewards of volunteering; developed for children ages four to seventeen in countries of the western hemisphere; designed in script format for read-aloud role-playing, 95pp, $2.95 plus $1.50 p/h (quantity discounts, leader/teacher guide available) **Little Red Hen** 7304 Beverly Street, Annandale, VA 22003 703-354-6270

TEENAGER'S GUIDE TO THE RECORD BUSINESS

(1990) - a compendium of the record industry written by a record producer to try to reach at-risk youth through the popular music field inspired by a survey to determine the number of well-known artists who rose to stardom from poverty backgrounds (includes interviews with some of them); covers many occupations in the record business, including artist, manager, producer, engineer, arranger, writer, music business attorney or accountant, etc.; uses lively conversational style and a paperback format to attract talented youth who may not relate to structured texts; appends self-tests to help determine individual feasibility for pursuit of such a career, and *A Word to the Youth Worker* to help maintain reality among youth who aspire to a career in music, 50pp, $6.50 *[proceeds from this book benefit a homeless-prevention program]* **Mortgage Burning Fund** PO Box 762, Annandale, VA 22003 703-354-6270

TRAINING HANDBOOK SERIES

(1989) - a series of handbooks addressing orchestra volunteers, but useful for any volunteer manager, including:
- Principles of Volunteerism ($8 members/$12 nonmembers)
- Fundraising Facts ($3/$5)
- Corporate Sponsorship ($9/$13)
- Annual Fund Drives ($8/$12)
- Evaluating Your Orchestra ($1/$2)
- Long Range Planning ($2/$3)

Ask for complete list **American Symphony Orchestra League** 777 Fourteenth Street, NW, Suite 500, Washington, DC 20005 202-628-0099

VOLUNTEERS!
(ENGLISH/SPANISH/FRENCH/PORTUGUESE)

(1990) - a translated version of the children's book of the same name with all four languages on each page; provides vignettes and line drawings of real-life community volunteer activities; designed for children ages four to seventeen in the countries of the western hemisphere, 95pp, $2.95 plus $1.25 p/h (quantity discounts; inquire) **Little Red Hen** 7304 Beverly Street, Annandale, VA 22003 703-354-6270

VOLUNTEERS IN INTERCULTURAL PROGRAMS

(1989) - a series of training videos and manuals supported by the *W.K. Kellogg Foundation* and originally designed to improve the skills of the Youth For Understanding volunteers who work with students and host families participating in international exchanges, but now adapted by other youth organizations (Boys Clubs, Girl Scouts, Special Olympics, YMCA and 4-H); focuses on heightening the volunteer's intercultural awareness and interpersonal skills by using a variety of training techniques in three series: (1) *Cultural Communication Series,* (2) *Interpersonal Communication Series,* and (3) *Promotion and Marketing Series*; includes in its techniques role playing, case studies and simulation, 30-40 hours per series, $599/series plus $15 postage/handling (Units within series may be purchased separately, inquire) **Youth For Understanding International Exchange** International Center, 3501 Newark Street, NW, Washington, DC 20016-3167 202-966-2800

VOLUNTEERS IN THE ARTS

(1980) - proceedings and other information resulting from a conference on setting up a Volunteers in the Arts program in areas of jobs that can be done, skills needed to administer the program, board members as volunteers; includes forms and other practical materials, $2.50/packet (ask about related tape/slide presentation, same title) **Voluntary Action Center of Greater Milwaukee** 600 East Mason Street, Milwaukee, WI 53202 414-273-7887

WASHINGTON INTERNATIONAL ARTS LETTER

(monthly) - service providing information on 20th century patronage, support programs, and developments in the arts and government, Av. 4pp, $24.50/year individuals; $30.00/year organizations **Washington International Arts Letter** PO Box 12010, Des Moines, IA 50312 515-243-8691

YOUTH ORCHESTRA HANDBOOK

(1989) - an examination of the concerns of volunteers and others committed to ensuring orchestral opportunities for young people in their communities; includes in-depth chapters on the problems of volunteers, managers and board members of youth orchestras - fundraising, marketing, administration, touring, repertoire, etc., 329pp, $25.00 (members), $35.00 (nonmembers) **American Symphony Orchestra League** 777 Fourteenth Street, NW, Suite 500, Washington, DC 20005 202-628-0099

BUSINESS ASSISTANCE

BUSINESS BUILDING IDEAS FOR FRANCHISES AND SMALL BUSINESS
(1977) - promotion ideas designed to help small business owners understand the importance of a well-planned and executed promotional program, 48pp, $2.50 **Pilot Books** 103 Cooper Street, Babylon, NY 11702 516-422-2225

DIRECTORY OF STATE AND FEDERAL FUNDS FOR BUSINESS DEVELOPMENT
(1977) - compilation of information on business financing assistance available from state and federal governments for starting or relocating a business, 64pp, $5.00 **Pilot Books** 103 Cooper Street, Babylon, NY 11702 516-422-2225

ECONOMICS FOR YOUNG AMERICANS (EYA)
(kept current) - a program for instructing secondary and junior college students in the basics of economics; includes Phase I, Phase II, and Phase III, each containing four filmstrips, audio cassettes, scripts, teaching guides, and student activity masters in areas such as natural resource conservation, competition, investments, etc., inquire about cost (ask about companion piece in production, *How Two Local Chambers Worked With Communities on the EYA Program*) **Chamber of Commerce of the United States** 1615 H Street, NW, Washington , DC 20230 202-659-6000

FACTS: SCORE/ACE
(1978) - brief history of the dual program linking seasoned volunteer business people with owners/managers of small businesses needing management counseling; offers this free service to all small businesses - with or without SBA loans; includes state-by-state listing of cities with ACE/SCORE chapters (ACE volunteers are currently active businesspersons; SCORE volunteers are retired persons), #16, 4pp, free **US/SBA - Service Corps of Retired Executives/Active Corps of Executives** 1441 L Street, NW, Washington, DC 20416 202-653-6579

HANDBOOK FOR SMALL BUSINESS FINANCE
(kept current) - descriptions of a few of the many techniques in financial management that can help the small business owner, 63pp, $4.50 **US/GSA - Government Printing Office** Superintendent of Documents, Washington, DC 20402 202-783-3238

HOW TO DO BUSINESS WITH THE GOVERNMENT
(1979) - a guide to help businesses determine when it is wise to do business with the government; discusses problems, procedures, and effect on the overall business, 34pp, $2.50 **Pilot Books** 103 Cooper Street, Babylon, NY 11702 516-422-2225

HOW TO START A PROFITABLE RETIREMENT BUSINESS
(1975) - guide to businesses that can be started with a small investment and, in some cases, supplement an inadequate fixed income or solve the problem of resistance to hiring older persons in the job market, 56pp, $2.50 **Pilot Books** 103 Cooper Street, Babylon, NY 11702 516-422-2225

JOBS: HOW PEOPLE CREATE THEIR OWN
(1977) - a practical guide for those who want to own their own businesses, or have major control of their responsibilities on the job; discusses crafts as a business as well as the conventional small business operation; provides brief profiles of existing efforts, illustrations, and other aids to clarify the text, 228pp, $4.95 **Beacon Press** 25 Beacon Street, Boston, MA 02108 617-742-2110

MANAGEMENT ASSISTANCE
(1979) - brief profiles of SBA programs including: The Small Business Institute (university involvement); The Call Contracting Program (involving management and technical assistance firms); Management Training (courses, problem clinics, prebusiness workshops and conferences); Small Business Development Center (private sector initiative), and other programs, 13pp, free **US/SBA - Office of Management Assistance** 1441 L Street, NW, Washington , DC 20416 202-653-6579

SBA PILOT MINI-LOAN PROGRAM FOR WOMEN
(undated) - outline of the Executive Order creating a policy and setting in motion a program for women's business enterprise; includes complete details on eligibility, terms and other factors of the program, 4pp, free **US/SBA - Office for Women** 1441 L Street, NW, Washington, DC 20416 202-653-6579

SCORE/ACE COUNSELOR'S GUIDEBOOK
(1975) - manual developed to point up some of the more common problems encountered by small business owners/managers, and suggest a basis for their solution; covers general areas such as

"Sources of Information" and "Overall Considerations," and specific areas such as "A Small Retailer," "Service Organizations;" appends listing of pamphlets, forms, and other resources; useful for anyone providing management assistance, 48pp, single copy free **US/SBA - Service Corps of Retired Executives/Active Corps of Executives** 1441 L Street, NW, Washington, DC 20416 202-653-6579

SINGLE-ENTRY BOOKKEEPING SYSTEM FOR SMALL-SCALE MANUFACTURING BUSINESSES
(1979) - a tool providing illustrations and step-by-step directions for constructing the bookkeeping kit, with reminders and hints inserted in vulnerable instruction areas; includes eight questions and answers on analyzing the business, sample forms and letters, and a glossary of bookkeeping terms (developed by a volunteer), 54pp, $4.95 **Volunteers in Technical Assistance** 1815 North Lynn Street, Arlington, VA 22209 703-276-1800

SMALL BUSINESS GOES TO COLLEGE
(1979) - samples of courses offered by some 200 colleges and universities to assist the small business person, 82pp, $4.75 **US/GSA - Government Printing Office** Superintendent of Documents, Washington, DC 20402 202-783-3238

SMALL BUSINESS GUIDE TO GOVERNMENT
(1980) - a handbook designed to enable small business owners and potential owners to identify quickly the proper government agency or person to handle their needs, help solve problems, and point to available resources, 73pp, single copy free **US/SBA - Office of Advocacy** 1441 L Street, NW, Washington, DC 20416 202-653-6579

SMALL BUSINESS IDEAS FOR WOMEN - HOW TO GET STARTED
(1975) - details on businesses in and outside of the home which are flexible in the amount of time and commitment required, and depend on the requirements and abilities of the individual, 32pp, $2.00 **Pilot Books** 103 Cooper Street, Babylon, NY 11702 526-422-2225

SMALL BUSINESS REPORTER BULLETIN
(intermittent) - public service bulletin to keep small business owners and managers informed of trends and issues that may affect their businesses, and to reflect and respond to requests from readers, av. 8pp, $2.00 (available free at Bank of America branches in California), free listing of available titles **Small Business Reporter** Department 3401, PO Box 37000, San Francisco, CA 94137 415-622-3456

SO YOU'RE GOING INTO BUSINESS
(undated) - basic information on the initial steps and problems that a new business owner or manager will encounter in the early stages of establishing the business, 16pp, single copy free **Chamber of Commerce of the United States** Domestic Distribution Department, 1615 H Street, NW, Washington, DC 20230 202-659-6000

STARTING A BUSINESS AFTER 50
(1977) - examples and guidelines for older persons wishing to own their own businesses; takes into consideration some of the limitations of the elderly, 46pp, $2.50 **Pilot Books** 103 Cooper Street, Babylon, NY 11702 516-422-2225

STARTING AND MANAGING A SMALL BUSINESS OF YOUR OWN
(1974) - coverage of every aspect of a small business from the initial idea to the profit monitoring areas, PB 282-705, 125pp,

$9.00 **National Technical Information Service** 5285 Port Royal Road, Springfield, VA 22151 703-557-4650

STRATEGIES & TECHNIQUES/SAVING THE FINANCIALLY-DISTRESSED SMALL BUSINESS
(1976) - an overview of some of the remedies available to the small business owner in financial difficulties, 48pp, $6.00 **Pilot Books** 103 Cooper Street, Babylon, NY 11702 516-422-2225

TRAINING TO MANAGE A PROFITABLE SMALL BUSINESS
(1980) - a directory of 189 colleges and universities in 43 states which provide instruction in small business management, 24pp, $2.50 **Reymont Associates** 6556 Southwest Maple, Boca Raton, FL 33433 305-391-3929

WANT TO BE YOUR OWN BOSS?
(undated) - practical advice and resource information for the individual seeking to start a business; also useful for current business owners/managers seeking a checkpoint for their operations, 16pp, single copy free **US/DoL - Office of Information** 200 Constitution Avenue, NW, Washington , DC 20210 202-523-7304

WHAT THEY REALLY TEACH YOU AT HARVARD BUSINESS SCHOOL
(1986) - a "serious spoof" written from the human side, and portraying emotional experiences as well as the educational guidelines used at Harvard in areas of marketing, employee relations, finance, interviewing, and other aspects of running a business; includes a detailed course-by-course description of the general business curriculum required of all students, 260pp, $9.95 plus postage and handling ($.50 per order and $.50 per book) **Warner Books** 75 Rockefeller Plaza, New York, NY 10019 212-484-7056

A WOMAN'S GUIDE TO HER OWN FRANCHISED BUSINESS
(1979) - details on a type of business that provides the satisfaction of owning a business, and the experience to enable independence at a later time, 40pp, $2.50 **Pilot Books** 103 Cooper Street, Babylon, NY 11702 516-422-2225

WOMEN AND THE SMALL BUSINESS ADMINISTRATION
(1979) - overview of SBA's assistance to women, describing services in general, and those of particular interest to women, such as the National Women's Business Ownership Campaign started in 1977, 6pp, free **US/SBA - Office for Women** 1441 L Street, NW, Washington, DC 20416 202-653-6579

YOUR BUSINESS TAX KIT
(kept current) - kit containing tax forms, instructions, and sample notices sent to businesses; kit is designed to meet the needs of new businesses and, to the extent possible, contents are based upon the needs of the type of business to which the kit is being given, single kit free **Internal Revenue Service** Taxpayer Service Division, 1111 Constitution Avenue, NW, Washington, DC 20225 202-566-4904

BUSINESS/INDUSTRY INVOLVEMENT

THE BEST ENVIRONMENTAL CONSERVATION EDUCATION PROGRAMS IN AMERICA
(1982) - profiles of award winners in a project co-sponsored by Allis-Chalmers and the National Association of Conservation Districts, which seeks outstanding programs in conservation education; provides detailed profiles of winners and programs in schools at all grade levels (elementary, intermediate, and high school), 16pp, free **Allis-Chalmers Corporation** 1101 Seventeenth Street, NW, Washington, DC 20036 202-659-2500

BLOOD PRESSURE CONTROL AT THE WORKSITE
(1979) - a manual of procedures for blood pressure control programs in industrial settings; includes step-by-step procedures and protocols; appends sample forms, 83pp, $5.00; 10 or more, $4.00/copy **Institute of Labor and Industrial Relations** 401 Fourth Street, Ann Arbor, MI 48103 313-764-1817

BOEING EMPLOYEES GOOD NEIGHBOR FUND
(kept current) - overview of a project which is supported by contributions from Boeing employees to provide funds to non-profit social and welfare agencies to carry out programs of benefit to the community; includes profiles of groups receiving the awards (a $1,500 award by Boeing Computer Services in Vienna, Virginia, to the Northern Virginia Youth Services Coalition, for example), free information kit **Boeing Company** PO Box 3707, Seattle, WA 98124-2207 206-655-2121

BUSINESS AND ENVIRONMENT: TOWARD COMMON GROUND
(1977) - overview of issues that divide the business and environmental communities; includes views, ideas and suggestions from leaders on both sides of the issue; draws together the major points to effect a "merger" of ideas that could suggest solutions to this persistent debate, 450pp, $10.00 **Conservation Foundation** 1250 24th Street, NW, Washington, DC 20037 202-293-4800

BUSINESS ISSUES IN THE CLASSROOM
(1990) - a videotape which provides information on curriculum materials and business volunteers for the *Business Issues in the Classroom* program presented to schools across the country, 12 minutes, inquire about cost **Constitutional Rights Foundation** 601 South Kingsley Drive, Los Angeles, CA 90005 213-487-5590

THE BUSINESS SECTOR ROLE IN EMPLOYMENT POLICY
(1979) - compilation of information on ways that business has been and can become involved in helping to establish equitable employment policy at local, regional, and national levels, 26pp, single copy free **National Commission for Employment Policy** 1522 K Street, NW, Washington, DC 20005 202-724-1545

"C DAY"
(undated) - profile of one company's volunteer effort in which 1,500 workers voluntarily report to work on a free Saturday and give their days' earnings to the United Way ($240,000 in 1982); stresses that employees usually could not afford as much out-of-pocket (program is almost 40 years old), other information available **McCormick and Company** 414 Light Street, Baltimore, MD 21202 301-547-6000

CITIZEN VOLUNTEER PROGRAM
(1983) - key "how-to" steps in identifying community problems, determining which needs best suit the volunteer's talents, and gaining cooperation from others; addresses those who: have never volunteered, have wanted to volunteer but have never been asked, don't want to volunteer, but could get others to volunteer, are looking for ways to involve employees, want to develop personal skills, are concerned about families, communities and people in need, but don't know how to help, or have other reasons for getting involved. Includes sections such as:
- Fourteen Questions You Should Ask Yourself
- Key Questions for Organizations - Especially Businesses
- Benefits of Volunteering
- Where to Get Started - 20 People Who Need You Now and Talents They Can Use
- Actions for Individuals - 23 Things You Can Do
- Actions for Senior Management - 14 Ways to Learn What Needs to Be Done; How to Support Employee Involvement
- Where To Go For More Help
- "Private Initiatives Now!" (speech)
- "A Call to Social Involvement" (speech)

Bases information partially on the success of Rexnord's ongoing "Activate Someone" project initiated in the 1970's, and the under-used pool of expertise available through the company, single copy of the booklet is free **Rexnord Resource Center** 200 Executive Drive, Brookfield, WI 53005 414-643-3000

CLEAN TEAM
(undated) - a manual for initiating an in-plant program to solve the problem of mismanagement of waste in business and industry through a cooperative effort by workers and management; includes information for recruiting a "clean team," preparing a solid waste energy survey, and training the team members, $30 (request free background and order form for the "Clean Team") **Keep America Beautiful** Mill River Plaza, 9 West Broad Street, Stamford, CT 06902 203-323-8987

COMPANIES SHOW GREATER CONCERN: HEALTH INITIATIVE SURVEY
(October 1983) - special issue of *Roundtable Report* reflecting a survey that shows increased insurer-community cooperative activity, Av. 4pp, #83-9, single copy free **Business Roundtable** 200 Park Avenue, Suite 2222, New York, NY 10166 212-682-6370

COMPANY PROGRAM ON ALCOHOLISM
(1974) - an aid to management in formulating a program for rehabilitation of alcoholic employees (prepared by Christopher D. Smithers Foundation with 35 leading U.S. firms), 42pp, $1.30 **National Council on Alcoholism** 12 West 21st Street, New York, NY 10010 212-206-6770

CONTROLLING CHOLESTEROL: AFTER 50
(1989) - a video developed by RJR Nabisco through its subsidiary, the Fleischmann Corporation, to address the issue of high cholesterol, which affects one out of four adults who risk heart disease; includes case histories involving older persons, the role of diet, exercise and heredity in cholesterol control, and other information for persons age 50 and over, 30 minutes, VHF, $8.99 **RJR Nabisco Corporation** 300 Galleria Parkway, Atlanta, GA 30339 404-852-3000

CONTROLLING CHOLESTEROL THROUGH DIET AND NUTRITION
(1989) - a video developed by the Fleischmann subsidiary, of RJR Nabisco Corporation to address the issue of high cholesterol, which affects one out of four adults who risk heart disease; includes shopping with a nutritionist, low cholesterol cooking tips, foods that can help lower cholesterol levels, and a low saturated fat, low cholesterol diet, 30 minutes, VHF, $8.99 **RJR Nabisco Corporation** 300 Galleria Parkway, Atlanta, GA 30339 404-852-3000

CORPORATE/COMMUNITY INVOLVEMENT (IL)
(kept current) - an overview of the involvement of McDonald's Corporation and McDonald's individual restaurants in the nation's communities; includes information about Ronald McDonald House (where parents of seriously ill children can stay in the area of the hospital); various campaigns in local restaurants, such as "Sponsor An Athlete" (to offset expenses for local Special Olympians); the Child Restraint Seats program providing "free on loan" seats to parents, etc. (in cooperation with the American Automobile Association); the Blue Chip-In summer jobs program (in cooperation with the local mayor); the 1984 Olympic Games Gymnastic Program sponsorship, and other efforts, single kit free **McDonald's Corporation** One McDonald's Plaza, Oak Brook, IL 60521 312-887-3200

CORPORATE COMMUNITY INVOLVEMENT (VA)
(1986) - a bibliography of selected abstracts on corporate community involvement in areas of research, cash and non-cash giving, education, employment, model programming, etc. from 1980 to 1986; appends involvement from 1950 to 1979, and listings of organizational and other resources, 92pp, $10.00 **United Way of America** 701 North Fairfax Street, Alexandria, VA 22314 703-836-7100

CORPORATE GUIDE TO THE HOLIDAYS
(1989) - an outgrowth of the *Make It Home for the Holidays* campaign launched each December through a joint venture of business/industry, local government, and the private sector; offers responsible party giving tips aimed at reducing highway fatalities due to drunk driving; developed for members, but available to others while supply lasts, inquire **Greater Washington Board of Trade** 1129 Twentieth Street, NW, Washington, DC 20036 202-857-5900

CREATING AND MANAGING A CORPORATE SCHOOL VOLUNTEER PROGRAM
(undated) - comprehensive resource manual designed to take individuals through a thirteen-stage process resulting in a business and education partnership volunteer program (available in duplicated version only), $30.00 **National Association of Partners in Education** 601 Wythe Street, Suite 200, Alexandria, VA 22314 703-836-4880

CREATING CORPORATE-CAMPUS PARTNERSHIPS
(1988) - a special issue of *Currents* which explains the basis of corporate-education relationships; includes points to consider in promoting and maintaining the partnership in several areas of concern such as philanthropy, shared research parks, etc., 72pp, $6 (members); $7.50 (nonmembers) **Council for Advancement and Support of Education** 80 South Early Street, Alexandria, VA 22304 703-823-6966

DC CVC ACCOMPLISHMENTS
(updated as needed) - a fact sheet on the accomplishments of the DC Corporate Volunteer Council; includes projects such as a senior citizen talent show, a nonprofit/business partnership workshop, a consultant service to employee volunteer programs nationwide, monthly meetings on community issues, a joint business/volunteer initiative focused on hunger and homelessness, etc., one page, free **District of Columbia Corporate Volunteer Council** 1313 New York Avenue, NW, Suite 303, Washington, DC 20005 202-638-2664

DRINKING ON THE JOB: THE $15-BILLION HANGOVER
(1983) - an exploration of the cost to employers, and thus the general public, of maintaining drinking employees without taking steps to mount a program that helps the employee while solving the company's fiscal problem, 28pp, $.50 (quantity discounts) **Public Affairs Committee** 381 Park Avenue, New York, NY 10016 212-683-4331

EAP MANUAL
(1983) - an outline of the nature and extent of the problem of alcoholism in industry, some attempts to deal with the problem, the key role of labor, and a proven approach to establishing an effective employee alcoholism/assistance program; includes a review of the key elements, and an explanation of how these elements are integrated with existing policies and procedures; covers employee education, insurance, training (including union staff), design of the information system, and statistical information about savings through employee assistance programs (New York Transit Authority effected savings of over $1,000,000 per year in paid sick leave, for example), $6.00 (request complete list of pamphlets, books and handouts for employee/alcoholism assistance programs, including: *Henry's Loaded Again... I Say, Let's Fire Him* (reprint) and *Company/Union Programs for Alcoholics* (pamphlet) **National Council on Alcoholism** 12 West 21st Street, New York , NY 10010 212-206-6770

AN EFFECTIVE APPROACH TO EMPLOYEE ALCOHOLISM
(1972) - detailed outline on how to install and implement an

employee alcoholism program, 4pp reprint, $.30 **National Council on Alcoholism** 12 West 21st Street, New York, NY 10010 212-206-6770

EMPLOYEE AND RETIREE VOLUNTEER INVOLVEMENT: INFORMATION PACKET

(1983) - an overview of the ways in which Honeywell supports and encourages volunteerism, including:
- **Community Service Awards:** once in a lifetime grants of $500 to organizations with which Honeywell employees are active volunteers.
- Management Assistance Project (MAP):

a program in which volunteers provide technical and management assistance to area nonprofit organizations.
- **HELP (Honeywell Employee Launched Projects):** a program in which departments or groups of employees use their skills and energies to respond to community needs.
- **Honeywell Retiree Volunteer Program:** a program in which retired employees coordinate recruitment activities, organize and develop the programs, administer the office and train and place other retired volunteers.

Provides information on the above award-winning programs, and other materials on the company's involvement in voluntary action, single packet free [Honeywell is one of the recipients of the 1983 President's Volunteer Action Awards] **Honeywell** PO Box 524, Minneapolis, MN 55440 612-870-5200

EMPLOYEE ASSISTANCE PROGRAM

(undated) - information about the company's successful efforts to alleviate the problems arising from the bankruptcy of Braniff Airlines, which resulted in 5,000 workers entering the already tight job market; describes the communications center established by the company, which involved 34 company volunteers to operate the round-the-clock service; provides an overview of the three-day job readiness seminar sponsored by the company to assist former Braniff employees with resume writing, interviewing and job counseling, and three Job Fairs for the Dallas-Fort Worth area (a program that was absorbed by the community's permanent employment service when the urgency subsided), single packet free **Frito-Lay, Inc.** Box 35034, Dallas, TX 75235 214-351-7000

EMPLOYEE ASSISTANCE PROGRAMS (EAP)

(1983) - one of a series of "Strategic Issue Briefs" reviewing the history and current status of development of employee assistance programs; examines potential implications and issues of this work service program, #0341, $2.00 members; $2.50 non-members **United Way of America** 701 North Fairfax Street, Alexandria, VA 22314-2045 703-836-7100

EMPLOYERS AND CHILD CARE: ESTABLISHING SERVICES THROUGH THE WORKPLACE

(1982) - a comprehensive overview of child care programs in the workplace; covers:
- The Child Care Need and Services Available
- Employer/Labor Involvement in Programs
- Establishing a Task Force
- Planning and Cost Analysis
- Funding Sources
- Tax Issues
- Program Components
- Implementing the Program Plan

Includes a detailed summary and references for additional information; appends a partial list of employer-sponsored child care programs in the United States, 83pp, single copy free **US/DoL - Women's Bureau** 200 Constitution Avenue, NW, Washington, DC 20210 202-523-6611

EMPLOYMENT DISCRIMINATION BASED ON CRIMINAL RECORDS

(1978) - overview of progress being made through cooperative efforts of business/industry to eliminate the practice of immediate rejection in the job market for ex-prisoners, #24,959, 8pp, $1.25 (must use stock number) **National Clearinghouse for Legal Services** 407 South Dearborn Street, Suite 600, Chicago, IL 60605 312-939-3830

ENERGY CONSERVATION

(kept current) - description of the Company's free speakers' service designed as a public service to help local groups as they plan programs to pursue solutions to energy problems; topics covered by Virginia Power speakers include energy conservation, nuclear power, environmental effects of electricity generation, radiation, natural gas, fuel cost, inflation and others; makes speakers available for energy fairs, conventions, local radio and TV talk shows, and related activities; provides speakers with slide shows or films, depending on the subject matter; includes schools in its speaker program, 4-panel foldout, free **Virginia Power** Community Affairs Department, PO Box 2666, Richmond, VA 23261 804-771-3000

EXECUTIVE LOAN PROGRAM

(undated) - an overview of a national technical assistance program in which companies offer experts in the field of ridesharing to organizations to assist them in developing, organizing, and/or expanding a ridesharing program, free **US/DoT - National Ridesharing Information Center** 400 Seventh Street, SW, Washington, DC 20590 202-426-0210

4-H SALUTE TO EXCELLENCE PROGRAM

(1983) - overview of a program designed to recognize and enhance the skills of volunteer leaders who work with the nearly five million youth in the 4-H program; describes sponsorship by R.J. Reynolds of the five-day national event (the first corporation to salute the leadership of the more than 620,000 volunteer leaders working daily with 4-H youth); lists objectives of the program as follows:
- increase leadership abilities through communications skills
- increase the effectiveness of volunteer leadership in 4-H
- gain a greater understanding of the legislative process
- enhance abilities to teach and formulate programs
- design plans of action to expand volunteerism within each state
- recognize 4-H volunteer leaders

States overall goal as "combining recognition and education in one substantial program;" 14pp, single copy free **R. J. Reynolds Industries** World Headquarters Building, Winston-Salem, NC 27102 919-773-2000

GOLDEN RULE AWARDS PROGRAM

(annually) - a packet of information describing an awards program that provides five grants in three categories of volunteerism:
- individuals who have been cited for outstanding volunteer services;
- volunteer organizations that have been honored for performing exceptional service; and
- J.C. Penney employees who have contributed exemplary volunteer service.

Lists award winners who receive an engraved Golden Rule award and a bronze sculpture designed by artist Greg Wyat, plus the opportunity to designate a volunteer organization to receive $2,000 from J.C. Penney; describes composition of the panel of judges, which is composed of community leaders, single packet free **J.C. Penney Company** 14041 Dallas Parkway, Dallas, TX 75240 214-591-1000

GOOD NEIGHBOR FUND

(undated) - fact sheet describing a program in which register tapes display a figure totaling five percent of the purchase amount and designate it as a contribution for a nonprofit group; enables purchaser to pass tapes along to a favorite charity, who then submits them to the company and receives a contribution equaling five percent of the total of all tickets, 2pp, free **Fantle's** 3301 Pennsy Drive, Landover, MD 20785 301-772-6000

GUIDELINES FOR BUSINESS SPONSORED CONSUMER EDUCATION MATERIALS

(1982) - a discussion of the differences among consumer education materials, promotion materials, and information materials, emphasizing that consumer education materials are without commercialization; provides guidelines for developing appropriate education materials, the necessity for accuracy and objectivity, the selection of format and media, and ways to ensure quality and credibility; includes insert describing ways the Society can assist corporations so that the intended beneficiary of the materials, the general public, receives the best possible information, 8pp and insert, single copy free **Society of Consumer Affairs Professionals in Business** 400 Leesburg Pike, Suite 311, Alexandria, VA 22302 703-998-7371

HOW RIDESHARING CAN HELP YOUR COMPANY: A MANUAL FOR EMPLOYERS

(1980) - a "how-to" manual for employers wishing to organize a company ridesharing program; includes sample forms and letters, and facts and statistics to aid in establishing a program, free **US/DoT - National Ridesharing Information Center** 400 Seventh Street, SW, Washington, DC 20590 202-426-0210

INVOLVEMENT CORPS IMPLEMENTATION REPORT

(undated) - detailed report on the beginnings and current operation of a local Involvement Corps; covers program objectives, implementation, relationships with involvement, corporations, and agencies, impact of corporate volunteerism program on regular VAC activities, several forms, checklists, and other aids, 23pp, $4.00 **Involvement Corps** 161 West Wisconsin Avenue, Milwaukee, WI 53203 414-273-7887

INVOLVEMENT CORPS RESOURCE COORDINATOR HANDBOOK

(1979) - description of the corporate volunteer program with background and benefits; includes key elements of the program, responsibilities of the coordinator, selection of the community involvement team (CIT), management liaison suggestions, project ideas, volunteer recognition ideas, sample forms, and other aids, unpaged, $5.00 **Involvement Corps** 161 West Wisconsin Avenue, Milwaukee, WI 53203 414-273-7887

JOB STRATEGIES FOR URBAN YOUTH: SIXTEEN PILOT PROGRAMS FOR ACTION

(1979) - reports on cooperative programs initiated and successfully completed to help solve the urgent problems of urban youth employment, 112pp report $7.95; 18pp executive summary $3.95 **Work in America Institute** 700 White Plains Road, Scarsdale, NY 10583 914-472-9600

JOB TRAINING OPPORTUNITIES

(annually) - a handbook based on input from major corporations in a large city describing job training opportunities that are funded under the Job Training Partnership Act (JTPA); covers numerous job areas (auto mechanic, accounting assistant, bank teller, chef, computer programmer, etc.), and special programs for Asian, handicapped, Hispanic, Indochinese, offenders, older workers and youth; includes sections on direct job placement and educational

development, 36pp, single copy free **District of Columbia Corporate Volunteer Council** 1313 New York Avenue, NW, Suite 303, Washington, DC 20005 202-638-2664

KAB CASE STUDIES

(dates vary) - selected two to four-page accounts of volunteer efforts in localities across the country ($.50/set; Av. four per set); titles on business involvement:

- *PRIDE: A Bank's Concern* (undated) - profile of a program that grew out of a local bank's concern about the center-city's litter problem; discusses development of program, which involved 4,000 volunteers. 2pp
- *Beverage Industry Recycling Program in Arizona* (undated) - story of *BIRP (Beverage Industry Recycling Program)* formed by two beverage companies; describes the six mini-centers in the statewide operation, 2pp

(request by case study title; sets are random selections) **Keep America Beautiful** Mill River Plaza, Nine West Broad Street, Stamford, CT 06902 203-323-8987

LIFESAVER TAGS

(1989) - brochure describing a free service of Coors which provides lifesaver tags with important medical data which can save lives in emergency situations; describes types of emergencies that might require the tags (injuries while jogging, cycling, running, walking, etc.), and emphasizes the special urgency when an injured person is unidentified and in need of medical aid; includes instructions on filling out (with indelible ink) and attaching these machine-washable tags to clothing, shoes, wallet, neckchains, etc.; appends order blank, free (two sent; if more needed, specify) **Adolph Coors Company** Community Affairs Office, Golden, CO 80401-1295 303-277-2197

MAYORS' AWARDS PROGRAM IN RECOGNITION OF OUTSTANDING LEADERSHIP IN CITIZEN VOLUNTEERISM

(annually) - an overview of the Mayors' Awards Program sponsored by Xerox, covering the focus, the presenters, national awards winners, those singled out for special recognition, and the recipient of the Michael A. deNunzio Award presented for distinguished achievement, Av. 24pp, single copy free **Xerox Corporation** Community Affairs Office, Stamford, CT 06904 203-329-8700

THE MENTALLY RETARDED WORKER: AN ECONOMIC DISCOVERY

(1983) - a report to the President presenting findings demonstrating that mentally retarded persons can be productive workers; covers three areas:

- First Section introduces the subject, discusses retardation, and describes why the retarded worker is an economic discovery.
- Second Section counters misconceptions of some employers with testimony from employers who have profited from hiring people who are mentally retarded.
- Third Section identifies training and employment issues and recommends changes for the decade of the 80's.

Structures guidelines for application to parents of retarded workers, trainers, policymakers, and the mentally retarded themselves, as well as the employer; closes with "Post Script: The Future," 26pp, single copy free **US/President's Committee on Mental Retardation** Office of Human Development, Washington, DC 20201 202-245-7634

NATIONAL ALLIANCE OF BUSINESS: ANNUAL REPORT

(undated) - more than an annual report in its detailed descriptions of programs designed to help alleviate employment pressures on certain population groups (single copy free); includes:

- The Private Sector Initiative Program - concerted efforts at closer collaboration between government and the private sector.

- Raising the Level of Leadership - the loaned executive program.
- College Cluster Program - an effort to bring together business and the historically black colleges.
- Youth Motivation Task Force - several programs for motivating, training, and placing youth.
- Assistance to Education - work with educational organizations, high schools and colleges to improve vocational education and counseling techniques.
- Business Awareness - a program designed to raise the level of business understanding about job training partnerships at local and state levels.

National Alliance of Business 1015 Fifteenth Street, NW, Washington, DC 20005 202-457-0040

NATIONAL DIRECTORY OF ARTS AND EDUCATION SUPPORT BY BUSINESS CORPORATIONS

(1981) - a compilation that shows what areas of the arts have interested the business world over the years; lists by location to give aid-seekers data on sources on their own home grounds; includes over 700 main bodies and over 2800 subsidiaries, approx. 228pp, $75.00 **Washington International Arts Letter** PO Box 12010, Des Moines, IA 50312 515-243-8691

1990 VOLUNTEER PROJECTS: UNITED WAY AT WORK PROGRAM

(1990) - a guide for employees providing categorized "shopping lists" of volunteer projects in the community in need of volunteer assistance; includes program ideas in areas of health, crisis intervention, family services, emergency services, recreation, staff support, basic services, etc., single copy free **Volunteer Center of the Greater Quad Cities** 1417 Sixth Avenue, Moline , IL 61265 309-764-6804

NON PROFITS ARE BUSINESSES THAT HELP THEIR COMMUNITY

(1990) - a dual-message to businesses, pointing out the benefits of community service to business on the one hand, and providing suggestions for giving on the other (both in-kind and money), 6-panel foldout, free **Volunteer Boulder County** 3305 North Broadway, Suite One, Boulder, CO 80304 303-444-4904

POTENTIAL COSTS AND ECONOMIC BENEFITS OF INDUSTRIAL DAY CARE

(1971) - pros and cons to help leaders in business and industry decide on the issue of day care for employees, 26pp, single copy free **US/DoL - Women's Bureau** 200 Constitution Avenue, NW, Washington, DC 20210 202-523-6611

RESPOND TO: MENTALLY RESTORED WORKERS

(undated) - a look at the experience of employers with mentally-restored workers; emphasizes positive results in areas of productivity, absences due to illness, attitudes of supervisors and fellow-workers, etc.; cites federal programs providing incentives, and other information helpful to employers on the subject, 6-panel foldout [currently out of print; request photocopy] **National Mental Health Association** 1021 Prince Street, Alexandria, VA 22314 703-684-7722

RETIREMENT - A NEW DIMENSION

(1980) - packet of materials used in the Center's pre-retirement program in its work with business/industry and the community; emphasizes volunteer services and recreational and educational programs for the retired person, $1.50/packet **Volunteer Resources Division** 484 Main Street, Suite 300, Worcester, MA 01608 617-757-5631

RIDESHARING PROGRAMS OF BUSINESS AND INDUSTRY

(1983) - descriptions of 25 successful ridesharing programs listing companies involved, and discussing ridesharing modes such as carpools, vanpools, buspools and transit; cites key program elements including matching, preferential parking, overtime and flextime policies, promotional activities, technical assistance and program costs as they relate to company savings; appends ridesharing program profiles for the 25 companies, 55pp, free **US/DoT - National Ridesharing Information Center** 400 Seventh Street, SW, Washington, DC 20590 202-426-0210

SPEAKERS!

(kept current) - an overview of the Company's free speakers' service, involving volunteer speakers who are ecomonists, geologists, engineers, and other professionals; covers issues in areas of Careers in Energy, Conservation - Saving the Way to Tomorrow, Wilderness - A Choice for the Future, The Need for Energy Alternatives, Corporation and Society, ARCO and the '84 Olympics, Solar Electricity - Energy for Our Time, and others; provides slide shows and films for many of the talks, 8-panel foldout, free [Also available from Atlantic Richfield Company, 515 South Flower Street, Los Angeles, CA 90071 213-486-3511] **Atlantic Richfield Company** 1333 New Hampshire Avenue, NW, Suite 1001, Washington, DC 20036 202-457-6200

TIME, INC. AND ITS COMMUNITIES: A SPECIAL REPORT

(1982) - a special edition of *Equal Time* to report on Time's activities toward improving the nation's communities; includes information on the company's commitment to equal opportunity in three ways:

Affirmative Action mandates each department and subsidiary to set internal hiring and promotion goals for minorities and women.
Corporate Contributions - gives 2% of previous year's pretax profits annually to educational, civic, welfare, cultural and environmental institutions (plans to increase the amount gradually to 5% of previous year's pretax profits).
Community Development - channels corporate resources and talent to essential institutions in communities through its Community Relations Office, establishing diverse community involvement priorities such as:

- Business and Community Partnerships
- Scholarship Assistance
- Loaned Executives
- Managerial and Financial Assistance to Small Businesses
- Plan for Purchasing Goods and Services from Minority- and Women-Owned Businesses
- Involvement in Public Policy Debates on the revitalization of the nation's cities.

Highlights special programs for which the Corporation is sole sponsor, often lending employees and technical assistance to them; examples of these discrete programs are:

- **Program 3** - a high school equivalency and work program for urban youth;
- **Time-Life Academy of Transition** - a community-based "street academy" or storefront school;
- **Project Partnership** - a corporate partnership to employ the disabled;
- **Summer Editorial Intern Program** - a project for college journalism students; and
- **Summer Jobs for Youth** - a project for high school students.

Includes a column describing community involvement of Time's wholly-owned activities across the country, such as the examples below:

- **Temple Eastex** - Minority Recruitment and Relocation; Engineering Internships; and Bilingual Education.
- **Inland Container** - Minority Purchasing.
- **American Television and Communications** - Seed Money to

Community-based Programs; Community Programming; Training Center for the Unemployed; and Job Training at a Prison.
- **Home Box Office** - Museum Open to Schools; Cable Car Day; Cash for Cancer; and Aid to Black Culture.
- **Time-Life Books** - Publishing Courses for Minorities.
- **Little, Brown** - Jobs for the Mentally Retarded.
- **Book-of-the-Month-Club** - Training for the Disabled.
- **Pioneer Press** - Technical Assistance for Non Profits.

Provides an overview of corporate activities in the area of committing financial resources through direct corporate contributions to over 200 institutions and organizations each year, representing interests in education, cultural activities, civic affairs, social welfare, and environment; provides name of grantee and number of years supported (ranging from two years for a neighborhood economic development group and five years for an employment service for the disabled to 38 years for the National Urban League and the New York Public Library).
Discusses individual volunteer efforts as an unofficial "company standard," with top management setting examples by serving on boards of community organizations and in other capacities, 8pp, single copy free (inquire about a full subscription to Equal Time, a quarterly newsletter focusing on equal employment opportunity and including articles such as "Unemployed Vietnam-era Veterans" and "Inland's Minority Purchasing Program," as well as updates on Time's Community Relations Office activities) **Time Incorporated, Community Relations Office** Time and Life Building, Rockefeller Center, New York, NY 10010 212-841-2526

'TIS THE SEASON
(1990) - information packet about the *Neighbor Helping Neighbor* program in which the *Washington Post, Giant Foods,* and the *Capital Area Community Food Bank* joined forces to raise food and money to feed 160,000 people in the District of Columbia, southern and central Maryland, and northern Virginia; may include reprints, sample printed grocery bag, etc., but contents change as materials are depleted, single packet free **Washington Post** Promotion Department, 1150 Fifteenth Street, NW, Washington, DC 20071 202-334-4371

UNITED WAY AT WORK
(1990) - a collection of profiles of business/industry involvement in volunteerism in the Joaquin County area; includes programs of *J.C. Penney, Contel, Owens-Brockway, Pacific Gas and Electric,* and the *Stockton Development Center;* subject areas include shelters, fairs, food drives, recycling, Special Olympics, stop-smoking events, handicapped, child abuse, etc., 6pp, single copy free **Volunteer Center/United Way At Work** 12 East Park Street, PO Box 1585, Stockton, CA 95201 209-943-0870

V.I.C.E. SQUAD
(kept current) - brochure describing the Adolph Coors Company Volunteers In Community Enrichment (V.I.C.E.) program, including when and how it began, the scope of the service, and the type of assistance it can provide to other companies interested in mounting corporate volunteer programs, 8-panel foldout, free **Adolph Coors Company** Community Affairs Office, Golden, CO 80401-1295 303-277-2197

V.I.C.E. SQUAD MONTHLY ACTIVITY GUIDE
(monthly) - a listing of approved projects for V.I.C.E. and A.D.V.I.C.E. squads of the Coors community involvement program; includes upcoming activities, ongoing activities, and a photo page of Coors volunteers in action, Av. 4pp, single copy free **Adolph Coors Company** Community Affairs Office, Golden, CO 80401-1295 303-277-2197

VIP INFORMATION PACKET
(1990) - overview of ways in which a utility company has not only provided release-time volunteers, but has assisted with the development of a countywide volunteer center and recruitment of citizen volunteers from its eight-county service area, unpaged, single copy free **Atlantic Electric Company** 1199 Black Horse Pike, Pleasantville, NJ 08232 609-645-4100

VOLUNTEERS FROM THE WORKPLACE
(undated) - brief profile of a program involving some 200 volunteer employees from a local company (the Bankers Life "It's Up to Me" group); lists examples of projects such a group can mount, and benefits to the volunteer, the corporation, the community and the person or group being served, 6-panel foldout and application card, $.50 + $.25 handling **Volunteer Center of United Way of Central Iowa** 1100 Ninth Street, Suite 300, Des Moines, IA 50314 515-246-6545

VOLUNTEERS FROM THE WORKPLACE
(1979) - an overview of employee volunteer programs based on a 1978 survey; covers issues of corporate volunteerism such as released time practices, group volunteer projects, union counseling programs, internal employee matching systems, loaned executives, corporate funding, etc.; appends directories of corporate and union activities and a glossary of organizations which involve the employees as volunteers, 312pp, **VOLUNTEER - The National Center** 1111 North 19th Street, Suite 500, Arlington, VA 22209 703-276-0542

VOLUNTEERS IN ASSISTANCE
(kept current) - kit of materials on a program that has been designed to help employees, retirees and members of their immediate families to match their interests, skills and time with volunteer projects for children, teenagers, young adults, adults, elderly, physically handicapped, mentally retarded, and others; includes an overview of the program and its personalized consultation, placement and follow-up, its Volunteers in Assistance Community Involvement fund (where employee volunteers initiate funding to eligible organizations); its listing of responsibilities (such as, "Go to your volunteer placement a minimum of three times."); its listing of sample activities for volunteers ("Advise a minority businessman," "Feed babies in the hospital nursery," etc.); sample forms, copies of the newsletter, *Tenneco Topics,* etc., single kit free **Tenneco, Incorporated** Commerce Building, PO Box 2511, Houston, TX 77001 713-757-2058

VOLUNTEERS IN COMMUNITY ENRICHMENT CALENDAR
(annually) - a wall calendar designed for appointments, notes and memos regarding volunteer assignments and noting holidays and other dates to remember when planning volunteer activities; contains full-color photographs of community involvement efforts of the volunteer program of Adolph Coors Company - Volunteers in Community Enrichment (V.I.C.E.) and Additional Duties for Volunteers in Community Enrichment (A.D.V.I.C.E.) Squads, 28pp, single copy free **Adolph Coors Company** Community Affairs Department, Golden, CO 80401-1295 303-277-2197

VOLUNTEERS UNDER THIRTY
(1989) - a booklet cautioning and advising volunteers to make sure that what they're getting into is going to be rewarding; lists several questions that potential volunteers should ask themselves before making contacts; lists a sampling of national organizations that offer volunteer opportunities; includes sections on ways to make the assignment work, local opportunities, and "creative volunteer ideas" describing volunteer roles, 24pp, single copy free **Adolph Coors Company** Community Affairs Department, Golden, CO 80401-1295 214-277-2197

THE WICHITA EXPERIENCE: MOBILIZING CORPORATE RESOURCES TO MEET COMMUNITY NEEDS

(1978) - an in-depth look at one of the models described in *Volunteers from the Workplace,* described elsewhere, which involved 14 corporations and the local Voluntary Action Center, and operates with an "in-plant volunteer coordinator" (a company employee given released time to operate the volunteer program); explores all aspects of the effort, from support by the corporation to the placement of volunteers, 51pp, $3.65 **VOLUNTEER - The National Center** 1111 North 19th Street, Suite 500, Arlington, VA 22209 703-276-0542

WORKING WITH EMPLOYED VOLUNTEERS

(1980) - help for all involved in the corporate volunteer program to assure smooth operation and open channels of communication, unpaged, $2.00 **Involvement Corps** 161 West Wisconsin Avenue, Milwaukee, WI 53203 414-273-7887

WORKPLACE SERIES ON DRUG/ALCOHOL ABUSE

(1988-89) - a series of videotapes to serve as educational tools for supervisor training and employee education, or in job training programs, all available in two versions - one addressing the employer, and one addressing the employee; includes:

- **Drugs At Work** (employer version 23 minutes, employee version 23-1/2 minutes) - information about the nature and scope of alcohol and government and other initiatives available for assistance (employer); employee version same as employer version with employees' comments added reflecting their perception of their companies' policies in this area.
- **Getting Help** (employer version 24 minutes; employee version 23 minutes) - benefits of an effective employee assistance program (EAP) to employees and employers through comments from business, labor, and government leaders (employer); employee version same but with more employee interviews than leader comments.
- **Drug Testing: Handle With Care** (employer version 22 minutes; employee version 22 minutes) - descriptions of options available for designing a drug testing component as part of a drug-free workplace program (employer); employee version same except that a few employee comments have been added.
- **Finding Solutions** (for both employer and employee, 19 minutes) - depiction of drug abuse in the workplace as a community-wide problem, with solutions offered through education and prevention as personal, workplace, and community responsibilities.

The above videotapes may be purchased, also; users in loan program pay only return postage. **US/HHS - National Clearinghouse for Alcohol and Drug Information** PO Box 2345, Rockville, MD 20852 301-468-2600

WORKSETTING HBP CONTROL MATERIALS

(undated) - a series of publications to assist employers in dealing with the high blood pressure problem among employees; includes:

- Re: High Blood Pressure Control in the Worksetting (seven program profiles, 12pp)
- High Blood Pressure in the Workplace (fact sheet, one page)
- High Blood Pressure Control in the Worksetting (bibliography, 5pp)
- High Blood Pressure in the Worksetting (conference proceedings, 102pp)
- Cost of Worksite Hypertension Treatment (a guide to costs, 46pp)
- Cardiovascular Primer for the Workplace (an introduction for business/industry, including knowns and unknowns, facts to consider for specific employee grouping, and descriptions of programs, 88pp)

Single copies of any or all publications are free. **US/HHS - High Blood Pressure Information Center** 4733 Bethesda Avenue, Suite 530, Bethesda, MD 20814 301-652-7700

XEROX ADOPTION ASSISTANCE PLAN

(undated) - a case for "balancing the scales" by providing financial assistance to offset the cost of adoption as well as assisting with medical payments when a child is born to an employee; offers up to $1,000 to help with agency and lawyer fees; covers 55,000 employees (similar programs in Pitney-Bowes, Hallmark Cards, IBM, and other companies), free profile **Xerox Corporation** Library Services, 300 North Zeeb Road, Ann Arbor, MI 48013 313-761-4700

YOU AND YOUTH: WHAT AMERICAN BUSINESS IS DOING TO EMPLOY AND TRAIN YOUNG PEOPLE

(monthly) - newsletter developed for those groups and individuals seeking ways to involve business in helping to solve community employment problems, Av. 12pp, $18.50/year for public and nonprofit organizations; $37/year for others **Vocational Foundation** 902 Broadway, 15th Floor, New York, NY 10010 212-777-0700

YOU CAN SEE TOMORROW

(1983) - a film developed by the Company's Foundation for individuals and groups concerned with children's health; demonstrates how parents, teachers, health professionals, and childcare workers can work together to observe, detect and help prevent health problems in children in the early elementary school years; covers many areas of cooperation between all parties concerned; includes examples from urban and rural areas; from north, south, east, and west, and from a full range of socioeconomic circumstances; demonstrates that improved observation/detection of children's health problems frequently requires no more than a change in attitude; includes guide for teachers or other leaders of children's groups, 16mm sound and color, 24 minutes, free on loan (also request the Company's free Health and Safety Educational Materials Catalog) **Metropolitan Life Insurance Company** One Madison Avenue, New York, NY 10010 212-578-2211

YOUR EMPLOYEES: THE COMMUNITY NEEDS THEM FOR VOLUNTEER PROJECTS

(undated) - recruitment piece to businesses/industries describing the benefits to company, employee and community from company volunteer efforts; lists project ideas tailored to corporate volunteerism, 6-panel foldout, free **Involvement Corps** 161 West Wisconsin Avenue, Milwaukee, WI 53203 414-273-7887

CIVIC AFFAIRS

CEA CONGRESSIONAL LEDGER: RATING CONGRESS ON BLACK & HISPANIC INTERESTS
(annually) - voting records and ratings for all Congressmen on issues involving civil rights, human and community development, the federal budget, consumer rights, government tax and spending priorities and other areas most directly affecting Black and Hispanic interests, $5.00 (quantity discounts) **Congressional Education Associates** PO Box 2996, Washington, DC 20013 202-547-9000

CHOOSING THE PRESIDENT
(kept current) - step-by-step process of nominating and electing the President of the United States; analyzes inner workings of entire system (including state-by-state chart), voter behavior, and the parties themselves, #420, 106pp, $1.95 **League of Women Voters of the US** 1730 M Street, NW, Washington, DC 20036 202-429-1965

COMMON FUTURE ACTION PLAN
(1988) - an educational tool to increase public awareness about the concept of "sustainability" (development that meets the needs of the present without compromising the needs of the future) and to suggest an agenda for action; emphasizes that solutions are limited only by the imaginations of those who choose to use it, 44pp, inquire about cost **Sierra Club** 730 Polk Street, San Francisco, CA 94109 415-776-2211

COMMUNITY GUIDE
(intermittent) - newsletter-type pamphlets each of which focuses on a single issue; e.g., "Monitoring Your Program," 6pp, $.40 **League of Women Voters of the US** 1730 M Street, NW, Washington, DC 20036 202-429-1965

CONGRESS WATCHER
(bimonthly) - facts on key consumer bills in Congress and how individual members of Congress voted on them; includes information on how to become active in your community; covers current issues, and includes section on "Issues to Watch" to address matters that have the potential for future problems, 16pp, $8.00/year **Public Citizen** 215 Pennsylvania Avenue, SE, Washington, DC 20003 202-546-4996

CURRENT FOCUS
(intermittent) - a series of booklets, each focusing on a specific issue regarding the voting/legislative process, 8pp, $.40 **League of Women Voters of the US** 1730 M Street, NW, Washington, DC 20036 202-429-1965

EDUCATING WOMEN FOR PUBLIC LIFE: REPORT FROM THE VISITING PROGRAM IN PRACTICAL POLITICS
(1974) - projections and recommendations based on an experimental course taught at Douglass College in New Jersey by politicians-in-residence to better equip women interested in public life as a career, 50pp, $2.00 **Center for the American Woman and Politics** Rutgers University, New Brunswick, NJ 08901 201-828-2210

ELECTION KIT
(kept current) - background information on the national issues that candidates will be talking about; includes eight publications on jobs, urban options, energy, the general welfare and other areas, #452, $2.75 **League of Women Voters of the US** 1730 M Street, NW, Washington, DC 20036 202-429-1965

FAIRFIELD 2000
(1986) - a special supplement placed in four daily newspapers as a public service in the Fairfield County area to inform citizens of the work of the task forces and over 800 citizen volunteers of *Fairfield 2000,* formed to study problems in the community and recommend solutions, 16pp, limited supply, single copy free **Regional Plan Association** Connecticut Committee, 500 Summer Street, Stamford, CT 06901 203-356-0390

GIANT KILLING
(quarterly) - a newsletter covering public interest advocacy success stories, training events, awards announcements, and advocate/Congress interaction, 12pp, single copy free **Advocacy Institute** 1730 M Street, NW, Suite 600, Washington, DC 20036 202-659-8475

HOW TO GET SERVICES BY BEING ASSERTIVE
(1980) - an assertiveness training manual specifically designed for parents, to teach them assertiveness skills, negotiating skills and advocacy skills to enable them to become confident, effective participants at staffings, meetings, due process hearings, special

education meetings, etc.; contains many special assertiveness training exercises and techniques, and success stories, 100pp, $5.00 plus $1.00 p/h, quantity discounts **Coordinating Council for Handicapped Children** 220 South State Street, Room 412, Chicago, IL 60604 312-939-3513

IF WORKING FOR CHANGE ISN'T WORKING
(kept current) - a portfolio of information on a university's project designed to help citizens deal with the establishment and bring about change that will benefit the community; includes workshop descriptions, faculty biographies, publication descriptions, and other materials, single portfolio free **Citizen Involvement Training Program** 381 Hills South, Room 381, Amherst, MA 01003 413-545-2038

KNOW YOUR COMMUNITY
(1972) - a guide to help citizens take a good look at the structure and functions of their local government; designed to help uncover needs in all areas of the human services, 48pp, $.75 plus $.50 handling charge per order (quantity discounts) **League of Women Voters of the US** 1730 M Street, NW, Washington, DC 20036 202-429-2965

LISTENING TO THE METROPOLIS
(1974) - an evaluation of the *Choices '76* program of the New York region, with strengths and weaknesses identified and related to the program goals, unpaged, $5.00 (members $3.00) **Regional Plan Association** 1040 Avenue of the Americas, New York, NY 10018 212-398-1140

LOBBY? YOU? OF COURSE YOU CAN...AND YOU SHOULD!
(undated) - "how-to" guidelines for advancing your cause by letting your legislators know what you want and why it is needed, 9pp pamphlet, $.50 **Independent Sector** 1828 L Street, NW, Washington, DC 20036 202-223-8100

LOBBYING FOR YOUR CAUSE
(1986) - a guide to establishing an effective advocacy group; outlines the essentials of organization and operation, how to get more exposure and positive publicity, and how to establish good relations with government agencies, legislators, media, administrators, and other groups; appends financial management and funding sources, 48pp, $3.95 plus $1.00 postage/handling **Pilot Books** 103 Cooper Street, Babylon, NY 11702 516-422-2225

MEDIA ADVOCACY COOKBOOK
(1990) - a catalog addressing public interest advocacy, outlining successful media advocacy campaigns, and designed to create a self-help aid for individuals and groups working in the area of advocacy, in press, inquire **Advocacy Institute** 1730 M Street, NW, Suite 600, Washington, DC 20036 202-659-8475

MORRIS 2000
(1985) - a special edition of *Regional Plan News* describing in detail the accomplishments of hundreds of citizen volunteers who formed task forces, held public forums, debates, and county-wide conventions to develop recommendations and action steps for a "balanced growth strategy" for Morris; edition published by *The Star Ledger* (daily newspaper) and distributed to 77,000 residents as a public service, 16pp, limited copies available, single copy free **Regional Plan Association** 60 Park Place, Suite 1603, Newark, NJ 07102 201-623-1133

NEW DIRECTIONS FOR THE BRONX
(1990) - A special supplement to the *New York Daily News* (printed as a public service) reporting on the progress of several

hundred volunteers in four task forces who made initial recommendations for consideration by the wider community in matters of growth and development of the area, 16pp, limited supply, single copy free **Regional Plan Association** 1040 Avenue of the Americas, New York, NY 10018 212-398-1140

PEACE GARDEN NEWSLETTER
(intermittent) - news of the progress of the *National Peace Garden Project* to be constructed on 12 acres of land in Washington, DC, following a bill enacted in Congress in 1987 setting aside the land; includes information on the goals of the project; fundraising efforts, in-kind contributors, etc., free **National Peace Garden** 806 Fifteenth Street, NW, #218, PO Box 27558, Washington, DC 20038-7558 202-393-6248

PEACE GARDEN PRESS KIT
(undated) - a packet of materials that is updated as the *Peace Garden Project* progresses; includes information on how the design was selected, the Congressional bill setting aside 12 acres of land in Washington, DC, for the project, sketches of the winning design, progress reports on its 1992 goal of $12 million, etc., unpaged, single copy free **National Peace Garden** 806 Fifteenth Street, NW #218, PO Box 27558, Washington, DC 20038-7558 202-393-6248

PLAYING THEIR GAME OUR WAY
(1990) - helps citizens and citizen groups understand federal, state and local governmental structures, as well as *work* those processes; includes information on how to lobby, and how to hold agencies and elected officials accountable, 32pp, $10.00 plus $2.50 postage **Citizen Involvement Training Program** 381 Hills South, Room 381, Amherst, MA 01003 413-545-2038

POLITICAL ACCOUNTABILITY RATING
(kept current) - voting records of members of Congress on issues tackled by the League and its local community members, #379, 6pp, $.40 **League of Women Voters of the US** 1730 M Street, NW, Washington, DC 20036 202-429-1965

THE POLITICAL PARTICIPATION OF WOMEN IN THE UNITED STATES: A SELECTED BIBLIOGRAPHY
(1977) - comprehensive overview of publications on the subject in a format that facilitates quick reference and enables the user to develop a solid base for working in this area, 169pp, $11.00 **Scarecrow Press** PO Box 656, Metuchen, NJ 08840 201-5448-8600

POWER: A REPOSSESSION MANUAL
(undated) - a comparison of six major approaches to community organizing; includes a series of steps necessary to organize successfully for power, 36pp, $10.00 plus $2.50 postage **Citizen Involvement Training Program** 381 Hills South, Room 381, Amherst, MA 01003 413-545-2038

PUBLIC ACTION KIT (PAK)
(1979) - packet of materials described by LWV as "everything you always wanted to know about political action and didn't know who to ask;" includes a number of League pamphlets and booklets which, together, form a step-by-step process for action, #629, approx. 130pp, $4.00 plus $.50 handling per order **League of Women Voters of the US** 1730 M Street, NW, Washington, DC 20036 202-429-1965

THE RIGHT TO WRITE
(undated) - reprint of an article by a U.S. Congressman in a newsletter prepared for his constituents offering some suggestions for writing to your representative in Congress; cites that very few people actually write to their Congressmen due to the

misconception that Congressmen do not take time to read their letters, 2pp, $.20 + $1.00 postage (pay postage only once when ordering multiple publications) **Sierra Club** Public Affairs, 730 Polk Street, San Francisco, CA 94109 415-776-2211

SANE WORLD
(monthly) - a vehicle for reporting on monitoring of hill activities to keep the public informed especially in the area of peace and disarmament, 4pp, $4.00/year (free to SANE/FREEZE members) **SANE/FREEZE** 711 G Street, SE, Washington, DC 20003 202-546-7100

SECOND CENTURY INITIATIVE - A FIVE-YEAR PLAN
(1987) - a blueprint of the agency's five-year plan listing nearly 90 recommendations made by a special *Second Century Initiative* Committee to help launch the United Way of America's second century; includes commitment to several areas including: 1) the homeless, 2) housing, 3) drug abuse prevention, 4) minority leadership development, 5) school support, 6) employment training, includes details on initiating programs in the above and other areas, 16pp, inquire about availability and cost **Valley of the Sun United Way** 1515 East Osborn Road, PO Box 10748, Phoenix, AZ 85064-0748 602-263-7701

SOCIAL ACTION FOR SENIOR CENTERS
(1974) - guide to involving the elderly in social action on their own behalf in areas of housing, transportation, reduced public assistance, rent control, tax relief and home care; emphasizes staff role and other organizational support to help seniors "fight city hall" and win, 56pp, $3.75 **National Council on the Aging** 600 Maryland Avenue, SW, West Wing 100, Washington, DC 20024 202-479-1200

TEACHING ABOUT SPACESHIP EARTH
(1973) - a role-playing experience for children with practical ideas and useful as a tool for international understanding and peace education, 68pp, $1.00 **Association for Childhood Education International** 11141 Georgia Avenue , Suite 200, Wheaton, MD 20902 301-942-2443

TELL IT TO WASHINGTON
(kept current) - tips on getting involved in the government process through letters, calls, and personal visits; includes current Congressional Directory with separate listings of Senate and House Committees, #349, 24pp, $.35 **League of Women Voters of the US** 1730 M Street, NW, Washington, DC 20036 202-429-1965

TOOL CATALOG: TECHNIQUES AND STRATEGIES FOR SUCCESSFUL ACTION PROGRAMS
(kept current) - comprehensive guide for planning any kind of action program or project; includes organization and planning, publicity and information techniques, with detailed descriptions of and instructions for each technique, 248pp, $9.00 **American Association of University Women** 1111 Sixteenth Street, NW, Washington, DC 20036 202-785-7700

VITAL ISSUES
(10/yr) - illustrated mini-guide to practical politics relating to a specific issue in each edition, using a newsletter format and including references for in-depth information on the subject presented, 6pp, $.95 issue, $6.00/year **Center for Information on America** , Washington, CT 06793 203-868-2602

VOLUNTEERING AT COMMON CAUSE
(kept current) - descriptions of jobs handled by volunteers, including the staffing of a national telephone network, research, congressional monitoring, operating the "sunset" program

(reviewing programs for ongoing usefulness), and many other areas of concern to citizens, 6-panel foldout, single copy free **Common Cause** Volunteer Office, 2030 M Street, NW, Washington, DC 20036 202-833-1200

WESTCHESTER 2000
(1985) - a special supplement in two local daily newspapers as a public service to help involve the entire County in *Westchester 2000,* a group of task forces formed to look ahead to avoid problems of growth and other problems for the county, 16pp, limited supply, single copy free [Also inquire about copies from the Regional Plan Association, 1040 Avenue of the Americas, New York, NY 10018 (212-398-1140)] **Westchester County Association** 235 Mamaroneck Avenue, White Plains, NY 10605 914-958-6444

COMMUNICATIONS & PUBLIC RELATIONS

ABC'S OF PUBLIC RELATIONS
(1972) - an illustrated, quick-reference basic guide to help foster better groundwork within the organization before approaching the media; addresses the responsible PR person in the organization as the "key" to success in this area, 15pp, write for pricing and quantity discounts to PR Department, Channing L. Bete Company, 200 State Road, South Deerfield, MA 01373 or call 800-628-7733 **Channing L. Bete Company** South Deerfield, MA 01373

AIDS 101 SLIDESHOW
(1989) - a 'speaker support' presentation using words, photos and illustrations to give viewers basic information on what causes AIDS, how HIV affects the body, transmission and prevention, the AIDS antibody test, etc.; considers a wide range of audiences, but is especially suitable for those requiring a simple, easy-to-understand presentation, 35 slides and script guidelines, $50.00 **San Francisco AIDS Foundation** 333 Valencia Street, PO Box 6182, San Francisco, CA 94101-6182 415-861-3397

CLASS OF 2000: THE PREJUDICE PUZZLE
(1990) - audiotapes from a weeklong series based on *National Public Radio's* new *Specials Project,* in which issues of national concern which affect our communities are aired over a week's time frame; initial series features young people talking about their feelings about prejudice (has air dates of September 9-15, 1990), 5- to 22-minute segments, inquire about availability of transcripts or tapes **National Public Radio** 2025 M Street, NW, Washington, DC 20036 202-822-2000

CLIP 'N COPY - COPYRIGHT-FREE ART WITH THE VOLUNTEER MANAGER IN MIND
(1989) - cartoons, graphic images, words and phrases especially designed with volunteer themes; contains three sections:
Chapter 1: The Starter Kit, 100 cartoons by five different artists and 60 words/phrases in both calligraphy and type styles, $8.95 + $1.50 shipping
Chapter 2: Recognition and Borders, over 175 cartoons, generic images and borders and 50 words and phrases geared to awards, certificates, invitations, announcements, etc., $8.95 + $1.50 shipping
Chapter 3: Holidays and Seasons, page headers and banners to help celebrate seasons, children at play, holiday images, etc., $9.50 + $1.50 shipping **Association for Volunteer Administration** PO Box 4584, Boulder, CO 80306 303-492-8630

COMMUNICATION RESOURCE HANDBOOK SERIES
(1982) - two remaining handbooks of a six-book series designed to assist local program leaders in understanding the media coverage needed to keep the community informed about program activities:
● *Community Resource Handbook IV: Guide for Building Employee Understanding* (of media coverage)
● *Community Resource Handbook V: Creating a Media Resource Guide*
Provides details in catalog; contact librarian or historian for information about remaining out-of-print handbooks on basic elements, media relations, and two on "listening to the community," $2.50 each guide/members; $3.00 each guide/non-members (quantity discounts) **United Way of America** 701 North Fairfax Street, Alexandria, VA 223-4-2045 703-836-7100

COMPREHENSIVE GUIDE TO SUCCESSFUL CONFERENCES AND MEETINGS
(1987) - detailed advice on every facet of planning and running conferences, meetings and similar events; draws on fifty years of combined experience in this field by the authors; includes areas ranging from food and beverages to evaluation and follow up, 466pp, $37.95 **Jossey Bass, Publishers** 350 Sansome Street, San Francisco, CA 94104 415-433-1767

CORPORATION FOR PUBLIC BROADCASTING ANNUAL REPORT
(annually) - a look back each year at the services provided by CPB station services, program services, education services, personal development services, and system support services; appends financial statements and a listing of stations receiving grants, contracts, and awards from CPB, Av. 48pp, single copy free **Corporation for Public Broadcasting** 1111 Sixteenth Street, NW, Washington, DC 20036 202-293-6160

DEVELOPING A PR PLAN
(1988) - advice from eight experts showing how to use a mission and goals statement to structure PR activities; leads user to its most important constitutents, how to separate the committed from the undecided, and how to select the appropriate media format and message, 22pp, $5.00 (members); $6.26 (nonmembers) #28211 **Council for Advancement and Support of Education** Publications Order Department, 80 South Early Street, Alexandria, VA 22304 703-82-6966

DIRECTORY OF PUBLIC BROADCASTING INFORMATION RESOURCES

(1979) - a compilation of organizations monitoring, advocating, evaluating, programming, and providing other checks and public interest services in public broadcasting areas, 73pp, single copy free **Corporation for Public Broadcasting** 1111 Sixteenth Street, NW, Washington, DC 20036 202-293-6160

EASY/ACCESS

(quarterly) - newsletter of the state department charged with monitoring and keeping the public informed on the rights of the disabled; includes legislative updates, guest columns, reports on tools and resources for advocates and others, new product lines for the disabled, case studies, calendar, etc., 8pp, free subscription **Virginia Department for Rights of the Disabled** James Monroe Building, 17th Floor, 101 North 14th Street, Richmond, VA 23219 804-225-2042

EDITING AND WRITING SERIES

(1979-83) - two guides to help those responsible for getting the word out about the organization:

- *Creative Editing and Writing* - collection of articles covering editing "from A to Z" and a workbook of writing and editing exercises (format useful for workshops for staff), 279pp, $40 (members); $50 (nonmembers)
- *How to Improve Your Writing* - technniques for clear, effective writing with suggestions for nonsexist language, a list of misused and overused words, and tips on better communication through simple, direct language, 11pp, $5.00 (members); $6.25 (nonmembers) **Council for Advancement and Support of Education** Publications Order Department, 80 South Early Street, Alexandria, VA 22304 703-823-6966

GA-SK NEWSLETTER

(quarterly) - a communications vehicle for TDD users and other interested persons; includes articles on legislation, equipment, travel facilities, volunteer services, new on-line systems, etc., 32pp, includes free annual international directory, $15.00/year (residential), $30.00/year (business/organization) **Telecommunications for the Deaf** 814 Thayer Avenue, Silver Spring, MD 20910 301-589-3786

GETTING YOUR PUBLIC RELATIONS STORY ON TV AND RADIO

(1986) - a basic manual written by a veteran reporter and publicist showing the kinds of newsworthy material radio and television news editors, as well as talk show hosts, are looking for, and how to mold your presentation to fit these needs, 30pp, $3.95 plus $1.00 postage/handling **Pilot Books** 103 Cooper Street, Babylon, NY 11702 516-422-2225

GETTING YOURS: PUBLICITY AND FUNDING PRIMER FOR NONPROFIT VOLUNTARY ORGANIZATIONS

(1983) - guidelines for generating both publicity and funding; advises on how to handle the media, the right medium, news releases, public service announcements, feature stories, press conferences and interviews; includes section on non-media publicity (brochures, newsletters, annual reports, posters, community events, public speaking, etc.); examines funding sources, including government funding, foundations and corporate grants; discusses keys to forming coalitions with other groups, corporate volunteerism, emergency cash-flow loan funds, proposal writing, and a variety of fund-raising ideas; intersperses checklists and examples throughout, 88pp, inquire about cost **Contact Center** PO Box 81826, Lincoln, NE 68501 402-464-0602

GUIDE TO DOCUMENTING A LOCAL PROGRAM

(1979) - a detailed handbook on how to document a program - from identification of the best person to carry out the effort, to the preparation and completion of the document; appends a sample completed program documentation, 59pp, single copy free **US/HHS - Children's Bureau** , Washington, DC 20201 202-755-7762

HOW ADVERTISERS, MEDIA REACT TO OLDER MARKET

(5/12/89) - special issue of the *Tempo* section tracing the change of attitude in the media from portrayal of the elderly as "folksy" advice-givers who were ignored, or in a "cartoony" light - shown as hard of hearing, walking slowly, etc., to current media portrayal of older persons as sexy, aware, sharp-witted go-getters; outlines reasons for this phenomenon, 4pp, single copy free while supply lasts **The Journal** 6883 Commercial Drive, Springfield, VA 22151 703-750-2000

HOW TO DO LEAFLETS, NEWSLETTERS AND NEWSPAPERS

(1976) - a manual designed to help those responsible for communication to become more aware of what attracts attention and interest in written and other media; emphasizes in-house efforts and provides illustrated, step-by-step instructions; discusses ways of gathering information, interviewing, designing layout, scheduling procedures, etc.; includes glossary of printing terms, chart of editor's correction marks, etc., 45pp, $2.50 **New England Free Press** 60 Union Square, Somerville, MA 02143

HOW TO USE THE MEDIA EFFECTIVELY: A LAYMAN'S GUIDE FOR VOLUNTEER ORGANIZATIONS

(1978) - a handbook designed to inform organizations on how to involve the media in serving the public interest; discusses weekly columns, public service announcements, press releases, and the timing and deadlines necessary to make these and other techniques effective; includes state list of organizations that can be helpful, 12pp, single copy free **Lincoln Filene Center for Citizenship & Public Affairs** , Medford, MA 02155 617-628-5000

IF YOU WANT AIR TIME

(Rev. 1979) - a guide aimed at clarifying the distinct and separate functions of publicity, promotion, and public relations, and helping organizations select the appropriate approach to get the most benefit out of a station's assistance; includes sample news releases for radio and TV, 18pp, $.15 **National Association of Broadcasters** 1771 N Street, NW, Washington, DC 20036 202-429-5300

INDIVIDUAL GIVING/VOLUNTEERING CAMPAIGN

(1984) - a packet of information on a nationwide campaign conducted by a partnership (Ad Council, President's Office on Private Sector Initiatives, and Independent Sector) to increase public awareness on the benefits of voluntary action, both volunteering and voluntary giving, single packet free **Advertising Council** 825 Third Avenue, New York, NY 10022 212-758-0400

AN INTRODUCTION TO PUBLIC BROADCASTING

(kept current) - an educational piece on public broadcasting in the U.S.; covers the diverse uses of public broadcasting in meeting unusual and specific audience needs without the primary objective of profitability; introduces the reader to other national and regional organizations created by CPB and the stations, but now belonging solely to the stations, 6-panel foldout, single copy free **Corporation for Public Broadcasting** 1111 Sixteenth Street, NW, Washington, DC 20036 202-293-6160

MEDIA KIT
(1980) - a portfolio of materials on reaching the public, getting into print, speakers bureau, broadcast media, slide show production, newsletters, etc., to help make the public more acutely aware of voting responsibility and other civic matters, #163, $2.00/kit plus $.50 handling charge per order **League of Women Voters of the US** 1730 M Street, NW, Washington, DC 20036 202-429-1965

MEDIA RELATIONS HANDBOOK: TIPS ON HOW TO GET YOUR STORY ACROSS
(undated) - a guide to writing news releases and feature stories, addressing the various TV news categories, learning who is who at radio and TV stations, public speaking and other areas; includes a checklist for use before media contact, 24pp, $1.35 **National Council on the Aging** 600 Maryland Avenue, SW, West Wing 100, Washington, DC 20024 202-479-1200

NEW GUIDE TO EFFECTIVE MEDIA RELATIONS
(1988) - summaries from 45 PR professionals that worked for them; includes insights from both triumphs and disasters; focuses on nitty-gritty problems faced every day, 101pp, $18.50 (members); $23.25 (nonmembers) #26701 **Council for Advancement and Support of Education** Publications Order Department, 80 South Early Street, Alexandria, VA 22304 703-823-6966

OLDER PEOPLE ARE PEOPLE TOO!
(1977) - appeal to TV producers, directors, and writers to deal with facts, not stereotypes, to portray older persons more realistically on their programs; heavily illustrated, 15pp, $2.70 **National Council on the Aging** 600 Maryland Avenue, SW, West Wing 100, Washington, DC 20024 202-479-1200

ORGANIZING SPECIAL EVENTS AND CONFERENCES: GUIDE FOR VOLUNTEERS & STAFF
(1989) - A reference book for both volunteer and staff event managers containing step-by-step instructions, checklists, and schedules; information on budgeting, committees, evaluation, media, and site selection; and lists of organizations, addresses, and publications; includes hints and anecdotes from professionals and volunteers in the field, 250pp, $16.95 **Pineapple Press** PO Drawer 16008, Southside Station, Sarasota, FL 34239 813-952-1085

PLAIN TALK
(1981) - presents guidelines for clear communication for writers, translators, field workers, and anyone interested in better, simpler ways of communicating ideas and information; learn to fight bureaucratic gobbledygook! 76pp, $5.95 **Volunteers in Technical Assistance** 1815 North Lynn Street, Arlington, VA 22209 703-276-1800

PLANNING AND MARKETING CONFERENCES AND WORKSHOPS
(1990) - more than 170 practical tools, tips, and techniques for planning and marketing all kinds of conferences and workshops; includes sections on image, costs, design and printing, mailing, achieving goals, expectations, and others, 220pp, $24.95 **Jossey Bass, Publishers** 350 Sansome Street, San Francisco, CA 94104 415-433-1767

PLANNING AND SETTING OBJECTIVES
(1977) - a basic guide beginning with an inventory of needs, problems, objectives, etc., on which to base a well-thought-out public relations program; emphasizes the value of a good public relations program in reaching goals, 22pp, $3.00 **Foundation for Public Relations, Research & Education** 310 Madison Avenue, Suite 1710, New York, NY 10017 212-370-9353

A PRIMER
(1972) - a layman's guide to publicity tricks, the mass media, press releases, brochures, open houses, tours and other public relations techniques; includes a comprehensive 8-page *PR Checklist* for use before launching a media program, 46pp, $3.00 **Volunteer Center of the Greater Quad Cities** 1417 Sixth Avenue, Moline, IL 61265 309-764-6804

PRINTING IT*
(1976) - a guide to in-house printing based on the philosophy that "it is possible to make pennilessness and some simple skills work as powerfully as lots of dough and snazzy studies;" presents the publication itself as an example of this philosophy, 127pp, $3.50 **Book People** 2940 Seventh Street, Berkeley, CA 94710 415-549-3030

PRODUCING, DESIGNING & WRITING NEWSLETTERS
(undated) - overview of a one-day course in newsletter production which sends participants home with an extensive package of tools (publications, diskettes, layouts, etc.), or provides the same package with a six-hour seminar video for those who cannot attend (brochure itself is in newsletter style using techniques taught at the seminar), 4pp, brochure free **Newsletter Factory** 3036 Roswell Road, Marietta, GA 30062 404-977-9800

PUBLIC PARTICIPATION IN PUBLIC BROADCASTING
(1978) - details on a Task Force on Public Participation in Public Broadcasting, composed of citizens and created to identify ways to improve citizen involvement within all sectors of the public broadcasting system; includes section on involvement of volunteers at the local level, 48pp, single copy free **Corporation for Public Broadcasting** 1111 Sixteenth Street, NW, Washington, DC 20036 202-293-6160

PUBLIC RELATIONS MANUAL FOR WORKSHOPS
(undated) - a desk guide for starting, expanding or improving a sheltered workshop public relations program, 32pp, $1.00 **National Association of Rehabilitation Facilities** PO Box 17675, Washington, DC 20041 703-556-8848

PUBLICITY PORTFOLIO
(4th ed. 1978) - a handbook using "the right material, the right form, the right person, the right time" approach to mounting an effective publicity program; includes numerous examples, photos, forms and other aids for dealing with all media, 57pp, $12.00 **Fund-Raising Institute** Box 365, Ambler, PA 19002 215-646-7019

SLIDE SHOWS ON A SHOESTRING
(1990) - an explanation of an inexpensive way of telling the story of the agency - through a synchronized slide/tape presentation for less than $100; includes sections on scripting, photography, taping, graphic slide production, and copyright considerations; appends forms and other tools designed to enhance production capability, 54pp, $7.95 (mail $11.00) **Macduff/Bunt Associates** 821 Lincoln Street, Walla Walla, WA 99362 509-529-0244

THE S.O.A.P.S.
(1987) - a "tongue-in-cheek" tabloid featuring condensed soap opera plots based on actual health and social problems of Akron women, and written by a syndicated columnist who synopsizes network soaps for 200 newspapers, with companion articles written by local staff and volunteers of an Akron coalition of health agencies that explains the kinds of services available to women in the Akron area, 12pp, single copy free while supply lasts **Social Services of Akron Project** 245 South High Street, Akron, OH 44308 216-535-2999

SPECIALS PROJECT INFORMATION PACKET

(1990) - an overview of a new concept by *National Public Radio* to rally citizens and organizations across the country to join with their member stations and mount projects that address national issues that affect our communities; includes fact sheet, letter to potential partners, schedule for the first special (how youth feel about prejudice), and other materials as they become available, single packet free **National Public Radio** 2025 M Street, NW, Washington, DC 20036 202-822-2000

TEEN RAP PSAS

(1989) - part of an outreach campaign to urban teens; covers topics of concern to teenagers such as safe sex, peer pressure, sexual negotiations, fear, casual contagion and compassion for people with AIDS; set to rap music and can be used as discussion-starters in classes and workshops as well as on the radio, five 60-second spots, $25.00 **San Francisco AIDS Foundation** 333 Valencia Street, PO Box 6182, San Francisco, CA 94101-6182 415-861-3397

THE 10 COMMANDMENTS FOR ON-CAMERA APPEARANCE

(1990) - tips for before, during and after an on-camera interview; includes hints on dressing for men and women, unpaged, free with SASE **Susan Peterson Productions** 1211 Connecticut Avenue, NW, Washington, DC 20036 202-463-0505

THROWAWAY PEOPLE

(1990) - an audiovisual that walks the viewer through a typical inner-city neighborhood afflicted with drugs and crack problems; discusses the relationship among the neighborhood's drug trade, economy, murders of young black men (by young black men - more murders than days in the year), and the civil rights movement; focuses on a few "obstinate people" who refuse to give up on the community or the people who live there, one hour, inquire about availability and cost **Frontline - Channels 22 and 26** PO Box 2626, Washington, DC 20013 202-998-2600

TRIPLE JEOPARDY

(1984) - an audiovisual presentation discussing the plight of many Hispanic elderly (old, poor, and members of a minority); cites the study that prompted the presentation; 3/4" and 1/2" video tape, $65; filmstrip with 119 frames and cassette with cue signals, $40 **National Association for Hispanic Elderly** 3325 Wilshire Boulevard, Suite 800, Los Angeles, CA 90010-1724 213-487-1922

VOLUNTEERS IN ACTION & FUNDRAISING THEMES

(kept current) - one of the *Clip 'N Copy* series providing 150 cartoon, realistic, and botanical style art by eight different artists, and key words and phrases in calligraphy and type; includes borders and corners, "conversation bubbles," and other artwork to reinforce messages in newsletters, flyers and brochures+, unpaged, $9.50 (8-panel foldout describing this and three other collections in the series: *Starter Kit, Recognition and Borders,* and *Holidays and Seasons,* free) **Association for Volunteer Administration** PO Box 4585, Boulder, CO 80306 303-497-0238

WE INTERRUPT THIS PROGRAM

(1990) - a manual for groups interested in knowing more about using the media as a community organizing tool, and media directions and applications for social change, 50pp, $10.00 plus $2.50 postage **Citizen Involvement Training Program** 381 Hills South, Room 381, Amherst, MA 01003 413-545-2038

YOUR PERSONAL GUIDE TO MARKETING A NONPROFIT ORGANIZATION

(1988) - a simple, skills-oriented workbook to show nonprofit organizers how to put marketing concepts into action; explains marketing principles in an easy-to-understand format; focuses attention on individual skills development; leads reader through the complex process of marketing a nonprofit, 153pp, $18.50 (members); $23.25 (nonmembers) #24201 **Council for Advancement and Support of Education** Publications Order Department, 80 South Early Street, Alexandria, VA 22304 703-823-6966

COMMUNITY SERVICES

BUILDING A MOVEMENT: RESOURCE BOOK/STUDENTS IN COMMUNITY SERVICE
(1989) - a comprehensive manual giving practical advice on how to start and run a campus-based community service organization; includes ideas on fundraising, program development, recruitment and promotion plans, 200pp, $35.00 **Campus Outreach Opportunity League (COOL)** 386 McNeal Hall, University of Minnesota, St. Paul, MN 55108-1011 612-624-3018

CENTER FOR PUBLIC SERVICE PORTFOLIO
(1989) - a pocketed portfolio containing the *Center's* Annual Report; newsletters *Public Works* and *Community Matters);* fact sheets on workshops, fellowships, etc.; project descriptions, etc., upaged, single portfolio free **Brown University Center for Public Service** 25 George Street, PO Box 1974, Providence, RI 02912 401-863-2338

COMMUNITY
(6/year) - a magazine designed to assist program leaders in examining a broad range of views significant to volunteerism in the functional areas of the United Way; includes descriptions of innovative programs and activities in the community, single copy #0090 $1.50; subscription #0304 $8.00 (ask about quantity discounts on multiple specific copies) **United Way of America** 701 North Fairfax Street, Alexandria, VA 22314-2045 703-836-7100

COMMUNITY COLLABORATION: MANUAL FOR VOLUNTARY SECTOR ORGANIZATIONS
(1991) - step-by-step instructions on how to build successful collaborations to avoid duplication of effort and better serve the community; elaborates on two development tasks that must be accomplished in the first phase of development: (1) assessment of community interest and readiness; and (2) enlistment of key community members necessary for success, 76pp, $10.95 **National Assembly of Voluntary Health and Social Welfare Organizations** 1319 F Street, NW, Suite 601, Washington, DC 20004 202-347-2080

COMMUNITY DREAMS
(1984) - ideas, mostly small in scale and low in cost, for improving community life; culled from the author's and his friends' experience and imagination; ranges from sensible to whimsical ideas, 223pp, $8.95 **Community Service, Inc.** PO Box 243, Yellow Springs, OH 45387 513-767-1461

COMMUNITY OPTIONS: PROJECTS YOU CAN DO TO REGENERATE YOUR COMMUNITY
(1987) - a citizens' guide to starting the "think big, start small" process by beginning with the community's heritage and building upon it, and by realizing that people are the only ones who can decide what is best for them, 27pp, $6.95 **Community Regeneration** 222 Main Street, Emmaus, PA 18098 215-967-5171

COMMUNITY VOLUNTEER SERVICES HANDBOOK
(undated) - overview of what volunteers can do in the community in areas of advocacy, older adults, drug abuse, health care, crime prevention, energy, the handicapped, housing, ex-prisoners, etc., 63pp, $1.75 (quantity discounts) **B'nai B'rith Community Volunteer Services** 1640 Rhode Island Avenue, NW , Washington, DC 20036 202-857-6600

DIFFERENCES: A BRIDGE OR A WALL
(1990) - a guide designed to help groups and organizations gain a clearer understanding of differences in our society, why they exist, and how to deal with them effectively, 107pp, $10.00 plus $2.50 postage **Citizen Involvement Training Program** 381 Hills South, Room 381, Amherst, MA 01003 413-545-2038

EFFECTIVE SOCIAL ACTION BY COMMUNITY GROUPS
(1990) - guide to ways in which individual citizens, with little vested authority, can generate meaningful changes in their communities; describes eleven techniques community groups use to exert influence, about 265pp (in press), $25.95 **Jossey Bass, Publishers** 350 Sansome Street, San Francisco, CA 94104 415-433-1767

FOCUS
(3/year) - information on volunteer efforts by members of the *Jesuit Volunteer Corps,* which provides opportunities for the volunteers to serve up to a year in various parts of the country to assist the needy, 12pp, single copy free **Jesuit Volunteer Corps: Northwest** PO Box 3928, Portland, OR 97208 503-228-2457

GREENFIELD, IOWA: AMERICA'S #1 REGENERATION TOWN
(1989) - a special Greenfield issue of the newsletter, *Regeneration,* and a series of clippings describing ways in which one town was improved by citizen action, unpaged, $3.00 **Community Regeneration** 222 Main Street, Emmaus, PA 18098 215-967-5171

HOW TO MAKE CITIZEN INVOLVEMENT WORK
(undated) - an examination of involvement forms of the past, and what citizen action can become; includes a planning guide and a checklist for suggested strategies, 36pp, $10.00 plus $2.50 postage **Citizen Involvement Training Program** 381 Hills South, Room 381, Amherst, MA 01003 413-545-2038

HOW TO MAKE THE WORLD A BETTER PLACE: A GUIDE TO DOING GOOD
(1990) - more than 100 quick and easy actions an individual can take to improve the community, and thus the world; appends *Twelve Essential Resources* to help potential volunteers stay "informed, inspired, and ready for action," 303pp, $9.95 **Quill/William Morrow** 105 Madison Avenue, New York, NY 10016 212-889-3050

HOW TO START A COMMUNITY VOLUNTEER SERVICES PROJECT
(undated) - step-by-step guide beginning with a determination of community needs and discussing ideas for specific projects, selecting a chairman, committees, publicity, evaluation, etc., 5pp, single copy free **B'nai B'rith Community Volunteer Services** 1640 Rhode Island Avenue, NW , Washington, DC 20036 202-857-6600

NEW VISIONS: SUCCESS STORIES OF PERSONAL AND COMMUNITY REGENERATION
(1989) - ten common activities for community regeneration, ranging from health and fitness to gardening, recreation and art; includes specific examples of how ordinary people have been able to accomplish extraordinary things, 32pp, single copy free **Community Regeneration** 222 Main Street, Emmaus, PA 18098 215-967-5171

ON YOUR MARK, GO! GET SET: CAMPUS IDEALS TO COMMUNITY INVOLVEMENT
(1989) - a detailed guide provides a pragmatic action-oriented approach on how to begin or rejuvenate a comprehensive campus community service organization, $13.40 **Campus Outreach Opportunity League (COOL)** 386 McNeal Hall, University of Minnesota, St. Paul, MN 55108-1011 612-624-3018

PARTNERSHIPS FOR COMMUNITY DEVELOPMENT
(1990) - help for organizations and individuals working in associations, task forces, networks, councils, consortia and partnerships; addresses both beginning and seasoned practitioners; provides a conceptual framework for analyzing collaborative efforts; helps develop strategies to avoid common pitfalls and create, strengthen and sustain effective partnerships, 125pp, $15.00 plus $2.50 postage **Citizen Involvement Training Program** 381 Hills South, Room 381, Amherst, MA 01003 413-545-2038

PEOPLE AND EVENTS
(1983) - a unique account of the development of community services; traces the development of community services; traces the growth of the United Way movement from its beginning in 1887 to the present, deluxe edition with slip cover #0162 $30.00; standard #0163 $25.00 **United Way of America** 701 North Fairfax Street, Alexandria, VA 22314-2045 703-836-7100

PEOPLE APPROACH: NINE NEW STRATEGIES FOR CITIZEN INVOLVEMENT
(1979) by Ivan H. Scheier - a discussion of the position that volunteering will re-emerge through specific approaches related to people's natural ways of being helpful, including methods such as the Resource Exchange Process (MINIMAX); Need Analysis; Recognition, Recruiting, Self-Help and Helping (SHAH) and others, 116pp, $5.55 **VOLUNTEER - The National Center** 1111 North 19th Street, Suite 500, Arlington, VA 22209 703-276-0542

PLANNING, FOR A CHANGE
(1981) - an aid for citizen groups who want to plan creatively in order to come up with innovative programs and strategies; provides specific methods in a step-by-step format, 36pp, $10.00 plus $2.50 postage **Citizen Involvement Training Program** 381 Hills South, Room 381, Amherst, MA 01003 413-545-2038

PROGRAM DESCRIPTIONS
(undated) - four projects for the *Access California* program: Advisory Board, Operation Alert (hotline), Services, and Telecom D; volunteer roles are cited, 6pp, single copy free **San Bernardino County Board of Supervisors** 686 East Mill Street, San Bernardino, CA 92408 714-383-3805

PROGRAM PLANNING CALENDAR WORKBOOK
(yearly) - ideas for programming in calendar format with programs of community service for every month including both Jewish and secular holidays and the means by which to plan a program as well as the "how-to" in carrying out these programs, $1.00 **B'nai B'rith Community Volunteer Services** 1640 Rhode Island Avenue, NW , Washington, DC 20036 202-857-6600

REGENERATING AMERICA: OPPORTUNITIES TO BUILD ON
(1989) - a variety of innovative, practical examples of community regeneration that apply directly to a variety of localities and regions where regeneration workshops have been conducted, and which can be applied to any community; includes bibliography, 30pp, $7.50 **Community Regeneration** 222 Main Street, Emmaus, PA 18098 215-967-5171

URBAN VOLUNTEERS
(1980) - a research and demonstration project to study the nature of volunteer efforts in minority communities, answering questions that have been studied before but given little space in the literature; appends an extensive Urban Volunteers Bibliography, 25pp, inquire about availability (worth requesting photocopy) **Institute for Neighborhood Initiative** 1055 Thomas Jefferson Street, Washington, DC 20007 202-342-5000

VIDEOTAPE SERIES
(various dates) - an award-winning series of videotapes dealing with issues that affect every community, most running from seven to ten minutes, various formats, specify format and inquire about cost:
- *Volunteering: The Road to Glory,* 8 minutes
- *Aging: The Graying of America,* 8 minutes
- *America's New Homeless,* 10-1/2 minutes
- *Day Care: Close to the Heart,* 8 minutes
- *Early Retirement: To Be or Not To Be ... And How,* 9 minutes
- *Illiteracy: America's Quiet Tragedy,* 8-1/2 minutes
- *Kids & Drugs: A Family Crisis,* 11 minutes
- *Reach Out (Information & Referral Services),* 9 minutes
- *Stress,* 8 minutes
- *Superwoman,* 8 minutes
- *Teen Pregnancy: Childhood Robbery,* 10 minutes
- *Teenagers: The Pressured Generation,* 7 minutes
- *Unemployment: The Changing Workplace,* 7 minutes

[Ask about the free 26-minute videotape, *Second Century Initiative,* narrated by United Way of America President, William Aramony, and the free-with-purchase 28-minute TV special, *The Changing American Family.*] **United Way of America** 701 North Fairfax Street, Alexandria, VA 22314-2045 703-836-7100

YES I CAN! A PRACTICAL GUIDE TO DISCOVERING HOW GREAT YOU ARE
(1989) - hints as to using your "hidden" talents and discovering how interests and ideas you might have thought were insignificant can be used to successfully enrich you and your entire community, 36pp, $6.95 **Community Regeneration** 222 Main Street, Emmaus, PA 18098 215-967-5171

CONSUMER SERVICES

ACT GUIDE TO CHILDREN'S TELEVISION
(Rev. 1979) - handbook designed to assist consumers in fostering TV advertising and program reform to continue the trend toward eliminating all manipulative advertising practices; includes a 20-page "Children's Workbook" to involve the young themselves in the process, 226pp, $5.95 **Beacon Press** 25 Beacon Street, Boston, MA 02108 617-742-2110

BEING OUR AGE AND LEARNING TO LIKE IT
(undated) - suggestions to older persons on building programs for "fighting back" in areas of inadequate services and opportunities - and enjoying the process, 18pp, $2.50 **Unitarian Universalist Women's Federation** 25 Beacon Street, Boston, MA 02108 617-742-2100

BUYERS UP COOPERATIVE MEMBERSHIP KIT
(undated) - an overview of an oil-buying cooperative designed to cut fuel costs through group discount prices, even with regular, automatic delivery; includes graphics to demonstrate savings, and a membership application form, 4pp, free **Buyers Up** PO Box 33757, Washington, DC 20033-0757 202-328-3800

THE BUYING CLUB
(undated) - simple outline on how to get a buying club underway, factors of initial operation, and a look at other ways of saving through group efforts, brochure, $4.75 per 100 **National Cooperative Business Association** 1407 New York Avenue, NW, Suite 100, Washington, DC 20005 202-638-6222

CONSUMER INFORMATION CATALOG
(quarterly) - a listing of more than 200 selected federal consumer publications based on the Center's cooperative working arrangement with other federal agencies; includes topics such as health, food, energy, housing, automobiles, etc., 16pp, single copy free (also Spanish) **US Consumer Information Center** Department 579L, Pueblo, CO 81009 202-492-5713

CONSUMER PRODUCT SAFETY COMMISSION
(kept current) - a fact sheet listing the federal sources to which the consumer can turn for information and assistance, 10 copies or less free (over ten from Superintendent of Documents, U.S. Government Printing Office, Washington, DC 20402, fact sheet #52, 50/$3.65) **US/Office of Consumer Affairs** 111 Eighteenth Street, NW, Room 303, Washington, DC 20207 202-492-5713

CONSUMER PROTECTION PROGRAMS
(1979) - description of a service by and for the elderly covering money management, fraud, consumer education, etc. (one of the "Senior Peer Employment Programs" series on innovations in providing jobs for older persons), 19pp, $2.15 **National Council on the Aging** 600 Maryland Avenue, SW, West Wing 100, Washington, DC 20024 202-479-1200

CONSUMER REPORTS
(monthly) - product quality ratings to increase the consumer's chances of getting his/her money's worth (tests are made on products bought by Consumers Union staff on the open market), Av. 60pp, $14/year **Consumers Union of the United States** 256 Washington Street, Mount Vernon, NY 10550 914-667-9400

CONSUMER SOURCEBOOK
(3rd Ed. 1981) - comprehensive listings of live and print sources of information for consumer protection and guidance; covers federal, state, and local government agencies, associations, centers, institutes, and similar bodies; newspaper, radio, and television services; books, periodicals and audiovisual materials; companies and their trade names, etc., in areas such as health, safety, social welfare, law, finances, economics, transportation, consumer fraud, communications, and others subjects (36 in all), 850pp, two volumes, $125/set **Gale Research Company** Book Tower, Detroit, MI 48226 313-961-2242

CONSUMER'S RESOURCE HANDBOOK
(1989) - a manual to help citizens locate the right source of assistance - from both governmental and nongovernmental sources - for resolving problems with products and services; includes state and local government offices (developed by The White House Office of the Special Assistant for Consumer Affairs), 91pp, single copy free **US Consumer Information Center** Department 579 L, Pueblo, CO 81009 202-566-1794

CURRENT CONSUMER AND LIFE STUDIES
(9/year) magazine for children and youth cautioning them about the marketplace, consumer law, sports equipment ratings, and other consumer issues pertinent to specific age groups, av. 32pp, $3.95/school year (for 15 or more subscriptions; otherwise inquire) **Curriculum Innovations** PO Box 310, Highwood, IL 60040 312-432-2700

DON'T BE SWINDLED...HERE ARE NINE WAYS YOU COULD BE
(1977) - details on some of the most common con games and swindles in use today; provides insight into the methods used and points out some of the warning signs often overlooked, 8pp, $.13 (minimum order usually 500) **American Bankers Association** 1120 Connecticut Avenue, NW, Washington, DC 20036 202-663-5000

FINAL REPORT TO THE PRESIDENT ON NATIONAL CONSUMER WEEK
(annually) - summaries of the current year's National Consumer Week (NCW), which covers activities sponsored by more than 500 organizations each year (NCW solicits slogans for each year's National Consumer Week and provides posters, flyers, and ideas around the selected slogan to assist participants in their presentations), 20pp, single copy free **US/Office of Consumer Affairs** , Washington, DC 20201 202-634-4329

FRAUD ADVERTISING HANDBOOK
(kept current) - names and addresses of people and organizations who can help confirm suspicions of fraudulent ads and answer questions for consumers, newspapers, etc., number of pages varies, single copy free **US/Office of Consumer Affairs** , Washington, DC 20201 202-634-4329

FRAUD ALERT ON JOINT VENTURES INVOLVING MEDICARE PATIENT REFERRALS
(1989) - fact sheet on arrangements between those referring Medicare and Medicaid patients and those providing Medicaid and Medicare services, and the implications that these joint ventures may violate an anti-kickback law, 2pp, free **US/HHS - Inspector General Hotline** PO Box 1182, Washington, DC 20201

THE FUTURE OF LEGAL SERVICES FOR MENTALLY RETARDED PERSONS
(undated) - exploration of what has happened and what can be done in the area of legal rights for the mentally retarded; discusses the need for a strong citizen advocacy program, 24pp, single copy free **US/President's Committee on Mental Retardation** RO Building, 7th and D Streets, SW, Washington, DC 20402 202-245-7634

GETTING YOUR DAY IN COURT
(1989) - a public service booklet developed with the assistance of the *General District Court* and the *Fairfax Bar Association;* outlines steps to take (negotiation, binding arbitration, letter, etc.) before considering a lawsuit; includes information on which court applies, eligibility for free or reduced rate legal services; where to sue, preparing to sue, evidence, witnesses, how to get started, the difference in suing businesses and corporations, filing, the trial, appeal, etc., 13pp, single copy free **Fairfax County Department of Consumer Affairs** 3959 Pender Drive, Fairfax, VA 22030 703-359-9161

GUIDE TO CONSUMER SERVICE
(kept current) - practical advice on financial, professional, legal, and other consumer services to help develop an awareness of the difference between a "good" and "poor" service; includes illustrations, charts, etc., #AO7, 127pp, $7.00 **Consumers Union of the United States** 256 Washington Street, Mount Vernon, NY 10550 914-667-9400

GUIDE TO COURT IN THE PUBLIC INTEREST: A GUIDE FOR COMMUNITY GROUPS
(1983) - guide to help community groups realize that any citizen concern is suitable for litigation; emphasizes that, although lobbying, picketing, conducting public education campaigns, etc.,

may work for some concerns, others require more drastic action; includes rationale for suing, how to choose and work with a lawyer, how the court system works, glossary, resources, etc., 16pp, $.85 plus $.50 handling per order **League of Women Voters of the US** 1730 M Street, NW, Washington, DC 20036 202-429-1965

HELP FOR LIFE'S FINANCIAL PHASES
(1989) - a series of booklets jointly developed by USDA and American Express to help consumers cope with financial questions at different phases in their lives: *Getting Started* #436V, *Settling Down* #464V, and *Keeping Pace* #468V, 6pp each, $.50 each (must use item number) **US/Consumer Information Center** , Pueblo, CO 81009

HOME SHOPPING
(1988) - special report on the emerging phenomenon of video shopping developed by the Council of Better Business Bureaus (CBBB) as a forerunner to a planned survey on the subject, and a CBBB consumer education program in cooperation with the Federal Trade Commission and Direct Marketing Association, single copy free **US/Office of Consumer Affairs** , Washington, DC 20201 202-634-4329

HOW TO GET (AND KEEP) THE CREDIT YOU DESERVE
(1979) - detailed examination for consumers of the lender's criteria for extending credit, correct procedures for seeking and obtaining credit, and the rights and responsibilities of the credit user; addresses high school juniors and seniors, 6-panel foldout, $.15 (minimum normally 50 copies; see notation on ABA materials, above, for ordering fewer copies) **American Bankers Association** 1120 Connecticut Avenue, NW, Washington, DC 20036 202-467-4871

AN IDEA WHOSE TIME IS ALWAYS
(1975) - compilation of the "Cooperation" column distributed as special features of the Cooperative News Service to keep readers informed on the various types of cooperatives and their benefits, number of columns varies, unpaged, $.85 **National Cooperative Business Association** 1407 New York Avenue, NW, Suite 100, Washington, DC 20005 202-638-6222

LAW AND LEGAL INFORMATION DIRECTORY
(2nd ed. 1982) - comprehensive coverage of live and print sources of legal information of all kinds; covers the continuing legal education, para-legal education, scholarships and grants, the federal court system, bar associations, special libraries, research centers, national and international organizations, periodicals, and other areas, 648pp, $170.00 **Gale Research Company** Book Tower, Detroit, MI 48226 313-961-2242

LAWYER IN THE CLASSROOM
(undated) - outline of a program where volunteer lawyers visit the school to inform students of their rights and answer questions, serve as a "Hot Line Lawyer" to be available for questions at any time, develop a lesson plan, etc., 8- panel foldout, free **Constitutional Rights Foundation** PO Box 2362, Texas City, TX 77592 713-668-5727

LEGAL SERVICES FOR THE ELDERLY
(1975) - overview of the need for improved legal services for the elderly, and ways for organizers to initiate or improve this type of service, 38pp, $2.15 **National Council on the Aging** 600 Maryland Avenue, SW, West Wing 100, Washington, DC 20024 202-479-1200

MAKING DEPOSITS

(1989) - answer to the frequently-asked question, "How long can financial institutions hold funds before making them available to the depositor?" 4pp, #584V, free (must use item number) **US/Consumer Information Center** , Pueblo, CO 81009

MONEY MANAGEMENT TEACHER'S GUIDE

(1980) - a guide to aid teachers in adapting the "To The Point" cluster to the individual needs of each student; includes explanation of objectives and preparation for each unit, suggestions for increasing students' chances of success, and concept and skill development for each study unit, 48pp, $2.25 **New Readers Press** Box 131, Syracuse, NY 13210 315-422-9121

MOVIES FOR TV

(1978) - Consumers Union's own ratings of 8166 TV movies as they relate to the best interests of consumers, unpaged, $1.50 plus $.25 postage/handling **Consumers Union of the United States** 256 Washington Street, Mount Vernon, NY 10550 914-667-9400

NAD CASE REPORTS

(monthly) - news items on BBB investigations, responses to inquiries, and other BBB activities of interest to the consumer, subscription (inquire about cost) **Council of Better Business Bureaus** 115 Wilson Boulevard, Arlington, VA 22209 703-276-0218

THE NAME OF THE GAME IS MONEY

(1972) - consumer education package for a group of 30 people, including manuals, crossword puzzles, leader's manual, and three overhead slides; addresses students in grades six to eight on personal money management and other consumer issues, $25/package **American Bankers Association** 1120 Connecticut Avenue, NW, Washington, DC 20036 202-663-5000

NSCLC NEWSLETTER

(weekly) - newsletter reporting on legal issues affecting the elderly poor, technical assistance available to nursing homes and others working with the elderly, advocacy efforts on behalf of the older poor, and training and other events designed to assist workers with the elderly, 8pp, single copy free **National Senior Citizens Law Center** 2025 M Street, NW, Suite 400, Washington, DC 20036 202-887-5280

NURSING HOME LAW LETTER

(monthly) - a newsletter specifically oriented toward nursing home law to inform administrators and others working with the elderly poor of current issues in the legal aspects of services to older persons in nursing homes; includes information on training and other assistance available to nursing home staff, volunteers, advocates, etc., 12pp, single copy free **National Senior Citizens Law Center** 2025 M Street, NW, Suite 400, Washington, DC 20036 202-887-5280

PRACTICAL LAW FOR THE LAYMAN

(1980) - coverage of the whole spectrum of consumer services, including: condominiums and cooperatives, taxes, bill collections, consumer protection, money management, starting a small business, investments, retirement, when NOT to act as your own lawyer, etc., 225pp, $6.95 **Acropolis Books** 2400 Seventeenth Street, NW, Washington, DC 20009 800-972-5855

THE REPRESENTATIVE PAYEE PROJECT: A VOLUNTEER FINANCIAL PROTECTIVE SERVICE PROJECT

(1986) - Results of a program mounted by the American Association of Retired Persons (AARP) and Legal Council for the Elderly (LCE) to: (1) test the feasibility of using volunteer representative payees to provide financial protective services to individuals who are incapable of managing their own affairs and have no friends or relatives; and (2) provide these services in a cost-effective manner that can be replicated nationwide; uses three project models developed for this study: (1) the Washington, DC, model used a paid staff working half time to manage the volunteer payees; (2) the Baltimore/Harrisonburg model used volunteers to manage the volunteer payees and the volunteer managers were supervised by AARP/LCE; and (3) the corporate model used an executive from a private business enterprise to manage the volunteer payees; provides findings of ongoing monitoring, bi-weekly logs and statistical data which determined the most-to-least feasible model for replication, 87pp, inquire about cost **US/DoC - National Technical Information Service** 5285 Port Royal Road, Springfield, VA 22151 703-557-4650

TARGET THE ELDERLY

(3rd pr., kept current) - information on how to deal with the consumer fraud schemes to which the elderly are particularly vulnerable (developed by the Better Business Bureau), 34pp, $1.00 (quantity discounts) **Consumer Affairs Foundation** PO Box 70, Boston, MA 02112 617-482-6914

TEACHER'S GUIDE TO THE CONSUMER RESOURCE HANDBOOK

(1988) - a companion piece to the *Consumer's Resource Handbook* containing suggestions for lessons based on the handbook's consumer tip sections, plus follow-up activities; includes suggested teaching units on making purchasing decisions, etc. (though written for secondary level, adaptable for elementary and adult education levels), 8pp, single copy free **US/Office of Consumer Affairs** , Washington, DC 20201 202-634-4329

TIPS BOOKLETS

(intermittent) - consumer information series of some 70 booklets on a variety of subjects such as consumer credit, shopping for food, saving energy, work-at-home schemes, etc.; includes applicable laws, buying alternatives, and other pertinent information, Av. 9pp, single copy $.25 with #10 self-addressed stamped envelope (write for list), additional copies vary from $12 to $20 per hundred **Council of Better Business Bureaus** 115 Wilson Boulevard, Arlington, VA 22209 703-276-0218

TIPS FOR CONSUMERS

(monthly) - copies of columns published in daily and weekly papers and other publications, free subscription **Council of Better Business Bureaus** 115 Wilson Boulevard, Arlington, VA 22209 703-276-0218

TO THE POINT ON MONEY MANAGEMENT

(1980) - five books covering the essentials of personal money management; titles include: Saving and Investing; Using a Checking Account; Making a Budget; Using Credit; Insuring Yourself, Approx. 48pp each, $2.25 **New Readers Press** Box 131, Syracuse, NY 13210 315-422-9121

20 WAYS NOT TO BE "GYPPED"

(1978) - illustrated guide cautioning against 20 of the more than 800 identified "gyps" in the marketplace, including contests, selling out sales, "deals" on a car, neighbor's COD package, fuel-saving devices, free inspections, quick cures, bait and switch, etc.; identifies the warning signs and offers do's and don't's to alert the consumer; lists several sources whose purpose is to hear complaints, 15pp, $.75 (bulk discounts) **Channing L. Bete Company** , South Deerfield, MA 01373

URBAN HOUSING COURTS AND LANDLORD-TENANT JUSTICE

(1977) - assistance for individuals, groups, and communities seeking better housing justice through the court process; includes profiles of three Housing Courts - how they came about, their jurisdictions, powers, operations, etc., and a section on landlord-tenant disputes in small claims courts, 36pp, single copy free **American Bar Association** 750 North Lake Shore Drive, Chicago, IL 60611 312-988-5000

USE AND ABUSE OF MONEY

(1978) - advice to consumers on money management, including credit, retirement investment, estate planning, etc.; includes 3-page work sheet to help project long-term financial goals and objectives for individual or family, 8pp, $.40 ($2.95/dozen) **Augsburg Fortress** 426 South Fifth Street, Box 1209, Minneapolis, MN 55440 612-330-3300

USE AND ABUSE OF TV TIME

(1978) - overview of the adverse effects on consumers of some of the TV advertising practices, e.g., junk food ads, instant toll-free purchasing, etc.; suggests ways in which consumers can launch a monitoring and letter-writing campaign; lists major active resource groups such as Action for Children's Television, 8pp, $.40 ($2.95/dozen) **Augsburg Fortress** 426 South Fifth Street, Box 1209, Minneapolis, MN 55440 612-330-3300

WHAT CONSUMERS SHOULD KNOW ABOUT SERVICE CONTRACTS

(1989) - a guide published jointly by the Federal Trade Commission and Electronic Industries Association to help consumers ask the right questions about a service contract or extended warranty, 4pp, single copy free **US/Office of Consumer Affairs** , Washington, DC 20201 202-634-4229

WHAT IS A CO-OP?

(undated) - description of a co-op and its people-oriented philosophy; discusses marketing, service, purchasing co-ops, and other areas, with illustrations, brochure, $.05 each (quantity discounts) **National Cooperative Business Association** 1407 New York Avenue, NW, Suite 100, Washington, DC 20005 202-638-6222

WHERE TO GO, WHO TO SEE, WHAT TO DO

(1973) - guide to consumer services in areas such as money management, child care, employment, and other sources in the community, 26pp, $1.44 **Steck-Vaughn Company** PO Box 2028, Austin, TX 78768 512-476-6721

A WOMAN'S GUIDE TO PERSONAL AND BUSINESS CREDIT

(1978)- information for women on their credit rights and how to assert and protect them; identifies credit obstacles that continue to face women, 48pp, $2.95 **Pilot Books** 103 Cooper Street, Babylon, NY 11702 516-422-2225

YOUR RIGHTS WHEN YOU'RE YOUNG

(1979) - a guide describing the general legal rights of minors as members of families, schools and communities; includes photos and interesting case histories, set in an easy-to-read design, that focus on a young person's role in the complex laws regarding medical, legal and social services, 96pp, $2.65 **New Readers Press** Box 131, Syracuse, NY 13210 315-422-9121

ZILLIONS

(bimonthly) - children's version of Consumer Reports with quick-reference charts and illustrations designed to give youngsters an early start as wise buyers, av. 22pp, $11.95/year (bulk rates available) **Consumers Union of the United States** 256 Washington Street, Mount Vernon, NY 10550 914-667-9400

DAY CARE/HEAD START

THE ABC'S OF QUALITY DAY CARE
(3rd Pr. 1982) - information based on the premise that finding quality day care for children is a difficult task; includes sections on the choices of styles, providers, safety, curriculum, the parents' role, and points for discussion and consideration, 16pp, single copy free **Virginia Division for Children** 805 East Broad Street, 11th Floor, Richmond, VA 23219 804-786-5507

AIDES TO TEACHERS AND CHILDREN
(1968) - exploration of who they are, what they do, how to find them, and how to train and work with them; includes bibliography, 64pp, $.75 (members 10% discount) **Association for Childhood Education International** 11141 Georgia Avenue, Wheaton, MD 20902 301-942-2443

BEING A DAY CARE AIDE
(1972) - a look at all aspects of working with very young children to serve as a reference for child care workers in day care centers, 208pp, inquire about cost **Prentice-Hall** , Englewood Cliffs, NJ 07632 201-592-2000

BUSINESS INCENTIVES FOR PROVIDING CHILDCARE AS A BENEFIT TO EMPLOYEES
(1982) - a compilation of sources for information on employer-sponsored child care; including where to find details about tax incentives that encourage industry to support child care, #503, single copy free with SASE, additional $.25 each (quantity discounts) **National Association for the Education of Young Children** 1834 Connecticut Avenue, NW, Washington, DC 20009 202-232-8777

CARING FOR A CHILD
(1982) - a comprehensive handbook on caring for children under preschool age (5 or 6 years old); for use by parents, relatives and babysitters as well as day care workers; covers everyday care, feeding, clothing, mental and emotional development, safety and health information, inquire about cost **Washington State University** Bulletin Department, Pullman, WA 99163 509-335-3564

THE CHANGING DIMENSIONS OF DAY CARE
(1970) - the case for keeping pace with the changing times as they affect the most vital aspects of the quality of day care; presents

highlights from Child Welfare and other hints for updating and upgrading the day care program, 62pp, $4.00 **Child Welfare League of America** 440 First Street, NW, Washington, DC 20001 202-638-2952

CHILD CARE CENTERS: INDOOR LIGHTING - OUTDOOR PLAY SPACE
(1973) - practical, constructive, money-saving advice for those who plan and design child care facilities, 28pp, $3.45 **Child Welfare League of America** 440 First Street, NW, Washington, DC 20001 202-638-2952

CHILD'S POTENTIAL TO LEARN
(1980) - illustrated guide for parents and others working with preschool children, suggesting ways to stimulate the child's imagination, sensory perception, physical capabilities, etc., emphasizes the importance of the early learning years, 15pp, $.75 **Channing L. Bete Company** , South Deerfield, MA 01373

THE CHILD'S RIGHT TO QUALITY DAY CARE
(1970) - overview of what should be included in a quality program; includes discussions on licensing and responsibility as well, 8pp, $.35 (10/$3.00) **Association for Childhood Education International** 11141 Georgia Avenue , Suite 200, Wheaton, MD 20902 301-942-2443

COMMUNITY SOLUTIONS FOR CHILD CARE
(1979) - proceedings of a conference convened to examine solutions provided by communities to help solve child care problems; provides case studies of supportive services like California's network of 34 I&R agencies for parents seeking child care arrangements, Washington, D.C.'s day care center at the courthouse for parents who must appear in court, a "parent rap session" at an industry in Texas which provides lunches so parents can share problems and solutions on child care, etc.; addresses the volunteer element where it exists, 105pp, single copy free **US/DoL - Women's Bureau** 200 Constitution Avenue, NW, Washington, DC 20210 202-523-6611

CONFRONTING THE CHILD CARE CRISIS
(1979) - an examination of the new needs arising from the increased incidence of separation and divorce, single parenthood and working mothers; reports on federal, state and local response

over the past decade, including the red tape, overlapping services, mismanagement, wasted resources, and lack of interest that has stalled legislation for infants, preschool and school-age children; outlines ways industry, business, universities, hospitals, and other institutions can help, 127pp, $10.50 **Beacon Press** 25 Beacon Street, Boston, MA 02108 617-742-2110

CWLA STANDARDS FOR DAY CARE SERVICE

(2nd ed.) - standards intended to be goals for continuous improvement of services to children; represents practices considered by CWLA to be most desirable, 123pp, $7.50 **Child Welfare League of America** 440 First Street, NW, Washington, DC 20001 202-638-2952

DAY CARE: HOW TO PLAN, DEVELOP, AND OPERATE A DAY CARE CENTER

(1971) - complete guide starting with needs assessment and including funding, budgeting, leadership, site location, staff, curriculum, play areas, health services, etc., 337pp, out of print, will republish if demand warrants, inquire about availability and cost **Beacon Press** 25 Beacon Street, Boston, MA 02108 617-742-2110

DAY CARE LEGAL HANDBOOK: LEGAL ASPECTS OF ORGANIZING AND OPERATING DAY CARE PROGRAMS

(1977) - a guide to insurance, taxes, contracts and other procedures for organizing a day care center, 177pp, $4.00 **ERIC Clearinghouse on Early Childhood Education** Kenyon Road, Urbana, IL 61801 217-328-3870

DAY CARE LICENSING POLICIES AND PRACTICE

(1976) - a state survey to determine the variations in licensing for day care across the state, and the attitudes and implementation of those in licensed day care operations, 72pp, $4.00 **Education Commission of the States** 707 Seventeenth Street, Suite 2700, Denver, CO 80202-3427 303-830-3600

DAY CARE: PLANNING AND IMPLEMENTING

(1973) - a case for assuring that each day care center reflect the unique needs of its community; presents broad guidelines on goals, staff, curriculum, parents, volunteers, etc.; appends list of resources, 28pp, $2.00 **National Education Association** 1201 Sixteenth Street, NW, Washington, DC 20036 202-8833-4233

DESIGNING A DAY CARE CENTER

(1975) - techniques for building a day care center that will reflect the educational philosophy of the program; discusses renovation, indoor design, furniture construction; detailed drawings, 176pp,$3.45 **Beacon Press** 25 Beacon Street, Boston, MA 02108 617-742-2110

DESIGNING THE CHILD DEVELOPMENT CENTER

(1968) - detailed drawings, instructions, resources, and suggestions for both external and internal design of a center that will foster maximum learning among young children, 24pp, single copy free **US/DEd - Office for Children and Youth** 400 Maryland Avenue, SW, Washington, DC 20202 202-245-8707

EARLY CHILDHOOD EDUCATION: AN INTRODUCTION TO THE PROFESSION

(undated) - orientation for child care workers and others covering the whole spectrum of education for the young child, 103pp, $1.10 **National Association for the Education of Young Children** 1834 Connecticut Avenue, NW, Washington, DC 20009 202-232-8777

EVALUATING CHILDREN'S PROGRESS: A RATING SCALE FOR CHILDREN IN DAY CARE

(undated) - provides rating scales, related to specific ages, for use in correcting information about individual children in groups. **Day Care Council of America** 1602 Seventeenth Street, NW, Washington, DC 20009 202-745-0220

FAMILY DAY CARE

(1977) - a guidebook to help professionals and laypeople to work as partners in developing the cooperative neighborhood approach to the care of young children; emphasizes involving parents, caregivers, organizers, and the total community in the effort, 143pp, $9.50 **Beacon Press** 25 Beacon Street, Boston, MA 02108 617-742-2110

FAMILY DAY CARE: RESOURCES FOR PROVIDERS

(1976) - overview of public/private resources at local, state, and national levels for family day care providers, 177pp, $3.50 **Squibb Publications** Shaker Road, Harvard, MA 02451 617-772-3535

FEDERAL CHILD CARE LEGISLATION

(1979) - overview of legislation enacted during 1976, 1977, and 1978 to give administrators and others some insight into the legal trends in the area of child care, 14pp, single copy free **US/DoL - Women's Bureau** 200 Constitution Avenue, NW, Washington, DC 20210 202-523-6611

FEDERAL FUNDS FOR DAY CARE

(1972) - outline of programs offered by federal agencies that provide funds for day care projects, 91pp, single copy free **US/DoL - Women's Bureau** 200 Constitution Avenue, NW, Washington, DC 20210 202-523-6611

FEEDING BABIES AND LITTLE KIDS

(1976) - series of fact sheets on feeding children from birth to age three; addressed to mothers, but useful for workers with infants, inquire about cost **Washington State University** Bulletin Department, Pullman, WA 99163 509-335-3564

FOOD BUYING GUIDE FOR CHILD CARE CENTERS

(1974) - handbook that considers all aspects of the nutrition needs of very young children, and provides information on planning and acquisition, 43pp, single copy free **US/DoA - Food and Nutrition Service** 3101 Park Center Drive, Alexandria , VA 22303 703-756-3281

FOOD FARE FOR CHILD DAY CARE

(1974) - manual for those responsible for planning and acquiring food for child care programs; covers costs, quantities, and other specific aspects of the task, 50pp, $.97 + postage **Florida Department of Health and Rehabilitative Services** PO Box 210, Jacksonville, FL 32201 804-725-3080

FOOD GUIDE FOR THE FIRST FIVE YEARS

(1983) - hints for parents and workers with very young children to help make mealtime both nutritious and a pleasant experience for all concerned, 20pp, $.25 (quantity discounts) **National Live Stock and Meat Board** 444 Michigan Avenue, Chicago, IL 60611 312-467-5520

FOOD SELECTION FOR GOOD NUTRITION IN GROUP FEEDING

(1972) - guide based on extensive study of a system that will do the best job in meeting the nutrition needs of groups, 32pp, single copy free **US/DoA - Consumer and Food Economics Institute** Federal Building, Hyattsville, MD 20782 301-436-8221

GAO SURVEY ON CHILD CARE SERVICES IN THE ARMED FORCES
(1989) - a survey to determine the level of child care services available to military single and/or working parents; discusses percentage of bases with services, adequacy of services, number of children needing services, etc., single copy free **US/GAO - General Accounting Office** 441 G Street, NW, Washington, DC 20548 202-275-2812

A GOOD BEGINNING FOR BABIES: GUIDELINES FOR GROUP CARE
(1975) - comprehensive guide covering all aspects of providing group care on a daily basis for infants, 189pp, $5.75 **National Association for the Education of Young Children** 1834 Connecticut Avenue, NW, Washington, DC 20009 202-232-8777

GUIDE FOR ESTABLISHING AND OPERATING DAY CARE CENTERS FOR YOUNG CHILDREN
(undated) - planning and operating guide for organizers covering all aspects from the talking stage to implementation and evaluation, 100pp, $6.50 **Child Welfare League of America** 440 First Street, NW, Washington, DC 20001 202-638-2952

GUIDE FOR THE CARE OF INFANTS IN GROUPS
(undated) - handbook outlining criteria for safeguarding infants, with suggestions for initial planning steps to make the overall task more efficient and effective, 104pp, $4.50 **Child Welfare League of America** 440 First Street, NW, Washington, DC 20001 202-638-2952

GUIDELINES: EVALUATING THE LEARNING ENVIRONMENT OF A DAY CARE CENTER
(1974) - a comprehensive premise for effective monitoring and evaluation in both physical interactional and program settings; includes evaluation model, 134pp, $3.75 **Day Care Council of America** 1602 Seventeenth Street, NW, Washington, DC 20009 202-745-0220

HEALTH SERVICES
(1971) - manual to help day care planners carry out services to meet the needs of young children and their parents; includes utilization of existing community resources, record keeping and budgeting, preventive measures in dental/speech/hearing/language and mental health services, 187pp, $1.50 **Day Care Council of America** 1602 Seventeenth Street, NW, Washington, DC 20009 202-745-0220

HOW TO DEVELOP A CRISIS NURSERY
(1979) - overview of the growth of the 24-hour nursery to fill the natural need of parents for periods of relief from their children; discusses types of nurseries, funding, staff, and other aspects, 23pp, single copy free **National Center on Child Abuse and Neglect** U.S. Dept. of Health & Human Svcs., PO Box 1182, Washington, DC 20201 202-755-7500

IDEAS THAT WORK WITH YOUNG CHILDREN
(1979) - an idea-bank for curriculum planners on teaching with impact, language arts, learning activities, helping children cope, and other areas affecting the learning environment of young children, 297pp, $4.75 **National Association for the Education of Young Children** 1834 Connecticut Avenue, NW, Washington, DC 20009 202-232-8777

THE INFANT DAY CARE DEBATE: NOT WHETHER BUT HOW?
(undated) - exploration of the stimulation, and other concerns, in the option for infant day care - considering babysitting and parent

co-ops as well as day care centers, 163pp, $2.25 **Day Care Council of America** 1602 Seventeenth Street, NW, Washington, DC 20009 202-745-0220

A LAP TO SIT ON AND MUCH MORE
(1971) - one of a series of helps for day care workers; includes insights into child behavior, ideas for activities, etc., 96pp, $3.00 (members 10% discount) **Association for Childhood Education International** 11141 Georgia Avenue , Suite 200, Wheaton, MD 20902 301-942-2443

LEARNING GAMES FOR INFANTS AND TODDLERS
(1977) - playtime handbook for caregivers of very small children designed to help them use their bodies, learn the language, begin to think, and feel good about themselves and the caregiver, 80pp, $2.95 **New Readers Press** Box 131, Syracuse, NY 13210 315-422-9121

THE MAGIC YEARS
(undated) - comprehensive aid for workers with young children covering the whole spectrum of potential, problems, learning capabilities, and other facets of the earliest years of childhood, 302pp, $4.95 **Child Welfare League of America** 440 First Street, NW, Washington, DC 20001 202-638-2952

MIGRANT CHILDREN: THEIR EDUCATION
(1971) - overview of "children on the move" with help in providing smooth integration into the learning program, and bridging the gap between classroom and the child's family, 64pp, $1.00 **Association for Childhood Education International** 11141 Georgia Avenue , Suite 200, Wheaton, MD 20902 301-942-2443

MORE THAN GRAHAM CRACKERS: NUTRITION EDUCATION AND FOOD PREPARATION WITH YOUNG CHILDREN
(1979) - recipes, finger plays, teaching ideas, and resources "beyond the kitchen cupboard" to help children select, prepare and enjoy nutritious foods, 100pp, $4.25 **National Association for the Education of Young Children** 1834 Connecticut Avenue, NW, Washington, DC 20009 202-232-8777

NUTRITION AND EDUCATIONAL GROWTH IN CHILDREN
(undated) - results of a survey of educators and nutritionists giving evidence of the grave interrelationship between food and education, 64pp, $2.00 (members 10% discount) **Association for Childhood Education International** 11141 Georgia Avenue , Suite 200, Wheaton, MD 20902 301-942-2443

OPENING, MIXING, MATCHING
(1973) - descriptions of nine programs where curriculum was opened up to mix age groups (0-8), utilize the bus and other external facilities for learning, etc., 44pp, $1.50 **Association for Childhood Education International** 11141 Georgia Avenue , Suite 200, Wheaton, MD 20902 301-942-2443

ORGANIZING DAY CARE
(1983) - comprehensive manual covering all day care areas, including: board, funding, community support, differences between "bad, marginal and good day care," budgets for 35 and for 55 children, outline for proposal, staffing and job descriptions, equipment list, sample floor plans, sample by-laws, and more, 30pp, $2.00 **National Child Day Care Association** 1501 Benning Road, NE, Washington, DC 20002 202-397-3800

PERSPECTIVES IN CHILD CARE
(1973) - account of a national debate on the need of major

investment of federal funds in child care legislation, 64pp, $.85 **National Association for the Education of Young Children** 1834 Connecticut Avenue, NW, Washington, DC 20009 202-232-8777

PHYSICAL EDUCATION FOR CHILDREN'S HEALTHFUL LIVING

(1973) - support for the importance to the health of growing children of a good program of physical education; includes formulas for play, 80pp, $.75 **Association for Childhood Education International** 11141 Georgia Avenue , Suite 200, Wheaton, MD 20902 301-942-2443

PLANNING ENVIRONMENTS FOR YOUNG CHILDREN: PHYSICAL SPACE

(1969) - overview of how facilities can either invite or inhibit a responsive atmosphere; includes techniques for analyzing any facility; offers detailed diagrams, 48pp, $2.00 **National Association for the Education of Young Children** 1834 Connecticut Avenue, NW, Washington, DC 20009 202-232-8777

PRIME TIME: CHILDREN'S EARLY LEARNING YEARS

(1973) - recounted experiences of a director of a nursery school discussing methods and techniques through which teachers, teacher aides, and parents can help young children overcome physical, behavioral, and emotional learning problems, 198pp, $2.85 **Citation Press** 50 West 44th Street, New York, NY 10036 212-867-7700

THE PRIMER

(1972) - an introduction to understanding teaching goals and classroom practices in a group day care setting for three-, four- and five-year-old children, 30pp, $1.50 **National Child Day Care Association** 1501 Benning Road, NE, Washington, DC 20002 202-397-3800

REACHING PARENTS SERIES

(kept current) - collection of booklets in the area of parent cooperation in nursery schools; cites workshops and other programs to keep parents involved for the benefit of their children, $10.00/kit (members $7.00) (booklets sold separately also; inquire) **Parent Cooperative Pre-Schools International** PO Box 90410, Indianapolis, IN 46290 317-849-0992

SELECTED READING: ISSUES OF CHILD CARE

(1972) - selections from federally-sponsored reports and studies discussing the purpose of day care, the various types of programs, family involvement, etc.; recommends use as a training manual for day care staff and volunteers, 84pp, $3.50 **Day Care Council of America** 1602 Seventeenth Street, NW, Washington, DC 20009 202-745-0220

SO YOU'RE GOING TO RUN A DAY CARE SERVICE!

(1975) - a comprehensive guide for the new day care operator covering procedures ranging from how to conduct the initial meeting to methods of evaluating the operation, 114pp, $3.00 **Day Care Council of New York** 205 East 42nd Street, New York, NY 10003 212-687-9052

SOME WAYS OF DISTINGUISHING A GOOD EARLY CHILDHOOD PROGRAM

(1975) - eighteen points to help parents answer such questions as "How can we tell a good early childhood program from a poor one?" providing information on specific points of comparison, 16pp, $.25 (also Spanish) single copies free with self-addressed stamped envelope) **National Association for the Education of Young Children** 1834 Connecticut Avenue, NW, Washington, DC 20009 202-232-8777

TENDER LOVING CARE

(1972) - account of a program designed to employ older people as aides to work with very young people, 29pp, $.80 **National Council on the Aging** 600 Maryland Avenue, SW, West Wing 100, Washington, DC 20024 202-479-1200

TOWARD BETTER KINDERGARTEN

(undated) - attention to the priorities and responsibilities inherent in providing quality facilities, and the learning experiences and freedom a young child needs; includes many ideas directly applicable to day care, 64pp, $1.25 (members 10% discount) **Association for Childhood Education International** 11141 Georgia Avenue , Suite 200, Wheaton, MD 20902 301-942-2443

TRAINING FOR CHILD CARE WORK: PROJECT FRESH START

(undated) - a model, JTPA-supported child care project providing a framework through which communities can work to meet the critical shortage of trained child care workers, while having an impact on the employability of disadvantaged women, 48pp, $2.75 **US/DoL - Women's Bureau** 200 Constitution Avenue, NW, Washington, DC 20210 202-523-6611

WINDOWS ON DAY CARE

(undated) - a set of basic standards for day care centers which resulted from a nationwide survey; includes other general recommendations for administrators, 248pp, $2.50 **National Council of Jewish Women** 15 East 26th Street, New York, NY 10010 212-532-1740

DISASTER RESPONSE/EMERGENCY PREPAREDNESS

ANIMAL RESCUE VOLUNTEER TRAINING
(1989) - two training films, developed on-site, to assist volunteers about to start helping with the cleanup of oiled otters and birds resulting from the *Exxon Valdez* oil spill; includes step-by-step instructions from an animal's arrival to completed cleanup, with experts talking over the footage, and much technical information provided; features a closing shot of the release of a rescued and rehabilitated bird who flies off in a burst of energy, inquire about length and cost. **Exxon** 800 Bell Street, Houston, TX 77002 713-656-3636

DISASTER VOLUNTEERS
(undated) - a report on a national volunteer program to secure disaster volunteers, which began in 1980 as a joint venture of *Tenneco* and the *American Red Cross;* includes information on the six areas of cooperation, including mutual planning, training, cooperative service projects and other activities, unpaged, single copy free **Tenneco, Incorporated** Commerce Building, PO Box 2511, Houston, TX 77001 713-757-2058

THE HEART OF AIRLIFELINE
(undated) - a packet of information describing a service that involves over 600 volunteer pilots, physicians, and interested citizens who provide emergency air transportation in medical emergencies; includes general information, application for membership and/or volunteer involvement, and other information, single packet free **Airlifeline** 1772 J Street, Suite 14, Sacramento, CA 95814 916-442-6230

HERE'S LOOKING AT YOU KID
(1990) - a videotape telling the story of a child and how he adjusted to an accident that severely burned over three quarters of his body; includes description of adjustment the child and parent had to make at home, at school and in public; provides information on how to remove hazards to prevent burn injuries to children; offers help to parents whose child must endure a similar traumatic ordeal, indicate format, rental/3 days, $50.00; purchase $300 **Virginia Department for Rights of the Disabled** James Monroe Building, 17th Floor, 101 North 14th Street, Richmond, VA 23219 804-225-2042

HOW TO MOBILIZE COMMUNITY VOLUNTEER RESOURCES
(1978) - guide to the area-wide coordination of volunteers for an immunization or disaster relief program by linking the Board of Health, the central volunteer-providing facility, and the community at large; details the role of each of these participants; includes resource list and other helpful information for other volunteer health programs, 105pp, inquire about cost **Volunteer Action Center of Broward County** 1300 Andrews Avenue, Fort Lauderdale, FL 33315 305-522-6761

DRUG ABUSE/ALCOHOLISM

ABC'S OF DRINKING & DRIVING
(1980) - facts about a leading safety problem in the U.S. - alcohol-related driving accidents; discusses legal implications (breath test, etc.), effects of alcohol on reaction time, etc., 15pp, $.75 **Channing L. Bete Company** , South Deerfield, MA 01373

ABSTINENCE: A VIABLE CHOICE
(1980) - an account of the problems irresponsible drinking causes communities, and an appeal to the church community to join the total community in an effort to alleviate the problem, llpp, $.30 ($15/100) **Board of Church and Society** 100 Maryland Avenue, NE, Washington, DC 20002 202-488-5600

ALCOHOL AND DRUGS ARE WOMEN'S ISSUES
(1990) - a look at the tendency to emphasize men in treatment for drug and alcohol addiction; an overview of the problem as it relates to women, in process at press time, inquire **Women's Action Alliance** 370 Lexington Avenue, Suite 603, New York, NY 10017 212-779-2846

ALCOHOL: DISEASE/DRINK/DRUNK
(1978) - comprehensive question/answer overview of the topic most often thrown back at adults confronting their children on marijuana - alcohol; covers the subject with complete chapters in each of the title areas, using an easy-reference format touching on government involvement, cultural influence, preventive programs, and many other categories, 78pp, $2.95 **TANE Press** 6778 Greenville Avenue, Dallas, TX 73231 214-363-5305

ALCOHOLISM SERIES
(1988) - a listing of 30 inexpensive publications on all aspects of alcoholism, ranging from halfway houses to multiple addictions, and from *Flare Up: Stress Time* to *Humor, Health and Spirit Lifters,* and from brochures and fact sheets to directories and textbooks, free list (most publications are under a dollar) **Association of Halfway House Alcoholism Programs of North America** 786 East Seventh Street, St. Paul, MN 55105 612-771-0933

ALCOHOLISM: THE NEEDS OF MINORITIES
(1973) - overview of special alcoholism programs among poverty and minority groups, and the importance of continuing these programs, 10pp, $.35 **National Council on Alcoholism** 12 West 21st Street, New York, NY 10010 212-206-6770

CATCHING ON
(1980) - a comic book for the 8-11 age group with games, puzzles and basic drug information, single copy free **US/HHS - National Clearinghouse for Alcohol and Drug Information** PO Box 416, Kensington, MD 20795 301-443-6500

CHEMICAL SURVIVAL: A PRIMER FOR WESTERN MAN AND WOMAN
(1979) - a brief history of drug use in the U.S., including alcohol, coffee and tobacco, followed by specific "trips" and their effects/dangers; includes perspectives on safety and driving, cleaning up (kicking the habit), recommended reading, and a "bummer chart" (emergency information), $1.50 (quantity discounts) **Do It Now Foundation** PO Box 21126, Phoenix, AZ 85036 602-257-0797

CHOICES ABOUT DRUGS AND DRINKING
(Rev. 1987) - drug education kit developed for use with pre-teenage groups (grades 4-6) but useful for older youth and adult education programs as well; includes teacher/leader guide and eight 200-copy duplicating masters on decisions, alternatives and other choices about drugs, including alcohol and smoking; schools can contact local Kiwanis Club to request kits **Kiwanis International** 3636 Woodview Trace, Indianapolis, IN 46268 317-875-8755

COMIX
(1981) - a blend of lively drawings and easy-to-read text that points out the effects and dangers of drugs (for grades 3 to 6), 12pp, $.25 **Do It Now Foundation** PO Box 21126, Phoenix, AZ 85036 602-257-0797

COMMAND GUIDANCE FOR "CAMPAIGN DRUG FREE"
(1989) - A comprehensive guide for Unit Commanding Officers in the U.S. Navy to administering *Campaign Drug Free,* a voluntary program aimed at the demand side of the national drug problem; includes information on dual leadership (civilian and military) and ways in which Navy, Marine Corps, and Coast Guard Reservists are helping by visiting fifth- and sixth-grade classes with the Campaign's program; appends evaluation form, news articles, window decals, and other materials as available, 11pp, single copy free **US/DoD - Naval Reserve Force** Office of the Secretary, The Pentagon, Washington, DC 20350-1000 202-695-2486

COMMUNITY ORGANIZATION WORKBOOK

(1976) - a tool for training personnel of volunteer alcoholism organizations to improve their programs, 68pp, $5.00 **National Council on Alcoholism** 12 West 21st Street, New York, NY 10010 212-206-6770

CONSUMER INFORMATION ABOUT DRUGS

(undated) - compilation of materials on drugs as they pertain to health care, medications, nonprescribed drugging effects, symptoms of drug abuse, school performance, etc.; includes list of available consumer publications, single kit free **Pharmaceutical Manufacturers Association** 1100 Fifteenth Street, NW, Washington, DC 20005 202-835-4300

DRUG ABUSE: A REALISTIC PRIMER FOR PARENTS

(1980) - straight talk to parents reminding them that all young people between the ages of 5 and 20 will be exposed to drugs at some point - and that knowing the answers to some of their questions without hesitation could satisfy their natural curiosity and eliminate experimentation; provides information in most potential problem areas, 14pp, $.50 **Do It Now Foundation** PO Box 5115, Phoenix, AZ 85010 602-257-0797

DRUG ABUSE - ADVISOR SUPPLEMENT

(updated) - handbook for the adult worker with youth groups - professional or volunteer; suggests community and family activities of a nonjudgmental supportive nature to keep the door to communication open, 8pp, $.10 **B'nai B'rith Youth Organization** 1640 Rhode Island Avenue, NW, Washington, DC 20036 202-857-6585

DRUG ABUSE: MEETING THE CHALLENGE

(1987) - an overview of the drug problems in the U.S.; includes illustrated descriptions of programs of the *National Institute of Drug Abuse;* addresses prevention, drugs in the workplace, treatment, and research, with special attention given to AIDS and IV drug use, VHS22A, 23 minutes, free for maximum one-month loan (accompanied by viewer feedback form; borrowers pay return postage only) **US/HHS - National Clearinghouse for Alcohol and Drug Information** Box 2345, Rockville, MD 20852 301-468-2600

DRUG ABUSE PAMPHLET SERIES

(various dates) - facts and recommendations on specific aspects of alcohol abuse, 6- to 8-panel foldouts, $.15 each:
- *All About Alcohol*
- *The Co-Alcoholic Wife*
- *Alcohol: Simple Facts About Combinations with Other Drugs*
- *Denial: The Defense that Disables*
- *Cause and Defect: Fetal Alcohol Syndrome*
- *DWI: Facts About Drunk Driving*

Do It Now Foundation PO Box 5115, Phoenix, AZ 85010 602-257-0797

DRUG ABUSE PREVENTION NEEDS ASSESSMENT

(1989) - a survey of the community to determine factors that contribute to drug abuse; reflects responses from 204 of 450 people (education, law enforcement, community and youth representatives) receiving the questionnaire in one of the *InTouch* prevention service areas in the county; determines scope and areas of concentration by *InHouse* staff and volunteers for the ensuing year, single copy free **InTouch** Cook County Sheriff's Office, 1401 Maybrook Drive, Maywood, IL 60153 312-865-2900

DRUG ABUSE: TEENAGE HANGUP

(1976) - comprehensive question/answer format developed to help teachers understand the drug pressures facing students, but useful for anyone working to prevent or treat drug abuse among young people; includes Q/A sections on commonly-used drugs, special problems, laws, treatment, rehabilitation, resources, 140pp, $2.95 **TANE Press** 6778 Greenville Avenue, Dallas, TX 75231 214-363-5305

DRUG FREE SCHOOLS AND COMMUNITIES ACT

(1989) - packet of information compiled by the Illinois Board of Education for non-competitive Drug Free Schools and Communities money, which is set at $4.00 per student; includes provisions for private schools to work through public schools to mount programs; describes a wide range of prevention activities, including school programs, parent/community programs, and youth leadership activities eligible for use of the funds, unpaged, free **InTouch Program** Cook County Sheriff's Office, Youth Services Department , Maywood, IL 60153 312-865-2900

DRUG-FREE SCHOOLS SERIES

(1988-89) - a series of publications and other materials to assist teachers, parents, and others involved in the schools in creating drug-free zones; includes:
- *What Works. Schools Without Drugs* - a guide for educators and other members of the community developed by the *U.S. Department of Education* with the latest information about alcohol and other drugs and their effects, examples of successful school-based programs, etc., 87pp
- *The Fact Is... You Can Prevent Alcohol and Other Drug Use Among Junior and Senior High School Students* and *The Fact Is... You Can Prevent Alcohol and Other Drug Problems Among Elementary School Children* - resources such as audiovisuals, program descriptions, and professional and organizational aids for educators and parents; includes intervention and prevention programs, each 17pp
- *Drug Prevention Curricula: A Guide to Selection and Implementation* - what to look for and what to avoid, unpaged
- *The Fact Is... You Can Form a Student Assistance Program* - types of student assistance programs, and where to obtain further information, 9pp
- *It's Elementary. Meeting the Needs of High-Risk Youth in the School Setting* - problems and special needs faced by children of alcohol abusing or other drug using parents; includes resource list for elementary school age children of alcoholics, 29pp
- *If a Child from an Alcoholic Home Comes to You* - guidance for adults on how to best help children who approach them with problems of parental alcohol abuse, one page
- *The Challenge* - selected issues of a bimonthly newsletter published by the *U.S. Department of Education* containing information about alcohol and other drug prevention activities, request list of issues available.

Single copies of all publications are free; request complete list. **US/HHS - National Clearinghouse for Alcohol and Drug Information** PO Box 2345, Rockville, MD 20852 301-468-2600

DRUG TRAFFICKING STUDY TASK FORCE REPORT TO THE GOVERNOR

(1991) - results of a two-year study commissioned in the 1988-89 General Assembly to develop a formula for escalating the war on drugs by coordinating the state's educational, medical and law enforcement resources, in process, available late 1991, inquire about cost **Drug Trafficking Study Task Force** Virginia Crime Commission, 223 Governor Street, Richmond, VA 23219 804-786-1431

DRUGS & ALCOHOL: A HANDBOOK FOR YOUNG PEOPLE

(1981) - up-to-date information on the actions and effects of drugs and alcohol, and problems associated with abuse; examines reasons for drug misuse and discusses constructive, healthy alternatives;

includes a two-question quiz that explores what kids know - and what they think they know - about drugs and alcohol, for grades 5-8, 30pp, $.75 **Do It Now Foundation** PO Box 21126, Phoenix, AZ 85036 602-257-0797

DRUGS AND YOU
(1980) - a guide for young people to provide all of the facts and myths about drug abuse to allow them to make a decision based on knowledge, not peer pressure, 15pp, $.75 **Channing L. Bete Company** , South Deerfield, MA 01373

DRUGS ARE NOT THE PROBLEM
(undated) - a look at the drug problem as only a symptom of the more general problems of teenagers growing up; suggests ways to deal with the basic problems rather than the symptoms (developed by youth for youth), 23pp, $.25 **B'nai B'rith Youth Organization** 1640 Rhode Island Avenue, NW, Washington, DC 20036 202-857-6585

DRUGS ARE STILL NOT THE PROBLEM... BUT...
(undated) - a modification of the philosophy in its companion piece above, conceding that drug abuse - although still not the total problem - has become an increasingly acceptable teenage fad affecting "normal" a well as troubled youngsters; suggests ways to reverse or redirect this trend, 8pp, $.10 **B'nai B'rith Youth Organization** 1640 Rhode Island Avenue, NW, Washington, DC 20036 202-857-6585

EDUCATIONAL OFF-PRINT SERIES
(various dates) - reprints of articles from the Journal of Psychedelic Drugs selected for practical application and accuracy (request complete list):
- A Rational Approach to Drug Abuse Prevention (1973), $1.00
- Drugs: Information for Crisis Treatment (Rev. 1979), $.90
- Drugs of Abuse: An Introduction to their Actions and Potential Hazards (Rev.1979), $.90
- Downers: The Central Nervous System Depressant Drug (Rev. 1980), $.90

[Also available from Do It Now Foundation, separate entry] **U.S. Journal of Drug and Alcohol Dependence** 2119A Hollywood Boulevard, Hollywood, FL 33020 305-920-9433

EMERGENCY OVERDOSE, POISON AND BUMMER CHART
(1980) - two-sided medicine cabinet chart listing emergency procedures and antidotes, with spaces for emergency phone numbers, etc.; lists licit as well as illicit chemicals, 8-1/2"x11" (suggestion: order two to post both sides), $15 (bulk rates available) **Do It Now Foundation** PO Box 21126, Phoenix, AZ 85036 602-257-0797

AN EMERGING ISSUE: THE FEMALE ALCOHOLIC
(1977) - a look at the problems in treating the female alcoholic, and how they differ from those of the male alcoholic; discusses the implications for existing treatment facilities, the rise in alcoholism among women, etc., 10pp, $.35 **National Council on Alcoholism** 12 West 21st Street, New York, NY 10010 212-206-6770

FAMILY AND FRIENDS SERIES ON DRUG/ALCOHOL ABUSE
(1987-89) - a series of publications and other materials addressing families and friends of drug/alcohol abusers or potential abusers; includes:
- 10 Steps to Help Your Child Say No. A Parent's Guide - assistance for parents in guiding their children away from alcohol, tobacco, marijuana, and other drugs, 12pp
- What You Can Do About Drug Use in America - an overview

of drugs and information for preventing problems caused by alcohol and other drugs, 32pp
- Drug-Free Communities: Turning Awareness Into Action - help for parents and other adult groups in sharing an understanding of alcohol and other drug problems as a community problem that requires a community respponse, 34pp
- When Cocaine Affects Someone You Love - guide for family members covering cocaine's physical and emotional signs, how families are affected, and the recovery process, 12pp
- Cocaine/Crack. The Big Lie - commonly-asked questions about cocaine and crack, 9pp
- Alcohol and Youth: Fact Sheet - answers to questions about young people and alcohol, and information on prevention efforts, 5pp
- Pointers for Parents Card - a 3-1/2"x8-1/2" card for quick reference by parents on preventing their child from using alcohol or other drugs (used as handout at fairs, workshops, conferences)
- Snappy Answers Card for Kids - 3-1/2# x 8-1/2" card with responses kids can use to say "no"
- Alcohol Problems and Youth: Reading List - list of resources for teaching preteens and teenagers about alcohol, 3pp
- When Your Parent Drinks Too Much - reprint from Seventeen providing coping strategies, 3pp
- Are You a Drug Quiz Whiz? - tests for knowledge about alcohol and other drugs (20 questions), 2pp
- Why Eddie Murphy Won't Do Drugs - explanation by the star about his choice of a drug-free lifestyle, one page
- If a Child from an Alcoholic Home Comes to You - guidance for adults on how to best help children who approach them for help with problems of parental alcohol abuse, one page
- Questions and Answers About Alcohol Problems - answers to questions asked by children, one page
- Children of Alcoholics Kits - four separate kits with background and referral information (Kit for Helpers, Kit for Kids, Kit for Parents, Kit for Therapists)

Single copies of all publications free; request complete catalog. **US/HHS - National Clearinghouse for Alcohol and Drug Information** PO Box 2345, Rockville, MD 20852 301-468-2600

FOR PARENTS ONLY: WHAT YOU NEED TO KNOW ABOUT MARIJUANA
(1981) - orientation on marijuana's uses, effects and medical uses to help parents compete with their children's peers on the subject of marijuana; provide suggestions on how to establish rules, say no, eliminate guilt, talk with other parents, and develop acceptable alternatives to drug use; includes drug chart and glossary of terms, 28pp, single copy free **US/HHS - National Clearinghouse for Alcohol and Drug Information** PO Box 416, Kensington, MD 20795 301-443-6500

GET INVOLVED BEFORE YOUR KIDS DO
(1990) - a videotape featuring well-known actors role-playing family situations to help parents communicate more effectively with their children about drugs and alcohol; designed for use with an award-winning training program/discussion group of the same name, inquire about format and cost **AAL Drug and Alcohol Use Prevention Program** 4321 North Ballard Road, Appleton, WI 54919-0001 414-734-5721

GLUE SNIFFING: BIG TROUBLE IN A TUBE
(1972) - facts on the most misunderstood and underestimated form of drug abuse - inhalation of glue vapor; emphasizes the risks of moving on to more potent drugs, failure in school, bizarre behavior and death, 31pp, $1.00 **TANE Press** 6778 Greenville, Dallas, TX 75231 214-363-5305

GRASSROOTS: THE TOTAL DRUG INFORMATION SERVICE

(monthly) - selection of articles, meeting announcements, film and literature reviews based on a scanning of journals and newsletters to provide a central place for views of the experts and other drug-related information (formerly a binder with 20 sections and 12 monthly supplements; now a monthly journal), inquire about cost (distributes selected materials from the new STASH, formerly of Madison, Wisconsin) **U.S. Journal of Drug and Alcohol Dependence** 2119-A Hollywood Boulevard , Hollywood, FL 33020 305-920-9433

GROUP PROCESS IN ALCOHOL EDUCATION WITH STRATEGIES IN THE CLASSROOM

(1978) - techniques for role playing to allow students to present both sides of the drinking issue; presents a pilot study of a process combining alcohol education with driver training, 40pp, $5.50 (member $4.50) **American Driver and Traffic Safety Education Association** 123 North Pitt Street, Suite 511, Alexandria, VA 22314 703-836-4748

HERE ARE 101 THINGS YOU CAN DO ABOUT THE DRUG PROBLEM

(1990) - literally 101 things parents can do, including things you can do in the community, about your own behavior, to be a better parent, within your family, with other parents, with kids, to get support from the media, with school personnel, to influence legislation, and in cooperation with your local police; presents a bulleted list with descriptive statements, 8-panel foldout, single copy free **Regional Youth Substance Abuse Project (RYSAP)** 75 Washington Avenue, Bridgeport, CT 06604-4001 203-333-333

HOW TO HELP: WHAT YOU CAN DO TO HELP YOUR COMMUNITY HELP ALCOHOLIC PEOPLE

(1979) - overview of what has been done so far, what still needs to be done, the problem of jailing drunk drivers without treatment, the case of the reluctance of hospitals and doctors to treat the alcoholic patient, the need for full community participation in prevention and treatment programs, etc., 16pp, single copy free (order #PH111) **US/HHS - National Clearinghouse for Alcohol and Drug Information** Box 2345, Rockville, MD 20852 301-468-2600

I DIDN'T KNOW...AN ADULT APPROACH TO DRUG ABUSE

(undated) - a primer on ways in which community education and community action can help determine the nature of a community drug problem and work toward a solution; e.g., sponsor a "store-front drug central" for information and referral and other services; includes a glossary of terms and selected resources, 22pp, $.20 **B'nai B'rith International** Community Volunteer Services, 1640 Rhode Island Avenue, NW, Washington, DC 20036 202-857-6600

IT STARTS WITH PEOPLE

(1979) - guide for anyone who wants to be involved with youth and drug abuse prevention; includes prevention strategies and organizational models (school, community, minority groups); provides three program profiles (Massachusetts, California, Nevada); lists other resources, 76pp, single copy free **US/HHS - National Clearinghouse for Alcohol and Drug Information** P.O. Box 416, Kensington, MD 20795 301-443-6500

LET'S GET THE PROBLEM DRINKER OFF OUR HIGHWAYS THROUGH CONCERTED COMMUNITY ACTION

(1980) - case for involving the entire community in a campaign to implement programs that will identify and rehabilitate problem drinkers and address their driving privileges; discusses Alcohol Safety Action Projects (ASAPs) that are increasing in numbers in communities across the country, 15pp, $.75 (quantity discounts) **Channing L. Bete Company** , South Deerfield, MA 01373

LET'S THINK ABOUT DRUGS

(1972) - alternating in-depth real-life examples and question-and-answer sections on the major drugs, their effects and dangers; includes list of other resources (includes alcohol and tobacco), 14pp, $.25 **TANE Press** 6778 Greenville, Dallas, TX 75231 214-363-5305

MADD PUBLICATIONS

(1990) - MADD provides a number of publications to keep the public informed of its activities, and to assist victims of drunk drivers and their advocates with resource and support information; publications include:
- *MADD in Action* - national newsletter
- *MADDvocate* - a magazine for victims and their advocates
- *No Time for Goodbye* and *Beyond Sympathy* - victim brochures (available in both English and Spanish)

Inquire about additional, more specific materials, and cost and availability of those listed above. **Mothers Against Drunk Driving** PO Box 1217, Hurst, TX 76053 817-268-MADD

MAJOR DRUGS: THEIR USES AND EFFECTS

(kept current) - colorful poster providing both common and street names for major drugs, medical use, effects of average dose, effects of large doses, long-term effects of abuse; uses reverse side for information on drug deaths, the cost of abusing drugs, and other factual and amusing items, 12"x22" (folded 8"x12"), one free (add'l 20/$2.50) **Playboy Foundation** 919 North Michigan Avenue, Chicago, IL 60611 312-751-8000

MCGRUFF SERIES FOR CHILDREN

(1990) - a comic book (**McGruff's Surprise Party**) for ages 8-10, and a coloring book also featuring McGruff (**Crack Down on Drugs**) both teaching the importance of saying "no" to alcohol and other drugs for ages 5-8, single copies free **US/HHS - National Clearinghouse for Alcohol and Drug Information** PO Box 2345, Rockville, MD 20852 301-468-2600

MEDIA-ADVERTISING PARTNERSHIP FOR A DRUG-FREE AMERICA PSAS

(undated) - a series of more than 100 public service announcements (PSAs) which combine frightening statistics about illegal drug use with stark emotional portraits targeted to youth, parents, employees, employers, and the general public, information packet free, print PSAs $5/set, video PSAs $10/set (specify target audience) **United Way of America** 701 North Fairfax Street, Alexandria, VA 22314-2045 703-836-7100

THE MEDICINES YOUR DOCTOR PRESCRIBES: A GUIDE FOR CONSUMERS

(1983) - brochure offering practical information on the safe and effective use of prescription medicines, 10pp, first 25 copies free (additional, $10/100) **Pharmaceutical Manufacturers Association** 1100 Fifteenth Street, NW, Washington, DC 20005 202-835-4300

MILTON AND HIS MAGIC MOTORCYCLE

(1972) - an aid used in a drug abuse prevention program at the elementary level; uses the story book technique in which the youngsters can relate to the hero - in this case a boy who is pressured by his peers to try drugs, 109pp, $2.95 **TANE Press** 6778 Greenville Avenue, Dallas, TX 75231 214-363-5305

MONTGOMERY COUNTY ANTI-ABUSE STUDY

(1989) - a report detailing a year-long study by a 32-member panel from business, government and community and recommending what one large county can do to combat drug abuse, 136pp, inquire about cost **Montgomery County Panel on Drug Problems** Montgomery County Executive Office, 100 Maryland Avenue, Rockville, MD 20850 301-217-1000

NCADI MONOGRAPH/FACT SHEET SERIES

(1986-90) - a series of monographs, fact sheets, posters, etc., on abuse of alcohol and other drugs, prevention, driving, employment, treatment, testing, model programs, etc., including:

- *Stopping Alcohol and Other Drug Use Before It Starts: The Future of Prevention* (100pp monograph)
- *Prevention of Psychiatric Disorders in Children and Adolescents* (478pp monograph)
- *Research, Action and the Community: Experiences in the Prevention of Alcohol and Other Drug Problems* (29 papers)
- *Seventh Special Report to the U.S. Congress on Alcohol and Health* (in process at press time)
- *Third Triennial Report to Congress: Drug Abuse and Drug Abuse Research III* (in process at press time)
- *Treatment for Alcoholic Substance Abusers* (238pp monograph)
- *Survey of Employer Anti-Drug Programs* (32pp paper)
- *Drinking and Driving and Health Promotion* (131pp special issue of journal)
- *Cocaine: The Big Lie 1986-1988* (2pp fact sheet)
- *Guide to Mobilizing Ethnic Minority Communities for Drug Abuse Prevention* (39pp)
- *Growing Up Drug Free: A Parent's Guide to Prevention* (52pp)
- *Play It Smart Don't Start* (a full-color poster featuring Herschel Walker, football star (22"x27")
- *Project Descriptions. Model Curricula for Alcohol and Other Drug Abuse Physician and Nurse Education* (12 model projects for curriculum enrichment)
- *Substance Abuse Among Blacks* (overview)
- *Remarks by the President to Students* (a personal message from President George Bush)
- *Crack Shatters Lives* (22"x34" color poster, two-sided)

Not a complete list; request free catalog containing dozens of other posters, fact sheets, monographs, books, etc.; all publications single copy free **US/HHS - National Clearinghouse for Alcohol and Drug Information** PO Box 2345, Rockville, MD 20852 301-468-2600

NOT ON MY WATCH... NOT ON MY SHIP... NOT IN MY NAVY...

(1989) - a compilation of drug abuse information defining the various substances of abuse, a check-off sheet listing symptoms that profile a drug abuser, and a list of Navy Officers around the country designated to provide *Campaign Drug Free* public affairs support; appends articles, window decals, and other materials as available related to the Campaign, 16pp, single copy free **US/DoD - Naval Reserve Force** Office of the Secretary, The Pentagon, Washington, DC 20350-1000 202-695-2486

PAMPHLET SERIES

(various dates) - coverage of specific drug topics, 6- to 8-panel foldouts, $.25 each unless noted otherwise:

- *Comprehensive Drug Knowledge Test*, $.35
- *Garbage: A Report on Street Ripoffs*
- *Cleaning Yourself Up - for People Who Don't Think They're Addicts*
- *The Magic Mushroom*
- *Junk: Getting Yourself Together*
- *What Senior Citizens Should Know About Drugs and Alcohol*
- *Sniffing: Good Smells and Bad Smells*

(Request complete catalog) **Do It Now Foundation** PO Box 21126, Phoenix, AZ 85056 602-257-0797

PARENTS, PEERS, AND POT

(1979) - a strategy for parents to prevent marijuana use by their children; emphasizes the easy access to marijuana for children and teenagers and the peer pressure facing them daily; provides suggestions for working with family, neighborhood, school and community, 98pp, single copy free **US/HHS - National Clearinghouse for Alcohol and Drug Information** PO Box 416, Kensington, MD 20795 301-443-6500

PREVENTION/EVALUATION/TREATMENT SERIES ON DRUG/ALCOHOL ABUSE

(1981-89) - materials for community leaders and others on prevention, evaluation and treatment in areas of alcohol and drug abuse; includes:

- *Prevention Plus II: Tools for Creating and Sustaining a Drug-Free Community* (a framework for organizing or expanding community activities for youth), 560pp
- *Working With Evaluation: A Guide for Drug Abuse Prevention Program Managers* (helps program staff work effectively with evaluators), 110pp
- *A Community Solution, Drug Abuse Treatment* (introduction to the elements of treatment through personal statements of recovering persons), 4-panel foldout
- *Drugs and Alcohol Abuse: Implications for Treatment* (clinical issues and management issues), 151pp
- *Prevention Networks - Cocaine Use in America* (ideas on preventing cocaine abuse in the U.S.), 16pp
- *Adolescent Peer Pressure* (insights and ideas for program planners concerned with peer programs)
- *Stopping Alcohol and Other Drug Use Before It Starts: The Future of Prevention* (a look at future directions), 100pp
- *Handbook on Evaluating Drug and Alcohol Prevention Programs* (the STEPP, Staff/Team Evaluation of Prevention Programs, approach), 113pp

Single copies of all publications are free. Request complete catalog. **US/HHS - National Clearinghouse for Alcohol and Drug Information** PO Box 2345, Rockville, MD 20852 301-468-2600

PREVENTION PLUS II: TOOLS FOR CREATING AND SUSTAINING A DRUG-FREE COMMUNITY

(1990) - fourth in a series providing a framework for organizing or expanding community alcohol and other drug problem prevention activities for youth; addresses persons throughout the community who are serious about prevention and in a position to assist in organizing a community effort; includes three other titles in the series: *One by One: Helping Communities to Help Themselves, What You Can Do About Drug Use In America*, and *Drug-Free Communities: Turning Awareness Into Action*, 541pp, single copy free **US/HHS - National Clearinghouse for Alcohol and Drug Information** PO Box 2345, Rockville, MD 20852 301-468-2600

PREVENTION PROGRAMS FOR YOUTH

(1985-89) - a series of videotapes sponsored by the *National Clearinghouse for Alcohol and Drug Information (NCDAI)* for kindergarten to twelfth grade; available through NCDAI's free loan program, including:

- **Drug Avengers** (grades 1-6) - 10 five-minute animated episodes set in the year 2050, with students being sent back to the 20th century to teach children about the dangers of drugs.
- **Fast Forward Future** (grades 4-6) - three 15-minute episodes allowing youngsters to peer into the future and see what will happen if they use drugs, and if they don't use drugs.
- **Straight Up** (grades 4-6) - Six 15-minute episodes about a boy who faces peer pressure to use alcohol and drugs.
- **Straight At Ya** (grades 7-9) - 44-minute tape set in a junior

high classroom and deals with peer pressure and a healthy life style.

- **Lookin' Good** (grades 7-9) - two 29-minute episodes based on actual events involving alcohol and drug use, and spotlighting refusal skills.
- **Hard Facts About Alcohol, Marijuana and Crack; Speak Up, Speak Out; Learning to Say No to Drugs, Dare to be Different; Resisting Drug Related Pressure** (grades 10-12) - three 15- to 22-minute episodes dramatizing effects of drugs, techniques against peer pressure, and goals and values in resisting pressures to use drugs.
- **Private Victories** (grades 10-12) - four 29-minute episodes emphasizing that young people can succeed if they care enough about themselves.
- **Downfall** (grades 7-12) - 29 minutes, profiling athletes whose careers were disrupted by drugs.
- **President Bush Speaks to The Nation's Schools** (grades 9-12) - 15 minutes on the importance of staying drug free.
- **Schoolyard** (12-14 years) - 3-1/2 minutes, depicts a youth being offered drugs by an older boy after school, and the helpful intervention of another student.
- **The NO Show - McGruff Goes Rock Video** (6-12 years) - 23 minutes, helps kids learn that saying no to drugs is not just OK - it's cool; lists fun things to do if you don't use drugs, using animated cartoon characters to spread the word.

Most of the above videotapes are also available for purchase, inquire. On loan program, user pays return postage only. **US/HHS - National Clearinghouse for Alcohol and Drug Information** PO Box 2345, Rockville, MD 20852 301-468-2600

QUESTIONS AND ANSWERS ABOUT DRUG ABUSE

(1976) - three-part, pocket-sized guide to measure the reader's knowledge about drugs, their uses and consequences, and to provide insight into, and specific examples of prevention efforts that can be mounted by family/community, 64pp, $.50 (also in Spanish) **Benjamin Company** 485 Madison Avenue, New York, NY 10022 212-759-6920

SERIES ON DRUGS AND ALCOHOL AND THE ELDERLY

(1983-88) - a series of fact sheets and booklets addressing the problems of alcohol and the aging; includes:

- *Age Page: Aging and Alcohol Abuse* - physical affects (2pp)
- *Alcohol Alert #2: Alcohol and Aging* - overview of drinking patterns, etc. (4pp)
- *Nature and Extent of Alcohol Problems Among the Elderly* - NIAAA Research Monograph (331pp)
- *Alcohol and the Elderly: Update* - reading list on prevalence, special characteristics, prevention, intervention, treatment (6pp)
- *Special Focus: Alcohol and the Elderly* - reprint containing nine articles with profiles of special programs (51pp)
- *The Fact Is... It's Dangerous to Drink Alcohol While Taking Certain Medicines* - kinds of reactions that can occur from mixing alcohol with commonly-used medications (2pp)

Single copies of all publications are free; request complete catalog. **US/HHS - National Clearinghouse for Alcohol and Drug Information** PO Box 2345, Rockville, MD 20852 301-468-2600

SERIES ON MINORITIES AND WOMEN AND DRUG/ALCOHOL ABUSE

(1984-89) - fact sheets, guides, monographs, studies, etc., on the abuse of alcohol and drugs by women and minorities; includes:

- *Women and Alcohol Problems: Tools for Prevention* (three levels of prevention and 12 strategies for program planners), 27pp
- *Women and Drugs: A New Era for Research* (Research Monograph 65 of a series based on papers and discussions), 105pp
- *Treatment Services for Drug Dependent Women, Vols. 1 and*

2 (descriptions of basic treatment services, counseling techniques, vocational rehabilitation, family therapy, child care, parenting, etc.), 504pp
- *Women and Alcohol* (presentation by an expert in the field), 4pp
- *Prevention Networks: Multicultural Perspectives in Drug Abuse Prevention* (newsletter with articles, interviewes, etc.), 14pp
- *Alcohol and Black Americans: Update* (resource list of publications), 7pp
- *Alcohol and Hispanics: Update* (resource list of publications), 6pp
- *Alcohol and Other Drug Use in Three Hispanic Populations: Mexican Americans, Puerto Ricans, and Cuban Americans* (findings of survey), 4pp
- *Hispanic Parents Can Help Their Children Avoid Alcohol and Drugs* (how parents can create an environment to protect their children), 6pp
- *Substance Abuse Among Hispanic Americans* (overview of the problem in English and Spanish), 2pp
- *Alcohol Topics in Brief: Alcohol and Native Americans* (historical perspective of alcohol use among this group, and the problem today), 8pp
- *The Fact Is... Alcohol and Other Drug Proglems Are a Major Concern in Native American Communities* (special concerns of Native American communities), 14pp

Single copies of all publications free; request complete list, including several publications printed in Spanish only. **US/HHS - National Clearinghouse for Alcohol and Drug Information** PO Box 2345, Rockville, MD 20852 301-468-2600

SIGNS OF USE FOR SUBSTANCES FOR DRUGGING EFFECTS

(1978) - descriptions of general behavioral symptoms as well as symptoms resulting from use of specific substances for nonmedical purposes, 6-panel foldout, first 200 free (additional $2/100) **Pharmaceutical Manufacturers Association** 1100 Fifteenth Street, NW, Washington, DC 20005 202-835-4300

SOMEONE CLOSE DRINKS TOO MUCH

(1979) - help for the family which doesn't know what to do about an alcoholic family member; presents do's and don't's for the family to implement while waiting for the "right time" (when the alcoholic seeks help); includes information on chances of recovery based on today's statistics, 15pp, single copy free (order #PH104) **US/HHS - National Clearinghouse for Alcohol and Drug Information** Box 2345, Rockville, MD 20852 301-468-2600

SUBSTANCE ABUSE: A FOCUS ON MINORITIES

(1979) - compilation of information obtained from various sources to give the reader a better understanding of substance abuse, particularly among racial minorities; describes types, methods of abuse, incidence of abuse, and knowledge gap that exists today, 46pp, $3.00 (bulk rates) **Board of Church and Society** Office of Drug & Alcohol Concerns, 100 Maryland Avenue, NE, Washington, DC 20002 202-488-5600

SUBSTANCE ABUSE - DRUG AND CHEMICAL CHART

(1983) - chart of information on substances used for nonmedical purposes, substances such as alcohol, marijuana, narcotics, stimulants, depressants, inhalants, hallucinogens, "Angel Dust," and other substances, first 50 copies free (additional copies $5/100) **Pharmaceutical Manufacturers Association** 1100 Fifteenth Street, Washington, DC 20005 202-835-4300

SUBSTANCE ABUSE - SIGNS AND SYMPTOMS

(1983) - a list of physical signs and behavioral characteristics associated with abuse of substances such as alcohol, marijuana, narcotics, stimulants, depressants, inhalants, hallucinogens, "Angel Dust," and other substances, first 50 copies free (additional, $5/100) **Pharmaceutical Manufacturers Association** 1100 Fifteenth Street, NW, Washington, DC 20005 202-835-4300

SURGEON GENERAL'S WORKSHOP ON DRUNK DRIVING PROCEEDINGS

(1989) - more than 100 recommendations developed by 11 panels of experts and forwarded to the Surgeon General; includes key recommendations such as excise taxes on alcoholic beverages, providing counter-advertising of alcoholic beverages, etc., 106pp, single copy free [also request *Surgeon General's Workshop on Drunk Driving Background Papers,* which provided a foundation for launching the workshop for the 11 panels cited above.] **US/HHS - National Clearinghouse for Alcohol and Drug Information** PO Box 2345, Rockville, MD 20852 301-468-2600

TV PUBLIC SERVICE ANNOUNCEMENTS SERIES

(1986-88) - a series of public service announcements (PSAs) for various age groups developed by the *National Clearinghouse for Alcohol and Drug Information (NCADI)* and available for free loan; includes:

- **Be Smart! Don't Start! PSAs** (8-12 years, one minute)
- **Partnership for a Drug-Free America TV Spots** (youth and adult, 12 minutes)
- **Preventing Alcohol and Other Drug Problems: Selected PSAs** (youth and adult, 18 minutes)
- **Stay Smart! Don't Start! ...Using Alcohol or Other Drugs** (10-14 years, 1-1/2 minutes)

The *Stay Smart* message is part of a 1987 program, *Be Smart! Don't Start! - Just Say No!.* All PSAs are available for purchase, also; users in loan program pay return postage only. **US/HHS - National Clearinghouse for Alcohol and Drug Information** PO Box 2345, Rockville, MD 20852 301-468-2600

UNDERSTANDING AMERICA'S DRINKING PROBLEM

(1987) - information on the prevalence of the alcohol problem, national drinking practices, government efforts to control alcohol problems, public health policy, and the effectiveness of prevention and treatment programs, 254pp, $24.95 **Jossey Bass, Publishers** 350 Samsone Street, San Francisco, CA 94104-1310 415-433-1767

UNDERSTANDING AND DEALING WITH ALCOHOLISM

(1980) - the tracking of alcohol after it is swallowed to every part of the body, including the brain, to demonstrate the cause of its effects on behavior, health, driving, etc.; defines alcoholism, withdrawal, treatment, sources of help, 24pp, $.50 (quantity discounts) **Public Affairs Pamphlets** 381 Park Avenue South, New York, NY 10016 212-683-4331

WHAT EVERY PARENT SHOULD KNOW ABOUT DRUGS AND DRUG ABUSE

(1980) - illustrated guide to help parents react to their child's curiosity about or use of drugs; provides charts and drawings to help make parents more knowledgeable of the symptoms, methods, and dangers of the various types of drugs, as well as legal implications; emphasizes the wisdom of seeking professional help if family efforts fall short, 13pp, $.75 **Channing L. Bete Company** , South Deerfield, MA 01373

WHAT EVERY TEENAGER SHOULD KNOW ABOUT ALCOHOLISM

(1980) - an appeal to young people to learn all the facts before making the decision to drink; describes alternatives open to youth, effects on the body, problems in alcohol abuse, major dangers (driving and mixing drugs), answers to questions frequently asked by teenagers, 15pp, $.75 (quantity discounts) **Channing L. Bete Company** , South Deerfield, MA 01373

WHAT EVERYONE SHOULD KNOW ABOUT ALCOHOL

(1980) - one of a series of illustrated guides beginning with the question, "What is alcohol?" and taking the reader through a number of other question areas on alcohol abuse, why people drink, effects on health, crime, and driving, symptoms, and what a person who wants to stop drinking can do, 15pp, $.75 (Other Booklets in this Series: *What Everyone Should Know About Alcoholism, About Alcoholism Services, About Women and Alcohol,* $.75 each, quantity discounts) **Channing L. Bete Company** , South Deerfield, MA 01373

WHAT EVERYONE SHOULD KNOW ABOUT DRUG ABUSE

(1980) - illustrated guide on how drugs affect people medically, economically, legally, and socially; includes centerfold drug chart on commonly-used drugs, 15pp, $.75 (quantity discounts) **Channing L. Bete Company** , South Deerfield, MA 01373

WHAT SENIOR CITIZENS SHOULD KNOW ABOUT DRUGS AND ALCOHOL

(1982) - An appeal to older persons to monitor their drug-taking and avoid the inadvertent addiction to drugs frequently found among the elderly; includes precautions against equating more leisure time and less responsibility (retirement) with uselessness - a situation which often initiates drinking problems; provides mini-checklist for quick-reference when taking medication, 8-panel foldout, $.20 ($1.40/ten, $8.00/hundred, $70.00/thousand) **Do It Now Foundation** PO Box 21126, Phoenix, AZ 85036 602-257-0797

WHAT TO DO IF YOUR CHILD IS IN TROUBLE WITH DRUGS

(1990) - a guide to help parents face the problem of a child involved with drugs or alcohol; includes sections on some parents' tendency to minimize the situation, denial, taking the blame, getting help, support groups, emergency help, long-term programs and evaluation, student assistance teams, counseling options, employee assistance programs, involvement with the law, family support, recovery, etc.; appends warning signs and resources available for help (Connecticut groups, but booklet relevant to all parents), 10pp, single copy free **Regional Youth Substance Abuse Project (RYSAP)** 75 Washington Avenue, Bridgeport, CT 06604-4001 203-333-3333

WHEN YOU SAY L'CHAIM...IS IT TO LIFE?

(undated) - a guide for local volunteer groups to mount a program of information and action to deal with community problems of alcohol abuse (addressed to B'nai B'rith chapters, but useful for any volunteer group), 16pp, $.20 **B'nai B'rith International** Community Volunteer Services, 1640 Rhode Island Avenue, NW, Washington, DC 20036 202-857-6535

WHO TOOK THE DRUGS?

(1979) - a family in turmoil and a job-related near tragedy in comic book format to provide older youth and adults with a simplified view of drug effects, 32pp, $1.00 (also available from Do It Now Foundation, separate entry) **U.S. Journal of Drug and Alcohol Dependence** 2119A Hollywood Boulevard, Hollywood, FL 33020 305-920-9433

WHY NOT MARIJUANA?

1976 - platform for both advocates and opponents of marijuana, with a conclusion based on the arguments presented - that more research and educational programs should be mounted before decisions are made regarding legalization or stiffer penalties, 47pp, $1 **TANE Press** 6778 Greenville Avenue, Dallas, TX 75231 214-363-5305

EDUCATION

A TO ZOO
(Third Ed. 1989) - a listing of more than 11,500 fiction and nonfiction picture books for preschoolers through second graders, arranged under 600 subject headings "from aardvarks to zoos," 896pp, $44.95, also available from book dealers **R. R. Bowker** PO Box 762, New York, NY 10011

ABC'S OF SCHOOL VOLUNTEERS
(1973) - quick-reference guide to the needs and objectives of school volunteer programs; outlines some of the duties volunteers perform, 15pp, $.75 (bulk discounts) **Channing L. Bete Company** , South Deerfield, MA 01373

ABOUT CONTINUING EDUCATION
(1977) - illustrated overview of ongoing education programs for adults; includes checklist for selecting school, costs to expect, etc., 15pp, $.75 **Channing L. Bete Company** , South Deerfield, MA 01373

ACCEPT ME AS I AM
(1985) - a guide to best books of juvenile nonfiction on impairments and disabilities, developed for people working with children age two and up, 363pp, $29.95, also available from book dealers [an *ALA Outstanding Reference* source] **R. R. Bowker** PO Box 762, New York, NY 10011

ADULT EDUCATION CLEARINGHOUSE NEWSLETTER
(monthly) - ongoing coverage of programs, publications, government action, and other activities in the field; includes calendar of relevant workshops/meetings/conferences across the country (grant writing, adult tutoring, the elderly, etc.), Av. 10pp, $14.50/year (prepaid) **US/DEd - National Adult Education Clearinghouse** Adult Continuing Education Center, Montclair, NJ 07043 201-895-4353

ALL ABOUT CLEO
(kept current) - comprehensive booklet about the program which provides economically disadvantaged students - many of them having marginal or less than conventional admissions credentials - with an opportunity to attend an accredited law school with necessary financial and other assistance, 26pp, single copy free **Council on Legal Education Opportunity** 1800 M Street, NW, Suite 200, Washington, DC 20036 202-785-4840

ALL ABOUT SCHOOL VOLUNTEERS (FOR TEACHERS ONLY!)
(1980) - a reference for teachers to pinpoint some of the tasks volunteers can perform in the classroom; includes list of assignments a volunteer should not do, and the additional planning the teacher will need to do in exchange for the volunteer assistance, 7pp, $1.00 **Zanesville City Schools** Volunteer Services, 200 North Sixth Street, Zanesville, OH 43701 614-454-9751

BECOMING A SCHOOL PARTNER
(1989) - overview of a new program of the Association providing detailed information on how older persons can help enrich the school curriculum and assist in the classroom; includes 17 specific suggestions, e.g., help students write and produce plays, or hold group discussions about groups and films; includes sections on *How You Can Help, and How to Volunteer,* with numerous details to help give the older volunteer a full understanding of what is involved, 8-panel foldout, free **American Association of Retired Persons** Special Projects/Program Department, 1909 K Street, NW, Washington, DC 20049 202-872-4700

BECOMING A SCHOOL PARTNER: A GUIDE FOR OLDER VOLUNTEERS
(1989) - a comprehensive guide for the older person considering becoming a volunteer in the schools; includes sections on preparing students, easing pressures of overburdened schools, benefits to schools and communities, bringing the generations together, working directly with students, working behind the scenes, and how to get started; appends a listing of other resource organizations, 36pp, single copy free [order brochure of same name first to determine interest] **American Association of Retired Persons** AARP Fulfillment Section, 1909 K Street, NW, Washington, DC 20049 202-872-4700

BEGINNING EQUAL: A MANUAL ABOUT NONSEXIST CHILDREARING FOR INFANTS & TODDLERS
(1983) - *Trainer's Workshop* materials and background readings for caregivers and parents of children from birth to age three in identifying and reducing sex-role stereotyping; includes workshop handouts (both English and Spanish), 241pp, $9.75 **Project BE** 370 Lexington Avenue, Suite 603, New York, NY 10017 212-779-2846

THE B.E.S.T. PROJECT (OVERVIEW)

(1990) - an overview of a program in which *Brown University* students teach English as a Second Language to learners from all over the world; includes some handwritten stories by the immigrants, 6-panel foldout, free **Brown University** 25 George Street, PO Box 1974, Providence, RI 02912 401-863-2338

BIBLIOGRAPHY OF MATERIALS ON SEXISM IN CHILDREN'S BOOKS

(kept current) - A listing of children's books and other materials that demonstrate sexism (developed by a publisher of nonsexist, nonracist books for children), number of pages varies, inquire about cost and other materials **Lollipop Power Books** PO Box 277, Carrboro, NC 27510 919-933-9679

BILINGUAL EDUCATION RESOURCE GUIDE

(1977) - summaries of legislation, civil rights activities, state programs, and other topics of interest to those involved in bilingual education programs; includes bibliographies of resources useful in Mexican American and Native American education, 120pp, $7.25 **National Education Association** The Academic Building, Saw Mill Road, West Haven, CT 06516 203-934-2669

THE BILINGUAL TEACHER AIDE: COMPETENCIES AND TRAINING

(1979) - story of the evolvement of the nonprofessional bilingual teacher aide to a trained professional with major responsibilities in the teaching program, 110pp, $3.25 **Dissemination and Assessment Center for Bilingual Education** 7703 North Lamar Boulevard, Austin, TX 78752 512-458-9131

BOOKLET SERIES

(1980) - illustrated guides for quick-reference overviews of various areas (15pp each, $.75 each); two in the handicapped area:
- *What Everyone Should Know About Educating the Handicapped Child*
- *What Every Parent Should Know About Learning Disabilities*

Channing L. Bete Company , South Deerfield, MA 01373

BOOKS TO HELP CHILDREN COPE WITH SEPARATION AND LOSS

(Third Ed. 1988) - a continuation of an in-depth analysis and of books divided into categories of separation and loss that affect children, such as: new school, new neighborhood, losing a friend, working parents (25 others); lists over 600 books, 532pp, $39.95 (second edition also available, 439pp, $39.95) **R. R. Bowker** PO Box 762, New York, NY 10011

BUSINESS IN THE CLASSROOM: ISSUES FOR DEBATE

(undated) - a volunteer program headed by a Business Advisory Council composed of local senior-level executives; schedules classroom visits for open-ended discussions for grades 7-12 to analyze problems and misconceptions about the business world, and create a foundation of reality, 8pp, single copy free **Constitutional Rights Foundation** 601 South Kingsley Drive, Los Angeles , CA 90005 213-487-5590

CLEO: ADVANCING LEGAL EDUCATION

(1989-90) - an overview of the *Council On Education Opportunity (CLEO)* providing a brief history, funding sources, program structure, training descriptions, eligibility, financial assistance, service to veterans, law school assistance, the performance of CLEO students, etc.; appends references to other scholarships and federal, state and special loan programs, 16pp, free **Council on Legal Education Opportunity** 1800 M Street, NW, Suite 290, North Lobby, Washington, DC 20036 202-785-4840

COLOR OR CHARACTER: HOW WILL OUR CHILDREN BE JUDGED

(annually) - a special Martin Luther King, Jr. Day section of *The Washington Times* featuring essays written by distinguished Americans, particularly those of African-American descent [5th annual edition contributors: President George Bush, Secretary of HUD Jack Kemp, Governor L. Douglas Wilder, actors Malcolm Jamal Warner and Jaime Escalante, and others]; features artwork finalists from schools on *What does Martin Luther King Jr. Day Mean to me?*, available for classroom use, limited back issues, inquire about cost **Washington Times** Newspaper In Education Program, 3600 New York Avenue, NE, Washington, DC 20002 301-345-0240

COMMUNITY INVOLVEMENT WORKS

(undated) - a motivational illustrated booklet depicting community resource volunteers in learning activities with school children; interweaves quotes of students and volunteers with the story of the Community Resource Volunteers program, 20pp, inquire about availability and cost **WISE & GISE/CRV Volunteer Services** 807 NE Broadway, Minneapolis, MN 55413 612-348-6152

COMMUNITY RESOURCE VOLUNTEERS CATALOG

(kept current) - "shopping list" for teachers/students listing hundreds of subject areas for which community resource volunteers are available; states responsibilities of requesting class to provide needs outlined by volunteer in advance, provides checklist for class, emphasizes the combining of classes with similar interests, and lists appropriate procedures for visit, 10pp (inquire about cost) **WISE & GISE/CRV Volunteer Services** 807 NE Broadway, Minneapolis, MN 55413 612-348-6152

COMMUNITY RESOURCES CATALOG

(1979) - one example of a reference listing of volunteers offering curriculum enrichment and adult learning programs; covers more than 130 subject areas, 23pp, inquire about cost **Volunteer Service Bureau/VAC** 431 Olympian Boulevard, Beloit, WI 53511 608-365-1278

COMMUNITY SCHOOL FOLIOS

(1979) - program descriptions (single copy free) including the following areas:
- *Arts and Crafts*
- *Big Brothers*
- *Business Education*
- *Career Planning*
- *Comunity Services Occupations*
- *Consumer & Home Economics Education*
- *Foreign Languages*
- *The Home School Counselor*
- *Industrial Technical Education*
- *Music-Youth Enrichment*
- *Police School Cadets*
- *Preschool Story Hour*
- *Play Ball! (recreation)*
- *Reach (runaways)*
- *Scholarships*
- *Science Enrichment*
- *Senior Citizens*
- *Speech and Drama*
- *Stepping Stones (school clubs)*
- *Urban Environment*

Flint Community Schools 923 East Kearsley Street, Flint, MI 48502 313-762-1256 (elementary)

CROSS AGE TUTORIALS

(undated) - fact sheet on older student volunteers who tutor younger students; includes information about the whole-class method of cross-age tutoring, free **Los Angeles Unified School District** 450 North Grand Avenue, Los Angeles, CA 90012 213-625-6900

CRV OPERATION MATERIALS
(various dates) - brochures, booklets and fact sheets on recruitment and recognition, list of 15-minute kinescopes, latest evaluation summary, usage/evaluation data, tip sheet (newsletter), etc. (inquire about cost) **WISE & GISE/CRV Volunteer Services** 807 NE Broadway, Minneapolis, MN 55413 612-348-6152

DO YOUR FEMALE STUDENTS SAY "NO THANKS" TO THE COMPUTER?
(1987) - a brochure designed by *Apple Computer's* graphics department to introduce computer equity for girls to faculty, staff, administrators, and others administering training programs; shows where to see the computer gender gap, why it matters, and how it can be closed, 8-page foldout, single copy free, $1.00 each additional **Women's Action Alliance** 370 Lexington Avenue, Suite 603, New York, NY 10017 212-779-2846

DOES YOUR DAUGHTER SAY "NO, THANKS" TO THE COMPUTER?
(1989) - a companion brochure to one designed for teachers and others administering training programs; addresses parents who want to make sure their daughters become and remain computer-skilled; explains where parents can see the computer gender gap happening, why it matters, and what they can do to encourage their daughters' computer skills, 8-page foldout, single copy free, additional $1.00 each **Women's Action Alliance** 370 Lexington Avenue, Suite 603, New York, NY 10017 212-779-2846

EACH ONE TEACH ONE
(1984) - guide for volunteers tutoring elementary school children in an after-school program at a community center; includes philosophy and goals, job descriptions, sections on reading and math, "All About Me" section for children, general suggestions for tutoring, and a self-evaluation checklist for volunteers, 83pp, $2.50 **Zanesville City Schools** Volunteer Services, 200 North Sixth Street, Zanesville, OH 43701 614-454-9751

EDUCATION OF YOUNG ADOLESCENTS: A STUDY
(1989) - a report recommending far-reaching changes in the way teenagers are treated during the middle grades, including a core academic program that promotes community service; cites an emphasis on high school or early education, with the middle schools left out; touches on drug, sex, driving, suicide and other issues affecting this age group, single copy free **Carnegie Council on Adolescent Development** Task Force on Adolescent Education, 170 East 64th Street, New York, NY 10021 212-838-4120

EDUCATION THAT WORKS: AN ACTION PLAN FOR THE EDUCATION OF MINORITIES
(1990) - the result of nearly two years of work by a group of educators and social scientists who analyzed programs that are successfully educating minority youth; describes a 10-principle plan designed to make all schools work for minority students through bridges between communities, work and schools, **National Education Association** 1201 Sixteenth Street, NW, Washington, DC 20036 202-822-7200

EDUCATIONAL OPPORTUNITIES FOR OLDER PERSONS
(1978) - descriptions of organizations and services in the public and private sectors offering courses and other educational activities which are specifically for or include older persons, 5pp, single copy free **US/HHS - Administration on Aging** 200 C Street, SW, Washington, DC 20201 202-619-0724

EFFECTIVE SCHOOLS FOR POOR CHILDREN: A PARENT HANDBOOK
(1982) - a handbook about the concept of quality education for all children; summarizes research presented in *What Works?* (described elsewhere) in a question-and-answer format intended to help parents judge school quality and participate in making schools more effective; appends bibliographh, 25pp, $2.75 **National Clearinghouse for Legal Services** 407 South Dearborn Street, Suite 400, Chicago, IL 60605 312-939-3830

EMERGENCY ENGLISH FOR REFUGEES
(1979) - introduction to teaching English to speakers of other languages to assist volunteers in meeting emergency conversational needs of refugees; provides 20 lesson outlines, and about 30 ideas for developing a lesson from scratch, text of two Indochinese Refugee Education Guides, simple booklets on specific topics (e.g., How to Patch Holes in the Wall), a brief bibliography, and other resources, 120pp, $2.00 **Lutheran Church Women** 29 Queen Lane, Philadelphia, PA 19129 215-438-2200

EQUAL PLAY: A JOURNAL ON NONSEXIST EDUCATION
(semiannually) - a journal featuring major issues in educational equity for children through contributions from experts and specialists; reports on new research that has practical implications for the classroom; includes activities and curriculum materials, reviews of books, films, filmstrips and resource materials, and model programs and ideas for nonsexist childrearing and teaching, $12.50/year for individuals; $20.00/year for organizations; back issues still available include:
- Mainstreaming Young Children, $2.50
- Early Equal Education, $4.50
- Growing Up Free, $2.50
- Mainstreaming Disabled Children, $4.50
- Changing Roles, $2.50
- Positive and Negative Aspects of Toys, $2.50
- Access to Equality Conference, $4.50
- Beginning Equal, $4.50
- Computer Equity, $7.50
- Career Education, $7.50
- Sex Equity in Sport, $7.50
- Sex Equity Internationally, $7.50
- The Boys' Issue, $7.50
- Sexuality, Teen Pregnancy and Sex Equity, $7.50

(All 14 back issues, $60.00) **Women's Action Alliance** 370 Lexington Avenue, Suite 603, New York, NY 10017 212-779-2846

EQUAL THEIR CHANCES: CHILDREN'S ACTIVITIES FOR NONSEXIST LEARNING
(1981) - hundreds of creative and practical activities for promoting non-sexist learning in all curriculum areas; designed for teachers of elementary through junior high grades; appends list of resources, 164pp, $6.95 **Prentice-Hall** One Gulf & Western Plaza, New York, NY 10023 212-373-8500

FAMILIES LEARNING TOGETHER AT HOME AND IN THE COMMUNITY
(1980) - activities for the home that are fun and also help children achieve more in school; includes 24 reading and 24 math activities based on items found in the home; useful for anyone working with young children, 128pp, $12.00 (tax-deductible contribution) **Home and School Institute** , Washington, DC 20018 202-466-3633

FLASH FOX SUMMER READING GAME PACKET
(undated) - a packet of materials for youngsters who opt to join the library's summer reading program, which requires the reading of five or more books; includes a book log, a bookmark, and information about the certificate that can be earned and the end-of-summer party for children who reach the goal, unpaged,

single packet free **Fairfax County Public Library** 11216 Waples Mill Road, Fairfax, VA 22030 703-222-3155

FLEXIBLE PACING FOR ABLE LEARNERS
1988 - addresses the problem in challenging gifted children; discusses ways in finding the best possible match in a given setting, including activities ranging from early entrance to some form of acceleration and from program and curriculum design to credit by examination; describes *flexible pacing programs* being used across the country, 119pp, $10.00 (nonmembers $12.50) **Council for Exceptional Children** 1920 Association Drive, Reston, VA 22091-1589 703-620-3660

FLYER FILE ON GIFTED STUDENTS
(1990) - an easy-storage file folder packed with reprints, minibibliographies, and other quick-reference items covering topics for the gifted such as: summer experiences, mentors, language minority, advocacy, and stress management; includes 23 two- to four-page flyers to duplicate and use as handouts for teachers, parents and others where individuals are working with potentially gifted children, unpaged, $18.00 (nonmembers $22.50) **Council for Exceptional Children** 1920 Association Drive, Reston, VA 22091-1589 703-620-3660

GUIDELINES FOR COMMUNITY RESOURCE VOLUNTEERS
(kept current) - an aid to enable the volunteer to plan his/her visit to the school with assurance that the prearranged schedule will be respected, 7pp (inquire about cost) **WISE & GISE/CRV Volunteer Services** 807 NE Broadway, Minneapolis, MN 55413 612-348-6152

GUIDELINES FOR INVOLVING OLDER SCHOOL VOLUNTEERS
(undated) - experiences of school volunteer programs in seven cities which pioneered in promoting participation of older adults as school volunteers; includes experiences in recruiting, training, and enjoying older school volunteers from the basis of these guidelines, $3.00 **National Association of Partners in Education** 601 Wythe Street, Suite 200, Alexandria, VA 22314 703-836-4880

HELP (HANDBOOK FOR ENGLISH LANGUAGE PARAPROFESSIONALS)
(1982) - a guide for tutors of English as a Second Language; includes a collection of creative ideas and activities, organized by levels and topics; addresses the tutor's role of creating a learning environment; includes a variety of instructional approaches, designed in the following "overlapping" system for a better transition between levels of instruction: *Lessons for Beginning Students, Lessons for Beginning and Intermediate Students, Lessons for Intermediate Students, Lessons for Intermediate and Advanced Students,* and *Lessons for Advanced Students,* three-ring binder, unpaged, inquire about cost **Oakton Community College/MONNACEP** 7701 North Lincoln Avenue, Skokie, IL 60077 705-635-1426

HELPING CHILDREN LEARN AT HOME AND IN SCHOOL
(1982) - an aid for parent volunteers to help them continue their classroom tutoring at home with their own children; includes general guidelines and reading lessons and activity ideas, 21pp, $2.50 (also in Spanish) **Los Angeles Unified School District** 450 North Grand Avenue, Los Angeles, CA 90012 213-625-6900

HELPING CHILDREN LEARN AT SCHOOL AND AT HOME
(kept current) - a handbook adapted from three NAPE guides:

Effective Listening Skills, Hand book for Volunteers Who Help Children Learn, and Activities to Enhance Learning; provides parents, teachers, volunteers and others with a tool for reading development adaptable to home, school or community facility, 68pp, $4.50 (members $3.75) **National Association of Partners in Education** 601 Wythe Street, Suite 200, Alexandria, VA 22314 703-836-4880

HELPING HANDS: VOLUNTEER WORK IN EDUCATION
(undated) - overview of roles of volunteers in the field of education; includes section on after school child care, 126pp, $6.00 **University of Chicago Press** 5801 Ellis Avenue, Chicago, IL 60637 312-962-7733

HOSTS AWARENESS BROCHURE
(kept current) - detailed history and overview of the HOSTS program, including funding sources, evaluation statistics and other information, 8pp, free **HOSTS (Help One Student To Succeed)** 450 West Grand Avenue, Los Angeles , CA 90012 213-625-6900

HOSTS TUTOR TRAINING MANUAL
(in revision) - comprehensive guide for training volunteers in the school system's remedial reading program; emphasizes what tutors can do to improve the self-concept of the under-achieving student, $20.00 **HOSTS (Help One Student To Succeed)** 5802 MacArthur Boulevard, Vancouver, WA 98661 206-694-1705

HOW TO IMPROVE YOUR READING SKILLS
(1974) - illustrated guide highlighting areas of reading habits that may be preventing full enjoyment of reading; includes self-test and other aids to measure progress, 15pp, $.75 (bulk rates) **Channing L. Bete Company** , South Deerfield, MA 01373 413-665-7611

HOW TO INITIATE AND ADMINISTER A COMMUNITY RESOURCE VOLUNTEER PROGRAM
(1974) - a detailed description of the methods and techniques of one school system in bringing together capable citizens with time to spare, and a need within the school sysem for curriculum enrichment; uses a color-coding technique and includes questionnaires, forms, maps, and other aids for clarification throughout the guide, 102pp (inquire about cost) **WISE & GISE/CRV Volunteer Services** 807 NE Broadway, Minneapolis, MN 55413 612-348-6152

KIDS IN TROUBLE
(1979) - account of how a year-round camp sponsored by a salesmen's club helped boys from six to sixteen years of age who could not make it in the public school system; covers reasons for referral, average length of stay (16-18 months), program techniques, counselor training, and other aspects, 94pp, $3.95 **Wildwood Books** PO Box 7263, Tyler, TX 75711 214-839-4782

THE KINDERGARTEN CHILD AND READING
(1977) - a guide for those interested in helping children become acquainted with reading and prepare for formal reading instruction in grade one; discusses past/present attitudes toward preschool reading, the diversity in children of this age group, ways to foster interest, individualized instruction, and efficient ways to use instructional materials, 82pp, $4.00 (members $2.50) **International Reading Association** PO Box 8139, 800 Barksdale Road, Newark, DE 19714 302-731-1600

KNOW YOUR SCHOOLS
(1974) - a step-by-step guide to help citizens make an orderly study of their school system to determine its effectiveness and benefit to those it is intended to serve, 31pp, $1.00, plus $.50 handling per order **League of Women Voters of the US** 1730 M Street, NW, Washington, DC 20036 202-429-1965

LEARNING DISABILITIES: PROBLEMS AND PROGRESS
(1979) - a definition of the problem describing causes, signs of trouble, prevention, testing, treatment, ways parents/teachers/others can help and the outlook for the future, 28pp, $.50 (quantity discounts) **Public Affairs Committee** 381 Park Avenue South, New York, NY 10016 212-683-4331

LITERATURE, CREATIVITY, AND IMAGINATION
(1973) - tips from three children's book authors on providing some new "magic" for children's education program that will stimulate their minds and help them reach their fullest potentials, 20pp, $.75 **Association for Childhood Education International** 11141 Georgia Avenue , Suite 200, Wheaton, MD 20902 301-942-2443

THE MOST ENABLING ENVIRONMENT: EDUCATION IS FOR ALL CHILDREN
(undated) - an illustrated bulletin to help meet the needs of teachers, parents and child care workers who must face "mainstreaming" of children with handicaps into classrooms and other group activities; relates to Public Law 94-142, examining all aspects of the mandate; discusses obstacles, successes, and other elements of efforts in this area, 64pp, $4.00 (members, 10% discount) **Association for Childhood Education International** 11141 Georgia Avenue , Suite 200, Wheaton, MD 20902 301-942-2443

NATIONAL PARTNERSHIPS IN EDUCATION PROGRAM INFORMATION
(1983) - a pocketed portfolio containing an overview of the partnership program, advice for schools, businesses, and community organizations regarding roles in the partnership, program examples, meeting agendae and participants, speeches, statements of endorsement, question/answer brochures, press releases, etc., single copy free **National Partnerships in Education Program** Office of National Service, Washington, DC 20500 202-456-6676

THE NEUTER COMPUTER: COMPUTERS FOR GIRLS AND BOYS
(1986) - an overview of ways to encourage computer use by girls and close the computer gender gap; includes 56 computer activities, 96 computer equity strategies for teachers, administrators, parents, and students, and guidance on planning and evaluating a computer equity program in a school; appends resource listings, forms and questionnaires for copying, 279pp, $24.95 **Neal-Schuman Publications** 23 Leonard Street, New York, NY 10013 212-925-8650

NEW YORK CITY SCHOOL VOLUNTEER PROGRAM INFORMATION
(1981-82) - report on the history, financing, volunteer recruitment, screening, training, and supervision, specific programs, and other details about the program (will include current annual report on request), 5pp, single copy free **New York City School Volunteer Program** 20 West 40th Street, New York, NY 10018 212-921-5622

NONSEXIST EDUCATION FOR YOUNG CHILDREN: A PRACTICAL GUIDE
(1975) - a look at sex fairness in early education in areas of learning and play environments, toys and materials, and how to secure the support of staff and parents for nonsexist education, 115pp, $4.95 **Citation Press** 730 Broadway, New York, NY 10003

NONSEXIST EDUCATION SERIES
(undated) - a series of smaller publications developed for quick reference in the area of equity in education, including:
- The Nonsexist Classroom Checklist, 4pp, $.75
- Checklist for Evaluating Sexism in Children's Books, $2.50

- Bibliography of Materials for Equal Early Education, 8pp, $2.50
- Creating an Inclusionary Early Childhood Classroom Environment, 5pp, $2.00

Women's Action Alliance 370 Lexington Avenue, Suite 603, New York, NY 10017 212-779-2846

NOTES FROM A DIFFERENT DRUMMER
(1977) - an award-winning guide to juvenile fiction portraying the handicapped, developed for people who work with children ages five to eighteen, 375pp, $29.95, also available from book dealers (inquire about follow-up edition, *More Notes From A Different Drummer*, 1984, 495pp, $39.95) **R. R. Bowker** PO Box 762, New York, NY 10011

PARENT/COMMUNITY INVOLVEMENT LEAFLET ASSORTMENT
(various dates) - series of pamphlets designed to help the community understand and work more closely with the school system $3.95/set/25 of same title; Examination Kit (one of each title) $4.95; titles available:
- *Discipline at Home*
- *Discipline at Work*
- *Doing Well in School*
- *Get Involved in Your Child's School*
- *Gifted and Talented Children: How Parents Can Help*
- *Know Your Teacher*
- *Let's Have a Conference: You and Your Child's Teacher*
- *Motivation for Learning: How Parents Can Help*
- *Reading at School and at Home*
- *The Schools Are Yours: Help Take Care of Them*
- *Spelling: How It Is Taught and How Parents Can Help*
- *Talking With Your Child*
- *Those Kids Who Got Promoted Anyway*
- *Values and Valuing Parents and Students*
- *TV, Reading and Writing*

National Education Association The Academic Building, Saw Mill Road, West Haven, CT 06516 203-934-2669

PARENTS: ACTIVE PARTNERS IN EDUCATION
(1971) a guide attempting to reverse the trend of home and school growing further apart; establishes a case for the need of home/school/community cooperation to prevent confusion and anxieties among the children, 32pp, $3.50 **National Education Association** The Academic Building, Saw Mill Road, West Haven, CT 06516 203-934-2669

PARTNERS IN LEARNING: THE STORY OF THE NYC/ETP PROGRAM
(undated) - overview of a program with dual benefits - meaningful experiences for Neighborhood Youth Corps enrollees, and academic assistance for early elementary school children through a one-to-one tutoring relationship, 6-panel foldout, single copy free **Partners in Learning** 923 East Kearsley Street, Flint, MI 48502 313-762-1256 (elementary)

PAUL ROBESON SCHOLARSHIP AWARD
(kept current) - kit of materials about a scholarship program that encourages academic excellence and the correct use of written and spoken English among black students in the Washington area (the first award, $43,557, 1989), unpaged, free **Project Excellence Scholarship Program** c/o Carl Rowan, 1703 Kaiser Avenue, Irvine, CA 92714 714-250-4000

PRACTICAL GUIDE TO COUNSELING THE GIFTED IN A SCHOOL SETTING
(2nd Ed. 1990) - a guide that builds on the first edition adding

100% more information; stresses the importance of helping gifted children through the often stressful experience of being an accelerated learner; describes the writing, reading, and counseling connection, plus counseling gifted children in small groups, and the need to cultivate the *gift* to assure that the gifted child reaches his or her full potential, $10.00 (nonmembers $12.50) **Council for Exceptional Children** 1920 Association Drive, Reston, VA 22901-1589 703-620-3660

THE PRIVATE & PERSONAL READING JOURNAL OF (NAME OF CHILD)

(1989) concept by Marion Sader - a lively and colorful illustrated journal designed to encourage reading by the very young; provides space for reading habits (favorite books, authors, characters, subjects, etc.), books recently read, books recommended to others, thoughts about books, etc., as well as a "blank" table of contents to locate all of these notes over and over again; includes poems, quotes, tips to use when visiting the library, and a listing of favorite children's books by celebrities, including President Bush, Barbara Bush, Bill Cosby, Jim Henson, Ann Landers, and others, 16pp, $3.50 (quantity discounts available for some groups) **R. R. Bowker** Department R-90, PO Box 762, New York, NY 10011

PUBLIC RELATIONS TOOLS FOR SCHOOL VOLUNTEERS

(kept current) - guidelines on dealing with the news media, setting up exhibits, taking photographs, designing publications, and other techniques needed for a well-rounded PR program; includes a number of examples, a checklist, a list of "freebies and cheapies" on the subject, etc.; addresses school volunteers, but information is basic to any PR program, 39pp, $5.50 (members $4.50) **National Association of Partners in Education** 601 Wythe Street, Alexandria, VA 22314 703-836-4880

QUALITY EDUCATION FOR MINORITIES PROJECT

(1990) - a plan designed to meet the educational needs and interests of Alaska Native, American Indian, Black American, Mexican American, and Puerto Rican peoples in the United States, five groups historically undereducated in America; includes a set of goals for the year 2000, myths about education of minority Americans, recommended strategies, and the roles of family, community, public and private sectors; includes charts, graphs and other tools for quick reference; appends resources, definitions, and roles and responsibilities in the action plan, 132pp, free for SASE with $2.40 postage (quantity discounts) **Massachusetts Institute of Technology** Room 26-153, Cambridge, MA 02139 617-253-4417

READING AND THE BLACK ENGLISH SPEAKING CHILD

(1978) - listing of annotated publications selected for their relevance and currency in the area of the Black English speaking child in the education system that uses standard English for measurement; includes a word list demonstrating some of the major differences between standard and Black English, 47pp, $2.50 (members $1.75) **International Reading Association** 800 Barksdale Road, PO Box 8139, Newark, DE 19714 302-731-1600

RECIPES FOR READING: A GUIDE FOR PARENTS

(undated) - illustrated handbook in a "cookbook" format to help parents provide pre-reading readiness for their children; uses drawings of items found in the home as a base for each exercise; addressed to parents, but helpful to all working with young children, 28pp, single copy free **National Urban Coalition** 1201 Connecticut Avenue, NW, Washington, DC 20036 202-331-2400

SCHOOL VOLUNTEER PROGRAMS: EVERYTHING YOU NEED TO KNOW TO START OR IMPROVE YOUR PROGRAM

(1982) - tips for setting up a district-wide program, recruiting,

orienting, training, working with teachers, maintaining volunteer morale, and evaluating the program; includes sample, 36pp, $4.50 **National Association of Partners in Education** 601 Wythe Street, Alexandria, VA 22314 703-836-4880

SCHOOL VOLUNTEER SONG

(1973) - a 58-second tape designed by the Des Moines Public School System as a public service announcement, reel $3.50; cassette $3.00 **Ozark Opry Records** PO Box 242, Osage Beach, MO 65065 314-348-3383

SEX DIFFERENCES AND READING

(1976) - selected annotated publications approaching the problem of sex differences in reading from different points of view to foster better understanding among workers in this field, 40pp, $2.00 (members $1.50) **Dissemination Center for Bilingual Education** 7703 North Lamar Boulevard, Austin, TX 78752 512-458-9131

SPECIAL AAACE PUBLICATIONS

(various dates) - a basic library for adult education programs:
- *Teaching the Disadvantaged Adult,* $2.00
- *How Adults Can Learn More*
- *Faster,* $2.00
- *Teaching Reading to Adults,* $2.95
- *A Treasury of Techniques for Teaching Adults,* $2.00
- *Second Treasury,* $2.00
- *When You're Teaching Adults,* $1.00
- *Tested Techniques for Teachers of Adults,* $3.00
- *You Can Be a Successful Teacher of Adults,* $6.00
- *Training Teachers of Adults: Models and Innovative Programs,* $3.50
- *Guidance Function and Counseling Roles in Adult Education,* $4.00

American Association for Adult and Continuing Education 1112 Sixteenth Street, NW, Suite 420, Washington, DC 20036 202-463-6333

STANDARDS FOR PROGRAMS INVOLVING THE GIFTED AND TALENTED

(1989) - a guide to help those who work with gifted children on standards developed with the assistance of hundreds of professionals involved in the field; describes minimum characteristics that should be found in all programs for able learners if they are to be identified, evaluated, and helped to reach their potential, 16pp, $5.00 (nonmembers $6.25) **Council for Exceptional Children** 1920 Association Drive, Reston, VA 22091-1589 703-620-3660

SUMMER READING CALENDAR OF EVENTS

(quarterly) - a listing of hundreds of events including puppet shows, trail hikes, visiting pets, magic shows, as well as reading and other programs sponsored by the library system; specific to Fairfax County, but ideas are useful to any library's children's program, 16pp, single copy free **Fairfax County Public Library** 11216 Waples Mill Road, Fairfax, VA 22030 703-222-3155

TEACHER'S GUIDE

(1979) - a guide to help teachers aid readers in discovering what job satisfaction can mean to them; includes suggestions for transferral of the personal and interpersonal incidents of the books into concrete learning activities, 32pp, $1.25 **New Readers Press** Box 131, 1320 Jamesville Avenue, Syracuse, NY 13210 315-422-9121

TEACHER'S GUIDELINES FOR USING COMMUNITY RESOURCE VOLUNTEERS

(kept current) - quick-reference instructions to take the teacher from the initial selection of a volunteer to the guidebooks to the thank you letter from the children, 7pp (inquire about cost) **WISE & GISE/CRV Volunteer Services** 807 NE Broadway, Minneapolis, MN 55413 612-348-6152

TOTAL COMMUNITY LIBRARY SERVICE
(1973) - a case for involving all interested community agencies and organizations in planning for library services that will meet the needs of those being served; includes overviews of two successful projects (Action Library, Philadelphia; Olney Merger Project, Olney, Texas) and an extensive background reading list, 148pp, $6.00 **American Library Association** 50 East Huron Street, Chicago, IL 60611 312-944-6780

TOYS TO GO
(1976) - criteria for the selection, acquisition, storing, and suggested uses for toys that will address the social, mental and emotional growth of children, 24pp, $4.00 **American Library Association** 50 East Huron Street, Chicago, IL 60611 312-944-6780

TUTORING TIPS
(1984) - insight for the volunteer tutor into the sensitivity of such a one-to-one situation; covers record-keeping and other practical areas, with an emphasis on helping the tutee to overcome feelings of inadequacy, 4pp, single copy free **Los Angeles Unified School District** 450 North Grand Avenue, Los Angeles, CA 90012 213-625-6900

THE UNDERSERVED: OUR YOUNG GIFTED CHILDREN
(1983) - a guide for teachers, parents and others who work with young children to help them recognize potentially gifted children and follow through with appropriate action; presents models of existing programs, and competencies needed to help these special youngsters develop their abilities, 228pp, $16.00 (nonmembers $20) **Council for Exceptional Children** 1920 Association Drive, Reston, VA 22091-1589 703-620-3660

USING LANGUAGE-EXPERIENCE APPROACH
(1975) - guide to a classroom-tested method of teaching reading which develops the stories that students tell or write into reading materials; includes four basic ways to create a curriculum using the language-experience approach, 40pp, $2.00 **New Readers Press** Box 131, 1320 Jamesville Avenue, Syracuse, NY 23210 315-422-9131

VOLUNTEERS AND CHILDREN WITH SPECIAL NEEDS
(1983) - comprehensive program designed to help the mildly handicapped child succeed by avoiding the frustration of attempting activities beyond his/her capabilities, 25pp, $4.50 (members $2.00) **National Association of Partners in Education** 601 Wythe Street, Suite 200, Alexandria, VA 22314 703-836-4880

VOLUNTEERS IN SPECIAL EDUCATION
(1983) - a look at the functions of volunteers in five special education areas: essential education, learning disabilities/severe behavior disorders, health, handicapped, hearing impaired, and visually impaired; includes task list for volunteer and teacher, 23pp, $1.00 **Zanesville City Schools** Volunteer Services, 200 North Sixth Street, Zanesville, OH 43701 614-454-9751

A WALK THROUGH WILLIAMS
(1977) - illustrated story of one community's successful effort in the development of a community education center; includes grounds and floor plans throughout the guide as each component is discussed to give the reader a feeling of "walking through" the facility, 16pp, single copy free **Flint Community Schools** 923 East Kearsley Street, Flint, MI 48502 313-762-1256 (elementary)

WHAT WORKS? AN EXAMINATION OF EFFECTIVE SCHOOLS FOR BLACK CHILDREN
(1981) - an examination of the social context in which effective schools operate to provide quality education to poor black children; evaluates the steps taken to provide equal access to quality schooling for poor people; describes effective schools, the process that effective schools use, and factors that cause these schools to be effective; appends list of references, 183pp, $15.50 (see follow-up publication, *Effective Schools for Poor Children*, described elsewhere) **National Clearinghouse for Legal Services** 475 South Dearborn, Suite 400, Chicago, IL 60605 312-939-3830

WORK-EDUCATION COUNCILS: PROFILES OF COLLABORATIVE EFFORTS
(1979) - case studies demonstrating the effectiveness of cooperative programs between labor and education sectors designed to lead to successful attainment of employment goals, 112pp, $8.50 **National Institute for Work and Learning** 1200 Eighteenth Street, NW, Washington, DC 20036 202-887-6800

YOU CAN HELP YOUR CHILD READ
(updated as needed) - a handbook for parents, tutors and others working with children in areas of education on defining and analyzing the problem, selecting exercises and readings, making simple reading games, etc., 69pp, $3.95 **ADER** PO Box 364, Norwich, CT 06360

EMPLOYMENT

ABOUT BABY-SITTING
(1978) - illustrated guide for youth who may be considering baby-sitting as a means of income; includes qualities that make a good sitter, and guidelines for emergency and medical information needed to assure maximum security, 15pp, $.75 (quantity discounts) **Channing L. Bete Company** , South Deerfield, MA 01373

AGE-BASED EMPLOYMENT DISCRIMINATION
(1977) - view of employment problems of the elderly that can be traced to age discrimination (developed by National Senior Citizens Law Center), 3pp, $.75 **National Clearinghouse for Legal Services** 407 South Dearborn Street, Suite 400, Chicago, IL 60605 312-939-3830

BROCHURE SERIES: EMPLOYEES WITH EPILEPSY
(undated) - informative materials developed by the Foundation with The President's Committee on Employment of the Handicapped, and the U.S. Department of Labor (single copies free):
  ◗ *Epilepsy: The Employer's Role*
  ● *Employers... Julie, Mary and Steve can fill your job needs, TAPS will show you how!*
  ● *Employment Action on Epilepsy: A Guide for Employers and Employees*
  ● *Respond to: Workers with Epilepsy*
TAPS (Training and Placement Service) 4351 Garden City Drive, Suite 406, Landover, MD 20785 301-459-3700

COMMUNITY BASED ORGANIZATIONS IN MANPOWER PROGRAMS AND POLICY
(undated) - overview of sources of information for communities seeking to improve or establish manpower programs, 42pp, single copy free **National Commission for Employment Policy** 1522 K Street, NW, Washington, DC 20005

COUNSELING FOR CAREERS IN THE 1980'S
(1980) - help for those with responsibility for counseling job-seekers; provides information on the heightened competition for jobs, the ever-changing job requirements, and the need for more cooperation between education and labor, 186pp, $6.95 ($5.95 prepaid) **Garrett Park Press** , Garrett Park, MD 20896 301-946-2553

DEVELOPING A PROFESSIONAL VITAE OR RESUME
(1978) - discussion of the increasing importance of providing a summary of education, past employment and other information to compete for jobs in today's economy; includes several sample resumes, and a set of worksheets to help the reader get started, 110pp, $5.95 ($4.95 prepaid) **Garrett Park Press** , Garrett Park, MD 20896 301-946-2553

DIRECTORY OF SPECIAL PROGRAMS FOR MINORITY GROUP MEMBERS
(1980) - includes sections on "Career Information Services," "Employment Skills Bank," and "Financial Aid Sources" as well as thousands of job training opportunities, talent banks, summer jobs, employment services, etc.; emphasizes aid to Black, Hispanic, Asian and Native Americans, 612pp, $20.00 ($19.00 prepaid) **Garrett Park Press** , Garrett Park, MD 20896 301-946-2553

ECONOMIC DISLOCATION AND WORKER ADJUSTMENT ASSISTANCE ACT
(1990) - overview of the replacement for Title III of the *Job Training Partnership Act,* which provides a comprehensive approach to assisting dislocated workers that also includes provisions of the *Worker Adjustment and Notification Act (WARN);* covers all aspects of the Title, such as rapid response, retraining services, needs-related payments, reemployment, continuing certificates of eligibility, etc., appends a copy of the 1989 Amendment, a guide to advance notice of closings and layoffs, and other materials as they become available, unpaged, free **US/DoL - Employment and Training Administration** 200 Constitution Avenue, NW, Washington, DC 20210 202-535-0525

FEDERAL HIRING INITIATIVES: NEW WAYS TO HOLD DOWN TAXES AND TRAINING COSTS
(1979) - brief account of the federal government's efforts to coordinate, consolidate, and otherwise devise more efficient hiring practices, 22pp, $1.00 **National Institute for Work and Learning** 1200 Eighteenth Street, NW, Washington, DC 20036 202-887-6800

FOR STARTERS
(1981) - white collar and blue collar federal jobs requiring high school diploma or six months of work experience; up to two years of college or the equivalent of work experience; lists types of positions and the ratio of applicants/job openings by area, 10-panel

foldout, free (other specific information available on request) **US/OPM - Office of Information** 1900 E Street, NW, Washington, DC 20415 202-737-9616

GOODWILL IS GOOD NEWS: EMPLOYMENT OPPORTUNITIES
(undated) - account of the Industries' commitment to providing rehabilitation services, training, employment, placement in industry, and personal growth for the handicapped; invites the handicapped to apply for administrative positions in local Goodwill Industries, including job descriptions for these positions, and information about additional opportunities at other levels within the organization, 8pp, free **Goodwill Industries of America** Department of Human Resources, 9200 Wisconsin Avenue, Bethesda, MD 20814-3896 301-530-6500

HOW NONDISCRIMINATION AND EQUAL OPPORTUNITY PROGRAMS IMPACT ON THE PRIVATE SECTOR
(1979) - Information on 57 of the major laws and orders affecting recipients of federal financial assistance; cites the government's growing concern over discrimination and the need for program managers to constantly monitor activities in this regard, 24pp, $5.00 **Reymont Associates** PO Box 2013, Boca Raton, FL 33427-2013 305-391-3929

INVOLVING SCHOOLS IN EMPLOYMENT AND TRAINING PROGRAMS FOR YOUTH
(1979) - insight into the need for education and employment to work hand-in-hand to help solve problems of youth unemployment, 24pp, single copy free **National Council on Employment Policy** 1730 K Street, Suite 701, Washington, DC 20006 202-833-2532

JOB-SEEKING GUIDE FOR SENIORS
(undated) - hard facts and straight talk to the older person on fighting the persistent myths about older workers through positive thinking and perseverence, 28pp, $2.15 **National Council on the Aging** 600 Maryland Avenue, NW, West Wing 100, Washington, DC 20024 202-479-1200

JOBS: HOW PEOPLE CREATE THEIR OWN
(1977) - discussion of the failure of the job market to provide enough - or "creative enough" - jobs to enable people to do the kind of work they want to do; provides overview of alternatives as an individual, in a participatory work group, and in the labor market itself, 228pp, $4.95 **Beacon Press** 25 Beacon Street, Boston, MA 02109 617-742-2110

LIFE CENTERED CAREER EDUCATION
(1989) - a videotape presenting a discussion among two special educators experienced in the *Life Centered Career Education* curriculum, which provides special activities to be used with students at the elementary and secondary levels (originally designed for instruction with mildly mentally retarded secondary students, but found useful at other levels), 30 minutes, $50.00 (nonmembers $62.50) [Two activity books and a trainer's manual are available for use separately or with the videotape, inquire.] **Council for Exceptional Children** 1920 Association Drive, Reston, VA 22091-1589 703-620-3660

LOCATING, RECRUITING, AND EMPLOYING WOMEN: EQUAL OPPORTUNITY APPROACH
(1980) - information on more than 300 women's organizations with talent banks and other employment or career assistance, 600 women's counseling and placement centers, a model affirmative action plan, and an extensive bibliography on the subject, $8.50

($7.50 prepaid) **Garrett Park Press**, Garrett Park, MD 20896 301-946-2553

NOTICE: JTPA; STATE DESIGNATION OF ENTITIES AS DISLOCATED WORKER UNITS
(1989) - a summary of a change in the *Job Training Partnership Act* regarding dislocated worker units under Title III, as amended by *Economic Dislocation and Worker Adjustment Assistance Act (EDWAA)*; includes updated list of names, addresses, and telephone numbers of entities designed by States as *Dislocated Worker Units (agencies charged with assisting employees after plant closures, etc.)*, 4pp, free *US/DoL - Employment and Training Administration* 200 Constitution Avenue, NW, Washington, DC 20210 202-535-0525

THE NUTS AND BOLTS OF NTO: HOW TO HELP WOMEN ENTER NON-TRADITIONAL OCCUPATIONS
(2nd Ed. 1986) - a guide for recruiting, training, and placing girls and women in male-intensive vocational courses and programs; designed for program coordinators and others working at the junior high school through adult levels; includes nationally field-tested guidelines from program planning through follow-up; appends resource listings, sample outreach materials, forms and questionnaires, and other information, 204pp, $18.50 **Scarecrow Press** 52 Liberty Street, Box 4167, Metuchen, NJ 08840

PREPARING FOR AFFIRMATIVE ACTION: A WORKBOOK FOR PRACTICAL TRAINING
(1980) - seventeen exercises to help program managers understand the laws of equal employment, become more sensitive to prejudice around them, and more effectively use the talents of minorities and women, workbook and leader's guide, $10.00 **Garrett Park Press**, Garrett Park, MD 20896 301-946-2553

PUBLICATIONS OF THE DEPARTMENT OF LABOR
(intermittent) - materials on training for employment, youth employment, employment safety, wages, cost of living, etc. - some free from the Department, others available at nominal cost from the Government Printing Office; ask to put on mailing list for free updates **US/DoL - Office of Information** 200 Constitution Avenue, NW, Washington, DC 29210 202-331-2400

RENT-A-KID
(1982) - a description of a program designed to provide odd job employment opportunities for young teenagers; includes hand-out fact sheets for both the potential employer and the teenager, free packet **Citizens Committee on Youth** 2147 Central Avenue, Cincinnati, OH 45214 513-632-5200

SELF-EVALUATION CAREER GUIDE
(1978) - a guide that grew out of the concern for the high career aspirations of teenagers in the face of today's tight job market; includes survey data that indicates (1) teenagers rarely discuss future job plans with any adult; (2) teenagers rarely pick jobs that match skills, 79pp, $3.50 **Pilot Books** 103 Cooper Street, Babylon, NY 11702 516-422-2225

SENIOR COMMUNITY SERVICE PROJECT
(1978) - a look at the operations, responsibilities and progress of a program designed to combat employment and income-related problems of older, economically-disadvantaged individuals through satisfying jobs, 58pp, single copy free **National Council on the Aging** 600 Maryland Avenue, NW, West Wing 100, Washington, DC 20024 202-479-1200

SENIOR PEER EMPLOYMENT PROGRAMS
(1979) - continuing series of profiles on some of the innovative

approaches to employing older workers in programs that benefit the elderly; e.g., consumer and crime protection programs (described under those sections), Av. 18pp, $2.15 each profile **National Council on the Aging** 600 Maryland Avenue, NW, West Wing 100, Washington, DC 20024 202-479-1200

SENIOR WORKER ACTION PROGRAM: PROJECT SWAP
(1972) - overview of a program designed to supplement the inadequate incomes of older people by promoting their employment - particularly in part-time and temporary jobs, 29pp, $.80 **National Council on the Aging** 600 Maryland Avenue, NW, West Wing 100, Washington, DC 20024 202-479-1200

STAYING POOR: HOW THE *JOB TRAINING PARTNERSHIP ACT* FAILS WOMEN
(1988) - results of a national study on women in programs of the *Job Training Partnership Act (JTPA)* that was sponsored by the *Ford Foundation*; describes how this federal employment program prepares women for female-stereotyped jobs paying such low wages that *JTPA* is not a promising route out of poverty; addresses issues of training and employment, support services and job benefits, program administration, the contract application process, and conclusions and recommendations; appends data findings, annotated bibliography, and other information, 181pp, $17.50 **Scarecrow Press** 52 Liberty Street, Box 4167, Metuchen, NJ 08840

20 WAYS TO GET MORE DONE
(1976) - illustrated quick-reference guide to help improve effectiveness and production on the job and in other areas of day-to-day living, 15pp, $.75 **Channing L. Bete Company** , South Deerfield, MA 01373 413-665-7611

WHAT IS THE JOB TRAINING PARTNERSHIP ACT?
(1990) - a comprehensive packet of information designed to answer questions regarding the *Job Training Partnership Act* (replaces CETA), which transfers responsibility for the program to the states; includes answers to questions such as "What is meant by partnership? What training services are available? How can I get further information?; appends a copy of the 1983 *Job Training Partnership Act* and other materials as they become available, 79+pp, free **US/DoL - Employment and Training Commission** 200 Constitution Avenue, NW, Washington, DC 20210 202-535-0525

WORKING FOR THE USA
(kept current) - detailed guide explaining the federal government's employment system, and including a section on volunteer experience, 26pp, free **US/OPM - Office of Information** 1900 E Street, NW, Washington, DC 20415 202-737-9616

"YOU AND OTHERS ON THE JOB" SERIES
(1979) - a series of novels portraying realistic incidents in the lives of Carlos, a beginning woodworker; Melanie, a legal secretary trainee; and Paul, a salesclerk in a large department store; designed to help those new in the working world to handle challenging personal and interpersonal problems on the job, to have more confidence in their own abilities, and to be successful at work, 48pp, $4.00/set **New Readers Press** Box 131, 1320 Jamesville Avenue, Syracuse, NY 13210 315-442-9121

YOU AND YOUTH: WHAT AMERICAN BUSINESS IS DOING TO EMPLOY AND TRAIN YOUNG PEOPLE
(monthly) - newsletter developed for those groups and individuals seeking ways to involve business in helping to solve community employment problems, av. 12pp, $18.50/year for public and nonprofit organizations, $37/year for others **Vocational Foundation** 902 Broadway, Fifteenth Floor, New York, NY 10010 212-777-0700

YOUR RETIREMENT JOB GUIDE
(undated) - ideas and suggestions on possible job opportunities for ambulatory and homebound elderly, 46pp, single copy free **American Association of Retired Persons** 1909 K Street, NW, Washington, DC 20006 202-872-4700

YOUTH EMPLOYMENT PROGRAM: A GUIDE FOR YOUTH WORKERS
(1979) - examples of programs involving employed youth which resulted from community initiative and collaborative efforts from all community factions, 186pp, $5.00 (inquire about newsletter, Youth Alternatives) **American Youth Work Center** 1522 Connecticut Avenue, NW, Fourth Floor, Washington, DC 20036 202-785-0764

YOUTH PERSPECTIVES: EMPLOYABILITY DEVELOPMENT PROGRAMS AND THE WORLD OF WORK
(undated) - report on four regional conferences mounted to obtain the views of young people on barriers to youth employment, effectiveness of youth employment programs, attitudes toward work, and the relationship between work and education; covers National Youth Councils, which are an outgrowth of the seminars, 24pp, single copy free **National Urban Coalition** 1120 G Street, NW, Suite 900, Washington, DC 20005 202-628-2990

YOUTH UNEMPLOYMENT: PROBLEMS AND PROGRAMS
(1979) - special issue of "Vital Issues" devoted to a discussion of the lack of job opportunities for youth, and some of the consequences if this situation is not reversed; uses the experience of the City of Boston as a check against statistics at the national level, 4pp, 45c (discounts) **Center for Information on America** , Washington, CT 06793 203-868-2602

INFORMATION INTERVIEWING: WHAT IT IS AND HOW TO USE IT IN YOUR CAREER
(1990) - a guide to the technique of *information interviewing,* which helps the individual learn more about occupations, identify potential employers, build confidence for job interviews, and develop new career contacts; includes sections on using libraries, one-minute introductions, getting beyond the receptionist, interview scripts, tips for midlife career changers, getting promoted, etc., 125pp, $10.95 ($9.95 prepaid) **Garrett Park Press** PO Box 190, Garrett Park, MD 20896 301-946-2553

FUNDING/FUND-RAISING/RELATED SERVICES

ACCENT ON HUMOR: A LOOK AT THE LIGHTER SIDE OF PHILANTHROPY
(1988) - a collection of quips, cartoons, and quotations relating to philanthropy designed for use in thanking donors, praising volunteers, and entertaining staff in humorous way, 85pp, $5.50 (quantity discounts) #20018 **Council for Advancement and Support of Education** Publications Order Department, 80 South Early Street, Alexandria, VA 22304 703-823-6966

THE ART OF ASKING: A VOLUNTEER'S GUIDE TO ASKING FOR THE MAJOR GIFT
(1982) - reprint of an often-requested *Currents* article giving guidelines that volunteers can use in preparing for prospect calls and in asking for gifts; addresses both new and experienced volunteers, 2pp, $50.00/100 copies (members); $62.50/100 copies (nonmembers) #22801 **Council for Advancement and Support of Education** Publications Order Department, 80 South Early Street, Alexandria, VA 22304 703-823-6966

THE ART OF WINNING GOVERNMENT GRANTS
(1977) - a guide through the maze of government offices to find the appropriate grant for an individual program; provides advice on filling out application forms, approaching the correct agency, being aware of one's own influence with those in Washington who represent the public; includes extensive additional information sources, 246pp, $10.00 **Vanguard Press** 424 Madison Avenue, New York, NY 10017 212-753-3906

ARTS SUPPORT BY PRIVATE FOUNDATIONS
(updated as needed) - history of activities of more than 1200 foundations in relation to the arts; points to areas of the arts most frequently funded by foundations; includes foundations which do not participate in larger directories, **Washington International Newsletter** Box 9005, Washington, DC 20003 202-488-0880

THE BREAD GAME
(Rev. 1981, 4th rev., 3rd pr.) - provides information for non-profit organizations on the ways and means of tapping public and private foundation coffers; explores what women's organizations can expect from foundations, and how organizations can develop self-support systems, as well as information on how to write a proposal, set up an accounting system, and how to research foundations, $9.95 plus $1.25 postage and handling **Volcano Press** 330 Ellis Street, San Francisco, CA 94102 415-775-0918

THE CARD CARRYING VOLUNTEER
(1989) - overview of a program designed to utilize the BankCard system to add a dimension of fundraising and outreach to small and medium size nonprofit organizations (formerly available only to large groups), 6-panel foldout, free **Partnership BankCard Systems** 3344 14th Street, Boulder, CO 80302 303-447-1718

CATALOG OF FEDERAL DOMESTIC ASSISTANCE
(updated as needed) - provides assistance to communities by categorizing and describing the types of federal assistance available; includes information on eligibility requirements for specific programs, and guidance on how to file an application for a particular program; serves as the reference point for FAPRS (Federal Assistance Programs Retrieval System described in Funding section); increases and improves communication/coordination between the federal government and state/local governments, looseleaf manual and one update $30.00 (foreign $37.50) **US/GSA - Government Printing Office** Superintendent of Documents, Washington, DC 20402 202-783-3238

CHANGING DEMOGRAPHICS: FUND RAISING IN THE 1990S
(1990) - a guide discussing the "four emerging majorities" (baby boomers, working women, Hispanics, and older Americans), and how they will affect future funding efforts; demonstrates how each of these groups is undersolicited and overlooked, and provides details on ways to reach these new prospective donor groups; discusses the rapid increase in nonprofit organizations in the U.S., and their continuous solicitation to a donor group that is becoming increasingly narrow due to changing demographics, 267pp, hardback, $34.95 **Bonus Books** 160 East Illinois Street, PO Box 11403, Chicago, IL 60611 312-467-0424

CHRONICLE OF PHILANTHROPY
(biweekly) - a newsletter/journal covering the latest developments of large foundations in areas of fundraising, boards and volunteers, corporate giving, grants, ideas that have worked for others, new books, statistics, tax and court rulings, updates on federal/state regulations, calendar of conferences and other events, job opportunities, etc., Av. 44pp, $47.50/year or $24.00/six months introductory subscriptions; $57.50/year thereafter **Chronicle of Higher Education** Subscription Office, PO Box 1989, Marion, OH 43306-4089 202-466-1200 (Wash., DC)

COMMERCE BUSINESS DAILY
(daily) - information on proposed U.S. Government procurements, sales, and contract awards (of particular interest to subscribers seeking contracts or subcontracts, or federal surplus property), $100/year (priority mailing, $175/year) **US/GSA - Government Printing Office** Superintendent of Documents, Washington, DC 20402 202-783-3238

THE COMPLETE FUND RAISING GUIDE
(1975) - outline of specifics for conducting all kinds of fund-raising campaigns; discusses sources of funds as well as operational details, 159pp, $13.50 **Public Service Materials Center** 415 Lexington Avenue, New York, NY 10017 212-687-0645

COMSEARCH PRINTOUTS
(1982) - information in over 75 specific subject areas; e.g., Community Funds, Citizen Participation, Youth Programs; covers over 400 foundations reporting on grants of $5,000 or more; two formats: 8x11 paper printouts $11.00 each; 3x5 microfiche cards $5.00 each, broad special topics, $28.00 **Foundation Center** 79 Fifth Avenue, New York, NY 10003 212-628-4230

CORPORATE FOUNDATION PROFILES
(6th Ed. 1990) - in-depth, multi-page profiles of the largest company-sponsored foundations in the country; includes for each foundation:
- portrait of sponsoring company; history of foundation
- address, purpose statement, giving limitations, key staff
- financial data
- statistical analysis of recently-awarded grants, list of grants
- application guidelines, funding schedule

Includes extensive indexing system designed to target grantmakers by subject fields funded, geographic location, and types of support preferred; covers 600 additional foundations - almost 900 foundations in all, $125 plus $2.00 postage and handling **Foundation Center** 79 Fifth Avenue, New York, NY 10003 212-620-4230

DIRECTORY OF STATE AND FEDERAL FUNDS FOR BUSINESS DEVELOPMENT
(1977) - a starting point for those seeking information about federal and state financial assistance; emphasizes the importance of "shopping" and "comparing" to obtain the maximum benefit from funding efforts (which is not always the "most money"), 63pp, $5.00 **Pilot Books** 103 Cooper Street, Babylon, NY 11702 516-422-2225

EFFECTIVE CORPORATE FUND RAISING
(1982) - a systematic approach to raising money from business; uses real-life situation as case example; assists fund raisers in any location and any type of nonprofit fund raising (published with assistance from Shell Companies Foundation), 74pp, $14.95 **American Council for the Arts** 570 Seventh Avenue, New York, NY 10018 212-354-6655

FABULOUS FANTASY TRIATHLON (THE NON-EVENT OF 1990)
(1990) - overview of an imaginary event where entrants pay an "entry fee" (donation) in several athletic classes, including *Company Team, Olympic Hopeful, Expert, Amateur, and Couch Potato,* but do not run, swim, or bike to win one of the 25 prizes offered; uses "registrations" in a drawing administered by the *Race Committee* for the prizes, while "non-runners, non-swimmers, and non-bikers" sit home and wait for the results, 6-panel foldout, free **Volunteer Boulder County** 3305 North Broadway, Suite One, Boulder, CO 80304 303-444-4904

FINANCIAL INCENTIVES IN CHARITABLE GIVING
(1988) - an approach for staff members and volunteer solicitors that outlines donor benefits and helps donors understand the tax and other financial incentives of charitable giving, single copy free, bulk rates on quantities **Council for Advancement and Support of Education** 80 South Early Street, Alexandria, VA 22304 703-823-6966 (VA)

501(C)(3)
(monthly) - newsletter of an organization that brings together nonprofit organizations and the corporate community in the area of fundraising - especially in-kind contributions, 8pp, inquire about cost **American Association for Corporate Contributions** PO Box 6401, Evanston, IL 60204

FOUNDATION CENTER NATIONAL DATA BANK
(1982) - information on over 22,000 nonprofit organizations which are classified as private foundations; provides immediate access to small and geographically limited grant-making private foundations - two volumes, $45.00 **Foundation Center** 79 Fifth Avenue, New York, NY 10003 212-628-4230

FOUNDATION FUNDAMENTALS
(1981) - information which takes the reader step-by-step through the funding research process, 148pp, $6.50 **Foundation Center** 79 Fifth Avenue, New York, NY 10003 212-628-4230

FOUNDATION GRANTS TO INDIVIDUALS
(1979) - profiles of programs of over 12,000 foundations which make grants to individuals; includes fund sources for scholarships, internships, travel grants, etc., 236pp, $15.00 **Foundation Center** 79 Fifth Avenue, New York, NY 10003 212-628-4230

FOUNDATION NEWS
(bimonthly) - feature articles on developments in the field; includes "Foundation Grants Index" (latest reported grants of $5,000 or more), $24.00/year (2 years/$44.00) **Council on Foundations** 1828 L Street, NW, Washington, DC 20036 202-466-6512

FRI CAPITAL IDEAS
(1979) - in-depth description of how to solicit major gifts from private sources, detailing how to prepare for, launch and run a capital fund-raising campaign or a major-gift program; includes many case histories and examples, 320pp, $49.95 **Fund-Raising Institute** Box 365, Ambler, PA 19002 215-646-7019

FRI MONTHLY PORTFOLIO
(monthly) - fund-raising techniques that are applicable to most types of organizations; includes many illustrated articles, with most edited to contain just the key how-to ideas; contains three sections: Newsletter, Letter Clinic, and a Bulletin citing a specific area, unpaged, $48/year **Fund-Raising Institute** Box 365, Ambler, PA 19002 215-646-7019

FRM WEEKLY
(weekly) - newsletter-style reports on the different funding topics, legislation, meetings, activities, etc., length varies, $98/year **Fund Raising Management (FRM)** 224 Seventh Street, Garden City, NY 11530 516-746-6700

FUND RAISING MANAGEMENT
(monthly) - reports on grantsmanship, fund-raising, government and corporate funding, related conferences, case histories, etc.; index available, $45.00/year **Fund Raising Management** 224 Seventh Street, Garden City, NY 11530 516-746-6700

FUND-RAISING: THE GUIDE TO RAISING MONEY FROM PRIVATE SOURCES

(1979) - guidelines for the "eager volunteer" or the "professional fund raiser" who needs to come up with new ideas and approaches to compete for foundation funds; addresses the professional but presented so that the nonprofessional can obtain a better understanding of the process and develop appropriate questions to upgrade skills, 254pp, $15.95 **University of Oklahoma Press** , Norman, OK 73019 405-325-5111

FUNDING FOR TRAINING: A SURVEY OF RESOURCES FOR DEVELOPMENTALLY DISABLED PERSONNEL

(undated) - identification of sources of federal funding, and description of the procurement of funds from state and private sector resources for the purpose of staff training; contains a section on how to utilize periodicals in searching for training support; includes bibliography, 38pp (microfiche only available), $.15 **Clearinghouse of Rehabilitation Training Materials** 115 Old USDA Building, Oklahoma State University, Stillwater, OK 74074 405-624-7650

FUNDING SOURCES AND TECHNICAL ASSISTANCE FOR MUSEUMS AND HISTORICAL AGENCIES

(1979) - traditional sources of arts funding as well as those applicable to arts that are available to "educational organizations" - a legitimate category for the arts that is seldom explored by arts organizations, 138pp, $7.50 to members; $10.00 to others **American Association for State and Local History** 708 Berry Road, Nashville, TN 37204 615-383-5991

GETTING YOUR SHARE: AN INTRODUCTION TO FUNDRAISING

(1976) - a guide designed to take nonprofessional grant seekers through all the steps of fundraising; includes a proposal checklist, an annotated resource listing of helpful groups and publications, and a list of change-oriented foundations, 36pp, $2.50 **Women's Action Alliance** 370 Lexington Avenue, Suite 603, New York, NY 10017 212-779-2846

GIFT-IN-KIND SEMINAR PLANNING GUIDE

(1986) - a step-by-step guide to developing a gift-in-kind seminar to attract corporate gifts of merchandise, business sponsored employee volunteers and free expertise, and donations of services from companies (companion piece to *Give and Take,* a 105-page overview of approved methods of donating, accepting donated gifts of inventory based on tax codes, described separately), the planning guide is free with the purchase of the book, but otherwise not available, $20.50 for both items **American Association for Corporate Contributions** c/o Newsletters By Design, Old Courthouse, 601 Trap Street, Ontonagon, MI 49953 906-884-2397

GIFTS CATALOG HANDBOOK

(1978) - list of project needs (cash, materials, equipment, services) for distribution to all segments of the community; presents how-to instructions, 13pp, free **US/DoI - National Park Service** Information Exchange, 18th & C Streets, NW, Washington, DC 20240 202-343-4747

GIVE AND TAKE

(4th Pr. 1986) by Thomas Graham Lee and Margaret Stewart Carr - a comprehensive guide to approved methods of donating corporate inventory; includes overview and explanation of section 170(E)(3) of the tax code relating to in-kind donations; has sections on how it works, what can be given, what can't be given, how to go about it, etc., 105+pp, includes companion seminar guide (see separate entry), 100pp, $20.50 **American Association for Corporate Contributions** c/o Newsletters By Design, Old Courthouse, 601 Trap Street, Ontonagon, MI 49953 906-884-2397

GIVING: BIG BUCKS, BARE BASICS AND BLUE SKIES

(undated) - an inspirational speech by David Rockefeller with guidelines for expanding the substantial philanthropic resources you already have at hand, 7pp paperback keynote address, $2.00 **Independent Sector** 1828 L Street, NW, Washington, DC 20036 202-223-8100

GIVING USA

(annual) - a compilation of facts and trends of American philanthropy for a given year, 160pp, $45.00 (or $75.00 combined cost if ordered with *Giving USA Update,* described separately) **AAFRC Trust for Philanthropy** 25 West 43rd Street, New York, NY 10036 212-354-5799

GIVING USA UPDATE

(10/year) overview of current trends and other information that affects philanthropy and nonprofit organizations and institutions, $35.00/year (or $75.00 combined cost with *Giving USA,* described in separate entry) **AAFRC Trust for Philanthropy** 25 West 43rd Street, New York, NY 10036 212-354-5799

GOAL 1: FUND RAISING - CATALOG 83

(1983) - three remaining handbooks of a nine-book series on fund raising and related subjects:
- *Corporate Contributions: Understanding the Decision-Making Process*
- *Loaned Executive's Program for Smaller Communities*
- *Donor Option: A Consideration*

Request catalog containing these and other materials on taxes, training, benefits, etc. Contact librarian or historian for information about out-of-print handbooks on personal gifts, direct mail, group solicitation, loaned executive recruitment, training programs, and United Way allocations to agencies, free catalog **United Way of America** 701 North Fairfax Street, Alexandria, VA 223-4-2045 703-836-7100

GOLD BOOK: DIRECTORY OF SUCCESSFUL PROJECTS BY VOLUNTEERS

(1990) - descriptions of fundraising projects mounted by orchestra volunteers; includes name, address, and phone number of each project chairperson; features volunteer education projects, ticket sales campaigns, and comparative statistical reports, $22/members; $35/nonmembers **American Symphony Orchestra League** 777 Fourteenth Street, NW, Suite 500 , Washington, DC 20005 202-628-0099

GRANTSMANSHIP RESOURCES FOR REHABILITATION PROGRAMS

(undated) - a compilation of materials recommended by experts in the field for those who plan programs, develop proposals, administer organizations and raise funds; describes 50 publications and 16 organizations, 14pp, $1.25 (ask about quantity discounts) **Grantsmanship Center** 1031 South Grand Avenue, Los Angeles, CA 90015 213-749-4721

GUIDE FOR STATE AND LOCAL GOVERNMENT AGENCIES

(1976) - help for agencies seeking grants and contracts with the federal government; presents cost principles and procedures for establishing cost allocation plans and indirect cost rates, 88pp, $5.50 **US/GSA - Government Printing Office** Superintendent of Documents, Washington, DC 20402 202-783-3238

GUIDE TO CORPORATE GIVING IN THE ARTS

(1978) - a casebook describing the arts support policies and practices of 359 U.S. corporations; includes financial data, decision criteria, levels of giving, contact persons for querying, etc.;

emphasizes the ability to compare arts activities by corporations through the case book, 402pp, $13.75 **American Council for the Arts** 570 Seventh Avenue, New York, NY 10018 212-354-6655

HOW TO GET GOVERNMENT GRANTS
(1977) - guide to specific federal agencies to approach for grants in a given area; explains the process used in approving the grants, and gives information on writing proposals and administering the grants, 160pp, $13.50 **Public Service Materials Center** 355 Lexington Avenue, New York, NY 10017 212-687-0646

HOW TO ORGANIZE AND PRODUCE A RADIOTHON
(1989) - a manual offering ideas and experiences from the creator of the original radio fundraiser for orchestras; guides the user to producing a successful radiothon that reaches the entire community; specifies orchestras, but has basic principles of a radiothon useful to any program, 59pp, $10.00 (members); $15.00 (non-members) **American Symphony Orchestra League** 777 Fourteenth Street, NW, Suite 500, Washington, DC 20005 202-628-0099

HOW TO RAISE MONEY: SPECIAL EVENTS FOR ARTS ORGANIZATIONS
(1977) - a compilation of fund raising ideas from around the country (including Canada) intended to answer the question, "What kind of event shall we have this year?" Includes over 20 examples, 32pp, $3.00 **American Council for the Arts** 570 Seventh Avenue, New York, NY 10018 212-354-6655

HOW TO SUCCEED IN FUND-RAISING TODAY
(1975) - instructions on how to conduct successful community events, how to publicize them, and how other groups have found ways to raise funds for their programs, 205pp, $9.95 paperback, $16.95 cloth **Alan C. Hood & Company** 28 Country Hill, Brattleboro, VT 05301 802-254-2200

HOW TO WRITE A SUCCESSFUL PROPOSAL
(kept current) - a complete course including eight hours of instructions on tape cassettes, a 142-page textbook coordinated with the tapes, an album of sample fund-raising letters keyed to the textbook and a review book, $97.00 **Fund-Raising Institute** Box 365, Ambler, PA 19002 215-646-7019

HOW TO WRITE POWERFUL FUND RAISING LETTERS
(1990) - a guide that uses "the mistakes of others" to guide readers through a process that is designed to help tailor letters to an organization's individual needs; includes sample fundraising letters in fields of the arts, health, older persons, environment, and others, 206pp, hardcover, $29.95 **Bonus Books** 160 East Illinois Street, PO Box 11403, Chicago, IL 60611 312-467-0424

HOW TO WRITE SUCCESSFUL FOUNDATION PRESENTATIONS
(1979) - guidelines on written foundation presentations, and examples of actual grant-winning presentations for general operating expenses, renewal and increases of grants, etc.; includes letters for requesting initial appointments, 98pp, $9.95 **Public Service Materials Center** 415 Lexington Avenue, New York, NY 10017 212-687-0646

THE HUMAN RACE: PEOPLE IN MOTION
(1990) - a packet of materials including an illustrated overview of an annual race (first Saturday in May) developed to help assure that the 1,043 nonprofits operating in California (all of whom participate in some way in the success of the event) are assured of resources to help the people who need their services, a fact sheet, and a listing of Volunteer Center sponsors across the state, business/industry and community participants, and an update of participation statistics (exceeding 20,000 in 1990), insertions vary based on available materials, unpaged kit, free **Volunteer Center/United Way At Work** United Way of San Joaquin County, 12 East Park Street, PO Box 1585, Stockton, CA 95201 209-943-0870

INDIVIDUAL GIVING/VOLUNTEERING CAMPAIGN
(1983-84) - a packet of information on an advertising campaign developed to increase public awareness on the benefits of volunteering; discusses joint venture with sponsors from the volunteer community (both public and private sectors), the Advertising Council, and the donor of the logo design and slogan for the campaign, single packet free **Ogilvy and Mather** 230 Park Avenue, New York, NY 10169 212-867-8200

LOCAL GOVERNMENT FUNDING REPORT
(weekly) - provides a comprehensive overview of federal funding for local programs; focuses on concerns of local governments, but is useful to people in nonprofit organizations as well - especially if the program is working in more than one area of concern; details coverage of pending legislation, provides analyses of new program regulations and includes other current information, $138.00/year **Government Information Services** 1611 North Kent Street, Suite 308, Arlington, VA 22209 703-528-1082

MATCHING GIFT LEAFLET SERIES: 1989-90
(1989-90) - leaflets providing brief explanations of how companies match employees' contributions to a nonprofit organization; lists corporations that participate in such a program and shows donors how to get their gifts matched by their companies; includes four leaflets covering areas of
- higher education;
- secondary and elementary schools;
- nonprofit cultural organizations and public television and radio;
- nonprofit hospitals, health and social service, environmental, and civic organizations; and the United Way.

Each leaflet lists firms donating in the specific category, single copy free; bulk rates on quantities **Council for Advancement and Support of Education** Publications Order Department, 80 South Early Street, Alexandria, VA 22304 703-823-6966

MEGA GIFTS: WHO GIVES THEM, WHO GETS THEM
(1989) - provides forum for 25 prominent donors to tell why they gave $1 million or more to a variety of institutions; traces the history of these and other gifts to help fundraisers understand the motivation behind large gifts, 224pp, $28.95 plus $3.00 postage and handling **Bonus Books** 160 East Illinois Street, PO Box 11403, Chicago, IL 60611 312-467-0424

MORE DIALING, MORE DOLLARS
(1990) - a twelve-step guide for managers of organizations interested in using telemarking to raise money for programs; shows how to set up and conduct a telemarketing campaign, 93pp, $9.00 (both members and non-members) **American Symphony Orchestra League** 777 Fourteenth Street, NW, Suite 500, Washington, DC 20005 202-628-0099

NATIONAL DIRECTORY OF ARTS & EDUCATION SUPPORT BY BUSINESS CORPORATIONS
(1981) - lists 703 major corporations with 2812 divisions, subsidiaries and affiliates; includes addresses, officers, and programs supported, unpaged, $75.00 **Washington International Arts Letter** PO Box 12010, Des Moines, IA 50312 515-243-8691

NATIONAL DIRECTORY OF ARTS SUPPORT BY PRIVATE FOUNDATIONS, VOL. 4

(1981) - lists 1,687 foundations, typical grants, and subject areas subsidized, 264pp, $65.00 **Washington International Arts Letter** PO Box 12010, Des Moines, IA 50312 515-243-8691

NATIONAL DIRECTORY OF GRANTS AND AID TO INDIVIDUALS IN THE ARTS

(1982) - lists over 1,800 sources of financial assistance in all of the arts, coded by subject; includes restrictions, amounts over $1,000, deadlines and addresses, 221pp, $15.95 **Washington International Arts Letter** PO Box 12010, Des Moines, IA 50312 515-243-8691

NATIONAL ENDOWMENT FOR THE HUMANITIES: OVERVIEW

(annually) - summarizes all program funding areas; lists areas not funded; provides eligibility guidelines, program deadlines, State Humanities Councils, etc., 19pp, single copy free **National Endowment for the Humanities** 1100 Pennsylvania Avenue, NW, Washington, DC 20506 202-786-0438

NCIB STANDARDS IN PHILANTHROPY

(1982) - describes how National Charities Information Bureau (NCIB) evaluates national not-for-profit organizations through application of its eight standards in philanthropy; designed to help grantmakers, contributors and not-for-profit agencies understand the considerations on which NCIB bases its comments and conclusions and to provide a tool for use in evaluating agencies that NCIB does not review, 40pp, $4.00 (bulk rates) **National Charities Information Bureau** 19 Union Square, West, Sixth Floor, New York, NY 10003 212-929-6300

NEW APPROACHES TO FUNDING IN PARKS AND RECREATION

(1970) - tips on how to involve citizens in organizing boards and obtaining funds for parks through government grants; describes the model community efforts that created a park in a Minnesota community, 126pp, $3.95 **National Recreation and Park Association** 3101 Park Center Drive, Alexandria, VA 22302 703-820-4940

THE NEW HOW TO RAISE FUNDS FROM FOUNDATIONS

(1979) - guidelines for approaching a foundation through written contact; includes sample letters and presentations, 92pp, $9.95 **Public Service Materials Center** 415 Lexington Avenue, New York, NY 10017 212-687-0646

OFFICIAL FUNDRAISING ALMANAC

(1990) - a guide designed to assist those with fundraising responsibilities through more than 100 charts, graphs, tables and other planning tools; includes information on fundraising software and other special equipment that can expedite the fundraising program; lists largest donors and their interests, a fundraising bibliography, fundraising quotations, history of fundraising, major leaders in the field, etc., 410pp, clothbound, $39.95 **Bonus Books** 160 East Illinois Street, PO Box 11403, Chicago, IL 60611 312-467-0424

101 WAYS TO RAISE RESOURCES

(1990) - more than 900 ideas in 45 categories including general advice, solicitation of individuals, corporations and foundations, volunteers, non-cash fund-raising, publicity, special events, etc., to help the board or individual in charge of raising funds for programs, unpaged, $8.00 **VMS/Heritage Arts** 1807 Prairie Aenue, Downers Grove, IL 60515 312-964-1194

OUTREACH PLAN: FOCUS ON THE HISPANIC COMMUNITY

(1989) - a videotape featuring a popular Hispanic musician designed to reach the Hispanic community and increase its involvement in the United Way as contributors, and as applicant organizations for United Way funding, 23 minutes, inquire about cost **United Way of the Capital Area (Hartford)** 99 Woodland Street, Hartford , CT 06105-1207 203-249-2300

PART OF THE SOLUTION: INNOVATIVE APPROACHES TO NONPROFIT FUNDING

(2nd Pr. 1989) - overview of the results of the *Exploratory Project on Financing the Nonprofit Sector* conducted in 1987 by the *Center for Public Policy;* addresses two major purposes of the study: (1) to examine the state of the funding base of nonprofit organizations; and (2) to identify major new mechanisms to help finance these organizations; appends selected references, committees and panels involved and papers on taxes, methodology, etc., 132pp, $15.00 (prepaid) **Union Institute Center for Public Policy** 1731 Connecticut Avenue, NW, Suite 300, Washington, DC 20009 202-667-1313

PHILANTHROPY IN ACTION

(1990) - overview of ways philanthropy can make contributions in nine areas of concern to all fund raisers, including relieving human misery, preserving and enhancing institutions, nourishing the spirit, creating tolerance, understanding, and peace among people, etc., 337pp, $19.95 (paperback), $29.95 (hardback) **Independent Sector** 1828 L Street, NW, Washington, DC 20036 202-223-8100

PHILANTHROPY: VOLUNTARY ACTION FOR THE PUBLIC GOOD

(1988) - discusses the unique role of philanthropic giving in our society; includes ethics and tactics of giving and new models of management for voluntary organizations; appends a summary of research on philanthropy, 282pp, $19.95 #20012 **Council for Advancement and Support of Education** Publications Order Department, 80 South Early Street, Alexandria, VA 22304 703-823-6966 (VA)

POPULATION REFERENCE BUREAU

(bimonthly) - two of the bulletins in this series that allude to the importance of accurate population counts in the allocation of federal funds each year:

- *The 1980 Census: The Counting of America* - an appeal for cooperation by all in the census-taking activity to assure accurate apportionment of seats in the House of Representatives, and the appropriate apportionment of more than $50 billion each year from the federal government for services to the people; explains the consequences of the constant 2.5% undercount; discusses the new law mandating a census every five years after 1980, 40pp, $2.00
- *How America Studies Itself: The U.S. Census* - a highly readable teaching module geared to the upper high school and college undergraduate level; describes the U.S. census as an important sociologic tool and outlines its current uses and benefits to Americans, including the need for accuracy in the population count to assure appropriate apportionment of $50 million annually for services to the people, 13pp, $1.00

Population Reference Bureau 777 Fourteenth Street, NW, Suite 800, Washington, DC 20005 202-639-8040

PROFILE: IN-KIND GIVING

(bimonthly) - descriptions of in-kind programs instituted by companies and businesses to assist voluntary human services, arts and education organizations; provides information on the benefits of this kind of supplement to financial support to both the company and the recipient organization, 12pp, single copy free

Gifts In Kind 700 North Fairfax Street, Suite 610, Alexandria, VA 22314 703-836-2121

PROFILES OF EFFECTIVE CORPORATE GIVING PROGRAMS

(1989) - a general overview of a research study of 48 of the nation's most well-established corporate giving programs, including why grant-making in many companies is *reactive* instead of *proactive*, 14pp research paper, $2.00 **Independent Sector** 1828 L Street, NW, Washington, DC 20036 202-223-8100

PROPOSAL WRITING

(1988) - a special issue of *Currents* giving the basics of effective proposal writing, from content to structure to length, advice on dealing with problem situations, how to learn about prospects before approaching them, etc.; appends basic bibliography, 80pp, $6 (members); $7.50 (nonmembers) #22903 **Council for Advancement and Support of Education** Publications Order Department, 80 South Early Street, Alexandria, VA 22304 703-823-6966 (VA)

PROSPECT RESEARCH: A HOW-TO GUIDE

(1989) - recommendations on how to locate and investigate potential major donors; helps user process raw information; discusses the 10% of potential donor base who will contribute 90% of gift dollars received, 150pp, $18.50 (members); $23.25 (nonmembers) #26701 **Council for Advancement and Support of Education** Publications Order Department, 80 South Early Street, Alexandria, VA 22304 703-823-6966 (VA)

PROSPECTING: SEARCHING OUT THE PHILANTHROPIC DOLLAR

(1979) - the case for considering the funding activity as a principal part of the organizational structure rather than merely a peripheral to the development process; instructs on locating the most useful information, generating new prospects, and devising a record-keeping system that will be most beneficial, 69pp plus forms kit, $19.95 **Taft Group** 5138 McArthur Boulevard, Washington, DC 20037 202-966-7086

RAISING MONEY FOR THE ARTS

(1979) - proceedings of conference strictly on fundraising which was conducted with the help of the United Way; includes recruiting and training of volunteers, and developing a case for giving, 42pp, $10.00 **American Council for the Arts** 570 Seventh Avenue, New York, NY 10018 212-354-6655

REACH OUT AND RAISE MORE FUNDS: PHONATHON TRAINING VIDEOTAPE

(1986) - an audiovisual designed to help organizations improve their phonathon techniques; takes callers through all of the steps, from greeting to closing; includes administrative guide to help plan and conduct a phonothon, and cards to be used by volunteers while at the phones as reminders of steps to a successful call, 15 minutes, $29.95 (members); $37.50 (nonmembers) **Council for Advancement and Support of Education** Publications Order Department, 80 South Early Street, Alexandria, VA 22304 703-823-6966 (VA)

RESEARCH, DEMONSTRATION, AND EVALUATION STUDIES

(1977) - description of the research program of the Administration for Children, Youth and Families for Fiscal Year 1977; lists specific projects funded by this agency in the context of eight long-range goals, 123pp, complimentary until limited supply is exhausted **US/HHS - Office of Information** Box 1182, Washington, DC 20013 202-475-0257

RESOURCE RAISING: THE ROLE OF NON-CASH ASSISTANCE IN CORPORATE PHILANTHROPY

(1990) - a look at other corporate contributions such as products, services and personnel, which is becoming a trend across the country; includes how-to information for attracting these resources, 56pp, $10.00 **Independent Sector** 1828 L Street, NW, Washington, DC 20036 202-223-8100

THE RICH GET RICHER, THE POOR WRITE PROPOSALS

(1990) - a training manual that makes proposal-writing and other aspects of the fund-raising process more understandable and manageable; includes proposal-writing, researching and potential funding sources, and other fund-raising approaches, 40pp, $10.00 plus $2.50 postage **Citizen Involvement Training Program** 381 Hills South, Room 381, Amherst, MA 01003 413-545-2038

ROAD MAP THROUGH TITLE XX

(1979) - analysis of the issues of regulations governing Title XX funding; allows readers to teach themselves methods of analyzing regulations and to acquire a logical and detailed understanding of Title XX regulations, 138pp, $6.00 **Child Welfare League of America** 440 First Street, NW, Washington, DC 20001 202-638-2952

SOLICITATION SYSTEM

(1980) - help for executives and volunteers in preparing a fund-raising effort; includes the *Handbook for Fund-Raising Executives,* which tells how to use the system and gives detailed guidance on key steps, the instruction booklet, *How to Make Your Mark as a Solicitor of Gifts,* record-keeping, evaluation, and other materials designed for quick reference and immediate use, $15.00/kit **Fund-Raising Institute** Box 365, Ambler, PA 19002 215-646-7019

STRUGGLING THROUGH TIGHT TIMES: A HANDBOOK FOR WOMEN'S AND OTHER NONPROFITS

(1984) - an introductory handbook for women's and other nonprofit organizations; covers diversifying an organization's funding base, improving management, assessing an organization for undertaking income-generating activities, and preliminary feasibility analysis for income-generating projects, 28pp, $4.75 **Women's Action Alliance** 370 Lexington Avenue, Suite 603, New York, NY 10017 212-779-2846

STUDENT GUIDE TO FINANCIAL AID

(annually) - explanation of grant, loan and work-study programs for college, vocational and technical school students, #516V, free (must use item number) **US/Consumer Information Center** , Pueblo, CO 81009

THE SUCCESSFUL GRANTSMANSHIP KIT

(1980) - step-by-step instructions in all areas of grant development - from internal procedures to prospecting and proposal writing; includes "inside tips" from the experts; contains *The Guide to Successful Grantsmanship* (comprehensive manual), *Grant Writing Made Easy* (steps to easier proposal writing), and *Successful Grantsmanship Supplement* (column reprints), $21.00/kit if prepaid; otherwise $25.00 (booklet, *Grant Writing Made Easy,* available separately, $3.50) **Grant Development Institute** 2525 West Main, Littleton, CO 80120 303-795-3000

TOP FUND-RAISING VOLUNTEERS

(1984) - a special issue of *Currents* providing profiles of six top volunteer fund raisers and a volunteer's guide to asking for major gifts; covers training volunteers, common donor questions, and responding to nongivers, 72pp, $6 (members); $7.50 (nonmembers) #22852 **Council for Advancement and Support of Education**

Publications Order Department, 80 South Early Street,
Alexandria, VA 22304 703-823-6966 (VA)

UNO, DOS, TRES, CUATRO...

(1984) - an overview of the Association's survey service, including
a data base on the nation's Hispanic population to provide
assistance to groups needing population information for proposals,
to help assure an accurate population count for allocated funds for
social services, to sample Hispanic populations on specific subject
matter, etc., 6-panel foldout, free **National Association for
Hispanic Elderly** 2727 West Sixth Street, Suite 270 , Los Angeles,
CA 90057 213-487-1922

UP YOUR ACCOUNTABILITY

(1973) - overview of the importance of sound accounting practices
in establishing funding credibility and improving organization's
efficiency, 66pp, $9.95 **Taft Group** 5138 McArthur Boulevard,
Washington, DC 20037 202-966-7086

WHAT MAKES A GOOD PROPOSAL?

(1977) - annotated checklist to help proposal writers, providing
advice based on successful proposals, 8-panel foldout, single copy
free **Foundation Center** 79 Fifth Avenue, New York, NY 10003
212-620-4230

WHAT WILL A FOUNDATION LOOK FOR WHEN YOU
SUBMIT A GRANT PROPOSAL?

(1977) - information for proposal writers based on the Center's
grant file, 8-panel foldout, single copy free **Foundation Center** 79
Fifth Avenue, New York, NY 10003 212-628-4230

WHERE AMERICA'S LARGE FOUNDATIONS MAKE
THEIR GRANTS

(1988) - listing of grants made by more than 600 foundations, most
with assets of more than $10 million who make 80% of foundation
grants; includes address, grant amount and, in many cases, the
purpose of the grant, App. 300pp, $34.50 **Public Service Materials
Center** 415 Lexington Avenue, New York, NY 10017
215-687-0646

WINNING WORDS: A VOLUNTEER'S GUIDE TO ASKING
FOR MAJOR GIFTS

(1984) - a guide created specifically for volunteers explaining
duties of the asker and the civic obligations of the potential donor;
includes most common questions asked by donors, 8pp, $1.50
(quantity discounts; special discounts for members) #22802
Council for Advancement and Support of Education Publications
Order Department, 80 South Early Street, Alexandria, VA 22304
703-823-6966 (VA)

WISE GIVING GUIDE

(monthly) - ratings of nationwide nonprofit organizations based on
National Charities Information Bureau's *Basic Standards of
Philanthropy;* lists according to those who meet standards, have
not provided adequate information, waiting for unresolved
question, being updated; includes list of standards, 20-panel
foldout, single copy free (subscription $20/year) **National Charities
Information Bureau** 19 Union Square West, Sixth Floor, New
York, NY 10003 212-929-6300

GOVERNORS' OFFICES ON VOLUNTEERISM

ALTERNATIVE PROGRAM EVALUATION TECHNIQUES: A HANDBOOK*
(1979) - a comprehensive compilation of information based on the assumption that "whatever you are doing in a program is based on a choice which was decided upon from among many possible alternatives," and having a primary focus on the applicability of program evaluation under conditions where resources are scarce and expert assistance lacking; includes a list of evaluation resources, 182pp, inquire about cost **Virginia Division for Children** 805 East Broad Street, Richmond, VA 23219 804-786-5507

DON'T THINK ABOUT IT... DO IT!
(undated) - recruitment brochure describing the procedure for requesting volunteers or volunteer opportunities, and listing staffed and satellite offices across the state, 6-panel foldout, free **Volunteer Link** Department of Community Affairs , 156 S. State Street, Dover, DE 19903 302-736-4456

GOVERNOR'S VOLUNTEER AWARDS
(annually) - program descriptions and achievements of individual and group recipients of the annual Governor's Volunteer Awards; includes an overview by the Governor and listings of staff and committees involved in the selection process, winners from previous years, and information on nominating volunteers for future awards, 17pp, single copy free **New Jersey Office of Volunteerism** 101 South Broad Street, CN 800, Trenton, NJ 08625-0800 609-292-9069

GUIDEBOOK FOR VOLUNTEERS
(1983) - a quick-reference handbook to answer questions about the State's volunteer program, covering local projects, assignments, supervision, training, recognition, references, confidentiality, and other aspects of the program; includes a glossary of terms and acronyms that are frequently used in the program and other information, 11pp, single copy free **Oregon Volunteer Services Program** Adult & Family Services Division, 415 Public Service Building, Salem, OR 97310 503-373-1561

NEW JERSEY OFFICE OF VOLUNTEERISM
(kept current) - details on the purpose, objectives and services of New Jersey's Office on Volunteerism; includes lists of Voluntary Action Centers (VACs), Directors of Volunteers in Agencies (DOVIAs), and the Governor's Advisory Committee on Private/Public Volunteer Partnerships, 12pp, single copy free **New Jersey Office of Volunteerism** 101 South Broad Street, CN 800, Trenton, NJ 08625-0800 609-292-9069

SPECIAL TASK FORCES AND MEETINGS/OFFICE OF CHILDREN AND YOUTH*
(kept current) - a schedule of titles, purposes, membership, and attendees covering task forces and meetings of the State Office of Children and Youth which include volunteers from both the professional child-worker community, and from the general public, 8 sheets, single packet free (also request a copy of the State law which set up the Office and enabled establishment of the task forces) **Hawaii Office of Children and Youth** PO Box 3044, Kana'ina Building, Honolulu, HI 96802 808-548-7582

VOLUNTEER HANDBOOK
(1982) - a guide providing general information about volunteer opportunities at the Department of Social and Health Services (DSHS), basic information about registration, supervision and benefits for volunteers, and an overview of the kinds of human service activities in which volunteers may be involved, 38pp, single copy free **Washington Office of Volunteerism** OB-44R, Olympia, WA 98504 206-753-5983

VOLUNTEER PROGRAMS OF THE IOWA DEPARTMENT OF SOCIAL SERVICES: STATEWIDE MANUAL
(1980) - one-page descriptions of thirty volunteer programs across the state covering areas of adult corrections, mental health, juvenile institutions, mental retardation, veterans, and the general programs in the individual districts that encompass many areas (requires each of the districts and institutions to develop a program manual based on the format of statewide manual), 51pp, inquire about cost **Iowa Department of Social Services** Hoover State Office Building, Fifth Floor, Des Moines, IA 50319 515-281-4598

HEALTH

...AND ACCESS FOR ALL
(1990) - a comprehensive study on Hispanics and the Medicaid program, which is designed to work in tandem with states to provide medical care to the nation's poor without health insurance; addresses the performance of the program in the seven contiguous states where 84 percent of Hispanics live (Arizona, California, Florida, Illinois, New Jersey, New York and Texas), and ways in which it discriminates against Hispanics, inquire about availability and cost **National Coalition of Hispanic Health & Human Service Organizations** 1030 Fifteenth Street, NW, Suite 1053, Washington, DC 20005 202-371-2100

BECOME A VOLUNTEER IN A CANCER CARE CHAPTER
(undated) - a recruitment brochure explaining the goals and objectives of a Cancer Care Chapter, what volunteers do, and how to start a new chapter, 4-page foldout, free **Cancer Care** Chapters Department, One Park Avenue, New York, NY 10016 212-679-5700

BETTER HEALTH IN LATER YEARS
(1970) - advice on keeping fit at 60, 65, 70, and older through an individually-planned health program for older persons, 28pp, $.50 (quantity discounts) **Public Affairs Committee** 381 Park Avenue, New York, NY 10016 212-683-4331

CANCER CARE: CHAPTER INFORMATION PACKET
(kept current) - a series of manuals covering the various activities and duties of Cancer Care Chapters, such as communications, membership, the program, information, education, and social services; includes guides for the Chapter manager, the fund-raising vice president, and the treasurer, inquire about cost **Cancer Care** Chapters Department, One Park Avenue, New York, NY 10016 212-679-5700

CANCER: FACTS YOU SHOULD KNOW
(undated) - guide on the seven warning signals, detection, treatment and cures, presented in an easy-to-read reference format, 11pp, $.25 **American Medical Association** 535 North Dearborn Street, Chicago, IL 60610 312-645-5000

CONSUMER HEALTH EDUCATION: A DIRECTORY
(1975) - an overview of resources available to assist community groups and individuals needing information to mount or improve health efforts in the community, 45pp, single copy free **US/HHS - Public Health Service** 5600 Fishers Lane, Rockville, MD 20857 301-245-6867

CONTROL YOURSELF
(1990) - a quick-reference brochure designed to encourage patients to follow physician's advice in controlling high blood pressure through medication, diet, exercise, etc., 3-panel foldout, $10.00/100 **Health Education Services** PO Box 7126, Albany, NY 12224 518-474-2121

CRISIS IN HEALTH CARE
(1980) - detailed overview of all aspects of American health care, past mistakes, what can be expected in the future, etc., includes section on where to go for health information, and a comparison of proposed national health plans, 400pp, $6.95 **Acropolis Books** 2400 Seventeenth Street, NW, Washington, DC 20009 202-387-6800

CROSSROADS
(undated) - a packet of information about the hospital's volunteer program for persons coping with incurable illness; includes three-page program description, two brochures (*Crossroads* and *Christian Affirmation to Life: A Statement on Terminal Illness*), and other materials as available, single packet free **Crossroads Program** 4520 Twelfth Street, NE, Washington , DC 20017 202-269-7470

THE FAMILY AND HEALTH CARE
(1985) - overview of the critical interface between families, the health of their members and the health care system designed to support families; includes discussions of recent theory/practice activities, 148pp, FR8501, $15.00 **National Council on Family Relations** 3989 Central Avenue, NE, Suite 550, Minneapolis, MN 55421-3921 612-781-9331

FOCUS ON HEALTH
(quarterly) - a newsletter providing news on health issues, conferences, hospital programs, and other information of interest to the consumer in areas of health and physical fitness, 8pp, free subscription **Wellness Center** Alexandria Hospital, 4320 Seminary Road, Alexandria, VA 22304 703-379-3494

GUIDE FOR VOLUNTEERS

(undated) - a handbook for hospital volunteers covering volunteer department services, getting started, on-the-job hints, courtesies for volunteers, code of ethics, etc., 16pp, single copy free (Also request the 4-panel foldout brochure, *Make Your Day Count!* which answers questions that a new or potential volunteer might have) **Washington Hospital Center** 110 Irving Street, NW, Washington, DC 20010 202-541-6207

GUIDELINES FOR THE USE OF VOLUNTEERS FOR HIGH BLOOD PRESSURE EDUCATION, DETECTION AND CONTROL

(1976) - the basic elements of a volunteer effort to reach the greatest possible number of citizens for blood pressure measurement; covers planning, resource development, publicity and education, recruitment and training of volunteers, operation, follow-up, and further resources, 17pp, single copy free **US/HHS High Blood Pressure Information Center** 4733 Bethesda Avenue, Suite 530, Bethesda, MD 20814 301-951-3260

HEALING AT HOME: A GUIDE TO HEALTH CARE FOR CHILDREN

(1973) - tools to assess health and decide when children show symptoms of illness; cautions against making judgments beyond the framework of the book or when in doubt; includes resource appendix; useful for any child care situation, 192pp, $5.95 **Beacon Press** 25 Beacon Street, Boston, MA 02108 617-742-2110

HEALTH, AGING, ILLNESS AND POVERTY: SOS-2

(1970) - details on how federal programs can bring some relief to the problems of aging; includes guidelines for community programs, 45pp, $2.15 **National Council on the Aging** 600 Maryland Avenue, SW, West Wing 100, Washington, DC 20024 202-479-1200

HEALTH BOOKLET SERIES

(1979/1980) - illustrated guides in areas of health, 15pp each, $.75 each:
- *Shots for Tots* - immunization information (how early, which age groups, community-wide involvement)
- *You and Your Heart* - workings of the heart, importance of exercise, regular checkups; damage smoking, worry, inappropriate diet can do
- *You Should Take a CPR Course (1979)* - case for making as many people as possible proficient in CPR (cardiopulmonary resuscitation), since victim must be revived in 4-6 minutes

Channing L. Bete Company , South Deerfield, MA 01373

HEALTH CARE REPORT

(1971) - tips on what to consider when organizing a health fair; who to involve, what services to offer, roles of coordinator, doctor, community people, 10pp, single copy free **Volunteers in Mission** Division of Voluntary Service, 475 Riverside Drive, New York, NY 10027 212-870-2515

HEALTH FAIR MANUAL

(undated) - description of a low-cost project to bring community health resources to a central location; includes guide for developing a health fair and follow-up suggestions, 16pp, $1.00 **Health Fair Project** Community Activities Department, 15 East 26th Street, New York, NY 10010 212-532-1740

HEALTH MAINTENANCE SERVICE FOR THE OLDER ADULT

(1972) - account of a model program designed to establish a coordinated neighborhood-based health service for older people who are poor or whose health needs may make them poor; includes reminder to employ older people on project staff whenever possible, with suggestions for this purpose, 37pp, $1.10 **National Council on the Aging** 600 Maryland Avenue, SW, West Wing 100, Washington, DC 20024 212-479-1200

HEALTH ORGANIZATIONS OF THE UNITED STATES, CANADA, AND THE WORLD

(1981) - details for more than 1,600 voluntary associations, professional societies, and other groups concerned with health and related fields; lists by geographic location and by subject area, 411pp, $85.00 **Gale Research Company** Book Tower, Detroit, MI 48226 313-961-2242

HEALTH REACH

(bimonthly) - an overview of hospital services, including training programs for the community, *Arlington Foundation* activities and accomplishments, community partnership, and other information to assistant residents in participating in good health practices (geared to Northern Virginia, but a good example of hospital/community interaction), 4pp, single copy free **Arlington Hospital** 1701 North George Mason Drive, Arlington, VA 22205 703-558-6595

HEALTH SERVICES DIRECTORY

(1981) - a comprehensive directory of 20,000 clinics, centers, programs, and services available in the U.S. to treat major areas of health and social concern; arranges information by health or social problem, with 33 chapters covering aging, alcoholism, burns, cancer, deafness, mental health, runaways, smoking, battered women, and other areas, 620pp, $84.00 **Gale Research Company** Book Tower, Detroit, MI 48226 313-961-2242

HELP YOURSELF TO HEALTH

(1980) - an exploration of four major areas of health information: staying healthy and feeling good about oneself; how to get more out of doctor visits; common health problems, including home treatments and determining when to call a doctor; how to buy and take store medicines, 80pp, $2.95 **New Readers Press** Box 131, Syracuse, NY 13210 315-422-9121

HELP YOURSELF TO HEALTH WORKBOOK

(1982) - a tool to reinforce the information presented in *Help Yourself to Health;* includes exercises and suggested projects for each chapter, such as fill-ins, true-false, matching, multiple choice, crossword puzzles, answer keys, 48pp, $2.25 **New Readers Press** Box 131, Syracuse, NY 13210 315-422-9121

HIGH BLOOD PRESSURE PAMPHLET SERIES

(1980) - quick-reference information in both Spanish and English, 4-panel foldouts, free:
- *High Blood Pressure Facts and Fiction*
- *If You're Black, Here Are Some Facts You Should Know about High Blood Pressure*
- *What You Should Know about the National Program to Control High Blood Pressure*

US/HHS - High Blood Pressure Information Center 4733 Bethesda Avenue, Suite 530, Bethesda, MD 20814 301-951-3260

HIGH BLOOD PRESSURE - YOU CAN SAVE LIVES

(1980) - an appeal to community volunteers to mount public awareness, detection and follow-up programs to intervene in cases of high blood pressure and possibly save lives, 4pp, single copy free **B'nai B'rith International** Community Volunteer Services, 1640 Rhode Island Avenue, NW, Washington, DC 20036 202-857-6580

HOME HEALTH SERVICES FOR THE OLDER POOR

(1972) - description of a program presenting a general procedure for organizations/agencies to use in assisting their communities in organizing a home health service for the older poor; includes bibliography, 48pp, $1.10 **National Council on the Aging** 600 Maryland Avenue, SW, West Wing 100, Washington, DC 20024 202-479-1200

HOSPICE: DIVINE REDEEMER MEMORIAL HOSPITAL INFORMATION PACKET

(1984) - packet of information on a program that provides trained volunteers to work with the patient and the family of the patient during the advanced stages of terminal illness; includes 11-page manual in pocketed binder with inserts as available, such as a brochure on the state hospice organization, training curricula, and other materials, single packet free **Divine Redeemer Memorial Hospital** 724 Nineteenth Avenue North, St. Paul, MN 55075 612-450-4500

HOSPITAL AUXILIARY HANDBOOK

(1977) - a guide for operating an auxiliary of unpaid citizens from the community; includes section on the hospital volunteer program, describing the volunteer director's relationship with the auxiliary chairman of volunteers, the hospital, the community, student volunteers, volunteer insurance and recognition, and an idea bank of internal (emergency room, crafts, etc.) and external (blood procurement, patient transportation, etc.) services by volunteers, 94pp, $4.00 **Hospital Association of Pennsylvania** PO Box 608, 1200 Camp Hill Bypass, Camp Hill, PA 17011 717-763-7053

I CAN COPE

(1990) - a brochure describing a program designed to give cancer patients and their families a better understanding of the disease so that they can make informed inquiries to their doctor, and can communicate better as a family; includes details of this free service of the *American Cancer Society,* and information on how a hospital or other health facility can bring the program to the facility, 6-panel foldout (request from your local *American Cancer Society* office) **American Cancer Society, Ohio Division** 3085 West Market Street, Akron , OH 44303 216-867-9445

INJURY PREVENTION: MEETING THE CHALLENGE

(1989) - guidelines from the *National Committee for Injury Prevention and Control* on defining the local injury problem, exercising injury control, and evaluating the effectiveness of injury prevention methods, 304pp, single copy free **US/HHS - National Clearinghouse for Alcohol and Drug Information** PO Box 2345, Rockville, MD 20852 301-468-2600

KINDERGARTEN SCREENING INSTRUMENT

(1975) - comprehensive manual for a volunteer program in identifying problems that may require medical attention, observation, or other treatment; includes job descriptions, training information, record-keeping aids, basic medical measuring instruments instruction, notes to parents in both English and Spanish, etc., 80pp, $12.00 (free information brochure) **Volunteers in Public Schools** 3830 Richmond Avenue, Houston, TX 77027 713-892-6384

MANUAL FOR HOSPICE VOLUNTEERS

(kept current) - overview of the Hospice program, requirements for volunteering, areas of hospice care, and certification for the hospice volunteer; includes guidelines and directives as well as information in insurance coverage and resources, 11pp, single copy free in packet described elsewhere, inquire about cost of additional copies **Divine Redeemer Memorial Hospital** 724 Nineteenth Street, South St. Paul, MN 55075 612-450-4500

MEDICAL AND HEALTH INFORMATION DIRECTORY

(1980) - descriptive coverage of modern health care activity with more than 16,000 entries providing basic data on agencies, institutions, companies and associations concerned with health care at state and national levels, arranged by subject, 850pp, $160.00 **Gale Research Company** Book Tower, Detroit, MI 48226 313-961-2242

PEOPLE HELPING PEOPLE

(1989) - A guide for the youth leader in areas of administrative roles and relationships, starting a Red Cross youth involvement program, programs and services for youth, national resources, chapter and station program examples, awards and recognition, and the five key commitments and aspects of career development for youth (although addressed to Red Cross youth leaders, adaptable to any youth-oriented volunteer program), 9pp, single copy free **American Red Cross** National Headquarters, 430 Seventeenth Street, NW, Washington, DC 20006 202-737-8300

PEOPLE'S GUIDE TO HEALTH CARE: HOW TO ORGANIZE A HOSPITAL GRIEVANCE COMMITTEE

(undated) - a model for groups challenging the power structure of medical institutions such as hospitals; tells how to make initial community survey, and describes one group's first confrontations with administrators, 10pp, single copy free **Legal Aid Society** 2108 Payne Avenue, Cleveland, OH 44144 216-621-4415

PLANNING HEALTH SERVICES FOR THE ELDERLY: SOS-8

(1971) - a guide for community planners, aging residents, and providers of health services emphasizing the importance of developing health care programs only when the older people need and want them; includes specific recommendations and funding sources, 29pp, $2.15 **National Council on the Aging** 600 Maryland Avenue, SW, West Wing 100, Washington, DC 20024 202-479-1200

PRISON HEALTH

(1973) - special issue of monthly newsletter for those trying to understand the facts and politics behind prison health; emphasizes the urgent need for community support and discusses the struggles of groups in New York and San Francisco, 12pp, $.60 **Health/PAC Bulletin** 17 Murray Street, New York, NY 10007 212-267-8890

THE PULSE OF LIFE

(1976) - guide for establishing a volunteer blood donor program to assure a sufficient supply of blood when needed; sums up the advantage of giving blood over buying insurance to guarantee the cost of blood with program slogan, "You can't transfuse dollars"; prefaced with a letter from a Red Cross official on the subject, 6pp, $.25 **B'nai B'rith International** Community Volunteer Services, 1640 Rhode Island Avenue, NW, Washington, DC 20036 202-857-6580

REGULATIONS AND HEALTH: UNDERSTANDING AND INFLUENCING THE PROCESS

(1979) - straight talk to those concerned with health on the consequences of waiting too long to challenge a federal regulation; states the difference between a law (stated in broad terms and relatively permanent) and a regulation (strategy to implement the law) and the four stages of possible intervention, progressively more difficult and costly, 66pp, $8.00 (members $7.00) **National Health Council** 622 Third Avenue, 34th Floor, New York, NY 10017 212-972-2700

THE SENIOR CITIZEN'S 10-MINUTES-A-DAY FITNESS PLAN

(1989) - a plan for an exercise program that requires no equipment or complicated exercises, developed with an awareness of senior limitations to build muscle tone, promote cardiovascular health and stimulate blood flow; includes two dozen hidden excercises in everyday activities, and sensible eating patterns, $3.50 **Pilot Books** 103 Cooper Street, Babylon, NY 11702 516-422-2225

SICK FOR JUSTICE: HEALTH CARE AND UNHEALTHY CONDITIONS

(1978) - activist's handbook centered around development of a base for legislation including areas of profit motive, community and consumer control/input, attaching occupational/environmental causes, and providing cradle-to-grave health coverage; uses the south as an example of health care inadequacy that has not changed for thirty years, 128pp, $3.00 (2/$4.50) **Southern Exposure** PO Box 230, Chapel Hill, NC 27514 919-929-2141

SMOKING OR HEALTH

(1971) - a summary of the Surgeon General's comprehensive report in simple understandable language with many illustrations included to hold the interest of those not likely to read available detailed reports; uses a slight change in the title - from Smoking and Health - to further emphasize the message of the federal report, 39pp, $1.50 **TANE Press** 6778 Greenville, Dallas, TX 75231 214-363-5305

SO YOU'VE GOT HIGH BLOOD PRESSURE

(1990) - a guide that reinforces physician recommendations for controlling hypertension; includes a blood pressure recording chart; uses cartoon graphics and simple, straightforward language (both Spanish and English), 22pp, pocket-size (poster with same theme, 17"x22", $1.50) **Health Education Services** PO Box 7126, Albany, NY 12224 518-474-2121

SOME QUESTIONS AND ANSWERS ABOUT VD

(1980) - the case for using "Very Dangerous" synonymously with Venereal Disease - seeking immediate help from the nearest possible source; includes numbers for the VD National Hotline operated by the Association, and the 12 most frequently asked questions on VD today, 8-panel foldout, single pamphlet free, additional $9.00/100; $70.00/1,000 [Also request similar leaflets on herpes, AIDS, NGU and PID, and related materials] **American Social Health Association** Box 13827, Research Triangle Pk, NC 27709 919-361-2742

SOUTH BAY FREE CLINIC: CHECK US OUT

(undated) - an overview of a clinic founded in 1969 by concerned citizens; includes information on satellite clinics, services offered, funding sources, and other information, 6-panel foldout, single copy free **South Bay Free Clinic** 1807 Manhattan Boulevard, Manhattan Beach, CA 90266 213-376-2149

SPIRIT AND BREATH: A LUNG CANCER REHABILITATION PROGRAM VISITOR'S MANUAL

(undated) - a training manual providing suggestions to the volunteer for visiting patients who have or have had lung cancer; includes sections on guidelines, preparation, the visit, a message to the physician, follow-up, and questions and answers, 11pp, free on request **Spirit and Breath Association** 8210 Elmwood Avenue, Suite 209, Skokie, IL 60077 708-673-1384

SPIRIT AND BREATH: A REHABILITATION PROGRAM FOR LUNG CANCER PEOPLE

(undated) - a brochure describing the overall Spirit and Breath program, 6-panel foldout, free on request **Spirit and Breath Association** 8210 Elmwood Avenue, Suite 209, Skokie, IL 60077 708-673-1384

SPIRIT AND BREATH AFTER SURGERY

(undated) - guide published by American Cancer Society's Patient-to-Patient Service describing the Spirit and Breath program and offering hints for making the transition from surgery to home, 36pp, single copy free (also available from local offices of the American Cancer Society) **Spirit and Breath Association** 8210 Elmwood Avenue, Suite 209, Skokie, IL 60077 708-673-1384

SPIRIT AND BREATH: COORDINATOR-TRAINER'S GUIDE AND PROCEDURE MANUAL

(1983) - a guide for the leader of a program developed to provide a supportive atmosphere for persons who have or have had lung cancer (often a veteran from the Volunteer Patient Visitors Group); includes information such as: Overview of the American Cancer Society, Medical Update by a Doctor or Surgeon, a detailed outline of the Coordinator's duties, an other information, 10pp, free on request **Spirit and Breath Association** 821 Elmwood Avenue, Suite 209, Skokie, IL 60077 708-673-1384

SPIRIT AND BREATH: PATIENT TO PATIENT EXERCISE MANUAL

(undated) - a manual describing exercises effective in rehabilitation, unpaged, free on request [also available free from the Illinois Division of the American Cancer Society in Chicago] **Spirit and Breath Association** 8210 Elmwood Avenue, Suite 209, Skokie, IL 60077 708-673-1384

STROKE: NEW APPROACHES TO PREVENTION AND TREATMENT

(1979) - explanation of the causes of a stroke, warning signs, the importance of treating "little strokes" treatment/rehabilitation, etc., 20pp, $.50 (quantity discounts) **Public Affairs Committee** 381 Park Avenue South, New York, NY 10016 212-683-4331

TO SMOKE OR NOT TO SMOKE

(1980) - insight into why people start to smoke, good reasons for not smoking, the damage that is done to the body, ways to kick the habit, the negative image presented to children and youth, etc., 15pp, $.75 **Channing L. Bete Company** , South Deerfield, MA 01373

TOBACCO ABUSE

(1978) - reasons for not starting, advice for kicking the habit; uses "straight talk" geared to youth on health effects (from depleting stored vitamins to brain damage), and social aspects (bad breath, ventilation problems when nonsmokers present); presents a program for quitting, but emphasizes that willpower is the only sure method, 6-panel foldout, $.15 **Do It Now Foundation** PO Box 5115, Phoenix, AZ 85010 602-257-0797

VD BEGETS VD

(1979) - an educational test on things a teenager should know about VD; written to be useful for junior high school age and older, 8-panel foldout, $.15 (quantity discounts) **Do It Now Foundation** PO Box 21126, Phoenix, AZ 85036 602-257-0797

VD DOESN'T HAVE TO BE...IF YOU KNOW WHAT IT'S ABOUT

(undated) - program ideas and examples on how to implement speakers bureaus, hotlines, a print campaign, etc., to assist the community in educating the public about VD, 16pp, $.20 **B'nai B'rith International** Community Volunteer Services, 1640 Rhode Island Avenue, NW, Washington, DC 20036 202-857-6580

VOLUNTEER PROGRAM: INFORMATION PACKET
(undated) - an overview of a program involving volunteers in
activities relating to lung problems, such as Stop Smoking Clinic,
Community and School Health Education (speakers), Medical
Presentations, and other programs; includes sample forms and a
bill of rights for volunteers, single packet free **Lung Association of
Northern Virginia** 9735 Main Street, Fairfax, VA 22031
703-591-4131

A VOLUNTEER SERVICE DEPARTMENT
(1973) - guidelines for hospital administrators on establishing and
maintaining a program involving volunteers in the hospital;
includes purposes and planning, organizing, managing and
evaluating the program, 8pp, $1.50 **Hospital Association of
Pennsylvania** PO Box 608, 1200 Camp Hill Bypass, Camp Hill,
PA 17011 717-763-7653

**VOLUNTEER STAFFING FOR COMMUNITY HEALTH
PLANNING**
(1982) - a manual for people involved in the "new realities of
health planning" to help them mobilize their volunteer workers to
offset funding restrictions; discusses how volunteers have
participated in health planning in the past through boards,
committees, and councils, and how that role will be expanded in
an era of reduced resources; addresses agency self-assessment,
motivational factors, job design, volunteer recruitment, volunteer
training and coordination, and committee development; examines
functional areas in which volunteers can play important roles;
appends annotated bibliography **Institute for Health Planning** Two
East Mifflin Street, Madison, WI 53705 608-255-8891

VOLUNTEERS OF AMERICA CLINIC
(undated) - overview of a clinic for senior citizens involving
volunteers from the local Volunteer Center, and through personal
contacts of the staff with people who have had experience in the
medical field; describes medical, nursing and footcare services,
6-panel foldout, single copy free **Senior Clinic** 537 SE Adler,
Portland, OR 97214 503-232-2233

THE WAY TO WELLNESS
(quarterly) - a calendar of free lectures, free classes, and classes
offered for a nominal fee with discounts for seniors in many areas
of health, parenting, aging, physical fitness, self-image, investment
planning, etc., 12-panel foldout, free subscription **Wellness Center**
Alexandria Hospital, 4320 Seminary Road, Alexandria, VA 22304
703-379-3494

WHAT EVERYONE SHOULD KNOW ABOUT CANCER
(1979) - illustrated guide to inform individuals and groups about
ways to increase the chances of cancer cures; presents both fact
and fiction with rationales and reference to other resources which
both provide information and use volunteer help for public
awareness programs, 115pp, $.75 **Channing L. Bete Company** ,
South Deerfield, MA 01373

WHAT EVERYONE SHOULD KNOW ABOUT VD
(1980) - discussion of the escalation of VD as a health problem,
some of the reasons for this rise, the symptoms, and the need for
more public education campaigns, 15pp, $.75 (quantity discounts)
Channing L. Bete Company , South Deerfield, MA 01373

WHY, CHARLIE BROWN, WHY? (VIDEO)
(1990) - an audivisual using cartoon characters popular with
children to help youngsters understand pediatric cancer and enable
them to cope when a playmate or classmate is diagnosed with the
disease, 30 minutes, inquire about availability and cost **Columbia
Broadcasting System** 51 West 52nd Street, New York, NY 10019
212-975-3285

HOUSING

ANSWERS TO QUESTIONS ON SECTION 8: LOWER INCOME HOUSING ASSISTANCE
(kept current) - a guidebook describing the existing Section 8 program, who is eligible, what housing is eligible, advantages and disadvantages, etc.; includes a "key word list" leading the user to specific information; e.g., the elderly, the handicapped, 50pp, $8.00 (members $5.00) **National Association of Housing & Redevelopment Officials** 1320 Eighteenth Street, NW, Washington, DC 20036 202-429-2960

AOA FACT SHEET: HOUSING FOR OLDER PEOPLE
(kept current) - overview of some of the possibilities for providing housing that will meet the needs and preferences of older people; includes directory of retirement housing facilities, 4pp, free **US/HHS - Administration on Aging** 330 Independence Avenue, SW, Washington, DC 20201 202-619-0724

BLACK SUBURBANIZATION IN THE MID-1970'S
(1978) - a look at the results of the Federal Fair Housing Act of 1968 and the alteration in suburban racial patterns in the ten-year period following its passage; describes the new black suburbanite and explores the implications of this trend for equal opportunity policies and programs in the future (summary report; inquire about full report), 17pp, $1.00 (quantity discounts) **National Committee Against Discrimination in Housing** 1425 H Street, NW Washington, DC 20005 202-783-8250

BUILDING HOUSES IN PARTNERSHIP WITH GOD'S PEOPLE IN NEED
(kept current) - a packet of brochures, fact sheets, and other materials as available describing a nonprofit Christian housing ministry which builds and renovates homes for the needy; describes its policy of *no profit/no interest* and the requirement for 500 hours of *sweat equity* required from the potential owner and family (affiliated with the international organization), single packet free **Habitat for Humanity of Rhode Island** Box 3265, Elmwood Station, Providence, RI 02907 401-831-5424

BUILDING HOUSING FOR SENIOR CITIZENS OF LIMITED INCOME
(1979) - basic manual for local volunteer services groups on initiating and operating a building/managing program of housing for senior citizens (serves all races, religions, national origins),
12pp, single copy free (inquire about related slide and sound program) **B'nai B'rith International** Senior Citizens Housing Committee, 1640 Rhode Island Avenue, NW, Washington, DC 20036 202-857-6580

BUILDING SOUTH
(1980) - overview of building trends in the South, with emphasis on community design centers created to stem the flow of overnight communities by developers and work to retain some of the architectural character of the deeply traditional South; cites volunteer role in centers, 128pp, $3.00 (2/$4.50) **Southern Exposure** Box 531, Durham, NC 27702 919-688-8167

CHISS INFORMATION PACKET
(kept current) - packet of materials that describe the advantages and disadvantages of various housing options, as well as guidelines for each option; appends description of the CHISS (Consumer Housing Information Service for Seniors) information and referral program sponsored nationally by the American Association of Retired Persons (AARP) and locally by various organizations and agencies on aging, unpaged, single copy free **Fairfax Area Agency on Aging** 11242 Waples Mill Road, Suite 100, Fairfax , VA 22030-6036 703-246-5411

COMMON QUESTIONS AND ANSWERS ON SELF-HELP HOUSING
(1978) - answers to 35 general and technical questions on self-help housing; covers participation of female heads of households, city employees building country homes, etc., 5pp, one copy free (additional, $.75 each) **Rural America** 725 Fifteenth Street, NW, Suite 900, Washington, DC 20005 202-628-1480

COOPERATIVE HOUSING IN THE USA
(undated) - facts about the advantages of co-operative housing for low-income families and the benefits to communities in providing good housing at low cost; excludes reference to luxury co-ops such as Watergate, which are not considered representative of the cooperative housing movement as originally intended, 22pp, $.50 **Cooperative Housing Foundation** 2501 M Street, NW, Suite 450, Washington, DC 20037 202-887-0700

COOPERATIVE HOUSING: PEOPLE HELPING EACH OTHER

(undated) - facts about the advantages of co-operative housing for low-income families and the benefits to communities in providing good housing at low cost; excludes reference to luxury co-ops such as Watergate, which are not considered representative of the cooperative housing movement as originally intended, 22pp, $.50 **National Association of Housing Cooperatives** 2501 M Street, NW, Suite 451, Washington, DC 20037 202-887-0706

DELIVERY OF HUMAN RESOURCES UNDER THE TARGET PROJECTS PROGRAM
(1977) - comprehensive overview of how 142 housing authorities spent 91 million dollars in HUD's Target Projects Program funds to improve conditions for the poor in housing projects; discusses involvement of resident committees and councils in the planning and evaluation process, the emergence of strong resident leaders, and the community resources that were mobilized from public/private sectors; program areas included tenant economic development, security and safety, I&R, recreation, employment, and many other areas, 136pp, $7.50 (members $4.50) **National Association of Housing & Redevelopment Officials** 1320 Eighteenth Street, NW, Washington , DC 20036 202-429-2960

DO IT YOURSELF
(1978) - illustrated, quick-reference handbook to assist homeowners in weatherizing their homes to decrease costs and increase family comfort; includes guidelines on weatherstripping, caulking, windows, underpinning, roof patching, vents, etc., and concludes with a number of specific energy tips, and a list of additional resources, 22pp, single copy free **Combined Community Action** PO Box 753, 4th and Harris, Smithville, TX 78957 412-237-2434

FAIR HOUSING AND FUNDING: A LOCAL STRATEGY
(1976) - a manual providing basic information necessary to seek and gain funding for those interested in fair housing at every level of the community; combines the manual with an offer of assistance every step of the way; e.g., determining which of the techniques outlined in the manual apply to a particular community situation, 200pp, single copy free **US/HUD - Office of Policy Development** 400 Seventh Street, SW, Washington, DC 20410 202-755-6417

FAIR MORTGAGE LENDING: A HANDBOOK FOR COMMUNITY GROUPS
(1978) - a description of the new enforcement program on race and sex discrimination in home finance; suggestions for fair housing, civil rights, and community groups for specific action steps to take to see that local lenders are complying with fair housing laws, 21pp, single copy free **Center for National Policy Review** 620 Michigan Avenue, NE, Washington , DC 20064 202-832-8525

GRANNY FLATS LOAN PROGRAM
(1983) - a packet of materials describing the county's low-interest loan program for the home owner who wishes to construct a separate dwelling unit in the home for elderly or handicapped persons; emphasizes the benefits of the "reverse" situation in which the elderly or handicapped become the landlords under this program and rent to tenants to acquire extra income, services, security or companionship [operates the granny program under the Home Improvement Loan Program (HILP) offering loans of up to $15,000 at 9.99% interest], single packet free **Fairfax County Redevelopment and Housing Authority** Municipal Building, 10455 Main Street, Fairfax, VA 22030 703-691-2914

GUIDE TO FAIR HOUSING LAW ENFORCEMENT
(1979) - a manual that describes the first effort of a federal agency (HUD) to encourage the use of "testers" by private fair housing groups to collect evidence against real estate practitioners

suspected of violating the law; includes guidelines that permit all concerned citizens to participate in a national law enforcement effort, 64pp, single copy free **National Committee Against Discrimination in Housing** 1425 H Street, NW , Washington, DC 20005 202-783-8250

GUIDELINES: DEVELOPING A CHORE SERVICE & MINOR HOME REPAIR MAINTENANCE PROGRAM
(undated) - a guide for developing a handyman service which provides employment for older persons, and volunteer opportunities for older persons, youth, and others while improving the living conditions of the elderly, 9pp, $.80 **National Voluntary Organizations for Independent Living for the Aging** 600 Maryland Avenue, SW, West Wing 100, Washington, DC 20024 202-479-1200

HOME BUYER'S CHECK LIST
(kept current) - yes/no questions for the potential home buyer on neighborhood, house, energy checkpoints, expenses, and budgetary limitations, 9pp, single copy free **U.S. League of Savings Institutions** 111 East Wacker Drive, Chicago, IL 60601 312-644-3100

HOME MAINTENANCE AND REPAIR PROGRAM FOR THE ELDERLY
(1973) - description of a repair and maintenance service to assist the older poor while hiring other poor to perform the service, 34pp, $1.10 **National Council on the Aging** 600 Maryland Avenue, NW, West Wing 100, Washington, DC 20024 202-479-1200

HOUSING FOR ALL UNDER LAW
(1978) - recommendations of the American Bar Association Advisory Commission on Housing and Urban Growth regarding a plan that would consider housing for all - particularly low- and moderate-income households; advocates the involvement of citizen groups with representatives of the public and private sector in all phases of any future plan, 8pp executive summary, single copy free **US/HUD - Office of Policy Development** 400 Seventh Street, SW, Washington, DC 20410 202-755-6417

HOUSING FOR THE POOR: A NEGLECTED NEED
(kept current) - overview of one of the major priorities of the Community Services Administration; provides facts on funding for housing by CSA itself, and through CSA's efforts to mobilize funds from agencies with large sums to spend on housing for the rural poor; lists types of services (self-help housing, rural home repair, rental management, home ownership, construction, planning, water and sewer programs, technical assistance), 6-panel foldout, free [Responsibilities for the former Community Services Administration are now in the Office of Community Services, D-HHS; if above not available, related materials will be substituted] **US/HHS - Office of Community Services** PO Box 1182, Washington, DC 20201 202-653-2010

HOUSING JUSTICE IN SMALL CLAIMS COURTS
(1979) - executive summary of a report on the use of small claims courts for housing-related issues, the prohibition by some states of the use of an attorney, efforts by 33 states to speed up, simplify and/or reduce the expense of the process, and more, 31pp, single copy free (inquire about full report) **American Bar Association** 750 North Lake Shore Drive, Chicago, IL 60611 312-988-5000

HOW THE FEDERAL GOVERNMENT BUILDS GHETTOS
(1968) - a tracing of the "ghetto system" from the 1930's to the late 1960's with 17 charges and recommendations for federal housing authorities; includes information on ways the federal government tried to reverse the alienation and tension created by

this dual housing system (this booklet now most useful as a companion guide to *Black Suburbanization in the Mid 1970's*, separate entry) **National Committee Against Discrimination in Housing** 1425 H Street, NW , Washington, DC 20005 202-783-8250

IMPROVING THE LIVING ENVIRONMENT OF THE ELDERLY POOR: SOS-7

(1971) - manual for community groups on housing assistance programs and related services such as safety to demonstrate that supportive environments are inseparable from the housing requirements of the elderly; includes bibliography, 24pp, $2.15 **National Council on the Aging** 600 Maryland Avenue, SW, West Wing 100, Washington, DC 20024 202-479-1200

INSULATE YOUR HOME

(1979) - guide to selecting the right insulation based on climate, (resistance) ratings, etc.; cautions about rendering insulation less effective by neglect of necessary vapor barriers, ventilation, caulking, etc. 15pp, $.75 (quantity discounts) **Channing L. Bete Company** , South Deerfield, MA 01373

LIMITED ACCESS

(1977) - discussion of the small nonmetropolitan areas where the need for participation in the Community Development Block Grant (CDBG) program is greatest, but actual participation very minimal due to lack of funds to maintain the application process; includes comprehensive recommendations to increase benefits of the program to the poor - addressed separately to Congress, HUD, and the Community Services Administration, 67pp, single copy free [Responsibilities for the former Community Services Administration are now in the Office of Community Services, D-HHS; if above not available, related materials will be substituted] **US/HHS - Office of Community Services** PO Box 1182, Washington, DC 20201 202-653-2020

MEDIA ACTION HANDBOOK

(1975) - practical, step-by-step suggestions for planning, initiating, and carrying forward an overall information program involving television, radio, and the press, 57pp, $4.00 **National Committee Against Discrimination in Housing** 1425 H Street, NW , Washington, DC 20005 202-223-6250

MONITORING YOUR CDBG PROGRAM

(1977) - guidelines on organizing a monitoring project to oversee the Community Development Block Grant Program to assure maximum opportunity for communities with the greatest need, 6pp, $.40 **League of Women Voters of the US** 1730 M Street, NW, Washington, DC 20036 202-429-1965

MORTGAGE BURNING FUND INFORMATION PACKET

(1990) - information on a program that sprung up when the media uncovered more and more stories about the elderly losing their homes because of "small print" in equity loans; includes steps being taken to change legislation while raising funds for excessive interest and other charges now levied "within legal parameters," unpaged, free with $1.69 postage (stamps OK) **Mortgage Burning Fund** PO Box 762, Annandale, VA 22003 703-354-6270

NO MORE SHACKS: THE DARING VISION OF HABITAT FOR HUMANITY

(1986) - history and overview of *Habitat for Humanity,* a program founded in 1976 by the book's author, Millard Fuller, which builds homes for purchase by low-income families, at minimal cost, without interest or profit, and involves the families themselves in "sweat equity" to help with their new dwellings (usually 500 hours required), 220pp, available free with promise to "pass it on" once

read (contributions accepted) **Habitat for Humanity International** Habitat and Church Streets, Americus, GA 31709-3423 912-924-6935

OF THE PEOPLE, BY THE PEOPLE, FOR THE PEOPLE: COOPERATIVE HOUSING FOR RURAL AMERICA

(1979) - a handbook for developing small and low-income housing cooperatives; includes a survey of cooperatives with fewer than 100 members, new observations on benefits of cooperative housing (political power, transportation assistance, etc.), 157pp, $5.00 donation (to be used to finance a Spanish translation) **Rural America** 725 Fifteenth Street, NW, Suite 900, Washington, DC 20005 202-628-1480

PLANNING AND DEVELOPING A SHARED LIVING PROJECT

(1979) - a guide for neighborhood and grassroots community groups on starting and maintaining congregate housing projects for older people (an arrangement for from three to forty people to share space but maintain needed privacy); includes sections on funding, evaluation, and national resources, 12Opp, $2.00 **Action for Boston Community Development** 178 Tremont Street, Boston, MA 02111 617-597-3000

SELECTING AND BUYING A MOBILE HOME

(1974) - pictorial script to provide facts about homes that cost from $5,000 to $21,000 and include major appliances and other furnishings; includes questions important to purchasers - especially the elderly who are retiring to mobile homes in increasing numbers, 28pp, single copy free (ask about related slides and filmstrips) **US/DoA - Photography Division** Independence Avenue, (Between 12th & 14th Sts.), Washington, DC 20250 202-447-2791

10 QUESTIONS AND ANSWERS FOR LANDLORDS & TENANTS

(undated) - help for tenants on filing a complaint, rights and responsibilities of landlord and tenant, handling of problems in areas of heat, insect infestation, peeling lead paint, etc.; includes information on how local civic groups can work with city hall, 17pp, single copy free **Chicago Building Department** Complaint and Information Section, City Hall, 8th Floor, Chicago, IL 60602 312-922-7925

TENANTS' RIGHTS

(3rd ed. 1990) - handbook aimed at informing tenants of their rights, and providing hints to assist them in dealing with landlords; includes problems involving rent increases, poor housing, evictions, "repair and deduct," etc., 15pp, single copy free **North Shore Community Action Programs** 98 Main Street, Peabody, MA 01960 617-531-0767

TRENDS IN HOUSING

(bimonthly) - ongoing news on developments in housing, including fair housing activities, across the U.S., 12pp, $10/year **National Committee Against Discrimination in Housing** 1425 H Street, NW Washington, DC 20005 202-783-8250

UNDERSTANDING FAIR HOUSING

(1973) - overview of the influence of a variety of public and private forces on patterns of residency in the U.S; discusses prospects for the future in solving the dual housing market dilemma; includes background reading list, 19pp, single copy free **Civil Rights Clearinghouse** 1121 Vermont Avenue, NW, Washington, DC 20005 202-254-6600

WISE HOME BUYING
(1975) - guide to precautionary measures that should be taken to avoid "getting in over your head," relying on a broker's oral promises, finding hidden defects, being overwhelmed by glitter, etc.; includes financing and credit information, HUD Regional Offices, etc., 36pp, single copy free **US/HUD - Office of Information** 451 Seventh Street, SW, Washington, DC 20410 202-755-5735

INFORMATION & REFERRAL

ADOLESCENT SUICIDE: MENTAL HEALTH CHALLENGE
(1979) - appeal to families, counselors and others to become more aware and understanding of the turbulence of adolescence, and take steps that will help reverse the trend toward sharp increases in suicide among teenagers; cites the heavier increase among black teenagers, and some of the factors involved; refers to the 200 suicide prevention centers around the country where emergency advice, help, referral are offered, and the 700 federally-sponsored community mental health centers, 20pp, $.50 (bulk rates) **Public Affairs Committee** 381 Park Avenue South, New York, NY 10016 212-683-4331

AIDS EASY-TO-READ BROCHURE SERIES
(1989) - a series of brochures addressing specific areas of concern regarding AIDS (foldout brochures; $.30 each; quantity discounts):
- *AIDS Lifeline: The Best Defense Against AIDS is Information* - basic facts, prevention, cause, risk, transmission, symptoms, treatment and diagnosis.
- *When a Friend Has AIDS* - specific ways to communicate, consider, listen and touch.
- *Straight Talk about Sex and AIDS* - a guide to promoting open communication between partners.
- *Your Child and AIDS* - answers to questions about AIDS risk through bites, cuts, bruises or contact with other children who have AIDS (National Center for Disease Control Guidelines).
- *Women and AIDS* - guidelines on AIDS prevention for women; addresses concerns about pregnancy and breastfeeding.
- *Fact vs Fiction* - ten 'true' or 'false' statements about AIDS transmission, diagnosis, and who can get the disease.

San Francisco AIDS Foundation 333 Valencia Street, PO Box 6182, San Francisco, CA 94101-6182 415-861-3397

AIRS
(six/year) - newsletter providing current news on areas affecting information and referral operations, free to members; others inquire **Alliance of Information and Referral Systems** 47 South Pennsylvania Street, #405, Indianapolis, IN 46204 317-637-6101

CALMWORD
(quarterly) - newsletter reporting on new developments and information resources in the area of child abuse, free subscription **Child Abuse Listening Mediation** PO Box 718, Santa Barbara, CA 93102 805-682-1366 (offices)

CHALLENGE TO UNITED WAY: INFORMATION & REFERRAL
(1978) - a resource for new and established information and referral (I&R) services; discusses the issues, definitions, and basic program elements of I&R services; covers the network concept and other areas; provides examples of I&R services and a challenge to volunteer and public agencies to provide workable programs between recipients and providers of services, 12pp, #UCR0182, $2.50 **United Way of America** 701 North Fairfax Street, Alexandria, VA 22314-2045 703-836-7100

CHILD ABUSE AND NEGLECT HELPLINES
(1978) - description of a helpline program, and a listing of programs by region with telephone numbers; includes bibliography, 8pp, single copy free **US/HHS - National Center on Child Abuse and Neglect** PO Box 1182, Washington, DC 20201 202-755-7500

CHILD PROTECTIVE SERVICES ANNUAL REPORT
(annually) - a view of child abuse and neglect in the Commonwealth and a statement of what the Department is doing to help families provide a safe environment for children who are at risk; appends statistical charts on disposition of complaints, and types of maltreatment, 24pp, single copy free **Child Protective Services** 8007 Discovery Drive, Richmond, VA 23229-8699 804-662-9204 (office)

CHILD PROTECTIVE SERVICES IN VIRGINIA
(kept current) - a widely-distributed brochure explaining Virginia's *Child Abuse and Neglect Act,* local social service agency responsibility, community responsibility, and the rights of accused parents, 8-panel foldout, free **Child Protective Services** Virginia Dept. of Social Services, 8007 Discovery Drive, Richmond, VA 23229-8699 804-662-9204 (office)

COMMUNICATION-HELP CENTER PROCEDURES MANUAL
(1979) - manual used in student volunteer center on a college campus; includes program description, mechanics of operation, areas covered and theories/ethics in each area, evaluation, etc., 73pp, $5.00 **Communication-Help Center** Morris Avenue, Union, NJ 07083 201-289-2100

COMMUNITY INFORMATION SERVICE: A DIRECTORY OF PUBLIC LIBRARY INVOLVEMENT

(1974) - results of a questionnaire sent to state libraries plus 62 individual libraries; provides information on type of information-providing activity, date opened, staffing, funding, etc., 92pp, $5.00 **University of Maryland Book Store** University Boulevard, College Park, MD 20740 301-454-5447

CONTEMPORARY ISSUES

(various dates) - an ongoing series of booklets covering topics such as substance abuse, child abuse, youth suicide, growing-up female, and education; addresses adults working with girls and designed to complement Girl Scout handbooks and other program materials; includes suggested activities for different age groups, program links that tie the booklet in with other materials, and comprehensive bibliographies and lists of national and regional resources, lengths vary, inquire about availability and cost **Girl Scouts of the USA** 830 Third Avenue, New York, NY 10022 212-940-7800

CRISIS CENTER/HOTLINE: A GUIDEBOOK TO BEGINNING AND OPERATING

(1972) - covers all aspects of establishing a service, including legal considerations, financing tips, evaluation, etc., 144pp, $14.75 **Charles C. Thomas, Publisher** 2600 South First Street, Springfield, IL 62717 217-789-8980

CRISIS COUNSELLING: EMOTIONAL FIRST AID

(Rev. 1990) - a comprehensive guide designed to assist crisis interveners - both professionals and volunteers - in every phase of their work with people in crisis and in those in emergency situations; includes several fields across this area, including law enforcement, mental health and education; bases contents on nearly a decade and a half of experience in conducting forums and other training exercises, 419pp, inquire about cost **American Academy of Crisis Interveners** c/o Edward S. Rosenbluh, Ph.D. , 218 Breckenridge Lane, Suite 102, Louisville, KY 40207 502-896-0200

CRISIS SERVICES FOR CAMPUS AND COMMUNITY: A HANDBOOK FOR THE VOLUNTEER

(2nd Pr. 1989) - handbook designed to prepare untrained volunteers in crisis intervention; describes evolution of a number of volunteer programs from the perspective of experience and participation, including training, consultation and supervision; discusses volunteer feelings and needs, results by volunteers after training, community resources, public agencies available for referral, volunteer retention, and evaluation; appends reference lists for each chapter, tables, footnotes and an index, 248pp, inquire about cost **Charles C. Thomas, Publisher** 2600 First Street, PO Box 4709, Springfield , IL 62708-4709 217-789-8990

DIRECTORY OF INFORMATION AND REFERRAL SERVICES

(annually) - a guide to information and referral services in the U.S. and Canada including names, addresses, telephone numbers, contact persons, hours of operation, type of I&R, and geographic area served; includes Call for Action (radio) and Federal Information Centers, $15.00/members; $17.00/non-members, plus $2.50 postage/handling for each **AIRS Directory Project** 47 South Pennsylvania Avenue, Suite 405, Indianapolis, IN 46204 317-637-6101

DIRECTORY OF UNITED WAY AFFILIATED INFORMATION AND REFERRAL SERVICES

(1981) - a listing of more than 300 information and referral services that meet the criteria outlined in National Standards for Information and Referral Services; includes the county served, organizational auspices, Metro size, contact person and address for each I&R service, #0201, $2.00 **United Way of America** 701 North Fairfax Street, Alexandria, VA 22314-2045 703-836-7100

GRASSROOTS TRAINING MANUAL: GUIDE TO AN EXPERIENTIAL PROGRAM

(undated) - a comprehensive orientation handbook providing an overview of the program and a two-part text:
- **Part One:** *Training and Screening, Communication, Communications Techniques, EIAG: A Theory of Learning, Recognizing and Dealing with Persons in Crisis, Carl Rogers: Helping Relationships,* and *The Eight Dimensions of Effective Counseling Behavior.*
- **Part Two:** *Transference-Counter Transference Summary, Grassroots Counseling Model, Suicide Calls,* and *Drug Counseling.*

Lists total services of the mental health center in its introduction, 56pp, inquire about cost **Grassroots Crisis Intervention Center** 6700 Freetown Road, Columbia, MD 21044 301-531-6006

HELP FOR EMOTIONAL AND MENTAL PROBLEMS

(1979) - the case for community action to increase the number of *Information and Referral Centers,* mental health centers, hotlines, etc., to help families, workers, and others with mental and emotional problems that do not incapacitate them but could lead to more severe disorders; cites the heavy use of these facilities where they exist; refers to United Way and other sources for information on locating or starting a center in the community, 28pp, $.50 **Public Affairs Committee** 381 Park Avenue South, New York, NY 10016 212-683-4331

HELPING PEOPLE IN CRISIS

(1979) by Douglas A. Puryear - suggestions for an approach to effective crisis intervention; includes seven chapters of case examples to illustrate techniques recommended for crisis work, 237pp, $22.95 **Jossey Bass, Publishers** 350 Sansome Street, San Francisco, CA 94104-1310 415-433-1767

HELPING TRAUMATIZED FAMILIES

(1989) - a guide to building rapport and trust, supportiveness and communication, and to approaching that first question the family asks - "Why did it happen?" - with sensitivity; details ways to improve cost-effectiveness of volunteer-based programs, approx. 175pp (in press), $22.95 **Jossey Bass, Publishers** 350 Sansome Street, San Francisco, CA 94104 415-433-1767

HOW TO START A RAPE CRISIS CENTER

(2nd ed., 1977) - handbook to help those seeking to establish a rape crisis center in their communities; offers comprehensive guidelines in all steps of the operation, 55pp, $4.00 (plus $.75 postage) **Rape Crisis Center** PO Box 21005, Washington, DC 20009 202-333-7273

IASP

(undated) - overview of the constitution, rights and responsibilities of participants, administration, and other aspects of an international association for suicide prevention programs; describes services to centers - including VITA, a bulletin for exchange of experiences and information, meetings, and other activities, 12pp, single copy free (English/Spanish/French) **International Association for Suicide Prevention** 455 Virginia Avenue, San Mateo, CA 94402 415-877-5600

INFORMATION AND REFERRAL CENTERS: A FUNCTIONAL ANALYSIS

(Rep. 1974) - analysis of services and planning in I&R Centers, and the integration of the findings into a single model, 47pp, single copy free **US/HHS - Administration on Aging** 330 C Street, SW, Washington, DC 20201 202-619-0724

INFORMATION AND REFERRAL: HOW TO DO IT

(1975) - a documentary discussion of information and referral as performed at the Information Center of Hampton Roads, located in Norfolk, Virginia, and serving 1,160,000 people in Southeastern Virginia; includes two volumes:

Volume I, Part I - Before Beginning, Development Concerns - introduces the I&R concept; includes detailed account of a model program in Virginia and, based on this model, information on pre-development activities, personnel, facilities, budgets, controls, storage and retrieval; appends 48 pages of forms and other aids, 152pp

Volume I, Part II - The First Step: Establishing the Resource Data Base - discusses the concept and the reality of a community human services delivery system; includes details on what you should know about a service provider, how to establish the resource data base (survey management concerns), and how to maintain the resource data base; appends survey instrument, approved abbreviations, facility codes, sample printout, etc., in actual use at the model program, 225pp

Volume I, Part III - ICSIS - Information Center Services Identification System - the complete sytem of identifying descriptors and codes as used in the model program, with contact information for direct contact with the program

Volume I, Part IV - Operating the I&R Center - step-by-step description of the model program's operation, emphasizing the need to train referral specialists to respond very quickly and accurately; describes the aids provided to staff, including service provider suspension files by computer number and access to an alphabetical rolodex to supplement the computer when more details about a provider are needed; discusses individual searches using finer consumer eligibility factors, tracking and outreach functions, follow-up, publicity, etc.; appends samples of every step of the operation, 130pp

Volume II - the complete technical documentation for the Automated Community Services Information System (ACSIS) of the Hampton Roads program, single copy free

I&R Guide: Interdepartmental Task Force on Information and Referral (undated) - a baseline criteria in relation to other common elements of any I&R service, 6pp, single copy free **US/HHS - Administration on Aging** Administration on Aging, 330 Independence Avenue, NW, Washington, DC 20201 202-783-3238

INFORMATION AND REFERRAL SERVICES

(three/year) - journal of Information and Referral Systems, Inc., providing articles by the experts, information on I&R-related resources, etc., sample issue $5.00; subscription $10/year for members, others $20/year/individual, $30/year/institution **Alliance of Information and Referral Systems** 47 South Pennsylvania Street, #405, Indianapolis, IN 46204 317-637-6101

INFORMATION AND REFERRAL SERVICES: NATIONAL STANDARDS

(kept current) - guidelines for local managers and potential managers to mount new programs on a solid footing, or improve existing local I&R efforts, $4.00 ($3.00 members) **Alliance of Information and Referral Systems** 47 South Pennsylvania Street, #405, Indianapolis, IN 46204 317-637-6101

INFORMATION AND REFERRAL SERVICES: REACHING OUT

(updated as needed) - practical guide for I&R Center managers, administrative staff, and outreach workers that takes the services of information and referral out of the I&R center and into the community, 51pp, single copy free **US/HHS - Administration on Aging** 200 C Street, SW, Washington, DC 20201 202-783-3238

INFORMATION FOR EVERYDAY SURVIVAL: WHAT YOU NEED AND WHERE TO GET IT

(1976) - an annotated list of free or inexpensive materials to bring help for solving everyday problems; arranges information under Aging, Children, Free Time, Housing, and numerous other basic categories (some items out of print, but usually replaced with a current similar item), 416pp, $10.00 **American Library Association** 50 East Huron Street, Chicago, IL 606111 312-944-6780

INFORMATION FOR THE COMMUNITY

(1976) - compilation of new and revised papers devoted to the management of I&R centers as well as to the description of efficient external information paths; describes the conditions that gave rise to the information and referral services concept and discusses information needs, 292pp, $10.00 **American Library Association** 50 East Huron Street, Chicago, IL 60611 312-944-6780

JOURNAL OF CRISIS INTERVENTION

(periodically) - coverage of the field of crisis intervention in a new journal with the hallmark issue scheduled for October 1991; plans to include guest articles, regular columns, news of resources, training events, and other items of interest to professionals and volunteers working with those in crisis, cost not determined (inquire about submission of articles) **American Academy of Crisis Interveners** c/o Edward S. Rosenbluh, 218 Breckenridge Lane, Suite 102, Louisville, KY 40207 502-895-0200

NATIONAL DIRECTORY OF CHILDREN & YOUTH SERVICES

(1990-91) - a compilation of agencies and organizations throughout the U.S. that offer services for children and youth; organizes information by state and county; covers social services, health services, juvenile justice agencies, and others, 718pp, $59.00 plus $4.00 shipping **Network Directory** PO Box 1837, Longmont, CO 80502-1837 800-343-6681

NATIONAL DIRECTORY OF RUNAWAY CENTERS

(1979) - listing based on responses to questionnaire regarding clients served, services, staff, funding, management, advocacy, etc.; includes sample questionnaire, unpaged, $9.95 **Runaway Project** 1522 Connecticut Avenue, NW, Fourth Floor, Washington, DC 20036 202-785-0764

NATIONAL DOMESTIC HOTLINE INFORMATION PACKET

(1990) - a selection of fact sheets, flyers and mini-posters on domestic abuse prevention and intervention; includes a comprehensive article on *Signs to Look for in a Battered Personality,* a quick-reference pie chart defining domestic violence, a mini-poster entitled *My Husband Hit Me* (also called the *faces* flyer), a letter from a battered woman, etc., single copy free (requests, in return, *your* information for sharing) **Michigan Coalition Against Domestic Violence** PO Box 7032, Huntington Woods, MI 48070 800-333-SAFE/873-6363-TTY

NATIONAL STANDARDS FOR INFORMATION & REFERRAL SERVICES

(1973) - a basic tool representing the combined input from numerous organizations to help assure quality I&R services; emphasizes the accountability of such a service to the entire community; provides practical steps from the "talking stage" through the planning and implementation process; includes glossary of terms, and list of participating agencies and information contributors, 16pp, $2.00 ($1.50 for members) **United Way of America** 701 North Fairfax Street, Alexandria, VA 22314-2045 703-836-7100

PASS IT ON
(1983) - overviews and mission statements for Rape Crisis Center, The Washington Free Clinic and Washington Women's Self-Help programs, 12pp, single copy free **Rape Crisis Center** PO Box 21005, Washington, DC 20009 202-333-7273

RAPE: A REFERENCE FOR WOMEN IN DC
(1983) - an overview of the Rape Crisis Center and sections on myths, rape prevention tactics and medical needs, 5pp, $.75 **Rape Crisis Center** PO Box 21005, Washington, DC 20009 202-333-7273

REPORT OF THE INTERDEPARTMENTAL TASK FORCE ON INFORMATION & REFERRAL
(1978) - report on the functions, activities, programs and accomplishments of the Task Force formed to improve, expand, monitor and evaluate the role of federal agencies in I&R services for older people, 24pp, single copy free **US/HHS - Administration on Aging** 200 C Street, SW, Washington, DC 20201 202-619-0724

RUNAWAYS
(1976) - exploration of the reasons why young people run away from home, the problems they face, where and how they can find help and what parents and counselors can do; includes a guide to hotlines and halfway houses, 186pp, $6.95 **Beacon Press** 25 Beacon Street, Boston, MA 02108 617-742-2110

SUICIDE: PREVENTION, INTERVENTION, POSTVENTION
(1971) - a look at the theories, what has been done, clues to aid prevention, several types of helpers (the family, the church, the professional), and the unfortunate delay in expanding the suicide prevention center movement, 140pp, $5.50 **Beacon Press** 25 Beacon Street, Boston, MA 02108 617-742-2110

TELE-CARE
1987) - comprehensive manual addressing four broad skill areas of telephone counseling:
Chapters 1-5 - establishing the local referral database;
Chapters 6-8 - confrontation, referral and crisis intervention;
Chapters 9-11 - some of the difficulties of dealing with suicidal callers, persons who are bereaved, and the manipulative sex caller;
Chapters 12-14 - contracting, supervision and certain theological insights, 72pp, $4.00 **CONTACT USA** Pouch A, Harrisburg, PA 17105 717-232-3501

TELL ME WHERE TO TURN
(1983) - full color film using the documentary technique to show how information and referral centers help people in trouble by telling them where to go to solve their problems and, in doing so, serve as clearinghouses for a myriad of health and welfare services in a community; includes a discussion guide, 16mm, 26-1/2 minutes, $170/print; $15/rental (developed under U.S. Public Health Service Grant) **Public Affairs Committee** 381 Park Avenue South, New York, NY 10016 212-683-4331

TOLL FREE HOTLINE DIRECTORY
(1990) - a listing of over a hundred hotlines with *800 numbers* and, where needed, in-state and collect numbers, other sources of information, a discussion of government and private sector hotlines, a brief history and overview of *Public Citizen,* and a listing of organizations founded by Ralph Nader, including areas of disability, pensions, banking, trial lawyers, auto safety, and others, 16-panel foldout, single copy free, additional copies $1.00 plus SASE **Public Citizen** PO Box 19404, Washington, DC 20036 202-546-4996

TRAINING THE VOLUNTEERS: PUBLICATIONS
(various dates) - program materials to train volunteers for intense telephone counseling work; materials include:
- *CONTACT Training manual* (1989) $40.00
- *Maxwell's Mulberrybush Manual,* $5.00
- *Text: Preparing to Listen,* $4.00
- *You Only Have to Ask,* $.75
- *Becoming Whole,* $1.00

Not a complete list; inquire about others **CONTACT USA** Pouch A, Harrisburg, PA 17105 717-232-3501

TROUBLED? LET'S TALK
(kept current) - brief overview of a 20-year-old crisis intervention hotline; defines role of volunteer listeners, speaker services, kinds of calls received, kinds of referrals made, etc., 4pp, free **Northern Virginia Hotline** PO Box 187, Arlington, VA 22210 703-527-4077

UNITED WAY REFERRAL AGENT PROGRAM
(1974) - a handbook for employers sponsoring a volunteer referral agent among employees who is trained to refer company employees to services in the community that will help them solve their problems; provides step-by-step guide to selection of referral agent, training preparation and implementation, operation of a one-day community awareness event, etc.; includes sample recruitment and other forms, 13pp, $2.50 **United Way of America** 701 North Fairfax Street, Alexandria, VA 22314-2045 703-836-7100

WHAT YOU NEED TO KNOW ABOUT RAPE
(1977) - an appeal to the rape victim to take steps toward counseling and help immediately to increase the chances of catching the attacker; offers checklist for walking, driving, staying home; covers counseling, investigation, charges, VD, other areas of concern, 40pp, single copy free **Citizens Information Service** 67 East Madison Street, Chicago, IL 60603 312-236-0315

WHERE DO YOU LOOK? WHOM DO YOU ASK? HOW DO YOU KNOW? RESOURCES FOR CHILD ADVOCATES
(1980) - suggestions on how to use existing resources and sources of information - many of them public and free - to work on behalf of children at the state and local level, 128pp, $5.50 **Children's Defense Fund** 1520 New Hampshire Avenue, NW, Washington, DC 20036 202-483-1470

YOU AND THE HELPING RELATIONSHIP
(kept current) - handbook for paraprofessionals (trained nonprofessionals) discussing some of the areas of training, including: Crisis Theory, Empathy, How to Communicate Sympathy, Things NOT To Do, Things Not to be Afraid of, and a checklist of ten pointers to keep in mind when working with people, 20pp, single copy free **Interdivisional Volunteer Program** PO Box 628, Hillsboro, OR 97123 503-648-0711

YOUTH-SERVING ORGANIZATIONS DIRECTORY
(1980) - a "one-stop source of information" on organizations, research groups, and special libraries that serve the interest of today's youth in America (drawn from Gale's Encyclopedia of Associations, Research Centers Directory, and Directory of Special Libraries), 1179pp, $65.00 **Gale Research Company** Book Tower, Detroit, MI 48226 313-961-2242

YOUTH YELLOW PAGES
(kept current) - a pocket-size booklet that tells youngsters and
their families where to get information and assistance in cases of
child abuse, sexual assault, mental health, unplanned pregnancies,
substance abuse, eating disorders, and other problems; designed by
a coalition of agencies and organizations for students from seventh
to twelfth grades; based on the *Kansas City Youth Yellow Pages,*
size varies, single copy free as available **AFL-CIO Community
Services** 3625 Douglas, Kalamazoo, MI 49007 616-343-0348

LAW ENFORCEMENT/CRIME PREVENTION

ALTERNATIVE SENTENCING
(1989) - video dramatization of a repeat offender who receives an opportunity to participate in a community-based volunteer program; demonstrates the basic 'one-to-one' volunteer concept, detailing a progressive rehabilitation program for repeat offenders, VHS, inquire about preview copy and cost, color, 30 minutes [produced for VIP by *Golden Rule Insurance Company*] **Volunteers in Prevention, Probation, Prisons** VIP Video, 527 North Main , Royal Oak, MI 48067 313-398-8550

ASSAULTS ON WOMEN: RAPE AND WIFE BEATING
(1980) - overview of where women can turn after becoming victims of the two most underreported and least punished crimes in America; includes suggestions on ways to help for authorities, the woman herself, counselors, and the concerned citizen, 28pp, $.50 (quantity discounts) **Public Affairs Committee** 381 Park Avenue, New York, NY 10016 212-683-4331

BREAKING INTO PRISON: A GUIDE TO VOLUNTEER ACTION
(1974) - advice for citizens who want to help improve prison life through direct action in prison volunteer programs; includes overview of what volunteers can expect, how to start useful programs, special problems of women inmates, alternatives to children's prisons, courts, prevention, and volunteer tasks outside prison walls, 194pp, $8.25 **Beacon Press** 25 Beacon Street, Boston, MA 02108 617-742-2110

CHILDREN IN JAIL
(1977) - case studies of the home lives of children prior to their incarceration, the implications for their present situations - with an appeal to the child advocate to continue trying to help, even without the support of law and social structure, 178pp, $4.95 **Beacon Press** 25 Beacon Street, Boston, MA 02108 617-742-2110

COMMUNITY PRE-SENTENCE PROGRAM
(undated) - description of a program that utilizes volunteers to provide investigative social services in adult criminal courts, 15pp, single copy free **Hennepin County Court Services** Volunteer Services, A-506 Government Center, Minneapolis, MN 55487 612-348-7919

CONFERENCE COMMITTEE DIVERSION PROGRAM REPORT
(1989) - an extensive research project on the *Conference Committee Diversion Program,* which diverts juvenile first offenders from the formal juvenile justice system; includes community service as one of the recommendations of the *Committees,* single copy free **Conference Committee** 1211 East Alder M.S. 2L, Seattle, WA 98122 206-296-1134

COURT VOLUNTEERS
(kept current) - brief job descriptions for volunteers in eight areas of court services; includes prepaid mail-back card for contact information and choice of volunteer job, 8-panel foldout, single copy free **Hennepin County Court Services** Volunteer Services, A-506 Government Center, Minneapolis, MN 55487 612-348-7919

CRIME AND THE LAW
(1981) - overview of the criminal justice system, including the rights of suspects, recourse for victims, and the duties of witnesses and jurors; presents information on the Constitution and criminal law, the rights of suspects and defendants, and aid for witnesses and victims of crime; each chapter begins with a summary of its contents and ends with a glossary of key terms, 64pp, $2.95 **New Readers Press** Box 131, Syracuse, NY 13210 315-422-9121

CRIME AND THE LAW WORKBOOK
(1982) - a workbook to reinforce information in *Crime and the Law;* presents extra practice in legal terms and thought-provoking questions about the criminal justice system, along with actual newspaper stories about court cases, illustrations of legal forms, and answer key, 40pp, $2.00 **New Readers Press** Box 131, Syracuse, NY 13210 315-422-9121

CRIME AWARENESS PAMPHLET SERIES
(1980) - illustrated guides in areas of crime awareness and prevention, 15pp each, $.75 each (quantity discounts):
- *30 Ways You Can Prevent Crime*
- *What Every Woman Should Know About Self-Protection*
- *What Every Woman Should Know About Rape*
[not a complete list; request catalog] **Channing L. Bete Company**, South Deerfield, MA 01373

CRIME PREVENTION
(Rev. 1982) - crime prevention program outlining techniques and means of preventing crime against neighborhoods, homes, elderly and all individuals; free **B'nai B'rith International** Community Volunteer Services, 1640 Rhode Island Avenue, NW, Washington, DC 20036 202-857-6580

CRIMINAL VICTIMIZATION IN THE UNITED STATES
(1980) - report on the extent and nature of selected crimes and their impact on citizens; data are based on citizen reporting of crimes reported to police; examines various aspect of victimization as seen through the eyes of victims; 98pp, NCJRS Document Loan Program, NCJ84015; limited number of copies available on first-come, first-served basis **National Criminal Justice Reference Service** 1015 Twentieth Street, NW, Washington, DC 20036 301-251-5500

EFFECTIVE COORDINATION OF VOLUNTEERS
(1980) - manual designed to assist managers of victim assistance programs in recruiting, screening, training, and supervising a volunteer staff; emphasizes practical information and training techniques applicable to any agency seeking volunteers; covers all aspects of volunteer management, with special attention to the timing of training, and the continuation of the learning process through ongoing inservice training; cautions managers to watch for signs of burnout; appends sample training materials, program descriptions, schedules, exercises and an outline of the criminal justice system (prepared by the Domestic Violence Project of Rockville, Maryland, and the Washington, DC, Office on Domestic Violence), 141pp, $12.50 (a summary is available for $3.50) **US/DOC - National Technical Information Service** 5285 Port Royal Road, Springfield, VA 22151 703-557-4650

EFFECTIVE DESIGN & MANAGEMENT OF VOLUNTEER INVOLVEMENT IN JUVENILE & CRIMINAL JUSTICE
(1988) - a joint attempt by the University of Wisconsin and the International Association of Justice Volunteerism (formerly, National Association of Volunteers in Criminal Justice) to "pull together the best thinking on volunteer management" to help communities achieve the goal of increased and more effective citizen involvement in criminal justice; includes sections on philosophy (a complete partnership of paid staff and volunteer), training, management, and examples of volunteer involvement, 77pp, inquire about cost **International Association of Justice Volunteerism** Criminal Justice Institute, PO Box 786, Milwaukee, WI 63201 414-229-5630

HANDBOOK FOR VOLUNTEERS IN CORRECTIONS
(Rev. 1987) - an overview of the Department of Corrections, a section on the role of the volunteer, guidelines to assist the volunteer, and *Connecticut Prison Association's Bill of Rights for Volunteers,* with space for notes to keep the volunteer current on developments, 12pp, single copy free **Connecticut Department of Corrections** Volunteer Services, 90 Brainard Road, Hartford, CT 06114 203-566-3685

HANDLING THE CRISIS
(1990) - a handbook that is provided to participants of OAR's *Family Assistance Program,* which offers family and inmate support groups and individual counseling, inquire about availability and cost **Offender Aid and Restoration of Fairfax County** 4153 Chain Bridge Road , Fairfax, VA 22030 703-273-7552

HCCS VOLUNTEER PROGRAM MANUAL
(kept current) - orientation developed by staff and volunteers to provide entry information for incoming volunteers and staff in the court volunteer program; includes information on the goals of the program, the client, volunteer/staff teamwork, adult and juvenile criminal justice systems, volunteer client relationships, background reading, etc., 37pp, $3.00 **Hennepin County Court Services** Volunteer Services, A-506 Government Center, Minneapolis, MN 55487 612-348-7919

"HE TOLD ME NOT TO TELL"
(1979) - a guide for parents and childcare workers to promote better communication with young children about sexual assult; discusses when and how to talk to children, what they are up against, how to help them protect themselves, ways kids can tell someone they need help, what to do besides talk, steps to take when a child has been assaulted, etc.; appends a copy of the laws in Washington State relevant to this issue, and information on incest and the sex offender, 28pp, single copy free while supply lasts [also available in limited supply from Child Protective Services, Virginia Department of Social Services, 8001 Discovery Drive, Richmond, VA 23229-8699 800-552-7096] **King County Rape Relief** 305 South 43rd, Renton, WA 98055 206-226-RAPE (24-hr)

HOME DETENTION: AN ALTERNATIVE
1977 - details on the use of volunteers in programs that allows certain juvenile offenders to remain at home, or in a home atmosphere, under the supervision of a volunteer; includes recruitment, screening, evaluation, etc., of this volunteer-staffed program, 32pp, $1.50 **Hennepin County Court Services** Volunteer Services, A-506 Government Center, Minneapolis, MN 55487 612-348-7919

IS THERE A BETTER WAY? A PERSPECTIVE ON AMERICAN PRISONS
(undated) - an overview of alternative punishments for crimes, such as restitution, community service orders, house arrest, probation and contract probation, deferred sentencing, suspended sentencing, fines, alcohol/drug treatment, employment assistance, pre-trial intervention, and community dispute (or citizen dispute) settlement; covers alternatives involving some incarceration (shorter sentences, weekend sentences, increased "good time" credit, etc.); discusses the benefits of alternative punishments, and how citizens can help, 30pp, single copy free **Prison Fellowship Ministries** PO Box 17500, Washington, DC 20041 202-478-0100

JAIL MINISTRY IS GOOD BUSINESS?
(undated) - an appeal to business and industry citing the good investment of preventing crime, and the advantages of giving jobs to men and women released from correctional institutions; provides examples of employers who have hired ex-offenders, 6-panel foldout, free **Good News Jail and Prison Ministries International** 1036 S. Highland Street, Arlington, VA 22204 703-979-2200

JUSTICE: EYEWITNESS ACCOUNTS
(1974) - reports by volunteer student observers and others of incidences of the "other justice" administered by police on the street, municipal court judges, job supervisors, teachers, health care, mental institutions, etc.; cites ways some groups - minorities, renters, former mental patients - have fought back by organizing, 275pp, $4.50 **Beacon Press** 25 Beacon Street, Boston, MA 02108 617-742-2110

LIFTS: LOW-INCOME FAMILY TRAINING AND SUPPORT
(1989) - a how-to manual for setting up low-income family support activities to prevent child abuse and strengthen the family unit in the high-risk population; bases learnings on a two-year polit project conducted in Boise, Idaho; includes parenting workshops and family events and focuses on relieving stress and improving basic self-esteem, unpaged, $5.00 **Idaho Hunger Action Council** 205 North Tenth, Suite 602, Boise, ID 83702 208-336-7010

NATIONAL ASSOCIATION OF TOWN WATCH OVERVIEW
(1990) - institutional brochure describing this crime and drug prevention network, which emphasizes citizen involvement in their own communities to help prevent crime and drug abuse, with information on its *National Night Out* neighborhood program, 6-panel foldout, free **National Town Watch Association** PO Box 303, Wynnewood, PA 19096 215-649-8055

NEW SPIRIT
(quarterly) - the newsletter of the *National Town Watch Association* providing news of town awards, the *National Night Out* program (where everyone in the country turns on outside lights in support of crime prevention - August 7th for the 1990 effort), local profiles of neighborhood watch programs, etc., 8pp, single copy free, inquire about subscriptions **National Town Watch Association** PO Box 303, Wynnewood, PA 19096 215-649-7055

PAMPHLET SERIES
(1980) - illustrated guides for citizens providing basic information on how citizens can get involved, 15pp each, $.75 each:
- *About Child Abuse*
- *About Wife Abuse*

Channing L. Bete Company , South Deerfield, MA 01373

PLANNING FOR JUVENILE JUSTICE
(1975 w/updates) - comprehensive handbook bringing together four years of experience in juvenile justice programs in local YMCAs across the country; includes section on volunteer support covering tasks, recruiting, training and recognizing volunteer efforts; provides detailed steps designed to lay out the process for developing a sound base from which to foster a rallying of all community resources; describes various types of programs, funding, evaluation, etc.; offers updates on request, 96pp, $6.00 (quantity discounts) **Juvenile Justice Services** Urban Action & Program Division, 101 North Wacker Drive, Chicago, IL 60606 312-977-0031

PRISONER VOLUNTEER SERIES
(undated) - components of an ongoing series designed to assist the community service volunteer in working with prisoners; titles change, $.10 each:
- *Meeting the Human Needs of Prisoners,* 14pp
- *The Atlanta Story,* 11pp
- *What's a Nice Jewish Boy Doing in a Place Like That,* 5pp

[not a complete list; request catalog] **B'nai B'rith International** Community Volunteer Services, 1640 Rhode Island Avenue, Washington, DC 20036 202-857-6580

REACH OUT TO WOMEN IN PRISON
(1976) - overview of a program attempting to "balance the scales" by providing the type of attention to women that is most often given to men in prison; uses a role-play format with hard-hitting dialogue to create an awareness in the participants of the consequences of prison life; mentions other ways to help such as court-watching, prison library, help for prisoners' families, etc., 12pp, $.40 ($2.95/dozen) (developed by The American Lutheran Church Women) **Augsburg Publishing House** 426 South Fifth Street, Box 1209, Minneapolis , MN 55440 612-330-3300

REACHING OUT: THE VOLUNTEER IN CHILD ABUSE AND NEGLECT PROGRAMS
(1979) - comprehensive handbook to help citizens make a decision regarding volunteer work in the field; covers existing volunteer activities, information for volunteer work directly with families, finding, training and keeping volunteers, and where to go to volunteer; appends a number of forms and other exhibits, 57pp, single copy free **National Center on Child Abuse and Neglect** U.S. Dept. of Health & Human Svcs., PO Box 1182, Washington, DC 20201 202-755-7500

REGENERATION THEN... REHABILITATION
(undated) - institutional booklet providing an overview of a program that sends Chaplains into jails and prisons to offer both pastoral and social services; includes articles by key figures in the organization and articles on "The Local Chaplain," services provided, prisoners who return to become volunteer Chaplains, and the organization's correspondence courses, 10pp, single copy free **Good News Jail and Prison Ministries International** 1036 S. Highland Street, Arlington, VA 22204 703-979-2200

SELECTED NOTIFICATIONS OF INFORMATION (SNI)
(bimonthly) - announcements of additions to the NCJRS collection of publications designed for the practitioner in criminal justice programs and projects; includes calendar of events of interest to those involved in this field; permits user-interest selections through application form in 80 areas, free subscription **National Criminal Justice Reference Service** Box 6000, Rockville, MD 20850 301-251-5500

SENTENCING GUIDELINES
(1990) - a study based on more than 30,000 Circuit Court cases that showed a kind of "luck-of-the-draw" system in which sentences could be influenced by a defendant's sex, race and socioeconomic status or by whichever judge happened to be sitting behind the bench; cites cases such as those where offenders with similar criminal backgrounds who committed almost identical burglaries received prison sentencing ranging from one to 20 years, inquire about availability and cost **Virginia Circuit Court** John Marshall Courts Building, 800 East Marshal Street, Richmond, VA 23219 804-780-6505

SOURCES OF INFORMATION ABOUT AND DESCRIPTIONS OF CRIME PREVENTION PROGRAMS FOR THE ELDERLY
(1977) - overview of local efforts to provide information on prevention of crime against the elderly; describes national projects on prevention, aid to elderly victims and witnesses, and others, 4pp plus attached resource lists, free **US/HHS - Department of Health & Human Services** Administration on Aging , 330 Independence Avenue, NW, Washington, DC 20201 202-245-2158

STATUS OFFENDERS
(1976) - discussion of some of the problems facing community organizations in their efforts to design and implement action programs for status offenders; includes sections on advocacy, fund-raising, proposal writing, use of the media, etc., and provides several case studies of active projects for juvenile status offenders, 94pp, $1.00 **National Council of Jewish Women** 15 East 26th Street, New York, NY 10010 212-532-1740

STOP! THE MADNESS INFORMATION PACKET
(kept current) - brochures, posters, fact sheets, statistics, and other information designed to assist volunteer groups in reducing violence and murder among youth in their communities, unpaged, single copy free **Stop! The Madness** 1325 W Street, NW, Washington, DC 20009 202-483-2771

TEACHING-TRAINING MODULES ON VOLUNTEERS IN CRIMINAL JUSTICE
(1983) - a series of twelve booklets used in a nationwide training program, but designed for use in any setting involving volunteers in the juvenile and criminal justice systems; titles are:
- History of Volunteers in Juvenile and Criminal Justice.
- Value Base of Volunteerism
- Volunteer Resource Development
- Management and Administration of Volunteer Programs
- Dynamics of Individual and Group Counseling by Volunteers

- Many Uses of Volunteers
- Volunteers in Institutions & Alternatives, Juvenile Diversion, Probation, Detention
- Volunteers & Adult Misdemeanant Courts
- Volunteers with the Adult Felon
- Issues, Trends and Directions in the 1980's
- Volunteer Information Portfolio (Scheier)
- Index to free Audio-Visual Resources

A sample booklet can be ordered for $3.00, at which time complete ordering and other information will be forwarded. **Volunteers in Prevention, Probation, Prisons** 527 North Main Street, Royal Oak, MI 48067 313-398-8550

TWENTY-FIVE YEAR PRESIDENTIAL CERTIFICATE PROGRAM FOR VOLUNTEERS IN JUVENILE CRIMINAL JUSTICE

(undated) - a packet of materials describing a program for the criminal justice volunteer community that awards supervisors of volunteers (paid or unpaid), who have supervised 50 or more volunteers for at least a year (or equivalent), and volunteers who have donated at least 50 hours a month for a year with a certificate signed by the President (now a tradition that has involved four consecutive Presidents), single packet free **US/White House** , Washington, DC 20500 202-456-1414

TWENTY-TWO STEPS TO SAFER NEIGHBORHOODS

(undated) - project descriptions outlining some of the ways people are working to create safer neighborhoods schools; includes crime watch, buddy system, crime insurance, jail visitation, volunteer police station receptionist, volunteer student patrol, troubled youth, and other programs (developed by CETA staff), 29pp, $.50 (quantity discounts) **National Alliance for Safer Cities** 500 East 62nd Street, New York, NY 10021 212-310-9000

UNDERSTANDING THE DRUG AND CRIME CONNECTION

(undated) - overview of the relationship between drugs and crime, with recommendations for future policies and action, 22pp, $1.00 [Also available from the Do-It-Now Foundation, separate entry] **U.S. Journal of Drug and Alcohol Dependence** 2119A Hollywood Boulevard, Hollywood, FL 33020 305-920-9433

VIP VIDEO: PARTNERSHIP MODEL

(1990) - a video developed for judges, probation officers, community leaders and concerned citizens designed to address the lack of resources available to fight high rates of recidivism in the justice system, free review with request on letterhead, inquire about cost **Volunteers in Prevention, Probation, Prisons** 527 North Main Street, Royal Oak, MI 48067 313-398-8550

VIRGINIA'S CHILD ABUSE/NEGLECT PROGRAM

(undated) - special report designed to answer all inquiries for information on Virginia's child abuse and neglect programs; includes an overview of the Division, a listing of accomplishments, suggestions for the community, quiz for citizens on their knowledge of the issue, warning signals, *The Three Elements in Abuse,* available help, types of injuries, *Code of Virginia,* sexual abuse facts, characteristics of the abuser, etc., unpaged, single copy free **Child Protective Services** Virginia Dept. of Social Services, 8007 Discovery Drive, Richmond, VA 23229-8699 804-662-9204

VOLUNTEER INFORMATION PACKET

(undated) - a collection of materials designed to orient the volunteer to the Department of Corrections Volunteer Program; includes a handbook (described elsewhere), a *Catalog of Opportunities for Volunteers in Corrections,* a listing of internships available, a "welcome letter" from the Director, and miscellaneous

fact sheets as they become available, unpaged, single copy free **Connecticut Department of Corrections** 90 Brainard Road, Hartford, CT 06114 203-566-3685

THE VOLUNTEER INVESTIGATES

(undated) - a manual for the training of volunteers to conduct pre-sentence investigations for the court; includes orientation, volunteer/staff relationships, the offender, interviewing/communications skill, use of community resources, effective report writing and presentation to the court, etc., 51pp, $3.00 **Hennepin County Court Services** Volunteer Services, A-506 Government Center, Minneapolis, MN 55487 612-348-7919

VOLUNTEER SERVICES GUIDELINES

(1978) - guidelines in areas crucial to a successful volunteer program in juvenile justice; presents four detailed chapters: (1) volunteer program design, organizational structure, potential program applications and public relations; (2) the volunteer: who s/he is, motives for volunteering, suggestions for recruiting, screening, training, matching; (3) legal issues involved in using volunteers, including agency liability and volunteer insurance; (4) financial aspects, 25pp, single copy free **National Criminal Justice Reference Service** 1600 Research Boulevard, Box 6000, Rockville, MD 20850 301-251-5500

VOLUNTEERS IN JUVENILE JUSTICE

(1977) - details on current innovative uses of volunteers in the juvenile justice system; presents model guidelines for a volunteer program, descriptions of innovative programs in existence, involvement of volunteers in setting standards, development of training for volunteer supervisors, guidance for volunteer/staff relations, etc., 113pp, single copy free **National Criminal Justice Reference Service** 1015 Twentieth Street, NW, Washington, DC 20036 202-251-5500

WHO CARES FOR KIDS? AND WHERE DO THEY GO AFTER JUVENILE COURT?

(1979) - overview of services the courts have available for abused, neglected, homeless, delinquent, emotionally disturbed, mentally ill, ungovernable, drug-abusive, and other troubled children; uses Illinois as an example of statewide resources for these children, 8pp, $.50 **Citizens Information Service** 67 East Madison Street, Chicago, IL 60603 312-236-0315

WHY BOTHER?

(undated) - recruitment brochure covering the cost of crime, the Correctional Chaplaincy, the challenge to the church, and ways citizen volunteers can help, 6-panel foldout, free **Good News Jail and Prison Ministries International** 1036 S. Highland Street, Arlington, VA 22204 703-979-2200

WITH JUSTICE FOR SOME: AN INDICTMENT OF THE LAW BY YOUNG ADVOCATES

(1972) - case studies selected by young lawyers and law students to demonstrate some of the blatant violations of the rights of disadvantaged people; includes descriptions of cases in areas of education, women, minorities, poverty, industry, courts, public interest law, etc.; introduction by Ralph Nader, 400pp, $3.95 **Beacon Press** 25 Beacon Street, Boston, MA 02108 617-742-2110

YOUR PATH TO PERSONAL SAFETY

(undated) - a public service brochure produced and distributed by the *Fairfax County Police Department* following incidents of crime on the pathways that entwine throughout the area; includes more than a dozen safety tips regarding pathway useage, parked car precautions, attackers, and devices that can help in the event of an emergency, 6-panel foldout, free **Fairfax County Police**

Department Mason District Station, 6507 Columbia Pike, Annandale, VA 22003 703-256-8035

YOUR POLICEMAN
(undated) - picture story in the form of a coloring book for young children to intercept the process that creates negative feelings in youth toward police officers, 12pp, $.20 **B'nai B'rith International** Community Volunteer Services, 1640 Rhode Island Avenue, NW, Washington, DC 20036 202-857-6580

YOUTH AND THE LAW IN THE DISTRICT OF COLUMBIA
(Rev. 1988) - information for those under 18 years old to introduce them to the local laws that might affect them (entering/destroying property, stealing, personal behavior, their own rights, Children Centers, a juvenile record, etc.); includes excerpts from some 40 essays written by junior high school children, and youngsters in the Human Resources system, one free; additional $1.00 each **District of Columbia Women's Commission for Crime Prevention** 945 G Street, NW, Washington, DC 20001 202-347-2696

LEADERSHIP DEVELOPMENT/BOARDS

THE A-B-C'S OF PARLIAMENTARY PROCEDURE
(1990) - a basic, illustrated guide taking the new leader step-by-step through the "order of business" procedure of a meeting; includes quick-reference charts, a glossary, and other aids, 15pp, write for pricing and quantity discounts **Channing L. Bete Company** , South Deerfield, MA 01373

AN APPROACH TO YOUTH PARTICIPATION
(1975) - (part of an ongoing series entitled "A Source Catalog on Youth Participation") a strategy designed to mobilize youth to share community concerns, become involved, and thereby decrease or eliminate the exclusion of youth from the decision-making process; addresses the effects of compelling youth to obey rules over which they have no control - alienation, resentment, hostility; emphasizes the contribution the viewpoint of youth can make toward an effective and responsive community, 22pp, single copy free **US/HHS - Department of Health & Human Services** Division of Youth Activities, 300 Independence Avenue, Washington, DC 20201 202-245-2870

BOARD MANUAL WORKBOOK
(1979; 10th Anniversary Revision, 1989) - a tool to assist organizations in developing an orientation manual, assessing board strengths and weaknesses, preparing a meeting agenda, writing welcome letters to new board members, identifying jobs and skills for effective action, strengthening organizational structure, editing constitution and by-laws, personalizing the use of resource materials, etc.; appends a resource list of publications, 54pp, $8.95 **Volunteer Consultants** 9015 Cliffside Drive, Clarence, NY 14031-1408

BOARD MANUAL WORKBOOK: INSTRUCTORS' GUIDE
(1981) - course planner for use with the *Board Manual Workbook;* includes actual session plans, pre-meeting packet designs, quizzes and instructional and evaluation tools, unpaged, $16.95 **Volunteer Consultants** 9015 Cliffside Drive, Clarence, NY 14031-1408

THE BOARD MEMBER'S BOOK
(1990) by Brian O'Connell - guidance on handling legal responsibilities, budgeting and financial accountability, relationship with other board members and staff, proven tips for making the most of board and committee meetings, etc., 208pp, $21.95 **Independent Sector** 1828 L Street, NW, Washington, DC 20036 202-223-8100

BOARDS AND ADVISORY COUNCILS: A KEY TO EFFECTIVE MANAGEMENT
(1979) -an overview and examination of the distribution of authority between citizen boards/councils and organization staff, and suggestions on bringing about clear understanding and cooperative efforts in such relationships, 59pp, single copy free **National Council on the Aging** 1828 L Street, NW, Washington, DC 20036 202-223-6250

BOARDS THAT MAKE A DIFFERENCE
(1990) - guide to ways a board can "hammer out" clear, concise, and practical policy statements that support the overall purpose of its organization; guides board members in working with managers to accomplish that purpose; details processes for delegating authority, establishing parameters, and evaluating performance, 272pp, $22.95 **Jossey Bass, Publishers** 350 Sansome Street, San Francisco, CA 94104 415-433-1767

BOARDWALK: WORKING AT LEADERSHIP KNOWLEDGE
(1989) - a series designed to develop board-level skills; contains four integrated components:
I - How to Bring VLDP to Your Community: explains the VLDP concept
II - "Train the Trainer" Institute: teaches background and skills needed by BoardWALK workshop leaders and group facilitors
III - Organizational Training Needs Survey Instrument (OTNS): analyzes each organization's unique requirements and steers participants toward the workshops best for them
IV - Workshops: gives an in-depth look at various facets of the board member's role (12 different workshops), looseleaf, unpaged, inquire about cost **United Way of America** Volunteer Leadership Development, 701 North Fairfax Street, Alexandria, VA 22314-3045 703-836-7100

BREAKING THE BOARDOM
(1990) - an annotated bibliography of books, journal articles, manuals and more on all issues necessary for board and council effectiveness, 19pp, $10.00 plus $2.50 postage **Citizen Involvement Training Program** 381 Hills South, Room 381, Amherst, MA 01003 413-545-2038

BUILDING A STRONG BOARD
(undated) - outline of a training program for board members provided by the Volunteer Center for any interested board;

training topics include roles and responsibilities, board structure, staff relations, purpose and goal-setting, organizational planning, evaluation, funding, team building, legal/fiscal issues, and others; a minimal fee is charged for the training, $2.00/packet **Volunteer Center of Central Florida** 1900 North Mills Street, Suite #1, Orlando, FL 32803 305-896-0945

BUILDING EFFECTIVE VOLUNTEER COMMITTEES

(1990) - ten steps to building effective committees, with detailed explanations on recruiting the right people, writing guidelines, establishing annual work plans, holding members accountable for their responsibilities, evaluating individuals and committee work; appends forms for copying and use, 82pp, $11.95 (by mail, $15.00) **Macduff/Bunt Associates** 821 Lincoln Street, Walla Walla, WA 99362 509-529-0244

BUILDING NEIGHBORHOOD ORGANIZATIONS: A GUIDEBOOK

(1983) - a study of ways to build more effective neighborhoods, examining 15 neighborhood organizations with different degrees of success in three categories - low-budget volunteer groups, big-budget neighborhood organizations, and neighborhood groups tied to government and politics; describes visits, interviews, and the key documents examined during the visit; focuses on the building and rebuilding of techniques of putting the organization together, seeking power, and the ways it operates to receive attention; includes in study areas: administration, fundraising, recruiting, training and leadership development, problem-solving, evaluation, participation, strategizing, negotiating, etc., 214pp, inquire about cost **CRG Press** PO Box 42120, 1000 Sixteenth Street, NW, Washington, DC 20015 202-223-2400

BUILDING SECOND CENTURY VOLUNTEER LEADERSHIP EXCELLENCE IN UNITED WAY

(1989) - an exercise to help generate a better understanding among volunteers about the composition of the Board (or committee) and to stimulate ideas for making changes, 4pp, inquire about cost **United Way of America** 701 North Fairfax Street, Alexandria, VA 22314-2045 703-836-7100

BUILDING THE COLLABORATIVE COMMUNITY

(1980)- a new handbook by Eva Schindler-Rainman to provide guidance in mobilizing citizens for action; inquire about cost **University of California Extension** 1138 Administration Building, Riverside, CA 92521 714-787-4105

BUT A NIGHT...

(1990) - recruitment piece to match professional skills and interests of applicants with available positions on the boards of community organizations and public agencies, 6-panel foldout, free **Volunteer Boulder** 3305 North Broadway, Suite One, Boulder, CO 80304 303-444-4904

CHIEF EXECUTIVE'S ROLE IN DEVELOPING THE NONPROFIT BOARD

(1988) - identification of eight ways the new or less experienced chief staff officer can strengthen the governing board so that both the board and chief executive work effectively to fulfill the organization's mission; includes practical grid to help identify and select new board members, 16pp, $4.95 **National Center for Nonprofit Boards** 1225 Nineteenth Street, NW, Suite 340, Washington, DC 20036 202-452-6262

CITIZEN PARTICIPATION

(undated) - discussion of citizen involvement in decision-making and the use of citizen advisory groups on a regular and meaningful basis, 11pp, $.75 **National League of Cities** 1301 Pennsylvania Avenue, NW, Washington, DC 20004 202-626-3000

COMMUNITY LEADER TRAINING LIBRARY

(undated) by Donald R. Fessler - a series of guides to assist leaders in training citizens to work effectively together toward chosen goals:
- *Leadership and the Effective Group,* 44pp, $1.50
- *A Logical Approach to Community Problem Solving,* 14pp, $1.00
- *How to Be a Leader,* 21pp, $1.00
- *Guidelines for Neighborhood-Community Organization,* 33pp, $1.00
- *Meetings That Get Results,* 17pp, $1.00
- *Motivating the Disadvantaged,* 14pp, $1.00

Entire set, $6.00 (Shelf box is included when entire set is ordered); 10% discount when 10 or more of a single title or of the boxed set are ordered; add $.69 postage for single manual, $1.59 for boxed set (stamps OK for postage) **Mortgage Burning Fund** PO Box 762, Annandale, VA 22003 703-354-6270

COMMUNITY LEADERSHIP DEVELOPMENT PROGRAM

(1979) - a program that grew out of two identifiable needs:
- to broaden current leadership in all areas of community life;
- to ensure leadership for the future;

Includes an outline of the two-day program, suggests eliminating some of the "games and climate-setting exercises" and focusing on group organization and problem-solving areas at the outset, 13pp, single copy free **Volunteer Bureau of United Way of San Diego County** 4699 Murphy Canyon Road, PO Box 23543, San Diego, CA 92123 714-492-2090

THE DECISION-MAKING PROCESS

(1979) - a program kit designed to help those with leadership responsibilities become more skilled in deciding issues and setting goals; includes a practical exercise suitable for small group units of from 5 to 8 persons, #15, $2.25/kit **Unitarian Universalist Women's Federation** 25 Beacon Street, Boston, MA 02108 617-742-2100

EFFECTIVE LEADERSHIP IN VOLUNTARY ORGANIZATIONS

(1990) by Brian O'Connell - a sharing of many hard-earned lessons about ways to develop staff and volunteer leadership in voluntary organizations, 202pp, $5.95 **Independent Sector** 1828 L Street, NW, Washington, DC 20036 202-223-8100

THE EFFECTIVE VOLUNTARY BOARD OF DIRECTORS

(1976) - a look at ways in which board roles are performed, creating a hypothetical organization to demonstrate board activities such as policy determination, resource development, and other functions, 185pp, $6.95 **Swallow Press** 811 West Junior Terrace, Chicago, IL 60613 312-871-2760

FACILITATING COMMUNITY CHANGE

(1976) by Donald R. Fessler - a basic guide for those with leadership responsibilities at the community level; discusses group meetings, involving the disadvantaged, the power structure, past change efforts, and numerous other activities and concerns, 146pp, $11.50 **University Associates** 8517 Production Avenue, San Diego, CA 92121 619-578-5900

FUND RAISING AND THE NONPROFIT BOARD MEMBER

(1988) - five principles that each board member should understand so that the full board can carry out its responsibility to raise funds for the organization; includes useful checklist to help board members - including those reluctant to ask others for money - do as much as possible to help raise funds, 13pp, $5.95 (author is executive with Lavender/Howe & Associates) **National Center for Nonprofit Boards** 1225 Nineteenth Street, NW, Suite 340, Washington, DC 20036 202-452-6262

GAINING MOMENTUM FOR BOARD ACTION

(1981) - a how-to guide on forming, joining or leading a board; includes four parts: *Understanding the Basics, Accomplishing Tasks, Working Together,* and *Continuing Board Development;* provides in each section a general discussion and practical examples; appends worksheets, charts, diagrams, and other tools to guide beginning and experienced board members toward building better boards, $10.50 **Marlborough Publications** PO Box 16406, San Diego, CA 92116 619-280-8310

GOVERNING BOARDS: THEIR NATURE AND NURTURE

(1989) by Cyril O. Houle - a guide for boards governing nonprofit and public-sector organizations; discusses the common issues, challenges and problems faced by boards; includes chapters on: How to Think About a Board; The Human Potential of the Board; The Structure of a Board; The Board, the Executive, and the Staff; The Operation of the Board; and The External Relationships of a Board; appends essays by leaders, a rating scale for boards, and other information, 248pp, $19.95 (developed by the National Center for Nonprofit Boards) **Jossey Bass, Publishers** 350 Sansome Street, San Francisco, CA 94104-1310 415-433-1767

A GRAPHIC LOOK AT BOARD COMPOSITION

(1989) - a worksheet to assist program leaders in balancing and improving the composition of their boards; considers minority representation and years of service; provides space for listing steps to be taken to bring about desired change, 4pp, inquire about cost **United Way of America** 701 North Fairfax Street, Alexandria, VA 22314-2045 703-836-7100

HANDBOOK FOR ADVISORY BODY MEMBERS

(1982) - a manual designed to explain to members and others the policies, procedures, and statutory requirements of DSHS (Dept. of Social & Health Services) in relation to the advisory bodies; includes information on the kinds of information and support the committees may expect from the department, and the ways the committees can assist the department (DSHS has over 35 advisory bodies with more than 500 members), 36pp, single copy free **Washington Office of Volunteerism** Mailstop OB-44R, Olympia, WA 98504 206-753-5983

HOW TO ORGANIZE AN EFFECTIVE PARENT/ADVOCACY GROUP AND MOVE BUREAUCRACIES

(1980) - step-by-step process for motivating parents and providing training that will enable them to get results when dealing with the bueaucracy; addressed to parents of handicapped children, but useful as a general leadership development tool, 130 pp, $5.00 plus $1.00 postage/handling, special quantity discounts available, inquire **Co-Ordinating Council for Handicapped Children** 220 South State Street, Room 412, Chicago, IL 60604 312-939-3513

LEADERSHIP AND SOCIAL CHANGE

(Rev. 1976) - an overview of tested leadership techniques and how they apply and effect specific leadership situations; cites real-life examples, 368pp, $13.50 **University Associates** 8517 Production Avenue, San Diego, CA 92121 619-578-5900

THE LEADERSHIP CHALLENGE

(1990) - an examination of the experiences of five hundred middle- and senior-level managers performing at their personal best; demonstrates that leadership is not the private preserve of a few charismatic men and women; details some of the practices common to successful leaders, 394pp, $12.95 (paper); $22,95 (cloth) **Jossey Bass, Publishers** 350 Sansome Street, San Francisco, CA 94104 415-433-1767

LEADERSHIP SERIES

(1990) by John W. Gardner - a series of videotapes addressing leadership issues, currently including two releases:
- *The Release of Human Possibilities*
- *The Task of Motivating*

Each videotape covers several unique areas of leadership, $45.00 (1-3 copies; bulk discounts available) **Independent Sector** 1828 L Street, NW, Washington, DC 20036 202-223-8100

NONPROFIT BOARD SERIES

(1989) - a series of booklets developed by a national organization whose prime concern is the nonprofit board:
- *Ten Basic Responsibilities of Nonprofit Boards*
- *The Chief Executive's Role in Developing the Nonprofit Board Member*
- *Fund Raising and the Nonprofit Board*

Av. 18pp, $4.95 each **National Center for Nonprofit Boards** 1225 Nineteenth Street, NW, Suite 340, Washington, DC 20036 202-452-6262

ON LEADERSHIP

(1990) by John Gardner - a focus on the elements of motivation, shared values, social cohesion and institutional renewal; includes section on how to make large scale systems flexible and adaptive; demonstrates how leaders must understand the needs of their people both large and small in order to gain their trust, 220pp, $19.95 **Independent Sector** 1828 L Street, NW, Washington, DC 20036 202-223-8100

ORGANIZING A BETTER YOUTH INVOLVEMENT UNIT

(1977) - organization manual for the development of a youth advisory board that provides youth with the opportunity to plan, operate, monitor, and evaluate programs by youth for the benefit of youth; identifies resources and focuses on some specific areas of concern to youth, 54pp, $2.00 **National Network of Youth Advisory Boards** PO Box 402036, Ocean View Branch, Miami, FL 33140 305-532-2607

ORIENTATION PACKET

(kept current) - ongoing information for board and committee members to clarify program goals, and keep them informed of the progress that is being made toward these goals, $2.00/packet **Volunteer Center of Lincoln** 215 Centennial Mall South, Lincoln, NE 68508 402-474-6218

PEOPLE POWER: A GUIDE TO GOOD BOARD MEMBERSHIP

(1980) - overview of what the board is, what the board does, what the board needs, legal responsibilities, board-staff relationships, board evaluation, and what makes a good board member in a quick-reference, easy-to-read format, $2.00 plus $.50 handling **Volunteer Center of United Way** 1111 Ninth Street, Suite 300, Des Moines , IA 50314 515-246-6545

POVERTY ALCOHOLISM PROGRAMS' SURVIVAL: ACTIONS FOR ADVISORY BOARDS

(1973) - guidelines for developing successful advisory boards for poverty alcoholism programs; draws on author's experience in "NIAAA Community Services Poverty Alcoholism Programs," 8pp, $.25 **National Council on Alcoholism** 12 West 21st Street, New York, NY 10010 212-206-6770

PROCEDURES SERIES

(1979) - help in some of the specific areas of decision-making: Simplified Parliamentary Procedure, #19; Nominating Committee Procedures, #22, request complete list, costs range from $.25 to $1.00 **Unitarian Universalist Women's Federation** 25 Beacon Street, Boston, MA 02108 617-742-2100

PROJECT LEAD

(kept current) - brochure describing in detail the four steps in the Project LEAD program, which is a development process for teenage volunteers who wish to learn leadership skills to apply to a local community need, 8-panel foldout, free **Quest International** 537 Jones Road, PO Box 566, Granville, OH 43023-0566 614-522-6400 (AK, HI)

PROJECT LEAD ADULT MENTOR MANUAL

(kept current) - orientation to a program designed to provide adult mentors to help teenagers increase their abilities at problem solving, personal communication, and group interaction, free with initiation of local Project LEAD **Quest International** 537 Jones Road, PO Box 566, Granville, OH 43023-0566 614-522-6400

PROJECT LEAD NEWSLETTER

(monthly) - information on new developments, activities of other teams across the country, and other aspects of Project LEAD that can help to keep team members informed and encouraged in their local problem-solving projects, Av. 8pp, free with initiation of a local Project LEAD **Quest International** 537 Jones Road, PO Box 566, Granville, OH 43023-0566 614-522-6400

PROJECT LEAD STUDENT VOLUNTEER HANDBOOK

(kept current) - handbook for teen volunteers to accompany a weekend-long leadership conference; contains an overview of the goals of the program, practice exercises, planning techniques, etc., free with initiation of local Project LEAD **Quest International** 537 Jones Road, PO Box 566, Granville, OH 43023-0566 614-522-6400

RESIDENT COUNCILS

(1978) - complete guide on establishing a council to give more power to the residents of nursing homes; includes information on the need, purpose, training program, operation, and continuing effectiveness, 46pp, $8.95 (member $13.90) **American Health Care Association** 1200 Fifteenth Street, NW, Washington , DC 20005 202-833-2050

SELF-CONTAINED BOARD TRAINING KITS

(1980) - two four-hour units of instruction geared toward smaller communities; focuses on responsibilities of board membership; includes instructor's kit consisting of manual, audiocassettes, and 16mm films, as well as one participant's kit with workbooks covering key learning concepts, workshops activities, and reference readings:
- *Unit I: Functions and Responsibilities of Board and Staff in Nonprofit Organizations* - duties of board, committee and chair; meeting effectiveness; board recruitment, selection, and development; evaluation of board and CEO, 41pp, #UC10603, $350.00
- *Unit II: Financial Development and Accountability in Nonprofit Organizations* - legal obligations, social accountability, finance, strategy, fundraising, etc., 48pp, #UC10604, $275.00

United Way of America 701 North Fairfax Street, Alexandria, VA 22314-2045 703-836-7100

SO...YOU SERVE ON A BOARD

(Rev. 1978) - quick-reference itemization of board functions, member roles, selection and term procedures, training obligations, board/staff relationships and responsibilities, evaluation by/of board, etc., 25pp, $1.50 ($15.00/dozen) **Volunteer Center of San Gabriel Valley** 3301 Thorndale Road, Pasadena, CA 91107 213-792-6118

TEN BASIC RESPONSIBILITIES OF NONPROFIT BOARDS

(1988) - describes the fundamental responsibilities of boards, focusing primarily on the whole board as one entity; includes list of responsibilities of individual board members, 22pp, $5.95 (author is vice president of Association of Governing Boards of Universities and Colleges) **National Center for Nonprofit Boards** 1225 Nineteenth Street, NW, Suite 340, Washington, DC 20036 202-452-6262

TRAINING VOLUNTEER LEADERS

(1974) - a manual that grew out of the need for more specific training techniques for YMCA group leaders to become a comprehensive training guide for developing leadership in any organization in which persons come together in groups to achieve their objectives; includes steps for establishing a climate for learning, diagnosing needs, defining training objectives, designing the training unit and evaluating and re-diagnosing the program; provides extensive guidance for helping the group get organized, 189pp, $8.00 plus $1.00 postage/handling, prepaid **Young Men's Christian Association of the U.S.** Programs Materials Division, 291 Broadway, New York, NY 10007 202-374-2000

VOLUNTEER DEVELOPMENT TRAINING PACKAGES (VLDP)

(1986) - a comprehensive series providing tools for the training of boards, volunteer managers, citizen leaders and others; major components include:

The BoardWALK Series: Tools for the Training and Development of Nonprofit Boards (Boards Working At Leadership Knowledge) - the latest series of training materials available through *United Way of America's Volunteer Leadership Development Program (VLDP)*; offers tools designed to help leaders stage board-training sessions; includes twelve binders containing materials for conducting the twelve individual workshops that are *BoardWALK's* core; includes three handbooks that address the how-to's of an effective board development program:

The manuals:
- *VDLP Organization Handbook - How to Bring VLDP to Your Community* - introductory manual explaining the VLDP concept and offering step-by-step advice on how to establish and operate a board training program; appends worksheets and forms, 255 pages.
- *Training Institute Facilitator Handbook - How to Conduct VLDP Training Sessions* - special curriculum guide for teaching *BoardWALK* workshop leaders the skills needed for conducting training sessions; includes ways of adapting curriculum to formats ranging from two days to a full-retreat model, 415 pages+.
- *Organizational Needs Assessment Handbook - Techniques for Analyzing Agency Training Needs* - a survey tool to analyze the organization's unique requirements and steer participants toward those workshops that will prove most effective for them, 191 pages.

The Twelve Workshop Binders:
- *Operational Strategies for Boards* - understanding the board skills needed, 436+ pages.
- *Planning* - recognizing the critical role of planning in an organization's viability, 298+ pages.
- *Legal Issues* - exploration of the nonprofit as a corporate entity, and protection of reputation, 210 pages.
- *Managing Change* - strategies board members can use to adapt to internal and external changes, 238 pages.
- *Cooperative Action in the Community* - relationship between agencies and other community groups; dynamics of cooperative action, 314 pages.
- *Personnel* - board's role in personnel policies, hiring and evaluating Executive Director. 412+ pages.
- *Financial Decision Making* - ways board members can fulfill their financial responsibilities, 390+ pages.
- *Fund Raising* - role of philanthropy in nonprofit organizations - options, strategies, techniques, 425+ pages.

- *Public and Community Relations* - communicating through advertising, advocacy, networks, recognition, 213 pages.
- *Marketing* - definition of marketing mix, and development of marketing plan, 201 pages.
- *Evaluation* - ways of ensuring that organization meets its goals, 387 pages.

[This is an intensive training program tailored to the individual organization's needs. Inquire about cost and other details. Also see individual publications, self-contained board training kits, videotapes and other United Way of America leadership development materials described elsewhere in this book.] **United Way of America** 701 North Fairfax Street, Alexandria, VA 22314-2045 703-836-7100

VOLUNTEER LEADERSHIP DEVELOPMENT PROGRAM SERIES

(1979-83) - guides that address the roles and responsibilities of volunteers who serve on boards of nonprofit organizations, including:
- *Volunteer and Staff Responsibilities*, 14pp, $2.00
- *Personnel Administration in the Voluntary Agency*, 15pp, $2.00
- *Quick Evaluation Models for Assessing Organizational Performance*, 18pp, $2.00
- *The Board and Its Responsibilities*, 34pp, $5.00
- *The Effective Use of Committees*, 8pp, $2.00
- *The Agency and the Community*, 8pp, $2.00
- *The Crucial Relationship: Community Agencies and Community Structure*, 12pp, $2.00
- *Evaluation Concepts and Agency Self-Evaluation Methods: A Handbook*, 45pp, $2.00
- *The Citizen Board in Voluntary Agencies*, 71pp, $2.50 (100 or more, $1.50 each)

United Way of America 701 North Fairfax Street, Alexandria, VA 22314-2045 701-836-7100

YOUTH INVOLVEMENT: A CHALLENGE FOR COMMUNITIES

(1980) - a guide developed for communities by three teenagers in the Wisconsin Association for Youth to examine youth involvement in service to the community, and how leaders can work with youth to resolve problems and gain the maximum benefit from a community-youth partnership, 50pp, inquire about cost **Wisconsin Clearinghouse** 1954 East Washington Avenue, Madison, WI 53704 608-263-2797

YOUTH PARTICIPATION IN ORGANIZATIONS

(1976) - the case for involving youth in organizations with which they can identify, or helping them to form new ones, 47pp, single copy free **US/HHS - Division of Youth Activities** PO Box 1182, Washington, DC 20201 202-245-7000

LITERACY

BASIC LITERACY TUTOR HANDBOOK
(Rev. 1988) - a guide to the teaching of reading and writing to
adults; chapters include:
- Discovering Student Goals
- Techniques for Reading with Beginners
- Using the Language Experience Approach
- Teaching Reading Strategies
- Develooping Comprehension
- Teaching Writing
- Teaching Spelling and Increasing Vocabulary
- Teaching Basic Math
- Computer-Assisted Learning
- Putting It All Together
- Evaluating Progress

Includes bibliography and index, 56pp, $10 [*Supplement* published
in 1989, $5] plus $1.50 shipping and handling for one or both
Center for Literacy 3723 Chestnut Street, Philadelphia, PA 19104
215-382-3700

BEYOND PICTURE BOOKS
(1989) - a guide to first readers geared to the literacy crisis facing
the nation today; provides a selection of quality first readers for
children in kindergarten through second grade, compiled by
practicing specialists in children's literature; appends reading-level
indexes, 300pp, $39.95 **R. R. Bowker** PO Box 762, New York, NY
10011

EVEN START
(1989) - overview of a new program to promote family
involvement through adult literacy, parent education and early
childhood education projects, single copy free **US/DoE - Office of
Information** 400 Maryland Avenue, SW, Washington, DC 20024
202-732-4682

HANDBOOK FOR VOLUNTEER READING AIDES
(1975) - step-by-step description of the organization of a
community literacy program to assist groups wishing to mount
such a program, and to provide comprehensive background
information and tutoring helps for the volunteer reading aide,
86pp, $2.00 **Lutheran Church Women** 2900 Queen Lane,
Philadelphia, PA 19129 215-438-2200

HIGH/LOW HANDBOOK
(1990) - a comprehensive listing of books, materials, and services

for problem readers, designed for people who work with problem
readers age thirteen and up, 304pp, $39.95, also available from
book dealers **R. R. Bowker** PO Box 762, New York, NY 10011

**IMAGINE WHAT IT IS LIKE FOR SOMEONE WHO
CANNOT READ**
(1990) - overview of Brown University's *Adult Literacy Program;*
includes a discussion about adult literacy, and a description of the
program, 4-panel foldout, free **Brown University** 25 George Street,
PO Box 1974, Providence, RI 02912 401-863-2338

**LITERACY ACTION: COLLEGE/UNIVERSITY RESOURCE
BOOK**
(1989) - a resource book for campus leaders interested in
increasing awareness about literacy and building
campus/community literacy programs, 192pp, $13.40 **Campus
Outreach Opportunity League (COOL)** 386 McNeal Hall,
University of Minnesota, St. Paul, MN 55108-1011 612-624-3018

LITERACY POSTER
(1990) - a poster which encourages older persons to get involved
with their local literacy program; designed for use in public places;
i.e., Senior Centers, dining sites, congregate housing, libraries, etc.
(must be involved with one of these audiences to request poster),
17x24, single copy free **Institute of Lifetime Learning** 1909 K
Street, NW, Washington, DC 20049 202-872-4700

MAKING AMERICA LITERATE: HOW YOU CAN HELP
(1990) - a brochure designed to encourage and direct older persons
to get involved in the national fight against illiteracy; lists
organizations which are working to combat this problem, foldout
brochure, single copy free **Institute of Lifetime Learning** 1909 K
Street, NW, Washington, DC 20049 202-872-4700

ORGANIZATION HANDBOOK
(1981) - survey, development and management techniques for local
literacy groups, with models for organization, by-laws and
record-keeping for the organizing and sustaining of a volunteer
literacy program, 100pp, unbound, 3-hole punched, $5.00 **New
Readers Press** Box 131, 1320 Jamesville Avenue, Syracuse, NY
23210 315-422-9131

PARTICIPATORY LITERACY EDUCATION
(1989) - overview of literacy programs that actively involve the learners themselves in shaping program content and development; discusses how this practice enhances the effectiveness of adult literacy education; shows how to use different techniques to enhance adult participation; includes case histories from both the community and the workplace, $12.95 **Jossey Bass, Publishers** 350 Sansome Street, San Francisco, CA 94104-1310 415-433-1767

READER DEVELOPMENT BIBLIOGRAPHY
(1982) - a comprehensive list of books published for use with adult new readers; includes books with readability levels of grades 2 through 8, recommended by the head librarian of the Reader Development Program of the Philadelphia Free Library, 122pp, $9.95 **New Readers Press** Box 131, 1320 Jamesville Avenue, Syracuse, NY 23210 315-422-9131

READING AND THE ADULT LEARNER
(1980) - description of adult reading programs in the U.S.; includes programs in a nursing home, a jail, a business, through television, computers, etc., 76pp, $4.00, (members $2.50) **International Reading Association** 800 Barksdale Road, PO Box 8139, Newark, DE 19714 302-731-1600

SPORTS ILLUSTRATED FOR KIDS
(monthly) - a youth-oriented version of *Sports Illustrated* designed to help curb the illiteracy of America's youth; incorporates a newly-created comic strip character, *Buzz Beamer,* to supplement articles and stories and help maintain interest; includes teaching guide with each issue; number of pages vary; available at nominal cost but provided free to school districts in impoverished areas, inquire **Time, Inc.** Corporate Community Involvement, Rockefeller Center, New York, NY 10020 212-522-1212

THE TIME TO READ APPROACH TO LITERACY
(kept current) - details about the theory and practice behind a national literacy program for learners 12 to adult who read at fourth-grade level or above but cannot read fluently; designed to utilize newspapers, magazines, job applications, etc., as well as instructional materials to bridge the gap between the basic programs for nonreaders and the high school equivalency program, unpaged, free **Time, Inc.** Corporate Community Relations, Rockefeller Center, New York, NY 10020 212-522-1212

TIME TO READ: THE TIME, INC. LITERACY PROGRAM
(kept current) - a comprehensive packet about a national literacy program designed to bridge the gap between basic programs for nonreaders and high school equivalency programs; includes a question and answer brochure, sample newsletter, news clips from around the country, ad photostats, and other materials, unpaged, free to those interested after receiving the initial overview publication, *Time To Read Approach to Reading,* described above. **Time, Inc.** Corporate Community Relations, Rockefeller Center, New York, NY 10020 212-522-1212

USING READABILITY
(1977) - a guide for writing or evaluating materials for adult new readers; explanation of factors that affect reading ease; guide to the use of Gunning and Fry readability formulae, 40pp, $2.00 **New Readers Press** Box 131, 1320 Jamesville Avenue, Syracuse, NY 23210 315-422-9131

WRITERS' VOICES; NEW WRITERS' VOICES
(1989-90) - two series of books created to give adults literacy students a chance to read what they see other people reading on the subway, in libraries and at home; includes works of Erdrich, Anaya, Angelou, entertainers Burnett and Cosby and others who

adapted the books themselves in cooperation with LVA, 30 books in all, write for list, $2.95 each plus $2.00 shipping **Literacy Volunteers of America** LVNYC, 121 Sixth Avenue, New York, NY 10013 212-925-3001

MENTAL HEALTH

ABOUT THE VOLUNTEER PROGRAM OF PRAIRIE VIEW
(undated) - a packet of materials describing a program that is designed to involve volunteers as a way of increasing community involvement in the treatment of the mentally ill, and increase patient contact with the outside community; includes a descriptive brochure, job descriptions, reprints (*Volunteers Play a Supporting Role in Psychodrama, Volunteers Key to Mental Health Center's Philosophy*, and *Developing Effective Volunteer Services*), and other items, single packet free **Prairie View Mental Health Center** 1901 East First Street, Box 467, Newton, KS 67114 316-283-2400

BLUEPRINT...A VOLUNTEER PROGRAM
(1973) - comprehensive handbook for development of a volunteer program in a mental health setting; covers identification of leadership, recruitment and interviewing, placement, orientation, training; describes practical applications for hospitals, schools and related agencies, 135pp, $5.00 **St. Lawrence Hospital** Community Services/Education, 1201 West Oakland, Lansing, MI 48915 517-372-3610

COMMUNITY FRIENDS
(undated) - a portfolio of information about a program designed to bring together trained volunteers and lonely, isolated and depressed people, giving the support of friendship; lists ideas for activities that lead to a successful relationship; includes sample forms, fact sheets and other materials, single portfolio free **Community Friends** 95 Mahalani Street, Wailuku, HI 96793 808-242-6461

COMPEER INFORMATION PACKET
(undated) - information about a program developed to match community volunteers in a one-to-one supportive, rehabilitative relationship with mental health patients as an adjunct to therapy; includes a fact sheet, reprints, and other items as available, single packet free **Compeer, The Health Association** 973 East Avenue, Rochester, NY 14607 716-271-3540

CREATIVE MENTAL HEALTH SERVICES FOR THE ELDERLY
(1977) - case studies of ten programs, ranging from the most primary effort to notable accomplishments - all selected for their innovations in prevention of emotional dysfunction in the elderly, 190pp, $9.50 **American Psychiatric Association** 1400 K Street, NW, Washington, DC 20005 202-682-6000

FRIENDS
(undated) - packet of information about a program utilizing hundreds of volunteers who have faced stressful times to help others who are presently under stress; uses theme "voice of experience" to motivate those under stress to participate, free packet **Lutheran Social Services of North Dakota** 1325 South Eleventh Street, Fargo, ND 58102 701-235-7341

GUIDE FOR VOLUNTEERS AT THE WEST-ROS-PARK MENTAL HEALTH CENTER
(kept current) - orientation/educational manual for the mental health case aide working on a one-to-one relationship basis with those both in the hospital and in the community, 25pp, $2.00 **Volunteer Case Aide Program** 780 American Legion Highway, Roslindale, MA 02131 617-325-6700

GUIDELINES FOR THE TRANSITIONAL VOLUNTEER PROGRAM
(1979) - overview of the basic necessity to initiate, develop, and operate a program for transitional volunteers; includes sample forms, 11pp, $1.00 **Volunteer Center of Lincoln** 215 Centennial Mall South, Lincoln, NE 68508 402-474-6218

HALFWAY HOUSES FOR THE MENTALLY ILL
(1971) - case studies of 17 halfway houses for people who are or have been mentally ill; represents widely differing sizes and styles which, along with a chapter on establishing halfway houses, are intended to provide a base for persons interested in developing such programs in their communities, 224pp, $7.00 **American Psychiatric Association** 1400 K Street, NW, Washington, DC 20005 202-682-6000

HELPING THE MENTAL PATIENT AT HOME
(1979) - practical information and suggestions which families can use to help mental patients who have returned from mental hospitals, and which program leaders can use to help those receiving care in the community, 15pp, $1.00 **National Mental Health Association** 1021 Prince Street, Alexandria, VA 22314 703-684-7722

IN AND OUT THE WINDOWS
(1982) - the moving story of Kit Ferris, a schizophrenic who learns to accept and eventually recover from her illness, 64pp,

$2.25 **New Readers Press** Box 131, Syracuse, NY 13210
315-422-9121

LECTURES TO RELATIVES OF FORMER PATIENTS
(undated) - ongoing discussions with families prior to a patient's
release to head off circumstances in the family environment that
may have caused the original breakdown; includes guidelines
following each lecture to further assist persons working with
mental patients and their families, 229pp, $5.00 (ask about
directory of group meetings) **Recovery, Inc.** 802 North Dearborn
Street, Chicago, IL 60610 312-337-5661

LONELINESS CAN KILL PEOPLE
(undated) - recuitment brochure with questions and answers about
the West-Ros-Park Center's operation and volunteer case aide
program, 8-panel foldout, free **Volunteer Case Aide Program**
West-Ros-Park Mental Health Center, 780 American Legion
Highway, Roslindale, MA 02131 617-325-6700

MENTAL/EMOTIONAL HEALTH BOOKLET SERIES
(1987-89) - three booklets addressing emotional health, including:
About Your Child's Emotional Health, About Self Esteem, and
Emotional Abuse: Words Can Hurt; explains the value of a good
self image at home, school and on the job; details the harm to
children of emotional abuse, and the value of good emotional
health, 16pp each, single copies free [first two booklets also
available from Channing L. Bete Company 200 State Road, South
Deerfield, MA 01373 800-628-7733] **Child Protective Services**
Virginia Dept. of Social Services, 8007 Discovery Drive,
Richmond, VA 23229-8699

MENTAL HEALTH INFORMATION BOOKLET SERIES
(1980) - illustrated guides in mental health areas, 15pp each, $.75
each:
  ● *What Every One Should Know About Mental Health*
  ● *What Everyone Should Know About Mental Health Services*
  ● *What Everyone Should Know About Stress*
  ● *About Your Child's Emotional Health*
Channing L. Bete Company , South Deerfield, MA 01373

**MENTAL HEALTH PROGRAMS FOR PRESCHOOL
CHILDREN: A FIELD STUDY**
(1974) - descriptions of seven programs serving the mental health
needs of children under six years of age; outlines volunteer
involvement and types of programs that differ regarding the kinds
of children and families served, 182pp, $8.00 **American Psychiatric
Association** 1400 K Street, NW, Washington, DC 20005
202-682-6000

NMHA PAMPHLET SERIES
(1979) - brief overviews of mental health subjects, quantity
discounts:
  ● *Mental Health is 1-2-3, $.35*
  ● *Some Things You Should Know about Mental and Emotional
    Illness, $.40*
  ● *How to Deal with Mental Problems, $.40*
  ● *When Things Go Wrong, $.40*
  ● *Depression: What You Should Know About It, $.40*
  ● *How to Deal with Your Tensions, $.40*
  ● *What Every Child Needs for Better Mental Health, $.40*
  ● *Mental Illness May Be Prevented, $.35*
  ● *Respond to: Mentally Restored Workers, $.35*
[all titles not available at all times] **National Mental Health
Association** 1021 Prince Street, Alexandria, VA 22314
703-684-7722

**PROGRAMS IN RECOGNIZING EMOTIONAL
DISTURBANCE IN CHILDREN**
(undated) - overview of the many facets of a child's behavior and
how this contributes to early identification of emotional problems,
15pp, $1.50 **Child Welfare League of America** 440 First Street,
NW, Washington, DC 20001 202-638-2942

REACH OUT TO THE MENTALLY ILL
(1976) - guide for a session with people who recognize that they
are under stress and want to do something about it; presents case
studies, a narration for three readers, and references to relevant
books, 8pp, $.40 ($2.95/dozen) **Augsburg Fortress** 426 South Fifth
Avenue, Box 1209, Minneapolis, MN 55440 612-330-3300

**REHABILITATING THE MENTALLY ILL IN THE
COMMUNITY**
(2nd pr. 1973) - overview of problems and practices of developing
and operating rehabilitation programs in the community for the
mentally ill; includes six program descriptions, each a full chapter
with complete information on how the facility involves volunteers
(five extensively and one on a casual basis); appends additional
brief program descriptions and a viewpoint on the future of
community-based mental health rehabilitation, 213pp, $7.00
American Psychiatric Association 1400 K Street, NW,
Washington, DC 20005 202-682-6000

**SIBLINGS COPING: WRITTEN BY BROTHERS AND
SISTERS OF MENTALLY ILL PERSONS**
(undated) - the result of the work of a group of siblings of
mentally ill persons written in an issue-by-issue format to help
themselves and others to understand feelings such as guilt and
anger in relation to the plight of the mentally ill family member,
8-panel foldout, single copy free **Alliance for the Mentally Ill of
Greater Milwaukee** PO Box 18818, Milwaukee, WI 53216
414-442-9424

TAKE CARE OF MILLIE
(1980) - story of a widow, unaccustomed to being alone, who
learns to be assertive and make her own decisions, 64pp, $2.00
New Readers Press , Box 131, Syracuse, NY 13210 315-422-9121

THERAPEUTIC SERVICES AT OUR CENTER
(undated) - a handbook covering all divisions of the center,
including the Volunteer Services division and how it interfaces
with all of the others; presents a quick-reference format with an
introduction providing basic information about the overall
program, 14pp, inquire about cost **Cambridge Mental Health and
Developmental Center** , Cambridge, OH 43725 614-439-1371

THIS WAY TO REALITY
(undated) - guide for a modest in-service training program to
develop skills for communicating with older people suffering from
confusion and faulty memory to help them increase their potential,
233pp, $8.50 (ask about five related filmstrips) **American Health
Care Association** 1200 Fifteenth Street, NW, Washington , DC
20005 202-833-2050

TRANSITIONAL VOLUNTEERS! WHO ARE THEY?
(1980)- packet of information on how one VAC planned and
established an ongoing volunteer program in concert with the
trend toward greater deinstitutionalization of psychiatric patients;
includes project brochure, workshop format, development outline,
release for information on potential transitional volunteers, etc.,
$1.50/packet **Volunteer Resources Division** 484 Main Street, Suite
300, Worcester, MA 01608 617-757-5631

VOLUNTEER PROGRAM: MOUNT VERNON MENTAL HEALTH CENTER
(undated) - a packet of information describing the volunteer program and its relationship to the Center's overall efforts to assist people experiencing depression, fears, marital problems and other emotional problems; includes leaflets on volunteer opportunities and facts about the program, a newsletter, and other materials as available, single packet free **Mount Vernon Center for Community Mental Health** 8119 Holland Road, Alexandria, VA 22306 703-360-6910

WOODBURN CENTER FOR COMMUNITY MENTAL HEALTH
(undated) - a packet of information on a program that enlists and trains volunteers and graduate school trainees to work with psychiatrists, psychologists, psychiatric social workers, psychiatric nurses, counselors and therapists to assist citizens who are experiencing stress and other emotional problems, single packet free **Woodburn Center for Community Mental Health** 3340 Woodburn Road, Annandale, VA 22003 703-573-0523

NATIONAL SERVICE/POINTS OF LIGHT INITIATIVE

CITIZENSHIP THROUGH SERVICE: YOUTH AND AMERICA'S FUTURE
(1988) - a reprint of a chapter, "Pathways to Success: Citizenship through Service," from the book, *The Forgotten Half: Pathways to Success for American Youth;* addresses varied opportunities every community's voluntary sector has to offer young people to work on their own or with adults to promote community service; includes sections on the benefits of service, school-based volunteer requirement, youth volunteer corps, National Service, and other issues, 16pp, single copy free **William T. Grant Foundation** Work/Family/Citizenship Committee, 1001 Connecticut Avenue NW, #301, Washington, DC 20036-5541 202-775-9731

NATIONAL SERVICE: A PROMISE TO KEEP
(1989) - background information detailing early National Service activities, proposals, and writings; includes sections on the 1950s, the 1960s, the 1970s and the 1980s, tracing the work of a pioneer in developing the idea for National Service, and addressing the present Administration's proposals and bills, 247pp, hardcover, $17.95 **John Alden Books** PO Box 26668, Rochester, NY 14626 716-225-8534

NATIONAL SERVICE AND "POINTS OF LIGHT" IN THE NEWS
(1989) - fact sheet providing a comprehensive overview of the National Service legislation, legislators, and individual sections of the program; includes discussion of the YES (Youth Engaged in Service) program and the Points of Light initiative; appends AVA Region I's definition of National Service, and the policy of Community Service outlined by the National Governors' Association, 2pp, free **Association for Volunteer Administration** PO Box 4584, Boulder, CO 80306 303-497-0238

NATIONAL SERVICE BRIEFING PAPER
(1990) - an overview of the objectives and plans of the *Office of National Service,* formerly *Office of Private Sector Initiatives,* of The White House, which is charged with keeping the President advised on community service policy and strategy, among other functions, unpaged, free **US/White House - Office of National Service** Old Executive Office Building, Room 100, Washington, DC 20500 202-456-6266

POINTS OF LIGHT INITIATIVE: COMMUNITY SERVICE AS NATIONAL POLICY
(1990) - a comprehensive briefing paper providing detailed information on the President's *Points of Light Initiative;* describes the challenge and the mission, and addresses the three-part strategy developed to help the nation accomplish the mission (claiming society's problems as one's own; identifying, enlarging and multiplying what is working; discovering, encouraging and developing leaders), 9pp, free **US/White House - Office of National Service** Old Executive Office Building, Room 100, Washington, DC 20500 202-456-6266

PRESIDENT'S NEW LEADERSHP STRUCTURES FOR POINTS OF LIGHT INITIATIVE
(1990) - descriptions of the three institutions that enable the President to play a personal leadership role in the growing nationwide community service movement (*Points of Light Initiative Foundation, Daily Point of Light, Office of National Service*), 7pp, free **US/White House - Office of National Service** Old Executive Office Building, Room 100, Washington, DC 20500 202-456-6266

SERVICE OPPORTUNITIES FOR YOUTH
(1989) - summaries of federal legislation affecting national service for youth; overview for educators, social workers, business groups, religious congregations, and community organizations wishing to establish youth service components; provides profiles of successful youth service programs, names of national organizations, and other information, $4.50 **Children's Defense Fund** 122 C Street, NW, Suite 400, Washington, DC 20001 202-628-8787

A THOUSAND POINTS OF LIGHT: THE FIRST ONE HUNDRED
(1990) - a listing of the first 100 individuals, organizations, groups, and business/industry honorees recognized by the President as part of the *Thousand Points of Light Initiative* (from November 22, 1989 to March 26, 1990); provides a brief outlines of programs or services in which the honorees are involved, 36pp, single copy free **US/White House - Office of National Service** , Washington, DC 20500 202-456-6266

NUTRITION

ABC'S OF GOOD NUTRITION
(1980) - heavily illustrated guide on what good nutrition means in terms of health, energy, disease, etc.; includes comparison of food needs for young children, teenagers, young adults, older people, etc., 15pp, $.75 (quantity discounts) **Channing L. Bete Company** , South Deerfield, MA 01373

BAG IT! A GUIDE TO PACKING NUTRITIOUS LUNCHES
(undated) - illustrated guide presenting the case for packing instead of buying a lunch to have better control over nutritious content; includes a chart enabling numerous possibilities in putting together a balanced lunch, 24pp, single copy free **Giant Food** Consumer Affairs Department, PO Box 1804, Washington, DC 20013 202-341-4100

BREAKFAST AND THE BRIGHT LIFE
(1970) - pictorial script emphasizing the importance of breakfast and its contribution to daily food needs, the relative ease in its preparation, and good selections of food for starting the day; developed for use with a slide presentation, but useful in itself as a training tool, 8pp, single copy free (request slide/filmstrip information) **US/DoA - Photography Division** Independence Avenue, (Between 12th & 14th Sts.), Washington, DC 20250 202-447-2791

CAMP FOOD SERVICES SUPERVISOR
(1979) - specific help for those responsible for preparing food for children in camping programs; details techniques of preparation, service, equipment care and maintenance, as well as interaction with other staff and campers, 39pp, $1.95 **American Camping Association** Bradford Woods, Martinsville, IN 46151-7902 317-342-8456

COMMUNITY FOOD AND NUTRITION PROGRAM: FOOD FOR THE POOR
(kept current) - overview of the program which seeks to reduce hunger among the poor by both direct service and institutional change; provides an account of the scope of the program, the types of funding, and several brief profiles of existing programs (Feed the Babies, Vermont Garden Project, others), 6-panel foldout, free **Community Food and Nutrition Program** Office of Community Services, Office of the Secretary, Washington, DC 20201 202-653-2010

CONSUMER'S GUIDE TO COMMUNITY SERVICE
(1989) - a booklet sent in response to telephone calls in response to the *Prime Time to End Hunger* campaign in the fall of 1989; includes contact information for local *Volunteer Center, United Way,* or *Emergency Food and Shelter Board,* single copy free while supply lasts **VOLUNTEER - The National Center** 1111 North 19th Street, Suite 500, Arlington, VA 22209 703-276-0542

CREATIVE FOOD EXPERIENCES FOR CHILDREN
(1981) - activities, games, facts and recipes for use with children to enable them to learn by helping with preparation of food, 191pp, $5.95 **Center for Science in the Public Interest** 1501 Sixteenth Street, NW, Washington, DC 20036 202-332-9110

EATING BETTER AT SCHOOL: AN ORGANIZER'S GUIDE
(1980) - handbook for parents, volunteers, and others concerned with the quality of foods served in the schools; outlines steps for a successful monitoring and improvement campaign and tells of other people's victories; includes an overview of the school lunch program, facts on health and nutrition, and a list of local and national organizations available for help, 32pp, $2.50 (50 or more $1.00 each; also available from Children's Foundation, separate entry) **Center for Science in the Public Interest** 1501 Sixteenth Street, NW, Washington, DC 20036 202-332-9110

FOOD
(1980) - one of a series of the *Home and Garden Bulletin* focusing on the relationship of food and nutrition to the kind of health that enables people to participate fully in chosen occupations and leisure activities, 16pp, single copy free **US/DoA - Food and Nutrition Service** Independence Avenue, (Between 12th & 14th Sts.), Washington, DC 20251 202-447-2791

FOOD BANK INFORMATION PACKET
(undated) - a packet of materials describing a food bank operation (a clearinghouse which collects food from food donors, and sorts and allocates to agencies serving the needy); includes specific information, articles, newsletters, and other materials about the Blue Ridge operation, the supporting produce, retail, and other food suppliers, and other items, single packet free **Blue Ridge Area Food Bank** Box 1365, Staunton, VA 24401 703-886-3003

FOOD BANK INFORMATION PACKET
(undated) - overview of a program designed to provide emergency food assistance to the needy by salvaging foodstuffs that would otherwise be wasted; includes volunteer job descriptions, protocol for volunteers, record-keeping forms, and information on how to start a food bank, single packet free **Gallatin Valley Emergency Food Bank** 317 Mendenhall, Bozeman, MT 59175 406-587-4486

FOOD CO-OPS: AN ALTERNATIVE TO SHOPPING IN SUPERMARKETS
(1974) - manual for starting "genuine people's organizations" - food co-ops; covers initial meetings, space acquisition, financing, book keeping, etc., based on a real-life successful operation; includes other program descriptions, the history of co-ops, and three appendices listing co-op newsletters, wholesalers recommended by co-ops, and a directory of co-ops across the country, 188pp, $3.95 **Beacon Press** 25 Beacon Street, Boston, MA 02108 617-742-2110

FOOD: WHERE NUTRITION, POLITICS AND CULTURE MEET
(1976) - an "assertively unconventional" food and nutrition book designed to involve children and young people in projects and activities that deviate from the normal technique (tracking down the foodways of parents and grandparents; interviewing patrons of fast-food restaurants), but hold their interest and teach them to investigate, communicate, and effect change, 214pp, $5.50 (quantity discounts) **Center for Science in the Public Interest** 1501 Sixteenth Street, NW, Washington, DC 20036 202-332-9110

HANDBOOK FOR MEALS ON WHEELS VOLUNTEERS
(undated) - organizational information for operating a meals on wheels program from more than one location; includes brief history of program, job descriptions, and other details, 20pp, $2.50 **Meals on Wheels of Central Maryland** 1729 York Road, Baltimore, MD 21212 301-561-1100

HOW FOOD AFFECTS YOU
(undated) - illustrated script on the basic nutritional values of food as it affects growth, unborn babies, muscles, blood, nerves, teeth, etc.; developed for use with a slide presentation, but very effective by itself as a training tool, 12pp, single copy free (request slide/filmstrip information) **US/DOA - Photography Division** Independence Avenue, (Between 12th & 14th Sts.), Washington, DC 20250 202-447-2791

HOW TO START A FOOD DISTRIBUTION PROGRAM
(1990) - overview of getting started, from "discussing your idea with a friend" to surveying the community, finding the right individuals to help, establishing a funding base, and setting up the nonprofit organization; includes both challenges and hardships of such a venture, 4pp, free **City Harvest** 139 West 25th Street, Tenth Floor, New York, NY 10001-7201 212-463-0456

AN INTRODUCTION TO GLEANING: INFORMATION PACKET
(1983) - a set of manuals and other information used in a program designed to harvest the leftovers in Idaho fields (1.8 million tons of food) through the use of volunteer gleaners/partners (gleaners are people who cannot adequately meet their food needs who share their harvest with partners and partner organizations, who are either disabled, senior citizens, provide child care for the gleaners, or are Head Start, Senior Meals on Wheels, soup kitchens or other nonprofit free food programs); includes a manual for the team captain, for the food donor, and for the individual or group wishing to know more about the gleaning process; appends sample forms and other aids, unpaged, $1.00 **Idaho Hunger Action**

Council 205 North Tenth, Suite 602, Boise, ID 83702 208-336-7010

KID CUISINE INFORMATION KIT
1990) - information about eight nutritious dinners developed for children ages three to ten, with clear microwave instructions for the older ages; includes activity items such as games and puzzles, unpaged, free **ConAgra Frozen Foods** Banquet Division, Route 1, Box 24-A, Crozet, VA 22932 804-823-3200

KID'S KITCHEN CLUB
(1990) - a packet of nutrition information aimed at "latchkey children" to accompany a new line of nutritious, *child-tested* shelf-stable entrees with full microwave instructions to counteract the 'cold cereal/fast food' habits of these children; includes newsletter, membership card, insignia patch, and a *Kidalogue* describing the entrees and other products, unpaged, free **George A. Hormel & Company** 500 Fourteenth Avenue, NE, Austin, MN 55912 507-437-5611

MARTHA'S TABLE: INFORMATION PACKET
(undated) - a packet of information on a program operated by volunteers to feed the hungry in Washington, DC's poorest and toughest neighborhoods; includes information on "Kid's Kitchen" (a program with small tables, children's books, and other considerations for hungry children), McKenna's Wagon (a mobile kitchen distributing soup and sandwiches to hungry people around the city), and Martha's Table, the basic program, single packet free **Martha's Table** 2124 Fourteenth Street, NW, Washington, DC 20009 202-328-6608

MEALS ON WHEELS PROGRAM INFORMATION
(1976) - instructions to the driver and the patient to facilitate an effective meals program; includes set of guidelines for program operation, 7pp, single copy free (send self-addressed stamped envelope) **Meals on Wheels Program of Rochester** 1609 East Main Street, Rochester , NY 14609 716-482-0120

MY OWN MEALS INFORMATION PACKET
(1990) - information about five nutritious entrees developed for children from two to eight, with microwave instructions for the older ages, and accompanying activity items such as games and puzzles, unpaged, free **My Own Meals, Inc.** 400 Lake Cook Road, Deerfield, IL 60015 708-948-1118

NEWS FROM S.O.S.
(quarterly) - newsletter of a national and international organization whose purpose is to raise public awareness and raise funds to help fight hunger in the U.S. and other countries, 8pp, single copy free **Share Our Strength (SOS)** 733 Fifteenth Street, NW, Suite 700, Washington, DC 20005 202-393-2925

NUTRITION AND YOUR HEALTH: DIETARY GUIDELINES FOR AMERICANS
(1980) - colorful, heavily illustrated booklet addressing seven dietary areas that affect health: food variety, ideal weight, saturated fat, fiber content, sugar, sodium, alcohol, 20pp, single copy free **US/DoA - Food and Nutrition Service** Independence Avenue, (Between 12th & 14th Sts.), Washington, DC 20251 202-447-2791

REPORT ON NEW DIRECTIONS: SENIOR GROWING PROJECT
(1983) - an overview of a gardening program that involves older volunteers in growing vegetables on lots of several acres to provide vegetables to local meals preparation sites; includes a small plot set aside for the volunteer's own personal garden, 8-panel foldout, free

National Gardening Association 180 Flynn Avenue, Burlington, VT 05401 802-863-1308

SUMMER FOOD SERVICE FOR CHILDREN
(1976) - facts about federal efforts to provide nutrition to school children during the months between regular school sessions, 2pp, single copy free **US/DoA - Food and Nutrition Service** 3101 Park Center Drive, Alexandria, VA 22302 703-756-3281

TWO MEALS A DAY... FIVE DAYS A WEEK
(undated) - a packet of information about a program designed to improve the nutritional status of homebound people through well-balanced meals, nutrition counseling and education, and to improve their emotional and social wellbeing, as well as to refer them, when necessary, to other helping sources; includes annual report, a recruitment brochure, a pocket guide to services and other materials as available, single packet free **Meals on Wheels of Buffalo and Erie County** 775 Main Street, Suite 510, Buffalo, NY 14203 716-852-2626

TYSON LOONEY TUNE MEALS
(1990) - information about eight nutritious entrees developed with "latchkey" children in mind which include simple microwave instructions, and nutrition-oriented puzzles, stickers, games, stories, etc., unpaged, free **Warner Brothers** 4000 Warner Boulevard, Burbank, CA 91505 818-954-6000

USDA ANNOUNCES COMMODITIES/HUNGER PREVENTION ACT PROVISIONS
(1989) - a listing of commodities to be purchased under the Act based on mandate to spend $40 million to purchase, process and distribute commodities to soup kitchens and food banks, free information packet **US/DoA - Food and Nutrition Service** Food Distribution Branch, Alexandria, VA 22302 703-756-3660

WELCOME TO OUR SENIOR MEALS PROGRAM
(undated) - an overview and information brochure designed to inform senior participants in a program designed to help provide nutritious meals and nutrition education for the elderly; lists seven steps to help the participant get the most out of the program, 6-panel foldout, single copy free (also request overall brochure to learn of other St. Joseph Community Services programs) **St. Joseph Community Services** Continental Boulevard, PO Box 910, Merrimack, NH 03054 603-424-9967

PHYSICAL ENVIRONMENT

ACID RAIN: THE INVISIBLE POLLUTANT
(1982) - detailed description of the sources of acid precipitation, its effects on aquatic and terrestrial ecosystems, and the debate over its control; self-mailing foldout, $1.00 (100/$50) **Concern** 1794 Columbia Road, NW, Washington, DC 20009 202-328-8160

ACTION ON THE 9 FOR 90S
(1990) - nine personal steps one can take to support nine national and global issues: The Greenhouse Effect, Wildlife and Habitat, Ozone Depletion, Saving the Rainforests, Acid Rain, Water, Toxics, Antartica, and Recycling, inquire about availability and cost **Environmental Defense Fund** 257 Park Avenue, South, New York, NY 10010 212-505-2100

AIR POLLUTION: THE FACTS ABOUT YOUR LUNGS
(kept current) - straight talk about the harmful effects of polluted air on all forms of life and matter; includes a list of the major pollutants, how to get rid of air pollution, and community activities to help strengthen local efforts, 8-panel foldout, single copy free **American Lung Association** 1740 Broadway, New York, NY 10019 212-315-8700

ANTHROZOOS
(quarterly) - the professional journal of the society offering articles by authorities in the field of animal/human interaction and the environment; includes resource information and conference proceedings summaries, Av. 36pp, inquire about availability and cost **Delta Society** 321 Burnett Avenue, South #303, PO Box 1080, Renton, WA 98057-1080 206-226-7357

AUDUBON NATURALIST NEWS
(10/year) - newsletter designed to keep citizens informed of projects, training events, school programs, legislation, and other activities and materials developed to increase public understanding of natural history and the basic importance of preserving and renewing our natural resources, 12pp, free subscription **Audubon Naturalist Society** Woodend, 8940 Jones Mill Road, Chevy Chase, MD 20815 301-652-9188

BAYBOOK
(1990) - a guide to reducing water pollution at home; includes dozens of tips that citizens can use to help keep their area's water free of pollution, unpaged, single copy free **Citizens Program for the Chesapeake Bay** 6600 York Road, Baltimore, MD 21212

BOOKLETS ON ENERGY
(various dates) - illustrated guides on saving resources and money through care in using energy, 15pp each, $.75 each:
- *How to Conserve Energy at Home (1980)*
- *Energy Crisis (1978)*
- *How YOU Can Save Energy Every Day (1979)*

(quantity discounts) **Channing L. Bete Company** , South Deerfield, MA 01373

CATALOG OF ENVIRONMENTAL FILMS
(undated) - brief profiles of films in all areas of environmental improvement (air, land, water, noise, energy, solid waste, litter, attitudes, etc.); includes source/rental-purchase information, 12pp, $.50 **Keep America Beautiful** Mill River Plaza, 9 West Broad Street, Stamford, CT 06092 203-323-8987

CCS MULTI-MATERIAL RECYCLING MANUAL
(1983) - comprehensive handbook for establishing cost-effective, voluntary recycling programs at the local level by working with business, industry and government; covers recycling of aluminum, paper, glass, plastics, iron and steel; also lays out how to encourage citizen involvement, increase volumes of recyclables available for collection and stabilizing markets for various kinds of recyclables, 101pp, $25.00, plus $2.00 postage and handling **Keep America Beautiful** Mill River Plaza, 9 West Broad Street, Stamford, CT 06902 203-323-8987

CHESAPEAKE CLEAN-UP CAMPAIGN (AUDIOVISUAL)
(1989) - a slide show and presentation to recruit groups for tree planting, stream clearnance, habitat enhancement, etc.; provides tools, gloves, bio-degradable trash bags, monitoring equipment, research on soil and tree compatibility, 12 minutes, inquire about availability and cost **Maryland Governor's Office** One State Circle, Annapolis, MD 21401 301-225-4500

CITIZEN MONITORING PROGRAM REPORTS
(kept current) - a series of reports to keep citizens informed and involved based on the monitoring of volunteer efforts to keep the Chesapeake Bay free from pollution and litter; also serves as data for scientists researching water quality, inquire about availability and cost **Alliance for the Chesapeake Bay** c/o Kathy Elett, 410 Severn Avenue, Annapolis, MD 21403 301-377-6270

CLEAN AIR

(1990) - an overview of the 20 years since the Clean Air Act was passed (health standards for breathable air have not been met), what Congress can do, what the citizen can do, 4pp, $.40+$1.00 postage (pay postage only once when ordering multiple Sierra Club materials) **Sierra Club** Information Service, 730 Polk Street, San Francisco, CA 94109 415-776-2211

CLEAN AIR: COSTS AND TRADE-OFFS

(1974) - statement of concern about the growing costs of improving the environment - as measured by taxes, prices, etc.; discusses regulations as they involve emissions from power plants and cars, complaints from plants and drivers, unemployment due to plant closings, carpools, etc., 6pp, $.25 **Citizens Information Service** 67 East Madison Street, Chicago, IL 60603 312-236-0315

DIRECTORY OF NATIONAL CITIZEN VOLUNTEER ENVIRONMENT MONITORING PROGRAMS

(1989) - a directory of volunteer monitoring programs from around the country, with a focus on water quality monitoring programs; includes name, address, contact person, telephone, and a brief description of each program; includes both national, state, regional and local programs; updated as new materials are received, 20pp, single copy free **US/EPA - Environment Monitoring Programs** 401 M Street, SW, Washington, DC 20460 202-475-7751

DRACONS VISIT EARTH TO STUDY FOOD AND THE LAND

(1983) - tells the story of man's climb from a subsistence society to one in which a single farmer can supply the needs of many and ex⁻!ains the role conservation has in maintaining agricultural production; for students in grades four through junior high school, 16pp cartoon booklet, $.75 (inquire about teacher's guide, 10 other booklets, and quantity discounts) **Soil and Water Conservation Society of America** 7515 NE Ankeny Road, Ankeny, IA 50021 515-289-2331

DRINKING WATER: A COMMUNITY ACTION GUIDE

(2nd Pr. 1988) - a guide for citizens to the importance of community attention to drinking water quality and protection, testing and treatment, supply and conservation and innovative state programs; includes examples of innovative reference list, 31pp, $3.00 (bulk rates of same title for nonprofits: 10/$12, 25/$18, 50/$32, 100/$50) **Concern** 1794 Columbia Road, NW, Washington, DC 20009 202-328-8160

ECOLOGY BEGINS AT HOME

(3rd ed., undated) - a household environmental handbook making suggestions that are categorized according to rooms and areas of the home, from the kitchen with its luxury small appliances to the garden and its compost pile, 16pp, $.65 **Sierra Club** Information Service, 730 Polk Street, San Francisco, CA 94109 415-776-2211

ECOLOGY COLORING BOOK

(undated) - a selection of environmental areas easily understood by the very young, designed in a coloring book format to add interest, 24pp, $.20 **B'nai B'rith International** Community Volunteer Services, 1640 Rhode Island Avenue, NW, Washington, DC 20036 202-857-6580

THE END OF AFFLUENCE: A BLUEPRINT FOR YOUR FUTURE

(1974) - descriptions of adaptations needed for an era of limited resources, 288pp **Zero Population Growth** 1601 Connecticut Avenue, NW, Suite 400, Washington, DC 20009 202-332-2200

ENERGY AND THE POOR: CONTINUING CRISIS

(1979) - overview of CSA's program of emergency help to the poor in crisis energy situations (threats of utility cutoff, furnace repair, etc.) and its experimental program of alternative sources of energy to reduce costs for the poor; discusses a series of energy research projects on behalf of the poor, 6-panel foldout, free [NOTE: Responsibilities for the former Community Services Administration are now in the Office of Community Services, D-HHS; if above are not available, related materials will be substituted] **US/HHS - Office of Community Services** PO Box 1182, Washington, DC 20201 202-653-2010

ENERGY CONSERVATION STRATEGIES

(undated) - training manual initially used in "Citizen Training for Energy Conservation," attended by a diverse group of citizen leaders; examines the possible consequences of energy waste, and identifies strategies that show citizens how to evaluate proposals brought before the public on saving energy, 50pp, $3.00 **Conservation Foundation** 1250 24th Street, NW, Washington, DC 20037 202-293-4800

ENERGY: USE IT WISELY AROUND THE HOME

(1975) - narrative guide demonstrating the many ways energy can be saved in America, where 6% of the world's population uses 30% of the world's supply of energy (can be used alone or with related set of slides; inquire about cost of slides), 14pp, single copy free **US/DoA - Photography Division** Independence Avenue, SW, (Between 12th & 14th Sts.), Washington, DC 20250 202-447-2791

ENVIRONMENTAL QUALITY AND THE CITIZEN

(1971) - training manual designed to be used with local resource people assisting the instructor to foster a more localized approach and generate a "community pride" atmosphere in the training session; states course objective of increased awareness by local citizens of their roles in maintaining environmental quality, 40pp, $2.00 **Soil and Water Conservation Society of America** 7515 NE Ankeny Road, Ankeny, IA 50021 515-289-2331

FARMLAND: A COMMUNITY ISSUE

(1987) - a manual explaining the implications of agricultural chemicals and public health, soil and water contamination, resource conservation, and environmentally-sound farming; includes profiles of innovative programs, guidelines for action, and detailed resource and reference lists, 22pp, $3.00 (bulk rates of same title for nonprofits: 10/$12, 25/$18, 50/$32, 100/$50) **Concern** 1794 Columbia Road, NW, Suite #6, Washington, DC 20009 202-328-8160

15 WAYS TO SAVE ENERGY AND MONEY

(1977) - ways citizens can be prudent while giving America time to develop new resources, 40pp, $2.50 **Pilot Books** 103 Cooper Street, Babylon, NY 11702 516-422-2225

FOREST SERVICE VOLUNTEER

(kept current) - details on the volunteer program of the Forest Service that is available to all ages, from youngsters under 18 to retirees; includes information on the *Volunteers in the National Forests Act of 1972* and information on applying, working for college credits, etc.; appends address list of worksites across the country, 6-panel foldout, free **US/DoA - Forest Service** 1375 K Street, NW, #613, PO Box 96090, Washington, DC 20013-6090 202-535-0927

FREE CHECKLISTS ON THE ENVIRONMENT

(kept current) - a series of 2-page outlines to provide ideas for citizens of all ages; some titles:
• *Community Clean-up Campaign Check List*

- *You take the first step...ways to improve the environment;*
- *Pollution Pointers for Elementary Students*

(ask about posters, litterbags and other materials) **Keep America Beautiful** Mill River Plaza, Stamford, CT 06092 203-323-8987

FRESHWATER WETLANDS: THEIR NATURE AND IMPORTANCE TO MAN
(1978) - the case for enacting laws to protect wetlands (natural flood storage areas) such as most of the New England states have done to prevent further "reclaiming" of the lands for industrial, commercial and residential development; includes information on the value of these wetlands to flood control, periods of heavy evaporation, etc., 8pp, single copy free **New England Environmental Network** Tufts University, Medford, MA 02155 617-628-5000

THE FUTURE OF THE ENVIRONMENTAL MOVEMENT
(1979) - an overview of subjects that well-intentioned Americans have avoided (expert knowledge of political infighting, how tough enforceable legislation must be written, etc.), and the need to eliminate sloppy management and lack of communication among environmental organizations, 8pp, single copy free **New England Environmental Leadership Network** Tufts University, Medford, VA 02155 617-628-5000

GROUNDWATER: A COMMUNITY ACTION GUIDE
(4th Pr. 1989) - a definition of "groundwater" and an explanation and call for action by citizens to observe groundwater as to availability and depletion, quality and contamination, public health, and detection and monitoring; appends selected readings, citizen organizations, and state groundwater contacts, 23pp, $3.00 (bulk rates of same title for nonprofits: 10/#12, 25/$18, 50/$32, 100/$50) **Concern** 1794 Columbia Road, NW, Washington, DC 20009 202-328-8160

GUIDE TO IMPROVING THE COMMUNITY: HOW TO RUN A LOCAL AWARDS PROGRAM
(undated) - assistance for any organization considering development of an awards program on improvement of the environment; includes basic steps, awards criteria and judging procedures, sample news release and 30-second radio spot; discusses benefits to the community, sponsorship, etc., 12pp, $.50 **Keep America Beautiful** Mill River Plaza, 9 West Broad Street, Stamford, CT 06092 203-323-8987

GUIDE TO MECHANICAL LITTER REMOVAL EQUIPMENT
(undated) - basic information about mechanical devices currently available for removing litter from highways and urban areas; identifies manufacturers and approximate costs, 19pp, free **Keep America Beautiful** Mill River Plaza, 9 West Broad Street, Stamford, CT 06092 203-323-8987

GUIDE TO PRESERVING THE NATURAL ENVIRONMENT
(1989) - a brochure developed jointly by the *Fairfax County Park Authority, Fairfax County Department of Environmental Management* and *Friends of Huntley Meadows Park,* a citizens' group dedicated to preservation of the natural environment and to park volunteerism; describes ways in which the citizen can make a critical difference in preserving natural resources, including oil/antifreeze disposal, erosion control, effective landscaping, use of natural pesticides, recycling, etc., lists numbers for reporting observed environmental hazards, 8-panel foldout, free **Fairfax County Park Authority** 3701 Pender Drive, Fairfax, VA 22030-6067 703-246-5700

HAZARDOUS WASTE: A COMMUNITY ACTION GUIDE
(1982) - a citizen's handbook including the definition of and origins of hazardous waste, examples of the effects of incorrect disposal, descriptions of current available methods of disposal, a summary of federal legislation and regulations, guidelines for citizens to act in their own communities, and a comprehensive list, with addresses and telephone numbers, of all state solid and hazardous waste agencies and of the Environmental Protection Agency's 10 regional solid waste offices, 22pp, $3.00 (quantity discounts) **Concern** 1794 Columbia Road, NW, Washington, DC 20009 202-328-8160

HIGH SCHOOL WORK GROUP PROGRAM/LISTING OF VOLUNTEER CONSERVATION JOBS
(1990) - overview of the high school work group program, with detailed listings of summer volunteer positions in national parks and forests; provides brief descriptions, time commitments, number of persons needed at location, etc., 12pp, single copy free **Student Conservation Association** Box 550, Charlestown, NH 03603 603-826-4301

HOME ENERGY CONSERVATION CHECKLIST
(undated) - quick reference guide to cost-saving energy practices in existing homes, and things to look for in buying new homes; includes U.S. map showing minimum insulation recommendations in specific areas of the country, 15pp, single copy free **U.S. League of Savings Institutions** 111 East Wacker Drive, Chicago, IL 60601 312-644-3100

HOUSEHOLD HAZARDOUS WASTE WHEEL
(1990) - a tool to identify toxic chemicals in common household products; explains how to dispose properly of household toxins, and recommends non-toxic alternatives, $2.75 **EHMI Company** 10 Newmarket Road, PO Box 932, Durham, NH 03824 603-868-1496

HOUSEHOLD WASTE: A CITIZEN'S ACTION GUIDE
(1989) - a detailed explanation of ways in which every citizen can contribute to the reduction of household waste by recycling, adopting new habits, making informed choices, and taking action in the community, 30pp, $3.00 (bulk rates of same title for nonprofits: 10/$15, 25/$30, 50/$50, 100/$75) **Concern** 1794 Columbia Road, NW, Washington, DC 20009 202-328-8160

HOW TO BECOME AN ENVIRONMENTAL ACTIVIST
(1984) - a reprint from *Citizen Participation,* the magazine of the Lincoln Filene Center at Tufts University; emphasizes the importance of "deciding if you want to lead or follow" before joining a citizen effort; lists 12 lessons that activists have learned over the years, such as "Learn from experienced activists," and "Always tell the truth," 4pp, $.40 + $1.00 postage (pay postage only once when ordering multiple publications) **Sierra Club** Information Service, 730 Polk Street, San Francisco, CA 94109 415-776-2211

HOW TO PLAN AN ENERGY FAIR
(1982) - a guide on how to educate the community in which we live on energy efficiency; outlines basic organizational skills and steps in planning an energy fair, as well as helpful hints and sample materials; single copy free (additional $.20 each) **B'nai B'rith International** Community Volunteer Services, 1640 Rhode Island Avenue, NW, Washington, DC 20036 202-857-6580

HOW TO PLAN AN ENVIRONMENTAL CONFERENCE: A TECHNIQUE FOR DEVELOPING CITIZEN LEADERSHIP
(undated) - handbook to provide assistance in bringing together diverse groups of citizens to survey the many aspects of an environmental problem; covers initial steps, responsibilities of the

Planning Committee and subcommittees, conducting the seminar, and following up by reconvening at a later time (applicable to a conference on any topic), single copy free **League of Women Voters of the US** 1730 M Street, NW, Washington, DC 20036 202-429-1965

HOW TO SAVE YOUR RIVER: A CITIZEN'S GUIDE TO WATER PROJECTS

(1977) - guide to the ingredients of a good project - especially cooperation among citizen groups, government agencies, local Congressmen, and others; takes the reader from the survey stage through a guide for developing political strength, legal action, and project alternatives, 8pp, $.25 **Sierra Club** Information Service, 730 Polk Street, San Francisco, CA 94109 415-776-2211

HUMAN RESOURCE PROGRAMS HOSTED BY THE FOREST SERVICE

(kept current) - description of *Hosted Human Resource Programs* - work programs funded by other agencies, but providing people to do the work of the Forest Service; provides details on the major programs and a listing of dozens of others; includes alternative programs which are non-federal; appends references to additional information, 12pp, free **US/DoA - Forest Service** 1375 K Street, NW, #613, PO Box 96080, Washington, DC 20013-6090 202-535-0927

INTERACTION

(semiannually) - newsletter designed to keep interested individuals and organizations current on pet therapy programs and other areas of interaction between animals, people and the environment, Av. 16pp, single copy free **Delta Society** 321 Burnett Avenue, South #303, PO Box 1080, Renton, WA 98057-1080 206-226-7357

JOB CORPS INFORMATION PACKET

(kept current) - series of brochures providing an overview of a conservation program for youth ages 17-22, including: *Tell Them About Job Corps,* a vehicle for teachers counselors and others working with disadvantaged youth (8-panel foldout); *Job Corps Works; So Do Its Graduates,* an pictorial foldout poster with an overview of the Job Corps program (12-panel foldout) and a bulleted overview for quick reference (4-panel foldout); and *Job Corps Civilian Conservation Centers,* a listing of Centers across the country, with map, and a brief overview of the program (12pp), free **US/DoA - Forest Service** 1375 K Street, NW, #613, PO Box 96090, Washington, DC 20013-6090 202-535-0927

KAB CASE STUDIES II

(dates vary) - selected two- to four-page accounts of volunteer efforts in localities across the country, $.50/set (based on current studies on hand, av. 4/set); some titles:
- *Volunteers from All Sectors Participate in Zelienople (PA) Recycling*
- *A Community-wide Citizen Action Program to Improve Detroit*
- *The River Rat Society*
- *Students to Overcome Pollution (STOP)*
- *Millers Creek (NC) Elementary School*

Keep America Beautiful Mill River Plaza, 9 West Broad Street, Stamford, CT 06902 203-323-8987

LAND USE

(1975) - the case for considering land as a "resource" and not a "commodity;" cites the effects of large highway networks, extended sewer lines, strip mining, government ownership of land, etc., on recreation, conservation, and other open land needs, Eco-Tips #8, 6-panel foldout, $1.00 ($50/100) **Concern** 1794 Columbia Road, NW, Washington, DC 20009 202-328-8160

LEAF COMPOSTING GUIDE

(undated) - information on the substitution of composting for the previous practice of burning leaves by communities concerned with air pollution, and how it is done, one-page fact sheet, first five copies free, extra copies $.05 each **Keep America Beautiful** Mill River Plaza, 9 West Broad Street, Stamford, CT 06902 203-323-8987

LIMITS

(1975) - narrative guide tracing land abuse activities from the beginning of the country and outlining emergency measures taken to renew the land; addresses the limits to land and other resources and the necessity to protect them (can be used alone or with slide set; ask about slide set cost), 19pp, single copy free **US/DoA - Photography Division** Independence Avenue, (Between 12th & 14th Sts.), Washington, DC 20250 202-447-2791

LISTING OF AVAILABLE EPA DOCUMENTS ON NOISE ABATEMENT AND CONTROL

(1974) - compilation of publications developed by EPA and available through the National Technical Information Service and/or the Government Printing Office, 4pp list free **US/EPA - Office of Noise Abatement and Control** 401 M Street, SW, Washington, DC 20460 202-382-4700

MAKE ROOM FOR MONSTORS...AND WILDLIFE ON THE LAND

(1982) - describes value of wildlife, explains wildlife habitat needs; focuses on beneficial and detrimental land uses and management affecting habitat; and describes how children can attract wildlife to their homes; for students in grades four through junior high school, 16pp cartoon booklet, $.75 (inquire about teacher's guide, 10 other booklets, and quantity discounts) **Soil and Water Conservation Society of America** 7515 NE Ankeny Road, Ankeny, IA 50021 515-289-2331

NEEDED: CLEAN AIR

(1979) - illustrated guide emphasizing that, although pure air is as important as pure water, fervent effort is expended in one (water) while casual efforts are directed toward the other (air); outlines costs of dirty air in money and lives; suggests ways everyone can get involved, 15pp, $.75 **Channing L. Bete Company** , South Deerfield, MA 01373 800-628-7733

NOISE AND YOU

(1979) - illustrated guide on the effects of too much noise for long periods of time (and certain types of noise for shorter periods) on hearing, safety, efficiency, etc.; cites steps being taken to reduce noise output, and provides a checklist for determining the need for noise protection, 15pp, $.75 (discounts) **Channing L. Bete Company** , South Deerfield, MA 01373

NUCLEAR POWER: THE BARGAIN WE CAN'T AFFORD

(1980) - a nuts-and-bolts primer on the economics of nuclear power; explains why nuclear energy causes your electric bills to skyrocket and tells you what you can do about it - through the courts, through citizen organizing and through your state public service commission, 100pp, $5.95 postpaid **Environmental Action Foundation** 1525 New Hampshire Avenue, NW, Washington, DC 20036 202-745-4870

ONE MILLION MARYLANDERS

(1990) - information packet on the Governor's campaign to keep the Chesapeake Bay clean; includes ten ways citizens can help by proper use of water, household products and pesticides, and proper maintenance of lawns and cars, unpaged, single copy free **Maryland Governor's Campaign** One State Circle, Annapolis, MD 21401 301-974-5300

ORGANIZING A VOLUNTEER HOME ENERGY ASSESSMENT PROGRAM

(1982) - demonstrates ways in which to save on fuel costs, heating bills and gasoline prices; also explains basic tools necessary to perform home energy assessments; single copy free, additional copies $.20 each **B'nai B'rith International** Community Volunteer Services, 1640 Rhode Island Avenue, NW, Washington, DC 20036 202-857-6580

PEOPLE, ANIMALS AND THE ENVIRONMENT

(biannual) - a magazine offering articles, profiles, resources, research reports, and other information regarding the animal/human bond and the environment, Av. 36pp, inquire about subscription rates **Delta Society** 321 Burnett Avenue, South #303, PO Box 1080, Renton, WA 98057-1080 206-226-7357

PESTICIDES: A COMMUNITY ACTION GUIDE

(Rev. 1987) - a serious look at the effects of pesticides in areas of agricultural pesticides, pesticides and health, pesticides in forests, and pesticides in cities and towns; includes comprehensive community action guidelines and appends detailed resources and bibliography, 23pp, $3.00 (bulk rates of same title for nonprofits: 10/$12, 25/$18, 50/$32, 100/$50) **Concern** 1794 Columbia Road, NW, Washington, DC 20009 202-328-8160

PITCH IN FOR A CLEANER COMMUNITY

(undated) - narrative guide to serve as a starting point for a community cleanup campaign meeting (use alone or with slides #C-165), single guide free; inquire about cost of slide set **US/DoA - Photography Division** Independence Avenue, SW, (Between 12th & 14th Sts.), Washington, DC 20250 202-447-2791

PLANNING AND ORGANIZING AN ADULT ENVIRONMENTAL EDUCATION PROGRAM

(1973) - compilation of practical examples based on actual environmenal programs, and theoretical information on planning and organizing effective training programs; includes programs set up by citizens' groups, a community college, an adult education facility and others, 43pp, $2.00 **Soil and Water Conservation Society of America** 7515 NE Ankeny Road, Ankeny, IA 50021 515-289-2331

PLANTS, ANIMALS, AND MAN - SHARING THE EARTH: AN ECOLOGY STORY

(1975) - a basic primer on ecology for children, explaining how soil, water, air, and solar energy interact to create food, also outlines needs for conservation, pollution control, and proper planning; for students in grades four through junior high school, 16pp cartoon booklet, $.75 (inquire about teacher's guide, 10 other booklets, and quantity discounts) **Soil and Water Conservation Society of America** 7515 NE Ankeny Road, Ankeny, IA 50021 515-289-2331

PLANTS, HOW THEY IMPROVE OUR ENVIRONMENT

(1972) - explains how plants of all types improve environmental quality by guarding against soil erosion, absorbing pollutants, and reducing noise; provides do-it-yourself projects that encourage children to get involved to help them understand these plant functions; for students in grades four through junior high school, 16pp cartoon booklet, $.75 (inquire about teacher's guide, 10 other booklets and quantity discounts) **Soil and Water Conservation Society of America** 7515 NE Ankeny Road, Ankeny, IA 50021 515-289-2331

POPULATION BULLETIN SERIES

(quarterly) - current information from the authorities on specific population subjects of interest to the general public, $3.00 each

(quantity discounts) **Population Reference Bureau** 777 Fourteenth Street, NW, Washington, DC 20005 202-639-0040

POPULATION-ENVIRONMENT BALANCE FACT SHEET SERIES

(monthly) - a series of fact sheets designed to keep the public informed of the effects of an imbalance between the population and the environment; includes:
- *Have You Heard?* which provides quick-reading vignettes on water shortages, global warming, etc., 2pp
- *Balance Data* which takes one issue and expands on it, 2pp
- *Balance Report* which is a newsletter with graphics, legislation updates, immigration information, etc., 6pp

Single copy free, inquire about subscriptions
Population-Environment Balance 1325 G Street, NW, Washington, DC 20005 202-879-3000

POPULATION HANDBOOK

(1978) - a quick-reference guide to simplify the dynamics of population - how it affects the price of baby food, the sale of pop records, government retirement funds - every facet of life; stresses the importance of population in SMSA (Standard Metropolitan Statistical Area) computations by the Office of Management of Budget in relation to delivery of medical, educational, law enforcement, and other services; appends a glossary and a listing of other resources, 64pp, $4.00 **Population Reference Bureau** 777 14th Street, NW, Washington, DC 20005 202-639-8040

POWER AND LIGHT: POLITICAL STRATEGIES FOR THE SOLAR TRANSITION

(1980) - this timely book tells how citizens can work with city councils, state legislators and utility regulators to make solar energy and conservation happen at the local level, 262pp, $7.95 postpaid **Environmental Action Foundation** 1525 New Hampshire Avenue, NW, Washington, DC 20036 202-745-4870

PRIDE OF PLACE: COMMUNITY ENVIRONMENTAL PROGRAMS FOR YOUNG PEOPLE

(1979) - nationally applicable guidebook designed to help young people develop pride in their environment and a sense of responsibility for the place in which they live; covers every step of the planning process; includes numerous program profiles, how to choose intelligently, other resources, etc.; presents an extensive case study of a model water quality program, 91pp, single copy free **Action for Boston Community Development** 178 Tremont Street, Boston, MA 02111 617-357-6000

QUESTIONS AND ANSWERS ABOUT THE RECLAMATION AND RECYCLING OF GLASS CONTAINERS

(undated) - overview of the need for used glass containers by manufacturers for recycling, the reduction in energy when reclaiming glass, the reduction of the use of natural resources, etc.; provides state-by-state list of glass recycling centers, and a section on organizing a community reclamation program (with centerfold equipment and traffic flow chart), 16pp, single copy free **Glass Packaging Institute** 1133 20th Street, NW, Suite 321, Washington, DC 20036 202-887-4850

RECYCLING NONFERROUS SCRAP METALS

(1990) - overview of how all non-iron-based metals are processed for recycling; includes descriptions of the 20 most recycled metals, 16pp brochure, single copy free (send SASE) **Institute of Scrap Recycling Industries** PR Department, 1627 K Street, NW, Washington, DC 20006 202-466-4050

RECYCLING PAPER
(1990) - identification of commonly recycled types of scrap paper and products made from recycled paper; provides an overview of how the scrap paper dealer prepares paper for recycling, 16pp brochure, single copy free (send SASE) **Institute of Scrap Recycling Industries** PR Department, 1627 K Street, NW, Washington, DC 20006 202-466-4050

RECYCLING QUESTIONS AND ANSWERS
(Rev. 1979) - quick-reference guide to the paper recycling process; provides information on waste paper dealers, overpackaging, etc., 12pp, single copy free (additional $.20 each) **American Forest Council** 1250 Connecticut Avenue, NW, Suite 320, Washington, DC 20036 202-463-2455

RECYCLING SCRAP IRON AND STEEL
(1990) - explanation of how scrap iron and steel are purchased, processed for recycling and returned to the marketplace, 16pp brochure, single copy free (send SASE) **Institute of Scrap Recycling Industries** PR Division, 1627 K Street, NW , Washington, DC 20006 202-466-4050

RECYCLING SCRAP MATERIALS CONTRIBUTES TO A BETTER ENVIRONMENT
(1989) - explanation of energy savings and other evirnomental benefits that result from commonly recycled materials, including metals, paper and plastics; 8-1/2"x11" 2pp flyer, single copy free (send SASE) **Institute of Scrap Recycling Industries** PR Department, 1627 K Street, NW, Washington, DC 20006 202-466-4050

REGENERATION: YOU AND YOUR ENVIRONMENT
(1989) - a manual of classroom activities on environmental regeneration for grades K-12; includes reproducible worksheets for students and a full-size color poster for display; adapts to after-school programs, nature centers and home use, unpaged, $5.00 **Community Regeneration** 222 Main Street, Emmaus, PA 18098 215-967-5171

RESOURCE ASSISTANT PROGRAM: VOLUNTEER POSITIONS
(quarterly) - listing of volunteer programs in natural resource management open to individuals 18 or older who have graduated from high school (no upper age limit); includes full descriptions of positions, details such as length of commitment, requirements, duties, category of assignment, etc.; includes positions appropriate for disabled persons, with some adapted to help provide this opportunity; appends full set of application materials, 69pp, $4.00/copy (subscriptions available) **Student Conservation Association** Box 550, Charlestown, NH 03603 603-826-4301

RESOURCE RECOVERY AND YOU!
(1976) - illustrated guide discussing the need for recycling, and ways that government, industry and the private citizen can work toward an effective solution to the problem of turning mounting wastes into usable resources, 15pp, $.75 (quantity discounts) **Channing L. Bete Company** , South Deerfield, MA 01373

REWARDS OF VOLUNTEER TRAILS WORK
(undated) - a report documenting experiences of people who have participated in the Society's Volunteer Service Corps program; gives reasons why volunteerism is the most effective way to get trails built, No. 6, $1.50 **American Hiking Society** 1015 31st Street, NW, Washington, DC 20007 703-385-3252

SAVING ENERGY IN THE HOME: SOME SUGGESTIONS FOR OLDER AMERICANS
(1975) - step-by-step guide for homeowners on low-cost improvements, selecting contractors, tax credits, crisis assistance, winterizing, help with fuel bills, and other services and aids for low-income persons, 12pp, single copy free **National Clearinghouse on Aging** Administration on Aging, 330 C Street, SW, Washington, DC 20201 202-245-2158

SCHOOL GARDENS: EARTHCARE IN THE DOORYARD GARDEN
(1976) - a handbook detailing the many benefits to the environment of natural gardening - use of neglected lots, recycling through composting, decreased pollution, energy savings, food production, etc., 11pp, $.70 + $1.00 postage and handling (pay postage only when ordering multiple Sierra Club materials) **Sierra Club** Information Service, 730 Polk Street, San Francisco, CA 94109 415-776-2211

SENIOR CONSERVATION EMPLOYMENT PROGRAM
(kept current) - overview of a community service/employment program for disadvantaged senior citizens administered by the Forest Service in cooperation with the U.S. Department of Labor; describes counseling, free physical examinations, training and other benefits supplementing the work experience provided through the program; cites some cases where placement was made in unsubsidized jobs; describes types of work and how to apply, 6-panel foldout **US/DoA - Forest Service** 1375 K Street, NW, #613, PO Box 96090, Washington, DC 20013-6090 202-535-0927

SIERRA CLUB PUBLIC LANDS BOOKLET SERIES
(1988) - full listings of parks, refuges, wilderness areas, rivers and trails with maps, acreage and mileage figures, addresses and background information; definitions and usages for each type of public land to help end the confusion often encountered by environmental activists and others, $1.50/booklet members; $2.00/booklet others:
- *National Park System*
- *National Wilderness Preservation*
- *National Trails System*
- *National Wild and Scenic Rivers System*

Owners of one or more of this series receive periodic updates **Sierra Club** Information Service, 730 Polk Street, San Francisco, CA 94109 415-776-2211

...SO MACHAR WILL BE A BRIGHT TOMORROW: A B'NAI B'RITH GUIDE FOR ENERGY PROGRAMS
(1977) - the case for sacrificing certain comforts to help America toward "energy independence" includes basic energy facts, alternative resources, and examples of energy conservation programs for groups working in this field (addressed to B'nai B'rith Lodges, but useful for any group), 22pp booklet and other materials, $.20/packet **B'nai B'rith International** Community Volunteer Services, 1640 Rhode Island Avenue, NW, Washington, DC 20036 202-857-6580

32 WAYS YOU CAN FIGHT POLLUTION AND PROTECT THE ENVIRONMENT
(1978) - illustrated guide on abuse of water, power, waste, motor vehicles, fuels, chemicals, goods, contribute to the declining quality of the environment; lists ways in these and other areas that each individual can help to reverse this trend, 15pp, $.75 (bulk rates) **Channing L. Bete Company** , South Deerfield, MA 01373

TOWARD CLEAN WATER: A GUIDE TO CITIZEN ACTION
(undated) - guide to the major opportunities for citizen participation under the 1972 Federal Water Pollution Control Act Amendments; focuses on the direct needs of citizens working at the neighborhood, state, regional, national levels with an emphasis

on helping citizen leaders understand why certain decisions are made, 328pp $8.00 **Conservation Foundation** 1250 24th Street, Washington, DC 20037 202-293-4800

UTILITY UPDATE NO. 278
(1990) - overview of ways in which climbing vines can save energy by providing shade and lowering air temperature near house walls by 10 degrees or more, improving the environment by consuming carbon dioxide and producing oxygen, and defoliating in the fall to allow the sun to save heat consumption energy; includes list of 50 climbing vines, a sun angle chart for every day of the year, and several characteristics about the vines (length, flowering/nonflowering, etc.) so that personal choices can be made, $1.00 plus SASE (inquire about other *Utility Bills Updates*) **Journal Newspapers** ATT: James Dulley, 6906 Royalgreen Drive, Cincinnati , OH 45244 513-231-6034

VOLUNTEER CONSERVATION POSITIONS
(1983) - overview of the 1983 Park and Forest Assistants program, which enables over 900 college students to work side by side with professional staff and learn to perform conservation assignments based on the same standards that apply to other employees; includes profiles of over 200 park and forest sites from which a volunteer can make a selection for application, 16pp, single copy free (Request information about high school volunteer program) **Student Conservation Association** PO Box 550, Charleston, NH 03603 603-826-5206

VOLUNTEERING AT THE STRANDING CENTER
(kept current) - information on opportunities for volunteers interested in assisting marine mammals and sea turtles stranded on New Jersey's beaches through injury, illness or disorientation; includes overview of the program, unpaged, single copy free **Marine Mammal Stranding Center** 3625 Atlantic Brigantine Blvd, Brigantine, NJ 08203 609-266-0538

WASTE AND TOXIC SUBSTANCES RESOURCE GROUP
(constantly updated) - lists books, pamphlets, films, packets, and educational materials for people working on solid and hazardous waste, and toxic exposure issues; resource covers such topics as hazardous waste recycling technologies, dump sites, model legislation, materials conservation and occupational health and safety, 35pp, $2.00 postpaid **Environmental Action Foundation** 1525 New Hampshire Avenue, NW, Washington, DC 20036 202-745-4870

WASTE: CHOICES FOR COMMUNITIES
(1988) - overview of costs to communities as landfill space diminishes; describes the problem, outlines current management options and alternatives and suggests actions that everyone can take to achieve a nationwide commitment to waste reduction, recycling and cause, 30pp, $3.00 (bulk rates of same title to nonprofits: 10/$12, 25/$18, 50/$32, 100/$50) **Concern** 1794 Columbia Road, NW, Washington, DC 20009 202-328-8160

WATER SENSE WHEEL
(1990) - a tool which gives tips on how to determine water quality in one's home or office, $2.75 **EHMI Company** 10 Newmarket Road, PO Box 932, Durham, NH 03824 603-868-1496

WATER SUPPLY: CONSTRAINTS AND OPPORTUNITIES
(1977) - a look at the national water situation in relation to costs, regulations, and what is being done to improve the situation; includes several case studies (California, Florida, New York City); bibliography, 52pp, $1.25 **Sierra Club** Information Service, 730 Park Street, San Francisco, CA 94109 415-776-2211

WATER - THE BASIS OF LIFE
(1979) - explanation of the importance of good water quality and adequate water quantity to life on earth; addresses students in grades four through junior high school, 16pp cartoon booklet,$.75 (inquire about teacher's guide and 10 other booklets, and quantity discounts) **Soil and Water Conservation Society of America** 7515 NE Ankeny Road, Ankeny, IA 50021 515-289-2331

WHAT IS RECYCLING? WHY DO COMMUNITY RECYCLING PROGRAMS SOMETIMES FAIL?
(1989) - explanation of what constitutes true recycling as opposed to mere separation and collection of recyclables; describes the significance of market development to recycling, 8-1/2"x11" 2pp flyer, single copy free (send SASE) **Institute of Scrap Recycling Industries** PR Department, 1627 K Street, NW, Washington, DC 20006 202-466-4050

WHAT THE FOREST SERVICE DOES
(kept current) - detailed information on the Forest Service's responsibilities in matters of land, water, wildlife, minerals and energy, wood, forage, fire management, pest management, engineering, recreation, cooperative resource management, and other areas; includes overview of volunteer and employment programs in these areas; appends related legislation outlines, and a quick-reference chart of the Agency's major activities, 35pp, free **US/DoA - Forest Service** 1375 K Street, NW, #613, PO Box 96090, Washington, DC 20013-6090 202-535-0927

WHAT YOU CAN DO TO RECYCLE MORE PAPER
(1975) - a look at the conservation value of recycled paper - saves trees, decreases pollution, cuts down on solid waste, etc.; appeals to consumers to demand recycled paper from merchants, utility companies, banks, corporations, etc.; lists ways citizens, students, teachers, employees, and others can alter current lackadaisical practices in the total community, 12-panel foldout, free **US/EPA - Office of Solid Waste Management** 401 M Street, NW, Washington , DC 20460 202-382-4700

WILDLIFE NEEDS YOU
(1983) - a booklet for children describing problems of wildlife survival and listing several actions that children can take through school, youth group and/or at home, including writing to Congress; appends glossary, 8pp, $.80 **Sierra Club** Information Service, 730 Polk Street, San Francisco, CA 94109 415-776-2211

THE WORLD POPULATION PROBLEM: MAKING A DIFFERENCE
(undated) - question/answer overview of some of the misconceptions in family planning and population crisis areas; includes information on the work of staff and volunteers in a high-level advocacy capacity on a wide range of topics including employment, food, and other programs as they relate to population issues, 12-panel foldout, single copy free [Also has office at 435 East 52nd Street, New York, NY 10022 212-751-9511] **Population Crisis Committee/Draper Fund** 1120 Nineteenth Street, NW, Washington, DC 20036 202-659-1833

YOUR COMMUNITY IS AN ENVIRONMENTAL RESOURCE
(undated) - a guide to help citizens treat their community as a living laboratory in which to observe and apply sound conservation principles; includes suggestions on determining physical assets, cultural assets, liabilities, attitudes, local programs, etc.; outlines procedures for setting up a conservation center (from a simple library corner to an elaborate center with bird feeders, a "closed ecosystem" in a terrarium model of a town, etc.), 8pp, $1.00 **Keep America Beautiful** Mill River Plaza, 9 West Broad Street, Stamford, CT 06902 203-323-8987

YOUR ENVIRONMENTAL ACTION STARTS HERE
(undated) - comprehensive guide beginning with a neighborhood
survey to provide a basis for a series of projects that will help meet
environmental needs of a neighborhood; includes sample news
releases and guidelines for several projects, 10pp, $.50 **Keep
America Beautiful** Mill River Plaza, 9 West Broad Street,
Stamford, CT 06092 203-323-8987

YOUR INDEPENDENCE GARDEN
(1980) - a step-by-step guide for beginners from selecting the site
and preparing the soil to weeding and getting the bugs out;
discusses areas as small as 2' x 2' as well as standard-size areas;
includes quick-reference charts, and contact information for those
interested in starting a community garden, $1.00 (covers
postage/handling only; quantity discounts) **National Gardening
Association** 180 Flynn Avenue, Burlington, VT 05401
802-863-1308

**YOUTH GARDENS SPROUTING WITH COMMUNITY
SUPPORT**
(1972) - overview of the successful efforts of one community in
securing vacant lots and other unused land for use by youth in
gardening projects; cites the dual value: cleaning up otherwise
neglected land providing productive activities for youth, 6pp,
single copy free **Washington Youth Gardens** 1250 Eye Street, NW,
Suite 500, Washington, DC 20005 202-789-2900

PRIVATE SECTOR INITIATIVES OFFICES

COMMERCE DEPARTMENT REPORT ON PRIVATE SECTOR INITIATIVES
(1982) - an overview of the department's activities in identifying and pursuing incentive programs, partnerships, and services that might best be performed by the private sector, 6pp, single copy free **US/DoC - Private Sector Initiatives Program** Office of the Secretary, 14th St. between E & Constitution, Washington, DC 20230 202-377-2000

COMMUNICATIONS INDUSTRY PROJECT UPDATE
(1983) - an executive summary of reports from HHS Regional Offices on partnership activities by the communications industry on behalf of the developmentally disabled; includes for each activity the region, state, and estimated value of the service provided (e.g., in New York the Ad Club is designing a brochure on community living for developmentally disabled persons at a cost to the Club of $50,000; a TV documentary in Hawaii cost the station about $20,000; other programs range from $5,000 to $786,800); appends a list of individuals and their exceptional volunteer contributions through the media on behalf of developmentally disabled persons), 8pp, single copy free **Working Group on Private Sector Initiatives** Office of Human Development, Washington, DC 20201 202-245-2874

PRESIDENT'S PRIVATE SECTOR INITIATIVES STATUS REPORTS
(1982) - an overview of the general status of the organization for private sector initiatives support within the Department of Defense; covers implementation of four objectives:
- Objective #1: *Increasing Private Sector Participation*
- Objective #2: *Forming Public-Private Partnerships*
- Objective #3: *Increasing Employee Volunteer Activity*
- Objective #4: *Promoting the Program*

Includes a brief history of the *President's Private Sector Initiatives Program* (as released by the Special Assistant to the President in 1983); appends a number of letters, schedules, contact lists, and other items to help clarify DoD's work in this area of voluntary action, unpaged, single copy free **US/DoD - Office of Economic Adjustment** Army-Navy Drive, Third Floor, Arlington, VA 22202 703-695-1800

THE PRIVATE SECTOR IN STATE SERVICE DELIVERY: EXAMPLES OF INNOVATIVE PRACTICES
(1989) - examples designed to encourage state officials to consider opportunities for greater use of the private sector by giving examples of actual experiences drawn from a wide variety of states, addressing public/private partnerships, the use of volunteers, contracting, concessions, and others; includes *minuses* as well as *pluses* and highlights problems that must be overcome; covers services to corrections, parks and recreation, human services, employment and training, and transportation, 172pp, $12.75 (paper); $24.50 (cloth) **Urban Institute Press** 4720 Boston Way, Lanham, MD 20706 301-459-3366

PRIVATE SECTOR INITIATIVES AND VOLUNTEERISM IN THE PRIVATE SECTOR
(1982) - an overview of NCUA's efforts to emphasize activities having a strong focus on involvement in the private sector, 3pp, single copy free **US/NCUA - Private Sector Initiatives and Volunteerism** NCUA Administration Board, 1776 G Street, NW, Washington, DC 20456 202-356-1000

PRIVATE SECTOR INITIATIVES PROGRAMS OF THE DEPARTMENT OF TRANSPORTATION
(1982) - an overview of DoT's efforts to promote and encourage the private sector to decrease dependence on government; covers all offices of the department with summaries of active and proposed initiatives, 10pp, single copy free **US/DoT - Private Sector Initiatives Programs** Office of the Secretary, 400 Seventh Street, SW, Washington, DC 20590 202-426-4000

PRIVATE SECTOR INITIATIVES: USEPA
(1982) - an overview of the agency's efforts to make maximum use of the ingenuity and energy of the American people in protecting the environment, 8pp, single copy free **US/EPA - Private Sector Initiatives Efforts** Office of the Administrator, 401 M Street, SW, Washington, DC 20640 202-382-4700

PRIVATE SECTOR INVOLVEMENT WORKBOOK
(1979) - strategies for gaining the voluntary assistance of all elements of the private sector - community groups, industry, foundations, individuals, etc.; details several "private sector involvement mechanisms" such as volunteerism, employee recreation, private sector resource councils, neighborhood initiative, income tax effects, etc.; includes listing of management tools and HCRS programs, 84pp, single copy free **US/DoI - National Park Service** Information Exchange, Washington, DC 20240 202-343-1100

REPORT ON OPM ACTIVITIES...ON PRIVATE SECTOR INITIATIVES
(1982) - an overview of OPM's efforts to emphasize programs that bear on the private sector and indicate initiative in the area of public/private partnerships, 4pp, single copy free **US/OPM - Private Sector Initiatives in OPM** Office of the Director, 1900 E Street, NW, Washington, DC 20415 202-632-6106

REPORT TO THE WHITE HOUSE ON PRIVATE SECTOR INITIATIVES
(1982) - an overview of SBA's activities that utilize the private sector to obtain leverage from all programs in achievement of goals and meeting small business community needs, 10pp, single copy free **US/SBA - Private Sector Initiatives Activities** Office of the Administrator, 1441 L Street, NW, Washington, DC 20416 202-653-6365

SERIES OF REPORTS ON PRIVATE SECTOR INITIATIVES PROGRAMS IN FEDERAL AGENCIES
(1982) - overviews of federal agency response to the Administration's proposal to work more closely with the private sector in addressing community needs, including reports from the following agencies:
- Department of Agriculture
- Department of Commerce
- Department of Defense
- Department of Education
- Department of Health and Human Services
- Department of the Interior
- Department of Justice
- Department of Labor
- Department of Transportation
- Department of the Treasury
- Environmental Protection Agency
- Federal Communications
- Federal Emergency Management Agency
- Federal Home Loan Bank Board
- Federal Trade Commission
- General Services Administration
- National Aeronautics and Space Administration
- National Credit Union Administration
- National Endowment for the Humanities
- National Science Foundation
- Nuclear Regulatory Commission
- Office of Personnel Management
- Securities and Exchange Commission
- Small Business Administration
- Veterans Administration

Describes activities reflecting cooperation between the reporting agency and organizations in the private sector (see appropriate sections of this book for detailed descriptions); also request copies of the Proclamation, *National Year of Voluntarism* (copies are free). **US/White House - Office of National Service** 1600 Pennsylvania Avenue, NW, Washington, DC 20500 202-456-6266

TREASURY'S INVOLVEMENT IN PRIVATE SECTOR INITIATIVES PROGRAMS
(1982) - an overview of the Treasury Department's efforts to apply its programs when possible to the private sector initiatives concept, 10pp, single copy free **US/DTreas - Treasury's Involvement in Private Sector Initiatives** Office of the Secretary, 15th & Pennsylvania Avenue, NW, Washington, DC 20220 202-566-2000

VETERANS ADMINISTRATION PRIVATE SECTOR INITIATIVES REPORT
(1982) - an overview of the VA's efforts to increase participation of staff at the local level to enhance the public/private initiatives concept, 11pp, single copy free **US/VA - Private Sector Initiatives**

Program Office of the Secretary, 810 Vermont Avenue, NW, Washington, DC 20420 202-393-4120

VOLUNTARISM: PRIVATE SECTOR INITIATIVES, DOD ACTION PLAN
(1983) - a follow-up of earlier reports to update the PSI implementation plan at DoD; encompasses a set of goals and objectives that link DoD with communities and other public and private groups; involves a planning process as well as an implementation program; appends principles, facts and premises undergirding the *Action Plan,* 12pp, single copy free **US/DoD - Office of Economic Adjustment** Army-Navy Drive, Third Floor, Arlington, VA 22202 703-695-1800

VOLUNTEERISM (DOD)
(1983) - a report prepared by the Assistant Secretary of Defense for *Manpower, Reserve Affairs and Logistics;* addresses reimbursement for volunteers called for by the *House Armed Services Committee Report 97-552,* accompanying the *Uniformed Services Pay Act of 1982;* includes sections in areas of:
- Programs and Roles of Volunteers;
- Position on Reimbursement; and
- Major Problems Relative to Volunteerism.

Includes an executive summary, recommendations, and a legislative appendix, 25pp, single copy free **US/DoD - Office of Economic Adjustment** Army-Navy Drive, Third Floor, Arlington, VA 22202 703-695-1800

PSYCHOSOCIAL SUPPORT SERVICES

BASKET OF JOY INFORMATION PACKET
(undated) - information on a program designed to address the
psychosocial needs of elderly homebound persons at holiday time
through fruit baskets and visits by volunteers; includes steps to
getting started, funding source, etc., unpaged, free **Basket of Joy
Campaign** Volunteers of America, 1550 Yates Street, Denver , CO
80204 303-623-8052

CARE FOR THE CAREGIVER
(1989) - an audiovisual narrated by Sue Vineyard designed to help
caregivers identify pressures, diagnose demands, look realistically
at five dimensions (physical, emotional, spiritual, mental and
relational), and map a course toward better balance and health in
life, 37 minutes, $12.95 **VMS/Heritage Arts** 1807 Prairie Avenue,
Downers Grove, IL 60515 708-964-1194

CHILDREN'S VIEW OF THEMSELVES
(1972) - appeal to child care workers to perceive the feelings and
ego-building needs of children and work to provide room in the
curriculum for this consideration; includes ways in which adults
can develop the sensitivity needed, 40pp, $3.00 **Association for
Childhood Education International** 11141 Georgia Avenue , Suite
200, Wheaton, MD 20902 301-942-2443

EMPLOYEE ASSISTANCE PROGRAMS (EAPS)
(undated) - overview of a company program offering referral to
company-financed professional counseling for troubled workers
and their dependents; stresses saving to company as well as benefit
to the employees, free report **McDonnell Douglas Corporation**
1150 Sixteenth Street, NW, Washington, DC 20036 202-466-4600

EXPLORING THE HEART OF HEALING
(1986) - a two-part video series exploring the healing process
within a community living and dying with AIDS; addresses those
personally involved in AIDS in Part I, including a message to
grieving parents, questions and answers, etc.; deals with caregivers
supporting themselves and others, burnout and other issues facing
caregivers in Part II; serves as a training tool for volunteers,
students, people with AIDS and their loved ones, Part I (2 hours),
$50.00; Part II (1 hour), $50.00; both tapes, $80.00 (also available
in a three-hour audiotape, $18.00) **San Francisco AIDS
Foundation** 333 Valencia Street, PO Box 6182, San Francisco, CA
94101-6182 415-861-3397

**FAMILIES IN RURAL AMERICA: STRESS, ADAPTATION
AND REVITALIZATION**
(1988) - an overview of the hardships faced by rural American
families, their coping strategies, and resources for their support,
297pp, OP8803, $18.50 **National Council on Family Relations**
3989 Central Avenue, NE, Suite 550, Minneapolis, MN
55421-3921 612-781-9331

FAMILIES IN STRESS
(1979) - an appeal to family members to use the resources
available to them when the family situation becomes too stressful
to be handled within the home; provides insight into ways to
locate community, church, and other services for this purpose, and
some tips and tension relievers for immediate use, 24pp, single
copy free **US/HHS - National Center on Child Abuse and Neglect**
PO Box 1182, Washington, DC 20013 703-558-8222

FAMILY STRESS, COPING AND ADAPTATION
(1980) - the work of clinics in the area of intervention in family
stress and coping; includes articles on dual-career family stress,
unemployment, drug dependency, ill health and divorce, 177pp,
FR8010, $10.50 **National Council on Family Relations** 3989
Central Avenue, NE, Suite 550, Minneapolis, MN 55421
612-781-9331

**FREEDOM THROUGH DIGNITY: A GUIDE FOR
VOLUNTEERS WORKING WITH PRISONERS**
(1979) - exploration of the ways in which the offender can have
exposure to persons who have been successful in dealing with the
problems of daily living; covers goals of volunteers, necessary
qualities, areas of involvement, rules for volunteers, resources, etc.,
11pp, $.20 **B'nai B'rith International** Community Volunteer
Services, 1640 Rhode Island Avenue, NW, Washington, DC 20036
202-857-6580

**FRIEND TO FRIEND PROGRAM: A SPECIAL KIND OF
FRIENDSHIP**
(1985) - a monograph developed for presentation at the
International Conference on Volunteerism in Jerusalem, Israel, in
March 1985; provides a brief history of the program which
matches teenage volunteers with physically and mentally
handicapped youngsters of the same age, vignettes about the
friendships, the families, the volunteers, the training, the matching,

the supervision, the recognition, and the termination of the two-year commitment by the young volunteers (usually beginning the service at age 16); appends quotes from parents and volunteers about the experience, 6pp, single copy free **Jewish Social Service Agency** 6127 Montrose Road, Rockville, MD 20852 301-881-3700

FRIENDLY VISITORS: GUIDELINES FOR DEVELOPING QUALITY SERVICE

(updated as needed) - organization and training information for mounting or improving a friendly visitor service for the elderly; includes specific suggestions for some problems (blind, deaf), 17pp, $1.10 **National Voluntary Organizations for Independent Living for the Aged** 600 Maryland Avenue, SW, West Wing 200, Washington, DC 20024 202-479-1200

GUIDE FOR FRIENDLY VISITORS

(1983) - an overview of a program that offers volunteer visitors to nursing homes on a regular basis to help counteract the problems of isolation and aging; includes sections on ways the community can help, ideas for volunteers, qualifications of the Friendly Visitor, rights and responsibilities of all parties concerned, and "guideposts" of dos and don'ts; appends glossary of terms and acronyms frequently used, 13pp, single copy free **Oregon Volunteer Services Program** Adult and Family Services Division, 415 Public Service Building, Salem, OR 97310 503-373-1561

HEALING WITH TIME AND LOVE: A GUIDE TO VISITING THE ELDERLY

(1979) - a discussion of the home and the resident, and guidelines for the visitor to help him/her understand such problems as depression, confusion, sensory losses, etc., 47pp, single copy free **Ethel Percy Andrus Gerontology Center** , Los Angeles, CA 90007 213-743-6060

MUSIC THERAPY FOR MOMS

(1990) - a collection of songs and poems written over the years by a mother at times when she felt tempted to become an enabler for her children; shows how another outlet can help parents resist giving "too much help" to their children instead of letting some things be learned - with a little pain - by experience, 50pp, $9.00 (proceeds from this publication will benefit a homelessness program) **Mortgage Burning Fund** PO Box 762, Annandale, VA 22003 703-354-6270

PARENT AIDE PROGRAM

(1983) - a packet of materials describing the Parent Aide Program of volunteers, including job description, sample training curricula and bibliography, a paper on perspectives of the Parent Aide Program, sample forms, and other materials, single packet free **Washington Department of Social & Health Services** , Olympia, WA 98504 206-753-4215

SAFEGUARDING THE EMOTIONAL HEALTH OF OUR CHILDREN

(undated) - coverage of some of the factors disturbing the emotional balance of children, with special focus on the rejecting mother, 16pp, $1.50 **Child Welfare League of America** 440 First Street, NW, Washington, DC 20001 202-638-2952

STUDENTS AT RISK

(1988) - a special issue of *Teaching Exceptional Children* which provides approaches for working with children identified "At Risk;" includes articles on youth suicide, medically fragile children, youngsters with chemical dependencies, infants, migrant and rural exceptional children, and gifted and talented children, 96pp, $7.00 **Council for Exceptional Children** 1920 Association Drive, Reston, VA 22091-1589 703-620-3660

SURVIVAL TIPS FOR PARENTS AND KIDS

(1989 ed.) - an edition of *Children, Our Greatest Natural Resource* that walks parents through the normal growth and developmental stages for children and helps them deal with stress, and provides child safety tips for when parent and child are apart; includes activity pages for children, survival information checklist for babysitters, babysitter checklist for parents, survival information checklist for kids, and a chart of communication tips for parents and kids, 14pp, single copy free [local *Boards of Realtors* provided development funds for initial printing; a grant from National Center on Child Abuse and Neglect and Virginia Dept. of Social Services funded the current printing] **Child Protective Services** Virginia Dept. of Social Services, 8007 Discovery Drive, Richmond, VA 23229-8699 804-662-9204 (office)

SURVIVING BURNOUT

(1989) - an audiovisual narrated by Sue Vineyard designed to lead viewers through ways of diagnosing pressure points and reducing them; includes options for getting work, personal, social and family life back into balance and returning to the joy of living and giving, 45 minutes, $12.95 **VMS/Heritage Arts** 1807 Prairie Avenue, Downers Grove, IL 60515 708-964-1194

TELEPHONE REASSURANCE SERVICE: GLUIDELINES FOR DEVELOPING QUALITY SERVICES

(updated as needed) - overview of program development, volunteer training, cost and other information for a program providing a regular check on socially isolated persons includes hints on how to limit a call, emergency procedures, etc., 13pp, $1.10 **National Council on the Aging** 600 Maryland Avenue, SW, West Wing 100, Washington, DC 20024 202-479-1200

USE AND ABUSE OF PEOPLE

(1978) - first-person narratives by the abused, the abuser, the caregiver; cites volunteer services where they exist in each case, 16pp, $.60 or $6.60/dozen (developed by American Lutheran Church Women) **Augsburg Fortress** 426 South Fifth Avenue, Box 1209, Minneapolis, MN 55440 612-330-3300

WRITECONNECTION PROGRAM

(1990) - a starter kit of materials for a program developed with the assistance of Navy chaplains for the married and single sailor to begin and maintain a weekly writing program with his or her own children and/or a little brother or sister; includes colorful stationery, monthly calendars, return mailers for the child, "quick mailers" for times when a long letter is not possible, activity projects to share, correspondence tracking chart, and a sturdy binder to keep everything together, $24.95 (military price, others inquire); refills, $14.95 (military price, others inquire) **Positive Parenting** 2644 East Indian School Road, Suite 400, Phoenix, AZ 85016 602-956-0070

RECIPIENTS - SPECIAL GROUPS

ABILITY IS AGELESS
(kept current) - a series of brochures for prospective employee and potential employer describing the services of SER, a full-service employment program for persons 55 years of age or older where staff are supplemented by volunteers, often the clients themselves as they await positions, unpaged, free **Senior Employment Resources** 4201 John Marr Drive, Suite 236, Annandale, VA 22003 703-750-1936

ABOUT LATCHKEY CHILDREN
(1989 ed.) - a guide to help parents decide whether their children are ready for the challenges of being home alone; lists ways to fill child's time to avoid boredom or wandering (chores, homework, reading, hobbies), how to set up a telephone network, making the child part of the discussion of arrangements, etc.; encourages support of after-school programs whenever possible; appends national and local resources for further information and assistance, 16pp, single copy free [Also available from Channing L. Bete Company 200 State Road, South Deerfield, MA 01373-0200 800-628-7733] **Child Protective Services** Virginia Dept. of Social Services, 8007 Discovery Drive, Richmond, VA 23229-8699

ADDRESS UNKNOWN: THE HOMELESS IN AMERICA
(1989) - overview of multiple causes of homelessness (decreased demand for unskilled labor, lack of affordable housing, etc.); recommends solutions with affordable costs; stresses that the homeless are not a homogeneous group needing the same type of assistance (written by former director of research at the *Social and Demographic Research Institute, University of Massachusetts),* 189pp, $36.95 hardcover; $14.95 paperback **Aldine de Gruyter** Div. of Walter de Gruyter, 200 Saw Mill River Road, Hawthorne, NY 10532 914-747-0110

ADOLESCENCE BOOKLET SERIES
(1989 ed.) - two booklets addressing the difficult period of transition from childhood to adulthood, including: *Child Development: from 9 to 12 years old* and *Understanding Adolescence;* addresses this "most misunderstood age group" in matters of their struggle for independence, body image, discipline problems, emotional health, changing family patterns, availabity of drugs and alcohol, etc., 16pp each, single copy free while supply lasts [also available from Channing L. Bete Company 200 State Road, South Deerfield, MA 01373 800-628-7733] **Child Protective Services** Virginia Dept. of Social Services, 8007 Discovery Drive, Richmond, VA 23229-8699

ADRDA NEWSLETTER
(quarterly) - newsletter reporting on research, legislation, chapter activities, local support groups, educational programs, nursing homes, awards, etc., Av. 8pp, single copy free **Alzheimer's Disease & Related Disorders Association** 70 East Lake Street, Suite 600, Chicago, IL 60601 312-853-3060

ADVOCACY IN THE FIELD OF AGING: SOS-7
(1972) - an appeal to emphasize that the advocate's role is to "inform," while the selection process and the decision to act must be left to the target population; includes needs assessment, planning, evaluation, elder's role, etc., 38pp, $2.15 **National Council on the Aging** 600 Maryland Avenue, West Wing 100, Washington, DC 20024 202-479-1200

ADVOCATE'S GUIDE TO HOME CARE FOR THE ELDERLY
(undated) - basic knowledge necessary to represent persons seeking home care; includes eligibility requirements for Medicare home health and Medicaid home health services, and a variety of programs that help with nonmedical daily activities (bathing, housekeeping, shopping, home delivery of meals, etc.); provides other facts on alternatives to institutional care, 132pp, $15.00 **National Clearinghouse for Legal Services** 4075 South Dearborn, Suite 400, Chicago, IL 60605 312-939-3830

AGEISM - DISCRIMINATION AGAINST OLDER PEOPLE
(1979) - a comparison of ageism to racism and sexism - a bias that thrives best in the absence of facts; explodes myths perpetuated by words like "toothless," "senile," etc., 28pp, $.50 (quantity discounts) **Public Affairs Committee** 381 Park Avenue South, New York, NY 10016 212-683-4331

AIM'S LEISURE GUIDE TO INDEPENDENT LIVING
(1972) - suggestions to the older person on using leisure time for pleasure and constructive activities, 14pp, single copy free **Action for Independent Maturity** 1909 K Street, NW, Washington, DC 20006 202-872-4700

ALTERNATIVE HOUSE VOLUNTEER MANUAL
(1984) - an overview of a program for adolescent runaway youth and their families; includes sections on listening, confidentiality, rights and rules for volunteer counselors, the hotline, house rules,

training and orientation, etc., 30pp, inquire about cost **Alternative House** Box 637, McLean, VA 22101 703-356-8385

AMERICA'S CHILDREN AND FAMILIES/KEY FACTS
(1982) - facts on the current condition of American children, youth and families, including family structure and income, employment, children without families, child care and development, health and medical services, education, social services and welfare status, housing conditions, victimization, delinquency, etc., 81pp, $5.50 **Children's Defense Fund** 122 C Street, NW, Washington, DC 20001 202-628-8787

ANTI-CRIME PROGRAMS
(1978) - description of a service by and for the elderly covering home security, street security, victim assistance, educational programs, etc. (one of the Senior Peer Employment Programs series on innovations in providing jobs for older persons) 16pp, $2.15 **National Council on the Aging** 600 Maryland Avenue, NW, West Wing 100, Washington, DC 20024 202-479-1200

ASIAN-PACIFIC HUMAN SERVICE NEEDS STUDY
(1989) - a study of the needs of Cambodian, Chinese, Japanese, Korean, Lao, Filipino, Samoan, Thai, Tongan, and Vietnamese families in Los Angeles County; lists concerns such as cultural traditions, languages, the absence of volunteerism as an Asian tradition, family pride (containing problems within the family), etc.; describes alternatives to these concerns to enable services to reach the distressed, inquire about cost and availability **United Way of Los Angeles** 621 South Virgil Avenue, Los Angeles, CA 90005-4046 213-736-1300

THE AT RISK ELDERLY: COMMUNITY SERVICE APPROACHES
(1979) - report on a three-year project designed to demonstrate that in-home and supportive services can be both increased and improved through coopertive efforts among local voluntary, private and public agencies; includes brief appended community profiles from 25 communities, 86pp, $3.75 **United Services for Older Adults** 212 Davie Street, Greensboro, NC 27401 919-373-1545

AUDITORY HANDICAPS AND READING
(1980) - a guide developed to assist educators and others working in deaf children's programs in complying with the law on education for all handicapped children; lists approaches currently advocated for these children in bibliographic form, 56pp, cost not determined, inquire **International Reading Association** PO Box 8139, 800 Barksdale Road, Newark, DE 19711 302-731-1600

AWARENESS COLORING BOOK
(undated) - a coloring book for Spanish-speaking children - both handicapped and non-handicapped - to help them understand what it means for a child to have a handicap, unpaged, inquire about cost **Association for Retarded Citizens** 1851 Ram Runway, Suite 104, College Park, GA 30337 404-761-2745

BARRIERS
(1984) - an audiovisual presentation addressing the gap between the need of the Hispanic elderly for social assistance, and their actual use of social services, 3/4" and 1/2" videotape, $65; filmstrip with 97 frames and cassette with cue signals, $40 **National Association for Hispanic Elderly** 2727 West Sixth Street, Suite 270 , Los Angeles, CA 90057 213-487-1922

BOYS & GIRLS CLUBS INFORMATION PACKET
(kept current) - a packet of information on the activities of the clubs, listing its specific programs, such as Summer in the Parks,

Aquatic Intervention, Photo-Journalism, Youth Helping Youth, Food Service, Older American Program, and others; includes the program of the first **Youth Volunteer Fair** offered by the Greater Washington Clubs, and other materials as available, single packet free **Boys & Girls Clubs of Greater Washington** PO Box 39063, Washington, DC 20016 202-462-4438

BOYS & GIRLS CLUBS OF GREATER WASHINGTON
(undated) - current information on programs and services of a youth-development agency with eight branch *Clubs* and ten emergency and residential group homes which serve neglected, abused and homeless youth; works from locations in the District of Columbia, Montgomery County, Annapolis, Alexandria, and Prince William County; provides job training and career development, tutoring; publishes a special handbook describing an outreach program for teenage parents, and other materials as available, single packet free **Boys & Girls Clubs of Greater Washington** 1320 Fenwick Lane, Suite 800, Silver Spring, MD 20910 301-587-4315

BUYING POWER
(1980) - special issue of "Prime Times" the newsletter of ACTION's Older American Volunteer Programs, on what is being done for the older consumer; includes examples of ways in which some communities have helped the elderly stretch dollars, advice from top-level resource persons, and references to other resources, 20pp, single copy free **US/ACTION - Older Americans Volunteer Programs (OAVP)** 1100 Vermont Avenue, NW, Suite 1100, Washington, DC 20525 202-634-9108

CAPITAL CONNECTION
(quarterly) - the newsletter of the *Boys & Girls Club of Greater Washington* providing an overview of activities and programs, new grants, *Club* profiles, etc., 6pp, free, contributions welcome **Boys & Girls Clubs of Greater Washington** 1320 Fenwick Lane, Suite 800, Silver Spring, MD 20910 301-587-4315

CARRIER ALERT PROGRAM
(kept current) - a packet of information on a program that trains postal carriers to recognize signs of problems regarding the homebound, the elderly, and the handicapped along mail routes, and take action (usually through reports to social agencies) to help alleviate the problems; includes a joint statement of support for the all-volunteer program (National Association of Letter Carriers, the United Way, and the United States Postal Service), reprints, news releases, speeches, project profiles, and other materials, single packet free **US/PS - Office of News and Public Affairs** 475 L'Enfant Plaza, Washington, DC 20260 202-245-4000

CHECKPOINTS FOR CHILDREN
(monthly) - current information in areas of protective services, residential care, childcare co-ops, youth hotlines, etc., AV. 20pp, $10/year **National Institute of Social Welfare Research** 455 North Milledge Avenue, PO Box 152, Athens, GA 30603 404-542-7614

CHILD ABUSE BOOKLET SERIES
(1989 ed.) - series of booklets addressing the issue of child abuse and neglect, including: *About Child Abuse; About Alcohol, Child Abuse and Child Neglect; About Child Neglect; About the Sexual Abuse of Children,* and *About Incest;* addresses each issue with definitions, warning signs, responsibility in reporting, ways of prevention, services and resources for assistance, etc., 16pp each, single copies free while supply lasts [also available from Channing L. Bete Company 200 State Road, South Deerfield, MA 01373 800-628-7733] **Child Protective Services** Virginia Dept. of Social Services, 8007 Discovery Drive, Richmond, VA 23229-8699

CHILD ABUSE: EDUCATION AND ACTION TOWARD PREVENTION

(1976) - detailed guidelines for mounting a local program in the area of child abuse; presents a composite of successful procedures of six B'nai B'rith pilot programs which mobilized their communities to help in their efforts, 6pp, single copy free **B'nai B'rith International** Community Volunteer Services, 1640 Rhode Island Avenue, NW, Washington, DC 20036 202-857-6535

CHILD ADVOCATE'S GUIDE TO CAPITOL HILL AND FEDERAL AGENCIES

(1981) - information on key members of Congress and committees with jurisdiction over children's programs, and federal agencies responsible for children's programs; analyzes how child advocates can effectively monitor and work with government, 52pp, $2.75 **Children's Defense Fund** 122 C Street, NW, Washington, DC 20001 202-628-8787

CHILD FIND OF AMERICA NEWS

(quarterly) - news on every aspect of missing children, from raising funds to mediation; includes articles on *Friends of Child Find,* student interns, business/industry involvement, etc., children found through TV, etc. 4pp, free **Child Find of America** PO Box 277, New Paltz, NY 12561-9277 914-255-1848

CHILDREN WITHOUT HOMES

(1978) - a tracking of patterns and decisions that subject children and their families to public abuse and neglect by removing children from their families and placing them long distances away from their communities; includes recommendations for change at all levels of government, 278pp, $5.50 **Children's Defense Fund** 122 C Street, NW, Washington, DC 20001 202-628-8787

CHILDREN'S PLACE: CREATING A FAMILY RESOURCE CENTER

(1983) - handbook describing how the Children's Place identified community needs, organized, found a site, developed financing, staffed, and set up policy and programs; discusses activities of the program including short-term child care, learning environment for small children, support activities for parents, and special needs and crisis care for families; appends tables for quick reference, 56pp, inquire about cost **Project SHARE** 7830 Old Georgetown Road, Suite 204, Bethesda, MD 20814 301-231-9539

CHRISTMAS WISH INFORMATION PACKET

(1990) - a packet of newspaper clippings, job descriptions, a newspaper tabloid, training outline, etc., to provide an overview of the Saginaw County DSS *Christmas Wish* program, which caught them by surprise the first year with 6,000 "wishes" (of which they were able to fill 3,000 through donor recruitment); includes steps taken to avoid such problems in the future with this popular program, unpaged, single copy free (contents change based on available materials) **Saginaw County Department of Social Services** 411 East Genesee, PO Box 5070, Saginaw, MI 48605 517-771-1614

CITIZEN ADVOCACY

(undated) - an overview of the numerous ways in which individual citizens and citizen groups can represent the interests of the handicapped, SN 040-000-00286-3, $1.00 **US/GSA - Government Printing Office** Superintendent of Documents, Washington, DC 20402 202-783-3238

CITIZEN ADVOCACY RESOURCES

(1979) - an annotated reference to literature, training materials, and other resources relevant to citizen advocacy for developmentally disabled persons; includes areas of administration, rights and benefits, access and travel, community living, and others, 170pp, $6.00 **Research and Training Center in Mental Retardation** Box 4510, Lubbock, TX 79409 806-742-3131

COMMITMENT & COMPASSION: BOSTON'S COMPREHENSIVE POLICY FOR THE HOMELESS

(1988-89) - a report on homeless services in Boston, Massachusetts, laying out the extent of homelessness in that city and explaining available services; provides information on programs for families, the mentally ill, veterans, AIDS patients and other special needs populations, as well as an accounting of federal and city funds available to Boston programs [prepared by the City of Boston], free copy from the National Coalition on the Homeless, Washington office **National Coalition for the Homeless** 1439 Rhode Island Avenue, NW, Washington, DC 20005 202-659-3310

COMMUNITY ORGANIZATION, PLANNING AND RESOURCES FOR THE OLDER POOR: SOS-1

(1970) - assistance for community organizations working to help the older poor gain some control over their lives, 72pp, $2.15 **United Services for Older Adults** 212 Davie Street, Greensboro, NC 27401 919-373-1545

COMMUNITY REORGANIZATION, PLANNING AND RESOURCES FOR OLDER PEOPLE

(1970) - assistance to community organizations working to help the older poor gain some control over their lives, 72pp, $2.15 **National Council on the Aging** 600 Maryland Avenue, SW, West Wing 100, Washington, DC 20024 202-479-1200

COMPENDIUM OF 1,500 RESOURCES FOR PEOPLE WITH DISABILITIES

(1989) - a comprehensive desk-top information and referral resource which draws upon experience in special recreation reflected in 3,800 programs, 4,500 abstracts, 35 national databases, and extensive research-program-training projects; includes foundation information, commercial sources, government resources, and other aids for the professional, consumer, or others working with the handicapped, 500pp, $49.95 **Special Recreation** 362 Koser Avenue, Iowa City, IA 52246-3038 319-337-7578

COMPENDIUM OF RESPONSES TO THE HOMELESS/AFFORDABLE HOUSING CRISIS IN AMERICA

(1989) - summary examples of the work that mortgage bankers are currently engaged in to assist the homeless and provide affordable housing across the country; includes award-winning examples and other exemplary initiatives as well as a list of members providing assistance, 20pp, single copy free **Mortgage Bankers Association of America** 1125 Fifteenth Street, NW, Washington, DC 20005-2766 202-861-6987

COMPREHENSIVE PROGRAM FOR THE ELDERLY IN RURAL AREAS

(1972) - overview of a model program designed to inform community groups in ways they can act as catalysts for involving the older poor in improving the quality of their lives; covers areas of nutrition, consumer problems, employment, etc., 36pp, $1.10 **National Council on the Aging** 600 Maryland Avenue, SW, West Wing 100, Washington, DC 20024 202-479-1200

CONSUMER GUIDE FOR OLDER PEOPLE

(undated) - mini-guide which folds to wallet size for quick reference on fraud schemes and swindles, "bargain prices" and other pitfalls in consumer areas, 16-panel foldout, single copy free **US/HHS - Administration on Aging** 200 C Street, SW, Washington, DC 20201 202-619-0724

CONTINUING CHOICES

(1975) - guide for volunteers to ideas for programs that benefit the elderly; provides 48 brief program profiles in areas such as information and referral, legal assistance, transportation, oral history, health, older volunteer opportunities, etc.; includes list of government subsidized programs, 50pp, $1.00 **National Council of Jewish Women** 15 East 26th Street, New York, NY 10010 212-532-1740

CULTURALLY DIVERSE/BILINGUAL EDUCATION SERIES

(1984-89) - a series of publications relating to education and other needs of culturally and lingually exceptional pupils, including:

- Education Services to Handicapped Students with Limited English Proficiency: A California Statewide Study, 1986, 122pp, $8.00 (nonmembers $10)
- Education of Culturally and Linguistically Different Exceptional Children, 1984, 123pp, $8.00 (nonmembers $10)
- Exceptional Asian Children and Youth, 1986, 69pp, $8.00 (nonmembers $10)
- American Indian Exceptional Children and Youth, 1987, 70pp, $6.80 (nonmembers $8.50)
- Meeting the Multicultural Needs of the Hispanic Students in Special Education, 1989, 96pp, $7.00 (nonmembers, same)
- Schools and the Culturally Diverse Student: Promising Practices and Future Directions, 1988, 143pp, $14.40 (nonmembers $18.00)

Computer Search reprints in these and other areas also are available for $12.80 per search (nonmembers $16), inquire about subject areas **Council for Exceptional Children** 1920 Association Drive, Reston, VA 22091-1589 703-620-3660

DEVELOPING DAY CARE FOR OLDER PEOPLE: SOS-11

(1974) - guidelines for a program to ensure a pleasant and safe environment, supervision, activities, rest periods, and at least one nutritious meal; differs from senior center concept only in the fact that seniors are more handicapped by physical, mental and/or social problems, 70pp, $2.15 **National Council on the Aging** 600 Maryland Avenue, SW, West Wing 100, Washington, DC 20024 202-479-1200

DIFFERENT USE OF VOLUNTEERS IN PUBLIC WELFARE SETTINGS: A PILOT STUDY

(1972) - overview of the uses and limitations of volunteers as service providers in three county-level public welfare programs, 96pp, $2.50 **Regional Institute of Social Welfare Research** PO Box 152, Athens, GA 30603 404-546-0798

DROP-IN CENTER: FOOD SERVICES TO THE HOMELESS

(undated) - a packet of information describing a service to the homeless that includes free dinners along with other basic services; includes an 8-panel foldout brochure and reprints about the service, single packet free **Committee for Creative Non-Violence** 1345 Euclid Street, NW, Washington , DC 20009 202-332-4332

DYNAMICS OF GROUP PROGRAMS IN SENIOR CENTERS

(1973) - overview with emphasis on the volunteer as a prominent figure in the establishment and continuation of most centers, and the training of both volunteers and paid staff in working with groups of older citizens, 39pp, $2.15 **National Council on the Aging** 600 Maryland Avenue, SW, West Wing 100, Washington, DC 20024 202-479-1200

"EACH LIFE IS PRECIOUS UNTO ITSELF"

(kept current) - a recruitment piece describing the role of LUVS in the overall Youth Haven program; includes statistical and other information to inform potential volunteers of the services provided to abused, neglected, abandoned, and dependent children, 12-panel foldout, free (also request copy of the project's institutional brochure, and a special recruitment flyer covering the LUVS program) **Let Us Volunteer Service (LUVS) Program** PO Box 7997, Naples, FL 33941 813-262-3327

EARLY CHILDHOOD SPECIAL EDUCATION: BIRTH TO THREE

(1988) - a guide to providing educational services to very young children; responds to P.I. 99-457, the mandate that requires participation of many disciplines; represents the nature of the "new territory" through the experience of qualified professionals in the field; includes chapters on early intervention, model programs, curriculum, parent involvement, team approaches, evaluation, etc., 257pp, $21.60 (nonmembers $27) [Inquire about related computer search reprints] **Council for Exceptional Children** 1920 Association Drive, Reston, VA 22091-1589 703-620-3660

EDUCATING STUDENTS WITH LEARNING PROBLEMS: A SHARED RESPONSIBILITY

(1990) - a report by the Assistant Secretary which describes what an OSERS Task Force perceives to be weaknesses in current approaches to the education of students with learning problems, and strategies for correcting these weaknesses, in preparation, free when available **US/DEd - Clearinghouse on Disability Information** Switzer Building, Room 3132, Washington, DC 20202-2524 202-732-1241

EDUCATION FOR OLDER ADULTS

(1983) - an overview describing 16 educational programs for older adults operated by colleges, community colleges, nonprofit independent educational organizations, unions, libraries and units of the aging network; covers educational activities, staffing, costs, and characteristics of the older learners, 62pp, $5.50 **National Council on the Aging** 600 Maryland Avenue, SW, West Wing 100, Washington, DC 20024 202-479-1200

EMPLOYEE TRAINING MODULES

(kept current) - materials developed by teachers from Flint area schools who work with business/industry during summer months in the *Quality Education Program* at the Flint and Lansing UAW-GM Human Resources Centers to prepare modules, which are used nationwide by GM, in exchange for the opportunity to take back to the classroom some insight into potential career opportunities for their students, unpaged, single copy free **UAW-GM National Human Resource Center** Region 1-C, 2636 Featherstone, Auburn Hills, MI 48321 313-377-2400

ENRICHED BY THEIR PRESENCE

(undated) - in-house information source for local offices on legislative issues and policy development, but useful to any group working with immigrants and refugees, inquire about availability and cost **Migration and Refugee Service** c/o US Catholic Charities, 1312 Massachusetts Avenue, NW, Washington, DC 20005 202-659-6630

EPILEPSY SCHOOL ALERT

(1980) - kit of materials addressed to school administrators but containing materials of interest to any concerned individual or group on recognition and first aid, medications, the nurse, the parent, tips for teachers, learning disabilities combined with other handicaps, etc.; includes evaluation vehicle, $2.00/kit **Epilepsy Foundation of America** 4351 Garden City Drive, Landover, MD 20785 301-459-3700

EPILEPSY: YOU AND YOUR CHILD
(1980) - parent's information kit containing a guide to help parents examine their own feelings and help the child deal with visiting relatives, school children, and his own self-concept; includes a booklet of answers to questions that may be asked by other people, a first-person narrative in child-type print (Because You Are My Friend) to help other children understand, and other materials, single packet free **Epilepsy Foundation of America** 4351 Garden City Drive, Landover, MD 20785 301-459-3700

EXPLORE YOUR VOLUNTEER OPPORTUNITIES
(kept current) - a job description describing the role of the volunteer in the *Ombudsman Program* and a brief overview of the origins of the program; includes mail-back inquiry form, 6-panel foldout, free **Ombudsman Program** Northern Virginia Long-Term Care, 11242 Waples Mill Road, #100, Fairfax, VA 22030 703-246-5411

THE FAMILY AND HANDICAPPED MEMBERS
(1984) - a look at the reactions of the family to the diagnosis of a handicapping condition, stress in the family, family organization, etc., 204pp, FR8501, $12.00 **National Council on Family Relations** 3989 Central Avenue, NE, Suite 550, Minneapolis, MN 55421-3921 612-781-9331

FAMILY SUPPORT ACT: AN EARLY IMPLEMENTATION GUIDE
(1989) - identifies and recommends implementation practices to design humane and effective programs to assist welfare recipients out of poverty, as offered in the *Family Support Act of 1988;* covers areas of work, education and training, childcare, AFDC-UP family issues, and health care, inquire about cost **Coalition on Human Needs** Att: Lisa Murray, 1000 Wisconsin Avenue, NW, Washington, DC 20007 202-342-0726

FAMILY THEMES ON CASSETTE
(1985-90) - a series of cassettes on family issues designed to assist with conferences, meetings, group discussions, and other with a focus on the family; titles include: *Children and Their Families, Families and Addictions,* and *Enriching Families/Ethnic, Cultural, and Religious Networks,* hundreds of tapes, write for complete list with annotations, $7.00/tape (every 8th tape free) **Custom Audio Tapes** 888 Corporation Street, Bridgeport, IL 62417 618-945-8751

FEDERAL PROGRAMS THAT RELATE TO CHILDREN
(1979) - a compilation submitted by government agencies to demonstrate efforts on behalf of children; presents programs that benefit children from 28 agencies, ranging from money-handling programs by the Treasury Department to "artists in schools" programs by the National Endowment for the Arts, 125pp, single copy free **US/HHS - Administration for Children, Youth and Families** U.S. Dept. of Health & Human Svcs., PO Box 1182, Washington, DC 20201 202-755-7500

FEDERAL PROGRAMS TO ASSIST THE ELDERLY
(1979) - facts on information and referral, medical, nutrition, employment, and other programs to meet the needs of the elderly, 4pp, free **US/HHS - Administration on Aging** 200 C Street, SW, Washington, DC 20201 202-619-0724

THE FINANCIAL SIDE OF RETIREMENT PLANNING
(1979) - illustrated guide cautioning retirement planners of the need to determine the cost of retirement before firm plans are made, 15pp, $.75 **Channing L. Bete Company** , South Deerfield, MA 01373

FIRST PLACE EDUCATION PACKET
(1990) - information about an elementary school for the homeless from the conception of the idea by a former schoolteacher to its present level with volunteer assistance for a paid staff, unpaged, free (send #10 SASE) **First Place** Department P, PO Box 15112, Seattle, WA 98115-0112 206-323-6715

FOR THE WELFARE OF CHILDREN
(1978) - appeal to child advocates to examine current issues being debated on welfare reform for the impact any changes will have on children; presents overview on welfare and children, 40pp, $2.50 **Children's Defense Fund** 122 C Street, NW, Washington, DC 20001 202-628-8787

GROUP CARE OF CHILDREN: CROSSROADS AND TRANSITIONS
(1977) - review of care currently available in the U.S. and Canada to children needing residential services; includes questionnaire for an on-site survey of the actual conditions as they are, discussion of what they should be, and a challenge to the field to redefine and reorganize, 327pp, $8.45 **Child Welfare League of America** 440 First Street, NW, Washington, DC 20013 202-638-2952

GUIDE TO ESTABLISHING AN ACTIVITY CENTER FOR MENTALLY RETARDED PERSONS
(undated) - assistance for program and operational planning for the development of a work activities program, 90pp, single copy free ($1.50 postage and handling) **National Association of Rehabilitation Facilities** PO Box 17675, Washington, DC 20041 703-556-8848

GUIDE TO HEALTH INSURANCE FOR PEOPLE WITH MEDICARE
(1980) - a discussion of the reasons why people who get Medicare benefits should be careful when they shop for health insurance, what is covered under Medicare, whether or not additional coverage is needed, shopping hints, 24pp, single copy free **US/OMB - Health Care Planning Administration** 6325 Security Boulevard, Baltimore, MD 21235 301-597-3000

GUIDEBOOK FOR LOCAL COMMUNITIES PARTICIPATING IN OPERATION INDEPENDENCE
(1975) - manual for a program designed to stimulate development of services within the community for the most vulnerable older persons who need supportive services to live alone or return to their homes; emphasizes cooperative efforts among all sectors of the community, 55pp, $1.10 **National Voluntary Organizations for Independent Living for the Aging** 600 Maryland Avenue, SW, West Wing 100, Washington, DC 20024 202-479-1200

A GUIDEBOOK FOR VOLUNTEERS
(undated) - basic information about the volunteers within the Adult and Family Services and Children's Services Division of the Oregon Department of Human Services; includes sections on the mission of the program, local programs, volunteers' expectations, and agency expectations, as well as a glossary of terms, a list of ethics and information on reporting forms, 11pp, single copy free **Interdivisional Volunteer Program** PO Box 628, Hillsboro, OR 97123 503-648-0711

GUIDELINES FOR A TELEPHONE REASSURANCE SERVICE
(1975) - manual for setting goals, beginning, operating, and evaluating a program for keeping in contact with isolated older persons; includes guidelines for training volunteers, 23pp, single copy free **US/HHS - Administration on Aging** 200 C Street, SW, Washington, DC 20201 202-619-0724

HANDBOOK FOR DEVELOPING A VOLUNTEER/RETIREE PROGRAM: SECOND CAREERS VOLUNTEER PROGRAM

(1980) - a step-by-step guide outlining the procedures for setting up a volunteer program for retirees in the community; comes complete with model forms, brochure information, and public service announcements; has a primary focus on the skilled retiree, inquire about availability and cost **Mayor's Voluntary Action Center** 61 Chambers Street, New York, NY 10007 212-566-5950

THE HANDICAPPED DRIVER'S MOBILITY GUIDE

(1978) - an aid for handicapped drivers and those working in programs for the handicapped to help provide more freedom in travel; includes information about adaptive equipment, driver training, and related services, 78pp, available from local AAA offices (some underwrite cost; inquire) **American Automobile Association** 1111 Gatehouse Road, Falls Church, VA 22042 703-AAA-6000

HANDICAPPED REQUIREMENTS HANDBOOK

(kept current) - looseleaf guide consisting of two sections:
- *Volume 1:* The Basic 504 Compliance guide that outlines and analyzes fundamental requirements and standards applicable to all federal fund recipients;
- *Volume 2:* the Agency Requirement Chapters to augment the Basic Guide by presenting and analyzing the differing requirements issued by some federal agencies under section 504.

Subscription includes newsletter, 6-page monthly supplements, and individualized phone/mail/visit advisory service, initial guide approximately 300pp, two volumes, $95.00/year **Federal Programs Advisory Service** 2120 L Street, NW, Washington, DC 20037 202-872-1766

HAVE A GOOD DAY: A VISITING AND TELEPHONE SERVICE FOR THE ELDERLY

(updated) - description of a cooperative service of groups and agencies in one county seeking to improve the lives of their isolated or lonely senior citizens; includes a checklist for potential volunteers to help them understand the volunteer role, 24pp, inquire about cost **Volunteer Center of Memphis** 263 South McLean Boulevard, Memphis, TN 38104 901-452-8655

HELLO WORLD!

(1979) - vignettes on mentally retarded persons in various settings to help foster better understanding, programs, preventive measures, etc.; addresses volunteers and others in an appeal for a "fresh start" in improving the image and services for the mentally retarded, 24pp, free **US/President's Committee on Mental Retardation** RO Building, Seventh & D Streets, SW, Washington, DC 20201 202-245-7634

HELPING OURSELVES: FAMILIES AND THE HUMAN NETWORK

(1976) - ways family members can relate to each other, kin, friends, neighbors, and the total community before turning to the "experts" for assistance in family life, 176pp, $4.95 **Beacon Press** 25 Beacon Street, Boston, MA 02108 617-742-2110

HELPING TO MAKE DREAMS COME TRUE

(1989) - a pictorial brochure briefly describing Gallaudet's volunteer program, roles volunteers play, and the achievements volunteers help to make possible for Gallaudet; gives details on qualifications for the free sign language training classes (four hours minimum weekly commitment), and provides other details on participation, 6-panel foldout, free **National Information Center on Deafness** 800 Florida Avenue, NE, Washington, DC 20002 202-651-5606

HOME DELIVERED MEALS PROGRAM FOR THE ELDERLY

(1973) - description of a demonstration program established to help determine the most effective methods of providing hot meals to the elderly, 34pp, single copy free **US/HHS - Administration on Aging** 330 Independence Avenue, SW, Washington, DC 20201 202-619-0724

HOMELESS CHILDREN AND THEIR FAMILIES

(1989) - a study of the plight of homeless families and single adults, preliminary report, unpaged, $14.00 [prepared jointly by the Child Welfare League of America and Travelers Aid International] Specify #2864 **Child Welfare League of America** c/o CSSC, 300 Raritan Center Parkway, Edison, NJ 08818 201-225-5555

HOMELESSNESS IN AMERICA: A SUMMARY

(1989) - a special report dealing with several aspects of homelessness - what it means, how many people, causes, solutions, and what citizens can do; includes other sources of information and a brief bibliography, 8pp, single copy free [also available from New York office: 105 East 22nd Street, New York, NY 10010 - 212-460-8110] **National Coalition for the Homeless** 1439 Rhode Island Avenue, NW, Washington, DC 20005 202-659-3310

HOSPITALS AND HOME CARE FOR THE ELDERLY

(1978) - overview of efforts to help the aging keep their independence by remaining in their own homes or other places of residence as long as possible; emphasizes the need for hospitals and community agencies to improve communications, and establish a mutual goal, 36pp, $3.20 **National Voluntary Organizations for Independent Living for the Aging** 600 Maryland Avenue, SW, West Wing 100, Washington, DC 20024 202-479-1200

THE HOST POST

(monthly) - newsletter of a program that brings together young and old for a companionship and social services program to assist the elderly; includes news of education, health, and recreation programs, columns by officials and members reporting on the progress of the program and local activities, membership updates, etc., 8pp, Minimum $5.00 donation for yearly subscription **Montgomery General Hospital** 3438 Olney-Laytonsville Road, Olney, MD 20832 301-774-6114

HOST: RECRUITMENT BROCHURE

(undated) - an overview of the program including eligibility for becoming a volunteer, rewards of volunteering, cooperative agencies working with HOST, and other facts of interest to potential volunteers, 8-panel foldout, free **Montgomery General Hospital** 3438 Olney-Laytonsville Road, Olney, MD 20832 301-774-6114

HOUSING FOR THE HANDICAPPED AND DISABLED: GUIDE FOR LOCAL ACTION

(1977) - comprehensive guide that local groups can use to mount programs for developing residential living environments with special design and service components for physically and mentally handicapped persons; helps speed up the process through its step-by-step format that treats each aspect of the housing development process as it will most likely be encountered by a local group, 176pp, $7.00 **National Association of Housing & Redevelopment Officials** 1320 Eighteenth Street, NW, Washington , DC 20036 202-429-2980

HOW TO ORGANIZE AND PROMOTE A REMINISCENCE WRITING CONTEST

(1980) - detailed guidelines for mounting a program by and for the elderly which gives them pleasure in relating memories and knowledge while giving them an opportunity to volunteer their services for a cultural/historical contribution through an activity like the University's "Yarns of Yesteryear" contest, 20pp, $3.00 (inquire about Home Study Course) **Yarns of Yesteryear Project** 610 Langden Street, Madison, WI 53706 608-263-3494

HOW TO PUBLISH A DIRECTORY OF SERVICES FOR OLDER ADULTS

(undated) - detailed instructions for compiling a directory to help individual senior citizens cut through the maze of social welfare, health, counseling, leisure time, and other programs; provides "how-to's" on establishing need, organizing, budgeting, acquiring funding and co-sponsors, training volunteers, gathering information, and producing, publicizing, and distributing the directory; includes sample news release, radio spot, and other aids, 30pp, $1.00 **National Council of Jewish Women** 15 East 26th Street, New York, NY 10010 212-532-1740

HUNGER/HOMELESSNESS ACTION: COLLEGE/UNIVERSITY RESOURCE BOOK

(1990) - articles, profiles, directories and ideas for programs on community service, fundraising, and education around the issues of hunger and homelessness both in the U.S. and abroad, $13.40 **Campus Outreach Opportunity League (COOL)** 386 McNeal Hall, University of Minnesota, St. Paul, MN 55108-1011 612-624-3018

THE ILLUSION OF CARING

(1976) - a look at the children in foster homes and institutions, and the false picture that is often presented about their care; illustrated with children's art, 124pp, $3.95 **Beacon Press** 25 Beacon Street, Boston, MA 02108 617-742-2110

INDEPENDENT LIVING FOR PHYSICALLY DISABLED PEOPLE

(1983) - advice on developing, implementing and evaluating self-help rehabilitation programs; shows how the lives of disabled people are enriched through independent living programs that promote full community involvement; offers detailed descriptions of actual programs throughout the world, 429pp, $32.95 **Jossey Bass, Publishers** 350 Sansome Street, San Francisco, CA 94104-1310 415-433-1767

INNOCENT VICTIMS: NCJW MANUAL ON CHILD ABUSE AND NEGLECT

(1978) - program models in areas of taking a community survey, establishing a hotline, starting a parents anonymous program, establishing family outreach and crisis care centers, building a coalition for monitoring/advocacy; includes overview of the problem, and an extensive resource listing, 108pp, $2.50 **National Council of Jewish Women** 15 East 26th Street, New York, NY 10010 202-532-1740

INNOVATIVE APPROACHES TO YOUTH SERVICES

(1973) - a look at programs which offer a large number of services to youth who are having a variety of problems; covers funding, facilities, program development, special programs (runaways, parent education, etc.), staff and volunteers, training and orientation, community relations, political involvement, etc., 131pp, $5.00 (also available from Do It Now Foundation, separate entry) **U.S. Journal of Drug and Alcohol Dependence** 2119A Hollywood Boulevard, Hollywood, FL 35020 305-925-9433

INSTITUTE OF LIFETIME LEARNING PUBLICATIONS

(undated) - a series of publications available from the *Institute* on education topics for older persons; single copy of each free, write for quantity costs:

- *Learning Opportunities for Older Persons* D171
- *Making America Literate: How You Can Help* D12755
- *College Centers for Older Learners* D12489
- *Tuition Policies in Higher Education for Older Adults* D12401
- *Minicourse Series Order Form* D168
- *Minicourse Discussion Leader's Guide* D12197
- *How to Write for Publication* D12290
- *Museum Opportunities for Older Persons* D12211
- *Community Television: A Handbook for Production* D12761
- *Elderhostel Brochure* D1178
- *The Constitution Brochure* D1178
- *GED Brochure: "Wish You Had Finished High School?"* D13048

For annotations of these publications, request Catalog Sheet, 2pp, free **Institute of Lifetime Learning** AARP Fulfillment, 1909 K Street, NW, Washington, DC 20049 202-662-4895

INTERNATIONAL TELEPHONE DIRECTORY FOR TDD USERS

(annually) - TDD phone numbers of businesses, travel services, residential listings, medical services, and many more, all organized by states; includes quarterly *GA-SK Newsletter* and a free listing in the directory, annual subscription, $15.00 (residential), $30.00 (business/organizational) **Telecommunications for the Deaf** 814 Thayer Avenue, Silver Spring, MD 20910 301-589-3006

IT TAKES MANY HANDS

(kept current) - annual report of Youth Haven, a child care program for neglected and abused children; covers the volunteer program at the Haven, LUVS (Let Us Volunteer Service), as well as a history and background, and a step-by-step report of the year's activities, 40pp, single copy free **Let Us Volunteer Service (LUVS) Program** PO Box 7007, Naples, FL 33941 813-262-3327

JEWISH BRAILLE INSTITUTE *VOICE*

(monthly) - a sound-scriber disc containing the newsletter of the *Jewish Braille Institute* providing current information on the Institute's services to Jewish blind persons and other individuals, inquire about cost **Jewish Braille Institute** 110 East 30th Street, New York, NY 10016 212-889-2525

JOB SUCCESS FOR HANDICAPPED YOUTH: A SOCIAL PROTOCOL CURRICULUM

(1987) - a model addressing the principal that it is inappropriate social behavior rather than lack of skills that prevents handicapped workers from competing successfully in the work place; includes sections on teaching social skills, and actual lessons to use in school and on the job; appends forms for duplication on social skills, interviewing employers, and observing the worker on the job, 62pp, $10.00 (nonmembers $12.50) **Council for Exceptional Children** 1920 Association Drive, Reston, VA 22091-1589 703-620-3660

THE LEADING EDGE: SERVICE PROGRAMS THAT WORK

(1978) - descriptions of successful service programs for the mentally retarded throughout the U.S. in areas of family, education, residences, the mentally retarded offender, mental health, prevention, self-assertion;, etc.; includes section on "some new directions" distilled for quick reference from the programs described, 76pp, single copy free **US/President's Committee on Mental Retardation** RO Building, 7th & D Streets, SW, Washington, DC 20201 202-245-7634

LEARNING DISABILITIES WITH EMPHASIS ON READING

(1978) - a representative listing of printed materials on reading and learning disabilities published during the 1970's and reflecting areas of child development, general education, linguistics, speech/hearing, etc., as they related to reading instruction for LD persons, 57pp, $2.50 (members $1.75) **International Reading Association** PO Box 8139, 800 Barksdale Road, Newark, DE 19711 302-731-1600

THE LEGAL FRAMEWORK FOR ENDING FOSTER CARE DRIFT
(1983) - a guide to evaluating and improving state laws, regulations and court rules, single copy free (request complete list) **National Legal Resource Center for Child Advocacy and Protection** 1800 M Street, NW, Washington, DC 20036 202-331-2250

LET'S END ISOLATION
(undated) - examples of services in all areas for the elderly - employment, transportation, nutrition, volunteer work, etc.; includes overview of funding possibilities for community programs, 46pp, single copy free **US/HHS - Administration on Aging** 200 C Street, SW, Washington, DC 20201 202-619-0724

LIFE CENTERED CAREER EDUCATION: A COMPETENCY BASED APPROACH
(1989) - some specific examples of how *Life Centered Career Education* can be taught; provides a framework for building a comprehensive curriculum effort, and a means of student assessment; bases revisions in the current edition on developments over the ten-year period of the program, 179pp, $15.60 (nonmembers $19.50) **Council for Exceptional Children** 1920 Association Drive, Reston, VA 22091-1589 703-620-3660

LOVE IS AGELESS MATERIALS
(1979) - a variety of oversized puzzles, bingo games, needlepoint canvasses, etc., for the elderly, write for complete information and price list **American Health Care Association** 1200 Fifteenth Street, NW, Washington , DC 20005 202-833-2050

MEALS ON WHEELS
(1979) - detailed handbook providing steps for action, methods of operation and guides for projected budgeting and management, sample forms, and other aids, 21pp, $1.00 **National Council of Jewish Women** 15 East 26th Street, New York, NY 10010 212-532-1740

MEDICAL ADVANCES HAVE MADE IT POSSIBLE FOR MORE PEOPLE TO REACH OLD AGE...BUT FOR WHAT?
(undated) - a guide for organizers covering numerous program areas for assistance to the elderly (meals on wheels, minibus service, telephone reassurance, etc.); includes program sheet on the older adult as a volunteer leading readers to the local Voluntary Action Center where one exists for help in getting started, 36pp, $.25 **B'nai B'rith International** Community Volunteer Services, 2640 Rhode Island Avenue, NW, Washington, DC 20036 202-393-5284

MEDICARE AND YOU
(1980) - illustrated guide on Medicare coverage to help users get the most out of the program; helps to avoid confusion by listing services NOT covered, 15pp, $.75 **Channing L. Bete Company** , South Deerfield, MA 01373

MEDICARE PROBLEMS
(1977) - a look at some of the inadequacies and inconveniences of using the Medicare system; includes listing of other resources, 23pp, $2.25 **National Clearinghouse for Legal Services** 407 South Dearborn, Suite 400 , Chicago, IL 60605 312-939-3830

MENTAL HEALTH: COPING WITH STRESS
(1979) - a retirement planning guide published for older employees nearing retirement, 16pp, single copy free (if requested on organization letterhead) **Retirement Advisors** 919 Third Avenue, New York, NY 10022 212-421-2400

THE MENTAL HEALTH NEEDS OF HOMELESS PERSONS
(1986) - analysis of the mental health needs of the increasing population of homeless persons, including adults, adolescents, battered women, and whole families; analyzes shortcomings in the current system of care - both emergency and long term - and discusses ways in which comprehensive care for the homeless can be provided, $14.95 **Jossey Bass, Publishers** 350 Sansome Street, San Francisco, CA 94104-1310 415-433-1767

MENTAL RETARDATION - A CHANGING WORLD
(1979) - defines mental retardation, emphasizing the wide range of differences among mentally retarded persons (mild, moderate, severe, profound levels of retardation); discusses causes, attitudes, effects on families, available services, residential and community facilities, and rights of the retarded, 28pp, $.50 (quantity discounts) **Public Affairs Committee** 381 Park Avenue South, New York, NY 10016 212-683-4331

MENTAL RETARDATION: THE LEADING EDGE
(1978) - a collection of illustrated program descriptions reporting on programs that have proven successful for the mentally retarded, including several on employment, 76pp, single copy free **US/President's Committee on Mental Retardation** RO Building, 7th and D Streets, SW, Washington, DC 20201 202-245-7634

MOBILE MEALS: GUIDELINES FOR DEVELOPING QUALITY SERVICES
(undated) - overview of the types of meal delivery plans available to a community group, administration and organization, meal preparation, sample menus, etc., 17pp, $1.10 **National Council on the Aging** 600 Maryland Avenue, SW, West Wing 100, Washington, DC 20024 202-479-1200

MRS RESETTLEMENT & IMMIGRATION DIRECTORY
(annually) - a comprehensive listing of orientation, training, health, housing, employment and other services available to immigrants and refugees coming to the U.S., inquire about availability and cost **Migration and Refugee Service** c/o US Catholic Charities, 1312 Massachusetts Avenue, NW, Washington, DC 20005 202-659-6630

MY CHILD IN CRISIS? ... NEVER!!!
(1989) - a brochure describing a local all-volunteer program of the national Child Security Network in which child identification and health information is stored in a computer for instant recall in case of a crisis; file includes blood type, allergies, pre-existing conditions, family physician, insurance information, and contact information for parents and three alternative contacts, 6-panel foldout, free **Child Security Network** Southwest Regional Division, Milford, CT 06460 203-783-3036

MY LEFT FOOT: THE GLORIOUS RAGE OF CHRISTY BROWN
(1990) - a dramatization of the life of a victim of cerebral palsy, how he coped, the growing up years, his rage at the attitudes and bias around him toward the handicapped, how he forced people to deal with him (eating in the best restaurants, for example), his despair and alcoholism, and his rise above diversity to become a leader and family man, inquire about format, availability and cost **Virginia Department for Rights of the Disabled** James Monroe

Building, 17th Floor, 101 North 14th Street, Richmond, VA 23219
804-225-2042

**NATIONAL VOLUNTARY ORGANIZATIONS: A
RESOURCE FOR THE VULNERABLE AGING**
(1978) - overview and case studies on participation by 27 national
voluntary organizations in "Operation Independence," a project
calling for better in-home and supportive services for certain
elderly persons in the community, 80pp, $3.20 **National Voluntary
Organizations for Independent Living for the Aging** 600 Maryland
Avenue, SW, West Wing 100, Washington, DC 20024
202-679-1200

NEIGHBORHOOD CONSERVATION AND THE ELDERLY
(1978) - discussion of the effects of relocation due to urban
renewal on the elderly poor; presents case studies of neighborhood
efforts to deal with this problem, 72pp, $4.00 **Conservation
Foundation** 1250 24th Street, NW, Washington, DC 20037
202-293-4800

NEW ENVIRONMENTS FOR RETARDED PEOPLE
(1975) - an album of facility designs developed to help those
planning, adapting, or rehabilitating facilities for use by mentally
retarded persons; includes drawings and photographs for designs
from the U.S. and other countries, SN 017-000041-8, $1.15
US/GSA - Government Printing Office Superintendent of
Documents, Washington, DC 20402 202-783-3238

NEW LIFE IN THE NEIGHBORHOOD
(1980) - subtitled *How persons with disabilities can help make a
good neighborhood better,* this book explains "normalization," and
why people with disabilities and those without benefit from
community integration; addresses commonplace fears (such as
impact on property values), and other myths surrounding people
with mental retardation, inquire about cost **Abingdon Press** 201
Eighth Avenue, South, PO Box 801, Nashville, TN 37202
615-749-6290

NEW LIGHT ON AN OLD PROBLEM
(1979) - nine frequently asked questions about child abuse, with
answers in chart, narrative, and other forms to provide
quick-reference clarification, 19pp, single copy free **National
Center on Child Abuse and Neglect** U.S. Dept. of Health &
Human Svcs., PO Box 1182, Washington, DC 20201 202-755-7500

NEW NEIGHBORS
(1974) - an aid for those who advocate new homes in the
community for the mentally retarded; includes practical advice
from fourteen experts in the field, SN 040-000-00310-0, $2.60
US/GSA - Government Printing Office Superintendent of
Documents, Washington, DC 20402 202-783-3238

NOT BY BREAD ALONE
(1982) - a B'nai B'rith guide for working with handicapped people;
explains how to help people with disabilities achieve as much
independence as possible in order to participate in society to the
fullest extent; $.20 each **B'nai B'rith International** Community
Volunteer Services, 1640 Rhode Island Avenue, NW, Washington,
DC 20036 202-857-6580

**NOT SINCE THE GREAT DEPRESSION HAVE SO MANY
HOMELESS AMERICANS LIVED ON THE STREETS...**
(1990) - a brochure describing the homeless problem, identifying
the homeless, offering reasons for increasing numbers of homeless
Americans, outlining what is being done and plans for the future,
and providing an overview of the National Coalition, 6-panel
foldout, free *[also available from New York office: 105 East 22nd
Street, New York, NY 10010 - 212-460-8110]* **National Coalition
for the Homeless** 1439 Rhode Island Avenue, NW, Washington,
DC 20005 202-659-3310

**NURSING HOME SURVEY: HOW TO DEVELOP AND
PUBLISH A NURSING HOME GUIDE**
(1979) - help for consumers confronted with the need to make an
informed choice regarding nursing home placement; offers a single
source of information about homes in a specific community/area
and their specific strengths and weaknesses; provides guidelines for
organizing, staffing, developing a budget, planning training,
promoting, publishing, etc.; appends numerous forms, other aids,
29pp, $1.00 **National Council of Jewish Women** 15 East 26th
Street, New York, NY 10010 212-532-1740

NURSING HOMES: STRATEGY FOR REFORM
(1979) - step-by-step analysis of the nursing home scandals,
discussing the "geriatric gold rush" syndrome (since
Medicare/Medicaid), the timidity of law enforcement, alternatives
to homes, etc.; offers comprehensive evaluation checklist, and some
ideas for preventing future scandals, 28pp, $.50 (quantity
discounts) **Public Affairs Committee** 381 Park Avenue South, New
York, NY 10016 212-683-4311

NUTRITION EDUCATION FOR THE ELDERLY
(1982) - a variety of methods for educating the elderly on the
importance of good eating habits, 129pp, $5.00 **Virginia Council
on Health and Medical Care** PO Box 12363, Central Stations,
Richmond, VA 23241 703-649-0323

NUTRITION FOR THE ELDERLY
(1975) - a guide to menu planning, buying and the care of food for
community programs, 44pp, single copy free **Consumer and Food
Economics Institute** , Washington, DC 20250 202-447-2791

NUTRITION PROGRAM FOR THE ELDERLY
(1972) - informative guide for setting up a meals program that uses
preparation techniques that allow the meal to be eaten where it is
purchased (at very low cost), carried home, or - when necessary -
delivered to the homebound, 41pp, $1.10 **National Voluntary
Organizations for Independent Living for the Aging** 600 Maryland
Avenue, SW, West Wing 100, Washington, DC 20024
202-479-1200

OBTAINING FEDERAL MONEY FOR CHILDREN
(1976) - steps that must be taken to obtain needed funds, with
sections on the development of program concepts, efficient
organizations, and how to understand state and county budget
cycles; includes individual state analyses, 66pp, $6.00 **Child
Welfare League of America** 440 First Street, NW, Washington,
DC 20001 202-638-2952

OLD FOLKS AT HOMES
(1976) - a graphic view of a cross section of nursing homes across
the country, citing unsafe, unsanitary practices as well as
outstanding, beneficial procedures; discusses the role of the
volunteer, providing details when possible, 148pp, $7.50 **American
Psychiatric Association** 1400 K Street, NW, Washington, DC
20005 202-682-6000

OLDER AMERICANS AND THE ARTS
(1976) - ideas for encouraging active participation by the elderly in
the arts; includes suggestions for community approaches; provides
a list of national and other resources, 64pp, $3.20 **National
Council on the Aging** 600 Maryland Avenue, SW, West Wing 100,
Washington, DC 20024 202-479-1200

OLDER TREES STILL BLOSSOM...

(1984) - an overview of Project AYUDA, a senior community service employment program for the Hispanic elderly, which is funded by the U.S. Department of Labor under Title V of the Older Americans Act; involves part-time subsidized employment in community service work in public and private nonprofit agencies, training and job development, and eventual placement in jobs outside the program, 6-panel foldout, free **National Association for Hispanic Elderly** 2727 West Sixth Street, Suite 270 , Los Angeles, CA 90057 213-487-1922

OMBUDSMAN PROGRAM INFORMATION PACKET

(kept current) - packet of materials describing a program of advocacy for residents of long-term care facilities; includes fact sheets, program description, job description, and general information for both volunteer and patient, unpaged, free **Ombudsman Program** Northern Virginia Long-Term Care, 11242 Waples Mill Road, #100, Fairfax, VA 22030 703-246-5411

OSERS NEWS IN PRINT

(monthly) - a newsletter which focuses on Federal activities affecting people with disabilities and new developments in the information field, length varies, free **US/DEd - Clearinghouse on Disability Information** Switzer Building, Room 3132, Washington, DC 20202-2524 202-732-1241

OUT-LINE

(occasionally) - information on national and local efforts to improve communication technology for the hearing impaired; free subscription (ask about other materials) **Organization for the Use of the Telephone (OUT)** PO Box 175, Owings Mill, MD 21117 301-655-1827

OUTREACH TO THE AGING BLIND: SOME STRATEGIES FOR COMMUNITY ACTION

(1977) - guide to ways in which local communities can reach out to their aging blind members who are often "hidden;" includes guidelines for "consciousness raising" meetings and what to include in them, funding sources, and tips on promotion and evaluation of local outreach programs, 168pp, $5.00 **American Foundation for the Blind** 15 West 16th Street, New York, NY 10011 212-620-2000

PAMPHLETS ON EMPLOYMENT

(1980) - information for employers and employees to put employment of epileptics in the proper perspective, single copy of each free:
- Employment Action on Epilepsy
- Respond to: Workers with Epilepsy
- Employers... Julie, Mary and Steve can fill your job needs. TAPS will show you how!
- The Employer's Role

Epilepsy Foundation of America 4351 Garden City Drive, Landover, MD 20785 301-459-3700

PENDING HOMELESS LEGISLATION

(kept current) - detailed overviews of pending legislation and related implications; includes sample letter to Congress, 2pp, free [also available from New York office: 105 East 22nd Street, New York, NY 10010 - 212-460-8110] **National Coalition for the Homeless** 1439 Rhode Island Avenue, NW, Washington, DC 20005 202-659-3310

PEOPLE HELPING PEOPLE: MARYVALE

(undated) - a packet of information on a program that serves girls ages two to 18, and boys ages two to seven, who are experiencing problems in their current living situations; includes a fact sheet, volunteer job descriptions (Recreation Aide, Child Care Aide, and Tutor), statistical information, and an organizational brochure, single packet free **Maryvale** 7600 East Graves Avenue, Rosemead, CA 91770 213-280-6510

PEOPLE LIVE IN HOUSES

(1975) - descriptions of group homes, foster homes, and other types of residential settings for retarded children and adults, SN 017-000-00143-4, $1.70 **US/GSA - Government Printing Office** Superintendent of Documents, Washington, DC 20402 202-783-3238

PHONE PAL INFORMATION PACKET

(1990) - information about Phone Pal, a program that matches older volunteers and "latchkey children" (children who are home alone before or after school) for a daily telephone contact to provide the child and the parent with an added sense of security, unpaged, free **Southwestern Bell** 1010 Pine, Room 921, St. Louis, MO 63101 314-235-9800

P.L. 99-457 - THE NEXT STEP FORWARD FOR HANDICAPPED CHILDREN

(1987) - a video training program to help advocates, educators and others who work with handicapped children understand the federal legislation passed in October 1986; describes how services for handicapped children from birth through age five have been strengthened, and how interagency support will help enhance service delivery; includes a 23-minute videocassette, masters for 21 overhead transparencies, copies of the *Act*, and the *Report*, fact sheets, and a *User's Guide*, $125.00 (nonmembers $156.25) **Council for Exceptional Children** 1920 Association Drive, Reston, VA 22091 703-620-3660

PLANNING AND ORGANIZING A SHELTERED WORKSHOP FOR MENTALLY RETARDED PERSONS

(undated) - how-to guide to assessing community needs for a workshop, and basic operational principles, 79pp, single copy free ($1.50 postage/handling) **National Association of Rehabilitation Facilities** PO Box 17675, Washington, DC 20041 703-556-8848

PLANNING EFFECTIVE ADVOCACY PROGRAMS

(1979) - information on organizing, media relations, consumer participation, fundraising, etc., in the development of community advocacy programs; discusses some of the pitfalls, and suggests ways to avoid them, 61pp, $4.00 plus $1.00 postage **American Coalition of Citizens with Disabilities** 346 Connecticut Avenue, NW, Washington, DC 20036 202-785-4265

PLANNING FOR RETIREMENT: INFORMATION SOURCES

(1974) - a compilation of resource information for near-retirees to help avoid some of the inherent problems in poorly-planned use of time and resources; lists national, academic, community, church, local government, and other sources of planning help, 14pp, free **US/HHS - Administration on Aging** 330 Independence Avenue, SW, Washington, DC 20201 202-619-0724

PLANNING FOR YOUR RETIREMENT YEARS

(1979) - a question/answer guide for the potential retiree leading to an individualized plan for retirement years; questions based on actual inquiries to a retirement guidance counselor, 59pp, $2.50 **Pilot Books** 103 Cooper Street, Babylon, NY 11702 516-422-2225

PLANNING HOUSING ENVIRONMENTS FOR THE ELDERLY

(1974) - a tool for those concerned with planning, building, and maintaining housing for the elderly (written by an architect and a planner); emphasizes considering the health, living habits and other conditions and activities of target group before finalizing plans, 120pp, $8.00 **National Council on the Aging** 600 Maryland Avenue, SW, West Wing 100, Washington, DC 20024 202-479-1200

PLANNING WITH THE AGING: A PROCESS APPROACH: SOS-6
(1971) - suggested action that can be taken to explode myths about the aging, determine realistic needs, and find resources to meet these needs, 31pp, $2.15 **National Council on the Aging** 600 Maryland Avenue, SW, West Wing 100, Washington, DC 20024 202-479-1200

POCKET GUIDE TO FEDERAL HELP FOR INDIVIDUALS WITH DISABILITIES
(1990) - a quick-reference summary of benefits and services available to qualified individuals, unpaged, free **US/DEd - Clearinghouse on Disability Information** Switzer Building, Room 3132, Washington, DC 20202-2524 202-732-1241

THE PROBLEM OF MENTAL RETARDATION
(1979) - overview of current developments on behalf of the mentally retarded in areas including community services, manpower, residential care, special education, rehabilitation, prevention, etc.; includes extensive checklist on preventive measures to help concerned persons/groups determine where their communities stand, 24pp, free **US/President's Committee on Mental Retardation** RO Building, Seventh & D Streets, SW, Washington, DC 20201 202-245-7634

PRODUCTIVE LEISURE (TENTATIVE TITLE)
(In process) by Regina Kessler - a comprehensive guide to retirement leisure addressing the 15-20 healthy active years after retirement faced by today's retirees; uses experiential exercises to assist retirees in making the best choices based on their interests and needs; details many of the options open to retirees, discusses how to get involved in an interest area, and presents real-life stories of successful retirees; includes chapters on volunteering, education, travel, second careers, sports and fitness, hobbies and the arts, expected publication date 1992, inquire about availability and cost **Pharos Books** 200 Park Avenue, New York, NY 10166 212-692-3830

PROGRAM PLANNING: ACCOUNTABILITY, CREDIBILITY, TRUST
(1975) - a guide to assist planners and managers of senior centers in setting goals and priorities, fostering community support, operating, monitoring and evaluating the program; emphasizes involvement of center participants in the planning and operation, 16pp, $1.10 [addressed to senior centers, but useful for accountability of any program] **National Council on the Aging** 600 Maryland Avenue, NW, West Wing 100, Washington, DC 20024 202-479-1200

PUBLIC/VOLUNTARY COLLABORATION: A PARTNERSHIP IN INDEPENDENT LIVING FOR THE AGED
(1981) - overview of a mini-White House Conference on Aging convened by NVOILA; covers issue areas such as: health maintenance/wellbeing, long-term care, family/social services and other support systems, physical/social environment and quality of life, age-integrated society (family) and research, 16pp, $2.00 **National Council on the Aging** 600 Maryland Avenue, SW, West Wing 100, Washington, DC 22024 202-479-1200

THE PURSUIT OF DIGNITY
(1977) - a look at new living alternatives for the elderly in areas of day care, health, housing, nutrition, etc.; includes information on volunteers in hospitals, housing, and direct services as well as on the elderly themselves as volunteers, 154pp, $4.95 **Beacon Press** 25 Beacon Street, Boston, MA 02109 617-742-2110

REACH OUT TO ABUSED CHILDREN
(1976) - an awareness vehicle in a script format to involve a group of concerned citizens in a direct dialogue regarding the problem of child abuse and ways they can become involved in helping alleviate the problem, 12pp, $.40 (developed by American Lutheran Church Women) **Augsburg Fortress** 426 South Fifth Avenue, Box 1209, Minneapolis, MN 55440 612-330-3300

READER'S GUIDE FOR PARENTS OF CHILDREN WITH MENTAL PHYSICAL OR EMOTIONAL DISABILITIES
(1980) - guide for parents to help them understand the reading problems of their handicapped children, and inform them on what can and is being done to help, 46pp, single copy free **US/HHS - Bureau of Community Health Services** 5600 Fishers Lane, Rockville, MD 20857 301-443-2330

RECREATION AND THE BLIND ADULT
(1971) - answers to common questions about the participation of blind adults in recreation activities; identifies activities in which adaptations are necessary and those that need none, 10pp, single copy free **American Foundation for the Blind** 15 West 16th Street, New York, NY 10011 212-620-2000

RECREATION FOR DISABLED PERSONS
(1979) - a guide for those advocating sports as a pastime for the disabled; lists numerous activities now including handicapped, an awareness campaign for nonhandicapped participants, role of service organizations, and the need for volunteers every step of the way, 28pp, $.50 (quantity discounts) **Public Affairs Committee** 381 Park Avenue South, New York, NY 10016 212-683-4331

REFLECTIONS ON GROWING UP DISABLED
(1983) - a sharing of the childhood feelings, insights, and self-perceptions of disabled people; includes frustrations related to learning and socialization; provides insight into the problems, fears, and triumphs of handicapped children, both in the community and in learning settings, 112pp, $10.00 (nonmembers $12.50) **Council for Exceptional Children** 1920 Association Drive, Reston, VA 22091-1589 703-620-3660

RETIREMENT PLANNING: A B'NAI B'RITH PROGRAM
(undated) - a portfolio of information on activities that retirees can mount to provide a better base for their retirement years; includes program profiles on consciousness-raising, citizen action and legislation, income planning, second careers, psychological adjustment, physical fitness and health maintenance, $1.25/kit **B'nai B'rith International** Community Volunteer Services, 1640 Rhode Island Avenue, NW, Washington, DC 20036 202-856-6580

RETIREMENT REHEARSAL GUIDEBOOK
(undated) - workbook for planning the retirement future; offers charts, illustrations and other aids in areas of record-keeping, income, where to locate for retirement, and others, 214pp, inquire about cost **Pictorial, Inc.** 1718 Lafayette Road, Indianapolis, IN 46222 317-299-7220

ROSIE'S PATROL NEWSLETTER
(intermittent) - a new vehicle by a group formed after a child was abducted and later murdered in a quiet Virginia community, *Rosie's Patrol*, which works with a volunteer Board of Directors.

hundreds of local volunteers, and national and local organizations across the country to find ways to make neighborhoods and homes safer for children, in process at press time, inquire **Rosie's Patrol** PO Box 306, Burke, VA 22015-0306 703-978-5243

RUNAWAY TEENAGERS
(1977) - discussion of the growing trend among youth to leave home, and some possible solutions to the problem, 28pp, $.50 (bulk rates) **Public Affairs Committee** 381 Park Avenue South, New York, NY 10016 212-683-4311

SAFETY NETWORK
(monthly) - newsletter reporting on activities relating to the homeless in areas of legislation, drugs, housing, local activities, coming events, model projects, etc., 4pp, free subscription [also available from New York office: 105 East 22nd Street, New York, NY 10010 - 212-460-8110] **National Coalition for the Homeless** 1439 Rhode Island Avenue, NW, Washington, DC 20005 202-659-3310

SATURATION WORK INITIATIVE MODEL (SWIM): FINAL REPORT
(1989) - final report on a demonstration of a welfare employment initiative (SWIM) operated in San Diego, California, between 1985 and 1987, when it was replaced by the *Greater Avenues for Independence (GAIN)* program; includes findings on the maximum level of monthly participation feasible in such a program, whether the SWIM program had an impact on employment and welfare dependence, and whether the approach proved cost-effective, 159pp, $12.50 (full copy), $2.50 (executive summary) **Manpower Demonstration Research Corporation** Three Park Avenue, New York, NY 10016 212-532-3200

THE SCAN VOLUNTEER
(undated) - an overview of the responsibilities of a volunteer assigned to a provide one-to-one assistance to parents who have abused their children, or who are categorized as "high risk" (experiencing difficulty handling the role as parent), 4pp, single copy free (also request a copy of "SCAN Center of Spokane County," an informational brochure on the overall program) **East Central Community Center** South 500 Stone, Spokane, WA 99202 509-548-7445

SELF-HELP GROUPS IN REHABILITATION
(undated) - reports on what self-help groups throughout the country have done to help disabled people help themselves; discusses policy implications of this movement, 36pp, single copy free ($1.25 postage and handling) **American Coalition of Citizens with Disabilities** 1200 Fifteenth Street, NW, Washington, DC 20005 202-785-4265

SELF-STUDY AND EVALUATION GUIDE: PERSONNEL ADMINISTRATION AND VOLUNTEER SERVICE
(Rev. 1980) - a tool keyed to realistic attainable levels of performance rather than perfection; designed for use with other guides for additional agency areas, inquire about cost **National Accreditation Council for Agencies Serving the Blind and Physically Handicapped** 232 Madison Avenue, Suite 907, New York, NY 10016 212-779-8080

THE SENIOR ADVOCATE PROGRAM
(undated) - details of program designed to help the elderly navigate through complicated bureaucratic structures and obtain the benefits they deserve; includes volunteer job description for the senior advocate and an outline of the steps necessary to become an effective advocate, 5pp report, 4pp fact sheet, brochure, single packet free **United Services for Older Adults** 212 Davie Street, Greensboro, NC 27401 919-373-1545

SKY RANCH LOG
(quarterly) - a newsletter describing activities at *Sky Ranch,* and profiling some of the boys, ages 10 to 18, who have been outstanding residents; includes information on sponsors, activities, and overall accomplishments of the young residents, 16pp, single copy free **Sky Ranch for Boys** , Sky Ranch, SD 57724 605-797-4422

SOCIAL SERVICE ORGANIZATIONS AND AGENCIES DIRECTORY
(1982) - a guide to "live" sources of information on a range of social concerns, from adoption and alcoholism to sexuality, vocational education, and youth; provides names, addresses, phone numbers, purposes, services, and publications of more than 3,000 national voluntary and professional associations, 900 state and regional associations, 2,100 state governmental agencies, and 300 federal agencies, 540pp, $95.00 **Gale Research Company** Book Tower, Detroit, MI 48226 313-961-2242

SOURCES OF INFORMATION ABOUT AND DESCRIPTIONS OF CRIME PREVENTION PROGRAMS FOR THE ELDERLY
(1977) - overview of local efforts to provide information on prevention of crime against the elderly; describes national projects on prevention, aid to elderly victims and witnesses, and others, 4pp plus resource lists, free **US/HHS - Administration on Aging** 200 C Street, SW, Washington, DC 20201 202-619-0724

SPECIAL RECREATION DIGEST
(quarterly) - a journal/newsletter that provides information on activities, recreation programs, support groups and resources, with seven goals to which to apply this information: recreation participation, adjustment, written plans, recreation skills/competence, recreation independence, recreation fulfillment, and treatment and meet the organizations objective of self-determination in recreation for all people with disabilities, 320pp (all issues), $39.95/year **Special Recreation** 362 Koser Avenue, Iowa City, IA 52246 319-337-7578

STATEWIDE ADVOCACY SYSTEMS FOR THE DEVELOPMENTALLY DISABLED - PROFILES IN INNOVATION
(1978) - descriptions of what states have been and could be doing in programs of protection and advocacy for children and adults afflicted with mental retardation, epilepsy, cerebral palsy, autism and certain learning disabilities (an estimated national population of five million); addresses state planners, but useful for consumers who need information for related programs, 24pp, single copy free **ABA Commission on the Mentally Disabled** DD Protection & Advocacy Review, 1155 East 60th Street, Chicago, IL 60637 312-947-4000

STEWART B. MCKINNEY HOMELESS ASSISTANCE ACT OF 1987
(1987) - the Act passed in July 1987 that enables funding for programs that help meet the needs of the homeless, unpaged, free **US/House of Representatives** Librarian, House Office Building, Washington, DC 20515 202-224-3121

SUMMARY OF EXISTING LEGISLATION AFFECTING PERSONS WITH DISABILITIES
(1987) - a history and description of all relevant laws affecting disabled persons through 1987, unpaged, free **US/DEd - Clearinghouse on Disability Information** Switzer Building, Room 3132, Washington, DC 20202-2524 202-732-1241

SUMMER MAGIC
(1982) - a Seniors Camp Vacation Program; a summer program to enrich the life of the senior citizen; an education, a vacation, a sharing and learning about Jewish life; a how to on planning such a program; free **B'nai B'rith International** Community Volunteer Services, 1640 Rhode Island Avenue, NW, Washington, DC 20036 202-343-4747

TACTS VOLUNTEER SHELTER: INFORMATION PACKET
(undated) - a packet of information on a program designed to serve people in crisis by providing a temporary shelter; includes job descriptions for volunteers in areas of shelter manager, administrative aide, transportation aide, special projects manager, children's aide, computer program, and food committee (cooks, if necessary), code of ethics, training goals and objectives, and other materials, 10pp, single copy free **The Arlington County Temporary Shelter (TACTS)** PO Box 1285, Arlington, VA 22210 703-237-0881

TELECARE
(undated) - a question-and-answer handbook to inform interested groups and individuals about a volunteer-run telephone reassurance program operated from a hospital, and how they can help by becoming Telecare volunteers, 6pp, single copy free **Telecare, Center for Life, Providence Hospital,** Center for Life, 1150 Varnum Street, NE, Washington, DC 20017 202-269-7439

TIME OF TRANSITION: THE GROWTH OF FAMILIES HEADED BY WOMEN
(1975) - the case for viewing female-headed families as transitional entities between one traditional family structure and another; discusses the consequences of children being raised in single-parent families, the implications for economic independence of women, the role of welfare, society, public policy, etc., 223pp, $6.50 **Urban Institute Press** 2100 M Street, NW, Washington, DC 20037 202-833-7200

TRAINING GUIDE FOR VOLUNTEERS WORKING WITH OLDER PEOPLE
(1979) - a manual based on the premise that - to be an effective volunteer with the aging - volunteers must examine their attitudes and develop an awareness of the aging process, and a knowledge of community resources and the type of advocacy necessary to close the gaps in services to the elderly; stresses the need to work effectively with resource people in both planning and implementing programs, 26pp, $1.50 **Education/Social Action Service** 15 East 26th Street, New York, NY 10010 212-532-1740

TRANSITION FROM SCHOOL TO ADULT LIFE
(1987) - special issue of *Exceptional Children* documenting the progress in the transition movement; provides a combination of historical perspective with current reports on research and programs, 96pp, $7.00 **Council for Exceptional Children** 1920 Association Drive, Reston, VA 22091-1589 703-620-3660

TRANSPORTATION AND THE MENTALLY RETARDED
(1972) - details on the results of a study of special transportation needs and problems of mentally retarded persons, SN 040-000-00285, $1.00 **US/GSA - Government Printing Office** Superintendent of Documents, Washington, DC 20402 202-783-3238

UNDERSTANDING DEVELOPMENTAL DISABILITIES
(1990) - a video designed for respite and homecare providers to people with mental retardation and developmental disabilities which stars staff and participants from YAI's respite, evening programs, day treatment programs, and residential programs;

includes workbook, in process with second tape, *Understanding Families,* planned, inquire **Young Adult Institute** 460 West 34th Street, New York, NY 10001-2382 212-563-7474

UNDERSTANDING LEARNING DISABILITIES: A PARENT GUIDE AND WORKBOOK
(1990) - a guide written by parents who have a child with a learning disability and professionals; includes topic areas covering the learning disabilities, coping strategies for parents, helping the child in home and school environments, and planning for the future, unpaged looseleaf format, $14.00 (without binder), $19 (with binder) **Virginia Department for Rights of the Disabled** James Monroe Building, 17th Floor, 101 North 14th Street, Richmond, VA 23219 804-225-2242

A UNIQUE ONE-TO-ONE EXPERIENCE
(undated) - an overview of a program that was developed after a community survey to determine the greatest need resulted in an expressed need for a one-to-one youth-oriented program; covers the application and interview process, costs per match ($400/year compared to $1500/year in the juvenile justice system), requirements to become a big brother or sister, and other areas, 4-page foldout, single copy free **Big Brothers/Big Sisters of Waynesboro** PO Box 897, Waynesboro, VA 22980 703-943-7871

UNITED WAY TEACH SHIRT
(1987 - a T-shirt designed to provide parents with a simple way of teaching their children how to deal with strangers, how to respond to emergencies, and how to remember important information like home telephone numbers and addresses (especially useful at festivals, conferences and other large gatherings where children might wander); displays colorful pictographs accompanied by appropriate statements; available in bilingual versions for several languages, others can be arranged, inquire about cost and other details at local United Way offices **United Way of America** 701 North Fairfax Street, Alexandria, VA 22314-2045 703-836-7100

UPDATE
(monthly) - newsletter reporting on services provided to immigrants and refugees, both sponsored and those needing sponsors; covers employment assistance, housing allowances, orientation, social security and school registration assistance, etc., 12pp, single copy free **Migration and Refugee Service** c/o US Catholic Charities, 1312 Massachusetts Avenue, NW, Washington, DC 20005 202-659-6630

THE U.S. DEPARTMENT OF LABOR REPORTS TO OLDER AMERICANS
(kept current) - details on job training, placement programs, and protection from age discrimination in employment through the Department's programs, 14pp, free **US/DoL - Office of the Secretary** 200 Constitution Avenue, NW, Washington, DC 20210 202-523-7304

USE AND ABUSE OF THE PHYSICALLY HANDICAPPED
(1979) - overview with brief case studies on problems facing the handicapped, especially being viewed as an object of pity instead of a fully accepted person; includes section on possible actions in areas of attitudes, transportation, legislation, 8pp, $.40 ($2.95/dozen) (developed by American Lutheran Church Women) **Augsburg Fortress** 426 South Fifth Street, Box 1206, Minneapolis, MN 55440 612-330-3300

USING TITLE XX TO SERVE CHILDREN/YOUTH
(1976) - help for advocates of children and youth in understanding the opportunities in Title XX, and in preparing them to participate in the planning process, 76pp, single copy free **US/HHS -**

Administration for Children, Youth and Families PO Box 1182, Washington, DC 20201 202-755-7750

USING YOUR TTY/TDD
(1990) - an audiovisual designed to assist with training of personnel to use TDDs/TTYs; covers *learning how to us TDDs/TTYs, teaching others to use TDDs/TTYs at their own pace,* and *publicizing your TDD/TTY accessibility,* open-captioned, 30 minutes, $29.95 plus $3.00 shipping and handling **Sign Media, Inc.** 4020 Blackburn Lane, Burtonsville, MD 20866 301-421-0268

THE VOLUNTEER IN AGENCIES FOR BLIND AND VISUALLY HANDICAPPED PERSONS
(1971) - questions and answers about the opportunities for volunteers in agencies serving the blind, 8pp, single copy free **American Foundation for the Blind** 15 West 16th Street, New York, NY 10011 212-620-2000

VOLUNTEER PROGRAMS: EMPLOYEES' MANUAL
(undated) - a handbook designed as an appendix to the *Statewide Manual* described separately; includes samples of all forms necessary to operate a volunteer services program, ranging from the initial form requesting volunteers through the evaluation steps, unpaged, inquire about cost
Also request copies of recruitment brochures, *How to become a DSS Volunteer* and *One-on-One: Making Two People Happy,* statistical reports, and other materials **Iowa Department of Social Services** Hoover State Office Building, Fifth Avenue, Des Moines, IA 50319 515-281-4598

VOLUNTEERS FOR PEOPLE IN NEED
(1972) - formal papers and the summaries of informal discussions from a knowledge utilization conference on the use of volunteers in vocational rehabilitation and public welfare agencies, 159pp, $2.00 **Goodwill Industries of America** 9200 Wisconsin Avenue, Bethesda, MD 20814 301-530-6500

VOLUNTEERS: GALLAUDET UNIVERSITY
(1989) - a handbook for volunteers providing a brief history of the University in general and the volunteer program in particular; includes sections on responsibilities and rights of all parties to the volunteer relationship, opportunities, procedures, benefits, and other information for the volunteer; appends form for free sign language classes, and a statement of understanding, unpaged, single copy free when available **National Information Center on Deafness** 800 Florida Avenue, NE, Washington, DC 20002 202-651-5606

VOLUNTEERS IN CHILD ABUSE AND NEGLECT PROGRAMS
(1980) - report on traditional and innovative roles for volunteers in child abuse prevention and other social service programs; includes information on existing efforts: the involvement of volunteer professionals, volunteers in direct service to families, etc.; appends bibliography and extensive list of child abuse prevention programs that use volunteers, 49pp, single copy free **US/HHS - National Center on Child Abuse and Neglect** U.S. Dept. of Health & Human Svcs, PO Box 1182, Washington, DC 20201 202-755-7500

VOLUNTEERS IN REHABILITATION HANDBOOK
(1973) - a comprehensive management tool for volunteer leaders/administrators to develop and strengthen the effectiveness of their volunteer programs; draws from results of a three-year study in cooperation with the U.S. Department of Health & Human Services, set of 12 handbooks $11.00:
- *Why Involve Volunteers*

- *How Volunteers Can Help*
- *How to Organize a Volunteer Program*
- *How to Administer a Volunteer Program*
- *How to Recruit Volunteers*
- *How to Interview and Place Volunteers*
- *How to Prepare Volunteers to Help*
- *How to Supervise and Evaluate Volunteers*
- *How to Motivate Volunteers*
- *How to Incorporate Group Volunteering*
- *How to Assure Responsible Volunteering*
- *Catalog of Resources*

Goodwill Industries of America 9200 Wisconsin Avenue, Bethesda, MD 20814 301-530-6500

WE DELIVER: ERIC SPECIAL EDUCATION INFORMATION
(1990) - an overview of the *ERIC Clearinghouse on Handicapped and Gifted Children* in a question and answer format; includes answers to questions such as: *What is ERIC? What is the Connection Between ERIC and CEC? How can you access ERIC?* and *What information is available from ERIC-CEC?*; appends a partial list of related ERIC Clearinghouses (which are databases of a federally-funded information system), 10-panel foldout, free **Council for Exceptional Children** 1920 Association Drive, Reston, VA 22091 703-620-3660

WE WERE CHILDREN THEN: VOLUME I
(4th Pr. 1982) - a compilation of more than 90 stories (entries to the University of Wisconsin's *Yarns of Yesteryear* contest, see separate entry); includes sections on: *Growing Up, Remembered Places, Hard Times, Gypsies,* etc.; uses large type, 187pp, $11.95; VOLUME II (1982) now available, $13.95 **Stanton and Lee Publishers** 44 East Mifflin Street, Madison, WI 53703 608-255-3254

WELFARE EMPLOYMENT PROGRAMS: PUBLICATIONS
(various dates) - monographs, reports, and other publications in the area of welfare employment programs; titles include:
- Work Initiatives for Welfare Recipients: Lessons from a multi-state experiment
- Reforming Welfare With Work (1986)
- Arizona: Preliminary Management Lessons from Arizona's WIN Demonstration Program (1984)
- Arkansas: Interim Findings from the Arkansas WIN Demonstration Program (1984)
- Arkansas: Employment and Welfare Impacts of the Arkansas WORK Program (1989)
- California: Findings from the San Mateo County Employment Preparation Program (1985)
- California: Final Report on the San Diego Job Search and Work Experience Program (1986)
- Illinois: Final Report on Job Search and Work Experience in Cook County (1987)
- Maine: Interim Findings from a Grant Diversion Program (1985)
- Maine: Final Report on the Training Opportunities in the Private Sector Program (1988)
- Maryland: Final Report on the Employment Initiatives Evaluation (1985)
- Maryland: Supplemental Report on the Baltimor Options Program (1987)
- New Jersey: Final Report on the Grant Diversion Project (1988)
- Virginia: Final Report on the Employment Services Program (1986)
- West Virginia: Final Report on the Community Work Experience Demonstrations (1986)
- Welfare Grant Diversion: Early Observations from Programs in Six States (1985)

- Welfare Grant Diversion: Lessons and Prospects (1986)
- Relationships Between Earnings and Benefits for Working Recipients: Four Area Case Studies (1985)
- A Study of Performance Measures and Subgroup Impacts in Three Welfare Employment Programs (1987)
- Subgroup Impacts and Performance Indicators for Seleected Welfare Employment Programs (1988)
- Findings on State Welfare Employment Programs (1987)
- Final Report on the Saturation Work Initiative Model in San Diego (1989)
- GAIN: Planning and Early Implementation (1987)
- GAIN: Early Implementation Experiences and Lessons (1989)
- GAIN: Child Care in Welfare Employment (1989)

Not a complete list; request catalog and inquire about availability and cost. **Manpower Demonstration Research Corporation** 1669 Bush Street, San Francisco, CA 94109 415-441-7607

WHAT ARE WE LEARNING ABOUT CIRCLES OF SUPPORT?

(1988) - overview of experiences of several *circles of support* in Connecticut - a group of people who agree to meet on a regular basis to help a person with a disabil;ity accomplish certain personal visions or goals; encompasses the concept of "personal futures planning," 50pp, inquire about cost **Communitas, Inc.** 73 Indian Drive, Manchester, CT 60640 203-645-6976

WHAT EVERYONE SHOULD KNOW ABOUT EPILEPSY

(1980) - illustrated guide giving details on causes, patterns, symptoms, seizures, treatment, emergency aid, attitudes, and available resources; includes Q/A page exploding outmoded myths about epilepsy and responding to questions that have caused undue concern, 15pp, $.75 (bulk rates) (This publication included in school alert kit above.) **Channing L. Bete Company** , South Deerfield, MA 01373

WHAT EVERYONE SHOULD KNOW ABOUT MENTAL RETARDATION

(1980) - illustrated guide for persons concerned about preventive measures and services being provided to the retarded; includes charts, listings, and other information on progress to date and what can be done in the next decade, 15pp, $.75 (quantity discounts) **Channing L. Bete Company** , South Deerfield, MA 01373

WHAT MAKES PEOPLE WITH DISABILITIES DISABLED?

(undated) - brochure giving suggestions on how to relate to people with disabilities, how to look beyond the disability and look at the individual's ability and the personality; includes sections on communication as a two-way street; "no-no" words; and detailed information on deafness/hearing impairment, blindness/visual impairment, mobility impairments, mental retardation, cerebral palsy, mental illness, epilepsy, and neurological disorders, 8-panel foldout, single copy free **New York Office of Advocate for the Disabled** Office of the Governor, State Capitol Building, Albany, NY 12202 518-474-8390

WHAT SENIOR CITIZENS SHOULD KNOW ABOUT CRIME PREVENTION

(1980) - illustrated guide to self protection in various situations (at home, on a trip, in the car, etc.) discussing the need for the elderly to know how criminals operate, and how to foil them, 15pp, $.75 **Channing L. Bete Company** , South Deerfield, MA 01373

WHAT'S A FAMILY

(1980) - illustrated guide to provide a general view of the inter-relationships among family members, and ways in which harmony can be maintained by considering rights and feelings of all members, 15pp, $.75 **Channing L. Bete Company** , South Deerfield, MA 01373

A WHOLE LOT OF LOVE

(undated) - a coloring book providing a brief story about the origin of the telephone, and its original purpose (to learn how sound traveled so that Alexander Graham Bell could improve his teaching of deaf children); includes information about the Telephone Pioneers of America and the assistance they provide, with an emphasis on the equipment they develop for the hearing impaired, 32pp, single copy free **Telephone Pioneers of America** 22 Cortland Street, Room C-2575, New York, NY 10007 212-393-3252

WORKING WITH HOMELESS PEOPLE: A GUIDE FOR STAFF AND VOLUNTEER

(1989) - guidance for volunteers and staff working in shelters and other programs for the homeless, 115pp, free **Columbia University** Community Services, Broadway & 116th Street, West, New York, NY 10027 212-854-5746

YAI INFORMATION KIT

(undated) - a compilation of brochures, reports, fact sheets, flyers, etc., providing information about the *Young Adult Institute's* services to persons with mental retardation and developmental disabilities; may include information on its *Alumni Club*, family training, statistics, etc. (contents change based on materials available at time of request), unpaged, single copy free **Young Adult Institute** 460 West 34th Street, New York, NY 10001-2382 212-563-7474

YOUNG ADULTS AND THEIR PARENTS

(1976) - overview of common problems arising between young adults and their parents, and some suggestions for trying to work them out within the family before seeking counseling, 28pp, $.50 (bulk rates) **Public Affairs Committee** 381 Park Avenue South, New York, NY 10016 212-683-4311

YOUR CAMP AND THE HANDICAPPED CHILD

(undated) - explanation of how the handicapped child can be "just another camper" when attitudes of camp leaders and parents are supportive and based on fact, 16pp, $.75 **American Camping Association** Bradford Woods, Martinsville, IN 46151 317-342-8456

YOUR RETIREMENT HOBBY GUIDE

(undated) - how-to guide on unusual hobbies using shells, tape recorders, tinted bottles, apples, vegetables, marbles, plaster pieces, metals, etc., 32pp, single copy free **American Association of Retired Persons** 1909 K Street, NW, Washington, DC 20006 202-872-4700

YOUR RETIREMENT HOUSING GUIDE

(1975) - an appeal to retirees to give a lot of thought to the selection of a retirement home; provides in-depth information on options available - including the option of "staying put," 47pp, single copy free **American Association of Retired Persons** 1909 K Street, NW, Washington , DC 20006 202-479-1200

YOUTH VOLUNTEERS AND THE DISABLED: GETTING IT TOGETHER

(1979) - a discussion of the general need for youth volunteer activities involving disabled persons; includes an overview of the role assumed by the Office of Handicapped Individuals, and reports on 4-H and Girl Scouts seminars on the subject, 3lpp, single copy free **US/DoE - Office of Handicapped Individuals** Special Education & Rehabilitation, Washington, DC 20201 202-245-1961

RECREATION & SPORTS

AIR PRODUCTS DEVELOPMENTAL CYCLING PROGRAM
(undated) - an overview of a program in which volunteer expert instructors (including a former world champion) teach bicycle safety, maintenance, and the fundamentals of riding and racing at no cost to participants; includes people eight years of age and older in the program, with continuing opportunities to compete at more advanced levels (two graduates of the program became U.S. Junior National Champions), 6-panel foldout, single copy free **Air Products and Chemicals** PO Box 538, Allentown, PA 18105 215-481-8079

AMC WORKSHOPS AND SEMINARS
(1990) - a detailed list of workshops and seminars offered by *Appalachian Mountain Club* crew members and volunteers; includes: *Learn, Discover and Explore; Understanding Natural Systems: Field Seminars; Fighting Forest Fires in the White Mountains,* etc., 20-panel foldout, free **Appalachian Mountain Club** Regional Office, PO Box 298-V, Gorham, NH 03581 603-466-2721

AQUATIC RESOURCE EDUCATION PROGRAM: INSTRUCTOR'S MANUAL AND OTHER MATERIALS
(kept current) - a packet of materials describing a program in which volunteer instructors receive certification to teach the art of fishing in a way that will help create responsible attitudes toward the environment; appends job description, 12pp (manual) and other materials, single copy free **Massachusetts Division of Fisheries and Wildlife** Field Headquarters, Westborough, MA 01581 617-366-4479

CARRY THE TORCH
(1984) - information on the Torch Relay Program which offers all Americans an opportunity to participate in the Olympiad XXIII through an 80-day, 19,000-kilometer (12,000-mile) walk across the country hand-carrying the Olympic torch, and heralding the beginning of the games upon arrival at its final destination (begins New York May 8, 1984; ends Los Angeles July 28, 1984); includes information about sponsorship of "Youth Legacy Kilometers" to launch a new "Legacy for Youth" fund (sponsorship reservations made on a first-come, first-served basis); includes reservation application, 16-panel foldout, single copy free **Los Angeles Olympic Organizing Committee** , Los Angeles, CA 90084 213-305-1984

DIRECTORY OF LOW-COST VACATIONS WITH A DIFFERENCE
(undated) - a guide providing alternatives to ordinary vacations; includes people-to-people programs, senior citizen programs, farm vacations, home exchanges, study groups, vacation work programs, bed and breakfast programs, etc.; provides brief descriptions of the organizations offering these free and low-cost vacation opportunities for every age group, $5.95 **Pilot Books** 103 Cooper Street, Babylon, NY 11702 516-422-2225

EVALUATION AND SELF-STUDY OF PUBLIC RECREATION AND PARK AGENCIES
(1972) - guide to help recreation and park professionals and lay citizenry to evaluate their park and recreation department operation to be sure that it is fulfilling its obligation to the community, 70pp, $4.00 **National Recreation and Park Association** 3101 Park Center Drive, 12th Floor, Alexandria, VA 22202 202-820-4940

FACTS ON SPECIAL OLYMPICS
(kept current) - description of the program of physical fitness sports training and athletic competition for mentally retarded children and adults; includes purpose, eligibility (8 years old or older), type of sports and games, training, volunteers, etc.; emphasizes that it is run entirely by volunteers; includes *How You Can Help Checklist,* 16pp, single copy free **Special Olympics International** 1350 New York Avenue, NW, Suite 500, Washington, DC 20005 202-628-3630

FUNDRAISING
(1979) - handbook to help agencies facing problems of operating on a limited and inadequate budget; takes the reader through a strategy-planning and implementation process, and includes case examples of local efforts that were mounted by volunteers and other community and nonprofessional fundraisers, with amounts ranging from $2,000 to $6,000,000; includes list of other information sources, 30pp, free **US/DoI - National Park Service** Information Exchange, 18th & C Streets, NW, Washington, DC 20240 202-485-9666

GIVING A LIFT TO OLYMPIC CYCLISTS: SPECIAL EDITION OF "YOU"
(August 1983) - an overview of the involvement of company

employees as volunteers in the pre-Olympic events held in the summer of 1983; includes information on the tasks assigned to the volunteers (drivers, receptionists, parking attendants, training run guides for the 12-hour practice runs, etc.), the benefits they derived through association with athletes from various cultures, the knowledge about cycling gained through participation, improvement of their conversational French (the universal language of cycling); and the comaraderie that developed among the volunteers, 8pp, single copy free **TransAmerica Occidental Life Insurance Company** 1150 South Olive Street , Los Angeles, CA 90015 213-742-2111

GOLDEN EAGLE/GOLDEN AGE PASSPORTS

(kept current) - description of two programs that allows entrance to federal parks, monuments, and recreation areas that charge admission: (1) *Golden Age Passport,* which allows persons 62 years of age or older to have a free lifetime entrance permit; admits permit holder and a carload of accompanying people, or, if not by car, accompanying spouse and children; also provides a 50% discount on rental of boats, etc. (2) *Golden Eagle* is for those under 62 and costs $10.00, a descriptive brochure is free **US/DoI - National Park Service** Information Exchange, Washington, DC 20243 202-343-4747

GUIDE TO AMC HUTS AND LODGES

(1990) - colorfully illustrated booklet showing settings and describing huts and lodges in the Appalachian Mountain Club's (AMC) system, where volunteers provide service, vacationers enjoy the areas and learn about the natural sciences, environmental research projects, and important conservation issues, and trail maintenance techniques used by AMC crews and volunteers, 16pp, single copy free **Appalachian Mountain Club** Regional Office, PO Box 298-V, Gorham, NH 03581 603-466-2721

HELPING OUT IN THE OUTDOORS

(19th Pr. 1990; annual publication) - a directory of volunteer work and internships on America's public lands; includes programs, locations, descriptions, age requirements, phone numbers, etc., 94pp, $3.00 **American Hiking Society** 1015 31st Street, NW, Washington, DC 20007 703-385-3252

LET'S PLAY TO GROW

(undated) - a supplement to Special Olympics so that the very young and profoundly retarded can participate; serves also as lead-up activities in preparation for Special Olympics; includes a manual and 12 Play Guides for specific sports; describes awards presented to the participant, parents, siblings and volunteers assisting in the shared play program, $2.50/kit **Special Olympics International** 1350 New York Avenue, NW, Suite 500, Washington, DC 20005 202-628-3630

OLYMPIC DAY FOR YOUTH

(1990) - a ring binder containing detailed information on how to organize an *Olympic Day for Youth;* focuses attention on the ideals and spirit of the Olympic games. and places emphasis on concepts of cooperation, non-discrimination, and non-sexism; helps youth to work together to set goals and, in so doing, develop a positive image, unpaged, inquire about cost **U.S. Olympic Committee** 1750 East Boulder Street, Colorado Springs, CO 80909 719-578-4575

OLYMPIC DAY IN THE SCHOOLS

(1990) - a ring binder with complete information on how to plan, organize and administer a day-long program that uses the excitement and drama of the Olympic Games to inspire young people in all areas of education; includes posters, handbooks, fact sheets, reading lists, etc., unpaged, inquire about cost **U.S. Olympic Committee** 1750 East Boulder Street, Colorado Springs, CO 80909 719-578-4575

OUTDOOR RECREATION IN AMERICA: TRENDS, PROBLEMS AND OPPORTUNITIES

(2nd ed. 1978) - roles and cooperative efforts among agencies and organizations to identify and act upon current and potential problems in out door recreation, conservation, etc.; includes illustrations to clarify efforts, case studies, etc., 296pp, $7.50 **Burgess Publishing Company** 7108 Ohms Lane, Minneapolis, MN 55435 612-831-1344

PLAYGROUND MANUAL

(1969) - specifications for a playground developed from available resources; includes designs for constructions more natural to wood, rope, brick, etc., rather than steel; includes detailed drawings for the adaptation of discarded cable spools, old tires, 55-gallon drums, etc., $2.95 (developed by a volunteer) **Volunteers in Technical Assistance** 1815 North Lynn Street, Suite 200, Arlington, VA 22209 703-276-1800

RECREATION FOR SENIOR CITIZENS

(undated) - overview of how older adults can get involved in leisure activities according to their interests, income and capabilities, 12pp, single copy free **Kentucky Commission on Aging** 207 Holmes Street, Frankfort, KY 40601 502-564-2500

RECREATION FOR URBAN AMERICA

(1979) - assistance for urban citizens and action groups to work effectively with local, state and federal officials, elected representatives, and private organizations to help create better recreational opportunities for disadvantaged urban citizens in the bleakest neighborhoods, 38pp, single copy free **National Urban Coalition** 1120 G Street, NW, Suite 900, Washington, DC 20005 202-628-2990

SCROUNGING

(1980) - a unique acquisition project catching on across the country to benefit both the recreation programs and the givers as well as the environment; describes programs which have scrounged items ranging from plastic hose material to unused freight cars; presents guidelines for locating and soliciting usable materials, stockpiling, recognizing donors, scrounging from the feds, and other basic scrounging ideas; includes chart with possible sources/resources/uses for scrounging efforts, 8pp, single copy free **US/DoI - National Park Service** Information Exchange, Washington, DC 20240 202-343-4747

SENIOR ADULT CAMPING

(1979) - guidance on philosophy, goals, administration, health/safety, emergency procedures, food management, etc., to meet the needs of the growing activity of camping for older persons; includes section on fund-raising to help offset costs in certain senior camp programs, 46pp, $1.25 **American Camping Association** Bradford Woods, Martinsville, IN 46151 317-342-8456

SPECIAL OLYMPICS INTERNS IN RECREATION: A PROGRAM THAT WORKS

(1983) - description of an employment and training project for mentally retarded youth, which is sponsored by the Department of Labor, the Joseph P. Kennedy, Jr., Foundation, others, 4-panel foldout, free **Kennedy Interns in Recreation** Route 3, Box 165P, Hammond, LA 70401 504-567-3111

SPECIAL SATURDAY: STAFF HANDBOOK

(1983) - a comprehensive guide outlining steps involved in providing a Saturday program for children on the waiting list of the Big Brother/Big Sister volunteer program; includes sections on the volunteers, counselors, children's needs, supervision, emergency procedures, first aid, and other guidelines, 21pp, inquire about cost **Big Brothers/Big Sisters** 470 Mamaroneck Avenue, White Plains, NY 10605 914-948-8004

UNITED STATES OLYMPIC TRAINING CENTER
(1984) - an overview of the activities of the Training Center which trains the nation's Olympic hopefuls chosen by the National Governing Bodies for each sport; includes details on the Center's activities, the responsibilities of the Center and the athlete, etc.; includes photographs of the Center and activities, a list of Olympic trainees, and other information, 12pp, single copy free [also request the full-color brochure by the same name, which lists other Training Centers in the U.S. and abroad]
[NOTE: Those receiving this information after the Games, request available back issues for educational value, especially where children's groups are involved] **U.S. Olympic Committee** Office of Communications, 1790 East Boulder Street, Colorado Springs, CO 80909 719-578-4575

VIEWS AND NEWS
(bimonthly) - a newsletter describing leisure and recreation activities for senior citizens; includes information on training and technical assistance available to senior centers and camps working with older persons, 12pp, single copy free **Vacation and Senior Citizens Association** 275 Seventh Avenue, 15th Floor, New York, NY 10001 212-645-6590

VOLUNTEER HANDBOOK
(1978) - a resource guide on volunteerism for park and recreation and heritage conservation organizations to help them establish a volunteer program; cites benefits to recreation agency, community and volunteer; provides detailed case studies of successful volunteer recreation programs nationwide; includes additional resources, 44pp, single copy free **US/DoI - National Park Service** Information Exchange, Washington, DC 20240 202-889-3800

VOLUNTEER IN THE MOUNTAINS
(1990) A listing of 1990 Appalachian Mountain Club volunteer trails opportunities; includes location, dates, job description, and contact information for programs in several parts of the country; e.g. *Upper Goose Pond (MA) Volunteer Caretaker Program* and *White Mountain (NH) Volunteer Crews,* 12-panel foldout, free **Appalachian Mountain Club** Regional Office, PO Box 298-V, Gorham, NH 03581 603-466-2721

VOLUNTEER "VACATIONS" ON AMERICA'S PUBLIC LANDS
(1978) - overview of a program that enables families, individuals, groups to enjoy a vacation while contributing time and energy to help maintain and improve public lands; includes state-by-state list of opportunities, 48pp, $2.95 (free to member) **American Hiking Society** 1015 31st Street, NW, Washington, DC 20007 703-385-3252

WHAT IS VASCA?
(kept current) - brochure detailing the recreation and camping services provided by an umbrella group for senior citizens centers and vacation camps; describes technical assistance and other services designed to enhance the quality of life of older persons through leisure activities, foldout brochure, free **Vacation and Senior Citizens Association** 275 Seventh Avenue, 15th Floor, New York, NY 10001 212-645-6590

SELF-HELP

BE SMART AND PLAY IT SAFE: YOU CAN REDUCE FEAR AND CRIME IN YOUR NEIGHBORHOOD
(1978) - a practical guide for crime prevention and apprehension of criminals in neighborhoods and apartment buildings; covers home/car security, protection for the elderly, rape, etc.; profiles solutions such as a neighborhood directory, tenant patrols and block watches, etc., 10pp, $.50 **Citizens Information Service** 67 East Madison Street, Chicago, IL 60603 312-236-0315

CABRILLO ECONOMIC DEVELOPMENT CORPORATION
(undated) - newsletters, reports, magazines, and other materials reporting on the development and activities of a corporation that began with one project by its determined owners in a self-help effort to preserve their homes (Cabrillo Village) and expanded into a comprehensive group helping other communities with techniques and knowledge learned through the initial project, unpaged packet of materials, single copy free **Cabrillo Economic Development Corporation** PO Box 4216, Saticoy, CA 93004 805-659-3791

CHILD ABUSE: WHAT RESOURCES FOR MEETING THE PROBLEM?
(1978) - a special edition of "Vital Issues" providing an overview of the problem, and discussing identification, treatment, and prevention - including the use of volunteers, self-help groups, and community councils, 4pp, $.45 (quantity discounts) **Center for Information on America** , Washington, CT 06793 203-868-2602

COMPREHENSIVE PROGRAM FOR THE ELDERLY IN RURAL AREAS
(1072) - overview of a model program designed to inform community groups in ways they can act as catalysts for involving the older poor in improving the quality of their lives; covers areas of nutrition, consumer problems, employment, etc., 36pp, $1.10 **National Council on the Aging** 600 Maryland Avenue, SW, West Wing 100, Washington, DC 20024 202-479-1200

THE DRINKING GAME AND HOW TO BEAT IT
(1976) - a first person account by a recovered alcoholic written as a motivational piece for heavy drinkers, but useful for anyone working with people with alcohol problems, 48pp, single copy free, additional $.46 each (100 minimum) **Benjamin Company** One Westchester Plaza, Elmsford, NY 10523 914-592-8088

NUSA CONFERENCE REPORT
(annually) - a detailed report of an annual conference designed to keep neighborhood activists informed of activities around the country - both successful and unsuccessful - to assist them as they form and work with partnerships from public and private sectors in their communities to improve their neighborhoods, number of pages vary, inquire about cost **Neighborhoods USA** 4643 Amesborough, Dayton, OH 45420 513-222-2889

NUSA NEWSLETTER
(quarterly) - a newsletter reporting on activities from around the country by neighborhood activists and other members of NUSA, including local government staff and elected officials; provides articles and other information to help neighborhood groups improve their communities, 12pp, single copy free **Neighborhoods USA** 4643 Amesborough, Dayton, OH 45420 513-222-2889

ORGANIZING A SELF-HELP CLEARINGHOUSE
(1982) - a step-by-step guide to establishing a local self-help clearinghouse to serve the needs of tenants and other consumers; bases information on experiences of successful local clearinghouses across the country, $5.00 **National Self-Help Clearinghouse** Graduate School/University Center, 33 West 42nd Street, New York, NY 10036 212-642-2944

TEENAGE PREGNANCY/PARENTING

AIDS KILLS WOMEN AND BABIES
(1987) - graphic explanations about AIDS risk and prevention; covers IV needle, sexual and maternal transmission (developed for use in San Francisco jails, but can be used to reach any low-literacy population; third grade reading level with multi-ethnic graphics), foldout brochure, $.30 (English or Spanish) **San Francisco AIDS Foundation** 333 Valencia Street, PO Box 6182, San Francisco, CA 94104-6182 415-861-3397

ALCOHOL AND YOUR UNBORN BABY
(1979) - facts about the effects of heavy drinking on unborn babies, the risk factor, alternatives, where to get help, etc., 14pp, single copy free (order #PH90) **US/HHS - National Clearinghouse for Alcohol and Drug Information** Box 2345, Rockville, MD 20852 301-468-2600

ALCOHOL: FACTS BEHIND THE RUMORS BEHIND THE MYTHS
(1979) - an examination of the widely accepted "facts" - and myths - about alcohol; discusses alcohol's health effects and relationship to other drugs; explores alcohol abuse and alcoholism and other problem areas, including fetal alcohol syndrome, rehabilitation, etc., 24pp, $2.50 **Do It Now Foundation** PO Box 21126, Phoenix, AZ 85036 602-257-0797

AS A CHILD GROWS
(1979) - descriptions and illustrations of children under five years of age, their likes, needs and activities at each stage of growth; an easy book about discipline and needs of young children (designed for parents, but useful for child care workers), 32pp, $1.00 **New Readers Press** Box 131, 1320 Jamesville Avenue, Syracuse, NY 13210 315-442-9121

BEAUTIFUL BABIES AND HEALTH COUPON BOOK
(kept current) - a book of information and free coupons for discounts on a variety of maternity and infant-related items, such as baby furniture, photograph packages, maternity and infant clothes; contains prenatal and health information which encourages women to seek early and continuous prenatal care, and assists the process by validating the coupons during regular pre- and postnatal visits only (distributed 100,000 books throughout the Washington, DC metropolitan area in 1989), size varies, free (This is a project of March of Dimes, Blue Cross/Blue Shield of DC, and WRC-TV Channel 4.) **March of Dimes Birth Defects**

Foundation National Capital Area Chapter, 2700 South Quincy Street, Suite 220, Arlington, VA 22206 703-824-0111

CHILDCARE AND THE FAMILY
(1989) - articles on fathers' participation, single parents' needs, day care, and care of handicapped children, 120pp, FR8910, $15.00 **National Council on Family Relations** 3989 Central Avenue, NE, Suite 550, Minneapolis, MN 55421-3921 612-781-9331

CHILDREN OF SINGLE PARENTS AND THE SCHOOLS
(1990) - a look at the subtle differences in the school experience of a child with both parents, and one with a single parent, in process at press time, inquire **Women's Action Alliance** 370 Lexington Avenue, Suite 603, New York, NY 10017 212-779-2846

CURRENT RESEARCH ON THE CONSEQUENCES OF MATERNAL DRUG ABUSE
(1985) - *Monograph 59* of a series of studies on effects of maternal substance abuse; discusses effects of marijuana, methadone, phencyclidine, and alcohol, 113pp, single copy free **US/HHS - National Clearinghouse for Alcohol and Drug Information** PO Box 2345, Rockville, MD 20852 301-468-2600

CWLA STANDARDS FOR SERVICES TO UNMARRIED PARENTS
(1971) - a guide for professionals and citizen groups developed in response to the need of communities and agencies for ways of measuring the quality of their services, 89pp, $7.50 **Child Welfare League of America** 440 First Street, NW, Washington, DC 20001 202-638-2952

EDUCATION FOR PARENTHOOD
(1978) - description of a program designed to help teenagers prepare for effective parenthood through working with young children and learning about child development and the role of parents, 8-panel foldout, single copy free **US/HHS - Administration for Children, Youth and Families** PO Box 1182, Washington, DC 20013 202-755-7750

THE FACT IS... ALCOHOL AND OTHER DRUGS CAN HARM AN UNBORN BABY
(Rev. 1989) - background information on the effects of alcohol, illegal drugs, and other substances on a developing baby; appends

list of resources for patient and professional education, 13pp, single copy free **US/HHS - National Clearinghouse for Alcohol and Drug Information** PO Box 2345, Rockville, MD 20852 301-468-2600

FOR YOU, FOR YOUR CHILDREN
(kept current) - brochure for parents describing the Parent-to-Parent Program where volunteers make weekly home visits to work with parents and infants or young children in play activities and child development education, and where "parent meetings" are convened to enable sharing of experiences and ideas in parenting, 6-panel foldout, free **US/DoD - Navy Family Service Center** Parent-to-Parent Program, Naval Training Center Bldg. 42, Great Lakes, IL 60088-5123 312-688-3603

HAVING A BABY
(1975) - a thorough, reassuring discussion of every aspect of pregnancy; a comprehensive guide for parents-to-be; reliable medical information presented in an easy-to-understand, straight-forward format, 168pp, $3.50 **New Readers Press** Box 131, 1320 Jamesville Avenue, Syracuse, NY 13210 315-442-9121

MAKING RESPONSIBLE CHOICES ABOUT SEX
(1989 ed.) - a guide for young people on making values an important part of decisions about sex; encourages self-questions about readiness, reasons, and potential consequences; shows other ways to build relationships and offers advice on peer pressure, 16pp, $.79, minimum 25 (quantity discounts) **Channing L. Bete Company** 200 State Road, South Deerfield, MA 01373-0200

MATERNAL NUTRITION: A CONTEMPORARY APPROACH TO INTERDISCIPLINARY CARE
(1989) - a curriculum designed to help pregnant women learn the value of good nutrition; includes instructors' outlines, slides, participant handouts, a videotape, and bibliographies; distributes the information through local March of Dimes chapters, state health departments and academic institutions, which in turn make the materials available to health professionals caring for pregnant women nationwide, single packet free to qualified requestors (distribution made possible by a $185,000 grant from Kraft Foods) **March of Dimes** National Capital Area Chapter, 2700 South Quincy Street, Suite 220, Arlington, VA 22206 703-824-0111

MEN'S ROLES IN THE FAMILY
(1979) - strategies for changing male family roles, effects of traditional roles, household and children participation, men's caregiving roles, fathering, unmarried fathers, and economic roles, 227pp, FR7910, $12.00 **National Council on Family Relations** 3989 Central Avenue, NE, Suite 550, Minneapolis, MN 55421-3921 612-781-9331

OUR YOUNGEST PARENTS: A STUDY OF THE USE OF SUPPORT SERVICES BY ADOLESCENT MOTHERS
(1980) - overview of the problems faced by today's teen-aged parent, and what is being done and can be done to help them make appropriate decisions for their future and the future of their children, 96pp, $5.50 **Child Welfare League of America** 440 First Street, NW, Washington, DC 20001 202-638-2952

PARENTING
(1987) - topics on first year parenting experience, stresses of parenting, exceptional children, adoption, and three stages of child rearing, 116pp, FR8701, $15.00 **National Council on Family Relations** 3989 Central Avenue, NE, Suite 1250, Minneapolis, MN 55421-3921 612-781-9331

PARENTING BOOKLET SERIES
(1989 ed.) - a series of booklets including *Teen Parenthood, Parenting,* and *Single Parenting;* explains responsibilities, care requirements, medical/physical/emotional needs of infants and young children, cost of raising a child, the parent's or parents' own needs, involving the father, dealing with stress, seeking help, communication with extended family, etc; appends resources and services available, 16pp each, single copies free while supply lasts [also available from Channing L. Bete Company 200 State Road, South Deerfield, MA 01373-0200 800-628-7733] **Child Protective Services** Virginia Dept. of Social Services, 8007 Discovery Drive, Richmond, VA 23229-8699

PREGNANCY AND AIDS
1988 - overview of issues relating to pregnancy, including common routes of transmission, risk to unborn child, needle and condom use, the antibody test, and casual contagion, foldout brochure, $.30 (quantity discounts) **San Francisco AIDS Foundation** 333 Valencia Street, PO Box 6182, San Francisco, CA 94101-6182 415-861-3397

SINGLE AND PREGNANT
(1979) - a guide to provide counselors and other workers with teens a practical view of the alternatives open to single, pregnant women that will be best for all parties concerned, 120pp, $1.95 **Beacon Press** 25 Beacon Street,, Boston, MA 02108 617-742-2110

THE SINGLE PARENT FAMILY
(1986) - overview of the multiple job and home life responsibilities, social and economic profile, life cycle states, changing legal status, teenage mothers, handicapped children, temporary singles (prisoners' families), life as a single father, how children from single parent families fare as young adults, etc., 224 pages, FR8601, $15.00 **National Council on Family Relations** 3989 Central Avenue, NE, Suite 550, Minneapolis, MN 55421-3921 612-781-9331

SPECIAL FOCUS: PREVENTING ALCOHOL-RELATED BIRTH DEFECTS
(1985) - a reprint from *Alcohol Health & Research World* providing articles on the current knowledge of the effects of alcohol on pregnancy outcome and prevention strategies that have been developed in the area of alcohol-related birth defects, 75pp, single copy free **US/HHS - National Clearinghouse for Alcohol and Drug Information** PO Box 2345, Rockville, MD 20852 301-468-2600

SUBSTANCE ABUSE AMONG PREGNANT WOMEN
(1989) - a study of 36 hospitals in Virginia to determine the degree of substance abuse among pregnant women; discusses the greater risks in low birth weights and birth defects, including defects that are invisible at birth such as low IQ and behavioral problems, inquire about cost **Center for Perinatal Addiction** 2111 West Main Street, Richmond, VA 23220 804-355-8846

TAKE CHARGE OF YOUR PREGNANCY
(1989) - a video divided into five segments, covering medical, emotional and lifestyle aspects of pregnancy, from conception through delivery; provides a comprehensive overview of the intricacies of fetal development, and key topics to a healthy pregnancy and delivery - nutrition, exercise, diagnostic tests, use of drugs and alcohol, medical problems that can complicate pregnancy, childbirth preparation, and post delivery care (narrated by Candice Bergen and Dr. John Long), 90 minutes, color, $29.98 (CBS-Fox makes contribution to March of Dimes for every copy sold), also available at local video and specialty outlets **CBS/Fox Video** 1800 M Street, NW, Washington, DC 20036

TAPP: NATIONAL DIRECTORY OF TEENAGE PREGNANCY PREVENTION PROGRAMS
(1989) - a comprehensive overview of programs across the country addressing the problems inherent in cases of pregnancy among adolescent girls; includes descriptions and contact information, 557pp, $29.95 **Women's Action Alliance** 370 Lexington Avenue, New York, NY 10017 212-532-8330

TEENAGE MOTHERHOOD: SOCIAL AND ECONOMIC CONSEQUENCES
(1979) - a study of the effects of early childbearing on education, family size, marriage and marital instability, employment, poverty, etc.; explores indirect as well as direct effects; appends resource list, 50pp, $7.00 **Urban Institute Press** 2100 M Street, NW, Washington, DC 20037 202-223-1950

TEENAGE PREGNANCY: A MAJOR PROBLEM FOR MINORS
(1979) - overview of incidence, outcomes, problems of teenage pregnancy; includes information on contraceptive use, clinic services, legal rights, information barriers, action programs, etc., 4pp, one free with SASE **Zero Population Growth** 1601 Connecticut Avenue, NW, Washington, DC 20009 202-332-2200

VITAL INFORMATION FOR ANYONE WHO MAY EVER HAVE A BABY
(undated) - discussion of the need to begin preparing for pregnancy *before* conception by developing good health habits and exploring birthing options, hospitals, doctors, etc.; includes detailed answers to the most frequently asked questions on pregnancy; describes the *MOM (Matters on Maternity)* program offered by the hospital to work with women before, during, and after pregnancy, and information about prenatal courses (free or at nominal cost) and hospital tours, 4pp, free **Alexandria Hospital** Great Expectations, 4320 Seminary Road, Alexandria, VA 22304 703-379-3636

WHEN A BABY IS NEW
(1979) - three reading selections with touching illustrations that help convey the joys - and tribulations - of life with a baby; helps new parents become aware of a baby's need to be loved and nurtured (written on a second-grade level), 48pp, $1.25 **New Readers Press** Box 131, 1320 Jamesville Avenue, Syracuse, NY 13210 315-442-9121

WIC DIRECTORY OF SPECIAL SUPPLEMENTAL FOOD PROGRAMS FOR WOMEN, INFANTS AND CHILDREN
(1979) - state-by-state list of WIC programs (in all 50 states) to enable local communities to make referrals to local people, and for those in the program who have moved to another location; includes map for each state indicating Center locations, 115pp, $2.50 **WIC (Women, Infants and Children) Advocacy Staff** 815 Fifteenth Street, NW, Suite 928, Washington, DC 20005 202-347-3300

WORKING FOR WOMEN AND CHILDREN: THE WIC ORGANIZING GUIDE
(undated) - manual for organizing an advocacy project on food and nutrition for women, infants and children in the community; based on nineteen-year-old program, 63pp, $2.50 (free to low-income organizations and individuals who cannot afford to purchase) **WIC (Women, Infants and Children) Advocacy Staff** 815 Fifteenth Street, NW, Suite 928, Washington, DC 20005 202-347-3300

TRAINING/CONFERENCES/TEACHING

AVC WORKSHOPS PROCEEDINGS INDEX
(1978) - a means of access to information on fund raising, public relations, training, volunteer-staff relations, business/industry involvement, the board of directors, volunteer administration, and many more areas resulting from brainstorming sessions by experts in the field; lists some 200 workshop transcripts by author and subject attainable for $.10/page to AVC members, $.20/page to others, 16pp, $4.00 **Association of Volunteer Centers** c/o VOLUNTEER - The National Center, 1111 Nineteenth Street, Arlington, VA 22209 703-276-0542

BEYOND EXPERTS: A GUIDE FOR CITIZEN TRAINING
(undated) - an overview of specific options for citizen group training; involves a seven-step sequence of planning and carrying out training activities; contains a cumulative index of CITP's eight manuals, 36pp, $10.00 plus $2.50 postage **Citizen Involvement Training Program** 381 Hills South, Room 381, Amherst, MA 01003 413-545-2038

EDUCATIONAL NEEDS IN VOLUNTEER ADMINISTRATION
(1990) - a survey packet sent to volunteer organizations across the country and in some other countries to help assess the needs for training in the field, and to elicit comments on the proposed *Institute for Volunteer Administration,* which is being considered to provide more depth and consistency in training volunteer leaders, unpaged, single packet free **Association for Volunteer Administration** PO Box 4584, Boulder, CO 80306 303-497-0238

HOW TO PLAN BETTER MEETINGS AND TRAINING PROGRAMS: SOS-10
(1972) - comprehensive guide providing information on methods and techniques in areas of planning, physical setup, layouts, audiovisual aids, discussions, role playing, buzz groups, plays for living, etc., 28pp, $2.15 **National Council on the Aging** 600 Maryland Avenue, NW, West Wing 100, Washington, DC 20024 202-479-1200

INFORMATION AND REFERRAL PROGRAMMED RESOURCE & TRAINING COURSE
(1979) - details of a service provided through the National Academy of Voluntarism and the Services Outrach Division of the United Way to assist groups in upgrading I&R Services; includes in the self contained course: Section I - information on organizing an I&R service; Section II - a series of training exercises using a workbook and cassette. The course can be adapted to meet specific needs and is provided with consultation and followup services on request, free 6-panel foldout, $100/course **United Way of America** 701 North Fairfax Street, Alexandria, VA 22314-2045 703-836-7100

INTERNATIONAL DIRECTORY FOR YOUTH INTERNSHIPS
(kept current) - descriptions of volunteer and intern positions available at the UN and its related agencies, and nongovernmental organization-related programs; provides background information for each program, and outlines the rights and responsibilities of the volunteer and intern, 22pp, single copy free **UNA-USA Publications** 300 East 42nd Street, New York, NY 10017 212-697-3232

MAKING MEETINGS WORK
(1976) - a manual describing an approach to meetings that is designed to foster maximum participation by attendees; includes extensive appendix of checklists, forms and other aids, 121pp, $13.95 **University Associates** 8517 Production Avenue, San Diego, CA 92121 619-578-5900

MAP (MANAGEMENT ASSISTANCE PROGRAM)
(1980) - a free service providing training and consultation for agencies with volunteer programs, 38pp, single copy free **United Way of San Diego County** 4699 Murphy Canyon Road, PO Box 23543, San Diego, CA 92123-0543 619-292-0993

PLANNING AND CONDUCTING EDUCATION AND TRAINING PROGRAMS: A SEVEN STEP PROCESS
(1977) - a two-part guide first outlining the seven basic steps in any training process (from establishing the need to assessing the effectiveness) and then providing a real life example of how this technique works, 62pp, $1.00 **Center for Youth Development and Research** 48 McNeal Hall, 1985 Buford Avenue, St. Paul, MN 55108 612-376-7624

PROGRAM PLANNER: DESIGNING A CONFERENCE
(1979) - step-by-step listing of tasks, including people and organizations to be involved, decisions for the planning committee

publicity, packet for participants, registration procedures, and evaluation (with list of possible evaluation questions), 4pp, $1.00 **Unitarian Universalist Women's Federation** 25 Beacon Street, Boston, MA 02108 617-742-2100

REGIONAL CONFERENCE PLANNING GUIDE
(1981) - a handbook full of step-by-step ideas and suggestions for organizing, carrying out and evaluating conferences and meetings; includes lists of pre-conference tasks, budget guidelines, sample job descriptions, letters and time tables, 28pp, $15.00 ($12.50 for members) **Association for Volunteer Administration** PO Box 4584, Boulder, CO 80306 303-497-0238

TAKING YOUR MEETINGS OUT OF THE DOLDRUMS
(1975) by Eva Schindler-Rainman and Ronald Lippett - an informal approach to meeting preparation designed to lessen the rigidity often associated with conferences and meetings; emphasizes human interaction without standardized rituals to facilitate freedom of expression; includes a 40-page "tool kit," checklists, and other aids, 100pp, $10.50 **University Associates** 8517 Production Avenue, San Diego, CA 92121 619-578-5900

TRAINING AND CERTIFYING YOUR VOLUNTEERS
(1985) - study guide designed for the activity/volunteer director who works with the frail elderly; acclimates volunteers to the setting and provides a step-by-step process for conducting experiential exercises to help volunteers understand the disabled and older adult; outlines a three-week volunteer training and certification program, focusing the first week on the philosophy of care, the purpose of the program, the importance of volunteering, and the problems of the elderly, the second week on specific problems such as stress, senility, strokes, special diets, wheelchair techniques, etc., and the third week on volunteer rights and policy, resident rights, compassion, recordkeeping, meeting attendance, and concluding with a recognition banquet; appends exercises designed for the program; explores the benfits of certification; includes a bibliography, 71pp, inquire about cost **Educational Parameters** 83 Industrial Lane, Agawam, MA 01001 413-789-1124

TRAINING TECHNIQUES IN BRIEF
(1990) - a guide covering the basic training techniques: lecture, nominal group, panel, and others; presents information on synetics and computerized instruction; includes definitions, descriptions in use, and examples of each technique; appends list of materials needed and space for notes, 37pp, $10.95 (by mail, $14.00) **Macduff/Bunt Associates** 821 Lincoln Street, Walla Walla, WA 99362 509-529-0244

TRAINING WHEELS
(bimonthly) - newsletter "for and about trainers and their work;" includes articles on methods of presentation, requirements of successful workshops, marketing, etc.; reviews relevant books and other materials; solicits articles from the volunteer field, Av. 4pp, $29.00/year **VMS/Heritage Arts** 1807 Prairie Avenue, Downers Grove, IL 60515

VOLUNTARISM: CONFRONTATION & OPPORTUNITY
(1975) - proceedings of a seminar designed to help responsible staff and volunteers in strengthening voluntarism in their organizations; discusses the advantages of advance planning in blending staff and volunteer talents, and other methods and techniques often overlooked by the organization, 39pp, $2.00 **Young Men's Christian Association of the US** 101 North Wacker Drive, Chicago, IL 60606 312-977-0031

VOLUNTEER FIELD EXPERIENCE PACKET
(1980) - set of forms developed for record-keeping in student volunteer field placement programs; includes site location form, time sheet, and evaluation forms for both student and agency, 5pp, single packet free **United Way of San Diego County** 4699 Murphy Canyon Road, PO Box 23543, San Diego, CA 92123-0543 619-492-2000

WORN PATHS AND UNBROKEN TRAILS
(1989) - proceedings of the 1989 conference of the Association for Voluntary Action Scholars (see organizational listing), $25.00 plus $2.00 postage/handling **Macduff/Bunt Associates** 821 Lincoln Street, Walla Walla, WA 99362

TRANSPORTATION & SAFETY

BICYCLING FOR RECREATION AND COMMUTING
(1972) - the case for bicycling whenever possible instead of driving; includes an overview of citizen action, federal promotion, long distance routes, reserved lanes, national trails system, theft problem, funding from federal and other sources, and what public-spirited citizen groups can do to move bureaucracies in this area, 26pp, single copy free **US/DoT - Office of Information** 400 Seventh Street, SW, Washington, DC 20590 202-426-0660

CHECKLIST FOR IMPROVING PEDESTRIAN SAFETY IN YOUR COMMUNITY
(1982) - a compilation of policies and practices that have proven effective in pedestrian accident data gathering and use, laws and enforcement, traffic engineering, public information, school pedestrian safety, and comprehensive community pedestrian safety programs, 16pp, $.30 single copy **Highway Users Federation for Safety and Mobility** 1776 Massachusetts Avenue, NW, Washington, DC 20036 202-857-1200

COMMUNITY RIDESHARING: A LEADERSHIP ROLE
(1979) - a challenge to citizen leaders to take advantage of federal funds and program support available to communities for ridesharing programs; points out the benefits to individuals, business and the community; details the type of assistance available and how to acquire it, 10pp, single copy free **US/DoT - National Ridesharing Information Center** 400 Seventh Street, SW, Room 3215, Washington, DC 20590 202-426-2953

DISCOVERING TRAFFIC SAFETY: FOR CHILDREN
(1979) - details about an audiovisual program designed for children is grades K-9 to help them accept responsibility as a pedestrian, a passenger, and later as a driver to help remove one of the persistent problems in driving - accidents involving children; involves a series of films and a leaders' guide, 4-panel brochure, $.50 **Highway Users Federation for Safety and Mobility** 1776 Massachusetts Avenue, NW, Washington, DC 20036 202-857-1200

DRIVER SAFETY
(1982) - a guide to develop a safe drivers public education and action program to make highways safer; single copy free **B'nai B'rith International** Community Volunteer Services, 1640 Rhode Island Avenue, NW, Washington, DC 20036 202-857-6580

DRIVERS! THE VOLUNTEER WORLD NEEDS YOU!
(1990) - a look at a problem that plagues volunteer programs that require transportation (meals-on-wheels, visitation, errands for the homebound, children's outings, etc.), to the point where they must either limit the help they can provide, or hire drivers for part of the service - both options having adverse affects on the individuals who need assistance - and the community; describes ways to approach experienced drivers (couriers, bus drivers, truckers, etc.) to encourage an "extra day of driving" to help improve the quality of life for the less fortunate; includes insurance and liability information, 20pp, $6.00 (proceeds from this book benefit a homelessness prevention program) **Mortgage Burning Fund** PO Box 762, Annandale, VA 22003 703-354-6270

THE END OF THE ROAD: A CITIZEN'S GUIDE TO TRANSPORTATION PROBLEM SOLVING
(1977) - suggestions for concerned individuals and groups on getting involved in shaping the transportation policy of the community and the state (...they will respond to the "Citizens' Coalition on the Transportation Crisis" even if it consists of only you and a neighbor); appends a real-life case study, guidelines for commenting on stated policy, etc., 159pp, $3.50 **Environmental Action Foundation** 1525 New Hampshire Avenue, NW, Washington, DC 20036 202-745-4870

GUIDE TO MORE EFFECTIVE DRUNK DRIVING LEGISLATION IN THE STATES
(1982) - pamphlet explaining the illegal per se law and other provisions connected with drunk driving legislation, listing per se and presumptive laws for each state, 4-panel brochure, $.25 **Highway Users Federation for Safety and Mobility** 1776 Massachusetts Avenue, NW, Washington, DC 20036 202-857-1200

GUIDELINES FOR THE ORGANIZATION OF COMMUTER VAN PROGRAMS
(1979) - follows development of a company-sponsored commuter van program from feasibility study to administration of the ongoing operations; serves as background information for citizens seeking this type of help, 18pp, single copy free **US/DoT - Federal Highway Admistration** 400 Seventh Street, SW, Washington, DC 20590 202-426-0660

HERTZ FEDERAL VANPOOL PROGRAM

(1979) - overview of the cooperative program between Hertz and the Employee Transportation Coordinator in each federal installation; provides maintenance, insurance, service, special equipment, and other elements of a lease agreement; describes financial and energy benefits (each van saves 5,000 gallons of gas annually), and presents guidelines from Hertz on establishing vanpool programs, 6-panel foldout, free (also distributed by Department of Transportation; inquire at local federal offices) **Hertz Government Sales Office** 8319 Ardwick-Ardmore Road, Landover, MD 20785 301-322-2877

HIGH COST TO PUBLIC OF MOTOR VEHICLE CRASHES

(1989) - overview of the cost of motor vehicle crashes to consumers ($74 billion in 1986); suggestions for ending this drain on financial resources (increasing seat belt use, enforcing posted speed limits, cracking down on drunk driving, etc.), single copy free **US/DoT - National Highway Traffic Safety Administration** 400 Seventh Street, SW, Washington, DC 20590 202-366-4570

MOBILITY, TRANSPORTATION AND AGING

(undated) - a discussion of the relationship between the local travel network and the capabilities of older persons to use services and enjoy leisure activities intended for them; includes suggestions for alleviating the problem, 26pp, single copy free **US/HHS - Administration on Aging** 200 C Street, SW, Washington, DC 20201 202-619-0724

NORTH AMERICAN BICYCLE ATLAS

(kept current) - information for the cycler within the community or the long distance bicycle traveler; provides tips on all aspects of bicycle use, and logistical information vital "on the road," 68pp, $6.25 plus $1.80 shipping **American Youth Hostels** PO Box 37613, Washington, DC 20013 202-783-6161

OUTLINE AND SUGGESTED METHODOLOGY FOR NEW TRANSPORTATION PROGRAMS

(1977) - overview of the need for improving transportation services for non-emergency situations involving the elderly and disabled; provides guidelines for establishing a door-to-door program, 14pp, $1.00 **Pioneers on Wheels** PO Box 278, Belvedere, NJ 07823 07823

PARA-TRANSIT: NEGLECTED OPTION FOR URBAN MOBILITY

(1974) - a detailed overview of alternative transportation methods that are or could be used on secondary roads in urban areas, their implications for the elderly, the handicapped, and others needing special consideration; covers dial-a-ride, jitney, ride-sharing and other alternative services as compared to conventional modes; presents case studies on jitney, dial-a-ride and other services, and some innovations in recent legislation, 319pp, $4.95 **Urban Institute Press** 2100 M Street, NW, Washington, DC 20037 202-833-7200

PRESCHOOL CHILDREN IN TRAFFIC

(1980) - a set of five booklets designed to assist parents and others working with small children (2-1/2 to 6) to prepare them to meet the challenge of traffic in residential neighborhoods, five 15pp booklets (inquire at local office regarding cost and acquisition) **American Automobile Association** 12600 Fair Lakes Circle, Fairfax, VA 22033-4907 703-AAA-6000

RIDE REVIEW

(kept current) - overview of five commuter alternatives for county residents as well as ridematching and vanpool-forming assistance; includes low-cost and no-cost connecting lines designed to encourage use of public transportation, 6-panel foldout, free **RIDESOURCES** County Office of Transportation, 4050 Legato Road, 9th Floor, Fairfax, VA 22033 703-246-3311 (offices)

RIDESHARE AND SAVE

(1979) - a guide and workbook developed to strengthen the case for ridesharing; provides chart comparing costs of driving alone and ridesharing one way, including standard and subcompact cars in 10-, 20-, and 40-mile one-way commute situations; provides detailed worksheets to help driver allow for any variables unique to his situation, 10pp, single copy free **National Ridesharing Information Center** Federal Highway Administration , Room 3215, Washington, DC 20590 202-426-2953

RIDESHARING: AN EASY WAY TO SAVE GAS AND MONEY

(1979) - hard facts about the cost of owning and operating automobiles, and how ridesharing can reduce this expense, 10pp, single copy free **National Ridesharing Information Center** Federal Highway Administration , Room 3215, Washington, DC 20590 202-426-2953

SEE ONE DRUNK TOO MANY

(1982) - description of an audiovisual program available from new car, truck and tire dealers designed to help communities solve the drunk driving problem, foldover flyer, single copy free **Highway Users Federation for Safety and Mobility** 1776 Massachusetts Avenue, NW, Washington, DC 20036 202-857-1200

TRANSPORTATION AND THE ELDERLY AND HANDICAPPED

(1977) - information on resource materials in the area of alternative forms of transportation in the community for the elderly and the handicapped; includes listings for door-to-door van service, specially equipped buses to accommodate wheelchairs or feeble elderly, etc., 83pp, single copy free **US/DoT - Office of Technology Sharing** Kendall Square, Cambridge, MA 02142 617-494-2846

TRANSPORTATION FOR THE HANDICAPPED

(1975) - indexed, annotated bibliography including sections on accessibility, air travel, mass transit, automobiles, special equipment, transportation for the blind, elderly, etc., 26pp, single copy free **US/DoT - Library Service Division** 400 Seventh Street, NW, Washington, DC 20590 202-426-8058

TRANSPORTATION: GUIDELINE FOR DEVELOPING QUALITY SERVICE

(undated) - overview of what can be done about the third leading problem of the elderly - inadequate transportation; covers types of services, sponsorship, eligibility, development, and other aspects to assist in establishing a community transportation system, 10pp, $.80 **National Voluntary Organizations for Independent Living for the Aging** 600 Maryland Avenue, NW, West Wing 100, Washington, DC 20024 202-479-1200

TRANSPORTATION POLICY AND ENERGY CONSERVATION

(1980) - a report written for a citizen training program mounted to deal with the legislative and regulatory gaps in the area of transportation services; discusses the lack of intercity and rural service, and the impact on the environment of the resistance to car pools and other ride-sharing activities, 71pp, $3.50 **Conservation Foundation** 1250 24th Street, NW, Washington, DC 20037 202-293-4800

VOLUNTEER DRIVER GUIDE: GLOVE COMPARTMENT COMPANION

(undated) - quick-reference pocket-sized booklet outlining transportation assignments, insurance, accidents (including on-the-spot report form), unusual requests by clients, and other helpful tips for volunteer drivers, 8pp, $1.00 **Volunteer Service of Santa Cruz County** 1111 Emeline Avenue, Santa Cruz , CA 95060 408-423-0554

VOLUNTEERS INSURANCE SERVICE ASSOCIATION/CIMA

(1980) - general description of the insurance coverages that can be provided to protect volunteers who drive; includes guidelines to pinpoint limitations (e.g., sports clubs, volunteer firemen among those not eligible), includes application form, 8-panel foldout **Volunteers Insurance Service Association/CIMA** 216 South Peyton Street, Alexandria, VA 22314 703-739-9300

WHEELS SERIES

(various dates) - five manuals developed for slow readers, and a teacher's guide for use by leaders of transportation and youth programs; manuals include:

- *Studying for a Driver's License* (1973) - simple outline of a driver's manual, for use with individual state manuals; includes 100 multiple-choice practice questions and a glossary of terms and words used in manuals, 56pp, $2.00
- *Becoming a Car Owner* (1976) - consumer tips on buying new or used cars; information on financing, insurance and registration; operational costs of service and repairs, 64pp, $2.65
- *Maintaining Your Car* (1979) - explanation of car systems; hints on how to tell when a system is not working correctly and who should fix it; do-it-yourself instructions for many simple repairs and maintenance functions, 80pp, $3.25
- *Taking the Wheel* (1978) - explanation of safe driving skills, attitudes, and concepts; driving techniques for different road and weather conditions; driving under the influence of drugs or alcohol, 96pp, $3.95
- *Wheels Workbook* (1980) - pre-tests and post-tests for Becoming a Car Owner, Maintaining Your Car, and Taking the Wheel, 64pp, $2.50
- *Wheels Teacher's Guide* (1980) - methods of teaching the Wheels series; techniques for individual instruction; suggestions for helping students with reading problems; activities, games, and ready-to-use exercises; appends skills evaluation sheet to assess students' abilities and progress, a list of resources and bibliography, 64pp, $2.65

New Readers Press Box 131, Syracuse, NY 13210 315-422-9121

WHO NEEDS HIGH SCHOOL DRIVER EDUCATION

(1980) - an explanation, in question and answer format, of the costs, benefits, and instructional nature of high school driver education courses, designed to assist community groups in improving the quality of existing driver education programs or obtaining such programs in their schools, 4-panel brochure, $.50 **Highway Users Federation for Safety and Mobility** 1776 Massachusetts Avenue, NW, Washington, DC 20036 202-857-1200

VOLUNTEERS - SPECIAL GROUPS

ACTORS AND OTHERS NEWSLETTER
(annually) - a report on the year's activities by actors and others in areas wildlife conservation, endangered species, zero pet population, pet adoption, and others, 12pp, single copy free **Actors and Others for Animals** 5510 Cahuenga Road, North Hollywood, CA 91601 818-985-6263

ALL HANDS: SPECIAL ISSUE ON VOLUNTEERISM
(Fall 1989) - a special issue of *All Hands,* a magazine of the U.S. Navy, highlighting some of the many worldwide volunteer services provided by men and women of the Navy; includes numerous photographs of the Navy members performing a wide variety of volunteer activities, single copy free as supply lasts **US/DoD - Naval Internal Relations Activity** 601 North Fairfax Street, Alexandria, VA 22314-2007 703-696-6874

AMERICAN BAR ASSOCIATION PUBLIC SERVICES GROUP
(1979) - description of the many human service areas covered by the Division, including mental disability, housing, the elderly, child abuse, energy, environment, jobs for the disadvantaged, etc., 44pp, single copy free **American Bar Association** 750 North Lake Shore Drive, Chicago, IL 606-1 312-988-5000

ART FOR ART'S SAKE
(1987) - a series of printed materials created in an original collection by the best-known cartoonists in the U.S. (Gary Trudeau, Johnny Hart, Jim Davis, Bill Keane, and others) to call attention to the needs of the nation's children; includes posters, note cards, and signed limited editions, inquire about styles and costs **Child Welfare League of America** 440 First Street, NW, Suite 310, Washington, DC 20001-2085 202-638-2952

AUTUMN STAGES/LIFESTORY THEATRE: INFORMATION PACKET
(kept current) - overview of a troupe of older volunteer actors and actresses who have developed the *Lifestory Theater* to utilize extensive audience participation in instant improvisation of life stories of older persons in nursing homes, nutritional sites, churches and synagogues, geriatric wings of hospitals, libraries, senior centers, festivals and other sites for older adults; includes details of other activities of the group, unpaged, single copy free **Autumn Stages** , Upper Montclair, NJ 07042 201-746-7710

AVANZANDO
(quarterly) - a newsletter printed for Spanish-speaking Americans providing information on training, resources, networking, and other services of the Association, single copy free, inquire about subscription **Association for Retarded Citizens of Georgia** 1851 Ram Runway, Suite 104 , College Park, GA 30337 404-761-2745

BELOIT VAC'S RSVP PROGRAM
(1979) - annual report of a program using 1,111 volunteers in 68 area stations; lists some 150 assignments ranging from board members to artists, and reports on the program's PR, consultation, conference, and special activities; includes funding and budget information, 13pp, single copy free **Volunteer Service Bureau/VAC** 431 Olympian Boulevard, Beloit, WI 53511 608-365-1278

BIG BROTHERS/BIG SISTERS OF AMERICA
(undated) - kit of materials describing the service and its two arms - Big Brothers and Big Sisters; includes current newsletter, annual report, and informational brochures, single kit free **Big Brothers/Big Sisters of America** 230 North 13th Street, Philadelphia, PA 19107 215-567-7000

BREAK AWAY: A GUIDE TO ORGANIZING AN ALTERNATIVE SPRING BREAK
(1990) - a guide for campus leaders who are establishing or expanding a spring break or extra-curricular service trip - community service; Includes profiles of existing programs, ideas for initiating reflective components and suggestions for fundraising, $7.50 **Campus Outreach Opportunity League (COOL)** 386 McNeal Hall, University of Minnesota, St. Paul, MN 55108-1011 612-624-3018

BUILDING ON FAITH
(1990) - a listing of dozens of church efforts ranging from the restoration of housing units by a single church to interfaith, multi-unit projects; includes development histories of various projects, describing their organizations, resources and impacts; appends suggestions for similar efforts elsewhere, 67pp, inquire about cost **Conference on Shelter and Housing** c/o AME Zion Church, 1511 K Street, NW, Washington, DC 20005 292-347-1419

CAREGIVERS QUARTERLY

(quarterly) - newsletter for local caregivers volunteer programs to keep them informed of meetings, conferences, workshops, resources, administrative activities, awards, publications, etc., 6-8pp, inquire about cost **National Federation of Interfaith Volunteer Caregivers** 105 Mary's Avenue, PO Box 1939, Kingston, NY 12401-1939 914-331-1358

CASA: A CHILD'S VOICE IN COURT

(1989) - annual report of the *National CASA Association* for the year 1988-89; include overview of the organization and its goals, objectives, projections, support base, statistics, balance sheet, etc.; appends list of committee members, board members, advisory council members, and staff, 12pp, single copy free **National CASA Association** 2722 Eastlake Avenue, East, Seattle, WA 98102 206-328-8588

A CHANCE TO CONTRIBUTE TO YOUR COMMUNITY...

(kept current) - a recruitment brochure to enlist volunteers as home visitors to work with parents and very young children in play activities and child development education, and to help plan "parent meetings" for sharing experiences and ideas on parenting, 6-panel foldout, free **US/DoD - Navy Family Service Center** Parent-to-Parent Program, Naval Training Center Bldg. 42, Great Lakes, IL 60088 312-688-3603

CHILDREN AS VOLUNTEERS

(1983) - encouragement for directors of volunteers, organization officers, teachers and youth group leaders to develop opportunities for youngsters to serve their communities; provides examples and models of individual and group involvement by children; offers techniques for designing assignments, recruiting and training children; includes legal and insurance-related concerns, 68pp, $8.75 **ENERGIZE** 5450 Wissahickon Avenue, Philadelphia, PA 19144 215-436-8342

THE CHOICE IS YOURS

(1989) - a videotape based on a program begun by a death row inmate attempting to help deter young people from breaking the law; takes the viewer inside the cell and describes in detail the grinding daily routine on death row, 22 minutes, $20 **Catholic Communications Center** c/o Bob Edwards, Director, 811-D Cathedral Place, Richmond, VA 23220-4898

THE CHURCH PUZZLE GAME

(1989) - a tool to help leaders begin an organizational analysis - to understand what's happening in the group, to analyze member involvement and identify areas that deserve further attention, 40pp, $9.50 **ENERGIZE** 5450 Wissahickon Avenue, Philadelphia, PA 19144 215-438-8342

CIRCLES OF FRIENDS

(1988) - overview of several friendship circles - referred to as *living documents* - showing the possibilities of friendship between people with disabilities and those without; addresses both those within and those outside of the field of mental retardation, inquire about cost **Abingdon Press** 201 Eighth Avenue South, PO Box 801, Nashville, TN 37202 615-749-6290

A CLOSE ENCOUNTER OF A SPECIAL KIND: A LITTLE BROTHER OR SISTER NEEDS YOU

(undated) - handbook for volunteers and potential volunteers describing a program that matches adult volunteers and children in need of a positive role model; sections include: How You Can Help, Commitment, Dos and Don'ts, Goals, Some Suggestions (for activities), and Responsibility to the Agency; appends a glossary of terms and acronyms to assist the volunteer in understanding

frequently-used terms, 9pp, single copy free Also request sample forms, job descriptions, fact sheets, project profiles, etc. **Interdivisional Volunteer Program** PO Box 628, Hillsboro, OR 97123 503-648-0711

THE CONNECTION

(quarterly) - the newsletter of the *National CASA Association*, providing news on legislation, statistics, program profiles, guest articles, "kid quotes," training, etc., 16pp, $25/year **National CASA Association** 2722 Eastlake Avenue, East, Suite 220, Seattle , WA 98102 206-328-8588

CORPORATE-COMMUNITY INVOLVEMENT

(1983) - a survey providing an overview of how small and large American corporations are responding to their contention that the demand for greater business involvement is strongest from inside the business community; includes a distillation of some of the principles of effective corporate community involvement, such as:
- Two fundamentals of success: involvement of top executive; and, the firm's "bottom line" economic interests);
- The myth that only large corporations can involve themselves;
- What business executives must learn to work with representatives of the communities;
- The policy, planning, priorities, management structure, and evaluation needed in a program of involvement (just like any other business undertaking).

[This is the second of a series; also request a copy of the first, *Investing in America,* which is a comprehensive report on the President's Task Force on Private Sector Initiatives. A third in the series is in press, and describes the principal national organizations working with the White House Office on Private Sector Initiatives to increase public/private partnerships] **Civitex** 55 West 44th Street, 6th Floor, New York, NY 10036 212-730-7930

CORPORATE VOLUNTEERISM - THE INVOLVEMENT CORPS

(undated) - description of the program, what it offers all concerned, the skills needed to run a good corporate volunteer program - one that will meet community needs while affording the corporation the satisfaction of contributing vital assistance to society; includes list of branch offices, 8pp, single copy free **Involvement, Inc.** 1366 Las Canoas Road, Pacific Palisades, CA 90272 213-459-1022

DEVELOPING LEADERSHIP FOR PARENT/CITIZEN GROUPS

(1976) - guidelines for developing leaders in the community to increase citizen participation; covers styles of leadership, being a leader, making your group work, and motivating others; addressed to involvement in education, but basic to any program of group- or self-leadership training, 59pp, $3.50 **National Committee for Citizens in Education** 410 Wilde Lake Village Green, Columbia, MD 21044 301-997-9300

DEVELOPMENT OF AN ECUMENICAL VOLUNTEER PROGRAM

(1984) - overview of an ecumenical volunteer program in Alabama designed to help people become self-sufficient; acknowledges the successes of the program and discusses some of the weaknesses; makes recommendations such as assisting the volunteers, many of whom were retired persons or homemakers with no experience in providing services to clients, through guidance by skilled professional support staff; cites areas in which professional assistance is most needed - screening for emergency aid, advocacy and referral, teaching of self-help skills, food distribution, etc.; appends training materials and sample volunteer records, 16pp, inquire about cost **Project SHARE** 7830 Old Georgetown Road, Suite 204, Bethesda, MD 20814 301-231-9539

THE EDUCATION UPDATE
(quarterly) - newsletter of the Association for Retarded Citizens of Georgia to provide continuing education to parents and professionals working with handicapped children, single copy free, inquire about subscription cost **Association for Retarded Citizens of Georgia** 1851 Ram Runway, Suite 104 , College Park, GA 30337 404-761-2745

EMPLOYMENT AND VOLUNTEER OPPORTUNITIES FOR OLDER PEOPLE
(1970) - overview of the increasing number of opportunities available to older persons - due in part to recent legislation on behalf of the elderly, and partly to a rising awareness of the contributions the "most experienced segment of the population" can make; outlines the options in both job and volunteer areas (in both public and private sectors) and profiles some of the federal programs (JTPA, SBA, ACTION, Bureau of the Census, Teacher Corps, etc.), 6pp, single copy free **US/HHS - Administration on Aging** 200 C Street, SW, Washington, DC 20201 202-619-0724

FROM BELIEF TO COMMITMENT: FINDINGS FROM A NATIONAL SURVEY
(1990) - a study by the *Gallup Organization* commissioned by the *Independent Sector* on how religious congregations contribute money and services; includes sections on programs, number of people volunteering, total revenues and sources, etc., based on a survey of some 4,200 local congregations, 52pp, $25.00 ($17.50 members) **Independent Sector** 1828 L Street, NW, Washington, DC 20036 202-223-8100

FROM BELIEF TO COMMITMENT: THE ACTIVITIES AND FINANCES OF RELIGIOUS CONGREGATIONS IN THE US
(1988) - a study undertaken by The Gallup Organization for Independent Sector that looks at religious congregations and the significant role they play in the voluntary sector, 52pp, $25 **Independent Sector** 1828 L Street, NW, Washington, DC 20036 202-223-8100

FSC/COLORADO FACT SHEETS
(kept current) - a series of fact sheets with brief descriptions of programs offered by VOA in Colorado; with contact information for youth services in areas of shelters, ranches, teenage pregnancy, and other areas; and for services to the elderly in areas of nutrition, recreation, and volunteer opportunities, etc., one-page formats, free **Family Service Center/Colorado Branch** 1865 Larimer Street, Denver, CO 80202 303-297-0408

FULL PARDON
(monthly) - overview of the month's work in jails and prisons assisting prisoners in areas of education, counseling, family contact, and pastoral counseling; includes articles by prisoners who have returned to the community or have become Chaplains in the program that helped them, 4pp, free **Good News Jail and Prison Ministries International** 1036 S. Highland Street, Arlington, VA 22204 703-979-2200

GRAY PANTHER MANUAL FOR ORGANIZING: VOLUMES I AND II
(undated) - basic steps to take in organizing volunteers around issues affecting isolated populations, and guidelines for operating and maintaining interest in action programs, $6.00 each volume; $11.00 for both **Gray Panthers** 311 South Juniper Street, Suite 601, Philadelphia, PA 19107 215-382-3300

GROWING OLDER: OPTIONS AND OPPORTUNITIES
(kept current) - tips for older persons on creating interest in their concerns, finding resource people and publications, and other ways of getting involved in activities to improve life for older Americans, 4pp, $1.00 **Unitarian Universalist Women's Federation** 25 Beacon Street, Boston, MA 02108 617-742-2100

HOST: A MANUAL FOR CREATING AN INTERGENERATIONAL VOLUNTEER PROGRAM TO ASSIST OLDER ADULTS
(kept current) - a step-by-step guide to assist other communities in replicating the HOST program, which brings together young and old in an interfaith-intergenerational volunteer project to provide supportive services for isolated older persons, 5pp, inquire about cost **Montgomery General Hospital** 3438 Olney-Laytonsville Road, Olney, MD 20832 301-774-6114

HOST INFORMATION PACKET
(undated) - a pocketed portfolio with fact sheets, brochures, sample newsletter, sample training program, etc., providing an overview of a program that brings together young and old in an interfaith/intergenerational volunteer program that provides companions and helpers for older persons in their own homes and in nursing homes, unpaged, single packet free [contents change as program grows and changes] **Montgomery General Hospital** 3438 Olney-Laytonsville Road, Olney, MD 20832 301-774-6114

HOW TO MOBILIZE CHURCH VOLUNTEERS
(1983) - a guide covering topics such as: the *Theology of Volunteerism,* current trends, tools and organizational essentials, recruiting and placement, pillars and pew-sitters, etc.; includes worksheets, sample reports, and problem-solving exercises, 156pp, $9.95 **Volunteer Management Associates** 320 South Cedar Brook Road, Department VRC1, Boulder, CO 80304 303-447-0558

HOW TO WORK EFFECTIVELY WITH ALUMNI BOARDS
(1981) - a look at the leadership role of alumni boards, qualifications of board members, relationships with the institution's president and other administrators, and board involvement in various issues, (addressed to universities, but useful to anyone concerned with boards), 81pp, $14.50 **Council for Advancement and Support of Education** 80 South Early Street, Alexandria, VA 22304 703-836-4776

IDEAS FOR ACTION - "THERE OUGHT TO BE A PROGRAM"
(undated) - detailed planning manual detailing program development steps for those having difficulty getting started; covers publicity, fund raising, resource people, evaluation, and other areas; includes check lists and other aids to facilitate the learning process, as well as hundreds of ideas (prison visits, cleanup, etc.) for youth programs, 32pp, $.50 **B'nai B'rith Youth Organization** 1640 Rhode Island Avenue, NW, Washington, DC 20036 202-857-6585

IF YOU ARE A PROFESSIONAL...A.A. WANTS TO WORK WITH YOU
(1978) - a call to those persons working in treatment programs or medical facilities for alcoholics to cooperate with A.A. by providing the technical service that is not part of the A.A. program, 8-panel foldout, free (ask for free brochure, "A Brief Guide to Alcoholics Anonymous") **Alcoholics Anonymous World Services** PO Box 459, Grand Central Station, New York, NY 10163 212-686-1100

I'M BLIND, LET ME HELP YOU - THE OLDER VISUALLY HANDICAPPED VOLUNTEER
(1974) - a description in words and pictures of the experiences of several older visually handicapped volunteers in RSVP programs; includes tips on training and placement of these volunteers, 20pp,

single copy free **American Foundation for the Blind** 15 West 16th Street, New York, NY 10011 212-620-2000

INTERGENERATIONAL SERVICE-LEARNING PROJECT: A NATIONAL DEMONSTRATION

(undated) - a program to expand services for older people while providing off-campus learning opportunities for students; emphasizes increasing advocacy, improving access to health care, etc., 6-panel foldout, single copy free **Intergenerational Service-Learning Project** 1828 L Street, NW, Washington, DC 20036 202-223-6250

INTERN PROGRAM

(kept current) - overview of a program which offers 30 internship positions to college students from across the country; provides experience in legislation, issue development, legislative correspondence, litigation, and other areas, 6-panel foldout, single copy free **Common Cause** Volunteer Office, 2030 M Street, NW, Washington, DC 20036 202-833-1200

INVOLVING PARENTS

(1989) - information about a school system that improved dramatically after parenting courses and volunteer opportunities were offered to parents, unpaged, single copy free **Orangeburg School System** 578 Ellis Street, NE, Orangeburg, SC 29115 803-534-5454

IT'S TIME TO STAND UP FOR YOUR CHILDREN: A PARENT'S GUIDE TO CHILD ADVOCACY

(1982) - answers to questions such as: What is child advocacy? How can parents be effective advocates for their children? What are the steps to take? What obstacles will parents encounter? and others in a quick-reference handbook format, 48pp, $2.50 **Child Welfare League of America** 122 C Street, NW, Washington, DC 20001 202-628-8787

JFK LIBRARY CORPS OVERVIEW

(kept current) - details on a program designed to "help young people develop a commitment to public service that will continue through their lives;" provides information on program content, types of projects, resource persons and groups, and the ultimate goal of the program, 8-panel foldout (opens into 17"x22" poster), free **JFK Library Corps** Columbia Point, Boston, MA 02125 617-929-4500

JUNIOR VOLUNTEERS: A VITAL LINK

(1989) - a manual in response to problems hospitals are finding in recruiting junior volunteers: too few juniors; too many activities; competition from paying jobs; no transportation; AIDS scare, competition from other agencies; includes "answers" in model programs with job descriptions, etc.; model scholarships for health careers; legal guidelines for volunteers under 14; volunteer/staff relations featuring program descriptions linking nursing and the volunteer department, 166pp, hardback, $35.00 **New Jersey Association Directors of Volunteer Services** c/o Judy Janas, DVS, 175 Madison Ave., Mount Holly, NJ 08060 609-267-0700

K OF C ROUNDTABLE

(monthly) - newsletter of a *Knights of Columbus* local Council for procedural reporting, but designed also to keep members informed of the progress of the Council's projects, programs, and other activities to assist the community, and to recruit volunteers among the members to fill the volunteer needs of these efforts, Av. 2pp, single copy free **St. Matthias of Somerset Council No. 9925** PO Box 5183, Somerset, NJ 08875 201-560-3589

LEND-A-HAND: THE HOW, WHERE, AND WHY OF VOLUNTEERING

(1988) - a listing of more than 100 national and international organizations that welcome young volunteers, arranged by 15 areas of involvement - from animal welfare and the arts to helping young people get involved in politics or world peace; describes each group's goals and activities, the range of volunteer opportunities that exist, and whom to contact; includes practical suggestions for finding the right cause and organization, and getting the most out of the volunteer experience, 160pp, $11.95 **Morrow Junior Books** William Morrow & Company, 105 Madison Avenue, New York, NY 10016 212-889-3050

MEALS ON WHEELS INFORMATION PACKAGE

(kept current) - questions and answers regarding the meals on wheels efforts in one large county; includes area served, contact information, clientele served, etc., free **Annandale Christian Community for Action (ACCA)** 7200 Columbia Pike, Annandale, VA 22003 703-256-1378

MILITARY FAMILY

(monthly) - authorized unofficial newsletter of the Department of Defense developed to provide information to those involved in family programs, family advocacy matters, and other activities related to military family issues; includes interviews, guest columns, legislative issues, publication and film reviews, etc., 8pp, free subscription **Military Family Resource Center** Assistant Secretary of Defense, 4015 Wilson Boulevard, Arlington, VA 22203-5190 202-696-4555

MULTIDISCIPLINARY CHILD ABUSE AND NEGLECT TEAM MANUAL

(1978) - guidelines for setting up teams which include agencies, professionals, and citizens and allow each team to inject its own ideas and concepts; provides detailed steps in all phases of the process, and includes hypothetical and actual models of CAN (Child Abuse and Neglect) teams, 77pp, $3.50 **National Institute of Social Welfare Research** 455 North Milledge Avenue, PO Box 152, Athens, GA 30603 404-542-7614

THE NAME OF THE GAME IS CARING

(kept current) - course materials designed to help young people in grades 7 through 12 acquire skills necessary to become effective volunteer recreation leaders with children, teenagers, the elderly, the disabled, the ill, or the convalescent in a variety of settings; includes 24 activity sheets; a 16-page facilitator's guide, and four two-sided posters, $8.15 (Inquire first at local Red Cross Chapter) **American Red Cross** Youth Services, 17th and D Streets, NW, Washington, DC 20006 202-737-8300

THE NAVY CHAPLAIN: VOLUNTEERS IN THE CRP

(1990) - a special issue of the annual magazine featuring volunteerism; includes program descriptions, resources (in both public and private sectors), reviews, essays, poems, award announcements, and articles titled *How to Mobilize Chapel Volunteers, The Reward of A Thing Well Done: A Volunteer Profession,* and *Lay Involvement As An Expression Of Religious Commitment,* Vol. 4, No. 3, single copy free **Chaplain Resource Board** 6500 Hampton Boulevard, Norfolk, VA 23508-1296 804-444-7655

OLDER VOLUNTEERS: A FACT SHEET

(kept current) - a summary of data from five national surveys containing information on the nature and extent of older persons' involvement in volunteer activities; provides highlights of: "The Numbers and Proportions of Older Persons Who Volunteer," "The Demography of Volunteers 65 and Over," and "What Older Volunteers Do and Why," 12pp, $$2.00 **National Council on the**

Aging 600 Maryland Avenue, SW, West Wing 100, Washington, DC 20024 202-467-1200

PARENT AIDES IN CHILD ABUSE AND NEGLECT

(1979) - the case for using parents of nonabused children - both volunteer and paid - to serve as "special friends" to abusive and neglectful parents to help them experience the warmth and understanding that they need, and have been trying to get from their children without success and with dire results; offers detailed guidelines for setting up, maintaining a program, 70pp, single copy free **National Center on Child Abuse and Neglect** U.S. Dept. of Health & Human Svcs., PO Box 1182, Washington, DC 20201 202-755-7500

PARENT TO PARENT (VIDEOTAPE)

(1989) - a videotape describing a program that puts volunteer parents (*Parent Partners*) in touch with other parents to help them work toward the independence, productivity and community integration of children with disabilities; features parents expressing their experiences with their special needs children and the organization, 15 minutes, inquire about cost and availability **Virginia Institute for Developmental Disabilities** Virginia Commonwealth University, 910 West Franklin Street, Richmond, VA 23220 804-225-3825 (TDD Access)

PARTICIPATION OF THE ELDERLY POOR IN SENIOR CENTERS: SOS-3

(1970) - ways of helping the older poor person become an asset rather than a liability through involvement in the Center's operation, 26pp, $2.15 **National Council on the Aging** 600 Maryland Avenue, SW, West Wing 100, Washington, DC 20024 202-479-1200

PARTNERS IN COPING: GROUPS FOR SELF AND MUTUAL HELP

(1978) - guide based on the premise that people who come together with others similarly situated can help themselves and each other; provides a look at the existing self-help groups like Recovery (ex-mental patients) and Alcoholics Anonymous, but encourages smaller, grassroots efforts like Project Release, started by a former mental patient in New York City in one room in a church; includes guidelines for starting such a group, 28pp, $.50 **Public Affairs Committee** 1400 K Street, NW, Washington, DC 20005 202-683-4331

PATERSON HABITAT FOR HUMANITY PACKET

(kept current) - information on a housing program for the poor that began in 1984 to meet a severe housing shortage in an eastern city, unpaged, single packet free **Paterson Habitat for Humanity** 511 22nd Street, East, Paterson, NJ 07514 201-278-4280

PATIENTS IN NURSING HOMES AND DANCING

(1971) - comprehensive guide based on a program of dance therapy administered by a 73-year-old instructor (the author of the guide); details all phases of the operation, affects on patients, games and equipment used, role of therapist, evaluation, etc., 34pp, $2.75 **Unitarian Universalist Women's Federation** 25 Beacon Street, Boston, MA 02108 617-742-2100

PEP TALK

(quarterly) - a newsletter for parents and others who have completed the PEP training program for parents and professionals working with handicapped children, free to training participants, others inquire **Association for Retarded Citizens of Georgia** 1851 Ram Runway, Suite 102 , College Park, GA 30337 404-761-2745

PRESIDENT'S COMMUNITY SERVICE FELLOWSHIP

(1990) - overview and application for the *President's Community Service Fellowship,* a program designed to encourage *Brown* undergraduates to participate in productive and rewarding full-time public service while addressing real community needs. The *Fellowship* allows students to identify a community need at the local, national, or international level, to develop an innovative, practical project that addresses that need, and to implement the project during the summer months, 8pp, free **Brown University** 25 George Street, PO Box 1974, Providence, RI 02912 401-863-2338

PROGRAM CALENDAR WORKBOOK

(undated) - a companion piece to the *Ideas for Action* manual in calendar format with ideas for programming for major holidays - both Jewish and secular - and the facility to keep track of events as the planning progresses, when the program is underway, etc., 32pp, $.20 **B'nai B'rith Youth Organization** 1640 Rhode Island Avenue, NW, Washington, DC 20036 202-857-6585

PROJECTS: BRETHREN VOLUNTEER SERVICE

(annually) - a compehensive listing of opportunities for volunteers serving individually or in groups both across the U.S. and abroad; includes project areas of youth counseling, community development, care of children and the elderly, health care, agriculture, education, carpentry and construction, houseparenting, office and secretarial tasks, refugee work, environmental projects, peace, and prison reform (volunteers receive room, board, medical expenses, and a monthly allowance, and may live in group situations, in single apartments, or with a local family), 44pp, single copy free (also request the institutional brochure providing additional detail on this program) **Brethren Volunteer Service** General Board, 1451 Dundee Avenue, Elgin, IL 60120 312-742-5100

PUTTING IT TOGETHER: LEARNING AND DEVELOPING THROUGH VOLUNTEER SERVICE

(1974) - special issue of the Center's newsletter discussing the educational value of volunteer service when social agencies and schools combine internal instruction and field activity in programs, 6pp, $.25 **Center for Youth Development and Research** 48 McNeal Hall, 1985 Buford Avenue, St. Paul, MN 55108 612-336-7624

REACHING OUT: SCHOOL-BASED COMMUNITY SERVICE PROGRAMS

(1988) - an overview of the concepts underlying youth in community service, rationales and structural options for school-based service programs, the range of service opportunities, and the nuts and bolts of starting and running a secondary school service program; includes sections on getting started, expectations, evaluation, operating, and getting advice; appends 33 school-based service programs, a bibliography, and national resources; serves as an affirmation of the ability of young people to help solve problems confronting their schools and communities, 109pp, $15.00 **National Crime Prevention Council** 1700 K Street, NW, Second Floor, Washington, DC 20006-3817 202-393-7141

RED CROSS TEEN VOLUNTEER DIRECTORY

(1990) - more than a directory, in addition to 450 specific volunteer opportunities for teens (ages 13-18), this guide includes a description of services that each agency provides, the types of activities teens would be needed for, age limits, whether the volunteer opportunity is on a bus line, and specific days and times the volunteer would be needed; includes sections on *Things to Think About Before Making a Volunteer Commitment, How to be a Successful Volunteer on the Job, What a Volunteer Can Expect from an Agency,* and *What an Agency Can Expect of a Volunteer,* inquire about availability and cost **American Red Cross** 50 Prince Street, Rochester, NY 14607-1097 716-461-9800

RELEASING THE POTENTIAL OF THE OLDER VOLUNTEER

(1976) - case studies on programs involving the older volunteer, with full details on such a program at the Ethel Percy Andrus Gerontology Center; includes suggestions and recommendations for including the older volunteer, 96pp, $3.50 **Andrus Gerontology Center** University Park, MCO191, Los Angeles, CA 90084-0191 213-741-5160

REPORT OF TASK FORCE ON TRANSITIONAL VOLUNTEERS

(undated) - definition, background, and recommendations for working with persons recovering from mental illness who are seeking volunteer involvement; appends reporting forms and other information, 5pp, single copy free **Task Force on Transitional Volunteers** 7510 Clairemont Mesa Boulevard, PO Box 2761, San Diego, CA 92112 714-292-0993

RESOURCES FOR YOUTH

(quarterly) - newsletter designed to help youth improve their volunteer programs; provides information on seed money sources, youth leadership, innovative programs, relevant publications, and other areas reflecting the extensive activity by youth across the country in service programs, Av. 6pp, free (ask to be placed on mailing list) **Institute for Responsive Education** 605 Commonwealth Avenue, Boston, MA 02215 617-353-3309

SENIOR OPPORTUNITIES AND SERVICES: DIGNITY FOR THE ELDERLY

(kept current) - overview of efforts by senior citizen information and advocacy projects aimed at improving all aspects of needs and services for the elderly; includes brief profiles of several active senior citizen organizations, 6-panel foldout, free (formerly available from the now-defunct Community Services Administration) **US/HHS - Department of Health and Human Services** Office of Community Services, Office of the Secretary, Washington, DC 20201 202-653-2010

SERVE: OLDER VOLUNTEERS IN COMMUNITY SERVICE

(1971) - account of the program used as a model for today's RSVP concept; discusses program establishment, community support, retaining volunteers, evaluation, etc., 347pp, $14.00 **Community Services Society of New York** 105 East 22nd Street, New York , NY 10010 212-254-8900

SERVICE OPPORTUNITIES FOR YOUTH

(1989) - a report advocating a change in providing opportunities for teenagers to serve as volunteers - involving "at-risk" youth who may need some of the services volunteers have to offer, but also need the opportunity to serve; praises the resurgence of youth service after two decades of self-absorption, but sees it also as a means of involving disadvantaged youth in the skills training, exposure to work environment, and opportunities for resume-building, and the renewed sense of self-worth resulting from volunteer involvement; cites several such programs in existence, including San Antonio's *Valued Youth Partnership Program* and Baltimore's *Magic Me* program - both focusing on youngsters not doing well in school; appends a number of private, public, federal and local service programs for youth, inquire about cost **Adolescent Pregnancy Prevention Clearinghouse** Children's Defense Fund, 120 C Street, NW, Washington, DC 20001 202-628-8787

SILVER HAIRED LEGISLATIVE SESSION REPORT

(biannual) - a report on the Silver Haired Legislative Session (SHLS), a program which enables older persons to become delegates at a special session at the State Capitol, and write bills, work in committees, speak on the floor of the House Chamber, and vote their opinion; includes copies of all of their bills that were passed, unpaged, inquire about cost [1988 copies available; 1990 copies available October 1990] **Arkansas Division of Aging and Adult Services** PO Box 1437, Slot 1412, Little Rock, AR 72203-1437 501-682-2411

SPEAK UP FOR A CHILD

(1990) - a portfolio of fact sheets, question/answer sheets, newspaper articles, a newsletter issue, charts, etc., to provide a broad overview of this the *National CASA Association,* unpaged, single copy free **National CASA Association** 2722 Eastlake Avenue, East, Suite 220, Seattle , WA 98102 206-328-8588

SPECIAL SATURDAY: PARENT'S FACT BOOK

(1983) - an aid for parents to inform them of a special activity which was developed to compensate for the lack of volunteers to serve as big brothers and big sisters (involves the children on the waiting list in group activities once a week), 5pp, single copy free **Big Brothers/Big Sisters** 470 Mamaroneck Avenue, White Plains, NY 10605 914-948-8004

STIMULATING THE DEVELOPMENT OF OLDER VOLUNTEER PROGRAMS

(Vol. I, 1983) - guide for putting volunteers into place in areas that lack extensive service resources for older people; outlines how a central resource organization can provide the knowledge and expertise to help volunteer programs develop in local communities, 72pp, $6.50 **National Council on the Aging** 600 Maryland Avenue, SE, West Wing 100, Washington, DC 20024 202-479-1200

STOPOUT! WORKING WAYS TO LEARN

(1978) - volunteer opportunities, internships, and short-term jobs for the college student who must drop out of college for money reasons, or is unmotivated but hopes to finish his/her education at a later time; describes over 200 programs in areas of arts, communications, education, health, consumer protection, religion, the environment, women and minorities; includes "Stopout for Money," a section with special focus for those needing money to return to school, 214pp **Garrett Park Press** , Garrett Park, MD 20896 301-946-2553

STUDENT IMPACT

(monthly) - periodical which functions as the student voice in higher education as well as a forum for students advocating early involvement in human relations, political action, leadership training, and other programs that will serve to complement the educational curriculum, $5.00/year (free to members) **Student National Education Association** 1201 Sixteenth Street, NW, Washington, DC 20036 202-833-4000

STUDENT VOLUNTEER SERVICES BUREAU

(1971) - advantages to youth and community in having a volunteer bureau affiliated with the school; information on staffing, organization, funding, etc., 20pp, $1.82 **ERIC Document Reproduction Service** PO Box 190, Arlington, VA 22210 703-841-1212

SUPER VOLUNTEERS!

(1985) - a story introducing the *Super Volunteers!* who are four children of mixed heritage (one mentally retarded) who stumble and fall and make mistakes, but pick themselves up, learn from the experience, and find out what fun it is to do things for other people; presents story in a script format to encourage reading aloud by several children in the group; includes page to send back giving the child's views on volunteerism and an optional drawing (T-shirt transfer sent upon receipt of this page), 95pp, $1.95 plus

$.69 postage (leader/teacher guide, $.50 if ordered with book; quantity discounts available) **Four-One-One (411)** 7304 Beverly Street, Annandale, VA 22003 703-354-6270

SUPER VOLUNTEERS! GLENN, GINGER, CHARLIE AND LACY SAY... COME ON!! JOIN THE CLUB!!
(1985) - a detailed overview of *Super Volunteers!,* a program begun in 1985 to harness the enthusiasm and energy of the very young (ages 4-17) to meet expressed needs in the community; includes photographs of several teams, and information on materials to form a club (minimum 12 volunteers), 6-panel foldout, free **Little Red Hen** 7304 Beverly Street, Annandale, VA 22003 703-354-6270

SUPER VOLUNTEERS! SONG
(1985) - the marching song of the award-winning *Super Volunteers!,* which are teams of young people ages four to seventeen who work with school and community leaders to fill unmet needs, sung by former *Annie* cast member, cassette, $3.00 plus $1.00 handling **Little Red Hen** 7304 Beverly Street, Annandale, VA 22003 703-354-6270

SUPER VOLUNTEERS! (VIDEOCASSETTE)
(1990) - videocassette based on book of the same name, which is a story of four children and a dog who get into and out of trouble and learn along the way what fun it is to volunteer; designed for children and youth ages four to seventeen; includes leader/teacher guide, 25 minutes, $19.95 (slides and cassette tape also available, same price) **Little Red Hen** 7304 Beverly Street, Annandale, VA 22003 703-354-6270

TAP FOR TAP
(kept current) - a comprehensive packet of materials providing details on a program for youth ages 14-17 in conservation settings; includes fact sheets, reprographics, applications, bumper stickers and buttons, and other materials to assist a community in installing a TAP program, unpaged, single copy free **Touch America Project (TAP)** 1319 Eighteenth Street, NW, Washington, DC 20036

THESE ARE NOT STRANGERS
(undated) - a kit of materials in a quick-reference but comprehensive format to aid in the development of a youth volunteer program in a community college; covers staffing (paid and volunteer), role of the college, benefits of the program to the youth as well as the community, finance sources, leadership, etc., $1.00/kit (6 for $5.00) **Young Men's Christian Association of the U.S.** 101 North Wacker Drive, Chicago, IL 60606 312-977-0031

TO FIND THE WAY...TO OPPORTUNITIES AND SERVICES FOR OLDER AMERICANS
(1975) - guide addressed to senior citizens, outlining services available to them, but reminding them of the potential to improve the quality of these services through "senior power;" describes several volunteer programs involving older persons, and lists public agencies and private voluntary organizations with relevant local programs, 45pp, free **US/HHS - Administration on Aging** 330 C Street, SW, Washington, DC 20201 202-619-0724

TOUCH AMERICA PROJECT FOR YOUTH VOLUNTEERS
(kept current) - overview of a volunteer conservation program offered to young people ages 14-17; includes job descriptions, guidelines, legislation, and how to get a TAP program started in the community, 8-panel foldout, free **American Conservation Volunteers** 1319 Eighteenth Street, NW, Washington, DC 20036

TOWARDS BETTER COMMUNICATION THROUGH RESOURCE IDENTIFICATION

(1977) - a compilation of youth program resources in areas of youth involvement boards, action-learning schools, youth rights, consumer issues, etc.; includes extensive bibliography, 72pp, $2.00 **National Network of Youth Advisory Boards** PO Box 402036, Ocean View Branch, Miami Beach, FL 33140 305-532-2607

VOLUNTARY ACTION AND CONTRIBUTIVE ROLES FOR ELDERS
(1982) - an overview of issues related to older persons as volunteers, the future potential of the issues, government policy, the roles of corporations and organized labor, and institutional barriers to older volunteers, 27pp, $3.00 **National Council on the Aging** 600 Maryland Avenue, SW, West Wing 100, Washington, DC 20024 202-479-1200

VOLUNTARY ACTION AND OLDER AMERICANS
(1983) - a catalog of program profiles describing 28 programs involving older volunteers or conducting self-help mutual aid activities involving older people; includes programs operated by government at organizations, educational and cultural institutions, and religious organizations; covers staffing, recruitment and orientation, funding, and a general description of activities, 92pp, $6.50 **National Council on the Aging** 600 Maryland Avenue, SW, West Wing 100, Washington, DC 20024 212-479-1200

VOLUNTARY ACTION AND OLDER PEOPLE
(1983) - an annotated bibliography of more than 100 articles and monographs on the subject of voluntarism and self-help as related to older people; gives special emphasis to materials having broad or policy implications, 26pp, $3.00 **National Council on the Aging** 600 Maryland Avenue, SW, West Wing 100, Washington, DC 20024 202-479-1200

VOLUNTEENS ARE INCREDIBLE
(undated) - brochure describing a program utilizing young teenagers (13 years old or older, but including 12-year-olds entering eighth grade) to assist in a center for mentally retarded children and adults, 6-panel foldout, free **Western Carolina Center** Volunteer Services, Enola Road, Morganton, NC 28655 704-433-2614

VOLUNTEER JOBS IN PARKS AND FORESTS: THE STUDENT CONSERVATION PROGRAM
(1980) - overview of a program developed to enable agencies responsible for conservation/recreation to expand their services, and to offer young persons an outdoor educational experience with many benefits - skill development, career exploration, etc.; includes information on both high school and college programs, and a location directory, kit of publications and posters, free **Student Conservation Association** PO Box 550, Charleston, NH 03603 603-826-5203

VOLUNTEER OPPORTUNITIES
(kept current) - brief descriptions of volunteer opportunities in three of the clinic's service divisions: Administrative Services (eight positions); Medical Services (13 positions); and Educational Services (six positions), 6-panel foldout, free **Howard Brown Memorial Clinic** 945 West George Street, Chicago, IL 60657 312-871-5777

VOLUNTEERS!
(1985) - a factual account of one-to-one volunteer activities in line drawings taken from photographs in local volunteer programs in the community, most featuring children (with a volunteer coach, with a hospital volunteer, with a school resource volunteer, with a day care volunteer, with the First Lady at the circus, etc.); includes a narrative with each drawing, a page to send back with

the child's views on volunteerism and an optional drawing (a T-shirt transfer is sent upon receipt of this page); appends volunteer-related activity pages (dot-to-dot, color-by-number, etc.), 95 pages, $1.95 plus $.69 postage (teacher/leader guide, $.50 if ordered with book; quantity discounts available) **Four-One-One (411)** 7304 Beverly Street, Annandale, VA 22003 703-354-6270

VOLUNTEERS! (VIDEOCASSETTE)

(1990) - an audiocassette based on the book of the same time developed to provide vignettes of community volunteers for children and youth ages four to seventeen, to be used with or without book; includes leader/teacher guide, 25 minutes, $19.95 (slides and cassette tape also available, same price) **Little Red Hen** 7304 Beverly Street, Annandale, VA 22003 703-354-6270

WORKING WITH ALUMNI VOLUNTEERS

(1986) - a reprint from *Currents,* discussing recruitment training, retaining, and recognizes volunteers; includes section on how to establish good rapport between volunteers and staff, and how to spot danger signs and deal with troublesome volunteers before it is too late, 64pp, #22867, $6 (members); $7.50 (nonmembers) **Council for Advancement and Support of Education** Publications Order Department, 80 South Early Street, Alexandria, VA 22304 703-823-6966

YOUTH EXPLORING SERVICE (YES) PROGRAM

(kept current) - a booklet listing over 250 volunteer opportunities for youths at over 80 agencies for distribution to schools, and for use in soliciting PSAs (geared to Louisville, but a good example for other communities), unpaged, single copy free **Metro United Way** 334 East Broadway, PO Box 4488, Louisville, KY 40204-0488 502-583-2821

ORGANIZATION
NAME INDEX

A

A, B, and C on Burglary, pgs. 426, 716

AAA Michigan See Project Graduation

AAFRC Trust for Philanthropy, pg. 1016

AAL Drug and Alcohol Use Prevention Program, pg. 999

AAUW Educational Foundation, pgs. 431, 615

AAUW Group Effectiveness Team See Conference on Volunteerism

AAUW Legal Advocacy Fund, pgs. 431, 580

ABA Commission on the Mentally Disabled, pg. 1078

Abell Foundation See Homework Hotline

Ability Is Ageless, pgs. 54, 901

Abingdon Press, pgs. 1075, 1095

Abused Adult Resource Center (AARC), pgs. 333, 834

Acacia Federal Savings Bank, pgs. 35, 915

Academy for Educational Development, pg. 955

ACCA (Annandale Christian Community for Action) See Van Ministry

ACCESS, Inc. See The S.O.A.P.S.

Acropolis Books, pgs. 990, 1022

Action for Boston Community Development, pgs. 1029, 1059

Action for Independent Maturity, pg. 1067

Action Support Center for Ending Hunger See End Hunger Network

Actors and Others for Animals, pgs. 354, 782, 1094

AD Support Group of Greater Alabama, pgs. 453, 680

Adams' Express: A Mini-Grant Program, pgs. 111, 639

ADDitions School Volunteers, pgs. 299, 619, 641

Adelphi University, pgs. 161, 221, 241, 666, 872 See also The Systematic Involvement of Volunteers in Human Services

ADER, pg. 1010

Administration of Volunteer Programs and Operation of Social Agencies, pg. 183

Administration of Volunteer Services, pg. 228

Administration on Aging See Teaching Senior Center

Adolescent Pregnancy Prevention Clearinghouse, pg. 1099

Adolph Coors Company, pgs. 25, 975, 977

Adopt-A-Family, pgs. 117, 385, 683, 840

Adopt-A-School, pgs. 31, 621, 622 See also Partnerships

Adopt-A-School Dance Program, pgs. 32, 525

Adopt-A-Stream, pg. 780

Adult Career Center for Exceptional Persons See Garden of Young Hearts

Adult Foster Care, pgs. 385, 902

Adult Literacy Project, pg. 733

Adult Tutorial Program, pg. 624

Advanced Seminars in Volunteer Administration, pg. 228

Advertising Council, pgs. 61, 983

Advocacy By and For The Blind, pgs. 393, 847

Advocacy for Action: A New Role for Volunteers, pgs. 286, 554

Advocacy Institute, pgs. 556, 979, 980

AFB Mid-Atlantic Regional Center, pgs. 393, 847

Affordable Housing Project, pgs. 358, 687

Affordable Meetings, pg. 229

AFL-CIO, pg. 396

AFL-CIO Central Labor Council See Union Retirees Resources

AFL-CIO Community Services, pg. 1035

AFL-CIO Community Services Committee, pgs. 502, 919

African-American Festival of Academic Excellence, pgs. 296, 631

Aging Futures Project, pgs. 8, 896, 952

Aid to End AIDS Committee, pgs. 105, 519

Aid to Incarcerated Mothers, pg. 719

Aid to Victims of Crime*, pg. 729

AIDS Action Committee, pgs. 120, 519

AIDS Arms Network, Inc., pgs. 509, 959

AIDS Chronic Care Unit Volunteer Program, pgs. 494, 511

AIDS Hotline, pgs. 160, 520

AIDS in the Workplace, pgs. 31, 41, 516, 517

AIDS Prevention Program for Youth, pg. 510

AIDS Program, pg. 512

AIDS Project: Friendly Visitors, pg. 522

AIDS Public Education Program, pg. 515

AIDS-Walk New York, pgs. 119, 518

Air and Waste Management Association, pg. 762

Air Crash Drill, pgs. 434, 591

Air Force Members as Volunteers*, pg. 342

Air Products and Chemicals, pgs. 55, 919, 1082

Air Products Developmental Cycling Program, pgs. 55, 919

Airlifeline, pg. 996

AIRS Directory Project, pg. 1032

Alabama Children's Trust Fund See Blount County Children's Center

Alan C. Hood & Company, pg. 1017

Alan Young Buick See Help the Homeless Million Dollar Shootout

Albuquerque Public Schools See Rainbow Sunshine School

ALCOA See Recycling for Ravi

Alcoa Foundation See Orchestra Management Seminar

Alcohol Education for Youth and Community*, pg. 601

Alcoholics Anonymous (AA), pgs. 432, 602

Alcoholics Anonymous World Services, pgs. 598, 1096

Alcoholism and Substance Abuse - AIDS Program, pg. 601

Aldine de Gruyter, pg. 1067

Alexander Graham Bell Association for the Deaf, pg. 854

Alexander Human Development Center Volunteer Council, pgs. 415, 852

Alexander Parents Organization See Alexander Human Development Center Volunteer Council

Alexandria Chamber of Commerce See Employee Assistance Programs

Alexandria Community Mental Health Center, pg. 740

Alexandria Community Shelter See Substance Abuse Treatment Center and Shelter

Alexandria Hospital, pgs. 670, 1088 See also Ask the Doctor; Fairfax Alternative Services Workshop

Alexandria Memorial Baptist Church See Black Georgetown Reunion Group

Alexandria Mental Health and Substance Abuse Board, pgs. 459, 876

Alexandria Parent-Teachers Association See Good Neighbor Exchange Program

Alexandria Police Department See Drunk-Driving Simulator Program and Forum

Alexandria Public Schools, pgs. 438, 829

Alexandria Volunteer Bureau See Volunteer Program Management

Alexis de Tocqueville Society, pg. 101

Alexis de Tocqueville Society Program, pg. 15

All Saints Episcopal Church See Free Hotline

All Souls Church, pgs. 450, 727

Allegheny County Community College, pgs. 186, 255, 261, 279, 286, 554, 656

ALLGO, pgs. 384, 518

Alliance for a Living Ocean See Beachfront Volunteers

Alliance for Neighborhood Government See National Association of Neighborhoods

Alliance for the Chesapeake Bay, pg. 1055

Alliance for the Mentally Ill of Greater Milwaukee, pg. 1049

Alliance for Volunteerism, pgs. 14, 555

Alliance of Guardian Angels, pgs. 496, 710

Alliance of Information and Referral Systems, pgs. 155, 1031, 1033

Alliance to Save Energy See Performance Contracting

Allis-Chalmers Corporation, pg. 972

Alpine Rescue Team, pgs. 495, 592

Alston Wilkes Society, pg. 661

Alternative Education and Work Center, pgs. 429, 649

Alternative House, pgs. 312, 814, 1067

Aluminum Company of America See Recycling for Ravi

Alzheimer's Disease & Related Disorders Association, pgs. 453, 680, 902, 1067

Amateur Radio Emergency Service (ARES), pgs. 47, 591

Ameribanc Adopt-A-School Program, pgs. 38, 622

Ameribanc Savings Bank, pgs. 38, 622

America Responds to AIDS, pgs. 67, 513

America The Beautiful Fund, pg. 760

American Academy of Crisis Interveners, pgs. 174, 744, 1032, 1033

American Academy of Ophthalmology Foundation, pgs. 172, 679

American Academy of Pediatrics See Art for Kids' Sake

American Association for Adult and Continuing Education, pgs. 623, 1009

American Association for Corporate Contributions, pgs. 97, 1015, 1016

American Association for Leisure and Recreation, pg. 917

American Association for State and Local History, pg. 1016

American Association of Counseling & Development See Military Educators and Counselors Association

American Association of Retired Persons, pgs. 396, 895, 901, 1004, 1013, 1081 See also Bluegrass Medicare-Medicaid Assistance Program; Conference on Nonprofit Leadership and Management; Legal Counsel for the Elderly; ROVERS (Retired and Older Volunteers: An Educational Resource Service)

American Association of University Women, pgs. 431, 580, 615, 981 See also Volunteers: Empowerment Today and Tomorrow

American Athletic Association for the Deaf*, pg. 854

American Automobile Association, pgs. 1072, 1092

American BankCard Services See Partnership BankCard Systems*

American Bankers Association, pgs. 989, 990

American Bar Association, pgs. 332, 433, 439, 573, 813, 881, 991, 1028, 1094 See also Council on Legal Education Opportunity

American Blind Bowling Association, pg. 845

American Camping Association, pgs. 917, 1052, 1081, 1083

American Cancer Society, pgs. 469, 665

American Cancer Society, Ohio Division, pgs. 666, 1024

American Chamber of Commerce Executives See National Association of Community Leadership Organizations

American Civil Liberties Union, pgs. 433, 717

American Coalition of Citizens with Disabilities*, pgs. 857, 1076, 1078

American Community Cultural Center Association, pg. 524

American Conservation Volunteers, pgs. 488, 776, 1100

American Council for the Arts, pgs. 524, 966, 967, 1015, 1016, 1017, 1019

American Council of the Blind, pgs. 330, 845

American Council on Alcohol Problems, pg. 602

American Craft Council, pgs. 188, 526

American Driver and Traffic Safety Education Association, pg. 1000

American Farmland Trust See National Celebration of the Outdoors

American Federation of Arts, pgs. 68, 528

American Federation of Police, pgs. 494, 708

American Forest Council, pg. 1060

American Forestry Association See Touch America Project (TAP)

American Foundation for AIDS Research, pgs. 105, 508, 962

American Foundation for the Blind, pgs. 845, 1076, 1077, 1080, 1096

American Greeting Card Company See Art for Kids' Sake

American Health Care Association, pgs. 398, 906, 947, 1044, 1049, 1074

American Heart Association See National Coalition for Volunteer Protection; Volunteer Leadership: Challenges For The Nineties

American Hiking Society, pgs. 1060, 1083, 1084 See also National Celebration of the Outdoors

American Hospital Association, pgs. 3, 663

American Humane Association, pgs. 171, 782

American Indian Partnerships with United Ways*, pg. 300

American Institute of Cooperation, pg. 576

American Library Association, pgs. 636, 966, 968, 1010, 1033 See also Institute on Federal Library Resources

American Lung Association, pgs. 678, 762, 1055 See also Conference on Volunteerism

American Lung Association of New Hampshire See Lakes Region Conference on Volunteerism - Volunteers: A Caring Resource; A Practical Perspective

American Lung Association of Northern Virginia, pgs. 114, 678

The American Lutheran Church See Lutheran Social Services Volunteer Program

American Medical Association, pgs. 197, 599, 612, 1022 See also Mission House

American Nutrition Society, pg. 749

American Parents Committee, pgs. 413, 796

American Plant Food Company See School Ecology Project

American Psychiatric Association, pgs. 174, 744, 1048, 1049, 1075

American Radio Relay See Wheelchair Race Communications Services

American Reading Council, pg. 639

American Red Cross, pgs. 60, 172, 232, 235, 261, 342, 403, 410, 436, 443, 465, 477, 493, 590, 592, 593, 595, 672, 677, 786, 812, 893, 919, 956, 958, 1024, 1097, 1098 See also Buddies for Life; Everyday Heroes; Homelessness Prevention Program; National Coalition for Volunteer Protection; Navy Volunteers at Guantanamo Bay; Volunteer Training

American Red Cross, Mid-America Chapter See Disaster Professional Volunteer Network

American Red Cross of Greater Central New Hampshire See Lakes Region Conference on Volunteerism - Volunteers: A Caring Resource; A Practical Perspective

American Red Cross Office of HIV/AIDS Education, pgs. 31, 105, 509, 510, 514, 515, 517, 518, 960, 961, 962, 963, 964, 965

American Red Cross/Saratoga County See Maplewood Manor RSVP Program

American Red Cross, Syracuse Chapter See Bloodmobile

American Red Cross/Virginia Capital Chapter See Youth Services

American Social Health Association, pgs. 178, 680, 681, 1025

American Society for the Prevention of Cruelty to Animals, pg. 782

American Society of Association Executives See National Coalition for Volunteer Protection

American Society of Composers, Authors and Publishers (ASCAP) See James Madison National Council

American Society of Directors of Volunteer Services, pgs. 3, 663

American Stock Exchange See James Madison National Council

American Symphony Orchestra League, pgs. 189, 277, 539, 967, 968, 969, 1016, 1017

American Television and Communications Corporation See Cablevision by the People*

American University, pgs. 253, 264 See also Champ Bakery

American Values: The Community Action Network, pg. 79

American Youth Hostels, pg. 1092

American Youth Work Center, pg. 1013

AmFar, pgs. 105, 508

Amherst Wilder Foundation, pgs. 318, 785

Amherst Y.E.S. (Youth Engaged in Service), pg. 466

Amherst Youth Board, pg. 466

Andrus Gerontology Center, pg. 1099

Annandale Christian Community for Action (ACCA), pgs. 113, 358, 360, 362, 364, 365, 369, 374, 584, 641, 831, 832, 836, 873, 886, 936, 1097
See also Bailey's Crossroads Community Shelter; Van Ministry

Annandale Lions Club, pgs. 390, 847

Anti-Drug Teams, pgs. 499, 609

Appalachian Mountain Club, pgs. 917, 928, 1082, 1083, 1084

Appalachian Search and Rescue Conference See Six Friends Memorial Fund

Apples for the Students, pgs. 38, 626

ARC Covenant, pgs. 358, 882

Archaeological Volunteer Program, pg. 525

Archdiocese of Detroit See Prevention through Action

Arden Publications, pg. 950

Area Agency on Aging, pg. 267 See also Senior Connection

Area VII Senior Companion Program See Volunteer Training

ArHA/Council on Volunteer Training Events, pgs. 304, 675

ArHA Council on Volunteers See ArHA/Council on Volunteer Training Events

The Arizona Department of Economic Security See The Volunteerism Project; Women Off Welfare (WOW)

Arizona Hospital Association, pgs. 304, 675

Arizona State University See Communications Workshop/Perspectives for Volunteers

Arkansas Convalescent Center, pg. 904

Arkansas Department of Human Services, pg. 556

Arkansas Division of Aging and Adult Services, pgs. 124, 562, 1099

Arkansas Division of Volunteerism, pg. 124

Arkansas Elks Association See Alexander Human Development Center Volunteer Council

Arkansas Office of Volunteerism, pg. 89 See also Certified Volunteer Manager Program; Institute on Volunteer Administration: A Proposal; Volunteer Consultant Services Program

Arkansas Office of Volunteers, pg. 947

Arkansas Public Administration Consortium, pg. 234

Arkansas State University See Certified Volunteer Manager Program

Arlington County Police Department See Drunk-Driving Simulator Program and Forum

Arlington County Public Schools See Principal on the Roof*

The Arlington County Temporary Shelter (TACTS), pgs. 170, 307, 833, 884, 1079

Arlington Hospital, pgs. 114, 671, 1023

Arlington Hospital Foundation, pgs. 114, 671

Arlington Volunteer Services See Volunteer Program Management

Army Child Care Technical Assistance Conference, pg. 889

Army Community Service, pgs. 344, 890

Army Community Service Volunteer Training, pg. 275

Arrowhead 22: Future Challenges: A Universal Perspective, pg. 320

Arrowhead United Way See Social Action Corps

Art Against AIDS, pgs. 75, 105, 528, 540

Art Against AIDS Exhibit, pgs. 105, 528

Art for Kids' Sake, pgs. 434, 801

Art Vistas Docents See Young Authors' Faire

Arthur Anderson & Company See Business/Industry Advisory Council (BIAC)

Arts and Business Council, pgs. 32, 526

Arts Council of Greater Grand Rapids, pgs. 387, 530

Ask the Doctor, pgs. 434, 678

Asociacion Nacional Por Personas Mayores, pg. 901

Aspects of Administrative Functions for Managers of Volunteer Programs, pg. 229

Assembly of State Offices on Volunteerism, pg. 122

Assistance League of Pasadena See California House

Assistance to Earthquake Victims, pgs. 349, 592

Associated Services for the Blind, pg. 845

Association for Childhood Education International, pgs. 586, 966, 981, 992, 994, 995, 1008, 1065

Association for Children and Adults with Learning Disabilities See Learning Disabilities Association of America

Association for Commuter Transportation, pg. 937

Association for Jewish Children of Philadelphia, pg. 956

Association for Retarded Citizens, pgs. 47, 863, 864, 1068

Association for Retarded Citizens of Georgia, pgs. 453, 1094, 1096, 1098

Association for Retarded Citizens of Northern Virginia See Citizen Advocacy

Association for Volunteer Administration, pgs. 3, 188, 229, 243, 245, 250, 252, 258, 271, 274, 509, 568, 945, 950, 952, 982, 985, 1051, 1089, 1090 See also AYE SHARE; Volunteer & Community Partnerships Institute; Volunteer Program Management; Volunteers in Great Britain: A Study Tour

Association for Volunteer Administration, Region IV, pgs. 65, 246, 945

Association for Volunteer Administration, Region X, pg. 244

Association of American Law Schools See Council on Legal Education Opportunity

Association of Certified Servers, pgs. 382, 602
Association of Community Organizations for Reform Now (ACORN), pgs. 451, 582
Association of Evangelical Lutheran Churches See Lutheran Social Services Volunteer Program
Association of Halfway House Alcoholism Programs of North America, pgs. 602, 997
Association of Junior Leagues, pgs. 197, 322, 623 See also Minority Volunteers: Pluralism in the Volunteer Arena; Project LEAD
Association of Ladies of Charity of the US, pgs. 354, 824 See also Catholic Charities USA
Association of Nervous & Former Mental Patients, pgs. 453, 745
Association of Retired Faculty (NC State) See ROVERS (Retired and Older Volunteers: An Educational Resource Service)
Association of Voluntary Action Scholars, pgs. 3, 230, 615 See also AYE SHARE; Conference on Nonprofit Leadership and Management; Credit and Degree Programs in Voluntary Association Administration in Colleges and Universities; National Conference on Volunteerism
Association of Volunteer Centers, pgs. 3, 949, 1089 See also Interconnections
Association of Volunteer Centers (AVC) See National Conference on Volunteerism
Association Press, pg. 947
Associations for the Education of the Deaf See Special Materials Project*
Athletics Congress See Junior National Track and Field
Atlanta Community Food Bank, pg. 751
Atlanta Public Schools, pg. 473
Atlantic Electric Company, pgs. 30, 977
Atlantic Richfield Company, pg. 976
Atlantic Richfield Foundation See California Literacy*
Audience Arts, pg. 966
Audubon Naturalist Society, pgs. 443, 770, 771, 776, 956, 1055
Augsburg Fortress, pgs. 991, 1049, 1066, 1077, 1079
Augsburg Publishing House, pg. 1038
Augusta Mental Health Institute, pgs. 341, 726
Austin Family Court See CASA (Court Appointed Special Advocates)
Automotive Consumer Action Program (AUTOCAP), pgs. 451, 582
Autumn Stages, pgs. 402, 534, 1094
AVA Certification Program, pg. 229
AVAS Annual Conference, pg. 230
Avenues to Awareness: A Program for the Volunteer, pg. 230
AYE SHARE, pg. 231

B

B. Dalton Bookseller See Adult Literacy Project; California Literacy*
Back Roads Bike Trek, pgs. 114, 678
Bailey's Crossroads Community Shelter, pgs. 359, 885
Bain & Company See City Year
Balanced Budgets for Consumers, pg. 578
Ball State University, pg. 243
Baltimore City Health Department, pg. 406
Baltimore City School System See Homework Hotline
Bank of Boston See City Year; From All Walks of Life
Bank of New England See From All Walks of Life
Bank Street College of Education, pg. 930

The Barn Players See Senior Acting Program of the Barn Players*
Baroque Music Festival of Corona del Mar, pg. 529
Basic Accounting Assistance, pg. 9
Basic Leader Training Course, pgs. 296, 639
Basic Management of Volunteer Programs, pg. 231
Basic Managerial Skills for Directors of Volunteers, pg. 232
Basics of Volunteer Program Management*, pg. 147
Basket of Joy Campaign, pgs. 467, 909, 1065
Battered Women's Shelter See The S.O.A.P.S.
Bay Area SCORE Program, pgs. 435, 544
Bay Ridge Nutrition and Home Care Programs, pgs. 379, 757
Be Alive in 2005: Promoting Wellness into the 21st Century, pgs. 344, 671
Beachfront Volunteers, pgs. 467, 762
Beacon Press, pgs. 970, 988, 992, 993, 1012, 1023, 1034, 1036, 1037, 1039, 1053, 1072, 1073, 1077, 1087
Beaver County Day School, pg. 471
Beaver County Federated Library System, pg. 733
Bechtel Group, Inc., pgs. 440, 626
Beery Middle School See Adopt-A-Family
Befriender Training, pgs. 318, 785
Befrienders International Samaritans Worldwide See Samaritans; The Samaritans; The Samaritans USA
The Belknap Mill See Lakes Region Conference on Volunteerism - Volunteers: A Caring Resource; A Practical Perspective
Bell Atlantic See Business/Industry Advisory Council (BIAC)
Bell Laboratories See Street News Homeless Vendors Program
Bell of Pennsylvania, pg. 855
Beloit Daily News See United Way Editorial Board
Benjamin Banneker High School, pg. 471
Benjamin Company, pgs. 1002, 1085
Bergen County Bar Association See Record Debate Classic
Bergen County Board of Education See Record Debate Classic
Berks Community Television, pg. 64
Berks County Chamber of Commerce See Berks Schoolcasting*
Berks County Schools See Berks Schoolcasting*
Berks Schoolcasting*, pgs. 64, 619
Berks-Suburban Cable Company See Berks Schoolcasting*
Bernardsville Business Alliance See Litterthon
Bernardsville Environmental Commission See Litterthon
Bernie's Modern Formal Shop See CPSS Fashion Show
Bespak Corporation See CATCH Program
The B.E.S.T. Project, pgs. 467, 632
The Best Years, pgs. 74, 897
Betances School See Home-Based Child Care in Hartford
Bethel AME Church, pgs. 173, 755
Bethel Love Kitchen, pgs. 173, 755
Bethel New Life See Statewide Leadership Symposium: Working Together to Make Visions Realities
Bethesda HELP, pg. 157
Beverly Hospital See Looking Ahead: Managing Tomorrow's Volunteers
Bicycle Safety and Seat Belt Awareness Programs, pgs. 56, 937
Big Brothers/Big Sisters, pgs. 1083, 1099 See also Special Saturday

Big Brothers/Big Sisters of America, pgs. 447, 820, 1094 See also National Coalition for Volunteer Protection; National Collaboration for Youth
Big Brothers/Big Sisters of Nassau County*, pgs. 447, 820
Big Brothers/Big Sisters of Waynesboro, pg. 1079
Big Brothers/Big Sisters Program, pgs. 448, 820
Big Brothers/Big Sisters Program-Child Psychiatry*, pgs. 448, 821
Big Country Retired Senior Volunteer Program, pgs. 7, 402, 691
Bioregional Project, pg. 770
Birmingham Area Alliance of Business, pgs. 42, 658
Bishop Airport Authority, pgs. 113, 859
Black Georgetown Reunion Group, pgs. 359, 533
Black Hawk College See Volunteers: Empowerment Today and Tomorrow
Black Hawk County Extension See Volunteer Training
Black Hawk County Retired Senior Volunteer Program See Volunteer Training
Blockbuster Community Service Program, pg. 24
Blockbuster Entertainment Corporation, pg. 24
Bloodmobile, pgs. 468, 664
Blount County Children's Center, pg. 815
Blue Cross of Southern California See Public Relations on a Shoestring*
Blue Ridge Area Food Bank*, pgs. 51, 751, 1052
Blue Ridge to the White House: Wheelchair Race of Champions, pgs. 47, 868
Bluegrass Medicare-Medicaid Assistance Program, pgs. 399, 903
Blueprint, pg. 740
B'nai B'rith Community Volunteer Services, pgs. 986, 987
B'nai B'rith International, pgs. 946, 1000, 1003, 1023, 1024, 1025, 1027, 1037, 1038, 1040, 1056, 1057, 1059, 1060, 1065, 1069, 1074, 1075, 1077, 1079, 1091
B'nai B'rith Youth Organization, pgs. 998, 999, 1096, 1098
Board Development Consultation Service, pg. 183
Board Leadership and Development, pg. 183
Board Management Training Workshop, pg. 183
Board of Church and Society, pgs. 997, 1002
Boarder Baby Project, pgs. 33, 798
Boardsmanship Seminar*, pg. 184
Boeing Company, pg. 972 See also Governors' School
Boise Peace Quilt Project, pg. 565
Bonus Books, pgs. 1014, 1017, 1018
Book People, pg. 984
Bordeaux Hospital See Partners in Caring
Boston Bar Association See City Year
Boston College See Looking Ahead: Managing Tomorrow's Volunteers
Boston Foundation See Teens as Community Resources*
Boston Globe Foundation See From All Walks of Life
Boston University, pg. 265
Bostrom Alternative Center for Education*, pg. 650
Boulder Public Library, pg. 636
Boulder Valley Public Schools, pg. 957
Boy Scouts; Law Engineering See Tampa Causeway Beautification Project
Boy Scouts of America, pgs. 57, 59, 60, 422, 613, 809, 851, 852 See also National Celebration of the Outdoors; National Collaboration for Youth; Ottawa River "Fighting Back" Campaign; Project Bravo

Boys & Girls Clubs of Greater Washington, pgs. 58, 608, 798, 874, 1068 *See also Project Right Start*

Bread and Roses, pgs. 106, 538

Breakthrough Foundation, pgs. 94, 566

Brethren Volunteer Service, pg. 1098

The Bridge, pgs. 34, 232, 874

Bridgeport Post *See Fairfield 2000*

Bridging Volunteer Resources, pg. 232

Bronx AIDS Volunteer Organization, pgs. 388, 513

Bronx Development Council *See New Directions for the Bronx*

Brookdale Community College, pgs. 399, 545

Brookdale-SCORE Program, pgs. 399, 545

Brooklyn AIDS Task Force, pgs. 468, 517

Broome County Department of Social Services, pgs. 458, 834

Broward Community College *See Volunteers In Action*

Broward County Parks & Recreation Division *See Horses and the Handicapped of South Florida*

Brown Program in Leadership, pg. 192

Brown University, pgs. 191, 192, 309, 467, 485, 491, 537, 632, 738, 775, 1005, 1046, 1098

Brown University Center for Public Service, pg. 986

Browning Ferris Industries *See Ottawa River "Fighting Back" Campaign*

Bruce-Monroe Elementary School, pgs. 436, 547

Bruner, Middleton & Associates *See Give Me Shelter: Designs for Urban Survival*

Bryant Adult Community Education Center, pgs. 458, 933

Buddies for Life, pg. 664

Buehler Products *See CATCH Program*

Buffalo Department of Human Resources *See Conference on Volunteerism*

Building an Effective Board, pg. 184

Building and Construction Trades Council of Rochester *See Camp Good Days and Special Times Rebuilding Project*

Building Better Boards, pg. 184

Building Better Boards: Legal Liability and Responsibilities, pg. 184

Building Creative Organizations*, pg. 185

Building Momentum for a Responsive America, pgs. 287, 558

Building Partnerships with Corporations, pg. 23

Building Seismic Safety Council, pgs. 432, 591

Bureau of Drug Abuse Services Grants Program, pgs. 110, 607

Burgess Publishing Company, pg. 1083

Business Committee for the Arts, pgs. 32, 526

Business/Community Involvement Program, pg. 46

Business Concentration Toward Charities, pg. 24

Business/Industry Advisory Council (BIAC), pgs. 38, 619

Business/Industry Program, pg. 22

Business Information and Resource Council, pg. 139

Business Issues in the Classroom, pgs. 37, 626

Business Management/Junior Achievement, pgs. 43, 546

Business Roundtable, pg. 973

Business/School Partnership Program, pgs. 25, 622

But I'm Different..., pgs. 69, 931

Buyers Up, pgs. 577, 988

C

Cabarrus County Schools, pg. 650

Cable-Wiedemer, Inc. *See Camp Good Days and Special Times Rebuilding Project*

Cablevision by the People*, pg. 64

Cabrillo Economic Development Corporation, pg. 1085

Cabrillo Improvement Association, pgs. 454, 692

Cabrillo Village, pgs. 454, 692

California Board of Education *See FOCUS (Families of Children United for Safety)*

California Council for Veterans Affairs, pgs. 378, 894

California Department of Education, pgs. 416, 931

California Hospital Association, pg. 272

California House, pgs. 83, 911

California Literacy*, pg. 733

California Park and Recreation Society *See Morro Bay Harbor Festival*

California State University, pgs. 228, 474

Call for Action, pg. 155

CALM *See Child Abuse Listening Mediation*

Cambridge Mental Health and Developmental Center, pg. 1049

Camp Fire, pgs. 57, 809

Camp Good Days and Special Times, pgs. 469, 665

Camp Good Days and Special Times Rebuilding Project, pgs. 502, 919

Campaign Drug Free, pgs. 348, 610

Campaign for Human Development, pg. 226

Campbell Soup Company *See 4-H Specific Forums: Adult Volunteer Training*

Campus Literacy Awareness Month Program, pgs. 469, 733

Campus Ministry, pg. 360

Campus Outreach Opportunity League (COOL), pgs. 291, 324, 461, 946, 953, 987, 1046, 1073, 1094 *See also Volunteers: Empowerment Today and Tomorrow*

Cancer Care, pg. 1022

Cancer Task Force *See Help-On-Wheels*

Candle Lighters, pg. 101

Candle Lighters' Proposal Lunch, pg. 101

Canton Middle School *See Homework Hotline*

Cape May County Volunteers and Resources, pgs. 169, 837

Cape May County Welfare Board *See Cape May County Volunteers and Resources*

Capital Area Community Food Bank, pgs. 52, 751 *See also Neighbors Helping Neighbors*

Capital Associates *See CATCH Program*

Capital Centre *See People Need People Volunteer Fair*

Capital Metropolitan Transportation Authority, pgs. 34, 936

Capitol Hill Association of Merchants and Professionals, pgs. 173, 880

Cardinal Gibbons High School, pg. 647

Care About the Strays, pg. 782

The Care and Nourishment of Volunteers*, pg. 232

Career Development for Volunteer Leadership, pg. 277

Carkhuff Institute of Human Technology, pgs. 284, 789

Carnegie Council on Adolescent Development, pg. 1006

Carnegie Foundation *See Student Volunteers*

Carondelet Community Betterment Federation, pgs. 50, 693

Carondelet Management Institute, pg. 6

Carrier Alert, pg. 382

Cary High School PTSA *See CATCH Program*

CASA, pgs. 331, 807

Casa Colina Hospital *See Organization for After-Stroke Resources*

CASA (Court Appointed Special Advocates), pgs. 334, 800

CASA National *See Court Appointed Special Advocates (CASA)*

CASA of Travis County, pgs. 334, 800

CASA Project (Court Appointed Special Advocates), pgs. 334, 575

CATCH Program, pgs. 415, 635

Catholic Charities, pgs. 366, 654 *See also Continental Homeless Assistance Program*

Catholic Charities USA, pgs. 97, 952

Catholic Committee of Appalachia, pgs. 355, 838

Catholic Communications Center, pg. 1095

Catholic Family Services *See Family AIDS Education Project*

Catholic University of America, pgs. 156, 636

Catholic Youth Organization, pgs. 482, 604

CAUSE (Community and University Services in Education), pgs. 469, 625

CB Radio Patrol, pgs. 494, 708

CB Radio Posse *See CB Radio Patrol*

CBS/Fox Video, pg. 1087

CE-2, pgs. 41, 625

CEC Special Project: ERIC Clearinghouse on Handicapped and Gifted Children, pgs. 170, 860

Cecil County Public Schools, pg. 642

Cecil County Public Schools Volunteer Program, pg. 642

Celebration of Volunteerism: Annual Statewide Conference, pg. 147

Celebrity Auction*, pg. 107

Centennial School District Wellness Committee, pgs. 305, 667

Center for Arts Information, pg. 524

Center for Auto Safety, pgs. 330, 937

Center for Community Change, pgs. 204, 552

Center for Corporate Public Involvement, pg. 22

Center for Creative Community, pgs. 4, 15, 243, 569, 948, 949, 953, 954, 955 *See also Career Development for Volunteer Leadership; DOVIA Skill Development Workshops*; Institute on Volunteer Administration: A Proposal*

Center for Early Adolescence, pgs. 283, 796

Center for Environmental Education *See Clean the Bay Day*

Center for Family and Child Enrichment *See Family AIDS Education Project*

Center for Information on America, pgs. 561, 981, 1013, 1085

Center for Literacy, pgs. 733, 734, 1046

Center for Marine Conservation, pg. 781

Center for National Policy Review, pg. 1028

Center for Organizational and Community Development, pgs. 94, 566

Center for Perinatal Addiction, pg. 1087

Center for Prevention and Treatment of Sexual Abuse, pgs. 146, 726

Center for Public Policy, pg. 954

Center for Public Service, pg. 309

Center for Religion, Ethics and Social Policy, pg. 313

Center for Science in the Public Interest, pgs. 750, 1052, 1053

Center for Study of Responsive Law, pg. 571

Center for the American Woman and Politics, pgs. 955, 979

Center for the Study of Parent Involvement, pgs. 204, 638

Center for the Study of Social Administration *See Minority Volunteers: Pluralism in the Volunteer Arena*

Center for Voluntary Action *See Volunteerism: A Bridge to the Future*

Center for Volunteer Development, pgs. 14, 99

Center for Youth Development and Research, pgs. 1089, 1098

Center for Youth Service, pgs. 59, 811

Center on Budget and Policy Priorities, pg. 952

Central Fairfax Services, pg. 858

Central Florida Association of Health and Social Services See More Than Meets The Ear - A Listening Skills Seminar

Central Lutheran Church, pgs. 360, 632

Central Michigan University See Michigan Special Olympics State Games

Central Naugatuck Valley Retired Senior Volunteer Program, pg. 399

Central Summer School, pgs. 360, 632

Central Wisconsin Association of Volunteer Administrators, pg. 241 See also Volunteer Administrator's Conference

Centrum of Hollywood See CHIP-IN

Cerebral Palsy of the South Shore, pgs. 394, 850

Cerebral Palsy Sports Program, pg. 850

Certificate in Volunteer Management, pg. 233

Certificate Program in Volunteer Administration, pg. 234

Certified Volunteer Manager Program, pg. 234

CETA See The Shed Project*; Voluntary Action Center of South Lake Tahoe; WMNR Radio - Access Broadcasting Company*

Chairman of Volunteers Gallery, pg. 16

Challenge International, pgs. 71, 842

Challenges for Alternative Sentencing in Our Communities, pg. 723

Chamber of Commerce, pgs. 40, 415, 635, 791

Chamber of Commerce Literacy Council, pgs. 50, 734

Chamber of Commerce of the United States, pgs. 542, 970, 971

Champ Bakery, pgs. 426, 802

Champions Run For Life Torch Relay, pgs. 120, 665

Champlain Valley Union High School, pg. 473

CHAMPS See Give Them A Hand, Not A Handout

Changing Values in Experiential Education*, pg. 310

Changing Ways We Do Business: New Roles and Responsibilities, pg. 301

Channel 4 See Child Identification Program

Channing L. Bete Company, pgs. 959, 961, 982, 990, 992, 997, 999, 1000, 1003, 1004, 1005, 1007, 1011, 1013, 1023, 1025, 1026, 1029, 1036, 1038, 1041, 1049, 1052, 1055, 1058, 1060, 1071, 1074, 1081, 1087

Chapel Hill Training Outreach Project, pgs. 298, 618

Chaplain Resource Board, pg. 1097

Chaplin Education System See Senior Course on Volunteerism

Chapter Grants Program, pgs. 105, 518

Chapter II Block Grant See Project OASES

Chapter Ten Services Board See Central Fairfax Services

Charity Plane Ride for Orange Grove, pg. 101

Charity Sports, pgs. 115, 878 See also Loaves & Fishes

Charles C. Thomas, Publisher, pgs. 947, 1032

Chateau Gardens See Polish Legion of American Veterans Auxiliary

Chatham College, pg. 235

Chatham Management Seminar, pg. 235

Chattanooga Nature Center, pg. 771

Chemeketa Community College, pg. 268

Cherokee United Way See American Indian Partnerships with United Ways*

Chesapeake Campaign, pg. 769

Chesapeake College, pg. 322

Chicago Board of Education, pgs. 351, 647

Chicago Building Department, pg. 1029

Chicago City-Wide College, pg. 290

Chicago Community Trust See Community Programs

Chicago Education Corps See Saturday Scholars

Chicago Public Library, pg. 636 See also Volunteer Leadership: Challenges For The Nineties; Volunteers: Empowerment Today and Tomorrow

Chicago Public Library Volunteer Services, pg. 636

Chicago Runaway Switchboard, pgs. 162, 805

Child Abuse Hotline, pgs. 165, 812

Child Abuse Listening Mediation, pgs. 165, 812, 1031

Child Abuse Services Team (CAST), pgs. 427, 815

Child and Family Services See Young Volunteers in Action*

Child and Family Services of Knox County, pg. 841

Child Assault Prevention Team, pgs. 495, 815

Child Development Centers of ACCA, pgs. 360, 584

Child Find of America, pgs. 812, 1069

Child Identification Program, pgs. 33, 815

Child Protective Services, pgs. 816, 1031, 1039, 1049, 1066, 1067, 1068, 1087

Child Security Network, pg. 1074

Child Security Network of Connecticut, pgs. 162, 816

Child Welfare League of America, pgs. 330, 434, 561, 800, 801, 930, 992, 993, 994, 1019, 1049, 1066, 1071, 1072, 1075, 1086, 1087, 1094, 1097 See also Art for Kids' Sake

Children as Peacemakers, pgs. 461, 563

Children: The Time is Now, pgs. 333, 807

Children's Defense Fund, pgs. 330, 557, 1034, 1051, 1068, 1069, 1071

Children's Foundation, pg. 586

Children's Literacy Initiative, pgs. 318, 734

Children's Memorial Hospital of Oklahoma See Teenline

Children's Miracle Network Telethon, pgs. 109, 804

Children's Quilt Project, pgs. 400, 511

Children's Room, pg. 636

CHIP/AHIP (Charlottesville Housing Improvement Program/Albemarle Housing Improvement Program), pgs. 469, 693

CHIP-IN, pgs. 361, 885

CHISS (Consumer Housing Information Service for Seniors), pgs. 174, 689

The Choice is Yours, pgs. 429, 703

Christ Episcopal Church, pgs. 373, 745

Christian Family Services of Lapeer County See Project Graduation

Christian Involvement, pg. 361

Christian Service Department, pg. 361

Christian Service Program, pg. 362

Christmas Basket Program, pgs. 386, 835

Christmas Clearing House, pgs. 45, 835

Christmas Toy Shop, pg. 919

Christmas Wishes, pg. 836

Christopher D. Smithers Foundation, pg. 598

Chronicle Guidance Publications, pg. 956

Chronicle of Higher Education, pg. 1014

Chrysalis House, pg. 612

Church People for Change and Reconciliation, pgs. 372, 693

Church Volunteer Administration, pg. 308

CIPED (Community Involvement Personal Education Development), pgs. 470, 625

Citadel Retirement Community, pgs. 305, 902

Citation Press, pgs. 995, 1008

Citibank See Student Volunteer/Work Project (SV/WP)

Citizen Advocacy, pgs. 334, 844

Citizen Advocates for Justice, pgs. 335, 701

Citizen Involvement Training Program, pgs. 980, 985, 986, 987, 1019, 1041, 1089 See also Center for Organizational and Community Development

Citizen Involvement Training Project (CITP), pg. 290

Citizen/Labor Energy Coalition, pg. 772

Citizens Advisory Commission See North Shore Civil Defense Team

Citizens Against Substance Abuse (CASA) See Kids Helping Kids

Citizens Committee on Youth, pgs. 40, 656, 1012

Citizens Communication Center, pg. 61

Citizens' Crime Watch of Dade County, pgs. 454, 709

Citizens for a Better Bernardsville (CBB), pg. 779

Citizens for Safe Drivers Against Drunk Drivers/Chronic Offenders, pgs. 451, 938

Citizens Forum on Self-Government, pgs. 287, 567

Citizens Information Service*, pgs. 79, 552, 1034, 1039, 1056, 1085

Citizens Organized Patrol Efforts (COPE), pgs. 455, 709

Citizens Program for the Chesapeake Bay, pg. 1055

Citizens' Scholarship Foundation of America, pgs. 102, 641

City Harvest, pg. 1053

City of Alexandria See Alexandria Community Mental Health Center

City of Austin See Roadrunner Program

City of Boulder See Children's Room

City of Charlottesville See CHIP/AHIP (Charlottesville Housing Improvement Program/Albemarle Housing Improvement Program)

City of Chicago See Local Volunteer School Councils

City of Dallas See AIDS Arms Network, Inc.

City of Flint See FEAT Foundation; Flint Airshow; Parking Posse

City of Hartford See The Courant's Youth Leadership Awards Program

City of Lapeer, pg. 870

City of Memphis Hospital See Fund for Needy School Children

City of Minneapolis See Fresh Force

City of New Orleans, pg. 642

City of New York See City Volunteer Corps

City of Pacifica See Youth-In-Action Auction

City of Pittsburgh See Project OASES

City of Raleigh See Retired Senior Volunteer Program; Voluntary Action Center of Wake County*

City of St. Paul See Community Projects in Saint Paul

City of St. Petersburg, pgs. 499, 609

City of San Antonio See Health Care for the Homeless Coalition

City of San Diego See Interfaith Shelter Network; Project HELP (Help Expedite Legal Problems for the Homeless)

City of South Lake Tahoe See Voluntary Action Center of South Lake Tahoe

City of Southfield, pgs. 429, 781

City of Sparks See Committee to Aid Abused Women

City of Stamford See Seventh Grade Social Problems Course

City of Versailles, pg. 525

City Spirit Cultural Arts Festival, pg. 530

City University of New York See Minority Volunteers: Pluralism in the Volunteer Arena

City Volunteer Corps, pg. 95

City Year, pg. 93
Civic Partnership: Initiative, Innovation*, pgs. 287, 567
Civil Rights Clearinghouse, pg. 1029
Civitex, pg. 1095
Clara Barton Camp for Girls with Diabetes, pg. 668
Clara Barton Council, pg. 664
Clarion Press, pg. 961
A Class Act, pg. 83
Class Action Suit, pg. 102
Class of 2000: The Prejudice Puzzle, pgs. 74, 823
Clean Community System, pg. 779
Clean Michigan Fund See FEAT Foundation
Clean the Bay Day, pg. 781
Clean Water Action Project, pg. 780
Clearinghouse of Rehabilitation Training Materials, pg. 1016
Clearinghouse on Disability Information, pgs. 170, 860
Clearinghouse on the Handicapped*, pgs. 170, 860
Cleburne County Cares, pg. 83
Cleburne County Department of Human Services, pg. 83
Cleveland Foundation See The Greater Cleveland Connection
Cleveland Public Schools See Student Care Day
Cleveland State University, pg. 477
Close Up Foundation, pg. 560
Clyde's Restaurant Group See School Ecology Project
Co-ordinating Council for Handicapped Children, pgs. 199, 851, 1043
Coalition for a National Health System*, pg. 663
Coalition for Literacy, pgs. 202, 732
Coalition for Volunteer Support, pg. 140
Coalition on Human Needs, pg. 1071
Coalition on Voluntarism See Volunteers Do Make a Difference!
Coalition on Volunteerism See Volunteer Link
Coca Cola Company See Georgia Special Olympics Summer Games
Coca Cola USA See Valued Youth Partnership Program
College Entrance Examination Board See Veterans Counseling and Guidance Center
College-In-Residence Volunteers (CIRV), pgs. 470, 862
College of the Emeriti, pgs. 438, 660
College of Wooster, pgs. 486, 695
Colorado Department of Health, Alcohol and Drug Abuse See Youth Who Care
Colorado Office of Volunteerism, pg. 124 See also The Bridge
Colorado Springs Police Department, pgs. 497, 730
Columbia Broadcasting System, pg. 1026
Columbia Experimental Theatre See Stay the Night on My Street
Columbia University, pg. 1081
Columbus Board of Education See Project Passage
Columbus Board of Realtors, pgs. 117, 683
Columbus Developmental Center, pgs. 395, 787
Columbus Recreation and Parks Department See Junior National Track and Field
Columbus Zoo, pgs. 50, 883
Combined Community Action, pg. 1028
Commission for the Advancement of Public Interest Organizations, pg. 571
Commission of Public Health See AIDS Program
Commission on Self-Sufficiency, pgs. 199, 842
Commission on Voluntary Service and Action, pgs. 461, 946, 956
Committee for Creative Non-Violence, pg. 1070

Committee on Aging, pg. 967
Committee on Cooperation with the Professional Community, pgs. 432, 602
Committee to Aid Abused Women, pgs. 165, 831
Common Cause, pgs. 309, 552, 981, 1097 See also Catholic Committee of Appalachia
Common Ground, Common Good, pg. 291
Commonwealth of Kentucky See Governor's Conference on Volunteerism
Communicating Human Needs, pg. 69
Communication-Help Center, pgs. 157, 1031
Communications Skills for the College Bound, pgs. 190, 560
Communications Workshop/Perspectives for Volunteers, pg. 289
Communitas, Inc., pg. 1081
Community Action Agency See Milton Cares Telephone Reassurance
Community Action Training*, pg. 181
Community Action Training (CAT), pg. 291
Community Activities Council, pg. 762
Community Advisement Board, pgs. 35, 915
Community Advisory Boards, pg. 195
Community Betterment Program, pgs. 50, 693
Community Block Homes, pgs. 34, 816
Community Board Training Day, pg. 185
Community Careers Resource Center, pgs. 79, 652
Community College of Allegheny County See Short Courses and Seminars for Administrators of Volunteers; The Untapped Resource: Disabled Persons as Volunteers; Volunteer Experience: Change, Challenge, Choices; Working Effectively with Boards and Committees
Community Coordinating Council of Lee County, pg. 232
Community Council, Inc. See The Volunteerism Project
Community Development, Neighborhood Self-Sufficiency and Volunteerism/Volunteer Program Management, pg. 291
Community Economics, pg. 684
Community Education Resource Center See Center for Organizational and Community Development
Community Education Services of Chinatown, pg. 735 See also Literacy and Life Skills
Community Environmental Program*, pg. 760
Community Family Life Services, pgs. 374, 717
Community Field Work, pg. 471
Community Food and Nutrition Program, pgs. 119, 750, 1052
Community for Creative Non-Violence, pgs. 73, 687
Community Forum on the Proposed Harlem on the Hudson Project, pgs. 328, 778
Community Friends*, pgs. 745, 1048
Community Housing Resources Board, pgs. 202, 685
Community INFO Line, pg. 157
Community Information Center, pg. 571
Community Involvement Program, pg. 324
Community Laboratory Project, pg. 471
Community Leader Training Associates, pg. 181
Community Learning Program, pg. 471
Community Mental Health Center See Blueprint
Community Partners Program*, pgs. 49, 668
Community Problem Solving Committee, pg. 84
Community Programs, pgs. 84, 758
Community Projects in Saint Paul, pg. 84
Community Regeneration, pgs. 181, 552, 986, 987, 1060
Community Relations, pgs. 25, 622
Community Renewal Team See Home-Based Child Care in Hartford

Community Research Forum*, pgs. 79, 702
Community Resource Center, pg. 187
Community Resource Volunteers, pgs. 435, 627
Community Service, pg. 284
Community Service/Awareness Action, pg. 472
Community Service Block Grant See Gleaning*
Community Service Council of Broward County, pgs. 176, 904
Community Service Council of Greater Tulsa See Bridging Volunteer Resources
Community Service, Inc., pg. 986
Community Service Planning Council of Greenville County, pg. 254
Community Service Program, pg. 464
Community Service Requirement, pg. 93
Community Services, pg. 324
Community Services Administration See Free The Children (FTC)
Community Services Block Grant Funds See Volunteer Services/CAC
Community Services of Portales See Small Town Survival Workshops
Community Services Project, pg. 94
Community Services Society of New York, pg. 1099
Community Training and Development, pg. 181
Community Volunteer Service, pgs. 239, 244, 252
Community Volunteer Service of the St. Croix Valley Area See Building Creative Organizations*; Lake Sylvia V.I.P. (Very Important Person) Conference*
Community Workshop and Training Center, pgs. 72, 853
Community Youth Gang Services See Alternative Education and Work Center
Companion Animal Hospital See Refuge for Injured Wildlife
Companions of Alameda County, pgs. 448, 821
Companionship/Therapy Program, pgs. 472, 786
Compeer, pg. 739
Compeer, The Health Association, pg. 1048
Complete Volunteer Legal Liability Workshop, pg. 148
Comprehensive Accounting Corporation, pg. 542
COMSAT See Master Builder Game
ConAgra Frozen Foods, pg. 1053
Concern, pgs. 1055, 1056, 1057, 1058, 1059, 1061
Concern, Inc., pg. 760
Concern of Durham, pg. 743
Concerned Christians of Livingston County See Livingston County RSVP Program
Concord-Cabarrus Community Schools Program See School Community Relations Program
Conejo Valley Retired Senior Volunteer Program, pg. 400
Conference Committee, pg. 1036
Conference on Nonprofit Leadership and Management, pg. 278
Conference on Philosophical Issues in Volunteerism, pg. 320
Conference on Shelter and Housing, pg. 1094
Conference on Volunteerism, pg. 235
Conflict Resolution/Alternatives to Violence Center, pgs. 451, 723
Congressional Education Associates, pg. 979
Connecticut Alcohol and Drug Abuse Commission See Regional Youth Substance Abuse Project (RYSAP); Youth Leadership Venture Funding Program
Connecticut Department of Corrections, pgs. 294, 716, 1037, 1039
Connecticut Leadership Conference, pg. 125
Connecticut Master Gardeners, pg. 755
Conner-Harris Mini Mall, pgs. 427, 547
Connexion, pgs. 420, 604

Conservation Foundation, pgs. 766, 769, 972, 1056, 1060, 1075, 1092

Conservation Tillage Information Center*, pg. 766

Consortium of Peace Research, Education & Development, pgs. 462, 563

Constitutional Rights Foundation, pgs. 37, 90, 626, 972, 989, 1005

Consumer Affairs Foundation, pg. 990

Consumer and Food Economics Institute, pg. 1075

Consumer Coalition for Health, pg. 664

Consumer Deputy Program, pg. 571

Consumer Education and Protective Association International, pg. 571

Consumer Energy Council of America Research Foundation, pg. 772

Consumer Federation of America, pg. 571

Consumer Information Service, pgs. 164, 574

Consumers Union of the United States, pgs. 988, 989, 990, 991

Contact Center, pg. 983

CONTACT USA, pgs. 155, 1034

Continental Airlines, pgs. 49, 878

Continental Homeless Assistance Program, pgs. 49, 878

Cook County Sheriff's Office, pgs. 295, 296, 600, 606

COOL IT!, pgs. 472, 769

COOL National Conference, pg. 324

"Cool School Video" Contest, pgs. 354, 629

Cooperative Housing Foundation*, pgs. 684, 1027

Coordinating Council for Handicapped Children, pg. 979

Coors V.I.C.E. Squad, pg. 25

COPE Retiree Program, pg. 396

COPRED Students Peace Network, pgs. 462, 563

Core Curriculum - The Volunteer, pg. 236

Corporate Retirees Information and Assistance Program, pgs. 176, 900

Corporate Volunteer Council See Volunteer Connection Telethon

Corporation for Public Broadcasting, pgs. 61, 195, 982, 983, 984

Corpus Christi Catholic Church, pgs. 366, 520

Correctional Mini-Courses, pgs. 294, 716

Costa Mesa Police Department, pgs. 459, 913

Council for Advancement and Support of Education, pgs. 973, 982, 983, 984, 985, 1014, 1015, 1017, 1018, 1019, 1020, 1096, 1101

Council for Exceptional Children, pgs. 170, 634, 860, 947, 960, 1007, 1008, 1009, 1010, 1012, 1066, 1070, 1073, 1074, 1076, 1077, 1079, 1080

Council of Agencies to Coordinate Homebound Services See Handicapped Volunteer/Volunteering for the Handicapped

Council of Better Business Bureaus, pgs. 22, 572, 963, 990

Council of National Organizations for Adult Education, pgs. 197, 623

Council of the Southern Mountains See Catholic Committee of Appalachia

Council of Volunteer Directors See Volunteer Connection Telethon

Council on Aging of Warren County, Inc. See Retired Senior Volunteer Program

Council on Economic Priorities, pg. 22

Council on Environmental Alternatives*, pg. 772

Council on Foundations, pgs. 97, 1015

Council on Legal Education Opportunity, pgs. 110, 625, 1004, 1005

Council on Voluntary Action See Volunteerism: A Bridge to the Future

Country Gathering, pgs. 400, 757

County Information Center, pg. 158

County of Albemarle See CHIP/AHIP (Charlottesville Housing Improvement Program/Albemarle Housing Improvement Program)

County of Onondaga See Diversion to Community Service*

County of San Diego See Interfaith Shelter Network

The Courant's Youth Leadership Awards Program, pg. 16

Court Appointed Special Advocates (CASA), pgs. 335, 808

Court Employment Project, pgs. 338, 720

Court Referral Program, pgs. 338, 725

Court Referred Volunteer Program of Rensselaer County, pgs. 338, 725

Cousteau Society, pgs. 447, 538

C&P Telephone Company See Management Workshops for Nonprofit Organizations

CPSS Fashion Show, pgs. 394, 850

CRACKDOWN, pgs. 499, 609

Creative Involvement for Productive Communities, pg. 281

Credit and Degree Programs in Voluntary Association Administration in Colleges and Universities, pg. 236

CRG Press, pg. 1042

Crime Justice Foundation, pg. 193

Crime, Law and Community: A Student Service Curriculum, pgs. 314, 713

Crime Prevention Coalition See National Town Watch Association

Crime Prevention Committee of Contra Costa County, pgs. 427, 709

Crisis Line Information & Referrals, pg. 158

Critical Mass Energy Project, pg. 772

Cross-Cultural Community Workshop, pgs. 191, 537

Crossroads Program, pg. 1022

CRY, Inc. (Citizens Redirecting Youth), pgs. 415, 795

Cuban American Association of Austin, pgs. 384, 531

Culpeper Community Services See Fairfax Alternative Services Workshop

Culpeper Senior Center, pgs. 412, 541

Cultural Arts Commission, pg. 530

Curb It!, pgs. 338, 777

Curriculum Development for Volunteer Administrators, pg. 236

Curriculum Innovations, pg. 988

Custom Audio Tapes, pg. 1071

Cuyahoga Community College See The Greater Cleveland Connection

Cuyahoga Falls Cancer Club, pg. 665

C.V. Starr National Service Fellowship Program, pg. 208

D

Daily News See Fighting Dirty!

Daisy (Friend-Raiser) Ball, pgs. 113, 859

Dakota Area Referral and Transportation for Seniors, pgs. 405, 910

Dallas Jewish Coalition for the Homeless, pgs. 445, 874

Danbury News-Times See Fairfield 2000

Danville Volunteer Council See Basics of Volunteer Program Management*

Darien Book Aid Plan, pg. 639

DARTS See Peer Counselor Program*

Data Systems Unlimited, pgs. 53, 658

Daughters of the American Colonists, pg. 534

Davis Information Group, pg. 951

Davis Nursery, pgs. 442, 784

Day Care Council of America, pgs. 583, 993, 994, 995

Day Care Council of New York, pg. 995

Dayton-Hudson Foundation See Adult Literacy Project

The Deaf Way, pgs. 393, 529

Debt and Credit Counseling Service, pg. 577

Delaware Department of Community Affairs See RSVP of New Castle County

Delaware Department of Health and Social Services, pg. 127 See also 24-Hour Child Abuse/Neglect Telephone Report Line; Adopt-A-Family; Preschool Diagnostic and Developmental Education Nurseries; Volunteer Service Program; Work Incentive Demonstration Program/Job Factory

Delaware Division for the Visually Impaired, pg. 849

Delaware Division of Mental Retardation See Volunteer Services

Delaware Division of State Service Centers, pgs. 385, 840

Delaware Division of Volunteer Services, pg. 126

Delaware Humanities Forum See Volunteers Do Make a Difference!

Delaware State Hospital, pgs. 167, 389, 742, 806

Delaware Valley Eye Bank See White Cane Drive

Delaware Volunteer Coordinators, pg. 238

Delta Lions Club See LaFreniere Park Special Recreation Programming Division

Delta Society, pgs. 782, 1055, 1058, 1059

Democratic National Committee See Stop! The Madness Foundation

Demonstration Program, pg. 97

Demystifying the Internship Experience, pg. 310

Denise Reich Real Estate, pgs. 414, 702

Denison Campus Government Association See Denison Community Association

Denison Community Association, pg. 473

Denison University, pg. 473

Denver Post Newspaper See Basket of Joy Campaign

Department of Children and Youth Services See Regional Youth Substance Abuse Project (RYSAP)

Department of Natural Resources See Maryland Hunter Education Program

Department of Public Works See Making the Volunteer Experience Count

Des Moines Area Community College, pgs. 239, 261, 269

Desegregation Monitoring and Advisory Committee, pgs. 298, 632

Design Center See Support for Public Television

Design for Change, pgs. 198, 638

Design Industries Foundation for AIDS See Heart Strings - Memphis Stop

Detroit Health Department See Prevention through Action

Detroit Lions See Michigan Special Olympics State Games

Detroit Public Schools, pgs. 27, 549

Developing Your Perspective: A Seminar in Volunteer Administration Today, pg. 237

Developing Your Perspective: Recruiting Volunteers, pg. 321

Development Career Guidance Program See Minority Entrepreneurship Program*

Devils Lake Public Schools See RSVP of Ramsey County

Dickerson Associates, pg. 688

Digital Equipment Corporation See From All Walks of Life; U.S. National Senior Olympics

Direct Line, pgs. 164, 579

Directors of Volunteers in Agencies, pg. 237 See also DOVIA Skill Development Workshops*

Disaster Professional Volunteer Network, pgs. 436, 592

Disaster Service Volunteers, pg. 593
Discount Mart Shopping Center II, pgs. 436, 547
Discover Center of Idaho, pg. 533
Discover Graphics, pg. 534
Dissemination and Assessment Center for Bilingual Education, pgs. 631, 1005
Dissemination Center for Bilingual Education, pg. 1009
Distributive Education Clubs of America, pgs. 42, 546
District of Columbia AIDS Information Line, pgs. 160, 521
District of Columbia Board of Education, pg. 646
District of Columbia Building Inspections Division See School Fire Safety Monitoring Program
District of Columbia City Council, pgs. 501, 610 See also School Fire Safety Monitoring Program
District of Columbia Corporate Volunteer Council, pgs. 25, 973, 975
District of Columbia Department of Consumer and Regulatory Affairs See School Fire Safety Monitoring Program
District of Columbia Department of Corrections See HITS (High Intensity Treatment Supervision)
District of Columbia Department of Human Services See AIDS Program
District of Columbia Department of Recreation See Senior Craftsman Showcase*
District of Columbia Family Services Administration See F.A.C.T. Hotline (Families and Children in Trouble)
District of Columbia Fire Department See School Fire Safety Monitoring Program
District of Columbia Government, pg. 670
District of Columbia Home Purchase Assistance Program See Manna, Inc.*
District of Columbia Independent Living Program See But I'm Different...
District of Columbia Office on Aging See Friendship House; Senior Craftsman Showcase*
District of Columbia Police Department, pgs. 382, 426, 427, 547, 708, 802
District of Columbia Public Schools, pgs. 354, 418, 610, 620, 629, 646
District of Columbia School System See Community Laboratory Project
District of Columbia Schools See Conner-Harris Mini Mall
District of Columbia Superior Court, pgs. 339, 726 See also Friends of the Superior Court
District of Columbia Women's Commission for Crime Prevention, pgs. 196, 703, 1040
Diversion to Community Service*, pgs. 339, 725
Divine Redeemer Memorial Hospital, pgs. 305, 674, 1024 See also Hospice - Divine Redeemer Memorial Hospital
Division of Volunteer Services, pg. 126
Do It Now Foundation, pgs. 598, 997, 998, 999, 1001, 1003, 1025, 1086
Docent Council of Philadelphia See Docent Education Workshop
Docent Council of the Zoological Society of Philadelphia See Docent Education Workshop
Docent Education Workshop, pgs. 276, 532
Dodd, Mead & Company, pg. 968
Dodge Motor Company See Drunk-Driving Simulator Program and Forum
Dogs for the Deaf, pg. 854
Dollars for Scholars, pgs. 102, 641
Dollywood Foundation, pgs. 39, 633

Domestic Abuse Project of Delaware County, pgs. 166, 831
Dominican College See National Academy for Volunteers in Education
Doncaster Youth Challenge, a.k.a. Sneaker Camp, pgs. 222, 704
Donor Involvement, pg. 102
Douglas N. Lawson Associates, Inc., pg. 98
Douglass College, pgs. 476, 794
DOVE, Inc., pg. 85
Dover Public Library See Volunteer Link
DOVIA (Directors of Volunteers in Agencies), pg. 320
DOVIA Meetings for Volunteer Administrators, pg. 237
DOVIA Skill Development Workshops*, pg. 237
DOVIA Training Programs, pg. 237
Downtown Senior Center See Teaching Senior Center
Drug Abuse Information Hotline*, pgs. 168, 605
Drug Alliance, pg. 605
Drug Trafficking Study Task Force, pgs. 295, 607, 998
Drunk-Driving Simulator Program and Forum, pgs. 425, 613
Dryden Associates, pgs. 950, 958
DSS Volunteer Services Program, pg. 829
Duke Ellington School of the Arts, pgs. 69, 931
DUO, pg. 473
DuPage County Health Department See Volunteer Leadership: Challenges For The Nineties
Dutchman Correctional Institute School See Spartanburg Adult Writing and Reading (AWARE)
Duties to the Community, pg. 473
Dutton Fire Department See High-Rise Fire Response Training
Duvall/Hendricks See Give Me Shelter: Designs for Urban Survival
DVC Workshops and Conferences, pg. 238
Dwight-Englewood School, pg. 85
Dwight-Englewood School Volunteer Program, pg. 85
The Dynamics of a Successful Volunteer Program, pg. 238
The Dynamics of a Successful Volunteer Program: Correspondence Course, pg. 238
Dynamite Planning... Explode Into Action!, pg. 239
Dynasty Enterprises of Virginia See Business/Industry Advisory Council (BIAC)
D'Youville College See You Are The Board*

E

Earl's Hamburgers, pg. 28
Early Home Education, pgs. 474, 588
Earth Day 1990, pg. 770
Earth Day 1990/EPA, pg. 770
Earth First See Econet
Earth Island Institute See Econet
Earth Team, pg. 767
EarthSave See First Annual Soviet-American Youth Summit
East Central Community Center, pg. 1078
East Ramapo Central School District, pg. 484
East Tennessee Community Design Center, pgs. 436, 778
East Texas Association for Abused Families See Women's Center of East Texas
Easter Seal Society of Pennsylvania, pg. 303
Eastern High School's 500 Club, pgs. 38, 641
Eastern Iowa Community College District, pg. 186
Eastern Sussex Family YMCA See Volunteer Link

Eastwood Civic Association See Roberts Park and Playground/Lantrip School Park*
Easy Riders Medical Transportation, pgs. 379, 938
Easy Riders Volunteer Program*, pgs. 379, 938
Ebensburg Center, pgs. 405, 867
Echoes of the Past, pg. 534
Eckerd College See Adams' Express: A Mini-Grant Program
Eckerd Foundation See Doncaster Youth Challenge, a.k.a. Sneaker Camp
ECO, pg. 719
Econet, pgs. 44, 769
Education and Employment Resource Center, pgs. 344, 890
Education and Human Services Course, pg. 325
Education & Prevention Services: AIDS Program, pgs. 67, 516
Education Commission of the States, pg. 993
Education Foundation See Adams' Express: A Mini-Grant Program
Education/Social Action Service, pg. 1079
Education Support Program, pgs. 39, 633
Educational Information and Resource Center, pg. 703
Educational Parameters, pg. 1090
Educational Participation in Communities, pg. 474
Effective Boardsmanship, pg. 148
Effective Management of Volunteer Programs, pg. 239
The Effective Volunteer, pg. 239
Effective Volunteer Administration, pg. 239
EHMI Company, pgs. 1057, 1061
El Dorado County Justice System See Voluntary Action Center of South Lake Tahoe
Elderhostel, pg. 900
Elders and Voluntarism*, pg. 319
Elim Lutheran Church See ARC Covenant
Emergency Food Program, pg. 751
Emergency Infant Nutrition Program: Free Breakfast Project, pgs. 474, 748
Emergency Services Program, pg. 593
Emergency Shelter Council, pgs. 73, 875
Emeriti Women's Council See Jobs for Older Women*
Emory University See Georgia Special Olympics Summer Games
Employee Assistance Program Consortium, pgs. 40, 790
Employee Assistance Programs, pgs. 40, 791
Employee Assistance Society of North America, pgs. 40, 790
Employment Skills for Homeless Youth, pg. 874
End Hunger Network, pgs. 73, 756, 875 See also Prime Time to End Hunger
End Hunger Project, pg. 76, 752
Energize, pgs. 240, 277, 946, 948, 951, 953, 954, 956, 1095
Energize Volunteer Management Training Program, pg. 240
Energy Action Education Project, pg. 772
Energy Committed to Offenders, pg. 719
Entering the Community: Summer Volunteer Service and Career Opportunities for Students, pg. 311
Entertainment Industries Council, pgs. 354, 605
Environment Information Center, pg. 760
Environmental Action, pg. 760
Environmental Action Foundation, pgs. 761, 1058, 1059, 1061, 1091
Environmental Defense Fund, pg. 1055
Environmental Policy Institute, pg. 761
Environmental Scan Task Force, pg. 187
Epilepsy Foundation of America, pgs. 331, 859, 1070, 1071, 1076

Epiphany Roman Catholic Church *See Black Georgetown Reunion Group*
Episcopal Church of the Good Shepherd *See ARC Covenant*
Epsilon Sigma Alpha International, pg. 101
Equitable *See City Year*
ERIC Clearinghouse on Early Childhood Education, pg. 993
ERIC Document Reproduction Service, pg. 1099
Erie County Department of Senior Services *See Meals on Wheels of Buffalo and Erie County*
Ethel Percy Andrus Gerontology Center, pg. 1066
Ethnic American Art Slide Library, pg. 967
Evaluation and Change, pg. 947
Everyday Heroes, pg. 593
Executive High School Internship Association *See Changing Values in Experiential Education**
Experiential Learning - Working with Student Volunteers, pg. 465
Exploring New Frontiers in Volunteerism, pg. 240
Exxon, pgs. 36, 596, 996 *See also Performance Contracting*

F

F.A.C.T. Hotline (Families and Children in Trouble), pgs. 169, 832
Fair Oaks Hospital *See Adopt-A-School*
Fairfax Alternative Services Workshop, pgs. 315, 724
Fairfax Area Agency on Aging, pgs. 174, 689, 1027
Fairfax County *See Senior Employment Resources; Teen Center*
Fairfax County Department of Consumer Affairs, pg. 989
Fairfax County Department of Extension and Continuing Education *See Celebrity Auction**
Fairfax County Park Authority, pg. 1057
Fairfax County Park/Conservation Division *See Fairfax Alternative Services Workshop*
Fairfax County Police Department, pg. 1039 *See also Drunk-Driving Simulator Program and Forum*
Fairfax County Public Health Services *See Bailey's Crossroads Community Shelter*
Fairfax County Public Library, pgs. 1006, 1009
Fairfax County Public Schools, pgs. 38, 297, 616, 619, 621 *See also Training for Disabled Students*
Fairfax County Redevelopment and Housing Authority, pg. 1028
Fairfax County Schools, pgs. 43, 546
Fairfield County Courts *See Regional Youth Substance Abuse Project (RYSAP)*
Fairfield 2000, pg. 568
Fairfield University, pg. 360
Fairleigh Dickinson University, pgs. 239, 449, 630
Families in Action National Drug Information Center, pgs. 413, 603
Family AIDS Education Project, pgs. 362, 516
Family Assistance Program *See Family Assistance Project of Hollywood (FAP)*
Family Assistance Project of Hollywood (FAP), pgs. 386, 877
Family Counseling Services of Greater Miami *See Family AIDS Education Project*
Family Crisis Center, pgs. 166, 838
Family Day Care Technical Assistance Conference, pg. 588
Family Emergency Committee of ACCA, pgs. 362, 832
Family Friends Project, pgs. 401, 851

Family Life and AIDS Instruction Program, pgs. 39, 516
Family Life/Community and Government, pgs. 325, 561
Family Resource and Referral Center*, pgs. 169, 837
Family Service America, pgs. 490, 577, 840, 899, 955 *See also Youth Evaluation Services (Y.E.S.)*
Family Service Center/Colorado Branch, pg. 1096
Family Service of Westchester, pgs. 486, 921
Family Services of Knox County *See Southeast Resource Center for Children and Youth Services*
Family Services-Woodfield, pgs. 9, 608
Family Stress Services of DC, pgs. 169, 832
Family Support Group, pgs. 455, 730
Fantle's, pg. 975
Far Northwest Caregivers, pgs. 363, 905
Fare SHARE, pgs. 455, 752
Fargo-Morehead Directors of Volunteer Services *See Metamorphosis: Growth and Change in the Administration of Volunteer Services*
Fatherhood Project, pg. 930
FBI Academy, pgs. 450, 700
FDA Experimental AIDS Treatment Hotline, pgs. 160, 521
FEAT Foundation, pg. 762
Federal Assistance Programs Retrieval System (FAPRS), pg. 97
Federal Emergency Management Agency (FEMA) *See Independent Living/Homeless Youth*
Federal Express *See Art for Kids' Sake*
Federal Information Policies: Access is the Key, pgs. 307, 554
Federal Library Committee *See Federal Information Policies: Access is the Key*
Federal Programs Advisory Service, pg. 1072
Federation of Protestant Welfare Agencies, pgs. 22, 182, 248 *See also Minority Volunteers: Pluralism in the Volunteer Arena*
Federation of Southern Cooperatives and Land Assistance Fund, pg. 576
Female Offender Rehabilitation Program, pg. 661
FEST (Fort Eustis Soldiers Theatre), pgs. 345, 539
Festival, pgs. 387, 530
Field Education Program, pg. 363
Field Experience Education, pg. 475
Fifth Avenue Center, pg. 13
Fighting Dirty!, pgs. 44, 763
Finding and Preparing New Board Members for Service, pg. 185
Findlay Area Native American Indian Center, pgs. 173, 880
First American Bank, pgs. 103, 596
First Annual Soviet-American Youth Summit, pgs. 284, 564
First Call for Help/Fort Worth, pg. 158
First Call for Help/Wichita, pg. 158
FIRST (Factual Information Regarding Sex and Teens), pgs. 162, 805
First Family Volunteer Program, pg. 26
First Lutheran Church, pgs. 368, 758
First National Bank of Hot Springs, pg. 26
First Parish Church (Universalist-Unitarian) *See Sundial Volunteers*
First Place, pgs. 876, 1071
First Presbyterian Church, pgs. 371, 764
First Presbyterian Church of Hollywood *See CHIP-IN*
First State Conference on School Volunteers, pgs. 297, 616
First Trinity Lutheran Church *See Van Ministry*

Flame of Hope, pgs. 428, 868
Flight Attendant Volunteer Corps, pgs. 446, 629
Flint Airshow, pgs. 113, 859
Flint Community Schools, pgs. 649, 1005, 1010
Flint Police Department *See Parking Posse*
Flint Township/Flint Police *See Flint Airshow*
Florence Crittenton Association of America, pg. 930
Florida Department of Health and Rehabilitative Services, pg. 993
Florida Department of Transportation *See Tampa Causeway Beautification Project*
Florida Freshwater Fish and Game Commission *See Refuge for Injured Wildlife*
Florida Power, pg. 27
Florida Public Relations Association/Jacksonville *See Growing with Public Relations**
Florida Sheriffs Association *See Florida Sheriffs Youth Villa*
Florida Sheriffs Youth Ranches, pgs. 496, 817
Florida Sheriffs Youth Villa, pgs. 496, 817
Flying Senior Citizens of the USA*, pgs. 396, 939
FOCUS (Families of Children United for Safety), pgs. 416, 931
Food Research and Action Center, pgs. 76, 331, 748, 756
Food Safety Hotline, pgs. 176, 580
Ford Foundation *See Youth Community Service*
The Ford Group *See Spare Change Project*
Ford Motor Company *See Blue Ridge to the White House: Wheelchair Race of Champions; Friends of the Rouge; Wheelchair Race Communications Services*
Forest Service Volunteer Program, pg. 767
Forging Partnerships*, pgs. 292, 713
Fort Campbell High School, pg. 471
Fort Dix Volunteers, pgs. 345, 890
Fort Gordon Volunteer Program, pgs. 345, 891
Fort Sill Volunteers, pgs. 346, 891
Fort Worth Adolescent Pregnancy Board *See New Lives*
Fort Worth Independent School District, pg. 932 *See also New Lives*
Fort Worth School District *See SNAP (Students Need A Pat)*
48 Hours on Capitol Hill, pgs. 287, 554
Forum 90: Backward Glances... Forward Visions, pgs. 292, 699
Forum on School Vandalism, pgs. 315, 703
Forum 90: Pre-Conference Agenda (tentative), pg. 714
Foster Grandparent Program (FGP), pgs. 396, 866
Foundation Center, pgs. 98, 957, 1015, 1020
Foundation for Children with Learning Disabilities, pgs. 112, 862
Foundation for Hospice and Homecare, pgs. 172, 674, 836
Foundation for Public Relations, Research & Education, pg. 984
Foundation for Success*, pgs. 293, 714
Foundation Research Service (FRS), pg. 98
4-H General Forums: Adult Volunteer Training, pgs. 240, 810
4-H Program *See National Collaboration for Youth*
4-H Specific Forums: Adult Volunteer Training, pgs. 317, 810
Four-One-One (411), pgs. 4, 463, 951, 954, 957, 958, 1099, 1100
Fox Photo *See Communicating Human Needs*
FOX Television - WTTG, pg. 961
Franconia District Citizens Advisory Committee, pgs. 426, 716

Franconia Police Department *See A, B, and C on Burglary*

Fraternal Benefits & Financial Services for Lutherans *See Get Involved Before Your Kids Do*

Fraternal Order of Police Lodge 182 *See Curb It!*

Fred Pryor Seminars, pg. 62

Fred Ruffing Memorial Scholarship, pgs. 113, 641

Free Hotline, pg. 159

Free The Children (FTC), pgs. 112, 940

Freedom from Hunger Foundation, pg. 756

Freihofer's Bakery *See Regional Youth Substance Abuse Project (RYSAP)*

Fremont Chamber of Commerce, pgs. 435, 544

Fresh Force, pg. 476

Fresno Bee *See End Hunger Project*

Friend to Friend Program*, pgs. 363, 786

Friends Committee on National Legislation, pgs. 195, 553

Friends of Handicapped Readers, pg. 637

Friends of Libraries USA*, pg. 635

Friends of Linden Place, pgs. 144, 535

Friends of the Rouge, pgs. 429, 781

Friends of the Superior Court, pgs. 437, 728

Friends of the Vietnam Veterans Memorial, pg. 893

Friends Peace Committee, pgs. 355, 563

Friendship House, pg. 86

Frito-Lay, Inc., pg. 974

From All Walks of Life, pgs. 120, 519

From Me to We: A Funny Reason to Have a Conference, pg. 241

Frontline - Channels 22 and 26, pg. 985

FTC Vacation Travel Hotline, pgs. 163, 582

Fund for Advancement of Camping, pgs. 119, 923

Fund for Needy School Children, pgs. 109, 799

Fund-Raising Institute, pgs. 98, 984, 1015, 1017, 1019

Fund Raising Management, pg. 1015

Fund Raising Management (FRM), pg. 1015

Fund-Raising Success Seminar, pg. 100

Fundamentals of Volunteer Program Management, pg. 241

Furniture Committee of ACCA, pgs. 364, 836

Future Generations, pg. 688

The Future of Volunteerism: Shapes and Scenarios, pg. 14

Futures for Youth, pg. 657

G

Gadsden Board of Education *See PALS Program*

Gadsden Chamber of Commerce, pgs. 50, 734

Gadsden United Way *See Chamber of Commerce Literacy Council; PALS Program*

GAIN (Greater Achievement Through Involvement Now), pg. 144

Gaines Township Fire Department *See High-Rise Fire Response Training*

Gainesville Voluntary Action Center *See Volunteer Management Certification*

Gale Research Company, pgs. 988, 989, 1023, 1024, 1034, 1078

Gallatin County Council on Aging *See Gallatin Valley Emergency Food Bank*

Gallatin Valley Emergency Food Bank, pgs. 52, 752, 1053

Gallaudet Board of Trustees, pgs. 200, 855

Gallaudet College, pgs. 393, 529

Gallaudet University, pgs. 200, 855 *See also Management Workshops for Nonprofit Organizations; Volunteer Orientation Program*

Galveston Historical Foundation, pg. 536

Gamma Omicron Chapter/Phi Mu, pg. 391

Gannett Foundation *See Stop! The Madness Foundation*

Gannett Outdoors *See Friends of the Rouge*

Gannett Westchester Newspapers *See Westchester 2000*

Garden of Young Hearts, pgs. 476, 868

Garrett Park Press, pgs. 948, 1011, 1012, 1013, 1099

Gartenhaus Furs, pgs. 33, 798

The Gatehouse: The Cook/Douglass Peer Counseling Center, pgs. 476, 794

Gateway Foundation *See Volunteer Leadership: Challenges For The Nineties*

Gay and Lesbian Community Service Center *See CHIP-IN*

Gay Men's Health Crisis, pgs. 508, 962, 963, 964 *See also AIDS-Walk New York*

General Atlantic Partners *See City Year*

General Cinemas *See City Year*

General Communication Company of America *See Public Relations on a Shoestring**

General Motors *See Quality Education Program*

Genesee County Commission on Substance Abuse Services *See Project Graduation*

Genesee County Sheriff's Department *See Flint Airshow*

George A. Hormel & Company, pg. 1053

George Mason University *See COPRED Students Peace Network; Phi Mu Sorority Community Service Chapter; Study War No More; Tau Kappa Epsilon (TKE) Community Projects*

George Washington University, pgs. 462, 548

Georgetown Public Library *See Volunteer Link*

Georgetown University, pg. 291 *See also Black Georgetown Reunion Group*

Georgetown University Law Center, pg. 61

Georgia Association for Retarded Citizens *See Parents Educating Parents*

Georgia Department of Human Resources *See Volunteer Transportation Program*

Georgia Special Olympics Summer Games, pg. 868

Georgia State University, pgs. 273, 282

Geraldine R. Dodge Foundation *See Basic Managerial Skills for Directors of Volunteers*

Get Away Clean, pgs. 284, 789

Get Involved Before Your Kids Do, pgs. 414, 600

Gettysburg College, pgs. 450, 822

Giant Food, pgs. 38, 626, 1052

Gibbs P.A.C.E. *See Troop 400 and Troop 391*

Gift to the City, pgs. 364, 694

Gifts In Kind, pgs. 117, 1018

Gifts In Kind America, pg. 117

Giraffe Project, pgs. 16, 948

Girl Scout Council *See Conference on Volunteerism*

Girl Scouting in the Inner City, pgs. 551, 920

Girl Scouts of DuPage County *See Volunteers: Empowerment Today and Tomorrow*

Girl Scouts of the Milwaukee Area, pgs. 480, 778

Girl Scouts of the USA, pgs. 58, 60, 551, 809, 843, 920, 1032 *See also Institute on Volunteer Administration: A Proposal; National Celebration of the Outdoors; Project Bravo*

Girls Clubs of America, pgs. 58, 810

Give Five Alabama, pg. 123

Give Five Campaign, pg. 18

Give Me Shelter: Designs for Urban Survival, pgs. 306, 884

Give Them A Hand, Not A Handout, pgs. 173, 880

Given Opportunities..., pgs. 72, 853

Glass Packaging Institute, pg. 1059

Gleaning*, pgs. 455, 759

GMHC Walkathon, pgs. 119, 518, 964

GMI Engineering & Management Institute *See Youth Volunteer Services*

Goals for Dallas*, pgs. 86, 559

God's Love We Deliver (GLWD), pgs. 379, 521

Going with the Current: Volunteer Management Workshop, pg. 241

Golden Rule Awards Program, pg. 15

Golden Triangle Radio Information Center, pgs. 72, 849

Goldwater Memorial Hospital, pgs. 494, 511

Gonzaga Action Program (GAP), pg. 364

Gonzaga University, pg. 364

Good Hope Senior Center, pg. 719

Good Neighbor Exchange Program, pgs. 438, 829

Good News Jail and Prison Ministries International, pgs. 226, 723, 1037, 1038, 1039, 1096

Good Samaritan Recognition Ceremony, pgs. 17, 755

Goodner Brothers Aircraft, pgs. 37, 597

Goodwill Industries of America, pgs. 1012, 1080 *See also Data Systems Unlimited*

Goodwill Industries of San Francisco, pgs. 53, 658

Goucher College, pg. 267

Government Contracts Clinic, pgs. 462, 548

Government Information Services, pgs. 98, 553, 1017

Governor's Advisory Committee on Child Abuse and Neglect/VA, pgs. 151, 817

Governor's Advisory Committee on Child Abuse & Neglect *See Child Abuse Hotline; Child Protective Services*

Governor's Advisory Committee on Private/Public Volunteer Partnerships/NJ, pg. 209

Governor's Alliance for a Drug-Free Tennessee *See Shaving Cream Lesson - Drug Prevention Seminar*

Governor's Conference on Volunteerism, pg. 132

Governor's Conference on Volunteers in Energy*, pgs. 125, 773

Governor's Council on Voluntary Action/CT, pgs. 125, 126, 773 *See also Major Certificate Program for Volunteer Managers*

Governor's Council on Voluntary Action/Youth Action Committee *See Governor's Youth Action Conference*

Governor's Office for Voluntary Service/NY, pg. 142

Governor's Office for Volunteer Services/TX, pg. 145

Governor's Office for Volunteers/IA *See Regional Seminars and a State Conference on Volunteerism*

Governor's Office of Voluntary Action/IL, pgs. 210, 268

Governor's Office of Voluntary Action, pg. 130

Governor's Office of Volunteer Services *See Visitor Hospitality Center**

Governor's Office of Volunteer Services/MN, pg. 134

The Governor's Office of Volunteer Services/NM *See Save Our Water**

Governor's Office on Voluntary Action/IL *See LIVE '89 (Leadership in Volunteerism Experience)*

Governor's Office on Volunteer Services/KY, pg. 132

Governor's Office on Volunteer Services/NM, pgs. 82, 140 *See also Volunteers: Our Greatest Natural Resource*

Governor's Office on Volunteerism *See Virginia Division of Volunteerism*

Governor's Office on Volunteerism/AL, pgs. 122, 123, 256, 270

Governor's Office on Volunteerism and Citizen Affairs/NC, pg. 142

Governor's Office on Volunteerism/IL, pgs. 130, 131 See also Media Relations for Nonprofit and Volunteer Organizations

Governor's Office on Volunteerism/NH, pgs. 137, 138

Governor's Office on Volunteerism/NH, pgs. 138, 139, 254 See also Governor's Office on Volunteerism/NH

Governor's Office on Volunteerism/RI See Tea and Treasures

Governors' School, pgs. 151, 797

Governors' Statewide Advisory Board/WA See Governors' School

Governor's Task Force on Child Abuse and Neglect/NJ See Child Assault Prevention Team

Governor's Youth Action Conference, pg. 126

G.P. Putnam's Sons, pg. 962

Grace Baptist Church, pgs. 370, 753

GRADS Program, pgs. 416, 932

Graduate Certificate Program for Management of Volunteer Services, pg. 241

Graduate Program in Public Policy and Citizen Participation, pgs. 287, 554

Grafton School, pgs. 200, 856

Grafton School Volunteer Board, pgs. 200, 856

Grand Blanc School District, pg. 493

Grand Isle Erosion Fight, pgs. 500, 593

Grand People, Inc., pg. 401

Grand People's Retired Senior Volunteer Program, pg. 401

Grand Rapids Symphony Orchestra, pgs. 106, 539

Grant Development Institute, pg. 1019

Grant Information System, pg. 98

Grantsmanship Center, pgs. 98, 100, 302, 1016 See also Grantsmanship Training Program

Grantsmanship Training Program, pg. 302

Grantsmanship Training Program (short course), pg. 100

Grassroots Crisis Intervention & Peer Counseling Center, pgs. 175, 741

Grassroots Crisis Intervention Center, pg. 1032

Grassroots Crisis Intervention Center Training Program, pg. 308

Graterford Prison See Graterfriends

Graterford State Correctional Institution, pgs. 401, 720

Graterfriends, pgs. 401, 720

Gray Panthers, pgs. 225, 887, 1096

Great Books Foundation, pg. 639 See also Basic Leader Training Course

Great Neck & Manhasset Public Schools, BOCES of Nassau County See Parent-Child Home Program

Great Plains Volunteer, pg. 957

The Greater Cleveland Connection, pg. 477

Greater Hartford Association of Realtors, pgs. 202, 685

Greater Kansas City Section See CASA Project (Court Appointed Special Advocates)

Greater Louisville Organization for Health See Mission House

Greater Milwaukee Voluntary Action Center, pg. 945 See also Involvement Corps*; Student Volunteer Programs: A New Resource for Community Agencies*

Greater Rochester International Airport, pgs. 434, 591

Greater Southeast Community Center for the Aging, pg. 911

Greater Washington Board of Trade, pg. 973

Greek Festival, pgs. 364, 530

Green Countrie Towne Program, pgs. 500, 763

Green Line Action Association, pgs. 43, 549

Greenhouse, pg. 743

Greenville Technical College, pgs. 239, 263

Greenwich Time See Fairfield 2000

Grissom Middle School, pgs. 192, 627

Grocery Manufacturers Representatives Organization See End Hunger Project

Group Safety Association, pg. 9

Group W Westinghouse Broadcasting See Art for Kids' Sake

Growing Up With Nature, pgs. 416, 783

Growing with Public Relations*, pg. 289

Grubbs Oldsmobile See Help the Homeless Million Dollar Shootout

Guadalupe Elementary School, pgs. 424, 532

Guardian Ad Litem Program, pgs. 336, 701

Guardian Angels, pgs. 496, 710

Gulf State Steel, pgs. 51, 737

H

H-CAP (Community Action Program) See Volunteer Training Program for Volunteer Advocates

Habitat for Humanity See Habitat for Humanity International; Operation Clean Sweep; Student Habitat for Humanity

Habitat for Humanity International, pgs. 355, 687, 1029 See also Habitat for Humanity of Rhode Island; Paterson Habitat for Humanity

Habitat for Humanity of Rhode Island, pgs. 365, 695, 1027

Habitat for Humanity of San Antonio, pgs. 370, 688

Habitat for Humanity/Philadelphia, pgs. 364, 694

Haddon Township Council, pgs. 486, 762, 765

Handicapped Learner Materials, pg. 856

Handicapped Parking Enforcement Team, pgs. 428, 863

Handicapped Volunteer/Volunteering for the Handicapped, pgs. 221, 872

Happy Trails To You: A Workshop for Volunteers, pg. 774

Hardee's Restaurants See Wheelchair Race Communications Services

Harriet Tubman Center, pgs. 175, 741

Harris Bank, pgs. 39, 620

The Hartford Courant, pg. 16

Hartford School System See The Courant's Youth Leadership Awards Program

Hartford Superior Court, pgs. 460, 914

Harvard University See A Class Act

Hasbro Foundation See Volunteers in Providence Schools

Hastings High School, pgs. 481, 647

Hawaii Office of Children and Youth, pg. 1021

Hawaii Office of the Governor, pgs. 129, 817

Hawaii Office on Aging See Volunteer Training Program for Volunteer Advocates

Hawaii Protection and Advocacy Agency, pgs. 128, 844

Hawaii State Agency See Office of Children and Youth (OCY)

Hawaii State Youth Volunteer Board*, pg. 128

Hawaii Youth At Risk, pgs. 438, 704

Hawkeye Institute of Technology, pg. 267

Hazardous Waste Volunteer Program, pg. 594

Hazzard Foundation See Volunteers in Providence Schools

H.B. Zachry Company See Miracle Week

Head Start See Young Volunteers in Action*

Head Start - Family Day Care, pgs. 108, 586

Head Start Program, pg. 583

Health and Safety Circus, pgs. 477, 672

Health Care for the Homeless Coalition, pg. 879

Health Crisis Network See The Response Pool

Health Education Services, pgs. 960, 961, 962, 963, 964, 1022, 1025

Health Fair, pgs. 349, 672

Health Fair Project, pg. 1023

Health/PAC Bulletin, pg. 1024

Healthcare Volunteer Program, pgs. 313, 663

Hearing Dogs, Inc. See International Hearing Dog, Inc.

Hearing Ear Dog Program, pg. 854

The Heart of Compassion, pg. 6

Heart Strings - Memphis Stop, pgs. 105, 519

Heartline*, pgs. 73, 895

Hechinger Foundation See School Ecology Project

Heiskell Awards For Community Service, pg. 949

Help for You!, pg. 242

Help-On-Wheels, pgs. 365, 666

Help the Homeless Million Dollar Shootout, pgs. 115, 878

Helping Hand, pgs. 41, 654

Hennepin County Court Services, pgs. 1036, 1037, 1039

Henry J. Kaiser Family Foundation See Free The Children (FTC)

Heritage Arts/VMS Systems, pg. 953

Herner & Company See Institute on Federal Library Resources

Hertz Government Sales Office, pg. 1092

High-Rise Fire Response Training, pgs. 26, 594

Highland Park High School, pgs. 485, 794

Highway Beautification Council See Tampa Causeway Beautification Project

Highway Users Federation for Safety and Mobility, pgs. 1091, 1092, 1093

Hilcher Ford See Help the Homeless Million Dollar Shootout

Hispanic Family Day Care Network See Home-Based Child Care in Hartford

Hispanic National Bar Association See Council on Legal Education Opportunity

HITS (High Intensity Treatment Supervision), pgs. 339, 726

HIV/AIDS Prevention Program for African American Youth and Families, pg. 518

HIV/AIDS Prevention Program for Hispanic Youth and Families, pg. 518

HIV/AIDS Workplace Program, pgs. 31, 517

Hogan's Alley, Virginia, pgs. 450, 700

Holiday Inn See U.S. National Senior Olympics

Holy Ghost Church See Continental Homeless Assistance Program

Holy Redeemer College, pg. 363

Home and School Institute, pgs. 634, 1006 See also CATCH Program

Home-Based Child Care in Hartford, pg. 588

Home Health and Hospice Care See NH State Conference on Volunteerism

Home League, pgs. 402, 793

Home Repairs Project, pgs. 402, 691

Home Town Awards, pg. 130

Homeless Advocacy Program See Project HELP (Help Expedite Legal Problems for the Homeless)

Homelessness Prevention Program, pgs. 140, 686

Homes of Hope See Operation Clean Sweep

Homework Hotline, pgs. 416, 645

Honeywell, pg. 974

Honeywell Foundation, pgs. 44, 688

Honeywell Neighborhood Improvement Program, pgs. 44, 688

HOPE, pg. 663

Hope Lutheran Church See Meals on Wheels Program of ACCA

Hopkins High School See Community Involvement Program

Horses and the Handicapped of South Florida, pg. 869

Hospice - Divine Redeemer Memorial Hospital, pg. 675

Hospice, Inc. *See The Response Pool*

Hospice Organization, pg. 675

Hospice Volunteer Training Program*, pgs. 305, 674

Hospital Association of Pennsylvania, pgs. 1024, 1026

HOST (Hands Of Shared Time), pgs. 327, 477, 906, 909

Hosted Programs and Youth Conservation Corps, pg. 774

HOSTS (Help One Student To Succeed), pg. 1007

Hot Line for the Homeless*, pgs. 173, 880

Hotel Sales & Marketing Association International, pg. 229

House of Ruth *See Give Me Shelter: Designs for Urban Survival*

Housing Now!, pgs. 73, 687

Housing Program of ACCA, pgs. 365, 886

Housing Services: AIDS Program, pg. 684

Houston Ex-Offender Program, pgs. 41, 720

Houston Independent School District *See Business/School Partnership Program*

How to Effectively Manage People Who Have AIDS as Volunteers, pgs. 274, 509

The How-To of Working with Volunteers - TLC (Teaching/Learning/Caring), pg. 278

How to Proofread, pg. 62

How to Work Effectively with Volunteers, pg. 242

Howard Brown Memorial Clinic, pgs. 425, 512, 963, 1100

Howard County Grant-in-Aid *See Grassroots Crisis Intervention & Peer Counseling Center*

Howrey & Simon *See Give Me Shelter: Designs for Urban Survival*

Hudson High School, pg. 193

Hudson State Service Center, pgs. 127, 788

Hug-A-Tree And Survive, pg. 813

Hug In, pgs. 72, 853

Human Development Commission *See Project Graduation*

Human Relations Skills for Volunteers, pg. 242

Human Resource Development Council District IX *See Gallatin Valley Emergency Food Bank*

Human Resources Center, pgs. 112, 857 *See also Handicapped Volunteer/Volunteering for the Handicapped*

Human Service Programs: Volunteer Leadership Emphasis Area, pg. 134

Hunter College, pgs. 301, 829

Hunter College School of Social Work, pg. 384

Huron County Mental Health Services, pg. 744

H.W. Fry Realty Corporation *See Operation Clean Sweep*

I

I Am Involved, pg. 27

I Can Cope, pg. 666

I Have a Dream Foundation, pgs. 111, 640

I. Ricchi Restaurant *See Taste of the Nation*

IBM *See Data Systems Unlimited*

Idaho Hunger Action Council, pgs. 455, 759, 1037, 1053

Idaho Volunteer, pg. 129

/I/D/E/A/, pg. 626

IDRA *See Valued Youth Partnership Program*

Illinois Bell *See LIVE '89 (Leadership in Volunteerism Experience)*

Illinois Bell Telephone Company *See Statewide Leadership Symposium: Working Together to Make Visions Realities*

Illinois Chamber of Commerce *See Statewide Leadership Symposium: Working Together to Make Visions Realities*

Illinois Department of Alcohol and Substance *See InTouch*

Illinois Retail Merchant Association *See Governor's Office of Voluntary Action*

Illinois State Board of Education, pgs. 34, 816

Immaculate Heart Community *See CHIP-IN*

Improving Museum Volunteer Performance, pgs. 276, 533

In-Home Detention Program, pgs. 340, 913

In-Service Training/Statewide Volunteer Development, pgs. 133, 828

"In the Trenches" Author Search Program, pg. 65

Independence Isle, Inc. *See LaFreniere Park Special Recreation Programming Division*

Independence Neighborhood Councils, pg. 87

Independent Living for the Handicapped, pg. 861

Independent Living/Homeless Youth, pgs. 34, 874

Independent Sector, pgs. 4, 18, 301, 945, 947, 948, 950, 951, 955, 958, 980, 1016, 1018, 1019, 1041, 1042, 1043, 1096

Indian Arts and Crafts Board, pgs. 383, 527

Individual Giving/Volunteering Campaign*, pg. 61

Indochina Resource Action Center, pgs. 383, 825

Industrial Home for the Blind, pg. 849

Informal Steering Committee on Prescription Drug Abuse, pg. 612

Information and Referral Resource and Training Course, pg. 155

Information and Volunteer Services of Allegheny County *See Short Courses and Seminars for Administrators of Volunteers*

Information Center for Individuals with Disabilities, pg. 171

Information Center on Children's Cultures*, pgs. 161, 527

Information Exchange*, pgs. 177, 925

Information Resources Training Program, pg. 308

Information Service*, pgs. 174, 744

Informe SIDA, pgs. 384, 518

Ingraham Volunteers*, pg. 159

Inmate Spruce-Up Teams, pgs. 430, 763

Inside/Out*, pgs. 394, 872

Institute for Creative Conflict Management, pgs. 288, 565

Institute for Development of Educational Activities, pg. 626

Institute for Health Planning, pg. 1026

Institute for Neighborhood Initiative, pg. 987

Institute for Noetic Sciences, pg. 16

Institute for Responsive Education, pgs. 462, 1099

Institute for the Advanced Study of Volunteerism, pg. 243

Institute of Labor and Industrial Relations, pg. 972

Institute of Lifetime Learning, pgs. 901, 966, 967, 1046, 1073

Institute of Marriage and Family Relations, pg. 840

Institute of Scrap Recycling Industries, pgs. 1059, 1060, 1061

Institute on Federal Library Resources, pgs. 156, 636

Institute on Volunteer Administration: A Proposal, pg. 243

Institute on Volunteerism, pg. 243

Inter-Agency Volunteer Quarterly Forums, pg. 146

Interact Club, pgs. 467, 762

Interconnections, pg. 244

Intercultural Development Research Association (IDRA), pgs. 488, 630

Interdivisional Volunteer Program, pgs. 143, 829, 1034, 1071, 1095

Interfaith Center on Corporate Responsibility, pg. 22

Interfaith Council of Jacksonville, pg. 309

Interfaith Justice and Peace Center, pgs. 288, 565

Interfaith Shelter Network, pgs. 366, 886

Interfaith Volunteer Caregiving Workshop, pg. 357

Intergenerational Project for Service Learning, pg. 462

Intergenerational Service-Learning Project, pgs. 225, 888, 1097

Internal Revenue Service, pg. 971

International Association for Suicide Prevention, pgs. 179, 744, 1032

International Association of Justice Volunteerism, pgs. 697, 950, 1037 *See also Forum 90: Backward Glances... Forward Visions; Pre-Forum 90 Training Institutes*

International Association of Volunteer Effort, pgs. 5, 537

International AVA Leadership Bank, pg. 188

International Cultural Centers for Youth, pg. 528

International Guiding Eyes, pg. 846

International Hearing Dog, Inc., pg. 854

International Reading Association, pgs. 1007, 1009, 1047, 1068, 1073

International Very Special Arts Festival, pgs. 394, 530

Interracial Council for Business Opportunity, pg. 548

InTouch, pgs. 296, 600, 998

InTouch Program, pg. 998 *See also Prevention Makers*

Introduction to Volunteering, Etc., pg. 244

Introduction to Volunteerism in the Juvenile Justice System (Sociology 195: WX and WX2), pgs. 315, 714

Involvement Corps*, pgs. 27, 975, 978

Involvement, Inc., pgs. 23, 1095

Iowa Crime Commission/Scott County *See In-Home Detention Program*

Iowa Department of Social Services, pgs. 132, 826, 1021, 1080

Iowa Governor's Office for Volunteers, pg. 132

IRM Corporation *See Wholeffects Education: National Conference*

Isaiah House, pgs. 366, 520

Issues on Volunteerism: Service Learning in the Community, pg. 325

Ithaca City School District *See The Learning Web*

J

Jackie Robinson Foundation, pgs. 189, 803

Jackson Communications Management *See Statewide Leadership Symposium: Working Together to Make Visions Realities*

Jail 'N Bail on Capitol Hill, pgs. 113, 859

James Madison National Council, pgs. 197, 637

JANGO (Junior Army Navy Guild Organization)*, pgs. 341, 676

Japanese American Service Committee *See Governor's Office of Voluntary Action*

Jaycees *See Children's Miracle Network Telethon*

J.C. Penney Company, pgs. 15, 974

Jefferson County Medical Society, pgs. 440, 879

Jersey City Cultural Arts Commission See City Spirit Cultural Arts Festival
Jersey City Government See City Spirit Cultural Arts Festival
Jesse Cosby Neighborhood Center See Volunteer Training
Jesuit High School, pg. 478
Jesuit Service Project, pg. 478
Jesuit Volunteer Corps: Northwest, pgs. 80, 986
Jewish Braille Institute, pg. 1073
Jewish Braille Institute of America, pgs. 355, 846
Jewish Child Care Association of New York See Two Together*
Jewish Community Federation of Louisville, pg. 10
Jewish Family Services, pgs. 362, 516
Jewish Federation See Conference on Volunteerism
Jewish Guild for the Blind, pgs. 355, 846
Jewish Social Service Agency, pgs. 363, 786, 1065
Jewish Vocational Service, pgs. 387, 734
Jewish Volunteer Association, pg. 10
JFK Library Corps, pgs. 478, 1097
Jhoon Rhee Institute of Tae Kwon Do, pgs. 32, 918
Job Corps, pg. 656
Job Search, pgs. 366, 654
Job Therapy, Inc. (Ex-Offender Program: Project Start)*, pgs. 340, 662
Jobs for Older Women*, pgs. 438, 660
Jobs for Older Women Action Project, pg. 659
John Alden Books, pg. 1051
John Carroll University, pg. 230
John F. Kennedy Center for the Performing Arts See International Very Special Arts Festival
John F. Kennedy High School, pgs. 314, 713
John F. Kennedy Library Foundation, pg. 478
Johns Hopkins Tutorial Project, pg. 646
Johns Hopkins University, pgs. 646, 769
Joint Action in Community Service, pg. 957
Joint Advocacy Coalition for the Mentally Disabled, pgs. 331, 739
Joint Center for Political Studies, pg. 561
Joint Educational Project, pgs. 225, 888
Jonathan Jaques Children's Cancer Center, pgs. 120, 665
Jossey Bass, Publishers, pgs. 946, 947, 948, 951, 954, 982, 984, 986, 1003, 1032, 1041, 1043, 1047, 1073, 1074
The Journal, pg. 983
Journal Newspapers, pg. 1061
Junior Achievement (JA), pgs. 43, 546 See also Business Management/Junior Achievement
Junior League See 24-Hour Child Abuse/Neglect Telephone Report Line; Corporate Retirees Information and Assistance Program; Making the Volunteer Experience Count; The S.O.A.P.S.; Youth Volunteer Services
Junior League of Boston See Conference on Nonprofit Leadership and Management
Junior League of Chattanooga See Volunteer Training and Recruitment Conference
Junior League of Detroit, pgs. 87, 510
Junior League of Elizabeth/Plainfield See STS (Sharing Talents and Skills)
Junior League of Fort Smith, pg. 262
Junior League of Minneapolis See Market-Ability: Marketing Strategies for Nonprofits
Junior League of Pittsburgh See Volunteer Experience: Change, Challenge, Choices
Junior League of Reading See Community Board Training Day

Junior League of Topeka See Board Management Training Workshop
Junior League of Tuscaloosa See Boardsmanship Seminar*
Junior League of York See Volunteer Center of York County
Junior National Track and Field, pg. 927
Just Say No Clubs See Within You, Inc./Just Say No Clubs
Juvenile Arbitration Program of South Carolina, pgs. 336, 705
Juvenile Assistance, McLean, Ltd (JAM), pgs. 312, 814
Juvenile Justice Services, pg. 1038
Juvenile Reception and Diagnostic Center (JRDC), pgs. 366, 705
JVS Volunteer Tutorial Program, pgs. 387, 734

K

Kairos House, pgs. 21, 520
Kaiser Roll, pgs. 47, 869
Kansas City Department of Parks and Recreation, pgs. 55, 776
Kapolani Community College See Volunteer Training Program for Volunteer Advocates
Kappa Alpha Psi Fraternity See Young Black Scholars Program (YBS)
KCTS-TV, pg. 963
Kean College, pg. 157
Keene State College, pg. 624
Keep America Beautiful, pgs. 779, 973, 975, 1055, 1056, 1057, 1058, 1061, 1062
Keep Perrysburg Beautiful, pgs. 338, 777
Kellogg Foundation See Building Better Boards
Kennebec Valley Community Action Program, pg. 13
Kennedy Interns in Recreation*, pgs. 393, 863, 1083
Kent County Mental Hygiene Clinic/Day Hospital Volunteers*, pg. 741
Kentucky Commission on Aging, pg. 1083
Kentucky Dept. of Human Resources See Country Gathering
Kentwood Fire Department See High-Rise Fire Response Training
Kessler Institute for Rehabilitation Auxiliary, pgs. 113, 859
KFSN-TV Channel 30 (ABC affiliate) See End Hunger Project
Kids Helping Kids, pgs. 223, 612
King County Juvenile Judges Committee, pgs. 498, 722
King County Rape Relief, pg. 1037
King County Superior Court, pgs. 336, 701
Kirtland Community College, pgs. 413, 903
Kiwanis Club See Children's Miracle Network Telethon; Ramapo Key Club*
Kiwanis International, pgs. 92, 997
KMOL-TV, pgs. 109, 804
Knights of Columbus, pgs. 92, 392 See also Children's Miracle Network Telethon; Garden of Young Hearts
Knox County Child and Family Services, pgs. 163, 805
Knox County Schools See Adopt-A-School*; Recycling for Ravi
Knox County Schools Drug Prevention Office, pgs. 197, 606
Knoxville Child and Family Services, pg. 491
Knoxville City Schools See Adopt-A-School*
Knoxville Junior League See Adopt-A-School*
Knoxville Volunteer Coordinating Center, pg. 622
Knoxville Zoo Tiger Team, pgs. 484, 777
Knoxville Zoological Gardens, pg. 967 See also Recycling for Ravi

Kornreich Organization See Group Safety Association
KVIE-TV See Support for Public Television
KVIQ-TV See The Best Years
KYW-TV See Fighting Dirty!

L

La Brasserie Restaurant See Taste of the Nation
La Casa de Puerto Rico See Home-Based Child Care in Hartford
Labor Editors Roundtable, pg. 65
Labor Temple, pgs. 502, 691
LaFreniere Park Special Recreation Programming Division, pgs. 376, 924
Lake Arrowhead Conference for Volunteer Program Administrators, pg. 320
Lake Erie Marine Trades Association See Ottawa River "Fighting Back" Campaign
Lake Sylvia Conferences See Dynamite Planning... Explode Into Action!; Planning Today for Tomorrow's Volunteers*
Lake Sylvia V.I.P. (Very Important Person) Conference*, pg. 244
Lakes Region Conference on Volunteerism - Volunteers: A Caring Resource; A Practical Perspective, pg. 138
Lakes Region United Way See Lakes Region Conference on Volunteerism - Volunteers: A Caring Resource; A Practical Perspective
Lakeside School, pg. 278
Lamar University, pgs. 298, 617
Lancaster Information and Referral See Transitional Volunteer Program
Lapeer Board of Education See Special Olympics - Lapeer
Laramie County United Way See Recruiting, Training and Retention of Volunteers
Laramie County Voluntary Action Center See Recruiting, Training and Retention of Volunteers
Laramie County Volunteer Information/Action Center See Publicity Workshop
Larchmont Homes, pg. 103
Latino Outreach See Prevention through Action
Laubach Literacy See Time to Read
Laubach Literacy Action, pg. 732 See also Spartanburg Adult Writing and Reading (AWARE)
Laubach Literacy International, pg. 732
Laubach Literary Action See Memphis Literacy Council
Laurel Crest Manor See A Perfect Match
Law Enforcement Assistance Administration See Aid to Victims of Crime*
Law Enforcement Assistance Program, pgs. 118, 697
Law School Admission Council See Council on Legal Education Opportunity
Lead Poisoning Prevention Program, pg. 670
Leader Dogs for the Blind, pg. 846
Leadership: A Capital Investment, pg. 245
Leadership and Management of Volunteer Programs*, pg. 246
Leadership for the Nineties*, pg. 186
League of Conservation Voters*, pg. 761
League of Women Voters Education Fund, pgs. 376, 569
League of Women Voters of the US, pgs. 561, 760, 979, 980, 981, 984, 989, 1007, 1029, 1057 See also Virginia Volunteers - Health of the Commonwealth
Learning Disabilities Association of America, pg. 862
The Learning Web, pg. 313
Leave Bank, pgs. 49, 669
Lee County Restitution Program, pgs. 340, 730

Lee County Youth Services, pgs. 449, 822 *See also FIRST (Factual Information Regarding Sex and Teens)*

Leeward Community College *See Volunteer Training Program for Volunteer Advocates*

Legal Aid Society, pg. 1024 *See also Project HELP (Help Expedite Legal Problems for the Homeless)*

Legal Counsel for the Elderly, pgs. 439, 581

Legal Programs for the Homeless, pgs. 439, 881

Legal Services Corporation*, pg. 572

Legal Services for Children*, pgs. 432, 575

Legal Services for the Elderly, pgs. 432, 906

Legal Services for the Elderly Poor, pg. 581

Leisure Information Service, pgs. 177, 925

LeMoyne College, pg. 483

Let Us Volunteer Service (LUVS) Program, pgs. 1070, 1073

Lexington Senior Citizens Center, pgs. 399, 903

Lifestory Theater, pgs. 402, 534

Lifework Associates *See Help for You!*

Lillick & McHose, pgs. 442, 881

Lilly Foundation *See Mindstretchers; Youth As Resources; Youth as Resources/YMCA; Youth Resources of Southwestern Indiana*

Lincoln Action Program *See Youth Development Program*

Lincoln County Council on Aging *See Lincoln County Senior Companion Program*

Lincoln County Senior Companion Program, pgs. 395, 910

Lincoln Del/Storer Cable Communications, pgs. 47, 869

Lincoln Filene Center, pgs. 3, 615

Lincoln Filene Center for Citizenship & Public Affairs, pgs. 278, 946, 983

Lincoln School System, pgs. 111, 768

Linden School, pgs. 296, 639

Lindenwood Colleges, pg. 259

Lions Club *See Cape May County Volunteers and Resources; Children's Miracle Network Telethon*

Lions Club International, pg. 92

Lions International *See Lions Club International*

Literacy and Life Skills, pg. 735

Literacy Incentive Program (No Read, No Release), pgs. 430, 735

Literacy Volunteers of America, pgs. 732, 1047 *See also Time to Read; Volunteer Initiative Program (VIP)*

Literacy Volunteers of Chicago, pg. 735

Literacy Volunteers of New York State, pg. 735

Litterthon, pg. 779

Little City Foundation, pgs. 72, 853

Little League *See National Coalition for Volunteer Protection*

Little Red Hen, pgs. 968, 1100, 1101

Little Rock Animal Control, pgs. 383, 787

LIVE '89 (Leadership in Volunteerism Experience), pg. 130

Livingston County RSVP Program, pg. 402

Loaves & Fishes, pgs. 367, 882 *See also Help the Homeless Million Dollar Shootout*

Local Initiatives Support Corporation *See Manna, Inc.**

Local Volunteer School Councils, pgs. 198, 638

Logan Regional Hospital, pgs. 115, 903

Lollipop Power Books, pg. 1005

Long Beach Aquatic Park *See Champions Run For Life Torch Relay*

Long Beach Memorial Medical Center *See Champions Run For Life Torch Relay*

Long Beach Township Department of Public Works *See Beachfront Volunteers*

Long Beach Unified School District, pg. 88

Long Island Lighting Company, pgs. 54, 901

Longhorn Dodge *See Help the Homeless Million Dollar Shootout*

Looking Ahead: Managing Tomorrow's Volunteers, pg. 246

Los Angeles County Area Agency on Aging *See Senior Nutrition Program*

Los Angeles Department of Corrections *See Juvenile Reception and Diagnostic Center (JRDC)*

Los Angeles Olympic Organizing Committee, pg. 1082

Los Angeles Police Department, pgs. 455, 730

Los Angeles Poverty Department (LAPD), pgs. 75, 540

Los Angeles Unified School District, pgs. 429, 649, 1005, 1007, 1010

Los Gatos Mission Oaks Hospital *See Family Life and AIDS Instruction Program*

Los Gatos Union School District, pgs. 39, 516

Loudoun County Extension Services *See Virginia Volunteers - Health of the Commonwealth*

Loudoun House, pgs. 456, 690

Louisiana Nature and Science Center, pgs. 416, 783

Louisiana State Special Olympics Summer Games, pg. 869

Louisiana State University *See Louisiana State Special Olympics Summer Games*

Louisiana Training Institute*, pgs. 367, 705

Louisville Youth Involvement Committee, pg. 19

Lourdes College *See Peace Conference*

Low-Income Apartments Program, pgs. 355, 690

Lower Columbia Community Action Council, pg. 91

Loyal Order of Moose, pg. 92

Lung Association of Northern Virginia, pg. 1026

Luther Place Memorial Church, pgs. 367, 886

Luther Place Women's Shelter, pgs. 367, 886

Lutheran Church in America *See Lutheran Social Services Volunteer Program*

Lutheran Church/Missouri Synod *See Lutheran Social Services Volunteer Program*

Lutheran Church Women, pgs. 1006, 1046

Lutheran Metropolitan Ministry, pgs. 365, 666

Lutheran Resources Commission/Washington, pg. 303

Lutheran Social Service of Minnesota, pg. 950

Lutheran Social Services of North Dakota, pg. 1048

Lutheran Social Services Volunteer Program, pg. 368

M

M.A. in Volunteer Administration: The Goddard Graduate Program, pg. 246

MacDonald Media Services *See Public Relations on a Shoestring**

Macduff/Bunt Associates, pgs. 947, 953, 956, 984, 1042, 1090

Madison House, pgs. 164, 448, 469, 472, 474, 479, 489, 493, 574, 588, 648, 676, 693, 786, 820, 922

Magnolia Tree Earth Center, pgs. 480, 775

Mailer Education Seminars, pg. 8

Mainstream, pgs. 46, 857

Major Certificate Program for Volunteer Managers, pg. 247

Make-A-Wish Foundation *See Make-A-Wish Foundation of America*

Make-A-Wish Foundation of America, pg. 667

Make it Home for the Holidays, pgs. 37, 605

Making the Grade: A Report Card on American Youth, pgs. 192, 799

Making the Volunteer Experience Count, pgs. 281, 655

Mall Walkers, pg. 670

Management Development Seminar for Directors of Volunteer Services, pg. 247

Management of Volunteer Programs in the Armed Forces, pgs. 341, 889

Management of Volunteer Programs/Norwich, pg. 7

Management of Volunteer Programs/Sinclair, pg. 247

Management of Volunteer Services, pg. 248

Management Skills for Volunteer Leaders, pg. 248

Management Workshops for Nonprofit Organizations, pg. 248

Managing Volunteers for Results, pg. 249

Managing Your Fiscal Responsibilities as a Nonprofit: How to Avoid Financial Pitfalls, pg. 274

Manassas Municipal Airport *See Six Friends Memorial Fund*

Manchester Board of Mayor & Aldermen *See Youth Affairs Task Force*

Manchester School Board *See Youth Affairs Task Force*

Manchester School Committee *See Youth Affairs Task Force*

Manhattan Court Employment Project *See Court Employment Project*

Manna Bowl, pgs. 368, 758

Manna, Inc.*, pgs. 368, 683

Manpower Demonstration Research Corporation, pgs. 1078, 1080

Manteno Veterans Home, pgs. 403, 892

Manteno Veterans Home Volunteer Program, pgs. 403, 892

Maplewood Manor RSVP Program, pgs. 403, 786

March of Dimes, pgs. 113, 149, 667, 859, 961, 1087 *See also Center for Youth Service*

March of Dimes Birth Defects Foundation, pgs. 120, 860, 1086

Maricopa County Environmental Services, pg. 594

Maricopa County Private Industry Council *See Women Off Welfare (WOW)*

Marillac House, pgs. 84, 758

Marillac Social Center, pgs. 474, 748

Marine Mammal Stranding Center, pgs. 783, 1061

Market-Ability: Marketing Strategies for Nonprofits, pg. 62

Marketing for Voluntary Service Organizations, pg. 289

Marketing Strategies for Nonprofit Organizations, pg. 62

Marlborough Publications, pg. 1043

Marnie Holbrook Roberson Consultant Services *See Looking Ahead: Managing Tomorrow's Volunteers*

Marriott Corporation *See School Ecology Project; Training for Disabled Students*

Marshall School, pg. 326

The Marshall Service Unit and Volunteer Outreach, pg. 326

Martha's Table, pg. 1053

Martial Arts for Seniors, pg. 719

Mary Hitchcock Memorial Hospital *See NH State Conference on Volunteerism*

Maryland Department of Juvenile Services, pgs. 222, 704

Maryland Department of Natural Resources, pg. 780

Maryland Governor's Campaign, pg. 1058

Maryland Governor's Office, pg. 1055

Maryland Hunter Education Program, pgs. 133, 783

Maryland Nursing Home Ombudsmen *See Recruiting Techniques for Volunteer Organizations*

Maryland Save Our Streams (SOS) *See Adopt-A-Stream*

Maryland Tidewater Administration *See Adopt-A-Stream*

Maryvale, pg. 1076

Masonic Temple *See CPSS Fashion Show*

Massachusetts Aquatic Resource Education Program (AREP), pg. 928

Massachusetts Association for the Blind*, pg. 849

Massachusetts Department of Corrections *See Inmate Spruce-Up Teams*

Massachusetts Department of Public Works, pgs. 430, 763

Massachusetts Division of Fisheries and Wildlife, pgs. 928, 1082

Massachusetts General Hospital, pg. 247

Massachusetts Hospital Association *See Management Development Seminar for Directors of Volunteer Services*

Massachusetts Institute of Technology, pg. 1009

Master Builder Game, pgs. 440, 626

Master Chemical Company *See Curb It!*

Master of Professional Studies Degree: Fund Raising Management, pg. 302

Masuk High School, pgs. 66, 853

Matching Funds Project, pg. 102

Mature Outlook, pgs. 331, 898

Maxima Corporation *See Champ Bakery*

May Department Stores *See U.S. National Senior Olympics*

Mayor's Voluntary Action Center, pgs. 949, 1072

McClellan AFB Health Fair, pgs. 343, 672

McCormick and Company, pg. 972

McDonald's Corporation, pg. 973

McDonald's of Paragould, Arkansas, pgs. 56, 937

McDonald's Restaurants *See Community Block Homes; Helping Hand*

McDonnell Douglas Corporation, pg. 1065

McGraw-Hill Book Store, pg. 951

McNeil Pharmaceutical, Division of McNeilab, pgs. 37, 599

Meals on Wheels of Birmingham, pgs. 369, 908

Meals on Wheels of Buffalo and Erie County, pgs. 380, 748, 1054

Meals on Wheels of Central Maryland, pg. 1053

Meals on Wheels Program of ACCA, pgs. 369, 873

Meals on Wheels Program of Rochester, pg. 1053

Mecklenburg Correctional Center, pgs. 429, 703

Media Access Project, pg. 61

Media General *See Adopt-A-School*

Media Relations for Nonprofit and Volunteer Organizations, pg. 290

Medical Services - AIDS Program, pg. 513

Medical Services Program, pgs. 479, 676

Mega Foods *See Conner-Harris Mini Mall*

Memphis AIDS Coalition *See Heart Strings - Memphis Stop*

Memphis Board of Education *See Fund for Needy School Children*

Memphis Health Department *See Fund for Needy School Children*

Memphis Literacy Council, pg. 736

Mended Hearts, pgs. 456, 673

Mennonite Urban Ministry *See Continental Homeless Assistance Program*

Mental Health Association, pg. 739

Mental Health Association in Maui, pg. 745

Mental Health Association of Rhode Island *See Volunteers with Special Needs*

Mental Health Players, pgs. 76, 743

Mental Retardation Association of America, pg. 863

Merrimack County RSVP *See Lakes Region Conference on Volunteerism - Volunteers: A Caring Resource; A Practical Perspective*

Mervyn's Department Stores *See Communicating Human Needs*

Mesa Chamber of Commerce *See Women Off Welfare (WOW)*

Mesa United Way, pgs. 396, 940

A Message for the Future - The Voluntas Time Capsule, pgs. 15, 569

Metamorphosis: Growth and Change in the Administration of Volunteer Services, pg. 250

Metro Alternative Shelter House (MASH), pgs. 35, 818

Metro-HELP, pgs. 162, 805

Metro High School, pg. 93

Metro United Way, pgs. 19, 1101

Metromedia *See James Madison National Council*

Metropolitan Community College *See Human Service Programs: Volunteer Leadership Emphasis Area*

Metropolitan Council for Community Services, pg. 323 *See also Voluntary Action Center of Chattanooga*

Metropolitan Council of Directors of Volunteers, pgs. 285, 797

Metropolitan Life Insurance Company, pg. 978 *See also Seaside Health Promotion Conference*

Metropolitan State University *See University Programs for Volunteers and Administrators of Volunteers*

Metropolitan Washington Council of Governments *See But I'm Different...*

Mexican-American Legal Defense and Educational Fund, pg. 578

Miami County Cooperative Extension Service, pg. 842

Miami County Extension Service and Health Department *See Wednesday Morning Mothers*

Michigan Board of Education *See Quality Education Program*

Michigan Coalition Against Domestic Violence, pgs. 165, 837, 1033

Michigan Department of Natural Resources *See Friends of the Rouge*

Michigan Department of Social Services, pgs. 301, 828 *See also In-Service Training/Statewide Volunteer Development*

Michigan Special Olympics State Games, pgs. 479, 869

Michigan State Police *See Project Graduation*

Michigan State University, pgs. 260, 485

Michigan Statewide Volunteer Development, pgs. 133, 828

Mid-Atlantic Center for Community Education *See First State Conference on School Volunteers*

Mid-Atlantic Regional Council *See Community Partners Program**

Mid-Cumberland Community Action Agency (CAA), pg. 407

Mid-South Industries *See Chamber of Commerce Literacy Council*

Mid-Valley Adolescent Center*, pgs. 35, 706

MIDAS Touch, pgs. 108, 548

Middletown Public Schools *See Basic Leader Training Course*

Migrant Recreation Program, pgs. 479, 922

Migration and Refugee Service, pgs. 356, 825, 1070, 1074, 1079

Military Educators and Counselors Association, pgs. 377, 793

Military Family Resource Center, pg. 1097

Milton Cares Telephone Reassurance, pgs. 404, 787

Milton Eisenhower Foundation *See Project Right Start*

Milton Police Department *See Milton Cares Telephone Reassurance*

Milwaukee and the Single Girl*, pgs. 480, 778

Mindstretchers, pgs. 192, 627

Mini-Grant Program, pg. 99

Mini-Grants: Research in Volunteerism, pg. 99

Minneapolis Community College *See The Supervisory Cycle*

Minneapolis Public Schools, pgs. 435, 476, 627, 644

Minneapolis Urban League Volunteer Services*, pg. 95

Minnesota Association for Field Experience Learning *See Demystifying the Internship Experience*

Minnesota Association of Volunteer Centers *See Dynamite Planning... Explode Into Action!; Planning Today for Tomorrow's Volunteers**

Minnesota Association of Volunteer Directors *See Dynamite Planning... Explode Into Action!; Regional Volunteer Workshops*

Minnesota Correctional Facility-Red Wing, pgs. 498, 708

Minnesota Department of Human Services *See Virginia Volunteers - Health of the Commonwealth*

Minnesota Extension Service/Anoka County, pg. 578

Minnesota Office of Volunteer Services, pgs. 134, 135

Minorities Caucus of Family Service America, pgs. 331, 835

Minority Entrepreneurship Program*, pgs. 27, 549

Minority Volunteers: Pluralism in the Volunteer Arena, pg. 384

Miracle Week, pgs. 370, 688

Miss Michigan Pageant *See Michigan Special Olympics State Games*

Mission House, pgs. 440, 879

Missionary Sisters of Charity *See Continental Homeless Assistance Program*

Mississippi Library Commission, pg. 637

Mississippi Office of Volunteerism, pg. 136

Missouri Division of Family Services *See Show-Me Seminars*

Missouri Office for Volunteer Effectiveness (MOVE) *See Statewide Conference on Volunteerism*

Missouri School System *See Show-Me Seminars*

Missouri Volunteer Office *See Show-Me Seminars*

Missouri Volunteers, pgs. 136, 617

Mobil Oil *See Adopt-A-School*

Mobile School System *See Schoolmate Handicraft Volunteers*

Model Mugging, pgs. 450, 727

M.O.M.S. (Mothers On the Move Spiritually), pgs. 417, 706

Monmouth County Child Assault Prevention Division *See Child Assault Prevention Team*

Monroe County Government *See Air Crash Drill*

Montefiore Medical Center *See Project BRAVO*

Montgomery Anti-Drug Conference, pgs. 295, 606

Montgomery County Department of Recreation *See Martial Arts for Seniors*

Montgomery County Department of Social Services, pgs. 294, 813

Montgomery County (MD) Health *See AIDS Program*

Montgomery County Panel on Drug Problems, pgs. 295, 606, 1001

Montgomery County Public Schools, pg. 642

Montgomery County School Volunteer Program, pg. 642

Montgomery General Hospital, pgs. 477, 906, 1072, 1096 *See also Taking a Trip to Friendship*

Montgomery Ward *See Women Off Welfare (WOW)*

More Than Meets The Ear - A Listening Skills Seminar, pg. 308

Morris 2000, pg. 559

Morris County Board of Chosen Freeholders *See Morris County Chaplaincy Council*

Morris County Chaplaincy Council, pgs. 370, 721

Morris County Department of Human Services, pg. 757

Morris County Nutrition Program, pg. 757

Morro Bay Harbor Festival, pg. 531

Morrow Junior Books, pg. 1097

Mortgage Bankers Association of America, pg. 1069

Mortgage Burning Fund, pgs. 116, 686, 961, 968, 1029, 1042, 1066, 1091

Most Incomprehensive Government Regulation Award Program, pg. 542

Mothers Against Drunk Driving, pgs. 413, 602, 1000 *See also Drunk-Driving Simulator Program and Forum*

Mothers of PWAs (Persons With AIDS), pgs. 226, 522

Motor Voters, pgs. 457, 567

Mott Foundation *See FEAT Foundation; Training for the Municipal Volunteer Coordinator*; Youth Volunteer Services*

Mount Carmel Guild in Newark *See White Cane Drive*

Mount Hood National Forest, pg. 597

Mount Vernon Center for Community Mental Health, pg. 1050

Mount Zion United Methodist Church, pgs. 359, 533

MOVE (Mobilization of Volunteers), pg. 480

Movement for Economic Justice, pg. 553

Mt. Adams Ministerial Association Food Bank, pgs. 370, 753

Mt. Garfield Plumbing and Heating *See Youth Who Care*

Mu Omega Chapter/TKE, pg. 392

Multi-Phasic Health Screening, pgs. 404, 680

Multiple Sclerosis Society of Orange County, pgs. 394, 866

Multnomah County Sheriff's Office, pg. 595

Murphy Oil Corporation *See James Madison National Council*

Muscular Dystrophy Association *See Seacoast Conference on Volunteerism: A Time for Growth; A Time for Change*

Museum of History and Industry *See Seattle-King County RSVP (Retired Senior Volunteer Program)*

My Own Meals, Inc., pg. 1053

Mynderse Academy *See Seneca Falls Concerned Parents*

N

NAACP, pgs. 296, 631

The Name of the Game is Caring, pgs. 465, 919

The NAMES Project/AIDS Memorial Quilt, pgs. 67, 513

The NAMES Project Foundation, pgs. 67, 513, 515, 963

NASA *See Master Builder Game*

Nassau County Youth Board *See Big Brothers/Big Sisters of Nassau County**

National Academy for Voluntarism, pg. 181

National Academy for Volunteerism, pg. 155

National Academy for Volunteers in Education, pgs. 297, 617

National Accreditation Council for Agencies Serving the Blind and Physically Handicapped, pg. 1078

National AIDS Information Campaign, pgs. 67, 513

National AIDS Network, pg. 508

National Air Conservation Commission, pg. 762

National Alliance for Safer Cities, pg. 1039

National Alliance of Blind Students, pgs. 393, 846

National Alliance of Business, pgs. 23, 975 *See also Student Volunteer/Work Project (SV/WP)*

National Alliance of Business/Houston, pgs. 41, 720

National Alliance of Senior Citizens, pgs. 397, 898

National Assembly of Voluntary Health and Social Welfare Organizations, pgs. 5, 951, 986

National Association for Child Care Management, pg. 583

National Association for Creative Children and Adults, pgs. 524, 967

National Association for Hispanic Elderly, pgs. 901, 985, 1020, 1068, 1076

National Association for Human Development, pg. 902

National Association for Parents of the Visually Impaired, pgs. 225, 785

National Association for Partners in Education, pgs. 297, 617

National Association for the Education of Young Children, pgs. 583, 992, 993, 994, 995

National Association for the Physically Handicapped*, pgs. 452, 842

National Association for the Southern Poor, pgs. 452, 566

National Association of Alcoholism and Drug Abuse Counselors, pg. 598

National Association of Alcoholism Counselors *See National Association of Alcoholism and Drug Abuse Counselors*

National Association of Broadcasters, pgs. 61, 983

National Association of Citizens' Crime Commissions, pgs. 195, 697

National Association of Community Leadership Organizations, pgs. 204, 566

National Association of Conservation Districts, pgs. 189, 766

National Association of Extension Home Economists, pgs. 432, 825

National Association of Foreign Student Affairs *See Cross-Cultural Community Workshop*

National Association of Housing & Redevelopment Officials, pgs. 682, 946, 1027, 1028, 1072

National Association of Housing Cooperatives, pgs. 685, 1027

National Association of Investment Companies, pgs. 99, 548

National Association of Neighborhoods, pg. 80

National Association of Older Americans*, pgs. 73, 397, 895

National Association of Partners in Education, pgs. 42, 298, 618, 620, 657, 973, 1007, 1009, 1010

National Association of People with AIDS, pgs. 424, 523

National Association of Perinatal Addiction Research and Education, pgs. 295, 931

National Association of Police Athletic Leagues, pgs. 425, 918

National Association of Rehabilitation Facilities, pgs. 984, 1071, 1076

National Association of Secondary School Principals, pg. 616

National Association of Town Watch, pg. 452 *See also National Town Watch Association*

National Association of Volunteers in Criminal Justice, pgs. 292, 293, 316, 317, 713, 714, 715 *See also International Association of Justice Volunteerism (IAJV)*

National Association of Women Business Owners, pgs. 107, 548, 549

National Association of Women Highway Safety Leaders, pgs. 205, 935

National Association on Drug Abuse Problems, pg. 606

National Audubon Society *See Clean the Bay Day*

National Automobile Dealers Association, pgs. 451, 582

National Bar Association *See Council on Legal Education Opportunity*

National Black Child Development Institute, pg. 586

National Board of YMCAs, pgs. 285, 797

National Braille Association, pg. 846

National Business League, pg. 549

National CASA Association, pgs. 333, 807, 1095, 1099

National Catholic Disaster Relief Committee, pgs. 356, 591

National Catholic Rural Life Conference *See Catholic Committee of Appalachia*

National Celebration of the Outdoors, pg. 769

National Center for a Barrier Free Environment, pg. 844

National Center for Appropriate Technology, pg. 772

National Center for Community Action*, pg. 91

National Center for Community Crime Prevention, pgs. 75, 713

National Center for Hearing Dog Information, pgs. 171, 782

National Center for Missing and Exploited Children, pg. 813

National Center for Nonprofit Boards, pgs. 183, 951, 1042, 1043, 1044

National Center for Therapeutic Riding, pg. 870

National Center for Voluntary Action *See VOLUNTEER - The National Center*

National Center on Child Abuse and Neglect, pgs. 108, 813, 994, 1038, 1075, 1098

National Challenge Committee on Disability *See Challenge International*

National Charities Information Bureau, pgs. 952, 1018, 1020

National Child Day Care Association, pgs. 994, 995

National Child Labor Committee, pg. 586

National Children's Center *See Troop 400 and Troop 391*

National Civic League*, pg. 553

National Clean Air Coalition, pg. 762

National Clearinghouse for Criminal Justice Planning and Architecture, pg. 717

National Clearinghouse for Improving the Management of Human Services, pg. 5

National Clearinghouse for Legal Services, pgs. 974, 1006, 1010, 1011, 1067, 1074

National Clearinghouse for Poison Control Centers, pgs. 171, 670

National Clearinghouse on Aging, pg. 1060

National Clearinghouse on Volunteerism, pg. 4

National Clients Council, pgs. 331, 572

National Coalition for Parent Involvement in Education *See National Academy for Volunteers in Education*

National Coalition for the Homeless, pgs. 201, 873, 881, 1069, 1072, 1075, 1076, 1078

National Coalition for Volunteer Protection, pgs. 7, 553, 956

National Coalition of Christian Volunteers in Criminal Justice *See Problems Facing Volunteer Leaders Today**

National Coalition of Hispanic Health and Human Services Organizations, pgs. 959, 1022 *See also AIDS Public Education Program*

National Collaboration for Youth, pgs. 68, 796

National Commission for Employment Policy, pgs. 972, 1011

National Commission on Resources for Youth, pg. 462

National Committee Against Discrimination in Housing, pgs. 685, 1027, 1028, 1029

National Committee for Citizens in Education, pg. 1095

National Committee for Prevention of Alcoholism and Drug Dependency, pg. 598

National Committee for Prevention of Child Abuse, pgs. 70, 813 *See also Child Protective Services*

National Committee on Art Education for the Elderly, pgs. 188, 899

National Committee on the Education of Migrant Children, pg. 586

National Community Action Foundation, pgs. 91, 825

National Community Education *See ROVERS (Retired and Older Volunteers: An Educational Resource Service)*

National Community Organizing Project (NCOP), pgs. 201, 873

National Community Service Sentencing Association, pg. 723

National Conference for Volunteer Leadership*, pg. 136

National Conference of Black Lawyers, pgs. 432, 580

National Conference of Catholic Charities *See Catholic Charities USA*

National Conference on Drug Abuse and Parenting*, pgs. 295, 931

National Conference on Neighborhood Concerns *See Neighborhoods USA*

National Conference on Parent Involvement, pgs. 414, 638

National Conference on Volunteerism, pg. 250

National Consumers League, pg. 572

National Cooperative Business Association, pgs. 576, 988, 989, 991

National Correctional Recreational Association, pg. 723

National Council for Equal Business Opportunity, pg. 549

National Council of Catholic Women *See Association of Ladies of Charity of the US*

National Council of Community Mental Health Centers*, pg. 740

National Council of Jewish Women, pgs. 257, 945, 995, 1038, 1070, 1073, 1074, 1075 *See also CASA Project (Court Appointed Special Advocates)*

National Council of Puerto Rican Volunteers, pg. 5

National Council of Senior Citizens, pgs. 397, 895

National Council of the YMCAs *See Young Men's Christian Association of the U.S.*

National Council on Alcoholism, pgs. 602, 973, 997, 998, 999, 1043

National Council on Employment Policy, pg. 1012

National Council on Family Relations, pgs. 169, 837, 1022, 1065, 1071, 1086, 1087

National Council on the Aging, pgs. 74, 203, 225, 332, 462, 464, 888, 896, 898, 900, 903, 905, 966, 981, 984, 988, 989, 995, 1012, 1013, 1023, 1024, 1028, 1029, 1041, 1066, 1067, 1068, 1069, 1070, 1074, 1075, 1076, 1077, 1085, 1089, 1097, 1098, 1099, 1100 *See also Family Friends Project*

National Council on the Black Aging, pg. 562

National Court Appointed Special Advocate Association, pgs. 331, 807

National Crime Prevention Council, pgs. 100, 196, 697, 718, 1098 *See also Crime, Law and Community: A Student Service Curriculum; National Town Watch Association; Teens as Community Resources*; Youth As Resources; Youth as Resources/YMCA; Youth Resources of Southwestern Indiana*

National Criminal Justice Reference Service, pgs. 1037, 1038, 1039

National Dance Institute, pgs. 32, 525

National Domestic Violence Hotline, pgs. 165, 837

National Down Syndrome Congress, pgs. 199, 864

National Easter Seal Society, pg. 843

National Education Association, pgs. 967, 993, 1005, 1006, 1008

National Education-Training Program: Volunteer Court-Corrections Movement, pgs. 316, 700

National Emergency Food and Shelter Board *See Prime Time to End Hunger*

National Employment and Training Association, pg. 652

National Endowment for the Arts, pg. 525 *See also East Tennessee Community Design Center*

National Endowment for the Humanities, pg. 1018

National Energy Foundation, pg. 773

National Energy Resources Organization, pg. 773

National Extension Homemakers Council, pg. 825

National Eye Care Project, pgs. 172, 679

National Federation of Interfaith Volunteer Caregivers, pgs. 356, 357, 861, 1095

National Federation of State High School Associations, pg. 604

National Forum on a Commission on Volunteerism: The Federal Government and Future of Volunteerism*, pgs. 14, 555

National Foundation for Consumer Credit, pg. 577

National Friends of Public Broadcasting, pg. 62

National Gallery of Art, pg. 528

National Gallery of Art Extension Programs, pg. 528

National Gardening Association, pgs. 923, 1053, 1062

National Geographic Society *See National Celebration of the Outdoors*

National Governors' Association, pgs. 122, 949

National Governors' Conference *See National Governors' Association*

National Head Start Association*, pg. 583

National Health Council*, pgs. 664, 1024

National Health Screening Council *See Be Alive in 2005: Promoting Wellness into the 21st Century*

National Health Screening Council for Volunteer Organizations*, pgs. 200, 671

National Home Demonstration Council *See National Extension Homemakers Council*

National HomeCaring Council, pgs. 172, 836

National Hospice Organization, pg. 674

National Housing Conference, pgs. 201, 682

National Housing Partnership, pgs. 116, 686 *See also Loudoun House*

National Hunger Coalition, pgs. 76, 756

National Indian Youth Council, pg. 198

National Information Center for Children and Youth with Handicaps, pgs. 171, 861

National Information Center on Deafness, pgs. 20, 855, 1072, 1080

National Injury Information Center, pgs. 163, 670

National Institute for Work and Learning, pgs. 1010, 1011

National Institute of Social Welfare Research, pgs. 1068, 1097

National League of Cities, pgs. 557, 1042

National Legal Aid and Defender Association, pg. 572

National Legal Resource Center for Child Advocacy and Protection, pgs. 332, 813, 1074

National Library Service for the Blind, pgs. 397, 846

National Listen America Club, pgs. 462, 603

National Live Stock and Meat Board, pg. 993

National Media Resource Center on the Aging, pgs. 74, 900

National Mental Health Association, pgs. 76, 740, 976, 1048, 1049

National Military Family Association, pgs. 332, 838

National Multiple Sclerosis Society *See Multiple Sclerosis Society of Orange County*

National Municipal League *See Civic Partnership: Initiative, Innovation**

National Network of Runaway and Youth Services *See Youth Development*

National Network of Youth Advisory Boards, pgs. 189, 796, 1043, 1100

National Organization of Adolescent Pregnancy and Parenting, pg. 930

National Organization on Disability (NOD), pgs. 71, 843

National Parent Teachers Association *See National Coalition for Volunteer Protection; Statewide Drug Task Force Conference*

National Partnerships in Education Program, pg. 1008

National Peace Garden, pgs. 565, 980

National Peace Institute Foundation, pg. 563

National Peer Helpers Association, pgs. 452, 794

National Police Athletic League *See National Association of Police Athletic Leagues*

National Priorities Project, pg. 553

National Prison Project, pgs. 433, 717

National Public Radio, pgs. 65, 74, 823, 982, 985

National Recreation and Park Association, pgs. 917, 1018, 1082

National Resource Center for Consumers of Legal Services*, pgs. 164, 572

National Ridesharing Information Center, pg. 1092

National Runaway Switchboard, pgs. 161, 804

National Rural Health Association, pg. 669

National Safety Council, pg. 935

National School Volunteer Program *See Show-Me Seminars*

National Self-Help Clearinghouse, pgs. 221, 1085

National Senior Citizens Law Center, pgs. 581, 990

National Society for Internships & Experiential Education, pg. 310

National Society of Black Engineering Students *See Young Black Scholars Program (YBS)*

National Society of the DAC *See Echoes of the Past*

National Solar Heating and Cooling Information Center, pg. 773

National Strategy in Marketing *See Champ Bakery*

National Support Center for Families of the Aging, pgs. 452, 791

National Technical Information Service, pg. 971

National Town Watch Association, pgs. 202, 708, 1038 *See also National Association of Town Watch*

National Training and Information Center*, pgs. 328, 567

National Urban Coalition, pgs. 558, 1009, 1013, 1083

National Urban League *See AIDS Public Education Program*

National Voluntary Organizations Active in Disaster, pg. 591

National Voluntary Organizations for Independent Living for the Aged, pgs. 905, 1028, 1066, 1071, 1072, 1075, 1092

National Volunteer Project*, pg. 917

National Water Project*, pg. 780

National Wheelchair Athletic Association, pgs. 47, 868

National Wildlife Federation, pgs. 472, 769

National Workshop on Voluntarism, pg. 251

National Youth Council on Civic Affairs, pgs. 462, 557

National Youth Service Day 1990, pg. 208

Nature Conservancy, pg. 766

Navajo United Way *See American Indian Partnerships with United Ways*

Navy Family Service Center, pg. 957

Navy League of the United States *See Campaign Drug Free*

Navy Volunteers at Guantanamo Bay, pgs. 350, 892

NAWBO Scholarship Fund, pgs. 107, 549

NCSL Job Skills Development Seminars, pgs. 282, 655

Neal-Schuman Publications, pg. 1008

Nebraska Organization of Volunteer Leaders *See Volunteers in Great Britain: A Study Tour*

Neighborhood Anti-Crime Rally/Community Forum, pgs. 382, 708

Neighborhood Councils Service Center, pg. 87

Neighborhood Development Services Center, pgs. 80, 777

Neighborhood Probation Unit, pgs. 496, 913

Neighborhood Tree Corps, pgs. 480, 775

Neighborhoods USA, pgs. 204, 288, 558, 828, 1085

Neighbors Helping Neighbors, pgs. 53, 753

Net Result Tennis Foundation, pgs. 441, 920

Network *See Catholic Committee of Appalachia*

Network Directory, pg. 1033

Neutrogena, Inc. *See James Madison National Council*

New Breed Drill Team, pgs. 481, 920

New Brunswick Board of Education *See Communications Skills for the College Bound*

New Brunswick High School, pgs. 190, 560

New Directions for the Bronx, pg. 559

New England Center for Continuing Education, pgs. 404, 851

New England Environmental Leadership Network, pg. 1057

New England Environmental Network, pg. 1057

New England Free Press, pg. 983

New England Medical Center *See From All Walks of Life*

New England Municipal Center, pgs. 258, 555

New Hampshire Association for the Blind *See Lakes Region Conference on Volunteerism - Volunteers: A Caring Resource; A Practical Perspective*

New Hampshire Foster Grandparent Program, pgs. 404, 851

New Hampshire Jaycees *See Seacoast Conference on Volunteerism: A Time for Growth; A Time for Change*

New Hampshire Public School District *See The Shed Project**

New Hampshire State Department *See The Shed Project**

New Hampshire Vocational Technical College *See Seacoast Conference on Volunteerism: A Time for Growth; A Time for Change*

New Heights Restaurant *See Taste of the Nation*

New Jersey Association Directors of Volunteer Services, pg. 1097

New Jersey Board of Education *See Beachfront Volunteers*

New Jersey Department of Human Services *See The Self-Help Movement: New Form of Volunteerism and a Resource for Professionals**

New Jersey Division of Youth & Family Services *See Volunteer Initiative Program (VIP)*

New Jersey NAACP, pg. 567

New Jersey Office of the Governor, pgs. 140, 686

New Jersey Office of Volunteerism, pgs. 139, 945, 1021

New Jersey Self-Help Clearinghouse, pg. 222

New Jersey Special Olympics *See White Cane Drive*

New Life Farm, pg. 770

New Lives, pg. 932

New Mexico Statewide Conference on Volunteerism, pg. 141

New Opportunities for Waterbury *See Central Naugatuck Valley Retired Senior Volunteer Program*

New Orleans Public Schools *See Growing Up With Nature*

New Orleans School System *See New Orleans Volunteers*

New Orleans Volunteers, pg. 642

New Readers Press, pgs. 732, 990, 991, 994, 1009, 1010, 1013, 1023, 1036, 1046, 1047, 1048, 1049, 1086, 1087, 1088, 1093

New St. Peter Baptist Church *See West St. John Ministry of Care*

New School for Social Research, pg. 302

New Volunteer Coordinator's Training, pg. 251

New York Avenue Meals on Wheels, pgs. 411, 749

New York Avenue Presbyterian Church *See Seniors: Special Delivery*

New York City Board of Education, pg. 631

New York City Human Resources Administration *See Minority Volunteers: Pluralism in the Volunteer Arena*

New York City School Volunteer Program*, pgs. 643, 1008

New York Daily News *See New Directions for the Bronx*

New York Giants *See Master Builder Game*

New York Giants School Speakers Program, pgs. 449, 630

New York Law Enforcement Division *See Flame of Hope*

New York Office of Advocate for the Disabled, pg. 1081

New York State Department of Corrections, pgs. 430, 707

New York State Division for Youth *See Amherst Y.E.S. (Youth Engaged in Service); Big Brothers/Big Sisters of Nassau County*; Court Referred Volunteer Program of Rensselaer County; The Learning Web*

New York State General Accounting Service *See Student Volunteer/Work Project (SV/WP)*

New York State School System *See Crime, Law and Community: A Student Service Curriculum*

Newark Board of Education *See Forum on School Vandalism*

Newark City Council, pgs. 315, 703

Newark Library League, pg. 641

Newark Library League Scholarship Program, pg. 641

Newark Police Department *See Forum on School Vandalism*

Newark Star-Ledger *See Morris 2000*

Newsday Newspapers, pg. 17

Newsday Volunteer Recognition Program, pg. 17

Newsletter Factory, pgs. 63, 984

NH State Conference on Volunteerism, pg. 138

NHTSA Hotline, pgs. 164, 582

No Greater Love, pg. 563

Noche Cubana (Cuban Night), pgs. 384, 531

Nonprofit Mailers Federation, pgs. 287, 554

Norfolk Catholic Christian Service Program, pg. 481

Norfolk Catholic High School, pg. 481

Norman Police Department, pg. 936

North American Family Campers Association, pg. 927

North American Riding for the Handicapped Association, pg. 870

North Carolina Department of Justice *See How to Work Effectively with Volunteers*

North Carolina Justice Academy, pg. 242

North Carolina/Virginia Exchange: Part One, pg. 142

North Conway Institute, pg. 598

North Dakota Association of Coordinators of Volunteer Services, pg. 250

North High Community Service Program, pg. 94

North High School, pg. 94

North Penn Senior Center *See Graterfriends*

North Shore Civil Defense Team, pgs. 128, 594

North Shore Community Action Programs, pg. 1029

North Shore Community College Volunteer Office, pg. 244

Northeast Kentucky Area Development Council, pgs. 400, 757

Northeast Service Center, pg. 655

Northeastern Bible College, pg. 361

Northern Illinois University *See Leadership and Management of Volunteer Programs**

Northern Virginia Association for Volunteer Administration, pg. 952

Northern Virginia Community College, pg. 481 *See also Get Away Clean*

Northern Virginia Hotline, pgs. 159, 1034

Northern Virginia Long-Term Care, pgs. 337, 899

Northport Veterans' Hospital *See Handicapped Volunteer/Volunteering for the Handicapped*

Northside Surgical Supply, pgs. 30, 872

Northwest Alabama Reading Aides, pg. 736

Northwest Ohio School District *See Health and Safety Circus*

Northwestern University *See Volunteers: Empowerment Today and Tomorrow*

Not on My Block, pgs. 501, 610

Notre Dame *See Study War No More*

Noxzema Extraordinary Teen Contest, pg. 27

Noxzema Skin Cream, pg. 27

Nursing Home Project, pgs. 405, 907

Nurturing Network, pg. 930

Nutrition Education and Information, pgs. 176, 750

Nutrition Foundation, pgs. 176, 750

Nutrition Institute of America, pg. 750

O

Oak Park and River Forest High School, pgs. 482, 771

Oakton Community College/MONNACEP, pgs. 624, 1007

O.A.R. of Roanoke See Offender Aid and Restoration of Roanoke, Virginia*

OAR/USA See Offender Aid and Restoration of Fairfax County

Ocala Volunteer Center See Volunteer Management Certification

Ocala Volunteer Service Center See Management Skills for Volunteer Leaders

Occidental Life Insurance Companies See Public Relations on a Shoestring*

Occidental Restaurant See Taste of the Nation

Ocean County College, pgs. 305, 674

Ocean County Tourism Advisory Council See Beachfront Volunteers

O'Connell High School, pgs. 425, 613

Odell Associates See Tampa Causeway Beautification Project

ODPHP National Health Information Center, pgs. 172, 677

ODT, Inc., pg. 950

Odyssey House, pg. 599

Offender Aid and Restoration, pg. 720

Offender Aid and Restoration of Fairfax County, pgs. 721, 1037

Offender Aid and Restoration of Roanoke, Virginia*, pg. 706

Office for Church In Society, pgs. 357, 554

Office for Special Constituencies, pg. 525

Office of Children and Youth (OCY), pgs. 129, 817

Office of Community Investment, pg. 692

Ogden Department of Aging and Volunteer Services See ARC Covenant

Ogilvy and Mather, pg. 1017

Ohio AFL-CIO See Labor Editors Roundtable

Ohio State Hospital See Project Passage

Ohio State Scenic Rivers Program See Ottawa River "Fighting Back" Campaign

Ohio State University, pg. 927

OIC National Shelter Program, pgs. 457, 887

OIC of America See OIC National Shelter Program

Oklahoma City Literacy Council, pgs. 202, 737

Oklahoma Department of Economic and Community Affairs See Bridging Volunteer Resources

Oklahoma Department of Mental Health See Teenline

Oklahoma Historical Society See Echoes of the Past

Oklahoma University Health Sciences Center, pgs. 163, 806

Old Dominion University, pgs. 315, 714

Older Adult Offender Project, pg. 661

Older Americans as a Growing National Resource*, pg. 320

Older Women's League (OWL), pgs. 74, 896

Olympic Day in the Schools/Olympic Day For Youth, pg. 926

Olympic Organizing Committee*, pg. 926

Ombudsman Program, pgs. 337, 899, 1071, 1076

On-Site Programs for Volunteer Organizations, pg. 279

One Hundred Black Men of Los Angeles, pgs. 384, 633

One Million Marylanders for the Bay See Adopt-A-Stream

Operation Child Watch, pg. 813

Operation Clean Sweep, pgs. 371, 764

Operation Cover Up, pgs. 405, 874

Operation Coverup, pgs. 428, 764

Operation Good Neighbor, pg. 744

Operation Outreach, pg. 646

Operation Rescue, pg. 646

Opportunities Industrialization Centers of America, pgs. 452, 457, 662, 887

Optimist Club See Children's Miracle Network Telethon

Orange County (CA) See Court Appointed Special Advocates (CASA)

Orange County District Attorney's Office See Child Abuse Services Team (CAST)

Orange County Public Schools See ADDitions School Volunteers*; Workshops for Volunteer Coordinators and Volunteers in Education*

Orange Empire Railway Museum, pgs. 378, 535

Orangeburg Public Schools, pgs. 418, 638

Orangeburg School System, pg. 1097 See also Parenting and School Volunteer Program

Orangewood Children's Home, pgs. 427, 815

Orchestra Management Seminar, pgs. 277, 539

Oregon Human Development Corporation, pgs. 18, 824

Oregon State University, pgs. 300, 631

Oregon State Volunteer Services Program, pg. 143

Oregon Volunteer Services Program, pgs. 1021, 1066

Organization for After-Stroke Resources, pg. 681

Organization for the Use of the Telephone (OUT), pgs. 71, 854, 1076

Organizational Dynamics, pgs. 183, 265, 279

Orphan Foundation of America, pgs. 357, 806

Oryx Press, pg. 98

Oswego County, pg. 491

Ottawa River "Fighting Back" Campaign, pg. 764

Ottawa River Improvement Association, pg. 764

Our Community Kitchen, pgs. 371, 758

Our Daily Bread, pg. 883

Out of Work: What Now? An Unemployment Clinic, pgs. 441, 654

Outings for Homeless Children, pgs. 50, 883

Outreach & Escort, pgs. 114, 862

Outreach Plan: Focus on the Hispanic Community, pgs. 77, 824

The OWL (Outreach-Working-Learning) Program, pg. 481

Ozark Opry Records, pg. 1009

P

Pacific Science Center See Seattle-King County RSVP (Retired Senior Volunteer Program)

Pacifica Chamber of Commerce See Youth-In-Action Auction

Padgett Thompson, pg. 62

Page Traditional Elementary School, pgs. 441, 640

Palma Ceia Methodist Church See Tampa Causeway Beautification Project

PALS Program, pgs. 51, 737

Panel on Drug Abuse/Panel on Alcoholism, pgs. 197, 599

Papillion Board of Education See Family Life/Community and Government

Papillion/La Vista High School, pgs. 325, 561

PAR Leadership Training Foundation, pg. 204

Paragould Police Department See Bicycle Safety and Seat Belt Awareness Programs

Paramus Fire Department See Paramus Heavy Rescue Squad

Paramus Heavy Rescue Squad, pg. 595

Parent Aide Program - Centralized Service Unit, pg. 833

Parent Aide Training, pgs. 294, 813

Parent-Child Home Program, pgs. 417, 588

Parent-Child Program*, pgs. 417, 932

Parent Cooperative Pre-Schools International, pg. 995

Parent Resources and Information on Drug Abuse (PRIDE) See PRIDE

Parent-Teachers Association (PTA) See Valentine School Art Show

Parent-Teen AIDS Education Project, pgs. 275, 515

Parent to Parent, pgs. 418, 852

Parent to Parent, Attention on Attendance, pgs. 418, 620

Parent-to-Parent Program, pgs. 350, 839

Parental Stress Center, pgs. 166, 933

Parenting and School Volunteer Program, pgs. 418, 638

Parents Anonymous, pgs. 414, 712 See also Child Protective Services; F.A.C.T. Hotline (Families and Children in Trouble)

Parents Educating Parents, pgs. 457, 856

Parents Educating Parents: Training Program, pg. 453

Parents for the Environment, pgs. 419, 780

Parents' Resource Institute on Drug Education, pgs. 168, 606

Parents United, pgs. 421, 596 See also Child Protective Services

Parish Hill High School, pg. 326

The Park People See Roberts Park and Playground/Lantrip School Park*

Parkersburg High School, pg. 324

Parkersburg School District See Community Services

Parking Posse, pgs. 428, 863

Parkinson's Institute for Caregivers, pgs. 305, 902

Parma-Hilton Playground Project, pgs. 501, 921

Parma Town Hall Park, pgs. 501, 921

Partners*, pgs. 36, 706

Partners For Livable Places, pg. 692

Partners in Caring, pgs. 54, 907

Partners in Learning, pg. 1008

Partnership BankCard Systems*, pgs. 99, 1014

Partnership Umbrella, pg. 945

Partnerships, pgs. 351, 623

PATC Volunteers, pg. 775

Paterson Habitat for Humanity, pgs. 371, 695, 1098

Pathways to Independence, pgs. 385, 744

Patowmack Herbal Farm: Summer Employment for the Handicapped, pgs. 47, 864

Peace Conference, pgs. 288, 565

Peace Garden Project, pg. 565

Peace Links Arkansas, pg. 565

Peace Links - Women Against Nuclear War, pg. 563

Peace Museum, pg. 564

Peekskill Star See Westchester 2000

Peer Counseling/Cross-Age Tutoring Program, pgs. 481, 647

Peer Counselor Program*, pgs. 405, 910

PennSERVE: The Governor's Office of Citizen Service, pg. 143

Pennsylvania Department of Education See Adult Literacy Project

Pennsylvania Developmental Disabilities Planning Council See The Untapped Resource: Disabled Persons as Volunteers

Pennsylvania Easter Seal Society See The Untapped Resource: Disabled Persons as Volunteers

Pennsylvania Horticultural Society See Green Countrie Towne Program

Pennsylvania State University, pgs. 185, 238, 264, 272, 279 See also The Untapped Resource: Disabled Persons as Volunteers; Volunteers: Facts and Fiction

Pennsylvania Statewide Symposium on Voluntarism & Education, pg. 321
People Helping People/Cheyenne, pg. 322
People Need People Volunteer Fair, pg. 19
People With AIDS See People With AIDS Coalition
People With AIDS Coalition, pgs. 425, 523
Pepsi-Cola See Child Identification Program
A Perfect Match, pgs. 405, 867
Performance Based Assessment Program for Certification in Volunteer Administration, pg. 252
Performance Contracting, pgs. 45, 773
Person to Person*, pgs. 419, 841
Pet Therapy, pgs. 383, 787
Pets for People, pgs. 54, 910
Pew Charitable Trusts See Health Care for the Homeless Coalition; National Federation of Interfaith Volunteer Caregivers
Pfizer Pharmaceuticals See U.S. National Senior Olympics
Pharmaceutical Manufacturers Association, pgs. 998, 1000, 1002
Pharmacists Against Drug Abuse, pgs. 37, 599
Pharos Books, pg. 1077
Phi Mu Sorority Community Service Chapter, pg. 391
Philadelphia Green Program See Green Countrie Towne Program
Philadelphia Licenses & Inspections Department See Fighting Dirty!
Philadelphia Police Department See Fighting Dirty!
Philadelphia Streets Department See Fighting Dirty!
Philadelphia 17th Police District See Green Countrie Towne Program
Philadelphia Zoo, pgs. 276, 532
PhilaPride, pgs. 44, 763
Phoenix Memorial Hospital, pg. 289
Phoenix Union High School District See Bostrom Alternative Center for Education*
Phone Pal, pgs. 34, 818
Phone-TTY, pg. 855
Pictorial, Inc., pg. 1077
Piedmont TEC See Building Better Boards
Pilot Books, pgs. 953, 970, 971, 980, 983, 991, 1012, 1015, 1025, 1056, 1076, 1082
Pineapple Press, pg. 984
Pinellas County School System See Adams' Express: A Mini-Grant Program
Pioneers on Wheels, pg. 1092
PIRG, pgs. 310, 572
Pittsburgh Middle Schools, pgs. 482, 650
Pittsburgh Public Schools See Project OASES
Pittsburgh Steelers Football Club See Helping Hand
Pittway Corporation See Statewide Leadership Symposium: Working Together to Make Visions Realities
Planet Drum Foundation, pg. 770
Planned Parenthood Federation of America, pg. 931
Planned Parenthood of Summit/Portage/Medina Counties See The S.O.A.P.S.
Planning Today for Tomorrow's Volunteers*, pg. 252
Play Schools Association*, pg. 584
Playboy Foundation, pg. 1000
Point Breeze Civic Association See Green Countrie Towne Program
Point Breeze Federation, pgs. 500, 763
Point Place Junior High School See Ottawa River "Fighting Back" Campaign
Points of Light Initiative, pg. 206
Police Department Volunteer Program, pgs. 459, 913

Polish Legion of American Veterans Auxiliary, pgs. 353, 893
Pollution Control Center, pgs. 482, 771
Pond Springs Baptist Church See Far Northwest Caregivers
Population Council, pg. 768
Population Crisis Committee, pg. 768
Population Crisis Committee/Draper Fund, pg. 1061
Population-Environment Balance, pgs. 768, 1059
Population Institute, pg. 768
Population Reference Bureau, pgs. 768, 1018, 1059
Portland Community College, pg. 266
Portland General Electric Company, pgs. 405, 874
Portland Mountain Rescue, pg. 595
Portland Park Bureau See TRIS (Trails Information System)
Portland Sheriff's Office See Portland Mountain Rescue
Positive Parenting, pgs. 352, 790, 1066
Post Natural Bran Flakes See U.S. National Senior Olympics
Potomac Appalachian Trail Club, pgs. 774, 775
PPG Industries See Helping Hand
Practice Excellence: National Conference on Volunteerism, pg. 252
Prairie View Mental Health Center, pgs. 390, 742, 1048
Pre-Forum 90 Training Institutes, pgs. 293, 700
Prentice-Hall, pgs. 992, 1006
Preparing for an Aging Society, pgs. 8, 896
Presbyterian Church USA See Gift to the City
Presbyterian Hunger Project See Gleaning*
Preschool Diagnostic and Developmental Education Nurseries, pgs. 127, 587
Presidential Classroom for Young Americans, pgs. 462, 557
President's Advisory Committee on Points of Light Initiatives Foundation, pg. 207
President's Committee on Employment of the Handicapped, pg. 658
President's Committee on Mental Retardation, pgs. 71, 864
President's Council on Physical Fitness, pg. 918
Prevention and Youth Services See Project Graduation
Prevention Makers, pgs. 295, 606
Prevention through Action, pgs. 482, 604
PRIDE, pgs. 168, 606
Primary/Secondary Peace Education Network, pg. 564
Prime Time to End Hunger, pgs. 73, 77, 875, 883
Prince George's Voluntary Action Center, pgs. 19, 951, 954
Prince William County Public Works Department See Parents for the Environment
Principal on the Roof*, pgs. 441, 640
Prison Fellowship Ministries, pgs. 357, 719, 1037
Private Sector Efforts Program, pgs. 215, 761
Private Sector Initiatives Program, pgs. 212, 616
Probation Volunteers, pgs. 460, 914
Problems Facing Volunteer Leaders Today*, pgs. 316, 715
Producing, Designing & Writing Newsletters, pg. 63
Professional Certification in Volunteer Management, pg. 253
Professional Development for Community Trainers, pg. 279
Program Development Assistance Package, pgs. 301, 828
Program Exchange Process (PEP), pgs. 172, 677
Project Any Baby Can, pgs. 401, 851
Project BE, pg. 1004

Project Blueprint, pg. 199
Project BRAVO, pgs. 388, 513, 630
Project Concern International, pgs. 463, 669
Project Concern Youth Program, pgs. 463, 669
Project Excellence Scholarship Program, pg. 1008
Project Graduation, pgs. 420, 604
Project HELP (Help Expedite Legal Problems for the Homeless), pgs. 442, 881
Project LEAD, pg. 190
Project NOVA - AIDS Program, pgs. 160, 521
Project OASES, pgs. 482, 650
Project Opportunity, pgs. 458, 933
Project Passage, pgs. 395, 787
Project Right Start, pgs. 223, 934
Project SHARE, pgs. 5, 950, 953, 958, 1069, 1095
Project Volunteer, pg. 453
Projects in the Community, pg. 483
Proposal Writing Institute*, pg. 303
Providence School System, pg. 645
Pryor Resources See How to Proofread
Psychological Services and Student Life See The Gatehouse: The Cook/Douglass Peer Counseling Center
Public Affairs Committee, pgs. 973, 1008, 1022, 1025, 1031, 1032, 1034, 1036, 1067, 1074, 1075, 1077, 1078, 1081, 1098
Public Affairs Pamphlets, pg. 1003
Public Assistance Clients Volunteer, pgs. 458, 834
Public Awareness About Child Care (PAACC), pgs. 414, 702
Public Citizen, pgs. 156, 332, 560, 772, 979, 1034
Public Citizen Health Research Group, pg. 664
Public Citizen Litigation Group, pg. 572
Public Interest Computer Association, pgs. 8, 952
Public Interest Research Group, pgs. 310, 572
Public Relations on a Shoestring*, pg. 290
Public Relations Society of America, pg. 290
Public Relations Student Society of America, pg. 69
Public Service Activities Division, pgs. 433, 573
Public Service Company of Oklahoma See Special Olympics Time
Public Service Institute See Media Relations for Nonprofit and Volunteer Organizations
Public Service Materials Center, pgs. 1015, 1017, 1018, 1020
Public Service Volunteers, pgs. 341, 726
The Public Welfare Foundation See Senior Program
Publicity Workshop, pg. 64
Pulaski Auxiliary Post No. 8, pgs. 353, 893

Q

Quality Education Program, pgs. 28, 657
The Quest for Community, pg. 148
Quest International, pgs. 190, 1044
Quill/William Morrow, pg. 987
The Quilt and AIDS Education, pg. 515

R

R. J. Reynolds Industries, pg. 974
R. R. Bowker, pgs. 957, 963, 968, 1004, 1005, 1008, 1009, 1046
R-T-P, INC.*, pg. 659
The RADAR Network, pg. 599
Radcliffe College See A Class Act
Radio Information Service (RIS), pgs. 72, 849
Ragan Henry Law Firm See Children's Literacy Initiative

Rainbow Center for Exceptional Children, pg. 587
Rainbow Sunshine School, pg. 635
Raleigh Parks and Recreation Division, pgs. 388, 924
Ralston Purina Company, pgs. 54, 910
Ramapo College, pgs. 442, 627
Ramapo High School, pg. 483
Ramapo Key Club*, pg. 483
Ramsey County See RSVP of Ramsey County
Random House, Inc., pg. 957
Rape and Domestic Violence Information Center, pgs. 177, 727
Rape Crisis Center, pgs. 177, 178, 727, 1032, 1034
Rape Crisis Service of Central Contra Costa County, pgs. 178, 728
Re-Entry Ministries, pgs. 372, 722
Read for Literacy, pg. 737
Reading and Berks County Chamber of Commerce, pgs. 64, 619
REAL Services, pg. 926
Record Debate Classic, pgs. 442, 627
Recording for the Blind, pg. 847
Recovery, Inc., pgs. 453, 745, 1049
Recreation Programs for Learning Disabled Teens & Adults, pgs. 420, 863
Recruiting Techniques for Volunteer Organizations, pg. 322
Recruiting, Training and Retention of Volunteers, pg. 322
Recycling for Ravi, pgs. 484, 777
Red Cross Disaster Aid, pg. 595
Redken Company See Women Off Welfare (WOW)
Refuge for Injured Wildlife, pgs. 442, 784
Refugee Volunteer Tutor Training, pgs. 300, 631
Regenerative Agriculture Association See Community Regeneration
Region VII Area Agency on Aging See Service Delivery for the Elderly*
Regional Bilingual Training Resource Center*, pg. 631
Regional Institute of Social Welfare Research, pg. 1070
Regional Plan Association, pgs. 559, 568, 951, 979, 980 See also Westchester 2000
Regional Seminars and a State Conference on Volunteerism, pg. 132
Regional Volunteer Workshops, pg. 134
Regional Youth Substance Abuse Project (RYSAP), pgs. 608, 1000, 1003
Rehab Project: Neighborhood Revitalization Through Home Ownership, pgs. 372, 693
Religious Society of Friends, pgs. 195, 355, 553, 563
Renaissance Youth Center See Prevention through Action
Renew America, pg. 773
Rensselaer County Department for Youth See Court Referred Volunteer Program of Rensselaer County
Rent-A-Kid Referral Service, pgs. 40, 656
Republican National Committee, pg. 271 See also Stop! The Madness Foundation
Requirement: Skip Classes, pg. 88
Research and Training Center in Mental Retardation, pg. 1069
Reserve Police Officer Corps, pgs. 460, 729
Reserve Police Program, pgs. 460, 729
Resource Development Conference*, pg. 303
Resource Development Seminars, pg. 253
Respite for AIDS Volunteers, pgs. 21, 520
The Response Pool, pgs. 106, 520

Retired Senior Volunteer Program, pgs. 68, 203, 397, 404, 405, 406, 407, 408, 540, 680, 787, 907 See also The Best Years; Friends of Handicapped Readers; Police Department Volunteer Program; ROVERS (Retired and Older Volunteers: An Educational Resource Service); Schoolmate Handicraft Volunteers
Retirement Advisors, pg. 1074
Rexnord Resource Center, pg. 972
Reymont Associates, pgs. 971, 1012
Rhode Island Foundation See Volunteers in Providence Schools
Rhode Island Historical Preservation Commission See Tea and Treasures
RIDESOURCES, pg. 1092
River Club Restaurant See Taste of the Nation
Riverside University High School, pg. 325
Riverside University School District See Education and Human Services Course
RJR Nabisco Corporation, pg. 973
Roadrunner Program, pgs. 34, 936
Roanoke Valley Council of Community Services See Voluntary Action Center Training (Blacksburg)*
Robert Wood Johnson Foundation, pgs. 49, 668, 950 See also National Federation of Interfaith Volunteer Caregivers; Regional Youth Substance Abuse Project (RYSAP); Youth Evaluation Services (Y.E.S.)
Robert Wood Johnson Trust See Health Care for the Homeless Coalition
Roberts Park and Playground/Lantrip School Park*, pgs. 55, 929
Rochester Gas and Electric Corporation See Parma-Hilton Playground Project
Rochester General Hospital Association See U.S. Open Volunteer Committee
Rochester Institute of Technology, pgs. 428, 868
Rock Creek Park Horse Centre See Therapeutic Riding Program
Rock Valley Community College, pg. 266
Rockingham Planning Commission See Seacoast Conference on Volunteerism: A Time for Growth; A Time for Change
Rocky Mountain Institute See Econet
Rodale Institute, pgs. 181, 552
Roddy Coca-Cola Bottling Company See Recycling for Ravi
Roman Catholic Diocese of San Diego, pgs. 373, 754
Ronald Reagan Presidential Materials Staff, pg. 957
Roses for Fallen Fathers, pg. 893
Rosie's Patrol, pgs. 420, 710, 1077
Rotary Club See Children's Miracle Network Telethon
Rotary Club of Demarest and Cresskill See Tenafly-Alpine Safe Rides Program and others
Rotary International, pg. 92 See also Beachfront Volunteers
ROTC See Flint Airshow
ROVERS (Retired and Older Volunteers: An Educational Resource Service), pgs. 408, 628
Roy Rogers Restaurants, pgs. 48, 659
RSVP - Nursing Home Project*, pg. 408
RSVP of Humboldt County, pgs. 74, 897
RSVP of Lake Region Community College See RSVP of Ramsey County
RSVP of Morris County, pgs. 176, 409, 900
RSVP of New Castle County, pgs. 127, 788
RSVP of Ramsey County, pg. 409
RSVP of Utah County, pg. 102
RSVP Thrift Shop*, pgs. 103, 836
Runaway Hotline, pgs. 162, 805
Runaway Project, pg. 1033
Runyon Saltzman Weagraff & Siegel See Support for Public Television

Rural Advancement Fund International*, pg. 577
Rural America, pgs. 694, 1027, 1029
Rural American Women See Catholic Committee of Appalachia
Rural Volunteer Services Network, pg. 152
Rutgers University, pg. 233 See also Homelessness Prevention Program
Rutgers University Press, pg. 963
Ryans' Nursing Home Volunteer Program, pgs. 484, 908
Ryland Mortgage Corporation See Support for Public Television

S

Sacramento Escrow Company See Support for Public Television
Safe House, pgs. 46, 833
Safe Place, pgs. 35, 818
Safe Streets, pgs. 428, 764 See also Operation Coverup
Safety Town (Where Children Learn to Live), pg. 936
Safeway Stores, pgs. 33, 815
Saginaw County Department of Social Services, pgs. 419, 829, 836, 841, 1069
Saginaw Veterans Hospial See Polish Legion of American Veterans Auxiliary
St. Anthony Medical Center See Future Generations
St. Augustine Historical Preservation Board, pg. 525
St. John the Baptist Church See West St. John Ministry of Care
St. John's University, pgs. 469, 625
St. Joseph Community Services, pgs. 749, 1054
St. Joseph Hospital See St. Joseph Community Services
St. Joseph Roman Catholic Church See ARC Covenant
St. Joseph's Home for the Blind See White Cane Drive
St. Joseph's House of Hospitality, pgs. 373, 883
St. Lawrence Hospital, pg. 1048
St. Lawrence Hospital & Healthcare Services, pg. 740
St. Louis County & Municipal Police Academy See Reserve Police Program
St. Louis County Police Department, pgs. 460, 729
St. Luke's-Roosevelt Hospital Center, pgs. 417, 448, 522, 821, 932
St. Mark's Episcopal Church See Re-Entry Ministries
St. Mary's High School, pg. 361
St. Matthias of Somerset Council No. 9925, pgs. 392, 1097
St. Paul/Office of the Mayor, pg. 84
St. Paul's Episcopal Cathedral, pgs. 17, 755
St. Petersburg Code Enforcement Division See CRACKDOWN
St. Petersburg Fire Department See CRACKDOWN
St. Petersburg Police Department See CRACKDOWN
St. Petersburg Public Works See CRACKDOWN
St. Petersburg Sanitation Department See CRACKDOWN
St. Stephens School See First Annual Soviet-American Youth Summit
St. Teresa of Avila Catholic Church, pgs. 417, 706
St. Thomas Episcopal Church, pg. 883
Sts. Constantine & Helen Greek Orthodox Cathedral, pgs. 364, 530

Salt Lake City School Volunteers, pg. 643
Salt Lake School District See Adopt-A-School
Salt River Project See School Ecology Project
Salvation Army, pgs. 357, 402, 793, 826 See also Bailey's Crossroads Community Shelter; Continental Homeless Assistance Program; Homelessness Prevention Program; Project OASES; Seventh Grade Social Problems Course; Substance Abuse Treatment Center and Shelter
Salvation Army Hamburger Sales Day, pg. 28
The Samaritans, pgs. 179, 788
Samaritans, pgs. 179, 793
Samaritans USA, pgs. 179, 792 See also Samaritans; The Samaritans
San Antonio Youth Literacy See Communicating Human Needs
San Bernardino County Board of Supervisors, pg. 987
San Diego County Board of Education See Partnerships
San Diego County Ecumenical Conference, pgs. 366, 886
San Fernando Valley Interfaith Council, pg. 88
San Francisco AIDS Foundation, pgs. 275, 515, 960, 961, 962, 964, 982, 985, 1031, 1065, 1086, 1087
San Francisco AIDS Foundation Speakers Bureau, pgs. 960, 964
San Francisco Department of Recreation & Parks See San Francisco Special Olympics Winter Games
San Francisco Education Fund See San Francisco Peer Resource Programs
San Francisco Peer Resource Programs, pgs. 484, 788
San Francisco Special Olympics Winter Games, pgs. 48, 864
San Jose Chamber of Commerce See Adopt-A-School
San Jose Children's Musical Theatre*, pg. 538
San Jose Unified School District, pgs. 31, 621
San Jose Water Company See Adopt-A-School
San Marino Schools, pgs. 423, 531
SANE/FREEZE, pg. 981
Santa Clara County, pgs. 110, 607
Santa Fe Preparatory School, pg. 488
Santa Julia Church See Informe SIDA
Saturday Scholars, pgs. 351, 647
Saunders B. Moon Child Development Center, pgs. 28, 584
Saunders B. Moon School Community Resource Advisory Program, pgs. 28, 584
Save Our Water*, pgs. 141, 781
Save the Children/Child Care Support Center, pg. 588
SCAN (Spokane Child Abuse and Neglect Prevention Center), pgs. 70, 818
SCAN (Stop Child Abuse Now) See Blount County Children's Center
Scarecrow Press, pgs. 980, 1012, 1013
SCAVA Workshops for Volunteer Administrators*, pg. 254
Schindler-Rainman Institutes, pg. 182
School and Community Service Program, pg. 484
School Community Relations Program, pg. 650
School Council Volunteers, pgs. 39, 620
School Ecology Project, pgs. 443, 771
School Fire Safety Monitoring Program, pgs. 421, 596
School of Library and Information Science See Institute on Federal Library Resources
School of the Holy Childhood, pgs. 114, 858 See also U.S. Open Volunteer Committee
School Tutoring Program, pg. 647
School Volunteers, pg. 621

Schoolmate Handicraft Volunteers, pgs. 409, 527
Schoolmate Program, pgs. 409, 527
Scott Community College See Leadership for the Nineties*
Scouting for the Handicapped, pgs. 60, 843, 851
Scurry County Senior Center, pgs. 413, 898
Seacoast Conference on Volunteerism: A Time for Growth; A Time for Change, pg. 254
Search for Shelter See Give Me Shelter: Designs for Urban Survival
Sears, Roebuck & Company See Governor's Office of Voluntary Action; Public Relations on a Shoestring*; United Way Editorial Board
Seaside Health Promotion Conference, pgs. 305, 667
Seattle Children's Museum See Seattle-King County RSVP (Retired Senior Volunteer Program)
Seattle-King County RSVP (Retired Senior Volunteer Program), pg. 410
Seattle Pacific University, pg. 488
Seattle Police Department See Seattle-King County RSVP (Retired Senior Volunteer Program)
Seattle Public Library See Seattle-King County RSVP (Retired Senior Volunteer Program)
Seattle University, pgs. 151, 797
Second African Baptist Church, pgs. 375, 830
Second Air Division Association of the Eighth Air Force, pgs. 353, 535
Second Careers Program, pg. 660
Second Judicial Circuit Court See Juvenile Arbitration Program of South Carolina
Secondary School Volunteers, pgs. 298, 617
Security Alert Group - Three Link Towers (SAG), pgs. 410, 711
Security Pacific Foundation See California Literacy*
Selecting and Training Volunteers, pg. 255
Self-Help Center, pg. 221
Self-Help Development Institute See Self-Help Center
Self-Help for Hard of Hearing People, pgs. 224, 855
The Self-Help Movement: New Form of Volunteerism and a Resource for Professionals*, pg. 222
Seneca Falls Central School District, pgs. 421, 707
Seneca Falls Concerned Parents, pgs. 421, 707
Senior Acting Program of the Barn Players*, pgs. 68, 540
Senior Citizen Internship Program, pgs. 314, 562
Senior Citizens Home Assistance Services, pg. 905
Senior Citizens United Community Services, pgs. 385, 902
Senior Clinic, pg. 1026
Senior Community Services See Family Friends Project
Senior Community Services, Inc. See Home Repairs Project; Volunteer Senior Leaders
Senior Companion Program (SCP), pgs. 398, 909
Senior Connection, pgs. 176, 904
Senior Course on Volunteerism, pg. 326
Senior Craftsman Showcase*, pgs. 410, 527
Senior Employment Resources, pgs. 443, 661, 1067
Senior Games of Indiana, pg. 926
Senior Nutrition Program, pg. 908
Senior Opportunities and Services, pg. 398
Senior Program, pgs. 225, 888
Senior Report, pgs. 177, 905
Senior Victim Assistance Team, pgs. 497, 730
Seniors and Children Together, pgs. 411, 585
Seniors: Special Delivery, pgs. 411, 749

Service Corps of Retired Executives (SCORE), pgs. 411, 545
Service Delivery for the Elderly*, pgs. 380, 912
Service-Learning Center, pg. 485
Service to Military Families/Service to Veterans (Ohio), pgs. 342, 443, 893
70001 Training and Employment Institute, pg. 657
Seventh Grade Social Problems Course, pg. 191
Seward Rescue Center, pgs. 36, 596
Shaklee Corporation See San Francisco Special Olympics Winter Games
Shalom Et Benedictus, pg. 600
Shalom Et Benedictus Substance Abuse Programs, pg. 600
Shanti Project, pg. 523
SHARE*, pg. 747
Share Our Strength (SOS), pgs. 433, 445, 756, 1053
Share Self-help and Resource Exchange, pgs. 373, 754
SHARE-USA See Fare SHARE
Sharing and Caring - A Food Pantry, pg. 754
Shaving Cream Lesson - Drug Prevention Seminar, pgs. 197, 606
Shaw Neighborhood Advisory Committee, pgs. 455, 709
Shawmut Bank See From All Walks of Life
The Shed Project*, pgs. 444, 858
Shelby County See Free The Children (FTC)
Shelter for Victims of Domestic Violence, pg. 635
Shelter House, pgs. 373, 887
Shenandoah National Park See PATC Volunteers
Sheraton Beach Inn See Virginia Volunteers - Health of the Commonwealth
SHHH, pgs. 224, 855
Shoreham-Wading Middle School, pg. 284
Shoreham-Wading School District See Community Service
Short Courses and Seminars for Administrators of Volunteers, pg. 255
A Shoulder to Cry On, pgs. 422, 934
Show-Me Seminars, pgs. 136, 617
Shrine of the Immaculate Conception, pgs. 226, 522
Sidwell Friends, pg. 472
Sierra Club, pgs. 979, 980, 1056, 1057, 1058, 1060, 1061 See also Clean the Bay Day
Sierra Western Insurance Agency See Support for Public Television
Sign Media, Inc., pg. 1080
Silver Haired Legislative Session, pgs. 124, 562
Sinclair Community College, pg. 247
Six Friends Memorial Fund, pgs. 103, 596
Sixteenth Street Community Health Center, pg. 663
60 Karats, pgs. 412, 541
Skills Expansion Through Resource Volunteers in Education (SERVE), pgs. 298, 618
Sky Ranch for Boys, pgs. 789, 1078
Small Business Assistance Center, pg. 542
Small Business Development Center See NH State Conference on Volunteerism
Small Business Development Program, pgs. 433, 542
Small Business Reporter, pg. 971
The Small Business Way: Small Businesses Supporting United Way, pg. 28
Small Town Survival Workshops, pg. 82
Smaller Business of America*, pg. 543
Smithsonian Institution, pg. 528 See also Discover Graphics
Smithsonian Institution Traveling Exhibition Service, pg. 528

Smithsonian Resident Associate Program, pg. 534

SNAP (Students Need A Pat), pgs. 444, 628

Snow Goose Gallery See School Ecology Project

SO SAD (Save Our Sons and Daughters), pgs. 422, 707

The S.O.A.P.S., pgs. 175, 916

Social Action Corps, pgs. 497, 668

Social Lab, pg. 311

Social Legislation Information Service/CWLA, pg. 561

Social Services of Akron Project, pgs. 175, 916, 984

Social Work Program: 60-Hour Volunteer Work Requirement, pg. 326

Society Bank, pgs. 45, 764

Society Bank/Wolf Creek Association Partnership, pgs. 45, 764

Society for Nonprofit Organizations, pgs. 5, 952, 953

Society for Nutrition Education*, pgs. 76, 750

Society of Consumer Affairs Professionals in Business, pgs. 433, 573, 975

Society of St. Vincent de Paul, pg. 80

Soil and Water Conservation Society of America, pgs. 774, 1056, 1058, 1059, 1061

Solving Community Problems by Building Community Partnerships, pg. 135

Sonoma State University, pg. 475

Sooner Fashion Mall Merchants See Safety Town (Where Children Learn to Live)

SOS (Serve Our Seniors) Student Volunteer Program, pgs. 485, 794

South Bay Free Clinic, pg. 1025

South Bronx Summer Project, pgs. 485, 775

South Brunswick High School, pgs. 470, 625

South Carolina Association for Volunteer Administration (SCAVA), pg. 23 See also SCAVA Workshops for Volunteer Administrators*

South Carolina Department of Corrections See Spartanburg Adult Writing and Reading (AWARE)

South Carolina Literacy Association See Spartanburg Adult Writing and Reading (AWARE)

South Dakota Association of Volunteer Leaders See Volunteer Leadership Conference

South Dakota Governor's Office, pg. 145

South High School, pgs. 416, 932

South Huntington School Volunteer Program, pg. 644

South Providence Tutorial, pg. 647

Southeast Bank See Workshop for Volunteers

Southeast Resource Center for Children and Youth Services, pgs. 163, 805

Southeastern University, pgs. 282, 653

Southern Exposure, pgs. 1025, 1027

Southern Illinois University See Governor's Office of Voluntary Action

Southern Methodist University, pg. 480

Southern Regional Task Force on Infant Mortality See Virginia Ecumenical Infant Mortality Prevention Project Conference

Southside Apothecary See Wheelchair Wash

Southwest Church of Christ, pg. 375

Southwest Virginia Black Lung Task Force, pg. 201

Southwestern Bell, pgs. 34, 818, 1076

S/OVCP Winter Conference, pg. 255

Sovran Bank See Business/Industry Advisory Council (BIAC)

SOWEGA Council on Aging See Nursing Home Project; RSVP - Nursing Home Project*

Spalding County Department of Children and Family Services See Volunteer Transportation

Spare Change Project, pgs. 115, 879

Sparkle Committee, pgs. 486, 765

Spartanburg Adult Writing and Reading (AWARE), pg. 737

Special Materials Project*, pg. 856

Special Mortgage Affordable Housing Program, pgs. 29, 689

Special Olympics, pg. 868 See also Louisiana State Special Olympics Summer Games

Special Olympics International, pgs. 867, 1082, 1083

Special Olympics - Lapeer, pg. 870

Special Olympics - Michigan, pgs. 479, 869

Special Olympics - New Orleans, pg. 869

Special Olympics Time, pgs. 346, 870

Special Populations Division, pgs. 476, 868

Special Populations Program, pgs. 388, 924

Special Recreation, pgs. 923, 1069, 1078

Special Saturday, pgs. 486, 921

Special Student Advisory Board, pg. 192

Specials Project, pg. 65

The Spice Program and Introduction, pg. 311

Spirit and Breath Association, pgs. 459, 679, 1025

Spirit and Breath Volunteer Program, pgs. 459, 679

The Spirit That Supports Alabama - Volunteers, pg. 256

Spokane Community Mental Health Center See SCAN (Spokane Child Abuse and Neglect Prevention Center)

Springfield College, pgs. 183, 280

Springville Griffith Central School, pg. 644

Squibb Corporation See Business/Industry Advisory Council (BIAC)

Squibb Publications, pg. 993

Stamford Advocate See Fairfield 2000

Stamford Emergency Shelter See Seventh Grade Social Problems Course

Stanford University, pgs. 44, 769

Stanton and Lee Publishers, pg. 1080

Star City Social Club, pgs. 373, 745

Starrett Elementary School, pgs. 444, 628

State Department of Social and Health Services See Parent Aide Program - Centralized Service Unit

State of Alabama See Blount County Children's Center

State of Connecticut See Youth Evaluation Services (Y.E.S.)

State of Florida See Archaeological Volunteer Program

State of Hawaii, pgs. 128, 594 See also Multi-Phasic Health Screening

State of Illinois See Home Town Awards; Manteno Veterans Home Volunteer Program

State of Louisiana See Louisiana Training Institute*

State of Michigan See Independent Living/Homeless Youth

State of Minnesota See Solving Community Problems by Building Community Partnerships; Volunteer Program Management

State of New Jersey See Beachfront Volunteers; Child Assault Prevention Team; Marine Mammal Stranding Center; Sparkle Committee

State of Oregon See Seaside Health Promotion Conference

State of Pennsylvania See PennSERVE: The Governor's Office of Citizen Service

State of South Carolina See Parenting and School Volunteer Program

State of Tennessee See Free The Children (FTC)

State of Vermont, pgs. 146, 726

State of Virginia See Virginia Ecumenical Infant Mortality Prevention Project Conference; Virginia Partnership Fund and Other Programs

State University of New York at Albany, pg. 464

State Volunteer Program, pgs. 132, 826

Stateline United Way, pg. 66

Statewide Conference on Volunteerism, pg. 137

Statewide Drug Task Force Conference, pgs. 295, 607

Statewide HIV/AIDS Network, pg. 509

Statewide Leadership Symposium: Working Together to Make Visions Realities, pg. 210

Statewide Volunteer Management Training Program, pg. 129

Stay the Night on My Street, pgs. 73, 875

STD National Hotline, pgs. 178, 680

Steck-Vaughn Company, pg. 991

Steelcase, Inc., pgs. 26, 594

Stockley Center, pgs. 377, 865

Stop! The Madness, pg. 1038

Stop! The Madness Foundation, pgs. 75, 731

Strategies of Volunteer Leadership, pg. 279

Stratocom See Street News Homeless Vendors Program

Street Aid, pg. 876

Street News Homeless Vendors Program, pg. 876

Stride Rite Children's Center, pgs. 29, 585

Stride Rite Corporation, pgs. 29, 585

STS (Sharing Talents and Skills), pgs. 376, 629

Student Care Day, pg. 108

Student Coalition for Action in Literacy Education (SCALE), pgs. 469, 733

Student Community Service (SCS) Program, pg. 463

Student Conservation Association, pgs. 463, 767, 928, 1057, 1060, 1061, 1100

Student Habitat for Humanity, pgs. 486, 695

Student National Education Association, pg. 1099

Student Organization, Inc. See Communication-Help Center

Student Volunteer Programs: A New Resource for Community Agencies*, pg. 327

Student Volunteer Services, pg. 487

Student Volunteer/Work Project (SV/WP), pgs. 42, 657

Student Volunteers, pg. 193

Students Against Driving Drunk (SADD), pgs. 463, 603

Study War No More, pgs. 288, 565

Substance Abuse Treatment Center and Shelter, pgs. 459, 876

Sugar Ray Robinson Youth Foundation*, pg. 538

Suicide Prevention Hotline, pgs. 179, 788

Summer Associates Program See Project HELP (Help Expedite Legal Problems for the Homeless)

Summer Master's Degree Program in Community Leadership and Development, pg. 280

Summerfest Art Faire, pgs. 115, 903

Summit Shock Incarceration Facility, pgs. 430, 707

Sun Company, pgs. 55, 929

Sundial Volunteers, pgs. 374, 904

Super Volunteers!, pg. 463

Superior Council, pg. 80

Superior Court Conference Committee Diversion Program, pgs. 498, 722

Supervising Volunteers*, pg. 256

Supervision Skill Series/MAP (Management Assistance Program), pg. 257

The Supervisory Cycle, pg. 257

Support Center of Washington, pg. 248

Support for Public Television, pg. 103

Support Services - AIDS Program, pgs. 106, 523

Surround*, pgs. 498, 708

Surry County Friends of Youth/Best Friends Program, pgs. 449, 821

Sursum Corda Village, pgs. 501, 690
Susan Peterson Productions, pg. 985
Swallow Press, pg. 1042
Sweet Briar College, pgs. 484, 488, 648, 908
SYCOM See Business/Industry Advisory Council (BIAC)
Syracuse University, pg. 624 See also Study War No More
Syracuse University Continuing Education Program, pg. 624
The Systematic Involvement of Volunteers in Human Services, pg. 257

T

Tacoma Police Department See Operation Coverup
TACTS Volunteer Program, pgs. 170, 833
TACTS Volunteer Shelter Manager Training, pgs. 307, 884
Tae Kwon Do Choreographic Performances, pgs. 32, 918
Taft Group, pgs. 99, 947, 1019, 1020
Taking a Trip to Friendship, pgs. 327, 909
Tampa Causeway Beautification Project, pg. 765
Tampa Electric; Critikon; Cigna See Tampa Causeway Beautification Project
Tampa Parks Department, pg. 765
Tandem Computers See Adopt-A-School
TANE Press, pgs. 997, 998, 999, 1000, 1003, 1025
Tapes for the Blind, pg. 847
TAPS (Training and Placement Service), pg. 1011
TARGET - Helping Students Cope with Alcohol and Drugs, pg. 604
Tarrant County Hospital District See New Lives
TASH: The Association for the Severely Handicapped, pg. 843
Task Force on Transitional Volunteers, pg. 1099
Taste of the Nation, pgs. 445, 756
Tattnall County Department of Family & Children Services See Volunteer Transportation Program
Tau Kappa Epsilon (TKE) Community Projects, pg. 392
TAVS (Teenage Volunteers), pgs. 487, 677
TDD/TTY Operator Services, pg. 855
Tea and Treasures, pgs. 144, 535
Teachers College, Columbia University See The Systematic Involvement of Volunteers in Human Services
Teaching-for-Excellence Mini-Grant Program, pgs. 111, 639
Teaching Senior Center, pgs. 311, 911
Team-Building, pg. 148
Technical Assistance Program (TAP), pg. 5
Technical Assistance to Cooperatives, pg. 577
Technical Information Center of the Office on Smoking and Health, pgs. 172, 678
Teen-Age Assembly of America*, pg. 190
Teen Center, pgs. 422, 823
Teen Complex, pg. 657
Teen Mothers Support Program See Project Right Start
Teen Opportunities Promote Success (TOPS), pgs. 42, 658
Teen Parents Self-Sufficiency Programs, pgs. 223, 934
Teenage Volunteers Working in Adolescent Program*, pgs. 487, 743
Teenline, pgs. 163, 806
Teens as Community Resources*, pg. 193
Telecare, Center for Life, Providence Hospital,, pg. 1079
Telecommunications for the Deaf, pgs. 983, 1073

Telephone Pioneers of America, pgs. 54, 907, 1081
Television Information Office*, pg. 62
Temple Awards for Creative Altruism, pg. 16
Ten Speed Press, pg. 948
Tenafly-Alpine Safe Rides Program and others, pgs. 422, 613
Tenant Ownership/Management Program, pgs. 501, 690
Tenneco, Incorporated, pgs. 977, 996
Tennessee Children's Services Commission See Tennessee Volunteers for Children Conference
Tennessee Department of Human Services See Child and Family Services of Knox County
Tennessee Volunteers for Children Conference, pgs. 285, 797
Texas A&M, pg. 236 See also Curriculum Development for Volunteer Administrators
Texas Department of Human Resources Grant See Women's Center of East Texas
Texas Employment Commission See Health Care for the Homeless Coalition
Texas Proud Voyage, pg. 536
Texas Tech Research and Training Center in Mental Retardation, pg. 953
Texas Volunteer Conference, pg. 145
Thank You Picket Lines, pg. 17
THANKS (Thoughtful, Helping Adults N' Kids Sharing), pgs. 449, 822
Theodore Roosevelt National Bank, pgs. 24, 29, 192, 689
Therapeutic Riding Program, pg. 870
Therapy on Horseback*, pg. 870
Third Sector Press, pg. 100
Thomas Jefferson Forum*, pg. 19
Three Link Towers See Security Alert Group - Three Link Towers (SAG)
Three Ways to Care, pg. 103
Thursday Afternoon Program (TAP), pg. 488
Tidy See Ottawa River "Fighting Back" Campaign
Tigard High School, pgs. 41, 625
Time, Inc., pgs. 51, 738, 1047
Time Incorporated, Community Relations Office, pgs. 947, 949, 976
Time to Read, pgs. 51, 738
Tiny Town Foundation, pg. 536
TIP Neighborhood House/Older Adult Volunteers, pg. 412
TIPS Program, pg. 703
Titcomb President Bishop's Fund See Gleaning*
Title I of the Higher Education Act See Volunteer Experience: Change, Challenge, Choices
T.J. Coolidge See Thomas Jefferson Forum*
Toll Free Hotline Information - A Program of Ralph Nader, pg. 156
Tompkins County Youth Bureau See The Learning Web
Topeka Public Library See Board Management Training Workshop
A Total Process, pg. 258
Touch America Project (TAP), pgs. 488, 776, 1100
Toward the Year 2000 - The Challenge, pgs. 258, 568
Town and Village of Groton See The Learning Web
Town Meeting for the Homeless, pgs. 307, 885
Townwide Census, pgs. 111, 768
Toyota Motor Sales USA, pg. 99
Training for Disabled Students, pgs. 48, 659
Training for the Municipal Volunteer Coordinator*, pgs. 258, 555
Training for Volunteers and Volunteer Agencies, pg. 282

Trans World Airlines See U.S. National Senior Olympics
TransAmerica Occidental Life Insurance Company, pg. 1082
Transitional Volunteer Program, pgs. 389, 745
Transitional Volunteers Are..., pg. 389
TransParent School Model Program, pgs. 416, 645
Transportation Committee of ACCA, pgs. 374, 936
Traveler's Aid See CHIP-IN
Trenton Board of Education, pgs. 481, 920
Tri-County Community Council See Grand People's Retired Senior Volunteer Program
Tri-State Drug Rehabilitation and Counseling Program, pgs. 223, 612
Trial Lawyers for Public Justice, pgs. 433, 573
Trident TEC See Building Better Boards
Trinity University See Miracle Week
TRIS (Trails Information System), pg. 597
Triton College, pgs. 441, 654
Troop 400 and Troop 391, pgs. 59, 852
Trust for Public Land See Econet
TRW Employees Charitable Organization (ECHO) See MIDAS Touch
Tufts University, pgs. 287, 554
Tulane University See Louisiana State Special Olympics Summer Games
Tulare County Food Resources, pgs. 381, 754
Tully Central School, pgs. 468, 664
Tulsa Association of Volunteer Administrators (TAVA) See Bridging Volunteer Resources
Tulsa County Historical Society See Echoes of the Past
Turn of River Middle School See Seventh Grade Social Problems Course
Turrell Fund, pgs. 119, 923
Tutorial Program, pgs. 445, 648
Tutoring Volunteer Program, pgs. 488, 648
Tuxedo Valet, pgs. 43, 549
Twenty-First Century Discussion Group, pgs. 376, 569
Twenty-Five Year Presidential Award Certificate Program for Volunteers in Juvenile Criminal Justice, pgs. 16, 698
24-Hour Child Abuse/Neglect Telephone Report Line, pgs. 167, 806
The Twin City of Texarkana, Arkansas-Texas See Retired Senior Volunteer Program
Twin City Urban Corps See Demystifying the Internship Experience
Two Together*, pg. 648

U

UAW-GM Human Resource Center, pgs. 28, 657
UAW-GM National Human Resource Center, pg. 1070
UNA-USA Publications, pg. 1089
Understanding is Progress, pg. 661
Une Soiree Parisienne (An Evening in Paris), pgs. 114, 862
Unified Community Resource Council, pg. 89
Union Carbide See CATCH Program
Union-Endicott School District, pg. 94
Union Institute Center for Public Policy, pg. 1018
Union Retirees Resources, pgs. 502, 691
Unitarian Universalist Housing Foundation, pgs. 358, 687
Unitarian Universalist Women's Federation, pgs. 988, 1042, 1043, 1089, 1096, 1098 See also Clara Barton Camp for Girls with Diabetes
United Auto Workers See Econet; Quality Education Program

United Automobile, Aerospace and Agricultural Implement Workers of America *See Labor Editors Roundtable*

United Black Fund *See Champ Bakery*

United Cerebral Palsy of Middle Tennessee, pg. 850

United Cerebral Palsy/Spastic Children's Foundation*, pg. 850

United Church of Christ, pgs. 357, 554

United Community Services of Johnson County *See Volunteer Center of Johnson County*

United Hospital Fund, pg. 964

United Illuminating *See Regional Youth Substance Abuse Project (RYSAP)*

United Methodist Social Services *See Interfaith Shelter Network*

United Ministries in Higher Education, pg. 260

United Planning Organization *See Friendship House*

United Services for Older Adults, pgs. 1068, 1069, 1078

United States Tennis Association *See Net Result Tennis Foundation*

United Steelworkers of America *See Helping Hand*

United Way *See Aspects of Administrative Functions for Managers of Volunteer Programs; Capital Area Community Food Bank; The Care and Nourishment of Volunteers*; Child and Family Services of Knox County; Citizen Advocacy; Corporate Retirees Information and Assistance Program; Developing Your Perspective: A Seminar in Volunteer Administration Today; Developing Your Perspective: Recruiting Volunteers; Emergency Food Program; Finding and Preparing New Board Members for Service; Friendship House; Fund for Needy School Children; Gallatin Valley Emergency Food Bank; Independent Living/Homeless Youth; Morris County Chaplaincy Council; Northwest Alabama Reading Aides; RSVP of Ramsey County; SCAN (Spokane Child Abuse and Neglect Prevention Center); The S.O.A.P.S.; Spartanburg Adult Writing and Reading (AWARE); Visitor Hospitality Center*; Volunteers in Providence Schools; Volunteers with Special Needs*

"United Way at Work" Conference, pg. 24

"United Way at Work" Program, pg. 29

United Way Board of Directors *See Youth Affairs Task Force*

United Way/Crusade of Mercy *See Direct Line; Leadership and Management of Volunteer Programs*; Supervising Volunteers*; Volunteer Staffing Workshops**

United Way Editorial Board, pg. 66

United Way of Adams County *See Volunteers for Youth*

United Way of Allegheny County & SW PA, pgs. 41, 654

United Way of America, pgs. 15, 29, 101, 104, 117, 181, 182, 199, 280, 286, 537, 945, 946, 949, 950, 952, 954, 955, 958, 960, 963, 964, 973, 974, 982, 986, 987, 1000, 1016, 1031, 1032, 1033, 1034, 1041, 1042, 1043, 1044, 1045, 1079, 1089 *See also Building Better Boards; Building Momentum for a Responsive America; Environmental Scan Task Force; Gifts In Kind; Information and Referral Resource and Training Course; Performance Contracting; Preparing for an Aging Society; Prime Time to End Hunger*

United Way of America Project Blueprint *See American Indian Partnerships with United Ways**

United Way of America's Management and Community Studies Institute *See Environmental Scan Task Force*

United Way of America's Resource Development Division *See "United Way at Work" Conference; "United Way at Work" Program*

United Way of Anchorage, pg. 300

United Way of Berks County *See Community Board Training Day*

United Way of Broward County *See Senior Connection*

United Way of Buffalo/Erie County *See You Are The Board**

United Way of California, pg. 9

United Way of Central Carolinas, pg. 24

United Way of Central Maryland, pgs. 41, 84, 517 *See also Grassroots Crisis Intervention & Peer Counseling Center*

United Way of Central Massachusetts *See Transitional Volunteers Are...*

United Way of Chicago, pg. 231 *See also Supervising Volunteers*; Volunteer Staffing Workshops**

United Way of Dade County, pgs. 106, 520 *See also Family AIDS Education Project*

United Way of Eastern Fairfield County, pg. 608 *See also Youth Evaluation Services (Y.E.S.)*

United Way of El Paso, pg. 12

United Way of Franklin County, pg. 65

United Way of Fresno County, pgs. 76, 752

United Way of Great Salt Lake Area, pgs. 411, 585

United Way of Greater Chattanooga *See Community INFO Line*

United Way of Greater Los Angeles, pgs. 187, 947

United Way of Greater Manchester, pgs. 198, 631

United Way of Greater Rochester *See Camp Good Days and Special Times Rebuilding Project*

United Way of Greater St. Louis, pg. 20 *See also Volunteer Connection Telethon*

United Way of Greater Topeka *See Board Management Training Workshop*

United Way of Greenville County, pg. 28

United Way of Licking County, pg. 17

United Way of Los Angeles, pg. 1068 *See also Group Safety Association*

United Way of Massachusetts *See Conference on Nonprofit Leadership and Management*

United Way of Massachusetts Bay *See Looking Ahead: Managing Tomorrow's Volunteers; New Volunteer Coordinator's Training*

United Way of Minneapolis *See DOVIA Training Programs; A Total Process*

United Way of Minneapolis Area *See Building an Effective Board; Demystifying the Internship Experience; Market-Ability: Marketing Strategies for Nonprofits; The Supervisory Cycle*

United Way of New Orleans *See Core Curriculum - The Volunteer*

United Way of North Central Massachusetts *See Massachusetts Association for the Blind**

United Way of Northern Nevada *See Voluntary Action Center of South Lake Tahoe*

United Way of Wake County, pg. 11

United Way of Redlands *See Social Action Corps*

United Way of San Antonio and Bexar County, pgs. 69, 879

United Way of San Diego, pg. 956

United Way of San Diego County, pgs. 237, 257, 630, 954, 1089, 1090

United Way of San Joaquin County, pg. 13

United Way of South Carolina, pg. 184

United Way of South Hampton Roads, pg. 102

United Way of Southeastern Pennsylvania, pg. 103

United Way of Southwestern New England *See Conference on Nonprofit Leadership and Management*

United Way of Stamford, pg. 191

United Way of Tarrant County, pg. 158

United Way of the Capital Area, pg. 90

United Way of the Capital Area (Hartford), pgs. 77, 194, 493, 588, 611, 803, 824, 1018

United Way of the Capital Area (Jackson), pgs. 104, 193, 803

United Way of the Coastal Empire *See Girl Scouting in the Inner City*

United Way of the Midlands *See Stay the Night on My Street*

United Way of the Plains, pgs. 158, 192, 799

United Way of Tompkins County *See The Learning Web*

United Way of Tuscaloosa County *See Boardsmanship Seminar**

United Way of Weld County, pg. 232

United Way of Westchester *See Special Saturday*

United Way of Wichita/Sedgwick County *See First Call for Help/Wichita*

United Way of Wyoming Valley, pgs. 45, 773

United Way Services of Cleveland, pg. 108

United Way Services of Las Vegas, pg. 102

United Way/Voluntary Action Center *See Transitional Volunteers Are...*

United Way Volunteer Center, pgs. 389, 745 *See also Youth Allocations Committee*

United Way Youth Leadership Advisors *See Youth Leadership Venture Funding Program*

United Way's Voluntary Action Center of the Minnesota Area *See Building Creative Organizations**

University Associates, pgs. 955, 1042, 1043, 1089, 1090

University Gerontology Center *See Teaching Senior Center*

University of Akron, pg. 241

University of Alabama, pg. 489 *See also Boardsmanship Seminar**

University of Arkansas at Little Rock *See Certified Volunteer Manager Program*

University of Arkansas, Fayetteville *See Certified Volunteer Manager Program*

University of California *See Arrowhood 22: Future Challenges: A Universal Perspective*

University of California Extension, pg. 1042

University of Chicago Press, pg. 1007

University of Colorado, pg. 263

University of Connecticut, pgs. 247, 755

University of Delaware, pgs. 228, 234, 276, 533

University of Detroit, pg. 249

University of Illinois *See Governor's Office of Voluntary Action; LIVE '89 (Leadership in Volunteerism Experience)*

University of Illinois Extension *See Volunteer Leadership: Challenges For The Nineties*

University of Maryland Book Store, pg. 1032

University of Massachusetts, pgs. 94, 290, 566 *See also National Priorities Project*

University of Minnesota *See Common Ground, Common Good*

University of Nebraska, pgs. 269, 281, 655

University of Nevada, pg. 311

University of New Hampshire *See NH State Conference on Volunteerism*

University of New Orleans *See Louisiana State Special Olympics Summer Games*

University of North Carolina, pgs. 283, 796 *See also Campus Literacy Awareness Month Program*

University of North Florida, pg. 262
University of Oklahoma Press, pg. 1016
University of Oregon, pg. 291
University of Pennsylvania, pg. 66
University of Rhode Island Extension *See Looking Ahead: Managing Tomorrow's Volunteers*
University of South Carolina Law School *See Stay the Night on My Street*
University of South Dakota, pg. 326
University of Southern California *See Senior Program*
University of Southern Mississippi *See National Conference for Volunteer Leadership**
University of Tennessee *See East Tennessee Community Design Center; Southeast Resource Center for Children and Youth Services*
University of Texas, pg. 487
University of Texas at Austin *See Wholeffects Education: National Conference*
University of Vermont, pg. 314
University of Washington, pg. 255 *See also The How-To of Working with Volunteers - TLC (Teaching/Learning/Caring)*
University of Wisconsin, pgs. 398, 489, 532, 536
University of Wisconsin/Milwaukee, pg. 697
University of Wisconsin-Stevens Point, pg. 325
University Programs for Volunteers and Administrators of Volunteers, pg. 135
The Untapped Resource: Disabled Persons as Volunteers, pg. 303
Urban Angler *See Massachusetts Aquatic Resource Education Program (AREP)*
Urban Coalition, pgs. 80, 777
Urban Drug-Free Schools Initiative, pg. 610
Urban Elderly Coalition, pgs. 332, 898
Urban Institute Press, pgs. 946, 947, 951, 952, 953, 1063, 1079, 1088, 1092
Urban Involvement, pg. 488
Urban Services Agency *See Johns Hopkins Tutorial Project*
Ursuline College *See The Greater Cleveland Connection*
Ursuline High School, pg. 362
US/ACTION *See Big Brothers/Big Sisters of Nassau County*; Central Naugatuck Valley Retired Senior Volunteer Program; Corporate Retirees Information and Assistance Program; GAIN (Greater Achievement Through Involvement Now); Governor's Conference on Volunteers in Energy*; Lincoln County Senior Companion Program; Livingston County RSVP Program; Milton Cares Telephone Reassurance; Nursing Home Project; Older Americans as a Growing National Resource*; Retired Senior Volunteer Program; RSVP - Nursing Home Project*; RSVP of Ramsey County; Rural Volunteer Services Network; Save Our Water*; The Spirit That Supports Alabama - Volunteers; Union Retirees Resources; Visitor Hospitality Center*; Volunteer Volunteer Coordinators*; Volunteers... OUR Caring Alabama; Young Volunteers in Action*; Youth Community Service*
US/ACTION; Chamber of Commerce *See RSVP Thrift Shop**
US/ACTION - Older Americans Volunteer Programs (OAVP), pg. 1068
US/ACTION - RSVP *See Milton Cares Telephone Reassurance*
US/ACTION (Senior Companion Program) *See Volunteer Training Program for Volunteer Advocates*
US/ACTION - The Federal Volunteer Agency, pgs. 5, 80, 97, 99, 251, 255, 273, 282, 396, 397, 398, 463, 605, 655, 866, 909, 950

US/ACTION - VISTA *See Adult Literacy Project; East Tennessee Community Design Center; Milton Cares Telephone Reassurance; Youth Who Care*
US/Administration: The President's Private Sector Initiatives Program, pg. 209
U.S. Association of Museum Volunteers *See Improving Museum Volunteer Performance*
U.S.-Based Japanese Corporations and the United Way, pgs. 104, 537
U.S. Catholic Charities, pgs. 356, 825
U.S. Catholic Conference, pg. 226
US/Civil Air Patrol *See Six Friends Memorial Fund*
US/Coast Guard Auxiliary, pg. 929
US/Commission on Civil Rights*, pg. 578
U.S. Committee for United Nations Children's Fund, pgs. 161, 527
U.S. Committee on UNICEF, pgs. 966, 967, 968
U.S. Conference of Mayors, pg. 558 *See also National Celebration of the Outdoors*
US/Congress, pg. 572 *See also U.S. Institute of Peace*
US Congress Staff *See Jail 'N Bail on Capitol Hill*
US Consumer Information Center, pgs. 988, 989, 990, 1019
US/Consumer Product Safety Commission, pgs. 163, 571, 670
US/DEd - Clearinghouse on Disability Information, pgs. 1070, 1076, 1077, 1078
US/DEd - Department of Education *See Clearinghouse on Disability Information; Clearinghouse on the Handicapped*; Private Sector Initiatives Program; Urban Drug-Free Schools Initiative*
US/DEd - Division for the Handicapped, pgs. 170, 860
US/DEd - National Adult Education Clearinghouse, pg. 1004
US/DEd - Office for Children and Youth, pg. 993
US/DEd - Office of Special Education and Rehabilitative Services, pgs. 170, 860
US/DEd - Office of the Secretary, pgs. 212, 616
US/DoA - Consumer and Food Economics Institute, pg. 993
US/DoA - Department of Agriculture *See Forest Service Volunteer Program; 4-H General Forums: Adult Volunteer Training; 4-H Specific Forums: Adult Volunteer Training; Hosted Programs and Youth Conservation Corps; Job Corps; Technical Assistance to Cooperatives; US/DoA - Farmers Home Administration*
US/DoA - Division of Cooperative Services, pg. 577
US/DoA - Farmers Home Administration, pg. 694
US/DoA - Food and Nutrition Service, pgs. 176, 580, 993, 1052, 1053, 1054
US/DoA - Forest Service, pgs. 656, 767, 774, 1056, 1058, 1060, 1061
US/DoA - Forestry Division *See Touch America Project (TAP)*
US/DoA - 4-H Youth/Extension Service, pgs. 58, 240, 317, 810
US/DoA - Mount Hood National Forest *See TRIS (Trails Information System)*
US/DoA - Photography Division, pgs. 1029, 1052, 1053, 1056, 1058, 1059
US/DoA - Soil Conservation Service, pg. 767

US/DoC - Department of Commerce *See US/DoC - Private Sector Initiatives Program; Washington for Minority Youth Awareness Day*
US/DoC - National Technical Information Service, pgs. 956, 990, 1037
US/DoC - Office of Minority Business Enterprise, pgs. 299, 546
US/DoC - Private Sector Initiatives Program, pgs. 210, 543, 1063
US/DoD - Air Force *See Flint Airshow*
US/DoD - Air Force Office of Public Affairs, pg. 342
US/DoD - Army Community Service, pgs. 275, 344, 890
US/DoD - Army Corps of Engineers *See Friends of the Rouge*
US/DoD - Army National Guard/Michigan *See Flint Airshow*
US/DoD - Army Preventive Medicine Activity, pgs. 344, 671
US/DoD - Army TRADOC, CFSC-FSC, pg. 889
US/DoD - Charleston Naval Base, pgs. 352, 840
US/DoD - Commander Naval Base San Diego, pgs. 351, 623
US/DoD - Department of Defense *See US/DoD - Private Sector Initiatives Program*
US/DoD - Department of the Air Force *See Air Force Members as Volunteers**
US/DoD - Department of the Army *See Army Child Care Technical Assistance Conference; Army Community Service; Army Community Service Volunteer Training; Be Alive in 2005: Promoting Wellness into the 21st Century; Education and Employment Resource Center; Fort Dix Volunteers; Special Olympics Time; Volunteer Program - Fort Benjamin Harrison*
US/DoD - Department of the Navy, pgs. 349, 350, 592, 892 *See also Campaign Drug Free; Health Fair; US/DoD - Navy Family Service Center; Welcome Baby*
US/DoD - Fort Belvoir *See Six Friends Memorial Fund*
US/DoD - Fort Benjamin Harrison, pgs. 347, 894
US/DoD - Fort Benning *See Volunteer Resource Center*
US/DoD - Fort Dix, pgs. 345, 890
US/DoD - Fort Eustis, pgs. 345, 539
US/DoD - Fort Gordon, pgs. 345, 891
US/DoD - Fort Leavenworth Combined Arms Center, pg. 348
US/DoD - Fort Sill, pgs. 346, 891
US/DoD - JANGO *See JANGO (Junior Army Navy Guild Organization)**
US/DoD - McClellan Air Force Base, pgs. 343, 672
US/DoD - Naval Academy *See Institute on Federal Library Resources*
US/DoD - Naval Internal Relations Activity, pg. 1094
US/DoD - Naval Regional Medical Clinic, pgs. 349, 672
US/DoD - Naval Reserve Force, pgs. 348, 610, 997, 1001
US/DoD - Naval Service School Command Post *See Saturday Scholars*
US/DoD - Navy Civil Engineers Corps *See Parma-Hilton Playground Project*
US/DoD - Navy Family Service Center, pgs. 348, 350, 839, 1087, 1095
US/DoD - Office of Economic Adjustment, pgs. 1063, 1064
US/DoD - Office of the Navy Chaplain *See WriteConnection Program: Love A Child By Mail*

US/DoD - Private Sector Initiatives Program, pg. 211

US/DoD - USS Kitty Hawk *See USS Kitty Hawk/Washington Square Partnership*

US/DoD - Warren Air Force Base *See Recruiting, Training and Retention of Volunteers*

US/DoE - Handicapped Personnel Preparation *See Parents Educating Parents; Parents Educating Parents: Training Program*

US/DoE - Office of Handicapped Individuals, pg. 1081

US/DoE - Office of Information, pg. 1046

US/DoI - Bureau of Indian Affairs, pgs. 383, 527 *See also AIDS Public Education Program*

US/DoI - Department of the Interior *See Indian Arts and Crafts Board; Information Exchange*; Private Sector Efforts Program*

US/DoI - Forest Service *See Portland Mountain Rescue*

US/DoI - Forestry Division *See Touch America Project (TAP)*

US/DoI - National Park Service, pgs. 177, 925, 956, 1016, 1063, 1082, 1083, 1084

US/DoI - Office of the Secretary, pgs. 215, 761

US/DoJ - Department of Justice *See Law Enforcement Assistance Program; US/DoJ - Private Sector Initiatives*

US/DoJ - District Court *See Fairfax Alternative Services Workshop; Volunteer Training - School Desegregation Monitoring**

US/DoJ - Law Enforcement Assistance Agency, pgs. 118, 697

US/DoJ - National Criminal Justice Reference Service, pgs. 174, 718

US/DoJ - Private Sector Initiatives, pgs. 216, 698

US/DoL - Department of Labor *See Operation Child Watch; US/DoL - Employment and Training Administration; US/DoL - Private Sector Involvement Program; US/DoL - Women's Bureau; Youth Community Service*

US/DoL - Employment and Training Administration, pgs. 652, 1011, 1012

US/DoL - Employment and Training Commission, pg. 1013

US/DoL - Green Thumb Program *See Adult Literacy Project*

US/DoL - Office of Information, pgs. 971, 1012

US/DoL - Office of the Secretary, pg. 1079

US/DoL - Private Sector Involvement Program, pgs. 216, 652

US/DoL - Women's Bureau, pgs. 659, 813, 974, 976, 992, 993, 995

US/DoL - Coast Guard *See Ottawa River "Fighting Back" Campaign; Volunteer Sailboat Navigators*

US/DoT - Department of Transportation *See US/DoT - Private Sector Initiatives Programs*

US/DoT - Federal Aviation Administration *See Air Crash Drill*

US/DoT - Federal Highway Admistration, pg. 1091

US/DoT - Library Service Division, pg. 1092

US/DoT - National Highway Traffic Safety Administration, pgs. 164, 582, 1092

US/DoT - National Ridesharing Information Center, pgs. 974, 975, 976, 1091

US/DoT - Office of Information, pg. 1091

US/DoT - Office of Technology Sharing, pg. 1092

US/DoT - Private Sector Initiatives Programs, pgs. 218, 935, 1063

US/DTreas - Bureau of Alcohol, Tobacco and Firearms, pgs. 499, 609

US/DTreas - Department of the Treasury *See Anti-Drug Teams; US/DTreas - Treasury's Involvement in Private Sector Initiatives; Volunteer Income Tax Assistance (VITA)*

US/DTreas - Internal Revenue Service, pgs. 434, 578

US/DTreas - Treasury's Involvement in Private Sector Initiatives, pgs. 219, 573, 1064

US/Engineering & Housing Support Center *See Adopt-A-School*

US/EPA - Earth Day, pg. 770

US/EPA - Environment Monitoring Programs, pg. 1056

US/EPA - Environmental Protection Agency *See Earth Day 1990/EPA; Waste Alert!*

US/EPA - Office of Noise Abatement and Control, pg. 1058

US/EPA - Office of Solid Waste Management, pgs. 779, 1061

US/EPA - Private Sector Initiatives Efforts, pg. 1063

US/Federal Aviation Administration *See Charity Plane Ride for Orange Grove*

US/Federal Home Loan Bank Board, pg. 692

US/Federal Library & Information Center Committee, pgs. 307, 554

US/Federal Library Committee *See Institute on Federal Library Resources*

US/FEMA - Federal Emergency Management Agency *See Building Seismic Safety Council*

US/FTC - Federal Trade Commission, pgs. 163, 582

US/GAO - General Accounting Office, pg. 994

US/GSA - General Services Administration *See US/GSA - Private Sector Initiatives*

US/GSA - Government Printing Office, pgs. 970, 971, 1014, 1015, 1016, 1069, 1075, 1076, 1079

US/GSA - Private Sector Initiatives, pgs. 212, 543

US/HHS - Administration for Children, Youth and Families, pgs. 108, 286, 584, 586, 813, 949, 1071, 1079, 1086

US/HHS - Administration on Aging, pgs. 319, 896, 897, 1006, 1027, 1032, 1033, 1034, 1069, 1071, 1072, 1074, 1076, 1078, 1092, 1096, 1100 *See also Preparing for an Aging Society*

US/HHS - Bureau of Community Health Services, pg. 1077

US/HHS - Cancer Information Clearinghouse, pgs. 161, 665

US/HHS - Center for Drug-Free Schools & Communities *See Urban Drug-Free Schools Initiative*

US/HHS - Centers for Disease Control *See Statewide HIV/AIDS Network; World Health Organization Collaborating Center on AIDS*

US/HHS - Children's Bureau, pg. 983 *See also Southeast Resource Center for Children and Youth Services*

US/HHS - Department of Health & Human Services, pgs. 1038, 1041, 1099 *See also FDA Experimental AIDS Treatment Hotline; Head Start Program; Milwaukee and the Single Girl*; National Center on Child Abuse and Neglect; National Clearinghouse for Poison Control Centers; Senior Opportunities and Services; US/HHS - Administration on Aging; US/HHS - Cancer Information Clearinghouse; US/HHS - High Blood Pressure Information Center; US/HHS - National AIDS Information Clearinghouse; US/HHS - National*

Clearinghouse for Alcohol and Drug Information; US/HHS - National Clearinghouse for Mental Health Information; US/HHS - Office of Community Services; US/HHS - Working Group on Private Sector Initiatives; Using Volunteers in Your Agency; Voluntarism: A Key to the Future; Volunteer & Community Partnerships Institute; The Volunteerism Project*

US/HHS - Division of Youth Activities, pg. 1045

US/HHS - Food and Drug Administration, pgs. 160, 171, 521, 670

US/HHS - High Blood Pressure Information Center, pgs. 180, 681, 978, 1023

US/HHS - Inspector General Hotline, pg. 989

US/HHS - National AIDS Information Clearinghouse, pgs. 160, 520, 960, 963, 964

US/HHS - National Cancer Institute, pgs. 161, 665

US/HHS - National Center on Child Abuse and Neglect, pgs. 1031, 1065, 1080

US/HHS - National Clearinghouse for Alcohol and Drug Information, pgs. 168, 599, 602, 959, 978, 997, 998, 999, 1000, 1001, 1002, 1003, 1024, 1086, 1087

US/HHS - National Clearinghouse for Health Information, pg. 283

US/HHS - National Clearinghouse for Mental Health Information, pgs. 175, 744

US/HHS - National Institutes of Health, pgs. 180, 681

US/HHS - Office of Community Services, pgs. 91, 398, 1028, 1029, 1056

US/HHS - Office of Human Development, pg. 583

US/HHS - Office of Information, pg. 1019

US/HHS - Office of the Secretary, pgs. 119, 214, 750, 826 *See also US/HHS - Office of Community Services*

US/HHS - Office on Smoking & Health, pgs. 172, 678

US/HHS - Public Health Service, pg. 1022

US/HHS - Working Group on Private Sector Initiatives, pgs. 214, 826

US/House of Representatives, pg. 1078

US/HUD - Department of Housing & Urban Development *See US/HUD - Private Sector Initiative Activities in HUD*

US/HUD - Federal National Mortgage Association (Fannie Mae) *See Manna, Inc.**

US/HUD - Office of Fair Housing and Equal Opportunity, pgs. 116, 685

US/HUD - Office of Information, pg. 1030

US/HUD - Office of Policy Development, pg. 1028

US/HUD - Office of the Secretary, pgs. 213, 682

US/HUD - Private Sector Initiative Activities in HUD, pgs. 213, 682

U.S. Institute of Peace, pg. 564

U.S. Jaycees, pg. 92

U.S. Journal of Drug and Alcohol Dependence, pgs. 999, 1000, 1003, 1039, 1073

U.S. Junior Chamber of Commerce *See U.S. Jaycees*

U.S. League of Savings Institutions, pgs. 1028, 1057

US/Library of Congress, pgs. 197, 397, 637, 846 *See also Federal Information Policies: Access is the Key; Friends of Handicapped Readers; Institute on Federal Library Resources*

US/National Endowment for the Arts *See Orchestra Management Seminar*

US/National Gallery of Art *See Orchestra Management Seminar*

U.S. National Senior Olympics, pg. 926

US/NCUA - National Credit Union Administration *See US/NCUA - Private Sector Initiatives and Volunteerism*

US/NCUA - Private Sector Initiatives and Volunteerism, pgs. 217, 574, 1063

US/Office of Consumer Affairs, pgs. 574, 988, 989, 990, 991

U.S. Olympic Committee, pgs. 926, 927, 1083, 1084

US/OMB - Federal Programs Information Branch, pg. 97

US/OMB - Health Care Planning Administration, pg. 1071

US/OMB - Office of Management and Budget *See Federal Assistance Programs Retrieval System (FAPRS)*

U.S. Open Golf Tournament *See U.S. Open Volunteer Committee*

U.S. Open Volunteer Committee, pgs. 114, 858

US/OPM - Office of Information, pgs. 49, 669, 1011, 1013

US/OPM - Office of Personnel Management *See Leave Bank; US/OPM - Private Sector Initiatives in OPM*

US/OPM - Private Sector Initiatives in OPM, pgs. 217, 653, 1064

US/Presidential Awards Programs, pgs. 16, 698

US/President's Committee on Mental Retardation, pgs. 975, 989, 1072, 1073, 1074, 1077

US/PS - Mailer Education Center, pgs. 8, 952

US/PS - Office of News and Public Affairs, pgs. 382, 1068

US/PS - Postal Service *See Carrier Alert; Mailer Education Seminars*

US/RTC - Resolution Trust Corporation *See Low-Income Apartments Program*

US/SBA - Office for Women, pgs. 970, 971

US/SBA - Office of Advocacy, pg. 971

US/SBA - Office of Management Assistance, pg. 970

US/SBA - Private Sector Initiatives Activities, pgs. 218, 543, 1064

US/SBA - SCORE/ACE, pgs. 398, 412, 544, 545

US/SBA - Service Corps of Retired Executives/Active Corps of Executives, pgs. 398, 412, 544, 545, 970

US/SBA - Small Business Administration *See Bay Area SCORE Program; Brookdale-SCORE Program; Service Corps of Retired Executives (SCORE); US/SBA - Private Sector Initiatives Activities; US/SBA - Service Corps of Retired Executives/Active Corps of Executives*

US/Senate, pgs. 314, 562

US/VA - Private Sector Initiatives Program, pgs. 220, 888, 1064

US/VA - VAVS Workshops, pgs. 276, 889

US/VA - Veterans Administration *See Institute on Federal Library Resources; US/VA - Private Sector Initiatives Program; US/VA - VAVS Workshops; Volunteer Leadership: Challenges For The Nineties*

US/VA - Veterans Administration Medical Center, pgs. 353, 893

US/White House, pgs. 168, 209, 605, 1039 *See also Twenty-Five Year Presidential Award Certificate Program for Volunteers in Juvenile Criminal Justice*

US/White House - Comment Line, pg. 556

US/White House - Office of National Service, pgs. 206, 207, 1051, 1064

US/White House - Partnerships in Education, pg. 620

Using Volunteers in Your Agency, pg. 283

USOC Education Committee, pg. 927

USS Kitty Hawk/Washington Square Partnership, pgs. 352, 765

Utah Department of Social Services, pg. 146

Utah Division of Wildlife Resources, pg. 784

Utah Second District Juvenile Court, pgs. 496, 913

Utah State University Chamber of Music *See Summerfest Art Faire*

V

VA Hospital *See Publicity Workshop*

VA Voluntary Services Board, pgs. 353, 893

VAC Board Education Program, pg. 186

VAC of the Minneapolis Area *See Lake Sylvia V.I.P. (Very Important Person) Conference**

VAC of the St. Paul Area *See Lake Sylvia V.I.P. (Very Important Person) Conference**

VAC Training, pg. 259

VAC Workshops*, pg. 280

Vacation and Senior Citizens Association, pgs. 925, 1084

Vacations for the Aging *See Vacation and Senior Citizens Association*

Valentine School Art Show, pgs. 423, 531

Valley Green Juvenile Drug Abuse Prevention Facility, pg. 608

Valley of the Sun United Way, pg. 981 *See also The Volunteerism Project*

Valued Youth Partnership Program, pgs. 488, 630

Van Ministry, pgs. 374, 717

Vanguard Press, pg. 1014

VD National Hotline, pgs. 178, 681

Vermont College, pg. 246

Vermont Internship Program, pg. 314

Very Special Arts, pgs. 394, 530

Veterans Counseling and Guidance Center, pgs. 378, 894

Veterans for Peace, pgs. 353, 564

Victim-Witness Assistance Center*, pg. 731

Vietnamese Community Services *See Governor's Office of Voluntary Action*

The Village Family Service Center *See Retired Senior Volunteer Program*

Virginia Association of Elementary School Principals *See First State Conference on School Volunteers*

Virginia Association of School Administrators *See First State Conference on School Volunteers*

Virginia Bureau of Insurance *See Virginia Citizens Consumer Council*

Virginia Circuit Court, pg. 1038

Virginia Citizens Consumer Council, pgs. 337, 574

Virginia Commonwealth University *See Marketing for Voluntary Service Organizations; Parent to Parent*

Virginia Community Development Organization *See National Association for the Southern Poor*

Virginia Congress of Parents and Teachers *See First State Conference on School Volunteers*

Virginia Council on Health and Medical Care, pg. 1075

Virginia Department for Rights of the Disabled, pgs. 199, 201, 842, 983, 996, 1074, 1079

Virginia Department of Corrections *See Virginia Volunteers - Health of the Commonwealth*

Virginia Department of Education Driver Safety Program *See Drunk-Driving Simulator Program and Forum*

Virginia Department of Health *See AIDS Program*

Virginia Department of Housing & Community Development, pgs. 116, 686

Virginia Department of Social Services, pgs. 151, 165, 812, 816, 817

Virginia Department of State Police *See VSPA Fund-Raising Programs*

Virginia Department of Volunteerism *See Celebration of Volunteerism: Annual Statewide Conference; Complete Volunteer Legal Liability Workshop; Effective Boardsmanship; Managing Your Fiscal Responsibilities as a Nonprofit; How to Avoid Financial Pitfalls; North Carolina/Virginia Exchange: Part One; The Quest for Community; Statewide Drug Task Force Conference; Team-Building; Virginia Volunteers - Health of the Commonwealth; Volunteer Management Series; Volunteer Program Management; Volunteering: A Celebration of Community*

Virginia Division for Children, pgs. 992, 1021

Virginia Division of Volunteerism, pgs. 146, 147, 148, 149, 150, 240, 289, 955 *See also Voluntary Action Center Training (Blacksburg)**

Virginia Ecumenical Infant Mortality Prevention Project Conference, pgs. 149, 667

Virginia Education Association *See First State Conference on School Volunteers*

Virginia Emergency Services *See Six Friends Memorial Fund*

Virginia Foundation for Humanities and Public Policy *See Conference on Philosophical Issues in Volunteerism*

Virginia Governor's Office, pgs. 430, 735

Virginia Group to Alleviate Smoking in Public, pg. 679

Virginia Institute for Developmental Disabilities, pgs. 418, 852, 1098

Virginia Office of the Attorney General *See Virginia Citizens Consumer Council*

Virginia Partnership Fund and Other Programs, pgs. 116, 686

Virginia Polytechnic Institute and State University, pgs. 236, 303, 320

Virginia Power, pg. 974

Virginia Society of Certified Public Accountants, pgs. 9, 274

Virginia State Chamber of Commerce *See First State Conference on School Volunteers*

Virginia State Police *See Six Friends Memorial Fund*

Virginia State Police Association, pgs. 110, 601

Virginia Tech *See Credit and Degree Programs in Voluntary Association Administration in Colleges and Universities; The Future of Volunteerism: Shapes and Scenarios; Mini-Grants: Research in Volunteerism; Proposal Writing Institute**

Virginia Volunteers - Health of the Commonwealth, pg. 149

VISA - Volunteers in School Action, pg. 644

VISCAP (Volunteer Incentive Service Credit Account Program), pgs. 413, 903

Vision, Planning & Partnership in Neighborhood Organizing, pgs. 288, 828

Visiting Friends*, pgs. 445, 673

Visiting Nurse Association *See The Response Pool*

Visiting Nurse Association of Milwaukee, pgs. 445, 673

Visitor Hospitality Center*, pgs. 381, 718

Visits Through Video, pg. 911

V.I.S.T.A. *See Voluntary Action Center of South Lake Tahoe*

VISTA (Volunteers In Service to America), pg. 80

VITA (Volunteers In Teaching Adults), pg. 624

VIVA (Very Important Volunteers in Action), pgs. 413, 898

VM Systems, pg. 253 *See also Institute on Volunteer Administration: A Proposal*

VMS/Heritage Arts, pgs. 946, 948, 952, 1018, 1065, 1066, 1090

VOA Symposium on Homelessness, pgs. 307, 873

VOCAL, pg. 137

Vocational Foundation, pgs. 978, 1013

Vogel Alcove, pgs. 445, 874

Volcano Press, pg. 1014

Voluntarism: A Key to the Future*, pgs. 319, 897

Voluntarism: Confrontation and Opportunity*, pgs. 285, 797

Voluntary Action Association Administration Program, pg. 259

Voluntary Action Center, pgs. 45, 76, 273, 487, 677, 743, 835 *See also The Care and Nourishment of Volunteers*; Court Referral Program; Volunteer Bureau of the Omaha United Way; Volunteer Bureau of the United Way*

Voluntary Action Center/Lynchburg *See The Quest for Community*

Voluntary Action Center of Boston, pg. 251

Voluntary Action Center of Chattanooga, pg. 10

Voluntary Action Center of Fairfax County *See Complete Volunteer Legal Liability Workshop; Volunteer Program Management*

Voluntary Action Center of Greater Milwaukee, pg. 968

Voluntary Action Center of Greater Richmond *See Volunteer Management Series*

Voluntary Action Center of Greensboro, pgs. 955, 958

Voluntary Action Center of Lynchburg *See Basics of Volunteer Program Management**

Voluntary Action Center of Montgomery, AL *See TAVS (Teenage Volunteers)*

Voluntary Action Center of Montgomery County, pg. 259

Voluntary Action Center of Morris County, pgs. 186, 232, 280, 955

The Voluntary Action Center of Muscatine, pgs. 386, 835

Voluntary Action Center of Norfolk *See Complete Volunteer Legal Liability Workshop*

Voluntary Action Center of Prince George's County *See People Need People Volunteer Fair*

Voluntary Action Center of South Lake Tahoe, pg. 10

Voluntary Action Center of the Fairfax County Area, pgs. 11, 259, 315, 724

Voluntary Action Center of the I&R Services of Allegheny County *See Volunteer Experience: Change, Challenge, Choices*

Voluntary Action Center of the Midlands *See Building Better Boards*

Voluntary Action Center of the Prince William Area, pg. 260 *See also Volunteer Management Series*

Voluntary Action Center of the St. Paul Area, pg. 185 *See also Demystifying the Internship Experience*

Voluntary Action Center of the Virginia Peninsula *See Complete Volunteer Legal Liability Workshop*

Voluntary Action Center of Tuscaloosa, pg. 184

Voluntary Action Center of United Way, pgs. 62, 184, 257, 258, 310 *See also DOVIA Training Programs*

Voluntary Action Center of Wake County*, pg. 11

Voluntary Action Center Training (Blacksburg)*, pg. 259

Voluntary Action Center Training (Manassas)*, pg. 260

Voluntary Action Centers of Blacksburg and Roanoke *See Voluntary Action Center Training (Blacksburg)**

Voluntary Center of the United Way of Greater Richmond *See Team-Building*

Voluntary Center of Thomas Jefferson Area *See Volunteer Management Series*

Voluntary Way of the Midlands *See Volunteer Bureau of the Omaha United Way*

Voluntas *See Institute on Volunteer Administration: A Proposal*

Volunteer Action Center, pg. 264

Volunteer Action Center of Broward County, pgs. 950, 996

Volunteer Action Center of Los Angeles, pg. 660

Volunteer Administration Specialization, pg. 260

Volunteer Administrator's Conference, pg. 260

Volunteer & Community Partnerships Institute, pgs. 286, 584

Volunteer and Information Agency, pg. 236

Volunteer and Paid Staff Working Together, pg. 261

Volunteer Awards Program, pgs. 18, 824

Volunteer Boulder, pg. 1042

Volunteer Boulder County, pgs. 951, 976, 1015

Volunteer Bureau *See Making the Volunteer Experience Count*

Volunteer Bureau of Greater Portland *See Volunteer Program Management Certificate Program*

Volunteer Bureau of the Omaha United Way, pg. 12

Volunteer Bureau of the United Way, pg. 12

Volunteer Bureau of United Way of San Diego County, pg. 1042

Volunteer Case Aide Program, pgs. 1048, 1049

Volunteer Center, pgs. 460, 914 *See also Victim-Witness Assistance Center*; Volunteer Training and Recruitment Conference*

Volunteer Center Division *See DOVIA Skill Development Workshops*; Supervision Skill Series/MAP (Management Assistance Program)*

Volunteer Center, Inc., pgs. 339, 725

Volunteer Center of Central Florida, pgs. 184, 241, 272, 308, 1041

Volunteer Center of Chicago, pgs. 246, 256, 323

Volunteer Center of Greater Milwaukee, pgs. 27, 949, 967

Volunteer Center of Johnson County, pg. 12

Volunteer Center of Licking County *See Thank You Picket Lines*

Volunteer Center of Lincoln*, pgs. 953, 1043, 1048

Volunteer Center of Maricopa County, pg. 269 *See also The Volunteerism Project*

Volunteer Center of Marion County, pg. 242

Volunteer Center of Memphis, pgs. 954, 1072

Volunteer Center of Orange County *See Police Department Volunteer Program*

Volunteer Center of Rensselaer County *See Court Referred Volunteer Program of Rensselaer County*

Volunteer Center of San Gabriel Valley, pg. 1044

Volunteer Center of the Greater Quad Cities, pgs. 958, 976, 984

Volunteer Center of the United Way, pg. 187

Volunteer Center of Topeka, pg. 183

Volunteer Center of United Way, pgs. 952, 967, 1043

Volunteer Center of United Way of Central Iowa, pgs. 949, 977

Volunteer Center of York County, pg. 12

Volunteer Center/United Way At Work, pgs. 13, 955, 977, 1017

Volunteer Clearinghouse *See Volunteer Link*

Volunteer Clearinghouse of the District of Columbia, pg. 25

Volunteer Community Betterment Project, pgs. 37, 597

Volunteer Connection Telethon, pg. 20

Volunteer Consultant Services Program, pg. 556

Volunteer Consultants, pg. 1041

Volunteer Coordination, pg. 261

Volunteer Coordinators' Roundtable of Fairfax County *See Complete Volunteer Legal Liability Workshop*

Volunteer Council, pg. 189

Volunteer Counseling Service of Rockland County, pgs. 378, 791

Volunteer Department, pgs. 389, 742

Volunteer Development Institute*, pg. 182

Volunteer Experience: Change, Challenge, Choices, pgs. 261, 656

Volunteer Forum, pg. 947

Volunteer Fund Raising Committee, pgs. 115, 879

Volunteer Greenville *See SCAVA Workshops for Volunteer Administrators**

Volunteer Income Tax Assistance (VITA), pgs. 434, 578

Volunteer Information Center, pg. 64

Volunteer Information Service *See Thursday Afternoon Program (TAP)*

Volunteer Initiative Program (VIP), pg. 30

Volunteer Intervening for Equity (VIE)*, pg. 322

Volunteer Jacksonville, pg. 289 *See also Volunteering in the Religious Setting*

Volunteer Lawyers for the Arts, pgs. 329, 575

Volunteer Lawyers Project, pgs. 446, 580

Volunteer Leaders Conference, pgs. 287, 558

Volunteer Leadership: Challenges For The Nineties, pg. 131

Volunteer Leadership Conference, pg. 145

Volunteer Leadership Development Program, pgs. 182, 280

Volunteer Leadership Program, pg. 182

Volunteer Leadership Workshop, pg. 262

Volunteer Link, pgs. 126, 1021

Volunteer Management Associates, pg. 1096

Volunteer Management Certification, pg. 262

Volunteer Management for the Non-Profit Professional*, pg. 262

Volunteer Management: Level I and Level II, pg. 263

Volunteer Management Program: First Level Workshop (1990), pg. 263

Volunteer Management Program: Second Level Workshop, pg. 263

Volunteer Management Program: Third Level Workshop, pg. 264

Volunteer Management Seminars, pg. 264

Volunteer Management Series, pg. 150

Volunteer Management Systems Course, pg. 264

Volunteer Network*, pg. 13

Volunteer Ombudsman Citizen Action League (VOCAL) *See Statewide Conference on Volunteerism*

Volunteer Orientation Program, pgs. 20, 855
Volunteer Paleontology Dig, pgs. 489, 536
Volunteer Prison League, pg. 698
Volunteer Program Administration and Voluntary Organization Management, pg. 264
Volunteer Program Efficiency in a Down-Sided Economy*, pgs. 317, 715
Volunteer Program - Fort Benjamin Harrison, pgs. 347, 894
Volunteer Program Management, pgs. 135, 150, 265
Volunteer Program Management Certificate Program, pg. 266
Volunteer Program of Prairie View, pgs. 390, 742
Volunteer Reading Aides Program, pgs. 357, 732
Volunteer Resource Center, pgs. 347, 894 See also The Bridge
Volunteer Resources - AIDS Program, pgs. 20, 510
Volunteer Resources Division, pgs. 389, 976, 1049
Volunteer Sailboat Navigators, pg. 929
Volunteer Senior Leaders, pg. 203
Volunteer Service Bureau, pgs. 248, 262, 958
Volunteer Service Bureau/VAC, pgs. 1005, 1094
Volunteer Service Center/United Way See Experiential Learning - Working with Student Volunteers
Volunteer Service Corps Committee, pgs. 398, 906
Volunteer Service of Santa Cruz County, pg. 1093
Volunteer Service Program, pg. 849
Volunteer Services, pgs. 377, 644, 865
Volunteer Services/CAC, pg. 91
Volunteer Services Curriculum, pg. 266
Volunteer Services Program/Social Services, pg. 830
Volunteer Services Program/UA, pg. 489
Volunteer Services Unlimited/UWM See Entering the Community: Summer Volunteer Service and Career Opportunities for Students
Volunteer Staffing Workshops*, pg. 323
VOLUNTEER - The National Center, pgs. 3, 6, 77, 281, 341, 466, 883, 889, 946, 948, 953, 955, 958, 977, 978, 987, 1052 See also Institute on Volunteer Administration: A Proposal; National Conference for Volunteer Leadership*; Prime Time to End Hunger
Volunteer Training, pg. 267
Volunteer Training and Recruitment Conference, pg. 323
Volunteer Training Program, pg. 267
Volunteer Training Program for Volunteer Advocates, pgs. 128, 844
Volunteer Training - School Desegregation Monitoring*, pgs. 298, 632
Volunteer Transportation, pgs. 381, 939
Volunteer Transportation Program, pgs. 381, 938
Volunteer Tutoring Program, pgs. 489, 648
Volunteer Vacation Program, pg. 928
Volunteer Volunteer Coordinators*, pg. 7
Volunteer Workshops in Maine, pg. 267
Volunteering: A Celebration of Community, pg. 150
Volunteering in the Religious Setting, pg. 309
Volunteering Your Way to a Successful Career, pgs. 282, 653
Volunteerism, pg. 268
Volunteerism: A Bridge to the Future, pg. 152
Volunteerism and Social Work Practice, pgs. 301, 829
The Volunteerism Project, pg. 123
Volunteers: A Capital Idea*, pgs. 298, 618
Volunteers at Fort Leavenworth, pg. 348
Volunteers Do Make a Difference!, pg. 127

Volunteers: Empowerment Today and Tomorrow, pg. 268
Volunteers: Facts and Fiction, pg. 321
Volunteers for Community Service See Metamorphosis: Growth and Change in the Administration of Volunteer Services
Volunteers for Volunteers See West Virginia Conference on Volunteerism
Volunteers for Youth, pgs. 450, 822
Volunteers: Heroes of the 80's*, pg. 269
Volunteers In Action, pgs. 13, 118, 185, 229, 237, 269, 304, 321, 633, 871
Volunteers in Great Britain: A Study Tour, pg. 269
Volunteers in Mission, pg. 1023
Volunteers in Parks (VIP), pgs. 55, 776
Volunteers in Prevention, Probation, Prisons, pgs. 6, 292, 293, 316, 699, 700, 714, 1036, 1038, 1039 See also Twenty-Five Year Presidential Award Certificate Program for Volunteers in Juvenile Criminal Justice
Volunteers in Providence Schools, pg. 645
Volunteers in Public Schools, pg. 1024
Volunteers In Service to America See VISTA (Volunteers In Service to America)
Volunteers in Technical Assistance, pgs. 81, 308, 433, 542, 945, 971, 984, 1083
Volunteers Insurance Service Association/CIMA, pgs. 950, 1093
Volunteers of America, pgs. 81, 270, 307, 355, 467, 690, 698, 873, 908, 909 See also CHIP-IN; Continental Homeless Assistance Program
Volunteers of America Annual Meeting, pg. 270
Volunteers of America Foodbank See Seattle-King County RSVP (Retired Senior Volunteer Program)
Volunteers of America of Delaware Valley, pgs. 307, 885
Volunteers of America of Los Angeles, pgs. 108, 548
Volunteers of America of Mesa See Parkinson's Institute for Caregivers
Volunteers of Cape Cod, pgs. 13, 394, 872
Volunteers... OUR Caring Alabama, pg. 270
Volunteers: Our Greatest Natural Resource, pg. 141
Volunteers: The Renewable Resource, pg. 271
Volunteers with Special Needs, pgs. 304, 871
Voter Registration Assistance, pg. 567
VSPA Fund-Raising Programs, pgs. 110, 601

W

Wake Area Mental Health Agency See Special Populations Program
Wake County Public School System See ROVERS (Retired and Older Volunteers: An Educational Resource Service)
WalkAmerica, pgs. 120, 860
Wallerstein Foundation for Geriatric Life Improvement See Youth Services to Frail, Homebound Elderly
Wallington Lions Club, pgs. 377, 850
Warner Books, pg. 971
Warner Brothers, pg. 1054
Warren Air Force Base See Recruiting, Training and Retention of Volunteers
Washington Consortium on HIV Infection in Youth See But I'm Different...
Washington Department of Social & Health Services, pgs. 152, 470, 862, 1066
Washington for Minority Youth Awareness Day, pgs. 299, 546
Washington Heights Ecumenical Food Pantry, pgs. 375, 754
Washington Historical Society See Black Georgetown Reunion Group

Washington Hospital Center, pg. 1023
Washington Informer See Champ Bakery
Washington International Arts Letter, pgs. 967, 968, 976, 1017, 1018
Washington International Newsletter, pg. 1014
Washington Metropolitan Police Department, pgs. 460, 729
Washington Office of Volunteerism, pgs. 152, 1021, 1043
Washington Post, pgs. 38, 53, 306, 641, 753, 884, 977 See also James Madison National Council
Washington Regional Alcohol Program, pgs. 37, 605
Washington Square Association, pgs. 352, 765
Washington State Center for Voluntary Action, pg. 152
Washington State University, pgs. 231, 992, 993 See also AYE SHARE
Washington Times, pg. 1005
Washington Urban League See Operation Rescue
Washington Workshops Foundation, pg. 568
Washington Youth Gardens, pg. 1062
Washtenaw County Department of Social Services, pg. 830
Waste Alert!, pg. 779
Waste Management of Knoxville See Recycling for Ravi
Watergate Restaurant See Taste of the Nation
WBBM Newsradio, pgs. 164, 579
WBEL Radio See United Way Editorial Board
We Care, pg. 375
Wednesday Morning Mothers, pg. 842
Welcome Baby, pgs. 352, 840
Welfare Reform Task Force See Women Off Welfare (WOW)
Wellness and Health Activation Networks, pgs. 173, 678
The Wellness Center, pgs. 434, 678, 1022, 1026
Wenatchee Valley College See Community Resource Center
WERZ-Radio See Seacoast Conference on Volunteerism: A Time for Growth; A Time for Change
West Harlem Coalition, pgs. 328, 778
West St. John Ministry of Care, pgs. 375, 830
West Virginia Conference on Volunteerism, pg. 153
West Virginia Department of Welfare Volunteer Program, pgs. 153, 830
West Virginia Office on Volunteerism, pg. 153
Westark Community College See Volunteer Leadership Workshop
Westchester 2000, pg. 569
Westchester Community College, pg. 465
Westchester County See County Information Center
Westchester County Association, pgs. 569, 981
Western Carolina Center, pgs. 490, 865, 1100
Western Carolina Center Volunteens, pgs. 490, 865
Western Gerontological Society*, pgs. 319, 398, 897
Western State Hospital, pgs. 487, 743
Western Texas College See VIVA (Very Important Volunteers in Action)
Western Wayne County Conservation Club See Friends of the Rouge
Westfield Board of Education See STS (Sharing Talents and Skills)
Westfield Public Schools See STS (Sharing Talents and Skills)
Westtown School, pg. 490
Westtown Service Network, pg. 490
WGEZ Radio See United Way Editorial Board
Wheelchair Race Communications Services, pgs. 47, 591

Wheelchair Wash, pgs. 30, 872
Where Do We Go From Here?, pg. 271
White Cane Drive, pgs. 377, 850
The White House See National Workshop on Voluntarism
Whitman College Center of Mexican Affairs See Public Relations on a Shoestring*
Whitman-Walker Clinic, pgs. 20, 67, 106, 160, 510, 512, 513, 516, 521, 523, 601, 684, 960
Wholeffects Education: National Conference, pgs. 299, 618
Wholeffects Institute, pgs. 299, 618
WIC (Women, Infants and Children) Advocacy Staff, pg. 1088
Wichita Crime Commission, pgs. 195, 697
Wichita State University, pgs. 311, 911
Wiehe Partnership See Give Me Shelter: Designs for Urban Survival
Wildlife Habitat Foundation See Friends of the Rouge
Wildlife Volunteers, pg. 784
Wildwood Books, pg. 1007
William Beaumont Hospital, pgs. 422, 934
William T. Grant Foundation, pg. 1051
Willing Workers of College Hill, pg. 904
Wilmorite Corporation See Camp Good Days and Special Times Rebuilding Project
Winthrop Rockefeller Foundation See Peace Links Arkansas
Wiping Out Drug Abuse Drug Free Teen Center, pgs. 423, 611
Wisconsin Clearinghouse, pg. 1045
WISE & GISE/CRV Volunteer Services, pgs. 1005, 1006, 1007, 1009
WISE Resources Volunteers See Volunteer Services
Wissahickon High School, pg. 311
Wissahickon School District See Social Lab
Within You, Inc./Just Say No Clubs, pg. 604
W.K. Kellogg Foundation See American Indian Partnerships with United Ways*; Project Blueprint; Project LEAD
WMNR Radio - Access Broadcasting Company*, pgs. 66, 853
WMUR-TV See Seacoast Conference on Volunteerism: A Time for Growth; A Time for Change
WNBC-TV See Ability Is Ageless
WOL-AM 140 Radio See Champ Bakery
Wolf Creek Association See Society Bank/Wolf Creek Association Partnership
Woman-to-Woman Hotline, pgs. 161, 666
Women Against Nuclear War, pg. 565
Women Against Rape See Child Assault Prevention Team
Women in Communications, Inc. See Communicating Human Needs
Women Off Welfare (WOW), pgs. 396, 940
Women's Action Alliance, pgs. 950, 964, 997, 1006, 1008, 1016, 1019, 1086, 1088
Women's Center of East Texas, pgs. 167, 834
Women's Community Leadership Institute Project Board See Leadership for the Nineties*
Women's Health Alliance of Long Island See Healthhouse Volunteer Program
Women's Health, Information and Resource Center See Healthhouse Volunteer Program
Woodburn Center for Community Mental Health, pg. 1050
Woodburn Mental Health Center See Bailey's Crossroads Community Shelter
Woodend Volunteer Program, pg. 776
Woodford County Bicentennial Celebration, pg. 525
Woodland Volunteer Center, pg. 751
Woodson Junior High School See Conner-Harris Mini Mall

Work in America Institute, pg. 975
Work Incentive Demonstration Program/Job Factory, pg. 655
Working Effectively with Boards and Committees, pg. 186
Working Group on Private Sector Initiatives, pg. 1063
Working Partners, pg. 271
Workshop for Volunteer Managers*, pg. 272
Workshop for Volunteers, pg. 272
Workshop Series on Volunteerism, pg. 272
Workshops for Volunteer Coordinators and Volunteers in Education*, pgs. 299, 619
Workshops for Volunteer Managers, pg. 273
Workshops in Effective Volunteer Utilization, pg. 273
World Classic Martial Arts See Martial Arts for Seniors
World Health Organization Collaborating Center on AIDS, pg. 509
World Resources Institute See Econet
WriteConnection Program: Love A Child By Mail, pgs. 352, 790
WTAE-TV See Helping Hand
WUST Radio, pgs. 177, 905
WXPN-FM Radio, pg. 66
Wyandotte House, Inc., pgs. 446, 819
Wyandotte House/Neutral Ground, pgs. 446, 819

X

X67 Student Volunteer Program, pg. 956
Xerox Corporation, pgs. 975, 978

Y

YAI Alumni Club Karate Program, pg. 921
Yale University See Statewide Leadership Symposium: Working Together to Make Visions Realities
Yarns of Yesteryear Project, pgs. 398, 532, 1072
Yellowfire Press See Career Development for Volunteer Leadership
YES Program (Youth-Elderly Services)*, pgs. 490, 899
YMCA, pgs. 81, 827
YMCA National Board See National Collaboration for Youth
YMCA Program Store, pg. 949
You Are The Board*, pg. 187
You Can Free A Mind: Adult Literacy Program, pgs. 491, 738
Young Adult Institute, pgs. 865, 921, 1079, 1081
Young Adult Services, pg. 636
Young Audiences, pg. 538
Young Authors' Faire, pgs. 424, 532
Young Black Scholars Program (YBS), pgs. 384, 633
Young Leaders Conference, pg. 286
Young Men's Christian Association of the U.S., pgs. 81, 827, 1044, 1090, 1100
Young Volunteers in Action, pgs. 311, 327, 491
Young Volunteers in Action: Training for Project Directors, pg. 273
Young Wings USA*, pgs. 446, 629
Young Women's Christian Association See Schoolmate Handicraft Volunteers
Young Women's Christian Association of the U.S., pgs. 81, 827
Youth Advisory Commission, pgs. 107, 194, 557, 766
Youth Affairs Task Force, pgs. 198, 631
Youth Allocations Committee, pgs. 104, 193, 803

Youth Ambassadors of America, pgs. 284, 564
Youth As Resources, pgs. 100, 193, 718
Youth as Resources/YMCA, pg. 194
Youth Community Service, pgs. 90, 466, 491
Youth Department-Diocese of Buffalo See Amherst Y.E.S. (Youth Engaged in Service)
Youth Development, pgs. 162, 789
Youth Development Program, pgs. 492, 649
Youth Evaluation Services (Y.E.S.), pgs. 9, 608
Youth For Understanding International Exchange, pg. 968
Youth Haven, pg. 819
Youth In Action, pg. 90
Youth-In-Action Auction, pgs. 107, 766
Youth in Action Program See Youth Allocations Committee
Youth-In-Government Day, pgs. 194, 557
Youth Involvement Committee See Louisville Youth Involvement Committee
Youth Leadership Venture Funding Program, pgs. 194, 493, 611, 803
Youth Ocean Explorer Program, pgs. 447, 538
Youth Recreation Program, pgs. 493, 922
Youth Resources of Southwestern Indiana, pg. 195
Youth Service America, pg. 208
Youth Services, pgs. 60, 493, 812
Youth Services to Frail, Homebound Elderly, pgs. 464, 903
Youth Train, pgs. 424, 799
Youth Volunteer Services, pg. 493
Youth Who Care, pgs. 494, 611
YWCA See Home-Based Child Care in Hartford; Management Workshops for Nonprofit Organizations; The S.O.A.P.S.
YWCA National Board See National Collaboration for Youth
YWCA of the National Capital Area, pgs. 420, 863

Z

Zanesville City Schools, pgs. 1004, 1006, 1010
Zero Population Growth, pgs. 768, 1056, 1088

GEOGRAPHIC INDEX

ALABAMA

BIRMINGHAM
Birmingham Area Alliance of Business,
pgs. 42, 658
Meals on Wheels of Birmingham, pgs. 369, 908
Re-Entry Ministries, pgs. 372, 722
Teen Opportunities Promote Success (TOPS),
pgs. 42, 658
University of Alabama, pg. 489
Volunteer Services Program/UA, pg. 489

FLORENCE
Northwest Alabama Reading Aides, pg. 736

GADSDEN
Chamber of Commerce Literacy Council,
pgs. 50, 734
Gadsden Chamber of Commerce, pgs. 50, 734
Gulf State Steel, pgs. 51, 737
PALS Program, pgs. 51, 737

MOBILE
AD Support Group of Greater Alabama,
pgs. 453, 680
Alzheimer's Disease & Related Disorders
Association, pgs. 453, 680
Ethnic American Art Slide Library, pg. 967
Schoolmate Handicraft Volunteers, pgs. 409, 527
Schoolmate Program, pgs. 409, 527

MONTGOMERY
Christmas Clearing House, pgs. 45, 835
Give Five Alabama, pg. 123
Governor's Office on Volunteerism/AL,
pgs. 122, 123, 256, 270
Mental Health Players, pgs. 76, 743
The Spirit That Supports Alabama - Volunteers,
pg. 256
TAVS (Teenage Volunteers), pgs. 487, 677
The Voluntary Action Center, pgs. 45, 76, 273,
487, 677, 743, 835
Volunteers... OUR Caring Alabama, pg. 270
Workshops for Volunteer Managers, pg. 273

ONEONTA
Blount County Children's Center, pg. 815

TUSCALOOSA
Boardsmanship Seminar*, pg. 184
Voluntary Action Center of Tuscaloosa, pg. 184

UNIVERSITY
Forging Partnerships*, pgs. 292, 713
Foundation for Success*, pgs. 293, 714
National Association of Volunteers in Criminal
Justice, pgs. 292, 293, 316, 317, 713, 714, 715
Problems Facing Volunteer Leaders Today*,
pgs. 316, 715
Volunteer Program Efficiency in a Down-Sided
Economy*, pgs. 317, 715

ALASKA

ANCHORAGE
American Indian Partnerships with United
Ways*, pg. 300
Exxon, pgs. 36, 596
National Association of Extension Home
Economists, pgs. 432, 825
Seward Rescue Center, pgs. 36, 596
United Way of Anchorage, pg. 300

ARIZONA

MESA
Citadel Retirement Community, pgs. 305, 902
Mesa United Way, pgs. 396, 940

Parkinson's Institute for Caregivers, pgs. 305,
902
Women Off Welfare (WOW), pgs. 396, 940

PARADISE VALLEY
ArHA/Council on Volunteer Training Events,
pgs. 304, 675
Arizona Hospital Association, pgs. 304, 675

PHOENIX
Bostrom Alternative Center for Education*,
pg. 650
Communications Workshop/Perspectives for
Volunteers, pg. 289
Do It Now Foundation, pgs. 997, 998, 999,
1001, 1003, 1025, 1086
DOVIA (Directors of Volunteers in Agencies),
pg. 320
Grant Information System, pg. 98
Hazardous Waste Volunteer Program, pg. 594
Make-A-Wish Foundation of America, pg. 667
Maricopa County Environmental Services,
pg. 594
National Association of Women Highway Safety
Leaders, pgs. 205, 935
Older Americans as a Growing National
Resource*, pg. 320
Oryx Press, pg. 98
Phoenix Memorial Hospital, pg. 289
Positive Parenting, pgs. 352, 790, 1066
Valley of the Sun United Way, pg. 981
Volunteer Center of Maricopa County, pg. 269
The Volunteerism Project, pg. 123
Volunteers: Heroes of the 80's*, pg. 269
WriteConnection Program: Love A Child By
Mail, pgs. 352, 790

TEMPE
Do It Now Foundation, pg. 598

TUCSON
Carondolet Management Institute, pg. 6
The Heart of Compassion, pg. 6

YUMA
Rainbow Center for Exceptional Children,
pg. 587

ARKANSAS

ALEXANDER
Alexander Human Development Center
Volunteer Council, pgs. 415, 852

DARDANELLE
Sharing and Caring - A Food Pantry, pg. 754

FORT SMITH
Junior League of Fort Smith, pg. 262
Volunteer Leadership Workshop, pg. 262

HEBER SPRINGS
Cleburne County Cares, pg. 83
Cleburne County Department of Human
Services, pg. 83

HOT SPRINGS
First Family Volunteer Program, pg. 26
First National Bank of Hot Springs, pg. 26

JONESBORO
Southwest Church of Christ, pg. 375
We Care, pg. 375

LITTLE ROCK
Arkansas Department of Human Services,
pg. 556
Arkansas Division of Aging and Adult Services,
pgs. 124, 562, 1099
Arkansas Division of Volunteerism, pg. 124

Arkansas Office of Volunteerism, pg. 89
Arkansas Office of Volunteers, pg. 947
Arkansas Public Administration Consortium,
pg. 234
Certified Volunteer Manager Program, pg. 234
Child Identification Program, pgs. 33, 815
Little Rock Animal Control, pgs. 383, 787
Peace Links Arkansas, pg. 565
Pet Therapy, pgs. 383, 787
Safeway Stores, pgs. 33, 815
Silver Haired Legislative Session, pgs. 124, 562
Unified Community Resource Council, pg. 89
Volunteer Consultant Services Program, pg. 556
Women Against Nuclear War, pg. 565

MENA
Goodner Brothers Aircraft, pgs. 37, 597
Volunteer Community Betterment Project,
pgs. 37, 597

PARAGOULD
Bicycle Safety and Seat Belt Awareness
Programs, pgs. 56, 937
McDonald's of Paragould, Arkansas, pgs. 56,
937

TEXARKANA
Arkansas Convalescent Center, pg. 904
Retired Senior Volunteer Program, pg. 407
Willing Workers of College Hill, pg. 904

CALIFORNIA

ALHAMBRA
California Literacy*, pg. 733

ARCATA
The Best Years, pgs. 74, 897
RSVP of Humboldt County, pgs. 74, 897

BAKER
Juvenile Reception and Diagnostic Center
(JRDC), pgs. 366, 705

BERKELEY
Book People, pg. 984
Children's Quilt Project, pgs. 400, 511
Jobs for Older Women Action Project, pg. 659
Ten Speed Press, pg. 948
Within You, Inc./Just Say No Clubs, pg. 604

BURBANK
Warner Brothers, pg. 1054

BURLINGAME
International Association for Suicide
Prevention, pgs. 179, 744

CONCORD
Crime Prevention Committee of Contra Costa
County, pgs. 427, 709
Rape Crisis Service of Central Contra Costa
County, pgs. 178, 728

CORONA DEL MAR
Baroque Music Festival of Corona del Mar,
pg. 529

COSTA MESA
Costa Mesa Police Department, pgs. 459, 913
Police Department Volunteer Program, pgs. 459,
913

DAVIS
Freedom from Hunger Foundation, pg. 756

DOWNEY
Tapes for the Blind, pg. 847

FORT ORD
Be Alive in 2005: Promoting Wellness into the 21st Century, pgs. 344, 671
US/DoD - Army Preventive Medicine Activity, pgs. 344, 671

FREMONT
Bay Area SCORE Program, pgs. 435, 544
Fremont Chamber of Commerce, pgs. 435, 544
National Youth Council on Civic Affairs, pgs. 462, 557

FRESNO
End Hunger Project, pgs. 76, 752
United Way of Fresno County, pgs. 76, 752

GLENDORA
Organization for After-Stroke Resources, pg. 681

HAYWARD
Companions of Alameda County, pgs. 448, 821

HOLLYWOOD
End Hunger Network, pgs. 73, 756, 875
Family Assistance Project of Hollywood (FAP), pgs. 386, 877
Prime Time to End Hunger, pgs. 73, 875

IRVINE
Multiple Sclerosis Society of Orange County, pgs. 394, 866
Project Excellence Scholarship Program, pg. 1008

LAKE ARROWHEAD
Arrowhead 22: Future Challenges: A Universal Perspective, pg. 320
Lake Arrowhead Conference for Volunteer Program Administrators, pg. 320

LOMA LINDA
Social Action Corps, pgs. 497, 668

LONG BEACH
Administration of Volunteer Services, pg. 228
California State University, pgs. 228, 474
Champions Run For Life Torch Relay, pgs. 120, 665
Educational Participation in Communities, pg. 474
Jonathan Jaques Children's Cancer Center, pgs. 120, 665
Long Beach Unified School District, pg. 88
Requirement: Skip Classes, pg. 88
Senior Nutrition Program, pg. 908
Volunteers of America, pg. 908

LOS ANGELES
Alternative Education and Work Center, pgs. 429, 649
American Foundation for AIDS Research, pgs. 105, 508, 962
AmFar, pgs. 105, 508
Andrus Gerontology Center, pg. 1099
Asociacion Nacional Por Personas Mayores, pg. 901
Business Issues in the Classroom, pgs. 37, 626
California Council for Veterans Affairs, pgs. 378, 894
CHIP-IN, pgs. 361, 885
Constitutional Rights Foundation, pgs. 37, 90, 626, 972, 1005
Environmental Scan Task Force, pg. 187
Ethel Percy Andrus Gerontology Center, pg. 1066
Family Support Group, pgs. 455, 730
Grantsmanship Center, pgs. 98, 100, 302, 1016
Grantsmanship Training Program, pg. 302
Grantsmanship Training Program (short course), pg. 100

HOSTS (Help One Student To Succeed), pg. 1007
International Association of Volunteer Effort, pgs. 5, 537
Joint Educational Project, pgs. 225, 888
Los Angeles Olympic Organizing Committee, pg. 1082
Los Angeles Police Department, pgs. 455, 730
Los Angeles Unified School District, pgs. 429, 649, 1005, 1007, 1010
Mexican-American Legal Defense and Educational Fund, pg. 578
MIDAS Touch, pgs. 108, 548
National Association for Hispanic Elderly, pgs. 901, 985, 1020, 1068, 1076
Olympic Organizing Committee*, pg. 926
Parents Anonymous, pgs. 414, 712
Public Relations on a Shoestring*, pg. 290
Public Relations Society of America, pg. 290
Ronald Reagan Presidential Materials Staff, pg. 957
San Fernando Valley Interfaith Council, pg. 88
Schindler-Rainman Institutes, pg. 182
Second Careers Program, pg. 660
Senior Program, pgs. 225, 888
Spare Change Project, pgs. 115, 879
Sugar Ray Robinson Youth Foundation*, pg. 538
TransAmerica Occidental Life Insurance Company, pg. 1082
United Way of Greater Los Angeles, pgs. 187, 947
United Way of Los Angeles, pg. 1068
Veterans Counseling and Guidance Center, pgs. 378, 894
Volunteer Action Center of Los Angeles, pg. 660
Volunteer Fund Raising Committee, pgs. 115, 879
Volunteers of America of Los Angeles, pgs. 108, 548
Youth Community Service, pg. 90

LOS GATOS
Family Life and AIDS Instruction Program, pgs. 39, 516
Los Gatos Union School District, pgs. 39, 516

MANHATTAN BEACH
South Bay Free Clinic, pg. 1025

MILL VALLEY
Bread and Roses, pgs. 106, 538

MORRO BAY
Morro Bay Harbor Festival, pg. 531

NEWARK
Newark Library League, pg. 641
Newark Library League Scholarship Program, pg. 641

NORTH HOLLYWOOD
Actors and Others for Animals, pgs. 354, 782, 1094

OAKLAND
Center for the Study of Parent Involvement, pgs. 204, 638
Community Economics, pg. 684
Project Volunteer, pg. 453
Society for Nutrition Education*, pgs. 76, 750

ORANGE
Child Abuse Services Team (CAST), pgs. 427, 815
Court Appointed Special Advocates (CASA), pgs. 335, 808
Orangewood Children's Home, pgs. 427, 815

PACIFIC PALISADES
Involvement, Inc., pgs. 23, 1095

PACIFICA
Youth Advisory Commission, pgs. 107, 194, 557, 766
Youth-In-Action Auction, pgs. 107, 766
Youth-In-Government Day, pgs. 194, 557

PALO ALTO
American Social Health Association, pgs. 178, 680
STD National Hotline, pgs. 178, 680

PASADENA
American Nutrition Society, pg. 749
California House, pgs. 83, 911
Primary/Secondary Peace Education Network, pg. 564
Volunteer Center of San Gabriel Valley, pg. 1044

PERRIS
Orange Empire Railway Museum, pgs. 378, 535

RICHMOND
Arden Publications, pg. 950

RIVERSIDE
University of California Extension, pg. 1042

ROHNERT PARK
Field Experience Education, pg. 475
Sonoma State University, pg. 475

ROSEMEAD
Maryvale, pg. 1076

SACRAMENTO
Airlifeline, pg. 996
California Department of Education, pgs. 416, 931
California Hospital Association, pg. 272
FOCUS (Families of Children United for Safety), pgs. 416, 931
Larchmont Homes, pg. 103
McClellan AFB Health Fair, pgs. 343, 672
Support for Public Television, pg. 103
US/DoD - McClellan Air Force Base, pgs. 343, 672
Workshop for Volunteer Managers*, pg. 272

SAN BERNARDINO
San Bernardino County Board of Supervisors, pg. 987

SAN DIEGO
College of the Emeriti, pgs. 438, 660
DOVIA Skill Development Workshops*, pg. 237
Hug-A-Tree And Survive, pg. 813
Interfaith Shelter Network, pgs. 366, 886
Jobs for Older Women*, pgs. 438, 660
Lillick & McHose, pgs. 442, 881
Marlborough Publications, pg. 1043
Partnerships, pgs. 351, 623
Project Bravo, pg. 630
Project Concern International, pgs. 463, 669
Project Concern Youth Program, pgs. 463, 669
Project HELP (Help Expedite Legal Problems for the Homeless), pgs. 442, 881
Roman Catholic Diocese of San Diego, pgs. 373, 754
San Diego County Ecumenical Conference, pgs. 366, 886
Share Self-help and Resource Exchange, pgs. 373, 754
Supervision Skill Series/MAP (Management Assistance Program), pg. 257
Task Force on Transitional Volunteers, pg. 1099
United Way of San Diego, pg. 956

United Way of San Diego County, pgs. 237, 257, 630, 954, 1089, 1090

University Associates, pgs. 955, 1042, 1043, 1089, 1090

US/DoD - Commander Naval Base San Diego, pgs. 351, 623

Volunteer Bureau of United Way of San Diego County, pg. 1042

Youth Development, pgs. 162, 789

SAN FRANCISCO

AIDS in the Workplace, pgs. 31, 516

American Academy of Ophthalmology Foundation, pgs. 172, 679

Bechtel Group, Inc., pgs. 440, 626

Breakthrough Foundation, pgs. 94, 566

Children as Peacemakers, pgs. 461, 563

Community Education Services of Chinatown, pg. 735

Data Systems Unlimited, pgs. 53, 658

Elders and Voluntarism*, pg. 319

Goodwill Industries of San Francisco, pgs. 53, 658

Group Safety Association, pg. 9

Jossey Bass, Publishers, pgs. 946, 947, 948, 951, 954, 982, 984, 986, 1003, 1032, 1041, 1043, 1047, 1073, 1074

Kairos House, pgs. 21, 520

Legal Services for Children*, pgs. 432, 575

Literacy and Life Skills, pg. 735

Manpower Demonstration Research Corporation, pg. 1080

Master Builder Game, pgs. 440, 626

The NAMES Project/AIDS Memorial Quilt, pgs. 67, 513

The NAMES Project Foundation, pgs. 67, 513, 515, 963

National Alliance of Blind Students, pgs. 393, 846

National Eye Care Project, pgs. 172, 679

National Peer Helpers Association, pgs. 452, 794

Parent-Teen AIDS Education Project, pgs. 275, 515

Planet Drum Foundation, pg. 770

The Quilt and AIDS Education, pg. 515

Respite for AIDS Volunteers, pgs. 21, 520

San Francisco AIDS Foundation, pgs. 275, 515, 960, 961, 962, 964, 982, 985, 1031, 1065, 1086, 1087

San Francisco AIDS Foundation Speakers Bureau, pgs. 960, 964

San Francisco Peer Resource Programs, pgs. 484, 788

San Francisco Special Olympics Winter Games, pgs. 48, 864

Shanti Project, pg. 523

Sierra Club, pgs. 979, 980, 1056, 1057, 1058, 1060, 1061

Small Business Reporter, pg. 971

United Way of California, pg. 9

Volcano Press, pg. 1014

Western Gerontological Society*, pgs. 319, 398, 897

SAN JOSE

Adopt-A-School, pgs. 31, 621

Bureau of Drug Abuse Services Grants Program, pgs. 110, 607

Candle Lighters, pg. 101

Candle Lighters' Proposal Lunch, pg. 101

Guadalupe Elementary School, pgs. 424, 532

Outreach & Escort, pgs. 114, 862

San Jose Children's Musical Theatre*, pg. 538

San Jose Unified School District, pgs. 31, 621

Santa Clara County, pgs. 110, 607

Une Soiree Parisienne (An Evening in Paris), pgs. 114, 862

Young Authors' Faire, pgs. 424, 532

SAN MARINO

San Marino Schools, pgs. 423, 531

Valentine School Art Show, pgs. 423, 531

SAN MATEO

International Association for Suicide Prevention, pg. 1032

SANTA BARBARA

Child Abuse Listening Mediation, pgs. 165, 812, 1031

SANTA CRUZ

Volunteer Service of Santa Cruz County, pg. 1093

SATICOY

Cabrillo Economic Development Corporation, pg. 1085

Cabrillo Improvement Association, pgs. 454, 692

Cabrillo Village, pgs. 454, 692

SAUSALITO

Institute for Noetic Sciences, pg. 16

Temple Awards for Creative Altruism, pg. 16

SOUTH LAKE TAHOE

Voluntary Action Center of South Lake Tahoe, pg. 10

STANFORD UNIVERSITY

Econet, pgs. 44, 769

Stanford University, pgs. 44, 769

STOCKTON

Christian Involvement, pg. 361

St. Mary's High School, pg. 361

United Way of San Joaquin County, pg. 13

Volunteer Center/United Way At Work, pgs. 13, 955, 977, 1017

SUNNYVALE

Our Daily Bread, pg. 883

St. Thomas Episcopal Church, pg. 883

SYLMAR

International Guiding Eyes, pg. 846

THOUSAND OAKS

Conejo Valley Retired Senior Volunteer Program, pg. 400

TORRANCE

Toyota Motor Sales USA, pg. 99

VAN NUYS

United Cerebral Palsy/Spastic Children's Foundation*, pg. 850

VISALIA

Tulare County Food Resources, pgs. 381, 754

WEST LOS ANGELES

One Hundred Black Men of Los Angeles, pgs. 384, 633

Young Black Scholars Program (YBS), pgs. 384, 633

WESTLAKE VILLAGE

National Listen America Club, pgs. 462, 603

WOODLAND

Emergency Food Program, pg. 751

Woodland Volunteer Center, pg. 751

COLORADO

BOULDER

Association for Volunteer Administration, pgs. 3, 188, 229, 243, 245, 250, 252, 258, 274, 509, 568, 945, 950, 952, 982, 985, 1051, 1089, 1090

AVA Certification Program, pg. 229

Boulder Public Library, pg. 636

Boulder Valley Public Schools, pg. 957

Children's Room, pg. 636

How to Effectively Manage People Who Have AIDS as Volunteers, pgs. 274, 509

Institute on Volunteer Administration: A Proposal, pg. 243

International AVA Leadership Bank, pg. 188

Leadership: A Capital Investment, pg. 245

National Conference on Volunteerism, pg. 250

Partnership BankCard Systems*, pgs. 99, 1014

Performance Based Assessment Program for Certification in Volunteer Administration, pg. 252

Practice Excellence: National Conference on Volunteerism, pg. 252

Toward the Year 2000 - The Challenge, pgs. 258, 568

University of Colorado, pg. 263

Volunteer Boulder, pg. 1042

Volunteer Boulder County, pgs. 951, 976, 1015

Volunteer Management Associates, pg. 1096

Volunteer Management Program: First Level Workshop (1990), pg. 263

Volunteer Management Program: Second Level Workshop, pg. 263

Volunteer Management Program: Third Level Workshop, pg. 264

X67 Student Volunteer Program, pg. 956

COLORADO SPRINGS

Blue Ridge to the White House: Wheelchair Race of Champions, pgs. 47, 868

Challenges for Alternative Sentencing in Our Communities, pg. 723

Colorado Springs Police Department, pgs. 497, 730

Junior Achievement (JA), pgs. 43, 546

National Community Service Sentencing Association, pg. 723

National Wheelchair Athletic Association, pgs. 47, 868

Olympic Day in the Schools/Olympic Day For Youth, pg. 926

Senior Victim Assistance Team, pgs. 497, 730

U.S. Olympic Committee, pgs. 926, 927, 1083, 1084

USOC Education Committee, pg. 927

DENVER

American Humane Association, pgs. 171, 782

Basket of Joy Campaign, pgs. 467, 909, 1065

Colorado Office of Volunteerism, pg. 124

Continental Airlines, pgs. 49, 878

Continental Homeless Assistance Program, pgs. 49, 878

Denise Reich Real Estate, pgs. 414, 702

Education Commission of the States, pg. 993

Family Service Center/Colorado Branch, pg. 1096

Help for You!, pg. 242

Lutheran Social Services Volunteer Program, pg. 368

National Center for Hearing Dog Information, pgs. 171, 782

Partners*, pgs. 36, 706

Public Awareness About Child Care (PAACC), pgs. 414, 702

Volunteers of America, pgs. 467, 909

Youth Train, pgs. 424, 799

EVERGREEN

Alpine Rescue Team, pgs. 495, 592

GOLDEN

Adolph Coors Company, pgs. 25, 975, 977

Coors V.I.C.E. Squad, pg. 25

GRAND JUNCTION
Youth Who Care, pgs. 494, 611

GREELEY
The Bridge, pg. 232
United Way of Weld County, pg. 232

HENDERSON
International Hearing Dog, Inc., pg. 854

LITTLETON
Grant Development Institute, pg. 1019

LONGMONT
Network Directory, pg. 1033

MORRISON
Tiny Town Foundation, pg. 536

PUEBLO
US Consumer Information Center, pgs. 988, 989, 990, 1019

CONNECTICUT

BRIDGEPORT
Family Services-Woodfield, pgs. 9, 608
Regional Youth Substance Abuse Project (RYSAP), pgs. 608, 1000, 1003
United Way of Eastern Fairfield County, pg. 608
Youth Evaluation Services (Y.E.S.), pgs. 9, 608

CHAPLIN
Parish Hill High School, pg. 326
Senior Course on Volunteerism, pg. 326

DARIEN
Darien Book Aid Plan, pg. 639

FAIRFIELD
Campus Ministry, pg. 360
Fairfield University, pg. 360

HARTFORD
Connecticut Department of Corrections, pgs. 294, 716, 1037, 1039
Connecticut Leadership Conference, pg. 125
Correctional Mini-Courses, pgs. 294, 716
The Courant's Youth Leadership Awards Program, pg. 16
Governor's Conference on Volunteers in Energy*, pgs. 125, 773
Governor's Council on Voluntary Action/CT, pgs. 125, 126, 773
Governor's Youth Action Conference, pg. 126
The Hartford Courant, pg. 16
Hartford Superior Court, pgs. 460, 914
Home-Based Child Care in Hartford, pg. 588
Outreach Plan: Focus on the Hispanic Community, pgs. 77, 824
Probation Volunteers, pgs. 460, 914
United Way of the Capital Area (Hartford), pgs. 77, 194, 493, 588, 611, 803, 824, 1018
Youth Leadership Venture Funding Program, pgs. 194, 493, 611, 803

MANCHESTER
Communitas, Inc., pg. 1081

MERIDEN
Child Security Network of Connecticut, pgs. 162, 816

MILFORD
Child Security Network, pg. 1074

MONROE
Masuk High School, pgs. 66, 853
WMNR Radio - Access Broadcasting Company*, pgs. 66, 853

NEW HAVEN
Knights of Columbus, pg. 92

NEWINGTON
Amateur Radio Emergency Service (ARES), pgs. 47, 591
US/VA - Veterans Administration Medical Center, pgs. 353, 893
VA Voluntary Services Board, pgs. 353, 893
Wheelchair Race Communications Services, pgs. 47, 591

NORWICH
ADER, pg. 1010

STAMFORD
Clean Community System, pg. 779
Fairfield 2000, pg. 568
Keep America Beautiful, pgs. 779, 973, 975, 1055, 1056, 1057, 1058, 1061, 1062
Regional Plan Association, pgs. 568, 979
Seventh Grade Social Problems Course, pg. 191
United Way of Stamford, pg. 191
Xerox Corporation, pg. 975

STORRS
Connecticut Master Gardeners, pg. 755
Major Certificate Program for Volunteer Managers, pg. 247
University of Connecticut, pgs. 247, 755

WASHINGTON
Center for Information on America, pgs. 561, 981, 1013, 1085

WATERBURY
Central Naugatuck Valley Retired Senior Volunteer Program, pg. 399

WEST HARTFORD
Community Housing Resources Board, pgs. 202, 685
Greater Hartford Association of Realtors, pgs. 202, 685

WEST HAVEN
National Education Association, pgs. 967, 1005, 1008

WINDSOR
Mailer Education Seminars, pg. 8
US/PS - Mailer Education Center, pgs. 8, 952

DELAWARE

DOVER
Delaware Division of Volunteer Services, pg. 126
Division of Volunteer Services, pg. 126
Kent County Mental Hygiene Clinic/Day Hospital Volunteers*, pg. 741
Preschool Diagnostic and Developmental Education Nurseries, pgs. 127, 587
Volunteer Link, pgs. 126, 1021

GEORGETOWN
Stockley Center, pgs. 377, 865
Volunteer Services, pgs. 377, 865

NEW CASTLE
Delaware Department of Health and Social Services, pg. 127
Delaware State Hospital, pgs. 167, 389, 742, 806
24-Hour Child Abuse/Neglect Telephone Report Line, pgs. 167, 806
Volunteer Department, pgs. 389, 742
Volunteers Do Make a Difference!, pg. 127

NEWARK
Adopt-A-Family, pgs. 385, 840
Delaware Division of State Service Centers, pgs. 385, 840

Delaware Volunteer Coordinators, pg. 238
DVC Workshops and Conferences, pg. 238
Hudson State Service Center, pgs. 127, 788
International Reading Association, pgs. 1007, 1009, 1047, 1068, 1073
RSVP of New Castle County, pgs. 127, 788

WILMINGTON
Advanced Seminars in Volunteer Administration, pg. 228
Certificate Program in Volunteer Administration, pg. 234
Delaware Division for the Visually Impaired, pg. 849
Improving Museum Volunteer Performance, pgs. 276, 533
Northeast Service Center, pg. 655
University of Delaware, pgs. 228, 234, 276, 533
Volunteer Service Program, pg. 849
Work Incentive Demonstration Program/Job Factory, pg. 655

DISTRICT OF COLUMBIA

WASHINGTON
AAUW Educational Foundation, pgs. 431, 615
AAUW Legal Advocacy Fund, pgs. 431, 580
Acropolis Books, pgs. 990, 1022
Action for Independent Maturity, pg. 1067
Adolescent Pregnancy Prevention Clearinghouse, pg. 1099
Advocacy By and For The Blind, pgs. 393, 847
Advocacy Institute, pgs. 556, 979, 980
AFB Mid-Atlantic Regional Center, pgs. 393, 847
AFL-CIO, pg. 396
AIDS Prevention Program for Youth, pg. 510
AIDS Program, pg. 512
AIDS Public Education Program, pg. 515
Alcoholism and Substance Abuse - AIDS Program, pg. 601
Alexander Graham Bell Association for the Deaf, pg. 854
All Souls Church, pgs. 450, 727
Allis-Chalmers Corporation, pg. 972
America The Beautiful Fund, pg. 760
American Association for Adult and Continuing Education, pgs. 623, 1009
American Association of Retired Persons, pgs. 396, 895, 901, 1004, 1013, 1081
American Association of University Women, pgs. 431, 580, 615, 981
American Bankers Association, pgs. 989, 990
American Bar Association, pgs. 332, 813
American Civil Liberties Union, pgs. 433, 717
American Coalition of Citizens with Disabilities*, pgs. 857, 1076, 1078
American Conservation Volunteers, pgs. 488, 776, 1100
American Council of the Blind, pgs. 330, 845
American Forest Council, pg. 1060
American Health Care Association, pgs. 398, 906, 947, 1044, 1049, 1074
American Hiking Society, pgs. 1060, 1083, 1084
American Institute of Cooperation, pg. 576
American Lung Association, pg. 762
American Parents Committee, pgs. 413, 796
American Psychiatric Association, pgs. 174, 744, 1048, 1049, 1075
American Red Cross, pgs. 172, 465, 590, 677, 919, 956, 958, 1024, 1097
American Red Cross Office of HIV/AIDS Education, pgs. 31, 105, 509, 510, 514, 515, 517, 518, 960, 961, 962, 963, 964, 965
American Symphony Orchestra League, pgs. 189, 277, 539, 967, 968, 969, 1016, 1017
American University, pgs. 253, 264

American Youth Hostels, pg. 1092
American Youth Work Center, pg. 1013
Anti-Drug Teams, pgs. 499, 609
Art Against AIDS, pgs. 75, 105, 528, 540
Art Against AIDS Exhibit, pgs. 105, 528
Art for Kids' Sake, pgs. 434, 801
Assistance to Earthquake Victims, pgs. 349, 592
Association for Commuter Transportation, pg. 937
Association of Certified Servers, pgs. 382, 602
Atlantic Richfield Company, pg. 976
Benjamin Banneker High School, pg. 471
Black Georgetown Reunion Group, pgs. 359, 533
B'nai B'rith Community Volunteer Services, pgs. 986, 987
B'nai B'rith International, pgs. 946, 1000, 1003, 1023, 1024, 1025, 1027, 1037, 1038, 1040, 1056, 1057, 1059, 1060, 1065, 1069, 1074, 1075, 1077, 1079, 1091
B'nai B'rith Youth Organization, pgs. 998, 999, 1096, 1098
Board Development Consultation Service, pg. 183
Board of Church and Society, pgs. 997, 1002
Boys & Girls Clubs of Greater Washington, pg. 1068
Bruce-Monroe Elementary School, pgs. 436, 547
Building Seismic Safety Council, pgs. 432, 591
Business Concentration Toward Charities, pg. 24
But I'm Different..., pgs. 69, 931
Buyers Up, pgs. 577, 988
Campaign Drug Free, pgs. 348, 610
Campaign for Human Development, pg. 226
Capital Area Community Food Bank, pgs. 52, 751
Capitol Hill Association of Merchants and Professionals, pgs. 173, 880
Carrier Alert, pg. 382
Catholic Charities USA, pgs. 97, 952
Catholic University of America, pgs. 156, 636
CBS/Fox Video, pg. 1087
Center for Auto Safety, pgs. 330, 937
Center for Community Change, pgs. 204, 552
Center for Corporate Public Involvement, pg. 22
Center for National Policy Review, pg. 1028
Center for Public Policy, pg. 954
Center for Science in the Public Interest, pgs. 750, 1052, 1053
Center for Study of Responsive Law, pg. 571
Center for Youth Service, pgs. 59, 811
Center on Budget and Policy Priorities, pg. 952
Chamber of Commerce of the United States, pgs. 542, 970, 971
Champ Bakery, pgs. 426, 802
Changing Ways We Do Business: New Roles and Responsibilities, pg. 301
Chapter Grants Program, pgs. 105, 518
Child Welfare League of America, pgs. 330, 434, 561, 800, 801, 930, 992, 993, 994, 1019, 1049, 1066, 1071, 1075, 1086, 1087, 1094, 1097
Children's Defense Fund, pgs. 330, 557, 1034, 1051, 1068, 1069, 1071
Children's Foundation, pg. 586
Citizen/Labor Energy Coalition, pg. 772
Citizens Communication Center, pg. 61
Citizens Organized Patrol Efforts (COPE), pgs. 455, 709
Civil Rights Clearinghouse, pg. 1029
Class of 2000: The Prejudice Puzzle, pgs. 74, 823
Clean Water Action Project, pg. 780
Clearinghouse on Disability Information, pgs. 170, 860
Clearinghouse on the Handicapped*, pgs. 170, 860
Coalition on Human Needs, pg. 1071

Commission for the Advancement of Public Interest Organizations, pg. 571
Committee for Creative Non-Violence, pg. 1070
Common Cause, pgs. 309, 552, 981, 1097
Community Action Training (CAT), pg. 291
Community Advisory Boards, pg. 195
Community Careers Resource Center, pgs. 79, 652
Community Environmental Program*, pg. 760
Community Family Life Services, pgs. 374, 717
Community Food and Nutrition Program, pgs. 119, 750, 1052
Community for Creative Non-Violence, pgs. 73, 687
Community Information Center, pg. 571
Community Laboratory Project, pg. 471
Community Service/Awareness Action, pg. 472
Concern, pgs. 1055, 1056, 1057, 1058, 1059, 1061
Concern, Inc., pg. 760
Conference on Shelter and Housing, pg. 1094
Congressional Education Associates, pg. 979
Conner-Harris Mini Mall, pgs. 427, 547
Conservation Foundation, pgs. 766, 769, 972, 1056, 1060, 1075, 1092
Conservation Tillage Information Center*, pg. 766
Consumer and Food Economics Institute, pg. 1075
Consumer Coalition for Health, pg. 664
Consumer Energy Council of America Research Foundation, pg. 772
Consumer Federation of America, pg. 571
COOL IT!, pgs. 472, 769
"Cool School Video" Contest, pgs. 354, 629
Cooperative Housing Foundation*, pgs. 684, 1027
COPE Retiree Program, pg. 396
Corporation for Public Broadcasting, pgs. 61, 195, 982, 983, 984
Council on Foundations, pgs. 97, 1015
Council on Legal Education Opportunity, pgs. 110, 625, 1004, 1005
CRG Press, pg. 1042
Critical Mass Energy Project, pg. 772
Crossroads Program, pg. 1022
CRY, Inc. (Citizens Redirecting Youth), pgs. 415, 795
Day Care Council of America, pgs. 583, 993, 994, 995
The Deaf Way, pgs. 393, 529
Demonstration Program, pg. 97
Discount Mart Shopping Center II, pgs. 436, 547
Discover Graphics, pg. 534
District of Columbia AIDS Information Line, pgs. 160, 521
District of Columbia Board of Education, pg. 646
District of Columbia City Council, pgs. 501, 610
District of Columbia Corporate Volunteer Council, pgs. 25, 973, 975
District of Columbia Government, pg. 670
District of Columbia Police Department, pgs. 382, 426, 427, 547, 708, 802
District of Columbia Public Schools, pgs. 354, 418, 610, 620, 629, 646
District of Columbia Superior Court, pgs. 339, 726
District of Columbia Women's Commission for Crime Prevention, pgs. 196, 703, 1040
Drug Abuse Information Hotline*, pgs. 168, 605
Drug Alliance, pg. 605
Duke Ellington School of the Arts, pgs. 69, 931
Earth Day 1990/EPA, pg. 770
Earth Team, pg. 767
Eastern High School's 500 Club, pgs. 38, 641

Education & Prevention Services: AIDS Program, pgs. 67, 516
Energy Action Education Project, pg. 772
Environmental Action, pg. 760
Environmental Action Foundation, pgs. 761, 1058, 1059, 1061, 1091
Environmental Policy Institute, pg. 761
F.A.C.T. Hotline (Families and Children in Trouble), pgs. 169, 832
Family Stress Services of DC, pgs. 169, 832
Federal Assistance Programs Retrieval System (FAPRS), pg. 97
Federal Information Policies: Access is the Key, pgs. 307, 554
Federal Programs Advisory Service, pg. 1072
Florence Crittenton Association of America, pg. 930
Food Research and Action Center, pgs. 76, 331, 748, 756
Food Safety Hotline, pgs. 176, 580
Forest Service Volunteer Program, pg. 767
48 Hours on Capitol Hill, pgs. 287, 554
Foster Grandparent Program (FGP), pgs. 396, 866
Foundation for Hospice and Homecare, pgs. 172, 674, 836
4-H General Forums: Adult Volunteer Training, pgs. 240, 810
4-H Specific Forums: Adult Volunteer Training, pgs. 317, 810
FOX Television - WTTG, pg. 961
Friends Committee on National Legislation, pgs. 195, 553
Friends of the Superior Court, pgs. 437, 728
Friends of the Vietnam Veterans Memorial, pg. 893
Friendship House, pg. 86
Frontline - Channels 22 and 26, pg. 985
FTC Vacation Travel Hotline, pgs. 163, 582
Gallaudet Board of Trustees, pgs. 200, 855
Gallaudet College, pgs. 393, 529
Gallaudet University, pgs. 200, 855
George Washington University, pgs. 462, 548
Georgetown University, pg. 291
Georgetown University Law Center, pg. 61
Giant Food, pg. 1052
Give Five Campaign, pg. 18
Give Me Shelter: Designs for Urban Survival, pgs. 306, 884
Give Them A Hand, Not A Handout, pgs. 173, 880
Glass Packaging Institute, pg. 1059
Government Contracts Clinic, pgs. 462, 548
Gray Panthers, pgs. 225, 887
Greater Washington Board of Trade, pg. 973
Green Line Action Association, pgs. 43, 549
Happy Trails To You: A Workshop for Volunteers, pg. 774
Head Start - Family Day Care, pgs. 108, 586
Head Start Program, pg. 583
Highway Users Federation for Safety and Mobility, pgs. 1091, 1092, 1093
HITS (High Intensity Treatment Supervision), pgs. 339, 726
HIV/AIDS Prevention Program for African American Youth and Families, pg. 518
HIV/AIDS Prevention Program for Hispanic Youth and Families, pg. 518
HIV/AIDS Workplace Program, pgs. 31, 517
Home and School Institute, pgs. 634, 1006
Hosted Programs and Youth Conservation Corps, pg. 774
Housing Now!, pgs. 73, 687
Housing Services: AIDS Program, pg. 684
Independent Living for the Handicapped, pg. 861

Independent Sector, pgs. 4, 18, 301, 945, 947, 948, 950, 951, 955, 958, 980, 1016, 1018, 1019, 1041, 1042, 1043, 1096

Indian Arts and Crafts Board, pgs. 383, 527

Indochina Resource Action Center, pgs. 383, 825

Information Exchange*, pgs. 177, 925

Information Service*, pgs. 174, 744

Institute for Neighborhood Initiative, pg. 987

Institute of Lifetime Learning, pgs. 901, 966, 967, 1046, 1073

Institute of Scrap Recycling Industries, pgs. 1059, 1060, 1061

Institute on Federal Library Resources, pgs. 156, 636

Intergenerational Project for Service Learning, pg. 462

Intergenerational Service-Learning Project, pgs. 225, 888, 1097

Internal Revenue Service, pg. 971

International Very Special Arts Festival, pgs. 394, 530

James Madison National Council, pgs. 197, 637

Jhoon Rhee Institute of Tae Kwon Do, pgs. 32, 918

Job Corps, pg. 656

Joint Action in Community Service, pg. 957

Joint Center for Political Studies, pg. 561

Law Enforcement Assistance Program, pgs. 118, 697

Lead Poisoning Prevention Program, pg. 670

League of Conservation Voters*, pg. 761

League of Women Voters Education Fund, pgs. 376, 569

League of Women Voters of the US, pgs. 561, 760, 979, 980, 981, 984, 989, 1007, 1029, 1057

Leave Bank, pgs. 49, 669

Legal Counsel for the Elderly, pgs. 439, 581

Leisure Information Service, pgs. 177, 925

Los Angeles Poverty Department (LAPD), pgs. 75, 540

Luther Place Memorial Church, pgs. 367, 886

Luther Place Women's Shelter, pgs. 367, 886

Lutheran Resources Commission/Washington, pg. 303

Mainstream, pgs. 46, 857

Management Workshops for Nonprofit Organizations, pg. 248

Manna, Inc.*, pgs. 368, 683

Martha's Table, pg. 1053

McDonnell Douglas Corporation, pg. 1065

Media Access Project, pg. 61

Medical Services - AIDS Program, pg. 513

Migration and Refugee Service, pgs. 356, 825, 1070, 1074, 1079

Mini-Grant Program, pg. 99

Model Mugging, pgs. 450, 727

M.O.M.S. (Mothers On the Move Spiritually), pgs. 417, 706

Mortgage Bankers Association of America, pg. 1069

Mothers of PWAs (Persons With AIDS), pgs. 226, 522

Mount Zion United Methodist Church, pgs. 359, 533

Movement for Economic Justice, pg. 553

The Name of the Game is Caring, pgs. 465, 919

National AIDS Network, pg. 508

National Air Conservation Commission, pg. 762

National Alliance of Business, pgs. 23, 975

National Assembly of Voluntary Health and Social Welfare Organizations, pgs. 5, 951, 986

National Association for Child Care Management, pg. 583

National Association for Human Development, pg. 902

National Association for the Education of Young Children, pgs. 583, 992, 993, 994, 995

National Association for the Southern Poor, pgs. 452, 566

National Association of Broadcasters, pgs. 61, 983

National Association of Conservation Districts, pgs. 189, 766

National Association of Housing & Redevelopment Officials, pgs. 682, 946, 1027, 1028, 1072

National Association of Housing Cooperatives, pgs. 685, 1027

National Association of Investment Companies, pgs. 99, 548

National Association of Neighborhoods, pg. 80

National Association of People with AIDS, pgs. 424, 523

National Association of Rehabilitation Facilities, pgs. 984, 1071, 1076

National Black Child Development Institute, pg. 586

National Business League, pg. 549

National Catholic Disaster Relief Committee, pgs. 356, 591

National Celebration of the Outdoors, pg. 769

National Center for a Barrier Free Environment, pg. 844

National Center for Community Action*, pg. 91

National Center for Community Crime Prevention, pgs. 75, 713

National Center for Missing and Exploited Children, pg. 813

National Center for Nonprofit Boards, pgs. 183, 951, 1042, 1043, 1044

National Center for Therapeutic Riding, pg. 870

National Center on Child Abuse and Neglect, pgs. 108, 813, 994, 1038, 1075, 1098

National Child Day Care Association, pgs. 994, 995

National Clean Air Coalition, pg. 762

National Clearinghouse on Aging, pg. 1060

National Coalition for the Homeless, pgs. 201, 873, 881, 1069, 1072, 1075, 1076, 1078

National Coalition for Volunteer Protection, pgs. 7, 553, 956

National Coalition of Hispanic Health & Human Service Organizations, pgs. 959, 1022

National Collaboration for Youth, pgs. 68, 796

National Commission for Employment Policy, pgs. 972, 1011

National Committee Against Discrimination in Housing, pgs. 685, 1027, 1028, 1029

National Community Action Foundation, pgs. 91, 825

National Community Organizing Project (NCOP), pgs. 201, 873

National Consumers League, pg. 572

National Cooperative Business Association, pgs. 576, 988, 989, 991

National Council for Equal Business Opportunity, pg. 549

National Council of Senior Citizens, pgs. 397, 895

National Council on Employment Policy, pg. 1012

National Council on the Aging, pgs. 74, 203, 225, 332, 462, 464, 888, 896, 898, 900, 903, 905, 966, 981, 984, 988, 989, 995, 1012, 1013, 1023, 1024, 1028, 1029, 1041, 1066, 1067, 1068, 1069, 1070, 1074, 1075, 1076, 1077, 1085, 1089, 1097, 1098, 1099, 1100

National Crime Prevention Council, pgs. 100, 196, 697, 718, 1098

National Criminal Justice Reference Service, pgs. 1037, 1039

National Education Association, pgs. 993, 1006

National Endowment for the Arts, pg. 525

National Endowment for the Humanities, pg. 1018

National Gallery of Art, pg. 528

National Gallery of Art Extension Programs, pg. 528

National Governors' Association, pgs. 122, 949

National Head Start Association*, pg. 583

National HomeCaring Council, pgs. 172, 836

National Housing Conference, pgs. 201, 682

National Housing Partnership, pgs. 116, 686

National Hunger Coalition, pgs. 76, 756

National Information Center for Children and Youth with Handicaps, pgs. 171, 861

National Information Center on Deafness, pgs. 20, 855, 1072, 1080

National Injury Information Center, pgs. 163, 670

National Institute for Work and Learning, pgs. 1010, 1011

National League of Cities, pgs. 557, 1042

National Legal Aid and Defender Association, pg. 572

National Legal Resource Center for Child Advocacy and Protection, pgs. 332, 813, 1074

National Library Service for the Blind, pgs. 397, 846

National Media Resource Center on the Aging, pgs. 74, 900

National Organization on Disability (NOD), pgs. 71, 843

National Partnerships in Education Program, pg. 1008

National Peace Garden, pgs. 565, 980

National Peace Institute Foundation, pg. 563

National Prison Project, pgs. 433, 717

National Public Radio, pgs. 65, 74, 823, 982, 985

National Ridesharing Information Center, pg. 1092

National Senior Citizens Law Center, pgs. 581, 990

National Urban Coalition, pgs. 558, 1009, 1013, 1083

National Voluntary Organizations Active in Disaster, pg. 591

National Voluntary Organizations for Independent Living for the Aged, pgs. 905, 1028, 1066, 1071, 1072, 1075, 1092

National Wildlife Federation, pgs. 472, 769

National Workshop on Voluntarism, pg. 251

National Youth Service Day 1990, pg. 208

NCSL Job Skills Development Seminars, pgs. 282, 655

Neighborhood Anti-Crime Rally/Community Forum, pgs. 382, 708

Neighborhood Development Services Center, pgs. 80, 777

Neighbors Helping Neighbors, pgs. 53, 753

New York Avenue Meals on Wheels, pgs. 411, 749

NHTSA Hotline, pgs. 164, 582

No Greater Love, pg. 563

Nonprofit Mailers Federation, pgs. 287, 554

Not on My Block, pgs. 501, 610

Nutrition Education and Information, pgs. 176, 750

Nutrition Foundation, pgs. 176, 750

ODPHP National Health Information Center, pgs. 172, 677

Offender Aid and Restoration, pg. 720

Office for Special Constituencies, pg. 525

Office of Community Investment, pg. 692

Older Women's League (OWL), pgs. 74, 896

Operation Child Watch, pg. 813

Operation Outreach, pg. 646
Operation Rescue, pg. 646
Orchestra Management Seminar, pgs. 277, 539
Orphan Foundation of America, pgs. 357, 806
Parent to Parent, Attention on Attendance, pgs. 418, 620
Parents United, pgs. 421, 596
Partners For Livable Places, pg. 692
PATC Volunteers, pg. 775
Peace Garden Project, pg. 565
Peace Links - Women Against Nuclear War, pg. 563
Pharmaceutical Manufacturers Association, pgs. 998, 1000, 1002
PIRG, pgs. 310, 572
Points of Light Initiative, pg. 206
Population Crisis Committee, pg. 768
Population Crisis Committee/Draper Fund, pg. 1061
Population-Environment Balance, pgs. 768, 1059
Population Institute, pg. 768
Population Reference Bureau, pgs. 768, 1018, 1059
Potomac Appalachian Trail Club, pgs. 774, 775
President's Advisory Committee on Points of Light Initiatives Foundation, pg. 207
President's Committee on Employment of the Handicapped, pg. 658
President's Committee on Mental Retardation, pgs. 71, 864
President's Council on Physical Fitness, pg. 918
Prison Fellowship Ministries, pgs. 357, 719, 1037
Private Sector Efforts Program, pgs. 215, 761
Private Sector Initiatives Program, pgs. 212, 616
Professional Certification in Volunteer Management, pg. 253
Program Exchange Process (PEP), pgs. 172, 677
Project NOVA - AIDS Program, pgs. 160, 521
Public Affairs Committee, pg. 1098
Public Citizen, pgs. 156, 332, 560, 772, 979, 1034
Public Citizen Health Research Group, pg. 664
Public Citizen Litigation Group, pg. 572
Public Interest Computer Association, pgs. 8, 952
Public Interest Research Group, pgs. 310, 572
Rape Crisis Center, pgs. 177, 727, 1032, 1034
Religious Society of Friends, pgs. 195, 553
Renew America, pg. 773
Republican National Committee, pg. 271
Reserve Police Officer Corps, pgs. 460, 729
Resource Development Conference*, pg. 303
Retired Senior Volunteer Program, pg. 397
Roses for Fallen Fathers, pg. 893
Roy Rogers Restaurants, pgs. 48, 659
Runaway Project, pg. 1033
Rural America, pgs. 694, 1027, 1029
St. Teresa of Avila Catholic Church, pgs. 417, 706
The Samaritans, pgs. 179, 788
The Samaritans USA, pgs. 179, 792
SANE/FREEZE, pg. 981
School Fire Safety Monitoring Program, pgs. 421, 596
Senior Citizen Internship Program, pgs. 314, 562
Senior Companion Program (SCP), pgs. 398, 909
Senior Craftsman Showcase*, pgs. 410, 527
Senior Opportunities and Services, pg. 398
Senior Report, pgs. 177, 905
Seniors: Special Delivery, pgs. 411, 749
70001 Training and Employment Institute, pg. 657
Share Our Strength (SOS), pgs. 433, 445, 756, 1053
Shaw Neighborhood Advisory Committee, pgs. 455, 709

Shrine of the Immaculate Conception, pgs. 226, 522
Sidwell Friends, pg. 472
Smithsonian Institution, pg. 528
Smithsonian Institution Traveling Exhibition Service, pg. 528
Smithsonian Resident Associate Program, pg. 534
Social Legislation Information Service/CWLA, pg. 561
Southeastern University, pgs. 282, 653
S/OVCP Winter Conference, pg. 255
Special Mortgage Affordable Housing Program, pgs. 29, 689
Special Olympics International, pgs. 867, 1082, 1083
Special Student Advisory Board, pg. 192
Specials Project, pg. 65
Statewide HIV/AIDS Network, pg. 509
Stop! The Madness, pg. 1038
Stop! The Madness Foundation, pgs. 75, 731
Student Community Service (SCS) Program, pg. 463
Student National Education Association, pg. 1099
Suicide Prevention Hotline, pgs. 179, 788
Support Center of Washington, pg. 248
Support Services - AIDS Program, pgs. 106, 523
Sursum Corda Village, pgs. 501, 690
Susan Peterson Productions, pg. 985
Tae Kwon Do Choreographic Performances, pgs. 32, 918
Taft Group, pgs. 947, 1019, 1020
Taste of the Nation, pgs. 445, 756
Technical Assistance Program (TAP), pg. 5
Technical Assistance to Cooperatives, pg. 577
Telecare, Center for Life, Providence Hospital,, pg. 1079
Tenant Ownership/Management Program, pgs. 501, 690
Theodore Roosevelt National Bank, pgs. 24, 29, 192, 689
Therapeutic Riding Program, pg. 870
Toll Free Hotline Information - A Program of Ralph Nader, pg. 156
Touch America Project (TAP), pgs. 488, 776, 1100
Training for Disabled Students, pgs. 48, 659
Trial Lawyers for Public Justice, pgs. 433, 573
Tuxedo Valet, pgs. 43, 549
Twenty-First Century Discussion Group, pgs. 376, 569
Twenty-Five Year Presidential Award Certificate Program for Volunteers in Juvenile Criminal Justice, pgs. 16, 698
Union Institute Center for Public Policy, pg. 1018
Urban Coalition, pgs. 80, 777
Urban Drug-Free Schools Initiative, pg. 610
Urban Elderly Coalition, pgs. 332, 898
Urban Institute Press, pgs. 947, 1079, 1088, 1092
US/ACTION - Older Americans Volunteer Programs (OAVP), pg. 1068
US/ACTION - The Federal Volunteer Agency, pgs. 5, 80, 97, 99, 251, 255, 273, 282, 396, 397, 398, 463, 605, 655, 866, 909, 950
US/Administration: The President's Private Sector Initiatives Program, pg. 209
U.S. Catholic Charities, pgs. 356, 825
U.S. Catholic Conference, pg. 226
US/Commission on Civil Rights*, pg. 578
U.S. Conference of Mayors, pg. 558
US/Congress, pg. 572
US/Consumer Product Safety Commission, pgs. 163, 670
US/DEd - Clearinghouse on Disability Information, pgs. 1070, 1076, 1077, 1078

US/DEd - Division for the Handicapped, pgs. 170, 860
US/DEd - Office for Children and Youth, pg. 993
US/DEd - Office of Special Education and Rehabilitative Services, pgs. 170, 860
US/DEd - Office of the Secretary, pgs. 212, 616
US/DoA - Division of Cooperative Services, pg. 577
US/DoA - Farmers Home Administration, pg. 694
US/DoA - Food and Nutrition Service, pgs. 176, 580, 1052, 1053
US/DoA - Forest Service, pgs. 656, 767, 774, 1056, 1058, 1060, 1061
US/DoA - 4-H Youth/Extension Service, pgs. 58, 240, 317, 810
US/DoA - Photography Division, pgs. 1029, 1052, 1053, 1056, 1058, 1059
US/DoA - Soil Conservation Service, pg. 767
US/DoC - Office of Minority Business Enterprise, pgs. 299, 546
US/DoC - Private Sector Initiatives Program, pgs. 210, 543, 1063
US/DoD - Department of the Navy, pgs. 349, 592
US/DoD - Naval Reserve Force, pgs. 348, 610, 997, 1001
US/DoD - Private Sector Initiatives Program, pg. 211
US/DoE - Office of Handicapped Individuals, pg. 1081
US/DoE - Office of Information, pg. 1046
US/DoI - Bureau of Indian Affairs, pgs. 383, 527
US/DoI - National Park Service, pgs. 177, 925, 956, 1016, 1063, 1082, 1083, 1084
US/DoI - Office of the Secretary, pgs. 215, 761
US/DoJ - Law Enforcement Assistance Agency, pgs. 118, 697
US/DoJ - Private Sector Initiatives, pgs. 216, 698
US/DoL - Employment and Training Administration, pgs. 652, 1011, 1012
US/DoL - Employment and Training Commission, pg. 1013
US/DoL - Office of Information, pgs. 971, 1012
US/DoL - Office of the Secretary, pg. 1079
US/DoL - Private Sector Involvement Program, pgs. 216, 652
US/DoL - Women's Bureau, pgs. 659, 813, 974, 976, 992, 993, 995
US/DoT - Federal Highway Admistration, pg. 1091
US/DoT - Library Service Division, pg. 1092
US/DoT - National Highway Traffic Safety Administration, pgs. 164, 582, 1092
US/DoT - National Ridesharing Information Center, pgs. 974, 975, 976, 1091
US/DoT - Office of Information, pg. 1091
US/DoT - Private Sector Initiatives Programs, pgs. 218, 935, 1063
US/DTreas - Bureau of Alcohol, Tobacco and Firearms, pgs. 499, 609
US/DTreas - Internal Revenue Service, pgs. 434, 578
US/DTreas - Treasury's Involvement in Private Sector Initiatives, pgs. 219, 573, 1064
US/EPA - Earth Day, pg. 770
US/EPA - Environment Monitoring Programs, pg. 1056
US/EPA - Office of Noise Abatement and Control, pg. 1058
US/EPA - Office of Solid Waste Management, pgs. 779, 1061

US/EPA - Private Sector Initiatives Efforts, pg. 1063
US/Federal Home Loan Bank Board, pg. 692
US/Federal Library & Information Center Committee, pgs. 307, 554
US/FTC - Federal Trade Commission, pgs. 163, 582
US/GAO - General Accounting Office, pg. 994
US/GSA - Government Printing Office, pgs. 970, 971, 1014, 1015, 1016, 1069, 1075, 1076, 1079
US/GSA - Private Sector Initiatives, pgs. 212, 543
US/HHS - Administration for Children, Youth and Families, pgs. 108, 286, 584, 586, 813, 949, 1071, 1079, 1086
US/HHS - Administration on Aging, pgs. 896, 1006, 1027, 1032, 1033, 1034, 1069, 1071, 1072, 1074, 1076, 1078, 1092, 1096, 1100
US/HHS - Children's Bureau, pg. 983
US/HHS - Department of Health & Human Services, pgs. 1038, 1041, 1099
US/HHS - Division of Youth Activities, pg. 1045
US/HHS - Inspector General Hotline, pg. 989
US/HHS - National Center on Child Abuse and Neglect, pgs. 1031, 1065, 1080
US/HHS* - Office of Community Services, pgs. 91, 398, 1028, 1029, 1056
US/HHS - Office of Human Development, pg. 583
US/HHS - Office of Information, pg. 1019
US/HHS - Office of the Secretary, pgs. 119, 214, 750, 826
US/HHS - Working Group on Private Sector Initiatives, pgs. 214, 826
US/House of Representatives, pg. 1078
US/HUD - Office of Fair Housing and Equal Opportunity, pgs. 116, 685
US/HUD - Office of Information, pg. 1030
US/HUD - Office of Policy Development, pg. 1028
US/HUD - Office of the Secretary, pgs. 213, 682
US/HUD - Private Sector Initiative Activities in HUD, pgs. 213, 682
U.S. Institute of Peace, pg. 564
US/Library of Congress, pgs. 197, 397, 637, 846
US/NCUA - Private Sector Initiatives and Volunteerism, pgs. 217, 574, 1063
US/Office of Consumer Affairs, pgs. 574, 988, 989, 990, 991
US/OMB - Federal Programs Information Branch, pg. 97
US/OPM - Office of Information, pgs. 49, 669, 1011, 1013
US/OPM - Private Sector Initiatives in OPM, pgs. 217, 653, 1064
US/Presidential Awards Programs, pgs. 16, 698
US/President's Committee on Mental Retardation, pgs. 975, 989, 1072, 1073, 1074, 1077
US/PS - Office of News and Public Affairs, pgs. 382, 1068
US/SBA - Office for Women, pgs. 970, 971
US/SBA - Office of Advocacy, pg. 971
US/SBA - Office of Management Assistance, pg. 970
US/SBA - Private Sector Initiatives Activities, pgs. 218, 543, 1064
US/SBA - SCORE/ACE, pgs. 398, 544
US/SBA - Service Corps of Retired Executives/Active Corps of Executives, pgs. 398, 544, 970
US/Senate, pgs. 314, 562
US/VA - Private Sector Initiatives Program, pgs. 220, 888, 1064
US/VA - VAVS Workshops, pgs. 276, 889

US/White House, pgs. 168, 209, 605, 1039
US/White House - Comment Line, pg. 556
US/White House - Office of National Service, pgs. 206, 207, 1051, 1064
US/White House - Partnerships in Education, pg. 620
Van Ministry, pgs. 374, 717
Very Special Arts, pgs. 394, 530
VISTA (Volunteers In Service to America), pg. 80
Volunteer & Community Partnerships Institute, pgs. 286, 584
Volunteer Clearinghouse of the District of Columbia, pg. 25
Volunteer Council, pg. 189
Volunteer Income Tax Assistance (VITA), pgs. 434, 578
Volunteer Management Seminars, pg. 264
Volunteer Orientation Program, pgs. 20, 855
Volunteer Resources - AIDS Program, pgs. 20, 510
Volunteer Service Corps Committee, pgs. 398, 906
Volunteering Your Way to a Successful Career, pgs. 282, 653
Washington for Minority Youth Awareness Day, pgs. 299, 546
Washington Hospital Center, pg. 1023
Washington International Newsletter, pg. 1014
Washington Metropolitan Police Department, pgs. 460, 729
Washington Post, pgs. 38, 53, 306, 641, 753, 884, 977
Washington Times, pg. 1005
Washington Workshops Foundation, pg. 568
Washington Youth Gardens, pg. 1062
Waste Alert!, pg. 779
Whitman-Walker Clinic, pgs. 20, 67, 106, 160, 510, 512, 513, 516, 521, 523, 601, 684, 960
WIC (Women, Infants and Children) Advocacy Staff, pg. 1088
William T. Grant Foundation, pg. 1051
Working Group on Private Sector Initiatives, pg. 1063
Working Partners, pg. 271
WUST Radio, pgs. 177, 905
Young Volunteers in Action: Training for Project Directors, pg. 273
Youth As Resources, pgs. 100, 718
Youth For Understanding International Exchange, pg. 968
Youth Service America, pg. 208
Youth Services to Frail, Homebound Elderly, pgs. 464, 903
Zero Population Growth, pgs. 768, 1056, 1088

FLORIDA

BOCA RATON
Reymont Associates, pgs. 971, 1012

BONIFAY
Grand People, Inc., pg. 401
Grand People's Retired Senior Volunteer Program, pg. 401

BOYS RANCH
Florida Sheriffs Youth Ranches, pgs. 496, 817
Florida Sheriffs Youth Villa, pgs. 496, 817

COCONUT CREEK
Horses and the Handicapped of South Florida, pg. 869
Volunteers In Action, pgs. 118, 633

DOVER
Davis Nursery, pgs. 442, 784
Refuge for Injured Wildlife, pgs. 442, 784

FORT LAUDERDALE
Community Service Council of Broward County, pgs. 176, 904
Senior Connection, pgs. 176, 904
Volunteer Action Center of Broward County, pgs. 950, 996

FORT MYERS
The Care and Nourishment of Volunteers*, pg. 232
Community Coordinating Council of Lee County, pg. 232

HASTINGS
Hastings High School, pgs. 481, 647
Peer Counseling/Cross-Age Tutoring Program, pgs. 481, 647

HOLLYWOOD
U.S. Journal of Drug and Alcohol Dependence, pgs. 999, 1000, 1003, 1039, 1073

JACKSONVILLE
Florida Department of Health and Rehabilitative Services, pg. 993
Growing with Public Relations*, pg. 289
Interfaith Council of Jacksonville, pg. 309
University of North Florida, pg. 262
Volunteer Jacksonville, pg. 289
Volunteer Management for the Non-Profit Professional*, pg. 262
Volunteering in the Religious Setting, pg. 309

KEY WEST
Health Fair, pgs. 349, 672
US/DoD - Naval Regional Medical Clinic, pgs. 349, 672

LANTANA
Crisis Line Information & Referrals, pg. 158

LIGHTHOUSE POINT
US/Coast Guard Auxiliary, pg. 929
Volunteer Sailboat Navigators, pg. 929

MIAMI
Citizens' Crime Watch of Dade County, pgs. 454, 709
Family AIDS Education Project, pgs. 362, 516
Jewish Family Services, pgs. 362, 516
National Network of Youth Advisory Boards, pg. 1043
The Response Pool, pgs. 106, 520
United Way of Dade County, pgs. 106, 520

MIAMI BEACH
National Network of Youth Advisory Boards, pgs. 189, 796, 1100

NAPLES
Let Us Volunteer Service (LUVS) Program, pgs. 1070, 1073
Youth Haven, pg. 819

NORTH MIAMI
American Federation of Police, pgs. 494, 708
CB Radio Patrol, pgs. 494, 708

NORTH PALM BEACH
National Association of Police Athletic Leagues, pgs. 425, 918

OCALA
Human Relations Skills for Volunteers, pg. 242
Management Skills for Volunteer Leaders, pg. 248
Volunteer Center of Marion County, pg. 242
Volunteer Management Certification, pg. 262

Volunteer Service Bureau, pgs. 248, 262, 958

ORLANDO
ADDitions School Volunteers, pgs. 299, 619, 641
Building Better Boards: Legal Liability and
  Responsibilities, pg. 184
Going with the Current: Volunteer Management
  Workshop, pg. 241
More Than Meets The Ear - A Listening Skills
  Seminar, pg. 308
Volunteer Center of Central Florida, pgs. 184,
  241, 272, 308, 1041
Workshop for Volunteers, pg. 272
Workshops for Volunteer Coordinators and
  Volunteers in Education*, pgs. 299, 619

PENSACOLA
Military Educators and Counselors Association,
  pgs. 377, 793

SAINT AUGUSTINE
Archaeological Volunteer Program, pg. 525
St. Augustine Historical Preservation Board,
  pg. 525

SAINT PETERSBURG
Adams' Express: A Mini-Grant Program,
  pgs. 111, 639
Christmas Toy Shop, pg. 919
City of St. Petersburg, pgs. 499, 609
CRACKDOWN, pgs. 499, 609
Florida Power, pg. 27
I Am Involved, pg. 27
Teaching-for-Excellence Mini-Grant Program,
  pgs. 111, 639

SARASOTA
Pineapple Press, pg. 984

STUART
American Red Cross, pg. 593
Emergency Services Program, pg. 593

TAMPA
Tampa Causeway Beautification Project, pg. 765
Tampa Parks Department, pg. 765

GEORGIA

ALBANY
Nursing Home Project, pgs. 405, 907
Retired Senior Volunteer Program, pgs. 405,
  408, 907
RSVP - Nursing Home Project*, pg. 408

AMERICUS
Habitat for Humanity International, pgs. 355,
  687, 1029

ATHENS
National Institute of Social Welfare Research,
  pgs. 1068, 1097
Regional Institute of Social Welfare Research,
  pg. 1070

ATLANTA
America Responds to AIDS, pgs. 67, 513
Atlanta Community Food Bank, pg. 751
Atlanta Public Schools, pg. 473
Duties to the Community, pg. 473
Family Day Care Technical Assistance
  Conference, pg. 588
Federation of Southern Cooperatives and Land
  Assistance Fund, pg. 576
Georgia State University, pgs. 273, 282
National AIDS Information Campaign, pgs. 67,
  513
Parents' Resource Institute on Drug Education,
  pgs. 168, 606
PRIDE, pgs. 168, 606

RJR Nabisco Corporation, pg. 973
Save the Children/Child Care Support Center,
  pg. 588
Training for Volunteers and Volunteer
  Agencies, pg. 282
Workshops in Effective Volunteer Utilization,
  pg. 273
World Health Organization Collaborating Center
  on AIDS, pg. 509

COLLEGE PARK
Association for Retarded Citizens, pg. 1068
Association for Retarded Citizens of Georgia,
  pgs. 453, 1094, 1096, 1098
Parents Educating Parents, pgs. 457, 856
Parents Educating Parents: Training Program,
  pg. 453

DECATUR
Families in Action National Drug Information
  Center, pgs. 413, 603

DORAVILLE
Georgia Special Olympics Summer Games,
  pg. 868
Special Olympics, pg. 868

FORT BENNING
Volunteer Resource Center, pgs. 347, 894

FORT GORDON
Fort Gordon Volunteer Program, pgs. 345, 891
US/DoD - Fort Gordon, pgs. 345, 891

GRIFFIN
Volunteer Transportation, pgs. 381, 939

MARIETTA
Newsletter Factory, pgs. 63, 984
Producing, Designing & Writing Newsletters,
  pg. 63

REIDSVILLE
Volunteer Transportation Program, pgs. 381, 938

SAVANNAH
Girl Scouting in the Inner City, pgs. 551, 920
Girl Scouts of the USA, pgs. 551, 920

HAWAII

HONOLULU
Hawaii Office of Children and Youth, pg. 1021
Hawaii Office of the Governor, pgs. 129, 817
Hawaii Protection and Advocacy Agency,
  pgs. 128, 844
Hawaii State Youth Volunteer Board*, pg. 128
Hawaii Youth At Risk, pgs. 438, 704
Multi-Phasic Health Screening, pgs. 404, 680
North Shore Civil Defense Team, pgs. 128, 594
Office of Children and Youth (OCY), pgs. 129,
  817
Retired Senior Volunteer Program, pgs. 404, 680
State of Hawaii, pgs. 128, 594
Teen-Age Assembly of America*, pg. 190
Volunteer Training Program for Volunteer
  Advocates, pgs. 128, 844

WAILUKU
Community Friends*, pgs. 745, 1048
Mental Health Association in Maui, pg. 745

IDAHO

BOISE
Boise Peace Quilt Project, pg. 565
Discover Center of Idaho, pg. 533
Gleaning*, pgs. 455, 759
Idaho Hunger Action Council, pgs. 455, 759,
  1037, 1053

Idaho Volunteer, pg. 129
Nurturing Network, pg. 930
Statewide Volunteer Management Training
  Program, pg. 129

ILLINOIS

ARLINGTON HEIGHTS
Mature Outlook, pgs. 331, 898

AURORA
Comprehensive Accounting Corporation, pg. 542
Most Incomprehensive Government Regulation
  Award Program, pg. 542

BRIDGEPORT
Custom Audio Tapes, pg. 1071

CHAMPAIGN
Community Research Forum*, pgs. 79, 702
National Clearinghouse for Criminal Justice
  Planning and Architecture, pg. 717
YMCA Program Store, pg. 949

CHICAGO
ABA Commission on the Mentally Disabled,
  pg. 1078
Alzheimer's Disease & Related Disorders
  Association, pgs. 902, 1067
American Bar Association, pgs. 433, 439, 573,
  881, 991, 1028, 1094
American Hospital Association, pgs. 3, 663
American Library Association, pgs. 636, 966,
  968, 1010, 1033
American Medical Association, pgs. 197, 599,
  612, 1022
American Red Cross, pgs. 436, 592
American Society of Directors of Volunteer
  Services, pgs. 3, 663
Association of Nervous & Former Mental
  Patients, pgs. 453, 745
Basic Management of Volunteer Programs,
  pg. 231
Bonus Books, pgs. 1014, 1017, 1018
Chicago Board of Education, pgs. 351, 647
Chicago Building Department, pg. 1029
Chicago City-Wide College, pg. 290
Chicago Public Library, pg. 636
Chicago Public Library Volunteer Services,
  pg. 636
Chicago Runaway Switchboard, pgs. 162, 805
Citizen/Labor Energy Coalition, pg. 772
Citizens Information Service*, pgs. 79, 552,
  1034, 1039, 1056, 1085
Co-ordinating Council for Handicapped
  Children, pgs. 199, 851, 1043
Coalition for Literacy, pgs. 202, 732
Community Programs, pgs. 84, 758
Coordinating Council for Handicapped
  Children, pg. 979
Design for Change, pgs. 198, 638
Direct Line, pgs. 164, 579
Disaster Professional Volunteer Network,
  pgs. 436, 592
Emergency Infant Nutrition Program: Free
  Breakfast Project, pgs. 474, 748
Female Offender Rehabilitation Program,
  pg. 661
Given Opportunities..., pgs. 72, 853
Governor's Office of Voluntary Action/IL,
  pgs. 210, 268
Governor's Office of Voluntary Action, pg. 130
Governor's Office on Volunteerism/IL, pgs. 130,
  131
Great Books Foundation, pg. 639
Howard Brown Memorial Clinic, pgs. 425, 512,
  963, 1100

Informal Steering Committee on Prescription Drug Abuse, pg. 612
Jewish Vocational Service, pgs. 387, 734
Juvenile Justice Services, pg. 1038
JVS Volunteer Tutorial Program, pgs. 387, 734
Leadership and Management of Volunteer Programs*, pg. 246
Legal Programs for the Homeless, pgs. 439, 881
Literacy Volunteers of Chicago, pg. 735
Little City Foundation, pgs. 72, 853
LIVE '89 (Leadership in Volunteerism Experience), pg. 130
Local Volunteer School Councils, pgs. 198, 638
Marillac House, pgs. 84, 758
Marillac Social Center, pgs. 474, 748
Media Relations for Nonprofit and Volunteer Organizations, pg. 290
Metro-HELP, pgs. 162, 805
National Association of Perinatal Addiction Research and Education, pgs. 295, 931
National Association of Women Business Owners, pgs. 107, 548, 549
National Clearinghouse for Legal Services, pgs. 974, 1006, 1010, 1011, 1067, 1074
National Committee for Prevention of Child Abuse, pgs. 70, 813
National Conference on Drug Abuse and Parenting*, pgs. 295, 931
National Easter Seal Society, pg. 843
National Live Stock and Meat Board, pg. 993
National Runaway Switchboard, pgs. 161, 804
National Safety Council, pg. 935
National Training and Information Center*, pgs. 328, 567
NAWBO Scholarship Fund, pgs. 107, 549
Panel on Drug Abuse/Panel on Alcoholism, pgs. 197, 599
Peace Museum, pg. 564
Playboy Foundation, pg. 1000
Public Service Activities Division, pgs. 433, 573
Recovery, Inc., pgs. 453, 745, 1049
Saturday Scholars, pgs. 351, 647
Statewide Leadership Symposium: Working Together to Make Visions Realities, pg. 210
Supervising Volunteers*, pg. 256
Swallow Press, pg. 1042
Understanding is Progress, pg. 661
United Way of Chicago, pg. 231
University of Chicago Press, pg. 1007
US/HHS - Administration on Aging, pgs. 319, 897
U.S. League of Savings Institutions, pgs. 1028, 1057
Voluntarism: A Key to the Future*, pgs. 319, 897
Volunteer Center of Chicago, pgs. 246, 256, 323
Volunteer Leadership: Challenges For The Nineties, pg. 131
Volunteer Staffing Workshops*, pg. 323
Volunteers: Empowerment Today and Tomorrow, pg. 268
WBBM Newsradio, pgs. 164, 579
YMCA, pgs. 81, 827
Young Adult Services, pg. 636
Young Men's Christian Association of the U.S., pgs. 81, 827, 1090, 1100

DECATUR
DOVE, Inc., pg. 85

DEERFIELD
My Own Meals, Inc., pg. 1053

DOWNERS GROVE
Heritage Arts/VMS Systems, pg. 953
Resource Development Seminars, pg. 253

VM Systems, pg. 253
VMS/Heritage Arts, pgs. 946, 948, 952, 1018, 1065, 1066, 1090

ELGIN
Brethren Volunteer Service, pg. 1098

EVANSTON
American Association for Corporate Contributions, pgs. 97, 1015
Rotary International, pg. 92
Self-Help Center, pg. 221

GREAT LAKES
Navy Family Service Center, pg. 957
Parent-to-Parent Program, pgs. 350, 839
US/DoD - Navy Family Service Center, pgs. 348, 350, 839, 1087, 1095

HIGHWOOD
Curriculum Innovations, pg. 988

LOVES PARK
Rock Valley Community College, pg. 266
Volunteer Services Curriculum, pg. 266

MANTENO
Manteno Veterans Home, pgs. 403, 892
Manteno Veterans Home Volunteer Program, pgs. 403, 892

MAYWOOD
Cook County Sheriff's Office, pgs. 295, 296, 600, 606
InTouch, pgs. 296, 600, 998
InTouch Program, pg. 998
Prevention Makers, pgs. 295, 606

MOLINE
Volunteer Center of the Greater Quad Cities, pgs. 958, 976, 984

MOOSEHEART
Loyal Order of Moose, pg. 92

NAPERVILLE
Harris Bank, pgs. 39, 620
School Council Volunteers, pgs. 39, 620

NORTHFIELD
PAR Leadership Training Foundation, pg. 204

OAK BROOK
Lions Club International, pg. 92
McDonald's Corporation, pg. 973

OAK PARK
Employee Assistance Society of North America, pgs. 40, 790
Oak Park and River Forest High School, pgs. 482, 771
Pollution Control Center, pgs. 482, 771

PARK RIDGE
National Down Syndrome Congress, pgs. 199, 864

PEORIA
Community Workshop and Training Center, pgs. 72, 853
Hug In, pgs. 72, 853

RIVER GROVE
Out of Work: What Now? An Unemployment Clinic, pgs. 441, 654
Triton College, pgs. 441, 654

SKOKIE
Oakton Community College/MONNACEP, pgs. 624, 1007
Spirit and Breath Association, pgs. 459, 679, 1025

Spirit and Breath Volunteer Program, pgs. 459, 679
VITA (Volunteers In Teaching Adults), pg. 624

SPRINGFIELD
Charles C. Thomas, Publisher, pgs. 947, 1032
Community Block Homes, pgs. 34, 816
Governor's Office on Volunteerism/IL, pg. 130
Home Town Awards, pg. 130
Illinois State Board of Education, pgs. 34, 816

URBANA
ERIC Clearinghouse on Early Childhood Education, pg. 993

WESTMONT
Mended Hearts, pgs. 456, 673

INDIANA

EVANSVILLE
Youth Resources of Southwestern Indiana, pg. 195

FORT BENJ HARRISON
US/DoD - Fort Benjamin Harrison, pgs. 347, 894
Volunteer Program - Fort Benjamin Harrison, pgs. 347, 894

FORT WAYNE
Youth as Resources/YMCA, pg. 194

INDIANAPOLIS
AIRS Directory Project, pg. 1032
Alliance of Information and Referral Systems, pgs. 155, 1031, 1033
Handicapped Learner Materials, pg. 856
Kiwanis International, pgs. 92, 997
Parent Cooperative Pre-Schools International, pg. 995
Pictorial, Inc., pg. 1077
Special Materials Project*, pg. 856
Youth As Resources, pg. 193

MARTINSVILLE
American Camping Association, pgs. 917, 1052, 1081, 1083

MISHAWAKA
Grissom Middle School, pgs. 192, 627
Mindstretchers, pgs. 192, 627

MUNCIE
Ball State University, pg. 243
Institute on Volunteerism, pg. 243

SOUTH BEND
REAL Services, pg. 926
Senior Games of Indiana, pg. 926

IOWA

ANKENY
Des Moines Area Community College, pgs. 239, 261, 269
Effective Management of Volunteer Programs, pg. 239
Soil and Water Conservation Society of America, pgs. 774, 1056, 1058, 1059, 1061
Volunteer Coordination, pg. 261
Volunteers in Action, pg. 269

DAVENPORT
Eastern Iowa Community College District, pg. 186
In-Home Detention Program, pgs. 340, 913
Leadership for the Nineties*, pg. 186

DES MOINES

Iowa Department of Social Services, pgs. 132, 826, 1021, 1080

Iowa Governor's Office for Volunteers, pg. 132

Our Community Kitchen, pgs. 371, 758

Regional Seminars and a State Conference on Volunteerism, pg. 132

State Volunteer Program, pgs. 132, 826

Volunteer Center of United Way, pgs. 952, 1043

Volunteer Center of United Way of Central Iowa, pgs. 949, 977

Washington International Arts Letter, pgs. 967, 968, 976, 1017, 1018

IOWA CITY

Special Recreation, pgs. 923, 1069, 1078

MUSCATINE

Christmas Basket Program, pgs. 386, 835

The Voluntary Action Center of Muscatine, pgs. 386, 835

WATERLOO

Hawkeye Institute of Technology, pg. 267

Volunteer Training, pg. 267

KANSAS

FORT LEAVENWORTH

US/DoD - Fort Leavenworth Combined Arms Center, pg. 348

Volunteers at Fort Leavenworth, pg. 348

KANSAS CITY

Wyandotte House, Inc., pgs. 446, 819

Wyandotte House/Neutral Ground, pgs. 446, 819

MERRIAM

Retired Senior Volunteer Program, pgs. 68, 540

Senior Acting Program of the Barn Players*, pgs. 68, 540

MISSION

Volunteer Center of Johnson County, pg. 12

NEWTON

Commission on Voluntary Service and Action, pg. 956

Prairie View Mental Health Center, pgs. 390, 742, 1048

Volunteer Program of Prairie View, pgs. 390, 742

OVERLAND PARK

Marketing Strategies for Nonprofit Organizations, pg. 62

Padgett Thompson, pg. 62

SHAWNEE MISSION

Fred Pryor Seminars, pg. 62

How to Proofread, pg. 62

TOPEKA

Board Management Training Workshop, pg. 183

Volunteer Center of Topeka, pg. 183

WICHITA

First Call for Help/Wichita, pg. 158

Making the Grade: A Report Card on American Youth, pgs. 192, 799

National Association of Citizens' Crime Commissions, pgs. 195, 697

Teaching Senior Center, pgs. 311, 911

United Way of the Plains, pgs. 158, 192, 799

Wichita Crime Commission, pgs. 195, 697

Wichita State University, pgs. 311, 911

KENTUCKY

FORT CAMPBELL

Community Learning Program, pg. 471

Fort Campbell High School, pg. 471

FRANKFORT

Assembly of State Offices on Volunteerism, pg. 122

Governor's Conference on Volunteerism, pg. 132

Governor's Office on Volunteer Services/KY, pg. 132

Kentucky Commission on Aging, pg. 1083

LEXINGTON

Bluegrass Medicare-Medicaid Assistance Program, pgs. 399, 903

Futures for Youth, pg. 657

Lexington Senior Citizens Center, pgs. 399, 903

Metro Alternative Shelter House (MASH), pgs. 35, 818

National Correctional Recreational Association, pg. 723

Safe Place, pgs. 35, 818

Teen Complex, pg. 657

LOUISVILLE

American Academy of Crisis Interveners, pgs. 174, 744, 1032, 1033

Jefferson County Medical Society, pgs. 440, 879

Jewish Community Federation of Louisville, pg. 10

Jewish Volunteer Association, pg. 10

Louisville Youth Involvement Committee, pg. 19

Metro United Way, pgs. 19, 1101

Mission House, pgs. 440, 879

US/SBA - SCORE/ACE, pgs. 412, 545

US/SBA - Service Corps of Retired Executives/Active Corps of Executives, pgs. 412, 545

OLIVE HILL

Country Gathering, pgs. 400, 757

Northeast Kentucky Area Development Council, pgs. 400, 757

OWENSBORO

Court Referral Program, pgs. 338, 725

Volunteer Probation Officer Program, pgs. 460, 914

VERSAILLES

City of Versailles, pg. 525

Woodford County Bicentennial Celebration, pg. 525

WHITESBURG

Catholic Committee of Appalachia, pgs. 355, 838

LOUISIANA

BATON ROUGE

Tutorial Program, pgs. 445, 648

EDGARD

Second African Baptist Church, pgs. 375, 830

West St. John Ministry of Care, pgs. 375, 830

GRAND ISLE

Grand Isle Erosion Fight, pgs. 500, 593

HAMMOND

Kennedy Interns in Recreation*, pgs. 393, 863, 1083

METAIRIE

LaFreniere Park Special Recreation Programming Division, pgs. 376, 924

Low-Income Apartments Program, pgs. 355, 690

VOA Symposium on Homelessness, pgs. 307, 873

Volunteer Prison League, pg. 698

Volunteers of America, pgs. 81, 270, 307, 355, 690, 698, 873

Volunteers of America Annual Meeting, pg. 270

MONROE

Louisiana Training Institute*, pgs. 367, 705

NEW ORLEANS

American Red Cross, pg. 595

Association of Community Organizations for Reform Now (ACORN), pgs. 451, 582

Catholic Charities, pgs. 366, 654

City of New Orleans, pg. 642

Core Curriculum - The Volunteer, pg. 236

Growing Up With Nature, pgs. 416, 783

Home League, pgs. 402, 793

Jesuit High School, pg. 478

Jesuit Service Project, pg. 478

Job Search, pgs. 366, 654

Louisiana Nature and Science Center, pgs. 416, 783

Louisiana State Special Olympics Summer Games, pg. 869

New Orleans Volunteers, pg. 642

Red Cross Disaster Aid, pg. 595

Salvation Army, pgs. 402, 793

Special Olympics - New Orleans, pg. 869

Volunteer and Information Agency, pg. 236

MAINE

AUGUSTA

Augusta Mental Health Institute, pgs. 341, 726

Public Service Volunteers, pgs. 341, 726

PORTLAND

Area Agency on Aging, pg. 267

Ingraham Volunteers*, pg. 159

Veterans for Peace, pgs. 353, 564

Volunteer Workshops in Maine, pg. 267

WATERVILLE

Kennebec Valley Community Action Program, pg. 13

Volunteers In Action, pg. 13

MARYLAND

ANNAPOLIS

Alliance for the Chesapeake Bay, pg. 1055

Doncaster Youth Challenge, a.k.a. Sneaker Camp, pgs. 222, 704

Maryland Department of Juvenile Services, pgs. 222, 704

Maryland Governor's Campaign, pg. 1058

Maryland Governor's Office, pg. 1055

Maryland Hunter Education Program, pgs. 133, 783

BALTIMORE

AIDS in the Workplace, pgs. 41, 517

Baltimore City Health Department, pg. 406

Chesapeake Campaign, pg. 769

Citizens Program for the Chesapeake Bay, pg. 1055

Community Problem Solving Committee, pg. 84

Homework Hotline, pgs. 416, 645

Johns Hopkins Tutorial Project, pg. 646

Johns Hopkins University, pgs. 646, 769

McCormick and Company, pg. 972

Meals on Wheels of Central Maryland, pg. 1053

Retired Senior Volunteer Program, pg. 406

TransParent School Model Program, pgs. 416, 645

United Way of Central Maryland, pgs. 41, 84, 517

US/OMB - Health Care Planning
Administration, pg. 1071

BELTSVILLE
National Energy Resources Organization,
pg. 773

BETHESDA
Affordable Housing Project, pgs. 358, 687
Boy Scouts of America, pgs. 59, 852
Citizens for Safe Drivers Against Drunk
Drivers/Chronic Offenders, pgs. 451, 938
Consumer Deputy Program, pg. 571
Goodwill Industries of America, pgs. 1012, 1080
National Clearinghouse for Improving the
Management of Human Services, pg. 5
National Clearinghouse for Poison Control
Centers, pgs. 171, 670
Project SHARE, pgs. 5, 950, 953, 958,
1069, 1095
Self-Help for Hard of Hearing People, pgs. 224,
855
SHHH, pgs. 224, 855
Troop 400 and Troop 391, pgs. 59, 852
Unitarian Universalist Housing Foundation,
pgs. 358, 687
US/Consumer Product Safety Commission,
pg. 571
US/HHS - Cancer Information Clearinghouse,
pgs. 161, 665
US/HHS - Food and Drug Administration,
pgs. 171, 670
US/HHS - High Blood Pressure Information
Center, pgs. 180, 681, 978, 1023
US/HHS - National Cancer Institute, pgs. 161,
665
US/HHS - National Institutes of Health,
pgs. 180, 681

BRANDYWINE
Adopt-A-Stream, pg. 780
Maryland Department of Natural Resources,
pg. 780

BURTONSVILLE
Sign Media, Inc., pg. 1080

CHERRYFIELD
Conflict Resolution/Alternatives to Violence
Center, pgs. 451, 723

CHEVY CHASE
Audubon Naturalist Society, pgs. 443, 770, 771,
776, 956, 1055
Boarder Baby Project, pgs. 33, 798
Earth Day 1990, pg. 770
Gartenhaus Furs, pgs. 33, 798
School Ecology Project, pgs. 443, 771
Woodend Volunteer Program, pg. 776

COLLEGE PARK
University of Maryland Book Store, pg. 1032

COLUMBIA
Grassroots Crisis Intervention & Peer
Counseling Center, pgs. 175, 741
Grassroots Crisis Intervention Center, pg. 1032
Grassroots Crisis Intervention Center Training
Program, pg. 308
Harriet Tubman Center, pgs. 175, 741
National Committee for Citizens in Education,
pg. 1095

ELKTON
Cecil County Public Schools, pg. 642
Cecil County Public Schools Volunteer
Program, pg. 642

GARRETT PARK
Garrett Park Press, pgs. 948, 1011, 1012, 1013,
1099

HYATTSVILLE
US/DoA - Consumer and Food Economics
Institute, pg. 993

KENSINGTON
National Health Screening Council for Volunteer
Organizations*, pgs. 200, 671
US/HHS - National Clearinghouse for Alcohol
and Drug Information, pgs. 997, 999, 1000,
1001

LANDOVER
Apples for the Students, pgs. 38, 626
Epilepsy Foundation of America, pgs. 331, 859,
1070, 1071, 1076
Fantle's, pg. 975
Giant Food, pgs. 38, 626
Hertz Government Sales Office, pg. 1092
TAPS (Training and Placement Service),
pg. 1011

LANHAM
Urban Institute Press, pgs. 946, 951, 952, 953,
1063

MT RANIER
Alliance for Volunteerism, pgs. 14, 555
National Forum on a Commission on
Volunteerism: The Federal Government and
Future of Volunteerism*, pgs. 14, 555

OLNEY
HOST (Hands Of Shared Time), pgs. 327, 477,
906, 909
Montgomery General Hospital, pgs. 477, 906,
1072, 1096
Taking a Trip to Friendship, pgs. 327, 909

OWINGS MILL
Organization for the Use of the Telephone
(OUT), pgs. 71, 854, 1076

PASADENA
Chrysalis House, pg. 612

RIVERDALE
People Need People Volunteer Fair, pg. 19
Prince George's Voluntary Action Center,
pgs. 19, 951, 954

ROCKVILLE
African-American Festival of Academic
Excellence, pgs. 296, 631
AIDS Hotline, pgs. 160, 520
Bethesda HELP, pg. 157
FDA Experimental AIDS Treatment Hotline,
pgs. 160, 521
Friend to Friend Program*, pgs. 363, 786
Jewish Social Service Agency, pgs. 363, 786,
1065
Montgomery Anti-Drug Conference, pgs. 295,
606
Montgomery County Department of Social
Services, pgs. 294, 813
Montgomery County Panel on Drug Problems,
pgs. 295, 606, 1001
Montgomery County Public Schools, pg. 642
Montgomery County School Volunteer
Program, pg. 642
NAACP, pgs. 296, 631
National Council of Community Mental Health
Centers*, pg. 740
National Criminal Justice Reference Service,
pgs. 1038, 1039
National Solar Heating and Cooling Information
Center, pg. 773
Parent Aide Training, pgs. 294, 813
The RADAR Network, pg. 599
Taft Group, pg. 99

Technical Information Center of the Office on
Smoking and Health, pgs. 172, 678
US/DoJ - National Criminal Justice Reference
Service, pgs. 174, 718
US/HHS - Bureau of Community Health
Services, pg. 1077
US/HHS - Food and Drug Administration,
pgs. 160, 521
US/HHS - National AIDS Information
Clearinghouse, pgs. 160, 520, 960, 963, 964
US/HHS - National Clearinghouse for Alcohol
and Drug Information, pgs. 168, 599, 602, 959,
978, 998, 999, 1000, 1001, 1002, 1003, 1024,
1086, 1087
US/HHS - National Clearinghouse for Health
Information, pg. 283
US/HHS - National Clearinghouse for Mental
Health Information, pgs. 175, 744
US/HHS - Office on Smoking & Health,
pgs. 172, 678
US/HHS - Public Health Service, pg. 1022
Using Volunteers in Your Agency, pg. 283

SILVER SPRING
Boys & Girls Clubs of Greater Washington,
pgs. 58, 608, 798, 874, 1068
Employment Skills for Homeless Youth, pg. 874
Good Hope Senior Center, pg. 719
Make it Home for the Holidays, pgs. 37, 605
Martial Arts for Seniors, pg. 719
National Foundation for Consumer Credit,
pg. 577
Project Right Start, pgs. 223, 934
Teen Parents Self-Sufficiency Programs,
pgs. 223, 934
Telecommunications for the Deaf, pgs. 983, 1073
Valley Green Juvenile Drug Abuse Prevention
Facility, pg. 608
Washington Regional Alcohol Program, pgs. 37,
605

TEMPLE HILLS
Greater Southeast Community Center for the
Aging, pg. 911
Visits Through Video, pg. 911

TOWSON
Goucher College, pg. 267
Volunteer Training Program, pg. 267

WHEATON
Association for Childhood Education
International, pgs. 586, 966, 981, 992, 994, 995,
1008, 1065

WYE MILLS
Chesapeake College, pg. 322
Recruiting Techniques for Volunteer
Organizations, pg. 322

MASSACHUSETTS

AGAWAM
Educational Parameters, pg. 1090

AMHERST
Center for Organizational and Community
Development, pgs. 94, 566
Citizen Involvement Training Program, pgs. 980,
985, 986, 987, 1019, 1041, 1089
Citizen Involvement Training Project (CITP),
pg. 290
National Priorities Project, pg. 553
ODT, Inc., pg. 950
University of Massachusetts, pgs. 94, 290, 566

BEVERLY
Introduction to Volunteering, Etc., pg. 244

North Shore Community College Volunteer Office, pg. 244

BOSTON
Action for Boston Community Development, pgs. 1029, 1059
Aid to Incarcerated Mothers, pg. 719
AIDS Action Committee, pgs. 120, 519
Beacon Press, pgs. 970, 988, 992, 993, 1012, 1023, 1034, 1036, 1037, 1039, 1053, 1072, 1073, 1077, 1087
Boston University, pg. 265
City Year, pg. 93
Committee on Aging, pg. 967
Consumer Affairs Foundation, pg. 990
Crime Justice Foundation, pg. 193
Elderhostel, pg. 900
From All Walks of Life, pgs. 120, 519
Information Center for Individuals with Disabilities, pg. 171
Inmate Spruce-Up Teams, pgs. 430, 763
Institute for Responsive Education, pgs. 462, 1099
JFK Library Corps, pgs. 478, 1097
John F. Kennedy Library Foundation, pg. 478
Management Development Seminar for Directors of Volunteer Services, pg. 247
Massachusetts Department of Public Works, pgs. 430, 763
Massachusetts General Hospital, pg. 247
Minorities Caucus of Family Service America, pgs. 331, 835
National Commission on Resources for Youth, pg. 462
New Volunteer Coordinator's Training, pg. 251
North Conway Institute, pg. 598
Samaritans, pgs. 179, 793
Stride Rite Children's Center, pgs. 29, 585
Stride Rite Corporation, pgs. 29, 585
Teens as Community Resources*, pg. 193
Thomas Jefferson Forum*, pg. 19
Unitarian Universalist Women's Federation, pgs. 988, 1042, 1043, 1089, 1096, 1098
Voluntary Action Center of Boston, pg. 251
Volunteer Program Management, pg. 265

BRIGHTON
A Class Act, pg. 83

CAMBRIDGE
Massachusetts Institute of Technology, pg. 1009
US/DoT - Office of Technology Sharing, pg. 1092

CHESTNUT HILL
Beaver County Day School, pg. 471
Community Field Work, pg. 471

DORCHESTER
Wiping Out Drug Abuse Drug Free Teen Center, pgs. 423, 611

FALL RIVER
Family Service America, pgs. 490, 899
YES Program (Youth-Elderly Services)*, pgs. 490, 899

FITCHBURG
Massachusetts Association for the Blind*, pg. 849
Sundial Volunteers, pgs. 374, 904

HARVARD
Squibb Publications, pg. 993

HYANNIS
Inside/Out*, pgs. 394, 872
Volunteers of Cape Cod, pgs. 13, 394, 872

MARLBORO
Students Against Driving Drunk (SADD), pgs. 463, 603

MEDFORD
Association of Voluntary Action Scholars, pgs. 3, 230, 615
AVAS Annual Conference, pg. 230
Conference on Nonprofit Leadership and Management, pg. 278
Graduate Program in Public Policy and Citizen Participation, pgs. 287, 554
Lincoln Filene Center, pgs. 3, 615
Lincoln Filene Center for Citizenship & Public Affairs, pgs. 278, 946, 983
New England Environmental Network, pg. 1057
Tufts University, pgs. 287, 554

NORTH OXFORD
Clara Barton Camp for Girls with Diabetes, pg. 668

PEABODY
North Shore Community Action Programs, pg. 1029

QUINCY
Cerebral Palsy of the South Shore, pgs. 394, 850
CPSS Fashion Show, pgs. 394, 850

ROSLINDALE
Volunteer Case Aide Program, pgs. 1048, 1049

SOMERVILLE
New England Free Press, pg. 983

SOUTH DEERFIELD
Channing L. Bete Company, pgs. 959, 961, 982, 990, 992, 997, 999, 1000, 1003, 1004, 1005, 1007, 1011, 1013, 1023, 1025, 1026, 1029, 1036, 1038, 1041, 1049, 1052, 1055, 1058, 1060, 1071, 1074, 1081, 1087

SPRINGFIELD
Administration of Volunteer Programs and Operation of Social Agencies, pg. 183
Springfield College, pgs. 183, 280
Summer Master's Degree Program in Community Leadership and Development, pg. 280

WEST BOYLSTON
Hearing Ear Dog Program, pg. 854

WESTBORO
Massachusetts Aquatic Resource Education Program (AREP), pg. 928
Massachusetts Division of Fisheries and Wildlife, pgs. 928, 1082

WORCESTER
Small Business Assistance Center, pg. 542
Transitional Volunteers Are..., pg. 389
Volunteer Resources Division, pgs. 389, 976, 1049

MICHIGAN

ANN ARBOR
Institute of Labor and Industrial Relations, pg. 972
Volunteer Services Program/Social Services, pg. 830
Washtenaw County Department of Social Services, pg. 830
Xerox Corporation, pg. 978

AUBURN HILLS
UAW-GM National Human Resource Center, pg. 1070

BAD AXE
Huron County Mental Health Services, pg. 744
Operation Good Neighbor, pg. 744

DETROIT
Catholic Youth Organization, pgs. 482, 604
Detroit Public Schools, pgs. 27, 549
Gale Research Company, pgs. 988, 989, 1023, 1024, 1034, 1078
Junior League of Detroit, pgs. 87, 510
Managing Volunteers for Results, pg. 249
Michigan Special Olympics State Games, pgs. 479, 869
Minority Entrepreneurship Program*, pgs. 27, 549
Prevention through Action, pgs. 482, 604
SO SAD (Save Our Sons and Daughters), pgs. 422, 707
Special Olympics - Michigan, pgs. 479, 869
University of Detroit, pg. 249

EAST LANSING
Michigan State University, pgs. 260, 485
Service-Learning Center, pg. 485
Volunteer Administration Specialization, pg. 260

FLINT
Bishop Airport Authority, pgs. 113, 859
Connexion, pgs. 420, 604
Flint Airshow, pgs. 113, 859
Flint Community Schools, pgs. 649, 1005, 1010
Handicapped Parking Enforcement Team, pgs. 428, 863
Parking Posse, pgs. 428, 863
Partners in Learning, pg. 1008
Project Graduation, pgs. 420, 604
Quality Education Program, pgs. 28, 657
UAW-GM Human Resource Center, pgs. 28, 657

GRAND BLANC
FEAT Foundation, pg. 762
Grand Blanc School District, pg. 493
Youth Volunteer Services, pg. 493

GRAND RAPIDS
Arts Council of Greater Grand Rapids, pgs. 387, 530
The Bridge, pgs. 34, 874
Festival, pgs. 387, 530
Grand Rapids Symphony Orchestra, pgs. 106, 539
High-Rise Fire Response Training, pgs. 26, 594
Independent Living/Homeless Youth, pgs. 34, 874
Steelcase, Inc., pgs. 26, 594

HUNTINGTON WOODS
Michigan Coalition Against Domestic Violence, pgs. 165, 837, 1033
National Domestic Violence Hotline, pgs. 165, 837

KALAMAZOO
AFL-CIO Community Services, pg. 1034

LANSING
Blueprint, pg. 740
In-Service Training/Statewide Volunteer Development, pgs. 133, 828
Michigan Department of Social Services, pgs. 301, 828
Michigan Statewide Volunteer Development, pgs. 133, 828
Program Development Assistance Package, pgs. 301, 828
St. Lawrence Hospital, pg. 1048
St. Lawrence Hospital & Healthcare Services, pg. 740

LAPEER
City of Lapeer, pg. 870
Special Olympics - Lapeer, pg. 870

ONTONAGON
American Association for Corporate
Contributions, pg. 1016

PONTIAC
National Conference on Parent Involvement,
pgs. 414, 638

PULASKI
Polish Legion of American Veterans Auxiliary,
pgs. 353, 893
Pulaski Auxiliary Post No. 8, pgs. 353, 893

ROCHESTER
Leader Dogs for the Blind, pg. 846

ROSCOMMON
Kirtland Community College, pgs. 413, 903
VISCAP (Volunteer Incentive Service Credit
Account Program), pgs. 413, 903

ROYAL OAK
Forum 90: Backward Glances... Forward
Visions, pgs. 292, 699
Forum 90: Pre-Conference Agenda (tentative),
pg. 714
National Education-Training Program:
Volunteer Court-Corrections Movement,
pgs. 316, 700
Pre-Forum 90 Training Institutes, pgs. 293, 700
A Shoulder to Cry On, pgs. 422, 934
Volunteers in Prevention, Probation, Prisons,
pgs. 6, 292, 293, 316, 699, 700, 714, 1036,
1038, 1039
William Beaumont Hospital, pgs. 422, 934

SAGINAW
Christmas Wishes, pg. 836
DSS Volunteer Services Program, pg. 829
Person to Person*, pgs. 419, 841
Saginaw County Department of Social Services,
pgs. 419, 829, 836, 841, 1069

SOUTHFIELD
City of Southfield, pgs. 429, 781
Friends of the Rouge, pgs. 429, 781

STANDISH
Service Delivery for the Elderly*, pgs. 380, 912

MINNESOTA

ANOKA
Balanced Budgets for Consumers, pg. 578
Minnesota Extension Service/Anoka County,
pg. 578

AUSTIN
George A. Hormel & Company, pg. 1053

BLOOMINGTON
Kaiser Roll, pgs. 47, 869
Lincoln Del/Storer Cable Communications,
pgs. 47, 869

DULUTH
Marshall School, pg. 326
The Marshall Service Unit and Volunteer
Outreach, pg. 326

MINNEAPOLIS
Augsburg Fortress, pgs. 991, 1049, 1066, 1077,
1079
Augsburg Publishing House, pg. 1038
Building an Effective Board, pg. 184
Burgess Publishing Company, pg. 1083
Central Lutheran Church, pgs. 360, 632

Central Summer School, pgs. 360, 632
Community Resource Volunteers, pgs. 435, 627
Demystifying the Internship Experience, pg. 310
Directors of Volunteers in Agencies, pg. 237
DOVIA Training Programs, pg. 237
Evaluation and Change, pg. 947
Family Resource and Referral Center*, pgs. 169,
837
Fresh Force, pg. 476
Hennepin County Court Services, pgs. 1036,
1037, 1039
Honeywell, pg. 974
Honeywell Foundation, pgs. 44, 688
Honeywell Neighborhood Improvement
Program, pgs. 44, 688
Lutheran Social Service of Minnesota, pg. 950
Market-Ability: Marketing Strategies for
Nonprofits, pg. 62
Minneapolis Public Schools, pgs. 435, 476, 627,
644
Minneapolis Urban League Volunteer Services*,
pg. 95
National Council on Family Relations, pgs. 169,
837, 1022, 1065, 1071, 1086, 1087
The Supervisory Cycle, pg. 257
A Total Process, pg. 258
Voluntary Action Center of United Way,
pgs. 62, 184, 257, 258, 310
Volunteer Services, pg. 644
WISE & GISE/CRV Volunteer Services,
pgs. 1005, 1006, 1007, 1009

MINNETONKA
Community Involvement Program, pg. 324

RED WING
Minnesota Correctional Facility-Red Wing,
pgs. 498, 708
Surround*, pgs. 498, 708

SAINT PAUL
Amherst Wilder Foundation, pgs. 318, 785
Association of Halfway House Alcoholism
Programs of North America, pgs. 602, 997
Befriender Training, pgs. 318, 785
Building Creative Organizations*, pg. 185
Campus Outreach Opportunity League
(COOL), pgs. 291, 324, 461, 946, 953,
986, 987, 1046, 1073, 1094
Center for Youth Development and Research,
pgs. 1089, 1098
Common Ground, Common Good, pg. 291
Community Projects in Saint Paul, pg. 84
COOL National Conference, pg. 324
Divine Redeemer Memorial Hospital, pg. 1024
Fare SHARE, pgs. 455, 752
Governor's Office of Volunteer Services/MN,
pg. 134
Human Service Programs: Volunteer Leadership
Emphasis Area, pg. 134
Minnesota Office of Volunteer Services, pgs. 134,
135
Regional Volunteer Workshops, pg. 134
St. Paul/Office of the Mayor, pg. 84
Solving Community Problems by Building
Community Partnerships, pg. 135
University Programs for Volunteers and
Administrators of Volunteers, pg. 135
Voluntary Action Center of the St. Paul Area,
pg. 185
Volunteer Program Management, pg. 135

SAINT PETER
Citizens' Scholarship Foundation of America,
pgs. 102, 641
Dollars for Scholars, pgs. 102, 641

SOUTH SAINT PAUL
Dakota Area Referral and Transportation for
Seniors, pgs. 405, 910
Divine Redeemer Memorial Hospital, pgs. 305,
674, 1024
Hospice - Divine Redeemer Memorial Hospital,
pg. 675
Hospice Volunteer Training Program*, pgs. 305,
674
Peer Counselor Program*, pgs. 405, 910

STILLWATER
Community Volunteer Service, pgs. 239, 244,
252
Dynamite Planning... Explode Into Action!,
pg. 239
Lake Sylvia V.I.P. (Very Important Person)
Conference*, pg. 244
Planning Today for Tomorrow's Volunteers*,
pg. 252

MISSISSIPPI

JACKSON
Friends of Handicapped Readers, pg. 637
Mississippi Library Commission, pg. 637
Mississippi Office of Volunteerism, pg. 136
National Conference for Volunteer Leadership*,
pg. 136
United Way of the Capital Area, pg. 90
United Way of the Capital Area (Jackson),
pgs. 104, 193, 803
Volunteer Center of United Way, pg. 967
Youth Allocations Committee, pgs. 104, 193,
803
Youth In Action, pg. 90

TUPELO
National Employment and Training
Association, pg. 652

MISSOURI

BRIDGETON
American Council on Alcohol Problems, pg. 602

BRIXEY
Bioregional Project, pg. 770
New Life Farm, pg. 770

CANTON
National Committee on Art Education for the
Elderly, pgs. 188, 899

CHILLICOTHE
Livingston County RSVP Program, pg. 402

EAST PRAIRIE
RSVP Thrift Shop*, pgs. 103, 836

INDEPENDENCE
Independence Neighborhood Councils, pg. 87
Neighborhood Councils Service Center, pg. 87

JEFFERSON CITY
Missouri Volunteers, pgs. 136, 617
Show-Me Seminars, pgs. 136, 617
Statewide Conference on Volunteerism, pg. 137
VOCAL, pg. 137

KANSAS CITY
Camp Fire, pgs. 57, 809
CASA Project (Court Appointed Special
Advocates), pgs. 334, 575
Community Partners Program*, pgs. 49, 668
Earl's Hamburgers, pg. 28
Kansas City Department of Parks and
Recreation, pgs. 55, 776

National Federation of State High School Associations, pg. 604
National Rural Health Association, pg. 669
Robert Wood Johnson Foundation, pgs. 49, 668
Salvation Army Hamburger Sales Day, pg. 28
TARGET - Helping Students Cope with Alcohol and Drugs, pg. 604
Volunteers in Parks (VIP), pgs. 55, 776

OSAGE BEACH
Ozark Opry Records, pg. 1009

SAINT CHARLES
Lindenwood Colleges, pg. 259
Voluntary Action Association Administration Program, pg. 259

SAINT LOUIS
Aid to Victims of Crime*, pg. 729
Carondelet Community Betterment Federation, pgs. 50, 693
Community Betterment Program, pgs. 50, 693
Community Service Requirement, pg. 93
Desegregation Monitoring and Advisory Committee, pgs. 298, 632
Metro High School, pg. 93
Pets for People, pgs. 54, 910
Phone Pal, pgs. 34, 818
Ralston Purina Company, pgs. 54, 910
Society of St. Vincent de Paul, pg. 80
Southwestern Bell, pgs. 34, 818, 1076
Superior Council, pg. 80
United Way of Greater St. Louis, pg. 20
U.S. National Senior Olympics, pg. 926
Volunteer Connection Telethon, pg. 20
Volunteer Training - School Desegregation Monitoring*, pgs. 298, 632

WELLSTON
Reserve Police Program, pgs. 460, 729
St. Louis County Police Department, pgs. 460, 729

MONTANA

BOZEMAN
Gallatin Valley Emergency Food Bank, pgs. 52, 752, 1053

BUTTE
National Center for Appropriate Technology, pg. 772

GREAT FALLS
American Red Cross, pg. 261
Volunteer and Paid Staff Working Together, pg. 261

NEBRASKA

LINCOLN
Contact Center, pg. 983
Employee Assistance Program Consortium, pgs. 40, 790
Making the Volunteer Experience Count, pgs. 281, 655
University of Nebraska, pgs. 269, 281, 655
Volunteer Center of Lincoln*, pgs. 953, 1043, 1048
Volunteers in Great Britain: A Study Tour, pg. 269
Youth Development Program, pgs. 492, 649

OMAHA
Hospice Organization, pg. 675
Volunteer Bureau of the Omaha United Way, pg. 12

PAPILLION
Family Life/Community and Government, pgs. 325, 561
Papillion/La Vista High School, pgs. 325, 561

NEVADA

LAS VEGAS
Class Action Suit, pg. 102
The Spice Program and Introduction, pg. 311
United Way Services of Las Vegas, pg. 102
University of Nevada, pg. 311

SPARKS
Committee to Aid Abused Women, pgs. 165, 831

NEW HAMPSHIRE

CHARLESTON
Student Conservation Association, pgs. 1061, 1100, 463, 767, 928, 1057, 1060

CONCORD
Business Information and Resource Council, pg. 139
Governor's Office on Volunteerism/NH, pgs. 137, 138, 139, 254
Lakes Region Conference on Volunteerism - Volunteers: A Caring Resource; A Practical Perspective, pg. 138
NH State Conference on Volunteerism, pg. 138
Seacoast Conference on Volunteerism: A Time for Growth; A Time for Change, pg. 254

DURHAM
EHMI Company, pgs. 1057, 1061
New England Center for Continuing Education, pgs. 404, 851
New England Municipal Center, pgs. 258, 555
New Hampshire Foster Grandparent Program, pgs. 404, 851
Training for the Municipal Volunteer Coordinator*, pgs. 258, 555

GORHAM
Appalachian Mountain Club, pgs. 917, 928, 1082, 1083, 1084
National Volunteer Project*, pg. 917
Volunteer Vacation Program, pg. 928

KEENE
Adult Tutorial Program, pg. 624
Keene State College, pg. 624

MANCHESTER
United Way of Greater Manchester, pgs. 198, 631
Youth Affairs Task Force, pgs. 198, 631

MERRIMACK
St. Joseph Community Services, pgs. 749, 1054

SANDOWN
The Shed Project*, pgs. 444, 858

NEW JERSEY

ALPINE
Boy Scouts of America, pgs. 422, 613
Tenafly-Alpine Safe Rides Program and others, pgs. 422, 613

ASBURY PARK
Child Assault Prevention Team, pgs. 495, 815

ATLANTIC CITY
Atlantic Electric Company, pg. 30
Volunteer Initiative Program (VIP), pg. 30

BELVEDERE
Pioneers on Wheels, pg. 1092

BERNARDSVILLE
Citizens for a Better Bernardsville (CBB), pg. 779
Litterthon, pg. 779

BRIGANTINE
Marine Mammal Stranding Center, pgs. 783, 1061

CAMDEN
Adult Foster Care, pgs. 385, 902
Community Activities Council, pg. 762
Haddon Township Council, pgs. 486, 762, 765
Senior Citizens United Community Services, pgs. 385, 902
Sparkle Committee, pgs. 486, 765

DENVILLE
New Jersey Self-Help Clearinghouse, pg. 222
The Self-Help Movement: New Form of Volunteerism and a Resource for Professionals*, pg. 222

EAST RUTHERFORD
G.P. Putnam's Sons, pg. 962

EDISON
Child Welfare League of America, pg. 1072

ENGLEWOOD
Dwight-Englewood School, pg. 85
Dwight-Englewood School Volunteer Program, pg. 85

ENGLEWOOD CLIFFS
Prentice-Hall, pg. 992

ESSEX FELLS
Christian Service Department, pg. 361
Northeastern Bible College, pg. 361

FORT DIX
Fort Dix Volunteers, pgs. 345, 890
US/DoD - Fort Dix, pgs. 345, 890

HACKENSACK
Fairleigh Dickinson University, pgs. 449, 630
New York Giants School Speakers Program, pgs. 449, 630
Phone-TTY, pg. 855

HIGHLAND PARK
Highland Park High School, pgs. 485, 794
SOS (Serve Our Seniors) Student Volunteer Program, pgs. 485, 794

JERSEY CITY
City Spirit Cultural Arts Festival, pg. 530
Cultural Arts Commission, pg. 530

KEAN
Communication-Help Center, pg. 157
Kean College, pg. 157

LINCROFT
Brookdale Community College, pgs. 399, 545
Brookdale-SCORE Program, pgs. 399, 545

MADISON
Effective Volunteer Administration, pg. 239
Fairleigh Dickinson University, pg. 239

MAHWAH
Ramapo College, pgs. 442, 627
Record Debate Classic, pgs. 442, 627

MANAHAWKIN
Beachfront Volunteers, pgs. 467, 762
Interact Club, pgs. 467, 762

METUCHEN
Scarecrow Press, pgs. 980, 1012, 1013

MIDDLETOWN
Net Result Tennis Foundation, pgs. 441, 920

MONMOUTH JUNCTION
CIPED (Community Involvement Personal
Education Development), pgs. 470, 625
South Brunswick High School, pgs. 470, 625

MONTCLAIR
US/DEd - National Adult Education
Clearinghouse, pg. 1004

MORRIS PLAINS
Corporate Retirees Information and Assistance
Program, pgs. 176, 900
RSVP of Morris County, pgs. 176, 409, 900

MORRISTOWN
Basic Managerial Skills for Directors of
Volunteers, pg. 232
Directors of Volunteers in Agencies, pg. 237
DOVIA Meetings for Volunteer Administrators,
pg. 237
Morris County Chaplaincy Council, pgs. 370,
721
Morris County Department of Human Services,
pg. 757
Morris County Nutrition Program, pg. 757
VAC Board Education Program, pg. 186
VAC Workshops*, pg. 280
Voluntary Action Center of Morris County,
pgs. 186, 232, 280, 955

MOUNT HOLLY
First Presbyterian Church, pgs. 371, 764
New Jersey Association Directors of Volunteer
Services, pg. 1097
Operation Clean Sweep, pgs. 371, 764

NEW BRUNSWICK
Center for the American Woman and Politics,
pgs. 955, 979
Certificate in Volunteer Management, pg. 233
Communications Skills for the College Bound,
pgs. 190, 560
Douglass College, pgs. 476, 794
The Gatehouse: The Cook/Douglass Peer
Counseling Center, pgs. 476, 794
New Brunswick High School, pgs. 190, 560
Rutgers University, pg. 233
Rutgers University Press, pg. 963

NEWARK
Forum on School Vandalism, pgs. 315, 703
Morris 2000, pg. 559
New Jersey NAACP, pg. 567
Newark City Council, pgs. 315, 703
Regional Plan Association, pgs. 559, 980
Voter Registration Assistance, pg. 567

ORANGE
Turrell Fund, pgs. 119, 923

PARAMUS
Paramus Heavy Rescue Squad, pg. 595

PATERSON
Paterson Habitat for Humanity, pgs. 371, 695,
1098

PLEASANTVILLE
Atlantic Electric Company, pg. 977

POMPTON PLAINS
American Community Cultural Center
Association, pg. 524

PRINCETON
American Red Cross, pgs. 60, 812
Recording for the Blind, pg. 847
Robert Wood Johnson Foundation, pg. 950
Youth Services, pgs. 60, 812

RIO GRANDE
Cape May County Volunteers and Resources,
pgs. 169, 837

SEWELL
Educational Information and Resource Center,
pg. 703
TIPS Program, pg. 703

SOMERSET
Knights of Columbus, pg. 392
St. Matthias of Somerset Council No. 9925,
pgs. 392, 1097

THOROFARE
Town Meeting for the Homeless, pgs. 307, 885
Volunteers of America of Delaware Valley,
pgs. 307, 885

TOMS RIVER
Hospice Volunteer Training Program*, pgs. 305,
674
Ocean County College, pgs. 305, 674

TRENTON
Community Action Training*, pg. 181
Governor's Advisory Committee on
Private/Public Volunteer Partnerships/NJ,
pg. 209
Homelessness Prevention Program, pgs. 140, 686
New Breed Drill Team, pgs. 481, 920
New Jersey Office of the Governor, pgs. 140,
686
New Jersey Office of Volunteerism, pgs. 139,
945, 1021
Trenton Board of Education, pgs. 481, 920

UNION
Communication-Help Center, pg. 1031

UPPER MONTCLAIR
Autumn Stages, pgs. 402, 534, 1094
Lifestory Theater, pgs. 402, 534

VERONA
Salvation Army, pgs. 357, 826

WALLINGTON
Wallington Lions Club, pgs. 377, 850
White Cane Drive, pgs. 377, 850

WEST ORANGE
Daisy (Friend-Raiser) Ball, pgs. 113, 859
Kessler Institute for Rehabilitation Auxiliary,
pgs. 113, 859

WESTFIELD
STS (Sharing Talents and Skills), pgs. 376, 629

NEW MEXICO

ALBUQUERQUE
National Indian Youth Council, pg. 198
Rainbow Sunshine School, pg. 635
Shelter for Victims of Domestic Violence,
pg. 635

SANTA FE
Center for Creative Community, pgs. 4, 15, 243,
569, 948, 949, 953, 954, 955
Coalition for Volunteer Support, pg. 140

Governor's Office on Volunteer Services/NM,
pgs. 82, 140
Institute for the Advanced Study of
Volunteerism, pg. 243
A Message for the Future - The Voluntas Time
Capsule, pgs. 15, 569
New Mexico Statewide Conference on
Volunteerism, pg. 141
Santa Fe Preparatory School, pg. 488
Save Our Water*, pgs. 141, 781
Small Town Survival Workshops, pg. 82
Thursday Afternoon Program (TAP), pg. 488
Visitor Hospitality Center*, pgs. 381, 718
Volunteers: Our Greatest Natural Resource,
pg. 141

NEW YORK

ALBANY
Alcohol Education for Youth and Community*,
pg. 601
Community Service Program, pg. 464
Health Education Services, pgs. 960, 961, 962,
963, 964, 1022, 1025
New York Office of Advocate for the Disabled,
pg. 1081
New York State Department of Corrections,
pgs. 430, 707
State University of New York at Albany, pg. 464
Summit Shock Incarceration Facility, pgs. 430,
707

ALBERTSON
Human Resources Center, pgs. 112, 857

AVERILL PARK
Coalition for a National Health System*, pg. 663

BABYLON
Pilot Books, pgs. 953, 970, 971, 980, 983, 991,
1012, 1015, 1025, 1056, 1076, 1082

BINGHAMTON
Broome County Department of Social Services,
pgs. 458, 834
Public Assistance Clients Volunteer, pgs. 458,
834

BRONX
Bronx AIDS Volunteer Organization, pgs. 388,
513
Project BRAVO, pgs. 388, 513
TIP Neighborhood House/Older Adult
Volunteers, pg. 412

BROOKLYN
Alliance of Guardian Angels, pgs. 496, 710
Bay Ridge Nutrition and Home Care Programs,
pgs. 379, 757
Brooklyn AIDS Task Force, pgs. 468, 517
Guardian Angels, pgs. 496, 710
Industrial Home for the Blind, pg. 849
Magnolia Tree Earth Center, pgs. 480, 775
Neighborhood Tree Corps, pgs. 480, 775

BUFFALO
American Blind Bowling Association, pg. 845
American Red Cross, pg. 235
Conference on Volunteerism, pg. 235
Flying Senior Citizens of the USA*, pgs. 396,
939
Literacy Volunteers of New York State, pg. 735
Meals on Wheels of Buffalo and Erie County,
pgs. 380, 748, 1054
Volunteer Center of the United Way, pg. 187
Volunteer Lawyers Project, pgs. 446, 580
You Are The Board*, pg. 187

CHITTENANGO
Good Samaritan Recognition Ceremony, pgs. 17, 755
St. Paul's Episcopal Cathedral, pgs. 17, 755

CLARENCE
Volunteer Consultants, pg. 1041

DRYDEN
Dryden Associates, pgs. 950, 958

ELMSFORD
Benjamin Company, pg. 1085

ENDICOTT
Community Services Project, pg. 94
Union-Endicott School District, pg. 94

FPO NEW YORK
Navy Volunteers at Guantanamo Bay, pgs. 350, 892
US/DoD - Department of the Navy, pgs. 350, 892

GARDEN CITY
Adelphi University, pgs. 161, 221, 241, 666, 872
Fund Raising Management, pg. 1015
Graduate Certificate Program for Management of Volunteer Services, pg. 241
Handicapped Volunteer/Volunteering for the Handicapped, pgs. 221, 872
Woman-to-Woman Hotline, pgs. 161, 666

HAWTHORNE
Aldine de Gruyter, pg. 1067

HEMPSTEAD
Big Brothers/Big Sisters of Nassau County*, pgs. 447, 820

HICKSVILLE
Ability Is Ageless, pgs. 54, 901
Long Island Lighting Company, pgs. 54, 901

HILTON
Parma-Hilton Playground Project, pgs. 501, 921
Parma Town Hall Park, pgs. 501, 921

HUNTINGTON STATION
South Huntington School Volunteer Program, pg. 644

ITHACA
Center for Religion, Ethics and Social Policy, pg. 313
The Learning Web, pg. 313

JAMAICA
CAUSE (Community and University Services in Education), pgs. 469, 625
St. John's University, pgs. 469, 625

KINGSTON
Interfaith Volunteer Caregiving Workshop, pg. 357
National Federation of Interfaith Volunteer Caregivers, pgs. 356, 357, 861, 1095

MELVILLE
Newsday Newspapers, pg. 17
Newsday Volunteer Recognition Program, pg. 17

MILL NECK
Christopher D. Smithers Foundation, pg. 598

MORAVIA
Chronicle Guidance Publications, pg. 956

MOUNT VERNON
Consumers Union of the United States, pgs. 988, 989, 990, 991

National Council of Puerto Rican Volunteers, pg. 5

NEW CITY
Volunteer Counseling Service of Rockland County, pgs. 378, 791

NEW HYDE PARK
Parent-Child Home Program, pgs. 417, 588

NEW PALTZ
Child Find of America, pgs. 812, 1069

NEW YORK
AAFRC Trust for Philanthropy, pg. 1016
Academy for Educational Development, pg. 955
Adopt-A-School Dance Program, pgs. 32, 525
Advertising Council, pgs. 61, 983
Affordable Meetings, pg. 229
AIDS Project: Friendly Visitors, pg. 522
AIDS-Walk New York, pgs. 119, 518
Alcoholics Anonymous (AA), pgs. 432, 602
Alcoholics Anonymous World Services, pgs. 598, 1096
American Council for the Arts, pgs. 524, 966, 967, 1015, 1016, 1017, 1019
American Craft Council, pgs. 188, 526
American Federation of Arts, pgs. 68, 528
American Foundation for the Blind, pgs. 845, 1076, 1077, 1080, 1096
American Lung Association, pgs. 678, 1055
American Reading Council, pg. 639
American Society for the Prevention of Cruelty to Animals, pg. 782
American Values: The Community Action Network, pg. 79
Arts and Business Council, pgs. 32, 526
Association of Junior Leagues, pgs. 197, 322, 623
Association Press, pg. 947
Audience Arts, pg. 966
Bank Street College of Education, pg. 930
Benjamin Company, pg. 1002
Big Brothers/Big Sisters Program-Child Psychiatry*, pgs. 448, 821
Business Committee for the Arts, pgs. 32, 526
Business/Industry Program, pg. 22
Business Roundtable, pg. 973
Call for Action, pg. 155
Cancer Care, pg. 1022
Carnegie Council on Adolescent Development, pg. 1006
Center for Arts Information, pg. 524
Citation Press, pgs. 995, 1008
Citizen Advocates for Justice, pgs. 335, 701
Citizens Forum on Self-Government, pgs. 287, 567
City Harvest, pg. 1053
City Volunteer Corps, pg. 95
Civic Partnership: Initiative, Innovation*, pgs. 287, 567
Civitex, pg. 1095
Clarion Press, pg. 961
Columbia Broadcasting System, pg. 1026
Columbia University, pg. 1081
Commission on Voluntary Service and Action, pgs. 461, 946
Committee on Cooperation with the Professional Community, pgs. 432, 602
Community Forum on the Proposed *Harlem on the Hudson* Project, pgs. 328, 778
Community Services Society of New York, pg. 1099
Council of National Organizations for Adult Education, pgs. 197, 623
Council on Economic Priorities, pg. 22
Council on Environmental Alternatives*, pg. 772
Court Employment Project, pgs. 338, 720
Day Care Council of New York, pg. 995

Dodd, Mead & Company, pg. 968
Douglas N. Lawson Associates, Inc., pg. 98
Education/Social Action Service, pg. 1079
Environment Information Center, pg. 760
Environmental Defense Fund, pg. 1055
Fatherhood Project, pg. 930
Federation of Protestant Welfare Agencies, pgs. 22, 182, 248
Flight Attendant Volunteer Corps, pgs. 446, 629
Foundation Center, pgs. 98, 957, 1015, 1020
Foundation for Children with Learning Disabilities, pgs. 112, 862
Foundation for Public Relations, Research & Education, pg. 984
Foundation Research Service (FRS), pg. 98
Gay Men's Health Crisis, pgs. 508, 962, 963, 964
Girl Scouts of the USA, pgs. 58, 60, 809, 843, 1032
Girls Clubs of America, pgs. 58, 810
GMHC Walkathon, pgs. 119, 518, 964
God's Love We Deliver (GLWD), pgs. 379, 521
Governor's Office for Voluntary Service/NY, pg. 142
Health Fair Project, pg. 1023
Health/PAC Bulletin, pg. 1024
Heiskell Awards For Community Service, pg. 507
Hotel Sales & Marketing Association International, pg. 229
Hunter College, pgs. 301, 829
Hunter College School of Social Work, pg. 384
I Have a Dream Foundation, pgs. 111, 640
Individual Giving/Volunteering Campaign*, pg. 61
Information Center on Children's Cultures*, pgs. 161, 527
Interfaith Center on Corporate Responsibility, pg. 22
International Cultural Centers for Youth, pg. 528
Interracial Council for Business Opportunity, pg. 548
Jackie Robinson Foundation, pgs. 189, 803
Jewish Braille Institute, pg. 1073
Jewish Braille Institute of America, pgs. 355, 846
Jewish Guild for the Blind, pgs. 355, 846
Legal Services for the Elderly, pgs. 432, 906
Legal Services for the Elderly Poor, pg. 581
Literacy Volunteers of America, pg. 1047
Management of Volunteer Services, pg. 248
Manpower Demonstration Research Corporation, pg. 1078
Master of Professional Studies Degree: Fund Raising Management, pg. 302
Mayor's Voluntary Action Center, pgs. 949, 1072
McGraw-Hill Book Store, pg. 951
Metropolitan Life Insurance Company, pg. 978
Minority Volunteers: Pluralism in the Volunteer Arena, pg. 384
Morrow Junior Books, pg. 1097
National Accreditation Council for Agencies Serving the Blind and Physically Handicapped, pg. 1078
National Alliance for Safer Cities, pg. 1039
National Association on Drug Abuse Problems, pg. 606
National Board of YMCAs, pgs. 285, 797
National Charities Information Bureau, pgs. 952, 1018, 1020
National Child Labor Committee, pg. 586
National Civic League*, pg. 553
National Committee on the Education of Migrant Children, pg. 586
National Conference of Black Lawyers, pgs. 432, 580

National Council of Jewish Women, pgs. 257, 945, 995, 1038, 1070, 1073, 1074, 1075
National Council on Alcoholism, pgs. 602, 973, 997, 998, 999, 1043
National Dance Institute, pgs. 32, 525
National Health Council*, pgs. 664, 1024
National Self-Help Clearinghouse, pgs. 221, 1085
Neal-Schuman Publications, pg. 1008
New Directions for the Bronx, pg. 559
New School for Social Research, pg. 302
New York City Board of Education, pg. 631
New York City School Volunteer Program*, pgs. 643, 1008
Noxzema Extraordinary Teen Contest, pg. 27
Noxzema Skin Cream, pg. 27
Nutrition Institute of America, pg. 750
Odyssey House, pg. 599
Office for Church In Society, pgs. 357, 554
Ogilvy and Mather, pg. 1017
Parent-Child Program*, pgs. 417, 932
People With AIDS Coalition, pgs. 425, 523
Pharos Books, pg. 1077
Planned Parenthood Federation of America, pg. 931
Play Schools Association*, pg. 584
Population Council, pg. 768
Prentice-Hall, pg. 1006
Project BE, pg. 1004
Public Affairs Committee, pgs. 973, 1008, 1022, 1025, 1031, 1032, 1034, 1036, 1067, 1074, 1075, 1077, 1078, 1081
Public Affairs Pamphlets, pg. 1003
Public Relations Student Society of America, pg. 69
Public Service Materials Center, pgs. 1015, 1017, 1018, 1020
Quill/William Morrow, pg. 987
R. R. Bowker, pgs. 957, 963, 968, 1004, 1005, 1008, 1009, 1046
R-T-P, INC.*, pg. 659
Random House, Inc., pg. 957
Regional Bilingual Training Resource Center*, pg. 631
Regional Plan Association, pgs. 559, 951, 980
Retirement Advisors, pg. 1074
St. Luke's-Roosevelt Hospital Center, pgs. 417, 448, 522, 821, 932
Scouting for the Handicapped, pgs. 60, 843
Street Aid, pg. 876
Street News Homeless Vendors Program, pg. 876
The Systematic Involvement of Volunteers in Human Services, pg. 257
Telephone Pioneers of America, pg. 1081
Television Information Office*, pg. 62
Time, Inc., pgs. 51, 738, 1047
Time Incorporated, Community Relations Office, pgs. 947, 949, 976
Time to Read, pgs. 51, 738
Two Together*, pg. 648
UNA-USA Publications, pg. 1089
United Church of Christ, pgs. 357, 554
United Hospital Fund, pg. 964
U.S. Committee for United Nations Children's Fund, pgs. 161, 527
U.S. Committee on UNICEF, pgs. 966, 967, 968
Vacation and Senior Citizens Association, pgs. 925, 1084
Vanguard Press, pg. 1014
Vocational Foundation, pgs. 978, 1013
Voluntarism: Confrontation and Opportunity*, pgs. 285, 797
Volunteer Intervening for Equity (VIE)*, pg. 322
Volunteer Lawyers for the Arts, pgs. 329, 575
Volunteer Leadership Program, pg. 182

Volunteerism and Social Work Practice, pgs. 301, 829
Volunteers in Mission, pg. 1023
Volunteers: The Renewable Resource, pg. 271
Warner Books, pg. 971
Washington Heights Ecumenical Food Pantry, pgs. 375, 754
West Harlem Coalition, pgs. 328, 778
Women's Action Alliance, pgs. 950, 964, 997, 1006, 1008, 1016, 1019, 1086, 1088
YAI Alumni Club Karate Program, pg. 921
Young Adult Institute, pgs. 865, 921, 1079, 1081
Young Audiences, pg. 538
Young Men's Christian Association of the U.S., pg. 1044
Young Wings USA*, pgs. 446, 629
Young Women's Christian Association of the U.S., pgs. 81, 827

NYACK
Wholeffects Education: National Conference, pgs. 299, 618
Wholeffects Institute, pgs. 299, 618

OSWEGO
Oswego County, pg. 491
Youth Community Service, pg. 491

PLAINVIEW
Crime, Law and Community: A Student Service Curriculum, pgs. 314, 713
John F. Kennedy High School, pgs. 314, 713

ROCHESTER
AFL-CIO Community Services Committee, pgs. 502, 919
Air Crash Drill, pgs. 434, 591
American Cancer Society, pgs. 469, 665
American Red Cross, pg. 1098
Camp Good Days and Special Times, pgs. 469, 665
Camp Good Days and Special Times Rebuilding Project, pgs. 502, 919
Compeer, The Health Association, pg. 1048
Corpus Christi Catholic Church, pgs. 366, 520
Flame of Hope, pgs. 428, 868
Greater Rochester International Airport, pgs. 434, 591
Isaiah House, pgs. 366, 520
John Alden Books, pg. 1051
Meals on Wheels Program of Rochester, pg. 1053
National Braille Association, pg. 846
Northside Surgical Supply, pgs. 30, 872
Rochester Institute of Technology, pgs. 428, 868
St. Joseph's House of Hospitality, pgs. 373, 883
School of the Holy Childhood, pgs. 114, 858
U.S. Open Volunteer Committee, pgs. 114, 858
Volunteer Forum, pg. 947
Wheelchair Wash, pgs. 30, 872

ROOSEVELT ISLAND
AIDS Chronic Care Unit Volunteer Program, pgs. 494, 511
Goldwater Memorial Hospital, pgs. 494, 511

SAINT JAMES
Healthouse Volunteer Program, pgs. 313, 663

SARATOGA
American Red Cross, pgs. 403, 786
Maplewood Manor RSVP Program, pgs. 403, 786

SCARSDALE
Work in America Institute, pg. 975

SENECA FALLS
Seneca Falls Central School District, pgs. 421, 707

Seneca Falls Concerned Parents, pgs. 421, 707

SHOREHAM
Community Service, pg. 284
Shoreham-Wading Middle School, pg. 284

SPRING VALLEY
East Ramapo Central School District, pg. 484
Ramapo High School, pg. 483
Ramapo Key Club*, pg. 483
School and Community Service Program, pg. 484

SPRINGVILLE
Springville Griffith Central School, pg. 644
VISA - Volunteers in School Action, pg. 644

SYRACUSE
Bloodmobile, pgs. 468, 664
Diversion to Community Service*, pgs. 339, 725
Institute for Creative Conflict Management, pgs. 288, 565
Laubach Literacy Action, pg. 732
Laubach Literacy International, pg. 732
LeMoyne College, pg. 483
Literacy Volunteers of America, pg. 732
New Readers Press, pgs. 732, 990, 991, 994, 1009, 1010, 1013, 1023, 1036, 1046, 1047, 1048, 1049, 1086, 1087, 1088, 1093
Projects in the Community, pg. 483
Rape Crisis Center, pgs. 178, 727
Study War No More, pgs. 288, 565
Syracuse University, pg. 624
Syracuse University Continuing Education Program, pg. 624
Tully Central School, pgs. 468, 664
Victim-Witness Assistance Center*, pg. 731
Volunteer Center, Inc., pgs. 339, 725

TROY
Court Referred Volunteer Program of Rensselaer County, pgs. 338, 725

VALHALLA
Experiential Learning - Working with Student Volunteers, pg. 465
Westchester Community College, pg. 465

WANTAGH
Davis Information Group, pg. 951

WHITE PLAINS
Big Brothers/Big Sisters, pgs. 1083, 1099
County Information Center, pg. 158
Family Service of Westchester, pgs. 486, 921
Special Saturday, pgs. 486, 921
Westchester 2000, pg. 569
Westchester County Association, pgs. 569, 981

WILLIAMSVILLE
Amherst Y.E.S. (Youth Engaged in Service), pg. 466
Amherst Youth Board, pg. 466

NORTH CAROLINA

CARRBORO
Lollipop Power Books, pg. 1005

CARY
CATCH Program, pgs. 415, 635
Chamber of Commerce, pgs. 415, 635

CHAPEL HILL
Campus Literacy Awareness Month Program, pgs. 469, 733
Center for Early Adolescence, pgs. 283, 796
Chapel Hill Training Outreach Project, pgs. 298, 618

Skills Expansion Through Resource Volunteers in Education (SERVE), pgs. 298, 618
Southern Exposure, pg. 1025
Student Coalition for Action in Literacy Education (SCALE), pgs. 469, 733
University of North Carolina, pgs. 283, 796

CHARLOTTE
ECO, pg. 719
Energy Committed to Offenders, pg. 719
"United Way at Work" Conference, pg. 24
United Way of Central Carolinas, pg. 24

CONCORD
Cabarrus County Schools, pg. 650
School Community Relations Program, pg. 650

DURHAM
Concern of Durham, pg. 743
Greenhouse, pg. 743
National Council on the Black Aging, pg. 562
Southern Exposure, pg. 1027

GREENSBORO
United Services for Older Adults, pgs. 1068, 1069, 1078
Voluntary Action Center of Greensboro, pgs. 955, 958

HATTERAS
Fund for Advancement of Camping, pgs. 119, 923

MORGANTON
Western Carolina Center, pgs. 490, 865, 1100
Western Carolina Center Volunteens, pgs. 490, 865

MT AIRY
Surry County Friends of Youth/Best Friends Program, pgs. 449, 821

PITTSBORO
Rural Advancement Fund International*, pg. 577

RALEIGH
Cardinal Gibbons High School, pg. 647
Changing Values in Experiential Education*, pg. 310
Governor's Office on Volunteerism and Citizen Affairs/NC, pg. 142
National Society for Internships & Experiential Education, pg. 310
North Carolina/Virginia Exchange: Part One, pg. 142
Raleigh Parks and Recreation Division, pgs. 388, 924
Retired Senior Volunteer Program, pg. 406
ROVERS (Retired and Older Volunteers: An Educational Resource Service), pgs. 408, 628
School Tutoring Program, pg. 647
Special Populations Program, pgs. 388, 924
United Way of of Wake County, pg. 11
Voluntary Action Center of Wake County*, pg. 11

RESEARCH TRIANGLE PK
American Social Health Association, pgs. 178, 681, 1025
VD National Hotline, pgs. 178, 681

SALEMBURG
How to Work Effectively with Volunteers, pg. 242
North Carolina Justice Academy, pg. 242

SANFORD
FIRST (Factual Information Regarding Sex and Teens), pgs. 162, 805
Lee County Restitution Program, pgs. 340, 730

Lee County Youth Services, pgs. 449, 822
THANKS (Thoughtful, Helping Adults N' Kids Sharing), pgs. 449, 822

WINSTON SALEM
R. J. Reynolds Industries, pg. 974

NORTH DAKOTA

BISMARCK
Abused Adult Resource Center (AARC), pgs. 333, 834

DEVILS LAKE
RSVP of Ramsey County, pg. 409

FARGO
Lutheran Social Services of North Dakota, pg. 1048
North High Community Service Program, pg. 94
North High School, pg. 94
Retired Senior Volunteer Program, pg. 406

GRAND FORKS
Metamorphosis: Growth and Change in the Administration of Volunteer Services, pg. 250
North Dakota Association of Coordinators of Volunteer Services, pg. 250

OHIO

AKRON
American Cancer Society, Ohio Division, pgs. 666, 1024
Fundamentals of Volunteer Program Management, pg. 241
I Can Cope, pg. 666
The S.O.A.P.S., pgs. 175, 916
Social Services of Akron Project, pgs. 175, 916, 984
University of Akron, pg. 241

BELLBROOK
Society Bank, pgs. 45, 764
Society Bank/Wolf Creek Association Partnership, pgs. 45, 764

CAMBRIDGE
Cambridge Mental Health and Developmental Center, pg. 1049

CINCINNATI
Association of Ladies of Charity of the US, pgs. 354, 824
Citizens Committee on Youth, pgs. 40, 656, 1012
Easy Riders Medical Transportation, pgs. 379, 938
Easy Riders Volunteer Program*, pgs. 379, 938
Journal Newspapers, pg. 1061
National Association for Creative Children and Adults, pgs. 524, 967
National Association for the Physically Handicapped*, pgs. 452, 842
Rent-A-Kid Referral Service, pgs. 40, 656

CLEVELAND
Cleveland State University, pg. 477
Fund-Raising Success Seminar, pg. 100
The Greater Cleveland Connection, pg. 477
Help-On-Wheels, pgs. 365, 666
Legal Aid Society, pg. 1024
Lutheran Metropolitan Ministry, pgs. 365, 666
Smaller Business of America*, pg. 543
Student Care Day, pg. 108
Third Sector Press, pg. 100
United Way Services of Cleveland, pg. 108

COLUMBUS
Adopt-A-Family, pgs. 117, 683

Columbus Board of Realtors, pgs. 117, 683
Columbus Developmental Center, pgs. 395, 787
Columbus Zoo, pgs. 50, 883
Dickerson Associates, pg. 688
Future Generations, pg. 688
GRADS Program, pgs. 416, 932
Junior National Track and Field, pg. 927
Labor Editors Roundtable, pg. 65
Ohio State University, pg. 927
Outings for Homeless Children, pgs. 50, 883
Project Passage, pgs. 395, 787
South High School, pgs. 416, 932
United Way of Franklin County, pg. 65
Volunteer Action Center, pg. 264
Volunteer Management Systems Course, pg. 264

CUYAHOGA FALLS
Cuyahoga Falls Cancer Club, pg. 665

DAYTON
/I/D/E/A/, pg. 626
Institute for Development of Educational Activities, pg. 626
Management of Volunteer Programs/Sinclair, pg. 247
Neighborhoods USA, pgs. 204, 288, 558, 828, 1085
Sinclair Community College, pg. 247
Vision, Planning & Partnership in Neighborhood Organizing, pgs. 288, 828

FINDLAY
Findlay Area Native American Indian Center, pgs. 173, 880
Hot Line for the Homeless*, pgs. 173, 880

GRANVILLE
Denison Community Association, pg. 473
Denison University, pg. 473
Project LEAD, pg. 190
Quest International, pgs. 190, 1044

HEBRON
Kids Helping Kids, pgs. 223, 612
Tri-State Drug Rehabilitation and Counseling Program, pgs. 223, 612

HUDSON
Hudson High School, pg. 193
Student Volunteers, pg. 193

LEBANON
Retired Senior Volunteer Program, pg. 407

LIMA
Church People for Change and Reconciliation, pgs. 372, 693
Rehab Project: Neighborhood Revitalization Through Home Ownership, pgs. 372, 693

MARION
Chronicle of Higher Education, pg. 1014

NEW ALBANY
Care About the Strays, pg. 782

NEWARK
Thank You Picket Lines, pg. 17
United Way of Licking County, pg. 17

PARMA
Free Hotline, pg. 159

PERRYSBURG
Curb It!, pgs. 338, 777
Keep Perrysburg Beautiful, pgs. 338, 777

SPRINGFIELD
American Red Cross, pgs. 342, 443, 893
Service to Military Families/Service to Veterans (Ohio), pgs. 342, 443, 893

TOLEDO
American Red Cross, pgs. 477, 672
Health and Safety Circus, pgs. 477, 672
Interfaith Justice and Peace Center, pgs. 288, 565
Ottawa River "Fighting Back" Campaign, pg. 764
Ottawa River Improvement Association, pg. 764
Peace Conference, pgs. 288, 565
Read for Literacy, pg. 737

TROY
Miami County Cooperative Extension Service, pg. 842
Wednesday Morning Mothers, pg. 842

UNIVERSITY HEIGHTS
Avenues to Awareness: A Program for the Volunteer, pg. 230
John Carroll University, pg. 230

WEST ALEXANDRIA
Heartline*, pgs. 73, 895
National Association of Older Americans*, pgs. 73, 397, 895

WOOSTER
College of Wooster, pgs. 486, 695
Student Habitat for Humanity, pgs. 486, 695

YELLOW SPRINGS
Community Service, Inc., pg. 986

YOUNGSTOWN
Christian Service Program, pg. 362
Ursuline High School, pg. 362

ZANESVILLE
Zanesville City Schools, pgs. 1004, 1006, 1010

OKLAHOMA

FORT SILL
Fort Sill Volunteers, pgs. 346, 891
Special Olympics Time, pgs. 346, 870
US/DoD - Fort Sill, pgs. 346, 891

NORMAN
Norman Police Department, pg. 936
Safety Town (Where Children Learn to Live), pg. 936
University of Oklahoma Press, pg. 1016

OKLAHOMA CITY
Oklahoma City Literacy Council, pgs. 202, 737
Oklahoma University Health Sciences Center, pgs. 163, 806
Teenline, pgs. 163, 806

STILLWATER
Clearinghouse of Rehabilitation Training Materials, pg. 1016

TULSA
American Red Cross, pg. 232
Bridging Volunteer Resources, pg. 232
Buddies for Life, pg. 664
Chairman of Volunteers Gallery, pg. 16
Clara Barton Council, pg. 664
Daughters of the American Colonists, pg. 534
Echoes of the Past, pg. 534
First Lutheran Church, pgs. 368, 758
Manna Bowl, pgs. 368, 758
U.S. Jaycees, pg. 92

OREGON

CORVALLIS
Oregon State University, pgs. 300, 631
Refugee Volunteer Tutor Training, pgs. 300, 631

EUGENE
Community Development, Neighborhood Self-Sufficiency and Volunteerism/Volunteer Program Management, pg. 291
University of Oregon, pg. 291

GRESHAM
Mount Hood National Forest, pg. 597
TRIS (Trails Information System), pg. 597

HILLSBORO
Interdivisional Volunteer Program, pgs. 143, 829, 1034, 1071, 1095

JACKSONVILLE
Dogs for the Deaf, pg. 854

NEWPORT
Lincoln County Senior Companion Program, pgs. 395, 910

PORTLAND
Centennial School District Wellness Committee, pgs. 305, 667
Jesuit Volunteer Corps: Northwest, pgs. 80, 986
Multnomah County Sheriff's Office, pg. 595
Oregon Human Development Corporation, pgs. 18, 824
Portland Community College, pg. 266
Portland Mountain Rescue, pg. 595
Seaside Health Promotion Conference, pgs. 305, 667
Senior Clinic, pg. 1026
Volunteer Awards Program, pgs. 18, 824
Volunteer Program Management Certificate Program, pg. 266

SALEM
Chemeketa Community College, pg. 268
Mid-Valley Adolescent Center*, pgs. 35, 706
Oregon State Volunteer Services Program, pg. 143
Oregon Volunteer Services Program, pgs. 1021, 1066
Volunteerism, pg. 268

SANDY
Board Leadership and Development, pg. 183
Operation Cover Up, pgs. 405, 874
Organizational Dynamics, pgs. 183, 265, 279
Portland General Electric Company, pgs. 405, 874
Professional Development for Community Trainers, pg. 279
Volunteer Program Management, pg. 265

TIGARD
CE-2, pgs. 41, 625
Tigard High School, pgs. 41, 625

PENNSYLVANIA

ALIQUIPPA
Adult Literacy Project, pg. 733
Beaver County Federated Library System, pg. 733

ALLENTOWN
Air Products and Chemicals, pgs. 55, 919, 1082
Air Products Developmental Cycling Program, pgs. 55, 919

AMBLER
Fund-Raising Institute, pgs. 98, 984, 1015, 1017, 1019
Social Lab, pg. 311
Wissahickon High School, pg. 311

CAMP HILL
Hospital Association of Pennsylvania, pgs. 1024, 1026

EBENSBURG
Ebensburg Center, pgs. 405, 867
A Perfect Match, pgs. 405, 867

EMMAUS
Community Regeneration, pgs. 181, 552, 986, 987, 1060
Rodale Institute, pgs. 181, 552

GETTYSBURG
Gettysburg College, pgs. 450, 822
Volunteers for Youth, pgs. 450, 822

GRATERFORD
Graterford State Correctional Institution, pgs. 401, 720
Graterfriends, pgs. 401, 720

HARRISBURG
CONTACT USA, pgs. 155, 1034
PennSERVE: The Governor's Office of Citizen Service, pg. 143

HOLLAND
Church Volunteer Administration, pg. 308

LANCASTER
Transitional Volunteer Program, pgs. 389, 745
United Way Volunteer Center, pgs. 389, 745

MEDIA
Domestic Abuse Project of Delaware County, pgs. 166, 831
Pennsylvania State University, pg. 279
Strategies of Volunteer Leadership, pg. 279

MIDDLETOWN
Easter Seal Society of Pennsylvania, pg. 303
The Untapped Resource: Disabled Persons as Volunteers, pg. 303

PHILADELPHIA
Associated Services for the Blind, pg. 845
Association for Jewish Children of Philadelphia, pg. 956
Bell of Pennsylvania, pg. 855
Big Brothers/Big Sisters of America, pgs. 447, 820, 1094
Career Development for Volunteer Leadership, pg. 277
Center for Literacy, pgs. 733, 734, 1046
Children's Literacy Initiative, pgs. 318, 734
Consumer Education and Protective Association International, pg. 571
Disaster Service Volunteers, pg. 593
Docent Education Workshop, pgs. 276, 532
Energize, pgs. 240, 277, 946, 948, 951, 953, 954, 956, 1095
Energize Volunteer Management Training Program, pg. 240
Everyday Heroes, pg. 593
Fighting Dirty!, pgs. 44, 763
Friends Peace Committee, pgs. 355, 563
Gift to the City, pgs. 364, 694
Gray Panthers, pg. 1096
Green Countrie Towne Program, pgs. 500, 763
Habitat for Humanity/Philadelphia, pgs. 364, 694
Lutheran Church Women, pgs. 1006, 1046
National Clients Council, pgs. 331, 572
OIC National Shelter Program, pgs. 457, 887
Opportunities Industrialization Centers of America, pgs. 452, 457, 662, 887
Philadelphia Zoo, pgs. 276, 532
PhilaPride, pgs. 44, 763
Point Breeze Federation, pgs. 500, 763
Religious Society of Friends, pgs. 355, 563

TDD/TTY Operator Services, pg. 855
Three Ways to Care, pg. 103
United Way of Southeastern Pennsylvania, pg. 103
University of Pennsylvania, pg. 66
USS Kitty Hawk/Washington Square Partnership, pgs. 352, 765
Volunteer Reading Aides Program, pgs. 357, 732
Washington Square Association, pgs. 352, 765
WXPN-FM Radio, pg. 66

PITTSBURGH
Advocacy for Action: A New Role for Volunteers, pgs. 286, 554
Air and Waste Management Association, pg. 762
Allegheny County Community College, pgs. 186, 255, 261, 279, 286, 554, 656
Chatham College, pg. 235
Chatham Management Seminar, pg. 235
Golden Triangle Radio Information Center, pgs. 72, 849
Helping Hand, pgs. 41, 654
Learning Disabilities Association of America, pg. 862
On-Site Programs for Volunteer Organizations, pg. 279
Parental Stress Center, pgs. 166, 933
Pittsburgh Middle Schools, pgs. 482, 650
Project OASES, pgs. 482, 650
Radio Information Service (RIS), pgs. 72, 849
Short Courses and Seminars for Administrators of Volunteers, pg. 255
United Way of Allegheny County & SW PA, pgs. 41, 654
Volunteer Experience: Change, Challenge, Choices, pgs. 261, 656
Working Effectively with Boards and Committees, pg. 186

READING
Berks Community Television, pg. 64
Berks Schoolcasting*, pgs. 64, 619
Cablevision by the People*, pg. 64
Community Board Training Day, pg. 185
Pennsylvania State University, pg. 185
Reading and Berks County Chamber of Commerce, pgs. 64, 619

SPRING HOUSE
McNeil Pharmaceutical, Division of McNeilab, pgs. 37, 599
Pharmacists Against Drug Abuse, pgs. 37, 599

SWARTHMORE
National Support Center for Families of the Aging, pgs. 452, 791

UNIVERSITY PARK
The Dynamics of a Successful Volunteer Program, pg. 238
The Dynamics of a Successful Volunteer Program: Correspondence Course, pg. 238
Pennsylvania State University, pgs. 238, 264, 272
Pennsylvania Statewide Symposium on Voluntarism & Education, pg. 321
Volunteer Program Administration and Voluntary Organization Management, pg. 264
Volunteers: Facts and Fiction, pg. 321
Workshop Series on Volunteerism, pg. 272

WESTTOWN
Westtown School, pg. 490
Westtown Service Network, pg. 490

WILKES BARRE
Performance Contracting, pgs. 45, 773
United Way of Wyoming Valley, pgs. 45, 773

WYNNEWOOD
National Association of Town Watch, pg. 452

National Town Watch Association, pgs. 202, 708, 1038

YORK
Volunteer Center of York County, pg. 12

RHODE ISLAND

BRISTOL
Friends of Linden Place, pgs. 144, 535
Tea and Treasures, pgs. 144, 535

KINGSTON
Association for Volunteer Administration, Region I, pg. 246
Looking Ahead: Managing Tomorrow's Volunteers, pg. 246

LINCOLN
Lincoln School System, pgs. 111, 768
Townwide Census, pgs. 111, 768

MIDDLETOWN
Basic Leader Training Course, pgs. 296, 639
Linden School, pgs. 296, 639

NARRAGANSETT
Habitat for Humanity of Rhode Island, pgs. 365, 695

PROVIDENCE
Aspects of Administrative Functions for Managers of Volunteer Programs, pg. 229
The B.E.S.T. Project, pgs. 467, 632
Brown Program in Leadership, pg. 192
Brown University, pgs. 191, 192, 309, 467, 485, 491, 537, 632, 738, 775, 1005, 1046, 1098
Brown University Center for Public Service, pg. 986
Center for Public Service, pg. 309
Cross-Cultural Community Workshop, pgs. 191, 537
C.V. Starr National Service Fellowship Program, pg. 208
Developing Your Perspective: A Seminar in Volunteer Administration Today, pg. 237
Developing Your Perspective: Recruiting Volunteers, pg. 321
Finding and Preparing New Board Members for Service, pg. 185
Habitat for Humanity of Rhode Island, pg. 1027
Providence School System, pg. 645
South Bronx Summer Project, pgs. 485, 775
South Providence Tutorial, pg. 647
Volunteers In Action, pgs. 185, 229, 237, 304, 321, 871
Volunteers in Providence Schools, pg. 645
Volunteers with Special Needs, pgs. 304, 871
You Can Free A Mind: Adult Literacy Program, pgs. 491, 738

SOUTH CAROLINA

AIKEN
Juvenile Arbitration Program of South Carolina, pgs. 336, 705

CHARLESTON
US/DoD - Charleston Naval Base, pgs. 352, 840
Welcome Baby, pgs. 352, 840

COLUMBIA
Alston Wilkes Society, pg. 661
Building Better Boards, pg. 184
Community Service Planning Council of Greenville County, pg. 254
Emergency Shelter Council, pgs. 73, 875
GAIN (Greater Achievement Through Involvement Now), pg. 144

Older Adult Offender Project, pg. 661
SCAVA Workshops for Volunteer Administrators*, pg. 254
Stay the Night on My Street, pgs. 73, 875
United Way of South Carolina, pg. 184

GREENVILLE
The Effective Volunteer, pg. 239
Greenville Technical College, pgs. 239, 263
The Small Business Way: Small Businesses Supporting United Way, pg. 28
United Way of Greenville County, pg. 28
Volunteer Management: Level I and Level II, pg. 263

HILTON HEAD ISLAND
Building Partnerships with Corporations, pg. 23
South Carolina Association for Volunteer Administration, pg. 23

ORANGEBURG
Orangeburg Public Schools, pgs. 418, 638
Orangeburg School System, pg. 1097
Parenting and School Volunteer Program, pgs. 418, 638

SPARTANBURG
Spartanburg Adult Writing and Reading (AWARE), pg. 737

SOUTH DAKOTA

PIERRE
South Dakota Governor's Office, pg. 145
Volunteer Leadership Conference, pg. 145

SIOUX FALLS
Great Plains Volunteer, pg. 957

SKY RANCH
Sky Ranch for Boys, pgs. 789, 1078

VERMILLION
Social Work Program: 60-Hour Volunteer Work Requirement, pg. 326
University of South Dakota, pg. 326

TENNESSEE

CHATTANOOGA
Chattanooga Nature Center, pg. 771
Community INFO Line, pg. 157
Compeer, pg. 739
Mental Health Association, pg. 739
Metropolitan Council for Community Services, pg. 323
Voluntary Action Center of Chattanooga, pg. 10
Volunteer Training and Recruitment Conference, pg. 323

HIXSON
Charity Plane Ride for Orange Grove, pg. 101
Epsilon Sigma Alpha International, pg. 101

KINGSPORT
Safe House, pgs. 46, 833

KNOXVILLE
Adopt-A-School*, pg. 622
Bethel AME Church, pgs. 173, 755
Bethel Love Kitchen, pgs. 173, 755
Child and Family Services of Knox County, pg. 841
East Tennessee Community Design Center, pgs. 436, 778
Knox County Child and Family Services, pgs. 163, 805
Knox County Schools Drug Prevention Office, pgs. 197, 606
Knoxville Child and Family Services, pg. 491

Knoxville Volunteer Coordinating Center, pg. 622
Knoxville Zoo Tiger Team, pgs. 484, 777
Knoxville Zoological Gardens, pg. 967
Recycling for Ravi, pgs. 484, 777
Senior Citizens Home Assistance Services, pg. 905
Shaving Cream Lesson - Drug Prevention Seminar, pgs. 197, 606
Southeast Resource Center for Children and Youth Services, pgs. 163, 805
Young Volunteers in Action*, pg. 491

MEMPHIS
Aid to End AIDS Committee, pgs. 105, 519
Free The Children (FTC), pgs. 112, 940
Fund for Needy School Children, pgs. 109, 799
Heart Strings - Memphis Stop, pgs. 105, 519
Memphis Literacy Council, pg. 736
Service Corps of Retired Executives (SCORE), pgs. 411, 545
Volunteer Center of Memphis, pgs. 954, 1072

NASHVILLE
Abingdon Press, pgs. 1075, 1095
American Association for State and Local History, pg. 1016
Cerebral Palsy Sports Program, pg. 850
Metropolitan Council of Directors of Volunteers, pgs. 285, 797
Partners in Caring, pgs. 54, 907
Telephone Pioneers of America, pgs. 54, 907
Tennessee Volunteers for Children Conference, pgs. 285, 797
United Cerebral Palsy of Middle Tennessee, pg. 850

PIGEON FORGE
Dollywood Foundation, pgs. 39, 633
Education Support Program, pgs. 39, 633

SMYRNA
Mid-Cumberland Community Action Agency (CAA), pg. 407
Retired Senior Volunteer Program, pg. 407

TEXAS

ABILENE
Big Country Retired Senior Volunteer Program, pgs. 7, 402, 691
Home Repairs Project, pgs. 402, 691
Volunteer Volunteer Coordinators*, pg. 7

ARLINGTON
Association for Retarded Citizens, pg. 863

AUSTIN
ALLGO, pgs. 384, 518
Capital Metropolitan Transportation Authority, pgs. 34, 936
CASA (Court Appointed Special Advocates), pgs. 334, 800
CASA of Travis County, pgs. 334, 800
Cuban American Association of Austin, pgs. 384, 531
Dissemination and Assessment Center for Bilingual Education, pgs. 631, 1005
Dissemination Center for Bilingual Education, pg. 1009
Far Northwest Caregivers, pgs. 363, 905
Governor's Office for Volunteer Services/TX, pg. 145
Informe SIDA, pgs. 384, 518
National Association for Parents of the Visually Impaired, pgs. 225, 785
Noche Cubana (Cuban Night), pgs. 384, 531
Roadrunner Program, pgs. 34, 936
Runaway Hotline, pgs. 162, 805

Steck-Vaughn Company, pg. 991
Student Volunteer Services, pg. 487
Texas Volunteer Conference, pg. 145
University of Texas, pg. 487

BEAUMONT
Lamar University, pgs. 298, 617
Secondary School Volunteers, pgs. 298, 617

COLLEGE STATION
Credit and Degree Programs in Voluntary Association Administration in Colleges and Universities, pg. 236
Texas A&M, pg. 236

DALLAS
AIDS Arms Network, Inc., pgs. 509, 959
Blockbuster Community Service Program, pg. 24
Blockbuster Entertainment Corporation, pg. 24
Dallas Jewish Coalition for the Homeless, pgs. 445, 874
Frito-Lay, Inc., pg. 974
Goals for Dallas*, pgs. 86, 559
Golden Rule Awards Program, pg. 15
J.C. Penney Company, pgs. 15, 974
MOVE (Mobilization of Volunteers), pg. 480
Southern Methodist University, pg. 480
TANE Press, pgs. 997, 998, 999, 1000, 1003, 1025
Vogel Alcove, pgs. 445, 874

EL PASO
United Way of El Paso, pg. 12
Volunteer Bureau of the United Way, pg. 12

FORT WORTH
Charity Sports, pgs. 115, 878
First Call for Help/Fort Worth, pg. 158
Fort Worth Independent School District, pg. 932
Help the Homeless Million Dollar Shootout, pgs. 115, 878
Loaves & Fishes, pgs. 367, 882
New Lives, pg. 932
SNAP (Students Need A Pat), pgs. 444, 628
Starrett Elementary School, pgs. 444, 628
United Way of Tarrant County, pg. 158

GALVESTON
Galveston Historical Foundation, pg. 536
Texas Proud Voyage, pg. 536

HOUSTON
Business/School Partnership Program, pgs. 25, 622
Community Relations, pgs. 25, 622
Exxon, pg. 996
Houston Ex-Offender Program, pgs. 41, 720
National Alliance of Business/Houston, pgs. 41, 720
Roberts Park and Playground/Lantrip School Park*, pgs. 55, 929
Sun Company, pgs. 55, 929
Tenneco, Incorporated, pgs. 977, 996
Volunteers in Public Schools, pg. 1024

HURST
Mothers Against Drunk Driving, pgs. 413, 602, 1000

IRVING
Boy Scouts of America, pgs. 57, 60, 809, 851
Scouting for the Handicapped, pgs. 60, 851

LONGVIEW
Women's Center of East Texas, pgs. 167, 834

LUBBOCK
Research and Training Center in Mental Retardation, pg. 1069
Texas Tech Research and Training Center in Mental Retardation, pg. 953

SAN ANTONIO
Children's Miracle Network Telethon, pgs. 109, 804
Communicating Human Needs, pg. 69
Family Friends Project, pgs. 401, 851
Habitat for Humanity of San Antonio, pgs. 370, 688
Health Care for the Homeless Coalition, pg. 879
Intercultural Development Research Association (IDRA), pgs. 488, 630
KMOL-TV, pgs. 109, 804
Miracle Week, pgs. 370, 688
Project Any Baby Can, pgs. 401, 851
Retired Senior Volunteer Program, pg. 203
United Way of San Antonio and Bexar County, pgs. 69, 879
Valued Youth Partnership Program, pgs. 488, 630
Volunteer Senior Leaders, pg. 203

SMITHVILLE
Combined Community Action, pg. 1028

SNYDER
Scurry County Senior Center, pgs. 413, 898
VIVA (Very Important Volunteers in Action), pgs. 413, 898

TEXAS CITY
Constitutional Rights Foundation, pg. 989

TYLER
Wildwood Books, pg. 1007

UTAH

LOGAN
Logan Regional Hospital, pgs. 115, 903
Summerfest Art Faire, pgs. 115, 903

OGDEN
American Athletic Association for the Deaf*, pg. 854
ARC Covenant, pgs. 358, 882
Security Alert Group - Three Link Towers (SAG), pgs. 410, 711
SHARE*, pg. 747

PROVO
Matching Funds Project, pg. 102
RSVP of Utah County, pg. 102

SALT LAKE CITY
Adopt-A-School, pg. 621
Inter-Agency Volunteer Quarterly Forums, pg. 146
Mental Retardation Association of America, pg. 863
National Energy Foundation, pg. 773
Neighborhood Probation Unit, pgs. 496, 913
Salt Lake City School Volunteers, pg. 643
School Volunteers, pg. 621
Seniors and Children Together, pgs. 411, 585
United Way of Great Salt Lake Area, pgs. 411, 585
Utah Department of Social Services, pg. 146
Utah Division of Wildlife Resources, pg. 784
Utah Second District Juvenile Court, pgs. 496, 913
Wildlife Volunteers, pg. 784

VERMONT

BRATTLEBORO
Alan C. Hood & Company, pg. 1017

BURLINGTON
Milton Cares Telephone Reassurance, pgs. 404, 787

National Gardening Association, pgs. 923, 1053, 1062
Retired Senior Volunteer Program, pgs. 404, 787

EAST HAVEN
North American Family Campers Association, pg. 927

HINESBURG
Champlain Valley Union High School, pg. 473
DUO, pg. 473

MONTPELIER
Center for Prevention and Treatment of Sexual Abuse, pgs. 146, 726
M.A. in Volunteer Administration: The Goddard Graduate Program, pg. 246
Management of Volunteer Programs/Norwich, pg. 7
State of Vermont, pgs. 146, 726
Vermont College, pg. 246

VIRGINIA

ALEXANDRIA
Aging Futures Project, pgs. 8, 896, 952
Alexandria Community Mental Health Center, pg. 740
Alexandria Hospital, pgs. 670, 1088
Alexandria Mental Health and Substance Abuse Board, pgs. 459, 876
Alexandria Public Schools, pgs. 438, 829
Alexis de Tocqueville Society, pg. 101
Alexis de Tocqueville Society Program, pg. 15
American Driver and Traffic Safety Education Association, pg. 1000
Army Child Care Technical Assistance Conference, pg. 889
Army Community Service, pgs. 344, 890
Army Community Service Volunteer Training, pg. 275
Ask the Doctor, pgs. 434, 678
Building Momentum for a Responsive America, pgs. 287, 558
Chamber of Commerce, pgs. 40, 791
Council for Advancement and Support of Education, pgs. 973, 982, 983, 984, 985, 1014, 1015, 1017, 1018, 1019, 1020, 1096, 1101
Employee Assistance Programs, pgs. 40, 791
First Annual Soviet-American Youth Summit, pgs. 284, 564
Gifts In Kind, pgs. 117, 1018
Gifts In Kind America, pg. 117
Good Neighbor Exchange Program, pgs. 438, 829
Information and Referral Resource and Training Course, pg. 155
Mall Walkers, pg. 670
Mount Vernon Center for Community Mental Health, pg. 1050
National Academy for Voluntarism, pg. 181
National Academy for Volunteerism, pg. 155
National Academy for Volunteers in Education, pgs. 297, 617
National Association for Partners in Education, pgs. 297, 617
National Association of Community Leadership Organizations, pgs. 204, 566
National Association of Partners in Education, pgs. 42, 298, 618, 620, 657, 973, 1007, 1009, 1010
National Mental Health Association, pgs. 76, 740, 976, 1048, 1049
National Military Family Association, pgs. 332, 838
National Recreation and Park Association, pgs. 917, 1018, 1082
Partnership Umbrella, pg. 945

Preparing for an Aging Society, pgs. 8, 896
Presidential Classroom for Young Americans, pgs. 462, 557
Project Blueprint, pg. 199
Saunders B. Moon Child Development Center, pgs. 28, 584
Saunders B. Moon School Community Resource Advisory Program, pgs. 28, 584
Society of Consumer Affairs Professionals in Business, pgs. 433, 573, 975
Student Volunteer/Work Project (SV/WP), pgs. 42, 657
Substance Abuse Treatment Center and Shelter, pgs. 459, 876
"United Way at Work" Program, pg. 29
United Way of America, pgs. 15, 29, 101, 104, 117, 181, 182, 199, 280, 286, 537, 945, 946, 949, 950, 952, 954, 955, 958, 960, 963, 964, 973, 974, 982, 986, 987, 1000, 1016, 1031, 1032, 1033, 1034, 1041, 1042, 1043, 1044, 1045, 1079, 1089
U.S.-Based Japanese Corporations and the United Way, pgs. 104, 537
US/DoA - Food and Nutrition Service, pgs. 993, 1054
US/DoD - Army Community Service, pgs. 275, 344, 890
US/DoD - Army TRADOC, CFSC-FSC, pg. 889
US/DoD - Naval Internal Relations Activity, pg. 1094
Volunteer Leaders Conference, pgs. 287, 558
Volunteer Leadership Development Program, pgs. 182, 280
Volunteers: A Capital Idea*, pgs. 298, 618
Volunteers Insurance Service Association/CIMA, pgs. 950, 1093
The Wellness Center, pgs. 434, 678, 1022, 1026
Young Leaders Conference, pg. 286
Youth Ambassadors of America, pgs. 284, 564

ANNANDALE
Acacia Federal Savings Bank, pgs. 35, 915
Ameribanc Adopt-A-School Program, pgs. 38, 622
Ameribanc Savings Bank, pgs. 38, 622
Annandale Christian Community for Action (ACCA), pgs. 113, 358, 360, 362, 364, 365, 369, 374, 584, 641, 831, 832, 836, 873, 886, 936, 1097
Annandale Lions Club, pgs. 390, 847
Central Fairfax Services, pg. 858
Child Development Centers of ACCA, pgs. 360, 584
Community Advisement Board, pgs. 35, 915
Fairfax County Police Department, pg. 1039
Fairfax County Public Schools, pgs. 297, 616
Family Emergency Committee of ACCA, pgs. 362, 832
First State Conference on School Volunteers, pgs. 297, 616
Four-One-One (411), pgs. 4, 463, 951, 954, 957, 958, 1099, 1100
Fred Ruffing Memorial Scholarship, pgs. 113, 641
Furniture Committee of ACCA, pgs. 364, 836
Housing Program of ACCA, pgs. 365, 886
Little Red Hen, pgs. 968, 1100, 1101
Meals on Wheels Program of ACCA, pgs. 369, 873
Mortgage Burning Fund, pgs. 116, 686, 961, 968, 1029, 1042, 1066, 1091
National Clearinghouse on Volunteerism, pg. 4
Northern Virginia Community College, pg. 481
The OWL (Outreach-Working-Learning) Program, pg. 481
Second Air Division Association of the Eighth Air Force, pgs. 353, 535

Senior Employment Resources, pgs. 443, 661, 1067
Super Volunteers!, pg. 463
Transportation Committee of ACCA, pgs. 374, 936
Woodburn Center for Community Mental Health, pg. 1050

APPOMATTOX
National Committee for Prevention of Alcoholism and Drug Dependency, pg. 598

ARLINGTON
Air Force Members as Volunteers*, pg. 342
The Arlington County Temporary Shelter (TACTS), pgs. 170, 307, 833, 884, 1079
Arlington Hospital, pgs. 114, 671, 1023
Arlington Hospital Foundation, pgs. 114, 671
Association of Volunteer Centers, pgs. 3, 949, 1089
c/o VOLUNTEER - The National Center, pg. 3
Close Up Foundation, pg. 560
Council of Better Business Bureaus, pgs. 22, 572, 963, 990
Creative Involvement for Productive Communities, pg. 281
Culpeper Senior Center, pgs. 412, 541
Drunk-Driving Simulator Program and Forum, pgs. 425, 613
ERIC Document Reproduction Service, pg. 1099
First American Bank, pgs. 103, 596
Good News Jail and Prison Ministries International, pgs. 226, 723, 1037, 1038, 1039, 1096
Government Information Services, pgs. 98, 553, 1017
Information Resources Training Program, pg. 308
Jail 'N Bail on Capitol Hill, pgs. 113, 859
JANGO (Junior Army Navy Guild Organization)*, pgs. 341, 676
Management of Volunteer Programs in the Armed Forces, pgs. 341, 889
March of Dimes, pgs. 113, 859, 961, 1087
March of Dimes Birth Defects Foundation, pgs. 120, 860, 1086
Military Family Resource Center, pg. 1097
National Alliance of Senior Citizens, pgs. 397, 898
National Association of Alcoholism and Drug Abuse Counselors, pg. 598
National Hospice Organization, pg. 674
National Water Project*, pg. 780
Nature Conservancy, pg. 766
Northern Virginia Hotline, pgs. 159, 1034
O'Connell High School, pgs. 425, 613
Page Traditional Elementary School, pgs. 441, 640
Prime Time to End Hunger, pgs. 77, 883
Principal on the Roof*, pgs. 441, 640
Six Friends Memorial Fund, pgs. 103, 596
60 Karats, pgs. 412, 541
Small Business Development Program, pgs. 433, 542
TACTS Volunteer Program, pgs. 170, 833
TACTS Volunteer Shelter Manager Training, pgs. 307, 884
US/DoD - Air Force Office of Public Affairs, pg. 342
US/DoD - Office of Economic Adjustment, pgs. 1063, 1064
Volunteer Development Institute*, pg. 182
VOLUNTEER - The National Center, pgs. 6, 77, 281, 341, 466, 883, 889, 946, 948, 953, 955, 958, 977, 978, 987, 1052
Volunteers in Technical Assistance, pgs. 81, 308, 433, 542, 945, 971, 984, 1083
WalkAmerica, pgs. 120, 860

Youth Community Service, pg. 466

AUBURN
North American Riding for the Handicapped Association, pg. 870
Therapy on Horseback*, pg. 870

BERRYVILLE
Grafton School, pgs. 200, 856
Grafton School Volunteer Board, pgs. 200, 856

BLACKSBURG
Center for Volunteer Development, pgs. 14, 99
Community Leader Training Associates, pg. 181
Conference on Philosophical Issues in Volunteerism, pg. 320
Curriculum Development for Volunteer Administrators, pg. 236
The Future of Volunteerism: Shapes and Scenarios, pg. 14
Mini-Grants: Research in Volunteerism, pg. 99
Proposal Writing Institute*, pg. 303
Virginia Polytechnic Institute and State University, pgs. 236, 303, 320
Voluntary Action Center of Montgomery County, pg. 259
Voluntary Action Center Training (Blacksburg)*, pg. 259

BOYDON
The Choice is Yours, pgs. 429, 703
Mecklenburg Correctional Center, pgs. 429, 703

BURKE
Mu Omega Chapter/TKE, pg. 392
Rosie's Patrol, pgs. 420, 710, 1077
Tau Kappa Epsilon (TKE) Community Projects, pg. 392

BURLINGTON
University of Vermont, pg. 314
Vermont Internship Program, pg. 314

CHARLOTTESVILLE
Big Brothers/Big Sisters Program, pgs. 448, 820
CHIP/AHIP (Charlottesville Housing Improvement Program/Albemarle Housing Improvement Program), pgs. 469, 693
Companionship/Therapy Program, pgs. 472, 786
Consumer Information Service, pgs. 164, 574
Early Home Education, pgs. 474, 588
Madison House, pgs. 164, 448, 469, 472, 474, 479, 489, 493, 574, 588, 648, 676, 693, 786, 820, 922
Medical Services Program, pgs. 479, 676
Migrant Recreation Program, pgs. 479, 922
Volunteer Tutoring Program, pgs. 489, 648
Youth Recreation Program, pgs. 493, 922

CROZET
ConAgra Frozen Foods, pg. 1053

DUNN LORING
Recreation Programs for Learning Disabled Teens & Adults, pgs. 420, 863
YWCA of the National Capital Area, pgs. 420, 863

FAIRFAX
Adopt-A-School, pg. 621
American Automobile Association, pg. 1092
American Lung Association of Northern Virginia, pgs. 114, 678
Back Roads Bike Trek, pgs. 114, 678
Business/Industry Advisory Council (BIAC), pgs. 38, 619
CHISS (Consumer Housing Information Service for Seniors), pgs. 174, 689
Consortium of Peace Research, Education & Development, pgs. 462, 563

COPRED Students Peace Network, pgs. 462, 563
Fairfax Alternative Services Workshop, pgs. 315, 724
Fairfax Area Agency on Aging, pgs. 174, 689, 1027
Fairfax County Department of Consumer Affairs, pg. 989
Fairfax County Park Authority, pg. 1057
Fairfax County Public Library, pgs. 1006, 1009
Fairfax County Public Schools, pgs. 38, 619, 621
Fairfax County Redevelopment and Housing Authority, pg. 1028
Lung Association of Northern Virginia, pg. 1026
Northern Virginia Long-Term Care, pgs. 337, 899
Offender Aid and Restoration of Fairfax County, pgs. 721, 1037
Ombudsman Program, pgs. 337, 899, 1071, 1076
RIDESOURCES, pg. 1092
VAC Training, pg. 259
Voluntary Action Center of the Fairfax County Area, pgs. 11, 259, 315, 724

FAIRFAX STATION
Celebrity Auction*, pg. 107

FALLS CHURCH
American Automobile Association, pg. 1072
Bailey's Crossroads Community Shelter, pgs. 359, 885
Business/Community Involvement Program, pg. 46
Business Management/Junior Achievement, pgs. 43, 546
Citizen Advocacy, pgs. 334, 844
Fairfax County Schools, pgs. 43, 546
Joint Advocacy Coalition for the Mentally Disabled, pgs. 331, 739
National Resource Center for Consumers of Legal Services*, pgs. 164, 572
Shelter House, pgs. 373, 887

FORT BELVOIR
Education and Employment Resource Center, pgs. 344, 890
US/DoD - Army Community Service, pgs. 344, 890

FORT EUSTIS
FEST (Fort Eustis Soldiers Theatre), pgs. 345, 539
US/DoD - Fort Eustis, pgs. 345, 539

HAMPTON
Association for Volunteer Administration, Region IV, pgs. 65, 945
Center for Marine Conservation, pg. 781
Clean the Bay Day, pg. 781
"In the Trenches" Author Search Program, pg. 65

HAYMARKET
Parents for the Environment, pgs. 419, 780

LEESBURG
Association for Retarded Citizens, pgs. 47, 864
Loudoun House, pgs. 456, 690
Patowmack Herbal Farm: Summer Employment for the Handicapped, pgs. 47, 864

MANASSAS
Voluntary Action Center of the Prince William Area, pg. 260
Voluntary Action Center Training (Manassas)*, pg. 260

MCLEAN
Alternative House, pgs. 312, 814, 1067

Automotive Consumer Action Program (AUTOCAP), pgs. 451, 582
Carkhuff Institute of Human Technology, pgs. 284, 789
Challenge International, pgs. 71, 842
Get Away Clean, pgs. 284, 789
Juvenile Assistance, McLean, Ltd (JAM), pgs. 312, 814
Motor Voters, pgs. 457, 567
National Automobile Dealers Association, pgs. 451, 582
Pathways to Independence, pgs. 385, 744
Teen Center, pgs. 422, 823

MEDFORD
New England Environmental Leadership Network, pg. 1057

MERRIFIELD
Northern Virginia Association for Volunteer Administration, pg. 952

MOUNT VERNON
Bryant Adult Community Education Center, pgs. 458, 933
Project Opportunity, pgs. 458, 933

NEWPORT NEWS
Virginia Citizens Consumer Council, pgs. 337, 574

NORFOLK
Chaplain Resource Board, pg. 1097
Cousteau Society, pgs. 447, 538
Donor Involvement, pg. 102
Introduction to Volunteerism in the Juvenile Justice System (Sociology 195: WX and WX2), pgs. 315, 714
Norfolk Catholic Christian Service Program, pg. 481
Norfolk Catholic High School, pg. 481
Old Dominion University, pgs. 315, 714
United Way of South Hampton Roads, pg. 102
Youth Ocean Explorer Program, pgs. 447, 538

QUANTICO
FBI Academy, pgs. 450, 700
Hogan's Alley, Virginia, pgs. 450, 700

RESTON
American Association for Leisure and Recreation, pg. 917
CEC Special Project: ERIC Clearinghouse on Handicapped and Gifted Children, pgs. 170, 860
Council for Exceptional Children, pgs. 170, 634, 860, 947, 960, 1007, 1008, 1009, 1010, 1012, 1066, 1070, 1073, 1074, 1076, 1077, 1079, 1080
Distributive Education Clubs of America, pgs. 42, 546
Entertainment Industries Council, pgs. 354, 605
National Association of Secondary School Principals, pg. 616
National Organization of Adolescent Pregnancy and Parenting, pg. 930

RICHMOND
American Red Cross, pg. 493
Basic Accounting Assistance, pg. 9
Basics of Volunteer Program Management*, pg. 147
Catholic Communications Center, pg. 1095
Celebration of Volunteerism: Annual Statewide Conference, pg. 147
Center for Perinatal Addiction, pg. 1087
Child Abuse Hotline, pgs. 165, 812
Child Protective Services, pgs. 816, 1031, 1039, 1049, 1066, 1067, 1068, 1087
Commission on Self-Sufficiency, pgs. 199, 842

Complete Volunteer Legal Liability Workshop, pg. 148

Drug Trafficking Study Task Force, pgs. 295, 607, 998

Effective Boardsmanship, pg. 148

Exploring New Frontiers in Volunteerism, pg. 240

Garden of Young Hearts, pgs. 476, 868

Governor's Advisory Committee on Child Abuse and Neglect/VA, pgs. 151, 817

Greek Festival, pgs. 364, 530

Literacy Incentive Program (No Read, No Release), pgs. 430, 735

Managing Your Fiscal Responsibilities as a Nonprofit: How to Avoid Financial Pitfalls, pg. 274

March of Dimes, pgs. 149, 667

Marketing for Voluntary Service Organizations, pg. 289

Parent to Parent, pgs. 418, 852

The Quest for Community, pg. 148

Sts. Constantine & Helen Greek Orthodox Cathedral, pgs. 364, 530

Southwest Virginia Black Lung Task Force, pg. 201

Special Populations Division, pgs. 476, 868

Statewide Drug Task Force Conference, pgs. 295, 607

Team-Building, pg. 148

Virginia Circuit Court, pg. 1038

Virginia Council on Health and Medical Care, pg. 1075

Virginia Department for Rights of the Disabled, pgs. 199, 201, 842, 983, 996, 1074, 1079

Virginia Department of Housing & Community Development, pgs. 116, 686

Virginia Department of Social Services, pgs. 151, 165, 812, 816, 817

Virginia Division for Children, pgs. 992, 1021

Virginia Division of Volunteerism, pgs. 146, 147, 148, 149, 150, 240, 289, 955

Virginia Ecumenical Infant Mortality Prevention Project Conference, pgs. 149, 667

Virginia Governor's Office, pgs. 430, 735

Virginia Institute for Developmental Disabilities, pgs. 418, 852, 1098

Virginia Partnership Fund and Other Programs, pgs. 116, 686

Virginia Power, pg. 974

Virginia Society of Certified Public Accountants, pgs. 9, 274

Virginia State Police Association, pgs. 110, 601

Virginia Volunteers - Health of the Commonwealth, pg. 149

Volunteer Management Series, pg. 150

Volunteer Program Management, pg. 150

Volunteering: A Celebration of Community, pg. 150

VSPA Fund-Raising Programs, pgs. 110, 601

Youth Services, pg. 493

ROANOKE

Christ Episcopal Church, pgs. 373, 745

Offender Aid and Restoration of Roanoke, Virginia*, pg. 706

Star City Social Club, pgs. 373, 745

SPRINGFIELD

A, B, and C on Burglary, pgs. 426, 716

Franconia District Citizens Advisory Committee, pgs. 426, 716

Gamma Omicron Chapter/Phi Mu, pg. 391

Institute of Marriage and Family Relations, pg. 840

The Journal, pg. 983

National Technical Information Service, pg. 971

Phi Mu Sorority Community Service Chapter, pg. 391

US/DoC - National Technical Information Service, pgs. 956, 990, 1037

STAUNTON

Blue Ridge Area Food Bank*, pgs. 51, 751, 1052

Teenage Volunteers Working in Adolescent Program*, pgs. 487, 743

Western State Hospital, pgs. 487, 743

STEPHENSON

Shalom Et Benedictus, pg. 600

Shalom Et Benedictus Substance Abuse Programs, pg. 600

SWEET BRIAR

Ryans' Nursing Home Volunteer Program, pgs. 484, 908

Sweet Briar College, pgs. 484, 488, 648, 908

Tutoring Volunteer Program, pgs. 488, 648

VERONA

Virginia Group to Alleviate Smoking in Public, pg. 679

VIENNA

Wellness and Health Activation Networks, pgs. 173, 678

WAYNESBORO

Big Brothers/Big Sisters of Waynesboro, pg. 1079

WASHINGTON

ELLENSBURG

Fifth Avenue Center, pg. 13

Volunteer Network*, pg. 13

LONGVIEW

Lower Columbia Community Action Council, pg. 91

Volunteer Services/CAC, pg. 91

MEDICAL LAKE

College-In-Residence Volunteers (CIRV), pgs. 470, 862

Washington Department of Social & Health Services, pgs. 470, 862

OLYMPIA

Rural Volunteer Services Network, pg. 152

Volunteerism: A Bridge to the Future, pg. 152

Washington Department of Social & Health Services, pgs. 152, 1066

Washington Office of Volunteerism, pgs. 152, 1021, 1043

Washington State Center for Voluntary Action, pg. 152

PULLMAN

AYE SHARE, pg. 231

Washington State University, pgs. 231, 992, 993

RENTON

Association for Volunteer Administration, Region X, pg. 244

Delta Society, pgs. 782, 1055, 1058, 1059

Interconnections, pg. 244

King County Rape Relief, pg. 1037

SEATTLE

American Red Cross, pg. 410

Boeing Company, pg. 972

CASA, pgs. 331, 807

Children: The Time is Now, pgs. 333, 807

Conference Committee, pg. 1036

First Place, pgs. 876, 1071

Governors' School, pgs. 151, 797

Guardian Ad Litem Program, pgs. 336, 701

The How-To of Working with Volunteers - TLC (Teaching/Learning/Caring), pg. 278

Job Therapy, Inc. (Ex-Offender Program: Project Start)*, pgs. 340, 662

KCTS-TV, pg. 963

King County Juvenile Judges Committee, pgs. 498, 722

King County Superior Court, pgs. 336, 701

Labor Temple, pgs. 502, 691

Lakeside School, pg. 278

National CASA Association, pgs. 333, 807, 1095, 1099

National Court Appointed Special Advocate Association, pgs. 331, 807

Parent Aide Program - Centralized Service Unit, pg. 833

Seattle-King County RSVP (Retired Senior Volunteer Program), pg. 410

Seattle Pacific University, pg. 488

Seattle University, pgs. 151, 797

Selecting and Training Volunteers, pg. 255

Superior Court Conference Committee Diversion Program, pgs. 498, 722

TASH: The Association for the Severely Handicapped, pg. 843

Union Retirees Resources, pgs. 502, 691

University of Washington, pg. 255

Urban Involvement, pg. 488

SPOKANE

East Central Community Center, pg. 1078

Gonzaga Action Program (GAP), pg. 364

Gonzaga University, pg. 364

SCAN (Spokane Child Abuse and Neglect Prevention Center), pgs. 70, 818

TACOMA

Operation Coverup, pgs. 428, 764

Safe Streets, pgs. 428, 764

VANCOUVER

HOSTS (Help One Student To Succeed), pg. 1007

VASHON

Association for Volunteer Administration, pg. 271

Where Do We Go From Here?, pg. 271

WALLA WALLA

Macduff/Bunt Associates, pgs. 947, 953, 956, 984, 1042, 1090

WENATCHEE

Community Resource Center, pg. 187

WHIDBEY ISLAND

Giraffe Project, pgs. 16, 948

WHITE SALMON

Grace Baptist Church, pgs. 370, 753

Mt. Adams Ministerial Association Food Bank, pgs. 370, 753

WEST VIRGINIA

CHARLESTON

West Virginia Conference on Volunteerism, pg. 153

West Virginia Department of Welfare Volunteer Program, pgs. 153, 830

West Virginia Office on Volunteerism, pg. 153

KEYSER

Family Crisis Center, pgs. 166, 838

MORGANTOWN

Rape and Domestic Violence Information Center, pgs. 177, 727

PARKERSBURG

Community Services, pg. 324

Parkersburg High School, pg. 324

WISCONSIN

APPLETON
AAL Drug and Alcohol Use Prevention Program, pg. 999
Get Involved Before Your Kids Do, pgs. 414, 600

BELOIT
Stateline United Way, pg. 66
United Way Editorial Board, pg. 66
Volunteer Service Bureau/VAC, pgs. 1005, 1094

BROOKFIELD
National Friends of Public Broadcasting, pg. 62
Rexnord Resource Center, pg. 972

FOND DU LAC
Community Training and Development, pg. 181

MADISON
Institute for Health Planning, pg. 1026
Society for Nonprofit Organizations, pgs. 5, 952, 953
Stanton and Lee Publishers, pg. 1080
University of Wisconsin, pgs. 398, 489, 532, 536
Volunteer Paleontology Dig, pgs. 489, 536
Wisconsin Clearinghouse, pg. 1045
Yarns of Yesteryear Project, pgs. 398, 532, 1072

MARSHFIELD
Central Wisconsin Association of Volunteer Administrators, pg. 241
From Me to We: A Funny Reason to Have a Conference, pg. 241

MILWAUKEE
Alliance for the Mentally Ill of Greater Milwaukee, pg. 1049
Debt and Credit Counseling Service, pg. 577
Education and Human Services Course, pg. 325
Entering the Community: Summer Volunteer Service and Career Opportunities for Students, pg. 311
Family Service America, pgs. 577, 840, 955
Friends of Libraries USA*, pg. 635
Girl Scouts of the Milwaukee Area, pgs. 480, 778
Greater Milwaukee Voluntary Action Center, pg. 945
HOPE, pg. 663
International Association of Justice Volunteerism (IAJV), pgs. 697, 950, 1037
Involvement Corps*, pgs. 27, 975, 978
Milwaukee and the Single Girl*, pgs. 480, 778
Riverside University High School, pg. 325
Sixteenth Street Community Health Center, pg. 663
Student Volunteer Programs: A New Resource for Community Agencies*, pg. 327
University of Wisconsin/Milwaukee, pg. 697
Visiting Friends*, pgs. 445, 673
Visiting Nurse Association of Milwaukee, pgs. 445, 673
Voluntary Action Center of Greater Milwaukee, pg. 968
Volunteer Center of Greater Milwaukee, pgs. 27, 949, 967
Young Volunteers in Action, pgs. 311, 327

STEVENS POINT
Issues on Volunteerism: Service Learning in the Community, pg. 325
United Ministries in Higher Education, pg. 260
University of Wisconsin-Stevens Point, pg. 325
Volunteer Administrator's Conference, pg. 260

STURGEON BAY
National Extension Homemakers Council, pg. 825

WATERFORD
Field Education Program, pg. 363
Holy Redeemer College, pg. 363

WYOMING

CHEYENNE
People Helping People/Cheyenne, pg. 322
Publicity Workshop, pg. 64
Recruiting, Training and Retention of Volunteers, pg. 322
Volunteer Information Center, pg. 64